AMERICAN
WHOLESALERS
AND
DISTRIBUTORS
DIRECTORY

AMERICAN WHOLESALERS AND DISTRIBUTORS DIRECTORY

*A comprehensive guide
offering industry
details on approximately
27,000 wholesalers
and distributors
in the United States.*

NINTH EDITION

Louise Gagné, Editor

Louise Gagne, *Editor*

Keith Jones, *Managing Editor*

Jenai Mynatt, *Contributing Editor*

Ronald D. Montgomery, *Data Capture Manger*
Gwendolyn S. Tucker, *Data Capture Project Admistrator*
Frances L. Monroe, *Data Capture Speciast*
Nikkita Bankston, *Data Capture Associe*
Katrina Coach, Cynthia Jones, Elizabeth Pilette, *Data apture Assistants*
Teresa Elsey, *Data Capture Summer Intn*

Evi Seoud, *Assistant Production Manaer*
Nekita M. McKee, *Buyer*
Mike Logusz, *Graphic Artist*

Theresa Rocklin, *Manager, Technical Suppo Services*
Dan Bono, *Programmer*

Kris Musial, *Senior Consultant*

ISBN 0-7876-3473-5
ISSN 1061-2114

Printed in the United States of America

CONTENTS

Highlights ix

Introduction xi

User's Guide xv

Abbreviations xix

Product Line Category Thesaurus xxi

Company Listings

Section 1 – Adhesives 1

Section 2 - Aeronautical Equipment and Supplies 3

Section 3 - Agricultural Equipment and Supplies 11

Section 4 - Alcoholic Beverages 61

Section 5 - Automotive 85

Section 6 - Books and Other Printed Materials 133

Section 7 - Chemicals 167

Section 8 - Cleaning and Janitorial Supplies 177

Section 9 – Clothing 185

Section 10 - Communications Systems and Equipment 213

Section 11 - Compressors 227

Section 12 - Computers and Software 229

Section 13 - Construction Materials and Machinery 269

Section 14 - Electrical and Electronic Equipment and Supplies 321

Section 15 - Explosives 375

Section 16 - Floorcovering Equipment and Supplies 377

Section 17 - Food 401

Section 18 - Furniture and Fixtures 501

Section 19 - Gifts and Novelties 511

Section 20 - Guns and Weapons 519

Section 21 - Hardware 521

Section 22 - Health and Beauty Aids 541

Section 23 - Heating and Cooling Equipment and Supplies 553

Section 24 - Horticultural Supplies 573

Section 25 - Household Appliances 581

Section 26 - Household Items 597

Section 27 - Industrial Machinery 611

Section 28 - Industrial Supplies 649

Section 29 - Jewelry 675

Section 30 - Livestock and Farm Products 689

Section 31 - Luggage and Leather Goods 715

Section 32 - Marine 719

Section 33 - Medical, Dental, and Optical Equipment 727

Section 34 - Medical, Dental, and Optical Supplies 745

Section 35 - Metals 767

Section 36 - Minerals and Ores 797

Section 37 - Motorized Vehicles 801

Section 38 - Office Equipment and Supplies 809

Section 39 - Paints and Varnishes 833

Section 40 - Paper and Paper Products 843

Section 41 - Petroleum, Fuels, and Related Equipment 861

Section 42 - Photographic Equipment and Supplies 891

Section 43 - Plastics 895

Section 44 - Plumbing Materials and Fixtures 901

Section 45 - Railroad Equipment and Supplies 919

Section 46 - Recreational and Sporting Goods 921

Section 47 - Restaurant and Commercial Foodservice Equipment and Supplies 943

Section 48 - Rubber 953

Section 49 - Scientific and Measurement Devices 955

Section 50 - Security and Safety Equipment 963

Section 51 - Shoes 971

Section 52 - Soft Drinks 979

Section 53 - Sound and Entertainment Equipment and Supplies 985

Section 54 - Specialty Equipment and Products 1005

Section 55 - Storage Equipment and Containers 1019

Section 56 - Textiles and Notions 1023

Section 57 - Tobacco Products 1035

Section 58 - Toys and Hobby Goods 1041

Section 59 - Used, Scrap, and Recycled Materials 1055

Section 60 - Veterinary Products 1067

Section 61 - Wood and Wood Products 1077

SIC Index 1083

Geographic Index 1235

Alphabetic Index 1467

Section 48 - Rubber 963

Section 49 - Scientific and Measurement Devices 968

Section 50 - Security and Safety Equipment 943

Section 51 - Shoes 921

Section 52 - Soft Drinks 979

Section 53 - Sound and Entertainment Equipment and Supplies 986

Section 54 - Specialty Equipment and Products 1008

Section 55 - Storage Equipment and Containers 1010

Section 56 - Textiles and Notions 1123

Section 57 - Tobacco Products 1035

Section 58 - Toys and Hobby Goods 1041

Section 59 - Used, Scrap, and Recycled Materials 1055

Section 60 - Veterinary Products 1061

Section 61 - Wood and Wood Products 1077

SIC Index 1064

Geographic Index 1239

Alphabetic Index 1451

HIGHLIGHTS

The eighth edition of *American Wholesalers and Distributors Directory* provides needed coverage of a major industry sector. It profiles approximately **27,000** large and small wholesalers and distributors throughout the United States and Puerto Rico.

Wholesalers covered serve all areas, including:

➢ 2,399 specializing in food or food related products
➢ 2,961 specializing in electrical and electronic goods
➢ 1,190 handling industrial machinery, equipment, and supplies
➢ 1,121 serving the automotive industry
➢ 1,603 covering recreational, sporting, and hobby goods
➢ 3,171 specializing in men's, women's, and children's clothing
➢ 1,094 focusing on the computer industry
➢ 857 focusing on the agricultural and farming industry

Key features and benefits of this edition include:

➢ **Organization.** Entries have been organized into 61 broad subject categories based on each company's product line. 1,000 new entries have been added to this edition.
➢ **Contact Information.** Complete contact information—including company name, address, and phone number, as well as fax number when available—is provided for each entry.
➢ **Principal product line information** is included for all companies profiled in this edition.
➢ **Employee** figures are included for a majority of wholesalers and distributors.
➢ **Sales** figures for 1999, or an estimate for 2000, are included when provided by the respondent.
➢ **E-mail addresses** and **URLs (Internet addresses)** are included to provide greater flexibility. This edition has a 61% increase in websites from 2,390 to 3,863; a 47% increase in company emails from 2,501 to 3,673; and a 45% increase in personal emails from 744 to 1,078.

This edition also provides four easy ways to access vital information on U.S. wholesalers and distributors:

➢ by broad subject terms derived from each company's principal product line, then alphabetically by company name
➢ by Standard Industrial Classification (SIC) Code (see **SIC Index**)
➢ by state and city (see **Geographic Index**)
➢ by company name (see **Alphabetic Index**)

Be sure to read the **Introduction** and **User's Guide** for more information about this edition.

INTRODUCTION

The role of wholesalers and distributors in the U.S. economy is vital. Each year, manufacturers produce hundreds of thousands of products from automobiles to zippers. Wholesalers and distributors buy these products from the manufacturer, then sort, assemble, grade, and store them for resale to retailers and commercial, agricultural, governmental, and industrial users.

The *American Wholesalers and Distributors Directory* (*AWDD*) provides direct, one-stop access to this market by profiling approximately 27,400 wholesalers and distributors across the United States and Puerto Rico. These companies include small businesses as well as large corporations, and they represent both the public and private sector.

The U.S. Department of Commerce classifies the industries in which these companies are active by these and other categories:

Apparel, Piece Goods, and Notions
Beer, Wine, and Distilled Alcoholic Beverages
Chemicals and Allied Products
Durable and Nondurable Goods
Drugs, Drug Proprietaries, and Druggists' Sundries
Electrical and Electronic Equipment
Farm Products
Furniture and Homefurnishings
Groceries and Related Products
Hardware
Lumber and Other Construction Materials
Machinery, Equipment, and Supplies
Metals and Minerals
Motor Vehicles, Parts, and Supplies
Paper and Paper Products
Petroleum and Petroleum Products
Plumbing and Heating Equipment
Scrap and Waste Materials

Arrangement

The directory has been organized into 61 sections and contains three indexes.

➤ **Sections 1-61** organize wholesalers and distributors by broad subject terms derived from each company's reported principal product line, then alphabetically by company name. Each individual product line is then grouped with like products based on where an individual might purchase those products. For example, a user looking for a nuts and bolts wholesaler would find the company listed under the subject category *hardware*; similarly, a user looking for a distributor of sofas and couches would find that company listed under the broad term *furniture*. This list provides vital information to help the user find companies within a specific range of products. For a complete list of product lines, see the **Product Line Category Thesaurus** immediately preceding Section 1.

➤ The **SIC Index** arranges each wholesaler and distributor numerically by both primary and secondary

Standard Industrial Classification (SIC) Codes, then alphabetically by company name. The entry number, rather than the page number, appears in brackets directly after each company name.

➢ The **Geographic Index** groups wholesalers and distributors by state and city, then alphabetically by company name. The entry number, rather than the page number, appears in brackets immediately following each company name.

➢ The **Alphabetic Index** arranges companies alphabetically by company name and provides the address and telephone number for each entry. The entry number, rather than the page number, appears in brackets directly after each company name.

For more information on how to use *American Wholesalers and Distributors Directory*, see the **User's Guide** following the **Introduction**.

Content of Listings

Entries in *AWDD* contain some or all of the following elements of information:

> Company name; address; phone, fax, and toll-free numbers; company e-mail addresses and URLs
> Product lines
> Standard Industrial Classification (SIC) codes
> Year established
> Annual estimated sales
> Number of employees
> Officers (names, titles and personal email addresses)

Estimated sales and employee information, listed here as reported by the company, are intended to be used as a method of gauging the relative size of profiled companies rather than representing exact figures.

Method of Compilation

Information for this directory was gathered in several ways. Wholesalers and distributors were directly contacted to verify their listings and gather new data. Additional entries were compiled from information contained in Gale databases, including the *Ward's Business Directory of U.S. Private and Public Companies*. Extensive original research was completed by The Gale Group staff to thoroughly update the wholesaler and distributor listings contained in the ninth edition and to obtain additional new listings.

Alternate Formats

American Wholesalers and Distributors Directory is available on the *Gale Business Resources* CD-ROM. In addition, this title is available for licensing on magnetic tape or diskette in fielded format. Either the complete database or a custom selection of entries may be ordered. The database is available for internal data processing and nonpublishing purposes only. For more information, call a Customer Services representative at 800-877-GALE.

Comments or Suggestions

Comments or suggestions about *American Wholesalers and Distributors Directory* and information on new wholesalers and distributors are always welcome. Please contact:

Editor
American Wholesalers and Distributors Directory
The Gale Group
27500 Drake Rd.
Farmington Hills, MI 48331-3535
Phone: (248) 699-4253
Toll-free: 800-877-GALE
Fax: (248) 699-8070

USER'S GUIDE

The *American Wholesalers and Distributors Directory* is organized into 61 sections and 3 indexes:

❖ **Sections 1-61** provide alphabetical listings by company name within broad subject categories derived from each company's principle product line. Each individual product line is then grouped with like products based on where an individual might purchase those products. This list provides vital information to help the user find companies within a specific range of products. For a complete list of product lines, see the **Product Line Category Thesaurus** immediately preceding Section 1.

❖ The **SIC Index** arranges companies alphabetically within each of their Standard Industrial Classification (SIC) codes.

❖ The **Geographic Index** groups companies geographically by state and city.

❖ The **Alphabetic Index** organizes entries alphabetically according to company name.

Sample Entry -- Sections 1- 61
Wholesalers and Distributors

Listings in Sections 1-61 are organized alphabetically by broad subject categories based on each company's principal product line, then alphabetically by company name. When the company name is a personal name, the company name is alphabetized by the surname unless the first name or initials are part of a trade name. The editor has made every effort to distinguish between first names, initials, acronyms, trade names, or multiple surnames; where the editor was unable to make the determination, the company name is alphabetized by the first element in its name. The user is advised to try to locate a company first by surname, and if unsuccessful, to try the first element in the name.

A fabricated sample entry illustrating the information that might be found in a typical listing is shown below. The number preceding each portion of the sample entry designates an item of information that is explained following the sample entry.

1)	**ENTRY NUMBER.** This number **does not** indicate page number.
2)	**COMPANY NAME.**
3)	**CONTACT INFORMATION.**
4)	**PRODUCT LINE.** Describes specific types of products the company wholesales or distributes within its particular industry.
5)	**SIC(s).** Lists the profiled company's Standard Industrial Classification (SIC) code(s) and its corresponding industry description. The SIC system was established by the Office of Budget and Management, which is part of the Executive Office of the President, in order to provide a uniform means of categorizing various types of businesses and services. For additional information, refer to the *Standard Industrial Classification Manual 1987*, available from the National Technical Information Service.
6)	**YEAR ESTABLISHED.**
7)	**SALES.** As reported by the company, this figure represents approximate annual sales.
8)	**NUMBER OF EMPLOYEES.**
9)	**OFFICERS.** The names and titles of the company's executive officers.
10)	**VARIANT NAMES.** Lists any variant names held by the company.

Sample Entry — SIC Index

This index is arranged numerically by Standard Industrial Classification (SIC) code; companies are organized alphabetically within each of their SICs. Each company's entry number appears in brackets immediately following the company name.

A fabricated entry is shown below.

┌───┐
│   │
│ **SIC 5064 – Electrical Appliances-Television and Radio**   │
│ 1) Reando Miquel Phillips Co.   2) [72499]   │
│   │
└───┘

1)	**COMPANY NAME.**
2)	**ENTRY NUMBER.** This number **does not** indicate page number.

Sample Entry — Geographic Index

Listings in this section are arranged alphabetically according to state, city, and company name. Each company name is followed, in parentheses, by the broad subject term derived from its principle product line. Each company's entry number appears in brackets immediately following this term.

A fabricated entry is shown below.

DETROIT

1) Dominguez & Associates **2)** (Household Items) **3)** [1989]

---

1)   **COMPANY NAME.**
2)   **BROAD SUBJECT CATEGORY.**
3)   **ENTRY NUMBER.** This number **does not** indicate page number.

Sample Entry — Alphabetic Index

Companies are arranged alphabetically by name within this index. For quick reference, the listings also contain the company's address and telephone number. An entry number, rather than a page number, appears in brackets following the contact information.

A sample fabricated entry is listed below.

---

1) Mariachi Productions **2)** 6969 Malaga Rd., Clinton Township 48035; **3)** (574)555-1748; **4)** [8649]

---

1)   **COMPANY NAME.**
2)   **ADDRESS.**
3)   **TELEPHONE NUMBER.**
4)   **ENTRY NUMBER.** This number **does not** indicate page number.

Sample Entry — Geographic Index

Listings in this section are arranged alphabetically by state, city and company name. Each company name is followed, in parentheses, by the broad subject term derived from its principle product line. (A bold company-entry number appears in brackets in italic type following this term.)

A fabricated entry is shown below.

DETROIT

1) Dominguez & Associates, 2) (Incorporation name) 3) [9999]

---

1) COMPANY NAME
2) BROAD SUBJECT CATEGORY
3) ENTRY NUMBER. This number does not indicate page number.

Sample Entry — Alphabetic Index

Companies are arranged alphabetically by name within this index. For quick reference, the listings also contain the company's address and telephone number. An entry number rather than a page number appears in brackets following the company name/line.

A sample fabricated entry is shown below.

---

1) Monarch Industries, 2) 1234 Maple Rd., Clinton Township, MI 48035 3) (313) 555-1234 4) [9999]

---

1) COMPANY NAME
2) ADDRESS
3) TELEPHONE NUMBER
4) ENTRY NUMBER. This number does not indicate page number.

ABBREVIATIONS

Address and Text Abbreviations

&	and
Actg	Acting
Admin	Administrator
Advt	Advertising
AFB	Air Force Base
APO	Army Post Office
Apt	Apartment
Archv	Archivist
Assn	Association
Assoc	Associate
Asst	Assistant
Ave	Avenue
Bldg	Building
Blvd	Boulevard
Ch	Chief
Chm	Chairman
Cir	Circle
c/o	Care of
Commnr	Commissioner
Commun	Communications
Consult	Consultant
Coord	Cordinator
Corp	Corporation
Couns	Counselor
Ct	Court
Dep	Deputy
Devel	Development
Dir	Director
Div	Division
Dr	Drive
E	East
Ed	Editor
Exec	Executive
Expy	Expressway
Fed	Federation
Fl	Floor
FPO	Fleet Post Office
Fwy	Freeway
Gen	General
Grp	Group
Hd	Head
Hwy	Highway
Inc	Incorporated
Info	Information
Intl	International
Libn	Librarian
Ln	Lane
Ltd	Limited
Mgr	Manager
Mktg	Marketing
Mng	Managing
N	North
NE	North East
No	Number
NW	North West
Off	Officer
Orgn	Organization
Pk	Park
Pke	Pike
Pkwy	Parkway
Pl	Place
PO	Post Office
Pres	President
Proj	Project
Pub	Publisher
Rd	Road
RD	Rural Delivery
Rel	Relations
Res	Research(er)
RFD	Rural Free Delivery
Rm	Room
RR	Rural Route
Rte	Route
S	South
SE	South East
Sec	Secretary
Sq	Square
SR	Star/State Route
St	Saint, Street
Sta	Station
Ste	Sainte, Suite
Sup(v)	Supervisor
Svc(s)	Service(s)
SW	South West
Terr	Terrace
Tpke	Turnpike
V	Vice
W	West

U.S. State and Territory Postal Codes

AK	Alaska	MT	Montana
AL	Alabama	NC	North Carolina
AR	Arkansas	ND	North Dakota
AZ	Arizona	NE	Nebraska
CA	California	NH	New Hampshire
CO	Colorado	NJ	New Jersey
CT	Connecticut	NM	New Mexico
DC	District of Columbia	NV	Nevada
DE	Delaware	NY	New York
FL	Florida	OH	Ohio
GA	Georgia	OK	Oklahoma
HI	Hawaii	OR	Oregon
IA	Iowa	PA	Pennsylvania
ID	Idaho	PR	Puerto Rico
IL	Illinois	RI	Rhode Island
IN	Indiana	SC	South Carolina
KS	Kansas	SD	South Dakota
KY	Kentucky	TN	Tennessee
LA	Louisiana	TX	Texas
MA	Massachusetts	UT	Utah
MD	Maryland	VA	Virginia
ME	Maine	VT	Vermont
MI	Michigan	WA	Washington
MN	Minnesota	WI	Wisconsin
MO	Missouri	WV	West Virginia
MS	Mississippi	WY	Wyoming

Product Line Category Thesaurus

Above Ground Storage Tanks
See: Storage Equipment and Containers

Abrasives
See: Industrial Supplies

Absorbents
See: Industrial Supplies

Academic Caps & Gowns
See: Clothing

Accounting Machines
See: Office Equipment and Supplies

Acetone
See: Chemicals

Acetylene
See: Industrial Supplies

Acids
See: Chemicals

Acrylic and Modacrylic
See: Plastics

Adding Machines
See: Office Equipment and Supplies

Additives
See: Chemicals

Addressing Machines
See: Office Equipment and Supplies

Adhesives

Adsorbents
See: Chemicals

Adult Books
See: Books and Other Printed Materials

Advertising Specialties
See: Specialty Equipment and Products

Adzes
See: Hardware

Aeronautical Equipment and Supplies

Aeronautical Hardware
See: Aeronautical Equipment and Supplies

Aeronautical, Nautical, and Navigational Instruments
See: Aeronautical Equipment and Supplies

Aggregate
See: Construction Materials and Machinery

Agricultural Chemicals
See: Chemicals

Agricultural Equipment and Supplies
(*See also:* Livestock and Farm Products; Veterinary Products)

Agricultural Equipment Stampings
See: Agricultural Equipment and Supplies

Agricultural Land Preparation Machinery
See: Agricultural Equipment and Supplies

Agricultural Tractors
See: Agricultural Equipment and Supplies

Air Compressors
See: Compressors

Air-conditioning Compressors
See: Heating and Cooling Equipment and Supplies

Air-conditioning Condensing Units
See: Heating and Cooling Equipment and Supplies

Air-conditioning Equipment
See: Heating and Cooling Equipment and Supplies

Air-conditioning Room Units
See: Heating and Cooling Equipment and Supplies

Air Filters
See: Specialty Equipment and Products

Air Pollution Control Equipment and Supplies
See: Heating and Cooling Equipment and Supplies

Air Purification Equipment for Heating and Cooling
See: Heating and Cooling Equipment and Supplies

Air Quality Monitors
See: Heating and Cooling Equipment and Supplies

Air Source Heat Pumps
See: Heating and Cooling Equipment and Supplies

Air Space Heaters
See: Heating and Cooling Equipment and Supplies

Aircraft
See: Aeronautical Equipment and Supplies

Aircraft Carpeting
See: Floorcovering Equipment and Supplies

Aircraft Fueling Services
See: Aeronautical Equipment and Supplies

Aircraft Fuels
See: Petroleum, Fuels, and Related Equipment

Aircraft Paints
See: Paints and Varnishes

Aircraft Parts
See: Aeronautical Equipment and Supplies

Alarm Systems
See: Security and Safety Equipment

Alcoholic Beverages
(*See also:* Soft Drinks)

Ale
See: Alcoholic Beverages

Alfalfa
See: Livestock and Farm Products

Alkalies
See: Chemicals

Allied Paint Products
See: Paints and Varnishes

Alloy Steel Castings
See: Metals

Alloys
See: Metals

Aluminum
See: Metals

Aluminum Alloy Castings
See: Metals

Aluminum Foil
See: Metals

Aluminum Oxide
See: Chemicals

Aluminum Plate
See: Metals

Aluminum Sheet and Strip
See: Metals

Amateur Radio Equipment
See: Communications Systems
and Equipment

Ambulances
See: Motorized Vehicles

Ammonia
See: Chemicals

Ammunition
See: Guns and Weapons

Animal Feeds
See: Agricultural Equipment and
Supplies

Animal Hair
See: Livestock and Farm Products

Animal Healthcare Products
See: Veterinary Products

Anthropology Books
See: Books and Other Printed
Materials

Antique Guns
See: Guns and Weapons

Antiques
See: Furniture and Fixtures

Appliance Parts
See: Household Appliances

Appliances
See: Household Appliances

Archery Equipment
See: Recreational and Sporting
Goods

Art Goods
See: Gifts and Novelties

Art Reference and Instruction Books
See: Books and Other Printed
Materials

Artificial Flowers
See: Horticultural Supplies

Artificial Turf
See: Recreational and Sporting
Goods

Artists' Equipment
See: Specialty Equipment and
Products

Arts and Crafts Books
See: Books and Other Printed
Materials

Asphalt Felts and Coatings
See: Construction Materials and
Machinery

Athletic Footwear
See: Shoes

Athletic Goods
See: Recreational and Sporting
Goods

Attache Cases
See: Luggage and Leather Goods

Audio Cabinets
See: Furniture and Fixtures

Audio Tapes for Recording
See: Sound and Entertainment
Equipment and Supplies

Auditorium Seating
See: Furniture and Fixtures

Automatic Controls
See: Scientific and Measurement
Devices

Automobile Carpeting
See: Floorcovering Equipment and
Supplies

Automobile Engines, New
See: Automotive

Automobile Engines, Used
See: Automotive

Automobile Parts, New
See: Automotive

Automobile Parts, Used
See: Automotive

Automobile Seat Covers
See: Automotive

Automobile Trimmings
See: Automotive

Automobiles
See: Motorized Vehicles

Automotive
(See also: Industrial Machinery;
Motorized Vehicles)

Automotive Accessories
See: Automotive

Automotive Air-Conditioning
Equipment
See: Automotive

Automotive Batteries
See: Automotive

Automotive Paints
See: Paints and Varnishes

Automotive Repair Books
See: Books and Other Printed
Materials

Automotive Stampings
See: Automotive

Automotive Switches, for Electrical
Circuitry
See: Automotive

Automotive Tools
See: Industrial Machinery

Awnings
See: Construction Materials and
Machinery

Axes
See: Hardware

Axial Fans
See: Electrical and Electronic
Equipment and Supplies

Baby Clothes
See: Clothing

Baby Furniture
See: Furniture and Fixtures

Baby Toys
See: Toys and Hobby Goods

Bags and Sacks
See: Storage Equipment and
Containers

Bakery Products
See: Food

Ball Bearings
See: Industrial Supplies

Balloons
See: Gifts and Novelties

Bandages and Tapes
See: Medical, Dental, and Optical
Supplies

Banjos
See: Sound and Entertainment
Equipment and Supplies

Banners
See: Gifts and Novelties

Barber and Beauty Shop Furniture and Equipment
See: Specialty Equipment and Products

Baseball Cards
See: Toys and Hobby Goods

Baseball and Softball Equipment
See: Recreational and Sporting Goods

Basketballs
See: Recreational and Sporting Goods

Baskets
See: Gifts and Novelties

Bathmats
See: Household Items

Bathroom Accessories
See: Household Items

Bathtub and Shower Fittings
See: Plumbing Materials and Fixtures

Bathtubs
See: Plumbing Materials and Fixtures

Batteries
See: Electrical and Electronic Equipment and Supplies

Battery Charging Alternators
See: Electrical and Electronic Equipment and Supplies

Batting
See: Textiles and Notions

Bayonets
See: Guns and Weapons

Beans
See: Food; Livestock and Farm Products

Bearings
See: Automotive

Beauty and Barber Shop Accessories
See: Health and Beauty Aids

Bedroom Furniture
See: Furniture and Fixtures

Beds
See: Furniture and Fixtures

Bedsets
See: Household Items

Bedsheets
See: Household Items

Bedspreads
See: Household Items

Bedsprings
See: Furniture and Fixtures

Beepers
See: Communications Systems and Equipment

Beer
See: Alcoholic Beverages

Belts
See: Clothing

Beverage Concentrates
See: Soft Drinks

Beverages
See: Soft Drinks; Alcoholic Beverages

Bicycle Carriers
See: Recreational and Sporting Goods

Bicycles and Parts
See: Recreational and Sporting Goods

Billiards Tables and Equipment
See: Recreational and Sporting Goods

Binding Machinery and Equipment
See: Specialty Equipment and Products

Binocular Cases
See: Luggage and Leather Goods

Binoculars
See: Scientific and Measurement Devices

Biscuits
See: Food

Black Powder Guns
See: Guns and Weapons

Blankets
See: Household Items

Blasting Accessories
See: Explosives

Bleachers
See: Furniture and Fixtures

Blinds
See: Household Items

Blood and Plasma
See: Medical, Dental, and Optical Supplies

Blouses
See: Clothing

Blowers and Fans, for Motor Vehicles
See: Automotive

Blueprinting Equipment
See: Specialty Equipment and Products

Board Games
See: Toys and Hobby Goods

Boating Equipment
See: Marine; Recreational and Sporting Goods

Boats
See: Marine

Boilers
See: Heating and Cooling Equipment and Supplies

Bolts
See: Hardware

Books and Other Printed Materials

Boring Machines
See: Industrial Machinery

Botanicals
See: Health and Beauty Aids

Bottled Drinks
See: Soft Drinks

Bottled Water
See: Soft Drinks

Bottles
See: Storage Equipment and Containers

Bovine Semen
See: Livestock and Farm Products

Bowling Alleys and Machinery
See: Recreational and Sporting Goods

Bowling Equipment
See: Recreational and Sporting Goods

Boxcars
See: Railroad Equipment and Supplies

Boxes

See: Paper and Paper Products;
Storage Equipment and
Containers

Braces, Orthopedic
(*See also:* Medical, Dental, and
Optical Equipment)

Braiding
See: Textiles and Notions

Brake Parts and Assemblies
See: Automotive

Brandy
See: Alcoholic Beverages

Brasses
See: Metals

Bread
See: Food

Breakfast Cereals
See: Food

Bridal Gowns
See: Clothing

Bridesmaids' Dresses
See: Clothing

Briefcases
See: Luggage and Leather Goods

Bristles
See: Livestock and Farm Products

Broadcast Equipment
See: Communications Systems
and Equipment

Bronze
See: Metals

Brooches
See: Jewelry

Broomcorn
See: Livestock and Farm Products

Brushes
See: Health and Beauty Aids;
Hardware

Buffers
See: Industrial Machinery

Builders' Hardware
See: Construction Materials and
Machinery; Hardware

Building Toys
See: Toys and Hobby Goods

Bullets
See: Guns and Weapons

Burlap

See: Textiles and Notions

Buses
See: Motorized Vehicles

Business and Economics Books
See: Books and Other Printed
Materials

Business Forms
See: Paper and Paper Products;
Office Equipment and Supplies

Business Machines
See: Office Equipment and
Supplies

Business Service Publications
See: Books and Other Printed
Materials

Butane Gas
See: Petroleum, Fuels, and
Related Equipment

Butter and Margarine
See: Food

Buttons
See: Textiles and Notions

Cabinetry Supplies
See: Construction Materials and
Machinery

Cabinets
See: Furniture and Fixtures

Cable Conduit
See: Electrical and Electronic
Equipment and Supplies

Cables
See: Electrical and Electronic
Equipment and Supplies; Industrial
Supplies

Cabooses
See: Railroad Equipment and
Supplies

Cake Decorations
See: Food

Calculators
See: Office Equipment and
Supplies

Calendars
See: Books and Other Printed
Materials

Camcorders
See: Photographic Equipment and
Supplies

Camera Cases

See: Luggage and Leather Goods;
Photographic Equipment and
Supplies

Cameras
See: Photographic Equipment and
Supplies

Camping Tents and Equipment
See: Recreational and Sporting
Goods

Candles
See: Household Items

Candy
See: Food

Canes
See: Gifts and Novelties

Canned Foods
See: Food

Canned Milk
See: Food

Canning Machinery
See: Specialty Equipment and
Products

Canvas and Related Products
See: Textiles and Notions

Capacitors
See: Electrical and Electronic
Equipment and Supplies

Caps
See: Clothing

Caps & Gowns
See: Clothing

Car Phones
See: Communications Systems
and Equipment

Carbon Black
See: Minerals and Ores

Carburetors
See: Automotive

Cards
See: Paper and Paper Products

**Carnival and Amusement Park
Equipment**
See: Recreational and Sporting
Goods

Carpet Cleaning Supplies
See: Floorcovering Equipment and
Supplies

Carpet Installation Supplies

See: Floorcovering Equipment and
Supplies

Carpet Supplies
See: Floorcovering Equipment and
Supplies

Carpet Tiles
See: Floorcovering Equipment and
Supplies

Carpeting
See: Floorcovering Equipment and
Supplies

Carpets
See: Floorcovering Equipment and
Supplies; Household Items

Cars
See: Motorized Vehicles

Cartons for Beverages
See: Paper and Paper Products

Carts
See: Industrial Machinery

Cash Registers
See: Office Equipment and
Supplies

Cast and Wrought Iron Hammocks
See: Furniture and Fixtures

Castings
See: Metals

Casual Shoes
See: Shoes

Cat Food
See: Veterinary Products

Catalogs
See: Books and Other Printed
Materials

Cattle
See: Livestock and Farm Products

Caulking Compounds
See: Adhesives

Caustic Soda
See: Minerals and Ores

CDRom Players
See: Sound and Entertainment
Equipment and Supplies

Cellular Telephones
See: Communications Systems
and Equipment

Cement

See: Construction Materials and
Machinery

Ceramic Wall and Floor Tiles
See: Floorcovering Equipment and
Supplies

Chain Saws
See: Hardware

Chairs
See: Furniture and Fixtures

Cheese, Natural and Process
See: Food

Chemical Fire Extinguishing
Equipment
See: Security and Safety
Equipment

Chemical Food Additives
See: Chemicals

Chemical Preparations
See: Chemicals

Chemical Products
See: Chemicals

Chemicals

Chests
See: Furniture and Fixtures

Chewing Gum
See: Food

Chewing Tobacco
See: Tobacco Products

Chickens
See: Livestock and Farm Products

Chicks
See: Livestock and Farm Products

Children's Books
See: Books and Other Printed
Materials

Children's Shoes
See: Shoes

China
See: Household Items

Chisels
See: Hardware

Chlorine
See: Chemicals

Chocolate
See: Food

Christmas Ornaments and

Decorations
See: Gifts and Novelties

Christmas Tree Lights
See: Gifts and Novelties

Christmas Trees
See: Wood and Wood Products

Chucks
See: Hardware

Cider
See: Food

Cigarettes
See: Tobacco Products

Cigars
See: Tobacco Products

Circuit Boards
See: Electrical and Electronic
Equipment and Supplies

Circuit Breakers
See: Electrical and Electronic
Equipment and Supplies

Citizens' Band Radios
See: Communications Systems
and Equipment

Civil War Items
See: Toys and Hobby Goods

Cleaning and Janitorial Supplies

Clocks
See: Household Items

Closet Organizers
See: Household Items

Clothes Dryers
See: Household Appliances

Clothes Washing Machines
See: Household Appliances

Clothing

Coal
See: Minerals and Ores

Coal Tar Products
See: Minerals and Ores

Coated Fabrics
See: Textiles and Notions

Coated Paper Rolls and Sheets
See: Paper and Paper Products

Coatings
See: Paints and Varnishes

Coats

See: Clothing

Cocktail Mixes
See: Alcoholic Beverages

Cocktails
See: Alcoholic Beverages

Cocoa Products
See: Food

Coffee
See: Food; Soft Drinks

Coin-Operated Game Machines
See: Recreational and Sporting
Goods

Coke
See: Minerals and Ores

Cold Remedies
See: Medical, Dental, and Optical
Supplies

Cold-Rolled Steel
See: Metals

Collectors' Miniatures
See: Gifts and Novelties

College Jewelry and Emblems
See: Jewelry

Combines
See: Agricultural Equipment and
Supplies

Combs
See: Health and Beauty Aids

Comic Books
See: Books and Other Printed
Materials

Commercial and Industrial Garbage
and Trash Compactors
See: Specialty Equipment and
Products

Commercial Cooking and Food
Warming Equipment
See: Restaurant and Commercial
Foodservice Equipment and
Supplies

Commercial Fishing Equipment
See: Marine

Commercial Food Products
Machinery
See: Restaurant and Commercial
Foodservice Equipment and
Supplies

Commercial Lighting Fixtures
See: Furniture and Fixtures

Commercial Refrigerators

See: Restaurant and Commercial
Foodservice Equipment and
Supplies

Communications Systems and
Equipment

Compact Disc Players
See: Sound and Entertainment
Equipment and Supplies

Compact Discs
See: Sound and Entertainment
Equipment and Supplies

Components for Stationary Buildings
See: Construction Materials and
Machinery

Compressed Air and Gas Dryers
See: Industrial Machinery

Compressors

Computer Accessories
See: Computers and Software

Computer Books
See: Books and Other Printed
Materials

Computer Paper
See: Paper and Paper Products

Computer Parts
See: Computers and Software

Computer Printers
See: Computers and Software

Computer Terminals
See: Computers and Software

Computers and Software

Concrete Additives
See: Construction Materials and
Machinery

Concrete Products Machinery
See: Industrial Machinery

Conduit and Conduit Fittings
See: Electrical and Electronic
Equipment and Supplies

Confections
See: Food

Construction Machinery
See: Construction Materials and
Machinery

Construction Materials and Machinery

Construction Paper

See: Paper and Paper Products

Control and Signal Wire and Cable
See: Industrial Supplies

Control System Instruments
See: Scientific and Measurement
Devices

Controlling Instruments and
Accessories
See: Scientific and Measurement
Devices

Conveyors and Conveying Equipment
See: Industrial Machinery

Cookbooks
See: Books and Other Printed
Materials

Cookies
See: Food

Cooking Appliances
See: Household Appliances

Copper and Copper-Based Alloy
Pipes and Tubes
See: Metals

Copper Ore
See: Minerals and Ores

Copper Sheets
See: Metals

Copying Machines and Supplies
See: Office Equipment and
Supplies

Cordials
See: Alcoholic Beverages

Corn
See: Livestock and Farm Products

Corrugated and Solid Fiber Boxes
See: Paper and Paper Products

Cosmetics
See: Health and Beauty Aids

Costume Jewelry
See: Jewelry

Costumes
See: Clothing

Cotton
See: Livestock and Farm Products

Cotton Fabrics, Finished
See: Textiles and Notions

Couches

See: Furniture and Fixtures

Countertops
See: Construction Materials and Machinery

Counting Devices
See: Scientific and Measurement Devices

Coveralls
See: Clothing

Crackers
See: Food

Craft Kits
See: Toys and Hobby Goods

Craft Supplies
See: Toys and Hobby Goods

Cranes
See: Industrial Machinery

Crates
See: Storage Equipment and Containers

Crayons
See: Office Equipment and Supplies

Cream
See: Food

Crepe and Machine-Creped Paper
See: Paper and Paper Products

Crop Preparation Machines
See: Agricultural Equipment and Supplies

Crude Oil
See: Petroleum, Fuels, and Related Equipment

Cured and Smoked Meats
See: Food

Curtains
See: Household Items

Custom Cabinets and Cabinetwork
See: Construction Materials and Machinery; Furniture and Fixtures

Custom Continuous Forms
See: Paper and Paper Products

Custom Fabricated Metal Tanks and Vessels
See: Metals; Storage Equipment and Containers

Cutlery
See: Household Items

Cutting Machine Tools

See: Industrial Machinery

Cyanide
See: Chemicals

Dairy Products
See: Food

Data Conversion Equipment
See: Computers and Software

Davenports
See: Furniture and Fixtures

Dehumidifiers
See: Household Appliances

Den Furniture
See: Furniture and Fixtures

Desks
See: Furniture and Fixtures; Office Equipment and Supplies

Detergents
See: Cleaning and Janitorial Supplies

Diagnostic Apparatus
See: Medical, Dental, and Optical Equipment; Scientific and Measurement Devices

Diamonds, for Jewelry Purposes
See: Jewelry

Dictaphones
See: Office Equipment and Supplies

Die-Cut Paper and Board
See: Paper and Paper Products

Dies
See: Industrial Supplies

Diesel
See: Petroleum, Fuels, and Related Equipment

Diesel Engines
See: Automotive

Dining Furniture
See: Furniture and Fixtures

Dishes
See: Household Items

Dishwashing Machines
See: Household Appliances

Disinfection Equipment
See: Medical, Dental, and Optical Equipment

Disposable Plastic Bags

See: Plastics

Disposable Plastic Cups
See: Plastics

Disposable Plastic Dishes
See: Plastics

Disposable Plastic Eating Utensils
See: Plastics

Disposable Plastic Shipping Supplies
See: Plastics

Distribution Panels
See: Electrical and Electronic Equipment and Supplies

Dog Food
See: Veterinary Products

Doll Clothes and Accessories
See: Toys and Hobby Goods

Dolls
See: Toys and Hobby Goods

Doors and Door Frames
See: Construction Materials and Machinery

Doughnuts
See: Food

Drafting Instruments and Tables
See: Specialty Equipment and Products

Draperies
See: Household Items

Drapery Material
See: Textiles and Notions

Dress Shoes
See: Shoes

Dressed Furs
See: Luggage and Leather Goods; Livestock and Farm Products

Dressers
See: Furniture and Fixtures

Dresses
See: Clothing

Dried and Dehydrated Food Products
See: Food

Dried and Dehydrated Fruits
See: Food

Dried Beet Pulp
See: Livestock and Farm Products
Dried Milk Products
See: Food

Drill Bits
See: Hardware

Drilling Machines
See: Industrial Machinery

Drilling Mud
See: Petroleum, Fuels, and
Related Equipment

Drills
See: Hardware; Industrial
Machinery

Drive Train Components
See: Automotive

Drums
See: Sound and Entertainment
Equipment and Supplies

Dry Bakery Products
See: Food

Dry Beans
See: Livestock and Farm Products;
Food

Dry Cleaning Chemicals
See: Cleaning and Janitorial
Supplies

Dry Cleaning Equipment
See: Cleaning and Janitorial
Supplies

Dry Ice
See: Chemicals

Dryers
See: Household Appliances

Dunnage
See: Marine

Dust Collection Equipment for
Heating and Cooling
See: Heating and Cooling
Equipment and Supplies

Dynamite
See: Explosives

Earrings
See: Jewelry

Educational Games and Toys
See: Toys and Hobby Goods

Eggs
See: Food

Electric Blankets
See: Household Items

Electric Fans
See: Electrical and Electronic
Equipment and Supplies

Electric Garbage Disposals
See: Household Appliances

Electric Hand Tools
See: Hardware

Electric Motors
See: Electrical and Electronic
Equipment and Supplies

Electric Water Heaters
See: Household Appliances

Electrical and Electronic Equipment
and Supplies

Electrical Housewares
See: Household Appliances

Electrical Insulators
See: Electrical and Electronic
Equipment and Supplies

Electronic Coils and Transformers
See: Electrical and Electronic
Equipment and Supplies

Electronic Components
See: Electrical and Electronic
Equipment and Supplies

Electronic Equipment and Supplies
See: Electrical and Electronic
Equipment and Supplies

Electronic Games
See: Toys and Hobby Goods

Electronic Ignitions
See: Automotive

Electronic Musical Instruments
See: Sound and Entertainment
Equipment and Supplies

Electronic Resistors
See: Electrical and Electronic
Equipment and Supplies

Electronic Security Systems
See: Security and Safety
Equipment

Electronic Systems and Equipment
See: Electrical and Electronic
Equipment and Supplies

Electronic Wire and Cable
See: Electrical and Electronic
Equipment and Supplies

Embossing Seals
See: Gifts and Novelties

Embroidery and Embroidery
Supplies
See: Textiles and Notions

Enameled Iron and Metal Plumbing
Fixtures
See: Plumbing Materials and
Fixtures

Enamels
See: Paints and Varnishes

Engine Electrical Equipment Parts
See: Automotive

Engineering Instruments
See: Scientific and Measurement
Devices

Engraving
See: Gifts and Novelties

Entertainment Center Cabinets
See: Furniture and Fixtures

Entertainment Lighting Equipment
See: Sound and Entertainment
Equipment and Supplies

Envelopes
See: Paper and Paper Products

Essential Oils
See: Health and Beauty Aids

Ethyl Alcohol
See: Chemicals

Evaporated Salt
See: Chemicals

Exercise Equipment
See: Recreational and Sporting
Goods

Exhaust System Parts
See: Automotive

Explosives

Extension Planks
See: Industrial Machinery

Extracts
See: Food

Extruded Aluminum Rod, Bar, and
Other Shapes
See: Metals

Eye Glasses
See: Medical, Dental, and Optical
Supplies

Fabricated Manmade Fiber Products
See: Textiles and Notions

Fabricated Rubber Products
See: Rubber

Fabricated Steel Plate
See: Metals

Fabrics
See: Textiles and Notions

Facsimile Machines
See: Office Equipment and
Supplies

Family Room Furniture
See: Furniture and Fixtures

Farm Equipment
See: Agricultural Equipment and
Supplies

Farm Machinery
See: Agricultural Equipment and
Supplies

Farm Supplies
See: Agricultural Equipment and
Supplies

Fasteners
See: Hardware

Fax Machines
See: Office Equipment and
Supplies

Feathers
See: Livestock and Farm Products

Feed
See: Veterinary Products;
Agricultural Equipment and
Supplies

Felt
See: Textiles and Notions

Fencing and Fence Gates
See: Agricultural Equipment and
Supplies; Construction Materials
and Machinery

Ferroalloys
See: Metals

Fertilizers
See: Agricultural Equipment and
Supplies

Fiber Optic Cable
See: Electrical and Electronic
Equipment and Supplies

Fiberglass
See: Construction Materials and
Machinery

Fiction Books
See: Books and Other Printed
Materials

Field Beans
See: Livestock and Farm Products

Fifth Wheel Travel Trailers
See: Motorized Vehicles

Figurines
See: Gifts and Novelties

Files
See: Medical, Dental, and Optical
Supplies; Office Equipment and
Supplies

Film
See: Photographic Equipment and
Supplies

Film Developing Equipment
See: Photographic Equipment and
Supplies

Films
See: Sound and Entertainment
Equipment and Supplies

Filters
See: Photographic Equipment and
Supplies; Paper and Paper
Products; Scientific and

Filters, for Internal Combustion
Engines
See: Automotive

Filtration Equipment
See: Specialty Equipment and
Products

Fire Alarms
See: Security and Safety
Equipment

Fire Control Equipment
See: Security and Safety
Equipment

Fire Extinguishers
See: Security and Safety
Equipment

Fire Sighting Equipment
See: Security and Safety
Equipment

Fire Tracking Equipment
See: Security and Safety
Equipment

Firearms
See: Guns and Weapons

Firefighting Equipment
See: Security and Safety
Equipment

Fireplaces
See: Construction Materials and
Machinery

Firewood
See: Wood and Wood Products

First-Aid Kits
See: Security and Safety
Equipment; Medical, Dental, and
Optical Supplies

Fish Locators
See: Marine

Fishing Tackle and Equipment
See: Recreational and Sporting
Goods; Marine

Fittings
See: Hardware

Flags
See: Gifts and Novelties

Flanges
See: Hardware

Flashlights
See: Hardware

Flat Metal Strapping
See: Metals

Flatware
See: Household Items

Flavorings
See: Food

Floor Tile, All Types
See: Floorcovering Equipment and
Supplies

Floor Underlayment
See: Floorcovering Equipment and
Supplies

Floorcovering Equipment and
Supplies
(*See also:* Household Items)

Floriculture
See: Horticultural Supplies

Florists' Supplies
See: Horticultural Supplies

Flour
See: Food

Flower Pots
See: Horticultural Supplies

Flowers
See: Horticultural Supplies

Fluorescent Lamp Ballasts
See: Furniture and Fixtures

Folding Boxes
See: Paper and Paper Products

Food

Food Additives
See: Chemicals

Food Broker
See: Food

Food Preparations
See: Food

Food Preservatives
See: Chemicals

Food Products Machinery
See: Restaurant and Commercial
Foodservice Equipment and
Supplies

Football Equipment and Clothing
See: Recreational and Sporting
Goods

Footwear
See: Shoes

Foreign Language Books
See: Books and Other Printed
Materials

Forklifts
See: Industrial Machinery

Foundry Supplies
See: Industrial Supplies

Fraternal Jewelry and Emblems
See: Jewelry

Fresh Flowers
See: Horticultural Supplies

Frozen Foods
See: Food

Frozen Juices
See: Food

Fruit
See: Food

Fruit and Berry Wines
See: Alcoholic Beverages

Fruit Juices
See: Food

Fuel Oil
See: Petroleum, Fuels, and
Related Equipment

Furniture and Fixtures

Furniture Hardware
See: Hardware

Furniture Wax
See: Petroleum, Fuels, and
Related Equipment

Furs
See: Luggage and Leather Goods;
Clothing

Furs, Raw
See: Livestock and Farm Products

Fuses and Fuse Equipment
See: Electrical and Electronic
Equipment and Supplies

Galvanized or Other Coated Sheets
See: Metals

Galvanized Steel
See: Metals

Game Machines
See: Recreational and Sporting
Goods

Garbage Compactors
See: Specialty Equipment and
Products

Garbage Disposals
See: Household Appliances

Garden Hose, Rubber and Plastic
See: Agricultural Equipment and
Supplies

Garden Tools
See: Agricultural Equipment and
Supplies

Gardening Books
See: Books and Other Printed
Materials

Gas Compressors
See: Compressors

Gas Cylinders
See: Industrial Supplies

Gas Generator Sets
See: Industrial Machinery

Gases
See: Industrial Supplies

Gaskets
See: Industrial Supplies

Gasoline
See: Petroleum, Fuels, and
Related Equipment

Gasoline Engines and Parts
See: Automotive

Gauges
See: Hardware; Scientific and
Measurement Devices

Gears
See: Industrial Supplies

Gelatin
See: Food

Gemstones
See: Jewelry

General Industrial Machinery
See: Industrial Machinery

Generators
See: Electrical and Electronic
Equipment and Supplies

Gift Wrap Paper
See: Paper and Paper Products

Gifts and Novelties

Glass
See: Construction Materials and
Machinery

Glass Containers
See: Storage Equipment and
Containers

Glass Products
See: Household Items

Glasses
See: Medical, Dental, and Optical
Supplies

Glassware
See: Household Items

Glazing Compounds
See: Adhesives

Gloves
See: Clothing

Glue
See: Adhesives

Goats
See: Livestock and Farm Products

Go-Carts
See: Recreational and Sporting
Goods

Gold Jewelry
See: Jewelry

Gold Ore
See: Minerals and Ores

Gold Plate Jewelry
See: Jewelry

Golf Equipment
See: Recreational and Sporting
Goods

Grain
See: Livestock and Farm Products

Grain Elevator
See: Livestock and Farm Products

Grains
See: Food

Graphic Arts Supplies
See: Specialty Equipment and
Products

Greases
See: Petroleum, Fuels, and
Related Equipment

Greeting Cards
See: Paper and Paper Products

Grinders
See: Industrial Machinery

Grocery Bags and Sacks
See: Paper and Paper Products

Grommets
See: Hardware

Guitars
See: Sound and Entertainment
Equipment and Supplies

Gum
See: Food

Gummed Products
See: Adhesives

Guns and Weapons

Gymnasium Equipment
See: Recreational and Sporting
Goods

Hair Accessories
See: Health and Beauty Aids

Hair Preparations
See: Health and Beauty Aids

Hairbrushes
See: Health and Beauty Aids

Hammers
See: Hardware

Hand Stamps
See: Office Equipment and
Supplies

Hand Tools
See: Hardware

Handbags
See: Luggage and Leather Goods

Handles
See: Hardware

Hardware
(See also: Industrial Machinery;
Industrial Supplies)

Hardwood Flooring
See: Floorcovering Equipment and
Supplies

Harness Equipment, Electronic
See: Electrical and Electronic
Equipment and Supplies

Hassocks
See: Furniture and Fixtures

Hatchets
See: Hardware

Hats
See: Clothing

Health and Beauty Aids
(See also: Medical, Dental, and
Optical Equipment; Medical,
Dental, and Optical

Health Foods
See: Food; Health and Beauty Aids

Heat Pumps
See: Heating and Cooling
Equipment and Supplies

Heating and Cooling Equipment and
Supplies
(See also: Automotive)

Heating Equipment
See: Heating and Cooling
Equipment and Supplies

Heavy Chemicals
See: Chemicals

Heavy Forged Tools
See: Industrial Machinery

Heavy Moving Equipment
See: Industrial Machinery

Helmets
See: Recreational and Sporting
Goods

Herbicides
See: Agricultural Equipment and
Supplies; Chemicals

Hides
See: Livestock and Farm Products;
Luggage and Leather Goods

History Books
See: Books and Other Printed
Materials

Hobby Kits
See: Toys and Hobby Goods

Hogs
See: Livestock and Farm Products

Hoists
See: Industrial Machinery

Holiday Decorations
See: Gifts and Novelties

Hominy
See: Food

Honers
See: Industrial Machinery

Hops
See: Livestock and Farm Products;
Food

Horses
See: Livestock and Farm Products

Horticultural Supplies

Hoses
See: Industrial Supplies

Hosiery
See: Clothing

Hospital Beds
See: Medical, Dental, and Optical
Equipment

Hospital Food
See: Food; Restaurant and
Commercial Foodservice
Equipment and Supplies

Hospital Furniture
See: Medical, Dental, and Optical
Equipment

Hospital Gowns
See: Clothing; Medical, Dental,
and Optical Supplies

Hospital Linens
See: Medical, Dental, and Optical
Supplies

Hot-Rolled Steel
See: Metals

Hot Tubs
See: Recreational and Sporting

Goods

Hotel and Motel Furniture
See: Furniture and Fixtures

Household Appliances
(See also: Sound and Entertainment Equipment and Supplies; Restaurant and Commercial

Household Carpeting
See: Floorcovering Equipment and Supplies

Household Chemicals
See: Chemicals

Household Items

Household Utensils
See: Household Items

Household Water Systems
See: Plumbing Materials and Fixtures

Humidifiers
See: Household Appliances

Humor Books
See: Books and Other Printed Materials

Hunting Equipment
See: Recreational and Sporting Goods

Hydraulic Barber and Beauty Shop Chairs
See: Specialty Equipment and Products

Hydraulic Fluid Power Systems
See: Industrial Machinery

Hydraulic Fluid Power Pumps, Motors, and Hydrostatic
See: Industrial Machinery

Hydraulic Generator Sets
See: Heating and Cooling Equipment and Supplies

Hydraulic Parts
See: Industrial Supplies

Ice
See: Soft Drinks

Ice Cream
See: Food

Ice Makers
See: Household Appliances

Incinerators
See: Specialty Equipment and

Products

Indicators
See: Scientific and Measurement Devices

Industrial Alcohol
See: Chemicals

Industrial Belting and Packing Hose
See: Industrial Supplies

Industrial Brushes
See: Industrial Supplies

Industrial Chemicals
See: Chemicals

Industrial Controls
See: Industrial Machinery; Scientific and Measurement Devices

Industrial Converting Paper
See: Paper and Paper Products

Industrial Diamonds
See: Industrial Supplies

Industrial Dryers
See: Industrial Machinery

Industrial Fabrics
See: Textiles and Notions

Industrial Gases
See: Industrial Supplies

Industrial Lighting Fixtures
See: Furniture and Fixtures

Industrial Machinery
(See also: Automotive; Compressors; Hardware; Industrial Supplies

Industrial Motor Controls
See: Industrial Machinery

Industrial Organic Chemicals
See: Chemicals

Industrial Rubber Products
See: Rubber

Industrial Safety Devices
See: Security and Safety Equipment; Industrial Supplies

Industrial Salts
See: Chemicals

Industrial Sewing Machinery
See: Industrial Machinery

Industrial Solvents
See: Chemicals

Industrial Supplies
(See also: Hardware; Industrial Machinery)

Industrial Transmissions
See: Industrial Machinery

Infants' Clothing
See: Clothing

Inflatable Athletic Balls
See: Recreational and Sporting Goods

Inflatable Boats
See: Marine

Ingots
See: Metals

Inked Ribbons
See: Office Equipment and Supplies

Insecticides
See: Agricultural Equipment and Supplies; Chemicals

Institutional Food
See: Food; Restaurant and Commercial Foodservice Equipment and Supplies

Insulation
See: Construction Materials and Machinery

Integrating Meters for Gas and Liquids
See: Scientific and Measurement Devices

Intercommunication Equipment
See: Communications Systems and Equipment

Iron and Steel Semi-Finished Products
See: Metals

Iron Ore
See: Minerals and Ores

Irons
See: Household Appliances

Irrigation Equipment and Supplies
See: Agricultural Equipment and Supplies

Italian Food Specialties
See: Food

Jackets
See: Clothing

Jams, Jellies, and Preserves
See: Food

Janitorial Supplies
See: Cleaning and Janitorial
Supplies

Jeans
See: Clothing

Jetskis
See: Marine

Jewelers' Findings
See: Jewelry

Jewelers' Materials
See: Jewelry

Jewelry

Jewelry Boxes and Cases
See: Jewelry

Journals
See: Books and Other Printed
Materials

Jumpsuits
See: Clothing

Karaoke Machines
See: Sound and Entertainment
Equipment and Supplies

Kerosene
See: Petroleum, Fuels, and
Related Equipment

Ketchup
See: Food

Kitchen Cabinets
See: Construction Materials and
Machinery

Kitchen Furniture
See: Furniture and Fixtures

Kitchenware
See: Household Items

Knives
See: Household Items; Industrial
Supplies

Kosher Foods
See: Food

Kraft Packaging and Converting
Paperboard
See: Paper and Paper Products

Labels
See: Paper and Paper Products

Laboratory Supplies
See: Scientific and Measurement
Devices

Lace and Net Goods
See: Textiles and Notions

Lacquers
See: Paints and Varnishes

Ladders
See: Industrial Supplies

Laminates
See: Construction Materials and
Machinery

Lamps
See: Household Items; Furniture
and Fixtures

Lampshades
See: Household Items

Land Transportation Motors
See: Automotive

Landscaping Equipment and
Supplies
See: Agricultural Equipment and
Supplies

Laser Disks
See: Sound and Entertainment
Equipment and Supplies

Lathes
See: Industrial Machinery

Laundry Equipment and Supplies
See: Cleaning and Janitorial
Supplies

Laundry Soap, Chips, and Powder
See: Cleaning and Janitorial
Supplies

Law Books
See: Books and Other Printed
Materials

Lawn and Garden Equipment
See: Agricultural Equipment and
Supplies

Lawn Furniture
See: Furniture and Fixtures

Lawn Games Equipment
See: Recreational and Sporting
Goods

Lawn Mowers
See: Agricultural Equipment and
Supplies

Lead Ore
See: Minerals and Ores

Leaded Brasses
See: Metals

Leaf Tobacco
See: Tobacco Products

Leather Clothing
See: Clothing; Luggage and
Leather Goods

Leather Coats and Jackets
See: Clothing; Luggage and
Leather Goods

Library Furniture
See: Furniture and Fixtures

Lighting Equipment
See: Electrical and Electronic
Equipment and Supplies

Limestone
See: Agricultural Equipment and
Supplies

Linens
See: Household Items

Lingerie
See: Clothing

Liquefied Petroleum Gas
See: Petroleum, Fuels, and
Related Equipment

Liqueurs
See: Alcoholic Beverages

Liquid Chillers
See: Household Appliances

Liquor
See: Alcoholic Beverages

Listers
See: Hardware

Livestock and Farm Products
(See also: Agricultural Equipment
and Supplies; Food)

Living Room Furniture
See: Furniture and Fixtures

Lockers
See: Furniture and Fixtures

Locks
See: Security and Safety
Equipment

Locomotives
See: Railroad Equipment and
Supplies

Logs
See: Wood and Wood Products

Looseleaf Binders
See: Office Equipment and
Supplies

Lotions
See: Medical, Dental, and Optical

Supplies

Loveseats
See: Furniture and Fixtures

LP Gas
See: Petroleum, Fuels, and
Related Equipment

Lubricants
See: Petroleum, Fuels, and
Related Equipment

Luggage and Leather Goods

Lumber
See: Construction Materials and
Machinery

Lunchboxes
See: Office Equipment and
Supplies

Machine Tools
See: Industrial Machinery

Magazines
See: Books and Other Printed
Materials

Magnesium
See: Metals

Malt Beverages
See: Alcoholic Beverages; Food

Mandolins
See: Sound and Entertainment
Equipment and Supplies

Manganese
See: Minerals and Ores

Manmade Fabrics
See: Textiles and Notions

Manmade Fiber Thread
See: Textiles and Notions

Maps
See: Books and Other Printed
Materials

Marine

Marine Paints
See: Paints and Varnishes

Marine Propulsion Machinery and
Equipment
See: Marine

Markers
See: Office Equipment and
Supplies

Masonry Cement
See: Construction Materials and

Machinery

Masonry Materials
See: Construction Materials and
Machinery

Material Handling Equipment
See: Industrial Machinery

Math Books
See: Books and Other Printed
Materials

Mattresses
See: Furniture and Fixtures

Mayonnaise
See: Food

Measuring Tools
See: Scientific and Measurement
Devices

Meat
See: Food

Media-to-Media Data Conversion
Equipment
See: Computers and Software

Medical Books
See: Books and Other Printed
Materials

Medical, Dental, and Optical
Equipment
(*See also:* Medical, Dental, and
Optical Supplies; Health and
Beauty

Medical Gases
See: Medical, Dental, and Optical
Supplies

Medical, Dental, and Optical
Supplies
(*See also:* Medical, Dental, and
Optical Equipment; Health and
Beauty

Medicinals
See: Medical, Dental, and Optical
Supplies

Medicine Cabinets
See: Furniture and Fixtures

Men's Shoes
See: Shoes

Metal Cleaning Machinery
See: Industrial Machinery

Metal Cutting Shears
See: Industrial Supplies

Metal Degreasing Machinery
See: Industrial Machinery

Metal Drying Machinery
See: Industrial Machinery

Metal Finishing Machinery
See: Industrial Machinery

Metal Furniture
See: Furniture and Fixtures

Metal Polishes
See: Paints and Varnishes

Metal Roofing
See: Construction Materials and
Machinery

Metal Salts
See: Chemicals

Metal Strapping
See: Metals

Metal Tubing
See: Metals

Metallic Concentrates
See: Metals

Metallic Ores
See: Minerals and Ores

Metals

Metaphysical Publications
See: Books and Other Printed
Materials

Mexican Food Specialties
See: Food

Microcomputers
See: Computers and Software

Microfilming Equipment
See: Photographic Equipment and
Supplies

Microphones
See: Communications Systems
and Equipment

Microprocessors
See: Computers and Software

Microscopes
See: Scientific and Measurement
Devices

Milk
See: Food

Milking Machinery
See: Agricultural Equipment and
Supplies

Milling Machines
See: Industrial Machinery

Milo
See: Livestock and Farm Products

Mimeograph Paper
See: Paper and Paper Products

Mineral Supplements
See: Health and Beauty Aids

Minerals and Ores

Mining Machinery
See: Specialty Equipment and Products

Mirror and Picture Frames
See: Gifts and Novelties

Mirrors
See: Gifts and Novelties

Miscellaneous End-use Chemicals
See: Chemicals

Mittens
See: Clothing

Mixers
See: Alcoholic Beverages

Mobile Home Decking
See: Construction Materials and Machinery

Mobile Telephones
See: Communications Systems and Equipment

Model Kits
See: Toys and Hobby Goods

Modems
See: Computers and Software

Mohair, raw
See: Livestock and Farm Products

Moss
See: Livestock and Farm Products

Mother-of-the-Bride Dresses
See: Clothing

Motion Picture Cameras
See: Photographic Equipment and Supplies

Motion Picture Equipment
See: Photographic Equipment and Supplies

Motor Scooters
See: Motorized Vehicles

Motor Vehicle Instruments
See: Automotive

Motor Vehicle Lighting Equipment
See: Automotive

Motor Vehicle Suspension Systems
See: Automotive

Motor Vehicle Wheels
See: Automotive

Motorcycle Parts
See: Automotive

Motorcycles
See: Motorized Vehicles

Motorized Vehicles
(See also: Automotive; Recreational and Sporting Goods)

Motors
See: Automotive

Mules
See: Livestock and Farm Products

Multicultural Studies Books
See: Books and Other Printed Materials

Music Books
See: Books and Other Printed Materials

Musical Instrument Cases
See: Luggage and Leather Goods

Musical Instruments and Parts
See: Sound and Entertainment Equipment and Supplies

Muskets
See: Guns and Weapons

Nails
See: Hardware

Naphtha
See: Petroleum, Fuels, and Related Equipment

Napkins
See: Household Items; Paper and Paper Products

Necklaces
See: Jewelry

Needles
See: Medical, Dental, and Optical Supplies; Textiles and Notions

Newspapers
See: Books and Other Printed Materials

Nickel
See: Metals

Nightwear
See: Clothing

Nitrous Oxide
See: Medical, Dental, and Optical Supplies

Non-Fiction Books
See: Books and Other Printed Materials

Nonalcoholic Beer
See: Alcoholic Beverages

Nonalcoholic Beverages
See: Soft Drinks

Nonelectric Heating Radiators and Parts
See: Heating and Cooling Equipment and Supplies

Nonelectronic Games
See: Toys and Hobby Goods

Nonmetallic Minerals and Concentrates
See: Minerals and Ores

Novelty Buttons and Pins
See: Gifts and Novelties

Novelty Glassware
See: Gifts and Novelties

Novelty T-Shirts
See: Gifts and Novelties

Nuts
See: Food; Hardware

O-Rings
See: Industrial Supplies

Oats
See: Livestock and Farm Products

Occupational Luggage
See: Luggage and Leather Goods

Odor Control Materials
See: Specialty Equipment and Products

Off-Highway Contractors' Wheeled Tractors
See: Motorized Vehicles

Office Equipment and Supplies
(See also: Computers and Software)

Office Furniture
See: Furniture and Fixtures; Office Equipment and Supplies

Office Machines
See: Office Equipment and

Supplies

Office Storage Units
See: Office Equipment and Supplies; Storage Equipment and Containers

Oil Kernals
See: Livestock and Farm Products

Oil Nuts
See: Livestock and Farm Products

Oil Refining Machinery, Equipment, and Supplies
See: Petroleum, Fuels, and Related Equipment

Oils
See: Petroleum, Fuels, and Related Equipment

Oils and Fats
See: Food

Oilseeds
See: Livestock and Farm Products

Ophthalmic Goods
See: Medical, Dental, and Optical Supplies

Organic Coatings, Enamels, and Lacquers
See: Paints and Varnishes

Orthodontic Brace Shields
See: Medical, Dental, and Optical Supplies

Orthopedic Appliances
See: Medical, Dental, and Optical Equipment

Orthopedic Braces
See: Medical, Dental, and Optical Equipment

Orthopedic Footwear
See: Shoes

Ottomans
See: Furniture and Fixtures

Outdoor Furniture
See: Furniture and Fixtures

Ovens
See: Household Appliances

Over-the-Counter Medications
See: Medical, Dental, and Optical Supplies

Overalls
See: Clothing

Overcoats
See: Clothing

Oxygen
See: Medical, Dental, and Optical Supplies

Packaging
See: Paper and Paper Products; Plastics

Paddings
See: Floorcovering Equipment and Supplies; Textiles and Notions

Pagers
See: Communications Systems and Equipment

Paint Brushes, Rollers, and Pads
See: Paints and Varnishes

Paint Spray Equipment
See: Paints and Varnishes

Paints and Varnishes

Pajamas
See: Clothing

Pallets
See: Storage Equipment and Containers

Panel Boards
See: Electrical and Electronic Equipment and Supplies

Paneling
See: Construction Materials and Machinery

Pans
See: Household Items

Paper and Paper Products

Paper Bags
See: Paper and Paper Products

Paper Business Machine Supplies
See: Paper and Paper Products

Paper Coating and Glazing
See: Paper and Paper Products

Paper Cups
See: Paper and Paper Products

Paper Napkins
See: Paper and Paper Products

Paper Novelties
See: Gifts and Novelties; Paper and Paper Products

Paper Plates
See: Paper and Paper Products

Paper Shipping Supplies
See: Paper and Paper Products

Paper Towels
See: Paper and Paper Products

Paperback Books
See: Books and Other Printed Materials

Parasols
See: Gifts and Novelties

Partitions and Fixtures
See: Furniture and Fixtures

Parts for Small Household Appliances
See: Household Appliances

Pasta
See: Food

Peanuts
See: Food

Pecans
See: Food

Pedometers
See: Scientific and Measurement Devices

Pelts
See: Livestock and Farm Products; Luggage and Leather Goods

Pencils
See: Office Equipment and Supplies

Pendants
See: Jewelry

Pens
See: Office Equipment and Supplies

Pepper
See: Food

Perfume
See: Health and Beauty Aids

Periodicals
See: Books and Other Printed Materials

Personal Computers
See: Computers and Software
Personal Goods
See: Health and Beauty Aids

Personal Industrial Safety Devices
See: Security and Safety Equipment; Industrial Supplies

Pesticides
See: Agricultural Equipment and Supplies

Pet Foods
See: Veterinary Products

Pet Supplies
See: Veterinary Products

Petroleum, Fuels, and Related Equipment

Pharmaceutical Preparations
See: Medical, Dental, and Optical Supplies

Phonograph Records
See: Sound and Entertainment Equipment and Supplies

Photo Albums
See: Gifts and Novelties

Photocopying Equipment and Supplies
See: Office Equipment and Supplies

Photographic Chemicals
See: Photographic Equipment and Supplies

Photographic Equipment and Supplies

Photographic Film, Plates, Paper, and Cloth
See: Photographic Equipment and Supplies

Photographic Printing Apparatus
See: Photographic Equipment and Supplies

Pianos
See: Sound and Entertainment Equipment and Supplies

Pickles and Pickled Products
See: Food

Picnic Tables
See: Furniture and Fixtures

Picks
See: Hardware

Picture Frames
See: Gifts and Novelties

Pies
See: Food

Pillows
See: Household Items

Pins

See: Textiles and Notions

Pipe and Fittings
See: Plumbing Materials and Fixtures

Pipe Tobacco
See: Tobacco Products

Pipes
See: Industrial Supplies; Tobacco Products; Plumbing Materials and Fixtures

Piping Unions
See: Plumbing Materials and Fixtures

Pistons
See: Automotive

Plant Food
See: Horticultural Supplies

Plasters
See: Construction Materials and Machinery

Plastic Belts and Belting
See: Plastics

Plastics

Plate Glass
See: Construction Materials and Machinery

Platinum Jewelry
See: Jewelry

Playground Equipment
See: Recreational and Sporting Goods

Pleasure Boats
See: Marine

Pliers
See: Hardware

Plows
See: Agricultural Equipment and Supplies

Plumbing and Heating Valves and Specialties
See: Plumbing Materials and Fixtures

Plumbing Fixtures
See: Plumbing Materials and Fixtures

Plumbing Materials and Fixtures

Plywood

See: Construction Materials and Machinery

Pneumatic Fluid Power Systems
See: Industrial Machinery

Pneumatic Parts
See: Industrial Supplies

Pneumatic Tires
See: Automotive

Poetry Books
See: Books and Other Printed Materials

Polishers
See: Industrial Machinery

Pollution Control Equipment
See: Specialty Equipment and Products

Polyester Fabrics
See: Textiles and Notions

Polyester Yarns
See: Textiles and Notions

Pool Equipment and Supplies
See: Recreational and Sporting Goods

Pool Tables and Equipment
See: Recreational and Sporting Goods

Pools
See: Recreational and Sporting Goods

Pop
See: Soft Drinks

Popcorn
See: Food

Porch Furniture
See: Furniture and Fixtures

Portable Sanitation Products
See: Cleaning and Janitorial Supplies

Postcards
See: Paper and Paper Products

Potato Chips
See: Food

Potatoes
See: Food

Potpourri
See: Gifts and Novelties

Pots

See: Household Items

Potted Plants
See: Horticultural Supplies

Pottery
See: Gifts and Novelties

Potting Soil
See: Horticultural Supplies

Poultry
See: Food

Power Hand Tools
See: Hardware

Power Regulators, Boosters,
Reactors
See: Electrical and Electronic
Equipment and Supplies

Power Roof Fans
See: Heating and Cooling
Equipment and Supplies

Power Roof Ventilation Systems
See: Heating and Cooling
Equipment and Supplies

Power Saw Blades
See: Industrial Supplies

Power Transmission Equipment and
Supplies
See: Automotive

Power Wire and Cable
See: Electrical and Electronic
Equipment

Precious Stones
See: Jewelry; Minerals and Ores

Precision Measuring Tools
See: Scientific and Measurement
Devices

Prefabricated Building Materials
See: Construction Materials and
Machinery

Prefabricated Wood Buildings and
Components
See: Construction Materials and
Machinery

Prepared Foods
See: Food

Prepared Sauces
See: Food

Prerecorded Audio Tapes
See: Sound and Entertainment
Equipment and Supplies

Prerecorded Cassettes
See: Sound and Entertainment
Equipment and Supplies

Prerecorded Video Disks
See: Sound and Entertainment
Equipment and Supplies

Prescription Sunglasses
See: Medical, Dental, and Optical
Supplies

Printers
See: Computers and Software

Printing Equipment and Supplies
See: Specialty Equipment and
Products

Printing Presses
See: Specialty Equipment and
Products

Product Finishes
See: Paints and Varnishes

Propeller Fans
See: Industrial Supplies

Protective Clothing
See: Clothing; Security and Safety
Equipment

Protective Equipment for Sports
See: Recreational and Sporting
Goods; Security and Safety
Equipment

Psychology Books
See: Books and Other Printed
Materials

Public Address Equipment
See: Communications Systems
and Equipment

Pumps, Valves, and Fittings
See: Industrial Machinery;
Plumbing Materials and Fixtures

Purses
See: Luggage and Leather Goods

Putty
See: Adhesives

Puzzles
See: Toys and Hobby Goods

Racks and Accessories
See: Storage Equipment and
Containers

Racquetball Equipment
See: Recreational and Sporting
Goods

Radiators
See: Automotive

Radio Parts and Accessories
See: Sound and Entertainment
Equipment and Supplies

Radio Receivers
See: Communications Systems
and Equipment; Sound and
Entertainment Equipment and
Supplies

Radios
See: Sound and Entertainment
Equipment and Supplies

Rags
See: Used, Scrap, and Recycled
Materials

Railroad Equipment and Supplies

Railroad Equipment
See: Railroad Equipment and
Supplies

Railroad Ties
See: Railroad Equipment and
Supplies

Railroad Track
See: Railroad Equipment and
Supplies

Rails and Accessories
See: Railroad Equipment and
Supplies; Metals

Raincoats
See: Clothing

Ranges
See: Household Appliances

Rasps
See: Hardware

Rayon
See: Textiles and Notions

Reamers
See: Hardware

Recording Cassettes
See: Sound and Entertainment
Equipment and Supplies

Recording Instruments and Accessories
See: Sound and Entertainment
Equipment and Supplies

Recording Machines
See: Sound and Entertainment

Equipment and Supplies

Recreational and Sporting Goods

Recreational Vehicle Air-Conditioning
Equipment
See: Automotive

Recreational Vehicle Stampings
See: Automotive

Recreational Vehicles
See: Motorized Vehicles; Automotive; Recreational and Sporting
Goods

Recycled Paper
See: Used, Scrap, and Recycled
Materials

Recycled Products
See: Used, Scrap, and Recycled
Materials

Recycled Oil
See: Used, Scrap, and Recycled
Materials

Recycling Equipment
See: Specialty Equipment and
Products; Used, Scrap, and
Recycled Materials

Reference Books
See: Books and Other Printed
Materials

Refrigeration and Air-Conditioning
Equipment
See: Heating and Cooling
Equipment and Supplies;
Household

Refrigerators
See: Household Appliances

Regulators
See: Electrical and Electronic
Equipment and Supplies

Reinforced Plastics
See: Plastics

Relays
See: Electrical and Electronic
Equipment and Supplies

Religious Books
See: Books and Other Printed
Materials

Residential Lighting Fixtures
See: Furniture and Fixtures

Resistance Welders
See: Industrial Machinery

Resistors

See: Electrical and Electronic
Equipment and Supplies

Restaurant, Cafeteria, and Bar
Furniture and Fixtures
See: Restaurant and Commercial
Foodservice Equipment and

Restaurant and Commercial
Foodservice Equipment and Supplies
(*See also:* Furniture and Fixtures)

Restaurant Equipment
See: Restaurant and Commercial
Foodservice Equipment and
Supplies

Restaurant Fixtures
See: Restaurant and Commercial
Foodservice Equipment and
Supplies

Restaurant Food
See: Food; Restaurant and
Commercial Foodservice
Equipment and Supplies

Restaurant Supplies
See: Restaurant and Commercial
Foodservice Equipment and
Supplies

RF Chokes
See: Electrical and Electronic
Equipment and Supplies

Ribbons
See: Textiles and Notions

Ribbons for Gifts
See: Gifts and Novelties

Rice
See: Food

Rifles
See: Guns and Weapons

Ring Mountings
See: Jewelry

Rings
See: Jewelry

Rivets
See: Hardware

Robes
See: Clothing

Rods
See: Hardware; Metals; Automotive

Rolled and Drawn Nonferrous Metals
See: Metals

Roof Drainage Equipment

See: Construction Materials and
Machinery

Roof Trusses
See: Construction Materials and
Machinery

Roofing Equipment and Supplies
See: Construction Materials and
Machinery

Roofing Felts and Coatings
See: Construction Materials and
Machinery

Room Air-conditioners
See: Heating and Cooling
Equipment and Supplies;
Household Appliances

Ropes and Cables
See: Industrial Supplies

Rosins
See: Paints and Varnishes

Rotary Actuators, Hydraulic and
Pneumatic
See: Automotive

Rubber

Rubber Balloons
See: Gifts and Novelties

Rubber Belts and Belting
See: Rubber

Rubber Goods
See: Rubber

Rulers
See: Office Equipment and
Supplies

Rustproofing Chemicals
See: Chemicals

Safes
See: Security and Safety
Equipment

Safety Equipment
See: Security and Safety
Equipment

Safety Products
See: Security and Safety
Equipment

Sailboats
See: Marine

Salad Dressings
See: Food

Salted Snacks
See: Food

Salts
See: Chemicals

Sample Cases
See: Luggage and Leather Goods

Sandals
See: Shoes

Sandwich Cookies
See: Food

Sandwiches
See: Food

Sanitary Food Trays, Plates, and Dishes
See: Paper and Paper Products

Sanitary Napkins and Tampons
See: Paper and Paper Products; Health and Beauty Aids

Sanitary Paper Products
See: Paper and Paper Products; Medical, Dental, and Optical Supplies

Sanitation Equipment and Products
See: Cleaning and Janitorial Supplies

Saw Blades
See: Hardware

Sawhorses
See: Hardware

Saws
See: Hardware

Scaffold Jacks
See: Industrial Machinery; Industrial Supplies

Scaffolding Equipment
See: Industrial Machinery; Industrial Supplies

Scales
See: Scientific and Measurement Devices

Scalpels
See: Medical, Dental, and Optical Supplies

Scanners
See: Computers and Software; Medical, Dental, and Optical Supplies

Scarves
See: Clothing

Scatter Rugs
See: Household Items

School Backpacks
See: Office Equipment and Supplies

School Furniture
See: Furniture and Fixtures

School Jewelry and Emblems
See: Jewelry

School Supplies
See: Office Equipment and Supplies

Science Books
See: Books and Other Printed Materials

Scientific and Measurement Devices

Scientific Instruments
See: Scientific and Measurement Devices

Scissors and Shears
See: Hardware; Health and Beauty Aids

Scrap Metals
See: Used, Scrap, and Recycled Materials

Scrap Paper
See: Used, Scrap, and Recycled Materials

Scrap Products
See: Used, Scrap, and Recycled Materials

Scrapbooks
See: Gifts and Novelties; Books and Other Printed Materials

Screens for Windows and Doors
See: Construction Materials and Machinery

Screws
See: Hardware

Seafood, Fresh and Canned
See: Food

Sealants
See: Adhesives

Seasonal Items
See: Gifts and Novelties

Seasonings
See: Food

Security and Safety Equipment

Seeds
See: Agricultural Equipment and Supplies; Livestock and Farm Products

Self-Help Books
See: Books and Other Printed Materials

Semiconductors and Related Devices
See: Electrical and Electronic Equipment and Supplies

Semiprecious Stones
See: Jewelry; Minerals and Ores

Semitrucks
See: Motorized Vehicles

Septic Tanks
See: Plumbing Materials and Fixtures

Settees
See: Furniture and Fixtures

Sewing Accessories
See: Textiles and Notions

Shades
See: Household Items

Shampoos
See: Health and Beauty Aids

Sheep
See: Livestock and Farm Products

Sheep-Lined Clothing
See: Clothing

Sheet Metal
See: Metals

Sheet Music
See: Books and Other Printed Materials

Sheets
See: Household Items

Shelving
See: Furniture and Fixtures; Storage Equipment and Containers

Shingles
See: Construction Materials and Machinery

Ships
See: Marine

Shirts
See: Clothing

Shoes

Shotguns
See: Guns and Weapons

Shorts
See: Clothing

Shoulder Pads
See: Textiles and Notions

Signaling Equipment
See: Specialty Equipment and Products

Signs and Advertising Displays
See: Specialty Equipment and Products

Silk
See: Textiles and Notions

Silk Flowers
See: Horticultural Supplies

Silk, raw
See: Livestock and Farm Products; Textiles and Notions

Silver Jewelry
See: Jewelry

Silver Ore
See: Minerals and Ores

Silverware
See: Household Items

Single Web Paper
See: Paper and Paper Products

Ski Racks
See: Recreational and Sporting Goods

Ski-Wear
See: Clothing

Skiing Equipment
See: Recreational and Sporting Goods

Skin Preparations and Lotions
See: Health and Beauty Aids

Skins, raw
See: Livestock and Farm Products; Luggage and Leather Goods

Skirts
See: Clothing

Small Game
See: Food; Livestock and Farm Products

Smoke Alarms
See: Security and Safety Equipment

Snap Fasteners

See: Textiles and Notions

Snow Removal Equipment
See: Specialty Equipment and Products

Snowmobiles
See: Recreational and Sporting Goods; Motorized Vehicles

Soaps
See: Cleaning and Janitorial Supplies; Health and Beauty Aids

Soccer Equipment
See: Recreational and Sporting Goods

Socks
See: Clothing

Soda
See: Soft Drinks

Sofas
See: Furniture and Fixtures

Soft Drinks
(*See also:* Food)

Software
See: Computers and Software

Softwood Flooring
See: Floorcovering Equipment and Supplies

Solar Heating Panels and Equipment
See: Heating and Cooling Equipment and Supplies

Solenoid Valves
See: Automotive

Solvent Recovery Equipment
See: Specialty Equipment and Products

Sound and Entertainment Equipment and Supplies
(*See also:* Electrical and Electronic Equipment and Supplies)

Soundproofing Tiles
See: Construction Materials and Machinery

Soups
See: Food

Souvenir Cards
See: Paper and Paper Products

Soybean Products
See: Food

Soybeans
See: Livestock and Farm Products; Food

Spaghetti Sauce
See: Food

Spark Plugs
See: Automotive

Speaker Systems
See: Communications Systems and Equipment

Special Industrial Paper
See: Paper and Paper Products

Specialty Bags and Liners
See: Paper and Paper Products

Specialty Cleaning Equipment and Products
See: Cleaning and Janitorial Supplies

Specialty Equipment and Products

Specialty Wines
See: Alcoholic Beverages

Speed Changers, Drives, and Gears
See: Automotive

Spices
See: Food

Spirits
See: Alcoholic Beverages

Sporting Goods
See: Recreational and Sporting Goods

Sports Books
See: Books and Other Printed Materials

Sportswear
See: Clothing

Stampers
See: Office Equipment and Supplies

Starches
See: Food

Stationery
See: Paper and Paper Products

Statuary
See: Gifts and Novelties

Steam Generator Sets
See: Plumbing Materials and Fixtures

Steel
See: Metals

Steel Pipes and Tubes
See: Metals

Steel Springs
See: Metals

Steel Wire
See: Metals

Stereo Equipment
See: Sound and Entertainment Equipment and Supplies

Sterling Silver
See: Jewelry

Stones
See: Jewelry

Stopwatches
See: Scientific and Measurement Devices

Storage Equipment and Containers

Storage Tanks
See: Storage Equipment and Containers

Store, Bank, and Office Fixtures
See: Furniture and Fixtures

Stoves
See: Household Appliances

Stuffed Toy Animals
See: Toys and Hobby Goods

Sugar
See: Food

Sugar, raw
See: Food; Livestock and Farm Products

Suits and Suit Coats
See: Clothing

Sun Glasses
See: Health and Beauty Aids

Sun Screens and Sun Lotions
See: Health and Beauty Aids

Sundries
See: Health and Beauty Aids

Surgical and Medical Instruments and Apparatus
See: Medical, Dental, and Optical Equipment

Surgical Shears
See: Medical, Dental, and Optical Supplies

Surgical Supplies
See: Medical, Dental, and Optical Supplies

Surveying Equipment

See: Scientific and Measurement Devices

Sutures
See: Medical, Dental, and Optical Supplies

Sweaters
See: Clothing

Sweatshirts
See: Clothing

Sweeteners
See: Food

Swimming Pools
See: Recreational and Sporting Goods

Swimwear
See: Clothing

Swine
See: Livestock and Farm Products

Switchboard Equipment
See: Communications Systems and Equipment

Switches
See: Electrical and Electronic Equipment and Supplies

Synthetic Fabrics
See: Textiles and Notions

Synthetic Turf
See: Recreational and Sporting Goods

Syringes
See: Medical, Dental, and Optical Supplies

T-shirts, Novelty
See: Clothing; Gifts and Novelties

T-Shirts
See: Clothing

Table Linens
See: Household Items

Tables
See: Furniture and Fixtures

Tableware
See: Household Items

Tanks
See: Storage Equipment and Containers

Tape Players and Recorders
See: Sound and Entertainment Equipment and Supplies

Tapes

See: Sound and Entertainment Equipment and Supplies; Adhesives

Tapping Attachments
See: Hardware

Taxis
See: Motorized Vehicles

Tea
See: Food

Telephone Answering Machines
See: Communications Systems and Equipment

Telephone Equipment
See: Communications Systems and Equipment

Telephone Switching Equipment
See: Communications Systems and Equipment

Telephones
See: Communications Systems and Equipment

Telescopes
See: Scientific and Measurement Devices

Television Sets
See: Sound and Entertainment Equipment and Supplies

Tennis Equipment
See: Recreational and Sporting Goods

Terminals
See: Computers and Software

Testing Equipment
See: Scientific and Measurement Devices

Textbooks
See: Books and Other Printed Materials

Textile Bags
See: Textiles and Notions

Textile Goods
See: Textiles and Notions

Textile Industries Machinery
See: Industrial Machinery

Textile Printers' Supplies
See: Industrial Supplies

Textile Tape
See: Adhesives; Textiles and Notions

Textiles and Notions

Theatrical Equipment
See: Specialty Equipment and Products

Therapeutic Appliances and Supplies
See: Medical, Dental, and Optical Equipment

Thread
See: Textiles and Notions

Throw Rugs
See: Household Items

Ties
See: Clothing

Tile Flooring
See: Floorcovering Equipment and Supplies

Timber
See: Wood and Wood Products

Tin
See: Metals

Tires
See: Automotive

Tissue Paper
See: Paper and Paper Products

Tobacco Products

Toilet Paper
See: Paper and Paper Products

Toilet Partitions
See: Furniture and Fixtures; Plumbing Materials and Fixtures

Toilet Seats
See: Plumbing Materials and Fixtures

Toiletries
See: Health and Beauty Aids

Tomato Sauces and Pastes
See: Food

Tool Cases
See: Hardware

Tool and Die Machinery and Parts
See: Industrial Machinery

Tool Holders
See: Hardware

Tools
See: Hardware; Industrial Machinery

Totalizing Meters for Gas and Liquids
See: Scientific and Measurement Devices

Towels
See: Household Items

Toys and Hobby Goods
(*See also:* Recreational and Sporting Goods)

Tractor-Mounting Equipment
See: Industrial Machinery

Tractors
See: Agricultural Equipment and Supplies

Trading Cards
See: Toys and Hobby Goods

Traffic Control Equipment
See: Specialty Equipment and Products

Trailers
See: Automotive; Motorized Vehicles

Trains
See: Railroad Equipment and Supplies

Transcription Machines
See: Office Equipment and Supplies

Transformers
See: Electrical and Electronic Equipment and Supplies

Transmission Equipment
See: Automotive

Transmissions, Industrial
See: Industrial Machinery

Trash Compactors
See: Specialty Equipment and Products

Travel and Camping Trailers, Parts and Components
See: Automotive; Recreational and Sporting Goods

Travel Books
See: Books and Other Printed Materials

Travel Cases
See: Luggage and Leather Goods

Trophies
See: Gifts and Novelties

Truck Parts and Accessories

See: Automotive

Truck Trailers and Chassis
See: Automotive; Motorized Vehicles

Trucks
See: Motorized Vehicles

Tubing
See: Industrial Supplies

Tufting
See: Textiles and Notions

Tungsten
See: Minerals and Ores

Turbines
See: Industrial Machinery

Turpentine
See: Paints and Varnishes; Chemicals

Turrets
See: Construction Materials and Machinery

Twine
See: Industrial Supplies

Type Holders
See: Office Equipment and Supplies

Typewriters
See: Office Equipment and Supplies

Ukuleles
See: Sound and Entertainment Equipment and Supplies

Umbrellas
See: Gifts and Novelties

Underwear
See: Clothing

Uniforms
See: Clothing

Unitary Air-Conditioners
See: Heating and Cooling Equipment and Supplies

Upholstered Furniture
See: Furniture and Fixtures

Upholstery Fabrics
See: Textiles and Notions

Upholstery Fillings
See: Textiles and Notions

Used, Scrap, and Recycled Materials

Used Automotive Parts
See: Used, Scrap, and Recycled Materials; Automotive

Used Cars
See: Used, Scrap, and Recycled Materials; Automotive

Utensils
See: Household Items

Vacuum Cleaners
See: Household Appliances

Vacuum Cleaning Systems
See: Specialty Equipment and Products

Vacuum Pumps
See: Industrial Machinery

Valves
See: Industrial Supplies; Plumbing Materials and Fixtures

Varnishes
See: Paints and Varnishes

Vaults
See: Security and Safety Equipment

VCRs
See: Sound and Entertainment Equipment and Supplies

Vegetable Fibers
See: Livestock and Farm Products

Vegetable Juices
See: Food

Vegetables
See: Food

Vehicular and Pedestrian Traffic Control Equipment
See: Specialty Equipment and Products

Vehicular Lighting Equipment
See: Automotive

Vending Machines
See: Specialty Equipment and Products

Venetian Blinds
See: Household Items

Ventilating Equipment and Supplies
See: Heating and Cooling Equipment and Supplies

Vests
See: Clothing

Veterinary Products
(See also: Agricultural Equipment and Supplies)
See: Breeding and Agricultural

Video Cassette Recorders
See: Sound and Entertainment Equipment and Supplies

Video Disk Players
See: Sound and Entertainment Equipment and Supplies

Video Disks
See: Sound and Entertainment Equipment and Supplies

Video Games
See: Toys and Hobby Goods

Video Tapes for Recording
See: Sound and Entertainment Equipment and Supplies

Videos
See: Sound and Entertainment Equipment and Supplies

Vinegar
See: Food

Vinyl Coated Fabrics
See: Textiles and Notions

Vitamins
See: Health and Beauty Aids

Wadding
See: Textiles and Notions

Wading Pools
See: Recreational and Sporting Goods

Wallcovering
See: Household Items

Wallets
See: Luggage and Leather Goods

Wallpaper
See: Household Items

Washcloths
See: Household Items

Washers
See: Hardware

Washing Machines
See: Household Appliances

Waste Products
See: Used, Scrap, and Recycled Materials

Wastewater Treatment Equipment
See: Specialty Equipment and Products

Watches and Parts

See: Jewelry

Water Beds
See: Furniture and Fixtures

Water, Bottled
See: Soft Drinks

Water Filters
See: Household Appliances; Specialty Equipment and Products

Water Heaters
See: Plumbing Materials and Fixtures

Water Treatment Systems
See: Specialty Equipment and Products

Waterpumps
See: Plumbing Materials and Fixtures

Waxes
See: Petroleum, Fuels, and Related Equipment

Weapons
See: Guns and Weapons

Welding Gases
See: Industrial Supplies

Welding Machinery and Equipment
See: Industrial Machinery

Welding Supplies
See: Industrial Supplies

Wheat
See: Livestock and Farm Products

Wheel Covers
See: Automotive

Wheelchairs
See: Medical, Dental, and Optical Equipment

Wheeled Tractors and Attachments
See: Agricultural Equipment and Supplies; Motorized Vehicles

Wheels
See: Automotive

Whirlpool Baths
See: Plumbing Materials and Fixtures; Recreational and Sporting Goods

Whiskey
See: Alcoholic Beverages

Whiteprinting Equipment
See: Specialty Equipment and

Products

Winches
See: Industrial Machinery

Window Blinds and Shades
See: Household Items

Window Sashes
See: Construction Materials and Machinery

Window Siding
See: Construction Materials and Machinery

Windows and Window Frames
See: Construction Materials and Machinery

Wine
See: Alcoholic Beverages

Wine Coolers
See: Alcoholic Beverages

Wipers, from Nonwoven Fabrics
See: Textiles and Notions

Wire Connectors
See: Electrical and Electronic Equipment and Supplies

Wire Rods
See: Metals

Wire Rope or Cable
See: Industrial Supplies

Wire Screening
See: Metals

Wiring Devices
See: Electrical and Electronic Equipment and Supplies

Women's Shoes
See: Shoes

Wood Carpet
See: Wood and Wood Products

Wood Chips
See: Wood and Wood Products

Wood Fillers and Sealers
See: Adhesives

Wood Pulp
See: Wood and Wood Products

Wood Siding
See: Construction Materials and Machinery

Wood and Wood Products

Wooden Furniture
See: Furniture and Fixtures

Wooden Reels for Wire and Cable
See: Industrial Supplies

Woodwinds
See: Sound and Entertainment Equipment and Supplies

Woodworking Machinery
See: Industrial Machinery

Wool and Wool Blends
See: Textiles and Notions

Wool, Raw
See: Livestock and Farm Products

Wool, Tops and Noils
See: Livestock and Farm Products

Work Gloves and Mittens

See: Clothing

Work Pants
See: Clothing

Work Shirts
See: Clothing

Wrought Iron Furniture
See: Furniture and Fixtures

X-Ray Apparatus
See: Medical, Dental, and Optical Equipment

Yachts
See: Marine

Yarns
See: Textiles and Notions

Yogurt
See: Food

Zinc
See: Minerals and Ores

Zinc Ore
See: Minerals and Ores

Zippers and Slide-In Fasteners
See: Textiles and Notions

Products

Windows
See Construction Materials and Machinery

Window Blinds and Shades
See Household Items

Window Glazing
See Construction Materials and Machinery

Window Sash
See Construction Materials and Machinery

Windows and Window Frames
See Construction Materials and Machinery

Wine
See Alcoholic Beverages

Wine Coolers
See Alcoholic Beverages

Wipes from Nonwoven Fabrics
See Textiles and Hosiery

Wire Conductors
See Electrical and Electronic Equipment and Supplies

Wire Rope
See Metals

Wire Rope & Cable
See Industrial Supplies

Wire Screening
See Metals

Wiring Devices
See Electrical and Electronic Equipment and Supplies

Women's Shoes
See Shoes

Wood Carpet
See Wood and Wood Products

Wood Chips
See Wood and Wood Products

Wood Fillers and Sealers
See Adhesives

Wood Pulp
See Wood and Wood Products

Wood Siding
See Construction Materials and Machinery

Wood and Wood Products

Wooden Furniture
See Furniture and Fixtures

Wooden Reels for Wire and Cable
See Electrical Supplies

Woodwind
See Sound and Entertainment Equipment and Supplies

Woodworking Machinery
See Industrial Machinery

Wool and Wool Blend
See Textiles and Hosiery

Wool Raw
See Livestock and Farm Products

Wool Tops and Noils
See Livestock and Farm Products

Work Gloves and Mittens

See Clothing

Workwear
See Clothing

Work Shirts
See Clothing

Wrought Iron Furniture
See Furniture and Fixtures

X-Ray Apparatus
See Medical, Dental, and Optical Equipment

Yachts
See Marine

Yarns
See Textiles and Hosiery

Yogurt
See Food

Zinc
See Minerals and Ores

Zinc Ore
See Minerals and Ores

Zippers and Slide Fasteners
See Textiles and Hosiery

(1) Adhesives

Entries in this section are arranged alphabetically by company name. When the company name is a personal name, the company name is alphabetized by the surname unless the first name or initial(s) are part of a trade name. See the User's Guide at the front of this directory for additional information.

■ 1 ■ **American Packing and Gasket Company**
PO Box 213
Houston, TX 77001
Phone: (713)675-5271 **Fax:** (713)675-2730
E-mail: info@apandg.com
URL: http://www.apandg.com/
Products: Adhesives and sealants; O-rings; Packing and gasket material; Glass; Plastic products. **SIC:** 5169 (Chemicals & Allied Products Nec).

■ 2 ■ **Associated Allied Industries Inc.**
5151 N 32nd St.
Milwaukee, WI 53209
Phone: (414)461-5050
Products: Three-part epoxies and plasticized sealants. **SIC:** 5169 (Chemicals & Allied Products Nec). **Sales:** $500,000 (1992). **Emp:** 7. **Officers:** Artur Wilhelm, VP of Admin.; M.J. Nemetz, Treasurer & Secty.

■ 3 ■ **Bender Wholesale Distributors**
2911 Moose Trail
Elkhart, IN 46514
Phone: (219)264-4409 **Fax:** (219)262-8799
Products: Adhesives; Rivets. **SICs:** 5169 (Chemicals & Allied Products Nec); 5072 (Hardware). **Est:** 1948.

■ 4 ■ **CourterCo**
5373 W 79th St.
Indianapolis, IN 46268-1631
Phone: (317)875-7550 **Free:** (800)837-7550
E-mail: sales@courterco.com
URL: http://www.couterco.com/
Products: Adhesives; Cabinet hardware; Tools. **SIC:** 5169 (Chemicals & Allied Products Nec). **Emp:** 90.

■ 5 ■ **Everitt & Ray Inc.**
1325 Johnson Dr.
La Puente, CA 91745
Phone: (626)961-3611 **Fax:** (626)333-7567
Products: Abrasives and adhesives, including sanding belts. **SICs:** 5085 (Industrial Supplies); 5169 (Chemicals & Allied Products Nec). **Sales:** $3,000,000 (2000). **Emp:** 15. **Officers:** David Everitt.

■ 6 ■ **Flexstik Adheso Graphics**
625 Main St.
Westbury, NY 11590
Phone: (516)333-3666 **Fax:** (516)333-1114
E-mail: sales@Adheso-Graphics.com
URL: http://www.adheso-graphics.com
Products: Adhesive tapes. **SIC:** 5169 (Chemicals & Allied Products Nec).

■ 7 ■ **Futura Adhesives & Chemicals**
795 Glendale Rd.
Scottdale, GA 30079
Phone: (404)296-8288
Free: (800)226-3003 **Fax:** (404)299-3420
Products: Adhesives and glues. **SIC:** 5169 (Chemicals & Allied Products Nec). **Est:** 1987. **Sales:** $1,500,000 (2000). **Emp:** 15. **Officers:** Sam Fahmie, President.

■ 8 ■ **Heigl Adhesive Sales**
7634 Washington Ave.
Eden Prairie, MN 55344
Free: (800)797-7728 **Fax:** (612)943-1255
E-mail: sales@heigladhesive.com
URL: http://www.heigladhesive.com
Products: Adhesives, sealants, coatings and potting compounds. **SIC:** 5169 (Chemicals & Allied Products Nec).

■ 9 ■ **J.E. Lenover & Son Inc.**
13420 Wayne Rd.
Livonia, MI 48150-1246
Phone: (734)427-0000
Free: (800)LEN-OVER **Fax:** (734)427-0986
Products: Caulking compounds and sealants; Adhesives and sealants; Wallboard. **SICs:** 5169 (Chemicals & Allied Products Nec); 5031 (Lumber, Plywood & Millwork). **Emp:** 5.

■ 10 ■ **Neely Industries**
2704 W Pioneer Pkwy.
Arlington, TX 76013
Phone: (817)226-2500
Free: (800)242-1483 **Fax:** (817)274-4504
E-mail: sales@neelyindustries.com
URL: http://www.neelyindustries.com/
Products: Adhesives, sealants, and lubricants. **SIC:** 5169 (Chemicals & Allied Products Nec).

■ 11 ■ **Riley Sales Inc.**
1719 Romano Dr.
Plymouth Meeting, PA 19462
Phone: (610)279-4500
Free: (800)345-7529 **Fax:** (610)279-2509
URL: http://www.rileysales.com/
Products: Adhesives, tapes, and sealants. **SIC:** 5169 (Chemicals & Allied Products Nec).

■ 12 ■ **R.S. Hughes Company Inc.**
PO Box 25061
Glendale, CA 91221
Phone: (818)563-1122
Products: Tapes, adhesives, abrasives, electrical insulation, shipping and packaging labels and signs, and safety equipment. **SICs:** 5169 (Chemicals & Allied Products Nec); 5131 (Piece Goods & Notions); 5099 (Durable Goods Nec). **Sales:** $100,000,000 (2000). **Emp:** 360. **Officers:** Robert McCollum, CEO & President; Rai Brendel, CFO.

■ 13 ■ **Sailor Corporation of America**
121 Bethea Rd., Ste. 307
Fayetteville, GA 30214
Phone: (770)461-9081
Free: (800)248-4583 **Fax:** (770)461-8452
E-mail: info@sailorpen.com
URL: http://www.sailorpen.com
Products: Adhesives and glues; Writing instruments, including pens and markers. **SIC:** 5169 (Chemicals & Allied Products Nec). **Est:** 1992. **Emp:** 44. **Officers:** Richard C. Egolf, CEO & President, e-mail: regolf@sailorpen.com; Michael Masuyama, Exec. VP, e-mail: mmasuyama@sailorpen.com; Karen Howard, VP of Finance, e-mail: khoward@sailorpen.com. **Former Name:** PDM Adhesives Corp.

■ 14 ■ **John G. Shelley Company Inc.**
16 Mica Ln.
Wellesley Hills, MA 02481
Phone: (781)237-0900
Free: (800)525-0202 **Fax:** (781)237-8978
E-mail: sales@johnshelley.com
URL: http://www.johnshelley.com
Products: Adhesives; Pressure sensitive tape; Urethane and silicone molding compounds; Die cut gaskets; Custom rubber molded products. **SICs:** 5169 (Chemicals & Allied Products Nec); 5085 (Industrial Supplies). **Est:** 1927. **Sales:** $6,000,000 (2000). **Emp:** 30. **Officers:** H. Chandler Shelley Jr., President; Warren R. Kelley, VP of Admin.

■ 15 ■ **Superior Epoxies & Coatings, Inc.**
2527 Lantrac Ct.
Decatur, GA 30035
Phone: (770)808-0023
Free: (800)240-1310 **Fax:** (770)808-6777
E-mail: supgloss@bellsouth.net
URL: http://www.superiorepoxies.com
Products: Adhesives and glues. **SIC:** 5169 (Chemicals & Allied Products Nec). **Est:** 1993. **Sales:** $2,000,000 (2000). **Emp:** 8. **Officers:** Donald A. Goldstein, President; John Malick, Vice President.

■ 16 ■ **Superior FomeBords Corp.**
2700 W Grand Ave.
Chicago, IL 60612
Phone: (773)278-9200
Free: (800)362-6267 **Fax:** (773)278-9466
URL: http://www.fomebords.com
Products: Self-adhesive boards. **SIC:** 5169 (Chemicals & Allied Products Nec).

■ 17 ■ **Tite Co.**
2896 Gant Quarters Cir.
Marietta, GA 30068
Phone: (770)565-4580
Products: Adhesives and glues. **SIC:** 5169 (Chemicals & Allied Products Nec).

■ 18 ■ **Versatile Industrial Products**
1371-4 Church St.
Bohemia, NY 11716
Phone: (631)567-8866 **Fax:** (631)567-8528
URL: http://www.versatileindustrial.com/
Products: Adhesives, sealants, silicones, and epoxies. **SIC:** 5169 (Chemicals & Allied Products Nec).

■ 19 ■ **Web Seal Inc.**
15 Oregon St.
Rochester, NY 14605-3094
Phone: (716)546-1320 **Fax:** (716)546-5746
Products: Sealing products. **SIC:** 5169 (Chemicals & Allied Products Nec). **Sales:** $3,500,000 (1992). **Emp:** 26. **Officers:** D.L. Hurley, President.

(2) Aeronautical Equipment and Supplies

Entries in this section are arranged alphabetically by company name. When the company name is a personal name, the company name is alphabetized by the surname unless the first name or initial(s) are part of a trade name. See the User's Guide at the front of this directory for additional information.

■ 20 ■ **AAA Interair Inc.**
PO Box 522230
Miami, FL 33152
Phone: (305)889-6111
Free: (800)327-9836 **Fax:** (305)887-0003
E-mail: sales@aaainterair.com
URL: http://www.aaainterair.com
Products: Aircraft parts. **SIC:** 5088 (Transportation Equipment & Supplies). **Est:** 1990. **Sales:** $20,000,000 (2000). **Emp:** 40. **Officers:** Douglas A. Potter, President; John J. Higgins, Treasurer; Eduardo Nunez, VP of Sales.

■ 21 ■ **AAR Corp.**
200 Saw Mill River Rd.
Hawthorne, NY 10532
Phone: (914)747-0500 **Fax:** (914)747-0696
Products: Airplane parts. **SIC:** 5088 (Transportation Equipment & Supplies). **Sales:** $15,000,000 (2000). **Emp:** 26.

■ 22 ■ **AAR Corp.**
1100 N Wood Dale Rd.
Wood Dale, IL 60191
Phone: (630)227-2000 **Fax:** (630)227-2019
Products: Transportation equipment and supplies. **SIC:** 5088 (Transportation Equipment & Supplies). **Est:** 1951. **Sales:** $589,300,000 (2000). **Officers:** David P. Storch, CEO & President; Timothy J. Romenesko, VP, CFO & Treasurer.

■ 23 ■ **ABSCOA Industries Inc.**
12774 Florence Ave.
Santa Fe Springs, CA 90670-3906
Phone: (562)903-7801 **Fax:** (562)903-7801
E-mail: sales@abscoa.com
URL: http://www.abscoa.com
Products: Aerospace fasteners, including nuts, bolts, and screws; Self-sealing fasteners. **SICs:** 5088 (Transportation Equipment & Supplies); 5072 (Hardware). **Est:** 1947. **Sales:** $32,000,000 (2000). **Emp:** 105. **Officers:** Gary North, President; Mel Clott, General Mgr. **Alternate Name:** AAR Hardware Inc.

■ 24 ■ **Aero Services International Inc.**
660 Newtown-Yardley Rd.
Newtown, PA 18940
Phone: (215)860-5600 **Fax:** (215)968-6010
Products: Airplane parts. **SIC:** 5088 (Transportation Equipment & Supplies). **Est:** 1948. **Sales:** $39,600,000 (2000). **Emp:** 326. **Officers:** John L. Pugh, CEO & Treasurer; John F. Sullivan, Exec. VP & CFO; Roberta V. Romberg, Secretary; Larry A. Ulrich, President & COO.

■ 25 ■ **Aero Systems Aviation Inc.**
PO Box 52-2221
Miami, FL 33152-2221
Phone: (305)871-1300 **Fax:** (305)884-1400
Products: Aviation equipment. **SIC:** 5088 (Transportation Equipment & Supplies). **Sales:** $75,000,000 (2000). **Emp:** 100. **Officers:** Jeffrey T. Stable, President; James Gorsuch, Controller.

■ 26 ■ **Aero Systems Inc.**
PO Box 52-2221
Miami, FL 33152-2221
Phone: (305)871-1300
Products: Aircraft parts. **SIC:** 5088 (Transportation Equipment & Supplies). **Est:** 1957. **Sales:** $22,700,000 (2000). **Emp:** 100. **Officers:** Robert G. Holmes Jr., President & Chairman of the Board; David A. Wayne, VP of Finance; Ronald E. Suihkonen, VP of Sales; C. Earl Ashton, VP of Information Systems; R. Edward Holmes, VP of Admin.

■ 27 ■ **Aerodynamics Inc.**
PO Box 270100
Waterford, MI 48327
Phone: (810)666-3500 **Fax:** (810)666-2307
Products: Aircraft and aircraft parts. **SIC:** 5088 (Transportation Equipment & Supplies). **Est:** 1959. **Sales:** $15,000,000 (2000). **Emp:** 95. **Officers:** Cheryl L. Minshall, President; Richard Petri, CFO; Ken Wade, Sales Mgr.

■ 28 ■ **Aeronca Inc.**
1712 Germantown Rd.
Middletown, OH 45042
Phone: (513)422-2751
Products: Component parts for aircraft. **SIC:** 5088 (Transportation Equipment & Supplies). **Est:** 1929. **Sales:** $48,000,000 (2000). **Emp:** 410. **Officers:** Bill J. Wade, President; J.N. Kreider, VP of Admin.; Keith Wyman, VP of Business Development; John Kramer, Dir. of Systems; David Caudill, Dir of Human Resources.

■ 29 ■ **Aerospace Products International Inc.**
3778 Distirplex Dr., N
Memphis, TN 38118
Phone: (901)365-3470
Free: (800)450-6777 **Fax:** (901)375-2603
E-mail: sales@apiparts.com
URL: http://www.apiparts.com
Products: Aircraft parts and accessories. **SIC:** 5088 (Transportation Equipment & Supplies). **Est:** 1988. **Sales:** $80,000,000 (1999). **Emp:** 175. **Officers:** Gerald Schlesinger, President, e-mail: jschlesinger@apiparts.com; Marc Greenberg, CEO & VP, e-mail: mgreenberg@apiparts.com. **Former Name:** AMR Combs/API.

■ 30 ■ **Aerotech World Trade Corp.**
11 New King St.
White Plains, NY 10604
Phone: (914)681-3000 **Fax:** (914)428-3621
Products: Airplane and helicopter productss. **SIC:** 5088 (Transportation Equipment & Supplies). **Sales:** $100,000,000 (1999). **Emp:** 100. **Officers:** Jan R. Enderson, President; Ann M. Rinaldi, VP of Marketing & Sales, e-mail: annr@aerotechworld.com; Neil Kelly, Director Distribution Svcs & Adm., e-mail: neilk@aerotechworld.com; John Dileo, Manager Commercial Sales, e-mail: johnd@aerotechworld.com; John Vittoria, Dir. of Finance, e-mail: johnv@aerotechworld.com.

■ 31 ■ **Agusta Aerospace Corp.**
PO Box 16002
Philadelphia, PA 19114
Phone: (215)281-1400 **Fax:** (215)281-1462
Products: Helicopters. **SIC:** 5088 (Transportation Equipment & Supplies). **Est:** 1981. **Sales:** $150,000,000 (2000). **Emp:** 90. **Officers:** Robert J. Budica, CEO & President; Vincent Genovese, Exec. VP of Finance & Admin.

■ 32 ■ **Aim Enterprises, Inc.**
10126 Residency Rd.
Manassas, VA 20110-2007
Phone: (703)361-7177 **Fax:** (703)361-1405
Products: Aircrafts, engines, and parts; Aeronautical equipment; Aircraft cleaning compounds. **SICs:** 5088 (Transportation Equipment & Supplies); 5169 (Chemicals & Allied Products Nec). **Est:** 1976. **Sales:** $7,000,000 (2000). **Emp:** 25. **Officers:** Luis Ambroggio, President.

■ 33 ■ **Air Comm Corp.**
3300 Airport Rd.
Boulder, CO 80301
Phone: (303)440-4075 **Fax:** (303)440-6355
Products: Heaters and air conditioners for helicopters. **SIC:** 5088 (Transportation Equipment & Supplies). **Officers:** Norman Steiner, President.

■ 34 ■ **Airbus Industry of North America Inc.**
198 Van Buren St., No. 300
Herndon, VA 20170-5338
Phone: (703)834-3400 **Fax:** (703)834-3340
Products: Aeronautical equipment and supplies. **SIC:** 5088 (Transportation Equipment & Supplies). **Sales:** $63,000,000 (2000). **Emp:** 200.

■ 35 ■ **Aircraft and Component Equipment Suppliers Inc.**
PO Box 60968
Pasadena, CA 91116-6968
Phone: (213)564-2421 **Fax:** (626)398-6846
Products: Aviation, military, and police equipment and spares. **SICs:** 5088 (Transportation Equipment & Supplies); 5099 (Durable Goods Nec). **Sales:** $8,000,000 (2000). **Emp:** 10. **Officers:** R.M. Vartanian, President.

■ 36 ■ **Aircraft Spruce and Specialty Co.**
225 Airport Cir.
Corona, CA 92880
Phone: (909)372-9555
Free: (877)477-7823 **Fax:** (909)372-0555
E-mail: info@aircraftspruce.com
URL: http://www.aircraftspruce.com
Products: Aircraft parts; Pilot supplies. **SIC:** 5088 (Transportation Equipment & Supplies). **Est:** 1965. **Sales:** $25,000,000 (2000). **Emp:** 130. **Officers:** Jim Irwin, President; Nanci Irwin, Vice President.

■ 37 ■ **Airmotive Inc.**
3400 Winona Ave.
Burbank, CA 91504
Phone: (818)845-7423
Products: Aircraft parts, including motors. **SIC:** 5088 (Transportation Equipment & Supplies). **Est:** 1943.

Sales: $28,000,000 (2000). Emp: 58. Officers: Chris Kreston, CFO; Robert Young, Dir. of Sales; Terry Inglis, Director.

■ 38 ■ Alamo Aircraft, Ltd.
PO Box 37343
San Antonio, TX 78237
Phone: (210)434-5577   Fax: (210)434-1030
E-mail: sales@alamoaircraft.com
URL: http://www.alamoaircraft.com
Products: Aircraft parts, including nuts, bolts, and frames. SIC: 5088 (Transportation Equipment & Supplies). Est: 1946. Sales: $12,000,000 (2000). Emp: 48. Officers: Jesse E. Wulfe, President; Carl Wulfe, Treasurer; Leon C. Wulfe Jr., VP of Marketing; Perry Wulfe, Dir. of Data Processing. Former Name: Alamo Aircraft Supply Inc.

■ 39 ■ Allied Screw Products
PO Box 543
Mishawaka, IN 46546-0543
Phone: (219)255-4718   Fax: (219)255-4173
URL: http://www.aspi-nc.com
Products: Aerospace items. SIC: 5088 (Transportation Equipment & Supplies). Est: 1954. Sales: $6,500,000 (1999). Emp: 70. Officers: Neil Silver, Chairman of the Board; Leah Silver, Treasurer; Pam Rubenstein, Vice President; K.E. Holderman, President; Patrick Szucs, Vice President.

■ 40 ■ Almerica Overseas Inc.
PO Box 2188
Tuscaloosa, AL 35403
Phone: (205)758-1311   Fax: (205)759-1962
Products: Aircraft parts; Fire extinguishers. SICs: 5088 (Transportation Equipment & Supplies); 5088 (Transportation Equipment & Supplies); 5099 (Durable Goods Nec); 5084 (Industrial Machinery & Equipment); 5078 (Refrigeration Equipment & Supplies). Est: 1985. Sales: $2,000,000 (2000). Emp: 5. Officers: K. Gordon Lawless, President.

■ 41 ■ American General Supplies Inc.
7840 Airpark Rd., No. 9200
Gaithersburg, MD 20879
Phone: (301)294-8900   Fax: (301)294-8905
Products: Aircraft parts. SIC: 5088 (Transportation Equipment & Supplies). Est: 1982. Sales: $15,000,000 (2000). Emp: 32. Officers: Kassa Maru, President; Melessie Maru, Treasurer; Giuseppe Chiappini, Dir. of Data Processing.

■ 42 ■ ASC Industries
PO Box 5068
Arlington, TX 76006
Phone: (817)640-1300
Free: (800)733-1580   Fax: (817)649-2685
E-mail: ascind@ascintl.com
URL: http://www.ascintl.com
Products: Aircraft hardware, including bolts, nuts, screws, washers, and inserts. SIC: 5088 (Transportation Equipment & Supplies). Est: 1951. Emp: 50. Officers: Ollin Taylor, President, e-mail: otaylor@ascintl.com; Dolores Barton, Accountant; Greg Vinson, Sales Mgr.

■ 43 ■ Associated Aircraft Supply Inc.
6020 Cedar Springs Rd.
PO Box 35788
Dallas, TX 75235-5788
Phone: (214)331-4381
Free: (800)369-3212   Fax: (214)339-9840
URL: http://www.associated-aircraft.com
Products: Electrical aircraft parts, including toggle switches, terminal boards, and circuit breakers. SIC: 5088 (Transportation Equipment & Supplies). Est: 1953. Sales: $12,000,000 (2000). Emp: 19. Officers: J.L. Mann, CEO.

■ 44 ■ ASW Aviation Services Inc.
6060 W Airport Dr.
North Canton, OH 44720
Phone: (216)494-6104   Fax: (216)733-8913
Products: Aviation supplies, including fuel. SICs: 5088 (Transportation Equipment & Supplies); 5172 (Petroleum Products Nec). Sales: $3,000,000 (2000). Emp: 15. Officers: Phil Maynard, President.

■ 45 ■ Atlantic Aviation Corp.
PO Box 15000
Wilmington, DE 19850
Phone: (302)322-7000
Free: (800)441-9390   Fax: (302)322-7227
Products: Aircraft and fueling parts. SIC: 5088 (Transportation Equipment & Supplies).

■ 46 ■ D. Austin Aircraft (HIE)
RR 1, Box 397
Whitefield, NH 03598
Phones: (603)837-2627   (603)846-7728
Fax: (603)837-2627
E-mail: daair@together.net
Products: Aircraft maintenance; Supplies; Parts; Service. SIC: 5088 (Transportation Equipment & Supplies). Est: 1983. Emp: 10. Officers: David Bicknell, Owner.

■ 47 ■ Auxiliary Power International Corp.
4400 Ruffin Rd.
PO Box 85757
San Diego, CA 92186-5757
Phone: (619)627-6501   Fax: (619)627-6502
Products: Aircraft auxiliary power engines. SIC: 5088 (Transportation Equipment & Supplies). Est: 1989. Sales: $2,000,000 (2000). Emp: 8. Officers: Timothy M. Morris, CEO & President; Bob Ridgeway, Controller. Alternate Name: Sandstrand Corp.

■ 48 ■ AvAlaska, Inc.
4340 Postmark Dr.
Anchorage, AK 99502
Phone: (907)248-7070
Free: (800)770-7069   Fax: (907)248-7771
Products: Aircraft parts. SIC: 5088 (Transportation Equipment & Supplies). Officers: Mark Johnson, President.

■ 49 ■ Avatar Alliance L.P.
PO Box 1238
Orange, CT 06477-7238
Phone: (203)380-9377
Products: Aircraft parts. SIC: 5088 (Transportation Equipment & Supplies).

■ 50 ■ Aviatech Corporation
912 Airport Rd.
Roanoke, TX 76262
Phone: (817)430-4784   Fax: (817)491-1181
E-mail: aviatech@flash.net
Products: Aviation equipment and supplies. SIC: 5088 (Transportation Equipment & Supplies). Est: 1970. Emp: 6. Officers: F. Patrick Carr Jr., President.

■ 51 ■ Aviation Distributors Inc.
1 Capital Dr.
Lake Forest, CA 92630
Phone: (949)586-7558
Products: Aircraft parts. SIC: 5088 (Transportation Equipment & Supplies). Sales: $39,000,000 (2000). Emp: 54. Officers: Saleem S. Naber, CEO & President; Gary L. Joslin, CFO.

■ 52 ■ Aviation Sales Co. (Miami, Florida)
6905 NW 25th St.
Miami, FL 33122-1898
Phone: (305)592-4055   Fax: (305)599-6626
Products: Aircraft parts. SIC: 5088 (Transportation Equipment & Supplies). Sales: $256,900,000 (2000). Emp: 850. Officers: Dale S. Baker, CEO & Chairman of the Board; Joseph E. Civiletto, VP & CFO.

■ 53 ■ AWS Companies Inc.
2113 Merrill Field Dr.
Anchorage, AK 99501-4117
Phone: (907)272-4397   Fax: (907)277-0175
Products: Transportation equipment; Aircraft parts and auxiliary equipment; Space vehicle equipment. SIC: 5088 (Transportation Equipment & Supplies). Officers: Scott Jones, President.

■ 54 ■ Azimuth Corp. (Orlando, Florida)
3600 Rio Vista Ave., Ste. A
Orlando, FL 32805-6005
Phone: (407)849-0480   Fax: (407)849-0625
Products: Aerospace components and electronic equipment. SICs: 5088 (Transportation Equipment & Supplies); 5065 (Electronic Parts & Equipment Nec).

Sales: $152,000,000 (2000). Emp: 200. Officers: Alexander Milley, President; David Doolittle, CFO.

■ 55 ■ BAI Inc.
21 Airport Blvd.
South San Francisco, CA 94080
Phone: (650)872-1955
Products: Specialty aerospace products. SIC: 5088 (Transportation Equipment & Supplies).

■ 56 ■ Banner Aerospace Inc.
PO Box 20260
Washington, DC 20041
Phone: (202)478-5790   Fax: (202)478-5795
URL: http://www.banner.com
Products: Aircraft supplies, including engines and rotables. SIC: 5088 (Transportation Equipment & Supplies). Est: 1990. Sales: $287,900,000 (2000). Emp: 550. Officers: Jeffrey J. Steiner, CEO & Chairman of the Board; Warren D. Persavich, Sr. VP & CFO.

■ 57 ■ Barfield Inc.
PO Box 025367
Miami, FL 33102-5367
Phone: (305)871-3900   Fax: (305)871-5629
Products: Aviation instruments. SIC: 5088 (Transportation Equipment & Supplies). Est: 1945. Sales: $35,000,000 (2000). Emp: 300. Officers: Marc Paganini, CEO & President; Jim Taylor, Controller; Morris Venezia, VP of Marketing; S. Lathrup.

■ 58 ■ Bayjet Inc.
410 W Thorpe Rd.
Las Cruces, NM 88005-5830
Phone: (505)526-3353
Free: (800)658-2774   Fax: (505)526-6003
Products: Transportation equipment and supplies, including aircraft and space vehicle supplies and parts. SIC: 5088 (Transportation Equipment & Supplies). Officers: Ed Bailey, CEO.

■ 59 ■ Bizjet International Sales and Support Inc.
3515 N Sheridan Rd.
Tulsa, OK 74115
Phone: (918)832-7733
E-mail: bizjet@bizjetinternational.com
URL: http://www.bizjetinternational.com
Products: Aviation equipment, installation, and repairs. SIC: 5088 (Transportation Equipment & Supplies). Est: 1986. Sales: $50,000,000 (2000). Emp: 230. Officers: W.L. Butch Walker, President.

■ 60 ■ BP America Inc.
200 Public Sq.
Cleveland, OH 44114
Phone: (216)586-4141
Free: (800)883-5527   Fax: (216)586-4050
Products: Jet and marine fuel. SIC: 5172 (Petroleum Products Nec). Sales: $11,550,000,000 (2000). Emp: 12,700. Officers: Steve Percy, CEO & Chairman of the Board; Thomas Gentile, Sr. VP & CFO.

■ 61 ■ Braden's Flying Service Inc.
3800 Sullivan Trail
Easton, PA 18040
Phone: (610)258-1706
Products: Aircraft parts. SIC: 5088 (Transportation Equipment & Supplies). Est: 1934. Sales: $3,000,000 (2000). Emp: 20. Officers: Paul Braden, President; Elizabeth Braden, Treasurer.

■ 62 ■ Brewer Associates Inc.
68 Franklin St.
Laconia, NH 03246-2322
Phone: (603)524-9225
Products: Transportation equipment and supplies; Aircraft and space vehicle supplies and parts; Aircraft engines and engine parts. SIC: 5088 (Transportation Equipment & Supplies). Officers: Donald Brewer, President.

■ 63 ■ Bridge Stone Aircraft Tire (USA), Inc.
7775 NW 12th St.
Miami, FL 33126
Phone: (305)592-3530   Fax: (305)592-0485
Products: Aircraft tires. SIC: 5088 (Transportation

Equipment & Supplies). **Sales:** $22,000,000 (2000). **Emp:** 150.

■ **64** ■ **Bridon Elm Inc.**
PO Box 10367
New Orleans, LA 70181-0367
Phone: (504)734-5871
Products: Aeronautical equipment. **SIC:** 5088 (Transportation Equipment & Supplies). **Est:** 1957. **Sales:** $9,000,000 (2000). **Emp:** 32. **Officers:** William Hobbs, President; E. Al Ulrich, Vice President.

■ **65** ■ **British Aerospace Holdings Inc.**
15000 Conference Center Dr., Ste
Chantilly, VA 20151-3819
Phone: (703)227-1500   **Fax:** (703)227-1505
Products: Aeronautical equipment and supplies. **SIC:** 5088 (Transportation Equipment & Supplies). **Sales:** $130,000,000 (2000). **Emp:** 200.

■ **66** ■ **British Aerospace North America Inc.**
15000 Conference Center Dr., Ste. 200
Chantilly, VA 20151-3819
Phone: (703)802-0080   **Fax:** (703)227-1610
Products: Commercial aircraft and aviation supplies. **SIC:** 5088 (Transportation Equipment & Supplies). **Est:** 1977. **Sales:** $130,000,000 (2000). **Emp:** 200. **Officers:** Paul Harris, Sr. VP & General Mgr.; Steve Masse, CFO. **Former Name:** British Aerospace Holdings Inc.

■ **67** ■ **Bruce Industries Inc.**
PO Box 1700
Dayton, NV 89403-1700
Phone: (702)246-0101   **Fax:** (702)246-0451
Products: Lighting systems for aircrafts. **SIC:** 5088 (Transportation Equipment & Supplies). **Est:** 1956. **Sales:** $26,000,000 (2000). **Emp:** 235. **Officers:** Frank B. Bruce, President; James Bradshaw, Finance Officer; Kurt Tella, Dir. of Marketing.

■ **68** ■ **Burbank Aircraft Supply Inc.**
2333 Utah Ave.
El Segundo, CA 90245
Phone: (310)727-5000
Products: Aircraft fasteners. **SIC:** 5072 (Hardware). **Sales:** $98,000,000 (2000). **Emp:** 300. **Officers:** Terry Brenner, President; Dennis McKinney, Sr. VP & CFO.

■ **69** ■ **Charlotte Aerospace Co. Inc.**
4801 E Independence Blvd., Ste. 1101
Charlotte, NC 28212
Phone: (704)536-1921   **Fax:** (704)536-1938
Products: Aircraft; Engine parts. **SIC:** 5088 (Transportation Equipment & Supplies). **Officers:** Harold J. Caldwell Sr., President. **Alternate Name:** Casco.

■ **70** ■ **Click Bond Inc.**
2151 Lockheed Way
Carson City, NV 89706
Phone: (702)885-8000   **Fax:** (702)883-0191
Products: Fasteners for aerospace equipment. **SICs:** 5072 (Hardware); 5088 (Transportation Equipment & Supplies). **Est:** 1987. **Sales:** $5,000,000 (2000). **Emp:** 65. **Officers:** Charles G. Hutter, President; Collie L. Hutter, Exec. VP & Treasurer; James F. Stemler, VP of Sales.

■ **71** ■ **Coast Air Inc.**
11134 Sepulveda Blvd.
Mission Hills, CA 91345
Phone: (818)898-2288
Free: (800)423-6092   **Fax:** (818)361-8918
E-mail: customerservice@coastair.com
URL: http://www.coastair.com
Products: Aerospace electromechanical hardware. **SIC:** 5088 (Transportation Equipment & Supplies). **Est:** 1953. **Sales:** $5,500,000 (2000). **Emp:** 20. **Officers:** F.W. Sutherland, CEO; Mariani Salmon, President.

■ **72** ■ **Commerce Overseas Corp.**
200 Saw Mill River Rd.
Hawthorne, NY 10532
Phone: (914)773-2100   **Fax:** (914)773-4214
E-mail: sales@commerceoverseas.com
URL: http://www.commerceoverseas.com
Products: Aerospace equipment; Electronic testing equipment; Industrial products. **SICs:** 5088 (Transportation Equipment & Supplies); 5065 (Electronic Parts & Equipment Nec); 5085 (Industrial Supplies). **Est:** 1967. **Sales:** $10,000,000 (2000). **Emp:** 25. **Officers:** Christopher Garville, CEO & Chairman of the Board.

■ **73** ■ **Commercial Aviation Support Inc.**
8550 W Flagler St., Ste. 101
Miami, FL 33144-2037
Phone: (305)594-0084   **Fax:** (305)594-0097
Products: Aircraft, engines, propellers, and parts. **SIC:** 5088 (Transportation Equipment & Supplies). **Officers:** E.T. Johnston, Vice President.

■ **74** ■ **Composite Technology Inc.**
1001 Avenue R.
Grand Prairie, TX 75050-1506
Phone: (972)556-0744   **Fax:** (972)556-0781
Products: Helicopter blades. **SIC:** 5088 (Transportation Equipment & Supplies). **Est:** 1972. **Sales:** $2,000,000 (2000). **Emp:** 40. **Officers:** John Niamtu, President; Mike Topa, VP of Finance; Don Russell, Dir. of Sales.

■ **75** ■ **Cooper Power Tools Division-Apex**
762 W Stewart St.
Dayton, OH 45408
Phone: (937)222-7871   **Fax:** (937)228-0422
Products: Hand tools; Aircraft aerospace fasteners. **SICs:** 5088 (Transportation Equipment & Supplies); 5072 (Hardware). **Emp:** 360. **Officers:** L.J. D'Aloisio.

■ **76** ■ **Corporate Rotable and Supply Inc.**
6701 NW 12th Ave.
Ft. Lauderdale, FL 33309
Phone: (954)972-2807
Products: Aircraft parts. **SIC:** 5088 (Transportation Equipment & Supplies). **Sales:** $12,000,000 (1992). **Emp:** 42. **Officers:** Armando Leighton, President.

■ **77** ■ **Crescent Airways Inc.**
7501 Pembroke Rd.
Hollywood, FL 33023-2579
Phone: (954)987-1900   **Fax:** (954)987-1912
Products: Helicopters and parts. **SIC:** 5088 (Transportation Equipment & Supplies). **Sales:** $10,000,000 (1993). **Emp:** 150. **Officers:** Tom Ramirez, President; Allen Suderman, CFO.

■ **78** ■ **D. Austin Aircraft**
RR 1, Box 397
Whitefield, NH 03598
Phone: (603)837-2627   **Fax:** (603)837-2627
Products: Aeronautical equipment and supplies. **SIC:** 5088 (Transportation Equipment & Supplies).

■ **79** ■ **Dallas Aerospace Inc.**
1875 N IH-35
Carrollton, TX 75006-3761
Phone: (214)539-1993
Products: Expandable aircraft equipment; Bearings; Lights; Aircraft skin. **SICs:** 5088 (Transportation Equipment & Supplies); 5063 (Electrical Apparatus & Equipment); 5085 (Industrial Supplies). **Sales:** $16,000,000 (2000). **Emp:** 50. **Officers:** Herman Schulz, President.

■ **80** ■ **Derco Industries Inc.**
PO Box 25549
Milwaukee, WI 53225
Phone: (414)355-3066
Products: Aircraft parts. **SIC:** 5088 (Transportation Equipment & Supplies). **Est:** 1979. **Sales:** $50,000,000 (2000). **Emp:** 120. **Officers:** Eric Dermond, President; Christine Meyer, Dir. of Data Processing; Sara J. Peterson, Dir. of Human Resources.

■ **81** ■ **Dunlop Aviation North America**
6573 Old Dixie Hwy., Ste. 120
Forest Park, GA 30297
Phone: (404)362-9900   **Fax:** (404)362-9911
Products: Aircraft wheel and brake components. **SIC:** 5088 (Transportation Equipment & Supplies). **Sales:** $2,000,000 (1991). **Emp:** 30. **Officers:** Mario Andreou, VP of Operations; R. T. Rice, VP of Finance & Controller.

■ **82** ■ **Eaton Corp.**
1640 Monrovia Ave.
Costa Mesa, CA 92627-4405
Phone: (949)642-2427   **Fax:** (949)722-4475
Products: Aerospace controls. **SIC:** 5088 (Transportation Equipment & Supplies). **Sales:** $27,000,000 (2000). **Emp:** 355. **Officers:** Kenneth T. Renaud.

■ **83** ■ **Elliott Aviation Inc.**
PO Box 100
Moline, IL 61266-0100
Phone: (309)799-3183   **Fax:** (309)799-3463
Products: Airplanes; Aviation equipment; Fuel. **SICs:** 5088 (Transportation Equipment & Supplies); 5172 (Petroleum Products Nec). **Est:** 1936. **Sales:** $60,000,000 (2000). **Emp:** 300. **Officers:** Wynn Elliott, President; Jeff M. Hyland, Finance Officer; Robert Hummel, Dir. of Marketing & Sales; Kevin Rostenbach, Dir. of Information Systems; Peggy Hull, Dir of Human Resources.

■ **84** ■ **Export Consultants Corp.**
250 Lackland Dr., No. 6
PO Box 308
Middlesex, NJ 08846
Phone: (732)469-0700   **Fax:** (732)469-9105
E-mail: eccfly@worldnet.att.net
URL: http://www.ecc-corp.com
Products: Aeronautical instruments and parts; Communication equipment; Helicopter and aircraft spare parts; Aircraft radio communication equipment; Mobile, hand-held communication equipment. **SICs:** 5088 (Transportation Equipment & Supplies); 5065 (Electronic Parts & Equipment Nec). **Est:** 1975. **Officers:** M.A. Althausen, Vice President.

■ **85** ■ **Eyak Aircraft**
PO Box 87
Willow, AK 99688-0087
Phones: (907)495-6428   (907)495-9000
Fax: (907)495-4000
Products: Aircraft restoration, maintenance and sales. **SIC:** 5088 (Transportation Equipment & Supplies). **Est:** 1968. **Emp:** 3. **Officers:** Maggie Stanger, Partner, e-mail: stanger@custommpu.com; Joseph E. Stanger, Partner.

■ **86** ■ **Far East Trading Company Inc.**
3911 Old Lee Highway, Ste. 42A
Fairfax, VA 22030
Phone: (703)591-0993   **Fax:** (703)591-0653
Products: Aircraft oil and lubricants; Aircraft spare parts. **SICs:** 5088 (Transportation Equipment & Supplies); 5172 (Petroleum Products Nec). **Officers:** Robert L. Abraham, Vice President.

■ **87** ■ **Federal Express Aviation Services Inc.**
2005 Corporate Ave.
Memphis, TN 38132
Phone: (901)395-3830   **Fax:** (901)395-3828
Products: Airplanes and stage 3 noise reduction kits for B-727 aircraft. **SIC:** 5088 (Transportation Equipment & Supplies). **Sales:** $250,000,000 (2000). **Emp:** 15. **Officers:** James R. Parker, President.

■ **88** ■ **Flight Products International**
PO Box 1558
Kalispell, MT 59903-1558
Phone: (406)752-8783   **Fax:** (406)257-7078
Products: Cockpit supplies. **SIC:** 5088 (Transportation Equipment & Supplies). **Officers:** James Fleming, President.

■ **89** ■ **Fortune Industries Inc.**
2153 Eagle Pkwy.
Ft. Worth, TX 76177-2311
Phone: (817)490-5700
Free: (800)989-9717   **Fax:** (817)490-5705
URL: http://www.questrontechnology.com
Products: Hardware for aircraft and missiles. **SICs:** 5088 (Transportation Equipment & Supplies); 5072 (Hardware). **Sales:** $14,000,000 (2000). **Emp:** 65. **Officers:** Malcom Tallman, President; Debra Alvey, Treasurer.

■ 90 ■ Fuses Unlimimted
9248 Eton Ave.
Chatsworth, CA 91311-5807
Phone: (818)786-8111
Products: Aircraft equipment and supplies, including fuses and hardware. **SIC:** 5088 (Transportation Equipment & Supplies). **Est:** 1950. **Sales:** $15,000,000 (2000). **Emp:** 35. **Officers:** Steve Hallapeter, Chairman of the Board; Nancy Ellington, Controller; Chris Leiker, Dir. of Marketing.

■ 91 ■ Future Metals Inc.
5400 NW 35th Ave.
Ft. Lauderdale, FL 33309
Phone: (954)739-5350
Free: (800)733-0960 **Fax:** (954)730-9543
URL: http://www.futuremetals.com
Products: Aircraft tubing. **SIC:** 5088 (Transportation Equipment & Supplies). **Est:** 1971. **Sales:** $45,000,000 (2000). **Emp:** 90. **Officers:** John F. Porfidio, President; Donald Ursini, Controller; Luis Benitez, VP of Sales; Clifford Bennett, Technical Dir.; e-mail: kperes@futuremetals.com

■ 92 ■ G-N Aircraft Inc.
1701 E Main St.
Griffith, IN 46319
Phone: (219)924-7110 **Fax:** (219)924-1059
Products: Piston aircraft engines. **SIC:** 5088 (Transportation Equipment & Supplies). **Est:** 1960. **Sales:** $2,300,000 (2000). **Emp:** 44. **Officers:** Paul Goldsmith, President; Richard Gilliland, CFO.

■ 93 ■ Gillette Air Inc.
2000 Airport Rd., Rm 5
Gillette, WY 82716-8105
Phone: (307)686-2900 **Fax:** (307)686-1471
Products: Transportation equipment; Aircraft parts and auxiliary equipment; Space vehicle equipment. **SIC:** 5088 (Transportation Equipment & Supplies). **Officers:** Arnold Erickson, President.

■ 94 ■ Hawker Pacific Inc.
11240 Sherman Way
Sun Valley, CA 91352
Phone: (818)765-6201
Free: (800)443-8302 **Fax:** (818)765-2065
E-mail: john.shade@hawker.com
URL: http://www.hawker.com
Products: Aircraft parts. **SIC:** 5088 (Transportation Equipment & Supplies). **Est:** 1978. **Sales:** $33,000,000 (2000). **Emp:** 210. **Officers:** David Lokken, President; Phil Panzera, CFO; Brian Carr; Mike Riley, VP of Operations; Richard Abey.

■ 95 ■ Hedrick Beechcraft Inc.
8402 Nelms Rd.
Houston, TX 77061
Phone: (713)567-5000 **Fax:** (713)567-5099
URL: htttp://www.raytheon.com
Products: Aircrafts and aircraft parts. **SIC:** 5088 (Transportation Equipment & Supplies). **Est:** 1938. **Sales:** $22,000,000 (2000). **Emp:** 125. **Officers:** David Vaughan, General Mgr.

■ 96 ■ Hermetic Aircraft International Corp.
100 Corporate Dr.
Holtsville, NY 11742
Phone: (516)758-4242
Products: Aircraft parts. **SIC:** 5088 (Transportation Equipment & Supplies). **Sales:** $20,000,000 (2000). **Emp:** 90. **Officers:** Roger Fauchon, CEO & President; Jeffrey Fausett, VP of Finance; Johm Minietta, Dir. of Sales.

■ 97 ■ Hoder-Rogers Inc.
885 Warren Ave.
East Providence, RI 02914-1423
Phone: (401)438-2725
Free: (800)431-4514 **Fax:** (401)438-8260
Products: Aeronautical equipment and supplies. **SIC:** 5088 (Transportation Equipment & Supplies). **Sales:** $2,000,000 (2000). **Emp:** 1.

■ 98 ■ Hoffmann Aircraft Inc.
427 Cr. 125
Texico, NM 88135-9776
Phone: (505)389-5505 **Fax:** (505)389-5504
Products: Transportation equipment; Aircraft parts and auxiliary equipment; Automotive parts and supplies, New. **SICs:** 5088 (Transportation Equipment & Supplies); 5013 (Motor Vehicle Supplies & New Parts). **Officers:** Karl Hoffmann, President.

■ 99 ■ Honeywell H.P.G.
11953 Challenger Ct.
Moorpark, CA 93021
Phone: (805)531-0001 **Fax:** (805)531-0005
Products: Aircraft bearings. **SIC:** 5085 (Industrial Supplies). **Est:** 1949. **Sales:** $21,000,000 (2000). **Emp:** 9. **Officers:** William C. Henning, Site Leader. **Former Name:** Aerospace Bearing Support Inc.

■ 100 ■ Intermountain Piper Inc.
301 N 2370 W
Salt Lake City, UT 84116
Phone: (801)322-1645
Products: Aircraft parts, including engines and plane frames. **SIC:** 5088 (Transportation Equipment & Supplies). **Est:** 1958. **Sales:** $2,900,000 (2000). **Emp:** 10. **Officers:** Steven E. Lindquist, President; John A. Lindquist, Treasurer & Secty.; Arnold Richens, Dir. of Marketing.

■ 101 ■ International Air Leases Inc.
PO Box 522230
Miami, FL 33152
Phone: (305)889-6000
Free: (800)327-9836 **Fax:** (305)887-9831
Products: Aircraft parts and leasing. **SIC:** 5088 (Transportation Equipment & Supplies). **Est:** 1971. **Sales:** $300,000,000 (2000). **Emp:** 377. **Officers:** George Batchelor, President; Raymond Walker, COO; Elizabeth Fagundo, Personnel Dir.

■ 102 ■ International Airline Support Group Inc.
3030 SW 42nd St.
Ft. Lauderdale, FL 33312-6809
Phone: (305)593-2658 **Fax:** (305)993-1751
Products: Aircraft; Aircraft engines and engine parts; Aircraft propellers and helicopter rotors. **SIC:** 5088 (Transportation Equipment & Supplies). **Est:** 1982. **Sales:** $250,000,000 (2000). **Emp:** 65. **Officers:** Richard Wellman, CEO; William Hartman, CFO; Bob Bender, VP of Marketing & Sales; Stan Switzer, Dir of Human Resources.

■ 103 ■ International Engine Parts Inc.
8950 Lurline Ave.
Chatsworth, CA 91311
Phone: (818)882-8803 **Fax:** (818)882-8623
E-mail: iepo@aol.com
Products: Airplane engines and parts. **SIC:** 5088 (Transportation Equipment & Supplies). **Est:** 1964. **Sales:** $6,000,000 (2000). **Emp:** 20. **Officers:** Elmo Iadevaia Sr., President; Rudy Aquino, Controller; Elmo Iadevaia Jr., Dir. of Marketing & Sales.

■ 104 ■ International Lease Finance Corp.
1999 Avenue of the Stars., 39th Fl.
Los Angeles, CA 90067
Phone: (310)788-1999 **Fax:** (310)788-1976
Products: Commercial jet aircraft. **SIC:** 5088 (Transportation Equipment & Supplies). **Sales:** $386,000,000 (2000). **Emp:** 75. **Officers:** Steven Udvar-Hazy, CEO & President.

■ 105 ■ Intertrade Ltd.
4700 N River Blvd. NE
Cedar Rapids, IA 52411
Phone: (319)378-3500
Products: Used avionics equipment. **SIC:** 5065 (Electronic Parts & Equipment Nec).

■ 106 ■ Irwin International Inc.
PO Box 4000
Corona, CA 91718
Phone: (909)372-9555 **Fax:** (909)372-0555
Products: Aircraft parts and pilot eyewear. **SICs:** 5088 (Transportation Equipment & Supplies); 5048 (Ophthalmic Goods). **Sales:** $15,000,000 (2000). **Emp:** 50. **Officers:** James Irwin, CEO; Nanci Irwin, Vice President.

■ 107 ■ Israel Aircraft Industries International
50 W 23rd St.
New York, NY 10010
Phone: (212)620-4400
Products: Aircraft and parts. **SIC:** 5088 (Transportation Equipment & Supplies).

■ 108 ■ Jet Equipment and Tools
PO Box 1349
Auburn, WA 98071
Phone: (206)351-6000 **Fax:** (206)804-5303
URL: http://www.jettools.com
Products: Jet equipment, including material handling products, metalworking machinery, woodworking machinery, airtools, metalforming machinery, and hand tools. **SIC:** 5088 (Transportation Equipment & Supplies). **Est:** 1959. **Sales:** $50,000,000 (2000). **Emp:** 100. **Officers:** Robert R. Skummer, President & COO; Reudi Temperli, Controller; David W. Loving, VP of Marketing & Sales.

■ 109 ■ Jonas Aircraft and Arms Company Inc.
225 Broadway
New York, NY 10005
Phone: (212)619-0330 **Fax:** (212)619-2743
E-mail: jonasny1@aol.com
Products: Aircraft parts and equipment; Chemical fire extinguishing equipment; Fishing tackle and equipment; Organic chemicals, including tear gas. Shotguns; Firearms; Batons; Uniforms; Helmets. **SICs:** 5088 (Transportation Equipment & Supplies); 5169 (Chemicals & Allied Products Nec); 5099 (Durable Goods Nec); 5091 (Sporting & Recreational Goods). **Est:** 1937. **Officers:** Geoffrey Steinemann, President; Magaly Osorio, Sales/Marketing Contact, e-mail: jonasaafl@aol.com; Mrs. Virginia Caban.

■ 110 ■ K-Tech Aviation, Inc.
5025 E Nebraska St.
Tucson, AZ 85706
Phone: (520)747-4417 **Fax:** (520)745-6139
URL: http://www.k-techav.com
Products: Aircraft parts. **SIC:** 5088 (Transportation Equipment & Supplies). **Est:** 1990. **Sales:** $1,000,000 (1999). **Emp:** 4. **Officers:** Larry Kotz, President, e-mail: lkotz@k-Techav.com; Sean Oseran, Sales/ Marketing Contact, e-mail: oseran@k-techav.com.

■ 111 ■ Kaman Industrial Technologies Inc.
1332 Blue Hills Ave.
Bloomfield, CT 06002
Phone: (203)243-8311 **Fax:** (203)286-4112
Products: Aeronautical equipment and supplies. **SIC:** 5085 (Industrial Supplies). **Sales:** $320,000,000 (2000). **Emp:** 1,350.

■ 112 ■ Kansas City Aviation Center Inc.
PO Box 1850
Olathe, KS 66063
Phone: (913)782-0530
Products: Aircrafts. **SIC:** 5088 (Transportation Equipment & Supplies). **Sales:** $13,000,000 (1994). **Emp:** 65. **Officers:** David Armacost, CEO.

■ 113 ■ Kirkhill Aircraft Parts Co.
PO Box 3500
Brea, CA 92821
Phone: (714)524-5520
Products: Plane seals and gaskets. **SIC:** 5088 (Transportation Equipment & Supplies). **Est:** 1977. **Sales:** $13,000,000 (2000). **Emp:** 55. **Officers:** Henry C. Ray, CEO; Marlin Summers, Exec. VP of Finance; Rhea Hooper, Mgr. of Admin.

■ 114 ■ Lake Aircraft Inc.
PO Box 5336
Laconia, NH 03247-5336
Phone: (603)524-5868 **Fax:** (603)524-5728
E-mail: wolf@amphib.com
URL: http://www.amphib.com
Products: Transportation equipment; Aircraft parts and auxiliary equipment; Space vehicle equipment. **SIC:** 5088 (Transportation Equipment & Supplies). **Officers:** Armand Rivard, President.

■ 115 ■ Lektro Inc.
1190 SE Flightline Dr.
Warrenton, OR 97146
Phone: (503)861-2288   Fax: (503)861-2283
Products: Aircraft ground support equipment; Aircraft tow vehicles; Custom electric vehicles. SIC: 5088 (Transportation Equipment & Supplies).

■ 116 ■ Lincoln Trading Co.
5925 Benjamin Center Dr., No. 113
Tampa, FL 33634-5239
Phone: (813)874-6620   Fax: (813)874-7204
Products: Computer software and hardware; Aviation parts and supplies. SICs: 5088 (Transportation Equipment & Supplies); 5045 (Computers, Peripherals & Software). Officers: C.J. Lanson, President.

■ 117 ■ Lindquist Investment Co.
3909 S Airport Rd.
Ogden, UT 84405
Phone: (801)399-4532
Products: Small aircraft. SIC: 5088 (Transportation Equipment & Supplies). Est: 1947. Sales: $15,500,000 (2000). Emp: 55. Officers: Steven E. Lindquist, President.

■ 118 ■ Londavia Inc.
399 Concord Tpke., Rte. 4
Barrington, NH 03825
Phone: (603)868-9900   Fax: (603)868-2672
Products: Transportation equipment and supplies; Aircraft and space vehicle supplies and parts. SIC: 5088 (Transportation Equipment & Supplies). Officers: John Raisbeck, President.

■ 119 ■ Lynton Group Inc.
9 Airport Rd.
Morristown, NJ 07960
Phone: (973)292-9000   Fax: (973)292-1529
Products: Aircraft and parts. SIC: 5088 (Transportation Equipment & Supplies). Sales: $26,000,000 (2000). Emp: 104. Officers: Christopher Tennant, CEO & President; Paul A. Boyd, CFO & Treasurer.

■ 120 ■ Matrix Aviation Inc.
1701 S Hoover Rd.
Wichita, KS 67209
Phone: (316)942-0844
Products: Avionics instruments; Airframe components. SIC: 5088 (Transportation Equipment & Supplies). Sales: $5,000,000 (1993). Emp: 15. Officers: Wayne Grossardt, President.

■ 121 ■ Ron McIntosh and Associates Inc.
853 26th St.
Santa Monica, CA 90403
Phone: (310)828-5694   Fax: (310)828-6830
Products: Aircraft and missile parts. SIC: 5088 (Transportation Equipment & Supplies). Est: 1966. Sales: $1,300,000 (2000). Emp: 3. Officers: James Gray, President; A. Farinet, Controller.

■ 122 ■ Memphis Group Inc.
3900 Willow Lake Blvd.
Memphis, TN 38118
Phone: (901)362-8600   Fax: (901)365-1482
Products: Aircraft parts and auxiliary equipment; Aircraft engine instruments. SIC: 5088 (Transportation Equipment & Supplies). Est: 1971. Sales: $65,000,000 (2000). Emp: 200. Officers: John A. Williams, President; John Temple, Exec. VP; Don Scott; Mike Justice, VP of Marketing; Cathy Hanking, VP of Sales.

■ 123 ■ Meridian Aerospace Group Ltd.
3796 Vest Mill Rd.
Winston-Salem, NC 27103
Phone: (919)765-5454   Fax: (919)765-5577
Products: Commercial and private aircraft. SIC: 5088 (Transportation Equipment & Supplies). Est: 1988. Sales: $25,000,000 (2000). Emp: 8. Officers: William D. Gardner, CEO & President.

■ 124 ■ Metro Crown International
PO Box 12238
Kansas City, MO 64152
Phone: (660)879-5514
Products: Aircraft parts and auxiliary equipment;

Aircraft engines and engine parts. SIC: 5088 (Transportation Equipment & Supplies).

■ 125 ■ Metro-Jasim, Inc.
39 Lloyd St.
New Hyde Park, NY 11040
Phone: (516)248-1177
Products: Aircraft equipment and supplies. SIC: 5088 (Transportation Equipment & Supplies).

■ 126 ■ Miami Aviation Corp.
14980 NW 44th Ct.
Opa Locka, FL 33054
Phone: (305)688-0511
Products: Aviation parts. SIC: 5088 (Transportation Equipment & Supplies). Est: 1962. Sales: $5,000,000 (2000). Emp: 55. Officers: Frank C. Hart Jr., President; Rachel Cardoso, Controller; Kermit Singer, Sales Mgr.

■ 127 ■ Michelle International, Ltd.
6622 Eastside Dr. NE, No. 31
Browns Point, WA 98422-1175
Phone: (253)924-0844   Fax: (253)924-0941
Products: New and used commercial aircrafts and parts; Medical equipment; International trading company. SICs: 5088 (Transportation Equipment & Supplies); 5047 (Medical & Hospital Equipment); 5012 (Automobiles & Other Motor Vehicles). Est: 1982. Officers: Michael R. Luttmer, President.

■ 128 ■ Mid Continent Aircraft Corp.
PO Box 540
Hayti, MO 63851
Phone: (314)359-0500   Fax: (314)359-0538
E-mail: sales@midcont.com
URL: http://www.midcont.com
Products: Aircraft vehicles and parts. SIC: 5088 (Transportation Equipment & Supplies). Est: 1949. Sales: $14,000,000 (2000). Emp: 50. Officers: Richard Reade, President; Chris Cobb, Controller; Larry Cookenboo, Exec. VP; Dennie Stokes, Sr. VP.

■ 129 ■ MidWest Air Motive Corp.
PO Box 1014
Bismarck, ND 58502-1014
Phone: (701)663-7747   Fax: (701)667-1296
E-mail: midwest1@uswest.net
Products: Retail aircraft and aircraft parts, new and used avonics. SIC: 5088 (Transportation Equipment & Supplies). Est: 1993. Sales: $2,500,000 (2000). Emp: 5. Officers: Monroe Chase, General Mgr., e-mail: Midwest@uswest.net.

■ 130 ■ Military Industrial Supply Co.
1720 Main St., Ste. 1
Palm Bay, FL 32905
Phones: (321)952-8877   (321)952-8811
Free: (800)738-6322
E-mail: multiinventory@aol.com
Products: Electro-mechanical parts for military and space shuttle use; industrial hardware. SIC: 5065 (Electronic Parts & Equipment Nec). Est: 1987. Sales: $1,000,000 (2000). Emp: 4. Officers: Jinelle Naylor, Human Resource Contact; Bill Taylor, Human Resource Contact.

■ 131 ■ National Airmotive Corp.
PO Box 6069
Oakland, CA 94614
Phone: (510)613-1000   Fax: (510)562-7426
Products: Aircraft engines. SIC: 5088 (Transportation Equipment & Supplies). Est: 1960. Sales: $119,000,000 (2000). Emp: 375. Officers: Gerry Roberts, President; John Viboch, VP of Finance; Dennis Bagwell, VP of Marketing & Sales; Richard Bowley, Dir. of Information Systems; Michael Rosen, Dir of Human Resources.

■ 132 ■ Northwest Parts & Equipment
PO Box 1205
Eagle, ID 83616-1205
Phone: (208)375-1500
Products: Transportation equipment and supplies. SIC: 5088 (Transportation Equipment & Supplies). Officers: Kenneth Whitney, Owner.

■ 133 ■ Ontario Air Parts Inc.
15042 Whittram Ave.
Fontana, CA 92335
Phone: (909)829-3031
Products: Aircraft and engine parts. SIC: 5088 (Transportation Equipment & Supplies). Sales: $12,000,000 (2000). Emp: 43. Officers: James A. Fishback, President.

■ 134 ■ Pac Aero
120 S Weber Dr.
Chandler, AZ 85226-3216
Phone: (602)365-2610
E-mail: burpacr@aol.com
Products: Aeronautical equipment; Chemicals. SICs: 5088 (Transportation Equipment & Supplies); 5169 (Chemicals & Allied Products Nec). Est: 1966. Sales: $18,000,000 (2000). Emp: 36. Officers: Tom Hodges, CEO & President; Ron Gall, VP of Operations; Craig Chelius, Controller.

■ 135 ■ Pacific Coast Air Tool and Supply Inc.
4560 Carter Ct.
Chino, CA 91710
Phone: (909)627-0948   Fax: (909)628-5290
E-mail: info@pacificcoasttools.com
URL: http://www.pacificcoasttools.com
Products: Airplane tools, including hand, air, electric, and construction tools; Industrial supplies; Pumps; Compactors; Generators. SICs: 5084 (Industrial Machinery & Equipment); 5072 (Hardware); 5085 (Industrial Supplies). Est: 1985. Sales: $2,200,000 (2000). Emp: 11. Officers: Ken Marquardt, Vice President.

■ 136 ■ PAS Div.
10540 Ridge Rd.
New Port Richey, FL 34654
Phone: (727)849-9240   Fax: (727)842-1740
E-mail: pas_pas@pall.com
Products: Aircraft filtration parts. SIC: 5088 (Transportation Equipment & Supplies). Est: 1993. Sales: $20,000,000 (2000). Emp: 12. Officers: Richard Haas, President; Michele Woodland, Vice President.

■ 137 ■ Pietsch Aircraft Restoration & Repair
2216 N Broadway
Minot, ND 58701-1011
Phone: (701)852-4092   Fax: (701)852-5343
Products: Transportation equipment; Aircraft parts and auxiliary equipment; Space vehicle equipment. SIC: 5088 (Transportation Equipment & Supplies). Est: 1957. Emp: 5. Officers: Warren Pietsch, President. Former Name: Peach Flying.

■ 138 ■ Precision Propeller Service Inc.
4777 Aeronca St.
Boise, ID 83705-5055
Phone: (208)344-5161
Free: (800)643-8379   Fax: (208)344-9503
Products: Aeronautical equipment and supplies. SIC: 5088 (Transportation Equipment & Supplies). Sales: $1,300,000 (2000). Emp: 7.

■ 139 ■ Professional Aviation Associates Inc.
4694 Aviation Pkwy., Ste. K
Atlanta, GA 30349
Phone: (404)767-0282
Free: (800)283-2105   Fax: (404)767-1467
Products: Avionics, landing gear, hydraulic components, engine accessories, electrical components, and airframe components. SICs: 5088 (Transportation Equipment & Supplies); 5084 (Industrial Machinery & Equipment); 5065 (Electronic Parts & Equipment Nec); 5085 (Industrial Supplies). Sales: $12,000,000 (2000). Emp: 30. Officers: Thomas J. Chastain, President.

■ 140 ■ Raytheon Aircraft Services
PO Box 51830
Indianapolis, IN 46251
Phone: (317)241-2893   Fax: (317)243-6752
Products: Aircraft. SIC: 5088 (Transportation Equipment & Supplies). Est: 1971. Sales: $15,000,000 (2000). Emp: 92. Officers: Mike Robinson, General Mgr. Alternate Name: United Beechcraft Inc.

■ 141 ■ **Reeve Aleutian Airways Inc.**
4700 W Intl. Airport Rd.
Anchorage, AK 99502-1091
Phone: (907)243-1112 **Fax:** (907)249-2317
Products: Airplanes. **SIC:** 5088 (Transportation
Equipment & Supplies). **Est:** 1932. **Sales:** $32,000,000
(2000). **Emp:** 250. **Officers:** Richard D. Reeve,
President; Morris W. Shephard, Controller.

■ 142 ■ **Rice Aircraft Inc.**
350 Motor Pkwy.
Hauppauge, NY 11788
Phone: (516)435-1500 **Fax:** (516)435-1665
Products: Aircraft fasteners. **SICs:** 5088
(Transportation Equipment & Supplies); 5072
(Hardware). **Est:** 1985. **Sales:** $11,000,000 (2000).
Emp: 35. **Officers:** Bruce J. Rice, Owner; Ann Dunn,
Controller.

■ 143 ■ **R.S.B.I. Aerospace Inc.**
3606 NE Independence
Lees Summit, MO 64063
Phone: (816)246-4800
Products: Aircraft parts. **SIC:** 5088 (Transportation
Equipment & Supplies). **Sales:** $1,000,000 (2000).
Emp: 5. **Officers:** Ross Barber, President.

■ 144 ■ **Ryder Aviall Inc.**
PO Box 549015
Dallas, TX 75354-9015
Phone: (214)353-7000
Products: Aviation parts and supplies. **SIC:** 5088
(Transportation Equipment & Supplies). **Est:** 1981.
Sales: $1,260,000,000 (2000). **Emp:** 4,079. **Officers:**
John Wallace, President.

■ 145 ■ **Saab Aircraft of America Inc.**
21300 Ridgetop Cir.
Sterling, VA 20163
Phone: (703)406-7200 **Fax:** (703)406-7224
Products: Airplanes. **SIC:** 5088 (Transportation
Equipment & Supplies). **Sales:** $25,000,000 (2000).
Emp: 70. **Officers:** Jack Faherty, President; Ron
Frederick, Vice President.

■ 146 ■ **Sacramento Sky Ranch Inc.**
PO Box 22610
Sacramento, CA 95822
Phone: (916)421-7672
Products: Airplane engines. **SIC:** 5088 (Transportation
Equipment & Supplies). **Sales:** $6,000,000 (2000).
Emp: 20. **Officers:** John Schwaner, President.

■ 147 ■ **Smiths Industries**
148 East Ave., Ste. 2-I
Norwalk, CT 06851-5726
Products: Aeronautical equipment. **SIC:** 5088
(Transportation Equipment & Supplies). **Est:** 1960.
Sales: $15,000,000 (2000). **Emp:** 25. **Officers:**
Jerome Hines, President; Michael Silinsky, VP of
Finance.

■ 148 ■ **Solair Inc.**
3380 SW 11th Ave.
Ft. Lauderdale, FL 33315
Phone: (954)523-9999 **Fax:** (954)523-6505
Products: Avionics, landing gear, hydraulic
components, and engine accessories and components.
SIC: 5088 (Transportation Equipment & Supplies).
Sales: $64,000,000 (2000). **Emp:** 85. **Officers:**
Timothy C. Daggett, President; David Alden, CFO.

■ 149 ■ **Spacecraft Components Corp.**
14137 Chadrow Ave.
Hawthorne, CA 90251-5027
Phone: (310)973-6400 **Fax:** (310)973-2820
E-mail: space@spacecraft.com
URL: http://www.spacecraft.com
Products: Aerospace and aircraft custom connectors;
Molded cable assemblies. **SIC:** 5088 (Transportation
Equipment & Supplies). **Est:** 1962. **Sales:** $6,000,000
(1999). **Emp:** 55. **Officers:** Irv Zeiger, President; Debra
Koza, Accounting Manager; Craig Wiseman,
Sales/Marketing Contact.

■ 150 ■ **Spencer Industries Inc. (Seattle, Washington)**
8410 Dallas Ave.
Seattle, WA 98108
Phone: (206)763-0210
Products: Aircraft fasteners and hydraulic systems and
components. **SICs:** 5088 (Transportation Equipment &
Supplies); 5085 (Industrial Supplies). **Sales:**
$151,000,000 (2000). **Emp:** 200. **Officers:** Charles
Harris, President; John Hoyt, VP & CFO.

■ 151 ■ **Stein Seal Company Inc.**
PO Box 316
Kulpsville, PA 19443
Phone: (215)256-0201
Products: Helicopter machine parts. **SIC:** 5088
(Transportation Equipment & Supplies). **Est:** 1955.
Sales: $9,000,000 (2000). **Emp:** 100. **Officers:** P.C.
Stein Jr., President.

■ 152 ■ **Summit Aviation Inc.**
Summit Airport
Middletown, DE 19709
Phone: (302)834-5400 **Fax:** (302)378-7035
Products: Used aircraft parts. **SIC:** 5088
(Transportation Equipment & Supplies). **Est:** 1960.
Sales: $27,000,000 (2000). **Emp:** 100. **Officers:**
Patrick J. Foley, President; Deborah Dragone,
Treasurer; Norman Lee, Dir. of Marketing; Joyce
Morales, Dir of Personnel.

■ 153 ■ **Sun Aviation Inc.**
PO Box 18290
Raytown, MO 64133-8290
Phone: (816)358-4925 **Fax:** (816)737-0658
Products: Aeronautical equipment and supplies. **SIC:**
5088 (Transportation Equipment & Supplies).

■ 154 ■ **Sun Valley Aviation Inc.**
PO Box 1085
Hailey, ID 83333-1085
Phone: (208)788-9511 **Fax:** (208)788-9653
Products: Transportation equipment and supplies;
Aircraft and space vehicle supplies and parts. **SIC:**
5088 (Transportation Equipment & Supplies). **Officers:**
Wayne Werner, President.

■ 155 ■ **Syban International Inc.**
PO Box 16132
Hooksett, NH 03106-6132
Phone: (603)645-6015 **Fax:** (603)225-5721
Products: Transportation equipment; Aircraft parts and
auxiliary equipment; Missile and space vehicle
components, parts; Aeronautical equipment and
supplies. **SIC:** 5088 (Transportation Equipment &
Supplies). **Officers:** Aphrodite Doulias, President.

■ 156 ■ **TD Materials Inc.**
2211 S Tubeway Ave.
Los Angeles, CA 90040-1615
Phone: (213)232-6171 **Fax:** (213)232-6195
URL: http://www.tdmaterials.com
Products: Aircraft parts. **SIC:** 5051 (Metals Service
Centers & Offices). **Est:** 1939. **Sales:** $22,000,000
(2000). **Emp:** 55. **Officers:** William A. Lippman, CEO;
Stephen R. Levet, CFO.

■ 157 ■ **Techrepco Inc.**
PO Box 15608
Albuquerque, NM 87174-0608
Phone: (505)898-1727 **Fax:** (505)898-2127
Products: Transportation equipment and supplies;
Aircraft and space vehicle supplies and parts. **SIC:**
5088 (Transportation Equipment & Supplies). **Officers:**
Richard Steward, President.

■ 158 ■ **Texas Turbo Jet Inc.**
7725 Waxwing Cir. W
Ft. Worth, TX 76137-1009
Products: Aircraft parts and engines. **SIC:** 5088
(Transportation Equipment & Supplies). **Est:** 1972.
Sales: $5,000,000 (2000). **Emp:** 20. **Officers:** W.F.
Jones, Owner; R. Jones, President.

■ 159 ■ **Thermion Technologies Inc.**
130 E Crescent Ave.
Mahwah, NJ 07430
Phone: (201)529-2275 **Fax:** (201)848-7882
Products: Aircraft de-icing equipment and supplies.
SIC: 5088 (Transportation Equipment & Supplies).

■ 160 ■ **TLD America**
812 Bloomfield Ave.
Windsor, CT 06095
Phone: (860)688-9520
Free: (800)526-5298 **Fax:** (860)688-7895
Products: Aircraft ground support equipment. **SIC:**
5088 (Transportation Equipment & Supplies). **Est:**
1966. **Sales:** $52,000,000 (2000). **Emp:** 178. **Officers:**
Antoine Maguin, CEO; Serge Bilcheck, CFO. **Former
Name:** Devtec Corp.

■ 161 ■ **Tower Aviation Services**
PO Box 2444
Oakland, CA 94614
Phone: (510)635-3500 **Fax:** (510)635-0885
Products: Aviation repair components. **SIC:** 5088
(Transportation Equipment & Supplies). **Est:** 1968.
Sales: $20,000,000 (2000). **Emp:** 70. **Officers:** C.
Archer, President.

■ 162 ■ **Toyota Aviation U.S.A. Inc.**
3250 Airflite Way
Long Beach, CA 90807
Phone: (562)490-6200
Products: Aviation items. **SIC:** 5088 (Transportation
Equipment & Supplies). **Est:** 1988. **Sales:** $22,900,000
(2000). **Emp:** 43. **Officers:** Alan E. Cabito, President;
Eugene Broscow, Controller; James E. Press,
President.

■ 163 ■ **Tronair Inc.**
S 1740 Eber Rd.
Holland, OH 43528
Phone: (419)866-6301
Free: (800)426-6301 **Fax:** (419)867-0634
E-mail: mail@tronair.com
URL: http://www.tronair.com
Products: Aircraft ground support and maintenance
equipment; Hydraulic jacks. **SIC:** 5088 (Transportation
Equipment & Supplies). **Est:** 1972. **Sales:** $18,000,000
(1999). **Emp:** 90. **Officers:** Kerry Hansen, President, e-
mail: khansen@tronair.com.

■ 164 ■ **Unirex Inc.**
9310 E 37th St. N
Wichita, KS 67226-2014
Phone: (316)636-1228
Free: (800)397-1257 **Fax:** (316)636-5482
E-mail: sales@unirexinc.com
URL: http://www.unirexinc.com
Products: Aircraft parts and auxiliary equipment; Bolts,
nuts, rivets, screws, and washers. **SIC:** 5088
(Transportation Equipment & Supplies). **Est:** 1968.
Sales: $10,000,000 (2000). **Emp:** 25. **Officers:** Rob
Crawford, President; Brian Anderson, VP of Marketing
& Sales; Mark Coffey, Sales/Marketing Contact, e-mail:
mark@unirexinc.com; David Crawford, Customer
Service Contact, e-mail: david@unirexinc.com.

■ 165 ■ **U.S. Aircraft Industries International Inc.**
30-A Field St.
West Babylon, NY 11704
Phone: (516)420-0064 **Fax:** (516)420-9470
Products: Aircraft and aircraft parts. **SIC:** 5088
(Transportation Equipment & Supplies). **Officers:** Larry
Horowitz, Vice President.

■ 166 ■ **US Airways Group Inc.**
2345 Crystal Dr.
Arlington, VA 22227
Phone: (703)872-5306
Products: Aircraft and aircraft parts. **SIC:** 5088
(Transportation Equipment & Supplies). **Sales:**
$8,513,800,000 (2000). **Emp:** 42,500. **Officers:**
Stephen M. Wolf, Chairman of the Board; Rakesh
Gangwal, President & CEO; Thomas Mutryn, Sr. VP &
CFO.

■ 167 ■ **Venada Aviation Inc.**
685 Trade Center Dr.
Las Vegas, NV 89119-3712
Phone: (702)897-1600 **Fax:** (702)897-1604
Products: Transportation equipment; Aircraft parts and auxiliary equipment; Space vehicle equipment. **SIC:** 5088 (Transportation Equipment & Supplies). **Officers:** Tracey Madsen, President.

■ 168 ■ **Washington Avionics Inc.**
8535 Perimeter Rd. S
Seattle, WA 98108-3802
Phone: (206)762-0190 **Fax:** (425)468-0661
Products: Aircraft electronics and service. **SIC:** 5088 (Transportation Equipment & Supplies). **Officers:** Lloyd Lonsberry, President.

■ 169 ■ **Watkins System Inc.**
PO Box 4000
Concordville, PA 19331
Phone: (610)358-3400 **Fax:** (215)459-0224
Products: Aircraft refueler trucks. **SIC:** 5084 (Industrial Machinery & Equipment). **Est:** 1952. **Sales:** $55,000,000 (2000). **Emp:** 250. **Officers:** George Watkins, President; Don R. Shipengrover, Treasurer & Secty.

■ 170 ■ **Way-Point Avionics Inc.**
2301 University Dr., No. 38
Bismarck, ND 58504-7595
Phone: (701)223-2055 **Fax:** (701)224-0985
Products: Transportation equipment; Aircraft parts and auxiliary equipment; Space vehicle equipment. **SIC:** 5088 (Transportation Equipment & Supplies). **Officers:** Linda Buller, Vice President.

■ 171 ■ **Weems & Plath, Inc.**
214 Eastern Ave.
Annapolis, MD 21403
Phone: (410)263-6700
Free: (800)638-0428 **Fax:** (410)268-8713
URL: http://www.weems-plath.com
Products: Nautical and navigational instruments. **SIC:** 5088 (Transportation Equipment & Supplies). **Est:** 1928. **Sales:** $4,200,000 (2000). **Emp:** 18. **Officers:**

Peter W. Trogdon, President. **Former Name:** C. #Plath North American.

■ 172 ■ **Western Aircraft Inc.**
4444 Aeronca St.
Boise, ID 83705-5090
Phone: (208)338-1800
Free: (800)333-3442 **Fax:** (208)338-1830
Products: Aircraft. **SIC:** 5088 (Transportation Equipment & Supplies). **Sales:** $20,000,000 (2000). **Emp:** 88. **Officers:** John Penn, CEO; Mike Maynard, Controller.

■ 173 ■ **Wiggins Airways Inc. Parts East**
PO Box 250
Norwood, MA 02062
Phone: (617)762-5690
Products: Aircraft parts. **SIC:** 5088 (Transportation Equipment & Supplies). **Est:** 1929. **Sales:** $17,900,000 (2000). **Emp:** 103. **Officers:** David Ladd, President; James Barry, VP & Treasurer.

■ 174 ■ **E.W. Wiggins Airways Inc. Parts East**
PO Box 708
Norwood, MA 02062
Phone: (781)762-3500 **Fax:** (781)762-7510
Products: Airplane parts. **SIC:** 5088 (Transportation Equipment & Supplies). **Est:** 1929. **Sales:** $2,000,000 (2000). **Emp:** 15. **Officers:** David L. Ladd, President; Jim Barry, CFO; Philip Douglas, Vice President.

■ 175 ■ **W.S. Wilson Corp.**
24 Harbor Park Dr.
Port Washington, NY 11050
Phone: (516)621-8800
Products: Airplane bearings. **SIC:** 5088 (Transportation Equipment & Supplies). **Est:** 1917. **Sales:** $25,000,000 (2000). **Emp:** 30. **Officers:** Harry L. Baugher, President; Robert Yule, Vice President.

■ 176 ■ **World Fuel Services Inc.**
700 S Royal Poinciana Blvd., Ste. 800
Miami Springs, FL 33166
Phone: (305)883-8554 **Fax:** (305)887-2642
Products: Jet fuel. **SIC:** 5172 (Petroleum Products

Nec). **Sales:** $418,000,000 (2000). **Emp:** 90. **Officers:** Raymond Rossman, President; Carlos Abaunza, CFO.

■ 177 ■ **WRG Corp.**
143B SW 153rd St.
PO Box 66557
Seattle, WA 98166
Phone: (206)242-9300 **Fax:** (206)241-2114
E-mail: wrgatsea@worldnet.att.net
Products: Communication equipment; Ammunition and armaments; Military vehicles, including armored and non-armored; Semi-finished metals; Aircraft and aerospace parts; Industrial products. **SICs:** 5088 (Transportation Equipment & Supplies); 5051 (Metals Service Centers & Offices); 5099 (Durable Goods Nec). **Est:** 1965. **Sales:** $5,000,000 (2000). **Emp:** 8. **Officers:** Stephen A. Gray, President; Sheri L. Goranson, VP of Operations; Larry L. Meacham, VP of Marketing & Sales.

■ 178 ■ **Yingling Aircraft Inc.**
PO Box 9248
Wichita, KS 67277
Phone: (316)943-3246
E-mail: yingling@feist.com
URL: http://www.yinglingaircraft.com
Products: Private aircraft parts and fuel. **SICs:** 5088 (Transportation Equipment & Supplies); 5172 (Petroleum Products Nec). **Est:** 1946. **Sales:** $20,000,000 (1999). **Emp:** 60. **Officers:** Jack Feiden, President; Rae Jean Barger, Treasurer & Secty.; Nancy Periolat, Data Processing Mgr.

■ 179 ■ **Zephyr Manufacturing Co., Inc.**
201 Hindry Ave.
Inglewood, CA 90301-1519
Phone: (310)410-4907 **Fax:** (310)410-2913
E-mail: zephyr@zephyrtool.com
URL: http://www.zephyrtool.com
Products: Aircraft and industrial hand tools. **SICs:** 5088 (Transportation Equipment & Supplies); 5072 (Hardware). **Est:** 1939. **Sales:** $10,000,000 (2000). **Emp:** 100. **Officers:** Bernard Kersulis, President; Rick Guerrero, VP of Sales; Ann Nakamura, Customer Service Mgr. **Alternate Name:** Rick #Guerrero.

(3) Agricultural Equipment and Supplies

Entries in this section are arranged alphabetically by company name. When the company name is a personal name, the company name is alphabetized by the surname unless the first name or initial(s) are part of a trade name. See the User's Guide at the front of this directory for additional information.

■ **180** ■ **AA Equipment**
10611 Ramona Ave.
Montclair, CA 91763
Phone: (714)626-8586 **Fax:** (714)624-0675
Products: Farm equipment including tractors, lawnmowers, and irrigation systems. **SIC:** 5083 (Farm & Garden Machinery).

■ **181** ■ **Abell Corp.**
PO Box 8056
Monroe, LA 71211
Phone: (318)345-2600
Free: (800)325-7204 **Fax:** (318)387-0115
Products: Fertilizers and polyurethane tanks. **SICs:** 5191 (Farm Supplies); 5162 (Plastics Materials & Basic Shapes). **Sales:** $125,000,000 (2000). **Emp:** 200. **Officers:** Dixon Abell, President; Kim Koker, VP of Finance.

■ **182** ■ **Ada Feed and Seed Inc.**
12 W Thorp Ave.
PO Box 231
Ada, MN 56510
Phone: (218)784-7158 **Fax:** (218)784-3024
E-mail: adafeed@means.net
Products: Agricultural supplies, including feed, seed, fertilizer, sunflower processors, and animal health products. **SICs:** 5191 (Farm Supplies); 5199 (Nondurable Goods Nec); 5083 (Farm & Garden Machinery). **Est:** 1930. **Sales:** $4,000,000 (2000). **Emp:** 10. **Officers:** Grant R. Wagner, Vice President; Tim Wagner, President.

■ **183** ■ **Adams County Co-operative Association Inc.**
109 E Andrews St.
Monroe, IN 46772
Phone: (219)692-6111
Products: Farm supplies; Feed; Fertilizer and fertilizer materials. **SICs:** 5153 (Grain & Field Beans); 5191 (Farm Supplies). **Est:** 1928. **Sales:** $25,000,000 (1999). **Emp:** 45. **Officers:** D. Piper, General Mgr.; Ben Bloom, Controller.

■ **184** ■ **Adams Hard-Facing Company of California**
10 Greg St.
Sparks, NV 89431-6276
Phone: (775)359-0399 **Fax:** (775)359-9638
Products: Farm implements. **SIC:** 5083 (Farm & Garden Machinery). **Sales:** $1,000,000 (2000). **Emp:** 3. **Officers:** Keith Vinnyard McQuire, CEO.

■ **185** ■ **Carroll Adams Tractor Co.**
902 W Rose St.
WalLa Walla, WA 99362
Phone: (509)525-4550 **Fax:** (509)525-8673
Products: Farm tractors and large lawn mowers. **SICs:** 5191 (Farm Supplies); 5172 (Petroleum Products Nec). **Est:** 1949. **Sales:** $5,000,000 (2000). **Emp:** 35. **Officers:** Robert D. Adams, President; Kim Croft, Office Mgr.

■ **186** ■ **Adams Tractor Company Inc.**
PO Box 3043
Spokane, WA 99202-3043
Phone: (509)535-1708 **Fax:** (509)536-1850
Products: Farm and mowing equipment; Light industrial machinery. **SICs:** 5083 (Farm & Garden Machinery); 5084 (Industrial Machinery & Equipment). **Est:** 1929. **Sales:** $5,000,000 (2000). **Emp:** 28. **Officers:** K.A. Adams, President; Linda Trimp, Office Mgr.; Gene Cory, Sales Mgr.

■ **187** ■ **J. & L. Adikes Inc.**
PO Box 310600
Jamaica, NY 11431-0600
Phone: (718)739-4400 **Fax:** (718)291-6141
Products: Fertilizers and chemicals; Grass seed. **SIC:** 5191 (Farm Supplies). **Est:** 1855.

■ **188** ■ **Adler Seeds Inc.**
6085 W 550 N
Sharpsville, IN 46068
Phone: (765)963-5397 **Fax:** (765)963-5398
Products: Corn and soybean seed. **SIC:** 5191 (Farm Supplies). **Est:** 1937. **Sales:** $2,000,000 (2000). **Emp:** 20. **Officers:** James Adler, President; Madonna Alderson, CFO; Michael Phillips, Dir. of Marketing & Sales.

■ **189** ■ **Adrian Wheat Growers Inc.**
PO Box 219
Adrian, TX 79001
Phone: (806)538-6222
Products: Wheat; Feed; Fertilizers; Chemicals; Tires. **SICs:** 5153 (Grain & Field Beans); 5191 (Farm Supplies); 5014 (Tires & Tubes); 5172 (Petroleum Products Nec). **Est:** 1934. **Sales:** $4,000,000 (2000). **Emp:** 9. **Officers:** John Perrin, President; Larry Webb, Treasurer.

■ **190** ■ **Aeon International Corp.**
459 6th Ave.
Marion, IA 52302-9122
Phone: (319)377-7415 **Fax:** (319)377-6514
E-mail: aeon@aeonintl.com
URL: http://www.aeonintl.com
Products: Automotive maintenance equipment; Industrial furnaces; Farm sprayers; Hydraulic cylinders; Feed ingredients for livestock; Industrial sweepers; Fast-food equipment and supplies. **SICs:** 5083 (Farm & Garden Machinery); 5013 (Motor Vehicle Supplies & New Parts); 5191 (Farm Supplies); 5084 (Industrial Machinery & Equipment). **Est:** 1946. **Officers:** C.M. Adams, President; H. Bob Barnes, Project Admin.

■ **191** ■ **AFI**
PO Box 7305
Kansas City, MO 64116
Phone: (816)459-6000
Products: Feed. **SIC:** 5191 (Farm Supplies).

■ **192** ■ **AG Distributors, Inc.**
6615 Robertson Ave.
Nashville, TN 37209
Phone: (615)356-9113
Products: Fertilizers. **SIC:** 5191 (Farm Supplies).

■ **193** ■ **Ag-Industrial Manufacturing**
PO Box 53
Lodi, CA 95241
Phone: (209)369-1994 **Fax:** (209)333-0736
Products: Grape harvesters, pre-pruning and vine trimming machines, vine lifting machines; Sprayer and pruning supplies. **SIC:** 5083 (Farm & Garden Machinery). **Sales:** $7,000,000 (1999). **Emp:** 40. **Officers:** Claude Brown, President.

■ **194** ■ **Ag-Land FS Inc.**
1505 Valle Vista
Pekin, IL 61554
Phone: (309)346-4145
Products: Farm supplies, including fertilizer, seeds, and feed. **SICs:** 5191 (Farm Supplies); 5172 (Petroleum Products Nec); 5198 (Paints, Varnishes & Supplies); 5013 (Motor Vehicle Supplies & New Parts). **Est:** 1928. **Sales:** $22,000,000 (2000). **Emp:** 60. **Officers:** Kendall Miller, General Mgr.; David Summers, Controller; Larry Dell, Dir. of Marketing & Sales.

■ **195** ■ **Ag-Land Inc.**
1819 McCloud Ave.
New Hampton, IA 50659
Phone: (515)394-4226
Products: Field, garden, and flower seeds. **SIC:** 5083 (Farm & Garden Machinery). **Est:** 1939. **Sales:** $1,000,000 (2000). **Emp:** 6. **Officers:** Steven P. McGrath, President.

■ **196** ■ **AG ONE CO-OP Inc.**
PO Box 2009
Anderson, IN 46018
Phone: (765)643-6639 **Fax:** (765)643-4396
Products: Agricultural supplies; Petroleum. **SICs:** 5191 (Farm Supplies); 5172 (Petroleum Products Nec). **Est:** 1930. **Sales:** $81,000,000 (2000). **Emp:** 100. **Officers:** Doug Brount, General Mgr.; Don Golden, Controller.

■ **197** ■ **AG Partners L.L.C.**
PO Box 38
Albert City, IA 50510
Phone: (712)843-2291
Products: Fertilizer; Feed; Diesel fuel; Animal food. **SICs:** 5153 (Grain & Field Beans); 5191 (Farm Supplies). **Sales:** $115,000,000 (2000). **Emp:** 120. **Officers:** Bruce G. Anderson, Manager. **Alternate Name:** Albert City Elevator Inc.

■ **198** ■ **Ag-Pro Inc.**
Hwy. 165 S
De Witt, AR 72042
Phone: (870)946-3564
Free: (800)467-8764 **Fax:** (870)946-3566
Products: Agricultural equipment and supplies. **SIC:** 5083 (Farm & Garden Machinery). **Est:** 1973. **Sales:** $8,000,000 (2000). **Emp:** 25.

■ **199** ■ **Ag Services of America Inc.**
PO Box 668
Cedar Falls, IA 50613
Phone: (319)277-0261 **Fax:** (319)277-0144
Products: Seeds; Agricultural chemicals, including

insecticides, herbicides, and fertilizers. **SIC:** 5191 (Farm Supplies). **Est:** 1985. **Sales:** $147,600,000 (2000). **Emp:** 133. **Officers:** Gaylen D. Miller, CEO & President; Brad D. Schlotfeldt, VP of Finance & Treasurer.

■ 200 ■ **AG Systems Inc.**
1100 Hwy. 7 E
Hutchinson, MN 55350
Phone: (612)587-4030 **Fax:** (612)587-8791
Products: Fertilizer machinery equipment and parts. **SICs:** 5191 (Farm Supplies); 5083 (Farm & Garden Machinery). **Est:** 1969. **Sales:** $20,000,000 (2000). **Emp:** 100. **Officers:** Craig Lenz, President; Roger Mumm, CFO.

■ 201 ■ **Ag Valley Cooperative**
PO Box 450
Arapahoe, NE 68922-0450
Phone: (308)962-7790
Free: (877)250-2049 **Fax:** (308)962-5321
Products: Grain; Feed; Fertilizer; Seed. **SIC:** 5191 (Farm Supplies). **Est:** 1997. **Sales:** $150,000,000 (2000). **Emp:** 250. **Officers:** Eldon Kroemer, Branch Mgr. **Former Name:** Koch Agriculture Company Inc. Agri Service Div.

■ 202 ■ **Agaland CO-OP Inc.**
PO Box 369
Canfield, OH 44406-0369
Phone: (216)533-5551
Products: Farm supplies, including fertilizer, chemicals, and feed. **SICs:** 5191 (Farm Supplies); 5153 (Grain & Field Beans); 5172 (Petroleum Products Nec). **Est:** 1933. **Sales:** $12,900,000 (2000). **Emp:** 35. **Officers:** Wendal Montgomery, General Mgr.; Bob Yoder, Controller.

■ 203 ■ **Agate Cooperative**
PO Box 10
Agate, ND 58310
Phone: (701)656-3213
Products: Grain, feed, and seed. **SIC:** 5153 (Grain & Field Beans). **Est:** 1915. **Sales:** $1,000,000 (2000). **Emp:** 2. **Officers:** Charles Peters, President; Daryl Stevens, General Mgr.

■ 204 ■ **Agco Inc.**
PO Box 668
Russell, KS 67665
Phone: (785)483-2128 **Fax:** (785)483-4872
E-mail: agco@russellks.net
Products: Grain; Feed and seed. **SICs:** 5191 (Farm Supplies); 5153 (Grain & Field Beans). **Est:** 1967. **Sales:** $14,000,000 (2000). **Emp:** 25. **Officers:** Kenneth Stielow, President; Bil Burton, General Mgr.

■ 205 ■ **Agland Coop**
PO Box 350
Scribner, NE 68057
Phone: (402)664-2256 **Free:** (800)875-6698
Products: Farm supplies, including feed, oil, plywood, light pine; Seed; Fertilizer; Chemicals. **SICs:** 5191 (Farm Supplies); 5172 (Petroleum Products Nec); 5031 (Lumber, Plywood & Millwork). **Est:** 1913. **Sales:** $8,400,000 (2000). **Emp:** 11. **Officers:** Dale J. Johnson, General Mgr. **Former Name:** Farmers Cooperative Mercantile Co.

■ 206 ■ **Agland Cooperative**
PO Box C
Parkston, SD 57366
Phone: (605)928-3381 **Fax:** (605)928-3653
Products: Farm supplies; Petroleum brokers. **SICs:** 5191 (Farm Supplies); 5172 (Petroleum Products Nec). **Est:** 1939. **Sales:** $9,100,000 (2000). **Emp:** 40. **Officers:** Lee Vanderwerff, President; Gail Sperlich, General Mgr.

■ 207 ■ **Agland Cooperative**
14 N Main St.
Alta, IA 51002
Phone: (712)284-2332
Products: Feed; Grain; Petroleum. **SICs:** 5153 (Grain & Field Beans); 5191 (Farm Supplies); 5172 (Petroleum Products Nec). **Est:** 1974. **Sales:** $8,000,000 (2000). **Emp:** 20. **Officers:** John Pruss, General Mgr.

■ 208 ■ **Agland Cooperative**
PO Box 125
Oakland, NE 68045
Phone: (402)685-5613 **Fax:** (402)685-5230
Products: Feed; Propane; Tires; Grain; Chemicals; Fertilizer; Gasoline; Oil; Diesel fuel. **SICs:** 5191 (Farm Supplies); 5153 (Grain & Field Beans); 5172 (Petroleum Products Nec). **Est:** 1915. **Sales:** $15,000,000 (2000). **Emp:** 32. **Officers:** Maurice Mederow, President; Dale Johnson, General Mgr.

■ 209 ■ **Agland Inc.**
260 Factory Rd.
Eaton, CO 80615
Phone: (303)454-3391
Products: Grains, fertilizers, chemicals, and feed. **SICs:** 5191 (Farm Supplies); 5172 (Petroleum Products Nec); 5031 (Lumber, Plywood & Millwork). **Est:** 1905. **Sales:** $75,000,000 (2000). **Emp:** 250. **Officers:** Bob Mekelburg, CFO; William McKay, President.

■ 210 ■ **Agri Cooperative Inc.**
310 Logan Rd.
Holdrege, NE 68949-0548
Phone: (308)995-8626 **Fax:** (308)995-5449
Products: Agricultural equipment and tools. **SIC:** 5171 (Petroleum Bulk Stations & Terminals). **Sales:** $60,000,000 (2000). **Emp:** 125. **Officers:** Ron Jurgens, CEO.

■ 211 ■ **Agri-Sales Associates Inc.**
209 Louise Ave.
Nashville, TN 37203
Phone: (615)329-1141 **Fax:** (615)329-2770
E-mail: bmountain@agri-sales.com
Products: Agricultural products; Veterinary medical supplies and equipment. **SICs:** 5191 (Farm Supplies); 5083 (Farm & Garden Machinery). **Sales:** $46,000,000 (2000). **Emp:** 40. **Officers:** Jerry R. Bellar, President; Jackie A. Bellar, Treasurer.

■ 212 ■ **Agri-Tech F.S. Inc.**
16119 Hwy. 81 W
Darlington, WI 53530
Phone: (608)776-4600 **Fax:** (608)776-3312
Products: Farm supplies including livestock feed; LPG dealer, home heating fuel, convenience store. **SIC:** 5191 (Farm Supplies). **Sales:** $32,000,000 (2000). **Emp:** 50. **Officers:** William Hanson, President; Jim Leitzinger, Controller.

■ 213 ■ **AgriBioTech Inc.**
120 Corporate Park Dr.
Henderson, NV 89014
Phone: (702)566-2440
Free: (800)308-8975 **Fax:** (702)566-2450
E-mail: info@agribiotech.com
URL: http://www.agribiotech.com
Products: Turf and forage seeds. **SIC:** 5191 (Farm Supplies). **Est:** 1995. **Sales:** $65,900,000 (2000). **Emp:** 325. **Officers:** Johnny R. Thomas, CEO & President; Henry A. Ingalls, VP & CFO.

■ 214 ■ **Agriculture Services Inc.**
PO Box 627
Blackfoot, ID 83221
Phone: (208)785-1717
Free: (800)287-1719 **Fax:** (208)785-5029
E-mail: agserv@srv.net
Products: Irrigation equipment and supplies. **SIC:** 5083 (Farm & Garden Machinery). **Est:** 1951. **Sales:** $3,000,000 (2000). **Emp:** 15. **Officers:** T.B. Slayton, President; Karl Slayton, Vice President; Ross Chaffin, Secretary.

■ 215 ■ **Agriland F.S. Inc.**
PO Box 680
Harlan, IA 51537
Phone: (712)755-5141
Products: Agricultural products, including fertilizer, feed, and grain. **SICs:** 5191 (Farm Supplies); 5153 (Grain & Field Beans). **Est:** 1985. **Sales:** $29,000,000 (2000). **Emp:** 45. **Officers:** Lud Buman, President; Bill Ridgely, General Mgr.; Dan Josefson, Dir. of Marketing.

■ 216 ■ **AgriPride F.S.**
PO Box 329
Nashville, IL 62263
Phone: (618)327-3046
Products: Farm products, including fertilizer and seeds. **SICs:** 5191 (Farm Supplies); 5153 (Grain & Field Beans). **Est:** 1941. **Sales:** $34,000,000 (2000). **Emp:** 84. **Officers:** Randy Newcomb, President.

■ 217 ■ **Agriturf Inc.**
59 Dwight St.
Hatfield, MA 01038
Phone: (413)247-5687 **Fax:** (413)247-9401
Products: Fertilizer; Grass seed. **SIC:** 5191 (Farm Supplies).

■ 218 ■ **Agsco Inc.**
PO Box 13458
Grand Forks, ND 58201
Phone: (701)775-5325
Free: (800)859-3047 **Fax:** (701)775-9587
E-mail: info@agsco-agdepot.com
URL: http://www.agsco-agdepot.com
Products: Agricultural chemicals. **SIC:** 5191 (Farm Supplies). **Est:** 1934. **Sales:** $50,000,000 (2000). **Emp:** 125. **Officers:** Randy Brown, President.

■ 219 ■ **Agway, Inc.**
333 Butternut Dr.
DeWitt, NY 13214-1803
Phone: (315)449-7061 **Fax:** (315)449-6078
Products: Farm and garden equipment, including tractors and lawn mowers. **SIC:** 5083 (Farm & Garden Machinery). **Est:** 1964.

■ 220 ■ **Albert City Elevator Inc.**
PO Box 38
Albert City, IA 50510
Phone: (712)843-2291
Products: Grain elevator. **SICs:** 5153 (Grain & Field Beans); 5191 (Farm Supplies). **Sales:** $75,000,000 (2000). **Emp:** 85. **Officers:** Bruce G. Anderson, Manager.

■ 221 ■ **Allamakee Implement Co.**
1736 Lansing Harpers Rd.
Lansing, IA 52151-7577
Phone: (319)568-3463
Products: Lawn and farm tractors. **SIC:** 5083 (Farm & Garden Machinery). **Est:** 1960. **Sales:** $3,000,000 (2000). **Emp:** 16. **Officers:** John Weber, President.

■ 222 ■ **Allen County Cooperative Association**
PO Box 97
New Haven, IN 46774
Phone: (219)749-5130 **Fax:** (219)493-2749
Products: Grass seed; Cat and dog food; Shovels and rakes; Insecticides. **SICs:** 5153 (Grain & Field Beans); 5191 (Farm Supplies). **Est:** 1930. **Sales:** $25,000,000 (2000). **Emp:** 45. **Officers:** Ronald DeLong, General Mgr.; Phyllis Lampe, Controller.

■ 223 ■ **Allen's Supply Co.**
7248 Ashville Hwy.
Knoxville, TN 37924
Phone: (865)525-9200
Free: (800)325-2048 **Fax:** (865)525-4040
E-mail: allensup@bellsouth.net
Products: Pet supplies; Veterinary instruments; Pharmaceutical preparations for veterinary use; Livestock equipment. **SICs:** 5199 (Nondurable Goods Nec); 5199 (Nondurable Goods Nec); 5122 (Drugs, Proprietaries & Sundries). **Est:** 1975. **Sales:** $3,000,000 (1999). **Emp:** 9. **Officers:** Allen Breeden, Contact.

■ 224 ■ **Allerton Implement Co.**
PO Box 80
Allerton, IL 61810
Phone: (217)834-3305 **Fax:** (217)834-3400
Products: Farm, lawn, and garden equipment, including tractors. **SIC:** 5083 (Farm & Garden Machinery). **Est:** 1936. **Sales:** $12,500,000 (2000). **Emp:** 36. **Officers:** David R. Mohr, President.

■ 225 ■ **Alliance Agronomics Inc.**
7104 Mechanicsville Tpk. Ste. 217
Mechanicsville, VA 23111
Phone: (804)730-2900
Products: Mixed fertilizers. **SIC:** 5191 (Farm Supplies).
Sales: $24,000,000 (1993). **Emp:** 90. **Officers:**
Garland W. Garrett, CEO; Ron Watson, Comptroller.

■ 226 ■ **Allied International Marketing Corp.**
380 Maple Ave., Ste. 202
Vienna, VA 22180
Phone: (703)255-6400   **Fax:** (703)255-0921
Products: Livestock and farm products. **SIC:** 5191
(Farm Supplies). **Sales:** $1,000,000 (2000).

■ 227 ■ **Allied Seed Co-Op, Inc.**
1917 E Fargo
Nampa, ID 83687
Phones: (208)466-9218   (208)467-9953
(208)467-9953
Products: Clover and alfalfa seed. **SIC:** 5191 (Farm
Supplies).

■ 228 ■ **Alltech Inc.**
3031 Catnip Hill Pike
Nicholasville, KY 40356
Phone: (606)885-9613   **Fax:** (606)885-6736
Products: Animal feed additives. **SIC:** 5191 (Farm
Supplies). **Sales:** $31,000,000 (2000). **Emp:** 100.
Officers: Pearse Lyons, President.

■ 229 ■ **Alma Farmers Cooperative
Association**
Clay and Collins St.
Alma, MO 64001
Phone: (660)674-2291
Products: Farm supplies, including grain, chemicals,
fertilizer, and feed. **SICs:** 5191 (Farm Supplies); 5153
(Grain & Field Beans). **Sales:** $10,000,000 (2000).
Emp: 20. **Officers:** Mike Dobson, General Mgr.

■ 230 ■ **Alma Farmers Union Cooperative**
1300 Main St. S
Alma, WI 54610
Phone: (608)685-4481
Products: Feed; Fuel. **SICs:** 5191 (Farm Supplies);
5172 (Petroleum Products Nec). **Est:** 1930. **Sales:**
$5,500,000 (2000). **Emp:** 30. **Officers:** Steven Nelson,
General Mgr.; Jim Feuling, Treasurer & Secty.; P.
Wenger, Dir. of Data Processing.

■ 231 ■ **Amazing Wind Machines Inc.**
7839 Greenwich Rd.
Lodi, OH 44254-9709
Phone: (978)952-2889
Products: Handmade kinetic wind sculptures. **SIC:**
5083 (Farm & Garden Machinery). **Est:** 1989. **Sales:**
$120,000 (2000). **Emp:** 2. **Officers:** Jane Corbus,
Owner, e-mail: jcorbuswil@aol.com.

■ 232 ■ **American Farm & Feed**
1533 Knox St.
Kansas City, MO 64116-3744
Phone: (816)842-1905
Products: Feed; Farm supplies. **SIC:** 5191 (Farm
Supplies).

■ 233 ■ **American Feed and Farm Supply Inc.**
PO Box 7218
Omaha, NE 68107
Phone: (402)731-1662   **Fax:** (402)731-2117
Products: Feed; Farm supplies. **SIC:** 5191 (Farm
Supplies). **Est:** 1988. **Sales:** $58,000,000 (1999).
Emp: 185. **Officers:** Joe Hohn, President.

■ 234 ■ **American Pride Coop**
55 W Bromley Ln.
Brighton, CO 80601
Phone: (303)659-1230   **Fax:** (303)659-7650
E-mail: ampride@amnix.com
URL: http://www.ampride-coop.com
Products: Animal feed; Fuels; Blended fertilizers. **SIC:**
5191 (Farm Supplies). **Est:** 1936. **Sales:** $32,000,000
(1999). **Emp:** 126. **Officers:** Al Shivley, President &
CEO.

■ 235 ■ **American Rice Growers Cooperative
Association**
PO Box 188
Raywood, TX 77582
Phone: (281)456-0788   **Fax:** (281)587-4851
Products: Rice; Grass seeds; Chemicals. **SICs:** 5153
(Grain & Field Beans); 5191 (Farm Supplies). **Est:**
1948. **Sales:** $1,200,000 (2000). **Emp:** 20. **Officers:**
Gene Nelson, President; James Hewitt, CFO.

■ 236 ■ **American Rice Growers Cooperative
Association**
PO Box 129
Dayton, TX 77535
Phone: (409)258-2681   **Fax:** (409)258-8569
Products: Rice; Seed; Chemical fertilizers; Farm
supplies. **SIC:** 5191 (Farm Supplies). **Est:** 1948. **Sales:**
$7,000,000 (2000). **Emp:** 25. **Officers:** F.M. Graves,
President & Chairman of the Board; Charles Lyons,
General Mgr.

■ 237 ■ **Ames Co.**
PO Box 1774
3801 Camden at Broadway
Parkersburg, WV 26101
Phone: (304)424-3000
Free: (800)624-2654   **Fax:** (304)424-3234
Products: Lawn and garden supplies, including rakes,
hoses, and wheel barrows; Heavy striking tools. **SIC:**
5191 (Farm Supplies). **Sales:** $120,000,000 (2000).
Emp: 999. **Officers:** R.E. Keup, President & CEO; I.R.
Phillips, VP of Operations; H.B. Martin, VP of Sales; R.
Moss, VP of Finance; M. Deitsch, Dir. of Marketing.

■ 238 ■ **Ampac Seed Co.**
PO Box 318
Tangent, OR 97389
Phone: (541)928-1651   **Fax:** (541)928-2430
Products: Agricultural equipment and supplies. **SIC:**
5191 (Farm Supplies).

■ 239 ■ **Amvac Chemical Corp.**
4100 E Washington Blvd.
Los Angeles, CA 90023
Phone: (213)264-3910   **Fax:** (213)268-1028
Products: Pesticides and insecticides. **SIC:** 5191
(Farm Supplies). **Sales:** $45,000,000 (2000). **Emp:**
126. **Officers:** Glenn Wintemute, Chairman of the
Board; James Barry, CFO.

■ 240 ■ **Andersen Turf Supply**
5462 Oceanus, Unit C
Huntington Beach, CA 92649
Phone: (714)897-0202   **Fax:** (714)373-1188
Products: Seed microorganisms; Turf grass. **SIC:**
5159 (Farm-Product Raw Materials Nec).

■ 241 ■ **Anderson Brothers Inc.**
PO Box 277
Edgeley, ND 58433
Phone: (701)493-2241
Products: Farm equipment; Cars and trucks. **SICs:**
5083 (Farm & Garden Machinery); 5012 (Automobiles
& Other Motor Vehicles). **Est:** 1964. **Sales:** $4,000,000
(2000). **Emp:** 10. **Officers:** Charles Anderson,
President.

■ 242 ■ **Andersons Inc.**
480 W Dussel Dr.
Maumee, OH 43537
Phone: (419)893-5050   **Fax:** (419)891-6655
Products: Farm and lawn fertilizer. **SICs:** 5153 (Grain
& Field Beans); 5191 (Farm Supplies). **Est:** 1987.
Sales: $1,154,900,000 (2000). **Emp:** 3,024. **Officers:**
Richard P. Anderson, CEO & President; Richard
George, Controller; Joe Christian, Dir of Human
Resources.

■ 243 ■ **Andgrow Fertilizer**
3150 Stoney Point Rd.
East Berlin, PA 17316
Phone: (717)259-9573   **Free:** (800)426-2827
Products: Fertilizer. **SIC:** 5191 (Farm Supplies). **Est:**
1901. **Sales:** $10,000,000 (2000). **Emp:** 25. **Officers:**
Phil Nell, General Mgr.; Greg Muchmore, Dir. of
Operations.

■ 244 ■ **Anfinson's Inc.**
1700 I94 Business Loop E
Dickinson, ND 58601-9802
Phone: (701)227-1226   **Fax:** (701)225-0358
Products: Farm and ranch supplies; Corrals and
fencing. **SIC:** 5191 (Farm Supplies). **Est:** 1961. **Sales:**
$5,000,000 (2000). **Emp:** 30. **Officers:** Richard Mitzel,
CEO.

■ 245 ■ **Apache Farmers Cooperative**
PO Box 332
Apache, OK 73006
Phone: (580)588-3351
Products: Seed; Fertilizer; Fuel; Animal health
products. **SIC:** 5191 (Farm Supplies). **Est:** 1920.
Sales: $19,000,000 (2000). **Emp:** 40. **Officers:** Dean
Hatfield, President; Kermit Gilbreath, CFO.

■ 246 ■ **Applied Hydroponics Inc.**
755 Southpoint Blvd.
Petaluma, CA 94954
Phone: (707)765-9990
URL: http://www.hydrofarm.com
Products: Indoor garden equipment; Hydroponic
gardens; High-intensity greenhouse lighting. **SICs:**
5083 (Farm & Garden Machinery); 5063 (Electrical
Apparatus & Equipment). **Est:** 1977. **Sales:**
$5,000,000 (2000). **Emp:** 25. **Officers:** Stuart R.
Dvorin, President.

■ 247 ■ **Arbordale Home and Garden
Showplace**
480 Dodge Rd.
Amherst, NY 14068
Phone: (716)688-9125
Products: Gardening supplies, including fertilizers,
sprinklers, hoses, and seeds; Plants and flowers. **SICs:**
5191 (Farm Supplies); 5193 (Flowers & Florists'
Supplies). **Est:** 1968. **Sales:** $3,000,000 (2000). **Emp:**
90. **Officers:** Richard A. Salmon, President.

■ 248 ■ **Archer Cooperative Grain Co.**
PO Box 147
Archer, IA 51231
Phone: (712)723-5233   **Fax:** (712)723-5266
E-mail: arcrcoop@netins.net
Products: Fertilizer and feed; Grain. **SICs:** 5153 (Grain
& Field Beans); 5191 (Farm Supplies). **Est:** 1907.
Sales: $8,000,000 (2000). **Emp:** 10. **Officers:** Dan
Noteboom, President; Galen Vollink, Treasurer &
Secty.; John Steensma, Dir. of Marketing.

■ 249 ■ **Arends Brothers Inc.**
Rte. 54 N
Melvin, IL 60952
Phone: (217)388-7717
Products: Farm equipment. **SIC:** 5083 (Farm &
Garden Machinery). **Est:** 1932. **Sales:** $17,000,000
(2000). **Emp:** 35. **Officers:** Kent Arends, President.

■ 250 ■ **Arends and Sons Inc.**
715 S Sangamon Ave.
Gibson City, IL 60936
Phone: (217)784-4241
Products: Tractors for farming, lawn, and garden;
Computers. **SICs:** 5083 (Farm & Garden Machinery);
5045 (Computers, Peripherals & Software). **Est:** 1930.
Sales: $20,000,000 (2000). **Emp:** 50. **Officers:** William
Arends, President; Steve Arends, VP & Treasurer.

■ 251 ■ **Argent Chemical Laboratories Inc.**
8702 152nd Ave. NW
Redmond, WA 98052
Phone: (425)885-3777
Products: Agricultural supplies, including feeds and
chemicals. **SIC:** 5191 (Farm Supplies). **Sales:**
$3,000,000 (2000). **Emp:** 11. **Officers:** Elliot
Lieberman, President.

■ 252 ■ **Arizona Bag Co. LLC**
PO Box 6650
Phoenix, AZ 85005-6650
Phone: (602)272-1333
Free: (800)257-2247   **Fax:** (602)278-7871
Products: Industrial and agricultural supplies. **SICs:**
5085 (Industrial Supplies); 5191 (Farm Supplies); 5083
(Farm & Garden Machinery). **Est:** 1946. **Sales:**
$8,000,000 (2000). **Emp:** 20. **Officers:** Steven R.
Matthews, President.

■ 253 ■ Arizona Machinery Co., Inc.
197 W Warner Rd.
Chandler, AZ 85224
Phone: (602)963-4531 **Fax:** (602)963-5079
Products: Tractor parts. **SIC:** 5083 (Farm & Garden Machinery).

■ 254 ■ Arkansas Valley Seed Co.
PO Box 16025
Denver, CO 80216
Phone: (303)320-7500 **Fax:** (303)320-7516
URL: http://www.avseeds.com
Products: Lawn seed, turf seed, native grasses, and forage seed. **SIC:** 5191 (Farm Supplies). **Est:** 1945. **Alternate Name:** AVSEEDS. **Alternate Name:** Colorado Seeds.

■ 255 ■ Arkfeld Manufacturing & Distributing Company Inc.
1230 Monroe Ave.
PO BOX 54
Norfolk, NE 68702-0054
Phone: (402)371-9430
Free: (800)533-0676 **Fax:** (402)371-5137
E-mail: arkfeldm@ncfcomm.com
Products: Livestock equipment and supplies; Automatic waterers; Animal scales; Feed and grain scales; Dial-digital scales; Prefabricated pumphouses; Security cabinets; Custom metal tail gates; Engine stands; Custom truck equipment; Custom metal fabricator. **SIC:** 5191 (Farm Supplies). **Est:** 1917. **Sales:** $600,000 (1999). **Emp:** 15. **Officers:** Robert J. Ackerfeld.

■ 256 ■ Arrow Truck Sales Inc.
3200 Manchester Traffic Way
Kansas City, MO 64129
Phone: (816)923-5000
Free: (800)827-7690 **Fax:** (816)923-9000
URL: http://www.arrowtruck.com
Products: Used vehicles, including trucks, vans and tractors; Trailers. **SICs:** 5083 (Farm & Garden Machinery); 5082 (Construction & Mining Machinery). **Est:** 1950. **Sales:** $200,000,000 (2000). **Emp:** 275. **Officers:** Lewis Nerman, President, e-mail: lnerman@arrowtruck.com; Steve Clough, CFO.

■ 257 ■ Arthur Companies Inc.
PO Box 145
Arthur, ND 58006
Phone: (701)967-8312 **Fax:** (701)967-8381
Products: Grain; Fertilizer; Chemicals. **SICs:** 5153 (Grain & Field Beans); 5191 (Farm Supplies); 5169 (Chemicals & Allied Products Nec). **Est:** 1906. **Sales:** $10,000,000 (2000). **Emp:** 40. **Officers:** Frederick W. Burgum, President; Scott Kroger, Controller; Joel Moore, Dir. of Marketing & Sales.

■ 258 ■ Ashby Equity Association
101 Main St.
Ashby, MN 56309
Phone: (218)747-2219
Products: Petroleum; Fertilizers; Chemicals. **SICs:** 5191 (Farm Supplies); 5172 (Petroleum Products Nec); 5169 (Chemicals & Allied Products Nec); 5014 (Tires & Tubes). **Est:** 1918. **Sales:** $2,800,000 (2000). **Emp:** 14. **Officers:** Jim Kloos, General Mgr.; Alison Rein, Manager.

■ 259 ■ Associated Farmers Cooperative
695 Exchange Ave.
Conway, AR 72032
Phone: (501)329-2971 **Fax:** (501)329-0320
Products: Feed and seed. **SIC:** 5191 (Farm Supplies). **Est:** 1967. **Sales:** $3,000,000 (2000). **Emp:** 20. **Officers:** Mike Davis, General Mgr.

■ 260 ■ Atwater Creamery Co.
PO Box 629
Atwater, MN 56209
Phone: (320)974-8820
Products: Farm supplies, including animal health products and feed; Dairy products, including milk, cheese, and butter. **SICs:** 5083 (Farm & Garden Machinery); 5143 (Dairy Products Except Dried or Canned). **Est:** 1891. **Sales:** $9,000,000 (2000). **Emp:** 12. **Officers:** Gerald Gratz, President; Larry Poe, General Mgr.

■ 261 ■ Auglaize Farmers Cooperative
PO Box 360
Wapakoneta, OH 45895
Phone: (419)738-2137
Products: Animal feed and grain; Fertilizer; Farm equipment. **SICs:** 5153 (Grain & Field Beans); 5191 (Farm Supplies); 5172 (Petroleum Products Nec). **Est:** 1933. **Sales:** $90,000,000 (2000). **Emp:** 150. **Officers:** Larry Hammond, General Mgr.; Darren Langhals, CFO; Kim Dauch, Dir. of Marketing & Sales; Keith Martin, Dir of Human Resources.

■ 262 ■ Augusta Cooperative Farm Bureau
1205-B Richmond Rd.
Staunton, VA 24401
Phone: (540)885-1265 **Fax:** (540)885-5582
E-mail: augcoop@cfw.com
URL: http://www.augcoop.com
Products: Farm supplies; Feed and fertilizer. **SICs:** 5153 (Grain & Field Beans); 5191 (Farm Supplies). **Est:** 1929. **Sales:** $19,000,000 (2000). **Emp:** 150. **Officers:** Dale C. Smith, General Mgr.

■ 263 ■ Aurora Cooperative Elevator Co.
PO Box 209
Aurora, NE 68818
Phone: (402)694-2106 **Fax:** (402)694-2060
E-mail: auroracoop@hamilton.net
URL: http://www.auroracoop.com
Products: Animal healthcare products; Chemicals; Grain, feed, and seed; Petroleum. **SICs:** 5191 (Farm Supplies); 5199 (Nondurable Goods Nec); 5169 (Chemicals & Allied Products Nec); 5172 (Petroleum Products Nec). **Est:** 1908. **Sales:** $140,000 (2000). **Emp:** 200. **Officers:** Rodney Schroeder, CEO & President; Ronald Becker, VP of Acctg. & Management Info. Systems; Donald Comer, VP of Grain Mktg./Merchandising/Transp.

■ 264 ■ Avon-Lakewood Nursery Inc.
39115 Detroit Rd.
Avon, OH 44011
Phone: (440)934-5832
Products: Nursery specializing in ornamentals suited for growing on the West Coast. **SIC:** 5193 (Flowers & Florists' Supplies).

■ 265 ■ B-M-B Company Inc.
9th & Vermont
Holton, KS 66436
Phone: (785)364-2186
Products: Farm and garden machinery. **SIC:** 5083 (Farm & Garden Machinery). **Officers:** Tim Gardner, CEO.

■ 266 ■ B and W Farm Center Inc.
PO Box 876
Cordele, GA 31015
Phone: (912)273-3398
Products: Feed, seed, and fertilizer. **SICs:** 5191 (Farm Supplies); 5153 (Grain & Field Beans). **Est:** 1960. **Sales:** $1,000,000 (2000). **Emp:** 6. **Officers:** C. Garwood, President; Sue Lindsey, Bookkeeper.

■ 267 ■ Bacon Products Co. Inc.
PO Box 22187
Chattanooga, TN 37422
Phone: (423)892-0414 **Fax:** (423)892-2065
Products: Insecticides and pesticides. **SIC:** 5191 (Farm Supplies). **Officers:** Reed Bacon, President.

■ 268 ■ Badger Farmers Cooperative
PO Box 97
Badger, SD 57214
Phone: (605)983-3241 **Fax:** (605)983-5831
Products: Feed; Seed; Fertilizers; Chemicals. **SICs:** 5153 (Grain & Field Beans); 5191 (Farm Supplies). **Est:** 1913. **Sales:** $5,000,000 (2000). **Emp:** 6. **Officers:** Tim Bjorklund, President; Chris Miller, General Mgr.

■ 269 ■ Badgerland Farm Center
PO Box 119
Whitewater, WI 53190
Phone: (414)473-2410
Products: Fertilizer; Grain; Petroleum products. **SICs:** 5191 (Farm Supplies); 5153 (Grain & Field Beans); 5171 (Petroleum Bulk Stations & Terminals). **Est:** 1934. **Sales:** $12,000,000 (2000). **Emp:** 30. **Officers:** Narbert Schleicher, General Mgr.; Larry Zell, Manager; David Neal, Operations Mgr.

■ 270 ■ Bailey Seed Company, Inc.
PO Box 13517
Salem, OR 97309
Phone: (503)362-9700
Free: (800)407-7713 **Fax:** (503)362-1705
E-mail: baileyseed@aol.com
URL: http://www.baileyseed.com
Products: Lawn seed. **SIC:** 5191 (Farm Supplies). **Est:** 1994. **Sales:** $1,600,000 (2000). **Emp:** 10. **Former Name:** R.H. Bailey Seeds, Inc.

■ 271 ■ H.J. Baker and Brother Inc.
595 Summer St.
Stamford, CT 06901-1407
Phone: (203)328-9200 **Fax:** (203)967-8412
Products: Fertilizer. **SIC:** 5191 (Farm Supplies). **Officers:** Jerry Skop, Export Sales Manager.

■ 272 ■ Baker Implement Co.
PO Box 787
Kennett, MO 63857-0787
Phone: (573)888-4646
Products: Farm implements; Tractors; Cotton pickers. **SIC:** 5083 (Farm & Garden Machinery). **Sales:** $47,000,000 (2000). **Emp:** 150. **Officers:** Jerry Kombs, President.

■ 273 ■ Baker Implement Co.
PO Box 787
Kennett, MO 63857
Phone: (573)888-4646 **Fax:** (573)888-2826
Products: Farm machinery and equipment. **SIC:** 5083 (Farm & Garden Machinery). **Sales:** $68,000,000 (2000). **Emp:** 150. **Officers:** Jerry Kombs, President.

■ 274 ■ Bakersfield AG Co. Inc.
34710 7th Standard Rd.
Bakersfield, CA 93312
Phone: (805)399-9191 **Fax:** (805)399-1063
Products: Agricultural chemicals; Fertilizers. **SIC:** 5191 (Farm Supplies). **Est:** 1965. **Sales:** $9,000,000 (2000). **Emp:** 30. **Officers:** Frank Waterman Jr., President.

■ 275 ■ Bar-H-Implement Inc.
Rte. 1
Stone Lake, WI 54876
Phone: (715)865-6211
Products: Farm equipment, including tractors. **SIC:** 5083 (Farm & Garden Machinery). **Est:** 1985. **Sales:** $2,000,000 (2000). **Emp:** 12. **Officers:** Roy Hendricks, President; Nancy Hendricks-Slayton, Treasurer & Secty.

■ 276 ■ Barbee-Neuhaus Implement Co.
2000 W Expwy. 83
Weslaco, TX 78596
Phone: (956)968-7502
Free: (800)357-7502 **Fax:** (956)968-4173
URL: http://www.barbeeneuhaus.com
Products: Farming equipment. **SIC:** 5083 (Farm & Garden Machinery). **Sales:** $23,000,000 (1993). **Emp:** 75. **Officers:** Earl Neuhaus, President; Kirk Bloomquist, Controller.

■ 277 ■ Barenbrug U.S.A.
PO Box 820
Boardman, OR 97818-0820
Phone: (503)481-4001
Products: Agricultural equipment and supplies. **SIC:** 5191 (Farm Supplies). **Sales:** $3,000,000 (2000). **Emp:** 15.

■ 278 ■ Barnett Implement Co. Inc.
PO Box 666
Mt. Vernon, WA 98273
Phone: (206)424-7995 **Fax:** (206)424-0403
Products: Lawn tractors and riding mowers; Garden tractors; Agricultural tractors. **SIC:** 5083 (Farm & Garden Machinery). **Sales:** $6,000,000 (2000). **Emp:** 29. **Officers:** Jerald Rindal, President.

■ 279 ■ **Barron Farmers Union Cooperative Services Inc.**
505 E Grove Ave.
Barron, WI 54812
Phone: (715)537-3181 **Fax:** (715)537-9322
Products: Feed. **SIC:** 5153 (Grain & Field Beans). **Est:** 1934. **Sales:** $6,500,000 (2000). **Emp:** 60. **Officers:** Arvid Herrmann, President; Todd Rosvold, General Mgr.

■ 280 ■ **Barry Grain and Feed Inc.**
PO Box 902
Hempstead, TX 77445
Phone: (409)826-6190
Products: Cattle feed; Corn grain; Seed; Fertilizer. **SICs:** 5191 (Farm Supplies); 5153 (Grain & Field Beans). **Est:** 1963. **Sales:** $5,500,000 (2000). **Emp:** 25. **Officers:** Hubert Barry, President.

■ 281 ■ **Bartlett Cooperative Association Inc.**
PO Box 4675
Bartlett, KS 67332
Phone: (316)226-3322
Products: Feed; Seed; Grain; Oil; Batteries; Fertilizer. **SICs:** 5153 (Grain & Field Beans); 5191 (Farm Supplies). **Est:** 1951. **Sales:** $21,000,000 (1999). **Emp:** 52. **Officers:** Kent Houston, President; Maxine Callahan, Treasurer & Secty.

■ 282 ■ **Bascom Elevator Supply Association**
PO Box 305
Bascom, OH 44809
Phone: (419)937-2233
Products: Agricultural equipment and supplies. **SIC:** 5191 (Farm Supplies). **Sales:** $10,000,000 (2000). **Emp:** 12.

■ 283 ■ **Battle Creek Farmers Cooperative**
PO Box 10
Battle Creek, NE 68715
Phone: (402)675-2375
Products: Grain; Feed and seed; Petroleum; Animal healthcare products. **SICs:** 5191 (Farm Supplies); 5153 (Grain & Field Beans). **Est:** 1937. **Sales:** $37,000,000 (2000). **Emp:** 45. **Officers:** Gary Maxwell, General Mgr.

■ 284 ■ **Bay Houston Towing Co.**
PO Box 3006
Houston, TX 77253
Phone: (713)529-3755 **Fax:** (713)529-2591
Products: Peat. **SIC:** 5193 (Flowers & Florists' Supplies). **Sales:** $38,500,000 (2000). **Emp:** 403. **Officers:** Mark E. Kuebler, President; Milow Klein, VP of Finance.

■ 285 ■ **BE Implemented Partners Ltd.**
PO Box 752
Brownfield, TX 79316
Phone: (806)637-3594 **Fax:** (806)637-8992
Products: Farm equipment, including tractors, riders, and mowers. **SIC:** 5083 (Farm & Garden Machinery). **Est:** 1964. **Sales:** $5,000,000 (2000). **Emp:** 25. **Officers:** Coffee Connor, President; Walter Bray, CFO; Chris Snodgrass, Sales Mgr.

■ 286 ■ **Beachley Hardy Seed Co.**
PO Box 3147
Shiremanstown, PA 17011
Phone: 800-442-7391
Products: Farming supplies, including grass seed. **SIC:** 5191 (Farm Supplies).

■ 287 ■ **Beardsley Farmers Elevator Co.**
PO Box 297
Beardsley, MN 56211
Phone: (612)265-6933 **Fax:** (612)265-6959
Products: Farm supplies, including grains, feed, fertilizers, and chemicals. **SICs:** 5153 (Grain & Field Beans); 5191 (Farm Supplies). **Est:** 1904. **Sales:** $12,000,000 (2000). **Emp:** 6. **Officers:** Harold Gibson, President; Mark Willand, Manager.

■ 288 ■ **Beattie Farmers Union Cooperative Association**
PO Box 79
Beattie, KS 66406
Phone: (785)353-2237 **Fax:** (785)353-2236
Products: Farm supplies. **SIC:** 5191 (Farm Supplies).

Sales: $15,000,000 (2000). **Emp:** 22. **Officers:** Ivan Wiench, President; Pamela Rush, Controller.

■ 289 ■ **Beatty Implement Co.**
PO Box 288
Auburn, IL 62615
Phone: (217)438-6111
Products: Farm equipment. **SIC:** 5083 (Farm & Garden Machinery). **Est:** 1953. **Sales:** $5,000,000 (2000). **Emp:** 20. **Officers:** L.B. Beatty, President; R. Keith Beatty, Dir. of Systems.

■ 290 ■ **Bedford Farm Bureau Cooperative**
102 Industrial Ave.
Bedford, PA 15522
Phone: (814)623-6194
Products: Seeds. **SIC:** 5191 (Farm Supplies). **Est:** 1942. **Sales:** $5,000,000 (2000). **Emp:** 25. **Officers:** Jim Wakefield, President; Pam Eagleson, Secretary.

■ 291 ■ **Bedford Farmers Cooperative**
PO Box 64
Shelbyville, TN 37160-0064
Phone: (931)684-3506
Products: Farm supplies, including chemicals, fertilizers, feed, seed, and fuels. **SIC:** 5191 (Farm Supplies). **Est:** 1956. **Sales:** $7,200,000 (2000). **Emp:** 30. **Officers:** Donald Taylor, Chairman of the Board; Vickey Stewart, Manager.

■ 292 ■ **Bee County Cooperative Association Inc.**
PO Box 128
Tynan, TX 78391
Phone: (512)547-3366
Products: Farm supplies including tillage machinery and feed; Gas and diesel fuel. **SICs:** 5153 (Grain & Field Beans); 5191 (Farm Supplies). **Est:** 1943. **Sales:** $9,500,000 (2000). **Emp:** 14. **Officers:** Bradley R. Johnson, CEO; Jill Cain, Controller.

■ 293 ■ **Belarus Machinery Inc.**
7075 W Parkland Ct.
Milwaukee, WI 53223
Phone: (414)355-2000 **Fax:** (414)355-8370
Products: Agricultural tractors. **SIC:** 5083 (Farm & Garden Machinery). **Est:** 1976. **Sales:** $2,000,000 (2000). **Emp:** 70. **Officers:** Edward Ossinski, President; Valery Zakharov, CFO; E.W. Muehlhausen, Sales/Marketing Contact; Bob Chriske, Customer Service Contact; Brian Bartman, Dir. of Admin.

■ 294 ■ **Bellamy's Inc.**
Box 106
Elwood, NE 68937
Phone: (308)785-3311
Products: Agricultural and outdoor equipment. **SIC:** 5083 (Farm & Garden Machinery). **Est:** 1959. **Sales:** $3,000,000 (2000). **Emp:** 20. **Officers:** Kenneth Bellamy, President; Bill Berens, Sales Mgr.

■ 295 ■ **Belle Plaine Cooperative**
820 E Main St.
Belle Plaine, MN 56011
Phone: (612)873-4244
Products: Agricultural chemicals and fertilizers; Petroleum and propane. **SICs:** 5191 (Farm Supplies); 5172 (Petroleum Products Nec). **Est:** 1965. **Sales:** $6,000,000 (2000). **Emp:** 20. **Officers:** John Nagel, President; Wilmer Schmidt, General Mgr.

■ 296 ■ **Belstra Milling Co. Inc.**
PO Box 460
Demotte, IN 46310
Phone: (219)987-4343 **Fax:** (219)987-5227
Products: Animal feed. **SIC:** 5191 (Farm Supplies). **Est:** 1956. **Sales:** $7,500,000 (2000). **Emp:** 13. **Officers:** Timothy K. Belstra, CEO.

■ 297 ■ **Beltrami Farmers Elevator**
PO Box 8
Beltrami, MN 56517
Phone: (218)926-5522
Products: Grain, feed, and seed; Chemicals. **SIC:** 5153 (Grain & Field Beans). **Est:** 1940. **Sales:** $9,000,000 (2000). **Emp:** 5. **Officers:** Jim Todahl, CEO; Thomas Nelson, Manager.

■ 298 ■ **Belzoni Tractor Co. Inc.**
PO Box 297
Belzoni, MS 39038
Phone: (601)247-3414
Products: Agricultural tractors and equipment. **SIC:** 5083 (Farm & Garden Machinery). **Est:** 1963. **Sales:** $4,000,000 (2000). **Emp:** 23. **Officers:** Larry E. Shurden, President; Jane Shurden, Treasurer & Secty.

■ 299 ■ **Benson Farmers Cooperative**
PO Box 407
Benson, IL 61516
Phone: (309)394-2293 **Fax:** (309)394-2670
Products: Grain; Propane. **SICs:** 5153 (Grain & Field Beans); 5169 (Chemicals & Allied Products Nec). **Est:** 1920. **Sales:** $17,000,000 (2000). **Emp:** 8. **Officers:** Dean Backer, President; Gerald McMillan, General Mgr.

■ 300 ■ **Benton County Cooperative**
PO Box 278
Ashland, MS 38603
Phone: (601)224-8933
Products: Fuels for farmers; Feed, seed, chemicals, and fertilizers. **SICs:** 5191 (Farm Supplies); 5172 (Petroleum Products Nec). **Est:** 1939. **Sales:** $4,000,000 (2000). **Emp:** 20. **Officers:** Denny Simpson, President; Sammie Ormon, General Mgr.

■ 301 ■ **Berchtold Equipment Company Inc.**
PO Box 3098
Bakersfield, CA 93385
Phone: (805)323-7818 **Fax:** (805)325-4059
E-mail: beco@berchtold.com
URL: http://www.berchtold.com
Products: Agriculture and industrial tractors and equipment. **SIC:** 5083 (Farm & Garden Machinery). **Est:** 1910. **Sales:** $12,000,000 (2000). **Emp:** 60. **Officers:** Mark Berchtold, President.

■ 302 ■ **Berlin Farmers Elevator**
PO Box 28
Berlin, ND 58415
Phone: (701)883-5347
Products: Grain, feed, and seed; Chemicals and fertilizers. **SICs:** 5153 (Grain & Field Beans); 5191 (Farm Supplies). **Est:** 1941. **Sales:** $6,000,000 (2000). **Emp:** 7. **Officers:** Roger Fiken, President; John Cisinski, General Mgr.

■ 303 ■ **Berry Tractor and Equipment Co.**
PO Box 12288
Wichita, KS 67277
Phone: (316)943-4246 **Fax:** (316)943-3903
Products: Tractors and other mining equipment. **SIC:** 5082 (Construction & Mining Machinery). **Est:** 1957. **Sales:** $30,000,000 (2000). **Emp:** 85. **Officers:** Dan Scheer, President; Judy Worrell, Treasurer & Secty.

■ 304 ■ **Berthold Farmers Elevator Co.**
PO Box 38
Berthold, ND 58718
Phone: (701)453-3431
Products: Agricultural products, including grain, feed, seed, chemicals, and fertilizers. **SIC:** 5191 (Farm Supplies). **Est:** 1915. **Sales:** $10,000,000 (2000). **Emp:** 11. **Officers:** Roger Haaland, President; Dan DeRouchey, General Mgr.

■ 305 ■ **Bertrand Cooperative**
PO Box 67
Bertrand, NE 68927
Phone: (308)472-3415 **Fax:** (308)995-8626
Products: Feed; Fertilizer and fertilizer materials; Grain. **SIC:** 5191 (Farm Supplies). **Est:** 1916. **Sales:** $6,000,000 (2000). **Emp:** 12. **Officers:** Mike Meier, President; Bud Fyfe, General Mgr.; Lloyd Stehl, Manager.

■ 306 ■ **Bethea Distributing Inc.**
500 S 1st Ave.
Dillon, SC 29536
Phone: (803)774-6891 **Fax:** (803)774-6891
Products: Hardware; Chemicals; Fertilizer. **SICs:** 5191 (Farm Supplies); 5083 (Farm & Garden Machinery). **Est:** 1947. **Sales:** $2,000,000 (2000). **Emp:** 11. **Officers:** Thomas C. Bethea Jr., President.

■ 307 ■ **Bickett Equipment Company Inc.**
PO Box 619
Morganfield, KY 42437
Phone: (502)389-1424 **Fax:** (502)899-1542
Products: Automobiles; Tractors. **SIC:** 5083 (Farm & Garden Machinery). **Est:** 1941. **Sales:** $3,500,000 (2000). **Emp:** 17. **Officers:** Royce Bickett, President.

■ 308 ■ **Big Corn Cooperative Marketing Association Inc.**
PO Box 591
Greybull, WY 82426
Phone: (307)765-2058
Products: Farm supplies. **SIC:** 5191 (Farm Supplies). **Est:** 1923. **Sales:** $21,000,000 (1999). **Emp:** 75. **Officers:** Darrell Horton, President; David Ramburg, Controller; Louis Pistulka, General Mgr.

■ 309 ■ **Big Horn Cooperative Market Association Inc.**
PO Box 591
Greybull, WY 82426
Phone: (307)765-2061 **Fax:** (307)459-2922
Products: Fertilizer; Fuel; Lumber. **SICs:** 5191 (Farm Supplies); 5172 (Petroleum Products Nec). **Est:** 1923. **Sales:** $13,000,000 (2000). **Emp:** 50. **Officers:** Darrel Horton, CEO; Louis Pistulka, CFO; David Ramberg, Dir. of Operations.

■ 310 ■ **Big Stone County Cooperative**
PO Box 362
Clinton, MN 56225
Phone: (612)325-5466
Products: Farm supplies, including fertilizer; Fuel; Tires. **SICs:** 5191 (Farm Supplies); 5172 (Petroleum Products Nec). **Est:** 1928. **Sales:** $5,000,000 (2000). **Emp:** 12. **Officers:** Tod Sandberg, President; Tim Sletten, General Mgr.; Gerald Folk, Vice President; Bruce Hoernmann.

■ 311 ■ **Big T Pump Company Inc.**
PO Drawer 2278
Hereford, TX 79045
Phone: (806)364-0353
Products: Irrigation pumps, parts, and drills. **SICs:** 5083 (Farm & Garden Machinery); 5084 (Industrial Machinery & Equipment). **Est:** 1946. **Sales:** $1,500,000 (2000). **Emp:** 20. **Officers:** Kenneth Christie, President; Kenneth Glenn, General Mgr.

■ 312 ■ **Big Tex Feed Co. Inc.**
3720 Lamar Ave.
Paris, TX 75460
Phone: (903)785-1681
Products: Feed. **SIC:** 5153 (Grain & Field Beans). **Est:** 1962. **Sales:** $8,600,000 (2000). **Emp:** 15. **Officers:** Charles Bryans, CEO; Kathleen Bryans, CFO.

■ 313 ■ **Big Tex Grain Company Inc.**
401 Blue Star St.
San Antonio, TX 78204
Phone: (210)227-3462
Products: Feed, including cattle, hog, and horse. **SICs:** 5153 (Grain & Field Beans); 5153 (Grain & Field Beans). **Est:** 1952. **Sales:** $3,000,000 (2000). **Emp:** 30. **Officers:** G. Richard Galloway, President.

■ 314 ■ **Big Valley AG Services Inc.**
PO Box 926
Gridley, CA 95948
Phone: (530)846-5612 **Fax:** (530)846-5639
Products: Fertilizer; Chemicals. **SIC:** 5191 (Farm Supplies). **Est:** 1985. **Sales:** $7,000,000 (2000). **Emp:** 15. **Officers:** Dean Miller, General Mgr.; Joel Bisson, Controller.

■ 315 ■ **K.M. Biggs Inc.**
PO Box 967
Lumberton, NC 28359
Phone: (919)738-5206
Products: Farm machinery. **SIC:** 5083 (Farm & Garden Machinery). **Sales:** $11,000,000 (1993). **Emp:** 50. **Officers:** I.M. Biggs, President.

■ 316 ■ **Binford Farmers Union Grain**
PO Box 165
Binford, ND 58416
Phone: (701)676-2481
Products: Agricultural products, including grain, feed, seed, chemicals, and fertilizers; Fencing supplies. **SICs:** 5153 (Grain & Field Beans); 5191 (Farm Supplies). **Est:** 1949. **Sales:** $5,000,000 (2000). **Emp:** 4. **Officers:** Peter Becherl, President; Lonnie Fiebiger, General Mgr.

■ 317 ■ **Bingham Equipment Co.**
815 Gila Bend Hwy.
Casa Grande, AZ 85222
Phone: (602)836-8700 **Fax:** (602)421-1316
Products: Agricultural equipment and parts; Industrial equipment and parts. **SICs:** 5084 (Industrial Machinery & Equipment); 5083 (Farm & Garden Machinery). **Est:** 1957. **Sales:** $47,000,000 (2000). **Emp:** 150. **Officers:** Blain Bingham, CEO.

■ 318 ■ **Bird-X, Inc.**
300 N Elizabeth St., 2N
Chicago, IL 60607
Phone: (312)226-2473
Free: (800)662-5021 **Fax:** (312)226-2480
E-mail: sales@bird-x.com
URL: http://www.bird-x.com
Products: Bird control devices. **SICs:** 5063 (Electrical Apparatus & Equipment); 5065 (Electronic Parts & Equipment Nec). **Emp:** 20. **Officers:** Ronald I. Schwarcz, President; Mona G. Zemsky, Manager, e-mail: mona@bird-x.com; Maria Ramirez, e-mail: mramirez@bird-x.com; Alison James, Human Resources Contact, e-mail: alison@bird-x.com.
Former Name: Indus-Tool Inc; Go For It Products; Yates & Bird; Motloid.

■ 319 ■ **Bixby Feed Mill Inc.**
Rte. 2
Blooming Prairie, MN 55917
Phone: (507)583-7231 **Fax:** (507)583-7041
Products: Feed; Twine; Feeder parts. **SIC:** 5191 (Farm Supplies). **Est:** 1958. **Sales:** $3,000,000 (2000). **Emp:** 10. **Officers:** Greg Johnson, President.

■ 320 ■ **Black Enterprises Inc.**
1807 Black Hwy.
York, SC 29745
Phone: (803)684-4971
Products: Farm equipment, including tractors and mowers. **SIC:** 5083 (Farm & Garden Machinery). **Est:** 1986. **Sales:** $2,000,000 (2000). **Emp:** 8. **Officers:** Edward Black, President.

■ 321 ■ **Tom Blackmon Auctions Inc.**
PO Box 7464
Little Rock, AR 72217
Phone: (501)664-4526
Products: Heavy farm equipment. **SIC:** 5083 (Farm & Garden Machinery). **Sales:** $9,000,000 (2000). **Emp:** 30. **Officers:** Tom Blackmon, President.

■ 322 ■ **Bleyhl Farm Service**
119 E Main
Grandview, WA 98930
Phone: (509)882-1225
Products: Feed; Fertilizer; Chemicals. **SIC:** 5191 (Farm Supplies). **Est:** 1964. **Sales:** $28,500,000 (2000). **Emp:** 80. **Officers:** Greg Robertson, General Mgr.

■ 323 ■ **Blount Farmers Cooperative**
1514 W Broadway Ave.
Maryville, TN 37801
Phone: (615)982-2761
Products: Feed, seed, and fertilizer; Hardware; Lawnmowers. **SICs:** 5191 (Farm Supplies); 5072 (Hardware). **Est:** 1947. **Sales:** $14,000,000 (2000). **Emp:** 55. **Officers:** Butch Loggins, General Mgr.

■ 324 ■ **Bluestem Farm and Ranch Supply Inc.**
2611 W 50 Hwy.
Emporia, KS 66801
Phone: (316)342-5502 **Fax:** (316)342-9314
Products: Animal veterinary supplies; Animal feed; Saddles; Clothing; Household appliances. **SICs:** 5191 (Farm Supplies); 5136 (Men's/Boys' Clothing); 5064 (Electrical Appliances—Television & Radio). **Est:** 1961. **Sales:** $12,000,000 (2000). **Emp:** 60. **Officers:** Lee Nelson, Owner; Edward Schneider, General Mgr.

■ 325 ■ **Bode Cooperative**
PO Box 155
Bode, IA 50519
Phone: (515)379-1754
Products: Farm supplies, including animal feed, fertilizer, and chemicals. **SICs:** 5153 (Grain & Field Beans); 5191 (Farm Supplies). **Est:** 1908. **Sales:** $25,000,000 (2000). **Emp:** 23. **Officers:** Peter Erpelbing, President; Kent Tigges, General Mgr.; Mark Schock, Dir. of Marketing.

■ 326 ■ **Boettcher Enterprises Inc.**
118 W Court St.
Beloit, KS 67420
Phone: (785)738-5761 **Fax:** (785)738-6513
Products: Agriculture and farm supplies. **SIC:** 5191 (Farm Supplies). **Sales:** $20,000,000 (1993). **Emp:** 26. **Officers:** Jarold Boettcher, President; Larry Golladay, CFO.

■ 327 ■ **Bolivar Farmers Exchange**
PO Box 27
Bolivar, MO 65613
Phone: (417)326-5231
Products: Farm supplies, including feed, seed, and fertilizer. **SIC:** 5191 (Farm Supplies). **Est:** 1920. **Sales:** $8,000,000 (2000). **Emp:** 37. **Officers:** Howard O'Connor, CEO.

■ 328 ■ **Bond County Services Co.**
822 S 2nd St.
Greenville, IL 62246
Phone: (618)664-2030
Products: Farm supplies. **SICs:** 5153 (Grain & Field Beans); 5191 (Farm Supplies); 5172 (Petroleum Products Nec). **Est:** 1936. **Sales:** $7,500,000 (2000). **Emp:** 18. **Officers:** William Chappell, President; Andrew Wagner, General Mgr.

■ 329 ■ **Bonus Crop Fertilizer Inc.**
PO Box 1725
Bay City, TX 77404-1725
Phone: (409)245-4825 **Fax:** (409)245-9454
Products: Fertilizer. **SIC:** 5191 (Farm Supplies). **Est:** 1973. **Sales:** $9,000,000 (2000). **Emp:** 49. **Officers:** W.D. Barton Jr., CEO.

■ 330 ■ **Booker Equity Union Exchange Inc.**
PO Box 230
Booker, TX 79005-0230
Phone: (806)658-4541
Products: Feed and fertilizer. **SICs:** 5153 (Grain & Field Beans); 5191 (Farm Supplies). **Est:** 1920. **Sales:** $1,900,000 (2000). **Emp:** 4. **Officers:** Ron Hilbig, General Mgr.

■ 331 ■ **Booneville Cooperative Elevator Co.**
PO Box 34
Booneville, IA 50038
Phone: (515)987-4533 **Fax:** (515)987-4307
Products: Field, garden, and flower seeds; Complete livestock feeds; Fertilizer and fertilizer materials; Petroleum and its products. **SICs:** 5153 (Grain & Field Beans); 5191 (Farm Supplies); 5172 (Petroleum Products Nec). **Est:** 1949. **Sales:** $6,900,000 (2000). **Emp:** 8. **Officers:** Michael Koch, President; Vincent Booge, General Mgr.

■ 332 ■ **Bowers Implement Co. Inc.**
338 Hwy. 24-27Bypass E
Albemarle, NC 28001
Phone: (704)983-2161
Products: Tractors and equipment. **SIC:** 5083 (Farm & Garden Machinery). **Est:** 1965. **Sales:** $4,000,000 (2000). **Emp:** 13. **Officers:** A.H. Bowers, President.

■ 333 ■ **Brandt Consolidated Inc.**
Rte. 125 W
Pleasant Plains, IL 62677
Phone: (217)626-1123 **Fax:** (217)626-1927
Products: Fertilizer. **SIC:** 5191 (Farm Supplies). **Est:** 1967. **Sales:** $25,000,000 (2000). **Emp:** 70. **Officers:** Glen Brandt, President; Fred Rice, Controller; Al Mallicoat, Dir. of Marketing.

■ 334 ■ **Braun & Son Implement Inc.**
1027 S Broadway St.
Hobart, OK 73651
Phone: (580)726-3337
Products: Agricultural equipment. SIC: 5083 (Farm & Garden Machinery). **Est:** 1946. **Sales:** $2,000,000 (2000). **Emp:** 18. **Officers:** Delbert Braun, President; Bill Braun, CFO; Jim Hebenspeger, Sales Mgr.

■ 335 ■ **Brewer Environmental Industries Inc.**
311 Pacific St.
Honolulu, HI 96817
Phone: (808)532-7400   **Fax:** (808)532-7521
Products: Fertilizer. SICs: 5169 (Chemicals & Allied Products Nec); 5191 (Farm Supplies). **Est:** 1890. **Sales:** $100,000,000 (2000). **Emp:** 191. **Officers:** Stephen W. Knoy, President; Marc Tilker, CFO; Joy Kono, VP of Marketing.

■ 336 ■ **Bridgeport Equipment Co. Inc.**
PO Box 310
Bridgeport, NE 69336
Phone: (308)262-1342
Products: Farming equipment. SICs: 5083 (Farm & Garden Machinery); 5031 (Lumber, Plywood & Millwork); 5072 (Hardware). **Est:** 1944. **Sales:** $3,000,000 (2000). **Emp:** 7. **Officers:** Adrian Goltl, CEO; Deb Alber, Treasurer.

■ 337 ■ **George F. Brocke and Sons Inc.**
PO Box 159
Kendrick, ID 83537
Phone: (208)289-4231   **Fax:** (208)289-4242
Products: Feed; Lentils. SICs: 5159 (Farm-Product Raw Materials Nec); 5153 (Grain & Field Beans). **Est:** 1948. **Sales:** $13,000,000 (2000). **Emp:** 35. **Officers:** George F. Brocke Jr., President; Dean H. Brocke, Manager.

■ 338 ■ **Brotherton Seed Company Inc.**
PO Box 1136
Moses Lake, WA 98837
Phone: (509)765-1816   **Fax:** (509)765-1817
E-mail: broseed@televar.com
Products: Pea and bean seeds. SIC: 5191 (Farm Supplies). **Est:** 1955. **Sales:** $4,000,000 (2000). **Emp:** 25. **Officers:** J. Brotherton, President.

■ 339 ■ **Brown County Co-op**
PO Box 8
Robinson, KS 66532-0008
Phone: (785)544-6512
Products: Grain, feed, and animal health care products. SICs: 5191 (Farm Supplies); 5153 (Grain & Field Beans); 5199 (Nondurable Goods Nec). **Est:** 1915. **Sales:** $7,600,000 (2000). **Emp:** 15. **Officers:** Jerry Hjetland, President; Donald Goltz, Vice President.

■ 340 ■ **Brown County Cooperative Association**
Rte. 5
Hiawatha, KS 66434
Phone: (913)742-2196
Products: Grain; Fertilizer; Batteries; Petroleum. SICs: 5159 (Farm-Product Raw Materials Nec); 5191 (Farm Supplies). **Est:** 1956. **Sales:** $25,000,000 (2000). **Emp:** 50. **Officers:** Harold Neher, President.

■ 341 ■ **Brown Motors Inc.**
PO Box 230
Grangeville, ID 83530-0230
Phone: (208)983-1730   **Fax:** (208)983-1930
Products: Tractors and plows. SIC: 5083 (Farm & Garden Machinery). **Est:** 1932. **Sales:** $4,100,000 (2000). **Emp:** 30. **Officers:** Pamela J. Eimers, Owner; Sharon Newby, Secretary; Richard Wessels, Dir. of Marketing; Jean Vanderwall, Dir. of Information Systems; Alan S. Humason, General Mgr.

■ 342 ■ **Brown Tractor and Implement Inc.**
269 W Main St.
Ashville, OH 43103
Phone: (740)983-2951
Products: Farm equipment; Tractor equipment. SIC: 5083 (Farm & Garden Machinery). **Est:** 1930. **Sales:** $5,000,000 (2000). **Emp:** 11. **Officers:** R.E. Brown, President & Treasurer.

■ 343 ■ **Browning Equipment Inc.**
800 E Main St.
Purcellville, VA 20132-3163
Phone: (540)338-7123   **Fax:** (540)338-5835
E-mail: Browningeq@aol.com
Products: Lawn and garden equipment; Farm equipment, including tractors and mowers; Portable and home standby generators. SICs: 5083 (Farm & Garden Machinery); 5191 (Farm Supplies). **Est:** 1980. **Sales:** $5,500,000 (2000). **Emp:** 32. **Officers:** R.E. Browning, President; J. Copeland, CFO.

■ 344 ■ **Browning Seed Inc.**
S Interstate 27
PO Box 1836
Plainview, TX 79073
Phone: (806)293-5271   **Fax:** (806)293-9050
Products: Seeds. SIC: 5191 (Farm Supplies).

■ 345 ■ **Brownton Cooperative Agriculture Center**
PO Box 189
Brownton, MN 55312
Phone: (320)328-5211
Products: Chemical fertilizer; Feed; Gasoline. SIC: 5191 (Farm Supplies). **Est:** 1916. **Sales:** $6,500,000 (2000). **Emp:** 9. **Officers:** Bruce Loeschen, General Mgr.

■ 346 ■ **Bruce Vehicle/Equipment Auction Services Inc.**
PO Box 3825
Greenville, SC 29608-3825
Phone: (864)242-3090   **Fax:** (864)271-6510
Products: Farm machinery. SIC: 5012 (Automobiles & Other Motor Vehicles). **Est:** 1938. **Sales:** $2,000,000 (2000). **Emp:** 50. **Officers:** Gary F. Bruce, CEO & President; C. Ray Powell, Finance Officer; Arline Bruce, Dir. of Marketing; Jeff Gidden, Dir. of Data Processing.

■ 347 ■ **Otis Bryant and Son Inc.**
PO Box 148
Caneyville, KY 42721
Phone: (502)879-3221
Products: Agricultural supplies, including feed and grain. SICs: 5191 (Farm Supplies); 5153 (Grain & Field Beans). **Est:** 1962. **Sales:** $9,000,000 (1999). **Emp:** 30. **Officers:** Otis Bryant, President; Paul Bryant, Manager.

■ 348 ■ **Buckeye Countrymark Corp.**
PO Box 189
Xenia, OH 45385
Phone: (513)372-3541   **Fax:** (513)372-3141
Products: Argricultural products, including seed, grain, feed, and pet food products. SICs: 5153 (Grain & Field Beans); 5191 (Farm Supplies); 5149 (Groceries & Related Products Nec). **Est:** 1937. **Sales:** $25,000,000 (2000). **Emp:** 50. **Officers:** Roger Stockwell, CEO; Gary Gottfried, Controller.

■ 349 ■ **Bucklin Tractor and Implement**
Hwy. 54
Bucklin, KS 67834
Phone: (316)826-3271
Products: Tractors and farming machinery. SIC: 5083 (Farm & Garden Machinery). **Est:** 1944. **Sales:** $23,000,000 (2000). **Emp:** 23. **Officers:** Kelly J. Estes, President; Letty A. Bachelor, Controller; Maynard L. Estes, Dir. of Marketing & Sales.

■ 350 ■ **Buckman Farmers Cooperative Creamery**
PO Box 458
Buckman, MN 56317
Phone: (612)468-6433
Products: Farm supplies and dairy products. SICs: 5143 (Dairy Products Except Dried or Canned); 5153 (Grain & Field Beans); 5191 (Farm Supplies). **Est:** 1912. **Sales:** $5,000,000 (2000). **Emp:** 20. **Officers:** Francis Dillenberg, President; Robert Virnig, General Mgr.

■ 351 ■ **Buhrman and Son Inc.**
PO Box 5305
Richmond, VA 23220
Phone: (804)358-6776   **Fax:** (804)353-8431
Products: Farming equipment; Weed eating products.

SICs: 5083 (Farm & Garden Machinery); 5191 (Farm Supplies). **Est:** 1926. **Sales:** $4,000,000 (2000). **Emp:** 38. **Officers:** Robert Buhrman, President; Mac B. Buhrman, Vice President; Hue Buhrman, Sales Mgr.

■ 352 ■ **Burchinal Cooperative Society**
11745 B. 2nd St.
Rockwell, IA 50469-8705
Phone: (515)822-4660
Products: Farm supplies, including fertilizer, animal feed, and chemicals. SICs: 5191 (Farm Supplies); 5191 (Farm Supplies). **Est:** 1904. **Sales:** $13,000,000 (1993). **Emp:** 12. **Officers:** Robert Bartlett, President; Ron Pumphrey, General Mgr.

■ 353 ■ **E.F. Burlingham and Sons**
PO Box 217
Forest Grove, OR 97116-0217
Phone: (503)357-2141
Products: Turfgrass seed. SIC: 5191 (Farm Supplies). **Sales:** $5,700,000 (2000). **Emp:** 41.

■ 354 ■ **C-D Farm Service Company Inc.**
PO Box 560
Spencer, IA 51301-0560
Phone: (712)262-4205
Products: Fertilizer; LP gas; Petroleum; Feed, including grain. SICs: 5191 (Farm Supplies); 5172 (Petroleum Products Nec). **Sales:** $13,000,000 (2000). **Emp:** 45. **Officers:** Elwin Tritle, President; Sheri Conrad, Controller.

■ 355 ■ **CADCO Div.**
2776 County Rd. 69
Gibsonburg, OH 43431
Phone: (419)665-2367   **Fax:** (419)665-2595
Products: Herbicides, plant growth regulators; Agricultural sprayers; Pavement marking products; Paints. SICs: 5191 (Farm Supplies); 5198 (Paints, Varnishes & Supplies). **Sales:** $4,000,000 (2000). **Emp:** 12. **Officers:** James Herl, General Mgr.; Kevin Lauch, Controller.

■ 356 ■ **Cairo Cooperative Equity Exchange**
265 S Penalosa St.
Penalosa, KS 67035
Phone: (316)532-5106
Products: Farm supplies, including feed, fertilizer, and chemicals; Grain elevators. SICs: 5083 (Farm & Garden Machinery); 5191 (Farm Supplies). **Est:** 1951. **Sales:** $6,000,000 (2000). **Emp:** 9. **Officers:** Charles McGregor, Branch Mgr.

■ 357 ■ **Cal-Coast Machinery**
617 S Blosser Rd.
Santa Maria, CA 93454
Phone: (805)925-0931   **Fax:** (805)925-8123
Products: Tractors; Industrial equipment; Lawn care equipment. SICs: 5083 (Farm & Garden Machinery); 5084 (Industrial Machinery & Equipment).

■ 358 ■ **Cal-West Seeds Inc.**
PO Box 1428
Woodland, CA 95776
Phone: (530)666-3331   **Fax:** (530)666-5317
Products: Seeds. SIC: 5191 (Farm Supplies). **Est:** 1939. **Sales:** $38,000,000 (1999). **Emp:** 100. **Officers:** Paul Baumer, CEO & President; William Fife, VP of Finance; Tom Hickman, Sales & Marketing Contact; Michelle Johnson, Customer Service Contact.

■ 359 ■ **Calarco Inc.**
PO Box 727
Corcoran, CA 93212
Phone: (209)992-3127
Products: Chemicals and fertilizer. SIC: 5191 (Farm Supplies). **Est:** 1954. **Sales:** $12,000,000 (2000). **Emp:** 30. **Officers:** George Fuller, President; Jerry Jordon, Controller.

■ 360 ■ **Caldwell Implement Co. Inc.**
PO Box 295
Burlington, KS 66839
Phone: (316)364-5327
Products: Outdoor equipment. SIC: 5083 (Farm & Garden Machinery). **Est:** 1934. **Sales:** $3,000,000 (2000). **Emp:** 15. **Officers:** Thomas Caldwell, President; I. Caldwell, Treasurer.

■ 361 ■ **Bradley Caldwell, Inc.**
200 Kiwanis Blvd.
PO Box T
Hazleton, PA 18201
Phone: (717)455-7511
Free: (800)257-9100 **Fax:** (717)455-0385
Products: Lawn and garden products. **SIC:** 5083 (Farm & Garden Machinery). **Est:** 1930. **Emp:** 360. **Officers:** James Bradley, Chairman of the Board; David Caldwell, COO; Ralph Caldwell, President; William Fisher, VP of Marketing.

■ 362 ■ **Caledonia Farmers Elevator Co., Lake Odessa Branch**
1018 3rd Ave.
Lake Odessa, MI 48849-1157
Phone: (616)374-8061 **Fax:** (616)374-0129
Products: Farm products, including fertilizer, chemicals, seed, and animal feeds. **SICs:** 5191 (Farm Supplies); 5153 (Grain & Field Beans). **Est:** 1919. **Sales:** $4,000,000 (2000). **Emp:** 9. **Officers:** Steve Buche, President; Robert Possehn, Controller.

■ 363 ■ **Calhoun County Cooperative**
PO Box 900
Calhoun City, MS 38916
Phone: (601)628-6682 **Fax:** (601)628-6026
Products: Farm supplies. **SIC:** 5191 (Farm Supplies). **Est:** 1935. **Sales:** $2,000,000 (2000). **Emp:** 9. **Officers:** Buddy Doler, President & Chairman of the Board; Eddie Helms, Manager.

■ 364 ■ **California Ammonia Co.**
PO Box 280
French Camp, CA 95231-0280
Phone: (209)982-1000
Free: (800)624-4200 **Fax:** (209)983-0822
Products: Ammonia-based fertilizer. **SIC:** 5191 (Farm Supplies). **Sales:** $58,600,000 (2000). **Emp:** 35. **Officers:** Bob Smith, Exec. VP & General Mgr.; Barry T. Powell, VP, CFO & Chief Acct. Officer.

■ 365 ■ **Calumet Industries Inc.**
Rte. 2, Box 30
Calumet, OK 73014
Phone: (405)262-2263
Products: Livestock and farm products. **SIC:** 5191 (Farm Supplies). **Sales:** $14,000,000 (2000). **Emp:** 40.

■ 366 ■ **Campbell Tractor and Equipment Co.**
PO Box 430
Summersville, WV 26651
Phone: (304)872-2611
Products: Wheel-loaders; Forklifts; Dozers; Skidders; Tractors and agricultural attachments. **SICs:** 5083 (Farm & Garden Machinery); 5084 (Industrial Machinery & Equipment). **Est:** 1950. **Sales:** $15,000,000 (2000). **Emp:** 32. **Officers:** George Harris, President; Gene Campbell, VP of Sales.

■ 367 ■ **Campbell Tractors and Implements Inc.**
2014 Franklin Blvd.
Nampa, ID 83687
Phone: (208)466-8414
Products: Tractors. **SIC:** 5083 (Farm & Garden Machinery). **Est:** 1930. **Sales:** $8,000,000 (2000). **Emp:** 60. **Officers:** Allan Nobel, President; Donna Knittel, Controller; Dan Campbell, Dir. of Marketing & Sales.

■ 368 ■ **Canadian Equity Cooperative**
302 S 1st St.
Canadian, TX 79014
Phone: (806)323-6428
Products: Seed. **SICs:** 5191 (Farm Supplies); 5153 (Grain & Field Beans). **Sales:** $1,000,000 (2000). **Emp:** 4. **Officers:** Larry Nelson, General Mgr.

■ 369 ■ **Cane Equipment Cooperative Inc.**
PO Box 556
Plaquemine, LA 70764
Phone: (504)687-2050
Products: Agricultural equipment. **SIC:** 5083 (Farm & Garden Machinery). **Est:** 1969. **Sales:** $1,000,000 (2000). **Emp:** 10. **Officers:** Donald Ancoin, President.

■ 370 ■ **Cannon Valley Cooperative**
PO Box 200
Northfield, MN 55057
Phone: (507)645-9556 **Fax:** (507)645-5985
Products: Agricultural supplies, including feed and fertilizer; Petroleum. **SICs:** 5191 (Farm Supplies); 5172 (Petroleum Products Nec). **Est:** 1921. **Sales:** $19,700,000 (2000). **Emp:** 39. **Officers:** Vern Coester, President; Cliff Gipp, Controller.

■ 371 ■ **Canton Mills Inc.**
PO Box 97
Minnesota City, MN 55959
Phone: (507)689-2131
Free: (800)328-5349 **Fax:** (507)689-2400
Products: Natural and phosphate fertilizers; Feeds. **SIC:** 5191 (Farm Supplies). **Est:** 1961. **Sales:** $1,200,000 (2000). **Emp:** 8. **Officers:** David C. Bunke, President. **Alternate Name:** Fertilizer by Shut-Gro.

■ 372 ■ **Carco International Inc.**
2721 Midland Blvd.
Ft. Smith, AR 72904
Phone: (501)441-3270 **Fax:** (501)783-1020
Products: Farm equipment; Agricultural equipment. **SICs:** 5083 (Farm & Garden Machinery); 5191 (Farm Supplies). **Est:** 1915. **Sales:** $12,000,000 (2000). **Emp:** 42. **Officers:** Carl M. Corley, CEO & Chairman of the Board.

■ 373 ■ **Carroll County Equipment Co.**
PO Box 610
Carrollton, MO 64633
Phone: (660)542-2485
Free: (800)214-3337 **Fax:** (660)542-0141
Products: Agricultural equipment and supplies. **SIC:** 5083 (Farm & Garden Machinery). **Sales:** $7,500,000 (2000). **Emp:** 21.

■ 374 ■ **Carroll Farmers Cooperative**
PO Box 546
Huntingdon, TN 38344
Phone: (901)986-8271 **Fax:** (901)986-9824
Products: Agricultural supplies, including chemicals and fertilizer; Seeds. **SIC:** 5191 (Farm Supplies). **Est:** 1940. **Sales:** $4,000,000 (2000). **Emp:** 20. **Officers:** Robert Lovett, General Mgr.

■ 375 ■ **Carter Service Center**
PO Box 213
Italy, TX 76651
Phone: (972)483-6027 **Fax:** (972)483-7504
Products: Fertilizer. **SIC:** 5191 (Farm Supplies). **Est:** 1973. **Sales:** $7,000,000 (2000). **Emp:** 90. **Officers:** James Carter, President.

■ 376 ■ **Cascade Seed Co.**
PO Box 2544 T.A.
Spokane, WA 99220
Phone: (509)534-9431 **Fax:** (509)534-9619
Products: Grass seed; Garden items; Pet supplies. **SICs:** 5191 (Farm Supplies); 5199 (Nondurable Goods Nec); 5193 (Flowers & Florists' Supplies). **Est:** 1956.

■ 377 ■ **Casey Implement Company Inc.**
PO Box 246
Casey, IL 62420
Phone: (217)932-5941
Products: Tractors, including farm, lawn, and garden. **SIC:** 5083 (Farm & Garden Machinery). **Est:** 1966. **Sales:** $6,000,000 (2000). **Emp:** 20. **Officers:** Jim Wilson, President; Mark Kibler, Sales Mgr.

■ 378 ■ **Cass County Service Co.**
342 N Main St.
Virginia, IL 62691
Phone: (217)452-7751 **Fax:** (217)452-7754
Products: Farm supplies, including gas, oil, and diesel fuel; Fertilizer and feed. **SICs:** 5153 (Grain & Field Beans); 5172 (Petroleum Products Nec); 5191 (Farm Supplies). **Est:** 1927. **Sales:** $22,000,000 (2000). **Emp:** 39. **Officers:** Leland Sweatman, President; David M. Mottet, General Mgr.; Bob Walker, Marketing Mgr.

■ 379 ■ **A.L. Castle of Stockton**
5700 Cherokee Rd.
Stockton, CA 95215
Phone: (209)931-0684
Free: (800)350-0684 **Fax:** (209)931-4010
E-mail: cstlesed@inreach.com
Products: Grass and bird seed; Chemicals; Turf fertilizers. **SIC:** 5191 (Farm Supplies). **Est:** 1975. **Emp:** 10. **Officers:** David Sheffield, President; Ken Pullman, Secretary; Jodie Sheffield, Vice President.

■ 380 ■ **Castongia's Inc.**
PO Box 157
Rensselaer, IN 47978
Phone: (219)866-5117 **Fax:** (219)866-2182
Products: Farming equipment. **SIC:** 5083 (Farm & Garden Machinery). **Sales:** $10,600,000 (1994). **Emp:** 32. **Officers:** Roger Castongia, President.

■ 381 ■ **Cedar Valley FS Inc.**
PO Box 409
New Hampton, IA 50659
Phone: (515)394-3031 **Fax:** (515)394-5849
Products: Feed; Grain; Seed; Fertilizer; Paint. **SICs:** 5191 (Farm Supplies); 5198 (Paints, Varnishes & Supplies); 5153 (Grain & Field Beans). **Est:** 1946. **Sales:** $18,000,000 (2000). **Emp:** 62. **Officers:** Randy Seligman, General Mgr.; Wade Mittelstadt, Controller.

■ 382 ■ **Cenex Harvest States**
PO Box A
Garretson, SD 57030
Phone: (605)594-3415
Free: (800)580-3415 **Fax:** (605)594-3471
E-mail: efckelly@splitrocktel.net
Products: Feed; Grain; Chemicals; Fertilizer; Seed. **SICs:** 5191 (Farm Supplies); 5153 (Grain & Field Beans). **Est:** 1918. **Sales:** $23,250,000 (2000). **Emp:** 23. **Officers:** Bud Hippe, General Mgr.; Kelly Bunde, Branch Mgr. **Former Name:** Eastern Farmers Co-op.

■ 383 ■ **Cenex Harvest States Cooperative**
PO Box 65
Corsica, SD 57328-0065
Phone: (605)946-5491 **Fax:** (605)946-5215
E-mail: aartsd@dignet.com
URL: http://www.corsica-chslol.com
Products: Fuel; Fertilizer; Feed. **SICs:** 5191 (Farm Supplies); 5172 (Petroleum Products Nec). **Est:** 1942. **Sales:** $27,000,000 (2000). **Emp:** 50. **Officers:** Don Oakland, President; Art Duerksen, General Mgr. **Alternate Name:** Corsica Cooperative Association Inc.

■ 384 ■ **Cenex/Land O'Lakes AG Services**
PO Box 64089
St. Paul, MN 55164-0089
Phone: (612)451-5151
Free: (800)232-3639 **Fax:** (612)451-5568
Products: Feed; Seed; Gas; Petroleum; Diary products, including butter, cream, and cheese. **SICs:** 5191 (Farm Supplies); 5191 (Farm Supplies); 5083 (Farm & Garden Machinery). **Est:** 1987. **Sales:** $2,900,000,000 (2000). **Emp:** 3,000. **Officers:** Noel Estenson, President; Maurice Miller, VP of Marketing; Michael R. McKeown, Dir. of Information Systems; Chuck Jones, VP of Human Resources.

■ 385 ■ **Centra Sota Cooperative**
PO Box 210
Buffalo, MN 55313
Phone: (612)682-1464
Products: Feed; Fertilizer; Petroleum. **SICs:** 5191 (Farm Supplies); 5153 (Grain & Field Beans). **Est:** 1922. **Sales:** $15,500,000 (2000). **Emp:** 30. **Officers:** James Simmons, General Mgr.; Robert Colebank, Finance Officer.

■ 386 ■ **Central Alabama Cooperative Farms Inc.**
PO Box 1079
Selma, AL 36701
Phone: (205)874-9083
Products: Agricultural supplies; Lawn and garden supplies. **SIC:** 5191 (Farm Supplies). **Est:** 1946. **Sales:** $4,600,000 (2000). **Emp:** 10. **Officers:** Tim Wood, General Mgr.

■ 387 ■ Central Cooperatives Inc.
PO Box 26
Pleasant Hill, MO 64080
Phone: (816)987-2196
Products: Feed and fertilizer mixing. **SIC:** 5191 (Farm Supplies). **Sales:** $19,500,000 (2000). **Emp:** 45.

■ 388 ■ Central Counties Cooperative
125 High St.
Kellogg, IA 50135
Phone: (515)526-8236 **Fax:** (515)526-8100
E-mail: coop@starovte.com
URL: http://www.centralcounties.com
Products: Grain, including corn, oats, and soybeans; Petroleum; Agricultural chemicals, including fertilizer. **SICs:** 5153 (Grain & Field Beans); 5191 (Farm Supplies). **Est:** 1940. **Sales:** $85,000,000 (2000). **Emp:** 80. **Officers:** Marc Melhus, General Mgr.; Stan Heidamann, Treasurer.

■ 389 ■ Central Farm Supply Inc.
PO Box 167
Wooster, OH 44691
Phone: (330)264-0282 **Fax:** (330)264-0409
Products: Farm supplies, including feed; Fences; Lawn and garden supplies. **SICs:** 5191 (Farm Supplies); 5083 (Farm & Garden Machinery). **Est:** 1964. **Sales:** $14,000,000 (2000). **Emp:** 36. **Officers:** Bill Jones, President & CEO.

■ 390 ■ Central Farmers Cooperative
Box 330
ONeill, NE 68763-0330
Phone: (402)843-2223
Products: Grain; Feed; Fertilizer; Lumber. **SICs:** 5153 (Grain & Field Beans); 5191 (Farm Supplies); 5141 (Groceries—General Line); 5031 (Lumber, Plywood & Millwork). **Sales:** $12,000,000 (2000). **Emp:** 30. **Officers:** Doug Derscheid, General Mgr.

■ 391 ■ Central Garden and Pet Co.
3697 Mt. Diablo Blvd., Ste. 310
Lafayette, CA 94549
Phone: (510)283-4573 **Fax:** (510)283-6165
Products: Gardening supplies; Pet supplies. **SICs:** 5191 (Farm Supplies); 5091 (Sporting & Recreational Goods); 5199 (Nondurable Goods Nec). **Est:** 1985. **Sales:** $841,000,000 (2000). **Emp:** 2,700. **Officers:** William E. Brown, CEO & Chairman of the Board; Robert B. Jones, VP & CFO; Allan E. Manseau, VP of Marketing.

■ 392 ■ Central Garden and Pet Supply Inc.
PO Box 27126
Salt Lake City, UT 84127
Phone: (801)973-7514 **Fax:** (801)972-8239
Products: Gardening and pet supplies. **SICs:** 5191 (Farm Supplies); 5199 (Nondurable Goods Nec); 5149 (Groceries & Related Products Nec).

■ 393 ■ Central Garden and Pet Supply Inc.
16179 SE 98th Ave.
Clackamas, OR 97015
Phone: (503)650-4400 **Fax:** (503)650-0636
Products: Garden and pet supplies. **SICs:** 5191 (Farm Supplies); 5199 (Nondurable Goods Nec).

■ 394 ■ Central Garden Supplies
925 E 66th St.
Lubbock, TX 79404
Phone: (806)745-8668 **Fax:** (806)748-1673
Products: Gardening supplies. **SIC:** 5191 (Farm Supplies).

■ 395 ■ Central Illinois Harvestore Inc.
208 N Rolla St.
Eureka, IL 61530
Phone: (309)467-2334
Products: Farming machinery for milk, corn, and fertilizer. **SIC:** 5083 (Farm & Garden Machinery). **Est:** 1958. **Sales:** $400,000 (2000). **Emp:** 8. **Officers:** Glenn Nichols, President.

■ 396 ■ Central Iowa Cooperative
PO Box 190
Jewell, IA 50130
Phone: (515)827-5431
Products: Grain, feed, fertilizer, and chemicals. **SICs:** 5153 (Grain & Field Beans); 5191 (Farm Supplies).

Est: 1975. **Sales:** $25,000,000 (2000). **Emp:** 26. **Officers:** David Olthoff, President; Ron Amundson, General Mgr.

■ 397 ■ Central Minnesota Cooperative
PO Box 192
Sauk Centre, MN 56378
Phone: (320)352-6533 **Fax:** (320)352-2846
Products: Grain; Feed; Fuel; Fertilizer. **SICs:** 5143 (Dairy Products Except Dried or Canned); 5191 (Farm Supplies). **Est:** 1917. **Sales:** $9,000,000 (2000). **Emp:** 20. **Officers:** Mike Goerdt, President; Stan Hanna, Dir. of Marketing.

■ 398 ■ Central Power Systems
1114 W Cass St.
Tampa, FL 33606
Phone: (813)253-6035 **Fax:** (813)251-8640
URL: http://www.centralpower.com
Products: Service engines and parts. **SIC:** 5083 (Farm & Garden Machinery). **Est:** 1996. **Sales:** $7,000,000 (2000). **Emp:** 30. **Officers:** Jeff Mergenthaler, Dir. of Sales & Marketing. **Former Name:** Spencer Engine Inc.

■ 399 ■ Central Rivers Cooperative
502 S 2nd St.
Princeton, MN 55371
Phone: (612)389-2582
Products: Mixed fertilizers. **SIC:** 5191 (Farm Supplies). **Sales:** $18,000,000 (1994). **Emp:** 60. **Officers:** Tim Kavanaugh, Finance General Manager.

■ 400 ■ Central Tractor Farm & Country, Inc.
PO Box 3330
Des Moines, IA 50316
Phone: (515)266-3101 **Fax:** (515)266-2952
Products: Lawn, garden, and household equipment. **SICs:** 5083 (Farm & Garden Machinery); 5023 (Homefurnishings).

■ 401 ■ Central Wisconsin Cooperative
PO Box 14
Stratford, WI 54484
Phone: (715)687-4443 **Fax:** (715)687-4126
Products: Lawn and garden equipment, including feed, seed, fertilizer, machinery, parts; Bulk fuel; LP fuel. **SIC:** 5191 (Farm Supplies). **Est:** 1926. **Sales:** $30,000,000 (1999). **Emp:** 120. **Officers:** Frank H. Brenner, General Mgr. **Former Name:** Stratford Farmers Cooperative.

■ 402 ■ Century Equipment Inc.
5959 Angola Rd.
Toledo, OH 43615
Phone: (419)865-7400 **Fax:** (419)865-8215
URL: http://www.centuryequip.com
Products: Lawnmowers and snowblowers. **SIC:** 5084 (Industrial Machinery & Equipment). **Est:** 1950. **Sales:** $25,000,000 (2000). **Emp:** 90. **Officers:** Robert O'Brien, Chairman of the Board; Tom Williams, Treasurer; Marty O'Brien, President.

■ 403 ■ Century Rain Aid
31691 Dequindre
Madison Heights, MI 48071
Phone: (248)588-2990
Free: (800)347-4272 **Fax:** (248)588-3528
E-mail: rainaid@rainaid.com
URL: http://www.rainaid.com
Products: Irrigation equipment. **SIC:** 5083 (Farm & Garden Machinery). **Sales:** $50,000,000 (1994). **Emp:** 200. **Officers:** Wayne Miller.

■ 404 ■ Cereal Byproducts Co.
763 New Ballas Rd. S
St. Louis, MO 63141
Phone: (314)569-2915
Free: (800)237-3258 **Fax:** (314)569-3537
Products: Animal feed and additives; Grain and field beans; Pet food; Bird feed. **SICs:** 5191 (Farm Supplies); 5153 (Grain & Field Beans); 5149 (Groceries & Related Products Nec). **Est:** 1917. **Sales:** $60,000,000 (2000). **Emp:** 40. **Officers:** Jan Wallach, Export Mgr.

■ 405 ■ Cereal Byproducts Co.
763 New Ballas Rd. S
St. Louis, MO 63141
Phone: (314)569-2915
Free: (800)237-3258 **Fax:** (314)569-3537
Products: Agricultural equipment and supplies. **SIC:** 5191 (Farm Supplies). **Sales:** $60,000,000 (2000). **Emp:** 40.

■ 406 ■ Charles River BRF Inc.
305 Almeda-Genoa Rd.
Houston, TX 77047
Phone: (713)433-5846 **Fax:** (713)433-6971
Products: Laboratory primates. **SIC:** 5199 (Nondurable Goods Nec). **Sales:** $9,000,000 (2000). **Emp:** 22. **Officers:** Raj Bhalla, President; Cheryl Katz, Controller.

■ 407 ■ Chase Trade, Inc.
One Chase Manhattan Plaza
New York, NY 10081
Phone: (212)552-1264
Products: Concrete; Agricultural chemicals, including fertilizer; Industrial inorganic chemicals, including ethanol. **SICs:** 5191 (Farm Supplies); 5032 (Brick, Stone & Related Materials); 5169 (Chemicals & Allied Products Nec). **Officers:** R. Michael Rice, President.

■ 408 ■ Chem Gro of Houghton Inc.
PO Box 76
Houghton, IA 52631
Phone: (319)469-2611 **Fax:** (319)469-2612
Products: Agricultural chemicals; Fertilizer. **SIC:** 5191 (Farm Supplies). **Est:** 1962. **Sales:** $7,000,000 (2000). **Emp:** 20. **Officers:** Harold H. Dyer, President.

■ 409 ■ Chem-Real Investment Corp.
12015 E 46th Ave., No. 460
Denver, CO 80239
Phone: (303)375-1203 **Fax:** (303)375-0044
E-mail: chemreal@henge.com
Products: Heaters; Industrial chemicals; Pesticides; Diesel additives; Sewage odor elimination products; Fish and shrimp production technology. **SICs:** 5169 (Chemicals & Allied Products Nec); 5141 (Groceries—General Line); 5084 (Industrial Machinery & Equipment). **Est:** 1958. **Sales:** $5,000,000 (1999). **Emp:** 10. **Officers:** Phillip C. Mozer, President; Allan G. Duey, Vice President.

■ 410 ■ Chemi-Trol Chemical Co.
2776 County Rd. 69
Gibsonburg, OH 43431
Phone: (419)665-2367 **Fax:** (419)334-5285
Products: Herbicides. **SIC:** 5191 (Farm Supplies). **Est:** 1999. **Sales:** $10,000,000 (1999). **Officers:** Ben Ammons, CEO & Chairman of the Board; John McFadden, Treasurer; Charles E. Adnea, President & COO.

■ 411 ■ Cheney Cooperative Elevator Association
PO Box 340
Cheney, KS 67025
Phone: (316)542-3181
Products: Grain; Fertilizer; Petroleum; Feed; Seed; Chemicals. **SICs:** 5153 (Grain & Field Beans); 5191 (Farm Supplies); 5172 (Petroleum Products Nec). **Est:** 1952. **Sales:** $10,000,000 (2000). **Emp:** 20. **Officers:** Dale Voran, President & Chairman of the Board.

■ 412 ■ Cherry Farms Inc.
PO Box 128
Lee, FL 32059
Phone: (850)971-5558
Products: Farm supplies, including feed, feeders, and fertilizer; Pipe supplies. **SIC:** 5191 (Farm Supplies). **Est:** 1949. **Sales:** $1,000,000 (2000). **Emp:** 10. **Officers:** Larrie J. Cherry Sr., President; Carson Cherry, Vice President; Virgina Cherry, Treasurer & Secty.

■ 413 ■ Mark Chesson and Sons Inc.
101 Chesson Dr.
Williamston, NC 27892
Phone: (919)792-1566 **Fax:** (919)792-2965
Products: Farm machinery and equipment; Agricultural tractors. **SIC:** 5083 (Farm & Garden

Machinery). **Sales:** $3,000,000 (2000). **Emp:** 18. **Officers:** W.E. Chesson, President.

■ **414** ■ **Chester Inc.**
PO Box 2237
Valparaiso, IN 46384
Phone: (219)462-1131 **Fax:** (219)464-8488
Products: Farm supplies; Computers; Tractors. **SICs:** 5191 (Farm Supplies); 5191 (Farm Supplies); 5153 (Grain & Field Beans). **Est:** 1951. **Sales:** $30,000,000 (2000). **Emp:** 100. **Officers:** C.F. Bowman, President.

■ **415** ■ **Chick Master International Inc.**
120 Sylvan Ave.
PO Box 1250
Englewood Cliffs, NJ 07632
Phone: (201)947-8810 **Fax:** (201)947-4608
URL: http://www.chickmaster.com
Products: Commercial poultry incubators. **SIC:** 5083 (Farm & Garden Machinery). **Officers:** Robert Holzer, President; Ralph Magrans, VP of International Sales/Marketing; Alan Shandler, VP of Finance & Admin.; Richard Burke, VP & Gen. Mgr., e-mail: cmrburke@worldnet.att.net; John Harbaugh, e-mail: cmjharbaugh@worldnet.att.net; Alan Shandler, e-mail: ashandler@worldnet.att.net.

■ **416** ■ **Christian County Farmers Supply Co.**
PO Box 377
Taylorville, IL 62568
Phone: (217)824-2205
Products: Agricultural chemicals, feed, seed, fertilizers and fuel oil; Gasoline service station. **SICs:** 5191 (Farm Supplies); 5172 (Petroleum Products Nec). **Est:** 1927. **Sales:** $16,000,000 (1999). **Emp:** 51. **Officers:** Stan Ryan, President; Fred Steffen, Treasurer & Secty.

■ **417** ■ **Chula Farmers Cooperative**
PO Box 10
Chula, MO 64635
Phone: (660)639-3125 **Fax:** (660)639-2104
Products: Farm supplies, including fertilizer and feed. **SIC:** 5083 (Farm & Garden Machinery). **Est:** 1952. **Sales:** $5,000,000 (1999). **Emp:** 11. **Officers:** Allan Tollson, President; Steve Meyer, General Mgr.

■ **418** ■ **Claiborne Farmers Cooperative**
PO Box 160
New Tazewell, TN 37824-0160
Phone: (423)626-5251 **Fax:** (423)626-7667
Products: Farming supplies. **SIC:** 5191 (Farm Supplies). **Est:** 1947. **Sales:** $6,600,000 (2000). **Emp:** 34. **Officers:** Gary Munday, President; Tim Day, General Mgr.; Jeana Owens, Bookkeeper.

■ **419** ■ **Clarence Cooperative Company Inc.**
619 Lombard St.
Clarence, IA 52216
Phone: (319)452-3805 **Fax:** (319)452-3837
Products: Feed; Fertilizer; Petroleum. **SICs:** 5153 (Grain & Field Beans); 5191 (Farm Supplies). **Est:** 1919. **Sales:** $40,000,000 (2000). **Emp:** 70. **Officers:** Robert Murrell, General Mgr.; Kathy West, CFO; David Holm, Dir. of Marketing.

■ **420** ■ **Clarenie Cooperative Elevator Co.**
29434 Allen Grove Rd.
Dixon, IA 52745
Phone: (319)843-2115
Free: (800)859-2115 **Fax:** (319)843-3901
E-mail: dixcoop@netins.net
Products: Grains; Feed; Seeds; Fertilizer; Chemicals; Farming supplies. **SICs:** 5153 (Grain & Field Beans); 5191 (Farm Supplies). **Est:** 1919. **Sales:** $8,900,000 (2000). **Emp:** 9. **Officers:** Phil Petersen, Branch Mgr., e-mail: philpetersen@hotmail.com.

■ **421** ■ **Clarion Farmers Elevator Cooperative**
PO Box 313
Clarion, IA 50525
Phone: (515)532-2881 **Fax:** (515)532-2273
Products: Grain, feed, and fertilizer. **SICs:** 5153 (Grain & Field Beans); 5191 (Farm Supplies). **Est:** 1912. **Sales:** $16,000,000 (2000). **Emp:** 15. **Officers:** Al Struthers, General Mgr.

■ **422** ■ **H.C. Clark Implement Company Inc.**
PO Box 1158
Aberdeen, SD 57402
Phone: (605)225-8170 **Fax:** (605)225-4671
Products: Agricultural equipment and supplies. **SIC:** 5083 (Farm & Garden Machinery). **Sales:** $5,000,000 (2000). **Emp:** 25.

■ **423** ■ **Clark Landmark Inc.**
PO Box 687
Springfield, OH 45501
Phone: (937)323-7536
Products: Agricultural supplies; Garden supplies. **SICs:** 5191 (Farm Supplies); 5153 (Grain & Field Beans). **Est:** 1934. **Sales:** $11,000,000 (2000). **Emp:** 50. **Officers:** Gordon Wallace, General Mgr.

■ **424** ■ **Clearwater Grain Co.**
PO Box 427
Clearwater, KS 67026
Phone: (316)584-2011
Products: Farm supplies, including grain, feed, and fertilizer. **SICs:** 5153 (Grain & Field Beans); 5191 (Farm Supplies). **Est:** 1959. **Sales:** $6,000,000 (2000). **Emp:** 7. **Officers:** Bill Garner, General Mgr.

■ **425** ■ **Clemons Tractor Co.**
PO Box 7707
Ft. Worth, TX 76111
Phone: (817)834-8131 **Fax:** (817)831-8775
Products: Tractors. **SICs:** 5083 (Farm & Garden Machinery); 5082 (Construction & Mining Machinery). **Est:** 1955. **Sales:** $5,000,000 (2000). **Emp:** 19. **Officers:** Lewis H. Clemons, President.

■ **426** ■ **Clerf Equipment Inc.**
228 Beachwood Ln.
Panama City, FL 32413-2791
Products: Farm tractors. **SIC:** 5083 (Farm & Garden Machinery). **Sales:** $1,000,000 (2000). **Emp:** 7. **Officers:** Howard Clerf, Owner.

■ **427** ■ **Clinton AG Service Inc.**
PO Box 24228
Clinton, MN 56225
Phone: (320)325-5203
Free: (800)879-3434 **Fax:** (320)325-5203
Products: Agricultural supplies, including feed, seed, liquid and dry fertilizer, and chemicals; Pet food; Grain handling equipment. **SIC:** 5191 (Farm Supplies). **Est:** 1985. **Sales:** $2,000,000 (1999). **Emp:** 10. **Officers:** Gary Dybdahl, Owner.

■ **428** ■ **Clyde Cooperative Association**
PO Box 86
Medford, OK 73759
Phone: (580)395-3341
Free: (800)725-3341 **Fax:** (580)395-2080
E-mail: clydcoop@kskc.net
URL: http://www.bcity.com/clydecoop
Products: Farming supplies. **SIC:** 5191 (Farm Supplies). **Est:** 1921. **Sales:** $20,000,000 (2000). **Emp:** 43. **Officers:** Pat Powell, President; Glen R. Schickedanz, General Mgr.; Arlie Goforth, Dir. of Marketing & Sales.

■ **429** ■ **Co-HG**
116 Misner, Mingo
Colby, KS 67701
Phone: (785)462-2033 **Fax:** (785)462-8250
Products: Fertilizer and fertilizer materials; Grain; Farm supplies. **SICs:** 5153 (Grain & Field Beans); 5191 (Farm Supplies). **Est:** 1948. **Sales:** $8,000,000 (2000). **Emp:** 9. **Officers:** J.J. Denny, Crop Production; Gary C. Runnells, Branch Mgr. **Former Name:** Mingo Cooperative Grain Co.

■ **430** ■ **Coast Grain Company Inc.**
5355 E Airport Dr.
Ontario, CA 91761-0961
Phone: (909)390-9766 **Fax:** (909)983-3822
Products: Grain; Feed. **SICs:** 5153 (Grain & Field Beans); 5153 (Grain & Field Beans). **Est:** 1938. **Sales:** $25,000,000 (2000). **Emp:** 200. **Officers:** Rhona Weinberg-Gewelber, President; Seiso Kawasaki, CFO; Tom Scaife, Dir. of Sales.

■ **431** ■ **Coastal Plains Farmers Co-op Inc.**
PO Box 590
Quitman, GA 31643
Phone: (912)263-7564
Products: Farm feed and supplies; Fertilizers; Insecticides; Herbicides. **SIC:** 5191 (Farm Supplies). **Est:** 1901. **Sales:** $6,000,000 (2000). **Emp:** 15. **Officers:** Billy Drew, General Mgr.; Greg Croft, Dir. of Sales.

■ **432** ■ **Cocke Farmers Cooperative Inc.**
PO Box 309
Newport, TN 37821
Phone: (423)623-2331
Products: Farming supplies; Gardening supplies; Pet supplies. **SICs:** 5191 (Farm Supplies); 5083 (Farm & Garden Machinery); 5199 (Nondurable Goods Nec). **Est:** 1947. **Sales:** $4,000,000 (2000). **Emp:** 18. **Officers:** Jimmy Hensley, Manager.

■ **433** ■ **Bill Coffey and Sons Inc.**
Rte. 16
Ashmore, IL 61912
Phone: (217)349-8338
Products: Tractors, including farm, lawn, and garden. **SICs:** 5083 (Farm & Garden Machinery); 5191 (Farm Supplies). **Est:** 1968. **Sales:** $4,000,000 (2000). **Emp:** 20. **Officers:** Bill Coffey Sr., President.

■ **434** ■ **Cold Spring Cooperative Creamery**
301 1st St. S
PO Box 423
Cold Spring, MN 56320
Phone: (320)685-8651 **Fax:** (320)685-7260
Products: Agriculture. **SICs:** 5191 (Farm Supplies); 5143 (Dairy Products Except Dried or Canned); 5172 (Petroleum Products Nec). **Est:** 1917. **Sales:** $6,000,000 (2000). **Emp:** 13. **Officers:** Dave Regnier, President; Ralph Schlangen, General Mgr.

■ **435** ■ **Collingwood Grain Inc.**
PO Box 2150
Hutchinson, KS 67504-2150
Phone: (316)663-7121 **Fax:** (316)669-5880
Products: Grain and feed; Fertilizers and chemicals. **SICs:** 5153 (Grain & Field Beans); 5191 (Farm Supplies). **Est:** 1890. **Sales:** $580,000,000 (2000). **Emp:** 700. **Officers:** Lowell Downey, President; John Bair, Controller; Randy Whisenhumt, VP of Fertilizer and Chemicals; Ken Sprinkle, Dir. of Systems.

■ **436** ■ **Columbus Tractor Machinery Co.**
PO Box 2407
Columbus, GA 31902
Phone: (706)687-0752
Products: Tractors parts and supplies. **SIC:** 5083 (Farm & Garden Machinery). **Est:** 1951. **Sales:** $2,000,000 (2000). **Emp:** 12. **Officers:** David R. Parkman Sr., President; David R. Parkman Jr., VP of Finance.

■ **437** ■ **Concordia Farmers Cooperative Co.**
708 Bismark St.
Concordia, MO 64020
Phone: (816)463-2256 **Fax:** (816)463-2230
Products: Fertilizer; Feed. **SICs:** 5153 (Grain & Field Beans); 5153 (Grain & Field Beans); 5191 (Farm Supplies). **Est:** 1912. **Sales:** $9,000,000 (2000). **Emp:** 33. **Officers:** Stan Oetting, President; Kelly B. Thorp, General Mgr.

■ **438** ■ **Conrad Cooperative**
PO Box 160
Conrad, IA 50621-0160
Phone: (515)366-2040 **Fax:** (515)366-2855
Products: Grain; Fertilizer and chemicals; Refined fuels; Livestock feed. **SICs:** 5153 (Grain & Field Beans); 5172 (Petroleum Products Nec); 5191 (Farm Supplies). **Est:** 1996. **Sales:** $56,600,000 (2000). **Emp:** 60.

■ **439** ■ **Conrad Implement Co.**
PO Box 1207
Conrad, MT 59425
Phone: (406)278-5531
Products: Agricultural equipment. **SICs:** 5191 (Farm Supplies); 5083 (Farm & Garden Machinery). **Est:** 1937. **Sales:** $5,000,000 (2000). **Emp:** 20. **Officers:** Vaughn D. Dutro, President & Treasurer.

■ 440 ■ **Consolidated Cooperatives Inc.**
PO Box 877
Worthington, MN 56187
Phone: (507)376-4113 **Fax:** (507)376-6331
Products: Farm supplies, including chemicals, feed, and fertilizer. **SICs:** 5153 (Grain & Field Beans); 5191 (Farm Supplies). **Est:** 1910. **Sales:** $30,000,000 (2000). **Emp:** 37. **Officers:** Voris Spittle, President; Doug Anton, Treasurer & Secty.; Marlin Mammen, General Mgr.

■ 441 ■ **Consumer Cooperative of Walworth County**
PO Box 377
Elkhorn, WI 53121
Phone: (414)723-3150 **Fax:** (414)723-2106
Products: Agricultural equipment and supplies. **SIC:** 5191 (Farm Supplies). **Est:** 1936. **Sales:** $6,500,000 (2000). **Emp:** 24.

■ 442 ■ **Consumer Oil and Supply Co.**
PO Box 38
Braymer, MO 64624
Phone: (816)645-2215
Products: Petroleum products; Feed; Chemicals; Farm supplies. **SICs:** 5172 (Petroleum Products Nec); 5172 (Petroleum Products Nec); 5191 (Farm Supplies). **Est:** 1929. **Sales:** $9,500,000 (2000). **Emp:** 18. **Officers:** Wayne Leamer, General Mgr.

■ 443 ■ **Consumers Cooperative**
PO Box 533
Richland Center, WI 53581
Phone: (608)647-6171 **Fax:** (608)647-6237
Products: Agricultural equipment and supplies. **SIC:** 5191 (Farm Supplies). **Est:** 1934. **Sales:** $9,000,000 (2000). **Emp:** 20.

■ 444 ■ **Consumers Cooperative Exchange**
1400 Logan St.
Merrill, WI 54452
Phone: (715)536-2491
Products: Farm supplies, including feed, fertilizer, and chemicals. **SIC:** 5191 (Farm Supplies). **Est:** 1937. **Sales:** $5,000,000 (2000). **Emp:** 20. **Officers:** James Gaeu, President; Lawrence Duginski, General Mgr.

■ 445 ■ **Coop Country Partners**
PO Box 517
Sauk City, WI 53583
Phone: (608)643-3345
Free: (800)572-2667 **Fax:** (608)643-7891
E-mail: edachen@cc-partners.com
Products: Animal health care products and feed; Seed; Grain; Fertilizer; Chemicals; Petroleum. **SICs:** 5191 (Farm Supplies); 5153 (Grain & Field Beans); 5169 (Chemicals & Allied Products Nec); 5199 (Nondurable Goods Nec). **Est:** 1997. **Sales:** $45,000,000 (2000). **Emp:** 200. **Officers:** Gene Larson, President; Al Sanow, General Mgr.

■ 446 ■ **Coop Services Inc.**
PO Box 2187
Lawton, OK 73502
Phone: (580)355-3700 **Fax:** (580)355-3705
E-mail: coopservicesinc@aol.com
Products: Farming and agricultural supplies; Pet supplies. **SICs:** 5153 (Grain & Field Beans); 5191 (Farm Supplies); 5083 (Farm & Garden Machinery). **Est:** 1924. **Sales:** $9,500,000 (2000). **Emp:** 18. **Officers:** Chester Fisher, President; Warren Devore, General Mgr. **Former Name:** Cooperative Services Inc.

■ 447 ■ **Cooperative Agricultural Center**
PO Box 770
Lakefield, MN 56150
Phone: (507)662-5285 **Fax:** (507)662-6761
Products: Agricultural supplies, including feed, fertilizer, chemicals, and petroleum. **SICs:** 5191 (Farm Supplies); 5172 (Petroleum Products Nec). **Est:** 1911. **Sales:** $6,200,000 (2000). **Emp:** 19.

■ 448 ■ **Cooperative Agricultural Services Inc.**
411 W 2nd
Oakley, KS 67748
Phone: (785)672-3300
Products: Grain and feed, fertilizers, and farm supplies. **SICs:** 5153 (Grain & Field Beans); 5191 (Farm Supplies). **Sales:** $25,000,000 (1993). **Emp:** 55.

Officers: William Kuhlman, President; Stan Stark, Finance Officer.

■ 449 ■ **Cooperative Association No. 1 Inc.**
201 E Front St.
Slater, MO 65349
Phone: (660)529-2244 **Fax:** (660)529-2877
Products: Farm supplies, including chemicals and feed. **SIC:** 5191 (Farm Supplies). **Est:** 1919. **Sales:** $10,000,000 (2000). **Emp:** 18. **Officers:** William Horgan, CEO; Esther Peel, Treasurer.

■ 450 ■ **Cooperative Elevator Co.**
7211 E Michigan Ave.
Pigeon, MI 48755
Phone: (517)453-4500
Free: (800)968-0601 **Fax:** (517)453-3942
Products: Grains; Feed; Seeds; Fertilizer; Chemicals. **SIC:** 5153 (Grain & Field Beans). **Est:** 1915. **Sales:** $92,000,000 (2000). **Emp:** 160. **Officers:** John P. Kohr, CEO; W. Boyle, VP of Finance; Mike Eisengruber, Vice President.

■ 451 ■ **Cooperative Elevator Co.**
PO Box 338
Francesville, IN 47946
Phone: (219)567-9132 **Fax:** (219)567-9132
Products: Grain elevator; Chemicals; Feed; Hardware; Fertilizer. **SICs:** 5153 (Grain & Field Beans); 5072 (Hardware); 5191 (Farm Supplies). **Est:** 1919. **Sales:** $10,000,000 (2000). **Emp:** 12. **Officers:** Stanley Boehning, President; Donald Markin, Manager.

■ 452 ■ **Cooperative Elevator Supply Co.**
PO Box 220
Meade, KS 67864
Phone: (316)873-2161
Products: Feed, fertilizer, and chemicals. **SICs:** 5191 (Farm Supplies); 5153 (Grain & Field Beans). **Sales:** $5,500,000 (2000). **Emp:** 20. **Officers:** Steve Edwards, President; Ed Hisson, Treasurer & Secty.; Randy Ackerman, Dir. of Marketing.

■ 453 ■ **Cooperative Exchange**
PO Box 156
Arlington, KS 67514
Phone: (316)538-2331
Products: Fertilizer; Insecticides; Herbicides; Feed; Cattle; Gasoline; Grains. **SICs:** 5153 (Grain & Field Beans); 5191 (Farm Supplies); 5172 (Petroleum Products Nec). **Est:** 1921. **Sales:** $3,000,000 (2000). **Emp:** 4. **Officers:** Sig Collins, President; Dale Ostmeyer, General Mgr.

■ 454 ■ **Cooperative Feed Dealer Inc.**
PO Box 670
Chenango Bridge, NY 13745
Phone: (607)648-4194 **Fax:** (607)648-8322
Products: Farm feed ingredients. **SICs:** 5191 (Farm Supplies); 5153 (Grain & Field Beans). **Est:** 1935. **Sales:** $40,000,000 (2000). **Emp:** 35. **Officers:** L. Stephens, General Mgr.; H.D. Larnerd, Treasurer.

■ 455 ■ **Cooperative Grain and Product Co.**
PO Box 128
Ringsted, IA 50578
Phone: (712)866-0581 **Fax:** (712)866-0580
Products: Agricultural chemicals, including herbicides and pesticides. **SICs:** 5153 (Grain & Field Beans); 5191 (Farm Supplies). **Est:** 1936. **Emp:** 70. **Officers:** Larry Bierstead, President; Larry Sterk, Mgr. of Finance.

■ 456 ■ **Cooperative Grain and Supply**
107 W Grand St.
Hillsboro, KS 67063
Phone: (316)947-3917
Products: Grain and feed; Fertilizers; Batteries. **SIC:** 5191 (Farm Supplies). **Est:** 1966. **Sales:** $20,000,000 (2000). **Emp:** 55. **Officers:** Lyman L. Adams Jr., General Mgr.

■ 457 ■ **Cooperative Grain and Supply**
107 W Grand St.
Hillsboro, KS 67063
Phone: (316)947-3917
Products: Agricultural equipment and supplies. **SIC:** 5191 (Farm Supplies). **Sales:** $20,000,000 (2000). **Emp:** 55.

■ 458 ■ **Cooperative Oil Co.**
PO Box 289
Alma, NE 68920
Phone: (308)928-2126 **Fax:** (308)928-2127
Products: Feed and fertilizer; Grain; Farm supplies; Batteries; Oil and fuel. **SICs:** 5191 (Farm Supplies); 5172 (Petroleum Products Nec); 5153 (Grain & Field Beans). **Est:** 1923. **Sales:** $6,000,000 (2000). **Emp:** 14. **Officers:** John Ehrke, President; Tom J. Keuton, General Mgr.

■ 459 ■ **Cooperative Service Oil Co.**
208 E Grand St.
Chilton, WI 53014
Phone: (920)849-2377
Free: (888)811-2667 **Fax:** (920)849-9060
Products: Fertilizer, feed, and seed; Grain; Petroleum. **SICs:** 5191 (Farm Supplies); 5172 (Petroleum Products Nec). **Est:** 1931. **Sales:** $14,000,000 (2000). **Emp:** 40. **Officers:** Steve Zutz, Manager; Dave Schneider, Board President.

■ 460 ■ **Cooperative Services of Clark County**
PO Box 260
Dorchester, WI 54425-0260
Phone: (715)267-6105
Products: Farm supplies, including tractors and feed. **SICs:** 5191 (Farm Supplies); 5083 (Farm & Garden Machinery). **Est:** 1935. **Sales:** $7,000,000 (2000). **Emp:** 40. **Officers:** Dennis Syth, President; Dianna Frame, Office Mgr.

■ 461 ■ **Cooperative Union Mercantile Co. Inc.**
PO Box 274
Grinnell, KS 67738
Phone: (785)824-3201
Products: Grain; Feed; Fertilizer and chemicals. **SICs:** 5153 (Grain & Field Beans); 5191 (Farm Supplies). **Sales:** $8,000,000 (2000). **Emp:** 40. **Officers:** Murray J. Barhman, President; Melvin Quint, General Mgr.

■ 462 ■ **Coos Grange Supply Co.**
1085 S 2nd St.
Coos Bay, OR 97420
Phone: (541)267-7051
Products: Farm supplies, including grains, seeds, feeds, and fertilizers. **SIC:** 5191 (Farm Supplies). **Est:** 1937. **Sales:** $2,000,000 (2000). **Emp:** 12. **Officers:** Otto Witt, President; Keith Johnson, Treasurer.

■ 463 ■ **Cornlea Auction Co.**
R.R. 1
Cornlea, NE 68642
Phone: (402)923-0894
Products: Farm equipment. **SIC:** 5083 (Farm & Garden Machinery). **Est:** 1953. **Sales:** $3,000,000 (2000). **Emp:** 15. **Officers:** Mylen Wegener, President; Jim Wegener, Vice President.

■ 464 ■ **Cory Orchard and Turf Div.**
6739 Guion Rd.
Indianapolis, IN 46268
Phone: (317)328-1000 **Fax:** (317)328-1111
Products: Agricultural chemicals and equipment. **SIC:** 5191 (Farm Supplies). **Sales:** $6,700,000 (2000). **Emp:** 17. **Officers:** Jon M. Cravens, General Mgr.

■ 465 ■ **Cottage Grove Cooperative**
203 W Cottage Grove Rd.
Cottage Grove, WI 53527
Phone: (608)839-4511
Free: (800)236-3276 **Fax:** (608)839-5144
URL: http://www.cgcoop.com
Products: Grain, feed, seed, and fertilizer; Petroleum and chemicals. C-Stores, LP Gas, Heating and Cooling, Hardware. **SICs:** 5153 (Grain & Field Beans); 5171 (Petroleum Bulk Stations & Terminals); 5191 (Farm Supplies). **Est:** 1933. **Sales:** $61,000,000 (2000). **Emp:** 250. **Officers:** John Blaska, President; Larry Swalheim, CFO. **Former Name:** Dane County Farmers Union Cooperative.

■ 466 ■ **Countrymark Cooperative Inc.**
950 N Meridian St.
Indianapolis, IN 46204-3909
Phone: (317)685-3000 **Fax:** (317)685-3191
Products: Grain; Farm supplies, including feed, seed, fertilizers, and chemicals. **SICs:** 5153 (Grain & Field Beans); 5191 (Farm Supplies). **Est:** 1926. **Sales:**

$2,000,000,000 (2000). **Emp:** 1,650. **Officers:** Philip French, CEO & President; Robert Werner, VP of Finance; Paul Weinstein, VP of Marketing; Ed Bryan, Dir. of Information Systems; Dean Denhart, VP of Human Resources.

■ **467** ■ **Countryside Marketing**
PO Box 80110
Billings, MT 59108-0110
Phone: (406)245-6627 **Fax:** (406)245-6737
Products: Farm products, including sprayers, hydraulics, bail sheetings, and lathes. **SIC:** 5083 (Farm & Garden Machinery). **Est:** 1951. **Sales:** $3,000,000 (2000). **Emp:** 10. **Officers:** D. Hove, President & Treasurer.

■ **468** ■ **County General**
RR 1, Box 500
Hettinger, ND 58639
Phone: (701)567-2412 **Fax:** (701)567-4265
Products: Farm supplies. **SIC:** 5191 (Farm Supplies). **Sales:** $15,000,000 (2000). **Emp:** 99.

■ **469** ■ **County Line Co-op**
555 Main St.
Rising Sun, OH 43457
Phone: (419)457-5711 **Fax:** (419)457-2000
Products: Farm supplies, including grain, seed, feed, and chemicals. **SICs:** 5153 (Grain & Field Beans); 5072 (Hardware); 5191 (Farm Supplies). **Est:** 1912. **Sales:** $13,000,000 (1999). **Emp:** 7. **Officers:** Donald Kline, President; Chris Chalfin, Treasurer.

■ **470** ■ **Cranston International Inc.**
PO Box 820
Woodland, CA 95776
Phone: (530)662-7373 **Fax:** (530)662-1387
E-mail: wilkintl@cs.com
Products: Tractors. **SIC:** 5083 (Farm & Garden Machinery). **Est:** 1934. **Sales:** $7,000,000 (2000). **Emp:** 21. **Officers:** J.T. Wilkinson, President; Dean Beall, Controller.

■ **471** ■ **Creameries Blending Inc.**
303 6th St. NE
Little Falls, MN 56345
Phone: (612)632-3631
Products: Petroleum; Feed; Fertilizer. **SICs:** 5191 (Farm Supplies); 5172 (Petroleum Products Nec). **Est:** 1965. **Sales:** $8,000,000 (2000). **Emp:** 23. **Officers:** J.E. Salvog, General Mgr.

■ **472** ■ **Crescent Cooperative Association**
PO Box 316
Crescent, OK 73028
Phone: (405)969-3334
Products: Farm supplies, including fertilizer, corn, and grain. **SICs:** 5191 (Farm Supplies); 5153 (Grain & Field Beans). **Est:** 1949. **Sales:** $4,500,000 (2000). **Emp:** 11. **Officers:** Don Hixon, President; John Wornbask, General Mgr.

■ **473** ■ **Crestland Cooperative**
PO Box 329
Creston, IA 50801-0329
Phone: (515)782-6411 **Fax:** (515)782-6869
Products: Grain; Feed; Fertilizer. **SICs:** 5153 (Grain & Field Beans); 5191 (Farm Supplies). **Est:** 1919. **Sales:** $100,000,000 (2000). **Emp:** 160. **Officers:** Larry E. Crosser, CEO; Douglas G. Elliot, CFO; Michael B. DeJong, Data Processing Mgr.; Juleen F. Loomis, Accounting Manager.

■ **474** ■ **Creston Feed and Grain Co.**
PO Box 603
Creston, IA 50801-0603
Phone: (515)782-7202
Products: Feed. **SIC:** 5191 (Farm Supplies). **Est:** 1963. **Sales:** $6,000,000 (2000). **Emp:** 12. **Officers:** Gary Bailey, President; Paul Baker, Secretary; Rex Daub, Sales Mgr.

■ **475** ■ **Crites-Moscow Growers Inc.**
PO Box 8912
Moscow, ID 83843
Phone: (208)882-5519 **Fax:** (208)882-6464
Products: Pea seed. **SIC:** 5191 (Farm Supplies). **Est:** 1933. **Sales:** $6,000,000 (2000). **Officers:**

John Hermann, CEO; David E. Jones, Treasurer; T.J. Druffel, General Mgr.

■ **476** ■ **Crockett Farmers Cooperative Co.**
359 W Main St.
Alamo, TN 38001
Phone: (901)696-5528 **Fax:** (901)696-2969
Products: Farming and agricultural supplies; Tires; Petroleum. **SICs:** 5191 (Farm Supplies); 5014 (Tires & Tubes). **Est:** 1945. **Sales:** $9,000,000 (2000). **Emp:** 28. **Officers:** Terry Sellers, Manager.

■ **477** ■ **Crookston Farmers Cooperative**
PO Box 398
Crookston, MN 56716
Phone: (218)281-2881 **Fax:** (218)281-3022
Products: Grain and feed; Chemicals; Seeds; Fuel; Fertilizer. **SICs:** 5153 (Grain & Field Beans); 5191 (Farm Supplies). **Est:** 1939. **Sales:** $18,000,000 (2000). **Emp:** 11. **Officers:** V Plante, President; Donald R. Staehnke, CFO.

■ **478** ■ **Croushorn Equipment Company Inc.**
PO Box 796
Harlan, KY 40831
Phone: (606)573-2454
Products: Heavy equipment, including tractors, lawnmowers, and plows. **SICs:** 5082 (Construction & Mining Machinery); 5082 (Construction & Mining Machinery). **Est:** 1930. **Sales:** $12,000,000 (2000). **Emp:** 17. **Officers:** James E. Croushorn, President; Earl Croushorn II, Vice President; Harold Sellers, Dir. of Sales.

■ **479** ■ **Crystal Cooperative Inc.**
PO Box 210
Lake Crystal, MN 56055
Phone: (507)726-6455
Products: Gas and propane; Fertilizer and insecticides; Grain; Hardware. **SICs:** 5153 (Grain & Field Beans); 5072 (Hardware); 5191 (Farm Supplies). **Est:** 1927. **Sales:** $22,500,000 (2000). **Emp:** 36. **Officers:** Dean Lee, President; Ron Held, General Mgr.

■ **480** ■ **CT Wholesale**
PO Box 31510
Stockton, CA 95213
Phone: (209)983-8484
Free: (800)221-2884 **Fax:** (209)983-8449
Products: Farm supplies. **SIC:** 5191 (Farm Supplies). **Est:** 1999. **Former Name:** H.C. Shaw Co.

■ **481** ■ **Cullman Seed and Feed Co.**
PO Box 548
Cullman, AL 35056
Phone: (205)734-3892 **Fax:** (205)734-3899
Products: Seed and grain. **SICs:** 5191 (Farm Supplies); 5153 (Grain & Field Beans). **Est:** 1944. **Sales:** $6,500,000 (2000). **Emp:** 17. **Officers:** Tim W. Chambers, President.

■ **482** ■ **Cumberland Farmers Union Cooperative**
PO Box 118
Almena, WI 54805-0118
Products: Farming supplies. **SIC:** 5191 (Farm Supplies). **Est:** 1920. **Sales:** $4,500,000 (2000). **Emp:** 20. **Officers:** Mike Thompson, President; Earl McClelland, General Mgr.

■ **483** ■ **Cumberland Valley Cooperative Association**
PO Box 350
Shippensburg, PA 17257
Phone: (717)532-2191
Products: Seed and fertilizer. **SIC:** 5191 (Farm Supplies). **Est:** 1929. **Sales:** $5,000,000 (2000). **Emp:** 30. **Officers:** Rene Lavoie, General Mgr.; Merle Harnish, Treasurer; Eddie A. Parsons, Dir. of Marketing.

■ **484** ■ **Curtis & Curtis, Inc.**
Star Rte., Box 8-A
Clovis, NM 88101
Phone: (505)762-4759
Free: (800)753-4649 **Fax:** (505)763-4213
E-mail: cci@3lefties.com
Products: Grass seed. **SIC:** 5191 (Farm Supplies).

Est: 1956. **Emp:** 15. **Officers:** Tye Curtis, Sales/Marketing Contact.

■ **485** ■ **Custer Grain Co.**
2006 Tony Country Rd.
Garrett, IN 46738
Phone: (219)357-5432
Products: Grain, feed, seed, fertilizer. **SICs:** 5153 (Grain & Field Beans); 5191 (Farm Supplies). **Est:** 1967. **Sales:** $10,000,000 (2000). **Emp:** 10. **Officers:** W.H. Custer, President.

■ **486** ■ **Dairyland Seed Company Inc.**
PO Box 958
West Bend, WI 53095
Phone: (414)338-0163
Free: (800)236-0163 **Fax:** (414)626-2281
Products: Corn, alfalfa and soybean seeds. **SIC:** 5191 (Farm Supplies). **Sales:** $82,000,000 (2000). **Emp:** 130. **Officers:** Steven Strachota, President.

■ **487** ■ **Dakota Pride Coop**
648 W 2nd St.
Winner, SD 57580
Phone: (605)842-2711
Free: (888)325-7743 **Fax:** (605)842-2715
E-mail: dakotapride@gwtc.net
URL: http://www.dakotapride.com
Products: Grain; Feed; Propane fuel; Batteries. **SICs:** 5191 (Farm Supplies); 5153 (Grain & Field Beans); 5172 (Petroleum Products Nec). **Est:** 1940. **Sales:** $36,000,000 (2000). **Emp:** 90. **Officers:** George Olson, Chairman of the Board; Mike Barfuss, Treasurer.

■ **488** ■ **Dallas County Farmers Exchange**
PO Box 1024
Buffalo, MO 65622
Phone: (417)345-2121
Products: Hardware; Feed for farms. **SICs:** 5191 (Farm Supplies); 5072 (Hardware). **Est:** 1950. **Sales:** $4,500,000 (2000). **Emp:** 30. **Officers:** Bob Howerton, President; Phil Perkins, General Mgr.

■ **489** ■ **Dallas Ford New Holland Inc.**
1351 S Loop 12
Irving, TX 75060
Phone: (972)579-9999 **Fax:** (972)579-7871
Products: Construction and farm equipment, including tractors, plows, and forklifts. **SICs:** 5083 (Farm & Garden Machinery); 5082 (Construction & Mining Machinery). **Est:** 1941. **Sales:** $9,500,000 (2000). **Emp:** 20. **Officers:** Mike Lyle, President.

■ **490** ■ **Dalton, Cooper Gates Corp.**
68 Forest Ave.
Locust Valley, NY 11560
Phone: (516)759-2011 **Fax:** (516)759-2055
Products: Agricultural and golf course equipment. **SIC:** 5083 (Farm & Garden Machinery). **Est:** 1953. **Emp:** 10. **Officers:** Pierre Gonthier, Dir. of Marketing.

■ **491** ■ **Dalton Cooperative Creamery Association**
PO Box 248
Dalton, MN 56324
Phone: (218)589-8806
Products: Feed. **SIC:** 5191 (Farm Supplies). **Est:** 1920. **Sales:** $2,600,000 (2000). **Emp:** 2. **Officers:** John Lindquist, President; Kristine Peterson, Controller.

■ **492** ■ **Danco Prairie FS Cooperative**
5371 Farmco Dr.
Madison, WI 53718-1425
Phone: (608)241-4181
Products: Farm supplies; Petroleum products. **SICs:** 5191 (Farm Supplies); 5172 (Petroleum Products Nec). **Est:** 1929. **Sales:** $14,000,000 (2000). **Emp:** 69. **Officers:** John Cullen, General Mgr.; Ernie Kitchen, Controller.

■ **493** ■ **Danvers Farmers Elevator Co.**
PO Box 160
Danvers, IL 61732
Phone: (309)963-4305
Products: Grain and fertilizer; Farm chemicals. **SICs:** 5191 (Farm Supplies); 5153 (Grain & Field Beans). **Est:** 1904. **Sales:** $11,000,000 (2000). **Emp:** 10.

Officers: Jim Vierling, CEO; Art Nafziger, Treasurer & Secty.

■ 494 ■ **Danville Cooperative Association**
PO Box 67
Danville, KS 67036
Phone: (316)962-5238
Products: Farm supplies, including chemicals, bearings, fertilizers, insecticides, and pesticides. SIC: 5191 (Farm Supplies). Est: 1952. Sales: $8,000,000 (2000). Emp: 10. Officers: Milford Coady, President; David Andra, General Mgr.

■ 495 ■ **Dassel Cooperative Dairy Association**
PO Box E
Dassel, MN 55325
Phone: (320)275-2257
Products: Feed; Diesel fuel; Dairy products; Seed; Gasoline. SICs: 5191 (Farm Supplies); 5172 (Petroleum Products Nec); 5143 (Dairy Products Except Dried or Canned). Est: 1894. Sales: $3,000,000 (2000). Emp: 6. Officers: Dennis Danielson, Manager.

■ 496 ■ **Datron Corp.**
5001 W 80th St.
Minneapolis, MN 55437
Phone: (612)831-1626
Products: Veterinary hospital supplies. SIC: 5199 (Nondurable Goods Nec). Sales: $4,000,000 (2000). Emp: 44. Officers: Michael Flom, President.

■ 497 ■ **Davidson Farmers Cooperative**
3511 Dickerson Rd.
Nashville, TN 37207-1705
Phone: (615)255-5797 Fax: (615)254-9092
Products: Complete livestock feeds; Field, garden, and flower seeds; Fertilizer and fertilizer materials; Insecticides; Pesticides. SIC: 5191 (Farm Supplies). Sales: $1,600,000 (2000). Emp: 9. Officers: Phillip Paul, President; Shelton Wasilewsky, Manager.

■ 498 ■ **Jo Davies Service Co.**
313 W Sycamore St.
Elizabeth, IL 61028
Phone: (815)858-2238
Products: Fertilizer. SICs: 5171 (Petroleum Bulk Stations & Terminals); 5191 (Farm Supplies). Est: 1931. Sales: $5,000,000 (2000). Emp: 13. Officers: Don Lawfer, President; Arlyn Henmen, Controller; Douglas Long, Manager.

■ 499 ■ **John Day Co.**
PO Box 3541
Omaha, NE 68103
Phone: (402)455-8000 Fax: (402)457-3812
Products: Farm equipment and industrial supplies. SICs: 5083 (Farm & Garden Machinery); 5085 (Industrial Supplies). Sales: $25,000,000 (2000). Emp: 120. Officers: John D. Fonda, CEO, President & Treasurer; Nancy Kurtenbach, Sr. VP & CFO.

■ 500 ■ **De Mott Tractor Company Inc.**
2235 E 25th St., Ste. 230
Idaho Falls, ID 83404-7538
Phone: (208)522-6372
Products: Tractor equipment. SIC: 5083 (Farm & Garden Machinery). Est: 1963. Sales: $4,000,000 (2000). Emp: 20. Officers: William J. De Mott, President.

■ 501 ■ **Dean-Henderson Equipment Co. Inc.**
Hwy. 165 S
England, AR 72046
Phone: (501)842-2521
Products: Farm equipment, including tractors and combines. SIC: 5083 (Farm & Garden Machinery). Est: 1968. Sales: $6,000,000 (2000). Emp: 18. Officers: Jimmy Dean, President.

■ 502 ■ **Dean Machinery Co.**
1201 W 31st St.
Kansas City, MO 64108
Phone: (816)753-5300 Fax: (816)753-6005
URL: http://www.deanmch.com
Products: Heavy equipment. SIC: 5083 (Farm & Garden Machinery). Est: 1958. Sales: $100,000,000 (1999). Emp: 280. Officers: Curt Stokes, President;

Jim Denny, CFO; Tim Lewis, VP of Sales, e-mail: tlewis@deanmch.com.

■ 503 ■ **Decker and Company Inc.**
16438 Felton Rd.
Lansing, MI 48906
Phone: (517)321-7231 Fax: (517)321-7424
Products: Lawn, garden, and farm equipment, including mowers and loaders. SIC: 5083 (Farm & Garden Machinery). Est: 1947. Sales: $3,500,000 (2000). Emp: 9. Officers: M. Decker, President; D. Upton, CFO.

■ 504 ■ **Decorative Plant Service Inc.**
1150 Phelps St.
San Francisco, CA 94124
Phone: (415)826-8181
Products: Landscaping equipment and supplies. SIC: 5193 (Flowers & Florists' Supplies). Est: 1948. Sales: $5,500,000 (2000). Emp: 95. Officers: Ed Rathbun, President; Harold Callahan, Controller.

■ 505 ■ **Dell Rapids Co-op Grain**
PO Box 70
Dell Rapids, SD 57022
Phone: (605)428-5494
Free: (800)589-1030 Fax: (605)428-5704
Products: Grain; Fertilizers; Gloves and overshoes. SICs: 5153 (Grain & Field Beans); 5191 (Farm Supplies); 5139 (Footwear); 5136 (Men's/Boys' Clothing). Sales: $6,900,000 (2000). Emp: 7. Officers: Greg Hauglid, President; Mark Lee, General Mgr.

■ 506 ■ **DeLong Company Inc.**
PO Box 552
Clinton, WI 53525
Phone: (608)676-2255
Products: Feed and farm equipment. SICs: 5191 (Farm Supplies); 5083 (Farm & Garden Machinery); 5153 (Grain & Field Beans). Est: 1956. Sales: $40,000,000 (1999). Emp: 65. Officers: David DeLong, President.

■ 507 ■ **Delphi Products Co.**
PO Box 149
Delphi, IN 46923
Phone: (765)564-3752
Free: (800)382-7903 Fax: (765)564-4970
Products: Hog equipment. SIC: 5083 (Farm & Garden Machinery). Est: 1963. Sales: $3,000,000 (2000). Emp: 25. Officers: Blair Underhill, President; Alan Girton, Vice President. Former Name: DPC Inc.

■ 508 ■ **Del's Farm Supply**
1856 Haleukana St.
Lihue, HI 96766-1459
Phone: (808)245-9200 Fax: (808)245-3781
Products: Field, garden, and flower seeds; Grain; Fencing and fence gates. SICs: 5191 (Farm Supplies); 5153 (Grain & Field Beans). Emp: 6.

■ 509 ■ **Delta Cotton Cooperative Inc.**
Hwy. 34 E
Marmaduke, AR 72443
Phone: (501)597-2741
Products: Agricultural equipment and supplies. SIC: 5083 (Farm & Garden Machinery). Est: 1965. Sales: $4,000,000 (2000). Emp: 15.

■ 510 ■ **Delta Implement Co.**
PO Box 460
Rolling Fork, MS 39159
Phone: (662)873-2661 Fax: (662)827-5944
Products: Tractors. SIC: 5083 (Farm & Garden Machinery). Est: 1924. Sales: $5,000,000 (2000). Emp: 17. Officers: J.B. Nash Jr., President.

■ 511 ■ **Delta Purchasing Federation**
PO Box 8177
Greenwood, MS 38930
Phone: (601)453-7374 Fax: (601)455-5831
Products: Chemicals; Tires; Fuels; Farm supplies. SICs: 5191 (Farm Supplies); 5172 (Petroleum Products Nec). Est: 1946. Sales: $51,000,000 (2000). Emp: 44. Officers: Ralph T. Hand Jr., President; Gerald Carpenter, VP & Comptroller.

■ 512 ■ **Delta Ridge Implement**
PO Box 240
Rayville, LA 71269
Phone: (318)728-6423
Products: Farm equipment. SIC: 5083 (Farm & Garden Machinery). Est: 1975. Sales: $10,000,000 (2000). Emp: 40. Officers: C.E. Prisock, President; Melvin N. Vidrine, Jr., Manager.

■ 513 ■ **Dent and Co.**
5800 E Mabry Dr.
Clovis, NM 88101
Phone: (505)763-5517
Products: Tractors; Lawn mowers. SIC: 5083 (Farm & Garden Machinery). Est: 1970. Sales: $8,000,000 (2000). Emp: 20. Officers: Ronnie Dent, CEO.

■ 514 ■ **Des Arc Implement Co.**
PO Box 250
Des Arc, AR 72040
Phone: (870)256-4121 Fax: (870)256-4256
Products: Farm tractors. SIC: 5083 (Farm & Garden Machinery). Est: 1950. Sales: $4,000,000 (2000). Emp: 15. Officers: James D. Norman, President; Robert E. Norman, VP of Finance.

■ 515 ■ **Desert Design Inc.**
7460 Ranch Destino
Las Vegas, NV 89123
Phone: (702)361-4677
Products: Landscaping machinery. SIC: 5083 (Farm & Garden Machinery). Officers: James Doyle, President.

■ 516 ■ **Desoto County Cooperative**
2425 Mount Pleasant Rd.
Hernando, MS 38632
Phone: (601)429-4407
Products: Fertilizer; Seed. SICs: 5191 (Farm Supplies); 5072 (Hardware). Est: 1927. Sales: $6,000,000 (2000). Emp: 16. Officers: David Bridgforth, President; Larry Darnell, Manager.

■ 517 ■ **Dewar Elevator Co.**
Box 80
Dewar, IA 50623
Phone: (319)234-1392 Fax: (319)233-1030
Products: Corn; Dry beans; Feed; Agricultural chemicals. SICs: 5153 (Grain & Field Beans); 5191 (Farm Supplies); 5169 (Chemicals & Allied Products Nec). Est: 1951. Sales: $3,000,000 (2000). Emp: 3. Officers: Bryan Shimp, Owner.

■ 518 ■ **Dexter Implement Co.**
PO Box 217
Dexter, MO 63841
Phone: (573)624-7467
Products: Outdoor equipment. SIC: 5083 (Farm & Garden Machinery). Est: 1987. Sales: $4,000,000 (2000). Emp: 14. Officers: Charles Chilcutt, CEO.

■ 519 ■ **Dickson Farmers Cooperative**
705 Henslee Dr.
Dickson, TN 37055
Phone: (615)446-2343
Free: (800)875-2342 Fax: (615)446-3600
E-mail: dfarmcoop@aol.com
Products: Farm supplies, including seed and fertilizer. SIC: 5191 (Farm Supplies). Est: 1946. Sales: $8,500,000 (2000). Emp: 43. Officers: Philip Buckner, General Mgr.; Paul Sullivan.

■ 520 ■ **Dodge City Implement Inc.**
PO Box 139
Dodge City, KS 67801
Phone: (316)227-2165
Products: Farming equipment. SIC: 5083 (Farm & Garden Machinery). Sales: $13,000,000 (1994). Emp: 30. Officers: Dan Hubbell, Controller.

■ 521 ■ **Dokken Implement Co. Inc.**
612 4th St. & Pine St.
Nezperce, ID 83543
Phone: (208)937-2422 Fax: (208)937-2324
Products: Farm equipment. SIC: 5083 (Farm & Garden Machinery). Est: 1931. Sales: $3,800,000 (2000). Emp: 22. Officers: David W. Branson, President; George Branson, Treasurer & Secty.

■ 522 ■ Dollar Farm Products Co.
1001 Dothan Hwy.
Bainbridge, GA 31717
Phone: (912)248-2750
Products: Chemicals; Seed. **SIC:** 5191 (Farm Supplies). **Sales:** $7,000,000 (2000). **Emp:** 25. **Officers:** Hubert Dollar, President.

■ 523 ■ Donley Seed Co.
2121 Cottage St.
Ashland, OH 44805
Phone: (419)289-7459 **Fax:** (419)281-7056
Products: Lawn seed. **SIC:** 5191 (Farm Supplies).

■ 524 ■ Donnellson Implement Inc.
PO Box 246
Donnellson, IA 52625
Phone: (319)835-5511
Products: Heavy equipment, including tractors and movers. **SIC:** 5083 (Farm & Garden Machinery). **Est:** 1941. **Sales:** $2,000,000 (2000). **Emp:** 15. **Officers:** David G. Reu, President; Angie Reu, Bookkeeper.

■ 525 ■ Door County Cooperative Inc.
92 E Maple St.
Sturgeon Bay, WI 54235
Phone: (920)743-6555 **Fax:** (920)743-6743
Products: Feed and fertilizer. **SIC:** 5191 (Farm Supplies). **Sales:** $12,000,000 (1994). **Emp:** 45. **Officers:** Charles Jarman, President; D. John Butterbrodt, CFO.

■ 526 ■ Drummond Cooperative Elevator Inc.
PO Box 56
Drummond, OK 73735
Phone: (580)493-2212
Products: Grains; Feed; Seed; Fertilizer; Chemicals; Petroleum. **SICs:** 5153 (Grain & Field Beans); 5191 (Farm Supplies); 5172 (Petroleum Products Nec). **Est:** 1932. **Sales:** $3,000,000 (2000). **Emp:** 5. **Officers:** Charles Buckminster, President.

■ 527 ■ Dubois County Farm Bureau Cooperative
901 Main St.
Huntingburg, IN 47542
Phone: (812)683-2809
Products: Feed, grain, seed, and fertilizer; Farm equipment. **SICs:** 5153 (Grain & Field Beans); 5191 (Farm Supplies); 5083 (Farm & Garden Machinery). **Est:** 1928. **Sales:** $10,000,000 (2000). **Emp:** 40. **Officers:** Dennis Ackerman, President.

■ 528 ■ DuBois Elevator Co.
4886 E 450 N
Dubois, IN 47527
Phone: (812)678-2891 **Fax:** (812)678-5931
Products: Poultry feed. **SIC:** 5191 (Farm Supplies). **Sales:** $21,000,000 (2000). **Emp:** 100. **Officers:** J.F Seger, President; Bradley Seger, Vice President.

■ 529 ■ W.A. DuBose and Son Co.
207 N John Redditt Dr.
Lufkin, TX 75904-2635
Phone: (409)632-3363
Products: Tractors; Mowers; Riders. **SIC:** 5083 (Farm & Garden Machinery). **Est:** 1953. **Sales:** $5,000,000 (2000). **Emp:** 23. **Officers:** W.A. DuBose, President.

■ 530 ■ H.B. Duvall Inc.
PO Box 70
Frederick, MD 21705-0070
Phone: (301)662-1125 **Fax:** (301)695-0265
Products: Farm equipment, including tractors; Lawn and garden equipment, including lawnmowers. **SIC:** 5083 (Farm & Garden Machinery). **Est:** 1944. **Sales:** $5,000,000 (2000). **Emp:** 30. **Officers:** John Bare, Owner.

■ 531 ■ Dye Seed Ranch
Rte. 1, Box 99
Pomeroy, WA 99347
Phone: (509)843-3591 **Fax:** (509)843-3594
Products: Grass seeds. **SIC:** 5191 (Farm Supplies).

■ 532 ■ Dyer Lauderdale Co-op
PO Box 550
Dyersburg, TN 38025
Phone: (901)285-7161 **Fax:** (901)285-7164
Products: Farm supplies and grain cooperative. **SICs:** 5191 (Farm Supplies); 5153 (Grain & Field Beans). **Est:** 1985. **Sales:** $25,000,000 (2000). **Emp:** 40. **Officers:** Tommy Dunlap, President; Stan Anderson, General Manager, Finance.

■ 533 ■ Early Tractor Co. Inc.
PO Box 588
Blakely, GA 31723
Phone: (912)723-3595 **Fax:** (912)723-3530
E-mail: earlytra@sowega.net
URL: http://www.sbshow.com/ga/early/earlytractor
Products: Tractors; Plows; Irrigation systems. **SIC:** 5083 (Farm & Garden Machinery). **Est:** 1965. **Sales:** $12,000,000 (2000). **Emp:** 25. **Officers:** Marty Howard, CEO; Pat Gentry, Treasurer & Secty.

■ 534 ■ East Central Cooperative Inc.
PO Box 128
Cleveland, WI 53015
Phone: (920)693-8220
Products: Feed machinery and fertilizer. **SICs:** 5191 (Farm Supplies); 5083 (Farm & Garden Machinery). **Est:** 1919. **Sales:** $10,000,000 (2000). **Emp:** 45. **Officers:** Bruce Trewin, President & Treasurer.

■ 535 ■ East West Connect Inc.
1862 Independence Sq.
Atlanta, GA 30338-5150
Phone: (404)396-3145 **Fax:** (404)396-2235
Products: Fertilizer and fertilizer materials. **SIC:** 5191 (Farm Supplies). **Officers:** Ava Lee, President.

■ 536 ■ Eastern Europe, Inc.
460 W 34th St., 12th Fl.
New York, NY 10001
Phone: (212)947-8585 **Fax:** (212)629-3147
E-mail: info@easteurinc.com
Products: Fertilizers; Wheat and corn; Chemicals; Coal; Steel and aluminum. **SICs:** 5191 (Farm Supplies); 5153 (Grain & Field Beans); 5051 (Metals Service Centers & Offices); 5052 (Coal, Other Minerals & Ores). **Officers:** Robert Ross, President. **Former Name:** International Farmers Grain.

■ 537 ■ Eastern Farmers Coop
PO Box 266
Jasper, MN 56144
Phone: (507)348-3911
Products: Corn; Oats; Feed; Fertilizer; Chemicals; Petroleum. **SICs:** 5153 (Grain & Field Beans); 5153 (Grain & Field Beans); 5191 (Farm Supplies). **Est:** 1907. **Sales:** $25,000,000 (1999). **Emp:** 11. **Officers:** Jim Morken, General Mgr. **Former Name:** Jasper Farmers Elevator.

■ 538 ■ Easy Gardener Inc.
PO Box 21025
Waco, TX 76702-1025
Phone: (254)753-5353
Free: (800)327-9462 **Fax:** (254)753-5372
Products: Nonwoven landscape fabrics, including shade cloth and landscape edging. **SIC:** 5072 (Hardware). **Sales:** $25,000,000 (2000). **Emp:** 65. **Officers:** Richard M. Grandy, President; Lynda Gustafson, CFO.

■ 539 ■ Eaton Equipment Corp.
PO Box 250
Blasdell, NY 14219
Phone: (716)822-2020 **Fax:** (716)822-8836
Products: Lawn and garden equipment. **SICs:** 5083 (Farm & Garden Machinery); 5084 (Industrial Machinery & Equipment). **Sales:** $14,000,000 (2000). **Emp:** 50. **Officers:** Wyndham Eaton, President.

■ 540 ■ Ebbert's Field Seed Inc.
6840 N State 48
Covington, OH 45318
Phones: (937)473-2521 (937)473-3710
Free: (888)802-5715
Products: Agricultural seeds. **SIC:** 5191 (Farm Supplies). **Sales:** $2,000,000 (2000). **Emp:** 9. **Officers:** M. Kenworthy, President.

■ 541 ■ Eckroat Seed Co.
PO Box 17610
Oklahoma City, OK 73136
Phone: (405)427-2484 **Fax:** (405)427-7174
Products: Seed; Fertilizer; Pesticide. **SIC:** 5191 (Farm Supplies). **Est:** 1927. **Sales:** $8,000,000 (2000). **Emp:** 15. **Officers:** Arthur V. Eckroat, President; Robert A. Eckroat, CFO; Donald E. Eckroat, Dir. of Marketing.

■ 542 ■ Edison Non-Stock Cooperative
PO Box 68
Edison, NE 68936
Phone: (308)927-3681 **Fax:** (308)927-2455
Products: Feed; Grain; Fertilizer; Fuel; Farming supplies. **SICs:** 5153 (Grain & Field Beans); 5191 (Farm Supplies); 5172 (Petroleum Products Nec). **Est:** 1953. **Sales:** $33,000,000 (2000). **Emp:** 55. **Officers:** Kenneth Shoen, President; Randy Gardner, Treasurer & Secty.; Bill Fitzke, General Mgr.

■ 543 ■ Edon Farmers Cooperative Association Inc.
PO Box 308
Edon, OH 43518
Phone: (419)272-2121 **Fax:** (419)272-2304
E-mail: edoncoop@bright.net
Products: Farm supplies. **SICs:** 5153 (Grain & Field Beans); 5191 (Farm Supplies). **Est:** 1919. **Sales:** $26,000,000 (2000). **Emp:** 42. **Officers:** Terry Hake, President; Randall K. Broady, General Manager and Treasurer.

■ 544 ■ Elberta Farmers Cooperative
Drawer B
Elberta, AL 36530
Phone: (205)986-8103
Products: Farm supplies, including fertilizer and feed. **SICs:** 5191 (Farm Supplies); 5072 (Hardware). **Est:** 1946. **Sales:** $3,100,000 (2000). **Emp:** 14. **Officers:** Curtis Cassebaum, President; Thomas Harrell, General Mgr.

■ 545 ■ Elbow Lake Cooperative Grain
PO Box 68
Elbow Lake, MN 56531
Phone: (218)685-5331
Products: Grain; Chemicals. **SICs:** 5153 (Grain & Field Beans); 5191 (Farm Supplies). **Est:** 1936. **Sales:** $17,000,000 (2000). **Emp:** 10. **Officers:** Dean Kjefbo, President.

■ 546 ■ Elkhart Farmers Cooperative Association Inc.
PO Box 903
Elkhart, TX 75839
Phone: (903)764-2298 **Fax:** (903)764-2247
Products: Chemicals; Fertilizers; Feed; Grains; Farm supplies. **SICs:** 5159 (Farm-Product Raw Materials Nec); 5191 (Farm Supplies). **Est:** 1946. **Sales:** $7,000,000 (2000). **Emp:** 19. **Officers:** George Beeler, President; Frank Wilson, General Mgr.

■ 547 ■ Ellis and Capp Equipment Co.
301 E 8th St.
Greeley, CO 80631
Phone: (970)352-9141 **Fax:** (970)352-9179
E-mail: elliscapp@aol.com
Products: Farm equipment. **SIC:** 5083 (Farm & Garden Machinery). **Est:** 1947. **Sales:** $8,000,000 (2000). **Emp:** 45. **Officers:** Pat Barnett, President.

■ 548 ■ Ellis Equipment Co. Inc.
701 S Main St.
Logan, UT 84321-5402
Phone: (435)752-4311 **Fax:** (435)752-4384
Products: Agricultural equipment. **SIC:** 5083 (Farm & Garden Machinery). **Est:** 1938. **Sales:** $7,000,000 (2000). **Emp:** 20. **Officers:** R.D. Ellis, President; J.C. Ellis, Treasurer & Secty.

■ 549 ■ Ellsworth Farmers Union Cooperative Oil Co.
610 E Main St.
Ellsworth, WI 54011
Phone: (715)273-4363
Products: Farm supplies; Hardware; Fuel. **SICs:** 5171 (Petroleum Bulk Stations & Terminals); 5191 (Farm Supplies); 5072 (Hardware). **Est:** 1931. **Sales:**

$3,000,000 (2000). **Emp:** 15. **Officers:** Mike Green, President; Larry Dokkestul, General Mgr.

■ 550 ■ **Elmco Distributors Inc.**
30 Estling Lake Rd.
Denville, NJ 07834-1907
Phone: (201)887-6600 **Fax:** (201)887-1354
Products: Lawn mowers. **SIC:** 5083 (Farm & Garden Machinery). **Est:** 1947. **Sales:** $15,000,000 (2000). **Emp:** 10. **Officers:** Hartley D. Bingham Jr., CEO & President; Chris Russell, Controller.

■ 551 ■ **Emma Cooperative Elevator Co.**
125 Lexington Ave.
Sweet Springs, MO 65351
Phone: (660)335-6355 **Fax:** (660)335-4279
Products: Poultry, hog and dairy feeds. **SICs:** 5083 (Farm & Garden Machinery); 5191 (Farm Supplies). **Sales:** $12,000,000 (2000). **Emp:** 14. **Officers:** Rick Alexander, President.

■ 552 ■ **Empire N.A. Inc.**
18284 N 1100th Ave.
Cambridge, IL 61238-9364
Phone: (309)944-5321
Products: Farm equipment and supplies. **SICs:** 5083 (Farm & Garden Machinery); 5191 (Farm Supplies). **Sales:** $13,000,000 (1994). **Emp:** 60. **Officers:** Robert Bottens, President; Marian Fairbanks, Controller.

■ 553 ■ **Equity Cooperative of Amery Inc.**
319 S Keller Ave.
Amery, WI 54001
Phone: (715)268-8177 **Fax:** (715)268-8200
E-mail: EqtiCoop@spacestar.net
Products: Farm supplies. **SIC:** 5191 (Farm Supplies). **Est:** 1920. **Sales:** $11,000,000 (2000). **Emp:** 55. **Officers:** Martin Binfet, President; Larry Wojchik, General Mgr.

■ 554 ■ **Equity Supply Co.**
PO Box 579
Kalispell, MT 59901
Phone: (406)755-7400
Products: Agricultural supplies, including tools, fertilizers, seeds, feed, and grain. **SICs:** 5153 (Grain & Field Beans); 5191 (Farm Supplies); 5143 (Dairy Products Except Dried or Canned). **Est:** 1917. **Sales:** $11,000,000 (2000). **Emp:** 65. **Officers:** Nathan Byrd, CEO.

■ 555 ■ **Erie Crawford Cooperative**
PO Box 312
Union City, PA 16438
Phone: (814)438-3881
Products: Feed, seeds, and fertilizer. **SIC:** 5191 (Farm Supplies). **Est:** 1941. **Sales:** $4,000,000 (2000). **Emp:** 20. **Officers:** George Peters, President.

■ 556 ■ **Evergreen Mills Inc.**
PO Box 548
Ada, OK 74820
Phone: (580)332-6611
Products: Animal and poultry feeds, including feed for horses, cattle, cats, dogs, and rabbits. **SIC:** 5191 (Farm Supplies). **Est:** 1902. **Sales:** $12,000,000 (2000). **Emp:** 75. **Officers:** Bob Waller, President; Lee Murphy, VP of Marketing.

■ 557 ■ **Ezell-Key Grain Company Inc.**
PO Box 1062
Snyder, TX 79550
Phone: (915)573-9373 **Fax:** (915)573-9374
Products: Feed. **SIC:** 5191 (Farm Supplies). **Est:** 1955. **Sales:** $6,000,000 (2000). **Emp:** 32. **Officers:** Bob Potter, General Mgr.; Kent Mills, Dir. of Marketing.

■ 558 ■ **FABCO Equipment Inc.**
11200 W Silver Spring Rd.
Milwaukee, WI 53225
Phone: (414)461-9100
Products: Tractors. **SIC:** 5082 (Construction & Mining Machinery). **Est:** 1982. **Sales:** $210,000,000 (2000). **Emp:** 300. **Officers:** Joseph Fabick, President; J. Gibbons, VP of Finance; David J. Barlin, Dir. of Marketing & Sales.

■ 559 ■ **Robert A. Fabel Inc.**
92283 Highway 70
Vinton, CA 96135
Phone: (530)993-4647
Free: (800)232-8607 **Fax:** (530)993-4627
E-mail: rfabel@psln.com
URL: http://www.psln.com/rfabel/
Products: Lawnmowers and tractors. **SIC:** 5083 (Farm & Garden Machinery). **Est:** 1954. **Sales:** $1,000,000 (2000). **Emp:** 5. **Officers:** R.A. Fabel, President; W. Hughes, CFO.

■ 560 ■ **Fairdale Farmers Cooperative Elevator Co.**
PO Box 102
Fairdale, ND 58229
Phone: (701)966-2515 **Fax:** (701)966-2203
Products: Grain; Fertilizer; Feed; Chemicals. **SICs:** 5153 (Grain & Field Beans); 5191 (Farm Supplies). **Est:** 1918. **Sales:** $6,500,000 (1999). **Emp:** 5. **Officers:** Marvin Moen, President.

■ 561 ■ **Farm Equipment Company of Asheville Inc.**
PO Box 2745
Asheville, NC 28802
Phone: (704)253-8483
Products: Tractors; Implements. **SICs:** 5084 (Industrial Machinery & Equipment); 5083 (Farm & Garden Machinery). **Est:** 1944. **Sales:** $1,600,000 (2000). **Emp:** 30. **Officers:** Paul B. Roberson, President.

■ 562 ■ **Farm Implement and Supply Company Inc.**
520 W Mill
Plainville, KS 67663
Phone: (785)434-4824
Free: (888)589-6930 **Fax:** (785)434-7390
Products: Farm equipment; Outdoor machinery. **SIC:** 5083 (Farm & Garden Machinery). **Est:** 1945. **Sales:** $6,000,000 (2000). **Emp:** 12. **Officers:** Ronald Gilliland, President.

■ 563 ■ **Farm-Oyl Company Inc.**
2333 Hampden Ave.
St. Paul, MN 55114
Phone: (612)646-7571
Products: Farming supplies; Fuel. **SICs:** 5172 (Petroleum Products Nec); 5083 (Farm & Garden Machinery). **Est:** 1929. **Sales:** $10,000,000 (2000). **Emp:** 30. **Officers:** Robert E. Larson, President; Robert Anderson, Controller; Richard Hill, VP of Marketing.

■ 564 ■ **Farm Service Company Inc.**
1020 S 8th St.
Council Bluffs, IA 51501
Phone: (712)323-7167
Products: Grains; Fertilizers; Chemicals; Seeds; Feeds. **SICs:** 5153 (Grain & Field Beans); 5191 (Farm Supplies). **Est:** 1931. **Sales:** $30,000,000 (2000). **Emp:** 60. **Officers:** Jerome Heuertz, General Mgr.; Terry Bahl, Dir. of Marketing.

■ 565 ■ **Farm Service Cooperative Inc.**
2308 Pine St.
Harlan, IA 51537
Phone: (712)755-3185 **Fax:** (712)755-2726
Products: Grain; Fertilizer; Seed; Feed. **SICs:** 5191 (Farm Supplies); 5172 (Petroleum Products Nec); 5153 (Grain & Field Beans). **Est:** 1931. **Sales:** $65,000,000 (2000). **Emp:** 110. **Officers:** Keith Heim, President.

■ 566 ■ **Farm Service Inc.**
PO Drawer M
Hoxie, AR 72433
Phone: (870)886-7779
Products: Garden supplies; Feed for livestock. **SIC:** 5191 (Farm Supplies). **Est:** 1965. **Sales:** $20,000,000 (2000). **Emp:** 100. **Officers:** L. Singleton, General Mgr.

■ 567 ■ **Farm Services Inc.**
PO Box 360
Vinton, IA 52349
Phone: (319)472-2394
Products: Fertilizer and fertilizer materials. **SIC:** 5191 (Farm Supplies). **Sales:** $15,000,000 (2000). **Emp:** 50.

Officers: John Swift, General Mgr.; Don Boddicker, Controller.

■ 568 ■ **Farmers Coop Association of Jackson, Sherburn, Spring Lake & Trimont**
PO Box 228
Jackson, MN 56143
Phone: (507)847-4160 **Fax:** (507)639-2051
Products: Grains; Seed. **SICs:** 5153 (Grain & Field Beans); 5191 (Farm Supplies). **Est:** 1905. **Sales:** $63,000,000 (2000). **Emp:** 35. **Officers:** Dennis Hunwardsen, General Mgr.

■ 569 ■ **Farmers Cooperative**
PO Box 47
Dayton, IA 50530
Phone: (515)547-2813 **Free:** (800)642-6815
Products: Grain, fertilizer, and animal health care products. **SICs:** 5153 (Grain & Field Beans); 5191 (Farm Supplies). **Est:** 1905. **Sales:** $85,000,000 (2000). **Emp:** 100. **Officers:** Roger Coppen, General Mgr.

■ 570 ■ **Farmers Cooperative**
201 S 10th St.
Ft. Smith, AR 72901
Phone: (501)783-8959
Products: Seed; Garden tools. **SICs:** 5191 (Farm Supplies); 5072 (Hardware). **Est:** 1944. **Sales:** $28,000,000 (2000). **Emp:** 70. **Officers:** Gene Bruick, CEO.

■ 571 ■ **Farmers Cooperative Association**
PO Box 3001
Gillette, WY 82717
Phone: (307)682-4468 **Fax:** (307)682-4846
Products: Garden equipment. **SIC:** 5153 (Grain & Field Beans). **Est:** 1927. **Sales:** $18,000,000 (2000). **Emp:** 80. **Officers:** Jerry Thorstad, General Mgr.; Terri Curtis, Controller.

■ 572 ■ **Farmers Cooperative Association**
PO Box 249
Vici, OK 73859
Phone: (580)995-4202
Products: Grains, including wheat, corn, and milo; Chemicals and fertilizer; Feed for cats, dogs, hogs, and cattle; Oil, gasoline, and diesel fuel. **SICs:** 5153 (Grain & Field Beans); 5172 (Petroleum Products Nec); 5191 (Farm Supplies). **Est:** 1920. **Sales:** $4,000,000 (2000). **Emp:** 14. **Officers:** Keven Day, General Mgr.

■ 573 ■ **Farmers Cooperative Association**
PO Box 2108
Broken Arrow, OK 74013
Phone: (918)251-5379 **Fax:** (918)251-2773
Products: Grains, including wheat and corn; Chemicals and fertilizer; Cattle and hog feed. **SICs:** 5191 (Farm Supplies); 5153 (Grain & Field Beans). **Est:** 1943. **Sales:** $4,500,000 (2000). **Emp:** 16. **Officers:** Paul Hayes, President; Celesta Mathias, Office Mgr.; Rolland McDaris, General Mgr.

■ 574 ■ **Farmers Cooperative Association**
PO Box 1015
Port Gibson, MS 39150
Phone: (601)437-4281
Products: Feed, seed, and fertilizer. **SIC:** 5191 (Farm Supplies). **Est:** 1950. **Sales:** $5,000,000 (2000). **Emp:** 13. **Officers:** Charles Barland, President; Jim Cassell, General Mgr.

■ 575 ■ **Farmers Cooperative Association**
900 E Jefferson St.
Siloam Springs, AR 72761
Phone: (501)524-6175 **Fax:** (501)524-6177
Products: Farm supplies; Vet supplies; Feed. **SICs:** 5191 (Farm Supplies); 5172 (Petroleum Products Nec). **Est:** 1965. **Sales:** $8,500,000 (2000). **Emp:** 30. **Officers:** Carol Walker, Office Mgr.

■ 576 ■ **Farmers Cooperative Association**
Hwy. 63 N
New Hampton, IA 50659
Phone: (515)394-3052
Products: Grain; Feed; Fertilizer. **SICs:** 5153 (Grain & Field Beans); 5191 (Farm Supplies). **Sales:** $30,000,000 (2000). **Emp:** 10. **Officers:** Darwin Sittit, CEO.

■ 577 ■ Farmers Cooperative Association
PO Box 187
Okarche, OK 73762
Phone: (405)263-7289
Products: Feed for hogs and cattle; Grain, including wheat and corn; Fertilizer and chemicals. **SIC:** 5191 (Farm Supplies). **Est:** 1906. **Sales:** $5,000,000 (2000). **Emp:** 14. **Officers:** Dean Anderson, General Mgr.

■ 578 ■ Farmers Cooperative Association
PO Box 1045
Manhattan, KS 66505-1045
Phone: (913)776-9467
Products: Farm products, including feed, fertilizer, and grain. **SICs:** 5153 (Grain & Field Beans); 5191 (Farm Supplies). **Sales:** $19,900,000 (2000). **Emp:** 50. **Officers:** Paul Irvine, President; Marsha Lowery, Controller.

■ 579 ■ Farmers Cooperative Association
PO Box 196
Meno, OK 73760
Phone: (580)776-2241   **Fax:** (580)776-2242
Products: Feed; Wheat; Chemicals; Fertilizers; Fuel. **SICs:** 5153 (Grain & Field Beans); 5191 (Farm Supplies). **Est:** 1916. **Sales:** $3,000,000 (2000). **Emp:** 11. **Officers:** Gary Jantzen, President; Vernon Hiebert, Treasurer & Secty.; Gene Wedel, Manager.

■ 580 ■ Farmers Cooperative Association
PO Box 220
Allen, NE 68710
Phone: (402)635-2312   **Fax:** (402)635-2433
Products: Grain; Feed; Fertilizer; Chemicals. **SICs:** 5153 (Grain & Field Beans); 5191 (Farm Supplies). **Est:** 1915. **Sales:** $2,000,000 (1999). **Emp:** 4. **Officers:** Bill Woods, General Mgr.

■ 581 ■ Farmers Cooperative Association
PO Box 390
Forest City, IA 50436
Phone: (515)582-2814
Products: Farm supplies; Fertilizer; Grain. **SICs:** 5153 (Grain & Field Beans); 5191 (Farm Supplies). **Est:** 1920. **Sales:** $15,000,000 (1999). **Emp:** 12. **Officers:** Kevin Lackore, President; Gary Sterling, General Mgr.

■ 582 ■ Farmers Cooperative Association
4th & Barnes
Alva, OK 73717
Phone: (405)327-3854
Products: Farming supplies; Grain elevator. **SICs:** 5191 (Farm Supplies); 5153 (Grain & Field Beans). **Est:** 1917. **Sales:** $16,000,000 (2000). **Emp:** 45. **Officers:** Randy Schwerdtfeger, President.

■ 583 ■ Farmers Cooperative Association
E Country Rd.
Columbus, KS 66725
Phone: (316)429-2296
Products: Farm supplies, including feed, fertilizer, and grain. **SIC:** 5191 (Farm Supplies). **Est:** 1950. **Sales:** $12,000,000 (2000). **Emp:** 29. **Officers:** Rich Reynolds, CEO; Scott Jarrett, President.

■ 584 ■ Farmers Cooperative Association
209 S Market St.
Eldorado, OK 73537
Phone: (580)633-2274   **Fax:** (580)633-2276
Products: Fertilizer; Wheat; Cotton. **SIC:** 5191 (Farm Supplies). **Est:** 1920. **Sales:** $5,486,000 (1999). **Emp:** 8. **Officers:** Buddy Thompson, President; Barney Trammel, Manager.

■ 585 ■ Farmers Cooperative Association
400 Walnut St.
Laurens, IA 50554
Phone: (712)845-4566
Products: Grain; Feed; Seed; Fertilizers. **SICs:** 5153 (Grain & Field Beans); 5191 (Farm Supplies). **Sales:** $45,000,000 (2000). **Emp:** 54. **Officers:** Keith Hoffman, CEO; Phil Dukes, General Mgr.

■ 586 ■ Farmers Cooperative Business Association
PO Box 38
Shelby, NE 68662
Phone: (402)527-5511   **Fax:** (402)527-5515
Products: Feed; Grain; Fertilizer; Chemicals. **SICs:** 5153 (Grain & Field Beans); 5191 (Farm Supplies). **Est:** 1921. **Sales:** $50,000,000 (2000). **Emp:** 50. **Officers:** Roland From, Chairman of the Board; Ron Golka, CFO.

■ 587 ■ Farmers Cooperative Co.
110 River Rd.
Akron, IA 51001
Phone: (712)568-2426
Free: (800)682-3979   **Fax:** (712)568-2427
Products: Grain elevator; Fertilizer; Seed; Feed; Agronomy sales; Chemicals. **SIC:** 5191 (Farm Supplies). **Est:** 1908. **Sales:** $10,000,000 (2000). **Emp:** 12. **Former Name:** Farmers Cooperative Association.

■ 588 ■ Farmers Cooperative Co.
PO Box 100
Carmen, OK 73726
Phone: (580)987-2234
Products: Farm products, including fertilizer, gasoline, and feed. **SICs:** 5153 (Grain & Field Beans); 5191 (Farm Supplies). **Est:** 1927. **Sales:** $13,000,000 (2000). **Emp:** 26. **Officers:** Jim Bourlon, General Mgr.

■ 589 ■ Farmers Cooperative Co.
103 N Blanch
Manly, IA 50456
Phone: (515)454-2282   **Fax:** (515)454-2313
Products: Chemicals; Seed; Fertilizer; Grain; Farm equipment; Gates; Feeders. **SICs:** 5153 (Grain & Field Beans); 5191 (Farm Supplies). **Est:** 1926. **Sales:** $14,000,000 (2000). **Emp:** 9. **Officers:** Larry Shuttler, President.

■ 590 ■ Farmers Cooperative Co.
PO Box 186
Clear Lake, IA 50428
Phone: (515)357-5274   **Fax:** (515)397-5275
Products: Feed and grain. **SICs:** 5153 (Grain & Field Beans); 5191 (Farm Supplies). **Est:** 1921. **Sales:** $5,000,000 (2000). **Emp:** 15. **Officers:** John Burgardt, President; Greg Tangemann, General Mgr.

■ 591 ■ Farmers Cooperative Co.
PO Box 127
Brookings, SD 57006
Phone: (605)692-6216
Products: Fertilizers; Grain and feed. **SICs:** 5153 (Grain & Field Beans); 5191 (Farm Supplies). **Est:** 1913. **Sales:** $15,000,000 (2000). **Emp:** 22. **Officers:** R.C. Lathrop, General Mgr.

■ 592 ■ Farmers Cooperative Co.
PO Box 505
Glidden, IA 51443
Phone: (712)659-2227   **Fax:** (712)659-2226
Products: Farm supplies, including feed, fertilizer, seed, grain, and chemicals. **SICs:** 5153 (Grain & Field Beans); 5191 (Farm Supplies). **Est:** 1933. **Sales:** $18,500,000 (2000). **Emp:** 25. **Officers:** Ron Kerwood, General Mgr.

■ 593 ■ Farmers Cooperative Co.
PO Box 70
Waverly, NE 68462
Phone: (402)786-2665
Products: Farm products, including grains, fertilizers, herbicides, and insecticides; Fuels, including gasoline, diesel fuel, and oil. **SICs:** 5153 (Grain & Field Beans); 5191 (Farm Supplies); 5172 (Petroleum Products Nec). **Est:** 1921. **Sales:** $48,000,000 (1999). **Emp:** 54. **Officers:** Michael Minchow, President; Harold R. Hummel, General Mgr.; Greg Carlson, Vice President; Rodney Otley, Secretary.

■ 594 ■ Farmers Cooperative Co.
PO Box 157
Woolstock, IA 50599
Phone: (515)839-5532
Products: Petroleum; Grains; Fertilizers. **SICs:** 5172 (Petroleum Products Nec); 5191 (Farm Supplies); 5153 (Grain & Field Beans). **Sales:** $12,000,000 (2000). **Emp:** 12. **Officers:** John Peterson, General Mgr.

■ 595 ■ Farmers Cooperative Co.
141 N Main
Paullina, IA 51046
Phone: (712)448-3412
Products: Grain; Seed; Fertilizer; Feed. **SICs:** 5191 (Farm Supplies); 5153 (Grain & Field Beans). **Est:** 1918. **Sales:** $4,000,000 (2000). **Emp:** 18. **Officers:** Earl Gimberg, President; Tracy Gathman, General Mgr.

■ 596 ■ Farmers Cooperative Co.
PO Box 308
Rudd, IA 50471
Phone: (515)395-2271   **Fax:** (515)395-2275
Products: Fertilizer; Lawn care products; Chemicals; Fuel. **SICs:** 5191 (Farm Supplies); 5169 (Chemicals & Allied Products Nec); 5172 (Petroleum Products Nec). **Est:** 1904. **Sales:** $10,000,000 (2000). **Emp:** 24. **Officers:** Bruce Penington, CEO; D.A. Straube, Manager.

■ 597 ■ Farmers Cooperative Co.
445 S Main St.
West Point, NE 68788
Phone: (402)372-5303
Products: Feed; Grain; Fertilizer; Chemicals. **SICs:** 5153 (Grain & Field Beans); 5191 (Farm Supplies). **Est:** 1915. **Sales:** $7,000,000 (2000). **Emp:** 12. **Officers:** Dan Slagel, General Mgr.; Jim Meier, Manager.

■ 598 ■ Farmers Cooperative Co.
PO Box 278
Lost Nation, IA 52254
Phone: (319)678-2506
Products: Grain; Feed; Seed; Fertilizer; Chemicals. **SICs:** 5153 (Grain & Field Beans); 5191 (Farm Supplies). **Est:** 1920. **Sales:** $2,000,000 (2000). **Emp:** 8. **Officers:** Chris Schroder, President; Dale Holtapp, General Mgr.

■ 599 ■ Farmers Cooperative Co.
PO Box 192
Mondamin, IA 51557
Phone: (712)646-2411
Products: Grain; Seed; Fertilizer; Gasoline; Petroleum. **SICs:** 5153 (Grain & Field Beans); 5191 (Farm Supplies); 5171 (Petroleum Bulk Stations & Terminals). **Est:** 1918. **Sales:** $10,400,000 (2000). **Emp:** 16. **Officers:** Oral E. Hillman, President; Jerry Carrier, General Mgr.

■ 600 ■ Farmers Cooperative Co.
Washington & North
Remsen, IA 51050
Phone: (712)786-1134   **Fax:** (712)786-2998
Products: Grain; Feed. **SICs:** 5153 (Grain & Field Beans); 5191 (Farm Supplies). **Est:** 1910. **Sales:** $18,000,000 (2000). **Emp:** 19. **Officers:** D.J. Pick, General Mgr.; Kenneth Maass, CFO.

■ 601 ■ Farmers Cooperative Co.
PO Box 339
Readlyn, IA 50668-0339
Phone: (319)279-3396
Products: Grain; Feed; Fertilizers; Chemicals. **SICs:** 5153 (Grain & Field Beans); 5191 (Farm Supplies). **Est:** 1942. **Sales:** $11,000,000 (2000). **Emp:** 25. **Officers:** Arnold Doepke, President.

■ 602 ■ Farmers Cooperative Co.
PO Box 399
Alton, IA 51003
Phone: (712)756-4121
Free: (800)732-9655   **Fax:** (712)756-4199
Products: Feed; Fertilizer; Gasoline; Oil; Diesel fuel; Grains; Corn; Beans. **SICs:** 5153 (Grain & Field Beans); 5172 (Petroleum Products Nec); 5191 (Farm Supplies). **Est:** 1908. **Sales:** $26,000,000 (2000). **Emp:** 100. **Officers:** Skip Ellis Hein, General Mgr.; John Feikema, Accountant.

■ 603 ■ Farmers Cooperative Co.
PO Box 35
Farnhamville, IA 50538
Phone: (515)544-3213   **Fax:** (515)439-2309
Products: Grain elevators; Fertilizer and fertilizer materials; Chemical preparations; Feed. **SICs:** 5153 (Grain & Field Beans); 5191 (Farm Supplies). **Est:** 1939. **Sales:** $240,000,000 (2000). **Emp:** 190.

Officers: Roger Koppen, General Mgr.; Robert Peterson, Controller.

■ 604 ■ Farmers Cooperative Company Inc.
111 N Weimer St.
Ventura, IA 50482
Phone: (515)829-3891
Products: Grains; Seeds; Fertilizer; Hardware; Feed; Chemicals; Oils. **SICs:** 5153 (Grain & Field Beans); 5191 (Farm Supplies); 5072 (Hardware); 5172 (Petroleum Products Nec). **Est:** 1905. **Sales:** $10,500,000 (2000). **Emp:** 8. **Officers:** Robert Olson, President; Roy Ziesmer, General Mgr.

■ 605 ■ Farmers Cooperative Elevator
PO Box 208
Ord, NE 68862
Phone: (308)728-3254 **Fax:** (308)728-5940
Products: Feed; Grain; Fertilizer; Chemicals; Grain elevator. **SICs:** 5153 (Grain & Field Beans); 5191 (Farm Supplies). **Est:** 1914. **Sales:** $30,000,000 (2000). **Emp:** 30. **Officers:** Jim Novotny, CEO; Angie Stalker, Controller.

■ 606 ■ Farmers Cooperative Elevator
PO Box 348
Buffalo Center, IA 50424
Phone: (515)562-2828 **Fax:** (515)562-2847
Products: Farm supplies, including seed, fertilizer, and lawn care products. **SICs:** 5153 (Grain & Field Beans); 5191 (Farm Supplies). **Est:** 1910. **Sales:** $34,000,000 (2000). **Emp:** 39. **Officers:** Tom Meyer, General Mgr.

■ 607 ■ Farmers Cooperative Elevator
Main St.
Stockton, IA 52769
Phone: (319)785-4436
Products: Feed; Fertilizer; Seed; Grain; Chemicals; Petroleum. **SICs:** 5153 (Grain & Field Beans); 5191 (Farm Supplies); 5083 (Farm & Garden Machinery); 5172 (Petroleum Products Nec). **Est:** 1937. **Sales:** $8,000,000 (2000). **Emp:** 18. **Officers:** Roger Schroeder, President; Keith Wall, Manager.

■ 608 ■ Farmers Cooperative Elevator
PO Box 67
Wakita, OK 73771
Phone: (580)594-2234
Products: Chemicals; Insecticides; Oil; Gasoline; Diesel; Grains, including wheat and corn. **SICs:** 5153 (Grain & Field Beans); 5172 (Petroleum Products Nec); 5191 (Farm Supplies). **Sales:** $10,000,000 (2000). **Emp:** 8. **Officers:** Richard Claflin, General Mgr.

■ 609 ■ Farmers Cooperative Elevator
PO Box 45
Thompson, IA 50478-0045
Phone: (515)584-2241
Products: Fertilizer; Lawn care products; Chemicals; Fuel. **SICs:** 5153 (Grain & Field Beans); 5191 (Farm Supplies). **Est:** 1927. **Sales:** $35,000,000 (2000). **Emp:** 29. **Officers:** Ronald G. Pyle, General Mgr.

■ 610 ■ Farmers Cooperative Elevator Association
401 Commercial St.
Greenleaf, KS 66943
Phone: (785)747-2236 **Fax:** (785)747-2438
Products: Agricultural products, including grain, livestock equipment, chemicals, and gasoline. **SICs:** 5153 (Grain & Field Beans); 5191 (Farm Supplies); 5172 (Petroleum Products Nec). **Est:** 1935. **Sales:** $14,000,000 (2000). **Emp:** 23. **Officers:** Ray K. Johnson, General Mgr.; Thomas Kantor, Controller.

■ 611 ■ Farmers Cooperative Elevator Association
1016 2nd Ave.
Sheldon, IA 51201
Phone: (712)324-2548 **Fax:** (712)324-5297
Products: Grain; Fertilizer; Seed; Feed. **SICs:** 5153 (Grain & Field Beans); 5191 (Farm Supplies). **Est:** 1914. **Sales:** $60,000,000 (1999). **Emp:** 110. **Officers:** Marlin Oostephus, President; Skip (Elis) Hein, Finance Officer & General Mgr.

■ 612 ■ Farmers Cooperative Elevator Co.
PO Box 604
Rushford, MN 55971
Phone: (507)864-7733
Products: Grain, fertilizer, feed, seed, and chemicals. **SICs:** 5153 (Grain & Field Beans); 5191 (Farm Supplies). **Est:** 1903. **Sales:** $10,000,000 (2000). **Emp:** 20. **Officers:** Eugene Hanson, President; Bill Grindland, General Mgr.

■ 613 ■ Farmers Cooperative Elevator Co.
PO Box 112
Winterset, IA 50273
Phone: (515)462-4611
Products: Farm supplies, including fertilizer, chemicals, feed, grains, corn, soybeans, and petroleum. **SICs:** 5191 (Farm Supplies); 5153 (Grain & Field Beans); 5172 (Petroleum Products Nec). **Est:** 1933. **Sales:** $4,000,000 (2000). **Emp:** 9. **Officers:** John Spera, President.

■ 614 ■ Farmers Cooperative Elevator Co.
PO Box 188
Ruthven, IA 51358
Phone: (712)837-5231
Products: Feed; Seed; Fertilizer; Chemicals. **SICs:** 5153 (Grain & Field Beans); 5191 (Farm Supplies). **Est:** 1911. **Sales:** $41,000,000 (2000). **Emp:** 51. **Officers:** Vergil Stettnicks, General Mgr.

■ 615 ■ Farmers Cooperative Elevator Co.
PO Box 200
Radcliffe, IA 50230
Phone: (515)899-2101 **Fax:** (515)899-2105
E-mail: radcoop@netins.net
Products: Farm supplies, including fertilizers, chemicals, feed, grains, corn, and soybeans. **SICs:** 5191 (Farm Supplies); 5191 (Farm Supplies); 5153 (Grain & Field Beans). **Est:** 1900. **Sales:** $15,000,000 (2000). **Emp:** 25. **Officers:** Robert Imsland, President; Jeff Ullestad, General Mgr.

■ 616 ■ Farmers Cooperative Elevator Co.
PO Box 518
Waukee, IA 50263
Phone: (515)987-4511
Products: Agricultural supplies, including fertilizers, chemicals, feed, seeds, and petroleum. **SICs:** 5153 (Grain & Field Beans); 5191 (Farm Supplies); 5172 (Petroleum Products Nec). **Est:** 1936. **Sales:** $23,000,000 (2000). **Emp:** 30. **Officers:** Tim Broderick, President; Clair Rew, Dir. of Marketing.

■ 617 ■ Farmers Cooperative Elevator Co.
509 A Ave.
Grundy Center, IA 50638
Phone: (319)824-5466
Products: Grain; Feed; Fertilizer. **SICs:** 5153 (Grain & Field Beans); 5191 (Farm Supplies). **Est:** 1919. **Sales:** $11,700,000 (2000). **Emp:** 14. **Officers:** Paul Harberts, President; Eldon Klaassen, General Mgr.

■ 618 ■ Farmers Cooperative Elevator Co.
533 Bradford St.
Marble Rock, IA 50653
Phone: (515)397-2515
Products: Grain; Feed; Fertilizer. **SICs:** 5153 (Grain & Field Beans); 5191 (Farm Supplies). **Est:** 1934. **Sales:** $8,500,000 (2000). **Emp:** 10. **Officers:** Larry Staudt, President; Steve Bodensteiner, General Mgr.

■ 619 ■ Farmers Cooperative Elevator Co.
N Main St.
Rake, IA 50465
Phone: (515)566-3351 **Fax:** (515)566-3311
Products: Fertilizer; Feed; Petroleum. **SICs:** 5191 (Farm Supplies); 5172 (Petroleum Products Nec). **Sales:** $15,000,000 (2000). **Emp:** 12. **Officers:** Roger Schaefer, President; Phil Benn, CFO; Mark Winter, Dir. of Systems.

■ 620 ■ Farmers Cooperative Elevator Co.
Hwy. 285
Arcadia, IA 51430
Phone: (712)689-2298
Products: Feed; Seed; Fertilizer; Grain; Lumber. **SICs:** 5191 (Farm Supplies); 5153 (Grain & Field Beans); 5031 (Lumber, Plywood & Millwork). **Est:** 1937. **Sales:**

$24,000,000 (2000). **Emp:** 26. **Officers:** Dennis Leiting, General Mgr.; Verl Massman, President.

■ 621 ■ Farmers Cooperative Elevator Co.
PO Box 66
Plymouth, NE 68424
Phone: (402)656-3615
Products: Grain; Feed; Fertilizer; Petroleum; Fuel; Hardware; Tires. **SICs:** 5153 (Grain & Field Beans); 5191 (Farm Supplies); 5172 (Petroleum Products Nec); 5014 (Tires & Tubes); 5072 (Hardware). **Est:** 1902. **Sales:** $50,000,000 (2000). **Emp:** 115. **Officers:** Doug Derscheid, General Mgr.

■ 622 ■ Farmers Cooperative Elevator Co. Lake Lillian Div.
Main St.
Lake Lillian, MN 56253
Phone: (612)664-4121
Products: Feed; Fertilizer; Fuel. **SICs:** 5153 (Grain & Field Beans); 5191 (Farm Supplies). **Est:** 1923. **Sales:** $6,000,000 (2000). **Emp:** 10. **Officers:** Jim Whittman, Manager.

■ 623 ■ Farmers Cooperative Exchange
109 South St.
Pella, IA 50219
Phone: (515)628-4167 **Fax:** (515)628-8195
Products: Farm supplies, including fertilizer and chemicals; Petroleum; Grain, including corn, soybeans, and oats. **SICs:** 5153 (Grain & Field Beans); 5191 (Farm Supplies); 5172 (Petroleum Products Nec). **Sales:** $12,000,000 (2000). **Emp:** 22. **Officers:** Larry N. Crozier, General Mgr.

■ 624 ■ Farmers Cooperative Exchange
PO Box 188
Weatherford, OK 73096
Phone: (580)772-3334
Products: Farm supplies, including feed. **SIC** 5191 (Farm Supplies). **Est:** 1917. **Sales:** $4,000,000 (2000). **Emp:** 11. **Officers:** Steve Sweeney, General Mgr.

■ 625 ■ Farmers Cooperative Exchange
PO Box 8
Otley, IA 50214
Phone: (515)627-5311 **Fax:** (515)627-5311
Products: Farm supplies, including fertilizer, chemicals, and feed; Corn, soybeans, and grain. **SICs:** 5153 (Grain & Field Beans); 5191 (Farm Supplies). **Est:** 1937. **Sales:** $10,000,000 (2000). **Emp:** 16. **Officers:** Pete Keuning, President; Craig Hetland, General Mgr.

■ 626 ■ Farmers Cooperative Exchange
PO Box 158
Bessie, OK 73622
Phone: (580)337-6343
Products: Grain; Fuel; Feed. **SICs:** 5153 (Grain & Field Beans); 5191 (Farm Supplies); 5172 (Petroleum Products Nec). **Est:** 1917. **Sales:** $3,000,000 (2000). **Emp:** 5. **Officers:** Jack Sawatsley, President; Bob Lindsey, Manager.

■ 627 ■ Farmers Cooperative Exchange
804 1st Ave. NW
Rockford, IA 50468
Phone: (515)756-3611
Products: Seed; Fertilizer; Grain; Refined fuel; Chemicals. **SICs:** 5191 (Farm Supplies); 5172 (Petroleum Products Nec); 5169 (Chemicals & Allied Products Nec). **Sales:** $6,700,000 (2000). **Emp:** 10. **Officers:** Jim Muller, President; Rick Kaduce, General Mgr.

■ 628 ■ Farmers Cooperative Grain Association
524 E Parallel St.
Conway Springs, KS 67031
Phone: (316)456-2222
Products: Farm products, including grain, feed, fertilizer, and chemicals. **SICs:** 5153 (Grain & Field Beans); 5191 (Farm Supplies). **Est:** 1954. **Sales:** $10,000,000 (2000). **Emp:** 10. **Officers:** Norbert Myer, President; Norbert Gerstenkorn, General Mgr.

■ **629** ■ **Farmers Cooperative Grain Association**
210 S Nebraska St.
Waterville, KS 66548
Phone: (913)785-2555
Products: Feed; Fertilizer; Grain. **SICs:** 5153 (Grain & Field Beans); 5191 (Farm Supplies). **Est:** 1951. **Sales:** $4,000,000 (2000). **Emp:** 10. **Officers:** Gail Roepke, President.

■ **630** ■ **Farmers Cooperative Grain and Seed Co.**
PO Box 88
Lamoni, IA 50140
Phone: (515)784-3326 **Fax:** (515)784-7926
Products: Agricultural supplies, including grain, feed, fertilizers, and chemicals. **SICs:** 5153 (Grain & Field Beans); 5191 (Farm Supplies). **Est:** 1920. **Sales:** $7,900,000 (2000). **Emp:** 16. **Officers:** Joe Hendren, President; Ron Schachtner, General Mgr.

■ **631** ■ **Farmers Cooperative Grain and Supply Co.**
815 N Brown St.
Minden, NE 68959
Phone: (308)832-2380 **Fax:** (308)832-2442
Products: Grain; Feed; Fertilizers; Chemicals; Farming supplies. **SICs:** 5153 (Grain & Field Beans); 5191 (Farm Supplies). **Est:** 1903. **Sales:** $25,000,000 (2000). **Emp:** 25. **Officers:** Ronald Hunt, General Mgr.

■ **632** ■ **Farmers Cooperative Grain and Supply Co.**
PO Box 245
Rocky, OK 73661
Phone: (580)666-2440
Products: Farming supplies; Grain. **SICs:** 5191 (Farm Supplies); 5153 (Grain & Field Beans). **Sales:** $3,000,000 (2000). **Emp:** 12. **Officers:** Eldon Cook, President.

■ **633** ■ **Farmers Cooperative Inc.**
312-16 W 3rd St.
Farmville, VA 23901
Phone: (804)392-4192
Products: Equipment, including lawn, garden, and farm. **SIC:** 5191 (Farm Supplies). **Est:** 1947. **Sales:** $3,000,000 (2000). **Emp:** 18. **Officers:** Charles Scott, Manager.

■ **634** ■ **Farmers Cooperative Market**
PO Box 187
Frisco City, AL 36445
Phone: (334)267-3175 **Fax:** (334)267-2760
Products: Farm supplies, including seed and fertilizer. **SIC:** 5191 (Farm Supplies). **Est:** 1949. **Sales:** $11,000,000 (2000). **Emp:** 46. **Officers:** Sam Carter, General Mgr.

■ **635** ■ **Farmers Cooperative Oil of Balaton**
PO Box 189
Balaton, MN 56115
Phone: (507)734-3331 **Fax:** (507)734-6241
Products: Farming supplies. **SIC:** 5171 (Petroleum Bulk Stations & Terminals). **Est:** 1955. **Sales:** $2,000,000 (2000). **Emp:** 8. **Officers:** John Sanow, General Mgr., e-mail: jsanow@frontiernet.net.

■ **636** ■ **Farmers Cooperative Oil Co.**
PO Box 310
Newman Grove, NE 68758
Phone: (402)447-6292
Products: Feed; Grain; Petroleum; Fertilizer; Chemicals. **SIC:** 5191 (Farm Supplies). **Est:** 1927. **Sales:** $9,900,000 (2000). **Emp:** 17. **Officers:** Roger Lyon, President; Allen Schroeder, General Mgr.; Dennis McCloud, Office Mgr.; Davolyn Nelson, Dir. of Data Processing.

■ **637** ■ **Farmers Cooperative Society**
390 E 5th St.
Garner, IA 50438
Phone: (515)923-2695 **Fax:** (515)923-2444
Products: Farm supplies, including seeds and lawn fertilizers; Lumber and building materials; Grain. **SICs:** 5153 (Grain & Field Beans); 5191 (Farm Supplies). **Est:** 1907. **Sales:** $30,000,000 (2000). **Emp:** 45. **Officers:** Sidney Heitmeyer, General Mgr.

■ **638** ■ **Farmers Cooperative Supply and Shipping Association**
136 E Elm St.
West Salem, WI 54669
Phone: (608)786-1100
Products: Farming supplies; Hardware. **SICs:** 5191 (Farm Supplies); 5072 (Hardware). **Est:** 1918. **Sales:** $29,000,000 (2000). **Emp:** 45. **Officers:** Donald Servais, President; Merlin Wehrs, Treasurer & Secty.

■ **639** ■ **Farmers Cooperative Trading Co.**
PO Box 135
Mooreland, OK 73852
Phone: (580)994-5375
Products: Chemicals and fertilizers; Grains, including wheat, corn, and milo; Gas, oil, and diesel fuel. **SICs:** 5153 (Grain & Field Beans); 5191 (Farm Supplies); 5172 (Petroleum Products Nec). **Est:** 1915. **Sales:** $7,000,000 (2000). **Emp:** 25. **Officers:** Ronnie Peach, President; Gene Newans, General Mgr.

■ **640** ■ **Farmers Cooperative Union**
PO Box 159
Sterling, KS 67579
Phone: (316)278-2141 **Fax:** (316)278-2147
Products: Farm products, including gasoline, diesel fuel, oil, and feed; Grains, including wheat, and milo; Soybeans. **SICs:** 5191 (Farm Supplies); 5153 (Grain & Field Beans); 5172 (Petroleum Products Nec). **Est:** 1917. **Sales:** $20,000,000 (2000). **Emp:** 52. **Officers:** Richard Fisher, General Mgr.

■ **641** ■ **Farmers Elevator Co.**
PO Box 399
Elk Point, SD 57025
Phone: (605)356-2657
Products: Feed; Seed; Fertilizers; Chemicals. **SICs:** 5153 (Grain & Field Beans); 5191 (Farm Supplies). **Est:** 1921. **Sales:** $8,000,000 (2000). **Emp:** 4. **Officers:** Bill Bowar, Manager.

■ **642** ■ **Farmers Elevator Co.**
PO Box 346
Kingsley, IA 51028
Phone: (712)378-2888
Products: Grain; Seed; Fertilizer. **SICs:** 5153 (Grain & Field Beans); 5191 (Farm Supplies). **Est:** 1905. **Sales:** $7,000,000 (2000). **Emp:** 12. **Officers:** Michael Grabe, President; Robert Honkomp, General Mgr.

■ **643** ■ **Farmers Elevator Co.**
PO Box 175
Waverly, IL 62692
Phone: (217)965-4004
Products: Grain; Seeds; Feed; Fertilizer; Chemicals. **SICs:** 5191 (Farm Supplies); 5153 (Grain & Field Beans); 5169 (Chemicals & Allied Products Nec). **Est:** 1905. **Sales:** $8,000,000 (2000). **Emp:** 13. **Officers:** Greg Dolbeare, General Mgr.

■ **644** ■ **Farmers Elevator Company of Avoca**
PO Box 157
Westbrook, MN 56183
Phone: (507)274-6141 **Fax:** (507)274-5561
Products: Grain; Fertilizer; Feed; Seed; Chemicals. **SICs:** 5153 (Grain & Field Beans); 5191 (Farm Supplies). **Est:** 1906. **Sales:** $9,000,000 (2000). **Emp:** 15. **Officers:** Leo Vortherms, President; Roger Knudsen, Treasurer & Secty.; Harold Johnson, General Mgr.

■ **645** ■ **Farmers Elevator Cooperative**
1204 Main St.
Scranton, IA 51462
Phone: (712)652-3321
Products: Fertilizer; Seeds; Feed; Chemicals; Grains. **SICs:** 5191 (Farm Supplies); 5169 (Chemicals & Allied Products Nec); 5153 (Grain & Field Beans). **Est:** 1907. **Sales:** $15,000,000 (2000). **Emp:** 20. **Officers:** Jerry Kunce, General Mgr.

■ **646** ■ **Farmers Elevator Grain and Supply**
16-973 Rd. B
New Bavaria, OH 43548
Phone: (419)653-4132 **Fax:** (419)653-4132
Products: Grain; Seed; Feed; Farm chemicals; Fertilizer. **SICs:** 5153 (Grain & Field Beans); 5191 (Farm Supplies). **Est:** 1912. **Sales:** $12,900,000

(2000). **Emp:** 15. **Officers:** Jim Sheeks, President; William Klear Jr. Jr., Manager.

■ **647** ■ **Farmers Elevator Supply Co.**
511 South Ctr.
Clinton, MO 64735
Phone: (660)885-5578 **Fax:** (660)885-5833
Products: Farm supplies; Grain; Chemical preparations; Fertilizer and fertilizer materials. **SICs:** 5191 (Farm Supplies); 5153 (Grain & Field Beans). **Est:** 1917. **Sales:** $4,000,000 (1999). **Emp:** 10. **Officers:** Jerry Helmick, Manager.

■ **648** ■ **Farmers Exchange**
115 Main St.
Stevensville, MT 59870
Phone: (406)777-5441
Products: Agricultural supplies, including feed, chemicals, and fertilizers; Grains, including oats, barley, and wheat. **SICs:** 5171 (Petroleum Bulk Stations & Terminals); 5171 (Petroleum Bulk Stations & Terminals); 5191 (Farm Supplies); 5072 (Hardware). **Est:** 1936. **Sales:** $7,700,000 (2000). **Emp:** 45. **Officers:** Will Dukart, General Mgr.

■ **649** ■ **Farmers Exchange Cooperative**
PO Box 38
Lake Park, IA 51347
Phone: (712)832-3621
Products: Chemicals; Fertilizer; Corn; Oats; Beans; Feed. **SICs:** 5153 (Grain & Field Beans); 5191 (Farm Supplies); 5171 (Petroleum Bulk Stations & Terminals). **Est:** 1905. **Sales:** $8,000,000 (2000). **Emp:** 12. **Officers:** Dennis Krier, Manager.

■ **650** ■ **Farmers Gin Co.**
PO Box 217
Bells, TN 38006
Phone: (901)663-2996 **Fax:** (901)663-3752
E-mail: farmgin@ibm.net
Products: Cotton gin. **SIC:** 5083 (Farm & Garden Machinery). **Est:** 1925. **Sales:** $500,000 (2000). **Emp:** 6. **Officers:** Ray Pearson, President; Eugene S. Permenter, Manager.

■ **651** ■ **Farmers Grain Co.**
PO Box 80
Palmer, IL 62556
Phone: (217)526-3114
Products: Grain; Seeds; Fertilizer; Feeds. **SICs:** 5153 (Grain & Field Beans); 5191 (Farm Supplies). **Est:** 1909. **Sales:** $8,000,000 (2000). **Emp:** 5. **Officers:** Laverne Crull, General Mgr.

■ **652** ■ **Farmers Grain Company of Charlotte**
R.R. 1
Chatsworth, IL 60921
Phone: (815)689-2673 **Fax:** (815)689-2161
Products: Feed; Fertilizers. **SIC:** 5191 (Farm Supplies). **Est:** 1907. **Sales:** $7,300,000 (2000). **Emp:** 12. **Officers:** L.C. Kerber, President.

■ **653** ■ **Farmers Grain Company Inc.**
PO Box 188
Kremlin, OK 73753-0188
Phone: (580)874-2219 **Fax:** (580)874-2400
Products: Farm supplies; Grain. **SICs:** 5153 (Grain & Field Beans); 5191 (Farm Supplies). **Est:** 1915. **Sales:** $10,000,000 (2000). **Emp:** 21. **Officers:** Richard Greary, President.

■ **654** ■ **Farmers Grain Cooperative**
PO Box 166
Colo, IA 50056
Phone: (515)377-2253
Products: Agricultural supplies, including chemicals, fertilizers, feed, and grains. **SICs:** 5191 (Farm Supplies); 5153 (Grain & Field Beans). **Est:** 1930. **Sales:** $10,000,000 (2000). **Emp:** 20. **Officers:** Robert Oswald, President; Paul Krzrzick, General Mgr.

■ **655** ■ **Farmers Grain Cooperative**
PO Box 177
Walton, KS 67151
Phone: (316)837-3313 **Fax:** (316)837-4781
Products: Grain; Fertilizer; Chemicals; Petroleum; Livestock equipment; Farm supplies, including feed. **SICs:** 5153 (Grain & Field Beans); 5191 (Farm Supplies); 5169 (Chemicals & Allied Products Nec).

Est: 1958. **Sales:** $38,000,000 (2000). **Emp:** 55. **Officers:** Terry Sauerwein, President; Larry Raskops, CFO.

■ 656 ■ **Farmers Grain Exchange**
PO Box 990
Havre, MT 59501
Phone: (406)265-2275 **Fax:** (406)265-8750
Products: Agricultural supplies, including grain elevators, feed, chemicals, and fertilizers; Wheat, barley, and oats. **SICs:** 5083 (Farm & Garden Machinery); 5191 (Farm Supplies). **Est:** 1926. **Sales:** $11,000,000 (2000). **Emp:** 6. **Officers:** Sam Shrauger, Chairman of the Board; Arleen Munson, Manager.

■ 657 ■ **Farmers Grain and Supply Company Inc.**
Rte. 1
Star City, IN 46985
Phone: (219)595-7101
Products: Farm supplies, including fencing, hog warmers, feed, and heat bulbs; Grain. **SICs:** 5153 (Grain & Field Beans); 5191 (Farm Supplies). **Est:** 1917. **Sales:** $5,000,000 (2000). **Emp:** 6. **Officers:** D. Mitchell, President; R. Sommer, Treasurer & Secty.

■ 658 ■ **Farmers Supply Cooperative-AAL**
PO Box 1799
Greenwood, MS 38930
Phone: (601)453-6341
Products: Seed; Fertilizer; Insecticides; Gas. **SICs:** 5191 (Farm Supplies); 5153 (Grain & Field Beans). **Est:** 1945. **Sales:** $30,000,000 (2000). **Emp:** 80. **Officers:** Joe L. Whicker, President; John L. Cheatham Jr., Treasurer & Secty.; Jerry Hovas, Manager.

■ 659 ■ **Farmers Supply Sales Inc.**
PO Box 1205
Kalona, IA 52247
Phone: (319)656-2291 **Fax:** (319)656-3873
E-mail: fssikl@jddealer.com
Products: Farm equipment, including cultivators, combines, and tractors; Lawn and garden tractors. **SIC:** 5083 (Farm & Garden Machinery). **Est:** 1953. **Sales:** $9,000,000 (2000). **Emp:** 30. **Officers:** Phil Ropp, President; Warren Ropp, Treasurer & Secty.; Myron Ropp, Vice President.

■ 660 ■ **Farmers Union Cooperative Association**
131 S Nebraska St.
Salem, SD 57058
Phone: (605)425-2691
Products: Farm supplies. **SIC:** 5191 (Farm Supplies). **Est:** 1937. **Sales:** $9,500,000 (2000). **Emp:** 23. **Officers:** Norman Peterson, President; Dean Koch, Manager.

■ 661 ■ **Farmers Union Cooperative Association of Howard County**
PO Box 237
St. Paul, NE 68873
Phone: (308)754-4431
Products: Fertilizer and animal feeds. **SIC:** 5191 (Farm Supplies). **Sales:** $3,000,000 (2000). **Emp:** 21. **Officers:** Bruce Rathman, President; Tom Mudloff, Mgr. of Finance.

■ 662 ■ **Farmers Union Cooperative Oil Co.**
PO Box 1018
Luverne, MN 56156-2518
Phone: (507)283-9571
Products: Agricultural products, including fertilizers and chemicals. **SIC:** 5171 (Petroleum Bulk Stations & Terminals). **Est:** 1954. **Sales:** $3,500,000 (2000). **Emp:** 11. **Officers:** L. Lindblom, General Mgr.

■ 663 ■ **Farmers Union Elevator**
PO Box 128
Buxton, ND 58218
Phone: (701)847-2646
Products: Farm products, including grain, feed, and seed. **SICs:** 5153 (Grain & Field Beans); 5191 (Farm Supplies). **Est:** 1930. **Sales:** $5,000,000 (2000). **Emp:** 6. **Officers:** Clyde Soderberg, President; Kerry M. Rice, CFO.

■ 664 ■ **Farmers Union Oil Co.**
PO Box B
Maddock, ND 58348
Phone: (701)438-2861
Products: Fertilizer; Chemicals; Grain. **SICs:** 5153 (Grain & Field Beans); 5191 (Farm Supplies); 5172 (Petroleum Products Nec). **Est:** 1931. **Sales:** $3,500,000 (2000). **Emp:** 14. **Officers:** Milton Erickson, President; John Halborsom, General Mgr.

■ 665 ■ **Farmers Union Oil Co.**
PO Box 347
Menno, SD 57045
Phone: (605)387-5151 **Fax:** (605)387-5645
Products: Farm supplies. **SIC:** 5191 (Farm Supplies). **Est:** 1937. **Sales:** $4,600,000 (2000). **Emp:** 24. **Officers:** Mark Schaeffer, Chairman of the Board.

■ 666 ■ **Farmers Union Oil Co.**
PO Box 67
Oslo, MN 56744
Phone: (218)695-2511
Products: Fertilizer; Chemicals. **SICs:** 5172 (Petroleum Products Nec); 5191 (Farm Supplies). **Est:** 1966. **Sales:** $8,000,000 (2000). **Emp:** 16. **Officers:** Robert Hjelnins, CEO.

■ 667 ■ **Farmers Union Oil Co.**
PO Box 129
Lake Bronson, MN 56734
Phone: (218)754-4300
Products: Petroleum, fuels, and related equipment. **SIC:** 5191 (Farm Supplies). **Sales:** $5,000,000 (2000). **Emp:** 14.

■ 668 ■ **Farmers Union Oil Co. (Crookston, Minnesota)**
PO Box 398
Crookston, MN 56716-0647
Phone: (218)281-1809 **Fax:** (218)281-3022
Products: Fertilizer, chemicals, gas and fuel. **SICs:** 5191 (Farm Supplies); 5172 (Petroleum Products Nec). **Sales:** $18,000,000 (2000). **Emp:** 20. **Officers:** Steve Jordan, General Mgr.

■ 669 ■ **Farmers Union Oil Company of Kenmare**
PO Box 726
Kenmare, ND 58746
Phone: (701)385-4277 **Fax:** (701)385-4279
Products: Farming equipment and supplies, including haulers, loaders, combines, chemicals, fertilizers, and petroleum. **SICs:** 5171 (Petroleum Bulk Stations & Terminals); 5172 (Petroleum Products Nec); 5169 (Chemicals & Allied Products Nec). **Est:** 1934. **Sales:** $9,000,000 (2000). **Emp:** 43. **Officers:** W. Weaver, General Mgr.

■ 670 ■ **Farmers Union Oil Co. (Starbuck, Minnesota)**
310 Wollan St.
Starbuck, MN 56381
Phone: (320)239-2233
Products: Mixed fertilizer and petroleum products. **SICs:** 5191 (Farm Supplies); 5172 (Petroleum Products Nec). **Sales:** $4,000,000 (2000). **Emp:** 20. **Officers:** Brad Manderschied, Mgr. of Finance.

■ 671 ■ **Farmers Union Oil Co. (Willmar, Minnesota)**
721 W Litchfield Ave.
Willmar, MN 56201
Phone: (612)235-3700 **Fax:** (612)235-7651
Products: Fertilizer. **SIC:** 5191 (Farm Supplies). **Sales:** $3,000,000 (1993). **Emp:** 20. **Officers:** Lynn Dokkebakken, General Mgr.

■ 672 ■ **Farmway Cooperative Inc.**
PO Box 568
Beloit, KS 67420
Phone: (785)738-2241 **Fax:** (785)738-5150
Products: Farm supplies, including fertilizer. **SIC:** 5191 (Farm Supplies). **Est:** 1911. **Sales:** $63,000,000 (2000). **Emp:** 118. **Officers:** Byron Ulery, General Mgr.; Phillip Kirchoff, Controller; Kent Miller, Dir. of Marketing.

■ 673 ■ **Farwest Equipment, Inc.**
1802 Pike NW
Auburn, WA 98001
Phone: (253)833-2060
Free: (800)926-8873 **Fax:** (253)833-3021
Products: Turf equipment. **SIC:** 5083 (Farm & Garden Machinery).

■ 674 ■ **Fayette County Cooperative Inc.**
PO Box 448
Connersville, IN 47331
Phone: (317)825-1131
Products: Agricultural supplies, including fertilizer, chemicals, feed, and grain. **SICs:** 5153 (Grain & Field Beans); 5191 (Farm Supplies). **Est:** 1927. **Sales:** $23,000,000 (2000). **Emp:** 42. **Officers:** Bill Sargeant, General Mgr.; Robert Hurst, Secretary.

■ 675 ■ **Federation Cooperative**
108 N Water St.
Black River Falls, WI 54615
Phone: (715)284-5354 **Fax:** (715)286-9672
Products: Farm supplies and petroleum bulk stations; Gasoline service stations. **SICs:** 5191 (Farm Supplies); 5171 (Petroleum Bulk Stations & Terminals). **Sales:** $5,000,000 (2000). **Emp:** 65. **Officers:** Leroy Wiersma, General Mgr.

■ 676 ■ **Feed Products Inc.**
1000 W 47th Ave.
Denver, CO 80211
Phone: (303)455-3646
Free: (800)332-8285 **Fax:** (303)477-6206
Products: Feed. **SIC:** 5191 (Farm Supplies). **Est:** 1945. **Sales:** $5,500,000 (2000). **Emp:** 16. **Officers:** W.H. Kieser Jr., President; M. Trumble, Dir. of Marketing.

■ 677 ■ **Feed Seed and Farm Supplies Inc.**
PO Box 536
Sylvania, GA 30467
Phone: (912)564-7758
Products: Feed; Fertilizer; Seed. **SIC:** 5191 (Farm Supplies). **Est:** 1951. **Sales:** $1,000,000 (2000). **Emp:** 9. **Officers:** George Boddiford Jr., President; Elise Boddiford, VP & Treasurer.

■ 678 ■ **Feldmann Engineering & Manufacturing Company, Inc.**
520 Forest Ave.
Sheboygan Falls, WI 53085-2513
Phone: (920)467-6167 **Fax:** (920)467-6169
E-mail: feldman.engineering@excel.net
URL: http://www.jiffy-on-ice.com
Products: Power and hand ice drills; Power earth augers; Core plug lawn aerators. **SICs:** 5083 (Farm & Garden Machinery); 5072 (Hardware). **Est:** 1947. **Emp:** 49. **Officers:** Marvin H. Feldmann, CEO; Cliff Feldmann, President, e-mail: feldmann.engineering@excel.net; Daniel Redman, Dir. of Marketing; Susan Walter, Office Mgr.

■ 679 ■ **Ferriday Farm Equipment Company Inc.**
PO Box 712
Ferriday, LA 71334
Phone: (318)757-4576 **Fax:** (318)757-4166
Products: Farm equipment. **SIC:** 5083 (Farm & Garden Machinery). **Est:** 1938. **Sales:** $4,000,000 (2000). **Emp:** 24. **Officers:** Mittie L. Schiele, President; Lynne Ashmore, Controller.

■ 680 ■ **Ferrin Cooperative Equity Exchange**
12805 Ferrin Rd.
Carlyle, IL 62231
Phone: (618)226-3275
Products: Grain; Feed; Field, garden, and flower seeds; Fertilizer and fertilizer materials; Chemical preparations. **SICs:** 5153 (Grain & Field Beans); 5191 (Farm Supplies). **Est:** 1921. **Sales:** $4,500,000 (2000). **Emp:** 8. **Officers:** Norman Kleiboeker, President; Robert Williams, General Mgr.

■ 681 ■ **Fey Inc.**
108 W Main
Ashley, ND 58413
Phone: (701)288-3471
Products: Farm machinery; Lawn and garden equipment. **SICs:** 5191 (Farm Supplies); 5083 (Farm &

Garden Machinery). **Est:** 1971. **Sales:** $3,000,000 (2000). **Emp:** 11. **Officers:** Leroy Fey, President.

■ **682** ■ **Jim Fiebiger and Son Inc.**
20909 Miami-Shelby Rd.
Conover, OH 45317
Phone: (937)368-3880
Products: Farm equipment, including chemicals, seeds, corn, beans, and grass. **SIC:** 5191 (Farm Supplies). **Est:** 1972. **Sales:** $5,000,000 (2000). **Emp:** 12. **Officers:** James Fiebiger, President; Annette Fiebiger, CFO.

■ **683** ■ **Fieldcrest Fertilizer Inc.**
Rte. 3, Box 1-C
Madison, MN 56256
Phone: (612)598-7567
Products: Fertilizer. **SIC:** 5191 (Farm Supplies). **Est:** 1952. **Sales:** $3,000,000 (2000). **Emp:** 13. **Officers:** Kevin Tollefson, President.

■ **684** ■ **Fields Equipment Company Inc.**
PO Box 113
Winter Haven, FL 33880
Phone: (813)967-0602
Products: Lawnmowers and tractors. **SIC:** 5083 (Farm & Garden Machinery). **Est:** 1957. **Sales:** $20,000,000 (2000). **Emp:** 66. **Officers:** C.E. Fields Jr. Jr., President.

■ **685** ■ **First Farmers Cooperative Elevator**
PO Box 187
Cleghorn, IA 51014
Phone: (712)436-2224
Products: Grain; Fertilizer; Seed; Chemicals. **SICs:** 5153 (Grain & Field Beans); 5191 (Farm Supplies). **Est:** 1887. **Sales:** $4,000,000 (2000). **Emp:** 30. **Officers:** Bob Webb, General Mgr.

■ **686** ■ **FirstMiss Fertilizer Inc.**
PO Box 1249
Jackson, MS 39215-1249
Phone: (601)948-7550
Products: Fertilizer. **SIC:** 5191 (Farm Supplies). **Officers:** Charles R. Gibson, President.

■ **687** ■ **Fiser Tractor and Equipment Co.**
9700 Hwy. 5 N
Alexander, AR 72002
Phone: (501)847-3677 **Fax:** (501)778-1052
Products: Trucks, tractors, mowers, riders and parts. **SIC:** 5083 (Farm & Garden Machinery). **Est:** 1992. **Sales:** $3,500,000 (2000). **Emp:** 28. **Officers:** J. Dee Fiser, President.

■ **688** ■ **Fisher Implement Co.**
PO Box 159
Albany, OR 97321
Phone: (541)926-1534
E-mail: info@fisherimplement.com
URL: http://www.fisherimplement.com
Products: Farm equipment, lawn and garden equipment, and commercial equipment. **SIC:** 5083 (Farm & Garden Machinery). **Est:** 1924. **Sales:** $50,000,000 (2000). **Emp:** 250. **Officers:** Jim Richards, President; Margo Collins, Controller.

■ **689** ■ **Fisher & Son Co. Inc.**
237 E King St.
Malvern, PA 19355
Phone: (215)644-3300
Products: Turf care supplies. **SIC:** 5191 (Farm Supplies).

■ **690** ■ **Fitzgerald Ltd.**
331 NE Mcwilliams Ct
Bremerton, WA 98311-2506
Phone: (360)792-1550 **Fax:** (360)479-8840
Products: Farm and garden machinery; Fresh fruits and vegetables; Grain and Field beans; Livestock; Farm supplies. **SICs:** 5191 (Farm Supplies); 5083 (Farm & Garden Machinery); 5148 (Fresh Fruits & Vegetables); 5153 (Grain & Field Beans); 5154 (Livestock). **Est:** 1990. **Sales:** $3,200,000 (2000). **Emp:** 1. **Officers:** Violette Fitzgerald, President, e-mail: violettefitz@home.com. **Former Name:** Noble Earth Inc.

■ **691** ■ **Five County Farmers Association**
PO Box 758
Clarksdale, MS 38614
Phone: (601)627-7301
Products: Farming supplies, including gasoline, fertilizer, feed, and tires. **SICs:** 5172 (Petroleum Products Nec); 5191 (Farm Supplies). **Est:** 1947. **Sales:** $6,200,000 (2000). **Emp:** 25. **Officers:** John Keesee, President; Scott Kraft, Finance Officer; J. Wayne Reed, General Mgr.

■ **692** ■ **Fleming Sales Company Inc.**
1020 W Fullerton Ave., Ste. B
Addison, IL 60101-4335
Phone: (630)627-4444 **Fax:** (312)627-7893
Products: Lawn and garden equipment; Safety equipment; Hardware. **SICs:** 5083 (Farm & Garden Machinery); 5063 (Electrical Apparatus & Equipment); 5072 (Hardware). **Est:** 1945. **Sales:** $3,000,000 (2000). **Emp:** 50. **Officers:** J.E. Grady, Chairman of the Board; Virginia Neubaur, Treasurer & Secty.

■ **693** ■ **Florida Seed Company Inc.**
4725 Lakeland Commerce Pkwy.
Lakeland, FL 33805
Phone: (863)669-1333 **Fax:** (863)669-1331
Products: Seed, fertilizer, and growth enhancement products. **SIC:** 5191 (Farm Supplies). **Est:** 1945. **Sales:** $16,000,000 (2000). **Emp:** 5. **Officers:** G. Allred, President; Scott Jernigan, VP & General Merchandising Mgr.

■ **694** ■ **Florie Corporation Turf Irrigation and Water Works Supply**
16012 N 32nd St.
Phoenix, AZ 85032
Phone: (602)867-2040
Products: Sprinkler systems. **SIC:** 5083 (Farm & Garden Machinery).

■ **695** ■ **Flusche Supply Inc.**
Hwy. 25 S
Electra, TX 76360
Phone: (940)495-2166
Products: Field supplies. **SIC:** 5191 (Farm Supplies). **Est:** 1955. **Sales:** $1,000,000 (2000). **Emp:** 25. **Officers:** Gene Flusche, President; John Prickett, CFO.

■ **696** ■ **Foley Equipment Co.**
1550 S West St.
Wichita, KS 67213
Phone: (316)943-4211 **Fax:** (316)943-5658
E-mail: getinfo@foleyeq.com
URL: http://www.foleyeq.com
Products: Tractors for farming and construction. **SICs:** 5082 (Construction & Mining Machinery); 5083 (Farm & Garden Machinery). **Est:** 1942. **Officers:** P.J. Foley Jr., Chairman of the Board; Ann Konecny, President & CEO; Bill Moody, VP of Sales; Gary Litzenberger, VP of Product Support; Gary Scott, Human Resources Contact. **Former Name:** Foley Tractor Company Inc.

■ **697** ■ **Keith Forbes Implement Supply Inc.**
4825 White Oak Ave. SE
Iowa City, IA 52240
Phone: (319)351-8341 **Fax:** (319)351-8341
Products: Farm equipment and supplies, including grains, seeds, cultivators, sprayers, chemicals, and fertilizers. **SICs:** 5191 (Farm Supplies); 5083 (Farm & Garden Machinery). **Est:** 1957. **Sales:** $2,500,000 (2000). **Emp:** 4. **Officers:** Keith Forbes, Owner.

■ **698** ■ **Forbes Seed & Grain**
PO Box 85
Junction City, OR 97448
Phone: (541)998-8086 **Fax:** (541)998-1091
E-mail: fsales@forbesinc.com
URL: http://www.forbesinc.com
Products: Grass and forage seeds. **SIC:** 5191 (Farm Supplies). **Est:** 1979. **Emp:** 30. **Officers:** Vaughn Forbes, Contact; Scott Ross, Sales/Marketing Contact, e-mail: scottr@forbesinc.com.

■ **699** ■ **C.D. Ford and Sons Inc.**
PO Box 300
Geneseo, IL 61254
Phone: (309)944-4661
Products: Lawn and garden products. **SIC:** 5191

(Farm Supplies). **Est:** 1935. **Sales:** $3,000,000 (2000). **Emp:** 20. **Officers:** Richard Ford, President; Jeff Ford, VP of Finance; Ronald Ford, Vice President.

■ **700** ■ **Foxhome Elevator Co.**
PO Box 69
Foxhome, MN 56543
Phone: (218)643-6079
Products: Agricultural equipment and supplies. **SIC:** 5191 (Farm Supplies). **Est:** 1973. **Sales:** $3,000,000 (2000). **Emp:** 5.

■ **701** ■ **Franklin County Grain Grower Inc.**
PO Box 32
Preston, ID 83263
Phone: (208)852-0384
Products: Grain; Barley; Feed. **SICs:** 5191 (Farm Supplies); 5153 (Grain & Field Beans). **Est:** 1934. **Sales:** $6,500,000 (2000). **Emp:** 22. **Officers:** B. Gamble, President; Lamont Doney, General Mgr.

■ **702** ■ **Franklin Farmers Cooperative**
PO Box 272
Decherd, TN 37324
Phone: (931)967-5511
Products: Farm supplies, including chemicals, fertilizers, and feed; Grain; Wheat; Corn. **SICs:** 5191 (Farm Supplies); 5153 (Grain & Field Beans). **Sales:** $10,000,000 (2000). **Emp:** 29. **Officers:** Ray Damron, CEO.

■ **703** ■ **Franklin Feed and Supply Co.**
1977 Philadelphia Ave.
Chambersburg, PA 17201
Phone: (717)264-6148
Products: Animal feed; Fertilizer; Chemicals. **SICs:** 5191 (Farm Supplies); 5172 (Petroleum Products Nec). **Est:** 1965. **Sales:** $5,000,000 (2000). **Emp:** 30. **Officers:** J. Wilbur Burkholder, President.

■ **704** ■ **Frederick Manufacturing Corp.**
4840 E 12th St.
Kansas City, MO 64127
Phone: (816)231-5007 **Fax:** (816)231-0178
URL: http://www.silverstreak.com
Products: Lawnmower blades; Power equipment parts and accessories. **SIC:** 5083 (Farm & Garden Machinery). **Est:** 1949. **Sales:** $35,000,000 (2000). **Emp:** 200. **Officers:** J. Lee, VP of Marketing; Kenneth R. Day, President.

■ **705** ■ **Fredericksburg Farmers Cooperative**
1905 Ivory Ave.
Waverly, IA 50677
Phone: (319)352-1354
Products: Feed, including corn, beans, and oats. **SICs:** 5153 (Grain & Field Beans); 5191 (Farm Supplies). **Est:** 1936. **Sales:** $10,000,000 (2000). **Emp:** 12. **Officers:** Rick Davis, General Mgr.; Tom Ludwig, Controller.

■ **706** ■ **Fremont Cooperative Produce Co.**
540 W Main St.
Fremont, MI 49412
Phone: (616)924-3851 **Fax:** (616)924-0121
Products: Cattle and swine feed; Grain; Fertilizer. **SICs:** 5191 (Farm Supplies); 5153 (Grain & Field Beans). **Est:** 1912. **Sales:** $7,000,000 (2000). **Emp:** 14. **Officers:** Marvin Witte, President; Steve Thatcher, General Mgr.

■ **707** ■ **French Implement Company Inc.**
PO Box 187
Charleston, MO 63834
Phone: (573)649-3021
Products: Tractors. **SIC:** 5083 (Farm & Garden Machinery). **Est:** 1945. **Sales:** $4,000,000 (2000). **Emp:** 25. **Officers:** Rene Dekriek, President; Dorothy Secoy, Secretary; Don French, Treasurer.

■ **708** ■ **Frenchman Valley Farmer's Cooperative**
143 Broadway Ave.
Imperial, NE 69033
Phone: (308)882-4381
Free: (800)538-2667 **Fax:** (308)882-3242
Products: Livestock and farm products. **SIC:** 5191 (Farm Supplies). **Sales:** $52,000,000 (2000). **Emp:** 130.

■ 709 ■ Frontier Hybrids
PO Box 177
Abernathy, TX 79311
Phone: (806)298-2595   Fax: (806)298-2116
Products: Garden and bedding plants; Grass seed;
Corn and wheat. SICs: 5191 (Farm Supplies); 5193
(Flowers & Florists' Supplies).

■ 710 ■ Frontier Inc.
PO Box 668
Wahpeton, ND 58074-0668
Phone: (701)642-6656
Products: Farm equipment; Truck boxes. SICs: 5083
(Farm & Garden Machinery); 5012 (Automobiles &
Other Motor Vehicles). Est: 1969. Sales: $800,000
(2000). Emp: 11. Officers: Jacob Gust, President;
William F. Sprung, Secretary; Douglas Hudson, CEO.

■ 711 ■ Frontier Inc.
730 Deere Dr.
New Richmond, WI 54017
Phone: (715)246-6565
Products: Tractors and lawn mowers. SIC: 5083
(Farm & Garden Machinery). Sales: $16,000,000
(1999). Emp: 52. Officers: Charles B. Polfus,
President; Carol Carlson, Contact; Greg Christenson,
Sales Mgr.

■ 712 ■ Frontier Inc.
PO Box 668
Wahpeton, ND 58074-0668
Phone: (701)642-6656
Products: Agricultural equipment and supplies. SIC:
5083 (Farm & Garden Machinery). Sales: $800,000
(2000). Emp: 11.

■ 713 ■ Frontier Inc. (New Richmond,
Wisconsin)
730 Deere Dr.
New Richmond, WI 54017
Phone: (715)246-6565
Products: Farming equipment. SIC: 5083 (Farm &
Garden Machinery). Sales: $10,000,000 (1993). Emp:
49. Officers: Carol Carlson, Bookkeeper.

■ 714 ■ Frontier Trading Inc.
PO Box 460
Roff, OK 74865
Phone: (580)456-7732
Free: (800)522-9310   Fax: (580)456-7309
Products: Grain, feed, seed, and fertilizer. SICs: 5153
(Grain & Field Beans); 5191 (Farm Supplies). Est:
1965. Sales: $30,000,000 (2000). Emp: 13. Officers:
Dub Tolliver, President; Dana Wyche.

■ 715 ■ Fruit Growers Supply Co.
14130 Riverside Dr.
Sherman Oaks, CA 91423
Phone: (818)986-6480   Fax: (818)783-1941
Products: Agricultural equipment and supplies for
citrus fruit orchards. SIC: 5191 (Farm Supplies). Est:
1907. Sales: $80,000,000 (2000). Emp: 200. Officers:
Timothy J. Lindgren, President; M.A. Ensey, VP of
Finance.

■ 716 ■ Fruita Consumers Cooperative
1650 Hwys. 6 & 50
Fruita, CO 81521
Phone: (970)858-3667   Fax: (970)858-9587
Products: Farm supplies, including fertilizer and feed;
Tires. SICs: 5191 (Farm Supplies); 5172 (Petroleum
Products Nec). Est: 1937. Sales: $10,500,000 (2000).
Emp: 34. Officers: Bill Mannel, President; Donal D.
Compton Jr., General Mgr.

■ 717 ■ F.S. Adams Inc.
PO Box 73
Paloma, IL 62359
Phone: (217)455-2811
Products: Agricultural chemicals, feeds and fertilizers.
SIC: 5191 (Farm Supplies). Sales: $16,000,000
(1993). Emp: 40. Officers: Lowell Tenhouse,
President; Mike Coulter, Comptroller.

■ 718 ■ FS Cooperative Inc.
PO Box 98
Amherst Junction, WI 54407
Phone: (715)824-3151
Products: Agricultural supplies. SIC: 5191 (Farm

Supplies). Est: 1969. Sales: $15,000,000 (2000).
Emp: 45. Officers: Ken Soda, President.

■ 719 ■ Full Circle, Inc.
PO Box 49
Madras, OR 97741
Phone: (541)475-2222   Fax: (541)475-6603
Products: Bluegrass seeds. SIC: 5191 (Farm
Supplies).

■ 720 ■ Galesberg Cooperative Elevator Co.
PO Box 115
Galesburg, ND 58035
Phone: (701)488-2216   Fax: (701)488-2280
Products: Farm products, including grain, feed,
fertilizer, and propane. SICs: 5153 (Grain & Field
Beans); 5191 (Farm Supplies); 5172 (Petroleum
Products Nec). Est: 1914. Sales: $25,000,000 (2000).
Emp: 15. Officers: Ron Flaten, CEO.

■ 721 ■ Garden Grove Nursery Inc.
PO Box 80889
Phoenix, AZ 85060
Phone: (602)942-7500
Products: Fertilizer for trees and grass. SIC: 5191
(Farm Supplies). Est: 1979. Sales: $2,000,000 (2000).
Emp: 35. Officers: James Ehmann, President.

■ 722 ■ Garden Grow Co
PO Box 280
Independence, OR 97351
Phone: (503)838-2811   Fax: (503)838-6805
Products: Garden products, including fertilizers,
manures and soil. SIC: 5191 (Farm Supplies).
Officers: Gary Pickett, CFO.

■ 723 ■ Garden Valley Coop.
PO Box 38
Waumandee, WI 54622
Phone: (608)626-2111
Free: (800)637-9846   Fax: (608)626-2101
Products: Feed. SIC: 5191 (Farm Supplies). Est:
1904. Sales: $4,000,000 (2000). Emp: 13. Officers:
Terry Radsek, General Mgr.

■ 724 ■ Gardner Distributing Co.
6840 Trade Center Ave.
Billings, MT 59101
Phone: (406)656-5000
Free: (800)742-8811   Fax: (406)656-9817
Products: Lawn and garden equipment; Pet supplies.
SICs: 5083 (Farm & Garden Machinery); 5199
(Nondurable Goods Nec). Est: 1980. Sales:
$14,000,000 (2000). Emp: 38. Officers: Gardner
Tonigan, CEO, e-mail: gardner@imt.net; Rob
Chouinard, President, e-mail: robc@imt.net.

■ 725 ■ Gardner Inc.
1150 Chesapeake Ave.
Columbus, OH 43212
Phone: (614)488-7951   Fax: (614)486-7122
Products: Lawn mower parts; Engines for small
outdoor equipment; Gasoline. SICs: 5084 (Industrial
Machinery & Equipment); 5084 (Industrial Machinery &
Equipment); 5172 (Petroleum Products Nec). Est:
1944. Sales: $15,000,000 (2000). Emp: 50. Officers:
J.F. Finn, President; P. Erickson, CFO; D. Thornton,
General Mgr.

■ 726 ■ Garroutte Products
Bldg No. 5 Darrschool, Box 2930
Ponca City, OK 74602
Phone: (580)767-1622   Fax: (580)767-1750
Products: Strap goods for horses, including bridles,
brass collars, and reins. SIC: 5191 (Farm Supplies).
Emp: 49. Officers: R. D. Garroutte.

■ 727 ■ Garton Ford Tractor Inc.
PO Box 1849
Turlock, CA 95381
Phone: (209)632-3931   Fax: (209)632-8006
Products: Tractors. SIC: 5083 (Farm & Garden
Machinery). Est: 1957. Sales: $16,000,000 (2000).
Emp: 45. Officers: William L. Garton, President; John
M. Simone, Controller.

■ 728 ■ Gaston Sealey Company Inc.
PO Box 428
Fairmont, NC 28340
Phone: (919)628-6761
Free: (800)542-9012   Fax: (919)628-5807
Products: Tractor equipment. SIC: 5083 (Farm &
Garden Machinery). Est: 1951. Sales: $3,000,000
(2000). Emp: 10. Officers: WAde Sealey, President;
Velvet Hardin, Vice President; Fitzhugh Sealy, Vice
President.

■ 729 ■ Gateway Seed Co.
510 Bittner St.
St. Louis, MO 63147
Phone: (314)381-8500   Fax: (314)381-9361
E-mail: gatewaysd@aol.com
Products: Lawn and garden equipment; Household
supplies; Sporting and athletic goods. SICs: 5083
(Farm & Garden Machinery); 5023 (Homefurnishings);
5091 (Sporting & Recreational Goods). Est: 1963.
Emp: 30. Officers: Lloyd G. Rupp, President; Daniel
G. Rupp, Vice President; Stephen Rupp, Treasurer &
Secty.

■ 730 ■ Thomas E. Geddie
314 Faulk St.
Athens, TX 75751
Phone: (903)675-2424
Products: Farming supplies. SIC: 5191 (Farm
Supplies). Est: 1955. Sales: $900,000 (2000). Emp: 4.
Officers: Thomas E. Geddie, Owner.

■ 731 ■ Gehman Feed Mill Inc.
44 N 3rd St.
Denver, PA 17517
Phone: (215)267-5585
Products: Prepared animal feeds. SIC: 5191 (Farm
Supplies). Est: 1947. Sales: $14,000,000 (2000).
Emp: 35. Officers: Samuel Beanesderfer, President.

■ 732 ■ Gem Equipment Inc.
PO Box 149
Twin Falls, ID 83303-0149
Phone: (208)733-7272   Fax: (208)733-7290
Products: Farm, lawn, and garden equipment. SIC:
5083 (Farm & Garden Machinery). Est: 1979. Sales:
$8,000,000 (2000). Emp: 35. Officers: A. Avalos,
General Mgr.; Tim Norris, Controller; Larry Walden,
Sales Mgr.

■ 733 ■ Geneva Elevator Co.
PO Box 49
Geneva, IA 50633
Phone: (515)458-8145   Fax: (515)458-8254
E-mail: genev@iowaconnect.com
Products: Grain; Feed; Fertilizer; Farming chemicals.
SICs: 5153 (Grain & Field Beans); 5191 (Farm
Supplies). Est: 1988. Sales: $22,000,000 (2000).
Emp: 7. Officers: David Decker, General Mgr.

■ 734 ■ George H. International Corp.
5705 W Fort St.
Detroit, MI 48209
Phone: (313)842-6100   Fax: (313)842-7800
Products: Farm equipment and machinery; Chemicals;
Groceries; Industrial machinery; Architectural float
glass; Metal strapping for packaging. SICs: 5083 (Farm
& Garden Machinery); 5169 (Chemicals & Allied
Products Nec); 5141 (Groceries—General Line); 5084
(Industrial Machinery & Equipment). Officers: Rajan N.
George, President.

■ 735 ■ L.E. German Implement Co.
624 W Spring St.
Princeville, IL 61559
Phone: (309)385-4316   Fax: (309)385-2540
Products: Tractors, mowers, and riders; Construction
equipment, including backhoes and excavators. SICs:
5083 (Farm & Garden Machinery); 5084 (Industrial
Machinery & Equipment). Est: 1940. Sales:
$8,000,000 (1999). Emp: 25. Officers: C.L. German,
President.

■ 736 ■ German's Outdoor Power Equipment
624 W Spring St.
Box 218
Princeville, IL 61559
Phone: (309)694-3700   Fax: (309)385-2540
Products: Lawn and garden equipment, including

mowers, tractors, trimmers, and hand tools. **SIC:** 5083 (Farm & Garden Machinery).

■ **737** ■ **Gettel and Co.**
91 N Caseville Rd.
Pigeon, MI 48755
Phone: (517)453-3332
Products: Lawn and garden equipment parts; Agricultural equipment parts. **SIC:** 5083 (Farm & Garden Machinery). **Est:** 1950. **Sales:** $8,000,000 (2000). **Emp:** 20. **Officers:** Kent Gettel, President; Mark Gettel, Dir. of Marketing.

■ **738** ■ **Gibson Farmers Cooperative**
PO Box 497
Trenton, TN 38382
Phone: (901)855-1891
Products: Farm equipment and supplies, including chemicals, feed, and fertilizer. **SIC:** 5191 (Farm Supplies). **Sales:** $13,000,000 (2000). **Emp:** 50. **Officers:** Larry Cochran, CEO & Treasurer.

■ **739** ■ **A.L. Gilbert Co.**
PO Box 38
Oakdale, CA 95361
Phone: (209)847-1721
Free: (800)847-1721 **Fax:** (209)847-3542
Products: Custom feed for deer and cattle. **SIC:** 5191 (Farm Supplies). **Est:** 1892. **Sales:** $100,000,000 (2000). **Emp:** 250. **Officers:** Robert T. Gilbert, President; Jack Ulrich, Controller.

■ **740** ■ **Giles Farmers Cooperative Inc.**
PO Box 295
Pulaski, TN 38478
Phone: (931)363-2563
Products: Feed; Lawn mowers. **SICs:** 5191 (Farm Supplies); 5083 (Farm & Garden Machinery). **Sales:** $6,000,000 (2000). **Emp:** 20. **Officers:** Dickson Marks, President; Joe Christopher, Treasurer & Secty.

■ **741** ■ **Glade and Grove Supply Inc.**
PO Drawer 760
Belle Glade, FL 33430
Phone: (561)996-3095
Products: Farm equipment. **SIC:** 5083 (Farm & Garden Machinery).

■ **742** ■ **Glasgow Cooperative Association**
102 2nd St.
Glasgow, MO 65254
Phone: (816)338-2251
Products: Farming supplies, including feed, fertilizers, chemicals, and seed. **SICs:** 5153 (Grain & Field Beans); 5191 (Farm Supplies). **Est:** 1923. **Sales:** $15,000,000 (2000). **Emp:** 30. **Officers:** Leon Hammon, President; Ken Brink, Manager.

■ **743** ■ **Globe Seed and Feed Company Inc.**
PO Box 445
Twin Falls, ID 83303
Phone: (208)733-1373 **Fax:** (208)733-4484
Products: Agricultural equipment and supplies. **SIC:** 5191 (Farm Supplies). **Sales:** $3,000,000 (2000). **Emp:** 20.

■ **744** ■ **Gold-Eagle Cooperative**
PO Box 280
Goldfield, IA 50542-0280
Phone: (515)825-3161 **Fax:** (515)825-3732
Products: Grain and fertilizers; Chemicals. **SICs:** 5153 (Grain & Field Beans); 5191 (Farm Supplies). **Est:** 1906. **Sales:** $36,000,000 (2000). **Emp:** 60. **Officers:** Brad Davis, General Mgr.; John Stelzer, Controller.

■ **745** ■ **Golden Spike Equipment Co.**
1352 W Main St.
Tremonton, UT 84337
Phone: (435)257-5346
Products: Tractors. **SIC:** 5083 (Farm & Garden Machinery). **Est:** 1947. **Sales:** $4,000,000 (2000). **Emp:** 10. **Officers:** John D. Fronk, President.

■ **746** ■ **Golden Sun Feeds Inc. Danville Div.**
621 485th Ave.
Searsboro, IA 50242
Products: Animal feed. **SIC:** 5191 (Farm Supplies). **Sales:** $11,000,000 (2000). **Emp:** 35. **Officers:** Orlynn Harms, Manager.

■ **747** ■ **Goldmar Sales Corp.**
Box 6398
Baltimore, MD 21230
Phone: (410)727-3922 **Fax:** (410)244-8633
Products: Grass seed. **SIC:** 5159 (Farm-Product Raw Materials Nec). **Est:** 1962. **Emp:** 30. **Officers:** Aaron Goldberg, President, e-mail: yas97@juno.com.

■ **748** ■ **Goldthwaites of Texas, Inc.**
6000 N O'Connor Blvd.
Irving, TX 75039
Phone: (972)910-0764 **Fax:** (972)910-0765
Products: Lawn mowers; Irrigation equipment. **SIC:** 5083 (Farm & Garden Machinery).

■ **749** ■ **Goldthwaites of Texas Inc.**
1401 Foch St.
Ft. Worth, TX 76101
Phone: (817)332-1521 **Fax:** (817)334-7924
Products: Lawn mowers. **SIC:** 5083 (Farm & Garden Machinery).

■ **750** ■ **Gooding Seed Co.**
PO Box 57
Gooding, ID 83330
Phone: (208)934-8441 **Fax:** (208)934-8584
Products: Seed; Fertilizer. **SICs:** 5191 (Farm Supplies); 5153 (Grain & Field Beans).

■ **751** ■ **Graco Fertilizer Co.**
PO Box 89
Cairo, GA 31728
Phone: (912)377-1602
Products: Farm supplies, including fertilizer and potting soil. **SIC:** 5191 (Farm Supplies). **Est:** 1953. **Sales:** $4,000,000 (2000). **Emp:** 25. **Officers:** Ken Legette, President; Steve Moye, Comptroller.

■ **752** ■ **Graico International**
5062 W Plano Pwky., No. 300
Plano, TX 75093-4409
Phone: (972)931-7272 **Fax:** (972)931-7274
Products: Cotton machinery and parts. **SIC:** 5083 (Farm & Garden Machinery). **Officers:** Al Martinez, President.

■ **753** ■ **Grain Processing Corp.**
1600 Oregon St.
Muscatine, IA 52761
Phone: (319)264-4265
Free: (800)448-4472 **Fax:** (319)264-4289
E-mail: sales@grainprocessing.com
URL: http://www.grainprocessing.com
Products: Maltodextrins; Corn syrup solids; Ethyl alcohol; Starches; Animal feed ingredients. **SIC:** 5191 (Farm Supplies). **Est:** 1953. **Officers:** G. A. Kent, President; J. T. Kautz, Chairman of the Board; Diane Rieke, Sales/Marketing Contact; Mike Shield, Customer Service Contact.

■ **754** ■ **Grain Storage Corp.**
Monroe & 2nd St.
Sturgis, KY 42459
Phone: (502)333-5506 **Fax:** (502)333-5505
Products: Fertilizer; Field seeds; Feed. **SIC:** 5191 (Farm Supplies). **Est:** 1974. **Sales:** $800,000 (2000). **Emp:** 8. **Officers:** Dennis O'Nan, President.

■ **755** ■ **Grand Forks Equipment Inc.**
5101 Gateway Dr.
Grand Forks, ND 58203
Phone: (701)746-4436 **Fax:** (701)780-9550
E-mail: gfequip@aol.com
Products: Farm equipment. **SIC:** 5083 (Farm & Garden Machinery). **Est:** 1986. **Sales:** $8,000,000 (1999). **Emp:** 28. **Officers:** Greg Christenson, President.

■ **756** ■ **Grand River Cooperative Inc.**
225 John St.
Markesan, WI 53946
Phone: (920)398-2301
Free: (800)472-5516 **Fax:** (920)398-2101
Products: Farming supplies. **SIC:** 5191 (Farm Supplies). **Est:** 1934. **Sales:** $7,500,000 (2000). **Emp:** 34. **Officers:** David Dillie, President; Linda Triemstra, Office Mgr.; Brad Gjermo, General Mgr.

■ **757** ■ **Grange Supply Company Inc.**
NW 355 State St.
Pullman, WA 99163
Phone: (509)332-2511
Products: Hardware; Feed; Chemicals. **SICs:** 5191 (Farm Supplies); 5072 (Hardware); 5169 (Chemicals & Allied Products Nec). **Est:** 1932. **Sales:** $4,500,000 (2000). **Emp:** 25. **Officers:** Dan Druffel, President; Randy Sexton, General Mgr.

■ **758** ■ **Granite Seed**
1697 West 2100 North
Lehi, UT 84043
Phone: (801)768-4422 **Fax:** (801)768-3967
E-mail: don@graniteseed.com
URL: http://www.graniteseed.com
Products: Seed for turf, grass, and wildflowers; Shrubs; Erosion control products. **SICs:** 5191 (Farm Supplies); 5193 (Flowers & Florists' Supplies).

■ **759** ■ **Grassland Equipment**
892-898 Troy-Schenectady Rd.
Latham, NY 12110
Phone: (518)785-5841 **Fax:** (518)785-5740
URL: http://www.grasslandcorp.com
Products: Lawn, garden, and irrigation equipment; Power equipment; Turf and garden machinery and supplies; Irrigation systems. **SIC:** 5083 (Farm & Garden Machinery). **Est:** 1961. **Sales:** $21,000,000 (2000). **Emp:** 72. **Officers:** Horst Pogge, Chairman of the Board; Hans J. Pogge, Secretary; Kirk H. Pogge, President.

■ **760** ■ **Grassland West**
908 Port Dr.
Clarkston, WA 99403-1845
Phone: (509)758-9100 **Fax:** (509)758-6601
Products: Seed. **SIC:** 5191 (Farm Supplies).

■ **761** ■ **Graymont Cooperative Association Inc.**
PO Box 98
Graymont, IL 61743
Phone: (815)743-5321 **Fax:** (815)743-5759
Products: Grain; Lumber; Feed; Fertilizer. **SICs:** 5153 (Grain & Field Beans); 5191 (Farm Supplies). **Est:** 1904. **Sales:** $15,000,000 (2000). **Emp:** 20. **Officers:** B. Roeschley, President; Alan Zehr, General Mgr.

■ **762** ■ **Green/Line Equipment Inc.**
John Deere Rd.
Farina, IL 62838
Phone: (618)245-6591
Products: Lawn and farm tractors. **SIC:** 5083 (Farm & Garden Machinery). **Est:** 1982. **Sales:** $3,000,000 (2000). **Emp:** 12. **Officers:** Robert Venturi, President; William Anderson, Treasurer & Secty.

■ **763** ■ **Green Mountain Tractor Inc.**
PO Box 229
Middlebury, VT 05753
Phone: (802)388-4951 **Fax:** (802)388-7807
Products: Agricultural tractors. **SIC:** 5083 (Farm & Garden Machinery). **Est:** 1945. **Sales:** $3,000,000 (2000). **Emp:** 12. **Officers:** Reginald Bishop, President & Treasurer.

■ **764** ■ **Green Seed Co.**
1730 NE Expy.
Atlanta, GA 30329
Phone: (404)633-2778 **Fax:** (404)633-1493
Products: Seeds, including grass, tomato, and cucumber. **SIC:** 5191 (Farm Supplies). **Est:** 1934. **Sales:** $34,000,000 (2000). **Emp:** 200. **Officers:** L.A. Green III, President; T.L. Little, Treasurer & Secty.

■ **765** ■ **Green Valley Seed**
PO Box 185
Canfield, OH 44406
Phone: (330)533-4353 **Fax:** (330)533-0618
E-mail: grasseed4u@aol.com
URL: http://www.greenvalleyseed.com
Products: Grass seed; Fertilizer; Erosion control products. **SIC:** 5191 (Farm Supplies). **Est:** 1966. **Sales:** $1,400,000 (1999). **Emp:** 7. **Officers:** Jeffrey L. Hum, President; William A. Bieber, Vice President.
Former Name: Green Valley Turf Farms.

■ 766 ■ Green Velvet Sod Farms
3640 Upper Bellbrook Rd.
Bellbrook, OH 45305
Phone: (937)848-2501 **Fax:** (937)376-1153
Products: Sod and fertilizer. **SIC:** 5191 (Farm Supplies).

■ 767 ■ Greene Farmers Cooperative
PO Box 430
Greeneville, TN 37744
Phone: (423)638-8101
Products: Chemicals and fertilizer; Feed; Tires. **SICs:** 5191 (Farm Supplies); 5014 (Tires & Tubes). **Est:** 1945. **Sales:** $10,000,000 (2000). **Emp:** 46. **Officers:** George Clamer, President; D. Otten, Treasurer & Secty.

■ 768 ■ Gries Seed Farms Inc.
2348 N 5th St.
Fremont, OH 43420
Phone: (419)332-5571
Free: (800)472-4797 **Fax:** (419)332-1817
E-mail: gsfeed@ezworks.net
Products: Field seed. **SIC:** 5191 (Farm Supplies). **Est:** 1935. **Sales:** $7,000,000 (2000). **Emp:** 30. **Officers:** B.J. Gries, President; Ed Thurn, General Mgr.

■ 769 ■ Grossenburg Implement Inc.
HC 59, Box 1
Winner, SD 57580
Phone: (605)842-2040 **Fax:** (605)842-3485
E-mail: grossenburgs@gwtc.net
URL: http://www.grossenburg.com
Products: Farm equipment. **SIC:** 5083 (Farm & Garden Machinery). **Est:** 1937. **Sales:** $18,000,000 (2000). **Emp:** 55. **Officers:** Barry Grossenburg, President; Blanche Grossenburg, Treasurer & Secty.; Barry Grossenberg, Vice President.

■ 770 ■ Leland Grosz
PO Box 472
Garrison, ND 58540-0152
Phone: (701)337-5438
Products: Tractor salvage; Farm supplies. **SICs:** 5191 (Farm Supplies); 5083 (Farm & Garden Machinery). **Officers:** Leland Grosz, Owner.

■ 771 ■ Grove City Farmers Exchange Co.
3937 Broadway
Grove City, OH 43123
Phone: (614)875-6311 **Fax:** (614)875-5140
Products: Feed, including cattle; Lumber. **SICs:** 5191 (Farm Supplies); 5031 (Lumber, Plywood & Millwork). **Est:** 1920. **Sales:** $13,000,000 (2000). **Emp:** 25. **Officers:** David Cohli, President.

■ 772 ■ Growers Cooperative Inc.
PO Box 2196
Terre Haute, IN 47802
Phone: (812)235-8123
Products: Grain; Chemical preparations; Feed. **SICs:** 5153 (Grain & Field Beans); 5169 (Chemicals & Allied Products Nec); 5191 (Farm Supplies). **Est:** 1930. **Sales:** $63,000,000 (2000). **Emp:** 95. **Officers:** Keith C. Bowers, Exec. VP; Jerry Potrawski, Controller.

■ 773 ■ Growers Fertilizer Corp.
PO Box 1407
Lake Alfred, FL 33850
Phone: (813)956-1101
Products: Yard fertilizers. **SIC:** 5191 (Farm Supplies). **Est:** 1934. **Sales:** $15,000,000 (2000). **Emp:** 50. **Officers:** Don K. Webb, General Mgr.; Douglas Bailey, Controller.

■ 774 ■ Growers Ford Tractor Co.
8501 NW 58th St.
Miami, FL 33166
Phone: (305)592-7890
Free: (800)592-7890 **Fax:** (305)477-1659
Products: Tractor implements. **SIC:** 5083 (Farm & Garden Machinery). **Est:** 1950. **Sales:** $9,000,000 (2000). **Emp:** 40. **Officers:** N. Horacio Lopez, President; Martin Lopez, VP of Finance.

■ 775 ■ Growmark
1701 Towanda Ave.
Bloomington, IL 61701
Phone: (309)557-6000 **Fax:** (309)829-8532
URL: http://www.fsstystem.com
Products: Agronomic goods and services, including precision farming, plant food, seed, fuels, lubricants, buildings, grain systems, grain handling equipment; grain merchandising. **SICs:** 5191 (Farm Supplies); 5154 (Livestock); 5171 (Petroleum Bulk Stations & Terminals); 5193 (Flowers & Florists' Supplies). **Est:** 1927. **Sales:** $1,160,000 (1999). **Emp:** 20. **Officers:** Bill Davison, CEO; Dave Striegel, Sales/Marketing Contact; Dennis Farmer, Customer Service Contact; Gary Swango, Human Resources Contact.

■ 776 ■ Growmark
PO Box 2500
Bloomington, IL 61702-2500
Phone: (217)423-9738 **Fax:** (217)423-9819
Products: Farm equipment and goods, including livestock, feed, petroleum, plant food, and seed. **SICs:** 5191 (Farm Supplies); 5154 (Livestock); 5171 (Petroleum Bulk Stations & Terminals); 5193 (Flowers & Florists' Supplies).

■ 777 ■ Gulbranson Equipment Inc.
Rte. 2
Park Rapids, MN 56470
Phone: (218)732-9744 **Fax:** (218)732-9745
Products: Farm supplies; Lawn and garden equipment; Sporting and athletic goods. **SICs:** 5083 (Farm & Garden Machinery); 5091 (Sporting & Recreational Goods). **Sales:** $2,500,000 (2000). **Emp:** 20. **Officers:** Kieth Gulbranson, President; M. Gulbranson, Treasurer.

■ 778 ■ Gully Tri-Coop Association
PO Box 29
Gully, MN 56646
Phone: (218)268-4185 **Fax:** (218)268-4181
Products: Grain; Feed; Fuel; Chemicals; Fertilizers; Animal health care products. **SICs:** 5191 (Farm Supplies); 5199 (Nondurable Goods Nec); 5153 (Grain & Field Beans). **Est:** 1946. **Sales:** $2,000,000 (2000). **Emp:** 16. **Officers:** G. Rinde, Manager.

■ 779 ■ HAACO Inc.
PO Box 7190
Madison, WI 53707
Phone: (608)221-6200
Products: Rodenticides. **SIC:** 5191 (Farm Supplies). **Sales:** $13,400,000 (2000). **Emp:** 40.

■ 780 ■ Hagan & Stone Wholesale
Hwy. 163 N
PO Box 158
Tompkinsville, KY 42167-0158
Phone: (270)487-6138
Free: (800)626-0202 **Fax:** (270)487-9124
E-mail: diamante@scrtc.com
Products: Fencing; Metal roofing; Nails and screws; Rebars; Concrete mesh. **SICs:** 5083 (Farm & Garden Machinery); 5082 (Construction & Mining Machinery). **Est:** 1954. **Sales:** $8,000,000 (1999). **Emp:** 36. **Officers:** Stephen R. Hagar; Anthony Poland, Sales/Marketing Contact; Terry Wells, Customer Service Contact; Brian Hammer, Human Resources Contact.

■ 781 ■ Hale Center Wheat Growers Inc.
PO Drawer F
Hale Center, TX 79041
Phone: (806)839-2426 **Fax:** (806)839-2136
Products: Grain, feed, and fertilizer. **SICs:** 5153 (Grain & Field Beans); 5191 (Farm Supplies). **Est:** 1934. **Sales:** $14,400,000 (2000). **Emp:** 10. **Officers:** Arden Davis, President; Douglas Adams, Mgr. of Finance.

■ 782 ■ H.H. Halferty and Sons Inc.
PO Box 298
Smithville, MO 64089
Phone: (816)532-0221
Products: Tractors. **SIC:** 5083 (Farm & Garden Machinery). **Est:** 1936. **Sales:** $6,000,000 (2000). **Emp:** 20. **Officers:** Walter Halferty, CEO.

■ 783 ■ Halsey Seed Co.
2059 State Rt. 96
Trumansburg, NY 14886-9129
Phone: (607)387-7303 **Free:** (800)892-3049
Products: Alfalfa, field seeds, and turf seeds. **SIC:** 5191 (Farm Supplies). **Sales:** $10,100,000 (2000). **Emp:** 41.

■ 784 ■ Hamilton County Farm Bureau
PO Box 1106
Noblesville, IN 46060
Phone: (317)773-0870
Products: Agricultural products, including grain, propane, fuel, and feed. **SICs:** 5153 (Grain & Field Beans); 5191 (Farm Supplies). **Sales:** $10,000,000 (2000). **Emp:** 34. **Officers:** Jim Crouch, General Mgr.

■ 785 ■ Hamilton Equipment Inc.
567 S Reading Rd.
Ephrata, PA 17522
Phone: (717)733-7951
Products: Farm machinery, including light industrial equipment, backhoes, front-end loaders, lawn, and garden equipment. **SICs:** 5083 (Farm & Garden Machinery); 5198 (Paints, Varnishes & Supplies). **Est:** 1935. **Sales:** $15,000,000 (2000). **Emp:** 70. **Officers:** Robert J. Hamilton Jr., President; George W. Boyer, Controller.

■ 786 ■ Hanley Company Inc.
641 W Main St.
Sun Prairie, WI 53590
Phone: (608)837-5111 **Fax:** (608)837-0818
Products: Agricultural and hardware pipes, pipe fittings, and compressors. **SIC:** 5083 (Farm & Garden Machinery). **Est:** 1928. **Sales:** $12,000,000 (2000). **Emp:** 55. **Officers:** Tom Hanley, President.

■ 787 ■ Hansen and Peterson Inc.
PO Box 345
Burlington, WA 98233
Phone: (206)755-9011
Products: Feed. **SIC:** 5191 (Farm Supplies). **Est:** 1947. **Sales:** $600,000 (2000). **Emp:** 3. **Officers:** David L. Hansen, President.

■ 788 ■ Hansmeier and Son Inc.
Main St.
Bristol, SD 57219
Phone: (605)492-3611 **Fax:** (605)492-3585
Products: Seeds. **SICs:** 5153 (Grain & Field Beans); 5191 (Farm Supplies). **Est:** 1960. **Sales:** $5,000,000 (2000). **Emp:** 25. **Officers:** Floyd Hansmeier, President.

■ 789 ■ Harcourt Equipment
PO Box 115
Harcourt, IA 50544
Phone: (515)354-5331
Products: Tractors; Lawn mowers. **SIC:** 5083 (Farm & Garden Machinery). **Est:** 1984. **Sales:** $9,000,000 (2000). **Emp:** 24. **Officers:** Joe Powers, President.

■ 790 ■ Hardeman Fayette Farmers Cooperative
PO Box 277
Somerville, TN 38068
Phone: (901)465-3655 **Fax:** (901)465-3491
Products: Farm supplies, including feed, gasoline, diesel fuel, chemicals, and fertilizers; Grain, including wheat and milo. **SICs:** 5191 (Farm Supplies); 5172 (Petroleum Products Nec); 5153 (Grain & Field Beans). **Est:** 1943. **Sales:** $9,000,000 (2000). **Emp:** 12. **Officers:** Charles Dacus Jr., CEO; James R. Barber, General Mgr.; Wayne Thomas, Vice President.

■ 791 ■ Harmony Agri Services
25 2nd St. NE
Harmony, MN 55939
Phone: (507)886-6062 **Fax:** (507)886-6092
Products: Feed. **SICs:** 5153 (Grain & Field Beans); 5191 (Farm Supplies). **Est:** 1895. **Sales:** $12,000,000 (2000). **Emp:** 25. **Officers:** Jeffrey A. Soma, President; Michael Wolsted, Vice President; Mike Cox, Dir. of Marketing & Sales.

■ 792 ■ Harmony Country Cooperatives
PO Box 407
Colby, WI 54421
Phone: (715)223-2306 **Fax:** (715)223-4526
Products: Feed; Fertilizer; Hardware; Petroleum.
SICs: 5191 (Farm Supplies); 5172 (Petroleum Products Nec); 5072 (Hardware). **Est:** 1915. **Sales:** $18,500,000 (2000). **Emp:** 65. **Officers:** Ronald Schmidt, President; Arleen Christophersen; James Hager, General Mgr.

■ 793 ■ Harnack Co.
6015 S Main St.
Cedar Falls, IA 50613
Phone: (319)277-0660 **Fax:** (319)277-2275
Products: Agricultural equipment and supplies. **SIC:** 5083 (Farm & Garden Machinery). **Est:** 1953. **Sales:** $10,000,000 (2000). **Emp:** 12.

■ 794 ■ Harney County Farm Supply Co.
53 E Industrial St.
Burns, OR 97720
Phone: (541)573-2031
Products: Agricultural supplies. **SIC:** 5083 (Farm & Garden Machinery). **Est:** 1950. **Sales:** $4,000,000 (2000). **Emp:** 15. **Officers:** Gail McAllister, President; J.W. McAllister, CFO; CFO.

■ 795 ■ Harrold Engineering Group
PO Box 385
Manhattan, KS 66502
Phone: (785)776-0550 **Fax:** (785)776-0563
Products: Farm machinery and equipment. **SIC:** 5083 (Farm & Garden Machinery). **Officers:** Eugene H. Knutson, President.

■ 796 ■ Charles C. Hart Seed Co.
PO Box 9169
Wethersfield, CT 06129-0169
Phone: (860)529-2537
Free: (800)326-HART **Fax:** (860)563-7221
E-mail: hartseed@juno.com
URL: http://www.hartseed.com
Products: Seeds, including lawn seed. **SICs:** 5191 (Farm Supplies); 5169 (Chemicals & Allied Products Nec). **Est:** 1892. **Sales:** $5,000,000 (1999). **Emp:** 24. **Officers:** Charles H. Hart, President.

■ 797 ■ Harvest Land Cooperative Inc.
PO Box 516
Richmond, IN 47375
Phone: (765)962-1527
Products: Agricultural supplies. **SIC:** 5191 (Farm Supplies). **Sales:** $50,000,000 (2000). **Emp:** 150. **Officers:** Marlin Larsen, CEO; Norman Goode, Controller.

■ 798 ■ Harvest States Cooperatives. Canton Div.
PO Box 236
Canton, SD 57013
Phone: (605)987-2791 **Fax:** (605)987-5437
Products: Fertilizer and fertilizer materials; Grain; Feed; Field, garden, and flower seeds. **SICs:** 5153 (Grain & Field Beans); 5191 (Farm Supplies). **Sales:** $35,000,000 (2000). **Emp:** 16. **Officers:** Craig Larson, General Mgr.

■ 799 ■ Tom Hassenfritz Equipment Co.
1300 W Washington
Mt. Pleasant, IA 52641
Phone: (319)385-3114
Free: (800)634-4885 **Fax:** (319)385-3731
E-mail: thecompa@interl.net
Products: Lawn and garden equipment; Industrial engines. **SIC:** 5083 (Farm & Garden Machinery). **Est:** 1958. **Sales:** $6,000,000 (2000). **Emp:** 17. **Officers:** T. Hassenfritz, President.

■ 800 ■ Tom Hassenfritz Equipment Co.
1300 W Washington
Mt. Pleasant, IA 52641
Phone: (319)385-3114
Free: (800)634-4885 **Fax:** (319)385-3731
Products: Agricultural equipment and supplies. **SIC:** 5083 (Farm & Garden Machinery). **Sales:** $6,000,000 (2000). **Emp:** 17.

■ 801 ■ H.F. Hauff Co.
1801 Presson Pl.
Yakima, WA 98903
Phone: (509)248-0318 **Fax:** (509)248-0914
Products: Agricultural sprayers and wind machines.
SIC: 5083 (Farm & Garden Machinery). **Est:** 1964.
Sales: $3,000,000 (2000). **Emp:** 10. **Officers:** H.F. Hauff, Owner.

■ 802 ■ Hawkeye Seed Company Inc.
900 2nd St. SE
Cedar Rapids, IA 52401
Phone: (319)364-7118
Products: Garden and pet supplies. **SICs:** 5191 (Farm Supplies); 5149 (Groceries & Related Products Nec). **Sales:** $25,000,000 (1999). **Emp:** 40. **Officers:** Howard L. Dubishar, President; Ronald Rimrodt, Treasurer & Secty.

■ 803 ■ Hawthorne Machinery Inc. Hawthorne Power Systems Div.
PO Box 708
San Diego, CA 92112
Phone: (619)674-7000 **Fax:** (619)278-8564
Products: Heavy farm equipment; Earth moving equipment. **SICs:** 5084 (Industrial Machinery & Equipment); 5083 (Farm & Garden Machinery). **Est:** 1956. **Sales:** $26,000,000 (2000). **Emp:** 90. **Officers:** Tom J. Hawthorne, CEO; Phil Nerhood, VP & Treasurer; John Quirin, Dir of Human Resources.

■ 804 ■ Hayward Cooperative
PO Box 337
Hayward, MN 56043
Phone: (507)373-6439
Products: Feed, fertilizer, grain, and chemicals. **SICs:** 5153 (Grain & Field Beans); 5191 (Farm Supplies). **Est:** 1911. **Sales:** $4,000,000 (2000). **Emp:** 10. **Officers:** Wayne Kromminga, General Mgr.; Bob Wittmer, Manager.

■ 805 ■ Heart of Iowa Cooperative
229 E Ash St.
Roland, IA 50236
Phone: (515)388-4341 **Fax:** (515)388-4657
URL: http://www.hoic.com
Products: Grain; Feed; Seed; Fertilizer; Chemicals; Petroleum. **SICs:** 5153 (Grain & Field Beans); 5169 (Chemicals & Allied Products Nec). **Est:** 1937. **Sales:** $57,000,000 (2000). **Emp:** 63. **Officers:** Jim Penney, General Mgr.

■ 806 ■ Heart Seed
PO Box 313
Fairfield, WA 99012
Phone: (509)283-2322
Products: Lawn seed. **SIC:** 5191 (Farm Supplies).

■ 807 ■ Heartland Co-op
2829 Westown Pkwy., No. 350
West Des Moines, IA 50266
Phone: (515)225-1334
Free: (800)513-3938 **Fax:** (515)225-8511
Products: Grain, including soy beans and corn; Chemicals; Fertilizers. **SICs:** 5153 (Grain & Field Beans); 5191 (Farm Supplies). **Est:** 1919. **Sales:** $140,000,000 (2000). **Emp:** 150. **Officers:** Larry Petersen, General Mgr.; Terry Frahm, Controller.

■ 808 ■ Heartland Cooperative Inc.
PO Box 432
Crawfordsville, IN 47933
Phone: (317)362-6700
Products: Agricultural supplies, including grain, fuel, and fertilizer. **SICs:** 5191 (Farm Supplies); 5153 (Grain & Field Beans). **Sales:** $48,000,000 (2000). **Emp:** 120. **Officers:** Kenneth Pearson, President; Vance Pyle, General Mgr.

■ 809 ■ Heberer Equipment Company Inc.
505 S Railway St.
Mascoutah, IL 62258
Phone: (618)566-2166 **Fax:** (618)566-7302
URL: http://www.heberer.com
Products: Motorized farm and lawn equipment. **SICs:** 5082 (Construction & Mining Machinery); 5083 (Farm & Garden Machinery). **Est:** 1959. **Sales:** $10,200,000 (2000). **Emp:** 34. **Officers:** Robert D. Heberer II, CEO; James Heberer, CFO.

■ 810 ■ Hector Turf
1301 NW 3rd St.
Deerfield Beach, FL 33442
Phone: (305)429-3200 **Fax:** (305)360-7657
Products: Irrigation supplies, including turf. **SICs:** 5083 (Farm & Garden Machinery); 5191 (Farm Supplies). **Est:** 1912. **Sales:** $25,000,000 (2000). **Emp:** 60. **Officers:** J.R. Mantey, CEO & President; Ralph Roth, Accounting Manager; Ralph Baxter, VP of Sales; Lee Bacall, Information Systems Mgr.; Sandra Mantey, VP of Operations.

■ 811 ■ Helena Chemical Company Hughes
PO Box 427
Hughes, AR 72348
Phone: (870)339-2363
Products: Agricultural chemicals and fertilizers. **SIC:** 5191 (Farm Supplies). **Sales:** $6,000,000 (1994). **Emp:** 20. **Officers:** Mosby Blanks, Manager.

■ 812 ■ Helland and Long Implement Co.
PO Box 246
Belmond, IA 50421
Phone: (515)444-3011 **Fax:** (515)444-7011
Products: Farm machinery and equipment. **SIC:** 5083 (Farm & Garden Machinery). **Est:** 1936. **Sales:** $3,500,000 (2000). **Emp:** 14. **Officers:** Mike Maulsby, President; Carroll Boward, General Mgr.

■ 813 ■ Hempstead County Farmers Association
1400 E 3rd St.
Hope, AR 71801
Phone: (870)777-5729
Products: Farm supplies. **SIC:** 5191 (Farm Supplies). **Est:** 1952. **Sales:** $10,000,000 (2000). **Emp:** 25. **Officers:** Thomas Wilson, General Mgr.

■ 814 ■ Henry Farmers Cooperative Inc.
1211 W Wood, No. 1058
Paris, TN 38242
Phone: (901)642-1385 **Fax:** (901)642-1387
Products: Farm supplies; Petroleum products. **SICs:** 5191 (Farm Supplies); 5172 (Petroleum Products Nec). **Est:** 1949. **Sales:** $7,500,000 (2000). **Emp:** 30. **Officers:** Rodney Gallimore, Manager.

■ 815 ■ Heritage FS Inc.
PO Box 318
Gilman, IL 60938
Phone: (815)265-4751
Products: Fertilizers; Chemicals; Petroleum. **SICs:** 5191 (Farm Supplies); 5172 (Petroleum Products Nec). **Est:** 1930. **Sales:** $33,000,000 (2000). **Emp:** 70. **Officers:** Charles Yohnka, President; Mark Weillbacher, Controller; Ronald Asher, General Mgr.

■ 816 ■ Hermann Implement Inc.
PO Box 69
Wanamingo, MN 55983-0069
Phone: (507)824-2256 **Fax:** (507)824-2668
Products: Agricultural equipment and supplies. **SIC:** 5083 (Farm & Garden Machinery). **Est:** 1959. **Sales:** $10,000,000 (2000). **Emp:** 25.

■ 817 ■ Hewitt Brothers Inc.
PO Box 147
Locke, NY 13092
Phone: (315)497-0900 **Fax:** (315)497-9260
Products: Fuel oil; Gasoline; Feed; Fertilizer; Heating & cooling systems. **SICs:** 5191 (Farm Supplies); 5172 (Petroleum Products Nec); 5075 (Warm Air Heating & Air-Conditioning). **Est:** 1918. **Sales:** $6,500,000 (2000). **Emp:** 35. **Officers:** G.L. Hewitt, President; Sandra L. Ripic, Treasurer & Secty.; Stuart W. Wood Jr., Treasurer.

■ 818 ■ HGS Power House, Inc.
7 W Albany St.
Huntington Station, NY 11746
Phone: (516)423-1348 **Fax:** (516)673-9080
Products: Outdoor power equipment; Janitorial equipment. **SICs:** 5083 (Farm & Garden Machinery); 5087 (Service Establishment Equipment).

■ 819 ■ **Hi-Line Fertilizer Inc.**
Main St.
Hingham, MT 59528
Phone: (406)397-3194
Products: Nitrogenous fertilizer. **SIC:** 5191 (Farm Supplies). **Sales:** $13,000,000 (2000). **Emp:** 50. **Officers:** RW McKinley, Vice President; J.J. Raunig, President.

■ 820 ■ **HIA Inc.**
4275 Forest St.
Denver, CO 80216
Phone: (303)394-6040   **Fax:** (303)744-8449
Products: Irrigation products. **SIC:** 5083 (Farm & Garden Machinery). **Est:** 1974. **Sales:** $17,000,000 (2000). **Emp:** 63. **Officers:** Carl J. Bentley, Chairman of the Board; Alan C. Bergold, President & Treasurer.

■ 821 ■ **High Plains Cooperative Association**
405 E 4th St.
Colby, KS 67701
Phone: (785)462-3351
Products: Grain; Fertilizer; Gasoline. **SICs:** 5153 (Grain & Field Beans); 5172 (Petroleum Products Nec); 5191 (Farm Supplies). **Est:** 1949. **Sales:** $9,200,000 (2000). **Emp:** 23. **Officers:** Lyle Saddler, President; John Strecker, CFO; Diana Luhman, Dir. of Marketing.

■ 822 ■ **Highway Agricultural Services Inc.**
PO Box 153
Le Center, MN 56057
Phone: (612)357-2245
Products: Fertilizer and fuel. **SICs:** 5191 (Farm Supplies); 5172 (Petroleum Products Nec). **Est:** 1916. **Sales:** $13,000,000 (2000). **Emp:** 30. **Officers:** Don Budin, Chairman of the Board; Bill Sexe, General Mgr.

■ 823 ■ **Geo. W. Hill and Co., Inc.**
PO Box 787
Florence, KY 41022-0787
Phone: (606)371-8423   **Fax:** (606)371-4769
Products: Lawn, garden, turfgrass, and seed supplies. **SIC:** 5191 (Farm Supplies). **Est:** 1863. **Sales:** $20,000,000 (2000). **Emp:** 60. **Officers:** Dave Hill, President; Jim Kinsler, Controller; Jack Finfrock, Sales Mgr.

■ 824 ■ **Hills Beaver Creek Coop Farm Service**
PO Box 69
Beaver Creek, MN 56116
Phone: (507)673-2388   **Fax:** (507)673-2412
Products: Farm supplies, including grain, feed, chemicals, and fertilizers. **SICs:** 5153 (Grain & Field Beans); 5191 (Farm Supplies); 5169 (Chemicals & Allied Products Nec). **Est:** 1941. **Sales:** $16,000,000 (2000). **Emp:** 5. **Officers:** David Broesder, Branch Mgr. **Former Name:** Beaver Creek Cooperative Elevator.

■ 825 ■ **Hills Beaver Creek Cooperative Farm Service**
3rd & Summit Ave.
Hills, MN 56138
Phone: (507)962-3221   **Fax:** (507)962-3332
Products: Grain elevators; Feed; Field, garden, and flower seeds. **SIC:** 5191 (Farm Supplies). **Est:** 1903. **Sales:** $12,000,000 (2000). **Emp:** 16. **Officers:** Steve Fagerness, General Mgr.

■ 826 ■ **Hillsboro Equipment Inc.**
PO Box 583
Hillsboro, WI 54634
Phone: (608)489-2275   **Fax:** (608)489-2717
E-mail: hillsboro@jddealer.com
URL: http://www.hillsboroequipment.com
Products: Farm and industrial machinery including tractors. **SICs:** 5083 (Farm & Garden Machinery); 5084 (Industrial Machinery & Equipment). **Est:** 1935. **Sales:** $13,500,000 (2000). **Emp:** 45. **Officers:** D. Slama, President.

■ 827 ■ **Hobbs Implement Company Inc.**
E Church St. Ext.
Edenton, NC 27932
Phone: (919)482-7411   **Fax:** (919)482-8192
Products: Tractors. **SIC:** 5083 (Farm & Garden Machinery). **Sales:** $5,000,000 (2000). **Emp:** 29. **Officers:** W. Chesson Jr., President.

■ 828 ■ **Hocott Implement Company Inc.**
1105 S 7th
Raymondville, TX 78580
Phone: (956)689-2481   **Fax:** (956)689-2111
Products: Tractors. **SIC:** 5083 (Farm & Garden Machinery). **Est:** 1972. **Sales:** $3,300,000 (2000). **Emp:** 18. **Officers:** Kendall Hocott, President.

■ 829 ■ **Hoffman Cooperative Oil Association**
PO Box 275
Hoffman, MN 56339
Phone: (612)986-2061
Products: Farm supplies, including fertilizer, chemicals, and petroleum. **SICs:** 5172 (Petroleum Products Nec); 5191 (Farm Supplies). **Est:** 1951. **Sales:** $4,200,000 (2000). **Emp:** 12. **Officers:** LeRoy Stark, President; Kenneth Johnson, General Mgr.

■ 830 ■ **Hoffman and Reed Inc.**
915 Shanklin Ave.
Trenton, MO 64683
Phone: (816)359-2258
Products: Feed and grain for animals. **SICs:** 5153 (Grain & Field Beans); 5191 (Farm Supplies). **Est:** 1950. **Sales:** $17,000,000 (2000). **Emp:** 32. **Officers:** Charles D. Hoffman, Vice President; Phillip Hoffman, Treasurer.

■ 831 ■ **Hog Inc.**
RR 2 Box 8
Greenfield, IL 62044-9603
Fax: (217)368-2888
URL: http://www.hoginc.org
Products: Farm coops; Hog feed; Fertilizer; Herbicides; Agriculture equipment. **SICs:** 5159 (Farm-Product Raw Materials Nec); 5083 (Farm & Garden Machinery). **Est:** 1962. **Sales:** $38,414,000 (2000). **Emp:** 12. **Officers:** Steve Ring, General Mgr.

■ 832 ■ **Holden's Foundation Seeds L.L.C.**
PO Box 839
Williamsburg, IA 52361
Phone: (319)668-1100
Products: Seed, including corn. **SIC:** 5191 (Farm Supplies). **Est:** 1937. **Emp:** 100. **Former Name:** Holden's Foundation Seeds Inc.

■ 833 ■ **Holdrege Seed and Farm Supply Inc.**
PO Box 530
Holdrege, NE 68949-0530
Phone: (308)995-4465
Products: Seeds. **SIC:** 5191 (Farm Supplies). **Est:** 1943. **Sales:** $3,000,000 (2000). **Emp:** 14. **Officers:** Marvin C. Westcott, President; Donnie Freitag, Treasurer & Secty.; Kelly Swanson, Vice President.

■ 834 ■ **Hollingsworths' Inc.**
1175 SW 30th St.
Ontario, OR 97914
Phone: (541)889-7254
Free: (800)541-1612   **Fax:** (541)889-8364
E-mail: hollings@cyberhighway.net
Products: Farm, lawn, and garden equipment. **SIC:** 5083 (Farm & Garden Machinery). **Est:** 1939. **Sales:** $8,000,000 (2000). **Emp:** 35. **Officers:** William Hollingsworth, President; Murlin Brock, Sec. & Treas.

■ 835 ■ **Home & Garden Innovations**
130 Intervale Rd.
Burlington, VT 05401
Phone: (802)660-3506   **Fax:** 888-833-1417
Products: Home and gardening supplies, including furniture, gifts, and accessories. **SICs:** 5193 (Flowers & Florists' Supplies); 5083 (Farm & Garden Machinery). **Est:** 1995. **Sales:** $6,000,000 (2000). **Emp:** 15. **Officers:** Jim Feinson, President; John Scott, VP & General Mgr. **Alternate Name:** Gardener's Supply Co.

■ 836 ■ **Hoover Tractor and Engine Co.**
224 N East St.
Woodland, CA 95695
Phone: (530)662-8612
Products: Tractors; Bailers; Wind rowers; Tomato harvesters; Planters. **SIC:** 5083 (Farm & Garden Machinery). **Est:** 1951. **Sales:** $5,000,000 (2000). **Emp:** 10. **Officers:** Phil Neu, Owner; Ron Seybold, Owner.

■ 837 ■ **Horizon**
5214 S 30th St.
Phoenix, AZ 85040
Phone: (602)276-7700
Free: (800)782-8873   **Fax:** (602)276-7800
URL: http://www.horizononline.com
Products: Fertilizers, landscape materials and equipment sprinkler systems Irrigation equipment; Lighting; Fertilizer. **SICs:** 5191 (Farm Supplies); 5087 (Service Establishment Equipment). **Est:** 1961. **Sales:** $167,000,000 (2000). **Emp:** 330. **Officers:** David Lang, CEO; Joe Hensey, CFO.

■ 838 ■ **Horn Seed Company Inc.**
1409 NW Expy.
Oklahoma City, OK 73118
Phone: (405)842-6607   **Fax:** (405)842-6600
Products: Lawn and garden supplies, including weed killers and snow blowers. **SICs:** 5083 (Farm & Garden Machinery); 5191 (Farm Supplies). **Est:** 1922. **Sales:** $3,000,000 (2000). **Emp:** 28. **Officers:** Dave Shumake, Vice President.

■ 839 ■ **House of Rock Inc.**
1725 Merriam Ln.
Kansas City, KS 66106
Phone: (913)432-5990
Products: Landscaping materials. **SIC:** 5193 (Flowers & Florists' Supplies). **Est:** 1966. **Sales:** $1,000,000 (2000). **Emp:** 6. **Officers:** Jack Robinson, President.

■ 840 ■ **Houston Moneycreek Cooperative**
PO Box 775
Houston, MN 55943
Phone: (507)896-3121   **Fax:** (507)896-2090
Products: Feed; Soil testing equipment; Fertilizer; Seed. **SIC:** 5191 (Farm Supplies). **Est:** 1923. **Sales:** $3,000,000 (2000). **Emp:** 13. **Officers:** John Van Westen, General Mgr.

■ 841 ■ **Howard County Equity Cooperative Inc.**
PO Box 489
Elma, IA 50628
Phone: (515)393-2260   **Fax:** (515)393-2480
Products: Feeds, seeds, fertilizers, and chemicals. **SICs:** 5191 (Farm Supplies); 5169 (Chemicals & Allied Products Nec). **Est:** 1920. **Sales:** $6,500,000 (2000). **Emp:** 12. **Officers:** Robert Pietan, President; Joe Thraenert Jr., Treasurer & Secty.; Bob Ballantine, General Mgr.

■ 842 ■ **Hoxie Implement Company Inc.**
933 Oak Ave.
Hoxie, KS 67740
Phone: (785)675-3201
Products: Agricultural equipment, including tractors and combines. **SIC:** 5083 (Farm & Garden Machinery). **Est:** 1962. **Sales:** $10,000,000 (2000). **Emp:** 30. **Officers:** Gerald Heim, Owner.

■ 843 ■ **Huffman Equipment Co.**
Rte. 1
Palestine, TX 75801
Phone: (903)729-6951
Products: Tractors and mowers. **SIC:** 5083 (Farm & Garden Machinery). **Sales:** $3,000,000 (2000). **Emp:** 10. **Officers:** Bob Huffman, President.

■ 844 ■ **Hultgren Implement Inc.**
PO Box 239
Ida Grove, IA 51445
Phone: (712)364-3105
Free: (800)827-1650   **Fax:** (712)364-2197
E-mail: info@Hultgrenimplement.com
Products: New and used farm equipment. **SIC:** 5083 (Farm & Garden Machinery). **Est:** 1940. **Sales:** $9,000,000 (2000). **Emp:** 23. **Officers:** Larry Hultgren, President; Diane Hemer, Controller.

■ 845 ■ **Hunter Grain Co.**
PO Box 97
Hunter, ND 58048
Phone: (701)874-2112   **Fax:** (701)874-2395
Products: Fuels; Chemicals; Fertilizers. **SICs:** 5153 (Grain & Field Beans); 5191 (Farm Supplies). **Est:** 1925. **Sales:** $18,000,000 (2000). **Emp:** 25. **Officers:** Paul Coppin, General Mgr.; Alan Richter, Office Mgr.

■ 846 ■ Huntington County Farm Cooperative
PO Box 388
Huntington, IN 46750
Phone: (219)356-8110 **Fax:** (219)356-7185
Products: Petroleum and its products; Animal feeds; Farm poultry equipment (incubators, feeders, brooders, egg graders, etc.); Hog equipment (hog feeders, farrowing crates, pens, waterers). **SICs:** 5191 (Farm Supplies); 5083 (Farm & Garden Machinery); 5172 (Petroleum Products Nec). **Est:** 1923. **Sales:** $10,000,000 (2000). **Emp:** 23. **Officers:** Carl Bonner, CEO; Mark Tullis, General Mgr.

■ 847 ■ Husch and Husch Inc.
PO Box 160
Harrah, WA 98933
Phone: (509)848-2951
Products: Fertilizers; Herbicides; Pesticides. **SICs:** 5191 (Farm Supplies); 5169 (Chemicals & Allied Products Nec). **Est:** 1937. **Sales:** $6,000,000 (2000). **Emp:** 18. **Officers:** Kelly Husch, President; Deanna Husch, Treasurer & Secty.

■ 848 ■ Huss Implement Co.
PO Box 68
La Motte, IA 52054
Phone: (319)773-2231
Products: Farm machinery and equipment; Agricultural tractors. **SIC:** 5083 (Farm & Garden Machinery). **Est:** 1980. **Sales:** $1,500,000 (2000). **Emp:** 7. **Officers:** Dennis Huss, President; Mike Bonafas, Manager.

■ 849 ■ Hydro Agri North America Inc.
100 N Tampa St., No. 3200
Tampa, FL 33602
Phone: (813)222-5700 **Fax:** (813)875-5735
Products: Fertilizer. **SIC:** 5191 (Farm Supplies). **Est:** 1972. **Sales:** $425,000,000 (1999). **Emp:** 130. **Officers:** Edward Cavazuti, President; Dag Birkelund, VP of Finance & Admin.; Tim Chrislip, Dir. of Marketing; Susan Land, Personnel Mgr.

■ 850 ■ Hydro-Scape Products, Inc.
5805 Kearny Villa Rd.
San Diego, CA 92123
Phone: (619)560-6611 **Fax:** (619)560-9578
Products: Landscaping and irrigation products. **SIC:** 5083 (Farm & Garden Machinery).

■ 851 ■ Illinois Agricultural Association
1701 Towanda Ave.
Bloomington, IL 61701
Phone: (309)557-2111 **Fax:** (309)557-2559
Products: Farm supplies. **SIC:** 5191 (Farm Supplies). **Sales:** $120,000,000 (2000). **Emp:** 300. **Officers:** Ronald Warfield, President; Robert Weldon, VP of Finance & Treasurer.

■ 852 ■ Implement Sales LLC
1574 Stone Ridge Dr.
Stone Mountain, GA 30083
Phone: (770)368-8648
E-mail: imsalesatl@aol.com
Products: Farm equipment. **SIC:** 5083 (Farm & Garden Machinery). **Est:** 1954. **Sales:** $9,000,000 (1999). **Emp:** 16. **Officers:** Mitch ELkins, Manager. **Former Name:** Implement Sales Company Inc.

■ 853 ■ Independent Rental, Inc.
2020 S Cushman St.
Fairbanks, AK 99701
Phone: (907)456-6595 **Fax:** (907)456-2927
Products: Lawn and garden tools; Construction equipment and supplies. **SICs:** 5191 (Farm Supplies); 5072 (Hardware); 5084 (Industrial Machinery & Equipment).

■ 854 ■ Indiana Farm Systems Inc.
PO Box 277
Russiaville, IN 46979
Phone: (765)883-5557 **Fax:** (765)883-7601
Products: Grain equipment, including farm fast dryers. **SIC:** 5083 (Farm & Garden Machinery). **Est:** 1974. **Sales:** $3,000,000 (2000). **Emp:** 20. **Officers:** Dan Trost, President.

■ 855 ■ Indiana Seed Co.
PO Box 1745
Noblesville, IN 46060
Phone: (317)773-5813
Products: Fertilizer; Chemicals; Vegetable seeds. **SIC:** 5191 (Farm Supplies).

■ 856 ■ Industrial Fumigant Co.
19745 W 159th Street
PO Box 1200
Olathe, KS 66062
Phone: (913)782-7600 **Fax:** (913)782-6299
URL: http://www.indfumco.com
Products: Rodenticides; Plant pest control chemicals; Structural fumigants. **SICs:** 5191 (Farm Supplies); 5169 (Chemicals & Allied Products Nec). **Est:** 1937. **Emp:** 100. **Officers:** Robert Blachly; Michelle Homlin, Sales/Marketing Contact, e-mail: michelle@indfumco.com; Chris Mueller, Customer Service Contact, e-mail: chris@indfumco.com.

■ 857 ■ Industrial Tractor Co.
6870 Phillips Hwy.
PO Box 17309
Jacksonville, FL 32245
Phone: (904)296-5000 **Fax:** (904)296-0525
URL: http://www.industrialtractor.com
Products: Construction equipment and parts. **SIC:** 5083 (Farm & Garden Machinery). **Officers:** B. Helms, Sales & Marketing Contact, e-mail: bhelms@industrialtractor.com.

■ 858 ■ Ingredient Resource Corp.
2401 Lower Hunters
Louisville, KY 40216
Phone: (502)448-4480 **Fax:** (502)448-0516
Products: Animal feeds. **SIC:** 5191 (Farm Supplies). **Est:** 1980. **Sales:** $30,000,000 (2000). **Emp:** 8. **Officers:** James W. Ford, President; Steven D. Ford, Treasurer & Secty.; Thomas K. Biedenharn, Vice President.

■ 859 ■ Integrated World Enterprises
8350 NW 66th St.
Miami, FL 33166
Phone: (305)591-7797 **Fax:** (305)592-4053
Products: Farm equipment, including poultry waterers and feeders; Agricultural feed additives, including mold inhibitors. **SICs:** 5083 (Farm & Garden Machinery); 5191 (Farm Supplies). **Officers:** Martin R. Moreira, Exec. VP.

■ 860 ■ Interchange Corp.
117 Garth Rd., Ste. 1A
Scarsdale, NY 10583
Phone: (914)472-7881 **Fax:** (914)472-6585
Products: Construction and mining machinery; Computers, peripherals, and software; Industrial machinery and equipment; Medical and hospital equipment; Farm and garden machinery. **SICs:** 5083 (Farm & Garden Machinery); 5082 (Construction & Mining Machinery); 5045 (Computers, Peripherals & Software); 5084 (Industrial Machinery & Equipment); 5047 (Medical & Hospital Equipment). **Officers:** Amir Farzam, Mgr. Dir.

■ 861 ■ Intermountain Farmers Association
1147 W 2100 S
Salt Lake City, UT 84119
Phone: (801)972-2122 **Fax:** (801)972-2186
Products: Fertilizer and fertilizer materials; Lawn and garden equipment; Feed. **SICs:** 5083 (Farm & Garden Machinery); 5191 (Farm Supplies). **Est:** 1923. **Sales:** $80,000,000 (2000). **Emp:** 400. **Officers:** Steven L. Palmer, President; Spence Lloyd, VP of Finance.

■ 862 ■ International Agricultural Associates, Inc.
PO Box 5153
New Britain, PA 18901-0939
Phone: (215)230-3476
Free: (888)462-4721 **Fax:** (215)230-3478
E-mail: inagrai@p3.net
Products: Vegetable seeds; Pet foods; Hay and forage; Agricultural equipment; Feed. **SICs:** 5191 (Farm Supplies); 5149 (Groceries & Related Products Nec); 5083 (Farm & Garden Machinery). **Est:** 1979. **Sales:** $500,000 (1999). **Emp:** 3. **Officers:** Alvin D. Schulman, President.

■ 863 ■ International Division, Inc.
PO Box 1275
Springfield, MO 65801
Phone: (417)862-2673 **Fax:** (417)862-5434
Products: Poultry raising and processing equipment, including breeder and layer facilities; Animal health products. **SIC:** 5083 (Farm & Garden Machinery). **Est:** 1964. **Sales:** $10,000,000 (2000). **Emp:** 22. **Officers:** Forest Lipscomb Jr., President; Jaime R. Gomez, Exec. VP; Jose L. Sala, Vice President. **Also Known by This Acronym:** INDIV.

■ 864 ■ International Marketing Systems Ltd.
PO Box 806
Fargo, ND 58107
Phone: (701)237-4699 **Fax:** (701)237-4701
E-mail: info@imsetc.com
URL: http://www.imsetc.com
Products: Farm and garden machinery; Truck trailers; Industrial equipment and parts. **SICs:** 5083 (Farm & Garden Machinery); 5012 (Automobiles & Other Motor Vehicles); 5084 (Industrial Machinery & Equipment). **Est:** 1979. **Officers:** Jon Golberg, President.

■ 865 ■ International Seeds, Inc.
PO Box 168
Halsey, OR 97348
Phone: (541)369-2251 **Fax:** (541)369-2640
Products: Turf and floral seeds. **SIC:** 5191 (Farm Supplies).

■ 866 ■ Interstate Payco Seed Co.
PO Box 338
West Fargo, ND 58078
Phone: (701)282-7338 **Fax:** (701)282-8218
Products: Seeds, including sunflower and corn. **SIC:** 5191 (Farm Supplies). **Est:** 1917. **Sales:** $14,000,000 (2000). **Emp:** 60. **Officers:** Bruce Hovland, President & General Mgr.; Monte Rutledge, Treasurer; William Weber, General Mgr.; Bruce Kallhoff, Dir. of Systems.

■ 867 ■ Iowa Export Import Trading Co.
512 Tuttle St.
Des Moines, IA 50309
Phone: (515)245-2464
Free: (800)831-4145 **Fax:** (515)245-2878
E-mail: info@iowaexportimport.com
URL: http://www.iowaexportimport.com
Products: Farm machinery and equipment; Automotive parts and accessories. **SICs:** 5083 (Farm & Garden Machinery); 5013 (Motor Vehicle Supplies & New Parts). **Est:** 1983. **Sales:** $30,000,000 (2000). **Emp:** 25. **Officers:** Craig Winters, President; David Winkels, Vice President; Brent Clark, Vice President.

■ 868 ■ Iowa River Farm Service Inc.
PO Box 99
Toledo, IA 52342
Phone: (515)752-4274 **Fax:** (515)484-5385
Products: Petroleum, oil, gasoline, and diesel fuel; Chemicals and fertilizers. **SICs:** 5191 (Farm Supplies); 5172 (Petroleum Products Nec). **Est:** 1980. **Sales:** $10,000,000 (2000). **Emp:** 38. **Officers:** Dwayne Jacobs, General Mgr.; Mike Miller, CFO; Tom Severson, Dir. of Marketing. **Former Name:** Iowa River Farm Service Inc.

■ 869 ■ Iowa Veterinary Supply Co.
PO Box 518
Iowa Falls, IA 50126
Phone: (515)648-2529
Products: Concrete products. **SICs:** 5083 (Farm & Garden Machinery); 5191 (Farm Supplies). **Sales:** $104,000,000 (2000). **Emp:** 157.

■ 870 ■ IPE Trade Inc.
704 Hillwood Dr.
PO Box 1250
Daphne, AL 36526
Phone: (205)626-3128 **Fax:** (205)626-4252
Products: Peanut plant cultivating and harvesting machinery; Tobacco harvesting machinery; New and used fork lift trucks; Agricultural machinery. **SICs:** 5083 (Farm & Garden Machinery); 5084 (Industrial Machinery & Equipment). **Officers:** Inman P. Ellis, President.

■ 871 ■ **Irrideco International Corp.**
PO Box 1615
Englewood Cliffs, NJ 07632
Phone: (201)569-3030 **Fax:** (201)569-9237
Products: Micro flappers. **SIC:** 5083 (Farm & Garden Machinery). **Est:** 1952. **Sales:** $15,000,000 (2000). **Emp:** 50. **Officers:** R.J. Gilbert, President; S.H. Lu, VP of Finance.

■ 872 ■ **J & E Feed Distributors Inc.**
1509 N Main St.
Muskogee, OK 74401
Phone: (918)687-7111 **Fax:** (918)687-1536
E-mail: champions@oknet1.net
Products: Animal feed; Pet feed; Hunting apparel; Work apparel; Tack. **SICs:** 5191 (Farm Supplies); 5136 (Men's/Boys' Clothing). **Est:** 1980. **Emp:** 12. **Officers:** Ed Johnson, Owner.

■ 873 ■ **Jacklin Seed Co.**
PO Box 218
Nezperce, ID 83543
Phone: (208)937-2481 **Fax:** (208)937-2440
Products: Grass seed. **SIC:** 5191 (Farm Supplies).

■ 874 ■ **Jacklin Seed Co.**
1490 Industrial Way SW
Albany, OR 97321
Phone: (541)928-3677 **Fax:** (541)926-9873
Products: Field, garden, and flower seeds. **SIC:** 5191 (Farm Supplies).

■ 875 ■ **Jacklin Seed Simplot Turf & Horticulture**
5300 W Riverbend Ave.
Post Falls, ID 83854-9499
Phone: (208)773-7581 **Fax:** (208)773-4846
Products: Forage grass; Turf grass seed. **SIC:** 5191 (Farm Supplies). **Est:** 1935. **Emp:** 140. **Officers:** Hiromi Yanagisawa, Mgr. Dir.; Gayle Jacklin, Sales/Marketing Contact, e-mail: Gaylej@jacklin.com; Brandie Champman,. Customer Service Contact, e-mail: bchapman@jacklin.com; Becky Clemens, Human Resources Contact.

■ 876 ■ **Jacobi Sales Inc.**
Hwy. 150
Palmyra, IN 47164
Phone: (812)364-6141
Products: Farm machinery, including tractors, loaders, and mowers. **SIC:** 5083 (Farm & Garden Machinery). **Est:** 1928. **Sales:** $12,000,000 (2000). **Emp:** 63. **Officers:** Brian Jacobi, President; Jerry Uhl, Treasurer & Secty.; Kevin R. Book, Dir. of Marketing.

■ 877 ■ **Jacob's Store Inc.**
204 Centennial St.
Carmine, TX 78932
Phone: (409)278-3242
Products: Grocery; Feed; Hardware. **SICs:** 5191 (Farm Supplies); 5141 (Groceries—General Line); 5072 (Hardware). **Est:** 1935. **Sales:** $9,000,000 (2000). **Emp:** 35. **Officers:** Jerry Jacob, President.

■ 878 ■ **James Agriculture Center Inc.**
PO Box 87
Neelyville, MO 63954
Phone: (573)989-3250
Products: Agricultural supplies. **SICs:** 5191 (Farm Supplies); 5153 (Grain & Field Beans). **Est:** 1970. **Sales:** $4,500,000 (2000). **Emp:** 10.

■ 879 ■ **Jamestown Implement Inc.**
PO Box 469
Jamestown, ND 58401
Phone: (701)252-0580
Products: Agricultural tractors; Farm machinery and equipment. **SIC:** 5083 (Farm & Garden Machinery). **Est:** 1966. **Sales:** $17,000,000 (2000). **Emp:** 65. **Officers:** Maynard Helgaas, President.

■ 880 ■ **Jasper Farmers Exchange Inc.**
308 W Morrison Ave.
Jasper, MO 64755
Phone: (417)394-2156
Products: Agricultural equipment and supplies. **SIC:** 5191 (Farm Supplies). **Sales:** $3,000,000 (2000). **Emp:** 6.

■ 881 ■ **Jefferson County Farmco Coop.**
PO Box 359
Jefferson, WI 53549
Phone: (920)674-7000
Products: Farming supplies, petroleum and petroleum products. **SICs:** 5191 (Farm Supplies); 5153 (Grain & Field Beans); 5171 (Petroleum Bulk Stations & Terminals). **Sales:** $38,000,000 (2000). **Emp:** 60. **Officers:** William Pranga, General Mgr.; Leroy Tucker, Controller.

■ 882 ■ **Jefferson Farmers Cooperative**
106 Highway 92 South
PO Box 1429
Dandridge, TN 37725
Phone: (423)397-3434 **Fax:** (423)397-0129
Products: Feed and seed; Chain saws; Chemical products; Fertilizer; Tillers and trimmers. **SICs:** 5191 (Farm Supplies); 5083 (Farm & Garden Machinery); 5169 (Chemicals & Allied Products Nec). **Est:** 1945. **Sales:** $4,500,000 (1999). **Emp:** 25. **Officers:** Mark Pettit, Manager; Bill Loy, President.

■ 883 ■ **Jeffrey's Seed Company Inc.**
PO Box 887
Goldsboro, NC 27530
Phone: (919)734-2985
Products: Seed; Garden equipment. **SICs:** 5191 (Farm Supplies); 5083 (Farm & Garden Machinery). **Est:** 1888. **Sales:** $8,000,000 (2000). **Emp:** 55. **Officers:** J.T. Jeffreys, President & Treasurer.

■ 884 ■ **Jennings Implement Company Inc.**
Hwy. 54 & Hwy. 154
Curryville, MO 63339
Phone: (573)594-6493
Products: Farm equipment, including tractors and plows. **SIC:** 5083 (Farm & Garden Machinery). **Sales:** $4,000,000 (2000). **Emp:** 20. **Officers:** Edward Jennings, President.

■ 885 ■ **Jerrine Company Inc.**
PO Box 53
Zumbrota, MN 55992
Phone: (507)732-7838 **Fax:** (507)732-7749
Products: Dairy equipment, including swivels. **SIC:** 5083 (Farm & Garden Machinery). **Officers:** Gerald L. Huneke, President.

■ 886 ■ **Jersey County Farm Supply Co.**
PO Box 367
Jerseyville, IL 62052
Phone: (618)498-5534 **Fax:** (618)498-3402
Products: Chemicals and fertilizer. **SIC:** 5191 (Farm Supplies). **Est:** 1935. **Sales:** $7,000,000 (2000). **Emp:** 33. **Officers:** Ronald Guilander, President; Frank Yocom, Treasurer & Secty.; Dave Kadell, Sales Mgr.

■ 887 ■ **Jim Jess Implements Inc.**
PO Box 788
Coulee City, WA 99115
Phone: (509)632-5547 **Fax:** (509)632-8702
Products: Tractors, riders, and mowers. **SIC:** 5083 (Farm & Garden Machinery). **Est:** 1968. **Sales:** $11,000,000 (2000). **Emp:** 18. **Officers:** James L. Jess, President & CFO.

■ 888 ■ **Johnson Cooperative Grain Co.**
PO Box 280
Johnson, KS 67855
Phone: (316)492-6210 **Fax:** (316)492-6829
Products: Grain; Fertilizer; Fuel. **SICs:** 5153 (Grain & Field Beans); 5191 (Farm Supplies); 5172 (Petroleum Products Nec); 5014 (Tires & Tubes). **Est:** 1930. **Sales:** $36,000,000 (1999). **Emp:** 36. **Officers:** Thomas P. Ryan, CEO; Roger Hurst, President.

■ 889 ■ **R.N. Johnson Inc.**
PO Box 448
Walpole, NH 03608
Phone: (603)756-3321 **Fax:** (603)756-3452
E-mail: RNJ@Sover.net
URL: http://www.rnjohnsoninc.com
Products: Agricultural tractors. **SIC:** 5083 (Farm & Garden Machinery). **Est:** 1929. **Sales:** $1,000,000 (1999). **Emp:** 55. **Officers:** Alan W. Johnson, President; Terry Robison, Dir. of Marketing & Sales; Alan W. Johnson, Dir. of Marketing & Sales; Edward Karman, Dir. of Information Systems.

■ 890 ■ **Johnston County Feed & Farm Supply**
PO Box 217
Tishomingo, OK 73460-0217
Phone: (580)371-3607 **Fax:** (580)371-9034
Products: Animal feed and supply. **SIC:** 5191 (Farm Supplies). **Officers:** Carl Atteberry, Owner.

■ 891 ■ **Jones Tractor Company Inc.**
PO Box 4187
Spartanburg, SC 29303
Phone: (864)582-1245 **Fax:** (864)582-7121
Products: Tractors; Lawnmowers. **SIC:** 5083 (Farm & Garden Machinery). **Est:** 1955. **Sales:** $4,900,000 (2000). **Emp:** 20. **Officers:** Thomas L. Arthur, President & Treasurer.

■ 892 ■ **J.S. Woodhouse Co.**
PO Box 1169
West Springfield, MA 01089
Phone: (413)736-5462 **Fax:** (413)732-3786
Products: Agricultural equipment and supplies. **SIC:** 5083 (Farm & Garden Machinery). **Sales:** $6,000,000 (2000). **Emp:** 28.

■ 893 ■ **Juergens Produce and Feed Co.**
PO Box 1027
Carroll, IA 51401
Phone: (712)792-3506
Products: Produce; Feed. **SICs:** 5159 (Farm-Product Raw Materials Nec); 5099 (Durable Goods Nec). **Sales:** $13,000,000 (2000). **Emp:** 45. **Officers:** Vernis Juergens, President; Merle R. Danner, CFO; Bob Raue, Dir. of Marketing.

■ 894 ■ **Justin Seed Company Inc.**
PO Box 6
Justin, TX 76247
Phone: (940)648-2751
URL: http://www.justinseed.com
Products: Seed; Feed; Fertilizer; Erosion products. **SICs:** 5191 (Farm Supplies); 5083 (Farm & Garden Machinery). **Est:** 1959. **Sales:** $4,500,000 (2000). **Emp:** 10. **Officers:** Curtis Tally, President; Tracy Tally, Vice President.

■ 895 ■ **K and L Feed Mill Corp.**
PO Box 52
North Franklin, CT 06254
Phone: (203)642-7555 **Fax:** (203)642-6801
Products: Animal feed. **SIC:** 5191 (Farm Supplies). **Est:** 1970. **Sales:** $19,000,000 (2000). **Emp:** 50. **Officers:** John Lombardi Jr., President; Paul Rak, CFO; James Gavitt, Dir. of Marketing.

■ 896 ■ **Kamp Implement Co.**
PO Box 629
Belgrade, MT 59714
Phone: (406)388-4295 **Fax:** (406)388-3465
Products: Farm equipment. **SIC:** 5083 (Farm & Garden Machinery). **Sales:** $11,000,000 (2000). **Emp:** 40. **Officers:** Tom J. Kamp, President; Robert Kamp, CFO.

■ 897 ■ **Kaser Implement Inc.**
PO Box 327
Osborne, KS 67473
Phone: (785)346-2126
Products: Farm machinery and parts. **SIC:** 5083 (Farm & Garden Machinery). **Est:** 1957. **Sales:** $5,500,000 (2000). **Emp:** 18. **Officers:** Leslie Kaser, President; Ronald L. Kaser, Vice President.

■ 898 ■ **Kaufman Seeds Inc.**
PO Box 398
Ashdown, AR 71822-0398
Phone: (870)898-3328 **Fax:** (870)898-3302
Products: Pasture grass seed, including bermuda, ryegrass, clover, fescue, and bahia. **SIC:** 5191 (Farm Supplies). **Est:** 1941. **Sales:** $5,000,000 (2000). **Emp:** 20. **Officers:** John Hearn, President; Dorothy Johnson, Treasurer.

■ 899 ■ Kaye Corp.
1910 Lookout Dr.
North Mankato, MN 56003
Phone: (507)625-5293 **Fax:** (507)625-3656
E-mail: kaye6782@mctcnet.net
URL: http://www.kayecorp.com
Products: Gardening and yardwork supplies, including tillers, trimmers, chipper shredders, lawn vacuums, lawn combers, aerators, seeders, sod cutters, sprayers, mowers, edgers, blowers, brushcutters, generators; chain saws, and powerbrooms; Vehicles, including utility vehicles, golf cars, 4wheelers, scooters, and dirt bikes; Skid loaders; Mini excavators; Trailers; Picnic tables; Gas grills;. **SIC:** 5083 (Farm & Garden Machinery). **Est:** 1945. **Sales:** $30,000,000 (2000). **Emp:** 30. **Officers:** Marlin Lloyd, President; Mike Lloyd; Kevin Lloyd.

■ 900 ■ Keller & Sons
PO Box 490
Quincy, IL 62306
Phone: (217)228-6700 **Fax:** (217)223-3801
Products: Lawn and garden products, including seed and fertilizer. **SIC:** 5191 (Farm Supplies).

■ 901 ■ Kendall-Grundy FS Inc.
4000 N Division St.
Morris, IL 60450
Phone: (815)942-3210
Products: Fertilizer and fertilizer materials; Insecticides; Herbicidal preparations. **SIC:** 5191 (Farm Supplies). **Est:** 1971. **Sales:** $20,000,000 (2000). **Emp:** 65. **Officers:** Richard Westphal, President; Joe Pierski, Sales Mgr.

■ 902 ■ Kennedy-Kuhn Inc.
1042 S Washington St.
Van Wert, OH 45891
Phone: (419)238-1299
Products: Farm equipment. **SIC:** 5083 (Farm & Garden Machinery). **Sales:** $3,000,000 (2000). **Emp:** 15. **Officers:** Bruce Kennedy, President; Julie Anne Kennedy, Treasurer.

■ 903 ■ Kennett Liquid Fertilizer Co.
PO Box 528
Kennett, MO 63857
Phone: (573)888-5361
Products: Farming fertilizer and chemicals. **SIC:** 5191 (Farm Supplies). **Est:** 1962. **Sales:** $7,000,000 (2000). **Emp:** 10. **Officers:** Jerry Wright, President.

■ 904 ■ Kenney Machinery Corp.
PO Box 681068
Indianapolis, IN 46268
Phone: (317)872-4793
Products: Outdoor maintenance equipment, including lawnmowers. **SIC:** 5083 (Farm & Garden Machinery). **Est:** 1895. **Sales:** $20,000,000 (2000). **Emp:** 48. **Officers:** James E. Kenney, President & Treasurer.

■ 905 ■ Kenosha-Racine FS Cooperative
4304 S Beaumont
Kansasville, WI 53139
Phone: (414)886-5613
Free: (800)528-4584 **Fax:** (414)878-0181
Products: Chemicals; Fertilizers; Seeds. **SIC:** 5191 (Farm Supplies). **Est:** 1945. **Sales:** $4,000,000 (2000). **Emp:** 12. **Officers:** Norman Wilks, President; W.R. Mattie, CFO.

■ 906 ■ Kensington Cooperative Association
PO Box 128
Kensington, KS 66951
Phone: (785)476-2211
Products: Grain; Feed. **SICs:** 5191 (Farm Supplies); 5153 (Grain & Field Beans). **Est:** 1953. **Sales:** $3,000,000 (2000). **Emp:** 13. **Officers:** Leland Rodgers, President; Eulonda Hagman, Treasurer; Eddie Long, General Mgr.

■ 907 ■ Kentucky Buying Cooperative Int.
140 Venture Ct., Suite 1
Lexington, KY 40511
Phone: (859)253-9688
Free: (800)928-7777 **Fax:** (859)253-9669
E-mail: info@kbcinternational.com
URL: www.kbcinternational
Products: Horse supplies; Barn and stall supplies;

Veterinary instruments; Pharmaceutical preparations for veterinary use; Pet supplies. **SICs:** 5191 (Farm Supplies); 5122 (Drugs, Proprietaries & Sundries); 5199 (Nondurable Goods Nec). **Est:** 1989. **Sales:** $4,000,000 (1999). **Emp:** 23. **Officers:** Jeff Cox, Contact; Thomas Gaines, President. **Former Name:** Kentucky Buyers Co-op.

■ 908 ■ Kerber Milling Co.
1817 E Main St.
Emmetsburg, IA 50536
Phone: (712)852-2712 **Fax:** (712)852-2714
Products: Feed. **SIC:** 5191 (Farm Supplies). **Est:** 1922. **Sales:** $2,500,000 (2000). **Emp:** 24. **Officers:** John Kerber, CEO.

■ 909 ■ Kettle-Lakes Cooperative
PO Box 305
Random Lake, WI 53075
Phone: (414)994-4316 **Fax:** (414)994-9077
Products: Agriculture and petroleum products. **SIC:** 5191 (Farm Supplies). **Est:** 1917. **Sales:** $18,000,000 (2000). **Emp:** 45. **Officers:** Thomas A. Rysavy, Chairman of the Board.

■ 910 ■ Keystone Mills
309 Martindale Rd.
Ephrata, PA 17522
Phone: (717)354-4616
Products: Animal feed. **SIC:** 5191 (Farm Supplies). **Sales:** $30,000,000 (2000). **Emp:** 75. **Officers:** H. Melvin, Partner.

■ 911 ■ Kinder Seed Co.
2202 Hangar Pl., No. 170
Allentown, PA 18109-9507
Products: Farming supplies, including grass seed. **SIC:** 5191 (Farm Supplies).

■ 912 ■ R.M. King Co.
315 N Marks Ave.
Fresno, CA 93706
Phone: (209)266-0258 **Fax:** (209)266-1672
URL: http://www.rmking.com
Products: Cotton picking machinery, equipment, and parts; Farm machinery and equipment. **SIC:** 5083 (Farm & Garden Machinery). **Est:** 1953. **Sales:** $4,000,000 (2000). **Emp:** 26. **Officers:** Drake King, President.

■ 913 ■ Kleberg County Farmers Cooperative
Rte. 1
Kingsville, TX 78363
Phone: (512)592-2621 **Fax:** (512)592-2131
Products: Lawn and gardening supplies. **SIC:** 5083 (Farm & Garden Machinery). **Est:** 1944. **Sales:** $5,000,000 (2000). **Emp:** 26. **Officers:** Gary Underbrink, President; James Massey, General Mgr.

■ 914 ■ Klemme Cooperative Grain Co.
PO Box 250
Klemme, IA 50449
Phone: (515)587-2161 **Fax:** (515)587-2168
Products: Feeds, seeds, fertilizers, and chemicals. **SICs:** 5153 (Grain & Field Beans); 5159 (Farm-Product Raw Materials Nec). **Est:** 1921. **Sales:** $14,000,000 (2000). **Emp:** 18. **Officers:** Daryl Schweer, Manager; Jerry Gunderson, Controller.

■ 915 ■ Knievel's Inc.
R.R. 1, Box 71
Ewing, NE 68735
Phone: (402)485-2598
Products: Farming supplies, including fertilizer and chemicals. **SICs:** 5191 (Farm Supplies); 5171 (Petroleum Bulk Stations & Terminals). **Est:** 1975. **Sales:** $6,000,000 (2000). **Emp:** 17. **Officers:** Joe L. Knievel, Manager.

■ 916 ■ Knowles Produce and Trading Co.
W 2189 County Trunk Y
Lomira, WI 53048
Phone: (920)583-3747
Products: Used farm equipment; Feeds; Grain, including corn and oats. **SICs:** 5153 (Grain & Field Beans); 5191 (Farm Supplies). **Est:** 1912. **Sales:** $3,000,000 (2000). **Emp:** 20. **Officers:** Bruce P. Sterr, President; Margaret Riese, Bookkeeper.

■ 917 ■ Knox County Farm Bureau Cooperative Association
PO Box 301
Vincennes, IN 47591
Phone: (812)882-6380
Products: Agricultural supplies, including fertilizers, feeds, and grains. **SIC:** 5191 (Farm Supplies). **Est:** 1926. **Sales:** $10,000,000 (2000). **Emp:** 30. **Officers:** William E. Schroeder, President; Dan Weber, CFO.

■ 918 ■ Korvan Industries Inc.
270 Birch Bay Lynden Rd.
Lynden, WA 98264
Phone: (360)354-1500 **Fax:** (360)354-1300
Products: Harvesting equipment for blueberries, raspberries, coffee and raisins. **SIC:** 5083 (Farm & Garden Machinery). **Officers:** Herb Korthuis, President.

■ 919 ■ Kova Fertilizer Inc.
1330 N Anderson St.
Greensburg, IN 47240
Phone: (812)663-5081 **Fax:** (812)663-5081
Products: Fertilizers; Chemicals; Herbicides; Insecticides. **SICs:** 5191 (Farm Supplies); 5169 (Chemicals & Allied Products Nec). **Est:** 1935. **Sales:** $30,000,000 (2000). **Emp:** 100. **Officers:** Richard C. Reed, President; Bradley Reed, Treasurer & Secty.; Brian Reed, Vice President.

■ 920 ■ F.J. Krob and Co.
PO Box 159
Ely, IA 52227
Phone: (319)848-4161
Products: Farming supplies, including feed and chemicals. **SICs:** 5153 (Grain & Field Beans); 5191 (Farm Supplies). **Est:** 1912. **Sales:** $37,000,000 (2000). **Emp:** 44. **Officers:** Dave Krob, President; Mike Krob, Treasurer.

■ 921 ■ Kubota Tractor Corp.
PO Box 2992
Torrance, CA 90509-2992
Phone: (310)370-3370 **Fax:** (310)370-2370
Products: Agricultural and construction equipment. **SICs:** 5083 (Farm & Garden Machinery); 5082 (Construction & Mining Machinery). **Sales:** $88,000,000 (2000). **Emp:** 400. **Officers:** S. Majima, President; Dennis Miller, Controller.

■ 922 ■ Kunau Implement Co.
PO Box 39
Preston, IA 52069
Phone: (319)689-3311 **Fax:** (319)689-4621
Products: Farm equipment, including tractors and plows. **SIC:** 5083 (Farm & Garden Machinery). **Est:** 1936. **Sales:** $6,000,000 (2000). **Emp:** 21. **Officers:** Dan Kunau, President.

■ 923 ■ L & L Implement Company Inc.
PO Box 307
Yuma, CO 80759
Phone: (970)848-5482 **Fax:** (970)848-5143
Products: Tractors, riders, and mowers. **SIC:** 5083 (Farm & Garden Machinery). **Est:** 1966. **Sales:** $4,500,000 (2000). **Emp:** 20. **Officers:** Lawrence R. Meis, President; Larry D. Pounds, Finance Officer.

■ 924 ■ L and L Nursery Supply Inc.
PO Box 249
Chino, CA 91710
Phone: (909)591-0461 **Fax:** (909)591-3280
Products: Lawn and garden supplies. **SIC:** 5193 (Flowers & Florists' Supplies). **Sales:** $49,000,000 (2000). **Emp:** 300. **Officers:** Tom Medhurst, President; Linda Clark, CFO.

■ 925 ■ La Salle County Farm Supply Co.
3107 N Ilinois, Rte. 23
Ottawa, IL 61350
Phone: (815)434-0131 **Fax:** (815)434-0227
Products: Farm supplies, including hydros, chemicals, and fertilizers. **SIC:** 5191 (Farm Supplies). **Sales:** $27,100,000 (2000). **Emp:** 50. **Officers:** Walt Pries, CEO.

■ 926 ■ La Salle Farmers Grain Co.
PO Box 8
La Salle, MN 56056
Phone: (507)375-3468 **Fax:** (507)642-3393
Products: Agricultural supplies, including fertilizer and chemicals. **SICs:** 5153 (Grain & Field Beans); 5191 (Farm Supplies). **Est:** 1919. **Sales:** $35,000,000 (2000). **Emp:** 45. **Officers:** J. Graff, General Mgr.

■ 927 ■ Bob Ladd, Inc.
764 Scott St.
Memphis, TN 38112
Phone: (901)324-8801 **Fax:** (901)324-6814
Products: Lawn mowers; Golf carts. **SICs:** 5083 (Farm & Garden Machinery); 5088 (Transportation Equipment & Supplies).

■ 928 ■ Laethem Farm Service Co.
5040 Center St.
Fairgrove, MI 48733
Phone: (517)693-6172
Products: Agricultural equipment, including tractors. **SIC:** 5083 (Farm & Garden Machinery). **Est:** 1944. **Sales:** $4,000,000 (2000). **Emp:** 12. **Officers:** Mark Laethem, Manager.

■ 929 ■ Lake Andes Farmers Cooperative Co.
PO Box 217
Lake Andes, SD 57356
Phone: (605)487-7681 **Fax:** (605)487-7495
E-mail: lacoop@charles-mix.com
Products: Farm products, including grain, feed, and fertilizer. **SICs:** 5153 (Grain & Field Beans); 5191 (Farm Supplies); 5171 (Petroleum Bulk Stations & Terminals). **Est:** 1909. **Sales:** $6,000,000 (2000). **Emp:** 9. **Officers:** Bill Evans, President; Dan Svatos, General Mgr.

■ 930 ■ Lake Benton Farmers Elevator Inc.
110 W Lincoln Ave.
Lake Benton, MN 56149
Phone: (507)368-4603
Products: Grain; Seed; Feed; Fertilizer; Chemicals. **SICs:** 5153 (Grain & Field Beans); 5191 (Farm Supplies). **Est:** 1905. **Sales:** $6,500,000 (2000). **Emp:** 12. **Officers:** Jim Best, President & CFO.

■ 931 ■ Lakeland FS, Inc.
PO Box 50
Shelbyville, IL 62565
Phone: (217)774-3901 **Fax:** (217)774-5657
URL: http://www.mailus@lakelandfs.fssystem.com
Products: Farm supplies. **SIC:** 5191 (Farm Supplies). **Est:** 1936. **Sales:** $12,000,000 (2000). **Emp:** 60. **Officers:** Dave Tice, President; Arville Thompson, Controller; Jeff Sullivan, General Mgr. **Former Name:** Moultrie-Shelby FS Inc.

■ 932 ■ Lambright's Inc.
PO Box 71
Lagrange, IN 46761
Phone: (219)463-2178
Products: Eggs; Feeds; Cat and dog food. **SICs:** 5144 (Poultry & Poultry Products); 5149 (Groceries & Related Products Nec); 5144 (Poultry & Poultry Products). **Est:** 1966. **Sales:** $24,000,000 (2000). **Emp:** 100. **Officers:** Richard D. Lambright, President.

■ 933 ■ Lampson Tractor and Equipment Company Inc.
PO Box 85
Geyserville, CA 95441
Phone: (707)857-3443
Free: (800)400-1877 **Fax:** (707)857-3983
E-mail: sales@lampsontractor.com
URL: http://www.lampsontractor.com
Products: Mechanized farm supplies, including tractors and parts. **SIC:** 5083 (Farm & Garden Machinery). **Est:** 1974. **Sales:** $13,000,000 (2000). **Emp:** 50. **Officers:** Keith Lampson, President; Terry Proschold, Treasurer & Secty.; Paul Pigoni, General Mgr.

■ 934 ■ Landiseed International, Ltd.
PO Box 25690
Portland, OR 97298-0690
Phone: (503)203-6956 **Fax:** (503)203-6965
E-mail: landiseed@aol.com
Products: Grass seeds; Forage seeds. **SIC:** 5191

(Farm Supplies). **Est:** 1974. **Sales:** $20,000,000 (2000). **Emp:** 3. **Officers:** John F. Landis, President.

■ 935 ■ Landmark Co-Op Inc.
PO Box 606
New Philadelphia, OH 44663
Phone: (216)339-1062
Products: Farming products, including feed, fertilizer, and seed; Petroleum products, including gasoline, fuel oil, and diesel fuel. **SIC:** 5191 (Farm Supplies). **Est:** 1934. **Sales:** $14,000,000 (2000). **Emp:** 37. **Officers:** Marvin Brown, President; Brian Amstutz, Treasurer.

■ 936 ■ Landmark Supply Company Inc.
N 58 W 6181 Columbia Rd.
Cedarburg, WI 53012
Phone: (414)375-2909
Products: Animal feeds. **SIC:** 5191 (Farm Supplies).

■ 937 ■ Lano Equipment Inc.
3021 W 133rd St.
Shakopee, MN 55379
Phone: (612)445-6310 **Fax:** (612)496-0263
Products: Earth-moving, lawn, and landscaping equipment. **SICs:** 5083 (Farm & Garden Machinery); 5084 (Industrial Machinery & Equipment). **Est:** 1946. **Sales:** $10,000,000 (2000). **Emp:** 22. **Officers:** Gerhard Lano, President; Joseph Lano, Dir. of Sales.

■ 938 ■ Lansdowne-Moody Company Inc.
8445 E Fwy.
Houston, TX 77029
Phone: (713)672-8366
Products: Tractors. **SIC:** 5083 (Farm & Garden Machinery). **Est:** 1936. **Sales:** $7,000,000 (2000). **Emp:** 40. **Officers:** Edwin H. Harris Sr., President; Edwin H. Harris Jr., General Mgr.

■ 939 ■ Larsen Cooperative Company Inc.
8290 Hwy. T
Larsen, WI 54947
Phone: (414)836-2113
Products: Farm supplies, including feed; Gasoline and fuel oil. **SICs:** 5191 (Farm Supplies); 5172 (Petroleum Products Nec); 5072 (Hardware). **Est:** 1819. **Sales:** $15,000,000 (2000). **Emp:** 50. **Officers:** Leroy Peterson, General Mgr.

■ 940 ■ Walter Lasley and Sons Inc.
PO Box 168
Stratford, TX 79084-0168
Phone: (806)753-4411 **Fax:** (806)753-4435
Products: Feed. **SIC:** 5153 (Grain & Field Beans). **Est:** 1947. **Sales:** $17,000,000 (2000). **Emp:** 25. **Officers:** Walter Lasley, President.

■ 941 ■ Latshaw Enterprises Inc.
PO Box 7710
Wichita, KS 67277
Phone: (316)942-7266
Products: Lawn and garden tools; Mechanical controls. **SICs:** 5083 (Farm & Garden Machinery); 5084 (Industrial Machinery & Equipment). **Est:** 1959. **Sales:** $51,600,000 (2000). **Emp:** 400. **Officers:** John Latshaw, CEO & Chairman of the Board; David G. Carr, Sr. VP & CFO.

■ 942 ■ Laughery Valley AG Co-Op Inc.
336 N Buckeye
Osgood, IN 47037
Phone: (812)689-4401 **Fax:** (812)689-6131
Products: Farm supplies, including fertilizers and chemicals. **SICs:** 5191 (Farm Supplies); 5153 (Grain & Field Beans). **Est:** 1989. **Sales:** $7,000,000 (2000). **Emp:** 25. **Officers:** Jerald Jahnigen, President; Richard Miller, Treasurer.

■ 943 ■ Lawes Coal Company Inc.
PO Box 258
Shrewsbury, NJ 07702
Phone: (732)741-6300 **Fax:** (732)741-8527
Products: Oil and fuel; Fertilizer. **SICs:** 5191 (Farm Supplies); 5172 (Petroleum Products Nec). **Est:** 1926. **Sales:** $10,000,000 (2000). **Emp:** 48. **Officers:** Donald E. Lawes Jr., President & Treasurer; Donald Lawes III, Vice President.

■ 944 ■ Lawn and Golf Supply Company Inc.
647 Nutt Rd.
Phoenixville, PA 19460
Phone: (215)933-5801 **Fax:** (215)933-8890
Products: Mowing equipment; Grass seed and chemicals; Golf course supplies. **SICs:** 5191 (Farm Supplies); 5193 (Flowers & Florists' Supplies); 5083 (Farm & Garden Machinery).

■ 945 ■ Lawn Hill Cooperative
PO Box 68
New Providence, IA 50206
Phone: (515)497-5291 **Fax:** (515)497-5211
Products: Farm products, including feed and fertilizer. **SICs:** 5191 (Farm Supplies); 5153 (Grain & Field Beans). **Est:** 1950. **Sales:** $16,500,000 (2000). **Emp:** 30. **Officers:** Dean Hart, General Mgr.; Ron Laursen, Controller.

■ 946 ■ Le Roy Farmers Cooperative Creamery Association
PO Box 306
Le Roy, MN 55951
Phone: (507)324-5361
Products: Agricultural supplies, including feed, fertilizer, and chemicals. **SIC:** 5191 (Farm Supplies). **Est:** 1910. **Sales:** $3,000,000 (2000). **Emp:** 5. **Officers:** Corliss Jacobsen, General Mgr.

■ 947 ■ Le Roy Farmers Cooperative Grain and Stock Co.
PO Box 120
Le Roy, MN 55951
Phone: (507)324-5605 **Fax:** (507)324-5861
Products: Grain elevator implements; Lumber. **SICs:** 5031 (Lumber, Plywood & Millwork); 5083 (Farm & Garden Machinery). **Est:** 1918. **Sales:** $5,000,000 (2000). **Emp:** 23. **Officers:** Dick Farrell, General Mgr.

■ 948 ■ Ray Lee Equipment Co.
910 N Date St.
Plainview, TX 79072
Phone: (806)293-2538
Products: Tractors and mowers. **SIC:** 5083 (Farm & Garden Machinery). **Est:** 1985. **Sales:** $3,000,000 (2000). **Emp:** 18. **Officers:** Ray Lee, President; Aaron Lee, CFO; Mark Lee, Dir. of Marketing.

■ 949 ■ Lee F.S. Inc.
1129 Lee Center Rd.
Amboy, IL 61310
Phone: (815)857-3535
Products: Farm supplies, including fertilizer, chemicals, and feed. **SICs:** 5191 (Farm Supplies); 5171 (Petroleum Bulk Stations & Terminals); 5083 (Farm & Garden Machinery). **Est:** 1929. **Sales:** $20,000,000 (2000). **Emp:** 45. **Officers:** Edward Gilmore, President; Dave Tippey, Controller.

■ 950 ■ Lefeld Implement Inc.
5228 State Rte. 118
Coldwater, OH 45828
Phone: (419)678-2375
Products: Agricultural equipment. **SIC:** 5083 (Farm & Garden Machinery). **Est:** 1975. **Sales:** $5,000,000 (2000). **Emp:** 28. **Officers:** Steve Lefeld, President; Judy Marbaugh, Treasurer.

■ 951 ■ W.G. Leffelman and Sons Inc.
340 N Metcalf Ave.
Amboy, IL 61310
Phone: (815)857-2513 **Fax:** (815)857-3105
Products: Agricultural tractors; Plows and listers, excluding turf and grounds machinery; Farm machinery and equipment. **SIC:** 5083 (Farm & Garden Machinery). **Est:** 1935. **Sales:** $7,500,000 (2000). **Emp:** 20. **Officers:** John H. Leffelman, President; Douglas O'Rourke; Sylvan Leffelman, Treasurer & Secty.

■ 952 ■ LESCO Inc.
20005 Lake Rd.
Rocky River, OH 44116
Phone: (440)333-9250 **Fax:** (440)333-7789
Products: Turf grass and lawn equipment. **SIC:** 5083 (Farm & Garden Machinery).

■ **953** ■ **Lewis International**
55 E Palatine Rd.
Prospect Heights, IL 60070
Phone: (847)537-6110 **Fax:** (847)537-5736
Products: Tractors, including lawn and industrial.
SICs: 5083 (Farm & Garden Machinery); 5082 (Construction & Mining Machinery).

■ **954** ■ **Lewis Seed and Feed Co.**
306 W Gertrude Ave.
Drew, MS 38737-3228
Phone: (601)745-8543 **Fax:** (601)745-8544
Products: Fertilizer and fertilizer materials; Feed; Agricultural chemicals. **SIC:** 5191 (Farm Supplies). **Est:** 1958. **Sales:** $2,500,000 (2000). **Emp:** 12. **Officers:** N.B. Lewis, Partner; W.P. Lewis, Partner.

■ **955** ■ **Lewiston AG Inc.**
R.R. 1
Lewistown, IL 61542
Phone: (309)547-3793
Products: Fertilizer. **SIC:** 5191 (Farm Supplies). **Est:** 1955. **Sales:** $1,000,000 (2000). **Emp:** 12. **Officers:** Ted Nixon, President; John B. Gorsuch, VP of Finance.

■ **956** ■ **Liechty Farm Equipment Inc.**
PO Box 67
Archbold, OH 43502
Phone: (419)445-1565
Products: Farm machinery and equipment. **SIC:** 5083 (Farm & Garden Machinery). **Sales:** $14,000,000 (1994). **Emp:** 65. **Officers:** Wayne J. Liechty, President & Treasurer; Jay Beck, Mgr. of Finance.

■ **957** ■ **Lillegard Inc.**
PO Box 1178
Wahpeton, ND 58074
Phone: (701)642-8424 **Fax:** (701)642-9514
Products: Farm equipment, including combines and tractors. **SIC:** 5083 (Farm & Garden Machinery). **Est:** 1913. **Sales:** $9,000,000 (2000). **Emp:** 21. **Officers:** William F. Sprung, President; Douglas Hudson, VP of Marketing & Sales; Colvin Bunren, Treasurer & Secty.

■ **958** ■ **Chas. H. Lilly Co.**
6000 E Marginal Way
Seattle, WA 98108
Phone: (206)762-1224 **Fax:** (206)762-9246
Products: Lawn and garden products. **SIC:** 5191 (Farm Supplies).

■ **959** ■ **Limestone Farmers Cooperative Inc.**
PO Box 429
Athens, AL 35611
Phone: (205)232-5500
Products: Farm equipment including seed, chemicals, and feed. **SIC:** 5191 (Farm Supplies). **Est:** 1932. **Sales:** $10,000,000 (2000). **Emp:** 20. **Officers:** H.L. King, President; J.W. Hudson, General Mgr.; Andy Vanschoiack, Dir. of Marketing & Sales.

■ **960** ■ **Lincoln County Farmers Cooperative**
811 E Cherry St.
Troy, MO 63379
Phone: (314)528-6141
Products: Farming supplies, including feed and seed; Petroleum; Chemicals. **SICs:** 5191 (Farm Supplies); 5172 (Petroleum Products Nec); 5169 (Chemicals & Allied Products Nec). **Est:** 1908. **Sales:** $6,200,000 (2000). **Emp:** 17. **Officers:** Dale Hahn, CEO; John Northcutt, CFO.

■ **961** ■ **Linder Equipment Co.**
PO Box 1139
Tulare, CA 93275
Phone: (209)685-5000 **Fax:** (209)685-0452
Products: Farm equipment, including tractors and cotton pickers. **SICs:** 5083 (Farm & Garden Machinery); 5012 (Automobiles & Other Motor Vehicles). **Est:** 1947. **Sales:** $13,000,000 (2000). **Emp:** 60. **Officers:** David Linder, President; Frances H. Linder, Treasurer & Secty.; Jim Dokken, Sales Mgr.

■ **962** ■ **Livingston Service Co.**
320 N Plum St.
Pontiac, IL 61764
Phone: (815)844-7185 **Fax:** (815)842-1733
Products: Farm supplies, including fertilizer, petroleum products, bins, and buildings, agricultural chemicals.

SIC: 5191 (Farm Supplies). **Est:** 1930. **Sales:** $18,000,000 (1999). **Emp:** 50. **Officers:** V. Maier, President; Tim King, Sales Mgr.; Keith Hufendick, General Mgr.

■ **963** ■ **Lobel Chemical Corp.**
100 Church St., Ste. 1608
New York, NY 10007-2682
Phone: (212)267-4265
Free: (800)227-5805 **Fax:** (212)349-0869
Products: Pesticides. **SIC:** 5191 (Farm Supplies). **Sales:** $6,000,000 (2000). **Emp:** 10. **Officers:** Sheldon Lobel, President.

■ **964** ■ **Lockbourne Farmers Exchange Co.**
PO Box 11
Lockbourne, OH 43137
Phone: (614)491-0635
Products: Feed and fertilizer. **SIC:** 5191 (Farm Supplies). **Est:** 1944. **Sales:** $1,000,000 (2000). **Emp:** 7. **Officers:** Carl Patzer, President; Marianne Smith, Bookkeeper.

■ **965** ■ **Lockwood Farmers Exchange Inc.**
107 W 6th St.
Lockwood, MO 65682
Phone: (417)232-4525
Products: Feed; Field, garden, and flower seeds; Fertilizer and fertilizer materials; Farm supplies. **SIC:** 5191 (Farm Supplies). **Est:** 1922. **Sales:** $5,000,000 (2000). **Emp:** 12. **Officers:** Doyle Daniel, CEO.

■ **966** ■ **Loft's Seed Inc.**
30 Southard Ave., Ste. 100
Farmingdale, NJ 07727-1213
Phone: (732)356-8700 **Fax:** (732)356-5607
Products: Grass seeds and fertilizers. **SIC:** 5191 (Farm Supplies). **Sales:** $70,000,000 (2000). **Emp:** 150. **Officers:** Jon D. Loft, President & Chairman of the Board; Mike Celletto, Controller.

■ **967** ■ **Long Equipment Co.**
2009 Constitution Ave.
Enid, OK 73703-2004
Phone: (580)237-2304
Products: Agricultural equipment, including tractors. **SIC:** 5083 (Farm & Garden Machinery). **Est:** 1965. **Sales:** $5,000,000 (2000). **Emp:** 25. **Officers:** Steve Long, President; Ed Long, Treasurer & Secty.; Eddie McDowell, Sales Mgr.

■ **968** ■ **Long Machinery**
PO Box 5508
Missoula, MT 59806
Phone: (406)721-4050
Free: (800)548-1512 **Fax:** (406)721-6394
Products: Construction machinery; Power generators. **SIC:** 5083 (Farm & Garden Machinery). **Est:** 1979. **Emp:** 140. **Officers:** T.E. Ritzheimer, Exec. VP & General Mgr.; C.J. Johnson, VP of Finance; William D. Schwenk, Sales Mgr.

■ **969** ■ **Long Machinery Inc. Lewiston**
PO Box 1900
Lewiston, ID 83501
Phone: (208)746-3301
Products: Tractors and tractor parts. **SIC:** 5083 (Farm & Garden Machinery). **Est:** 1979. **Sales:** $7,000,000 (2000). **Emp:** 26. **Officers:** Gary Anderson, General Mgr.

■ **970** ■ **Lorraine Grain Fuel and Stock Co.**
PO Box 20
Lorraine, KS 67459-0020
Phone: (785)472-5271 **Fax:** (785)472-3130
Products: Farm supplies, including feed. **SIC:** 5191 (Farm Supplies). **Est:** 1939. **Sales:** $7,000,000 (2000). **Emp:** 20. **Officers:** Ronald Rathburn, President; Darryl Roane, General Mgr.

■ **971** ■ **Lostant Hatchery and Milling Company Inc.**
PO Box 208
Lostant, IL 61334
Phone: (815)368-3221 **Fax:** (815)368-3221
Products: Feed, seed, and farm chemicals. **SIC:** 5191 (Farm Supplies). **Est:** 1944. **Sales:** $1,000,000 (2000). **Emp:** 5. **Officers:** John J. Mertel, President; Marlene M. Warnell, Treasurer & Secty.

■ **972** ■ **Loveland Industries**
PO Box 1289
Greeley, CO 80632-1289
Phone: (970)356-8920
Free: (800)356-8920 **Fax:** (970)356-8926
E-mail: atd@loveland.com
URL: http://www.lovelandindustries.com
Products: Animal health products; Rodenticides; Seed products; Insecticides; Veterinary supplies. **SICs:** 5191 (Farm Supplies); 5169 (Chemicals & Allied Products Nec). **Est:** 1969. **Sales:** $85,000,000 (1999). **Emp:** 102. **Officers:** David Reynolds, President; Troy Feese, Controller; Deb Kerns, Sales/Marketing Contact, e-mail: dkerns@loveland.uap.com; Vance Doddridge, Customer Service Contact, e-mail: vdoddridge@loveland.uap.com.

■ **973** ■ **Lowville Farmers Cooperative Inc.**
5500 Shady Ave.
Lowville, NY 13367
Phone: (315)376-6587 **Fax:** (315)376-8233
Products: Farm and garden supplies, including feed and seed; Building supplies, including hardware and insulation; Dairy equipment and animal health supplies. **SICs:** 5191 (Farm Supplies); 5072 (Hardware); 5039 (Construction Materials Nec). **Est:** 1920. **Sales:** $10,000,000 (2000). **Emp:** 43. **Officers:** John H. Ross, President; S. Szalach, Chairman of the Board.

■ **974** ■ **Lucky Distributing**
PO Box 18000
Portland, OR 97218
Phone: (503)252-1249 **Fax:** (503)252-8360
Products: Tractors; Lawn and garden equipment; Heating equipment. **SICs:** 5083 (Farm & Garden Machinery); 5075 (Warm Air Heating & Air-Conditioning). **Est:** 1948. **Sales:** $9,000,000 (2000). **Emp:** 45. **Officers:** Fred Stockton, President.

■ **975** ■ **Lucky Farmers Inc.**
PO Box 217
Woodville, OH 43469
Phone: (419)849-2711
Products: Farm supplies, including feed, seed, chemicals, and fertilizer. **SICs:** 5191 (Farm Supplies); 5153 (Grain & Field Beans). **Est:** 1919. **Sales:** $60,000,000 (2000). **Emp:** 115. **Officers:** Daniel Walski, General Mgr.; Clark Botman, CFO.

■ **976** ■ **Lyssy and Eckel Inc.**
PO Box 128
Poth, TX 78147
Phone: (830)484-3314
Products: Fertilizers, feed and agricultural chemicals. **SIC:** 5191 (Farm Supplies). **Sales:** $20,000,000 (1994). **Emp:** 50. **Officers:** Ronald Eckel, President & CFO.

■ **977** ■ **M-G Inc.**
300 E Main St.
Weimar, TX 78962
Phone: (409)725-8581
Free: (800)460-8581 **Fax:** (409)725-8767
E-mail: mb@cutv.net
Products: Farm supplies, including herbicides, fertilizer, seeds, and animal feeds. **SIC:** 5191 (Farm Supplies). **Est:** 1940. **Sales:** $25,000,000 (1999). **Emp:** 105. **Officers:** Mark Kloesel, President.

■ **978** ■ **M and L Industries Inc.**
1210 St. Charles St.
Houma, LA 70360
Phone: (504)876-2280 **Fax:** (504)872-9596
E-mail: mlind@mobiletel.com
URL: http://www.mlind.net
Products: Tractors. **SICs:** 5084 (Industrial Machinery & Equipment); 5083 (Farm & Garden Machinery). **Est:** 1953. **Sales:** $20,000,000 (2000). **Emp:** 112. **Officers:** M.V. Marmade, President; Charlie Williams, CFO; Steven Marmande, Vice President.

■ **979** ■ **M and M Chemical Products Inc.**
PO Box 27-56
Redwood City, CA 94063
Phone: (650)368-4900
Products: Chemical fertilizer. **SIC:** 5191 (Farm Supplies). **Est:** 1979. **Sales:** $3,000,000 (2000). **Emp:** 3. **Officers:** Jerry W. Mertens, President & Treasurer.

■ 980 ■ **Madison County Cooperative**
PO Box 587
Canton, MS 39046
Phone: (601)859-1271
Products: Feed; Fertilizer and fertilizer materials; Agricultural chemicals. **SIC:** 5191 (Farm Supplies). **Est:** 1931. **Sales:** $5,000,000 (2000). **Emp:** 25. **Officers:** Steve Patrick, President; Joe S. Hand, Manager.

■ 981 ■ **Madison County Cooperative Inc.**
PO Box 5345
Huntsville, AL 35814
Phone: (205)837-5031 **Fax:** (205)837-6020
Products: Dealers in raw farm products; Field, garden, and flower seeds; Feed; Fertilizer and fertilizer materials. **SICs:** 5191 (Farm Supplies); 5083 (Farm & Garden Machinery). **Sales:** $1,000,000 (2000). **Emp:** 14. **Officers:** F. Hanes, General Mgr.

■ 982 ■ **Madison Service Co.**
900 Hillsboro Ave.
Edwardsville, IL 62025
Phone: (618)656-3500 **Fax:** (618)692-7277
Products: Feed; Seed; Fertilizer. **SICs:** 5153 (Grain & Field Beans); 5191 (Farm Supplies). **Est:** 1935. **Sales:** $21,000,000 (2000). **Emp:** 40. **Officers:** Gaylan Brussen, General Mgr.; Pamela Moehle, Controller; David Smith, Dir. of Marketing & Sales.

■ 983 ■ **Malvese Equipment Company Inc.**
PO Box 295
Hicksville, NY 11802
Phone: (516)681-7600 **Fax:** (516)938-8962
Products: Construction equipment; Tractors; Turf maintenance equipment. **SIC:** 5082 (Construction & Mining Machinery). **Est:** 1912. **Sales:** $20,000,000 (2000). **Emp:** 60. **Officers:** Paul G. Malvese, Vice President; Albert Cooley, President; R. Del Prete, Controller. **Former Name:** George Malvese and Company Inc.

■ 984 ■ **Manna Pro Corp. Denver Div.**
4545 Madison St.
Denver, CO 80216
Phone: (303)296-8668
Products: Feed. **SIC:** 5191 (Farm Supplies). **Sales:** $31,000,000 (2000). **Emp:** 60. **Officers:** Buck Markley, President.

■ 985 ■ **Manning Grain Co.**
PO Box 217
Fairmont, NE 68354
Phone: (402)266-3701 **Fax:** (402)266-2169
Products: Farming supplies. **SIC:** 5191 (Farm Supplies). **Est:** 1924. **Sales:** $6,000,000 (2000). **Emp:** 7. **Officers:** Thomas B. Manning, Owner.

■ 986 ■ **Mark Seed Co.**
PO Box 67
Perry, IA 50220
Phone: (515)465-2122 **Fax:** (515)465-2471
Products: Agricultural and lawn seed. **SIC:** 5191 (Farm Supplies).

■ 987 ■ **D.F. Marks Co.**
8510 212th St. SE
Woodinville, WA 98072
Phone: (425)485-3802 **Fax:** (425)485-4285
Products: Turf and field seed; Lawn and garden supplies. **SICs:** 5191 (Farm Supplies); 5193 (Flowers & Florists' Supplies).

■ 988 ■ **Maroa Farmers Cooperative Elevator Co.**
PO Box 349
Maroa, IL 61756
Phone: (217)794-5533
Products: Grain elevator. **SICs:** 5083 (Farm & Garden Machinery); 5191 (Farm Supplies). **Sales:** $10,000,000 (2000). **Emp:** 6. **Officers:** Larry Clark, President; Phil Seaman, General Mgr.

■ 989 ■ **Marshall Farmers Cooperative**
615 Ellington Pkwy.
Lewisburg, TN 37091
Phone: (931)359-1558
Products: Farm supplies, including chemicals, fertilizers, feed. **SIC:** 5191 (Farm Supplies). **Est:** 1948.

Sales: $9,000,000 (2000). **Emp:** 35. **Officers:** Mark Posey, General Mgr.

■ 990 ■ **Martindale Feed Mill**
PO Box 245
Valley View, TX 76272
Phone: (940)726-3203 **Fax:** (940)726-5235
Products: Feed; Dairy products. **SICs:** 5191 (Farm Supplies); 5143 (Dairy Products Except Dried or Canned). **Est:** 1963. **Sales:** $13,500,000 (2000). **Emp:** 36. **Officers:** Don Huspeth, General Mgr.

■ 991 ■ **Master Feed and Grain Inc.**
Mulberry St.
Conneautville, PA 16406
Phone: (814)587-3645
Products: Feed; Grain. **SICs:** 5191 (Farm Supplies); 5153 (Grain & Field Beans). **Est:** 1950. **Sales:** $4,500,000 (2000). **Emp:** 7. **Officers:** Louise M. Johns, President; Dorothy A. Luckock, VP of Finance; Bernie Mook, Manager.

■ 992 ■ **Maury Farmers Cooperative**
PO Box 860
Columbia, TN 38401
Phone: (931)388-0714 **Fax:** (931)380-0285
Products: Chemicals, feed, and fertilizers. **SIC:** 5191 (Farm Supplies). **Est:** 1945. **Sales:** $7,000,000 (2000). **Emp:** 38. **Officers:** Pete Brooke, Manager.

■ 993 ■ **Mauston Farmers Cooperative**
310 Prairie St.
Mauston, WI 53948
Phone: (608)847-5679
Products: Hardware; Belts and filters; Dog and cat food. **SICs:** 5191 (Farm Supplies); 5149 (Groceries & Related Products Nec); 5072 (Hardware). **Est:** 1922. **Sales:** $23,000,000 (2000). **Emp:** 60. **Officers:** Ken Wilcox, General Mgr.

■ 994 ■ **D.R. Mayo Seed Co.**
PO Box 10247
Knoxville, TN 37939
Phone: (865)577-7568 **Fax:** (865)577-8063
Products: Seeds. **SIC:** 5191 (Farm Supplies). **Est:** 1878. **Sales:** $4,000,000 (2000). **Emp:** 30. **Officers:** D.R. Mayo, President.

■ 995 ■ **Maywood Cooperative Association**
103 Commercial St.
Maywood, NE 69038
Phone: (308)362-4244
Products: Petroleum and its products; Grain; Farm supplies. **SICs:** 5191 (Farm Supplies); 5172 (Petroleum Products Nec); 5153 (Grain & Field Beans). **Est:** 1923. **Sales:** $37,000,000 (2000). **Emp:** 75. **Officers:** Richard Jorgensen, President; Cheryl Teel, Controller.

■ 996 ■ **Mazon Farmers Elevator**
604 South St.
PO Box 361
Mazon, IL 60444
Phone: (815)448-2113 **Fax:** (815)448-2609
Products: Grain; Fertilizer and chemicals; Petroleum. **SICs:** 5153 (Grain & Field Beans); 5191 (Farm Supplies); 5172 (Petroleum Products Nec); 5169 (Chemicals & Allied Products Nec). **Est:** 1919. **Sales:** $42,000,000 (2000). **Emp:** 20. **Officers:** S. Lowry, President; Patrick M. Mino, General Mgr.

■ 997 ■ **McCabe Equipment Inc.**
PO Box 5550
Coralville, IA 52241-0550
Phone: (319)351-0828
Products: Tractors, mowers, and riders. **SIC:** 5083 (Farm & Garden Machinery). **Sales:** $6,000,000 (2000). **Emp:** 20. **Officers:** Lawrence McCabe, President; Janet McCabe, Treasurer & Secty.

■ 998 ■ **McClung Equipment Co.**
PO Box 1316
Mountain View, AR 72560
Phone: (870)269-3866
Products: Farming equipment. **SIC:** 5083 (Farm & Garden Machinery). **Est:** 1979. **Sales:** $2,000,000 (2000). **Emp:** 13. **Officers:** Gary McClung, Owner; Jeannie McClung, Bookkeeper.

■ 999 ■ **McCranie Motor and Tractor Inc.**
U.S. Hwy. 41 S
Unadilla, GA 31091-0408
Phone: (912)627-3291 **Fax:** (912)627-9224
Products: Tractors. **SIC:** 5083 (Farm & Garden Machinery). **Est:** 1956. **Sales:** $20,000,000 (2000). **Emp:** 60. **Officers:** J. W. Johnson, President & Chairman of the Board; Charles L. Ellison Jr., Treasurer & Secty.

■ 1000 ■ **McCranie Motor and Tractor Inc. McCranie Implement Co.**
Hwy. 341 N
Hawkinsville, GA 31036
Phone: (912)892-9046
Free: (800)245-9046 **Fax:** (912)783-0778
Products: Tractors and parts. **SIC:** 5083 (Farm & Garden Machinery). **Est:** 1939. **Sales:** $6,000,000 (1999). **Emp:** 21. **Officers:** J.W. Johnston, President; Walter S. Daniel, VP of Finance.

■ 1001 ■ **McCune Farmers Union Cooperative Association**
PO Box 58
McCune, KS 66753
Phone: (316)632-4226 **Fax:** (316)632-5236
E-mail: mccunecoop@ckt.net
Products: Feed; Fertilizer and fertilizer materials; Farm supplies. **SICs:** 5191 (Farm Supplies); 5153 (Grain & Field Beans). **Est:** 1940. **Sales:** $6,500,000 (2000). **Emp:** 11. **Officers:** Kevin Fox, President; Merlin Hiller, Treasurer; Gary McGown, General Mgr.

■ 1002 ■ **McFarlane Manufacturing Company Inc.**
PO Box 100
Sauk City, WI 53583-0100
Phone: (608)643-3321 **Fax:** (608)643-3976
Products: Farm machinery and equipment. **SIC:** 5191 (Farm Supplies). **Est:** 1939. **Sales:** $40,000,000 (2000). **Emp:** 100. **Officers:** John McFarlane, CEO.

■ 1003 ■ **McGinnis Farms Inc.**
5610 McGinnis Ferry Rd.
Alpharetta, GA 30022
Phone: (404)740-1874
Products: Nursery stock and landscaping supplies. **SIC:** 5193 (Flowers & Florists' Supplies). **Sales:** $11,000,000 (1994). **Emp:** 100. **Officers:** Stan Walker, President; Victor Logan, Controller.

■ 1004 ■ **McLean County Service Co.**
402 N Hershey Rd.
Bloomington, IL 61701-1367
Phone: (309)662-9321 **Fax:** (309)662-9325
Products: Agricultural supplies, including fertilizers, pesticides, herbicides, oil, and gasoline. **SICs:** 5191 (Farm Supplies); 5172 (Petroleum Products Nec). **Est:** 1926. **Sales:** $100,000,000 (2000). **Emp:** 100. **Officers:** Dan Kelley, President; Jim Gleeson, Controller; John Feit, Dir. of Marketing & Sales.

■ 1005 ■ **McMann Loudan Farmers Cooperative**
15 East Ave.
Athens, TN 37303-1619
Phone: (423)745-0443 **Fax:** (423)745-7086
Products: Agricultural fertilizers, chemicals, and feed. **SIC:** 5191 (Farm Supplies). **Est:** 1950. **Sales:** $8,000,000 (2000). **Emp:** 51. **Officers:** Freddie Brewster, General Mgr.

■ 1006 ■ **McNeil Marketing Co.**
709 Vista Ter. Dr.
Nampa, ID 83686
Phone: (208)466-7403 **Fax:** (208)465-6171
Products: Hay rakes; Balers; Bale wrappers; Seeding equipment; Tillage tools; Turf equipment; Compact tractors; Rotary cutters; Rock removal. **SICs:** 5083 (Farm & Garden Machinery); 5191 (Farm Supplies). **Est:** 1991. **Sales:** $1,200,000 (1999). **Emp:** 2. **Officers:** Louis McNeil, President; Myrleen McNeil, Secretary; Louis McNeil, Sales/Marketing Contact.

■ **1007** ■ **Ben Meadows Company Inc.**
PO Box 20200
Canton, GA 30114-1920
Phone: (404)455-0907
Free: (800)441-6401 **Fax:** (404)457-1841
E-mail: mail@benmeadows.com
URL: http://www.benmeadows.com
Products: Forestry, environmental and natural resource supplies. **SICs:** 5082 (Construction & Mining Machinery); 5049 (Professional Equipment Nec). **Est:** 1956. **Emp:** 40. **Officers:** F. Karl Hube, President; Margaret Sudderth, Controller; John Asaro, VP & General Mgr.

■ **1008** ■ **Medalist America Turfgrass Seed Co.**
1490 Industrial Way SW
Albany, OR 97321
Free: (800)568-8873 **Fax:** (541)926-0126
Products: Field, garden, and flower seeds. **SIC:** 5191 (Farm Supplies).

■ **1009** ■ **Medica International Ltd.**
360 N Michigan Ave., Ste. 2001
Chicago, IL 60601
Phone: (312)263-1117 **Fax:** (312)263-1036
Products: Farm supplies, including fertilizer, macronutrient, and swine veterinary biologicals; Food service equipment; Medical equipment; Pharmaceuticals. **SICs:** 5191 (Farm Supplies); 5199 (Nondurable Goods Nec); 5122 (Drugs, Proprietaries & Sundries); 5046 (Commercial Equipment Nec); 5047 (Medical & Hospital Equipment). **Officers:** Susan Gripentrog, Export Director.

■ **1010** ■ **Medina Farmers Exchange Co.**
320 S Court St.
Medina, OH 44256
Phone: (216)723-3607 **Fax:** (216)722-8145
Products: Agricultural products, including grain, feed, and seed. **SIC:** 5191 (Farm Supplies). **Est:** 1904. **Sales:** $8,000,000 (2000). **Emp:** 20. **Officers:** James Duffy, President.

■ **1011** ■ **Medina Landmark Inc.**
241 S State St.
Medina, OH 44256
Phone: (216)723-3208
Products: Seed; Fertilizer; Petroleum products. **SICs:** 5191 (Farm Supplies); 5172 (Petroleum Products Nec). **Est:** 1965. **Sales:** $8,000,000 (2000). **Emp:** 21. **Officers:** Bill Rohrbauth, General Mgr.

■ **1012** ■ **Meherrin Agricultural and Chemical Co.**
PO Box 200
Severn, NC 27877
Phone: (919)585-1744
Products: Insecticides, herbicides, and pesticides. **SIC:** 5191 (Farm Supplies). **Est:** 1958. **Sales:** $75,000,000 (2000). **Emp:** 100. **Officers:** Dalas Barnes, President; William E. McKeoun, VP & General Merchandising Mgr.

■ **1013** ■ **Meis Seed and Feed Co.**
PO Box 1406
Le Mars, IA 51031
Phone: (712)546-4131 **Fax:** (712)546-9605
Products: Livestock feed. **SICs:** 5191 (Farm Supplies); 5153 (Grain & Field Beans). **Est:** 1917. **Sales:** $9,000,000 (2000). **Emp:** 21. **Officers:** David Meis, President; John Meis, Treasurer.

■ **1014** ■ **Memphis Ford New Holland Inc.**
3849 Getwell Rd.
Memphis, TN 38118
Phone: (901)362-9200
Products: Tractors. **SIC:** 5083 (Farm & Garden Machinery). **Sales:** $7,000,000 (2000). **Emp:** 35. **Officers:** Simon Wadsworth, President.

■ **1015** ■ **Menomonie Farmers Union Cooperative**
PO Box 438
Menomonie, WI 54751
Phone: (715)232-6200 **Fax:** (715)232-6202
Products: Farm supplies; Petroleum products. **SICs:** 5172 (Petroleum Products Nec); 5191 (Farm Supplies). **Est:** 1933. **Sales:** $14,988,000 (2000). **Emp:** 74. **Officers:** R.L. Cook, General Mgr.

■ **1016** ■ **Merschman Inc.**
PO Box 67
West Point, IA 52656
Phone: (319)837-6111 **Fax:** (319)837-6104
Products: Seed. **SIC:** 5191 (Farm Supplies). **Sales:** $30,000,000 (2000). **Emp:** 45. **Officers:** Joseph Merschman, CEO.

■ **1017** ■ **Mesa Sprinkler Inc.**
201 W Juanita
Mesa, AZ 85210
Phone: (602)964-8888 **Fax:** (602)844-9732
Products: Indoor and outdoor sprinklers. **SIC:** 5083 (Farm & Garden Machinery). **Est:** 1977. **Sales:** $12,000,000 (2000). **Emp:** 40. **Officers:** David Lange, Owner.

■ **1018** ■ **Metamora Elevator Co.**
State Rte. 120
Metamora, OH 43540
Phone: (419)644-4711
Products: Farm supplies, including feed, seed, chemicals, and fertilizer. **SICs:** 5153 (Grain & Field Beans); 5191 (Farm Supplies). **Est:** 1906. **Sales:** $63,000,000 (2000). **Emp:** 50. **Officers:** Fred R. Duncan, President; David Duncan, Vice President.

■ **1019** ■ **Meyer Equipment Inc.**
PO Box 393
Lisbon, ND 58054
Phone: (701)683-4000 **Fax:** (701)683-5108
E-mail: ag@meyerequipment.com
URL: http://www.meyerequipment.com
Products: Farm equipment. **SIC:** 5083 (Farm & Garden Machinery). **Est:** 1977. **Sales:** $18,000,000 (2000). **Emp:** 75. **Officers:** David Meyer, President. **Former Name:** Ransom County Implement Inc.

■ **1020** ■ **Meyer Seed Co.**
600 S Caroline St.
Baltimore, MD 21231
Phone: (410)342-4224
Products: Lawn and garden supplies, including seeds, tools, and chemicals. **SIC:** 5191 (Farm Supplies).

■ **1021** ■ **L.W. Meyer and Son of Sullivan Inc.**
PO Box 37
Sullivan, WI 53178
Phone: (414)593-2244
Free: (877)596-3937 **Fax:** (414)593-2050
E-mail: LWMeyer@intaccess.com
Products: Mowers, trimmers, chainsaws, and snowblowers. **SIC:** 5084 (Industrial Machinery & Equipment). **Est:** 1956. **Sales:** $8,000,000 (2000). **Emp:** 22. **Officers:** David C. Meyer, President.

■ **1022** ■ **Meyer West**
PO Box 8250
Stockton, CA 95208
Phone: (209)473-2966 **Fax:** (209)473-2968
Products: Farm equipment parts and accessories. **SIC:** 5083 (Farm & Garden Machinery). **Est:** 1947. **Sales:** $5,000,000 (2000). **Emp:** 17. **Officers:** D.R. Meyer Sr., President; Mike O'Brien, VP & General Mgr.

■ **1023** ■ **MFA Agriservice**
PO Box 312
Lebanon, MO 65536
Phone: (417)532-3174 **Fax:** (417)588-3244
Products: Farm equipment and supplies; Feed; Hardware; Animal health care products. **SICs:** 5191 (Farm Supplies); 5072 (Hardware); 5083 (Farm & Garden Machinery). **Sales:** $5,000,000 (2000). **Emp:** 40. **Officers:** L. Evans, President.

■ **1024** ■ **MFA Inc.**
201 Ray Young Dr.
Columbia, MO 65201-3599
Phone: (573)874-5111 **Fax:** (573)876-5292
Products: Farm supplies. **SIC:** 5191 (Farm Supplies). **Sales:** $720,000,000 (2000). **Emp:** 1,600. **Officers:** Don Copenharer, CEO & President; Allen F. Floyd, VP & CFO.

■ **1025** ■ **Michigan Glass Lined Storage Inc.**
3587 W Tupperlake Rd.
Lake Odessa, MI 48849
Phone: (616)374-8803 **Fax:** (616)374-7050
Products: Farm service type buildings. **SIC:** 5191

(Farm Supplies). **Sales:** $4,000,000 (2000). **Emp:** 25. **Officers:** Alan Lettinga, President.

■ **1026** ■ **Michigan State Seed Co.**
717 N Clinton
Grand Ledge, MI 48837
Phone: (517)627-2164 **Fax:** (517)627-7838
Products: Turf grass; Farm seeds. **SIC:** 5191 (Farm Supplies).

■ **1027** ■ **Mid-Kansas Cooperative Association**
PO Box D
Moundridge, KS 67107
Phone: (316)345-6328 **Free:** (800)864-4428
Products: Farming supplies, including feed and fertilizer. **SICs:** 5153 (Grain & Field Beans); 5153 (Grain & Field Beans); 5191 (Farm Supplies). **Est:** 1965. **Sales:** $21,000,000 (2000). **Emp:** 100. **Officers:** Bob Nattier, General Mgr.; Dennis Teter, Accounting Manager.

■ **1028** ■ **Mid State Power and Equipment Inc.**
PO Box 389
Columbus, WI 53925
Phone: (920)623-4020 **Fax:** (920)623-4376
Products: Farm equipment, including tractors. **SIC:** 5083 (Farm & Garden Machinery). **Est:** 1974. **Sales:** $9,000,000 (2000). **Emp:** 40. **Officers:** Curt Hanson, President; Cliff Konkol, Controller.

■ **1029** ■ **Mid-States Wool Growers Cooperative**
9449 Basil Western Rd.
Canal Winchester, OH 43110
Phone: (614)837-9665 **Fax:** (614)834-2008
E-mail: info@midstateswoolgrowers.com
URL: http://www.midstateswoolgrowers.com
Products: Livestock supplies, including sheep clippers and wormers. **SIC:** 5153 (Grain & Field Beans). **Est:** 1918. **Sales:** $4,000,000 (2000). **Emp:** 40. **Officers:** Don Van Nostran, CEO; Robert G. Zerkle, CFO.

■ **1030** ■ **Midland Co-Op Inc.**
PO Box 560
Danville, IN 46122
Phone: (317)745-4491 **Fax:** (317)745-6779
Products: Lawn care supplies; Boots and jackets; Tools, including hammers and nails; Horse feed; Fence chargers. **SICs:** 5191 (Farm Supplies); 5072 (Hardware); 5136 (Men's/Boys' Clothing); 5083 (Farm & Garden Machinery). **Est:** 1930. **Sales:** $40,000,000 (2000). **Emp:** 145. **Officers:** Kevin Still, CEO.

■ **1031** ■ **Midland Cooperative Inc.**
101 Main St.
Axtell, NE 68924
Phone: (308)263-2441
URL: http://www.midlandcoop.com
Products: Grain elevator; Fertilizer; Chemicals; Petroleum; Feed; Batteries. **SICs:** 5153 (Grain & Field Beans); 5191 (Farm Supplies); 5172 (Petroleum Products Nec). **Est:** 1903. **Sales:** $55,000,000 (2000). **Emp:** 65. **Officers:** Dale Rohrer, General Mgr.

■ **1032** ■ **Midland Implement Co.**
PO Box 30358
Billings, MT 59107-0358
Phone: (406)248-7771 **Fax:** (406)252-5772
Products: Outdoor power equipment, including chainsaws, lawn mowers, aerators, water system pumps, irrigation supplies, and turf vehicles. **SICs:** 5083 (Farm & Garden Machinery); 5084 (Industrial Machinery & Equipment). **Est:** 1920. **Emp:** 58. **Officers:** Gary Pates, Vice President; Randall Pates, Vice President; Lyle Bender, Human Resources Contact, e-mail: l-lb@worldnet.att.net.

■ **1033** ■ **Midor Ltd.**
N 3503 County T
PO Box 168
Elroy, WI 53929-9605
Phone: (608)462-8275 **Fax:** (608)462-8955
E-mail: midor@mwt.net
Products: Animal feed dairy products, including whey, whey protein, skim milk, and dairy blends. **SIC:** 5191 (Farm Supplies). **Sales:** $15,000,000 (2000). **Emp:** 49. **Officers:** Milt Wiesner; Debra E. Parrish, Sales/Marketing Contact; Eugene J. Dougherty, Customer Service Contact.

■ 1034 ■ **Midwest Consolidated Cooperative**
PO Box 129
Cyrus, MN 56323-0129
Phone: (612)795-2714
Products: Grain and feed; Fertilizers. **SICs:** 5153 (Grain & Field Beans); 5191 (Farm Supplies). **Est:** 1920. **Sales:** $25,000,000 (2000). **Emp:** 19. **Officers:** Rodney Leinen, General Mgr.

■ 1035 ■ **Midwest Cooperative**
PO Box 366
Quinter, KS 67752
Phone: (785)754-3348   **Fax:** (785)754-3826
E-mail: midwest@midwestcoop.net
URL: http://www.midwestcoop.net
Products: Farming supplies. **SIC:** 5191 (Farm Supplies). **Est:** 1945. **Sales:** $46,000,000 (2000). **Emp:** 75. **Officers:** Ross L. Boone, President; Ron Koehn, General Mgr.

■ 1036 ■ **Midwest Distributing Inc.**
Rte. 1
PO Box 39
Linden, IN 47955
Phone: (765)339-7283
Free: (800)669-4601   **Fax:** (765)339-4602
E-mail: mwdfence@tctc.com
URL: http://www.national-vinyl.com; www.grainstorage.com
Products: Grain bins and tanks; Farm products; Vinyl fencing. **SIC:** 5083 (Farm & Garden Machinery). **Est:** 1952. **Sales:** $2,000,000 (2000). **Emp:** 8. **Officers:** D. Childress, Chairman of the Board; John Childress, President. **Former Name:** Childress Farm Service Inc.

■ 1037 ■ **Midwest Farmers Cooperative**
PO Box 65
Hospers, IA 51238
Phone: (712)752-8421   **Fax:** (712)752-8457
Products: Corn; Soybeans; Feed; Chemicals; Fertilizer; Lumber. **SICs:** 5153 (Grain & Field Beans); 5191 (Farm Supplies); 5169 (Chemicals & Allied Products Nec); 5031 (Lumber, Plywood & Millwork). **Est:** 1908. **Sales:** $100,000,000 (2000). **Emp:** 6. **Officers:** Dale Hansen, Chairman of the Board; Denny Ruden, Location Mgr.

■ 1038 ■ **Miles Farm Supply Inc.**
PO Box 22879
Owensboro, KY 42304
Phone: (502)926-2420
Products: Farming supplies. **SIC:** 5191 (Farm Supplies). **Sales:** $279,000,000 (2000). **Emp:** 450. **Officers:** Billy J. Miles, President; Ed Delaney, Controller.

■ 1039 ■ **Mille Lacs Agriculture Services Inc.**
10 1st St.
Pease, MN 56363
Phone: (320)369-4220   **Fax:** (320)369-4841
Products: Cat, dog, and hog feed; Fertilizers; Insecticides; Herbicides. **SICs:** 5191 (Farm Supplies); 5149 (Groceries & Related Products Nec). **Est:** 1905. **Sales:** $3,000,000 (2000). **Emp:** 12. **Officers:** Abdon Peterson Jr., President; Marty G. Ringham, CFO.

■ 1040 ■ **Miller Sellner Implement Inc.**
Hwy. 4 S
Sleepy Eye, MN 56085
Phone: (507)794-2131   **Fax:** (507)794-3056
Products: Farm equipment, including tractors, combines, and plows. **SIC:** 5083 (Farm & Garden Machinery). **Est:** 1964. **Sales:** $9,000,000 (2000). **Emp:** 28. **Officers:** G.A. Miller, President.

■ 1041 ■ **Mills Farmers Elevator**
14 Main Ave. S
New York Mills, MN 56567
Phone: (218)385-2366
Products: Dog, cat, and other pet food; Fertilizer and fertilizer materials; Agricultural chemicals; Insecticides; Herbicidal preparations. **SICs:** 5153 (Grain & Field Beans); 5149 (Groceries & Related Products Nec). **Est:** 1913. **Sales:** $3,900,000 (2000). **Emp:** 10. **Officers:** Douglas Storrusten, Manager; Gary Fisher, CFO.

■ 1042 ■ **Mimbres Valley Farmers Association Inc.**
811 S Platinum St.
Deming, NM 88030
Phone: (505)546-2769   **Fax:** (505)546-0640
Products: Clothing; Hardware; Groceries; Feed. **SICs:** 5191 (Farm Supplies); 5149 (Groceries & Related Products Nec); 5136 (Men's/Boys' Clothing); 5072 (Hardware). **Est:** 1913. **Sales:** $19,100,000 (2000). **Emp:** 152. **Officers:** Garry S. Carter, General Mgr.

■ 1043 ■ **Mitchellville Cooperative**
101 S Center Ave.
Mitchellville, IA 50169
Phone: (515)967-4288   **Fax:** (515)967-6903
Products: Farm supplies, including grain, fertilizer, and petroleum. **SICs:** 5153 (Grain & Field Beans); 5191 (Farm Supplies); 5172 (Petroleum Products Nec). **Est:** 1951. **Sales:** $7,000,000 (2000). **Emp:** 9. **Officers:** Jerry Kunze, President.

■ 1044 ■ **Modern Distributing Co.**
1610 N Topping Ave.
Kansas City, MO 64120
Phone: (816)231-8500
Products: Lawn mowers. **SIC:** 5083 (Farm & Garden Machinery). **Est:** 1953. **Sales:** $23,300,000 (2000). **Emp:** 95. **Officers:** Joe Frazier, VP & General Merchandising Mgr.

■ 1045 ■ **Mondovi Cooperative Equity Association Inc.**
735 E Main St.
Mondovi, WI 54755
Phone: (715)926-4212   **Fax:** (715)926-4550
Products: Farm equipment; Seeds; Fertilizer; Hardware. **SICs:** 5191 (Farm Supplies); 5072 (Hardware); 5083 (Farm & Garden Machinery). **Est:** 1910. **Sales:** $15,000,000 (2000). **Emp:** 84. **Officers:** Paul Adams, President; Tim Urness, Treasurer & Secty.; Ed Gunderson, General Mgr.

■ 1046 ■ **Monroe City Feed Mill Inc.**
PO Box 126
Monroe City, IN 47557
Phone: (812)743-5121
Products: Feed. **SIC:** 5191 (Farm Supplies). **Est:** 1964. **Sales:** $4,000,000 (1999). **Emp:** 5. **Officers:** James D. Williams, President.

■ 1047 ■ **Monroe Lawrence Farm Bureau Cooperative**
1305 W Bloomfield Rd.
Bloomington, IN 47403
Phone: (812)332-4471   **Fax:** (812)331-8324
Products: Farm supplies, fertilizer, feed, hardware, and pest control supplies. **SICs:** 5191 (Farm Supplies); 5153 (Grain & Field Beans). **Est:** 1931. **Sales:** $6,000,000 (2000). **Emp:** 25. **Officers:** Henry Daniel, President.

■ 1048 ■ **Monte Vista Cooperative Inc.**
E Hwy. 160
Monte Vista, CO 81144
Phone: (719)852-5181   **Fax:** (719)852-3418
Products: Feed; Fertilizer and fertilizer materials; Farm supplies; Tools; Fencing and fence gates; Farm machinery and equipment; Tires and inner tubes, new; Automotive accessories; Major appliance parts. **SIC:** 5191 (Farm Supplies). **Sales:** $2,000,000 (2000). **Emp:** 64. **Officers:** Gerald Palmgren, General Mgr.

■ 1049 ■ **Montgomery Farmers Cooperative**
Guthrie Hwy. 79
Clarksville, TN 37040
Phone: (931)648-0637   **Fax:** (615)244-4055
Products: Farm supplies, including fertilizer, chemicals, and feed. **SIC:** 5191 (Farm Supplies). **Est:** 1946. **Sales:** $10,000,000 (2000). **Emp:** 35. **Officers:** Edgar Brown, Manager.

■ 1050 ■ **Moodie Implement Co.**
3701 U.S Hwy. 14
Pierre, SD 57501-5747
Phone: (605)224-1631
Products: Tractors, loaders, mowers, and riders. **SIC:** 5083 (Farm & Garden Machinery). **Est:** 1963. **Sales:** $3,500,000 (2000). **Emp:** 18. **Officers:** David L. Moodie, President.

■ 1051 ■ **R.W. Moore Equipment Co.**
PO Box 25068
Raleigh, NC 27611
Phone: (919)772-2121
Products: Agricultural tractors; Parts for farm machinery; Petroleum and its products. **SIC:** 5083 (Farm & Garden Machinery). **Est:** 1961. **Sales:** $10,000,000 (2000). **Emp:** 100. **Officers:** R.W. Moore, President; John Meacham, Mgr. of Finance; Worth Goodwin, Sales Mgr.

■ 1052 ■ **Fred Morgan Wholesale Feed**
700 W Johnson Ave.
Terre Haute, IN 47802
Phone: (812)232-9613
Products: Feed. **SIC:** 5191 (Farm Supplies). **Est:** 1961. **Sales:** $2,000,000 (2000). **Emp:** 5. **Officers:** Tim Morgan, President.

■ 1053 ■ **Morris Cooperative Association**
PO Box 150
Morris, MN 56267
Phone: (612)589-4744
Products: Fertilizer; Fuel. **SICs:** 5191 (Farm Supplies); 5171 (Petroleum Bulk Stations & Terminals). **Est:** 1933. **Sales:** $4,000,000 (2000). **Emp:** 26. **Officers:** Roy Mills, General Mgr.; Kathy Wolbersen, Office Mgr.

■ 1054 ■ **Morris Grain Company Inc.**
Rte. 3
Morris, MN 56267
Phone: (320)589-4050
Free: (800)872-2501   **Fax:** (320)589-4058
URL: http://www.alexweb.net/mgc
Products: Seed; Pesticides, insecticides, and herbicides. **SIC:** 5191 (Farm Supplies). **Est:** 1946. **Sales:** $4,000,000 (2000). **Emp:** 4. **Officers:** D. Greiner, President.

■ 1055 ■ **Mountain View Coop.**
110 Main St. W
Dutton, MT 59433-9686
Phone: (406)476-3690   **Fax:** (406)476-3501
Products: Farming supplies, including feed, chemicals, and seed; Grain. **SICs:** 5191 (Farm Supplies); 5153 (Grain & Field Beans). **Est:** 1997. **Sales:** $30,000,000 (2000). **Emp:** 50. **Officers:** Bruce Clark, General Mgr.

■ 1056 ■ **Moyer and Son Inc.**
PO Box 198
Souderton, PA 18964
Phone: (215)723-6001   **Fax:** (215)721-2800
Products: Pet supplies; Bird seed; Horse and cow feed. **SIC:** 5191 (Farm Supplies). **Est:** 1869. **Sales:** $35,000,000 (2000). **Emp:** 175. **Officers:** J. Moyer, President; Paul Musselman, Controller.

■ 1057 ■ **Mueller Feed Mill Inc.**
PO Box 730
Martin, SD 57551
Phone: (605)685-6611   **Free:** (800)843-8896
Products: Feed. **SIC:** 5153 (Grain & Field Beans). **Est:** 1961. **Sales:** $3,000,000 (1999). **Emp:** 18. **Officers:** Fred W. Mueller, President; Bernice Mueller, Treasurer.

■ 1058 ■ **Mustang Tractor and Equipment Co.**
PO Box 1373
Houston, TX 77251
Phone: (713)460-2000   **Fax:** (713)460-8473
Products: Tractors. **SIC:** 5082 (Construction & Mining Machinery). **Est:** 1952. **Emp:** 750. **Officers:** F. Louis Tucker Jr., President; J.W. Slaughter, VP of Finance; Melody Bizego, Marketing Mgr.; Steve Ross, Controller; Anna Keyes, Dir of Personnel.

■ 1059 ■ **Mycogen Plant Sciences. Southern Div.**
3600 Columbia St.
Plainview, TX 79072-9327
Phone: (806)744-1408   **Fax:** (806)765-0392
Products: Seeds. **SIC:** 5191 (Farm Supplies). **Est:** 1943. **Sales:** $6,000,000 (2000). **Emp:** 50. **Officers:** J.O. Gilbreath Jr., President; Peggy Kinslow, Controller; Bobby George, Dir. of Marketing.

■ **1060** ■ **Mycogen Seeds**
5501 Oberlin Dr.
San Diego, CA 92121-1718
Phone: (619)453-8030 **Fax:** (619)453-5494
Products: Crop seeds. **SIC:** 5191 (Farm Supplies).
Est: 1993. **Sales:** $65,000,000 (2000). **Emp:** 1,050.
Officers: James W. Hopkins, VP & General
Merchandising Mgr.; James A. Baumker, Exec. VP &
CFO; Terry Wright, Dir. of Systems; Naomi Whitacre,
Dir of Human Resources.

■ **1061** ■ **Mycogen Seeds**
103 Tomaras Ave.
Savoy, IL 61874
Phone: (217)373-5300
Products: Corn seeds. **SIC:** 5191 (Farm Supplies).
Est: 1981. **Sales:** $26,000,000 (2000). **Emp:** 25.
Officers: Monte Miles, Manager; Tom Landmesser, Dir
of Human Resources.

■ **1062** ■ **Myer Brothers Implements Inc.**
2740 N Columbus St.
Ottawa, IL 61350-1096
Phone: (815)433-4461
Products: Farm power equipment, including tractors;
Lawn and garden equipment. **SIC:** 5083 (Farm &
Garden Machinery). **Est:** 1954. **Sales:** $4,000,000
(2000). **Emp:** 8. **Officers:** Everett Myer, CEO &
President.

■ **1063** ■ **Myers Inc.**
610 W Main St.
Lexington, IL 61753
Phone: (309)365-7201
Products: Fertilizer and chemicals for farmers. **SIC:**
5191 (Farm Supplies). **Est:** 1955. **Sales:** $11,000,000
(2000). **Emp:** 32. **Officers:** Denny Myers, President.

■ **1064** ■ **Nansemond Ford Tractor Inc.**
3750 Pruden Blvd.
Suffolk, VA 23434
Phone: (757)539-0248
Products: Tractors. **SIC:** 5083 (Farm & Garden
Machinery).

■ **1065** ■ **National Seed Co.**
5300 Katrine Ave.
Downers Grove, IL 60515
Phone: (630)963-8787
Products: Grass seed. **SIC:** 5191 (Farm Supplies).

■ **1066** ■ **Necessary Organics Inc.**
1 Nature's Way
New Castle, VA 24127-0305
Phone: (540)864-5103
Free: (800)447-5354 **Fax:** (540)864-5186
E-mail: concern@swva.net
Products: Garden products; Fertilizers; Pest control
products; Compost activator; Slug and snail barrier;
Weed control. **SIC:** 5191 (Farm Supplies). **Est:** 1978.
Sales: $2,000,000 (2000). **Emp:** 8. **Officers:** Francis
Addy, President; Peter Hagedorn, CEO.

■ **1067** ■ **Neff Co.**
112 N Main St.
Avon, IL 61415
Phone: (309)465-3184
Products: Farm equipment, including tractors. **SIC:**
5083 (Farm & Garden Machinery). **Sales:** $5,000,000
(2000). **Emp:** 26. **Officers:** Joseph W. Maloney,
President.

■ **1068** ■ **Nelson Laboratories L.P.**
4001 N Lewis Ave.
Sioux Falls, SD 57104-5544
Phone: (605)336-2451 **Fax:** (605)336-9354
Products: Veterinarian medical tools and supplies.
SIC: 5047 (Medical & Hospital Equipment). **Sales:**
$26,000,000 (2000). **Emp:** 30. **Officers:** Greg Daniel,
CEO.

■ **1069** ■ **Nemaha County Cooperative**
Association
PO Box 204
Seneca, KS 66538
Phone: (785)336-2153
Products: Farm products, including fertilizers, feed for
dogs, cats, and hogs; Insecticides; Herbicides. **SIC:**

5191 (Farm Supplies). **Sales:** $25,000,000 (2000).
Emp: 49. **Officers:** Galen Lueger, CEO.

■ **1070** ■ **New AG Center Inc.**
25516 S Rte. 45
Monee, IL 60449
Phone: (815)469-5688 **Fax:** (815)469-8749
Products: Farming chemicals and fertilizer. **SIC:** 5191
(Farm Supplies). **Est:** 1965. **Sales:** $5,900,000 (2000).
Emp: 24. **Officers:** Mike Corbin, Manager.

■ **1071** ■ **New Horizons Ag Services**
406 Pacific Ave. S
Herman, MN 56248
Phone: (612)677-2251 **Fax:** (612)677-2718
Products: Grain; Feed; Agronomy; Petroleum. **SICs:**
5153 (Grain & Field Beans); 5191 (Farm Supplies).
Est: 1909. **Sales:** $43,000,000 (2000). **Emp:** 25.
Officers: Daryl Amundson, CEO; Kelly Longtin,
General Mgr.; Mike LeClair, Grain and Feed Dept.
Mgr.; Allen Knollenberg, Dir. of Information Systems;
Terry Christians, Petroleum Dept. Mgr.; Lowell
Christians, Agronomy Dept. Mgr. **Former Name:**
Herman-Norcross AG Services.

■ **1072** ■ **New Horizons Supply Cooperative**
770 Lincoln Ave.
Fennimore, WI 53809
Phone: (608)822-3217 **Fax:** (608)822-3225
Products: Fuel oil and propane; Farm supplies
including feed. **SIC:** 5191 (Farm Supplies). **Sales:**
$17,200,000 (2000). **Emp:** 83. **Officers:** Dean Roth,
President; Dennis Bell, Treasurer & Secty.

■ **1073** ■ **Newsom Seeds**
14 Derwood Cir.
Rockville, MD 20850
Phone: (301)762-2096
Free: (800)553-2719 **Fax:** (301)762-9544
Products: Grass seed and fertilizer. **SIC:** 5191 (Farm
Supplies). **Est:** 1985. **Sales:** $4,000,000 (2000). **Emp:**
10. **Officers:** Allen Bohrer, President.

■ **1074** ■ **Nichol's Farm Supply Inc.**
PO Box 118
Nichols, SC 29581
Phone: (843)526-2105 **Fax:** (843)526-2271
E-mail: jdevers3@aol.com
Products: Fertilizer and fertilizer materials;
Insecticides; Feed; Hardware; Plumbing fixtures,
equipment, and supplies; Electrical equipment and
supplies. **SICs:** 5191 (Farm Supplies); 5072
(Hardware); 5065 (Electronic Parts & Equipment Nec).
Est: 1946. **Sales:** $3,000,000 (1999). **Emp:** 12.
Officers: Jim M. Devers III, President.

■ **1075** ■ **J.J. Nichting Company Inc.**
1342 Pilot Grove Rd.
Pilot Grove, IA 52648
Phone: (319)469-4461 **Fax:** (319)469-4703
Products: Farm equipment, including tractors. **SIC:**
5083 (Farm & Garden Machinery). **Est:** 1920. **Sales:**
$9,500,000 (2000). **Emp:** 47. **Officers:** S.J. Nichting,
President.

■ **1076** ■ **NK Lawn & Garden Co.**
PO Box 300
Tangent, OR 97389
Phone: (541)928-2393 **Fax:** (541)928-2396
Products: Lawn seed. **SIC:** 5191 (Farm Supplies).

■ **1077** ■ **Norseworthy and Wofford Inc.**
PO Box 336
Weiner, AR 72479
Phone: (870)684-2271
Products: Tractor parts. **SIC:** 5083 (Farm & Garden
Machinery). **Sales:** $6,000,000 (2000). **Emp:** 30.
Officers: Lloyd Wofford, President.

■ **1078** ■ **North Caddo Cooperative Inc.**
PO Box 669
Hinton, OK 73047
Phone: (405)542-3212 **Fax:** (405)542-3291
Products: Farm and agricultural supplies. **SICs:** 5191
(Farm Supplies); 5153 (Grain & Field Beans). **Est:**
1920. **Sales:** $5,000,000 (2000). **Emp:** 20. **Officers:**
Kevin Dorsey, President; Carl Coe, Treasurer & Secty.;
Jimmy W. Smith, General Mgr.; Jean Pankratz, Office
Mgr.

■ **1079** ■ **North Central Cooperative Inc.**
2055 S Wabash St.
Wabash, IN 46992
Phone: (219)563-8381 **Fax:** (219)563-3021
Products: Grain and feed; Farm chemicals; Animal
health care products. **SICs:** 5191 (Farm Supplies);
5172 (Petroleum Products Nec); 5153 (Grain & Field
Beans). **Est:** 1927. **Sales:** $55,000,000 (2000). **Emp:**
100. **Officers:** D.M. Byerly, President; Doug Bible,
Treasurer; Dean DeVoe, VP of Marketing & Sales.

■ **1080** ■ **North Central Grain Cooperative**
PO Box 8
Bisbee, ND 58317
Phone: (701)656-3263 **Fax:** (701)656-3371
Products: Grain, feed, and seed. **SIC:** 5153 (Grain &
Field Beans). **Est:** 1988. **Sales:** $10,000,000 (2000).
Emp: 17. **Officers:** Charles Peters, President; Daryl
Stevens, General Mgr.

■ **1081** ■ **North Iowa Cooperative Elevator**
PO Box 1275
Mason City, IA 50401
Phone: (515)423-5311
Products: Grain; Feed; Fertilizer. **SICs:** 5153 (Grain &
Field Beans); 5191 (Farm Supplies). **Sales:**
$11,500,000 (2000). **Emp:** 14. **Officers:** Bob Scott,
President; Mark Kistermacher, General Mgr.

■ **1082** ■ **Northampton County Seed**
PO Box 51
Bath, PA 18014
Phone: (610)837-6311
Products: Farm seed; Soybeans; Corn; Alfalfa seed;
Lawn seed; Lawn fertilizer. **SICs:** 5191 (Farm
Supplies); 5153 (Grain & Field Beans). **Est:** 1950.
Sales: $700,000 (2000). **Emp:** 5. **Officers:** H. Douglas
Walker, President; Agnes S. Walker, Vice President;
Kathy M. Walker, Treasurer.

■ **1083** ■ **Northampton Farm Bureau**
Cooperative
300 Bushkill St.
Tatamy, PA 18085
Phone: (610)258-2871 **Fax:** (610)250-0838
Products: Feed; Fertilizer and fertilizer materials; Farm
machinery and equipment; Petroleum and its products.
SICs: 5191 (Farm Supplies); 5172 (Petroleum
Products Nec). **Est:** 1934. **Sales:** $4,500,000 (2000).
Emp: 22. **Officers:** Richard Bickert, General Mgr.

■ **1084** ■ **Northern Lakes Co-op Inc.**
304 W 1st St.
Hayward, WI 54843
Phone: (715)634-3211
Products: Fuel and feed. **SICs:** 5171 (Petroleum Bulk
Stations & Terminals); 5191 (Farm Supplies). **Sales:**
$17,000,000 (1994). **Emp:** 225. **Officers:** Paul
Diemert, Finance General Manager.

■ **1085** ■ **Northern Seed Service**
Star Rte. Box 45
Conrad, MT 59425
Phone: (406)627-2327
Products: Small grains; Grass seeds. **SICs:** 5191
(Farm Supplies); 5153 (Grain & Field Beans).

■ **1086** ■ **Northrup King Co.**
7500 Olson Memorial Hy
Golden Valley, MN 55427
Phone: (612)593-7333 **Fax:** (612)593-7801
Products: Seeds. **SIC:** 5191 (Farm Supplies).

■ **1087** ■ **Northwest Iowa Co-op**
PO Box 67
George, IA 51237
Phone: (712)475-3347 **Fax:** (712)475-3009
Products: Feed. **SIC:** 5191 (Farm Supplies). **Est:**
1906. **Sales:** $60,000,000 (2000). **Emp:** 45. **Officers:**
Dennis Schrick, Chairman of the Board; Dave
Reinders, General Mgr. **Former Name:** Farmers
Cooperative Elevator.

■ **1088** ■ **Northwest Iowa Cooperative**
206 S Main St.
George, IA 51237-0067
PO Box 67
Phone: (712)724-6171
Products: Farm supplies. **SICs:** 5153 (Grain & Field

Beans); 5191 (Farm Supplies). **Est:** 1981. **Sales:** $17,000,000 (2000). **Emp:** 21.

■ **1089** ■ **Northwest Wholesale Inc.**
PO Box 1649
Wenatchee, WA 98807
Phone: (509)662-2141 **Fax:** (509)663-4540
Products: Fruit packing and orchard supplies. **SIC:** 5191 (Farm Supplies). **Est:** 1937. **Sales:** $45,000,000 (2000). **Emp:** 47. **Officers:** Jerry Kenoyer, President; Kenneth Knappert, Treasurer; Jim Standerford, General Mgr.

■ **1090** ■ **Northwestern Supply Co.**
PO Box 426
St. Cloud, MN 56302
Phone: (320)251-0812
Free: (800)397-6972 **Fax:** (320)251-6210
Products: Lawn and garden supplies; Farm supplies; Animal health supplies. **SICs:** 5191 (Farm Supplies); 5122 (Drugs, Proprietaries & Sundries); 5083 (Farm & Garden Machinery). **Est:** 1956. **Sales:** $30,000,000 (2000). **Emp:** 90. **Officers:** Herbert Jameson Jr., President.

■ **1091** ■ **Northwood Equipment Inc.**
PO Box 148
Northwood, IA 50459
Phone: (515)324-1154
Products: Farm machinery, including tractors. **SIC:** 5083 (Farm & Garden Machinery). **Est:** 1972. **Sales:** $5,000,000 (2000). **Emp:** 19. **Officers:** Lester Behne, President.

■ **1092** ■ **Novartis Seeds Inc.**
PO Box 4188
Boise, ID 83704-4188
Phone: (208)322-7272 **Fax:** (208)322-1436
Products: Seeds. **SICs:** 5191 (Farm Supplies); 5193 (Flowers & Florists' Supplies). **Est:** 1876. **Sales:** $140,000,000 (1999). **Emp:** 600. **Officers:** John Sorenson, CEO & President; Jess Wilson, Finance Officer; Matt Wineinger; Dan Malone, Data Processing Mgr.

■ **1093** ■ **Novartis Seeds Inc. (Golden Valley, Minnesota)**
7500 Olson Memorial Hwy.
Golden Valley, MN 55427
Phone: (612)593-7333
Free: (800)445-0956 **Fax:** (612)593-7801
Products: Farm seeds. **SIC:** 5191 (Farm Supplies). **Sales:** $206,700,000 (2000). **Emp:** 790. **Officers:** Ed Shonsey, CEO & President; Jerry Hoeh, CFO.

■ **1094** ■ **Nylander and Sorenson Inc.**
2173 Blossom St.
Dos Palos, CA 93620
Phone: (209)392-2161
Products: Wheel tractors and attachments (except contractors' off- highway type, garden tractors, turf tractors, tillers); Farm machinery and equipment. **SIC:** 5083 (Farm & Garden Machinery). **Est:** 1936. **Sales:** $11,000,000 (2000). **Emp:** 51. **Officers:** John J. Sorenson, President; Edmund Slevin, Treasurer & Secty.

■ **1095** ■ **Nyssa Cooperative Supply Inc.**
18 N 2nd St.
Nyssa, OR 97913
Phone: (503)372-2254
Products: Petroleum; Fertilizer; Hardware, including wrenches. **SICs:** 5191 (Farm Supplies); 5072 (Hardware); 5172 (Petroleum Products Nec). **Est:** 1953. **Sales:** $10,000,000 (2000). **Emp:** 27. **Officers:** Jim Farmer, President.

■ **1096** ■ **Oakville Feed and Grain Inc.**
PO Box 68
Oakville, IA 52646
Phone: (319)766-4411 **Fax:** (319)766-4602
Products: Feed; Grain; Fertilizers; Farm chemicals. **SIC:** 5191 (Farm Supplies). **Est:** 1950. **Sales:** $40,000,000 (2000). **Emp:** 50. **Officers:** Robert McCulley, President; Janet Shipman, Controller; Steven Sime, Sales Mgr.; Dave Rauenbuehler, Dir. of Data Processing.

■ **1097** ■ **Ochs Inc.**
PO Box 361
Otis, KS 67565
Phone: (785)387-2361 **Fax:** (785)387-2323
Products: Farm and lawn tractors. **SIC:** 5083 (Farm & Garden Machinery). **Sales:** $2,500,000 (2000). **Emp:** 20. **Officers:** R.L. Royer, President.

■ **1098** ■ **R.D. Offutt Co.**
PO Box 7160
Fargo, ND 58106-7160
Phone: (701)237-6062
Products: Tractors. **SIC:** 5148 (Fresh Fruits & Vegetables). **Est:** 1964. **Sales:** $720,000,000 (2000). **Emp:** 2,000. **Officers:** Ronald D. Offutt, President; Alan F. Knoll, Chairman of the Board & Finance Officer; Paul J. Horn, Dir. of Marketing & Sales.

■ **1099** ■ **R.D. Offutt Co.**
1650 Governors Rd.
Casselton, ND 58012
Phone: (701)347-4403
Free: (800)726-5384 **Fax:** (701)347-4302
URL: http://www.rdoequipment.com
Products: Tractors. **SIC:** 5083 (Farm & Garden Machinery). **Est:** 1968. **Sales:** $5,000,000 (2000). **Emp:** 22. **Officers:** Dave Dietz, General Mgr.

■ **1100** ■ **Ogle Service Co.**
PO Box 138
Amboy, IL 61310
Phone: (815)857-3535 **Fax:** (815)732-6141
Products: Gas; Feed; Seed; Fertilizer. **SICs:** 5169 (Chemicals & Allied Products Nec); 5191 (Farm Supplies); 5171 (Petroleum Bulk Stations & Terminals). **Est:** 1936. **Sales:** $25,000,000 (2000). **Emp:** 65. **Officers:** Rex Meyer, President; John Strawn, Controller.

■ **1101** ■ **Ohigro Inc.**
Gillette Rd.
PO Box 196
Waldo, OH 43356
Phone: (614)726-2429 **Fax:** (614)726-2574
Products: Fertilizer and fertilizer materials. **SICs:** 5191 (Farm Supplies); 5153 (Grain & Field Beans). **Est:** 1966. **Sales:** $12,000,000 (2000). **Emp:** 35. **Officers:** Jerry Ward, President; Jerry A. Ward, President.

■ **1102** ■ **Ohio Agriculture and Turf Systems Inc.**
666 Redna Terr.
Cincinnati, OH 45215
Phone: (513)771-2699 **Fax:** (513)771-4497
Products: Organic fertilizers. **SIC:** 5191 (Farm Supplies). **Est:** 1990. **Sales:** $1,000,000 (2000). **Emp:** 5. **Officers:** Rick Sawyer, President.

■ **1103** ■ **Ohio Seed Company Inc.**
8888 Parsons Rd.
Croton, OH 43013-9731
Phone: (614)879-8366
Free: (800)879-3556 **Fax:** (614)879-6823
Products: Grass seed. **SIC:** 5191 (Farm Supplies). **Sales:** $8,000,000 (2000). **Emp:** 45. **Officers:** H.W. Keckley, President & Treasurer.

■ **1104** ■ **L.L. Olds Seed Co.**
PO Box 7790
Madison, WI 53707
Phone: (608)249-9291
Free: (800)356-7333 **Fax:** (608)249-0695
Products: Turf grass; Alfalfa; Farm and garden seed. **SICs:** 5191 (Farm Supplies); 5083 (Farm & Garden Machinery).

■ **1105** ■ **Oliger Seed Co.**
89 Hanna Pkwy.
Akron, OH 44319-1166
Phone: (330)724-1266 **Fax:** (330)724-4810
Products: Lawn seed; Wild bird seed; Erosion control materials. **SIC:** 5191 (Farm Supplies). **Est:** 1960.

■ **1106** ■ **Olsen-Fennell Seeds, Inc.**
PO Box 15028
Salem, OR 97309
Phone: (503)371-2940 **Fax:** (503)399-7119
Products: Grass seed. **SIC:** 5191 (Farm Supplies).

■ **1107** ■ **Omni USA Inc.**
7502 Mesa Rd.
Houston, TX 77028
Phone: (713)635-6331 **Fax:** (713)635-6360
Products: Power transmissions for the agricultural and construction industries, trailer jacks and couplers. **SICs:** 5063 (Electrical Apparatus & Equipment); 5084 (Industrial Machinery & Equipment). **Sales:** $14,500,000 (2000). **Emp:** 155. **Officers:** Jeffrey K. Daniel, CEO & President; Michael A. Zahorik, Secretary.

■ **1108** ■ **OPICO**
PO Box 849
Mobile, AL 36601
Phone: (334)438-9881 **Fax:** (917)464-7982
E-mail: info@opico.com
URL: http://www.opico.com
Products: Planting and harvesting machinery; Soil preparation machinery; Farm fertilizing and irrigating machinery; Farm livestock machinery; Turf machinery. **SIC:** 5083 (Farm & Garden Machinery). **Est:** 1946. **Emp:** 7. **Officers:** Carmelita C. Hartley, Marketing Mgr.

■ **1109** ■ **Orscheln Farm and Home Supply Inc.**
339 N Williams
Moberly, MO 65270
Phone: (660)263-4335 **Fax:** (660)263-6053
URL: http://orschelnfarmhome.com
Products: Work and western clothing; Chain link and wooden fencing; Grills; Patio equipment; Pet food and supplies; Livestock food; Car and pick-up accessories; Seeds; Plants; Paint; Power Tools; Farm equipment; Tractor parts; Mowers and accessories. **SICs:** 5191 (Farm Supplies); 5137 (Women's/Children's Clothing); 5083 (Farm & Garden Machinery); 5099 (Durable Goods Nec); 5013 (Motor Vehicle Supplies & New Parts). **Est:** 1960. **Sales:** $100,000,000 (2000). **Emp:** 1,200. **Officers:** Barry Orscheln, President.

■ **1110** ■ **Osage Cooperative Elevator**
PO Box 358
Osage, IA 50461
Phone: (515)732-3768
Products: Grain; Feed; Fertilizer. **SICs:** 5153 (Grain & Field Beans); 5191 (Farm Supplies). **Sales:** $12,000,000 (2000). **Emp:** 15. **Officers:** Larry Herman, President; Jerry Herrick, General Mgr.

■ **1111** ■ **Osborne Distributing Company Inc.**
PO Box 2100
Vernon, TX 76384
Phone: (817)552-7711 **Fax:** (817)553-4056
Products: Household items, including machinery, clothing, tools, and lawn and garden items. **SICs:** 5191 (Farm Supplies); 5136 (Men's/Boys' Clothing); 5137 (Women's/Children's Clothing); 5072 (Hardware). **Sales:** $40,000,000 (2000). **Emp:** 100. **Officers:** Lloyd Osborne, President.

■ **1112** ■ **Ottawa Cooperative Association Inc.**
302 N Main St.
Ottawa, KS 66067
Phone: (785)242-5170
Products: Farm supplies and grain; Farm products warehouse. **SICs:** 5191 (Farm Supplies); 5153 (Grain & Field Beans). **Sales:** $28,000,000 (2000). **Emp:** 44. **Officers:** Adrian Derousseau, General Manager, Finance.

■ **1113** ■ **Ouachita Fertilizer Div.**
PO Box 4540
Monroe, LA 71211-4540
Phone: (318)388-0400
Products: Fertilizer and fertilizer materials. **SIC:** 5191 (Farm Supplies). **Est:** 1955. **Sales:** $21,000,000 (2000). **Emp:** 54. **Officers:** Dixon Abell, President; Dwaine Taylor, Controller; Charles Mike Venable, Dir. of Marketing & Sales.

■ **1114** ■ **Outdoor Equipment Co.**
17485 N Outer Forty Dr.
Chesterfield, MO 63005-1322
Phone: (314)532-6622 **Fax:** (314)537-3673
URL: http://www.outdoorequipment.com
Products: Lawn care equipment and supplies, including fertilizers, seed, and irrigation equipment; Golf

equipment. **SICs:** 5191 (Farm Supplies); 5083 (Farm & Garden Machinery).

■ **1115** ■ **Pacific Machinery Inc.**
94-025 Farrington Hwy.
Waipahu, HI 96797
Phone: (808)677-9111 **Fax:** (808)676-0323
Products: Tractors.s. **SIC:** 5083 (Farm & Garden Machinery).

■ **1116** ■ **Page Seed Co.**
1-A Greene St.
Greene, NY 13778
Phone: (607)656-4107 **Fax:** (607)656-8558
E-mail: pageseed@aol.com
Products: Garden supplies, including vegetable and flower seeds, fertilizers, hoses, tools, and seeds; Greenhouses; Greenhouse equipment and supplies, including cold frames, heaters, and fans. **SIC:** 5191 (Farm Supplies). **Est:** 1896. **Sales:** $5,000,000 (1999). **Emp:** 75. **Officers:** W.E. Page, President; Michael W. Page, Vice President; Norm Niggli, Sales & Marketing Contact.

■ **1117** ■ **Papillon Agricultural Products Inc.**
PO Box 1161
Easton, MD 21601
Phone: (410)820-7400
Products: Feed ingredients. **SIC:** 5191 (Farm Supplies). **Est:** 1981. **Sales:** $6,000,000 (2000). **Emp:** 7. **Officers:** Normand Saint-Pierre, President.

■ **1118** ■ **Paramount Feed and Supply Inc.**
19310 W Longmeadow Rd.
Hagerstown, MD 21742
Phone: (301)733-8150 **Fax:** (301)790-2468
Products: Farm supplies; Grain; Feed; Field, garden, and flower seeds. **SICs:** 5153 (Grain & Field Beans); 5191 (Farm Supplies). **Est:** 1964. **Sales:** $5,000,000 (2000). **Emp:** 50. **Officers:** D.R. Martin, President.

■ **1119** ■ **Parts Industries Corp.**
PO Box 429
Memphis, TN 38101
Phone: (901)523-7711 **Fax:** (901)526-2833
Products: Farm equipment and auto parts. **SIC:** 5083 (Farm & Garden Machinery). **Sales:** $300,000,000 (2000). **Emp:** 1,850. **Officers:** Kenneth Walker, President; Anthony Buttanshaw, Sr. VP & CFO.

■ **1120** ■ **Peine Inc.**
103 N Main St.
Minier, IL 61759
Phone: (309)392-2011
Products: Herbicides, fertilizer and insecticides. **SIC:** 5191 (Farm Supplies). **Est:** 1935. **Sales:** $5,000,000 (2000). **Emp:** 20. **Officers:** Morris E. Peine, President; Craig Peine, Vice President.

■ **1121** ■ **Pennington Seed Inc.**
PO Box 290
Madison, GA 30650
Phone: (706)342-1234 **Fax:** (706)342-9644
Products: Lawn and garden supplies, including fertilizer, potting soil, chemicals, and grass seed. **SICs:** 5191 (Farm Supplies); 5072 (Hardware). **Est:** 1949. **Sales:** $250,000,000 (2000). **Emp:** 700. **Officers:** Brooks Pennington III, President; Grady Gill, VP & Treasurer; Steve Triplett, Dir. of Marketing; Carol Seabolt, Dir. of Systems.

■ **1122** ■ **Peoria County Service Co.**
R.R. 1
Edwards, IL 61528
Phone: (309)692-8196
Products: Fertilizer and fertilizer materials; Agricultural chemicals; Petroleum and its products. **SICs:** 5191 (Farm Supplies); 5172 (Petroleum Products Nec). **Est:** 1927. **Sales:** $4,500,000 (2000). **Emp:** 30. **Officers:** John Rosenbalm, CEO; Todd McKey, CFO; Mark Pedigo, Sales Mgr.

■ **1123** ■ **C.J. Perry and Son Inc.**
8401 Ridge Rd.
Gasport, NY 14067
Phone: (716)772-2636
Products: Farm equipment, including tractors. **SIC:** 5083 (Farm & Garden Machinery). **Est:** 1914. **Sales:**

$4,000,000 (2000). **Emp:** 15. **Officers:** Ronald L. Perry, President.

■ **1124** ■ **Pestcon Systems Inc.**
1808 Firestone Pky.
Wilson, NC 27893-7991
Phone: (252)237-7923 **Fax:** (252)237-3259
E-mail: sunzon@bbnp.com
URL: http://www.pestcon.com
Products: Fumigants and related safety equipment. **SIC:** 5191 (Farm Supplies). **Est:** 1938. **Officers:** Betty Lilyquist, Dir. of Env. and Reg. Aff.; George Hunt, VP of Sales; Keith Hamm, Dir. of Fumigation Sales.

■ **1125** ■ **Pestorious Inc.**
R.R. 1
Albert Lea, MN 56007
Phone: (507)373-6758
Products: Fertilizers; Seeds; Chemicals. **SIC:** 5191 (Farm Supplies). **Est:** 1949. **Sales:** $6,000,000 (2000). **Emp:** 5. **Officers:** Gary Pestorius, President.

■ **1126** ■ **Peterson's North Branch Inc.**
PO Box 218
North Branch, MN 55056
Phone: (612)674-4425
Products: Feed; Seed; Fertilizer; Chemicals. **SIC:** 5191 (Farm Supplies). **Est:** 1956. **Sales:** $11,000,000 (2000). **Emp:** 23. **Officers:** Bert Peterson, CEO; Jerome Peterson, President.

■ **1127** ■ **Pettisville Grain Company Inc.**
PO Box 9
Pettisville, OH 43553
Phone: (419)446-2547 **Fax:** (419)445-0423
Products: Feed; Grain; Pet products; Horse products. **SICs:** 5153 (Grain & Field Beans); 5191 (Farm Supplies). **Est:** 1903. **Sales:** $25,000,000 (2000). **Emp:** 31. **Officers:** Rodney Nofziger, President; Neil Rupp, CFO; Robert Leu, Sales Mgr.

■ **1128** ■ **Pickseed West, Inc.**
PO Box 888
Tangent, OR 97389
Phone: (541)926-8886
Free: (800)547-4108 **Fax:** (541)928-1599
E-mail: info@pickseedwest.com
URL: http://www.pickseedwest.com
Products: Lawn seeds and flower seeds. **SIC:** 5191 (Farm Supplies). **Est:** 1969. **Officers:** Dr. Jerry Pepin, VP & General Mgr.; Chris McDowell, VP of Sales & Business Development, e-mail: chrism@dnc.net.

■ **1129** ■ **Piggott Tractor and Equipment Company Inc.**
PO Box 327
Piggott, AR 72454
Phone: (870)598-2221
Products: Tractors, mowers, and rider mowers. **SIC:** 5083 (Farm & Garden Machinery). **Est:** 1936. **Sales:** $4,000,000 (2000). **Emp:** 16. **Officers:** Kenneth Norred, President; Delaine Campbell, Finance Officer; Bobby Shanklin, Dir. of Sales; Larry Norred, Dir. of Data Processing.

■ **1130** ■ **Pike County Cooperative**
PO Box 937
McComb, MS 39648
Phone: (601)684-1651
Products: Fertilizers; Cloth. **SICs:** 5191 (Farm Supplies); 5131 (Piece Goods & Notions). **Est:** 1943. **Sales:** $1,000,000 (2000). **Emp:** 11. **Officers:** Emon Estess, President; Thomas Tolar, General Mgr.

■ **1131** ■ **Pine Valley Supply**
225 Gieger Rd.
Philadelphia, PA 19115
Phone: (215)676-8100 **Fax:** (215)676-6182
Products: Turf care products, including grass seeds and fertilizer. **SIC:** 5191 (Farm Supplies).

■ **1132** ■ **Pioneer Implement Corp.**
PO Box 1408
Pendleton, OR 97801
Phone: (541)276-6341 **Fax:** (541)276-0085
Products: Farm equipment. **SIC:** 5083 (Farm & Garden Machinery). **Est:** 1965. **Sales:** $7,000,000 (2000). **Emp:** 35. **Officers:** Robert Blanc, President.

■ **1133** ■ **Planters Cooperative Association**
PO Box 8
Lone Wolf, OK 73655-0008
Phone: (580)846-9008 **Fax:** (580)846-9009
Products: Fertilizer; Gasoline; Propane; Chemicals; Diesel fuel. **SICs:** 5191 (Farm Supplies); 5172 (Petroleum Products Nec). **Est:** 1929. **Sales:** $4,000,000 (2000). **Emp:** 23. **Officers:** Dennis Boelte, President; Kenneth Hahn, CFO.

■ **1134** ■ **Plasterer Equipment Company Inc.**
2550 E Cumberland St.
Lebanon, PA 17042
Phone: (717)867-4657
Products: Tractors, mowers, and riders. **SIC:** 5083 (Farm & Garden Machinery).

■ **1135** ■ **PM AG Products Inc.**
17475 Jovanna
Homewood, IL 60430
Phone: (708)206-2030 **Fax:** (708)206-1340
Products: Sweetening syrups and molasses; Farm supplies. **SICs:** 5191 (Farm Supplies); 5149 (Groceries & Related Products Nec). **Est:** 1929. **Sales:** $450,000,000 (2000). **Emp:** 1,055. **Officers:** Michael A. Reed, President; Jerry Daignalut, CFO; Ken Munsch, General Mgr.; Clair McGriff, Dir. of Data Processing; Robert Harschnek, VP of Admin.

■ **1136** ■ **Poag Grain Inc.**
PO Box 2037
Chickasha, OK 73023
Phone: (405)224-6350 **Fax:** (405)224-6352
Products: Fertilizer; Seeds. **SIC:** 5191 (Farm Supplies). **Est:** 1966. **Sales:** $14,700,000 (2000). **Emp:** 50. **Officers:** Stephen A. Poag, President; Patty L. Poag, Treasurer.

■ **1137** ■ **Polfus Implement Inc.**
730 Deere Dr.
New Richmond, WI 54017
Phone: (715)246-6565
Free: (888)533-3735 **Fax:** (715)246-6605
URL: http://www.polfus.com
Products: Farm equipment. **SIC:** 5083 (Farm & Garden Machinery). **Est:** 1941. **Sales:** $15,000,000 (2000). **Emp:** 49. **Officers:** Charles B. Polfus, President; Greg Christenson, Vice President; Chris Polfus, Vice President.

■ **1138** ■ **Polk County Farmers Cooperative**
PO Box 47
Rickreall, OR 97371
Phone: (503)623-2363 **Fax:** (503)363-5662
E-mail: agwestsupply@juno.com
URL: http://www.agwestsupply.com
Products: Agricultural products, including fertilizer and tractors. **SICs:** 5083 (Farm & Garden Machinery); 5191 (Farm Supplies); 5171 (Petroleum Bulk Stations & Terminals). **Est:** 1932. **Sales:** $31,000,000 (2000). **Emp:** 110. **Officers:** Larry Crook, General Mgr.; Marguerite Reich, Treasurer & Secty.

■ **1139** ■ **Polk County Fertilizer Co.**
PO Box 366
Haines City, FL 33845
Phone: (941)422-1186 **Fax:** (813)422-4414
Products: Fertilizer and fertilizer materials. **SIC:** 5191 (Farm Supplies). **Est:** 1936. **Sales:** $4,100,000 (2000). **Emp:** 20. **Officers:** Wykliffe C. Tunno, General Mgr.

■ **1140** ■ **Polyphase Corp.**
16885 Dallas Pkwy., Ste. 400
Dallas, TX 75248
Phone: (972)732-0010 **Fax:** (972)732-6430
Products: Industrial and commercial timber and logging equipment. **SIC:** 5082 (Construction & Mining Machinery). **Sales:** $151,900,000 (2000). **Emp:** 932. **Officers:** Paul A. Tanner, CEO & Chairman of the Board; William E. Shatley, Sr. VP & CFO.

■ **1141** ■ **Posey County Farm Bureau Cooperative Association Inc.**
PO Box 565
Mt. Vernon, IN 47620
Phone: (812)838-4468
Products: Fertilizer; Chemicals; Gasoline. **SICs:** 5153 (Grain & Field Beans); 5191 (Farm Supplies). **Est:**

1927. **Sales:** $25,000,000 (2000). **Emp:** 50. **Officers:** Jim Swinney, CEO.

■ **1142** ■ **Postville Farmers Cooperative**
PO Box 520
Postville, IA 52162
Phone: (319)864-7234　　**Fax:** (319)864-7823
Products: Feed; Fuel; Grain. **SICs:** 5191 (Farm Supplies); 5172 (Petroleum Products Nec). **Est:** 1904. **Sales:** $9,000,000 (2000). **Emp:** 20. **Officers:** Ken Meyer, President; Joe D. Public, Manager.

■ **1143** ■ **Pounds Motor Company Inc.**
PO Box 770248
Winter Garden, FL 34777
Phone: (407)656-1352　　**Fax:** (407)656-7275
Products: Farm machinery and equipment; Commercial turf and grounds mowing equipment. **SIC:** 5083 (Farm & Garden Machinery). **Est:** 1921. **Sales:** $2,000,000 (2000). **Emp:** 20. **Officers:** J.H. Pounds, President.

■ **1144** ■ **Prairie Land Cooperative**
PO Box 99
Windom, MN 56101
Phone: (507)831-2527　　**Fax:** (507)831-2240
Products: Grain; Feed; Seed; Fertilizer; Chemicals. **SICs:** 5153 (Grain & Field Beans); 5191 (Farm Supplies). **Est:** 1905. **Sales:** $40,000,000 (2000). **Emp:** 42. **Officers:** Steve Freking, President; Ken Ling, General Mgr.

■ **1145** ■ **Prairie Land Cooperative**
PO Box 67
Jeffers, MN 56145-0067
Phone: (507)628-5566　　**Fax:** (507)628-4944
Products: Feed; Grain; Fertilizer; Seed. **SIC:** 5191 (Farm Supplies). **Sales:** $25,000,000 (2000). **Emp:** 20. **Officers:** Steve Freking, Chairman of the Board; Alvin Muller, Vice President; Tim Carlblom, Dir. of Sales; Robert Schoper, Treasurer; Mike Gertsema, General Mgr.

■ **1146** ■ **Prairie Land Cooperative Co.**
PO Box 309
Hubbard, IA 50122
Phone: (515)864-2266　　**Fax:** (515)864-3221
Products: Grain, including corn and soybeans; Feed; Petroleum; Agricultural chemicals. **SICs:** 5191 (Farm Supplies); 5169 (Chemicals & Allied Products Nec); 5172 (Petroleum Products Nec). **Est:** 1948. **Sales:** $40,000,000 (2000). **Emp:** 50. **Officers:** Rick Vaughan, General Mgr.; Kevin Lunn, Controller.

■ **1147** ■ **Premier Cooperative**
PO Box 230
Mt. Horeb, WI 53572
Phone: (608)437-5536
Products: Farm supplies, including feed, grain, fertilizers, chemicals, petroleum; Hardware; Lumber; Convenience stores; Auto repair. **SICs:** 5191 (Farm Supplies); 5172 (Petroleum Products Nec). **Est:** 1893. **Sales:** $24,000,000 (2000). **Emp:** 140. **Officers:** Andy Fiene, General Mgr. **Former Name:** Patrons Mercantile Cooperative.

■ **1148** ■ **Price Brothers Equipment Co.**
PO Box 3207
Wichita, KS 67201-3207
Phone: (316)265-9577　　**Fax:** (316)265-1062
Products: Farm equipment, including hay rakes and sprayers; Construction equipment, including trench digging machines. **SICs:** 5083 (Farm & Garden Machinery); 5082 (Construction & Mining Machinery). **Est:** 1938. **Sales:** $8,000,000 (2000). **Emp:** 30. **Officers:** Richard Price Jr., President.

■ **1149** ■ **Price Milling Co.**
PO Box 398
Russellville, AR 72801
Phone: (501)968-1662
Products: Insecticides; Herbicides; Fertilizers; Livestock feed and equipment. **SIC:** 5191 (Farm Supplies). **Est:** 1926. **Sales:** $1,500,000 (1999). **Emp:** 7. **Officers:** Jack D. Price Sr., President.

■ **1150** ■ **Howard Price Turf Equipment Inc.**
18155 Edison Ave.
Chesterfield, MO 63005
Phone: (314)532-7000
Products: Commercial turf equipment. **SIC:** 5083 (Farm & Garden Machinery). **Est:** 1973. **Sales:** $14,000,000 (2000). **Emp:** 100. **Officers:** Howard Price, President; Jean Goodman, CFO.

■ **1151** ■ **Prince Corp.**
8351 E County Rd. H
Marshfield, WI 54449
Phone: (715)384-3105
Free: (800)777-2486　　**Fax:** (715)387-6924
Products: Builder's hardware; Lawn and garden equipment; Farm machinery and equipment; Wild bird seed; Feeds. **SICs:** 5083 (Farm & Garden Machinery); 5072 (Hardware). **Est:** 1909. **Sales:** $40,000,000 (2000). **Emp:** 90. **Officers:** Jay Emling, President; Dennis Wessel, Vice President.

■ **1152** ■ **Prinsburg Farmers Cooperative**
PO Box 56
Prinsburg, MN 56281-0056
Phone: (320)978-8100
Products: Feed; Fertilizer; Seed; Chemicals. **SICs:** 5191 (Farm Supplies); 5169 (Chemicals & Allied Products Nec). **Est:** 1927. **Emp:** 35. **Officers:** Duane Mulder, President; Clinton Marcus, Vice President; Arvin Brouwer, Secretary.

■ **1153** ■ **Pro-Ag Chem Inc.**
PO Box 579
Chickasha, OK 73023
Phone: (405)224-2254
Products: Fertilizer; Grain. **SIC:** 5191 (Farm Supplies). **Est:** 1985. **Sales:** $8,100,000 (2000). **Emp:** 10. **Officers:** Stephen A. Poag, President; Steve Poag, Exec. VP.

■ **1154** ■ **Pro AG Farmers Co-op**
PO Box 155
Miltona, MN 56354
Phone: (218)943-4001
Products: Agronomy supplies; Feed; Petroleum. **SICs:** 5191 (Farm Supplies); 5172 (Petroleum Products Nec). **Est:** 1919. **Sales:** $25,000,000 (2000). **Emp:** 40. **Officers:** Bruce Stone, President; Mark Jaskowiak, General Mgr.

■ **1155** ■ **Pro Cooperative**
PO Box 322
Gilmore City, IA 50541
Phone: (515)373-6532
Products: Farm supplies, including grain, fertilizer, feed, and seed; Clothing; Fuel and petroleum; Chemicals; Batteries; Hardware. **SICs:** 5191 (Farm Supplies); 5169 (Chemicals & Allied Products Nec); 5172 (Petroleum Products Nec); 5072 (Hardware). **Est:** 1969. **Sales:** $100,000,000 (2000). **Emp:** 50. **Officers:** Joe F. Boeckholt, Manager; Chris Pederson, Controller; Stanley Benjamin, General Mgr.

■ **1156** ■ **Producers Cooperative Association**
1800 N Hwy. 6
Bryan, TX 77806
Phone: (409)778-6000
Products: Farm equipment, including gates and feed. **SIC:** 5191 (Farm Supplies). **Est:** 1943. **Sales:** $18,000,000 (2000). **Emp:** 70. **Officers:** Bobby Kurten, President; James Deatherage, General Mgr.

■ **1157** ■ **Producers Tractor Co.**
614 E Cypress St.
Brinkley, AR 72021
Phone: (870)734-2231　　**Fax:** (870)734-2631
Products: Tractors. **SIC:** 5083 (Farm & Garden Machinery). **Est:** 1947. **Sales:** $5,000,000 (2000). **Emp:** 20. **Officers:** David Griffin, President.

■ **1158** ■ **Progressive Farmers Cooperative**
1221 Grant St.
De Pere, WI 54115
Phone: (920)336-6449
Products: Feed; Fertilizer; Petroleum; Hardware. **SICs:** 5171 (Petroleum Bulk Stations & Terminals); 5191 (Farm Supplies). **Est:** 1930. **Sales:** $11,000,000 (2000). **Emp:** 40. **Officers:** J. Schmidt, General Mgr.

■ **1159** ■ **Prosper Farmers Cooperative Elevator**
PO Box 226
Harwood, ND 58042
Phone: (701)282-4094
Products: Agricultural supplies, including feed, fertilizers, and chemicals; Grain; Wheat; Corn; Soybeans. **SICs:** 5153 (Grain & Field Beans); 5191 (Farm Supplies). **Est:** 1912. **Sales:** $9,000,000 (2000). **Emp:** 5. **Officers:** Robert Bergman, CEO; Jacob Bakke, General Mgr.

■ **1160** ■ **Puck Implement Co.**
Hwy. 141
Manning, IA 51455
Phone: (712)653-2574　　**Fax:** (712)653-2742
Products: Agricultural machinery. **SIC:** 5083 (Farm & Garden Machinery). **Est:** 1927. **Sales:** $11,000,000 (2000). **Emp:** 32. **Officers:** Warren Puck, President.

■ **1161** ■ **Pulaski Chase Cooperative**
PO Box 79
Pulaski, WI 54162
Phone: (920)822-3235
Products: Farm machinery and equipment; Hardware; Feed; Grain; Fertilizer and fertilizer materials. **SICs:** 5191 (Farm Supplies); 5153 (Grain & Field Beans); 5083 (Farm & Garden Machinery); 5072 (Hardware). **Est:** 1940. **Sales:** $12,000,000 (2000). **Emp:** 45. **Officers:** Richard Ferfecki, President; Kevin Tews, General Mgr.

■ **1162** ■ **Pulaski County Farm Bureau Cooperative**
PO Box 346
Winamac, IN 46996
Phone: (219)946-6671
Products: Fertilizer; Chemicals. **SICs:** 5153 (Grain & Field Beans); 5191 (Farm Supplies). **Est:** 1928. **Sales:** $20,800,000 (2000). **Emp:** 37. **Officers:** S. Fritz, President; Phil Scheidenhelm, Treasurer.

■ **1163** ■ **Pulaski Equipment Co., Inc.**
10600 Maybelline Dr.
North Little Rock, AR 72117
Phone: (501)945-4121　　**Fax:** (501)945-5125
Products: Tractors and lawn care equipment. **SIC:** 5083 (Farm & Garden Machinery).

■ **1164** ■ **Pure Line Seeds Inc.**
PO Box 8866
Moscow, ID 83843
Phone: (208)882-4422　　**Fax:** (208)882-4326
E-mail: pure@moscow.com
URL: http://www.purelineseeds.com
Products: Pea and bean seeds. **SIC:** 5191 (Farm Supplies). **Est:** 1948. **Sales:** $3,800,000 (2000). **Emp:** 20. **Officers:** C.M. Shaffer, President; C.M. Shaffer, VP & General Merchandising Mgr.

■ **1165** ■ **Quitman County Farmers Association**
PO Box 160
Marks, MS 38646
Phone: (601)326-2391　　**Fax:** (601)326-2302
Products: Fertilizer; Feed. **SIC:** 5191 (Farm Supplies). **Est:** 1946. **Sales:** $3,500,000 (2000). **Emp:** 12. **Officers:** Robert A. Carson, President; Jeff Lambert, General Mgr.

■ **1166** ■ **R and L Supply Co-op**
300 Vine St.
Reedsburg, WI 53959
Phone: (608)524-6419
Products: Farm supplies. **SICs:** 5191 (Farm Supplies); 5153 (Grain & Field Beans); 5172 (Petroleum Products Nec). **Est:** 1930. **Sales:** $14,000,000 (2000). **Emp:** 64. **Officers:** Robert Bass, President; Allen Sanow, General Mgr.

■ **1167** ■ **Ramsey Seed, Inc.**
205 Stockton St.
Manteca, CA 95336
Phone: (209)823-1721　　**Fax:** (209)823-2582
Products: Seed. **SIC:** 5191 (Farm Supplies).

■ 1168 ■ **Ramy Seed Co.**
1329 N Riverfront St.
Mankato, MN 56001
Phone: (507)387-4091
Products: Seed corn. **SIC:** 5191 (Farm Supplies). **Est:** 1930. **Sales:** $5,000,000 (2000). **Emp:** 10. **Officers:** M.T. Ramy, President.

■ 1169 ■ **Ray-Carroll County Grain Growers Inc.**
PO Box 158
Richmond, MO 64085
Phone: (816)776-2291 **Fax:** (816)776-3213
Products: Grain; Petroleum; Fertilizer. **SICs:** 5191 (Farm Supplies); 5153 (Grain & Field Beans); 5172 (Petroleum Products Nec). **Est:** 1931. **Sales:** $65,000,000 (2000). **Emp:** 100. **Officers:** A. Kipping, President; M. Ritchason, General Mgr.

■ 1170 ■ **RCH Distributors Inc.**
3140 Carrier
Memphis, TN 38116
Phone: (901)345-3100
Products: Outdoor power equipment, including lawnmowers, trimmers, and fertilizers. **SICs:** 5083 (Farm & Garden Machinery); 5191 (Farm Supplies); 5082 (Construction & Mining Machinery). **Est:** 1895. **Sales:** $2,000,000 (2000). **Emp:** 15. **Officers:** Bill Wilkerson, President.

■ 1171 ■ **RDO Equipment Co.**
PO Box 7160
Fargo, ND 58109-7160
Phone: (701)237-6062
Free: (800)843-1865 **Fax:** (701)225-0207
URL: http://www.rdoequipment.com
Products: Tractors, including farm, lawn, and garden. **SICs:** 5083 (Farm & Garden Machinery); 5082 (Construction & Mining Machinery). **Est:** 1965. **Sales:** $140,000,000 (2000). **Emp:** 784. **Officers:** Ronald D. Offutt, CEO & Chairman of the Board; Allan Knowll, CFO.

■ 1172 ■ **RDO Equipment Co.**
PO Box 1069
Riverside, CA 92502
Phone: (909)682-5353
Products: Tractors. **SIC:** 5083 (Farm & Garden Machinery). **Est:** 1965. **Sales:** $43,000,000 (2000). **Emp:** 50. **Officers:** Dave Frambers, President.

■ 1173 ■ **Reading Feed and Grain Inc.**
313 S Ann St.
Reading, MI 49274
Phone: (517)283-2156 **Fax:** (517)283-2722
Products: Feed; Grain; Fertilizer. **SICs:** 5153 (Grain & Field Beans); 5191 (Farm Supplies). **Est:** 1944. **Sales:** $5,500,000 (2000). **Emp:** 18. **Officers:** Ronald E. Newton, President.

■ 1174 ■ **Real Veal Inc.**
N 8155 American St.
Ixonia, WI 53036
Phone: (414)567-8989
Products: Milk replacers. **SIC:** 5191 (Farm Supplies). **Sales:** $20,000,000 (2000). **Emp:** 50. **Officers:** Robert Gronevelt, President.

■ 1175 ■ **Recycled Wood Products**
PO Box 3517
Montebello, CA 90640
Phone: (213)727-7211 **Fax:** (213)727-7197
Products: Fertilizers and related products; Soil amendments; Wood products. **SICs:** 5199 (Nondurable Goods Nec); 5191 (Farm Supplies). **Est:** 1980. **Sales:** $17,000,000 (2000). **Emp:** 40. **Officers:** Chris Kiralla, President; Kathy Kiralla, Controller.

■ 1176 ■ **RedMax Komatsu Zenoah America Inc.**
4344 Shackleford Rd.
Norcross, GA 30093
Phone: (770)381-5147
Free: (800)291-8251 **Fax:** (770)381-5150
Products: Portable outdoor power equipment, including string trimmers, blowers, and hedge clippers. **SICs:** 5084 (Industrial Machinery & Equipment); 5083 (Farm & Garden Machinery). **Sales:** $20,000,000 (2000). **Emp:** 18. **Officers:** Takashi Nagata, CEO; Don

Kyle, VP of Marketing, e-mail: dkyle@redmax.com; David Vick, e-mail: dvick@redmax.com; K. Shimada, President, e-mail: saugustsou@redmax.com.

■ 1177 ■ **Reed Equipment Co.**
1551 Stimson St.
Stockton, CA 95206
Phone: (209)983-0100 **Fax:** (209)983-0658
E-mail: reedequip@earthlink.net
Products: Tractors; Turf equipment. **SICs:** 5083 (Farm & Garden Machinery); 5084 (Industrial Machinery & Equipment). **Officers:** Carl Reed; Steve Reed; Michael Lopez, Customer Service Contact.

■ 1178 ■ **Reeds Seeds Inc.**
PO Box 230
Chillicothe, MO 64601
Phone: (816)646-4426
Free: (800)279-8227 **Fax:** (816)646-4411
E-mail: sales@reedseed.com
URL: http://www.reedseed.com
Products: Seed and feed; Seed grower and processor. **SICs:** 5191 (Farm Supplies); 5153 (Grain & Field Beans). **Est:** 1956. **Sales:** $9,000,000 (2000). **Emp:** 35. **Officers:** Blackie D. Reed, President; James Trimble, CFO; E.L. Reed, Dir. of Marketing.

■ 1179 ■ **Reedsville Cooperative Association**
305 N 6th St.
Reedsville, WI 54230
Phone: (920)754-4321 **Fax:** (920)754-4536
Products: Farm supplies. **SIC:** 5191 (Farm Supplies). **Est:** 1923. **Sales:** $13,000,000 (2000). **Emp:** 80. **Officers:** Robert Lowe, CEO; John Glocke, Controller.

■ 1180 ■ **Steve Regan Co.**
4215 South 500 West
Murray, UT 84123
Phone: (801)268-4500 **Fax:** (801)268-4596
Products: Agricultural and greenhouse supplies; Pump supplies; Fencing. **SIC:** 5191 (Farm Supplies). **Est:** 1936. **Emp:** 50. **Officers:** Steve Westover, Manager.

■ 1181 ■ **Reinders, Inc.**
PO Box 825
Elm Grove, WI 53122-0825
Phone: (262)786-3300 **Fax:** (262)786-6111
Products: Turf and irrigation supplies. **SICs:** 5063 (Electrical Apparatus & Equipment); 5083 (Farm & Garden Machinery). **Est:** 1866. **Sales:** $7,000,000 (2000). **Emp:** 80. **Officers:** John Shurtleff, Controller; Lanita Beck, Personnel Mgr.

■ 1182 ■ **Research Seeds Inc.**
PO Box 1393
St. Joseph, MO 64502
Phone: (816)238-7333
Free: (800)821-7666 **Fax:** (816)238-7849
URL: http://www.researchseeds.com
Products: Seeds, including alfalfa, legumes, grass, and turf. **SIC:** 5191 (Farm Supplies).

■ 1183 ■ **Revels Tractor Company Inc.**
PO Box 339
Fuquay Varina, NC 27526
Phone: (919)552-5697 **Fax:** (919)552-9321
Products: Farm equipment; Lawn equipment; Golf equipment. **SICs:** 5083 (Farm & Garden Machinery); 5088 (Transportation Equipment & Supplies). **Sales:** $11,000,000 (2000). **Emp:** 50. **Officers:** C. Turner Revels Jr.; Charles T. Revels Sr., President; Kay Towell, Controller; Charles T. Revels Jr., General Mgr.

■ 1184 ■ **Revels Tractor Company Inc.**
PO Box 339
Fuquay Varina, NC 27526
Phone: (919)552-5697
Free: (800)849-5469 **Fax:** (919)552-9321
Products: Lawn and turf equipment; Farm equipment. **SIC:** 5083 (Farm & Garden Machinery). **Sales:** $16,000,000 (2000). **Emp:** 70. **Officers:** Charles Revels Jr., President; John Meacham, Vice President, General Manager, Finance.

■ 1185 ■ **Rhoads Mills Inc.**
PO Box 24
Selinsgrove, PA 17870-0024
Phone: (717)374-8141
Free: (800)326-8292 **Fax:** (717)374-8143
Products: Feed, for cattle and swine; Grains, including wheat, corn, and milo; Salts. **SICs:** 5191 (Farm Supplies); 5153 (Grain & Field Beans). **Est:** 1959. **Sales:** $4,500,000 (2000). **Emp:** 19. **Officers:** E.A. Rhoads, President; J.L. Rhoads, VP of Finance; R.T. Reich, Dir. of Marketing.

■ 1186 ■ **RHS Inc.**
PO Box 394
2005 W Oregon
Hiawatha, KS 66434
Phone: (785)742-2949
Free: (800)247-3808 **Fax:** (785)742-7174
E-mail: rhs-inc@rhs-inc.com
URL: http://www.rhs-inc.com
Products: Spraying systems; Agricultural and commercial sprayers. **SIC:** 5083 (Farm & Garden Machinery). **Est:** 1980. **Sales:** $5,100,000 (2000). **Emp:** 37. **Officers:** Richard W. Heiniger, CEO; S. Dean Ryerson, President; Bill Burdick, Sales Mgr., e-mail: bburdick@rhs-inc.com.

■ 1187 ■ **Rib River Valley Cooperative**
PO Box 215
409 Pine St.
Marathon, WI 54448
Phone: (715)443-2241 **Fax:** (715)443-3474
Products: Agricultural supplies, including fertilizer; Gas; Hardware. **SICs:** 5191 (Farm Supplies); 5013 (Motor Vehicle Supplies & New Parts); 5172 (Petroleum Products Nec). **Est:** 1935. **Sales:** $10,500,000 (2000). **Emp:** 45. **Officers:** Robert Dinkel, CEO; William Bruening, CFO; Jeff Johnson, Manager.

■ 1188 ■ **Rice Lake Farmers Union Cooperative**
PO Box 448
Rice Lake, WI 54868-0448
Phone: (715)234-8191
Products: Hardware; Feed and seed; Petroleum products. **SICs:** 5171 (Petroleum Bulk Stations & Terminals); 5171 (Petroleum Bulk Stations & Terminals); 5191 (Farm Supplies). **Est:** 1961. **Sales:** $11,300,000 (2000). **Emp:** 53. **Officers:** K. Goettl, Manager.

■ 1189 ■ **Richardson Seeds Inc.**
PO Box 60
Vega, TX 79092
Phone: (806)267-2379 **Fax:** (806)267-2820
Products: Seed. **SIC:** 5191 (Farm Supplies). **Sales:** $12,000,000 (2000). **Emp:** 40. **Officers:** Larry Richardson, CEO & President; Mike Richardson, COO & CFO.

■ 1190 ■ **Richter Fertilizer Co.**
Hwy. 100
Pleasant Hill, IL 62366
Phone: (217)285-4475
Products: Fertilizers. **SICs:** 5191 (Farm Supplies); 5172 (Petroleum Products Nec). **Officers:** Marvin Richter, President.

■ 1191 ■ **Richton International Corp.**
211 Sheffield St.
Mountainside, NJ 07092-2302
Phone: (973)966-0104 **Fax:** (973)966-7892
Products: Irrigation systems and decorative fountain equipment; Outdoor lighting. **SICs:** 5083 (Farm & Garden Machinery); 5063 (Electrical Apparatus & Equipment). **Sales:** $106,500,000 (2000). **Emp:** 425. **Officers:** Fred R. Sullivan, CEO & Chairman of the Board; Cornelius F. Griffin, VP & CFO.

■ 1192 ■ **Rickreall Farms Supply Inc.**
PO Box 67
Rickreall, OR 97371
Phone: (503)623-2366 **Fax:** (503)623-2367
Products: Tractors and accessories; Mowers; Turf products. **SICs:** 5083 (Farm & Garden Machinery); 5191 (Farm Supplies). **Est:** 1954. **Sales:** $4,000,000 (2000). **Emp:** 18. **Officers:** John Hochstetler, General Mgr., e-mail: RFSjohn@cs.com.

■ 1193 ■ Ridgeland Chetek Cooperative
PO Box 155
Ridgeland, WI 54763
Phone: (715)949-1165
Products: Hardware and feed; Petroleum; Fertilizer. **SICs:** 5191 (Farm Supplies); 5072 (Hardware). **Est:** 1931. **Sales:** $18,000,000 (2000). **Emp:** 75. **Officers:** Mark Hagedorn, President.

■ 1194 ■ Right of Way Equipment Co.
5500 Hillsborough Rd.
Raleigh, NC 27606
Phone: (919)851-1750
Products: Commercial landscape equipment, including earth-moving equipment, lawn mowers, and hedge trimmers. **SIC:** 5083 (Farm & Garden Machinery). **Sales:** $2,300,000 (2000). **Emp:** 13. **Officers:** Mike Holleman, President.

■ 1195 ■ Rippey Farmers Cooperative
Perseville St.
Rippey, IA 50235
Phone: (515)436-7411   **Fax:** (515)436-7633
Products: Agricultural supplies. **SIC:** 5191 (Farm Supplies). **Est:** 1958. **Sales:** $16,000,000 (2000). **Emp:** 12.

■ 1196 ■ E. Ritter Equipment Co.
116 Hwy. 63 W
Marked Tree, AR 72365
Phone: (870)358-2555
Products: Farm equipment, including tractors, combines, and cotton pickers. **SIC:** 5083 (Farm & Garden Machinery). **Est:** 1947. **Sales:** $3,000,000 (2000). **Emp:** 21. **Officers:** Ritter Arnold, President; Alan Wright, Finance Officer; Wayne Carter, Manager.

■ 1197 ■ River Country Cooperative
1080 W River St.
Chippewa Falls, WI 54729
Phone: (715)723-2828
Products: Petroleum; Fertilizer; Feed. **SICs:** 5191 (Farm Supplies); 5171 (Petroleum Bulk Stations & Terminals). **Est:** 1931. **Sales:** $27,000,000 (2000). **Emp:** 200. **Officers:** Bruce Milsna, General Mgr.

■ 1198 ■ River Valley Cooperative
PO Box 30
Watertown, WI 53094
Phone: (414)262-6760   **Fax:** (414)262-6777
Products: Feed, fertilizer, and chemicals; Fuel. **SICs:** 5191 (Farm Supplies); 5171 (Petroleum Bulk Stations & Terminals). **Est:** 1938. **Sales:** $10,000,000 (2000). **Emp:** 45. **Officers:** David Nehls, Chairman of the Board; Stephen Zillmer, President & General Mgr.

■ 1199 ■ Riverview FS Inc.
PO Box 5127
Rockford, IL 61125-0127
Phone: (815)332-4956
Products: Chemicals; Fertilizer; Propane and fuel oil. **SICs:** 5191 (Farm Supplies); 5171 (Petroleum Bulk Stations & Terminals); 5083 (Farm & Garden Machinery). **Est:** 1944. **Sales:** $22,000,000 (2000). **Emp:** 55. **Officers:** Ron R. Karlson, President; Daren Poppen, Controller; Neil Brandt, General Mgr.

■ 1200 ■ Roberts Seed Co.
PO Box 206
Tangent, OR 97389
Phone: (541)926-8891
Free: (800)258-4657   **Fax:** (541)926-8159
E-mail: robtseed@juno.com
Products: Grass seeds. **SIC:** 5191 (Farm Supplies). **Est:** 1973. **Sales:** $10,000,000 (2000). **Emp:** 20. **Officers:** Denise Dehart, Sales & Marketing Contact; Tony Steele; Brenda Landis; Walt Bryant.

■ 1201 ■ Clyde Robin Seed Co.
3670 Enterprise Ave.
Hayward, CA 94545
Phone: (510)785-0425   **Fax:** (510)785-6463
URL: http://www.clyderobin.com
Products: Lawn and flower seeds. **SIC:** 5191 (Farm Supplies). **Est:** 1934. **Emp:** 21. **Officers:** Steven Atwood, President, e-mail: stevenra@clyderobin.com; Susie Atwood, Sec. & Treas.

■ 1202 ■ Robstown Hardware Co.
PO Box 831
Robstown, TX 78380
Phone: (512)387-2564
Products: Tractors and mowers. **SIC:** 5083 (Farm & Garden Machinery). **Est:** 1913. **Sales:** $3,000,000 (2000). **Emp:** 25. **Officers:** Darwin Baucum, President; Pat Skull, Bookkeeper; Franklin Raska, Sales Mgr.

■ 1203 ■ Rock River Lumber and Grain Co.
406 Washington St.
Prophetstown, IL 61277
Phone: (815)537-5131
Products: Lumber; Grain, fertilizer, and seed. **SICs:** 5153 (Grain & Field Beans); 5191 (Farm Supplies). **Est:** 1931. **Sales:** $22,000,000 (2000). **Emp:** 45. **Officers:** Kent Gibson, CEO; Bob Peterson, Vice President.

■ 1204 ■ Rockbridge Farmers Cooperative
645 Waddell St.
Lexington, VA 24450
Phone: (703)463-7381   **Fax:** (703)463-2095
Products: Grain and feed; Chemicals and fertilizers. **SICs:** 5191 (Farm Supplies); 5153 (Grain & Field Beans). **Est:** 1927. **Sales:** $9,000,000 (2000). **Emp:** 51. **Officers:** M.M. Sterrett Jr., Chairman of the Board; Thomas Mueller, Treasurer & Secty.; Russell Elliott, Systems Mgr.

■ 1205 ■ Rockingham Cooperative Farm Bureau
101 Grace St.
Harrisonburg, VA 22801
Phone: (540)434-3856   **Fax:** (540)434-1217
URL: http://www.rockinghamcoop.com
Products: Farm products; Clothing; Hardware; Sporting goods. **SICs:** 5191 (Farm Supplies); 5136 (Men's/Boys' Clothing); 5072 (Hardware). **Est:** 1921. **Sales:** $22,000,000 (1999). **Emp:** 140. **Officers:** C.M. Wright, Exec. VP; Norman Wenger, VP of Operations; John Fleishman, VP of Sales.

■ 1206 ■ H. Rockwell and Son
PO Box 197
Canton, PA 17724
Phone: (717)673-5148
Products: Animal feed; Chemicals; Fertilizer; Wheat, corn, and grains. **SICs:** 5191 (Farm Supplies); 5153 (Grain & Field Beans). **Est:** 1852. **Sales:** $5,500,000 (2000). **Emp:** 20. **Officers:** J.H. Rockwell, Partner.

■ 1207 ■ Rockwood Chemical Co.
PO Box 34
Brawley, CA 92227
Phone: (760)344-0916
Products: Herbicides, pesticides, and fertilizer. **SIC:** 5191 (Farm Supplies). **Est:** 1960. **Sales:** $11,000,000 (2000). **Emp:** 12. **Officers:** Rich Waegner, President; Richard Elmer, Treasurer & Secty.

■ 1208 ■ Roeder Implement Company Inc.
1010 Skyline Dr.
Hopkinsville, KY 42240
Phone: (502)886-3994   **Fax:** (502)886-8752
Products: Tractors and supplies. **SIC:** 5083 (Farm & Garden Machinery). **Est:** 1964. **Sales:** $4,000,000 (2000). **Emp:** 15. **Officers:** Edwin Roeder, President.

■ 1209 ■ Roeder Implement Inc.
2550 Rockdale Rd.
Dubuque, IA 52003
Phone: (319)557-1184
Products: Agricultural equipment; Lawn and garden equipment; Machine shop tools. **SIC:** 5083 (Farm & Garden Machinery). **Est:** 1957. **Sales:** $8,600,000 (2000). **Emp:** 35. **Officers:** James V. Roeder, President.

■ 1210 ■ Rose Brothers Inc.
PO Box 319
Lingle, WY 82223
Phone: (307)837-2261   **Fax:** (307)837-2922
Products: Tractors; Agricultural equipment. **SIC:** 5083 (Farm & Garden Machinery). **Est:** 1953. **Sales:** $4,300,000 (1999). **Emp:** 14. **Officers:** Jeff Rose, CEO.

■ 1211 ■ Rosebud Farmers Union Cooperative Associates Inc.
PO Box 24 A
Gregory, SD 57533
Phone: (605)835-9656   **Fax:** (605)835-8372
Products: Farm supplies; Automotive supplies. **SICs:** 5191 (Farm Supplies); 5013 (Motor Vehicle Supplies & New Parts). **Est:** 1940. **Sales:** $7,500,000 (2000). **Emp:** 25. **Officers:** Robert Sperl Sr., President; Jerome Frasch, General Mgr.

■ 1212 ■ Rosenau Equipment Co.
Hwy. 281 N
Carrington, ND 58421
Phone: (701)652-3144
Products: Farm equipment. **SIC:** 5083 (Farm & Garden Machinery). **Est:** 1970. **Sales:** $3,000,000 (2000). **Emp:** 20. **Officers:** Jack Rosenau, President; Gaylen Rosenau, General Mgr.

■ 1213 ■ Rosen's Inc.
PO Box 933
Fairmont, MN 56031
Phone: (507)238-4201   **Fax:** (507)238-9966
Products: General-line of farm chemicals including insecticides. **SIC:** 5191 (Farm Supplies). **Sales:** $69,000,000 (1994). **Emp:** 130. **Officers:** Tom Rosen, CEO & President; Robert A. Hovde, CFO.

■ 1214 ■ Rotary Corp.
PO Box 947
Glennville, GA 30427
Phone: (912)654-3433   **Fax:** (912)654-3945
URL: http://www.rotarycorp.com
Products: Lawn and garden parts and supplies; Power equipment parts and accessories. **SIC:** 5083 (Farm & Garden Machinery). **Est:** 1954. **Sales:** $64,000,000 (2000). **Emp:** 485. **Officers:** Ed Nelson, CEO; Lee Woodcock, Finance Officer; Roy Fox, Marketing and Sales Officer; Dennis Lamb, Manufacturing Officer; Donalo Fountain, Operations Officer.

■ 1215 ■ Round Butte Seed Growers Inc.
PO Box 117
Culver, OR 97734
Phone: (541)546-5222   **Fax:** (541)546-2237
Products: Seed, fertilizer, grain, and chemicals. **SIC:** 5191 (Farm Supplies). **Est:** 1961. **Sales:** $8,000,000 (2000). **Emp:** 30. **Officers:** Britt Spaulding, General Mgr.; Pat Holechek, Controller.

■ 1216 ■ Rowland Nursery Inc.
7402 Menaul NE
Albuquerque, NM 87110
Phone: (505)883-5727
Products: Nurseries and garden products. **SIC:** 5193 (Flowers & Florists' Supplies). **Sales:** $12,000,000 (1992). **Emp:** 250. **Officers:** Reba K. Rowland, Owner; Sharon Rowland, Treasurer & Secty.

■ 1217 ■ Royal Seeds Inc.
PO Box 1393
St. Joseph, MO 64502
Phone: (816)238-0990   **Fax:** (816)238-7849
Products: Seed. **SICs:** 5148 (Fresh Fruits & Vegetables); 5191 (Farm Supplies). **Est:** 1972. **Sales:** $10,000,000 (2000). **Emp:** 20. **Officers:** William P. Junk, President; Ron Olinger, Controller; Ron Whiteley, Dir. of Marketing & Sales.

■ 1218 ■ Rugg Manufacturing Company Inc.
PO Box 507
Greenfield, MA 01302
Phone: (413)773-5471
Free: (800)633-8772   **Fax:** (413)774-4354
E-mail: sales@rugg.com
URL: http://www.rugg.com
Products: Consumer nonriding lawn, garden, and snow equipment, including forks, rakes, and shovels. **SICs:** 5083 (Farm & Garden Machinery); 5072 (Hardware). **Est:** 1842. **Sales:** $1,500,000 (2000). **Emp:** 12. **Officers:** Stephen Peck, President; Elizabeth Peck, Controller.

■ 1219 ■ Rush County Farm Bureau Cooperative
627 W 3rd St.
Rushville, IN 46173
Phone: (317)932-3921 **Fax:** (317)938-1522
Products: Farm equipment. **SICs:** 5153 (Grain & Field Beans); 5191 (Farm Supplies); 5072 (Hardware). **Est:** 1930. **Sales:** $11,000,000 (2000). **Emp:** 42. **Officers:** Robert Ging, President; Mark Webster, Treasurer.

■ 1220 ■ Rutherford Farmers Cooperative
210 Sanbyrn Dr.
Murfreesboro, TN 37130
Phone: (615)893-6212 **Fax:** (615)898-8805
E-mail: rfcoop@bellsouth.net
URL: http://www.truevalue.com/rutherford
Products: Seed; Chemical; Fertilizer; Hardware; Gas; Diesel; Oil; Lawn and garden products. **SIC:** 5191 (Farm Supplies). **Est:** 1945. **Sales:** $27,000,000 (2000). **Emp:** 130. **Officers:** Ralph Smith, President; Bill Bracy, General Mgr.

■ 1221 ■ Ryan Cooperative Inc.
PO Box 39
Ryan, IA 52330
Phone: (319)932-2101
Products: Agricultural supplies and equipment. **SIC:** 5191 (Farm Supplies). **Est:** 1918. **Sales:** $9,000,000 (2000). **Emp:** 12. **Officers:** Joe Kelchen, President; Arden Fischer, Vice President.

■ 1222 ■ Ryobi America Corp.
5201 Pearman Dairy Rd.
Anderson, SC 29625
Phone: (803)226-6511 **Fax:** (803)261-9435
Products: Outdoor products, including trimmers and lawnmowers; Power tools. **SIC:** 5072 (Hardware). **Est:** 1972. **Sales:** $49,000,000 (2000). **Emp:** 150. **Officers:** William S. McLay, President; Willie Holt, VP of Finance; Brian Sponsler, Director.

■ 1223 ■ S and H Tractor Co.
PO Box 729
Guymon, OK 73942
Phone: (580)338-2519 **Fax:** (580)338-2570
Products: Farm equipment, including combines, tractors, and haulers. **SIC:** 5083 (Farm & Garden Machinery). **Est:** 1961. **Sales:** $2,000,000 (2000). **Emp:** 8. **Officers:** Peter J. Hein, President.

■ 1224 ■ S & W Farm Equipment
PO Box 82182
Portland, OR 97282-0182
Phone: (503)234-0278 **Fax:** (503)234-0279
Products: Farm equipment, including sprayers and cultivators. **SIC:** 5083 (Farm & Garden Machinery). **Est:** 1955. **Sales:** $2,000,000 (2000). **Emp:** 7. **Officers:** J.R. Shotwell, President; Karen M. Moore, Office Mgr.

■ 1225 ■ S & W Supply Company Inc.
300 E 8th
Hays, KS 67601
Phone: (785)625-7363
Free: (800)777-1457 **Fax:** (785)625-4175
Products: Agricultural supplies; Automotive supplies; Industrial supplies. **SICs:** 5191 (Farm Supplies); 5013 (Motor Vehicle Supplies & New Parts); 5085 (Industrial Supplies); 5083 (Farm & Garden Machinery). **Est:** 1935. **Sales:** $5,000,000 (2000). **Emp:** 65. **Officers:** Don Bickle Sr., Chairman of the Board; Tim Bickle, President; Don G. Bickle Jr., Vice President.

■ 1226 ■ Sabina Farmers Exchange Inc.
PO Box 7
Sabina, OH 45169
Phone: (937)584-2411
Free: (800)521-5600 **Fax:** (937)584-4061
Products: Feed and grain; Seed; Fertilizer; Chemicals. **SICs:** 5191 (Farm Supplies); 5153 (Grain & Field Beans). **Est:** 1955. **Sales:** $38,000,000 (2000). **Emp:** 55. **Officers:** Edwin D. Kuehn, President.

■ 1227 ■ St. Clair Service Co.
PO Box 489
Belleville, IL 62222-0489
Phone: (618)233-1248
Products: Agricultural supplies, including chemicals and fertilzer. **SICs:** 5191 (Farm Supplies); 5083 (Farm

& Garden Machinery). **Est:** 1931. **Sales:** $1,300,000 (2000). **Emp:** 38. **Officers:** Greg Guenther, CEO; Robert Otten, Treasurer; Edward H. Schloz, General Mgr.

■ 1228 ■ St. Francis Mercantile Equity Exchange
PO Box 545
St. Francis, KS 67756
Phone: (913)332-2113
Products: Animal health care products; Feed; Grains; Fertilizers; Chemicals. **SICs:** 5153 (Grain & Field Beans); 5191 (Farm Supplies); 5172 (Petroleum Products Nec); 5013 (Motor Vehicle Supplies & New Parts). **Est:** 1911. **Sales:** $12,000,000 (2000). **Emp:** 25. **Officers:** D. Rath, President; Tim Burr, CFO.

■ 1229 ■ St. Paul Feed and Supply Inc.
PO Box 67
St. Paul, OR 97137
Phone: (503)633-4281
Products: Feed; Fertilizer and chemicals. **SIC:** 5191 (Farm Supplies). **Sales:** $4,000,000 (2000). **Emp:** 13. **Officers:** Robert Hockett, President.

■ 1230 ■ Sakata Seed America, Inc.
18095 Serene Dr.
Morgan Hill, CA 95037
Phone: (408)778-7758 **Fax:** (408)778-7751
Products: Vegetable and flower seeds. **SIC:** 5191 (Farm Supplies). **Est:** 1977. **Sales:** $50,000,000 (2000). **Emp:** 130. **Officers:** Paul G. Bennett, President; Koichi Matsunaga, CFO; John Nelson, Marketing & Sales Mgr.; Diana Blea, Dir of Human Resources; Bob Munger, Sales/Marketing Contact, e-mail: bmunger@sakata.com; Marci Huston, Customer Service Contact, e-mail: mhuston@sakata.com; Margaret Camarillo, Human Resources Contact, e-mail: mcamaril@sakata.com.

■ 1231 ■ Salem Farm Supply Inc.
Rte. 22
Salem, NY 12865
Phone: (518)854-7424
Free: (800)999-3276 **Fax:** (518)854-3057
E-mail: salemfarms@aol.com
Products: Farm equipment, including tractors. **SIC:** 5083 (Farm & Garden Machinery). **Est:** 1964. **Sales:** $10,000 (2000). **Emp:** 27. **Officers:** Philip T. Lewis, President.

■ 1232 ■ San Joaquin Valley Hay Growers Association
PO Box 1127
Tracy, CA 95378-1127
Phone: (209)835-1662 **Fax:** (209)835-0719
Products: Hay. **SIC:** 5191 (Farm Supplies). **Est:** 1940. **Sales:** $26,000,000 (2000). **Emp:** 18. **Officers:** M.M. Coelho, General Mgr.

■ 1233 ■ Sanborn Cooperative Grain Co.
309 W 1st St.
Sanborn, IA 51248
Phone: (712)729-3205 **Fax:** (712)729-3247
Products: Grain; Feed; Fertilizer and fertilizer materials. **SICs:** 5191 (Farm Supplies); 5153 (Grain & Field Beans). **Est:** 1906. **Sales:** $2,000,000 (2000). **Emp:** 17. **Officers:** John Cronin, General Mgr.

■ 1234 ■ Sand Livestock Systems Inc.
PO Box 948
Columbus, NE 68601
Phone: (402)564-1211 **Fax:** (402)564-1218
Products: Pig stalls. **SIC:** 5083 (Farm & Garden Machinery). **Sales:** $57,000,000 (2000). **Emp:** 300. **Officers:** Charles Sand, President; Tim Cumberland, Treasurer & Secty.; John Higgins, VP of Marketing.

■ 1235 ■ Sand Seed Service Inc.
Hwy. 143 N
Marcus, IA 51035
Phone: (712)376-4135 **Fax:** (712)376-4140
Products: Agricultural supplies. **SIC:** 5191 (Farm Supplies). **Est:** 1932. **Sales:** $24,000,000 (2000). **Emp:** 32. **Officers:** Charles Sand, President.

■ 1236 ■ Sauder and Rippel Inc.
Rte. 51
Minonk, IL 61760
Phone: (309)432-2531
Products: Farm equipment. **SIC:** 5083 (Farm & Garden Machinery). **Sales:** $4,200,000 (2000). **Emp:** 12. **Officers:** Frank Kandel, President.

■ 1237 ■ Schilling Brothers Inc.
R.R. 2
Mattoon, IL 61938
Phone: (217)234-6478
Products: Tractors; Forklifts. **SICs:** 5083 (Farm & Garden Machinery); 5084 (Industrial Machinery & Equipment). **Est:** 1985. **Sales:** $10,000,000 (2000). **Emp:** 15. **Officers:** Dwight Schilling, President; David Schilling, Treasurer & Secty.

■ 1238 ■ Schmidt Machine Co.
7013 State Hwy. 199
Upper Sandusky, OH 43351
Phone: (419)294-3814
Free: (800)589-3814 **Fax:** (419)294-2607
E-mail: info@schmidtmachine.com
URL: http://www.schmidtmachine.com
Products: Tractors; Combines. **SICs:** 5083 (Farm & Garden Machinery); 5084 (Industrial Machinery & Equipment). **Est:** 1935. **Sales:** $5,000,000 (2000). **Emp:** 40. **Officers:** Randy Schmidt, President; Darlene Mooney, Treasurer; Kevin Schmidt, Sales Mgr.

■ 1239 ■ Schuyler-Brown FS Inc.
PO Box 230
Rushville, IL 62681
Phone: (217)322-3306
Free: (800)648-6043 **Fax:** (217)322-2019
Products: Agricultural supplies. **SICs:** 5153 (Grain & Field Beans); 5153 (Grain & Field Beans); 5191 (Farm Supplies). **Est:** 1919. **Sales:** $50,000,000 (1999). **Emp:** 85. **Officers:** Glenn Koch, President; Brian Jallas, Controller; Brett Isley, Dir. of Marketing.

■ 1240 ■ Scott Cooperative Association
PO Box 340
Scott City, KS 67871
Phone: (316)872-5823
Products: Farm supplies; Grains; Fertilizers. **SICs:** 5153 (Grain & Field Beans); 5191 (Farm Supplies); 5172 (Petroleum Products Nec). **Est:** 1957. **Sales:** $24,000,000 (2000). **Emp:** 32. **Officers:** Junior Strecker, CEO; Gary Frienson, Office Mgr.

■ 1241 ■ Scott County Cooperative
PO Box 248
Forest, MS 39074
Phone: (601)469-1451
Products: Farm supplies, including feed, seed, and hardware. **SICs:** 5191 (Farm Supplies); 5191 (Farm Supplies); 5083 (Farm & Garden Machinery). **Est:** 1952. **Sales:** $4,000,000 (2000). **Emp:** 22. **Officers:** W.B. Madden, General Mgr.

■ 1242 ■ Scott Farm Service Inc.
N Commercial St.
Winchester, IL 62694
Phone: (217)742-3125
Products: Farm supplies, including fertilizer, chemicals, and feed. **SICs:** 5191 (Farm Supplies); 5171 (Petroleum Bulk Stations & Terminals). **Est:** 1937. **Sales:** $7,000,000 (2000). **Emp:** 25. **Officers:** Dwayne Martin, Manager.

■ 1243 ■ Scott-Hourigan Co.
511 S Lincoln Ave.
York, NE 68467-4211
Phone: (402)362-7711
Free: (800)284-7066 **Fax:** (402)362-7621
E-mail: scotthou@inebraska.com
URL: http://www.scotthourigancom
Products: Agricultural equipment, including grain dryers; Outdoor power equipment; Hard and soft hose travellers; Hoses; Lawn mowers. **SIC:** 5083 (Farm & Garden Machinery). **Est:** 1970. **Sales:** $2,000,000 (1999). **Emp:** 13. **Officers:** Dana Scott, President.

■ 1244 ■ Scott Seed Co.
PO Box 849
New Albany, IN 47150
Phone: (812)945-0229 **Fax:** (812)944-4941
Products: Seeds. SIC: 5191 (Farm Supplies).

■ 1245 ■ O.M. Scott and Sons Co.
14111 Scottslawn Rd.
Marysville, OH 43041
Phone: (937)644-0011 **Fax:** (937)644-7261
Products: Lawn fertilizer and grass seeds. SIC: 5191 (Farm Supplies).

■ 1246 ■ Scott Truck and Tractor Company Inc.
PO Box 4948
Monroe, LA 71211
Phone: (318)387-4160
Products: Farm equipment; Heavy equipment; Outdoor machinery. SICs: 5083 (Farm & Garden Machinery); 5082 (Construction & Mining Machinery). **Est:** 1940. **Sales:** $85,000,000 (2000). **Emp:** 500. **Officers:** T.H. Scott, Chairman of the Board; G.E. Bershen, CFO.

■ 1247 ■ Seaboard Seed Co.
PO Box 117
Bristol, IL 60512
Phone: (630)553-5800 **Fax:** (630)553-6735
Products: Seeds. SIC: 5191 (Farm Supplies).

■ 1248 ■ Seaman Grain Inc.
PO Box 93
Bowersville, OH 45307
Phone: (513)453-2343
Products: Farming supplies. SICs: 5153 (Grain & Field Beans); 5191 (Farm Supplies). **Est:** 1946. **Sales:** $12,000,000 (2000). **Emp:** 10. **Officers:** Brad Woods, President.

■ 1249 ■ Sedalia Implement Company Inc.
2205 S Limit
Sedalia, MO 65301
Phone: (660)826-0466
Products: Farm equipment. SIC: 5083 (Farm & Garden Machinery). **Est:** 1938. **Sales:** $5,000,000 (2000). **Emp:** 18. **Officers:** John Joy, President & Treasurer.

■ 1250 ■ Seed Corp. of America
4764 Hollins Ferry Rd.
Arbutus, MD 21227
Phone: (410)247-3000
Free: (800)666-5296 **Fax:** (410)247-2037
Products: Grass seed. SIC: 5191 (Farm Supplies).

■ 1251 ■ Seed Research of Oregon
27630 Llewellyn Road
Corvallis, OR 97333
Phone: (541)757-2663
Free: (800)253-5766 **Fax:** (541)758-5305
E-mail: info@sroseed.com
URL: http://www.sroseed.com
Products: Rye and bent grass seeds, including warm season grasses, bluegrass, and fescues. SIC: 5191 (Farm Supplies).

■ 1252 ■ Seedex Distributors, Inc.
9110 Waterville-Swanton
Waterville, OH 43566
Phone: (419)878-8561 **Fax:** (419)878-0693
Products: Lawn seed. SIC: 5191 (Farm Supplies).

■ 1253 ■ Seeds, Inc.
PO Box 866
Tekoa, WA 99033
Phone: (509)284-2848 **Fax:** (509)284-6464
Products: Turf grass seed. SIC: 5191 (Farm Supplies).

■ 1254 ■ Seedway
1734 Railroad Pl.
Hall, NY 14463
Phone: (716)526-6391 **Fax:** (716)526-6832
Products: Seeds. SIC: 5191 (Farm Supplies). **Sales:** $12,000,000 (2000). **Emp:** 30. **Officers:** Donald Wertman, CEO & President; Richard Snook, CFO.

■ 1255 ■ Seedway, Inc.
1734 Railroad Pl.
Hall, NY 14463
Phone: (716)526-5651 **Fax:** (716)526-6832
Products: Vegetable and turf seeds. SIC: 5191 (Farm Supplies). **Sales:** $14,000,000 (2000). **Emp:** 60. **Officers:** Donald Wertman, CEO; Richard Shook, CFO; H. Eugene Hohl, Dir. of Marketing.

■ 1256 ■ Seibert Equity Cooperative Association
PO Box 196
Seibert, CO 80834
Phone: (970)664-2211
Products: Hardware; Grains, fertilizers, and seeds. SICs: 5153 (Grain & Field Beans); 5191 (Farm Supplies); 5072 (Hardware). **Est:** 1915. **Sales:** $10,000,000 (2000). **Emp:** 8. **Officers:** Gene Hays, General Mgr.; Marilyn McCaffrey, Bookkeeper.

■ 1257 ■ Seifert Farm Supply
PO Box 54
Three Oaks, MI 49128
Phone: (616)756-9592
Products: Feed; Grain; Fertilizer; Chemicals; Pet food; Lawn and garden supplies. SICs: 5191 (Farm Supplies); 5153 (Grain & Field Beans). **Est:** 1974. **Sales:** $300,000 (2000). **Emp:** 3. **Officers:** Kenneth Seifert, Owner; Karen Seifert, CFO.

■ 1258 ■ Sellers Tractor Company Inc.
PO Box 1940
Salina, KS 67402-1940
Phone: (913)823-6378 **Fax:** (913)823-8083
Products: Tractors. SICs: 5082 (Construction & Mining Machinery); 5084 (Industrial Machinery & Equipment). **Est:** 1947. **Sales:** $15,000,000 (2000). **Emp:** 65. **Officers:** David P. Sellers, President; D.C. Sellers, Sr. VP; W. Euker, Exec. VP of Marketing.

■ 1259 ■ Selma Oil Mill Inc.
PO Box 632
Selma, AL 36702-0632
Phone: (334)875-3310 **Fax:** (334)875-3311
Products: Cotton seed for feed. SIC: 5191 (Farm Supplies). **Est:** 1971. **Sales:** $4,500,000 (2000). **Emp:** 11. **Officers:** Tim Currie, President; Robert Sanford, Exec. VP.

■ 1260 ■ Senesac Inc.
PO Box 592
Fowler, IN 47944
Phone: (765)884-1300 **Fax:** (765)884-8134
Products: Fertilizer and fertilizer materials. SIC: 5191 (Farm Supplies). **Est:** 1947. **Sales:** $7,000,000 (2000). **Emp:** 30. **Officers:** R.J. Puetz Sr., President & CFO; J. Pyle, Dir. of Marketing.

■ 1261 ■ Sharp Brothers Seed Co.
PO Box 140
Healy, KS 67850
Phone: (316)398-2231 **Fax:** (316)398-2220
E-mail: buffalo@midusa.net
URL: http://www.sharpseed.com
Products: Native grass seed and field seed; Turf; Forage. SIC: 5191 (Farm Supplies). **Est:** 1958. **Emp:** 50. **Officers:** Gail Sharp, President; Daniel Sharp, Vice President; David Sharp, Vice President.

■ 1262 ■ Shawano Equity Cooperative Inc.
660 E Seward St.
Shawano, WI 54166
Phone: (715)526-3197 **Fax:** (715)524-5300
Products: Farm supplies; Gas station. SIC: 5191 (Farm Supplies). **Sales:** $25,000,000 (2000). **Emp:** 40. **Officers:** Jon Kroenki, President.

■ 1263 ■ Shawneetown Feed and Seed
12778 U.S Hwy. 61
Jackson, MO 63755
Phone: (573)833-6262
Products: Grain and feed. SIC: 5191 (Farm Supplies). **Est:** 1946. **Sales:** $5,000,000 (2000). **Emp:** 20. **Officers:** Rex Meyr, President & CFO.

■ 1264 ■ Shelby Grain and Feed Co.
PO Box 49
Shelby, OH 44875
Phone: (419)342-6141
Products: Grain and feed. SICs: 5191 (Farm Supplies); 5153 (Grain & Field Beans). **Est:** 1990. **Sales:** $1,000,000 (2000). **Emp:** 5. **Officers:** Gerry Kraycraft, CEO.

■ 1265 ■ Shields Soil Service Inc.
1009 County Rd., Ste. 3000 N
Dewey, IL 61840
Phone: (217)897-1155
Products: Fertilizer. SIC: 5191 (Farm Supplies). **Sales:** $13,000,000 (1993). **Emp:** 50. **Officers:** F. Duane Shields, President.

■ 1266 ■ R.H. Shumway Seedsman
PO Box 1
Graniteville, SC 29829
Phone: (803)663-9771
Products: Vegetable and flower seeds. SIC: 5191 (Farm Supplies). **Est:** 1870. **Sales:** $1,600,000 (2000). **Emp:** 38. **Officers:** J. Wayne Hilton, President.

■ 1267 ■ SIGCO Sun Products Inc.
90 N 8th St.
Breckenridge, MN 56520
Phone: (218)643-8467
Free: (800)654-4145 **Fax:** (218)643-4555
E-mail: sigco@sigcosun.com
URL: http://www.sigco-sun.com
Products: Sunflower kernels; In-shell sunflower seeds; Confection sunflower; Toasted corn; Soy nuts. SIC: 5191 (Farm Supplies). **Est:** 1968. **Sales:** $30,000,000 (1999). **Emp:** 100. **Officers:** Jay Schuler, President; Ken Hodnefield; Nancy Nelson, Sales/Marketing Contact; Tim Mortensen, General Dir., e-mail: tim@sigcosun.com.

■ 1268 ■ Simpson Norton Corp.
4420 Andrews, Ste. A
North Las Vegas, NV 89031
Phone: (702)644-4066
Products: Turf equipment; Irrigation equipment. SIC: 5083 (Farm & Garden Machinery).

■ 1269 ■ Simpson Norton Corp.
PO Box 1295
Goodyear, AZ 85338
Phone: (623)932-5116 **Fax:** (623)932-5299
Products: Lawnmowers; Sprinkler systems. SIC: 5083 (Farm & Garden Machinery). **Est:** 1956. **Sales:** $42,000,000 (2000). **Emp:** 130. **Officers:** Roy W. Simpson, President.

■ 1270 ■ Sloan Implement Company Inc.
PO Box 80
Assumption, IL 62510-0080
Phone: (217)226-4411
Products: Tractors, forklifts, and plows. SIC: 5083 (Farm & Garden Machinery). **Est:** 1933. **Sales:** $32,000,000 (2000). **Emp:** 85. **Officers:** Tom Sloan, General Mgr.

■ 1271 ■ E.J. Smith Group Inc.
PO Box 7247
Charlotte, NC 28241-7247
Phone: (704)394-3361
Products: Lawn mowers. SIC: 5083 (Farm & Garden Machinery). **Est:** 1988. **Sales:** $4,000,000 (2000). **Emp:** 18. **Officers:** James A. Schilling, President.

■ 1272 ■ Smith Turf & Irrigation Co.
4355 Golf Acres Dr.
Charlotte, NC 28208
Phone: (704)393-8873
Free: (800)232-8676 **Fax:** (704)398-1428
Products: Turf equipment; Irrigation supplies. SIC: 5083 (Farm & Garden Machinery). **Est:** 1925. **Emp:** 120.

■ 1273 ■ Sommer Brothers Seed Co.
PO Box 248
Pekin, IL 61554
Phone: (309)346-2127 **Fax:** (309)346-5904
Products: Seed. SIC: 5191 (Farm Supplies).

■ 1274 ■ **South Central Co-op**
PO Box E
Fairfax, MN 55332
Phone: (507)426-8263 **Fax:** (507)426-8266
Products: Feed; Seed; Fertilizer; Gasoline. **SICs:** 5153 (Grain & Field Beans); 5172 (Petroleum Products Nec); 5191 (Farm Supplies). **Est:** 1906. **Sales:** $22,300,000 (2000). **Emp:** 30. **Officers:** Richard Graufman, President; Chuck Felton, General Mgr.

■ 1275 ■ **South Central Co-op**
118 N Meyers Ave.
Lacona, IA 50139
Phone: (515)534-4071
Products: Fertilizer and fertilizer materials; Agricultural chemicals; Petroleum brokers. **SICs:** 5191 (Farm Supplies); 5172 (Petroleum Products Nec). **Est:** 1930. **Sales:** $8,000,000 (2000). **Emp:** 21. **Officers:** Ramon D. Jacobson, General Mgr.; Neil Moon, Comptroller.

■ 1276 ■ **South Texas Implement Co.**
PO Box 35
Taft, TX 78390
Phone: (512)528-2535 **Fax:** (512)528-2966
Products: Lawnmowers. **SICs:** 5083 (Farm & Garden Machinery); 5072 (Hardware). **Est:** 1934. **Sales:** $2,000,000 (2000). **Emp:** 12. **Officers:** Ronie Setliss, President.

■ 1277 ■ **Southeast Cooperative Service Co.**
Hwy. 25 S
Advance, MO 63730
Phone: (573)722-3522 **Fax:** (573)722-3524
Products: Feed, fertilizers, agricultural chemicals and fuel oil; Gasoline service stations. **SICs:** 5191 (Farm Supplies); 5172 (Petroleum Products Nec). **Sales:** $11,000,000 (2000). **Emp:** 39. **Officers:** C.D. Stewart, President; Mike Galaway, CFO.

■ 1278 ■ **Southeastern Colorado Cooperative**
408 S 1st St.
Holly, CO 81047
Phone: (719)537-6514
Products: Agricultural supplies, including tires, animal health products, grains, and feed. **SICs:** 5191 (Farm Supplies); 5014 (Tires & Tubes); 5083 (Farm & Garden Machinery); 5199 (Nondurable Goods Nec). **Est:** 1945. **Sales:** $24,000,000 (2000). **Emp:** 33. **Officers:** Dale H. McWilson, Manager.

■ 1279 ■ **Southern Agriculture Insecticides Inc.**
PO Box 218
Palmetto, FL 34220
Phone: (813)722-3285
Free: (800)477-3285 **Fax:** (813)722-2974
URL: http://www.southernag.com
Products: Insecticides; Fertilizers. **SIC:** 5191 (Farm Supplies). **Est:** 1947. **Sales:** $35,000,000 (2000). **Emp:** 90. **Officers:** John R. Diem, President; William E. Diem, CFO.

■ 1280 ■ **Southern Farm and Home Center**
PO Box 1566
Hattiesburg, MS 39403
Phone: (601)582-3545
Products: Farm supplies and animal feed. **SIC:** 5191 (Farm Supplies). **Sales:** $30,000,000 (1994). **Emp:** 60. **Officers:** Bryan Watkins, President; Delbert L. Williams Jr., Finance Officer.

■ 1281 ■ **Southern Livestock Supply Co. Inc.**
7333 Town S Ave.
Baton Rouge, LA 70808-4141
Phone: (225)769-5811
Free: (800)231-4744 **Fax:** (225)767-0103
Products: Animal health supplies; Lawn and gardening supplies. **SICs:** 5191 (Farm Supplies); 5047 (Medical & Hospital Equipment); 5083 (Farm & Garden Machinery). **Est:** 1971. **Emp:** 26. **Officers:** Parry Richardson Jr., President.

■ 1282 ■ **Southern States Cooperative Inc.**
PO Box 26234
Richmond, VA 23260
Phone: (804)281-1000 **Fax:** (804)281-1141
URL: http://www.sscoop.com
Products: Agricultural products. **SIC:** 5191 (Farm Supplies). **Est:** 1923. **Sales:** $1,123,000,000 (2000).

Emp: 3,500. **Officers:** Wayne A. Boutwell, CEO & President; M. Terry Ragsdale, Exec. VP & COO; Jonathan A. Hawkins, Sr. VP & CFO; C.A. Miller III, VP of Information Systems.

■ 1283 ■ **Southern States Cooperative Inc.**
PO Box 26234
Richmond, VA 23260
Phone: (804)281-1000 **Fax:** (804)281-1141
Products: Animal feed and fertilizers. **SICs:** 5191 (Farm Supplies); 5153 (Grain & Field Beans). **Sales:** $1,120,000,000 (2000). **Emp:** 3,800.

■ 1284 ■ **Southern States Frederick Cooperative Inc.**
PO Box 694
Frederick, MD 21705
Phone: (301)663-6164
Free: (800)310-8903 **Fax:** (301)663-8173
Products: Seed; Feed; Fertilizer; Chemicals; Grain. **SICs:** 5153 (Grain & Field Beans); 5191 (Farm Supplies). **Est:** 1937. **Sales:** $4,500,000 (2000). **Emp:** 15. **Officers:** David Stas Jr., General Mgr.

■ 1285 ■ **Southworth-Milton Inc.**
100 Quarry Dr.
Milford, MA 01757
Phone: (508)634-3400 **Fax:** (508)634-5586
URL: http://www.southwork.milton.com
Products: Construction equipment, including loaders and telescopic handlers; Engines and generators. **SICs:** 5082 (Construction & Mining Machinery); 5083 (Farm & Garden Machinery). **Est:** 1940. **Emp:** 730. **Officers:** Chris Milton, President; Steve Boyd, Chairman of the Board & Finance Officer; Peter Zeras, VP of Sales; Dave Griffin, Vice President of Product Support; Dave Blackberry, Vice President of Power Systems.

■ 1286 ■ **Sovana, Inc.**
4500 Fuller Dr., Ste. 426
Irving, TX 75038
Phone: (972)541-1100 **Fax:** (972)541-1011
Products: Pesticides; Seeds; Irrigation equipment; Farm clearing machines; Agricultural equipment. **SICs:** 5083 (Farm & Garden Machinery); 5191 (Farm Supplies). **Officers:** Marwan M. Sakr, Vice President.

■ 1287 ■ **Spalding Cooperative Elevator Co.**
PO Box B
Spalding, NE 68665
Phone: (308)497-2266
Products: Feed. **SIC:** 5191 (Farm Supplies). **Sales:** $8,000,000 (2000). **Emp:** 20. **Officers:** Gerald Foltz, CEO; Tom Conelly, Manager.

■ 1288 ■ **Spartan Distributors Inc.**
487 W Division St.
Sparta, MI 49345
Phone: (616)887-7301
Products: Lawn mowers; Sprinkler systems. **SIC:** 5083 (Farm & Garden Machinery). **Est:** 1946. **Sales:** $50,000,000 (2000). **Emp:** 85. **Officers:** Dawn Johnson, President.

■ 1289 ■ **Spencer County Cooperative Associates Inc.**
PO Box 7
Chrisney, IN 47611
Phone: (812)362-7701
Products: Farm supplies, including seed, feed, and petroleum products. **SICs:** 5191 (Farm Supplies); 5172 (Petroleum Products Nec). **Est:** 1928. **Sales:** $6,000,000 (2000). **Emp:** 32. **Officers:** Tom Vaal, President; William Weisman, General Mgr.

■ 1290 ■ **Sphar & Co.**
PO Box 849
New Albany, IN 47151-0849
Phone: (812)744-1671
Products: Seed, including garden, grass, and corn. **SIC:** 5191 (Farm Supplies). **Officers:** Jack Buchanan.

■ 1291 ■ **Stacyville Cooperative Co.**
PO Box 217
Stacyville, IA 50476
Phone: (515)737-2348
Products: Feed; Field, garden, and flower seeds; Agricultural chemicals; Fertilizer and fertilizer materials.

SICs: 5153 (Grain & Field Beans); 5191 (Farm Supplies). **Est:** 1907. **Sales:** $14,000,000 (2000). **Emp:** 22. **Officers:** Richard Forey, General Mgr.

■ 1292 ■ **Standard Equipment Co.**
8411 Pulaski Hwy.
Baltimore, MD 21237
Phone: (410)687-1700 **Fax:** (410)391-6206
Products: John Deere construction equipment. **SIC:** 5083 (Farm & Garden Machinery). **Former Name:** Milton #James Co.

■ 1293 ■ **Stanislaus Farm Supply Co.**
624 E Service Rd.
Modesto, CA 95358
Phone: (209)538-7070 **Fax:** (209)541-3191
Products: Agricultural supplies, including feed, fertilizer, and hardware. **SIC:** 5191 (Farm Supplies). **Est:** 1949. **Sales:** $34,000,000 (2000). **Emp:** 80. **Officers:** Anselmo Bettencourt, CEO & President; Larry Carter, Treasurer; Espiridon Ixta, Dir. of Data Processing; Sam Bettencourt, Dir of Human Resources.

■ 1294 ■ **Carl F. Statz and Sons Inc.**
PO Box 38
Waunakee, WI 53597
Phone: (608)849-4101 **Fax:** (608)849-5699
Products: Farming supplies. **SICs:** 5083 (Farm & Garden Machinery); 5191 (Farm Supplies). **Est:** 1930. **Sales:** $12,000,000 (2000). **Emp:** 35. **Officers:** Ron Statz, President.

■ 1295 ■ **Stockton Feed and Milling Inc.**
PO Box 1446
Ft. Stockton, TX 79735
Phone: (915)336-3324 **Fax:** (915)336-7402
Products: Feed. **SIC:** 5191 (Farm Supplies). **Est:** 1958. **Sales:** $2,900,000 (2000). **Emp:** 9. **Officers:** Jeff Blackwell, Operations Mgr., e-mail: jeff@cmbresources.com; Charles Blackwell, President.

■ 1296 ■ **E.B. Stone and Son Inc.**
PO Box 550
Suisun City, CA 94585
Phone: (707)426-2500 **Fax:** (707)429-8960
Products: Fertilizers. **SIC:** 5191 (Farm Supplies). **Est:** 1936. **Sales:** $8,000,000 (2000). **Emp:** 48. **Officers:** B.G. Crandall, President; R. Picinini, Sales Mgr.

■ 1297 ■ **Stover Seed Company Inc.**
PO Box 21488
Los Angeles, CA 90021
Phones: (213)626-9669 (213)626-9669
Fax: (213)626-4920
Products: Lawn seed. **SIC:** 5191 (Farm Supplies). **Sales:** $400,000 (2000). **Emp:** 15. **Officers:** David L. Knutsen, President & Chairman of the Board.

■ 1298 ■ **Stratton Equity Cooperative**
98 Colorado Ave.
Stratton, CO 80836
Phone: (719)348-5326
Products: Farm supplies, including feed, chemicals, and fertilizer. **SIC:** 5191 (Farm Supplies). **Est:** 1915. **Sales:** $23,000,000 (2000). **Emp:** 60. **Officers:** Richard May, President.

■ 1299 ■ **Stratton Seed Co.**
PO Box 32
Stuttgart, AR 72160
Phone: (501)673-4433 **Fax:** (501)673-1577
E-mail: strattonseed@futura.net
Products: Seed, including rice and wheat. **SIC:** 5191 (Farm Supplies). **Est:** 1948. **Emp:** 85. **Officers:** Wendell Stratton, President; L.M. Stratton, Treasurer & Secty.; J. Craig, Dir. of Marketing; Jimmy Johnson, Production & Input Services.

■ 1300 ■ **Stribling Equipment Inc.**
PO Box 6038
Jackson, MS 39288
Phone: (601)939-1000 **Fax:** (601)932-3306
Products: Tractors, plows, and lawn mowers; Forklifts. **SICs:** 5082 (Construction & Mining Machinery); 5082 (Construction & Mining Machinery). **Est:** 1983. **Sales:** $25,000,000 (2000). **Emp:** 230. **Officers:** G.S. Swanson, President; Sam Everett, Secretary; Harold Hooper, VP of Marketing.

■ 1301 ■ **Stull Enterprises Inc.**
PO Box 887
Concordville, PA 19331-0887
Phone: (610)459-8406 **Fax:** (610)459-8032
URL: http://www.stullenterprises.com
Products: Turf maintenance equipment and supplies;
Outdoor power equipment; Gas grills. **SICs:** 5083
(Farm & Garden Machinery); 5088 (Transportation
Equipment & Supplies). **Est:** 1918. **Sales:** $29,000,000
(2000). **Emp:** 85. **Officers:** Rodman W. Smith,
President; Lee M. Sherman, VP & Treasurer, e-mail:
lsherman@stullenterprises.com; Woody Lesnett, Vice
President; Tom Yingling, General Mgr., e-mail:
stullbeltsville@erols.com.

■ 1302 ■ **Sunbelt Seeds Inc.**
PO Box 668
Norcross, GA 30091
Phone: (404)448-9932 **Fax:** (404)242-8332
Products: Grass seeds. **SIC:** 5191 (Farm Supplies).

■ 1303 ■ **Sunbrand Co.**
3900 Green Industrial Way
Atlanta, GA 30341
Phone: (404)455-0664 **Fax:** 800-228-7550
Products: Sowing equipment. **SIC:** 5083 (Farm &
Garden Machinery). **Est:** 1953. **Sales:** $48,000,000
(2000). **Emp:** 250. **Officers:** M. Tripp, President;
Earnest Arp, Controller; Ron Nipp, Dir. of Marketing;
Lamar Garrett, VP of Information Systems.

■ 1304 ■ **Sunray Cooperative**
PO Box 430
Sunray, TX 79086-0430
Phone: (806)948-4121
Products: Batteries; Boots; Gardening supplies; Feed;
Grain; Fertilizer; Fuel; Hardware. **SICs:** 5153 (Grain &
Field Beans); 5191 (Farm Supplies). **Est:** 1939. **Sales:**
$65,000,000 (1999). **Emp:** 70. **Officers:** Don
Wiseman, VP & General Merchandising Mgr.

■ 1305 ■ **Sunrise Cooperative Inc.**
82 Townsend Ave.
Norwalk, OH 44857
Phone: (419)668-3336 **Fax:** (419)663-3531
Products: Grain and farm supplies. **SICs:** 5153 (Grain
& Field Beans); 5191 (Farm Supplies). **Sales:**
$27,000,000 (1992). **Emp:** 50. **Officers:** Robert J.
Sunderman, President; Connie Jackson, Controller.

■ 1306 ■ **Superior-Deshler Inc.**
Main St.
Davenport, NE 68335
Phone: (402)364-2125
Products: Fertilizers; Chemicals. **SIC:** 5191 (Farm
Supplies). **Sales:** $5,000,000 (2000). **Emp:** 50.
Officers: Dennis Schardt, President.

■ 1307 ■ **Sutherland Farmers Cooperative**
201 1st St.
Sutherland, IA 51058
Phone: (712)446-3335
Products: Feed, fertilizer, and chemicals; Gasoline.
SICs: 5153 (Grain & Field Beans); 5191 (Farm
Supplies); 5172 (Petroleum Products Nec). **Est:** 1939.
Sales: $4,000,000 (2000). **Emp:** 17. **Officers:** Tim
Pepper, General Mgr.

■ 1308 ■ **Sweeney Brothers Tractor Co.**
4001 38th St., S
Fargo, ND 58104-6903
Phone: (701)492-7300 **Fax:** (701)492-7301
Products: Tractors. **SIC:** 5012 (Automobiles & Other
Motor Vehicles). **Est:** 1946. **Sales:** $5,000,000 (2000).
Emp: 25. **Officers:** L.F. Sweeney, President; P.
Fitzgerald, CFO; K. Sweeney, Dir. of Marketing.

■ 1309 ■ **Sweeney Seed Co.**
488 Drew Park
King of Prussia, PA 19406
Products: Field, garden, and flower seeds. **SIC:** 5191
(Farm Supplies).

■ 1310 ■ **Swift Co-op Oil Co.**
1020 Atlantic Ave.
Benson, MN 56215
Phone: (320)842-5311
Free: (800)697-5311 **Fax:** (320)843-2899
E-mail: Swiftcoopoil@Willmar.com
Products: Fertilizer; Fuel. **SIC:** 5191 (Farm Supplies).
Est: 1929. **Sales:** $9,300,000 (2000). **Emp:** 28.
Officers: Joel James, Manager.

■ 1311 ■ **Syrex, Inc.**
211 Wellington Rd.
Syracuse, NY 13214
Phone: (315)445-8008 **Fax:** (315)445-9422
Products: Organic and medicinal chemicals; Micro-
computers; Agricultural equipment; Construction
machinery; Canned fruits and vegetables. **SICs:** 5083
(Farm & Garden Machinery); 5169 (Chemicals & Allied
Products Nec); 5045 (Computers, Peripherals &
Software); 5149 (Groceries & Related Products Nec);
5082 (Construction & Mining Machinery). **Officers:**
Laurens Dorsey, President & Chairman of the Board.

■ 1312 ■ **T-Bone's Salvage and Equipment
Inc.**
Box N
Bovina, TX 79009
Phone: (806)238-1614
Products: Plows; Tractors; Rakes. **SIC:** 5083 (Farm &
Garden Machinery). **Sales:** $100,000 (2000). **Emp:** 1.
Officers: M.M. Trianen, President.

■ 1313 ■ **Tampico Farmers Elevator Co.**
PO Box 187
Tampico, IL 61283
Phone: (815)438-6155
Products: Fertilizers, feed, and chemicals. **SICs:** 5191
(Farm Supplies); 5153 (Grain & Field Beans). **Est:**
1912. **Sales:** $5,000,000 (2000). **Emp:** 6. **Officers:**
Laverne Mickley, President.

■ 1314 ■ **Taser International Inc.**
1314 Texas Ave., Ste. 1312
Houston, TX 77002
Phone: (713)224-0688 **Fax:** (713)224-0519
E-mail: taser@c-com.net
Products: Aquaculture feeds and supplies; Plastic
insulated and non-insulated containers; Industrial
supplies and equipment. **SICs:** 5191 (Farm Supplies);
5065 (Electronic Parts & Equipment Nec); 5083 (Farm
& Garden Machinery); 5013 (Motor Vehicle Supplies &
New Parts); 5084 (Industrial Machinery & Equipment).
Officers: Carlos R. Ortiz, President.

■ 1315 ■ **John Taylor Fertilizers Co.**
841 W Elkhorn Blvd.
Rio Linda, CA 95673
Phone: (916)991-4451
Products: Fertilizer. **SIC:** 5191 (Farm Supplies).

■ 1316 ■ **Taylor Rental Corp.**
PO Box 8000
New Britain, CT 06050
Phone: (860)229-9100 **Fax:** (860)826-3207
Products: Lawn tools; Party and banquet equipment
and supplies. **SICs:** 5072 (Hardware); 5113 (Industrial
& Personal Service Paper); 5199 (Nondurable Goods
Nec). **Est:** 1947. **Sales:** $43,000,000 (2000). **Emp:**
725. **Officers:** Richard Dandurand, President; D.
Seaborne, Controller; Bob Gautsch, Dir. of Marketing &
Sales; Ken Cesca, Dir of Human Resources.

■ 1317 ■ **Taylor and Sons Equipment Co.**
PO Box 40
Canal Winchester, OH 43110
Phone: (614)837-5516 **Fax:** (614)837-8011
Products: Gardening equipment, including tractors,
lawnmowers, and blades. **SIC:** 5083 (Farm & Garden
Machinery). **Est:** 1946. **Sales:** $2,500,000 (2000).
Emp: 16. **Officers:** Gayle Taylor, CEO.

■ 1318 ■ **Tazewell Farm Bureau Inc.**
PO Box 217
North Tazewell, VA 24630
Phone: (540)988-4131
Products: Farm supplies; Hardware; Clothing. **SICs:**
5191 (Farm Supplies); 5072 (Hardware); 5136
(Men's/Boys' Clothing). **Est:** 1917. **Sales:** $8,000,000
(2000). **Emp:** 50. **Officers:** T.C. Bowen Jr., President;

Mary-Anna Puckett, Treasurer & Secty.; David Farris,
General Mgr.

■ 1319 ■ **Tennessee Farmers Cooperative**
PO Box 3003
La Vergne, TN 37086
Phone: (615)793-8011 **Fax:** (615)793-8343
Products: Farm supplies, including fertilizer, feed, and
seed. **SIC:** 5083 (Farm & Garden Machinery). **Est:**
1945. **Sales:** $427,700,000 (2000). **Emp:** 700.
Officers: Vernon Glover, President; Tom Davis,
Treasurer & Controller; Charles Atkins, Sales Mgr.; Bill
Davis, Dir of Personnel.

■ 1320 ■ **Terra Industries Inc.**
600 4th St.
PO Box 6000
Sioux City, IA 51102-6000
Phone: (712)277-1340
Free: (800)831-1002 **Fax:** (712)233-3648
URL: http://www.terraindustries.com
Products: Farm supplies. **SIC:** 5191 (Farm Supplies).
Est: 1978. **Sales:** $2,542,400,000 (2000). **Emp:** 4,435.
Officers: Burton M. Joyce, CEO & President; Michael
L. Bennett, COO; Laurice Rauch, Chief Investment
Officer.

■ 1321 ■ **Terra International Inc.**
PO Box 6000
Sioux City, IA 51102-6000
Phone: (712)277-1340 **Fax:** (712)279-8700
Products: Chemicals, fertilizer, and insecticides. **SIC:**
5191 (Farm Supplies). **Est:** 1964. **Sales:**
$29,000,000,000 (2000). **Emp:** 4,000. **Officers:** Burton
M. Joyce, CEO & President; Francis G. Meyer, CFO;
Paul D. Foster, Sr. VP of Sales; Michael O'Brien, VP of
Information Systems; Gene Hallauer, VP of Human
Resources.

■ 1322 ■ **Terral-Norris Seed Company Inc.**
PO Box 826
Lake Providence, LA 71254
Phone: (318)559-2840
Products: Farm supplies, including seed. **SIC:** 5191
(Farm Supplies). **Est:** 1950. **Sales:** $24,000,000
(2000). **Emp:** 65. **Officers:** Thomas Terral, President;
Larry J. Mullen, Treasurer & Secty.

■ 1323 ■ **Terral Seed Inc.**
PO Box 826
Lake Providence, LA 71254
Phone: (318)559-2840 **Fax:** (318)559-2888
Products: Livestock and farm products. **SIC:** 5191
(Farm Supplies). **Sales:** $24,000,000 (2000). **Emp:** 65.

■ 1324 ■ **Terre Company of New Jersey Inc.**
PO Box 1000
Clifton, NJ 07014
Phone: (973)473-3393 **Fax:** (973)473-4402
Products: Seed fertilizer; Nursery stock. **SICs:** 5191
(Farm Supplies); 5193 (Flowers & Florists' Supplies).

■ 1325 ■ **Texhoma Wheat Growers Inc.**
PO Box 250
Texhoma, OK 73949
Phone: (405)827-7261
Products: Agricultural products; Hardware; Fertilizer.
SICs: 5191 (Farm Supplies); 5072 (Hardware); 5153
(Grain & Field Beans). **Est:** 1939. **Sales:** $9,000,000
(2000). **Emp:** 15. **Officers:** Mike Berry, President; Gary
Larson, General Mgr.

■ 1326 ■ **Theisen Farm and Home Stores**
4949 Chavenelle Rd.
Dubuque, IA 52004-0146
Phone: (319)556-4738 **Fax:** (319)556-7959
Products: Farm supplies; Lawn and garden
equipment; Building supplies. **SICs:** 5191 (Farm
Supplies); 5083 (Farm & Garden Machinery); 5039
(Construction Materials Nec). **Sales:** $20,000,000
(2000). **Emp:** 240. **Officers:** L.A. Theisen, President;
Julie Tujetsch, Dir. of Marketing; Chris Theisen, Dir. of
Operations; Tony Theisen, Director of Purchasing.

■ 1327 ■ **Thigpen Distributing Inc.**
PO Box 888
Tifton, GA 31793
Phone: (912)382-1396 **Fax:** (912)382-0749
E-mail: thigpen@planttel.net
Products: Commercial lawn care equipment. **SIC:** 5083 (Farm & Garden Machinery). **Est:** 1957. **Sales:** $6,000,000 (1999). **Emp:** 18. **Officers:** Jill Thigpen-Guess, President; Roger Guess, VP of Sales; Jackie Suhayda, Sales/Marketing Contact; Teresa Cravey, Customer Service Contact; Debbie Raulerson, Human Resources Contact.

■ 1328 ■ **Thompson Farmers Cooperative Elevator Co.**
PO Box 327
Thompson, ND 58278
Phone: (701)599-2740
Free: (877)354-1055 **Fax:** (701)599-2528
Products: Feed and seed; Chemicals; Fertilizers. **SIC:** 5191 (Farm Supplies). **Est:** 1915. **Sales:** $16,000,000 (2000). **Emp:** 7. **Officers:** Paul Galegher, President; Mike Morgan, General Mgr.

■ 1329 ■ **Joe Thompson Implement Co.**
PO Box 370
Abernathy, TX 79311
Phone: (806)298-2541 **Fax:** (806)298-2936
Products: Tractors. **SIC:** 5083 (Farm & Garden Machinery). **Est:** 1940. **Sales:** $4,000,000 (2000). **Emp:** 14. **Officers:** Harold Thompson, Mng. Partner; Doris Harris, Bookkeeper.

■ 1330 ■ **Thompson Implement Inc.**
PO Box 549
Olton, TX 79064
Phone: (806)285-2636
Products: Farm equipment, including tractors and irrigation systems. **SIC:** 5083 (Farm & Garden Machinery). **Est:** 1979. **Sales:** $3,000,000 (2000). **Emp:** 13. **Officers:** Michael Perry, President.

■ 1331 ■ **Larry Thompson Sales**
727 S Sherbrooke Cir.
Mt. Carmel, TN 37645
Phone: (423)246-7894
Products: Insecticides; Pesticides; Pet supplies. **SICs:** 5191 (Farm Supplies); 5199 (Nondurable Goods Nec). **Est:** 1975. **Sales:** $60,000 (2000). **Officers:** Larry Thompson, Owner.

■ 1332 ■ **Three Rivers FS Co.**
PO Box 248
Earlville, IA 52041
Phone: (319)923-2315
Products: Feed; Petroleum; Fertilizer. **SICs:** 5172 (Petroleum Products Nec); 5191 (Farm Supplies). **Est:** 1930. **Sales:** $21,000,000 (2000). **Emp:** 60. **Officers:** Don Albrecht, General Mgr.; D. Kirsch, Controller; Steve Schaller, Dir. of Marketing.

■ 1333 ■ **Thurmont Cooperative Inc.**
36 Walnut St.
Thurmont, MD 21788
Phone: (301)271-7321
Products: Feed; Fertilizer. **SIC:** 5191 (Farm Supplies). **Est:** 1934. **Sales:** $3,300,000 (2000). **Emp:** 14. **Officers:** Jerry R. Lillich, General Mgr.

■ 1334 ■ **Tidewater Companies Inc.**
PO Box 1116
Brunswick, GA 31521-1116
Phone: (912)638-7726 **Fax:** (912)638-5907
Products: Timber harvesting equipment; Yard equipment rental and supplies stores. **SIC:** 5083 (Farm & Garden Machinery). **Sales:** $109,000,000 (2000). **Emp:** 250. **Officers:** Ken S. Trowbridge Jr., Chairman of the Board; Earl C. Terry, CFO.

■ 1335 ■ **Tiffin Farmers Cooperative, Inc.**
585 S Seneca County Rd. 13
PO Box 576
Tiffin, OH 44883-0576
Phone: (419)447-0366 **Fax:** (419)447-2429
E-mail: tiffinfarmers@Tiffinohio.com
Products: Feed; Fertilizers; Crop and Yard chemicals; Grain; Seed; Farm Supply. **SICs:** 5153 (Grain & Field Beans); 5191 (Farm Supplies). **Est:** 1920. **Sales:** $7,000,000 (2000). **Emp:** 15. **Officers:** David Kiesel,

Board President; Steve Davis, General Mgr. **Former Name:** Tiffin Farms Inc.

■ 1336 ■ **Timberland Machines**
10A N Main St.
Lancaster, NH 03584
Phone: (603)788-4738
Products: Lawn and garden equipment. **SIC:** 5083 (Farm & Garden Machinery). **Sales:** $14,000,000 (2000). **Emp:** 40. **Officers:** Larry Connary, General Mgr.; Jim McMahon, Finance Officer.

■ 1337 ■ **Tindle Mills Inc.**
PO Box 733
Springfield, MO 65801
Phone: (417)862-7401 **Fax:** (417)862-7401
Products: Feed. **SIC:** 5191 (Farm Supplies). **Est:** 1896. **Sales:** $55,000,000 (2000). **Emp:** 200. **Officers:** J. Neil Ethridge, President; Thomas Rawlings, Controller; Dennis Hobbes, Dir. of Marketing.

■ 1338 ■ **Titgemeiers Feed, Inc.**
701 Western Ave.
Toledo, OH 43609
Phone: (419)243-3731 **Fax:** (419)243-3731
Products: Grass seed and fertilizers. **SIC:** 5191 (Farm Supplies). **Est:** 1887. **Sales:** $1,000,000 (2000). **Emp:** 7. **Officers:** Tom Stronbeck, Contact.

■ 1339 ■ **Todd Tractor Company Inc.**
PO Box 8
Seneca, KS 66538
Phone: (785)336-2138
Products: Lawn mowers; Tractors. **SIC:** 5083 (Farm & Garden Machinery). **Est:** 1951. **Sales:** $2,500,000 (2000). **Emp:** 12. **Officers:** Doug J. Todd, President; Elmer Schraad, Treasurer & Secty.; Melvin Gustin, Sales Mgr.

■ 1340 ■ **Toma International**
PO Box 523
Santa Cruz, CA 95061
Phone: (831)990-0326 **Fax:** (408)464-0556
Products: Vegetable and flower seeds; Farm equipment; Fertilizer; Fruit trees; Medical supplies and equipment. **SICs:** 5191 (Farm Supplies); 5047 (Medical & Hospital Equipment); 5083 (Farm & Garden Machinery); 5193 (Flowers & Florists' Supplies). **Est:** 1985. **Emp:** 5. **Officers:** Tony Livoti, President, e-mail: tony@tomainternational.com.

■ 1341 ■ **Top AG Inc.**
PO Box 284
Tipton, IN 46072
Phone: (317)675-8736
Free: (800)439-8126 **Fax:** (317)675-3080
E-mail: topag@netusa1.net
Products: Agricultural supplies, including grains and fertilizers; Petroleum. **SICs:** 5153 (Grain & Field Beans); 5153 (Grain & Field Beans). **Est:** 1931. **Sales:** $30,000,000 (2000). **Emp:** 57. **Officers:** James L. Rice, General Mgr.; John Graham, Controller.

■ 1342 ■ **Topeka Seed and Stove Inc.**
PO Box 400
Topeka, IN 46571
Phone: (219)593-2494
Products: Farm supplies, including feed, seeds, and heating stoves. **SIC:** 5191 (Farm Supplies). **Sales:** $2,000,000 (2000). **Emp:** 2. **Officers:** Bill Hochstetler, President.

■ 1343 ■ **Torrences Farm Implement**
PO Box C
Heber, CA 92249
Phone: (760)352-5355 **Fax:** (760)352-8707
Products: Tractors. **SIC:** 5083 (Farm & Garden Machinery). **Est:** 1938. **Sales:** $6,500,000 (2000). **Emp:** 38. **Officers:** L.B. Hester, President; S. Hester, CFO.

■ 1344 ■ **Toshin Trading Inc.**
PO Box 1226
Blythe, CA 92226
Phone: (760)922-4713
Products: Hay. **SIC:** 5191 (Farm Supplies).

■ 1345 ■ **Town and Country Coop.**
PO Box 250
Grafton, OH 44044
Phone: (440)926-2281
Products: Feed, fertilizer, grain and petroleum; Gasoline service stations. **SICs:** 5191 (Farm Supplies); 5153 (Grain & Field Beans); 5172 (Petroleum Products Nec). **Sales:** $21,000,000 (2000). **Emp:** 33. **Officers:** Tom Chester, General Mgr.

■ 1346 ■ **Tractor and Equipment Co.**
1835 Harnish Blvd.
Billings, MT 59101
Phone: (406)656-0202 **Fax:** (406)652-6865
Products: Tractors and tractor equipment. **SIC:** 5084 (Industrial Machinery & Equipment). **Est:** 1929. **Sales:** $48,000,000 (2000). **Emp:** 195. **Officers:** John J. Harnish, CEO; David L. Wendte, CFO; Jack Mercer, Dir. of Marketing & Sales; Howard C. Evans, Dir. of Data Processing; Connie Walker, Dir of Human Resources.

■ 1347 ■ **Tractor Place Inc.**
PO Box 689
Knightdale, NC 27545
Phone: (919)266-5846
Products: Farm and lawn tractors, parts, and accessories. **SIC:** 5083 (Farm & Garden Machinery).

■ 1348 ■ **Tracy-Garvin Cooperative**
PO Box 1098
Tracy, MN 56175
Phone: (507)629-3781 **Fax:** (507)629-3392
Products: Feed; Seed. **SIC:** 5191 (Farm Supplies). **Est:** 1920. **Sales:** $15,000,000 (2000). **Emp:** 23. **Officers:** B. Anderson, Manager.

■ 1349 ■ **Transammonia Inc.**
350 Park Ave.
New York, NY 10022
Phone: (212)223-3200 **Fax:** (212)759-1410
Products: Fertilizer. **SICs:** 5191 (Farm Supplies); 5172 (Petroleum Products Nec). **Est:** 1971. **Sales:** $2,478,000,000 (2000). **Emp:** 225. **Officers:** Ronald P. Stanton, CEO & Chairman of the Board; Edward Weiner, CFO; James Shroads, Information Systems Mgr.

■ 1350 ■ **Traylor Chemical and Supply Co.**
PO Box 547937
Orlando, FL 32854-7937
Phone: (407)422-6151 **Fax:** (407)423-5316
Products: Fertilizer. **SIC:** 5191 (Farm Supplies). **Sales:** $31,000,000 (2000). **Emp:** 50. **Officers:** William Traylor, President.

■ 1351 ■ **Treasure State Seed, Inc.**
Box 698
Fairfield, MT 59436
Phone: (406)467-2557
Free: (800)572-4769 **Fax:** (406)467-3377
E-mail: treasure@3rivers.net
Products: Seeds. **SIC:** 5191 (Farm Supplies). **Est:** 1980. **Emp:** 6. **Officers:** Donald L. Becker; Laurie M. Becker.

■ 1352 ■ **Tri-County Co-op**
107 Long Ave.
Lost Nation, IA 52254
Phone: (319)678-2231
Products: Agricultural products, including fertilizers. **SIC:** 5191 (Farm Supplies). **Est:** 1942. **Sales:** $5,900,000 (2000). **Emp:** 15. **Officers:** Lonnie Lullmann, CEO.

■ 1353 ■ **Tri-County Farmers Association**
416 E Cypress St.
Brinkley, AR 72021
Phone: (870)734-4874
Products: Farm supplies. **SIC:** 5191 (Farm Supplies). **Est:** 1960. **Sales:** $13,000,000 (2000). **Emp:** 27. **Officers:** Carl E. Geisler, President; Roland Warrington, General Mgr.

■ 1354 ■ **Tri-Parish Cooperative Inc.**
PO Box 89
Slaughter, LA 70777
Phone: (504)654-2727 **Fax:** (504)654-8500
Products: Fertilizer; Feed; Seed; Tractor parts; Gates;

Posts; Clothes; Pet supplies. **SICs:** 5191 (Farm Supplies); 5015 (Motor Vehicle Parts—Used); 5031 (Lumber, Plywood & Millwork); 5199 (Nondurable Goods Nec); 5136 (Men's/Boys' Clothing). **Est:** 1959. **Sales:** $6,000,000 (2000). **Emp:** 29. **Officers:** James C. Womack, President; Conrad L. Turner, CFO.

■ **1355** ■ **Tri Star Seed Co.**
20300 W 191st St.
Spring Hill, KS 66083-8982
Phone: (913)780-6186 **Fax:** (913)780-6280
Products: Garden, grass, and field seeds. **SIC:** 5191 (Farm Supplies).

■ **1356** ■ **Tri Valley Cooperative**
PO Box 227
St. Edward, NE 68660
Phone: (402)678-2251 **Fax:** (402)678-3458
Products: Feed; Grain; Fertilizer; Chemicals. **SICs:** 5153 (Grain & Field Beans); 5191 (Farm Supplies). **Est:** 1917. **Sales:** $29,000,000 (2000). **Emp:** 47. **Officers:** Larry Taylor, Manager.

■ **1357** ■ **Tricorp, Inc.**
PO Box 1009
Mobile, AL 36633-1009
Phone: (205)432-4800 **Fax:** (205)438-5500
Products: Lawnmowers; Farm equipment. **SIC:** 5083 (Farm & Garden Machinery). **Officers:** John Luard, President.

■ **1358** ■ **Troy BioSciences Inc.**
113 S 47th Ave.
Phoenix, AZ 85043
Phone: (602)233-9047
Free: (800)448-2843 **Fax:** (602)272-4155
URL: http://www.troybiosciences.com
Products: Biological pesticides. **SICs:** 5191 (Farm Supplies); 5169 (Chemicals & Allied Products Nec). **Officers:** F.G. Kennedy; Renee LaPuma, Sales/Marketing Contact, e-mail: renee@troybiosciences.com; Yolanda Harvey, Human Resources Contact, e-mail: yolanda@troybiosciences.com. **Former Name:** Fermone Corporation Inc.

■ **1359** ■ **Tru-Part Manufacturing Corp.**
232 Lothenbach Ave.
St. Paul, MN 55118
Phone: (612)455-6681 **Fax:** (612)455-2111
Products: Tractor replacement parts and accessories. **SIC:** 5083 (Farm & Garden Machinery). **Sales:** $65,000,000 (1994). **Emp:** 300. **Officers:** B.B. Calmenson, President; Lyle McCarty, CFO.

■ **1360** ■ **TruAl Inc.**
Rte. 1, Box 103
Lewisville, MN 56060
Phone: (507)435-4414
Products: Pig semen. **SIC:** 5159 (Farm-Product Raw Materials Nec).

■ **1361** ■ **Truman Farmers Elevator Co.**
PO Box 68
Truman, MN 56088
Phone: (507)776-2831 **Fax:** (507)776-2871
Products: Grain; Farm supplies, including fertilizer, fuel, and lumber. **SICs:** 5153 (Grain & Field Beans); 5031 (Lumber, Plywood & Millwork). **Est:** 1903. **Sales:** $38,000,000 (2000). **Emp:** 45. **Officers:** Bruce Stofferan, General Mgr.

■ **1362** ■ **Tulia Wheat Growers Inc.**
PO Box 787
Dimmitt, TX 79027-0787
Phone: (806)995-4176
Products: Farm equipment, including fuel, mowers and tractors. **SICs:** 5191 (Farm Supplies); 5172 (Petroleum Products Nec); 5083 (Farm & Garden Machinery). **Est:** 1934. **Sales:** $6,700,000 (2000). **Emp:** 11. **Officers:** Mark N. Thompson, President; Gary House, CFO; Don Russel, Manager.

■ **1363** ■ **Turf and Industrial Equipment Co.**
2715 Lafayette St.
PO Box 343
Santa Clara, CA 95052-0343
Phone: (408)727-5660 **Fax:** (408)727-5875
Products: Golf carts, lawnmowers, and tractors. **SICs:**

5083 (Farm & Garden Machinery); 5088 (Transportation Equipment & Supplies).

■ **1364** ■ **Turf Merchants**
33390 Tangent Loop
Tangent, OR 97389
Phone: (541)926-8649
Free: (800)421-1735 **Fax:** (541)926-4435
E-mail: spt@proaxis.com
URL: http://www.turfmerchants.com
Products: Grass seeds. **SIC:** 5191 (Farm Supplies). **Est:** 1984. **Sales:** $25,000,000 (2000). **Emp:** 10. **Officers:** Steven P. Tubbs, President; John L. Cochran, General Mgr.

■ **1365** ■ **Turf Products Corp.**
PO Box 1200
Enfield, CT 06083
Phone: (860)763-3581 **Fax:** (860)763-5550
Products: Lawn and garden equipment. **SIC:** 5083 (Farm & Garden Machinery). **Sales:** $33,000,000 (2000). **Emp:** 150. **Officers:** Frederick N. Zeytoonjian, President; John Motta, CFO.

■ **1366** ■ **Turf-Seed, Inc.**
PO Box 250
Hubbard, OR 97032
Phone: (503)651-2130 **Fax:** (503)651-2351
URL: http://www.turf-seed.com
Products: Seed. **SIC:** 5191 (Farm Supplies). **Est:** 1970. **Sales:** $25,000,000 (1999). **Emp:** 30. **Officers:** Bill Rose; Gordon Zielinski.

■ **1367** ■ **Twin City Implement Inc.**
2123 Memorial Hwy.
Mandan, ND 58554
Phone: (701)663-7505
Products: Farm equipment, including tractors and irrigation systems. **SIC:** 5083 (Farm & Garden Machinery). **Est:** 1964. **Sales:** $8,000,000 (2000). **Emp:** 17. **Officers:** Pete R. Deichert Jr., President; Don Deichert, Treasurer & Secty.

■ **1368** ■ **Twin County Service Co.**
PO Box 728
Marion, IL 62959
Phone: (618)993-5155 **Fax:** (618)997-2526
Products: Farm supplies, including seeds, fertilizer, chemicals, and feed; Animal health products; Oil filters; Gas and kerosene. **SICs:** 5191 (Farm Supplies); 5172 (Petroleum Products Nec). **Est:** 1931. **Sales:** $50,000,000 (2000). **Emp:** 80. **Officers:** Randy Handel, General Mgr.; Dan Brook, Controller; Gerald Witges, Sales Mgr.

■ **1369** ■ **Twin Falls Tractor and Implement Inc.**
1935 Kimberly Rd.
Twin Falls, ID 83301
Phone: (208)733-8687 **Fax:** (208)733-8047
Products: Farm implements, including tractors. **SIC:** 5083 (Farm & Garden Machinery). **Est:** 1952. **Sales:** $5,000,000 (2000). **Emp:** 26. **Officers:** Gene L. Glenn, President; Bob Wildman, General Mgr.; Gary Bratt, Sales/Marketing Contact; Linda Mortenson, Customer Service Contact.

■ **1370** ■ **UAP Northwest**
PO Box 506
Burlington, WA 98233
Phone: (360)757-6041
Products: Agricultural equipment and supplies. **SIC:** 5191 (Farm Supplies). **Sales:** $4,000,000 (2000). **Emp:** 12.

■ **1371** ■ **Union Fertilizer Co.**
4630 US Hwy. 60 E
Waverly, KY 42462-6900
Phone: (502)389-1241 **Fax:** (502)389-9456
Products: Agricultural supplies, including fertilizer, seed, and chemicals. **SIC:** 5191 (Farm Supplies). **Est:** 1951. **Sales:** $2,000,000 (2000). **Emp:** 7. **Officers:** Brian Clements, Manager.

■ **1372** ■ **Union Oil Mill Inc.**
PO Box 1320
Greenwood, MS 38935-1320
Products: Cottonseeds. **SIC:** 5153 (Grain & Field Beans). **Emp:** 6. **Officers:** T.S. Shuler, President.

■ **1373** ■ **Union Produce Cooperative**
PO Box 299
Ossian, IA 52161
Phone: (319)532-9381
Products: Feed. **SIC:** 5191 (Farm Supplies). **Est:** 1911. **Sales:** $7,400,000 (2000). **Emp:** 23. **Officers:** Richard Hendrickson, President; Dale Smith, General Mgr.

■ **1374** ■ **United Co-op Inc. (Hampton, Nebraska)**
PO Box 127
Hampton, NE 68843
Phone: (402)725-3131
Free: (800)245-4430 **Fax:** (402)725-3231
Products: Farm supplies, including grains. **SICs:** 5153 (Grain & Field Beans); 5191 (Farm Supplies); 5172 (Petroleum Products Nec). **Est:** 1910. **Sales:** $78,000,000 (2000). **Emp:** 100. **Officers:** Jay Larson, General Mgr.; Larry Hansen, Accounting Manager.

■ **1375** ■ **United Cooperative Farmers Inc.**
22 Kimball Pl.
Fitchburg, MA 01420
Phone: (508)345-4103
Free: (800)545-6655 **Fax:** (978)345-7187
Products: Grain; Feed, including bird feed. **SICs:** 5199 (Nondurable Goods Nec); 5153 (Grain & Field Beans); 5083 (Farm & Garden Machinery). **Est:** 1928. **Sales:** $31,000,000 (2000). **Emp:** 70. **Officers:** Donald Upton, CEO.

■ **1376** ■ **United Farmers Co-op**
PO Box 158
Rushmore, MN 56168
Phone: (507)478-4166
Free: (888)470-4166 **Fax:** (507)478-4502
URL: http://www.unitedfarmerscoop.com
Products: Feed; Fuel; Fertilizer; Chemicals. **SICs:** 5153 (Grain & Field Beans); 5172 (Petroleum Products Nec). **Sales:** $65,000,000 (2000). **Emp:** 60. **Officers:** Glenn Eben, Location Mgr. **Former Name:** United Co-op Rushmore.

■ **1377** ■ **United Farmers Cooperative**
PO Box 4
Lafayette, MN 56054
Phone: (507)228-8224
Free: (800)642-4104 **Fax:** (507)228-8766
E-mail: ufcasc@prairie.lakes.com
Products: Farm supplies, including seeds, feed, fertilizer, chemicals, and machinery; Grain. **SICs:** 5153 (Grain & Field Beans); 5191 (Farm Supplies); 5083 (Farm & Garden Machinery); 5172 (Petroleum Products Nec). **Est:** 1915. **Sales:** $52,000,000 (2000). **Emp:** 100. **Officers:** Steve Sjostrom, President; Lori Reimartf, Controller; Jeff Nielsen, General Mgr.

■ **1378** ■ **United Farmers Cooperative Inc.**
408 James St.
Stanton, IA 51573
Phone: (712)829-2117
Products: Fertilizer; Chemicals; Feed. **SIC:** 5191 (Farm Supplies). **Est:** 1940. **Sales:** $8,000,000 (2000). **Emp:** 18. **Officers:** Harold Rossander, General Mgr.

■ **1379** ■ **United Producers Consumers Cooperative**
1821 E Jackson St.
Phoenix, AZ 85034
Phone: (602)254-5644 **Fax:** (602)254-5644
Products: Hardware; Feed. **SIC:** 5191 (Farm Supplies). **Est:** 1934. **Sales:** $10,000,000 (2000). **Emp:** 65. **Officers:** Pauline Gentry, General Mgr.

■ **1380** ■ **United Service and Sales**
2808 S Main St.
Salt Lake City, UT 84115
Phone: (801)485-5770
Free: (800)203-8454 **Fax:** (801)485-5774
URL: http://www.unitedserviceandsales.com
Products: Lawn and garden equipment; Engines. **SIC:** 5083 (Farm & Garden Machinery).

■ **1381** ■ **United Services Association**
7025 Hickman Rd.
Des Moines, IA 50322
Phone: (515)276-6763 **Fax:** (515)276-0503
Products: Farm supplies. **SIC:** 5191 (Farm Supplies).

Est: 1972. Sales: $28,000,000 (2000). Emp: 6. Officers: Steve Bressler, President, e-mail: steve@unitedservices.net; Susan Lagneaux, VP & Dir. of Risk Management.

■ 1382 ■ U.S. Global Resources
10242 59th Ave. S
Seattle, WA 98178
Phone: (425)391-5646 Fax: (425)392-6713
E-mail: sharpdonn@aol.com
URL: http://www.usgr.com
Products: Greenhouse projects and equipment; Heating, air conditioning, coverings, agricultural poly, ventilation, sprayers, and fertilizer systems. SIC: 5083 (Farm & Garden Machinery). Est: 1941. Sales: $23,000,000 (2000). Emp: 68. Officers: Donn A. Sharp, President; Dorothy Darmody, Controller. Former Name: Sharp and Son Inc.

■ 1383 ■ U.S. Home and Garden Inc.
655 Montgomery St.
San Francisco, CA 94111
Phone: (415)616-8111
Products: Nonwoven landscape fabrics; Garden supplies and equipment; Agricultural fertilizers. SICs: 5072 (Hardware); 5191 (Farm Supplies). Sales: $52,000,000 (2000). Emp: 123. Officers: Robert L. Kassel, CEO, President & Chairman of the Board.

■ 1384 ■ United Suppliers Inc.
PO Box 538
Eldora, IA 50627
Phone: (515)858-2341 Fax: (515)858-5245
Products: Feed; Fertilizer; Chemicals. SIC: 5191 (Farm Supplies). Est: 1963. Sales: $130,000,000 (2000). Emp: 340. Officers: Maurice Hyde, President; Roger Krull, Comptroller.

■ 1385 ■ Universal Cooperative Inc.
1300 Corporate Center Curve
PO Box 460
Eagan, MN 55121
Phone: (651)239-1000 Fax: (651)239-1009
Products: Farming supplies. SICs: 5083 (Farm & Garden Machinery); 5072 (Hardware); 5169 (Chemicals & Allied Products Nec); 5153 (Grain & Field Beans). Est: 1972. Sales: $270,000,000 (2000). Emp: 155. Officers: Terrence Bohman, President; Dennis Gyolai, VP of Finance; L. Bryan Morrison, VP of Human Resources.

■ 1386 ■ Unverferth Manufacturing Company Inc.
PO Box 357
Kalida, OH 45853
Phone: (419)532-3121 Fax: (419)532-2468
Products: Farm equipment. SIC: 5083 (Farm & Garden Machinery). Est: 1948. Sales: $10,000,000 (2000). Emp: 100. Officers: Richard A. Unverferth, President; Dennis A. Kapcar, Controller; L. Daniel Fanger, Dir. of Marketing.

■ 1387 ■ Urwiler Oil and Fertilizer Inc.
Hwy. 20 N
Laurel, NE 68745
Phone: (402)256-3422
Products: Chemical fertilizers; Propane service; c-store. SICs: 5191 (Farm Supplies); 5172 (Petroleum Products Nec). Est: 1986. Sales: $6,000,000 (1999). Emp: 30. Officers: Greg Urwiler, President.

■ 1388 ■ U.S.A. Marketing Alliance Inc.
8570 Jewel Ave. N
Stillwater, MN 55082
Phone: (612)426-2164 Fax: (612)683-7295
Products: Farm machinery; Air pollution control products. SICs: 5083 (Farm & Garden Machinery); 5191 (Farm Supplies). Officers: Donald J. Heffernan, Director.

■ 1389 ■ UTECO Inc.
8504 Sanford Dr.
Richmond, VA 23228
Phone: (804)266-7807 Fax: (804)264-1196
Products: Parts for outdoor equipment, including lawn and garden supplies and lawnmower blades. SICs: 5083 (Farm & Garden Machinery); 5084 (Industrial Machinery & Equipment). Est: 1982. Sales:

$1,000,000 (2000). Emp: 7. Officers: Davis Bottom, President.

■ 1390 ■ Valley Crest Tree Co.
24121 Ventura Blvd.
Calabasas, CA 91302
Phone: (818)737-2600 Fax: (818)222-7307
Products: Nursery stock; Tree relocation. SIC: 5193 (Flowers & Florists' Supplies). Est: 1960. Sales: $40,000,000 (2000). Emp: 500. Officers: Stuart J. Sperber, President, e-mail: ssperber@rctree.com.

■ 1391 ■ Valley Farm Inc.
Hwy. 34 & Hwy. 61
Benkelman, NE 69021
Phone: (308)423-2515 Fax: (308)425-5615
Products: Farm equipment, including tractors. SIC: 5083 (Farm & Garden Machinery). Est: 1952. Sales: $3,400,000 (2000). Emp: 12. Officers: Tom Ham, President.

■ 1392 ■ Valley Farmers Cooperative (Natchitoches, Louisiana)
PO Box 2116
Natchitoches, LA 71457
Phone: (318)352-6426
Products: Farming equipment and supplies, including seed, feed, and fertilizer. SICs: 5191 (Farm Supplies); 5172 (Petroleum Products Nec). Est: 1951. Sales: $7,000,000 (2000). Emp: 25. Officers: John Aaron, General Mgr.

■ 1393 ■ Valley Feed Mill Inc.
315 W Center St.
Paris, TX 75460
Phone: (903)785-3501 Fax: (903)784-5829
Products: Fertilizers; Feed; Dog and cat products. SICs: 5191 (Farm Supplies); 5153 (Grain & Field Beans); 5199 (Nondurable Goods Nec). Est: 1953. Sales: $4,000,000 (2000). Emp: 45. Officers: Artis T. Edzards, President; Dorothy Edzards, Finance Officer.

■ 1394 ■ Valley Fertilizer and Chemical Company Inc.
PO Box 816
Mt. Jackson, VA 22842
Phone: (540)477-3121
Free: (800)571-3121 Fax: (540)477-3123
E-mail: vfsoil@shentel.net
Products: Fertilizer. SICs: 5191 (Farm Supplies); 5191 (Farm Supplies); 5084 (Industrial Machinery & Equipment). Est: 1937. Sales: $5,000,000 (2000). Emp: 18. Officers: Orville L. Smoot, President.

■ 1395 ■ VanderHave USA
PO Box 338
West Fargo, ND 58078
Phone: (701)282-7338
Products: Lawn and garden supplies. SIC: 5191 (Farm Supplies).

■ 1396 ■ Van's Supply and Equipment Inc.
1018 Circle Dr.
Green Bay, WI 54304
Phone: (920)499-5969 Fax: (920)499-5868
Products: Outdoor power equipment, including mowers and snowblowers. SIC: 5083 (Farm & Garden Machinery). Est: 1955. Sales: $10,000,000 (2000). Emp: 35. Officers: William Vanderperren, President; Roxanne Mueller, Vice President; Martin E. Young, General Mgr.

■ 1397 ■ Vater Implement Inc.
PO Box 749
Enid, OK 73702
Phone: (580)237-5051 Fax: (580)237-4021
Products: Farm equipment, including combines and tractors. SIC: 5083 (Farm & Garden Machinery). Est: 1933. Sales: $2,200,000 (2000). Emp: 8. Officers: George Traynor, President.

■ 1398 ■ Veterinary Companies of America Inc.
PO Box 148
Topeka, KS 66601-0148
Phone: (785)354-8523 Fax: (785)231-5775
Products: Animal feeds. SIC: 5191 (Farm Supplies). Est: 1975. Sales: $200,000,000 (2000). Emp: 1,000. Officers: Jim Keebler, CEO; Don Ford, CFO; Rick

Axelrod, Dir. of Marketing; Ned Luut, Dir. of Systems; George Behling.

■ 1399 ■ Vincent Implements Inc.
8258 Hwy 45
Martin, TN 38237
Phone: (901)587-3824
Free: (800)624-8754 Fax: (901)587-3827
Products: Farm equipment. SIC: 5083 (Farm & Garden Machinery). Est: 1963. Sales: $10,000,000 (2000). Emp: 35. Officers: John Vincent, President.

■ 1400 ■ Vita Plus Corp.
PO Box 259126
Madison, WI 53725-9126
Phone: (608)256-1988 Free: (800)362-8334
Products: Animal feed. SIC: 5191 (Farm Supplies). Est: 1948. Sales: $55,500,000 (2000). Emp: 200. Officers: Robert S. Tramburg, CEO.

■ 1401 ■ W-P Milling Company Inc.
1119 S Cherokee St.
Muskogee, OK 74402
Phone: (918)682-3388
Products: Animal feed. SIC: 5153 (Grain & Field Beans). Sales: $18,000,000 (2000). Emp: 100. Officers: J.W. Philbin, General Mgr.; M. Hudson, CFO.

■ 1402 ■ Wabash Valley Service Co.
909 N Court St.
Grayville, IL 62844
Phone: (618)375-2311
Products: Feed; Seed; Fertilizer; Farm fuels. SICs: 5191 (Farm Supplies); 5083 (Farm & Garden Machinery); 5172 (Petroleum Products Nec). Est: 1930. Sales: $36,000,000 (2000). Emp: 115. Officers: Charles Lynch, President; Todd Neibel, Controller.

■ 1403 ■ R.M. Wade and Co.
PO Box 23666
Portland, OR 97223
Phone: (503)641-1865 Fax: (503)692-9700
Products: Small tractors. SIC: 5083 (Farm & Garden Machinery). Sales: $22,000,000 (2000). Emp: 150. Officers: E.H. Newbegin, President; Dave Wendroff, CFO; Dave Steele, Dir. of Marketing.

■ 1404 ■ Walco International Inc. Cody Div.
PO Box 223
Cody, NE 69211
Phone: (402)823-4241
Products: Veterinary supplies and feed. SICs: 5122 (Drugs, Proprietaries & Sundries); 5191 (Farm Supplies).

■ 1405 ■ Cecil I. Walker Machinery Co.
PO Box 2427
Charleston, WV 25329
Phone: (304)949-6400 Fax: (304)949-5098
Products: Tractors. SIC: 5084 (Industrial Machinery & Equipment). Est: 1950. Sales: $130,000,000 (2000). Emp: 420. Officers: D. Stephen Walker, President; Andy Southworth, VP of Finance; Roger Lilly, Marketing Mgr.; Fred Michaels, Operations Mgr.

■ 1406 ■ Walla Walla Farmers Co-op Inc.
PO Box 928
WalLa Walla, WA 99362
Phone: (509)525-6690
Products: Fertilizers; Chemicals; Oils. SICs: 5191 (Farm Supplies); 5172 (Petroleum Products Nec). Est: 1933. Sales: $12,000,000 (2000). Emp: 45. Officers: Donald Meiners, President; Ed Meliah, Treasurer & Secty.

■ 1407 ■ Wallace County Cooperative Equity Exchange
PO Box 280
Sharon Springs, KS 67758
Phone: (785)852-4241 Fax: (785)852-4286
Products: Grain; Fertilizers; Fuels. SICs: 5153 (Grain & Field Beans); 5191 (Farm Supplies); 5172 (Petroleum Products Nec). Est: 1948. Sales: $29,000,000 (2000). Emp: 32. Officers: Dean Schemm, President; Ralph Stolz, CFO; Robert Waugh, President.

■ **1408** ■ **Wallace Grain Company Inc.**
PO Box 109
Sheridan, IN 46069-0109
Phone: (317)758-4434
Products: Horse feed. **SIC:** 5191 (Farm Supplies).
Est: 1935. **Sales:** $8,000,000 (2000). **Emp:** 14.
Officers: Phil G. Wallace, President; Craig Wallace,
Treasurer & Secty.; Fred Spencer, Dir. of Sales.

■ **1409** ■ **Wallace Hardware Co.**
PO Box 687
Morristown, TN 37815
Phone: (615)586-5650 **Fax:** (615)581-0766
Products: Farm equipment; Nuts and screws. **SICs:**
5072 (Hardware); 5083 (Farm & Garden Machinery);
5191 (Farm Supplies). **Est:** 1922. **Sales:** $50,000,000
(2000). **Emp:** 200. **Officers:** J.D. Wallace, President &
Treasurer; William A. Trusler, CFO; Richard Snowden,
VP of Sales; Kris Sigler, VP of Information Systems;
John Cahill, VP of Operations.

■ **1410** ■ **Walpeco**
1100 S 56th Ave.
Hollywood, FL 33023
Phone: (954)983-4511 **Fax:** (954)983-4995
E-mail: walpeco@bellsouth.net
Products: Farm machinery, including disc plows and
rotary cutters. **SIC:** 5083 (Farm & Garden Machinery).
Est: 1983. **Sales:** $2,000,000 (2000). **Emp:** 6.
Officers: Walter L. Petrovich, President.

■ **1411** ■ **Walters Cooperative Elevators**
Association
PO Box 7
Walters, OK 73572
Phone: (405)875-3344 **Fax:** (405)875-2065
Products: Feed; Animal health products; Seeds,
including lawn and garden; Chemical fertilizers. **SICs:**
5191 (Farm Supplies); 5153 (Grain & Field Beans).
Sales: $6,500,000 (2000). **Emp:** 7. **Officers:** Kenneth
Jones, President; Jim Kender Jr., Vice President.

■ **1412** ■ **Warner Fertilizer Company Inc.**
PO Box 796
Somerset, KY 42502
Phone: (606)679-8484 **Fax:** (606)679-6583
Products: Seed, fertilizer, and chemicals. **SIC:** 5191
(Farm Supplies). **Est:** 1965. **Sales:** $16,000,000
(2000). **Emp:** 25. **Officers:** Charles R. Warner,
President; J.C. Warner, Vice President.

■ **1413** ■ **Warren Farmers Cooperative**
PO Box 1
Mc Minnville, TN 37110
Phone: (931)668-4151 **Fax:** (931)668-3078
Products: Farm supplies, including grains, feeds,
fertilizers, mowers, feeders, and tires. **SICs:** 5191
(Farm Supplies); 5083 (Farm & Garden Machinery);
5153 (Grain & Field Beans); 5172 (Petroleum Products
Nec); 5014 (Tires & Tubes). **Est:** 1948. **Sales:**
$7,000,000 (2000). **Emp:** 36. **Officers:** Don Robins,
General Mgr.; James Bouldin, Controller.

■ **1414** ■ **Watertown Cooperative Elevator**
Association
810 Burlington Northern
Watertown, SD 57201
Phone: (605)886-3039
Products: Seed; Grain; Feed. **SICs:** 5153 (Grain &
Field Beans); 5191 (Farm Supplies). **Est:** 1945. **Sales:**
$35,000,000 (2000). **Emp:** 50. **Officers:** Ferdy Tesch,
President.

■ **1415** ■ **Wathena and Bendena Grain**
Company Inc.
PO Box 249
Wathena, KS 66090
Phone: (785)989-3322
Products: Fertilizer; Farm chemicals. **SIC:** 5191 (Farm
Supplies). **Est:** 1958. **Sales:** $6,000,000 (2000). **Emp:**
10. **Officers:** Dennis Ford, Partner.

■ **1416** ■ **Watonwan Farm Services**
Rte. 1, Box 4
Amboy, MN 56010
Phone: (507)674-3010
Products: Chemicals, fertilizers, and feed. **SIC:** 5191
(Farm Supplies). **Est:** 1937. **Sales:** $11,000,000

(2000). **Emp:** 25. **Officers:** Robert Schmieising,
President; Randy Reid, General Mgr.

■ **1417** ■ **Watseka Farmers Grain Company**
Cooperative
228 W Walnut St.
Watseka, IL 60970
Phone: (815)432-4169 **Fax:** (815)432-5299
Products: Farm products including fertilizer, grass
chemicals. **SIC:** 5191 (Farm Supplies). **Est:** 1909.
Sales: $6,600,000 (2000). **Emp:** 11. **Officers:** Richard
Arie, General Mgr.

■ **1418** ■ **Waukon Equity Cooperative**
8th Ave. NW
Waukon, IA 52172
Phone: (319)568-3456
Products: Agronomy supplies; Feed; Fuels. **SICs:**
5191 (Farm Supplies); 5172 (Petroleum Products Nec).
Est: 1916. **Sales:** $11,000,000 (2000). **Emp:** 24.
Officers: Gary A. Koschmeder, Manager; Don Lund,
Controller.

■ **1419** ■ **Weaks Martin Implement Co.**
PO Box 946
Mission, TX 78572
Phone: (210)585-1618 **Fax:** (210)585-3252
Products: Farm equipment, including tractors and
irrigation systems. **SIC:** 5083 (Farm & Garden
Machinery). **Est:** 1938. **Sales:** $18,000,000 (2000).
Emp: 44. **Officers:** Harvey Mutz, President; John
Morris, Treasurer; Jeff Richter, Sales Mgr.

■ **1420** ■ **Wedgworth's Inc.**
PO Box 2076
Belle Glade, FL 33430
Phone: (561)996-2076 **Fax:** (561)992-8917
Products: Fertilizers. **SIC:** 5191 (Farm Supplies).
Sales: $9,000,000 (2000). **Emp:** 20. **Officers:** Ruth S.
Wedgworth, President; E.J. McCroan, Comptroller.

■ **1421** ■ **Wesco Turf Inc.**
2101 Cantu Ct.
Sarasota, FL 34232
Phone: (941)377-6777
Free: (800)486-8873 **Fax:** (941)371-2967
E-mail: postmaster@wescoturf.com
Products: Irrigation products; Utility vehicles. **SIC:**
5083 (Farm & Garden Machinery). **Est:** 1987. **Sales:**
$31,000,000 (2000). **Emp:** 71. **Officers:** William
Gamble, President; Lenard Moore, VP of Finance.

■ **1422** ■ **West Bend Elevator Inc.**
PO Box 408
West Bend, WI 53095
Phone: (414)334-2337
Products: Feed; Salt. **SIC:** 5191 (Farm Supplies). **Est:**
1947. **Sales:** $6,000,000 (2000). **Emp:** 28. **Officers:**
David M. Gonring, President; Joyce Gonring, Treasurer
& Secty.; Allen T. Becker, VP of Marketing.

■ **1423** ■ **West Implement Company Inc.**
PO Box 1389
Cleveland, MS 38732
Phone: (662)843-5321 **Fax:** (662)843-1340
E-mail: westimplement@westimplement.com
URL: http://www.westimplement.com
Products: Farming implements, including tractors,
lawnmowers, and combines. **SIC:** 5083 (Farm &
Garden Machinery). **Est:** 1935. **Sales:** $48,000,000
(2000). **Emp:** 40. **Officers:** Rex Morgan, President;
Jeff L. Morgan, Vice President; Chip Otts, Sales &
Marketing Contact.

■ **1424** ■ **West Side Tractor Sales Inc.**
1400 W Ogden Ave.
Naperville, IL 60563
Phone: (708)355-7150
Products: Farm equipment, including tractors. **SIC:**
5082 (Construction & Mining Machinery). **Est:** 1962.
Sales: $44,000,000 (2000). **Emp:** 90. **Officers:** Steven
Benck, President; Laurie Champion, Controller; Tom
Stern, Dir. of Marketing.

■ **1425** ■ **West Texas Equipment Co.**
PO Box 61247
Midland, TX 79711
Phone: (915)563-1863 **Fax:** (915)561-9619
URL: http://www.wteat.com
Products: Heavy equipment; Agricultural products;
Engines. **SIC:** 5082 (Construction & Mining Machinery).
Sales: $70,000,000 (2000). **Emp:** 325. **Officers:** Scot
McKinney, Sales Mgr.

■ **1426** ■ **West Valley Farmers Inc.**
2741 N Hwy. 99 W
McMinnville, OR 97128
Phone: (503)472-6154
Products: Fertilizers; Flower, vegetable, and fruit
seeds. **SIC:** 5191 (Farm Supplies). **Sales:** $15,000,000
(2000). **Emp:** 105. **Officers:** Clarke Ellingson,
President; Robert Ober, Controller.

■ **1427** ■ **Westbay Equipment Co.**
Rte. 4
Galesburg, IL 61401
Phone: (309)342-8112 **Fax:** (309)342-2188
Products: Farm equipment, including tractors,
combines, and haulers. **SIC:** 5083 (Farm & Garden
Machinery). **Est:** 1959. **Sales:** $5,000,000 (2000).
Emp: 28. **Officers:** Charles D. Westbay, President;
Steven L. Westbay, Treasurer & Secty.

■ **1428** ■ **Westby Farmers Union Cooperative**
405 S Main St.
Westby, WI 54667
Phone: (608)634-3184
Products: Feed and seed. **SIC:** 5191 (Farm Supplies).
Est: 1941. **Sales:** $8,000,000 (2000). **Emp:** 40.
Officers: Richard Davig, General Mgr.

■ **1429** ■ **Western Farm Center**
21 W 7th St.
Santa Rosa, CA 95401
Phone: (707)545-0721 **Fax:** (707)545-4302
E-mail: westernfarm-retail@msn.com
Products: Pet supplies and food. **SICs:** 5191 (Farm
Supplies); 5149 (Groceries & Related Products Nec).

■ **1430** ■ **Western Farm Service/Cascade**
PO Box 269
Tangent, OR 97389
Phone: (541)928-3391 **Fax:** (541)926-8807
Products: Mixes fertilizers from purchased materials;
agricultural and industrial chemicals. **SIC:** 5191 (Farm
Supplies).

■ **1431** ■ **Western Farm Service Inc.**
3705 West Beechwood, Ste. 101
Fresno, CA 93711
Phone: (209)436-0450 **Fax:** (209)436-0515
Products: Fertilizers. **SIC:** 5191 (Farm Supplies). **Est:**
1968. **Sales:** $400,000,000 (2000). **Emp:** 1,000.
Officers: Herman T. Wilson Jr., President; John H.
Daugherty, CFO; Joe Davis, Dir. of Systems; Connie
Daugherty, Employee Relations Mgr.

■ **1432** ■ **Western Implement Co.**
2919 North Ave.
Grand Junction, CO 81504
Phone: (970)242-7960 **Fax:** (970)242-5241
Products: Farm equipment; Farm flower case
supplies; Hardware. **SIC:** 5083 (Farm & Garden
Machinery). **Sales:** $8,900,000 (2000). **Emp:** 40.
Officers: L. Coleman, President.

■ **1433** ■ **Western Seeds**
PO Box 850
Burley, ID 83318
Phone: (208)678-2268
Products: Agricultural seeds. **SIC:** 5191 (Farm
Supplies). **Est:** 1956. **Sales:** $3,500,000 (2000). **Emp:**
20. **Officers:** Robert Evans, President; George
Anderson, General Mgr.; Royce Otte, Manager.

■ **1434** ■ **Westland Seed, Inc.**
1308 Round Butte Rd. W
Ronan, MT 59864
Phone: (406)676-4100
Free: (800)547-3335 **Fax:** (406)676-4101
Products: Fertilizer; Chemicals; Seeds. **SIC:** 5191
(Farm Supplies). **Est:** 1973.

■ **1435** ■ **Wetsel, Inc.**
PO Box 791
Harrisonburg, VA 22801
Phone: (540)434-6753 **Fax:** (540)434-4894
E-mail: wetsel@shentel.net
URL: http://www.wetsel.com
Products: Lawn, garden, greenhouse, nursery, and golf course supplies. **SIC:** 5083 (Farm & Garden Machinery). **Sales:** $50,000,000 (2000). **Emp:** 180. **Officers:** Floyd Grigsby, President & CFO; Tom Wetsel, Dir. of Marketing; Connie Harouff, Customer Service Contact.

■ **1436** ■ **Whayne Supply Co.**
PO Box 35900
Louisville, KY 40232-5900
Phone: (502)774-4441 **Fax:** (502)774-1776
Products: Tractors. **SIC:** 5083 (Farm & Garden Machinery). **Est:** 1913. **Sales:** $500,000,000 (2000). **Emp:** 1,000. **Officers:** J. William Pullen, CEO & President; Mark A. Robinson, CFO; George E. Morsman, VP of Marketing & Sales; Richard Winsett, Information Systems Mgr.; James Davis, VP of Human Resources.

■ **1437** ■ **Harry J. Whelchel Co.**
PO Box 5022
Chattanooga, TN 37406
Phone: (423)698-4415 **Fax:** (423)629-7395
Products: Farm implements. **SIC:** 5083 (Farm & Garden Machinery). **Est:** 1954. **Sales:** $5,000,000 (2000). **Emp:** 20. **Officers:** Harry J. Whelchel Jr., President; Susan F. Whelchel, Vice President.

■ **1438** ■ **White Cloud Grain Co.**
PO Box 276
Hiawatha, KS 66434
Phone: (913)595-3254
Products: Farm chemicals, including insecticides, herbicides, and fertilizers. **SICs:** 5153 (Grain & Field Beans); 5191 (Farm Supplies). **Est:** 1962. **Sales:** $35,000,000 (2000). **Emp:** 50. **Officers:** Roger D. Wolf, President; Ernest C. Wolf, Controller; Warren L. Beavers, Dir. of Marketing.

■ **1439** ■ **White County Farmers Cooperative**
271 Mayberry St.
Sparta, TN 38583
Phone: (931)836-2278 **Fax:** (931)836-2270
Products: Farming and agricultural supplies. **SIC:** 5191 (Farm Supplies). **Est:** 1945. **Sales:** $5,300,000 (2000). **Emp:** 27. **Officers:** W.C. Dodson, President; David K. Glover, General Mgr.

■ **1440** ■ **White River Cooperative**
PO Box 232
Washington, IN 47501
Phone: (812)254-4250
Products: Fertilizer and fertilizer materials; Feed; Agricultural chemicals. **SICs:** 5191 (Farm Supplies); 5169 (Chemicals & Allied Products Nec). **Sales:** $7,000,000 (2000). **Emp:** 24. **Officers:** Harold Dant, CEO.

■ **1441** ■ **White Swan Ltd.**
2527 Camino Ramon Ste. 200
San Ramon, CA 94583-4409
Products: Seeds; Garden items. **SIC:** 5191 (Farm Supplies). **Sales:** $30,000,000 (2000). **Emp:** 95. **Officers:** Hal Saltzman, President.

■ **1442** ■ **White's Inc.**
4614 Navigation Blvd.
Houston, TX 77011
Phone: (713)928-2632 **Fax:** (713)928-5374
E-mail: whiteinc@wbell.net
URL: http://www.whitesinc.com
Products: Farm equipment, including plows and planters. **SIC:** 5083 (Farm & Garden Machinery). **Est:** 1918. **Sales:** $8,000,000 (2000). **Emp:** 23. **Officers:** S. White, President; Maywell Bunch, Treasurer.

■ **1443** ■ **Whittington Wholesale Company Inc.**
PO Box 67
Tunica, MS 38676
Phone: (601)363-2411
Products: Farming chemicals. **SIC:** 5191 (Farm Supplies). **Est:** 1922. **Sales:** $5,000,000 (2000). **Emp:** 10. **Officers:** A. Kenneth Whittington Jr., President; James Whittington, CFO.

■ **1444** ■ **WHO Manufacturing Co**
PO Box 1153
Lamar, CO 81052
Phone: (719)336-7433 **Fax:** (719)336-7052
Products: Farm machinery and industrial equipment. **SICs:** 5083 (Farm & Garden Machinery); 5084 (Industrial Machinery & Equipment).

■ **1445** ■ **Wilbro Inc.**
PO Box 400
Norway, SC 29113
Phone: (803)263-4201 **Fax:** (803)263-4200
E-mail: wilbro@tds.net
Products: Fertilizer. **SIC:** 5191 (Farm Supplies). **Sales:** $9,000,000 (2000). **Emp:** 35. **Officers:** Harvey M. Williamson Jr., President.

■ **1446** ■ **Wilbur-Ellis Co. Southern Div.**
PO Box 1020
Edinburg, TX 78540
Phone: (956)383-4901
Products: Chemicals and fertilizers. **SIC:** 5191 (Farm Supplies). **Est:** 1921. **Sales:** $70,000,000 (2000). **Emp:** 300. **Officers:** Noel Myers Jr., Controller.

■ **1447** ■ **Wilco Farmers Inc.**
PO Box 258
Mt. Angel, OR 97362
Phone: (503)845-6122 **Fax:** (503)845-9310
URL: http://www.wilcofarmers.com
Products: Livestock feed; Lawn and garden products; Pet food and supplies; Farm hardware; Fencing; Irrigation; Clothing; Automotive. **SICs:** 5191 (Farm Supplies); 5072 (Hardware). **Est:** 1967. **Sales:** $37,000,000 (2000). **Emp:** 170. **Officers:** Joseph Kirchner, President; Michael Jamison, Controller.

■ **1448** ■ **Wildhawk Inc.**
R.R. 2, Box 123
Warrens, WI 54666-9802
Phone: (608)378-4164 **Fax:** (608)378-4264
Products: Fertilizer and chemicals. **SIC:** 5191 (Farm Supplies). **Est:** 1983. **Sales:** $800,000 (2000). **Emp:** 3. **Officers:** Robert E. Hawk, President & COO.

■ **1449** ■ **Willamette Seed Co.**
PO Box 21120
Keizer, OR 97307-1120
Phone: (503)926-8883 **Fax:** (503)926-1975
Products: Grass, wildflower, and vegetable seeds. **SIC:** 5191 (Farm Supplies).

■ **1450** ■ **Willette Seed Farm Inc.**
41721 160th St.
Delavan, MN 56023
Phone: (507)854-3595 **Fax:** (507)854-3355
Products: Soybean seed; Soybeans for suet and food. **SIC:** 5191 (Farm Supplies). **Est:** 1960. **Sales:** $2,000,000 (1999). **Emp:** 8. **Officers:** T. Willette, Treasurer; P. Willette, President; Mike Hughes, Customer Service Contact.

■ **1451** ■ **Archie Williams Fertilizer Co.**
PO Box 1176
Carbondale, IL 62901
Phone: (618)549-0541
Products: Fertilizer. **SIC:** 5191 (Farm Supplies). **Est:** 1957. **Sales:** $5,000,000 (2000). **Emp:** 3. **Officers:** Archie Williams, Owner.

■ **1452** ■ **Williams Lawn Seed, Inc.**
PO Box 112
Maryville, MO 64468
Phone: (660)582-4614
Free: (800)457-9571 **Fax:** 888-682-4600
E-mail: leon@wls.com
URL: http://www.wls.com
Products: Turf grass seed and fertilizer. **SIC:** 5191 (Farm Supplies). **Est:** 1930. **Emp:** 12.

■ **1453** ■ **Ernie Williams Ltd.**
PO Box 737
Algona, IA 50511
Phone: (515)295-3561
Products: Farm and garden machinery. **SIC:** 5083 (Farm & Garden Machinery). **Est:** 1950. **Sales:** $12,000,000 (2000). **Emp:** 25. **Officers:** Ed Wilcox, President.

■ **1454** ■ **Wilson Supply Inc.**
4030 Howick St.
Salt Lake City, UT 84107-1454
Products: Grounds maintenance equipment and supplies. **SIC:** 5083 (Farm & Garden Machinery). **Est:** 1935. **Sales:** $8,000,000 (2000). **Emp:** 25. **Officers:** Brett Wilson, President; Scott Wilson, Controller.

■ **1455** ■ **Windom Cooperative Association**
251 1st Ave. S
Windom, MN 56101
Phone: (507)831-2580 **Fax:** (507)831-2583
Products: Fuel and fertilizer. **SICs:** 5153 (Grain & Field Beans); 5191 (Farm Supplies). **Est:** 1937. **Sales:** $25,000,000 (2000). **Emp:** 30. **Officers:** Willard Schroeder, President.

■ **1456** ■ **Winona River and Rail Inc.**
1000 East 3rd St.
Winona, MN 55987
Phone: (507)289-9321 **Fax:** (507)289-5810
Products: Mixed fertilizer. **SIC:** 5191 (Farm Supplies). **Sales:** $12,000,000 (1994). **Emp:** 13. **Officers:** Jeff Kuhn, General Mgr.

■ **1457** ■ **Witmer's Inc.**
PO Box 368
Columbiana, OH 44408
Phone: (330)427-2147
Products: Tractors and farm equipment. **SIC:** 5083 (Farm & Garden Machinery). **Est:** 1937. **Sales:** $5,900,000 (2000). **Emp:** 35. **Officers:** Ralph Witmer, President.

■ **1458** ■ **Wolf River Country Cooperative**
519 N Shawano St.
New London, WI 54961
Phone: (920)867-2176
Products: Farm supplies; Petroleum products. **SICs:** 5191 (Farm Supplies); 5172 (Petroleum Products Nec).

■ **1459** ■ **Wolverine Tractor and Equipment**
PO Box 19336
Detroit, MI 48219
Phone: (313)356-5200 **Fax:** (313)356-2029
Products: Tractors and parts. **SIC:** 5082 (Construction & Mining Machinery). **Est:** 1943. **Sales:** $40,000,000 (2000). **Emp:** 120. **Officers:** Robert McNutt, President; Michael McNutt, CFO; Eric Simon, Vice President.

■ **1460** ■ **Wood County Farm Supply**
PO Box 56
Arpin, WI 54410
Phone: (715)652-3835
Products: Farm supplies, including gas and feed. **SIC:** 5191 (Farm Supplies). **Est:** 1944. **Sales:** $11,000,000 (2000). **Emp:** 25. **Officers:** Brian Matthys, CEO.

■ **1461** ■ **P.L. Woodard and Company Inc.**
PO Box 877
Wilson, NC 27894
Phone: (919)243-3541
Products: Fertilizer. **SIC:** 5191 (Farm Supplies). **Est:** 1898. **Sales:** $4,800,000 (2000). **Emp:** 12. **Officers:** W. Dalton Sharp, President; A. Carroll Coleman, Treasurer & Secty.

■ **1462** ■ **Woodburn Fertilizer Inc.**
PO Box 7
Woodburn, OR 97071
Phone: (503)981-3521 **Fax:** (503)981-5747
Products: Fertilizer, feed, seed and chemicals. **SICs:** 5191 (Farm Supplies); 5169 (Chemicals & Allied Products Nec). **Sales:** $37,000,000 (2000). **Emp:** 60. **Officers:** Scott Burlingham, Payroll Mgr.; Scott Roerig, Controller.

■ **1463** ■ **J.S. Woodhouse Co.**
PO Box 1169
West Springfield, MA 01089
Phone: (413)736-5462 **Fax:** (413)732-3786
E-mail: info@jswoodhouse.com
URL: http://www.jswoodhouse.com
Products: Agricultural and forestry implements. **SIC:** 5083 (Farm & Garden Machinery). **Est:** 1843. **Sales:** $6,000,000 (2000). **Emp:** 28. **Officers:** William J.

Reilly, Vice President; Robert C. Reilly, President; Charles Reilly III, Vice President.

■ 1464 ■ **Wyatt-Quarles Seed Company Inc.**
PO Box 739
Garner, NC 27529
Phone: (919)772-4243 **Fax:** (919)772-4278
Products: Lawn and garden equipment and supplies. **SIC:** 5083 (Farm & Garden Machinery). **Sales:** $10,000,000 (2000). **Emp:** 48. **Officers:** V. Charles Wyatt, President; Joseph G. Moore, Vice President; Brenda G. Heinze, Secretary.

■ 1465 ■ **Wylie and Son Inc.**
PO Box 100
Petersburg, TX 79250-0100
Phone: (806)667-3566
Free: (800)722-4001 **Fax:** (806)667-3392
URL: http://www.wyliesprayers.com
Products: Spraying equipment. **SIC:** 5083 (Farm & Garden Machinery). **Est:** 1959. **Sales:** $7,000,000

(2000). **Emp:** 80. **Officers:** Scot Wylie, President; L.L. Wylie, Chairman of the Board & CFO; Jim Thompson, Customer Service Mgr., e-mail: jimt@ wyliesprayers.com; Mike Abbott, Controller.

■ 1466 ■ **Wyndmere Farmers Elevator Co.**
PO Box 67
Wyndmere, ND 58081
Phone: (701)439-2252 **Fax:** (701)439-2562
Products: Agricultural supplies, including feed, chemicals, and fertilizers; Grain elevators; Corn, soybeans, and wheat. **SICs:** 5153 (Grain & Field Beans); 5191 (Farm Supplies). **Est:** 1919. **Sales:** $9,000,000 (2000). **Emp:** 9. **Officers:** Tom Brosowske, President; Rich Mueller, General Mgr.

■ 1467 ■ **Zajac's Performance Seed**
33 Sicomac Rd.
North Haledon, NJ 07508
Phone: (973)423-1660 **Fax:** (973)423-6018
Products: Grass seed. **SIC:** 5191 (Farm Supplies).

■ 1468 ■ **Florein W. Zaloudek Co.**
PO Box 187
Kremlin, OK 73753-0187
Phone: (580)874-2211
Products: Tractors. **SIC:** 5083 (Farm & Garden Machinery). **Est:** 1920. **Sales:** $1,500,000 (2000). **Emp:** 18. **Officers:** Robert Zaloudek, Partner.

■ 1469 ■ **Zamzow's Inc.**
1201 Franklin Blvd.
Nampa, ID 83687-6744
Products: Garden supplies. **SICs:** 5191 (Farm Supplies); 5193 (Flowers & Florists' Supplies); 5083 (Farm & Garden Machinery). **Est:** 1933. **Sales:** $9,000,000 (2000). **Emp:** 50. **Officers:** Richard L. Zamzow, President; Debbie Carroell, Controller; Ken Kirkbride, Dir. of Marketing.

(4) Alcoholic Beverages

Entries in this section are arranged alphabetically by company name. When the company name is a personal name, the company name is alphabetized by the surname unless the first name or initial(s) are part of a trade name. See the User's Guide at the front of this directory for additional information.

■ **1470** ■ **800 Spirits Inc.**
385 Prospect Ave., Ste. 3
Hackensack, NJ 07601
Phone: (201)342-6330
Products: Wines and champagnes; Gourmet assessories. **SIC:** 5182 (Wines & Distilled Beverages). **Sales:** $6,000,000 (1994). **Emp:** 20. **Officers:** Robin Rucki, President.

■ **1471** ■ **A & B Distributors**
3901 Tull Ave.
Muskogee, OK 74403
Phone: (918)682-6331
Products: Beer. **SIC:** 5181 (Beer & Ale).

■ **1472** ■ **A-B Sales Inc.**
435 Eldora St.
Wichita, KS 67202
Phone: (316)264-1354   **Fax:** (316)264-0860
Products: Wine; Beer; Liquor. **SICs:** 5181 (Beer & Ale); 5182 (Wines & Distilled Beverages). **Est:** 1949. **Sales:** $10,000,000 (2000). **Emp:** 30. **Officers:** David W. Binter, President; Terry McEwan, General Mgr.; Steve Pratt, Sales Mgr.

■ **1473** ■ **A & L Coors Inc.**
PO Box 215
Durango, CO 81302
Phone: (970)247-3620   **Fax:** (970)385-6871
E-mail: anl@frontier.net
Products: Beer; Juice; Water. **SICs:** 5181 (Beer & Ale); 5149 (Groceries & Related Products Nec). **Est:** 1933. **Sales:** $7,000,000 (1999). **Emp:** 21. **Officers:** Bob Ariano, Owner; Jack Bergl, Dir. of Marketing; John Betka, General Mgr.

■ **1474** ■ **Admiral Wine and Liquor Co.**
603 S 21st St.
Irvington, NJ 07111
Phone: (973)371-2211
Free: (800)582-9463   **Fax:** (973)371-8521
E-mail: admiralcompuserve.com
URL: http://www.admiralwine.com
Products: Wine. **SIC:** 5182 (Wines & Distilled Beverages). **Est:** 1964. **Sales:** $15,000,000 (2000). **Emp:** 45. **Officers:** Michael Zeiger, President.

■ **1475** ■ **Airport Beer Distributors**
4850 W Lake Rd.
Erie, PA 16505-2920
Phone: (814)833-9781
Products: Beer. **SIC:** 5181 (Beer & Ale).

■ **1476** ■ **Alabama Crown**
421 Industrial Dr.
Birmingham, AL 35259
Phone: (205)941-1155   **Fax:** (205)942-3767
Products: Wine and beer. **SICs:** 5182 (Wines & Distilled Beverages); 5181 (Beer & Ale).

■ **1477** ■ **Alko Distributors Inc.**
PO Box 60757
Savannah, GA 31420
Phone: (912)920-9999
Products: Beer and wine. **SICs:** 5181 (Beer & Ale); 5182 (Wines & Distilled Beverages). **Sales:**

$15,000,000 (2000). **Emp:** 50. **Officers:** Micheal Kooden, President; Michael Kooden, President.

■ **1478** ■ **Allentown Beverage Company Inc.**
1249 N Quebec St.
Allentown, PA 18103
Phone: (610)432-4581
Free: (800)852-2337   **Fax:** (610)821-8311
Products: Beer. **SIC:** 5181 (Beer & Ale). **Est:** 1954. **Sales:** $5,000,000 (2000). **Emp:** 45. **Officers:** Carl Schwab, President; Seth Repko, Controller; David Schwab, Dir. of Marketing.

■ **1479** ■ **Allied Beverage Group, LLC**
7800 Browning Rd.
Pennsauken, NJ 08109
Phone: (609)486-4000   **Fax:** (609)665-2353
Products: Wine; Liquor. **SIC:** 5182 (Wines & Distilled Beverages). **Est:** 1996. **Officers:** Eric Perlmutter, Chairman of the Board; Jeffrey Altschuler, President; Jaime Lignana, Sales/Marketing Contact. **Former Name:** Baxter Warehouse.

■ **1480** ■ **Allied Distributing**
3810 Transport St.
Ventura, CA 93003
Phone: (805)644-2201   **Fax:** (805)644-4987
Products: Beer; Water; Wine. **SICs:** 5181 (Beer & Ale); 5182 (Wines & Distilled Beverages); 5149 (Groceries & Related Products Nec). **Est:** 1997. **Emp:** 75. **Officers:** Kevin Williams; Mike Dann; Danny Jovanovich. **Former Name:** Lagomarsino's.

■ **1481** ■ **Allstate Beverage Co.**
1580 Parallel St.
Montgomery, AL 36104
Phone: (334)265-0507
Products: Beer; Soft drinks; Bottled and flavored water. **SICs:** 5181 (Beer & Ale); 5149 (Groceries & Related Products Nec). **Est:** 1951. **Sales:** $30,000,000 (2000). **Emp:** 100. **Officers:** Charles B. Grant III, President; Norman Hamilton, Controller; Ed D. Fleming, Dir. of Marketing.

■ **1482** ■ **Alpena Beverage Co. Inc.**
1313 Kline Rd.
Alpena, MI 49707-8108
Phone: (517)354-4329   **Fax:** (517)356-3511
E-mail: alpbev@Voyager.net
Products: Beer; Wine; Liquor. **SICs:** 5181 (Beer & Ale); 5182 (Wines & Distilled Beverages). **Est:** 1976. **Emp:** 25. **Officers:** Wayne Lee.

■ **1483** ■ **Amoskeag Beverages Inc.**
PO Box 6540
Manchester, NH 03108
Phone: (603)622-9033   **Fax:** (603)622-7926
Products: Beer. **SIC:** 5181 (Beer & Ale). **Est:** 1946. **Sales:** $25,000,000 (2000). **Emp:** 85. **Officers:** Robert Dickerson, President; Richard Smalto, Controller; Bob Hanscom, Dir. of Marketing.

■ **1484** ■ **Anderson Distributing Co.**
144 W Porter St.
PO Box 752
Jackson, MI 49202
Phone: (517)782-8179   **Fax:** (517)782-5306
Products: Beer; Wine; Liquor. **SICs:** 5181 (Beer & Ale); 5182 (Wines & Distilled Beverages). **Est:** 1959. **Emp:** 49. **Officers:** James M. Anderson; Stephen D. Anderson.

■ **1485** ■ **Anheuser-Busch Inc.**
1 Busch Pl.
St. Louis, MO 63118
Phone: (314)577-2000   **Fax:** (314)577-2900
Products: Beer and specialty brews. **SIC:** 5181 (Beer & Ale). **Sales:** $12,800,000,000 (2000). **Emp:** 24,300. **Officers:** August A. Busch III, President & Chairman of the Board; Randy Baker, CFO.

■ **1486** ■ **Arizona Beverage Distributing Co. LLC**
1115 N 47th Ave.
Phoenix, AZ 85043-1801
Phone: (602)272-3751   **Fax:** (602)272-4099
Products: Beer, wine, and liquor. **SICs:** 5182 (Wines & Distilled Beverages); 5181 (Beer & Ale). **Est:** 1948. **Emp:** 365. **Officers:** Robert E. Smith, President.

■ **1487** ■ **Ben Arnold-Sunbelt Beverage Company L.P.**
PO Box 480
Ridgeway, SC 29130
Phone: (803)337-3500   **Fax:** (803)337-5310
Products: Beverages, including liquor, wine, and non-alcoholic mixes. **SICs:** 5182 (Wines & Distilled Beverages); 5149 (Groceries & Related Products Nec); 5181 (Beer & Ale). **Est:** 1927. **Sales:** $150,000,000 (2000). **Emp:** 365. **Officers:** Bill Tovell, President; Robert M. Sisk, VP & CFO; Larry Graves, Dir. of Data Processing; Ellen White, Dir of Human Resources. **Former Name:** Ben Arnold-Heritage Beverage Company L.P.

■ **1488** ■ **Aroostook Beverage Co.**
52 Rice St.
Presque Isle, ME 04769-2260
Phone: (207)769-2081   **Fax:** (207)769-2091
Products: Beer; Ale. **SIC:** 5181 (Beer & Ale). **Officers:** Peter Briggs, President.

■ **1489** ■ **Athens Distributing Co.**
1000 Herman
Nashville, TN 37208
Phone: (615)254-0101   **Fax:** (615)254-1749
Products: Wines; Liquors; Specialty items. **SIC:** 5182 (Wines & Distilled Beverages). **Est:** 1946. **Emp:** 40.

■ **1490** ■ **Atlanta Beverage Co.**
PO Box 44008
Atlanta, GA 30336
Phone: (404)699-6700   **Fax:** (404)699-6778
E-mail: atlantabev.com
URL: http://www.atlantabev.com
Products: Beer. **SIC:** 5181 (Beer & Ale). **Est:** 1954. **Emp:** 308. **Officers:** C. Mark Pirrung, CEO, e-mail: mpirrung@atlantabev.com.

■ **1491** ■ **Atlanta Wholesale Wine Co.**
275 Spring St. SW
Atlanta, GA 30303
Phone: (404)522-3358 **Fax:** (404)681-0633
URL: http://www.atlantawire.com
Products: Wine and liquor. **SIC:** 5182 (Wines & Distilled Beverages). **Est:** 1981. **Emp:** 85. **Officers:** Russ McCall, President, e-mail: rmccall@atlantawine.com; Greg Rusch, Sales/Marketing Contact, e-mail: rusch@atlantawine.com; Lorenia Vazquez, Sales/Marketing Contact, e-mail: lvazquez@atlantawine.com.

■ **1492** ■ **B & B Beer Distributing**
505 Ball NE
Grand Rapids, MI 49503-2011
Phone: (616)458-1177 **Fax:** (616)458-0270
Products: Beer. **SIC:** 5181 (Beer & Ale). **Emp:** 45.
Officers: T. A. Sullivan.

■ **1493** ■ **B & B Imports**
3020 N Piedras, Ste. B
El Paso, TX 79930
Phone: (915)562-0309
Products: Imported wine. **SIC:** 5182 (Wines & Distilled Beverages).

■ **1494** ■ **B & G Wholesalers Inc.**
337 28th Ave.
Nashville, TN 37209
Phone: (615)320-7292 **Fax:** (615)321-4173
URL: http://www.winespirits.com
Products: Imported and domestic wine and liquor. **SIC:** 5182 (Wines & Distilled Beverages). **Est:** 1949. **Emp:** 100. **Officers:** Thomas E. Bernard, President; Kim R. Conrad, Controller; Mac Armstrong, Sales Mgr.

■ **1495** ■ **B and J Sales Inc.**
1105 E Lafayette St.
Bloomington, IL 61701
Phone: (309)662-1373
Products: Beer. **SIC:** 5181 (Beer & Ale). **Est:** 1956.
Sales: $9,000,000 (2000). **Emp:** 30. **Officers:** Robert R. Wombacher, President; John W. Wombacher, VP of Finance.

■ **1496** ■ **Badger Liquor Company Inc.**
850 S Morris St.
Fond du Lac, WI 54936
Phone: (920)922-0550
Products: Wine and liquor. **SIC:** 5182 (Wines & Distilled Beverages). **Sales:** $54,000,000 (2000). **Emp:** 225. **Officers:** Gary Sadoff, President; Tom Knetter, Finance Officer.

■ **1497** ■ **Baker Distributing**
North Shrewsbury Rd.
North Clarendon, VT 05759
Phone: (802)773-3397 **Fax:** (802)775-4026
Products: Beer and wine. **SICs:** 5181 (Beer & Ale); 5182 (Wines & Distilled Beverages).

■ **1498** ■ **Banfi Products Corp.**
1111 Cedar Swamp Rd.
Glen Head, NY 11545-2121
Phone: (516)626-9200
Free: (800)645-6511 **Fax:** (516)626-6282
E-mail: mail@banfi.com
URL: http://www.banfivintners.com
Products: Wine. **SIC:** 5182 (Wines & Distilled Beverages). **Sales:** $251,000,000 (2000). **Emp:** 150. **Officers:** John Mariani, Chairman of the Board; Harry Mariani, President; Christina Mariani, Exec. VP; James Mariani, Exec. VP; Rick Condon, VP of Marketing; Alyssa Kalvar, Customer Service Contact, e-mail: akalvar@banfi.com; Judith Rifkin, Human Resources Contact, e-mail: jrifkin@banfi.com; Thomas Miles, VP of Sales. **Alternate Name:** VB Imports.

■ **1499** ■ **Banko Enterprises Inc.**
2124 Hanover Ave.
Allentown, PA 18103
Phone: (215)434-0147
Products: Beer; Flavored water. **SICs:** 5181 (Beer & Ale); 5149 (Groceries & Related Products Nec). **Sales:** $30,000,000 (2000). **Emp:** 100. **Officers:** Frank Banko, President.

■ **1500** ■ **Barcardi-Martini U.S.A., Inc.**
2100 Biscayne Blvd.
Miami, FL 33137
Phone: (305)573-8511 **Fax:** (305)576-2597
Products: Liquor. **SIC:** 5182 (Wines & Distilled Beverages). **Sales:** $602,000,000 (2000). **Emp:** 280.
Former Name: Barcardi Imports, Inc.

■ **1501** ■ **R.H. Barringer Distributing Company Inc.**
1620 Fairfax Rd.
Greensboro, NC 27407-4139
Phone: (336)854-0555 **Free:** (800)451-8272
Products: Beer; Snack foods. **SICs:** 5181 (Beer & Ale); 5145 (Confectionery). **Sales:** $66,000,000 (2000).
Emp: 220. **Officers:** Mark Craig, President; Danny Woosley, CFO.

■ **1502** ■ **Barton Brands California Inc.**
PO Box 6263
Carson, CA 90749-6263
Phone: (310)604-0017 **Fax:** (310)604-1495
Products: Distilled spirits. **SIC:** 5182 (Wines & Distilled Beverages). **Sales:** $10,000,000 (2000). **Emp:** 99.
Officers: Donald Hirsch.

■ **1503** ■ **Barton Inc.**
55 E Monroe St., Ste. 1700
Chicago, IL 60603
Phone: (312)346-9200
Products: Beer and wine. **SICs:** 5181 (Beer & Ale); 5182 (Wines & Distilled Beverages). **Est:** 1945. **Sales:** $140,000,000 (2000). **Emp:** 500. **Officers:** Alexander Berk, President.

■ **1504** ■ **Baton Rouge Wholesale**
PO Box 3928
Baton Rouge, LA 70821
Phone: (504)343-9551 **Fax:** (504)383-6636
Products: Liquor. **SIC:** 5182 (Wines & Distilled Beverages).

■ **1505** ■ **Bauer & Foss, Inc.**
3940 Gantz Rd.
Columbus, OH 43213-4845
Phone: (614)575-1112 **Fax:** (614)575-2585
URL: http://www.bfwine.com
Products: Wine and wine; Champagne; Water; Drink mixes. **SICs:** 5182 (Wines & Distilled Beverages); 5181 (Beer & Ale); 5149 (Groceries & Related Products Nec). **Est:** 1972. **Officers:** Gerry Zwayer.

■ **1506** ■ **Baum Wine Imports Inc.**
3870 Paris St., No. 3
Denver, CO 80239-3333
Phone: (303)322-3421
Products: Beer and wine. **SICs:** 5182 (Wines & Distilled Beverages); 5181 (Beer & Ale). **Emp:** 49.

■ **1507** ■ **Baumgarten Distributing Company, Inc.**
1618 W Detweiller Dr.
Peoria, IL 61615-1610
Phone: (309)691-4200 **Fax:** (309)691-4759
Products: Beer and wine. **SICs:** 5181 (Beer & Ale); 5182 (Wines & Distilled Beverages). **Est:** 1975. **Emp:** 36. **Officers:** Gary A. Baumgarten, President; Brice A. Baumgarten, Secretary.

■ **1508** ■ **Bavaria House Corp.**
1121 S Front St.
Wilmington, NC 28401
Phone: (910)251-0998 **Fax:** (910)251-9294
Products: Beer. **SIC:** 5181 (Beer & Ale). **Sales:** $1,200,000 (2000). **Emp:** 2. **Officers:** Gerhard Ritter, President; Jay Englehardt, Vice President.

■ **1509** ■ **Bayside Distributing Inc.**
PO Box 710
Epping, NH 03042-0710
Phone: (603)679-2302 **Fax:** (603)679-6749
Products: Beer; Ale; Malt beverages. **SIC:** 5181 (Beer & Ale). **Officers:** Mark Mc Caddin, President.

■ **1510** ■ **Beacon Distributing Co.**
325 E Nugget Ave.
Sparks, NV 89431
Phone: (702)323-3101
Products: Liquor and wine. **SIC:** 5182 (Wines & Distilled Beverages). **Est:** 1948. **Sales:** $11,000,000 (2000). **Emp:** 12. **Officers:** Keith Trader, Dir. of Operations; Alan Blach, Office Mgr.; Conrad Pugh, General Mgr.

■ **1511** ■ **Beacon Liquor and Wine**
325 E Nugget Ave.
Sparks, NV 89431
Phone: (702)331-3400 **Fax:** (702)331-3474
Products: Alcoholic beverages. **SIC:** 5182 (Wines & Distilled Beverages). **Sales:** $20,900,000 (2000). **Emp:** 57. **Officers:** Conrad Pugh, General Mgr.; Alan Blach, Finance Officer.

■ **1512** ■ **Beaverhead Bar Supply Inc.**
129 N Montana St.
Dillon, MT 59725-3307
Fax: (406)683-5161
Products: Wine; Snack foods; Candy; Paper and allied products. **SICs:** 5182 (Wines & Distilled Beverages); 5113 (Industrial & Personal Service Paper); 5145 (Confectionery). **Officers:** Dan Carpita, President.

■ **1513** ■ **Beck's North America**
1 Station Pl.
PO Box 120 007
Stamford, CT 06912-0007
Phone: (203)388-2325 **Fax:** (203)388-2400
E-mail: becksnorthamerica@juno.com
URL: http://www.becks-beer.com
Products: Beer. **SIC:** 5181 (Beer & Ale). **Est:** 1964.
Sales: $16,000,000 (2000). **Officers:** William J. Yetman, CEO & President; Thomas Angelo, Exec. VP of Finance; Leo Laughlin, Exec. VP of Sales; Rainer Meyrer, Exec. VP of Marketing. **Former Name:** Dribeck Importers Inc.

■ **1514** ■ **Beechwood Distributors Inc.**
PO Box 510946
New Berlin, WI 53151-0946
Phone: (414)821-1400 **Fax:** (414)821-1175
Products: Beer. **SIC:** 5181 (Beer & Ale). **Sales:** $24,000,000 (2000). **Emp:** 96. **Officers:** John Sheehan, President; Eileen Rossmiller, Controller.

■ **1515** ■ **Beer City**
Furnace Grove
Minersville, PA 17954-0126
Phone: (717)544-4701 **Fax:** (717)544-5743
Products: Beer; Pop. **SICs:** 5181 (Beer & Ale); 5149 (Groceries & Related Products Nec). **Emp:** 25.

■ **1516** ■ **Beer Import Company**
2536 Springfield Ave.
Union, NJ 07083
Phone: (908)686-0800 **Fax:** (908)686-0609
E-mail: bicsales@beer-import.com
Products: Imported beer, wine, and liquor. **SICs:** 5181 (Beer & Ale); 5182 (Wines & Distilled Beverages). **Est:** 1947. **Sales:** $11,300,000 (1999). **Emp:** 28. **Officers:** Robert L. Bischoff, President; Noel V. Bischoff, Vice President; Robert E. Bolig, VP of Operations; John Donahue, Sales Mgr. **Alternate Name:** International Wine and Spirits.

■ **1517** ■ **Beer World**
520 S 29th
Harrisburg, PA 17104-2105
Phone: (717)238-2337 **Fax:** (717)238-5942
Products: Beer, soda, and snacks. **SICs:** 5181 (Beer & Ale); 5149 (Groceries & Related Products Nec); 5145 (Confectionery). **Emp:** 49. **Officers:** Gary McGinnis, General Mgr.

■ **1518** ■ **Beitzell and Company Inc.**
705 Edgewood St. NE
Washington, DC 20017
Phone: (202)526-1234
Products: Liquor. **SIC:** 5182 (Wines & Distilled Beverages).

■ **1519** ■ **Beloit Beverage Company Inc.**
4059 W Bradley Rd.
Milwaukee, WI 53209-1796
Phone: (414)362-5000 **Free:** (800)345-0005
Products: Beer; Mineral water and fruit juices. **SICs:** 5181 (Beer & Ale); 5149 (Groceries & Related Products Nec). **Sales:** $39,000,000 (2000). **Emp:** 130. **Officers:** Don Morello, President; Steve Marks, Controller.

■ 1520 ■ **Bennett Distributing Co. Inc.**
320 Circle M Dr.
PO Box 142
Salisbury, NC 28145-0142
Phone: (704)636-7743
Free: (800)854-8533 **Fax:** (704)636-7747
E-mail: bennett@webkorner.com
Products: Wine; Beer. **SICs:** 5181 (Beer & Ale); 5182 (Wines & Distilled Beverages); 5149 (Groceries & Related Products Nec). **Est:** 1966. **Sales:** $1,200,000 (2000). **Emp:** 10. **Officers:** Vernon Bennett, President.

■ 1521 ■ **Bertolina Wholesale Co.**
520 Creek Ave.
Rock Springs, WY 82901-5244
Phone: (307)362-3482 **Fax:** (307)382-3482
Products: Beer; Ale; Malt beverages. **SIC:** 5181 (Beer & Ale). **Officers:** Paul Grasso, President.

■ 1522 ■ **Best Brands**
PO Box 290155
Nashville, TN 37229-0155
Phone: (615)350-8500 **Fax:** (615)350-8129
Products: Liquor and wine. **SIC:** 5182 (Wines & Distilled Beverages).

■ 1523 ■ **Best Way Distributing Co.**
13287 Ralston Ave.
Sylmar, CA 91342-1296
Phone: (818)362-9333 **Fax:** (818)362-7180
Products: Beer; Juices; Water. **SICs:** 5181 (Beer & Ale); 5149 (Groceries & Related Products Nec). **Emp:** 190.

■ 1524 ■ **Better Brands of Atlanta Inc.**
755 NW Jefferson St.
Atlanta, GA 30377
Phone: (404)872-4731 **Fax:** (404)892-0727
Products: Beverages, including beer. **SICs:** 5181 (Beer & Ale); 5149 (Groceries & Related Products Nec); 5182 (Wines & Distilled Beverages). **Est:** 1935. **Sales:** $70,000,000 (2000). **Emp:** 250. **Officers:** Bob Bailey, Exec. VP & General Mgr.; Scott Beaudin, CFO & Asst. General Mgr.

■ 1525 ■ **Better Brands of Milwaukee Inc.**
3241 S 20th St.
Milwaukee, WI 53215
Phone: (414)645-2900 **Fax:** (414)645-3036
Products: Beverages, including wine and liquor. **SICs:** 5182 (Wines & Distilled Beverages); 5149 (Groceries & Related Products Nec). **Est:** 1983. **Sales:** $2,500,000 (2000). **Emp:** 10. **Officers:** Robert Campbell, Sales Mgr. **Doing Business As:** Master Cellars of Milwaukee.

■ 1526 ■ **Better Brands of South Georgia**
103 Ave. B S
Valdosta, GA 31601-5153
Phone: (912)244-0447 **Fax:** (912)242-7182
Products: Beer. **SIC:** 5181 (Beer & Ale). **Emp:** 49. **Officers:** Dana Bailey.

■ 1527 ■ **Beverage Distributors Co.**
14200 E Montcrieff Pl., Ste. E
Aurora, CO 80011
Phone: (303)371-3421 **Fax:** (303)373-5295
Products: Beer; Liquor; Wine. **SICs:** 5182 (Wines & Distilled Beverages); 5181 (Beer & Ale). **Est:** 1974. **Sales:** $200,000,000 (2000). **Emp:** 380. **Officers:** Michael Geller, CEO, e-mail: MGeller@BeverageDistr.com; E.H. Hollman, CFO; Michael Mulligan, Dir. of Systems.

■ 1528 ■ **Beverage Wholesalers Inc.**
701 N 4th Ave.
Fargo, ND 58102
Phone: (701)293-7404 **Fax:** (701)235-1773
Products: Beer and ale. **SIC:** 5181 (Beer & Ale). **Officers:** Ronald Mitchell, President.

■ 1529 ■ **Gordon Biersch Brewing Co.**
33 E San Fernando St.
San Jose, CA 95113
Phone: (408)294-6785 **Fax:** (408)294-4052
Products: Beer. **SIC:** 5181 (Beer & Ale).

■ 1530 ■ **Bissman Company Inc.**
30 W 5th St.
Mansfield, OH 44901
Phone: (419)524-2337 **Fax:** (419)524-4858
Products: Beer. **SIC:** 5181 (Beer & Ale). **Est:** 1878. **Sales:** $8,000,000 (2000). **Emp:** 27. **Officers:** Ben F. Bissman IV, President.

■ 1531 ■ **Blach Distributing Co.**
PO Box 2690
Elko, NV 89803-2690
Phone: (702)738-5147
Free: (888)812-5224 **Fax:** (702)738-6731
Products: Beer and wine. **SICs:** 5181 (Beer & Ale); 5182 (Wines & Distilled Beverages). **Est:** 1974. **Sales:** $8,000,000 (2000). **Emp:** 25. **Officers:** Alan Blach, President; Robert Rosevear, Controller; E. Crapo, Dir. of Marketing; P. Keema, Information Systems Mgr.; Jeannie Blach, Dir of Human Resources.

■ 1532 ■ **Black Forest Distributors Ltd.**
Co. Rte. 84
PO Box 607
Cairo, NY 12413
Phone: (518)622-9888 **Fax:** (518)622-9889
Products: Beer and wine. **SICs:** 5181 (Beer & Ale); 5182 (Wines & Distilled Beverages). **Emp:** 9. **Officers:** Heinz Boedeker.

■ 1533 ■ **Black Hills Distributing Co. Inc.**
6080 SW Linderson Way
Tumwater, WA 98501-5229
Phone: (425)357-5579 **Fax:** (425)357-5578
Products: Nonalcoholic beverages; Beer; Wine. **SICs:** 5181 (Beer & Ale); 5182 (Wines & Distilled Beverages); 5149 (Groceries & Related Products Nec). **Emp:** 22. **Officers:** Jerry Bratton.

■ 1534 ■ **Block Distributing Co. Inc.**
PO Box 8157
San Antonio, TX 78208
Phone: (210)224-7531
Free: (800)749-7532 **Fax:** (210)225-2018
Products: Wine and liquor. **SIC:** 5182 (Wines & Distilled Beverages).

■ 1535 ■ **Block Distributing Co. Inc.**
PO Box 9429
Corpus Christi, TX 78469
Phone: (512)882-4273 **Fax:** (512)882-3526
Products: Wine; Hard liquor. **SIC:** 5182 (Wines & Distilled Beverages).

■ 1536 ■ **Block Distributing Co. Inc.**
2112 Rutland Dr., Ste. 140
Austin, TX 78758
Phone: (512)834-9742 **Fax:** (512)834-9792
Products: Liquor and wine. **SIC:** 5182 (Wines & Distilled Beverages).

■ 1537 ■ **Blue Rock Beverage Co.**
PO Box 1705
Sidney, MT 59270
Phone: (406)228-8249
Products: Beer; Soft drinks. **SICs:** 5181 (Beer & Ale); 5149 (Groceries & Related Products Nec).

■ 1538 ■ **Bob & Joe's Wholesale**
1011 E 2nd St.
Butte, MT 59701-2984
Phone: (406)723-5455 **Fax:** (406)723-5079
Products: Beer; Ale; Malt beverages. **SIC:** 5181 (Beer & Ale). **Officers:** Robert Koprivica, President.

■ 1539 ■ **Boisset U.S.A.**
650 5th St., Ste. 403
San Francisco, CA 94107
Phone: (415)979-0630
Free: (800)878-1123 **Fax:** (415)979-0305
Products: Beer and wine. **SICs:** 5181 (Beer & Ale); 5182 (Wines & Distilled Beverages). **Sales:** $13,000,000 (2000). **Emp:** 11. **Officers:** Jean-Charles Boisset, President; Alain Leonnet, VP & CFO.

■ 1540 ■ **Bologna Brothers**
PO Box 90737
Lafayette, LA 70509-0737
Phone: (318)235-8555 **Fax:** (318)234-1230
Products: Liquor. **SIC:** 5182 (Wines & Distilled Beverages).

■ 1541 ■ **Bologna Brothers**
6321 Humphreys St.
Harahan, LA 70123
Phone: (504)733-4361 **Fax:** (504)733-6043
Products: Liquor. **SIC:** 5182 (Wines & Distilled Beverages).

■ 1542 ■ **Bologna Brothers**
PO Box 8727
Shreveport, LA 71148
Phone: (318)869-2053 **Fax:** (318)868-4652
Products: Liquor. **SIC:** 5182 (Wines & Distilled Beverages).

■ 1543 ■ **Bonanza Beverage Co.**
6333 S Ensworth St.
Las Vegas, NV 89119
Phone: (702)361-4166 **Fax:** (702)361-6408
Products: Beer; Ale; Malt beverages. **SIC:** 5181 (Beer & Ale). **Officers:** William Gialketsis, President.

■ 1544 ■ **Bonded Spirits Corp.**
PO Box 265
Oconomowoc, WI 53066
Phone: (414)786-7770
Products: Alcoholic beverages, including wine, liquor, and beer. **SICs:** 5182 (Wines & Distilled Beverages); 5181 (Beer & Ale). **Officers:** Gary Binter.

■ 1545 ■ **Boone Distributing**
4300 Chateau Rd.
Columbia, MO 65202-6725
Phone: (573)474-6153 **Fax:** (573)474-7313
Products: Wine; Liquor. **SIC:** 5182 (Wines & Distilled Beverages). **Officers:** Ron Newman.

■ 1546 ■ **Bossi Sales Co. Inc.**
PO Box 3375
Springfield, MO 65802
Phone: (417)862-9351
Products: Liquor. **SIC:** 5182 (Wines & Distilled Beverages). **Sales:** $7,000,000 (2000). **Emp:** 25. **Officers:** Mary Lou Kayes, President; Lois Grouver, Controller; Joe Tindle, Sales Mgr.

■ 1547 ■ **Branded Liquors Inc.**
750 Everett St.
Norwood, MA 02062
Phone: (781)769-6500 **Fax:** (781)769-8472
Products: Wine; Beer. **SICs:** 5182 (Wines & Distilled Beverages); 5181 (Beer & Ale). **Est:** 1940. **Officers:** Marvin A. Gordon, CEO.

■ 1548 ■ **Brewery Products Co.**
1017 N Sherman
York, PA 17402-2130
Phone: (717)757-3515 **Fax:** (717)840-4328
Products: Beer. **SIC:** 5181 (Beer & Ale). **Emp:** 30.

■ 1549 ■ **Brewmaster**
2315 Verna Ct.
San Leandro, CA 94577-4205
Phone: (510)351-8920
Free: (800)288-8922 **Fax:** (510)351-4090
Products: Screenings and brewers' rice; Wine; Beer. **SICs:** 5181 (Beer & Ale); 5182 (Wines & Distilled Beverages); 5153 (Grain & Field Beans). **Est:** 1970. **Emp:** 7. **Officers:** T. E. Baird, President.

■ 1550 ■ **Briggs, Inc.**
PO Box 1403
Bangor, ME 04402-1403
Phone: (207)947-8671 **Fax:** (207)947-3310
Products: Beer; Ale; Malt beverages; Wine. **SICs:** 5181 (Beer & Ale); 5182 (Wines & Distilled Beverages). **Officers:** Allison Briggs, Chairman of the Board.

■ 1551 ■ Brotherhood America's Oldest Winery Ltd.
100 Brotherhood Plaza Dr.
PO Box 190
Washingtonville, NY 10992
Phone: (914)496-9101 **Fax:** (914)496-8720
Products: Wine. **SIC:** 5182 (Wines & Distilled Beverages). **Est:** 1839. **Sales:** $15,000,000 (2000). **Emp:** 50. **Officers:** Cesar Baeza, Exec. VP; Michael Vernieri, Treasurer; Silvana Spisany, Dir. of Tours; Robert Markouits, Secretary; James Cimino, Vice President.

■ 1552 ■ Broudy-Kantor Co. Inc.
3501 E Princess Anne Rd.
Norfolk, VA 23502
Phone: (757)855-6081 **Fax:** (757)855-9399
Products: Beverages, including imported and domestic wines, beers, specialty non-alcoholic beverages. **SIC:** 5182 (Wines & Distilled Beverages). **Est:** 1895. **Emp:** 250. **Officers:** J. Jerry Kantor, President; Mike Kantor, Exec. VP; Bill Handley, VP of Sales & Marketing.

■ 1553 ■ Brown Distributing
PO Box 056667
1300 Allendale Rd.
West Palm Beach, FL 33405
Phone: (561)655-3791 **Fax:** (561)833-8621
Products: Beer. **SIC:** 5181 (Beer & Ale). **Emp:** 140.

■ 1554 ■ Brown-Forman Beverage Div.
PO Box 1080
Louisville, KY 40201
Phone: (502)585-1100
Products: Wine; Hard liquor. **SIC:** 5182 (Wines & Distilled Beverages).

■ 1555 ■ Bryson Inc.
1301 E Highland
Tecumseh, OK 74873
Phone: (405)598-6514 **Fax:** (405)598-5414
Products: Beer. **SIC:** 5181 (Beer & Ale). **Emp:** 49.

■ 1556 ■ Buck Distributing Company Inc.
PO Box 1490
Upper Marlboro, MD 20773
Phone: (301)952-0400
Free: (800)750-2825 **Fax:** (301)627-5380
Products: Beer and ale. **SIC:** 5181 (Beer & Ale). **Est:** 1954. **Sales:** $38,000,000 (2000). **Emp:** 85. **Officers:** Betty J. Buck-Behney, President; Richard Kentula, Controller; David A. Cousemaker, VP & General Mgr.

■ 1557 ■ BudCo Incorporated of San Antonio
PO Box 937
San Antonio, TX 78294
Phone: (210)225-3044
Products: Beer. **SIC:** 5181 (Beer & Ale). **Est:** 1952. **Sales:** $50,000,000 (2000). **Emp:** 200. **Officers:** Berkley V. Dawson, President; James E. Dawson, Sr. VP; Vincent M. Dawson, Exec. VP.

■ 1558 ■ Budco of San Antonio Inc.
PO Box 937
San Antonio, TX 78294
Phone: (210)225-3044 **Fax:** (210)224-9802
Products: Beer. **SIC:** 5181 (Beer & Ale). **Sales:** $79,000,000 (2000). **Emp:** 220. **Officers:** Berkley V. Dawson, President; James E. Dawson, Sr. VP & Finance Officer.

■ 1559 ■ Buena Vista Winery Inc.
PO Box 182
Sonoma, CA 95476
Phone: (707)252-7117
Free: (800)678-8504 **Fax:** (707)252-0392
Products: Produces premium wines; imports wine and champagne. **SIC:** 5182 (Wines & Distilled Beverages). **Sales:** $22,000,000 (2000). **Emp:** 80. **Officers:** Harry Parsley, President; Peter Kasper, VP of Finance.

■ 1560 ■ Burke Beverage of California Inc.
31281 Wiegman Rd.
Hayward, CA 94544-7809
Phone: (510)489-1919 **Fax:** (510)489-9084
URL: http://www.burke.bev.com
Products: Beer. **SIC:** 5181 (Beer & Ale). **Est:** 1995. **Emp:** 185. **Officers:** Kevin Burke, Owner & Chairman of the Board, e-mail: kburke@burkebev.com; B. Neri, President, e-mail: bneri@burkebev.com; Paul Mungo, VP of Operations, e-mail: pmungo@burkebev.com. **Former Name:** Miller Brands of the East Bay.

■ 1561 ■ Burke Beverage Inc.
536 East Ave.
La Grange, IL 60525
Phone: (708)579-0333 **Fax:** (708)579-9808
Products: Beer. **SIC:** 5181 (Beer & Ale). **Est:** 1979. **Sales:** $55,000,000 (1999). **Emp:** 87. **Officers:** Kevin Burke, President; Doug Brooks, CFO.

■ 1562 ■ BYE Inc.
PO Box 31093
Billings, MT 59107-1093
Phone: (406)252-5391 **Fax:** (406)256-9491
Products: Soft drinks; Alcoholic cocktails. **SICs:** 5182 (Wines & Distilled Beverages); 5149 (Groceries & Related Products Nec). **Officers:** Gene Brosovich, President.

■ 1563 ■ C & G Distributing Co. Inc.
3535 St. Johns Rd.
Lima, OH 45804-4016
Phone: (419)221-2337
Products: Beer. **SIC:** 5181 (Beer & Ale). **Emp:** 99.
Officers: Samuel Guagenti.

■ 1564 ■ Cabo Distributing Co., Inc.
PO Box 10007
Newport Beach, CA 92658-0007
Phone: (626)575-8090 **Fax:** (626)350-3880
Products: Beer; Wine; Liquor. **SICs:** 5181 (Beer & Ale); 5182 (Wines & Distilled Beverages). **Emp:** 49.

■ 1565 ■ I.H. Caffey, Inc.
PO Box 410368
Charlotte, NC 28241-0368
Phone: (704)588-0930 **Fax:** (704)588-0935
Products: Beer. **SIC:** 5181 (Beer & Ale). **Est:** 1963. **Sales:** $33,000,000 (2000). **Emp:** 75. **Officers:** Chris Caffey, President; John Stritch, VP of Sales; Bill Richardson, VP of Finance. **Former Name:** Southern Wholesale Co.

■ 1566 ■ Calumet Breweries Inc.
6535 Osborn Ave.
Hammond, IN 46320
Phone: (219)845-2242 **Fax:** (219)845-2338
Products: Beer and non-alcoholic beverages. **SIC:** 5181 (Beer & Ale). **Est:** 1933. **Sales:** $15,000,000 (2000). **Emp:** 45. **Officers:** John J. Kiernan, President.

■ 1567 ■ Campari USA Inc.
6913 Fleet St.
Flushing, NY 11351
Phone: (212)753-8220 **Fax:** (212)688-8865
Products: Liquor and wine. **SIC:** 5182 (Wines & Distilled Beverages). **Emp:** 49.

■ 1568 ■ D. Canale Beverages Inc.
45 Eh Crump Blvd. W
Memphis, TN 38106
Phone: (901)948-4543 **Fax:** (901)948-0907
Products: Beer; Wine coolers. **SICs:** 5181 (Beer & Ale); 5182 (Wines & Distilled Beverages). **Sales:** $66,000,000 (2000). **Emp:** 220. **Officers:** Chris W. Canale, President; Donald L. Jordan, Comptroller.

■ 1569 ■ Capital Beverage Corp.
1111 E Tremont Ave.
Bronx, NY 10460
Phone: (718)409-2337 **Fax:** (718)597-3474
Products: Beer and malt liquor; Telephone cards. **SIC:** 5181 (Beer & Ale). **Est:** 1996. **Sales:** $17,000,000 (2000). **Emp:** 50. **Officers:** Carmine N. Stella, CEO, President & Chairman of the Board; Carol Macchiarulo, Treasurer & Secty.

■ 1570 ■ Capital Beverages Inc.
2333 Fairview Dr.
Carson City, NV 89701-5858
Phone: (702)882-2122 **Fax:** (702)882-2145
Products: Beer, ale, and fermented malt liquors. **SIC:** 5181 (Beer & Ale). **Officers:** Joe Brown, President.

■ 1571 ■ Capital Coors Co.
2424 Del Monte
West Sacramento, CA 95691-3808
Phone: (916)371-8164 **Fax:** (916)371-0385
Products: Beer. **SICs:** 5181 (Beer & Ale); 5182 (Wines & Distilled Beverages). **Emp:** 125. **Officers:** K. M. Adamson.

■ 1572 ■ Capitol Distributors Inc.
114 Hall St.
Concord, NH 03301-3425
Phone: (603)224-3348
Products: Beer and ale in barrels and kegs; Malt beverages and brewing byproducts. **SIC:** 5181 (Beer & Ale). **Officers:** James Shea, President.

■ 1573 ■ Cardinal Distributing
1750 Evergreen
Bozeman, MT 59715-1289
Phone: (406)586-0241 **Fax:** (406)587-1156
Products: Beer; Ale; Malt beverages; Wine; Fruit drinks, cocktails, and ades. **SICs:** 5181 (Beer & Ale); 5149 (Groceries & Related Products Nec); 5182 (Wines & Distilled Beverages). **Officers:** Edward Brandt, General Partner.

■ 1574 ■ Carenbauer Wholesale Corp.
1900 Jacob St.
Wheeling, WV 26003
Phone: (304)232-3000 **Fax:** (304)232-3630
Products: Beer. **SIC:** 5181 (Beer & Ale). **Est:** 1946. **Sales:** $9,000,000 (2000). **Emp:** 23. **Officers:** Carl Carenbauer, President; E. Carenbauer, Vice President.

■ 1575 ■ Carolina Beer Company Inc.
PO Box 938
Anderson, SC 29622
Phone: (803)225-1668 **Fax:** (864)224-9938
Products: Domestic and imported beer. **SIC:** 5181 (Beer & Ale). **Est:** 1941. **Sales:** $7,000,000 (2000). **Emp:** 24. **Officers:** William L. Lyles Jr., President, e-mail: larry.lyles@mindspring.com; Marian Lyles, Vice President; W.L. Lyles III, Vice President.

■ 1576 ■ Carolina Wine Co.
99 Rivermoor St.
West Roxbury, MA 02132
Phone: (617)327-1600 **Fax:** (617)327-1486
Products: Wine. **SIC:** 5182 (Wines & Distilled Beverages).

■ 1577 ■ Carriage House Imports Ltd.
99 Morris Ave.
Springfield, NJ 07081
Phone: (973)467-9646
Free: (800)899-0107 **Fax:** (973)467-7910
Products: Wine; Liquor. **SIC:** 5182 (Wines & Distilled Beverages). **Est:** 1987. **Sales:** $7,000,000 (2000). **Emp:** 4. **Officers:** Stephen Karp, President; David McGuire.

■ 1578 ■ Carter Distributing Co.
PO Box 388
Chattanooga, TN 37401-0349
Phone: (615)266-0056
Products: Beer; Bottled water; Wine coolers. **SICs:** 5181 (Beer & Ale); 5149 (Groceries & Related Products Nec); 5182 (Wines & Distilled Beverages). **Est:** 1959. **Sales:** $13,000,000 (2000). **Emp:** 70. **Officers:** W.L. Carter, Chairman of the Board; B.W. Carter, President; Robert N. Garrett, VP of Sales.

■ 1579 ■ Casa Nuestra Winery
3451 Silverado Trl. N
St. Helena, CA 94574-9721
Phone: (707)963-5783 **Fax:** (707)963-3174
E-mail: info@casanuestra.com
URL: http://www.casanuestra.com
Products: Wine. **SIC:** 5182 (Wines & Distilled Beverages). **Est:** 1979. **Sales:** $300,000 (2000). **Emp:** 5.

■ 1580 ■ Cash Distributing Co.
223 22nd St. N
PO Box 2687
Columbus, MS 39704
Phone: (601)328-3551 **Fax:** (601)327-8646
Products: Beer. **SIC:** 5181 (Beer & Ale). **Sales:** $10,000,000 (2000). **Emp:** 49. **Officers:** Marvin E.

Cash, President; Mike Cash, Vice President; Danny Cash, Vice President.

■ 1581 ■ Castleton Beverage Corp.
PO Box 26368
Jacksonville, FL 32226
Phone: (904)757-1290 **Fax:** (904)751-1397
Products: Rum; Soy sauce. **SICs** 5182 (Wines & Distilled Beverages); 5149 (Groceries & Related Products Nec). **Sales:** $69,000,000 (2000). **Emp:** 180. **Officers:** Felipe T. Lopez, VP & General Merchandising Mgr.; Charles Cauthen, Treasurer.

■ 1582 ■ Cellars Beverage Inc.
PO Box 1294
Bay City, MI 48706-0294
Phone: (517)754-6550 **Fax:** (517)754-5201
Products: Beer and wine. **SICs** 5182 (Wines & Distilled Beverages); 5181 (Beer & Ale). **Emp:** 24.
Officers: David B. Geelen.

■ 1583 ■ Centennial Beverage Corp.
PO Box 951
1850 Lefthand Cir.
Longmont, CO 80501-6720
Phone: (303)772-1955 **Fax:** (303)651-9690
Products: Beer; Bottled water. **SICs** 5181 (Beer & Ale); 5149 (Groceries & Related Products Nec). **Sales:** $12,000,000 (2000). **Emp:** 37. **Officers:** Mike Seavall.

■ 1584 ■ Central Beverage Corporation
PO Box 1427
123 Hopkins Hill Rd.
West Greenwich, RI 02817
Phone: (401)392-3580 **Fax:** (401)392-3595
Products: Wine, distilled beverages, and liquor. **SIC:** 5182 (Wines & Distilled Beverages). **Officers:** Paul M. Fradin; Charles S. Fradin.

■ 1585 ■ Central Distribution Co.
PO Box 165207
Little Rock, AR 72216
Phone: (501)372-3158 **Fax:** (501)372-2461
Products: Liquor; Wine. **SIC:** 5182 (Wines & Distilled Beverages).

■ 1586 ■ Central Distributors Inc.
PO Box 1936
Lewiston, ME 04241
Phone: (207)784-4026 **Fax:** (207)784-7869
Products: Beer, wine and ale. **SICs** 5181 (Beer & Ale); 5182 (Wines & Distilled Beverages). **Sales:** $17,000,000 (1994). **Emp:** 70. **Officers:** F.J. Barriault, Owner; Barbara Moud, Controller.

■ 1587 ■ Central Liquor Co.
PO Box 75447
Oklahoma City, OK 73147-0447
Phone: (405)947-8050 **Fax:** (405)949-1416
Products: Beer; Wine; Distilled liquor. **SICs** 5182 (Wines & Distilled Beverages); 5181 (Beer & Ale). **Emp:** 140.

■ 1588 ■ Chaddsford Winery
632 Baltimore Pike
Chadds Ford, PA 19317-9305
Phone: (610)388-6221 **Fax:** (610)388-0360
E-mail: cfwine@chaddsford.com
Products: Fine wines. **SIC:** 5182 (Wines & Distilled Beverages). **Est:** 1982. **Sales:** $3,500,000 (2000). **Emp:** 50. **Officers:** Eric Miller, President; Lee Miller, Vice President.

■ 1589 ■ Charmer Industries Inc.
1950 48th St.
Astoria, NY 11105
Phone: (718)726-2500 **Fax:** (718)726-3101
Products: Wine and liquor. **SIC:** 5182 (Wines & Distilled Beverages). **Sales:** $680,000,000 (2000). **Emp:** 1,300. **Officers:** Herman Merinoff, CEO; Steve Meresmen, CFO.

■ 1590 ■ Chateaux-Vineyards
6009 Goshen Springs Rd.
Norcross, GA 30071
Phone: (404)416-1880 **Fax:** (404)416-7803
E-mail: chateaux@worldnet.att.net
Products: Wines. **SIC:** 5182 (Wines & Distilled

Beverages). **Est:** 1981. **Emp:** 5. **Officers:** Perry Reale, Vice President.

■ 1591 ■ Chatham Imports Inc.
257 Park Ave. S
New York, NY 10010
Phone: (212)473-1100
Products: Beer, wine, and spirits; Soda and health beverages. **SICs:** 5181 (Beer & Ale); 5182 (Wines & Distilled Beverages); 5149 (Groceries & Related Products Nec).

■ 1592 ■ Chicago Beer Distributing
2064 W 167th St.
Markham, IL 60426
Phone: (708)333-4360
Products: Beer. **SIC:** 5181 (Beer & Ale). **Est:** 1943.
Sales: $13,000,000 (2000). **Emp:** 45. **Officers:** Cecil Troutwine, President; Allan Stojak, Controller; Kurt Kitchell, Sales Mgr.

■ 1593 ■ Choice Brands, Inc.
310 Powell Ave.
Monroe, LA 71211
Phone: (318)387-0432 **Fax:** (318)387-0456
Products: Beer. **SIC:** 5181 (Beer & Ale). **Est:** 1954.
Sales: $12,000,000 (2000). **Emp:** 50. **Officers:** Frank Elkins Jr., President & CFO.

■ 1594 ■ Churchill Distributors
7621 Energy Pkwy.
Baltimore, MD 21226-1734
Phone: (410)536-5500 **Fax:** (410)536-5672
Products: Wine and liquor. **SIC:** 5182 (Wines & Distilled Beverages).

■ 1595 ■ City Beverage Co.
Box 432
Defiance, OH 43512-0432
Phone: (419)782-7065
Free: (888)283-2739 **Fax:** (419)782-9426
Products: Beer. **SICs:** 5181 (Beer & Ale); 5182 (Wines & Distilled Beverages). **Est:** 1933. **Sales:** $10,000,000 (2000). **Emp:** 25. **Officers:** Carl Offerle, Chairman of the Board; Thomas L. Sauer; Philip A. Hoag.

■ 1596 ■ City Beverage Co.
PO Box 1036
Elizabeth City, NC 27909
Phone: (919)330-5539 **Fax:** (919)330-4880
Products: Beer and wine; Bottled water. **SICs** 5182 (Wines & Distilled Beverages); 5181 (Beer & Ale); 5149 (Groceries & Related Products Nec). **Est:** 1939. **Sales:** $18,000,000 (2000). **Emp:** 75. **Officers:** Jimmie Dixon, President.

■ 1597 ■ City Beverage Inc.
1103 Riverside Dr.
Huntington, IN 46750
Phone: (219)356-6910 **Fax:** (219)356-0273
Products: Beer. **SIC:** 5181 (Beer & Ale). **Sales:** $13,000,000 (2000). **Emp:** 45. **Officers:** Mike Fisher, President; Lani Thorn, Accountant.

■ 1598 ■ City Beverages
PO Box 620006
Orlando, FL 32862-0006
Phone: (407)851-7100 **Fax:** (407)826-0088
Products: Beer. **SIC:** 5181 (Beer & Ale). **Emp:** 200.

■ 1599 ■ Clarke Distributors Inc.
PO Box 624
Keene, NH 03431
Phone: (603)352-0344 **Fax:** (603)352-0988
Products: Beer and ale. **SIC:** 5181 (Beer & Ale).
Officers: Jeffrey Clarke, President.

■ 1600 ■ Classic City Beverages Inc.
PO Box 549
Athens, GA 30603
Phone: (706)353-1650 **Fax:** (706)353-1655
Products: Beer. **SIC:** 5181 (Beer & Ale). **Sales:** $22,000,000 (2000). **Emp:** 72. **Officers:** Robert L. O'Rear, President; David Werts, Controller.

■ 1601 ■ Classic Wine Imports Inc.
1356 Commonwealth Ave.
Boston, MA 02134
Phone: (617)731-6644 **Fax:** (617)566-4967
Products: Alcoholic beverages, including wine. **SIC:**

5182 (Wines & Distilled Beverages). **Est:** 1969. **Sales:** $20,000,000 (2000). **Emp:** 40. **Officers:** Burton Milles; Robert Hoffman; F. Ek.

■ 1602 ■ Clausen Distributing
PO Box 238
Helena, MT 59624
Phone: (406)442-2675 **Fax:** (406)442-2678
Products: Beer and wine. **SICs:** 5182 (Wines & Distilled Beverages); 5181 (Beer & Ale).

■ 1603 ■ Clement and Muller Inc.
2800 Grand Ave.
Philadelphia, PA 19114
Phone: (215)676-7575 **Fax:** (215)698-1414
E-mail: muller@mbcbpn.com
Products: Beer. **SIC:** 5181 (Beer & Ale). **Emp:** 165.
Officers: Sandra Muller.

■ 1604 ■ Coast Distributing Co.
PO Box 80758
San Diego, CA 92138
Phone: (619)275-4600
Products: Beer. **SIC:** 5181 (Beer & Ale). **Est:** 1979.
Sales: $55,000,000 (2000). **Emp:** 180. **Officers:** Leon Parma, President.

■ 1605 ■ Coastal Beverage Company Inc.
PO Box 10159
Wilmington, NC 28405
Phone: (910)799-3011 **Fax:** (910)392-3674
Products: Beer. **SIC:** 5181 (Beer & Ale). **Est:** 1960.
Sales: $15,000,000 (2000). **Emp:** 50. **Officers:** Lewis T. Nunnelee III, President; Emerson Surles, Office Mgr.

■ 1606 ■ Colonial Distributors Inc.
PO Box 378
Waterville, ME 04903-0378
Phone: (207)873-1143 **Fax:** (207)873-0768
Products: Beer; Ale; Malt beverages; Wine. **SICs:** 5181 (Beer & Ale); 5182 (Wines & Distilled Beverages).
Officers: Walter Simcock, President.

■ 1607 ■ Columbia Distributing Co./Henry Hirsdale/Admiralty Beverage Co.
PO Box 17195
Portland, OR 97217-0195
Phone: (503)289-9600 **Fax:** (503)240-8389
URL: http://www.columbia-dist.com
Products: Beer, wine, champagne, and natural beverages. **SICs:** 5181 (Beer & Ale); 5182 (Wines & Distilled Beverages); 5149 (Groceries & Related Products Nec). **Est:** 1935. **Sales:** $146,800,000 (1999). **Emp:** 475. **Officers:** Edward L. Maletis, President; Shirley Braunstein, CFO; Dave Torrance, VP of Retail; Chris Sarles, Vice President. **Former Name:** Columbia Distributing Co.

■ 1608 ■ Columbus Distributing Co.
4949 Freeway Dr. E
Columbus, OH 43229-5401
Phone: (614)846-1000 **Fax:** (614)846-5293
Products: Beer. **SIC:** 5181 (Beer & Ale). **Est:** 1933.
Emp: 250. **Officers:** Paul A. Jenkins Jr., President; Robert W. North, Exec. VP; Jeffrey H. Jenkins, Exec. VP.

■ 1609 ■ Commercial Distributing Co.
PO Box 1476
Westfield, MA 01086
Phone: (413)562-9691
Products: Beer. **SIC:** 5181 (Beer & Ale). **Est:** 1935.
Sales: $18,000,000 (2000). **Emp:** 60. **Officers:** Richard C. Placek, President & CFO.

■ 1610 ■ John A. Conkling Distributing Co.
44414 SD Hwy. S
Yankton, SD 57078-6454
Phone: (605)665-9351 **Fax:** (605)665-0274
Products: Beer. **SIC:** 5181 (Beer & Ale). **Est:** 1939.
Sales: $5,000,000 (2000). **Emp:** 10. **Officers:** Dan Conkling, President.

■ 1611 ■ John A. Conkling Distributing Co.
44414 SD Hwy. S
Yankton, SD 57078-6454
Phone: (605)665-9351 **Fax:** (605)665-0274
Products: Alcoholic beverages. **SIC:** 5181 (Beer & Ale). **Sales:** $5,000,000 (2000). **Emp:** 10.

■ 1612 ■ Considine Sales Co. Inc.
45 Sharpe Dr.
Cranston, RI 02920-4408
Phone: (401)463-7020 Fax: (401)463-3466
Products: Wine and distilled beverages; Beer. SICs: 5182 (Wines & Distilled Beverages); 5181 (Beer & Ale).
Officers: William Considine, President.

■ 1613 ■ Consolidated Beverages Inc.
PO Box C
Auburn, MA 01501
Phone: (508)832-5311 Fax: (508)832-9831
Products: Beer. SIC: 5181 (Beer & Ale). Sales: $17,000,000 (2000). Emp: 100. Officers: Ronald Fields, President.

■ 1614 ■ Constantine Wine
5320 L Enterprise St.
Sykesville, MD 21784
Phone: (410)549-9463 Fax: (410)549-9465
Products: Wine. SIC: 5182 (Wines & Distilled Beverages).

■ 1615 ■ Consumers of La Salle
1701 5th Ave.
Moline, IL 61265-7908
Phone: (815)223-2480 Fax: (815)223-7704
Products: Liquor, beer, and wine. SICs: 5181 (Beer & Ale); 5182 (Wines & Distilled Beverages). Emp: 24.
Officers: Gerry Doering.

■ 1616 ■ Continental Distributing Company Inc.
9800 W Balmoral Ave.
Rosemont, IL 60018
Phone: (847)671-7700 Fax: (708)671-1368
Products: Liquor, including vodka and whiskey. SIC: 5182 (Wines & Distilled Beverages). Est: 1933. Sales: $160,000,000 (2000). Emp: 400. Officers: Fred Cooper, President; Howard Rappin, VP of Finance; Charles Margolis, General Mgr.; Jack Jeffreys, Operations Mgr.

■ 1617 ■ Coors Distributing Co.
12th & Ford Sts.
Golden, CO 80401
Phone: (303)433-6541
Products: Beer. SIC: 5181 (Beer & Ale).

■ 1618 ■ Coors West
2700 Middlefield Rd., Bldg. B
PO Box 5036
Redwood City, CA 94063-3404
Phone: (650)367-7070 Fax: (650)368-6596
Products: Beer; Soft drinks; water, new age beverages. SICs: 5181 (Beer & Ale); 5149 (Groceries & Related Products Nec). Est: 1933. Emp: 85. Officers: Bob Franceschini Jr., President; Tom DelSarto, Vice President; Dave Espinoza, Sales Mgr.; Mike Carr, Operations Mgr.; Jane Lee, Controller.

■ 1619 ■ Copley Distributors Inc.
PO Box 1427
123 Hopkins Hill Rd.
West Greenwich, RI 02817
Phone: (401)392-3580 Fax: (401)342-3595
Products: Non-alcoholic and alcoholic beverages. SICs: 5182 (Wines & Distilled Beverages); 5149 (Groceries & Related Products Nec). Officers: Charles S. Fradin; Paul M. Fradin.

■ 1620 ■ J.W. Costello Beverage Co.
PO Box 95007
Las Vegas, NV 89193-5007
Phone: (702)876-4000 Fax: (702)876-3386
Products: Alcoholic beverages. SICs: 5182 (Wines & Distilled Beverages); 5181 (Beer & Ale). Est: 1945. Sales: $46,000,000 (2000). Emp: 150. Officers: J.W. Costello, President; Dennis Brennan, CFO.

■ 1621 ■ H. Cox & Son Inc.
1402 Sawyer Rd.
Traverse City, MI 49684
Phone: (616)943-4730
Products: Beer. SIC: 5181 (Beer & Ale).

■ 1622 ■ Crawford Sales Co.
1377 Hamilton Circle
Olathe, KS 66061-4526
Phone: (913)782-0801 Fax: (913)782-6590
Products: Beer. SIC: 5181 (Beer & Ale). Emp: 54.
Officers: R.G. Rossman, President; Ann E. McCort, Secretary; Kathryn E. Rossman, Treasurer.

■ 1623 ■ Crest Beverage Co.
PO Box 26640
San Diego, CA 92126
Phone: (619)566-1010 Fax: (619)566-1308
Products: Beer; Fresh fruit juices and nectars; Bottled water. SICs: 5181 (Beer & Ale); 5149 (Groceries & Related Products Nec). Est: 1956. Sales: $37,000,000 (2000). Emp: 125. Officers: Steve S. Sourapas, President; Sue Lyerly, Controller; Herb Prechtl, Dir. of Marketing & Sales.

■ 1624 ■ Crown Beer Distributors Inc.
PO Box 1255
Wall, NJ 07719
Phone: (908)223-9100
Products: Beer, wine, and liquor. SICs: 5181 (Beer & Ale); 5182 (Wines & Distilled Beverages). Est: 1969. Sales: $23,000,000 (2000). Emp: 75. Officers: Paul Rapisardi, President.

■ 1625 ■ Crown Beverages Inc.
1650 Linda Way
Sparks, NV 89431-6159
Phone: (702)358-2428 Fax: (702)358-2435
Products: Beer; Ale; Distilled liquor; Soft drinks. SICs: 5181 (Beer & Ale); 5182 (Wines & Distilled Beverages); 5149 (Groceries & Related Products Nec). Officers: Lawrence Ginochio, President.

■ 1626 ■ Crown Bottling Co.
PO Box 1906
Mankato, MN 56002-1906
Phone: (507)345-4715
Products: Beer. SIC: 5181 (Beer & Ale). Emp: 7.
Officers: Sonny LeDuc.

■ 1627 ■ Crown Distributing Co.
3409 McDougal Ave.
Everett, WA 98201-5040
Phone: (425)252-4192 Fax: (425)258-3016
Products: Beer; Soft drinks. SICs: 5181 (Beer & Ale); 5149 (Groceries & Related Products Nec). Emp: 75.
Officers: Kim R. Blunt, President & General Mgr.

■ 1628 ■ Crown Inc. Beverage Div.
2321 Bluebell Dr.
Livermore, CA 94550-1007
Phone: (310)404-7452 Fax: (310)926-6255
Products: Wines; Juices; Beer. SICs: 5182 (Wines & Distilled Beverages); 5149 (Groceries & Related Products Nec); 5181 (Beer & Ale). Sales: $5,000,000 (2000). Emp: 11. Officers: Jack Maydon, Vice President.

■ 1629 ■ Cunningham Wholesale Company Inc.
PO Box 32651
Charlotte, NC 28232
Phone: (704)392-8371
Products: Beverages, including beer, soft drinks, and flavored water. SICs: 5181 (Beer & Ale); 5149 (Groceries & Related Products Nec). Est: 1941. Sales: $2,000,000 (2000). Emp: 70. Officers: Thomas E. Cunningham, President; Al Kneeland, General Mgr.

■ 1630 ■ D & D Distributing
5840 N 70th St.
Lincoln, NE 68507
Phone: (402)467-3573
E-mail: dandddist@aol.com
Products: Beer and ale. SIC: 5181 (Beer & Ale). Est: 1973. Emp: 52.

■ 1631 ■ J.A. Dady Distributing Inc.
PO Box 40
Sisseton, SD 57262-0040
Phone: (605)698-3261 Fax: (605)698-4244
Products: Beer; Ale. SIC: 5181 (Beer & Ale). Officers: J. Dady, President.

■ 1632 ■ Dakota Beverage Co.
PO Box 967
Sioux Falls, SD 57101
Phone: (605)339-2337 Fax: (605)339-0982
Products: Beer and ale in barrels and kegs; Malt beverages. SIC: 5181 (Beer & Ale). Officers: John Gores, President.

■ 1633 ■ Dakota Sales Co. Inc.
PO Box 12209
Grand Forks, ND 58208-2209
Phone: (701)746-0341 Fax: (701)772-1811
Products: Beer; Ale; Malt beverages. SIC: 5181 (Beer & Ale). Officers: Roger Kieffer, President.

■ 1634 ■ William L. Damour
PO Box 426
Henniker, NH 03242-0426
Phone: (603)428-9463
Products: Wine. SIC: 5182 (Wines & Distilled Beverages). Officers: William Damour, Owner.

■ 1635 ■ Dana Distributors Inc.
1750 Rte. 211 E
Middletown, NY 10940
Phone: (914)692-6766 Fax: (914)692-2464
Products: Beer. SIC: 5181 (Beer & Ale). Est: 1970. Sales: $2,000,000 (2000). Emp: 49. Officers: James F. English, President; Kerry J. English, Vice President; Fred Dana Jr., Sec. & Treas.

■ 1636 ■ De Luca Liquor and Wine Ltd.
2548 W Desert Inn Rd.
Las Vegas, NV 89109
Phone: (702)735-9144 Fax: (702)732-0684
URL: http://www.vegasdrinks.com
Products: Beer, wine and liquor. SICs: 5181 (Beer & Ale); 5182 (Wines & Distilled Beverages). Sales: $120,000,000 (2000). Emp: 150. Officers: Ray Norvell, Exec. VP; Kenneth Leslie, Controller.

■ 1637 ■ Dearing Beverage Company Inc.
1520 Commerce St.
Winchester, VA 22601
Phone: (540)662-0561
Free: (800)552-9550 Fax: (540)662-0595
Products: Beer. SIC: 5181 (Beer & Ale). Est: 1933. Sales: $11,000,000 (2000). Emp: 29. Officers: Eugene F. Dearing III, President.

■ 1638 ■ DeBauge Brothers Inc.
2915 W 15th
Emporia, KS 66801
Phone: (316)342-4663
Products: Beer. SIC: 5181 (Beer & Ale). Est: 1938. Sales: $5,000,000 (2000). Emp: 15. Officers: Paul F. De Bauge, President; Dennis Carpenter, Controller.

■ 1639 ■ Delaney Management Corp.
PO Box 1185
Williston, ND 58802-1185
Phone: (701)572-1827 Fax: (701)572-0066
Products: Beer; Ale; Malt beverages. SIC: 5181 (Beer & Ale). Officers: Daniel Delaney, President.

■ 1640 ■ Delaware Importers Inc.
PO Box 271
New Castle, DE 19720
Phone: (302)656-4487 Fax: (302)656-0291
Products: Liquor, wine, and beer. SICs: 5182 (Wines & Distilled Beverages); 5181 (Beer & Ale). Est: 1933. Sales: $35,000,000 (2000). Emp: 97. Officers: E.J. Stegemeier, President; R.B. Hart, Vice President; K. Beach, Treasurer.

■ 1641 ■ H. Dennert Distributing Corp.
351 Wilmer Ave.
Cincinnati, OH 45226-1831
Phone: (513)871-7272
Free: (800)837-5659 Fax: (513)871-4432
Products: Beer, ale, seltzer and nonalcoholic beer. SICs: 5181 (Beer & Ale); 5149 (Groceries & Related Products Nec). Sales: $34,000,000 (1999). Emp: 100. Officers: Ronald J. Plattner, President; Jack R. Gardner, CFO.

■ 1642 ■ **Robert Denton and Company Ltd.**
2724 Auburn Rd.
Auburn Hills, MI 48326
Phone: (313)299-0600
Products: Liquor. **SIC:** 5182 (Wines & Distilled Beverages). **Sales:** $800,000 (2000). **Emp:** 3. **Officers:** Robert Denton, President.

■ 1643 ■ **Desert Beverage Co. Inc.**
908 E Cedar St.
Rawlins, WY 82301-5847
Phone: (307)324-5003
Products: Beer; Ale; Malt beverages. **SIC:** 5181 (Beer & Ale). **Officers:** Sid Davis, President.

■ 1644 ■ **Desert Eagle Distributing Co.**
6949 Market St.
El Paso, TX 79915
Phone: (915)772-4246 **Fax:** (915)775-0985
Products: Beer. **SIC:** 5181 (Beer & Ale). **Est:** 1956. **Sales:** $50,000,000 (2000). **Emp:** 160. **Officers:** Robert Brown, President; Clyde Scott, Vice President; Joe Damian, General Mgr.

■ 1645 ■ **DET Distributing Co.**
35 Conalco Dr.
Jackson, TN 38301-3665
Phone: (901)423-3344 **Fax:** (901)427-2466
Products: Beer. **SIC:** 5181 (Beer & Ale). **Est:** 1994. **Emp:** 25. **Officers:** Tim Estes, Sales Mgr.

■ 1646 ■ **DET Distributing Co.**
301 Great Circle Rd.
Nashville, TN 37228
Phone: (615)244-4113 **Fax:** (615)255-0122
E-mail: shattingly@detdist.com
URL: http://www.detdist.com
Products: Beer; Water. **SIC:** 5181 (Beer & Ale). **Est:** 1951. **Sales:** $68,000,000 (2000). **Emp:** 200. **Officers:** F. Dettwiller, President; David Earls, VP of Construction; David Earls, Dir. of Sales.

■ 1647 ■ **Dettor, Edwards & Morris**
PO Box 443
Grimstead, VA 23064-0443
Phone: (804)295-7526 **Fax:** (804)295-5316
Products: Wine; Groceries. **SICs:** 5182 (Wines & Distilled Beverages); 5141 (Groceries—General Line).

■ 1648 ■ **DeWitt Beverage**
PO Box 596
Brattleboro, VT 05302
Phone: (802)254-6063
Free: (800)287-6063 **Fax:** (802)254-4744
Products: Beer. **SIC:** 5181 (Beer & Ale). **Officers:** Allan Fisher.

■ 1649 ■ **Diamond Distributors**
1918 Bible Rd.
Lima, OH 45801
Phone: (419)227-5132 **Fax:** (419)227-0678
Products: Bottled liquors; Beer; Wine; Soft drinks; Tea. **SICs:** 5182 (Wines & Distilled Beverages); 5181 (Beer & Ale); 5149 (Groceries & Related Products Nec).

■ 1650 ■ **Diamond State Distributors**
PO Box 1223
Wilmington, DE 19899-1223
Phone: (302)888-2511 **Fax:** (302)888-2518
Products: Wine; Beer; Spirits. **SICs:** 5182 (Wines & Distilled Beverages); 5181 (Beer & Ale). **Est:** 1987. **Sales:** $5,000,000 (2000). **Emp:** 13. **Officers:** J.D. Guckert, President.

■ 1651 ■ **Dimitri Wine & Spirits**
PO Box 5046
Rock Island, IL 61204
Phone: (309)793-0055 **Fax:** (309)793-0086
Products: Beer, wine, and liquor; Soda. **SICs:** 5182 (Wines & Distilled Beverages); 5181 (Beer & Ale); 5149 (Groceries & Related Products Nec).

■ 1652 ■ **Diversified Imports**
3215 Lind Ave. SW
Renton, WA 98055
Phones: (206)251-8099 (206)251-8099
Fax: (206)251-5954
Products: Wine. **SIC:** 5182 (Wines & Distilled

Beverages). **Est:** 1972. **Sales:** $4,000,000 (2000). **Emp:** 10. **Officers:** Tim Martin.

■ 1653 ■ **Divine Brothers Distributing Inc.**
PO Box 3445
Great Falls, MT 59403-3445
Phone: (406)453-5457 **Fax:** (406)771-7635
Products: Beer, ale, and other fermented malt liquors. **SIC:** 5181 (Beer & Ale). **Officers:** Kevin Devine, President.

■ 1654 ■ **Dixie Beverage Co.**
2705 S Pleasant Valley Rd.
Winchester, VA 22601
Phone: (540)667-1656 **Fax:** (540)722-9773
Products: Beer and wine. **SICs:** 5181 (Beer & Ale); 5182 (Wines & Distilled Beverages). **Emp:** 49. **Officers:** Al Gregory.

■ 1655 ■ **D.M. Distributing Company Inc.**
7976 Long Hill Rd.
Pasadena, MD 21122-1053
Phone: (410)437-0900 **Fax:** (410)437-5180
Products: Beer. **SIC:** 5181 (Beer & Ale). **Emp:** 49.

■ 1656 ■ **Domecq Importers Inc.**
355 Riverside Ave.
Westport, CT 06880-4810
Phone: (203)637-6500 **Fax:** (203)637-6595
Products: Tequila, wines, sherries, and rums. **SIC:** 5182 (Wines & Distilled Beverages). **Est:** 1981. **Sales:** $22,000,000 (2000). **Emp:** 73. **Officers:** Martin Jones, CEO & President; Eric Barnes, Controller; Gabe Sagaz, VP of Marketing; Tom Kominsky, VP of Sales.

■ 1657 ■ **Dops, Inc.**
116 Pates Dr.
Ft. Washington, MD 20744-4841
Phone: (301)839-8650 **Fax:** (301)839-8658
Products: Wine and liquor. **SIC:** 5182 (Wines & Distilled Beverages).

■ 1658 ■ **Drinks Galore Inc.**
1331 Jerome Ave.
Bronx, NY 10452-3320
Phone: (212)681-0500 **Fax:** (212)992-4606
Products: Soft drinks; Beer. **SICs:** 5181 (Beer & Ale); 5149 (Groceries & Related Products Nec). **Emp:** 49.

■ 1659 ■ **Duplin Wine Cellars**
Hwy. 117 N
Rose Hill, NC 28458-9526
Phone: (910)289-3888
Free: (800)774-9634 **Fax:** (910)289-3094
Products: Wine. **SIC:** 5182 (Wines & Distilled Beverages). **Est:** 1975. **Sales:** $6,000,000 (2000). **Emp:** 49. **Officers:** David Fussell.

■ 1660 ■ **Dutchess Beer Distributors**
5 Laurel St.
Poughkeepsie, NY 12603
Phone: (914)452-0940
Products: Beer. **SIC:** 5181 (Beer & Ale). **Est:** 1933. **Sales:** $30,000,000 (2000). **Emp:** 70. **Officers:** D. Capillino, President; S. Kondysar, Vice President.

■ 1661 ■ **Dwan and Company Inc.**
PO Box 96
Torrington, CT 06790
Phone: (860)489-3149 **Fax:** (860)489-4805
Products: Beer. **SIC:** 5181 (Beer & Ale). **Est:** 1928. **Sales:** $10,000,000 (2000). **Emp:** 35. **Officers:** William J. Sweetman, President.

■ 1662 ■ **E-Corp, Inc.**
6152 S Forest Ct.
Littleton, CO 80121
Phone: (303)220-0250 **Fax:** (303)220-0251
Products: Imported beer, wine, and spirits. **SICs:** 5182 (Wines & Distilled Beverages); 5181 (Beer & Ale). **Est:** 1990. **Sales:** $975,000 (2000). **Emp:** 5. **Officers:** Dale S. Gale, President; George Gale, General Mgr.

■ 1663 ■ **Eagle Beverage Co.**
PO Box 1492
Springfield, OH 45501
Phone: (513)322-2082
Products: Beer, bottled water, and iced tea. **SICs:** 5181 (Beer & Ale); 5149 (Groceries & Related Products

Nec). **Sales:** $21,000,000 (2000). **Emp:** 70. **Officers:** James Acra, President.

■ 1664 ■ **Eagle Distributing Co.**
PO Box 1286
Lumberton, NC 28359-1286
Phone: (919)738-8165 **Fax:** (919)671-0422
Products: Beer. **SIC:** 5181 (Beer & Ale). **Est:** 1978. **Sales:** $12,500,000 (2000). **Emp:** 27.

■ 1665 ■ **Eagle Distributing Co. Inc.**
PO Box 27190
Knoxville, TN 37927
Phone: (423)637-3311
Products: Beer. **SIC:** 5181 (Beer & Ale). **Est:** 1957. **Sales:** $39,000,000 (2000). **Emp:** 130. **Officers:** Ray Hand, President.

■ 1666 ■ **Eagle Distributors Inc.**
169 Kolepa Pl.
Kahului, HI 96732-2433
Phone: (808)877-2520 **Fax:** (808)871-7024
Products: Alcoholic beverages; Soft drinks. **SICs:** 5181 (Beer & Ale); 5182 (Wines & Distilled Beverages); 5149 (Groceries & Related Products Nec). **Emp:** 35. **Officers:** Robert Elliott.

■ 1667 ■ **Eagle River Distributing**
120 Jack Frost Dr.
Eagle River, WI 54521
Phone: (715)479-9060 **Fax:** (715)479-6916
Products: Beer. **SIC:** 5181 (Beer & Ale). **Emp:** 25.

■ 1668 ■ **East Side Beverage Co.**
1260 Grey Fox Rd.
Arden Hills, MN 55112
Phone: (612)482-1133 **Fax:** (612)482-9810
Products: Beer. **SIC:** 5181 (Beer & Ale). **Est:** 1931. **Sales:** $120,000,000 (2000). **Emp:** 200. **Officers:** Todd Knipping, President; Craig Kascht, Controller.

■ 1669 ■ **Eber Brothers Wine and Liquor Corp.**
155 Paragon Dr.
Rochester, NY 14624-1167
Phone: (716)349-7700 **Free:** (800)776-3237
Products: Liquor and wines. **SIC:** 5182 (Wines & Distilled Beverages). **Est:** 1934. **Sales:** $62,000,000 (2000). **Emp:** 600. **Officers:** Lester Eber, President; John T. Ryan, CFO.

■ 1670 ■ **Edison Liquor Corp.**
PO Box 609
Brookfield, WI 53045
Phone: (414)821-0600 **Fax:** (414)821-0363
Products: Liquor. **SIC:** 5182 (Wines & Distilled Beverages). **Emp:** 104. **Officers:** E. Keierleber.

■ 1671 ■ **Edison West Liquor**
4454 Robertson Rd.
Madison, WI 53714
Phone: (608)246-8868
Free: (800)362-7364 **Fax:** (608)246-0863
Products: Liquor and wine. **SIC:** 5182 (Wines & Distilled Beverages).

■ 1672 ■ **El Ray Distributing Company Inc.**
PO Box 750
Napa, CA 94559
Phone: (707)252-8600 **Fax:** (707)252-8938
Products: Beer; Water. **SICs:** 5181 (Beer & Ale); 5149 (Groceries & Related Products Nec). **Est:** 1933. **Sales:** $10,000,000 (2000). **Emp:** 35. **Officers:** Steve Tramburelli, President & CFO; A.L. Tramburelli, Dir. of Marketing.

■ 1673 ■ **Elmer's Distributing Co.**
E Hwy. 28
Morris, MN 56267
Phone: (320)589-1191 **Fax:** (320)589-1979
Products: Beer; Bottled water. **SICs:** 5181 (Beer & Ale); 5149 (Groceries & Related Products Nec). **Est:** 1949. **Sales:** $1,900,000 (2000). **Emp:** 7. **Officers:** Jeffrey Anderson, Manager; Ronald Anderson.

■ 1674 ■ **Elmira Distributing**
374 Upper Oakwood Ave.
Elmira, NY 14903
Phone: (607)734-6231
Free: (800)724-2150 **Fax:** (607)733-6989
Products: Wine; Beer; Tobacco; Candy; Beverages.
SICs: 5182 (Wines & Distilled Beverages); 5194
(Tobacco & Tobacco Products); 5145 (Confectionery);
5149 (Groceries & Related Products Nec); 5141
(Groceries—General Line). **Est:** 1904. **Emp:** 28.
Officers: Toby Lagonegro, President; Richard Rinde,
Vice President; Stefano Ringer, Sales/Marketing
Contact.

■ 1675 ■ **Elmwood Beer Distributor**
2609 Elmwood Ave.
Erie, PA 16508
Phone: (814)864-6112
Products: Beer. **SIC:** 5181 (Beer & Ale).

■ 1676 ■ **Empire Distributing**
6100 Emmanuel Dr. SW
Atlanta, GA 30336
Phone: (404)349-1780
Free: (800)262-9395 **Fax:** (404)346-4624
Products: Beer, wine, and liquor; Non-alcoholic
beverages. **SICs:** 5182 (Wines & Distilled Beverages);
5181 (Beer & Ale); 5149 (Groceries & Related Products
Nec). **Est:** 1940. **Sales:** $150,000,000 (2000). **Emp:**
650. **Officers:** M. Kahn; D. Kahn; K. Applewhite; R.
Coleman, Sales/Marketing Contact; N. Schmuckler,
Human Resources Contact; J. Swarzkopf, CFO; D.
Heltch, Operations Mgr.

■ 1677 ■ **Empire Distributors of NC Inc.**
10 Walden Dr.
Arden, NC 28704
Phone: (828)687-8662
Products: Beer and ale; Soft drinks; Wines. **SIC:** 5181
(Beer & Ale).

■ 1678 ■ **Erie Beer Co.**
812 W 14th St.
Erie, PA 16501
Phone: (814)459-7777 **Fax:** (814)456-7412
Products: Beer. **SIC:** 5181 (Beer & Ale). **Est:** 1933.
Emp: 40. **Officers:** Michael A. McCormick; J. Phillip
McCormick; Edward T. McCormick.

■ 1679 ■ **Erwin Distributing Co.**
530 Monocacy Blvd.
Frederick, MD 21701
Phone: (301)662-0372 **Fax:** (301)663-9488
E-mail: rock1201@erols.com
Products: Beer; Water; Juice. **SICs:** 5181 (Beer &
Ale); 5182 (Wines & Distilled Beverages); 5149
(Groceries & Related Products Nec). **Est:** 1945. **Sales:**
$12,500,000 (2000). **Emp:** 25. **Officers:** Frank L.
Erwin, President; Frank A. Erwin, Vice President; Betty
G. Erwin, Secretary; Steve Grossnickle, Manager; Larry
Fritz, Customer Service Contact.

■ 1680 ■ **Evans Distributing Company Inc.**
PO Box 266
Marion, VA 24354
Phone: (703)783-4262 **Fax:** (703)783-6902
Products: Beer; Wine; Non-alcoholic beverages. **SICs:**
5181 (Beer & Ale); 5149 (Groceries & Related Products
Nec); 5182 (Wines & Distilled Beverages). **Est:** 1948.
Sales: $3,000,000 (2000). **Emp:** 23. **Officers:** William
Evans, President.

■ 1681 ■ **Evanston Wholesale Inc.**
PO Box 28
Evanston, WY 82931-0028
Phone: (307)789-3526
Products: Beer, ale, and fermented malt liquors. **SIC:**
5181 (Beer & Ale). **Officers:** Dusty Lym, President.

■ 1682 ■ **Fabiano Brothers Inc.**
PO 469
Mt. Pleasant, MI 48858
Phone: (517)752-2186 **Fax:** (517)773-6323
Products: Beer; Bottled water; Wine and spirits. **SICs:**
5181 (Beer & Ale); 5149 (Groceries & Related Products
Nec); 5182 (Wines & Distilled Beverages). **Est:** 1919.
Sales: $300,000 (2000). **Emp:** 75. **Officers:** J.
Fabiano, President.

■ 1683 ■ **Famous Brands Distributors Inc.**
2910 SW Topeka Blvd.
Topeka, KS 66611
Phone: (785)267-6622 **Fax:** (785)267-3336
Products: Wine and liquor. **SIC:** 5182 (Wines &
Distilled Beverages). **Sales:** $25,000,000 (2000). **Emp:**
99. **Officers:** Jim Dorsey, President; Russ Flynn, Vice
President.

■ 1684 ■ **Leon Farmer and Co.**
PO Drawer 1352
Athens, GA 30603
Phone: (706)353-1166 **Fax:** (706)369-8922
Products: Beer. **SIC:** 5181 (Beer & Ale). **Est:** 1960.
Sales: $45,000,000 (2000). **Emp:** 115. **Officers:** H.
Leon Farmer Jr., President; T. Mackey, CFO.

■ 1685 ■ **Farrell Distributing**
5 Holmes Rd.
South Burlington, VT 05403
Phone: (802)864-4422 **Fax:** (802)864-9878
Products: Wine; Distilled liquor; Beer; Soft drinks.
SICs: 5182 (Wines & Distilled Beverages); 5149
(Groceries & Related Products Nec); 5181 (Beer &
Ale). **Officers:** David Farrell, President.

■ 1686 ■ **Federal Wine and Liquor Co.**
PO Box 519
Kearny, NJ 07032
Phone: (973)624-6444
Products: Wine, liquor, and beer. **SICs:** 5182 (Wines
& Distilled Beverages); 5181 (Beer & Ale). **Sales:**
$4,000,000 (2000). **Emp:** 40. **Officers:** Richard
Leventhal, President; Peter Heck.

■ 1687 ■ **Fedway Associates Inc.**
PO Box 519
Kearny, NJ 07032
Phone: (973)624-6444 **Fax:** (973)344-3336
Products: Wines and spirits. **SIC:** 5182 (Wines &
Distilled Beverages). **Sales:** $150,000,000 (2000).
Emp: 500. **Officers:** Richard Leventhal, President;
Michael Dokachez, CFO.

■ 1688 ■ **Fetzer Vineyards**
4040 Civic Center Dr.Ste. 525
San Rafael, CA 94903
Phone: (415)444-7400 **Fax:** (415)444-7480
Products: Wine. **SIC:** 5182 (Wines & Distilled
Beverages). **Sales:** $100,000,000 (2000). **Emp:** 300.
Officers: Paul Dolan, President.

■ 1689 ■ **Fine Wine Brokers Inc.**
4621 N Lincoln Ave.
Chicago, IL 60625
Phone: (773)989-8166
Products: Wines. **SIC:** 5182 (Wines & Distilled
Beverages).

■ 1690 ■ **Finger Lakes Bottling Co.**
Wright Ave. Ext.
Auburn, NY 13021
Phone: (315)253-6561 **Fax:** (315)253-5661
Products: Beer. **SIC:** 5181 (Beer & Ale). **Est:** 1933.
Emp: 49. **Officers:** Mary Pisciotti.

■ 1691 ■ **Finnish National Distillers Inc.**
30 Rockefeller Plz. 4300
New York, NY 10112
Phone: (212)757-4440
Products: Liquor. **SIC:** 5182 (Wines & Distilled
Beverages). **Sales:** $45,000,000 (2000). **Emp:** 5.
Officers: Chester Brandes, President.

■ 1692 ■ **F.L.D. Distributors Inc.**
1 W 6th St.
Medford, OR 97501-2704
Phone: (541)779-9491 **Fax:** (541)776-8493
Products: Nonalcoholic beverages; Beer; Wine. **SICs:**
5181 (Beer & Ale); 5182 (Wines & Distilled Beverages);
5149 (Groceries & Related Products Nec). **Est:** 1958.
Sales: $6,500,000 (2000). **Emp:** 49. **Officers:** Jim
Pearson, General Mgr. **Alternate Name:** F.L.D./Empire
Beverages.

■ 1693 ■ **Food and Spirits Distributing
Company Inc.**
PO Box 363127
San Juan, PR 00936
Phone: (787)788-7070
Products: Liquor; Canned foods. **SICs:** 5182 (Wines &
Distilled Beverages); 5149 (Groceries & Related
Products Nec).

■ 1694 ■ **Forester Beverage Inc.**
Rte. 5, Box 2A
River Rd.
North Wilkesboro, NC 28659-9805
Phone: (919)667-6272
Free: (800)255-6571 **Fax:** (919)667-5532
Products: Beer. **SIC:** 5181 (Beer & Ale). **Est:** 1936.
Sales: $12,000,000 (2000). **Emp:** 30.

■ 1695 ■ **Forman Distributing Co.**
7550 Accotink Park Rd.
Springfield, VA 22150
Phone: (703)644-2425 **Fax:** (703)644-6842
Products: Alcoholic beverages, including wine and
beer. **SICs:** 5182 (Wines & Distilled Beverages); 5181
(Beer & Ale).

■ 1696 ■ **Henry A. Fox Sales Co.**
4494 36th St. SE
Grand Rapids, MI 49512
Phone: (616)949-1210 **Fax:** (616)848-0633
Products: Beer and wine. **SICs:** 5181 (Beer & Ale);
5182 (Wines & Distilled Beverages). **Est:** 1952. **Sales:**
$20,000,000 (2000). **Emp:** 107. **Officers:** H.A. Fox Jr.,
President; Joanne Fiedler, Treasurer; R. Drieborg, VP
of Marketing; P. Fox, Exec. VP of Operations.

■ 1697 ■ **Frank Distributing**
507 S Murray Ave.
Anderson, SC 29624-1520
Phone: (864)225-7071 **Fax:** (864)224-0730
Products: Beer. **SIC:** 5181 (Beer & Ale). **Emp:** 19.

■ 1698 ■ **Friendly Distributors**
6501 Rainier Dr.
Everett, WA 98201
Phone: (425)355-1900 **Fax:** (425)347-8543
Products: Beer; Liquor; Wine; Bottling mineral or
spring water. **SICs:** 5181 (Beer & Ale); 5182 (Wines &
Distilled Beverages); 5149 (Groceries & Related
Products Nec). **Emp:** 24. **Officers:** Kim Blunt; Jim
Stephanson, General Mgr.

■ 1699 ■ **Frank Fuhrer Holdings Inc.**
3100 E Carson St.
Pittsburgh, PA 15203
Phone: (412)488-8444
Products: Beer. **SIC:** 5181 (Beer & Ale). **Sales:**
$36,000,000 (2000). **Emp:** 120. **Officers:** Frank B.
Fuhrer, CEO & Chairman of the Board; Tom Pontzloff,
Controller.

■ 1700 ■ **Frank B. Fuhrer Wholesale Co.**
3100 E Carson St.
Pittsburgh, PA 15203
Phone: (412)488-8444
Free: (800)837-2212 **Fax:** (412)488-0195
Products: Beer. **SIC:** 5181 (Beer & Ale). **Est:** 1982.
Sales: $95,000,000 (2000). **Emp:** 130. **Officers:** Frank
B. Fuhrer, CEO & Chairman of the Board; David
Fuhrer, President.

■ 1701 ■ **G and G Enterprises Inc.**
PO Box 1206
Laramie, WY 82073
Phone: (307)745-3236 **Fax:** (307)742-5375
Products: Beer. **SIC:** 5181 (Beer & Ale). **Est:** 1949.
Sales: $1,500,000 (2000). **Emp:** 6. **Officers:** Eugene
Smith, President; Stacy L. Smith, Human Resources
Contact; Eugene P. Smith III, Customer Service
Contact. **Doing Business As:** Smith Beverages.

■ 1702 ■ **Gallup Sales Co. Inc.**
530 E 66 Ave.
Gallup, NM 87301-6028
Phone: (505)863-5241 **Fax:** (505)863-4219
Products: Wine and distilled beverages. **SIC:** 5182
(Wines & Distilled Beverages). **Officers:** Reed Ferrari,
President.

■ 1703 ■ Gambrinus Co.
14800 San Pedro, No. 310
San Antonio, TX 78232
Phone: (210)490-9128
Products: Beer. **SIC:** 5181 (Beer & Ale). **Est:** 1986.
Sales: $125,000,000 (2000). **Emp:** 95. **Officers:**
Carlos Alvarez, President; James Bolz, Controller; Ron
Christesson, Dir. of Marketing.

■ 1704 ■ Garco Wine
4017 Folsom
St. Louis, MO 63110
Phone: (314)664-8300   **Fax:** (314)664-0036
E-mail: garcowineman@msn.com
Products: Wine. **SIC:** 5182 (Wines & Distilled
Beverages). **Est:** 1946. **Emp:** 25. **Officers:** Stanley
Cohen; Michael Cohen, Human Resources Contact;
Anthony Barbieri, Sales/Marketing Contact; Barb
Dowdy, Customer Service Contact; Wendy Hempen,
Customer Service Contact.

■ 1705 ■ Gate City Beverage Distributors
PO Box 8458
San Bernardino, CA 92412
Phone: (909)799-1600   **Fax:** (909)799-1615
Products: Beer. **SIC:** 5181 (Beer & Ale). **Est:** 1946.
Sales: $38,000,000 (2000). **Emp:** 150. **Officers:**
Morton Aronoff, Chairman of the Board; David
Dempsey, Controller; Mike George, Dir. of Marketing.

■ 1706 ■ General Beer Distributors
6169 Mckee Rd.
Madison, WI 53701
Phone: (608)271-1234
Products: Beer. **SIC:** 5181 (Beer & Ale).

■ 1707 ■ General Beverage Sales Co.
PO Box 44326
Madison, WI 53744
Phone: (608)271-1234   **Fax:** (608)271-8625
Products: Beer, wine and distilled beverages. **SICs:**
5181 (Beer & Ale); 5182 (Wines & Distilled Beverages).
Sales: $30,000,000 (1994). **Emp:** 150. **Officers:**
Lawrence Weinstein, CEO & Chairman of the Board;
Dick Karls, Sr. VP & Finance Officer.

■ 1708 ■ General Distributing Co.
PO Box 16070
Salt Lake City, UT 84116
Phone: (801)531-7895   **Fax:** (801)363-4924
Products: Beer; Wine coolers. **SICs:** 5181 (Beer &
Ale); 5182 (Wines & Distilled Beverages). **Est:** 1968.
Sales: $51,000,000 (2000). **Emp:** 90. **Officers:** M.
Brennan, President; M. Purdie, VP of Finance; J.
Twiss, Sales Mgr.

■ 1709 ■ General Wholesale Co.
1271-A Tacoma Dr.
Atlanta, GA 30318
Phone: (404)351-3626   **Fax:** (404)350-6550
Products: Beer, liquor, and wine. **SICs:** 5181 (Beer &
Ale); 5182 (Wines & Distilled Beverages). **Est:** 1951.
Sales: $92,000,000 (2000). **Emp:** 300. **Officers:**
William D. Young Sr., President; William Murman,
Controller.

■ 1710 ■ General Wine Co.
373 Victor Ave.
Highland Park, MI 48203
Phone: (313)867-0521   **Fax:** (313)867-4039
URL: http://www.gwlc.com
Products: Wine, beer, and liquor. **SICs:** 5182 (Wines
& Distilled Beverages); 5181 (Beer & Ale). **Emp:** 300.
Officers: Sydney L. Ross, President.

■ 1711 ■ Georgia Crown Distributing
255 Villanova Dr.
Atlanta, GA 30336
Phone: (404)344-9550   **Fax:** (404)346-7638
Products: Liquor and wine. **SIC:** 5182 (Wines &
Distilled Beverages).

■ 1712 ■ Georgia Crown Distributing Co.
PO Box 7908
Columbus, GA 31908
Phone: (706)568-4580   **Fax:** (706)563-3905
Products: Liquor; Beer; Wine; Bottled water. **SICs:**
5181 (Beer & Ale); 5182 (Wines & Distilled Beverages);
5149 (Groceries & Related Products Nec). **Est:** 1938.

■ 1713 ■ Gibson Wine Company Inc.
1720 Academy
Sanger, CA 93657
Phone: (209)875-2505   **Fax:** (209)875-4761
Products: Wine, including table and fruit. **SIC:** 5182
(Wines & Distilled Beverages). **Est:** 1939. **Sales:**
$10,000,000 (2000). **Emp:** 51. **Officers:** Kim
Spruance, General Mgr.

■ 1714 ■ Gidden Distributing
PO Box 449
Temple, TX 76503
Phone: (254)773-9933   **Fax:** (254)773-2134
Products: Beer. **SIC:** 5181 (Beer & Ale).

■ 1715 ■ Gideon Distributing Inc.
5355 Ohio St.
PO Box 3645
Beaumont, TX 77704
Phone: (409)833-3361   **Fax:** (409)833-2775
Products: Beer. **SIC:** 5181 (Beer & Ale). **Officers:**
Tom Johnson.

■ 1716 ■ Giglio Distributing Company Inc.
PO Box 4046
Beaumont, TX 77704
Phone: (409)838-1654
Free: (800)725-2337   **Fax:** (409)838-4018
Products: Liquor. **SIC:** 5182 (Wines & Distilled
Beverages).

■ 1717 ■ Girardi Distributors Corp.
PO Box 967
Athol, MA 01331
Phone: (978)249-3581   **Fax:** (978)249-7894
Products: Beer. **SIC:** 5181 (Beer & Ale). **Est:** 1927.
Sales: $20,000,000 (2000). **Emp:** 35. **Officers:**
George R. Girardi Jr., President & Treasurer.

■ 1718 ■ Glasgow Distributors Inc.
PO Box 146
Glasgow, MT 59230-0146
Phone: (406)228-8277
Free: (800)559-8277   **Fax:** (406)228-8773
Products: Beer; Ale; Malt beverages; Soft drinks;
Chips. **SICs:** 5181 (Beer & Ale); 5149 (Groceries &
Related Products Nec); 5145 (Confectionery).
Officers: John Swanson, President.

■ 1719 ■ Glazer's of Iowa
4401 NW 112th St.
Urbandale, IA 50322
Phone: (515)252-7173
Free: (800)475-9463   **Fax:** (515)252-8681
Products: Wine and beer; Juices, soft drinks. **SICs:**
5182 (Wines & Distilled Beverages); 5181 (Beer & Ale);
5149 (Groceries & Related Products Nec). **Est:** 1988.
Emp: 60. **Officers:** Doug Nease, General Mgr. **Doing
Business As:** Messer Distributing Co.

■ 1720 ■ Glazer's Wholesale Drug Co. Inc.
14860 Landmark Blvd.
Dallas, TX 75240
Phone: (972)702-0900   **Fax:** (972)702-8508
Products: Alcoholic beverages, including ales and
wines. **SICs:** 5182 (Wines & Distilled Beverages); 5181
(Beer & Ale). **Sales:** $758,000,000 (2000). **Officers:**
Bennett Glazer, CEO; Cary Rossel, CFO.

■ 1721 ■ Globil Inc.
PO Box 50456
2350 Hemmert Ave.
Idaho Falls, ID 83405-0456
Phone: (208)522-5121   **Fax:** (208)523-8639
Products: Beers; Ale; Malt; Wines; Non-alcoholic
beverages. **SICs:** 5181 (Beer & Ale); 5182 (Wines &
Distilled Beverages); 5149 (Groceries & Related
Products Nec). **Est:** 1987. **Sales:** $3,000,000 (2000).
Emp: 20. **Officers:** Bill Cottle, President; Dusty Cottle,
Vice President; Doug Wessel, Sales Mgr.

Sales: $200,000,000 (2000). **Emp:** 675. **Officers:** Don
Leebern III, President; Lynn Robinson, Dir. of Data
Processing; Linda Greggory, Dir of Human Resources.

■ 1722 ■ Gold Coast Beverage Distributors
3325 NW 70th Ave.
Miami, FL 33122
Phone: (305)591-9800   **Fax:** (305)593-2393
Products: Beverages, including beer and
sparkling/spring water. **SICs:** 5181 (Beer & Ale); 5149
(Groceries & Related Products Nec). **Est:** 1938. **Sales:**
$220,000,000 (2000). **Emp:** 500. **Officers:** Steve
Levin, Chairman of the Board; Art Friedman, President
& CEO; Alfonso Fernandez, COO; Christy Yasi, Dir. of
Marketing & Sales; Carlos Gato, Dir of Human
Resources; Alan Okun, Exec. VP. **Former Name:**
Universal Brands Inc.

■ 1723 ■ Gold Coast Distributors Inc.
837 Robinwood Ct.
Traverse City, MI 49686
Phone: (616)929-7003
Products: Beer. **SIC:** 5181 (Beer & Ale).

■ 1724 ■ Golden Eagle of Arkansas Inc.
1900 E 15th St.
Little Rock, AR 72202
Phone: (501)372-2800
Products: Beer. **SIC:** 5181 (Beer & Ale). **Est:** 1945.
Sales: $18,000,000 (2000). **Emp:** 75. **Officers:** W.G.
Bray, President; J. Folen, Treasurer & Secty.; Bill
Wilkerson, Dir. of Sales; Grant Bray, Dir. of Marketing.

■ 1725 ■ Golden Eagle Distributors
PO Box 27506
Tucson, AZ 85726
Phone: (520)884-5999   **Fax:** (520)628-7377
Products: Beer. **SIC:** 5181 (Beer & Ale). **Est:** 1947.
Sales: $115,000,000 (2000). **Emp:** 300. **Officers:**
Virginia Lee Clements, CEO, Chairman of the Board &
Treasurer.

■ 1726 ■ C.R. Goodman
2906 Cavitt
Bryan, TX 77801
Phone: (409)822-9460
Products: Beer. **SIC:** 5181 (Beer & Ale).

■ 1727 ■ Goody-Goody Liquor Store Inc.
10301 Harry Hines Blvd.
Dallas, TX 75220
Phone: (214)350-5806   **Fax:** (214)350-4258
Products: Liquor. **SICs:** 5182 (Wines & Distilled
Beverages); 5181 (Beer & Ale). **Sales:** $16,000,000
(1994). **Emp:** 50. **Officers:** Mary J. Jansen, Treasurer.

■ 1728 ■ Gourmet Wine & Spirits
4445 Walzem St.
San Antonio, TX 78218
Phone: (210)654-1123
Products: Wine and liquor. **SIC:** 5182 (Wines &
Distilled Beverages).

■ 1729 ■ William Grant and Sons Inc.
130 Fieldcrest Ave.
Raritan Center
Edison, NJ 08837
Phone: (732)225-9000   **Fax:** (732)225-0950
Products: Wine; Distilled liquor. **SIC:** 5182 (Wines &
Distilled Beverages). **Est:** 1897. **Emp:** 104. **Officers:**
Derek H. Anderson, e-mail: danderson@
wgrantusa.com; Joel Gosler, Sales & Marketing
Contact, e-mail: jgosler@wgrantusa.com; Mark
Teasdale, e-mail: mteasdale@wgrantusa.com; Steven
Klauber, e-mail: sklauber@wgrantusa.com.

■ 1730 ■ Grantham Distributing Company Inc.
2685 Hansrob Rd.
Orlando, FL 32804
Phone: (407)299-6446   **Fax:** (407)295-7104
Products: Beer, wine, and distilled liquors. **SICs:** 5181
(Beer & Ale); 5182 (Wines & Distilled Beverages).
Sales: $54,300,000 (2000). **Emp:** 130. **Officers:**
Varley Grantham, CEO; Gary Tinbrook, Mgr. of Admin.

■ 1731 ■ Greene Beverage Company Inc.
PO Box 1699
Tuscaloosa, AL 35406
Phone: (205)345-6950
Products: Beer. **SIC:** 5181 (Beer & Ale). **Est:** 1937.
Sales: $8,000,000 (2000). **Emp:** 62. **Officers:** Grover
L. Burchfield III, CEO; Spencer Burchfield, Partner.

■ 1732 ■ Green's/Pine Avenue Beer
    Distibuting
3030 Pine Ave.
Erie, PA 16504
Phone: (814)453-2094
Products: Beer. **SIC:** 5181 (Beer & Ale). **Est:** 1999.
Former Name: Central Beer Distributing.

■ 1733 ■ Grey Eagle Distributors Inc.
2340 Millpark Dr.
Maryland Heights, MO 63043
Phone: (314)429-9100
Products: Beer. **SIC:** 5181 (Beer & Ale). **Est:** 1963.
Sales: $75,000,000 (2000). **Emp:** 185. **Officers:** Jerry
G. Clinton, President & Chairman of the Board; Jeffrey
M. Clinton, President & COO.

■ 1734 ■ Grosslein Beverages Inc.
13554 Tungsten St. NW
Anoka, MN 55303
Phone: (612)421-5804   **Fax:** (612)427-5555
Products: Beer. **SICs:** 5181 (Beer & Ale); 5149
(Groceries & Related Products Nec). **Est:** 1994. **Sales:**
$15,000,000 (1994). **Emp:** 45. **Officers:** Dana A.
Grosslein, President; Tom Blaska, VP & General Mgr.

■ 1735 ■ Tony Guiffre Distributing Co.
6839 Industrial Rd.
Springfield, VA 22151-4289
Phone: (703)642-1700
Products: Beer; Juice; Flavored water. **SICs:** 5181
(Beer & Ale); 5149 (Groceries & Related Products
Nec). **Est:** 1934. **Sales:** $19,000,000 (1999). **Emp:** 70.
Officers: J.M. Guiffre, President; Janet Mills,
Controller; Wayne Biggs, Exec. VP.

■ 1736 ■ Guinness America Inc.
6 Landmark Sq.
Stamford, CT 06901
Phone: (203)359-7100
Products: Beer and ale. **SIC:** 5181 (Beer & Ale).
Sales: $90,000,000 (1992). **Emp:** 300. **Officers:**
William Olson, President.

■ 1737 ■ Guinness Import Co.
6 Landmark Sq.
Stamford, CT 06901
Phone: (203)323-3311
Products: Beer and hard liquor. **SICs:** 5181 (Beer &
Ale); 5182 (Wines & Distilled Beverages). **Sales:**
$30,000,000 (2000). **Emp:** 100. **Officers:** William
Olson, CEO & President; Roger Little, VP of Finance &
Admin.; Paul Block, VP of Marketing.

■ 1738 ■ Gusto Brands Inc.
PO Box 278
Lagrange, GA 30241
Phone: (706)882-2573   **Fax:** (706)882-2412
Products: Beverages, including beer and non-
alcoholic drinks. **SICs:** 5181 (Beer & Ale); 5149
(Groceries & Related Products Nec). **Est:** 1945. **Sales:**
$15,000,000 (1999). **Emp:** 50. **Officers:** L.A. Haralson,
President; Tracy Alford, Vice President; Mike Ford,
Sales Mgr.; Betty Ann Carruth, Dir. of Systems.

■ 1739 ■ H-H of Savannah, Inc.
2501 E President St.
Savannah, GA 31404
Phone: (912)236-8284   **Fax:** (912)236-7034
E-mail: hhsav@aol.com
Products: Beer. **SIC:** 5181 (Beer & Ale). **Est:** 1968.
Sales: $16,000,000 (2000). **Emp:** 55. **Officers:** Fred
Hughes III, President.

■ 1740 ■ Bob Hall Inc.
5600 SE Crane Hwy.
Upper Marlboro, MD 20772
Phone: (301)627-1900
Products: Beer. **SIC:** 5181 (Beer & Ale). **Est:** 1934.
Sales: $40,000,000 (2000). **Emp:** 100. **Officers:**
Evalina S. Mitchell, CEO; Alan Horton, General Mgr.

■ 1741 ■ Halliday-Smith Inc.
1st St. & Holiday Dr.
Cairo, IL 62914
Phone: (618)734-0447
Products: Beer. **SIC:** 5181 (Beer & Ale). **Est:** 1901.
Sales: $700,000 (2000). **Emp:** 5. **Officers:** Stephen
Clifford, CEO.

■ 1742 ■ Halo Distributing Co.
PO Box 7370
San Antonio, TX 78207-0370
Phone: (210)735-1111   **Fax:** (210)737-2139
Products: Beer; Wine coolers. **SICs:** 5181 (Beer &
Ale); 5182 (Wines & Distilled Beverages). **Sales:**
$76,000,000 (2000). **Emp:** 205. **Officers:** Dennis
O'Malley, President; Gerard Kolodejcak, Controller.

■ 1743 ■ Hamburg
3104 Farber Dr.
Champaign, IL 61821
Phone: (217)352-7911
Free: (800)373-7911   **Fax:** (217)352-6723
Products: Liquor; Wine; Beer. **SICs:** 5182 (Wines &
Distilled Beverages); 5181 (Beer & Ale).

■ 1744 ■ Harbor Distributing Co.
1515 E 4th St.
Little Rock, AR 72202-2808
Phone: (501)372-0185   **Fax:** (501)372-2228
Products: Beer. **SIC:** 5181 (Beer & Ale). **Emp:** 100.
Officers: Nick Pierce, President.

■ 1745 ■ Harbor Distributing Co.
2824 E 208th
Long Beach, CA 90810-1101
Phone: (310)632-5483   **Fax:** (310)635-5483
Products: Beer. **SIC:** 5181 (Beer & Ale). **Emp:** 160.
Officers: M. Jude Reyes.

■ 1746 ■ Hartford Distributors Inc.
131 Chapel Rd.
Manchester, CT 06040
Phone: (860)643-2337
Free: (800)832-7211   **Fax:** (860)646-3780
Products: Beer; Snack foods. **SICs:** 5181 (Beer &
Ale); 5145 (Confectionery). **Sales:** $46,000,000 (2000).
Emp: 150. **Officers:** Ross Hollander, President;
Bernard Baker, Controller.

■ 1747 ■ Haubrich Enterprises Inc.
1901 Seminary Rd.
Quincy, IL 62301-1484
Phone: (217)223-1183
Products: Beer; Liquor. **SICs:** 5181 (Beer & Ale); 5182
(Wines & Distilled Beverages). **Sales:** $900,000
(2000). **Emp:** 15. **Officers:** Joseph Haubrich, CEO.

■ 1748 ■ Havre Distributors Inc.
935 1st St.
Havre, MT 59501-3705
Phone: (406)265-6212   **Fax:** (406)265-7262
Products: Beer; Ale; Malt beverages. **SIC:** 5181 (Beer
& Ale). **Officers:** Kenneth Myers, President.

■ 1749 ■ Heidelberg Distributing Co.
912 3rd St.
Perrysburg, OH 43551
Phone: (419)666-9782   **Fax:** (419)661-5975
Products: Beer; Ale. **SIC:** 5181 (Beer & Ale). **Est:**
1939. **Sales:** $30,000,000 (2000). **Emp:** 100. **Officers:**
John Roberts, CEO; Phyllis Jarvis, CFO.

■ 1750 ■ Heineken USA Inc.
50 Main St.
White Plains, NY 10606
Phone: (914)681-4100   **Fax:** (914)681-4110
Products: Beer. **SIC:** 5181 (Beer & Ale). **Est:** 1995.
Emp: 280. **Officers:** Michael Foley, CEO & President;
Daniel Walsh, VP of Finance.

■ 1751 ■ Hensley and Co.
4201 N 45th Ave.
Phoenix, AZ 85031
Phone: (602)264-1635
Products: Beer. **SIC:** 5181 (Beer & Ale). **Sales:**
$81,000,000 (2000). **Emp:** 350. **Officers:** Robert
Delgado, President.

■ 1752 ■ Heritage House Wines
809 Jefferson Hwy.
Jefferson, LA 70121
Phone: (504)837-6464   **Fax:** (504)830-0114
Products: Imported wines. **SIC:** 5182 (Wines &
Distilled Beverages).

■ 1753 ■ High Country Sales Inc.
4110 High Country Rd.
Colorado Springs, CO 80907-4319
Phone: (719)598-9200   **Fax:** (719)598-6380
Products: Beer. **SIC:** 5181 (Beer & Ale). **Sales:**
$25,000,000 (2000). **Emp:** 82. **Officers:** Bill Bliss;
Michael Spiger; John Simons. **Doing Business As:**
Better Brands.

■ 1754 ■ High Grade Beverage
PO Box 7092
North Brunswick, NJ 08902
Phone: (732)821-7600
Free: (800)221-1194   **Fax:** (732)821-5953
Products: Beer; Bottled water. **SICs:** 5181 (Beer &
Ale); 5149 (Groceries & Related Products Nec). **Est:**
1947. **Sales:** $2,000,000 (2000). **Emp:** 100. **Officers:**
Joe De Marco, CEO; Herbert Schloss, CFO; Anthony
De Marco, Corp. Sr. VP.

■ 1755 ■ High Life Sales Co.
1325 N Topping
Kansas City, MO 64120
Phone: (816)483-3700   **Fax:** (816)241-1789
Products: Beer. **SIC:** 5181 (Beer & Ale). **Est:** 1932.
Sales: $29,000,000 (2000). **Emp:** 80. **Officers:** G.J.
Mos III, CEO & President; Kris Patton, CFO; John
Kane, VP & Gen. Mgr., e-mail: johnkane@
cysource.com.

■ 1756 ■ Highland Distributing Co.
213 Blount
Fayetteville, NC 28302
Phone: (919)483-4168   **Fax:** (919)483-4169
Products: Beer and wine. **SICs:** 5181 (Beer & Ale);
5182 (Wines & Distilled Beverages). **Emp:** 49.
Officers: Pat Herrera; Melissa Herrera.

■ 1757 ■ Hillman International Brands, Ltd.
1441 Seamist Dr.
Houston, TX 77008
Phone: (713)869-5441   **Fax:** (713)862-5845
Products: Beer. **SIC:** 5181 (Beer & Ale). **Est:** 1992.
Emp: 150. **Officers:** M.H. Hillman, CEO.

■ 1758 ■ Hilltop Beer Distributing
4535 Buffalo Rd.
Erie, PA 16510
Phone: (814)899-6157
Products: Beer. **SIC:** 5181 (Beer & Ale).

■ 1759 ■ Hirst Imports
1080 Metropolitan Ave.
Oklahoma City, OK 73108-2032
Phone: (405)949-9393   **Fax:** (405)949-9825
Products: Wine, beer, and liquor. **SICs:** 5182 (Wines
& Distilled Beverages); 5181 (Beer & Ale). **Officers:**
Wayne Hirst.

■ 1760 ■ Hitchcock Distributing Inc.
2901 W Arkansas
Durant, OK 74701-4847
Phone: (580)924-3350   **Fax:** (580)924-3350
Products: Beer. **SIC:** 5181 (Beer & Ale). **Emp:** 19.
Officers: Tommy Hitchcock.

■ 1761 ■ Holsten Import Corp.
75 N Saw Mill River Rd., Ste. C
Elmsford, NY 10523
Phone: (914)345-8900   **Fax:** (914)245-9019
Products: Imported beer and ale. **SIC:** 5181 (Beer &
Ale). **Sales:** $3,500,000 (2000). **Emp:** 5. **Officers:**
Matthias Neidhart, President.

■ 1762 ■ Holston Distributing Co.
310 Lafcox Dr.
Johnson City, TN 37604
Phone: (423)928-6571
Products: Beer. **SIC:** 5181 (Beer & Ale).

■ 1763 ■ House of Schwan Inc.
PO Box 782950
Wichita, KS 67278
Phone: (316)636-9100   **Fax:** (316)636-6210
Products: Beer; Water. **SICs:** 5181 (Beer & Ale); 5149
(Groceries & Related Products Nec). **Est:** 1960. **Sales:**
$11,000,000 (2000). **Emp:** 60. **Officers:** Barry
Schwan, President; Dale Baalman, Finance Officer.

■ 1764 ■ House of Wines Inc.
6500 Chillum Pl. NW
Washington, DC 20012-2136
Phone: (202)882-3333 **Fax:** (202)722-2493
E-mail: 162how@aol.com
Products: Wine; Beer. **SICs:** 5182 (Wines & Distilled Beverages); 5181 (Beer & Ale). **Est:** 1946. **Sales:** $4,500,000 (2000). **Emp:** 30. **Officers:** Howard Rosenberg; Norman Nezin, Sales Contact.

■ 1765 ■ G. Housen and Co. Inc.
PO Box 687
Keene, NH 03431-0687
Phone: (603)357-4171 **Free:** (800)439-4171
Products: Beer, ale, and other fermented malt liquors.
SIC: 5181 (Beer & Ale). **Sales:** $5,000,000 (2000).
Emp: 16. **Officers:** Kevin Watterson, President.

■ 1766 ■ Hub City Distributors Inc.
PO Box 5124
Trenton, NJ 08648
Phone: (609)844-9600 **Fax:** (609)844-9669
Products: Beer. **SIC:** 5181 (Beer & Ale). **Est:** 1937.
Sales: $14,000,000 (2000). **Emp:** 55. **Officers:** Jim Sigler, President; Sidney Mayer, VP of Finance; Bob Arbitell, Dir. of Marketing.

■ 1767 ■ Joseph Huber Brewing Co., Inc.
1208 14th Ave.
PO Box 277
Monroe, WI 53566
Phone: (608)325-3191 **Fax:** (608)325-3198
E-mail: jpulizzano@tds.net
URL: http://www.berghoffbeer.com
Products: Beer; Root beer contract brews. **SIC:** 5181 (Beer & Ale). **Est:** 1845. **Sales:** $15,000,000 (2000).
Emp: 45. **Officers:** Steve Preston, VP & Treasurer; David Ferrino, Sales/Marketing Contact.

■ 1768 ■ Hubert Distributors Inc.
1200 Auburn Rd.
Pontiac, MI 48342
Phone: (810)858-2340
Products: Beer. **SIC:** 5181 (Beer & Ale). **Sales:** $47,000,000 (2000). **Emp:** 140. **Officers:** A.S. Gustafson, President; P. Ferguson, Sr. VP & Asst. CFO; Thomas A. Vella, Sr. VP & General Mgr.; Ann Demres, Dir. of Systems.

■ 1769 ■ Huntsville Beverage Co.
2327 Meridian St.
Huntsville, AL 35811
Phone: (205)536-8966 **Fax:** (205)533-6912
E-mail: hnk@hiwaay.com
Products: Beer and Wine. **SIC:** 5181 (Beer & Ale).
Est: 1980. **Emp:** 25.

■ 1770 ■ Ideal Wine & Spirits Co., Inc.
3890 Mystic Valley Pkwy.
Medford, MA 02155
Phone: (781)395-3300 **Fax:** (781)395-3138
Products: Wines and liquor. **SIC:** 5182 (Wines & Distilled Beverages).

■ 1771 ■ Imperial Beverage Co.
4124 Manchester
Kalamazoo, MI 49001-3275
Phone: (616)382-4200 **Fax:** (616)382-1109
E-mail: Imperial@Imperialbev.com
Products: Beer; Wine. **SICs:** 5181 (Beer & Ale); 5182 (Wines & Distilled Beverages). **Est:** 1982. **Emp:** 49.
Officers: Joe Cekola, e-mail: Cekolaj@ Imperialbev.com.

■ 1772 ■ Inlet Distributors
4142 Kingston Dr.
Anchorage, AK 99504-4441
Phone: (907)337-0963 **Fax:** (907)337-0963
Products: Wine and distilled beverages. **SIC:** 5182 (Wines & Distilled Beverages). **Officers:** Branka Pekich, Owner.

■ 1773 ■ Intermountain Beverage Company
PO Box 429
Pocatello, ID 83204-0429
Phone: (208)237-4711 **Fax:** (208)238-1781
Products: Beer; Ale; Malt beverages. **SIC:** 5181 (Beer & Ale). **Officers:** Paul Villano, President.

■ 1774 ■ Intermountain Distributing Co.
PO Box 1772
Billings, MT 59103-1772
Phone: (406)245-7744 **Fax:** (406)245-4143
Products: Beer; Ale; Malt beverages. **SIC:** 5181 (Beer & Ale). **Officers:** Ralph Nelles, President.

■ 1775 ■ International Brands West
915 Shelly St.
Springfield, OR 97477
Phone: (541)726-5561
Products: Beverages, including wine. **SIC:** 5181 (Beer & Ale).

■ 1776 ■ Iron City Distributing Company Inc.
2670 Commercial Ave.
Mingo Junction, OH 43938
Phone: (614)598-4171 **Fax:** (614)598-3977
Products: Beer and wine. **SICs:** 5181 (Beer & Ale); 5182 (Wines & Distilled Beverages). **Est:** 1937. **Sales:** $6,000,000 (2000). **Emp:** 25. **Officers:** Michael Bellas, President; R. Chapman, Sr. VP; Nick Latousakis, General Mgr.; Nick Riley, Dir. of Data Processing.

■ 1777 ■ Jackson Hole Distributing
PO Box 7503
Jackson, WY 83001
Phone: (307)733-5609 **Fax:** (307)734-0060
Products: Beer; Ale; Malt beverages. **SIC:** 5181 (Beer & Ale). **Officers:** Lee Garlach, General Mgr.

■ 1778 ■ Jarboe Sales Co.
PO Box 580130
Tulsa, OK 74158
Phone: (918)836-2511 **Fax:** (918)836-6688
Products: Liquor. **SIC:** 5182 (Wines & Distilled Beverages). **Emp:** 99.

■ 1779 ■ Jaydor Corp.
16 Bleeker St.
Millburn, NJ 07041
Phone: (973)379-1234 **Fax:** (973)379-1913
Products: Liquor. **SIC:** 5182 (Wines & Distilled Beverages). **Est:** 1933. **Sales:** $140,000,000 (2000).
Emp: 300. **Officers:** Michael D. Silverman, President; Louis Healey, CFO; Louis T. DeMarino, Sr. VP of Sales & Marketing; Jeffrey S. Silverman, VP & Operations Mgr.

■ 1780 ■ Paul Jerabek Wholesalers, Inc.
407 9th Ave. SE
Cedar Rapids, IA 52401
Phone: (319)365-7591 **Fax:** (319)365-5750
Products: Beer and wine. **SICs:** 5182 (Wines & Distilled Beverages); 5181 (Beer & Ale).

■ 1781 ■ Jerome Distribution Inc.
PO Box 227
Dickinson, ND 58602-0227
Phone: (701)225-3187 **Fax:** (701)227-0638
Products: Beer; Ale; Malt beverages; Paper and allied products. **SICs:** 5181 (Beer & Ale); 5113 (Industrial & Personal Service Paper). **Officers:** Arthur Jerome, President.

■ 1782 ■ Jerome Wholesales Inc.
PO Box 550
Devils Lake, ND 58301-0550
Phone: (701)662-5366 **Fax:** (701)662-7994
Products: Beer; Malt beverages. **SIC:** 5181 (Beer & Ale). **Officers:** Charles Jerome, President.

■ 1783 ■ Jet Wine and Spirits Inc.
PO Box 1113
Manchester, NH 03105-1113
Phone: (603)669-5884 **Fax:** (603)644-7845
Products: Wine; Distilled liquor. **SIC:** 5182 (Wines & Distilled Beverages). **Officers:** Carmine Martignetti.

■ 1784 ■ JMD Beverages
99-1269 Iwaena St.
Aiea, HI 96701
Phone: (808)487-9985 **Fax:** (808)487-2043
Products: Beer and wine. **SICs:** 5182 (Wines & Distilled Beverages); 5181 (Beer & Ale). **Est:** 1988.
Sales: $3,000,000 (2000). **Emp:** 16.

■ 1785 ■ Johnson Brothers Co. (St. Paul, Minnesota)
2341 University Ave.
St. Paul, MN 55114
Phone: (612)649-5800
Products: Wine and distilled alcohol. **SIC:** 5182 (Wines & Distilled Beverages). **Sales:** $250,000,000 (2000). **Emp:** 800. **Officers:** Lynn Johnson, President; Rich Ackerman, Controller.

■ 1786 ■ Johnson Brothers Liquor Co.
4520 S Church Ave.
Tampa, FL 33611-2201
Phone: (813)884-0451 **Fax:** (813)884-9717
Products: Liquor. **SIC:** 5182 (Wines & Distilled Beverages).

■ 1787 ■ Johnson Brothers Wholesale Liquor
2341 University Ave. W
St. Paul, MN 55114
Phone: (651)649-5800 **Fax:** (651)649-5894
Products: Liquor. **SIC:** 5182 (Wines & Distilled Beverages). **Sales:** $525,000,000 (2000). **Emp:** 1,100.
Officers: Lynn Johnson, President; Scott Belsass, CFO.

■ 1788 ■ Johnson Brothers Wholesale Liquor Co.
2341 University Ave. W
St. Paul, MN 55114
Phone: (612)649-5800 **Fax:** (612)649-5894
Products: Wine and liquor. **SIC:** 5182 (Wines & Distilled Beverages). **Sales:** $525,000,000 (2000).
Officers: Lynn Johnson, CEO; Scott Belsass, CFO; Susan Ewers, Human Resources Contact; Mitchell Johnson, President.

■ 1789 ■ Bill Jones Distributors Inc.
PO Box 97
Sandpoint, ID 83864-0097
Phone: (208)263-5912
Products: Beer; Ale; Malt beverages. **SIC:** 5181 (Beer & Ale). **Officers:** E. Jones, President.

■ 1790 ■ JRB Corp of Lynchburg
PO Box 1240
Verona, VA 24482-1240
Products: Beverages, including beer and wine. **SICs:** 5181 (Beer & Ale); 5182 (Wines & Distilled Beverages).
Est: 1956. **Sales:** $15,000,000 (2000). **Emp:** 46.
Officers: Randy Laird, President. **Former Name:** J and B Distributing Co.

■ 1791 ■ JT Beverage Inc.
PO Box 1526
Jamestown, ND 58402-1526
Phone: (701)252-3040
Products: Beer, ale, and other fermented malt liquors.
SIC: 5181 (Beer & Ale). **Officers:** Jay Thompson, President.

■ 1792 ■ Junction City Distributing Company Inc.
PO Box 186
Junction City, KS 66441
Phone: (785)238-6137
Free: (800)555-6137 **Fax:** (785)238-7892
Products: Beer and ale. **SIC:** 5181 (Beer & Ale). **Est:** 1950. **Sales:** $4,100,000 (2000). **Emp:** 11. **Officers:** Kelly T. Frakes, President; Bill Jones, Finance Officer.

■ 1793 ■ Robert Kacher Selections
3015 V St. NE
Washington, DC 20018
Phone: (202)832-9083
Products: Imported wine. **SIC:** 5182 (Wines & Distilled Beverages).

■ 1794 ■ Katcef Brothers Inc.
2404 A & Eagle Blvd.
Annapolis, MD 21401
Phone: (410)224-2391 **Fax:** (410)224-2399
Products: Beer. **SIC:** 5181 (Beer & Ale). **Est:** 1936.
Sales: $32,000,000 (2000). **Emp:** 76. **Officers:** Sylvia Katcef, President; Lawrie Gardner, Controller; Neal Katcef, VP of Marketing; Gary Jackson, Dir. of Systems.

■ 1795 ■ Kem Distributing Inc.
2604 Causton Bluff Rd.
Savannah, GA 31404
Phone: (912)233-1176   **Fax:** (912)236-1643
E-mail: kem@kemdist.com
Products: Beer; Soft drinks. **SICs:** 5181 (Beer & Ale);
5149 (Groceries & Related Products Nec). **Est:** 1961.
Sales: $16,000,000 (1999). **Emp:** 72. **Officers:** James
Powell, CEO; Dan Smith, Sales Mgr.; Bob Keys, CFO.

■ 1796 ■ Kent
650 36th St. SE
Wyoming, MI 49548
Phone: (616)241-5022   **Fax:** (616)241-5022
Products: Beer, wine, and wine coolers; Soft drinks.s.
SICs: 5182 (Wines & Distilled Beverages); 5181 (Beer
& Ale); 5149 (Groceries & Related Products Nec).

■ 1797 ■ Kings Liquor Inc.
6659 Camp Bowie Blvd.
Ft. Worth, TX 76116
Phone: (817)732-8091   **Fax:** (817)763-5835
Products: Liquor. **SIC:** 5182 (Wines & Distilled
Beverages). **Sales:** $12,000,000 (2000). **Emp:** 55.

■ 1798 ■ Kiva Direct Distribution Inc.
821 W San Mato
Santa Fe, NM 87505-9802
Phone: (505)982-1523   **Fax:** (505)986-1434
Products: Wine. **SIC:** 5182 (Wines & Distilled
Beverages). **Officers:** James Brady, President.

■ 1799 ■ KMC Corp.
2670 Commercial Ave.
Mingo Junction, OH 43938
Phone: (740)598-4171   **Fax:** (740)598-4677
Products: Beer, ale, and wine. **SICs:** 5181 (Beer &
Ale); 5182 (Wines & Distilled Beverages). **Sales:**
$14,000,000 (2000). **Emp:** 50. **Officers:** Michael
Bellas, President; R. Chapman, Sr. VP & CFO.

■ 1800 ■ John Knobel & Son Inc.
3010 Wheatland Terr.
Freeport, IL 61032-2996
Phone: (815)232-4138
Products: Beer. **SIC:** 5181 (Beer & Ale). **Emp:** 5.
Officers: John K. Knobel.

■ 1801 ■ Knoxville Beverage Co.
PO Box 51628
Knoxville, TN 37950-1628
Phone: (423)637-9411   **Fax:** (423)637-9414
Products: Liquor and wine. **SIC:** 5182 (Wines &
Distilled Beverages). **Est:** 1961. **Sales:** $10,000,000
(2000). **Emp:** 25. **Officers:** Orvis Milner, CEO; Michael
B. Milner, President; Nancy Parkos Duthey, Sec. &
Treas.

■ 1802 ■ Kobrand Corp.
134 E 40th St.
New York, NY 10016
Phone: (212)490-9300   **Fax:** (212)867-7916
Products: Spirits; Wine; Champagne; Olive oil. **SICs:**
5182 (Wines & Distilled Beverages); 5149 (Groceries &
Related Products Nec). **Emp:** 150. **Officers:** Charles J.
Palombini, President.

■ 1803 ■ F. Korbel and Bros. Inc.
13250 River Rd.
Guerneville, CA 95446
Phone: (707)887-2294   **Fax:** (707)869-2981
E-mail: info@korbel.com
URL: http://www.korbel.com
Products: Champagne, wine, and brandy. **SIC:** 5182
(Wines & Distilled Beverages). **Est:** 1882. **Sales:**
$80,000,000 (2000). **Emp:** 255. **Officers:** Gary B.
Heck, CEO & President; Dan Baker, Exec. VP; Harold
Duncan, VP of Operations; Margie Healy, Director of
Public Relations.

■ 1804 ■ Kramer Beverage Company Inc.
PO Box 1100
Pleasantville, NJ 08232
Phone: (609)645-2444
Free: (800)321-4522   **Fax:** (609)272-1047
E-mail: info@kramerbeverage.com
URL: http://kramerbeverage.com
Products: Beer. **SIC:** 5181 (Beer & Ale). **Est:** 1924.
Sales: $30,000,000 (2000). **Emp:** 90. **Officers:**

Charles W. Kramer, CEO & President; Lynn P. Kramer,
VP of Finance; Bill Critchfield, Sales Mgr.

■ 1805 ■ Milton S. Kronheim and Co.
2900 V St. NE
Washington, DC 20018
Phone: (202)526-8000
Products: Alcoholic beverages. **SIC:** 5182 (Wines &
Distilled Beverages). **Sales:** $38,000,000 (2000). **Emp:**
90.

■ 1806 ■ Kubota Inc.
4-1300 Kuhio Hwy.
Kapaa, HI 96746
Phone: (808)822-4581
Products: Liquor; Candy; Flowers. **SICs:** 5182 (Wines
& Distilled Beverages); 5193 (Flowers & Florists'
Supplies); 5145 (Confectionery).

■ 1807 ■ Watson Kunda and Sons Inc.
349 S Henderson Rd.
King of Prussia, PA 19406
Phone: (610)265-3113   **Fax:** (610)265-3190
URL: http://www.kundabev.com
Products: Beer; Soda. **SICs:** 5181 (Beer & Ale); 5149
(Groceries & Related Products Nec). **Est:** 1919. **Sales:**
$11,000,000 (2000). **Emp:** 40. **Officers:** W.B. Kunda,
President; Walter E. Kunda Jr., Dir. of Marketing;
Timothy W. Kunda, Dir. of Systems.

■ 1808 ■ L & L Wine & Liquor Corp.
1410 Allen Dr.
Troy, MI 48083-4001
Phone: (248)588-9200
Free: (800)767-1015   **Fax:** (248)588-3363
Products: Wine; Beer. **SICs:** 5182 (Wines & Distilled
Beverages); 5181 (Beer & Ale). **Est:** 1935.

■ 1809 ■ Labatt USA Inc.
23 Old King's Hwy. S
Darien, CT 06820
Phone: (203)750-6600   **Fax:** (203)750-6649
Products: Beer. **SIC:** 5181 (Beer & Ale). **Sales:**
$300,000,000 (2000). **Emp:** 500. **Officers:** Thaine
Preston, President; John Franzino, Finance Officer.

■ 1810 ■ Lagomarsino's Inc.
3810 Transport St.
Ventura, CA 93003
Products: Beverages including beer, soft drinks and
bottled water. **SICs:** 5181 (Beer & Ale); 5149
(Groceries & Related Products Nec). **Sales:**
$25,000,000 (2000). **Emp:** 85. **Officers:** Richard
Lagomarsino, CEO & President; Patricia Bobbitt,
Controller.

■ 1811 ■ Lake Beverage Corp.
900 John St.
West Henrietta, NY 14586-9797
Phone: (716)427-0090   **Fax:** (716)427-0693
Products: Beer and ale. **SIC:** 5181 (Beer & Ale).
Sales: $26,000,000 (2000). **Emp:** 90. **Officers:** Horst
H. Schroeder, President.

■ 1812 ■ Lake Erie Distributors
22 Simon Ave.
Lackawanna, NY 14218-1015
Phone: (716)822-0949   **Fax:** (716)822-0963
Products: Beer. **SIC:** 5181 (Beer & Ale). **Emp:** 49.

**■ 1813 ■ Larrabee Brothers Distributing
   Company Inc.**
PO Box 1850
815 S Blosser Rd.
Santa Maria, CA 93456
Phone: (805)922-2108   **Fax:** (805)925-9214
Products: Beer; Water; Juice. **SICs:** 5181 (Beer &
Ale); 5149 (Groceries & Related Products Nec). **Est:**
1961. **Sales:** $13,000,000 (2000). **Emp:** 55. **Officers:**
Michael Larrabee, President.

■ 1814 ■ Latah Distributors Inc.
220 W Morton St.
Moscow, ID 83843-2004
Phone: (208)882-4021
Products: Beer; Ale; Malt beverages. **SIC:** 5181 (Beer
& Ale). **Officers:** Paul Groves, President.

■ 1815 ■ Latrobe Brewing Company Inc.
119 Jefferson St.
Latrobe, PA 15650
Phone: (412)537-5545   **Fax:** (412)537-4035
Products: Beer. **SIC:** 5181 (Beer & Ale). **Officers:**
Richard Fogarty, President; Richard Vassos, VP of
Marketing; William Lewis, VP of Sales; Robert
Barghaus, VP of Finance & Admin.; Albert Spinelli, VP
of Operations; James Kissock, Controller.

■ 1816 ■ Ledo-Dionysus
PO Box 5708
Denver, CO 80217
Phone: (303)734-2400   **Fax:** (303)734-2662
Products: Liquor; Wine; Beer. **SICs:** 5182 (Wines &
Distilled Beverages); 5181 (Beer & Ale). **Est:** 1980.
Sales: $240,000,000 (2000). **Emp:** 310. **Officers:** Pat
Vogel, President.

■ 1817 ■ Lehrkinds Inc.
PO Box 399
Bozeman, MT 59771-0399
Phone: (406)586-2029   **Fax:** (406)586-7479
Products: Alcoholic beverages. **SIC:** 5181 (Beer &
Ale). **Sales:** $15,000,000 (2000). **Emp:** 50.

■ 1818 ■ Lemma Wine Co.
120 E Market
Portland, OR 97204
Phone: (503)231-4033   **Fax:** (503)231-4040
Products: Wine. **SIC:** 5182 (Wines & Distilled
Beverages).

■ 1819 ■ John Lenore & Co.
1250 Delevan Dr.
San Diego, CA 92102-2437
Phone: (619)232-6136   **Fax:** (619)232-1437
Products: Beverages. **SICs:** 5181 (Beer & Ale); 5182
(Wines & Distilled Beverages). **Emp:** 50.

■ 1820 ■ M. Lichtman and Company Inc.
4529 Crown Rd.
Liverpool, NY 13088
Phone: (315)457-7711   **Fax:** (315)457-6070
Products: Liquor; Wine. **SIC:** 5182 (Wines & Distilled
Beverages). **Sales:** $23,300,000 (2000). **Emp:** 65.
Officers: Lester Eber, CEO.

■ 1821 ■ The Lion Brewery, Inc.
700 N Pennsylvania
Wilkes Barre, PA 18702
Phone: (570)823-8801
Free: (800)233-8327   **Fax:** (570)823-6686
URL: http://www.lionbrewery.com
Products: Malt beverages and specialty soft drinks.
SICs: 5181 (Beer & Ale); 5149 (Groceries & Related
Products Nec). **Est:** 1933. **Sales:** $30,000,000 (2000).
Emp: 125. **Officers:** Charles E. Laswon Jr.; Patrick E.
Belard; Robert Covert, Customer Service Contact.
Former Name: Lion Inc.

■ 1822 ■ Liquid Town
6802 McArdle
Corpus Christi, TX 78412
Phone: (512)991-7932   **Fax:** (512)991-0642
Products: Beverages, including liquor, wine, and beer;
Gift baskets. **SICs:** 5182 (Wines & Distilled
Beverages); 5181 (Beer & Ale).

■ 1823 ■ Litter Distributing Co.
656 Hospital Rd.
Chillicothe, OH 45601
Phone: (740)774-4600   **Fax:** (740)773-2196
Products: Beer. **SIC:** 5181 (Beer & Ale). **Est:** 1951.
Sales: $1,100,000 (2000). **Emp:** 28. **Officers:** Robert
E. Litter, President; Kathleen Litter-Overly, CFO; Auna
Litter-Roseberry, Marketing Mgr.; Bryce Leachman,
Manager.

■ 1824 ■ Litter Industries Inc.
PO Box 297
Chillicothe, OH 45601
Phone: (740)773-2196   **Fax:** (740)773-2196
Products: Beer. **SIC:** 5181 (Beer & Ale). **Sales:**
$13,000,000 (1993). **Emp:** 100. **Officers:** Robert E.
Litter, President; Kathleen Litter-Overly, Finance
Officer.

■ **1825** ■ **Little Rock Distributing Co.**
PO Box 3417
Little Rock, AR 72203
Phone: (501)490-1506
Products: Wine, liquor, and beer. **SICs:** 5182 (Wines & Distilled Beverages); 5181 (Beer & Ale). **Sales:** $15,000,000 (2000). **Emp:** 50. **Officers:** Richard Levi, Vice President.

■ **1826** ■ **J. Lohr Winery**
1000 Lenzen Ave.
San Jose, CA 95126-2739
Phone: (408)288-5057   **Fax:** (408)993-2276
Products: Wine. **SIC:** 5182 (Wines & Distilled Beverages). **Sales:** $7,000,000 (2000). **Emp:** 49. **Officers:** Jerry Lohr.

■ **1827** ■ **Longhorn Liquors, Ltd.**
PO Box 5567
Arlington, TX 76005
Phone: (817)640-5555
Free: (800)777-5415   **Fax:** (817)640-3119
Products: Wine and liquor. **SIC:** 5182 (Wines & Distilled Beverages).

■ **1828** ■ **Lookout Beverages**
PO Box 23448
Chattanooga, TN 37422
Phone: (423)899-3962   **Fax:** (423)892-6127
Products: Liquor, wine, and water products. **SICs:** 5182 (Wines & Distilled Beverages); 5149 (Groceries & Related Products Nec).

■ **1829** ■ **Lovotti Brothers**
1275 Vine St.
Sacramento, CA 95814
Phone: (916)441-3911   **Fax:** (916)441-1426
Products: Wine, juices, and soda. **SICs:** 5182 (Wines & Distilled Beverages); 5149 (Groceries & Related Products Nec). **Officers:** Bob Biko.

■ **1830** ■ **Luce and Son Inc.**
2399 Valley Rd.
Reno, NV 89512
Phone: (702)785-7810   **Fax:** (702)785-7834
Products: Wine and distilled beverages. **SIC:** 5182 (Wines & Distilled Beverages). **Officers:** Cherry Luce, Chairman of the Board.

■ **1831** ■ **Luce and Son Inc.**
2399 Valley Rd.
Reno, NV 89512
Phone: (775)785-7810   **Fax:** (775)785-7834
Products: Beer, wine and liquor. **SICs:** 5181 (Beer & Ale); 5182 (Wines & Distilled Beverages). **Sales:** $30,000,000 (2000). **Emp:** 100. **Officers:** Gerald F. Hicks, President; Garry Hicks, Controller.

■ **1832** ■ **A.M. Lutheran Distributors Inc.**
1130 Lebanon Rd.
West Mifflin, PA 15122
Phone: (412)461-3133
Products: Beer; Soda; Water; Chips; Peanuts. **SICs:** 5181 (Beer & Ale); 5149 (Groceries & Related Products Nec); 5145 (Confectionery).

■ **1833** ■ **M and M Distributors Inc.**
PO Box 80077
Lansing, MI 48908
Phone: (517)322-9010   **Fax:** (517)322-0359
Products: Beer. **SIC:** 5181 (Beer & Ale). **Sales:** $30,000,000 (2000). **Emp:** 100. **Officers:** Andy McMillan, Owner; Doug Barr, General Mgr.

■ **1834** ■ **Maddalena Vineyard/San Antonio Winery**
737 Lamar St.
Los Angeles, CA 90031
Phone: (323)223-1401   **Fax:** (323)221-5957
Products: Wine. **SIC:** 5182 (Wines & Distilled Beverages). **Officers:** Robert Michero, Director.

■ **1835** ■ **Madison Bottling Co.**
616 8th St.
Madison, MN 56256
Phone: (320)598-7573   **Fax:** (320)598-3738
Products: Soft drinks; Beer; Nuts and seeds. **SICs:** 5181 (Beer & Ale); 5182 (Wines & Distilled Beverages). **Est:** 1917. **Sales:** $4,500,000 (2000). **Emp:** 12.

Officers: Roland Roth, President; Tim Roth, Treasurer & Secty.

■ **1836** ■ **Magic City Beverage Co.**
PO Box 1208
Minot, ND 58702-1208
Phone: (701)852-4031   **Fax:** (701)852-2297
Products: Beer; Ale; Malt beverages. **SIC:** 5181 (Beer & Ale). **Officers:** Cyrel Butz, Chairman of the Board.

■ **1837** ■ **Magnolia Distributing Co.**
249 N State Route 2
New Martinsville, WV 26155-2203
Phone: (304)455-2581   **Fax:** (304)455-2583
Products: Beer. **SIC:** 5181 (Beer & Ale). **Emp:** 3.

■ **1838** ■ **Magnolia Liquor Lafayette Inc.**
209 Lucille Ave.
PO Box 3587
Lafayette, LA 70502
Phone: (318)233-9244   **Fax:** (318)261-1870
Products: Liquor; Wine; Beer. **SICs:** 5182 (Wines & Distilled Beverages); 5181 (Beer & Ale). **Est:** 1946. **Emp:** 136. **Officers:** Forrest K. Dowty; William Goldring; Tom Cole; Tom Dailey.

■ **1839** ■ **Magnolia Marketing Co.**
PO Box 53333
New Orleans, LA 70153
Phone: (504)837-1500   **Fax:** (504)830-0114
Products: Liquor; Non-alcoholic beverages. **SICs:** 5182 (Wines & Distilled Beverages); 5149 (Groceries & Related Products Nec). **Sales:** $290,000,000 (2000). **Emp:** 950. **Officers:** Tom Cole, President; Clyde Giesenchlag, Treasurer; Fred Goodyear, Sr. VP of Marketing & Sales; Ed Umbenstock, Dir. of Data Processing; Erick May, Dir of Human Resources.

■ **1840** ■ **Maine Distributing Co.**
5 Coffey St.
Bangor, ME 04401
Phone: (207)947-4563
Products: Beer. **SIC:** 5181 (Beer & Ale).

■ **1841** ■ **Maisons Marques and Domaines USA Inc.**
383 4th St., Ste. 400
Oakland, CA 94607
Phone: (510)286-2000   **Fax:** (510)286-2010
URL: http://www.mmdusa.net
Products: Wine. **SIC:** 5182 (Wines & Distilled Beverages). **Est:** 1987. **Sales:** $40,000,000 (2000). **Emp:** 26. **Officers:** Jean Claude Rouzaud, President & Chairman of the Board; Guillaume Fouilleron, CFO & Treasurer; Gregory Balogh, COO & VP.

■ **1842** ■ **Major Brands**
6701 Southwest Ave.
St. Louis, MO 63143
Phone: (314)645-1843   **Fax:** (314)647-0027
Products: Wines, liquor, and beer. **SICs:** 5182 (Wines & Distilled Beverages); 5181 (Beer & Ale).

■ **1843** ■ **Major Brands**
1502 Old Hwy. 40 W
Columbia, MO 65202
Phone: (573)443-3169   **Fax:** (573)874-1035
Products: Wine and liquor; Water. **SICs:** 5182 (Wines & Distilled Beverages); 5149 (Groceries & Related Products Nec).

■ **1844** ■ **Major Brands**
550 E 13th Ave.
Kansas City, MO 64116
Phone: (816)221-1070   **Fax:** (816)421-1062
E-mail: spirits@unicom.net
Products: Alcoholic beverages, including beer, wine, liquor, and mixes; Bottled water. **SICs:** 5182 (Wines & Distilled Beverages); 5181 (Beer & Ale); 5149 (Groceries & Related Products Nec). **Officers:** Brad Epsten, Exec. VP & COO.

■ **1845** ■ **Major Brands-Cape Girardeau**
PO Box 818
Cape Girardeau, MO 63702-0818
Phone: (314)335-8079
Free: (800)264-8079   **Fax:** (314)335-2192
Products: Wine and liquor. **SIC:** 5182 (Wines & Distilled Beverages). **Sales:** $6,000,000 (2000). **Emp:**

16. **Officers:** Ken Tallent, General Mgr.; Teresa Crump, Customer Service Contact; Robin Balsmann, Dir of Human Resources.

■ **1846** ■ **Joe G. Maloof & Co.**
523 Commercial NE
PO Box 1086
Albuquerque, NM 87103-1086
Phone: (505)243-2293   **Fax:** (505)768-1552
Products: Beer; Ale; Malt beverages. **SIC:** 5181 (Beer & Ale). **Officers:** Joseph Maloof, President.

■ **1847** ■ **Manhattan Distributing Co.**
11675 Fairgrove Industrial Blvd.
Maryland Heights, MO 63043
Phone: (314)567-1400   **Fax:** (314)567-4541
Products: Wine and liquor. **SIC:** 5182 (Wines & Distilled Beverages). **Sales:** $41,500,000 (2000). **Emp:** 100. **Officers:** Nolan Crane, President; Doug Corley, Controller.

■ **1848** ■ **Maple City Ice Co.**
370 Cleveland Rd.
Norwalk, OH 44857
Phone: (419)668-2531   **Fax:** (419)668-5291
Products: Beer. **SIC:** 5181 (Beer & Ale). **Est:** 1917. **Sales:** $30,000,000 (2000). **Emp:** 90. **Officers:** Patricia A. Hipp, President; Jeffrey Hipp, Treasurer & Secty.

■ **1849** ■ **Maris Distributing Co.**
3820 NE 49th Rd.
Gainesville, FL 32609-1606
Phone: (352)378-2431   **Fax:** (352)378-5155
Products: Beer. **SIC:** 5181 (Beer & Ale). **Est:** 1968. **Sales:** $50,000,000 (2000). **Emp:** 100. **Officers:** Rudolph M. Maris.

■ **1850** ■ **Mark V Distributors Inc.**
3093 Kennesaw St.
Ft. Myers, FL 33916
Phone: (941)334-3511
Products: Beer; Wine. **SICs:** 5181 (Beer & Ale); 5149 (Groceries & Related Products Nec). **Est:** 1971. **Sales:** $23,000,000 (2000). **Emp:** 100. **Officers:** William G. Magerum, CEO; Alan Okun, Vice President.

■ **1851** ■ **Markstein Beverage Co.**
505 S Pacific St.
San Marcos, CA 92069
Phone: (760)744-9100   **Fax:** (760)744-0082
Products: Beer. **SIC:** 5181 (Beer & Ale). **Est:** 1918. **Sales:** $30,000,000 (2000). **Emp:** 95. **Officers:** Kenneth Markstein, President; Don Bale, VP of Marketing & Sales.

■ **1852** ■ **Markstein Beverage Company of Sacramento**
60 Main Ave.
Sacramento, CA 95838
Phone: (916)920-9070
Products: Beer; Bottled water. **SICs:** 5181 (Beer & Ale); 5149 (Groceries & Related Products Nec).

■ **1853** ■ **Martini and Prati Wines Inc.**
2191 Laguna Rd.
Santa Rosa, CA 95401
Phone: (707)823-2404   **Fax:** (707)829-8662
Products: Wine. **SIC:** 5182 (Wines & Distilled Beverages). **Est:** 1951. **Sales:** $1,500,000 (2000). **Emp:** 49.

■ **1854** ■ **Mason Distributing Company**
PO Box 183
Soda Springs, ID 83276-0183
Phone: (208)547-4516   **Fax:** (208)547-4522
Products: Beer and ale. **SIC:** 5181 (Beer & Ale). **Officers:** David Mason, President.

■ **1855** ■ **Mautino Distributing Company Inc.**
500 N Richard St.
Spring Valley, IL 61362
Phone: (815)664-4311   **Fax:** (815)664-2224
Products: Beer; Soda; Glassware. **SICs:** 5181 (Beer & Ale); 5149 (Groceries & Related Products Nec); 5023 (Homefurnishings). **Sales:** $15,000,000 (2000). **Emp:** 30. **Officers:** Anton Mautino, CEO.

■ **1856** ■ **Mayflower Wines & Spirits**
3201 New Mexico Ave. NW
Washington, DC 20016
Phone: (202)363-5800   **Fax:** (202)363-7060
Products: Beer; Wine. **SICs:** 5182 (Wines & Distilled Beverages); 5181 (Beer & Ale).

■ **1857** ■ **McBride Distributing Co.**
PO Box 1403
Fayetteville, AR 72702-0336
Phone: (501)521-2500   **Fax:** (501)521-5350
Products: Beer. **SIC:** 5181 (Beer & Ale). **Est:** 1949. **Sales:** $16,000,000 (2000). **Emp:** 40. **Officers:** Robert O. McBride, CEO; Debbie West, CFO; Angela Ryan, Dir. of Marketing; Ben Thompson, Dir. of Systems; Cheryl McBride.

■ **1858** ■ **McClaskeys Wine Spirits & Cigars Distributor**
930 NW 14th Ave.
Portland, OR 97209-2704
Phone: (503)224-3150   **Fax:** (503)224-2447
E-mail: mcwine@teleport.com
Products: Wine and liquor. **SIC:** 5182 (Wines & Distilled Beverages). **Est:** 1975. **Emp:** 38. **Officers:** Mike McClaskey, President; Donna McClaskey, Vice President; Dale Rouse, General Mgr.; Kim McClaskey-Dowdall, Manager; Pat McClaskey, Triad Downstate Gen. Mgr.; Randy Webster, District Mgr.

■ **1859** ■ **McCormick Beverage Co.**
PO Box 1346
Woodland, CA 95776-1346
Phone: (916)666-3263
Products: Beer. **SIC:** 5181 (Beer & Ale). **Sales:** $9,000,000 (2000). **Emp:** 30. **Officers:** Chuck Santoni, President.

■ **1860** ■ **McCormick Distilling Company Inc.**
1 McCormick Ln.
Weston, MO 64098
Phone: (816)386-2276   **Fax:** (816)386-2402
Products: Liquor; Distilled liquor. **SIC:** 5182 (Wines & Distilled Beverages). **Sales:** $5,000,000 (2000). **Emp:** 80. **Officers:** J. Hosier, President; Russel A. French, VP of Finance & Admin.; Charles A. Wittwer, VP of Sales.

■ **1861** ■ **Wilson McGinley Inc.**
36th & Allegheny R. R.
Pittsburgh, PA 15201
Phone: (412)621-4420
Products: Beer. **SIC:** 5181 (Beer & Ale). **Sales:** $5,000,000 (2000). **Emp:** 45. **Officers:** J.R. McGinley, President.

■ **1862** ■ **McLaughlin and Moran Inc.**
PO Box 20217
Cranston, RI 02920
Phone: (401)463-5454
Products: Beer. **SIC:** 5181 (Beer & Ale). **Est:** 1936. **Sales:** $37,000,000 (2000). **Emp:** 125. **Officers:** Paul P. Moran, President; Jeff Wingare, Comptroller; Charles Borkoski, Dir. of Marketing.

■ **1863** ■ **McQuade Distributing Company, Inc.**
1150 Industrial Dr.
Bismarck, ND 58501
Phone: (701)223-6850   **Fax:** (701)223-6624
Products: Beer. **SIC:** 5181 (Beer & Ale). **Est:** 1947. **Sales:** $8,000,000 (2000). **Emp:** 21. **Officers:** Sam McQuade, President.

■ **1864** ■ **McQuade Distributing Company Inc.**
1150 Industrial Dr.
Bismarck, ND 58501
Phone: (701)223-6850   **Fax:** (701)223-6624
Products: Alcoholic beverages. **SIC:** 5181 (Beer & Ale). **Sales:** $8,000,000 (2000). **Emp:** 21.

■ **1865** ■ **Mendez & Co. Inc.**
PO Box 3348
San Juan, PR 00936-3348
Phone: (787)793-8888   **Fax:** (787)783-9498
Products: Liquor, beer, groceries and construction materials. **SICs:** 5182 (Wines & Distilled Beverages); 5181 (Beer & Ale); 5141 (Groceries—General Line); 5039 (Construction Materials Nec). **Est:** 1912. **Sales:**

$175,000,000 (2000). **Emp:** 500. **Officers:** Jose A. Alvarez, President; Pablo J. Alvarez, Treasurer.

■ **1866** ■ **Merchant du Vin Corp.**
18436 Cascade Ave., S, No. 140
Tukwila, WA 98188-4729
Phone: (206)322-5022   **Fax:** (206)322-5185
Products: Beer. **SIC:** 5181 (Beer & Ale). **Sales:** $25,000,000 (2000). **Emp:** 70. **Officers:** Rich Hamilton, President; Chris Britton, CFO.

■ **1867** ■ **Merrimack Valley Distributing Company Inc.**
PO Box 417
Danvers, MA 01923
Phone: (978)777-2213
Products: Beer, liquor, and wine. **SICs:** 5181 (Beer & Ale); 5182 (Wines & Distilled Beverages). **Est:** 1933. **Sales:** $45,000,000 (2000). **Emp:** 100. **Officers:** Richard Tatelman, President & CFO; Jack Tatelman, Dir. of Marketing & Sales.

■ **1868** ■ **Metabran**
94-501 Kau St.
Waipahu, HI 96797
Phone: (808)676-6111   **Fax:** (808)676-6199
Products: Liquor; Wine. **SIC:** 5182 (Wines & Distilled Beverages).

■ **1869** ■ **Metz Beverage Company Inc.**
302 N Custer St.
Sheridan, WY 82801
Phone: (307)672-5848   **Fax:** (307)672-6405
Products: Beer; Ale; Malt beverages. **SIC:** 5181 (Beer & Ale). **Officers:** Diana Metz, President.

■ **1870** ■ **Metz Beverage Company Inc.**
302 N Custer St.
Sheridan, WY 82801
Phone: (307)672-5848
Products: Beer, ale and soda. **SICs:** 5181 (Beer & Ale); 5149 (Groceries & Related Products Nec). **Sales:** $18,000,000 (2000). **Emp:** 50. **Officers:** Diana Metz, President.

■ **1871** ■ **Mid-America Wine Co.**
3705 N Kenmore
Chicago, IL 60613
Phone: (773)327-7160   **Fax:** (773)327-7168
Products: Wine. **SIC:** 5182 (Wines & Distilled Beverages). **Officers:** Dennis Styck.

■ **1872** ■ **Mid-South Malts/Memphis Brews Inc.**
2537 Broad Ave.
Memphis, TN 38112
Phone: (901)324-2739
Products: Malts and home brewing ingredients. **SICs:** 5181 (Beer & Ale); 5149 (Groceries & Related Products Nec); 5153 (Grain & Field Beans). **Sales:** $500,000 (2000). **Emp:** 2. **Officers:** Ed Porter, President; Chuck Skypeck, Treasurer & Secty.

■ **1873** ■ **Mid State Distributors Inc.**
PO Box 5886
Columbia, SC 29250
Phone: (803)771-6100
Products: Beer. **SIC:** 5181 (Beer & Ale). **Sales:** $6,000,000 (1994). **Emp:** 23. **Officers:** Tally A. Easler Jr., President & Chairman of the Board.

■ **1874** ■ **Midland Bottling Co.**
1422 S 6th
St. Joseph, MO 64501-3638
Phone: (816)232-8477
Free: (800)799-4899   **Fax:** (816)364-3794
Products: Beer. **SIC:** 5181 (Beer & Ale). **Emp:** 21. **Officers:** Delbert Harvey.

■ **1875** ■ **Midstate Beverage Inc.**
5200 Franklin Ave.
Waco, TX 76710-6924
Phone: (254)753-0305   **Fax:** (254)753-4957
Products: Beer. **SIC:** 5181 (Beer & Ale). **Est:** 1963. **Sales:** $10,000,000 (2000). **Emp:** 40. **Officers:** Michael W. Dicorte, President; Stan Tindell, Treasurer & Secty.

■ **1876** ■ **Midwest Beverage Company Inc.**
14200 E Moncrieff Pl.
Aurora, CO 80011
Phone: (303)371-0832   **Fax:** (303)371-8106
Products: Wine; Liquor; Beer. **SICs:** 5182 (Wines & Distilled Beverages); 5181 (Beer & Ale). **Former Name:** Rocky Mountain Wine & Spirits.

■ **1877** ■ **Miller Brands**
31281 Wiegman Rd.
Hayward, CA 94544-7809
Phone: (510)489-1919   **Fax:** (510)489-9084
Products: Beer. **SIC:** 5181 (Beer & Ale). **Emp:** 49. **Officers:** Mike McKay; Walter Markstein.

■ **1878** ■ **Miller-Brands-Milwaukee L.L.C.**
1400 N 113th St.
Wauwatosa, WI 53226
Phone: (414)258-2337   **Fax:** (414)443-2100
Products: Beer. **SIC:** 5181 (Beer & Ale). **Est:** 1994. **Sales:** $45,000,000 (2000). **Emp:** 150. **Officers:** Paul Roller, President; Bruce Bolander, Accountant.

■ **1879** ■ **Miller of Dallas Inc.**
2730 Irving Blvd.
Dallas, TX 75207
Phone: (214)630-0777
Products: Beer. **SIC:** 5181 (Beer & Ale). **Sales:** $55,000,000 (2000). **Emp:** 185. **Officers:** Barry Andrews, President.

■ **1880** ■ **Miller Distributing Ft. Worth**
PO Box 3062
Ft. Worth, TX 76113
Phone: (817)877-5960
Products: Beer. **SIC:** 5181 (Beer & Ale).

■ **1881** ■ **Mirabile Beverage Company Inc.**
710 E Main St.
Norristown, PA 19401
Phone: (215)275-0285   **Fax:** (215)275-8562
Products: Beer. **SIC:** 5181 (Beer & Ale). **Emp:** 499. **Officers:** A. J. Mirabile; J. A. Mirabile; P. J. Mirabile; H. P. Mirabile.

■ **1882** ■ **Miramar Trading International Inc.**
400 Foam St., Ste. 210
Monterey, CA 93940
Phone: (831)655-5450   **Fax:** (831)655-1449
Products: Distilled spirits. **SIC:** 5182 (Wines & Distilled Beverages).

■ **1883** ■ **Mirassou Sales Co.**
3000 Aborn Rd.
San Jose, CA 95135
Phone: (408)274-4000
Free: (888)647-2776   **Fax:** (408)270-5881
E-mail: email@mirassou.com
URL: http://www.mirassou.com
Products: Wine. **SIC:** 5182 (Wines & Distilled Beverages). **Est:** 1964. **Sales:** $13,000,000 (1999). **Emp:** 80. **Officers:** Daniel Mirassou, President; James Mirassou, VP of Finance & Admin.; Peter Mirassou, VP of Production; Heather Mirassou, Dir. of Marketing; John Corcoran, Sales Mgr.

■ **1884** ■ **Missouri Conrad Liquors**
1200 Taney
Kansas City, MO 64116-4413
Phone: (816)421-1145   **Fax:** (816)421-1336
Products: Liquor; Wine. **SIC:** 5182 (Wines & Distilled Beverages). **Emp:** 49. **Officers:** M. A. Rhoades.

■ **1885** ■ **Mobile Beer & Wine Co.**
966 N Beltline Hwy.
Mobile, AL 36607-1109
Phone: (205)471-3486
Products: Beer; Wine. **SICs:** 5181 (Beer & Ale); 5182 (Wines & Distilled Beverages). **Sales:** $30,000,000 (2000). **Emp:** 99. **Officers:** Pat Looney.

■ **1886** ■ **Preston I. Moffett Co.**
PO Box 2870
Winchester, VA 22604
Phone: (540)662-7724   **Fax:** (540)722-2687
Products: Beer. **SIC:** 5181 (Beer & Ale). **Emp:** 49.

■ 1887 ■   **Mohawk Distilled Products L.P.**
11900 Biscayne Blvd., No. 600
North Miami, FL 33181-2726
Phone: (305)893-3394   **Fax:** (305)891-6577
E-mail: mariebrizard@worldnet.att.net
URL: http://www.mariebrizard.com
Products: Wine; Liquor. **SIC:** 5182 (Wines & Distilled
Beverages). **Est:** 1989. **Sales:** $45,000,000 (2000).
Emp: 25. **Officers:** Hubert Surville, President; Edward
Brozic, Exec. VP & CFO; Michael Avitable, VP of
Marketing Director; Albert Biehler, Dir. of MIS; Paul
Berkowitz, Sr. VP. **Doing Business As:** Marie #Brizard
Wine & Spirits, USA.

■ 1888 ■   **Monarch Beverage Inc.**
PO Box 18434
Las Vegas, NV 89114-8434
Phone: (702)731-1040   **Fax:** (702)732-8719
Products: Beer and ale; Fermented malt liquors;
Beverages. **SICs:** 5181 (Beer & Ale); 5182 (Wines &
Distilled Beverages); 5149 (Groceries & Related
Products Nec). **Officers:** W. Wirtz, President.

■ 1889 ■   **Monarch Wine Company of Georgia**
6300 Powers Ferry Rd., NW, No. 600-147
Atlanta, GA 30339-2946
Phone: (404)622-4661   **Fax:** (404)622-5421
Products: Fruit and berry wines; Specialty wines;
Wine. **SIC:** 5182 (Wines & Distilled Beverages). **Sales:**
$15,000,000 (2000). **Emp:** 55. **Officers:** H. J.
Weinstein; David Paszamant; Jack Griffin.

■ 1890 ■   **Monsieur Touton Selections, LTD**
129 W 27th St. 9th Flr.
New York, NY 10001
Phone: (212)255-0674   **Fax:** (212)255-2628
E-mail: touton@msn.com
Products: Imported wine and spirits. **SIC:** 5182 (Wines
& Distilled Beverages). **Est:** 1983. **Sales:** $30,000,000
(1999). **Emp:** 95. **Officers:** Alain Trelford,
Sales/Marketing Contact; Marie Helena, Customer
Service Contact; Neil Amaruso, Human Resources
Contact.

■ 1891 ■   **Montgomery Beverage Co.**
3181 Selma Hwy.
Montgomery, AL 36108-5003
Phone: (205)284-0550   **Fax:** (205)284-5149
Products: Beer; Wine; Liquor. **SICs:** 5181 (Beer &
Ale); 5182 (Wines & Distilled Beverages). **Emp:** 49.

■ 1892 ■   **Moon Distributors Inc.**
2800 Vance St.
Little Rock, AR 72206
Phone: (501)375-8291
Products: Liquor. **SICs:** 5181 (Beer & Ale); 5182
(Wines & Distilled Beverages). **Est:** 1935. **Sales:**
$30,000,000 (2000). **Emp:** 100. **Officers:** Stanley
Hastings, President; Phil Holder, Controller.

■ 1893 ■   **James Moroney, Inc.**
243-47 N 63rd St.
Philadelphia, PA 19139
Phone: (215)471-5300   **Fax:** (215)471-5336
Products: Wine. **SIC:** 5182 (Wines & Distilled
Beverages).

■ 1894 ■   **Morrey Distributing Co.**
1850 E Lincoln Way
Sparks, NV 89434-8944
Phone: (702)352-6000   **Fax:** (702)352-6010
Products: Beer and ale. **SIC:** 5181 (Beer & Ale).
Officers: Joseph Morrey, Chairman of the Board.

■ 1895 ■   **Mounthood Beverage Co.**
3601 NW Yeon Ave.
Portland, OR 97210
Phone: (503)274-9990
Free: (800)788-9992   **Fax:** (503)727-3234
URL: http://www.mhbco.com
Products: Beer, ale, wine and bottled water. **SICs:**
5181 (Beer & Ale); 5182 (Wines & Distilled Beverages);
5149 (Groceries & Related Products Nec). **Est:** 1990.
Sales: $145,000,000 (2000). **Emp:** 535. **Officers:**
Richard Lytle, President; Lou Wood, CFO.

■ 1896 ■   **MRR Traders, Ltd.**
69 Inner Belt Rd.
Somerville, MA 02143
Phone: (617)666-5939   **Fax:** (617)666-8713
Products: Wine. **SIC:** 5182 (Wines & Distilled
Beverages). **Officers:** William D. Friedberg.

■ 1897 ■   **Mutual Distributing Co.**
2233 Capital Blvd.
PO Box 26446
Raleigh, NC 27611
Phone: (919)828-3842
Free: (800)662-7609   **Fax:** (919)832-2813
URL: http://www.MutualDistributing.com
Products: Wine and malt liquor. **SICs:** 5182 (Wines &
Distilled Beverages); 5181 (Beer & Ale). **Est:** 1946.
Emp: 500. **Officers:** William T. Kennedy, CEO &
President,   e-mail: WKennedy@Mutual-
Distributing.com.

■ 1898 ■   **Ben Myerson Candy Co.**
928 Towne Ave.
Los Angeles, CA 90021
Phone: (213)623-6266
Free: (800)421-8448   **Fax:** (213)688-7571
Products: Candy; Wine. **SIC:** 5182 (Wines & Distilled
Beverages). **Sales:** $12,000,000 (2000). **Emp:** 120.
Officers: Robert Myerson, Chairman of the Board.

■ 1899 ■   **Fred Nackard Wholesale Beverage
Co.**
4900 E Railhead Ave.
Flagstaff, AZ 86001
Phone: (602)526-2229
Products: Beverages, including liquor, wine, beer, and
water. **SICs:** 5181 (Beer & Ale); 5182 (Wines & Distilled
Beverages); 5149 (Groceries & Related Products Nec).
Sales: $10,000,000 (2000). **Emp:** 35. **Officers:** P.
Nackard, President.

■ 1900 ■   **Fred Nackard Wholesale Beverage
Co.**
4900 E Railhead Ave.
Flagstaff, AZ 86001
Phone: (602)526-2229
Products: Alcoholic beverages. **SIC:** 5181 (Beer &
Ale). **Sales:** $10,000,000 (2000). **Emp:** 35.

■ 1901 ■   **National Beverage Company Inc.**
310 Back St.
Thibodaux, LA 70301
Phone: (504)447-4179
Products: Beer. **SIC:** 5181 (Beer & Ale). **Est:** 1958.
Sales: $10,000,000 (2000). **Emp:** 35. **Officers:** Joseph
A. Badeaux, Chairman of the Board; Thomas L.
Badeaux, President; Thomas B. Goulas, Sales Mgr.

■ 1902 ■   **National Distributing Co.**
4901 Savarese Circle N
Tampa, FL 33634
Phone: (813)885-3200
Free: (800)223-0201   **Fax:** (813)884-6063
URL: http://www.ndcweb.com
Products: Liquor, beer, and wine; Cigarss. **SICs:** 5182
(Wines & Distilled Beverages); 5181 (Beer & Ale); 5194
(Tobacco & Tobacco Products). **Emp:** 280. **Officers:**
Shai Froelich, e-mail: shari.froelich@natdistco.com.

■ 1903 ■   **National Distributing Co.**
3601 Silver Star Rd.
Orlando, FL 32808
Phone: (407)298-2300
Free: (800)522-2026   **Fax:** (407)291-8497
Products: Liquor and wine. **SIC:** 5182 (Wines &
Distilled Beverages). **Officers:** Jerry Alexander.

■ 1904 ■   **National Distributing Co.**
6256 N W St.
Pensacola, FL 32505
Phone: (850)476-1118
Free: (800)342-5208   **Fax:** (850)477-7323
Products: Liquor and wine. **SIC:** 5182 (Wines &
Distilled Beverages). **Officers:** Curtis Flower.

■ 1905 ■   **National Distributing Co.**
9423 N Main St.
Jacksonville, FL 32218
Phone: (904)751-0090
Free: (800)342-9490   **Fax:** (904)757-7276
Products: Liquor and wine. **SIC:** 5182 (Wines &
Distilled Beverages). **Officers:** Debbie Humphries.

■ 1906 ■   **National Distributing Company, Inc.**
4235 Sheriff Rd. NE
Washington, DC 20019
Phone: (202)388-8400   **Fax:** (202)396-0810
URL: http://www.ndcweb.com
Products: Wine, liquor, beer, and champagne. **SICs:**
5182 (Wines & Distilled Beverages); 5181 (Beer & Ale).
Est: 1935. **Sales:** $100,000,000 (2000). **Emp:** 230.
Officers: Michael C. Carlos, CEO. **Former Name:**
Forman Brothers Inc.

■ 1907 ■   **National Distributing Company Inc.**
PO Box 44127
Atlanta, GA 30336
Phone: (404)696-9440
Free: (800)282-3548   **Fax:** (404)691-0364
URL: http://www.natdistco.com
Products: Wine; Liquor. **SICs:** 5182 (Wines & Distilled
Beverages); 5181 (Beer & Ale). **Est:** 1942. **Sales:**
$310,000,000 (2000). **Emp:** 1,000. **Officers:** Michael
C. Carlos, CEO & Chairman of the Board; Andrew
Carlos, Exec. VP & Treasurer; John C. Carlos, Exec.
VP & COO; J.M. Davis, Chairman of the Board &
President.

■ 1908 ■   **National Distributing Co. Inc.**
441 SW 12th Ave.
Deerfield Beach, FL 33442
Free: (800)432-8814   **Fax:** (954)425-7777
Products: Liquor and wine. **SIC:** 5182 (Wines &
Distilled Beverages). **Officers:** Chris Kearney.

■ 1909 ■   **National Distributing Company Inc.**
PO Box 27227
Albuquerque, NM 87125
Phone: (505)345-4492   **Fax:** (505)344-7299
Products: Spirits, wine, and beer. **SICs:** 5182 (Wines
& Distilled Beverages); 5181 (Beer & Ale). **Officers:**
Patrick Vogel.

■ 1910 ■   **National Distributing Inc.**
116 Wallace Ave.
South Portland, ME 04106
Phone: (207)773-1719   **Fax:** (207)775-4413
URL: http://www.nat-dist.com
Products: Beer; Wine. **SICs:** 5182 (Wines & Distilled
Beverages); 5181 (Beer & Ale). **Est:** 1960. **Emp:** 125.
Officers: Frank Gaziano, Chairman of the Board;
Jeffrey Kane, President.

■ 1911 ■   **Nebraska Wine & Spirits Inc.**
4444 S 94th St.
Omaha, NE 68127-1209
Phone: (402)339-9444   **Fax:** (402)593-0209
Products: Wines and spirits, including non-alcoholic
beverages. **SICs:** 5182 (Wines & Distilled Beverages);
5149 (Groceries & Related Products Nec). **Emp:** 71.
Officers: Harold Epstein; Paul Epstein; Gary Epstein.

■ 1912 ■   **Nevada Beverage Co.**
PO Box 93538
Las Vegas, NV 89193
Phone: (702)739-9474   **Fax:** (702)739-7345
Products: Beer; Ale; Bottled water. **SICs:** 5181 (Beer
& Ale); 5149 (Groceries & Related Products Nec). **Est:**
1945. **Sales:** $61,000,000 (2000). **Emp:** 200. **Officers:**
Pat Clark, President.

■ 1913 ■   **New Belgium Brewing Co**
500 Linden St.
Ft. Collins, CO 80524
Phone: (970)221-0524   **Fax:** (970)221-0535
Products: Ale. **SIC:** 5181 (Beer & Ale). **Officers:** Jeff
Lebesch, President.

■ 1914 ■ New England Wine & Spirits
29 Ciro Rd.
PO Box 660
North Branford, CT 06471-0660
Phone: (203)488-7155 **Fax:** (203)483-1496
Products: Wine. **SIC:** 5182 (Wines & Distilled Beverages).

■ 1915 ■ New Hampshire Distributor Inc.
PO Box 267
Concord, NH 03302-0267
Phone: (603)224-9991 **Fax:** (603)224-8306
Products: Beer. **SIC:** 5181 (Beer & Ale). **Est:** 1946.
Emp: 100. **Officers:** C. Thomas Brown, President & CEO; Robert C. Hayes, VP of Finance; Jack A. Philbrick, Sr. VP of Marketing & Sales; Jack A. Philbrick Sr., Sr. VP of Marketing & Sales.

■ 1916 ■ New World Wines
2 Henry Adams St., Ste. M58
San Francisco, CA 94103
Phone: (415)863-2220
Free: (800)334-9463 **Fax:** (415)863-7176
Products: Wine, beer, and spirits. **SICs:** 5182 (Wines & Distilled Beverages); 5181 (Beer & Ale). **Sales:** $4,200,000 (2000). **Emp:** 7. **Officers:** Anna D. Everett, Treasurer.

■ 1917 ■ Austin Nichols and Company Inc.
156 East 46th St.
New York, NY 10017
Phone: (212)455-9400 **Fax:** (212)455-9421
Products: Beverages, including wine, liquor, and soft drinks. **SICs:** 5182 (Wines & Distilled Beverages); 5149 (Groceries & Related Products Nec). **Est:** 1855. **Sales:** $50,000,000 (2000). **Emp:** 170. **Officers:** M Bord, CEO & President; A Gold, VP & CFO; Bruce Schwartz, VP of Marketing.

■ 1918 ■ Nittany Beverage Co.
139 N Patterson
State College, PA 16801-3757
Phone: (814)238-3031 **Fax:** (814)238-4534
E-mail: www.nittanybeverage.com
Products: Beer; Beverages. **SICs:** 5181 (Beer & Ale); 5149 (Groceries & Related Products Nec). **Est:** 1968. **Emp:** 25. **Officers:** Jim Reeder, President.

■ 1919 ■ N.K.S. Distributors Inc.
PO Box 758
New Castle, DE 19720
Phone: (302)322-1811 **Free:** (800)292-9509
Products: Beer; Alcoholic wine coolers; Wine; Liquor. **SICs:** 5181 (Beer & Ale); 5182 (Wines & Distilled Beverages). **Est:** 1950. **Sales:** $45,000,000 (2000). **Emp:** 150. **Officers:** James V. Tigani Jr., President; Leo Renzette, Controller; Robert Tigani, VP & General Merchandising Mgr.

■ 1920 ■ Northern Beverage
250 Anton St.
Coeur D Alene, ID 83815
Phone: (208)765-8100 **Fax:** (208)765-6999
E-mail: northbev@televar.com
Products: Beer and wine. **SICs:** 5182 (Wines & Distilled Beverages); 5181 (Beer & Ale). **Est:** 1985. **Sales:** $5,000,000 (1999). **Emp:** 23. **Officers:** G. Dale Scarlett.

■ 1921 ■ Northern Distributing Co.
PO Box 315
Glens Falls, NY 12801
Phone: (518)792-3112
Products: Beer; Soda; Wine; Wine coolers. **SICs:** 5181 (Beer & Ale); 5149 (Groceries & Related Products Nec). **Est:** 1938. **Sales:** $20,000,000 (2000). **Emp:** 150. **Officers:** J.J. Carey, President; Maureen Wells, VP & General Merchandising Mgr.

■ 1922 ■ Northern Eagle Beverages Inc.
PO Box 827
Oneonta, NY 13820
Phone: (607)432-0400 **Fax:** (607)432-0401
Products: Beer; Juice; Soda. **SICs:** 5181 (Beer & Ale); 5149 (Groceries & Related Products Nec). **Est:** 1949. **Sales:** $9,000,000 (2000). **Emp:** 33. **Officers:** Louis B. Hagger, President; Matt Curley, Operations Mgr.

■ 1923 ■ Northern Virginia Beverage Co.
6605 Springfield Ctr.
Box 5266
Springfield, VA 22150
Phone: (703)922-9190 **Fax:** (703)922-7193
Products: Beer. **SIC:** 5181 (Beer & Ale). **Est:** 1960.
Sales: $12,000,000 (2000). **Emp:** 48.

■ 1924 ■ Northstar Distributors
10395A Democracy Ln.
Fairfax, VA 22030
Phone: (703)591-0897 **Fax:** (703)246-9540
E-mail: act@dgs.dgsys.com
Products: Beer. **SIC:** 5181 (Beer & Ale). **Est:** 1989.
Sales: $1,000,000 (1999). **Emp:** 10. **Officers:** Spencer Brand, President.

■ 1925 ■ Oak Distributing Company Inc.
5600 Williams Lake Rd.
Waterford, MI 48329-3571
Phone: (248)674-3171 **Fax:** (248)674-2699
Products: Beer. **SIC:** 5181 (Beer & Ale). **Emp:** 90.
Officers: Robert H. Baetens, Chairman of the Board; Ronald J. Baetens, President; David W. Baetens, Vice President.

■ 1926 ■ Odell Brewing Co.
800 E Lincoln Ave.
Ft. Collins, CO 80524
Phone: (970)498-9070
Products: Ale. **SIC:** 5181 (Beer & Ale). **Sales:** $4,700,000 (2000). **Emp:** 22. **Officers:** Doug Odell, CEO; Wynne Odell, Treasurer.

■ 1927 ■ Odom Corp.
PO Box 24627
Seattle, WA 98124
Phone: (206)623-3256 **Fax:** (206)467-5827
Products: Beverages, including wine, beer, and soft drinks; Groceries. **SICs:** 5182 (Wines & Distilled Beverages); 5149 (Groceries & Related Products Nec); 5181 (Beer & Ale). **Est:** 1938. **Sales:** $93,000,000 (2000). **Emp:** 300. **Officers:** John P. Odom, CEO & President; Gary Mills, CFO.

■ 1928 ■ Odom Northwest Beverages
517 Snake River Ave.
Lewiston, ID 83501-2262
Phone: (208)746-0114
Products: Beer and ale. **SIC:** 5181 (Beer & Ale).
Officers: Jay Dougherty, General Mgr. **Former Name:** K-K Distributors Inc.

■ 1929 ■ Old South Distributors Company Inc.
216 N Main St.
Winchester, KY 40391-1516
Phone: (606)744-6666 **Fax:** (606)744-2400
Products: Beer. **SIC:** 5181 (Beer & Ale). **Officers:** David Stubblefield.

■ 1930 ■ Oley Distributing Co.
920 N Main
PO Box 4660
Ft. Worth, TX 76106-9421
Phone: (817)625-8251 **Fax:** (817)626-7269
Products: Beer. **SIC:** 5181 (Beer & Ale). **Emp:** 100.
Officers: Pat O'Neal, President.

■ 1931 ■ B. Olinde and Sons Company Inc.
9536 Airline Hwy.
Baton Rouge, LA 70815
Phone: (504)926-3380
Products: Beer. **SIC:** 5181 (Beer & Ale). **Sales:** $60,000,000 (2000). **Emp:** 200. **Officers:** J.B. Olinde, President; H.T. Olinde Jr., CFO.

■ 1932 ■ Olinger Distributing Co.
9951 Heddon Rd.
Evansville, IN 47711-9660
Phone: (812)867-7481 **Fax:** (812)867-2581
Products: Liquor and wine. **SIC:** 5182 (Wines & Distilled Beverages). **Sales:** $10,000,000 (2000). **Emp:** 30.

■ 1933 ■ Olinger Distributing Co.
5337 W 78th St.
Indianapolis, IN 46268
Phone: (317)876-1188
Free: (800)366-1090 **Fax:** (317)876-3638
Products: Wine and distilled alcoholic beverages. **SIC:** 5182 (Wines & Distilled Beverages). **Sales:** $104,000,000 (2000). **Emp:** 365. **Officers:** Ray Dorulla, Exec. VP of Operations; Kelly Morris, VP & Controller.

■ 1934 ■ Antonio Origlio Inc.
2000 Bennett Rd.
Philadelphia, PA 19116
Phone: (215)698-9500 **Fax:** (215)698-1278
Products: Beer. **SIC:** 5181 (Beer & Ale). **Emp:** 135.

■ 1935 ■ John P. O'Sullivan Distributor Inc.
4047 Market Pl.
Flint, MI 48507
Phone: (810)733-7090
Products: Beer and ale. **SIC:** 5181 (Beer & Ale).

■ 1936 ■ Ourrison Inc.
PO Box 5266
Cheyenne, WY 82003-5266
Phone: (307)632-5628
Products: Beer; Ale; Malt beverages. **SIC:** 5181 (Beer & Ale). **Officers:** Rick Orrison, President.

■ 1937 ■ P & F Distributors Inc.
PO Box 354
Lewiston, ID 83501-0354
Phone: (208)743-5901
Free: (800)950-0226 **Fax:** (208)746-1615
Products: Beer; Ale; Malt beverages. **SIC:** 5181 (Beer & Ale). **Officers:** Bernita Pomeroy, President.

■ 1938 ■ Pacific Wine Co.
2701 S Western Ave.
Chicago, IL 60608
Phone: (773)247-8000
Products: Beverages, including beer, wine, and soft drinks. **SICs:** 5181 (Beer & Ale); 5149 (Groceries & Related Products Nec); 5182 (Wines & Distilled Beverages). **Sales:** $35,000,000 (2000). **Emp:** 95. **Officers:** John Terlato, President.

■ 1939 ■ Pacini Wines
3001 S State, Ste. 34
Ukiah, CA 95482
Phone: (707)468-0950 **Fax:** (707)463-8791
Products: Wine; Beer. **SICs:** 5182 (Wines & Distilled Beverages); 5181 (Beer & Ale). **Est:** 1980. **Emp:** 8.
Officers: Lorie Pacini, Owner.

■ 1940 ■ Paddington Corp.
1 Parker Plz.
Ft. Lee, NJ 07024
Phone: (201)592-5700 **Fax:** (201)592-0821
Products: Liquor. **SIC:** 5182 (Wines & Distilled Beverages). **Est:** 1980. **Emp:** 170. **Officers:** G. William Seawright, President; Roger L. Bush, VP of Finance; Roger Slone, VP of Marketing; Joseph McKenna, VP of Human Resources.

■ 1941 ■ Paramount Brands, Inc.
305 S Regent St.
PO Box 351
Port Chester, NY 10573
Phone: (914)937-5007
Free: (800)999-2903 **Fax:** (914)937-6055
Products: Wine and spirits. **SIC:** 5182 (Wines & Distilled Beverages).

■ 1942 ■ Paramount Liquor Co.
400 N Rangeline
Columbia, MO 65201
Phone: (573)474-6702 **Fax:** (573)474-6802
Products: Liquor. **SIC:** 5182 (Wines & Distilled Beverages). **Emp:** 15. **Officers:** Lindsay McConachie.

■ 1943 ■ Paw Paw Wine Distributors
816 S Kalamazoo
Paw Paw, MI 49079-9230
Phone: (616)657-5518 **Fax:** (616)657-3816
Products: Beer and wine; Champagne; Vermouth; Water; Soda; Mixers. **SICs:** 5181 (Beer & Ale); 5182 (Wines & Distilled Beverages). **Est:** 1945. **Sales:**

$12,000,000 (2000). **Emp:** 55. **Officers:** Raymond Schincariol, President; John Schincariol, Vice President; Casey Kopel, Sales/Marketing Contact; Don Schlueter, Customer Service Contact; Ron Schincariol, Human Resources Contact.

■ **1944** ■ **Pearce Co.**
PO Box 1239
Mesa, AZ 85211
Phone: (602)834-5527 **Fax:** (602)644-2941
Products: Beer. **SIC:** 5181 (Beer & Ale). **Est:** 1911.
Sales: $69,000,000 (2000). **Emp:** 235. **Officers:** Art Pearce, President; Roger DeMinor, Vice President; Jim Murphy, Marketing Mgr.

■ **1945** ■ **Pearlstine Distributors Inc.**
PO Box 72301
Charleston, SC 29415
Phone: (843)554-1022
Free: (800)922-1048 **Fax:** (843)745-1808
Products: Beer; Wine; Flavored water. **SICs:** 5181 (Beer & Ale); 5182 (Wines & Distilled Beverages); 5149 (Groceries & Related Products Nec). **Est:** 1865. **Sales:** $30,000,000 (2000). **Emp:** 200. **Officers:** Edwin Pearlstine, President; Chuck Marquardt, Controller.

■ **1946** ■ **Peerless Importers Inc.**
16 Bridgewater St.
Brooklyn, NY 11222
Phone: (718)383-5500
Products: Wine and Liquor. **SIC:** 5182 (Wines & Distilled Beverages). **Sales:** $310,000,000 (2000). **Emp:** 1,000. **Officers:** John Magliocco, CEO; Terrence Arlotta, CFO.

■ **1947** ■ **Pehler Brothers, Inc.**
700 S Clydesdale Dr.
Arcadia, WI 54612
Phone: (608)323-3440 **Fax:** (608)323-3547
E-mail: rkdbud@win.bright.net
Products: Beer. **SIC:** 5181 (Beer & Ale). **Est:** 1973.
Emp: 11. **Officers:** Aurelius J. Pehler.

■ **1948** ■ **Penn Distributors Inc.**
401 Domino Ln.
Philadelphia, PA 19128
Phone: (215)487-0300 **Fax:** (215)487-0352
Products: Beer. **SIC:** 5181 (Beer & Ale). **Sales:** $30,000,000 (2000). **Emp:** 100. **Officers:** Stanley Engle, President.

■ **1949** ■ **Pepin Distributing Co.**
6401 N 54th St.
Tampa, FL 33610
Phone: (813)626-6176 **Fax:** (813)626-5800
Products: Beer and other alcoholic beverages. **SICs:** 5181 (Beer & Ale); 5182 (Wines & Distilled Beverages). **Est:** 1960. **Sales:** $61,000,000 (2000). **Emp:** 200.
Officers: Thomas Pepin, Owner.

■ **1950** ■ **L.W. Peraldo Co. Inc.**
PO Box 350
Winnemucca, NV 89446-0350
Phone: (702)623-2553 **Fax:** (702)623-2726
Products: Beer; Ale. **SIC:** 5181 (Beer & Ale). **Officers:** Randy Peraldo, President.

■ **1951** ■ **Peterson Distributing Co.**
315 Railroad Ave.
Riverton, WY 82501-3561
Phone: (307)856-3397 **Fax:** (307)856-2644
E-mail: rich_ex@excite.com
Products: Beer; Ale; Malt beverages. **SIC:** 5181 (Beer & Ale). **Est:** 1935. **Sales:** $1,700,000 (2000). **Emp:** 5.
Officers: Richard Bennett, President.

■ **1952** ■ **Phillips Beverage Co.**
25 Main St. SE
Minneapolis, MN 55414
Phone: (612)331-6161 **Fax:** (612)623-1644
Products: Alcoholic beverages. **SICs:** 5182 (Wines & Distilled Beverages); 5181 (Beer & Ale). **Former Name:** Ed #Phillips & Sons.

■ **1953** ■ **Phillips Distributing Corp.**
PO Box 7725
Madison, WI 53707-7725
Phone: (608)222-9177
Free: (800)236-7269 **Fax:** (608)222-0558
Products: Liquor; Wine. **SIC:** 5182 (Wines & Distilled Beverages). **Est:** 1962. **Sales:** $12,500,000 (2000).
Emp: 40. **Officers:** Irving Levy, CEO & President; Marvin Levy, Controller.

■ **1954** ■ **Ed Phillips and Sons (Eau Claire, Wisconsin)**
PO Box 869
Eau Claire, WI 54701
Phone: (715)836-8600 **Fax:** (715)836-8609
Products: Liquor and wine. **SIC:** 5182 (Wines & Distilled Beverages). **Sales:** $15,000,000 (2000). **Emp:** 34. **Officers:** Timothy P. Horan, President; Sandra J. Thompson, Finance Officer.

■ **1955** ■ **Ed Phillips and Sons**
PO Box 869
Eau Claire, WI 54701
Phone: (715)836-8600 **Fax:** (715)836-8609
Products: Liquor and wine. **SIC:** 5182 (Wines & Distilled Beverages).

■ **1956** ■ **Ed Phillips & Sons of N.D.**
PO Box 1978
Fargo, ND 58107
Phone: (701)277-1499 **Fax:** (701)282-8869
Products: Liquor and wine. **SIC:** 5182 (Wines & Distilled Beverages). **Officers:** Robert L. Hansen, President.

■ **1957** ■ **Phoenix Imports Ltd.**
2925 Montclair Dr.
Ellicott City, MD 21043
Phone: (410)465-1155
Free: (800)700-4253 **Fax:** (410)465-1197
E-mail: mythbird@aol.com
URL: http://www.mythbirdbeer.com
Products: Foreign ales. **SIC:** 5181 (Beer & Ale). **Est:** 1985. **Emp:** 2. **Officers:** George Saxon, President; Pat Saxon, Vice President.

■ **1958** ■ **Pike Distributors Inc.**
401 E John St.
Newberry, MI 49868
Phone: (906)293-8611
Products: Beer. **SIC:** 5181 (Beer & Ale). **Est:** 1955.
Sales: $8,500,000 (2000). **Emp:** 40. **Officers:** S.J. Ketvirtis, President.

■ **1959** ■ **Pinnacle Distributing Co.**
14200 E Moncrieff
Aurora, CO 80011
Phone: (303)371-5890 **Fax:** (303)371-3975
Products: Alcoholic beverages, including beer, wine, and liquor. **SICs:** 5182 (Wines & Distilled Beverages); 5181 (Beer & Ale).

■ **1960** ■ **Pistoresi Distributing Inc.**
325 Columbia
Omak, WA 98841
Phone: (509)826-5900 **Fax:** (509)826-6400
Products: Beer and wine; Non-alcoholic beverages. **SICs:** 5181 (Beer & Ale); 5182 (Wines & Distilled Beverages); 5149 (Groceries & Related Products Nec). **Est:** 1919. **Sales:** $6,000,000 (2000). **Emp:** 20.
Officers: Ralph L. Pistoresi, Owner; Frances Pistoresi, VP of Finance; Lynn Lublin, Dir. of Marketing.

■ **1961** ■ **Plattsburgh Distributing**
215 Sharron Ave.
Plattsburgh, NY 12901
Phone: (518)561-3800 **Fax:** (518)561-0348
Products: Beer. **SIC:** 5181 (Beer & Ale). **Emp:** 17.
Officers: John Fisher.

■ **1962** ■ **Porter Distributing Co.**
PO Box 187
Mitchell, SD 57301-0187
Phone: (605)996-7465 **Fax:** (605)996-1606
Products: Beer. **SIC:** 5181 (Beer & Ale). **Officers:** James Porter, President.

■ **1963** ■ **Portland Distributing Co.**
PO Box 2812
Kirkland, WA 98083-2812
Products: Beer. **SIC:** 5181 (Beer & Ale). **Est:** 1949.
Sales: $8,000,000 (2000). **Emp:** 26. **Officers:** Wolfgang Werner, General Mgr.; Neil Benaroya, President.

■ **1964** ■ **Post Familie Vineyards and Winery**
Rte. 1, Box 1
Altus, AR 72821
Phone: (501)468-2741 **Fax:** (501)468-2740
Products: Wine. **SIC:** 5182 (Wines & Distilled Beverages).

■ **1965** ■ **Powers Distributing Company Inc.**
3700 Giddings Rd.
Lake Orion, MI 48359-1306
Phone: (248)393-3700 **Fax:** (248)393-1503
Products: Beer. **SIC:** 5181 (Beer & Ale). **Est:** 1939.
Sales: $66,000,000 (2000). **Emp:** 220. **Officers:** Gerald B. Powers, Co-President, e-mail: gpowers@powers-dist.com; Gary L. Thompson, VP of Operations, e-mail: gthompson@powers-dist.com; Robert J. Powers, Co-President, e-mail: rpowers@powers-dist.com; William Brazier, VP/General Manager, e-mail: wbrazier@powers-dist.com.

■ **1966** ■ **Premier Beverage**
PO Box 592248
Orlando, FL 32859
Phone: (407)240-4631 **Fax:** (407)240-0530
Products: Wine and liquor. **SIC:** 5182 (Wines & Distilled Beverages).

■ **1967** ■ **Premier Beverage**
PO Box 1630
Pensacola, FL 32597
Phone: (850)433-3151 **Fax:** (850)434-5163
Products: Wine, beer, and liquor. **SICs:** 5182 (Wines & Distilled Beverages); 5181 (Beer & Ale).

■ **1968** ■ **Premier Beverage**
8221 Eagle Palm Dr.
Riverview, FL 33569-8893
Phone: (813)623-6161 **Fax:** (813)621-6461
Products: Wine and spirits. **SICs:** 5182 (Wines & Distilled Beverages); 5181 (Beer & Ale).

■ **1969** ■ **Premier Distributors**
2600 Prairie Rd.
Eugene, OR 97402-9747
Phone: (541)688-6161 **Fax:** (541)688-6184
Products: Beer; Soft drinks; Bottling mineral or spring water; Fruit drinks, cocktails, and ades. **SICs:** 5181 (Beer & Ale); 5149 (Groceries & Related Products Nec). **Emp:** 49. **Officers:** John Morgan.

■ **1970** ■ **Premium Beverage Company Inc.**
922 N Railroad St.
Opelika, AL 36801
Phone: (205)745-4521
Products: Beer; Wine; Soft drinks. **SICs:** 5181 (Beer & Ale); 5182 (Wines & Distilled Beverages); 5149 (Groceries & Related Products Nec). **Est:** 1968. **Sales:** $10,800,000 (2000). **Emp:** 59. **Officers:** Billy A. Hall, President.

■ **1971** ■ **Premium Distributors Incorporated of Washington, D.C. L.L.C.**
3350 New York Ave. NE
Washington, DC 20002
Phone: (202)526-3900
Free: (888)524-5483 **Fax:** (202)526-7417
Products: Beer. **SIC:** 5181 (Beer & Ale). **Est:** 1982.
Sales: $21,000,000 (2000). **Emp:** 70. **Officers:** James Reyes, President; Michael Rickie, Controller.

■ **1972** ■ **Preston Premium Wines**
502 E Vineyard Dr.
Pasco, WA 99301
Phone: (509)545-1990 **Fax:** (509)545-1098
Products: Winery; Services include wine tasting, gourmet foods, self-guided tours, picnic facilities and gift shop. **SIC:** 5182 (Wines & Distilled Beverages).
Officers: Cathy Preston-Mouncer, Owner.

■ 1973 ■ Purity Products Inc.
4001 Washington Blvd.
Baltimore, MD 21227
Phone: (410)242-7200
Free: (800)935-1366 **Fax:** (410)247-5750
E-mail: sesh@erols.com
Products: Cocktail mixes and related items, including liquor. **SICs:** 5182 (Wines & Distilled Beverages); 5149 (Groceries & Related Products Nec). **Est:** 1973. **Sales:** $7,000,000 (2000). **Emp:** 22. **Officers:** Ivan Goldstein, President; Scott H. Goldstein, Dir. of Sales.

■ 1974 ■ Quality Beverage Limited Partnership
PO Box 671
Taunton, MA 02780
Phone: (508)822-6200
Free: (800)822-6252 **Fax:** (508)823-9092
Products: Beer. **SIC:** 5181 (Beer & Ale). **Est:** 1994. **Sales:** $61,000,000 (2000). **Emp:** 120. **Officers:** T. Conrad Wetterall, CEO. **Former Name:** Quality Beverage Inc.

■ 1975 ■ Quality Brands Inc.
226 Dover Rd.
Glen Burnie, MD 21060
Phone: (410)787-5656 **Fax:** (410)787-1716
Products: Spirits, wines and beer. **SIC:** 5182 (Wines & Distilled Beverages). **Est:** 1955. **Sales:** $60,000,000 (1994). **Emp:** 165. **Officers:** Herbert S. Kasoff, President; George Lee, Controller.

■ 1976 ■ Racine Vineyard Products
1439 Junction Ave.
Racine, WI 53403
Phone: (414)634-7300 **Fax:** (414)634-5788
Products: Wine. **SIC:** 5182 (Wines & Distilled Beverages).

■ 1977 ■ G. Raden and Sons Inc.
3215 Lind Ave. SW
Renton, WA 98055
Phone: (425)251-9300 **Fax:** (425)251-5954
Products: Wine. **SIC:** 5182 (Wines & Distilled Beverages). **Est:** 1972. **Sales:** $89,000,000 (2000). **Emp:** 300. **Officers:** Gary Raden, President.

■ 1978 ■ Rave Associates
6071 Jackson Rd.
Ann Arbor, MI 48103-9504
Phone: (734)761-7702 **Fax:** (734)761-8609
Products: Wine and beer. **SICs:** 5182 (Wines & Distilled Beverages); 5181 (Beer & Ale). **Est:** 1974. **Sales:** $9,000,000 (1999). **Emp:** 30. **Officers:** Gregg Mitchell, President; Martin Friedburg, Sr. VP.

■ 1979 ■ Rays Beverage Co.
4218 N Coronado Ave.
Stockton, CA 95204-2328
Phone: (209)466-6883 **Fax:** (209)948-1924
E-mail: raysbev@3l.wac.com
Products: Wine. **SIC:** 5182 (Wines & Distilled Beverages). **Est:** 1956. **Emp:** 17. **Officers:** Sandra L. Guidi, e-mail: sguidi@3l.wac.com.

■ 1980 ■ Redwood Vintners
12 Harbor Dr.
PO Box 685
Black Point
Novato, CA 94948
Phone: (415)892-6949
Free: (800)962-3764 **Fax:** (415)892-7469
Products: Wine; Distilled spirits. **SICs:** 5182 (Wines & Distilled Beverages); 5181 (Beer & Ale). **Est:** 1933. **Emp:** 174. **Officers:** Charles I. Daniels Jr., President & CEO; Peter L. Daniels, Exec. VP & COO; Steven Wyngard, Sales Mgr.; Michelle Clayworth, Human Resources Contact.

■ 1981 ■ Reitman Industries
10 Patton Dr.
West Caldwell, NJ 07006
Phone: (201)228-5100 **Fax:** (201)403-8679
Products: Liquor and wine. **SIC:** 5182 (Wines & Distilled Beverages). **Est:** 1933. **Sales:** $164,000,000 (2000). **Emp:** 325. **Officers:** Howard Jacobs, President; David C. Lowenstein, Exec. VP; Dennis Resnick, VP of Marketing; Rafael Ramos, Sales Mgr.; Joan Speer, Dir of Personnel.

■ 1982 ■ Reliance Wine & Spirits
4677 S 83rd East Ave.
Tulsa, OK 74145-6901
Phone: (918)664-3347
Products: Alcoholic beverages, including beer, wine, and liquor. **SICs:** 5182 (Wines & Distilled Beverages); 5181 (Beer & Ale).

■ 1983 ■ Remy Amerique Inc.
1350 Ave. of the Amer.
New York, NY 10019
Phone: (212)399-0200 **Fax:** (212)399-6909
Products: Wine and liquor. **SIC:** 5182 (Wines & Distilled Beverages). **Est:** 1980. **Sales:** $46,000,000 (2000). **Emp:** 150. **Officers:** Herve Zeller, President; Roy Singh, Controller.

■ 1984 ■ Republic Beverage Co.
9835 Genard Rd.
Houston, TX 77041
Phone: (713)690-8888
Free: (800)292-3303 **Fax:** (713)690-1169
URL: http://www.republicbeverage.com
Products: Liquor. **SIC:** 5182 (Wines & Distilled Beverages). **Est:** 1996. **Emp:** 800.

■ 1985 ■ Reuben's Wines & Spirits
107 W Stassney
Austin, TX 78745
Phone: (512)442-8395
Free: (800)982-7598 **Fax:** (512)447-8844
Products: Liquor; Beverages; Bar supplies; Cigars. **SICs:** 5182 (Wines & Distilled Beverages); 5149 (Groceries & Related Products Nec); 5194 (Tobacco & Tobacco Products). **Est:** 1980. **Sales:** $25,000,000 (2000). **Emp:** 90. **Officers:** Reuben Kogut, Chairman of the Board. **Former Name:** Reuben's Bottle Shop.

■ 1986 ■ Rheinpfalz Imports Ltd.
PO Box 49
Underhill Center, VT 05490-0049
Phone: (802)899-3905
Products: Wine; Distilled liquor. **SIC:** 5182 (Wines & Distilled Beverages). **Officers:** B. Kelley, President.

■ 1987 ■ Rhoades Wine Group, Inc.
PO Box 985
Plainfield, IN 46168
Phone: (317)839-2504 **Fax:** (317)838-3583
Products: Wine. **SIC:** 5182 (Wines & Distilled Beverages).

■ 1988 ■ Rhode Island Distributing Co.
PO Box 1437
Coventry, RI 02816
Phone: (401)392-3390 **Fax:** (401)392-3478
Products: Wine; Distilled liquor. **SIC:** 5182 (Wines & Distilled Beverages). **Officers:** Raymond Mancini, President.

■ 1989 ■ Richard Distributing Co.
1601 Commercial NE
Albuquerque, NM 87102-1572
Phone: (505)247-4186 **Fax:** (505)243-2438
Products: Beer; Wine; Spirits. **SICs:** 5182 (Wines & Distilled Beverages); 5181 (Beer & Ale). **Emp:** 99.

■ 1990 ■ C. Riffel & Sons Inc.
1253 S Water
Saginaw, MI 48601-2560
Phone: (517)752-8365 **Fax:** (517)752-5859
Products: Beer and wine. **SICs:** 5181 (Beer & Ale); 5182 (Wines & Distilled Beverages). **Emp:** 23. **Officers:** Richard Riffel.

■ 1991 ■ Rinella Beverage Co.
915 Tower Rd.
Mundelein, IL 60060
Phone: (847)949-7777 **Fax:** (847)949-9043
Products: Beer. **SIC:** 5181 (Beer & Ale). **Est:** 1983. **Emp:** 40. **Officers:** Sam C. Rinella; Mike Rinella, Sales & Marketing Contact.

■ 1992 ■ Ritchie and Page Distributing Company Inc.
292 3rd St.
Trenton, NJ 08611
Phone: (609)392-1146
Free: (800)257-9360 **Fax:** (609)392-8541
Products: Beer. **SIC:** 5181 (Beer & Ale). **Sales:** $29,000,000 (2000). **Emp:** 60. **Officers:** T.J. Ryan, CEO; William Morris, Controller.

■ 1993 ■ Riverside Liquors & Wine
17 Connor Ave.
Mt. Morris, NY 14510
Phone: (716)658-4701 **Fax:** (716)658-9175
Products: Wine. **SIC:** 5182 (Wines & Distilled Beverages).

■ 1994 ■ Roach and Smith Distributors, Inc.
1005 S Montana St.
Butte, MT 59701
Phone: (406)782-9158
Products: Cigars and cigarettes; Beer; Wine. **SICs:** 5181 (Beer & Ale); 5182 (Wines & Distilled Beverages); 5194 (Tobacco & Tobacco Products).

■ 1995 ■ Roanoke Distributing Company Inc.
PO Box 4210
Roanoke, VA 24015-0210
Phone: (540)342-3105 **Fax:** (540)345-1738
Products: Beer and wine; Soft drinks. **SICs:** 5181 (Beer & Ale); 5182 (Wines & Distilled Beverages); 5149 (Groceries & Related Products Nec). **Est:** 1932. **Sales:** $16,000,000 (2000). **Emp:** 80. **Officers:** S. Kime Patsel, President; Maryann Newbower, Controller.

■ 1996 ■ Robertson Distributing
PO Box 748
Norfolk, NE 68702-0748
Phone: (402)371-1891
Products: Beer. **SIC:** 5181 (Beer & Ale). **Emp:** 8. **Officers:** Roy Robertson.

■ 1997 ■ Rochester Liquor Corp.
PO Box 20596
Rochester, NY 14602-0596
Phone: (716)586-4911 **Fax:** (716)586-4048
Products: Liquor, including spirits and wine. **SIC:** 5182 (Wines & Distilled Beverages). **Est:** 1934. **Sales:** $10,000,000 (2000). **Emp:** 30. **Officers:** William Crandall, General Mgr.

■ 1998 ■ Romano Brothers Beverage Co.
7575 S Kostner Ave., No. 100
Chicago, IL 60652-1141
Phone: (773)767-9500
Products: Liquor. **SIC:** 5182 (Wines & Distilled Beverages). **Sales:** $2,000,000 (2000). **Emp:** 600. **Officers:** Michael Romano III, President & COO; D.J. Romano, Chairman of the Board; D.M. Romano, Exec. VP.

■ 1999 ■ Clare Rose Inc.
72 West Ave.
Patchogue, NY 11772
Phone: (516)475-1840
Products: Beer. **SIC:** 5181 (Beer & Ale). **Est:** 1936. **Sales:** $63,000,000 (2000). **Emp:** 90. **Officers:** F. Rose, CEO; Bob Wertley, VP & CFO.

■ 2000 ■ Royal Hill Co.
130 S Trade Center Pkwy.
Conroe, TX 77385-8215
Phone: (409)273-3500 **Fax:** (281)353-1121
Products: Beer. **SIC:** 5181 (Beer & Ale). **Emp:** 30. **Officers:** John Major.

■ 2001 ■ Royal Wine Co.
420 Kent Ave.
Brooklyn, NY 11211
Phone: (718)384-2400
Free: (800)382-8299 **Fax:** (718)486-8943
E-mail: wineinfo@royalwines.com
URL: http://www.royalwines.com
Products: Wine and grape juices. **SICs:** 5182 (Wines & Distilled Beverages); 5149 (Groceries & Related Products Nec). **Est:** 1950. **Sales:** $5,000,000 (2000). **Emp:** 50. **Officers:** David Herzog, CEO & President; Aaron Herzog, CFO.

■ **2002** ■ **Rudisill Enterprises Inc.**
PO Box 190
Gastonia, NC 28053
Phone: (704)824-9597
Products: Beer and malt beverages. **SIC:** 5181 (Beer & Ale). **Sales:** $5,000,000 (2000). **Emp:** 15. **Officers:** Sandra McPherson, Accountant.

■ **2003** ■ **S & C Importing**
PO Box 420
Sun Valley, ID 83353
Phone: (208)726-4316   **Fax:** (208)726-7212
Products: Wine. **SIC:** 5182 (Wines & Distilled Beverages).

■ **2004** ■ **Saelens Beverages Inc.**
PO Box 669
Galesburg, IL 61402-0669
Phone: (309)787-4546   **Fax:** (309)787-0863
Products: Beer, liquor, wine, and sodas. **SICs:** 5181 (Beer & Ale); 5182 (Wines & Distilled Beverages); 5149 (Groceries & Related Products Nec). **Emp:** 49.

■ **2005** ■ **St. Louis Beverage Co.**
PO Box 765
Ottawa, IL 61350-0765
Phone: (815)433-0365
Free: (800)345-0365   **Fax:** (815)433-4018
E-mail: slbco@sainet.net
Products: Beer. **SICs:** 5181 (Beer & Ale); 5145 (Confectionery). **Est:** 1921. **Sales:** $11,000,000 (2000). **Emp:** 25. **Officers:** Pat Reinhardt.

■ **2006** ■ **San Joaquin Beverage Co.**
PO Box 1138
Stockton, CA 95201
Phone: (209)948-9400
Free: (800)523-9103   **Fax:** (209)948-0946
E-mail: sjbeverage@mindspring.com
Products: Beer. **SIC:** 5181 (Beer & Ale). **Est:** 1986. **Emp:** 52. **Officers:** Bob Garibaldi; Jim Plunkett; Dick Klein; Tom Klein.

■ **2007** ■ **V. Santoni and Co.**
PO Box 1236
Woodland, CA 95776-1346
Phone: (530)666-4447
Products: Beer and wine. **SICs:** 5181 (Beer & Ale); 5182 (Wines & Distilled Beverages). **Sales:** $9,000,000 (2000). **Emp:** 30. **Officers:** Chuck Santoni, President.

■ **2008** ■ **Sapporo U.S.A. Inc.**
666 3rd Ave., 82th Fl.
New York, NY 10017
Phone: (212)922-9165   **Fax:** (212)765-2179
Products: Beer. **SIC:** 5181 (Beer & Ale). **Est:** 1984. **Sales:** $180,000,000 (2000). **Emp:** 29. **Officers:** Mike Yazawa, President; T. Mizokami, Treasurer & Secty.

■ **2009** ■ **Savannah Distributing Company Inc.**
PO Box 1388
Savannah, GA 31402
Phone: (912)233-1167
Free: (800)551-0777   **Fax:** (912)233-1157
Products: Alcoholic beverages, including beer, wine, and liquor. **SICs:** 5181 (Beer & Ale); 5182 (Wines & Distilled Beverages). **Est:** 1939. **Sales:** $15,000,000 (2000). **Emp:** 50. **Officers:** John A. Peters Jr., CEO; William Girardeau, CFO.

■ **2010** ■ **Sazerac Company Inc.**
PO Box 52821
New Orleans, LA 70152-2821
Phone: (504)831-9450   **Fax:** (504)831-2383
Products: Liquor; Cordials, liqueurs. **SIC:** 5182 (Wines & Distilled Beverages). **Emp:** 1,850. **Officers:** Mark Brown, President & CEO.

■ **2011** ■ **N.H. Scheppers Distributing**
1736 Southridge Dr.
Jefferson City, MO 65109-2046
Phone: (573)636-4831   **Fax:** (573)635-0526
Products: Beer. **SICs:** 5181 (Beer & Ale); 5145 (Confectionery). **Est:** 1954. **Emp:** 49. **Officers:** Joseph N. Scheppers.

■ **2012** ■ **Schieffelin and Somerset Co.**
2 Park Ave.
New York, NY 10016
Phone: (212)251-8200
Products: Wine and liquor. **SIC:** 5182 (Wines & Distilled Beverages). **Sales:** $82,000,000 (2000). **Emp:** 260. **Officers:** John P. Esposito, President & COO; Clint Rodenburg, Sr. VP of Marketing.

■ **2013** ■ **Schott Distributing Co.**
5245 W 6th St.
Goodview
Winona, MN 55987-1250
Phone: (507)452-5772   **Fax:** (507)452-5937
Products: Beer. **SIC:** 5181 (Beer & Ale). **Emp:** 15. **Officers:** Bruce Schott, Vice President; Mary Kay Peshon, Treasurer & Secty.

■ **2014** ■ **Scott Laboratories Inc.**
PO Box 4559
Petaluma, CA 94955-4559
Phone: (707)765-6666
Products: Filtering machinery for wine industry. **SIC:** 5084 (Industrial Machinery & Equipment). **Sales:** $21,000,000 (2000). **Emp:** 40. **Officers:** Bruce Scott, President; Rich W. Weishaar, Sr. VP & CFO.

■ **2015** ■ **Seago Distributing Co.**
800 Airport Rd.
Rockingham, NC 28379-4708
Phone: (919)997-5676   **Fax:** (919)895-7439
Products: Beer. **SIC:** 5181 (Beer & Ale). **Emp:** 40. **Officers:** William T. Seago; Vera R. Seago.

■ **2016** ■ **Seagram Classics Wine Co.**
2600 Campus Dr., Ste. 160
San Mateo, CA 94403
Phone: (650)378-3800
Free: (800)999-3801   **Fax:** (650)378-3820
Products: Wine. **SIC:** 5182 (Wines & Distilled Beverages). **Officers:** Samuel Bronsman II, President; Ray Chadwick, Exec. VP & CFO.

■ **2017** ■ **Select Wines & Spirits Co.**
2200 S 13th St.
Milwaukee, WI 53215-2774
Phone: (414)643-5444   **Fax:** (414)643-7661
Products: Wine; Liquor; Restaurant supplies. **SICs:** 5182 (Wines & Distilled Beverages); 5087 (Service Establishment Equipment). **Est:** 1934. **Emp:** 49. **Officers:** Larry Bornstein.

■ **2018** ■ **Seneca Beverage Corp.**
PO Box 148
Elmira, NY 14902
Phone: (607)734-6111   **Fax:** (607)734-2415
Products: Beer. **SIC:** 5181 (Beer & Ale). **Sales:** $32,000,000 (2000). **Emp:** 110. **Officers:** John Potter, President; Patty Santarone, Office Manager, Finance.

■ **2019** ■ **Service Distributing**
8397 Paris St.
Lorton, VA 22079
Phone: (703)339-6886   **Fax:** (703)339-6366
Products: Wine, liquor, and beer. **SICs:** 5182 (Wines & Distilled Beverages); 5181 (Beer & Ale).

■ **2020** ■ **Servidio Beverage Distributing Co.**
5160 Fulton Dr.
Suisun City, CA 94585-1639
Phone: (707)864-1741   **Fax:** (707)864-3330
Products: Beer. **SIC:** 5181 (Beer & Ale). **Emp:** 42. **Former Name:** Napa Valley Beverage Co.

■ **2021** ■ **Shaw-Ross International Inc.**
1600 NW 163rd St.
Miami, FL 33169
Phone: (305)625-6561
Products: Wine; Spirits. **SIC:** 5182 (Wines & Distilled Beverages).

■ **2022** ■ **Shestokas Distributing Inc.**
12970 McCarthy Rd.
Lemont, IL 60439
Phone: (312)229-8700
Products: Beer. **SIC:** 5181 (Beer & Ale).

■ **2023** ■ **Shore Point Distributing Co.**
PO Box 275
Adelphia, NJ 07710
Phone: (732)308-3334
Products: Beer; Wine. **SICs:** 5181 (Beer & Ale); 5182 (Wines & Distilled Beverages).

■ **2024** ■ **Sigel Liquor Stores Inc.**
2960 Anode Ln.
Dallas, TX 75220
Phone: (214)350-1271   **Fax:** (214)357-3490
Products: Liquor, beer, and wine; Soda; Flavored water. **SICs:** 5182 (Wines & Distilled Beverages); 5181 (Beer & Ale); 5149 (Groceries & Related Products Nec). **Est:** 1905. **Sales:** $71,000,000 (2000). **Emp:** 230. **Officers:** Louis Glazer, President; Al Miller, VP of Finance; David Dolan, Dir. of Marketing; Mike Ivie, Dir of Personnel.

■ **2025** ■ **Silverstate Co.**
325 E Nugget Ave.
Sparks, NV 89431
Phone: (702)331-3400   **Fax:** (702)331-3474
Products: Alcoholic beverages. **SIC:** 5182 (Wines & Distilled Beverages). **Sales:** $9,000,000 (2000). **Emp:** 30. **Officers:** Eric Anderson, General Mgr.; Alan Blach, Controller.

■ **2026** ■ **Sinclair Produce Distributing**
PO Box 432
Glasgow, MT 59230-0432
Phone: (406)228-2454   **Fax:** (406)228-8521
Products: Beer; Ale; Malt beverages. **SIC:** 5181 (Beer & Ale). **Officers:** Kelly Jennings, President.

■ **2027** ■ **SJL Beverage Co.**
901 N Belcrest
Springfield, MO 65802
Phone: (417)866-8226   **Fax:** (417)866-2887
Products: Wine; Liquor. **SIC:** 5182 (Wines & Distilled Beverages). **Emp:** 40. **Officers:** Joe Dellegrazio, Sales/Marketing Contact, e-mail: jdellegrazio@glazers.com; Stact Sherman, Customer Service Contact, e-mail: ssherman@glazers.com. **Former Name:** SJL Liquor Co.

■ **2028** ■ **Skokie Valley Beverage Co.**
199 Shepard Ave.
Wheeling, IL 60090
Phone: (847)541-1500   **Fax:** (847)541-2059
Products: Beer and non-alcoholic beverages. **SICs:** 5181 (Beer & Ale); 5149 (Groceries & Related Products Nec). **Est:** 1946. **Sales:** $21,000,000 (2000). **Emp:** 75. **Officers:** William A. Schirmang, President; Tony Schirmang, Comptroller.

■ **2029** ■ **Slocum & Sons Co.**
25 Industry
West Haven, CT 06516
Phone: (203)932-3688   **Fax:** (203)937-6430
Products: Wine. **SIC:** 5182 (Wines & Distilled Beverages).

■ **2030** ■ **Smoky Mountain Distributors**
7 Roberts Rd.
Asheville, NC 28803
Phone: (828)274-3606
Products: Beer and ale. **SIC:** 5181 (Beer & Ale).

■ **2031** ■ **Sodak Distributing Co.**
1710 N M Ave.
Sioux Falls, SD 57104-0274
Phone: (605)336-3320
Free: (800)658-3533   **Fax:** (605)336-3322
E-mail: sodakdist@hotmail.com
Products: Liquor, wine, and beer. **SICs:** 5182 (Wines & Distilled Beverages); 5181 (Beer & Ale). **Est:** 1956. **Sales:** $21,000,000. **Emp:** 42. **Officers:** M. Brzica.

■ **2032** ■ **Solman Distributors Inc.**
59 York St.
Caribou, ME 04736-2227
Phone: (207)493-3389   **Fax:** (207)492-0303
Products: Beer; Ale; Malt beverages. **SIC:** 5181 (Beer & Ale). **Officers:** Robert Solman, President.

■ **2033** ■ **Southern Illinois Wholesale Company Inc.**
Rte. 2, Box 234-A
Carterville, IL 62918
Phone: (618)985-3767 **Fax:** (618)985-3768
Products: Beer and liquor. **SICs:** 5182 (Wines & Distilled Beverages); 5181 (Beer & Ale). **Est:** 1925. **Sales:** $6,000,000 (2000). **Emp:** 18. **Officers:** John H. Murray, President.

■ **2034** ■ **Southern Wine Co.**
2614 3rd
Tuscaloosa, AL 35401-1024
Phone: (205)752-2596 **Fax:** (205)752-3888
Products: Wine. **SIC:** 5182 (Wines & Distilled Beverages). **Emp:** 16.

■ **2035** ■ **Southern Wine & Spirits**
1600 NW 163rd St.
Miami, FL 33169-5641
Phone: (305)625-4171 **Fax:** (305)620-5762
Products: Liquor, wine, and juices. **SICs:** 5182 (Wines & Distilled Beverages); 5149 (Groceries & Related Products Nec). **Emp:** 999. **Officers:** Harvey Chaplin.

■ **2036** ■ **Southern Wine & Spirits**
1099 Rocket Blvd.
Orlando, FL 32824
Phone: (407)855-7610 **Fax:** (407)855-6732
Products: Wine and liquor. **SIC:** 5182 (Wines & Distilled Beverages).

■ **2037** ■ **Southern Wine & Spirits**
5210 16th Ave. S
Tampa, FL 33619
Phone: (813)623-1288 **Fax:** (813)620-4071
Products: Wine and liquor. **SIC:** 5182 (Wines & Distilled Beverages).

■ **2038** ■ **Southern Wine & Spirits**
4500 Wynn Rd.
Las Vegas, NV 89103
Phone: (702)876-4500
Products: Beer, wine, and liquor; Water. **SICs:** 5182 (Wines & Distilled Beverages); 5149 (Groceries & Related Products Nec); 5181 (Beer & Ale).

■ **2039** ■ **Southern Wine & Spirits**
960 United Cir.
Sparks, NV 89431
Phone: (702)355-4500 **Fax:** (702)355-4509
Products: Beer, wine, and liquor; Sparkling water. **SICs:** 5182 (Wines & Distilled Beverages); 5181 (Beer & Ale); 5149 (Groceries & Related Products Nec).

■ **2040** ■ **Southern Wine and Spirits of America**
1600 NW 163rd St.
Miami, FL 33169
Phone: (305)652-4171 **Fax:** (305)625-4720
Products: Wine and spirits. **SIC:** 5182 (Wines & Distilled Beverages). **Sales:** $2,500,000,000 (2000). **Emp:** 4,400. **Officers:** Harvey Chaplin, CEO & President; Ken Merlin, Controller.

■ **2041** ■ **Southern Wine and Spirits of California Inc.**
17101 Valley View Rd.
Cerritos, CA 90701
Phone: (562)926-2000
Products: Liquor, wine, and beer; Water. **SICs:** 5182 (Wines & Distilled Beverages); 5181 (Beer & Ale); 5149 (Groceries & Related Products Nec). **Officers:** Harvy Chaplin, President.

■ **2042** ■ **Spadafore Distributing Co.**
635 Filley St.
Lansing, MI 48906
Phone: (517)485-4300 **Fax:** (517)485-1042
Products: Wine; Mixed spirits. **SIC:** 5182 (Wines & Distilled Beverages). **Est:** 1957. **Sales:** $1,000,000 (2000). **Emp:** 11. **Officers:** Andrew P. Spadafore, President; Charles C. Spadafore, Vice President; Nicholas Spadafore, Treasurer & Secty.

■ **2043** ■ **Spirit Distributing Co.**
5656 Morris Hill Rd.
Boise, ID 83706
Phone: (208)378-0550 **Fax:** (208)377-1626
Products: Beverages, including beer, ale, malt beverages, wine, and beverages. **SIC:** 5181 (Beer & Ale). **Sales:** $18,000,000 (2000). **Emp:** 91. **Officers:** Craig Stein, President. **Former Name:** Spirit II Distributing Inc.

■ **2044** ■ **Standard Beverage Corp.**
PO Box 968
Wichita, KS 67201
Phone: (316)838-7707 **Fax:** (316)838-5249
Products: Liquor; Beer; and Wine. **SIC:** 5182 (Wines & Distilled Beverages). **Est:** 1949. **Sales:** $87,000,000 (2000). **Emp:** 150. **Officers:** L. Rudd, President; Elizabeth Groce, Controller; Ross Schimmels, Executive Director.

■ **2045** ■ **Standard Crown Distributing Co.**
PO Box 1077
Macon, GA 31202
Phone: (912)746-7694 **Fax:** (912)746-1852
Products: Liquor, beer, and wine. **SICs:** 5182 (Wines & Distilled Beverages); 5181 (Beer & Ale). **Sales:** $19,000,000 (2000). **Emp:** 45. **Officers:** Jack Kugelman, President; Jimmy Chambers, General Mgr.

■ **2046** ■ **Standard Distributing Company Inc.**
601 E Dodge St.
Fremont, NE 68025
Phone: (402)721-9723 **Fax:** (402)721-0620
Products: Beer. **SIC:** 5181 (Beer & Ale). **Est:** 1950. **Sales:** $10,500,000 (2000). **Emp:** 22. **Officers:** Donald F. Dolejs, CEO; D. Bradley Dolejs, President; D. Christopher Dolejs, Vice President.

■ **2047** ■ **Standard Distributing Company Inc. (Waterloo, Iowa)**
2991 W Airline Cir.
Waterloo, IA 50703
Phone: (319)234-7571 **Fax:** (319)234-5099
Products: Beer, wine and natural beverages. **SICs:** 5181 (Beer & Ale); 5182 (Wines & Distilled Beverages); 5149 (Groceries & Related Products Nec). **Sales:** $8,000,000 (2000). **Emp:** 35. **Officers:** Joan Poe, Owner; David Poe, Vice President.

■ **2048** ■ **Star Distributors**
3543 Lamar Ave.
Memphis, TN 38118
Phone: (901)363-5555 **Fax:** (901)362-0880
Products: Wine and liquor. **SIC:** 5182 (Wines & Distilled Beverages).

■ **2049** ■ **Stash Distributing Inc.**
2138 Fair
Chico, CA 95928-6746
Phone: (530)891-6000
Products: Beer; Bottled water. **SICs:** 5181 (Beer & Ale); 5149 (Groceries & Related Products Nec). **Emp:** 34. **Officers:** Pat W. Lawing.

■ **2050** ■ **Jim Staton Distributing Co.**
149 S Walnut Cir.
Greensboro, NC 27409
Phone: (919)294-2714 **Fax:** (919)294-8107
Products: Wine; Mineral water; Imported beer. **SICs:** 5182 (Wines & Distilled Beverages); 5181 (Beer & Ale); 5149 (Groceries & Related Products Nec).

■ **2051** ■ **Stefanelli Distributing**
1945 W Yale Ave.
Fresno, CA 93705-4328
Phone: (559)233-7138
Free: (800)HAS-WINE **Fax:** (559)233-1146
URL: http://www.stefanelli-wine.com
Products: Beverages, including wine, micro brews, and liquor. **SIC:** 5182 (Wines & Distilled Beverages). **Est:** 1951. **Emp:** 20. **Officers:** Carla Stefanelli Rana, e-mail: carl@stefanelli-wine.com.

■ **2052** ■ **Stein Distributing Co.**
PO Box 9367
Boise, ID 83707
Phone: (208)375-1450 **Fax:** (208)375-0040
Products: Beer. **SIC:** 5181 (Beer & Ale). **Sales:** $20,000,000 (2000). **Emp:** 80. **Officers:** Keith Stein, CEO; Charley Jones, President, e-mail: stein-cj@rmci.net; John A. Grizzaffi, Vice President, e-mail: stein-jg@rmci.net.

■ **2053** ■ **Sterling Distributing Co.**
4433 S 96th St.
Omaha, NE 68127
Phone: (402)339-2300
Products: Liquor and wine. **SIC:** 5182 (Wines & Distilled Beverages). **Est:** 1942. **Sales:** $20,000,000 (2000). **Emp:** 43. **Officers:** Gene Pace, President; Rick Bokart, Vice President.

■ **2054** ■ **Stimson Lane Wine and Spirits Ltd.**
PO Box 1976
Woodinville, WA 98072
Phone: (425)488-1133 **Fax:** (425)488-4657
Products: Wine; Liquor. **SIC:** 5182 (Wines & Distilled Beverages). **Est:** 1934. **Sales:** $120,000,000 (2000). **Emp:** 450. **Officers:** Ted Baseler, Chief Operating Officer; Sheila Newlands, Exec. VP & CFO; Glenn Yaffa, Sr. VP of Sales.

■ **2055** ■ **Stoudt Distributing Co.**
PO Box 4147
Longview, TX 75606
Phone: (903)753-7239 **Fax:** (903)758-6479
Products: Beer. **SIC:** 5181 (Beer & Ale). **Est:** 1968. **Sales:** $10,000,000 (2000). **Emp:** 45. **Officers:** W.K. Stoudt, President & CFO.

■ **2056** ■ **Strathman Sales Company Inc.**
2127 SE Lakewood Blvd.
Topeka, KS 66605-1188
Phone: (785)354-8537 **Fax:** (785)354-8772
Products: Beer. **SIC:** 5181 (Beer & Ale). **Emp:** 24. **Officers:** Art Strathman, President.

■ **2057** ■ **Straub Brewery Company Inc.**
303 Sorg
St. Marys, PA 15857-1537
Phone: (814)834-2875 **Fax:** (814)834-7628
Products: Beer. **SIC:** 5181 (Beer & Ale). **Sales:** $4,000,000 (2000). **Emp:** 45. **Officers:** Daniel A. Straub, President; Thomas J. Straub, Vice President.

■ **2058** ■ **Strauss Distributing**
PO Box 191518
Little Rock, AR 72219
Phone: (501)565-0121 **Fax:** (501)565-0124
Products: Wine and liquor. **SIC:** 5182 (Wines & Distilled Beverages). **Officers:** David Cone.

■ **2059** ■ **Streva Distributing Co.**
4512 W Admiral Doyle
New Iberia, LA 70560-9770
Phone: (337)369-3838 **Fax:** (337)369-7461
E-mail: strevani@bellsouth.net
Products: Beverages, including beer and soft drinks. **SICs:** 5181 (Beer & Ale); 5149 (Groceries & Related Products Nec). **Est:** 1966. **Sales:** $9,000,000 (2000). **Emp:** 25. **Officers:** Jerry Streva, President.

■ **2060** ■ **Sun Imports Inc.**
PO Box 11618
Kansas City, MO 64138
Phone: (816)358-7077
Products: Wines and beer. **SICs:** 5182 (Wines & Distilled Beverages); 5181 (Beer & Ale).

■ **2061** ■ **Sunbelt Beverage Company L.L.C.**
4601 Hollins Ferry Rd.
Baltimore, MD 21227
Phone: (410)536-5000 **Fax:** (410)536-5599
Products: Wine and spirits. **SIC:** 5182 (Wines & Distilled Beverages). **Sales:** $560,000,000 (2000). **Emp:** 1,800. **Officers:** Todd Gardner, Controller.

■ **2062** ■ **Superior Distributing Co.**
PO Box 107
Fostoria, OH 44830
Phone: (419)435-1938
Products: Beer. **SIC:** 5181 (Beer & Ale). **Est:** 1949. **Sales:** $20,000,000 (2000). **Emp:** 90. **Officers:** Kris Klepper, CEO; Scott Harlow, Controller; Dan Diem, General Mgr.; Al Schank, Operations Mgr.

■ **2063** ■ **Superior Wines and Liquors Inc.**
PO Box 165790
Kansas City, MO 64116-5790
Phone: (816)421-1772 **Fax:** (816)421-0730
Products: Beer; Wine. **SICs:** 5182 (Wines & Distilled Beverages); 5181 (Beer & Ale). **Est:** 1933. **Sales:** $7,000,000 (2000). **Emp:** 30. **Officers:** E.L. Blando, Owner; Dave Kahmann, Controller.

■ **2064** ■ **Supreme Beverage Co. Inc.**
3217 Airport Hwy.
Birmingham, AL 35222-1259
Phone: (205)251-8010 **Fax:** (205)250-7160
Products: Beer. **SIC:** 5181 (Beer & Ale). **Sales:** $10,000,000 (2000). **Emp:** 200. **Officers:** Charles A. Schilleci; J.B. Schilleci Jr.

■ **2065** ■ **Sweetwater Distributors Inc.**
2300 Hoover Ave.
Modesto, CA 95354
Phone: (209)521-2350
Products: Beer, wine, and liquor. **SICs:** 5181 (Beer & Ale); 5182 (Wines & Distilled Beverages). **Est:** 1964. **Sales:** $11,000,000 (2000). **Emp:** 30. **Officers:** George Manatos, President; Peter Mamalis, Controller.

■ **2066** ■ **Sweetwood Distributing Inc.**
PO Box 1859
Rapid City, SD 57709-1859
Phone: (605)342-9011 **Fax:** (605)342-0938
Products: Beer; Ale; Malt beverages. **SIC:** 5181 (Beer & Ale). **Officers:** Don Sweetwood, President.

■ **2067** ■ **T & M Inc.**
PO Box 627
Dunseith, ND 58329-0627
Phone: (701)244-5149
Products: Distilled liquor; Soft drinks; Fresh fruit juices and nectars. **SICs:** 5182 (Wines & Distilled Beverages); 5149 (Groceries & Related Products Nec). **Officers:** Ray Trotter, Owner.

■ **2068** ■ **Talladega Beverage Co.**
928 N Railroad Ave.
Opelika, AL 36801-4368
Phone: (205)358-0068 **Fax:** (205)358-0070
Products: Wine; Bottled water; Beer. **SICs:** 5182 (Wines & Distilled Beverages); 5149 (Groceries & Related Products Nec); 5181 (Beer & Ale). **Emp:** 20.

■ **2069** ■ **Tarrant Distributors Inc.**
9835 Genard Rd.
Houston, TX 77041-7623
Phone: (713)690-8888
Products: Wine and distilled spirits. **SIC:** 5182 (Wines & Distilled Beverages). **Sales:** $355,500,000 (2000). **Emp:** 800. **Officers:** Jeff Goldring, Mng. Partner; David Ritch, Exec. VP & CFO.

■ **2070** ■ **Jim Taylor Corp.**
133 Atlantic Dr.
Maitland, FL 32751
Phone: (407)831-7800
Products: Malt beverages and soft drinks. **SICs:** 5181 (Beer & Ale); 5149 (Groceries & Related Products Nec). **Est:** 1974. **Sales:** $22,000,000 (2000). **Emp:** 74. **Officers:** James D. Taylor, President; Dennis Bryson, Exec. VP; Alex Taylor, Vice President.

■ **2071** ■ **J.J. Taylor Distributing Co.**
PO Box 70098
North Dartmouth, MA 02747
Phone: (508)999-1266
Products: Beer. **SIC:** 5181 (Beer & Ale). **Est:** 1958. **Sales:** $24,000,000 (2000). **Emp:** 70. **Officers:** John J. Taylor, President.

■ **2072** ■ **J.J. Taylor Distributing Miami Key-West**
3505 NW 107th St.
Miami, FL 33167
Phone: (305)688-4286 **Fax:** (305)769-1699
Products: Beer. **SIC:** 5181 (Beer & Ale). **Emp:** 160. **Officers:** Manuel Portuondo, President & General Mgr.; Carlos Smith, Sales/Marketing Contact; Sonia Barge, Human Resources Contact.

■ **2073** ■ **Terk Distributing**
4621 Maple St.
Abilene, TX 79602
Phone: (915)695-3430 **Fax:** (915)695-9920
Products: Liquor; Wine; Beer. **SICs:** 5182 (Wines & Distilled Beverages); 5181 (Beer & Ale).

■ **2074** ■ **Terk Distributing**
PO Box 32148
Amarillo, TX 79120
Phone: (806)376-4183 **Fax:** (806)376-1401
Products: Liquor; Wine; Beer. **SICs:** 5182 (Wines & Distilled Beverages); 5181 (Beer & Ale).

■ **2075** ■ **Terk Distributing**
1001 Pearl St.
Odessa, TX 79761
Phone: (915)332-9183 **Fax:** (915)334-8847
Products: Liquor. **SIC:** 5182 (Wines & Distilled Beverages).

■ **2076** ■ **Thames America Trading Company Ltd.**
714 Penny Royal Ln.
San Rafael, CA 94903
Phone: (415)492-2204 **Fax:** (415)492-2207
Products: Beer, ale, fermented cider, and California wine. **SICs:** 5181 (Beer & Ale); 5182 (Wines & Distilled Beverages). **Sales:** $2,000,000 (2000). **Emp:** 6. **Officers:** Jeffrey House, President; Gloria French, Dir. of Operations.

■ **2077** ■ **William Thies and Sons Inc.**
1335 NE 26th St.
Ft. Lauderdale, FL 33305
Phone: (954)566-1000
Products: Beer. **SIC:** 5181 (Beer & Ale).

■ **2078** ■ **Thompson Distributing**
PO Box 1702
Pocatello, ID 83204-1702
Phone: (208)232-2279
Products: Beer. **SIC:** 5181 (Beer & Ale). **Emp:** 22. **Officers:** Herbert D. Nickerson.

■ **2079** ■ **Thompson Distributing Inc.**
845 S Wyoming St.
Butte, MT 59701-2970
Phone: (406)723-6528 **Fax:** (406)782-1723
Products: Beer; Ale; Malt beverages. **SIC:** 5181 (Beer & Ale). **Officers:** James Thompson, President.

■ **2080** ■ **J.W. Thornton Wine Imports**
PO Box 2289
Ketchum, ID 83340
Phone: (208)726-3876 **Fax:** (208)726-3877
Products: Wine. **SIC:** 5182 (Wines & Distilled Beverages). **Est:** 1982. **Emp:** 6. **Officers:** Robert Gertschen, President.

■ **2081** ■ **Thorpe Distributing Co.**
600 Clydesdale Tr.
PO Box 337
Medina, MN 55340
Phone: (612)478-8502 **Fax:** (612)478-8503
Products: Beer. **SIC:** 5181 (Beer & Ale). **Emp:** 34. **Officers:** Jack Reis.

■ **2082** ■ **Three Lakes Distributing Co.**
111 Overton St.
Hot Springs, AR 71901
Phone: (501)623-8201 **Fax:** (501)624-4499
Products: Beer. **SIC:** 5181 (Beer & Ale). **Sales:** $8,000,000 (2000). **Emp:** 20. **Officers:** George R. O'Connor, President, e-mail: groc288@3lakesdisteb.com; Steve Fruti, Vice President. **Former Name:** Nance Frazer Sales Co.

■ **2083** ■ **Tippecanoe Beverages Inc.**
100 W Michigan St.
PO Box 247
Winamac, IN 46996-0247
Phone: (219)946-6666 **Fax:** (219)946-6612
Products: Beer. **SIC:** 5181 (Beer & Ale). **Est:** 1954. **Sales:** $6,000,000 (2000). **Emp:** 22. **Officers:** Fred Zahrt; Lillian Zahrt; David Zahrt.

■ **2084** ■ **Todhunter Imports Ltd.**
222 Lakeview Ave., Ste. 1500
West Palm Beach, FL 33401
Phone: (561)837-6300 **Fax:** (561)832-4556
E-mail: mcuomo@todhunter.com
URL: http://www.todhunter.com
Products: Spirits. **SIC:** 5182 (Wines & Distilled Beverages). **Est:** 1961. **Emp:** 15.

■ **2085** ■ **Tri County Coors**
PO Box 1053
Torrington, WY 82240-1053
Phone: (307)532-2932
Products: Beer; Ale; Malt beverages. **SIC:** 5181 (Beer & Ale). **Officers:** Randy Baugh, President.

■ **2086** ■ **Tryon Distributors**
136 E 36th St.
Charlotte, NC 28206
Phone: (704)334-0849 **Fax:** (704)334-2563
Products: Beer and wine. **SICs:** 5182 (Wines & Distilled Beverages); 5181 (Beer & Ale).

■ **2087** ■ **United Beverage, Inc.**
78 Regional Dr.
Concord, NH 03301
Phone: (603)223-2323 **Fax:** (603)228-6531
E-mail: ubi.nh@internetmci.com
Products: Wine; Beer. **SICs:** 5182 (Wines & Distilled Beverages); 5181 (Beer & Ale). **Est:** 1984. **Emp:** 38. **Officers:** Joe La Rocca, President.

■ **2088** ■ **United Distillers Group Inc.**
6 Landmark Sq.
Stamford, CT 06901
Phone: (203)359-7100 **Fax:** (203)359-7196
Products: Liquor; Beer. **SICs:** 5182 (Wines & Distilled Beverages); 5181 (Beer & Ale). **Est:** 1950. **Sales:** $580,000,000 (2000). **Emp:** 4,000. **Officers:** Joseph Heid, CEO; Stuart Fletcher, CFO; David Bryce, VP of Sales; Alec Vint, Dir. of Information Systems; Joseph A. Hudek, Dir of Human Resources.

■ **2089** ■ **United Distillers North America**
6 Landmark Sq.
Stamford, CT 06901
Phone: (203)359-7100
Products: Alcoholic beverages. **SICs:** 5182 (Wines & Distilled Beverages); 5181 (Beer & Ale). **Sales:** $93,000,000 (1994). **Emp:** 1,284. **Officers:** Walter Caldwell, CEO & President; Frank McMorrow, CFO.

■ **2090** ■ **United Distributors, Inc.**
2627 Collins Springs Dr.
Smyrna, GA 30080
Phone: (404)799-0333 **Fax:** (404)799-2222
Products: Liquor. **SIC:** 5182 (Wines & Distilled Beverages).

■ **2091** ■ **United Liquors Corp.**
4009 Airpark Cove
Memphis, TN 38188
Phone: (901)794-5540 **Fax:** (901)365-7129
Products: Alcoholic beverages. **SICs:** 5182 (Wines & Distilled Beverages); 5181 (Beer & Ale). **Officers:** John Caradonna.

■ **2092** ■ **United Liquors Ltd.**
1 United Dr.
West Bridgewater, MA 02379
Phone: (508)588-2300 **Fax:** (508)586-2546
URL: http://www.unitedliquors.com
Products: Beer; Wine; Liquor; Non-alcoholic. **SICs:** 5182 (Wines & Distilled Beverages); 5149 (Groceries & Related Products Nec); 5181 (Beer & Ale). **Est:** 1934. **Sales:** $240,000,000 (2000). **Emp:** 600. **Officers:** A. Raymond Tye, Chairman of the Board; David J. Roberts, CEO; Michael Tye, President; Karen Burns, Dir of Human Resources.

■ **2093** ■ **Valley Distributors**
15 11th St.
Elkins, WV 26241
Phone: (304)636-1330
Products: Beer. **SIC:** 5181 (Beer & Ale). **Emp:** 7.

■ 2094 ■ **Valley Distributors Inc.**
PO Box 548
Dillonvale, OH 43917
Phone: (740)769-2311
Free: (800)589-4989 **Fax:** (740)764-2013
E-mail: vald@1st.net
Products: Beer and wine. **SICs:** 5181 (Beer & Ale); 5182 (Wines & Distilled Beverages). **Est:** 1921. **Sales:** $4,000,000 (1999). **Emp:** 15. **Officers:** Delayne Charvat, President.

■ 2095 ■ **Valley Distributors Inc.**
534 Belgrade Rd.
Oakland, ME 04963-0008
Phone: (207)465-2121 **Fax:** (207)465-2119
URL: http://www.valley-dist.com
Products: Alcoholic beverages and soft drinks. **SICs:** 5181 (Beer & Ale); 5149 (Groceries & Related Products Nec). **Est:** 1974. **Officers:** Bernard Runser, President; Michael Runser, VP of Marketing & Sales, e-mail: m.runser@valley-dist.com.

■ 2096 ■ **Valley Distributors Inc.**
880 E Front St.
Fallon, NV 89406-8151
Phone: (702)423-3432 **Fax:** (702)423-2701
Products: Beer; Ale; Malt beverages. **SIC:** 5181 (Beer & Ale). **Officers:** Jerome Moretto, President.

■ 2097 ■ **Valley Sales Company Inc.**
PO Box 429
Jamestown, ND 58402-0429
Phone: (701)252-3950 **Fax:** (701)252-0069
Products: Beer and ale. **SIC:** 5181 (Beer & Ale). **Officers:** Greg Spenningsby, President.

■ 2098 ■ **Valley View Vineyard**
1000 Upper Applegate Rd.
Jacksonville, OR 97530
Phone: (541)899-8468 **Fax:** (541)899-8468
E-mail: vvvwine@cdsnet.net
URL: http://www.valleyviewwinery.com
Products: Wine; Corkscrews. **SICs:** 5182 (Wines & Distilled Beverages); 5199 (Nondurable Goods Nec). **Est:** 1972. **Emp:** 8. **Officers:** Ann Wisnovsky, Owner; Mark Wisnovsky, Operating Manager; Michael Wisnovsky, Sales Manager.

■ 2099 ■ **Valley Vintners Inc.**
PO Box 4284
Ketchum, ID 83340-4284
Phone: (208)837-4413
Products: Wine; Distilled liquor. **SIC:** 5182 (Wines & Distilled Beverages). **Officers:** Jamie Martin, President.

■ 2100 ■ **Vehrs Wine Inc.**
1702 Rankin St.
Missoula, MT 59802-1630
Phone: (406)543-6634
Free: (800)879-3481 **Fax:** (406)728-4405
E-mail: wine@bigsky.net
Products: Bottling wines and liquors; Beer. **SICs:** 5182 (Wines & Distilled Beverages); 5181 (Beer & Ale). **Est:** 1979. **Sales:** $2,000,000 (2000). **Emp:** 8. **Officers:** Tei Nash, President; Greg Carter.

■ 2101 ■ **Venture South Distributors**
1640 Kimberly Rd.
Twin Falls, ID 83301-7323
Phone: (208)733-5705
Free: (800)333-5705 **Fax:** (208)733-5745
Products: Beer, ale, and fermented malt liquors. **SIC:** 5181 (Beer & Ale). **Officers:** Mitch Watkins, President.

■ 2102 ■ **Vertner Smith Co.**
2300 Gault Pkwy.
Louisville, KY 40233-4174
Phone: (502)361-8421
Products: Wine; Liquor, including whiskey and scotch. **SIC:** 5182 (Wines & Distilled Beverages). **Est:** 1946. **Sales:** $24,000,000 (2000). **Emp:** 78. **Officers:** Vertner Smith III., President; Lisa Piercy, Treasurer & Secty.

■ 2103 ■ **Vintage House Merchants**
1090 A Bailey Hill Rd.
Eugene, OR 97402
Phone: (541)485-6868 **Fax:** (541)485-3191
E-mail: vhmeug@earthlink.com
Products: Wine. **SIC:** 5182 (Wines & Distilled Beverages). **Est:** 1979. **Sales:** $6,000,000 (1999). **Emp:** 24. **Officers:** Peter S. Wood, President; Donald L. Duwe, Sec. & Treas.

■ 2104 ■ **Vintage House Merchants, Inc.**
624 NE Everett
Portland, OR 97232
Phone: (503)231-1020
Free: (888)231-1020 **Fax:** (503)231-1615
E-mail: vhmpdx@earthlink.net
Products: Wine. **SIC:** 5182 (Wines & Distilled Beverages). **Est:** 1980. **Sales:** $5,500,000 (2000). **Emp:** 25. **Officers:** Peter S. Wood, President, e-mail: peter@vintagehousemerchants.com; Donald L. Duwe, Sec. & Treas.

■ 2105 ■ **Vintwood International Ltd.**
40 Prospect St.
Huntington, NY 11743
Phone: (516)424-9777
Free: (800)397-9737 **Fax:** (516)424-9749
E-mail: vintwood@earthlink.net
URL: http://www.vintwood.com
Products: Wine. **SIC:** 5182 (Wines & Distilled Beverages). **Est:** 1989. **Sales:** $15,000,000 (2000). **Emp:** 20. **Officers:** Frank A. Gentile, President; Robert Musorofiti, Exec. VP; Janine Judice, Customer Service Contact; Bob Musso, Human Resources Contact; Frank Pisano, General Mgr.

■ 2106 ■ **Virginia Imports**
881 S Pickett St.
Alexandria, VA 22304
Phone: (703)823-1230 **Fax:** (703)751-8077
Products: Imported beer; Domestic and imported wine; Champagne; Still and sparkling waters. **SICs:** 5182 (Wines & Distilled Beverages); 5181 (Beer & Ale); 5149 (Groceries & Related Products Nec).

■ 2107 ■ **Viva Vino Import Corp.**
1021 1/2 Saville Ave.
Eddystone, PA 19022
Phone: (215)872-1500 **Fax:** (215)872-1568
Products: Wine. **SIC:** 5182 (Wines & Distilled Beverages). **Est:** 1978. **Emp:** 10.

■ 2108 ■ **M.S. Walker Inc.**
20 3rd Ave.
Somerville, MA 02143
Phone: (617)776-6700 **Fax:** (617)776-5808
Products: Wine and distilled liquor. **SIC:** 5182 (Wines & Distilled Beverages). **Emp:** 200. **Officers:** Harvey Allen, President; Richard Sandler, CFO.

■ 2109 ■ **Dan Wallbaum Distributing**
PO Box 199
Yankton, SD 57078-0199
Phone: (605)665-2436
Products: Beer and ale in barrels and kegs; Malt beverages. **SIC:** 5181 (Beer & Ale). **Officers:** Daniel Wallbaum, President.

■ 2110 ■ **Wayne Densch Inc.**
2900 W 1st St.
Sanford, FL 32771
Phone: (407)323-5600 **Fax:** (407)324-9991
Products: Beer. **SIC:** 5181 (Beer & Ale). **Sales:** $36,000,000 (2000). **Emp:** 100. **Officers:** Leonard Williams, President; Len Williams, CFO.

■ 2111 ■ **Wayne Distributing Co.**
45 Sharpe Dr.
Cranston, RI 02920
Phone: (401)463-7020 **Fax:** (401)463-3466
Products: Beer. **SIC:** 5181 (Beer & Ale).

■ 2112 ■ **Weatherhead Distributing Co.**
PO Box 306
Oakes, ND 58474-0306
Phone: (701)742-2685 **Fax:** (701)742-2798
Products: Beer; Ale; Malt beverages. **SIC:** 5181 (Beer & Ale). **Officers:** Tim Weatherhead, President.

■ 2113 ■ **Western Beverage Company Inc.**
PO Box 941
Taylors, SC 29687
Phone: (864)268-6036
Products: Beer. **SIC:** 5181 (Beer & Ale). **Sales:** $9,000,000 (2000). **Emp:** 26. **Officers:** Jack E. Mullinax, President; Billy Rhodes, Controller.

■ 2114 ■ **Western Distributing Co.**
PO Box 5542
Denver, CO 80217
Phone: (303)292-1711 **Fax:** (303)297-9967
Products: Liquor; Beer. **SICs:** 5182 (Wines & Distilled Beverages); 5181 (Beer & Ale). **Est:** 1933. **Sales:** $160,000,000 (2000). **Emp:** 700. **Officers:** Vieri Gaines, COO; Christopher Boggs, CFO; Barry W. Swenson, VP of Sales; John DeForie, Operations Mgr.

■ 2115 ■ **Western Distributing Company Inc.**
PO Box 1969
Casper, WY 82602-1969
Phone: (307)265-8414 **Fax:** (307)265-8418
Products: Malt beverages, including bottled beer and ale. **SIC:** 5181 (Beer & Ale). **Emp:** 9. **Officers:** Kirk L. Klungness, President.

■ 2116 ■ **Western Maryland Distributing**
101 Winston St.
PO Box 33
Cumberland, MD 21502-2106
Phone: (301)722-8050 **Fax:** (301)724-0204
Products: Beer. **SIC:** 5181 (Beer & Ale). **Emp:** 16.

■ 2117 ■ **Whitehall Company Ltd.**
750 Everett St.
Norwood, MA 02062
Phone: (617)769-6500 **Fax:** (617)769-8472
E-mail: sales@ewhitehall.com
URL: http://www.ewhitehall.com
Products: Wine and beer. **SICs:** 5182 (Wines & Distilled Beverages); 5181 (Beer & Ale). **Est:** 1934. **Sales:** $98,000,000 (1999). **Emp:** 250. **Officers:** Marvin A. Gordon, CEO & Chairman of the Board; Gerald Freid, President; Kevin McCahn, VP of Sales.

■ 2118 ■ **Whitley Central Distributing Co.**
PO Box 436
Winner, SD 57580-0436
Phone: (605)842-1948 **Fax:** (605)842-1433
Products: Beer; Ale; Malt beverages. **SIC:** 5181 (Beer & Ale). **Est:** 1973. **Officers:** Russell Whitley, President.

■ 2119 ■ **Frederick Wildman and Sons Ltd.**
307 E 53rd St., No. 2
New York, NY 10022
Phone: (212)355-0700 **Fax:** (212)355-4723
Products: Wines. **SIC:** 5182 (Wines & Distilled Beverages). **Est:** 1938. **Sales:** $70,000,000 (2000). **Emp:** 60. **Officers:** Richard Cacciato, President; Enzo Marino, Sr. VP; Roger Bohmrich, Sr. VP.

■ 2120 ■ **Williams Distributing Corp.**
372 Pasco Rd.
Springfield, MA 01119
Phone: (413)783-1266
Products: Beer. **SIC:** 5181 (Beer & Ale). **Est:** 1950. **Sales:** $27,000,000 (2000). **Emp:** 90. **Officers:** James Sadowsky, President; Peter Leone, Controller; Moe Cavanaugh, Dir. of Sales.

■ 2121 ■ **Willow Distributors Inc.**
PO Box 153169
Dallas, TX 75315-3169
Phone: (214)426-5636 **Fax:** (214)426-1414
Products: Beer. **SIC:** 5181 (Beer & Ale). **Sales:** $60,000,000 (2000). **Emp:** 200. **Officers:** Dennis Nausler, President; Larry Huchtel, CFO.

■ 2122 ■ **Wilsbach Distributors Inc.**
PO Box 6148
Harrisburg, PA 17112
Phone: (717)561-3760
Free: (800)242-2337 **Fax:** (717)561-3766
E-mail: frsourbeer@wilsbach.com
Products: Beverages, including beer, soda, and spring water. **SICs:** 5181 (Beer & Ale); 5149 (Groceries & Related Products Nec). **Est:** 1933. **Sales:** $18,000,000 (2000). **Emp:** 65. **Officers:** Frank Sourbeer, President;

Charles Sourbeer, Vice President; Tim Waechter, Human Resources Contact.

■ 2123 ■ **The Wine Co.**
2222 Elm St. SE
Minneapolis, MN 55414
Phone: (612)331-6422 **Fax:** (612)331-6022
Products: Wine and beer. **SICs:** 5182 (Wines & Distilled Beverages); 5181 (Beer & Ale). **Est:** 1985. **Emp:** 12. **Officers:** Larry Colbeck.

■ 2124 ■ **Wine Distributors Inc.**
5800 Pennsylvania Ave.
Maple Heights, OH 44137
Phone: (216)587-9463
Products: Wine; Fresh fruit juices and nectars; Beer. **SICs:** 5182 (Wines & Distilled Beverages); 5149 (Groceries & Related Products Nec); 5181 (Beer & Ale). **Est:** 1971. **Emp:** 49. **Officers:** Jerry Tomb, Vice President; Marshall Reisman, President.

■ 2125 ■ **The Wine Merchant**
PO Box 401
Ardmore, PA 19003
Phone: (610)239-7400 **Fax:** (610)239-7077
Products: Wine and cognac. **SIC:** 5182 (Wines & Distilled Beverages).

■ 2126 ■ **Wine Trends, Inc.**
331 Tremorth Blvd.
Broadview Heights, OH 44147
Phone: (440)526-0943 **Fax:** (440)526-2129
Products: Wine. **SIC:** 5182 (Wines & Distilled Beverages).

■ 2127 ■ **Wine Warehouse**
6550 Washington Blvd.
City of Commerce, CA 90040
Phone: (213)724-1700 **Fax:** (213)724-4700
Products: Wine, beer, and liquor. **SICs:** 5182 (Wines & Distilled Beverages); 5181 (Beer & Ale).

■ 2128 ■ **Winebow, Inc.**
22 Hollywood Ave., Ste. C
Ho Ho Kus, NJ 07423
Phone: (201)445-0620
Free: (800)445-0620 **Fax:** (201)445-9869
Products: Wine. **SIC:** 5182 (Wines & Distilled Beverages).

■ 2129 ■ **Wines and Spirits International**
700 Anderson Hill Rd.
Purchase, NY 10577
Phone: (914)253-3777
Products: Wine; Distilled alcoholic beverages. **SIC:** 5182 (Wines & Distilled Beverages).

■ 2130 ■ **Winesellers Ltd.**
9933 N Lawler Ave., Ste. 355
Skokie, IL 60077
Phone: (847)679-0121 **Fax:** (847)679-2017
E-mail: info@winesellersltd.com
URL: http://www.winesellersltd.com
Products: Wine. **SIC:** 5182 (Wines & Distilled Beverages). **Est:** 1977. **Sales:** $20,000,000 (2000). **Emp:** 5. **Officers:** Yale Sager, President; Hattie Stewart, Finance Officer.

■ 2131 ■ **Winneva Distributing Co. Inc.**
PO Box 250
Winnemucca, NV 89446-0250
Phone: (702)623-2118 **Fax:** (702)623-2124
Products: Beer; Ale. **SIC:** 5181 (Beer & Ale). **Officers:** Louis Peraldo, President.

■ 2132 ■ **Wirtz Corp.**
680 N Lakeshore Dr., 16th Fl.
Chicago, IL 60611
Phone: (312)943-7000 **Fax:** (312)943-9017
Products: Beer, ale and wine. **SICs:** 5181 (Beer & Ale); 5182 (Wines & Distilled Beverages). **Sales:** $90,000,000 (2000). **Emp:** 300. **Officers:** William Wirtz, President; Linda Bescalli, Controller.

■ 2133 ■ **Wis WetGoods Co.**
607 S Arch St.
Janesville, WI 53545
Phone: (608)755-4961 **Fax:** (608)755-4970
Products: Beer. **SIC:** 5181 (Beer & Ale). **Est:** 1978. **Emp:** 16. **Officers:** Steve Bysted, President.

■ 2134 ■ **Wisconsin Distributors Inc.**
2921 Syene Rd.
Madison, WI 53713
Phone: (608)274-2337 **Fax:** (608)273-5666
Products: Beer; Juices; Mineral water. **SICs:** 5181 (Beer & Ale); 5149 (Groceries & Related Products Nec). **Sales:** $30,000,000 (2000). **Emp:** 100. **Officers:** Daryl Hanson, President.

■ 2135 ■ **Wisconsin Wholesale Beer Distributor**
2805 E Washington Ave.
Madison, WI 53701
Phone: (608)249-6464
Products: Beer. **SIC:** 5181 (Beer & Ale).

■ 2136 ■ **Wolfe Distributing Co.**
PO Box 711
Terrell, TX 75160
Phone: (972)563-6489
Products: Beer. **SIC:** 5181 (Beer & Ale). **Est:** 1967. **Sales:** $6,500,000 (2000). **Emp:** 21. **Officers:** Tracy D. Wolfe, President; Truett Cox, Accountant.

■ 2137 ■ **World Wide Wine and Spirit Importers Inc.**
40 Oak St.
Norwood, NJ 07648
Phone: (201)784-1990
Products: Wine; Brandy. **SIC:** 5182 (Wines & Distilled Beverages). **Est:** 1987. **Sales:** $1,000,000 (2000). **Emp:** 3. **Officers:** Thomas Coppini, President.

■ 2138 ■ **Worldwide Wines, Inc.**
155 Schoolhouse Rd.
Cheshire, CT 06410
Phone: (203)272-2980 **Fax:** (203)272-2942
URL: http://www.worldwide-wines.com
Products: Wine and champagne. **SIC:** 5182 (Wines & Distilled Beverages). **Est:** 1977. **Sales:** $18,000,000 (2000). **Emp:** 50. **Officers:** Howard S. Weiss; Henry Sandifer.

■ 2139 ■ **W.O.W. Distributing Company Inc.**
W 238 N 1777 Rockwood Dr.
Waukesha, WI 53188
Phone: (414)547-2337 **Fax:** (414)549-8282
Products: Beer. **SIC:** 5181 (Beer & Ale). **Sales:** $22,000,000 (2000). **Emp:** 75. **Officers:** Aldo Madrigrano, President.

■ 2140 ■ **Wright Wisner Distributing Corp.**
3165 Brighton Henrietta Town Lin
Rochester, NY 14623
Phone: (716)427-2880 **Fax:** (716)272-1216
Products: Beverages, including beer, juices, and pop. **SICs:** 5181 (Beer & Ale); 5149 (Groceries & Related Products Nec). **Est:** 1953. **Sales:** $30,000,000 (2000). **Emp:** 100. **Officers:** Claude H. Wright, President; Brian Lambert, VP of Finance; Larry Smith, VP of Sales & Operations.

■ 2141 ■ **Wyoming Liquor Division**
1520 E 5th St.
Cheyenne, WY 82002
Phone: (307)777-7120 **Fax:** (307)777-5872
URL: http://www.revenue.state.wy.us.
Products: Distilled spirits and wine. **SIC:** 5182 (Wines & Distilled Beverages). **Est:** 1935. **Emp:** 33. **Officers:** Lisa K. Burgess.

■ 2142 ■ **Young's Market Co.**
2164 N Batavia
Orange, CA 92865
Phone: (714)283-4933
Free: (800)317-6150 **Fax:** (714)283-6176
URL: http://www.youngsmkt.com
Products: Wine and liquor. **SIC:** 5182 (Wines & Distilled Beverages). **Est:** 1888. **Sales:** $910,000,000 (2000). **Emp:** 1,500. **Officers:** Vernon O. Underwood Jr., CEO & President; Dennis Hamann, Sr. VP & CFO; Mark Sneed, VP of Marketing; Steven Schaad, Sr. VP & COO; Karen Eaton, VP & CIO.

■ 2143 ■ **Young's Market Co.**
30740 Santana St.
Hayward, CA 94544
Phone: (510)475-2278
Products: Wine. **SIC:** 5182 (Wines & Distilled Beverages).

■ 2144 ■ **Zeb Pearce Cos.**
PO Box 1239
Mesa, AZ 85211-1239
Phone: (602)834-5527 **Fax:** (602)644-0525
Products: Beer and ale. **SIC:** 5181 (Beer & Ale). **Sales:** $98,000,000 (2000). **Emp:** 325. **Officers:** Art Pearce, President; John Grootveld, Controller.

■ 2145 ■ **Zekes Distributing Co.**
PO Box 145
Helena, MT 59624-0145
Phone: (406)442-7249 **Fax:** (406)449-4637
Products: Beer, ale, and malt beverages; Wine; Soft drinks. **SICs:** 5181 (Beer & Ale); 5149 (Groceries & Related Products Nec); 5182 (Wines & Distilled Beverages). **Est:** 1975. **Sales:** $3,000,000 (2000). **Emp:** 12. **Officers:** Robert Zucconi, President.

■ 2146 ■ **Zumot and Son**
7710 Old Spring House Rd.
McLean, VA 22102
Phone: (703)893-7233
Products: Liquor. **SIC:** 5182 (Wines & Distilled Beverages).

(5) Automotive

Entries in this section are arranged alphabetically by company name. When the company name is a personal name, the company name is alphabetized by the surname unless the first name or initial(s) are part of a trade name. See the User's Guide at the front of this directory for additional information.

■ 2147 ■ **4 Wheel Center Inc.**
7210 Gateway Blvd. E
El Paso, TX 79915-1301
Phones: (915)593-4848   (915)593-4849
Fax: (915)598-9915
Products: Motor vehicle wheels; Automotive accessories. **SIC:** 5013 (Motor Vehicle Supplies & New Parts). **Est:** 1977. **Emp:** 15. **Officers:** Carlos Enriquez, President.

■ 2148 ■ **A 1 Accredited Batteries**
714 Central Ave.
Billings, MT 59102-5817
Phone: (406)245-9839
Products: Automobile parts, used. **SIC:** 5015 (Motor Vehicle Parts—Used). **Officers:** Roxie Houchen, Owner.

■ 2149 ■ **A-1 Battery Distributors**
3220 A Ave.
Gulfport, MS 39507
Phone: (228)868-6482
Products: Batteries; Scrap metal. **SICs:** 5013 (Motor Vehicle Supplies & New Parts); 5093 (Scrap & Waste Materials).

■ 2150 ■ **A-1 New & Used Auto Parts, Inc.**
PO Box 1087
Williston, ND 58802-1087
Phone: (701)774-8315   **Fax:** (701)774-0310
E-mail: a1auto@dia.net
Products: Used automotive parts and supplies. **SIC:** 5015 (Motor Vehicle Parts—Used). **Officers:** Bob Kaelzer, President. **Former Name:** AA-1 Used Auto Parts Inc.

■ 2151 ■ **A & A Brake Service Co. Inc.**
224 3rd Ave.
Brooklyn, NY 11217-3036
Phones: (718)624-4488   (718)935-9327
Fax: (718)522-0268
Products: Automotive parts and supplies, New. **SIC:** 5013 (Motor Vehicle Supplies & New Parts). **Emp:** 49. **Officers:** A. Abatemarco.

■ 2152 ■ **A & A Midwest Distributing Inc.**
2580 N Commerce St.
North Las Vegas, NV 89030-3876
Phone: (702)649-7776
Free: (800)426-8771   **Fax:** (702)649-6777
E-mail: engquest@aol.com
Products: Used motor vehicle parts. **SIC:** 5015 (Motor Vehicle Parts—Used). **Officers:** Aaron Stolberg, President.

■ 2153 ■ **A C Auto Recycling**
6705 Juniper Dr.
Missoula, MT 59802-5751
Phone: (406)258-6141
Free: (800)452-5125   **Fax:** (406)258-7278
Products: Automobile parts, used. **SIC:** 5015 (Motor Vehicle Parts—Used). **Officers:** Archie Cram, Owner.

■ 2154 ■ **A-City Auto Glass**
2220 N Commerce St.
North Las Vegas, NV 89030-4147
Phone: (702)649-3905
Products: Used motor vehicle parts; Used automotive supplies. **SIC:** 5015 (Motor Vehicle Parts—Used). **Officers:** Joseph Cannavo, Owner.

■ 2155 ■ **A and D Auto Parts Inc.**
12166 York Rd.
Cleveland, OH 44133-3601
Phone: (440)237-9300   **Fax:** (440)243-8958
Products: Automobile parts. **SIC:** 5013 (Motor Vehicle Supplies & New Parts). **Est:** 1983. **Sales:** $800,000 (2000). **Emp:** 2. **Officers:** Doug Baldwin, President.

■ 2156 ■ **A & D Enterprises, Import-Export**
1128 Collingwood Lane
Bolingbrook, IL 60440
Phone: (630)378-1944   **Fax:** (630)378-1946
Products: Food service machinery and equipment; Farm machinery; Automobiles; Automotive parts and equipment; Wood and metalworking machinery. **SICs:** 5013 (Motor Vehicle Supplies & New Parts); 5012 (Automobiles & Other Motor Vehicles); 5046 (Commercial Equipment Nec); 5083 (Farm & Garden Machinery); 5084 (Industrial Machinery & Equipment). **Officers:** Augustyn M. Mardyla, President.

■ 2157 ■ **A & M Trading Company Inc.**
25 Austin Blvd.
Commack, NY 11725
Phone: (631)543-4490
Free: (800)669-3962   **Fax:** (631)543-4496
URL: http://www.dynabrite.com
Products: Automotive parts and supplies. **SIC:** 5013 (Motor Vehicle Supplies & New Parts). **Est:** 1948. **Sales:** $5,000,000 (2000). **Emp:** 15. **Officers:** M. Foster, President; B. Smith, Treasurer & Secty.; G. Smith, CEO, e-mail: gary@li.net.

■ 2158 ■ **A & P Auto Parts Inc.**
8572 Brewezton Rd.
Cicero, NY 13039
Phone: (315)699-2728
Free: (800)962-7222   **Fax:** (315)699-4617
E-mail: apauto@earthlink.net
URL: http://www.apautoparts.com
Products: Automotive parts. **SIC:** 5013 (Motor Vehicle Supplies & New Parts). **Est:** 1969. **Sales:** $4,000,000 (2000). **Emp:** 44. **Officers:** William Abold. **Former Name:** A-P-A Auto Parts.

■ 2159 ■ **A to Z Tire & Battery Inc.**
613 Broadway Blvd. SE
Albuquerque, NM 87101
Phone: (505)247-0134
Products: Tires; Batteries. **SIC:** 5014 (Tires & Tubes).

■ 2160 ■ **AAA Parts of Biltmore Inc.**
5 Brook St.
Asheville, NC 28803
Phone: (828)274-3781
Products: Brake lining. **SIC:** 5013 (Motor Vehicle Supplies & New Parts).

■ 2161 ■ **Aamco Transmissions Inc.**
1 Presidential Blvd.
Bala Cynwyd, PA 19004
Phone: (610)668-2900   **Fax:** (610)664-4570
Products: Automotive parts and supplies, including transmissions. **SIC:** 5013 (Motor Vehicle Supplies & New Parts). **Est:** 1963. **Sales:** $449,280,000 (1999). **Emp:** 235. **Officers:** Keith Morgan, CEO; Mark Wurth, President; Greg Matecki, Dir. of Finance; Bruce Schmiot, Dir. of Marketing.

■ 2162 ■ **Aargus Truck & Auto**
6145 D Wall St.
Sterling Heights, MI 48312
Phone: (810)979-2114   **Fax:** (810)979-2112
E-mail: interlog@gateway.net
Products: Automotive parts and supplies. **SIC:** 5013 (Motor Vehicle Supplies & New Parts). **Est:** 1976. **Sales:** $14,000,000 (2000). **Emp:** 27. **Officers:** T.J. Henke, President; B.A. Henke, Vice President; J. Howell, General Mgr.; J. Howell, General Mgr. **Alternate Name:** Guardian Automotive.

■ 2163 ■ **ABC Marketing**
RR 2 Box 123-A
Stratford, OK 74872-9400
Phone: (580)332-0110   **Fax:** (580)332-9955
Products: Used automobiles. **SIC:** 5012 (Automobiles & Other Motor Vehicles). **Officers:** Donald Akers, Owner.

■ 2164 ■ **Abc Mobile Brake**
105 Rains Ave.
Nashville, TN 37203
Phone: (615)254-2223
Products: Brakes. **SIC:** 5013 (Motor Vehicle Supplies & New Parts).

■ 2165 ■ **Able Welding Co.**
1527 42nd St.
Brooklyn, NY 11219
Phone: (718)259-3616   **Fax:** (718)236-6938
Products: Automotive parts and supplies, New. **SIC:** 5013 (Motor Vehicle Supplies & New Parts). **Est:** 1949. **Sales:** $1,000,000 (2000). **Emp:** 10. **Officers:** Dominick Colasanto, Contact.

■ 2166 ■ **AC-Delco/GM Service Parts Operation**
PO Box 6020
Grand Blanc, MI 48439
Phone: (810)606-2000
Products: Automotive parts and accessories. **SIC:** 5013 (Motor Vehicle Supplies & New Parts). **Sales:** $3,160,000,000 (2000). **Emp:** 13,000. **Officers:** W.J. Lovejoy, VP & General Merchandising Mgr.; R J. McCabe, Finance Officer.

■ 2167 ■ **Acarex Inc.**
91-31 Queens Blvd.
Elmhurst, NY 11373
Phone: (718)424-5551   **Fax:** (718)424-8668
E-mail: acarex@compuserve.com
URL: http://www.acarex.com
Products: Automotive parts and accessories; Equipment and accessories for the gas industry. **SICs:**

5013 (Motor Vehicle Supplies & New Parts); 5084 (Industrial Machinery & Equipment). **Est:** 1986. **Sales:** $2,000,000 (2000). **Emp:** 4. **Officers:** J. Acar, President.

■ **2168** ■ **Accupart International**
11 Black Rock Rd.
Carson City, NV 89706
Phone: (775)246-5990
Products: Brakess. **SIC:** 5013 (Motor Vehicle Supplies & New Parts).

■ **2169** ■ **Ace Auto Salvage**
10131 Garrymoore Ln.
Missoula, MT 59802-5674
Phone: (406)543-7614
Free: (888)500-7614 **Fax:** (406)543-1576
Products: Used motor vehicle parts. **SIC:** 5015 (Motor Vehicle Parts—Used). **Est:** 1996. **Emp:** 2. **Officers:** Larry Middlestead; Roy Middlestead.

■ **2170** ■ **Ace Battery Inc.**
2166 Bluff Rd.
Indianapolis, IN 46225
Phone: (317)786-2717 **Fax:** (317)783-4844
Products: Commercial and automotive batteries. **SIC:** 5013 (Motor Vehicle Supplies & New Parts). **Est:** 1945. **Sales:** $1,500,000 (2000). **Emp:** 7. **Officers:** James A. Kirkham, President; Shirley A. Kirkham, CFO; Thomas F. Clouse, Dir. of Marketing.

■ **2171** ■ **Ace Truck Body, Inc.**
1600 Thrailkill Rd.
PO Box 459
Grove City, OH 43123
Phone: (614)871-3100 **Fax:** (614)871-3860
Products: Automotive parts and supplies, New. **SIC:** 5013 (Motor Vehicle Supplies & New Parts). **Est:** 1978. **Sales:** $4,500,000 (2000). **Emp:** 22. **Officers:** Gary L. Leasure, Manager.

■ **2172** ■ **Ace Truck Equipment Co.**
PO Box 2605
Zanesville, OH 43702-2605
Phone: (740)453-0551 **Fax:** (740)453-7023
Products: Automotive parts and supplies, New. **SIC:** 5013 (Motor Vehicle Supplies & New Parts). **Officers:** David Beitzel, President.

■ **2173** ■ **Acme Auto Inc.**
PO Box 330666
West Hartford, CT 06133-0666
Phone: (860)246-2540
Products: Automotive parts and equipment. **SIC:** 5013 (Motor Vehicle Supplies & New Parts). **Est:** 1941. **Sales:** $28,000,000 (2000). **Emp:** 225. **Officers:** James Fine, President; Tom Moore, Finance Officer; William Starks, VP of Operations.

■ **2174** ■ **ACME Automotive Accessories Group**
17103 SR-4 E
Goshen, IN 46526
Phone: (219)534-1516
Free: (800)522-2263 **Fax:** (219)533-4452
URL: http://www.acmeair.com
Products: Automotive air conditioning systems. **SIC:** 5013 (Motor Vehicle Supplies & New Parts). **Est:** 1929. **Sales:** $6,000,000 (2000). **Emp:** 30. **Officers:** David Gratton, Vice President; Bill McCarthy, Sales/Marketing Contact; Mike Hiles, Customer Service Contact.

■ **2175** ■ **Acme Group**
5151 Loraine Ave.
Detroit, MI 48208
Phone: (313)894-7110 **Fax:** (313)894-8190
Products: Industrial textiles; Seating suspensions; Industrial filtration products; Automotive products. **SICs:** 5013 (Motor Vehicle Supplies & New Parts); 5085 (Industrial Supplies). **Est:** 1917. **Sales:** $70,000,000 (1999). **Emp:** 225. **Officers:** James Colman, President; G.E. Brumm, CFO; Neil Gross, Sales/Marketing Contact, e-mail: ngross@acmemill.com; Genevieve Dobroczynski, Customer Service Contact, e-mail: geneviev@memimill.com; Joan Caleo, HRCT, e-mail: joan@acmemill.com.

■ **2176** ■ **Acra Custom Wheel**
PO Box 1292
2310 N Foundation Dr.
South Bend, IN 46624
Phone: (219)233-3114
Free: (800)348-2803 **Fax:** (219)233-8856
Products: Motor vehicle wheels; Tires and inner tubes, new. **SICs:** 5013 (Motor Vehicle Supplies & New Parts); 5014 (Tires & Tubes). **Sales:** $6,000,000 (2000). **Emp:** 20. **Officers:** Steve Sulentic, President; Duane Bevis, Vice President.

■ **2177** ■ **A.C.T. Vehicle Equipment, Inc.**
946 Southampton Rd.
Westfield, MA 01085-1364
Phone: (413)568-6173
Products: Automotive parts and supplies, New. **SIC:** 5013 (Motor Vehicle Supplies & New Parts). **Officers:** Martin Mendes, Contact.

■ **2178** ■ **Action Auto Parts**
2606 N 10th St.
Dalton Gardens, ID 83815-4926
Phone: (208)664-9126
Products: Automobile parts, used. **SIC:** 5015 (Motor Vehicle Parts—Used). **Officers:** Ed Green, Owner.

■ **2179** ■ **Action Fabrication & Truck Equipment, Inc.**
4481 107th Cir. N
Clearwater, FL 33762-5029
Phone: (813)572-6319
Free: (800)330-1229 **Fax:** (813)572-4918
Products: Truck bodies; Trucking equipment. **SIC:** 5013 (Motor Vehicle Supplies & New Parts). **Est:** 1982. **Sales:** $4,000,000 (2000). **Emp:** 28. **Officers:** Mike Wool, President.

■ **2180** ■ **Addison Auto Parts Co.**
3908 Pennsylvania Ave.
Washington, DC 20020
Phone: (202)581-2900 **Fax:** (202)575-1353
Products: Automotive parts. **SIC:** 5013 (Motor Vehicle Supplies & New Parts). **Est:** 1987. **Sales:** $900,000 (2000). **Emp:** 4. **Officers:** James D. Addison, President; Marie Y. Addison, CFO.

■ **2181** ■ **ADESA Corp.**
2 Parkwood Crossing, Ste. 400
310 E 96th St.
Indianapolis, IN 46240
Phone: (317)815-1100
Free: (800)862-7882 **Fax:** (317)815-0500
URL: http://www.adesa.com
Products: Automobiles. **SIC:** 5012 (Automobiles & Other Motor Vehicles). **Est:** 1991. **Sales:** $250,000,000 (2000). **Emp:** 4,800. **Officers:** Jim Hallet, CEO & President; Bill Stackhouse, CFO.

■ **2182** ■ **ADT Automotive Inc.**
435 Metroplex Dr.
Nashville, TN 37211
Phone: (615)333-1400 **Fax:** (615)837-7811
Products: Automobiles. **SIC:** 5012 (Automobiles & Other Motor Vehicles). **Sales:** $297,800,000 (2000). **Emp:** 6,800. **Officers:** Tony Moorby, CEO & President; Larry C. Reese, Sr. VP & CFO.

■ **2183** ■ **Advance Stores Company Inc.**
PO Box 2710
Roanoke, VA 24001
Phone: (540)345-4911 **Fax:** (540)343-5559
Products: Automotive parts. **SIC:** 5013 (Motor Vehicle Supplies & New Parts). **Est:** 1929. **Sales:** $220,000,000 (2000). **Emp:** 4,000. **Officers:** Garnett Smith, President; Dick Hough, CFO; Chad Tilley, Sr. VP of Marketing; Ken Wirth, VP of Operations; Darrell Porter, Dir of Human Resources.

■ **2184** ■ **AEA Distributors**
2947 Prosperity Ave.
Fairfax, VA 22031
Phone: (703)560-0404
E-mail: aea@bordens.net
Products: Automotive parts and supplies. **SIC:** 5013 (Motor Vehicle Supplies & New Parts). **Est:** 1969.

■ **2185** ■ **AER Inc.**
7103 E 47 Ave. Dr.
Denver, CO 80216
Phone: (303)399-3673
Free: (800)348-3673 **Fax:** (303)355-8800
Products: Automobile parts. **SIC:** 5013 (Motor Vehicle Supplies & New Parts). **Est:** 1939. **Sales:** $15,600,000 (2000). **Emp:** 16. **Officers:** Robert McGraw, President; Chris Mantzuranis, Finance Officer.

■ **2186** ■ **AF & T Salvage**
6125 Jackrabbit Ln.
Belgrade, MT 59714-9021
Phone: (406)388-4735 **Free:** (800)821-5213
Products: Rebuilt parts for motor vehicles; Automobile parts, used; Automotive wrecking for scrap. **SIC:** 5015 (Motor Vehicle Parts—Used). **Officers:** Linda Marshall, Owner.

■ **2187** ■ **AG Truck Equipment Co.**
2256 West 1500 South
PO Box 359
Salt Lake City, UT 84110
Phone: (801)975-0400 **Fax:** (801)975-7567
Products: Automotive parts and supplies, New. **SIC:** 5013 (Motor Vehicle Supplies & New Parts). **Officers:** James Gianelo, Vice President.

■ **2188** ■ **AGR Warehouse Distributors**
135 Barnstable Rd.
Hyannis, MA 02601
Phone: (508)771-0443
Products: Automotive parts and supplies. **SIC:** 5013 (Motor Vehicle Supplies & New Parts).

■ **2189** ■ **AI Automotive Corp.**
414 E 75th St.
New York, NY 10021
Phone: (212)737-3000
Free: (800)377-0657 **Fax:** (212)249-4255
Products: Automotive parts and supplies. **SIC:** 5013 (Motor Vehicle Supplies & New Parts). **Est:** 1982. **Sales:** $18,000,000 (2000). **Emp:** 150. **Officers:** Steven R. Korf, President & CFO; Richard Mall, VP of Store Operations; Moe Catino, General Mgr.; Michael Pollier, Controller; Craig Shea, Sales/Marketing Contact, e-mail: csaiac@aol.com. **Alternate Name:** Bumper to Bumper. **Alternate Name:** General Automotive Supply.

■ **2190** ■ **AI International Corp.**
414 E 75th St.
New York, NY 10021
Phone: (212)245-6262 **Fax:** (212)249-4255
Products: Auto parts and supplies. **SIC:** 5013 (Motor Vehicle Supplies & New Parts). **Sales:** $82,000,000 (1992). **Emp:** 750. **Officers:** Stewart Baxter, President; Steve Korf, VP of Finance.

■ **2191** ■ **Air-Ax Suspension Systems**
PO Box 64
Edgerton, MN 56128
Phone: (507)442-8201
Free: (800)742-6868 **Fax:** (507)442-3917
Products: Motor vehicle suspension systems. **SIC:** 5013 (Motor Vehicle Supplies & New Parts). **Est:** 1984. **Sales:** $500,000 (2000). **Emp:** 4. **Officers:** Bob Roclofs, President.

■ **2192** ■ **Air Flow Systems Inc.**
5272 SE International Way
Portland, OR 97222
Phone: (503)659-9120
Free: (800)762-9876 **Fax:** (503)654-2418
URL: http://www.airflo.com
Products: Diesel truck parts. **SICs:** 5084 (Industrial Machinery & Equipment); 5013 (Motor Vehicle Supplies & New Parts). **Est:** 1971. **Sales:** $3,000,000 (2000). **Emp:** 18. **Officers:** N. Streitmatter, President; L. Westfall, VP of Finance.

■ **2193** ■ **Aisin World Corporation of America**
24330 Garnier St.
Torrance, CA 90505
Phone: (310)326-8681 **Fax:** (310)533-8271
Products: Auto parts. **SIC:** 5013 (Motor Vehicle Supplies & New Parts). **Est:** 1970. **Sales:** $590,000,000 (2000). **Emp:** 1,100. **Officers:** Tetsuro

Senga, President; Junichi Nishimura, CFO; Russell Koets, VP of Sales; Andy Tsui.

■ 2194 ■ AL-KO KOBER Corp.
25784 Borg Rd.
Elkhart, IN 46514
Phone: (219)264-0631 Fax: (219)264-5136
Products: Axles. SIC: 5013 (Motor Vehicle Supplies & New Parts). Est: 1984. Sales: $20,000,000 (2000). Emp: 120. Officers: Elwood Smith, President; Roland Kober, Vice President; John F. Juliano, VP of Sales.

■ 2195 ■ Alabama Crankshaft and Engine
1900-B S Broad St., Unit 3
Mobile, AL 36615-1821
Phone: (205)433-3691 Fax: (205)432-1159
Products: Automotive parts. SIC: 5013 (Motor Vehicle Supplies & New Parts). Sales: $6,000,000 (2000). Emp: 49. Officers: Charles Fincher; Denise Billitz.

■ 2196 ■ Alabama Crankshaft and Engine Warehouse Inc.
1432 Mims Ave. SW
Birmingham, AL 35211
Phone: (205)925-4616 Fax: (205)923-5634
Products: Brake shoes and drums; Crankshaft parts; Gaskets. SIC: 5013 (Motor Vehicle Supplies & New Parts). Est: 1958. Sales: $28,000,000 (2000). Emp: 100. Officers: Bert Siegel, President; Lennie Siegel, CFO; Eric Siegel, Dir. of Sales; Bernice Black, Dir. of Data Processing.

■ 2197 ■ Alabama Truck Body & Equipment, Inc.
190 Industrial Park Rd.
Oneonta, AL 35121
Phone: (205)274-4900
Free: (800)749-3238 Fax: (205)274-4903
URL: http://www.alabamatruckbody.com
Products: Automotive parts and supplies, New. SIC: 5013 (Motor Vehicle Supplies & New Parts). Est: 1990. Emp: 10. Officers: Leo Prince, Contact.

■ 2198 ■ Alban Engine Power Systems
6455 Washington Blvd.
Elkridge, MD 21075-5398
Phone: (410)796-8000
Free: (800)443-9813 Fax: (410)379-0911
E-mail: engine@albancat.com
URL: http://www.albancat.com
Products: CAT engine/Generator sales, parts and service. SIC: 5013 (Motor Vehicle Supplies & New Parts). Est: 1921. Sales: $44,000,000 (1999). Emp: 95. Officers: James C. Alban IV, President; Frank Izzo, VP of Finance; Michael E. Lewis, VP & General Mgr.

■ 2199 ■ Albuquerque Foreign Auto Parts
5028 Broadway Blvd. SE
Albuquerque, NM 87105-7414
Phone: (505)877-4856
Free: (800)733-7550 Fax: (505)877-5822
Products: Automobile parts, used. SIC: 5015 (Motor Vehicle Parts—Used). Est: 1989. Emp: 6. Officers: Bill Proffer, President.

■ 2200 ■ Alco Equipment Inc.
PO Box 386
Agawam, MA 01001-0386
Phone: (413)789-0330
Products: Trucks, truck bodies, trailers, and trailer parts. SIC: 5088 (Transportation Equipment & Supplies). Sales: $27,000,000 (1994). Emp: 150. Officers: David Townsend, President; Donna N. Frankel, Controller.

■ 2201 ■ Alcoa Conductors Products Co.
105 Westpark Dr.
Brentwood, TN 37027
Phone: (615)370-4300
Products: Automotive electrical circuits and fiber optics. SIC: 5063 (Electrical Apparatus & Equipment). Sales: $8,000,000 (2000). Emp: 35. Officers: Robert H. Barton, President.

■ 2202 ■ Alden Autoparts Warehouse Inc.
535 Grand Army Hwy.
Somerset, MA 02725
Phone: (508)673-4233
Products: Automotive products, including exhaust

systems, belts, hoses, filters, and chemicals. SICs: 5013 (Motor Vehicle Supplies & New Parts); 5169 (Chemicals & Allied Products Nec). Sales: $20,000,000 (2000). Emp: 110. Officers: Paul Kachapis, President; Vincent Ranucci, CFO; Sal Caizzaro, Dir. of Marketing.

■ 2203 ■ All-Car Distributors Inc.
PO Box 27
Antigo, WI 54409-0027
Phone: (715)623-3791
Free: (800)729-9974 Fax: (715)623-7239
URL: http://www.allcar.com
Products: Automotive parts and accessories. SICs: 5013 (Motor Vehicle Supplies & New Parts); 5014 (Tires & Tubes). Est: 1972. Sales: $36,000,000 (2000). Officers: Craig Cigel, Vice President, e-mail: craig@ allcar.com. Alternate Name: Allcar Automotive Centers.

■ 2204 ■ All Foreign Used Auto Parts
916 N Kings Rd.
Nampa, ID 83687-3193
Phone: (208)465-3272 Free: (800)834-8854
Products: Used motor vehicle parts and supplies. SIC: 5015 (Motor Vehicle Parts—Used). Officers: James Berlin, President.

■ 2205 ■ All Hours Auto Salvage
3110 Caldwell Blvd.
Nampa, ID 83651-6418
Phone: (208)466-9848 Fax: 800-223-7794
Products: Automobile parts, used. SIC: 5015 (Motor Vehicle Parts—Used). Officers: Leo Taylor, Owner.

■ 2206 ■ All Parts Brokers
3515 Cleveland Blvd.
Caldwell, ID 83605-6043
Phone: (208)454-0713 Free: (800)678-7474
Products: Used small truck parts. SIC: 5015 (Motor Vehicle Parts—Used). Officers: Terry Gilbert, Owner.

■ 2207 ■ All-Power Inc.
3435 S Racine Ave.
Chicago, IL 60608
Phone: (773)650-7400 Fax: (773)650-7388
Products: Truck engine parts. SIC: 5013 (Motor Vehicle Supplies & New Parts). Est: 1944. Sales: $5,100,000 (2000). Emp: 43. Officers: J. Carter Sr., Chairman of the Board; J. Carter Jr., President.

■ 2208 ■ All Products Automotive Inc.
4701 W Courtland Ave.
Chicago, IL 60639
Phone: (312)889-4500
Products: Automotive parts. SIC: 5013 (Motor Vehicle Supplies & New Parts). Sales: $12,000,000 (2000). Emp: 50. Officers: Greg Winthrop, President.

■ 2209 ■ Allied Bearing
3525 W Lincoln Ave.
PO Box 340066
Milwaukee, WI 53215
Phone: (414)672-3111 Fax: (414)672-9717
Products: Power transmission materials. SICs: 5084 (Industrial Machinery & Equipment); 5013 (Motor Vehicle Supplies & New Parts).

■ 2210 ■ Allied Bearings & Supply
932 8th Ave.
Nashville, TN 37203
Phone: (615)255-1204
Products: Auto parts and supplies, including motors and power transmission equipment. SIC: 5013 (Motor Vehicle Supplies & New Parts).

■ 2211 ■ Allied Belting and Transmission Inc.
PO Box 565713
Dallas, TX 75356
Phone: (214)631-7670
Free: (800)492-9664 Fax: (214)630-4354
Products: Conveyor belts, motor controls, and power transmission equipment. SIC: 5063 (Electrical Apparatus & Equipment). Est: 1947. Sales: $3,000,000 (2000). Emp: 8. Officers: Jon Hoggatt, President; Peggie Wright, Accounting Manager.

■ 2212 ■ Allied Body Works Inc.
625 S 96th St.
Seattle, WA 98108-4914
Phone: (206)763-7811 Fax: (206)244-2302
Products: Automotive parts and supplies, New. SIC: 5013 (Motor Vehicle Supplies & New Parts). Officers: Richard L. Minice Sr., Contact.

■ 2213 ■ Allied Inc.
260 Metty Dr.
Ann Arbor, MI 48106
Phone: (734)665-4419
Products: Auto parts. SIC: 5013 (Motor Vehicle Supplies & New Parts).

■ 2214 ■ Allied Tire and Auto Services
4749 US Highway 50 E
Carson City, NV 89701
Phone: (775)883-3101
Products: Tires. SIC: 5014 (Tires & Tubes).

■ 2215 ■ Allied Truck Equipment Corp.
4821 Massachusetts Ave.
Indianapolis, IN 46218
Phone: (317)545-1227 Fax: (317)542-7402
Products: Automotive parts and supplies, New. SIC: 5013 (Motor Vehicle Supplies & New Parts). Officers: John Schlenk, Contact.

■ 2216 ■ AlliedSignal Automotive Aftermarket
105 Pawtucket Ave.
Rumford, RI 02916-2422
Phone: (401)434-7000 Fax: (401)431-3253
Products: Automobile electrical parts, oil and air filters, brakes, spark plugs, and wiring cable. SIC: 5013 (Motor Vehicle Supplies & New Parts). Sales: $210,000,000 (2000). Emp: 500. Officers: Brad Hays, Sr. VP; Greg Perry, Controller.

■ 2217 ■ AlliedSignal Automotive Catalyst Co.
PO Box 580970
Tulsa, OK 74158-0970
Phone: (918)266-1400 Fax: (918)272-4314
Products: Automotive products, including catalytic converters; Industrial supplies. SICs: 5013 (Motor Vehicle Supplies & New Parts); 5085 (Industrial Supplies). Est: 1973. Sales: $250,000,000 (2000). Emp: 410. Officers: Thomas K. Walker, President; J. Famula, Finance Officer; J. Hiera, Dir. of Marketing; E. Burger, Dir. of Information Systems; R. Perrin, Dir of Human Resources.

■ 2218 ■ Allparts Inc.
RR 2 Box 153-A
Louisiana, MO 63353-9802
Free: (800)467-2505 Fax: (573)754-5858
Products: Brake and clutch hydraulic systems and brake hardware products for cars and light trucks. SIC: 5013 (Motor Vehicle Supplies & New Parts).

■ 2219 ■ Allstate Sales and Leasing Corp.
558 E Villaume Ave.
South St. Paul, MN 55075
Phone: (612)455-6500
Free: (800)328-0104 Fax: (612)450-8176
Products: Motorized vehicles. SIC: 5012 (Automobiles & Other Motor Vehicles). Sales: $100,000,000 (2000). Emp: 120.

■ 2220 ■ Allston Street Used Auto Parts
72 Allston St.
Providence, RI 02908-5311
Phone: (401)273-6739
Products: Used motor vehicle parts and supplies. SIC: 5015 (Motor Vehicle Parts—Used). Officers: Matthew Ray, Partner.

■ 2221 ■ Allyn Air Seat Co.
18 Millstream Rd.
Woodstock, NY 12498
Phone: (914)679-2051
Products: Motorcycle and automobile parts and accessories; Lawn and garden accessories; Bicycle accessories. SICs: 5013 (Motor Vehicle Supplies & New Parts); 5083 (Farm & Garden Machinery). Est: 1978. Sales: $500,000 (2000). Emp: 4. Officers: Ed Allyn, President, e-mail: edallyn@worldnet.att.net.

■ 2222 ■ **Alretta Truck Parts Inc.**
207 A St.
Boston, MA 02210
Phone: (617)268-8116
Products: Truck equipment and parts. SIC: 5013 (Motor Vehicle Supplies & New Parts).

■ 2223 ■ **Aluminum Line Products Co.**
24460 Sperry Circle
Westlake, OH 44145
Phone: (440)835-8880
Free: (800)321-3154 **Fax:** (440)835-8879
URL: http://www.aluminumline.com
Products: Aluminum parts, including coils, sheets, and panels for truck trailers. SIC: 5013 (Motor Vehicle Supplies & New Parts). **Est:** 1958. **Sales:** $50,000,000 (1999). **Emp:** 35. **Officers:** K.C. Wessel, President.

■ 2224 ■ **Amalgamated Automotive Industries Inc.**
PO Box 149
Camp Hill, PA 17001-0149
Phone: (717)939-7893
Products: Auto parts; Spark plugs; Starters; Brakes. SIC: 5013 (Motor Vehicle Supplies & New Parts). **Est:** 1969. **Sales:** $9,400,000 (2000). **Emp:** 92. **Officers:** Kurt J. Myers Jr., CEO & President; Janet P. Lebkicher, Controller.

■ 2225 ■ **Amarillo Clutch & Driveshaft Co.**
4420 I-40 E
Amarillo, TX 79103
Phone: (806)372-3893 **Fax:** (806)372-3408
Products: Driveshafts and clutches. SIC: 5013 (Motor Vehicle Supplies & New Parts).

■ 2226 ■ **American Auto Salvage**
PO Box 925
Clovis, NM 88102-0925
Phone: (505)763-4812
E-mail: todndeb@3lefties.com
Products: Automobile parts, new and used. SICs: 5015 (Motor Vehicle Parts—Used); 5013 (Motor Vehicle Supplies & New Parts). **Emp:** 3. **Officers:** Glen Fuller, General Mgr.

■ 2227 ■ **American Bus Sales**
195 Defense Hwy.
Annapolis, MD 21401
Phone: (410)269-0251
Products: Buses; Bus parts. SIC: 5012 (Automobiles & Other Motor Vehicles).

■ 2228 ■ **American Carrier Systems, Inc.**
2285 E Date Ave.
Fresno, CA 93706-5477
Phone: (559)442-1500
Free: (800)344-2174 **Fax:** (559)442-3618
E-mail: trailer1@thegrid.net
Products: Motor vehicle suspension systems. SIC: 5013 (Motor Vehicle Supplies & New Parts). **Est:** 1970. **Emp:** 31. **Officers:** Philip Sweet, President; Dave Sweet. **Alternate Name:** Superide Air Suspensions.

■ 2229 ■ **American Isuzu Motors Inc.**
41280 Bridge St.
Novi, MI 48375-1301
Phone: (248)426-4200
Free: (800)492-5665 **Fax:** (248)426-4228
URL: http://www.isuzuengines.com
Products: Diesel engines. SIC: 5084 (Industrial Machinery & Equipment). **Est:** 1976. **Sales:** $15,000,000 (2000). **Emp:** 48. **Officers:** Daniel Cleary; Joseph F. Okla, Marketing Mgr. **Former Name:** Isuzu Diesel of North America.

■ 2230 ■ **American Ladders & Scaffolds, Inc.**
129 Kreiger Ln.
Glastonbury, CT 06033
Phone: (860)657-9252
Free: (800)55C-LIMB **Fax:** (860)657-3543
Products: Automotive parts and supplies, New. SIC: 5013 (Motor Vehicle Supplies & New Parts). **Officers:** Kevin Prior, VP & Treasurer.

■ 2231 ■ **American Marketing International**
150 Engineers Rd.
Hauppauge, NY 11788
Phone: (516)435-4555 **Fax:** (516)435-4576
Products: Automotive parts and accessories, including motor vehicle rebuilt engine parts. SICs: 5013 (Motor Vehicle Supplies & New Parts); 5015 (Motor Vehicle Parts—Used). **Officers:** Holly Napolitano, Export Supervisor.

■ 2232 ■ **American Mobile Home Products Inc.**
817 E Maiden St.
Washington, PA 15301
Phone: (412)225-7200
Free: (800)258-2800 **Fax:** (412)225-3290
Products: Recreational Vehicle accessories. SIC: 5013 (Motor Vehicle Supplies & New Parts). **Est:** 1973. **Officers:** Richard W. Gubanish, President; Betty J. Gunbanish, VP, Sec. & Treas.

■ 2233 ■ **American Performance**
1799 Marietta Blvd., NW
Atlanta, GA 30318-3690
Phone: (404)355-8711
Free: (800)888-1111 **Fax:** (404)355-1115
Products: Automotive parts and supplies, New. SIC: 5013 (Motor Vehicle Supplies & New Parts). **Emp:** 49.

■ 2234 ■ **American Suzuki Motor Corp.**
PO Box 1100
Brea, CA 92822-1100
Phone: (714)996-7040 **Fax:** (714)970-6005
Products: Motorized vehicles. SIC: 5013 (Motor Vehicle Supplies & New Parts). **Sales:** $1,000,000,000 (2000). **Emp:** 450.

■ 2235 ■ **American Tire Distributors**
PO Box 515
Nitro, WV 25143
Phone: (304)755-8473
Products: Tires. SICs: 5014 (Tires & Tubes); 5013 (Motor Vehicle Supplies & New Parts). **Est:** 1943. **Sales:** $5,000,000 (2000). **Emp:** 19. **Officers:** Dennis Maroney, General Mgr.

■ 2236 ■ **American United Global Inc.**
11634 Patton Rd.
Downey, CA 90241
Phone: (562)862-8163 **Fax:** (562)861-4955
Products: O-rings and metal-to-rubber bonded sealing devices. SIC: 5082 (Construction & Mining Machinery). **Sales:** $154,500,000 (2000). **Emp:** 414. **Officers:** Robert M. Rubin, CEO, President & Chairman of the Board; David M. Barnes, VP & CFO.

■ 2237 ■ **Americas Trade & Supply Co.**
7630 NW 63rd St.
Miami, FL 33166
Phone: (305)594-0797 **Fax:** (305)592-8210
Products: Motor vehicle parts; Lumber and millwork; Construction materials; Office equipment; Computers and accounting software. SICs: 5013 (Motor Vehicle Supplies & New Parts); 5031 (Lumber, Plywood & Millwork); 5039 (Construction Materials Nec); 5044 (Office Equipment); 5045 (Computers, Peripherals & Software). **Officers:** Paul H. Butler.

■ 2238 ■ **Ample Technology**
2442 NW Market St., No. 43
Seattle, WA 98107
Phone: (206)789-0827
Free: (800)541-7789 **Fax:** (206)789-9003
E-mail: info@amplepower.com
URL: http://www.amplepower.com
Products: Motor vehicle instruments; Automotive batteries; Battery management and regulation for boats, RVs, and remote homes. SIC: 5013 (Motor Vehicle Supplies & New Parts). **Est:** 1987. **Sales:** $1,000,000 (2000). **Emp:** 5. **Officers:** Ruth Ishihara, President; David Smead, VP of Engineering; Dennis Kimmel, Sales/Marketing Contact, e-mail: kimmel@amplepower.com; Ruth Ishihara, Customer Service Contact, e-mail: ruth@amplepower.com; Ruth Ishihara, Human Resources Contact.

■ 2239 ■ **Anderson Auto Parts Co.**
PO Box 767
Anderson, SC 29622
Phone: (803)224-0388
URL: http://www.NAPAonline.com
Products: Automotive parts. SIC: 5013 (Motor Vehicle Supplies & New Parts). **Est:** 1929. **Sales:** $19,000,000 (2000). **Emp:** 180. **Officers:** Bannister A. Anderson, President; Hampton G. Anderson III, Treasurer.

■ 2240 ■ **Anderson & Spring Firestone**
5471 17th Ave. W
Virginia, MN 55792-3368
Phone: (218)741-1646 **Fax:** (218)741-8630
Products: Automotive springs; Automobile tires. SICs: 5014 (Tires & Tubes); 5013 (Motor Vehicle Supplies & New Parts). **Est:** 1921. **Sales:** $4,000,000 (2000). **Emp:** 9. **Officers:** Theodore Spanner, CEO & President.

■ 2241 ■ **Antelope Truck Stop**
4850 I-80 Service Rd.
Burns, WY 82053
Phone: (307)547-3334 **Fax:** (307)547-3644
Products: Truck accessories and supplies. SIC: 5013 (Motor Vehicle Supplies & New Parts).

■ 2242 ■ **Any & All Auto Parts Inc.**
755 W Sunset Rd.
Henderson, NV 89015-2601
Phone: (702)564-1212
Products: Automobile parts, used. SIC: 5015 (Motor Vehicle Parts—Used). **Officers:** Allen Rothstein, President.

■ 2243 ■ **AP Parts Co.**
PO Box 64010
Toledo, OH 43612-0010
Phone: (419)891-8400 **Fax:** (419)891-8460
Products: Mufflers. SIC: 5013 (Motor Vehicle Supplies & New Parts). **Sales:** $250,000,000 (2000). **Emp:** 2,000. **Officers:** T.R. Thibert.

■ 2244 ■ **APD Transmission Parts**
824 Memorial Dr. SE
Atlanta, GA 30316-1232
Phone: (404)688-1517
Free: (800)241-2910 **Fax:** (404)688-8816
Products: Automatic transmission parts; Rack and pinion parts; Power transmission equipment and supplies; Clutches. SIC: 5013 (Motor Vehicle Supplies & New Parts). **Emp:** 60. **Officers:** Michael Habif, President.

■ 2245 ■ **Apollo Tire Co. Inc.**
21339 Saticoy
Canoga Park, CA 91304
Phone: (818)348-6142
Products: Tires and wheels. SIC: 5014 (Tires & Tubes). **Est:** 1970. **Sales:** $18,000,000 (2000). **Emp:** 100. **Officers:** S. Bostanian, Vice President.

■ 2246 ■ **Applied Industrial Technologies**
900 E 2nd St.
Owensboro, KY 42303-3304
Phone: (270)684-9601 **Fax:** (270)685-1779
Products: Power transmission products, including bearings and chains. SIC: 5013 (Motor Vehicle Supplies & New Parts). **Former Name:** Kentucky Bearings Service.

■ 2247 ■ **Applied Industrial Technologies Inc.**
PO Box 6925
Cleveland, OH 44101-9986
Phone: (216)881-8900 **Fax:** (216)881-8988
Products: Replacement bearings; Power transmission components. SIC: 5085 (Industrial Supplies). **Sales:** $1,160,300,000 (2000). **Emp:** 4,101. **Officers:** John C. Dannemiller, CEO & President; John R. Whitten, VP of Finance & Treasurer.

■ 2248 ■ **A.P.S. Inc.**
3000 Pawnee St.
Houston, TX 77054-3301
Phone: (713)507-1100 **Fax:** (713)507-1310
Products: Auto accessories. SIC: 5013 (Motor Vehicle Supplies & New Parts). **Est:** 1957. **Sales:** $603,700,000 (2000). **Emp:** 6,833. **Officers:** Mark S. Hoffman, CEO & President; John Hendrix, VP & CFO.

■ 2249 ■ **Area Distributors, Inc.**
61-02 31st Ave.
Woodside, NY 11377
Phone: (718)726-9200
Products: Power transmissions equipment. **SICs:** 5084 (Industrial Machinery & Equipment); 5013 (Motor Vehicle Supplies & New Parts).

■ 2250 ■ **Area Wholesale Tire Co., Inc.**
5620 Airline Hwy.
PO Box 2723
Baton Rouge, LA 70821-2723
Phone: (504)356-2548
Free: (800)272-3067 **Fax:** (504)356-6727
Products: Tires and inner tubes, new. **SIC:** 5014 (Tires & Tubes). **Est:** 1961. **Emp:** 87. **Officers:** C.R. Potter, CEO & President.

■ 2251 ■ **S.M. Arnold Inc.**
7901 Michigan Ave.
St. Louis, MO 63111-3594
Phone: (314)544-4103 **Fax:** (314)544-3159
E-mail: smarnold97@aol.com
URL: http://www.smarnoldinc.com
Products: Car cleaning products. **SIC:** 5013 (Motor Vehicle Supplies & New Parts). **Est:** 1928. **Sales:** $10,000,000 (2000). **Emp:** 60. **Officers:** T. Arnold, Chairman of the Board; S. Arnold, CFO; J. Arnold, Dir. of Marketing; R. Moroni, Dir. of Data Processing.

■ 2252 ■ **Arnold Motor Supply Co.**
PO Box 320
Spencer, IA 51301-0320
Phone: (712)262-4885
Products: Automotive parts and supplies, including starters and converters. **SIC:** 5013 (Motor Vehicle Supplies & New Parts). **Est:** 1927. **Sales:** $20,000,000 (2000). **Emp:** 180. **Officers:** Milo Allen, General Mgr.; Steve Lansing, Controller.

■ 2253 ■ **Aronson Tire Co. Inc.**
510 Washington St.
Auburn, MA 01501
Phone: (508)832-3244
Products: Recapped and new tires. **SIC:** 5014 (Tires & Tubes). **Est:** 1928. **Sales:** $9,600,000 (2000). **Emp:** 50. **Officers:** Robert J. Aronson, President; Thomas Severance, Controller; Albert Bonavita, Dir. of Operations.

■ 2254 ■ **Arrow Safety Device Co.**
301 S DuPont Hwy.
PO Box 299
Georgetown, DE 19947-0299
Phone: (302)856-2516
Free: (800)327-2514 **Fax:** (302)856-1549
E-mail: arrow@jersey.net
URL: http://www.arrowsafetydevice.com
Products: Automotive and truck lighting and accessories. **SIC:** 5013 (Motor Vehicle Supplies & New Parts). **Est:** 1930. **Sales:** $5,000,000 (2000). **Emp:** 50. **Officers:** A.W. Hopkin Jr., CEO; Richard W. Workman, President; Robert L. Littleton, Sales Service Mgr.

■ 2255 ■ **Arrow Speed Warehouse**
686 S Adams
Kansas City, KS 66105
Phone: (913)321-1200 **Fax:** (913)321-7729
Products: Foreign and domestic automotive parts. **SIC:** 5013 (Motor Vehicle Supplies & New Parts). **Est:** 1957. **Sales:** $14,500,000 (2000). **Emp:** 100. **Officers:** Ron Coppaken, President; Bob Faltermeier, Controller; Bryan Foster, Dir. of Marketing & Sales; John Wyly, Marketing Mgr.

■ 2256 ■ **Arrow Trucks and Parts Co.**
2637 W Fort St.
Detroit, MI 48216
Phone: (313)496-0900
Free: (800)521-0645 **Fax:** (313)496-0937
Products: Drive train components, new, except wheels and brakes; Parts and attachments for industrial trucks and tractors. **SICs:** 5013 (Motor Vehicle Supplies & New Parts); 5085 (Industrial Supplies). **Est:** 1931. **Emp:** 31. **Officers:** L. Neuder, President; K. Kurtz, Vice President; W. Neuder, Vice President.

■ 2257 ■ **Arvin Industries Inc.**
PO Box 3000
Columbus, IN 47202-3000
Phone: (812)379-3000 **Fax:** (812)379-3688
Products: Automotive equipment; Laminated metals. **SICs:** 5085 (Industrial Supplies); 5013 (Motor Vehicle Supplies & New Parts). **Est:** 1919. **Sales:** $2,349,000,000 (2000). **Emp:** 14,324. **Officers:** Byron O. Pond, CEO & Chairman of the Board; Richard A. Smith, VP & CFO; W. Frederick Meyer, President & Dir. of Research.

■ 2258 ■ **Arvin Industries Inc. North American Automotive Div.**
1531 13th St.
Columbus, IN 47201
Phone: (812)379-3000
Products: Automotive parts. **SIC:** 5013 (Motor Vehicle Supplies & New Parts). **Est:** 1919. **Sales:** $400,000,000 (2000). **Emp:** 4,000. **Officers:** J.T. Atkins, President; Larry D. Blair, VP of Finance; Donald L. Scheidt, VP of Marketing & Sales; Dan Moore, Dir. of Information Systems; Richard L. Hendricks, VP of Human Resources.

■ 2259 ■ **Asbury Automotive Group**
One Tower Bridge, Ste. 1440
Conshohocken, PA 19428
Phone: (610)260-9800
Products: Automobile dealerships. **SIC:** 5012 (Automobiles & Other Motor Vehicles). **Sales:** $3,100,000,000 (2000). **Emp:** 5,100. **Officers:** Thomas R. Gibson, Chairman of the Board & COO; Allen Westergard, CFO.

■ 2260 ■ **ASEC Manufacturing**
PO Box 580970
Tulsa, OK 74158-0970
Phone: (918)266-1400 **Fax:** (918)272-4314
Products: Motor vehicle supplies and new parts. **SIC:** 5013 (Motor Vehicle Supplies & New Parts). **Sales:** $325,000,000 (2000). **Emp:** 650. **Officers:** Edwin L. Yoder, VP & General Merchandising Mgr.; Sean Purdy, Finance Officer.

■ 2261 ■ **ASI Erie**
345 E 16th St.
Erie, PA 16503-1902
Phone: (814)459-3000 **Fax:** (814)297-3940
Products: Exhaust and lube chassis. **SIC:** 5013 (Motor Vehicle Supplies & New Parts). **Emp:** 6. **Officers:** Mike Shultz, Manager.

■ 2262 ■ **ATC International**
16000 Memorial Dr., Ste. 210
Houston, TX 77079-4008
Phone: (713)622-3047 **Fax:** (713)622-1864
Products: Gas turbines; Automotive supplies; Aircraft equipment; Oilfield and pipeline equipment. **SICs:** 5013 (Motor Vehicle Supplies & New Parts); 5088 (Transportation Equipment & Supplies); 5084 (Industrial Machinery & Equipment). **Officers:** Pat Carpenter, Project Coordinator.

■ 2263 ■ **Atlanta Commercial Tire Inc.**
1495 Northside NW
Atlanta, GA 30318
Phone: (404)351-9016
Products: Truck tires. **SIC:** 5014 (Tires & Tubes).

■ 2264 ■ **Atlanta Wheels & Accessories, Inc.**
777 11th St. NW
Atlanta, GA 30318-5523
Phone: (404)876-5847
Free: (800)453-6247 **Fax:** (404)876-0097
Products: Motor vehicle wheels. **SIC:** 5013 (Motor Vehicle Supplies & New Parts). **Emp:** 24. **Officers:** Albert R. Rooken.

■ 2265 ■ **Atlantic Detroit Diesel-Allison Inc.**
PO Box 950
Lodi, NJ 07644
Phone: (201)489-5800
Products: Diesel engines and transmissions. **SIC:** 5084 (Industrial Machinery & Equipment). **Sales:** $86,400,000 (2000). **Emp:** 275. **Officers:** Richard Diegnan, Chairman of the Board; David Newingham, Controller.

■ 2266 ■ **Atlantic Mobile Homes and RV Supplies Corp.**
PO Box 7853
Greensboro, NC 27407
Phone: (910)299-4691
Products: Mobile home and RV supplies. **SIC:** 5013 (Motor Vehicle Supplies & New Parts). **Est:** 1953. **Sales:** $16,000,000 (2000). **Emp:** 24. **Officers:** Gary W. Myers, President; Geraldine Burch, Treasurer; Richard Gibson, General Mgr.

■ 2267 ■ **Atlantic Tire Wholesaler**
7307 Pulaski Hwy.
Baltimore, MD 21237
Phone: (410)866-6400
Products: Tires. **SIC:** 5014 (Tires & Tubes).

■ 2268 ■ **Authorized Motor Parts**
525 S Jefferson Ave.
St. Louis, MO 63103
Phone: (314)533-0243
Products: Foreign and domestic auto parts; Industrial, agricultural, and custom machinery parts. **SICs:** 5013 (Motor Vehicle Supplies & New Parts); 5084 (Industrial Machinery & Equipment); 5083 (Farm & Garden Machinery). **Sales:** $15,000,000 (2000). **Emp:** 100. **Officers:** W. Looney, Vice President.

■ 2269 ■ **Auto Clutch/All Brake Inc.**
5551 W Ogden Ave.
Cicero, IL 60804-3507
Phone: (708)656-2100
Free: (800)334-4654 **Fax:** (708)656-2080
Products: Truck parts. **SIC:** 5013 (Motor Vehicle Supplies & New Parts). **Est:** 1936. **Sales:** $8,000,000 (2000). **Emp:** 50. **Officers:** Frank R. Raidl. **Former Name:** Auto Clutch & Parts Service Inc.

■ 2270 ■ **Auto Collision Inc.**
PO Box 354
Jessup, MD 20794
Phone: (410)799-5680 **Fax:** (410)799-3042
URL: http://www.autocollisioninc.com
Products: Auto repair parts and supplies. **SICs:** 5013 (Motor Vehicle Supplies & New Parts); 5015 (Motor Vehicle Parts—Used). **Est:** 1971. **Sales:** $2,500,000 (2000). **Emp:** 33. **Officers:** Carl E. Nanney, President.

■ 2271 ■ **Auto Components Inc.**
1950 N Mannheim Rd.
Melrose Park, IL 60160
Phone: (708)345-8675 **Fax:** (708)345-8704
Products: Nonelectric heating radiators and parts; Blowers and fans; Automotive parts and supplies, New. **SIC:** 5013 (Motor Vehicle Supplies & New Parts). **Est:** 1972. **Sales:** $10,000,000 (2000). **Emp:** 150. **Officers:** J. P. Sheehan, President; Ben P. Barton, Marketing & Sales Mgr.

■ 2272 ■ **Auto Electric Sales and Service Co.**
PO Box 609
Ardmore, OK 73402
Phone: (580)223-8000 **Fax:** (580)223-8114
E-mail: ae609@brightok.net
Products: Automobile parts, including belts, spark plugs, clutches, and oil filters. **SIC:** 5013 (Motor Vehicle Supplies & New Parts). **Est:** 1921. **Sales:** $1,400,000 (2000). **Emp:** 12. **Officers:** Marc Dickinson, President; Lawrence Scott, Controller; David C. Dickinson, Vice President.

■ 2273 ■ **Auto Parts Association**
1170 W Riverdale Rd.
Ogden, UT 84405
Phone: (801)394-4700
Products: Brake lining. **SIC:** 5013 (Motor Vehicle Supplies & New Parts).

■ 2274 ■ **Auto Parts Club Inc.**
5825 Oberlin Dr., No. 100
San Diego, CA 92121
Phone: (619)622-5050 **Fax:** (619)622-5062
Products: Auto parts. **SICs:** 5013 (Motor Vehicle Supplies & New Parts); 5015 (Motor Vehicle Parts—Used). **Est:** 1989. **Sales:** $100,000,000 (2000). **Emp:** 700. **Officers:** Steve Kirby, CEO & President; Debbie Bosse, Controller; Robert Ames, Dir. of Marketing; David Watson, Dir. of Admin.; Gaylynn Bowes, Human Resources Mgr.

■ 2275 ■ Auto Parts Depot Inc.
741 Windsor St.
Hartford, CT 06120
Phone: (860)522-1104 **Fax:** (860)247-2801
Products: Used auto parts. **SIC:** 5015 (Motor Vehicle Parts—Used). **Est:** 1996. **Emp:** 6. **Officers:** Jacquelyne Treiber, President. **Former Name:** Blonders of Hartford.

■ 2276 ■ Auto Parts Wholesale
PO Box 3289
Bakersfield, CA 93385
Phone: (661)322-5011 **Fax:** (661)322-4478
Products: Automotive parts. **SIC:** 5013 (Motor Vehicle Supplies & New Parts). **Est:** 1956. **Sales:** $130,000,000 (1999). **Emp:** 1,400. **Officers:** Jon McMurtrey, President; Don McMurtrey, Finance Officer. **Former Name:** Henderson Brothers Stores.

■ 2277 ■ Auto Safety House Inc.
2630 W Buckeye Rd.
Phoenix, AZ 85009
Phone: (602)269-9721 **Fax:** (602)278-3916
Products: Trailer, truck, and bus parts. **SIC:** 5013 (Motor Vehicle Supplies & New Parts). **Est:** 1940. **Officers:** Harry Amster, Pres.; Kirk Amster, V.P.; Phil Polizzato, Mgr.

■ 2278 ■ Auto Service and Tire Supermarts Inc.
5861 Roswell Rd. NE
Atlanta, GA 30328
Phone: (404)252-1603
Products: Tires and automobile parts. **SIC:** 5014 (Tires & Tubes). **Est:** 1970. **Sales:** $2,500,000 (2000). **Emp:** 18. **Officers:** Leroy Lashley, President.

■ 2279 ■ Auto Trends Inc.
9818 Grinnell
Detroit, MI 48213
Phone: (313)571-7300 **Fax:** (313)571-1950
Products: Automobile trimmings; Automotive accessories; Automotive parts and supplies, New. **SIC:** 5013 (Motor Vehicle Supplies & New Parts). **Sales:** $3,000,000 (2000). **Emp:** 35. **Officers:** Charles D. Ninowski.

■ 2280 ■ Auto Truck Inc.
1160 N Ellis St.
Bensenville, IL 60106
Phone: (708)860-5600 **Fax:** (708)860-5631
Products: Automotive parts and supplies, New. **SIC:** 5013 (Motor Vehicle Supplies & New Parts). **Officers:** James Dondlinger, Contact.

■ 2281 ■ Auto Wares Inc.
440 Kirtland St. SW
Grand Rapids, MI 49507
Phone: (616)243-2125
Products: Commercial and passenger auto and truck parts. **SIC:** 5013 (Motor Vehicle Supplies & New Parts). **Est:** 1976. **Sales:** $240,000,000 (2000). **Emp:** 450. **Officers:** Fred Bunting, President; Greg Hinkle, Treasurer.

■ 2282 ■ Auto Wheel Service Inc.
1400 NW Raleigh St.
Portland, OR 97209
Phone: (503)228-9346 **Fax:** (503)273-2887
Products: Trailer parts; Auto and truck wheels. **SIC:** 5013 (Motor Vehicle Supplies & New Parts). **Est:** 1935. **Sales:** $6,500,000 (2000). **Emp:** 32. **Officers:** R.J. Diller, President; Tim Madden, Controller.

■ 2283 ■ Autoline Industries Inc.
625 Enterprise Dr.
Oak Brook, IL 60523-8813
Phone: (630)990-3200 **Fax:** (630)990-0500
E-mail: autoline@autolineonline.com
URL: http://www.autolineonline.com
Products: Rebuilt and new automotive parts and supplies, including water pumps, master cylinders, calipers, clutches, brake boosters, windshield wiper motors, window lift motors, ignition distributors, smog air pumps, powersteering pumps, gear boxes, rack and pinion units, and cv drive axles. **SICs:** 5015 (Motor Vehicle Parts—Used); 5013 (Motor Vehicle Supplies & New Parts). **Est:** 1947. **Emp:** 700. **Officers:** Michael J.

Winter, President; Steve Hoane, VP of Marketing & Sales; Donato A. Savini, Exec. VP & COO.

■ 2284 ■ Automoco Corp.
9142 Independance Ave.
Chatsworth, CA 91311-5902
Phone: (818)882-6422 **Fax:** (818)882-3616
Products: Automotive transmission parts. **SIC:** 5013 (Motor Vehicle Supplies & New Parts). **Est:** 1961. **Sales:** $15,600,000 (2000). **Emp:** 90. **Officers:** Don Spar, President; Steve Potter, VP of Finance.

■ 2285 ■ Automotive Diagnostics
8001 Angling Rd.
Kalamazoo, MI 49002
Phone: (616)329-7600 **Fax:** (616)329-7614
Products: Automotive equipment and parts. **SIC:** 5013 (Motor Vehicle Supplies & New Parts). **Est:** 1917. **Sales:** $160,000,000 (2000). **Emp:** 1,650. **Officers:** Ron Ortiz, President; Mark Kehlenbeck, VP of Finance; Russell Bailey, VP of Sales; Tom Minor, Dir. of Information Systems; Clyde Rundle, Human Resources Mgr.

■ 2286 ■ Automotive Distributors Inc.
10 Liberty Dr.
Bangor, ME 04401
Phone: (207)848-2233
Free: (800)699-6959 **Fax:** (207)848-2899
Products: Car wash and detail supply; Wiper rags and paper. **SIC:** 5087 (Service Establishment Equipment). **Est:** 1992. **Sales:** $500,000 (1999). **Emp:** 1. **Officers:** Anthony Carnay, anthonycarnay@msn.com.

■ 2287 ■ Automotive Dryers Inc.
PO Box 170
Cumming, GA 30028
Phone: (404)781-6653
Products: Automotive parts. **SIC:** 5013 (Motor Vehicle Supplies & New Parts).

■ 2288 ■ Automotive Electric and Supply Co.
935 Lindsay Blvd.
Idaho Falls, ID 83402-1817
Phone: (208)523-1442
Products: Used automotive parts and supplies. **SIC:** 5015 (Motor Vehicle Parts—Used). **Officers:** Kirk Hansen, President.

■ 2289 ■ Automotive Ignition Company Inc.
301 Meade St.
PO Box 91039
Pittsburgh, PA 15221
Phone: (412)243-3080
Free: (800)472-2463 **Fax:** (412)241-8843
E-mail: salesautomobileomotiveignitioncom
URL: http://www.automotiveignition.com
Products: Diesel fuel injection; Industrial ignitions; Heavy duty electrical equipment. **SIC:** 5013 (Motor Vehicle Supplies & New Parts). **Est:** 1926. **Sales:** $5,000,000 (2000). **Emp:** 25. **Officers:** P.V. Logue, President; Kevin Garland, Controller; James G. Logue, Dir. of Marketing; George Phillips, Sales & Marketing Contact; William Weil, Customer Service Contact.

■ 2290 ■ Automotive Importing Manufacturing Inc.
3920 Security Park Dr.
Rancho Cordova, CA 95742
Phone: (916)985-8505
Free: (800)366-3246 **Fax:** (916)985-0366
URL: http://www.aim.soft.com
Products: Automotive parts, including alternators, starters, and bearings. **SIC:** 5013 (Motor Vehicle Supplies & New Parts). **Sales:** $22,000,000 (2000). **Emp:** 300. **Officers:** Frank Seabourne, President; Steve Seabourne, Vice President, e-mail: steves@aim-soft.com.

■ 2291 ■ Automotive Industries Inc.
2021 Sunnydale Blvd.
Clearwater, FL 33765-1202
Phone: (904)355-7511 **Fax:** (904)355-9236
Products: Tires and inner tubes, new; Automotive parts and supplies, New. **SICs:** 5014 (Tires & Tubes); 5013 (Motor Vehicle Supplies & New Parts). **Est:** 1988. **Sales:** $30,000,000 (2000). **Emp:** 300. **Officers:** Jim Hallford, Warehouse Manager.

■ 2292 ■ Automotive Parts Distributors
900b South St.
Nashville, TN 37203
Phone: (615)259-2725
Products: Automotive parts and supplies. **SIC:** 5013 (Motor Vehicle Supplies & New Parts).

■ 2293 ■ Automotive Parts Headquarters Inc.
125 29th Ave. S
St. Cloud, MN 56301
Phone: (612)252-5411
Products: Automotive parts and accessories. **SIC:** 5013 (Motor Vehicle Supplies & New Parts). **Est:** 1978. **Sales:** $18,000,000 (2000). **Emp:** 275. **Officers:** John Bartlett Jr., President.

■ 2294 ■ Automotive Parts Wholesaler
131 Holton St.
Brighton, MA 02135-1313
Phone: (617)437-8433 **Fax:** (617)437-1223
Products: Drive line products and exhaust systems. **SIC:** 5013 (Motor Vehicle Supplies & New Parts).

■ 2295 ■ Automotive Sales Co.
1801 N Black Cnyn Hwy.
Phoenix, AZ 85009
Phone: (602)258-8851 **Fax:** (602)271-4459
Products: Auto parts, including power steering equipment, engines, hoses, filters, belts, and brakes. **SIC:** 5013 (Motor Vehicle Supplies & New Parts). **Est:** 1935. **Sales:** $24,000,000 (2000). **Emp:** 150. **Officers:** Osh Tadros, Area Mgr.; Tim Szkatulski, Controller; Howard Bartels, Sales Mgr., e-mail: howardbartels@fleetprisis.com; Lisa Anderson, Human Resources Mgr.

■ 2296 ■ Automotive Supply Associates
129 Manchester
Concord, NH 03301
Phone: (603)225-4000
Products: Automotive supplies. **SIC:** 5013 (Motor Vehicle Supplies & New Parts). **Sales:** $97,000,000 (1992). **Emp:** 400. **Officers:** George Segal, President.

■ 2297 ■ Automotive Supply Co.
PO Box 145
Appleton, WI 54912
Phone: (920)734-2651
Products: Automobile parts. **SIC:** 5013 (Motor Vehicle Supplies & New Parts). **Sales:** $30,000,000 (1994). **Emp:** 125. **Officers:** Casey Wewerka, President; Chris Borchardt, Controller.

■ 2298 ■ Automotive Trades Div.
3M Center Bldg. 223-6NW-01
St. Paul, MN 55144
Phone: (612)733-5547
Products: Automotive parts and supplies, New. **SIC:** 5013 (Motor Vehicle Supplies & New Parts).

■ 2299 ■ Automotive Wholesalers Co.
PO Box 1676
Goldsboro, NC 27533
Phone: (919)735-3236
Products: New automotive parts and supplies. **SIC:** 5013 (Motor Vehicle Supplies & New Parts). **Est:** 1948. **Sales:** $3,000,000 (2000). **Emp:** 29. **Officers:** Leon Bryant.

■ 2300 ■ Autoxport Inc.
111 Mill River Rd.
Oyster Bay, NY 11771-2736
Phone: (212)349-1168 **Fax:** (212)349-1329
Products: Motor vehicle parts; New and used motor vehicles. **SICs:** 5013 (Motor Vehicle Supplies & New Parts); 5012 (Automobiles & Other Motor Vehicles). **Officers:** Carlos H. Suazo, V.P.

■ 2301 ■ Awalt Wholesale Inc.
PO Box 907
Fairfield, TX 75840
Phone: (903)389-2159 **Fax:** (903)389-2493
Products: Automotive parts; Motor fuels; Lubricants. **SICs:** 5013 (Motor Vehicle Supplies & New Parts); 5172 (Petroleum Products Nec). **Est:** 1958. **Sales:** $8,000,000 (2000). **Emp:** 22. **Officers:** John Awalt, President, e-mail: awalt@attmail.com.

■ 2302 ■ **Axelrods Tire Inc.**
Rte. 66
Portland, CT 06480
Phone: (860)342-0102
Products: Tires. **SIC:** 5014 (Tires & Tubes). **Est:** 1970.
Sales: $700,000 (2000). **Emp:** 6. **Officers:** Jack Axelrod, CEO & President; Sharon Floyd.

■ 2303 ■ **B and B Motor and Control Inc.**
39-40 Cresent St.
Long Island City, NY 11101
Phone: (718)784-1313
Products: Motors. **SIC:** 5013 (Motor Vehicle Supplies & New Parts). **Est:** 1921. **Sales:** $19,000,000 (2000). **Emp:** 80. **Officers:** Paul Berson, President; J.T. Wallace, VP of Marketing.

■ 2304 ■ **B & B Parts Distributing**
1805 W 34th St.
Houston, TX 77018-6105
Phone: (713)222-6633   **Fax:** (713)222-6781
Products: Automotive supplies. **SIC:** 5013 (Motor Vehicle Supplies & New Parts). **Est:** 1974. **Emp:** 20.
Officers: Bobby Belyeu.

■ 2305 ■ **B and C Auto Supply**
5491 Minnesota Dr.
Anchorage, AK 99518
Phone: (907)562-2047
Products: Auto parts. **SIC:** 5013 (Motor Vehicle Supplies & New Parts). **Sales:** $12,000,000 (2000).
Emp: 100. **Officers:** Tom Wacker, General Mgr.

■ 2306 ■ **B & D Auto Salvage & Repair**
PO Box 456
Winner, SD 57580-0456
Phone: (605)842-2877
Products: Used automotive parts and supplies. **SIC:** 5015 (Motor Vehicle Parts—Used). **Officers:** Bob Herman, Partner.

■ 2307 ■ **B/T Western Corp.**
4 Upper Newport Plz., No. 200
Newport Beach, CA 92660
Phone: (714)476-8424   **Fax:** (714)476-1224
Products: Automobile parts and accessories. **SIC:** 5012 (Automobiles & Other Motor Vehicles). **Est:** 1976.
Sales: $100,000,000 (2000). **Emp:** 19. **Officers:** Ronald W. Barley, CEO & President.

■ 2308 ■ **Badger Body and Truck Equipment Co.**
6336 Grover St.
Omaha, NE 68106
Phone: (402)558-5300
Products: Truck platforms and boxes. **SICs:** 5012 (Automobiles & Other Motor Vehicles); 5013 (Motor Vehicle Supplies & New Parts). **Est:** 1917. **Sales:** $3,000,000 (1999). **Emp:** 13. **Officers:** Arthur M. Jacobs, President; Marion Epperson, Controller; Greg Siedelmann, Dir. of Marketing.

■ 2309 ■ **Badger Trailer and Equipment Corp.**
415 S 3rd St.
Milwaukee, WI 53204
Phone: (414)271-8273   **Fax:** (414)271-8277
Products: Truck and trailer repair supplies. **SIC:** 5013 (Motor Vehicle Supplies & New Parts). **Est:** 1940.
Sales: $5,000,000 (2000). **Emp:** 29. **Officers:** Gordon F. Lee, President & Treasurer.

■ 2310 ■ **Baker-Stephens Tire Co.**
305 N 1st St.
Artesia, NM 88210
Phone: (505)734-6001
Products: Tires. **SIC:** 5014 (Tires & Tubes).

■ 2311 ■ **Baker Truck Equipment**
State Rte. 60 at Mynes Rd.
PO Box 482
Hurricane, WV 25526
Phone: (304)722-3814   **Fax:** (304)722-3829
Products: Automotive parts and supplies, New. **SIC:** 5013 (Motor Vehicle Supplies & New Parts). **Officers:** Charlie Flowers, Contact.

■ 2312 ■ **Ball Tire and Gas Inc.**
620 Ripley Blvd.
Alpena, MI 49707
Phone: (517)354-4186   **Fax:** (517)356-2080
Products: Tires and petroleum. **SICs:** 5014 (Tires & Tubes); 5172 (Petroleum Products Nec). **Sales:** $15,000,000 (1993). **Emp:** 100. **Officers:** James Ball, President; Francis M.C. Ball, Treasurer.

■ 2313 ■ **Ballenger Automotive Service**
125 W Pierce
Council Bluffs, IA 51503-4396
Phone: (712)322-6636
Free: (800)831-8469   **Fax:** (712)322-6047
Products: Brake parts and assemblies; Automotive air-conditioning equipment; Spark plugs; Fuses and fuse equipment; Bearings; Switches, for electrical circuitry; Washers, hardware; Filters; Gasoline engines and gasoline engine parts for motor vehicles; Carburetors, pistons, rings, and valves; Automotive batteries. **SIC:** 5013 (Motor Vehicle Supplies & New Parts). **Est:** 1926. **Emp:** 18.

■ 2314 ■ **Baltimore & Washington Truck Equipment, Inc.**
1001 E Ridgeville Blvd.
PO Box 450
Mt. Airy, MD 21771
Phones: (301)831-7020   (301)442-1188
Free: (800)468-9290   **Fax:** (301)831-0170
Products: Automotive parts and supplies, New. **SIC:** 5013 (Motor Vehicle Supplies & New Parts). **Est:** 1994.
Emp: 17. **Officers:** Kevin Keller, President.

■ 2315 ■ **Banjo's Performancenter Inc.**
64 Cabinwood Dr.
Hendersonville, NC 28792-7644
Phone: (704)684-7814   **Fax:** (704)684-2523
Products: Racing car parts. **SIC:** 5013 (Motor Vehicle Supplies & New Parts). **Est:** 1970. **Sales:** $3,500,000 (2000). **Emp:** 20. **Officers:** Edwin K. Matthews Jr., President; Bob Dyer, Controller.

■ 2316 ■ **Barjan Products, L.P.**
2751 Morton Dr.
East Moline, IL 61244-1802
Phones: (309)755-4546   (312)595-3933
Fax: (309)755-5506
Products: Truck parts, accessories, and novelties.
SIC: 5013 (Motor Vehicle Supplies & New Parts).

■ 2317 ■ **Barker-Jennings Corp.**
PO Box 11289
Lynchburg, VA 24506
Phone: (804)846-8471   **Fax:** (804)846-8169
Products: Automotive parts and supplies, New; Hardware; Industrial supplies. **SICs:** 5013 (Motor Vehicle Supplies & New Parts); 5085 (Industrial Supplies); 5072 (Hardware). **Est:** 1885. **Sales:** $13,000,000 (2000). **Emp:** 90.

■ 2318 ■ **Barnes Motor and Parts Co.**
PO Box 1207
Wilson, NC 27893
Phone: (252)243-2161   **Fax:** (252)243-0720
URL: http://www.barnesmotorparts.com
Products: Automotive parts and paint. **SIC:** 5013 (Motor Vehicle Supplies & New Parts). **Est:** 1923.
Sales: $35,000,000 (1999). **Emp:** 350. **Officers:** Robert Kirkland Jr., President; Robert Kirland III., Treasurer & Secty.

■ 2319 ■ **Barneys Auto Salvage Inc.**
2700 N Cliff Ave.
Sioux Falls, SD 57104-0972
Phone: (605)338-7041
Products: Motor vehicle parts and accessories. **SIC:** 5015 (Motor Vehicle Parts—Used). **Officers:** Barney Cain, President.

■ 2320 ■ **Baron**
15321 Transistor Ln.
Huntington Beach, CA 92649-1143
Phone: (714)898-1255
Free: (800)232-2766   **Fax:** (714)895-5105
E-mail: lficathy@aol.com
Products: Automotive accessories. **SIC:** 5013 (Motor Vehicle Supplies & New Parts). **Est:** 1970. **Sales:** $1,200,000 (2000). **Emp:** 10.

■ 2321 ■ **Barron Motor Inc.**
PO Box 1327
Cedar Rapids, IA 52406
Phone: (319)393-6220   **Fax:** (319)393-4864
Products: Automotive parts. **SIC:** 5013 (Motor Vehicle Supplies & New Parts). **Est:** 1930. **Sales:** $30,000,000 (2000). **Emp:** 55. **Officers:** William J. Barron, President.

■ 2322 ■ **Barrows Used Auto Parts**
49 Townfarm
Monmouth, ME 04259-9801
Phone: (207)268-4262
Products: Automobile parts, used. **SIC:** 5015 (Motor Vehicle Parts—Used). **Officers:** David Barrows, Owner.

■ 2323 ■ **Barstad and Donicht Inc.**
795 Aladdin Ave.
San Leandro, CA 94577
Phone: (510)357-0777   **Fax:** (510)357-3777
Products: Parts and components for travel and camping trailers. **SIC:** 5088 (Transportation Equipment & Supplies). **Est:** 1950. **Sales:** $1,200,000 (2000).
Emp: 20. **Officers:** M. Dorn, President.

■ 2324 ■ **Barstow Truck Parts and Equipment Co.**
2431 W Main St.
Barstow, CA 92311
Phone: (760)256-1086
Products: Truck parts and equipment. **SIC:** 5013 (Motor Vehicle Supplies & New Parts). **Est:** 1968.
Sales: $7,500,000 (2000). **Emp:** 65. **Officers:** James Rajacich, President; Joyce Jaska, Controller.

■ 2325 ■ **Basic Convenience Foods**
2675 Industrial Dr., No. 202
Ogden, UT 84401
Phone: (801)399-0440
Products: Food, including garlic. **SIC:** 5013 (Motor Vehicle Supplies & New Parts).

■ 2326 ■ **Batteries Plus L.P.**
625 Walnut Ridge Dr.Ste. 106
Hartland, WI 53029
Phone: (414)369-0690   **Fax:** (414)369-0680
Products: Wet and dry batteries. **SIC:** 5013 (Motor Vehicle Supplies & New Parts). **Sales:** $18,000,000 (2000). **Emp:** 53. **Officers:** Ronald C. Rezetco, President.

■ 2327 ■ **Battery and Tire Warehouse Inc.**
625 N Fairview Ave.
St. Paul, MN 55104
Phone: (612)646-2265   **Fax:** (612)646-1390
Products: Tires and retread tires; Automotive parts and accessories, including batteries. **SICs:** 5014 (Tires & Tubes); 5013 (Motor Vehicle Supplies & New Parts).
Est: 1948. **Sales:** $12,000,000 (2000). **Emp:** 48.
Officers: C.J. Bodenstab, President; Patrick Fitschen, Controller.

■ 2328 ■ **Bauer Built Inc.**
Hwy. 25 S
PO Box 248
Durand, WI 54736-0248
Phone: (715)672-4295   **Fax:** (715)672-4675
Products: Tires. **SIC:** 5014 (Tires & Tubes). **Est:** 1944.
Sales: $127,000,000 (1999). **Emp:** 550. **Officers:** Jerry M. Bauer, President; Larry J. Weber, Exec. VP; Bill Yingst, Human Resources.

■ 2329 ■ **Beall Transport Equipment Co**
PO Box 17095
Portland, OR 97217
Phone: (503)285-5959   **Fax:** (503)285-1866
Products: New and used trailers, parts and services; Light manufacturing. **SIC:** 5012 (Automobiles & Other Motor Vehicles).

■ 2330 ■ **Beardslee Transmission Equipment Company Inc.**
27-22 Jackson Ave.
Long Island City, NY 11101
Phone: (718)784-4100   **Fax:** (516)747-9307
Products: Transmission equipment. **SIC:** 5013 (Motor Vehicle Supplies & New Parts). **Est:** 1951. **Sales:**

$4,000,000 (2000). **Emp:** 23. **Officers:** E.B. Beardslee, President.

■ 2331 ■ **Bearing Distributors Inc.**
140 Eastern Ave.
Bensenville, IL 60106
Phone: (708)595-9034 **Fax:** (708)595-4631
Products: Bearings; Power transmissions. **SICs:** 5084 (Industrial Machinery & Equipment); 5085 (Industrial Supplies); 5013 (Motor Vehicle Supplies & New Parts).

■ 2332 ■ **Bearing Distributors Inc.**
3002 Executive Dr.
PO Box 16364
Greensboro, NC 27406
Phone: (919)724-8401
Products: Transmission parts and bearings. **SICs:** 5013 (Motor Vehicle Supplies & New Parts); 5085 (Industrial Supplies).

■ 2333 ■ **Bearing Distributors Inc.**
4400 Indiana Ave., Ste. B
PO Box 4453
Winston-Salem, NC 27105
Phone: (919)661-1199 **Fax:** (919)661-1030
Products: Bearings; Power transmission equipment. **SIC:** 5013 (Motor Vehicle Supplies & New Parts).

■ 2334 ■ **Bearing Distributors, Inc.**
2039 Meeting St.
PO Box 7527
Charleston, SC 29405
Phone: (803)747-0473 **Fax:** (803)744-4201
Products: Bearings; Power transmission parts. **SICs:** 5013 (Motor Vehicle Supplies & New Parts); 5085 (Industrial Supplies).

■ 2335 ■ **Bearing Distributors Inc.**
930 Stadium Rd.
PO Box 2347
Columbia, SC 29202
Phone: (803)799-0834 **Fax:** (803)256-3824
Products: Bearings; Power transmission parts. **SICs:** 5013 (Motor Vehicle Supplies & New Parts); 5085 (Industrial Supplies).

■ 2336 ■ **Bearing Distributors Inc.**
1814 Trade St.
PO Box 4109
Florence, SC 29502
Phone: (803)665-1500 **Fax:** (803)664-9363
Products: Bearings; Power transmission parts. **SICs:** 5013 (Motor Vehicle Supplies & New Parts); 5085 (Industrial Supplies).

■ 2337 ■ **Bearing and Drivers Inc.**
PO Box 4325
Macon, GA 31201
Phone: (912)743-6711
Products: Bearings. **SIC:** 5085 (Industrial Supplies). **Sales:** $72,000,000 (2000). **Emp:** 220. **Officers:** Andrew H. Nations, CEO & President; Dan Martin, Controller.

■ 2338 ■ **Bearing Engineering**
5861 Christie Ave.
Emeryville, CA 94608
Phone: (510)653-3913 **Fax:** (510)653-0255
Products: Bearings; Electric motors; Power transmission equipment. **SICs:** 5085 (Industrial Supplies); 5013 (Motor Vehicle Supplies & New Parts). **Est:** 1936. **Emp:** 30.

■ 2339 ■ **Bearings & Drives, Inc.**
2216 Toledo Dr.
Albany, GA 31705
Phone: (912)432-5158 **Fax:** (912)432-7196
Products: Power transmission parts. **SIC:** 5013 (Motor Vehicle Supplies & New Parts).

■ 2340 ■ **Bearings & Drives, Inc.**
607 Lower Poplar St.
PO Box 4325
Macon, GA 31213
Phone: (912)743-6711 **Fax:** (912)743-0403
Products: Power transmission parts. **SICs:** 5085 (Industrial Supplies); 5013 (Motor Vehicle Supplies & New Parts).

■ 2341 ■ **Bearings & Drives, Inc.**
Hwy. 41 S
PO Box 828
Tifton, GA 31793
Phone: (912)382-2125 **Fax:** (912)382-2050
Products: Power transmission parts. **SICs:** 5085 (Industrial Supplies); 5013 (Motor Vehicle Supplies & New Parts).

■ 2342 ■ **Bearings & Drives, Inc.**
206 S Toombs St.
PO Box 1225
Valdosta, GA 31601
Phone: (912)242-0214 **Fax:** (912)247-2518
Products: Power transmission parts. **SICs:** 5085 (Industrial Supplies); 5013 (Motor Vehicle Supplies & New Parts).

■ 2343 ■ **Bearings & Transmission**
1301 E Voorhies
Danville, IL 61832
Phone: (217)443-2460 **Fax:** (217)443-8269
Products: Bearings, transmissions, and belts. **SICs:** 5084 (Industrial Machinery & Equipment); 5013 (Motor Vehicle Supplies & New Parts); 5085 (Industrial Supplies).

■ 2344 ■ **Beck-Arnley Worldparts Corp.**
PO Box 110910
Nashville, TN 37222
Phone: (615)834-8080
Products: Foreign automotive parts. **SIC:** 5013 (Motor Vehicle Supplies & New Parts). **Est:** 1927. **Sales:** $150,000,000 (2000). **Emp:** 600. **Officers:** Ira Davis, CEO & President; Joe Bagwell, Dir. of Sales; Wayne Houser, Dir. of Information Systems; Becky Barton, Dir of Human Resources.

■ 2345 ■ **Beerman Auto Supply Inc.**
86 Bridge St.
Johnstown, PA 15902
Phone: (814)536-3583
Products: Auto body supplies and glass. **SIC:** 5013 (Motor Vehicle Supplies & New Parts). **Sales:** $6,000,000 (2000). **Emp:** 25. **Officers:** Bill Horner, President.

■ 2346 ■ **Behrens Supply Co.**
211 Main St.
PO Box 61
Red Wing, MN 55066-0061
Phones: (612)388-9443 (612)388-2837
Fax: (612)388-7960
Products: Automotive and industrial parts and supplies. **SICs:** 5013 (Motor Vehicle Supplies & New Parts); 5085 (Industrial Supplies). **Est:** 1936. **Emp:** 49. **Officers:** Robert H. Behrens, President.

■ 2347 ■ **Belmont Automotive Co.**
1918 Pitkin Ave.
Brooklyn, NY 11207-3327
Phone: (718)385-4343 **Fax:** (718)385-0051
Products: Automobile parts, used. **SIC:** 5015 (Motor Vehicle Parts—Used). **Emp:** 49. **Officers:** Philip Sucher.

■ 2348 ■ **J.C. Bennington Co.**
66 Southgate Blvd.
New Castle, DE 19720
Phone: (302)322-3700 **Fax:** (302)323-0977
Products: Power transmission products. **SIC:** 5013 (Motor Vehicle Supplies & New Parts).

■ 2349 ■ **Bens Inc.**
3311 N Cliff Ave.
Sioux Falls, SD 57104-0847
Phone: (605)334-6944
Free: (800)658-3505 **Fax:** (605)334-3685
Products: Motor vehicle parts and accessories; Used tires. **SICs:** 5015 (Motor Vehicle Parts—Used); 5014 (Tires & Tubes). **Officers:** Ben Nordturdt, President.

■ 2350 ■ **Berg Fargo Motor Supply Inc.**
324 N Pacific Ave.
Fargo, ND 58108
Phone: (701)232-8821 **Fax:** (701)237-6159
Products: Automobile parts and supplies; Auto body supplies, including paint; Tractor parts and supplies. **SICs:** 5013 (Motor Vehicle Supplies & New Parts);

5198 (Paints, Varnishes & Supplies); 5083 (Farm & Garden Machinery). **Est:** 1946. **Sales:** $9,000,000 (2000). **Emp:** 40. **Officers:** David R. Berg, President.

■ 2351 ■ **Berry Tire Company Inc.**
9229 W Grand
Franklin Park, IL 60131
Phone: (708)451-2200 **Fax:** (708)451-2205
Products: Automotive parts, including tires. **SICs:** 5014 (Tires & Tubes); 5013 (Motor Vehicle Supplies & New Parts). **Est:** 1921. **Sales:** $20,000,000 (2000). **Emp:** 100. **Officers:** R.L. Berry, Owner; G. Fettel, Controller; D. Eugene, VP of Marketing.

■ 2352 ■ **Best Battery Company Inc.**
4015 Fleet St.
Baltimore, MD 21224
Phone: (410)342-8060
Products: Car batteries. **SIC:** 5013 (Motor Vehicle Supplies & New Parts). **Est:** 1953. **Sales:** $8,000,000 (2000). **Emp:** 35. **Officers:** Roland Best, President; B. Jones, Controller; Bruce Duncan, Dir. of Marketing.

■ 2353 ■ **Best Bilt Parts**
2527 E Kearney
Springfield, MO 65803
Phones: (417)831-4470 (417)869-0703
Free: (800)552-0036 **Fax:** (417)869-9686
E-mail: sales@best-bilt.com
URL: http://www.best-bilt.com
Products: Clutches; Drivelines; Engine parts. **SIC:** 5013 (Motor Vehicle Supplies & New Parts). **Emp:** 25. **Officers:** Mark A. Hagan, President; Barry D. Hagan, Vice President.

■ 2354 ■ **Best Plastics Inc.**
19300 Grange St.
Cassopolis, MI 49031
Phone: (616)641-5811 **Fax:** (616)641-5732
Products: Automotive accessories; Automotive parts and supplies, New. **SIC:** 5013 (Motor Vehicle Supplies & New Parts). **Est:** 1969. **Emp:** 100. **Officers:** Melvin Stewart, CEO; Douglas Stewart, President; Jim Stewart, Vice President; Michael O' Bryant, General Mgr.; Lee Karn, Production Supv.

■ 2355 ■ **Bestop Inc.**
PO Box 307
Broomfield, CO 80038
Phone: (303)465-1755 **Fax:** (303)466-3436
Products: Convertible tops and accessories for small sport utility vehicles. **SIC:** 5013 (Motor Vehicle Supplies & New Parts). **Sales:** $46,000,000 (2000). **Emp:** 780.

■ 2356 ■ **Better Brake Parts Inc.**
915 Shawnee Rd.
Lima, OH 45801
Phone: (419)227-0685
Products: Brake lining. **SIC:** 5013 (Motor Vehicle Supplies & New Parts).

■ 2357 ■ **Big A Auto Parts**
7751 Nieman Rd.
Shawnee, KS 66214-1406
Phone: (316)792-3553 **Fax:** (316)792-5641
Products: Foreign and domestic automotive parts. **SIC:** 5013 (Motor Vehicle Supplies & New Parts). **Est:** 1963. **Sales:** $18,000,000 (2000). **Emp:** 45. **Officers:** Mark S. Hoffman, President; William DeLaney, VP & CFO.

■ 2358 ■ **Big B Automotive Warehouse**
489 Grant St.
Akron, OH 44311-1156
Phone: (330)376-7121 **Fax:** (330)376-6317
Products: Automotive parts. **SIC:** 5013 (Motor Vehicle Supplies & New Parts). **Emp:** 999. **Officers:** David Valentine.

■ 2359 ■ **Big Boys Toys**
Rte. 67 A, RD No. 1, Box 174A
North Bennington, VT 05257
Phone: (802)447-1721
Free: (800)286-1721 **Fax:** (802)447-0962
Products: Automotive and truck accessories. **SIC:** 5013 (Motor Vehicle Supplies & New Parts). **Sales:** $200,000 (2000). **Emp:** 4. **Officers:** Richard Boutin, Owner.

■ 2360 ■ Big Sky Auto Auction Inc.
1236 Cordova St.
Billings, MT 59101
Phone: (406)259-5999
Free: (800)726-6786 Fax: (406)259-2776
Products: Auto auctions. SIC: 5012 (Automobiles & Other Motor Vehicles). Sales: $95,000,000 (2000). Emp: 100. Officers: Ted Becker, CEO.

■ 2361 ■ Biglow Industrial Company Inc.
PO Box 1251
Mountainside, NJ 07092-0251
Phone: (908)233-6500 Fax: (908)233-0921
Products: Power transmission equipment, including pneumatics, motors, and controls. SIC: 5013 (Motor Vehicle Supplies & New Parts). Est: 1921. Emp: 10. Officers: Robert S. Biglow Jr., CEO; Meghan Webb, Controller; Rich Hill, Dir. of Marketing; Pat Falino, Customer Service Contact.

■ 2362 ■ Bill's Battery Co. Inc.
5221 Crookshank Rd.
Cincinnati, OH 45238
Phone: (513)922-0100 Fax: (513)922-2566
Products: Batteries, starters, and air-conditioner parts; Chemicals. SICs: 5013 (Motor Vehicle Supplies & New Parts); 5169 (Chemicals & Allied Products Nec). Est: 1968. Sales: $6,500,000 (2000). Emp: 27. Officers: William J. Hartoin, President; Dennis Hartoin, General Mgr.

■ 2363 ■ Binghamton Truck Body & Equipment Corp.
25 Alice St.
PO Box 27
Binghamton, NY 13904
Phone: (607)723-8993 Fax: (607)771-0157
E-mail: bingtrkbod@mindspring.com
Products: Automotive parts and supplies; Truck bodies and equipment. SIC: 5013 (Motor Vehicle Supplies & New Parts). Est: 1960. Sales: $1,700,000 (2000). Emp: 8. Officers: William J. O'Brien, President.

■ 2364 ■ Birmingham Electric Battery Co.
2230 2nd Ave.
Birmingham, AL 35233
Phone: (205)251-3211
Products: Small engine parts. SICs: 5013 (Motor Vehicle Supplies & New Parts); 5084 (Industrial Machinery & Equipment). Est: 1913. Sales: $14,700,000 (2000). Emp: 75. Officers: Tom W. Henley, Chairman of the Board & Treasurer.

■ 2365 ■ J.R. Bisho Company, Inc.
564 Market St.
San Francisco, CA 94104
Phone: (415)397-0767 Fax: (415)397-0835
E-mail: bisho@bisho.com
URL: http://www.bisho.com
Products: Tractor equipment; Truck equipment; Emergency equipment lighting; Spot lights. SICs: 5088 (Transportation Equipment & Supplies); 5082 (Construction & Mining Machinery); 5083 (Farm & Garden Machinery); 5013 (Motor Vehicle Supplies & New Parts). Est: 1955. Sales: $7,000,000 (2000). Emp: 9. Officers: J.R. Bisho, President; M.L. Secoquian, Treasurer & Secty.

■ 2366 ■ J. Bittle American Inc.
7149 Mission Gorge Rd.
San Diego, CA 92120-1130
Phone: (619)560-2030
Products: Auto parts. SIC: 5013 (Motor Vehicle Supplies & New Parts). Est: 1985. Sales: $13,000,000 (2000). Emp: 35. Officers: J. Bittle, President; William Browning, CFO; Forrest Byas, Dir. of Marketing & Sales; Doug Baker, Dir. of Data Processing; Vickie Bittle, Dir of Human Resources.

■ 2367 ■ Blanchard Auto Electric Co.
PO Box 24626
Seattle, WA 98124
Phone: (206)682-2981
Free: (800)234-2981 Fax: (206)682-0248
E-mail: bae@seanet.com
URL: http://www.blanchardelectric.com
Products: Electrical tune-up products; Starters and alternators. SIC: 5013 (Motor Vehicle Supplies & New

Parts). Est: 1947. Sales: $2,500,000 (2000). Emp: 15. Officers: Bob Yates, President.

■ 2368 ■ E. Blankenship and Company Inc.
704 W Main St.
Marion, IL 62959
Phone: (618)993-2643
Products: Auto replacement parts. SIC: 5013 (Motor Vehicle Supplies & New Parts). Est: 1928. Sales: $8,000,000 (2000). Emp: 110. Officers: Clarence Bagby Jr., Exec. VP.

■ 2369 ■ Blue Hen Spring Works, Inc.
112 N Rehoboth Blvd.
Milford, DE 19963
Phone: (302)422-6600 Fax: (302)422-2478
Products: Truck parts. SIC: 5013 (Motor Vehicle Supplies & New Parts).

■ 2370 ■ Bluegrass Bandag, Inc.
1101 Enterprise Dr.
PO Box 756
Winchester, KY 40392-0756
Phone: (606)745-2850 Fax: (606)745-5800
Products: New and re-tread truck tires. SIC: 5014 (Tires & Tubes). Officers: Charles Roberts.

■ 2371 ■ Bonded Motors, Inc.
7522 S Maie Ave.
Los Angeles, CA 90001
Phone: (323)583-8631 Fax: (213)589-2900
Products: Automobile replacement engines. SIC: 5013 (Motor Vehicle Supplies & New Parts). Officers: Aaron Landon, CEO; Richard Funk, President; Paul Sullivan, CFO; Buddy Mercer, COO.

■ 2372 ■ Borg Warner Automotive Friction Products
6700 18 1/2 Mile Rd.
PO Box 8023
Sterling Heights, MI 48311-8023
Phone: (810)726-4470 Fax: (810)726-6708
Products: Transmission parts. SIC: 5013 (Motor Vehicle Supplies & New Parts). Sales: $1,200,000,000 (2000). Emp: 250. Officers: Chuck Dover.

■ 2373 ■ Bornell Supply
180 Eastom Cir.
Lima, OH 45804
Phone: (419)221-2080 Fax: (419)221-2822
Products: Power transmission supplies. SICs: 5084 (Industrial Machinery & Equipment); 5013 (Motor Vehicle Supplies & New Parts). Est: 1967. Sales: $1,000,000 (2000). Emp: 4. Officers: C.G. Wander Jr.

■ 2374 ■ Boulevard Truck Sales and Service Inc.
PMB 109
119 N Parker St.
Olathe, KS 66061-3139
Products: Industrial trucks. SIC: 5084 (Industrial Machinery & Equipment).

■ 2375 ■ Bowes Industries Inc.
PO Box 18802
Indianapolis, IN 46218-0802
Phone: (317)547-5245 Fax: (317)545-7683
Products: Small automotive parts. SIC: 5013 (Motor Vehicle Supplies & New Parts). Est: 1919. Sales: $20,000,000 (2000). Emp: 150. Officers: Wayne A. Smith, Chairman of the Board; John R. Gilligan, Finance Officer; G.L. Susdorf, Dir. of Marketing.

■ 2376 ■ Bozeman Distributors
5341 I 55 N
Jackson, MS 39206
Phone: (601)368-9274
Products: Car wash equipment supplies. SIC: 5087 (Service Establishment Equipment).

■ 2377 ■ Brake & Clutch, Inc.
63 Bridge St.
Salem, MA 01970
Phone: (978)745-2500
Free: (800)322-1111 Fax: (978)745-4484
Products: Automotive parts and supplies, New. SIC: 5013 (Motor Vehicle Supplies & New Parts). Officers: Frank J. Livas, President.

■ 2378 ■ Brake Sales Co. Inc.
999 N La Brea Ave.
Los Angeles, CA 90038-2321
Phone: (213)874-8880 Fax: (213)874-8057
Products: Brake products and supplies. SIC: 5013 (Motor Vehicle Supplies & New Parts). Est: 1963. Emp: 10.

■ 2379 ■ Brake and Wheel Parts Industries
2415 W 21st St.
Chicago, IL 60608
Phone: (773)847-7000
Products: Truck parts. SIC: 5013 (Motor Vehicle Supplies & New Parts). Sales: $12,000,000 (2000). Emp: 35. Officers: E. Goldberg, President; S. Cohen, Treasurer & Secty.

■ 2380 ■ Brand Co.
10560 Main St.
Fairfax, VA 22030
Phone: (703)385-2817 Fax: (703)352-4324
E-mail: brandinc@aol.com
Products: Tires. SIC: 5014 (Tires & Tubes).

■ 2381 ■ Brandywine Auto Parts Inc.
PO Box 68
Brandywine, MD 20613
Phone: (301)372-1000 Fax: (301)782-4227
Products: Automotive parts and supplies, New. SIC: 5013 (Motor Vehicle Supplies & New Parts). Est: 1962. Sales: $50,000,000 (2000). Emp: 400. Officers: Walter Meinhardt, President; John Lex, CFO.

■ 2382 ■ Brannon Tire Corp.
PO Box 2496
Stockton, CA 95201
Phone: (209)943-2771 Fax: (209)465-0609
Products: Tires, wheels, and brakes. SICs: 5013 (Motor Vehicle Supplies & New Parts); 5014 (Tires & Tubes). Est: 1981. Sales: $25,000,000 (2000). Emp: 185. Officers: Jerold F. Brannon, President; Judith Brannon, CFO; Mel Pechart, Dir. of Marketing & Sales.

■ 2383 ■ Brattleboro Auto Parts
RR 6, Box 32
Brattleboro, VT 05301-8542
Phone: (802)254-9034
Products: Used automotive parts and supplies. SIC: 5015 (Motor Vehicle Parts—Used). Officers: Gladys Pierson, Owner.

■ 2384 ■ Bridgestone Firestone, Inc.
50 Century Blvd.
Nashville, TN 37214
Phone: (615)872-5000
Products: Tires. SIC: 5014 (Tires & Tubes).

■ 2385 ■ Bridgestone/Firestone Tire Sales Co.
1 Bridgestone Park
Nashville, TN 37214
Phone: (615)391-0088
Products: Tires. SIC: 5014 (Tires & Tubes). Est: 1972. Sales: $58,000,000 (2000). Emp: 600. Officers: John Lampe, President; Glenn Atkinson, Controller; Shu Ishibashi, Dir. of Marketing.

■ 2386 ■ Brithinee Electric
620 S Rancho Ave.
Colton, CA 92324
Phone: (909)825-7971 Fax: (909)825-2044
Products: Electric motors. SIC: 5063 (Electrical Apparatus & Equipment). Sales: $4,000,000 (2000). Emp: 40. Officers: Wallace Brithinee, President & Chairman of the Board.

■ 2387 ■ Brittain Brothers Inc.
700 S Western
Oklahoma City, OK 73125
Phone: (405)235-1785
Products: Auto parts. SIC: 5013 (Motor Vehicle Supplies & New Parts). Sales: $41,000,000 (2000). Emp: 325. Officers: Robert C. Saunders, President.

■ 2388 ■ Broadway Tire Inc.
588 Broadway
Pawtucket, RI 02860
Phone: (401)725-3535
Products: Tires. SIC: 5014 (Tires & Tubes). Est: 1940. Sales: $3,000,000 (2000). Emp: 30. Officers: Gary L.

Orleck, CEO; Bob Paige, Sales Mgr.; Dale Aguiar, Vice President.

■ 2389 ■ Brock Supply Co.
2150 E Rio Salado Pkwy.
PO Box 1000
Tempe, AZ 85280-1000
Phone: (602)968-2222
Free: (800)528-4400 **Fax:** 800-889-0431
Products: Automotive parts and supplies, New. **SIC:** 5013 (Motor Vehicle Supplies & New Parts). **Sales:** $6,000,000 (2000). **Emp:** 35. **Officers:** Jerry W. Brock.

■ 2390 ■ Brocks Auto Supply
221 Hamilton
Houston, TX 77002-2333
Phone: (713)222-9928 **Fax:** (713)222-6781
Products: Automotive supplies. **SIC:** 5013 (Motor Vehicle Supplies & New Parts). **Est:** 1937. **Emp:** 20. **Officers:** Bobby Belyeu.

■ 2391 ■ Brookline Machine Co.
131 Holton St.
Boston, MA 02135
Phone: (617)782-4018 **Fax:** (617)787-5187
Products: Truck parts. **SIC:** 5013 (Motor Vehicle Supplies & New Parts). **Est:** 1938.

■ 2392 ■ Brookline Machine Co.
1870 Fillmore Ave.
Buffalo, NY 14214
Phone: (716)891-5611 **Fax:** (716)891-5614
Products: Heavy-duty truck parts. **SIC:** 5013 (Motor Vehicle Supplies & New Parts). **Former Name:** Automotive Parts Wholesaler.

■ 2393 ■ Brookline Machine Co.
333 Waterman Ave.
East Providence, RI 02914
Phone: (401)438-3650 **Fax:** (401)434-0549
Products: Truck parts. **SIC:** 5013 (Motor Vehicle Supplies & New Parts). **Doing Business As:** Cockcroft Co.

■ 2394 ■ Brookline Machine Company, Inc.
535 Sweetland Ave.
Hillside, NJ 07205
Phone: (908)688-6050
Free: (800)228-7861 **Fax:** (908)688-8450
Products: Heavy duty truck parts and hydraulics. **SIC:** 5013 (Motor Vehicle Supplies & New Parts). **Est:** 1938. **Emp:** 6.

■ 2395 ■ Brookline Machine Co. Williams Brothers Div.
296 Warren Ave.
Portland, ME 04103
Phone: (207)878-2994 **Fax:** (207)878-2996
Products: Truck parts. **SIC:** 5013 (Motor Vehicle Supplies & New Parts).

■ 2396 ■ Roger G. Brown Associates Inc.
PO Box 275
Bomoseen, VT 05732-0275
Phone: (802)265-4548
Products: Automobile parts, used; Automotive accessories. **SIC:** 5015 (Motor Vehicle Parts—Used). **Officers:** Mark Brown, President.

■ 2397 ■ Brown and Sons Co. Inc.
1720 Davison Rd.
Flint, MI 48506
Phone: (810)238-3242 **Fax:** (810)238-4255
Products: Filters; Automotive batteries; Automotive accessories; Rubber and plastic transmission belts and belting; Hydraulic and pneumatic rotary actuators, accumulators, cushions, and nonvehicular shock absorbers; Brake parts and assemblies; Gasoline engines and gasoline engine parts for motor vehicles; Miscellaneous allied paint products; Carburetors, new and rebuilt; Speed changers, drives, and gears. **SIC:** 5013 (Motor Vehicle Supplies & New Parts). **Est:** 1940. **Emp:** 9. **Officers:** George Brown, President; Pete Brown, Treasurer & Secty.

■ 2398 ■ Brown & Sons NAPA Auto Parts
1001 College Rd.
Fairbanks, AK 99701
Phone: (907)456-7312 **Fax:** (907)452-8881
Products: Auto parts. **SIC:** 5013 (Motor Vehicle Supplies & New Parts).

■ 2399 ■ Bruces Tire Ltd.
PO Box 276
Beecher Falls, VT 05902-0276
Phone: (802)266-7734 **Fax:** (802)266-3316
Products: Tires. **SIC:** 5014 (Tires & Tubes). **Officers:** Bruce Tibbetts, Owner.

■ 2400 ■ Burnstine's Distributing Corp.
PO Box 2367
Elkhart, IN 46515
Phone: (219)293-1571 **Fax:** (219)522-0827
Products: Electrical items for recreational vehicles, marine equipment, and automobiles. **SICs:** 5064 (Electrical Appliances—Television & Radio); 5063 (Electrical Apparatus & Equipment); 5013 (Motor Vehicle Supplies & New Parts). **Est:** 1904. **Sales:** $10,000,000 (2000). **Emp:** 28. **Officers:** Harry Burnstine, President; Andrew Mills, Dir. of Data Processing.

■ 2401 ■ Burquip Truck Bodies & Equipment
235 Adams St.
PO Box 769
Bedford Hills, NY 10507
Phone: (914)241-0950 **Fax:** (914)666-4790
Products: Automotive parts and supplies, New. **SIC:** 5013 (Motor Vehicle Supplies & New Parts). **Officers:** Todd Burbank, Vice President.

■ 2402 ■ Burton Auto Supply Inc.
PO Box 297
Weslaco, TX 78596
Phone: (210)968-3121
Products: Auto parts; Brake systems; Shocks; Exhaust systems; Engines; Lubricants; Industrial supplies; Automotive equipment; Air compressors; Hydraulic parts. **SIC:** 5013 (Motor Vehicle Supplies & New Parts). **Est:** 1926. **Sales:** $15,000,000 (2000). **Emp:** 160. **Officers:** E.R. Vaughan, President; Brian Humphreys, Controller.

■ 2403 ■ Burton-Rogers Company Inc.
220 Grove St.
Waltham, MA 02453
Phone: (781)894-6440
Free: (800)225-4678 **Fax:** (781)893-8393
Products: Automotive test equipment. **SIC:** 5065 (Electronic Parts & Equipment Nec). **Sales:** $4,000,000 (2000). **Emp:** 10. **Officers:** William de K. Burton, President & Treasurer.

■ 2404 ■ Butler County Motor Company Inc.
PO Box 1028
Butler, PA 16003
Phone: (724)287-2766
Products: Auto parts. **SIC:** 5013 (Motor Vehicle Supplies & New Parts). **Sales:** $20,000,000 (2000). **Emp:** 50. **Officers:** Anthony G. Johns, President; Wayne Barker, Accountant.

■ 2405 ■ BWD Automotive Corp.
11045 Gage Ave.
Franklin Park, IL 60131
Phone: (708)455-3120 **Fax:** (708)455-0618
Products: Automotive parts, including clutches, tune-up parts, wire, cable, and fuel pumps. **SIC:** 5013 (Motor Vehicle Supplies & New Parts). **Est:** 1924. **Sales:** $110,000,000 (2000). **Emp:** 300. **Officers:** R. Daley, President; William Kotzum, Controller; Pete Anderson, VP of Sales; Bruce Tartallione, VP of Marketing; Jeff Hagberg, VP of Operations.

■ 2406 ■ C R Laurence Company Inc.
PO Box 58923
Los Angeles, CA 90058
Phone: (323)588-1281
Products: Sealants and glaziers' supplies; Automotive accessories. **SIC:** 5169 (Chemicals & Allied Products Nec). **Officers:** Donald Friese, President.

■ 2407 ■ Cadillac Motor Car
PO Box 5018
Westlake Village, CA 91359
Phone: (805)373-9787 **Fax:** (805)373-9587
Products: Motor vehicles and car bodies. **SIC:** 5012 (Automobiles & Other Motor Vehicles).

■ 2408 ■ Cal-North Auto Brokers Inc.
PO Box 7305
Santa Rosa, CA 95407
Phone: (707)578-9245
Products: Automotive parts. **SIC:** 5013 (Motor Vehicle Supplies & New Parts). **Est:** 1983. **Sales:** $3,000,000 (2000). **Emp:** 10. **Officers:** David Snowden, President; Bonnie Madson, Dir. of Systems.

■ 2409 ■ California Affiliated Representative Inc.
9420 Reseda Blvd., No. 224
Northridge, CA 91324-2932
Phone: (213)589-6566 **Fax:** (213)589-6513
Products: Automotive products. **SIC:** 5013 (Motor Vehicle Supplies & New Parts). **Emp:** 26. **Officers:** C. M. Wright.

■ 2410 ■ California Tire Co.
2295 Davis Ct.
Hayward, CA 94545
Phone: (510)487-5777
Products: Tires. **SIC:** 5014 (Tires & Tubes). **Sales:** $45,000,000 (2000). **Emp:** 70. **Officers:** Michael C. Largent, President; Mike Kempel, Controller.

■ 2411 ■ S.X. Callahan Inc.
824 S Laredo St.
San Antonio, TX 78204
Phone: (210)224-1625 **Fax:** (210)227-0411
Products: Auto parts. **SIC:** 5013 (Motor Vehicle Supplies & New Parts). **Est:** 1909. **Sales:** $4,500,000 (2000). **Emp:** 28. **Officers:** Sam W. Callahan Sr., President; S.X. Callahan III, Exec. VP.

■ 2412 ■ CalMark Custom Covers
1617 Pacific Ave., Ste. 111
Oxnard, CA 93033
Phone: (805)486-3863 **Fax:** (805)486-4760
E-mail: covers@calmarkinc.com
URL: http://www.calmarkinc.com
Products: Custom RV and industrial covers; Lawn and garden rakes; Wheelbarrow extenders; EPA bags, covers, and sacks. **SICs:** 5013 (Motor Vehicle Supplies & New Parts); 5083 (Farm & Garden Machinery). **Est:** 1985. **Sales:** $750,000 (2000). **Emp:** 10. **Officers:** Arthur S. Miller, President; Fred Bennett, Sales Mgr. **Alternate Name:** Calmark Resources Inc.

■ 2413 ■ Calmini Products Inc.
6600-B McDivitt Dr.
Bakersfield, CA 93313
Phone: (805)398-9500 **Fax:** (818)988-8899
Products: Automotive parts and accessories. **SIC:** 5013 (Motor Vehicle Supplies & New Parts). **Est:** 1984. **Sales:** $2,000,000 (2000). **Emp:** 5. **Officers:** Randy Kramer, President; Steve Kramer, Vice President.

■ 2414 ■ Calumet Auto Recycling and Sales Inc.
6205 Indianapolis Blvd.
Hammond, IN 46320
Phone: (219)844-6600
Products: Auto parts, including body parts, engines, and batteries. **SIC:** 5013 (Motor Vehicle Supplies & New Parts). **Est:** 1926. **Sales:** $4,000,000 (2000). **Emp:** 17. **Officers:** Jill Rosenstein, President; Jerry Rosenstein, Vice President.

■ 2415 ■ Cantrell Auto Supply Company Inc.
2411 Alameda Ave.
El Paso, TX 79942
Phone: (915)542-1575 **Fax:** (915)542-3882
Products: Auto parts. **SIC:** 5013 (Motor Vehicle Supplies & New Parts). **Est:** 1943. **Sales:** $5,000,000 (2000). **Emp:** 35. **Officers:** Louis Cantrell Jr., President.

■ **2416** ■ **Capital Tire Inc.**
1001 Cherry St.
Toledo, OH 43608
Phone: (419)241-5111
Products: Tires. **SIC:** 5014 (Tires & Tubes). **Est:** 1919.
Sales: $35,300,000 (2000). **Emp:** 135. **Officers:**
Thomas B. Geiger Sr., President; Thomas B. Geiger
Jr., CFO.

■ **2417** ■ **Capitol Tire Shop**
414 W Main Cross St.
Findlay, OH 45839
Phone: (419)422-4554
Products: Tires. **SIC:** 5014 (Tires & Tubes).

■ **2418** ■ **Caple-Shaw Industries Inc.**
1112 NE 29th St.
Ft. Worth, TX 76106
Phone: (817)626-2816 **Fax:** (817)625-9442
E-mail: sales@capleshaw.com
URL: http://www.capleshaw.com
Products: Trailer and truck parts, including splash
guards, tail gates, running boards, and bed liners. **SIC:**
5013 (Motor Vehicle Supplies & New Parts). **Est:** 1957.
Sales: $5,000,000 (2000). **Emp:** 14. **Officers:** Bill
Shaw, President.

■ **2419** ■ **Capos Auto Parts Inc.**
5701 Broadway Blvd. SE
Albuquerque, NM 87105-7427
Phone: (505)873-0665 **Fax:** (505)873-1889
Products: Automobile parts, used. **SIC:** 5015 (Motor
Vehicle Parts—Used). **Officers:** James Capo,
President.

■ **2420** ■ **Capriotto and Sons Inc.**
S-3100 Abbott Rd.
Orchard Park, NY 14127
Phone: (716)823-5024 **Fax:** (716)823-4922
Products: Auto parts; Farming supplies. **SICs:** 5013
(Motor Vehicle Supplies & New Parts); 5083 (Farm &
Garden Machinery). **Est:** 1952. **Sales:** $14,000,000
(2000). **Emp:** 60. **Officers:** John Capriotto, President;
Carmen Capriotto, VP of Finance.

■ **2421** ■ **Car-Go Battery Co.**
3860 Blake St.
Denver, CO 80205
Phone: (303)296-8763
Free: (800)727-4100 **Fax:** (303)295-7125
Products: Complete battery pack and battery related
assembly. **SICs:** 5013 (Motor Vehicle Supplies & New
Parts); 5063 (Electrical Apparatus & Equipment).
Sales: $10,000,000 (2000). **Emp:** 50.

■ **2422** ■ **Car Parts Inc.**
613 N 36th St.
Milwaukee, WI 53208
Phone: (414)342-7070 **Fax:** (414)342-6440
E-mail: cpartsplus@aol.com
Products: Auto parts. **SIC:** 5013 (Motor Vehicle
Supplies & New Parts). **Est:** 1966. **Sales:** $15,000,000
(2000). **Emp:** 145. **Officers:** Phil Wisniewski,
President; Guy Theune, Vice President; Greg
Lehrkamp, Purchasing Mgr.

■ **2423** ■ **Car Quest Auto Parts Co.**
1818 Franklin St.
Waco, TX 76701
Phone: (254)752-5556
Products: Automotive parts and supplies, New; Tools
for automotive use. **SIC:** 5013 (Motor Vehicle Supplies
& New Parts). **Est:** 1872. **Sales:** $3,000,000 (2000).
Emp: 20. **Officers:** Jack Trawick, President; Jerry Hart,
Manager.

■ **2424** ■ **Cardillo Brothers Inc.**
1757 Plainfield Pike
Johnston, RI 02919-5919
Phone: (401)942-0331
Products: Motor vehicle parts, including used auto
parts. **SIC:** 5015 (Motor Vehicle Parts—Used).
Officers: Alfred Cardillo, President.

■ **2425** ■ **Carnegie Body Co.**
9500 Brookpark Rd.
Cleveland, OH 44129
Phone: (216)749-5000 **Fax:** (216)749-5640
Products: Truck parts. **SICs:** 5012 (Automobiles &

Other Motor Vehicles); 5013 (Motor Vehicle Supplies &
New Parts). **Est:** 1922. **Sales:** $14,000,000 (2000).
Emp: 90. **Officers:** Howard A. Weisblat, President;
Marcia J. Sabol, CFO.

■ **2426** ■ **Carolina's Auto Supply House, Inc.**
PO Box 36409
Charlotte, NC 28236
Phone: (704)334-4646
Free: (800)438-4070 **Fax:** (704)377-7016
URL: http://www.autosupplyhouse.com
Products: Automotive parts and supplies, including
radiators, axle assemblies, auto-body clips and
hardware, engine parts, and chemicals and paints. **SIC:**
5013 (Motor Vehicle Supplies & New Parts). **Est:** 1915.
Sales: $25,000,000 (2000). **Emp:** 70. **Officers:** E.
White, President.

■ **2427** ■ **Carquest**
5307 W Market St.
Greensboro, NC 27409-2809
Phone: (910)294-5632
Products: Automotive parts and supplies, New. **SIC:**
5013 (Motor Vehicle Supplies & New Parts). **Emp:** 49.
Officers: Chuck Clark.

■ **2428** ■ **CARQUEST Corp.**
12596 W Bayaud Ave., No. 400
Lakewood, CO 80228
Phone: (303)984-2000 **Fax:** (303)984-2001
Products: Automotive supplies. **SIC:** 5013 (Motor
Vehicle Supplies & New Parts). **Est:** 1974. **Sales:**
$1,614,000,000 (2000). **Emp:** 14,000. **Officers:** Peter
Kornafel, President; Tannis Watts, Accountant.

■ **2429** ■ **Carquest Distribution Co.**
PO Box 31437
Billings, MT 59107
Phone: (406)259-4577 **Fax:** (406)245-4074
Products: Automotive parts. **SIC:** 5013 (Motor Vehicle
Supplies & New Parts). **Sales:** $40,000,000 (2000).
Emp: 375. **Officers:** Allen Dedman, President; Lenore
Swenson, Controller; William Ball, Marketing & Sales
Mgr.; John Turcotte, Dir. of Data Processing; Dave
Rickell, Personnel Mgr.

■ **2430** ■ **Carquest Distribution Co. Cleaner
and Equipment Div.**
208 E 3 Notch St.
Andalusia, AL 36420
Phone: (205)222-6534 **Fax:** (205)222-2742
Products: Tools; Automotive supplies. **SIC:** 5013
(Motor Vehicle Supplies & New Parts). **Est:** 1908.
Sales: $18,000,000 (2000). **Emp:** 150. **Officers:**
James M. Taylor II, Chairman of the Board; Alen Till,
Controller; Ralph Wells, Sales Mgr.; Riley Taylor,
Operations Mgr.; Bill King, Dir of Human Resources.

■ **2431** ■ **Carrington Distributing Company Inc.**
1905 Trevilian Way
Louisville, KY 40205
Phone: (502)366-2913
Products: Seat covers. **SIC:** 5013 (Motor Vehicle
Supplies & New Parts).

■ **2432** ■ **Casale Engineering Inc.**
161 8th Ave.
La Puente, CA 91746
Phone: (626)330-6830 **Fax:** (626)330-2835
Products: Motor vehicle supplies and parts; V-drive for
boats. **SICs:** 5013 (Motor Vehicle Supplies & New
Parts); 5091 (Sporting & Recreational Goods). **Est:**
1964. **Sales:** $1,500,000 (2000). **Emp:** 15. **Officers:**
E.R. Casale, President; Diane Casale, CFO; Mitch
Casale, VP of Marketing.

■ **2433** ■ **Castriota Chevrolet Inc.**
1701 W Liberty Ave.
Pittsburgh, PA 15226
Phone: (412)343-2100
Free: (800)243-8987 **Fax:** (412)344-0198
Products: New and used vehicle auto parts. **SIC:** 5012
(Automobiles & Other Motor Vehicles). **Sales:**
$20,000,000 (2000). **Emp:** 50. **Officers:** A. Castriota,
CEO & President; Bob Yaggi, CFO.

■ **2434** ■ **Catamount North**
Dorset Lane Pk.
Williston, VT 05495
Phone: (802)879-7172 **Fax:** (802)878-6543
Products: Automotive parts and supplies, New. **SIC:**
5013 (Motor Vehicle Supplies & New Parts). **Officers:**
Tom Frechette, Contact.

■ **2435** ■ **Cate-McLaurin Company Inc.**
1001 Idlewild Blvd.
Columbia, SC 29201
Phone: (803)799-1955
Products: Tires for farm machinery, automobiles, and
bicycles. **SIC:** 5014 (Tires & Tubes). **Est:** 1932. **Sales:**
$6,000,000 (2000). **Emp:** 50. **Officers:** William P.
Cate, Chairman of the Board; Frank T. Clayton, CFO;
Charles H. Cate, President.

■ **2436** ■ **CCC Heavy Duty Trucks Co.**
3955 Bristol Pke.
Bensalem, PA 19020
Phone: (215)638-1474
Products: Trucks. **SIC:** 5012 (Automobiles & Other
Motor Vehicles).

■ **2437** ■ **Central Atlantic Toyota Distributors
Inc.**
6710 Baymeadow Dr.
Glen Burnie, MD 21060
Phone: (410)760-1500 **Fax:** (410)787-8000
Products: Automotive parts. **SIC:** 5012 (Automobiles &
Other Motor Vehicles). **Sales:** $410,000,000 (2000).
Emp: 260. **Officers:** Dennis Clemens, President &
General Mgr.; Colleen Eder, Controller.

■ **2438** ■ **Central Diesel, Inc.**
1422 Commerce Rd.
Richmond, VA 23224
Phone: (804)233-9814 **Fax:** (804)233-7084
Products: Truck engine parts. **SIC:** 5013 (Motor
Vehicle Supplies & New Parts).

■ **2439** ■ **Centurion Vehicles Inc.**
69651 US 131 S
PO Box 715
White Pigeon, MI 49099
Phone: (616)483-9659
Free: (800)483-9659 **Fax:** (616)483-7419
E-mail: infor@centurionvehicles.com
Products: Truck, van, and specialty vehicle conversion
supplies. **SIC:** 5013 (Motor Vehicle Supplies & New
Parts). **Est:** 1977. **Sales:** $30,000,000 (2000). **Emp:**
250. **Officers:** Robert J. Froschauer, President;
Frederick Duell, Exec. VP; Andrew Porritt, VP & Gen.
Sales Mgr.; Brett Doberenz, VP & Gen. Sales Mgr.;
Larry Olsiewicz, Customer Service Mgr.

■ **2440** ■ **Century Wheel & Rim Corp.**
1550 Gage Rd.
Montebello, CA 90640-6600
Phone: (323)728-3901
Free: (800)624-1715 **Fax:** (323)722-4177
E-mail: centurywheel@wman.com
URL: http://www.wman.com/~centurywheel
Products: Wheel rims; Axles; Brakes; Undercarriage
parts and supplies. **SIC:** 5013 (Motor Vehicle Supplies
& New Parts). **Est:** 1982. **Sales:** $38,000,000 (2000).
Emp: 94. **Officers:** Gene DiSano, Exec. VP; Gary
DiSano, VP & General Mgr.; Larry DiSano, Vice
President.

■ **2441** ■ **Cenweld Corp.**
230 E Portage Trail
Cuyahoga Falls, OH 44221
Phone: (216)923-9717 **Fax:** (216)923-5872
Products: Automotive parts and supplies, New. **SIC:**
5013 (Motor Vehicle Supplies & New Parts). **Est:** 1964.
Sales: $5,000,000 (2000). **Emp:** 25. **Officers:** James
M. Lay, President.

■ **2442** ■ **Certified Automotive Warehouse Inc.**
2301 S Ashland Ave.
Chicago, IL 60608
Phone: (312)829-6440 **Fax:** (312)829-3409
Products: Auto parts. **SIC:** 5013 (Motor Vehicle
Supplies & New Parts). **Est:** 1987. **Sales:** $60,000,000
(2000). **Emp:** 110. **Officers:** Timothy Lee, President;
Milton J. Jaffe, VP of Sales & Marketing.

■ 2443 ■ Champion Auto Stores Inc.
101 5th St. E
St. Paul, MN 55101-1820
Phone: (612)391-6655 **Fax:** (612)535-2854
Products: Automobile parts. **SIC:** 5013 (Motor Vehicle Supplies & New Parts). **Sales:** $336,000,000 (2000).
Emp: 800. **Officers:** Gary D. Bebeau, President.

■ 2444 ■ J.T. Chapman Co.
310 Armour Rd.
North Kansas City, MO 64116
Phone: (816)842-4488
Products: Gear boxes; Clutches; Brakes. **SIC:** 5013 (Motor Vehicle Supplies & New Parts). **Sales:** $6,000,000 (2000). **Emp:** 25. **Officers:** Louis Dennis, President.

■ 2445 ■ Charleston Auto Parts Company Inc.
PO Box 15291
Las Vegas, NV 89114
Phone: (702)642-5557 **Fax:** (702)642-9174
Products: Automobile parts. **SIC:** 5013 (Motor Vehicle Supplies & New Parts). **Sales:** $40,000,000 (1993).
Emp: 120. **Officers:** Ronald Cannon, President.

■ 2446 ■ Chesapeake Rim and Wheel Distributors
2730 Dorr St.
Fairfax, VA 22031
Phone: (703)560-4900 **Fax:** (703)560-9353
URL: http://www.crw.com
Products: Auto parts and supplies. **SIC:** 5013 (Motor Vehicle Supplies & New Parts). **Est:** 1960. **Emp:** 100.
Officers: Dave Willis, President.

■ 2447 ■ Chesapeake Rim & Wheel Distributors Inc.
7601 Pulaski Hwy.
Baltimore, MD 21237-2605
Phone: (410)866-3337
Free: (800)638-5418 **Fax:** (410)866-3284
Products: Motor vehicle wheels; Exhaust system parts; Automotive parts and supplies, New. **SIC:** 5013 (Motor Vehicle Supplies & New Parts). **Emp:** 49.
Officers: Ralph Willis.

■ 2448 ■ Chicago Chain & Transmission
650 E Plainfield Rd.
PO Box 705
Countryside, IL 60525
Phone: (312)482-9000 **Fax:** (708)482-3021
Products: Power transmissions. **SICs:** 5084 (Industrial Machinery & Equipment); 5013 (Motor Vehicle Supplies & New Parts).

■ 2449 ■ Cincinnati Belt & Transmission
737 W 6th St.
Cincinnati, OH 45203
Phone: (513)621-9050 **Fax:** (513)621-0549
E-mail: info@cinbelt.com
URL: http://www.cinbelt.com
Products: Power transmission equipment. **SICs:** 5084 (Industrial Machinery & Equipment); 5013 (Motor Vehicle Supplies & New Parts). **Emp:** 100. **Officers:** James E. Stahl Jr., President.

■ 2450 ■ Clarion Sales Corp.
661 W Redondo Beach Blvd.
Gardena, CA 90247
Phone: (310)327-9100 **Fax:** (310)327-1999
Products: car audio, stereo, electronic and multimedia products. **SICs:** 5013 (Motor Vehicle Supplies & New Parts); 5065 (Electronic Parts & Equipment Nec).
Sales: $22,000,000 (2000). **Emp:** 200. **Officers:** Jim Minarik, President.

■ 2451 ■ Clark Brothers Instrument Co.
56680 Mound Rd.
Shelby Township, MI 48316
Phone: (810)781-7000
Free: (800)622-5275 **Fax:** (810)781-7005
E-mail: gettings@clarkbrothers.net
URL: http://www.clarkbrothers.net
Products: Automotive instruments and heavy duty instruments, including speedometer and tachometer cables, ratio adaptors, right angle drives, and control cables. **SIC:** 5013 (Motor Vehicle Supplies & New Parts). **Est:** 1971. **Sales:** $5,000,000 (2000). **Emp:** 35.

Officers: Thomas F. Wright Sr., VP and General Mgr.; Eric Gettings, National Sales Mgr.

■ 2452 ■ Clark County Wholesale Inc.
PO Box 2018
Las Vegas, NV 89125-2018
Phone: (702)382-7700
Free: (800)574-5782 **Fax:** (702)382-5057
Products: Brakes; Asbestos; Engine parts. **SIC:** 5013 (Motor Vehicle Supplies & New Parts). **Est:** 1905.
Sales: $3,000,000 (2000). **Emp:** 41. **Officers:** Michael Hayden, President.

■ 2453 ■ Clarke Detroit Diesel-Allison Inc.
3133 E Kemper Rd.
Cincinnati, OH 45241
Phone: (513)771-2200 **Fax:** (513)771-0520
Products: Diesel engines, parts, automatic transmissions and parts. **SIC:** 5084 (Industrial Machinery & Equipment). **Est:** 1964. **Sales:** $100,000,000 (2000). **Emp:** 300. **Officers:** Mark M. Andreae, Exec. VP; Terry McMahon, Treasurer & Secty.; Don Bixler, VP of Marketing; Paula Brown, VP of Operations.

■ 2454 ■ Clark's Wholesale Tire Co.
3578 Sweeten Creek Rd.
Arden, NC 28704
Phone: (828)681-8100
Products: Tires. **SIC:** 5014 (Tires & Tubes).

■ 2455 ■ Clover Auto Supply Inc.
412 S 9th
Lincoln, NE 68508-2217
Phone: (402)474-1741
Free: (800)742-7384 **Fax:** (402)474-6716
Products: Automotive parts. **SIC:** 5013 (Motor Vehicle Supplies & New Parts). **Sales:** $3,000,000 (2000).
Emp: 42. **Officers:** A. J. Bell; Bill Buchmeier, Manager.

■ 2456 ■ CNEAD Division
1 Jacques St.
Worcester, MA 01603-1901
Phone: (508)755-0840 **Fax:** (508)756-8936
Products: Automotive parts and supplies, New. **SIC:** 5013 (Motor Vehicle Supplies & New Parts). **Emp:** 7.

■ 2457 ■ C.O. Tools Inc.
25837 Borg Rd.
PO Box 988
Elkhart, IN 46515
Phone: (219)262-1527
Free: (800)535-7164 **Fax:** (219)262-1529
Products: Automotive accessories. **SIC:** 5013 (Motor Vehicle Supplies & New Parts). **Est:** 1971. **Sales:** $10,000,000 (2000). **Emp:** 71. **Officers:** Stephen M. Abernathy, President.

■ 2458 ■ Coach House Products
484 Main St.
West Chicago, IL 60185-2864
Phone: (630)231-5770
Free: (888)793-1300 **Fax:** (630)231-5779
Products: Accessories for cars, trucks, and vans, including seat covers, cushions, curtains, floor mats, floor consoles, and tire covers. **SIC:** 5013 (Motor Vehicle Supplies & New Parts). **Est:** 1961. **Emp:** 7.
Officers: Lloyd J. Gorence, CEO; K.D. Gorence, Sales; J.C. Wayne, Administrator.

■ 2459 ■ Coast Counties Truck and Equipment Co.
1740 N 4th St.
San Jose, CA 95112
Phone: (408)453-5510 **Fax:** (408)453-7637
Products: Industrial trucks and equipment. **SICs:** 5084 (Industrial Machinery & Equipment); 5013 (Motor Vehicle Supplies & New Parts). **Sales:** $39,000,000 (1992). **Emp:** 100. **Officers:** Robert Archer, President.

■ 2460 ■ Coast Distribution System
1982 Zanker Rd.
San Jose, CA 95112
Phone: (408)436-8611
Products: Recreation vehicle parts and accessories.
SIC: 5013 (Motor Vehicle Supplies & New Parts).
Sales: $135,900,000 (2000). **Emp:** 345. **Officers:** Thomas R. McGuire, CEO & Chairman of the Board; Sandra A. Knell, Exec. VP & CFO.

■ 2461 ■ Coastal Energy Co.
PO Box 1269
Gulfport, MS 39502-1269
Phone: (228)863-0041
Products: Tires. **SIC:** 5014 (Tires & Tubes).

■ 2462 ■ Commercial Body Corp.
5601 Edith NE
Albuquerque, NM 87107
Phone: (505)344-8411 **Fax:** (505)344-8734
Products: Automotive parts and supplies, New. **SIC:** 5013 (Motor Vehicle Supplies & New Parts). **Officers:** Preston Wright, Contact.

■ 2463 ■ Commercial Body Corp.
1005 Commercial Blvd. S
Arlington, TX 76017
Phone: (817)467-1005 **Fax:** (817)472-8380
Products: Automotive parts and supplies, New. **SIC:** 5013 (Motor Vehicle Supplies & New Parts). **Officers:** Ruben Garcia, Branch Manager.

■ 2464 ■ Commercial Body Corp.
10800 Northwest Fwy.
Houston, TX 77092-7304
Phone: (713)688-7990
Free: (800)292-1931 **Fax:** (713)688-6430
E-mail: weherrin@juno.com
Products: Automotive parts and supplies, New. **SIC:** 5013 (Motor Vehicle Supplies & New Parts). **Officers:** Bill Herrin.

■ 2465 ■ Commercial Body Corp.
PO Box 1119
San Antonio, TX 78219
Phone: (210)476-7777
Free: (800)292-1931 **Fax:** (210)224-6885
URL: http://www.commercialbodycorp.com
Products: Automotive parts and supplies, New. **SIC:** 5013 (Motor Vehicle Supplies & New Parts). **Est:** 1934.
Emp: 100. **Officers:** Kent Grist, Contact, e-mail: kgrist@commercialbodycorp.com.

■ 2466 ■ Commercial Body Corp.
6010 Milwee
Houston, TX 77092
Phone: (713)688-7990
Free: (800)292-1931 **Fax:** (713)688-6430
Products: Automotive. **SIC:** 5013 (Motor Vehicle Supplies & New Parts).

■ 2467 ■ Commercial Motors
2101 Auiki St.
Honolulu, HI 96819-2254
Phone: (808)845-6421 **Fax:** (808)845-7717
Products: Automotive parts. **SIC:** 5013 (Motor Vehicle Supplies & New Parts). **Est:** 1947. **Sales:** $2,000,000 (2000). **Emp:** 60. **Officers:** Arthur Tedeschi, Vice President.

■ 2468 ■ Community Tire Co. Inc.
1307 N 7th St.
St. Louis, MO 63147
Phone: (314)241-3737
Products: Tires. **SIC:** 5014 (Tires & Tubes). **Est:** 1942.
Sales: $10,000,000 (2000). **Emp:** 100. **Officers:** Michael A. Berra, President; Phil Berra, CFO.

■ 2469 ■ Compact Performance Inc.
931 Hartz Way
Danville, CA 94526-3413
Phone: (510)831-1050 **Fax:** (510)838-5838
Products: Engine parts; Rebuilt engines. **SICs:** 5015 (Motor Vehicle Parts—Used); 5013 (Motor Vehicle Supplies & New Parts). **Est:** 1977. **Sales:** $2,800,000 (2000). **Emp:** 3. **Officers:** Keith Bigelow, President.

■ 2470 ■ Competition Parts Warehouse Inc.
1140 Campbell Ave.
San Jose, CA 95126
Phone: (408)243-3400 **Fax:** (408)243-9900
Products: Automobile parts, tires, and equipment. **SIC:** 5013 (Motor Vehicle Supplies & New Parts). **Est:** 1971.
Sales: $4,200,000,000 (2000). **Emp:** 550. **Officers:** Ray Barney, President.

■ 2471 ■ Complete Auto & Truck Parts
4510 Broadway Blvd. SE
Albuquerque, NM 87105-7404
Phone: (505)877-5960
Free: (800)423-3732 **Fax:** (505)873-1642
Products: Used auto parts. **SICs:** 5015 (Motor Vehicle Parts—Used); 5013 (Motor Vehicle Supplies & New Parts).

■ 2472 ■ Connecticut Driveshaft Inc.
470 Naugatuck Ave.
Milford, CT 06460
Phone: (203)877-2716 **Fax:** (203)877-7486
Products: Drive shafts. **SIC:** 5013 (Motor Vehicle Supplies & New Parts). **Est:** 1971. **Sales:** $18,000,000 (2000). **Emp:** 100. **Officers:** J.A. Honek, President; A.P. Honek, VP of Finance; Andrew Mirmina, Sales Mgr.; F. Honek, Dir. of Systems.

■ 2473 ■ Connecticut Driveshaft Inc.
59 Kelso Ave.
West Springfield, MA 01089-3701
Phone: (413)736-7207
Free: (800)443-4013 **Fax:** (413)733-6713
Products: Automotive and truck parts. **SIC:** 5013 (Motor Vehicle Supplies & New Parts).

■ 2474 ■ Consolidated Bearing Co.
10 Wing Dr.
Cedar Knolls, NJ 07927
Phone: (973)539-8300 **Fax:** (973)539-5902
Products: Wheel bearings. **SIC:** 5085 (Industrial Supplies). **Est:** 1934. **Sales:** $9,000,000 (2000). **Emp:** 45. **Officers:** Ralph Meerwarth, President.

■ 2475 ■ Consolidated Service Corp.
2500 Devon Ave.
Elk Grove Village, IL 60007
Phone: (708)640-2600 **Free:** (800)323-6644
Products: Tires and automobile parts. **SICs:** 5014 (Tires & Tubes); 5013 (Motor Vehicle Supplies & New Parts). **Sales:** $2,000 (2000). **Emp:** 365. **Officers:** Pat Starr, Chairman of the Board.

■ 2476 ■ Consolidated Truck Parts Inc.
PO Box 4844
Monroe, LA 71211
Phone: (318)325-1948
Free: (800)551-5195 **Fax:** (318)388-0947
URL: http://www.consolidatedtruckparts.com
Products: Truck parts; Drivetrain parts and equipment. **SIC:** 5013 (Motor Vehicle Supplies & New Parts). **Est:** 1957. **Sales:** $2,600,000 (2000). **Emp:** 10. **Officers:** O. Ray Niswanger, President; Danny Schulyer, Controller; Johnny Green, Sales Contact, e-mail: prtbrddg@bayou.com.

■ 2477 ■ Consolidated Utility & Equipment Service
53 Lebanon Rd.
Franklin, CT 06254
Phone: (860)886-7081 **Fax:** (860)886-6546
Products: Automotive parts and supplies, New. **SIC:** 5013 (Motor Vehicle Supplies & New Parts). **Officers:** Terry Harrison, VP of Operations.

■ 2478 ■ Consolidated Utility Equipment Service, Inc.
14 Caldwell Dr.
Amherst, NH 03031
Phone: (603)889-4071 **Fax:** (603)886-5909
URL: http://www.cuesnet.com
Products: Aerial lifts and truck bodies, new, used, and rentals. **SIC:** 5046 (Commercial Equipment Nec). **Est:** 1968. **Sales:** $15,000,000 (2000). **Emp:** 70. **Officers:** Al Morrison, President.

■ 2479 ■ Consulier Engineering Inc.
2391 Old Dixie Hwy.
Riviera Beach, FL 33404-5456
Phone: (561)842-2492 **Fax:** (561)845-3237
Products: Automotive parts. **SIC:** 5013 (Motor Vehicle Supplies & New Parts). **Sales:** $3,500,000 (2000). **Emp:** 15. **Officers:** Charles E. Spaeth, CEO; Thomas G. Weber, VP, CFO & Treasurer.

■ 2480 ■ Consumers Financial Corp.
PO Box 26
Camp Hill, PA 17001-0026
Phone: (717)761-4230
Products: Automobiles. **SIC:** 5012 (Automobiles & Other Motor Vehicles). **Sales:** $114,600,000 (2000). **Emp:** 54. **Officers:** James C. Robertson, CEO, President & Chairman of the Board; R. Fredric Zullinger, Sr. VP & CFO.

■ 2481 ■ Control Associates Inc.
20 Commerce Dr.
Allendale, NJ 07401-1600
Phone: (201)568-5513
Products: Valves, regulators, and alternators. **SICs:** 5085 (Industrial Supplies); 5013 (Motor Vehicle Supplies & New Parts). **Est:** 1956. **Sales:** $10,000,000 (2000). **Emp:** 47. **Officers:** J. Gary Gensheimer, President; Judith Metcalfe, Treasurer & Secty.

■ 2482 ■ Conversion Components Inc.
PO Box 429
23537 CR-106
Elkhart, IN 46515-0429
Phone: (219)264-4181 **Fax:** (219)264-2823
Products: Automotive accessories; Automotive parts and supplies, New. **SIC:** 5013 (Motor Vehicle Supplies & New Parts). **Est:** 1984. **Emp:** 7. **Officers:** James M. Shreve, President; Max E. Reeder, Vice President; Peggy Peterson, Vice President.

■ 2483 ■ Cooper Tire & Rubber Co.
701 Lima Ave.
Findlay, OH 45839
Phone: (419)423-1321
Products: Tires. **SIC:** 5014 (Tires & Tubes).

■ 2484 ■ Coronado Auto Recyclers Inc.
9320 San Pedro Dr. NE
Albuquerque, NM 87113-2123
Phone: (505)821-0440
Products: Used motor vehicle parts and supplies. **SIC:** 5015 (Motor Vehicle Parts—Used). **Officers:** Richard Loucks, President.

■ 2485 ■ Coronet Parts Manufacturing Co. Inc.
883-93 Elton St.
Brooklyn, NY 11208-5315
Phone: (718)649-1750
Free: (800)428-0015 **Fax:** (718)272-2956
Products: Valves and fittings. **SIC:** 5013 (Motor Vehicle Supplies & New Parts). **Est:** 1947. **Officers:** A.C. Salvati, Sales Mgr., e-mail: corbrass@aol.com; Janet Donato, Customer Service Contact; Joan Pipia, Human Resources Contact. **Alternate Name:** Janet #Donato.

■ 2486 ■ Corts Truck Equipment, Inc.
145 Mohawk St.
Whitesboro, NY 13492
Phones: (315)736-6641 (315)736-4850
Fax: (315)736-0655
Products: Automotive parts and supplies, New. **SIC:** 5013 (Motor Vehicle Supplies & New Parts). **Officers:** W. Barron Wilson, Contact.

■ 2487 ■ Cosmos Enterprises, Inc.
15 12th Ave. SE
Elbow Lake, MN 56531-4734
Phone: (218)685-4403
Free: (800)726-1965 **Fax:** (218)685-4404
E-mail: cosmos@runestone.net
URL: http://www.runestone.net/~cosmos
Products: Automotive products and tools. **SIC:** 5013 (Motor Vehicle Supplies & New Parts). **Est:** 1960. **Emp:** 30. **Officers:** Clint Grove, President; Evie Grove, Vice President; Kelly Chandler, Sales Mgr.; Bob Grove, Vice President.

■ 2488 ■ Covington Detroit Diesel Inc.
PO Box 18949
Greensboro, NC 27419
Phone: (336)292-9240 **Fax:** (252)292-9268
Products: Diesel engines. **SIC:** 5084 (Industrial Machinery & Equipment). **Sales:** $50,000,000 (1994). **Emp:** 243. **Officers:** Phillip Fowler, President; Donna Floyd, Controller.

■ 2489 ■ Covington Diesel Inc.
PO Box 18949
Greensboro, NC 27419
Phone: (919)292-9240 **Fax:** (919)292-9268
Products: Engines and engine parts. **SIC:** 5013 (Motor Vehicle Supplies & New Parts). **Est:** 1966. **Sales:** $76,000,000 (2000). **Emp:** 243. **Officers:** Tom Lanier, President; Phillip Denny, Controller; Jim Waye, Dir. of Marketing.

■ 2490 ■ Cox Enterprises Inc.
PO Box 105357
Atlanta, GA 30348
Phone: (404)843-5000 **Fax:** (404)843-5109
Products: Automobiles. **SIC:** 5012 (Automobiles & Other Motor Vehicles). **Sales:** $6,000,000 (1999). **Emp:** 60,000. **Officers:** James C. Kennedy, CEO & Chairman of the Board; Robert C. O'Leary, Exec. VP & CFO.

■ 2491 ■ Crain Automotive Inc.
PO Box 15178
Little Rock, AR 72231-5178
Phone: (501)945-8383
Products: Automotive parts. **SIC:** 5013 (Motor Vehicle Supplies & New Parts). **Est:** 1957. **Sales:** $35,000,000 (1999). **Emp:** 300. **Officers:** L. Crain Sr., President; Tom Tunnel, CFO; Keith Childers, VP of Operations; Chris Crain, VP & General Mgr.

■ 2492 ■ Crain M-M Sales Inc.
765 PickensInd'l DrExt
Marietta, GA 30062
Phone: (404)428-4421 **Fax:** (404)421-8292
Products: Automobiles. **SIC:** 5012 (Automobiles & Other Motor Vehicles). **Est:** 1958. **Sales:** $18,800,000 (2000). **Emp:** 42. **Officers:** Carl Myers, President; Rebecca Moss, Controller.

■ 2493 ■ Creger Auto Company Inc.
PO Box 7281
Shreveport, LA 71137-7281
Phone: (318)425-4292 **Fax:** (318)221-2796
Products: Automotive parts, including brakes. **SIC:** 5013 (Motor Vehicle Supplies & New Parts). **Est:** 1931. **Sales:** $1,000,000 (2000). **Emp:** 24. **Officers:** C.D. Creger, President.

■ 2494 ■ Crenshaw Corp.
1700 Commerce Rd.
PO Box 24217
Richmond, VA 23224
Phone: (804)231-6241
Free: (800)552-1930 **Fax:** (804)231-5455
Products: Bodies, equipment, and parts for trucks. **SIC:** 5013 (Motor Vehicle Supplies & New Parts). **Est:** 1946. **Sales:** $8,500,000 (2000). **Emp:** 56. **Officers:** Lee Crenshaw III, Vice President; C. Walford Crenshaw, President.

■ 2495 ■ Crest Truck Equipment Co. Inc.
Rte. 625, Bowmansville Rd.
PO Box 555
Bowmansville, PA 17507
Phone: (717)445-6746 **Fax:** (717)445-7967
Products: Truck accessories and parts. **SIC:** 5013 (Motor Vehicle Supplies & New Parts). **Officers:** Norman Ziegler Jr., President.

■ 2496 ■ Cross Co.
PO Box 18508
Greensboro, NC 27419-8508
Phone: (336)856-6000 **Fax:** (336)856-6999
E-mail: info@crossco.com
URL: http://www.crossco.com
Products: Fluid power equipment; Motion control equipment; Fluid instrumentation equipment; Factory automation equipment; Hoses and fittings. **SICs:** 5084 (Industrial Machinery & Equipment); 5085 (Industrial Supplies). **Est:** 1954. **Sales:** $100,000,000 (2000). **Emp:** 275. **Officers:** William S. Cross III, CEO & President; Ashley James, Chief Financial Officer. **Former Name:** Cross Sales and Engineering Co.

■ 2497 ■ Crotty Corp.
PO Box 37
Quincy, MI 49082
Phone: (517)639-8787
Free: (800)927-4009 **Fax:** (517)639-4309
Products: Automotive interior trim, including sunvisors.
SIC: 5013 (Motor Vehicle Supplies & New Parts).
Sales: $55,000,000 (2000). **Emp:** 900. **Officers:**
Willard E. Crotty Jr., President; Ron Dooley, Controller.

■ 2498 ■ CRW Parts, Inc.
3 James Ct.
Wilmington, DE 19801
Phone: (302)651-9300 **Fax:** (302)651-9479
Products: Automobile and truck parts. **SIC:** 5013
(Motor Vehicle Supplies & New Parts).

■ 2499 ■ CS Battery Inc.
4555 W 59th St.
Chicago, IL 60629
Phone: (773)582-3050 **Fax:** (773)582-3051
Products: Automotive batteries. **SIC:** 5013 (Motor
Vehicle Supplies & New Parts). **Est:** 1927. **Sales:**
$300,000 (2000). **Emp:** 3. **Officers:** Edward Kubiak,
President.

■ 2500 ■ CTR Used Parts & Equipment
12867 Hwy. 44
Middleton, ID 83644
Phone: (208)454-8878 **Fax:** (208)454-2139
Products: Used automotive parts and supplies,
including tractor parts. **SIC:** 5015 (Motor Vehicle
Parts—Used). **Officers:** Duane Shupe, Owner.

■ 2501 ■ Cumming-Henderson Inc.
PO Box 330
Santa Clara, CA 95052
Phone: (408)727-4440 **Fax:** (408)727-1542
Products: Automobile tires. **SIC:** 5014 (Tires & Tubes).
Est: 1952. **Sales:** $12,500,000 (2000). **Emp:** 60.
Officers: Gerald J. Regan, President; Rod Miller,
Controller; Rod Hall, VP of Sales.

■ 2502 ■ Cummins Alabama Inc.
PO Box 1147
Birmingham, AL 35201
Phone: (205)841-0421 **Fax:** (205)849-5926
Products: Diesel engines, parts, and generator sets.
SICs: 5084 (Industrial Machinery & Equipment); 5063
(Electrical Apparatus & Equipment). **Sales:**
$30,000,000 (1992). **Emp:** 120. **Officers:** K.B.
McDonald, President; D. Jones, CFO.

■ 2503 ■ Cummins Connecticut Inc.
260 Murphy Rd.
Hartford, CT 06114
Phone: (203)527-9156
Products: Diesel engines and generators. **SICs:** 5084
(Industrial Machinery & Equipment); 5063 (Electrical
Apparatus & Equipment). **Est:** 1935. **Sales:**
$10,000,000 (2000). **Emp:** 65. **Officers:** Mark Madden,
President; Edison B. Phillips, CFO.

■ 2504 ■ Cummins Cumberland Inc.
9822 Bluegrass Pkwy.
Louisville, KY 40299
Phone: (502)491-6060 **Fax:** (502)499-2908
Products: Engines. **SICs:** 5084 (Industrial Machinery
& Equipment); 5013 (Motor Vehicle Supplies & New
Parts). **Est:** 1946. **Sales:** $100,000,000 (2000). **Emp:**
325. **Officers:** Jack Apple, President; Andrew Willinger,
CFO.

■ 2505 ■ Cummins Gateway Inc.
7210 Hall St.
St. Louis, MO 63147
Phone: (314)389-5400 **Fax:** (314)389-9671
Products: Diesel engines. **SICs:** 5084 (Industrial
Machinery & Equipment); 5013 (Motor Vehicle Supplies
& New Parts). **Sales:** $25,000,000 (2000). **Emp:** 125.
Officers: John Wagner, President; David M. Keach,
Exec. VP & CFO; Ron Foster, VP of Marketing.

■ 2506 ■ Cummins Great Lakes Inc.
PO Box 530
De Pere, WI 54115
Phone: (414)337-1991 **Fax:** (414)337-9747
Products: Truck and generator engines. **SICs:** 5084
(Industrial Machinery & Equipment); 5063 (Electrical

Apparatus & Equipment). **Est:** 1983. **Sales:**
$35,000,000 (2000). **Emp:** 135. **Officers:** William
Maynard, President; Robin Last, CFO & VP; John
Laka, VP of Industrial; Mike Brandenburg, Information
Systems Mgr.; Rick Vohl, VP of Power Generation.

■ 2507 ■ Cummins Great Plains Diesel Inc.
PO Box 6068
Omaha, NE 68106
Phone: (402)551-7678 **Fax:** (402)551-1952
Products: Diesel engines; Diesel engine parts;
Generators; Motors. **SICs:** 5084 (Industrial Machinery
& Equipment); 5013 (Motor Vehicle Supplies & New
Parts); 5063 (Electrical Apparatus & Equipment).
Sales: $63,000,000 (2000). **Emp:** 200. **Officers:**
William Hanley, President.

■ 2508 ■ Cummins Intermountain Inc.
PO Box 25428
Salt Lake City, UT 84125
Phone: (801)355-6500 **Fax:** (801)524-1351
Products: Diesel engines. **SICs:** 5084 (Industrial
Machinery & Equipment); 5013 (Motor Vehicle Supplies
& New Parts). **Est:** 1945. **Sales:** $60,000,000 (2000).
Emp: 310. **Officers:** Lorin K. Pugh, CEO & President;
Frank Spilker, VP of Finance; Mark B. Zimmerer, VP of
Marketing & Sales; Bayne McMillan, Exec. VP &
General Mgr.

■ 2509 ■ Cummins Michigan Inc.
41216 Vincenti Ct.
Novi, MI 48375
Phone: (313)478-9700 **Fax:** (313)478-1570
Products: Diesel engines and diesel engine parts.
SICs: 5084 (Industrial Machinery & Equipment); 5013
(Motor Vehicle Supplies & New Parts). **Est:** 1971.
Sales: $46,000,000 (2000). **Emp:** 200. **Officers:** G.M.
Boll, President; Doug Miller, Controller.

■ 2510 ■ Cummins Midstates Power Inc.
3762 W Morris St.
Indianapolis, IN 46242
Phone: (317)243-7979 **Fax:** (317)240-1925
Products: Diesel engines. **SICs:** 5084 (Industrial
Machinery & Equipment); 5013 (Motor Vehicle Supplies
& New Parts). **Est:** 1981. **Sales:** $25,000,000 (2000).
Emp: 195. **Officers:** Hal A. Smitson Jr., President;
Eugene R. Hull, VP of Admin.; E.A. Friel, VP of
Marketing; D.D. Spence, Dir. of Systems.

■ 2511 ■ Cummins North Central Inc.
2690 Cleveland Ave. N
St. Paul, MN 55113
Phone: (651)636-1000
Free: (800)642-0085 **Fax:** (651)638-2442
Products: Engines and generators. **SICs:** 5084
(Industrial Machinery & Equipment); 5013 (Motor
Vehicle Supplies & New Parts). **Est:** 1974. **Sales:**
$60,000,000 (2000). **Emp:** 200. **Officers:** Jim
Andrews, President; Jefferey R. Boelsen, VP of
Finance; Russell Sheaffer, VP of Marketing & Sales, e-
mail: rwsheaffer@minn.cummins.com; William Mealey,
Information Systems Mgr.; Betty J. Aschenbrener,
Human Resources Mgr.

■ 2512 ■ Cummins Ohio Inc.
4000 Lyman Dr.
Hilliard, OH 43026
Phone: (614)771-1000 **Fax:** (440)439-7390
Products: Diesel engines and regulators. **SICs:** 5084
(Industrial Machinery & Equipment); 5013 (Motor
Vehicle Supplies & New Parts). **Sales:** $47,000,000
(2000). **Emp:** 289. **Officers:** Larry Stavnicky, General
Mgr.; G. Bank, CFO.

■ 2513 ■ Cummins Power Systems Inc.
2727 Ford Rd.
Bristol, PA 19007
Phone: (215)781-2955
Products: Cummins engines. **SIC:** 5084 (Industrial
Machinery & Equipment).

■ 2514 ■ Cummins Rocky Mountain, Inc.
5100 E 58th Ave.
Commerce City, CO 80022
Phone: (303)287-0201 **Fax:** (303)288-7080
URL: http://www.cumminrmi.com
Products: Engines, generators, parts, service. **SICs:**
5084 (Industrial Machinery & Equipment); 5013 (Motor

Vehicle Supplies & New Parts). **Emp:** 200. **Officers:**
John B. Dunn, Owner & Pres. **Former Name:**
Cummins Power Inc.

■ 2515 ■ Cummins Southern Plains Inc.
600 Watson Dr.
Arlington, TX 76011
Phone: (817)640-6801 **Fax:** (817)640-6852
Products: Engine generators and diesel parts. **SICs:**
5084 (Industrial Machinery & Equipment); 5013 (Motor
Vehicle Supplies & New Parts). **Est:** 1934. **Sales:**
$95,000,000 (2000). **Emp:** 500. **Officers:** R.D. Gillikin,
President; A.C. Funai, VP & CFO; J.D. Gatten, Dir. of
Marketing.

■ 2516 ■ Cummins Southwest Inc.
2239 N Black Canyon Hwy.
Phoenix, AZ 85009-2706
Phone: (602)252-8021
Products: Diesel engines, generator and transport
refrigeration equipment. **SICs:** 5084 (Industrial
Machinery & Equipment); 5078 (Refrigeration
Equipment & Supplies). **Sales:** $50,000,000 (1994).
Emp: 280. **Officers:** Frank Thomas, CEO & President;
Vickie Hauser, CFO.

■ 2517 ■ Cummins West Inc.
14775 Wicks Blvd.
San Leandro, CA 94577
Phone: (510)351-6101
Free: (800)595-5050 **Fax:** (510)357-3432
URL: http://www.cummins.com
Products: Diesel engines. **SIC:** 5084 (Industrial
Machinery & Equipment). **Est:** 1935. **Sales:**
$52,000,000 (2000). **Emp:** 250. **Officers:** Kevin
Shanahan, President; M. Doherty, CFO.

■ 2518 ■ Custom Trim of America
777 E Market St.
Akron, OH 44305
Phone: (330)253-6893
Free: (800)837-7633 **Fax:** (330)258-1469
Products: Automotive parts and supplies, New. **SIC:**
5013 (Motor Vehicle Supplies & New Parts). **Est:** 1971.
Sales: $5,000,000 (2000). **Emp:** 49. **Officers:** Alex
Kallas, President. **Former Name:** Custom Trim of
Akron.

■ 2519 ■ D & A Distributing
PO Box 1199
Lebanon, MO 65536-3213
Phone: (417)532-6198
Free: (800)492-4333 **Fax:** (417)532-2232
Products: Auto parts, including paint, bumpers, sand
papers, bed liners, and side railers. **SICs:** 5013 (Motor
Vehicle Supplies & New Parts); 5198 (Paints,
Varnishes & Supplies). **Emp:** 19. **Officers:** Doyal Allan.

■ 2520 ■ D & H Tire Service
919 Troup St.
Kansas City, KS 66104
Phone: (913)621-1155
Products: Tires, brakes, and shocks. **SICs:** 5014
(Tires & Tubes); 5013 (Motor Vehicle Supplies & New
Parts). **Est:** 1946. **Sales:** $4,500,000 (2000). **Emp:** 22.
Officers: Luther D. White, Partner.

■ 2521 ■ D & M Distributing
3970 E Olympic Blvd.
Los Angeles, CA 90023-3248
Phone: (213)268-9958 **Fax:** (213)266-3283
Products: Automotive parts. **SIC:** 5013 (Motor Vehicle
Supplies & New Parts). **Emp:** 49. **Officers:** Marco A.
Franco Sr.

■ 2522 ■ D-M Tire Supply
1259 Manheim Pke.
Lancaster, PA 17601
Phone: (717)291-4493
Products: Tires. **SIC:** 5014 (Tires & Tubes).

■ 2523 ■ D & W Distributing Co. Inc.
309 Mechanic St.
Pekin, IL 61554
Phone: (309)347-6194 **Fax:** (309)347-8493
Products: Automotive parts. **SIC:** 5013 (Motor Vehicle
Supplies & New Parts). **Sales:** $5,000,000 (2000).
Emp: 32. **Officers:** W.L. Heitzman, President; Devon

Hoerr, Vice President; Tom Hudson, Dir. of Marketing & Sales.

■ 2524 ■ **Dallas Peterbilt Inc.**
PO Box 560228
Dallas, TX 75356
Phone: (972)445-7505
Free: (800)256-7383 **Fax:** (972)438-5196
Products: Truck parts and service equipment. **SIC:** 5013 (Motor Vehicle Supplies & New Parts). **Est:** 1978. **Sales:** $140,000,000 (2000). **Emp:** 475. **Officers:** Jesse Kirk, Chairman of the Board; Bill Ballew, CFO; Jeff Houldey, Sales Mgr.; Leah Stout, Dir. of Data Processing; Dianne Neal, Dir of Human Resources.

■ 2525 ■ **Dallas Wheels & Accessories, Inc.**
3510 Dalworth
Arlington, TX 76011
Phone: (817)640-7575
Free: (800)937-5847 **Fax:** (817)633-6344
Products: Wheels. **SIC:** 5013 (Motor Vehicle Supplies & New Parts).

■ 2526 ■ **Dana World Trade Div.**
10800 NW 103rd St., Ste. 11
Miami, FL 33178
Phone: (305)499-5100 **Fax:** (305)499-4480
Products: Vehicular engine, driveline and chassis components and fluid power systems. **SIC:** 5013 (Motor Vehicle Supplies & New Parts). **Sales:** $10,000,000 (1999). **Emp:** 90. **Officers:** Paula Schaff, VP & General Mgr.

■ 2527 ■ **Danzey Oil and Tire Co. Inc.**
PO Box 1646
Dothan, AL 36302
Phone: (205)792-4159
Products: Tires. **SIC:** 5014 (Tires & Tubes). **Est:** 1936. **Sales:** $10,000,000 (2000). **Emp:** 20. **Officers:** R.M. Kennedy, President.

■ 2528 ■ **Dave's Auto Inc.**
PO Box 2292
Bismarck, ND 58502-0932
Phone: (701)255-1194 **Fax:** (701)223-6988
Products: Used motor vehicle parts and supplies. **SIC:** 5015 (Motor Vehicle Parts—Used). **Officers:** David Wahl, President.

■ 2529 ■ **Dave's Used Auto Parts Inc.**
PO Box 7118
Cumberland, RI 02864-0892
Phone: (401)334-2900
Products: Used motor vehicle parts; Automotive parts and supplies. **SICs:** 5015 (Motor Vehicle Parts—Used); 5013 (Motor Vehicle Supplies & New Parts). **Officers:** Dave Le Mayer, President.

■ 2530 ■ **Davey Motor Co.**
PO Box 1249
Columbus, MT 59019-1249
Phone: (406)322-5346 **Fax:** (406)322-4757
Products: Motors. **SIC:** 5013 (Motor Vehicle Supplies & New Parts). **Est:** 1928. **Sales:** $6,000,000 (2000). **Emp:** 20. **Officers:** M.E. Davey, President; Stanley C. Grotbo, General Mgr.

■ 2531 ■ **David Tire Co. Inc.**
PO Box 2284
Birmingham, AL 35201
Phone: (205)251-8473
Products: Tires. **SIC:** 5014 (Tires & Tubes). **Est:** 1947. **Sales:** $4,000,000 (2000). **Emp:** 12. **Officers:** John David, CEO.

■ 2532 ■ **S.A. Day Manufacturing Co.**
1489 Niagara St.
Buffalo, NY 14213
Phone: (716)881-3030 **Fax:** (716)881-4353
Products: Automobile radiator supplies. **SIC:** 5013 (Motor Vehicle Supplies & New Parts). **Est:** 1902. **Sales:** $7,500,000 (2000). **Emp:** 50. **Officers:** J.L. Martin, CEO & Chairman of the Board; Jackson Bowling, VP of Finance.

■ 2533 ■ **Dealer Chemical Corp.**
PO Box 460462
St. Louis, MO 63146
Phone: (314)576-1333
Products: Automobile rustproofing and undercoating. **SIC:** 5013 (Motor Vehicle Supplies & New Parts). **Sales:** $1,000,000 (2000). **Emp:** 15. **Officers:** Robert Parsons, President.

■ 2534 ■ **Dealers Truck Equipment Company Inc.**
PO Box 31435
Shreveport, LA 71130
Phone: (318)635-7567 **Fax:** (318)635-3144
Products: Transportation and construction equipment. **SICs:** 5088 (Transportation Equipment & Supplies); 5082 (Construction & Mining Machinery). **Sales:** $17,000,000 (1994). **Emp:** 160. **Officers:** R.F. Kayser III, President; B. Kayser, CFO.

■ 2535 ■ **Deas Tire Co.**
PO Box 1678
Gulfport, MS 39502-1678
Phone: (228)863-5072
Products: Tires. **SIC:** 5014 (Tires & Tubes). **Sales:** $27,000,000 (2000). **Emp:** 50. **Officers:** Louise Deas, Owner.

■ 2536 ■ **Dega Technologies**
1530 Monterey St.
San Luis Obispo, CA 93401-2928
Phone: (805)546-0444 **Fax:** (805)546-8046
Products: Internet Auto Parts Distribution Network for parts suppliers and buyers that enables all members in the supply chain to do business on line. **SIC:** 5013 (Motor Vehicle Supplies & New Parts). **Officers:** J.P. Makeyer, CEO; Dawn Legg, VP of Corp. Communications.

■ 2537 ■ **Delphi Saginaw Steering Systems**
3900 Hallond Rd.
Saginaw, MI 48601-9494
Phone: (517)757-4005
Products: Steering systems. **SIC:** 5013 (Motor Vehicle Supplies & New Parts).

■ 2538 ■ **Denman Tire Corp.**
400 Diehl South Rd.
Leavittsburg, OH 44430-9741
Phone: (330)675-4242
Free: (800)334-5543 **Fax:** (330)675-4232
URL: http://www.denmantire.com
Products: Tires. **SICs:** 5014 (Tires & Tubes); 5013 (Motor Vehicle Supplies & New Parts). **Est:** 1917. **Sales:** $70,000,000 (2000). **Emp:** 350. **Officers:** Charles Wright, President & COO.

■ 2539 ■ **Dependable Motor Parts**
PO Box 1746
Bay City, TX 77404-1746
Phone: (409)245-5506
Products: Motor parts. **SIC:** 5013 (Motor Vehicle Supplies & New Parts). **Est:** 1943. **Sales:** $4,300,000 (2000). **Emp:** 40. **Officers:** Mike Wade, President.

■ 2540 ■ **Desert Sky Wrecking**
2742 Hwy. 46
Wendell, ID 83355
Phone: (208)536-6606
Products: Used automotive parts and supplies. **SIC:** 5015 (Motor Vehicle Parts—Used). **Officers:** Larry Harms, Owner.

■ 2541 ■ **Detroit Diesel Overseas Corp.**
13400 W Outer Dr.
Detroit, MI 48239
Phone: (313)592-5000
Products: Diesel engines; Generators. **SICs:** 5013 (Motor Vehicle Supplies & New Parts); 5063 (Electrical Apparatus & Equipment).

■ 2542 ■ **Diamond Prairie Ranch Company Inc.**
1254 S 9th St.
Las Vegas, NV 89104-1503
Phone: (702)384-6478
Products: Used motor vehicle parts. **SIC:** 5015 (Motor Vehicle Parts—Used). **Officers:** G. Luzier, President.

■ 2543 ■ **Dickinson Supply Inc.**
37 3rd Ave. E
PO Box 1151
Dickinson, ND 58601
Phone: (701)225-8591
Free: (800)924-8591 **Fax:** (701)225-9868
Products: Automotive parts and supplies, New. **SIC:** 5013 (Motor Vehicle Supplies & New Parts). **Emp:** 7. **Officers:** Bill Plagge, President; Shirley Plagge, Secretary; Herb Decker, Manager.

■ 2544 ■ **Diesel Equipment Specialists**
Rt. 13
Bridgeville, DE 19933
Phone: (302)337-8742 **Fax:** (302)337-3201
Products: Diesel equipment parts. **SIC:** 5013 (Motor Vehicle Supplies & New Parts).

■ 2545 ■ **Diesel Power Equipment Co.**
15225 Industrial Rd.
Omaha, NE 68144
Phone: (402)330-5100
Free: (800)999-5689 **Fax:** (402)330-5100
E-mail: dpec@neonramp.com
Products: Engines. **SIC:** 5013 (Motor Vehicle Supplies & New Parts). **Est:** 1976. **Sales:** $16,000,000 (2000). **Emp:** 65. **Officers:** Walter Price Sr. Jr., President; Bill Engler, Comptroller; Steve Lamb, Sales Mgr.

■ 2546 ■ **Diesel Power Supply Co.**
2525 University Parks
Waco, TX 76707
Phone: (254)753-1587 **Fax:** (254)755-0100
E-mail: dieselpower@msn.com
Products: Engines and parts, including exhaust accessories, fans, gauges, generators, hoses, pumps, starters, alternators, transmissions, batteries, belts, cables and controls; Environmental products; Hard hats; Air tools and accessories; Chemicals and additives. **SIC:** 5084 (Industrial Machinery & Equipment). **Est:** 1960.

■ 2547 ■ **Discount Engine Exchange Inc.**
2112 W Main St.
Farmington, NM 87401-3221
Phone: (505)327-0319 **Fax:** (505)325-3256
Products: Motors. **SIC:** 5013 (Motor Vehicle Supplies & New Parts). **Officers:** Jerry Symonds, President.

■ 2548 ■ **Distributors Warehouse Inc.**
PO Box 7239
Paducah, KY 42002-7239
Phone: (502)442-8201 **Fax:** (502)442-4914
Products: Automotive supplies; Automotive parts. **SIC:** 5013 (Motor Vehicle Supplies & New Parts). **Est:** 1934. **Sales:** $13,000,000 (2000). **Emp:** 90. **Officers:** Walter Korte, President; Lisa Pullen, Controller; Steve Korte, Dir. of Marketing; Sarah McIntosh, Dir. of Data Processing.

■ 2549 ■ **Dixie Bearings, Inc.**
1005 S A St.
Ft. Smith, AR 72901
Phone: (501)782-9128 **Fax:** (501)783-4534
Products: Bearings; Power transmissions. **SICs:** 5085 (Industrial Supplies); 5013 (Motor Vehicle Supplies & New Parts). **Emp:** 10.

■ 2550 ■ **Dixie Bearings Inc.**
PO Box 93803
Cleveland, OH 44101
Phone: (216)881-2828 **Fax:** (216)881-7744
Products: Bearings. **SIC:** 5085 (Industrial Supplies). **Sales:** $250,000,000 (2000). **Emp:** 1,000. **Officers:** John C. Dannemiller, CEO & Chairman of the Board; John Whitten, VP of Finance.

■ 2551 ■ **Dixie International Co.**
3636 Indianola Ave.
Columbus, OH 43214
Phone: (614)262-0102 **Fax:** (614)267-0509
Products: Motorcycle parts and accessories. **SIC:** 5013 (Motor Vehicle Supplies & New Parts). **Est:** 1963. **Sales:** $10,000,000 (2000). **Emp:** 100. **Officers:** Joe L. Baca Sr., President.

■ 2552 ■ **Dixie Parts and Equipment Co.**
PO Box 929
Sidney, OH 45365
Phone: (937)492-6133
Products: Automotive supplies, including lighting equipment and brake fuses. **SIC:** 5013 (Motor Vehicle Supplies & New Parts). **Est** 1942. **Sales:** $2,000,000 (2000). **Emp:** 18. **Officers:** Tom Krupp, President.

■ 2553 ■ **D.N. Motors Ltd.**
531 Van Cortland Park
Yonkers, NY 10705
Phone: (914)476-7451
Products: Automotive motors. **SICs:** 5012 (Automobiles & Other Motor Vehicles); 5013 (Motor Vehicle Supplies & New Parts). **Sales:** $2,500,000 (2000). **Emp:** 4. **Officers:** A. Desai, Vice President.

■ 2554 ■ **Dodge City Cooperative Exchange Inc.**
PO Box 610
Dodge City, KS 67801
Phone: (316)225-4193
Products: Automotive products, including brakes and mufflers; Hardware; Fertilizers; Animal feed. **SICs:** 5013 (Motor Vehicle Supplies & New Parts); 5191 (Farm Supplies); 5072 (Hardware). **Est:** 1915. **Sales:** $35,900,000 (2000). **Emp:** 88. **Officers:** Dennis Spohr, President; David Stegall, CFO.

■ 2555 ■ **Domestic & International Technology**
115 West Ave.
Jenkintown, PA 19046
Phone: (215)885-7670 **Fax:** (215)884-1385
Products: Food processing equipment; Electrical generators; Industrial machinery and equipment; Motor vehicle supplies and parts. **SICs:** 5013 (Motor Vehicle Supplies & New Parts); 5046 (Commercial Equipment Nec); 5063 (Electrical Apparatus & Equipment); 5084 (Industrial Machinery & Equipment). **Officers:** R. Stollman, President.

■ 2556 ■ **Dorfman Auto Supply Inc.**
PO Box 611
Waverly, IA 50677-0611
Phone: (319)352-2180
Products: Automobile products. **SIC:** 5013 (Motor Vehicle Supplies & New Parts). **Est:** 1921. **Sales:** $1,500,000 (2000). **Emp:** 20. **Officers:** Herbert L. Dorfman, President & Treasurer.

■ 2557 ■ **Dorman Products Div.**
1 Dorman Dr.
Warsaw, KY 41095
Phone: (606)567-7000 **Fax:** (606)567-7010
Products: Automotive parts, including engines and brakes. **SIC:** 5013 (Motor Vehicle Supplies & New Parts). **Est:** 1927. **Sales:** $32,000,000 (2000). **Emp:** 250. **Officers:** Richard Berman, President; Malcolm Walter, CFO; Bob Bryant, Exec. VP of Marketing & Sales.

■ 2558 ■ **Dow-Hammond Trucks Co.**
720 G St.
Modesto, CA 95354
Phone: (209)524-4861 **Fax:** (209)524-3282
Products: Pickups and heavy trucks. **SIC:** 5012 (Automobiles & Other Motor Vehicles). **Est:** 1949. **Sales:** $16,000,000 (2000). **Emp:** 40. **Officers:** Russ Jones, President; Breck Austin, CFO.

■ 2559 ■ **Drake America Div.**
2 Gannett Dr.
White Plains, NY 10604
Phone: (914)697-9800 **Fax:** (914)697-9658
Products: Automotive parts; Restaurant supplies. **SICs:** 5013 (Motor Vehicle Supplies & New Parts); 5149 (Groceries & Related Products Nec). **Est:** 1947. **Sales:** $26,000,000 (2000). **Emp:** 35. **Officers:** Edward S. Dorian Jr., President; John Mott, Controller; Rudy C. Bruckenthal, Dir. of Marketing.

■ 2560 ■ **Fred Drake's Salvage**
4195 Dupont Pky.
Townsend, DE 19734
Phone: (302)378-4877
Free: (800)626-1159 **Fax:** (302)378-8679
Products: Automobile parts, used. **SIC:** 5015 (Motor Vehicle Parts—Used).

■ 2561 ■ **Dreyco Inc.**
263 Veterans Blvd.
Carlstadt, NJ 07072-2792
Phone: (201)896-9000 **Fax:** (201)896-1378
Products: Automotive parts, hand tools, and garage equipment and machinery. **SICs:** 5013 (Motor Vehicle Supplies & New Parts); 5072 (Hardware); 5084 (Industrial Machinery & Equipment). **Sales:** $16,000,000 (2000). **Emp:** 41. **Officers:** Jack Dreyfus, President; F. Dreyfus, Treasurer & Secty.

■ 2562 ■ **Dreyfus & Assoc.**
305 Madison Ave., Ste. 966
New York, NY 10165-0026
Phone: (212)867-7700 **Fax:** (212)867-7820
Products: Motor vehicle engine rebuilding equipment; Automotive accessories; Garage and service station equipment. **SICs:** 5013 (Motor Vehicle Supplies & New Parts); 5087 (Service Establishment Equipment). **Officers:** Louis J. Agnesini, Manager.

■ 2563 ■ **Drive Train Industries Inc.**
3301 Brighton Blvd.
Denver, CO 80216
Phone: (303)292-5176
Products: Truck parts. **SIC:** 5013 (Motor Vehicle Supplies & New Parts). **Est:** 1945. **Sales:** $18,000,000 (2000). **Emp:** 160. **Officers:** Jim Burke, President.

■ 2564 ■ **Drive Train Industries Inc.**
3350 E Yellowstone
Casper, WY 82609
Phone: (307)266-4390
Free: (800)442-3700 **Fax:** (307)234-0450
Products: Automotive and truck parts. **SIC:** 5013 (Motor Vehicle Supplies & New Parts).

■ 2565 ■ **Drivetrain Specialists**
1308 W 2nd St.
Odessa, TX 79763
Phone: (915)333-3241 **Fax:** (915)333-3666
Products: Drive train parts, including transmissions and clutches. **SIC:** 5013 (Motor Vehicle Supplies & New Parts).

■ 2566 ■ **Drucker Associates, Inc.**
PO Box 36219
Grosse Pointe Woods, MI 48236
Phone: (313)882-8228
Products: Industrial truck and trailer parts; Conveyors and conveying equipment; Automotive parts and accessories, including automotive maintenance equipment. **SICs:** 5013 (Motor Vehicle Supplies & New Parts); 5084 (Industrial Machinery & Equipment). **Officers:** Aaron Drucker, President.

■ 2567 ■ **Dunlop Tire Corp.**
PO Box 1109
Buffalo, NY 14240
Phone: (716)879-8200
Free: (800)253-6702 **Fax:** (716)879-8222
Products: Tires. **SIC:** 5014 (Tires & Tubes). **Sales:** $200,000,000 (2000). **Emp:** 2,000. **Officers:** Randall L. Clark.

■ 2568 ■ **Duromotive Industries**
241 41st St.
Brooklyn, NY 11232-2811
Phone: (718)499-3838 **Fax:** (718)788-8754
E-mail: sales@duromotive.com
URL: http://www.sales@duromotive.com
Products: Automotive parts. **SIC:** 5013 (Motor Vehicle Supplies & New Parts). **Est:** 1969. **Emp:** 19. **Officers:** Albert Dwek, President; Roger Seti, Customer Service Contact.

■ 2569 ■ **DVH Co.**
PO Box 560604
Dallas, TX 75356-0604
Phone: (214)631-0200 **Fax:** (214)631-0907
Products: Trailer components, including axles, forks, wheels, and springs. **SIC:** 5013 (Motor Vehicle Supplies & New Parts). **Est:** 1921. **Sales:** $4,000,000 (2000). **Emp:** 20. **Officers:** Dallas Hensley, President; Mike Phillips, Dir. of Marketing.

■ 2570 ■ **E & G Auto Parts Inc.**
211 W Long Ave.
Du Bois, PA 15801-2105
Phone: (814)371-3350
Products: Motor vehicle parts and accessories. **SIC:** 5013 (Motor Vehicle Supplies & New Parts). **Emp:** 12. **Officers:** Ernie Burkes, Manager.

■ 2571 ■ **East Jordan Cooperative Co.**
PO Box 377
East Jordan, MI 49727
Phone: (616)536-2275
Products: Hardware and farm supplies; Auto parts, including, batteries, starters, and brakes; Gasoline. **SICs:** 5013 (Motor Vehicle Supplies & New Parts); 5172 (Petroleum Products Nec); 5072 (Hardware). **Sales:** $2,000,000 (2000). **Emp:** 14. **Officers:** D. Graham, President; R.F. Massey, Dir. of Marketing.

■ 2572 ■ **Eastern Auto Parts Company Inc.**
795 Eastern Ave.
Malden, MA 02148
Products: Automobile parts, including mufflers, shocks, brakes, batteries, electrical, and rubber products. **SICs:** 5013 (Motor Vehicle Supplies & New Parts); 5014 (Tires & Tubes). **Est:** 1924. **Sales:** $2,000,000 (2000). **Emp:** 50. **Officers:** Donna Stieglitz, President; Matthew Stieglitz, Treasurer.

■ 2573 ■ **Eastern Bearings Inc.**
158 Lexington St.
Waltham, MA 02454
Phone: (781)899-3952
Free: (800)427-1014 **Fax:** (781)647-3227
E-mail: bob@ebearings.com
URL: http://www.ebearings.com
Products: Bearings; Electrical transmission equipment; Mechanical power transmission equipment; Lubrication systems. **SICs:** 5063 (Electrical Apparatus & Equipment); 5013 (Motor Vehicle Supplies & New Parts). **Est:** 1963. **Sales:** $40,000,000 (2000). **Emp:** 110. **Officers:** Richard Gorsey, President; Geoffrey Filker, COO, e-mail: geoff@ebearings.com.

■ 2574 ■ **Eastern Tool Warehouse Corp.**
20 Fairfield Pl.
West Caldwell, NJ 07006
Phone: (201)808-4637 **Fax:** (201)227-7029
Products: Automotive tools and equipment. **SIC:** 5013 (Motor Vehicle Supplies & New Parts). **Est:** 1946. **Sales:** $14,000,000 (2000). **Emp:** 55. **Officers:** Aaron Berkowitz, CEO; Mario Brassini, President; Jay Gartman, Vice President.

■ 2575 ■ **Eddie's Tire Service Inc.**
Rte. 6, Box 12460
Berkeley Springs, WV 25411
Phone: (304)258-1368 **Fax:** (304)258-1777
Products: Tires and wheels. **SIC:** 5014 (Tires & Tubes). **Est:** 1951. **Sales:** $20,000,000 (2000). **Emp:** 60. **Officers:** D.L. Stotler, President; D.J. Dhayer, Sec. & Treas.; G.D. Dhayer, Vice President.

■ 2576 ■ **Frank Edwards Co.**
110 S 3rd W
Salt Lake City, UT 84110
Phone: (801)363-8851 **Fax:** (801)364-2670
Products: Auto parts and supplies. **SIC:** 5013 (Motor Vehicle Supplies & New Parts). **Est:** 1915. **Sales:** $63,000,000 (2000). **Emp:** 150. **Officers:** Robert Edwards Jr., President; Bruce Hart, Exec. VP of Finance.

■ 2577 ■ **Eggimann Motor and Equipment Sales Inc.**
1813 W Beltline Hwy.
Madison, WI 53713
Phone: (608)271-5544
Free: (800)236-3941 **Fax:** (608)271-6308
E-mail: Eggiman@Eggimann.com
URL: http://www.Eggimann.com
Products: Parts for medium and heavy trucks. **SIC:** 5013 (Motor Vehicle Supplies & New Parts). **Est:** 1946. **Sales:** $6,000,000 (2000). **Emp:** 43. **Officers:** Steven Beecraft, CEO; Lloyd Ravet, Controller; Robert Sturdevant, Dir. of Marketing; Bob Messinger, General Mgr.; Sanford Moore, Controller; Rocky Shores, Payroll Mgr.

■ 2578 ■ El Mexicano Auto Salvage
1200 Coors Blvd. SW
Albuquerque, NM 87121-3406
Phone: (505)242-2131
Products: Automobile parts, used. **SIC:** 5015 (Motor Vehicle Parts—Used). **Officers:** Jesus Carrete, Owner.

■ 2579 ■ Electric Garage Supply Co.
204 N 9th St.
Brainerd, MN 56401
Phone: (218)829-2879
Products: Automotive supplies. **SIC:** 5013 (Motor Vehicle Supplies & New Parts). **Sales:** $1,000,000 (1994). **Emp:** 12. **Officers:** Milo Johnson, President.

■ 2580 ■ Electric Specialties Inc.
11536 W 4 A Rd.
Plymouth, IN 46563
Phone: (219)936-5725   **Fax:** (219)936-9481
Products: Ignition harness and cable sets. **SIC:** 5013 (Motor Vehicle Supplies & New Parts). **Est:** 1986.

■ 2581 ■ Elizabethtown Distributing Co. Inc.
PO Box 664
Elizabethtown, KY 42702-0664
Phone: (502)765-4117   **Fax:** (502)769-6798
Products: Automotive parts. **SIC:** 5013 (Motor Vehicle Supplies & New Parts). **Emp:** 49.

■ 2582 ■ Elliff Motors Inc.
1307 W Harrison St.
Harlingen, TX 78550
Phone: (210)423-3434
Products: Automotive motors. **SIC:** 5015 (Motor Vehicle Parts—Used). **Est:** 1944. **Sales:** $11,000,000 (2000). **Emp:** 7. **Officers:** Larry Elliff, President; Joe Elliff, VP of Finance; Bill Elliff, Dir. of Marketing.

■ 2583 ■ Elliott Auto Supply Company Inc.
2855 Eagandale Blvd.
St. Paul, MN 55121
Phone: (612)454-5184
Products: Auto parts and supplies. **SIC:** 5013 (Motor Vehicle Supplies & New Parts). **Sales:** $20,000,000 (1992). **Emp:** 100.

■ 2584 ■ Ellis Inc.
1001 Commonwealth Ave.
Boston, MA 02215
Phone: (617)782-4777
Free: (800)445-6437   **Fax:** (617)782-1462
URL: http://www.ellistherimman.com
Products: Automobile, truck, and van accessories. **SIC:** 5013 (Motor Vehicle Supplies & New Parts). **Est:** 1917. **Sales:** $4,000,000 (2000). **Emp:** 20. **Officers:** Edward Ellis, President & Treasurer; Steven Ellis, Sales Mgr.; Jason Grossman, General Mgr.

■ 2585 ■ Ely Auto Dismantlers
PO Box 71
Ely, NV 89301-0071
Phone: (702)289-8242
Products: Automobile parts, used. **SIC:** 5015 (Motor Vehicle Parts—Used). **Officers:** K. Hermansen.

■ 2586 ■ Emanuel Tire Co.
1300 Moreland Ave.
Baltimore, MD 21216
Phone: (410)947-0660   **Fax:** (410)947-3708
E-mail: emantire@aol.com
Products: Used tires. **SIC:** 5014 (Tires & Tubes). **Est:** 1958. **Sales:** $2,500,000 (2000). **Emp:** 35. **Officers:** Norman Emanuel, President.

■ 2587 ■ Emco Inc.
1310 Glenwood Ave.
PO Box 3114
Greensboro, NC 27403
Phone: (919)272-3146   **Fax:** (919)370-1038
Products: Transmission equipment. **SIC:** 5013 (Motor Vehicle Supplies & New Parts).

■ 2588 ■ Stuart Emery
261 Emery's Bridge Rd.
South Berwick, ME 03908-1935
Phone: (207)384-2115
Products: Used motor vehicle parts. **SIC:** 5015 (Motor Vehicle Parts—Used). **Officers:** Stuart Emery, Owner.

■ 2589 ■ Empire Power Systems Inc.
2211 W McDowell Rd.
Phoenix, AZ 85009-3074
Phone: (602)333-5600
Products: Trucks. **SIC:** 5084 (Industrial Machinery & Equipment). **Sales:** $50,000,000 (2000). **Emp:** 75. **Officers:** Gale L. Plummer, General Mgr.

■ 2590 ■ Engine & Performance Warehouse Inc.
955 Decatur St., Unit D
Denver, CO 80204-3365
Phone: (303)572-8844
Free: (800)888-8970   **Fax:** (303)825-7619
Products: Gasoline engines and gasoline engine parts for motor vehicles. **SIC:** 5013 (Motor Vehicle Supplies & New Parts). **Est:** 1972. **Emp:** 40.

■ 2591 ■ Engineered Drives
131 Lloyd St.
Allentown, PA 18103
Phone: (215)264-9368
Products: Power transmission products. **SICs:** 5013 (Motor Vehicle Supplies & New Parts); 5085 (Industrial Supplies).

■ 2592 ■ Engs Motor Truck Co.
1550 S McCarran Blvd.
Sparks, NV 89431
Phone: (702)359-8840
Products: Trucks and tractors. **SIC:** 5012 (Automobiles & Other Motor Vehicles). **Sales:** $85,000,000 (1994). **Emp:** 300. **Officers:** Edward W. Engs III, President; Stuart R. Engs, Treasurer & Secty.

■ 2593 ■ EPR Automotive Warehouse
831 Gretna Blvd.
Gretna, LA 70053-6939
Phone: (504)362-1380   **Fax:** (504)536-9345
Products: Automobile alternators and starters. **SIC:** 5013 (Motor Vehicle Supplies & New Parts). **Emp:** 21. **Officers:** Pedro de La Torre Jr.

■ 2594 ■ Equipment and Parts Export Inc.
745 5th Ave., Ste. 1114
New York, NY 10151
Phone: (212)753-9730   **Fax:** (212)826-0906
Products: Used motor vehicle parts; Office equipment; Electrical apparatus and equipment; Electronic parts and equipment; Tires and tubes. **SICs:** 5015 (Motor Vehicle Parts—Used); 5014 (Tires & Tubes); 5044 (Office Equipment); 5063 (Electrical Apparatus & Equipment); 5065 (Electronic Parts & Equipment Nec). **Officers:** Behic Tiryakioglu, Sales Mgr.

■ 2595 ■ Equipment Rental
4788 1st Ave. N
Duluth, MN 55803
Phone: (218)728-4441   **Fax:** (218)728-4442
Products: Automotive parts and supplies, New. **SIC:** 5013 (Motor Vehicle Supplies & New Parts). **Officers:** Bill Raymond, Contact.

■ 2596 ■ Ertel Products Inc.
1436 E 19th St.
Indianapolis, IN 46218-4228
Products: Automobile engine parts. **SIC:** 5013 (Motor Vehicle Supplies & New Parts). **Sales:** $4,000,000 (2000). **Emp:** 100. **Officers:** William B. Ertel, President; Donald Nachtigall, VP of Finance.

■ 2597 ■ ESCO Industries
955 Grand Oak Dr.
Howell, MI 48843
Phone: (517)546-6200
Products: Alternators; Starters. **SIC:** 5013 (Motor Vehicle Supplies & New Parts).

■ 2598 ■ E.W. Tire & Service Centers
718 Hope Hollow Rd.
Carnegie, PA 15106-3627
Phone: (412)276-2141   **Fax:** (412)429-1085
Products: Tires. **SIC:** 5014 (Tires & Tubes). **Emp:** 130. **Officers:** J. M. Smith, President.

■ 2599 ■ Exhaust Specialties II
700 SE Belmont St.
Portland, OR 97214
Phone: (503)233-5151   **Fax:** (503)283-6824
Products: Car exhaust systems and brakes. **SIC:** 5013 (Motor Vehicle Supplies & New Parts). **Est:** 1955. **Sales:** $1,000,000 (2000). **Emp:** 3. **Officers:** Floyd Boyle, President.

■ 2600 ■ Export Division of Gordon E. Hansen Agency Inc.
PO Box 98
Hampton, CT 06247
Phone: (860)455-9903   **Fax:** (860)455-9146
E-mail: exportdivisiongh@gyral.com
Products: Motor vehicle accessories, including air deflectors, rain and wind deflectors, bug deflectors, floor mats, cargo liners, bike racks, and tow straps; Teflon oil additives. **SIC:** 5013 (Motor Vehicle Supplies & New Parts). **Officers:** Gordon Hansen, President. **Former Name:** Gordon E. #Hansen Agency Inc.

■ 2601 ■ Ezon Inc.
1900 Exeter Rd.
Germantown, TN 38138
Phone: (901)755-5555   **Fax:** (901)754-3698
Products: Auto parts, including brakes. **SIC:** 5013 (Motor Vehicle Supplies & New Parts). **Est:** 1957. **Sales:** $250,000,000 (2000). **Emp:** 500. **Officers:** Barry Gomez, President; Jack Tackett, Dir. of Admin.

■ 2602 ■ F & W Rallye Engineering
39W960 Midan Dr.
Elburn, IL 60119
Phone: (630)232-6063
Free: (800)323-5251   **Fax:** (630)232-8702
Products: Automotive parts and supplies, New. **SIC:** 5013 (Motor Vehicle Supplies & New Parts). **Est:** 1974. **Sales:** $200,000 (2000). **Emp:** 1. **Officers:** Kern L. Fischer, General Mgr.

■ 2603 ■ Fabco Industries, Inc.
8406 W Loop, No. 338
Odessa, TX 79764
Phone: (915)367-4988
Free: (800)767-4988   **Fax:** (915)367-4980
Products: Automotive parts and supplies, New. **SIC:** 5013 (Motor Vehicle Supplies & New Parts). **Officers:** Danny Barlau, President.

■ 2604 ■ Factory Motor Parts
5605 F St.
Omaha, NE 68117-2820
Phone: (402)341-6318
Products: Automotive parts. **SIC:** 5013 (Motor Vehicle Supplies & New Parts). **Est:** 1980. **Sales:** $1,800,000 (2000). **Emp:** 6. **Officers:** David Durick, President; Gary Flury, Treasurer & Secty.

■ 2605 ■ R.E. Fair Company Inc.
5601 Huberville Rd.
Dayton, OH 45431
Phone: (937)253-1170
Free: (800)253-1170   **Fax:** (937)253-7936
Products: Automotive parts, including spark plugs, brakes, and filters; Oil; Electrical parts. **SIC:** 5013 (Motor Vehicle Supplies & New Parts). **Est:** 1948. **Sales:** $4,000,000 (1999). **Emp:** 12. **Officers:** Richard Fair, President.

■ 2606 ■ Fairfield Supply Co.
1675 S Sandusky
PO Box 429
Bucyrus, OH 44820
Phone: (419)562-4015   **Fax:** (419)562-9700
Products: Power transmission tools. **SIC:** 5013 (Motor Vehicle Supplies & New Parts).

■ 2607 ■ Falken Tire Corp.
10404 6th St.
Rancho Cucamonga, CA 91730
Phone: (909)466-1116
Free: (800)723-2553   **Fax:** (909)466-1169
E-mail: falkentire@earthlink.net
URL: http://www.falkentire.com
Products: Tires. **SIC:** 5014 (Tires & Tubes). **Est:** 1955. **Sales:** $45,000,000 (1999). **Emp:** 35. **Officers:** Hideo Honda, President; Roy Dickinson, Controller.

■ 2608 ■ Fayetteville Automotive Warehouse
226 Cool Spring
Fayetteville, NC 28301-5136
Phone: (910)483-6196
Free: (800)283-9445 **Fax:** (910)483-7039
Products: Automotive parts and supplies, New. **SIC:** 5013 (Motor Vehicle Supplies & New Parts). **Emp:** 49.

■ 2609 ■ Felt Auto Supply
645 S State
Salt Lake City, UT 84111-3819
Phone: (801)364-1977
Products: Automotive parts and supplies, New. **SIC:** 5013 (Motor Vehicle Supplies & New Parts). **Emp:** 13.

■ 2610 ■ Fenders and More Inc.
PO Box 2088
Brentwood, TN 37024-2088
Phone: (615)373-2050
Products: Automotive parts. **SIC:** 5013 (Motor Vehicle Supplies & New Parts).

■ 2611 ■ Ferguson Tire Service Inc.
1139 Main St.
Weirton, WV 26062
Phone: (304)748-5260
Products: Tires. **SIC:** 5014 (Tires & Tubes). **Est:** 1949. **Sales:** $3,500,000 (2000). **Emp:** 18. **Officers:** Gene Ferguson Jr., President; Gene Ferguson, Vice President.

■ 2612 ■ Ferodo America
1 Grizzly Ln.
Smithville, TN 37166-9979
Phone: (615)597-6700
Free: (800)251-3228 **Fax:** (615)597-5243
Products: Brake lines; Brake shoes. **SIC:** 5013 (Motor Vehicle Supplies & New Parts). **Sales:** $100,000,000 (2000). **Emp:** 499. **Officers:** J. L. Battle.

■ 2613 ■ Ferrari North America Inc.
250 Sylvan Ave.
Englewood Cliffs, NJ 07632
Phone: (201)816-2600
Products: Automobiles. **SICs:** 5012 (Automobiles & Other Motor Vehicles); 5013 (Motor Vehicle Supplies & New Parts). **Sales:** $44,000,000 (1994). **Emp:** 28. **Officers:** Gian L. Longinotti-Buitoni, President; T. Heffernan, CFO.

■ 2614 ■ Fiamm Technologies
Cadillac, MI 49601
Phone: (616)775-1373 **Fax:** (616)775-4402
Products: Car horns. **SIC:** 5013 (Motor Vehicle Supplies & New Parts). **Sales:** $6,000,000 (2000). **Emp:** 230. **Officers:** Glenn Bathrick, Plant Mgr. **Former Name:** Signaltone.

■ 2615 ■ Filter Supply Co.
1210 N Knollwood Cir.
Anaheim, CA 92801
Phone: (714)527-8221
Products: Filters for oil, water, and fuel. **SICs:** 5085 (Industrial Supplies); 5013 (Motor Vehicle Supplies & New Parts). **Est:** 1943. **Sales:** $4,000,000 (2000). **Emp:** 21. **Officers:** W.J. De Ranek, President; W.R. De Ranek, Treasurer & Secty.; K. Cathey, Dir. of Marketing; E.M. De Ranek, Vice President.

■ 2616 ■ Filtran Div.
PO Box 328
Des Plaines, IL 60016
Phone: (708)635-6670 **Fax:** (708)635-7724
Products: Filters for automatic transmissions. **SIC:** 5013 (Motor Vehicle Supplies & New Parts). **Est:** 1884. **Sales:** $69,000,000 (2000). **Emp:** 350. **Officers:** Kenneth V. Nelson, General Mgr.; William Smolik, Mgr. of Finance; Ken V. Nelson, Dir. of Marketing & Sales.

■ 2617 ■ FinishMaster Inc.
4259 40th St. SE
Kentwood, MI 49512
Phone: (616)949-7604
Products: Automotive paint supplies. **SIC:** 5198 (Paints, Varnishes & Supplies). **Est:** 1968. **Sales:** $107,500,000 (2000). **Emp:** 650. **Officers:** Andre B. Lacy, CEO & Chairman of the Board; Roger A. Sorokin, VP of Finance.

■ 2618 ■ First Automotive Inc.
103 S Dean
Bay City, MI 48706
Phone: (517)893-6521
Products: Automotive parts and supplies, including paint, ignition parts, and front end parts. **SICs:** 5013 (Motor Vehicle Supplies & New Parts); 5198 (Paints, Varnishes & Supplies). **Est:** 1914. **Sales:** $2,000,000 (2000). **Emp:** 30. **Officers:** Fred Bunting, President; Daniel L. Bond, Sales Mgr.

■ 2619 ■ Fisher Auto Parts
PO Box 148
Braceville, IL 60407
Phone: (815)237-2166
Products: Automotive supplies. **SIC:** 5013 (Motor Vehicle Supplies & New Parts). **Est:** 1960. **Sales:** $5,000,000 (2000). **Emp:** 25. **Officers:** Bill G. Daniels, President; Michael Daniels, Vice President. **Former Name:** Dabro Supply Co.

■ 2620 ■ Fisher Auto Parts Inc.
523 Edmunds
South Boston, VA 24592-3005
Phone: (804)572-3978
Products: Automotive parts. **SIC:** 5013 (Motor Vehicle Supplies & New Parts). **Emp:** 499. **Officers:** Ray Gosney.

■ 2621 ■ Fisher Auto Parts Inc.
512 Greenville Ave.
Staunton, VA 24401
Phone: (703)885-8905 **Fax:** (703)885-1808
Products: Auto parts. **SIC:** 5013 (Motor Vehicle Supplies & New Parts). **Est:** 1929. **Sales:** $550,000,000 (2000). **Emp:** 1,100. **Officers:** Art Fisher, President; Paul Mott, Treasurer & Secty.; Gary Shifflett, COO; Herb Godschalk, Data Processing Mgr.

■ 2622 ■ Fisher Auto Parts Inc. Manlove Div.
PO Box 479
Seaford, DE 19973
Phone: (302)629-9185
Products: Automotive supplies, including engine parts. **SIC:** 5013 (Motor Vehicle Supplies & New Parts). **Est:** 1941. **Sales:** $12,000,000 (2000). **Emp:** 60. **Officers:** Wanda Shorter, General Mgr.; Robert H. Norwood, Manager.

■ 2623 ■ Fisher Auto Parts Professionals
1830 SE 3rd Ave.
Rochester, MN 55904-7922
Phone: (507)285-9976 **Fax:** (507)288-1893
Products: Oil; Automobile parts; Machine parts. **SICs:** 5013 (Motor Vehicle Supplies & New Parts); 5172 (Petroleum Products Nec); 5085 (Industrial Supplies). **Sales:** $8,000,000 (2000). **Emp:** 130. **Officers:** Arthur Birdseye.

■ 2624 ■ Fisher Electric Motor Service
2025 Wayne Haven St.
Ft. Wayne, IN 46803
Phone: (219)493-0521 **Fax:** (219)493-4165
Products: Electric motors. **SIC:** 5063 (Electrical Apparatus & Equipment). **Sales:** $1,500,000 (1993). **Emp:** 17. **Officers:** Wayne Hoffman, President; Richard Farrar, CFO.

■ 2625 ■ Five Foreign Auto Salvage
601 Haines Ave. NW
Albuquerque, NM 87102-1225
Phone: (505)247-2227
Products: Automobile parts, used. **SIC:** 5015 (Motor Vehicle Parts—Used). **Officers:** Mark Warren, Owner.

■ 2626 ■ Five JS Auto Parts Inc.
5404 Broadway Blvd. SE
Albuquerque, NM 87105-7422
Phone: (505)877-6270
Free: (800)456-0065 **Fax:** (505)877-6270
Products: Automobile parts, used. **SIC:** 5015 (Motor Vehicle Parts—Used). **Officers:** Ron Mc Cullock, President.

■ 2627 ■ L.H. Flaherty Company Inc.
1577 Jefferson Ave. S
PO Box 7409
Grand Rapids, MI 49510
Phone: (616)245-9266 **Fax:** (616)241-0954
Products: Gear motors and boxes; Brakes. **SICs:** 5084 (Industrial Machinery & Equipment); 5013 (Motor Vehicle Supplies & New Parts).

■ 2628 ■ Fleet Parts Distributor
1630 S Dupont Hwy.
Dover, DE 19901
Phone: (302)674-5911
Products: Truck parts. **SIC:** 5013 (Motor Vehicle Supplies & New Parts).

■ 2629 ■ Fleet Pride
520 Lake Cook Rd.
Bradley, IL 60915
Phone: (847)444-1095 **Fax:** (847)444-1096
Products: Heavy duty truck parts; Truck repair. **SIC:** 5013 (Motor Vehicle Supplies & New Parts). **Sales:** $1,054,000,000 (2000). **Emp:** 2,500. **Officers:** John Greisch, CEO & President; John P. Miller, CFO.

■ 2630 ■ Fleet Specialties Div.
PO Box 4575
Thousand Oaks, CA 91359
Phone: (818)889-1716
Products: Tire inflation monitoring systems. **SIC:** 5013 (Motor Vehicle Supplies & New Parts).

■ 2631 ■ Flex-a-Lite Consolidated
PO Box 580
Milton, WA 98354
Phone: (253)922-2700
Free: (800)851-1510 **Fax:** (253)922-0026
E-mail: flex@flex-a-lite.com
URL: http://www.flex-a-lite.com
Products: Automotive parts, including electric engine fans, transmission coolers, and fan clutches. **SIC:** 5013 (Motor Vehicle Supplies & New Parts). **Est:** 1962. **Emp:** 30.

■ 2632 ■ Florida Detroit Diesel-Allison North Inc.
5105 Bowden Rd.
Jacksonville, FL 32216
Phone: (904)737-7330 **Fax:** (904)739-9097
Products: Engines and parts. **SICs:** 5084 (Industrial Machinery & Equipment); 5013 (Motor Vehicle Supplies & New Parts). **Est:** 1971. **Sales:** $40,000,000 (2000). **Emp:** 153. **Officers:** Micheal Catto, President; H.P. Littlefield, VP & CFO; Ron Zdanciewicz, Dir. of Marketing; John Hecker, Dir. of Data Processing; Rose Kozsey, Dir of Personnel.

■ 2633 ■ Florig Equipment
3202 Lanvale Ave.
Richmond, VA 23230
Phone: (804)353-9966 **Fax:** (804)353-4734
Products: Truck hydraulics. **SIC:** 5013 (Motor Vehicle Supplies & New Parts).

■ 2634 ■ Flowers Auto Parts Co.
PO Box 1118
Hickory, NC 28603
Phone: (828)345-2133
Products: Auto parts, including brakes, starters, batteries, and spark plugs. **SIC:** 5013 (Motor Vehicle Supplies & New Parts). **Est:** 1922. **Sales:** $14,000,000 (2000). **Emp:** 110. **Officers:** John R. Flowers Jr., President.

■ 2635 ■ Fontaine Fifth Wheel Co.
171 Cleage Dr.
Birmingham, AL 35217
Phone: (205)856-1100 **Fax:** (205)854-1211
Products: 5th wheel connectors. **SIC:** 5012 (Automobiles & Other Motor Vehicles). **Sales:** $16,000,000 (2000). **Emp:** 200. **Officers:** Ken Dickson, President.

■ 2636 ■ Fontaine Modification Co.
5325 Prosperity Dr.
Springfield, OH 45502
Phone: (937)399-3319 **Fax:** (937)399-2351
Products: Automotive parts and supplies, New. **SIC:**

5013 (Motor Vehicle Supplies & New Parts). **Officers:** Barry Krampe, Contact.

■ **2637** ■ **Forbes & Co.**
PO Box 750
Alexandria, VA 22313
Phone: (703)548-8833 **Fax:** (703)548-1038
Products: Motor vehicle parts and accessories; Electric and electronic equipment. **SICs:** 5013 (Motor Vehicle Supplies & New Parts); 5065 (Electronic Parts & Equipment Nec). **Est:** 1958. **Emp:** 4. **Officers:** Harlan B. Forbes Jr., President.

■ **2638** ■ **Foreign Car Parts Inc.**
2390 5th Ave. S
St. Petersburg, FL 33712
Phone: (813)327-6161 **Fax:** (813)327-3099
Products: Foreign car parts. **SIC:** 5013 (Motor Vehicle Supplies & New Parts). **Emp:** 49.

■ **2639** ■ **Foreign Car Parts Inc.**
5214 Quesenberry Ln
Las Cruces, NM 88005-4812
Phone: (505)526-5883 **Free:** (800)222-2613
Products: Used motor vehicle parts. **SIC:** 5015 (Motor Vehicle Parts—Used). **Officers:** Allen Chapman, President.

■ **2640** ■ **Foreign Tire Sales Inc.**
2204 Morris Ave.
Union, NJ 07083
Phone: (908)687-0559
Products: Tires. **SIC:** 5014 (Tires & Tubes).

■ **2641** ■ **John M. Forster Co.**
300 Commerce Dr.
Rochester, NY 14623
Phone: (716)334-0590 **Fax:** (716)334-3135
Products: Power transmissions. **SICs:** 5084 (Industrial Machinery & Equipment); 5013 (Motor Vehicle Supplies & New Parts).

■ **2642** ■ **Fort Wayne Fleet Equipment**
13710 Lower Huntington Rd.
Roanoke, IN 46783
Phone: (219)493-1800 **Fax:** (219)672-9110
Products: Automotive parts and supplies, New. **SIC:** 5013 (Motor Vehicle Supplies & New Parts). **Officers:** Denny Jones, President.

■ **2643** ■ **Four M Parts Warehouse**
402 E Chambers
Cleburne, TX 76031-5626
Phone: (817)645-7222 **Fax:** (817)645-4650
Products: Automotive parts. **SIC:** 5013 (Motor Vehicle Supplies & New Parts). **Est:** 1977. **Emp:** 70. **Officers:** Bill Martindale.

■ **2644** ■ **Johnny Frank's Auto Parts Co.**
1225 Sawyer St.
Houston, TX 77007
Phone: (713)869-6200
Products: Automotive salvage parts, including motors, beds, doors, brakes, and starters. **SIC:** 5015 (Motor Vehicle Parts—Used). **Sales:** $6,000,000 (2000). **Emp:** 12. **Officers:** Carter Frank, President; Vernon Frank, Owner.

■ **2645** ■ **Free Service Tire Company Inc.**
126 Buffalo St.
Johnson City, TN 37601
Phone: (423)928-6476 **Fax:** (423)461-1617
Products: Tires. **SIC:** 5014 (Tires & Tubes). **Est:** 1919. **Sales:** $35,000,000 (2000). **Emp:** 185. **Officers:** Lewis P. Wexler, President; Jim Luneke, Comptroller; Lewis P. Wexler Jr., Vice President.

■ **2646** ■ **Freedland Industries Corp.**
PO Box 278
Dearborn, MI 48121
Phone: (313)584-3033 **Fax:** (313)584-7195
Products: Automotive parts. **SIC:** 5013 (Motor Vehicle Supplies & New Parts). **Est:** 1974. **Sales:** $30,000,000 (2000). **Emp:** 100. **Officers:** R. Freedland, President; Sukumar Joshipura, Controller; Neil Waldman, Dir of Human Resources.

■ **2647** ■ **Freedman Seating Co.**
4043 N Ravenswood
Chicago, IL 60613
Phone: (773)929-6100 **Fax:** (773)929-8942
Products: Automotive parts and supplies, New. **SIC:** 5013 (Motor Vehicle Supplies & New Parts). **Est:** 1892. **Sales:** $1,000,000 (2000). **Emp:** 50.

■ **2648** ■ **Fremont Electric Company Inc.**
744 N 34th St.
Seattle, WA 98103
Phone: (206)633-2323
Products: Automobile parts. **SICs:** 5013 (Motor Vehicle Supplies & New Parts); 5088 (Transportation Equipment & Supplies). **Est:** 1915. **Sales:** $18,000,000 (2000). **Emp:** 164. **Officers:** M.M. McKinley Jr., President; J. Korbein, CFO.

■ **2649** ■ **Frey the Wheelman Inc.**
41-51 E Tupper St.
Buffalo, NY 14203
Phone: (716)854-3830
Products: Brake drums, wheels, and rims. **SIC:** 5013 (Motor Vehicle Supplies & New Parts). **Est:** 1907. **Sales:** $4,800,000 (2000). **Emp:** 50. **Officers:** Grace M. Fritz, President & Treasurer.

■ **2650** ■ **Friend Tire Co.**
11 Industrial Dr.
Monett, MO 65708
Phone: (417)235-7836
Products: Tires for cars and heavy industrial equipment. **SIC:** 5014 (Tires & Tubes). **Est:** 1925. **Sales:** $89,000,000 (2000). **Emp:** 230. **Officers:** Donald L. Isbell, President; Pats Kojima, CFO; Larry Balmas, Dir. of Marketing & Sales.

■ **2651** ■ **Matt Friend Truck Equipment, Inc.**
Hastings Industrial Park E, Bldg. SH66
PO Box 1083
Hastings, NE 68902-1083
Phone: (402)463-5675
Free: (800)444-7647 **Fax:** (402)463-5639
Products: Truck equipment. **SIC:** 5013 (Motor Vehicle Supplies & New Parts). **Est:** 1993. **Sales:** $1,500,000 (2000). **Emp:** 9. **Officers:** Matt Friend, President.

■ **2652** ■ **Frigi-Cool/RVAC Inc.**
PO Box 116968
Carrollton, TX 75007
Phone: (972)446-9497
Free: (800)527-0839 **Fax:** (972)446-0370
Products: Automotive air-conditioning equipment; Recreational vehicle air conditioners. **SIC:** 5013 (Motor Vehicle Supplies & New Parts). **Est:** 1981. **Sales:** $20,000,000 (2000). **Emp:** 65. **Officers:** Bobby Panner, President; Jo Sisme, VP of Finance; Bill Marcom, VP of Marketing. **Former Name:** Frigi-Cool Inc.

■ **2653** ■ **Frontier Truck Equipment and Parts Co.**
7167 E 53rd Pl.
Commerce City, CO 80022
Phone: (303)289-4311
Free: (800)289-4311 **Fax:** (303)286-7188
URL: http://www.frontiertruck.com
Products: Automotive maintenance equipment; New automotive parts and supplies. **SIC:** 5013 (Motor Vehicle Supplies & New Parts). **Est:** 1982. **Sales:** $5,500,000 (2000). **Emp:** 30. **Officers:** Robert H. Abel, President; Midge B. Abel, Treasurer & Secty.; Bill Forbes, Sales Mgr.; Bill Forbes, Sales Mgr.

■ **2654** ■ **FTC Corp.**
31700 Bainbrook Rd.
Westlake Village, CA 91361
Phone: (818)879-0229
Products: Automobile equipment. **SIC:** 5013 (Motor Vehicle Supplies & New Parts).

■ **2655** ■ **Full Bore - Cycle Lines USA**
9515 51st Ave., Unit 12
College Park, MD 20740
Phone: (301)474-9119
Free: (800)333-9119 **Fax:** (301)345-3231
Products: Motorized vehicles. **SIC:** 5013 (Motor Vehicle Supplies & New Parts).

■ **2656** ■ **Fullwell Products Inc.**
6140 Parkland Blvd.
Cleveland, OH 44124-4187
Phone: (440)942-1200
Products: Automobile parts; Hardware; Chemicals; Electrical equipment. **SICs:** 5013 (Motor Vehicle Supplies & New Parts); 5072 (Hardware); 5169 (Chemicals & Allied Products Nec); 5063 (Electrical Apparatus & Equipment). **Sales:** $12,000,000 (1994). **Emp:** 350. **Officers:** Keith Drewett, President; Idell Wolf, CFO.

■ **2657** ■ **Fumoto Engineering of America**
12328 Northrup Way
Bellevue, WA 98005
Phone: (425)869-7771 **Fax:** (425)869-2558
URL: http://www.fumotovalve.com
Products: Automotive parts and supplies, new. **SIC:** 5013 (Motor Vehicle Supplies & New Parts). **Est:** 1986. **Sales:** $1,000,000 (2000). **Emp:** 1. **Officers:** Norio Mitsuoka, General Mgr.

■ **2658** ■ **Gainesville Industrial Supply**
280 High St. SW
PO Box 423
Gainesville, GA 30503
Phone: (404)536-1271 **Fax:** (404)531-3214
Products: Powertrain equipment. **SICs:** 5084 (Industrial Machinery & Equipment); 5013 (Motor Vehicle Supplies & New Parts).

■ **2659** ■ **Ganin Tire Company Inc.**
1421 38th St.
Brooklyn, NY 11218
Phone: (718)633-0600 **Fax:** (718)633-1990
Products: Tires. **SIC:** 5014 (Tires & Tubes). **Sales:** $150,000,000 (2000). **Emp:** 150. **Officers:** Saul Ganin, President; John Woods, CFO.

■ **2660** ■ **Ganin Tire Inc.**
1421 38th St.
Brooklyn, NY 11218
Phone: (718)633-0600
Free: (800)344-2788 **Fax:** (718)633-1990
Products: Tires. **SIC:** 5014 (Tires & Tubes). **Est:** 1924. **Sales:** $30,000,000 (2000). **Emp:** 164.

■ **2661** ■ **Gans Tire Company Inc.**
PO Box 70
Malden, MA 02148-0001
Phone: (617)321-3910
Free: (800)343-3276 **Fax:** (617)322-2147
E-mail: dganz@galaxytire.com
URL: http://www.galaxytire.com
Products: Tires. **SIC:** 5014 (Tires & Tubes). **Est:** 1922. **Sales:** $60,000,000 (2000). **Emp:** 50. **Officers:** David Gans, President; Leo Browne, VP of Operations.

■ **2662** ■ **Gateway Auto Parts**
Rte. 20, PO Box 9
Huntington, MA 01050
Phone: (413)667-3101
Free: (800)992-1054 **Fax:** (413)667-3101
Products: Automotive parts and supplies, New. **SIC:** 5013 (Motor Vehicle Supplies & New Parts). **Officers:** Rick Dugre, Owner.

■ **2663** ■ **Gateway Tire Company Inc.**
4 W Crescentville Rd.
Cincinnati, OH 45246
Phone: (513)874-2500
Free: (800)837-1405 **Fax:** (513)874-7412
Products: Tires; Wheels; Tubes. **SICs:** 5014 (Tires & Tubes); 5013 (Motor Vehicle Supplies & New Parts). **Est:** 1973. **Sales:** $14,400,000 (2000). **Emp:** 35. **Officers:** William Patton.

■ **2664** ■ **Gay Johnson's Inc.**
PO Box 1829
Grand Junction, CO 81502
Phone: (970)245-7992 **Fax:** (970)242-5663
Products: Tires. **SIC:** 5014 (Tires & Tubes). **Est:** 1941. **Sales:** $20,000,000 (1999). **Emp:** 65. **Officers:** Bert Johnson, President; Dee A. Brinegar, CFO.

■ 2665 ■ GCR Rose Truck Tire Center
17051 I-35 N
Schertz, TX 78154
Phone: (210)533-7138
Free: (800)805-9320 Fax: (210)533-1255
Products: Truck, farm, and industrial tires. SIC: 5014
(Tires & Tubes). Est: 1968. Sales: $5,000,000 (2000).
Emp: 24. Officers: R.L. Heines, Manager.

■ 2666 ■ GCR Truck Tire Center
4160 Reardon Rd.
Forest, WI 54012
Phone: (608)846-2494
Products: Truck tires. SIC: 5014 (Tires & Tubes).

■ 2667 ■ Gear Clutch & Joint
124 E Broadway
Lubbock, TX 79403
Phone: (806)763-5329
Free: (800)999-9425 Fax: (806)765-6529
E-mail: gcjoi@aol.com
URL: http://www.ujointsinc.com
Products: Truck parts, including clutches. SIC: 5013
(Motor Vehicle Supplies & New Parts).

■ 2668 ■ Gear & Wheel Corp.
1965 Stan Home Way
Orlando, FL 32804
Phone: (407)843-1900 Fax: (407)422-9013
Products: Truck parts. SIC: 5013 (Motor Vehicle
Supplies & New Parts).

■ 2669 ■ General Auto Parts Inc.
384 King Rd.
Tiverton, RI 02878-2721
Phone: (401)624-6687 Fax: (401)625-1040
Products: Used motor vehicle parts; Automotive parts
and supplies. SICs: 5015 (Motor Vehicle Parts—Used);
5013 (Motor Vehicle Supplies & New Parts). Officers:
Anthony Russo, President.

■ 2670 ■ General Auto Sales Company Inc.
PO Box 177
Claremont, NH 03743-0177
Phone: (603)542-9595
Products: Used automotive parts and supplies. SIC:
5015 (Motor Vehicle Parts—Used). Officers: Allen
Whipple, President.

■ 2671 ■ General Parts Corp.
7 Emory Pl.
Knoxville, TN 37917
Phone: (615)525-6191 Fax: (423)637-4110
Products: Auto parts and supplies, including batteries,
brakes, starters, and spark plugs. SIC: 5013 (Motor
Vehicle Supplies & New Parts). Est: 1921. Sales:
$13,000,000 (2000). Emp: 24. Officers: Hamilton S.
Burnett Jr., President.

■ 2672 ■ General Parts, Inc.
PO Box 19268
Shawnee, KS 66214
Phone: (913)248-4200 Fax: (913)248-4201
Products: Automotive parts. SIC: 5013 (Motor Vehicle
Supplies & New Parts). Sales: $15,000,000 (1999).
Emp: 72. Officers: Temple Sloan, President; David
McCartney, Vice President; Al Minnis, Vice President;
Beverly Moretina, Farm Mgr.

■ 2673 ■ General Parts Inc.
PO Box 26006
Raleigh, NC 27611
Phone: (919)573-3000 Fax: (919)790-0411
Products: Auto parts, including brakes, mufflers,
starters, and spark plugs. SIC: 5013 (Motor Vehicle
Supplies & New Parts). Est: 1961. Sales:
$850,000,000 (2000). Emp: 3,500. Officers: N. Joe
Owen, President; John W. Gardner, CFO.

■ 2674 ■ General Tire Inc.
2550 Lukens Ln.
Carson City, NV 89706
Phone: (775)882-3454
Products: Tires. SIC: 5014 (Tires & Tubes).

■ 2675 ■ General Truck Body Co.
1919 10th St. NW
Roanoke, VA 24012
Phone: (540)362-1861 Fax: (540)362-5328
Products: Truck bodies and equipment. SIC: 5013
(Motor Vehicle Supplies & New Parts). Est: 1949.
Sales: $2,000,000 (2000). Emp: 12. Officers: J.
Bernard Young, President.

■ 2676 ■ General Truck Parts and Equipment
Co.
3835 W 42nd St.
Chicago, IL 60632
Phone: (773)247-6900
Products: Truck parts and accessories. SIC: 5013
(Motor Vehicle Supplies & New Parts). Sales:
$15,000,000 (2000). Emp: 35. Officers: Robert Smith,
President; Jeffery Kritzman, Controller.

■ 2677 ■ Genuine Auto Parts Co.
415 W Main St.
Rochester, NY 14608
Phone: (716)235-1595
Products: Automobile parts and supplies. SIC: 5013
(Motor Vehicle Supplies & New Parts). Officers: Max
Williams, Director; Al Van Erp, Controller.

■ 2678 ■ Genuine Parts Co.
2999 Circle 75 Pkwy.
Atlanta, GA 30339
Phone: (770)953-1700 Fax: (770)956-2212
Products: Automotive parts. SIC: 5013 (Motor Vehicle
Supplies & New Parts). Est: 1928. Sales:
$6,005,000,000 (2000). Emp: 24,500. Officers: Larry
L. Prince, CEO & Chairman of the Board; George W.
Kalafut, Exec. VP of Finance & Admin.; Robert J.
Susor, Sr. VP of Business Development; Thomas C.
Gallagher, President & COO; Louis W. Rice Jr., Sr. VP
of Personnel.

■ 2679 ■ Genuine Parts Company of West
Virginia Inc.
PO Box 670
Wheeling, WV 26003
Phone: (304)233-0300
Products: Automotive parts, including starters, brakes,
and spark plugs; Paint. SICs: 5013 (Motor Vehicle
Supplies & New Parts); 5198 (Paints, Varnishes &
Supplies). Est: 1925. Sales: $4,000,000 (2000). Emp:
80. Officers: William A. King Jr., President; Greg
Stuart, CFO.

■ 2680 ■ Gerhardt's Inc.
PO Box 10161
New Orleans, LA 70181-0161
Phone: (504)733-2500 Fax: (504)734-7730
E-mail: info@gerhardts.com
URL: http://www.gerhardts.com
Products: Diesel engines. SICs: 5013 (Motor Vehicle
Supplies & New Parts); 5084 (Industrial Machinery &
Equipment). Est: 1948. Sales: $25,000,000 (1999).
Emp: 173. Officers: A. Bruce Gerhardt, President;
Randall Nunmaker, Sales Mgr.

■ 2681 ■ Gillespie Oil Company Inc.
706 W Sandusky Ave.
Bellefontaine, OH 43311
Phone: (937)599-2085
Free: (800)686-3835 Fax: (937)592-2380
E-mail: gillespie.oil@logau.net
Products: Gasoline, diesel oil, filters, and windshield
washer solvent; Convenience store items. SICs: 5172
(Petroleum Products Nec); 5013 (Motor Vehicle
Supplies & New Parts). Est: 1954. Sales: $40,000,000
(2000). Emp: 100. Officers: Randy Diener, CEO;
Thomas Gillespie, President.

■ 2682 ■ Glasparts Inc.
PO Box 30116
Portland, OR 97294-3116
Phone: (503)254-9694
Free: (888)454-9694 Fax: 888-843-8856
URL: http://www.glasparts.com
Products: RV windshields. SIC: 5013 (Motor Vehicle
Supplies & New Parts). Est: 1987. Emp: 2. Officers:
Doug Wickham, Owner; Dian Lea, Sales/Marketing
Contact, e-mail: dianl@prodigy.net.

■ 2683 ■ Glass Specialty Inc.
2439 S Main St.
Box 737
Bloomington, IL 61701
Phone: (309)827-8087
Free: (800)322-6141 Fax: (309)828-4875
Products: Windshields. SIC: 5013 (Motor Vehicle
Supplies & New Parts). Est: 1957. Sales: $15,000,000
(2000). Emp: 499.

■ 2684 ■ Global Metrics Inc.
519 J. Marine View Ave.
Belmont, CA 94002-0843
Phone: (650)592-2722
Free: (800)227-9981 Fax: (650)591-5396
Products: Foreign auto parts. SIC: 5013 (Motor
Vehicle Supplies & New Parts). Est: 1977. Sales:
$2,000,000 (2000). Emp: 49. Officers: George Yaron.

■ 2685 ■ Global Motorsport Group Inc.
16100 Jacqueline Court
Morgan Hill, CA 95037
Phone: (408)778-0500 Fax: (408)778-0520
URL: http://www.customchrome.com
Products: Motorcycle parts and accessories. SIC:
5013 (Motor Vehicle Supplies & New Parts). Est: 1970.
Sales: $160,000,000 (2000). Emp: 450. Officers:
Joseph F. Keenan, President & CEO; James J. Kelly,
Exec. VP & CFO; Frances Mora, Human Resources
Contact.

■ 2686 ■ Globe Motorist Supply Company Inc.
121-123 E 3rd St.
Mt. Vernon, NY 10550
Phone: (914)668-6430 Fax: (914)668-0376
Products: Automotive parts and supplies, New. SIC:
5013 (Motor Vehicle Supplies & New Parts). Sales:
$50,000,000 (2000). Emp: 49. Officers: Alvin G.
Cutler, President & Treasurer.

■ 2687 ■ GM Service Parts Operations
6060 W Bristol Rd.
Flint, MI 48554
Phone: (734)635-5412
Products: Auto parts. SIC: 5013 (Motor Vehicle
Supplies & New Parts). Sales: $5,000,000,000 (1994).
Emp: 15,000. Officers: W.J. Lovejoy, VP & General
Merchandising Mgr.; D.C. Campion, CFO.

■ 2688 ■ Gold Eagle Co.
4400 S Kildare Ave.
Chicago, IL 60632
Phone: (773)376-4400
Free: (800)621-1251 Fax: (773)376-5749
URL: http://www.goldeagleco.com
Products: Automotive fluids. SICs: 5013 (Motor
Vehicle Supplies & New Parts); 5172 (Petroleum
Products Nec). Est: 1934. Emp: 250. Officers: Robert
Hirsch, CEO; Richard Hirsch, President; John M.
Yesensky, Sr. VP of Sales; Marc Blackman,
Sales/Marketing Contact; Alice Leverett, Customer
Service Contact; Vito Demario, Human Resources
Contact.

■ 2689 ■ Gold Rush Wrecking
PO Box 729
Osburn, ID 83849-0729
Phone: (208)784-9795
Products: Automobile parts, used. SIC: 5015 (Motor
Vehicle Parts—Used). Officers: Elmer Christman,
Owner.

■ 2690 ■ Gooch Brake and Equipment Co.
506-12 Grand Blvd.
Kansas City, MO 64106
Phone: (816)421-3085
Free: (800)444-3216 Fax: (816)421-7970
E-mail: gbrake@msn.com
Products: Brakes and brake equipment for heavy
trucks. SIC: 5013 (Motor Vehicle Supplies & New
Parts). Est: 1961. Sales: $5,000,000 (2000). Emp: 44.
Officers: O.G. Phillips Jr., Chairman of the Board;
Michael Humar, Vice President; Larry Smith, President.

■ 2691 ■ Goodyear Tire & Rubber Co.
300 S Salem Church Rd.
York, PA 17404-5537
Products: Tires. SIC: 5014 (Tires & Tubes).

■ **2692** ■ **Gopher Bearing**
2490 Territorial Rd.
St. Paul, MN 55114
Phone: (612)645-5871 **Fax:** (612)645-8572
Products: Power transmission products. **SICs:** 5013
(Motor Vehicle Supplies & New Parts); 5085 (Industrial
Supplies).

■ **2693** ■ **Gor-den Industries Inc.**
50 Commerce Pkwy.
Buffalo, NY 14224
Phone: (716)675-5600
Products: Auto parts. **SIC:** 5013 (Motor Vehicle
Supplies & New Parts). **Est:** 1965. **Sales:** $4,000,000
(2000). **Emp:** 30. **Officers:** Richard J. Deney,
President; Mike Russo, Controller; Paul Felser, Sales
Mgr.

■ **2694** ■ **Gorence Mobile Marketing
Distribution**
484 Main St.
West Chicago, IL 60185-2864
Phone: (630)231-5770
Free: (888)793-1300 **Fax:** (630)231-5779
Products: Van conversion equipment and supplies;
SUV, truck, automobile, and recreational vehicle
accessories. **SIC:** 5013 (Motor Vehicle Supplies & New
Parts). **Est:** 1975. **Emp:** 10. **Officers:** Lloyd J.
Gorence, CEO; K.D. Gorence. **Doing Business As:**
GMM Van Dock Distributors.

■ **2695** ■ **Grant Manufacturing & Equipment
Co.**
4009 W 49th St.
Tulsa, OK 74107
Phone: (918)446-4009 **Fax:** (918)446-4123
Products: Automotive parts and supplies, New. **SIC:**
5013 (Motor Vehicle Supplies & New Parts). **Officers:**
Craig Conway, General Mgr.

■ **2696** ■ **Grant Truck Equipment Co.**
1828 NW 4th St.
Oklahoma City, OK 73106-2611
Phone: (405)236-1494 **Fax:** (405)236-1472
Products: Automotive parts and supplies, New. **SIC:**
5013 (Motor Vehicle Supplies & New Parts). **Officers:**
Charles Redbird, General Mgr. **Former Name:** M.R.
Equipment Co., Inc.

■ **2697** ■ **Graves Automotive Supply**
645 W Holt Blvd.
Ontario, CA 91762
Phone: (909)984-2401 **Fax:** (909)983-5933
Products: Automobile parts. **SIC:** 5013 (Motor Vehicle
Supplies & New Parts). **Est:** 1928. **Sales:** $5,100,000
(2000). **Emp:** 41. **Officers:** Charles Stokke, President;
William T. Dingle, Chairman of the Board; Jennie
Violet, Dir of Human Resources.

■ **2698** ■ **Graywell Equipment Corp.**
50 Pond Rd.
PO Box 464
Oakdale, NY 11769
Phone: (516)563-2880 **Fax:** (516)563-8536
Products: Automotive parts and supplies, New. **SIC:**
5013 (Motor Vehicle Supplies & New Parts). **Officers:**
Lenny Graber, President.

■ **2699** ■ **Great Lakes Power Products**
2006 Tobsal Ct.
Warren, MI 48091
Phone: (810)759-5500
Free: (800)759-5438 **Fax:** (810)759-0879
URL: http://www.glpower.com
Products: Truck parts and equipment, including
clutches, transmissions, converters, and pump drives.
SIC: 5013 (Motor Vehicle Supplies & New Parts). **Est:**
1973. **Emp:** 200. **Alternate Name:** Great Lakes Power
Service. **Alternate Name:** Great Lakes Power Lift.

■ **2700** ■ **Great Lakes Power Products**
340 Bilmar Dr.
Pittsburgh, PA 15205
Phone: (412)937-0076 **Fax:** (412)937-0081
Products: Twin disc items for power transmission
clutches and brakes. **SIC:** 5013 (Motor Vehicle
Supplies & New Parts).

■ **2701** ■ **Great West Truck and Auto Inc.**
PO Box 3697
Kingman, AZ 86402
Phone: (520)757-7936 **Fax:** (520)757-1573
Products: Tires. **SIC:** 5014 (Tires & Tubes). **Est:** 1970.
Sales: $5,000,000 (2000). **Emp:** 63. **Officers:** A.
Lamont Wolsey, President; Eric Wolsey, Secretary;
Bob Chicoine, General Mgr.

■ **2702** ■ **Greater Mobile Auto Auction Div.**
1400 Lake Hearn Dr. NE Ste. D
Atlanta, GA 30319-1464
Phone: (678)649-9800
Products: Automobiless. **SIC:** 5012 (Automobiles &
Other Motor Vehicles). **Sales:** $47,000,000 (1992).
Emp: 30. **Officers:** Linda Aultman, President.

■ **2703** ■ **Green Manufacturing Company Inc.**
PO Box 26
Terrell, TX 75160
Phone: (972)524-1919
Products: Automotive batteries. **SIC:** 5013 (Motor
Vehicle Supplies & New Parts). **Sales:** $700,000
(2000). **Emp:** 3. **Officers:** J. Ronnie Green, CEO.

■ **2704** ■ **Green Meadow Auto Salvage, Inc.**
7313 Green Meadow Dr.
Helena, MT 59601-9381
Phone: (406)458-9204
Free: (800)345-5695 **Fax:** (406)458-9940
E-mail: grnmeadw@initco.net
Products: Motor vehicle parts and accessories; Used
automobile parts. **SICs:** 5015 (Motor Vehicle Parts—
Used); 5013 (Motor Vehicle Supplies & New Parts).
Est: 1984. **Emp:** 5. **Officers:** Ron Miller, Partner;
Loretta Miller, Partner.

■ **2705** ■ **Green Point Inc.**
221 Green Point Rd.
Brewer, ME 04412-9721
Phone: (207)989-3903
Free: (207)989-3842 **Fax:** (207)989-3842
E-mail: vickspain@aol.com
Products: New and used automobile parts. **SICs:**
5015 (Motor Vehicle Parts—Used); 5013 (Motor
Vehicle Supplies & New Parts). **Est:** 1981. **Sales:**
$3,000,000 (2000). **Emp:** 16. **Officers:** Randy Spain,
President.

■ **2706** ■ **Greene Equipment Co.**
PO Box 565
Halifax, PA 17032
Phone: (215)834-6161
Free: (800)227-0286 **Fax:** (215)834-6166
Products: Military vehicles. **SIC:** 5088 (Transportation
Equipment & Supplies).

■ **2707** ■ **Grismer Tire Co.**
PO Box 337
Dayton, OH 45401
Phone: (937)224-9815
Products: Tires; Automotive repair. **SIC:** 5014 (Tires &
Tubes). **Sales:** $30,000,000 (2000). **Emp:** 70.
Officers: Charles L. Marshall, President.

■ **2708** ■ **Gross and Hecht Trucking Corp.**
35 Brunswick Ave.
Edison, NJ 08818
Phone: (732)572-1500
Products: Trucks and automobiles. **SIC:** 5012
(Automobiles & Other Motor Vehicles). **Sales:**
$18,000,000 (1993). **Emp:** 200. **Officers:** Dennis
Abruzzi, President.

■ **2709** ■ **Gruener Sales Inc.**
1830 Kelso St.
Flint, MI 48503
Phone: (810)744-3141
Products: Truck equipment and parts. **SIC:** 5013
(Motor Vehicle Supplies & New Parts).

■ **2710** ■ **GTR Truck Equipment**
Division of Grand Traverse Rubber Supply
2098 M 37 S
Traverse City, MI 49684
Phone: (616)943-9640 **Fax:** (616)943-9790
Products: Truck equipment and accessories. **SIC:**
5013 (Motor Vehicle Supplies & New Parts). **Officers:**
Alan Lardie, Contact.

■ **2711** ■ **Gulf States Toyota Inc.**
PO Box 40306
Houston, TX 77040
Phone: (713)744-3300 **Fax:** (713)744-3332
Products: Automobiles and parts. **SICs:** 5012
(Automobiles & Other Motor Vehicles); 5013 (Motor
Vehicle Supplies & New Parts). **Est:** 1969. **Sales:**
$2,500,000,000 (2000). **Emp:** 1,600. **Officers:** Jerry
Pyle, President; Frank Gruen, CFO.

■ **2712** ■ **GWS Automotive and Truck
Equipment Sales Inc.**
2813 Agate St.
Bakersfield, CA 93304
Phone: (805)832-3860
Products: Automotive and truck equipment and
supplies. **SIC:** 5013 (Motor Vehicle Supplies & New
Parts).

■ **2713** ■ **H & D Transmission**
31-40 Whitestone Pkwy.
Flushing, NY 11354
Phone: (718)961-9666 **Fax:** (718)762-7876
Products: Bus and truck transmissions. **SIC:** 5013
(Motor Vehicle Supplies & New Parts).

■ **2714** ■ **H and H Distributors Inc.**
4015 Washington Rd.
McMurray, PA 15317
Phone: (412)621-8444
Products: Sound systems, air-conditioning, and cruise
control equipment for automobiles. **SIC:** 5013 (Motor
Vehicle Supplies & New Parts). **Est:** 1937. **Sales:**
$5,000,000 (2000). **Emp:** 50. **Officers:** Harold
Garfinkel, President; Theresa Oliver, Controller.

■ **2715** ■ **H & H Sales Company, Inc.**
PO Box 686
Huntertown, IN 46748-0686
Phone: (219)637-3177 **Fax:** (219)637-6880
E-mail: hhequip@gte.net
URL: http://www.qtesupersite.com/hhequip
Products: Custom truck bodies. **SIC:** 5013 (Motor
Vehicle Supplies & New Parts). **Est:** 1951. **Sales:**
$3,600,000 (2000). **Emp:** 38. **Officers:** John L.
Hawkins, CEO; Bill W. Gipson, Sales/Marketing
Contact; Pat Grogg, Customer Service Contact; Phil
Randall, Human Resources Contact.

■ **2716** ■ **Hadon Security Company Inc.**
PO Box 247
SR-82
Langley, OK 74350
Phone: (918)782-2709 **Fax:** (918)782-2709
Products: Safes and vaults; Recreational Vehicle
accessories. **SICs:** 5013 (Motor Vehicle Supplies &
New Parts); 5044 (Office Equipment). **Est:** 1979.
Officers: Don W. Seeger, Partner & Product Mgr.; H.
D. Paulsell, Partner.

■ **2717** ■ **Hahn Automotive Warehouse Inc.**
415 W Main St.
Rochester, NY 14608
Phone: (716)235-1595 **Fax:** (716)235-7134
Products: Automobile parts. **SIC:** 5013 (Motor Vehicle
Supplies & New Parts). **Est:** 1958. **Sales:**
$142,200,000 (2000). **Emp:** 1,109. **Officers:** Eli
Futerman, President & CEO; Peter Adamski, VP of
Finance; Michael Bonacci, Dir. of Marketing; Tim
Vergo, VP of Operations; Donald T. Hiller, Mgr. of
Admin.

■ **2718** ■ **Halasz from Dallas**
3775 West Bay
Dallas, TX 75214
Phone: (214)826-1422 **Fax:** (214)826-1422
Products: Recreational vehicles; Truck and van
components. **SIC:** 5013 (Motor Vehicle Supplies & New
Parts). **Est:** 1953. **Sales:** $1,500,000 (1999). **Emp:** 3.
Officers: William R. Halasz, General Mgr., e-mail:
whalasz@aol.com; Rick Halasz, President; D. L.
Halasz, Treasurer & Secty.

■ **2719** ■ **Hale Trailer Brake & Wheel**
PO Box 3305
Allentown, PA 18106-0305
Phone: (610)395-0371 **Fax:** (610)395-7868
Products: New automotive parts and supplies;
Trailers. **SICs:** 5013 (Motor Vehicle Supplies & New

Parts); 5012 (Automobiles & Other Motor Vehicles). **Est:** 1952. **Sales:** $38,000,000 (2000). **Emp:** 70. **Officers:** Barry Hale, President; Gerald S. Palguta, VP of Marketing.

■ 2720 ■ Tim Halpin Equipment Corp.
5670 NW 78th Ave.
Miami, FL 33166
Phone: (305)591-3164
Products: Automotive parts and supplies, New. **SIC:** 5013 (Motor Vehicle Supplies & New Parts). **Officers:** Tim Halpin, President.

■ 2721 ■ Hanco Corp.
3650 Dodd Rd.
Eagan, MN 55123-1305
Phone: (612)456-5600
Products: Tire equipment and supplies. **SIC:** 5013 (Motor Vehicle Supplies & New Parts). **Est:** 1928. **Sales:** $8,500,000 (2000). **Emp:** 30. **Officers:** J.N. Wright, President; L. Michaels, VP of Finance; Allen Vires, General Mgr.

■ 2722 ■ Hanser Automotive Co.
430 S Billings Blvd.
Billings, MT 59101
Phone: (406)248-7795
Free: (800)345-1754 **Fax:** (406)248-6180
E-mail: hanser1@juno.com
URL: http://www.autotranssystems.com
Products: Automobile parts, used. **SIC:** 5015 (Motor Vehicle Parts—Used). **Est:** 1967. **Sales:** $6,000,000 (2000). **Emp:** 80. **Officers:** Ralph Hanser, President.

■ 2723 ■ Hanser's Pick A Part Inc.
430 S Billing Blvd.
Billings, MT 59101-9364
Phone: (406)248-6073 **Fax:** (406)248-6180
Products: Automobile parts, used. **SIC:** 5015 (Motor Vehicle Parts—Used). **Officers:** Ralph Hanser, President.

■ 2724 ■ Hanson Tire Service Inc.
R.R. 2, Box A-1
Le Roy, MN 55951
Phone: (507)324-5638 **Fax:** (507)324-5966
Products: Auto parts, including tires and rims. **SICs:** 5014 (Tires & Tubes); 5013 (Motor Vehicle Supplies & New Parts). **Est:** 1950. **Sales:** $10,400,000 (2000). **Emp:** 40. **Officers:** Ronnie Eastvold, President; Greg Rollins, Treasurer & Secty.; R. Eastvold, President.

■ 2725 ■ Harlow International
2307 North Champlain St.
Arlington Heights, IL 60004
Phone: (847)870-0198 **Fax:** (847)934-6292
Products: Industrial motor controls, including environmental; Ornamental nursery products; Motor vehicle parts and equipment. **SICs:** 5013 (Motor Vehicle Supplies & New Parts); 5084 (Industrial Machinery & Equipment); 5193 (Flowers & Florists' Supplies). **Officers:** Donald J. Harlow, President.

■ 2726 ■ Harold's Tire and Auto
709 Liberty Dr.
Easley, SC 29640
Phone: (843)859-3741
Products: Tires. **SIC:** 5014 (Tires & Tubes).

■ 2727 ■ Harris Tire Co.
PO Box 888
Troy, AL 36081
Phone: (205)566-2691
Products: Automotive tires. **SIC:** 5014 (Tires & Tubes). **Est:** 1982. **Sales:** $6,000,000 (2000). **Emp:** 60. **Officers:** Gary B. Berry, President; Ace Coley, General Mgr.

■ 2728 ■ Harris Tire Co.
4355 Industrial Dr.
Jackson, MS 39209
Phone: (601)948-7401
Products: Tires. **SIC:** 5014 (Tires & Tubes).

■ 2729 ■ Harvey Chevrolet Corp.
PO Box 972
Radford, VA 24141
Phone: (703)639-3923
Products: Automobiles. **SIC:** 5012 (Automobiles & Other Motor Vehicles). **Sales:** $21,000,000 (1993). **Emp:** 75. **Officers:** George M. Harvey, President; John Campbell, Controller.

■ 2730 ■ Hatch Grinding Co.
320 S Lipan St.
Denver, CO 80223
Phone: (303)744-7114
Products: Auto parts. **SIC:** 5013 (Motor Vehicle Supplies & New Parts). **Est:** 1940. **Sales:** $15,000,000 (2000). **Emp:** 120. **Officers:** Peter R. Kornafel, President; Mike Everett, CFO; Phil May, Dir. of Marketing; Jay Dahl, Dir. of Systems.

■ 2731 ■ Hawkins Auto Parts
PO Box 740
Calhoun City, MS 38916-0740
Phone: (601)628-5168 **Fax:** (601)628-8399
Products: Automotive parts and equipment. **SIC:** 5013 (Motor Vehicle Supplies & New Parts).

■ 2732 ■ Hawthorne Machinery Inc.
PO Box 708
San Diego, CA 92112
Phone: (619)674-7000
Products: Gas engines and generators. **SICs:** 5084 (Industrial Machinery & Equipment); 5063 (Electrical Apparatus & Equipment). **Sales:** $158,000,000 (2000). **Emp:** 529. **Officers:** Tom J. Hawthorne, CEO; Richard Moss, VP & Treasurer.

■ 2733 ■ Haynes Manuals Inc.
PO Box 978
Newbury Park, CA 91319
Phone: (805)498-6703 **Fax:** (805)498-2867
Products: Publishers of automotive history, repair manuals and general interest books. **SIC:** 5192 (Books, Periodicals & Newspapers). **Officers:** Eric Oakley, President.

■ 2734 ■ J.H. Heafner Company Inc.
PO Box 837
Lincolnton, NC 28092
Phone: (704)735-3003 **Fax:** (704)735-0125
Products: Tires; Automotive tools and equipment. **SICs:** 5014 (Tires & Tubes); 5013 (Motor Vehicle Supplies & New Parts). **Est:** 1935. **Sales:** $250,000,000 (2000). **Emp:** 500. **Officers:** William H. Gaither, CEO & President; Donald C. Roof, Sr. VP & CFO; Dan Brown, Sr. VP of Sales & Marketing; Nancy Shupp, VP of Information Systems; J. Michael Gaither, Sr. VP of Administration & Gen. Counselor; Thomas J. Bonburg, Sr. VP of Strategic Planning.

■ 2735 ■ Heafner Tires & Products
712 N Main St.
Mauldin, SC 29662-1918
Phone: (864)675-9600
Free: (800)476-0877 **Fax:** (864)675-9605
Products: Tires and inner tubes, new; Automobile service station equipment. **SICs:** 5014 (Tires & Tubes); 5013 (Motor Vehicle Supplies & New Parts). **Emp:** 10.

■ 2736 ■ Heavy Parts International
19651 Bruce B. Downs Blvd.
Tampa, FL 33647
Phone: (813)991-7001 **Fax:** (813)991-7273
Products: Heavy truck parts. **SIC:** 5013 (Motor Vehicle Supplies & New Parts). **Sales:** $1,000,000 (2000). **Emp:** 4. **Officers:** Stephen J. Kin, President.

■ 2737 ■ Hebes Motor Co.
2226 W 800 S
Sterling, ID 83210-0022
Phone: (208)328-2221 **Fax:** (208)328-2222
Products: Used automotive parts and supplies. **SIC:** 5015 (Motor Vehicle Parts—Used). **Officers:** Heber Thelin, Owner.

■ 2738 ■ Hedahl's Auto Parts
PO Box 1038
Bismarck, ND 58502-1038
Phone: (701)223-8393 **Fax:** (701)221-4251
Products: Automobile parts, including batteries, brakes, starters, and spark plugs. **SIC:** 5013 (Motor Vehicle Supplies & New Parts). **Est:** 1916. **Sales:** $18,000,000 (2000). **Emp:** 165. **Officers:** Richard Hedahls, President; Charles Claremont, CFO; Larry Lysengen, Dir. of Marketing; Paul Barth, Dir. of Information Systems.

■ 2739 ■ Hedahl's Automotive Center
Hwy. 10 E & Jackson Ave.
Detroit Lakes, MN 56501
Phone: (218)847-1355
Free: (800)492-4808 **Fax:** (218)847-2178
URL: http://www.hedahls.com
Products: New automotive parts and supplies. **SIC:** 5013 (Motor Vehicle Supplies & New Parts). **Sales:** $1,000,000 (2000). **Emp:** 49. **Officers:** Kevin Klein.

■ 2740 ■ Hella Inc.
PO Box 2665
Peachtree City, GA 30269-0665
Phone: (770)631-7500
Free: (800)247-5924 **Fax:** (770)631-7575
E-mail: hella.faq@hellausa.com
URL: http://www.hellausa.com
Products: Vehicular lighting equipment. **SIC:** 5013 (Motor Vehicle Supplies & New Parts). **Est:** 1983. **Emp:** 65.

■ 2741 ■ Henderson Wheel and Warehouse Supply
1825 S 300 W
Salt Lake City, UT 84115
Phone: (801)486-2073
Products: Automotive parts. **SIC:** 5013 (Motor Vehicle Supplies & New Parts). **Est:** 1930. **Sales:** $23,900,000 (2000). **Emp:** 98. **Officers:** Michael S. Henderson, President.

■ 2742 ■ Hercules/CEDCO
1300 Morrical Blvd.
Findlay, OH 45840
Phone: (419)425-6400
Free: (800)677-9535 **Fax:** (419)425-6453
Products: Tires. **SIC:** 5014 (Tires & Tubes). **Sales:** $265,000,000 (2000). **Emp:** 280. **Officers:** Craig Anderson, CEO; Larry Seawell, CFO.

■ 2743 ■ Hercules Tire & Rubber Products
477 Main St.
Sanford, ME 04073
Phone: (207)324-4211
Products: Tires; Rubber products. **SIC:** 5014 (Tires & Tubes).

■ 2744 ■ Herzogs Auto Parts Inc.
2301 Julia
New Orleans, LA 70119-7534
Phone: (504)827-2886 **Fax:** (504)827-5362
E-mail: herzogjr@c$.com
Products: Automotive parts. **SIC:** 5013 (Motor Vehicle Supplies & New Parts). **Est:** 1971. **Sales:** $30,000,000 (2000). **Emp:** 68. **Officers:** C.L. Herzog Sr., CEO; C.L. Herzog Jr., President; Terri Sue Sampey, Treasurer & Secty.; Lynn Guignard, Vice President.

■ 2745 ■ Hesco Parts Corp.
PO Box 3008
Louisville, KY 40201
Phone: (502)589-9600
Products: Car parts, including engines. **SIC:** 5013 (Motor Vehicle Supplies & New Parts). **Est:** 1950. **Sales:** $45,000,000 (2000). **Emp:** 250. **Officers:** C.F. Ensor, President; Barbara Sullivan, Treasurer & Secty.

■ 2746 ■ Charles Hess
La Porte Rd.
RR No. 2, Box 6830
Morrisville, VT 05661
Phone: (802)888-4078
Products: Automobile parts, used. **SIC:** 5015 (Motor Vehicle Parts—Used). **Officers:** Charles Hess, Owner.

■ 2747 ■ Hesselbein Tire Company Inc.
3004 Lynch St.
Jackson, MS 39209
Phone: (601)352-3611 **Fax:** (601)353-1863
Products: Tires and inner tubes, new. **SIC:** 5014 (Tires & Tubes). **Est:** 1967. **Sales:** $24,000,000 (2000). **Emp:** 44. **Officers:** Denny King, President; R.B. Draper, CFO.

■ **2748** ■ **Hibdon Tire Center Inc.**
828 SE 29th St.
Oklahoma City, OK 73129
Phone: (405)632-5521 **Fax:** (405)632-0757
Products: Automotive parts and supplies, New; Pneumatic tires; Motor vehicle suspension systems; Brake parts and assemblies. **SICs:** 5014 (Tires & Tubes); 5013 (Motor Vehicle Supplies & New Parts). **Sales:** $12,000,000 (2000). **Emp:** 100. **Officers:** Mark Hibdon, President; Diane Hibdon, Controller.

■ **2749** ■ **Hickory Auto Parts Inc.**
PO Drawer 729
Hickory, NC 28603
Phone: (704)322-1325 **Fax:** (704)322-5540
Products: Auto parts and accessories, including brakes, starters, paints, and spray guns. **SIC:** 5013 (Motor Vehicle Supplies & New Parts). **Est:** 1926. **Sales:** $2,000,000 (2000). **Emp:** 50. **Officers:** R. Hord Jr., CEO; Rob Hord, VP of Finance.

■ **2750** ■ **High Performance Distributors**
1755 Mission Rd.
South San Francisco, CA 94080
Phone: (650)755-3350 **Fax:** (650)756-3350
E-mail: Hpd1755@aol.com
Products: Automotive parts and supplies. **SIC:** 5013 (Motor Vehicle Supplies & New Parts). **Est:** 1958. **Sales:** $3,000,000 (2000). **Emp:** 11. **Officers:** D.C. Smith, President; Melanie J. Parks.

■ **2751** ■ **Highland Auto and Truck Inc.**
1536 N Indiana St.
Los Angeles, CA 90063
Phone: (323)268-1311 **Fax:** (323)268-0215
Products: Automotive parts and supplies, New. **SIC:** 5013 (Motor Vehicle Supplies & New Parts). **Est:** 1950. **Sales:** $2,000,000 (2000). **Emp:** 22. **Officers:** George W. Piercy, President; Gerald Gubser, Treasurer & Secty.; John J. Collins, VP of Marketing.

■ **2752** ■ **Highland Auto and Truck Inc.**
1536 N Indiana St.
Los Angeles, CA 90063
Phone: (323)268-1311 **Fax:** (323)268-0215
Products: Automotive. **SIC:** 5013 (Motor Vehicle Supplies & New Parts). **Sales:** $2,000,000 (2000). **Emp:** 22.

■ **2753** ■ **Highway Auto Parts Inc.**
5 Lake Dr.
West Greenwich, RI 02817
Phone: (401)397-3000
Products: New and used automotive parts and supplies. **SICs:** 5015 (Motor Vehicle Parts—Used); 5013 (Motor Vehicle Supplies & New Parts). **Officers:** Norman Carpenter, President.

■ **2754** ■ **Hinojosa Parts Warehouse**
1416 Roosevelt
Brownsville, TX 78521-3110
Phone: (956)546-4513 **Fax:** (956)546-6507
Products: Automotive parts. **SIC:** 5013 (Motor Vehicle Supplies & New Parts). **Emp:** 49.

■ **2755** ■ **Hirsh Precision Products Inc.**
6420 Odell Pl
Boulder, CO 80301
Phone: (303)530-3131 **Fax:** (303)530-5242
Products: General machine shop (job work); Specializing in CNC turning and milling of automotive specialty tools and custom medical components. **SICs:** 5047 (Medical & Hospital Equipment); 5084 (Industrial Machinery & Equipment). **Officers:** Steve Hirsh, President.

■ **2756** ■ **Hiway 30 Auto Salvage**
960 Sunset Strip
Mountain Home, ID 83647-0118
Phone: (208)587-4429 **Free:** (800)540-4073
Products: Automobile parts, used. **SIC:** 5015 (Motor Vehicle Parts—Used). **Officers:** Cort Braithwaite, Owner.

■ **2757** ■ **H.L. Gage Sales Inc.**
PO 5170
Albany, NY 12205
Phone: (518)456-8871
Products: Industrial trucks. **SIC:** 5084 (Industrial Machinery & Equipment).

■ **2758** ■ **Hoekstra Truck Equipment Company, Inc.**
260 36th St. SE
PO Box 2246
Grand Rapids, MI 49501
Phone: (616)241-6664 **Fax:** (616)241-1111
Products: Truck equipment, accessories, and parts; Bus parts. **SIC:** 5013 (Motor Vehicle Supplies & New Parts). **Officers:** John Hoekstra, President.

■ **2759** ■ **Hoffmeyer Co.**
1600 Factor Ave.
San Leandro, CA 94577
Phone: (510)895-9955 **Fax:** (510)895-9014
URL: http://www.hoffmeyerco.com
Products: Conveyor belts and hoses. **SIC:** 5013 (Motor Vehicle Supplies & New Parts). **Est:** 1921. **Sales:** $6,000,000 (2000). **Emp:** 30. **Officers:** Frederick Oshay, Chairman of the Board; Todd Tippin, President.

■ **2760** ■ **T.J. Hogan and Associates Inc.**
34272 Doreka Ave.
Fraser, MI 48026
Phone: (810)296-5160 **Fax:** (810)296-5242
Products: Tools for automotive use. **SIC:** 5013 (Motor Vehicle Supplies & New Parts). **Est:** 1969. **Sales:** $38,000,000 (2000). **Emp:** 400. **Officers:** T.J. Hogan, President; Lynn A. Devantier, CFO; Mark A. Fritz, Dir. of Marketing & Sales; Joseph Grippe, Dir. of Data Processing.

■ **2761** ■ **Horsepower Control System**
906 Lydia
Kansas City, MO 64106
Phone: (816)471-6362
Free: (800)678-0152 **Fax:** (816)421-2302
E-mail: admin@hcskc.com
URL: http://www.horsepowercontrol.com
Products: Power transmissions, bearings, and belts for industrial equipment. **SICs:** 5084 (Industrial Machinery & Equipment); 5013 (Motor Vehicle Supplies & New Parts); 5085 (Industrial Supplies). **Est:** 1963. **Sales:** $6,500,000 (2000). **Emp:** 14. **Officers:** Francis Stevens, e-mail: fstevens@hcskc.com.

■ **2762** ■ **House of Hubcaps**
PO Box 6038
Great Falls, MT 59406-6038
Phone: (406)761-3288 **Fax:** (406)761-8137
Products: Wheel covers; Hubcaps. **SIC:** 5015 (Motor Vehicle Parts—Used). **Est:** 1990. **Sales:** $40,000 (2000). **Emp:** 1. **Officers:** Fritz Kummert, Owner.

■ **2763** ■ **Houston Peterbilt Inc.**
10200 N Loop E
Houston, TX 77029
Phone: (713)495-6323
Free: (800)580-7383 **Fax:** (713)495-6334
E-mail: banaitist@rush-enterprises.com
URL: http://www.rushtruckcenters.com
Products: Trucks for construction purposes. **SIC:** 5012 (Automobiles & Other Motor Vehicles). **Sales:** $160,000,000 (2000). **Emp:** 300. **Officers:** David Orf, President.

■ **2764** ■ **Howard Tire Service Inc.**
120 El Camino Real
Belmont, CA 94002
Phone: (415)592-3200 **Fax:** (415)592-2086
Products: Tires, rims, wheels, and shocks. **SICs:** 5014 (Tires & Tubes); 5013 (Motor Vehicle Supplies & New Parts). **Est:** 1961. **Sales:** $34,000,000 (2000). **Emp:** 80. **Officers:** Alfred Howard, President.

■ **2765** ■ **HT and T Company**
PO Box 4190
Hilo, HI 96720-0190
Phone: (808)933-7700 **Fax:** (808)933-7768
Products: Motorized vehicles. **SIC:** 5012 (Automobiles & Other Motor Vehicles). **Sales:** $20,000,000 (2000). **Emp:** 146.

■ **2766** ■ **C.P. Hunt Co.**
2406-10 Webster St.
Oakland, CA 94604
Phone: (510)444-1333 **Fax:** (510)832-1533
URL: http://www.cphunt.com
Products: Auto parts and accessories, including carburetors, hoses, spark plugs, and brakes. **SIC:** 5013 (Motor Vehicle Supplies & New Parts). **Est:** 1926. **Sales:** $18,000,000 (2000). **Emp:** 92. **Officers:** J. Hunt, President.

■ **2767** ■ **C.P. Hunt Co.**
2406-10 Webster St.
Oakland, CA 94604
Phone: (510)444-1333 **Fax:** (510)832-1533
Products: Automotive. **SIC:** 5013 (Motor Vehicle Supplies & New Parts). **Sales:** $18,000,000 (2000). **Emp:** 92.

■ **2768** ■ **I-90 Auto Salvage & Sales**
Munich & Vienna
Butte, MT 59701
Phone: (406)723-5711
Products: Automobile parts, used. **SIC:** 5015 (Motor Vehicle Parts—Used). **Officers:** James Martin, Owner.

■ **2769** ■ **Ichikoh America Inc.**
41650 Gardenbrook Rd., Ste. 120
Novi, MI 48375-1319
Phone: (248)380-7878 **Fax:** (248)380-8941
E-mail: ichikohmi@aol.com
Products: Rearview mirrors. **SIC:** 5013 (Motor Vehicle Supplies & New Parts). **Est:** 1987. **Sales:** $85,000,000 (2000). **Emp:** 9. **Officers:** Larry W. Wittenmyer, VP of Sales, e-mail: lwittenmyer@ichikoh-usa.com.

■ **2770** ■ **Ideal Sales and Distributing Company Inc.**
6811 E Slausen Ave.
City of Commerce, CA 90040
Phone: (213)726-8031
Products: Air-conditioning units for trucks. **SIC:** 5013 (Motor Vehicle Supplies & New Parts). **Est:** 1977. **Sales:** $4,000,000 (2000). **Emp:** 21. **Officers:** Mark Gross, President.

■ **2771** ■ **Im-Pruv-All**
2660 US Highway 50 E
Carson City, NV 89701
Phone: (775)883-1314
Products: Tires. **SIC:** 5014 (Tires & Tubes).

■ **2772** ■ **Impulse Merchandisers Inc.**
PO Box 77030
Baton Rouge, LA 70879-0809
Phone: (504)752-4800 **Fax:** (504)753-5055
URL: http://www.impulsemerchandisers.com
Products: Automotive supplies and accessories; Greeting cards; Sunglasses; Novelties; Toys. **SICs:** 5013 (Motor Vehicle Supplies & New Parts); 5048 (Ophthalmic Goods); 5092 (Toys & Hobby Goods & Supplies); 5199 (Nondurable Goods Nec). **Sales:** $7,000,000 (2000). **Emp:** 25. **Officers:** Joseph A. Palumbo Jr., President; Chris D. Wade, VP of Sales; Chris Schimmel III, General Mgr.; Diane Bradley, Contact.

■ **2773** ■ **Indus-Tool Inc.**
300 N Elizabeth St., 2N
Chicago, IL 60607
Phone: (312)226-2473
Free: (800)662-5021 **Fax:** (312)226-2480
E-mail: indus-tool@aol.com
URL: http://www.indus-tool.com
Products: Vehicle warning lights; Back-up alarms and batteries for automobiles. **SICs:** 5063 (Electrical Apparatus & Equipment); 5065 (Electronic Parts & Equipment Nec). **Sales:** $2,000,000 (2000). **Emp:** 15. **Officers:** Richard Seid, President; Ronald I. Schwarcz, General Mgr.

■ **2774** ■ **Industrial Parts Distributors Inc.**
522 Locust St.
Kansas City, MO 64106
Phone: (816)471-8049
Products: Automobile parts, including brake shoes, engines, and starters. **SIC:** 5013 (Motor Vehicle Supplies & New Parts). **Sales:** $4,000,000 (2000).

Emp: 30. Officers: William J. George, President; Kathy Dollar, CFO.

■ 2775 ■ Industrial Supply Solutions, Inc.
1531 S Main St.
Salisbury, NC 28144
Phone: (704)636-4241   Fax: (704)636-2093
E-mail: issi@cbiinternet.com
URL: http://www.indssi.com
Products: Power transmission equipment and supplies. SIC: 5085 (Industrial Supplies). Est: 1946. Sales: $35,000,000 (1999). Emp: 100. Officers: Frank Carmazzi; Mike Lear, Sales/Marketing Contact; Perry Bernhardt. Former Name: Piedmont Mill Supply Co.

■ 2776 ■ Industrial Transmission Inc.
N Green St. Ext
Greenville, NC 27834
Phone: (919)752-1353   Fax: (919)752-0528
Products: Transmissions. SIC: 5013 (Motor Vehicle Supplies & New Parts).

■ 2777 ■ Industrial Transmission Inc.
305 Friendship Dr.
Greensboro, NC 27409
Phone: (919)668-3200   Fax: (919)668-7672
Products: Power transmission equipment. SIC: 5013 (Motor Vehicle Supplies & New Parts).

■ 2778 ■ Inland Detroit Diesel/Allison
PO Box 5942
Carol Stream, IL 60197-5942
Phone: (630)871-1111
Products: Diesel engines, transmissions, and parts. SIC: 5013 (Motor Vehicle Supplies & New Parts). Est: 1970. Sales: $40,000,000 (2000). Emp: 135. Officers: John Baumer, General Mgr.

■ 2779 ■ Inland Detroit Diesel-Allison Inc.
13015 W Custer Ave.
Butler, WI 53007
Phone: (414)781-7100
Free: (800)236-6667   Fax: (414)781-0357
E-mail: dieseltoday@inland-dda.com
URL: http://www.inland-dda.com
Products: Detroit diesel engines; Allison automatic transmissions; Spectrum generator sets. SIC: 5013 (Motor Vehicle Supplies & New Parts). Est: 1958. Sales: $127,000,000 (2000). Emp: 300. Officers: Gregory W. Cole, CEO; Don Stacy, VP of Finance; Richard Bossert, VP of Sales.

■ 2780 ■ Inland Truck Parts
5678 NE 14th St.
Des Moines, IA 50313
Phone: (515)265-9901
Free: (800)362-2970   Fax: (515)265-8035
Products: Truck parts. SIC: 5013 (Motor Vehicle Supplies & New Parts).

■ 2781 ■ Inland Truck Parts
1313 S Young Ave.
Wichita, KS 67209
Phone: (316)945-0255
Free: (800)362-2219   Fax: (316)942-0537
Products: Truck parts. SIC: 5013 (Motor Vehicle Supplies & New Parts).

■ 2782 ■ Inland Truck Parts
3380 Mike Collins Dr.
Eden Prairie, MN 55344
Phone: (651)454-1100
Free: (800)552-1230   Fax: (651)454-1313
URL: http://www.inlandtruck.com
Products: Truck parts. SIC: 5013 (Motor Vehicle Supplies & New Parts).

■ 2783 ■ Inland Truck Parts
1620 Troost Ave.
Kansas City, MO 64108
Phone: (660)471-3154
Free: (800)892-5806   Fax: (660)221-8061
Products: Truck parts. SIC: 5013 (Motor Vehicle Supplies & New Parts).

■ 2784 ■ Inland Truck Parts
115 N 16th St.
Billings, MT 59101
Phone: (406)248-7340
Free: (800)332-7077   Fax: (406)245-3053
Products: Truck parts. SIC: 5013 (Motor Vehicle Supplies & New Parts).

■ 2785 ■ Inland Truck Parts
2300 Palmer
Missoula, MT 59802
Phone: (406)728-7413
Free: (800)332-2692   Fax: (406)728-9194
Products: Truck parts. SIC: 5013 (Motor Vehicle Supplies & New Parts).

■ 2786 ■ Inland Truck Parts
704 E 8th St.
North Platte, NE 69101
Phone: (308)532-4188
Free: (800)662-2963   Fax: (308)532-4153
Products: Truck parts. SIC: 5013 (Motor Vehicle Supplies & New Parts).

■ 2787 ■ Inland Truck Parts
9944 S 136th St.
Omaha, NE 68138
Phone: (402)331-1222
Free: (800)642-9353   Fax: (402)331-7444
Products: Truck parts. SIC: 5013 (Motor Vehicle Supplies & New Parts).

■ 2788 ■ Inland Truck Parts
1330 Deadwood Ave.
Rapid City, SD 57702
Phone: (605)348-4344
Free: (800)348-4344   Fax: (605)348-6926
URL: http://www.inlandtruck.com
Products: Truck parts. SIC: 5013 (Motor Vehicle Supplies & New Parts).

■ 2789 ■ Integrated Sensor Solutions
625 River Oaks Pkwy
San Jose, CA 95134
Phone: (408)324-1044   Fax: (408)324-1054
Products: Sensor signal integrated circuits and modules for the automotive and industrial industries. SIC: 5065 (Electronic Parts & Equipment Nec). Officers: Manher Naik, CEO.

■ 2790 ■ Interamerican Motor Corp.
PO Box 3939
Chatsworth, CA 91313-3939
Phone: (818)775-5028
Products: Automotive parts, including starters and motors. SIC: 5013 (Motor Vehicle Supplies & New Parts). Est: 1962. Sales: $100,000,000 (1999). Emp: 349. Officers: H. Hederer, President; W. Baur, Exec. VP of Finance.

■ 2791 ■ Intercon, Inc.
501 A Upland Ave.
Upland, PA 19015
Phone: (215)874-2100   Fax: (215)497-5181
Products: Automotive parts and supplies, New. SIC: 5013 (Motor Vehicle Supplies & New Parts). Officers: Jerry Southern Sr., President.

■ 2792 ■ International Brake Industries Inc.
1840 McCullough St.
Lima, OH 45801
Phone: (419)227-4421
Free: (888)424-1061   Fax: (419)224-1696
URL: http://www.ibilimo.com
Products: Automotive and truck brake hardware. SIC: 5013 (Motor Vehicle Supplies & New Parts). Sales: $32,000,000 (2000). Emp: 200. Officers: Skip Carroll, General Mgr.; Gregory Andes, VP of Finance.

■ 2793 ■ International Hi-Tech Trading Corp.
PO Box 7579
Burbank, CA 91510
Phone: (818)841-5453   Fax: (818)841-5453
Products: Diesel engines and parts; Motor vehicle supplies; Air conditioning equipment; Refrigeration equipment; Aircraft parts. SICs: 5013 (Motor Vehicle Supplies & New Parts); 5075 (Warm Air Heating & Air-Conditioning); 5078 (Refrigeration Equipment & Supplies); 5084 (Industrial Machinery & Equipment);

5088 (Transportation Equipment & Supplies). Officers: M. Aram, President.

■ 2794 ■ Interstate Bearing Co.
2501 E 80th St.
Bloomington, MN 55425-1319
Phone: (612)854-0836   Fax: (612)854-2999
Products: Bearings and power transmission products. SIC: 5085 (Industrial Supplies). Sales: $10,000,000 (2000). Emp: 45. Officers: Jeff Caswell, CEO; Harry Lindstrom, VP of Finance.

■ 2795 ■ Interstate Bearing Technologies
244-A W Pioneer Rd.
Fond du Lac, WI 54936
Phone: (920)921-8816
Free: (800)236-8405   Fax: (920)921-1928
Products: Power transmissions. SICs: 5084 (Industrial Machinery & Equipment); 5013 (Motor Vehicle Supplies & New Parts). Former Name: Badger Bearing.

■ 2796 ■ Intraco Corp.
530 Stephenson Hwy.
Troy, MI 48083-1131
Phone: (248)585-6900   Fax: (248)585-6920
Products: Construction glass; Automotive spare parts; Lubricants; Radiators, and air-conditioning parts; Automotive glass; Additives. SICs: 5013 (Motor Vehicle Supplies & New Parts); 5039 (Construction Materials Nec); 5075 (Warm Air Heating & Air-Conditioning); 5172 (Petroleum Products Nec). Est: 1971. Sales: $25,000,000 (2000). Emp: 30. Officers: Sam Antakli, VP of Sales.

■ 2797 ■ IPD Co., Inc.
11744 NE Ainsworth Cir.
PO Box 20339
Portland, OR 97220
Phone: (503)257-7500   Fax: (503)257-7596
URL: http://www.ipdusa.com
Products: Motor vehicle suspension systems; Automotive parts and supplies, New. SIC: 5013 (Motor Vehicle Supplies & New Parts). Est: 1963. Sales: $6,500,000 (2000). Emp: 29. Officers: Richard Gordon, President; David Precechtil, Vice President; Sue Hart, Vice President.

■ 2798 ■ IQ Products Co.
16212 State Hwy. 249
Houston, TX 77086
Phone: (281)444-6454   Fax: (281)444-0185
Products: Automotive products; Personal care products; Insecticide. SICs: 5013 (Motor Vehicle Supplies & New Parts); 5122 (Drugs, Proprietaries & Sundries); 5191 (Farm Supplies). Est: 1984. Sales: $80,000,000 (2000). Emp: 300. Officers: Yohanne Gupta, CEO; Cary Rutland, President; Pravin Gohel, Vice President; John T. Brogan.

■ 2799 ■ Iroquois Manufacturing Company, Inc.
596 Richmond Rd.
Hinesburg, VT 05461
Phone: (802)482-2155   Fax: (802)482-2962
E-mail: iroquois@accessvt.com
Products: Truck bodies and related truck equipment. SIC: 5012 (Automobiles & Other Motor Vehicles). Est: 1925. Sales: $6,000,000 (1999). Emp: 39. Officers: Shawn Lyman, Vice President; Joe Bodette, Customer Service Contact; Rob Schryer, Human Resources Contact.

■ 2800 ■ Irv Seaver Motorcycles
607 W Katella Ave.
Orange, CA 92867
Phone: (714)532-3700
Products: Motorcycles parts, service, accessories, and apparel. SIC: 5012 (Automobiles & Other Motor Vehicles). Sales: $11,000,000 (1999). Emp: 12. Officers: Brian Bell, Manager.

■ 2801 ■ Isspro Inc.
2515 NE Riverside Way
Portland, OR 97211
Phone: (503)288-4488
Free: (800)888-8065   Fax: (503)249-2999
Products: Instrumentation and electronics for industrial vehicles. SICs: 5013 (Motor Vehicle Supplies & New Parts); 5084 (Industrial Machinery & Equipment). Est:

1949. **Sales:** $25,000,000 (2000). **Emp:** 175. **Officers:** K. Ross, CEO, President & Chairman of the Board; D. Cromwell, Secty. & Controller; P. Wendlick, Vice President; D. Wendlick, Vice President; R. Hayden, Marketing & Sales Mgr.; Jan Leeding, Customer Service Contact.

■ 2802 ■ Itco Tire Co.
PO Box 641
Wilson, NC 27893
Phone: (919)291-8900 **Fax:** (919)237-0504
Products: Tires. **SIC:** 5014 (Tires & Tubes). **Est:** 1966. **Sales:** $200,000,000 (2000). **Emp:** 500. **Officers:** Armistead Burwell Jr., CEO; William E. Berry, VP of Finance; John N. Salamon, Vice President; C.D. Flowers, VP of Data Processing.

■ 2803 ■ Itco Tire Co.
485 Stafford Umberger Rd.
Wytheville, VA 24382
Phone: (540)228-4353
Products: Tires. **SIC:** 5014 (Tires & Tubes).

■ 2804 ■ ITM, Inc.
6386 Corley Rd.
Norcross, GA 30071
Phone: (404)446-0925 **Fax:** (404)446-1015
Products: Automotive parts. **SIC:** 5013 (Motor Vehicle Supplies & New Parts).

■ 2805 ■ ITTCO Sales Co., Inc.
181 Remington Blvd.
Ronkonkoma, NY 11779-6939
Phone: (516)737-6800
Free: (800)645-1404 **Fax:** (516)737-6805
E-mail: sales@ittco.com
URL: http://www.ittco.com
Products: Automotive parts, supplies, and accessories. **SIC:** 5013 (Motor Vehicle Supplies & New Parts). **Est:** 1978. **Emp:** 17. **Officers:** Neil A. Rosenberg, President, e-mail: nrosenberg@ittco.com; Richard W. Scherer, Vice President.

■ 2806 ■ J-Mark
2790 Ranchview Ln.
Minneapolis, MN 55447
Phone: (612)559-3300
Free: (800)328-6274 **Fax:** (612)559-4806
E-mail: j-mark@j-markproducts.com
Products: Automotive accessories. **SIC:** 5013 (Motor Vehicle Supplies & New Parts). **Est:** 1962. **Sales:** $12,000,000 (2000). **Emp:** 25. **Officers:** Gary Henriksen, Owner & Pres.; Jerry Moore, Sales/Marketing Contact.

■ 2807 ■ Jack's Salvage & Auto Parts Inc.
625 Metacom Ave.
Bristol, RI 02809-5131
Phone: (401)253-3478
Products: Automobile parts, used. **SIC:** 5015 (Motor Vehicle Parts—Used). **Officers:** Jack Francis, President.

■ 2808 ■ Mylon C. Jacobs Supply Co.
PO Box 1469
Broken Arrow, OK 74013
Phone: (918)455-8811
Free: (800)423-1138 **Fax:** (918)455-8853
Products: Valves; Fittings and related products. **SIC:** 5085 (Industrial Supplies). **Est:** 1964. **Emp:** 26. **Officers:** Jean A. Cook, Controller, e-mail: jcook@ mcjsupply.com; L.O. Morris III, President.

■ 2809 ■ Jaguar Cars
555 MacArthur Blvd.
Mahwah, NJ 07430-2327
Phone: (201)818-8500 **Fax:** (201)818-9770
Products: Automotive parts and supplies, New. **SIC:** 5013 (Motor Vehicle Supplies & New Parts). **Emp:** 250. **Officers:** Michael H. Dale, President; George J. Frame, VP of Finance & Admin.; John Crawford, President & Dir. of Research; William Morris, Information Systems Mgr.; Steven M. Valvano, Human Resources Mgr.

■ 2810 ■ Jahm Inc.
1155 E Whitcomb Ave.
Madison Heights, MI 48071
Phone: (313)583-2710 **Fax:** (313)583-2723
Products: Automobile lighting products. **SIC:** 5013

(Motor Vehicle Supplies & New Parts). **Est:** 1989. **Sales:** $20,000,000 (2000). **Emp:** 200. **Officers:** Tom Wall, President; Sid Barnwell, CFO; John B. Molesa, Dir. of Marketing & Sales.

■ 2811 ■ Jalopy Jungle Inc.
7804 S Hwy. 79
Rapid City, SD 57701
Phone: (605)348-8442
Free: (800)456-0715 **Fax:** (605)348-8167
Products: Automobile parts, used. **SIC:** 5015 (Motor Vehicle Parts—Used). **Officers:** Ed Griffith, President.

■ 2812 ■ Jarvis Supply Co.
117 E Sherman
Hutchinson, KS 67501-7160
Phone: (316)221-3113
Products: Automotive. **SIC:** 5013 (Motor Vehicle Supplies & New Parts). **Sales:** $12,000,000 (2000). **Emp:** 108.

■ 2813 ■ JB Junk & Salvage Inc.
2535 9th Ave. NW
Great Falls, MT 59404-5312
Phone: (406)454-1917
Products: Automobile parts, used; Motor vehicle parts and accessories. **SIC:** 5015 (Motor Vehicle Parts—Used). **Officers:** John Bowlin, President.

■ 2814 ■ JBA Headers
7149 Mission Gorge Rd.
San Diego, CA 92120-1130
Phone: (619)229-7797
Free: (800)830-3377 **Fax:** (619)229-7761
URL: http://www.jbaracing.com
Products: Exhaust headers. **SIC:** 5013 (Motor Vehicle Supplies & New Parts). **Est:** 1985. **Sales:** $13,000,000 (2000). **Emp:** 35. **Officers:** J. Bittle, President; Fred Galloway, General Mgr.; Jon Towers, Sales Mgr. **Alternate Name:** J. #Bittle American Inc.

■ 2815 ■ JC Whitney & Co.
225 N Michigan Ave.
Chicago, IL 60601
Phones: (312)431-6000 (312)431-6000
Fax: 800-537-2700
E-mail: jewhitney@jcwhitneyco.com
URL: http://www.jcwhitney.com
Products: Automotive parts. **SIC:** 5013 (Motor Vehicle Supplies & New Parts). **Est:** 1915. **Sales:** $120,000,000 (2000). **Emp:** 500. **Officers:** Tim Ford, President. **Former Name:** Warshawsky and Co.

■ 2816 ■ JDB Merchandising
PO Box 4032
St. Johnsbury, VT 05819
Phone: (802)748-1123 **Fax:** (802)748-6521
Products: Automotive parts and accessories. **SIC:** 5013 (Motor Vehicle Supplies & New Parts).

■ 2817 ■ Jenik Automotive Distributors Inc.
3385 Seneca Dr.
Las Vegas, NV 89109-3136
Phone: (702)736-6556 **Fax:** (702)736-3491
Products: Automobile parts, used. **SIC:** 5015 (Motor Vehicle Parts—Used). **Officers:** Nicholas Tierno, President.

■ 2818 ■ Jersey Truck Equipment Co.
5018 Industrial Rd.
Wall, NJ 07719
Phone: (732)938-6688 **Fax:** (732)938-3735
Products: Automotive parts and supplies, New. **SIC:** 5013 (Motor Vehicle Supplies & New Parts). **Officers:** David Hirsch, President.

■ 2819 ■ Jetzon Tire and Rubber Company Inc.
1050 Bethelem Pike, Box 249
Montgomeryville, PA 18936-0249
Phone: (215)643-2300 **Fax:** (215)628-8473
Products: Tires. **SIC:** 5014 (Tires & Tubes). **Sales:** $42,000,000 (1994). **Emp:** 65. **Officers:** Marc Hoffman, President; Michael Schwartz, VP & Controller.

■ 2820 ■ Jideco of Bardstown Inc.
901 Withrow Ct.
Bardstown, KY 40004
Phone: (502)348-3100 **Fax:** (502)348-3204
Products: Automotive cruise control; Windshield wiper motors. **SIC:** 5013 (Motor Vehicle Supplies & New Parts). **Est:** 1986. **Sales:** $130,000,000 (2000). **Emp:** 475.

■ 2821 ■ Jiffy Metal Products Co.
5025 W Lake St.
Chicago, IL 60644
Phone: (773)626-8090
Free: (800)548-2227 **Fax:** (773)626-1529
Products: Wheel covers; Metal stampings. **SIC:** 5013 (Motor Vehicle Supplies & New Parts). **Est:** 1939. **Sales:** $1,000,000 (2000). **Emp:** 20. **Officers:** Stanley Cag, Owner.

■ 2822 ■ Jilnance Corp.
PO Box 20534
Rochester, NY 14602
Phone: (716)235-1662 **Fax:** (716)436-5578
Products: Automotivee. **SIC:** 5063 (Electrical Apparatus & Equipment). **Sales:** $1,000,000 (2000). **Emp:** 12.

■ 2823 ■ Joe's Firestone Inc.
819 Hwy. 1 S
Greenville, MS 38701
Phone: (601)335-9221 **Fax:** (601)335-9223
Products: Tires and inner tubes, new; Small electrical appliances. **SICs:** 5014 (Tires & Tubes); 5063 (Electrical Apparatus & Equipment). **Est:** 1973. **Sales:** $6,000,000 (2000). **Emp:** 25. **Officers:** Joe Muzzi Jr., President; Lnda Muzzi, Office Mgr.

■ 2824 ■ Johnson Distributing, Inc.
1021 3rd St. NW
Great Falls, MT 59404-2360
Phone: (406)453-6541
Free: (800)332-7302 **Fax:** (406)727-5937
E-mail: johnsondist@worldnet.att.net
Products: Truck accessories and golf carts. **SIC:** 5013 (Motor Vehicle Supplies & New Parts). **Est:** 1950. **Sales:** $3,000,000 (2000). **Emp:** 13. **Officers:** Michael S. Henderson, President; William L. Henderson, Vice President. **Former Name:** Johnson Distributors Truck Equipment.

■ 2825 ■ Johnson Motor Sales Inc.
620 Deere Dr.
New Richmond, WI 54017
Phone: (715)246-2261
Products: Auto supplies. **SIC:** 5013 (Motor Vehicle Supplies & New Parts). **Sales:** $23,000,000 (2000). **Emp:** 45. **Officers:** Curtiss A. Anderson, President.

■ 2826 ■ Johnson and Towers Inc.
PO Box 4000
Mt. Laurel, NJ 08054
Phone: (609)234-6990 **Fax:** (609)234-3635
Products: Diesel engines. **SICs:** 5084 (Industrial Machinery & Equipment); 5013 (Motor Vehicle Supplies & New Parts). **Est:** 1926. **Sales:** $75,000,000 (2000). **Emp:** 300. **Officers:** W.F. Johnson Jr., President; T. Dutterer, Treasurer; A. Harris, Dir. of Marketing.

■ 2827 ■ Johnston Distributing Co.
6523 Merle Hay Rd.
PO Box 345
Johnston, IA 50131-0345
Phone: (515)276-5485 **Fax:** (515)276-1251
Products: Automotive parts. **SIC:** 5013 (Motor Vehicle Supplies & New Parts). **Est:** 1960. **Sales:** $5,000,000 (2000). **Emp:** 60. **Officers:** David A. Goss Jr.; Judy Mertens. **Former Name:** Big A Auto Parts.

■ 2828 ■ Johnstown Axle Works Inc.
100 Iron St.
Johnstown, PA 15906
Phone: (814)533-2910 **Fax:** (814)533-2929
Products: Axles. **SIC:** 5013 (Motor Vehicle Supplies & New Parts). **Sales:** $21,000,000 (2000). **Emp:** 100. **Officers:** James Duncan, Manager.

■ 2829 ■ **Joint Clutch and Gear Service Inc.**
1325 Howard
Detroit, MI 48226
Phone: (734)641-7575
Free: (800)572-8249 **Fax:** (734)641-7599
Products: Drive train components, new, except wheels
and brakes; Bearings; Cables; Clutches; Differential
parts; Exhaust systems; Hose, fittings, and belts;
Hydraulic pumps; Lighting; Snow plows and parts;
Transmission parts; Joints and drive shafts. **SIC:** 5013
(Motor Vehicle Supplies & New Parts). **Est:** 1946.
Sales: $5,000,000 (2000). **Emp:** 45. **Officers:** Larry
Lees, President.

■ 2830 ■ **Joint and Clutch Service Inc.**
PO Box 21089
Indianapolis, IN 46221
Phone: (317)634-2428
Products: Clutches, bearings, and seals. **SICs:** 5013
(Motor Vehicle Supplies & New Parts); 5085 (Industrial
Supplies). **Est:** 1950. **Sales:** $5,000,000 (2000). **Emp:**
17. **Officers:** Carl Ramser, VP & General
Merchandising Mgr.

■ 2831 ■ **Joint and Clutch Service Inc.**
PO Box 30282
Charlotte, NC 28230
Phone: (704)334-6883
Products: Auto body parts. **SIC:** 5013 (Motor Vehicle
Supplies & New Parts). **Est:** 1954. **Sales:** $15,000,000
(2000). **Emp:** 70. **Officers:** Fred A. Phillips, President;
Shelton Smith, Controller; John M. Phillips, VP of
Marketing.

■ 2832 ■ **Joliet Equipment Corp.**
PO Box 114
Joliet, IL 60434
Phone: (815)727-6606
Free: (800)435-9350 **Fax:** (815)727-6626
E-mail: motors@joliet-equipment.com
URL: http://www.joliet-equipment.com
Products: New and remanufactured electric motors;
Reducers; AC and DC motor drives. **SICs:** 5063
(Electrical Apparatus & Equipment); 5015 (Motor
Vehicle Parts—Used); 5014 (Tires & Tubes). **Est:**
1954. **Sales:** $12,000,000 (2000). **Emp:** 80. **Officers:**
J. Keck, President; R. Taylor, Controller; David R.
Hufford, VP of Marketing & Sales, e-mail: dhufford@
joliet-equipment.com.

■ 2833 ■ **G.E. Jones Electric Company Inc.**
204 N Polk St.
Amarillo, TX 79105
Phone: (806)372-5505
Products: Electric motor parts. **SIC:** 5063 (Electrical
Apparatus & Equipment). **Est:** 1926. **Sales:**
$3,000,000 (2000). **Emp:** 30. **Officers:** K.A. Stratton,
President; Sam F. Wands, Treasurer & Secty.; George
Stratton, Vice President.

■ 2834 ■ **Charlie C. Jones Inc.**
4041 E Thomas Rd., Ste. 200
Phoenix, AZ 85018-7530
Phone: (602)272-5621
Products: Auto parts. **SIC:** 5013 (Motor Vehicle
Supplies & New Parts). **Est:** 1922. **Sales:** $400,000
(2000). **Emp:** 2. **Officers:** K. John, President; Nancy
John, Treasurer & Secty.; Scott Schneider, Vice
President.

■ 2835 ■ **Ken Jones Inc.**
73 Chandler St.
Worcester, MA 01609
Phone: (508)755-5255
Products: Tires and inner tubes, new. **SIC:** 5014 (Tires
& Tubes). **Est:** 1938. **Sales:** $5,000,000 (2000). **Emp:**
16. **Officers:** G.K. Jones, President.

■ 2836 ■ **Jordan Research Corp.**
6244 Clark Center Ave., No. 4
Sarasota, FL 34238
Phone: (941)923-9707
Free: (800)533-0306 **Fax:** (941)925-1029
Products: Brake parts and assemblies. **SIC:** 5013
(Motor Vehicle Supplies & New Parts). **Sales:**
$800,000 (2000). **Emp:** 2. **Officers:** Jordan J.
Pokrinchak, President.

■ 2837 ■ **K & W Tire Co.**
735 N Prince St.
Lancaster, PA 17603
Phone: (717)397-3596
Products: Tires. **SIC:** 5014 (Tires & Tubes).

■ 2838 ■ **Kansas City Auto Auction Inc.**
3901 N Skiles
Kansas City, MO 64161
Phone: (816)452-4084 **Fax:** (816)459-4711
Products: Automobile auction firm. **SIC:** 5012
(Automobiles & Other Motor Vehicles). **Sales:**
$141,000,000 (2000). **Emp:** 150. **Officers:** Denis
Berry, President; Bob Gartner, Controller.

■ 2839 ■ **Kato Radiator Diesel Systems**
2200 4th Ave.
Mankato, MN 56001
Phone: (507)625-4118
Products: Radiators. **SIC:** 5013 (Motor Vehicle
Supplies & New Parts). **Sales:** $21,000,000 (2000).
Emp: 40. **Officers:** Robert Chesley, President; Jim
Trucker, General Mgr.

■ 2840 ■ **Kauffman Tire Service Inc.**
4847 Clark-Howell Hwy.
College Park, GA 30349
Phone: (404)762-8433
Free: (800)334-3321 **Fax:** (404)767-5332
Products: Tires. **SIC:** 5014 (Tires & Tubes). **Sales:**
$50,000,000 (2000). **Emp:** 25. **Officers:** John
Kauffman.

■ 2841 ■ **Kawasaki Motors Corporation U.S.A.
Engine Div.**
PO Box 888285
Grand Rapids, MI 49588-8285
Phone: (616)949-6500
Products: Engines. **SIC:** 5084 (Industrial Machinery &
Equipment). **Sales:** $8,000,000 (2000). **Emp:** 20.
Officers: Kent Murakami, General Mgr.

■ 2842 ■ **Kay Automotive Graphics**
PO Box 1000
Lake Orion, MI 48361
Phone: (810)377-4949 **Fax:** (810)377-2097
Products: Car decals; Pinstriping. **SIC:** 5013 (Motor
Vehicle Supplies & New Parts). **Est:** 1969. **Sales:**
$30,000,000 (2000). **Emp:** 265. **Officers:** J. Kay,
President; A.H. Bonnell, Exec. VP; W.J. Farnen, VP of
Marketing & Sales; K. McDonough, Dir. of Data
Processing; W. Burton, Dir of Human Resources.

■ 2843 ■ **KD Lamp Co.**
1910 Elm St.
Cincinnati, OH 45210
Phone: (513)621-4211
Free: (800)543-1943 **Fax:** (513)621-6088
E-mail: bmosby@kdlamp.com
URL: http://www.kdlamp.com
Products: Truck safety lighting. **SIC:** 5013 (Motor
Vehicle Supplies & New Parts). **Est:** 1914. **Sales:**
$12,000,000 (2000). **Emp:** 100. **Officers:** E Craig
Stone, President; Bill Mosey, VP of Marketing & Sales.

■ 2844 ■ **Keeter Manufacturing, Inc.**
PO Box 1227
Sisters, OR 97759-1227
Phone: (541)967-8400
Free: (800)336-1177 **Fax:** (541)967-8133
Products: Automotive parts. **SIC:** 5013 (Motor Vehicle
Supplies & New Parts). **Est:** 1979. **Sales:** $3,000,000
(2000). **Emp:** 60. **Officers:** Pamela Harris, President.

■ 2845 ■ **Kelly Springfield Tire**
6650 Ramsey St.
Fayetteville, NC 28311
Phone: (910)488-9295
Free: (800)638-5112 **Fax:** (910)630-5253
Products: Tires. **SIC:** 5014 (Tires & Tubes). **Sales:**
$200,000,000 (2000). **Emp:** 1,000. **Officers:** W. W.
Masters III.

■ 2846 ■ **Keltner Enterprises Inc.**
2829 S Scenic Ave.
Springfield, MO 65807
Phone: (417)882-8844
Free: (800)666-3311 **Fax:** (417)882-9536
E-mail: sales@keltners.com
URL: http://www.keltners.com
Products: Automotive parts; Chemicals; Lubricants.
SICs: 5172 (Petroleum Products Nec); 5013 (Motor
Vehicle Supplies & New Parts); 5169 (Chemicals &
Allied Products Nec). **Est:** 1952. **Sales:** $40,000,000
(2000). **Emp:** 75. **Officers:** Ken C. Keltner, President.

■ 2847 ■ **Kenco**
PO Box 1385
Raton, NM 87740-1385
Free: (800)227-3833
Products: Motor vehicle parts and accessories. **SIC:**
5013 (Motor Vehicle Supplies & New Parts).

■ 2848 ■ **Kennedy Engine Co.**
980 Motsie Rd.
Biloxi, MS 39532
Phone: (228)392-2200 **Fax:** (228)392-9507
Products: Diesel engines and parts. **SICs:** 5013
(Motor Vehicle Supplies & New Parts); 5084 (Industrial
Machinery & Equipment).

■ 2849 ■ **Kentucky Bearings Service**
PO Box 35157
Louisville, KY 40232-5157
Phone: (502)636-2571 **Fax:** (502)635-2268
Products: Power transmissions. **SICs:** 5084 (Industrial
Machinery & Equipment); 5013 (Motor Vehicle Supplies
& New Parts).

■ 2850 ■ **Kenworth of Tennessee Inc.**
Spence Ln. & I-40 E
Nashville, TN 37210
Phone: (615)366-5454
Products: Trucks. **SIC:** 5012 (Automobiles & Other
Motor Vehicles). **Sales:** $67,600,000 (1993). **Emp:**
245. **Officers:** Lester Turner Jr., President.

■ 2851 ■ **Keystone Automotive Industries Inc.**
700 E Bonita Ave.
Pomona, CA 91767
Phone: (909)624-8041 **Fax:** (909)624-9136
URL: http://www.keystone-auto.com
Products: Automotive parts. **SIC:** 5013 (Motor Vehicle
Supplies & New Parts). **Est:** 1947. **Sales:**
$350,000,000 (2000). **Emp:** 1,537. **Officers:** Charles
Hogarty, CEO & President, e-mail: chogarty@
keystone-auto.com; John M. Palumbo, CFO;
Christopher Northrup, Dir. of Marketing.

■ 2852 ■ **Keystone Automotive Operations Inc.**
44 Tunkhannock Ave.
Exeter, PA 18643
Phone: (570)655-4514
Free: (800)233-8321 **Fax:** (570)655-4005
URL: http://www.key-stone.com
Products: Automotive supplies, including domestic
and import parts and custom accessories; Truck and
SUV accessories, including custom wheels; Chemicals.
SICs: 5013 (Motor Vehicle Supplies & New Parts);
5169 (Chemicals & Allied Products Nec). **Est:** 1972.
Sales: $170,000,000 (2000). **Emp:** 950. **Officers:**
Ronald E. Elquist, CEO & President; Rick Kovalick, VP
of Purchasing. **Alternate Name:** Keystone Automotive
Warehouse.

■ 2853 ■ **Keystone Detroit Diesel Allison Inc.**
Cranberry Industrial
11 Progress Ave.
Zelienople, PA 16063
Phone: (412)776-3237 **Fax:** (412)776-9290
Products: Diesel engines; Transmissions. **SICs:** 5084
(Industrial Machinery & Equipment); 5013 (Motor
Vehicle Supplies & New Parts). **Est:** 1983. **Sales:**
$17,900,000 (2000). **Emp:** 75. **Officers:** Arthur E.
Bosetti, President & Chairman of the Board; A. Towne,
CFO; R. Carter, Dir. of Sales.

■ 2854 ■ **Ellwood Kieser and Sons**
5201 Comly St.
Philadelphia, PA 19135
Phone: (215)744-6666
Products: Automobile parts, including batteries,

brakes, and carburetors. **SIC:** 5013 (Motor Vehicle Supplies & New Parts). **Est:** 1917. **Sales:** $5,000,000 (2000). **Emp:** 20. **Officers:** Curtis W. Kieser, Chairman of the Board; Valerie Kieser, CFO; Rome Carpino, Sales Mgr.

■ **2855** ■ **Kimmel Automotive Inc.**
505 Kane St.
Baltimore, MD 21224
Phone: (410)633-3300 **Fax:** (410)633-2516
Products: Tires. **SIC:** 5014 (Tires & Tubes). **Est:** 1937. **Sales:** $81,000,000 (2000). **Emp:** 360. **Officers:** James R. Hartman, President; Ron Rhodes, VP & CFO; Jack Pearce, Vice President.

■ **2856** ■ **King Auto Parts Inc.**
935 High St.
Central Falls, RI 02863-1505
Phone: (401)725-1298
Products: Used automotive parts and supplies. **SIC:** 5015 (Motor Vehicle Parts—Used). **Officers:** Sanford Fink, President.

■ **2857** ■ **King Bearing Div.**
2641 Irving Blvd.
Dallas, TX 75207
Phone: (214)631-3270 **Fax:** (214)905-9113
Products: Bearings. **SIC:** 5085 (Industrial Supplies). **Sales:** $5,000,000 (2000). **Emp:** 15. **Officers:** Joe Hauk, Manager.

■ **2858** ■ **KK Motorcycle Supply**
431 E 3rd St.
Dayton, OH 45401
Phone: (937)222-1303 **Fax:** (937)222-9387
Products: Motorcycle parts and accessories. **SIC:** 5013 (Motor Vehicle Supplies & New Parts).

■ **2859** ■ **J. Korber and Co.**
PO Box 30548
Albuquerque, NM 87190
Phone: (505)884-4652 **Fax:** (505)884-4681
Products: Automobile parts. **SIC:** 5013 (Motor Vehicle Supplies & New Parts). **Est:** 1890. **Sales:** $13,200,000 (2000). **Emp:** 55. **Officers:** Al Korber, President.

■ **2860** ■ **Kostelecky's Fiberglass**
RR 2, Box 46
Jamestown, ND 58401-9505
Phone: (701)252-6725
Products: Motor home parts. **SIC:** 5013 (Motor Vehicle Supplies & New Parts). **Officers:** Dexter Kostelecky, Owner.

■ **2861** ■ **KPK Truck Body Manufacturing and Equipment Distributing Company Inc.**
3045 Verdugo Rd.
Los Angeles, CA 90065
Phone: (213)221-9167 **Fax:** (213)221-9170
Products: Truck body equipment. **SIC:** 5013 (Motor Vehicle Supplies & New Parts). **Est:** 1968. **Sales:** $500,000 (2000). **Emp:** 7. **Officers:** R.A. Kiner, President & CFO.

■ **2862** ■ **Kraco Enterprises Inc.**
505 E Euclid Ave.
Compton, CA 90224
Phone: (213)774-2550 **Fax:** (310)603-2260
Products: Auto accessories. **SIC:** 5013 (Motor Vehicle Supplies & New Parts). **Est:** 1955. **Sales:** $120,000,000 (2000). **Emp:** 500. **Officers:** Lawrence M. Kraines, Chairman of the Board; Bob Brocoff, President; Kent Friend, Sr. VP of Marketing & Sales; Roger Melanison, Dir. of Purchasing; Clara Krotzer, VP of Admin.

■ **2863** ■ **Kranz Automotive Supply**
300 Russell Blvd.
PO Box 13300A
St. Louis, MO 63157
Phone: (314)776-3787 **Fax:** (314)776-5089
Products: Automotive parts and supplies, New. **SIC:** 5013 (Motor Vehicle Supplies & New Parts). **Officers:** Gene Kohler Sr., President.

■ **2864** ■ **Kumho U.S.A. Inc.**
14605 Miller Ave.
Fontana, CA 92336-1695
Phone: (909)428-3300
Free: (800)445-8646 **Fax:** (909)428-3989
URL: http://www.kumhousa.com
Products: Tires for passenger cars, light trucks and trucks. **SIC:** 5014 (Tires & Tubes). **Est:** 1975. **Sales:** $175,000,000 (2000). **Emp:** 50. **Officers:** Jong G. Kahng, President.

■ **2865** ■ **Kunkel Services Co.**
PO Box 708
Bel Air, MD 21014
Phone: (410)838-3344
Free: (800)627-6573 **Fax:** (410)879-1053
Products: Automobile parts, including small engine parts. **SIC:** 5013 (Motor Vehicle Supplies & New Parts). **Sales:** $13,000,000 (2000). **Emp:** 160.

■ **2866** ■ **Kustom Fit**
8990 S Atlantic
South Gate, CA 90280
Phone: (323)564-4481 **Fax:** (323)564-5754
E-mail: kustom@kustomfit.com
URL: http://www.kustomfit.com
Products: Specialty seating for RVs, heavy trucks, and pickup trucks. **SIC:** 5013 (Motor Vehicle Supplies & New Parts). **Est:** 1961. **Sales:** $10,000,000 (2000). **Emp:** 200. **Officers:** Earl H. Belk, Chairman of the Board; Ron D. Belk, President; Jose Gonzalez; Ruben Garcia, Marketing & Sales Mgr.; Teri Porras, Customer Service Contact.

■ **2867** ■ **KYB Corporation of America**
140 N Mitchell Ct.
Addison, IL 60101-1490
Phone: (708)620-5555 **Fax:** (708)620-8133
Products: Shocks; Hydraulic motors. **SICs:** 5013 (Motor Vehicle Supplies & New Parts); 5084 (Industrial Machinery & Equipment). **Est:** 1974. **Sales:** $30,000,000 (2000). **Emp:** 34. **Officers:** Takashi Sanada, President & CFO; Osamu Kunihara, CFO; Verne Tiffany, VP of Marketing & Sales; Gail E. Rose, VP of Admin.

■ **2868** ■ **L-Z Truck Equipment Co., Inc.**
1881 Rice St.
Roseville, MN 55113
Phone: (612)488-2571
Free: (800)247-1082 **Fax:** (612)488-9857
Products: Automotive parts and supplies, New. **SIC:** 5013 (Motor Vehicle Supplies & New Parts). **Est:** 1952. **Sales:** $2,500,000 (2000). **Emp:** 30. **Officers:** Steve Zeece Sr., President; Steve Zeece Jr., Vice President.

■ **2869** ■ **Laforza Automobiles Inc.**
PO Box 461077
Escondido, CA 92046
Free: (800)523-6792 **Fax:** (760)738-7593
Products: Sport utility vehicles. **SIC:** 5012 (Automobiles & Other Motor Vehicles). **Officers:** Dave Hops, President & Chairman of the Board.

■ **2870** ■ **W.E. Lahr Co.**
PO Box 8158
St. Paul, MN 55108-0158
Phone: (612)644-6448 **Fax:** (612)644-7204
Products: Automotive parts. **SIC:** 5013 (Motor Vehicle Supplies & New Parts). **Sales:** $25,000,000 (1993). **Emp:** 150. **Officers:** William V. Lahr, Chairman of the Board; Herb Lohse, President.

■ **2871** ■ **Lakeland Enterprises, Inc.**
3809 Broadway
Lorain, OH 44052
Phone: (440)233-7266 **Fax:** (440)233-7891
Products: Automotive parts and supplies, New. **SIC:** 5013 (Motor Vehicle Supplies & New Parts). **Officers:** Greg Mead, Contact.

■ **2872** ■ **Land Rover North America Inc.**
PO Box 1503
Lanham Seabrook, MD 20706
Phone: (301)731-6523 **Fax:** (301)731-9054
Products: Imported four-wheel drive vehicles. **SIC:** 5012 (Automobiles & Other Motor Vehicles). **Est:** 1986. **Sales:** $230,000,000 (2000). **Emp:** 150. **Officers:**

Charles R. Hughes, President; Joel D. Scharfer, VP of Finance.

■ **2873** ■ **Laramie Tire Distributors**
PO Box 28
Norristown, PA 19404-0028
Phone: (215)275-6480 **Fax:** (215)275-3980
Products: Tires. **SIC:** 5014 (Tires & Tubes). **Est:** 1971. **Sales:** $80,000,000 (2000). **Emp:** 86. **Officers:** Wayne Reichman, President; Skip Viola, Exec. VP.

■ **2874** ■ **LaVanture Products Co.**
PO Box 2088
Elkhart, IN 46515
Phone: (219)264-0658
Free: (800)348-7625 **Fax:** 800-348-7629
E-mail: sales@lavanture.com
URL: http://www.lavanture.com
Products: Products for recreational vehicles, including hardware and electrical supplies. **SIC:** 5013 (Motor Vehicle Supplies & New Parts). **Est:** 1969. **Emp:** 146. **Officers:** Richard A. LaVanture, President; Steve Fulton, COO; Wayne Cooper, VP & General Mgr.; Rick Neff, VP of Sales; Shari Huston, Customer Service Contact; Steffanie Donnell, Human Resources Contact.

■ **2875** ■ **L.B. Industries Inc.**
PO Box 2797
Boise, ID 83701
Phone: (208)345-7515
Products: Automotive parts and supplies, New. **SIC:** 5013 (Motor Vehicle Supplies & New Parts). **Est:** 1956. **Sales:** $12,000,000 (2000). **Emp:** 50. **Officers:** Lawrence B. Barnes, CEO; Jerry Bartels, Treasurer; Joe D. Davis, President.

■ **2876** ■ **Philip Lebzelter and Son Co.**
300 N Queen St.
Lancaster, PA 17603
Phone: (717)397-0372
Products: Tires and rims. **SIC:** 5014 (Tires & Tubes). **Est:** 1854. **Sales:** $6,100,000 (2000). **Emp:** 51. **Officers:** C.C. McCormick, President; D.A. Miller III, VP of Marketing.

■ **2877** ■ **Lee/Star Tire Co.**
Willow Brook Rd.
Cumberland, MD 21502-2599
Phone: (301)777-6000 **Fax:** (301)777-6060
Products: Tires. **SIC:** 5014 (Tires & Tubes). **Est:** 1965. **Sales:** $15,000,000 (2000). **Emp:** 28. **Officers:** L.N. Fiedler, CEO & President; Gary L. Sutherland, VP of Finance; F.N. James, Vice President; J.A. Glover, Dir. of Data Processing; G.A. Ernest, VP of Investor Relations.

■ **2878** ■ **Leisure Components/SF Technology**
16730 Gridley Rd.
Cerritos, CA 90703
Phone: (562)924-5763
Free: (800)865-0401 **Fax:** (562)924-0846
E-mail: sftsales@aol.com
URL: http://www.sftech.com
Products: Recreational vehicle accessories, including hand pumps, battery isolators, and tail light converters. **SIC:** 5013 (Motor Vehicle Supplies & New Parts). **Est:** 1974. **Sales:** $2,200,000 (2000). **Emp:** 35. **Officers:** Red Fraser, President; Mike Retherford; Suzanne Rollins, Customer Service Contact.

■ **2879** ■ **Letts Equipment Div.**
1111 Bellevue Ave.
Detroit, MI 48207
Phone: (313)579-1100
Products: Tractor parts; Forged products. **SIC:** 5084 (Industrial Machinery & Equipment). **Est:** 1970. **Sales:** $1,000,000 (2000). **Emp:** 4. **Officers:** C.E. Letts Jr., President.

■ **2880** ■ **Lexus Div.**
19001 S Western Ave.
Torrance, CA 90509
Phone: (310)328-2075 **Fax:** (310)781-3207
Products: Automobiles. **SIC:** 5012 (Automobiles & Other Motor Vehicles). **Sales:** $2,380,000,000 (2000). **Emp:** 1,500. **Officers:** Bryan Bergsteinsson, VP & General Merchandising Mgr.

■ 2881 ■ Lightbourn Equipment Co.
PO Box 801870
Dallas, TX 75380
Phone: (972)233-5151 **Fax:** (972)661-0738
Products: Automobile service equipment. **SIC:** 5013
(Motor Vehicle Supplies & New Parts). **Est:** 1945.
Sales: $8,000,000 (2000). **Emp:** 25. **Officers:** Walt J.
Lightbourn Jr., CEO; Ted Landrum, Controller; W.S.
Lightbourn III, Dir. of Marketing.

■ 2882 ■ Liland Trade & Radiator Service Inc.
220 E 2nd
East Syracuse, NY 13057-2930
Phone: (315)432-0745
Free: (800)300-2367 **Fax:** (315)432-0627
Products: Radiators; Air conditioning parts; Gas tanks.
SIC: 5013 (Motor Vehicle Supplies & New Parts). **Est:**
1980. **Sales:** $6,000,000 (2000). **Emp:** 28. **Officers:**
Charles T. Li.

■ 2883 ■ Lincoln Clutch and Brake Supply
211 S 20th St.
Lincoln, NE 68510
Phone: (402)475-1439
Free: (800)927-2207 **Fax:** (402)475-1536
Products: Automotive parts and supplies. **SIC:** 5013
(Motor Vehicle Supplies & New Parts). **Est:** 1974.
Sales: $1,800,000 (1999). **Emp:** 12. **Officers:** Virgil A.
Meints, President; Mary K. Meintz, Sec. & Treas.

■ 2884 ■ Lindeco International Corp.
10600 NW 37th Ter.
Miami, FL 33178
Phone: (305)477-4446 **Fax:** (305)477-8116
E-mail: lindeco@msn.com
Products: Automobile parts, including engines,
suspensions, and engine parts. **SIC:** 5013 (Motor
Vehicle Supplies & New Parts). **Est:** 1957. **Sales:**
$8,000,000 (2000). **Emp:** 7. **Officers:** G. Lindenstraus,
President; Enrique Escobar, Exec. VP.

■ 2885 ■ Lisac's Inc.
2200 Yale Ave.
Butte, MT 59701
Phone: (406)494-7056
Products: Tires. **SIC:** 5014 (Tires & Tubes).

■ 2886 ■ Lister-Petter Inc.
815 E 56 Hwy.
Olathe, KS 66061-4914
Phone: (913)764-3512 **Fax:** (913)764-5493
E-mail: lpinfo@lister-petter.com
URL: http://www.lister-petter.com
Products: Diesel and gaseous fueled engines;
Generating sets; Light tower and trash pumps. **SICs:**
5084 (Industrial Machinery & Equipment); 5063
(Electrical Apparatus & Equipment). **Est:** 1867. **Emp:**
60. **Officers:** Philip L. Cantrill, President; Dan Thelen,
Controller; Alfie Pearson, Marketing Mgr.; Carol Holm,
Human Resources Contact, e-mail: carolh@lister-
petter.com.

■ 2887 ■ LoJack of California Corp.
9911 W Pico Blvd., No. 1000
Los Angeles, CA 90035
Phone: (310)286-2610
Free: (800)929-2000 **Fax:** (310)286-2853
Products: Stolen vehicle recovery devices. **SIC:** 5013
(Motor Vehicle Supplies & New Parts). **Est:** 1990.
Sales: $100,000,000 (1999). **Emp:** 110. **Officers:**
John Raber, Div. VP; Garrett Garland, Exec.Dir., Sales.

■ 2888 ■ LoJack of New Jersey Corp.
12 Rte. 17 N
Paramus, NJ 07652
Phone: (201)368-8716
Products: Auto theft recovery devices. **SIC:** 5013
(Motor Vehicle Supplies & New Parts). **Emp:** 40.
Officers: Michael Daly, President; Joseph Abely, CFO.

■ 2889 ■ Lombard Management Inc.
12015 Mora Dr., Unit 4
Santa Fe Springs, CA 90670
Phone: (562)944-9494 **Fax:** (562)944-8596
Products: Automotive accessories. **SIC:** 5013 (Motor
Vehicle Supplies & New Parts). **Officers:** B.J. Fazeli,
President.

■ 2890 ■ Long Motor Corp.
PO Box 14991
Shawnee Mission, KS 66286-4991
Phone: (913)541-1525 **Fax:** (913)541-9231
Products: Automotive parts. **SIC:** 5013 (Motor Vehicle
Supplies & New Parts). **Est:** 1984. **Sales:** $23,000,000
(2000). **Emp:** 100. **Officers:** Leo William Long,
President & CEO; Janet Dahl, Vice President.

■ 2891 ■ Long Trailer & Body Service, Inc.
5817 Augusta Rd.
PO Box 5105, Sta. B
Greenville, SC 29606
Phone: (864)277-7555
Products: Automotive parts and supplies, New. **SIC:**
5013 (Motor Vehicle Supplies & New Parts). **Officers:**
Karen Mullinnix, Contact.

■ 2892 ■ R.J. Loock & Company Inc.
343 N Gay St.
Baltimore, MD 21202-4837
Phones: (410)685-1771 (410)685-4711
(410)685-4712
Free: (800)435-6625 **Fax:** (410)837-1334
Products: Automotive, marine, and industrial parts;
Chemicals; Auto paint. **SICs:** 5013 (Motor Vehicle
Supplies & New Parts); 5088 (Transportation
Equipment & Supplies); 5169 (Chemicals & Allied
Products Nec); 5198 (Paints, Varnishes & Supplies).
Est: 1920. **Sales:** $2,000,000 (2000). **Officers:** Robert
R. Loock, President.

■ 2893 ■ Lotus Cars USA Inc.
500 Marathon Pkwy.
Lawrenceville, GA 30045-2800
Phone: (404)822-4566
Products: Lotus automobiles. **SIC:** 5012 (Automobiles
& Other Motor Vehicles).

■ 2894 ■ Louisiana Lift & Equipment, Inc.
6847 Greenwood Rd.
PO Box 3869
Shreveport, LA 71119
Phone: (318)631-5100 **Fax:** (318)635-1653
Products: Automotive parts, including bumpers and
panels. **SIC:** 5013 (Motor Vehicle Supplies & New
Parts). **Est:** 1980. **Emp:** 170. **Officers:** Kurt Tape;
John Bean; Bob Lumley; Ken Edwards.

**■ 2895 ■ Lucas Industries Inc. Aftermarket
Operations Div.**
1624 Meijer Dr.
Troy, MI 48084
Phone: (313)288-2000 **Fax:** (313)280-8280
Products: Aftermarket automotive parts. **SIC:** 5013
(Motor Vehicle Supplies & New Parts). **Est:** 1948.
Sales: $65,000,000 (2000). **Emp:** 150. **Officers:** Alan
Naisby, VP & General Merchandising Mgr.; David Neef,
Controller.

■ 2896 ■ Lucas Tire Inc.
810 Neville St.
Beckley, WV 25801
Phone: (304)253-3305 **Fax:** (304)252-8131
Products: Tires. **SIC:** 5014 (Tires & Tubes). **Est:** 1945.
Sales: $2,500,000 (1999). **Emp:** 16. **Officers:** Charles
F. Lucas, President; Van S. Lucas, Vice President.

■ 2897 ■ Lund Truck Parts Inc.
PO Box 386
Tea, SD 57064-0386
Phone: (605)368-5611
Products: Automobile parts, used. **SIC:** 5015 (Motor
Vehicle Parts—Used). **Officers:** Douglas Lund,
President.

■ 2898 ■ Warner T. Lundahl Inc.
42-23 Francis Lewis Blvd.
Bayside, NY 11361
Phone: (718)279-8586 **Fax:** (718)279-9228
Products: Automotive equipment; Electrical
equipment; Construction equipment. **SICs:** 5013 (Motor
Vehicle Supplies & New Parts); 5063 (Electrical
Apparatus & Equipment); 5082 (Construction & Mining
Machinery). **Est:** 1959. **Sales:** $1,000,000 (2000).
Emp: 4. **Officers:** Warner T. Lundahl, President.

■ 2899 ■ Lynwood Battery Manufacturing Co.
4505 E Washington Blvd.
Los Angeles, CA 90040-1023
Phone: (213)263-8866
Products: Batteries for automobile, RV, and industrial
use. **SICs:** 5013 (Motor Vehicle Supplies & New Parts);
5084 (Industrial Machinery & Equipment). **Est:** 1935.
Sales: $100,000 (2000). **Emp:** 1. **Officers:** T.W. Kirk,
President; Mary F. Leite, Treasurer.

■ 2900 ■ M & L Motor Supply Co.
1606 S Hastings Way
Eau Claire, WI 54701-4620
Phone: (715)832-1647
Products: Automotive parts and supplies, New. **SIC:**
5013 (Motor Vehicle Supplies & New Parts). **Emp:** 49.

■ 2901 ■ M & R Distributors Inc.
4232 S Saginaw St.
Flint, MI 48507
Phone: (810)744-9008
Products: Automobile radio and stereos; Auto alarm
systems. **SIC:** 5013 (Motor Vehicle Supplies & New
Parts).

■ 2902 ■ Machine Service, Inc.
1000 Ashwaubenon St.
Green Bay, WI 54303
Phone: (920)339-3000 **Fax:** (920)339-3001
Products: Heavy-duty truck parts. **SIC:** 5013 (Motor
Vehicle Supplies & New Parts).

■ 2903 ■ Machine Service Inc.
1954 S Stoughton Rd.
Madison, WI 53716
Phone: (608)221-9122 **Fax:** (608)221-8552
Products: Clutches; Drive line transmission; Bearings;
Seals. **SICs:** 5085 (Industrial Supplies); 5013 (Motor
Vehicle Supplies & New Parts).

■ 2904 ■ Machine Service, Inc.
4750 S 10th St.
Milwaukee, WI 53221
Phone: (414)483-8338 **Fax:** (414)483-8672
Products: Heavy-duty truck parts. **SIC:** 5013 (Motor
Vehicle Supplies & New Parts).

■ 2905 ■ Madisonville Tire and Retreading Inc.
PO Box 1593
48 Fedeeral St.
Madisonville, KY 42431
Phone: (502)821-2954
Products: Tires. **SIC:** 5014 (Tires & Tubes). **Est:** 1944.
Sales: $3,000,000 (2000). **Emp:** 32. **Officers:** Donald
E. Robinson, President.

■ 2906 ■ Magna Automotive Industries
999 Central Ave.
Woodmere, NY 11598-1205
Phone: (516)295-0188 **Fax:** (516)295-0625
E-mail: magnauto@prodigy.com
Products: Domestic automobile parts. **SIC:** 5013
(Motor Vehicle Supplies & New Parts). **Est:** 1966.
Sales: $2,000,000 (2000). **Emp:** 2. **Officers:** Manuel
Davidson, CEO; William Davidson, Dir. of Data
Processing.

■ 2907 ■ Magna Graphics
PO Box 1015
Lakeland, FL 33802-1015
Phone: (941)688-8515 **Fax:** (941)665-2759
Products: Automobile accessories, including air-
brushed auto tags. **SIC:** 5013 (Motor Vehicle Supplies
& New Parts).

■ 2908 ■ Magneto Diesel Injector Service Inc.
6931 Navigation Blvd.
Houston, TX 77011
Phone: (713)928-5686 **Fax:** (713)928-8154
Products: Diesel engine parts. **SIC:** 5084 (Industrial
Machinery & Equipment). **Est:** 1948. **Sales:**
$4,000,000 (2000). **Emp:** 100. **Officers:** Bruce Ingram
Jr., President.

■ 2909 ■ Magnum Tire Corp.
724 N 1st St.
Minneapolis, MN 55401
Phone: (612)338-8861 **Fax:** (612)338-8104
Products: Tires and inner tubes, new. **SIC:** 5014 (Tires

& Tubes). **Est:** 1977. **Sales:** $18,000,000 (2000). **Emp:** 35. **Officers:** Steven Wallack, Owner.

■ **2910** ■ **Maier Manufacturing**
416 Crown Point Cir.
Grass Valley, CA 95945-9389
Phone: (530)272-9036 **Fax:** (530)272-4306
E-mail: maier@oro.net
URL: http://www.maier-mfg.com
Products: Motorcycle parts. **SIC:** 5013 (Motor Vehicle Supplies & New Parts). **Est:** 1972. **Emp:** 55. **Officers:** Charles A. Maier; George W. Maier; Mark R. Maier.

■ **2911** ■ **Maine Equipment Company, Inc.**
RFD No. 2, Box 580
Bangor, ME 04401
Phone: (207)848-5738 **Fax:** (207)848-7448
Products: Automotive parts and supplies, New. **SIC:** 5013 (Motor Vehicle Supplies & New Parts). **Officers:** Lee Summer, Contact.

■ **2912** ■ **Maine Ladder & Staging Co., Inc.**
13 Portland Rd.
Box 899
Gray, ME 04039
Phone: (207)657-2070
Free: (800)492-0829 **Fax:** (207)657-2034
Products: Automotive parts and supplies, New. **SIC:** 5013 (Motor Vehicle Supplies & New Parts). **Officers:** Jim Oswald, Manager.

■ **2913** ■ **Maldaver Company Inc.**
1791 Bellevue
Detroit, MI 48207
Phone: (313)579-2110 **Fax:** (313)579-1217
Products: Automotive parts. **SIC:** 5013 (Motor Vehicle Supplies & New Parts). **Est:** 1948. **Emp:** 35. **Officers:** Suzanne Maldaver, President; George Ellis, Vice President; Bradley Ellis, Vice President. **Former Name:** American Dismantlers & Recycling, Inc.

■ **2914** ■ **Manlove Auto Parts**
117 E Market St.
Georgetown, DE 19947-1405
Phone: (302)856-2507
Products: Automotive parts. **SIC:** 5013 (Motor Vehicle Supplies & New Parts).

■ **2915** ■ **Manning Equipment Inc.**
PO Box 23229
Louisville, KY 40223
Phone: (502)426-5210
Free: (800)876-8768 **Fax:** (502)426-5213
Products: Automotive parts and supplies, New. **SIC:** 5013 (Motor Vehicle Supplies & New Parts). **Sales:** $15,000,000 (2000). **Emp:** 150. **Officers:** Randy Sirko, Sales Mgr.

■ **2916** ■ **Marietta Ignition Inc.**
PO Box 737
Marietta, OH 45750
Phone: (740)374-6746 **Fax:** (740)674-6746
Products: Automotive parts and supplies, New. **SIC:** 5013 (Motor Vehicle Supplies & New Parts). **Est:** 1920. **Sales:** $5,000,000 (2000). **Emp:** 48. **Officers:** Charles W. Wesel, President.

■ **2917** ■ **Marine Systems Inc.**
116 Capital Blvd.
Houma, LA 70360
Phone: (504)851-4990 **Fax:** (504)872-5302
Products: Diesel engines and engine parts. **SIC:** 5084 (Industrial Machinery & Equipment). **Sales:** $35,900,000 (1992). **Emp:** 110. **Officers:** Dorman L. Strahan, President.

■ **2918** ■ **Marnal Corp.**
501 Industrial Park Dr.
La Habra, CA 90631
Phone: (562)691-4443
Free: (800)522-2061 **Fax:** (562)691-7773
E-mail: marnal@marnal.com
URL: http://www.marnal.com
Products: Automotive parts. **SIC:** 5013 (Motor Vehicle Supplies & New Parts). **Est:** 1981. **Sales:** $7,000,000 (2000). **Emp:** 13. **Officers:** Reynaldo D'Angelo, President, e-mail: reysr@marnal.com; Francisco D'Angelo, Vice President, e-mail: fdangelo@marnal.com.

■ **2919** ■ **Marvin Land Systems, Inc.**
12637 Beatrice St.
Los Angeles, CA 90066
Phone: (310)306-2800 **Fax:** (310)306-5108
E-mail: sales@marvinland.com
URL: http://www.marvingroup.com
Products: Military vehicle equipment. **SIC:** 5013 (Motor Vehicle Supplies & New Parts). **Est:** 1963. **Sales:** $56,000,000 (2000). **Emp:** 45. **Officers:** Jerry Friedman, CEO. **Former Name:** FMS Corp.

■ **2920** ■ **Marwil Products Co.**
PO Box 287
Ft. Loramie, OH 45845-0287
Phone: (937)295-3651 **Fax:** (937)295-2835
Products: Exhaust system parts. **SIC:** 5013 (Motor Vehicle Supplies & New Parts). **Sales:** $13,000,000 (2000). **Emp:** 85. **Officers:** William Marwil.

■ **2921** ■ **Masek Distributing Inc.**
PO Box 130
Gering, NE 69341-0130
Phone: (308)436-2100
Free: (800)800-8987 **Fax:** (308)436-2800
Products: New and used golf cars. **SIC:** 5012 (Automobiles & Other Motor Vehicles). **Sales:** $15,000,000 (2000). **Emp:** 30. **Officers:** Joe Masek, CEO; Randy K. Hays, VP of Finance.

■ **2922** ■ **Matco Tools Corp.**
4403 Allen Rd.
Stow, OH 44224
Phone: (330)929-4949 **Fax:** (330)926-5320
Products: Hand tools for mechanics. **SICs:** 5013 (Motor Vehicle Supplies & New Parts); 5072 (Hardware). **Est:** 1979. **Sales:** $60,000,000 (2000). **Emp:** 565. **Officers:** Thomas N. Willis, President; Raymond J. Michaud, VP of Finance.

■ **2923** ■ **Matheny Motor Truck Co.**
3rd St. & Anne St.
Parkersburg, WV 26101
Phone: (304)485-4418
Products: Automotive parts. **SIC:** 5013 (Motor Vehicle Supplies & New Parts). **Est:** 1922. **Sales:** $42,000,000 (2000). **Emp:** 70. **Officers:** Mike Matheny, President; Tim Matheny, Sales Mgr.

■ **2924** ■ **R.B. Matheson Trucking Inc.**
10519 E Stockton Blvd., No. 125
Elk Grove, CA 95624
Phone: (916)685-2330 **Fax:** (916)685-8875
Products: Trucking equipment and supplies. **SIC:** 5013 (Motor Vehicle Supplies & New Parts). **Est:** 1964. **Sales:** $35,000,000 (2000). **Emp:** 425. **Officers:** Robert B. Matheson, CEO & President; Laurie Johnson, Controller.

■ **2925** ■ **George A. Mathewson Co.**
415 Raymond Blvd.
Newark, NJ 07105
Phone: (973)344-0081 **Fax:** (973)344-8376
Products: Power transmission. **SICs:** 5084 (Industrial Machinery & Equipment); 5013 (Motor Vehicle Supplies & New Parts).

■ **2926** ■ **Matt Friend Truck Equipment Inc.**
Hastings Industrial Park E, Bldg. SH66
Hastings, NE 68902-1083
Phone: (402)463-5675
Free: (800)444-7647 **Fax:** (402)463-5639
Products: Automotive. **SIC:** 5013 (Motor Vehicle Supplies & New Parts). **Sales:** $1,500,000 (2000). **Emp:** 9.

■ **2927** ■ **Maz Auto**
3800 San Pablo Ave.
Emeryville, CA 94608-3814
Phone: (510)428-3950 **Fax:** (510)601-8411
Products: Automotive glass and accessories. **SIC:** 5013 (Motor Vehicle Supplies & New Parts). **Est:** 1987. **Emp:** 49. **Officers:** Ed Hemmat; Mori Maroufi.

■ **2928** ■ **McCallum Motor Supply Co.**
PO Box 216
Unionville, CT 06085
Phone: (860)677-2611 **Fax:** (860)676-8404
Products: Motor parts, including starters. **SIC:** 5013 (Motor Vehicle Supplies & New Parts). **Est:** 1928.

Sales: $3,000,000 (2000). **Emp:** 15. **Officers:** Edmond Kowronk, General Mgr.; Jerry Gosselin, General Mgr.

■ **2929** ■ **McCarthy Tire Service**
987 Stony Battery Rd.
Lancaster, PA 17603
Phone: (717)898-0114
Products: Tires. **SIC:** 5014 (Tires & Tubes).

■ **2930** ■ **McCord Auto Supply Inc.**
PO Box 743
Monticello, IN 47960
Phone: (219)583-4136
Free: (800)348-2396 **Fax:** (219)583-7267
E-mail: mccord@monti.net
Products: Tires for agricultural equipment and trucks. **SIC:** 5014 (Tires & Tubes). **Est:** 1959. **Sales:** $8,500,000 (2000). **Emp:** 34. **Officers:** Ross M. Fischer, President.

■ **2931** ■ **McCullough Distributing Company, Inc.**
5613-23 Tulip St.
Philadelphia, PA 19124-1626
Phone: (215)288-9700
Free: (800)523-3522 **Fax:** (215)289-0389
Products: Automotive parts and supplies. **SIC:** 5013 (Motor Vehicle Supplies & New Parts). **Est:** 1956. **Emp:** 15.

■ **2932** ■ **V.H. McDow & Sons Salvage**
PO Box 208
Grafton, NH 03240-0208
Phone: (603)523-4555
Products: Used motor vehicle parts and supplies. **SIC:** 5015 (Motor Vehicle Parts—Used). **Officers:** Vincent Mc Dow, Owner.

■ **2933** ■ **McGuire Bearing**
2611 BW 5th Ave.
Eugene, OR 97402
Phone: (541)343-0820 **Fax:** (541)343-9216
Products: Power transmission products. **SICs:** 5084 (Industrial Machinery & Equipment); 5013 (Motor Vehicle Supplies & New Parts); 5085 (Industrial Supplies).

■ **2934** ■ **McGuire Bearing**
947 SE Market St.
Portland, OR 97214
Phone: (503)238-1570
Free: (800)547-6045 **Fax:** (503)232-1478
Products: Car transmission products; Bearings. **SICs:** 5013 (Motor Vehicle Supplies & New Parts); 5085 (Industrial Supplies).

■ **2935** ■ **MCM Enterprise**
PO Box 1001
Reno, NV 89504
Phone: (702)356-5601 **Fax:** (702)356-5603
Products: Automobile parts and accessories; Medical equipment; Used automobiles. **SICs:** 5013 (Motor Vehicle Supplies & New Parts); 5047 (Medical & Hospital Equipment); 5012 (Automobiles & Other Motor Vehicles). **Officers:** Michael A. Rodas, President.

■ **2936** ■ **Mechanical Drives Co.**
3015 Leonis Blvd.
Los Angeles, CA 90058
Phone: (323)587-7901 **Fax:** (323)587-8236
E-mail: mechdrives@aol.com
Products: Power transmission equipment and supplies; Motors; Valves. **SICs:** 5085 (Industrial Supplies); 5013 (Motor Vehicle Supplies & New Parts). **Est:** 1958. **Sales:** $7,000,000 (2000). **Emp:** 35. **Officers:** T. Wayne Gehan, President.

■ **2937** ■ **Mechanic's Auto Parts, Inc.**
1041 Glassboro Rd., Ste. F1
Williamstown, NJ 08094-0741
Phone: (856)875-6700 **Fax:** (856)875-0741
Products: Auto parts and supplies. **SIC:** 5013 (Motor Vehicle Supplies & New Parts). **Est:** 1976. **Sales:** $30,000,000 (1999). **Emp:** 400. **Officers:** Joseph M. York, President; Joseph M. Rossini, Exec. VP; Michael Bell, Vice President.

■ 2938 ■ **Medart Inc.**
124 Manufacturers Dr.
Arnold, MO 63010-4727
Phone: (636)282-2300 **Fax:** 888-510-3100
E-mail: postmaster@medartinc.com
URL: http://www.medartinc.com
Products: Air-cooled engines and parts; Marine accessories and parts. **SIC:** 5013 (Motor Vehicle Supplies & New Parts). **Est:** 1912. **Sales:** $35,000,000 (2000). **Emp:** 100. **Officers:** J. Michael Medart, President; David A. Strubberg, VP & CFO; Mike Medart, Dir. of Marketing.

■ 2939 ■ **Mega Company**
2501 K St. NW, Ste. 9C
Washington, DC 20037
Phone: (202)338-2112 **Fax:** (202)338-2128
E-mail: kamil@erols.com
Products: Motor oil; Tires; Lumber; Metal buildings. **SICs:** 5014 (Tires & Tubes); 5031 (Lumber, Plywood & Millwork); 5172 (Petroleum Products Nec). **Est:** 1983. **Emp:** 15. **Officers:** Salah Turkmani, President.

■ 2940 ■ **Mellen Parts Company Inc.**
126 Renaissance Pkwy.
Atlanta, GA 30308
Phone: (404)876-4331 **Fax:** (404)876-1078
Products: Automotive parts and supplies, New. **SIC:** 5013 (Motor Vehicle Supplies & New Parts). **Est:** 1922. **Sales:** $2,000,000 (2000). **Emp:** 12. **Officers:** S.B. Mellen Jr., President; Janice Cohran, Treasurer.

■ 2941 ■ **Menco Corp.**
PO Box 1300
Springfield, IL 62705
Phone: (217)544-7485 **Fax:** (217)527-1329
Products: Auto parts. **SIC:** 5013 (Motor Vehicle Supplies & New Parts). **Est:** 1946. **Sales:** $5,100,000 (2000). **Emp:** 28. **Officers:** William Maggs, President; Ken Bollin, VP of Finance.

■ 2942 ■ **Mendon Leasing Corp.**
362 Kingsland Ave.
Brooklyn, NY 11222
Phone: (718)391-5300
Free: (800)229-6022 **Fax:** (718)389-2149
Products: Truck rental, leasing; and maintenance programs; New truck sales. **SIC:** 5012 (Automobiles & Other Motor Vehicles). **Sales:** $82,000,000 (2000). **Emp:** 250. **Officers:** Don Resnicoff, President; Barry Haskell, VP of Finance.

■ 2943 ■ **Merchants Inc.**
9073 Euclid Ave.
Manassas, VA 20110-5306
Phone: (703)368-3171
Free: (800)368-3130 **Fax:** 800-255-9159
Products: Tires; Automotive repair equipment. **SICs:** 5014 (Tires & Tubes); 5013 (Motor Vehicle Supplies & New Parts). **Est:** 1943. **Sales:** $250,000,000 (2000). **Emp:** 1,800. **Officers:** James L. Matthews, President; James R. Cato, CFO; Tara Rosenberger, Dir. of Advertising; Paul Hawkins, Dir. of Information Systems; Robert Barnes, VP ofWholesale Operations. **Doing Business As:** American Tire Distributors.

■ 2944 ■ **Merrill Co.**
601 1st Ave. SW
Spencer, IA 51301
Phone: (712)262-1141 **Fax:** (712)262-1255
Products: Metallic gaskets and machined seals; Bearings; Spark plugs. **SICs:** 5013 (Motor Vehicle Supplies & New Parts); 5085 (Industrial Supplies). **Est:** 1964. **Sales:** $8,400,000 (2000). **Emp:** 35. **Officers:** Milo Allen, General Mgr.

■ 2945 ■ **Merritts Auto Salvage**
532 Hwy. 95
Weiser, ID 83672-5720
Phone: (208)549-1076 **Fax:** 800-286-1076
Products: Automobile parts, used. **SIC:** 5015 (Motor Vehicle Parts—Used). **Officers:** Wayne Merritt, Owner.

■ 2946 ■ **Mesabi Radial Tire Co.**
18th St. at 5th Ave. E
Hibbing, MN 55746
Phone: (218)263-6865
Products: Tires. **SIC:** 5014 (Tires & Tubes). **Est:** 1953.

Sales: $3,500,000 (2000). **Emp:** 7. **Officers:** Carl M. D'Aquila, President; Dolores D'Aquila, Controller.

■ 2947 ■ **Metrix South Inc.**
6501 NW 12th Ave.
Ft. Lauderdale, FL 33309-1109
Phone: (954)979-5660
Free: (800)765-0000 **Fax:** (954)979-0159
E-mail: mbrent@bellsouth.net
URL: http://www.metrixtpw.com
Products: Automotive parts and supplies, New. **SIC:** 5013 (Motor Vehicle Supplies & New Parts). **Est:** 1974. **Emp:** 100. **Officers:** Michael Birnholz, Sales/Marketing Contact.

■ 2948 ■ **Metropolitan Diesel Supply Co.**
18211 Weaver Ave.
Detroit, MI 48228
Phone: (313)272-6370 **Fax:** (313)272-9280
Products: Automotive parts and supplies, New. **SIC:** 5013 (Motor Vehicle Supplies & New Parts). **Est:** 1978. **Sales:** $1,200,000 (2000). **Emp:** 8.

■ 2949 ■ **Mid-Ark Salvage Pool Inc.**
703 Hwy. 64 E
Conway, AR 72032
Phone: (501)796-2812
Products: Salvaged automobiles. **SIC:** 5093 (Scrap & Waste Materials).

■ 2950 ■ **Mid-City Automotive Warehouse Inc.**
3450 N Kostner Ave.
Chicago, IL 60641
Phone: (773)282-9393 **Fax:** (773)282-5045
Products: Automotive parts and supplies, New. **SIC:** 5013 (Motor Vehicle Supplies & New Parts). **Est:** 1960. **Sales:** $9,000,000 (2000). **Emp:** 45. **Officers:** Mike Warshawsky, President.

■ 2951 ■ **Mid Michigan Trailer & Truck Equipment, Inc.**
327 Lansing Rd.
PO Box 427
Potterville, MI 48876
Phone: (517)645-8011 **Fax:** (517)645-8016
Products: Automotive parts and supplies, New. **SIC:** 5013 (Motor Vehicle Supplies & New Parts). **Officers:** Larry Eckstein, Vice President.

■ 2952 ■ **Mid-State Automotive**
915 N Cherry
Knoxville, TN 37917-7012
Phone: (423)523-5123
Free: (800)288-1783 **Fax:** (423)523-5123
Products: Automotive parts and supplies, New. **SIC:** 5013 (Motor Vehicle Supplies & New Parts). **Emp:** 49. **Officers:** Marvin Neal.

■ 2953 ■ **Mid States Classic Cars**
835 W Grant St.
Hooper, NE 68031
Phone: (402)654-2772 **Fax:** (402)654-2332
E-mail: mscobra@htcnet.com
URL: http://www.cobracounty.com/midstates
Products: Cobra replica kits and parts. **SIC:** 5012 (Automobiles & Other Motor Vehicles). **Est:** 1986. **Emp:** 8. **Officers:** Robert W. Kallio, General Mgr.

■ 2954 ■ **MidAmerican Metals Company Inc.**
519 E Third St.
Owensboro, KY 42303
Phone: (502)926-3515
Free: (800)280-3515 **Fax:** (502)684-8445
Products: Used and rebuilt automobile parts. **SIC:** 5015 (Motor Vehicle Parts—Used). **Est:** 1987. **Sales:** $700,000 (2000). **Emp:** 5. **Officers:** Paul J. Busse, President; Mary M. Busse, Vice President.

■ 2955 ■ **Midway Inc.**
220 Sandusky St.
Monroeville, OH 44847
Phone: (419)465-2551
Products: Freightliners. **SIC:** 5084 (Industrial Machinery & Equipment). **Est:** 1945. **Sales:** $25,000,000 (2000). **Emp:** 200. **Officers:** Gary R. Scherz, President; Stanley Drabik, VP of Finance.

■ 2956 ■ **Midway Motor Supply Core Supplier**
68 W Sheffield
Pontiac, MI 48340
Phone: (248)332-4755 **Fax:** (248)332-4630
Products: Automobile engines, used; Parts and accessories for internal combustion engines. **SIC:** 5015 (Motor Vehicle Parts—Used). **Est:** 1963. **Sales:** $1,000,000 (2000). **Emp:** 3. **Officers:** Lloyd C. Haack, Owner.

■ 2957 ■ **Midway Parts Inc.**
708 E Highway 212
Gettysburg, SD 57442-1814
Phone: (605)765-2466 **Fax:** (605)765-2466
Products: Rebuilt parts for motor vehicles; Motor vehicle parts and accessories. **SIC:** 5015 (Motor Vehicle Parts—Used). **Est:** 1959. **Sales:** $600,000 (2000). **Emp:** 2. **Officers:** Bryan Hause, President.

■ 2958 ■ **Midway Trading, Inc.**
PO Box 2128
Reston, VA 20195
Phone: (703)471-4020 **Fax:** (703)471-4218
E-mail: satch@midwaytrading.com
Products: Commercial equipment; Industrial supplies; Chemicals and allied products; Petroleum products; New motor vehicle parts. **SICs:** 5013 (Motor Vehicle Supplies & New Parts); 5046 (Commercial Equipment Nec); 5085 (Industrial Supplies); 5169 (Chemicals & Allied Products Nec); 5172 (Petroleum Products Nec). **Officers:** S.W. Baumgart, President; J. Parr, Sales/Marketing Contact. **Former Name:** Trident International Ltd.

■ 2959 ■ **Midwest Auto Parts Distributors Inc.**
PO Box 8158
St. Paul, MN 55108-0158
Phone: (612)644-6448 **Fax:** (612)644-7204
Products: Automotive parts. **SIC:** 5013 (Motor Vehicle Supplies & New Parts). **Est:** 1963. **Sales:** $23,000,000 (2000). **Emp:** 150. **Officers:** W.E. Lahr Jr., CEO & Chairman of the Board; Steve Schmidt, Controller; H. Lohse, Dir. of Marketing; P. McBain, Dir. of Systems.

■ 2960 ■ **Midwest Truck and Auto Parts Inc.**
4200 S Morgan St.
Chicago, IL 60609-2517
Phone: (312)225-1550
Free: (800)934-2727 **Fax:** (312)225-1615
E-mail: info@midwesttruck.com
URL: http://www.midwesttruck.com
Products: Automotive and truck parts. **SIC:** 5013 (Motor Vehicle Supplies & New Parts). **Est:** 1943. **Emp:** 75. **Officers:** Don Chudacoff, CEO; Mark Chudacoff, President; Tom Antonson, Vice President.

■ 2961 ■ **Midwest Wrecking Co.**
PO Box 3757
Edmond, OK 73083
Phone: (405)478-8833
Products: Used auto parts. **SIC:** 5015 (Motor Vehicle Parts—Used).

■ 2962 ■ **Mighty Distributing System of America Inc.**
650 Engineering Dr.
Norcross, GA 30092
Phone: (770)448-3900
Free: (800)829-3900 **Fax:** (770)446-8627
URL: http://www.mightyautoparts.com
Products: Auto parts. **SIC:** 5013 (Motor Vehicle Supplies & New Parts). **Est:** 1963. **Officers:** Ken Voelker, President; Pelham Wilder, VP & CFO; Gary Vann, VP of Marketing & Sales, e-mail: gary.vann@mightyautoparts.com;Mark Spruil, Information Systems Mgr.; Shannon Sanderson, Human Resources Contact, e-mail: shannonsanderson@mightyautoparts.com.

■ 2963 ■ **Mill Supply Corp.**
PO Box 12216
Salem, OR 97309
Phone: (503)585-7411
Free: (800)645-6608 **Fax:** (503)581-4894
E-mail: msc@mill-supply.com
URL: http://www.mill-supply.com
Products: Rubber products; Power transmission. **SIC:** 5013 (Motor Vehicle Supplies & New Parts). **Est:** 1946. **Sales:** $17,000,000 (1999). **Emp:** 53. **Officers:** George Steelhammer, CEO; Geoff Steelhammer,

Sales/Marketing Contact, e-mail: geoffsteel@ sprintmail.com; Ron Wilson, Customer Service Contact, e-mail: ron@mill-supply.com; Steve Zahradnik, Human Resources Contact, e-mail: stevez@teleport.com.

■ 2964 ■ Miller Bearings Inc.
17 S Westmoreland Dr.
Orlando, FL 32805
Phone: (407)425-9078   Fax: (407)648-4474
E-mail: benge@magicnet.net
URL: http://www.millerbearings.com
Products: Bearings; Mechanical and electrical power transmissions. SICs: 5013 (Motor Vehicle Supplies & New Parts); 5085 (Industrial Supplies). Est: 1947. Emp: 120. Officers: Lynne R. Etheridge, CEO.

■ 2965 ■ Miller Bearings Inc.
3210 Power Ave.
Jacksonville, FL 32207
Phone: (904)737-9919   Fax: (904)737-9969
Products: Ball and roller bearings; Power transmission equipment and supplies. SICs: 5013 (Motor Vehicle Supplies & New Parts); 5085 (Industrial Supplies).

■ 2966 ■ Miller Bearings Inc.
6681 NW 82nd Ave.
Miami, FL 33166
Phone: (305)593-1724   Fax: (305)593-9423
URL: http://www.millerbearings.com
Products: Bearings; Power transmission equipment. SICs: 5085 (Industrial Supplies); 5013 (Motor Vehicle Supplies & New Parts). Est: 1947. Emp: 118.

■ 2967 ■ Miller Bearings Inc.
1132 53rd Court N
West Palm Beach, FL 33407
Phone: (561)863-5111   Fax: (561)842-8158
Products: Ball and roller bearings; Power transmission equipment and supplies. SICs: 5085 (Industrial Supplies); 5013 (Motor Vehicle Supplies & New Parts).

■ 2968 ■ Miller Brothers Giant Tire Service Inc.
PO Box 3965
Cayce, SC 29033
Phone: (803)796-8880   Fax: (803)794-4346
Products: Tires; Tubes. SIC: 5014 (Tires & Tubes). Est: 1984. Sales: $6,000,000 (2000). Emp: 12. Officers: Y.M. Miller, President; Rick Miller, VP of Finance.

■ 2969 ■ Miller Tire Co. Inc.
3801 N Broadway Ave.
Muncie, IN 47303
Phone: (765)282-4322
Products: Tires. SIC: 5014 (Tires & Tubes).

■ 2970 ■ Miller Tire Distributors
3822 N Broadway Ave.
Muncie, IN 47303
Phone: (765)282-7405
Products: Tires. SIC: 5014 (Tires & Tubes).

■ 2971 ■ Miller Tire Service Inc.
PO Box 883
Columbia, SC 29203-6436
Phone: (803)252-5675   Fax: (803)252-7254
Products: Tires. SIC: 5014 (Tires & Tubes). Est: 1930. Sales: $2,000,000 (2000). Emp: 20. Officers: Theron Markell Miller Jr., President.

■ 2972 ■ Millersburg Tire Service Inc.
7375 State Rte. 39 E
Millersburg, OH 44654
Phone: (330)674-1085   Fax: (330)674-6598
Products: Farm tires. SIC: 5014 (Tires & Tubes). Est: 1953. Sales: $13,000,000 (2000). Emp: 30. Officers: Brad Schmucker, President.

■ 2973 ■ Mirly Truck Center Inc.
PO Box 9
Advance, MO 63730-0009
Phone: (573)722-3574   Fax: (573)722-3189
Products: Motor vehicle parts and accessories. SIC: 5013 (Motor Vehicle Supplies & New Parts). Est: 1938. Sales: $20,000,000 (2000). Emp: 20. Officers: Tim Middleton, President; J.R. Middleton, Treasurer & Secty.

■ 2974 ■ Mission Valley Ford Trucks Sales Inc.
PO Box 611150
San Jose, CA 95161
Phone: (408)436-2920
Products: Trucks. SIC: 5012 (Automobiles & Other Motor Vehicles).

■ 2975 ■ Missouri Power Transmission
1801 Santa Fe Pl.
Columbia, MO 65202-1935
Phone: (573)474-1446   Fax: (573)474-9927
Products: Power transmissions. SICs: 5084 (Industrial Machinery & Equipment); 5013 (Motor Vehicle Supplies & New Parts).

■ 2976 ■ Missouri Power Transmission
3226 Blair Ave.
St. Louis, MO 63107
Phone: (314)421-0919   Fax: (314)421-1512
Products: Power transmissions. SICs: 5084 (Industrial Machinery & Equipment); 5013 (Motor Vehicle Supplies & New Parts). Est: 1970. Sales: $30,000,000 (2000). Emp: 100. Officers: Alfred Dressing, President; Chad Dressing, Vice President; Emma Roth, Secretary. Alternate Name: Fleck Bearing. Former Name: Riverside Bearing. Alternate Name: Hi-Tec Industrial Supply.

■ 2977 ■ Mitchell Industrial Tire Co.
PO Box 71839
Chattanooga, TN 37407
Phone: (615)698-4442   Fax: (615)698-4294
Products: Industrial tires. SIC: 5014 (Tires & Tubes). Est: 1953. Sales: $11,000,000 (2000). Emp: 60. Officers: Benton Hood, President.

■ 2978 ■ Mobile Automotive Diagnostic
309 Boston Rd.
North Billerica, MA 01862-2621
Phone: (978)667-1934   Fax: (978)667-1011
Products: Automotive accessories, including radios, alarms, and air-conditioning. SIC: 5013 (Motor Vehicle Supplies & New Parts). Officers: John Mac Kenzie, President.

■ 2979 ■ Modi Rubber Ltd.
10560 Main St.
Fairfax, VA 22030
Phone: (703)273-0123
Products: Tires. SIC: 5014 (Tires & Tubes).

■ 2980 ■ Monroe Truck Equipment Inc.
1051 W 7th St.
Monroe, WI 53566
Phone: (608)328-8127
Free: (800)356-8134   Fax: (608)329-8180
URL: http://www.monroetruck.com
Products: Truck equipment and accessories; Snow and ice equipment. SIC: 5013 (Motor Vehicle Supplies & New Parts). Est: 1958. Sales: $30,000,000 (1999). Emp: 950. Officers: Richard L. Feller, Chairman of the Board; David J. Quade, President; Rick F. Rufenacht, VP of Marketing & Sales; John Robertson, Customer Service Contact; Lynn Daniels, Human Resoyrces Contact, e-mail: ldaniels@mobroetruck.com.

■ 2981 ■ Montana Truck Parts
PO Box 123
Milltown, MT 59851-0123
Phone: (406)258-6221   Free: (800)742-7650
Products: Used motor vehicle parts and supplies. SIC: 5015 (Motor Vehicle Parts—Used). Officers: Ralph Rambo, Owner.

■ 2982 ■ Moog Louisville Wholesale
1421 W Magazine
Louisville, KY 40203-2063
Phone: (502)583-7795   Fax: (502)589-4960
Products: Automotive parts, including carburetors and engine parts. SIC: 5013 (Motor Vehicle Supplies & New Parts). Emp: 60. Officers: Douglas R. Washbish.

■ 2983 ■ Moore's Wholesale Tire Sales
88 Railroad Ave. Exit
Albany, NY 12205
Phone: (518)446-9027
Products: Tires. SIC: 5014 (Tires & Tubes).

■ 2984 ■ Morgan Tire and Auto Inc.
2021 Sunnydale Blvd.
Clearwater, FL 33765
Phone: (727)441-3727   Fax: (727)443-2401
Products: Tires and automobile supplies. SIC: 5014 (Tires & Tubes). Sales: $436,000,000 (2000). Emp: 1,000. Officers: Larry Morgan, CEO & Chairman of the Board; Bill Long, CFO.

■ 2985 ■ Morgan's Auto Parts
415 Airport Rd. No. B
New Castle, DE 19720
Phone: (302)322-2229   Fax: (302)322-0490
Products: Automobile parts. SIC: 5013 (Motor Vehicle Supplies & New Parts).

■ 2986 ■ Morgantown Tire Wholesalers
111 Maple St.
Morgantown, KY 42261
Phone: (502)526-5570
Products: Tires. SIC: 5014 (Tires & Tubes).

■ 2987 ■ Morse Parker Motor Supply
809 High St.
Portsmouth, VA 23704-3333
Phone: (757)393-4051   Fax: (757)393-4056
Products: Automotive supplies. SIC: 5013 (Motor Vehicle Supplies & New Parts). Emp: 33.

■ 2988 ■ Moss Dynamics
1050 St. John St.
Easton, PA 18042
Phone: (215)253-9385   Fax: (215)253-3210
Products: Automotive equipment and supplies, including lubricating oils, tires and tubes, chemicals, and waxes. SICs: 5013 (Motor Vehicle Supplies & New Parts); 5172 (Petroleum Products Nec); 5014 (Tires & Tubes); 5169 (Chemicals & Allied Products Nec). Officers: Terry Champion, Vice President.

■ 2989 ■ Motion Ind.
PO Box 764
East Windsor, CT 06088-0764
Phone: (860)292-6091   Fax: (860)292-6087
Products: Power transmission equipment and supplies; Bearings. SICs: 5013 (Motor Vehicle Supplies & New Parts); 5085 (Industrial Supplies). Emp: 7. Former Name: Atlantic Tracy, Inc.

■ 2990 ■ Motion Industries
80 Access Rd.
Warwick, RI 02886-1002
Phone: (401)736-0515   Fax: (401)736-5245
URL: http://www.motion-industries.com
Products: Power transmissions and electrical drives; Bearings. SICs: 5013 (Motor Vehicle Supplies & New Parts); 5085 (Industrial Supplies). Alternate Name: Atlantic Tracy Inc.

■ 2991 ■ Motion Industries
7130 Packer Dr.
Wausau, WI 54401
Phone: (715)848-2994   Fax: (715)848-7135
E-mail: wbc706@dwave.net
Products: Power transmission products; Bearings. SICs: 5085 (Industrial Supplies); 5084 (Industrial Machinery & Equipment); 5013 (Motor Vehicle Supplies & New Parts). Est: 1965. Sales: $6,500,000 (2000). Emp: 14. Officers: Bob Heckendorf, Branch Mgr.; Joe Friday, Operations Mgr. Former Name: Wisconsin Bearing.

■ 2992 ■ Motion Industries, Inc.
2222 Nordale Dr.
Appleton, WI 54911
Phone: (920)731-4121   Fax: (920)734-9138
Products: Power transmission products, including bearings; Fluid power, linear, electrical, and hose specialists. SICs: 5085 (Industrial Supplies); 5013 (Motor Vehicle Supplies & New Parts). Emp: 20. Officers: Robert Walczak, Branch Mgr. Former Name: Wisconsin Bearing.

■ 2993 ■ Motor Master Products
1307 Baltimore St.
Defiance, OH 43512-1903
Phone: (419)782-7131
Free: (800)537-9623   Fax: (419)784-4992
Products: Drive link components. SIC: 5013 (Motor

Vehicle Supplies & New Parts). **Est:** 1923. **Sales:** $5,000,000 (2000). **Emp:** 10. **Officers:** Greg Riley, President; Roger Boff, Sec. & Treas.; Dilbert Schwab, Sales Mgr.

■ 2994 ■ **Motor Parts & Bearing Co.**
221 S Main
Bolivar, TN 38008-2705
Phone: (901)658-5263
Products: Automotive parts and supplies, New; Industrial supplies; Farm supplies. **SICs:** 5013 (Motor Vehicle Supplies & New Parts); 5085 (Industrial Supplies); 5083 (Farm & Garden Machinery). **Emp:** 49.

■ 2995 ■ **Motor Parts and Supply Inc.**
750 Abbott Ln.
Colorado Springs, CO 80905
Phone: (719)632-4276
Products: Automotive parts, including engines and starters. **SIC:** 5013 (Motor Vehicle Supplies & New Parts). **Est:** 1945. **Sales:** $9,000,000 (2000). **Emp:** 80. **Officers:** B.W. Cameron, President.

■ 2996 ■ **Motor Products Company Inc.**
733 N 5th Ave.
PO Box 3640
Knoxville, TN 37917-6722
Phone: (423)525-5321
Free: (800)667-5321 **Fax:** (423)637-5821
Products: Automotive parts and supplies, New. **SIC:** 5013 (Motor Vehicle Supplies & New Parts). **Sales:** $2,000,000 (2000). **Emp:** 99. **Officers:** Eddie Sanford, President; John Freels, Vice President.

■ 2997 ■ **Motorcycle Stuff Inc.**
PO Box 1179
Cape Girardeau, MO 63701
Phone: (573)243-1111 **Fax:** (573)243-1888
Products: Motorcycle parts. **SIC:** 5013 (Motor Vehicle Supplies & New Parts).

■ 2998 ■ **Mt. Kisco Truck & Auto Parts**
135 Kisco Ave.
Mt. Kisco, NY 10549
Phone: (914)666-3155 **Fax:** (914)241-3399
E-mail: mtkiscotruck@msm.com
Products: Automotive parts and supplies. **SIC:** 5013 (Motor Vehicle Supplies & New Parts). **Est:** 1916. **Sales:** $5,000,000 (2000). **Emp:** 30. **Officers:** Steve Finklestein, Contact. **Former Name:** Mt. Kisco Truck & Fleet Supply.

■ 2999 ■ **Mt. Kisco Truck and Fleet Supply**
135 Kisco Ave.
Mt. Kisco, NY 10549
Phone: (914)666-3155 **Fax:** (914)241-3399
Products: Automotive. **SIC:** 5013 (Motor Vehicle Supplies & New Parts). **Sales:** $5,000,000 (2000). **Emp:** 30.

■ 3000 ■ **Mount Vernon Auto Parts**
8351 Richmond Hwy.
Alexandria, VA 22309
Phone: (703)780-3445 **Fax:** (703)780-4106
Products: Wheels and brakes. **SIC:** 5013 (Motor Vehicle Supplies & New Parts). **Est:** 1962. **Sales:** $1,000,000 (2000). **Emp:** 15. **Officers:** Jay L. Thomas, Manager.

■ 3001 ■ **Mountain Muffler**
1605 Hwy. 201 N
PO Box 374
Mountain Home, AR 72653-0374
Phone: (870)425-8868
Free: (800)844-8868 **Fax:** (870)425-3688
E-mail: info@mountainmuffler.com
URL: http://www.mountainmuffler.com
Products: Automotive exhaust products. **SIC:** 5013 (Motor Vehicle Supplies & New Parts). **Est:** 1981. **Sales:** $14,000,000 (2000). **Emp:** 90. **Officers:** Mack Butterfield, President; Dave Butterfield, Sales/Marketing Contact; Dave Butterfield, Customer Service Contact; Jennifer Stahlman, Human Resources Contact. **Former Name:** Wright-Way Inc.

■ 3002 ■ **Mr. Hub Cap**
499 W San Carlos St.
San Jose, CA 95110
Phone: (408)294-4304
Products: Hub caps. **SIC:** 5013 (Motor Vehicle Supplies & New Parts). **Est:** 1979. **Sales:** $200,000 (2000). **Emp:** 2. **Officers:** Ernie Breit, Owner.

■ 3003 ■ **K.C. Mundy Enterprises, Inc.**
4 Florence Ct.
Jackson, NJ 08527-2913
Phone: (732)574-3202
Free: (888)667-0088 **Fax:** (732)363-7522
E-mail: kcm0909@csn.com
URL: http://www.kcmundy.com
Products: Motor vehicle supplies and parts; Medical and hospital equipment; Industrial machinery and equipment; Industrial supplies; Drugs, proprietaries, and sundries. **SICs:** 5013 (Motor Vehicle Supplies & New Parts); 5047 (Medical & Hospital Equipment); 5084 (Industrial Machinery & Equipment); 5085 (Industrial Supplies); 5122 (Drugs, Proprietaries & Sundries). **Emp:** 13. **Officers:** Kenneth C. Mundy, CEO.

■ 3004 ■ **Thomas W. Murray**
PO Box 214
Dover, DE 19903
Phone: (302)736-1790
Free: (877)736-1790 **Fax:** (302)674-8230
E-mail: murco@dmv.com
Products: Military vehicle parts, including jeep parts and trucks. **SIC:** 5013 (Motor Vehicle Supplies & New Parts). **Est:** 1942. **Officers:** John S. Murray.

■ 3005 ■ **Mustang Power Systems**
7777 Washington Ave.
Houston, TX 77007
Phone: (713)861-0777 **Fax:** (713)861-0500
Products: Diesel engines and generators. **SIC:** 5013 (Motor Vehicle Supplies & New Parts). **Sales:** $11,000,000 (1993). **Emp:** 76. **Officers:** F. Louis Tucker, President; J.W. Slaughter, VP of Finance.

■ 3006 ■ **Mutual Truck Parts Co.**
2000-04 S Wabash Ave.
Chicago, IL 60616
Phone: (312)225-3500 **Fax:** (312)225-6586
Products: Automotive parts and supplies, New; Spark plugs. **SIC:** 5013 (Motor Vehicle Supplies & New Parts). **Est:** 1934. **Sales:** $900,000 (2000). **Emp:** 10. **Officers:** Marilyn B. Hochberg, President.

■ 3007 ■ **Mutual Wheel Co.**
2345 4th Ave.
Moline, IL 61265
Phone: (309)757-1200
Products: Industrial truck parts. **SIC:** 5084 (Industrial Machinery & Equipment). **Sales:** $24,000,000 (1993). **Emp:** 78. **Officers:** David Engstrom, President; Alan Johnson, CFO.

■ 3008 ■ **MVR Auto Refinishing Supplies**
891 Alua, No. B3
Wailuku, HI 96793
Phone: (808)242-8175 **Fax:** (808)242-7488
Products: Paints and varnishes. **SIC:** 5013 (Motor Vehicle Supplies & New Parts). **Sales:** $400,000 (2000). **Emp:** 4.

■ 3009 ■ **Myco Plastics**
1550 5th St. SW
Winter Haven, FL 33880
Phone: (941)299-7580
Free: (800)749-MYCO **Fax:** (941)299-1593
Products: Automobile accessories, including tags and plastic letters. **SIC:** 5013 (Motor Vehicle Supplies & New Parts).

■ 3010 ■ **Myers Equipment Corp.**
8860 Akron-Canfield Rd.
Canfield, OH 44406
Phone: (330)533-5556 **Fax:** (330)533-2784
Products: Thomas bus body parts and supplies, new and used. **SIC:** 5013 (Motor Vehicle Supplies & New Parts). **Est:** 1947. **Emp:** 39. **Officers:** David Myers, President & Owner; James Drotleff, Sales Mgr.

■ 3011 ■ **Myers Industries Inc.**
1293 S Main St.
Akron, OH 44301
Phone: (330)253-5592 **Fax:** (330)253-6568
E-mail: sales@po.myerstiresupply.com
URL: http://www.myertiresupply.com
Products: Tire repair and car underbody service products. **SIC:** 5013 (Motor Vehicle Supplies & New Parts). **Est:** 1933. **Sales:** $392,000,000 (2000). **Emp:** 2,503. **Officers:** Stephen E. Myers, CEO & President; Gregory J. Stodnick, VP & CFO.

■ 3012 ■ **Myers Industries Inc. Myers Tire Supply**
PO Box 1029
Akron, OH 44309
Phone: (330)253-5592
Products: Tire repair supplies. **SIC:** 5014 (Tires & Tubes). **Sales:** $308,000,000 (2000). **Emp:** 480. **Officers:** Steven Myers, President.

■ 3013 ■ **Nalley Cos.**
87 W Paces Ferry Rd.
Atlanta, GA 30305
Phone: (404)261-3130 **Fax:** (404)261-8742
Products: Automobiles and heavy trucks. **SIC:** 5012 (Automobiles & Other Motor Vehicles). **Sales:** $350,000,000 (2000). **Emp:** 600. **Officers:** C.V. Nalley III, President; Larry Davis, CFO.

■ 3014 ■ **Nankang USA Inc.**
300 W Artesia Blvd.
Compton, CA 90220-5530
Phone: (310)604-8760
Free: (800)227-8925 **Fax:** (310)637-8952
E-mail: sales@nankangusa.com
URL: http://www.nankangusa.com
Products: Tires, wheels, and tubes. **SICs:** 5014 (Tires & Tubes); 5013 (Motor Vehicle Supplies & New Parts). **Est:** 1972. **Officers:** Robert W. Liu; Mimi W. Liu; Dave Jones, Sales/Marketing Contact. **Alternate Name:** SenDel Wheel.

■ 3015 ■ **National Bushing and Parts Company Inc.**
PO Box 7007
St. Cloud, MN 56302
Phone: (320)251-3221
Products: Automobile parts, including carburetors and transmissions. **SIC:** 5013 (Motor Vehicle Supplies & New Parts). **Est:** 1921. **Sales:** $6,400,000 (2000). **Emp:** 61. **Officers:** Timothy Feddema, CEO; James Albers, CFO; Donald Kussman, Sales Mgr.

■ 3016 ■ **National Impala Association**
2928 4th Ave.
PO Box 968
Spearfish, SD 57783
Phone: (605)642-5864 **Fax:** (605)642-5868
E-mail: impala@blackhills.com
URL: http://www.impala.blackhills.com
Products: Classic automobile parts. **SIC:** 5013 (Motor Vehicle Supplies & New Parts). **Est:** 1980. **Emp:** 2. **Officers:** Dennis L. Naasz, President.

■ 3017 ■ **National Wine and Spirits Corp.**
PO Box 1602
Indianapolis, IN 46206-1607
Phone: (317)636-6092 **Fax:** (317)685-8810
Products: Wine, spirits, and non-alcoholic beverages. **SICs:** 5182 (Wines & Distilled Beverages); 5149 (Groceries & Related Products Nec). **Sales:** $168,000,000 (2000). **Emp:** 525. **Officers:** James Beck, President; Pat Trefun, VP of Finance.

■ 3018 ■ **NBC Truck Equipment Inc.**
28130 Groesbeck Hwy.
Roseville, MI 48066
Phone: (810)774-4900 **Fax:** (810)772-1280
E-mail: nbctrk@rust.net
URL: http://www.nbctruckequip.com
Products: Automotive parts and supplies, New. **SIC:** 5013 (Motor Vehicle Supplies & New Parts). **Est:** 1968. **Emp:** 63. **Officers:** Bill Roland, President; Tom DeSchryver, Sales/Marketing Contact; Daniel A. Sabedra Jr., Human Resources Contact.

■ 3019 ■ **Neapco Inc.**
Queen St. & Bailey St.
Pottstown, PA 19464
Phone: (610)323-6000 **Fax:** (610)324-2551
Products: Automotive parts, including original parts.
SICs: 5013 (Motor Vehicle Supplies & New Parts);
5015 (Motor Vehicle Parts—Used). **Sales:**
$30,000,000 (2000). **Emp:** 499. **Officers:** Ronald H.
Vaughn.

■ 3020 ■ **Neely TBA**
6940 Clinton
Houston, TX 77020
Phone: (713)675-0924 **Fax:** (713)675-9162
Products: Automobile and truck parts. **SIC:** 5013
(Motor Vehicle Supplies & New Parts). **Est:** 1959.
Emp: 6.

■ 3021 ■ **Neil Parts Distribution Corp.**
1900 Route 112
Medford, NY 11763-0787
Phone: (516)758-1144
Products: Auto parts. **SIC:** 5015 (Motor Vehicle
Parts—Used). **Sales:** $52,000,000 (1993). **Emp:** 100.
Officers: Neil Feldstein, President.

■ 3022 ■ **Neil's Automotive Service, Inc.**
167 E Kalamazoo
Kalamazoo, MI 49007
Phone: (616)342-9855 **Fax:** (616)342-4261
Products: Automotive parts and supplies, New. **SIC:**
5013 (Motor Vehicle Supplies & New Parts). **Officers:**
Stephanie Peters, Contact.

■ 3023 ■ **Neil's Automotive Service, Inc.**
62915 Red Arrow Hwy.
Hartford, MI 49057
Phone: (616)621-2434 **Fax:** (616)621-2105
Products: Automotive parts and supplies, New. **SIC:**
5013 (Motor Vehicle Supplies & New Parts). **Officers:**
Pat Peters, Contact.

■ 3024 ■ **Nelson Leasing Inc.**
PO Box 993
Willmar, MN 56201
Phone: (320)235-2770
Free: (800)247-9002 **Fax:** (320)235-7780
Products: Trucks and truck parts; Truck rentals. **SICs:**
5012 (Automobiles & Other Motor Vehicles); 5013
(Motor Vehicle Supplies & New Parts). **Sales:**
$37,000,000 (1999). **Emp:** 110. **Officers:** Dale Nelson,
President & CFO.

■ 3025 ■ **Ness Company Inc.**
PO Box 667
York, PA 17405
Phone: (717)792-9791 **Fax:** (717)792-9794
Products: Parts and attachments for industrial trucks
and tractors; Motor vehicle parts and accessories.
SICs: 5088 (Transportation Equipment & Supplies);
5013 (Motor Vehicle Supplies & New Parts). **Est:** 1892.
Sales: $1,700,000 (2000). **Emp:** 14. **Officers:** Thomas
C. Wozniak, CEO & President; Beulah R. Odorfer,
Treasurer; William S. McElhiney, Exec. VP.

■ 3026 ■ **Ness Trading Co.**
5730 Natural Bridge Ave.
St. Louis, MO 63120
Phone: (314)381-4900
Free: (800)769-6377 **Fax:** (314)381-2941
E-mail: nesstrade@aol.com
URL: http://www.nesstrading.com
Products: Automotive parts and accessories. **SIC:**
5013 (Motor Vehicle Supplies & New Parts). **Est:** 1984.
Sales: $3,000,000 (2000). **Emp:** 8. **Officers:** Bonnie
Laiderman, Vice President; Howard Laiderman,
President.

■ 3027 ■ **New Haven Body, Inc.**
395 State St.
PO Box 474
North Haven, CT 06473
Phone: (203)248-6388 **Fax:** (203)281-0060
Products: Truck equipment. **SIC:** 5013 (Motor Vehicle
Supplies & New Parts). **Est:** 1992. **Emp:** 9. **Officers:**
Dave Cataldo, Contact.

■ 3028 ■ **New Haven Filter Co.**
PO Box 16
New Haven, MO 63068
Phone: (573)237-3081 **Fax:** (573)237-3083
Products: Filters for large diesel trucks. **SIC:** 5013
(Motor Vehicle Supplies & New Parts). **Est:** 1961.
Sales: $5,000,000 (2000). **Emp:** 15. **Officers:** Thomas
Plummer, President; Clyde Ruegge, Treasurer.

■ 3029 ■ **New Mexico Salvage Pool**
7705 Broadway Blvd. SE
Albuquerque, NM 87105-7455
Phone: (505)877-2424 **Fax:** (505)873-1152
Products: Automobile parts, used. **SIC:** 5015 (Motor
Vehicle Parts—Used). **Officers:** Ray Auge, Owner.

■ 3030 ■ **New World Research Corp.**
50 Broad Street, Suite 412
New York, NY 10004
Phone: (212)509-9091 **Fax:** (212)509-9221
Products: Office equipment; Medical and hospital
equipment; Electrical apparatus and equipment;
Hardware; Motor vehicle supplies and parts. **SICs:**
5013 (Motor Vehicle Supplies & New Parts); 5044
(Office Equipment); 5047 (Medical & Hospital
Equipment); 5063 (Electrical Apparatus & Equipment);
5072 (Hardware). **Est:** 1945. **Officers:** B.L. Light,
President.

■ 3031 ■ **Nichols Fleet Equipment**
2919 8th Ave.
PO Box 72638
Chattanooga, TN 37407
Phone: (423)622-7528 **Fax:** (423)622-7809
Products: Automotive parts and supplies, New. **SIC:**
5013 (Motor Vehicle Supplies & New Parts). **Officers:**
David Nichols, President.

■ 3032 ■ **Nick's Junk Inc.**
PO Box 3392
Casper, WY 82602-3392
Phone: (307)265-5833
Products: Automobile parts, used. **SIC:** 5015 (Motor
Vehicle Parts—Used). **Officers:** Mohsen Amir,
President.

■ 3033 ■ **Nikzak**
6924 Valjean Ave.
Van Nuys, CA 91406
Phone: (818)901-9031 **Fax:** (818)901-0218
Products: Automotive seat covers. **SIC:** 5013 (Motor
Vehicle Supplies & New Parts).

■ 3034 ■ **Nippondenso of Los Angeles Inc.**
3900 Via Oro Ave.
Long Beach, CA 90810
Phone: (310)834-6352
Products: Electronic automotive parts. **SIC:** 5013
(Motor Vehicle Supplies & New Parts). **Est:** 1971.
Sales: $81,000,000 (2000). **Emp:** 335. **Officers:** K.
Amano, President; Don Ohira, Controller; Dennis
Taylor, Marketing Mgr.; Mark Jonas, Information
Systems Mgr.; Jona Hester, Human Resources Mgr.

■ 3035 ■ **Nitto Tires**
10805 Holder St., Ste. 175
Cypress, CA 90630
Phone: (714)236-1863
Free: (888)648-8652 **Fax:** (714)252-0008
E-mail: http://www.nittotire.com
Products: Tires. **SIC:** 5014 (Tires & Tubes). **Emp:** 12.

■ 3036 ■ **Noel's Automotive Warehouse**
605 S Gallatin
PO Box 3487
Jackson, MS 39207
Phone: (601)948-4381 **Fax:** (601)948-4386
Products: Automobile parts. **SIC:** 5013 (Motor Vehicle
Supplies & New Parts). **Emp:** 70. **Officers:** Mack T.
Morgan; Joseph Kenneth Long. **Alternate Name:**
Brandon Auto Supply. **Alternate Name:** Professional
Auto Parts. **Alternate Name:** Super Parts Place.

■ 3037 ■ **Noleen Racing Inc.**
17525 Alder St., Ste. 16
Hesperia, CA 92345-5005
Phone: (760)246-5000
Products: Automotive suspensions. **SIC:** 5013 (Motor

Vehicle Supplies & New Parts). **Sales:** $3,000,000
(2000). **Emp:** 15. **Officers:** Clark Jones, President.

■ 3038 ■ **Nordstroms**
25513 480th Ave.
Garretson, SD 57030-9340
Phone: (605)594-3910
Products: Automobile parts, used. **SIC:** 5015 (Motor
Vehicle Parts—Used). **Officers:** Art Nordstrom, Owner.

■ 3039 ■ **Norse Motors Inc.**
255 Lafayette St.
London, OH 43140
Phone: (614)852-1122
Products: Automobiles. **SIC:** 5012 (Automobiles &
Other Motor Vehicles). **Est:** 1980. **Sales:** $21,000,000
(2000). **Emp:** 50. **Officers:** Barbara Sanford,
President.

■ 3040 ■ **North 54 Salvage Yard**
PO Box 387
Alamogordo, NM 88311-0387
Phone: (505)437-4188
Products: Automobile parts, used. **SIC:** 5015 (Motor
Vehicle Parts—Used). **Officers:** Truitt Smith,
President.

■ 3041 ■ **North American Cylinders Inc.**
PO Box 128
Citronelle, AL 36522
Phone: (205)866-2400
Products: Gasoline cylinders. **SIC:** 5013 (Motor
Vehicle Supplies & New Parts). **Sales:** $24,000,000
(2000). **Emp:** 40. **Officers:** Michael Rabren, President.

■ 3042 ■ **North Penn Equipment**
903 Lambson Ln.
New Castle, DE 19720
Phone: (302)654-1990 **Fax:** (302)654-3429
Products: Truck parts and supplies. **SIC:** 5013 (Motor
Vehicle Supplies & New Parts).

■ 3043 ■ **North Providence Auto Salvation**
940 Smithfield Rd.
Providence, RI 02904-2911
Phone: (401)353-6720
Products: Automobile parts, used. **SIC:** 5015 (Motor
Vehicle Parts—Used). **Officers:** William Breault,
Owner.

■ 3044 ■ **North Riverside Venture Inc.**
50 Technology Park
Norcross, GA 30092
Phone: (404)446-5556
Products: Automotive parts. **SIC:** 5013 (Motor Vehicle
Supplies & New Parts). **Sales:** $61,000,000 (1993).
Emp: 251. **Officers:** Ken Voelker, President.

■ 3045 ■ **Northeast Tire of Maine**
1178 Hammond St.
Bangor, ME 04401
Phone: (207)945-4517
Products: Tires. **SIC:** 5014 (Tires & Tubes).

■ 3046 ■ **Northern Auto Supply Co.**
1906 N Peach Ave.
Marshfield, WI 54449
Phone: (715)384-2124
Products: Automotive parts and supplies, New. **SIC:**
5013 (Motor Vehicle Supplies & New Parts). **Est:** 1918.
Sales: $18,000,000 (2000). **Emp:** 169. **Officers:** Don
Komis, CEO & President; David Lockwood, CFO; Ron
Kranning, VP of Marketing.

■ 3047 ■ **Northland Equipment Company, Inc.**
306 W State St.
Janesville, WI 53546
Phone: (608)754-6608
Free: (800)362-0731 **Fax:** (608)754-0675
Products: Automotive parts and supplies, New. **SIC:**
5013 (Motor Vehicle Supplies & New Parts). **Officers:**
James Shebiel, Vice President.

■ 3048 ■ **Norwood Auto Parts Co.**
624 Broadway
Long Branch, NJ 07740-4007
Phone: (732)222-3833
Products: Auto body supplies, including paint and
tools. **SICs:** 5013 (Motor Vehicle Supplies & New
Parts); 5198 (Paints, Varnishes & Supplies). **Est:** 1942.

Sales: $15,000,000 (2000). **Emp:** 150. **Officers:** Patrick McElduff, CEO; Chris Browne, Dir. of Marketing.

■ 3049 ■ Nova Clutch Inc.
39 Front St.
Brooklyn, NY 11201-1063
Phone: (718)858-8282
Free: (800)600-1521 **Fax:** (718)935-0885
E-mail: novaclutch@novaclutch.com
Products: Automotive clutches. **SIC:** 5013 (Motor Vehicle Supplies & New Parts). **Est:** 1974. **Emp:** 49.

■ 3050 ■ Number One International
1775 S Redwood Rd.
Salt Lake City, UT 84104
Phone: (801)975-5900
Products: Automotive engine parts; Diesel engine parts. **SICs:** 5013 (Motor Vehicle Supplies & New Parts); 5084 (Industrial Machinery & Equipment). **Est:** 1973. **Sales:** $10,000,000 (2000). **Emp:** 42. **Officers:** Rex Falkenrath, President; Ray Falkenrath, Vice President.

■ 3051 ■ Nylen Products Inc.
1436 E 19th St.
Indianapolis, IN 46218-4228
Products: Engine parts, including pistons, pins, and sleeves. **SIC:** 5013 (Motor Vehicle Supplies & New Parts). **Sales:** $2,000,000 (2000). **Emp:** 99. **Officers:** William Ertel Sr.

■ 3052 ■ Ochterbeck Distributing Company Inc.
2405 Jackson St.
Houston, TX 77004
Phone: (713)659-4922 **Fax:** (713)659-3309
Products: Automotive and truck accessories. **SIC:** 5013 (Motor Vehicle Supplies & New Parts). **Sales:** $4,000,000 (2000). **Emp:** 29. **Officers:** Lloyd Ochterbeck, President; Charles Ochterbeck, CFO; Chris Castleberry, Dir. of Operations.

■ 3053 ■ O'Connor Truck Sales Inc.
H St & Hunting Park Av
Philadelphia, PA 19124
Phone: (215)744-8500 **Fax:** (215)288-5430
Products: Trucks and parts. **SICs:** 5012 (Automobiles & Other Motor Vehicles); 5015 (Motor Vehicle Parts—Used). **Sales:** $52,000,000 (2000). **Emp:** 54. **Officers:** Jack Corr, President; John Clark, CFO.

■ 3054 ■ OEM Parts Center Inc.
110 S Sherman St.
Spokane, WA 99202-1529
Phone: (509)838-3525 **Fax:** (509)838-0105
Products: Automobile, truck, and industrial vehicle parts. **SIC:** 5013 (Motor Vehicle Supplies & New Parts). **Est:** 1964. **Sales:** $3,000,000 (2000). **Emp:** 35. **Officers:** Kenneth Dunlap, President.

■ 3055 ■ Off Road Specialty
4866 Fenton St.
Boise, ID 83714-1411
Phone: (208)376-3974 **Fax:** (208)376-3967
Products: Automobile parts, used. **SIC:** 5015 (Motor Vehicle Parts—Used). **Officers:** Lamont Kouba, Owner.

■ 3056 ■ Offenhauser Sales Corp.
PO Box 32218
Los Angeles, CA 90032
Phone: (213)225-1307 **Fax:** (213)225-2789
Products: Automotive parts and supplies, New. **SIC:** 5013 (Motor Vehicle Supplies & New Parts). **Est:** 1946. **Sales:** $1,000,000 (2000). **Emp:** 13. **Officers:** Fred C Offenhauser Jr.; Jim Offenhauser.

■ 3057 ■ Ohio Auto Rebuilders Supply, Inc.
2389 Refugee Pk.
Columbus, OH 43207-2173
Phone: (614)443-0526 **Fax:** (614)443-0590
Products: Automobile engines, used; Automobile parts, used. **SIC:** 5015 (Motor Vehicle Parts—Used). **Est:** 1958. **Emp:** 19. **Officers:** William E. Harris Sr., President; William E. Harris Jr., Sec. & Treas.

■ 3058 ■ Ohio Light Truck Parts Co.
217 W 3rd St.
Dover, OH 44622
Phone: (330)364-1881 **Fax:** (330)364-3616
Products: Light truck parts, including running boards and hubcaps. **SIC:** 5013 (Motor Vehicle Supplies & New Parts). **Est:** 1980. **Sales:** $1,000,000 (2000). **Emp:** 3. **Officers:** Mel Zook, President; Bruce Goedel, Manager.

■ 3059 ■ Ohio Truck Equipment, Inc.
4100 Rev Dr.
Cincinnati, OH 45232
Phone: (513)541-4700
Free: (800)543-4411 **Fax:** (513)542-0526
Products: Automotive parts and supplies, New. **SIC:** 5013 (Motor Vehicle Supplies & New Parts). **Officers:** Ken Revelson, President.

■ 3060 ■ O.K. Auto Parts
1730 W Michigan St.
Duluth, MN 55806
Phone: (218)722-6233
Products: Automotive parts, including alternators, starters, and spark plugs. **SIC:** 5013 (Motor Vehicle Supplies & New Parts). **Est:** 1947. **Sales:** $600,000 (2000). **Emp:** 90. **Officers:** Jim Karvonen, General Mgr.

■ 3061 ■ OK Hafens Tire Store Inc.
505 W Lake Mead Dr.
Henderson, NV 89015-7015
Phone: (702)564-5312
Products: Used motor vehicle parts, including used tires. **SICs:** 5015 (Motor Vehicle Parts—Used); 5014 (Tires & Tubes). **Officers:** Kathleen Hafen, President.

■ 3062 ■ Oldsmobile Div.
920 Townsend St.
Lansing, MI 48921
Phone: (517)377-5000 **Fax:** (517)377-2833
Products: Motor vehicles. **SIC:** 5012 (Automobiles & Other Motor Vehicles). **Sales:** $110,000,000 (2000). **Emp:** 600. **Officers:** Darwin E. Clark, General Mgr.; Christopher Y. Meyer, Comptroller.

■ 3063 ■ Orange Motor Company Inc.
799 Central Ave.
Albany, NY 12206
Phone: (518)489-5414
Products: Car parts, including motors. **SIC:** 5013 (Motor Vehicle Supplies & New Parts). **Est:** 1916. **Sales:** $52,000,000 (2000). **Emp:** 130. **Officers:** Carl E. Touhey, President & Treasurer.

■ 3064 ■ O'Reilly Automotive Inc.
233 S Patterson Ave.
Springfield, MO 65801
Phone: (417)862-6708 **Fax:** (417)869-8903
Products: Auto parts and supplies. **SIC:** 5013 (Motor Vehicle Supplies & New Parts). **Sales:** $316,400,000 (2000). **Emp:** 3,945. **Officers:** David E. O'Reilly, CEO & President; James R. Batten, CFO & Treasurer.

■ 3065 ■ Ost and Ost Inc.
1265 W Laurel Blvd.
Pottsville, PA 17901
Phone: (717)622-4330 **Fax:** (717)622-9416
Products: Automotive parts and supplies, New; Industrial supplies. **SICs:** 5013 (Motor Vehicle Supplies & New Parts); 5085 (Industrial Supplies). **Est:** 1925. **Sales:** $2,400,000 (2000). **Emp:** 38. **Officers:** Daniel C. Ost, President; Clayton F. Ost, VP & Treasurer.

■ 3066 ■ Ozark Automotive Distributors Inc.
233 S Patterson Ave.
Springfield, MO 65802
Phone: (417)862-6708 **Fax:** (417)369-8903
Products: Auto parts, including spark plugs and carburetors. **SIC:** 5013 (Motor Vehicle Supplies & New Parts). **Est:** 1957. **Sales:** $72,000,000 (2000). **Emp:** 500. **Officers:** David O'Reilly, President; Ann Drennan, CFO; Larry Pryor, Dir. of Marketing; Mike Williams, Dir. of Information Systems; Steve Pope, Dir of Human Resources.

■ 3067 ■ P & B Truck Accessories
2122 S Stoughton Rd.
Madison, WI 53716
Phone: (608)222-4499 **Fax:** (608)221-0915
Products: Automotive parts and supplies, New. **SIC:** 5013 (Motor Vehicle Supplies & New Parts). **Officers:** Steve Clausen, Contact.

■ 3068 ■ P and E Inc.
709 Two Mile Pkwy.
Goodlettsville, TN 37072-2315
Phone: (615)327-1210
Products: Automobile parts and equipment, including seats, carburetors, brakes, starters, and racing equipment. **SIC:** 5013 (Motor Vehicle Supplies & New Parts).

■ 3069 ■ P-G Products Inc.
2831 Stanton Ave.
Cincinnati, OH 45206
Phone: (513)961-5500 **Fax:** (513)961-2045
Products: Recycled automobile bumpers. **SIC:** 5013 (Motor Vehicle Supplies & New Parts). **Est:** 1958. **Sales:** $5,000,000 (2000). **Emp:** 60. **Officers:** Don R. Gorman, President.

■ 3070 ■ PACCAR Inc. Parts Div.
750 Houser Way N
Renton, WA 98055
Phone: (425)251-7400 **Fax:** (425)254-6200
Products: Truck parts, including brakes, axles, and bumpers. **SIC:** 5013 (Motor Vehicle Supplies & New Parts). **Sales:** $420,000,000 (2000). **Emp:** 650. **Officers:** Bob Christensen, General Mgr.

■ 3071 ■ PACCAR International
777 106th Ave. NE
PO Box 1518
Bellevue, WA 98009
Phone: (425)828-8872 **Fax:** (425)828-8882
E-mail: paccint@ibm.net
URL: http://www.paccar.com
Products: Heavy-duty trucks; Motor vehicle parts for trucks; Construction machinery, including winches. **SICs:** 5013 (Motor Vehicle Supplies & New Parts); 5012 (Automobiles & Other Motor Vehicles); 5082 (Construction & Mining Machinery).

■ 3072 ■ PACCAR Leasing Corp.
PO Box 1518
Bellevue, WA 98009
Phone: (425)455-7400
Free: (800)426-1420 **Fax:** (425)637-5046
Products: Heavy-duty trucks and industrial winches; Automotive parts and related services. **SIC:** 5013 (Motor Vehicle Supplies & New Parts). **Sales:** $24,000,000 (2000). **Emp:** 170.

■ 3073 ■ Paccar Technical Ctr.
1261 Farm To Market Rd.
Mt. Vernon, WA 98273
Phone: (360)757-8311
Products: Trucks. **SIC:** 5012 (Automobiles & Other Motor Vehicles).

■ 3074 ■ Pacific Dualies, Inc.
13637 Cimarron Ave.
Gardena, CA 90249
Phone: (310)516-9898
Free: (800)426-0584 **Fax:** (310)516-8797
E-mail: pdi@pacific-dualies.com
URL: http://www.pacific-dualies.com
Products: Automotive parts. **SIC:** 5013 (Motor Vehicle Supplies & New Parts). **Est:** 1969. **Sales:** $15,000,000 (2000). **Emp:** 15. **Officers:** Steve Wang, President; Mike Wang, Vice President; Danny Dudas, Sales/Marketing Contact; Anna Gutierrez, Customer Service Contact; Angela Griffith.

■ 3075 ■ Pacific Supply Co.
900 Arlee Pl.
Anaheim, CA 92805
Phone: (714)778-3313
Products: Automotive parts. **SIC:** 5013 (Motor Vehicle Supplies & New Parts). **Sales:** $60,000,000 (2000). **Emp:** 350. **Officers:** Brad Wayne, President; Jim Lane, CFO; Pat Winters, Dir. of Marketing.

■ 3076 ■ **PAFCO Truck Bodies Inc.**
1954 E Washington St.
East Peoria, IL 61611
Phone: (309)699-4613
Free: (800)257-2580   **Fax:** (309)699-5360
Products: Automotive parts and supplies, New. **SIC:**
5013 (Motor Vehicle Supplies & New Parts). **Officers:**
Max Pfaffmann, President.

■ 3077 ■ **Palmetto Ford Truck Sales Inc.**
7245 NW 36th St.
Miami, FL 33166
Phone: (305)592-3673
Products: Interior and exterior truck parts, including
brakes, axles, and truck beds. **SIC:** 5013 (Motor
Vehicle Supplies & New Parts). **Est:** 1966. **Sales:**
$28,000,000 (2000). **Emp:** 80. **Officers:** H. William
Grant, President; Robert Yglesias, Finance Officer.

■ 3078 ■ **Pam Oil Inc.**
PO Box 5200
Sioux Falls, SD 57117-5200
Phone: (605)336-1788   **Fax:** (605)339-9909
Products: Automotive supplies including antifreeze
and oil. **SIC:** 5013 (Motor Vehicle Supplies & New
Parts). **Sales:** $150,000,000 (2000). **Emp:** 400.
Officers: William G. Pederson, President; Dennis
Schulte, CFO.

■ 3079 ■ **Jim Paris Tire City of Montbello Inc.**
1150 E 58th Ave.
Denver, CO 80216
Phone: (303)297-3600
Products: Tires. **SIC:** 5014 (Tires & Tubes). **Sales:**
$22,500,000 (1992). **Emp:** 135. **Officers:** James T.
Paris, President & CFO.

■ 3080 ■ **Parker Brothers and Company Inc.**
PO Box 107
Houston, TX 77001
Phone: (713)928-8400   **Fax:** (713)928-8490
Products: Truck equipment and supplies. **SIC:** 5013
(Motor Vehicle Supplies & New Parts). **Est:** 1928.
Sales: $9,000,000 (2000). **Emp:** 38. **Officers:** Timothy
H. Parker, CEO & President; James Trimble, Exec. VP
of Finance; Jill Devoti, Dir. of Marketing; Terry
Carberry, Controller.

■ 3081 ■ **Parkway Automotive Warehouse**
640 W Brooks St.
Ontario, CA 91762
Phone: (714)983-2651   **Fax:** (714)983-5933
E-mail: pawgra@gte.net
Products: Automotive parts and supplies, New. **SIC:**
5013 (Motor Vehicle Supplies & New Parts). **Est:** 1973.
Sales: $3,200,000 (2000). **Emp:** 9. **Officers:** Charles
Stokke, President.

■ 3082 ■ **Parts Depot Company L.P.**
PO Box 13785
Roanoke, VA 24037
Phone: (540)345-1001   **Fax:** (540)983-7924
URL: http://www.allprobumpertobumper.com
Products: Automotive and truck parts. **SIC:** 5013
(Motor Vehicle Supplies & New Parts). **Est:** 1948.
Sales: $110,000,000 (1999). **Emp:** 800. **Officers:**
Rollie Olson, CEO & Chairman of the Board; Willi
Alexander, President & COO.

■ 3083 ■ **Parts Inc.**
PO Box 429
Memphis, TN 38101
Phone: (901)523-7711   **Fax:** (901)524-5582
Products: Automobile parts and supplies, including
paint, wax, and oil. **SICs:** 5013 (Motor Vehicle Supplies
& New Parts); 5198 (Paints, Varnishes & Supplies);
5172 (Petroleum Products Nec). **Sales:** $270,000,000
(2000). **Emp:** 2,500. **Officers:** Kenneth Walker,
President; Anthony Buttanshaw, VP & CFO; Mike
Crawford, Dir. of Marketing; Jim Meeks, Dir. of
Information Systems; Ronald Polk, VP of Human
Resources.

■ 3084 ■ **Parts Plus of Dearborn**
PO Box 429
Memphis, TN 38101-0429
Phone: (901)582-3300
Products: Automotive parts. **SIC:** 5013 (Motor Vehicle

Supplies & New Parts). **Sales:** $12,000,000 (2000).
Emp: 27. **Officers:** Frank Abrams, Manager.

■ 3085 ■ **Parts Warehouse Inc.**
1901 E Roosevelt Rd.
Little Rock, AR 72206
Phone: (501)375-1215
Products: Automobile parts. **SIC:** 5013 (Motor Vehicle
Supplies & New Parts). **Est:** 1957. **Sales:** $30,000,000
(2000). **Emp:** 140. **Officers:** Bob Raff, President; Bill
Kuykendall, Vice President.

■ 3086 ■ **Pasha Group Co.**
802 S Fries St.
Wilmington, CA 90744
Phone: (562)437-0911
Products: Automobile accessories. **SIC:** 5013 (Motor
Vehicle Supplies & New Parts). **Sales:** $36,000,000
(1993). **Emp:** 150. **Officers:** George Pasha III,
President.

■ 3087 ■ **Patron Transmission**
394 1st St.
Hackensack, NJ 07601
Phone: (201)343-2200   **Fax:** (201)343-0808
Products: Power transmissions. **SICs:** 5084 (Industrial
Machinery & Equipment); 5013 (Motor Vehicle Supplies
& New Parts).

■ 3088 ■ **Peach State Truck Centers**
I-85 Jimmy Carter Blvd.
Norcross, GA 30091
Phone: (770)449-5300
Free: (800)367-3878   **Fax:** (770)447-0984
Products: Heavy-duty trucks. **SIC:** 5012 (Automobiles
& Other Motor Vehicles). **Est:** 1974. **Sales:**
$50,000,000 (2000). **Emp:** 140. **Officers:** Thomas B.
Reynolds, President; Dennis Worrall, VP & CFO.
Former Name: Peach State Ford Trucks Inc.

■ 3089 ■ **Penn Detroit Diesel**
Rte. 222
Fleetwood, PA 19522
Phone: (215)944-0451   **Fax:** (215)944-6019
Products: Truck parts. **SIC:** 5013 (Motor Vehicle
Supplies & New Parts).

■ 3090 ■ **Penn Detroit Diesel Allison Inc.**
8330 State Rd.
Philadelphia, PA 19136-2996
Phone: (215)335-0500   **Fax:** (215)335-2760
Products: Diesel engines and parts. **SIC:** 5084
(Industrial Machinery & Equipment). **Est:** 1935. **Sales:**
$50,000,000 (2000). **Emp:** 205. **Officers:** Christopher
Cannon, President; Don Nedorostek, Treasurer &
Secty.; G.L. Tiffan, Dir. of Marketing & Sales; Don
Bryan, Dir. of Data Processing.

■ 3091 ■ **Performance Products**
8000 Haskell Ave.
Van Nuys, CA 91406
Phone: (818)787-7500   **Fax:** (818)787-2396
URL: http://www.performanceproducts.com
Products: Truck parts and accessories; Automotive
parts and accessories. **SIC:** 5013 (Motor Vehicle
Supplies & New Parts). **Est:** 1964. **Sales:** $24,000,000
(1999). **Emp:** 94. **Officers:** Ron Rowen, CEO &
President; Richard Sweeney, Sales/Marketing Contact;
David Palmer, Customer Service Contact.

■ 3092 ■ **The Performance Shop Inc.**
747 Gaffney Rd.
Fairbanks, AK 99701
Phone: (907)479-6125   **Fax:** (907)479-7125
E-mail: a4x4shop@alaska.net
Products: Auto parts and accessories. **SIC:** 5013
(Motor Vehicle Supplies & New Parts). **Est:** 1992.
Sales: $400,000 (2000). **Emp:** 3. **Former Name:**
Alaskan Paint & Paper.

■ 3093 ■ **Michael E. Perpall Enterprises**
455 Quaker Ln.
West Warwick, RI 02893-2114
Phone: (401)823-8500   **Fax:** (401)828-9330
Products: Automotive electronics. **SIC:** 5013 (Motor
Vehicle Supplies & New Parts). **Officers:** Michael
Perpall, President.

■ 3094 ■ **Peterbilt of Knoxville Inc.**
5218 Rutledge Pike
Knoxville, TN 37924
Phone: (615)546-9553
Products: Trucks and other vehicles. **SIC:** 5012
(Automobiles & Other Motor Vehicles). **Sales:**
$38,000,000 (1993). **Emp:** 77. **Officers:** J.T. Bailey,
CEO & Chairman of the Board.

■ 3095 ■ **Peugeot Citroen Engines**
150 Clove Rd.
Little Falls, NJ 07424-2138
Phone: (201)438-5559
Products: Automobile engines and drive train
components. **SIC:** 5013 (Motor Vehicle Supplies & New
Parts). **Sales:** $5,000,000 (1993). **Emp:** 5. **Officers:**
Richard A. Darienzo, Director.

■ 3096 ■ **Pfeiffer Hijet**
2424 28th St. SE
Grand Rapids, MI 49512
Phone: (616)949-7800
Free: (800)968-3366   **Fax:** (616)949-2656
Products: Automobiles and automobile parts. **SICs:**
5012 (Automobiles & Other Motor Vehicles); 5013
(Motor Vehicle Supplies & New Parts).

■ 3097 ■ **Phillips and Temro Industries**
9700 W 7th St.
Eden Prairie, MN 55344
Phone: (612)941-9700
Free: (800)328-6108   **Fax:** (612)941-2285
E-mail: sales@zerostart.com
URL: http://www.zerostart.com
Products: Automotive heaters and accessories. **SIC:**
5013 (Motor Vehicle Supplies & New Parts). **Est:** 1920.
Sales: $50,000,000 (1999). **Emp:** 550. **Officers:** Bill
Rose, President; Gary Edwards, Dir. of Business
Development; Kirk Nelson, Quality Assurance
Manager; Gary Markham, Controller; Greg Renberg, e-
mail: Renberg@ptibuddcompany.com; Ervin Sandul,
Customer Service Contact, e-mail: Sandul@
ptibuddcompany.com; Susan Warkentin, Human
Resources Contact, e-mail: Warkentin@
ptibuddcompany.com. **Alternate Name:** Thyssen
Krupp Automotive.

■ 3098 ■ **Pioneer Mercantile Co.**
PO Box 1709
Bakersfield, CA 93302
Phone: (805)327-8545   **Fax:** (805)327-3293
Products: Automotive parts and supplies, New;
Electronic ignitions; Carburetors, new and rebuilt. **SICs:**
5013 (Motor Vehicle Supplies & New Parts); 5015
(Motor Vehicle Parts—Used). **Est:** 1899. **Sales:**
$3,000,000 (2000). **Emp:** 41. **Officers:** Leo A.
Schamblin Sr., President.

■ 3099 ■ **Plaza Fleet Parts**
1520 S Broadway
St. Louis, MO 63104
Phone: (314)231-5047
Products: Truck parts and supplies. **SIC:** 5013 (Motor
Vehicle Supplies & New Parts). **Est:** 1946. **Sales:**
$19,000,000 (2000). **Emp:** 120. **Officers:** Louis J.
Boggeman, President; Mark Wilson, CFO; Skip Steffen,
Dir. of Marketing & Sales.

■ 3100 ■ **Point Spring Co.**
7307 Grand Ave.
Pittsburgh, PA 15225-1043
Phone: (412)264-3152   **Fax:** (412)264-4325
E-mail: ngva@pointspring.com
URL: http://www.pointspring.com
Products: Equipment for heavy duty trucks, including
springs, drive shafts, and transmissions. **SIC:** 5013
(Motor Vehicle Supplies & New Parts). **Est:** 1974.
Emp: 165. **Officers:** John W. Reder, Sales Mgr.

■ 3101 ■ **C.E. Pollard Co.**
13575 Auburn
Detroit, MI 48223
Phone: (313)837-6776   **Fax:** (313)837-5374
Products: Motorized vehicles. **SIC:** 5012 (Automobiles
& Other Motor Vehicles). **Sales:** $4,000,000 (2000).
Emp: 8.

■ **3102** ■ **Pomps Tire Service Inc.**
1123 Cedar St.
Green Bay, WI 54301
Phone: (920)435-8301
Products: Tires and inner tubes. **SIC:** 5014 (Tires & Tubes). **Est:** 1965. **Sales:** $80,000,000 (2000). **Emp:** 400. **Officers:** Jim Wochinske, CEO; T. Snyder, CFO; Tom Strehl, Dir. of Marketing.

■ **3103** ■ **Popes Parts Inc.**
PO Drawer 740
Thibodaux, LA 70302
Phone: (504)446-8485   **Fax:** (504)446-2869
Products: Automobile parts. **SIC:** 5013 (Motor Vehicle Supplies & New Parts). **Est:** 1955. **Sales:** $5,000,000 (2000). **Emp:** 47. **Officers:** Al Diez Jr., President & CFO.

■ **3104** ■ **Pos-A-Traction Inc.**
2400 S Wilmington Ave.
Compton, CA 90224-8010
Phone: (310)637-8600   **Fax:** (310)608-1536
Products: Motor vehicle tires. **SIC:** 5014 (Tires & Tubes). **Est:** 1939. **Sales:** $13,000,000 (2000). **Emp:** 20. **Officers:** Jay Krech, President; Tim Lowe, Dir. of Operations.

■ **3105** ■ **Potter-Webster Co.**
130 SE 7th Ave.
Portland, OR 97214
Phone: (503)232-8146   **Fax:** (503)232-3367
Products: Heavy-duty truck parts. **SIC:** 5013 (Motor Vehicle Supplies & New Parts).

■ **3106** ■ **Power Drive & Equipment**
3333 Locust Dr.
St. Louis, MO 63103
Phone: (314)533-3401
Free: (800)325-0626   **Fax:** (314)533-0159
Products: Drive shafts and truck equipment. **SICs:** 5013 (Motor Vehicle Supplies & New Parts); 5084 (Industrial Machinery & Equipment).

■ **3107** ■ **Power Drive, Inc.**
4401 W Esthner
Wichita, KS 67209
Phone: (316)942-4227
Free: (800)362-2680   **Fax:** (316)942-1311
E-mail: powerdrive@feist.com
URL: http://www.tpe-pdi.com
SICs: 5084 (Industrial Machinery & Equipment); 5013 (Motor Vehicle Supplies & New Parts). **Est:** 1970. **Emp:** 9. **Officers:** Jim Carpenter, Manager.

■ **3108** ■ **Power Drives, Inc.**
8031 Pence Rd.
PO Box 25427
Charlotte, NC 28229
Phone: (704)568-7480   **Fax:** (704)568-7256
E-mail: powerdrv@bellsouth.net
URL: http://www.power-drives.com
Products: Power transmissions. **SICs:** 5084 (Industrial Machinery & Equipment); 5013 (Motor Vehicle Supplies & New Parts). **Est:** 1969. **Emp:** 6.

■ **3109** ■ **Power Equipment Co.**
PO Box 20534
Rochester, NY 14602
Phone: (716)235-1662   **Fax:** (716)436-5578
E-mail: powermark@netacc.net
Products: Rebuilt electric motors and drives. **SIC:** 5063 (Electrical Apparatus & Equipment). **Est:** 1941. **Sales:** $1,000,000 (2000). **Emp:** 9. **Officers:** Mark Kolko, President. **Former Name:** Jilnance Corp.

■ **3110** ■ **Power Industries**
926 Kaiser Dr.
Napa, CA 94558-6206
Phone: (707)252-7333   **Fax:** (707)257-8547
Products: Power transmissions. **SICs:** 5084 (Industrial Machinery & Equipment); 5013 (Motor Vehicle Supplies & New Parts).

■ **3111** ■ **Power & Pumps Inc.**
3402 SW 26th Ter., No. B-11
Ft. Lauderdale, FL 33312-5071
Phone: (954)563-5627
Free: (800)918-7867   **Fax:** (954)566-3302
Products: Bearings; Electric motors; Pumps; Rubber

and plastic belts and belting, flat; Machine chain; Industrial supplies. **SICs:** 5085 (Industrial Supplies); 5013 (Motor Vehicle Supplies & New Parts). **Emp:** 15.

■ **3112** ■ **Power Torque**
1741 Rudder Industrial Park Dr.
Fenton, MO 63026
Phone: (314)343-2250   **Fax:** (314)343-4374
Products: Power transmissions; Ball bearings; Belts. **SICs:** 5084 (Industrial Machinery & Equipment); 5013 (Motor Vehicle Supplies & New Parts); 5085 (Industrial Supplies).

■ **3113** ■ **Powertron Battery Co.**
2218 W 2nd St.
Santa Ana, CA 92703
Phone: (714)543-4858
Free: (800)400-4858   **Fax:** (714)543-9211
E-mail: powertron@juno.com
Products: Batteries for commercial, marine, camcorder, cellphone, ups, alarms. Also offer alkaline, ni-cad, ni-mh, and lithium batteries. **SIC:** 5013 (Motor Vehicle Supplies & New Parts). **Est:** 1962. **Sales:** $1,000,000 (1999). **Emp:** 7. **Officers:** William L. Leonhardt, President; Dina E. Leonhardt, CFO; Craig Koehly, VP of Marketing, e-mail: powertron@juno.com; Drew Leonhardt, VP of Sales, e-mail: powertron@juno.com. **Doing Business As:** W.L. #Leonhardt Company Inc.

■ **3114** ■ **Precision Bearing Co.**
2050 Delaware
Des Moines, IA 50317
Phone: (515)265-9811   **Fax:** (515)262-5765
Products: Power transmission equipment and bearings. **SICs:** 5084 (Industrial Machinery & Equipment); 5013 (Motor Vehicle Supplies & New Parts).

■ **3115** ■ **Precision Built Parts**
1819 Troost Ave.
Kansas City, MO 64108
Phone: (816)471-1552   **Fax:** (816)471-0813
Products: Truck parts. **SIC:** 5013 (Motor Vehicle Supplies & New Parts).

■ **3116** ■ **Precision Industries Inc.**
4611 S 96th St.
Omaha, NE 68127
Phone: (402)593-7000   **Fax:** (402)593-7054
Products: Bearings, hydraulics, pneumatics, pumps, conveyors, power transmissions, pipe valve fittings and fastners. **SICs:** 5085 (Industrial Supplies); 5084 (Industrial Machinery & Equipment). **Sales:** $133,000,000 (2000). **Emp:** 600. **Officers:** Dennis Circo, President; Ron Haasee, Accounting Vice President.

■ **3117** ■ **Premier Industrial Corp.**
PO Box 94884
Cleveland, OH 44101
Phone: (216)391-8300   **Fax:** (216)391-8327
Products: Fasteners, welding equipment and supplies; Automotive replacement electronic components. **SIC:** 5065 (Electronic Parts & Equipment Nec). **Sales:** $818,200,000 (2000). **Emp:** 4,500. **Officers:** Peter Costello, CEO.

■ **3118** ■ **John Prior Inc.**
1600 Stewart Ave.
Westbury, NY 11590
Phone: (516)683-1020   **Fax:** (516)683-1024
Products: Automotive supplies and parts. **SIC:** 5013 (Motor Vehicle Supplies & New Parts). **Officers:** Ronald G. Prior, President.

■ **3119** ■ **Privilege Auto Parts**
95 Privilege Rd.
Woonsocket, RI 02895-0779
Phone: (401)766-8456
Products: Automobile parts, used. **SIC:** 5015 (Motor Vehicle Parts—Used). **Officers:** George Fontaine, Owner.

■ **3120** ■ **ProDiesel**
922 Main St.
Nashville, TN 37206
Phone: (615)227-2242
Free: (800)327-4373   **Fax:** (615)228-8259
E-mail: prodiesel@worldnet.att.net
Products: Diesel engines. **SIC:** 5084 (Industrial Machinery & Equipment). **Est:** 1958. **Sales:** $15,000,000 (2000). **Emp:** 170. **Officers:** Victoria Jackson, President; William A. Gregoricus, Exec. VP & General Mgr.

■ **3121** ■ **Progressive Tire**
3000 35th Ave. N
Birmingham, AL 35207
Phone: (205)841-3336
Products: Tires. **SIC:** 5014 (Tires & Tubes).

■ **3122** ■ **Progressive Tire Group**
950 Businesss Park Rd.
Wisconsin Dells, MI 53094
Products: Tires. **SIC:** 5014 (Tires & Tubes).

■ **3123** ■ **PullRite/Pulliam Enterprise Inc.**
13790 E Jefferson Blvd.
Mishawaka, IN 46545
Phone: (219)259-1520
Free: (800)443-2307   **Fax:** (219)258-0289
E-mail: info@pullrite.com
URL: http://www.pullrite.com
Products: Trailer towing systems, including weight equalizing and wheel hitches. **SICs:** 5088 (Transportation Equipment & Supplies); 5013 (Motor Vehicle Supplies & New Parts). **Est:** 1978. **Emp:** 30. **Officers:** Randall Pulliam, President.

■ **3124** ■ **Purolator Products**
3 Miracle Mile
Elmira, NY 14903-1031
Phone: (607)737-8011   **Fax:** (607)737-8335
Products: Clutches, brakes, fuel pumps, and starters. **SIC:** 5013 (Motor Vehicle Supplies & New Parts). **Sales:** $30,000,000 (2000). **Emp:** 400. **Officers:** Roman Boruta.

■ **3125** ■ **Purvis Bearing Service**
1315 S 7th St.
Corsicana, TX 75110
Phone: (903)874-4721   **Fax:** (903)872-7953
Products: Bearings; Power transmissions. **SICs:** 5084 (Industrial Machinery & Equipment); 5013 (Motor Vehicle Supplies & New Parts).

■ **3126** ■ **Purvis Bearing Service**
2413-17 Franklin Ave.
Box 797
Waco, TX 76708
Phone: (254)753-6477   **Fax:** (254)753-7122
Products: Power transmission equipment. **SICs:** 5084 (Industrial Machinery & Equipment); 5013 (Motor Vehicle Supplies & New Parts).

■ **3127** ■ **Putnam Truck Parts**
PO Box 157
Letcher, SD 57359-0157
Phone: (605)248-2648   **Fax:** (605)248-2650
Products: Truck parts; Trailers. **SICs:** 5015 (Motor Vehicle Parts—Used); 5012 (Automobiles & Other Motor Vehicles). **Est:** 1983. **Emp:** 5. **Officers:** Douglas Putnam, Owner; Linda Putnam, Owner. **Doing Business As:** Putnam Auto Sales.

■ **3128** ■ **Quaker City Motor Parts Co.**
PO Box 5000
Middletown, DE 19709
Phone: (302)378-9834   **Fax:** (302)378-0726
Products: Auto parts. **SIC:** 5013 (Motor Vehicle Supplies & New Parts). **Sales:** $48,000,000 (2000). **Emp:** 200. **Officers:** Michael Schwarz, President; James Duckworth, Exec. VP; Dennis Carruth, Sales Mgr.; Nita McBride, Data Processing Mgr.

■ **3129** ■ **Quality Truck Bodies & Repair, Inc.**
Firestone Pkwy.
PO Box 1669
Wilson, NC 27893
Phone: (919)291-5795
Free: (800)334-5182   **Fax:** (919)291-5367
Products: Automotive parts and supplies, New. **SIC:**

5013 (Motor Vehicle Supplies & New Parts). **Officers:** Gary Williams, Contact.

■ **3130** ■ **Quinsig Automotive Warehouse Inc.**
13 Quinsigamond Ave.
Worcester, MA 01608
Phone: (508)756-3536
Products: Automotive parts, including transmissions, motors, and starters. **SIC:** 5013 (Motor Vehicle Supplies & New Parts). **Est:** 1965. **Sales:** $7,000,000 (2000). **Emp:** 44. **Officers:** Bernard Minahan, President; Stephen Hodes, Treasurer; Gerald Ryan, Dir. of Marketing.

■ **3131** ■ **Brad Ragan Inc.**
PO Box 240587
Charlotte, NC 28224
Phone: (704)521-2100
Products: Tires. **SIC:** 5014 (Tires & Tubes). **Est:** 1943. **Sales:** $252,000,000 (2000). **Emp:** 1,750. **Officers:** William Brophey, CEO & President; Ronald J. Carr, VP, CFO & Treasurer.

■ **3132** ■ **Rahn Industries, Inc.**
7720 Maie Ave.
Los Angeles, CA 90001-2693
Phone: (213)588-1291
Free: (800)421-7070 **Fax:** (213)589-9485
Products: Automotive air-conditioning condensers. **SIC:** 5013 (Motor Vehicle Supplies & New Parts). **Officers:** William R. Hahn, President.

■ **3133** ■ **Ram Motors and Controls Inc.**
PO Box 629
Leesport, PA 19533-0629
Phone: (215)376-7102
Products: Electrical motors and controls. **SIC:** 5063 (Electrical Apparatus & Equipment). **Sales:** $25,000,000 (1992). **Emp:** 200. **Officers:** David Walton, President; Jeffrey Musser, VP of Finance.

■ **3134** ■ **Ram Turbos Inc.**
2300 N Miami Ave.
Miami, FL 33137
Phone: (305)576-4550 **Fax:** (305)576-4612
Products: Automotive industrial supplies. **SIC:** 5013 (Motor Vehicle Supplies & New Parts). **Est:** 1978. **Officers:** D. Ramirez, President.

■ **3135** ■ **Rapac Network International**
291 S Van Brunt St.
Englewood, NJ 07631
Phone: (201)871-9300 **Fax:** (201)871-3931
URL: http://www.rni-2000.com
Products: Fuel management systems; Taxi meters; On-board triplog computers. **SIC:** 5013 (Motor Vehicle Supplies & New Parts). **Sales:** $5,000,000 (1999). **Emp:** 16. **Officers:** S. Weinreich, President; Jon Schwaarg, Sales & Marketing Contact, e-mail: rnijons@aol.com.

■ **3136** ■ **Rayside Truck & Trailer**
2983 S Military Tr.
West Palm Beach, FL 33415
Phone: (561)965-7950
Free: (800)272-7950 **Fax:** (561)965-7998
E-mail: charles@rayside.com
URL: http://www.rayside.com
Products: Automotive parts and supplies, New. **SIC:** 5013 (Motor Vehicle Supplies & New Parts). **Est:** 1979. **Emp:** 34. **Officers:** Charles Rayside, President.

■ **3137** ■ **RBI Corp.**
101 Cedar Ridge Dr.
Ashland, VA 23005
Phone: (804)550-2210 **Fax:** (804)550-2386
Products: Small engine parts. **SIC:** 5013 (Motor Vehicle Supplies & New Parts). **Sales:** $12,000,000 (1992). **Emp:** 50. **Officers:** William T. Miller, President & Treasurer.

■ **3138** ■ **Recycled Auto Parts of Brattleboro Inc.**
R.R. 6
Brattleboro, VT 05301
Phone: (802)254-9034
Products: Used automobile parts. **SIC:** 5015 (Motor Vehicle Parts—Used). **Sales:** $3,000,000 (2000). **Emp:** 7. **Officers:** Robert Johnson, President.

■ **3139** ■ **Red Stone Inc.**
114 Ashaway Rd.
Westerly, RI 02891-1437
Phone: (401)596-5283
Products: Automobile parts, used; Used tires. **SICs:** 5015 (Motor Vehicle Parts—Used); 5014 (Tires & Tubes). **Officers:** Richard Cofoni, President.

■ **3140** ■ **Redburn Tire**
3801 W Clarendon Ave.
Phoenix, AZ 85019
Phone: (602)272-7601
Products: Tires. **SIC:** 5014 (Tires & Tubes). **Sales:** $25,000,000 (2000). **Emp:** 135. **Officers:** A. Wigg, President; Don Leffer, CFO.

■ **3141** ■ **Redlands Auto Parts**
402 W Stuart Ave.
Redlands, CA 92374-3138
Phone: (949)793-2101 **Fax:** (714)335-2861
Products: Automotive parts and paint. **SICs:** 5013 (Motor Vehicle Supplies & New Parts); 5198 (Paints, Varnishes & Supplies). **Est:** 1981. **Emp:** 17. **Officers:** Dave Golder.

■ **3142** ■ **Reinalt-Thomas Corp.**
14631 N Scottsdale Rd.
Scottsdale, AZ 85254
Phone: (602)951-1938 **Fax:** (602)443-5374
Products: Tires, wheels, and accessories. **SIC:** 5014 (Tires & Tubes). **Sales:** $810,000,000 (2000). **Emp:** 5,000. **Officers:** Bruce T. Halle, President; Robert H. Holman, Exec. VP of Finance.

■ **3143** ■ **Relco Corp.**
10600 Mastin St.
Overland Park, KS 66212
Phone: (913)894-9090
URL: http://www.reliableautomotive.com
Products: Automotive parts and supplies, including engines, spark plugs, alternators, and brakes. **SIC:** 5013 (Motor Vehicle Supplies & New Parts). **Est:** 1929. **Emp:** 300. **Officers:** Bob Price, President; Greg Doyle, COO; Dave Tuggle, Customer Service Contact; Susan Biggs, Human Resources Contact, e-mail: sbiggs@relconet.com.

■ **3144** ■ **Reliable Automotive of Kansas Inc.**
10600 Mastin
Overland Park, KS 66212
Phone: (913)894-9090
Products: Automotive parts and accessories. **SIC:** 5013 (Motor Vehicle Supplies & New Parts). **Emp:** 50. **Officers:** Bob Price, President; Greg Doyle, COO.

■ **3145** ■ **Reliable Belt & Transmission**
1120 Cherry
Toledo, OH 43608
Phone: (419)248-2695 **Fax:** (419)248-2011
Products: Power transmission products. **SICs:** 5084 (Industrial Machinery & Equipment); 5013 (Motor Vehicle Supplies & New Parts).

■ **3146** ■ **Reliable Tire Co.**
2420 Greenleaf Ave.
Elk Grove Village, IL 60007-5510
Phone: (847)593-0090
Free: (800)331-9898 **Fax:** (847)593-0476
Products: Pneumatic tires. **SIC:** 5014 (Tires & Tubes). **Emp:** 9.

■ **3147** ■ **Reliable Tire Distributors Inc.**
PO Box 560
Camden, NJ 08101
Phone: (609)365-6500
Free: (800)342-3426 **Fax:** (609)365-8717
Products: Tires and inner tubes, new. **SIC:** 5014 (Tires & Tubes). **Est:** 1956. **Emp:** 105.

■ **3148** ■ **Reno Auto Wrecking Inc.**
2429 W 4th St.
Reno, NV 89503-8807
Phone: (702)329-8671 **Fax:** (702)329-9210
Products: Automobile parts, used. **SIC:** 5015 (Motor Vehicle Parts—Used). **Officers:** Dick Mills, President.

■ **3149** ■ **Republic Automotive**
2550 W 5th Ave.
Denver, CO 80204-4803
Phone: (303)534-6133 **Fax:** (303)572-1025
Products: Automotive parts. **SIC:** 5013 (Motor Vehicle Supplies & New Parts). **Sales:** $8,000,000 (2000). **Emp:** 40. **Officers:** Ben Warren.

■ **3150** ■ **Republic Automotive Parts Inc.**
500 Wilson Pike Cir., Ste. 115
Brentwood, TN 37027-3225
Phone: (615)373-2050 **Fax:** (615)373-1629
Products: Automotive parts. **SIC:** 5013 (Motor Vehicle Supplies & New Parts). **Est:** 1923. **Sales:** $154,600,000 (2000). **Emp:** 1,300. **Officers:** Keith M. Thompson, CEO & President; Donald B. Hauk, Exec. VP & CFO.

■ **3151** ■ **Revco Products, Inc.**
7221 Acacia Ave.
Garden Grove, CA 92841-3908
Phone: (714)891-6688 **Fax:** (714)891-2705
Products: Recreational Vehicle accessories; Testing equipment. **SICs:** 5013 (Motor Vehicle Supplies & New Parts); 5049 (Professional Equipment Nec). **Est:** 1977. **Emp:** 16. **Officers:** David Gonzales, President.

■ **3152** ■ **Rex Auto Parts**
1233 Gordon Park Rd.
Augusta, GA 30901
Phone: (706)722-7526 **Fax:** (706)724-0181
Products: Auto parts. **SIC:** 5013 (Motor Vehicle Supplies & New Parts). **Sales:** $14,000,000 (2000). **Emp:** 60. **Officers:** Harold Mays, Owner.

■ **3153** ■ **Reynolds Tire and Rubber Div.**
1421 38th St.
Brooklyn, NY 11218
Phone: (718)633-0600 **Fax:** (718)633-1990
E-mail: ganinman@aol.com
URL: http://www.ganintire.com
Products: Tires. **SIC:** 5014 (Tires & Tubes). **Est:** 1923. **Sales:** $100,000,000 (2000). **Emp:** 100. **Officers:** Saul Ganin, President; John Woods, Controller; Thomas Fettes, VP of Sales.

■ **3154** ■ **RGA Tire Shop**
9 Ledge Rd.
Pelham, NH 03076
Phone: (603)898-9077
Products: Automobile parts, used. **SIC:** 5015 (Motor Vehicle Parts—Used). **Officers:** Arthur Croteau, Owner.

■ **3155** ■ **Rheuban Associates**
3180 S Ocean Dr., No. 606
Hallandale, FL 33009
Phone: (954)454-9787 **Fax:** (954)454-9787
Products: Motor vehicle parts and accessories. **SIC:** 5013 (Motor Vehicle Supplies & New Parts). **Officers:** Frances Rheuban, President.

■ **3156** ■ **Donald B. Rice Tire Co.**
909 East St.
Frederick, MD 21701
Phone: (301)662-0166 **Fax:** (301)695-3882
URL: http://www.ricetire.com
Products: Tires. **SIC:** 5014 (Tires & Tubes). **Est:** 1956. **Sales:** $30,000,000 (2000). **Emp:** 150. **Officers:** K. Rice, President, e-mail: kenrice@ricetire.com; Jim Hammond, Sales/Marketing Contact; Chris Chase, Customer Service Contact; Gordon Nizer, Human Resources Contact.

■ **3157** ■ **Richland Ltd.**
PO Box 489
Spring Green, WI 53588
Phone: (608)588-7779 **Fax:** (608)647-6395
Products: Cylinder sleeves. **SIC:** 5013 (Motor Vehicle Supplies & New Parts). **Sales:** $2,000,000 (2000). **Emp:** 49. **Officers:** W. J. Dallman.

■ **3158** ■ **Ridge Auto Parts Company Inc.**
714 S Thomas Rd.
Ft. Wayne, IN 46804
Phone: (219)456-6913
Products: Motor vehicle suspension systems; Gasoline engines and gasoline engine parts for motor vehicles; Automotive parts and supplies, New. **SIC:**

5013 (Motor Vehicle Supplies & New Parts). **Sales:** $2,000,000 (2000). **Emp:** 49. **Officers:** Joe Thomas; Jim Thomas.

■ **3159** ■ **Ridge Co.**
PO Box 2859
South Bend, IN 46680
Phone: (219)234-3143
Products: Automotive parts. **SIC:** 5013 (Motor Vehicle Supplies & New Parts). **Est:** 1928. **Sales:** $48,000,000 (2000). **Emp:** 200. **Officers:** Jim Goodhew, President; Dave Hegyi, Controller.

■ **3160** ■ **Rim and Wheel Service Inc.**
1014 Gest St.
Cincinnati, OH 45203
Phone: (513)721-6940   **Fax:** (513)721-4160
Products: Automotive parts, including rims, wheels, lights, and drums. **SICs:** 5013 (Motor Vehicle Supplies & New Parts); 5014 (Tires & Tubes). **Est:** 1929. **Sales:** $15,000,000 (2000). **Emp:** 82. **Officers:** Richard Broxon, President; James Otten, Finance Officer.

■ **3161** ■ **Rippey Auto Parts Company Inc.**
117 E 6th St.
Columbia, TN 38401
Phone: (931)388-0723   **Fax:** (931)388-9069
Products: Auto parts. **SIC:** 5013 (Motor Vehicle Supplies & New Parts). **Est:** 1932. **Sales:** $2,000,000 (2000). **Emp:** 20. **Officers:** James M. Rippey Jr., President; Linda L. Rippey, Treasurer; T. Rippey, Dir. of Marketing & Sales.

■ **3162** ■ **Rising Sun Import Parts Inc.**
8983 Mira Mesa Blvd.
San Diego, CA 92126
Phone: (619)693-0044
Products: Parts for Japanese automobiles. **SIC:** 5013 (Motor Vehicle Supplies & New Parts). **Sales:** $3,000,000 (2000). **Emp:** 30. **Officers:** Dan Hahlbohm, President.

■ **3163** ■ **Rivers Body Co., Inc.**
10626 General Ave.
PO Box 6009
Jacksonville, FL 32236
Phone: (904)781-5622
Free: (888)781-5622   **Fax:** (904)786-1553
Products: Automotive parts and supplies, New. **SIC:** 5013 (Motor Vehicle Supplies & New Parts). **Emp:** 15. **Officers:** John Murray, President; Blake Murray, General Mgr.; Patrick Murray, Parts and Purchasing.

■ **3164** ■ **Riverside Drives Inc.**
4509 W 160th St.
PO Box 35166
Cleveland, OH 44135
Phone: (216)362-1211   **Fax:** (216)362-6836
Products: Power transmissions. **SICs:** 5084 (Industrial Machinery & Equipment); 5013 (Motor Vehicle Supplies & New Parts).

■ **3165** ■ **Road Rescue Inc.**
1133 Rankin St.
St. Paul, MN 55116
Phone: (612)699-5588   **Fax:** (612)699-9899
Products: Ambulance supplies and parts. **SIC:** 5047 (Medical & Hospital Equipment). **Est:** 1976. **Sales:** $18,000,000 (2000). **Emp:** 140. **Officers:** Norbert J. Conzemius, President; Loren Prairie, CFO; Craig F. Schauffert, VP of Sales; James R. Grossman, VP of Admin.

■ **3166** ■ **Road-Runner Tire Service**
33960 Old Willamette Hwy. S
Eugene, OR 97405
Phone: (541)744-2000
Products: Tires. **SIC:** 5014 (Tires & Tubes).

■ **3167** ■ **Road Tested Recycled Auto Parts Inc.**
4544 Woodson Rd.
St. Louis, MO 63134-3704
Phone: (314)427-3900
Products: Wheels; Tires; Wheel covers; Motors; Transmissions; Brakes; Rear ends. **SICs:** 5015 (Motor Vehicle Parts—Used); 5014 (Tires & Tubes). **Sales:** $2,000,000 (2000). **Emp:** 5. **Officers:** Mike Weinhause, President.

■ **3168** ■ **Robbins Auto Parts Inc.**
110 Washington St.
Dover, NH 03820
Phone: (603)742-2880
Products: Automotive parts. **SIC:** 5013 (Motor Vehicle Supplies & New Parts). **Sales:** $200,000,000 (2000). **Emp:** 500. **Officers:** Stanley Robbins, President & Treasurer; Doug Dupuis, Controller; Sandra Heald, Dir of Personnel.

■ **3169** ■ **Fred Roberts Auto Parts**
320 Main
Arcade, NY 14009-1115
Phone: (716)492-5114   **Fax:** (716)492-5115
Products: Automotive parts. **SIC:** 5013 (Motor Vehicle Supplies & New Parts). **Emp:** 13. **Officers:** Al Mosher.

■ **3170** ■ **Rockland Tire and Service Co.**
109 Rte. 59
Monsey, NY 10952
Phone: (914)356-7100
Products: Tires. **SIC:** 5014 (Tires & Tubes). **Est:** 1985. **Sales:** $1,300,000 (2000). **Emp:** 12. **Officers:** G. Michael Wallace, President.

■ **3171** ■ **Rodefeld Company Inc.**
96 W Main St.
Richmond, IN 47374
Phone: (765)966-1571   **Fax:** (765)966-1574
Products: Automotive repair products. **SIC:** 5013 (Motor Vehicle Supplies & New Parts). **Est:** 1900. **Sales:** $21,000,000 (2000). **Emp:** 175. **Officers:** Charles Rodefeld, President; Jim Breckenridge, Controller; Jim McPherson, VP of Marketing.

■ **3172** ■ **Rodi Automotive Inc.**
13 Harbor Park Dr.
Port Washington, NY 11050
Phone: (516)484-9500   **Fax:** (516)484-4341
E-mail: autobarn1@worldnet.att.net
Products: Auto parts. **SIC:** 5013 (Motor Vehicle Supplies & New Parts). **Est:** 1957. **Sales:** $27,000,000 (2000). **Emp:** 250. **Officers:** Herb Blumberg, President; David Blumberg, Vice President.

■ **3173** ■ **Rol-Lift Corp.**
12300 Amelia Dr.
Houston, TX 77045
Phone: (713)434-3400   **Fax:** (713)433-9710
Products: Pallet trucks. **SIC:** 5012 (Automobiles & Other Motor Vehicles). **Sales:** $17,000,000 (2000). **Officers:** D.M. Buchanan, President; D.E. Peters, Exec. VP of Finance.

■ **3174** ■ **Roppel Industries Inc.**
829 Logan St.
Louisville, KY 40204
Phone: (502)581-1004   **Fax:** (502)581-1028
Products: Radiators and air-conditioners. **SIC:** 5013 (Motor Vehicle Supplies & New Parts). **Est:** 1947. **Sales:** $15,000,000 (2000). **Emp:** 62. **Officers:** Thomas V. Roppel, President; Mike Eisenback, Controller; Steve Yankowy, Manager; Brian Denseford, Sales Contact; Venita Brown, Human Resources Contact.

■ **3175** ■ **Rott-Keller Supply Co.**
PO Box 390
Fargo, ND 58107-0390
Phone: (701)235-0563
Free: (800)437-4604   **Fax:** (701)232-7900
Products: Tires, electrical appliances, household plants. **SICs:** 5014 (Tires & Tubes); 5064 (Electrical Appliances—Television & Radio); 5193 (Flowers & Florists' Supplies). **Sales:** $19,000,000 (2000). **Emp:** 30. **Officers:** Herb F. Rott Jr., President; Dean Rott, CFO.

■ **3176** ■ **Rowland Equipment, Inc.**
2900 NW 73rd St.
Miami, FL 33147
Phones: (305)691-9280   (305)691-6211
Fax: (305)693-8267
E-mail: RowTrukInc@aol.com
Products: Service Bodies; Liftgates; Winches; and Tankers. **SIC:** 5013 (Motor Vehicle Supplies & New Parts). **Est:** 1982. **Sales:** $25,000,000 (1999). **Emp:** 16. **Officers:** Joyce Cobb, Contact.

■ **3177** ■ **Royal Auto Supply Inc.**
300 Enterprise Ln.
Colmar, PA 18915
Phone: (215)643-7670   **Fax:** (215)822-1768
Products: Auto parts, including starters, alternators, spark plugs, and master cylinders. **SIC:** 5013 (Motor Vehicle Supplies & New Parts). **Est:** 1938. **Sales:** $42,000,000 (2000). **Emp:** 175. **Officers:** Jon Slenn, President; Dan Gregson, Controller.

■ **3178** ■ **Sadisco of Florence**
PO Box 6525
Florence, SC 29502
Phone: (843)669-1941
Products: Used automobiles. **SIC:** 5012 (Automobiles & Other Motor Vehicles). **Sales:** $54,000,000 (1994). **Emp:** 100.

■ **3179** ■ **Safety Industries Inc.**
1st and K Aves.
PO Box 1137
Mc Gill, NV 89318
Phone: (702)235-7766
Products: Automotive parts and supplies, New; Signs and advertising displays. **SICs:** 5013 (Motor Vehicle Supplies & New Parts); 5099 (Durable Goods Nec). **Sales:** $2,000,000 (2000). **Emp:** 8. **Officers:** Lionel K. Hastings, President.

■ **3180** ■ **Safety Service Co.**
835 Fesslers Pkwy.
Nashville, TN 37210
Phone: (615)244-2853   **Fax:** (615)726-3916
Products: Truck brakes and carburetors. **SIC:** 5013 (Motor Vehicle Supplies & New Parts). **Est:** 1971. **Sales:** $6,500,000 (2000). **Emp:** 14. **Officers:** Larry Clarton, President; John Cash, Controller; Ray Johnson, Sales Mgr.

■ **3181** ■ **Safety Truck Equipment Inc.**
669 Market St.
Paterson, NJ 07513
Phone: (973)684-3668   **Fax:** (973)881-9129
Products: Parts for air brake systems in trucks. **SIC:** 5013 (Motor Vehicle Supplies & New Parts). **Sales:** $4,000,000 (2000). **Emp:** 20. **Officers:** H. Zachary, President.

■ **3182** ■ **Safeway Tire Co.**
4623 Superior Ave.
Cleveland, OH 44103
Phone: (216)881-1737
Products: Tires, wheels, shocks, and brakes. **SICs:** 5014 (Tires & Tubes); 5013 (Motor Vehicle Supplies & New Parts). **Est:** 1949. **Sales:** $6,000,000 (2000). **Emp:** 75. **Officers:** Lynn Adamic, Office Mgr.; Larry Adamic, President.

■ **3183** ■ **Salazar International, Inc.**
23800 Commerce Park
Beachwood, OH 44122
Phone: (216)464-2420   **Fax:** (216)464-9084
Products: Truck and trailer parts. **SIC:** 5013 (Motor Vehicle Supplies & New Parts). **Est:** 1960. **Sales:** $4,000,000 (2000). **Emp:** 5. **Officers:** Harold B. Mendes, President.

■ **3184** ■ **Sam Yanen Ford Sales Inc.**
PO Box 534
Moundsville, WV 26041
Phone: (304)845-4244
Products: Motor vehicles. **SIC:** 5012 (Automobiles & Other Motor Vehicles). **Sales:** $12,000,000 (1994). **Emp:** 39. **Officers:** Rod A. Yanen, President.

■ **3185** ■ **San Antonio Brake and Clutch Service Inc.**
PO Box 976
San Antonio, TX 78294
Phone: (210)226-0254   **Fax:** (210)226-2043
Products: Automotive parts. **SIC:** 5013 (Motor Vehicle Supplies & New Parts). **Est:** 1939. **Sales:** $3,300,000 (2000). **Emp:** 48. **Officers:** J.L. McCormick, President.

■ **3186** ■ **Sandusky Industrial Supply**
2000 Superior St.
Box 2190
Sandusky, OH 44870
Phone: (419)626-4467
Products: Power transmission equipment. **SICs:** 5084 (Industrial Machinery & Equipment); 5013 (Motor Vehicle Supplies & New Parts).

■ **3187** ■ **Sanel Auto Parts Inc.**
PO Box 1254
Concord, NH 03301
Phone: (603)225-4100
Products: Automobile parts and supplies. **SIC:** 5013 (Motor Vehicle Supplies & New Parts). **Sales:** $21,000,000 (1992). **Emp:** 90. **Officers:** George Segal, President; Bob Schadee, VP of Finance.

■ **3188** ■ **Santa Maria Tire Inc.**
PO Box 6007
Santa Maria, CA 93456
Phone: (805)928-2501
Products: Tires for trucks, buses, and utility vehicles. **SIC:** 5014 (Tires & Tubes). **Est:** 1965. **Sales:** $5,500,000 (2000). **Emp:** 51. **Officers:** C.F. Stephens, CEO & President; C Haberstich, CFO.

■ **3189** ■ **Santa Rosa Bearing**
1100 Santa Rosa Ave.
Santa Rosa, CA 95403
Phone: (707)545-7904   **Fax:** (707)545-0837
Products: Power transmissions. **SIC:** 5013 (Motor Vehicle Supplies & New Parts).

■ **3190** ■ **Saw Mill Auto Wreckers**
12 Worth St.
Yonkers, NY 10701
Phone: (914)968-5300
Products: Automobile parts, including doors, motors, and transmissions. **SIC:** 5015 (Motor Vehicle Parts—Used). **Est:** 1946. **Sales:** $1,000,000 (2000). **Emp:** 10. **Officers:** Joseph Americo, President.

■ **3191** ■ **R.H. Scales Company Inc.**
240 University Ave.
Westwood, MA 02090-2393
Phone: (781)320-0005   **Fax:** (781)320-0632
Products: Automobile and truck parts and accessories. **SIC:** 5013 (Motor Vehicle Supplies & New Parts). **Est:** 1933. **Sales:** $10,000,000 (2000). **Emp:** 35. **Officers:** Robert H. Scales Jr., CEO & President; Richard L. Scales, Treasurer; David A. Scales, Sales Mgr.

■ **3192** ■ **Scarborough Auto Parts Inc.**
40 Holmes Rd.
Scarborough, ME 04074-9565
Phone: (207)883-4161   **Fax:** (207)883-4257
Products: Used motor vehicle parts and supplies. **SIC:** 5015 (Motor Vehicle Parts—Used). **Officers:** John Dickinson, President.

■ **3193** ■ **Scherer Truck Equipment, Inc.**
6105 NW River Park Dr.
Kansas City, MO 64150
Phone: (816)587-0190
Free: (800)373-TRCK   **Fax:** (816)587-5127
Products: Automotive parts and supplies, New. **SIC:** 5013 (Motor Vehicle Supplies & New Parts). **Officers:** Walter Thomas, President.

■ **3194** ■ **Scherer Truck Equipment, Inc.**
2670 Auburn Rd.
Auburn Hills, MI 48326
Phone: (248)853-7277   **Fax:** (248)853-7487
E-mail: scherer@qni.com
URL: http://www.scherertruck.com
Products: Automotive parts and supplies, New. **SIC:** 5013 (Motor Vehicle Supplies & New Parts). **Officers:** Gene Short, Contact.

■ **3195** ■ **Schmann Auto Parts**
701 Clairton Blvd.
Pittsburgh, PA 15236
Phone: (412)655-3434
Products: Automotive parts and accessories, including brake pads, starters, wax, and mufflers. **SIC:** 5013 (Motor Vehicle Supplies & New Parts). **Est:** 1988.

Sales: $1,000,000 (2000). **Emp:** 16. **Officers:** Michael Bloom, Manager.

■ **3196** ■ **Schrader-Bridgeport International**
500 S 45th St. E
Muskogee, OK 74403
Phone: (918)687-5427
Free: (800)331-4062   **Fax:** (918)682-1635
URL: http://www.schrader-bridgeport.net
Products: Tire repair supplies, including patches and tools; Airline accessories. **SICs:** 5085 (Industrial Supplies); 5088 (Transportation Equipment & Supplies). **Est:** 1923. **Sales:** $52,000,000 (2000). **Emp:** 150. **Officers:** Richard Shindel, Plant Mgr.; Larry Chapins, Controller; Jesse Wilkerson, Marketing Mgr., e-mail: jwilkerson@schrader-bridgeport.net; Bob Holton, Information Systems Mgr.; Carol May, Customer Service Contact, e-mail: cmay@schrader-bridgeport.net. **Former Name:** Camel Products Div.

■ **3197** ■ **Schukei Chevrolet Inc.**
PO Box 1525
Mason City, IA 50401
Phone: (515)423-5402
Products: Automotive parts, supplies and accessories. **SIC:** 5013 (Motor Vehicle Supplies & New Parts). **Sales:** $19,000,000 (2000). **Emp:** 55. **Officers:** Robert A. Schukei, President; Steve Schukei, Treasurer.

■ **3198** ■ **Les Schwab Warehouse Center Inc.**
PO Box 667
Prineville, OR 97754
Phone: (503)447-4136   **Fax:** (503)447-8118
Products: Tires and related products. **SIC:** 5014 (Tires & Tubes). **Est:** 1952. **Sales:** $352,000,000 (2000). **Emp:** 2,200. **Officers:** G. Phil Wick, President; Tom Freedman, Sr. VP & Treasurer; Jerry Harper, Dir. of Marketing; Larry Henderson, VP of Data Processing; Larry Smith, Human Resources Mgr.

■ **3199** ■ **Scientific Brake and Equipment Co.**
702 Dickerson Rd.
PO Box 1023
Gaylord, MI 49735
Phone: (517)732-7507
Free: (800)292-3081   **Fax:** (517)732-6124
Products: Automotive parts and supplies, New. **SIC:** 5013 (Motor Vehicle Supplies & New Parts). **Officers:** Ken Hasty, Contact.

■ **3200** ■ **Scientific Brake and Equipment Co.**
314 W Genesee Ave.
PO Box 840
Saginaw, MI 48602
Phone: (517)755-4411
Free: (800)292-0235   **Fax:** (517)755-4469
E-mail: info@scientificbrake.com
URL: http://www.scientificbrake.com
Products: Automotive parts and supplies, New. **SIC:** 5013 (Motor Vehicle Supplies & New Parts). **Est:** 1928. **Sales:** $18,000,000 (2000). **Emp:** 75. **Officers:** Thomas T. Princing, President, e-mail: tprincing@scientificbrake.com; John T. Princing, Vice President, e-mail: jprincing@scientificbrake.com.

■ **3201** ■ **Scruggs Equipment Company Inc.**
1940 Channel Ave.
PO Box 13284
Memphis, TN 38113
Phone: (901)942-9312   **Fax:** (901)942-4595
Products: Automotive parts and supplies, New. **SIC:** 5013 (Motor Vehicle Supplies & New Parts). **Est:** 1936. **Emp:** 12. **Officers:** Bud Scruggs Jr., Contact.

■ **3202** ■ **Seaboard Automotive Inc.**
721 Blackhorse Pike
Blackwood, NJ 08012
Phone: (609)227-2252
Products: Automotive parts. **SIC:** 5013 (Motor Vehicle Supplies & New Parts).

■ **3203** ■ **Sehman Tire Service Inc.**
PO Box 889
Franklin, PA 16323
Phone: (814)437-7878   **Fax:** (814)432-7578
Products: Tires. **SIC:** 5014 (Tires & Tubes). **Est:** 1957. **Sales:** $7,000,000 (2000). **Emp:** 47. **Officers:** Larry W. Sehman, President; Teresa Hovis, Controller.

■ **3204** ■ **Semix Inc.**
4160 Technology Dr.
Fremont, CA 94538
Phone: (510)659-8800   **Fax:** (510)659-8444
Products: Motor drivers. **SIC:** 5063 (Electrical Apparatus & Equipment). **Sales:** $5,000,000 (1993). **Emp:** 18. **Officers:** Norio Sugano, CEO & President.

■ **3205** ■ **Servco Pacific Inc.**
PO Box 2788
Honolulu, HI 96803
Phone: (808)521-6511   **Fax:** (808)523-3937
URL: http://www.servco.com
Products: Automobile supplies; Office supplies; Appliances and electronics. **SICs:** 5013 (Motor Vehicle Supplies & New Parts); 5112 (Stationery & Office Supplies); 5064 (Electrical Appliances—Television & Radio). **Est:** 1919. **Emp:** 980.

■ **3206** ■ **Service Motor Parts**
2741 Turnpike Industrial Dr.
Middletown, PA 17057
Phone: (717)939-1344
Free: (800)222-1822   **Fax:** (717)939-1977
Products: Engine and chassis parts for light trucks and cars; Tools and automotive equipment. **SIC:** 5013 (Motor Vehicle Supplies & New Parts). **Est:** 1956. **Emp:** 34. **Officers:** Melvin Brownold, Vice President; David Brownold, President.

■ **3207** ■ **Service Tire Co.**
2737 W Vernor Hwy.
Detroit, MI 48216
Phone: (313)237-0050
Products: Tires. **SIC:** 5014 (Tires & Tubes). **Est:** 1929. **Sales:** $10,000,000 (2000). **Emp:** 25. **Officers:** Gerald Rosenthal, President.

■ **3208** ■ **Service Unlimited**
PO Box 304
Mendon, MI 49072
Phones: (616)463-2958   (616)649-1188
Fax: (616)649-4088
E-mail: tlreauto@aol.com
Products: Shoelaces; Visors; Interstate utility trailers and haulers. **SICs:** 5012 (Automobiles & Other Motor Vehicles); 5137 (Women's/Children's Clothing); 5131 (Piece Goods & Notions); 5199 (Nondurable Goods Nec); 5136 (Men's/Boys' Clothing). **Est:** 1989. **Emp:** 2.

■ **3209** ■ **Setco Solid Tire and Rim**
2300 SE Washington St.
Idabel, OK 74745
Phone: (580)286-6531
Free: (800)634-2381   **Fax:** (580)286-6743
E-mail: setco@oio.net
URL: http://www.setcojyd.com
Products: Solid tires. **SIC:** 5014 (Tires & Tubes). **Est:** 1968. **Emp:** 85. **Officers:** Buck Hill, President; Sharon Birdsong, Marketing; Duane Birdsong, Complex Mgr.

■ **3210** ■ **Shamrock Auto Parts Inc.**
2560 E 4th St.
Reno, NV 89512-0867
Phone: (775)329-1606   **Fax:** (775)329-5607
Products: Tires and wheels. **SIC:** 5014 (Tires & Tubes). **Est:** 1956. **Sales:** $500,000 (1999). **Emp:** 4. **Officers:** Harvey Kaye, President.

■ **3211** ■ **Shamrock Custom Truck Caps, Inc.**
1820 N Black Horse Pke.
Williamstown, NJ 08094
Phone: (609)629-1411   **Fax:** (609)728-5463
Products: Truck caps and accessories. **SIC:** 5013 (Motor Vehicle Supplies & New Parts). **Est:** 1983. **Officers:** John Bombara, President; Jane Bombara, Vice President.

■ **3212** ■ **Earle Shankle Co. Inc.**
5200 46th Ave.
Hyattsville, MD 20781
Phone: (301)699-8500   **Fax:** (301)927-1554
Products: Automotive parts and supplies, New. **SIC:** 5013 (Motor Vehicle Supplies & New Parts). **Officers:** Edith Shankle, Contact.

■ 3213 ■ Shaub Ellison Co.
1121 Court C
Tacoma, WA 98402
Phone: (253)272-4119 **Fax:** (253)926-1174
Products: Tires; Automotive systems, including brakes and shocks. **SICs:** 5014 (Tires & Tubes); 5013 (Motor Vehicle Supplies & New Parts). **Est:** 1920. **Sales:** $10,000,000 (2000). **Emp:** 85. **Officers:** Steven T. Shaub, President.

■ 3214 ■ Shaw Auto Parts Inc.
PO Box 4729
Pocatello, ID 83205-4729
Phone: (208)232-5952 **Fax:** (208)233-0904
Products: Automobile parts, used. **SIC:** 5015 (Motor Vehicle Parts—Used). **Officers:** Larry Shaw, President.

■ 3215 ■ Shelby Industries Inc.
PO Box 308
Shelbyville, KY 40066
Phone: (502)633-2040 **Fax:** (502)633-2186
Products: Parts and components for travel and camping trailers. **SIC:** 5013 (Motor Vehicle Supplies & New Parts). **Est:** 1972. **Emp:** 65. **Officers:** Lalit K. Sarin, CEO & President; Vivek K. Sarin; Keith Price; Bill Steinberger, Sales/Marketing Contact.

■ 3216 ■ Shepherd's Auto Supply Inc.
1001 Williamson SE
Roanoke, VA 24034
Phone: (540)344-6666 **Fax:** (540)347-0314
Products: Automotive parts. **SIC:** 5013 (Motor Vehicle Supplies & New Parts). **Est:** 1921. **Sales:** $7,500,000 (2000). **Emp:** 92. **Officers:** Jacob D. Hoback, President; Terrance N. Neate, CFO; R.A. Argabright, Vice President.

■ 3217 ■ Sibco Enterprises Incorporated
87 Wedgemere Rd.
Stamford, CT 06905
Phone: (203)322-4891 **Fax:** (203)329-2671
Products: New automotive replacement parts; Industrial and automotive lubricants; Metal cutting tools. **SICs:** 5013 (Motor Vehicle Supplies & New Parts); 5084 (Industrial Machinery & Equipment); 5172 (Petroleum Products Nec). **Officers:** S.J. Buccheri, President.

■ 3218 ■ Sidney Auto Wrecking Inc.
RR 8C89, Box 5178
Sidney, MT 59270
Phone: (406)482-1406
Products: Used motor vehicle parts; Used automotive parts and supplies. **SIC:** 5015 (Motor Vehicle Parts—Used). **Officers:** Maynard Baisch, President.

■ 3219 ■ Siemens Automotive Corp.
PO Box 217017
Auburn Hills, MI 48326
Phone: (248)253-1000 **Fax:** (248)253-2999
Products: Electronic and electromechanical automobile parts. **SIC:** 5013 (Motor Vehicle Supplies & New Parts). **Sales:** $2,700,000,000 (2000). **Emp:** 15,555. **Officers:** George R. Perry, CEO & President; Steve McGinnis, CFO.

■ 3220 ■ Sierra Detroit Diesel Allison Inc.
1755 Adams Ave.
San Leandro, CA 94577-1001
Phone: (510)526-0521
Products: Diesel engines; Diesel engine parts. **SICs:** 5013 (Motor Vehicle Supplies & New Parts); 5084 (Industrial Machinery & Equipment). **Est:** 1982. **Sales:** $40,000,000 (2000). **Emp:** 150. **Officers:** Roger L. Howsmon, CEO & Chairman of the Board; Peggy Hetlage, CFO; Steven P. Kerns, Dir. of Marketing.

■ 3221 ■ Siferd-Hossellman Co.
PO Box 450
Lima, OH 45802-0450
Phone: (419)228-1221 **Fax:** (419)228-2949
Products: Automotive parts. **SIC:** 5013 (Motor Vehicle Supplies & New Parts). **Est:** 1919. **Sales:** $6,000,000 (2000). **Emp:** 45. **Officers:** Andrew Burneson, President.

■ 3222 ■ Siliconix Inc.
PO Box 54951
Santa Clara, CA 95056
Phone: (408)988-8000 **Fax:** (408)567-8950
Products: Semiconductor products for computer, communications, automotive, industrial and hi-tech markets. **SIC:** 5065 (Electronic Parts & Equipment Nec). **Sales:** $383,300,000 (1999). **Emp:** 1,642. **Officers:** King Owyang, CEO & President; Jens Meyerhoff, Sr. VP of Finance & Admin.

■ 3223 ■ Simpson Equipment Corp.
PO Box 2229
Wilson, NC 27894
Phone: (919)291-4105 **Fax:** (919)237-9950
Products: Truck bodies, cranes, and truck equipment. **SIC:** 5013 (Motor Vehicle Supplies & New Parts). **Est:** 1948. **Sales:** $3,000,000 (2000). **Emp:** 20. **Officers:** J.R. Simpson, Chairman of the Board; Grady L. Barnes, President; Frankie Reaves, VP of Sales & Operations.

■ 3224 ■ Singer Products Export Company Inc.
250 E Hartsdale Ave.
Hartsdale, NY 10530
Phone: (914)722-0400 **Fax:** (914)722-0404
Products: Automotive parts and electrical machinery. **SICs:** 5013 (Motor Vehicle Supplies & New Parts); 5063 (Electrical Apparatus & Equipment). **Sales:** $4,000,000 (2000). **Emp:** 10.

■ 3225 ■ Six Robblees Inc.
PO Box 3703
Seattle, WA 98124
Phone: (206)767-7970 **Fax:** (206)763-7416
Products: Wheels; Trailer parts; Undercarriage parts; Truck parts; Tire chains. **SIC:** 5014 (Tires & Tubes). **Est:** 1913. **Sales:** $30,000,000 (1999). **Emp:** 140. **Officers:** J. David Robblee, CEO; Richard Metcalf, VP of Finance; Thomas R. Ogren, President.

■ 3226 ■ Six States Distributors
247 W 1700 S
Salt Lake City, UT 84115
Phone: (801)488-4666 **Fax:** (801)488-4690
Products: Clutches; Transmissions; Rear bumpers. **SIC:** 5013 (Motor Vehicle Supplies & New Parts). **Est:** 1956. **Sales:** $28,000,000 (2000). **Emp:** 170. **Officers:** R.C. Hafer, President; M.A. Sollis, CFO.

■ 3227 ■ Six States Distributors Inc.
4432 Franklin Blvd.
Eugene, OR 97403
Phone: (541)747-9944 **Fax:** (541)747-9947
E-mail: eugene@sixstates.com
Products: Hydraulic pumps; Drive shafts; 4x4 and H.D. truck parts. **SIC:** 5013 (Motor Vehicle Supplies & New Parts). **Est:** 1956. **Officers:** Bill Usher, Manager, e-mail: billusher@sixstates.com.

■ 3228 ■ Skaggs Automotive Inc.
110 S Sherman St.
Spokane, WA 99202-1529
Phone: (509)838-3529
Products: Automotive parts. **SIC:** 5013 (Motor Vehicle Supplies & New Parts). **Est:** 1949. **Sales:** $7,000,000 (2000). **Emp:** 57. **Officers:** C.R. Skaggs, CEO & Chairman of the Board; Don Castle, Dir. of Marketing; Charles Thill, Dir. of Systems.

■ 3229 ■ Slingman Industries
5 Shirley Ave.
PO Box 6870
Somerset, NJ 08875
Phone: (732)249-3500 **Fax:** (732)249-3676
Products: Power transmission equipment; Pumps; Motors. **SICs:** 5084 (Industrial Machinery & Equipment); 5013 (Motor Vehicle Supplies & New Parts).

■ 3230 ■ SLM Power Group Inc.
PO Box 9156
Corpus Christi, TX 78469
Phone: (512)883-4358 **Fax:** (512)887-6439
Products: Semi-truck parts. **SIC:** 5013 (Motor Vehicle Supplies & New Parts). **Est:** 1971. **Sales:** $50,000,000 (2000). **Emp:** 400. **Officers:** Wayne Stockseth, CEO & President; Steven Stockseth, VP of Finance; Mark Stockseth, Vice President; Terrie Steen, Dir of Personnel.

■ 3231 ■ Smith Detroit Diesel
8 Glendale Ave.
Sparks, NV 89431
Phone: (702)359-1713
Free: (800)574-1713 **Fax:** (702)359-6579
Products: Heavy-duty diesel parts; Air-conditioning supplies. **SICs:** 5013 (Motor Vehicle Supplies & New Parts); 5075 (Warm Air Heating & Air-Conditioning). **Est:** 1978. **Sales:** $35,000,000 (2000). **Emp:** 193. **Officers:** M.B. Smith, President; C.W. Fleming, Vice President.

■ 3232 ■ Smith Detroit Diesel Allison Inc.
PO Box 27527
Salt Lake City, UT 84127
Phone: (801)262-2631 **Fax:** (801)262-0078
Products: Diesel engines; Transmissions. **SICs:** 5084 (Industrial Machinery & Equipment); 5013 (Motor Vehicle Supplies & New Parts). **Est:** 1960. **Sales:** $32,000,000 (2000). **Emp:** 150. **Officers:** Michael B. Smith, President; Brent D. Sandberg, VP of Admin.; Steve Baker, Sales Mgr.; Alan Tomlinson, Data Processing Mgr.

■ 3233 ■ Smith Motor Sales
PO Box 692050
San Antonio, TX 78269-2050
Phone: (210)223-4281
Products: Auto dealer. **SIC:** 5012 (Automobiles & Other Motor Vehicles). **Sales:** $54,000,000 (2000). **Emp:** 148. **Officers:** Roy F. Smith, President.

■ 3234 ■ Smyrna Truck Body & Equipment, Inc.
2158 Atlanta St.
Smyrna, GA 30080
Phone: (404)433-0112 **Fax:** (404)432-8770
Products: Automotive parts and supplies, New. **SIC:** 5013 (Motor Vehicle Supplies & New Parts). **Officers:** Barry Fouts, General Mgr.

■ 3235 ■ Snap Products Inc.
PO Box 2967
Houston, TX 77252-2967
Phone: (713)546-4000
Free: (800)248-6688 **Fax:** (713)546-3628
E-mail: info@pennzoil-quakerstate.com
URL: http://www.pennzoil.com
Products: Automotive products. **SIC:** 5013 (Motor Vehicle Supplies & New Parts). **Est:** 1963. **Sales:** $50,000,000 (2000). **Emp:** 125. **Officers:** Caryn Crump, Sr. VP & General Mgr., e-mail: caryncrump@pzlqs.com; Tim Russell, Dir. of Business Operations, e-mail: timrussell@pzlqs.com; John J. Harvey, VP of Sales, e-mail: johnharvey@pzlqs.com.

■ 3236 ■ Sound Warehouse Inc.
516 Elm St.
Manchester, NH 03101-2511
Phone: (603)668-4979
Products: Automotive electrical equipment. **SIC:** 5013 (Motor Vehicle Supplies & New Parts). **Officers:** Stephen Beken, President.

■ 3237 ■ South Gateway Tire Co.
65 Market St.
Shreveport, LA 71101-2826
Phone: (318)222-8415
Free: (800)647-9340 **Fax:** (318)222-0632
Products: Industrial wheels; Motor vehicle wheels; Tires and inner tubes, new. **SICs:** 5014 (Tires & Tubes); 5013 (Motor Vehicle Supplies & New Parts). **Emp:** 18. **Officers:** Fred R. Russell.

■ 3238 ■ South Kentucky Trucks Inc.
PO Box 1369
Somerset, KY 42502
Phone: (606)679-4321 **Fax:** (606)679-8423
Products: Truck parts. **SIC:** 5013 (Motor Vehicle Supplies & New Parts). **Est:** 1969. **Sales:** $14,000,000 (2000). **Emp:** 56. **Officers:** Jerry S. Ikerd, President & CFO.

■ 3239 ■ **Southern Automotive Inc.**
597 N Saginaw St.
Pontiac, MI 48342
Phone: (810)335-5555 **Fax:** (810)355-1564
Products: Automotive parts and supplies, New; Generators. **SICs:** 5013 (Motor Vehicle Supplies & New Parts); 5063 (Electrical Apparatus & Equipment). **Est:** 1980. **Sales:** $4,100,000 (2000). **Emp:** 30. **Officers:** Tom Tyson, President.

■ 3240 ■ **Southern Motorcycle Supply**
3670 Ruffin Rd.
San Diego, CA 92123-1810
Phone: (858)560-5005 **Fax:** (858)560-4626
E-mail: southern@southernms.com
URL: http://www.southernms.com
Products: Motorcycle, watercraft, and ATV parts and accessories. **SIC:** 5013 (Motor Vehicle Supplies & New Parts). **Est:** 1969. **Emp:** 30.

■ 3241 ■ **Southern Nevada Auto Parts Inc.**
2221 Losee Rd.
North Las Vegas, NV 89030-4106
Phone: (702)642-1333 **Fax:** (702)649-9261
Products: Automobile parts, used. **SIC:** 5015 (Motor Vehicle Parts—Used). **Officers:** William Ellis, President.

■ 3242 ■ **Southern Nevada T.B.A. Supply Inc.**
1701 Las Vegas Blvd S
Las Vegas, NV 89104
Phone: (702)732-2382 **Fax:** (702)735-4061
Products: Tires. **SIC:** 5014 (Tires & Tubes). **Est:** 1948. **Sales:** $20,300,000 (2000). **Emp:** 200. **Officers:** Ted Wiens Jr., President; Kathy Mevius, Controller; Chris Publow, General Mgr. **Doing Business As:** Ted #Wiens Tire.

■ 3243 ■ **Southern Power Inc.**
2001 Oak Mountain Dr.
Pelham, AL 35124
Phone: (205)664-2001
Free: (800)782-7253 **Fax:** (205)663-9911
Products: Brake parts and assemblies. **SIC:** 5013 (Motor Vehicle Supplies & New Parts).

■ 3244 ■ **Southford Garage Truck Equippers**
Rte. Jct. 67 & 188
PO Box 174
Southbury, CT 06488
Phone: (203)264-5343
Free: (800)457-5697 **Fax:** (203)262-1405
Products: Truck equipment, including truck bodies, hitches, trailers, and hoists; Toolboxes; Van shelving; Bedliners; Snow removal equipment and snow plow parts. **SIC:** 5013 (Motor Vehicle Supplies & New Parts). **Est:** 1954. **Officers:** Mel Tomlinson, Owner.

■ 3245 ■ **Special Fleet Service**
875 Waterman Dr.
PO Box 990
Harrisonburg, VA 22801
Phone: (540)434-4488 **Fax:** (540)434-2244
Products: Automotive parts and supplies, New. **SIC:** 5013 (Motor Vehicle Supplies & New Parts). **Officers:** Greg Weaver, President.

■ 3246 ■ **Specialized Sales and Service Inc.**
PO Box 968
Klamath Falls, OR 97601
Phone: (541)884-5103
Products: Automotive parts. **SIC:** 5013 (Motor Vehicle Supplies & New Parts). **Est:** 1932. **Sales:** $5,100,000 (2000). **Emp:** 40. **Officers:** Wayne Stockstech, President; Wayne Sorenson, General Mgr.

■ 3247 ■ **Specialty Hearse and Ambulance Sales Corp.**
180 Dupont St.
Plainview, NY 11803
Phone: (516)349-7700 **Fax:** (516)349-0482
Products: Motorized Vehicless. **SIC:** 5012 (Automobiles & Other Motor Vehicles). **Sales:** $14,000,000 (2000). **Emp:** 16.

■ 3248 ■ **Specialty Vehicles Inc.**
16351 Gothard St., Ste. C.
Huntington Beach, CA 92647
Phone: (714)848-8455
Free: (800)784-8726 **Fax:** (714)848-2114
Products: Motorized vehicles. **SIC:** 5012 (Automobiles & Other Motor Vehicles).

■ 3249 ■ **Speed-O-Motive**
12061 E Slauson Ave.
Santa Fe Springs, CA 90670
Phone: (562)945-3444 **Fax:** (562)698-5210
Products: Car parts. **SIC:** 5013 (Motor Vehicle Supplies & New Parts). **Est:** 1946. **Emp:** 8.

■ 3250 ■ **Spencer Chain Gear Co.**
8410 Dallas Ave. S
Seattle, WA 98108-4423
Phone: (206)762-6767
Products: Power transmissions. **SIC:** 5085 (Industrial Supplies). **Sales:** $200,000 (1993). **Emp:** 4. **Officers:** Loren Williams, General Mgr.

■ 3251 ■ **Spencer Industries Inc. Chain Gear Div.**
Chain Gear Div.
1229 S Orr
Seattle, WA 98108
Phone: (206)762-6767 **Fax:** (206)767-2514
Products: Automobile parts. **SIC:** 5013 (Motor Vehicle Supplies & New Parts).

■ 3252 ■ **Spitzer Electrical Co.**
43 W 9th Ave.
Denver, CO 80204
Phone: (303)629-7221 **Fax:** (303)573-1059
Products: Auto parts, including electrical emissions and fuel systems. **SIC:** 5013 (Motor Vehicle Supplies & New Parts). **Est:** 1936. **Sales:** $1,000,000 (2000). **Emp:** 6. **Officers:** Thomas A. Spitzer, President; Nelson Tompkins, Treasurer; Kevin Best, Sales Mgr.

■ 3253 ■ **Spokane Diesel Inc.**
E 6615 Mallon
Spokane, WA 99220
Phone: (509)535-3663 **Fax:** (509)535-3734
Products: Transmissions and fuel systems. **SICs:** 5084 (Industrial Machinery & Equipment); 5013 (Motor Vehicle Supplies & New Parts). **Est:** 1953. **Sales:** $17,000,000 (2000). **Emp:** 80. **Officers:** Doug Burpee, President; Sue Price, Controller.

■ 3254 ■ **Spradling Originals**
PO Box 96
6841 Gadsen Hwy.
Trussville, AL 35173-0096
Phone: (205)655-7404
Free: (800)338-5484 **Fax:** (205)655-7406
E-mail: spradorig1@aol.com
URL: http://www.spradlingoriginals.com
Products: Trimmings for automobiles and others. **SIC:** 5013 (Motor Vehicle Supplies & New Parts). **Est:** 1981. **Sales:** $3,000,000 (2000). **Emp:** 16.

■ 3255 ■ **Sprague Devices Inc.**
107 Eastwood Rd.
Michigan City, IN 46360
Phone: (219)872-7295 **Fax:** (219)879-4748
Products: Windshield wiper motors. **SIC:** 5013 (Motor Vehicle Supplies & New Parts). **Est:** 1946. **Sales:** $30,000,000 (2000). **Emp:** 300. **Officers:** James D. Davis, President; John Heffelfinger, Controller; Theodore J. Gawronski, VP of Marketing & Sales; Tim Kent, Dir. of Information Systems; Tom Alexander, Dir of Human Resources.

■ 3256 ■ **SSF Imported Auto Parts Inc.**
466 Forbes Blvd.
South San Francisco, CA 94080
Phone: (650)873-9280
Products: Foreign auto parts. **SIC:** 5013 (Motor Vehicle Supplies & New Parts). **Est:** 1979. **Sales:** $9,000,000 (2000). **Emp:** 40. **Officers:** Olaf H. Siemers, President; Barry Fabro, Controller.

■ 3257 ■ **SSR Pump Co.**
PO Box 149
Michigan, ND 58259-9743
Phone: (701)259-2331
Products: Transportation equipment and supplies; Pumps; Fuel tanks; Sunflower pans; Gates. **SICs:** 5088 (Transportation Equipment & Supplies); 5015 (Motor Vehicle Parts—Used). **Officers:** Daniel Shirek, President.

■ 3258 ■ **Standard Automotive Parts Corp.**
25 West St.
Lawrence, MA 01841-3497
Phone: (978)683-5731
Products: Automotive parts and supplies, New. **SIC:** 5013 (Motor Vehicle Supplies & New Parts). **Emp:** 37. **Officers:** Leonard Richards.

■ 3259 ■ **Standard Battery and Electric Co.**
PO Box 28
Waterloo, IA 50704
Phone: (319)235-1455 **Fax:** (319)233-8932
E-mail: sbatt91546@aol.com
Products: Automotive parts and supplies; Industrial abrasive and bonding products. **SIC:** 5013 (Motor Vehicle Supplies & New Parts). **Est:** 1916. **Sales:** $2,200,000 (2000). **Emp:** 23. **Officers:** W.R. Layman, President.

■ 3260 ■ **Standard Parts Corp.**
500 Commerce Rd.
Richmond, VA 23224
Phone: (804)233-8321 **Free:** (800)445-8815
Products: Heavy-duty truck parts. **SIC:** 5013 (Motor Vehicle Supplies & New Parts). **Est:** 1922. **Sales:** $13,000,000 (2000). **Emp:** 90. **Officers:** William Kirby, President; Ken Tilman, Controller.

■ 3261 ■ **Stan's Towing & Repair**
Huckel Hill Rd.
RR 1, Box 684
Vernon, VT 05354
Phone: (802)257-1032
Products: Used automotive parts and supplies; Used cars. **SICs:** 5015 (Motor Vehicle Parts—Used); 5012 (Automobiles & Other Motor Vehicles). **Est:** 1982. **Emp:** 2. **Officers:** Stanley Sage, Owner.

■ 3262 ■ **Stant Corp.**
1620 Columbia Ave.
Connersville, IN 47331-1696
Phone: (765)962-6655 **Fax:** (765)962-6866
Products: Automotive parts. **SIC:** 5013 (Motor Vehicle Supplies & New Parts). **Sales:** $100,000,000 (2000). **Emp:** 2,400. **Officers:** David R. Paridy, President; M. Whetter, Dir. of Marketing & Sales; W.T. Margetts, Dir of Human Resources.

■ 3263 ■ **State Electric Company Inc.**
PO Box 28589
St. Louis, MO 63146
Phone: (314)569-2140
Free: (800)325-4258 **Fax:** (314)569-2488
E-mail: scott@state-electric.com
URL: http://www.state-electric.com
Products: Motors and motor controls. **SICs:** 5063 (Electrical Apparatus & Equipment); 5013 (Motor Vehicle Supplies & New Parts). **Est:** 1952. **Sales:** $7,000,000 (1999). **Emp:** 27. **Officers:** J.R. Baum, President.

■ 3264 ■ **Statler Body Works**
5573 Main St.
Box D
Marion, PA 17235
Phone: (717)375-2251 **Fax:** (717)375-2645
Products: Automotive parts and supplies, New. **SIC:** 5013 (Motor Vehicle Supplies & New Parts). **Officers:** Garry Wenger, Manager.

■ 3265 ■ **Steelfab**
500 Marshall St.
Paterson, NJ 07503
Phone: (973)278-0350 **Fax:** (973)345-7633
Products: Automotive parts and supplies, New. **SIC:** 5013 (Motor Vehicle Supplies & New Parts). **Officers:** Peter Garafano III, Contact.

■ **3266** ■ **Steepleton Tire Co.**
PO Box 90
Memphis, TN 38101
Phone: (901)774-6440 **Fax:** (901)774-6445
Products: Tires. **SIC:** 5014 (Tires & Tubes). **Est:** 1945.
Sales: $6,000,000 (2000). **Emp:** 45. **Officers:**
Steepleton, Chairman of the Board.

■ **3267** ■ **Stewart & Stevenson**
2929 Vassar Dr. NE
Albuquerque, NM 87107
Phone: (505)881-3511
Free: (800)733-3511 **Fax:** (505)881-3511
Products: Diesel engines; Generators. **SICs:** 5084
(Industrial Machinery & Equipment); 5013 (Motor
Vehicle Supplies & New Parts).

■ **3268** ■ **Stewart & Stevenson**
1515 W Murray Dr.
Farmington, NM 87401
Phone: (505)325-5071
Free: (800)767-5071 **Fax:** (505)325-5073
Products: Diesel engines; Transmissions. **SICs:** 5084
(Industrial Machinery & Equipment); 5013 (Motor
Vehicle Supplies & New Parts).

■ **3269** ■ **Stewart & Stevenson**
3919 Irving Blvd.
Dallas, TX 75247
Phone: (214)631-5370 **Fax:** (214)634-2811
Products: Diesel engines; Transmissions; Fan belts;
Spark plugs; Filters; Batteries. **SICs:** 5013 (Motor
Vehicle Supplies & New Parts); 5084 (Industrial
Machinery & Equipment).

■ **3270** ■ **Stewart and Stevenson Services Inc.**
PO Box 1637
Houston, TX 77251-1637
Phone: (713)868-7700 **Fax:** (713)868-7692
Products: Diesel engines; Aircraft ground support and
aircraft tow and baggage tractors; Drilling products,
including power generation equipment. **SICs:** 5084
(Industrial Machinery & Equipment); 5088
(Transportation Equipment & Supplies). **Sales:**
$1,206,800,000 (2000). **Emp:** 4,240. **Officers:** Michael
L. Grimes, CEO & President; John Doster, CFO.

■ **3271** ■ **Stone Heavy Vehicle Specialists Inc.**
PO Box 25518
Raleigh, NC 27611
Phone: (919)779-2351
Free: (800)334-3002 **Fax:** (919)772-8531
Products: Truck parts and accessories. **SIC:** 5013
(Motor Vehicle Supplies & New Parts). **Officers:**
Ronnie Mason, Operations Mgr.

■ **3272** ■ **Strafco Inc.**
PO Box 600
San Antonio, TX 78292-0600
Phone: (210)226-0101 **Fax:** (210)271-7495
Products: Automotive parts, paint and related
products. **SICs:** 5013 (Motor Vehicle Supplies & New
Parts); 5198 (Paints, Varnishes & Supplies); 5084
(Industrial Machinery & Equipment). **Sales:**
$113,000,000 (2000). **Emp:** 1,080. **Officers:** Jack D.
Trawick, President; Huey Rhudy, Treasurer & Secty.

■ **3273** ■ **Stratham Tire Inc.**
17 Portsmouth Ave.
Stratham, NH 03885
Phone: (603)772-3783
Products: Tires. **SIC:** 5014 (Tires & Tubes). **Est:** 1960.
Sales: $17,000,000 (2000). **Emp:** 160. **Officers:** Lionel
LaBonte, CEO & President.

■ **3274** ■ **Straus Frank Co.**
1964 S Alamo St.
San Antonio, TX 78204-1689
Phone: (210)226-0101 **Fax:** (210)226-0803
Products: Tires and inner tubes, new. **SIC:** 5014 (Tires
& Tubes). **Est:** 1870. **Sales:** $110,000,000 (2000).
Emp: 1,130. **Officers:** David J. Straus, Chairman of
the Board; Jack D. Trawick, President; Huey J. Rhudy,
Treasurer.

■ **3275** ■ **Stringfellow, Inc.**
2710 Locust St.
Nashville, TN 37207-4036
Phone: (615)226-4900
Free: (800)832-4404 **Fax:** (615)226-8685
Products: Automotive parts and supplies, New. **SIC:**
5013 (Motor Vehicle Supplies & New Parts). **Officers:**
John Reetz, President.

■ **3276** ■ **STS Truck Equipment and Trailer
Sales**
6680 Manlius Center Rd.
East Syracuse, NY 13057
Phone: (315)437-5406 **Fax:** (315)437-5615
Products: Trailers; Truck equipment and parts. **SIC:**
5013 (Motor Vehicle Supplies & New Parts). **Est:** 1949.
Emp: 52. **Officers:** Shawn Jacobs, General Mgr.

■ **3277** ■ **Stull Industries Inc.**
12155 Magnolia, Bldg. 5
Riverside, CA 92503
Phone: (909)343-2181 **Fax:** (909)343-2127
Products: Truck accessories. **SIC:** 5013 (Motor
Vehicle Supplies & New Parts). **Officers:** William S.
Stull.

■ **3278** ■ **Sturdevant Auto Supply**
100 Smith
Rock Rapids, IA 51246-1767
Phone: (712)472-3651
Products: Automotive parts and supplies, New. **SIC:**
5013 (Motor Vehicle Supplies & New Parts). **Emp:** 49.

■ **3279** ■ **Sturdevant Auto Supply**
505 E Main
Luverne, MN 56156-1905
Phone: (507)283-2371
Products: Automobile parts, used. **SIC:** 5015 (Motor
Vehicle Parts—Used). **Emp:** 49. **Officers:** Steve Popp.

■ **3280** ■ **Sturdevant Auto Supply**
501 Broadway
Box 398
Wheaton, MN 56296
Phone: (320)563-8209 **Free:** (800)950-0289
Products: Automotive parts and supplies. **SIC:** 5013
(Motor Vehicle Supplies & New Parts). **Sales:**
$500,000 (2000). **Emp:** 2. **Officers:** Mike Fox,
Manager.

■ **3281** ■ **Sumitok America Inc.**
23326 Hawthorne Blvd., Ste. 360
Torrance, CA 90505
Phone: (310)378-7886 **Fax:** (310)378-0108
Products: Electronic materials for autos, computers,
and VCR's; Motor generators; Metallic magnets. PDL
Lumber and building materials. **SIC:** 5065 (Electronic
Parts & Equipment Nec). **Sales:** $6,500,000 (1993).
Emp: 74. **Officers:** Susumu Hashimoto, President;
Hisashi Maruyama, Treasurer.

■ **3282** ■ **Summit of New England**
386 Hill St.
Biddeford, ME 04005
Phone: (207)283-1463
Products: Tires. **SIC:** 5014 (Tires & Tubes).

■ **3283** ■ **Sunnyside Auto Finance**
2424 W Montrose Ave.
Chicago, IL 60618
Phone: (773)267-8200
Products: Automobile parts, including tires and
mufflers. **SICs:** 5013 (Motor Vehicle Supplies & New
Parts); 5014 (Tires & Tubes). **Est:** 1929. **Sales:**
$8,500,000 (2000). **Emp:** 30. **Officers:** Leonard
Demichele, President; Sam Monteleone, General Mgr.

■ **3284** ■ **Superior Auto Electric**
1847 Highland Ave.
New Hyde Park, NY 11040-4049
Phone: (516)437-1267 **Fax:** (516)437-1754
Products: Automotive parts and supplies, new and
rebuilt. **SIC:** 5013 (Motor Vehicle Supplies & New
Parts). **Est:** 1965. **Sales:** $3,750,000 (2000). **Emp:** 42.
Officers: Paul Burstein.

■ **3285** ■ **Superior Auto Sales Inc.**
5201 Camp Rd.
Hamburg, NY 14075
Phone: (716)649-6695
Free: (800)732-3275 **Fax:** (716)649-2375
Products: Automobiles. **SIC:** 5012 (Automobiles &
Other Motor Vehicles). **Sales:** $27,000,000 (2000).
Emp: 28. **Officers:** Richard J. Izzo, President; Donald
Baldwin, Controller.

■ **3286** ■ **Superior Pump Exchange Co.**
12901 Crenshaw Blvd.
Hawthorne, CA 90250-5511
Phone: (310)676-4995 **Fax:** (310)676-9430
Products: Water pumps for cars and trucks. **SIC:** 5013
(Motor Vehicle Supplies & New Parts). **Est:** 1944.
Sales: $500,000 (2000). **Emp:** 5. **Officers:** Ed Wisse,
Owner; Sharon Wisse Magruder, Manager.

■ **3287** ■ **Superior Tire Inc.**
2320 Western Ave.
Las Vegas, NV 89102
Phone: (702)384-2937
Products: Tires. **SIC:** 5014 (Tires & Tubes). **Est:** 1952.
Sales: $15,000,000 (2000). **Emp:** 100. **Officers:** Marlo
O. Reimer, President; Robert Wright, Treasurer &
Secty.; Steven Reimer, VP of Marketing.

■ **3288** ■ **Sussen Inc.**
6000 Carnegie Ave.
Cleveland, OH 44103
Phone: (216)361-1700 **Fax:** (216)361-0843
Products: Automobile parts. **SIC:** 5013 (Motor Vehicle
Supplies & New Parts). **Est:** 1921. **Sales:** $37,000,000
(2000). **Emp:** 200. **Officers:** Daniel C. Sussen,
President; John Pippin, VP of Finance; William G.
Fording, Dir. of Marketing.

■ **3289** ■ **Swansons Tire Company Inc.**
PO Box 1342
Oklahoma City, OK 73101
Phone: (405)235-8305 **Fax:** (405)235-0111
Products: Pneumatic tires. **SIC:** 5014 (Tires & Tubes).
Emp: 19. **Officers:** Mary H. Swanson.

■ **3290** ■ **T & L Industries Co.**
300 Quaker Ln., Ste. 7 (PMB 151)
Warwick, RI 02886-6682
Phone: (401)884-1504
Free: (800)524-1504 **Fax:** (401)946-6299
URL: http://www.gojacks.com
Products: Automotive line. Vehicle moving jacks used
to lift cars. **SIC:** 5013 (Motor Vehicle Supplies & New
Parts). **Est:** 1992. **Sales:** $3,000,000 (1999). **Emp:** 10.
Officers: Robert V. Jackvony, President, e-mail: bob@
ezgojaks.com. **Former Name:** ABA-Tron Industries
Inc.

■ **3291** ■ **T-W Truck Equippers, Inc.**
590 Elk St.
Buffalo, NY 14210-2237
Phone: (716)683-2250 **Fax:** (716)683-2257
Products: Automotive parts and supplies, New. **SIC:**
5013 (Motor Vehicle Supplies & New Parts). **Officers:**
Tom Ogden, Contact.

■ **3292** ■ **Target Tire and Automotive Corp.**
2221 Lejeune Blvd.
Jacksonville, NC 28540
Phone: (919)353-4300
Products: Tires; Automotive accessories. **SICs:** 5014
(Tires & Tubes); 5013 (Motor Vehicle Supplies & New
Parts). **Sales:** $60,000,000 (2000). **Emp:** 170.
Officers: L.B. Stein, President; Howard M. Stein, Vice
President; Dave Puckett, Vice President.

■ **3293** ■ **TBC Corp.**
PO Box 18342
Memphis, TN 38181-0342
Phone: (901)363-8030 **Fax:** (901)541-3625
Products: New wheels, motor vehicle. **SIC:** 5014
(Tires & Tubes). **Est:** 1956. **Sales:** $136,920,000
(2000). **Emp:** 200. **Officers:** Marvin E. Bruce, CEO &
Chairman of the Board; Louis S. DiPasqua, COO &
President; Kenneth P. Dick, Sr. VP of Sales; Bob M.
Hubbard, Sr. VP of Purchasing & Engineering.

■ **3294** ■ **Tech Distributing/Supply**
28300 Industrial Blvd.
Hayward, CA 94545
Phone: (510)783-7085
Products: Tires. **SIC:** 5014 (Tires & Tubes). **Est:** 1980.
Sales: $1,000,000 (2000). **Emp:** 24. **Officers:** Don
Zavattero, Vice President.

■ **3295** ■ **Tech Inc.**
PO Box 14310
Shawnee Mission, KS 66285-4310
Phone: (913)492-6440 **Fax:** (913)492-8159
Products: Tire and tire repair materials, including
tread. **SIC:** 5014 (Tires & Tubes). **Est:** 1952. **Sales:**
$12,000,000 (2000). **Emp:** 46. **Officers:** Jack Clifford,
President; Robert Bjorseth, CFO.

■ **3296** ■ **Technical Sales Inc.**
433 Clyde Ave.
Mountain View, CA 94043-2209
Phone: (650)969-6308
Free: (800)346-3441 **Fax:** (650)964-3407
Products: Dupont vespel parts and supplies. **SIC:**
5065 (Electronic Parts & Equipment Nec). **Sales:**
$10,800,000 (2000). **Emp:** 56. **Officers:** Walter G.
Chew, President; David L. Chew, Accountant.

■ **3297** ■ **Technovance Corp.**
956 W Hyde Park Blvd.
Inglewood, CA 90302-3308
Phone: (310)674-5130 **Fax:** (562)694-0011
Products: Automotive engine cylinderhead repair
components. **SIC:** 5013 (Motor Vehicle Supplies & New
Parts). **Sales:** $2,000,000 (2000). **Emp:** 49. **Officers:**
R. A. Hermann.

■ **3298** ■ **Teleparts, Inc.**
763-C Susquehanna Ave.
Franklin Lakes, NJ 07417
Phone: (201)847-9509 **Fax:** (201)847-9511
E-mail: teleparts@aol.com
Products: Mining equipment parts; Electrical engine
equipment; Motor vehicle parts; Truck trailer axles;
Tractor and loader parts and attachments. **SICs:** 5013
(Motor Vehicle Supplies & New Parts); 5082
(Construction & Mining Machinery); 5063 (Electrical
Apparatus & Equipment). **Est:** 1990. **Officers:** Doron
Miller, President.

■ **3299** ■ **Temple Products of Indiana Inc.**
4511 Pine Creek Rd.
Elkhart, IN 46516
Phone: (219)294-3621 **Fax:** (219)293-9827
Products: Mobile home and RV accessories. **SIC:**
5013 (Motor Vehicle Supplies & New Parts). **Est:** 1970.
Sales: $10,000,000 (2000). **Emp:** 15. **Officers:** John
Loomis, General Mgr.

■ **3300** ■ **Texas Kenworth Co.**
PO Box 560049
Dallas, TX 75356-0049
Phone: (214)920-7300 **Fax:** (214)920-7318
Products: Truck parts, including steering wheels, oil
filters, and beds. **SIC:** 5013 (Motor Vehicle Supplies &
New Parts). **Sales:** $70,000,000 (2000). **Emp:** 250.
Officers: V.E. Salvino, President; Charles Masterson,
Controller.

■ **3301** ■ **Textron Automotive**
2100 Dove St.
Port Huron, MI 48060
Phone: (810)989-3900
Products: Automotive parts and supplies. **SIC:** 5013
(Motor Vehicle Supplies & New Parts).

■ **3302** ■ **W.B. Thompson Company Inc.**
PO Box 709
Iron Mountain, MI 49801
Phone: (906)774-6543 **Fax:** (906)774-0110
Products: Off-highway truck parts and supplies. **SIC:**
5013 (Motor Vehicle Supplies & New Parts). **Est:** 1940.
Sales: $11,000,000 (2000). **Emp:** 30. **Officers:** W.
Barton Berg Jr., President; Jerry Brian, Mgr. of Finance
& Admin.; W. Barton Berg Sr., Sales Mgr.

■ **3303** ■ **Throwbot Inc.**
955 Fee Dr.
Sacramento, CA 95815
Phone: (916)923-0505
Products: Automobile parts. **SIC:** 5013 (Motor Vehicle
Supplies & New Parts).

■ **3304** ■ **Time Equipment**
311 N Campbell
Rapid City, SD 57701
Phone: (605)348-2360 **Fax:** (605)348-0058
Products: Automotive parts and supplies, New. **SIC:**
5013 (Motor Vehicle Supplies & New Parts). **Officers:**
Phil Swaney, Contact.

■ **3305** ■ **Tire Corral Inc.**
800 Ash Ave.
McAllen, TX 78501
Phone: (956)631-8473 **Fax:** (956)630-2742
Products: Tires; Custom wheels. **SIC:** 5014 (Tires &
Tubes). **Sales:** $9,000,000 (2000). **Emp:** 18. **Officers:**
Scott Mathews, President.

■ **3306** ■ **The Tire Rack Wholesale**
777 W Chippewa Ave.
South Bend, IN 46614
Phone: (219)287-2316
Free: (800)445-0179 **Fax:** (219)236-7700
Products: Tires and wheels. **SIC:** 5014 (Tires &
Tubes). **Officers:** Peter Veldman; Wilma Veldman.

■ **3307** ■ **Tire Welder Inc.**
3428 Pan America Fwy NE
Albuquerque, NM 87107-4741
Phone: (505)884-3550 **Fax:** (505)884-1480
Products: Used tires. **SIC:** 5014 (Tires & Tubes).
Officers: Steve Wenk, President.

■ **3308** ■ **Tires Inc.**
5951 Ames Ave.
Omaha, NE 68104-2705
Phone: 800-228-2241 **Fax:** (402)392-2176
Products: Pneumatic tires. **SIC:** 5014 (Tires & Tubes).
Est: 1969. **Sales:** $10,000,000 (2000). **Emp:** 70.
Officers: Jerry Hoberman, President.

■ **3309** ■ **Tires, Wheels, Etc. Wholesale Inc.**
3910 Cherry Ave., No. 17038
Long Beach, CA 90807-3727
Phone: (310)981-2686
Products: Tires for automobiles. **SIC:** 5014 (Tires &
Tubes). **Sales:** $32,000,000 (2000). **Emp:** 60.
Officers: Hank Feldman, Owner.

■ **3310** ■ **Tires Wholesale Inc.**
4540 E Hammer Ln.
Las Vegas, NV 89115-1402
Phone: (702)644-5544
Products: Automobile engines, used. **SIC:** 5015
(Motor Vehicle Parts—Used). **Officers:** Richard
RousseII, President.

■ **3311** ■ **Tisdale Used Auto Parts**
PO Box 1213
Gardiner, ME 04345-1213
Phone: (207)582-7542 **Fax:** (207)582-8233
Products: Automobile parts, used. **SIC:** 5015 (Motor
Vehicle Parts—Used). **Officers:** Robert Miville,
President.

■ **3312** ■ **Titan Technologies Inc.**
(Albuquerque, New Mexico)
3202 Candelaria Rd. NE
Albuquerque, NM 87107
Phone: (505)884-0272
Products: Recycled tires. **SIC:** 5093 (Scrap & Waste
Materials).

■ **3313** ■ **TNT Insured Towing Auto Salvage**
PO Box 8184
Boise, ID 83707-2184
Phone: (208)362-4418 **Fax:** (208)362-9632
Products: Automobile parts, used. **SIC:** 5015 (Motor
Vehicle Parts—Used). **Officers:** Tommy Thompson,
Owner.

■ **3314** ■ **T.O. Haas Holding Co.**
PO Box 81067
Lincoln, NE 68501
Phone: (402)474-3211
Products: Tires and automobile supplies. **SICs:** 5014
(Tires & Tubes); 5013 (Motor Vehicle Supplies & New
Parts).

■ **3315** ■ **T.O. Haas Tire Company Inc.**
PO Box 81067
Lincoln, NE 68501
Phone: (402)473-1415
Free: (800)876-0191 **Fax:** (402)473-1402
Products: Tires. **SICs:** 5014 (Tires & Tubes); 5013
(Motor Vehicle Supplies & New Parts). **Sales:**
$80,000,000 (2000). **Emp:** 265. **Officers:** Randall
Haas, President; Dave Scott, Mgr. of Finance.

■ **3316** ■ **Tokico (USA) Inc.**
17225 Federal Dr.
Allen Park, MI 48101-3613
Phone: (313)336-5310
Products: Master cylinders and shocks. **SIC:** 5013
(Motor Vehicle Supplies & New Parts). **Emp:** 400.

■ **3317** ■ **Tomasco Mulciber Inc.**
2001 Courtright Rd.
Columbus, OH 43232-4210
Phone: (614)231-0075 **Fax:** (614)231-9910
Products: Automotive parts. **SIC:** 5013 (Motor Vehicle
Supplies & New Parts). **Emp:** 170. **Officers:** K.
Shirasaki.

■ **3318** ■ **Tomco Auto Products Inc.**
4330 E 26th St.
Los Angeles, CA 90023-4770
Phone: (213)268-4830
Free: (800)858-3458 **Fax:** (213)269-4148
URL: http://www.tomcoautoproducts.com
Products: Carburetors, new and rebuilt. **SIC:** 5013
(Motor Vehicle Supplies & New Parts). **Est:** 1947.
Sales: $24,000,000 (2000). **Emp:** 370. **Officers:** Victor
Moss, President; Donald H. Maltzman, Chairman of the
Board; Richard A. Schoenfeld, Exec. VP; Bob Miller,
VP of Sales. **Former Name:** Tomco Carburetor
Company.

■ **3319** ■ **Top Source Technologies Inc.**
7108 Fairway Dr., No. 200
Palm Beach Gardens, FL 33418-3769
Phone: (561)775-5756 **Fax:** (561)775-5938
Products: Automotive parts. **SIC:** 5013 (Motor Vehicle
Supplies & New Parts). **Est:** 1986. **Sales:** $16,900,000
(2000). **Emp:** 62. **Officers:** William C. Willis Jr., CEO &
President; David Natan, VP of Finance; William E.
Somerville, Controller.

■ **3320** ■ **F. Torello and Son Machine Co.**
206 Orange Ave.
West Haven, CT 06516
Phone: (203)933-1684
Products: Mechanical auto parts. **SIC:** 5013 (Motor
Vehicle Supplies & New Parts). **Sales:** $3,000,000
(2000). **Emp:** 12. **Officers:** Thomas Torello, CEO.

■ **3321** ■ **Torque Drive**
317 S Park Ave.
Warren, OH 44483
Phone: (330)399-1000 **Fax:** (330)394-7564
Products: Power transmissions. **SICs:** 5084 (Industrial
Machinery & Equipment); 5013 (Motor Vehicle Supplies
& New Parts).

■ **3322** ■ **Toyota Motor Distributors Inc.**
440 Forbes Blvd.
Mansfield, MA 02048
Phone: (508)339-5701
Products: Automotive parts. **SIC:** 5013 (Motor Vehicle
Supplies & New Parts). **Sales:** $18,000,000 (2000).
Emp: 75. **Officers:** Bill Fay, General Mgr.

■ **3323** ■ **Trace Engineering**
5916 195th NE
Arlington, WA 98223
Phone: (253)435-8826 **Fax:** (253)435-2229
Products: Power inverters. **SIC:** 5013 (Motor Vehicle
Supplies & New Parts). **Est:** 1985. **Sales:** $7,000,000
(2000). **Emp:** 65. **Officers:** Ken Cox, President; John
Vilitch, CEO; Bob Summers, Marketing Dir.

■ **3324** ■ **Tracom Inc.**
932 S Ayers Ave.
Ft. Worth, TX 76103
Phone: (817)534-6566
Free: (800)423-2536 **Fax:** (817)534-4064
Products: Diesel engines and component parts. **SICs:** 5084 (Industrial Machinery & Equipment); 5013 (Motor Vehicle Supplies & New Parts). **Est:** 1987. **Sales:** $4,500,000 (2000). **Emp:** 20. **Officers:** William T. Rucker, CEO & President, e-mail: billr@tracominc.com; Michele Grogan, Controller; Brendon Hand, Vice President; Elizabeth A. Owens, Dir. of Internal Sales.

■ **3325** ■ **Trailer Craft**
1031 E 64th Ave.
Anchorage, AK 99518
Phone: (907)563-3238 **Fax:** (907)561-4995
Products: Trailer parts. **SIC:** 5013 (Motor Vehicle Supplies & New Parts). **Est:** 1969. **Emp:** 50. **Officers:** John A. Lutz, President.

■ **3326** ■ **Transmission Engineering Co.**
PO Box 580
1851 N Penn Rd.
Hatfield, PA 19440
Phone: (215)822-6737
Free: (800)521-3285 **Fax:** (215)822-5608
E-mail: ptsales@transengr.com
URL: http://www.transengr.com
Products: Power transmission, motion control and electrical supplies for marine and material handling industries. **SICs:** 5084 (Industrial Machinery & Equipment); 5085 (Industrial Supplies). **Est:** 1936. **Sales:** $1,600,000 (2000). **Emp:** 53. **Officers:** C. Bishop, Chairman of the Board; Scott Bishop, CEO & President; Tony Sandor, Dir. of Data Processing; Tony Sandor, Dir. of Data Processing.

■ **3327** ■ **Transmission Exchange Co.**
1803 NE ML King Jr. Blvd.
Portland, OR 97212
Phone: (503)284-0768
Free: (800)776-1191 **Fax:** (503)280-1655
E-mail: mail@txchange.com
URL: http://www.txchange.com
Products: Power transmission equipment and supplies. **SIC:** 5013 (Motor Vehicle Supplies & New Parts). **Est:** 1952. **Emp:** 19. **Officers:** Stanley Hodes; Gregory Hodes.

■ **3328** ■ **Transply Inc.**
PO Box 7727
York, PA 17404-0727
Phones: (717)767-1005 (717)845-2685
Fax: (717)767-9410
Products: Automotive equipment, including power transmissions, belts, brake shoes, and motors. **SICs:** 5085 (Industrial Supplies); 5063 (Electrical Apparatus & Equipment). **Est:** 1972. **Sales:** $19,000,000 (2000). **Emp:** 82. **Officers:** Ray Gross, President.

■ **3329** ■ **Transport Equipment, Inc.**
637 Elmdale Rd.
Toledo, OH 43609
Phone: (419)385-4641
Free: (800)685-4641 **Fax:** (419)385-9447
Products: Automotive parts and supplies, New. **SIC:** 5013 (Motor Vehicle Supplies & New Parts). **Officers:** Scott Tuttle, Vice President.

■ **3330** ■ **Transtar Industries Inc.**
7350 Young Dr.
Walton Hills, OH 44146-5390
Phone: (216)232-5100
Products: Power transmission equipment and supplies; Electrical transmission equipment. **SIC:** 5013 (Motor Vehicle Supplies & New Parts). **Sales:** $24,000,000 (2000). **Emp:** 100. **Officers:** Monte Ahuja, President.

■ **3331** ■ **Transtat Equipment, Inc.**
PO Box 593865
Orlando, FL 32859
Phone: (407)857-2040
Free: (800)331-2377 **Fax:** (407)855-7127
Products: Automotive parts and supplies, New. **SIC:** 5013 (Motor Vehicle Supplies & New Parts). **Officers:** Leroy C. Peterson, Contact.

■ **3332** ■ **Treadways Corp.**
601 Gateway, Ste. 650
South San Francisco, CA 94080
Phone: (650)583-5555
Free: (800)688-8889 **Fax:** (650)872-0187
Products: Tires. **SIC:** 5014 (Tires & Tubes). **Emp:** 170. **Officers:** D. Wire; K. Iwsawa; M. Ueno.

■ **3333** ■ **Tri Citi Auto Warehouse**
6715 66th St. N
Pinellas Park, FL 33781-5035
Phone: (813)544-8856 **Fax:** (813)541-5480
Products: Automotive parts, including mufflers, gaskets, and carburetors. **SIC:** 5013 (Motor Vehicle Supplies & New Parts). **Emp:** 49. **Officers:** Steven Carlisle.

■ **3334** ■ **Tri-County Truck Tops, Inc.**
Rtes. 62 & 25 PO Box 201
Algonquin, IL 60102
Phone: (847)658-7200 **Fax:** (847)658-0940
Products: Automotive parts and supplies, New. **SIC:** 5013 (Motor Vehicle Supplies & New Parts). **Officers:** Carl Silva, President.

■ **3335** ■ **Tri-Power, Inc.**
358 Milling Rd.
Mocksville, NC 27028
Phone: (704)634-5348 **Fax:** (704)634-0237
Products: Power transmission equipment. **SIC:** 5013 (Motor Vehicle Supplies & New Parts).

■ **3336** ■ **Tri-State Auction Company Inc.**
PO Box 772
West Fargo, ND 58078-0772
Phone: (701)282-8203 **Fax:** (701)281-0888
Products: Automobiles. **SIC:** 5012 (Automobiles & Other Motor Vehicles). **Officers:** Kent Zabel, President.

■ **3337** ■ **Tri-State Bearing Co.**
3418 E 25th St.
Minneapolis, MN 55406
Phone: (612)721-2463
Products: Power transmission products. **SICs:** 5013 (Motor Vehicle Supplies & New Parts); 5085 (Industrial Supplies).

■ **3338** ■ **Tri-State Ladder & Scaffolding Company, Inc.**
26 Colton St.
Worcester, MA 01610
Phone: (508)754-3030
Free: (800)462-8001 **Fax:** (508)831-9992
Products: Automotive parts and supplies, New. **SIC:** 5013 (Motor Vehicle Supplies & New Parts). **Officers:** David Wauczinski, Contact.

■ **3339** ■ **Tri State Warehouse Inc.**
PO Box 1719
Sioux Falls, SD 57101-1719
Phone: (605)336-1482 **Fax:** (605)336-0340
Products: Auto parts, including starters and transmissions. **SIC:** 5013 (Motor Vehicle Supplies & New Parts). **Est:** 1936. **Sales:** $5,000,000 (2000). **Emp:** 35. **Officers:** M.G. Maurer, President.

■ **3340** ■ **Triangle Inc.**
51 Fernwood Ln.
Roslyn, NY 11576
Phone: (516)365-8143 **Fax:** (516)365-8429
E-mail: trngl@aol.com
URL: http://www.nauticalworld.com/triangle
Products: Automotive accessories; Boating accessories. **SICs:** 5013 (Motor Vehicle Supplies & New Parts); 5088 (Transportation Equipment & Supplies). **Est:** 1977. **Sales:** $2,000,000 (2000). **Emp:** 4. **Officers:** Arthur Einhorn, President; Judith Evans, Secretary.

■ **3341** ■ **Tricon Industries Inc.**
Electromechanical Div.
1600 Eisenhower Ln.
Lisle, IL 60532-2167
Phone: (630)964-2330 **Fax:** (630)964-5179
E-mail: saks@triconinc.com
URL: http://www.triconinc.com
Products: Molded plastics products; Automotive parts and supplies, New. **SICs:** 5013 (Motor Vehicle Supplies & New Parts); 5162 (Plastics Materials & Basic Shapes). **Est:** 1944. **Sales:** $50,000,000 (2000). **Emp:** 575. **Officers:** Ralph W. Grandle, President; Susan Grandle, Treasurer; Patricia L. Grandle, Secretary.

■ **3342** ■ **Triumph Motorcycles America Ltd.**
403 Dividend Dr.
Peachtree City, GA 30269
Phone: (404)631-9500
Products: Motorcycles. **SIC:** 5012 (Automobiles & Other Motor Vehicles).

■ **3343** ■ **Truck Body Manufacturing Company, Inc.**
48 Hunter Ave.
Johnston, RI 02919-4006
Phone: (401)351-0711 **Fax:** (401)331-5955
Products: Automotive parts and supplies, New. **SIC:** 5013 (Motor Vehicle Supplies & New Parts). **Officers:** Albert R. Payette, President.

■ **3344** ■ **Truck Equipment Boston, Inc.**
316 N Beacon St.
Brighton, MA 02135
Phone: (617)782-4320 **Fax:** (617)254-5112
Products: Automotive parts and supplies, New. **SIC:** 5013 (Motor Vehicle Supplies & New Parts). **Officers:** Emil A. Florio, Contact.

■ **3345** ■ **Truck Equipment Co.**
511 N Channing Ave.
St. Louis, MO 63103
Phone: (314)533-6200 **Fax:** (314)533-0159
Products: Truck equipment. **SIC:** 5013 (Motor Vehicle Supplies & New Parts).

■ **3346** ■ **Truck Equipment Distributors**
2020 SW Blvd.
Tulsa, OK 74107
Phone: (918)584-4733 **Fax:** (918)584-6019
Products: Truck parts and equipment, including chains, bodies, mirrors, lenses, and tables. **SIC:** 5013 (Motor Vehicle Supplies & New Parts).

■ **3347** ■ **Truck Equipment Inc.**
680 Potts Ave.
Green Bay, WI 54304
Phone: (414)494-7451
Free: (800)242-7337 **Fax:** (920)494-2130
Products: Truck and trailer parts. **SICs:** 5012 (Automobiles & Other Motor Vehicles); 5013 (Motor Vehicle Supplies & New Parts). **Est:** 1958. **Sales:** $71,000,000 (2000). **Emp:** 45. **Officers:** Isadore L. Kwaterski, CEO; Tom Kwaterski, Treasurer & Secty.

■ **3348** ■ **Truck Equipment Sales Inc.**
PO Box 1987
Dothan, AL 36302
Phone: (205)792-4124
Products: Beds, gates, and packers for trucks. **SICs:** 5012 (Automobiles & Other Motor Vehicles); 5013 (Motor Vehicle Supplies & New Parts). **Est:** 1964. **Sales:** $4,800,000 (2000). **Emp:** 40. **Officers:** R.C. Frey, President.

■ **3349** ■ **Truck Parts and Equipment Inc.**
4501 Esthner St.
Wichita, KS 67209
Phone: (316)942-4251
Products: Truck parts. **SIC:** 5013 (Motor Vehicle Supplies & New Parts). **Est:** 1925. **Sales:** $8,000,000 (2000). **Emp:** 62. **Officers:** Zeke Pinaire, President; Winston Abraham, Controller.

■ **3350** ■ **Truck Pro**
818 Division
Evansville, IN 47711
Phone: (812)424-2900 **Fax:** (812)422-2428
Products: Heavy-duty truck products. **SIC:** 5013 (Motor Vehicle Supplies & New Parts).

■ **3351** ■ **Truckways Inc.**
PO Box 911
Mills, WY 82644-0911
Phone: (307)234-0756
Products: Automobile parts, used; Motor vehicle parts and accessories. **SIC:** 5015 (Motor Vehicle Parts—Used). **Officers:** Delores Choyeski, President.

■ 3352 ■ **Truckwell of Alaska**
11221 Olive Ln.
Anchorage, AK 99515
Phone: (907)349-8845
Free: (800)478-8845 **Fax:** (907)344-0644
Products: Automotive parts and supplies, New. **SIC:** 5013 (Motor Vehicle Supplies & New Parts). **Officers:** Arnie Swanson, Contact.

■ 3353 ■ **TRW. Inc**
11202 E Germann Rd.
Queen Creek, AZ 85242
Phone: (480)987-4000 **Fax:** (480)987-4742
Products: Driver and passenger side air bag inflators, modules and gas generators. **SIC:** 5013 (Motor Vehicle Supplies & New Parts).

■ 3354 ■ **TRW Replacement**
3717 Pipestone Rd.
Dallas, TX 75212-6111
Phone: (214)637-2831 **Fax:** (214)637-2207
Products: Auto parts. **SIC:** 5013 (Motor Vehicle Supplies & New Parts). **Emp:** 49.

■ 3355 ■ **Tuckers Tire & Oil Company Inc.**
844 S Main
PO Box 1149
Dyersburg, TN 38025-1149
Phone: (901)285-8520
Free: (800)443-0802 **Fax:** (901)285-5889
Products: Tires and inner tubes, new. **SIC:** 5014 (Tires & Tubes). **Sales:** $6,000,000 (2000). **Emp:** 49. **Officers:** J. R. Tucker.

■ 3356 ■ **Twinco Romax Inc.**
4635 Willow Dr.
Hamel, MN 55340
Phone: (612)478-2360
Free: (800)682-3800 **Fax:** (612)478-3411
Products: Automobile parts. **SIC:** 5013 (Motor Vehicle Supplies & New Parts). **Sales:** $21,000,000 (2000). **Emp:** 50. **Officers:** D. Ribnick, President.

■ 3357 ■ **U-Joints, Inc.**
4220 Edith NE
Albuquerque, NM 87107
Phone: (505)345-2666
Products: Drive line parts. **SIC:** 5013 (Motor Vehicle Supplies & New Parts).

■ 3358 ■ **U-Joints, Inc.**
11213 Rojas
El Paso, TX 79926
Phone: (915)593-8215 **Fax:** (915)593-8688
Products: Transmission parts; Truck parts; Brakes. **SIC:** 5013 (Motor Vehicle Supplies & New Parts).

■ 3359 ■ **Ultraseal International Inc.**
1100 N Wilcox Ave.
Los Angeles, CA 90038
Phone: (323)466-1226
Free: (800)346-9090 **Fax:** (323)465-9456
E-mail: tirelife@ultraseal.com
URL: http://www.ultraseal.com
Products: Tire sealant. **SIC:** 5013 (Motor Vehicle Supplies & New Parts). **Est:** 1968. **Emp:** 10. **Officers:** Liz Aguirre, President; Ron Aguirre, Vice President.

■ 3360 ■ **Uni Filter Inc.**
1468 S Manhattan Ave.
Fullerton, CA 92831
Phone: (714)535-6933 **Fax:** (714)535-6927
E-mail: unifilter@aol.com
URL: http://www.unifilter.com
Products: Washable foam air filters for motorcycles, light trucks, and cars. **SIC:** 5013 (Motor Vehicle Supplies & New Parts). **Est:** 1971. **Emp:** 55. **Officers:** Tom Gross, Vice President.

■ 3361 ■ **Union Bearing & Transmission**
505 Bryant St.
Denver, CO 80204-4809
Phone: (303)825-1540 **Fax:** (303)825-1599
Products: Power transmission products, including bearings. **SICs:** 5084 (Industrial Machinery & Equipment); 5085 (Industrial Supplies); 5013 (Motor Vehicle Supplies & New Parts).

■ 3362 ■ **United Auto Parts Inc.**
301 W 1st
Mitchell, SD 57301-2514
Phone: (605)996-5585 **Fax:** (605)996-0831
Products: Electrical parts for automobiles, including ignitions and filters. **SIC:** 5013 (Motor Vehicle Supplies & New Parts). **Emp:** 49. **Officers:** L. L. Hildebrandt, President; Ruth Brane.

■ 3363 ■ **United Automotive Supply Co.**
2637 E 10 Mile Rd.
Warren, MI 48091-6800
Phone: (248)399-3900 **Fax:** (248)399-5841
Products: Gas engines; Hydraulic and pneumatic rotary actuators, accumulators, cushions, and nonvehicular shock absorbers. **SIC:** 5013 (Motor Vehicle Supplies & New Parts). **Est:** 1930. **Emp:** 35. **Officers:** Robert C. Rosenfeld, President.

■ 3364 ■ **United Engines**
7454 E 41st St.
Tulsa, OK 74145
Phone: (918)627-8080 **Fax:** (918)663-0467
Products: Diesel engines. **SIC:** 5013 (Motor Vehicle Supplies & New Parts).

■ 3365 ■ **United Engines Inc.**
7255 Greenwood Rd.
Shreveport, LA 71119
Phone: (318)635-8022 **Fax:** (318)635-8093
Products: Engines. **SIC:** 5013 (Motor Vehicle Supplies & New Parts).

■ 3366 ■ **United Engines Inc.**
PO Box 75079
Oklahoma City, OK 73147
Phone: (405)947-3321
Free: (800)955-3321 **Fax:** (405)947-3406
Products: Diesel engines, transmissions, and natural gas engines. **SICs:** 5063 (Electrical Apparatus & Equipment); 5013 (Motor Vehicle Supplies & New Parts); 5084 (Industrial Machinery & Equipment).

■ 3367 ■ **United Industrial Tire Inc.**
PO Box 689
Lebanon, IN 46052
Phone: (765)482-9603 **Fax:** (317)841-2214
Products: Tires. **SIC:** 5014 (Tires & Tubes). **Sales:** $4,000,000 (2000). **Emp:** 8. **Officers:** Al Harker, President.

■ 3368 ■ **United Manufacturers Service**
403 N Court St.
Marion, IL 62959
Phone: (618)997-1375
Products: Car parts, including mufflers and tires. **SIC:** 5013 (Motor Vehicle Supplies & New Parts). **Est:** 1966. **Sales:** $7,000,000 (2000). **Emp:** 22. **Officers:** Edward H. Aikman, President.

■ 3369 ■ **United School Bus Seat Services**
116 Depew Dr.
Branson, MO 65616
Phone: (417)334-3100
Products: Buses. **SIC:** 5012 (Automobiles & Other Motor Vehicles).

■ 3370 ■ **U.S. Manufacturing Corp.**
2401 16th St.
Port Huron, MI 48060
Phone: (810)984-4145
Products: Automotive parts and supplies; Industrial machinery. **SICs:** 5013 (Motor Vehicle Supplies & New Parts); 5084 (Industrial Machinery & Equipment).

■ 3371 ■ **U.S. Oil Company Inc.**
425 S Washington St.
Combined Locks, WI 54113
Phone: (920)739-6100
Free: (800)444-0202 **Fax:** (920)788-5910
URL: http://www.usoil.com
Products: Gasoline; Fuel oil; Tires; Automotive parts, including exhaust systems and brakes. **SICs:** 5013 (Motor Vehicle Supplies & New Parts); 5171 (Petroleum Bulk Stations & Terminals). **Est:** 1957. **Sales:** $440,000,000 (2000). **Emp:** 900. **Officers:** Tom Schmidt, President; Paul Bachman, CFO; Fred Pennings, Information Systems Mgr.; Jack McCool, Dir of Human Resources.

■ 3372 ■ **United Tire Distributors Inc.**
3224 C Ave.
Gulfport, MS 39507
Phone: (228)863-6193
Products: Tires. **SIC:** 5014 (Tires & Tubes).

■ 3373 ■ **Unity Manufacturing Co.**
1260 N Clybourn Ave.
Chicago, IL 60610
Phone: (312)943-5200 **Fax:** (312)943-5681
E-mail: unitymfg@aol.com
Products: Lights for motor vehicles, including spotlights, foglights, and worklights. **SIC:** 5013 (Motor Vehicle Supplies & New Parts). **Est:** 1918. **Sales:** $12,000,000 (2000). **Emp:** 180. **Officers:** Louis E. Gross; William E. Gross, Sales/Marketing Contact; Timothy S. Gross, Customer Service Contact.

■ 3374 ■ **Universal Coach Parts Inc.**
105 E Oakton St.
Des Plaines, IL 60018
Phones: (847)803-8900 800-323-1238
Fax: 800-525-4569
URL: http://www.ucpparts.com
Products: Bus and coach parts. **SIC:** 5013 (Motor Vehicle Supplies & New Parts). **Est:** 1977. **Sales:** $200,000,000 (2000). **Emp:** 300. **Officers:** Pedro Ferro, Vice President.

■ 3375 ■ **Universal Joint Specialists Inc.**
PO Box 9605
Tulsa, OK 74157-0605
Phone: (918)585-5785
Free: (800)666-4246 **Fax:** (918)599-7758
Products: Joints. **SIC:** 5013 (Motor Vehicle Supplies & New Parts). **Sales:** $19,000,000 (2000). **Emp:** 35. **Officers:** Rick Schafer, President.

■ 3376 ■ **University Motors Ltd.**
60 S University Ave.
Morgantown, WV 26505
Phone: (304)296-4401 **Fax:** (304)296-5399
Products: Automobiles. **SIC:** 5012 (Automobiles & Other Motor Vehicles). **Sales:** $25,000,000 (1993). **Emp:** 70. **Officers:** Andrew Claydon, CEO; Jeff LeMasters, Finance Officer.

■ 3377 ■ **US Farathane Inc.**
3905 Rochester Rd.
Royal Oak, MI 48073
Phone: (248)585-1888
Products: Automobile parts. **SIC:** 5013 (Motor Vehicle Supplies & New Parts).

■ 3378 ■ **US Reflector**
144 Canterbury St.
Worcester, MA 01603
Phone: (508)753-6373
Free: (800)414-5024 **Fax:** (508)753-2142
E-mail: ecu@ix.netcom.com
URL: http://www.usreflector.com
Products: Automotive polishing products and lubricants; Highway safety/reflector products. **SICs:** 5013 (Motor Vehicle Supplies & New Parts); 5046 (Commercial Equipment Nec); 5199 (Nondurable Goods Nec). **Est:** 1989. **Sales:** $100,000,000 (2000). **Emp:** 5. **Officers:** Joseph P. Cancelmo Jr., President; George J. Cancelmo, Vice President.

■ 3379 ■ **Utility Trailer Sales Co.**
PO Box 1510
Fontana, CA 92334
Phone: (909)428-8300
Free: (800)766-4887 **Fax:** (909)823-9662
Products: Semi-truck trailers. **SIC:** 5084 (Industrial Machinery & Equipment). **Sales:** $50,000,000 (2000). **Emp:** 80. **Officers:** Thayne Stanger, General Mgr.; George Tietze, Controller.

■ 3380 ■ **Utility Trailer Sales Company of Arizona**
1402 N 22nd Ave.
Phoenix, AZ 85009
Phone: (602)254-7213 **Fax:** (602)271-4128
URL: http://www.utilityaz.com
Products: Trailer parts; Truck equipment parts. **SICs:** 5013 (Motor Vehicle Supplies & New Parts); 5014 (Tires & Tubes). **Est:** 1944. **Sales:** $20,000,000 (2000). **Emp:** 75. **Officers:** Robert B. Cravens, Chairman of

the Board; George Cravens, President; Douglas Hansen, Secretary.

■ 3381 ■ Utility Truck Equipment Sales
PO Box 15357
Boise, ID 83715
Phone: (208)384-5242
Free: (800)627-3642   **Fax:** (208)336-8068
E-mail: utility@utilityboise.com
URL: http://www.utilityboise.com
Products: Dump bodies; Hoists; Van bodies; Snowplows; Service bodies; Sanders; Truck equipment. **SIC:** 5013 (Motor Vehicle Supplies & New Parts). **Est:** 1973. **Emp:** 30. **Officers:** Steve Bowman.

■ 3382 ■ Valley Auto Parts
365 W Hwy. 14
Spearfish, SD 57783-9513
Phone: (605)642-4695
Products: Automobile parts, used. **SIC:** 5015 (Motor Vehicle Parts—Used). **Officers:** Jim Lee, Owner.

■ 3383 ■ Valley Auto and Truck Wrecking Inc.
PO Box 586
Bakersfield, CA 93302
Phone: (805)831-8171
Products: Automotive parts and supplies, New; Automobile parts, used. **SICs:** 5013 (Motor Vehicle Supplies & New Parts); 5015 (Motor Vehicle Parts—Used). **Sales:** $10,000,000 (2000). **Emp:** 19. **Officers:** Ken Thayer, President.

■ 3384 ■ Valley Detroit Diesel Allison Inc.
425 S Hacienda Blvd.
City of Industry, CA 91745-1123
Phone: (626)333-1243
Free: (800)924-4265   **Fax:** (626)369-7096
E-mail: inquiries@vdda.com
URL: http://www.valleydda.com
Products: Diesel truck and alternative fuel engines. **SIC:** 5013 (Motor Vehicle Supplies & New Parts). **Est:** 1949. **Sales:** $100,000,000 (2000). **Emp:** 300. **Officers:** Clark Lee, President.

■ 3385 ■ Valley Ford Truck Sales
5715 Canal Rd.
Cleveland, OH 44125
Phone: (216)524-2400
Products: Truck parts, including tires and mufflers. **SIC:** 5013 (Motor Vehicle Supplies & New Parts). **Est:** 1964. **Sales:** $52,000,000 (2000). **Emp:** 67. **Officers:** J.W. Drakesmith, President; Georgina Imbrigiotta, VP of Finance; Brian O'Donnell, Dir. of Marketing & Sales.

■ 3386 ■ Valley Motor Supply Inc.
101 2nd St.
Havre, MT 59501-3507
Phone: (406)265-2231
Products: Car parts. **SIC:** 5013 (Motor Vehicle Supplies & New Parts). **Est:** 1930. **Sales:** $600,000 (2000). **Emp:** 6. **Officers:** Gary Cady, General Mgr.

■ 3387 ■ VantageParts Inc.
PO Box 20015
Portland, OR 97294-0015
Phone: (503)224-5904
Products: Vehicle component parts. **SIC:** 5013 (Motor Vehicle Supplies & New Parts). **Sales:** $63,000,000 (2000). **Emp:** 150. **Officers:** Steve Furnlund, General Mgr.; Mark Gumpenberger, Controller.

■ 3388 ■ Vasso Systems, Inc.
159 Cook St.
Brooklyn, NY 11206
Phone: (718)417-5303   **Fax:** (718)456-9760
Products: Automotive parts and supplies, New. **SIC:** 5013 (Motor Vehicle Supplies & New Parts). **Officers:** Anthony Vasso, President.

■ 3389 ■ Vehicle Services/Commercial Truck & Van Equipment
Baltimore Pike & Marple Ave.
Clifton Heights, PA 19018
Phone: (610)259-2260   **Fax:** (610)622-1735
E-mail: alvehicl@concentric.net
Products: Automotive parts and supplies. **SIC:** 5013 (Motor Vehicle Supplies & New Parts). **Officers:** Sam Horn, Contact, e-mail: samhorn@icdc.com.

■ 3390 ■ Venturian Corp.
1600 2nd St. S
Hopkins, MN 55343
Phone: (612)931-2500   **Fax:** (612)931-2402
Products: Military spare parts. **SICs:** 5013 (Motor Vehicle Supplies & New Parts); 5088 (Transportation Equipment & Supplies); 5065 (Electronic Parts & Equipment Nec). **Est:** 1983. **Sales:** $28,300,000 (2000). **Emp:** 128. **Officers:** Gary B. Rappaport, CEO, President & Chairman of the Board; Mary F. Jensen, CFO & Treasurer; Reinhild D. Hinze, VP of Operations.

■ 3391 ■ Vernitron Corp. AST Bearings Div.
115 Main Rd.
Montville, NJ 07045
Phone: (973)335-2230   **Fax:** (973)335-6987
URL: http://www.astrbearings.com
Products: Bearings. **SIC:** 5013 (Motor Vehicle Supplies & New Parts). **Sales:** $28,000,000 (2000). **Emp:** 60. **Officers:** Mitchell Dutton, President.

■ 3392 ■ Viam Manufacturing Inc.
9440 Norwalk Blvd.
Santa Fe Springs, CA 90670
Phone: (310)695-0651   **Fax:** (310)695-1043
Products: Automobile floor mats. **SIC:** 5013 (Motor Vehicle Supplies & New Parts). **Est:** 1984. **Sales:** $18,000,000 (2000). **Emp:** 147. **Officers:** Hiroo Nakayama, President; James R. Kelso, CFO; Munehiro Takagi, VP of Marketing & Sales; Jackie Cuenca, Dir. of Information Systems; Barbara Ryan, Personnel Mgr.

■ 3393 ■ V.I.P. Discount Auto Center
12 Lexington St.
Lewiston, ME 04240
Phone: (207)784-5423   **Fax:** (207)784-9178
Products: Automotive parts. **SIC:** 5013 (Motor Vehicle Supplies & New Parts). **Est:** 1962. **Sales:** $100,000,000 (2000). **Emp:** 200. **Officers:** Thomas O. Auger, President; Allen Kurtlin, Controller; Janet McCarthy, Dir. of Marketing; Mike Sweeney, VP of Operations; Nancy Hunt, VP of Human Resources.

■ 3394 ■ L.W. Volz Truck Equipment, Inc.
1704 Rockwell Rd.
Abington, PA 19001
Phone: (215)659-4164   **Fax:** (215)659-3945
Products: Automotive parts and supplies, New. **SIC:** 5013 (Motor Vehicle Supplies & New Parts). **Officers:** Joseph F. Volz, President.

■ 3395 ■ W & W Body
219 Industrial Park South Blvd.
Hwy. 31 S
Southside Industrial Park
Florence, SC 29505
Phone: (803)661-6339   **Fax:** (803)661-6343
Products: Automotive parts and supplies, New. **SIC:** 5013 (Motor Vehicle Supplies & New Parts). **Officers:** Barry Weatherford, Contact.

■ 3396 ■ Wahlberg-McCreary Inc.
PO Box 920780
Houston, TX 77292
Phone: (713)684-0000
Products: Automotive parts, including brakes, spark plugs, and starters. **SIC:** 5013 (Motor Vehicle Supplies & New Parts). **Sales:** $14,000,000 (2000). **Emp:** 45. **Officers:** Michael McCreary, President.

■ 3397 ■ John M. Wallock
616 Warwick Rd.
Winchester, NH 03470
Phone: (603)239-8882
Products: Automobile parts, used. **SIC:** 5015 (Motor Vehicle Parts—Used). **Officers:** John Wallock, Owner.

■ 3398 ■ Wareheim Air Brakes
3100 Washington Blvd.
Baltimore, MD 21230
Phone: (410)644-0400
Free: (800)645-6447   **Fax:** (410)644-1341
Products: Tractor trailer parts, including belts, hoses, and spark plugs. **SIC:** 5013 (Motor Vehicle Supplies & New Parts).

■ 3399 ■ Warehouse Service Co.
PO Box 666
Richmond, IN 47374
Phone: (765)962-4577   **Fax:** (765)962-4570
Products: Automotive parts. **SIC:** 5013 (Motor Vehicle Supplies & New Parts). **Est:** 1963. **Sales:** $10,300,000 (2000). **Emp:** 22. **Officers:** Dean Robinson, President.

■ 3400 ■ Warner Fruehauf Trailer Co.
5710 Dupont Pky.
Smyrna, DE 19977
Phone: (302)653-8561   **Fax:** (302)653-0250
Products: Engines. **SIC:** 5013 (Motor Vehicle Supplies & New Parts).

■ 3401 ■ Warren Distributing Inc.
1750 22nd
Santa Monica, CA 90404-3921
Phone: (310)828-3362   **Fax:** (310)829-3883
E-mail: sales@warrendist.com
URL: http://www.warrendist.com
Products: Automobile parts and accessories. **SIC:** 5013 (Motor Vehicle Supplies & New Parts). **Est:** 1963. **Sales:** $31,000,000 (2000). **Emp:** 165. **Officers:** Warren Weiss, President; Brian Weiss, Vice President.

■ 3402 ■ Waters Truck and Tractor Company Inc.
PO Box 831
Columbus, MS 39701
Phone: (601)328-1575   **Fax:** (601)327-7945
Products: Trucks. **SIC:** 5012 (Automobiles & Other Motor Vehicles). **Sales:** $54,000,000 (1994). **Emp:** 170. **Officers:** Michael Waters, President; Richard Duston, Controller.

■ 3403 ■ O.J. Watson Company, Inc.
5335 Franklin St.
Denver, CO 80216-6213
Phone: (303)295-2885
Free: (800)332-2124   **Fax:** (303)296-8049
Products: Automotive parts and supplies, New. **SIC:** 5013 (Motor Vehicle Supplies & New Parts). **Officers:** Dick Eckrich, General Mgr.

■ 3404 ■ Ray V. Watson Co.
PO Box 4886
Baltimore, MD 21211
Phone: (410)467-0878   **Fax:** (410)467-6891
Products: Power transmissions. **SICs:** 5084 (Industrial Machinery & Equipment); 5013 (Motor Vehicle Supplies & New Parts).

■ 3405 ■ Watson Truck and Supply Inc.
PO Box 10
Hobbs, NM 88240
Phone: (505)397-2411
Free: (800)992-8766   **Fax:** (505)397-1679
E-mail: ravenp@wtaccess.com
Products: Trucks. **SIC:** 5012 (Automobiles & Other Motor Vehicles). **Est:** 1943. **Sales:** $39,000,000 (2000). **Emp:** 175. **Officers:** Charley R. Smith, Chairman of the Board; R. Kenneth A. Shelton, President; Mike Miller, Sec. & Treas.

■ 3406 ■ WDI United Warehouse Inc.
10 Randolph St.
Montgomery, AL 36101
Phone: (205)265-0728
Products: Automotive parts. **SIC:** 5013 (Motor Vehicle Supplies & New Parts). **Est:** 1959. **Sales:** $7,000,000 (2000). **Emp:** 30. **Officers:** B.T. Brooks Jr., President.

■ 3407 ■ Weekley Auto Parts Inc.
7600 Gateway Dr.
Grand Forks, ND 58203-9608
Phone: (701)772-2112   **Fax:** (701)772-0393
Products: Automobile and truck parts. **SIC:** 5015 (Motor Vehicle Parts—Used). **Est:** 1950. **Sales:** $400,000 (2000). **Emp:** 5. **Officers:** Scott Weekley, President.

■ 3408 ■ Wesco Auto Parts
1705 West Garvey N
West Covina, CA 91790
Phone: (562)692-9844
Products: Auto parts. **SIC:** 5013 (Motor Vehicle Supplies & New Parts).

■ 3409 ■ **West Side Distributors Ltd.**
41839 Michigan Ave.
Canton, MI 48188
Phone: (313)397-2500
Products: Automotive parts and supplies. **SIC:** 5013 (Motor Vehicle Supplies & New Parts). **Est:** 1952. **Sales:** $17,000,000 (2000). **Emp:** 70. **Officers:** M. Mazur, CEO; Jacqueline Wichert, Accountant.

■ 3410 ■ **West Virginia Ohio Motor Sales Inc.**
PO Box 71
Wheeling, WV 26003
Phone: (304)232-7515   **Fax:** (304)232-6719
Products: Tractor trailer supplies. **SIC:** 5013 (Motor Vehicle Supplies & New Parts). **Est:** 1939. **Sales:** $10,000,000 (2000). **Emp:** 42. **Officers:** R.W. Mendenhall, President; T. Mendenhall, VP of Marketing.

■ 3411 ■ **Western Power Sports, Inc.**
5272 Irving St.
Boise, ID 83706-1210
Phone: (208)376-8400   **Fax:** (208)375-8901
E-mail: dealer@wps-inc.com
URL: http://www.wps-inc.com
Products: Snowmobile, ATV, motorcycle, and watercraft parts. **SICs:** 5013 (Motor Vehicle Supplies & New Parts); 5091 (Sporting & Recreational Goods). **Est:** 1960.

■ 3412 ■ **Western States Manufacturing Company, Inc.**
PO Box 3655
Sioux City, IA 51102
Phone: (712)252-4248   **Fax:** (712)258-4368
E-mail: patchit@westernweld.com
Products: Tire repair products. **SIC:** 5014 (Tires & Tubes). **Est:** 1924. **Sales:** $2,000,000 (2000). **Emp:** 18. **Officers:** Jim Levich, General Mgr.; Lou Jensen, Sales Mgr.

■ 3413 ■ **Western Truck Equipment Company Inc.**
PO Box 20723
Phoenix, AZ 85036
Phone: (602)257-0777   **Fax:** (602)340-1534
E-mail: elmer@wteco.com
URL: http://www.wteco.com
Products: Truck equipment and bodies. **SIC:** 5013 (Motor Vehicle Supplies & New Parts). **Est:** 1958. **Sales:** $4,000,000 (2000). **Emp:** 18. **Officers:** Jon C. Campbell, President; Elmer Waddell, Sales/Marketing Contact; Scott Campbell, Sales/Marketing Contact.

■ 3414 ■ **Westex Automotive Corp.**
40880 Encyclopedia Circle
Fremont, CA 94538-2470
Phone: (510)659-1700
Free: (800)228-5090   **Fax:** (510)490-7352
Products: Automotive parts, including foreign parts. **SIC:** 5013 (Motor Vehicle Supplies & New Parts). **Emp:** 49. **Officers:** Gary Evans.

■ 3415 ■ **Westlake Inc.**
40 N Water St.
Lititz, PA 17543-1609
Phone: (717)626-0272
Products: Upholstered products for recreational vehicles. **SIC:** 5013 (Motor Vehicle Supplies & New Parts). **Est:** 1984. **Officers:** William J. Westlake, President; Shirley I. Westlake, Vice President.

■ 3416 ■ **George C. Wetherbee and Co.**
2566 E Grand Blvd.
Detroit, MI 48211
Phone: (313)871-3200   **Fax:** (313)871-8614
Products: Automotive parts; Hardware. **SIC:** 5013 (Motor Vehicle Supplies & New Parts). **Est:** 1860. **Sales:** $13,000,000 (2000). **Emp:** 50. **Officers:** Albert Zimmerman II, President; George Williamson, Controller; Leonard Dorazio, Dir. of Data Processing.

■ 3417 ■ **Wetherill Associates Inc.**
1101 Enterprise Dr.
Royersford, PA 19468
Phone: (610)495-2200   **Fax:** (610)495-4000
Products: Automotive parts for starters and alternators for use by aftermarket rebuilders. **SIC:** 5013 (Motor Vehicle Supplies & New Parts). **Sales:** $127,000,000

(2000). **Emp:** 450. **Officers:** E. Marie Bothe, President; Kevin K. Kraft, Treasurer.

■ 3418 ■ **Whalen Tire**
845 Nevada Ave.
Butte, MT 59701
Phone: (406)723-6170
Products: Tires. **SIC:** 5014 (Tires & Tubes).

■ 3419 ■ **Wharton and Barnard Inc.**
PO Box 179
Milford, DE 19963
Phone: (302)422-4571
Products: Automotive parts. **SIC:** 5013 (Motor Vehicle Supplies & New Parts). **Est:** 1924. **Sales:** $28,000,000 (2000). **Emp:** 115. **Officers:** Robert Hermann, President; Ron Hall, Controller; William P. Barnard, VP of Sales; Ronald Ward, Dir. of Information Systems.

■ 3420 ■ **Wheel City Inc.**
244 Constitution Way
Idaho Falls, ID 83402-3541
Phone: (208)524-3193   **Fax:** (208)524-3195
Products: Motor vehicle parts and accessories. **SIC:** 5013 (Motor Vehicle Supplies & New Parts). **Officers:** Mark Nelson, President.

■ 3421 ■ **Wheel Masters Inc.**
PO Box 60910
Reno, NV 89506-0910
Phone: (775)972-7888
Free: (800)325-9484   **Fax:** (775)972-7975
Products: Stainless steel wheel cover systems and accessories. **SIC:** 5013 (Motor Vehicle Supplies & New Parts). **Est:** 1984. **Sales:** $6,000,000 (2000). **Emp:** 15. **Officers:** Jerry Edwards, President.

■ 3422 ■ **Wheeler Brothers Inc.**
PO Box 737
Somerset, PA 15501
Phone: (814)443-7000   **Fax:** (814)443-7100
E-mail: sales@teamllv.com
URL: http://www.teamllv.com
Products: Automotive parts and accessories. **SIC:** 5013 (Motor Vehicle Supplies & New Parts). **Est:** 1960. **Sales:** $48,000,000 (2000). **Emp:** 120. **Officers:** Harold W. Wheeler Jr., President; Joan M. Wheeler, VP of Finance; Charles Thompson, Dir. of Information Systems; Barbara Davies, Dir of Human Resources.

■ 3423 ■ **White Bear Equipment, Inc.**
4 Anderson Dr.
PO Box 5450
Albany, NY 12205
Phone: (518)438-4462   **Fax:** (518)438-4396
Products: Automotive parts and supplies, New. **SIC:** 5013 (Motor Vehicle Supplies & New Parts). **Officers:** Earl Greenleaf Jr., President.

■ 3424 ■ **White Brothers Inc.**
24845 Corbit Pl.
Yorba Linda, CA 92887
Phone: (714)692-3404   **Fax:** (714)692-3409
URL: http://www.whitebros.com
Products: Motorcycle parts. **SIC:** 5013 (Motor Vehicle Supplies & New Parts). **Est:** 1976. **Emp:** 90.

■ 3425 ■ **The C.E. White Co.**
PO Box 308
417 N Kibler St.
New Washington, OH 44854
Phone: (419)492-2157   **Fax:** (419)492-2544
Products: Seating; Automotive parts and supplies, New. **SIC:** 5013 (Motor Vehicle Supplies & New Parts). **Est:** 1937. **Sales:** $5,800,000 (2000). **Emp:** 60. **Officers:** Clayton White, Chairman of the Board; Edward White, President; Al White, Treasurer & Secty.; Pam Latino, Vice President.

■ 3426 ■ **Billy D. White Inc.**
PO Box 3466
Odessa, TX 79762
Phone: (915)362-0326   **Fax:** (915)367-7210
Products: Rig building, repairing and dismantling. **SIC:** 5084 (Industrial Machinery & Equipment). **Sales:** $1,000,000 (2000). **Emp:** 20. **Officers:** Billy D. White, President.

■ 3427 ■ **White's Herring Tractor and Truck Inc.**
PO Box 3817
Wilson, NC 27893
Phone: (252)291-0131   **Fax:** (252)291-7745
Products: Heavy trucks and tractors. **SICs:** 5084 (Industrial Machinery & Equipment); 5083 (Farm & Garden Machinery). **Sales:** $31,000,000 (2000). **Emp:** 100. **Officers:** D. Steve White, CEO & President; Sandra S. Pridgen, Secretary.

■ 3428 ■ **Wholesale Tire Company Auto Centers**
PO Box 5430
Bay Shore, NY 11706-0307
Phone: (516)665-7100
Products: Tires. **SIC:** 5014 (Tires & Tubes).

■ 3429 ■ **Wholesale Tire Inc.**
PO Box 1660
Clarksburg, WV 26302
Phone: (304)624-8465
Products: Tires; Automotive parts, including brakes. **SICs:** 5014 (Tires & Tubes); 5013 (Motor Vehicle Supplies & New Parts). **Est:** 1950. **Sales:** $54,000,000 (2000). **Emp:** 100. **Officers:** William C. Wymer, President & Treasurer.

■ 3430 ■ **Wilcox Brothers Co.**
PO Box 86245
Pittsburgh, PA 15221-0245
Phone: (412)243-3604
Products: Automotive parts, including spark plugs and engines. **SIC:** 5013 (Motor Vehicle Supplies & New Parts). **Est:** 1960. **Sales:** $8,000,000 (2000). **Emp:** 35. **Officers:** John Fitchwell, President.

■ 3431 ■ **Wilks Tire and Battery Service**
428 N Broad St.
Albertville, AL 35950
Phone: (256)878-0211
Products: Tires; Batteries. **SICs:** 5014 (Tires & Tubes); 5013 (Motor Vehicle Supplies & New Parts).

■ 3432 ■ **Williams Auto Parts**
PO Box 1269
Decatur, AL 35602
Phone: (205)353-0811   **Fax:** (205)350-0306
Products: Automotive parts. **SIC:** 5013 (Motor Vehicle Supplies & New Parts). **Sales:** $4,000,000 (2000). **Emp:** 49. **Officers:** E.J. Briscoe; W.E. Briscoe.

■ 3433 ■ **Williams Detroit Diesel Allison**
2849 Moreland Ave., SE
Atlanta, GA 30315
Phone: (404)366-1070
Free: (800)545-7116   **Fax:** (404)361-4015
E-mail: salesberry@wddase.com
Products: Engines. **SICs:** 5084 (Industrial Machinery & Equipment); 5013 (Motor Vehicle Supplies & New Parts). **Est:** 1912. **Sales:** $25,000,000 (2000). **Emp:** 100. **Officers:** H.R. Watson, President & General Mgr.; W.S. Williams, VP & CFO; William D. Bizjak, Sales Mgr.; Ken Katz, Data Processing Mgr.

■ 3434 ■ **Williams Detroit Diesel Allison**
869 W Goodale
Columbus, OH 43212
Phone: (614)228-6651   **Fax:** (614)228-6027
Products: Diesel engine parts. **SIC:** 5084 (Industrial Machinery & Equipment).

■ 3435 ■ **Williams Detroit Diesel Allison**
3325 Libby Rd.
Lemoyne, OH 43441
Phone: (419)837-5067
Free: (800)758-8785   **Fax:** (419)837-5229
Products: Diesel engine parts; Transmissions. **SICs:** 5084 (Industrial Machinery & Equipment); 5013 (Motor Vehicle Supplies & New Parts).

■ 3436 ■ **Williams Detroit Diesel Allison**
1835 S Hwy. 101
Greer, SC 29651
Phone: (864)877-0935   **Fax:** (864)848-1176
Products: Diesel parts. **SIC:** 5013 (Motor Vehicle Supplies & New Parts).

■ 3437 ■ **Williams Detroit Diesel Allison**
2610 Augusta Rd.
U.S 1 & I-26
West Columbia, SC 29169
Phone: (803)791-5910 **Fax:** (803)794-2527
Products: Engines and transmissions. **SIC:** 5013
(Motor Vehicle Supplies & New Parts).

■ 3438 ■ **Jack Williams Tire Co.**
PO Box 3655
Scranton, PA 18505
Phone: (717)457-5000
Products: Automotive accessories, including tires.
SICs: 5014 (Tires & Tubes); 5013 (Motor Vehicle
Supplies & New Parts). **Est:** 1929. **Sales:** $29,000,000
(2000). **Emp:** 200. **Officers:** William C. Williams,
President; Caroline O'Rourke, Controller; Michael
Salak, Dir. of Marketing & Sales.

■ 3439 ■ **Wilson Brothers Co.**
212 Atlantic Ave. N
Thief River Falls, MN 56701-2059
Phone: (218)681-1880 **Fax:** (218)681-4910
Products: Auto parts. **SIC:** 5013 (Motor Vehicle
Supplies & New Parts). **Emp:** 49. **Officers:** John
Bartlett.

■ 3440 ■ **Jim Wilson Co.**
PO Box 970
Cape Girardeau, MO 63702-0970
Phone: (314)334-4477 **Fax:** (314)335-4316
Products: Automotive parts; Tires; Service equipment;
Truck parts. **SICs:** 5013 (Motor Vehicle Supplies &
New Parts); 5014 (Tires & Tubes). **Est:** 1947. **Sales:**
$19,000,000 (2000). **Emp:** 85. **Officers:** James B.
Wilson, President; J.A. Thrower, Treasurer & Secty.;
Donna Schener, Sec. & Treas.

■ 3441 ■ **WirthCo Engineering Inc.**
6519 Cecilia Cir.
Bloomington, MN 55439
Phone: (612)941-9073
Free: (800)959-0879 **Fax:** (612)941-0659
E-mail: sales@wirthco.com
URL: http://www.wirthco.com
Products: 12-volt parts and accessories; Funnels;
Plastic shovels; Plastic parts and accessories; Battery
maintainers. **SICs:** 5013 (Motor Vehicle Supplies &
New Parts); 5083 (Farm & Garden Machinery). **Est:**
1980. **Emp:** 12. **Officers:** Steve Wirth; Kathy Wirth;
Steve Wirth, Sales/Marketing Contact; Suzanne
Stenquist, Customer Service Contact; Roger Bowman,
Human Resources Contact.

■ 3442 ■ **Wisconsin Bearing**
PO Box 5635
De Pere, WI 54115-5635
Phone: (920)437-6591
Products: Power transmisssion products. **SICs:** 5085
(Industrial Supplies); 5013 (Motor Vehicle Supplies &
New Parts).

■ 3443 ■ **Wisconsin Brake and Wheel Inc.**
4700 N 124th St.
Milwaukee, WI 53225
Phone: (414)536-2060 **Fax:** (414)781-8287
Products: Truck parts. **SIC:** 5013 (Motor Vehicle
Supplies & New Parts). **Est:** 1920. **Sales:** $9,000,000
(2000). **Emp:** 18. **Officers:** Peter D. Lund, President;
Bruce Nuemann, Treasurer; Jeff Mead, Vice President.

■ 3444 ■ **Womack Machine**
8808 E Admiral Pl.
Tulsa, OK 74115
Phone: (918)836-7763 **Fax:** (918)838-2759
Products: Pumps; Motors; Tires. **SICs:** 5084
(Industrial Machinery & Equipment); 5013 (Motor
Vehicle Supplies & New Parts); 5014 (Tires & Tubes).

■ 3445 ■ **Woody Tire Company Inc.**
1606 50th St.
Lubbock, TX 79412
Phone: (806)747-4556
Products: Tires. **SIC:** 5014 (Tires & Tubes). **Est:** 1935.
Sales: $3,000,000 (2000). **Emp:** 26. **Officers:** David E.
Woody, President & CFO.

■ 3446 ■ **Worldwide Environmental Products Inc.**
430 S Cataract Ave.
San Dimas, CA 91773
Phone: (909)599-6431 **Fax:** (909)599-8253
Products: Automotive emissions test equipment. **SIC:**
5013 (Motor Vehicle Supplies & New Parts). **Est:** 1984.
Sales: $6,000,000 (2000). **Emp:** 25. **Officers:** William
Delaney, President; Arthur Vasquez Jr., Controller.

■ 3447 ■ **Wrangler Power Products Inc.**
1500 Willow Way
Prescott, AZ 86304
Free: (800)962-2616
Products: Electrical components for automobiles. **SIC:**
5012 (Automobiles & Other Motor Vehicles). **Sales:**
$500,000 (2000). **Emp:** 3. **Officers:** Marilyn J. Jones,
President; Ronald C. Jones, VP of Finance.

■ 3448 ■ **Wright Supplier**
14 Marlboro Ave.
Brattleboro, VT 05301-3522
Phone: (802)254-4718
Products: Automotive parts. **SIC:** 5013 (Motor Vehicle
Supplies & New Parts). **Officers:** Stephen Wright,
Owner.

■ 3449 ■ **Wright Tool Co.**
PO Box 1239
Troy, MI 48099
Phone: (248)643-6666 **Fax:** (313)643-6530
Products: Automotive service tools. **SIC:** 5013 (Motor
Vehicle Supplies & New Parts). **Est:** 1948. **Sales:**
$5,000,000 (2000). **Emp:** 22. **Officers:** William Wright,
CEO; Nancy Wright, CFO; Jody Nelson, Dir. of Data
Processing.

■ 3450 ■ **Yankee Custom, Inc.**
1271 Main St.
Tewksbury, MA 01876
Phone: (978)851-9024 **Fax:** (978)851-4983
Products: Automotive parts and supplies, New. **SIC:**
5013 (Motor Vehicle Supplies & New Parts). **Est:** 1969.
Sales: $4,000,000 (2000). **Emp:** 14. **Officers:** Bill
Cole, Contact.

■ 3451 ■ **A.R. Young Company Inc.**
PO Box 11135
Indianapolis, IN 46201
Phone: (317)263-3800 **Fax:** (317)263-3806
Products: Power transmission equipment. **SIC:** 5013
(Motor Vehicle Supplies & New Parts). **Est:** 1929.
Sales: $2,000,000 (2000). **Emp:** 8. **Officers:** Elizabeth
Young, President; Robert M. Reynolds, VP of Sales.

■ 3452 ■ **Young Windows Inc.**
PO Box 387
Conshohocken, PA 19428
Phone: (610)828-5422 **Fax:** (610)828-2144
Products: Windows for commercial vehicles. **SIC:**
5013 (Motor Vehicle Supplies & New Parts). **Est:** 1950.
Sales: $5,000,000 (2000). **Emp:** 55. **Officers:** L.H.
Cook, President; Edmund T. Opielski, Dir. of Marketing.

■ 3453 ■ **Zeller Electric Inc.**
4250 Hoffmeister Ave.
St. Louis, MO 63125
Phone: (314)638-9641
Free: (800)530-5810 **Fax:** (314)638-6318
Products: Electric motors. **SIC:** 5063 (Electrical
Apparatus & Equipment). **Sales:** $4,000,000 (1992).
Emp: 50. **Officers:** Linda Jamieson, President; Linda
Medlin, CFO.

■ 3454 ■ **ZEXEL USA Corp.**
625 Southside Dr.
Decatur, IL 62521
Phone: (217)362-2300
Products: Farm car products; Air-conditioning; Diesel
fuel injection parts and supplies. **SICs:** 5013 (Motor
Vehicle Supplies & New Parts); 5064 (Electrical
Appliances—Television & Radio); 5084 (Industrial
Machinery & Equipment). **Est:** 1975. **Sales:**
$235,000,000 (2000). **Emp:** 1,100. **Officers:** A.
Tanaka, CEO; G. Clinch, Vice President; R. Yamagiwa,
Exec. VP of Sales; M. Caldwell, Dir. of Data
Processing; J. Sullivan, Human Resources Mgr.

■ 3455 ■ **Ziegler Tire and Supply Co.**
4150 Millennium Blvd. SE
Massillon, OH 44646
Phone: (330)477-2747 **Fax:** (330)477-4318
Products: Tires, rims, automobile service retreading.
SICs: 5014 (Tires & Tubes); 5013 (Motor Vehicle
Supplies & New Parts); 5172 (Petroleum Products
Nec). **Est:** 1919. **Sales:** $10,000,000 (2000). **Emp:** 98.
Officers: Harold E. Ziegler Jr., President; William
Ziegler, CFO; John Ziegler Jr., Dir. of Marketing.

■ 3456 ■ **Zinc Positive Inc.**
PO Box 64157
Tacoma, WA 98464
Phone: (253)566-0869
Products: Engine parts. **SIC:** 5013 (Motor Vehicle
Supplies & New Parts). **Est:** 1989.

(6) Books and Other Printed Materials

Entries in this section are arranged alphabetically by company name. When the company name is a personal name, the company name is alphabetized by the surname unless the first name or initial(s) are part of a trade name. See the User's Guide at the front of this directory for additional information.

■ **3457** ■ **A-C Book Service**
60 St. Felix St.
Brooklyn, NY 11217-1206
Phone: (718)855-0600
Products: Books, including philosophy and theology.
SIC: 5192 (Books, Periodicals & Newspapers). **Est:** 1958. **Sales:** $40,000 (1999). **Emp:** 2. **Officers:** Albert J. Berube, Dir. of Marketing.

■ **3458** ■ **Abingdon Press**
PO Box 801
Nashville, TN 37202
Phone: (615)749-6451
Free: (800)251-3320 **Fax:** (615)749-6372
E-mail: cwilliams@abingdon.org
Products: Trade, religious, reference, and children's books. **SIC:** 5192 (Books, Periodicals & Newspapers). **Sales:** $7,000,000 (2000). **Officers:** Niel Alexander, President, e-mail: nalexander@umpublishing.org; Don Sherwood, VP of Sales, e-mail: dsherrod@umpublishing.org.

■ **3459** ■ **Abranovic Associates Inc.**
161 S McKean St.
Kittanning, PA 16201
Phone: (412)543-2005 **Fax:** (412)543-3477
Products: Magazines. **SIC:** 5192 (Books, Periodicals & Newspapers). **Est:** 1971.

■ **3460** ■ **Academi-Text Medical Wholesalers**
330 N Superior
Toledo, OH 43604-1422
Phone: (419)255-9755
Free: (800)552-8398 **Fax:** (419)255-9606
E-mail: academi-text@worldnet.att.net
URL: http://www.academi-text.com
Products: Technical books; Software and videos; Multimedia engineering text. **SICs:** 5192 (Books, Periodicals & Newspapers); 5065 (Electronic Parts & Equipment Nec); 5045 (Computers, Peripherals & Software). **Est:** 1983. **Emp:** 10. **Officers:** Daryl Yourist, e-mail: dyourist@worldnet.att.net.

■ **3461** ■ **Academic Enterprises Ltd.**
20 Simmons Dr.
Milford, MA 01757
Phone: (508)473-8034 **Fax:** (508)478-6964
Products: Books. **SIC:** 5192 (Books, Periodicals & Newspapers). **Est:** 1972. **Sales:** $1,000,000 (2000). **Emp:** 2. **Officers:** Carol Benke, President.

■ **3462** ■ **Academic Therapy Publications**
High Noon Bks/Arena Press
20 Commercial Blvd.
Novato, CA 94949-6191
Phone: (415)883-3314
Free: (800)422-7249 **Fax:** (415)883-3720
URL: http://www.atpub.com
Products: Educational materials including diagnostic tests and curriculum and resource materials for teachers and parents. **SIC:** 5192 (Books, Periodicals & Newspapers). **Est:** 1965. **Sales:** $2,000,000 (2000). **Emp:** 12. **Officers:** Anna M. Arena, President; Jim Arena, Vice President.

■ **3463** ■ **Academy Chicago Publishers Ltd.**
363 W Erie St.
Chicago, IL 60610
Phone: (312)751-7300
Free: (800)248-7323 **Fax:** (312)751-7306
Products: Trade books. **SIC:** 5192 (Books, Periodicals & Newspapers). **Est:** 1975. **Emp:** 12. **Officers:** Anita Miller, President; Jordan Miller, Vice President.

■ **3464** ■ **Accent Books**
PO Box 15337
Denver, CO 80215
Phone: (303)988-5300
Free: (800)525-5550 **Fax:** (303)989-7737
Products: Religious publications. **SIC:** 5192 (Books, Periodicals & Newspapers).

■ **3465** ■ **Accents Publications Service, Inc.**
4611 Assembly Dr., Ste. F
Lanham, MD 20706-4843
Phone: (301)588-5496 **Fax:** (301)588-5249
E-mail: accents@iamdigex.net
Products: Government publications from the United States, Canada, Ireland, and Australia; International organization and association publications from Australia, Canada, and New Zealand. **SIC:** 5192 (Books, Periodicals & Newspapers). **Est:** 1984. **Officers:** Nadav Katz, Dir.

■ **3466** ■ **Access Publishers Network**
6893 Sullivan Rd.
Grawn, MI 49637
Phone: (616)276-5196
Free: (800)345-0096 **Fax:** (616)276-5197
E-mail: accessmi@aol.com
Products: Books. **SIC:** 5192 (Books, Periodicals & Newspapers). **Est:** 1989. **Sales:** $5,000,000 (2000). **Emp:** 23. **Officers:** David Reecher, CEO; Terry Jones, Dir. of Sales; Margaret Anne Slawsin, Acquisition Dir. **Former Name:** Publishers Distribution Service.

■ **3467** ■ **Accura Music, Inc.**
13398 Mansfield Rd.
PO Box 4260
Athens, OH 45701-4260
E-mail: accura@accuramusic.com
URL: http://www.accuramusic.com
Products: Sheet music; Books about music. **SICs:** 5192 (Books, Periodicals & Newspapers); 5199 (Nondurable Goods Nec). **Est:** 1968.

■ **3468** ■ **ACS Publications**
PO Box 34487
San Diego, CA 92163-4487
Phone: (619)297-9203
Free: (800)888-9983 **Fax:** (619)297-9251
Products: Text books, including astrological and metaphysical. **SIC:** 5192 (Books, Periodicals & Newspapers). **Est:** 1973. **Officers:** Maria Kay Simms, President; Maritha Pottenger, CFO; Linda L. Harris, Sales Manager.

■ **3469** ■ **Adams Book Company, Inc.**
537 Sackett St.
Brooklyn, NY 11211
Phone: (718)875-5464 **Fax:** (718)852-3212
E-mail: sales@adamsbook.com
URL: http://www.adamsbook.com
Products: Textbooks; Paperbacks; Software. **SICs:** 5192 (Books, Periodicals & Newspapers); 5045 (Computers, Peripherals & Software). **Est:** 1945.

■ **3470** ■ **Adams News Co. Inc.**
1555 W Galer St.
Seattle, WA 98119-3166
Phone: (206)284-7617
Free: (800)533-7617 **Fax:** (206)284-7599
Products: Hardbacks; Puzzles and games; Magazines. **SICs:** 5192 (Books, Periodicals & Newspapers); 5092 (Toys & Hobby Goods & Supplies). **Est:** 1927.

■ **3471** ■ **Addor Associates, Inc.**
115 Roseville Rd.
PO Box 2128
Westport, CT 06880
Phone: (203)226-9791 **Fax:** (203)221-1844
Products: Books. **SIC:** 5192 (Books, Periodicals & Newspapers). **Est:** 1981.

■ **3472** ■ **Adler's Foreign Books Inc.**
915 Foster St.
Evanston, IL 60201-3199
Phone: (847)866-6329
Free: (800)433-9229 **Fax:** (847)866-6287
Products: Foreign language books. **SIC:** 5192 (Books, Periodicals & Newspapers). **Est:** 1970. **Sales:** $1,500,000 (2000). **Emp:** 16. **Officers:** Hubert Mengin, President.

■ **3473** ■ **Advanced Marketing Services Inc.**
5880 Oberlin Dr., Ste. 400
San Diego, CA 92121
Phone: (619)457-2500 **Fax:** (619)452-2237
Products: Books. **SIC:** 5192 (Books, Periodicals & Newspapers). **Est:** 1982. **Sales:** $385,600,000 (2000). **Emp:** 428. **Officers:** Michael M. Nicita, CEO & President; Charles C. Tillinghast, Chairman of the Board.

■ **3474** ■ **Adventures Unlimited Press**
PO Box 74
Kempton, IL 60946-0074
Phone: (815)253-6390 **Fax:** (815)256-2299
E-mail: auphq@frontiernet.net
URL: http://www.adventuresunlimited.co.nz
Products: Books, including exotic travel, ancient sciences, alternative energy, and alternative health. **SICs:** 5192 (Books, Periodicals & Newspapers); 5065 (Electronic Parts & Equipment Nec); 5099 (Durable Goods Nec). **Est:** 1983. **Sales:** $800,000 (2000). **Emp:** 4. **Officers:** David H. Childress, President.

■ **3475** ■ **Aerial Photography Services Inc.**
2511 S Tryon St.
Charlotte, NC 28203
Phone: (704)333-5143 **Fax:** (704)333-5148
Products: Postcards; Aerial photos. **SIC:** 5192 (Books,

Periodicals & Newspapers). **Est:** 1965. **Emp:** 25. **Officers:** James Doane, President; Charles E. Guenzi, CEO.

■ **3476** ■ **African & Caribbean Imprint Library Services**
PO Box 350
West Falmouth, MA 02574
Phone: (508)540-5378 **Fax:** (508)548-6801
E-mail: ailscils@sprintmail.com
URL: http://www.africanbooks.com
Products: Publications, including periodicals and newspapers; Microfilm and microfiche; Monographs; Maps; Government documents. **SIC:** 5192 (Books, Periodicals & Newspapers). **Est:** 1970.

■ **3477** ■ **AIDS Impact Inc.**
PO Box 9443
Seattle, WA 98109
Phone: (206)284-3865 **Fax:** (206)284-3879
Products: AIDS instructional materials. **SIC:** 5192 (Books, Periodicals & Newspapers). **Sales:** $1,000,000 (2000). **Emp:** 7. **Officers:** Madiline P. Beery, President.

■ **3478** ■ **AIMS International Books, Inc.**
7709 Hamilton Ave.
Cincinnati, OH 45231-3103
Phone: (513)521-5590
Free: (800)733-2067 **Fax:** (513)521-5592
E-mail: aimsbooks@fuse.net
URL: http://www.aimsbooks.com
Products: Children's and adult's books in Spanish, Arabic, Italian, Korean, Japanese, Russian, Vietnamese, and Chinese. **SIC:** 5192 (Books, Periodicals & Newspapers). **Est:** 1984. **Alternate Name:** Another Language Press.

■ **3479** ■ **Akiba Press**
5949 Estates Dr.
Oakland, CA 94611
Phone: (510)339-1283
E-mail: irenapn@aol.com
Products: History books. **SIC:** 5192 (Books, Periodicals & Newspapers). **Est:** 1978. **Sales:** $2,000 (2000). **Emp:** 2. **Officers:** Sheila Baker, President.

■ **3480** ■ **AKJ Educational Services, Inc.**
5609-2A Fishers Ln.
Rockville, MD 20852
Phone: (301)770-4030
Free: (800)922-6066 **Fax:** (301)770-2338
E-mail: info@akjedsvcs.com
URL: http://www.akjedsvcs.com
Products: Paperback books. **SIC:** 5192 (Books, Periodicals & Newspapers). **Est:** 1978. **Sales:** $2,500,000 (2000). **Emp:** 7. **Officers:** Edward S. Mandel, President.

■ **3481** ■ **Al-WaLi Inc.**
401 Thornton Rd.
Lithia Springs, GA 30122
Phone: (770)948-7845
Free: (800)326-2665 **Fax:** (770)944-2313
E-mail: newleaf@newleaf-dist.com
URL: http://www.newleaf-dist.com
Products: Metaphysical, holistic health, and conscious living books and periodicals; Prerecorded audio/video cassettes. **SICs:** 5192 (Books, Periodicals & Newspapers); 5099 (Durable Goods Nec). **Est:** 1975. **Sales:** $25,000,000 (1999). **Emp:** 70. **Officers:** Rich Bellezza, CEO, President & Treasurer.

■ **3482** ■ **Alabama Book Store**
PO Box 1279
Tuscaloosa, AL 35403-1279
Phone: (205)758-4532
Free: (800)382-2665 **Fax:** (205)758-5525
E-mail: abs@alabamabook.com
URL: http://www.alabamabook.com; www.bamastuff.com
Products: College text books. **SIC:** 5192 (Books, Periodicals & Newspapers). **Est:** 1939. **Sales:** $2,920,000 (2000). **Emp:** 35. **Officers:** Richard L. Zeanah, President; William W. Deal III, Secretary; David M. Jones, Treasurer.

■ **3483** ■ **Alamo Square Distributors**
4530 19th St.
PO Box 14543
San Francisco, CA 94114
Phone: (415)863-7410 **Fax:** (415)863-7456
E-mail: alamosqdist@earthlink.net
Products: Books from gay and lesbian presses. **SIC:** 5192 (Books, Periodicals & Newspapers). **Est:** 1992. **Sales:** $600,000 (1999). **Emp:** 2. **Officers:** Steve Cautine, Partner; Bert Herrman, Partner.

■ **3484** ■ **Alamo Square Distributors**
4530 18th St.
San Francisco, CA 94114
Phone: (415)863-7410 **Fax:** (415)863-7456
E-mail: alamosquardist@earthlink.net
Products: Books. **SIC:** 5192 (Books, Periodicals & Newspapers). **Sales:** $750,000 (2000). **Emp:** 2. **Officers:** Steve Cantine, Partner.

■ **3485** ■ **Alamo Square Distributors**
4530 18th St.
San Francisco, CA 94114
Phone: (415)863-7410 **Fax:** (415)863-7456
Products: Books and other printed materials. **SIC:** 5192 (Books, Periodicals & Newspapers). **Sales:** $800,000 (2000). **Emp:** 2.

■ **3486** ■ **Alaska News Agency Inc.**
325 W Potter Dr.
Anchorage, AK 99518
Phone: (907)563-3251 **Fax:** (907)261-8523
Products: Books; Magazines. **SIC:** 5192 (Books, Periodicals & Newspapers).

■ **3487** ■ **Alaska Pacific University Press**
Alaska Pacific University
4101 University Dr.
Anchorage, AK 99508
Phone: (907)564-8218 **Fax:** (907)562-4276
Products: Books. **SIC:** 5192 (Books, Periodicals & Newspapers). **Est:** 1963. **Emp:** 1. **Officers:** Douglas North, President; Erin Downey, Manager.

■ **3488** ■ **Alfred Publishing Company Inc.**
PO Box 10003
Van Nuys, CA 91410-0003
Phone: (818)891-5999
Free: (800)292-6122 **Fax:** (818)891-2369
URL: http://www.alfredpub.com
Products: Musical education books. **SIC:** 5192 (Books, Periodicals & Newspapers). **Est:** 1928. **Sales:** $23,000,000 (2000). **Emp:** 145. **Officers:** Morton Manus, President; John Handlos, CFO; Danny Rocks, Exec. VP of Sales; Steven Manus, CEO; Andrew Surmani, VP of Marketing.

■ **3489** ■ **Alfreda's Film Works c/o Continnuus**
PO Box 416
Denver, CO 80201-0416
Phone: (303)575-5676
Products: Films; Videos. **SICs:** 5192 (Books, Periodicals & Newspapers); 5099 (Durable Goods Nec). **Est:** 1998. **Sales:** $499,000 (2000). **Emp:** 1. **Officers:** A. Doyle, Founder. **Alternate Name:** Prosperity & Profits Unlimited.

■ **3490** ■ **All America Distributors Corp.**
8431 Melrose Pl.
Los Angeles, CA 90069
Phone: (323)651-2650 **Fax:** (323)655-9452
E-mail: psi@loop.com
Products: Magazines, books, calendars, postcards, and posters. **SIC:** 5192 (Books, Periodicals & Newspapers). **Est:** 1960. **Emp:** 27. **Officers:** Bentley Morriss, President; Ralph Weinstock, Dir. of Sales; Marc K. Morriss, Treasurer.

■ **3491** ■ **Alec R. Allenson, Inc.**
1307 Highway 179A
Westville, FL 32464
Phone: (850)956-2817
E-mail: allenson@wfeca.net
Products: Out-of-print and antiquarian theological books. **SIC:** 5192 (Books, Periodicals & Newspapers). **Est:** 1924. **Sales:** $100,000 (2000). **Emp:** 3. **Officers:** Robert D. Allenson, President, e-mail: allenson@wfeca.com.

■ **3492** ■ **Allentown News Agency Inc.**
719-723 Liberty St.
Allentown, PA 18105-0446
Phone: (610)432-4441 **Fax:** (610)432-2708
Products: Periodicals. **SIC:** 5192 (Books, Periodicals & Newspapers). **Est:** 1911. **Sales:** $7,000,000 (2000). **Emp:** 50. **Officers:** Rick Lentz, President.

■ **3493** ■ **Ally Press**
524 Orleans St.
St. Paul, MN 55107
Phone: (612)291-2652 **Fax:** (612)291-2652
URL: http://www.catalog.com/ally
Products: Books; Videos. **SICs:** 5192 (Books, Periodicals & Newspapers); 5065 (Electronic Parts & Equipment Nec). **Est:** 1973. **Sales:** $50,000 (2000). **Emp:** 1. **Officers:** Paul Feroe, Owner, e-mail: pferoe@pclink.com.

■ **3494** ■ **Bryant Altman Map, Inc.**
Norwood Commerce Center, Bldg. 26
Endicott St.
Norwood, MA 02062
Phone: (781)762-3339
Free: (800)480-MAPS **Fax:** (781)769-9080
Products: Books; Maps; Atlases. **SIC:** 5192 (Books, Periodicals & Newspapers). **Est:** 1976. **Sales:** $4,500,000 (2000). **Emp:** 10. **Officers:** John P. Grady, President, e-mail: jpg63@aol.com; Robert Gallo; Mark Linnane.

■ **3495** ■ **Ambassador Book Service, Inc.**
42 Chasner St.
Hempstead, NY 11550
Phone: (516)489-4011
Free: (800)431-8913 **Fax:** (516)489-5661
E-mail: ambassador@absbook.com
URL: http://www.absbook.com
Products: Scientific, technical, business, university press, scholarly, and medical publications; Non-print media; Journals. **SIC:** 5192 (Books, Periodicals & Newspapers). **Est:** 1973. **Sales:** $25,000,000 (2000). **Emp:** 74. **Officers:** Gary Herald, President & CEO; Stuart Grinell, Domestic Sales Mgr.; David Ungar, VP of International Sales; Steven Blicht, COO.

■ **3496** ■ **America West Distributors**
PO Box 3300
Bozeman, MT 59772
Phone: (406)585-0700
Free: (800)729-4131 **Fax:** (406)585-0703
Products: Books on UFO's, political conspiracy, and metaphysical information. **SIC:** 5192 (Books, Periodicals & Newspapers). **Est:** 1986.

■ **3497** ■ **American Audio Prose Library**
PO Box 842
Columbia, MO 65205-0842
Phone: (573)443-0361
Free: (800)447-2275 **Fax:** (573)499-0579
E-mail: aaplinc@compuserve.com
URL: http://www.americanaudioprose.com
Products: Audio cassettes. **SIC:** 5099 (Durable Goods Nec). **Est:** 1980. **Sales:** $85,000 (1999). **Emp:** 2. **Officers:** Kay Callison, Editor.

■ **3498** ■ **American Book Center**
Brooklyn Navy Yard, Bldg. 3
Brooklyn, NY 11205
Phone: (718)834-0170 **Fax:** (718)935-9647
Products: Books. **SIC:** 5192 (Books, Periodicals & Newspapers). **Est:** 1947. **Emp:** 70. **Officers:** Kenneth Gomez, Contact.

■ **3499** ■ **American Cooking Guild**
3600-K S Congress Ave.
Boynton Beach, FL 33426
Phone: (561)732-8111
Free: (800)367-9388 **Fax:** (561)732-8183
Products: Cookbooks. **SIC:** 5192 (Books, Periodicals & Newspapers). **Est:** 1981. **Officers:** Douglas Greenhut, President. **Alternate Name:** Powerline Publishing Co.

■ 3500 ■ **American Educational Services**
2101 NW Topeka Blvd.
Topeka, KS 66608
Phone: (785)233-4252
Free: (800)255-3502 **Fax:** (785)233-3129
URL: http://www.elonoclad.com
Products: Paperback books, including juvenile books; Software. **SICs:** 5192 (Books, Periodicals & Newspapers); 5045 (Computers, Peripherals & Software). **Est:** 1948.

■ 3501 ■ **American Mathematical Society**
PO Box 6248
Providence, RI 02940
Phone: (401)455-4000
Free: (800)321-4267 **Fax:** (401)331-3842
E-mail: cust-serv@ams.org
URL: http://www.ams.org
Products: Mathematical books. **SIC:** 5192 (Books, Periodicals & Newspapers). **Est:** 1888. **Sales:** $22,000,000 (1999). **Emp:** 250. **Officers:** Dr. John Ewing, Exec. Dir.; Paul Chambers, Sales Marketing Contact, e-mail: pgc@ams.org.

■ 3502 ■ **American Overseas Book Company Inc.**
550 Walnut St.
Norwood, NJ 07648
Phone: (201)767-7600 **Fax:** (201)784-0263
E-mail: books@aobc.com
URL: http://www.aobc.com
Products: Audio-visual materials; Journals; Books; Computer software. **SICs:** 5192 (Books, Periodicals & Newspapers); 5045 (Computers, Peripherals & Software). **Est:** 1969. **Sales:** $17,000,000 (2000). **Emp:** 27. **Officers:** Suzanne Gaffney, President.

■ 3503 ■ **American Printing House for the Blind, Inc.**
PO Box 6085
Louisville, KY 40206-0085
Phone: (502)895-2405
Free: (800)223-1839 **Fax:** (502)899-2274
E-mail: info@aph.org
URL: http://www.aph.org
Products: Books in braille; Large print books; Visual aids, Cassette recording duplication. **SIC:** 5192 (Books, Periodicals & Newspapers). **Est:** 1858. **Sales:** $14,000,000 (2000). **Emp:** 300. **Officers:** Tuck Tinsley III, President; Tony Grantz, Sales & Marketing Contact, e-mail: tgrantz@aph.org; Roseanne Broome, Customer Services Contact, e-mail: rbroome@aph.org; Norma Fletcher, Human Resources Contact, e-mail: nfletcher@aph.org.

■ 3504 ■ **American Wholesale Book Co.**
Helton Dr.
PO Box 219
Florence, AL 35630
Phone: (205)766-3789 **Fax:** (205)764-2511
Products: Mass market paperbacks; Software; Audio books on tape; Maps; Hardback and trade books. **SICs:** 5192 (Books, Periodicals & Newspapers); 5045 (Computers, Peripherals & Software); 5099 (Durable Goods Nec). **Est:** 1917.

■ 3505 ■ **Americans for the Arts**
1 E 53rd St., 2nd Fl.
New York, NY 10022
Phone: (212)223-2787
Free: (800)321-4510 **Fax:** (212)980-4857
URL: http://www.artsusa.org
Products: Art reference and instruction books. **SIC:** 5192 (Books, Periodicals & Newspapers). **Est:** 1996. **Sales:** $120,000 (2000). **Emp:** 23. **Officers:** Robert Lynch, President; Randy Cohen, VP of Information & Research; Mara Walker, VP of Programs & Member Services. **Former Name:** American Council for the Arts.

■ 3506 ■ **AMG Publications**
6815 Shallowford Rd.
Chattanooga, TN 37421
Phone: (423)894-6060
Free: (800)251-7206 **Fax:** (423)894-6863
URL: http://www.amgintional.org
Products: Books; Magazines. **SIC:** 5192 (Books, Periodicals & Newspapers). **Est:** 1945. **Sales:**

$3,500,000 (2000). **Emp:** 15. **Officers:** Dale Anderson, Vice President, e-mail: dalea@amginternational.org.

■ 3507 ■ **AMREP Corp.**
641 Lexington Ave.
New York, NY 10022
Phone: (212)541-7300
Products: Magazines. **SIC:** 5192 (Books, Periodicals & Newspapers). **Sales:** $152,500,000 (2000). **Emp:** 1,700. **Officers:** Anthony B. Gliedman, CEO, President & Chairman of the Board; Mohan Vachani, Sr. VP & CFO.

■ 3508 ■ **Ancient Future Music**
PO Box 264
Kentfield, CA 94914
Phone: (415)459-1892 **Free:** (888)823-8887
E-mail: info@ancient-future.com
URL: http://www.ancient-future.com/index.html
Products: Books of sheet music; World music CDs, LPs, and cassettes. **SICs:** 5192 (Books, Periodicals & Newspapers); 5099 (Durable Goods Nec); 5065 (Electronic Parts & Equipment Nec). **Est:** 1978. **Sales:** $30,000 (2000). **Emp:** 1. **Officers:** Matthew Montfort, Director.

■ 3509 ■ **Anco Management Services Inc.**
202 N Court St.
Florence, AL 35630
Phone: (256)766-3824
Products: Books and magazines; Fireworks. **SICs:** 5192 (Books, Periodicals & Newspapers); 5092 (Toys & Hobby Goods & Supplies). **Sales:** $740,000,000 (1992). **Emp:** 3,000. **Officers:** Joel Anderson, President.

■ 3510 ■ **Anderson Austin News**
499 Merritt Ave.
Nashville, TN 37203
Phone: (615)242-7603
Products: Books and magazines. **SIC:** 5192 (Books, Periodicals & Newspapers).

■ 3511 ■ **Anderson-Gemco**
1444 34th St.
Gulfport, MS 39501
Phone: (228)864-1044
Products: Books; Magazines. **SIC:** 5192 (Books, Periodicals & Newspapers).

■ 3512 ■ **Anderson News**
106 N Link
PO Box 2105
Ft. Collins, CO 80524
Phone: (970)221-2330
Free: (800)869-1161 **Fax:** (970)221-1251
Products: Magazines; Newspapers; Books. **SIC:** 5192 (Books, Periodicals & Newspapers). **Emp:** 45.
Alternate Name: Mountain States News Distributor.

■ 3513 ■ **Anderson News Co.**
1709 N East St.
Flagstaff, AZ 86004-4910
Phone: (520)774-6171 **Fax:** (520)779-1958
Products: Books. **SIC:** 5192 (Books, Periodicals & Newspapers). **Emp:** 24. **Former Name:** Northern Arizona News Co.

■ 3514 ■ **Anderson News Company**
1324 Coldwell Ave.
Modesto, CA 95350-5702
Phone: (209)577-5551 **Fax:** (209)577-4194
Products: Magazines; Paperback books. **SIC:** 5192 (Books, Periodicals & Newspapers). **Est:** 1917. **Emp:** 300. **Officers:** Frank Timpano, Vice President, e-mail: timpanof@andersonnews.com. **Former Name:** Medesto News Co.

■ 3515 ■ **Anderson News Co.**
5501 Park Ave.
PO Box 1297
Des Moines, IA 50305
Phone: (515)244-0044 **Fax:** (515)244-1144
Products: Books. **SIC:** 5192 (Books, Periodicals & Newspapers). **Est:** 1917.

■ 3516 ■ **Anderson News Co. Southwest**
11325 Gemini Ln.
Dallas, TX 75229
Phone: (972)501-5500
Products: Magazines; Books; Trading cards. **SIC:** 5192 (Books, Periodicals & Newspapers). **Sales:** $47,000,000 (2000). **Emp:** 150. **Officers:** Bennett T. Martin, President. **Former Name:** Martin News Agency Inc.

■ 3517 ■ **Anderson News Service Center**
26545 Danti Ct.
Hayward, CA 94545-3917
Phone: (650)349-7023 **Fax:** (650)349-7025
Products: Magazines; Books; Trading cards; T-shirts and caps; Maps, atlases, and almanacs; Comics. **SICs:** 5192 (Books, Periodicals & Newspapers); 5136 (Men's/Boys' Clothing); 5137 (Women's/Children's Clothing). **Est:** 1947. **Emp:** 295. **Former Name:** ETD-West.

■ 3518 ■ **Anderson News of Yuma**
PO Box 4427
Yuma, AZ 85366-4427
Phone: (520)782-1822 **Fax:** (520)782-1823
Products: Magazines. **SIC:** 5192 (Books, Periodicals & Newspapers). **Est:** 1986. **Sales:** $4,000,000 (2000). **Emp:** 25. **Officers:** Ken Ivie, General Mgr.

■ 3519 ■ **Antara Music Group**
468 McNally Dr.
Nashville, TN 37211-3318
Phone: (615)361-3053
Free: (800)877-7732 **Fax:** (615)781-8767
Products: Sheet music. **SIC:** 5199 (Nondurable Goods Nec). **Est:** 1987. **Sales:** $1,200,000 (2000). **Emp:** 10. **Officers:** Dr. Timothy Sharp, Director; Valerie Cameron, Asst. Dir.

■ 3520 ■ **Apollo Book**
PO Box 3839
Poughkeepsie, NY 12603
Phone: (914)462-0040
Free: (800)431-5003 **Fax:** (914)462-0119
Products: Art books; Antique books; Gardening books. **SIC:** 5192 (Books, Periodicals & Newspapers). **Est:** 1981. **Emp:** 2. **Officers:** Adam Opitz, President; Kimberly Renta, Manager.

■ 3521 ■ **Appalachian Distributors**
522 Princeton Rd.
Johnson City, TN 37601
Phone: (423)282-9475
Free: (800)289-2772 **Fax:** (423)282-9110
E-mail: appainc@aol.com
Products: Bibles; Books; Music; Gifts; Videos. **SICs:** 5192 (Books, Periodicals & Newspapers); 5099 (Durable Goods Nec); 5199 (Nondurable Goods Nec). **Est:** 1974. **Emp:** 96. **Officers:** H. Thomas Torbett, President; Hanes Torbett, Sales/Marketing Contact, e-mail: hltorb@aol.com; Kim Dawson, Customer Service Contact; Leon Overbay, Human Resources Contact, e-mail: rleono@aol.com; Robbie Edgar, VP of Operations. **Former Name:** Appalachian Bible Co. & Christian Books.

■ 3522 ■ **Applied Geographics Inc.**
100 Franklin St., Fl. 7
Boston, MA 02110
Phone: (617)292-7125
Products: Maps. **SIC:** 5192 (Books, Periodicals & Newspapers).

■ 3523 ■ **Aramark Magazines and Books**
2970 N Ontario St.
Burbank, CA 91504-2016
Phone: (213)857-7634 **Fax:** (213)930-4485
Products: Books; Magazines. **SIC:** 5192 (Books, Periodicals & Newspapers). **Officers:** Michael Gummeson, President.

■ 3524 ■ **Arch Hunter Books and Canyon Country Distribution Services**
PO Box 400034
18 Ballard Ct.
Thompson, UT 84540-0034
Phone: (435)285-2210 **Fax:** (435)285-2252
E-mail: archhunt@lasal.net
URL: http://www.archhunter.com
Products: Maps; Books; Travel books. **SIC:** 5192 (Books, Periodicals & Newspapers). **Est:** 1989.
Officers: Chris Moore, Owner. **Former Name:** Canyon Country Distribution.

■ 3525 ■ **Arrow Map Inc.**
50 Scotland Blvd.
Bridgewater, MA 02324
Phone: (508)880-2880
Free: (800)343-7500 **Fax:** (508)824-1735
Products: Maps, atlases, street guides, and zip code directories. **SIC:** 5192 (Books, Periodicals & Newspapers). **Est:** 1970.

■ 3526 ■ **Ashgate Publishing Co.**
Old Post Rd.
Brookfield, VT 05036
Phone: (802)276-3162
Free: (800)535-9544 **Fax:** (802)276-3837
E-mail: info@ashgate.com
URL: http://www.ashgate.com
Products: Books about the social sciences and humanities. **SIC:** 5192 (Books, Periodicals & Newspapers). **Est:** 1970. **Officers:** Richard Slappey, President; Barbara Church, Sales/Marketing Contact, e-mail: bchurch@ashgate.com; Suzanne Sprague, Customer Service Mgr., e-mail: ssprague@ashgate.com. **Former Name:** Cower Publishing Company Ltd.

■ 3527 ■ **Aspen West Publishing Co. Inc.**
PO Box 1245
Sandy, UT 84091
Phone: (801)565-1370
Free: (800)222-9133 **Fax:** (801)565-1373
Products: Books. **SIC:** 5192 (Books, Periodicals & Newspapers). **Est:** 1983.

■ 3528 ■ **Assorted Book Co.**
230 5th Ave., Ste. 1811
New York, NY 10001
Phone: (212)684-9000 **Fax:** (212)684-0590
Products: Books, including books on tape; Software; Music. **SICs:** 5192 (Books, Periodicals & Newspapers); 5045 (Computers, Peripherals & Software); 5199 (Nondurable Goods Nec). **Est:** 1992.

■ 3529 ■ **Astran Inc.**
591 SW 8th St.
Miami, FL 33130
Phone: (305)858-4300 **Fax:** (305)858-0405
E-mail: sales@astranbooks.com
Products: Books. **SIC:** 5192 (Books, Periodicals & Newspapers). **Est:** 1976. **Sales:** $700,000 (2000). **Emp:** 6. **Officers:** Rene Navarro, President.

■ 3530 ■ **Astran Inc.**
591 SW 8th St.
Miami, FL 33130
Phone: (305)858-4300 **Fax:** (305)858-0405
Products: Books and other printed materials. **SIC:** 5192 (Books, Periodicals & Newspapers). **Sales:** $700,000 (2000). **Emp:** 6.

■ 3531 ■ **Astronomical Society of the Pacific**
390 Ashton Ave.
San Francisco, CA 94112
Phone: (415)337-1100
Free: (800)962-3412 **Fax:** (415)337-5205
E-mail: catalog@aspsky.ord
URL: http://www.aspsky.org
Products: Astronomy books and multi-media materials, including posters, CD-ROMs, slide sets, globes, and audio and video tapes. **SIC:** 5192 (Books, Periodicals & Newspapers). **Est:** 1889. **Sales:** $1,750,000 (2000). **Emp:** 20. **Officers:** Wendy Sturley, Dir. of Marketing; Glenn Eaton, Marketing Coordinator.

■ 3532 ■ **Audubon Prints & Books**
9720 Spring Ridge Ln.
Vienna, VA 22182
Phone: (703)759-5567
Products: Natural history and antique prints; Books. **SIC:** 5192 (Books, Periodicals & Newspapers). **Est:** 1976.

■ 3533 ■ **Augsburg Fortress Publishers**
PO Box 1209
PO Box 1209
Minneapolis, MN 55440
Phone: (612)330-3300
Free: (800)426-0115 **Fax:** (612)330-3455
URL: http://www.augsburgfortress.org
Products: Religious books. **SIC:** 5192 (Books, Periodicals & Newspapers).

■ 3534 ■ **Auto-Bound, Inc.**
909 Marina Village Pky., No. 678
Alameda, CA 94501
Phone: (510)521-8630 **Fax:** (510)521-8755
URL: http://www.auto-bound.com
Products: Automotive and motorcycle manuals and books. **SIC:** 5192 (Books, Periodicals & Newspapers). **Est:** 1978.

■ 3535 ■ **Avery Book Stores, Inc.**
308 Livingston St.
Brooklyn, NY 11217
Phone: (718)858-3606
Products: New, used, and rare books. **SIC:** 5192 (Books, Periodicals & Newspapers). **Est:** 1953.

■ 3536 ■ **Avonlea Books**
PO Box 74, Main Sta.
White Plains, NY 10602-0074
Phone: (914)946-5923
Free: (800)423-0622 **Fax:** (914)946-5924
Products: Out-of-print books. **SIC:** 5192 (Books, Periodicals & Newspapers). **Est:** 1979. **Officers:** Leone E. Bushkin, Proprietor.

■ 3537 ■ **Back Bay News Distributors**
51 Melcher St.
Boston, MA 02210
Phone: (617)350-7170
Products: Newspapers. **SIC:** 5192 (Books, Periodicals & Newspapers).

■ 3538 ■ **Bacon Pamphlet Service, Inc.**
187 Hand Hollow Rd.
East Chatham, NY 12060
Phone: (518)794-7722 **Fax:** (518)794-3042
E-mail: bps@taconic.net
URL: http://www.baconpamphletservice.com
Products: Pamphlets and paperbound materials; Cd's and cassettes; Posters; Maps. **SIC:** 5192 (Books, Periodicals & Newspapers). **Est:** 1937. **Emp:** 1. **Officers:** Deborah Dodge.

■ 3539 ■ **Baker Book House Co.**
6030 E Fulton SE
Ada, MI 49301
Phone: (616)676-9185
Free: (800)877-2665 **Fax:** (616)676-9573
URL: http://www.bakerbooks.com
Products: Religious books. **SIC:** 5192 (Books, Periodicals & Newspapers).

■ 3540 ■ **Baker and Taylor**
2709 Water Ridge Pkwy.
Charlotte, NC 28217
Phone: (704)357-3500
Free: (800)775-1800 **Fax:** (704)329-8989
E-mail: btinfo@btol.com
URL: http://www.btol.com
Products: Books; Videos; Music products. **SIC:** 5192 (Books, Periodicals & Newspapers). **Est:** 1828. **Emp:** 2,500. **Officers:** Craig M. Richards, CEO; Gary Rautenstrauch, President; James Ulsamer, President; Connie Koury, VP of Marketing.

■ 3541 ■ **Baker and Taylor Inc.**
2709 Water Ridge Pky.
Charlotte, NC 28217
Phone: (704)357-3500
Free: (800)775-1800 **Fax:** (704)329-9105
Products: Books, video and music audio cassettes, and compact discs and accessories. **SIC:** 5099 (Durable Goods Nec). **Sales:** $880,000,000 (2000). **Emp:** 2,000. **Officers:** Craig M. Richards, CEO; Edward H. Gross, CFO.

■ 3542 ■ **Banner of Truth**
63 E Louther St.
PO Box 621
Carlisle, PA 17013
Phone: (717)249-5747 **Fax:** (717)249-0604
E-mail: banneroftruth@cs.com
URL: http://www.banneroftruth.co.uk
Products: Religious books. **SIC:** 5192 (Books, Periodicals & Newspapers). **Est:** 1957.

■ 3543 ■ **Baptist Spanish Publishing House**
PO Box 4255
El Paso, TX 79914
Phone: (915)566-9656 **Fax:** (915)562-6502
Products: Religious books and calendars. **SIC:** 5192 (Books, Periodicals & Newspapers).

■ 3544 ■ **Barclay Press**
110 S Elliott Rd.
Newberg, OR 97132-2144
Phone: (503)538-7345
Free: (800)962-4014 **Fax:** (503)538-7033
E-mail: info@barclaypress.com
URL: http://www.barclaypress.com
Products: Books, pamphlets, and church curriculum. **SIC:** 5192 (Books, Periodicals & Newspapers). **Est:** 1930. **Sales:** $108,000 (2000). **Emp:** 12. **Officers:** Dan McCracken, Manager.

■ 3545 ■ **Barrett & Co. Publishers**
PO Box 2008
Learned, MS 39154
Phone: (601)885-2288
E-mail: publitics@hotmail.com
Products: Books. **SIC:** 5192 (Books, Periodicals & Newspapers). **Est:** 1966.

■ 3546 ■ **Beekman Publishers, Inc.**
2626 Rte. 212
PO Box 888
Woodstock, NY 12498
Phone: (914)679-2300
Free: (800)233-5626 **Fax:** (914)679-2301
E-mail: beekman@beekman.net
URL: http://www.beekman.net
Products: Welsh and Celtic books; Alternative medicine books. **SIC:** 5192 (Books, Periodicals & Newspapers). **Est:** 1972. **Officers:** Kathy Nolan, e-mail: manager@beekman.net.

■ 3547 ■ **Beeman Jorgensen Inc.**
7510 Allisonville Rd.
Indianapolis, IN 46250
Phone: (317)841-7677 **Fax:** (317)849-2001
Products: Books. **SIC:** 5192 (Books, Periodicals & Newspapers). **Est:** 1987. **Sales:** $100,000 (2000). **Emp:** 3. **Officers:** Brett Johnson, CEO; Julie Johnson, CFO.

■ 3548 ■ **Before Columbus Foundation**
American Ethnic Studies, GN-80
University of Washington
Seattle, WA 98195
Phone: (206)543-4264
Products: Books. **SIC:** 5192 (Books, Periodicals & Newspapers).

■ 3549 ■ **Beijing Book Co. Inc.**
701 E Linden Ave.
Linden, NJ 07036-2495
Phone: (908)862-0909 **Fax:** (908)862-4201
Products: Books. **SIC:** 5192 (Books, Periodicals & Newspapers). **Est:** 1981. **Sales:** $7,000,000 (2000). **Emp:** 20.

■ 3550 ■ **Benjamin News Group**
219 E Park St.
Butte, MT 59701
Phone: (406)782-6995
Products: Magazines; Newspapers. **SIC:** 5192 (Books, Periodicals & Newspapers).

■ 3551 ■ **Bergano Book Co., Inc.**
PO Box 190
Fairfield, CT 06430
Phone: (203)254-2054 **Fax:** (203)255-3817
E-mail: bergano@aol.com
URL: http://www.bergano.com
Products: Books; Software; Training materials. **SICs:** 5192 (Books, Periodicals & Newspapers); 5045 (Computers, Peripherals & Software). **Est:** 1984. **Emp:** 5. **Officers:** Al Palmisano, President; Adrienne Fishman, Manager.

■ 3552 ■ **Bernan**
4611-F Assembly Dr.
Lanham, MD 20706-4391
Phone: (301)459-7666
Free: (800)274-4447 **Fax:** 800-865-3450
Products: Books. **SIC:** 5192 (Books, Periodicals & Newspapers). **Est:** 1952. **Officers:** Donald Hagen, Dir.

■ 3553 ■ **Beyda & Associates, Inc.**
6943 Valjean Ave.
Van Nuys, CA 91406
Phone: (818)988-3102
Free: (800)422-3932 **Fax:** (818)994-8724
Products: Books; Videos; Prerecorded audio tapes. **SICs:** 5192 (Books, Periodicals & Newspapers); 5099 (Durable Goods Nec); 5065 (Electronic Parts & Equipment Nec). **Est:** 1974.

■ 3554 ■ **Beyda & Associates, Inc.**
2150 Premier Row
Orlando, FL 32809
Phone: (407)438-6700 **Fax:** (407)438-0669
Products: Books, videos, CD's and cassettes. **SICs:** 5192 (Books, Periodicals & Newspapers); 5099 (Durable Goods Nec).

■ 3555 ■ **Big Horn Booksellers Inc.**
1813 E Mulberry
Ft. Collins, CO 80524
Phone: (970)224-1579
Free: (800)433-5995 **Fax:** (970)224-1394
Products: Books and other printed materials. **SIC:** 5192 (Books, Periodicals & Newspapers).

■ 3556 ■ **Bilingual Educational Services, Inc.**
2514 S Grand Ave.
Los Angeles, CA 90007-2688
Phone: (213)749-6213
Free: (800)448-6032 **Fax:** (213)749-1820
Products: Spanish-language books. **SIC:** 5192 (Books, Periodicals & Newspapers). **Est:** 1971.

■ 3557 ■ **Bilingual Publications Co.**
270 Lafayette St.
New York, NY 10012
Phone: (212)431-3500 **Fax:** (212)431-3567
E-mail: lindagoodman@juno.com
Products: Spanish books. **SIC:** 5192 (Books, Periodicals & Newspapers). **Est:** 1974. **Officers:** Linda E. Goodman, Owner.

■ 3558 ■ **Blacast Entertainment**
PO Box 175
Cambria Heights, NY 11411
Phone: (718)712-2300
E-mail: blacast@aol.com
URL: http://www.blacast.com
Products: African American videos and books; Cultural computer software and clipart. **SICs:** 5192 (Books, Periodicals & Newspapers); 5099 (Durable Goods Nec). **Est:** 1987. **Sales:** $1,000,000 (2000). **Emp:** 3. **Officers:** Edna Swan, President, e-mail: eswan@ladylaptop.com.

■ 3559 ■ **Black Gold Comics & Graphics**
2130 S Sheridan Rd.
Tulsa, OK 74129-1002
Products: Comic books. **SIC:** 5192 (Books, Periodicals & Newspapers). **Officers:** John Harper, Partner.

■ 3560 ■ **Blackwell North America Inc.**
6024 SW Jean Rd.
Lake Oswego, OR 97035
Phone: (503)684-1140
Free: (800)547-6426 **Fax:** (503)639-2481
Products: Supplier of books and other materials to academic and research libraries. **SIC:** 5192 (Books, Periodicals & Newspapers). **Est:** 1975. **Sales:** $110,000,000 (2000). **Emp:** 400. **Officers:** Fred A. Philipp, CEO & President; Gary Nees, Sr. VP & CFO.

■ 3561 ■ **Blackwell's Delaware Inc.**
6024 SW Jean Rd.
Lake Oswego, OR 97035
Phone: (503)684-1140
Products: Books. **SIC:** 5192 (Books, Periodicals & Newspapers). **Sales:** $77,000,000 (2000). **Emp:** 330. **Officers:** Fred Philipp, President; Gary Nees, CFO.

■ 3562 ■ **BMI Educational Services**
26 Hay Press Rd.
PO Box 800
Dayton, NJ 08810-0800
Phone: (732)329-6991 **Fax:** (732)329-6994
E-mail: bmiedserv@aol.com
Products: Books, including paperback; Audio and visual multicultural materials. **SICs:** 5192 (Books, Periodicals & Newspapers); 5099 (Durable Goods Nec); 5065 (Electronic Parts & Equipment Nec). **Est:** 1964. **Sales:** $6,000,000 (2000). **Emp:** 30. **Officers:** Gerald Wagner, CEO; Greta Einig, VP & Treasurer.

■ 3563 ■ **Bonneville News Co. Inc.**
965 Beardsley Pl.
Salt Lake City, UT 84119
Phone: (801)972-5454 **Fax:** (801)972-1075
Products: Paperback books; Magazines. **SIC:** 5192 (Books, Periodicals & Newspapers). **Sales:** $15,000,000 (2000). **Emp:** 49. **Officers:** Terry Watson, General Mgr.; E.L. Madsen Sr., President; E.L. Madsen Jr., Treasurer & Secty.

■ 3564 ■ **Bonus Books Inc.**
160 E Illinois St.
Chicago, IL 60611
Phone: (312)467-0580
Free: (800)225-3775 **Fax:** (312)467-9271
URL: http://www.bonus-books.com
Products: Sports books; Books. **SIC:** 5192 (Books, Periodicals & Newspapers). **Est:** 1985. **Emp:** 10. **Officers:** Aaron Cohodes, Marketing Mgr.; Kate Hawley, Sales & Marketing Contact, e-mail: kate@bonus-books.com; Richard Williams, Customer Service Contact, e-mail: richard@bonus-books.com.

■ 3565 ■ **Book Box, Inc.**
3126 Purdue Ave.
Los Angeles, CA 90066
Phone: (310)391-2313
Products: Children's books. **SIC:** 5192 (Books, Periodicals & Newspapers). **Est:** 1974.

■ 3566 ■ **Book Centers Inc.**
5600 NE Hassalo St.
Portland, OR 97213
Phone: (503)287-6657
Free: (800)547-7704 **Fax:** (503)284-8859
E-mail: info@acbc.com
URL: http://www.acbc.com
Products: Books. **SIC:** 5192 (Books, Periodicals & Newspapers). **Est:** 1975. **Sales:** $35,000,000 (2000). **Emp:** 120. **Officers:** Dan P. Halloran, President & Chairman of the Board.

■ 3567 ■ **Book Distribution Center**
PO Box 31669
Houston, TX 77235
Phone: (713)721-1980 **Fax:** (713)723-0099
Products: Books on socio-political affairs of the Muslim world and Islamic studies. **SIC:** 5192 (Books, Periodicals & Newspapers). **Est:** 1974.

■ 3568 ■ **Book Distribution Center, Inc.**
4617 N Witchduck Rd.
Virginia Beach, VA 23455
Phone: (757)456-0005 **Fax:** (757)552-0837
E-mail: sales@bookdist.com
URL: http://www.bookdist.com
Products: Books. **SIC:** 5192 (Books, Periodicals & Newspapers). **Est:** 1974. **Emp:** 6. **Officers:** Harvey D. Eluto, President; Harriett S. Eluto, Treasurer & Secty.; Cindy Everton, General Mgr. **Former Name:** Paperback Books, Inc.

■ 3569 ■ **Book Dynamics, Inc.**
26 Kennedy Blvd.
East Brunswick, NJ 08816
Phone: (732)545-5151
Free: (800)441-4510 **Fax:** (732)545-5949
Products: Hardcover titles; Trade and mass market paperbacks. **SIC:** 5192 (Books, Periodicals & Newspapers).

■ 3570 ■ **Book Home, Inc.**
119 E Dale St.
PO Box 825
Colorado Springs, CO 80901
Phone: (719)634-5885
Products: Scientific and technical publications. **SIC:** 5192 (Books, Periodicals & Newspapers). **Est:** 1942. **Emp:** 2.

■ 3571 ■ **The Book House Inc.**
208 W Chicago St.
Jonesville, MI 49250-0125
Phone: (517)849-2117
Free: (800)248-1146 **Fax:** (517)849-4060
E-mail: bhinfo@thebookhouse.com
URL: http://www.thebookhouse.com
Products: University press books, including sci-tech and trade. **SIC:** 5192 (Books, Periodicals & Newspapers). **Est:** 1962. **Officers:** John Ansett, President; James Marsh, Vice President.

■ 3572 ■ **Book Warehouse Inc.**
5154 NW 165th St.
Palmetto Lakes Industrial Pk.
Hialeah, FL 33014-6335
Phone: (305)624-4545
Free: (800)766-3254 **Fax:** (305)621-0425
URL: http://www.southernbook.com
Products: Books, including foreign language, current releases, standard backstock, and school titles; Audio books. **SICs:** 5192 (Books, Periodicals & Newspapers); 5099 (Durable Goods Nec). **Est:** 1996. **Sales:** $10,000,000 (2000). **Emp:** 20. **Officers:** Bruce Sardinia, President; Barbara Franzen, Marketing Contact, e-mail: bfranzen@southernbook.com. **Doing Business As:** Southern Book Service.

■ 3573 ■ **Book Wholesalers, Inc.**
1847 Mercer Rd.
Lexington, KY 40511
Phone: (606)231-9789
Products: Books. **SIC:** 5192 (Books, Periodicals & Newspapers). **Officers:** Joe Neri, Contact.

■ 3574 ■ **Bookazine Co., Inc.**
75 Hook Rd.
Bayonne, NJ 07002
Phone: (201)339-7777
Products: Books; Magazines. **SIC:** 5192 (Books, Periodicals & Newspapers). **Officers:** Fran Stone, Contact.

■ 3575 ■ **Bookcraft Inc.**
40 E South Temple
Salt Lake City, UT 84111-1003
Phone: (801)908-3400 **Fax:** (801)908-3401
Products: Religious books. **SIC:** 5192 (Books, Periodicals & Newspapers). **Est:** 1942. **Emp:** 58. **Officers:** Brad Pelo, President; Dave Harkness, Treasurer & Secty.

■ 3576 ■ **Booklegger**
PO Box 2626
Grass Valley, CA 95945
Phone: (530)272-1556
Free: (800)262-1556 **Fax:** (530)272-2133
Products: Golf books and videos; Training aids; Audios; Art prints; Greeting cards; Calendars. **SICs:** 5192 (Books, Periodicals & Newspapers); 5065 (Electronic Parts & Equipment Nec). **Est:** 1974. **Emp:** 19. **Officers:** Robert Kraut, President, e-mail: rkraut@booklegger.com; Susan Kraut, CEO, e-mail: skraut@booklegger.com; Linda Reed, Customer Service Contact.

■ 3577 ■ **BookLink Distributors**
PO Box 840
Arroyo Grande, CA 93421-0840
Phone: (805)473-1947
Products: Books, including California-Nevada travel

and history, architecture, business, cooking, collectibles, juvenile and spiritual titles. **SIC:** 5192 (Books, Periodicals & Newspapers). **Est:** 1982.

■ **3578** ■ **Bookmark, Inc.**
14643 W 95th St.
Lenexa, KS 66215
Phone: (913)894-1288
Free: (800)642-1288 **Fax:** (913)894-1842
E-mail: bookmark@sound.net
URL: http://www.bookmarki.com
Products: Books. **SIC:** 5192 (Books, Periodicals & Newspapers). **Est:** 1984. **Sales:** $1,000,000 (2000). **Emp:** 3. **Officers:** Patricia Monteiro, President; Mary Schneider.

■ **3579** ■ **Bookmen, Inc.**
525 N 3rd St.
Minneapolis, MN 55401
Phone: (612)359-5757
Free: (800)328-8411 **Fax:** (612)341-2903
URL: http://www.bookmen.com
Products: Trade, paperback, juvenile, hardcover books. **SIC:** 5192 (Books, Periodicals & Newspapers). **Est:** 1962. **Officers:** Bill Roth, Sales/Marketing Contact, e-mail: billr@bookmen.com; Jeffrey Vavra, Customer Service Contact, e-mail: service@bookmen.com; Diana Johnson, Human Resources Contact, e-mail: dianaj@bookmen.com.

■ **3580** ■ **Bookpeople**
7900 Edgewater Dr.
Oakland, CA 94621
Phone: (510)632-4700
Free: (800)999-4650 **Fax:** (510)632-1281
E-mail: custserv@bponline.com
URL: http://www.bponline.com
Products: Books; Calendars; Audio and video cassettes. **SIC:** 5192 (Books, Periodicals & Newspapers). **Est:** 1971. **Sales:** $25,000,000 (2000). **Emp:** 85. **Officers:** Joel Bernstein, General Mgr.; Gene Taback, President.

■ **3581** ■ **Books Nippan**
1123K Dominguez St.
Carson, CA 90746
Phone: (310)604-9701
Free: (800)562-1410 **Fax:** (310)604-1134
Products: Visual arts books. **SIC:** 5192 (Books, Periodicals & Newspapers). **Est:** 1976. **Sales:** $12,000,000 (2000). **Emp:** 40. **Officers:** T. Iwasaki, General Mgr.

■ **3582** ■ **Booksmith Promotional Co.**
100 Paterson Plank Rd.
Jersey City, NJ 07307
Phone: (201)659-2768 **Fax:** (201)659-3631
Products: Books. **SIC:** 5192 (Books, Periodicals & Newspapers). **Est:** 1973. **Officers:** Annette Hochberg, Sales/Marketing Contact, e-mail: hochberga@aol.com; Dalila Garcia. **Alternate Name:** Little Dania's Juvenile Promotions.

■ **3583** ■ **The Booksource**
1230 Macklind Ave.
St. Louis, MO 63110
Phone: (314)647-0600
Products: Books; Periodicals. **SIC:** 5192 (Books, Periodicals & Newspapers). **Officers:** Gary Jaffe, Contact.

■ **3584** ■ **BookWorld Services Inc.**
1933 Whitfield Park Loop
Sarasota, FL 34243
Phone: (941)758-8094
Free: (800)444-2524 **Fax:** (941)753-9396
E-mail: sales@bookworld.com
URL: http://www.bookworld.com
Products: Books. **SIC:** 5192 (Books, Periodicals & Newspapers). **Est:** 1963. **Sales:** $15,000,000 (2000). **Emp:** 28. **Officers:** Ronald Ted Smith, President; Wilfred Niquette, Exec. VP.

■ **3585** ■ **The Bookworm**
417 Monmouth Dr.
Cherry Hill, NJ 08002
Phone: (609)667-5884
Products: Textbooks, including teachers' editions.

SIC: 5192 (Books, Periodicals & Newspapers). **Est:** 1973. **Officers:** Herbert Nelson, President.

■ **3586** ■ **Bouregy, Thomas & Co. Inc.**
160 Madison Ave., 5th Fl.
New York, NY 10016-5412
Phone: (212)598-0222
Free: (800)223-5251 **Fax:** (212)979-1862
Products: Books, including westerns, mysteries, and romances. **SIC:** 5192 (Books, Periodicals & Newspapers). **Est:** 1950. **Officers:** Wilhelm H. Mickelsen, President.

■ **3587** ■ **Bradford Publishing Co.**
PO Box 448
Denver, CO 80201
Phone: (303)292-2500 **Fax:** (303)298-5014
Products: Publishes legal forms and law books. **SIC:** 5192 (Books, Periodicals & Newspapers). **Sales:** $2,000,000 (2000). **Emp:** 16.

■ **3588** ■ **Brady News and Recycling**
3240 Schuette Rd.
Midland, MI 48642
Phone: (517)496-9900
Products: Newspapers. **SIC:** 5192 (Books, Periodicals & Newspapers).

■ **3589** ■ **Branden Publishing Co.**
PO Box 094
Wellesley, MA 02482
Phone: (781)235-3634 **Fax:** (781)790-1056
E-mail: branden@branden.com
URL: http://www.branden.com
Products: Fiction and nonfiction books. **SIC:** 5192 (Books, Periodicals & Newspapers). **Est:** 1903. **Emp:** 7. **Officers:** Adolph Caso.

■ **3590** ■ **Brethren Press**
1451 Dundee Ave.
Elgin, IL 60120
Phone: (708)742-5100
Free: (800)323-8039 **Fax:** (708)742-6103
Products: Religious books. **SIC:** 5192 (Books, Periodicals & Newspapers).

■ **3591** ■ **Bridge-Logos Publishers**
PO Box 141630
Gainesville, FL 32614-1630
Phone: (352)472-7900
Free: (800)631-5802 **Fax:** (352)472-7908
E-mail: info@bridgelogos.com
URL: http://www.bridgelogos.com
Products: Religious books. **SIC:** 5192 (Books, Periodicals & Newspapers). **Est:** 1995. **Sales:** $1,400,000 (1999). **Emp:** 9. **Officers:** Guy J. Morrell, President.

■ **3592** ■ **Bridge Publications Inc.**
4751 Fountain Ave.
Los Angeles, CA 90029
Phone: (323)953-3320 **Free:** (800)722-1733
Products: Self help books; Math and science books; Literature books; Tapes audio and video recording. **SICs:** 5192 (Books, Periodicals & Newspapers); 5065 (Electronic Parts & Equipment Nec). **Est:** 1982. **Emp:** 90.

■ **3593** ■ **Brodart Co.**
500 Arch St.
Williamsport, PA 17705
Phone: (570)326-2461
Free: (800)233-8467 **Fax:** (570)326-1479
URL: http://www.brodart.com
Products: Books; Furniture. **SIC:** 5192 (Books, Periodicals & Newspapers). **Emp:** 1,100. **Officers:** George F. Coe, Contact.

■ **3594** ■ **Brotherhood of Life, Inc.**
110 Dartmouth SE
Albuquerque, NM 87106
Phone: (505)265-0888 **Fax:** (505)265-0888
E-mail: brohood@thuntek.net
URL: http://www.brotherhoodoflife.com
Products: Metaphysical, New Age, and occult books. **SIC:** 5192 (Books, Periodicals & Newspapers). **Est:** 1969. **Emp:** 6.

■ **3595** ■ **Brownlow Corp.**
6309 Airport Fwy.
Ft. Worth, TX 76117
Phone: (817)831-3831 **Fax:** (817)831-7025
URL: http://www.brownlowgift.com
Products: Gift books; Stationery; Gourmet beverages. **SICs:** 5192 (Books, Periodicals & Newspapers); 5149 (Groceries & Related Products Nec). **Former Name:** Brownlow Publishing Company, Inc.

■ **3596** ■ **Albert E. Brumley & Sons**
100 Albert E Brumley Pkwy.
Powell, MO 65730
Phone: (417)435-2225
Free: (800)435-3725 **Fax:** (417)435-2227
E-mail: info@brumleymusic.com
URL: http://www.brumleymusic.com
Products: Gospel, country, and bluegrass songbooks. **SIC:** 5192 (Books, Periodicals & Newspapers). **Est:** 1949. **Emp:** 3. **Officers:** Robert B. Brumley, President; Sharon K. Boles, Office Mgr.; Duane Garren, Sales/Marketing Contact. **Alternate Name:** Hartford Music Co.

■ **3597** ■ **Brunner News Agency**
217 Flanders Ave.
PO Box 598
Lima, OH 45802
Phone: (419)225-5826 **Fax:** (419)225-5537
E-mail: brunnews@aol.com
Products: Magazines; Books. **SIC:** 5192 (Books, Periodicals & Newspapers). **Est:** 1950. **Officers:** Thomas Brunner, Vice President.

■ **3598** ■ **BSC Litho Inc.**
3000 Canby St.
Harrisburg, PA 17103
Phone: (717)238-9469
Free: (800)272-5484 **Fax:** (717)232-4151
E-mail: bscprint@aol.com
URL: http://www.bsclitho.com
Products: Magazines; Brochures; Newsletters. **SICs:** 5192 (Books, Periodicals & Newspapers); 5112 (Stationery & Office Supplies). **Est:** 1921. **Sales:** $7,500,000 (2000). **Emp:** 75. **Officers:** Dave Hiatt, President; Joe Pizzo, General Mgr.; Jeff Kreuer, Marketing & Sales Mgr.; Mark Zampelli, Mgr. of Finance.

■ **3599** ■ **Bud Plant Comic Art**
13393 Grass Valley Ave., No. 7
PO Box 1689
Grass Valley, CA 95945
Phone: (530)273-2166
Free: (800)242-6642 **Fax:** (530)273-0915
E-mail: cs@budplant.com
URL: http://www.budplant.com
Products: Illustrated books, including graphic novels, art books, art instruction, children's books, and comics; Trading cards and specialty items. **SICs:** 5192 (Books, Periodicals & Newspapers); 5092 (Toys & Hobby Goods & Supplies). **Est:** 1972. **Sales:** $3,700,000 (1999). **Emp:** 23. **Officers:** Bud Plant, Owner; Betty Towne, Sales & Marketing Contact, e-mail: betty@budplant.com; Todd Wulf, Customer Service Contact.

■ **3600** ■ **BUDGEText Corporation**
1936 N Shiloh Dr.
PO Box 1487
Fayetteville, AR 72702-1487
Phone: (501)443-9205
Free: (800)643-3432 **Fax:** (501)442-3064
E-mail: sales@budgetext.com
URL: http://www.budgetext.com
Products: Used textbooks and computerized bookstore management systems. **SIC:** 5192 (Books, Periodicals & Newspapers). **Est:** 1968. **Emp:** 238. **Officers:** S.P. Anders, Owner; Whitney Morgan, President, e-mail: wmorgan@budgetext.com. **Former Name:** ABS Corp.

■ **3601** ■ **Butterworth Co. of Cape Cod**
89 Willow St.
Yarmouth Port, MA 02675-1742
Phone: (508)790-1111
Products: Maps; Printers. **SIC:** 5192 (Books, Periodicals & Newspapers).

■ 3602 ■ C and W Zabel Co.
PO Box 41
Leonia, NJ 07605-0041
Phone: (732)254-1000 **Fax:** (732)254-0121
Products: Books and other printed materials. **SIC:** 5192 (Books, Periodicals & Newspapers). **Sales:** $600,000 (2000). **Emp:** 8.

■ 3603 ■ Cambridge Educational
PO Box 2153
Charleston, WV 25328
Free: (888)744-0100
Products: Vendor of wide range of educational materials, including books, videos, CD-ROMs, and posters. **SIC:** 5192 (Books, Periodicals & Newspapers). **Officers:** Rich Hopkins, CEO & President.

■ 3604 ■ Cambridge Law Study Aids, Inc.
4814 S Pulaski Rd.
Chicago, IL 60632-4194
Phones: (773)376-1713 (773)376-1711
Free: (800)628-1160 **Fax:** (773)376-1110
Products: Law books. **SIC:** 5192 (Books, Periodicals & Newspapers). **Est:** 1961. **Sales:** $650,000 (2000). **Emp:** 4. **Officers:** Joseph J. Gasior; Bernadine Dziedzic.

■ 3605 ■ Cambridge University Press
40 W 20th St.
New York, NY 10011
Phone: (212)924-3900 **Free:** (800)221-4512
Products: Books and journals. **SIC:** 5192 (Books, Periodicals & Newspapers).

■ 3606 ■ Capeway News
2 Hinckley Rd.
Hyannis, MA 02601
Phone: (508)790-4103
Products: Newspapers; Magazines. **SIC:** 5192 (Books, Periodicals & Newspapers).

■ 3607 ■ Capital City Distribution Inc.
3702 E Roeser Rd., Unit 26
Phoenix, AZ 85040
Phone: (602)437-2502 **Fax:** (602)437-0470
Products: Comic books. **SIC:** 5192 (Books, Periodicals & Newspapers).

■ 3608 ■ Capital City Distribution Inc.
16643 Valley View Ave.
Cerritos, CA 90701
Phone: (562)802-5222 **Fax:** (562)802-5220
Products: Cards and comics. **SIC:** 5192 (Books, Periodicals & Newspapers).

■ 3609 ■ Capital City Distribution Inc.
107 Leland Ct.
Bensenville, IL 60106
Phone: (708)595-1100 **Fax:** (708)595-1514
Products: Comic books. **SIC:** 5192 (Books, Periodicals & Newspapers).

■ 3610 ■ Capitol News Distributors
1960 Washington St.
Boston, MA 02118
Phone: (617)427-5578
Products: Newspapers. **SIC:** 5192 (Books, Periodicals & Newspapers).

■ 3611 ■ Capra Press Inc.
PO Box 2068
Santa Barbara, CA 93120
Phone: (805)966-4590 **Fax:** (805)965-8020
Products: Adult trade and juvenile books; Fiction books; Literature books; Books. **SIC:** 5192 (Books, Periodicals & Newspapers). **Est:** 1969. **Sales:** $400,000 (2000). **Emp:** 1. **Officers:** Noel Young, President; David Dahl, Assistant.

■ 3612 ■ Carolina Biological Supply Co.
2700 York Rd.
Burlington, NC 27215
Phone: (919)584-0381 **Fax:** (919)584-3399
Products: Books, charts, and videos. **SIC:** 5192 (Books, Periodicals & Newspapers). **Est:** 1927.

■ 3613 ■ Carolina News Co.
245 Tillinghast St.
Fayetteville, NC 28301
Phone: (919)483-4135 **Fax:** (919)483-3080
Products: Magazines and paperbacks. **SIC:** 5192 (Books, Periodicals & Newspapers). **Est:** 1935.

■ 3614 ■ E. Castellon Inc.
PO Box 505
Mahwah, NJ 07430-0505
Phone: (973)772-7712
Products: Newspapers; Magazines. **SIC:** 5192 (Books, Periodicals & Newspapers). **Sales:** $900,000 (2000). **Emp:** 4. **Officers:** E. Castellon, President.

■ 3615 ■ Catholic Reading Society
997 Macarthur Blvd.
Mahwah, NJ 07430
Phone: (201)825-7300
Free: (800)218-1903 **Fax:** (201)825-8345
E-mail: info@paulistpress.com
URL: http://www.paulistpress.com
Products: Religious books. **SIC:** 5192 (Books, Periodicals & Newspapers). **Est:** 1960. **Emp:** 1. **Officers:** Sr. Marie de Lourdes. **Former Name:** National Catholic Reading Distributor.

■ 3616 ■ Caxton Printers Ltd.
312 Main St.
Caldwell, ID 83605
Phone: (208)459-7421 **Fax:** (208)459-7450
Products: Educational textbooks; Printers. **SICs:** 5192 (Books, Periodicals & Newspapers); 5045 (Computers, Peripherals & Software). **Est:** 1904. **Sales:** $13,000,000 (2000). **Emp:** 50. **Officers:** Gordon Gipson, President.

■ 3617 ■ CCS Printing
111 Oak Lawn Ave.
Dallas, TX 75207
Phone: (214)748-6622 **Fax:** (214)748-9922
Products: Brochures; Music related paper products. **SIC:** 5192 (Books, Periodicals & Newspapers).

■ 3618 ■ Celestial Arts Publishing Co.
PO Box 7123
Berkeley, CA 94707
Phone: (510)559-1600
Free: (800)841-2665 **Fax:** (510)559-1629
E-mail: order@tenspeed.com
URL: http://www.tenspeed.com
Products: Books on women's health, nutrition, cooking, parenting, self-help, and new age. **SIC:** 5192 (Books, Periodicals & Newspapers). **Est:** 1971. **Emp:** 45. **Officers:** Phil Wood, Publisher; JoAnn Deek, Sales/Marketing Contact, e-mail: joann@tenspeed.com; Shelli Moore, Customer Service Contact, e-mail: shelli@tenspeed.com; Susan Engle, Human Resources Contact, e-mail: susan@tenspeed.com.

■ 3619 ■ Cellar Book Shop
18090 Wyoming
Detroit, MI 48221
Phone: (313)861-1776 **Fax:** (313)861-1776
E-mail: cellarbook@aol.com
Products: Books on and from Southeast Asia and the Pacific Islands. **SIC:** 5192 (Books, Periodicals & Newspapers). **Est:** 1946.

■ 3620 ■ Central Arizona Distributing Co.
4932 W Pasadena Ave.
Glendale, AZ 85301-1466
Phone: (602)939-6511 **Fax:** (602)252-4983
Products: Books and magazines, including hard and soft back; Trading cards. **SICs:** 5192 (Books, Periodicals & Newspapers); 5092 (Toys & Hobby Goods & Supplies). **Emp:** 140. **Officers:** Tom Lieberman.

■ 3621 ■ Central Kentucky News Distributing Co.
808 Newtown Cir. No. B
Lexington, KY 40511-1230
Phone: (606)254-2765 **Fax:** (606)254-2767
Products: Paperback books, children's books, Bibles, best-selling hardcover and trade titles; Magazines. **SIC:** 5192 (Books, Periodicals & Newspapers). **Est:** 1948.

■ 3622 ■ Central News Co.
920 Hemlock Dr.
Columbia, SC 29201
Phone: (803)799-3414 **Fax:** (803)799-8858
Products: Magazines; Books. **SIC:** 5192 (Books, Periodicals & Newspapers). **Est:** 1940. **Emp:** 35.

■ 3623 ■ Central States/Multiplex Business Forms
4685 Merle Hay Rd., Ste. 205
Des Moines, IA 50322
Phone: (515)270-8382 **Fax:** (515)253-0711
Products: Health claim forms and business forms. **SIC:** 5112 (Stationery & Office Supplies). **Sales:** $800,000 (1994). **Emp:** 4. **Officers:** Kenneth Adams, Owner.

■ 3624 ■ Chalice Press
PO Box 179
St. Louis, MO 63166-0179
Phones: (314)231-8500 800-451-2665
Free: (800)366-3383 **Fax:** (314)231-8524
E-mail: customerservice@cbp21.com
URL: http://www.cbp21.com
Products: Books. **SIC:** 5192 (Books, Periodicals & Newspapers). **Est:** 1911. **Sales:** $5,000,000 (2000). **Emp:** 60. **Officers:** Cyrus White, Publisher; Susan Burgess, Sales/Marketing Contact, e-mail: sburgess@cbp21.com; Joyce Luker, Customer Service Contact.

■ 3625 ■ Bev Chaney, Jr. Books
73 Croton Ave.
Ossining, NY 10562
Phone: (914)941-1002
Products: Books. **SIC:** 5192 (Books, Periodicals & Newspapers). **Est:** 1980. **Sales:** $100,000 (2000).

■ 3626 ■ Chatsworth Press
9135 Alabama Ave., Ste. B
Chatsworth, CA 91311
Phone: (818)341-3156
Free: (800)262-7367 **Fax:** (818)341-3562
E-mail: info@pacificmediaent.com
URL: http://www.pacficmediaent.com
Products: Sexual information books and erotica. **SIC:** 5192 (Books, Periodicals & Newspapers). **Est:** 1973. **Officers:** Scott S. Brastow, President; William Kjontvedt, Sales/Marketing Contact, e-mail: william@pacificmediaent.com.

■ 3627 ■ Cheng & Tsui Company
25 West St.
Boston, MA 02111-1213
Phone: (617)988-2401
Free: (800)554-1963 **Fax:** (617)426-3669
E-mail: service@cheng-tsui.com
URL: http://www.cheng-tsui.com
Products: Asian literature in translation; Asian language learning products. **SIC:** 5192 (Books, Periodicals & Newspapers). **Est:** 1979. **Emp:** 13.

■ 3628 ■ Chidvilas, Inc.
PO Box 3849
Sedona, AZ 86340
Free: (800)777-7743
Products: Books and cassettes. **SICs:** 5192 (Books, Periodicals & Newspapers); 5099 (Durable Goods Nec). **Est:** 1977.

■ 3629 ■ Children's Media Center, Inc.
2878 Bayview Ave.
Wantagh, NY 11793
Phone: (516)826-0901 **Fax:** (516)785-6570
Products: Children's, videos, books, and cassettes; CDs; CD-Roms; Activity books; Board books. **SICs:** 5192 (Books, Periodicals & Newspapers); 5099 (Durable Goods Nec). **Est:** 1993.

■ 3630 ■ Children's Small Press Collection
719 N 4th Ave.
Ann Arbor, MI 48104
Phone: (734)668-8056
Free: (800)221-8056 **Fax:** (734)668-6308
Products: Books and tapes for children, parents, teachers, and family support professionals. **SIC:** 5192 (Books, Periodicals & Newspapers). **Est:** 1985.

■ **3631** ■ **Chilton Co.**
201 King of Prussia Rd.
Radnor, PA 19087
Phone: (610)964-4000
Free: (800)695-1214 **Fax:** (610)964-4100
Products: Automotive books; Craft and hobby books; Sewing and quilting books. **SIC:** 5192 (Books, Periodicals & Newspapers). **Est:** 1925.

■ **3632** ■ **C.H.I.P.S.**
10777 Mazoch Rd.
Weimar, TX 78962-5022
Phone: (979)263-5683 **Fax:** (979)263-5685
E-mail: orderdept@chipsbooks.com
URL: http://www.chipsbooks.com
Products: Books. **SIC:** 5192 (Books, Periodicals & Newspapers). **Est:** 1985. **Emp:** 4.

■ **3633** ■ **Choice Books**
2387 Grace Chapel Rd.
Harrisonburg, VA 22801
Phone: (540)434-1827
Free: (800)224-5006 **Fax:** (540)434-9894
E-mail: info@choicebooks.org
URL: http://www.choicebooks.org
Products: Books, including audio books; Videos; Calendars; Notecards. **SIC:** 5192 (Books, Periodicals & Newspapers). **Est:** 1962. **Sales:** $23,000,000 (2000). **Emp:** 136. **Officers:** John M. Bomberger, Director.

■ **3634** ■ **Christ for the World, Inc.**
PO Box 3428
Orlando, FL 32802
Phone: (407)423-3172 **Fax:** (407)843-7941
Products: Christian books and audio and video tapes. **SICs:** 5192 (Books, Periodicals & Newspapers); 5065 (Electronic Parts & Equipment Nec).

■ **3635** ■ **The Christian Broadcasting Network, Inc.**
700 CBN Center
Virginia Beach, VA 23463
Phone: (757)424-7777 **Fax:** (757)523-7990
Products: Christian educational products. **SICs:** 5192 (Books, Periodicals & Newspapers); 5099 (Durable Goods Nec).

■ **3636** ■ **Christian Destiny Inc.**
902 E D St.
PO Box C
Hillsboro, KS 67063
Phone: (316)947-2345 **Fax:** (316)947-5560
Products: Religious publications, including books, pamphlets, and newsletters. **SIC:** 5192 (Books, Periodicals & Newspapers).

■ **3637** ■ **Christian Publications Inc.**
3825 Hartzdale Dr.
Camp Hill, PA 17011
Phone: (717)761-7044
Free: (800)233-4443 **Fax:** (717)761-7273
E-mail: salemktg@cpi-horizon.com
URL: http://www.christianpublications.com
Products: Christian books and audio cassettes. **SIC:** 5192 (Books, Periodicals & Newspapers). **Est:** 1883. **Sales:** $12,000,000 (2000). **Emp:** 80. **Officers:** K. Neill Foster, Exec. VP.

■ **3638** ■ **Church Doctor Resource Center**
1230 U.S Hwy. 6
PO Box 145
Corunna, IN 46730-0145
Phone: (219)281-2452
Free: (800)626-8515 **Fax:** (219)281-2167
E-mail: churchdoctor@juno.com
URL: http://www.churchdoctor.org
Products: Church growth materials, including books and audio and video tapes. **SICs:** 5192 (Books, Periodicals & Newspapers); 5099 (Durable Goods Nec). **Est:** 1978. **Emp:** 12. **Officers:** Michael Brown, Sales/Marketing Contact; Shelly Hinkley, Customer Service Contact; Kent R. Hunter, Human Resources Contact; Kelly Hahn; Tom Hamel.

■ **3639** ■ **City and Suburban Delivery Systems East**
4725 34th St.
Long Island City, NY 11101
Phone: (718)349-5378 **Fax:** (718)349-5234
Products: Newspapers. **SIC:** 5192 (Books, Periodicals & Newspapers). **Sales:** $140,000,000 (2000). **Emp:** 600. **Officers:** David Thurm, President.

■ **3640** ■ **Claitor's Publishing Division**
3165 S Acadian at Interstate 10
PO Box 261333
Baton Rouge, LA 70826-1333
Phone: (504)344-0476
Free: (800)274-1403 **Fax:** (504)344-0480
E-mail: claitors@claitors.com
URL: http://www.claitors.com
Products: Textbooks, including teachers' editions; Books, including literature, business and economics, and art reference and instruction books. **SIC:** 5192 (Books, Periodicals & Newspapers). **Est:** 1922. **Sales:** $2,200,000 (2000). **Emp:** 14. **Officers:** Robert G. Claitor, President; Jon Claitor, VP of Operations; R.G. Claitor Jr., VP of Production; Anthony Cassards, Sales/Marketing Contact; Desmond Carrington, Customer Service Contact.

■ **3641** ■ **C.C. Clark Inc.**
PO Box 966
Starkville, MS 39760
Phone: (601)323-4317 **Fax:** (601)323-6461
Products: Bottled and canned soft drinks. **SIC:** 5149 (Groceries & Related Products Nec). **Sales:** $110,000,000 (2000). **Emp:** 560. **Officers:** Albert Clark, President & Treasurer.

■ **3642** ■ **Classroom Reading Service**
9830 Norwalk Blvd., Ste. 174
Santa Fe Springs, CA 90670
Phone: (562)906-1366
Free: (800)422-6657 **Fax:** (562)906-1370
E-mail: crsbooks@aol.com
URL: http://www.crsbooks.com
Products: Books, including non-fiction, fiction, poetry, and textbooks, including teacher's editions; Software. **SIC:** 5192 (Books, Periodicals & Newspapers). **Est:** 1975. **Sales:** $2,000,000 (2000). **Emp:** 7. **Officers:** Gus Pappas, President; Hope Pappas, Vice President.

■ **3643** ■ **Claymont Communications**
RR 1 Box 279
CharLes Town, WV 25414-9765
Phone: (304)725-1523
Products: Books. **SIC:** 5192 (Books, Periodicals & Newspapers). **Est:** 1978.

■ **3644** ■ **CLEARVUE**
6465 N Avondale
Chicago, IL 60631
Phone: (773)775-9433 **Fax:** (773)775-9999
Products: Educational materials. **SIC:** 5192 (Books, Periodicals & Newspapers). **Est:** 1953.

■ **3645** ■ **Coca-Cola Twin Falls Bottling Co.**
Box 86
Twin Falls, ID 83303-0086
Phone: (208)733-3833
Products: Soft drinks. **SIC:** 5149 (Groceries & Related Products Nec). **Sales:** $10,000,000 (2000). **Emp:** 30. **Officers:** Jack Pelo, CEO; Laurie Ekins, CFO.

■ **3646** ■ **Cogan Books**
15020 Desman Rd.
La Mirada, CA 90638
Phone: (562)941-5017
Free: (800)733-3630 **Fax:** (562)523-0796
URL: http://www.coganbooks.com
Products: Books. **SIC:** 5192 (Books, Periodicals & Newspapers). **Est:** 1972. **Emp:** 18. **Officers:** Annette Cogan, President; Nancy Cogan, Vice President; Barbara Cogan, Sales Mgr.

■ **3647** ■ **Columbia News Agency Inc.**
135 Warren
Hudson, NY 12534-3118
Phone: (518)828-1017 **Fax:** (518)828-3393
Products: Newpapers and magazines. **SIC:** 5192 (Books, Periodicals & Newspapers). **Est:** 1946. **Emp:** 20.

■ **3648** ■ **Common Ground Distributors Inc.**
115 Fairview Rd.
Asheville, NC 28803
Phone: (828)274-5575
Free: (800)654-0626 **Fax:** (828)274-1955
E-mail: orders@comground.com
URL: http://www.comground.com
Products: Nature books; Videos; Bird and small animal feeders. **SICs:** 5192 (Books, Periodicals & Newspapers); 5099 (Durable Goods Nec); 5065 (Electronic Parts & Equipment Nec). **Est:** 1986.

■ **3649** ■ **Como Sales Co., Inc.**
799 Broadway
New York, NY 10003
Phone: (212)677-1720 **Fax:** (212)533-9385
E-mail: como@idi.net
Products: Books. **SIC:** 5192 (Books, Periodicals & Newspapers). **Est:** 1966.

■ **3650** ■ **Compassion Book Service**
477 Hannah Branch Rd.
Burnsville, NC 28714
Phone: (828)675-9670 **Fax:** (828)675-9687
E-mail: heal2grow@aol.com
URL: http://www.compassionbook.com
Products: Self help books, videos, and audiotapes related to death and dying, loss and grief, bereavement and hope. **SIC:** 5192 (Books, Periodicals & Newspapers). **Est:** 1984. **Sales:** $300,000 (2000). **Emp:** 4. **Officers:** Donna O'Toole, Owner.

■ **3651** ■ **Concordia Publishing House**
3558 S Jefferson Ave.
St. Louis, MO 63118
Phone: (314)664-7000 **Fax:** (314)268-1329
Products: Religious materials. **SIC:** 5192 (Books, Periodicals & Newspapers).

■ **3652** ■ **Conkey's Bookstore**
226 E College Ave.
Appleton, WI 54911
Phone: (920)735-6223 **Fax:** (920)735-6227
Products: Books; Gifts and novelties. **SICs:** 5192 (Books, Periodicals & Newspapers); 5199 (Nondurable Goods Nec). **Est:** 1896. **Sales:** $3,000,000 (2000). **Emp:** 60. **Officers:** John Zimmerman, Owner.

■ **3653** ■ **Connors Associates, Inc.**
15 Lilac Ter.
Boston, MA 02131
Phone: (617)323-7029
Free: (800)950-5012 **Fax:** (617)327-4770
Products: Trade books. **SIC:** 5192 (Books, Periodicals & Newspapers). **Est:** 1979.

■ **3654** ■ **Consortium Book Sales and Distribution Inc.**
1045 Westgate Dr., No. 90
St. Paul, MN 55114
Phone: (612)221-9035
Free: (800)283-3572 **Fax:** (612)221-0124
E-mail: cnsrtm@aol.com
URL: http://www.cbsd.com
Products: Books. **SIC:** 5192 (Books, Periodicals & Newspapers). **Est:** 1985. **Sales:** $8,000,000 (2000). **Officers:** Randall Beek, President.

■ **3655** ■ **Contemporary Arts Press Distribution**
PO Box 3123, Rincon Annex
San Francisco, CA 94119
Phone: (415)431-7524 **Fax:** (415)431-7841
Products: Art books; VHS cassettes; Video discs; Computer art software. **SICs:** 5192 (Books, Periodicals & Newspapers); 5099 (Durable Goods Nec); 5045 (Computers, Peripherals & Software). **Est:** 1975.

■ **3656** ■ **Continental Book Co.**
80-00 Cooper Ave., Bldg. 29
Glendale, NY 11385
Phone: (718)326-0560 **Fax:** (718)326-4276
Products: Books. **SIC:** 5192 (Books, Periodicals & Newspapers).

■ **3657** ■ **Continnuus**
PO Box 416
Denver, CO 80201-0416
Phone: (303)575-5676
Products: Books, including workbooks. **SIC:** 5192 (Books, Periodicals & Newspapers). **Est:** 1989. **Sales:** $149,000 (2000). **Emp:** 1. **Officers:** A. Doyle.

■ **3658** ■ **Cook Communications Ministries**
4050 Lee Vance View
Colorado Springs, CO 80918
Phone: (719)535-2905
Products: Bibles, greeting cards, and religious toys. **SICs:** 5192 (Books, Periodicals & Newspapers); 5112 (Stationery & Office Supplies). **Sales:** $107,000,000 (2000). **Emp:** 1,050. **Officers:** David Mehlis, President; David Hachtel, VP & CFO.

■ **3659** ■ **David C. Cook Publishing Co.**
850 N Grove Ave.
Elgin, IL 60120
Phone: (708)741-2400
Free: (800)437-4337 **Fax:** (708)741-2444
Products: Religious books. **SIC:** 5192 (Books, Periodicals & Newspapers). **Est:** 1876.

■ **3660** ■ **Cookbook Collection, Inc.**
2500 E 195th St.
Belton, MO 64012
Phone: (816)322-2122 **Fax:** (816)322-3033
URL: http://www.cookbookstore.com
Products: Cookbooks; Cookbook software. **SIC:** 5192 (Books, Periodicals & Newspapers). **Est:** 1979. **Sales:** $1,000,000 (2000). **Emp:** 6. **Officers:** Larry L. Eveler, President; Waunita M. Eveler, VP & Secty. **Former Name:** The Collection.

■ **3661** ■ **Coronet Books, Inc.**
311 Bainbridge St.
Philadelphia, PA 19147
Phone: (215)925-2762 **Fax:** (215)925-1912
URL: http://www.coronetbooks.com
Products: Books. **SIC:** 5192 (Books, Periodicals & Newspapers). **Est:** 1986.

■ **3662** ■ **Coutts Library Services Inc.**
736 Cayuga St.
Lewiston, NY 14092
Phone: (716)754-4304
Free: (800)772-4304 **Fax:** (716)356-5064
Products: Books. **SIC:** 5192 (Books, Periodicals & Newspapers). **Est:** 1969. **Emp:** 150. **Officers:** K. Schmiedl, President; K. Gostlow, Vice President; C. Urquhart, Vice President.

■ **3663** ■ **Cover To Cover**
439 Norfolk Ave.
Norfolk, NE 68701
Phone: (402)371-1600
Products: Magazines. **SIC:** 5192 (Books, Periodicals & Newspapers). **Emp:** 2.

■ **3664** ■ **W.T. Cox Subscriptions, Inc.**
411 Marcia Dr.
Goldsboro, NC 27530
Phone: (919)735-1001
Free: (800)553-8088 **Fax:** (919)734-3332
URL: http://www.wtcox.com
Products: Periodicals and magazines; CD-ROM products. **SICs:** 5192 (Books, Periodicals & Newspapers); 5045 (Computers, Peripherals & Software). **Est:** 1974. **Officers:** Denise Nason, Sales/Mktg.; Ruby Sutton, Customer Service; Wendy Upchurch, Human Resources.

■ **3665** ■ **CPP-Belwin Inc.**
15800 NW 48th Ave.
PO Box 4340
Hialeah, FL 33014
Phone: (305)620-1500
Free: (800)327-7643 **Fax:** (305)621-4869
Products: Music books; Sheet music; Prerecorded audio tapes; Videos. **SICs:** 5199 (Nondurable Goods Nec); 5192 (Books, Periodicals & Newspapers); 5065 (Electronic Parts & Equipment Nec). **Est:** 1971. **Emp:** 220. **Officers:** Saul Feldstein, President.

■ **3666** ■ **Crandall Associates**
6107 Waltway Dr.
Houston, TX 77008-6259
Phone: (713)681-4376
Products: Books. **SIC:** 5192 (Books, Periodicals & Newspapers). **Est:** 1969.

■ **3667** ■ **Creative Arts Book Co.**
833 Bancroft Way
Berkeley, CA 94710
Phone: (510)848-4777
Free: (800)848-7789 **Fax:** (510)848-4844
E-mail: staff@creativeartsbooks.com
URL: http://www.creativeartsbooks.com
Products: Trade books. **SIC:** 5192 (Books, Periodicals & Newspapers). **Est:** 1968. **Sales:** $2,500,000 (1999). **Emp:** 12. **Officers:** D. Ellis; Elizabeth Ellis, Customer Service Contact.

■ **3668** ■ **Creative Healthcare Resources**
1701 E 79th St., Ste. 1
Minneapolis, MN 55425-1151
Phone: (612)854-9389
Free: (800)264-3246 **Fax:** (612)854-1866
E-mail: chem@chem.com
URL: http://www.chem.com
Products: Books, videos, and audio tapes on nursing and the healthcare industry. **SICs:** 5192 (Books, Periodicals & Newspapers); 5099 (Durable Goods Nec). **Est:** 1987.

■ **3669** ■ **Creative Homeowner Press**
24 Park Way
Upper Saddle River, NJ 07458
Phone: (201)934-7100
Free: (800)631-7795 **Fax:** (201)934-8971
E-mail: info@chp-publisher.com
URL: http://www.chp-publisher.com/
Products: Home improvement books. **SIC:** 5192 (Books, Periodicals & Newspapers). **Est:** 1926.

■ **3670** ■ **Creative Joys Inc.**
Southern Eagle Cartway
Brewster, MA 02631
Phone: (508)255-4685
Free: (800)451-5006 **Fax:** (508)255-5705
E-mail: mail@paraclete-press.com
URL: http://www.paraclete-press.com
Products: Sheet music; Books; CDs; Videos. **SICs:** 5192 (Books, Periodicals & Newspapers); 5099 (Durable Goods Nec); 5065 (Electronic Parts & Equipment Nec). **Est:** 1983. **Emp:** 50. **Officers:** Lillian Miao, CEO; Loretta Jack, Sales Mgr., e-mail: loretta@paraclete-press.com. **Doing Business As:** Paraclete Press.

■ **3671** ■ **Creative Source**
20702 El Toro Rd., Ste. 555
El Toro, CA 92630
Phone: (714)458-7971
Products: Books; Tapes; Compact discs; Videos. **SICs:** 5192 (Books, Periodicals & Newspapers); 5099 (Durable Goods Nec); 5065 (Electronic Parts & Equipment Nec). **Est:** 1980. **Sales:** $200,000 (2000). **Emp:** 1. **Officers:** Joe Moriarty.

■ **3672** ■ **Crescent Imports & Publications**
PO Box 7827
Ann Arbor, MI 48107-7827
Phone: (734)665-3492
Free: (800)521-9744 **Fax:** (734)677-1717
E-mail: Message@crescentimports.com
URL: http://www.crescentimports.com
Products: African American and Islamic books and supplies. **SIC:** 5192 (Books, Periodicals & Newspapers). **Est:** 1978. **Sales:** $500,000 (2000). **Emp:** 5. **Officers:** Mr. A. Ibrahim, CEO.

■ **3673** ■ **Cromland, Inc.**
1995 Highland Ave., Ste. 200
Bethlehem, PA 18020
Phone: (610)997-3000
Free: (800)944-5554 **Fax:** (610)997-8880
E-mail: info@cromland.com
URL: http://www.cromland.com
Products: Computer books, software, and magazines. **SIC:** 5192 (Books, Periodicals & Newspapers). **Est:** 1982.

■ **3674** ■ **Crossing Press**
1201 Shaffer Rd. No. B
Santa Cruz, CA 95060-5729
Phone: (831)420-1110
Free: (800)777-1048 **Fax:** (831)420-1114
E-mail: crossing@aol.com
URL: http://www.crossingpress.com
Products: Cookbooks; Alternative health, non-fiction, self-help, and metaphysical books. **SIC:** 5192 (Books, Periodicals & Newspapers). **Est:** 1972. **Sales:** $2,500,000 (2000). **Emp:** 15. **Officers:** Elaine Gill, Owner; Shauna Gunderson, Sales/Marketing Contact.

■ **3675** ■ **C.S.S. Publishing Co.**
517 S Main St.
PO Box 4503
Lima, OH 45802-4503
Phone: (419)227-1818
Free: (800)537-1030 **Fax:** (419)228-9184
E-mail: info@csspub.com
URL: http://www.csspub.com
Products: Religious publications; Short run printing. **SIC:** 5192 (Books, Periodicals & Newspapers). **Est:** 1970. **Sales:** $4,000,000 (2000). **Emp:** 57. **Officers:** Wesley T. Runk, President; Wesley D. Runk, Vice President; B. Ellen Shockey, Vice President; Timothy Allen Runk, Vice President.

■ **3676** ■ **Cuerno Largo Publications**
6406 Old Harbor Ln.
Austin, TX 78739
Phone: (512)288-3478
Free: (800)373-4726 **Fax:** (512)476-0925
E-mail: texas66@aol.com
Products: Booklets. **SIC:** 5192 (Books, Periodicals & Newspapers). **Est:** 1980. **Emp:** 2. **Officers:** Ken Rigsbee, President.

■ **3677** ■ **Cultural Hispana/Ameriketakoa**
PO Box 7729
Silver Spring, MD 20907
Phone: (301)585-0134 **Fax:** (301)585-0134
E-mail: mokordo@erols.com
Products: Reference, including literature, history; Books on Basque subjects. **SIC:** 5192 (Books, Periodicals & Newspapers). **Est:** 1980. **Sales:** $65,000 (2000). **Emp:** 1. **Officers:** J.M. Guerricagoitia, Owner, e-mail: jguerricagoitia@yahoo.com.

■ **3678** ■ **Cypress Book (USA) Co., Inc.**
3450 3rd St., Unit 4B
San Francisco, CA 94124
Phone: (415)821-3582
Free: (800)383-1688 **Fax:** (415)821-3523
E-mail: cypress1@sprintmail.com
Products: Books. **SIC:** 5192 (Books, Periodicals & Newspapers). **Est:** 1985. **Sales:** $700,000 (2000). **Emp:** 3. **Officers:** Guaqing Li, President.

■ **3679** ■ **Daedalus Books**
4601 Decatur St.
Hyattsville, MD 20781
Phone: (410)309-2705 **Free:** (800)395-2665
URL: http://www.daedalusbooks.com
Products: Books. **SIC:** 5192 (Books, Periodicals & Newspapers). **Est:** 1980. **Officers:** Tamara Stock, Sales & Marketing Contact, e-mail: tsock@daedalus-books.com.

■ **3680** ■ **The Daily Astorian**
PO Box 210
Astoria, OR 97103
Phone: (503)325-3211 **Fax:** (503)325-6573
Products: Publishes daily newspapers. **SIC:** 5192 (Books, Periodicals & Newspapers).

■ **3681** ■ **M. Damien Educational Services**
4810 Mahalo Dr.
Eugene, OR 97405
Phone: (541)687-9055
Products: Learning guides, teaching manuals, and study skills programs. **SIC:** 5192 (Books, Periodicals & Newspapers). **Est:** 1984. **Sales:** $30,000 (2000).

■ 3682 ■ **Dearborn Trade**
155 N Wacker Dr.
Chicago, IL 60606-1719
Phone: (312)836-4400
Free: (800)245-2665 **Fax:** (312)836-1021
Products: Business books, including real estate, insurance, investing, and small business. **SIC:** 5192 (Books, Periodicals & Newspapers). **Est:** 1977. **Officers:** Robert C. Kyle, Chairman of the Board; Dennis Blitz, President.

■ 3683 ■ **Delmar News Agency Inc.**
7120 Grand Blvd.
Houston, TX 77054-3408
Phone: (713)654-9921
Products: Magazines and newspapers. **SIC:** 5192 (Books, Periodicals & Newspapers). **Est:** 1932. **Sales:** $18,000,000 (2000). **Emp:** 100. **Officers:** Mike Dubb, President.

■ 3684 ■ **Delta Systems Company, Inc.**
1400 Miller Pkwy.
McHenry, IL 60050-7030
Phone: (815)363-3582
Free: (800)323-8270 **Fax:** 800-909-9901
URL: http://www.delta-systems.com
Products: English-as-a-second-language and foreign language materials. **SIC:** 5192 (Books, Periodicals & Newspapers). **Est:** 1979.

■ 3685 ■ **Deltiologists of America**
PO Box 8
Norwood, PA 19074
Phone: (610)485-8572
Products: Collection equipment; Books. **SIC:** 5192 (Books, Periodicals & Newspapers). **Est:** 1960. **Sales:** $60,000 (1999). **Emp:** 2. **Officers:** Dr. James Lewis Lowe, Director, e-mail: jlewislowe@juno.com.

■ 3686 ■ **Denver Business Journal Inc.**
1700 Broadway Ste. 515
Denver, CO 80290
Phone: (303)837-3500 **Fax:** (303)837-3535
Products: Publishes weekly newspaper. **SIC:** 5192 (Books, Periodicals & Newspapers).

■ 3687 ■ **Roy Derstine Book Co.**
14 Birch Rd.
Kinnelon, NJ 07405
Phone: (201)838-1109
Products: Nonfiction reference materials. **SIC:** 5192 (Books, Periodicals & Newspapers). **Est:** 1965.

■ 3688 ■ **DeRu's Fine Art Books**
1590 S Coast Hwy.
Laguna Beach, CA 92651
Phone: (714)376-3785 **Fax:** (714)376-9915
Products: Library prebound art catalogs and books dealing with early California art. **SIC:** 5192 (Books, Periodicals & Newspapers). **Est:** 1969. **Sales:** $100,000 (2000). **Emp:** 4. **Officers:** Dewitt C. McCall, Director.

■ 3689 ■ **Detroit Free Press Agency**
1117 Bancroft St.
Port Huron, MI 48060
Phone: (810)984-8767
Products: Newspapers. **SIC:** 5192 (Books, Periodicals & Newspapers).

■ 3690 ■ **Devin-Adair Publishers, Inc.**
Box A
Old Greenwich, CT 06870
Phone: (203)531-7755 **Fax:** (203)359-8568
Products: Books. **SIC:** 5192 (Books, Periodicals & Newspapers). **Est:** 1911. **Emp:** 8. **Officers:** R.H. Lourie.

■ 3691 ■ **DeVorss & Co.**
1046 Princeton Dr.
Marina del Rey, CA 90295-0550
Phone: (310)822-8940
Free: (800)843-5743 **Fax:** (310)821-6290
E-mail: service@devorss.com
URL: http://www.devorss.com
Products: Books. **SICs:** 5192 (Books, Periodicals & Newspapers); 5065 (Electronic Parts & Equipment Nec); 5099 (Durable Goods Nec). **Est:** 1929. **Emp:** 16.

Officers: Arthur Vergara, Publisher; Gary R. Peattie, President.

■ 3692 ■ **Dialogue Systems Inc.**
33 Irving Pl., Fl. 11
New York, NY 10003-2332
Phone: (212)647-1000 **Fax:** (212)647-0188
Products: Educational materials. **SIC:** 5192 (Books, Periodicals & Newspapers).

■ 3693 ■ **Diamond Comic Distributors Inc.**
101 Nob Hill Rd.
Madison, WI 53701
Phone: (608)274-5010
Products: Comic books. **SIC:** 5192 (Books, Periodicals & Newspapers).

■ 3694 ■ **Discipleship Resources**
1908 Grand Ave.
PO Box 840
Nashville, TN 37202
Phone: (615)340-7068
Free: (800)685-4370 **Fax:** (615)340-1789
E-mail: discipleshipresources@gbod.org
URL: http://www.discipleshipresources.org
Products: Printed and audio-visual program resources on evangelism, Christian education, worship, leadership development, ministry of the Laity, Covenant discipleship, and stewardship. **SICs:** 5192 (Books, Periodicals & Newspapers); 5099 (Durable Goods Nec). **Est:** 1968.

■ 3695 ■ **Distribution Services Inc.**
Brandywine Ctr. 580
West Palm Beach, FL 33409
Phone: (561)688-0097 **Fax:** (561)688-9795
Products: Magazines. **SIC:** 5192 (Books, Periodicals & Newspapers). **Est:** 1975. **Sales:** $27,000,000 (2000). **Emp:** 1,100. **Officers:** Michael R. Roscoe, CEO & Chairman of the Board; Michael J. Porche, President & COO; Charles J. MacDonald, VP, Client Services.

■ 3696 ■ **Distribution Systems of America**
600 W John St.
Hicksville, NY 11801
Phone: (516)465-0211 **Fax:** (516)688-6245
Products: Circulars; Magazines; Newspapers. **SIC:** 5192 (Books, Periodicals & Newspapers). **Est:** 1990. **Sales:** $55,000,000 (2000). **Emp:** 250. **Officers:** Richard Czark, General Mgr., e-mail: rczark@limedia.com.

■ 3697 ■ **Distribution Systems of America**
31 Grand Blvd. N
Brentwood, NY 11717
Phone: (516)952-1041
Products: Books. **SIC:** 5192 (Books, Periodicals & Newspapers). **Sales:** $55,000,000 (2000). **Emp:** 225. **Officers:** Lewis Sito, President.

■ 3698 ■ **Dixie News Co.**
900 Atando Ave.
Charlotte, NC 28206
Phone: (704)376-0140 **Fax:** (704)335-8604
Products: Books and other printed materials. **SIC:** 5192 (Books, Periodicals & Newspapers). **Sales:** $156,000,000 (2000). **Emp:** 216.

■ 3699 ■ **Document Center**
111 Industrial Way Ste. 9
Belmont, CA 94002
Phone: (650)591-7600
Products: Technical library; Documents and original works. **SIC:** 5192 (Books, Periodicals & Newspapers). **Officers:** Claudia Bach, Owner.

■ 3700 ■ **Dosik International**
9519 Evergreen St.
Silver Spring, MD 20901
Phone: (301)585-4259
Products: Scientific and technical books; Scientific instruments. **SICs:** 5192 (Books, Periodicals & Newspapers); 5049 (Professional Equipment Nec). **Est:** 1982. **Sales:** $1,000,000 (2000). **Emp:** 2. **Officers:** Stanley Dosik, President.

■ 3701 ■ **Ron Doussard & Associates, Inc.**
6 Castle Pines Ct.
Lake in the Hills, IL 60102
Phone: (847)854-6090
Free: (800)635-6795 **Fax:** 800-635-6791
E-mail: rondous426@aol.com
Products: Books. **SIC:** 5192 (Books, Periodicals & Newspapers). **Est:** 1977. **Emp:** 6. **Officers:** Ron Doussard.

■ 3702 ■ **Dufour Editions, Inc.**
PO Box 7
Chester Springs, PA 19425-0007
Phone: (610)458-5005 **Fax:** (610)458-7103
E-mail: dufour8023@aol.com
Products: Books in the humanities, including poetry, fiction, literature, social and political theory; Educational books. **SIC:** 5192 (Books, Periodicals & Newspapers). **Est:** 1949.

■ 3703 ■ **Duke University Press**
Box 90660
Durham, NC 27708-0660
Phone: (919)687-3600 **Fax:** (919)688-4574
URL: http://www.duke.edu/web/dupress
Products: Books. **SIC:** 5192 (Books, Periodicals & Newspapers). **Sales:** $2,700,000 (2000). **Emp:** 40. **Officers:** Steve Cohn, Dir. of Publishing Operations.

■ 3704 ■ **Durkin Hayes Publishing**
2221 Niagara Falls Blvd.
Niagara Falls, NY 14304
Phone: (716)731-9177
Free: (800)962-5200 **Fax:** (716)731-9180
URL: http://www.dhaudio.com
Products: Books; Prerecorded audio tapes; Compact discs. **SICs:** 5192 (Books, Periodicals & Newspapers); 5099 (Durable Goods Nec); 5065 (Electronic Parts & Equipment Nec). **Est:** 1981. **Sales:** $5,300,000 (2000). **Emp:** 27. **Officers:** Don Matheson, President; Dino Divito, Chairman of the Board & Finance Officer.

■ 3705 ■ **E-Heart Press, Inc.**
3700 Mockingbird Ln.
Dallas, TX 75205
Phone: (214)741-6915
Products: Books. **SIC:** 5192 (Books, Periodicals & Newspapers). **Est:** 1979.

■ 3706 ■ **Ryan East Distributors Ltd.**
6325 Erdman Ave.
Baltimore, MD 21205
Phone: (410)325-1298
Free: (800)622-5656 **Fax:** (410)325-7718
Products: Books. **SICs:** 5192 (Books, Periodicals & Newspapers); 5199 (Nondurable Goods Nec). **Est:** 1968. **Emp:** 15. **Officers:** Oscak Lebowitz, President. **Alternate Name:** Cove Distributors.

■ 3707 ■ **East Kentucky News Inc.**
416 Teays Rd.
PO Box 510
Paintsville, KY 41240
Phone: (606)789-8169 **Fax:** (606)789-1473
Products: Magazines. **SIC:** 5192 (Books, Periodicals & Newspapers). **Est:** 1956. **Sales:** $3,000,000 (2000). **Emp:** 20. **Officers:** Robin Cooper, Owner.

■ 3708 ■ **East Texas Distributing Inc.**
7171 Grand Blvd.
Houston, TX 77054
Phone: (713)748-8120
Products: Videos; Magazines; Books. **SIC:** 5192 (Books, Periodicals & Newspapers). **Sales:** $250,000,000 (2000). **Emp:** 700. **Officers:** David Streusand, President; Jim Pollan, VP of Video; Jack Cross, VP of Magazines.

■ 3709 ■ **East-West Center**
1601 East-West Rd.
Honolulu, HI 96848-1601
Phone: (808)944-7145 **Fax:** (808)944-7376
E-mail: ewcbooks@eastwestcenter.org
URL: http://www.eastwestcenter.org/res-rp.asp
Products: Scholarly and program-related books, reports, and other materials. **SIC:** 5192 (Books, Periodicals & Newspapers). **Est:** 1960. **Officers:** Charles E. Morrison, President.

■ 3710 ■ **Eastern Book Co.**
131 Middle St.
Portland, ME 04101
Phone: (207)774-0331
Free: (800)937-0331 **Fax:** (207)774-4678
E-mail: info@ebc.com
Products: Books. **SIC:** 5192 (Books, Periodicals & Newspapers). **Est:** 1957.

■ 3711 ■ **Eastview Editions**
PO Box 247
Bernardsville, NJ 07924
Phone: (908)204-0535
Products: Books and magazines specializing in art. **SIC:** 5192 (Books, Periodicals & Newspapers). **Est:** 1979.

■ 3712 ■ **Eble Music Co.**
PO Box 2570
Iowa City, IA 52244
Phone: (319)338-0313 **Fax:** (319)338-0108
E-mail: information@eble.com
Products: Sheet music; Music books. **SICs:** 5192 (Books, Periodicals & Newspapers); 5199 (Nondurable Goods Nec). **Est:** 1950. **Emp:** 9. **Officers:** David Hempel, Owner.

■ 3713 ■ **E.C.A. Associates Press**
PO Box 15004
Chesapeake, VA 23328
Phone: (757)547-5542 **Fax:** (757)547-5542
E-mail: eca@melanet.com
URL: http://www.melanet.com/eca
Products: African heritage studies books; History books; African heritage children's books. **SIC:** 5192 (Books, Periodicals & Newspapers). **Est:** 1978. **Sales:** $100,000 (2000). **Emp:** 7. **Officers:** Dr. E. Curtis Alexander, CEO & President; Barbara E. Alexander, COO & VP; Edward C. Alexander II, Executive Director.

■ 3714 ■ **Economical Wholesale Co.**
6 King Philip Rd.
Worcester, MA 01606
Phone: (508)853-3127 **Fax:** (508)852-8329
Products: Coin and stamp supplies. **SIC:** 5192 (Books, Periodicals & Newspapers). **Est:** 1959.

■ 3715 ■ **ECS Publishing Corporation**
138 Ipswich St.
Boston, MA 02215
Phone: (617)236-1935
Free: (800)777-1919 **Fax:** (617)236-0261
E-mail: office@ecspublishing.com
URL: http://www.ecspublishing.com
Products: Sheet music; Music books. **SICs:** 5192 (Books, Periodicals & Newspapers); 5199 (Nondurable Goods Nec). **Est:** 1931. **Sales:** $1,100,000 (2000). **Emp:** 11. **Officers:** Robert Schuneman, President; Kay Dunlap, Sales Mgr.

■ 3716 ■ **Edelweiss Publishing Co.**
110 Main St.
PO Box 656
Nuremberg, PA 18241
Phone: (215)298-3437 **Fax:** (215)298-2628
Products: Foreign and multilingual books; Educational magazines. **SIC:** 5192 (Books, Periodicals & Newspapers). **Est:** 1969.

■ 3717 ■ **Ediciones del Norte**
PO Box A130
Hanover, NH 03755
Phone: 800-782-5422
Free: (800)782-5422 **Fax:** (603)543-1018
E-mail: sales@nortebooks.com
URL: http://www.nortebooks.com
Products: Spanish, books and videos. **SIC:** 5192 (Books, Periodicals & Newspapers). **Est:** 1981. **Sales:** $100,000 (2000). **Emp:** 4. **Officers:** Richard Honibal, Marketing & Sales, e-mail: rhonibal@cyberportal.net.

■ 3718 ■ **Ediciones Universal**
3090 SW 8th St.
Miami, FL 33135
Phone: (305)642-3355 **Fax:** (305)642-7978
E-mail: ediciones@edicones.com
URL: http://www.ediciones.com
Products: Spanish books. **SIC:** 5192 (Books,

Periodicals & Newspapers). **Est:** 1965. **Emp:** 4.
Officers: Marta Saluat-Golik.

■ 3719 ■ **Edu-Tech Corp.**
65 Bailey Rd.
Fairfield, CT 06432
Phone: (203)374-4212
Free: (800)338-5463 **Fax:** (203)374-8050
E-mail: edutcorp@aol.com
Products: Books, including adult nonfiction, juvenile, and large print; Video and audio cassettes. **SICs:** 5192 (Books, Periodicals & Newspapers); 5099 (Durable Goods Nec). **Est:** 1978. **Emp:** 3. **Officers:** R. Caston.

■ 3720 ■ **Education Guide Inc.**
PO Box 421
Randolph, MA 02368
Phone: (781)961-2217 **Fax:** (781)963-8268
Products: General reference books. **SIC:** 5192 (Books, Periodicals & Newspapers).

■ 3721 ■ **Education People, Inc.**
Box 378
Chappaqua, NY 10514
Phone: (914)666-5423 **Fax:** (914)666-3091
Products: Educational books and materials. **SIC:** 5192 (Books, Periodicals & Newspapers). **Est:** 1975.

■ 3722 ■ **Educational Book Distributors**
c/o Publishers Services
PO Box 2510
Novato, CA 94948
Phone: (415)883-3530
Products: Educational books and materials. **SIC:** 5192 (Books, Periodicals & Newspapers). **Est:** 1978.

■ 3723 ■ **Educational Geodesics Inc.**
1971 Lou Ann Dr.
New Braunfels, TX 78130-1213
Phone: (512)629-0123
Products: Books. **SIC:** 5192 (Books, Periodicals & Newspapers). **Est:** 1980.

■ 3724 ■ **William B. Eerdmans Publishing Co.**
255 Jefferson Ave. SE
Grand Rapids, MI 49503
Phone: (616)459-4591
Free: (800)253-7521 **Fax:** (616)459-6540
E-mail: sales@eerdmans.com
URL: http://www.eerdmans.com
Products: Religious and theological publications, including children's books. **SIC:** 5192 (Books, Periodicals & Newspapers). **Est:** 1911. **Officers:** Ray Triggs, Customer Service; S.E. Eerdmans.

■ 3725 ■ **Eisenbrauns**
PO Box 275
Winona Lake, IN 46590
Phone: (219)269-2011 **Fax:** (219)269-6788
E-mail: orders@eisenbrauns.com
URL: http://www.eisenbrauns.com
Products: Books. **SIC:** 5192 (Books, Periodicals & Newspapers). **Est:** 1975. **Sales:** $2,000,000 (2000). **Emp:** 21.

■ 3726 ■ **Elder's Bookstore**
2115 Elliston Pl.
Nashville, TN 37203
Phone: (615)327-1867
E-mail: elderbook@mail.telalink.net
Products: Civil war history books; Antique books, 1st editions; Childrens. **SIC:** 5192 (Books, Periodicals & Newspapers). **Est:** 1951. **Emp:** 3. **Officers:** John Elder.

■ 3727 ■ **Emery Pratt Co.**
1966 W Main St.
Owosso, MI 48867-1397
Phone: (517)723-5291
Free: (800)248-3887 **Fax:** (517)723-4677
Products: Books and other printed materials. **SIC:** 5192 (Books, Periodicals & Newspapers). **Sales:** $11,000,000 (2000). **Emp:** 50.

■ 3728 ■ **Empire Comicsl**
1176 Mt. Hope Ave.
Rochester, NY 14620
Phone: (716)442-0371 **Fax:** (716)442-7807
Products: Comic books. **SIC:** 5192 (Books,

Periodicals & Newspapers). **Est:** 1975. **Sales:** $450,000 (2000).

■ 3729 ■ **Empire Publishing Inc.**
PO Box 717
Madison, NC 27025
Phone: (336)427-5850 **Fax:** (336)427-7372
E-mail: movietv@pop.vnet.net
URL: http://www.empirepublishinginc.com
Products: Media books. **SIC:** 5192 (Books, Periodicals & Newspapers). **Est:** 1974. **Sales:** $300,000 (2000). **Emp:** 5.

■ 3730 ■ **Empire State News Corp.**
2800 Walden Ave.
Cheektowaga, NY 14225
Phone: (716)681-1100 **Fax:** (716)681-1120
E-mail: esn@esnc.com
URL: http://www.esnc.com
Products: Magazines. **SIC:** 5192 (Books, Periodicals & Newspapers). **Sales:** $21,000,000 (2000). **Emp:** 70. **Officers:** Lawrence M. Scheur, President.

■ 3731 ■ **Encyclopaedia Britannica Educational Corp.**
310 S Michigan Ave.
Chicago, IL 60604
Phone: (312)347-7000
Products: Books, reference materials, and audio-visual materials. **SICs:** 5192 (Books, Periodicals & Newspapers); 5099 (Durable Goods Nec). **Est:** 1966.

■ 3732 ■ **Enrica Fish Books Inc.**
814 Washington Ave. SE
Minneapolis, MN 55414
Phone: (612)623-0707
Free: (800)728-8398 **Fax:** (612)623-0539
URL: http://www.enricafish.com
Products: Health and medical books. **SIC:** 5192 (Books, Periodicals & Newspapers). **Est:** 1978.

■ 3733 ■ **Enslow Publishers, Inc.**
40 Industrial Rd.
Box 398
Berkeley Heights, NJ 07922-0398
Phone: (908)771-9400
Free: (800)398-2504 **Fax:** (908)771-0925
E-mail: enslow@enslow.com
URL: http://www.enslow.com
Products: Children's and young adult books. **SIC:** 5192 (Books, Periodicals & Newspapers). **Est:** 1976. **Officers:** Mark Enslow, President, e-mail: enslow@ enslow.com; Brian Enslow, Vice President.

■ 3734 ■ **ETD KroMar**
180 James Dr. E
St. Rose, LA 70087-9662
Phone: (504)467-5863
Free: (800)349-7323 **Fax:** (504)464-6196
Products: Magazines and books. **SIC:** 5192 (Books, Periodicals & Newspapers). **Est:** 1953. **Sales:** $23,000,000 (2000). **Emp:** 200. **Officers:** Robert Rowe; Linda Dubret, Human Resources Contact, e-mail: linda@bayou.gs.net. **Former Name:** Graham Services Inc.

■ 3735 ■ **European American Music Distributors Corp.**
PO Box 850
Valley Forge, PA 19482
Phone: (215)648-0506 **Fax:** (215)889-0242
Products: Music publications. **SIC:** 5192 (Books, Periodicals & Newspapers). **Est:** 1977.

■ 3736 ■ **European Book Company Inc.**
925 Larkin St.
San Francisco, CA 94109
Phone: (415)474-0626
Free: (877)746-3666 **Fax:** (415)474-0630
E-mail: info@europeanbook.com
URL: http://www.europeanbook.com
Products: Foreign books; Magazines specializing in French. **SIC:** 5192 (Books, Periodicals & Newspapers). **Est:** 1962. **Emp:** 10. **Officers:** Jean Henri Gabriel, President.

■ 3737 ■ **Evangel Publishing House**
2000 Evangel Way
PO Box 189
Nappanee, IN 46550-0189
Phone: (219)773-3164 **Fax:** (219)773-5934
E-mail: eph@tln.net
URL: http://www.evangelpublishing.com
Products: Religious books. **SIC:** 5192 (Books, Periodicals & Newspapers). **Officers:** Joe Allison, Sales/Marketing Contact, e-mail: josephallison@compuserve.com.

■ 3738 ■ **Evergreen Publishing & Stationery**
760 W Garvey Ave.
Monterey Park, CA 91754
Phone: (626)281-3622 **Fax:** (626)284-1571
Products: Chinese learning materials such as books, music tapes, and videotapes to libraries. **SICs:** 5192 (Books, Periodicals & Newspapers); 5099 (Durable Goods Nec). **Est:** 1978.

■ 3739 ■ **EZ Nature Books**
PO Box 4206
San Luis Obispo, CA 93403-4206
Phone: (805)528-5292
Free: (800)455-0666 **Fax:** (805)534-0307
Products: Non-fiction books, including history, nature, and Native American texts. **SIC:** 5192 (Books, Periodicals & Newspapers). **Est:** 1983. **Sales:** $100,000 (2000). **Emp:** 1. **Officers:** Edwin Zolkoski, Owner.

■ 3740 ■ **Fairfield Book Co., Inc.**
42 Obtuse Rd. N
Brookfield Center, CT 06804
Phone: (203)775-0053
Products: Books. **SIC:** 5192 (Books, Periodicals & Newspapers). **Est:** 1977.

■ 3741 ■ **Fairfield Book Service Co.**
150 Margherita Lawn
Stratford, CT 06497
Phone: (203)375-7607
Products: Books. **SIC:** 5192 (Books, Periodicals & Newspapers). **Est:** 1963. **Emp:** 1. **Officers:** Gary C. Smith, President.

■ 3742 ■ **Fall River News Company, Inc.**
144 Robeson St.
Fall River, MA 02720-4925
Phone: (508)679-5266
Products: Paperbacks, periodicals, and maps. **SIC:** 5192 (Books, Periodicals & Newspapers). **Est:** 1923.

■ 3743 ■ **Family Life Productions**
PO Box 357
Fallbrook, CA 92088-0357
Phone: (760)728-6437
Free: (800)748-5722 **Fax:** (760)728-5309
Products: Books and other printed materials. **SIC:** 5192 (Books, Periodicals & Newspapers). **Sales:** $500,000 (2000). **Emp:** 3.

■ 3744 ■ **Family Reading Service**
1209 Toledo Dr.
Albany, GA 31705
Phone: (912)439-2279
Free: (800)673-6379 **Fax:** (912)436-3874
Products: Books. **SIC:** 5192 (Books, Periodicals & Newspapers). **Est:** 1972.

■ 3745 ■ **Faxon Company Inc.**
15 Southwest Pkwy.
Westwood, MA 02090
Phone: (781)329-3350 **Fax:** (781)329-8987
Products: Books. **SIC:** 5192 (Books, Periodicals & Newspapers). **Est:** 1881.

■ 3746 ■ **Philipp Feldheim, Inc.**
200 Airport Executive Park
Nanuet, NY 10954
Phone: (914)356-2282
Free: (800)237-7149 **Fax:** (914)425-1908
E-mail: info@feldheim.com
URL: http://www.feldheim.com
Products: Contemporary Judaica books, including books for young readers. **SIC:** 5192 (Books, Periodicals & Newspapers). **Est:** 1939.

■ 3747 ■ **F.E.P. Inc.**
5405 Boran Pl.
Tampa, FL 33610
Phone: (813)621-6085
Free: (800)227-0121 **Fax:** (813)626-9782
Products: Books. **SIC:** 5192 (Books, Periodicals & Newspapers). **Est:** 1971.

■ 3748 ■ **Fiesta Book Co.**
PO Box 490641
Key Biscayne, FL 33149
Phone: (305)858-4843 **Fax:** (305)858-9934
Products: Foreign language books. **SIC:** 5192 (Books, Periodicals & Newspapers). **Sales:** $250,000 (2000). **Emp:** 5. **Officers:** Maria Victoria Navarro, President.

■ 3749 ■ **Fine Associates**
1 Farragut Sq. S
Washington, DC 20006
Phone: (202)628-2610
Products: Maps, atlases, and urban prints. **SIC:** 5192 (Books, Periodicals & Newspapers). **Est:** 1975.

■ 3750 ■ **Carl Fischer Inc.**
62 Cooper Sq.
New York, NY 10003
Phone: (212)777-0900
Free: (800)762-2328 **Fax:** (212)477-4129
URL: http://www.carlfisher.com
Products: Sheet music; Music books. **SICs:** 5192 (Books, Periodicals & Newspapers); 5199 (Nondurable Goods Nec). **Est:** 1872. **Emp:** 100. **Alternate Name:** Carl Fisher Music Distributors.

■ 3751 ■ **Fishing Hot Spots/FHS Maps**
2389 Air Park Rd.
PO Box 1167
Rhinelander, WI 54501-1167
Phone: (715)365-5555
Free: (800)338-5957 **Fax:** (715)365-5575
E-mail: sales@fishingmaps.com
URL: http://www.fishinghotspots.com
Products: Maps, including fishing lake maps. **SIC:** 5192 (Books, Periodicals & Newspapers). **Est:** 1975. **Emp:** 15. **Officers:** Martin Kunas, CEO; Mike Michalak, President.

■ 3752 ■ **Flannery Co.**
13123 Aerospace Dr.
Victorville, CA 92394
Free: (800)456-3400 **Fax:** 800-284-5600
URL: http://www.flannerycompany.com
Products: Textbooks, including teacher's editions; Educational products; Videos. **SICs:** 5192 (Books, Periodicals & Newspapers); 5099 (Durable Goods Nec); 5065 (Electronic Parts & Equipment Nec). **Est:** 1948. **Sales:** $10,000,000 (2000). **Officers:** Stephen Flannery, General Mgr.

■ 3753 ■ **Florida Classics Library**
PO Drawer 1657
Port Salerno, FL 34992-1657
Phone: (561)546-9380 **Fax:** (561)546-7545
Products: Books, including history books; Maps. **SIC:** 5192 (Books, Periodicals & Newspapers). **Est:** 1976. **Emp:** 1.

■ 3754 ■ **The Florida News Group, Ltd.**
PO Box 20209
West Palm Beach, FL 33416
Phone: (561)547-3000 **Fax:** (561)547-3080
Products: Magazines, books, and newspapers. **SIC:** 5192 (Books, Periodicals & Newspapers). **Emp:** 260.

■ 3755 ■ **Flynt Distribution Company Inc.**
9171 Wilshire Blvd., No. 300
Beverly Hills, CA 90210
Phone: (310)858-7100 **Fax:** (310)275-3857
Products: Magazines. **SIC:** 5192 (Books, Periodicals & Newspapers). **Est:** 1975. **Sales:** $74,000,000 (2000). **Emp:** 300. **Officers:** James Kohls, President; Tom Candy, VP of Finance; James Gustafson, Vice President.

■ 3756 ■ **Follett Campus Resources**
2211 N West St.
River Grove, IL 60171-1800
Phone: (708)583-2000 **Fax:** (708)452-9203
Products: New and used college books. **SIC:** 5192

(Books, Periodicals & Newspapers). **Sales:** $30,000,000 (2000). **Emp:** 400. **Officers:** George Carr, President; Ken Carbonetti, Finance Officer.

■ 3757 ■ **Follett Corp.**
2233 West St.
River Grove, IL 60171-1895
Phone: (708)583-2000
Free: (800)621-4345 **Fax:** (708)452-9347
E-mail: infor@follett.com
URL: http://www.follett.com
Products: Elementary, high school, and college textbooks. **SIC:** 5192 (Books, Periodicals & Newspapers). **Est:** 1873. **Sales:** $1,400,000,000 (2000). **Emp:** 10,205. **Officers:** Kenneth J. Hull, President, e-mail: khull@follett.com; Kathryn Stanton, VP of Finance, e-mail: kstanton@follett.com; Christopher Trout, Dir. of Product Development, e-mail: ctraut@follett.com; Dick Waichler, VP of Human Resources.

■ 3758 ■ **Follett Library Book Co.**
1340 Ridgeview Dr.
McHenry, IL 60050
Phone: (815)759-1700
Free: (800)435-6170 **Fax:** 800-852-5458
E-mail: flr@follett.com
URL: http://www.titlewave.com
Products: Books, including fiction, non-fiction, and educational; Videos; CD-ROMs. **SIC:** 5192 (Books, Periodicals & Newspapers). **Est:** 1940. **Emp:** 665. **Officers:** Thomas Salvetti, President.

■ 3759 ■ **Follett Library Resources**
1340 Ridgeview Dr.
McHenry, IL 60050
Phone: (815)455-1100
Products: Books. **SIC:** 5192 (Books, Periodicals & Newspapers). **Officers:** Patricia Hall, Contact.

■ 3760 ■ **Ford & Bailie**
20 Carleton Cir.
PO Box 138
Belmont, MA 02478
Phone: (617)489-6635 **Fax:** (617)489-6388
Products: Publications relating to Celtic studies. **SIC:** 5192 (Books, Periodicals & Newspapers). **Est:** 1988. **Officers:** Patrick Ford, President; Chadine Bailie, Managing Dir.

■ 3761 ■ **Fortress Press**
PO Box 1209
Minneapolis, MN 55440
Phone: (612)330-3433
Free: (800)328-4648 **Fax:** (612)330-3215
URL: http://www.augsburgfortress.org
Products: Academic and professional books. **SIC:** 5192 (Books, Periodicals & Newspapers). **Est:** 1960.

■ 3762 ■ **Franciscan Press**
Quincy Univ.
1800 University
Quincy, IL 62301-2670
Phone: (217)228-5670 **Fax:** (217)228-5672
URL: http://www.quincy.edu@quincy.edu
Products: Religious books. **SIC:** 5192 (Books, Periodicals & Newspapers). **Est:** 1991. **Sales:** $150,000 (1999). **Officers:** Marsha Adams, Dir. of Operations and Marketing, e-mail: adamsma@quincy.edu; Jaime Uidal.

■ 3763 ■ **Franklin Book Company, Inc.**
7804 Montgomery Ave.
Elkins Park, PA 19027
Phone: (215)635-5252 **Fax:** (215)635-6155
E-mail: franklinbook@mindspring.com
URL: http://www.franklinbook.com
Products: Book distribution. **SIC:** 5192 (Books, Periodicals & Newspapers). **Est:** 1969. **Emp:** 30. **Officers:** Manny Deckter, President; Ed Merkel, General Mgr.; Linda Moran, Customer Service Contact, e-mail: lmoran@franklinbook.com.

■ **3764** ■ **Frederick Fell Publishers, Inc.**
2131 Hollywood Blvd.
Hollywood, FL 33020
Phone: (954)925-0555
Free: (800)771-3355 **Fax:** (954)925-5244
E-mail: fellpub@aol.com
URL: http://www.fellpub.com
Products: Books, including business, reference, self-help, health, finance, psychology, and inspirational. **SIC:** 5192 (Books, Periodicals & Newspapers). **Est:** 1943. **Sales:** $1,200,000 (2000). **Emp:** 29. **Officers:** Donald L. Lessne, Publisher; Barbara Newman, Vice President. **Former Name:** Lifetime Books Inc.

■ **3765** ■ **Friendly Frank's Distribution Inc.**
3990 Broadway
Gary, IN 46408
Phone: (219)884-5052 **Fax:** (219)887-2205
Products: Comic books. **SIC:** 5192 (Books, Periodicals & Newspapers). **Est:** 1978. **Sales:** $6,000,000 (2000). **Emp:** 35.

■ **3766** ■ **Friendship Press**
475 Riverside Dr., Rm. 860
New York, NY 10115
Phone: (212)870-2496 **Fax:** (212)870-2550
Products: Religious books and videos. **SICs:** 5192 (Books, Periodicals & Newspapers); 5065 (Electronic Parts & Equipment Nec). **Est:** 1935. **Emp:** 15. **Officers:** Audrey A. Miller.

■ **3767** ■ **Theodore Front Musical Literature**
16122 Cohasset St.
Van Nuys, CA 91406
Phone: (818)994-1902 **Fax:** (818)994-0419
E-mail: music@tfront.com
URL: http://www.tfront.com
Products: Music books; Sheet music; Compact discs; Musicological editions. **SICs:** 5192 (Books, Periodicals & Newspapers); 5199 (Nondurable Goods Nec). **Est:** 1961. **Sales:** $1,000,000 (2000). **Emp:** 7. **Officers:** Theodore Front; Christine Clark; Albert Statti, Customer Service Contact.

■ **3768** ■ **FSC Educational Inc.**
223 S Illinois Ave.
Mansfield, OH 44905
Phone: (419)589-8222
Products: Educational industrial arts products. **SICs:** 5085 (Industrial Supplies); 5199 (Nondurable Goods Nec). **Sales:** $54,000,000 (1992). **Emp:** 250. **Officers:** James D. Miller, President; Doug Dever, Controller.

■ **3769** ■ **Fujii Associates, Inc.**
120 E Burlington
La Grange, IL 60525
Phone: (708)354-2555 **Fax:** (708)354-6534
E-mail: fujiiassoc@msn.com
Products: Books. **SIC:** 5192 (Books, Periodicals & Newspapers). **Est:** 1972. **Emp:** 9. **Officers:** Don Sturtz, President.

■ **3770** ■ **Gardner's Book Service, Inc.**
4303 W Van Buren, No. 3
Phoenix, AZ 85043
Phone: (602)233-9424 **Fax:** (602)233-1992
Products: Books. **SIC:** 5192 (Books, Periodicals & Newspapers). **Est:** 1983.

■ **3771** ■ **Garrett Educational Corp.**
PO Box 1588
Ada, OK 74820
Phone: (580)332-6884
Free: (800)654-9366 **Fax:** (580)332-1560
E-mail: mail@garrettbooks.com
URL: http://www.garrettbooks.com
Products: Children's books. **SIC:** 5192 (Books, Periodicals & Newspapers). **Est:** 1965. **Sales:** $6,000,000 (2000). **Emp:** 100. **Officers:** Lionel H. Garrett, President; John Garrett, Sec. & Treas.

■ **3772** ■ **Gavilanes Books from Indoamerica**
PO Box 850286
New Orleans, LA 70185
Phone: (504)837-5806 **Fax:** (504)837-5806
E-mail: gavbooks@aol.com
Products: Cultural books. **SIC:** 5192 (Books, Periodicals & Newspapers). **Est:** 1986. **Sales:** $800,000 (1999). **Emp:** 6. **Officers:** Patrick Gavilanes,

OWN; Tony Lopez, SLM; Walter Fernandez, Dir. of Admin.

■ **3773** ■ **Geiger Bros.**
Mount Hope Ave.
PO Box 1609
Lewiston, ME 04241
Phone: (207)755-5000 **Fax:** (207)755-2423
E-mail: geiger@geiger.com
URL: http://www.geiger.com
Products: Calendars; Diaries; Farmers almanacs; Books. **SIC:** 5192 (Books, Periodicals & Newspapers). **Est:** 1878. **Sales:** $105,000,000 (2000). **Emp:** 550. **Officers:** Eugene Geiger, President; Barry Gates, Controller; J.G. Lantz, VP of Marketing & Sales; David Cutter, VP of Human Resources; Gary Biron, Sales & Marketing Mgr.; Ginny Theriault, Customer Service Mgr.; Laura Bosse, Human Resources Mgr.

■ **3774** ■ **Gem Guides Book Co.**
315 Cloverleaf Dr., No. F
Baldwin Park, CA 91706-6510
Phone: (626)855-1611 **Fax:** (626)855-1610
E-mail: gembooks@aol.com
Products: Guides to nature and hiking trails, rock collecting trails, and local interest for the West and Southwest. **SIC:** 5192 (Books, Periodicals & Newspapers).

■ **3775** ■ **Genealogical Sources Unlimited**
407 Ascot Ct.
Knoxville, TN 37923-5807
Phone: (423)690-7831
Products: Genealogical books. **SIC:** 5192 (Books, Periodicals & Newspapers). **Est:** 1976. **Sales:** $110,000 (1999). **Emp:** 2. **Officers:** George K. Schweitzer.

■ **3776** ■ **General Medical Publishers**
318 Lincoln Blvd., No. 117
Venice, CA 90291
Phone: (213)392-4911 **Fax:** (213)392-8734
Products: Nursing and psychology publications. **SIC:** 5192 (Books, Periodicals & Newspapers). **Est:** 1985.

■ **3777** ■ **George Washington University Press**
Academic Center, Rm. T-308
Washington, DC 20052
Phone: (202)676-5116
Free: (800)932-2337 **Fax:** (202)785-3382
Products: Textbooks, video cassettes, and audio cassettes. **SICs:** 5192 (Books, Periodicals & Newspapers); 5099 (Durable Goods Nec). **Est:** 1986.

■ **3778** ■ **Gessler Publishing Company, Inc.**
15 E Salem Ave.
Roanoke, VA 24011
Phone: (540)345-1429
Free: (800)456-5825 **Fax:** (540)342-7172
E-mail: gesslerq@qgroupplc.com
URL: http://www.gesslerq.com
Products: Foreign-language educational materials. **SIC:** 5192 (Books, Periodicals & Newspapers). **Est:** 1932. **Former Name:** Q U.S.A.

■ **3779** ■ **Gibson Dot Publications**
PO Box 117
Waycross, GA 31502-0117
Phone: (912)285-2848 **Fax:** (912)285-0349
E-mail: info@dotgibson.com
URL: http://www.dotgibson.com
Products: Cookbooks, gift books, children's bookss. **SIC:** 5192 (Books, Periodicals & Newspapers). **Est:** 1975. **Emp:** 9. **Officers:** N.G. Gibson, President; Dot Gibson, CEO.

■ **3780** ■ **David J. Gingery Publishing**
PO Box 75
Fordland, MO 65652
Phone: (417)890-1965
E-mail: gingery@cland.net
Products: Instructional books on metalworking. **SIC:** 5192 (Books, Periodicals & Newspapers). **Est:** 1979. **Sales:** $60,000,000 (2000). **Officers:** Vincent R. Gingerly, Owner.

■ **3781** ■ **Global Directions Inc.**
PO Box 470098
San Francisco, CA 94147-0098
Phone: (415)982-8811 **Fax:** (415)982-8817
Products: Periodicals. **SIC:** 5192 (Books, Periodicals & Newspapers). **Sales:** $2,000,000 (2000). **Emp:** 15. **Officers:** Lisa Spivey, President.

■ **3782** ■ **Gnomon Inc.**
1601 Fairview Dr.
Carson City, NV 89701
Phone: (775)885-2305
Products: Maps. **SIC:** 5192 (Books, Periodicals & Newspapers).

■ **3783** ■ **Gnomon Press**
PO Box 475
Frankfort, KY 40602-0475
Phone: (502)223-1858 **Fax:** (502)223-1858
E-mail: jgnomon@aol.com
Products: Books, including photography books. **SIC:** 5192 (Books, Periodicals & Newspapers). **Est:** 1965. **Sales:** $66,000 (2000). **Emp:** 2. **Officers:** Jonathan Greene, President; Dobree Adams, Vice President.

■ **3784** ■ **Golden-Lee Book Distributors, Inc.**
399 Thornall St., Ste. 3
Edison, NJ 08837-2238
Phone: (732)857-6333
Free: (800)473-7475 **Fax:** (732)857-5997
Products: Books and audio cassettes. **SICs:** 5192 (Books, Periodicals & Newspapers); 5099 (Durable Goods Nec).

■ **3785** ■ **Good Apple**
PO Box 2649
Columbus, OH 43216-2649
Phone: (614)357-3981
Free: (800)435-7234 **Fax:** (614)357-3987
Products: Books, including educational materials on elementary and high school levels. **SIC:** 5192 (Books, Periodicals & Newspapers). **Est:** 1973. **Emp:** 70.

■ **3786** ■ **Good Karma Publishing Inc.**
202 Main St.
PO Box 511
Ft. Yates, ND 58538
Phone: (701)854-7459
Free: (888)540-7459 **Fax:** (701)854-2004
URL: http://www.taichichih.org
Products: Books, videotapes, and audiotapes. **SICs:** 5192 (Books, Periodicals & Newspapers); 5099 (Durable Goods Nec); 5065 (Electronic Parts & Equipment Nec). **Est:** 1988. **Sales:** $106,000 (2000). **Emp:** 1. **Officers:** Jean Katus, CEO.

■ **3787** ■ **Good News Communications, Inc.**
3554 Strait St. E
Atlanta, GA 30340
Phone: (404)454-9445 **Fax:** (404)454-9225
Products: Magazines. **SIC:** 5192 (Books, Periodicals & Newspapers).

■ **3788** ■ **Gopher News Co.**
9000 10th Ave. N
Minneapolis, MN 55427-4322
Phone: (612)546-5300 **Fax:** (612)525-3100
Products: Periodicals, including magazines and books. **SIC:** 5192 (Books, Periodicals & Newspapers). **Est:** 1905. **Emp:** 175. **Officers:** R. St. Marie, Chairman of the Board; Donald O. Weber, President, e-mail: dow@gophernews.com; Scott Andrus, Dir. of Sales, e-mail: swa@gophernews.com; Candace Lofgren, Customer Service Mgr., e-mail: ccl@gophernews.com; Janis Kaufenberg, Human Resources Mgr., e-mail: ddk@gophernews.com.

■ **3789** ■ **Gospel Light Publications**
2300 Knoll Dr.
Ventura, CA 93003
Phone: (805)644-9721
Free: (800)235-3415 **Fax:** (805)650-8713
URL: http://www.gospellight.com
Products: Religious Books. **SIC:** 5192 (Books, Periodicals & Newspapers). **Est:** 1933. **Emp:** 125. **Officers:** Bill Greig III, President; Ronnie McDougall, Sales/Marketing Contact, e-mail: ronniemcdougall@gospellight.com; Marie Schlater, Customer Service Contact, e-mail: marieschlater@gospellight.com.

■ 3790 ■ Gospel Light Publications
PO Box 3875
Ventura, CA 93006
Phone: (805)644-9721 **Fax:** (805)658-3388
Products: Publishes Christian education curriculum, books and videos. **SIC:** 5192 (Books, Periodicals & Newspapers). **Sales:** $18,000,000 (2000). **Emp:** 180. **Officers:** Bill Greig, CEO & President; Terry Donnelly, CFO.

■ 3791 ■ Gospel Publishing House
1445 Boonville Ave.
Springfield, MO 65802
Phone: (417)831-8000 **Fax:** (417)862-7566
URL: http://www.gph.org
Products: Religious books. **SIC:** 5192 (Books, Periodicals & Newspapers). **Est:** 1914. **Former Name:** Logion Press.

■ 3792 ■ Graham Services Inc.
180 James Dr. E
St. Rose, LA 70087
Phone: (504)467-5863
Products: Books and magazines. **SIC:** 5192 (Books, Periodicals & Newspapers).

■ 3793 ■ Grail Foundation of America
2081 Partridge Ln.
Binghamton, NY 13903
Phone: (607)723-5163
Products: Books. **SIC:** 5192 (Books, Periodicals & Newspapers). **Est:** 1958.

■ 3794 ■ Granary Books, Inc.
307 Seventh Ave., 1401
New York, NY 10001
Phone: (212)337-9979 **Fax:** (212)337-9774
E-mail: info@granarybooks.com
URL: http://www.granarybooks.com
Products: Artists' books. **SIC:** 5192 (Books, Periodicals & Newspapers). **Est:** 1980. **Emp:** 2.

■ 3795 ■ Graphic Arts Center Publishing Co.
PO Box 10306
Portland, OR 97210
Phone: (503)226-2402
Free: (800)452-3032 **Fax:** (503)223-1410
Products: Travel books; Children's books; Calendars; Books. **SIC:** 5192 (Books, Periodicals & Newspapers). **Est:** 1974. **Emp:** 34. **Officers:** Charles Hopkins, President; Doug Pfeifer, Vice President; Ross Eberman; Ken Rowe.

■ 3796 ■ Great Northern Distributors, Inc.
935 N Washington Ave.
Scranton, PA 18501
Phone: (717)342-8159
Products: Books. **SIC:** 5192 (Books, Periodicals & Newspapers). **Est:** 1930.

■ 3797 ■ Great Outdoors Publishing Co.
4747 28th St. N
St. Petersburg, FL 33714
Phones: (813)525-6609 (813)552-3453
Free: (800)869-6609 **Fax:** (813)527-4870
Products: Cook books; Gardening books; Sports books. **SIC:** 5192 (Books, Periodicals & Newspapers). **Est:** 1947. **Sales:** $330,000 (2000). **Emp:** 4. **Officers:** Jan Allyn, President; Joyce Allyn, Vice President.

■ 3798 ■ Greeley Publishing Co.
PO Box 1138
Greeley, CO 80632
Phone: (970)352-0211 **Fax:** (970)356-5780
Products: Publishes daily newspaper. **SIC:** 5192 (Books, Periodicals & Newspapers). **Sales:** $11,000,000 (2000). **Emp:** 170.

■ 3799 ■ Green Gate Books
PO Box 934
Lima, OH 45802
Phone: (419)222-3816
Free: (800)228-3816 **Fax:** (419)227-3816
E-mail: ggb@wcoil.com
URL: http://www.greengatebooks.com
Products: New and out of print books on antiques and collectibles. **SIC:** 5192 (Books, Periodicals & Newspapers). **Est:** 1977. **Sales:** $500,000 (2000).

Emp: 5. **Officers:** Frank L. Hahn, Owner; Karen M. Nester, Manager.

■ 3800 ■ Green Leaf Press
PO Box 880
Alhambra, CA 91802-0880
Phones: (626)281-7221 (626)283-1313
Fax: (408)374-9683
Products: Christian books. **SIC:** 5192 (Books, Periodicals & Newspapers). **Est:** 1982. **Sales:** $15,000 (1999). **Emp:** 1. **Officers:** Dr. Foster H. Shannon, President.

■ 3801 ■ Group Publishing, Inc.
1515 Cascade Ave.
PO Box 481
Loveland, CO 80539
Phone: (970)669-3836 **Fax:** (970)669-3269
E-mail: info@grouppublishing.com
URL: http://www.grouppublishing.com
Products: Religious educational materials. **SIC:** 5192 (Books, Periodicals & Newspapers). **Est:** 1974. **Emp:** 300. **Officers:** Thom Schultz, CEO; Bill Korte, VP of Marketing & Sales, e-mail: bkorte@grouppublishing.com; Troy Stromme, VP Staff Servics, e-mail: tstromme@grouppublishing.com.

■ 3802 ■ Gryphon House, Inc.
10726 Tucker St.
PO Box 207
Beltsville, MD 20704-0207
Phone: (301)595-9500
Free: (800)638-0928 **Fax:** (301)595-0051
URL: http://www.gryphonhouse.com
Products: Early childhood teacher resource books; Books for children. **SIC:** 5192 (Books, Periodicals & Newspapers). **Est:** 1972. **Officers:** Cathy Calliotte Schwebel, Sales/Marketing Contact, e-mail: cathy@ghbooks.com; Faustino Nunez, Customer Service Contact, e-mail: faustino@ghbooks.com; Larry Rood, e-mail: larry@ghbooks.com.

■ 3803 ■ Guardian Book Co.
8464 Brown St.
Ottawa Lake, MI 49267
Phone: (734)856-1765 **Fax:** (734)854-7638
E-mail: gbcbooks@aol.com
Products: Educational and trade books. **SIC:** 5192 (Books, Periodicals & Newspapers). **Est:** 1981. **Sales:** $1,500,000 (2000). **Emp:** 3. **Officers:** Norm Black, e-mail: Nblack726@aol.com.

■ 3804 ■ Guidelines Inc.
26076 Getty Dr.
Laguna Niguel, CA 92677
Phone: (949)582-5001 **Fax:** (949)582-5026
URL: http://www.guidelines.org
Products: Books and magazines. **SIC:** 5192 (Books, Periodicals & Newspapers).

■ 3805 ■ Hacker Art Books Inc.
45 W 57th St.
New York, NY 10019
Phone: (212)688-7600 **Fax:** (212)754-2554
Products: Art books. **SIC:** 5192 (Books, Periodicals & Newspapers). **Sales:** $4,800,000 (2000). **Emp:** 12. **Officers:** Seymour Hacker, President.

■ 3806 ■ Hadley Cos.
11001 Hampshire Ave. S
Bloomington, MN 55438
Phone: (612)943-8474
Products: Artwork, including paintings. **SIC:** 5199 (Nondurable Goods Nec). **Sales:** $26,000,000 (1994). **Emp:** 200. **Officers:** Gary Schmidt, President; Michael Amundson, VP of Finance & Controller.

■ 3807 ■ Hamakor Judaica Inc.
PO Box 48836
Niles, IL 60714-0836
Phone: (847)966-4040
Free: (800)426-2567 **Fax:** (847)966-4033
E-mail: service@jewishsource.com
URL: http://www.jewishsource.com
Products: Jewish gifts and novelties; Religious books. **SICs:** 5192 (Books, Periodicals & Newspapers); 5199 (Nondurable Goods Nec). **Est:** 1975. **Sales:** $1,000,000 (2000). **Emp:** 15. **Officers:** Herschel Strauss, President.

■ 3808 ■ Bernard H. Hamel Spanish Book Corp.
10977 Santa Monica Blvd.
Los Angeles, CA 90025
Phone: (310)475-0453 **Fax:** (310)473-6132
E-mail: bernardhamel@spanishbooksusa.com
URL: http://www.bernardhamel.com
Products: Spanish books. **SIC:** 5192 (Books, Periodicals & Newspapers). **Est:** 1967. **Sales:** $400,000 (2000). **Officers:** Bernard Hamel, Sales/Marketing Contact.

■ 3809 ■ Gerard Hamon Inc.
PO Box 758
Mamaroneck, NY 10543
Phone: (914)381-4649 **Fax:** (914)381-2607
Products: French and Spanish books, including French periodicals. **SIC:** 5192 (Books, Periodicals & Newspapers). **Est:** 1986. **Sales:** $1,000,000 (1994). **Emp:** 3. **Officers:** Gerard Hamon, President.

■ 3810 ■ Hancock House Publishers
98231 Harrison Ave., X-1
Blaine, WA 98231
Phones: (360)538-1114 (425)354-6953
Free: (800)938-1114 **Fax:** (360)538-2262
E-mail: sales@hancockhouse.com
URL: http://www.hancockwildlife.org
Products: Books, on topics including nature, Native Americans, birds, regional history, cookbooks, western guidebooks, biographies, fishing, rhymes, stories, and sports. **SIC:** 5192 (Books, Periodicals & Newspapers). **Est:** 1968. **Sales:** $900,000 (1999). **Emp:** 10. **Officers:** David Hancock, President, e-mail: david@hancockwildlife.org.

■ 3811 ■ Handleman Co.
PO Box 7045
Troy, MI 48084-4142
Phone: (248)362-4400
Products: Music distribution and category management, operations; Music, video and licensing. **SICs:** 5192 (Books, Periodicals & Newspapers); 5045 (Computers, Peripherals & Software). **Sales:** $1,058,600,000 (1999). **Emp:** 2,300. **Officers:** Stephen Strome, CEO & President; Leonard A. Brams, Sr. VP & CFO.

■ 3812 ■ Harcourt Brace Professional Publishing
525 B St., Ste. 1900
San Diego, CA 92101-4495
Phone: (619)699-6716
Free: (800)831-7799 **Fax:** (619)699-6542
URL: http://www.hbpp.com
Products: Accounting, financial, tax-related, and general business books. **SICs:** 5192 (Books, Periodicals & Newspapers); 5045 (Computers, Peripherals & Software). **Est:** 1980. **Emp:** 75. **Officers:** Ken Rethmeier; Sid Bemstein; Andrew ODonnell, Sales/Marketing Contact; John Losavio, Customer Service Contact; Marilyn Bailin, Human Resources Contact. **Former Name:** CPA Services Inc.

■ 3813 ■ Harper San Francisco
353 Sacramento St., Ste. 500
San Francisco, CA 94111
Phone: (415)477-4400
Free: (800)242-7737 **Fax:** (415)477-4444
URL: http://www.harpercollins.com
Products: Books. **SIC:** 5192 (Books, Periodicals & Newspapers). **Est:** 1817.

■ 3814 ■ Harris-Teller, Inc.
7400 S Mason Ave.
Chicago, IL 60638
Phone: (708)496-2100
Free: (800)252-4004 **Fax:** (708)496-2130
E-mail: harristell@aol.com
Products: Musical accessories, including sheet music and music books. **SICs:** 5192 (Books, Periodicals & Newspapers); 5099 (Durable Goods Nec).

■ **3815** ■ **Harrowood Books**
3943 N Providence Rd.
Newtown Square, PA 19073
Phone: (610)353-5585
Free: (800)747-8356 **Fax:** (610)353-5585
E-mail: birdbook@philly.infi.net
Products: Books. **SIC:** 5192 (Books, Periodicals & Newspapers). **Sales:** $200,000 (2000). **Emp:** 4. **Officers:** Paul N. Harris.

■ **3816** ■ **Harvest House Publishers, Inc.**
1075 Arrowsmith St.
Eugene, OR 97402
Phone: (541)343-0123
Free: (888)501-6991 **Fax:** (541)342-6410
URL: http://www.harvesthousepubl.com
Products: Christian books and gifts. **SIC:** 5192 (Books, Periodicals & Newspapers). **Est:** 1972.

■ **3817** ■ **Harvest Publications**
2002 S Arlington Heights Rd.
Arlington Heights, IL 60005
Phone: (847)228-1471 **Fax:** (847)228-5376
Products: Religious books. **SIC:** 5192 (Books, Periodicals & Newspapers).

■ **3818** ■ **The Haworth Press Inc.**
10 Alice St.
Binghamton, NY 13904-1580
Phone: (607)722-5857
Free: (800)429-6784 **Fax:** (607)722-1424
E-mail: getinfo@haworthpressinc.com
Products: Books; Journals. **SIC:** 5192 (Books, Periodicals & Newspapers). **Est:** 1975. **Emp:** 130. **Officers:** William Cohen, President.

■ **3819** ■ **HCIA Inc.**
300 E Lumbard St.
Baltimore, MD 21202
Phone: (410)576-9600
Free: (800)568-3282 **Fax:** (410)547-8297
URL: http://www.hcia.com
Products: Medical information, including books and tapes. **SIC:** 5192 (Books, Periodicals & Newspapers). **Emp:** 700.

■ **3820** ■ **Healthcare Press**
PO Box 4784
Rollingbay, WA 98061
Phone: (206)842-5243
Products: Alzheimer's disease books. **SIC:** 5192 (Books, Periodicals & Newspapers). **Est:** 1983. **Emp:** 1. **Officers:** Joe Ringland, President.

■ **3821** ■ **William S. Hein and Co., Inc.**
1285 Main St.
Buffalo, NY 14209
Phone: (716)882-2600
Free: (800)828-7571 **Fax:** (716)883-8100
E-mail: mail@wshein.com
Products: Books, microforms, and CD-Roms in law and related fields. **SICs:** 5192 (Books, Periodicals & Newspapers); 5065 (Electronic Parts & Equipment Nec). **Est:** 1961. **Emp:** 125. **Officers:** Kevin Marmion, President; Brian Jablonski, Sales/Marketing Contact, e-mail: mail@wshein.com; Christine Tricoli, Human Resources Contact. **Former Name:** Fred B. #Rothman & Co.

■ **3822** ■ **Heirloom Bible Publications**
PO Box 780189
Wichita, KS 67278-0189
Phone: (316)267-3211
Free: (800)676-2448 **Fax:** (316)267-1850
E-mail: dandsinc@swbell.net
URL: http://www.biblebinding.com
Products: Bibles and reading materials. **SIC:** 5192 (Books, Periodicals & Newspapers). **Est:** 1948.

■ **3823** ■ **Herald House/Independence Press**
PO Box 1770
Independence, MO 64055
Phone: (816)252-5010
Free: (800)767-8181 **Fax:** (816)252-3976
E-mail: hhmark@heraldhouse.org
URL: http://www.heraldhouse.org
Products: Religious publications; Substance abuse resources. **SIC:** 5192 (Books, Periodicals & Newspapers). **Est:** 1860.

■ **3824** ■ **Herald Press**
616 Walnut Ave.
Scottdale, PA 15683
Phone: (724)887-8500
Free: (800)245-7894 **Fax:** (724)887-3111
E-mail: hp@mph.org
URL: http://www.mph.org
Products: Religious books. **SIC:** 5192 (Books, Periodicals & Newspapers). **Est:** 1908. **Officers:** Paul M. Schrock, Director; Patty Weaver, Dir. of Marketing; Patty Weaver, Sales/Marketing Contact, e-mail: patricia@mph.org; Kermit Roth, Customer Service Contact, e-mail: kermit@mph.org; Awanda Pritts, Human Resources Contact, e-mail: apritts@mph.org.

■ **3825** ■ **Hermitage Publishing Co.**
PO Box 310
Tenafly, NJ 07670
Phone: (201)894-8247 **Fax:** (201)894-5591
URL: http://lexiconbridge.com/hermitage
Products: Books in Russian; Books in English connected with Russian history and culture. **SIC:** 5192 (Books, Periodicals & Newspapers). **Est:** 1981. **Officers:** Igor Yefimov, Director, e-mail: yefimovim@aol.com.

■ **3826** ■ **Heroes World Distribution, Inc.**
1639 Rte. 10 E
Parsippany, NJ 07054
Phone: (973)984-8776 **Fax:** (973)984-7684
Products: Comic books. **SIC:** 5192 (Books, Periodicals & Newspapers). **Est:** 1995. **Sales:** $15,000,000 (2000). **Emp:** 150. **Officers:** Ivan Snyder, President; Tom Greenbaum, Sr. VP.

■ **3827** ■ **Himber's Books**
PO Box 41509
Eugene, OR 97404-0367
Phone: (541)686-8003
Products: Paperback books. **SIC:** 5192 (Books, Periodicals & Newspapers). **Est:** 1928.

■ **3828** ■ **E. Louis Hinrichs**
PO Box 1090
Lompoc, CA 93438-1090
Phone: (805)736-7512 **Fax:** (805)736-7512
E-mail: booklompoc@aol.com
URL: http://www.abe.com/home/wantablebooks
Products: Out-of-print and scarce technical, scientific, and professional books; General reference books; Hungarian books; General catalogs. **SIC:** 5192 (Books, Periodicals & Newspapers). **Est:** 1987.

■ **3829** ■ **Hispanic Books Distributors, Inc.**
1665 W Grant Rd.
Tucson, AZ 85745
Phone: (520)882-9484 **Fax:** (520)882-7696
Products: Spanish-language books and periodicals. **SIC:** 5192 (Books, Periodicals & Newspapers). **Est:** 1980.

■ **3830** ■ **Hobby Book Distributors**
3150 State Line Rd.
North Bend, OH 45052
Phone: (513)353-3390
Free: (800)543-1834 **Fax:** (513)353-3933
E-mail: dees@one.net
Products: Books; Dollhouses and miniatures. **SICs:** 5192 (Books, Periodicals & Newspapers); 5092 (Toys & Hobby Goods & Supplies). **Est:** 1969. **Emp:** 35. **Officers:** Jerry W. Hacker, President.

■ **3831** ■ **Holmgangers Press**
Shelter Cove
95 Carson Ct.
Whitethorn, CA 95589
Phone: (707)986-7700
Products: Literature, poetry, and history books. **SIC:** 5192 (Books, Periodicals & Newspapers). **Est:** 1974.

■ **3832** ■ **Homestead Book Co.**
6101 22nd Ave. NW
Seattle, WA 98107
Phone: (206)782-4532
Free: (800)426-6777 **Fax:** (206)784-9328
E-mail: davet@homesteadbook.com
URL: http://www.homesteadbook.com
Products: Books and magazines. **SIC:** 5192 (Books, Periodicals & Newspapers). **Est:** 1972. **Sales:** $2,000,000 (2000). **Emp:** 5. **Officers:** David Tatelman, President, e-mail: davet@homesteadbook.com; Jane Spreine, Sales Mgr.

■ **3833** ■ **Horizon Publishers & Distributors, Inc.**
50 South 500 West
Bountiful, UT 84011-0490
Phone: (801)295-9451
Free: (800)453-0812 **Fax:** (801)295-0196
E-mail: horizonp@burgoyne.com
URL: http://www.horizonpublishers.com
Products: Books for cooking, food preparation and storage, family relations, health, and cross-stitch patterns; Religious books on history, scriptural studies, and scriptural totes. **SIC:** 5192 (Books, Periodicals & Newspapers). **Est:** 1971. **Sales:** $1,000,000 (2000). **Emp:** 32. **Officers:** Duane S. Crowther, President; Jean D. Crowther, Vice President; Richard Hopkins, Sales Mgr.

■ **3834** ■ **Horizons Publishers and Dstbrs**
PO Box 490
Bountiful, UT 84010
Phone: (801)295-9451 **Fax:** (801)295-0196
Products: Publishes and distributes Christian books. **SIC:** 5192 (Books, Periodicals & Newspapers). **Officers:** Duane Crowther, President.

■ **3835** ■ **Hotho & Co.**
916 Norwood
Ft. Worth, TX 76107
Phone: (817)335-1833 **Fax:** (817)335-2300
Products: Books; Audio and video cassettes. **SICs:** 5192 (Books, Periodicals & Newspapers); 5099 (Durable Goods Nec). **Est:** 1961.

■ **3836** ■ **Hudson News Co.**
1305 Paterson Plank Rd.
North Bergen, NJ 07047
Phone: (201)867-3600 **Fax:** (201)867-0067
Products: Magazines and books. **SIC:** 5192 (Books, Periodicals & Newspapers). **Sales:** $340,000,000 (2000). **Emp:** 1,400. **Officers:** James Cohen, President; Howard Joroff, CFO.

■ **3837** ■ **Ideal Foreign Books, Inc.**
132-10 Hillside Ave.
Richmond Hill, NY 11418
Phone: (718)297-7477
Free: (800)284-2490 **Fax:** (718)297-7645
E-mail: idealforeignbooks@worldnet.att.net
URL: http://www.idealforeignbooks.com
Products: Imported Spanish and French language materials. **SIC:** 5192 (Books, Periodicals & Newspapers). **Est:** 1977. **Officers:** Andre Fetaya, President; Alain Fetaya, Marketing & Sales Mgr.

■ **3838** ■ **Ideal Foreign Books Inc.**
132-10 Hillside Ave.
Richmond Hill, NY 11418
Phone: (718)297-7477
Free: (800)284-2490 **Fax:** (718)297-7645
Products: Books and other printed materials. **SIC:** 5192 (Books, Periodicals & Newspapers).

■ **3839** ■ **Impact Christian Books Inc.**
332 Leffingwell Ave., Ste. 101
Kirkwood, MO 63122
Phone: (314)822-3309 **Fax:** (314)822-3325
URL: http://www.impactchristianbooks.com
Products: Christian books and inspirational literature. **SIC:** 5192 (Books, Periodicals & Newspapers). **Est:** 1972. **Emp:** 8. **Officers:** W.D. Banks, Marketing & Sales Mgr.

■ **3840** ■ **Imperial Delivery Service Inc.**
303 Smith St.
East Farmingdale, NY 11735
Phone: (516)752-2255
Products: Newspapers. **SIC:** 5192 (Books, Periodicals & Newspapers). **Sales:** $24,000,000 (2000). **Emp:** 100. **Officers:** Arthur Imperatore, President.

■ **3841** ■ **Imported Books**
2025 W Clarendon Ave.
PO Box 4414
Dallas, TX 75208
Phone: (214)941-6497
Products: Foreign-language books, including Spanish; Books and dictionaries in many languages. **SIC:** 5192 (Books, Periodicals & Newspapers). **Est:** 1975.

■ **3842** ■ **Independent Publishers Group Inc.**
814 N Franklin St.
Chicago, IL 60610
Phone: (312)337-0747
Free: (800)888-4741 **Fax:** (312)337-5985
Products: Adult fiction and nonfiction. **SIC:** 5192 (Books, Periodicals & Newspapers). **Est:** 1971. **Emp:** 30.

■ **3843** ■ **Ingham Publishing, Inc.**
5650 1st Ave., N
PO Box 12642
St. Petersburg, FL 33733-2642
Phone: (727)343-4811 **Fax:** (727)381-2807
E-mail: ftreflex@concentric.net
URL: http://www.reflexology-usa.net
Products: Health and medical books. **SIC:** 5192 (Books, Periodicals & Newspapers). **Est:** 1978. **Emp:** 6.

■ **3844** ■ **Ingram Book Group Inc.**
1 Ingram Blvd.
La Vergne, TN 37086
Phone: (615)793-5000 **Fax:** (615)793-3939
Products: Books, audio and video tapes. **SICs:** 5045 (Computers, Peripherals & Software); 5192 (Books, Periodicals & Newspapers). **Sales:** $1,820,000,000 (1993). **Emp:** 2,500. **Officers:** Lee Synnott, CEO; Mike Lovett, CFO.

■ **3845** ■ **International Book Centre**
2007 Laurel St.
PO Box 295
Troy, MI 48099
Phone: (248)879-8436 **Fax:** (248)879-8436
E-mail: ibc@ibcbooks.com
URL: http://www.ibcbooks.com
Products: Foreign language dictionaries, primarily English-Arabic; Middle Eastern history books. **SIC:** 5192 (Books, Periodicals & Newspapers). **Est:** 1973. **Sales:** $250,000 (2000). **Emp:** 7.

■ **3846** ■ **International Book Distributors Ltd.**
24 Hudson St.
Kinderhook, NY 12106
Phone: (518)758-1755
Free: (800)343-3531 **Fax:** (518)758-6702
URL: http://www.ibdltd.com
Products: Dictionaries; Books; Foreign language books. **SIC:** 5192 (Books, Periodicals & Newspapers). **Est:** 1989. **Sales:** $500,000 (2000). **Emp:** 5. **Officers:** Freek Lankhof, President, e-mail: lankhof@ibdltd.com.

■ **3847** ■ **International Business & Management Institute**
PO Box 3271
Tustin, CA 92781-3271
Phone: (949)552-8494 **Fax:** (949)423-5112
E-mail: ibmi-1@juno.com
Products: Business handbooks and seminar materials. **SIC:** 5192 (Books, Periodicals & Newspapers). **Est:** 1965. **Emp:** 27. **Officers:** D.H. Harquail, Dir. of Marketing.

■ **3848** ■ **International Marine Publishing Co.**
PO Box 545
Blacklick, OH 43004
Phone: 800-722-4726 **Fax:** (614)755-5645
Products: How-to books for boaters and outdoorspeople. **SIC:** 5192 (Books, Periodicals & Newspapers). **Est:** 1969. **Emp:** 10.

■ **3849** ■ **International Periodical Distributors**
674 Via De La Valle, Ste. 200
Solana Beach, CA 92075
Phone: (858)481-5928
Free: (800)999-1170 **Fax:** (858)259-7580
URL: http://www.ipd.com
Products: Magazines. **SIC:** 5192 (Books, Periodicals

& Newspapers). **Est:** 1981. **Officers:** Jim Gustafson, VP of Marketing & Sales.

■ **3850** ■ **International Service Co.**
International Service Building
333 4th Ave.
Indialantic, FL 32903
Phone: (321)724-1443 **Fax:** (321)724-1443
Products: Technical, scientific, and professional books. **SIC:** 5192 (Books, Periodicals & Newspapers). **Est:** 1958. **Emp:** 15. **Officers:** Dennis Samuels, President; Katherine Swanberg, Managing Dir.; F. Schneider, Comptroller; Robert Cohen, Assistant to the President.

■ **3851** ■ **International Specialized Book Services**
5804 NE Hassalo St.
Portland, OR 97213-3644
Phone: (503)287-3093
Free: (800)944-6190 **Fax:** (503)280-8832
E-mail: orders@isbs.com
Products: Books. **SIC:** 5192 (Books, Periodicals & Newspapers). **Est:** 1967.

■ **3852** ■ **International Wealth Success Inc.**
24 Canterbury Rd.
Rockville Centre, NY 11570
Phone: (516)766-5919
Free: (800)323-0548 **Fax:** (516)766-5850
E-mail: admin@iwsmoney.com
URL: http://www.iwsmoney.com
Products: Business and economics books. **SIC:** 5192 (Books, Periodicals & Newspapers). **Est:** 1967. **Emp:** 2. **Officers:** Tyler G. Hicks, President; Sean C. Beach, Vice President.

■ **3853** ■ **Interstate Distributors Inc.**
199 Commander Shea Blvd.
North Quincy, MA 02171
Phone: (617)328-9500
Free: (800)365-6430 **Fax:** (617)328-3026
Products: Trade books, mass market paperbacks, calendars, and maps. **SIC:** 5192 (Books, Periodicals & Newspapers). **Est:** 1947.

■ **3854** ■ **Interstate Periodical Distributors Inc.**
201 E Badger Rd.
Madison, WI 53713
Phone: (608)271-3600
Products: Magazines and books. **SIC:** 5192 (Books, Periodicals & Newspapers). **Sales:** $61,000,000 (2000). **Emp:** 250. **Officers:** Harry Tobias, President.

■ **3855** ■ **Irish Books & Media, Inc.**
Franklin Business Center
1433 Franklin Ave. E
Minneapolis, MN 55404-2135
Phone: (612)871-3505
Free: (800)229-3505 **Fax:** (612)871-3358
E-mail: irishbook@aol.com
URL: http://www.irishbook.com
Products: Irish-published and Irish-interest books. **SIC:** 5192 (Books, Periodicals & Newspapers). **Est:** 1971. **Sales:** $1,000,000 (2000). **Emp:** 5. **Officers:** Ethna McKiernan, President; Larry Burke, Sales/Marketing Contact; Liadan McKiernan, Customer Service Contact.

■ **3856** ■ **ISHK Book Services**
PO Box 1062
Cambridge, MA 02238
Phone: (781)289-5798
Free: (800)222-4745 **Fax:** 800-223-4200
Products: Books. **SIC:** 5192 (Books, Periodicals & Newspapers).

■ **3857** ■ **J & L Book Co.**
PO Box 1300
Spokane, WA 99213
Phone: (509)535-3360
Free: (800)288-9756 **Fax:** (509)535-3360
Products: Children's books. **SIC:** 5192 (Books, Periodicals & Newspapers). **Sales:** $700,000 (2000). **Emp:** 7.

■ **3858** ■ **Jain Publishing Co.**
PO Box 3523
Fremont, CA 94539
Phone: (510)659-8272 **Fax:** (510)659-0501
E-mail: mail@jainpub.com
URL: http://www.jainpub.com
Products: Books. **SIC:** 5192 (Books, Periodicals & Newspapers). **Est:** 1989. **Officers:** M.K. Jain, President.

■ **3859** ■ **Jalmar Press/Innerchoice Publishing**
24426 S Main St., No. 702
Carson, CA 90745
Phone: (310)816-3085
Free: (800)662-9662 **Fax:** (310)816-3092
E-mail: jalmarpress@att.net
URL: http://www.jalmarpress.com
Products: Books, including self-esteem, emotional intelligence, stress management, violence prevention, alcohol and drug abuse prevention. **SIC:** 5192 (Books, Periodicals & Newspapers). **Est:** 1971. **Emp:** 5. **Officers:** Bradley L. Winch Sr., President, e-mail: blwjalmar@worldnet.att.net; Cathy Winch, Operations Mgr.

■ **3860** ■ **Jeanie's Classics**
2123 Oxford St.
Rockford, IL 61103-4160
Phone: (815)968-4544
Products: Books. **SIC:** 5192 (Books, Periodicals & Newspapers). **Est:** 1982.

■ **3861** ■ **Jean's Dulcimer Shop and Crying Creek Publishers**
Hwy. 32
PO Box 8
Cosby, TN 37722
Phone: (423)487-5543
Products: Books related to folk and traditional music. **SIC:** 5192 (Books, Periodicals & Newspapers). **Est:** 1965.

■ **3862** ■ **Jellyroll Productions**
PO Box 255
Port Townsend, WA 98368
Phone: (360)385-1200 **Fax:** (360)385-6572
E-mail: jpo@olympus.net
URL: http://www.jerryosborne.com
Products: Books for music collectors. **SIC:** 5192 (Books, Periodicals & Newspapers). **Est:** 1975. **Emp:** 4. **Officers:** Jerry P. Osborne, e-mail: jo@jerryosborne.com.

■ **3863** ■ **Jenkins Trading Inc.**
PO Box 6059
Chelsea, MA 02150-0006
Phone: (617)387-7300
Free: (800)622-6612 **Fax:** (617)387-6379
E-mail: sormani@mindspring.com
URL: http://www.sormanicalendars.com
Products: Calendars; Posters; Greeting cards; Note cards. **SICs:** 5112 (Stationery & Office Supplies); 5192 (Books, Periodicals & Newspapers). **Est:** 1972. **Sales:** $3,000,000 (2000). **Emp:** 6. **Officers:** Judith S. Jenkins, President; Alexander Jenkins, Treasurer. **Doing Business As:** Sormani Calendars.

■ **3864** ■ **Jethro Publications**
2105 Nighthawk Dr.
Laramie, WY 82072-1900
Products: Books. **SIC:** 5192 (Books, Periodicals & Newspapers). **Est:** 1977.

■ **3865** ■ **JO-D Books**
81 Willard Terr.
Stamford, CT 06903
Phone: (203)322-0568
Products: Reference books. **SIC:** 5192 (Books, Periodicals & Newspapers). **Est:** 1980. **Sales:** $125,000 (2000). **Emp:** 1.

■ **3866** ■ **Johnson Books**
1880 S 57th Ct.
Boulder, CO 80301
Phone: (303)443-9766
Free: (800)258-5830 **Fax:** (303)443-1106
E-mail: books@jpcolorado.com
Products: Books. **SIC:** 5192 (Books, Periodicals & Newspapers). **Est:** 1978. **Emp:** 5. **Officers:** Mira

Perrizo, Associate Publisher; Richard Croog, Marketing & Sales Mgr.; Stephanie White, Accounts Coordinator; Stephen Topping, Editorial Dir.

■ 3867 ■ **Johnston Coca-Cola**
PO Box 207
Rockwood, TN 37854
Phone: (615)354-1631
Products: Canned and bottled soft drinks. **SIC:** 5149 (Groceries & Related Products Nec). **Sales:** $28,000,000 (2000). **Emp:** 60. **Officers:** Ken Jones, Mgr. of Finance.

■ 3868 ■ **Jones & Bartlett Publishers Inc.**
40 Tall Pine Dr.
Sudbury, MA 01776
Phone: (978)443-5000
Free: (800)832-0034   **Fax:** (978)443-8000
E-mail: info@jbpub.com
URL: http://www.jbpub.com
Products: College textbooks; Reference books for basic and health sciences; Videos. **SICs:** 5192 (Books, Periodicals & Newspapers); 5065 (Electronic Parts & Equipment Nec). **Est:** 1984. **Emp:** 25.

■ 3869 ■ **Joyce Media Inc.**
2654 Diamond St.
PO Box 848
Rosamond, CA 93560
Phone: (661)256-0149   **Fax:** (661)269-2139
URL: http://www.joycemediainc.com
Products: Newspapers; Magazines; Catalog and directory publishing. **SIC:** 5192 (Books, Periodicals & Newspapers). **Est:** 1969. **Sales:** $5,000,000 (2000). **Emp:** 7. **Officers:** John Joyce, President, e-mail: joycemed@pacbell.net.

■ 3870 ■ **Judson Press**
PO Box 851
Valley Forge, PA 19482-0851
Free: (800)331-1053   **Fax:** (610)768-2107
URL: http://www.judsonpress.com
Products: Religious books. **SIC:** 5192 (Books, Periodicals & Newspapers). **Est:** 1824.

■ 3871 ■ **C.G. Jung Foundation**
28 E 39th St.
New York, NY 10016
Phones: (212)697-6433   (212)697-6430
Free: (800)356-5864   **Fax:** (212)953-3989
E-mail: cgjungny@aol.com
Products: Psychology books. **SIC:** 5192 (Books, Periodicals & Newspapers). **Emp:** 3. **Officers:** Arnold DeVera, Book Service Manager.

■ 3872 ■ **K & S Militaria Books**
PO Box 9630
Alpine, TX 79831
Phone: (915)837-5053   **Fax:** (915)837-5021
Products: Books. **SIC:** 5192 (Books, Periodicals & Newspapers). **Est:** 1966.

■ 3873 ■ **Kable News Company Inc.**
641 Lexington Ave., 6th Fl.
New York, NY 10022
Phone: (212)705-4600   **Fax:** (212)705-4666
URL: http://www.kable.com
Products: Magazines and comic books. **SIC:** 5192 (Books, Periodicals & Newspapers). **Est:** 1932. **Sales:** $370,000,000 (2000). **Emp:** 1,500. **Officers:** Michael Duloc, President; Bruce Obendorf, Sr. VP & Finance Officer.

■ 3874 ■ **Kansas City Periodical Distributing Co.**
PO Box 14948
Shawnee Mission, KS 66285-4948
Phone: (913)541-8600   **Fax:** (913)541-9413
Products: Magazines and paperback books. **SIC:** 5192 (Books, Periodicals & Newspapers). **Sales:** $17,000,000 (2000). **Emp:** 50. **Officers:** James Brunkhardt, President.

■ 3875 ■ **Jean Karr & Company, Inc.**
5656 3rd St. NE
Washington, DC 20011
Products: Books. **SIC:** 5192 (Books, Periodicals & Newspapers).

■ 3876 ■ **Kazi Publications**
3023 W Belmont Ave.
Chicago, IL 60618
Phone: (773)267-7001   **Fax:** (773)267-7002
E-mail: kazibooks@kazi.org
URL: http://www.kazi.org
Products: Foreign language books, including Islam and middleeast books. **SIC:** 5192 (Books, Periodicals & Newspapers). **Est:** 1970. **Sales:** $500,000 (2000). **Emp:** 5. **Officers:** Liaquat Ali; Muhammad Munir Chaudry; Pervez Hanif.

■ 3877 ■ **Keith Distributors Inc.**
1055 S Ballenger Hwy.
Flint, MI 48532
Phone: (810)238-9104
Free: (800)373-2366   **Fax:** (810)238-9028
URL: http://www.KeithDistributors.com
Products: Books. **SIC:** 5192 (Books, Periodicals & Newspapers). **Est:** 1983. **Officers:** David Huellmantel, Contact.

■ 3878 ■ **Key Curriculum Press Inc.**
PO Box 2304
Berkeley, CA 94702
Phone: (510)595-7000
Free: (800)338-7638   **Fax:** (510)595-7040
E-mail: info@keypress.com
URL: http://www.keypress.com
Products: Math books; Videos; Software. **SICs:** 5192 (Books, Periodicals & Newspapers); 5065 (Electronic Parts & Equipment Nec); 5045 (Computers, Peripherals & Software). **Est:** 1971. **Sales:** $13,000,000 (2000). **Emp:** 95. **Officers:** Steven Rasmussen, President.

■ 3879 ■ **Kinokuniya Publications Service of New York**
10 W 49th St.
New York, NY 10020
Phone: (212)765-1465   **Fax:** (212)307-5593
Products: Books. **SIC:** 5192 (Books, Periodicals & Newspapers). **Est:** 1972. **Sales:** $25,000,000 (2000). **Emp:** 4. **Officers:** Shigeharu Ono, Vice President.

■ 3880 ■ **B.B. Kirkbride Bible Co.**
PO Box 606
Indianapolis, IN 46206
Phone: (317)633-1900
Free: (800)428-4385   **Fax:** (317)633-1444
E-mail: sales@kirkbride.com
URL: http://www.kirkbride.com
Products: Bibles and related products; Bible cases; Religious software. **SIC:** 5192 (Books, Periodicals & Newspapers). **Est:** 1915. **Sales:** $7,000,000 (2000). **Emp:** 13. **Officers:** J. Marshall Gage, President; Darrell Weitner, CFO; Jeff Wanat, Dir. of Mktg. & Sales; Sonja Gage, Treasurer; Michael B. Gage, Sales/Marketing Contact, e-mail: gage@kirkbride.com.

■ 3881 ■ **Kissen News Agency Inc.**
672 Rt., 211 E
Middletown, NY 10940-1718
Phone: (914)692-5222   **Fax:** (914)692-4767
Products: Newspapers; Magazines. **SIC:** 5192 (Books, Periodicals & Newspapers). **Est:** 1935. **Emp:** 15. **Officers:** Lewis Kornish.

■ 3882 ■ **George R. Klein News Co.**
5131 Post Rd.
Dublin, OH 43017-1160
Phone: (216)623-0370
Products: Books; Magazines. **SIC:** 5192 (Books, Periodicals & Newspapers). **Est:** 1927. **Sales:** $24,000,000 (2000). **Emp:** 100. **Officers:** Ronald Clark, President; Sam Boswell, Controller; Cheri Natali, VP of Marketing; Georgia Dorsey, Dir of Human Resources.

■ 3883 ■ **Klein's Booklein**
108 N Grand Ave.
PO Box 968
Fowlerville, MI 48836
Phone: (517)223-3964
Free: (800)266-5534   **Fax:** (517)223-1314
E-mail: Booklein@ismi.net
Products: Books. **SIC:** 5192 (Books, Periodicals & Newspapers). **Est:** 1993. **Sales:** $85,000 (2000). **Emp:**

3. **Officers:** Clayton Klein; Marjorie Klein; Crystal Hutchins.

■ 3884 ■ **Koen Book Distributors, Inc.**
10 Twosome Dr.
PO Box 600
Moorestown, NJ 08057
Phone: (609)235-4444
Products: Books. **SIC:** 5192 (Books, Periodicals & Newspapers). **Officers:** Robert H. Koen, Contact.

■ 3885 ■ **Kornish Distributors Co.**
672 Rt. 211 E
Middletown, NY 10940-1718
Phone: (914)692-4321   **Fax:** (914)692-4767
Products: Newspapers; magazines. **SIC:** 5192 (Books, Periodicals & Newspapers). **Est:** 1965. **Emp:** 20. **Officers:** Lewis Kornish.

■ 3886 ■ **Kregel Publications & Bookstores**
PO Box 2607
Grand Rapids, MI 49501-2607
Phone: (616)451-4775
Free: (800)733-2607   **Fax:** (616)451-9330
E-mail: kregelbooks@kregel.com
URL: http://www.kregel.com
Products: Theological books. **SIC:** 5192 (Books, Periodicals & Newspapers). **Est:** 1949. **Sales:** $5,000,000 (2000). **Emp:** 70. **Officers:** James Kregel; Jerold Kregel; Kenneth Kregel.

■ 3887 ■ **Krieger Publishing Co.**
PO Box 9542
Melbourne, FL 32902-9542
Phone: (321)724-9542
Free: (800)724-0025   **Fax:** (321)951-3671
E-mail: info@krieger-publishing.com
URL: http://www.krieger-publishing.com
Products: Scientific and technical textbooks. **SIC:** 5192 (Books, Periodicals & Newspapers). **Est:** 1970. **Emp:** 28. **Officers:** Donald E. Krieger, President; Robert E. Krieger, CEO.

■ 3888 ■ **George Kurian Reference Books**
PO Box 519
Baldwin Place, NY 10505
Phone: (914)962-3287
Products: Encyclopedias; Dictionaries; Atlases. **SIC:** 5192 (Books, Periodicals & Newspapers). **Est:** 1972. **Sales:** $100,000 (2000). **Emp:** 3. **Officers:** George Kurian, President.

■ 3889 ■ **Kurtzman Book Sales, Inc.**
1263 W Square Lake Rd.
Bloomfield Hills, MI 48302
Free: (800)869-0505   **Fax:** (248)335-4605
Products: Books from France, Germany, Spain, Italy, and Japan. **SIC:** 5192 (Books, Periodicals & Newspapers). **Est:** 1983.

■ 3890 ■ **Kuykendall's Press**
506 Chandler St.
PO Box 627
Athens, AL 35612
Phone: (256)232-1754   **Free:** (800)781-1754
Products: Adult Bible workbooks; College-level chemistry manuals. **SIC:** 5192 (Books, Periodicals & Newspapers). **Est:** 1948. **Officers:** Frances K. Owen, Owner.

■ 3891 ■ **La Cite**
2306 Westwood Blvd.
PO Box 64504
Los Angeles, CA 90064
Phone: (310)475-0658   **Fax:** (310)470-0610
E-mail: lacite@aol.com
URL: http://www.france.com/lacite/
Products: French books. **SIC:** 5192 (Books, Periodicals & Newspapers). **Est:** 1948.

■ 3892 ■ **Lake Martin Living**
375 Windy Wood
Alexander City, AL 35010
Phone: (256)329-2460
Products: Magazines. **SIC:** 5192 (Books, Periodicals & Newspapers).

■ 3893 ■ Landrum News Agency—Cincinnati Div.
7115 Dillward Ave.
Cincinnati, OH 45216
Phone: (513)821-5552 **Fax:** (513)821-1532
Products: Newspapers. **SIC:** 5192 (Books, Periodicals & Newspapers). **Sales:** $700,000 (2000).

■ 3894 ■ Landrum News Agency Inc.
4100 Fisher Rd.
Columbus, OH 43228
Phone: (614)272-0388 **Fax:** (614)272-9853
Products: Newspapers; Magazines; Paperback books.
SIC: 5192 (Books, Periodicals & Newspapers). **Est:** 1972. **Sales:** $3,000,000 (2000). **Emp:** 60. **Officers:** H. E. Landrum.

■ 3895 ■ Langley Press, Inc.
821 Georgia St.
Key West, FL 33040
Phone: (305)294-3156 **Fax:** (305)292-2174
Products: Books on Key West and the Florida Keys.
SIC: 5192 (Books, Periodicals & Newspapers). **Est:** 1982. **Emp:** 2. **Officers:** Wright Wangley, President; Joan K. Wangley, Sec. & Treas.

■ 3896 ■ Larry's News
Empire State Plz.
Albany, NY 12223
Phone: (518)462-3765
Products: Newspapers. **SIC:** 5192 (Books, Periodicals & Newspapers).

■ 3897 ■ Last Gasp of San Francisco
777 Florida
San Francisco, CA 94110
Phone: (415)824-6636
Free: (800)366-5121 **Fax:** (415)824-1836
E-mail: lastgasp@hooked.net
URL: http://www.lastgasp.com
Products: Trade books about beatniks, drugs, comics, tattoos, popculture, and graphic novels; Lumber jack wooden puzzles; T-shirts. **SICs:** 5192 (Books, Periodicals & Newspapers); 5136 (Men's/Boys' Clothing); 5092 (Toys & Hobby Goods & Supplies). **Est:** 1970. **Sales:** $3,100,000 (2000). **Emp:** 25. **Officers:** Ronald E. Turner, Owner.

■ 3898 ■ Latin Trading Corp.
539 H St., Ste. B
Chula Vista, CA 91910-7505
Phone: (619)427-7867
Free: (800)257-7248 **Fax:** (619)476-1817
E-mail: latintr@flash.net
Products: Audio and video tapes; Textbooks; Large supply of books in Spanish language. **SICs:** 5192 (Books, Periodicals & Newspapers); 5099 (Durable Goods Nec); 5065 (Electronic Parts & Equipment Nec). **Est:** 1984. **Sales:** $200,000 (1999). **Emp:** 3. **Officers:** Jose Figueroa, President; Jorge L. Gaona, Vice President; Alfredo Figueroa, Secretary.

■ 3899 ■ Law Distributors
14415 S Main St.
Gardena, CA 90248
Phone: (213)321-3275 **Fax:** (213)324-6381
Products: Educational material. **SIC:** 5192 (Books, Periodicals & Newspapers). **Est:** 1974.

■ 3900 ■ LEA Book Distributors
170-23 83rd Ave.
Jamaica, NY 11432
Phone: (718)291-9891 **Fax:** (718)291-9830
E-mail: leabook@mail.idt.net
URL: http://www.leabooks.com
Products: Books, including Spanish language and out-of-print; CD-Roms; Software; Spanish multimedia products. **SICs:** 5192 (Books, Periodicals & Newspapers); 5045 (Computers, Peripherals & Software). **Est:** 1978. **Sales:** $500,000 (2000). **Emp:** 3. **Officers:** Dr. Angel Capellan, President; Carmen I. Jaipersaud, Asst. to the President. **Alternate Name:** Libros De Espania Y America.

■ 3901 ■ Leader Newspapers
PO Box 991
Glendale, CA 91209
Phone: (818)241-4141 **Fax:** (818)243-5944
Products: Publishes Glendale Community News; distributes newspapers. **SIC:** 5192 (Books, Periodicals & Newspapers).

■ 3902 ■ The Learning Plant
PO Box 17233
West Palm Beach, FL 33416
Phone: (561)686-9456 **Fax:** (561)686-2415
E-mail: lrmplant@bellsouth.net
URL: http://www.learningplant.com
Products: Educational supplies, including books, puzzles, videocassettes, and posters; Cassette tapes; CD's. **SICs:** 5192 (Books, Periodicals & Newspapers); 5099 (Durable Goods Nec); 5092 (Toys & Hobby Goods & Supplies); 5065 (Electronic Parts & Equipment Nec). **Est:** 1978. **Officers:** Ruth T. Levow, President.

■ 3903 ■ Lectorum Publications Inc.
111 8th Ave., Ste. 804
New York, NY 10011
Phone: (212)929-2833
Free: (800)345-5946 **Fax:** (212)727-3035
E-mail: info@lectorum.com
URL: http://www.lectorum.com
Products: Spanish language books. **SIC:** 5192 (Books, Periodicals & Newspapers). **Est:** 1971. **Sales:** $12,000,000 (1994). **Emp:** 50. **Officers:** Teresa Mlawer, President; Fernando Febus, Controller; Carmen Rivera, Sales Mgr., e-mail: crivera@scholastic.com; Lisa Stein, Customer Service Contact, e-mail: lstein@scholastic.com.

■ 3904 ■ Legal Books Distributing
4247 Whiteside St.
Los Angeles, CA 90063
Phone: (213)526-7110
Free: (800)200-7110 **Fax:** (213)526-7112
E-mail: legalbooks@earthlink.net
URL: http://www.discovery-press.com
Products: Law books and law school study aids. **SIC:** 5192 (Books, Periodicals & Newspapers). **Est:** 1994. **Sales:** $2,500,000 (2000). **Emp:** 5. **Officers:** William A. Gehr.

■ 3905 ■ Leisure Arts, Inc.
PO Box 55595
Little Rock, AR 72215
Phone: (501)868-8800
Free: (800)643-8030 **Fax:** (501)868-8937
URL: http://www.leisurearts.com
Products: Books. **SIC:** 5192 (Books, Periodicals & Newspapers). **Est:** 1971. **Emp:** 400. **Officers:** Rick Barton, Publisher; Tom Sicbenmorgen, VP of Finance.

■ 3906 ■ J. Levine Books & Judaica
5 W 30th St.
New York, NY 10001
Phone: (212)695-6888
Free: (800)5JE-WISH **Fax:** (212)643-1044
E-mail: sales@levinejudaica.ca
URL: http://www.levinejudaica.com
Products: Religious books and supplies. **SIC:** 5192 (Books, Periodicals & Newspapers). **Est:** 1890. **Emp:** 10.

■ 3907 ■ Charles Levy Co.
1200 N North Branch St.
Chicago, IL 60622
Phone: (312)440-4400 **Fax:** (312)440-7414
Products: Magazines; Sports trading cards. **SIC:** 5192 (Books, Periodicals & Newspapers). **Est:** 1893. **Sales:** $285,000,000 (2000). **Emp:** 2,100. **Officers:** Carol G. Kloster, CEO & President; Thomas Halverson, Sr. VP & CFO; Judy Cotton, VP of Sales & Merchandising; Dennis Abboud, VP & General Merchandising Mgr.; Francis Lefkow, VP of Human Resources.

■ 3908 ■ Levy Home Entertainment
4201 Raymond Dr.
Hillside, IL 60162
Phone: (708)547-4400
Free: (800)497-0235 **Fax:** (708)547-4503
Products: Videos; Prerecorded audio tapes; Books. **SICs:** 5192 (Books, Periodicals & Newspapers); 5099 (Durable Goods Nec); 5065 (Electronic Parts & Equipment Nec). **Est:** 1969.

■ 3909 ■ Liberation Distributors
PO Box 5341
Chicago, IL 60680
Phone: (773)248-3442 **Fax:** (773)248-3442
Products: Books, including the writings of Communist party leaders; Literature. **SIC:** 5192 (Books, Periodicals & Newspapers). **Est:** 1979.

■ 3910 ■ Liberty Publishing Co. Inc.
PO BOX 4248
Deerfield Beach, FL 33442
Phone: (954)360-9000
URL: http://www.libertypub.com
Products: Nonfiction books, including software and how-to books. **SICs:** 5192 (Books, Periodicals & Newspapers); 5045 (Computers, Peripherals & Software). **Est:** 1977. **Sales:** $1,000,000 (1999). **Officers:** Jeffrey B. Little, President, e-mail: JBLittle@bellsouth.net.

■ 3911 ■ Library Book Selection Service, Inc.
2714 McGraw Dr.
PO Box 277
Bloomington, IL 61704
Phone: (309)663-1411
Free: (877)663-6434 **Fax:** (309)664-0059
E-mail: lbss@davesworld.net
Products: Books. **SIC:** 5192 (Books, Periodicals & Newspapers). **Est:** 1887. **Sales:** $1,000,000 (2000). **Emp:** 7.

■ 3912 ■ Library Research Associates Inc.
474 Dunderberg Rd.
Monroe, NY 10950
Phone: (914)783-1144
Free: (800)914-3379 **Fax:** (914)782-3953
Products: Books. **SIC:** 5192 (Books, Periodicals & Newspapers). **Est:** 1968. **Sales:** $150,000 (2000). **Emp:** 3. **Officers:** Matilda A. Gocek, CEO & President; John J. Gocek, Vice President; Dianne D. McKinstrie.

■ 3913 ■ Life Unlimited
800 N Ben Maddox, Ste. 204
Visalia, CA 93292
Phone: (209)733-1940
Products: Books related to enlightenment, self improvement, computers, and software; Audio cassette tapes. **SICs:** 5192 (Books, Periodicals & Newspapers); 5045 (Computers, Peripherals & Software); 5099 (Durable Goods Nec). **Est:** 1973.

■ 3914 ■ Lincoln Industries Inc.
PO Box 80269
Lincoln, NE 68501
Phone: (402)421-7300 **Fax:** (402)421-7507
Products: Textbooks, including teachers' editions; Used books. **SIC:** 5192 (Books, Periodicals & Newspapers). **Est:** 1973. **Sales:** $200,000,000 (2000). **Emp:** 1,100. **Officers:** George Lincoln, President; Bill Macy, Treasurer; Frank Condello, Dir. of Marketing; Larry Rempe, Dir. of Systems; Ed Phillips, Dir of Human Resources.

■ 3915 ■ Linden Tree Children's Records & Books
170 State St.
Los Altos, CA 94022
Phone: (650)949-3390 **Fax:** (650)949-0346
Products: Children's books; Prerecorded audio tapes; Videos; Compact discs; Toys; Nonelectronic games. **SICs:** 5192 (Books, Periodicals & Newspapers); 5099 (Durable Goods Nec); 5065 (Electronic Parts & Equipment Nec); 5092 (Toys & Hobby Goods & Supplies). **Est:** 1982. **Sales:** $950,000 (2000). **Emp:** 12. **Officers:** Dennis Ronberg.

■ 3916 ■ Ling's International Books
7531 Convoy Ct.
San Diego, CA 92111
Phone: (619)292-8104 **Fax:** (619)292-8207
Products: Spanish, Latin American, and French books. **SIC:** 5192 (Books, Periodicals & Newspapers). **Est:** 1974.

■ 3917 ■ Listening Library Inc.
1 Park Ave.
Old Greenwich, CT 06870
Phone: (203)637-3616
Free: (800)243-4504 **Fax:** 800-454-0606
E-mail: moreinfo@listeninglib.com
URL: http://www.listeninglib.com
Products: Audiobooks; Books. **SIC:** 5192 (Books, Periodicals & Newspapers). **Est:** 1956. **Emp:** 20.
Officers: Tim Ditlow, President.

■ 3918 ■ Literal Books
7705 Georgia Ave. NW, No. 102
Washington, DC 20012
Phone: (202)723-8688
Free: (800)366-8680 **Fax:** (202)882-6592
Products: Books in Spanish. **SIC:** 5192 (Books, Periodicals & Newspapers). **Est:** 1984. **Sales:** $250,000 (2000). **Emp:** 6. **Officers:** Jose Valencia; Leopoldo Rodriguez.

■ 3919 ■ Llewellyn Publications
PO Box 64383
St. Paul, MN 55164
Phone: (651)291-1970
Free: (800)843-6666 **Fax:** (651)291-1908
E-mail: lwlpc@llewellyn.com
URL: http://www.llewellyn.com
Products: Books, including new age, occult, and metaphysical books. **SIC:** 5192 (Books, Periodicals & Newspapers). **Est:** 1901. **Sales:** $17,000,000 (2000). **Emp:** 116. **Officers:** Carl Weschcke.

■ 3920 ■ Login Brothers Book Co.
1436 W Randolph St.
Chicago, IL 60607
Phone: (312)432-7700 **Free:** (800)680-2889
E-mail: sales@lb.com
URL: http://www.lb.com
Products: Books and software, including health sciences, scientific and technical, complementary medecine, and business. **SIC:** 5192 (Books, Periodicals & Newspapers). **Est:** 1966. **Emp:** 200.

■ 3921 ■ Longman Publishing Group
10 Bank St.
White Plains, NY 10606-1951
Phone: (914)993-5000
Free: (800)862-7778 **Fax:** (914)997-8115
Products: Books, including high school, college, and second-language text books. **SIC:** 5192 (Books, Periodicals & Newspapers). **Emp:** 85. **Officers:** Bruce S. Butterfield, President; Frank T. Demello, VP of Marketing & Sales; Arley Gray, VP of Products & Product Dvlpmt.; Vidya Tejwani, CFO.

■ 3922 ■ LPC
1436 W Randolph
Chicago, IL 60607
Phone: (312)432-7650
Free: (800)626-4330 **Fax:** (312)432-7601
E-mail: lpc-info@lb.com
URL: http://www.coolbooks.com
Products: Books; Presses. **SIC:** 5192 (Books, Periodicals & Newspapers). **Est:** 1991. **Emp:** 75.
Officers: Susan Shaw, VP of Sales; David Wilk, President; Jay Clark, Sales/Marketing Contact, e-mail: jay@lb.com; Linda Robinson, Customer Service Contact, e-mail: lr@lb.com; Cathy Costourous, Human Resources Contact, e-mail: cc@lb.com. **Alternate Name:** Login Publishers Consortium.

■ 3923 ■ Lutz News Co.
601 Abbott
Detroit, MI 48226-2556
Phone: (313)961-2615 **Fax:** (313)961-3752
Products: Newspapers. **SIC:** 5192 (Books, Periodicals & Newspapers). **Est:** 1931. **Sales:** $4,000,000 (2000). **Emp:** 49. **Officers:** Joseph Kass; Howard Lutz.

■ 3924 ■ M & M News Agency
Civic Industrial Pk.
PO Box 1129
La Salle, IL 61301
Phone: (815)223-2754 **Fax:** (815)223-2828
Products: News magazines; Collectors cards; Books. **SIC:** 5192 (Books, Periodicals & Newspapers).

■ 3925 ■ Mabon Business Equipment
2965 Spaatz Rd.
Monument, CO 80132
Phone: (970)481-2313
Products: Library and bookstore software. **SIC:** 5192 (Books, Periodicals & Newspapers). **Est:** 1974.

■ 3926 ■ MacAlester Park Publishing Co.
7317 Cahill Rd.
Minneapolis, MN 55439
Phone: (952)562-1234
Free: (800)407-9078 **Fax:** (952)941-3010
E-mail: publisher@mcchronicle.com
Products: Books; Magazines. **SIC:** 5192 (Books, Periodicals & Newspapers). **Est:** 1930. **Sales:** $300,000 (2000). **Emp:** 6. **Officers:** Michael Beard.

■ 3927 ■ MacRae's Indian Book Distributors
1605 Cole St.
PO Box 652
Enumclaw, WA 98022
Phone: (206)825-3737
Products: Books about American Indians. **SIC:** 5192 (Books, Periodicals & Newspapers). **Est:** 1997. **Sales:** $80,000 (2000). **Emp:** 1. **Officers:** Ken MacRae, Owner.

■ 3928 ■ Magazines Inc.
1135 Hammond St.
Bangor, ME 04401
Phone: (207)942-8237
Free: (800)649-9224 **Fax:** (207)942-9226
Products: Magazines; Books; Newspapers. **SIC:** 5192 (Books, Periodicals & Newspapers). **Est:** 1960.

■ 3929 ■ Main Court Book Fair
30 S 6th Ave.
PO Box 109
Mt. Vernon, NY 10550
Phone: (914)664-1633 **Fax:** (914)664-9508
Products: Books. **SIC:** 5192 (Books, Periodicals & Newspapers). **Est:** 1966. **Emp:** 15. **Officers:** Joshua H. Makanoff.

■ 3930 ■ Main Line Book Company Inc.
1974 Sproul Rd., Ste. 400
PO Box 914
Broomall, PA 19008
Phone: (215)353-5166 **Fax:** (215)359-1439
Products: Books. **SIC:** 5192 (Books, Periodicals & Newspapers). **Est:** 1974. **Sales:** $15,000,000 (2000). **Emp:** 130. **Officers:** Philip Cohen, CEO; Daniel Hilferty, Chief Operating Officer; William Touey, Controller; Kenneth Butkus, Sales Director.

■ 3931 ■ Maine Writers & Publishers Alliance
12 Pleasant St.
Brunswick, ME 04011
Phones: (207)729-6333 (207)725-0690
Fax: (207)725-1014
URL: http://www.mainewriters.org
Products: Books and literary journals. **SIC:** 5192 (Books, Periodicals & Newspapers). **Est:** 1974. **Emp:** 5. **Officers:** Sarah Cecil, Exec. Dir., e-mail: sarah@mainewriters.org; Trudy Chambers Price; Jill Schultz; John Cole, Editor; Jenny Hall; Arleen Rancourt.

■ 3932 ■ Majors Scientific Books Inc.
PO Box 819074
Dallas, TX 75381-9074
Phone: (972)353-1100
Free: (800)633-1851 **Fax:** (972)353-1300
URL: http://www.majors.com
Products: Health science books and software. **SICs:** 5192 (Books, Periodicals & Newspapers); 5045 (Computers, Peripherals & Software). **Est:** 1909. **Emp:** 300. **Officers:** John A. Majors Jr., Chairman of the Board; William H. Majors, Chairman of the Board.

■ 3933 ■ Manson News Distributors
1177 Avenue of the Americas, Ste. 36
New York, NY 10036-2714
Phone: (716)244-3880 **Fax:** (716)461-1388
Products: Magazines, newspapers, and books. **SIC:** 5192 (Books, Periodicals & Newspapers). **Emp:** 70.

■ 3934 ■ Many Feathers Books and Maps
2626 W Indian School Rd.
Phoenix, AZ 85017
Phone: (602)266-1043
Free: (800)279-7652 **Fax:** (602)279-2350
Products: Books and other printed materials. **SIC:** 5192 (Books, Periodicals & Newspapers). **Sales:** $900,000 (2000). **Emp:** 7.

■ 3935 ■ Map Link Inc.
30 S La Patera Ln. Unit #5
Santa Barbara, CA 93117
Phone: (805)692-6777
Free: (800)962-1397 **Fax:** (805)692-6787
E-mail: custserv@maplink.com
URL: http://www.maplink.com
Products: International travel maps; Folding maps; Wall maps; Travel guides; Globes. **SIC:** 5192 (Books, Periodicals & Newspapers). **Est:** 1985. **Sales:** $13,000,000 (1999). **Emp:** 70. **Officers:** Bill Hunt, President; James Ridgway, Sales/Marketing Contact, e-mail: bridgway@maplink.com; David Benson, Customer Service Contact, e-mail: dbenson@maplink.com; Tekle Menelik, Human Resources Contact, e-mail: tmenelik@maplink.com.

■ 3936 ■ Marquette Bottling Works Inc.
120 W Furnace St.
Marquette, MI 49855
Phone: (906)225-1209
Products: Bottled and canned soft drinks. **SIC:** 5149 (Groceries & Related Products Nec). **Sales:** $10,000,000 (1993). **Emp:** 30. **Officers:** William Larsh, Manager.

■ 3937 ■ Maryland Historical Press
9205 Tuckerman St.
Lanham, MD 20706
Phone: (301)577-5308 **Fax:** (301)577-8711
E-mail: mhpress@erols.com
Products: History books. **SIC:** 5192 (Books, Periodicals & Newspapers). **Est:** 1964. **Sales:** $100,000 (2000). **Emp:** 1. **Officers:** Vera F. Rollo Ph.D., Publisher.

■ 3938 ■ Maryland News Distributing Co.
4000 Coolidge Ave.
Baltimore, MD 21229
Phone: (301)536-4545
Products: Books; Magazines; Out-of-town newspapers; Periodicals. **SIC:** 5192 (Books, Periodicals & Newspapers). **Est:** 1923.

■ 3939 ■ Marysville Newspaper Distributor
1117 Bancroft St.
Port Huron, MI 48060
Phone: (810)984-5171
Products: Newspapers. **SIC:** 5192 (Books, Periodicals & Newspapers).

■ 3940 ■ Matthews Book Co.
11559 Rock Island Ct.
Maryland Heights, MO 63043
Phone: (314)432-1400
Free: (800)633-2665 **Fax:** (314)432-7044
URL: http://www.mattmccoy.com
Products: Health science books; Software; Medical supplies. **SICs:** 5192 (Books, Periodicals & Newspapers); 5045 (Computers, Peripherals & Software); 5047 (Medical & Hospital Equipment). **Est:** 1889. **Sales:** $58,000,000 (1999). **Emp:** 100. **Officers:** John Marcus, CEO & Chairman of the Board; Jim Klund, CFO; Linda Nash, Sr. VP, e-mail: lsn@mattmccoy.com; Mary Copley, Customer Service Contact, e-mail: mic@mattmccoy.com; Ella Knoepp, Human Resources Contact. **Former Name:** Matthews Medical Books. **Former Name:** Matthews-McCoy.

■ 3941 ■ MBS Textbook Exchange Inc.
2711 W Ash St.
Columbia, MO 65203
Phone: (573)445-2243
Free: (800)325-0577 **Fax:** (573)446-5256
Products: New and used college textbooks. **SIC:** 5192 (Books, Periodicals & Newspapers). **Est:** 1909. **Sales:** $127,200,000 (2000). **Emp:** 530. **Officers:** R.K. Pugh, CEO; Andrew Gingrich, CFO.

■ 3942 ■ McClain Printing Co.
PO Box 403
Parsons, WV 26287
Phone: (304)478-2881
Free: (800)654-7179   **Fax:** (304)478-4658
E-mail: mcclain@access.mountain.net
URL: http://www.McClainPrinting.com
Products: Books, including history, poetry, and genealogy books; Brochures, magazines, pamphlets, newsletters, flyers, and posters. **SIC:** 5192 (Books, Periodicals & Newspapers). **Est:** 1958. **Sales:** $250,000 (2000). **Emp:** 30. **Officers:** Ken Smith, Vice President; George Smith, President; Michelle Mullenax, Vice President of Publishing.

■ 3943 ■ McDonald & Woodward Publishing
PO Box 10308
Blacksburg, VA 24062-0308
Phone: (540)951-9465   **Fax:** (540)552-0210
Products: Books, including natural and cultural history books. **SIC:** 5192 (Books, Periodicals & Newspapers).

■ 3944 ■ McKnight Sales Company Inc.
540 California Ave.
PO Box 4138
Pittsburgh, PA 15202
Phone: (412)761-4443   **Fax:** (412)761-0122
E-mail: sales@mscmags.com
URL: http://www.mscmags.com
Products: Magazines; Paperback books. **SIC:** 5192 (Books, Periodicals & Newspapers). **Est:** 1961. **Sales:** $3,063,000 (2000). **Emp:** 6. **Officers:** David P. McKnight Sr., President; Richard R. McKnight, Vice President; David P. McKnight Jr., Vice President.

■ 3945 ■ McPherson & Co. Publishers
PO Box 1126
Kingston, NY 12402
Phone: (914)331-5807
Free: (800)613-8219   **Fax:** (914)331-5807
E-mail: gmcpher@ulser.net
URL: http://www.mcphersonco.com
Products: Books and books on tape. **SICs:** 5192 (Books, Periodicals & Newspapers); 5099 (Durable Goods Nec). **Est:** 1974. **Officers:** Bruce R. McPherson, Publisher & Owner, e-mail: bmcpher@ulster.net. **Alternate Name:** Treacle Press. **Alternate Name:** Documentext. **Alternate Name:** Recovered Classics.

■ 3946 ■ Melman-Moster Associates, Inc.
361 Clinton Ave.
Wyckoff, NJ 07481
Phone: (201)847-0100   **Fax:** (201)847-7675
E-mail: books@melman-moster.com
Products: Books. **SIC:** 5192 (Books, Periodicals & Newspapers). **Est:** 1983.

■ 3947 ■ Melton Book Company Inc.
PO Box 140990
Donelson, TN 37214-0990
Phone: (615)391-3917
Free: (800)441-0511   **Fax:** (615)391-5225
Products: Religious products, including books and Bibles. **SIC:** 5192 (Books, Periodicals & Newspapers). **Est:** 1948.

■ 3948 ■ Meriwether Publishing, Ltd.
885 Elkton Dr.
Colorado Springs, CO 80907-3576
Phone: (719)594-4422
Free: (800)937-5297   **Fax:** (719)594-9916
E-mail: merpcds@aol.com
URL: http://www.meriwetherpublishing.com
Products: Books, including plays and scripts. **SIC:** 5192 (Books, Periodicals & Newspapers). **Est:** 1968. **Officers:** Arthur Zapel, Chairman of the Board; A. Mark Zapel, President; Ted O. Zapel, Vice President; Mark Zapel, Sales/Marketing Contact; Diana Short, Customer Service Contact, e-mail: mpdshort@aol.com.

■ 3949 ■ Metamorphous Advances Product Services
PO Box 10616
Portland, OR 97296-0616
Phone: (503)228-4972   **Fax:** (503)223-9117
E-mail: maps@metamodels.com
URL: http://www.metamodels.com/maps/maps.html
Products: Books; Tapes; Videos; Software. **SICs:** 5192 (Books, Periodicals & Newspapers); 5065 (Electronic Parts & Equipment Nec); 5045 (Computers, Peripherals & Software); 5099 (Durable Goods Nec). **Est:** 1992. **Officers:** David Cottrell, Sales/Marketing Contact, e-mail: dc@metamodels.com. **Also Known by This Acronym:** MAPS.

■ 3950 ■ Michiana News Service, Inc.
2232 S 11th St.
Niles, MI 49120
Phone: (616)684-3013
Free: (800)633-0176   **Fax:** (616)684-8740
Products: Books. **SIC:** 5192 (Books, Periodicals & Newspapers). **Est:** 1955.

■ 3951 ■ Michigan Church Supply Company Inc.
PO Box 279
Mt. Morris, MI 48458
Phone: (810)686-8877
Free: (800)521-3440   **Fax:** (810)686-0561
Products: Bibles and testaments; Electric fans; Gifts and novelties. **SICs:** 5192 (Books, Periodicals & Newspapers); 5199 (Nondurable Goods Nec); 5099 (Durable Goods Nec). **Est:** 1960. **Emp:** 20. **Officers:** Leo Flynn, President.

■ 3952 ■ Michigan State University Press
1405 S Harrison Rd., Ste. 25
East Lansing, MI 48823-5202
Phone: (517)355-9543
Free: (800)678-2120   **Fax:** (517)432-2611
E-mail: msupress@msu.edu
URL: http://www.msu.edu/unit/msupress
Products: Books and scholarly journals. **SIC:** 5192 (Books, Periodicals & Newspapers). **Est:** 1947. **Sales:** $1,000,000 (2000). **Emp:** 12. **Officers:** Fred C. Bohm, e-mail: bohm@msu.edu; Julie L. Loehr, Dir. of Advertising, e-mail: loehr@msu.com; Laura Carantza, e-mail: carantza@msu.edu.

■ 3953 ■ Mickler's Floridiana, Inc.
PO Box 621450
Oviedo, FL 32762-1450
Phone: (407)365-6425
Free: (800)250-4054   **Fax:** (407)365-6425
Products: Books; Videos; Maps. **SICs:** 5192 (Books, Periodicals & Newspapers); 5065 (Electronic Parts & Equipment Nec). **Est:** 1963. **Emp:** 4. **Officers:** Lori Mott, President.

■ 3954 ■ Mid-Penn Magazine Distributors
935 N Washington Ave.
Scranton, PA 18509-2924
Products: Magazines. **SIC:** 5192 (Books, Periodicals & Newspapers).

■ 3955 ■ Mid-State Distributors
1201 Sheffler Dr.
Chambersburg, PA 17201-6004
Phone: (717)263-2413
Free: (800)967-3748   **Fax:** (717)263-7742
Products: Weekly newspapers, books, and magazines. **SIC:** 5192 (Books, Periodicals & Newspapers). **Sales:** $15,000 (2000). **Emp:** 75. **Officers:** Steven Greenwald, President.

■ 3956 ■ Mid-State Periodicals Inc.
2516 W Schneidman Dr.
PO Box 3455
Quincy, IL 62305
Phone: (217)222-0833   **Fax:** (217)222-1256
Products: Books; Magazines. **SIC:** 5192 (Books, Periodicals & Newspapers). **Emp:** 27. **Officers:** Clarence Davis, General Mgr.; Jimmie Stone, Assistant Manager.

■ 3957 ■ Midmarch Arts Press
300 Riverside Dr.
New York, NY 10025
Phone: (212)666-6990
Products: Art and poetry books. **SIC:** 5192 (Books, Periodicals & Newspapers). **Est:** 1972. **Sales:** $50,000 (2000). **Emp:** 3. **Officers:** Judy Seigel, President; Cynthia Navaretta, Publisher.

■ 3958 ■ Midwest Distributors
PO Box 5224
Kansas City, KS 66119
Products: Books. **SIC:** 5192 (Books, Periodicals & Newspapers).

■ 3959 ■ Midwest Library Service
11443 St. Charles Rock Rd.
Bridgeton, MO 63044-2789
Phone: (314)739-3100
Free: (800)325-8833   **Fax:** (314)739-1326
E-mail: mail@midwestls.com
URL: http://www.midwestls.com
Products: Books for college, public, and special libraries. **SIC:** 5192 (Books, Periodicals & Newspapers). **Est:** 1959. **Sales:** $36,000,000 (2000). **Emp:** 140. **Officers:** Howard Lesser, President; Herbert Lesser, Vice President; Georgia Willen, Secretary.

■ 3960 ■ Milligan News Co., Inc.
150 N Autumn St.
San Jose, CA 95110
Phone: (408)298-3322
Free: (800)873-2387   **Fax:** (408)298-0235
E-mail: milligan@milligannews.com
Products: Comic books; Magazines; Trading cards. **SIC:** 5192 (Books, Periodicals & Newspapers). **Est:** 1935. **Emp:** 52. **Officers:** Jack Milligan, President; Jack Gillis, Vice President; Ron Nichols, General Mgr.; Hank Leimas, Sales/Marketing Contact.

■ 3961 ■ MILTCO Corp.
PO Box 1321
Harrisburg, PA 17105
Phone: (717)541-8130
Products: Books, periodicals, and newspapers. **SIC:** 5192 (Books, Periodicals & Newspapers). **Sales:** $7,600,000 (2000). **Emp:** 115. **Officers:** Ken Quigley, President; Bob Marsh, Controller.

■ 3962 ■ Missouri Archaeological Society Inc.
PO Box 958
Columbia, MO 65205
Phone: (573)882-3544
Free: (800)472-3223   **Fax:** (573)882-9410
URL: http://web.missouri.edu/~moarch/
Products: Archaeology books. **SIC:** 5192 (Books, Periodicals & Newspapers). **Est:** 1935. **Sales:** $33,150 (2000). **Emp:** 1. **Officers:** Melody Galen, Associate Editor, e-mail: galenm@missouri.edu.

■ 3963 ■ Missouri Archaeological Society Inc.
PO Box 958
Columbia, MO 65205
Phone: (573)882-3544
Free: (800)472-3223   **Fax:** (573)882-9410
Products: Books and other printed materials. **SIC:** 5192 (Books, Periodicals & Newspapers). **Emp:** 1.

■ 3964 ■ Mix Bookshelf
6400 Hollis St., No. 12
Emeryville, CA 94608
Phone: (510)653-3307
Free: (800)233-9604   **Fax:** (510)653-5142
Products: Technical, scientific, and professional books; Prerecorded audio tapes; Video discs prerecorded for home entertainment; Books. **SICs:** 5192 (Books, Periodicals & Newspapers); 5099 (Durable Goods Nec); 5065 (Electronic Parts & Equipment Nec). **Est:** 1982. **Emp:** 7. **Officers:** Brad Smith, General Mgr.; Todd Souvignier, Operations Manager.

■ 3965 ■ Montfort Publications
26 S Saxon Ave.
Bay Shore, NY 11706-8993
Phone: (631)665-0726   **Fax:** (631)665-4349
URL: http://www.montfortmissionaries.com
Products: Religious books. **SIC:** 5192 (Books, Periodicals & Newspapers). **Est:** 1947. **Sales:** $150,000 (2000). **Officers:** Theresa Vaz, Sale & Marketing Contact.

■ 3966 ■ Mook & Blanchard Wholesale Library Books
546 S Hofgaarden
La Puente, CA 91744
Phone: (626)968-6424
Free: (800)875-9911 **Fax:** (626)968-6877
E-mail: custserv@mookandblanchard.com
URL: http://www.mookandblanchard.com
Products: Elementary and middle school books. **SIC:** 5192 (Books, Periodicals & Newspapers). **Est:** 1970. **Emp:** 30. **Officers:** Jerry J. Mook, President; Lori Morrelli, Vice President.

■ 3967 ■ Moonbeam Publications, Inc.
836 Hastings St.
Traverse City, MI 49686-3441
Phone: (231)922-0533
Free: (800)445-2391 **Fax:** (231)922-0544
E-mail: jpersing@gtii.com
URL: http://www.moonbeampublications.com
Products: General reference books and videos; Educational aptitude testing materials. **SICs:** 5192 (Books, Periodicals & Newspapers); 5099 (Durable Goods Nec). **Est:** 1987. **Sales:** $500,000 (2000). **Emp:** 5. **Officers:** Judith M. Persing, President.

■ 3968 ■ The Morehouse Group, Inc.
PO Box 1321
Harrisburg, PA 17105
Phone: (717)541-8130 **Fax:** (717)541-8128
E-mail: morehousegroup@morehousegroup.com
URL: http://www.morehousegroup.com
Products: Religious books. **SIC:** 5192 (Books, Periodicals & Newspapers). **Est:** 1884. **Emp:** 50. **Officers:** Kenneth H. Quigley, President; Robert Marsh, CFO; Leslie Merrell, Marketing & Sales Mgr. **Former Name:** Morehouse Publishing Div.

■ 3969 ■ Moshy Brothers Inc.
127 W 25th St.
New York, NY 10001
Phone: (212)255-0613 **Fax:** (212)691-7393
E-mail: moshybrothers@aol.com
Products: Imported religious gifts and books. **SICs:** 5192 (Books, Periodicals & Newspapers); 5199 (Nondurable Goods Nec). **Est:** 1893. **Sales:** $1,700,000 (2000). **Emp:** 10. **Officers:** Paul Moshy; Fred Moshy.

■ 3970 ■ Motorbooks International
729 Prospect Ave.
PO Box 1
Osceola, WI 54020-0001
Phone: (715)294-3345
Free: (800)458-0454 **Fax:** (715)294-4448
E-mail: trade@motorbooks.com
Products: Books on transportation and military history. **SIC:** 5192 (Books, Periodicals & Newspapers). **Est:** 1965.

■ 3971 ■ Mott Media L.L.C.
112 E Ellen St.
Fenton, MI 48430-2115
Phone: (810)714-4280 **Fax:** (810)714-2077
E-mail: sales@mottmedia.com
URL: http://www.mottmedia.com
Products: Christian and educational books. **SIC:** 5192 (Books, Periodicals & Newspapers). **Est:** 1970.

■ 3972 ■ Mountain West Printing and Publishing Ltd.
1150 W Custer Pl
Denver, CO 80223
Phone: (303)744-3313
Free: (800)230-9393 **Fax:** (303)744-1332
Products: Publishes and prints magazines and brochures; Mailing, ink jet printing and tabbing services. **SIC:** 5192 (Books, Periodicals & Newspapers). **Sales:** $8,000,000 (2000). **Emp:** 55. **Officers:** Martin Walker, President.

■ 3973 ■ Moznaim Publishing Corp.
4304 12th Ave.
Brooklyn, NY 11219
Phone: (718)438-7680 **Fax:** (718)438-1305
Products: Judaica books. **SIC:** 5192 (Books, Periodicals & Newspapers). **Est:** 1970. **Emp:** 5. **Alternate Name:** Maznaim Publishers.

■ 3974 ■ Mr. Paperback Publisher News
2224 S 11th St.
Niles, MI 49120-4410
Phone: (616)684-1551 **Free:** (800)872-0031
Products: Magazines; Books. **SIC:** 5192 (Books, Periodicals & Newspapers).

■ 3975 ■ Music for Percussion, Inc.
170 NE 33rd St.
Ft. Lauderdale, FL 33334
Phone: (954)563-1844 **Fax:** (954)563-1844
Products: Books. **SIC:** 5192 (Books, Periodicals & Newspapers). **Est:** 1955.

■ 3976 ■ Music Sales Corp.
257 Park Ave. S, 20th Fl.
New York, NY 10010
Phone: (212)254-2100
Free: (800)431-7187 **Fax:** (212)254-2013
URL: http://www.musicsales.com
Products: Sheet music folios; Instructional videos and audio cassettes; Music reference books and biographies. **SICs:** 5192 (Books, Periodicals & Newspapers); 5099 (Durable Goods Nec). **Est:** 1930. **Emp:** 100. **Officers:** Barrie Edwards, President; John Castaldo, CFO; Steven Wilson, Dir. of Sales & Marketing, e-mail: steve-wilson@musicsales.com.

■ 3977 ■ Mustang Publishing Co.
PO Box 770426
Memphis, TN 38177
Phone: (901)684-1200
Free: (800)250-8713 **Fax:** (901)684-1256
E-mail: mustangpub@aol.com
URL: http://www.mustangpublishing.com
Products: Books. **SIC:** 5192 (Books, Periodicals & Newspapers). **Est:** 1983. **Sales:** $400,000 (2000). **Emp:** 1. **Officers:** Rollin A. Riggs, President.

■ 3978 ■ NACSCORP
528 E Lorain St.
Oberlin, OH 44074-1294
Phone: (440)775-7777
Free: (800)622-7498 **Fax:** (440)775-4769
E-mail: info@nacs.org
URL: http://www.nacs.org
Products: Software; Books, including trade and mass market titles. **SICs:** 5192 (Books, Periodicals & Newspapers); 5045 (Computers, Peripherals & Software). **Est:** 1963. **Sales:** $100,000,000 (2000). **Emp:** 150. **Officers:** Brian E. Cartier, President; Pamela S. Sedmak, Exec. VP & COO; Michelle Markel, VP of Human Resources, e-mail: mmarkel@nacs.org; Frank Sulen, VP & CFO.

■ 3979 ■ Najarian Music Company Inc.
269 Lexington St.
Waltham, MA 02452
Phone: (781)899-2200 **Fax:** (781)899-0838
Products: Sheet music; Music books. **SICs:** 5192 (Books, Periodicals & Newspapers); 5199 (Nondurable Goods Nec). **Est:** 1980. **Officers:** Robert Najarian, President.

■ 3980 ■ Nanny Goat Productions
PO Box 845
Laguna Beach, CA 92652
Phone: (714)494-7930
Products: Books. **SIC:** 5192 (Books, Periodicals & Newspapers). **Est:** 1972.

■ 3981 ■ Napsac Reproductions
Rte. 4, Box 646
Marble Hill, MO 63764
Phone: (573)238-4273 **Fax:** (573)238-2010
E-mail: napsac@clas.net
Products: Books. **SIC:** 5192 (Books, Periodicals & Newspapers). **Est:** 1976. **Sales:** $100,000 (2000). **Emp:** 3.

■ 3982 ■ Nataraj Books
7073 Brookfield Plz.
Springfield, VA 22150
Phone: (703)455-4996 **Fax:** (703)912-9052
E-mail: nataraj@erols.com
URL: http://www.natarajbooks.com
Products: Books. **SIC:** 5192 (Books, Periodicals & Newspapers). **Est:** 1983. **Sales:** $400,000 (2000). **Emp:** 4. **Officers:** Vinnie Mahajan; Renu Mahajan.

■ 3983 ■ National Association of College Stores Inc.
528 E Lorain St.
Oberlin, OH 44074-1298
Phone: (440)775-7777
Free: (800)622-7498 **Fax:** (440)775-4769
Products: Educational books and software. **SICs:** 5192 (Books, Periodicals & Newspapers); 5045 (Computers, Peripherals & Software). **Sales:** $85,000,000 (2000). **Emp:** 150. **Officers:** Brian Cartier, CEO; Frank Sulen, Controller.

■ 3984 ■ National Book Network Inc.
4720 Boston Way
Lanham, MD 20706-4310
Phone: (301)459-3366
Free: (800)462-6420 **Fax:** (301)459-1705
E-mail: custserv@nbnbooks.com
URL: http://www.nbnbooks.com
Products: Books; Prerecorded audio tapes. **SICs:** 5192 (Books, Periodicals & Newspapers); 5099 (Durable Goods Nec). **Est:** 1986. **Sales:** $50,000,000 (2000). **Emp:** 350. **Officers:** James E. Lyons, President; Chip Franzak Jr., CFO; Irv Myers, COO; Richard Freese, VP of Marketing & Sales; Marianne Bohr, VP of Marketing, e-mail: mbohr@nbnbooks.com; Michael Sullivan, VP of Sales; Jen Linck, Contact. **Alternate Name:** NBN.

■ 3985 ■ National Braille Press Inc.
88 St. Stephen St.
Boston, MA 02115
Phone: (617)266-6160
Free: (800)548-7323 **Fax:** (617)437-0456
URL: http://www.nbp.org
Products: Braille books and magazines. **SIC:** 5192 (Books, Periodicals & Newspapers). **Est:** 1927. **Sales:** $2,000,000 (2000). **Emp:** 32. **Officers:** William M. Raeder, Exec. Dir.; Diane Croft, Sales/Marketing Contact, e-mail: dcroft@nbp.org; Joanne Griffis, Customer Service Contact, e-mail: orders@nbp.org.

■ 3986 ■ National Learning Corp.
212 Michael Dr.
Syosset, NY 11791
Phone: (516)921-8888
Free: (800)645-6337 **Fax:** (516)921-8743
E-mail: passbooks@aol.com
URL: http://www.passbooks.com
Products: Books. **SIC:** 5192 (Books, Periodicals & Newspapers). **Est:** 1967. **Officers:** Michael P. Rudman, President.

■ 3987 ■ Naturegraph Publishers Inc.
PO Box 1047
Happy Camp, CA 96039
Phone: (530)493-5353
Free: (800)390-5353 **Fax:** (530)493-5240
E-mail: nature@sisqtel.net
URL: http://www.naturegraph.com
Products: Natural history and Native American culture books. **SIC:** 5192 (Books, Periodicals & Newspapers). **Est:** 1946. **Sales:** $290,000 (1999). **Emp:** 5. **Officers:** Barbara Brown, President; Sandy Condon, Sales/Marketing Contact; Martha Garcia, Customer Service Contact.

■ 3988 ■ NavPress
7899 Lexington Dr.
Colorado Springs, CO 80920
Phone: (719)548-9222
Free: (800)366-7788 **Fax:** (719)260-7223
Products: Religious literature. **SIC:** 5192 (Books, Periodicals & Newspapers).

■ 3989 ■ Nazarene Publishing House
PO Box 419527
Kansas City, MO 64141
Phones: (816)931-1900 (816)753-4071
Free: (800)877-0700 **Fax:** (816)753-4071
E-mail: nphdirect@nph.com
URL: http://www.nphdirect.com
Products: Religious books. **SIC:** 5192 (Books, Periodicals & Newspapers). **Est:** 1912. **Sales:** $18,000,000 (2000). **Emp:** 280. **Officers:** C. Hardy Weathers, President.

■ 3990 ■ **NEA Professional Library**
PO Box 2035
Annapolis Junction, MD 20701
Free: (800)229-4200 **Fax:** (301)206-9789
E-mail: neapl@pmds.com
URL: http://www.nea.org/books
Products: Research-based resource materials for K-12 classroom teachers and paraprofessionals. **SIC:** 5192 (Books, Periodicals & Newspapers). **Sales:** $1,500,000 (2000).

■ 3991 ■ **Nebraska Book Company Inc.**
PO Box 80529
Lincoln, NE 68501
Phone: (402)421-7300 **Fax:** (402)421-0507
Products: Textbooks; School supplies. **SICs:** 5192 (Books, Periodicals & Newspapers); 5112 (Stationery & Office Supplies). **Sales:** $160,000,000 (2000). **Emp:** 550. **Officers:** Mark Oppegard, President; Bruce Nevius, CFO.

■ 3992 ■ **Ner Tamid Book Distributors**
PO Box 10401
Riviera Beach, FL 33419
Phone: (561)686-9095
Products: Religious books, including Judaica; Children's books; Adult books. **SIC:** 5192 (Books, Periodicals & Newspapers). **Est:** 1968. **Emp:** 2. **Officers:** Herbert Wilkenfeld, Owner.

■ 3993 ■ **New Concepts Books & Tapes Distributors**
9722 Pine Lake
PO Box 55068
Houston, TX 77055
Phone: (713)465-7736
Free: (800)842-4807 **Fax:** (713)465-7106
Products: Books; Tapes audio and video recording. **SICs:** 5192 (Books, Periodicals & Newspapers); 5099 (Durable Goods Nec); 5065 (Electronic Parts & Equipment Nec). **Est:** 1981. **Sales:** $125,000 (2000). **Emp:** 3. **Officers:** Jacqueline L. Ellis, President.

■ 3994 ■ **New Jersey Book Agency**
59 Leamoor Dr.
PO Box 144
Morris Plains, NJ 07950
Phone: (973)267-7093 **Fax:** (973)292-3177
E-mail: newjbook@aol.co
Products: Special-order books. **SIC:** 5192 (Books, Periodicals & Newspapers). **Est:** 1979. **Sales:** $500,000 (2000). **Emp:** 2. **Officers:** Linton Segal; Irene Segal.

■ 3995 ■ **New Leaf Distributing Co.**
401 Thornton Rd.
Lithia Springs, GA 30122
Phone: (770)948-7845
Free: (800)326-2665 **Fax:** (770)944-2313
E-mail: newleaf@newleaf-dist.com
URL: http://www.newleaf-dist.com
Products: Books; Magazines; Recordings; Sidelines. **SIC:** 5192 (Books, Periodicals & Newspapers). **Est:** 1975. **Sales:** $25,000,000 (2000). **Emp:** 70. **Officers:** Rich Bellezza, CEO; Karen Price.

■ 3996 ■ **New Leaf Distributors Inc.**
401 Thornton Rd.
Lithia Springs, GA 30122
Phone: (770)948-7845 **Free:** (800)326-2665
Products: Books. **SIC:** 5192 (Books, Periodicals & Newspapers). **Est:** 1975.

■ 3997 ■ **New Testament Christian Press**
PO Box 1694
Media, PA 19063
Phone: (215)544-2871
Products: Religious and philosophical materials. **SIC:** 5192 (Books, Periodicals & Newspapers). **Est:** 1984.

■ 3998 ■ **Newark Newsdealers Supply Company Inc.**
CN 910
Harrison, NJ 07029
Phone: (973)482-1500
Products: Newspapers. **SIC:** 5192 (Books, Periodicals & Newspapers).

■ 3999 ■ **Newborn Enterprises Inc.**
PO Box 1713
Altoona, PA 16603
Phone: (814)944-3593
Free: (800)227-0285 **Fax:** (814)944-1881
Products: Videos; Books; Magazines; Newspapers. **SICs:** 5192 (Books, Periodicals & Newspapers); 5065 (Electronic Parts & Equipment Nec). **Est:** 1971. **Sales:** $11,000,000 (2000). **Emp:** 120. **Officers:** Barry Newborn, President.

■ 4000 ■ **The News Group, III**
1301 SW Washington St.
Peoria, IL 61602
Phone: (309)673-4549 **Fax:** (309)673-8883
Products: Magazines, Books, Childrens Books, Maps. **SIC:** 5192 (Books, Periodicals & Newspapers). **Est:** 1999. **Emp:** 14. **Officers:** Debra Wood, General Mgr.; Terry Jermac, Sales/Marketing Contact; Debra Wood, Human Resources Contact. **Former Name:** Illinois News Service.

■ 4001 ■ **The News Group - Rocky Mount**
2 Great State Ln.
Rocky Mount, NC 27803
Phone: (919)443-3124
Free: (800)582-6175 **Fax:** (919)443-0988
Products: Magazines; Paperback books; Bibles and testaments. **SIC:** 5192 (Books, Periodicals & Newspapers). **Est:** 1996. **Sales:** $4,000,000 (2000). **Emp:** 21. **Officers:** Earle E. Batt, President; Calvert L. Batt, General Mgr.

■ 4002 ■ **NEWSouth Distributors**
PO Box 61297
Jacksonville, FL 32236
Phone: (904)783-2350 **Fax:** (904)786-6026
Products: Magazines. **SIC:** 5192 (Books, Periodicals & Newspapers). **Sales:** $14,000,000 (2000). **Emp:** 60. **Officers:** Gil Brechtel, President; Timothy Self, Exec. VP; Kenneth Shukin, Manager; Joe Castaux.

■ 4003 ■ **Niagara County News Company Inc.**
70 Nicholls St.
Lockport, NY 14094-4899
Phone: (716)433-6466 **Fax:** (716)434-3667
Products: Magazines; Paperback books. **SIC:** 5192 (Books, Periodicals & Newspapers). **Officers:** Robert E. Erb, President; Robert N. Erb, Vice President.

■ 4004 ■ **Nippan Shuppan Hanbai**
1123 Dominguez St., Ste. K
Carson, CA 90746
Phone: (310)604-9701
Free: (800)562-1410 **Fax:** (310)604-1134
E-mail: nippan@np.jpn.net
URL: http://www.club.nttca.com/nippan
Products: Books. **SIC:** 5192 (Books, Periodicals & Newspapers). **Est:** 1976. **Sales:** $12,000,000 (2000). **Emp:** 40. **Officers:** T. Iwasaki, General Mgr. **Doing Business As:** Books Nippan.

■ 4005 ■ **Nolo Press/Folklaw Inc.**
950 Parker St.
Berkeley, CA 94710
Phone: (510)549-1976
Free: (800)992-6656 **Fax:** (510)548-5902
E-mail: cs@nolo.com
URL: http://www.nolo.com
Products: Legal books and software. **SICs:** 5192 (Books, Periodicals & Newspapers); 5045 (Computers, Peripherals & Software). **Est:** 1971. **Emp:** 75. **Officers:** Ralph Warner, Publisher; Linda Hanger, President.

■ 4006 ■ **Nor-Del Productions Ltd.**
PO Box 93262
Rochester, NY 14692
Phone: (716)292-5550
Free: (800)581-2665 **Fax:** (716)292-6513
Products: Books; Philatelist stamps. **SICs:** 5192 (Books, Periodicals & Newspapers); 5092 (Toys & Hobby Goods & Supplies). **Est:** 1976.

■ 4007 ■ **North American Book Dealers Exchange**
PO Box 606
Cottage Grove, OR 97424
Phone: (541)942-7455 **Fax:** (541)258-2625
E-mail: nabe@bookmarketingprofits.com
URL: http://www.bookmarketingprofits.com
Products: Books. **SIC:** 5192 (Books, Periodicals & Newspapers). **Est:** 1980. **Officers:** Al Galasso, Exec. Dir.

■ 4008 ■ **North Central Book Distributors**
N57 W13636 Carmen Ave.
Menomonee Falls, WI 53051
Phone: (262)781-3299
Free: (800)966-3299 **Fax:** (262)781-4432
E-mail: NBCD@EXECPC.com
Products: Books. **SIC:** 5192 (Books, Periodicals & Newspapers). **Est:** 1969. **Officers:** Thomas J. Ziegler, President.

■ 4009 ■ **Northland Publishing**
PO Box 1389
Flagstaff, AZ 86002
Phone: (520)774-5251
Free: (800)346-3257 **Fax:** (520)774-0592
E-mail: info@northlandpub.com
URL: http://www.northlandpub.com
Products: Books. **SIC:** 5192 (Books, Periodicals & Newspapers). **Est:** 1958. **Emp:** 18. **Officers:** David Jenney, President; Rick Savitz, Vice President; Jen Andrews, Marketing, e-mail: jandrews@northlandpub.com; Karen Whitten, Customer Service, e-mail: whitten@northlandpub.com; Kay McConagha, Human Resources Contact. **Former Name:** Northland Press.

■ 4010 ■ **Northland Publishing Company**
PO Box 1389
Flagstaff, AZ 86002
Phone: (520)774-5251 **Fax:** (520)774-0592
Products: Publishes Southwestern books. **SIC:** 5192 (Books, Periodicals & Newspapers).

■ 4011 ■ **Novelty Advertising Co.**
1148 Walnut St.
Coshocton, OH 43812
Phone: (740)622-3113
Free: (800)848-9163 **Fax:** (740)622-5286
E-mail: sales@noveltyadv.com
Products: Calendars. **SIC:** 5199 (Nondurable Goods Nec). **Est:** 1903. **Sales:** $6,000,000 (2000). **Emp:** 70. **Officers:** R. Coffman, President.

■ 4012 ■ **NTC/Contemporary Publishing Group**
4255 W Touhy Ave.
Lincolnwood, IL 60646-7975
Phone: (847)679-5500
Free: (800)323-4900 **Fax:** (847)679-2494
Products: Textbooks, including teachers' editions; Foreign language books; Books. **SIC:** 5192 (Books, Periodicals & Newspapers). **Est:** 1962.

■ 4013 ■ **Nystrom Co.**
3333 Elston Ave.
Chicago, IL 60618
Phone: (773)463-1144
Free: (800)621-8086 **Fax:** (773)463-0515
Products: Educational multimedia lesson guides. **SIC:** 5199 (Nondurable Goods Nec). **Sales:** $24,700,000 (2000). **Emp:** 200. **Officers:** James Cerza, President; Paul Ferino, Controller.

■ 4014 ■ **Oberlin College Press-Field Magazine-Field Translation Series-Field Poetry Series-Field Editions**
Oberlin College
10 N Professor St.
Oberlin, OH 44074
Phone: (440)775-8408 **Fax:** (440)775-8124
E-mail: oc.press@oberlin.edu
URL: http://www.oberlin.edu/~ocpress
Products: Books; Magazine. **SIC:** 5192 (Books, Periodicals & Newspapers). **Est:** 1969. **Emp:** 2. **Officers:** Linda Slocum, Business Mgr.; David Walker, Editor; David P. Young, Editor; Pamela Alexander, Editor; Martha Collins, Editor; Alberta Turner, Editor.

■ **4015** ■ **Ocean Springs Distributors Inc.**
14369 Oneal Rd.
Gulfport, MS 39503
Phone: (228)832-6685
Products: Post cards. **SIC:** 5192 (Books, Periodicals & Newspapers).

■ **4016** ■ **Oceana Publications Inc.**
75 Main St.
Dobbs Ferry, NY 10522
Phone: (914)693-8100
Free: (800)831-0758   **Fax:** (914)693-0402
E-mail: info@oceanalaw.com
URL: http://www.oceanalaw.com
Products: International legal publications. **SIC:** 5192 (Books, Periodicals & Newspapers). **Est:** 1946. **Emp:** 52. **Officers:** David R. Cohen, President; Lois Cohen, Vice President; Susan Demaio, Sr. VP and General Counsel; Stephen Nussbaum, Sr. VP & CFO; James Newman, VP of Operations; Louise Ciero, e-mail: VP of Admin. Svcs.; Bob Zappa, VP of Marketing & Sales.

■ **4017** ■ **Old Saltbox Publishing House Inc.**
40 Felt St.
Salem, MA 01970
Phones: (978)741-3458   (978)741-8980
Fax: (978)744-1378
Products: History and mystery books, including fact and fiction about the North East. **SIC:** 5192 (Books, Periodicals & Newspapers). **Est:** 1988. **Sales:** $120,000 (2000). **Emp:** 2. **Officers:** Robert E. Cahill, Owner & Sec. & Treas.; James G. Cahill, Director.

■ **4018** ■ **Oliver Worldclass Labs**
44834 S Grimmer Blvd.
Fremont, CA 94538
Phone: (707)747-1537
Free: (800)877-6720   **Fax:** (707)747-5681
E-mail: mail@oliverlabs.com
URL: http://www.oliverlabs.com
Products: Books; Educational technology equipment, including furniture and interactive white boards. **SIC:** 5192 (Books, Periodicals & Newspapers). **Est:** 1974. **Sales:** $1,000,000 (2000). **Emp:** 4. **Officers:** Randy Oliver, President.

■ **4019** ■ **Omega Publications**
PO Box 4130
Medford, OR 97501
Phone: (541)826-4512
Free: (800)343-1111   **Fax:** (541)826-1023
E-mail: omega@the-cutting-edge.org
URL: http://www.the-cutting-edge.org
Products: Christian books, tapes, videos, music, and teaching materials. **SIC:** 5192 (Books, Periodicals & Newspapers). **Est:** 1980. **Officers:** Jeani McKeever-Harrouon, President, e-mail: jeani@the-cutting-edge.org; Jack Harrouon, Vice President, e-mail: harrounz@the-cutting-edge.org.

■ **4020** ■ **Omega Publications, Inc.**
256 Darrow Rd.
New Lebanon, NY 12125
Phone: (518)794-8181
Free: (888)443-7107   **Fax:** (518)794-8187
E-mail: omegapub@wisdomschild.com
URL: http://www.omegapub.com
Products: Books and music. **SICs:** 5192 (Books, Periodicals & Newspapers); 5099 (Durable Goods Nec). **Est:** 1977. **Emp:** 4.

■ **4021** ■ **Omnibooks**
456 Vista Del Mar
Aptos, CA 95003-4832
Phone: (408)688-4098
Free: (800)626-6671   **Fax:** (408)685-2236
Products: Books. **SIC:** 5192 (Books, Periodicals & Newspapers). **Est:** 1974.

■ **4022** ■ **Omnigraphics Inc.**
615 Griswold
Detroit, MI 48226
Phone: (313)961-1340
Free: (800)234-1340   **Fax:** (313)961-1383
E-mail: info@omnigraphics.com
URL: http://www.omnigraphics.com
Products: Books. **SIC:** 5192 (Books, Periodicals & Newspapers). **Est:** 1985. **Sales:** $5,000,000 (2000). **Emp:** 45. **Officers:** Frederick G. Ruffner Jr., President;

Tom Murphy, VP of Finance & Controller; Laurie L. Harris, VP of Editorial; Peter E. Ruffner, Sr. VP; Jane Steele, Sales/Marketing Contact, e-mail: jjrs@sprynet.com; Carolyn Stockdale, Customer Service Contact, e-mail: cstockdale@omnigraphics.com.

■ **4023** ■ **Opportunities for Learning, Inc.**
941 Hickory Ln.
PO Box 8103
Mansfield, OH 44901-8103
Phone: (419)589-1700
Free: (800)243-7116   **Fax:** (419)589-1522
Products: Books, software, videos, and multimedia materials for grades six through twelve. **SICs:** 5192 (Books, Periodicals & Newspapers); 5045 (Computers, Peripherals & Software); 5099 (Durable Goods Nec). **Est:** 1972.

■ **4024** ■ **Organ Literature Foundation**
45 Norfolk Rd.
Braintree, MA 02184-5918
Phone: (781)848-1388   **Fax:** (781)848-7655
E-mail: organlitfnd@juno.com
Products: Sheet music; Books; Video tapes; Prerecorded audio tapes. **SICs:** 5192 (Books, Periodicals & Newspapers); 5199 (Nondurable Goods Nec); 5065 (Electronic Parts & Equipment Nec). **Est:** 1950. **Officers:** Henry Baker, President.

■ **4025** ■ **Orient Book Distributors**
PO Box 100
Livingston, NJ 07039
Phone: (973)746-3874   **Fax:** (973)783-4369
Products: Books from India. **SIC:** 5192 (Books, Periodicals & Newspapers). **Est:** 1977.

■ **4026** ■ **O.S.S. Publishing Co.**
517 S Main St.
Lima, OH 45802
Phone: (419)227-1818
Free: (800)537-1030   **Fax:** (419)228-9184
Products: Books and other printed materials. **SIC:** 5192 (Books, Periodicals & Newspapers). **Sales:** $4,000,000 (2000). **Emp:** 57.

■ **4027** ■ **Other Publishers**
PO Box 35
Barrytown, NY 12507
Phone: (914)758-5840   **Fax:** (914)758-8163
E-mail: publishers@stationhill.org
URL: http://www.stationhill.org
Products: Books. **SIC:** 5192 (Books, Periodicals & Newspapers). **Est:** 1980. **Sales:** $30,000 (1999). **Emp:** 5. **Officers:** George Quaska, Publisher.

■ **4028** ■ **Overland West Press**
PO Box 17507
Portland, OR 97217
Phone: (503)289-4834
Products: Books about the American West, past and present. **SIC:** 5192 (Books, Periodicals & Newspapers). **Est:** 1963.

■ **4029** ■ **Jerome S. Ozer**
340 Tenafly Rd.
Englewood, NJ 07631
Phone: (201)567-7040   **Fax:** (201)567-8134
Products: Books for college classes, including film and ethnic studies. **SIC:** 5192 (Books, Periodicals & Newspapers). **Est:** 1970. **Emp:** 3.

■ **4030** ■ **Pacific Books**
2573 Treasure Dr.
Santa Barbara, CA 93105
Phone: (805)687-8340   **Fax:** (805)687-2514
Products: Local interest books on coastal California. **SIC:** 5192 (Books, Periodicals & Newspapers). **Est:** 1987.

■ **4031** ■ **Pacific Coca-Cola Tacoma**
3333 S 38th St.
Tacoma, WA 98409
Phone: (253)474-9567
Products: Soft drinks. **SIC:** 5149 (Groceries & Related Products Nec). **Sales:** $6,000,000 (2000). **Emp:** 100. **Officers:** Mike Deutsch, General Mgr.

■ **4032** ■ **Pacific Mountain Book Associates**
3882 S Newport Way
Denver, CO 80237
Phone: (303)758-0494   **Fax:** (303)758-0494
Products: Books. **SIC:** 5192 (Books, Periodicals & Newspapers). **Est:** 1986.

■ **4033** ■ **Pacific Northwest Books Co.**
PO Box 314
Medford, OR 97501
Phones: (541)664-5205   (541)664-5205
Fax: (541)664-9131
URL: http://www.pnwbooks.com
Products: Nonfiction books specific to the Pacific Northwest, Oregon Trail, and World War II. **SIC:** 5192 (Books, Periodicals & Newspapers). **Est:** 1973. **Emp:** 2. **Officers:** Bert Webber, Owner, e-mail: bert@pnwbooks.com.

■ **4034** ■ **Pacific Terminals Ltd.**
PO Box 81126
Seattle, WA 98108
Phone: (206)762-2933
Products: Newsprint. **SIC:** 5111 (Printing & Writing Paper).

■ **4035** ■ **Pacific Trade Group**
94-527 Puahi St.
Waipahu, HI 96797
Phone: (808)671-6735
Products: Hawaiian books. **SIC:** 5192 (Books, Periodicals & Newspapers). **Est:** 1976.

■ **4036** ■ **Paladin Press**
PO Box 1307
Boulder, CO 80306
Phone: (303)443-7250
Free: (800)392-2400   **Fax:** (303)442-8741
E-mail: service@paladin-press.com
URL: http://www.paladin-press.com
Products: Books; Videos. **SICs:** 5192 (Books, Periodicals & Newspapers); 5065 (Electronic Parts & Equipment Nec). **Est:** 1970. **Emp:** 30. **Officers:** Peder Lund, Tina Mills, Sales/Marketing Contact, e-mail: tina@paladin-press.com; Paula Garber, Customer Service Contact.

■ **4037** ■ **Palmer News Inc.**
PO Box 1400
Topeka, KS 66601
Phone: (785)234-6679
Products: Magazines. **SIC:** 5192 (Books, Periodicals & Newspapers). **Est:** 1937. **Sales:** $34,000,000 (2000). **Emp:** 110. **Officers:** William H. Palmer, Owner; Terry Nolte, Comptroller; John Franznick, Dir. of Marketing.

■ **4038** ■ **Paperbacks for Educators**
426 W Front St.
Washington, MO 63090-2103
Phone: (636)239-1999
Free: (800)227-2591   **Fax:** (636)239-4515
E-mail: paperbacks@usmo.com
URL: http://www.any-book-in-print.com
Products: Books. **SIC:** 5192 (Books, Periodicals & Newspapers). **Est:** 1978. **Sales:** $1,250,000 (2000). **Emp:** 11. **Officers:** David L. Craig, President, e-mail: davecraig@usmo.com.

■ **4039** ■ **Paradies and Co.**
5950 Fulton Industrial
Atlanta, GA 30336
Phones: (404)530-2300   (912)966-5392
Fax: (404)696-6818
Products: Newspapers; Magazines; Clothes; Candy; Gifts. **SICs:** 5192 (Books, Periodicals & Newspapers); 5199 (Nondurable Goods Nec); 5145 (Confectionery); 5136 (Men's/Boys' Clothing); 5137 (Women's/Children's Clothing). **Sales:** $60,000,000 (2000). **Emp:** 200. **Officers:** Jack R. McCaffrey, President; Mickey Campbell, Vice President.

■ **4040** ■ **Parks & History Association, Inc.**
PO Box 40060
Washington, DC 20016
Phone: (202)472-3083   **Fax:** (202)472-3422
Products: Books. **SIC:** 5192 (Books, Periodicals & Newspapers). **Est:** 1968.

■ 4041 ■ Partners Book Distributing Inc.
2325 Jarco Dr.
Holt, MI 48842
Phone: (517)694-3205
Products: Books. **SIC:** 5192 (Books, Periodicals & Newspapers).

■ 4042 ■ Passeggiata Press, Inc.
222 W B St.
Pueblo, CO 81003-3404
Phone: (719)544-1038 **Fax:** (719)544-7911
E-mail: passeggiata@compuserve.com
Products: Works of creative literature and literary scholarship from the non-Western world. **SIC:** 5192 (Books, Periodicals & Newspapers). **Est:** 1973. **Emp:** 2. **Officers:** D.E. Herdeck; Theresa Santillanes, Customer Service Contact. **Former Name:** Three Continents Press.

■ 4043 ■ Path Press Inc.
PO Box 2925
Chicago, IL 60690-2925
Phone: (847)424-1620
Free: (800)548-2600 **Fax:** (847)424-1623
E-mail: PathPressInc@aol.com
Products: Multicultural studies books; Fiction books; Books; Tapes audio and video recording; Calendars. **SICs:** 5192 (Books, Periodicals & Newspapers); 5099 (Durable Goods Nec); 5065 (Electronic Parts & Equipment Nec). **Est:** 1982. **Sales:** $250,000 (2000). **Emp:** 5. **Officers:** Bennett J. Johnson, President; Ethelyn J. Baker, Secretary.

■ 4044 ■ Pathfinder Press
410 West St.
New York, NY 10014
Phone: (212)741-0690 **Fax:** (212)727-0150
E-mail: pathfinderpress@compuserve.com
Products: Non-fiction books; Paperback books; Edition, library, and other hardcover bookbinding. **SIC:** 5192 (Books, Periodicals & Newspapers). **Est:** 1970.

■ 4045 ■ Pathway Book Service
4 White Brook Rd.
Gilsum, NH 03448
Phone: (603)357-0236
Free: (800)345-6665 **Fax:** (603)357-2073
E-mail: pbs@pathwaybook.com
URL: http://www.pathwaybook.com
Products: Books; Nonprint materials. **SIC:** 5192 (Books, Periodicals & Newspapers). **Est:** 1976. **Emp:** 15. **Officers:** Ernest N. Peter. **Alternate Name:** Pem Press.

■ 4046 ■ G. Paulsen Company Inc.
27 Sheep Davis Rd.
Pembroke, NH 03275
Phone: (603)225-9787 **Fax:** (603)229-1712
E-mail: gpcomags@aol.com
Products: Books; Magazines; Newspapers. **SIC:** 5192 (Books, Periodicals & Newspapers). **Est:** 1961.

■ 4047 ■ P.B.D. Worldwide Fulfillment Services
1650 Bluegrass Lakes Pkwy.
Alpharetta, GA 30004
Phone: (770)442-8633 **Fax:** (770)442-9742
E-mail: pbdinfo@pbd.com
URL: http://www.pbd.com
Products: Catalog fulfillment. **SIC:** 5192 (Books, Periodicals & Newspapers). **Est:** 1976. **Sales:** $40,000,000 (1999). **Emp:** 125. **Officers:** James Docleter, CEO; Scott Docleter, COO & President. **Former Name:** P.B.D. Inc.

■ 4048 ■ P.D. Music Headquarters Inc.
PO Box 252, Village Sta.
New York, NY 10014
Phone: (212)242-5322
Products: Music publications. **SIC:** 5192 (Books, Periodicals & Newspapers). **Est:** 1987.

■ 4049 ■ Pelican Publishing Company Inc.
PO Box 3110
Gretna, LA 70054
Phone: (504)368-1175
Free: (800)843-1724 **Fax:** (504)368-1195
E-mail: sales@pelicanpub.com
URL: http://www.e-pelican.com
Products: Books. **SIC:** 5192 (Books, Periodicals & Newspapers). **Est:** 1926. **Emp:** 30. **Officers:** Joseph Billingsley, Sales/Marketing Contact, e-mail: sales@pelicanpub.com.

■ 4050 ■ Penfield Press
215 Brown St.
Iowa City, IA 52245
Phone: (319)337-9998
Free: (800)728-9998 **Fax:** (319)351-6846
E-mail: penfield@penfield-press.com
URL: http://www.penfield-press.com
Products: Books from and about Scandinavia, Germany, Ireland, Scotland, Eastern Europe, and The Netherlands. **SIC:** 5192 (Books, Periodicals & Newspapers). **Est:** 1979. **Emp:** 1. **Officers:** Joan L. Liffring-Zug-Bourret, President; John Johnson, Sales/Marketing Contact; Connie Schnoebelen, Sales/Marketing Contact.

■ 4051 ■ Pennsylvania State University Press
University Support Bldg. 1, Ste. C
University Park, PA 16802-1003
Phone: (814)865-1327
Free: (800)326-9180 **Fax:** (814)863-1408
URL: http://www.psu.edu/psupress
Products: Books. **SIC:** 5192 (Books, Periodicals & Newspapers). **Est:** 1956. **Sales:** $2,000,000 (2000). **Emp:** 18. **Officers:** Sanford G. Thatcher, Director.

■ 4052 ■ PennWell Publishing Co.
PO Box 1260
Tulsa, OK 74101
Phone: (918)835-3161 **Fax:** (918)831-9497
Products: Magazines, books and maps. **SIC:** 5192 (Books, Periodicals & Newspapers). **Sales:** $160,000,000 (2000). **Emp:** 1,000. **Officers:** Joseph Wolking, CEO; John Maney, VP of Finance.

■ 4053 ■ Pentecostal Publishing House
8855 Dunn Rd.
Hazelwood, MO 63042
Phone: (314)837-7300 **Fax:** (314)837-6574
E-mail: pphpublish@upci.org
URL: http://www.upci.org.com/pph
Products: Religious texts. **SIC:** 5192 (Books, Periodicals & Newspapers). **Est:** 1945. **Sales:** $8,000,000 (2000). **Emp:** 60. **Officers:** Marvin Curry, Manager, e-mail: mcurry@upci.org; Jerry Mcnall, Purchasing Agent, e-mail: jmcnall@upci.org; Betty Whayne, Credit Manager, e-mail: bwhayne@upci.org.

■ 4054 ■ Pepsi-Cola Bottling Company of La Crosse
PO Box 998
La Crosse, WI 54602-0998
Phone: (608)785-0450
Products: Bottled and canned soft drinks. **SIC:** 5149 (Groceries & Related Products Nec). **Officers:** Norman Gillette, President.

■ 4055 ■ Pepsi-Cola of Washington, D.C. L.P.
3900 Penn Belt Pl.
Forestville, MD 20747
Phone: (301)420-1166
Products: Soft drinks. **SIC:** 5149 (Groceries & Related Products Nec). **Sales:** $57,000,000 (1994). **Emp:** 160. **Officers:** Earl Graves, CEO & Chairman of the Board.

■ 4056 ■ Perin Press
226 E College Ave.
Appleton, WI 54911
Phone: (920)735-6223 **Fax:** (920)735-6227
Products: Regional interest books. **SIC:** 5192 (Books, Periodicals & Newspapers). **Est:** 1964. **Sales:** $50,000 (2000). **Emp:** 2. **Officers:** John Wiley, President.

■ 4057 ■ Periodical Services
3231 F Ave.
Gulfport, MS 39507
Phone: (228)864-6953
Products: Magazines. **SIC:** 5192 (Books, Periodicals & Newspapers).

■ 4058 ■ Perma-Bound Books
E Vandalia Rd.
Jacksonville, IL 62650
Phone: (217)243-5451
Free: (800)637-6581 **Fax:** 800-551-1169
Products: Books. **SIC:** 5192 (Books, Periodicals & Newspapers). **Est:** 1961.

■ 4059 ■ Persona Press
PO Box 14022
San Francisco, CA 94114-0022
Phone: (415)775-6143 **Fax:** (707)922-1236
E-mail: personapro@aol.com
URL: http://www.members.aol.com/personapro
Products: Fiction books. **SIC:** 5192 (Books, Periodicals & Newspapers). **Est:** 1978. **Officers:** N.A. Diaman, Publisher.

■ 4060 ■ Albert J. Phiebig Inc., Services to Libraries
PO Box 352
White Plains, NY 10602-0352
Phone: (914)948-0138 **Fax:** (914)948-0784
E-mail: ajpeincabaa@aoal.com
Products: Foreign books and periodicals. **SIC:** 5192 (Books, Periodicals & Newspapers). **Est:** 1947. **Emp:** 4. **Officers:** Albert J. Phiebig, President.

■ 4061 ■ Philosophical Research Society, Inc.
3910 Los Feliz Blvd.
Los Angeles, CA 90027
Phone: (213)663-2167
Free: (800)548-4062 **Fax:** (213)663-9443
Products: Books. **SIC:** 5192 (Books, Periodicals & Newspapers).

■ 4062 ■ Phoenix Mapping Service
2626 W Glenrose Ave.
Phoenix, AZ 85017
Phone: (602)433-0616
Free: (888)622-2786 **Fax:** (602)433-0695
URL: http://www.maps4u.com
Products: Books and maps on southwestern topics. **SIC:** 5192 (Books, Periodicals & Newspapers). **Est:** 1952. **Sales:** $1,200,000 (1999). **Emp:** 7. **Officers:** Robert L. Molner, CEO; James L. Willinger, Vice President, e-mail: james@maps4u.com; Michael Bayne, Buyer. **Former Name:** Many Feathers Books & Maps.

■ 4063 ■ Pickering Publications
205 Crocus Ln.
Asheville, NC 28803-3379
Phone: (828)684-7353
E-mail: jcyfy@aol.com
Products: Books. **SIC:** 5192 (Books, Periodicals & Newspapers). **Est:** 1986. **Officers:** J. H. Pickering, Owner.

■ 4064 ■ Pictorial Histories Publishing Co.
713 S 3rd W
Missoula, MT 59801
Phone: (406)549-8488
Free: (888)763-8350 **Fax:** (406)728-9280
E-mail: phpc@montana.com
URL: http://www.montana.com/phpc/stancvr.htm
Products: Books on military history, aviation, and medicine; Cassette tapes; Videocassettes. **SICs:** 5192 (Books, Periodicals & Newspapers); 5099 (Durable Goods Nec); 5065 (Electronic Parts & Equipment Nec). **Est:** 1976. **Sales:** $700,000 (2000). **Emp:** 3. **Officers:** Stan Cohen, Owner.

■ 4065 ■ Pilgrim Way Press
350 Pearl St., No. 1108
Eugene, OR 97401
Phone: (503)686-9594 **Free:** (888)546-3634
Products: Nonfiction books. **SIC:** 5192 (Books, Periodicals & Newspapers). **Est:** 1990. **Officers:** Ruth Barton Davis, Owner.

■ **4066** ■ **Plains Distribution Service, Inc.**
PO Box 3112
Fargo, ND 58108
Products: Books. **SIC:** 5192 (Books, Periodicals & Newspapers).

■ **4067** ■ **Playboy Entertainment Group Inc.**
9242 Beverly Blvd.
Beverly Hills, CA 90210
Phone: (310)246-4000
Products: Magazines and Videos. **SICs:** 5065 (Electronic Parts & Equipment Nec); 5192 (Books, Periodicals & Newspapers). **Sales:** $68,000,000 (2000). **Emp:** 140. **Officers:** Tony Lynn, President; Cathy Zulfer, Controller.

■ **4068** ■ **Plough Publishing House**
Spring Valley Bruderhof
Rte. 381 N
Farmington, PA 15437-9506
Phone: (724)329-1100
Free: (800)521-8011 **Fax:** (724)329-0914
Products: Religious books; Prerecorded audio tapes; Compact discs. **SIC:** 5192 (Books, Periodicals & Newspapers). **Est:** 1963. **Sales:** $1,000,000 (2000). **Emp:** 30.

■ **4069** ■ **PMG International Inc.**
1011 N Frio St.
San Antonio, TX 78207
Phone: (210)226-6820 **Fax:** (210)226-5716
Products: Magazines and books. **SIC:** 5192 (Books, Periodicals & Newspapers). **Est:** 1930. **Sales:** $61,000,000 (1999). **Emp:** 250. **Officers:** Jack Cavaleri, President; Lorrie Leach, CFO; Richard Romo, Dir. of Marketing; William Salomon, Exec. VP of Systems; Steve Parma, VP of Human Resources.

■ **4070** ■ **Pocahontas Press Inc.**
PO Box F
Blacksburg, VA 24063-1020
Phone: (540)951-0467
Free: (800)446-0467 **Fax:** (540)961-2847
E-mail: pocahontas.press@vt.edu
Products: Books, including history, biography, memoirs, poetry, natural history, and textbooks. **SIC:** 5192 (Books, Periodicals & Newspapers). **Est:** 1984. **Sales:** $82,000 (2000). **Emp:** 2. **Officers:** Mary C. Holliman, President, e-mail: mchollim@vt.edu; Judy Elliott, Sales/Marketing Contact; David Bruce Wallace, Customer Service Contact; Mary C. Holliman, Human Resources Contact, e-mail: mchollim@vt.edu. **Alternate Name:** Manuscript Memories.

■ **4071** ■ **Polycrystal Book Service**
PO Box 3439
Dayton, OH 45401
Phone: (937)233-9070 **Fax:** (937)223-9070
E-mail: polybook@dnaco.net
Products: Science books. **SIC:** 5192 (Books, Periodicals & Newspapers). **Est:** 1947.

■ **4072** ■ **Pomona Valley News Agency Inc.**
10736 Fremont Ave.
Ontario, CA 91762-3909
Phone: (909)591-3885 **Fax:** (909)627-1319
Products: Books. **SIC:** 5192 (Books, Periodicals & Newspapers). **Est:** 1951. **Emp:** 6. **Officers:** Jack Gingold, President.

■ **4073** ■ **Portland News Co.**
10 Southgate Rd.
Scarborough, ME 04074
Phone: (207)883-1300
Products: Newspapers. **SIC:** 5192 (Books, Periodicals & Newspapers).

■ **4074** ■ **Portland State University, School of Extended Studies, Continuing Education Press**
PO Box 1394
Portland, OR 97207-1394
Phone: (503)725-4891
Free: (800)547-8887 **Fax:** (503)725-4840
E-mail: press@pdx.edu
URL: http://www.extended.pdx.edu/press
Products: Educational materials. **SIC:** 5192 (Books, Periodicals & Newspapers). **Est:** 1965. **Emp:** 4.

Officers: Alba M. Scholz, Manager, e-mail: scholza@pdx.edu.

■ **4075** ■ **Potomac Adventist Book Center**
12004 Cherry Hill Rd.
Silver Spring, MD 20904-1985
Phone: (301)572-0700
Free: (800)325-8492 **Fax:** (301)572-7700
E-mail: orders@potomacabc.com
Products: Religious books and Bibles; Religious videos; Health food. **SICs:** 5192 (Books, Periodicals & Newspapers); 5149 (Groceries & Related Products Nec); 5065 (Electronic Parts & Equipment Nec). **Est:** 1904. **Sales:** $7,800,000 (2000). **Emp:** 54. **Officers:** J.C. Kinder, e-mail: jckinder@potomacabc.com.

■ **4076** ■ **Potomac Adventist Book Center**
8400 Carroll Ave.
Takoma Park, MD 20912
Phone: (301)439-3547
Free: (800)325-8492 **Fax:** (301)439-1758
Products: Books and other printed materials. **SIC:** 5192 (Books, Periodicals & Newspapers). **Sales:** $7,100,000 (2000). **Emp:** 44.

■ **4077** ■ **Power Sewing**
95 5th Ave.
San Francisco, CA 94118
Phone: (415)386-0440
Free: (877)667-1196 **Fax:** (415)386-0441
E-mail: powersew@aol.com
URL: http://www.sandrabetzina.com
Products: Sewing books and videos. **SIC:** 5192 (Books, Periodicals & Newspapers). **Est:** 1981. **Sales:** $200,000 (2000). **Emp:** 1. **Officers:** Sandra Betzina.

■ **4078** ■ **Practical Cookbooks**
145 Malcolm Ave. SE
Minneapolis, MN 55414
Phone: (612)378-9697
E-mail: jon.and.lois.willand@worldnet.att.net
Products: Cook books. **SIC:** 5192 (Books, Periodicals & Newspapers). **Est:** 1985. **Sales:** $7,000 (2000). **Emp:** 1. **Officers:** Lois Carlson Willand, President, e-mail: jon.and.lois.willand@worldnet.att.net.

■ **4079** ■ **Emery Pratt Co.**
1966 W Main St.
Owosso, MI 48867-1397
Phone: (517)723-5291
Free: (800)248-3887 **Fax:** (517)723-4677
E-mail: office@emery-pratt.com
URL: http://www.emery-pratt.com
Products: Books. **SIC:** 5192 (Books, Periodicals & Newspapers). **Est:** 1873. **Sales:** $12,000,000 (2000). **Emp:** 50. **Officers:** Maurice B. Shattuck, President; Avery Weaver; Maurice B. Shattuck Jr., Marketing Mgr.

■ **4080** ■ **Presbyterian & Reformed Publishing Co.**
1102 Marble Hill Rd.
PO Box 817
Phillipsburg, NJ 08865
Phone: (908)454-0505 **Fax:** (908)859-2390
URL: http://www.prpboks.com
Products: Religious books. **SIC:** 5192 (Books, Periodicals & Newspapers). **Emp:** 10. **Officers:** Karen Gray, Marketing & Sales Mgr. **Alternate Name:** P&R Publishing.

■ **4081** ■ **Presidio Press Inc.**
505B San Marin Dr.
Novato, CA 94945-1340
Phone: (415)898-1081
Free: (800)966-5179 **Fax:** (415)898-1340
Products: Military books. **SIC:** 5192 (Books, Periodicals & Newspapers). **Est:** 1974. **Emp:** 16. **Officers:** Robert Kane, President.

■ **4082** ■ **Theodore Presser Co.**
Presser Pl.
Bryn Mawr, PA 19010
Phone: (610)525-3636 **Fax:** (610)527-7841
URL: http://www.Presser.com
Products: Sheet music. **SIC:** 5192 (Books, Periodicals & Newspapers). **Sales:** $3,000,000 (2000). **Emp:** 55. **Officers:** Thomas Broido, President; George Hotton, Vice President.

■ **4083** ■ **Price Stern Sloan Inc.**
345 Hudson St.
New York, NY 10014
Phone: (212)477-6100 **Fax:** (212)445-3933
Products: Books; Humorous books; Cookbooks; Games; Puzzles. **SICs:** 5192 (Books, Periodicals & Newspapers); 5099 (Durable Goods Nec). **Est:** 1965. **Sales:** $37,000,000 (2000). **Emp:** 164. **Officers:** Morton Mint, CEO & President; Dan P. Reavis, Exec. VP of Finance & Operations.

■ **4084** ■ **Princeton Book Company Publishers**
PO Box 831
Hightstown, NJ 08520
Phone: (609)426-0602
Free: (800)220-7149 **Fax:** (609)426-1344
E-mail: pbc@dancehorizons.com
URL: http://www.dancehorizons.com
Products: Books and video cassettes on dance; Travel books. **SICs:** 5192 (Books, Periodicals & Newspapers); 5099 (Durable Goods Nec). **Est:** 1975. **Emp:** 8. **Officers:** Charles H. Woodford, President; Jennifer Thorn, Customer Service Contact, e-mail: pbc@dancehorizons.com.

■ **4085** ■ **Printed Matter Inc.**
77 Wooster St.
New York, NY 10012
Phone: (212)925-0325 **Fax:** (212)925-0464
URL: http://www.printedmatter.org
Products: Artists' books and publications. **SIC:** 5192 (Books, Periodicals & Newspapers). **Est:** 1976. **Sales:** $750,000 (2000). **Emp:** 6. **Officers:** David Platzker, Director.

■ **4086** ■ **Pro/Am Music Resources, Inc.**
63 Prospect St.
White Plains, NY 10606
Phone: (914)948-7436
Products: Books, records, cassettes, and sheet music. **SICs:** 5192 (Books, Periodicals & Newspapers); 5099 (Durable Goods Nec); 5199 (Nondurable Goods Nec).

■ **4087** ■ **Professional Book Distributors, Inc.**
1650 Bluegrass Lake Pkwy.
Alpharetta, GA 30004
Phone: (770)442-8633 **Fax:** (770)442-9742
E-mail: scott.dockter@pbd.com
URL: http://www.pbd.com
Products: Catalog fulfillment. **SIC:** 5192 (Books, Periodicals & Newspapers). **Est:** 1976. **Sales:** $40,000,000 (1999). **Emp:** 125. **Officers:** James E. Dockter, CEO, e-mail: sdockter@pbd.com; Scott Dockter, President & COO. **Alternate Name:** PBD, Inc.

■ **4088** ■ **Professional Book Service**
PO Box 835
Horsham, PA 19044-0835
Phone: (215)674-8040
Free: (800)648-8040 **Fax:** (215)441-8034
Products: Personal computer, computer science, and business and electronics books; Computer repair, systems design, and engineering books. **SIC:** 5192 (Books, Periodicals & Newspapers). **Est:** 1985.

■ **4089** ■ **Professional's Library**
2763 Townsend Rd.
Watkins Glen, NY 14891-9581
Phone: (914)724-3000
Free: (800)368-READ **Fax:** (914)724-3063
Products: Books. **SIC:** 5192 (Books, Periodicals & Newspapers). **Est:** 1983. **Sales:** $1,200,000 (2000). **Emp:** 7. **Officers:** Michael D. Cooper, President.

■ **4090** ■ **Provident Music Group**
741 Cool Springs Blvd.
Franklin, TN 37067
Phone: (615)261-6500
Free: (800)333-9000 **Fax:** (615)261-5903
Products: Book and sheet music publisher; Records, compact discs and audio and video tapes. **SICs:** 5099 (Durable Goods Nec); 5065 (Electronic Parts & Equipment Nec). **Sales:** $80,000,000 (1999). **Emp:** 300. **Officers:** James Van Hook, CEO & President; Mike Craft, CFO.

■ **4091** ■ **Publishers Associates**
PO Box 140361
Irving, TX 75014-0361
Phone: (972)681-0361 **Fax:** (972)686-5332
E-mail: contact@publishers-associates.com
URL: http://www.publishers-associates.com
Products: Books. **SIC:** 5192 (Books, Periodicals & Newspapers). **Est:** 1984. **Emp:** 13. **Officers:** A.F. Ide, CEO; John Paul Smith, COO; Rick Donovon, Sr. VP.

■ **4092** ■ **Publishers Distributing Co.**
6922 Hollywood Blvd., 10th Fl.
Los Angeles, CA 90028
Phone: (213)860-6070
Free: (800)464-4574 **Fax:** (213)957-9219
E-mail: dcullina@pdcdist.com
Products: Magazines and books. **SIC:** 5192 (Books, Periodicals & Newspapers). **Est:** 1967. **Sales:** $2,000,000 (2000). **Emp:** 48. **Officers:** Sam Watters, President.

■ **4093** ■ **Publishers Group West Inc.**
4065 Hollis St.
Emeryville, CA 94608
Phone: (510)658-3453 **Fax:** (510)658-1834
Products: Books. **SIC:** 5192 (Books, Periodicals & Newspapers). **Est:** 1976.

■ **4094** ■ **Publishers Group West Inc.**
1700 4th St.
Berkeley, CA 94710
Phone: (510)528-1444 **Fax:** (510)528-3444
Products: Books. **SIC:** 5192 (Books, Periodicals & Newspapers). **Sales:** $55,000,000 (1994). **Emp:** 200. **Officers:** Charlie Winton, President; Paul Rooney, CFO.

■ **4095** ■ **The Publishers Mark**
PO Box 6300
Incline Village, NV 89450
Phone: (702)831-5139 **Fax:** (775)831-4852
E-mail: bajaerin@telnor.net
URL: http://www.eduvision.com
Products: Books. **SIC:** 5192 (Books, Periodicals & Newspapers). **Est:** 1981. **Officers:** Erin Linn, OWN, e-mail: erinlsienna.net.

■ **4096** ■ **Publishing Center for Cultural Resources**
50 W 29th St., No. 7E
New York, NY 10001-4205
Phone: (212)260-2010
Products: Nonprofit organization books. **SIC:** 5192 (Books, Periodicals & Newspapers). **Est:** 1973.

■ **4097** ■ **Pure Beverage Inc.**
3902 E 16th St., Ste. B
Indianapolis, IN 46201-1538
Phone: (317)375-9925
Products: Fruit flavored carbonated soft drinks. **SIC:** 5149 (Groceries & Related Products Nec). **Sales:** $3,000,000 (1994). **Emp:** 17. **Officers:** Rick Polston, President.

■ **4098** ■ **Quail Ridge Press Inc.**
PO Box 123
Brandon, MS 39043
Phone: (601)825-2063
Free: (800)343-1583 **Fax:** (601)825-3091
E-mail: info@quailridge.com
URL: http://www.quailridge.com
Products: Regional books and cookbooks. **SIC:** 5192 (Books, Periodicals & Newspapers). **Est:** 1978. **Sales:** $1,500,000 (2000). **Emp:** 8. **Officers:** Gwen McKee, Co-Owner & Director; Barney McKee, Co-Owner & Director.

■ **4099** ■ **Quality Books Inc.**
1003 W Pines Rd.
Oregon, IL 61061
Phone: (815)732-4450
Free: (800)323-4241 **Fax:** (815)732-4499
URL: http://www.quality-books.com
Products: Nonfiction small press books, audio tapes, and special interest video tapes. **SICs:** 5192 (Books, Periodicals & Newspapers); 5099 (Durable Goods Nec). **Est:** 1964. **Emp:** 35. **Officers:** Harold G. Sterling, Sr. VP.

■ **4100** ■ **Quality Resources**
1 Water St.
White Plains, NY 10601
Phone: (914)761-9600 **Fax:** (914)761-9467
Products: Books. **SIC:** 5192 (Books, Periodicals & Newspapers). **Est:** 1989. **Officers:** Sandra Athans, Dir.

■ **4101** ■ **The Quilt Digest Press — A division of NTC/Contemporary Publishing Group**
4255 W Touhy Ave.
Lincolnwood, IL 60646-1933
Phone: (847)679-5500
Free: (800)323-4900 **Fax:** (847)679-2494
E-mail: ntcpub@tribune.com
URL: http://www.quiltdigestpress.com
Products: Arts and crafts books. **SIC:** 5192 (Books, Periodicals & Newspapers). **Est:** 1982. **Officers:** John Nohan, Publisher; Greg Euson, VP of Marketing & Sales; Neal McNish, Dir. of Sales; Sharon Gilbert, Dir. of Marketing.

■ **4102** ■ **Quite Specific Media Group Ltd.**
260 5th Ave.
New York, NY 10001
Phone: (212)725-5377 **Fax:** (212)725-8506
E-mail: info@quitespecificmedia.com
URL: http://www.quitespecificmedia.com
Products: Performing arts books; Costume and fashion books; Entertainment technology. **SIC:** 5192 (Books, Periodicals & Newspapers). **Est:** 1967.

■ **4103** ■ **R & R Technical Bookfinders Inc.**
1224 W Littleton Blvd.
Littleton, CO 80120
Phone: (303)794-4518 **Fax:** (303)798-7094
Products: Books. **SIC:** 5192 (Books, Periodicals & Newspapers). **Est:** 1957. **Emp:** 7. **Officers:** Kathleen Fieselman, President.

■ **4104** ■ **R & W Distribution Inc.**
87 Bright St.
Jersey City, NJ 07302
Phone: (201)333-1540 **Fax:** (201)333-1541
E-mail: rwmag@idt.net
Products: Magazines, comics, and paperback books. **SIC:** 5192 (Books, Periodicals & Newspapers). **Est:** 1973. **Officers:** Bert Wartelsky, Owner; Julie Chandra, Vice President.

■ **4105** ■ **Rainbow Publishers**
PO Box 261129
San Diego, CA 92196-1129
Phone: (619)271-7600 **Free:** (800)323-7337
Products: Religious educational materials. **SIC:** 5192 (Books, Periodicals & Newspapers). **Est:** 1979. **Sales:** $1,000,000 (2000). **Emp:** 7. **Officers:** Dan Miley.

■ **4106** ■ **H. Ramer & Associates, Inc.**
41 Dunn St.
Laguna Niguel, CA 92677
Phone: (949)249-2107 **Fax:** (949)582-7758
URL: http://www.hramerandassoc.com
Products: Books; Videos; Toys; Games; Puzzles. **SICs:** 5192 (Books, Periodicals & Newspapers); 5099 (Durable Goods Nec); 5092 (Toys & Hobby Goods & Supplies). **Est:** 1985. **Emp:** 4.

■ **4107** ■ **Ransom Distributing Co.**
PO Box 2010
Sparks, NV 89432
Products: Books. **SIC:** 5192 (Books, Periodicals & Newspapers). **Est:** 1989. **Officers:** D.M. Ransom, Owner.

■ **4108** ■ **Readmore Inc.**
22 Cortlandt St.
New York, NY 10007
Phone: (212)349-5540 **Fax:** (212)233-0746
Products: Books. **SIC:** 5192 (Books, Periodicals & Newspapers). **Est:** 1958. **Sales:** $60,000,000 (2000). **Emp:** 100. **Officers:** Dan Tonkery, CEO & President; James A. Benjamin, VP & CFO; Stanley Nason, VP of Sales; Steve Morgenroth, Dir. of Data Processing; Mark Golden, Dir. of Admin.

■ **4109** ■ **Reco International Corp.**
150 Haven Ave.
Port Washington, NY 11050
Phone: (516)767-2400 **Fax:** (516)767-2409
E-mail: recoint@aol.com
Products: Plates; Table trays; Figurines; Dolls; Clay bakers. **SICs:** 5192 (Books, Periodicals & Newspapers); 5032 (Brick, Stone & Related Materials); 5092 (Toys & Hobby Goods & Supplies). **Est:** 1967. **Emp:** 20. **Officers:** Heio W. Reich, President; D. William Simon, VP of Operations; Leonor H. Hartinez, Sales/Marketing Contact; Christine Reich, Customer Service Contact.

■ **4110** ■ **Redwing Book Company, Inc.**
44 Linden St.
Brookline, MA 02446
Phone: (617)738-4664
Free: (800)873-3946 **Fax:** (617)738-4620
E-mail: info@redwingbooks.com
URL: http://www.redwingbooks.com
Products: Books. **SIC:** 5192 (Books, Periodicals & Newspapers). **Est:** 1974. **Sales:** $2,600,000 (2000). **Emp:** 8.

■ **4111** ■ **Thomas Reed Publications, Inc.**
13 B St.
South Boston, MA 02127
Phone: (617)268-5500
Free: (800)995-4995 **Fax:** (617)268-5905
E-mail: info@reedsalmanac.com
URL: http://www.reedsalmanac.com
Products: Nautical almanacs. **SIC:** 5192 (Books, Periodicals & Newspapers). **Est:** 1992. **Former Name:** Barnacle Marine, Inc.

■ **4112** ■ **Regent Book Co.**
101A, Rte. 46 W
Saddle Brook, NJ 07663
Phone: (201)368-2208 **Fax:** (201)368-9770
Products: Books. **SIC:** 5192 (Books, Periodicals & Newspapers).

■ **4113** ■ **Desmond A. Reid Enterprises**
33 Lafayette Ave.
Brooklyn, NY 11217
Phone: (718)625-4651 **Fax:** (718)625-0654
Products: Multicultural studies books; Educational products. **SICs:** 5192 (Books, Periodicals & Newspapers); 5099 (Durable Goods Nec). **Est:** 1982.

■ **4114** ■ **Research Books, Inc.**
38 Academy St.
PO Box 1507
Madison, CT 06443
Phone: (203)245-3279 **Fax:** (203)245-1830
URL: http://www.researchbooks.com
Products: Books. **SIC:** 5192 (Books, Periodicals & Newspapers). **Est:** 1963. **Sales:** $5,000,000 (2000). **Emp:** 19. **Officers:** Brad Purcell, e-mail: brad@researchbwks.com.

■ **4115** ■ **Resource Publications Inc.**
160 E Virginia St., No. 290
San Jose, CA 95112-5876
Phone: (408)286-8505 **Fax:** (408)287-8748
E-mail: info@rpinet.com
URL: http://www.rpinet.com
Products: Books and other resources for ministers, counselors, and educators. **SIC:** 5192 (Books, Periodicals & Newspapers). **Est:** 1973. **Sales:** $2,000,000 (2000). **Emp:** 25. **Officers:** William Burns, President.

■ **4116** ■ **Rhode Island Publications Society**
1445 Wampanoag Trail, No. 203
Riverside, RI 02915-1000
Phone: (401)272-1776 **Fax:** (401)273-1791
Products: Books about Rhode Island's history, economy, and cultural life. **SIC:** 5192 (Books, Periodicals & Newspapers). **Est:** 1974. **Sales:** $62,000 (2000). **Emp:** 2. **Officers:** Dr. Patrick T. Conley, Chairman of the Board.

■ **4117** ■ **Richardson's Educators Inc.**
2014 Lou Ellen Ln.
Houston, TX 77018
Phone: (713)688-2244
Free: (800)392-8562 **Fax:** (713)688-8420
Products: Books. **SIC:** 5192 (Books, Periodicals &
Newspapers). **Est:** 1969.

■ **4118** ■ **Rittenhouse Book Distributors, Inc.**
511 Feheley Dr.
King of Prussia, PA 19406
Phone: (215)277-1414
Free: (800)345-6425 **Fax:** 800-223-7488
E-mail: customer.service@rittenhouse.com
URL: http://www.rittenhouse.com
Products: Books on nursing, medical, and health
sciences; Non-print book products. **SIC:** 5192 (Books,
Periodicals & Newspapers). **Est:** 1946. **Officers:**
Timothy Foster, Contact.

■ **4119** ■ **Riverside Book and Bible House**
1500 Riverside Dr.
PO Box 370
Iowa Falls, IA 50126
Phone: (515)648-4271
Free: (800)247-5111 **Fax:** 800-822-4271
Products: Bibles and religious books. **SIC:** 5192
(Books, Periodicals & Newspapers). **Est:** 1960.

■ **4120** ■ **Riverside Distributors**
PO Box 370
Iowa Falls, IA 50126-0370
Phone: (515)648-4271
Free: (800)247-5111 **Fax:** 800-822-4271
Products: Religious books; Bibles and testaments.
SIC: 5192 (Books, Periodicals & Newspapers). **Est:**
1959.

■ **4121** ■ **Rizzoli International Inc.**
300 Park Ave. S
New York, NY 10010
Phone: (212)387-3400
Free: (800)221-7945 **Fax:** (212)387-3535
Products: Illustrated books; Calendars. **SIC:** 5192
(Books, Periodicals & Newspapers). **Est:** 1976.
Officers: Solveig Williams, Publisher; Charles Miers,
Publisher; Dan Tucker, Dir. of Marketing; Tom Rupulo,
Sales Mgr. **Alternate Name:** Universe Publishing.

■ **4122** ■ **Roberts Co. Inc.**
180 Franklin St.
Framingham, MA 01701
Phone: (508)875-8877 **Fax:** (508)879-3735
Products: Books. **SIC:** 5192 (Books, Periodicals &
Newspapers). **Est:** 1959. **Sales:** $1,000,000 (2000).
Emp: 20.

■ **4123** ■ **Will Rogers Heritage Trust**
W Will Rogers Blvd.
PO Box 157
Claremore, OK 74018
Phone: (918)341-0719
Free: (800)828-9643 **Fax:** (918)341-8246
Products: Books. **SIC:** 5192 (Books, Periodicals &
Newspapers). **Est:** 1979.

■ **4124** ■ **Rosenblum's World of Judaica, Inc.**
2906 W Devon Ave.
Chicago, IL 60659
Phone: (773)262-1700
Free: (800)626-6536 **Fax:** (773)262-1930
Products: Books for Judaica and Hebraica schools.
SIC: 5192 (Books, Periodicals & Newspapers). **Est:**
1940.

■ **4125** ■ **Ross-Erikson**
8471 Warwick Dr.
Desert Hot Springs, CA 92240-1124
Products: Books. **SIC:** 5192 (Books, Periodicals &
Newspapers).

■ **4126** ■ **Royal Publications, Inc.**
790 W Tennessee Ave.
Denver, CO 80223
Phone: (303)778-8383 **Fax:** (303)744-9383
Products: Books, magazines, video and audio
cassettes, charts, and appropriate display racks. **SICs:**
5192 (Books, Periodicals & Newspapers); 5099
(Durable Goods Nec). **Est:** 1955.

■ **4127** ■ **Rushwin Publishing**
c/o James Gibson, Manager
PO Box 1150
Buna, TX 77612
Phone: (409)423-2521
Products: Religious sheet music. **SIC:** 5192 (Books,
Periodicals & Newspapers).

■ **4128** ■ **Russica Book & Art Shop Inc.**
799 Broadway
New York, NY 10003
Phone: (212)473-7480 **Fax:** (212)473-7480
Products: Russian literature and art books published
in the Soviet Union. **SIC:** 5192 (Books, Periodicals &
Newspapers). **Est:** 1976.

■ **4129** ■ **Rutgers Book Center**
127 Raritan Ave.
Highland Park, NJ 08904
Phone: (732)545-4344 **Fax:** (732)545-6686
E-mail: gunbooks@rutgersgunbooks.com
URL: http://www.rutgersgunbooks.com
Products: Books. **SIC:** 5192 (Books, Periodicals &
Newspapers). **Est:** 1973. **Emp:** 8. **Officers:** Mark Aziz,
CEO & President; Rose Aziz, Secretary. **Alternate
Name:** The Gun Room Press.

■ **4130** ■ **Rutland News Co.**
PO Box 1211
Rochester, NY 14603-1211
Free: (800)678-2920
Products: Newspapers and magazines. **SIC:** 5192
(Books, Periodicals & Newspapers). **Est:** 1948.
Officers: Terry P. McQuillen, General Mgr.

■ **4131** ■ **Ryen, Re Associates**
585 Seminole St.
Oradell, NJ 07649
Phone: (201)261-7450 **Fax:** (201)261-6294
Products: Books. **SIC:** 5192 (Books, Periodicals &
Newspapers). **Est:** 1974.

■ **4132** ■ **S & L Sales Co., Inc.**
2165 Industrial Blvd.
Waycross, GA 31503
Phone: (912)283-0210
Free: (800)243-3699 **Fax:** (912)283-0261
URL: http://www.slsales.com
Products: Books including cookbooks, crafts, arts,
juvenile, how-to, general fiction, and non-fiction. **SIC:**
5192 (Books, Periodicals & Newspapers). **Est:** 1965.
Emp: 12. **Officers:** Rickey L. Perritt, President; Bryan
L. Perritt, Vice President; Tina Simpson, Treasurer;
Annette G. Perritt, Secretary, e-mail: annette@
slsales.com; Jim Cannister, Sales/Marketing Contact,
e-mail: jim@slsales.com; Vicky Rawlins, Human
Resources Contact, e-mail: vicky@slsales.com.

■ **4133** ■ **S & W Distributors Inc.**
PO Box 14689
Greensboro, NC 27415
Phone: (336)272-7394 **Fax:** (336)272-7394
Products: Children's books; General reference books;
Videos; Large print books. **SICs:** 5192 (Books,
Periodicals & Newspapers); 5065 (Electronic Parts &
Equipment Nec). **Est:** 1966. **Sales:** $1,000,000 (2000).
Emp: 20. **Officers:** William E. Sanders, President; M.F.
Foote, Vice President.

■ **4134** ■ **Safari Press Inc.**
15621 Chemical Ln., Ste. B
Huntington Beach, CA 92649
Phone: (714)894-9080 **Fax:** (714)894-4949
E-mail: info@safaripress.com
URL: http://www.safaripress.com
Products: Books, including big-game hunting,
wingshooting, sporting firearms, and Africana. **SIC:**
5192 (Books, Periodicals & Newspapers). **Est:** 1983.
Sales: $2,000,000 (2000). **Emp:** 12.

■ **4135** ■ **Saint Aepan's Press & Book
Distributors, Inc.**
PO Box 385
Hillsdale, NJ 07642-0385
Phone: (201)664-0127
E-mail: books@greatoldebooks.com
URL: http://www.greatoldebooks.com
Products: Academic books. **SIC:** 5192 (Books,
Periodicals & Newspapers). **Est:** 1975. **Officers:**

Michael V. Cordasco, President. **Former Name:** Junius
Book Distributors, Inc.

■ **4136** ■ **San Francisco Center for Visual
Studies**
49 Rivoli St.
San Francisco, CA 94117
Phone: (415)664-4699 **Fax:** (415)564-1143
Products: Books and video tapes related to fine art.
SICs: 5192 (Books, Periodicals & Newspapers); 5099
(Durable Goods Nec). **Est:** 1973.

■ **4137** ■ **Saphrograph Corp.**
4910-12 Ft. Hamilton Pkwy.
Brooklyn, NY 11219
Phone: (718)331-1233 **Fax:** (718)372-8890
Products: Foreign language dictionaries. **SIC:** 5192
(Books, Periodicals & Newspapers). **Est:** 1961.

■ **4138** ■ **S.A.V.E. Half Price Books for
Libraries**
303 N Main St.
PO Box 30
Schulenburg, TX 78956
Phone: (409)743-4147 **Fax:** (409)743-4147
E-mail: savehalf@cvtv.net
Products: Books. **SIC:** 5192 (Books, Periodicals &
Newspapers). **Est:** 1988. **Emp:** 13. **Officers:** Suzie
Barbee, President.

■ **4139** ■ **S.C.B. Distributors**
15608 S New Century Dr.
Gardena, CA 90248
Phone: (310)532-9400
Free: (800)729-6423 **Fax:** (310)532-7001
E-mail: scb@scdistributors.com
URL: http://www.scbdistributors.com
Products: Arts and crafts books; Business and
economics books; Children's books; Comic books;
Health and medical books; Law books; Multicultural
studies books; Religious books; Travel books; Self help
books; Outdoor and adventure books. **SIC:** 5192
(Books, Periodicals & Newspapers). **Est:** 1989. **Emp:**
8. **Officers:** Aaron Silverman, President; Victor Duran,
Manager.

■ **4140** ■ **Schoenhof's Foreign Books Inc.**
486 Green St.
Cambridge, MA 02139
Phone: (617)547-8855 **Fax:** (617)547-8551
E-mail: info@schoenhofs.com
URL: http://www.schoenhofs.com
Products: Foreign language books, dictionaries,
cassettes, and learning materials. **SICs:** 5192 (Books,
Periodicals & Newspapers); 5099 (Durable Goods
Nec). **Est:** 1856. **Officers:** Dan Cianfarini, Dir. of
Marketing, e-mail: marketing@schoenhofs.com.

■ **4141** ■ **Scholarly Publications**
14601 Bellaire Blvd., Ste. 60
Houston, TX 77083
Phone: (281)504-4646
Free: (800)275-7825 **Fax:** (281)504-4642
E-mail: scholarlyp@aol.com
URL: http://www.scholarlypublications.com
Products: Books; Journals. **SIC:** 5192 (Books,
Periodicals & Newspapers). **Est:** 1983. **Sales:**
$5,000,000 (2000). **Emp:** 20. **Officers:** Mr. S.C. Gupta,
Mgr. Dir.; Mrs. S. Gupta, President; I. Rahman,
Sales/Marketing Contact, e-mail: rahman@
scholarlypublications.com.

■ **4142** ■ **Scholium International, Inc.**
PO Box 1519
Port Washington, NY 11050
Phone: (516)767-7171 **Fax:** (516)944-9824
E-mail: info@scholium.com
URL: http://www.scholium.com
Products: Specialized technical, scientific, and medical
books. **SIC:** 5192 (Books, Periodicals & Newspapers).
Est: 1973. **Officers:** Arthur A. Candido, President;
Elena M. Candido, Vice President; Jane M. Candido,
Customer Service Mgr.

■ 4143 ■ School Book Service
3650 Coral Ridge Dr., Ste. 112
Coral Springs, FL 33065
Phone: (954)341-7207
Free: (800)228-7361 **Fax:** 888-782-6655
URL: http://www.book-service.com
Products: Paperback books. **SIC:** 5192 (Books, Periodicals & Newspapers). **Est:** 1978. **Sales:** $850,000 (2000). **Emp:** 4. **Officers:** Marvin Sirotowitz, President.

■ 4144 ■ Schroeder's Book Haven
104 Michigan Ave.
League City, TX 77573
Phone: (281)332-5226
Free: (800)894-5032 **Fax:** (281)332-1695
E-mail: info@bookhaventexas.com
URL: http://www.bookhaventexas.com
Products: Books. **SIC:** 5192 (Books, Periodicals & Newspapers). **Est:** 1968. **Sales:** $180,000 (1999). **Emp:** 3. **Officers:** Bert Schroeder, Manager.

■ 4145 ■ Arthur Schwartz & Co.
234 Meads Mountain Rd.
Woodstock, NY 12498
Phone: (914)679-4024
Free: (800)669-9080 **Fax:** (914)679-4093
E-mail: aschwartz@ulster.net
URL: http://www.aschwartz-booksngames.com
Products: Art, crafts, and museum books; Educational board games. **SICs:** 5192 (Books, Periodicals & Newspapers); 5092 (Toys & Hobby Goods & Supplies). **Est:** 1987. **Sales:** $600,000 (2000). **Emp:** 5. **Officers:** Arthur Schwartz, President; Jo Yanow-Schwartz, Vice President. **Alternate Name:** Woodstocker Books.

■ 4146 ■ Science and Spirit Resources, Inc.
171-B Rumford St.
Concord, NH 03301
Phone: (603)226-3328 **Fax:** (603)229-0953
E-mail: info@science-spirit.com
URL: http://www.science-spirit.com
Products: Magazines. **SIC:** 5192 (Books, Periodicals & Newspapers). **Est:** 1989. **Emp:** 11. **Officers:** Kevin Sharpe, Publisher, e-mail: ksharpe@science-spirit.com.

■ 4147 ■ Scientific & Medical Publications of France Inc.
100 E 42nd St., Ste. 1510
New York, NY 10017
Phone: (212)983-6278 **Fax:** (212)687-1407
Products: French books. **SIC:** 5192 (Books, Periodicals & Newspapers). **Est:** 1972. **Sales:** $250,000 (2000). **Emp:** 3. **Officers:** G. Juery, Customer Service Contact. **Also Known by This Acronym:** SPMF.

■ 4148 ■ Selective Books Inc.
PO Box 984
Oldsmar, FL 34677-0984
Phone: (813)891-6451 **Fax:** (813)855-5791
E-mail: sbooks@mindspring.com
Products: Books; Directories; Manuals. **SIC:** 5192 (Books, Periodicals & Newspapers). **Est:** 1969. **Officers:** Lee Howard, Founder; Eddie Howard, President.

■ 4149 ■ Seneca News Agency Inc.
800 Pre-Emption Rd.
Geneva, NY 14456-0631
Phone: (315)789-3551 **Fax:** (315)781-1015
Products: Paperback books; Magazines; Newspapers; Comic books; Trading cards. **SIC:** 5192 (Books, Periodicals & Newspapers). **Est:** 1949. **Emp:** 20. **Officers:** Barry Budgar, Owner.

■ 4150 ■ Sepher-Hermon Press
1153 45th St.
Brooklyn, NY 11219
Phone: (718)972-9010 **Fax:** (718)972-6935
Products: Cultural and academic books on Judaica. **SIC:** 5192 (Books, Periodicals & Newspapers). **Est:** 1974. **Sales:** $165,000 (1999). **Emp:** 2. **Officers:** Samuel Gross, President; Margaret Gross, Secretary.

■ 4151 ■ Serconia Press
30 St. Marks Pl.
Brooklyn, NY 11217
Phone: (718)875-7731
Products: Science fiction books. **SIC:** 5192 (Books, Periodicals & Newspapers). **Est:** 1984. **Sales:** $10,000 (2000).

■ 4152 ■ Serendipity Couriers, Inc.
470 Du Bois St.
San Rafael, CA 94901-3911
Phone: (415)459-4000 **Fax:** (415)459-0833
E-mail: dipity@ix.netcom.com
Products: Magazines. **SIC:** 5192 (Books, Periodicals & Newspapers). **Est:** 1974. **Sales:** $4,250,000 (2000). **Emp:** 38. **Officers:** Joan Solana, President; Sam Solana, Vice President; Larry Loudermilk, General Mgr.

■ 4153 ■ Serendipity Couriers Inc.
470 Du Bois St.
San Rafael, CA 94901-3911
Phone: (415)459-4000 **Fax:** (415)459-0833
Products: Books and other printed materials. **SIC:** 5192 (Books, Periodicals & Newspapers). **Sales:** $3,600,000 (2000). **Emp:** 34.

■ 4154 ■ Servant Publications
PO Box 8617
Ann Arbor, MI 48107
Phone: (734)761-8505 **Fax:** (734)761-1577
Products: Secular reading material. **SIC:** 5192 (Books, Periodicals & Newspapers).

■ 4155 ■ Seven Hills Book Distributors Inc.
1531 Tremont St.
Cincinnati, OH 45214
Phone: (513)471-4300
Free: (800)545-2005 **Fax:** (513)471-4311
E-mail: shcustomerservice@sevenhillsbooks.com
URL: http://www.sevenhillsbooks.com
Products: Books. **SIC:** 5192 (Books, Periodicals & Newspapers). **Est:** 1974. **Emp:** 20. **Officers:** Ion Itescu, President; Amy Itescu, VP & Customer Service Mgr.; Bob Raterman, Sales Mgr.; Greg Hatfield, Senior Publicist; Janet Kunkel, Credit Mgr.

■ 4156 ■ M.E. Sharpe Inc.
80 Business Park Dr.
Armonk, NY 10504
Phone: (914)273-1800
Free: (800)541-6563 **Fax:** (914)273-2106
E-mail: mesinfo@usa.net
URL: http://www.mesharpe.com
Products: Books; Journals. **SIC:** 5192 (Books, Periodicals & Newspapers). **Est:** 1958. **Sales:** $6,500,000 (2000). **Emp:** 50. **Officers:** Myron E. Sharpe, President; Vincent Fuentes, CFO; Carmen Chetti, Dir. of Production; Diana McDermott, Dir. of Mktg. & Sales.

■ 4157 ■ Harold Shaw Publishers
2375 TelStar Dr., Ste. 160
Colorado Springs, CO 80920
Phone: (719)590-4999
Free: (800)603-7051 **Fax:** (719)590-8977
URL: http://www.shawpub.com
Products: Religious books. **SIC:** 5192 (Books, Periodicals & Newspapers). **Est:** 1967. **Sales:** $1,500,000 (2000). **Emp:** 4.

■ 4158 ■ Shen's Books and Supplies
821 S 1st Ave.
Arcadia, CA 91006-3918
Phone: (626)445-6958
Free: (800)456-6660 **Fax:** (626)445-6940
Products: Books and other printed materials. **SIC:** 5192 (Books, Periodicals & Newspapers). **Sales:** $1,000,000 (2000). **Emp:** 5.

■ 4159 ■ Sher Distributing Co.
8 Vreeland Ave.
Totowa, NJ 07512
Phone: (973)256-4050
Free: (800)289-4050 **Fax:** (973)256-1314
Products: Books. **SIC:** 5192 (Books, Periodicals & Newspapers). **Est:** 1952. **Sales:** $200,000,000 (2000). **Emp:** 1,100. **Officers:** Ben Sher, President; Sharon Hails.

■ 4160 ■ Sheriar Books
807 34th Ave S
North Myrtle Beach, SC 29582
Phone: (843)272-1339 **Fax:** (843)361-1747
E-mail: sheriarbks@aol.com
URL: http://www.sheriarfoundation.org
Products: Books; Videos. **SIC:** 5192 (Books, Periodicals & Newspapers). **Est:** 1971. **Sales:** $120,000 (2000). **Emp:** 2. **Officers:** Sheila Kyrnski, e-mail: SheriarDeb@aol.com; Deborah Smith, Sales/Marketing Contact.

■ 4161 ■ Signature Books Inc.
564 West 400 North
Salt Lake City, UT 84116
Phone: (801)531-1483
Free: (800)356-5687 **Fax:** (801)531-1488
E-mail: signature@thegulf.com
URL: http://www.signaturebooksinc.com
Products: Books. **SIC:** 5192 (Books, Periodicals & Newspapers). **Est:** 1981. **Sales:** $500,000 (2000). **Emp:** 7. **Officers:** George D. Smith, President; Gary J. Bergera, Vice President; Boyd Payne, Sales/Marketing Contact.

■ 4162 ■ Sigo Press/Coventure
PO Box 1435
Ft. Collins, CO 80522-1435
Phone: (978)740-0113
Free: (800)338-0446 **Fax:** (978)740-0117
Products: Books; Videos; Prerecorded audio tapes. **SICs:** 5192 (Books, Periodicals & Newspapers); 5065 (Electronic Parts & Equipment Nec); 5099 (Durable Goods Nec). **Est:** 1980. **Sales:** $500,000 (2000). **Emp:** 5. **Officers:** Sisa M. Sternback.

■ 4163 ■ Silver Bow News Distributing Company Inc.
219 E Park St.
Butte, MT 59701
Phone: (406)782-6995
Products: Mass-market magazines and paperback books. **SIC:** 5192 (Books, Periodicals & Newspapers). **Est:** 1936.

■ 4164 ■ Sirak & Sirak Associates
20 Davenport Rd.
Montville, NJ 07045-9184
Phone: (973)299-0085 **Fax:** (973)263-2363
Products: Books. **SIC:** 5192 (Books, Periodicals & Newspapers). **Est:** 1981. **Emp:** 5.

■ 4165 ■ Ski America Enterprises Inc.
PO Box 1140
Pittsfield, MA 01202-1140
Phone: (413)637-9810 **Fax:** (413)637-9873
Products: Magazines. **SIC:** 5192 (Books, Periodicals & Newspapers). **Est:** 1966. **Sales:** $5,000,000 (2000). **Emp:** 31. **Officers:** Barry Hollister, President; B. Robert Wadsworth, Sr. VP.

■ 4166 ■ Slawson Communications, Inc.
165 Vallecitos de Oro
San Marcos, CA 92069
Phone: (760)744-2299 **Fax:** (760)744-0424
Products: Books. **SIC:** 5192 (Books, Periodicals & Newspapers). **Est:** 1960.

■ 4167 ■ Small Changes Inc.
316 Terry Ave. N
PO Box 19046
Seattle, WA 98109
Phone: (206)382-1980 **Fax:** (206)382-1514
E-mail: info@smallchanges.com
Products: Magazines and calendars. **SIC:** 5192 (Books, Periodicals & Newspapers). **Est:** 1977. **Emp:** 10. **Officers:** Shari Basom, President, e-mail: shari@smallchanges.com.

■ 4168 ■ Small Press Distribution Inc.
1341 7th St.
Berkeley, CA 94710
Phone: (510)524-1668
Free: (800)869-7553 **Fax:** (510)524-0852
E-mail: orders@spdbooks.org
URL: http://www.spdbooks.org
Products: Poetry, fiction, and cultural writing from independent presses. **SIC:** 5192 (Books, Periodicals & Newspapers). **Est:** 1969. **Emp:** 7. **Officers:** Don

Knaub, Executive Director, e-mail: don@spdbooks.org; Victoria Shoemaker, Board President; Laura Moriarty, Asst. Director, e-mail: laura@spdbooks.org; Martin Kelly, Customer Service Contact, e-mail: marty@spdbooks.org; Joe Marradino, Human Resources Contact, e-mail: joe@spdbooks.org.

■ **4169** ■ **Society of Petroleum Engineers**
222 Palisades Creek Dr.
Richardson, TX 75080
Phone: (972)952-9393 **Fax:** (972)952-9435
URL: http://www.spe.org
Products: Books covering engineering methods for oil and gas drilling, exploration, and production operations. **SIC:** 5192 (Books, Periodicals & Newspapers). **Est:** 1949. **Emp:** 111. **Officers:** Tom Pellet, e-mail: tpellet@spe.org.

■ **4170** ■ **SOM Publishing**
School of Metaphysics
World Headquarters
Windyville, MO 65783
Phone: (417)345-8411
E-mail: som@som.org
URL: http://www.som.org
Products: Books; Quarterly journals. **SIC:** 5192 (Books, Periodicals & Newspapers). **Est:** 1973. **Sales:** $125,000 (2000). **Officers:** Dr. Barbara Condron, CEO; Paul Blosser, Dir. of Merchandising.

■ **4171** ■ **Source Books**
20341 Sycamore Dr.
PO Box 794
Trabuco Canyon, CA 92678
Phone: (949)858-1420
Free: (800)695-4237 **Fax:** (949)858-1420
E-mail: studio185@earthlink.net
Products: Religious books and audiotapes. **SICs:** 5192 (Books, Periodicals & Newspapers); 5099 (Durable Goods Nec). **Est:** 1985. **Emp:** 4. **Officers:** Denis Clarke; Jane Hammond.

■ **4172** ■ **South Asia Books**
PO Box 502
Columbia, MO 65205
Phone: (573)474-0116 **Fax:** (314)747-8124
Products: Books from India. **SIC:** 5192 (Books, Periodicals & Newspapers). **Est:** 1969.

■ **4173** ■ **Southern Publishers Group, Inc.**
3918 Montclair Rd., Ste. 108
PO Box 130460
Birmingham, AL 35213
Phone: (205)870-9834
Free: (800)239-7774 **Fax:** (205)870-3629
Products: Books promoting Southern U.S. writing and publishing. **SIC:** 5192 (Books, Periodicals & Newspapers). **Est:** 1990.

■ **4174** ■ **Southern Territory Associates**
PO Box 13519
Arlington, TX 76094
Phone: (817)861-9644
Free: (800)331-7016 **Fax:** (817)277-3199
Products: Books; Cassettes; Software. **SICs:** 5192 (Books, Periodicals & Newspapers); 5099 (Durable Goods Nec); 5045 (Computers, Peripherals & Software). **Est:** 1976.

■ **4175** ■ **Southern Wisconsin News**
1858 Artisan Rd.
Rte. 3
Edgerton, WI 53534
Phone: (608)884-2600 **Fax:** (608)884-2636
Products: Magazines; Books. **SIC:** 5192 (Books, Periodicals & Newspapers). **Est:** 1933. **Sales:** $4,500,000 (2000). **Emp:** 33. **Officers:** Thomas W. Purnell, President & Owner; Robert J. Purnell III, VP & Owner.

■ **4176** ■ **Southwest Book Co.**
13003 H Murphy Rd.
Stafford, TX 77477
Phone: (281)498-2603
Products: Children's books. **SIC:** 5192 (Books, Periodicals & Newspapers). **Est:** 1980.

■ **4177** ■ **Southwest Cookbook Distributors, Inc.**
PO Box 707
Bonham, TX 75418
Phones: (903)583-8898 (903)583-2459
(903)725-8898 **Fax:** (903)725-2522
Products: Cook books. **SIC:** 5192 (Books, Periodicals & Newspapers). **Est:** 1983. **Sales:** $1,000,000 (2000). **Emp:** 5. **Officers:** Barbara C. Jones, Owner.

■ **4178** ■ **Spanish & European Bookstore Inc.**
3102 Wilshire Blvd.
Los Angeles, CA 90010
Phone: (213)739-8899 **Fax:** (213)739-0087
Products: Books. **SIC:** 5192 (Books, Periodicals & Newspapers). **Est:** 1986. **Emp:** 3. **Officers:** Gian-Carla Quiroga, President.

■ **4179** ■ **Sparrow-Star**
101 Winners Cir.
Brentwood, TN 37024
Phone: (615)371-6800
Free: (800)877-4443 **Fax:** (615)311-6999
Products: Religious books; Tapes audio and video recording; Videos. **SICs:** 5192 (Books, Periodicals & Newspapers); 5065 (Electronic Parts & Equipment Nec); 5099 (Durable Goods Nec). **Est:** 1976. **Emp:** 100.

■ **4180** ■ **Specialty Promotions Co., Inc.**
6841 S Cregier Ave.
Chicago, IL 60649
Phone: (773)493-6900 **Fax:** (773)921-9374
URL: http://www.islamandyoubooks.com
Products: Islamic literature. **SIC:** 5192 (Books, Periodicals & Newspapers). **Est:** 1959. **Sales:** $50,000 (2000). **Emp:** 2. **Officers:** Abdul Salaam, e-mail: Abdulibn@juno.com.

■ **4181** ■ **The Speech Bin, Inc.**
1965 25th Ave.
Vero Beach, FL 32960
Phone: (561)770-0007
Free: (800)4SP-EECH **Fax:** (561)770-0006
E-mail: info@speechbin.com
URL: http://www.speechbin.com
Products: Educational materials, textbooks, software, and related products in special education, speech-language pathology, and audiology. **SICs:** 5192 (Books, Periodicals & Newspapers); 5045 (Computers, Peripherals & Software). **Est:** 1984. **Officers:** Joseph Binney, President.

■ **4182** ■ **Speedimpex USA, Inc.**
35-02 48th Ave.
Long Island City, NY 11101
Phone: (718)392-7477
Free: (800)969-1258 **Fax:** (718)361-0815
E-mail: information@speedimpex.com
URL: http://www.speedimpex.com
Products: Newspapers and magazines. **SIC:** 5192 (Books, Periodicals & Newspapers). **Est:** 1962. **Emp:** 100. **Officers:** Francesco Calvelli; Marco Marchetti.

■ **4183** ■ **Spofford's Newspapers**
106 Summer St.
Kennebunk, ME 04043
Phone: (207)985-7588
Products: Newspapers. **SIC:** 5192 (Books, Periodicals & Newspapers).

■ **4184** ■ **Spring Arbor Distribution Company Inc.**
1 Ingram Blvd.
La Vergne, TN 37086-3629
Free: (800)395-5599
Products: Religious publications, music, and gifts. **SICs:** 5192 (Books, Periodicals & Newspapers); 5065 (Electronic Parts & Equipment Nec); 5199 (Nondurable Goods Nec). **Est:** 1978. **Sales:** $157,000,000 (2000). **Emp:** 660. **Officers:** Rick Pigott, President; Tim Williams, VP of Finance & Treasurer; Allen Knight, Sr. VP of Market Development.

■ **4185** ■ **Spring Publishing**
299 E Quasset Rd.
Woodstock, CT 06281-3308
Phone: (860)943-4093 **Fax:** (860)943-4520
Products: Psychology books. **SIC:** 5192 (Books, Periodicals & Newspapers). **Est:** 1978. **Emp:** 5. **Officers:** James Hillman, President.

■ **4186** ■ **Sri Aurobindo Association**
2288 Fulton St., Ste. 310
Berkeley, CA 94704-1449
Phone: (650)848-1841 **Fax:** (650)848-8531
Products: Books. **SIC:** 5192 (Books, Periodicals & Newspapers). **Est:** 1977.

■ **4187** ■ **Stackpole Books**
5067 Ritter Rd.
Mechanicsburg, PA 17055
Phone: (717)796-0411
Free: (800)732-3669 **Fax:** (717)796-0412
Products: Reference books on the outdoors, nature, gardening, crafts, fly fishing, woodworking, and history. **SIC:** 5192 (Books, Periodicals & Newspapers). **Emp:** 45. **Officers:** David Ritter, President; Frank Rampulla, VP of Sales.

■ **4188** ■ **Standard Publishing Co.**
8121 Hamilton Ave.
Cincinnati, OH 45231
Phones: (513)931-4050 800-582-1385
Free: (800)543-1353 **Fax:** (513)931-0904
Products: Religious literature, posters, and stickers. **SIC:** 5192 (Books, Periodicals & Newspapers).

■ **4189** ■ **State Mutual Book & Periodical Service Ltd.**
521 5th Ave., 17th Fl.
New York, NY 10175
Phones: (212)292-4444 (718)261-1704
Fax: (631)537-0412
Products: Books. **SIC:** 5192 (Books, Periodicals & Newspapers). **Est:** 1976.

■ **4190** ■ **Sterling Publishing Co., Inc.**
387 Park Ave. S
New York, NY 10016-8810
Phones: (212)532-7160 800-542-7567
Free: (800)367-9692 **Fax:** (212)213-2495
URL: http://www.sterlingpub.com
Products: Self help books; How to and do-it-yourself books. **SIC:** 5192 (Books, Periodicals & Newspapers). **Est:** 1949. **Emp:** 120. **Officers:** Burton H. Hobson, Chairman of the Board; Lincoln A. Boehm, President; Charles Nurnberg, Exec. VP.

■ **4191** ■ **Stoelting Co.**
620 Wheat Ln.
Wood Dale, IL 60191-1109
Phone: (708)860-9700 **Fax:** (708)860-9775
Products: Psychological tests and special education materials. **SIC:** 5192 (Books, Periodicals & Newspapers). **Est:** 1886.

■ **4192** ■ **Straight Talk Distributing**
75 Pasatiempo Dr.
Santa Cruz, CA 95060-1440
Products: Pamphlets, booklets, study kits, and some books. **SIC:** 5192 (Books, Periodicals & Newspapers). **Est:** 1978.

■ **4193** ■ **Strawberry Hill Press**
3848 SE Division St.
Portland, OR 97202-1641
Phone: (503)235-5989
Products: Books. **SIC:** 5192 (Books, Periodicals & Newspapers). **Est:** 1973. **Sales:** $2,000,000 (2000). **Emp:** 15.

■ **4194** ■ **Subterranean Co.**
265 S 5th St.
PO Box 160
Monroe, OR 97456
Phone: (541)847-5274
Free: (800)274-7826 **Fax:** (541)847-6018
E-mail: subeo@clipper.net
Products: Avant garde poetry and prose books. **SIC:** 5192 (Books, Periodicals & Newspapers). **Est:** 1977. **Emp:** 5. **Officers:** Morgan Broadley, Sales/Marketing Contact; Jessic Broadley, Customer Service Contact.

■ 4195 ■ **Sunbelt Publications**
1250 Fayette St.
El Cajon, CA 92020
Phone: (619)258-4911
Free: (800)626-6579 **Fax:** (619)258-4916
E-mail: sunbeltpub@prodigy.net
URL: http://www.sunbeltpub.com
Products: Regional books, including natural science, outdoor adventure, local interest, and travel; National calendars. **SIC:** 5192 (Books, Periodicals & Newspapers). **Est:** 1984. **Sales:** $6,000,000 (2000). **Emp:** 25. **Officers:** Diana Lindsay, President; Lowell Lindsay, CFO; Kathy Gouin, Sales/Marketing Contact, e-mail: kgouin@sunbeltpub.com.

■ 4196 ■ **Sundance Publishing**
234 Taylor St.
PO Box 1326
Littleton, MA 01460
Phone: (978)486-9201 **Fax:** (978)486-8759
URL: http://www.sundancepub.com
Products: Teaching materials; Paperback books. **SIC:** 5192 (Books, Periodicals & Newspapers). **Est:** 1971. **Emp:** 70.

■ 4197 ■ **Sunday School Publishing Board**
330 Charlotte Ave.
Nashville, TN 37201
Phone: (615)256-2480
Products: Religious books. **SIC:** 5192 (Books, Periodicals & Newspapers). **Est:** 1926. **Sales:** $3,204,000 (1999). **Emp:** 126.

■ 4198 ■ **Sunflower University Press**
1531 Yuma
Box 1009
Manhattan, KS 66502-4228
Phone: (785)539-1888
Free: (800)258-1232 **Fax:** (785)539-2233
URL: http://www.sunflower-univ-press.org
Products: Books, including history books. **SIC:** 5192 (Books, Periodicals & Newspapers). **Est:** 1977. **Emp:** 6. **Officers:** Robin Higham, Publisher; Carol A. Williams, Associate Publisher.

■ 4199 ■ **Superlearning**
450 7th Ave., Ste. 500
New York, NY 10213
Phone: (212)279-8450 **Fax:** (212)695-9288
E-mail: superlearning@worldnet.att.net
URL: http://www.superlearning.com
Products: Products to accelerate learning and expand memory. **SICs:** 5192 (Books, Periodicals & Newspapers); 5099 (Durable Goods Nec). **Est:** 1980. **Officers:** Lynn Schroeder, President; Sheila Ostrander, Chairman of the Board; Christina Vandenboorn, Director.

■ 4200 ■ **Swift Fulfillment Services**
290 Broadway
Lynbrook, NY 11563-3276
Phone: (516)593-1195 **Fax:** (516)596-2911
Products: Books; CD-roms. **SICs:** 5192 (Books, Periodicals & Newspapers); 5045 (Computers, Peripherals & Software). **Est:** 1949. **Officers:** Preston Treiber; Barbara Fiegas.

■ 4201 ■ **Swift Lizard Distributors**
PO Box A, New Mexico Tech
Socorro, NM 87801
Phone: (505)835-5200
Products: Books. **SIC:** 5192 (Books, Periodicals & Newspapers).

■ 4202 ■ **Syracuse University Press**
621 Skytop Rd., Ste. 110
Syracuse, NY 13244-5290
Phone: (315)443-5546
Free: (800)365-8929 **Fax:** (315)443-5545
E-mail: talitz@syr.edu
URL: http://www.sumweb.syr.edu/su-press/
Products: Books. **SIC:** 5192 (Books, Periodicals & Newspapers). **Est:** 1943. **Sales:** $1,700,000 (2000). **Emp:** 22.

■ 4203 ■ **Taylor & Francis, Inc.**
325 Chestnut St., Ste. 800
Philadelphia, PA 19106
Free: (800)354-1420 **Fax:** (215)625-8914
URL: http://www.tandf.co.uk/journals
Products: Books. **SIC:** 5192 (Books, Periodicals & Newspapers). **Est:** 1983.

■ 4204 ■ **Taylor Publishing Co.**
PO Box 597
Dallas, TX 75221
Phone: (214)637-2800
Free: (800)677-2800 **Fax:** (214)637-2800
Products: Books. **SIC:** 5192 (Books, Periodicals & Newspapers). **Est:** 1980.

■ 4205 ■ **Team Up**
PO Box 1115
Warrensburg, MO 64093
Phone: (660)747-3569 **Fax:** (660)747-9748
Products: Books and other printed materials. **SIC:** 5192 (Books, Periodicals & Newspapers).

■ 4206 ■ **Team Up Services**
PO Box 382607
Duncanville, TX 75138
Phone: (972)709-7192 **Fax:** (972)709-7192
E-mail: teamup@god-mind.com
Products: Spiritual growth books. **SIC:** 5192 (Books, Periodicals & Newspapers). **Est:** 1990. **Sales:** $14,000 (2000). **Officers:** Jean Foster, Co-President; Carl Foster, Co-President; Ron Knight, Sales/Marketing Contact, e-mail: rknight@metronet.com.

■ 4207 ■ **Ten Speed Press**
PO Box 7123
Berkeley, CA 94707
Phone: (510)559-1600
Free: (800)841-2665 **Fax:** (510)559-1629
E-mail: order@tenspeed.com
URL: http://www.tenspeed.com
Products: Books, including general non-fiction, cookbooks, career books, self-help, parenting, and children's. **SIC:** 5192 (Books, Periodicals & Newspapers). **Est:** 1971. **Emp:** 75. **Officers:** Phil Wood, Publisher; Kirsty Melville; JoAnn Deck, Sales/Marketing Contact, e-mail: joann@tenspeed.com; Shelli Moore, Customer Service Contact, e-mail: shelli@tenspeed.com; Susan Engle, Human Resources Contact, e-mail: susan@tenspeed.com.

■ 4208 ■ **Terra Nova Press**
1309 Redwood Ln.
Davis, CA 95616
Phone: (530)756-7417 **Fax:** (530)756-7418
Products: Advice books for teenagers. **SIC:** 5192 (Books, Periodicals & Newspapers). **Est:** 1988. **Emp:** 1. **Officers:** Susan Curry, Owner.

■ 4209 ■ **Tesla Book Co.**
PO Box 121873
Chula Vista, CA 91912
Phone: (619)561-0341 **Free:** (800)398-2056
Products: Books. **SIC:** 5192 (Books, Periodicals & Newspapers). **Est:** 1979. **Officers:** Robert Feuling, Owner; Robin Feuling, Owner.

■ 4210 ■ **Texas A & M University Press**
Lewis St., Lindsey Bldg.
4354 TAMU
College Station, TX 77843-4354
Phone: (409)845-1436
Free: (800)826-8911 **Fax:** (409)847-8752
E-mail: fdl@tampress.tamu.edu
URL: http://www.tamu.edu/upress/
Products: Books; Audiotapes. **SICs:** 5192 (Books, Periodicals & Newspapers); 5099 (Durable Goods Nec). **Est:** 1974. **Sales:** $1,500,000 (2000). **Emp:** 22. **Officers:** Charles Backus, Director; Gayla Christiansen, Marketing Mgr.; Sharon Pavlas-Mills, Order Fulfillment Mgr.

■ 4211 ■ **Texas Book Co.**
2601 King St.
Greenville, TX 75401
Phone: (903)455-6937
Free: (800)527-1016 **Fax:** (903)454-2442
Products: Books. **SIC:** 5192 (Books, Periodicals & Newspapers). **Est:** 1976.

■ 4212 ■ **Texas State Directory Press**
1800 Nueces St.
Austin, TX 78701
Phone: (512)477-5698
Free: (800)388-8075 **Fax:** (512)473-2447
E-mail: tsdpress@txdirectory.com
Products: Directories. **SIC:** 5192 (Books, Periodicals & Newspapers). **Est:** 1935. **Sales:** $650,000 (2000). **Emp:** 5. **Officers:** Deena Geltmeyer, Sales & Marketing Contact; Janet Miller, Customer Service Contact.

■ 4213 ■ **Thatcher Distributing Group**
5 Cotter Dr.
New Brunswick, NJ 08901-1506
Phone: (732)246-1357
Products: English local history books. **SIC:** 5192 (Books, Periodicals & Newspapers). **Est:** 1984. **Officers:** Avice R. Wilson, e-mail: avice@lfu.net.

■ 4214 ■ **the distributors**
702 S Michigan
South Bend, IN 46601
Phone: (219)232-8500 **Fax:** (219)577-0440
E-mail: sales@thedistributors.com
URL: http://www.thedistributors.com
Products: Books. **SIC:** 5192 (Books, Periodicals & Newspapers). **Est:** 1970. **Officers:** Marc T. Raymond, Dir. of Sales.

■ 4215 ■ **Thieme New York**
333 7th Ave.
New York, NY 10001
Phone: (212)760-0888
Free: (800)782-3488 **Fax:** (212)947-1112
E-mail: custserv@thieme.com
URL: http://www.thieme.com
Products: Journals and books. **SIC:** 5192 (Books, Periodicals & Newspapers). **Est:** 1979. **Emp:** 35. **Officers:** Brian D. Scanlan, President.

■ 4216 ■ **Thinker's Press**
PO Box 8
Davenport, IA 52805-0008
Phone: (319)323-7117
Free: (800)397-7117 **Fax:** (319)323-7117
Products: Mail order chess books. **SIC:** 5192 (Books, Periodicals & Newspapers). **Est:** 1973. **Sales:** $60,000 (2000). **Emp:** 2. **Officers:** Robert B. Long, Owner.

■ 4217 ■ **Thomson Corp.**
7625 Empire Dr.
Florence, KY 41042
Phone: (606)525-2230 **Fax:** (606)282-5732
Products: General reference books; Textbooks, including teachers' editions. **SIC:** 5192 (Books, Periodicals & Newspapers). **Est:** 1968. **Sales:** $250,000,000 (2000). **Emp:** 135. **Officers:** Brian Nealie, VP & General Mgr.; Ty Field, CFO; Jim Paxton, Distribution Mgr.

■ 4218 ■ **Time Distribution Services Inc.**
1271 Ave. of the Amer.
New York, NY 10020
Phone: (212)522-8437
Products: Magazines. **SIC:** 5192 (Books, Periodicals & Newspapers). **Est:** 1974. **Sales:** $140,000,000 (2000). **Emp:** 600. **Officers:** Rich Jacobsen, CEO & President; Cam Choeter, Sr. VP; Jeff Blatt, Sr. VP.

■ 4219 ■ **Time Life Inc.**
2000 Duke St.
Alexandria, VA 22314-3414
Phone: (703)838-7000
Products: Books; Tapes; Videos. **SICs:** 5192 (Books, Periodicals & Newspapers); 5099 (Durable Goods Nec). **Est:** 1961. **Sales:** $500,000,000 (2000). **Emp:** 1,500. **Officers:** George Artandi, CEO & President; Ralph Cuomo, CFO; Mary P. Donohoe, Dir. of Marketing; Joe Cipolla, Dir. of Data Processing; Steve Goldstein, Dir of Human Resources.

■ 4220 ■ Time Warner and Sony Direct Entertainment
1221 Avenue of the Americas
New York, NY 10020
Phone: (212)522-1212 **Fax:** (212)522-0893
Products: Magazines. **SIC:** 5192 (Books, Periodicals & Newspapers). **Est:** 1990. **Sales:** $500,000,000 (2000). **Emp:** 1,600. **Officers:** Ruth Shields, President; Mack Ruckman, VP & Treasurer.

■ 4221 ■ Torah Umesorah Publications
5723 18th Ave.
Brooklyn, NY 11204
Phone: (718)259-1223 **Fax:** (718)259-1795
Products: Religious books. **SIC:** 5192 (Books, Periodicals & Newspapers). **Est:** 1945. **Officers:** Rabbi Yaakov Fruchter, Dir. of Publications.

■ 4222 ■ Total Information
844 Dewey Ave.
Rochester, NY 14613
Phone: 800-876-4636
Free: (800)876-4636 **Fax:** (716)254-0209
E-mail: orders@totalinformation.com
URL: http://www.totalinformation.com
Products: Books. **SIC:** 5192 (Books, Periodicals & Newspapers).

■ 4223 ■ Tout de Suite a la Microwave Inc.
PO Box 60121
Lafayette, LA 70596-0121
Phone: (318)984-2903
Products: Cook books. **SIC:** 5192 (Books, Periodicals & Newspapers). **Est:** 1977. **Emp:** 1.

■ 4224 ■ Tower Publishing Co.
588 Saco Rd.
Standish, ME 04084
Phone: (207)642-5400
Free: (800)969-8693 **Fax:** (207)642-5463
E-mail: info@towerpub.com
URL: http://www.towerpub.com
Products: Business directories and databases. **SICs:** 5192 (Books, Periodicals & Newspapers); 5092 (Toys & Hobby Goods & Supplies). **Sales:** $800,000 (2000). **Emp:** 13. **Officers:** Michael L. Lyons, President. **Former Name:** Tower International Inc.

■ 4225 ■ The TRACOM Corporation
8773 S Ridgelane Blvd., Ste. 101
Highlands Ranch, CO 80126
Phone: (303)470-4900 **Fax:** (303)470-4901
Products: Human resource and training products. **SICs:** 5085 (Industrial Supplies); 5192 (Books, Periodicals & Newspapers). **Est:** 1957. **Sales:** $2,700,000 (2000). **Emp:** 25. **Officers:** Joe Ratway, President; Steve Harteker, CFO; Julie Bisgard, Dir. of Marketing.

■ 4226 ■ Trafalgar Square
PO Box 257
Howe Hill Rd
North Pomfret, VT 05053
Phone: (802)457-1911
Free: (800)423-4525 **Fax:** (802)457-1913
E-mail: tsquare@sover.net
URL: http://www.trafalgarsquarebooks.com
Products: Books. **SIC:** 5192 (Books, Periodicals & Newspapers). **Est:** 1973. **Emp:** 20. **Officers:** Paul Feldstein, Managing Dir.

■ 4227 ■ Transamerican & Export News Co.
591 Camino de la Reina St., Ste. 200
San Diego, CA 92108-3192
Phone: (619)297-8065 **Fax:** (619)297-5353
Products: Magazines. **SIC:** 5192 (Books, Periodicals & Newspapers). **Est:** 1938. **Sales:** $1,500,000 (2000). **Emp:** 35.

■ 4228 ■ Treasure Chest Books, LLC
451 N Bonita Ave.
Tucson, AZ 85745
Phone: (520)623-9558
Free: (800)969-9558 **Fax:** (520)624-5888
Products: Products from or about the southwestern United States, including books and arts and crafts. **SICs:** 5192 (Books, Periodicals & Newspapers); 5199 (Nondurable Goods Nec). **Est:** 1975. **Emp:** 12. **Officers:** Ross Humphreys, Manager.

■ 4229 ■ Tree Frog Trucking Co.
318 SW Taylor
Portland, OR 97204
Phone: (503)227-4760 **Fax:** (503)227-0829
E-mail: lookglas@teleport.com
Products: Magazines and books. **SIC:** 5192 (Books, Periodicals & Newspapers). **Est:** 1969. **Emp:** 8. **Officers:** Bill Kloster, President.

■ 4230 ■ Tri-State Periodicals, Inc.
9844 Heddon Rd.
PO Box 1110
Evansville, IN 47706
Phone: (812)867-7416 **Fax:** (812)867-7419
Products: Books. **SIC:** 5192 (Books, Periodicals & Newspapers). **Est:** 1982.

■ 4231 ■ Tribune Co.
435 N Michigan Ave.
Chicago, IL 60611
Phone: (312)222-9100
Products: Newspapers. **SIC:** 5093 (Scrap & Waste Materials). **Est:** 1847. **Sales:** $2,719,800,000 (2000). **Emp:** 10,700. **Officers:** John W. Madigan, CEO, President & Chairman of the Board; Donald C. Grenesko, Sr. VP & CFO; Jeff Scherb, VP/CTO; John T. Sloan, Sr. VP & Auditor.

■ 4232 ■ Triple D Publishing Inc.
1300 S Dekalb St.
Shelby, NC 28152
Phone: (704)482-9673
Products: Magazines. **SIC:** 5192 (Books, Periodicals & Newspapers).

■ 4233 ■ Troll Associates of Memphis
4600 Pleasant Hill Rd.
Memphis, TN 38118
Phone: (901)365-4900
Products: Books. **SIC:** 5192 (Books, Periodicals & Newspapers). **Sales:** $86,000,000 (2000). **Emp:** 350. **Officers:** Tony Grano, General Mgr.

■ 4234 ■ Charles E. Tuttle Co. Inc.
153 Milk St., 5th Fl.
Boston, MA 02109-4809
Phone: (617)951-4080 **Fax:** (617)951-4045
Products: Books. **SIC:** 5192 (Books, Periodicals & Newspapers). **Est:** 1832.

■ 4235 ■ Ubiquity Distributors
607 Degraw St.
Brooklyn, NY 11217
Phone: (718)875-5491 **Fax:** (718)875-8047
Products: Periodicals. **SIC:** 5192 (Books, Periodicals & Newspapers). **Est:** 1981. **Emp:** 23. **Officers:** Joseph Massey, Sales/Marketing Contact.

■ 4236 ■ Ultra Books, Inc.
PO Box 945
Oakland, NJ 07436
Phone: (201)337-8787
Products: Trade paperbacks about metaphysics and health. **SIC:** 5192 (Books, Periodicals & Newspapers). **Est:** 1980. **Officers:** Martin S. Ruback, President.

■ 4237 ■ Unicorn Books and Crafts
1338 Ross St.
Petaluma, CA 94954
Phone: (707)762-3362
Free: (800)289-9276 **Fax:** (707)762-0335
Products: Textile crafts books. **SIC:** 5192 (Books, Periodicals & Newspapers).

■ 4238 ■ Unipub
4611-F Assembly Dr.
Lanham, MD 20706-4391
Phone: (301)459-7666
Free: (800)274-4888 **Fax:** 800-865-3450
Products: Books. **SIC:** 5192 (Books, Periodicals & Newspapers). **Est:** 1955. **Officers:** Donald Hagen, Director.

■ 4239 ■ United Magazine Company
5131 Post Rd.
Dublin, OH 43017
Phone: (614)792-0777
Products: Magazines. **SIC:** 5192 (Books, Periodicals & Newspapers). **Est:** 1989. **Sales:** $330,000,000 (2000). **Emp:** 2,100. **Officers:** Ronald Scherer, Chairman of the Board; Dave Thompson, Vice Chairman of the Board. **Alternate Name:** Scherer Companies Inc.

■ 4240 ■ United Magazine Company
5131 Post Rd.
Dublin, OH 43017
Phone: (614)792-0777
Products: Books and other printed materials. **SIC:** 5192 (Books, Periodicals & Newspapers). **Sales:** $330,000,000 (2000). **Emp:** 2,100.

■ 4241 ■ United Magazine Co. Southern Michigan Division
2571 Saradan
Jackson, MI 49202-1211
Phone: (517)784-7163
Free: (800)248-2213 **Fax:** (517)784-0075
Products: Magazines and books. **SIC:** 5192 (Books, Periodicals & Newspapers). **Emp:** 130.

■ 4242 ■ United Methodist Publishing House
201 8th Ave. S
Nashville, TN 37203
Phone: (615)749-6000 **Fax:** (615)749-6079
Products: Christian reading material. **SIC:** 5192 (Books, Periodicals & Newspapers). **Sales:** $82,000,000 (2000). **Emp:** 1,064. **Officers:** Robert K. Feaster, President; Larry Wallace, VP of Finance; Mike Cunningham, Information Systems Mgr. .

■ 4243 ■ Univelt Inc.
PO Box 28130
San Diego, CA 92198-0130
Phone: (760)746-4005 **Fax:** (760)746-3139
E-mail: 76121.1532@compuserve.com
URL: http://www.univelt.staigerland.com
Products: Math and science books; Technical, scientific, and professional books; Publications of American Astronautical Society (AAS). **SIC:** 5192 (Books, Periodicals & Newspapers). **Est:** 1970. **Sales:** $236,000 (1999). **Emp:** 6. **Officers:** Robert H. Jacobs, President; Madeleine Bera, Customer Service Mgr.

■ 4244 ■ University of Alaska Press
Univ. of Alaska Fairbanks
Gruening Bldg., 1st Fl.
PO Box 756240
Fairbanks, AK 99775-6240
Phone: (907)474-5831
Free: (888)252-6657 **Fax:** (907)474-5502
E-mail: fypress@uaf.edu
URL: http://www.uaf.edu/uapress
Products: Books; University press books; Videos; CDs. **SICs:** 5192 (Books, Periodicals & Newspapers); 5065 (Electronic Parts & Equipment Nec). **Est:** 1927. **Sales:** $200,000 (1999). **Emp:** 3. **Officers:** Claus M. Nasze, Executive Dir.; Pamela Odom, Acquisitions Editor; Deirdre Helfferich, Dist. Coord.

■ 4245 ■ University Book Service
2219 Westbrooke Dr.
Columbus, OH 43228
Phone: (614)777-2336
Free: (800)634-4272 **Fax:** (614)777-2341
Products: Juvenile books. **SIC:** 5192 (Books, Periodicals & Newspapers). **Est:** 1957.

■ 4246 ■ University Marketing Group
62 Linden Ave., Apt. B
Branford, CT 06405-5205
Phone: (203)483-5761 **Fax:** (203)481-0869
Products: Books. **SIC:** 5192 (Books, Periodicals & Newspapers).

■ 4247 ■ University of Missouri Press
2910 LeMone Blvd.
Columbia, MO 65201-8291
Phone: (573)882-7641
Free: (800)828-1894 **Fax:** (573)884-4498
Products: Regional interest books. **SIC:** 5192 (Books, Periodicals & Newspapers).

■ 4248 ■ University Press of Colorado
PO Box 849
Niwot, CO 80544
Phone: (303)530-5337 **Fax:** (303)530-5306
Products: Books. **SIC:** 5192 (Books, Periodicals & Newspapers). **Est:** 1969. **Emp:** 8.

■ 4249 ■ University Press of Kansas
2501 W 15th St.
Lawrence, KS 66049-3904
Phone: (785)864-4154 **Fax:** (785)864-4586
E-mail: mail@newpress.upress.ukans.edu
URL: http://www.kansaspress.ku.edu
Products: Non-fiction publications. **SIC:** 5192 (Books, Periodicals & Newspapers). **Est:** 1946. **Sales:** $2,200,000 (2000). **Emp:** 17. **Officers:** Susan Schott, Marketing Mgr., e-mail: sschott@ukans.edu; John Garvin, Accounts Mgr., e-mail: jgarvin@upress.newpress.ukans.edu.

■ 4250 ■ University Press of Virginia
PO Box 400318
Charlottesville, VA 22904-4318
Phone: (804)924-3468
Free: (800)831-3406 **Fax:** (804)982-2655
E-mail: upressva@virginia.edu
URL: http://www.upress.virginia.edu
Products: Books. **SIC:** 5192 (Books, Periodicals & Newspapers). **Est:** 1963. **Emp:** 22. **Officers:** Brenda Fitzgerald, Customer Service Mgr., e-mail: bwf@virginia.edu; Mark H. Saunders, Dir. of Marketing, e-mail: mhs5u@virginia.edu.

■ 4251 ■ University of Texas Press
PO Box 7819
Austin, TX 78713-7819
Phone: (512)471-7233
Free: (800)252-3206 **Fax:** (512)320-0668
Products: Books, including American history, anthropology, art, architecture, and geography. **SIC:** 5192 (Books, Periodicals & Newspapers). **Est:** 1940.

■ 4252 ■ University of Washington Press
PO Box 50096
Seattle, WA 98145-5096
Phone: (206)543-4050
Free: (800)441-4115 **Fax:** (206)543-3932
URL: http://www.washington.edu/uwpress/
Products: Books. **SIC:** 5192 (Books, Periodicals & Newspapers). **Est:** 1919. **Sales:** $4,000,000 (2000). **Emp:** 40.

■ 4253 ■ Upper Access Books
PO Box 457
Hinesburg, VT 05461
Phone: (802)482-2988
Free: (800)356-9315 **Fax:** (802)482-3125
Products: Books. **SIC:** 5192 (Books, Periodicals & Newspapers). **Sales:** $200,000 (2000). **Emp:** 3. **Officers:** Stephen Carlson, Exec. VP; Elizabeth Carlson, Treasurer.

■ 4254 ■ Upper Access Inc.
1 Upper Access Rd.
PO Box 457
Hinesburg, VT 05461
Phone: (802)482-2988
Free: (800)356-9315 **Fax:** (802)482-3125
E-mail: info@upperaccess.com
URL: http://www.upperaccess.com
Products: Books, including nonfiction and small-press titles; Software for small publishers. **SICs:** 5192 (Books, Periodicals & Newspapers); 5045 (Computers, Peripherals & Software). **Est:** 1987. **Sales:** $300,000 (2000). **Emp:** 4. **Officers:** Elizabeth Carlson, President; Stephen Carlson, Exec. VP. **Alternate Name:** Upper Access Books.

■ 4255 ■ Upper Room
PO Box 189
Nashville, TN 37202-0189
Phone: (615)340-7200 **Fax:** (615)340-7006
URL: http://www.upperroom.org
Products: Religious books. **SIC:** 5192 (Books, Periodicals & Newspapers). **Est:** 1935. **Sales:** $17,000,000 (2000). **Emp:** 100.

■ 4256 ■ Upstart Publishing Company Inc.
155 N Wacker Dr.
Chicago, IL 60606
Phone: (312)836-4400 **Fax:** (312)742-9121
Products: Business books. **SIC:** 5192 (Books, Periodicals & Newspapers). **Est:** 1977. **Sales:** $1,000,000 (2000). **Emp:** 8. **Officers:** Dennis Blitz, President.

■ 4257 ■ Vantage Sales & Marketing, Inc.
12 Village Ct.
Hazlet, NJ 07730
Phone: (732)739-3313 **Fax:** (732)739-6404
Products: Books. **SIC:** 5192 (Books, Periodicals & Newspapers). **Est:** 1981.

■ 4258 ■ Vegetarian Resource Group
PO Box 1463
Baltimore, MD 21203
Phone: (410)366-8343 **Fax:** (410)366-8804
Products: Brochures; Cook books; Magazines. **SIC:** 5192 (Books, Periodicals & Newspapers). **Est:** 1982. **Officers:** Charles Stahler; Debra Wasserman.

■ 4259 ■ Vestal Press Ltd.
4720 Boston Way
Lanham, MD 20706-4310
Phone: (301)797-4872 **Fax:** (301)797-4898
Products: Books, audio tapes, and compact discs devoted to the field of band organs, player pianos, music boxes, carousels, radio and phonograph collecting, early film history, and wood carving. **SICs:** 5192 (Books, Periodicals & Newspapers); 5099 (Durable Goods Nec). **Est:** 1961.

■ 4260 ■ Vistabooks Publishing
0637 Blue Ridge Rd.
Silverthorne, CO 80498
Phone: (970)468-7673 **Fax:** (970)468-7673
E-mail: vistabooks@compuserve.com
URL: http://www.vistabooks.com
Products: Books. **SIC:** 5192 (Books, Periodicals & Newspapers). **Est:** 1972. **Sales:** $30,000 (1999). **Emp:** 2. **Officers:** William R. Jones, Editor; Elizabeth A. Kerr, Business Mgr.

■ 4261 ■ VMS Inc.
17600 S Williams St., No. 6
Thornton, IL 60476-1077
Phone: (708)877-2814
Free: (800)343-6430 **Fax:** (708)877-2819
URL: http://www.vms-online.com
Products: Educational materials for industrial and technical training; Home economics and business education, including books, videos, and software. **SICs:** 5192 (Books, Periodicals & Newspapers); 5045 (Computers, Peripherals & Software); 5065 (Electronic Parts & Equipment Nec). **Est:** 1986. **Emp:** 10. **Officers:** Michael S. Walsh, President; Lydia E. Walsh, Vice President. **Former Name:** Vocational Marketing Services.

■ 4262 ■ Volcano Press, Inc.
PO Box 270
Volcano, CA 95689-0270
Phone: (209)296-3445
Free: (800)879-9636 **Fax:** (209)296-4515
E-mail: sales@volcanopress.com
URL: http://www.volcanopress.com
Products: Books; Audio cassettes. **SICs:** 5192 (Books, Periodicals & Newspapers); 5099 (Durable Goods Nec). **Est:** 1976. **Emp:** 5. **Officers:** Ruth Gottstein.

■ 4263 ■ Volcano Press Inc.
PO Box 270
Volcano, CA 95689-0270
Phone: (209)296-3445
Free: (800)879-9636 **Fax:** (209)296-4515
Products: Books and other printed materials. **SIC:** 5192 (Books, Periodicals & Newspapers).

■ 4264 ■ Voyageur Press, Inc.
123 N 2nd St.
PO Box 338
Stillwater, MN 55082
Phone: (612)430-2210
Free: (800)888-9653 **Fax:** (612)430-2211
E-mail: books@voyageurpress.com
Products: Books. **SIC:** 5192 (Books, Periodicals & Newspapers). **Est:** 1973. **Emp:** 20. **Officers:** Tom Lebovsky, Publisher; Dave Hoffman, Director. **Alternate Name:** Town Square Books.

■ 4265 ■ O.G. Waffle Book Co.
897 13th St.
PO Box 586
Marion, IA 52302
Phone: (319)373-1832
E-mail: ogwaffle@aol.com
Products: Books, including children's fiction; Textbooks, including teacher's editions; General reference books. **SIC:** 5192 (Books, Periodicals & Newspapers). **Est:** 1880. **Emp:** 2. **Officers:** Nancy K. Jennings, Owner.

■ 4266 ■ Walk Thru the Bible Ministries Inc.
61 Perimeter Park
PO Box 80587
Atlanta, GA 30366
Phone: (404)458-9300 **Free:** (800)554-9300
Products: Religious books. **SIC:** 5192 (Books, Periodicals & Newspapers).

■ 4267 ■ Walker and Co.
435 Hudson St.
New York, NY 10014-3941
Phone: (212)727-8300
Free: (800)289-2537 **Fax:** (212)307-1764
Products: Children's books; Fiction books; Self help books; Religious books. **SIC:** 5192 (Books, Periodicals & Newspapers).

■ 4268 ■ Ward's Natural Science Establishment Inc.
PO Box 92912
Rochester, NY 14692-9012
Phone: (716)359-2502 **Fax:** (716)334-6174
Products: Science educational materials. **SIC:** 5192 (Books, Periodicals & Newspapers). **Sales:** $34,000,000 (2000). **Emp:** 146. **Officers:** Gerry Christian, President; R. Wiegand, VP of Finance.

■ 4269 ■ W. Warner Book Distributors
1763 Dutch Broadway
Elmont, NY 11003-5044
Phone: (718)949-5910 **Fax:** (718)949-0115
Products: Books. **SIC:** 5192 (Books, Periodicals & Newspapers).

■ 4270 ■ Warner Press Inc.
PO Box 2499
Anderson, IN 46018
Phone: (765)644-7721
Free: (800)741-7721 **Fax:** (765)640-8005
Products: Books; Bulletin boards; Posters; Certificates; Post Cards; Coloring and activity books for children. **SIC:** 5192 (Books, Periodicals & Newspapers). **Est:** 1906. **Emp:** 40.

■ 4271 ■ Weidner & Sons Publishing
Box 2178
Riverton, 11775, 08077
Phone: (856)486-1755 **Fax:** (856)486-7583
E-mail: weidner@waterw.com
URL: http://www.waterw.com/~weidner
Products: Books on science, medicine, law, environment, and natural sciences. **SIC:** 5192 (Books, Periodicals & Newspapers). **Est:** 1971. **Officers:** James H. Weidner, CEO.

■ 4272 ■ Samuel Weiser Inc.
PO Box 612
York Beach, ME 03910-0612
Phone: (207)363-4393
Free: (800)423-7087 **Fax:** (207)363-5799
E-mail: email@weiserbooks.com
URL: http://www.weiserbooks.com
Products: Esoteric, Eastern philosophy, and astrology books. **SIC:** 5192 (Books, Periodicals & Newspapers).

Est: 1956. Emp: 15. Officers: Donald Weiser, President.

■ 4273 ■ WellSpring Books
325-A New Boston St.
Woburn, MA 01801
Phone: (781)938-6001
Free: (800)262-2926 Fax: (781)938-6002
Products: Judaica books. SIC: 5192 (Books, Periodicals & Newspapers). Est: 1974.

■ 4274 ■ Wesleyan Publishing House
Box 50434
Indianapolis, IN 46250
Phone: (317)570-5300
Free: (800)493-7539 Fax: (317)570-5370
E-mail: wph@wesleyan.org
URL: http://www.wesleyan.org
Products: Religious books, including Bibles. SIC: 5192 (Books, Periodicals & Newspapers). Former Name: Wesley Press.

■ 4275 ■ West Texas News Co.
1214 Barranca Dr.
El Paso, TX 79935-4601
Phone: (915)594-7586 Fax: (915)594-7589
Products: Books and magazines. SIC: 5192 (Books, Periodicals & Newspapers). Emp: 49. Officers: Tom Rademacher.

■ 4276 ■ Western Book Distributors
18 Virginia Gdns
Berkeley, CA 94702-1428
Phone: (510)849-0100
Free: (800)825-0100 Fax: (510)849-9157
Products: Books. SIC: 5192 (Books, Periodicals & Newspapers). Est: 1978. Sales: $3,500,000 (2000). Emp: 40. Officers: Matt Wyse, President; Bruce Feldman, Vice President.

■ 4277 ■ Western Library Books
560 S San Vicente Blvd.
Los Angeles, CA 90048
Phone: (213)653-8880
Products: Children's books. SIC: 5192 (Books, Periodicals & Newspapers). Est: 1984. Emp: 3. Officers: Marc Rogell, General Mgr.

■ 4278 ■ Western Merchandisers Inc.
PO Box 32270
Amarillo, TX 79120
Phone: (806)376-6251 Fax: (806)379-8731
Products: Books; Music videos; Computer software. SICs: 5192 (Books, Periodicals & Newspapers); 5065 (Electronic Parts & Equipment Nec); 5045 (Computers, Peripherals & Software). Sales: $530,000,000 (2000). Emp: 3,000. Officers: John Marmaduke, President; Greg Skelton, Controller; Howard Miller, Dir. of Marketing; Don Taylor, Vice President.

■ 4279 ■ Westview Press
5500 Central Ave.
Boulder, CO 80301
Phone: (303)444-3541 Fax: (303)449-3356
Products: Publishes and distributes academic and scholarly books. SIC: 5192 (Books, Periodicals & Newspapers). Sales: $20,000,000 (2000). Emp: 60.

■ 4280 ■ Whitaker House
30 Hunt Valley Cir.
New Kensington, PA 15068-7069
Phone: (412)274-4440
Products: Books. SIC: 5192 (Books, Periodicals & Newspapers).

■ 4281 ■ White Dove International
PO Box 1000
Taos, NM 87571
Phone: (505)758-5400 Fax: (505)758-2265
URL: http://www.powersource.com/wilde
Products: Books; Audio tapes and compact discs. SIC: 5192 (Books, Periodicals & Newspapers). Est: 1986. Former Name: Crystal Cave Enterprises.

■ 4282 ■ Wilcher Associates
13547 Ventura Blvd., I98
Sherman Oaks, CA 91423
Phone: (818)784-0474 Fax: (818)784-3134
Products: Books. SIC: 5192 (Books, Periodicals &

Newspapers). Est: 1947. Emp: 4. Officers: Bob Arnold, Partner, e-mail: bobarnold@earthlink.net; Jeannie Dunham, Partner; Dan Skaggs, Partner; Christine Foye, Partner.

■ 4283 ■ Wildlife Publications, Inc.
1014 NW 14th Ave.
Gainesville, FL 32601
Products: Books. SIC: 5192 (Books, Periodicals & Newspapers).

■ 4284 ■ Robert Wilkie
PO Box 1491
Joshua Tree, CA 92252-0828
Phone: (760)366-3925 Fax: (760)366-9709
Products: Books. SIC: 5192 (Books, Periodicals & Newspapers). Est: 1980.

■ 4285 ■ Darcy Williamson
PO Box 717
Donnelly, ID 83615
Phone: (208)325-8606
Products: Cookbooks and health related books. SIC: 5192 (Books, Periodicals & Newspapers). Est: 1978.

■ 4286 ■ Williamson Publishing Co.
PO Box 185
Charlotte, VT 05445
Phone: (802)425-2102
Free: (800)234-8791 Fax: (802)425-2199
E-mail: info@williamsonbooks.com
URL: http://www.williamsonbooks.com
Products: Active learning books for children ages two and up. SIC: 5192 (Books, Periodicals & Newspapers). Est: 1982. Sales: $3,000,000 (1999). Emp: 10. Officers: Jack Williamson, Publisher & President; Susan Williamson, Publisher & Editorial Dir.

■ 4287 ■ Willis Music Co.
7380 Industrial Rd.
Florence, KY 41042
Phone: (606)283-2050
Free: (800)354-9799 Fax: (606)283-1784
Products: Sheet music. SIC: 5192 (Books, Periodicals & Newspapers). Est: 1899. Emp: 175. Officers: Kevin Cranley, President; Edward Cranley, CEO.

■ 4288 ■ Wilshire Book Co.
12015 Sherman Rd.
North Hollywood, CA 91605
Phone: (818)765-8529 Fax: (818)765-2922
URL: http://www.mpowers.com
Products: Books, including psychology, how-to, non-fiction, mail order, entrepreneurship, horse books, gambling, health, astrology, and new age. SIC: 5192 (Books, Periodicals & Newspapers). Est: 1947. Emp: 21. Officers: Melvin Powers, President, e-mail: mpowers@mpowers.com.

■ 4289 ■ Wilson & Sons
23264 SE 58th St.
Issaquah, WA 98029-8906
Products: Books. SIC: 5192 (Books, Periodicals & Newspapers).

■ 4290 ■ Wimmer Cookbook Distribution
4210 B. F. Goodrich Blvd.
Memphis, TN 38118
Phone: (901)362-8900
Free: (800)727-1034 Fax: (901)795-9806
E-mail: wimmer@wimmerco.com
URL: http://www.wimmerco.com
Products: Cookbooks. SIC: 5192 (Books, Periodicals & Newspapers). Est: 1973. Emp: 150. Officers: Bill Hyatt, President; Melanie Moore Tatum, Dir. of Marketing; Chuck Michls, Controller.

■ 4291 ■ Winston-Derek Publishers Group Inc.
PO Box 90883
Nashville, TN 37209
Phone: (615)256-0201
Free: (800)826-1888 Fax: (615)256-8571
Products: Books; Greeting cards; Art goods. SICs: 5192 (Books, Periodicals & Newspapers); 5199 (Nondurable Goods Nec). Est: 1974. Sales: $1,500,000 (2000). Emp: 14. Officers: James W. Peebles, President; Derek Peebles, Secretary; Matalynn R. Peebles, Vice President; Marcia Watson,

Customer Service Contact; Elaina G. Short, Human Resources Contact.

■ 4292 ■ Wolverine Distributing
305 S Fourth St.
Basin, WY 82410
Phone: (307)568-2434
Free: (800)967-1633 Fax: (307)568-3306
Products: Books and other printed materials. SIC: 5192 (Books, Periodicals & Newspapers). Sales: $1,000,000 (2000). Emp: 2.

■ 4293 ■ Woodcrafters Lumber Sales, Inc.
212 NE 6th Ave.
Portland, OR 97232
Phone: (503)231-0226
Free: (800)777-3709 Fax: (503)232-0511
Products: Books on woodcrafts. SIC: 5192 (Books, Periodicals & Newspapers). Est: 1973.

■ 4294 ■ Woolson Spice Co.
1555 Kalani St.
Honolulu, HI 96817
Phone: (808)847-3600 Fax: (808)847-7900
Products: Roasted coffee. SIC: 5149 (Groceries & Related Products Nec). Sales: $9,000,000 (2000). Emp: 61. Officers: James Delano, President.

■ 4295 ■ Words Distributing Company
7900 Edgewater Dr.
Oakland, CA 94621
Phone: (510)553-9673
Free: (800)593-9673 Fax: (510)632-1281
E-mail: words@wordsdistributing.com
URL: http://www.wordsdistributing.com
Products: Books and video cassettes on spirituality, health and healing, and gay and lesbian topics. SIC: 5192 (Books, Periodicals & Newspapers). Est: 1996. Officers: Joel Bernstein, General Mgr. & Leisa Mock, Acquisitions; Judy Wheeler, Dir. of Mktg. & Sales; Ryn Speich, Sales Mgr.

■ 4296 ■ Wordware Publishing Inc.
2320 Los Rios Blvd., Ste. 200
Plano, TX 75074
Phone: (972)423-0090
Free: (800)229-4949 Fax: (972)881-9147
E-mail: info@wordware.com
URL: http://www.wordware.com
Products: Southwest regional books; Computer and game books; Petcare books; City guides; Educational software. SICs: 5192 (Books, Periodicals & Newspapers); 5045 (Computers, Peripherals & Software). Est: 1982. Emp: 20. Officers: Russell A. Stultz, President; Jim Hill, Publisher; Tom Owens, VP of Finance.

■ 4297 ■ Worldwide Books
1001 W Seneca St.
Ithaca, NY 14850
Phone: (607)272-9200
Free: (800)473-8146 Fax: (607)272-0239
E-mail: info@worldwide-artbooks.com
URL: http://www.worldwide-artbooks.com
Products: Art books. SIC: 5192 (Books, Periodicals & Newspapers). Est: 1962. Emp: 18. Officers: Jean Libkind, Contact.

■ 4298 ■ Worldwide Media Service Inc.
1 Meadowlands Plaza, Ste. 900
East Rutherford, NJ 07073-2100
Phone: (201)332-7100
Products: Magazines and books. SIC: 5192 (Books, Periodicals & Newspapers). Est: 1967. Sales: $60,000,000 (2000). Emp: 50. Officers: Lee Selverne, President; Sandra Joseph, Sr. VP.

■ 4299 ■ Writers & Books
740 University Ave.
Rochester, NY 14607
Phone: (716)473-2590 Fax: (716)729-0982
Products: Books, including small press books. SIC: 5192 (Books, Periodicals & Newspapers). Est: 1973.

■ **4300** ■ **Wyoming Periodical Distributors**
5734 Old W Yellowstone
Casper, WY 82604
Phone: (307)266-5328 **Fax:** (307)266-5329
Products: Periodicals; Paperback books; Magazines.
SIC: 5192 (Books, Periodicals & Newspapers).

■ **4301** ■ **Yankee Book Peddler Inc.**
999 Maple St.
Contoocook, NH 03229
Phone: (603)746-3102
Free: (800)258-3774 **Fax:** (603)746-5628
Products: Academic books. **SIC:** 5192 (Books, Periodicals & Newspapers). **Est:** 1971. **Emp:** 180.
Officers: John Secor, CEO; Glen Secor, CFO.

■ **4302** ■ **Yankee Paperback & Textbook Co.**
PO Box 18880
Tucson, AZ 85731
Phone: (520)325-7229
Free: (800)340-2665 **Fax:** (520)325-7229
Products: Paperback, hardcover, and trade books; Used textbooks; Audio cassettes; Reference materials; Educational materials; Judaic material covering books on history; Chasidis(m)/Chabad; Prayer; Mussar; Stories. **SICs:** 5192 (Books, Periodicals & Newspapers); 5065 (Electronic Parts & Equipment Nec). **Est:** 1983. **Officers:** Jerry Polizzi, Owner.

■ **4303** ■ **Ye Olde Genealogie Shoppe**
9605 Vandergriff Rd.
PO Box 39128
Indianapolis, IN 46239
Phone: (317)862-3330
Free: (800)419-0200 **Fax:** (317)862-2599
E-mail: yogs@iquest.net
URL: http://www.yogs.com
Products: Genealogical and local history books; Marriage records; Will records. **SIC:** 5192 (Books, Periodicals & Newspapers). **Est:** 1975. **Sales:** $250,000 (2000). **Emp:** 4. **Officers:** Walter R; Pat Gooldy.

■ **4304** ■ **Samuel Yudkin & Associates**
A232 Woodber
3636 16th St, NW
Washington, DC 20010
Phone: (202)232-6249 **Fax:** (202)234-0786
Products: Books, including autobiographies, history, novels, non-fiction, and fictionn. **SIC:** 5192 (Books, Periodicals & Newspapers). **Est:** 1970. **Sales:** $50,000 (2000). **Emp:** 3. **Officers:** Samuel Yudkin, President.

■ **4305** ■ **C & W Zabel Co.**
PO Box 41
Leonia, NJ 07605-0041
Phone: (732)254-1000 **Fax:** (732)254-0121
Products: Books. **SIC:** 5192 (Books, Periodicals & Newspapers). **Est:** 1975. **Sales:** $600,000 (2000). **Emp:** 8. **Officers:** Andrew Zabel, Owner.

■ **4306** ■ **Zephyr Press, Inc.**
PO Box 66006
Tucson, AZ 85728-6006
Phone: (520)322-5090
Free: (800)232-2187 **Fax:** (520)323-9402
E-mail: neways2learn@zephyrpress.com
URL: http://www.zephyrpress.com
Products: Educational materials and resources. **SIC:** 5192 (Books, Periodicals & Newspapers). **Est:** 1979. **Emp:** 14. **Officers:** Joey Tanner, e-mail: jtanner@zephyrpress.com; Allen Wittenberg, Human Resources Contact.

■ **4307** ■ **The Zondervan Corp.**
5300 Patterson SE
Grand Rapids, MI 49530
Phone: (616)698-6900
Free: (800)727-1309 **Fax:** (616)698-3313
URL: http://www.zondervan.com
Products: Religious books; Audio tapes; Bibles; Gifts and gift product. **SICs:** 5192 (Books, Periodicals & Newspapers); 5065 (Electronic Parts & Equipment Nec); 5099 (Durable Goods Nec); 5199 (Nondurable Goods Nec). **Est:** 1930. **Emp:** 1,500. **Officers:** Tracy Danz, Marketing & Sales Mgr., e-mail: tracy.danz@zph.com; Claudia Ganzevoort, Customer Service Mgr., e-mail: tina.bedard@zph.com.

(7) Chemicals

Entries in this section are arranged alphabetically by company name. When the company name is a personal name, the company name is alphabetized by the surname unless the first name or initial(s) are part of a trade name. See the User's Guide at the front of this directory for additional information.

■ 4308 ■ **A and S Corp.**
819 Edwards Rd.
Parsippany, NJ 07054
Phone: (201)575-6330 **Fax:** (201)575-5375
Products: Chemicals. **SIC:** 5169 (Chemicals & Allied Products Nec). **Est:** 1979. **Sales:** $5,000,000 (2000). **Emp:** 10. **Officers:** Marc E. Andre, President.

■ 4309 ■ **Aanns Trading Co.**
1805 Crystal Dr., Ste. 809
Arlington, VA 22202
Phone: (703)920-2708 **Fax:** (703)920-4675
Products: Pharmaceuticals; Wood furniture; Lumber and millwork; Nuts; Chemicals. **SICs:** 5169 (Chemicals & Allied Products Nec); 5021 (Furniture); 5031 (Lumber, Plywood & Millwork); 5122 (Drugs, Proprietaries & Sundries); 5145 (Confectionery). **Officers:** Philip H. Anns, President.

■ 4310 ■ **ABA-tron Industries Inc.**
PO Box 6341
Beverly Hills, CA 90212-1341
Phone: (213)857-8358
Products: Chemicals. **SIC:** 5169 (Chemicals & Allied Products Nec). **Sales:** $500,000 (2000). **Emp:** 1.

■ 4311 ■ **Abel Carbonic Products Inc.**
315 Harbor Way
South San Francisco, CA 94080
Phone: (650)873-4212 **Fax:** (650)589-5614
Products: Dry ice. **SIC:** 5199 (Nondurable Goods Nec). **Officers:** James Aberer, President.

■ 4312 ■ **Accurate Chemical and Scientific Corp.**
300 Shames Dr.
Westbury, NY 11590
Phone: (516)333-2221
Free: (800)645-6264 **Fax:** (516)997-4948
Products: Biochemicals and immunochemicals. **SIC:** 5122 (Drugs, Proprietaries & Sundries). **Sales:** $4,000,000 (2000). **Emp:** 26. **Officers:** Rudy Rosenberg, President.

■ 4313 ■ **Aceto Corp.**
1 Hollow Ln., Ste. 201
New HyDe Park, NY 11042-1215
Phone: (516)627-6000 **Fax:** (516)627-6093
Products: Chemicals, including color-producing pharmaceutical coatings and polymer additives. **SIC:** 5169 (Chemicals & Allied Products Nec). **Sales:** $183,000,000 (2000). **Emp:** 75. **Officers:** Leonard S. Schwartz, CEO & President; Donald Horowitz, CFO & Treasurer.

■ 4314 ■ **Aeropres Corp.**
PO Box 78588
Shreveport, LA 71137-8588
Phone: (318)221-6282 **Fax:** (318)213-1270
E-mail: jbowen@aeropres.com
Products: Aerosol propellants; Blowing agents; High purity NGLs. **SIC:** 5169 (Chemicals & Allied Products Nec). **Est:** 1973. **Sales:** $55,000,000 (2000). **Emp:** 158. **Officers:** B.C. McKeever, COO; K. Odom, President.

■ 4315 ■ **Aetna Chemical Corp.**
PO Box 430
Elmwood Park, NJ 07407
Phone: (201)796-0230 **Fax:** (201)796-4845
Products: Industrial chemicals. **SIC:** 5169 (Chemicals & Allied Products Nec). **Sales:** $6,000,000 (2000). **Emp:** 25. **Officers:** R. Moore, General Mgr.; Claire Vargo, Controller.

■ 4316 ■ **A.I.D. Inc.**
PO Box 427
Pennsville, NJ 08070
Phone: (609)678-4142 **Fax:** (609)974-4211
Products: Provides regulatory compliance training concerning the transport, storage, and disposal of hazardous materials. **SICs:** 5169 (Chemicals & Allied Products Nec); 5162 (Plastics Materials & Basic Shapes). **Sales:** $1,200,000 (2000). **Emp:** 12.

■ 4317 ■ **Amalgamet Inc.**
1480 US Hwy. 9 N, Ste. 207
Woodbridge, NJ 07095-1401
Phone: (732)634-6034
Products: Chemicals. **SIC:** 5169 (Chemicals & Allied Products Nec).

■ 4318 ■ **American Chemet Corp.**
PO Box 1160
East Helena, MT 59635
Phone: (406)227-5302 **Fax:** (406)227-8522
Products: Copper and zinc oxides. **SIC:** 5169 (Chemicals & Allied Products Nec).

■ 4319 ■ **American Chemical Company Inc.**
49 Central Ave.
South Kearny, NJ 07032
Phone: (973)344-3600 **Fax:** (973)578-4513
Products: Industrial chemicals and supplies. **SIC:** 5169 (Chemicals & Allied Products Nec). **Sales:** $35,000,000 (2000). **Emp:** 55. **Officers:** Stephan B. Fiveson, President; Mark Klypka, CFO.

■ 4320 ■ **American Chemical Works Co.**
PO Box 6031
Providence, RI 02940
Phone: (401)421-0828 **Fax:** (401)421-5909
Products: Laboratory and industrial chemicals. **SIC:** 5169 (Chemicals & Allied Products Nec). **Sales:** $10,000,000 (2000). **Emp:** 20. **Officers:** Bruce Holland, President; Brad Johnson, Controller.

■ 4321 ■ **American Chemicals Co. Inc.**
49 Central Ave.
South Kearny, NJ 07032
Phone: (973)344-3600 **Fax:** (973)578-4513
URL: http://www.amchems.com
Products: Surface active agents, solvents, and acetates. **SIC:** 5169 (Chemicals & Allied Products Nec). **Est:** 1944. **Emp:** 60. **Officers:** Jim Gardner, Dir. of Operations.

■ 4322 ■ **Amrochem Inc.**
2975 Westchester Ave.
Purchase, NY 10577
Phone: (914)694-4788 **Fax:** (914)694-4823
Products: Chemicals. **SIC:** 5169 (Chemicals & Allied

Products Nec). **Sales:** $700,000 (1990). **Emp:** 6. **Officers:** Daniel Ambarus, President.

■ 4323 ■ **Andrews Paper and Chemical Co.**
PO Box 509, 1 Channel Dr.
Port Washington, NY 11050
Phone: (516)767-2800 **Fax:** (516)767-1632
E-mail: jjkroez@aol.com
Products: Chemicals. **SICs:** 5169 (Chemicals & Allied Products Nec); 5111 (Printing & Writing Paper); 5113 (Industrial & Personal Service Paper). **Est:** 1956. **Sales:** $25,000,000 (2000). **Emp:** 12. **Officers:** Peter Muller, Chairman of the Board; John J. Kroez, VP & Treasurer; Harold Kroez, President.

■ 4324 ■ **Apache Nitrogen Products Inc.**
PO Box 700
Benson, AZ 85602
Phone: (520)720-2217 **Fax:** (520)720-4158
Products: Nitrogen fertilizers, ammonium nitrate solution and prill; distributes blasting caps and boosters. **SIC:** 5169 (Chemicals & Allied Products Nec). **Sales:** $35,000,000 (2000). **Emp:** 112. **Officers:** Robert Cashdollar, CEO & President.

■ 4325 ■ **Applied Biochemists, Inc.**
11163 Stonewood Dr.
Germantown, WI 53022-6500
Phone: (262)255-4449
Free: (800)558-5106 **Fax:** (262)255-4268
E-mail: info@appliedbiochemists.com
URL: http://www.appliedbiochemists.com
Products: Chemicals. **SIC:** 5169 (Chemicals & Allied Products Nec).

■ 4326 ■ **Ashland Chemical Co.**
PO Box 2219
Columbus, OH 43216
Phone: (614)790-3333
Free: (888)274-2436 **Fax:** (614)790-4119
Products: Chemicals. **SIC:** 5169 (Chemicals & Allied Products Nec). **Est:** 1967. **Sales:** $5,346,000,000 (2000). **Officers:** David J. D'Antoni, President; James Wilson, VP & Comptroller.

■ 4327 ■ **Ashland Chemical Co. Industrial Chemicals and Solvents Div.**
5420 Speaker Rd.
Kansas City, KS 66106
Phone: (913)621-3388 **Fax:** (913)621-1146
Products: Fiberglass; Resins; Industrial chemicals and solvents. **SIC:** 5169 (Chemicals & Allied Products Nec). **Est:** 1902. **Sales:** $15,000,000 (2000). **Emp:** 10. **Officers:** M Milton, Manager.

■ 4328 ■ **Atlantic F.E.C. Inc.**
PO Box 1488
Homestead, FL 33090
Phone: (305)247-8800
Products: Fertilizer and agricultural chemicals. **SIC:** 5191 (Farm Supplies). **Sales:** $10,500,000 (2000). **Emp:** 44. **Officers:** Robert F. Wysemann, President; John Frederick, Treasurer & Secty.

■ 4329 ■ **Atlas Chemical Inc.**
2929 Commercial St.
San Diego, CA 92113-1393
Phone: (619)232-7391 **Fax:** (619)232-6129
Products: Industrial chemicals. **SIC:** 5169 (Chemicals & Allied Products Nec). **Est:** 1939. **Sales:** $2,100,000 (2000). **Emp:** 14. **Officers:** R.F. Ellery, Treasurer.

■ 4330 ■ **Atlas Supply Inc.**
1736 4th Ave. S
Seattle, WA 98134
Phone: (206)623-4697
Products: Silicone and sealants. **SIC:** 5169 (Chemicals & Allied Products Nec). **Est:** 1917. **Sales:** $6,000,000 (2000). **Emp:** 18. **Officers:** John Ittes, President; R. McDonald, CFO.

■ 4331 ■ **Atomergic Chemetals Corp.**
71 Carolyn Blvd.
Farmingdale, NY 11735-1527
Phone: (516)694-9000 **Fax:** (631)694-9177
E-mail: info@atomergic.com
URL: http://www.atomergic.com
Products: Special organic and inorganic industrial chemicals. **SIC:** 5169 (Chemicals & Allied Products Nec). **Est:** 1962. **Sales:** $5,000,000 (2000). **Emp:** 30. **Officers:** M. Roitberg, President; M. Blum, Vice President.

■ 4332 ■ **Automotive International Inc.**
11308 Tamarco Dr.
Cincinnati, OH 45242
Phone: (513)489-7883
Free: (800)543-7156 **Fax:** (513)489-1329
Products: Automotive chemicals. **SIC:** 5169 (Chemicals & Allied Products Nec). **Sales:** $25,000,000 (2000). **Emp:** 50. **Officers:** Richard Hallberg, President; Judy Adler, Controller.

■ 4333 ■ **Axchem Solutions Inc.**
317 Washington St.
Manistee, MI 49660-1259
Phone: (231)723-2521 **Fax:** (231)723-7417
Products: Water treatment chemicals. **SIC:** 5169 (Chemicals & Allied Products Nec). **Est:** 1980. **Sales:** $9,000,000 (2000). **Emp:** 42. **Officers:** John Walther; Mike Ennis. **Former Name:** Axchem Inc.

■ 4334 ■ **Axton-Cross Company Inc.**
PO Box 6529
Holliston, MA 01746
Phone: (508)429-6766 **Fax:** (508)429-8688
Products: Industrial chemicals, including water treatment chemicals. **SIC:** 5169 (Chemicals & Allied Products Nec). **Sales:** $15,000,000 (2000). **Emp:** 55. **Officers:** Roger Blanchette Jr., General Mgr.

■ 4335 ■ **Barton Solvents Inc.**
PO Box 221
Des Moines, IA 50301
Phone: (515)265-7998 **Fax:** (515)265-0259
Products: Industrial solvents and chemicals. **SIC:** 5169 (Chemicals & Allied Products Nec). **Sales:** $60,000,000 (2000). **Emp:** 148. **Officers:** Lee L. Casten, President; Ed Walls, Treasurer & Secty.

■ 4336 ■ **Bison Corp.**
1935 SE Allen Ave.
Canton, OH 44707
Phone: (330)455-0282
Products: Industrial chemicals. **SIC:** 5169 (Chemicals & Allied Products Nec). **Est:** 1949. **Sales:** $5,000,000 (1999). **Emp:** 20. **Officers:** W.K. Henry, President.

■ 4337 ■ **Bodman Chemicals, Inc.**
PO Box 2421
Aston, PA 19014
Phone: (610)459-5600
Free: (800)241-8774 **Fax:** (610)459-8036
Products: Photographic equipment and supplies; Photographic printing apparatus; Miscellaneous end-use chemicals and chemical products. **SICs:** 5169 (Chemicals & Allied Products Nec); 5043 (Photographic Equipment & Supplies). **Officers:** Kris Lind, President.

■ 4338 ■ **Bower Ammonia and Chemical**
5811 Tacony St.
Philadelphia, PA 19135
Phone: (215)535-7530 **Free:** (800)643-6226
Products: Ammonia and industrial chemicals. **SIC:** 5169 (Chemicals & Allied Products Nec). **Sales:** $3,000,000 (2000). **Emp:** 25. **Officers:** Steven B. Tanner, President & COO; Jack J. Bowen, Exec. VP of Finance.

■ 4339 ■ **Brenntag Inc.**
PO Box 13786
Reading, PA 19612
Phone: (610)926-6100 **Fax:** (610)926-0420
Products: Chemicals and related products. **SIC:** 5169 (Chemicals & Allied Products Nec). **Sales:** $840,000,000 (1999). **Emp:** 1,400. **Officers:** Steven Clark, President; H. Edward Boyadjian, Sr. VP & CFO.

■ 4340 ■ **Brewer Environmental Industries Inc.**
311 Pacific St.
Honolulu, HI 96817
Phone: (808)532-7400 **Fax:** (808)532-7521
Products: Agricultural equipment and supplies. **SIC:** 5169 (Chemicals & Allied Products Nec). **Sales:** $100,000,000 (2000). **Emp:** 191.

■ 4341 ■ **Calsol Inc.**
PO Box 3983
Pomona, CA 91769
Phone: (909)623-6426
Products: Chemicals and solvents. **SIC:** 5169 (Chemicals & Allied Products Nec). **Est:** 1948. **Sales:** $4,000,000 (2000). **Emp:** 12. **Officers:** John M. Faull, President; Margaret Roff, Comptroller.

■ 4342 ■ **Caravan Trading Corporation**
45 John St.
New York, NY 10038
Phone: (212)943-3257 **Fax:** (212)240-0208
Products: Tin and tin base metals, shapes, forms, etc.; Toiletries and cosmetics; Textured noncellulosic synthetic fibers; Sodium hydroxide (caustic soda); Tobacco. **SICs:** 5169 (Chemicals & Allied Products Nec); 5051 (Metals Service Centers & Offices); 5122 (Drugs, Proprietaries & Sundries); 5194 (Tobacco & Tobacco Products). **Officers:** Laura Fitzgerald, President.

■ 4343 ■ **Cargill Inc.**
PO Box 9300
Minneapolis, MN 55440
Phone: (612)475-7575 **Fax:** (612)475-7899
Products: Potassium, sodium compounds, excluding bleaches, alkalies, alums; Chemical preparations. **SIC:** 5169 (Chemicals & Allied Products Nec). **Officers:** Elaine Koyama, Marketing Mgr.

■ 4344 ■ **Carol Service Co.**
PO Box 25
Lanark, IL 61046
Phone: (815)493-2181 **Fax:** (815)493-6173
Products: Mixed fertilizers. **SIC:** 5169 (Chemicals & Allied Products Nec). **Sales:** $10,000,000 (2000). **Emp:** 45. **Officers:** Lloyd Heller, General Mgr.; Chris Markley, Comptroller.

■ 4345 ■ **Catawba Color and Chemical Company Inc.**
157 21st St. NW
Hickory, NC 28601
Phone: (704)322-3203 **Fax:** (704)322-3204
Products: Chemicals for dyeing and finishing. **SIC:** 5169 (Chemicals & Allied Products Nec). **Est:** 1940. **Sales:** $1,500,000 (2000). **Emp:** 7. **Officers:** R.W. Frye, President.

■ 4346 ■ **Central Scientific Co.**
3300 Cenco Pkwy.
Franklin Park, IL 60131
Phone: (847)451-0150
Products: Chemicals and science equipment for schools. **SICs:** 5169 (Chemicals & Allied Products Nec); 5049 (Professional Equipment Nec). **Sales:** $25,000,000 (2000). **Emp:** 50. **Officers:** Martin Taylor, President; Steve Janis, VP of Finance.

■ 4347 ■ **Century Labs Inc.**
3200 S 24th St.
Kansas City, KS 66106
Phone: (913)262-0227 **Fax:** (913)677-3160
Products: Cleaning chemicals. **SIC:** 5169 (Chemicals & Allied Products Nec). **Est:** 1969. **Sales:** $15,000,000 (2000). **Emp:** 60. **Officers:** Mel Cosner, President; Alan Cosner, Treasurer.

■ 4348 ■ **Chem-Central**
PO Box 9188
Wyoming, MI 49509
Phone: (616)245-9111
Products: Industrial chemicals, including zylene and acetone. **SIC:** 5169 (Chemicals & Allied Products Nec).

■ 4349 ■ **Chem-Serv Inc.**
715 SE 8th St.
Minneapolis, MN 55414
Phone: (612)379-4411 **Fax:** (612)297-8906
Products: Specialty chemicals, including silicas. **SIC:** 5169 (Chemicals & Allied Products Nec). **Est:** 1951. **Sales:** $26,000,000 (2000). **Emp:** 10. **Officers:** Michael H. Baker, Chairman of the Board; Edward Machek, CFO; Harry Fischman, Dir. of Marketing.

■ 4350 ■ **Chemapol USA Inc.**
560 Sylvan Ave.
Englewood Cliffs, NJ 07632
Phone: (201)816-1382 **Fax:** (201)816-1384
Products: Chemicals and pharmaceuticals. **SICs:** 5169 (Chemicals & Allied Products Nec); 5122 (Drugs, Proprietaries & Sundries). **Sales:** $1,000,000 (2000). **Emp:** 3. **Officers:** Tony Kozlik, President.

■ 4351 ■ **CHEMCENTRAL Corp.**
PO Box 730
Bedford Park, IL 60499
Phone: (708)594-7000 **Fax:** (708)594-6328
Products: Solvents; Chemicals. **SIC:** 5169 (Chemicals & Allied Products Nec). **Est:** 1926. **Sales:** $875,000,000 (2000). **Emp:** 900. **Officers:** David Courtney, President & CEO; Lloyd Tarrh, VP & Treasurer; William Hough, VP & Dir. of Marketing.

■ 4352 ■ **ChemDesign Corp.**
99 Development Rd.
Fitchburg, MA 01420
Phone: (978)345-9999 **Fax:** (978)342-9769
Products: Industrial inorganic and organic chemicals. **SIC:** 5169 (Chemicals & Allied Products Nec). **Est:** 1982. **Emp:** 400. **Officers:** Bill Scott, VP of Marketing.

■ 4353 ■ **Chemical Associates of Illinois, Inc.**
1270 S Cleveland Massillon Rd.
Copley, OH 44321
Phone: (330)666-5200 **Fax:** (330)666-2890
E-mail: chemassoc@aol.com
Products: Chemicals. **SIC:** 5169 (Chemicals & Allied Products Nec). **Est:** 1981. **Former Name:** Chemical Associates Inc.

■ 4354 ■ **Chemical Export Company, Inc.**
77 Summer St.
Boston, MA 02210
Phone: (617)292-7773 **Fax:** (617)292-7766
E-mail: cheminex@rcn.com
Products: Industrial inorganic chemicals; Chemical preparations. **SIC:** 5169 (Chemicals & Allied Products Nec). **Est:** 1945. **Sales:** $10,000,000 (2000). **Emp:** 6. **Officers:** Herbert Kimiatek, President.

■ 4355 ■ **Chemical Sales Company Inc.**
4661 Monaco St.
Denver, CO 80216
Phone: (303)333-8511 **Fax:** (303)333-8517
Products: Industrial and hazardous waste. **SIC:** 5169 (Chemicals & Allied Products Nec). **Sales:** $10,000,000 (2000). **Emp:** 25. **Officers:** Art Clark Phd, President; Ronald Schwab Phd, CFO.

■ 4356 ■ **Chemicals Inc.**
270 Osborne Dr.
Fairfield, OH 45014-2246
Phone: (513)682-2000
Free: (800)576-5444 **Fax:** (513)682-2008
E-mail: shellb@chemgroup.com
URL: http://www.chemgroup.com
Products: Chemicals. **SIC:** 5169 (Chemicals & Allied

Products Nec). **Est:** 1960. **Sales:** $18,000,000 (2000). **Emp:** 21. **Officers:** Rich Winans, General Mgr.; Barb Shell.

■ **4357** ■ **Chemisolv Inc.**
5200 Cedar Crest Blvd.
Houston, TX 77087
Phone: (713)644-3797   **Fax:** (713)644-7564
Products: Formulated chemicals for the food and pulp and paper industries. **SIC:** 5169 (Chemicals & Allied Products Nec). **Sales:** $3,000,000 (2000). **Emp:** 7.
Officers: Ralph Davies, President.

■ **4358** ■ **Chemply Div.**
PO Box 18049
Pittsburgh, PA 15236
Phone: (412)384-5353
Free: (800)678-5480   **Fax:** (412)384-4050
Products: Chemicals. **SIC:** 5169 (Chemicals & Allied Products Nec). **Est:** 1963. **Sales:** $50,000,000 (2000).
Emp: 85. **Officers:** R. Kevin Gooderham, President, e-mail: kgooderham@elliseverard.com; William Karns, Controller; Thomas Woodyard, Dir. of Marketing, e-mail: twoodyard@elliseverard.com.

■ **4359** ■ **Chevron Corp.**
PO Box 7753
San Francisco, CA 94120
Phone: (415)894-7700   **Fax:** (415)894-0583
Products: International petroleum exploration, production, refining and marketing; Chemicals, coal and crude oil products distributions. **SICs:** 5169 (Chemicals & Allied Products Nec); 5172 (Petroleum Products Nec). **Sales:** $26,187,000,000 (2000). **Emp:** 39,191. **Officers:** David J. O'Reilly, CEO & Chairman of the Board; Martin Klitten, CFO.

■ **4360** ■ **Citizen's Distributors**
377 Pine St.
Burlington, VT 05401
Phone: (802)865-6992
Products: Chemicals. **SIC:** 5169 (Chemicals & Allied Products Nec).

■ **4361** ■ **Cometals Inc.**
1 Penn Plz., Ste. 4330
New York, NY 10119
Phone: (212)760-1200   **Fax:** (212)564-7915
Products: Industial chemicals, minerals, and metals.
SICs: 5169 (Chemicals & Allied Products Nec); 5051 (Metals Service Centers & Offices). **Emp:** 35. **Officers:** Eli Skornicki, President; Richard Conk, Controller.

■ **4362** ■ **Connell Brothers Company Ltd.**
345 California St., 27th Fl.
San Francisco, CA 94104
Phone: (415)772-4000   **Fax:** (415)772-4011
E-mail: lsmith@wecocbc.com
URL: http://www.wilburellis.com
Products: Chemicals; Plastics. **SICs:** 5169 (Chemicals & Allied Products Nec); 5052 (Coal, Other Minerals & Ores). **Est:** 1898. **Sales:** $300,000,000 (2000). **Emp:** 400. **Officers:** Ted Eliot, President; Herbert Tully, CFO.

■ **4363** ■ **Control Solutions Inc.**
2739 Pasadena Blvd.
Pasadena, TX 77502
Phone: (713)473-4946   **Fax:** (713)473-6713
Products: Chemicals. **SIC:** 5169 (Chemicals & Allied Products Nec). **Est:** 1985. **Sales:** $6,000,000 (2000). **Emp:** 25. **Officers:** Mark Boyd, CEO; Phillip Hunter, Controller; Keith McCoy, Dir. of Marketing & Sales.

■ **4364** ■ **Cook Composites and Polymers Co.**
820 E 14th Ave.
North Kansas City, MO 64116
Phone: (816)391-6000   **Fax:** (816)391-6337
Products: Resins. **SIC:** 5169 (Chemicals & Allied Products Nec). **Est:** 1990. **Sales:** $260,000,000 (2000). **Emp:** 1,100. **Officers:** Werner Bruck, CEO; Jean J. Vanroyen, CFO; Becky Bierschwal, Dir. of Information Systems; Dennis Hercules, VP of Human Resources.

■ **4365** ■ **Coolant Management Services Co.**
11052 Via El Mercado
Los Alamitos, CA 90720
Phone: (562)795-0470   **Fax:** (562)795-0475
E-mail: sales@coolantmanagement.com
URL: http://www.coolantmanagement.com
Products: Miscellaneous end-use chemicals and chemical products; Filters; Industrial wheels; Absorbents. **SICs:** 5169 (Chemicals & Allied Products Nec); 5099 (Durable Goods Nec). **Est:** 1972. **Sales:** $2,900,000 (1999). **Emp:** 14. **Officers:** Patrick L. Cunningham, President, e-mail: pat@coolantmanagement.com.

■ **4366** ■ **Cornbelt Chemical Co.**
PO Box 410
McCook, NE 69001
Phone: (308)345-5057
Products: Agricultural chemicals. **SICs:** 5191 (Farm Supplies); 5169 (Chemicals & Allied Products Nec).
Est: 1975. **Sales:** $75,000,000 (2000). **Emp:** 100.
Officers: Sharon K. Snyder, President.

■ **4367** ■ **Crompton and Knowles Colors Inc.**
PO Box 33188
Charlotte, NC 28233
Phone: (704)372-5890   **Fax:** (704)376-3091
Products: Chemicals and textile dyes. **SIC:** 5169 (Chemicals & Allied Products Nec). **Sales:** $265,000,000 (2000). **Emp:** 650. **Officers:** James J. Conway, President; Richard Lipka, VP & Controller.

■ **4368** ■ **Cron Chemical Corp.**
PO Box 14042
Houston, TX 77221
Phone: (713)644-7561   **Fax:** (713)644-9369
Products: Chemicals. **SIC:** 5169 (Chemicals & Allied Products Nec). **Est:** 1951. **Sales:** $28,000,000 (2000).
Emp: 50. **Officers:** J.J. Sette, CEO; Paul Ochoa, CFO.

■ **4369** ■ **D-Chem Corp.**
PO Box 460462
St. Louis, MO 63146
Phone: (314)772-8700   **Fax:** (314)773-4644
Products: Rustproofing chemicals. **SIC:** 5169 (Chemicals & Allied Products Nec). **Sales:** $3,000,000 (2000). **Emp:** 6.

■ **4370** ■ **Degussa Huls**
65 Challenger Rd.
Ridgefield Park, NJ 07660-2100
Phone: (201)641-6100   **Fax:** (201)807-3183
Products: Specialty chemicals; Precious metal products. **SIC:** 5169 (Chemicals & Allied Products Nec). **Sales:** $2,152,000,000 (2000). **Emp:** 2,400.
Officers: Andrew Burke, CEO & President; Karl J. Schmidt, VP & CFO.

■ **4371** ■ **Delta Distributors Inc.**
610 Fisher Rd.
Longview, TX 75604
Phone: (903)759-7151   **Fax:** (903)759-7548
Products: Sulfuric acids; Mineral spirits; Tylene. **SIC:** 5169 (Chemicals & Allied Products Nec). **Est:** 1966.
Sales: $95,000,000 (2000). **Emp:** 200. **Officers:** Kevin Kessing, President; David Baker, Controller; Charley Peck, Vice President.

■ **4372** ■ **Diamond Chemical/Supply Co.**
524 S Walnut St. Plaza
Wilmington, DE 19801
Phone: (302)656-7786   **Fax:** (302)656-3039
E-mail: sales@diamondchemical.com
URL: http://www.diamondchemical.com
Products: Industrial chemicals; Floor and carpet maintenance equipment; Paper products; Dishwashing and laundry chemicals; Kitchen equipment; Odor control products. **SICs:** 5169 (Chemicals & Allied Products Nec); 5113 (Industrial & Personal Service Paper); 5087 (Service Establishment Equipment). **Est:** 1934. **Sales:** $4,500,000 (2000). **Emp:** 28. **Officers:** R.L. Ventresca, President; R.G. Ventresca, VP of Operations; G.A. Ventresca, Vice President of Equipment Division; Joan Winnington, Sales Mgr.; Speed Malik, Accounting Officer; Jessica Fatkin, Administration Assistant.

■ **4373** ■ **Dixie Chemical Co. Inc.**
PO Box 130410
Houston, TX 77219
Phone: (713)863-1947
E-mail: mail@dixiechemical.com
URL: http://www.dixiechemical.com
Products: Chemicals. **SIC:** 5169 (Chemicals & Allied Products Nec). **Est:** 1946. **Emp:** 200. **Officers:** Gary Mossman, President; Malcolm P. Johnson, Marketing Mgr.

■ **4374** ■ **Douglas Products and Packaging Co.**
1550 E Old 210 Hwy.
Liberty, MO 64068
Phone: (816)781-4250
Free: (800)223-3684   **Fax:** (816)781-1043
E-mail: douglasproducts@juno.com
Products: Agricultural sanitation products; Heat transfer fluids. **SICs:** 5169 (Chemicals & Allied Products Nec); 5191 (Farm Supplies). **Est:** 1916.
Sales: $4,000,000 (2000). **Emp:** 16. **Officers:** G.C. McCaslin, President; Marc C. McCaslin, Vice President; Julie D'Ambrosia, Customer Service Contact; Roberta M. Holt, Human Resources Contact.

■ **4375** ■ **Dover Sales Co. Inc.**
PO Box 2479
Berkeley, CA 94702
Phone: (510)527-4780
Products: Industrial chemicals, including glycerine.
SIC: 5169 (Chemicals & Allied Products Nec). **Est:** 1937. **Sales:** $1,000,000 (2000). **Emp:** 5. **Officers:** V. Emmerich, Owner.

■ **4376** ■ **E.I. Dupont de Nemours and Co.**
1007 Market St.
Wilmington, DE 19898
Free: (800)441-7515   **Fax:** (302)774-7321
Products: Chemicals; Polymer products, including plastics; Medical equipment, including diagnostic imagers, centrifuges, and laboratory instruments; Automotive paints and resins; Electronics; Textile and industrial fibers. **SICs:** 5169 (Chemicals & Allied Products Nec); 5047 (Medical & Hospital Equipment); 5065 (Electronic Parts & Equipment Nec); 5162 (Plastics Materials & Basic Shapes); 5198 (Paints, Varnishes & Supplies).

■ **4377** ■ **Eagle Chemical Co.**
125 Witman Rd.
Reading, PA 19605
Phone: (215)921-2301
Products: Industrial dye and water treatment systems.
SIC: 5169 (Chemicals & Allied Products Nec). **Est:** 1940. **Sales:** $10,000,000 (2000). **Emp:** 18. **Officers:** James R. Pacific, President.

■ **4378** ■ **ECCA America Inc.**
PO Box 330
Sylacauga, AL 35150
Phone: (205)249-4901   **Fax:** (205)208-4600
Products: Calcium carbonate. **SIC:** 5169 (Chemicals & Allied Products Nec). **Sales:** $50,000,000 (2000).
Emp: 300. **Officers:** Jeremy Croggan, President.

■ **4379** ■ **Ecolab Inc. Professional Products Div.**
Ecolab Center, 370 N Wabasha St.
St. Paul, MN 55102
Phone: (612)293-2233   **Free:** (800)247-5362
Products: Janitorial products such as floorcare products, hard-surface cleaners, hand soaps, carpet-care products and odor-control systems. **SIC:** 5169 (Chemicals & Allied Products Nec). **Sales:** $90,000,000 (2000). **Emp:** 650. **Officers:** Dean DeBuhr, VP & General Merchandising Mgr.

■ **4380** ■ **Ecological Laboratories**
3314 Bertha Dr.
Baldwin, NY 11510
Phone: (516)379-3441   **Fax:** (516)379-3434
Products: Chemical preparations. **SIC:** 5169 (Chemicals & Allied Products Nec). **Officers:** Mike Richter.

■ 4381 ■ Elan Chemical Co.
268 Doremus Ave.
Newark, NJ 07105
Phone: (201)344-8014 **Fax:** (201)344-5990
Products: Chemicals. **SIC:** 5169 (Chemicals & Allied Products Nec). **Est:** 1969. **Sales:** $36,000,000 (2000). **Emp:** 121. **Officers:** Ira B. Kapp, President; David R. Weisman, Finance Officer; Cynthia McRae-Sheard, Vice President.

■ 4382 ■ Ellis and Everard Inc.
700 Galleria Pkwy., No. 350
Atlanta, GA 30339
Phone: (404)956-5360 **Fax:** (404)618-0770
Products: Household and industrial chemicals. **SIC:** 5169 (Chemicals & Allied Products Nec). **Est:** 1982. **Sales:** $430,000,000 (2000). **Emp:** 1,000. **Officers:** William J. Gissendanner, CEO & President; Anthony Barber, CFO.

■ 4383 ■ Empire Airgas
1200 Sullivan St.
Elmira, NY 14901
Free: (800)666-6523 **Fax:** 800-333-6523
Products: Industrial supplies. **SIC:** 5169 (Chemicals & Allied Products Nec). **Sales:** $25,000,000 (2000). **Emp:** 135.

■ 4384 ■ Environmental Chemical Group Inc.
PO Box 9
Rogers, TX 76569
Phone: (254)642-3444
Products: Environmentally safe chemicals. **SIC:** 5169 (Chemicals & Allied Products Nec).

■ 4385 ■ EXSL/Ultra Labs Inc.
1767 National Ave.
Hayward, CA 94545
Phone: (510)786-4567 **Fax:** (510)786-1826
Products: soap and detergents. **SICs:** 5169 (Chemicals & Allied Products Nec); 5087 (Service Establishment Equipment). **Sales:** $5,000,000 (2000). **Emp:** 9. **Officers:** Jon Tooper, President.

■ 4386 ■ Farmers Cooperative Association (Okarche, Oklahoma)
PO Box 187
Okarche, OK 73762
Phone: (405)263-7289
Products: Agricultural chemicals and farm supplies. **SIC:** 5191 (Farm Supplies). **Sales:** $6,000,000 (1994). **Emp:** 14. **Officers:** Dean Anderson, General Mgr.

■ 4387 ■ Farmers Union Oil Co. (Great Falls, Montana)
1000 Snetter Ave.
Great Falls, MT 59404
Phone: (406)453-2435
Products: Chemicals, farm supplies, petroleum bulk station. **SICs:** 5169 (Chemicals & Allied Products Nec); 5191 (Farm Supplies); 5171 (Petroleum Bulk Stations & Terminals). **Sales:** $15,000,000 (1992). **Emp:** 35. **Officers:** David Shane, President; Jim McDonald, Controller.

■ 4388 ■ Farwest Corrosion Control Co.
1480 W Artesia Blvd.
Gardena, CA 90248-3215
Phone: (310)532-9524 **Fax:** (310)532-3934
E-mail: fwcc@farwst.com
URL: http://www.farwst.com
Products: Corrosion control products. **SIC:** 5169 (Chemicals & Allied Products Nec). **Est:** 1961. **Emp:** 75. **Officers:** Gordon Rankin, President; Frank Skaff, Controller; Troy Rankin, Vice President; Steve Susa, Sales/Marketing Contact, e-mail: steve@farwst.com.

■ 4389 ■ Fitz Chem Corp.
757 Larch Ave.
Elmhurst, IL 60126
Phone: (708)941-0410 **Fax:** (708)941-0439
Products: Chemicals; Raw materials. **SICs:** 5169 (Chemicals & Allied Products Nec); 5159 (Farm-Product Raw Materials Nec). **Est:** 1985. **Sales:** $22,000,000 (2000). **Emp:** 17. **Officers:** R.C. Becker, President; Laura Bodmer, Controller; E. Croco, VP of Marketing.

■ 4390 ■ Flame Spray Inc.
PO Box 600510
San Diego, CA 92160
Phone: (619)283-2007
Products: Thermal spray coatings. **SIC:** 5169 (Chemicals & Allied Products Nec). **Sales:** $6,000,000 (2000). **Emp:** 20. **Officers:** Larry Suhl, President; Adolpho Castellas, Dir. of Marketing.

■ 4391 ■ Flask Chemical Corp.
13226 Nelson Ave.
La Puente, CA 91746-1514
Phone: (626)336-6690 **Fax:** (626)369-6131
Products: Chemicals. **SIC:** 5169 (Chemicals & Allied Products Nec). **Est:** 1972. **Sales:** $4,000,000 (2000). **Emp:** 15. **Officers:** Gerald B. Shapiro, President; Graig Robitaille, Operations Mgr.; Suzan Szymanski, Mgr. of Admin.

■ 4392 ■ Fly Guard Systems Inc.
PO Box 805
Sweet Home, OR 97386-0805
Phone: (541)367-1600
Free: (800)811-1039 **Fax:** (541)259-3312
Products: Insecticides. **SIC:** 5191 (Farm Supplies). **Est:** 1983. **Officers:** Darryl Zucker, Chairman of the Board.

■ 4393 ■ Food Ingredients and Additives Group
620 Progress Ave.
Waukesha, WI 53186
Phone: (414)547-5531 **Fax:** (414)547-0587
Products: Cultures and enzymes. **SIC:** 5169 (Chemicals & Allied Products Nec). **Sales:** $70,000,000 (2000). **Emp:** 175. **Officers:** David Carpenter, VP & General Merchandising Mgr.; Karen Miller, Controller.

■ 4394 ■ Francis Drilling Fluids Ltd.
PO Box 1694
Crowley, LA 70526
Phone: (318)783-8685
Products: Drilling fluid. **SIC:** 5169 (Chemicals & Allied Products Nec). **Sales:** $43,000,000 (2000). **Emp:** 100. **Officers:** Mike Francis, President; Ken Mattaws, Controller.

■ 4395 ■ Fremont Chemical Company Inc.
203 E Main St.
Riverton, WY 82501
Phone: (307)856-6063
Products: Oil field chemicals. **SIC:** 5169 (Chemicals & Allied Products Nec).

■ 4396 ■ Gallard-Schlesinger Industries Inc.
777 Zeckenderf Blvd.
Garden City, NY 11530
Phone: (516)229-4000
Free: (800)645-3044 **Fax:** (516)229-4015
E-mail: info@gallard-schlesinger.com
URL: http://www.gallard-schlesinger.com
Products: Food grade phosphates; Nutritional supplement and flavor ingredients; Cheese/dairy ingredients; Baking ingredients; Meat, poultry, and seafood ingredients; Cosmetics; Hair care products; Industrial and biotechnology lab products. **SICs:** 5169 (Chemicals & Allied Products Nec); 5122 (Drugs, Proprietaries & Sundries). **Est:** 1950. **Sales:** $50,000,000 (2000). **Emp:** 45. **Officers:** Sheldon Silibiger, President; Frank Voce, Controller; Daphne Toyas, Office Mgr.

■ 4397 ■ G.M. Gannon Company Inc.
3134 Post Rd.
Warwick, RI 02886
Phone: (401)738-2200
Products: Industrial chemicals. **SIC:** 5169 (Chemicals & Allied Products Nec). **Est:** 1969. **Sales:** $13,000,000 (2000). **Emp:** 25. **Officers:** G.M. Gannon, President.

■ 4398 ■ GEO Drilling Fluids Inc.
1431 Union Ave.
Bakersfield, CA 93305
Phone: (805)325-5919
Products: Chemicals for oil wells. **SIC:** 5169 (Chemicals & Allied Products Nec). **Est:** 1981. **Sales:** $9,000,000 (2000). **Emp:** 50. **Officers:** James Clifford, President; Richard Phillips, CFO.

■ 4399 ■ Girindus Corp.
34650 U.S Hwy. 19 N, No. 208
Palm Harbor, FL 34684-2156
Phone: (813)781-8383 **Fax:** (813)287-0033
Products: Chemicals; Pharmaceuticals. **SICs:** 5169 (Chemicals & Allied Products Nec); 5122 (Drugs, Proprietaries & Sundries). **Sales:** $1,000,000 (2000). **Emp:** 3. **Officers:** Robert Link, President.

■ 4400 ■ G.J. Chemical Company Inc.
370-376 Adams St.
Newark, NJ 07114
Phone: (201)589-1450 **Fax:** (201)589-5786
Products: Ethyl alcohol and other industrial organic chemicals; Household and industrial chemicals. **SIC:** 5169 (Chemicals & Allied Products Nec). **Est:** 1975. **Sales:** $26,000,000 (2000). **Emp:** 49. **Officers:** Giosue Masci, President; Diane Colonna, CFO; T.G. Fenstermaker Jr., VP of Sales; Tushar Butala, Dir. of Data Processing; Flore Masci, Vice President; Paul DiMarco, Marketing & Sales Mgr.

■ 4401 ■ GNI Group Inc.
PO Box 220
Deer Park, TX 77536-0220
Phone: (281)930-0350 **Fax:** (281)930-0355
Products: Specialty chemicals. **SIC:** 5169 (Chemicals & Allied Products Nec). **Sales:** $68,500,000 (2000). **Emp:** 177. **Officers:** Carl V. Rush Jr., CEO & President; Titus H. Harris III, CFO.

■ 4402 ■ J.M. Grimstad, Inc.
2251 Hutson Rd.
Green Bay, WI 54303
Phone: (920)429-2040 **Fax:** (920)429-2050
Products: Fluid power components. **SIC:** 5169 (Chemicals & Allied Products Nec).

■ 4403 ■ J.M. Grimstad, Inc.
1100 Zane Ave. N
Minneapolis, MN 55422
Phone: (612)544-6100 **Fax:** (612)544-0282
Products: Fluid power components. **SIC:** 5169 (Chemicals & Allied Products Nec).

■ 4404 ■ J.M. Grimstad, Inc.
4792 Colt Rd.
Rockford, IL 61125
Phones: (815)874-6666 (847)364-4656
Fax: (815)874-4072
Products: Fluid power components. **SIC:** 5169 (Chemicals & Allied Products Nec).

■ 4405 ■ Hamler Industries
5811 Tacony St.
Philadelphia, PA 19135
Phone: (215)535-7530
Free: (800)643-6013 **Fax:** (215)743-7013
URL: http://www.tannerind.com
Products: Ammonia. **SIC:** 5169 (Chemicals & Allied Products Nec). **Est:** 1868. **Sales:** $10,000,000 (2000). **Emp:** 50. **Officers:** Stephen B. Tanner, President & COO; Jack J. Bowen, Exec. VP; John J. Bowen, Exec. VP.

■ 4406 ■ Harold Implement Company Inc.
1101 N Missouri
Corning, AR 72422
Phone: (870)857-3931
Products: Farm implements. **SIC:** 5083 (Farm & Garden Machinery).

■ 4407 ■ Harris Chemical Group Inc.
399 Park Ave., 32nd Fl.
New York, NY 10022
Phone: (212)750-3510
Products: Chemicals. **SIC:** 5169 (Chemicals & Allied Products Nec). **Sales:** $1,270,000,000 (2000). **Emp:** 2,951. **Officers:** D. George Harris, CEO; Manny DiTeresi, CFO.

■ 4408 ■ Harwell & Associates Inc. Chemical Div.
6507 E 42nd St.
Tulsa, OK 74145
Phone: (918)622-1212 **Fax:** (918)627-5416
Products: Household and industrial chemicals; Miscellaneous end-use chemicals and chemical products; Ethyl alcohol and other industrial organic

chemicals. **SIC:** 5169 (Chemicals & Allied Products Nec). **Est:** 1987. **Sales:** $1,000,000 (2000). **Emp:** 99. **Officers:** Mathew A. Brainerd.

■ **4409** ■ **Harwick Standard Distribution Corporation**
60 S Seiberling
Akron, OH 44305
Phone: (330)798-9300 **Fax:** (330)798-0214
URL: http://www.harwickstandard.com
Products: Raw materials for rubber and plastics compounds. **SIC:** 5169 (Chemicals & Allied Products Nec). **Est:** 1932. **Emp:** 110. **Officers:** J. J. Buda, CEO; K. S. Nygaard, VP of Marketing & Sales; J.E. Semonin, VP of Technology; E.M. Corbett, CEO; G.R. Hamrick, Sr. VP; R.C. Stambaugh.

■ **4410** ■ **Haviland Agricultural Inc.**
4160 Ten Mile Rd.
Sparta, MI 49345
Phone: (616)887-8333 **Fax:** (616)887-8333
Products: Agricultural chemicals. **SIC:** 5191 (Farm Supplies); 5169 (Chemicals & Allied Products Nec). **Est:** 1946. **Sales:** $18,000,000 (2000). **Emp:** 30. **Officers:** Dave Schwallier, General Mgr.; Tom Mollan, Director.

■ **4411** ■ **Haviland Products Co.**
421 Ann St. NW
Grand Rapids, MI 49504
Phone: (616)361-6691
Free: (800)456-1134 **Fax:** (616)361-9772
Products: General industrial and consumer chemical products. **SIC:** 5169 (Chemicals & Allied Products Nec). **Sales:** $52,000,000 (2000). **Emp:** 150. **Officers:** E. Bernard Haviland, President; T. Simmons, Controller.

■ **4412** ■ **hci Coastal Chemical Co., LLC**
PO Box 820
Abbeville, LA 70511-0820
Phone: (337)898-0001
Free: (800)535-3862 **Fax:** (337)892-1185
URL: http://www.hollandchemical.com
Products: Industrial chemicals. **SIC:** 5169 (Chemicals & Allied Products Nec). **Est:** 1958. **Sales:** $110,000,000 (2000). **Emp:** 221. **Officers:** J. Doyle, Group VP, e-mail: jdoyle@hciww.com; Scott Schwardt, Regional Mgr., e-mail: sschwardt@hciww.com. **Former Name:** Coastal Chemical Co., LLC.

■ **4413** ■ **HCI Great Lakes Region**
4801 S Austin
Chicago, IL 60638
Phone: (773)586-2000 **Fax:** (708)594-5678
URL: http://www.hciww.com
Products: Chemicals for industrial, food and personal care markets. **SICs:** 5169 (Chemicals & Allied Products Nec); 5122 (Drugs, Proprietaries & Sundries). **Est:** 1958. **Officers:** Gary Sauder, Regional Mgr.; Dan Arneson, Marketing Mgr. **Former Name:** Tab Chemicals Inc.

■ **4414** ■ **Henkel Corp. Chemicals Group**
5051 Estecreek Rd.
Cincinnati, OH 45232-1446
Phone: (513)482-3000
Products: Chemicals. **SIC:** 5169 (Chemicals & Allied Products Nec). **Est:** 1840. **Sales:** $300,000,000 (2000). **Emp:** 1,300. **Officers:** Robert Betz, President; Bill Land, Controller; Anthony Grybowski, Information Systems Mgr.; Michael Schubert, Dir of Human Resources.

■ **4415** ■ **John R. Hess and Company Inc.**
PO Box 3615
Cranston, RI 02910-0615
Phone: (401)785-9300
Products: Chemicals. **SIC:** 5169 (Chemicals & Allied Products Nec). **Est:** 1969. **Sales:** $26,000,000 (2000). **Emp:** 30. **Officers:** Peter Hess, President & Treasurer.

■ **4416** ■ **Hill Brothers Chemical Co.**
1675 N Main St.
Orange, CA 92867
Phone: (714)998-8800 **Fax:** (714)998-6310
SIC: 5169 (Chemicals & Allied Products Nec). **Est:** 1923. **Sales:** $21,800,000 (2000). **Emp:** 125. **Officers:**

Thomas A. Kipers, Exec. VP & CFO; Ronald R. Hill, President; Matt Thorne, Vice President.

■ **4417** ■ **HM Water Technologies Inc.**
PO Box 793
Barnegat, NJ 08005
Phone: (609)698-2468 **Fax:** (609)698-0121
Products: Specializes in industrial water treatment sales of chemicals and equipment, analytical testing of industrial water, and fuel oil treatment chemicals and testing. **SIC:** 5169 (Chemicals & Allied Products Nec). **Sales:** $300,000 (2000). **Emp:** 2.

■ **4418** ■ **E.T. Horn Co.**
16141 Heron Ave.
La Mirada, CA 90638
Phone: (714)523-8050 **Fax:** (714)670-6851
E-mail: ethorn@ethorn.com
Products: Food additives; Industrial materials. **SICs:** 5169 (Chemicals & Allied Products Nec); 5085 (Industrial Supplies). **Est:** 1961. **Sales:** $35,000,000 (2000). **Emp:** 70. **Officers:** Gene Alley, CEO; Patrick J. Marantette, President; James F. Calkin, VP of Marketing; Misty Carpenter, Data Processing Mgr.

■ **4419** ■ **Houghton Chemical Corp.**
PO Box 307
Allston, MA 02134
Phone: (617)254-1010 **Fax:** (617)254-2713
URL: http://www.houghton.com
Products: Industrial solvents; Chemicals; Water-treatment products; Antifreeze products. **SIC:** 5169 (Chemicals & Allied Products Nec). **Est:** 1927. **Sales:** $35,000,000 (2000). **Emp:** 75. **Officers:** Bruce Houghton, President; Mark Houghton, Exec. VP.

■ **4420** ■ **Hubbard-Hall Inc.**
563 S Leonard St.
Waterbury, CT 06708
Phone: (203)756-5521 **Fax:** (203)756-9017
URL: http://www.hubbardhall.com
Products: Industrial chemicals. **SIC:** 5169 (Chemicals & Allied Products Nec). **Est:** 1849. **Sales:** $50,000 (2000). **Emp:** 140. **Officers:** A.K. Skipp, President.

■ **4421** ■ **Hubbard Implement Inc.**
Hwy. 65 N
Hubbard, IA 50122
Phone: (515)864-2226
Products: Agricultural machinery. **SIC:** 5083 (Farm & Garden Machinery).

■ **4422** ■ **Humco Holding Group Inc.**
7400 Alumax Dr.
Texarkana, TX 75501
Phone: (903)831-7808
URL: http://www.humco.com
Products: Powder; Acetone. **SICs:** 5169 (Chemicals & Allied Products Nec); 5122 (Drugs, Proprietaries & Sundries). **Est:** 1947. **Sales:** $17,000,000 (2000). **Emp:** 150. **Officers:** Greg Pulido, President; John Thomas, Treasurer; Brenda P. Marshall, Dir. of Sales; Bernadette Howze, Data Processing Mgr.; Betty Rich, Dir of Human Resources.

■ **4423** ■ **HVC Inc.**
4600 Dues Dr.
Cincinnati, OH 45246
Phone: (513)874-9261 **Fax:** (513)874-0350
Products: Chemicals. **SIC:** 5169 (Chemicals & Allied Products Nec). **Est:** 1955. **Sales:** $47,000,000 (2000). **Emp:** 160. **Officers:** James B. Skelton, President; Richard P. Jones, Controller.

■ **4424** ■ **Hydrite Chemical Co.**
PO Box 0948
Brookfield, WI 53008-0948
Phone: (414)792-1450 **Fax:** (414)792-8721
Products: Chemicals. **SIC:** 5169 (Chemicals & Allied Products Nec). **Est:** 1926. **Sales:** $185,700,000 (2000). **Emp:** 650. **Officers:** John Honkamp, President; Dave Mueller, Finance Officer; Charles L. Terry, Dir. of Marketing; Jim Krueger, Dir. of Information Systems; Janine Arendj, Human Resources Mgr.; Paul Honkamp, Vice President.

■ **4425** ■ **ICI Fluoropolymers**
PO Box 15391
Wilmington, DE 19850-5391
Phone: (302)363-4746
Products: Thermoplastic resins. **SIC:** 5169 (Chemicals & Allied Products Nec). **Sales:** $65,000,000 (2000). **Emp:** 150. **Officers:** Charles D. Allen, Manager.

■ **4426** ■ **Ideal Chemical and Supply Co.**
4025 Air Park St.
Memphis, TN 38118
Phone: (901)363-7720
Free: (800)232-6776 **Fax:** (901)366-0864
E-mail: idealchem@worldnet.att.net
URL: http://www.idealchemical.com
SIC: 5169 (Chemicals & Allied Products Nec). **Est:** 1932. **Sales:** $35,000,000 (2000). **Emp:** 120. **Officers:** Sam Block Jr., CEO; Linda Wax, VP of Finance; Dennis Whipple, VP of Sales; Eloise McGee, Human Resources Contact, e-mail: emcgee@idealchem.com.

■ **4427** ■ **Industrial Adhesives Inc.**
PO Box 2489
Eugene, OR 97402
Phone: (541)683-6677 **Fax:** (541)343-4019
Products: Adhesives and sealants. **SIC:** 5169 (Chemicals & Allied Products Nec). **Officers:** Bernny Peters, President.

■ **4428** ■ **Industrial Environmental Products Inc.**
4035 Nine-Mcfarland Dr.
Alpharetta, GA 30022
Phone: (404)475-3993 **Fax:** 800-233-8550
Products: Adsorbents. **SIC:** 5169 (Chemicals & Allied Products Nec). **Emp:** 15.

■ **4429** ■ **Industrial Solvents Corp.**
411 Theodore Fremd Ave.
Rye, NY 10580
Phone: (914)967-7771
Products: Chemicals. **SIC:** 5169 (Chemicals & Allied Products Nec). **Est:** 1930. **Sales:** $30,000,000 (2000). **Emp:** 100. **Officers:** Edward Gardner, President.

■ **4430** ■ **Inland Leidy Inc.**
2225 Evergreen St.
Baltimore, MD 21216
Phone: (410)889-6600 **Fax:** (410)383-7826
Products: Chemicals; Dyes; Powders. **SIC:** 5169 (Chemicals & Allied Products Nec). **Est:** 1926. **Sales:** $34,000,000 (2000). **Emp:** 37. **Officers:** Samuel K. Himmelrich, CEO; Andrew D. Swanston, CFO; Thomas W. Lucas, VP of Sales.

■ **4431** ■ **Interconsal Associates Inc.**
544 E Weddell Dr., No. 9
Sunnyvale, CA 94089-2113
Phone: (408)745-0161 **Fax:** (408)745-6396
Products: Miscellaneous end-use chemicals and chemical products. **SIC:** 5169 (Chemicals & Allied Products Nec). **Est:** 1963. **Sales:** $6,000,000 (2000). **Emp:** 4. **Officers:** Patricia Ciano, President.

■ **4432** ■ **Interstate Chemical Co.**
2797 Freedland Rd.
Hermitage, PA 16148
Phone: (724)981-3771
Free: (800)422-2436 **Fax:** (724)981-3675
E-mail: lrazzano@interstatechemical.com
URL: http://www.interstatechemical.com
Products: Industrial chemicals. **SIC:** 5169 (Chemicals & Allied Products Nec). **Est:** 1968. **Sales:** $170,000,000 (1999). **Emp:** 260. **Officers:** Albert Puntureri, CEO, e-mail: apuntureri@interstatechemical.com.

■ **4433** ■ **JTS Enterprises Inc.**
4600 Post Oak Pl., Ste. 153
Houston, TX 77027
Phone: (713)621-6740 **Fax:** (713)621-2454
E-mail: 104636.1204@compuserve.com
Products: Industrial chemicals. **SIC:** 5169 (Chemicals & Allied Products Nec). **Est:** 1986. **Sales:** $50,000,000 (2000). **Emp:** 3. **Officers:** Forrest Henson Jr., President.

■ 4434 ■ **Keystone Aniline Corp.**
2501 W Fulton St.
Chicago, IL 60612
Phone: (312)666-2015
Products: Dyes. **SIC:** 5169 (Chemicals & Allied Products Nec). **Est:** 1921. **Sales:** $35,000,000 (2000). **Emp:** 50. **Officers:** Arthur J. Andrews, President; George A. Andrews, Dir. of Systems.

■ 4435 ■ **Keystone Chemical Supply Inc.**
PO Box 398
Wayne, MI 48184
Phone: (734)397-2600   **Fax:** (734)397-8111
Products: Chemicals and drugs. **SICs:** 5169 (Chemicals & Allied Products Nec); 5122 (Drugs, Proprietaries & Sundries). **Est:** 1947. **Sales:** $6,000,000 (2000). **Emp:** 12. **Officers:** Robert P. Goulet, CEO & President; Frank Vetere, Sales Mgr.

■ 4436 ■ **KMG Chemicals Inc.**
10611 Harwin Dr.
Houston, TX 77036
Phone: (713)988-9252   **Fax:** (713)988-9298
Products: Water filtration chemicals and systems. **SIC:** 5169 (Chemicals & Allied Products Nec). **Sales:** $22,700,000 (2000). **Emp:** 76. **Officers:** David L. Hatcher, President & Chairman of the Board; Jack Vernie, Controller.

■ 4437 ■ **Komp Equipment Company Inc.**
PO Box 1489
Hattiesburg, MS 39403-1489
Phone: (601)582-8215   **Fax:** (601)582-0100
Products: Industrial supplies. **SIC:** 5169 (Chemicals & Allied Products Nec). **Sales:** $10,000,000 (2000). **Emp:** 20. **Officers:** George P. Komp, CEO & President.

■ 4438 ■ **Larsen International, Inc.**
700 W Metro Park
Rochester, NY 14623
Phone: (716)272-7310   **Fax:** (716)272-0159
Products: Industrial organic chemicals; Chemical preparations; Electrical equipment; Environmental control instruments. **SICs:** 5169 (Chemicals & Allied Products Nec); 5049 (Professional Equipment Nec); 5063 (Electrical Apparatus & Equipment). **Officers:** Anant K. Upadhyaya, Exec. VP.

■ 4439 ■ **LCI Ltd.**
PO Box 4900
Jacksonville Beach, FL 32240-9000
Phone: (904)241-1200
Products: Chemicals. **SIC:** 5169 (Chemicals & Allied Products Nec).

■ 4440 ■ **LEK USA Inc.**
333 Sylvan Ave.
Englewood Cliffs, NJ 07632
Phone: (201)541-9310   **Fax:** (201)541-9314
Products: Active pharmaceutical ingredients. **SIC:** 5122 (Drugs, Proprietaries & Sundries). **Est:** 1995. **Sales:** $10,000,000 (2000). **Emp:** 3. **Officers:** Branko Huc Phd., President; Andrej Bertoncelj, President.

■ 4441 ■ **Loos and Dilworth Inc.**
61 E Green Ln.
Bristol, PA 19007
Phone: (215)785-3591
Free: (800)229-5667   **Fax:** (215)785-3597
Products: Chemicals; Motor oil. **SICs:** 5169 (Chemicals & Allied Products Nec); 5172 (Petroleum Products Nec). **Est:** 1893. **Emp:** 22. **Officers:** R. Campbell, President; Dave Tompkins, Sr. VP & General Mgr.; Linda Schepise, Dir. of Marketing.

■ 4442 ■ **Los Angeles Chemical Co.**
4545 Ardine St.
South Gate, CA 90280
Phone: (213)562-9500   **Fax:** (213)773-0909
Products: Chemicals, including acids and industrial chemicals. **SIC:** 5169 (Chemicals & Allied Products Nec). **Sales:** $15,000,000 (2000). **Emp:** 30. **Officers:** David Miller, President; Kosta Skovitis, CFO.

■ 4443 ■ **Lynde Co.**
3040 E Hennepin Ave.
Minneapolis, MN 55413
Phone: (612)331-2840
Products: Chemicals. **SIC:** 5169 (Chemicals & Allied Products Nec). **Sales:** $2,000,000 (2000). **Emp:** 6.

■ 4444 ■ **M and M Chemical Supply Inc.**
PO Box 1467
Casper, WY 82602-1467
Phone: (307)473-8818
Free: (800)585-8814   **Fax:** (307)473-8827
Products: Cleaning and janitorial supplies. **SIC:** 5169 (Chemicals & Allied Products Nec).

■ 4445 ■ **MacAlaster Bicknell Company of New Jersey Inc.**
Depot & North Sts.
Millville, NJ 08332
Phone: (609)825-3222   **Fax:** (609)825-3375
Products: Chemicals and additives. **SIC:** 5169 (Chemicals & Allied Products Nec). **Sales:** $5,000,000 (2000). **Emp:** 10. **Officers:** Karen Barsuglia, President; Kathleen Greenfield, Treasurer & Secty.

■ 4446 ■ **Magic American Corp.**
23700 Mercantile Rd.
Beachwood, OH 44122
Phone: (216)464-2353   **Fax:** (216)464-5895
Products: Household cleaners and polishes. **SIC:** 5169 (Chemicals & Allied Products Nec). **Sales:** $16,000,000 (2000). **Emp:** 32. **Officers:** Alan Zeilinger, President.

■ 4447 ■ **Magnolia Chemical and Solvents Inc.**
PO Box 10278
New Orleans, LA 70181
Phone: (504)733-6600
Free: (800)733-0066   **Fax:** (504)736-9200
E-mail: magchem@bellsouth.net
URL: http://www.magnoliachemicals.com
Products: Chemicals. **SIC:** 5169 (Chemicals & Allied Products Nec). **Est:** 1962. **Sales:** $15,000,000 (2000). **Emp:** 30. **Officers:** Richard E. Alberstadt, CEO & President.

■ 4448 ■ **Maintenance Engineering Corp.**
PO Box 1729
Houston, TX 77251
Phone: (713)222-2351   **Fax:** (713)222-1407
Products: Petrochemicals. **SIC:** 5169 (Chemicals & Allied Products Nec). **Sales:** $51,000,000 (1994). **Emp:** 150. **Officers:** Brad Hance, President; Brad Hance, Exec. VP of Finance.

■ 4449 ■ **Maltby Company Inc.**
11132-G Fleetwood St.
Sun Valley, CA 91352
Phone: (818)768-4426   **Fax:** (818)768-4429
Products: Automotive chemicals; Automotive and industrial adhesives and sealants. **SIC:** 5169 (Chemicals & Allied Products Nec). **Est:** 1982. **Sales:** $500,000 (2000). **Emp:** 3. **Officers:** Joe Pinto, President; Sheila M. Zacha, Treasurer & Secty.

■ 4450 ■ **George Mann and Company, Inc.**
PO Box 9066
Providence, RI 02940
Phone: (401)781-5600
Free: (800)556-2426   **Fax:** (401)785-1070
URL: http://www.georgemann.com
Products: Chemicals. **SIC:** 5169 (Chemicals & Allied Products Nec). **Est:** 1921. **Sales:** $35,000,000 (1999). **Emp:** 110. **Officers:** Richard D. Cleek, President; Louis R. Dolan, VP of Sales; Robert J. Marcotte, Sr. VP; Michael Duchesne, Sr. VP.

■ 4451 ■ **Market Actives, LLC**
8300 SW 71st Ave.
Portland, OR 97223
Phone: (503)244-0166
Free: (800)786-1609   **Fax:** (503)244-1555
URL: http://www.BitrexUSA@aol.com
Products: Bitrex bittering agents; Fragrances; Waxes; Essential oils. **SIC:** 5169 (Chemicals & Allied Products Nec). **Officers:** Mitchell Tracy. **Former Name:** B.I. Chemicals, Inc.

■ 4452 ■ **Paul Marsh Inc.**
654 Madison Ave.
New York, NY 10021
Phone: (212)759-9060   **Fax:** (212)319-6214
Products: Chemicals and allied products; Computers, peripherals, and software; Paintbrush bristles; Fine hair for artist brushes; Musical instruments. **SICs:** 5169 (Chemicals & Allied Products Nec); 5199 (Nondurable Goods Nec); 5045 (Computers, Peripherals & Software). **Officers:** Nelly Shoham, Purchasing Agent.

■ 4453 ■ **R.J. Marshall Co.**
26776 W 12 Mile Rd.
Southfield, MI 48034
Phone: (248)353-4100   **Fax:** (248)948-6460
E-mail: rjmarshco@aol.com
URL: http://www.rjmarshallco.com
Products: Industrial raw materials, including powders; Chemicals. **SICs:** 5169 (Chemicals & Allied Products Nec); 5085 (Industrial Supplies). **Est:** 1979. **Sales:** $20,000,000 (2000). **Emp:** 70. **Officers:** Richard J. Marshall, President; Joan E. Marshall, Exec. VP; Chris McLeod, COO & VP.

■ 4454 ■ **Martrex Inc.**
PO Box 1709
Minnetonka, MN 55345-3793
Phone: (612)933-5000   **Fax:** (612)933-1889
Products: Chemicals. **SIC:** 5169 (Chemicals & Allied Products Nec). **Est:** 1969. **Sales:** $40,000,000 (2000). **Emp:** 15. **Officers:** Bradley J. Boote, President; Scott Zachary, Controller.

■ 4455 ■ **Mega Systems Chemicals Inc**
450 N McKemy Ave.
Chandler, AZ 85226
Phone: (602)437-9105   **Fax:** (602)437-2613
Products: Chemicals for the semiconductor industry. **SIC:** 5169 (Chemicals & Allied Products Nec). **Officers:** Richard Roney, President; Pat Mehall, CFO.

■ 4456 ■ **Mega Systems Chemicals Inc.**
450 N McKerry Ave.
Chandler, AZ 85226
Phone: (602)437-9108   **Fax:** (602)437-2613
Products: Chemicals for the semiconductor industry. **SIC:** 5169 (Chemicals & Allied Products Nec). **Emp:** 170. **Officers:** Richard Honey, President; Pat Mehall, CFO.

■ 4457 ■ **Miller Machinery and Supply Company of Tampa**
PO Box 4039
Jacksonville, FL 32201-4039
Phone: (813)623-3553
Products: Chemicals; Dairy products. **SICs:** 5169 (Chemicals & Allied Products Nec); 5143 (Dairy Products Except Dried or Canned). **Est:** 1917. **Sales:** $2,000,000 (2000). **Emp:** 11. **Officers:** R.W. Decker, President; E.L. Decker Jr., Exec. VP.

■ 4458 ■ **Minnesota Chemical Co.**
2285 Hampden Ave.
St. Paul, MN 55114
Phone: (612)646-7521
Products: Chemicals. **SIC:** 5169 (Chemicals & Allied Products Nec). **Est:** 1915. **Sales:** $9,000,000 (2000). **Emp:** 35. **Officers:** Mike Baker, President; Steve Baker, VP & Treasurer.

■ 4459 ■ **Mon-Dak Chemical Inc.**
PO Box 1187
Washburn, ND 58577
Phone: (701)462-8588
Products: Chemicals. **SIC:** 5169 (Chemicals & Allied Products Nec). **Sales:** $2,000,000 (2000). **Emp:** 6. **Officers:** Howard J. Hawkins, CEO & Chairman of the Board.

■ 4460 ■ **Monson Chemicals Inc.**
154 Pioneer Dr.
Leominster, MA 01453
Phone: (508)534-1425   **Fax:** (508)840-1060
Products: Agricultural chemicals; Medicinal chemicals and botanical products. **SICs:** 5169 (Chemicals & Allied Products Nec); 5122 (Drugs, Proprietaries & Sundries). **Est:** 1961. **Sales:** $45,000,000 (2000). **Emp:** 75. **Officers:** Eugene P. McDonald, CEO & President;

Charles Walkovich, CFO; Normand W. Lafontaine, Vice President.

■ **4461** ■ **Monterey Chemical Co. Inc.**
PO Box 35000
Fresno, CA 93745-5000
Phone: (559)499-2100   **Fax:** (559)499-2100
URL: http://www.montereychemical.com
Products: Chemicals and chemical products. **SICs:** 5191 (Farm Supplies); 5169 (Chemicals & Allied Products Nec). **Est:** 1963. **Sales:** $14,000,000 (2000). **Emp:** 35. **Officers:** John F. Salmonson, President.

■ **4462** ■ **Moorhead and Company Inc.**
PO Box 8092
Van Nuys, CA 91409
Phone: (818)873-6640
Free: (800)290-2427   **Fax:** (818)787-2010
Products: Colloidal chemicals used in baking goods. **SIC:** 5169 (Chemicals & Allied Products Nec). **Sales:** $6,000,000 (2000). **Emp:** 11. **Officers:** Deborah Nichols, President; Betsy Nichols, Secretary.

■ **4463** ■ **Mozel Inc.**
4003 Park Ave.
St. Louis, MO 63110
Phone: (314)865-3115   **Fax:** (314)865-3129
Products: Chemicals. **SIC:** 5169 (Chemicals & Allied Products Nec). **Est:** 1931. **Sales:** $101,000,000 (1999). **Emp:** 107. **Officers:** David L. Watson, President; Don Kloppenburg, VP of Admin. & CFO; Jim O'Neill, VP of Sales; Steve Dollmon, VP of Sales; Mark Forthaus, VP of Operations.

■ **4464** ■ **Nalco Chemical Co.**
6991 E Camelback Rd.
Scottsdale, AZ 85251-2436
Phone: (480)941-3915   **Fax:** (480)945-1791
Products: Various chemical preparations for water treatment, industrial heating and cooling. **SIC:** 5169 (Chemicals & Allied Products Nec).

■ **4465** ■ **NanoMaterials, Inc.**
9 Preston Dr.
Barrington, RI 02806
Phone: (401)433-7022   **Fax:** (401)433-7001
E-mail: admin@nanomaterials.com
URL: http://www.nanomaterials.com
Products: Specialty chemicals; Metal, ceramic, composite, and fullerene nano-sized powders, including ultrafine, nanoparticles, nanocrystals, and nanophase. **SICs:** 5169 (Chemicals & Allied Products Nec); 5051 (Metals Service Centers & Offices). **Est:** 1996. **Sales:** $1,000,000 (2000). **Emp:** 12. **Officers:** Emily S. Reade, President; Charles Reade Jr., Sales Mgr.; Karen Ramos, Customer Service Contact.

■ **4466** ■ **Neutron Industries Inc.**
7107 N Black Canyon Hwy.
Phoenix, AZ 85021
Phone: (602)864-0090   **Fax:** (602)864-1790
Products: Cleaning supplies, polishing and sanitation preparations. **SIC:** 5169 (Chemicals & Allied Products Nec).

■ **4467** ■ **Neville Chemical Co.**
2800 Neville Rd.
Pittsburgh, PA 15225-1496
Phone: (412)331-4200   **Fax:** (412)777-4234
E-mail: neville@usaor.net
Products: Synthetic resins. **SIC:** 5169 (Chemicals & Allied Products Nec). **Est:** 1925. **Sales:** $120,000,000 (2000). **Emp:** 500. **Officers:** L. Van V. Dauler Jr. Jr., President & Chairman of the Board; William E. Moffitt, VP & Treasurer; George J. Willock, VP of Sales; John F. Kotow, Data Processing Mgr.

■ **4468** ■ **Nippon Steel Chemical Corporation of America**
345 Park Ave.
New York, NY 10154
Phone: (212)486-7150
Products: Chemicals. **SIC:** 5169 (Chemicals & Allied Products Nec).

■ **4469** ■ **Norco Inc.**
PO Box 15299
Boise, ID 83715
Phone: (208)336-1643   **Fax:** (208)384-1720
Products: Welding, safety, medical and specialty gases and supplies. **SIC:** 5169 (Chemicals & Allied Products Nec). **Officers:** Jim Kissler, CEO.

■ **4470** ■ **Norman, Fox & Co.**
PO Box 58727
Vernon, CA 90058
Phone: (323)583-0016
Free: (800)632-1777   **Fax:** (323)583-9769
E-mail: norfox@worldnet.att.net
URL: http://www.norfoxx.com
Products: Soaps; Surfactants; Chemicals and related items. **SIC:** 5169 (Chemicals & Allied Products Nec). **Est:** 1971. **Emp:** 42. **Officers:** Keith Johnson, President; Mary A. Luby, VP of Admin.; D.J. O'Shea, VP of Business Development; Jim Morgan, Dir. of Marketing; J. Michael Evans, Vice President; Norma S. Specht, Manager Customer Service; Mary A. Luby, VP Administration.

■ **4471** ■ **Odeen International, Inc.**
506 Cherry Rd.
Memphis, TN 38117
Phone: (901)682-6910   **Fax:** (901)767-2995
Products: Chemical surface active agents; Industrial organic chemicals. **SIC:** 5169 (Chemicals & Allied Products Nec). **Officers:** Marshall H. Odeen, President.

■ **4472** ■ **Old World Industries, Inc.**
4065 Commercial Ave.
Northbrook, IL 60062
Phone: (847)559-2000   **Free:** (800)323-5440
URL: http://www.oldworldind.com
Products: Anti-freeze and miscellaneous chemical products. **SIC:** 5169 (Chemicals & Allied Products Nec). **Est:** 1973. **Emp:** 135. **Officers:** Tom Hurvis, Chairman of the Board; Riaz Waraich, President. **Former Name:** Old World Trading Co.

■ **4473** ■ **Olin Corp.**
PO Box 4500
Norwalk, CT 06856-4500
Phone: (203)356-2000   **Fax:** (203)356-3595
Products: Chemicals; Copper ammunition. **SICs:** 5169 (Chemicals & Allied Products Nec); 5099 (Durable Goods Nec). **Est:** 1985. **Sales:** $2,000,000 (2000). **Emp:** 5. **Officers:** Jan Eveland, President; Hope Cortissoz, Controller.

■ **4474** ■ **Organic Dyestuffs Corp.**
PO Box 14258
East Providence, RI 02914
Phone: (401)434-3300   **Fax:** (401)438-8136
Products: Textile dyes processing. **SIC:** 5169 (Chemicals & Allied Products Nec). **Sales:** $7,000,000 (2000). **Emp:** 100. **Officers:** Robert Gormley, President.

■ **4475** ■ **Original Mink Oil Inc.**
PO Box 20191
Portland, OR 97220
Phone: (503)255-2814
Free: (800)547-5895   **Fax:** (503)255-2487
E-mail: omink@aol.com
Products: Waterproofers; Conditioners. **SIC:** 5169 (Chemicals & Allied Products Nec). **Est:** 1957. **Sales:** $1,000,000 (2000). **Emp:** 4. **Officers:** N.P. Wood, President; E.T. Wood, CFO; C.E. Wood, Dir. of Marketing & Sales; S.L. Stone, Dir. of Data Processing.

■ **4476** ■ **Osakagodo America Inc.**
600 3rd Ave.
New York, NY 10016
Phone: (212)867-0678
Products: Dyes and chemicals. **SIC:** 5169 (Chemicals & Allied Products Nec).

■ **4477** ■ **OSCA Inc.**
PO Box 80627
Lafayette, LA 70598
Phone: (318)837-6047
Products: Industrial chemicals for oil and gas. **SIC:** 5169 (Chemicals & Allied Products Nec). **Sales:**

$175,000,000 (2000). **Emp:** 600. **Officers:** Richard J Alario, CEO; John Jordan, President.

■ **4478** ■ **Overseas Capital Corp.**
3615 Euclid Ave.
Cleveland, OH 44115
Phone: (216)881-1322   **Fax:** (330)722-2281
Products: Solvents. **SIC:** 5169 (Chemicals & Allied Products Nec). **Est:** 1984. **Sales:** $90,000,000 (2000). **Emp:** 50. **Officers:** Vir K. Sondhi, CEO; Ijaz H. Shah, VP & CFO; Alvin McDaniel, VP of Marketing; Roger Herbold, Dir. of Data Processing.

■ **4479** ■ **P.A.T. Products Inc.**
44 Central St.
Bangor, ME 04401
Phone: (207)942-6348   **Fax:** (207)942-9662
Products: Chemical preparations. **SICs:** 5169 (Chemicals & Allied Products Nec); 5162 (Plastics Materials & Basic Shapes). **Sales:** $6,000,000 (2000). **Emp:** 8. **Officers:** Leo Coyle, President.

■ **4480** ■ **P.B. and S. Chemical Inc.**
PO Box 20
Henderson, KY 42420
Phone: (502)827-3545   **Fax:** (502)826-1486
Products: Chemicals, including chlorine, caustic and other acids, and copper sulfate. **SIC:** 5169 (Chemicals & Allied Products Nec). **Sales:** $180,000,000 (2000). **Emp:** 450. **Officers:** Tom McFarland, President; Al Bunpus, Controller; Ray Pemberton, Dir. of Marketing; Ken Curray, Dir of Human Resources.

■ **4481** ■ **Polysciences Inc.**
400 Valley Rd.
Warrington, PA 18976
Phone: (215)343-6484
Free: (800)523-2575   **Fax:** (215)343-0214
E-mail: polysci@tigger.jvnc.net
URL: http://www.polysciences.com
Products: Fine chemicals; Contract packaging; Custom synthesis. **SIC:** 5169 (Chemicals & Allied Products Nec). **Est:** 1961. **Sales:** $13,000,000 (1999). **Emp:** 80. **Officers:** Michael Ott, President; Mike Stehlin, Sales/Marketing Contact, e-mail: mstehlin@polysciences.com.

■ **4482** ■ **Potash Import and Chemical Corp.**
201 E 42nd St.
New York, NY 10017
Phone: (212)697-4994   **Fax:** (212)599-2778
E-mail: sales@picc-ny.com
Products: Chemicals and fertilizers, including magnesium sulphate, magnesium chloride, potassium sulphate, and potassium chloride. **SICs:** 5169 (Chemicals & Allied Products Nec); 5191 (Farm Supplies). **Est:** 1954. **Emp:** 7. **Officers:** Gerhard Horn, President; Mark Roberts, Vice President; Trey Few, Sales Mgr.

■ **4483** ■ **Power Chemical Company Inc.**
375 Rider Ave.
Bronx, NY 10451
Phone: (212)292-4320   **Fax:** (212)292-4322
Products: Industrial chemicals. **SIC:** 5169 (Chemicals & Allied Products Nec). **Est:** 1946. **Sales:** $4,500,000 (2000). **Emp:** 18. **Officers:** Harvey Schwartz, President.

■ **4484** ■ **PRC-DeSoto International Inc. Semco Application Systems**
PO Box 1800
Glendale, CA 91209
Phone: (818)247-7140   **Fax:** (818)549-7606
Products: Plastic cartridges for storing, mixing and applying chemicals; Sealant, coating and allied product distribution. **SIC:** 5169 (Chemicals & Allied Products Nec). **Sales:** $46,000,000 (1999). **Emp:** 234. **Officers:** Dennis Kovalsky, General Mgr.; David Johnson, Controller.

■ **4485** ■ **Princeton Lipids**
1 Research Way
Princeton, NJ 08540
Phone: (609)734-8457   **Fax:** (609)452-1890
Products: High purity phospholipids. **SIC:** 5122 (Drugs, Proprietaries & Sundries). **Sales:** $1,000,000 (1993). **Emp:** 3. **Officers:** Edward G. Silverman, COO.

■ 4486 ■ Pueblo Chemical and Supply Co.
PO Box 1279
Garden City, KS 67846
Phone: (316)275-6127
Products: Agricultural chemicals. **SICs:** 5191 (Farm Supplies); 5169 (Chemicals & Allied Products Nec). **Est:** 1965. **Sales:** $50,000,000 (2000). **Emp:** 100. **Officers:** Quentin Wilke, General Mgr.; Bob Brown, Controller.

■ 4487 ■ Puratex Co.
6714 Wayne Ave.
Pennsauken, NJ 08110-1699
Phone: (609)663-1050
Free: (800)698-6780   **Fax:** (609)663-1056
Products: Household and industrial chemicals. **SIC:** 5169 (Chemicals & Allied Products Nec). **Est:** 1928. **Sales:** $1,000,000 (2000). **Emp:** 10. **Officers:** R.F. Kuehne, President; W.T. Bounder, Secretary.

■ 4488 ■ Quickshine of America Inc.
277 Fairfield Dr.
Fairfield, NJ 07004
Phone: (973)227-4011   **Fax:** (973)227-5436
Products: Metal cleaners. **SIC:** 5169 (Chemicals & Allied Products Nec). **Est:** 1987. **Sales:** $3,000,000 (2000). **Emp:** 6. **Officers:** Joel Keoning, President.

■ 4489 ■ RAE Products and Chemical Inc.
11630 S Cicero Ave.
Alsip, IL 60803
Phone: (708)396-1984   **Fax:** (708)396-2332
Products: Industrial chemicals. **SIC:** 5169 (Chemicals & Allied Products Nec). **Est:** 1975. **Sales:** $5,500,000 (2000). **Emp:** 22. **Officers:** Donna Gurenberg, President; Fred Gruenberg, CFO; Guy Gurenberg, Dir. of Marketing.

■ 4490 ■ Rausch Naval Stores Company Inc.
PO Box 4085
New Orleans, LA 70178
Phone: (504)833-3754   **Fax:** (504)866-0502
Products: Pine chemicals. **SIC:** 5169 (Chemicals & Allied Products Nec). **Est:** 1932. **Sales:** $5,000,000 (2000). **Emp:** 25. **Officers:** Walter W. Rausch, President.

■ 4491 ■ Reade Advanced Materials
PO Box 15039
Riverside, RI 02915-0039
Phone: (401)433-7000   **Fax:** (401)433-7001
E-mail: ramsales@reade.com
URL: http://www.reade.com
Products: Specialty chemicals; Ceramic and metal powders, foils, wires, reagents, abrasives, fillers, reinforcements, nanomaterials, and sputtering targets. **SICs:** 5169 (Chemicals & Allied Products Nec); 5085 (Industrial Supplies). **Est:** 1881. **Sales:** $5,000,000 (2000). **Emp:** 25. **Officers:** Charles Reade Jr., Sales Mgr.; Emily S. Reade, General Mgr., e-mail: ereade@reade.com; Charles Reade, Sales/Marketing Contact, e-mail: sales@reade.com; Karen Ramos, Customer Service Contact, e-mail: kramos@reade.com; Bethany L. Cochran, Western Regional Manager.

■ 4492 ■ H. Reisman Corp.
377 Crane St.
PO Box 759
Orange, NJ 07051
Phone: (973)677-9200
Free: (800)631-3424   **Fax:** (973)675-2766
Products: Natural carotenoids; Herbals; Custom premixes; Palm tocotrienols; Natural antioxidants. **SICs:** 5169 (Chemicals & Allied Products Nec); 5122 (Drugs, Proprietaries & Sundries). **Est:** 1937. **Emp:** 50. **Officers:** David Holmes, President; William R. McLellan, Vice President; William R. McLellan, Sales/Marketing Contact; Pam Mistretta, Customer Service Contact.

■ 4493 ■ Research Biochemicals Inc.
1 Strathmore Rd.
Natick, MA 01760
Phone: (508)651-8151
Free: (800)736-3690   **Fax:** (508)655-1359
URL: http://www.callrbi.com
Products: Biochemical compounds, including neurochemicals, neuropeptides, and neurotoxins. **SIC:** 5169 (Chemicals & Allied Products Nec). **Est:** 1979.

Sales: $15,000,000 (2000). **Emp:** 50. **Officers:** Felice de Jong, CEO.

■ 4494 ■ Resin Management Corp.
2307 N 36th St.
Tampa, FL 33605
Phone: (813)242-4444   **Fax:** (813)241-2122
Products: Recycled plastics. **SIC:** 5169 (Chemicals & Allied Products Nec). **Sales:** $10,000,000 (2000). **Emp:** 20. **Officers:** Peter Blyth, President; Bo Hartley, CFO.

■ 4495 ■ Ribelin Sales Inc.
PO Box 461673
Garland, TX 75046
Phone: (214)272-1594   **Fax:** (214)272-1078
Products: Chemicals for making paint. **SIC:** 5169 (Chemicals & Allied Products Nec). **Est:** 1936. **Sales:** $8,000,000 (2000). **Emp:** 35. **Officers:** Michael Ribelin, President; Lloyd DeOrnellas, Controller; Steve Stephens, VP of Marketing.

■ 4496 ■ Riverside Chemical Company Inc.
PO Box 197
811 River Rd.
North Tonawanda, NY 14120
Phone: (716)692-1350   **Fax:** (716)692-1485
Products: Chemicals. **SIC:** 5169 (Chemicals & Allied Products Nec). **Est:** 1906. **Sales:** $8,000,000 (1999). **Emp:** 24. **Officers:** P.C. Rasch, President & Treasurer; John Jackson, Sales Mgr.; Gary Ryder, Office Mgr.; Lori Boulware, Personnel Mgr.; J.A. Rasch, Technical VP.

■ 4497 ■ Roebic Laboratories Inc.
25 Connair Rd.
Orange, CT 06477
Phone: (203)795-1283   **Fax:** (203)795-5227
Products: Specialty cleaning and sanitation products; Rustproofing chemicals; Treatment systems. **SIC:** 5169 (Chemicals & Allied Products Nec).

■ 4498 ■ Rosen's Diversified Inc.
PO Box 933
Fairmont, MN 56031
Phone: (507)238-4201
Products: Agricultural chemicals. **SICs:** 5169 (Chemicals & Allied Products Nec); 5191 (Farm Supplies). **Est:** 1947. **Sales:** $94,000,000 (2000). **Emp:** 300. **Officers:** Thomas Rosen, President; Rob Hovde, CFO.

■ 4499 ■ Safe Stride Non-Slip USA Inc.
PO Box 250093
West Bloomfield, MI 48325
Phone: (248)661-9176
Products: Chemicals for non-slip flooring. **SIC:** 5169 (Chemicals & Allied Products Nec). **Sales:** $800,000 (2000). **Emp:** 10. **Officers:** Hubert H. Barouch, CEO; Ike Englebaum, Dir. of Marketing & Sales.

■ 4500 ■ San Esters Corp.
55 E 59th St., Fl. 19
New York, NY 10022-1112
Phone: (212)972-1112   **Free:** (800)337-8377
Products: Chemical products for paints; Adhesives; Plastics. **SICs:** 5169 (Chemicals & Allied Products Nec); 5162 (Plastics Materials & Basic Shapes). **Est:** 1989. **Sales:** $6,000,000 (2000). **Emp:** 7. **Officers:** N. Fujita, President; B. Ito, Controller; Mark Smith, Sales Mgr.

■ 4501 ■ San Joaquin Sulphur Company Inc.
PO Box 700
Lodi, CA 95241
Phone: (209)368-6676
Products: Agricultural chemicals. **SICs:** 5191 (Farm Supplies); 5169 (Chemicals & Allied Products Nec). **Est:** 1941. **Sales:** $2,500,000 (1999). **Emp:** 13. **Officers:** Janet Chandler, President.

■ 4502 ■ Sattex Corp.
PO Box 2593
White City, OR 97503-0593
Phone: (541)826-8808   **Fax:** (541)836-4328
E-mail: sattex@aol.com
Products: Polishing compounds for metals, plastics, and cultured marble. **SIC:** 5169 (Chemicals & Allied Products Nec). **Est:** 1955. **Sales:** $1,000,000 (2000).

Emp: 10. **Officers:** Mary Warrick, CEO & President; Robert Te Selle, CFO; Karlene Larson, VP of Marketing & Sales.

■ 4503 ■ Savol Bleach Co.
15 Village St.
East Hartford, CT 06108-3924
Phone: (203)282-0878
Products: Industrial inorganic chemicals, soaps and detergents. **SIC:** 5169 (Chemicals & Allied Products Nec). **Sales:** $1,000,000 (1993). **Emp:** 5. **Officers:** Christopher Hatton, CEO.

■ 4504 ■ Seaforth Mineral and Ore Company Inc.
3690 Orange Pl., No. 495
Cleveland, OH 44122-4483
Phone: (216)292-5820   **Fax:** (216)292-1033
Products: Chemicals. **SIC:** 5169 (Chemicals & Allied Products Nec). **Est:** 1957. **Sales:** $15,000,000 (2000). **Emp:** 45. **Officers:** Gary McClurg, President; J. McClurg, President.

■ 4505 ■ Seegott Inc.
1675 D Holmes Rd.
Elgin, IL 60123
Phone: (847)468-6300
Free: (877)528-0808   **Fax:** (847)468-0424
URL: http://www.Seegot.com
Products: Chemical preparations. **SIC:** 5169 (Chemicals & Allied Products Nec). **Est:** 1985. **Sales:** $20,000,000 (1999). **Emp:** 15. **Officers:** David Meier, Vice President; Eric Barta, Sales Mgr., e-mail: ebarta@Seegot.com. **Former Name:** Votech, Inc.

■ 4506 ■ Seeler Industries Inc.
1 Genstar Ln.
Joliet, IL 60435-2668
Phone: (815)740-2645
Products: Chemicals, including hydrogen peroxide and hydrochloric acid. **SIC:** 5169 (Chemicals & Allied Products Nec). **Sales:** $10,000,000 (2000). **Emp:** 20. **Officers:** Joe Seeler, President.

■ 4507 ■ Semi-Gas Systems Inc.
625 Wool Creek Dr.
San Jose, CA 95112
Phone: (408)971-6500
Products: Cabinets; Purification products; Specialty gases and total site gas management. **SIC:** 5169 (Chemicals & Allied Products Nec). **Sales:** $17,000,000 (2000). **Emp:** 110. **Officers:** Don Ramlow, President.

■ 4508 ■ Sessions Specialty Co.
5090 Styers Ferry Rd.
Lewisville, NC 27023-9634
Phone: (919)722-7163
Products: Air fresheners. **SIC:** 5169 (Chemicals & Allied Products Nec). **Est:** 1946. **Sales:** $7,000,000 (2000). **Emp:** 25. **Officers:** Steve Sessions, President; Max Sessions, Finance Officer; Ron Hufman, Dir. of Marketing.

■ 4509 ■ Sewon America Inc.
2 University Plz., Ste. 202
Hackensack, NJ 07601
Phone: (201)343-1166   **Fax:** (201)343-3325
Products: Lysine for the animal feed and pharmaceuticals industries. **SIC:** 5122 (Drugs, Proprietaries & Sundries). **Sales:** $300,000 (2000). **Emp:** 2. **Officers:** Jhom Su Kim, President.

■ 4510 ■ Shin-Etsu Silicones of America Inc.
1150 Damar Dr.
Akron, OH 44305-1066
Phone: (330)630-9860   **Fax:** (330)630-9855
URL: http://www.shinetsusilicones.com
Products: Silicones. **SIC:** 5169 (Chemicals & Allied Products Nec). **Est:** 1985. **Emp:** 110. **Officers:** Nobuyuki Uesugi, President & CEO.

■ 4511 ■ Sierra Chemical Co
PO Box 50730
Sparks, NV 89435
Phone: (775)358-0888   **Fax:** (775)358-0987
Products: Explosives, bleach and chlorine; Hypochlorite. **SIC:** 5199 (Nondurable Goods Nec). **Officers:** Stanley Kinder, President.

■ **4512** ■ **Slack Chemical Company, Inc.**
PO Box 30
Carthage, NY 13619-0030
Phone: (315)493-0430 **Fax:** (315)493-3931
E-mail: slack@imcnet.net
Products: Industrial and heavy chemicals. **SIC:** 5169
(Chemicals & Allied Products Nec). **Est:** 1944. **Sales:**
$15,000,000 (2000). **Emp:** 75.

■ **4513** ■ **SOCO-Lynch Corp.**
10747 Patterson Pl.
Santa Fe Springs, CA 90670-4043
Phone: (323)269-0191 **Fax:** (323)264-9181
SIC: 5169 (Chemicals & Allied Products Nec). **Est:**
1937. **Sales:** $75,000,000 (2000). **Emp:** 90. **Officers:**
Anthony J. Gerace, President; William E. Huttner, VP of
Sales.

■ **4514** ■ **Soil Stabilization Products Company
Inc.**
PO Box 2779
Merced, CA 95344
Phone: (209)383-3296
Products: Environmentally sound product technology
for pavements, dust control, and soil stabilization in the
form of additives or retaining walls. **SICs:** 5169
(Chemicals & Allied Products Nec); 5039 (Construction
Materials Nec).

■ **4515** ■ **SOS Gases Inc.**
1100 Harrison Ave.
Kearny, NJ 07032
Phone: (201)998-7800
Free: (800)626-7998 **Fax:** (201)998-5243
E-mail: sosgases.inc@msn.com
Products: Research chemicals; Industrial and medical
gases. **SICs:** 5169 (Chemicals & Allied Products Nec);
5084 (Industrial Machinery & Equipment). **Est:** 1961.
Sales: $6,600,000 (2000). **Emp:** 39. **Officers:** Steven
C. DeFillipps, President; Carmen J. DeFillipps, Vice
President.

■ **4516** ■ **Southchem Inc.**
PO Box 1491
Durham, NC 27702
Phone: (919)596-0681
Products: Chemical products. **SIC:** 5169 (Chemicals &
Allied Products Nec). **Sales:** $58,000,000 (1992).
Emp: 119. **Officers:** Joseph H. Collie, President &
Treasurer.

■ **4517** ■ **SPAP Company LLC**
PO Box 680
Huntington Beach, CA 92648
Phone: (714)960-0586 **Fax:** (714)960-0587
E-mail: skipperbuzzy@earthlink.net
URL: http://www.home.earthlink.net/~skipperbuzzy
Products: Household supplies; Automotive
accessories; Electric and electronic equipment; Food;
Catalog products; DRTV products; Sports products;
Pest control products. **SICs:** 5169 (Chemicals & Allied
Products Nec); 5013 (Motor Vehicle Supplies & New
Parts); 5065 (Electronic Parts & Equipment Nec); 5149
(Groceries & Related Products Nec). **Est:** 1987. **Emp:**
1. **Officers:** Jeff Henderson, Owner. **Former Name:**
SPAP Company International.

■ **4518** ■ **Specialty Chemical Company, Inc.**
PO Box 2606
Cleveland, TN 37320-2606
Phone: (423)479-9664
Free: (800)356-9857 **Fax:** (423)472-7258
Products: Chemical preparations. **SIC:** 5169
(Chemicals & Allied Products Nec). **Est:** 1970. **Sales:**
$20,000,000 (2000). **Emp:** 37. **Officers:** Lester T.
Simerville, President; F. Joe Lee III, Vice President.

■ **4519** ■ **Spectrum Labs Inc.**
301 W County Rd., Ste. E2
New Brighton, MN 55112
Phone: (612)633-0101
Free: (800)447-5221 **Fax:** (612)633-1402
Products: Water conditioning chemicals. **SIC:** 5169
(Chemicals & Allied Products Nec). **Sales:** $5,000,000
(2000). **Emp:** 35. **Officers:** Duane Nowlin, President.

■ **4520** ■ **Sprayway Inc.**
484 Vista Ave.
Addison, IL 60101-4468
Phone: (630)628-3000
Free: (800)332-9000 **Fax:** (630)543-7797
E-mail: jbright@spraywayinc.com
URL: http://www.spraywayinc.com
Products: Aerosol products. **SIC:** 5169 (Chemicals &
Allied Products Nec). **Est:** 1946. **Emp:** 87. **Officers:**
Jim Bright, e-mail: jbright@spraywayinc.com.

■ **4521** ■ **Stafford County Flour Mills Co.**
PO Box 7
Hudson, KS 67545
Phone: (316)458-4121
Free: (800)530-5640 **Fax:** (316)458-5121
URL: http://www.flour.com
Products: Grain and agricultural chemicals; Flour.
SICs: 5153 (Grain & Field Beans); 5191 (Farm
Supplies). **Est:** 1905. **Sales:** $15,000,000 (2000).
Emp: 30. **Officers:** Alvin A. Brensing, President &
CFO; Alvin A. Brensing, President & CFO.

■ **4522** ■ **Summit Company**
PO Box 23337
Louisville, KY 40223
Phone: (502)245-9764 **Fax:** (502)244-1805
Products: Thinners for dopes, lacquers, and
oleoresinous thinners; Solvent recovery equipment;
Filters; Medical equipment. **SICs:** 5169 (Chemicals &
Allied Products Nec); 5047 (Medical & Hospital
Equipment); 5085 (Industrial Supplies). **Officers:**
Robert D. Schutz, President.

■ **4523** ■ **Sybron Chemicals Inc.**
PO Box 66
Birmingham, NJ 08011
Phone: (609)893-1100
Free: (800)678-0020 **Fax:** (609)893-2063
Products: Biochemical materials; Textile finishings;
Synthetic resins. **SIC:** 5169 (Chemicals & Allied
Products Nec).

■ **4524** ■ **Systematix Co.**
1700 E Walnut Ave, Ste. B
Fullerton, CA 92831
Phone: (714)879-2482 **Fax:** (714)562-2482
Products: Water systems; Filters; Water treatment
supplies. **SICs:** 5169 (Chemicals & Allied Products
Nec); 5099 (Durable Goods Nec).

■ **4525** ■ **Tanner Industries, Inc.**
735 Davisville Rd., 3rd Fl.
Southampton, PA 18966
Phone: (215)322-1238
Free: (800)643-6226 **Fax:** (215)322-7725
URL: http://www.tannerind.com
Products: Ammonia. **SIC:** 5169 (Chemicals & Allied
Products Nec). **Est:** 1890. **Sales:** $30,000,000 (2000).
Emp: 100. **Officers:** Stephen B. Tanner, President &
COO; Jack Bowen, Exec. VP; J. Thomas Lauria, Sales
Mgr.; Mark Tanner, Southern Regional VP; Marie
Shute, Human Resources Contact. **Former Name:**
National Ammonia Co.

■ **4526** ■ **Tetra Technologies Inc.**
25025 I-45 N
The Woodlands, TX 77380
Phone: (713)367-1983 **Fax:** (713)364-2240
Products: Gas, oil, waste, and chemical treatment
supplies. **SIC:** 5169 (Chemicals & Allied Products Nec).
Est: 1981. **Sales:** $178,500,000 (2000). **Emp:** 989.
Officers: Allen T. McInnes, CEO & President; Geoffrey
M. Hertel, Exec. VP of Finance & Admin.

■ **4527** ■ **Tex-Ag Co.**
PO Box 633
Mission, TX 78572
Phone: (956)585-4567
Products: Agricultural chemicals. **SIC:** 5191 (Farm
Supplies). **Sales:** $15,000,000 (1992). **Emp:** 35.
Officers: David Newman, Controller.

■ **4528** ■ **Texaco Additive Co.**
PO Box 27707
Houston, TX 77227-7707
Phones: (713)961-3711 (713)235-6254
Fax: (713)235-6166
Products: Chemicals. **SIC:** 5169 (Chemicals & Allied
Products Nec). **Est:** 1990. **Sales:** $301,200,000
(2000). **Emp:** 1,000. **Officers:** John I. Schell,
President; Jack B. Ziegler, Sales Mgr.

■ **4529** ■ **Texo Corp.**
2801 Highland Ave.
Cincinnati, OH 45212
Phone: (513)731-3400 **Fax:** (513)731-8113
Products: Chemicals. **SIC:** 5169 (Chemicals & Allied
Products Nec). **Est:** 1947. **Sales:** $30,000,000 (2000).
Emp: 185. **Officers:** Melvyn Fisher, CEO; Robert
Fisher, President; Michael A. Fisher, Exec. VP.

■ **4530** ■ **Textile Chemical Company Inc.**
PO Box 13788
Reading, PA 19612-3788
Phone: (610)926-4151
Products: Chemical supplies, including acids,
solvents, and food grade powders. **SIC:** 5169
(Chemicals & Allied Products Nec). **Sales:**
$100,000,000 (2000). **Emp:** 180. **Officers:** William E.
Huttner, CEO; Edward Boyadjian, VP & CFO.

■ **4531** ■ **Toray Industries (America) Inc.**
600 3rd Ave., 5th Fl.
New York, NY 10016-1902
Phone: (212)697-8150
Products: Chemical products and piece good fabrics.
SICs: 5169 (Chemicals & Allied Products Nec); 5131
(Piece Goods & Notions). **Sales:** $16,000,000 (2000).
Emp: 50. **Officers:** Kabe Junichi, President.

■ **4532** ■ **Transtech Industries Inc.**
200 Centennial Ave.
Piscataway, NJ 08855-1321
Phone: (732)981-0777
Products: Carbide lime and other high alkali products
used as neutralization agents in waste water treatment
plants. **SIC:** 5169 (Chemicals & Allied Products Nec).
Sales: $18,700,000 (1994). **Emp:** 163. **Officers:**
Robert V. Sliva, CEO & President; Andrew J. Mayer Jr.,
VP & CFO.

■ **4533** ■ **Triangle Chemical Co.**
PO Box 4528
Macon, GA 31213
Phone: (912)743-1548
Products: Agricultural chemicals. **SICs:** 5191 (Farm
Supplies); 5169 (Chemicals & Allied Products Nec).
Est: 1947. **Sales:** $5,000,000 (2000). **Emp:** 25.
Officers: Wycliffe E. Griffin, CEO.

■ **4534** ■ **Triple Crown America Inc.**
13 N 7th St.
Perkasie, PA 18944
Phone: (215)453-2500 **Fax:** (215)453-2508
E-mail: info@triplecrownamerica.com
URL: http://www.triplecrownamerica.com
Products: Industrial chemicals. **SIC:** 5169 (Chemicals
& Allied Products Nec). **Est:** 1986. **Sales:** $4,000,000
(2000). **Emp:** 15. **Officers:** Hokan Cederberg, CEO &
Chairman of the Board; Catherine Peklak, President.

■ **4535** ■ **Truesdale Company Inc.**
108 Holton St.
Brighton, MA 02135
Phone: (617)782-5300 **Fax:** (617)782-9924
URL: http://www.truesdaleco.com
Products: Chemicals. **SIC:** 5169 (Chemicals & Allied
Products Nec). **Est:** 1948. **Sales:** $30,000,000 (1999).
Emp: 20. **Officers:** Brenda Alpert, General Mgr.

■ **4536** ■ **Twinco Automotive Warehouse Inc.**
4635 Willow Dr.
Hamel, MN 55340
Phone: (612)478-2360
Products: Automotive chemicals. **SIC:** 5169
(Chemicals & Allied Products Nec). **Est:** 1927. **Sales:**
$27,000,000 (2000). **Emp:** 50. **Officers:** L. Ribnick,
President.

■ **4537** ■ **Ulrich Chemical Inc.**
3111 N Post Rd.
Indianapolis, IN 46226-6566
Phone: (317)898-8632 **Fax:** (317)895-0614
URL: http://www.ulrichchem.com
Products: Chemicals. **SIC:** 5169 (Chemicals & Allied
Products Nec). **Est:** 1919. **Sales:** $62,000,000 (2000).

Emp: 175. **Officers:** Edward M. Pitkin; Stephen J. Hiatt; James P. Fohl; Suzanne Shaw; James Collins.

■ 4538 ■ **UMPQUA Technology Co.**
PO Box 63
Chesterfield, MO 63006
Products: Iodization resins. **SIC:** 5169 (Chemicals & Allied Products Nec). **Officers:** George Rosenthal, Exec. VP.

■ 4539 ■ **Unelko Corp.**
14641 N 74th St.
Scottsdale, AZ 85260
Phone: (602)991-7272 **Fax:** (602)483-7674
Products: Water repellants, surface treatments and protective coatings. **SIC:** 5169 (Chemicals & Allied Products Nec). **Sales:** $7,000,000 (2000). **Emp:** 30. **Officers:** Howard Ohlhausen, President; Greg Anderson, CFO.

■ 4540 ■ **Universal Process Equipment Inc.**
PO Box 338
Roosevelt, NJ 08555-0338
Phone: (609)443-4545 **Fax:** (609)259-0644
Products: Chemical processing equipment. **SIC:** 5084 (Industrial Machinery & Equipment). **Sales:** $80,000,000 (2000). **Emp:** 150. **Officers:** Ronald H. Gale, President; Jeff Shapiro, VP & CFO.

■ 4541 ■ **US Chemical Corporation**
300 N Patrick Blvd.
Brookfield, WI 53045
Phone: (414)792-1555
Free: (800)558-9566 **Fax:** (414)792-8779
Products: Institutional chemicals; Cleanup systems. **SIC:** 5169 (Chemicals & Allied Products Nec). **Est:** 1962. **Sales:** $50,000,000 (2000). **Emp:** 215. **Officers:** Mark Laehn, President; Bruce Tressler, VP of Sales; Janine Spencer, Human Resources Contact.

■ 4542 ■ **Van Waters and Rogers**
PO Box 34325
Seattle, WA 98124-1325
Phone: (425)889-3400 **Fax:** (425)889-4100
URL: http://www.vwr-na.com
Products: Chemicals. **SIC:** 5169 (Chemicals & Allied Products Nec). **Est:** 1924. **Sales:** $1,923,280,816 (1999). **Emp:** 2,832. **Officers:** Paul H. Hough, President & CEO.

■ 4543 ■ **Van Waters & Rogers**
6100 Carillon Pt.
Kirkland, WA 98033
Phone: (425)889-3400
E-mail: vwr-inc.com
URL: http://www.vwr-inc.com
Products: Chemical compounding; Chemical manufacturing; Coatings, inks and adhesives; Electronics; Food and pharmaceuticals; Forest products; Mining; Oil, gas, and CPI; Waste management and waste treatment. **SIC:** 5169 (Chemicals & Allied Products Nec). **Est:** 1924. **Sales:** $1,600,447,789 (1999). **Emp:** 2,450. **Officers:** Paul Hough, CEO & President; Gary E. Pruitt, VP, CFO & Treasurer. **Former Name:** Univar Corp.

■ 4544 ■ **Van Waters and Rogers Inc.**
PO Box 34325
Seattle, WA 98124-1325
Phone: (425)889-3400 **Fax:** (425)889-4100
URL: http://www.vwr-inc.com
Products: Chemicals. **SIC:** 5169 (Chemicals & Allied Products Nec). **Est:** 1950. **Sales:** $1,276,700,000 (1999). **Emp:** 2,500. **Officers:** Paul Hough, CEO & President; Gary E. Pruitt, VP, CFO & Treasurer; Bevan A. Cates, Sr. VP of Marketing; H. Drew Macafee, VP of Human Resources.

■ 4545 ■ **Van Waters and Rogers Inc. Omaha**
3002 F St.
Omaha, NE 68107
Phone: (402)733-3266 **Fax:** (402)733-3152
Products: Chemical preparations. **SIC:** 5169 (Chemicals & Allied Products Nec). **Est:** 1924. **Sales:** $18,000,000 (2000). **Emp:** 35. **Officers:** Barry Kopf, Branch Mgr.

■ 4546 ■ **Vanguard Imaging Corp.**
55 Cabot Ct.
Hauppauge, NY 11788
Phone: (516)435-2100 **Fax:** (516)435-2293
Products: Film and film development chemicals for the cineagram used by medical labs. **SIC:** 5043 (Photographic Equipment & Supplies). **Sales:** $3,000,000 (2000). **Emp:** 10. **Officers:** Harry Warring, Controller.

■ 4547 ■ **Vic Supply Co.**
358 Romans Rd.
Elmhurst, IL 60126
Phone: (708)833-0033
Products: Electroplating chemicals. **SIC:** 5169 (Chemicals & Allied Products Nec).

■ 4548 ■ **Vie Americas Inc.**
PO Box 958
Glastonbury, CT 06033
Phone: (860)659-1397 **Fax:** (860)659-9679
E-mail: vie@worldnet.att.net
Products: Clays and materials for ceramics; Chemical resins; Chemical pigments; Brake parts and materials. **SICs:** 5169 (Chemicals & Allied Products Nec); 5013 (Motor Vehicle Supplies & New Parts). **Est:** 1982. **Officers:** Hugo Galarza, Director; Carlos Galarza, Dir. of Marketing; Nicolas Restrepo, Sales/Marketing Contact.

■ 4549 ■ **Wacker Chemicals (USA) Inc.**
3301 Sutton Rd.
Adrian, MI 49221-9397
Phone: (517)264-8791
Free: (800)485-3686 **Fax:** (517)264-8137
Products: Industrial chemicals. **SIC:** 5169 (Chemicals & Allied Products Nec). **Sales:** $18,000,000 (2000). **Emp:** 35. **Officers:** Detlev Berner, President; Jim McLarren, Accountant.

■ 4550 ■ **Water Source USA**
2929 N Prospect, Ste. 100
Colorado Springs, CO 80907
Phone: (719)630-0334
Products: Water absorbing polymers and super absorbents. **SIC:** 5169 (Chemicals & Allied Products Nec). **Sales:** $400,000 (1994). **Emp:** 2. **Officers:** Dan Zemler, President.

■ 4551 ■ **Welltep International Inc.**
138 Palm Coast Pkwy. NE, No. 192
Palm Coast, FL 32137-8241
Phone: (904)445-7160 **Fax:** (904)445-7169
Products: Fragrances; Aromatic chemicals; Essential oils and oleo resins; Chewing gum bases; Artificial and natural flavors. **SICs:** 5169 (Chemicals & Allied Products Nec); 5122 (Drugs, Proprietaries & Sundries). **Officers:** Luis A. Lopez, President.

■ 4552 ■ **West Agro Inc.**
11100 N Congress Ave.
Kansas City, MO 64153
Phone: (816)891-1600 **Fax:** (816)891-1595
E-mail: westagro@swbell.net
URL: http://www.westagro.com
Products: Chemicals for dairy farms. **SICs:** 5169 (Chemicals & Allied Products Nec); 5191 (Farm Supplies). **Est:** 1984. **Emp:** 215. **Officers:** W.M. Papineau, President; Dan Brookhart, Controller; Terry Mitchell, VSM; Tom Fahey, VIS.

■ 4553 ■ **Whittaker, Clark and Daniels**
1000 Coolidge St.
South Plainfield, NJ 07080
Phone: (908)561-6100
Free: (800)732-0562 **Fax:** (908)757-3488
URL: http://www.whcdinc.com
Products: Chemicals, including ether. **SIC:** 5169 (Chemicals & Allied Products Nec). **Est:** 1890. **Sales:** $23,000,000 (2000). **Emp:** 100. **Officers:** Michael Arguelan, President; Theodae Hubbard, Exec. VP; Brad Owens, Dir of Personnel.

■ 4554 ■ **Wilbur-Ellis Co.**
345 California St., 27th Fl.
San Francisco, CA 94104-2606
Phone: (415)772-4000 **Fax:** (415)772-4011
Products: Agricultural chemicals. **SICs:** 5191 (Farm Supplies); 5169 (Chemicals & Allied Products Nec). **Est:** 1921. **Sales:** $1,200,000,000 (2000). **Emp:** 2,000. **Officers:** Brayton Wilbur Jr., CEO & President; Herb Tully, Vice President; Keith Kuechmann, Dir. of Marketing; John Kirby, Dir. of Data Processing; Ofelia Uriarte, Personnel Mgr.

■ 4555 ■ **Wilbur-Ellis Co.**
215 N Summer St.
West Burlington, IA 52655-1191
Phone: (319)752-6324 **Fax:** (319)753-0404
Products: Agricultural chemicals. **SICs:** 5169 (Chemicals & Allied Products Nec); 5191 (Farm Supplies). **Est:** 1950. **Emp:** 15. **Officers:** Keith Boyer, President; Robert Christiensen, Dir. of Information Systems.

■ 4556 ■ **WILFARM L.L.C.**
215 N Summer St.
West Burlington, IA 52655-1191
Phone: (319)752-6329 **Fax:** (319)753-0404
Products: Agricultural chemicals. **SICs:** 5169 (Chemicals & Allied Products Nec); 5191 (Farm Supplies). **Est:** 1995. **Emp:** 12. **Officers:** Keith Boyer, President; Robert Christiensen, Dir. of Information Systems.

■ 4557 ■ **World Wide Chemnet Inc.**
2100 S Utica St.
Tulsa, OK 74114
Phone: (918)749-9060
Free: (800)988-5782 **Fax:** (918)747-1444
Products: Industrial chemicals sold through the Internet. **SIC:** 5169 (Chemicals & Allied Products Nec). **Sales:** $6,000,000 (2000). **Emp:** 8. **Officers:** Mark Nagle, President & CFO.

■ 4558 ■ **Xpedx-Birmingham**
PO Box 11367
Birmingham, AL 35202
Phone: (205)798-8380 **Fax:** (205)791-2675
URL: http://www.xpedx.com
Products: Chemicals. **SIC:** 5169 (Chemicals & Allied Products Nec). **Sales:** $11,000,000 (2000). **Emp:** 50. **Officers:** William M. Gravely, General Mgr.

■ 4559 ■ **Xport Port Authority Trading Co.**
One World Trade Center, 34 N
New York, NY 10048
Phone: (212)435-8499 **Fax:** (212)432-0297
Products: Industrial organic chemicals; Medical instruments and supplies; Industrial environmental control equipment; Telecommunication equipment; Groceries. **SICs:** 5169 (Chemicals & Allied Products Nec); 5047 (Medical & Hospital Equipment); 5063 (Electrical Apparatus & Equipment); 5149 (Groceries & Related Products Nec). **Officers:** Herbert Ouida, Director.

■ 4560 ■ **Zep Manufacturing Co., Springfield**
10 Fadem Rd.
Springfield, NJ 07081
Phone: (973)379-6545
Products: Chemicals. **SIC:** 5169 (Chemicals & Allied Products Nec). **Officers:** R Baldwin, General Mgr.

■ 4561 ■ **Zorbite Corp.**
612 Meyer Ln., No. 8
Redondo Beach, CA 90278
Phone: (310)374-6465
Free: (800)723-7672 **Fax:** (310)374-0167
E-mail: captfred@aol.com
URL: http://www.zorbite.com
Products: Absorbent substances, including vermiculite, zeolites, perlite, neutralizers, wood products, corn cob, and clay. **SICs:** 5169 (Chemicals & Allied Products Nec); 5193 (Flowers & Florists' Supplies). **Est:** 1974. **Sales:** $1,000,000 (2000). **Emp:** 6. **Officers:** Fred Babinski, President; Clive Fleissig, Vice President.

(8) Cleaning and Janitorial Supplies

Entries in this section are arranged alphabetically by company name. When the company name is a personal name, the company name is alphabetized by the surname unless the first name or initial(s) are part of a trade name. See the User's Guide at the front of this directory for additional information.

■ **4562** ■ **3-D Supply Inc.**
3540 W Sahara Ave., Ste. 290
Las Vegas, NV 89102-5816
Phone: (702)877-0805 **Fax:** (702)876-5843
Products: Service industry machinery; Specialty cleaning and sanitation products. **SICs:** 5087 (Service Establishment Equipment); 5169 (Chemicals & Allied Products Nec). **Officers:** Debra Johnson, President.

■ **4563** ■ **A-1 Chemical Inc.**
1197 Greg St.
Sparks, NV 89431-6004
Phone: (702)331-7627 **Fax:** (702)358-2082
Products: Service industry machinery; Specialty cleaning and sanitation products; Janitors' supplies. **SIC:** 5087 (Service Establishment Equipment). **Officers:** John Morton, President.

■ **4564** ■ **A & D Maintenance**
230 Moonbeam Dr.
Sparks, NV 89436-7262
Phone: (702)359-6394
Products: Service industry machinery; Laundry equipment and supplies; Dry cleaning equipment and clothing presses. **SICs:** 5087 (Service Establishment Equipment); 5169 (Chemicals & Allied Products Nec). **Officers:** Donald Johnson, Owner.

■ **4565** ■ **Able Trading Corp.**
2320 Keystone Dr.
Omaha, NE 68134
Phone: (402)391-4161 **Fax:** (402)391-7459
Products: Cleaning solutions. **SIC:** 5169 (Chemicals & Allied Products Nec). **Officers:** Jonathan M. Fixley, Chairman/President.

■ **4566** ■ **Advanced Maintenance Products Co.**
PO Box 6547
Manchester, NH 03108-6547
Phone: (603)669-9565
Products: Service industry machinery; Specialty cleaning and sanitation products; Janitors' supplies. **SICs:** 5087 (Service Establishment Equipment); 5169 (Chemicals & Allied Products Nec). **Officers:** Daniel Noury, President.

■ **4567** ■ **Aldelano Corp.**
24021 Lodge Pole Rd.
Diamond Bar, CA 91765
Phone: (909)861-3970
Products: Janitorial supplies; Corrugated supplies. **SICs:** 5087 (Service Establishment Equipment); 5113 (Industrial & Personal Service Paper). **Est:** 1985. **Sales:** $8,000,000 (2000). **Emp:** 100. **Officers:** A.D. Hollingsworth, President.

■ **4568** ■ **Alkota of Western Montana**
PO Box 18104
Missoula, MT 59808-8104
Free: (800)582-3942
Products: Cleaning and maintenance equipment and supplies; Pressure washers. **SICs:** 5087 (Service Establishment Equipment); 5169 (Chemicals & Allied Products Nec). **Officers:** Roy Hill, Owner.

■ **4569** ■ **Altimus Distributing**
PO Box 1724
Billings, MT 59103-1724
Phone: (406)259-9816
Free: (800)999-9816 **Fax:** (406)259-7632
E-mail: altimusd@aol.com
Products: Commercial laundry and dry cleaning equipment and supplies. **SIC:** 5087 (Service Establishment Equipment). **Est:** 1979. **Officers:** Ray Kunkel, Owner.

■ **4570** ■ **Amedem Enterprises, Inc.**
224 State St., Ste. 2
Portsmouth, NH 03801-4035
Phone: (603)436-7489 **Fax:** (603)436-7489
Products: Specialty cleaning and sanitation products; Janitors' supplies. **SICs:** 5087 (Service Establishment Equipment); 5169 (Chemicals & Allied Products Nec). **Officers:** Edward Walenta, President. **Former Name:** Pride Chemical, Inc.

■ **4571** ■ **American Homeware Inc.**
4715 McEwen Rd.
Dallas, TX 75244
Phone: (972)233-5541
Free: (800)922-5524 **Fax:** (972)702-0128
Products: Laundry products. **SIC:** 5169 (Chemicals & Allied Products Nec). **Emp:** 49. **Officers:** James L. Glenn; Doyal Perry.

■ **4572** ■ **American Wiping Rag**
51 Melcher St., No. 1
Boston, MA 02210
Phone: (617)426-4130
Products: Wiping cloths. **SIC:** 5087 (Service Establishment Equipment).

■ **4573** ■ **AMJ Inc.**
25 Precourt St.
Biddeford, ME 04005-4315
Phone: (207)284-5731 **Fax:** (207)282-4759
SICs: 5087 (Service Establishment Equipment); 5169 (Chemicals & Allied Products Nec). **Est:** 1926. **Sales:** $3,000,000 (2000). **Emp:** 10. **Officers:** John Jensen, President. **Doing Business As:** Biddeford & Saco Paper Co.

■ **4574** ■ **Aries Paper & Chemical Co. Inc.**
PO Box 1864
Lake Charles, LA 70602
Phone: (337)433-8794 **Fax:** (337)433-8891
E-mail: Ariespaper@Ariespaper.com
Products: Janitorial paper supplies; Janitorial chemicals; Restaurant paper supplies; Restaurant chemicals. **SICs:** 5087 (Service Establishment Equipment); 5113 (Industrial & Personal Service Paper); 5169 (Chemicals & Allied Products Nec). **Est:** 1982. **Sales:** $1,200,000 (2000). **Emp:** 8. **Officers:** James W. Butler, President; Warren Smith, Vice President; Charlotte Butler, Treasurer & Secty.

■ **4575** ■ **B-J Pac-A-Part**
410 25th Ave. S
Great Falls, MT 59405-7147
Phone: (406)761-4487
Free: (800)462-3543 **Fax:** (406)761-5725
Products: Specialty cleaning and sanitation products; Janitorial supplies; Car chemicals; Tire patching and car cleaning supplies; Brooms. **SICs:** 5087 (Service Establishment Equipment); 5169 (Chemicals & Allied Products Nec); 5199 (Nondurable Goods Nec). **Est:** 1976. **Sales:** $120,000 (2000). **Emp:** 3. **Officers:** A. Berniel Evenson, Partner; S. Jeanne Evenson, Partner.

■ **4576** ■ **W.P. Ballard and Co.**
PO Box 12246
Birmingham, AL 35202
Phone: (205)251-7272
Free: (800)457-2325 **Fax:** (205)251-7280
URL: http://www.wpballard.com
Products: Laundry and dry cleaning supplies. **SIC:** 5199 (Nondurable Goods Nec). **Est:** 1919. **Sales:** $30,000,000 (2000). **Emp:** 85. **Officers:** John Beeler Jr., President.

■ **4577** ■ **Banner Systems Inc.**
PO Box 3-302
Milford, CT 06460
Phone: (203)878-6524 **Fax:** (203)878-4747
Products: Janitorial supplies. **SICs:** 5087 (Service Establishment Equipment); 5169 (Chemicals & Allied Products Nec).

■ **4578** ■ **Best-Klean Products**
PO Box 127
5875 N Wayne St.
Fremont, IN 46737-0127
Phone: (219)495-9706 **Fax:** (219)495-1646
Products: Janitors' supplies; Paper and allied products; Protective clothing. **SICs:** 5087 (Service Establishment Equipment); 5113 (Industrial & Personal Service Paper); 5136 (Men's/Boys' Clothing); 5137 (Women's/Children's Clothing). **Est:** 1976. **Officers:** Ronald Keller, Owner.

■ **4579** ■ **Best Way Carpet Care Inc.**
PO Box 3693
Albuquerque, NM 87190-3693
Phone: (505)344-6838 **Fax:** (505)344-6838
Products: Commercial service establishment equipment, including cleaning, maintenance, and carpet and rug cleaning equipment and supplies. **SICs:** 5087 (Service Establishment Equipment); 5169 (Chemicals & Allied Products Nec). **Officers:** Nicholas Few, President.

■ **4580** ■ **Big Horn Wholesale**
231 Blackburn Ave.
Cody, WY 82414-8432
Phone: (307)587-4929 **Fax:** (307)587-4920
Products: Custodial supplies; Foodservice. **SICs:** 5087 (Service Establishment Equipment); 5113 (Industrial & Personal Service Paper); 5194 (Tobacco & Tobacco Products); 5141 (Groceries—General Line). **Est:** 1987. **Sales:** $1,200,000 (2000). **Emp:** 5. **Officers:** Greg Pendley.

■ **4581** ■ **Big W Supplies Inc.**
650 W 18th St.
Cheyenne, WY 82001-4305
Phone: (307)634-5502
Products: Service industry machinery; Specialty cleaning and sanitation products; Janitors' supplies. **SICs:** 5087 (Service Establishment Equipment); 5169 (Chemicals & Allied Products Nec). **Officers:** Gene Palen, President.

■ **4582** ■ **Black & Decker US Inc.**
3007 E Independence Blvd.
Charlotte, NC 28205-7036
Phone: (704)374-1779 **Fax:** (704)374-1225
Products: Vacuum cleaning systems; Power tools and parts. **SICs:** 5087 (Service Establishment Equipment); 5072 (Hardware). **Emp:** 49. **Officers:** Jack White.

■ **4583** ■ **Black Hills Chemical Co. Inc.**
PO Box 2082
Rapid City, SD 57709-2082
Phone: (605)342-0788
Free: (800)201-0788 **Fax:** (605)342-0830
Products: Service establishment equipment; Cleaning and maintenance equipment and supplies; Pool and spa chemicals. **SICs:** 5087 (Service Establishment Equipment); 5169 (Chemicals & Allied Products Nec). **Est:** 1959. **Sales:** $2,100,000 (2000). **Emp:** 12. **Officers:** Herman Blote, General Mgr.

■ **4584** ■ **Blue Lustre, LLC**
997 Horan Dr.
Fenton, MO 63026-2401
Phone: (314)343-5106
Free: (800)333-1232 **Fax:** (314)326-0621
URL: http://www.rugdoctor.com
Products: Carpet cleaning machinery and supplies. **SIC:** 5087 (Service Establishment Equipment). **Est:** 1956. **Emp:** 44. **Officers:** Tim Youngblood, General Mgr.

■ **4585** ■ **Blue Ribbon Linen Supply Inc.**
PO Box 798
Lewiston, ID 83501-0798
Phone: (208)743-5521 **Fax:** (208)743-6120
Products: Service establishment equipment, including cleaning and maintenance equipment and supplies. **SICs:** 5087 (Service Establishment Equipment); 5169 (Chemicals & Allied Products Nec). **Officers:** Gary Stachofsky, President.

■ **4586** ■ **Bockstanz Brothers Co.**
32553 Schoolcraft
Livonia, MI 48150-4307
Phone: (734)458-2006
Free: (800)462-9552 **Fax:** (734)458-4158
E-mail: bockstanz@aol.com
URL: http://www.bockstanz.com
Products: Janitorial supplies, including toilet paper and mops. **SICs:** 5087 (Service Establishment Equipment); 5113 (Industrial & Personal Service Paper). **Est:** 1906. **Sales:** $4,800,000 (2000). **Emp:** 19. **Officers:** Jack N. Bockstanz Jr., President; Domenic DeLagato, Sales/Marketing Contact; Sharon Kubany, Customer Service Contact.

■ **4587** ■ **BR Chemical Co. Inc.**
405 24th Ave. S
Grand Forks, ND 58201-7413
Phone: (701)775-5455
Products: Service establishment equipment; Cleaning and maintenance equipment and supplies; Janitors' supplies. **SIC:** 5087 (Service Establishment Equipment). **Officers:** Benton Rynestad, President.

■ **4588** ■ **Brady Industries Inc.**
4175 Arville St.
Las Vegas, NV 89103-3736
Phone: (702)876-3990 **Fax:** (702)876-1580
Products: Service industry machinery; Specialty cleaning and sanitation products; Janitors' supplies. **SICs:** 5087 (Service Establishment Equipment); 5169 (Chemicals & Allied Products Nec). **Officers:** William Brady, President.

■ **4589** ■ **Brissman-Kennedy Inc.**
295 Pennsylvania Ave. E
St. Paul, MN 55101-2455
Phone: (651)646-7933
Free: (800)327-3528 **Fax:** (651)645-6395
E-mail: bkinc@brissman-kennedy.com
URL: http://www.brissman-kennedy.com
Products: Janitorial supplies. Janitorial supplies, including chemicals, equipment, and floor matting. **SIC:** 5087 (Service Establishment Equipment). **Est:** 1947. **Emp:** 75.

■ **4590** ■ **Brulin and Co. Inc.**
PO Box 270
Indianapolis, IN 46206
Phone: (317)923-3211 **Fax:** (317)925-4596
E-mail: brulin@earthlink.net
URL: http://www.brulin.com
Products: Floor maintenance products; Carpet cleaners; Health supplies. **SICs:** 5169 (Chemicals & Allied Products Nec); 5122 (Drugs, Proprietaries & Sundries). **Est:** 1935. **Sales:** $20,000,000 (2000). **Emp:** 150. **Officers:** Charles Pollnow, President; Kim Essenburg, CFO; Michael Falkowski, VP of Marketing; Jolee Chartrand, Corporate VP; Jolee Plaggenburg, Dir of Human Resources.

■ **4591** ■ **C & W Distributing Inc.**
PO Box 22610
Santa Fe, NM 87502-2610
Phone: (505)982-3341 **Fax:** (505)982-3341
Products: Janitors' supplies. **SICs:** 5087 (Service Establishment Equipment); 5169 (Chemicals & Allied Products Nec). **Est:** 1985. **Officers:** Ken Whitney, President. **Doing Business As:** C & C Distributors.

■ **4592** ■ **Cameo Paper & Janitor Supply Co.**
433 Cypress Ln.
PO Box 1692
El Cajon, CA 92022
Phone: (619)442-2526 **Fax:** (619)442-2357
Products: Janitorial supplies, including toilet paper and paper towels. **SICs:** 5087 (Service Establishment Equipment); 5113 (Industrial & Personal Service Paper). **Est:** 1963. **Sales:** $3,000,000 (2000). **Emp:** 20. **Officers:** Patti Tuttle Shryock, President; Michael Tuttle, Vice President; David Ornelas, Secretary.

■ **4593** ■ **Capitol Chemical & Supply**
6600 Allied Way
Little Rock, AR 72209
Phone: (501)565-5288 **Fax:** (501)565-5289
Products: Laundry and dry cleaning supplies; Pool and water treatment chemicals. **SICs:** 5087 (Service Establishment Equipment); 5169 (Chemicals & Allied Products Nec). **Est:** 1946. **Emp:** 12. **Officers:** Gary W. Dunwoodel, President & CEO.

■ **4594** ■ **John R. Casey Inc.**
300 Station St.
Cranston, RI 02910-1322
Phone: (401)467-8020
Products: Service industry machinery; Janitors' supplies; Maintenance brushes including floor, scrub, dusting, and window. **SICs:** 5087 (Service Establishment Equipment); 5199 (Nondurable Goods Nec). **Officers:** Bernard Casey, President.

■ **4595** ■ **Central Vac International**
PO Box 160
Kimball, NE 69145-0160
Phone: (308)235-4139
Free: (800)666-3133 **Fax:** (308)235-4687
E-mail: sales@centralvac.com
URL: http://www.centralvac.com
Products: Vacuum cleaning systems. **SIC:** 5064 (Electrical Appliances—Television & Radio). **Est:** 1954. **Emp:** 15. **Officers:** Brian Wilson.

■ **4596** ■ **Century Papers Inc.**
PO Box 1908
Houston, TX 77251
Phone: (713)921-7800 **Fax:** (713)921-0913
Products: Janitorial supplies. **SICs:** 5113 (Industrial & Personal Service Paper); 5169 (Chemicals & Allied Products Nec). **Est:** 1919. **Sales:** $266,000,000 (2000). **Emp:** 500. **Officers:** W. Dwight Jackson, Exec. VP & General Mgr.; Ken Bourne, VP of Finance; Joe Giardina, VP of Marketing.

■ **4597** ■ **Chemed Corp.**
255 E 5th St.
Cincinnati, OH 45202-4726
Phone: (513)762-6900
Products: Sanitary products. **SIC:** 5113 (Industrial & Personal Service Paper). **Sales:** $341,800,000 (2000). **Emp:** 6,849. **Officers:** Edward L. Hutton, CEO & Chairman of the Board; Timothy S. O'Toole, Exec. VP & Treasurer.

■ **4598** ■ **Cherokee Chemical Company Inc.**
12600 S Daphne Ave.
Hawthorne, CA 90250
Phone: (213)757-8112
Free: (800)767-9112 **Fax:** (213)757-8527
Products: Industrial cleaning compounds; Wastewater treatment products. **SIC:** 5169 (Chemicals & Allied Products Nec). **Est:** 1964. **Sales:** $2,500,000 (2000). **Emp:** 41. **Officers:** D. Allen Criswell, President.

■ **4599** ■ **Clark's Store Fixtures Inc.**
1830 S Dort Hwy.
Flint, MI 48503
Phone: (810)239-4667
Products: Janitorial supplies; Refrigeration equipment; Steel. **SICs:** 5087 (Service Establishment Equipment); 5078 (Refrigeration Equipment & Supplies); 5051 (Metals Service Centers & Offices).

■ **4600** ■ **Colgate-Palmolive Co. Institutional Products Div.**
191 E Hanover Ave.
Morristown, NJ 07962-1905
Phone: (973)631-9000 **Fax:** (973)292-6028
E-mail: http://www.colpalipd.com
Products: Cleaning products. **SIC:** 5169 (Chemicals & Allied Products Nec). **Est:** 1887. **Sales:** $30,000,000 (2000). **Emp:** 15. **Officers:** Ed Gagliardi, Dir., IPO.

■ **4601** ■ **Columbus Paper Company Inc.**
PO Box 6369
Columbus, GA 31995-1699
Phone: (706)689-1361 **Fax:** (706)689-1452
Products: Janitorial and industrial supplies. **SICs:** 5085 (Industrial Supplies); 5087 (Service Establishment Equipment). **Est:** 1933. **Sales:** $19,000,000 (2000). **Emp:** 60. **Officers:** Michael Greenblatt, President & CFO.

■ **4602** ■ **Commercial Laundry Sales**
PO Box 391
Bozeman, MT 59771-0391
Phone: (406)587-5148 **Fax:** (406)587-4927
E-mail: cls391@compuserve.com
Products: Laundry equipment and supplies. **SIC:** 5087 (Service Establishment Equipment). **Emp:** 5. **Officers:** Mike Acuff, Owner & Pres.

■ **4603** ■ **Consolidated International Corp.**
333 Main St.
East Greenwich, RI 02818-3660
Phone: (401)884-0160 **Fax:** (401)885-1828
E-mail: info@cicus.com
URL: http://www.cicus.com
Products: Service establishment equipment; Laundry and dry cleaning equipment and supplies. **SIC:** 5087 (Service Establishment Equipment). **Est:** 1975. **Emp:** 7. **Officers:** Thomas Prunk, President.

■ **4604** ■ **Courtesy Sanitary Supply**
33533 Mound Rd.
Sterling Heights, MI 48310-6527
Phone: (810)979-8010 **Fax:** (810)979-8749
Products: Cleaning and sanitation products and equipment; Janitorial supplies, including brooms, vacuums, and scrubbers. **SICs:** 5169 (Chemicals & Allied Products Nec); 5087 (Service Establishment Equipment). **Est:** 1972. **Sales:** $3,000,000 (2000). **Emp:** 11. **Officers:** Robert Nasierowski, President.

■ **4605** ■ **Cowan Brothers Inc.**
809 State St.
Bristol, VA 24201
Phone: (703)669-8342
Products: Janitorial supplies; Candy; Cigarettes. **SICs:** 5169 (Chemicals & Allied Products Nec); 5145 (Confectionery); 5194 (Tobacco & Tobacco Products). **Est:** 1919. **Sales:** $2,500,000 (2000). **Emp:** 18.

Officers: Nell Banks, President; Russell Goyette, Treasurer & Secty.

■ **4606** ■ **Charles E. Cox**
PO Box 127
Carson City, NV 89702-0127
Phone: (702)883-9119
Products: Laundry and dry cleaning equipment. **SIC:** 5087 (Service Establishment Equipment). **Officers:** Charles Cox, Owner.

■ **4607** ■ **D & S Enterprises**
1901 Meadowlark
Farmington, NM 87401
Phone: (505)325-7445 **Fax:** (505)325-4229
Products: Service establishment equipment, including cleaning, maintenance, and carwashing equipment and supplies. **SICs:** 5087 (Service Establishment Equipment); 5169 (Chemicals & Allied Products Nec). **Est:** 1980. **Officers:** Daryl Boss, Owner.

■ **4608** ■ **Dakota Industrial Supply**
340 Main St. E
Valley City, ND 58072-3441
Phone: (701)845-2632
Free: (800)244-6391 **Fax:** (701)845-2632
E-mail: dakind@rrnet.com
Products: Service industry machinery; Specialty cleaning and sanitation products; Janitors' supplies. **SICs:** 5087 (Service Establishment Equipment); 5169 (Chemicals & Allied Products Nec). **Est:** 1940. **Sales:** $500,000 (2000). **Emp:** 8. **Officers:** Randy Swift, Owner.

■ **4609** ■ **Damon Industries, Inc.**
PO Box 2120
Alliance, OH 44601-0120
Phone: (330)821-5310
Free: (800)362-9850 **Fax:** (330)821-6355
Products: Janitorial supplies, including sanitary cleaners, paper products, toilet paper, dispensers, and floor strippers. **SICs:** 5087 (Service Establishment Equipment); 5113 (Industrial & Personal Service Paper); 5169 (Chemicals & Allied Products Nec). **Est:** 1938. **Sales:** $10,000,000 (2000). **Emp:** 100. **Officers:** A.J. Damon, President; R.C. Brumbaugh, Exec. VP. **Former Name:** Damon Chemical Co., Inc.

■ **4610** ■ **Darter Inc.**
1701 Crossroads Dr.
Joliet, IL 60431-9503
Phone: (708)534-7550 **Fax:** (708)534-7570
Products: Industrial cleaning solvents; Paper products, including towels. **SICs:** 5085 (Industrial Supplies); 5113 (Industrial & Personal Service Paper). **Est:** 1959. **Sales:** $25,000,000 (2000). **Emp:** 68. **Officers:** Bruce Fleischer, President; Paul Lowe, CFO; William R. Busby, Sales Mgr.

■ **4611** ■ **Decker's Inc.**
PO Box 51268
Idaho Falls, ID 83405-1268
Phone: (208)522-2551
Free: (800)227-2719 **Fax:** (208)522-2606
Products: Specialty cleaning and sanitation products; Janitors' supplies. **SICs:** 5087 (Service Establishment Equipment); 5169 (Chemicals & Allied Products Nec). **Officers:** Mac Taylor, Chairman of the Board.

■ **4612** ■ **Diamond Supply Company Inc.**
6101 Valley Jo St.
Emeryville, CA 94608
Phone: (510)655-3313
Free: (800)660-0313 **Fax:** (510)655-6443
Products: Janitorial supplies. **SIC:** 5087 (Service Establishment Equipment); 5169 (Chemicals & Allied Products Nec). **Est:** 1935. **Emp:** 300. **Former Name:** Diamond W Supply Co. Inc.

■ **4613** ■ **Easterday Janitorial Supply Co.**
17050 Margay Ave.
Carson, CA 90746
Phone: (310)762-1100
Free: (800)456-3329 **Fax:** (310)762-1074
Products: Janitorial and maintenance supplies. **SIC:** 5087 (Service Establishment Equipment). **Est:** 1935. **Emp:** 200. **Officers:** P. Ridgeway, President; Tom Sting, VP & Controller; Robert Hainley, Operations Mgr.

■ **4614** ■ **Ecolab Inc. Food and Beverage Div.**
Ecolab Center
370 Wabasha St.
St. Paul, MN 55102
Phone: (612)293-2233 **Free:** (800)392-3392
Products: Custom cleaning, sanitizing, dispensing and control systems, detergents, cleaners, sanitizers and lubricants, and water treatments for the dairy, farming, food and beverage processing and brewing industries. **SIC:** 5169 (Chemicals & Allied Products Nec). **Sales:** $54,900,000 (2000). **Emp:** 400. **Officers:** William A. Mathison, VP & General Merchandising Mgr.

■ **4615** ■ **Ecolab Inc. Institutional Div.**
Ecolab Center, 370 N Wabasha St.
St. Paul, MN 55102
Phone: (612)293-2233 **Free:** (800)352-5326
Products: Cleaners and sanitizers. **SIC:** 5169 (Chemicals & Allied Products Nec). **Sales:** $317,200,000 (2000). **Emp:** 2,315. **Officers:** Allan Schuman, CEO & President; Michael Shannon, CFO.

■ **4616** ■ **Ecolab Inc. Textile Care Div.**
Ecolab Center, 370 N Wabasha St.
St. Paul, MN 55102
Phone: (612)293-2233 **Free:** (800)553-8683
Products: Laundry products; Proprietary dispensing systems. **SICs:** 5087 (Service Establishment Equipment); 5169 (Chemicals & Allied Products Nec). **Sales:** $21,000,000 (2000). **Emp:** 150. **Officers:** William C. Crawford, VP & General Merchandising Mgr.

■ **4617** ■ **Edmer Sanitary Supply Co. Inc.**
519 E Meadow Ave.
East Meadow, NY 11554
Phone: (516)794-2000 **Fax:** (516)228-8759
SICs: 5087 (Service Establishment Equipment); 5113 (Industrial & Personal Service Paper). **Est:** 1957. **Sales:** $5,000,000 (2000). **Emp:** 30. **Officers:** Bill Zeitlin, President; Ed Zeitlin, Vice President; Randy Siegmann, VP of Operations; Glenn Rogers, VP of Operations.

■ **4618** ■ **Empire Corporation**
PO Box 1261
Burlington, VT 05402-1261
Phone: (802)862-5181 **Fax:** (802)862-5765
Products: Service industry machinery; Specialty cleaning and sanitation products; Janitors' supplies. **SICs:** 5087 (Service Establishment Equipment); 5169 (Chemicals & Allied Products Nec). **Officers:** Gregory Lovejoy, President.

■ **4619** ■ **Engberg Janitorial Supply & Service**
PO Box 222
Crosby, ND 58730-0222
Phone: (701)965-6803
Products: Service industry machinery; Specialty cleaning and sanitation products; Janitors' supplies. **SICs:** 5087 (Service Establishment Equipment); 5169 (Chemicals & Allied Products Nec). **Officers:** Herbert Engberg, Owner.

■ **4620** ■ **Karen Fisher**
21 E Maple St., No. B
Hailey, ID 83333-8401
Phone: (208)788-4970 **Fax:** (208)788-5791
Products: Service industry machinery; Specialty cleaning and sanitation products; Janitors' supplies. **SICs:** 5087 (Service Establishment Equipment); 5169 (Chemicals & Allied Products Nec). **Officers:** Karen Fisher, Owner.

■ **4621** ■ **Fitch Dustdown Co.**
2201 Russell St.
Baltimore, MD 21230-3198
Phone: (410)539-1953
Free: (800)933-4824 **Fax:** (410)727-2244
URL: http://www.fitchco.com
Products: Sanitation supplies. **SICs:** 5087 (Service Establishment Equipment); 5169 (Chemicals & Allied Products Nec). **Est:** 1898. **Sales:** $9,000,000 (1999). **Emp:** 50. **Officers:** Lynne Kirsner, CEO, e-mail: lynne@fitchco.com; Raymond Kirsner, President; Cordt Goldeisen, VP of Sales.

■ **4622** ■ **Henry Flack International, Inc.**
PO Box 865110
Plano, TX 75086-5110
Phone: (972)867-5677
Free: (800)527-4929 **Fax:** (972)867-8960
Products: Furniture wax. **SIC:** 5169 (Chemicals & Allied Products Nec). **Est:** 1986. **Emp:** 2. **Officers:** J.W. Bollom, Chairman of the Board; Jalea Himes, Operations Manager.

■ **4623** ■ **Flo-Pac Corp.**
700 N Washington Ave., No. 400
Minneapolis, MN 55401
Phone: (612)332-6240 **Fax:** (612)344-1663
E-mail: info@flo-pac.com
URL: http://www.flo-pac.com
Products: Brushes for maintenance. **SIC:** 5087 (Service Establishment Equipment). **Est:** 1913. **Sales:** $23,000,000 (2000). **Emp:** 200. **Officers:** J.A. Bowen, President.

■ **4624** ■ **Follum Supply**
1880 E Centre St.
Rapid City, SD 57701-4072
Phone: (605)343-3507 **Fax:** (605)348-5929
Products: Service industry machinery; Laundry equipment and supplies; Dry cleaning equipment and clothing presses. **SICs:** 5087 (Service Establishment Equipment); 5169 (Chemicals & Allied Products Nec). **Officers:** Roy Follum, Owner.

■ **4625** ■ **Foresight Inc.**
724 E 8th St.
Sioux Falls, SD 57103-1633
Phone: (605)334-4387
Products: Specialty cleaning and sanitation products; Janitors' supplies. **SICs:** 5087 (Service Establishment Equipment); 5169 (Chemicals & Allied Products Nec). **Officers:** Larry Snuttjer, President.

■ **4626** ■ **Forman Inc.**
2036 Lord Baltimore Dr.
Baltimore, MD 21244
Phone: (410)298-7500
Free: (800)638-9400 **Fax:** (410)298-2089
URL: http://www.formaninc.com/
Products: Food service disposables; Janitorial supplies; Food. **SICs:** 5087 (Service Establishment Equipment); 5113 (Industrial & Personal Service Paper); 5141 (Groceries—General Line). **Est:** 1945. **Emp:** 70. **Officers:** Joseph J. Mucha, Chairman of the Board; Frank A. Mucha, Treasurer; Wayne A. Littlefield, President; Giles F. Burns, Vice President; Robert J. Malone, Dir. of Sales; John G. Fitzpatrick, Dir. of Purchasing.

■ **4627** ■ **General Supply of Yakima Inc.**
PO Box 2217
Yakima, WA 98907-2217
Phone: (509)248-1241 **Fax:** (509)248-3664
Products: Janitorial supplies, including cleaners. **SICs:** 5087 (Service Establishment Equipment); 5169 (Chemicals & Allied Products Nec). **Emp:** 29. **Officers:** R. F. Sinclair, Owner; Fran DeVitis, General Mgr.; Carla Shubart, Office Mgr.

■ **4628** ■ **D.J. Giancola Exports, Inc.**
4317 E Genesee St.
PO Box 4
Syracuse, NY 13214
Phone: (315)446-1002 **Fax:** (315)446-2431
E-mail: sales@djgexports.com
URL: http://www.djgexports.com
Products: Commercial equipment, including drycleaning machines, pressing machines, and laundry machines; Spare parts and supplies. **SICs:** *5087 (Service Establishment Equipment); 5047 (Medical & Hospital Equipment). **Est:** 1959. **Sales:** $10,000,000 (1999). **Emp:** 16. **Officers:** Charles G. Giancola, President; Peter M. Kip Jr., e-mail: p.kip@djgexports.com.

■ **4629** ■ **Golden Products Co.**
6101 Washington Blvd.
Culver City, CA 90232-7470
Phone: (310)815-8283
Free: (800)900-8283 **Fax:** (310)815-8638
Products: Janitorial supplies; Landscaping supplies; Indoor plants. **SICs:** 5087 (Service Establishment

Equipment); 5193 (Flowers & Florists' Supplies). **Sales:** $75,000,000 (2000). **Emp:** 499. **Officers:** Tim Gilmore.

■ 4630 ■ **Goorland & Mann, Inc.**
825 N Union St.
Wilmington, DE 19805
Phone: (302)655-1514 **Fax:** (302)655-4519
Products: Janitorial supplies. **SIC:** 5087 (Service Establishment Equipment).

■ 4631 ■ **Great Lakes Air Systems Inc.**
1154 E Lincoln
Madison Heights, MI 48071
Phone: (248)546-9191 **Fax:** (248)541-6978
Products: Dry cleaning equipment. **SIC:** 5087 (Service Establishment Equipment).

■ 4632 ■ **Guss Cleaning & Supply**
240 Wyant Ln.
Hamilton, MT 59840-9371
Phone: (406)363-4427
Products: Service establishment equipment, including cleaning, maintenance, and carpet and rug cleaning equipment and supplies. **SICs:** 5087 (Service Establishment Equipment); 5169 (Chemicals & Allied Products Nec). **Officers:** Gus Schwarz, Owner.

■ 4633 ■ **Hercules Vacu-Maid**
3686 S Schwieder Ln.
Idaho Falls, ID 83406
Phone: (208)522-9666
Products: Service establishment equipment; Cleaning and maintenance equipment and supplies, including vacuum cleaning systems. **SIC:** 5087 (Service Establishment Equipment). **Officers:** Lloyd Cox, Partner.

■ 4634 ■ **HK Laundry Equipment Inc.**
530 Main St.
Armonk, NY 10504
Phone: (914)273-5757
Free: (800)229-4572 **Fax:** (914)273-5283
E-mail: info@hklaundry.com
URL: http://www.hklaundry.com
Products: Laundry equipment. **SIC:** 5087 (Service Establishment Equipment). **Est:** 1967. **Sales:** $3,000,000 (2000). **Emp:** 13. **Officers:** Karl Hinrichs, President.

■ 4635 ■ **Horizons Marketing Group Inc.**
W 62 N 228 Washington Ave.
Cedarburg, WI 53012
Phone: (414)375-1140
Products: Cleaning products; Car care products; Personal protection products, such as skin barriers and personal disinfectants. **SICs:** 5169 (Chemicals & Allied Products Nec); 5122 (Drugs, Proprietaries & Sundries). **Sales:** $14,500,000 (2000). **Emp:** 8. **Officers:** Robert W. Hahn, President; Vikki Hahn, CFO.

■ 4636 ■ **House of Clean Inc.**
PO Box 1203
Bozeman, MT 59771-1203
Phone: (406)587-5012 **Fax:** (406)586-9210
Products: Service establishment equipment; Cleaning and maintenance equipment and supplies; Janitors' supplies. **SICs:** 5087 (Service Establishment Equipment); 5169 (Chemicals & Allied Products Nec). **Officers:** Conrad Kradolfer, President.

■ 4637 ■ **HP Products**
4220 Saguaro Trl.
Indianapolis, IN 46268
Phone: (317)298-9950
Free: (800)382-5326 **Fax:** (317)387-9135
E-mail: ph3676@aol.com
URL: http://www.hpproducts.com
Products: Janitorial supplies; Safety supplies and equipment. **SICs:** 5087 (Service Establishment Equipment); 5099 (Durable Goods Nec). **Est:** 1964. **Sales:** $55,000,000 (1999). **Emp:** 280. **Officers:** Donald Ames Shuel, CEO & Chairman of the Board, e-mail: dshuel@aol.com; Jan Horton, Exec. VP & CFO; Bridget Walker, President & COO.

■ 4638 ■ **Hunt Cleaners Inc.**
PO Box 12
Cozad, NE 69130-0012
Phone: (308)784-3366
Free: (800)262-4568 **Fax:** (308)784-4169
E-mail: huntclea@nque.com
URL: http://www.huntcleaners.com
Products: Gloves and safety supplies; Industrial drycleaning equipment. **SICs:** 5087 (Service Establishment Equipment); 5085 (Industrial Supplies). **Est:** 1951. **Emp:** 18. **Officers:** Mike Neill, e-mail: mneill@nque.com; Jack Ortegren, Sales Mgr., e-mail: ortegren@nque.com.

■ 4639 ■ **Industrial Soap Co.**
2930 Market St.
St. Louis, MO 63103
Phone: (314)241-6363 **Fax:** (314)533-5556
Products: Janitors' supplies. **SICs:** 5087 (Service Establishment Equipment); 5169 (Chemicals & Allied Products Nec). **Est:** 1933. **Sales:** $7,000,000 (2000). **Emp:** 100. **Officers:** Robert D. Shapiro, Owner; Richard F. Shapiro, Owner; Mark S. Shapiro, Dir. of Marketing & Sales.

■ 4640 ■ **Interworld**
4161 Ingot St.
Fremont, CA 94538
Phone: (510)226-6080 **Fax:** (510)225-6089
E-mail: interworld@interworldgroup.com
Products: Cleanroom products, including latex, nitrile, and vinyl gloves, face masks, and shoe covers. **SICs:** 5087 (Service Establishment Equipment); 5169 (Chemicals & Allied Products Nec). **Est:** 1986. **Sales:** $28,000,000 (2000). **Emp:** 236. **Officers:** Phillip Loh, President; Terence Xavier, Marketing Executive; Lee Tay; Yvonne Ho; Yolanda Chu.

■ 4641 ■ **J & J Cleaning Service**
RR 62, Box 3121A
Livingston, MT 59047
Phone: (406)222-6231
Products: Service industry machinery; Specialty cleaning and sanitation products; Janitors' supplies. **SICs:** 5087 (Service Establishment Equipment); 5169 (Chemicals & Allied Products Nec). **Officers:** James Magone, Partner.

■ 4642 ■ **J & K Distributors**
451 Defense Hwy.
Annapolis, MD 21401
Products: Cleaning supplies. **SIC:** 5169 (Chemicals & Allied Products Nec).

■ 4643 ■ **Jackson Supply Co.**
1012 NE 3rd
Amarillo, TX 79107
Phone: (806)373-1888
Free: (800)288-9126 **Fax:** (806)373-5621
Products: Janitorial supplies and equipment. **SICs:** 5087 (Service Establishment Equipment); 5169 (Chemicals & Allied Products Nec). **Est:** 1964. **Sales:** $3,500,000 (2000). **Emp:** 22. **Officers:** E.C. Jackson; Richard Persall.

■ 4644 ■ **Jani-Serv**
5500 W Howard St.
Skokie, IL 60077-2699
Phone: (847)982-9000
Products: Janitorial supplies. **SICs:** 5087 (Service Establishment Equipment); 5169 (Chemicals & Allied Products Nec). **Est:** 1990. **Sales:** $50,000,000 (2000). **Emp:** 159. **Officers:** Dennis G. Ruth, President.

■ 4645 ■ **Janitor Supply Co.**
1100 S Main St.
Aberdeen, SD 57401-7030
Phone: (605)225-0444
Free: (800)225-6444 **Fax:** (605)225-0444
Products: Specialty cleaning and sanitation products; Janitors' supplies. **SICs:** 5087 (Service Establishment Equipment); 5169 (Chemicals & Allied Products Nec). **Est:** 1969. **Sales:** $80,000 (2000). **Emp:** 2. **Officers:** Tom Bakken, Owner, e-mail: bakken@adco2net.com.

■ 4646 ■ **I. Janvey and Sons Inc.**
218 Front St.
Hempstead, NY 11550
Phone: (516)489-9300
Products: Janitorial products, including floor waxes, glass cleaner, towels, and floor machines. **SICs:** 5087 (Service Establishment Equipment); 5169 (Chemicals & Allied Products Nec). **Est:** 1913. **Sales:** $11,100,000 (2000). **Emp:** 50. **Officers:** Bruce H. Janvey, CEO; Abraham Janvey, CFO; Henry Hammer, Sales Mgr.; Edward Jeffries, Dir. of Operations.

■ 4647 ■ **George T. Johnson Company Inc.**
141 Middlesex Tpk.
Burlington, MA 01803
Phone: (781)272-4900 **Fax:** (781)273-9002
Products: Janitors' supplies. **SIC:** 5087 (Service Establishment Equipment). **Est:** 1905. **Sales:** $25,000,000 (2000). **Emp:** 54. **Officers:** James Reider, President; Peter Vorvato, Treasurer.

■ 4648 ■ **Kay Chemical Co.**
8300 Capital Dr.
Greensboro, NC 27409-9790
Phone: (336)668-7290
Free: (800)333-4300 **Fax:** (336)668-9763
Products: Cleaning and sanitation supplies for the convenience industry. **SIC:** 5169 (Chemicals & Allied Products Nec). **Sales:** $163,600,000 (2000). **Emp:** 377. **Officers:** Randall Kaplan, President; George Harris, CFO.

■ 4649 ■ **Kellermeyer Co.**
PO Box 3357
Toledo, OH 43607
Phone: (419)255-3022 **Fax:** (419)255-2752
E-mail: info@kellermeyer.com
URL: http://www.kellermeyer.com
Products: Janitorial and cleaning supplies; Paper products; Packaging supplies and equipment. **SIC:** 5087 (Service Establishment Equipment). **Est:** 1944. **Sales:** $20,000,000 (2000). **Emp:** 92. **Officers:** Don V. Kellermeyer, President; Rebecca Berdue, Controller.

■ 4650 ■ **Kenway Distributors Inc.**
PO Box 14097
Louisville, KY 40214
Phone: (502)367-2201
Products: Janitorial supplies. **SIC:** 5087 (Service Establishment Equipment). **Est:** 1950. **Sales:** $14,000,000 (2000). **Emp:** 70. **Officers:** Kenneth R. Crutcher, President; Gene Vanderpool, Treasurer.

■ 4651 ■ **Kleen Supply Co.**
423 25th St.
Galveston, TX 77550
Phone: (409)762-0140
Products: Groceries and cleaning supplies. **SICs:** 5141 (Groceries—General Line); 5085 (Industrial Supplies). **Sales:** $400,000 (2000). **Emp:** 4. **Officers:** Carlos Pena, President.

■ 4652 ■ **Knight Marketing Corp.**
251 N Comrie Ave.
PO Box 290
Johnstown, NY 12095
Phone: (518)762-4591
Free: (800)477-7299 **Fax:** (518)762-2566
E-mail: admin@knightmkt.com
URL: http://www.knightmkt.com
Products: Speciality cleaning and sanitation products. **SICs:** 5087 (Service Establishment Equipment); 5169 (Chemicals & Allied Products Nec). **Est:** 1917. **Sales:** $11,000,000 (1999). **Emp:** 140. **Officers:** Michael Pozefsky, CEO; Edward Brown, President; Timothy Chace, Human Resources Contact, e-mail: tchace@knightmkt.com.

■ 4653 ■ **Knoll Motel**
1015 N Main St.
Barre, VT 05641
Phone: (802)479-3648
Products: Service industry machinery; Janitors' supplies; Vacuum cleaning systems. **SIC:** 5087 (Service Establishment Equipment). **Officers:** Stanley Sabens, Partner.

■ 4654 ■ Kranz Inc.
220 Decoven Ave.
Racine, WI 53403
Products: Cleaning supplies. SIC: 5087 (Service Establishment Equipment). Sales: $17,000,000 (1992). Emp: 70. Officers: Jeff Neubauer, President.

■ 4655 ■ Kwik Stop Car Wash Supply
3802 Pine View Dr.
Rapid City, SD 57702-6977
Phone: (605)341-1352
Products: Service industry machinery; Specialty cleaning and sanitation products; Carwash equipment and supplies; Electronic computing equipment. SICs: 5087 (Service Establishment Equipment); 5045 (Computers, Peripherals & Software); 5169 (Chemicals & Allied Products Nec). Officers: Jerry Anderson, Owner.

■ 4656 ■ Lake Tahoe Supplies
PO Box 7007
Incline Village, NV 89450-7007
Phone: (702)831-6395
Free: (800)332-3385   Fax: (702)831-0815
E-mail: tahosupply@aol.com
URL: http://www.laketahoesupply.com
Products: Janitorial supplies; Hotel equipment and supplies. SICs: 5087 (Service Establishment Equipment); 5046 (Commercial Equipment Nec). Est: 1980. Sales: $2,000,000 (2000). Emp: 8. Officers: Dominic Spallone, Owner.

■ 4657 ■ Laun-Dry Supply Company Inc.
3800 Durazno St.
El Paso, TX 79905
Phone: (915)533-8217
Free: (800)995-2863   Fax: (915)533-1301
E-mail: ldemployee@aol.com
Products: Janitors' supplies; Laundry equipment and supplies. SICs: 5087 (Service Establishment Equipment); 5169 (Chemicals & Allied Products Nec). Est: 1946. Sales: $11,000,000 (2000). Emp: 33. Officers: Lynn J. Gore, President; David Royalzy, VP of Marketing.

■ 4658 ■ Leading Products Co.
614 Diez Y Ocho Ct. SE
Rio Rancho, NM 87124-2235
Phone: (505)892-5740
Products: Service establishment equipment; Cleaning and maintenance equipment and supplies; Carwash equipment and supplies. SICs: 5087 (Service Establishment Equipment); 5169 (Chemicals & Allied Products Nec). Officers: Ronald Cepelak, Owner.

■ 4659 ■ J. Levin and Sons Co.
7610 W Chicago Ave.
Detroit, MI 48204
Phone: (313)834-6920   Fax: (313)834-0176
Products: Laundry equipment and supplies; Dry cleaning equipment and clothing presses. SIC: 5087 (Service Establishment Equipment). Est: 1884. Sales: $9,000,000 (2000). Emp: 40. Officers: Bernard Levin, CEO; Edwin Levin, VP & Treasurer.

■ 4660 ■ Lyk-Nu Inc.
1 Rotary Park Dr.
PO Box 3390
Clarksville, TN 37043-3390
Phone: (931)647-0139   Free: (800)245-9568
Products: Specialty cleaning and sanitation products; Waxes, except petroleum. SIC: 5169 (Chemicals & Allied Products Nec). Est: 1990. Sales: $600,000 (2000). Emp: 6. Officers: H. P. Batie, President; Bill Thompson, Warehouse Mgr. Former Name: Supersafe. Alternate Name: Car Care Products Inc.

■ 4661 ■ M & M Chemical Supply Inc.
PO Box 1467
Casper, WY 82602-1467
Phone: (307)473-8818
Free: (800)585-8814   Fax: (307)473-8827
E-mail: m_mchem@trib.com
Products: Janitorial and industrial chemicals. SICs: 5169 (Chemicals & Allied Products Nec); 5113 (Industrial & Personal Service Paper). Est: 1987. Officers: Mike Ridgeway, President.

■ 4662 ■ M & P Sales Inc.
3659 S Maryland Pkwy.
Las Vegas, NV 89109-3001
Phone: (702)734-9595
Products: Service establishment equipment; Laundry and dry cleaning equipment and supplies. SICs: 5087 (Service Establishment Equipment); 5169 (Chemicals & Allied Products Nec). Officers: Melvin Shapiro, President.

■ 4663 ■ A.J. Marshall Co.
6635 Sterling Dr. S
Sterling Heights, MI 48312
Phone: (810)939-1600   Fax: (810)939-7530
Products: Cleaning supplies; Restaurant supplies, including food and utensils. SICs: 5087 (Service Establishment Equipment); 5141 (Groceries—General Line); 5113 (Industrial & Personal Service Paper). Est: 1897. Sales: $2,000,000 (2000). Emp: 15. Officers: Nathan Greenberg, President.

■ 4664 ■ Master Cleaners Home Service
PO Box 1129
Helena, MT 59624-1129
Phone: (406)442-1964
Products: Service establishment equipment, including cleaning and maintenance equipment and supplies; Janitors' supplies. SIC: 5087 (Service Establishment Equipment). Officers: James Kathan, President.

■ 4665 ■ MCF Systems Atlanta Inc.
5353 Snapfinger Woods
Decatur, GA 30035
Phone: (404)593-9434
Products: Dry cleaning equipment. SIC: 5087 (Service Establishment Equipment). Est: 1989. Sales: $3,300,000 (2000). Emp: 25. Officers: Charles Mendez Jr., President.

■ 4666 ■ F.B. McFadden Wholesale Company Inc.
415 Railroad Ave.
Rock Springs, WY 82901
Phone: (307)362-5441   Fax: (307)382-8466
Products: Janitors' supplies. SIC: 5169 (Chemicals & Allied Products Nec). Est: 1936. Sales: $5,000,000 (1999). Emp: 15. Officers: E.H. McFadden, President; Pat McFadden, Finance Officer; J. McFadden, Dir. of Marketing.

■ 4667 ■ George M. Medek Inc.
216 W 36th St.
Boise, ID 83714-6531
Phone: (208)343-4343
Products: Service industry machinery; Specialty cleaning and sanitation products. SICs: 5087 (Service Establishment Equipment); 5169 (Chemicals & Allied Products Nec). Est: 1967. Sales: $150,000 (2000). Emp: 3. Officers: George Medek, Vice President; Zachary Medek, President.

■ 4668 ■ Memphis Chemical Janitorial Supply Inc.
PO Box 70512
Memphis, TN 38107
Phone: (901)521-1612
Free: (800)561-1612   Fax: (901)521-1613
Products: Janitorial supplies. SIC: 5087 (Service Establishment Equipment). Est: 1974. Sales: $501,224 (2000). Emp: 4.

■ 4669 ■ Mid City Hardware
130 W 25th St.
New York, NY 10001
Phone: (212)807-8713
Products: Janitorial supplies; Garbage liners; Cups, toilet paper, and paper towels. SICs: 5087 (Service Establishment Equipment); 5113 (Industrial & Personal Service Paper).

■ 4670 ■ Midwest Chemical and Supply Inc.
340 E 56th Ave.
Denver, CO 80216
Phone: (303)293-2122
Products: Janitorial equipment and chemicals. SICs: 5087 (Service Establishment Equipment); 5169 (Chemicals & Allied Products Nec). Sales: $12,000,000 (2000). Emp: 35. Officers: Karen Jean Bell, President.

■ 4671 ■ Midwest Cleaning Systems Inc.
E 1st St.
Alcester, SD 57001
Phone: (605)934-1711   Fax: (605)934-1708
Products: Service industry machinery; Specialty cleaning and sanitation products; Janitors' supplies. SICs: 5087 (Service Establishment Equipment); 5169 (Chemicals & Allied Products Nec). Officers: Todd Hakl, President.

■ 4672 ■ Mission Janitorial Supplies
9292 Activity Rd.
San Diego, CA 92126
Phone: (858)566-6700
Free: (800)733-1748   Fax: (858)271-5079
E-mail: sales@missionjanitorial.com
URL: http://www.missionjanitorial.com
Products: Janitorial supplies; Abrasive supplies. SIC: 5087 (Service Establishment Equipment). Est: 1939. Sales: $13,000,000 (2000). Emp: 50. Officers: Kevin J. Carlson, President.

■ 4673 ■ A.E. Moore, Inc.
State St.
Millsboro, DE 19966
Phone: (302)934-7055
Products: Paper; Janitorial supplies; Candy; Tobacco. SICs: 5087 (Service Establishment Equipment); 5113 (Industrial & Personal Service Paper); 5145 (Confectionery); 5194 (Tobacco & Tobacco Products).

■ 4674 ■ Nar Inc.
585 Riverside St.
Portland, ME 04103-1032
Phone: (207)797-8240   Fax: (207)878-3513
Products: Service industry machinery; Specialty cleaning and sanitation products; Janitors' supplies. SICs: 5087 (Service Establishment Equipment); 5169 (Chemicals & Allied Products Nec). Officers: James Russell, President.

■ 4675 ■ National Sanitary Supply Co. Portland Div.
2690 SE Mailwell Dr.
Milwaukie, OR 97222-7316
Phone: (503)234-0210   Fax: (503)239-7393
Products: Janitorial supplies, including soaps, detergents, and machines. SICs: 5087 (Service Establishment Equipment); 5169 (Chemicals & Allied Products Nec). Est: 1918. Sales: $7,000,000 (2000). Emp: 60. Officers: Larry G. Novinger, General Mgr.; Fred Stevens, Finance Officer; W. Pons, Manager.

■ 4676 ■ Walter E. Nelson Company Inc.
5937 N Cutter Cir.
Portland, OR 97217
Phone: (503)285-3037
Free: (800)929-2141   Fax: (503)285-4373
E-mail: wenelson@teleport.com
Products: Janitorial supplies; Building and maintenance supplies, including paper products. SICs: 5087 (Service Establishment Equipment); 5113 (Industrial & Personal Service Paper). Est: 1954. Sales: $20,000,000 (1999). Emp: 55. Officers: Robert Wakefield, CFO; Michael E. Nelson, CEO; Dave Henzi, VP of Operations; Dave Stegner, Sales Mgr.

■ 4677 ■ Northwest Arkansas Paper Co.
755 Gray Dr.
PO Box 729
Springdale, AR 72764
Phone: (501)751-7155
Free: (800)643-3068   Fax: (501)756-6301
Products: Janitorial equipment and supplies; Food service disposable supplies; Safety and first aid supplies; Packaging equipment and supplies. SICs: 5087 (Service Establishment Equipment); 5113 (Industrial & Personal Service Paper); 5122 (Drugs, Proprietaries & Sundries). Est: 1967. Emp: 120. Officers: William Gray, CEO & President; Ron H. Moore, Vice President. Also Known by This Acronym: NAPCO.

■ 4678 ■ NUCO Industries Inc.
110 Schmitt Blvd.
Farmingdale, NY 11735
Phone: (516)752-8600
Free: (800)645-9198 **Fax:** (516)752-7848
E-mail: nuco203@aol.com
URL: http://www.environmentalsupplies.com
Products: Cleaning chemicals; Sanitary products; Environmental clean-up supplies. **SICs:** 5087 (Service Establishment Equipment); 5169 (Chemicals & Allied Products Nec). **Est:** 1994. **Sales:** $5,000,000 (1999). **Emp:** 15. **Officers:** Sherry L. Sycoff, CEO; Alan R. Sycoff, Exec. VP of Marketing; Jeff Berlin, Sales Mgr.

■ 4679 ■ Okie Dokie Services
PO Box 668
Ketchum, ID 83340-0668
Phone: (208)726-3196 **Fax:** (208)726-3196
Products: Service industry machinery; Specialty cleaning and sanitation products; Janitors' supplies. **SICs:** 5087 (Service Establishment Equipment); 5169 (Chemicals & Allied Products Nec). **Officers:** Gregory Dale, Owner.

■ 4680 ■ Oliver Supply Co.
PO Box 430297
Pontiac, MI 48343-0297
Phone: (248)682-7222 **Fax:** (248)682-1786
Products: Janitorial supplies; Restaurant equipment. **SICs:** 5087 (Service Establishment Equipment); 5046 (Commercial Equipment Nec). **Est:** 1890. **Sales:** $1,500,000 (2000). **Emp:** 9.

■ 4681 ■ On Spot Janitor Supplies & Repair
5308 4th St. NW
Albuquerque, NM 87107-5206
Phone: (505)343-0215 **Fax:** (505)343-8731
Products: Vacuum cleaners; Janitorial equipment; Sewing machines. **SICs:** 5087 (Service Establishment Equipment); 5064 (Electrical Appliances—Television & Radio). **Officers:** Richard Gomez, Owner.

■ 4682 ■ PAMSCO Inc.
PO Box 309
Longview, WA 98632
Phone: (425)423-3500 **Fax:** (425)423-0897
Products: Janitors' supplies. **SICs:** 5087 (Service Establishment Equipment); 5113 (Industrial & Personal Service Paper). **Est:** 1955. **Sales:** $2,940,000 (2000). **Emp:** 18. **Officers:** Harry Brown, President; Charles House, Vice President.

■ 4683 ■ Paper Supply Co.
PO Box 11823
Winston-Salem, NC 27116-1823
Phone: (336)759-9647
Free: (800)722-2105 **Fax:** (336)759-2818
Products: Janitorial supplies, including paper. **SICs:** 5087 (Service Establishment Equipment); 5113 (Industrial & Personal Service Paper). **Est:** 1982. **Emp:** 17. **Officers:** Gary Miller, Vice President.

■ 4684 ■ Peerless Paper Mills Inc.
1122 Longford Rd.
Oaks, PA 19456
Phone: (215)933-9015 **Fax:** (215)933-6516
Products: Janitorial supplies; Industrial products. **SICs:** 5087 (Service Establishment Equipment); 5085 (Industrial Supplies). **Est:** 1898. **Sales:** $75,000,000 (2000). **Emp:** 150. **Officers:** W. Sheppard, CEO; W.J. Sheppard, President.

■ 4685 ■ Phenix Supply Co.
PO Box 6963
Atlanta, GA 30315
Phone: (404)622-8136
Products: Dry cleaning supplies, including detergents and hangers. **SICs:** 5087 (Service Establishment Equipment); 5169 (Chemicals & Allied Products Nec). **Est:** 1899. **Sales:** $13,000,000 (2000). **Emp:** 100. **Officers:** Robbie Freeman, President; Gary E. Akins, VP & CFO; Joel Dampier, Vice President; James Hartley, Vice President.

■ 4686 ■ Phillips Distribution Inc.
3000 E Houston
PO Box 200067
San Antonio, TX 78220
Phone: (512)227-2397
Free: (800)580-2397 **Fax:** (512)222-0790
Products: Packaging products for restaurants, supermarkets, and food processors; Sanitary and janitorial products. **SIC:** 5087 (Service Establishment Equipment). **Est:** 1945. **Sales:** $14,500,000 (2000). **Emp:** 38. **Officers:** Gil Phillips, President; Steve Meyer, Treasurer; Kelly Clifford, Secretary.

■ 4687 ■ Plant Maintenance Equipment
PO Box 48229
Seattle, WA 98148-0229
Phone: (206)242-5131 **Fax:** (206)244-1592
Products: Janitors' supplies; Vacuum cleaning systems; Specialty cleaning and sanitation products. **SICs:** 5087 (Service Establishment Equipment); 5169 (Chemicals & Allied Products Nec). **Officers:** Edward Louie, President.

■ 4688 ■ Portsmouth Paper Co.
PO Box 600
Portsmouth, NH 03802-0600
Phone: (603)436-1910 **Fax:** (603)436-0319
E-mail: admin@portsmouthpaper.com
URL: http://www.portsmouthpaper.com
Products: Service establishment equipment, including cleaning and maintenance equipment and supplies. **SIC:** 5087 (Service Establishment Equipment). **Est:** 1912. **Sales:** $30,000,000 (2000). **Emp:** 70. **Officers:** Steven M. Goodman, President; Cris T. Goodman, Vice President.

■ 4689 ■ Pressure Service Inc.
2361 S Plaza Dr.
Rapid City, SD 57702
Phone: (605)341-5154 **Fax:** (605)341-4843
Products: Service establishment equipment; Cleaning and maintenance equipment and supplies; Carwash equipment and supplies. **SICs:** 5087 (Service Establishment Equipment); 5169 (Chemicals & Allied Products Nec). **Officers:** Terry Bosma, President.

■ 4690 ■ PYA/Monarch Inc. Schloss and Kahn
U.S. Hwy. 80 W
Montgomery, AL 36108
Phone: (205)288-3111 **Fax:** (205)286-5299
Products: Cleaning supplies. **SIC:** 5169 (Chemicals & Allied Products Nec). **Est:** 1871. **Sales:** $100,000,000 (2000). **Emp:** 325. **Officers:** Steve Schloss, CEO; Scott Schwartz, Controller; James Hall, Manager; Ronnie Sargent, Vice President.

■ 4691 ■ R and D Products
PO Box 2365
Ft. Oglethorpe, GA 30742-2365
Phone: (706)867-4550
Products: Automotive cleaning supplies. **SIC:** 5169 (Chemicals & Allied Products Nec). **Sales:** $4,000,000 (2000). **Emp:** 10. **Officers:** Joe Proctor, Owner.

■ 4692 ■ Reed Distributors
PO Box 1704
Lewiston, ME 04241-1704
Phone: (207)784-1591 **Fax:** (207)784-3915
Products: Service industry machinery; Specialty cleaning and sanitation products; Paper and allied products. **SICs:** 5087 (Service Establishment Equipment); 5113 (Industrial & Personal Service Paper); 5169 (Chemicals & Allied Products Nec). **Officers:** John Campbell, President.

■ 4693 ■ Reedy International Corp.
25 E Front St.
Keyport, NJ 07735
Phone: (732)264-1777
Products: Footwear care products. **SIC:** 5099 (Durable Goods Nec).

■ 4694 ■ Rex Chemical Corp.
2270 NW 23rd St.
Miami, FL 33142
Phone: (305)634-2471 **Fax:** (305)634-5546
E-mail: rexchem@bellsouth.net
URL: http://www.rexchemical.com
Products: Janitorial and cleaning supplies. **SIC:** 5087

(Service Establishment Equipment). **Est:** 1965. **Sales:** $4,000,000 (2000). **Emp:** 50. **Officers:** R. Granja, Vice President; Betty Granja, President; A. Granja, Treasurer.

■ 4695 ■ RHO-Chem Div.
PO Box 6021
Inglewood, CA 90301
Phone: (213)776-6233 **Fax:** (213)645-6379
Products: Industrial cleaning products; Hazardous waste containers. **SICs:** 5169 (Chemicals & Allied Products Nec); 5099 (Durable Goods Nec). **Est:** 1951. **Sales:** $15,000,000 (2000). **Emp:** 61. **Officers:** Rocky Costello, General Mgr.; Mike Alessi, CFO; Moira Mahon, Dir of Human Resources.

■ 4696 ■ Richard-Ewing Equipment Co. Inc.
27121 Parklane Dr.
Sioux Falls, SD 57106-8000
Phone: (605)368-2528
Free: (800)658-3368 **Fax:** (605)368-5580
Products: Service industry machinery; Laundry equipment and supplies; Dry cleaning equipment and clothing presses. **SICs:** 5087 (Service Establishment Equipment); 5169 (Chemicals & Allied Products Nec). **Est:** 1960. **Officers:** Larry Jacobson, President.

■ 4697 ■ Ro-Vic Inc.
PO Box 1140
Manchester, CT 06045-1140
Phone: (860)646-3322
Free: (800)832-1013 **Fax:** (860)647-7057
Products: Industrial sanitation supplies. **SIC:** 5087 (Service Establishment Equipment). **Est:** 1956. **Sales:** $18,000,000 (2000). **Emp:** 77. **Officers:** R. Parrott Jr., President, e-mail: Rogparrott@aol.com; Karl L. Reichelt, Vice President, e-mail: Karl29@aol.com.

■ 4698 ■ Rochester Midland Corp.
PO Box 1515
Rochester, NY 14603
Phone: (716)336-2200
Free: (800)762-4448 **Fax:** (716)336-4406
Products: Janitor's supplies; Industrial chemicals; Water treatment systems; Feminine hygiene products; Printing equipment and chemicals. **SICs:** 5087 (Service Establishment Equipment); 5169 (Chemicals & Allied Products Nec); 5084 (Industrial Machinery & Equipment); 5122 (Drugs, Proprietaries & Sundries). **Sales:** $60,000,000 (2000). **Emp:** 1,073. **Officers:** H.D. Calkins, President; G.D. Kittredge; D.J. Vivian; J.O. Luthro.

■ 4699 ■ Rose Products and Services Inc.
545 Stimmel Rd.
Columbus, OH 43223
Phone: (614)443-7647
Products: Janitorial supplies, including mops and paper towels. **SICs:** 5087 (Service Establishment Equipment); 5113 (Industrial & Personal Service Paper). **Est:** 1926. **Sales:** $17,000,000 (2000). **Emp:** 55. **Officers:** Eldon L. Hall Sr., President.

■ 4700 ■ S & D Industrial Supply Inc.
PO Box 50252
Amarillo, TX 79159-0252
Products: Service industry machinery; Specialty cleaning and sanitation products; Janitors' supplies. **SICs:** 5087 (Service Establishment Equipment); 5169 (Chemicals & Allied Products Nec). **Officers:** David Davidson, President.

■ 4701 ■ Sadd Laundry and Dry Cleaning Supplies
1359 Colburn St.
Honolulu, HI 96817
Phone: (808)841-3818 **Fax:** (808)848-5088
E-mail: sudds2atsnpwt.net
Products: Laundry and dry cleaning supplies. **SIC:** 5087 (Service Establishment Equipment). **Est:** 1985. **Sales:** $1,100,000 (2000). **Emp:** 4. **Officers:** Michael C. Sadd, President.

■ 4702 ■ San Joaquin Supply Company Inc.
PO Box 7737
Fresno, CA 93747
Phone: (209)251-8455 **Fax:** (209)453-0921
Products: Cleaning products and equipment; Industrial chemicals. **SICs:** 5087 (Service Establishment

Equipment); 5113 (Industrial & Personal Service Paper); 5169 (Chemicals & Allied Products Nec). **Est:** 1938. **Sales:** $13,000,000 (2000). **Emp:** 100. **Officers:** James Knapp, President; Nancy Scheidt, Controller; Robert Albright, Sales/Marketing Contact.

■ **4703** ■ **Sani-Clean Distributors Inc.**
585 Riverside St.
Portland, ME 04103
Phone: (207)797-8240
Products: Janitorial supplies. **SIC:** 5087 (Service Establishment Equipment). **Est:** 1956. **Sales:** $1,000,000 (2000). **Emp:** 15. **Officers:** James Russell, President; Joe Kazilionis, Controller.

■ **4704** ■ **Schnaible Service and Supply Company Inc.**
231 Chestnut St.
PO Box 1453
Lafayette, IN 47902-1453
Phone: (765)742-0280   **Fax:** (765)423-5386
E-mail: schnaibl@schnaible.com
URL: http://www.schnaible.com
Products: Paper products, including industrial towels, tissue, and liners; Janitorial supplies. **SICs:** 5087 (Service Establishment Equipment); 5113 (Industrial & Personal Service Paper). **Est:** 1853. **Sales:** $7,000,000 (1999). **Emp:** 32. **Officers:** D.J. Stein, President; James Whelchel, Dir. of Systems; James Warr, Dir. of Marketing.

■ **4705** ■ **H. Schultz and Sons**
777 Lehigh Ave.
Union, NJ 07083
Phone: (908)687-5400   **Fax:** (908)687-1788
Products: Household cleaning products. **SIC:** 5169 (Chemicals & Allied Products Nec). **Est:** 1921. **Sales:** $25,000,000 (2000). **Emp:** 78. **Officers:** Robert Schultz, VP of Operations; Jerry Schultz, VP of Sales; Dave Schultz, VP of Marketing.

■ **4706** ■ **Seybold Co.**
107 Northeast Dr.
Loveland, OH 45140-7145
Phone: (513)683-8553
Free: (800)473-7604   **Fax:** (513)683-7128
E-mail: seybold@one.net
URL: http://www.seybold-company.com
Products: Janitorial supplies. **SICs:** 5113 (Industrial & Personal Service Paper); 5087 (Service Establishment Equipment); 5169 (Chemicals & Allied Products Nec). **Est:** 1922. **Sales:** $9,000,000 (1999). **Emp:** 30. **Officers:** T. J. Swigart, President & Chairman of the Board; J. Brookhart, Controller; David N. Reed, Vice President.

■ **4707** ■ **Shippers Supply Corp.**
2428 Crittenden Dr.
Louisville, KY 40217
Phones: (502)635-6368   (502)634-2800
Free: (800)557-2800   **Fax:** (502)635-7935
URL: http://www.shipperssupplyco.com
Products: Paper products. **SIC:** 5113 (Industrial & Personal Service Paper). **Est:** 1952. **Sales:** $26,000,000 (2000). **Emp:** 51. **Officers:** Henry Camp, President.

■ **4708** ■ **Ships Wheel Brand Corp.**
PO Box 544
Bristol, RI 02809-0544
Phone: (401)253-2882   **Fax:** (401)253-2975
Products: Service industry machinery; specialty cleaning and sanitation products. Paper products, cleaning chemicals, janitorial supplies, shipping supplies, food service supplies, and office products equipment. **SICs:** 5087 (Service Establishment Equipment); 5169 (Chemicals & Allied Products Nec). **Est:** 1971. **Sales:** $1,000,000 (2000). **Emp:** 6. **Officers:** Erik Warner, President. **Doing Business As:** T.J. #Russell Co.

■ **4709** ■ **Simplex Chemical Corp.**
6 Commercial St.
Sharon, MA 02067
Phone: (781)784-8484
Free: (800)222-2621   **Fax:** (781)784-8100
E-mail: aaasimplex@aol.com
Products: Janitorial supplies and cleaning chemicals. **SICs:** 5087 (Service Establishment Equipment); 5169

(Chemicals & Allied Products Nec). **Est:** 1977. **Sales:** $1,000,000 (2000). **Emp:** 26. **Officers:** Peter Brown, President.

■ **4710** ■ **Solutions and Cleaning Products**
208 W Brundage St.
Sheridan, WY 82801
Phone: (307)672-1846
Free: (888)672-1846   **Fax:** (307)672-0883
E-mail: capclean@cyberhighway.com
Products: Speciality cleaning and restoration products, for professional carpet cleaners. **SICs:** 5087 (Service Establishment Equipment); 5169 (Chemicals & Allied Products Nec). **Officers:** David Oakes, President. **Doing Business As:** Captain Clean Inc.

■ **4711** ■ **Speed Brite Inc.**
1810 W Innes St.
Salisbury, NC 28144-1766
Phone: (704)639-9771
Free: (800)874-2823   **Fax:** (704)637-5007
URL: http://www.speedbrite.com
Products: Jewelry cleaner; Ink jet cleaners. **SIC:** 5169 (Chemicals & Allied Products Nec). **Est:** 1991. **Sales:** $350,000 (2000). **Emp:** 8. **Officers:** Jimmy B. Rabon, President, e-mail: jim@speedbrite.com; Carol Rabon, Customer Service Contact. **Former Name:** Speed Brite Inc.

■ **4712** ■ **Star Brite**
4041 SW 47 Ave.
Ft. Lauderdale, FL 33314
Phone: (954)587-6280
Free: (800)327-8583   **Fax:** (954)587-2813
SIC: 5169 (Chemicals & Allied Products Nec). **Sales:** $16,000,000 (2000). **Emp:** 110. **Officers:** Peter G. Dornall, President.

■ **4713** ■ **State Janitorial Supply Co.**
24 Maggies Way
Dover, DE 19901
Phone: (302)734-4814   **Fax:** (302)734-8362
Products: Janitorial supplies. **SIC:** 5087 (Service Establishment Equipment).

■ **4714** ■ **Statewide Floor Waxing Distributors**
PO Box 718
Bangor, ME 04402-0718
Phone: (207)945-9591   **Fax:** (207)947-1000
Products: Service industry machinery; Specialty cleaning and sanitation products; Janitors' supplies. **SICs:** 5087 (Service Establishment Equipment); 5169 (Chemicals & Allied Products Nec). **Officers:** Aquelidio Redrigues, President.

■ **4715** ■ **Stein's Inc.**
PO Box 248
Moorhead, MN 56561-0248
Phone: (218)233-2727   **Fax:** (218)233-7586
Products: Janitorial and maintenance cleaning supplies. **SIC:** 5169 (Chemicals & Allied Products Nec). **Sales:** $18,000,000 (2000). **Emp:** 42. **Officers:** Kevin Stein, President; Craig Stein, CFO.

■ **4716** ■ **Thayer Inc.**
225 5th St.
PO Box 867
Benton Harbor, MI 49023-0867
Phone: (616)925-0633
Free: (800)870-0009   **Fax:** (616)925-0639
E-mail: thayer@qtm.net
Products: Janitoral supplies. **SICs:** 5087 (Service Establishment Equipment); 5113 (Industrial & Personal Service Paper). **Est:** 1946. **Sales:** $4,000,000 (1999). **Emp:** 17. **Officers:** Kay Varga Smith, President.

■ **4717** ■ **Tidewater Wholesalers Inc.**
708 W Constance Rd.
Suffolk, VA 23434
Phone: (757)539-3261   **Fax:** (757)925-4478
Products: Janitorial supplies; Candies; Tobacco products; Paper products. **SICs:** 5169 (Chemicals & Allied Products Nec); 5145 (Confectionery); 5194 (Tobacco & Tobacco Products). **Est:** 1948. **Sales:** $5,000,000 (2000). **Emp:** 15. **Officers:** John W. Orange, President & Chairman of the Board.

■ **4718** ■ **Turtle Plastics Co.**
7450 A Industrial Pk.
Lorain, OH 44053
Phone: (440)282-8008   **Fax:** (440)282-8822
E-mail: info@turtleplastics.com
URL: http://www.turtleplastics.com
Products: Janitorial supplies made from recycled plastic; Fatigue mats; Entrance mats; Pool decking. **SICs:** 5087 (Service Establishment Equipment); 5162 (Plastics Materials & Basic Shapes). **Est:** 1983. **Sales:** $3,000,000 (2000). **Emp:** 10. **Officers:** Thomas Norton, President. **Former Name:** Cleveland Reclaim Industries Inc.

■ **4719** ■ **TW Systems Ltd.**
99-1434 Koaha Pl.
Aiea, HI 96701
Phone: (808)486-2667   **Fax:** (808)486-2665
Products: Laundry equipment and supplies; Textiles. **SICs:** 5087 (Service Establishment Equipment); 5131 (Piece Goods & Notions). **Est:** 1955. **Sales:** $7,000,000 (2000). **Emp:** 30.

■ **4720** ■ **Unisource**
PO Box 1129
Bangor, ME 04402-1129
Phone: (207)947-7311   **Fax:** (207)947-8268
Products: Janitorial supplies, including paper napkins, towels, cups, and cleaners. **SIC:** 5113 (Industrial & Personal Service Paper). **Est:** 1919. **Sales:** $16,000,000 (2000). **Emp:** 45. **Officers:** Bill Leith, President; Norman Holcomb, CFO.

■ **4721** ■ **Urban Wholesale**
329 Saint Francis St.
Rapid City, SD 57701-5482
Phone: (605)343-0794
Products: Service establishment equipment, including cleaning and maintenance equipment and supplies. **SIC:** 5087 (Service Establishment Equipment). **Officers:** Gerald Urban, Owner.

■ **4722** ■ **Valley Coin Laundry Equipment Co.**
Woods Bay
Bigfork, MT 59911
Phone: (406)837-6616
Products: Service establishment equipment; Laundry and dry cleaning equipment and supplies. **SICs:** 5087 (Service Establishment Equipment); 5169 (Chemicals & Allied Products Nec). **Officers:** T Andrews, Owner.

■ **4723** ■ **Veterans Supply & Distributing Co.**
3225 Caniff Ave.
Hamtramck, MI 48212
Phone: (313)892-6660   **Fax:** (313)892-3044
Products: Janitors' supplies; Manufactured tobacco products. **SICs:** 5087 (Service Establishment Equipment); 5194 (Tobacco & Tobacco Products). **Est:** 1946. **Sales:** $1,500,000 (2000). **Emp:** 6. **Officers:** Louis Ray, President.

■ **4724** ■ **Virginia Industrial Cleaners and Equipment Co.**
PO Box 6248
Roanoke, VA 24017-0248
Phone: (540)366-8311   **Fax:** (540)563-9058
Products: Industrial steam cleaning equipment. **SIC:** 5087 (Service Establishment Equipment). **Officers:** R. Migliarese, President.

■ **4725** ■ **Wabash Independent Oil Co.**
707 E Fayette Ave.
Effingham, IL 62401
Phone: (217)342-9755
Products: Laundry and dry cleaning supplies. **SIC:** 5087 (Service Establishment Equipment). **Est:** 1947. **Sales:** $10,000,000 (2000). **Emp:** 45. **Officers:** John H. Bredenkamp Jr., President & Chairman of the Board; Charles W. Gebben, Treasurer; Darrill V. May, VP of Marketing.

■ **4726** ■ **Wards Cleaning & Supply**
PO Box 176
Burley, ID 83318-0176
Phone: (208)678-5105
Products: Service industry machinery; Specialty cleaning and sanitation products; Janitorial supplies; Carpets; Windows. **SICs:** 5087 (Service Establishment

Equipment); 5169 (Chemicals & Allied Products Nec). **Est:** 1983. **Emp:** 5. **Officers:** Ken Ward, Owner.

■ 4727 ■ **Warrenterprises Inc.**
1102 Ave. B NW
Great Falls, MT 59404
Phone: (406)761-5428
Products: Service establishment equipment; Cleaning and maintenance equipment and supplies. **SICs:** 5087 (Service Establishment Equipment); 5169 (Chemicals & Allied Products Nec). **Officers:** Warren O Keefe, President.

■ 4728 ■ **Waxie Sanitary Supply**
9353 Waxie Way
San Diego, CA 92123
Phone: (619)292-8111
Free: (800)544-8054 **Fax:** (619)541-7071
Products: Sanitary supplies. **SIC:** 5169 (Chemicals & Allied Products Nec). **Sales:** $253,000,000 (2000). **Emp:** 500. **Officers:** Charles Wax, President.

■ 4729 ■ **E. Weinberg Supply Company Inc.**
7434 W 27th St.
Minneapolis, MN 55426-3104
Phone: (612)920-0888
Free: (800)279-0888 **Fax:** (612)920-2911
Products: Chemicals, soaps, laundry detergents, and related products. **SICs:** 5169 (Chemicals & Allied Products Nec); 5122 (Drugs, Proprietaries & Sundries).

Sales: $13,000,000 (2000). **Emp:** 33. **Officers:** Henry E. Weinberg, President; Richard Duis, Controller.

■ 4730 ■ **Western Facilities Supply, Inc.**
PO Box 928
Everett, WA 98206-0928
Phone: (425)252-2105
Free: (800)448-9314 **Fax:** (425)259-5130
E-mail: sales@westfacsup.com
URL: http://www.westfacsup.com
Products: Janitorial supplies; Industrial paper products. **SICs:** 5087 (Service Establishment Equipment); 5113 (Industrial & Personal Service Paper). **Est:** 1950. **Emp:** 30. **Officers:** Peter A. Knehr, President.

■ 4731 ■ **Whalen Co.**
PO Box 1390
Easton, MD 21601
Phone: (410)822-9200
Products: HVAC equipment. **SIC:** 5075 (Warm Air Heating & Air-Conditioning).

■ 4732 ■ **A. Willets O'Neil Co.**
7200 Biscayne Blvd.
Miami, FL 33179
Phone: (305)759-2424 **Fax:** (305)754-6599
Products: Janitorial supplies; Industrial vacuum cleaners, floor cleaners, and carpet cleaners; Window cleaning supplies. **SICs:** 5087 (Service Establishment

Equipment); 5169 (Chemicals & Allied Products Nec). **Officers:** Steven B. Schemer, President.

■ 4733 ■ **Wink Davis Equipment Company Inc.**
800 Miami Cir., Ste. 220
Atlanta, GA 30324
Phone: (404)266-2290
Products: Laundry equipment and parts. **SIC:** 5087 (Service Establishment Equipment). **Sales:** $52,000,000 (2000). **Emp:** 98. **Officers:** Alex Davis, President.

■ 4734 ■ **With Enterprises Inc.**
4725 Lumber St. NE, Ste. 1
Albuquerque, NM 87109-2113
Phone: (505)889-3879 **Fax:** (505)889-9707
Products: Service establishment equipment, including cleaning and maintenance equipment and supplies. **SICs:** 5087 (Service Establishment Equipment); 5169 (Chemicals & Allied Products Nec). **Officers:** Doug With, President.

■ 4735 ■ **Yankton Janitorial Supply**
1116 W 9th St.
Yankton, SD 57078-3311
Phone: (605)665-6855
Products: Janitors' supplies, including specialty cleaning and sanitation products. **SICs:** 5087 (Service Establishment Equipment); 5169 (Chemicals & Allied Products Nec). **Est:** 1979. **Emp:** 3. **Officers:** Dixie Church, President.

(9) Clothing

Entries in this section are arranged alphabetically by company name. When the company name is a personal name, the company name is alphabetized by the surname unless the first name or initial(s) are part of a trade name. See the User's Guide at the front of this directory for additional information.

■ **4736** ■ **2BU-Wear**
188 Clayton St.
San Francisco, CA 94117
Phone: (415)752-9820
Products: Men's clothing, including leather shirts, denim shirts, T-shirts, and sweatshirts. **SIC:** 5136 (Men's/Boys' Clothing). **Officers:** Harald P. Stangl, Owner.

■ **4737** ■ **A and M Sales and Manufacturing Inc.**
3605 Hwy. 45 N
Henderson, TN 38340
Phone: (901)989-9925 **Fax:** (901)989-5221
Products: Clothing. **SIC:** 5136 (Men's/Boys' Clothing). **Sales:** $2,000,000 (2000). **Emp:** 15.

■ **4738** ■ **Aardvark Swim & Sports Inc.**
4212-F Technology Ct.
Chantilly, VA 20151-1214
Phone: (703)631-6045
Free: (800)729-1577 **Fax:** (703)968-3293
E-mail: aardart@ix.netcom.com
URL: http://www.aardvarkswim.com
Products: Swimwear. **SIC:** 5136 (Men's/Boys' Clothing). **Est:** 1985. **Sales:** $4,000,000 (2000). **Emp:** 40. **Officers:** Robert York, President.

■ **4739** ■ **AB Collections**
1466 Broadway, Ste. 1603
New York, NY 10036
Phone: (212)944-5950
Products: Children's clothing. **SIC:** 5137 (Women's/Children's Clothing).

■ **4740** ■ **A.B.A.C.O. Group**
Skypark Business Park
PO Box 4082
Irvine, CA 92616-4082
Phone: (949)552-8494 **Fax:** (949)423-5112
Products: Shoes; sporting and athletic goods, clothing, apparel, sportswear, camping supplies; Men's and women's casual apparel. **SICs:** 5139 (Footwear); 5091 (Sporting & Recreational Goods). **Est:** 1946. **Emp:** 79. **Officers:** B.E. Fisher, Merchandising Coordinator; R.T. Marlow, Head Buyer. **Former Name:** Abaco Group. **Former Name:** Abaco Buying Group.

■ **4741** ■ **Abbott Import-Export Co.**
2924 Sunset Ave.
Bakersfield, CA 93304
Phone: (805)324-2833 **Fax:** (805)324-4504
Products: Women's and children's clothing; Men's and boy's clothing. **SICs:** 5136 (Men's/Boys' Clothing); 5137 (Women's/Children's Clothing). **Officers:** Margaret Mitchell, Owner.

■ **4742** ■ **Joseph Abboud Apparel Corp.**
650 5th Ave., 27th Fl.
New York, NY 10019
Phone: (212)586-9140
Free: (800)999-0600
Products: Men's clothing. **SIC:** 5136 (Men's/Boys' Clothing). **Sales:** $28,000,000 (2000). **Emp:** 55. **Officers:** Bob Wisher, President; Marty Weinberg, VP of Finance.

■ **4743** ■ **ABC School Uniforms Inc.**
1085 E 31st St.
Hialeah, FL 33013-3589
Phone: (305)836-5000 **Fax:** (305)836-6147
E-mail: abc.uniform@juno.com
Products: Apparel, including uniforms and accessories. **SICs:** 5137 (Women's/Children's Clothing); 5136 (Men's/Boys' Clothing). **Est:** 1951. **Emp:** 49. **Officers:** David Baitinger; Kimberly Baitinger.

■ **4744** ■ **Abnormal Trees**
4 Copper Dr.
Wilmington, DE 19804-2413
Products: Men's and boys' clothing. **SIC:** 5136 (Men's/Boys' Clothing). **Officers:** Cory Comer, Owner. **Former Name:** Abnormalities.

■ **4745** ■ **Accessory Resource Gallery Inc.**
5 W 36th St., Ste. 500
New York, NY 10018
Phone: (212)971-7300 **Fax:** (212)714-2881
URL: http://www.accessorybrainstorms.com
Products: Women's accessories, including costume jewelry; Fashion, beauty, and lifestyle inventions; Hats, scarves, and hair accessories. **SICs:** 5137 (Women's/Children's Clothing); 5094 (Jewelry & Precious Stones). **Est:** 1983. **Sales:** $3,000,000 (2000). **Emp:** 5. **Officers:** Joan Lefkowitz, President. **Alternate Name:** Accessory Brainstorms.

■ **4746** ■ **Action Line/UniVogue, Inc.**
12091 Forestgate Dr.
Dallas, TX 75243
Phone: (214)341-7300
Free: (800)527-3374 **Fax:** (214)341-7306
E-mail: customerservice@univogue.com
URL: http://www.univogue.com
Products: Culinary, hospitality, health care and custom uniforms. **SIC:** 5136 (Men's/Boys' Clothing). **Est:** 1972. **Emp:** 46. **Officers:** Curtis Hougland, e-mail: chougland@univogue.com. **Former Name:** Action Line.

■ **4747** ■ **Action Sales Promotions**
PO Box 03-4044
Indialantic, FL 32903-0944
Phone: (407)639-0290
Products: Men's and women's apparel; General merchandise. **SICs:** 5137 (Women's/Children's Clothing); 5136 (Men's/Boys' Clothing). **Est:** 1982. **Sales:** $1,300,000 (2000). **Emp:** 3. **Officers:** Jeffrey Ashley.

■ **4748** ■ **Action Sport & Apparel**
532 W Dixie Ave.
Elizabethtown, KY 42701-2437
Phone: (502)769-3188 **Fax:** (502)737-0449
Products: Screen printing and embroidery for sports, industry, and specialty markets. **SICs:** 5136 (Men's/Boys' Clothing); 5137 (Women's/Children's Clothing). **Officers:** Tommy Bradbury, Partner.

■ **4749** ■ **Ad-Shir-Tizing Inc.**
PO Box 1122
Airway Heights, WA 99001-1122
Phone: (509)244-3363 **Fax:** (509)244-1964
Products: Men's and boys' clothing; Men's and boys' sportswear; Men's and boys' work clothing. **SIC:** 5136 (Men's/Boys' Clothing). **Officers:** Roy Best, President.

■ **4750** ■ **Adele Fashion Knit Corp.**
1370 Broadway
New York, NY 10018-7302
Phone: (212)695-3244 **Fax:** (212)695-1920
Products: Sweaters. **SICs:** 5136 (Men's/Boys' Clothing); 5137 (Women's/Children's Clothing). **Est:** 1950. **Emp:** 49. **Former Name:** Adele Accessories Corp.

■ **4751** ■ **Adidas America Inc./Intl Div**
541 NE 20th Ave Ste. 207
Portland, OR 97232
Phone: (503)230-2920 **Fax:** (503)797-4434
Products: Designs and footwear and apparel. **SIC:** 5139 (Footwear).

■ **4752** ■ **Marcus Adler Glove Co.**
32 W 39th
New York, NY 10018-3810
Phone: (212)840-8652 **Fax:** (212)768-8079
Products: Ladies' gloves and knit accessories. **SICs:** 5137 (Women's/Children's Clothing); 5136 (Men's/Boys' Clothing). **Est:** 1941.

■ **4753** ■ **Advanced Graphics**
421 Schatzel St.
Corpus Christi, TX 78401
Phone: (512)879-0019
Products: Shirts. **SIC:** 5131 (Piece Goods & Notions).

■ **4754** ■ **Patsy Aiken Designs Inc.**
PO Box 97457
Raleigh, NC 27624-7457
Phone: (919)872-8789 **Fax:** (919)872-9731
Products: Infants' and toddlers' play garments. **SIC:** 5137 (Women's/Children's Clothing). **Est:** 1979. **Sales:** $4,500,000 (2000). **Emp:** 125. **Officers:** Patsy Aiken; Joel Aiken.

■ **4755** ■ **Alba-Waldensian Inc.**
PO Box 100
Valdese, NC 28690
Phone: (828)874-2191 **Fax:** (828)879-6595
Products: Men's hosiery and sweaters. **SIC:** 5136 (Men's/Boys' Clothing). **Sales:** $75,200,000 (2000). **Emp:** 752. **Officers:** Lee N. Mortenson, CEO & President; Glenn J. Kennedy, CFO & Treasurer.

■ **4756** ■ **Albain Shirt Co.**
PO Box 429
Kinston, NC 28501
Phone: (919)523-2151 **Fax:** (919)523-7922
Products: Blouses; Dresses; Skirts and jackets; Men's shirts. **SICs:** 5137 (Women's/Children's Clothing); 5136 (Men's/Boys' Clothing). **Sales:** $12,000 (2000). **Emp:** 459. **Officers:** Fred A. Rouse.

■ 4757 ■ **All Dressed Up**
150 S Water
Batavia, IL 60510
Phone: (630)879-5130 **Fax:** (630)879-3374
E-mail: alldressedup@aol.com
URL: http://www.alldressedupcostumes.com
Products: Costumes for theatrical productions, corporate events, parties and theme weddings. **SICs:** 5136 (Men's/Boys' Clothing); 5137 (Women's/Children's Clothing). **Former Name:** Stage Rags.

■ 4758 ■ **All-In-One Monogramming**
909 W Garland Ave.
Spokane, WA 99205-2820
Phone: (509)325-4838 **Fax:** (509)325-1215
Products: Women's, children's, and infant's clothing, including hats and accessories. **SIC:** 5137 (Women's/Children's Clothing). **Officers:** Sandra Prince, Owner.

■ 4759 ■ **All Pro Championships Inc.**
2541 Holloway Rd.
Louisville, KY 40299-6104
Phone: (502)267-7836 **Fax:** (502)266-5867
Products: Men's and boys' sportswear; Men's and boys' work clothing. **SIC:** 5136 (Men's/Boys' Clothing). **Officers:** Nicholas Tabler, Chairman of the Board.

■ 4760 ■ **All That Jazz**
4505 Bandini Blvd.
Los Angeles, CA 90040
Phone: (213)869-1832 **Fax:** (213)780-5808
Products: Women's, misses', and juniors' dresses. **SIC:** 5137 (Women's/Children's Clothing). **Est:** 1975. **Sales:** $180,000,000 (2000). **Emp:** 550. **Officers:** Andrew Cohen, CEO & President; Ann Kennedy, Controller; Jay Balaban, Dir. of Marketing & Sales; Timothy Hart, Dir. of Data Processing; Mary Davies, Dir of Human Resources.

■ 4761 ■ **Allen Trading Company Inc.**
275 Dean Rd.
Brookline, MA 02445-4144
Phone: (617)232-7747 **Fax:** (617)232-0640
Products: Shoes. **SIC:** 5139 (Footwear).

■ 4762 ■ **Allimex International**
412 Washington St.
Lawrenceville, IL 62439-3159
Fax: (618)943-2902
Products: Women's lingerie and nightwear. **SIC:** 5137 (Women's/Children's Clothing). **Officers:** Richard K. Allison, President.

■ 4763 ■ **Alpena Screen Arts**
2577 US Hwy. 23 S
Alpena, MI 49707-4825
Phone: (517)354-5198 **Fax:** (517)354-5198
Products: Garment printing; Novelty and advertising specialties. **SICs:** 5136 (Men's/Boys' Clothing); 5199 (Nondurable Goods Nec); 5137 (Women's/Children's Clothing). **Est:** 1953. **Sales:** $228,000 (2000). **Emp:** 4. **Officers:** John A. Zbytowski, Owner.

■ 4764 ■ **Alpena Screen Arts**
2577 US Hwy. 23 S
Alpena, MI 49707-4825
Phone: (517)354-5198 **Fax:** (517)354-5198
Products: Clothing. **SIC:** 5136 (Men's/Boys' Clothing). **Sales:** $200,000 (2000). **Emp:** 4.

■ 4765 ■ **AmAsia International Ltd.**
34 3rd Ave.
Burlington, MA 01803
Phone: (781)229-6611 **Fax:** (781)229-9431
Products: Women's shoes. **SIC:** 5139 (Footwear). **Sales:** $100,000,000 (2000). **Emp:** 175. **Officers:** Norman Finn, CEO; Leslie Finn, CFO.

■ 4766 ■ **Amerex (USA) Inc.**
350 5th Ave., No. 7418
New York, NY 10118
Phone: (212)967-3330
Products: Outerwear, including jackets, hats, and gloves. **SICs:** 5137 (Women's/Children's Clothing); 5136 (Men's/Boys' Clothing). **Est:** 1946. **Sales:** $110,000,000 (2000). **Emp:** 200. **Officers:** Frederick R. Shretz, CEO; Stuart M. Cohen, Exec. VP; Ira

Gainger, Dir. of Marketing & Sales; Bruce Stein, Dir. of Data Processing; Lou Moreluzzi, Dir of Human Resources.

■ 4767 ■ **American Argo Corp. Sales and Distribution**
1385 Broadway, 24th Fl.
New York, NY 10018
Phone: (212)764-0700 **Fax:** (212)764-0709
Products: Men's and boys' sportswear. **SIC:** 5136 (Men's/Boys' Clothing). **Est:** 1962. **Sales:** $20,000,000 (2000). **Emp:** 60. **Officers:** Richard Lewis, General Mgr.

■ 4768 ■ **American Athletic Sales Inc.**
916 S Main St.
Salt Lake City, UT 84101-2923
Phone: (801)531-8032
Products: Men's and boys' clothing; Men's and boys' sportswear; Men's and boys' work clothing. **SIC:** 5136 (Men's/Boys' Clothing). **Officers:** R. Horsley, President.

■ 4769 ■ **American International Trading Co.**
604 W Bay St.
Costa Mesa, CA 92627
Phone: (949)645-2202 **Fax:** (949)645-1080
Products: Western clothing, cowboy boots, and accessories; English riding equipment, clothing, and accessories; Western furniture; Log homes. **SICs:** 5136 (Men's/Boys' Clothing); 5021 (Furniture); 5082 (Construction & Mining Machinery); 5137 (Women's/Children's Clothing). **Est:** 1969. **Sales:** $800,000 (2000). **Emp:** 25. **Officers:** William Viscome.

■ 4770 ■ **American Military Supply Inc.**
PO Box 2265
Macon, GA 31203-2265
Phone: (912)477-8206 **Fax:** (912)477-7905
Products: Men's and boys' clothing. **SIC:** 5136 (Men's/Boys' Clothing). **Officers:** David Hogg, President.

■ 4771 ■ **Amity Hosiery Company Inc.**
107 5th Ave.
Garden City Park, NY 11040
Phone: (516)741-2606
Free: (800)645-6024 **Fax:** (516)742-1978
E-mail: Amity107@aol.com
Products: Foot socks; Underwear; Hosiery. **SICs:** 5137 (Women's/Children's Clothing); 5136 (Men's/Boys' Clothing). **Est:** 1977. **Emp:** 20. **Officers:** Gershon Alter; Faizal Alter; Vincent Mingione.

■ 4772 ■ **Andrew Sports Club Inc.**
1407 Broadway, No. 1209
New York, NY 10018
Phone: (212)764-6225 **Fax:** (212)840-3078
Products: Casual shirts. **SIC:** 5137 (Women's/Children's Clothing). **Est:** 1983. **Sales:** $85,000,000 (2000). **Emp:** 75. **Officers:** Andrew Kirpalani, President; Anil Anand, CFO.

■ 4773 ■ **Anna Marie Designs Inc.**
811 3rd Ave. W
PO Box 777
Ashland, WI 54806-0777
Phone: (715)682-9569 **Fax:** (715)682-5986
Products: Clothing. **SICs:** 5137 (Women's/Children's Clothing); 5136 (Men's/Boys' Clothing). **Emp:** 99.

■ 4774 ■ **Annawear**
PO Box 2364
Highlands, NC 28741-2364
Phone: (704)526-4660 **Fax:** (704)526-2433
Products: Women's and children's clothing. **SIC:** 5137 (Women's/Children's Clothing). **Officers:** Anna Herz, Owner.

■ 4775 ■ **Anns Uniform Center Inc.**
2800 Lafayette Rd.
Portsmouth, NH 03801-5915
Phone: (603)431-6367 **Fax:** (603)431-7137
Products: Women's and children's clothing, including uniforms and footwear. **SICs:** 5137 (Women's/Children's Clothing); 5139 (Footwear). **Officers:** Paul Elliott, President.

■ 4776 ■ **Antler Uniform, Division of M. Rubin & Sons, Inc.**
34-01 38th Ave.
Long Island City, NY 11101
Phone: (718)361-2800
Free: (888)336-4687 **Fax:** (718)361-2680
E-mail: dblx10@aol.com
Products: Outerwear; Mens and womens shirts. **SICs:** 5136 (Men's/Boys' Clothing); 5137 (Women's/Children's Clothing). **Est:** 1944. **Sales:** $10,000,000 (2000). **Emp:** 50.

■ 4777 ■ **Apparel Exprex Inc.**
1184 Bonham Ave.
Columbus, OH 43211
Phone: (614)291-5651 **Fax:** (614)291-4650
Products: Sportswear, including t-shirts and baseball caps. **SICs:** 5136 (Men's/Boys' Clothing); 5137 (Women's/Children's Clothing).

■ 4778 ■ **Apple Graphics Ltd.**
1536 W Todd Dr., Ste. 105
Tempe, AZ 85283-4804
Phone: (602)731-9970
Free: (800)878-1557 **Fax:** (602)731-9520
Products: Custom screen printing; Sportswear. **SICs:** 5136 (Men's/Boys' Clothing); 5137 (Women's/Children's Clothing). **Est:** 1981. **Emp:** 12. **Officers:** Bruce Brierley, President.

■ 4779 ■ **Aquilla Fashions Inc.**
863 E Patterson St.
Lansford, PA 18232-1708
Phone: (717)645-7738 **Fax:** (717)645-7749
Products: Women's sportswear. **SIC:** 5137 (Women's/Children's Clothing). **Est:** 1981. **Sales:** $1,000,000 (2000). **Emp:** 99.

■ 4780 ■ **Archie's Sporting Goods of Gainesville**
1500 Brownsbridge Rd.
Gainesville, GA 30501
Phone: (404)532-9951
Free: (800)922-1468 **Fax:** (404)503-9293
Products: Women's and children's clothing, including sportswear and swimsuits. **SIC:** 5137 (Women's/Children's Clothing). **Officers:** Anthony Barrett, President.

■ 4781 ■ **Argus Buying Group**
California Ctr.
1st St.
PO Box 3271
Tustin, CA 92781-3271
Phone: (714)552-8494 **Fax:** (714)423-5112
Products: Sportswear, including jackets, t-shirts, sweats, and knitwear; Men's clothing; Sporting goods, including bags and accessories; Sports shoes. **SICs:** 5137 (Women's/Children's Clothing); 5136 (Men's/Boys' Clothing); 5091 (Sporting & Recreational Goods). **Est:** 1977. **Emp:** 19. **Officers:** R.T. Vasarlo, Dir. of Purchasing; N.B. Browning, Merchandising Mgr.

■ 4782 ■ **Arizona Mail Order Co.**
PO Box 27800
Tucson, AZ 85726
Phone: (520)745-4500 **Fax:** (520)750-6755
Products: Women's shoes and apparel; Homefurnishings; Jewelry. **SICs:** 5137 (Women's/Children's Clothing); 5023 (Homefurnishings); 5094 (Jewelry & Precious Stones).

■ 4783 ■ **Arizona Sport Shirts Inc.**
100 Gasoline Alley
Indianapolis, IN 46222-3965
Phone: (317)244-3905
Free: (800)922-9918 **Fax:** (317)247-4392
E-mail: azcompanies@arsworldnet.att.net
URL: http://www.azcompanies.com
Products: Sportswear, including racing apparel. **SICs:** 5136 (Men's/Boys' Clothing); 5137 (Women's/Children's Clothing). **Est:** 1974. **Sales:** $2,000,000(2000). **Emp:** 25. **Officers:** Karl Korbacher, President; Cherie Korbacher, VP & Secty.; Gerald Newton, VP of Operations; Geraw Newton, Customer Service Contact; Gerald Newton, Human Resources Contact.

■ **4784** ■ **Giorgio Armani Fashion Corp.**
11 W 42nd St., 19th Fl.
New York, NY 10036-8002
Phone: (212)265-2760
Products: Suits. **SICs:** 5136 (Men's/Boys' Clothing);
5137 (Women's/Children's Clothing).

■ **4785** ■ **Army & Navy Supplies**
2835 E 26th St.
Los Angeles, CA 90023
Phone: (213)263-8564   **Fax:** (213)263-9214
Products: Army and navy surplus. **SICs:** 5136
(Men's/Boys' Clothing); 5099 (Durable Goods Nec);
5199 (Nondurable Goods Nec).

■ **4786** ■ **ASAP**
PO Box 271393
Corpus Christi, TX 78427
Phone: (512)985-2727
Products: Hats. **SIC:** 5131 (Piece Goods & Notions).

■ **4787** ■ **Ashleys on Main**
PO Box 312
Brownsdale, MN 55918-0312
Phone: (507)433-8841
Products: Women's clothing. **SIC:** 5137
(Women's/Children's Clothing). **Officers:** Sue
Bartesch, President.

■ **4788** ■ **Athlon II Enterprises Inc.**
1684 SW 86th St.
Oklahoma City, OK 73159-6229
Phone: (405)685-3737   **Fax:** (405)685-5094
Products: Women's and children's clothing and
sportswear. **SIC:** 5137 (Women's/Children's Clothing).
Officers: Phil Boykin, President.

■ **4789** ■ **Atlanta Tees Inc.**
PO Box 264
Griffin, GA 30224-0264
Phone: (404)228-0940   **Fax:** (404)228-0995
Products: T-shirts. **SICs:** 5136 (Men's/Boys' Clothing);
5137 (Women's/Children's Clothing). **Officers:** Scott
Wheaton, President.

■ **4790** ■ **Australian Outback Collection**
PO Box 987
Evergreen, CO 80439-0987
Phone: (303)670-3933
Free: (800)688-2225   **Fax:** (303)670-3839
Products: Women's and men's clothing, including
outerwear and coats. **SICs:** 5137 (Women's/Children's
Clothing); 5136 (Men's/Boys' Clothing). **Officers:**
Christophe Blundell, President.

■ **4791** ■ **Authentic Sports Inc.**
372 5th Ave., Apt. 10H
New York, NY 10018-8110
Phone: (212)736-2121   **Fax:** (212)629-5107
Products: Men's outerwear. **SICs:** 5136 (Men's/Boys'
Clothing); 5137 (Women's/Children's Clothing). **Est:**
1959. **Sales:** $5,000,000 (2000). **Emp:** 24. **Officers:**
Jacques Haim, Exec. VP; George Grodzicki,
Sales/Marketing Contact. **Former Name:** Authentic
Imports Inc.

■ **4792** ■ **AVH Inc.**
PO Box 1887
Sioux City, IA 51102-1887
Phone: (712)277-4223   **Fax:** (712)277-2440
Products: Men's formalwear; Bridal supplies. **SICs:**
5136 (Men's/Boys' Clothing); 5137
(Women's/Children's Clothing). **Officers:** Adrian
Hanson, President.

■ **4793** ■ **Axon Import Export Corporation**
36 Compton Court
Basking Ridge, NJ 07920
Phone: (908)647-2346   **Fax:** (908)647-1936
Products: Computers, peripherals, and software;
Chemicals and allied products; Men's apparel;
Women's and children's apparel. **SICs:** 5136
(Men's/Boys' Clothing); 5169 (Chemicals & Allied
Products Nec); 5045 (Computers, Peripherals &
Software); 5137 (Women's/Children's Clothing).
Officers: Mihir Karia, President.

■ **4794** ■ **B & L Leather Co.**
8125 Winchester Rd.
New Market, AL 35761-7856
Phone: (205)379-3550
Products: Apparel belts. **SICs:** 5136 (Men's/Boys'
Clothing); 5137 (Women's/Children's Clothing).
Officers: Bill Ricketts, Owner.

■ **4795** ■ **B & W Hosiery, Inc.**
332 1st Ave. SW
Hickory, NC 28602-2939
Phone: (704)327-7005   **Fax:** (704)322-8140
Products: Ladies' knee highs. **SIC:** 5137
(Women's/Children's Clothing). **Emp:** 49. **Officers:**
Dan W. Reid.

■ **4796** ■ **Baby Bliss Inc.**
227 Spring St.
PO Box 9
Middleville, MI 49333
Phone: (616)795-3341
Free: (800)405-2229   **Fax:** (616)795-3343
E-mail: babyblissco@aol.com
URL: http://www.babybliss.com
Products: Newborn, infant, and toddler apparel. **SIC:**
5137 (Women's/Children's Clothing). **Est:** 1937. **Sales:**
$400,000 (1999). **Emp:** 8. **Officers:** C.L. Edkins,
President; C. Edkins, Sales/Marketing Contact.
Alternate Name: Middleville Apparel Co.

■ **4797** ■ **Baby Needs Inc.**
605 Cameron St.
Burlington, NC 27215-5915
Phone: (919)227-6202   **Fax:** (919)227-7593
Products: Knitted items; Rattles; Pacifiers; Booties;
Sheets. **SICs:** 5137 (Women's/Children's Clothing);
5023 (Homefurnishings). **Emp:** 49.

■ **4798** ■ **Bacon & Co. Inc.**
PO Box 78
Knoxville, TN 37901-0078
Phone: (865)523-9181   **Fax:** (865)546-2212
Products: Linens; Men's and women's clothing. **SICs:**
5137 (Women's/Children's Clothing); 5136
(Men's/Boys' Clothing); 5023 (Homefurnishings).
Officers: Jack Dance, President.

■ **4799** ■ **Ballantyne Cashmere USA Inc.**
499 7th Ave., 17th Fl.
New York, NY 10018
Phone: (212)736-4228
Products: Men's and women's cashmere sweaters.
SICs: 5131 (Piece Goods & Notions); 5136
(Men's/Boys' Clothing); 5137 (Women's/Children's
Clothing). **Sales:** $17,000,000 (1992). **Emp:** 9.
Officers: Jan Mehalick, Vice President.

■ **4800** ■ **David Banash and Son Inc.**
16 Rainbow Pond Dr.
Walpole, MA 02081-3454
Phone: (617)482-5478   **Fax:** (617)482-1684
Products: Women's fashion accessories. **SIC:** 5137
(Women's/Children's Clothing). **Officers:** Angel Algeri,
President.

■ **4801** ■ **Banian Trading Co.**
2252 Main St., Ste. 9 W
Chula Vista, CA 91911
Phone: (619)423-9975   **Fax:** (619)423-9980
E-mail: baniantrading@earthlink.ent
URL: http://www.baniantrading.com
Products: Women's clothing; Childrens' wear; Men's
wear; School uniforms; accessories; Toys; Giftware.
SICs: 5137 (Women's/Children's Clothing); 5092 (Toys
& Hobby Goods & Supplies); 5199 (Nondurable Goods
Nec). **Est:** 1987. **Officers:** Al Banian.

■ **4802** ■ **Jan Barboglio**
509 N Montclair Ave.
Dallas, TX 75208-5450
Phone: (214)688-0020   **Fax:** (214)688-0019
Products: Ladies' apparel. **SIC:** 5137
(Women's/Children's Clothing). **Emp:** 49. **Officers:** Jan
Barboglio.

■ **4803** ■ **Barborie Fashions**
490 W 18th St.
Hialeah, FL 33010-2622
Phone: (305)883-5089
Products: T-shirts. **SICs:** 5136 (Men's/Boys' Clothing);
5137 (Women's/Children's Clothing). **Est:** 1980. **Emp:**
49. **Officers:** Ishag S. Barouch, Manager.

■ **4804** ■ **Barbour Inc.**
55 Meadowbrook Dr.
Milford, NH 03055-4613
Phone: (603)673-1313   **Fax:** (603)673-6510
Products: Women's and children's clothing, including
unisex outerwear. **SICs:** 5136 (Men's/Boys' Clothing);
5137 (Women's/Children's Clothing). **Officers:** Thomas
Hooven, General Manager.

■ **4805** ■ **Bargain City**
14 Pinewood Dr.
Englishtown, NJ 07726
Phone: (732)536-7626   **Fax:** (732)972-6408
Products: Bandanas. **SICs:** 5136 (Men's/Boys'
Clothing); 5137 (Women's/Children's Clothing).

■ **4806** ■ **Barons Wholesale Clothiers**
27888 Orchard Lake Rd.
Farmington Hills, MI 48334-3756
Phone: (248)539-0525   **Fax:** (248)865-9265
Products: Men's and boy's clothing. **SIC:** 5136
(Men's/Boys' Clothing). **Est:** 1975. **Emp:** 12.

■ **4807** ■ **Baxter Knitting Co.**
1555 33rd St. SW
Hickory, NC 28602-4639
Phone: (704)327-0131
Products: Women's and children's clothing. **SIC:** 5137
(Women's/Children's Clothing). **Officers:** Danny
Huffman, Owner.

■ **4808** ■ **Bay Rag**
6250 NW 35th Ave.
Miami, FL 33147
Phone: (305)691-5502
Free: (800)321-0139   **Fax:** (305)693-8864
Products: Screen print T-shirts and active wear; Men's
and women's new and used clothing. **SICs:** 5137
(Women's/Children's Clothing); 5136 (Men's/Boys'
Clothing).

■ **4809** ■ **BCI Inc.**
1009 E Miracle Mile
Box 3961
McAllen, TX 78502
Phone: (956)630-2761   **Fax:** (956)630-4747
Products: Children's sportswear; Men's sportswear;
Women's sportswear; Outerwear. **SICs:** 5136
(Men's/Boys' Clothing); 5137 (Women's/Children's
Clothing). **Sales:** $1,500,000 (2000). **Emp:** 49.
Officers: Chris Freeland. **Former Name:** Rio Contract
Sewing.

■ **4810** ■ **BCVG Inc.**
2761 Fruitland Ave.
Vernon, CA 90058
Phone: (213)589-2224   **Fax:** (213)277-5459
Products: Women's clothing. **SICs:** 5137
(Women's/Children's Clothing); 5136 (Men's/Boys'
Clothing). **Sales:** $400,000,000 (2000). **Emp:** 1,200.
Officers: Max Azrie, Owner; Michael Cohen,
Controller.

■ **4811** ■ **Beco Helman Inc.**
801 Washington Ave. N
Minneapolis, MN 55401-1132
Phone: (612)338-5634   **Fax:** (612)338-1680
Products: Women's clothing. **SIC:** 5137
(Women's/Children's Clothing). **Est:** 1953. **Sales:**
$3,000,000 (2000). **Emp:** 60. **Officers:** Nip Thomas.

■ **4812** ■ **Bee Hat Co.**
2839 Olive St.
St. Louis, MO 63103-1427
Phone: (314)231-6631
Free: (800)325-7808   **Fax:** (314)231-5103
Products: Hats and caps, including dress felt hats,
straw hats, shop caps, and panama straw hats; Gloves;
Suspenders. **SICs:** 5136 (Men's/Boys' Clothing); 5137
(Women's/Children's Clothing). **Est:** 1926. **Sales:**

$1,000,000 (2000). **Emp:** 4. **Officers:** Mark Phillips, President.

■ **4813** ■ **Beeba's Creations Inc.**
10280 Camino Santa Fe
San Diego, CA 92121-3105
Phone: (619)549-2922 **Fax:** (619)549-6857
Products: Women's, misses', and juniors' dresses; Children's sportswear; Children's nightwear; Women's sportswear; Women's nightwear; Women's apparel belts. **SIC:** 5137 (Women's/Children's Clothing). **Est:** 1973. **Sales:** $158,000,000 (2000). **Emp:** 340.

■ **4814** ■ **P.M. Belt Corp.**
131 32nd St.
PO Box 320650
Brooklyn, NY 11232
Phone: (718)369-9800
Free: (800)762-3580 **Fax:** (718)369-9700
E-mail: pmbelt@aol.com
Products: Men's and boy's leather belts. **SIC:** 5136 (Men's/Boys' Clothing). **Est:** 1946.

■ **4815** ■ **Belts By Nadim, Inc.**
303 E 4th St., No. 2
Los Angeles, CA 90013-1575
Phone: (213)680-3483 **Fax:** (213)625-0991
Products: Belts. **SICs:** 5137 (Women's/Children's Clothing); 5136 (Men's/Boys' Clothing). **Sales:** $1,000,000 (2000). **Emp:** 49. **Officers:** G. Robinson.

■ **4816** ■ **Benben Sportswear**
8119 Rosehill Rd.
Shawnee Mission, KS 66215-2632
Phone: (913)541-0028
Products: Women's and children's clothing, including sportswear and swimsuits. **SIC:** 5137 (Women's/Children's Clothing). **Officers:** Richard Benben, Partner.

■ **4817** ■ **Benedict International Inc.**
8640-C Onyx Dr. SW
Lakewood, WA 98498-4880
Products: Women's and children's clothing, including outerwear and fur clothing. **SIC:** 5137 (Women's/Children's Clothing). **Officers:** Frank Benedict, President.

■ **4818** ■ **Benel Manufacturing Inc.**
Rfd. 1, PO Box 1301
Dunn, NC 28334-9801
Phone: (919)892-4925
Products: Garments, including children's clothing. **SICs:** 5137 (Women's/Children's Clothing); 5136 (Men's/Boys' Clothing). **Sales:** $500,000 (2000). **Emp:** 25. **Officers:** Bernard Bender; Cliff Bender.

■ **4819** ■ **Ben Berger L.L.C.**
15 W 37th St., 15th Fl.
New York, NY 10018
Phone: (212)220-8886
Free: (800)221-2593 **Fax:** (212)220-8887
E-mail: sales@benberger.com
Products: Gloves, hats, scarves, slippers, sockes, tights, Candies legware, Karen Newberger slippers. **SICs:** 5137 (Women's/Children's Clothing); 5136 (Men's/Boys' Clothing). **Est:** 1931. **Sales:** $35,000,000 (2000). **Emp:** 100. **Officers:** Morton Berger, President; Jeff Ring, Sr. VP; Michael Berger, Sr. VP. **Former Name:** Ben #Berger and Son Inc.

■ **4820** ■ **P.A. Bergner and Co.**
331 W Wisconsin Ave.
Milwaukee, WI 53203
Phone: (414)347-4141 **Fax:** (414)347-5337
Products: Clothing. **SICs:** 5137 (Women's/Children's Clothing); 5136 (Men's/Boys' Clothing). **Officers:** Mike McDonald, President of Finance.

■ **4821** ■ **Bernards Formal Wear Inc.**
734 9th St.
Durham, NC 27705-4803
Phone: (919)286-3633 **Fax:** (919)286-3633
Products: Men's and boys' clothing; Men's and boys' furnishings. **SIC:** 5136 (Men's/Boys' Clothing). **Officers:** Jean Lorenzo, President.

■ **4822** ■ **Best Style Formal Wear Inc.**
200 S 19th St.
Lincoln, NE 68510-1003
Phone: (402)474-0062
Products: Children's clothing accessories; Women's clothing; and Men's formal wear. **SICs:** 5137 (Women's/Children's Clothing); 5136 (Men's/Boys' Clothing). **Officers:** Carl Rohman, Chairman of the Board.

■ **4823** ■ **Biflex International Inc.**
183 Madison Ave.
New York, NY 10016
Phone: (212)725-2800 **Fax:** (212)683-8339
Products: Intimate apparel. **SIC:** 5137 (Women's/Children's Clothing). **Est:** 1946. **Sales:** $58,000,000 (1999). **Emp:** 300. **Officers:** Frank Darmante, CEO; Noel Kirchner, Controller; Dale Darmante, President; Michael Darmante, Exec. VP.

■ **4824** ■ **Billie's Fashion Hats**
2521 Wainwright St.
Corpus Christi, TX 78405
Phone: (512)887-6261
Products: Hats. **SIC:** 5131 (Piece Goods & Notions).

■ **4825** ■ **Black & Black Inc.**
3081 La Pietra Circle
Honolulu, HI 96815
Phone: (808)926-2626 **Fax:** 800-926-2636
Products: Clothing. **SICs:** 5137 (Women's/Children's Clothing); 5136 (Men's/Boys' Clothing). **Officers:** Cobey Black, President.

■ **4826** ■ **Blackbird Ltd.**
1143 E Broadmor
Tempe, AZ 85282
Phone: (602)966-7384 **Fax:** (602)894-6483
Products: Aircraft graphics on t-shirts. **SICs:** 5136 (Men's/Boys' Clothing); 5137 (Women's/Children's Clothing). **Est:** 1982. **Emp:** 30. **Officers:** John Breakey, President.

■ **4827** ■ **Bloom Brothers Co.**
15350 25th Ave. N, No. 114
Plymouth, MN 55447-2081
Phone: (612)832-3250 **Fax:** (612)832-3225
Products: Leather toys and dresses. **SIC:** 5137 (Women's/Children's Clothing); 5092 (Toys & Hobby Goods & Supplies). **Est:** 1906. **Sales:** $8,000,000 (2000). **Emp:** 25. **Officers:** William Dornbusch.

■ **4828** ■ **Bloomingdale's Inc.**
1000 3rd Ave.
New York, NY 10022
Phone: (212)705-2000
Products: Clothing. **SICs:** 5137 (Women's/Children's Clothing); 5136 (Men's/Boys' Clothing).

■ **4829** ■ **Blue Ridge Graphics Inc.**
550 Meade Ave.
Charlottesville, VA 22902-5461
Phone: (804)296-9746 **Fax:** (804)979-0523
Products: Men's and boys' clothing; Men's and boys' sportswear; Men's and boys' work clothing. **SIC:** 5136 (Men's/Boys' Clothing). **Officers:** John Kulick, President.

■ **4830** ■ **Bobtron International Inc.**
1101 Monterey Pass Rd.
Monterey Park, CA 91754
Phone: (213)748-9466 **Fax:** (213)748-9650
Products: Watches and parts; Men's and boys' clothing; Women's clothing. **SICs:** 5136 (Men's/Boys' Clothing); 5094 (Jewelry & Precious Stones); 5137 (Women's/Children's Clothing). **Sales:** $20,000,000 (2000). **Emp:** 34. **Officers:** Thomas Tsang, President.

■ **4831** ■ **Body Drama Inc.**
5840 Uplander Way, No. 202
Culver City, CA 90230-6620
Phone: (310)410-5090 **Fax:** (310)410-5099
E-mail: la_body@psinet.com
URL: http://www.nitches.com
Products: Women's sleepwear and lingerie. **SIC:** 5137 (Women's/Children's Clothing). **Est:** 1975. **Sales:** $21,331,334 (2000). **Emp:** 17. **Officers:** Steven P. Wyandt, Chairman of the Board; Sally Satterberg, Division Head.

■ **4832** ■ **Bogner of America Inc.**
PO Box 644
Newport, VT 05855
Phone: (802)334-6507 **Fax:** (802)334-6870
Products: Ski wear; Golf wear. **SICs:** 5137 (Women's/Children's Clothing); 5136 (Men's/Boys' Clothing). **Est:** 1972. **Sales:** $20,000,000 (2000). **Emp:** 200. **Officers:** Willy Bogner, President; Donald R. Schwamb, Exec. VP; Reginald Rhodes, Vice President; Tino Brandstetter, Vice President.

■ **4833** ■ **Bombay Industries Inc.**
989 6th Ave., 15th Fl.
New York, NY 10018
Phone: (212)564-3099
Products: Men's sportswear. **SIC:** 5136 (Men's/Boys' Clothing).

■ **4834** ■ **Borneo Group Inc.**
2317 E 34th St.
Minneapolis, MN 55406-2414
Phone: (612)331-6136
Free: (800)752-1190 **Fax:** (612)331-6255
Products: Men's and boys' sportswear; Women's sportswear. **SICs:** 5137 (Women's/Children's Clothing); 5136 (Men's/Boys' Clothing). **Est:** 1988. **Officers:** Susan Jacobsen, President.

■ **4835** ■ **Cy Boroff and Associates**
804 Apparel Ctr.
Chicago, IL 60654
Phone: (312)644-7020
Products: Men's clothing. **SIC:** 5136 (Men's/Boys' Clothing). **Sales:** $10,000,000 (2000). **Emp:** 4. **Officers:** Cy Boroff, President.

■ **4836** ■ **George Bosler Leather Co. Inc.**
3106 Sunny Ln.
Louisville, KY 40205-2825
Phone: (502)454-0416
Free: (800)624-9409 **Fax:** (502)454-0417
Products: Footwear and accessories. **SIC:** 5139 (Footwear). **Est:** 1899. **Officers:** R. Craven, President; R.J. Constantine Jr., VP & Treasurer.

■ **4837** ■ **Boss Manufacturing Co.**
221 W 1st St.
Kewanee, IL 61443
Phone: (309)852-2131
Free: (800)447-4581 **Fax:** (309)852-0848
E-mail: bossadmin@inw.net
Products: Gloves, protective clothing, and boots. **SIC:** 5136 (Men's/Boys' Clothing). **Est:** 1893. **Sales:** $40,000,000 (2000). **Emp:** 400. **Officers:** B. Lancaster, President; B. Wise, VP of Sales; J. DeClercq, Customer Service Contact; B. Williams, Human Resources.

■ **4838** ■ **Boston Trading Ltd. Inc.**
315 Washington St.
Lynn, MA 01902-4727
Phone: (781)592-4603
Free: (800)642-4463 **Fax:** (781)595-9937
Products: Women's and men's clothing. **SICs:** 5137 (Women's/Children's Clothing); 5136 (Men's/Boys' Clothing). **Officers:** Arnold Kline, President.

■ **4839** ■ **Boyt Harness Co./Bob Allen Sportswear**
220 S Main St.
Osceola, IA 50213
Phone: (515)342-6773
Free: (800)550-2698 **Fax:** (515)342-2703
Products: Shooting and hunting wear and accessories; canvas guncases. **SICs:** 5136 (Men's/Boys' Clothing); 5137 (Women's/Children's Clothing); 5091 (Sporting & Recreational Goods). **Est:** 1901. **Emp:** 150. **Officers:** Tony Caligiuri; Curt Borcherding; Rochelle Jones, Sales/Marketing Contact, e-mail: rjones@boytharness.com; Noreen Smith, Customer Service Contact, e-mail: pbradford@ boytharness.com. **Former Name:** Bob Allen Sportswear.

■ 4840 ■ **Brach Knitting Mills Inc.**
12 Roosevelt Ave.
Florida, NY 10921-1808
Phones: (914)651-4615   (914)651-4450
Fax: (914)651-1068
Products: Women's and misses' hosiery. **SIC:** 5137
(Women's/Children's Clothing). **Emp:** 25.

■ 4841 ■ **Branco Enterprises Inc.**
PO Box 280
Asheboro, NC 27204-0280
Phone: (910)629-1090   **Fax:** (910)629-0396
Products: Men's and boys' clothing; Women's
clothing. **SICs:** 5136 (Men's/Boys' Clothing); 5137
(Women's/Children's Clothing). **Officers:** Chester
Branson, President.

■ 4842 ■ **Brazabra Corp.**
8 Run Way
PO Box 698
Lee, MA 01238
Phone: (413)243-4690
Free: (800)251-3031   **Fax:** (413)243-4586
Products: Women's lingerie and undergarments. **SIC:**
5137 (Women's/Children's Clothing). **Officers:** Ted
Davis, President.

■ 4843 ■ **Ronna Bridges Accessories**
1852-F Wallace School Rd.
Charleston, SC 29407-4822
Phone: (803)763-7070
Free: (800)723-1182   **Fax:** (803)763-7072
Products: Women's and children's clothing. **SIC:** 5137
(Women's/Children's Clothing). **Officers:** Ronna
Bridges, CEO.

■ 4844 ■ **Bright Lights Sportswear Inc.**
1400 Broadway
New York, NY 10018
Phone: (212)354-0177   **Fax:** (212)354-0215
Products: Linen products; Skirts; Jackets; Blouses;
Dresses. **SICs:** 5136 (Men's/Boys' Clothing); 5137
(Women's/Children's Clothing). **Est:** 1975. **Officers:**
Scott Gins, President.

■ 4845 ■ **Brindar Design Inc.**
370 NE 219th Ave.
Gresham, OR 97030-8419
Phone: (503)661-5464   **Fax:** (503)667-4633
Products: Women's sportswear. **SIC:** 5137
(Women's/Children's Clothing). **Officers:** Laurie
Connelly, President.

■ 4846 ■ **Bristol Lettering of Hartford**
2034 Park St.
Hartford, CT 06106-2024
Phone: (860)232-5739   **Fax:** (860)232-3048
Products: Silk screened, embroidered, and printed t-
shirts. **SIC:** 5137 (Women's/Children's Clothing). **Est:**
1961. **Emp:** 6. **Officers:** Richard Case, Owner.

■ 4847 ■ **Brittania Sportswear**
1411 Broadway
New York, NY 10018-3403
Phone: (212)921-0060   **Fax:** (212)869-8060
Products: Men's and women's sportswear, including
casuals, jeans, denims, shorts, and tops. **SICs:** 5136
(Men's/Boys' Clothing); 5137 (Women's/Children's
Clothing). **Emp:** 49.

■ 4848 ■ **Broder Bros., Co.**
45555 Port St.
Plymouth, MI 48170
Phone: (734)454-4800
Free: (800)521-0850   **Fax:** 800-521-1251
E-mail: webmaster@broderbros.com
URL: http://www.broderbros.com
Products: Golf shirts; T-shirts; Sweatshirts; Outerwear;
Headwear; Ladies; Windshirts; Towels; Tote bags.
SICs: 5136 (Men's/Boys' Clothing); 5137
(Women's/Children's Clothing). **Est:** 1919. **Sales:**
$380,000,000 (2000). **Emp:** 700. **Officers:** Vince Tyra,
CEO; Howard Morof, CFO; Todd Turkin, President;
David Margolis, VP & Controller.

■ 4849 ■ **Broner Glove Co.**
1750 Harmon
Auburn Hills, MI 48326
Phone: (248)391-5006
Free: (800)521-1318   **Fax:** 800-276-6375
Products: Men's and boy's clothing, including
sportswear and work clothing; Safety clothing; Work
gloves. **SIC:** 5136 (Men's/Boys' Clothing). **Officers:**
David Broner, President.

■ 4850 ■ **Brooks Manufacturing Co.**
8439 Quivira
Lenexa, KS 66215
Phone: (913)492-1455   **Fax:** (913)492-8503
Products: Men's and boy's clothing, including caps,
jackets, t-shirts. **SICs:** 5136 (Men's/Boys' Clothing);
5137 (Women's/Children's Clothing). **Est:** 1975. **Emp:**
41. **Officers:** Al Yeddis, President.

■ 4851 ■ **Buffalo Inc.**
PO Box 2865
Spokane, WA 99202-0865
Phone: (509)534-1333
Free: (800)833-1845   **Fax:** (509)536-0287
URL: http://www.buffaloinc.com
Products: Printed and embroidered corporate apparel,
including T-shirts, shorts, and hats; Promotional
products. **SICs:** 5136 (Men's/Boys' Clothing); 5137
(Women's/Children's Clothing). **Est:** 1982. **Sales:**
$2,900,000 (1999). **Emp:** 33. **Officers:** Dan Fitzgerald,
CEO & President; Dave Cuplin, Sales/Marketing
Contact; Mike Roepker, Sales/Marketing Contact;
Sandy Cartwright, Human Resources Contact.

■ 4852 ■ **Burchs Fine Footwear Inc.**
223 1/2 Valley River Ctr.
Eugene, OR 97401-2176
Phone: (541)485-2070
Free: (800)201-2070   **Fax:** (541)484-1345
Products: Shoes. **SIC:** 5139 (Footwear). **Sales:**
$3,500,000 (2000). **Emp:** 12.

■ 4853 ■ **Burke Hosiery Mills Inc.**
PO Box 406
Hildebran, NC 28637-0406
Phone: (704)328-1725   **Fax:** (704)328-8373
Products: Infant's and children's socks and hoisery.
SIC: 5137 (Women's/Children's Clothing). **Est:** 1942.
Sales: $5,000,000 (2000). **Emp:** 125. **Officers:** David
L. Dale, President & Treasurer; David L. Dale Jr., Vice
President; Catherine M. Dale, Secretary.

■ 4854 ■ **Frederic H. Burnham Glove Co.**
1602 Tennessee St.
PO Box 276
Michigan City, IN 46360
Phone: (219)874-5205
Free: (800)535-2544   **Fax:** (219)874-5206
E-mail: 4gloves@burnhamglove.com
URL: http://www.burnhamglove.com
Products: Work gloves; Apparel. **SICs:** 5136
(Men's/Boys' Clothing); 5137 (Women's/Children's
Clothing). **Est:** 1891. **Sales:** $1,000,000 (2000). **Emp:**
6. **Officers:** Roger L. Frye, President; Esther Brown,
Dir. of Systems; Esther Brown, Sales/Marketing
Contact, e-mail: sales@burnhamglove.com; Charity
Seedorf, Customer Service Contact, e-mail: service@
burnhamglove.com.

■ 4855 ■ **Burtons Inc.**
800 Frederick St.
Cumberland, MD 21502
Phone: (301)777-3866
Products: Men's clothing. **SIC:** 5136 (Men's/Boys'
Clothing). **Est:** 1932. **Sales:** $1,000,000 (2000). **Emp:**
20. **Officers:** R.W. Burton, President.

■ 4856 ■ **Cabot Hosiery Mills Inc.**
35 N Main St.
Northfield, VT 05663
Phone: (802)485-6066
Products: Hosiery. **SIC:** 5137 (Women's/Children's
Clothing). **Officers:** Ronald Cabot, President.

■ 4857 ■ **California Manufacturing Co.**
Rte. 3
California, MO 65018-9416
Phone: (573)796-2133   **Fax:** (573)796-3875
Products: Men's and boy's jackets. **SIC:** 5136

(Men's/Boys' Clothing). **Sales:** $6,000,000 (2000).
Emp: 175. **Officers:** Darrell Sullivan.

■ 4858 ■ **Calvert Dry Goods Inc.**
409 W Baltimore St.
Baltimore, MD 21201-1716
Phone: (410)752-8253
Products: Men's and boys' clothing. **SIC:** 5136
(Men's/Boys' Clothing). **Officers:** Cynthia Rubinstein,
President.

■ 4859 ■ **Camo Distributors**
PO Box 863
Centre, AL 35960-9455
Phone: (205)475-3660   **Fax:** (205)475-5274
Products: Men's and boys' clothing. **SIC:** 5136
(Men's/Boys' Clothing). **Officers:** James Garmen,
President.

■ 4860 ■ **Captain TS**
PO Box 993
Port Angeles, WA 98362-0806
Phone: (425)452-6549
Free: (800)462-8593   **Fax:** (425)452-0884
Products: Men's and boys' clothing; Men's and boys'
sportswear; Men's and boys' work clothing. **SIC:** 5136
(Men's/Boys' Clothing). **Officers:** Johnnie Rector,
Owner.

■ 4861 ■ **Caring Concepts Inc.**
469 7th Ave.
New York, NY 10018
Phone: (212)564-3400
Products: Women's sportswear. **SICs:** 5137
(Women's/Children's   Clothing);   5137
(Women's/Children's Clothing). **Sales:** $4,000,000
(2000). **Emp:** 35. **Officers:** Lawrence C. Kaplan,
President; Richard Elman, Finance Officer.

■ 4862 ■ **Carolina Hosiery Connection**
525 Alleghany Ave.
Lynchburg, VA 24501-2609
Phone: (804)846-5099   **Fax:** (804)528-4905
Products: Hosiery. **SIC:** 5137 (Women's/Children's
Clothing). **Officers:** Elizabeth Harris, Owner.

■ 4863 ■ **Carolina Made Inc.**
400 Indian Trail Rd.
Indian Trail, NC 28079
Phone: (704)821-6425
Free: (800)222-1409   **Fax:** (704)821-6752
E-mail: caromade@vnet.net
URL: http://www.caromade.com
Products: T-shirts. **SIC:** 5136 (Men's/Boys' Clothing).
Est: 1967. **Emp:** 72. **Officers:** Jim Cherry, President &
Treasurer; Joanna Cherry Palunbo, Sr. VP; Joanna
Palunbo, Secretary.

■ 4864 ■ **Carolina Maid Products Inc.**
PO Box 308
Granite Quarry, NC 28072
Phone: (704)279-7221
Free: (800)332-5540   **Fax:** (704)279-7222
Products: Dresses. **SIC:** 5137 (Women's/Children's
Clothing). **Est:** 1935. **Sales:** $1,600,000 (2000). **Emp:**
50. **Officers:** David W. Swaim, President.

■ 4865 ■ **Carousel Fashions Inc.**
770 Dedham St.
Canton, MA 02021-1404
Phone: (781)821-0821   **Fax:** (781)821-2931
Products: Men's and boys' clothing; Women's
clothing. **SICs:** 5136 (Men's/Boys' Clothing); 5137
(Women's/Children's Clothing). **Officers:** Kevin
Harrington, President.

■ 4866 ■ **Carter Girls Fashions Inc.**
PO Box 4324
Meridian, MS 39304-4324
Phone: (601)693-1141   **Fax:** (601)483-7035
Products: Children's clothing. **SIC:** 5137
(Women's/Children's Clothing). **Officers:** Dee Carter,
President.

■ 4867 ■ **Castleberry Knits Ltd.**
530 7th Ave.
New York, NY 10018-4872
Phone: (212)221-4333   **Fax:** (212)221-2538
Products: Knits, including dresses and suits. **SICs:**

5137 (Women's/Children's Clothing); 5136 (Men's/Boys' Clothing). **Emp:** 49.

■ **4868** ■ **Tom Castleberry**
PO Box 140937
Nashville, TN 37214-0937
Phone: (615)367-9628
Free: (800)647-2258 **Fax:** (615)367-0067
Products: Men's and women's clothing. **SICs:** 5137 (Women's/Children's Clothing); 5136 (Men's/Boys' Clothing). **Officers:** Tom Castleberry, Owner.

■ **4869** ■ **Casual Apparel Inc.**
PO Box 544
Sparta, TN 38583-0544
Phone: (931)836-3004 **Fax:** (931)836-2393
Products: Men's and boys' clothing. **SIC:** 5136 (Men's/Boys' Clothing). **Officers:** Forest Cantrell, President.

■ **4870** ■ **S.D. Cattsa Inc.**
320 Calle Primera, Ste. E
San Ysidro, CA 92173
Phone: (619)428-4909 **Fax:** (619)428-0955
Products: Shirts; Blankets; Textiles. **SICs:** 5137 (Women's/Children's Clothing); 5136 (Men's/Boys' Clothing); 5131 (Piece Goods & Notions). **Est:** 1992. **Sales:** $2,000,000 (2000). **Emp:** 6.

■ **4871** ■ **Celebration Imports Inc.**
350 5th Ave.
New York, NY 10118
Phone: (212)239-6670
Products: Outerwear. **SICs:** 5136 (Men's/Boys' Clothing); 5137 (Women's/Children's Clothing).

■ **4872** ■ **Cellucap-Melco Manufacturing**
4626 N 15th St.
Philadelphia, PA 19019
Phone: (215)324-0213
Free: (800)441-9749 **Fax:** (215)324-1290
E-mail: sales@cellucap.com
URL: http://www.magpage.com/~melco
Products: Overalls; Jumpsuits; Shoe accessories; Disposable clothing. **SICs:** 5136 (Men's/Boys' Clothing); 5137 (Women's/Children's Clothing). **Est:** 1957. **Sales:** $5,000,000 (2000). **Emp:** 125. **Officers:** Jane Harris, President; Mark Davis, Exec. VP; Hank Wagenfeld, Exec. VP of Manufacturing. **Former Name:** Melco Inc.

■ **4873** ■ **Central Work Clothes**
2017 Fort St.
Lincoln Park, MI 48146-2402
Phone: (313)382-0988 **Fax:** (313)382-0350
Products: Work pants, excluding jeans; Work shirts; Work gloves and mittens. **SIC:** 5136 (Men's/Boys' Clothing). **Officers:** Nassef Abraham, President.

■ **4874** ■ **Centre Manufacturing Co. Inc.**
PO Box 579
Centre, AL 35960-0579
Phone: (205)927-5541 **Fax:** (205)927-4771
Products: Military and civilian coats. **SICs:** 5136 (Men's/Boys' Clothing); 5137 (Women's/Children's Clothing). **Sales:** $20,000,000 (2000). **Emp:** 625. **Officers:** Joseph C. Hays; William M. Hays; Robert N. Hays; Warren B. Dotson Jr.

■ **4875** ■ **Chandras**
1005 Kalahu Pl.
Honolulu, HI 96825-1331
Phone: (808)521-4068 **Fax:** (808)396-0938
Products: Dresses. **SIC:** 5137 (Women's/Children's Clothing). **Est:** 1975. **Emp:** 49. **Officers:** Maria E. Chandra.

■ **4876** ■ **Changing Colors**
1131 Bishop St., Unit 116
Honolulu, HI 96813-2822
Phone: (808)841-5607 **Fax:** (808)841-5607
Products: Men's and boy's clothing, including shirts. **SIC:** 5136 (Men's/Boys' Clothing). **Officers:** Serena Chen, Owner.

■ **4877** ■ **Chattanooga Manufacturing Inc.**
1407 3rd Fl.
New York, NY 10018
Phone: (212)921-1755 **Fax:** (212)921-4779
Products: Women's blouses. **SIC:** 5137 (Women's/Children's Clothing). **Emp:** 49. **Officers:** Jamshid Soufian.

■ **4878** ■ **Cherokee Hosiery Mills**
208 35th NE
Ft. Payne, AL 35967-3953
Phone: (205)845-0004 **Fax:** (205)845-0800
Products: Foot socks; Hosiery. **SICs:** 5136 (Men's/Boys' Clothing); 5137 (Women's/Children's Clothing). **Sales:** $36,000,000 (2000). **Emp:** 220. **Officers:** Jim Wilder.

■ **4879** ■ **Cherry Sticks Inc.**
1407 Broadway, No. 1503
New York, NY 10018
Phone: (212)947-9400
Products: Sportswear. **SICs:** 5136 (Men's/Boys' Clothing); 5137 (Women's/Children's Clothing). **Sales:** $13,000,000 (2000). **Emp:** 35. **Officers:** Charles Gammal, President; David Apperman, Controller.

■ **4880** ■ **Louis Chock Inc.**
74 Orchard
New York, NY 10002-4515
Phone: (212)473-1929 **Fax:** (212)473-6273
E-mail: chock1@juno.com
URL: http://www.chockcatalog.com
Products: Men's, women's, and children's hosiery, underwear, and sleepwear. **SICs:** 5136 (Men's/Boys' Clothing); 5137 (Women's/Children's Clothing). **Est:** 1921. **Emp:** 6.

■ **4881** ■ **Christie Brothers Fur Corp.**
333 7th Ave.
New York, NY 10001
Phone: (212)736-6944
Products: Fur coats. **SIC:** 5137 (Women's/Children's Clothing). **Officers:** Constantino Christie, President.

■ **4882** ■ **J.H. Churchwell Co.**
PO Box 1019
Jacksonville, FL 32201-1019
Phone: (904)356-5721
Free: (800)245-0075 **Fax:** (904)354-2436
E-mail: churchwells@worldnet.att.net
URL: http://www.churchillcompany.com
Products: Men's and boys' clothing; Women's clothing; Textiles; Advertising specialties; Screenprinting; Embroidery. **SICs:** 5136 (Men's/Boys' Clothing); 5131 (Piece Goods & Notions); 5137 (Women's/Children's Clothing). **Est:** 1911. **Sales:** $6,000,000 (2000). **Emp:** 11. **Officers:** Leonard R. Pavelka, President; Robert F. Pavelka, Sec. & Treas.

■ **4883** ■ **Vivian Clark Ltd.**
12111 The Apparel Center
Chicago, IL 60654
Phone: (312)222-1120
Free: (800)747-1120 **Fax:** (312)222-1718
Products: Women's clothing, including shirts, blouses, skirts, and dresses. **SIC:** 5137 (Women's/Children's Clothing). **Emp:** 8.

■ **4884** ■ **CMS Casuals Inc.**
13200 SE 30th St.
Bellevue, WA 98005-4403
Phone: (425)643-5270 **Fax:** (425)641-6342
Products: Apparel and accessories; Children's nightwear; Men's nightwear; Women's knit nightwear. **SICs:** 5137 (Women's/Children's Clothing); 5136 (Men's/Boys' Clothing). **Emp:** 99.

■ **4885** ■ **Coast Shoes Inc.**
13401 Saticoy St.
North Hollywood, CA 91605-3413
Phone: (818)786-0717
Free: (800)262-7851 **Fax:** (818)786-1227
Products: Shoes. **SIC:** 5139 (Footwear). **Sales:** $3,000,000 (2000). **Emp:** 6.

■ **4886** ■ **Cohan Berta Showroom**
214 W 39th St., Ste. 1003
New York, NY 10018
Phone: (212)840-0600
Products: Women's clothing. **SIC:** 5137 (Women's/Children's Clothing).

■ **4887** ■ **Paula Cohen Ltd.**
498 7th Ave.
New York, NY 10018
Phone: (212)947-8252
Products: Dress clothes; Formal attire. **SIC:** 5137 (Women's/Children's Clothing). **Sales:** $2,000,000 (2000). **Emp:** 8. **Officers:** Paula Cohen, President; Al Cohen, Vice President.

■ **4888** ■ **College Bowl Inc.**
333 W Baltimore St.
Baltimore, MD 21201-2512
Phone: (410)685-0661 **Fax:** (410)625-7503
Products: Men's and boys' sportswear. **SIC:** 5136 (Men's/Boys' Clothing). **Officers:** Joel Himmelfarb, President.

■ **4889** ■ **Columbia Sportswear Co.**
6635 N Baltimore Ave.
Portland, OR 97203-5402
Phone: (573)887-3681 **Fax:** (573)887-6268
Products: Men's sportswear; Women's sportswear. **SICs:** 5136 (Men's/Boys' Clothing); 5137 (Women's/Children's Clothing). **Est:** 1984. **Sales:** $5,000,000 (2000). **Emp:** 300.

■ **4890** ■ **Command Uniforms**
4545 Malsbary Rd.
Cincinnati, OH 45242-5624
Products: Men's clothing, sportswear, and work clothing; Uniforms. **SIC:** 5136 (Men's/Boys' Clothing). **Officers:** Gary Heldman, President; Devonne Campbell, Dir. of Marketing. **Former Name:** Farriors Inc.

■ **4891** ■ **The Company Logo Inc.**
PO Box 5042
Winston-Salem, NC 27113-5042
Phone: (336)722-6016 **Free:** (888)722-6016
Products: Embroidered jackets and hats; Casual clothing. **SICs:** 5136 (Men's/Boys' Clothing); 5137 (Women's/Children's Clothing). **Est:** 1983. **Sales:** $400,000 (2000). **Emp:** 6. **Officers:** Joseph Johnston, President.

■ **4892** ■ **Cooper Sportswear Manufacturing Company Inc.**
720 Frelinghuysen Ave.
Newark, NJ 07114
Phone: (201)824-3400 **Fax:** (201)824-0346
Products: Clothing. **SIC:** 5136 (Men's/Boys' Clothing). **Sales:** $30,000,000 (2000). **Emp:** 200.

■ **4893** ■ **Cop Shop**
1306 N Howard St.
Spokane, WA 99201-2412
Phone: (509)534-5068
Products: Uniforms and equipment. **SICs:** 5137 (Women's/Children's Clothing); 5136 (Men's/Boys' Clothing). **Officers:** Lynne Schierman, Owner.

■ **4894** ■ **Copy Cats Industries Inc.**
525 7th Ave.
New York, NY 10018-4999
Phone: (212)921-1595 **Fax:** (212)302-3815
Products: Women's blouses and sportswear. **SIC:** 5137 (Women's/Children's Clothing). **Emp:** 49.

■ **4895** ■ **Cornell Trading Inc.**
PO Box 1710
Williston, VT 05495-1710
Phone: (802)862-1144 **Fax:** (802)865-9769
Products: Housewares; Women's and children's clothing. **SICs:** 5137 (Women's/Children's Clothing); 5023 (Homefurnishings). **Officers:** Chris Cornell, President.

■ **4896** ■ **Corpus Christi Wholesale Mart**
3229 Ayers St.
Corpus Christi, TX 78415
Phone: (512)887-8184
Products: Shirts. **SIC:** 5131 (Piece Goods & Notions).

■ 4897 ■ Corral West Ranchwear Inc.
4519 Frontier Mall Dr.
Cheyenne, WY 82009
Phone: (307)632-0951 **Fax:** (307)638-0523
Products: Clothing, including western wear. **SICs:**
5136 (Men's/Boys' Clothing); 5137
(Women's/Children's Clothing); 5139 (Footwear).

■ 4898 ■ Victor Costa Inc.
5412 Vista Meadow Dr.
Dallas, TX 75248-2023
Phone: (214)634-1133 **Fax:** (214)630-2519
Products: Dresses; Suits. **SICs:** 5137
(Women's/Children's Clothing); 5136 (Men's/Boys'
Clothing). **Est:** 1974. **Sales:** $2,000,000 (2000). **Emp:**
499. **Officers:** Victor Costa.

■ 4899 ■ Cotton Caboodle Company Co.
203 W Thomas St.
Seattle, WA 98119-4213
Phone: (206)282-0075 **Fax:** (206)282-3795
E-mail: cottoncaboodle@seanet.com
Products: Children's and infant's clothing. **SIC:** 5137
(Women's/Children's Clothing). **Est:** 1985. **Sales:**
$2,000,000 (2000). **Emp:** 12. **Officers:** Sharon
Lagerberg, President; Charlotte Green, Sec. & Treas.

■ 4900 ■ The Cotton Exchange
PO Box 825
Wendell, NC 27591-0825
Phone: (919)365-5900 **Fax:** (919)365-5999
Products: Colthing and sportswear for men, women,
and children. **SICs:** 5136 (Men's/Boys' Clothing); 5137
(Women's/Children's Clothing). **Est:** 1985. **Sales:**
$25,000,000 (2000). **Emp:** 220. **Officers:** Bill Howard,
President.

■ 4901 ■ Country Miss Carrollton
Rte. 1, Box 67H
Carrollton, AL 35447-9784
Phone: (205)367-8171
Products: Women's jackets. **SIC:** 5137
(Women's/Children's Clothing). **Sales:** $6,000,000
(2000). **Emp:** 300. **Officers:** Nick Verzino.

■ 4902 ■ CRH International Inc.
15 Dan Rd.
Canton, MA 02021-2847
Phone: (781)821-1000 **Fax:** (781)821-2020
Products: Chidren's clothing. **SIC:** 5137
(Women's/Children's Clothing). **Officers:** Michael
Bozic, President.

■ 4903 ■ Cromer Co.
55 NE 7th St.
Miami, FL 33132
Phone: (305)373-5414 **Fax:** (305)358-5244
Products: Unisex sportswear. **SICs:** 5136
(Men's/Boys' Clothing); 5137 (Women's/Children's
Clothing). **Est:** 1913. **Sales:** $9,000,000 (2000). **Emp:**
40. **Officers:** Daniel Cromer, President; Thomas
Cromer, Vice President.

■ 4904 ■ Cullens Playland Inc.
8424 Florida Blvd.
Baton Rouge, LA 70806-4838
Phone: (504)927-9305 **Fax:** (504)927-9581
Products: Children's clothing. **SIC:** 5137
(Women's/Children's Clothing). **Officers:** Robert
Cullen, President.

■ 4905 ■ Cup Graphics and Screen Printing
4307 S Port Ave., No. 142
Corpus Christi, TX 78415
Phone: (512)992-5114
Products: Shirts. **SIC:** 5131 (Piece Goods & Notions).

■ 4906 ■ Custom Creations Sportswear
6950 NW 37th Ave.
Miami, FL 33147-6514
Phone: (305)693-7873 **Fax:** (305)694-1112
E-mail: ccsports@aol.com
URL: http://www.customcreations.net
Products: Men's and boys' clothing; Women's clothing
and sportswear; Uniforms. **SICs:** 5136 (Men's/Boys'
Clothing); 5137 (Women's/Children's Clothing). **Est:**
1996. **Sales:** $800,000 (2000). **Emp:** 15. **Officers:**
Minar Ajwani, e-mail: majwani@aol.com. **Former
Name:** Gim Tree Manufacturing.

■ 4907 ■ D and D Shoe Co.
200 S 5th St.
Mayfield, KY 42066
Phone: (502)251-2055 **Fax:** (502)251-0054
Products: Shoes. **SIC:** 5139 (Footwear).

■ 4908 ■ Daccord Inc.
545 NW 28th St.
Miami, FL 33127-4137
Phone: (305)576-0926 **Fax:** (305)576-0196
Products: Men's shirts. **SIC:** 5136 (Men's/Boys'
Clothing). **Emp:** 19.

■ 4909 ■ Damascus Worldwide, Inc.
PO Box 543
Rutland, VT 05702
Phone: (802)775-6062
Free: (800)451-4167 **Fax:** (802)773-3919
E-mail: gloves@damgloves.com
URL: http://www.damgloves.com
Products: Police and uniform gloves, including dress,
tactical and cut resistant gloves. **SIC:** 5136
(Men's/Boys' Clothing). **Est:** 1975. **Sales:** $1,000,000
(1999). **Emp:** 4. **Officers:** Lawrence J. Welton,
President; Ken Remhoff, Sales/Marketing Contact;
Lynn LaRock, Customer Service Contact; Donna
Blight, Human Resources Contact. **Former Name:**
Dakota Corp.

■ 4910 ■ Dan L. Davis Enterprises Inc.
402 Murray Rd.
Valdosta, GA 31602-4000
Phone: (912)247-4120 **Fax:** (912)242-1166
Products: Women's clothing accessories. **SIC:** 5137
(Women's/Children's Clothing). **Officers:** Dan Davis,
President.

■ 4911 ■ Del-Mar Industries Inc.
PO Box 496
Jacksonville, NC 28540
Phone: (919)347-1095 **Fax:** (910)347-7251
Products: Men's and boys' shirts; Men's and boys'
clothing. **SIC:** 5136 (Men's/Boys' Clothing). **Officers:**
Laran Houston, President.

■ 4912 ■ Denton Hosiery Mill
PO Box 476
Denton, NC 27239-0476
Phone: (336)859-2116 **Fax:** (336)859-5592
Products: Hosiery. **SICs:** 5137 (Women's/Children's
Clothing); 5136 (Men's/Boys' Clothing). **Est:** 1935.
Sales: $1,800,000 (2000). **Emp:** 22. **Officers:** M.W.
Carrick.

■ 4913 ■ Denver Waste Materials Inc.
2363 Larimer St.
Denver, CO 80205-2120
Phone: (303)295-7737 **Fax:** (303)297-8422
Products: Women's and children's clothing. **SIC:** 5137
(Women's/Children's Clothing). **Officers:** Gary Feder,
President.

■ 4914 ■ Design Tees Hawaii Inc.
PO Box 2515
Honolulu, HI 96804-2515
Phone: (808)848-4877
Products: Women's and children's clothing. **SIC:** 5137
(Women's/Children's Clothing). **Officers:** Spencer
Chapman, President.

■ 4915 ■ Diadora America
6419 S 228th St.
Kent, WA 98032-1874
Phone: (253)395-4644
Free: (800)423-9958 **Fax:** (253)395-4931
Products: Men's, women's and children's clothing,
including sportswear and swimsuits; Footwear. **SICs:**
5137 (Women's/Children's Clothing); 5136
(Men's/Boys' Clothing); 5139 (Footwear). **Officers:**
Galliano Mondin, President.

■ 4916 ■ Diamony International, Inc.
7670 Woodway, Ste. 160
Houston, TX 77063
Phone: (713)266-7604 **Fax:** (713)977-7177
Products: Women's clothing. **SIC:** 5137
(Women's/Children's Clothing).

■ 4917 ■ Dinorah's Sportswear
5101 NW 36th Ave.
Miami, FL 33142
Phone: (305)633-1488 **Fax:** (305)633-2785
Products: Adult's and children's clothing, including
shirts, shorts, and sweats. **SICs:** 5137
(Women's/Children's Clothing); 5136 (Men's/Boys'
Clothing).

■ 4918 ■ Direct Sales Inc.
212 S Garnett Rd.
Tulsa, OK 74128-1806
Phone: (918)438-2680
Products: Women's clothing. **SIC:** 5137
(Women's/Children's Clothing). **Officers:** Lester Belt,
President.

■ 4919 ■ Domsey Fiber Corp.
431 Kent Ave.
Brooklyn, NY 11211
Phone: (718)384-6000 **Fax:** (718)782-3962
Products: Used clothing. **SICs:** 5136 (Men's/Boys'
Clothing); 5137 (Women's/Children's Clothing). **Est:**
1953. **Sales:** $18,000,000 (2000). **Emp:** 400. **Officers:**
Arthur Salm, CEO; Albert Edery, Vice President.

■ 4920 ■ Don Overcast and Associates
250 Spring St.
Atlanta, GA 30303
Phone: (404)523-4082
Free: (800)527-6234 **Fax:** (404)527-6668
Products: Clothing. **SIC:** 5137 (Women's/Children's
Clothing). **Sales:** $10,000,000 (2000). **Emp:** 6.

■ 4921 ■ Dorfman-Pacific Company Inc.
PO Box 213005
Stockton, CA 95213-9005
Phone: (209)982-1400
Free: (800)DOR-FMAN **Fax:** (209)982-1596
E-mail: custservice@dorfman-pacific.com
URL: http://www.dorfman-pacific.com
Products: Hats. **SICs:** 5136 (Men's/Boys' Clothing);
5137 (Women's/Children'sClothing). **Est:** 1921. **Sales:**
$30,000,000 (2000). **Emp:** 130. **Officers:** Douglas
Highsmith, President, e-mail: dhighsmith@dorfman-
pacific.com; Bakul Patel, Controller, e-mail: bakulp@
dorfman-pacific.com; Art Gardner, Sr. VP of Marketing
& Sales, e-mail: artg@dorfman-pacific.com; Ed Weise,
Operations Mgr., e-mail: edw@dorfman-pacific.com.

■ 4922 ■ Dreyer & Associates Inc.
4408 Village Oaks Trail
Atlanta, GA 30338-5726
Phone: (404)577-5376
Products: Women's and children's clothing. **SIC:** 5137
(Women's/Children's Clothing). **Officers:** Robert
Dreyer, President.

■ 4923 ■ Driscoll Leather Company Inc.
714 S 15th St.
Omaha, NE 68102-3103
Phone: (402)341-4307
Free: (800)228-7012 **Fax:** (402)341-2774
Products: Shoes. **SIC:** 5139 (Footwear). **Sales:**
$1,600,000 (2000). **Emp:** 8.

■ 4924 ■ Dumans Custom Tailor Inc.
438 E Colfax Ave.
Denver, CO 80203-1909
Phone: (303)832-1701 **Fax:** (303)832-3535
Products: Men's and boys' clothing; Men's and boys'
sportswear; Men's and boys' work clothing. **SIC:** 5136
(Men's/Boys' Clothing). **Officers:** Maurice Duman,
President.

■ 4925 ■ Dyl-Chem Inc.
PO Box 4096
New Bedford, MA 02741-4096
Phone: (508)997-1960
Free: (800)887-3151 **Fax:** (508)992-6089
URL: http://www.whalerknits.com
Products: Sweaters. **SICs:** 5137 (Women's/Children's
Clothing); 5136 (Men's/Boys' Clothing). **Est:** 1972.
Emp: 15. **Officers:** Susan Frigault, President; Maureen
Baptista, Sales/Marketing Contact; Patricia Grime,
Customer Service Contact. **Doing Business As:**
Whalerknits.

■ 4926 ■ Eagle Pointe Inc.
Rte. 2, Box 117
Huddleston, VA 24104-9643
Phone: (540)297-1274 **Fax:** (540)297-1274
Products: Men's sweatshirts. **SIC:** 5136 (Men's/Boys' Clothing). **Emp:** 99. **Officers:** Shirley Owens; Ben L. Owens.

■ 4927 ■ East Coast Embroidery Inc.
375 Waterman Ave.
East Providence, RI 02914-0519
Phone: (401)434-9224
Free: (800)338-9224 **Fax:** (401)434-9238
E-mail: ecemb@gis.net
URL: http://www.eastcoastlogos.com
Products: Custom screen and embroidered sportswear and advertising products. **SICs:** 5136 (Men's/Boys' Clothing); 5137 (Women's/Children's Clothing). **Est:** 1986. **Emp:** 7. **Officers:** Constantin Vavolotis, President; Annemarie LaPorte, General Mgr.

■ 4928 ■ Eastland Screen Prints Inc.
9425 Mathy Dr.
Fairfax, VA 22031-4101
Phone: (703)250-2556 **Fax:** (703)978-2924
Products: Men's and boys' clothing; Printing on garments and apparel accessories. **SIC:** 5136 (Men's/Boys' Clothing). **Officers:** Alan Jackson, President.

■ 4929 ■ EBSCO Industries Inc. Western Region
920 41st Ave.
Santa Cruz, CA 95062
Phone: (408)475-5020 **Fax:** (408)475-4544
Products: Furniture; Apparel; Coffee mugs. **SICs:** 5136 (Men's/Boys' Clothing); 5021 (Furniture); 5023 (Homefurnishings); 5137 (Women's/Children's Clothing). **Est:** 1940. **Sales:** $17,000,000 (2000). **Emp:** 25. **Officers:** William Pumphrey, President; Billy Ceta, Dir. of Marketing.

■ 4930 ■ Ed-Burt Corp.
400 1st Ave. N
Minneapolis, MN 55401-1715
Phone: (612)333-3156
Products: Women's turtlenecks. **SIC:** 5137 (Women's/Children's Clothing). **Officers:** Edwin Neff, President.

■ 4931 ■ Eisenberg International Corp.
948 Giswold Ave.
San Fernando, CA 91340
Phone: (818)365-8161
Products: Men's suits. **SIC:** 5136 (Men's/Boys' Clothing). **Est:** 1966. **Sales:** $51,000,000 (2000). **Emp:** 75. **Officers:** Joel Eisenberg, President.

■ 4932 ■ Eisner Bros.
75 Essex St.
New York, NY 10002
Phone: (212)475-6868
Free: (800)426-7700 **Fax:** (212)475-6824
URL: http://www.eisnerbros.com
Products: Men's, women's and children's sportwear, including printables, licensed sportswear, t-shirts, sweatshirts, caps, jackets, coveralls, work clothing, tote bags, sport bags, aprons, reflective vests, team uniforms, and outfitting. **SICs:** 5136 (Men's/Boys' Clothing); 5137 (Women's/Children's Clothing). **Est:** 1971. **Sales:** $9,000,000 (2000). **Emp:** 25. **Officers:** Sholom Eisner; Charles Eisner.

■ 4933 ■ Elder Hosiery Mills Inc.
PO Box 2377
Burlington, NC 27216
Phone: (910)226-2229
Free: (800)745-0267 **Fax:** (910)226-5846
Products: Foot socks. **SICs:** 5136 (Men's/Boys' Clothing); 5137 (Women's/Children's Clothing). **Emp:** 110.

■ 4934 ■ Elem Corp.
225 W Trade St.
Burlington, NC 27215
Phone: (919)228-8725 **Fax:** (919)228-8354
Products: Socks. **SICs:** 5137 (Women's/Children's Clothing); 5136 (Men's/Boys' Clothing). **Sales:** $6,000,000 (2000). **Emp:** 99. **Officers:** Ben Lee.

■ 4935 ■ Walter Elson Import Export
270 Park Side Ave.
Brooklyn, NY 11226
Phone: (718)941-6670
Products: Men's pants and shirts; Electrical appliances; Cranes and earth movers; Groceries; Women's dresses. **SICs:** 5136 (Men's/Boys' Clothing); 5064 (Electrical Appliances—Television & Radio); 5082 (Construction & Mining Machinery); 5141 (Groceries—General Line); 5137 (Women's/Children's Clothing). **Officers:** Walter Elson, President.

■ 4936 ■ Ely & Walker
PO Box 1326
Lebanon, TN 37088-1326
Phone: (615)443-1878
Free: (800)359-1878 **Fax:** (615)443-2214
Products: Men's and women's western wear. **SICs:** 5136 (Men's/Boys' Clothing); 5137 (Women's/Children's Clothing). **Est:** 1878. **Officers:** Ivar Aavatsmark, President; Corey Rowe, VP of Marketing; Doug Soileau.

■ 4937 ■ Embroidery Services Inc.
1530 Interstate Dr.
PO Box 18040
Erlanger, KY 41018-0040
Phone: (606)283-6700
Free: (800)948-5454 **Fax:** (606)283-6706
Products: Decorated embroidered sportswear, hats, towels, jackets, and totes. **SICs:** 5136 (Men's/Boys' Clothing); 5137 (Women's/Children's Clothing). **Est:** 1982. **Sales:** $13,000,000 (2000). **Emp:** 130. **Officers:** George Riggs, President; Roger C. Marshall, General Mgr.; Bob Plott, Sales/Mktg.; Ralph Mitchell, Customer Service. **Doing Business As:** Oarsman Sportswear.

■ 4938 ■ The Empire Co.
6500 NE Halsey st.
Portland, OR 97213-0250
Phone: (503)227-6433 **Fax:** (503)227-4187
Products: Uniforms; Logoed apparel; Promotional products. **SICs:** 5136 (Men's/Boys' Clothing); 5137 (Women's/Children's Clothing); 5199 (Nondurable Goods Nec). **Officers:** Michael Menashe, CEO.

■ 4939 ■ Esprit International
PO Box 4025
Alameda, CA 94501-0425
Phone: (415)648-6900
Products: Young women's clothing and apparel. **SIC:** 5137 (Women's/Children's Clothing).

■ 4940 ■ Eudora Garment Corp.
PO Box B
Eudora, AR 71640
Phone: (870)355-8381 **Fax:** (870)355-2676
Products: Uniforms; Hospital uniforms; Workwear; Hospitality; Safety; Career apparel; Protective apparel. **SICs:** 5137 (Women's/Children's Clothing); 5136 (Men's/Boys' Clothing). **Est:** 1962. **Sales:** $164,000,000 (1999). **Emp:** 999. **Officers:** Alan Schwartz; Michael Benstock; Ray Anderson; Terry Lupo.

■ 4941 ■ Evans Inc.
36 S State St.
Chicago, IL 60603
Phone: (312)855-2000
Products: Furs and fine clothing. **SICs:** 5136 (Men's/Boys' Clothing); 5137 (Women's/Children's Clothing). **Est:** 1929. **Sales:** $82,700,000 (2000). **Emp:** 875. **Officers:** Patrick J. Regan, CEO & President; William E. Koziel, VP & CFO.

■ 4942 ■ F & R Sales Inc.
2101 S Dixie Rd.
Dalton, GA 30720-7565
Phone: (706)226-8564
Free: (800)635-5622 **Fax:** (706)226-7582
E-mail: bbro@ocsonline.com
URL: http://www.FandRsales.com
Products: Men's and boys' clothing, including shirts. **SIC:** 5136 (Men's/Boys' Clothing). **Est:** 1976. **Emp:** 8. **Officers:** Fred Hall, President.

■ 4943 ■ Fabric Art Inc.
3439 SW Dickinson St.
Portland, OR 97219-7555
Phone: (503)224-1303 **Fax:** (503)224-0027
Products: T-shirts. **SICs:** 5136 (Men's/Boys' Clothing); 5137 (Women's/Children's Clothing). **Sales:** $3,500,000 (2000). **Emp:** 30. **Officers:** Steve Lutz, President; Shari Jacobson, General Mgr.

■ 4944 ■ Fairfield Line Inc.
PO Box 500
Fairfield, IA 52556
Phone: (515)472-3191 **Fax:** (515)472-3194
Products: Work gloves. **SIC:** 5136 (Men's/Boys' Clothing). **Est:** 1905. **Sales:** $25,000,000 (2000). **Emp:** 200. **Officers:** F. Hunt, President; Larry Sheffler, Vice President; Richard W. Eland, Sales Mgr.; Joe Arndt, Dir. of Information Systems.

■ 4945 ■ Famous Mart Inc.
PO Box 220268
Charlotte, NC 28222
Phone: (704)333-5157 **Fax:** (704)333-5158
E-mail: lsinkor@famousmart.com
Products: Cologne; Men's, women's, and children's apparel, including shirts, sweaters, coats, and jackets; Sporting goods. **SICs:** 5136 (Men's/Boys' Clothing); 5091 (Sporting & Recreational Goods); 5122 (Drugs, Proprietaries & Sundries); 5137 (Women's/Children's Clothing). **Est:** 1954. **Sales:** $27,000,000 (2000). **Emp:** 40. **Officers:** G.P. Sinkoe, President. **Former Name:** Charlotte Salvage Co.

■ 4946 ■ Fashion Victim
3651 Clearview Pl.
Doraville, GA 30340-2129
Phone: (912)563-0111
Free: (800)522-7247 **Fax:** (912)455-0162
Products: T-shirts; Sculptures; Jewelry. **SICs:** 5137 (Women's/Children's Clothing); 5136 (Men's/Boys' Clothing); 5199 (Nondurable Goods Nec) (Jewelry & Precious Stones).

■ 4947 ■ Fashions Inc. Jackson
PO Box 604
Jackson, MS 39205-0604
Phone: (601)353-4490 **Fax:** (601)352-2010
E-mail: jxnfash@bellsouth.net
Products: Uniforms; Screen printing; Embroidery; Advertising specialties. **SICs:** 5137 (Women's/Children's Clothing); 5199 (Nondurable Goods Nec); 5136 (Men's/Boys' Clothing). **Est:** 1954. **Emp:** 5. **Officers:** Thomas Elzen, President; Les Kershner, Sales & Marketing Contact, e-mail: jxnsash@bellsouth.net.

■ 4948 ■ Felicia Grace and Co.
63 Willow Ave.
Larchmont, NY 10538-3640
Phone: (212)730-7004
Products: Women's clothing. **SIC:** 5137 (Women's/Children's Clothing).

■ 4949 ■ Felina Lingerie
180 Madison Ave., No. 1506
New York, NY 10016-5201
Phone: (212)683-9205 **Fax:** (212)213-6959
Products: Undergarments, including bras, panties, and bodyshapes. **SIC:** 5137 (Women's/Children's Clothing). **Emp:** 150.

■ 4950 ■ Fidelity Sportswear Co.
167 Bow St.
Everett, MA 02149
Phone: (617)389-7007 **Fax:** (617)389-8160
Products: Wool outerwear. **SICs:** 5136 (Men's/Boys' Clothing); 5137 (Women's/Children's Clothing). **Sales:** $9,000,000 (2000). **Emp:** 99. **Officers:** Edward Webber.

■ 4951 ■ Fiji Wear Inc.
72 Suttle St.
Durango, CO 81301-7978
Phone: (970)247-5581
Free: (800)262-9909 **Fax:** (970)259-3864
Products: Headbands; Hats. **SICs:** 5136 (Men's/Boys' Clothing); 5137 (Women's/Children's Clothing). **Emp:** 99.

■ 4952 ■ Finchers Findings Inc.
PO Box 289
Medicine Lodge, KS 67104-0289
Phone: (316)886-5952
Free: (800)362-0938 Fax: (316)886-3035
E-mail: finchers@cyberlodg.com
Products: Men's and boys' clothing; Women's clothing. SICs: 5136 (Men's/Boys' Clothing); 5137 (Women's/Children's Clothing). Est: 1976. Emp: 10. Officers: Ronnie Fincher, President; Brett Fincher, Sales Mgr.

■ 4953 ■ Fine-Line Products Inc.
738 10th Ave.
PO Box 43
Grafton, WI 53024
Phone: (414)375-0000
Free: (800)558-9850 Fax: (414)375-0030
E-mail: fineline@execpc.com
URL: http://www.fine-lineproducts.com
Products: T-shirts and sweatshirts; Caps; Costume jewelry; Decals; Patches; Incense and burners, candles, oil, and lamps; Posters; Cigarette cases. SICs: 5136 (Men's/Boys' Clothing); 5094 (Jewelry & Precious Stones); 5122 (Drugs, Proprietaries & Sundries); 5137 (Women's/Children's Clothing); 5199 (Nondurable Goods Nec). Est: 1974. Emp: 30. Officers: Dixie Randall.

■ 4954 ■ Fink Brothers Inc.
1385 Broadway
New York, NY 10018
Phone: (212)921-5683 Fax: (212)921-4036
Products: Bridal gowns. SIC: 5137 (Women's/Children's Clothing). Sales: $4,000,000 (2000). Emp: 80. Officers: Morris Fink.

■ 4955 ■ Fire-Dex Inc.
780 S Progress Dr.
Medina, OH 44256-1368
Phone: (330)723-0000
Free: (800)241-6563 Fax: (330)723-0035
Products: specialty equipment and products. SIC: 5136 (Men's/Boys' Clothing). Sales: $6,000,000 (2000). Emp: 65.

■ 4956 ■ Fit-All Sportswear Inc.
118 Fit-All Dr.
PO Box 1428
Pilot Mountain, NC 27041
Phone: (336)368-2227
Free: (800)348-8255 Fax: (336)368-5034
E-mail: fitall@surry.net
URL: http://www.fit-all.com
Products: Sport accessories, including headbands, wristbands, socks, hair accessories. SICs: 5137 (Women's/Children's Clothing); 5136 (Men's/Boys' Clothing). Est: 1983. Sales: $2,500,000 (1999). Emp: 50. Officers: Frank Badgett, Customer Service Contact; Rick Hunter, CEO & President; Charles Badgett, Exec. VP of Marketing & Sales; Lennis Worley, Dir of Human Resources.

■ 4957 ■ Fleurette California
336 S Anderson St.
Los Angeles, CA 90033
Phone: (213)269-5600 Fax: (213)269-5800
Products: Coats. SIC: 5137 (Women's/Children's Clothing). Sales: $5,500,000 (2000). Emp: 59. Officers: Mary L. Schwarz, President; Daniel J. Schwarz, CFO.

■ 4958 ■ Flexible Feat Sandals
2344 County Rd. 225
Durango, CO 81301-7034
Phone: (970)247-4628
Products: Shoes. SIC: 5139 (Footwear).

■ 4959 ■ Flirt Corp/Belldini
1428 Maple Ave.
Los Angeles, CA 90015-2526
Phone: (213)748-4442 Fax: (213)748-3243
E-mail: belldini@linkonline.net
URL: http://www.belldini.com
Products: Women's clothing including sweaters, suits, knit tops, and separates. SICs: 5137 (Women's/Children's Clothing); 5136 (Men's/Boys' Clothing). Est: 1986. Emp: 8. Officers: Robert Esshaghian; John Darbandi.

■ 4960 ■ Fontana & Fontana Inc.
PO Box 99
Indian Trail, NC 28079-0099
Phone: (704)882-1112 Fax: (704)882-2344
Products: Men's and boy's clothing, including sportswear and work attire; Footwear, including shoes. SICs: 5136 (Men's/Boys' Clothing); 5139 (Footwear). Officers: Robert Fontana, President.

■ 4961 ■ Foremost Athletic Apparel
1307 E Maple Rd.
Troy, MI 48083
Phone: (248)689-3850 Fax: (248)689-4653
Products: Sporting apparel. SICs: 5136 (Men's/Boys' Clothing); 5137 (Women's/Children's Clothing); 5139 (Footwear). Sales: $100,000,000 (2000). Emp: 200. Officers: John G. Levy, President; Michael Burns, Controller.

■ 4962 ■ Fortune Dogs Inc.
121 Gray Ave., Ste. 300
Santa Barbara, CA 93101
Phone: (805)963-8728
Products: Sporting apparel. SICs: 5136 (Men's/Boys' Clothing); 5137 (Women's/Children's Clothing).

■ 4963 ■ Forty Acres and A Mule Film Works
124 DeKalb Ave.
Brooklyn, NY 11217
Phone: (718)624-3703
Products: Clothing, including T-shirts, caps, and jackets. SICs: 5136 (Men's/Boys' Clothing); 5137 (Women's/Children's Clothing).

■ 4964 ■ M. Foster Associates Inc.
PO Box 585608
Dallas, TX 75258
Phone: (214)631-7732 Fax: (214)631-7765
Products: Women's and children's clothing. SIC: 5137 (Women's/Children's Clothing). Est: 1974. Sales: $15,000,000 (2000). Emp: 50. Officers: Bonnye N. Sherman, President; Cynthia D. Bietz, VP of Marketing; Glynda J. Davis, Dir. of Systems.

■ 4965 ■ Fox Point Sportswear Inc.
PO Box 1641
Waukesha, WI 53187-1641
Phone: (715)536-9461 Fax: (715)536-6971
Products: Sportswear, including jackets, bibs, wallets, gloves, duffel bags, and shorts. SICs: 5136 (Men's/Boys' Clothing); 5137 (Women's/Children's Clothing). Sales: $10,000,000 (2000). Emp: 250. Officers: John Bocke.

■ 4966 ■ Fox River Mills, Inc.
PO Box 298
Osage, IA 50461-0298
Phone: (515)732-3798 Fax: (515)732-5128
E-mail: foxsox@foxrivermills.com
URL: http://www.foxsox.com
Products: Socks, gloves, and mittens. SICs: 5137 (Women's/Children's Clothing); 5136 (Men's/Boys' Clothing). Emp: 300. Officers: Joel Anderson, Sales Mgr.; John Lessard, President; Hal Hofman, Dir. of Marketing; Jeff Lessard, Exec. VP of Sales.

■ 4967 ■ Fratzke Sales, Inc.
412 E 5th St.
Winona, MN 55987-3921
Phone: (507)452-6973
Free: (800)657-4473 Fax: (507)452-3182
Products: Work gloves, dress gloves, and mittens. SICs: 5136 (Men's/Boys' Clothing); 5137 (Women's/Children's Clothing). Est: 1996. Sales: $500,000 (2000). Emp: 2. Officers: Carl A. Fratzke, President. Former Name: Winona Sales Inc.

■ 4968 ■ French Toast
100 W 33rd St.
New York, NY 10001
Phone: (212)594-4740 Fax: (212)268-5160
URL: http://www.frenchtoast.com
Products: Children's clothing and school uniforms. SIC: 5137 (Women's/Children's Clothing). Est: 1955. Sales: $33,000,000 (2000). Emp: 100. Officers: Samuel Gindi, President; Joseph Sutton, Exec. VP.

■ 4969 ■ Fritzi of Utah
1350 Calpac Ave.
Spanish Fork, UT 84660-1805
Phone: (801)798-9811
Products: Girls' and women's clothing. SIC: 5137 (Women's/Children's Clothing). Est: 1972. Sales: $9,000,000 (2000). Emp: 30. Officers: Robert J. Pittelli, Dir. of Operations.

■ 4970 ■ Full Line Distributors
2650 Button at Winnett Dr., Ste. E
Doraville, GA 30340
Free: (800)385-5463 Fax: 800-432-0799
E-mail: fldmark@fullline.com
URL: http://www.fullline.com
Products: Undecorated garments for the imprinted sportswear industry. SICs: 5136 (Men's/Boys' Clothing); 5137 (Women's/Children's Clothing). Est: 1990. Sales: $78,000,000 (2000). Emp: 280. Officers: Isador Mitzner, CEO; John Hankinson, CFO.

■ 4971 ■ FW Sales
Box 664
Coraopolis, PA 15108
Phone: (724)457-8333 Fax: (724)457-8333
Products: Licensed apparel, including t-shirts, sweat shirts, and ball caps. SICs: 5136 (Men's/Boys' Clothing); 5137 (Women's/Children's Clothing). Est: 1973. Sales: $500,000 (2000).

■ 4972 ■ G-III Apparel Group Ltd.
512 7th Ave.
New York, NY 10018
Phone: (212)629-8830 Fax: (212)967-1487
Products: Leather and non-leather apparel. SICs: 5136 (Men's/Boys' Clothing); 5137 (Women's/Children's Clothing). Sales: $130,600,000 (2000). Emp: 239. Officers: Morris Goldfarb, CEO & President; Alan Feller, Exec. VP & CFO.

■ 4973 ■ Gachassin Inc.
PO Box 9068
New Iberia, LA 70562-9068
Phone: (318)369-7000
Free: (800)737-2986 Fax: (318)364-2493
E-mail: gach@mail.net-connect.net
Products: Men's and boys' sportswear; Men's and boys' uniforms; Men's and boys' work clothing. SIC: 5136 (Men's/Boys' Clothing). Est: 1963. Emp: 28. Officers: Richard Gachassin, CEO & Owner.

■ 4974 ■ Gallagher Industrial Laundry
151 McQuiston Dr.
Battle Creek, MI 49015-1076
Phone: (616)965-5171 Fax: (616)965-2810
Products: Men's and boy's clothing, including sportswear, work clothing, and uniforms; Entrance mats. SICs: 5136 (Men's/Boys' Clothing); 5023 (Homefurnishings). Officers: Ronald Gallagher, President.

■ 4975 ■ Gamco Manufacturing Co.
PO Box 964
422 Industrial Dr.
Jamestown, TN 38556
Phone: (931)879-9712 Fax: (931)879-9724
Products: Women's clothing. SIC: 5137 (Women's/Children's Clothing). Est: 1985. Sales: $3,600,000 (2000). Emp: 135. Officers: Hollis D. Gammon, President; Troy D. Gammon, Vice President.

■ 4976 ■ Garan, Inc.
115 Dorsky St.
Adamsville, TN 38310-2412
Phone: (901)632-3321 Fax: (901)632-3298
Products: Casual clothing for boys. SIC: 5136 (Men's/Boys' Clothing). Sales: $10,000,000 (2000). Emp: 200. Officers: Fred Watson.

■ 4977 ■ Garment District Inc.
200 Broadway
Cambridge, MA 02139-1944
Phone: (617)876-5230 Fax: (617)547-8477
Products: Men's and boys' clothing. SIC: 5136 (Men's/Boys' Clothing). Officers: Karen Friedman, President.

■ **4978** ■ **Susan Garment Inc.**
5601 Collins Ave., Apt. 1701
Miami Beach, FL 33140-2451
Phone: (305)272-6661 **Fax:** (305)272-9890
Products: Women's dresses. **SIC:** 5137
(Women's/Children's Clothing). **Emp:** 70. **Officers:**
Jesse Rich.

■ **4979** ■ **H.K. Garmirian Company Inc.**
20 Jones St.
New Rochelle, NY 10801
Phone: (914)645-0300 **Fax:** (914)654-0300
Products: Clothing. **SICs:** 5136 (Men's/Boys'
Clothing); 5137 (Women's/Children's Clothing). **Sales:**
$3,000,000 (2000). **Emp:** 20. **Officers:** Edwin
Garmirian, President; Paul Garmirian, Dir. of Marketing.

■ **4980** ■ **Garpac Corp.**
462 Seventh Ave.
New York, NY 10018
Phone: (212)760-0070 **Fax:** (212)564-2635
Products: Apparel; Home furnishings; Shoes. **SICs:**
5137 (Women's/Children's Clothing); 5023
(Homefurnishings); 5139 (Footwear). **Sales:**
$9,600,000 (2000). **Emp:** 54. **Officers:** David Roth,
CEO & President.

■ **4981** ■ **Genny USA Inc.**
650 5th Ave.
New York, NY 10019
Phone: (212)245-4860
Products: Men's and women's sportswear. **SICs:** 5137
(Women's/Children's Clothing); 5136 (Men's/Boys'
Clothing). **Sales:** $20,000,000 (2000). **Emp:** 30.
Officers: Lionel Jassy, CEO.

■ **4982** ■ **Genuine Rose Inc.**
1031 S Broadway, No. 934
Los Angeles, CA 90015-4006
Phone: (213)747-4120 **Fax:** (213)747-4939
Products: Girl's dresses and sportswear. **SIC:** 5137
(Women's/Children's Clothing). **Est:** 1982. **Sales:**
$4,000,000 (2000). **Emp:** 25. **Officers:** John Golshan;
Mike Golshan. **Alternate Name:** Jinelle. **Alternate
Name:** Clique.

■ **4983** ■ **GFT USA Corp.**
11 W 42nd St., 19th Fl.
New York, NY 10036-8002
Phone: (212)265-2788
Products: Women's clothing; Women's and misses'
suits, skirts, and jackets; Jackets; Blouses; Dresses.
SICs: 5137 (Women's/Children's Clothing); 5137
(Women's/Children's Clothing). **Sales:** $400,000,000
(2000). **Emp:** 600. **Officers:** Leopoldo Borzino,
President; John Colalillo, VP of Finance; Mary Ann
Ruggiero, Dir of Personnel.

■ **4984** ■ **S.L. Gilbert Company Inc.**
40 E 34th St.
New York, NY 10156-2031
Phone: (212)686-5145 **Fax:** (212)685-6318
Products: Men's socks. **SIC:** 5136 (Men's/Boys'
Clothing). **Est:** 1923. **Sales:** $10,000,000 (2000). **Emp:**
8. **Officers:** Thomas F. Gilbert, CEO.

■ **4985** ■ **Givenchy Corp.**
19 E 57th St.
New York, NY 10022-2508
Phone: (212)931-2550 **Fax:** (212)931-2558
Products: Men's and women's apparel and
acessories. **SICs:** 5137 (Women's/Children's Clothing);
5136 (Men's/Boys' Clothing). **Sales:** $5,000,000
(2000). **Emp:** 8. **Officers:** Beatrice DuPont, President;
Walter Price, Vice President.

■ **4986** ■ **Glamour Glove Corp.**
44-02 23rd St.
Long Island City, NY 11101-5000
Phone: (718)361-9881 **Fax:** (718)361-0833
Products: Dress and industrial gloves. **SICs:** 5136
(Men's/Boys' Clothing); 5137 (Women's/Children's
Clothing). **Est:** 1954. **Sales:** $1,000,000 (2000). **Emp:**
30. **Officers:** W. Le Bouvier, President.

■ **4987** ■ **H. Glaser and Son Inc.**
PO Box 5977
Holliston, MA 01746
Phone: (508)429-8381 **Fax:** (508)429-5321
Products: Hosiery. **SIC:** 5137 (Women's/Children's
Clothing). **Est:** 1895. **Sales:** $3,900,000 (2000). **Emp:**
12. **Officers:** Milton P. Cohen, CEO & President.

■ **4988** ■ **Glenco Hosiery Mills Inc.**
PO Box 1200
Cowpens, SC 29330-1200
Phone: (864)463-3295 **Fax:** (864)463-3012
Products: Foot socks; Hosiery. **SICs:** 5137
(Women's/Children's Clothing); 5136 (Men's/Boys'
Clothing). **Sales:** $6,000,000 (2000). **Emp:** 125.
Officers: Doug Cohen.

■ **4989** ■ **Glencraft Lingerie Inc.**
38 E 32nd
New York, NY 10016-5591
Phone: (212)689-5990 **Fax:** (212)545-0235
Products: Lingerie. **SIC:** 5137 (Women's/Children's
Clothing). **Sales:** $10,000,000 (2000). **Emp:** 499.
Officers: Harvey Jacobson.

■ **4990** ■ **Glentex Corp.**
417 5th Ave.
New York, NY 10016
Phone: (212)686-4424
Products: Women's accessories. **SIC:** 5137
(Women's/Children's Clothing). **Sales:** $100,000,000
(2000). **Emp:** 100. **Officers:** Alex Coleman, President;
Sid Hirsh, CFO; Henry Wasmuth, Dir. of Marketing;
Robert Staut, Dir. of Systems.

■ **4991** ■ **Glove Wagon Enterprises, Inc.**
705 Knollwood Cir.
Ft. Collins, CO 80524-1585
Phone: (970)490-1316 **Fax:** (970)482-6292
Products: Work gloves; Safety equipment. **SICs:** 5136
(Men's/Boys' Clothing); 5137 (Women's/Children's
Clothing); 5099 (Durable Goods Nec). **Est:** 1984.
Sales: $1,250,000 (2000). **Emp:** 2. **Officers:** Cliff
Buchholz, President.

■ **4992** ■ **Gold Bug**
4999 Oakland
Denver, CO 80239-2719
Phone: (303)371-2535 **Fax:** (303)371-2880
Products: Foot socks; Children's shoes. **SIC:** 5137
(Women's/Children's Clothing). **Sales:** $20,000,000
(2000). **Emp:** 135. **Officers:** William Gold.

■ **4993** ■ **Golden Goose**
39 Main St.
Bar Harbor, ME 04609-1845
Phone: (207)288-9901 **Fax:** (207)288-9901
Products: Men's and boys' clothing; Men's and boys'
work clothing; Children's sportswear; Men's
sportswear; Women's sportswear. **SICs:** 5136
(Men's/Boys' Clothing); 5137 (Women's/Children's
Clothing). **Officers:** David Ropp, Partner.

■ **4994** ■ **Golden Needles Knitting and Glove
Co. Monte Glove Div.**
PO Box 803
Wilkesboro, NC 28697
Phone: (919)667-5102 **Fax:** (919)838-2753
Products: Work gloves and mittens. **SIC:** 5136
(Men's/Boys' Clothing). **Est:** 1909. **Sales:** $8,000,000
(2000). **Emp:** 130. **Officers:** James Tollison, General
Mgr.

■ **4995** ■ **Goldman Brothers Inc.**
PO Box 23345
Honolulu, HI 96823-3345
Products: Children's sportswear; Men's sportswear;
Women's sportswear. **SICs:** 5137 (Women's/Children's
Clothing); 5136 (Men's/Boys' Clothing). **Officers:**
Joseph Yip, President.

■ **4996** ■ **Good Sports Inc.**
PO Box 840
Manchester, CT 06040
Phone: (860)647-0880 **Fax:** (860)647-0104
E-mail: goodsp1@aol.com
URL: http://www.hotleathers.com
Products: Clothing, including jackets and boots;
Leather accessories; Motorcycle gear. **SICs:** 5137
(Women's/Children's Clothing); 5136 (Men's/Boys'
Clothing); 5139 (Footwear). **Est:** 1979. **Emp:** 50.
Officers: Joe Aresco, Customer Service Contact.

■ **4997** ■ **Goodman Knitting Company Inc.**
300 Manley St.
Brockton, MA 02303
Phone: (508)588-7200
Products: Women's and men's apparel. **SICs:** 5136
(Men's/Boys' Clothing); 5137 (Women's/Children's
Clothing). **Est:** 1929. **Sales:** $36,000,000 (2000). **Emp:**
100. **Officers:** P. Goodman, President; B. Sylvetsky,
CFO.

■ **4998** ■ **Goulds Sports Textiles Inc.**
220 E Lafayette St.
Lagrange, IN 46761-1907
Phone: (219)463-7506 **Fax:** (219)463-4231
Products: Screen-printed clothing. **SICs:** 5137
(Women's/Children's Clothing); 5136 (Men's/Boys'
Clothing). **Officers:** Joe Gould, President.

■ **4999** ■ **Graham Sporting Goods Burlington**
2535 S Church St.
Burlington, NC 27215-5203
Phone: (910)226-5574 **Fax:** (910)226-5575
Products: Men's and boys' clothing. **SIC:** 5136
(Men's/Boys' Clothing). **Officers:** Earl Harrison,
Partner.

■ **5000** ■ **Gramex Corp.**
11966 St. Charles Rock Rd.
Bridgeton, MO 63044
Phone: (314)739-8300 **Fax:** (314)739-0023
Products: Clothing; Food; Electrical products. **SICs:**
5136 (Men's/Boys' Clothing); 5137
(Women's/Children's Clothing); 5149 (Groceries &
Related Products Nec); 5063 (Electrical Apparatus &
Equipment). **Est:** 1954. **Sales:** $170,000,000 (2000).
Emp: 1,400. **Officers:** Tom W. Holley, Chairman of the
Board; Fred Rudolph, CFO; Cathy Rancillo, Dir. of
Information Systems; Jane Gaitsch, Dir of Human
Resources.

■ **5001** ■ **Great American Wearhouse**
6750-H Jones Mill Ct.
Norcross, GA 30092
Phone: (404)447-4660
Free: (800)241-1151 **Fax:** (404)368-0316
Products: Men's sportswear; Children's sportswear;
Women's sportswear. **SICs:** 5136 (Men's/Boys'
Clothing); 5137 (Women's/Children's Clothing). **Emp:**
14. **Officers:** Gary Crouse.

■ **5002** ■ **Great Graphic Originals**
1297 McD Dr.
Dover, DE 19901
Phone: (302)734-7600
Free: (800)338-4018 **Fax:** (302)734-8394
E-mail: ggoltd@aol.com
URL: http://www.ggoltd.com
Products: Resort apparel and silk screened apparel.
SICs: 5137 (Women's/Children's Clothing); 5136
(Men's/Boys' Clothing). **Est:** 1978. **Emp:** 6. **Officers:**
Marsha Holler, President, e-mail: mrsaland@aol.com.

■ **5003** ■ **Greenwood Mills Inc.**
PO Box 1017
Greenwood, SC 29648
Phone: (864)229-2571 **Fax:** (864)229-1111
Products: Denim clothing. **SICs:** 5136 (Men's/Boys'
Clothing); 5137 (Women's/Children's Clothing). **Est:**
1889. **Sales:** $10,000,000 (2000). **Emp:** 335. **Officers:**
Jerry Hynche.

■ **5004** ■ **Gruner & Company, Inc.**
1350 Avenue Of The Americas, Ste. 804
New York, NY 10019-4702
Phone: (212)868-1484 **Fax:** (212)868-2008
Products: Raincoats and other waterproof outerwear.
SICs: 5136 (Men's/Boys' Clothing); 5137
(Women's/Children's Clothing). **Emp:** 49.

■ **5005** ■ **GSL Enterprises Inc.**
3113 Olu St.
Honolulu, HI 96816-1425
Phone: (808)735-1800 **Fax:** (808)735-7611
Products: Women's clothing. **SIC:** 5137

(Women's/Children's Clothing). **Officers:** Jeanie Chun, President.

■ **5006** ■ **The Guild**
2634 Georgia Ave. NW
Washington, DC 20001-3852
Phone: (202)745-0417 **Fax:** (202)790-0643
Products: T-shirts; Sweatshirts. **SICs:** 5136 (Men's/Boys' Clothing); 5137 (Women's/Children's Clothing). **Officers:** Alphonso Stanley, President.

■ **5007** ■ **Gulf Coast Sportswear Inc.**
PO Box 1498
Lake Jackson, TX 77566
Phone: (409)297-7552 **Fax:** (409)297-7355
Products: Men's and women's sportswear. **SICs:** 5136 (Men's/Boys' Clothing); 5137 (Women's/Children's Clothing). **Est:** 1974. **Sales:** $180,000,000 (2000). **Emp:** 500. **Officers:** Samuel T. McKnight, President; Randy Hale, VP & CFO; Eric Cuevas, Dir. of Information Systems.

■ **5008** ■ **Gussoff-Reslow & Associates**
250 Spring St. NW, Ste. 12N104B
Atlanta, GA 30303-1101
Phone: (404)221-0261 **Fax:** (404)524-7626
Products: Women's and children's clothing. **SIC:** 5137 (Women's/Children's Clothing). **Officers:** Barry Gussoff, President.

■ **5009** ■ **HA-LO**
3628 Walnut Hills Rd.
Cleveland, OH 44122
Phone: (216)292-2595 **Fax:** (216)292-4691
Products: Custom printed apparel; Ad specialty items. **SICs:** 5136 (Men's/Boys' Clothing); 5137 (Women's/Children's Clothing). **Officers:** John Herman, Managing Executive. **Former Name:** Ha-Lo Marketing.

■ **5010** ■ **Ha-Lo Marketing**
3628 Walnut Hills Rd.
Cleveland, OH 44122
Phone: (216)292-2595 **Fax:** (216)292-4691
Products: Clothing. **SIC:** 5136 (Men's/Boys' Clothing). **Sales:** $425,000,000 (2000). **Emp:** 12.

■ **5011** ■ **Haas Outdoors Inc.**
PO Box 757
West Point, MS 39773
Phone: (601)494-8859 **Fax:** (601)494-8879
Products: Camouflage clothing. **SIC:** 5136 (Men's/Boys' Clothing). **Est:** 1986. **Sales:** $10,000,000 (2000). **Emp:** 60. **Officers:** Toxey Haas, President.

■ **5012** ■ **Habitat Softwear**
PO Box 2086
Montrose, CO 81402
Phone: (970)249-3333 **Fax:** (970)249-0328
Products: Prints on T-shirts, sweatshirts and mugs; Embroidered garments. **SICs:** 5136 (Men's/Boys' Clothing); 5199 (Nondurable Goods Nec). **Officers:** Dean Rampy, CFO.

■ **5013** ■ **Hagale Industries Inc.**
601 E South St.
Ozark, MO 65721
Phone: (417)581-2351 **Fax:** (417)581-6092
Products: Clothing, including men's casual wear and sportswear; Women's and children's clothing. **SICs:** 5136 (Men's/Boys' Clothing); 5137 (Women's/Children's Clothing). **Sales:** $30,000,000 (2000). **Emp:** 1,000. **Officers:** James A. Hagale.

■ **5014** ■ **David Hamilton Inc.**
250 Spring St.
Atlanta, GA 30303
Phone: (404)681-2752
Products: Children's clothing. **SIC:** 5137 (Women's/Children's Clothing).

■ **5015** ■ **Hana Hou Corp.**
PO Box 3174
Honolulu, HI 96801-3174
Phone: (808)533-1944
Products: Men's, women's, and children's clothing, including uniforms. **SICs:** 5136 (Men's/Boys' Clothing); 5137 (Women's/Children's Clothing). **Officers:** Timothy Ching, President.

■ **5016** ■ **Pat Hanley Sales Inc.**
PO Box 1035
Fergus Falls, MN 56538-1035
Phone: (218)736-6958
Products: Men's and boys' clothing; Men's and boys' sportswear; Men's and boys' work clothing. **SIC:** 5136 (Men's/Boys' Clothing). **Officers:** Pat Hanley, President.

■ **5017** ■ **Happy Feet Plus**
18837 U.S 19 N
Clearwater, FL 33764
Phone: (813)539-7006
Free: (800)336-6657 **Fax:** (813)539-8550
Products: Shoes. **SIC:** 5139 (Footwear).

■ **5018** ■ **Happy Shirts Inc.**
1320 Liona St.
Honolulu, HI 96814-2352
Phone: (808)949-7575 **Fax:** (808)955-1017
Products: Women's and children's clothing, including sportswear and swimsuits. **SIC:** 5137 (Women's/Children's Clothing). **Officers:** Gulab Watumull, President.

■ **5019** ■ **Happy Valley Clothing Co.**
PO Box 168
Glen Arm, MD 21057-0168
Phone: (410)592-3500
Free: (800)787-7897 **Fax:** (410)592-3502
Products: Men's, women's and children's collegiate licensed clothing; Embroidered sportswear. **SICs:** 5137 (Women's/Children's Clothing); 5136 (Men's/Boys' Clothing). **Est:** 1985. **Sales:** $1,400,000 (1999). **Emp:** 6. **Officers:** Alan Woodman, President; Alicia Stewart, Sales & Marketing Contact.

■ **5020** ■ **J.M. Hardin Clothing Co. Inc.**
PO Box 138
Calhoun City, MS 38916-0138
Phone: (601)628-5311 **Fax:** (601)628-5311
Products: Women's and children's clothing. **SIC:** 5137 (Women's/Children's Clothing). **Officers:** John Hardin, President.

■ **5021** ■ **Hawaii ID Apparel**
930-C Austin Ln.
Honolulu, HI 96817
Phone: (808)848-5400 **Fax:** (808)841-2195
Products: Hawaiian print apparel and accessories. **SICs:** 5137 (Women's/Children's Clothing); 5136 (Men's/Boys' Clothing). **Est:** 1985. **Sales:** $750,000 (2000). **Emp:** 7. **Officers:** Hiro Furukawa.

■ **5022** ■ **Hawkins Fabrics**
111 Woodside Ave.
Gloversville, NY 12078
Phone: (518)773-9550 **Fax:** (518)773-9551
Products: Gloves. **SICs:** 5136 (Men's/Boys' Clothing); 5137 (Women's/Children's Clothing). **Sales:** $7,000,000 (2000). **Emp:** 100. **Officers:** J.F. Batty, President; Deb Wilde, Sales/Marketing Contact.

■ **5023** ■ **Hecht Manufacturing Co.**
8645 N Dean Cir.
River Hills, WI 53217-2038
Phone: (414)271-4650 **Fax:** (414)271-5277
Products: Skirts and jackets. **SIC:** 5137 (Women's/Children's Clothing). **Sales:** $3,000,000 (2000). **Emp:** 150. **Officers:** Richard Hecht, President; Marlene Hecht, Vice President.

■ **5024** ■ **Heikkinen Productions Inc.**
1410 W Michigan Ave.
Ypsilanti, MI 48197-5129
Phone: (734)485-4020
Products: Men's and boys' clothing; Men's and boys' sportswear; Men's and boys' work clothing; Shirts; Caps. **SIC:** 5136 (Men's/Boys' Clothing). **Officers:** Dan Heikkinen, President.

■ **5025** ■ **Hellam Hosiery Company Inc.**
198 Beaver St.
Hellam, PA 17406
Phone: (717)755-3831
Products: Women's and misses' hosiery; Men's hosiery. **SICs:** 5137 (Women's/Children's Clothing); 5136 (Men's/Boys' Clothing). **Sales:** $1,000,000 (2000). **Emp:** 50. **Officers:** Harry M. Gaubert.

■ **5026** ■ **Helman Corporation**
PO Box 56387
Atlanta, GA 30343-0387
Phone: (404)688-8231
Free: (800)682-8231 **Fax:** (404)584-5882
Products: Women's clothing. **SIC:** 5137 (Women's/Children's Clothing). **Officers:** Arnold Helman, President.

■ **5027** ■ **Henig Furs Inc.**
4135 Carmichael Rd.
Montgomery, AL 36106-3668
Phone: (205)277-7610 **Fax:** (205)272-3562
Products: Women's and children's clothing, including outerwear and fur clothing. **SIC:** 5137 (Women's/Children's Clothing). **Officers:** Michael Henig, President.

■ **5028** ■ **Henry Doneger Associates Inc.**
463 7th Ave.
New York, NY 10018
Phone: (212)564-1266
Products: Men's, women's, and children's apparel. **SICs:** 5136 (Men's/Boys' Clothing); 5137 (Women's/Children's Clothing). **Sales:** $15,000,000 (1994). **Emp:** 150. **Officers:** Abby Doneger, President; Frank Mercurio, Finance Officer.

■ **5029** ■ **Herman's Inc.**
PO Box 4748
Rock Island, IL 61204
Phone: (309)788-9568
Free: (800)447-1295 **Fax:** (309)786-8296
Products: Men's, boy's, and women's apparel. **SICs:** 5136 (Men's/Boys' Clothing); 5137 (Women's/Children's Clothing). **Est:** 1952. **Emp:** 40.

■ **5030** ■ **Highland Laundry Co.**
504-506 Pleasant St.
Holyoke, MA 01040
Phone: (413)534-7391
Free: (800)323-DUST **Fax:** (413)534-7444
URL: http://www.highlandlaundry.com
Products: Men's and boys' clothing; Men's and boys' sportswear; Men's and boys' work clothing; Uniform and mat rental service. **SIC:** 5136 (Men's/Boys' Clothing). **Est:** 1919. **Emp:** 35. **Officers:** Richard Lucchesi, President, e-mail: rlucchesi@highlandlaundry.com.

■ **5031** ■ **Highland Mills Inc.**
PO Box 33775
Charlotte, NC 28233
Phone: (704)375-3333 **Fax:** (704)342-0391
E-mail: highland@highlandmills.com
URL: http://www.highlandmills.com
Products: Ladies' and children's hosiery. **SIC:** 5137 (Women's/Children's Clothing). **Sales:** $47,000,000 (2000). **Emp:** 499. **Officers:** Saul Wojnowich. **Former Name:** Admiration Hosiery Mill.

■ **5032** ■ **Tommy Hilfiger USA Inc.**
25 W 39th St.
New York, NY 10018
Phone: (212)840-8888
Products: Men's sportswear. **SIC:** 5136 (Men's/Boys' Clothing). **Sales:** $501,000,000 (2000). **Emp:** 1,000. **Officers:** Edwin H. Lewis, CEO & Chairman of the Board; Steven A. Sorrillo, Sr. VP & CFO.

■ **5033** ■ **Holoubek Inc.**
W 238 N 1800
Waukesha, WI 53188-1198
Phone: (414)547-0500
Free: (800)558-0566 **Fax:** (414)547-5847
Products: T-shirts; Sweatshirts. **SIC:** 5136 (Men's/Boys' Clothing). **Est:** 1962. **Emp:** 150. **Officers:** Verne Holoubek, President; Jeffrey S. Witkowski, VP & General Mgr.

■ **5034** ■ **Honey Bee Fashions**
3912 S Broadway Pl.
Los Angeles, CA 90037
Phone: (213)231-3333 **Fax:** (213)231-0406
Products: Girls' clothing. **SIC:** 5137 (Women's/Children's Clothing). **Est:** 1978. **Emp:** 49. **Officers:** Mike Fraga.

■ **5035** ■ **Honey Fashions Ltd.**
417 5th Ave.
New York, NY 10016
Phone: (212)686-4424
Products: Women's apparel accessories. **SIC:** 5137
(Women's/Children's Clothing). **Sales:** $33,000,000
(2000). **Emp:** 100. **Officers:** Norman Elowitz,
President.

■ **5036** ■ **Hoosier Screen Printer Inc.**
6336 Travis Rd.
Greenwood, IN 46143-8625
Phone: (317)422-8231 **Fax:** (317)422-8231
Products: Contract printers. **SIC:** 5136 (Men's/Boys'
Clothing). **Officers:** Larry Knotts, President.

■ **5037** ■ **Horizon Impex**
430 Armor Cir. NE
Atlanta, GA 30324
Phone: (404)892-5544
Free: (800)822-2411 **Fax:** (404)724-0099
Products: Clothing. **SIC:** 5136 (Men's/Boys' Clothing).
Sales: $4,000,000 (2000). **Emp:** 4.

■ **5038** ■ **Hosiery Sales Inc.**
10 E 34th St.
New York, NY 10016
Phone: (212)889-2220 **Fax:** (212)889-5730
Products: Socks and hosiery. **SICs:** 5136
(Men's/Boys' Clothing); 5137 (Women's/Children's
Clothing). **Est:** 1958. **Sales:** $10,000,000 (2000). **Emp:**
100. **Officers:** Alan Stocknoff, President; Sonya
Vargas, Controller.

■ **5039** ■ **Host Apparel Inc.**
1430 Broadway
New York, NY 10018
Phone: (212)302-0800 **Fax:** (212)302-8570
Products: Men's pajamas, robes, and loungewear.
SIC: 5136 (Men's/Boys' Clothing). **Est:** 1959. **Sales:**
$87,000,000 (2000). **Emp:** 100. **Officers:** Howard F.
Cohen, President; Al Bomzer, Finance Officer; S.
Stephen Gould, Exec. VP, e-mail: steveg@
hostpj.usa.com.

■ **5040** ■ **House of Bianchi Inc.**
181 Canal St.
Lawrence, MA 01840-1802
Phone: (781)391-6111 **Fax:** (781)391-7447
Products: Bridal fashion. **SIC:** 5137
(Women's/Children's Clothing). **Sales:** $15,000,000
(2000). **Emp:** 250. **Officers:** Phylis Bianchi Lange.

■ **5041** ■ **I Play**
6 Chiles Ave.
Asheville, NC 28803
Phone: (704)254-9236 **Fax:** (704)258-9052
Products: Children's clothing. **SIC:** 5137
(Women's/Children's Clothing). **Est:** 1982. **Sales:**
$3,000,000 (2000). **Emp:** 16. **Officers:** Becky Cannon,
President. **Former Name:** Family Clubhouse, Inc.

■ **5042** ■ **IIRI International Inc.**
120 Webster St.
Pawtucket, RI 02861-1086
Phone: (401)272-8600 **Fax:** (401)273-5482
Products: Women's clothing. **SIC:** 5137
(Women's/Children's Clothing). **Est:** 1967. **Sales:**
$1,200,000 (2000). **Emp:** 6. **Officers:** Jagdish C.
Sachdev, President.

■ **5043** ■ **Ilani Shoes Ltd.**
47 W 34th St.
New York, NY 10001
Phone: (212)947-5830 **Fax:** (212)947-2319
Products: Shoes. **SIC:** 5139 (Footwear). **Sales:**
$5,000,000 (2000). **Emp:** 6.

■ **5044** ■ **Imar Industries Inc.**
13108 Greenwood Rd.
Minnetonka, MN 55343-8693
Phone: (612)938-2352 **Fax:** (612)938-3881
Products: Women's clothing accessories. **SIC:** 5137
(Women's/Children's Clothing). **Officers:** Paul Krause,
President.

■ **5045** ■ **Imex Corp.**
4846 Cranswick
Houston, TX 77041
Phone: (713)467-6899 **Fax:** (713)460-4815
Products: Men's, women's, and children's clothing,
including knit sweaters and pants. **SICs:** 5137
(Women's/Children's Clothing); 5136 (Men's/Boys'
Clothing). **Sales:** $5,000,000 (2000). **Emp:** 25.
Officers: C. Kuri, President; J. Olson, Controller.

■ **5046** ■ **Impo International Inc.**
PO Box 639
Santa Maria, CA 93456
Phone: (805)922-7753
Free: (800)367-4676 **Fax:** (805)925-0450
E-mail: webmaster@impo.com
Products: Women's fashion shoes. **SIC:** 5139
(Footwear). **Est:** 1969. **Officers:** Eric Kieler, President.

■ **5047** ■ **Imports Wholesale**
3900 Paradise Rd., Ste. V
Las Vegas, NV 89109-0930
Phone: (702)369-1040 **Fax:** (702)369-6454
Products: Men's and boys' clothing; Footwear. **SICs:**
5136 (Men's/Boys' Clothing); 5139 (Footwear).
Officers: Sam Mastroiannis, President.

■ **5048** ■ **India Hand Arts**
150 W Queen Ln.
PO Box 12271
Philadelphia, PA 19144-0371
Phone: (215)848-4040 **Fax:** (215)849-1234
URL: http://www.c-me.com/indiahandarts
Products: Women's clothing; Beachwear. **SIC:** 5137
(Women's/Children's Clothing). **Est:** 1970. **Emp:** 2.
Officers: Chuck Gupta, Owner, e-mail: cgupta@
worldnet.att.net.

■ **5049** ■ **Indiana Tees**
7260 Winton Dr.
Indianapolis, IN 46268
Phone: (317)387-8600
Free: (800)767-9696 **Fax:** (317)387-8601
Products: Apparel, including t-shirts, fleece, and
casual wear. **SICs:** 5137 (Women's/Children's
Clothing); 5136 (Men's/Boys' Clothing).

■ **5050** ■ **Industrial Uniform Company Inc.**
906 E Waterman St.
Wichita, KS 67202-4732
Phone: (316)264-2871 **Fax:** (316)264-2708
E-mail: uniform@southernind.net
Products: Uniforms; Corporate casual wear;
Promotional products. **SICs:** 5136 (Men's/Boys'
Clothing); 5137 (Women's/Children's Clothing). **Est:**
1938. **Emp:** 18. **Officers:** Anthony J. Taravella,
President; David L. Murfin, Chairman.

■ **5051** ■ **Infant To Teen Headwear**
112 W 34th St.
New York, NY 10120-0093
Phone: (212)564-7196 **Fax:** (212)564-7199
Products: Hats; Gloves and mittens. **SIC:** 5137
(Women's/Children's Clothing). **Emp:** 49.

■ **5052** ■ **InSport International Inc.**
1870 NW 173rd Ave.
Beaverton, OR 97006
Phone: (503)645-3552
Free: (800)652-5200 **Fax:** (503)629-9455
Products: Men's and women's activewear—bicycling
and running apparel. **SICs:** 5136 (Men's/Boys'
Clothing); 5137 (Women's/Children's Clothing). **Sales:**
$17,000,000 (2000). **Emp:** 45. **Officers:** Eric E. Merk,
President.

■ **5053** ■ **Intercontinental Importers Inc.**
PO Box 411
Southfield, MI 48037
Phone: (248)355-1770 **Fax:** (248)355-3873
Products: Men's and boys' apparel. **SIC:** 5136
(Men's/Boys' Clothing). **Est:** 1950. **Sales:** $10,000,000
(2000). **Emp:** 10. **Officers:** M.H. Rose, President &
Treasurer.

■ **5054** ■ **Intercontinental Industries**
710 Kakoi St.
Honolulu, HI 96819-2016
Phone: (808)836-1595 **Fax:** (808)833-5370
Products: General merchandise, including unisex T-
shirts. **SICs:** 5136 (Men's/Boys' Clothing); 5137
(Women's/Children's Clothing). **Officers:** Harry
Kaneta, Chairman of the Board.

■ **5055** ■ **Interknit Inc.**
645 Harrison St., 4th Fl.
San Francisco, CA 94107
Phone: (415)882-4680
Products: Knit clothing. **SIC:** 5137
(Women's/Children's Clothing). **Est:** 1994. **Sales:**
$3,000,000 (2000). **Emp:** 5. **Officers:** Sandra Lee,
President; John Ying, Controller.

■ **5056** ■ **Intermountain Lea Findings Co.**
1064 East 300 South
Salt Lake City, UT 84102-2513
Phone: (801)355-3737
Free: (800)658-8798 **Fax:** (801)521-4362
Products: Shoes. **SIC:** 5139 (Footwear). **Sales:**
$400,000 (2000). **Emp:** 4.

■ **5057** ■ **International Imports Inc.**
38741 Long St.
Harrison Township, MI 48045-2140
Phone: (248)349-8900
Products: Clothing, including shirts, shorts, hats, and
fleecewear. **SICs:** 5136 (Men's/Boys' Clothing); 5137
(Women's/Children's Clothing).

■ **5058** ■ **International Industries Inc.**
915 Hartford Tpke.
Shrewsbury, MA 01545-4148
Phone: (508)842-0393 **Fax:** (508)842-2344
Products: Men's clothing, including sportswear and
work clothing. **SIC:** 5136 (Men's/Boys' Clothing).
Officers: Chu Chun, President.

■ **5059** ■ **International Male**
741 F St.
San Diego, CA 92101
Phone: (619)544-9900 **Fax:** (619)544-9302
Products: Men's clothing. **SIC:** 5136 (Men's/Boys'
Clothing).

■ **5060** ■ **International Marketing Association
Ltd.**
10821 Lakeview
Lenexa, KS 66219-1327
Phone: (913)599-5995
Free: (800)321-1098 **Fax:** (913)599-2288
Products: Men's and unisex clothing. **SICs:** 5136
(Men's/Boys' Clothing); 5137 (Women's/Children's
Clothing). **Est:** 1982. **Emp:** 20. **Officers:** Steve
Robertson, CEO; A. Jerwidi, Sales/Marketing Contact.

■ **5061** ■ **International Waters**
989 Ave. of the Americas, 15th Fl.
New York, NY 10018-5410
Phone: (212)564-3099
Products: Men's, women's and children's sportswear.
SICs: 5136 (Men's/Boys' Clothing); 5137
(Women's/Children's Clothing). **Sales:** $10,000,000
(1993). **Emp:** 6. **Officers:** Don Wechsler, President;
Chandresa Mehta, Vice Chairman of the Board.

■ **5062** ■ **Intimate Fashions Inc.**
PO Box 375
Woodmere, NY 11598-0375
Phone: (212)686-1530
Products: Lingerie. **SIC:** 5137 (Women's/Children's
Clothing). **Est:** 1947. **Sales:** $13,000,000 (2000). **Emp:**
213. **Officers:** B. Segan, President; Judith Segan, VP
of Finance; Moshe Einav, VP of Marketing.

■ **5063** ■ **Island Snow Hawaii Inc.**
PO Box 364
Kailua, HI 96734-0364
Phone: (808)926-1815 **Fax:** (808)926-1817
Products: Men's and women's clothing. **SICs:** 5136
(Men's/Boys' Clothing); 5137 (Women's/Children's
Clothing). **Officers:** James Kodama, President.

■ 5064 ■ **Island Tee Shirt Sales Inc.**
29-D Hunter Rd.
Hilton Head Island, SC 29926-3715
Phone: (803)681-4133
Free: (800)338-0797 **Fax:** (803)689-2239
Products: Imprinted sportswear; Embroidered products, including sportswear, headwear, and towels. **SICs:** 5136 (Men's/Boys' Clothing); 5137 (Women's/Children's Clothing). **Est:** 1986. **Emp:** 20. **Officers:** John Calamari, President.

■ 5065 ■ **Ital Fashion Inc.**
1307 Santee
Los Angeles, CA 90015-2524
Phone: (213)748-8164 **Fax:** (213)748-9770
Products: Apparel, including dresses, pants, and suits. **SICs:** 5137 (Women's/Children's Clothing); 5136 (Men's/Boys' Clothing). **Emp:** 49.

■ 5066 ■ **Items Galore Inc.**
PO Box 1828
Warren, MI 48090-1828
Phone: (810)774-4800 **Fax:** (810)774-9711
SIC: 5137 (Women's/Children's Clothing). **Officers:** Larry Stevens, President.

■ 5067 ■ **ITI Interamericana Trade Inc.**
9201 SW 76 Ter.
Miami, FL 33173
Phone: (305)596-6288 **Fax:** (305)596-6388
Products: Clothing. **SIC:** 5136 (Men's/Boys' Clothing).

■ 5068 ■ **Ivars Sportswear Inc.**
PO Box 2449
Burlington, NC 27216-2449
Phone: (910)227-9683 **Fax:** (910)226-6330
Products: Men's and boys' clothing; Women's clothing; Girls' clothing. **SICs:** 5137 (Women's/Children's Clothing); 5136 (Men's/Boys' Clothing). **Officers:** Bennett Sapp, President.

■ 5069 ■ **Izod Lacoste**
200 Madison Ave.
New York, NY 10016-3903
Phone: (212)502-0349
Products: Men's sportswear, including shirts and jackets. **SIC:** 5136 (Men's/Boys' Clothing). **Est:** 1933. **Sales:** $140,000,000 (2000). **Emp:** 200. **Officers:** Bob Cosky, President; Pam Buck, Dir of Personnel.

■ 5070 ■ **J & B Wholesale Co.**
39 Grovers
Winthrop, MA 02152
Phone: (617)846-2188 **Fax:** (617)539-3470
Products: Used clothing. **SICs:** 5136 (Men's/Boys' Clothing); 5137 (Women's/Children's Clothing). **Officers:** Bill Passaro, General Mgr.

■ 5071 ■ **J & M Sportswear Inc.**
PO Box 23550
Shawnee Mission, KS 66223-0550
Phone: (913)897-5400
Free: (800)345-7379 **Fax:** (913)897-5448
Products: Men's and boys' clothing; Men's and boys' sportswear; Men's and boys' work clothing. **SIC:** 5136 (Men's/Boys' Clothing). **Officers:** Mike Mitchell, President.

■ 5072 ■ **J.A. Apparel Corp.**
650 5th Ave., 27th Fl.
New York, NY 10019
Phone: (212)586-9140
Products: Men's and women's clothing. **SICs:** 5136 (Men's/Boys' Clothing); 5137 (Women's/Children's Clothing). **Sales:** $27,000,000 (1991). **Emp:** 40. **Officers:** Joseph Abboud, President.

■ 5073 ■ **Jack's Tack International Distributors**
12607 Southeastern Ave.
Indianapolis, IN 46259-1151
Phone: (317)862-6842
Products: Women's English riding apparel and equine needs; Veterinary products and instruments. **SICs:** 5137 (Women's/Children's Clothing); 5091 (Sporting & Recreational Goods). **Officers:** Jack Sievers, President.

■ 5074 ■ **Jackster Inc.**
670 Surf Ave.
Stratford, CT 06497-6733
Phone: (203)378-4023
Free: (800)225-8370 **Fax:** (203)378-4605
Products: Belts, suspenders, handkerchiefs, and bandanas. **SIC:** 5136 (Men's/Boys' Clothing). **Est:** 1981.

■ 5075 ■ **Jansport Inc.**
PO Box 1817
Appleton, WI 54913
Phone: (920)734-5708
Free: (800)346-8239 **Fax:** (920)831-2372
Products: Printing on garments and apparel accessories; Embroideries. **SICs:** 5136 (Men's/Boys' Clothing); 5137 (Women's/Children's Clothing). **Est:** 1967. **Sales:** $50,000,000 (2000). **Emp:** 350. **Officers:** Paul Delany, President; N. J. Erickson, VP of Finance & CFO; Paul Delorey, President.

■ 5076 ■ **Jantzen Inc.**
101 Mountainview Dr.
Seneca, SC 29678
Phone: (864)882-3393 **Fax:** (864)882-0716
Products: Women's sportswear. **SIC:** 5137 (Women's/Children's Clothing). **Emp:** 550.

■ 5077 ■ **JCG Corp.**
501 Mokauea St. B
Honolulu, HI 96819-3232
Phone: (808)841-1882 **Fax:** (808)847-8818
Products: Unisex clothing. **SICs:** 5136 (Men's/Boys' Clothing); 5137 (Women's/Children's Clothing). **Officers:** Gordon Lau, President.

■ 5078 ■ **JCS Enterprises, Inc.**
99-061 Koaha Way
Aiea, HI 96701
Phone: (808)488-6195 **Fax:** (808)486-5742
Products: Screen printer and embroidery; Unisex t-shirts; Children's t-shirts; Caps. **SICs:** 5137 (Women's/Children's Clothing); 5136 (Men's/Boys' Clothing). **Officers:** Carmen Scelsa, President. **Doing Business As:** Sportcap/Rivaltees.

■ 5079 ■ **JDK Enterprises Inc.**
3948 Forest Oaks Ln.
Mebane, NC 27302-9625
Phone: (919)563-5068 **Fax:** (919)563-4182
E-mail: jdk@mebtel.net
Products: Clothing. **SICs:** 5136 (Men's/Boys' Clothing); 5137 (Women's/Children's Clothing). **Est:** 1978. **Sales:** $5,000,000 (2000). **Emp:** 30. **Officers:** David Scott, President, e-mail: dscott@mebtel.net.

■ 5080 ■ **Jefferies Socks**
PO Box 1680
Burlington, NC 27216-1680
Phone: (336)226-7315
Free: (800)334-6831 **Fax:** (336)226-8217
E-mail: jeffsock@netpath.net
Products: Socks. **SIC:** 5136 (Men's/Boys' Clothing). **Est:** 1937. **Emp:** 55. **Officers:** Kenneth M. Hamby, President.

■ 5081 ■ **Jelina International Ltd.**
530 7th Ave.
New York, NY 10018
Phone: (212)827-0228
Products: Women's, men's, and children's clothing. **SICs:** 5137 (Women's/Children's Clothing); 5136 (Men's/Boys' Clothing).

■ 5082 ■ **Jen-Mar Ltd.**
498 7th Ave.
New York, NY 10018
Phone: (212)594-3118 **Fax:** (212)594-2089
Products: Clothing. **SICs:** 5137 (Women's/Children's Clothing); 5136 (Men's/Boys' Clothing). **Est:** 1978. **Sales:** $11,500,000 (2000). **Emp:** 3. **Officers:** Jenny Collins, President; Marty Dennis, Vice President. **Former Name:** J.C.M.D. Inc.

■ 5083 ■ **Jewel and Co.**
9601 Apollo Dr.
Largo, MD 20774
Phone: (301)925-6200
Free: (800)638-8583 **Fax:** (301)925-6201
Products: Custom T-shirt screen printing. **SICs:** 5137 (Women's/Children's Clothing); 5136 (Men's/Boys' Clothing). **Sales:** $37,000,000 (2000). **Emp:** 103. **Officers:** Gary Gocken, VP of Finance.

■ 5084 ■ **Jim's Formal Wear Co.**
1 Tuxedo Park
Trenton, IL 62293
Phone: (618)224-9211 **Fax:** (618)224-7924
Products: Formal wear. **SIC:** 5136 (Men's/Boys' Clothing). **Sales:** $18,000,000 (2000). **Emp:** 220. **Officers:** Gary Davis, President; Kevin Litteken, VP of Finance.

■ 5085 ■ **JK Miami Corp.**
27000 NW 5th Ave., Ste. 13
Miami, FL 33127-4144
Phone: (305)576-1578 **Fax:** (305)576-4166
Products: Costume jewelry and costume novelties; Women's handbags and purses; Women's full-length and knee-length hosiery; Apparel belts; Underwear. **SICs:** 5137 (Women's/Children's Clothing); 5136 (Men's/Boys' Clothing). **Emp:** 49. **Officers:** Jae Wung.

■ 5086 ■ **JK Sports**
1801 W Lincoln Ave.
Fergus Falls, MN 56537
Phone: (218)739-5299 **Fax:** (218)739-9135
Products: Jackets, clothing, including sportswear. **SICs:** 5136 (Men's/Boys' Clothing); 5136 (Men's/Boys' Clothing). **Est:** 1987. **Sales:** $2,000,000 (2000). **Emp:** 25. **Officers:** John Klinnert, Owner.

■ 5087 ■ **JM/Ontario Tees**
847 S Wanamaker
Ontario, CA 91761
Phone: (909)390-0711
Free: (800)447-7794 **Fax:** (909)390-0719
Products: Men's sportswear; Women's sportswear. **SICs:** 5136 (Men's/Boys' Clothing); 5137 (Women's/Children's Clothing).

■ 5088 ■ **JMR Inc.**
9775 SW Commerce Cir., 3C
Wilsonville, OR 97070-9602
Phone: (503)682-1416 **Fax:** (503)682-5832
Products: Men's and boy's clothing, including screen printed and embroidered apparel. **SIC:** 5136 (Men's/Boys' Clothing). **Officers:** James Rogers, President.

■ 5089 ■ **JNT Corporation**
PO Box 1125
Newport News, VA 23601-0125
Phone: (757)599-0916
Free: (800)368-1011 **Fax:** (757)599-0860
Products: Women's clothing. **SIC:** 5137 (Women's/Children's Clothing). **Officers:** Theodore Goldfarb, President.

■ 5090 ■ **Johnson and Company Wilderness Products Inc.**
PO Box 2009
Bangor, ME 04402
Phone: (207)862-3373 **Fax:** (207)862-2267
Products: Cold weather and outdoor clothing. **SICs:** 5136 (Men's/Boys' Clothing); 5137 (Women's/Children's Clothing). **Sales:** $2,000,000 (2000). **Emp:** 10. **Officers:** Kenneth Johnson, President.

■ 5091 ■ **Johnson Garment Corp.**
3115 S Maple Ave.
PO Box 603
Marshfield, WI 54449-0603
Phone: (715)384-5272
Free: (800)274-5272 **Fax:** (715)384-4378
E-mail: jgc@commplusis.net
URL: http://www.johnsongarment.com
Products: Industrial and hunting outerwear. **SICs:** 5136 (Men's/Boys' Clothing); 5137 (Women's/Children's Clothing). **Est:** 1908. **Sales:** $3,000,000 (2000). **Emp:** 49. **Officers:** James S. Johnson, President.

■ 5092 ■ **Jones Sportswear Company Inc.**
1630 2nd Ave. S
Birmingham, AL 35233-1705
Phone: (205)326-6264
Free: (800)762-0719 **Fax:** (205)324-9647
E-mail: jsports@worldnet.att.net
URL: http://www.jonesportswear.com
Products: Men's and boy's clothing, including shirts, golf shirts, caps and jackets. **SIC:** 5136 (Men's/Boys' Clothing). **Est:** 1979. **Sales:** $5,000,000 (2000). **Emp:** 43. **Officers:** Bobby Jones, President.

■ 5093 ■ **Susan Brese Jones**
110 E Main St.
Thomaston, GA 30286-2920
Phone: (706)647-2178
Products: Adult's and children's sportswear; Athletic apparel. **SICs:** 5137 (Women's/Children's Clothing); 5136 (Men's/Boys' Clothing). **Officers:** Susie Jones, Owner.

■ 5094 ■ **Jordan Fashions Corp.**
1385 Broadway
New York, NY 10018-6002
Phone: (212)921-5560 **Fax:** (212)719-5975
Products: Bridesmaids and formal dresses. **SIC:** 5137 (Women's/Children's Clothing). **Sales:** $1,000,000 (2000). **Emp:** 49. **Officers:** Mariano Giordano.

■ 5095 ■ **Leslie Jordan Inc.**
1230 SW 1st Ave.
Portland, OR 97204-3234
Phone: (503)295-1987 **Fax:** (503)295-1989
Products: Men's, women's, and children's outerwear. **SICs:** 5137 (Women's/Children's Clothing); 5136 (Men's/Boys' Clothing). **Officers:** Leslie Jordan, President.

■ 5096 ■ **Jo's Designs**
PO Box 1930
Zephyr Cove, NV 89448-1930
Phone: (702)588-3100 **Fax:** (702)544-2811
Products: Printing on garments and apparel accessories; Commission embroidering. **SICs:** 5136 (Men's/Boys' Clothing); 5137 (Women's/Children's Clothing). **Officers:** David Sakas, President.

■ 5097 ■ **Joyce-Munden Co.**
PO Box 25025
Winston-Salem, NC 27114-5025
Phone: (336)765-0234
Free: (800)334-8752 **Fax:** (336)659-0200
E-mail: sales@joyce-munden.com
URL: http://www.joyce-munden.com
Products: Shirts, including t-shirts and sportshirts; Fleecewear; Jackets; Caps; Towels; Infant wear; Bags; Aprons; Underwear. **SICs:** 5136 (Men's/Boys' Clothing); 5137 (Women's/Children's Clothing). **Est:** 1947. **Sales:** $5,000,000 (2000). **Emp:** 15. **Officers:** Thomas C. Munden Jr., President.

■ 5098 ■ **Joyce Sportswear Co.**
1400 Calcutta Ln.
Naperville, IL 60563-2215
Phone: (630)883-9681 **Fax:** (630)882-9733
Products: Women's sportswear. **SIC:** 5137 (Women's/Children's Clothing). **Sales:** $25,000,000 (2000). **Emp:** 275. **Officers:** Raymond Cell.

■ 5099 ■ **JP Associates**
488 7th Ave., 4th Fl.
New York, NY 10018
Phone: (212)563-6663
Products: Women's clothing. **SIC:** 5137 (Women's/Children's Clothing).

■ 5100 ■ **JT Racing Inc.**
515 Otay Valley Rd.
Chula Vista, CA 91911-6059
Phone: (619)421-2660 **Fax:** (619)421-8160
Products: Sports apparel. **SICs:** 5136 (Men's/Boys' Clothing); 5137 (Women's/Children's Clothing). **Emp:** 99. **Officers:** John R. Gregory.

■ 5101 ■ **Karumit Associates Ltd.**
PO Box 11831
Winston-Salem, NC 27116
Phone: (336)765-8989 **Fax:** (336)765-9487
Products: Children's clothing and shoes; Women's lingerie. **SICs:** 5136 (Men's/Boys' Clothing); 5137 (Women's/Children's Clothing). **Est:** 1972. **Sales:** $1,345,000 (2000). **Emp:** 2. **Officers:** Hans R. Mittemeijer, President.

■ 5102 ■ **Kauai Screen Print**
3116 Houlako St.
Lihue, HI 96766-1432
Phone: (808)245-5123 **Fax:** (808)245-8730
Products: Screen print t-shirts. **SICs:** 5137 (Women's/Children's Clothing); 5136 (Men's/Boys' Clothing). **Officers:** Steve Hirano, Partner.

■ 5103 ■ **Kaufenberg Enterprises**
4301 S Valley View Blvd., Ste. 11
Las Vegas, NV 89103-4007
Phone: (702)891-0054 **Fax:** (702)894-8380
Products: Plain T-shirts. **SICs:** 5136 (Men's/Boys' Clothing); 5137 (Women's/Children's Clothing). **Emp:** 15.

■ 5104 ■ **Kays Enterprises Inc.**
13127 Trinity St.
Stafford, TX 77477-4297
Phone: (713)780-0808
Free: (800)848-5700 **Fax:** (713)780-0452
Products: T-shirts; Men's and boys' sportswear; Women's sportswear. **SICs:** 5136 (Men's/Boys' Clothing); 5137 (Women's/Children's Clothing). **Emp:** 38.

■ 5105 ■ **KBC Bargain Center Inc.**
4201 N Old State Rd. 3
Muncie, IN 47303-9512
Phone: (765)284-1000 **Fax:** (765)741-8857
Products: Clothing. **SICs:** 5136 (Men's/Boys' Clothing); 5137 (Women's/Children's Clothing). **Est:** 1977. **Emp:** 39. **Officers:** Richard Irwin, President. **Doing Business As:** Off Price World.

■ 5106 ■ **KD Sales Associates**
59 Bean Rd.
Merrimack, NH 03054-2406
Phone: (603)429-1298
Products: Clothing. **SICs:** 5136 (Men's/Boys' Clothing); 5137 (Women's/Children's Clothing). **Officers:** Kenneth De Cosmo, Partner.

■ 5107 ■ **Keddie Kreations of California**
11367 Sunrise Gold Cir., Ste. C-D
Rancho Cordova, CA 95742
Phone: (916)635-0113
Free: (888)338-1955 **Fax:** (916)635-8470
E-mail: keddie@cwnet.com
Products: Women's and men's tennis apparel. **SICs:** 5137 (Women's/Children's Clothing); 5136 (Men's/Boys' Clothing). **Est:** 1965. **Sales:** $1,000,000 (2000). **Emp:** 22. **Officers:** Barbara Keddie.

■ 5108 ■ **Kentucky Derby Hosiery**
314 S South St.
PO Box 987
Mt. Airy, NC 27030-4450
Phone: (919)786-4134 **Fax:** (919)786-4134
Products: Hosiery. **SIC:** 5137 (Women's/Children's Clothing). **Sales:** $14,000,000 (2000). **Emp:** 265. **Officers:** Bill Nichol. **Former Name:** Lynne Hosiery Mills Inc.

■ 5109 ■ **Kenwil Sales**
362 Industrial Park Rd.
Madisonville, TN 37354-6133
Phone: (423)442-3954
Products: Women's and misses' dresses. **SIC:** 5137 (Women's/Children's Clothing). **Est:** 1971. **Sales:** $3,000,000 (2000). **Emp:** 35. **Officers:** W. McConkey, CEO.

■ 5110 ■ **King Louie International Inc.**
13500 15th St.
Grandview, MO 64030-3000
Phone: (816)765-5212 **Fax:** (816)765-3228
Products: Women's clothing; Men's and boys' clothing. **SICs:** 5136 (Men's/Boys' Clothing); 5137 (Women's/Children's Clothing). **Emp:** 1,000.

■ 5111 ■ **Kiri Trading Co. Ltd.**
815 Myrtle Ave.
Natchez, MS 39120
Phone: (601)442-3388 **Fax:** (601)442-3811
Products: Men's and boys' clothing; Women's and children's clothing; Lumber, plywood, and millwork; Construction materials; Sporting and recreational goods. **SICs:** 5136 (Men's/Boys' Clothing); 5137 (Women's/Children's Clothing); 5091 (Sporting & Recreational Goods); 5031 (Lumber, Plywood & Millwork); 5039 (Construction Materials Nec). **Officers:** Patrick H. Mulvihill, President.

■ 5112 ■ **Jennifer Sly Kirk Artclothes**
648 E Huron St.
Milford, MI 48381
Phone: (248)684-7374
Products: Clothing. **SIC:** 5131 (Piece Goods & Notions).

■ 5113 ■ **Klear-Knit Sales Inc.**
64 Post Rd., W
Westport, CT 06880
Phone: (203)221-8650 **Fax:** (203)222-7331
Products: Men's, women's, and boys' knits and woven clothing. **SICs:** 5136 (Men's/Boys' Clothing); 5137 (Women's/Children's Clothing). **Est:** 1979. **Sales:** $10,000,000 (2000). **Emp:** 8. **Officers:** Joseph Sweedler, President.

■ 5114 ■ **Kolon America Inc.**
350 5th Ave., No. 5211
New York, NY 10118-0110
Phone: (212)736-0120
Products: Men's clothing; Women's blouses; Sneakers; Leather coats. **SICs:** 5136 (Men's/Boys' Clothing); 5137 (Women's/Children's Clothing); 5139 (Footwear). **Est:** 1950. **Sales:** $22,000,000 (2000). **Emp:** 20. **Officers:** I.Y. Ro, President; Gary Lim, CFO.

■ 5115 ■ **Kombi Ltd.**
102 Great Hill Rd.
Naugatuck, CT 06770
Phone: (203)723-7441
Free: (800)243-6117 **Fax:** (203)723-4980
URL: http://www.kswiss.com
Products: Gloves and mittens; Outerwear (ski and snowsuits, pants, etc.). **SICs:** 5136 (Men's/Boys' Clothing); 5137 (Women's/Children's Clothing). **Est:** 1972. **Sales:** $15,000,000 (2000). **Emp:** 25.

■ 5116 ■ **Kory Mercantile Company**
148 N Morley Ave.
Nogales, AZ 85621-3116
Phone: (520)287-2550 **Fax:** (520)287-5950
Products: Women's and children's clothing and accessories. **SIC:** 5137 (Women's/Children's Clothing).

■ 5117 ■ **L & L Shirt Shop**
5620 Fairview Ave.
Boise, ID 83706-1167
Phone: (208)376-8881 **Fax:** (208)376-0229
Products: Men's and boys' clothing; Men's and boys' shirts. **SIC:** 5136 (Men's/Boys' Clothing). **Officers:** Lyle Shockey, Owner.

■ 5118 ■ **L.A. Glo**
1662 S Long Beach Ave.
Los Angeles, CA 90021
Phone: (213)746-4140 **Fax:** (213)955-2004
Products: Special occasion dresses, including formal, prom, evening, and wedding gowns. **SIC:** 5137 (Women's/Children's Clothing).

■ 5119 ■ **L.A. T Sportswear Inc.**
PO Box 926
Canton, GA 30114
Phone: (770)479-1877 **Fax:** (770)479-4078
Products: Undecorated garments for the imprinted sportswear industry. **SICs:** 5136 (Men's/Boys' Clothing); 5137 (Women's/Children's Clothing). **Sales:** $72,600,000 (2000). **Emp:** 356. **Officers:** Isador E. Mitzner, CEO & Chairman of the Board; John F. Hankinson, CFO & Treasurer.

■ 5120 ■ **Lanahan Sales**
10325 SW 57th Pl.
Portland, OR 97219-5704
Phone: (503)244-6451 **Fax:** (503)245-7224
Products: Shoes. **SIC:** 5139 (Footwear). **Sales:** $1,000,000 (2000). **Emp:** 2.

■ 5121 ■ **Lanz Inc.**
8680 Hayden Pl.
Culver City, CA 90232
Phone: (310)558-0200 **Fax:** (310)558-0342
Products: Women's sleepwear, dresses, and sportswear. **SIC:** 5137 (Women's/Children's Clothing). **Est:** 1938. **Sales:** $30,000,000 (2000). **Emp:** 150. **Officers:** Alexis Scharff, President; R. Laret, Controller; Christopher Scharff, Dir. of Marketing; Robert Fiddler, Dir. of Information Systems; Jackie La Fave-Perkins, Dir of Human Resources.

■ 5122 ■ **LAT Sportswear, Inc.**
1200 Airport Dr.
Ball Ground, GA 30107
Phone: (404)409-8999
Free: (800)432-0802 **Fax:** 800-432-0799
E-mail: fldmark@fullline.com
URL: http://www.fullline.com
Products: Women's fashions, including tops, coverups, and tank tops; Infant and toddler imprintable active wear; Youth apparel; Undecorated garments for the imprinted sportswear industry. **SIC:** 5137 (Women's/Children's Clothing). **Est:** 1955. **Emp:** 173. **Officers:** David Keller, President. **Doing Business As:** Full-Line Distributors.

■ 5123 ■ **Ralph Lauren Hosiery Div.**
1 Rockefeller Plz.
New York, NY 10020-2002
Phone: (212)957-2000
Products: Socks and hosiery. **SIC:** 5137 (Women's/Children's Clothing).

■ 5124 ■ **LaVayne Distributors**
457 W Line St.
Calhoun, GA 30701
Phone: (706)625-4959
Products: Shirts and short sets for toddlers. **SIC:** 5137 (Women's/Children's Clothing).

■ 5125 ■ **Paul Lavitt Mills Inc.**
PO Box 1507
Hickory, NC 28602
Phone: (704)328-2463 **Fax:** (704)328-5908
Products: Socks. **SICs:** 5137 (Women's/Children's Clothing); 5136 (Men's/Boys' Clothing). **Sales:** $10,000,000 (2000). **Emp:** 145. **Officers:** Paul Lavitt; Arthur Lavitt.

■ 5126 ■ **The Leather Shop**
411 N Marion St., Ste. 1
Lake City, FL 32055
Phone: (904)752-7591 **Fax:** (904)752-4604
Products: Leather belts; Novelty items, including trucker wallets, buckles and key chains. **SICs:** 5136 (Men's/Boys' Clothing); 5137 (Women's/Children's Clothing); 5199 (Nondurable Goods Nec). **Officers:** Fred J. Lammers, Sales/Marketing Contact.

■ 5127 ■ **Legal Sportswear**
1450 Broadway
New York, NY 10018-2201
Phone: (212)398-2222
Products: Men's sportswear. **SIC:** 5136 (Men's/Boys' Clothing). **Sales:** $7,000,000 (2000). **Emp:** 20. **Officers:** Leo Zelkin, President.

■ 5128 ■ **Les Appel for Rex Lester Inc.**
127 E 9th St.
Los Angeles, CA 90015
Phone: (213)629-4539
Products: Men's and women's clothing, including sportswear. **SICs:** 5136 (Men's/Boys' Clothing); 5137 (Women's/Children's Clothing). **Sales:** $4,000,000 (2000). **Emp:** 4. **Officers:** Les Appel, President.

■ 5129 ■ **Richard A. Leslie Company Inc.**
7 Corporate Dr.
Orangeburg, NY 10962-2615
Phone: (914)359-5200
Free: (800)284-4445 **Fax:** (914)365-1456
E-mail: birdiejkt@aol.com
URL: http://www.birdiejackets.com
Products: Team sports jackets. **SICs:** 5136 (Men's/Boys' Clothing); 5137 (Women's/Children's Clothing). **Est:** 1946. **Emp:** 181. **Officers:** Lou Solomon; Robert Solomon; Eric Solomon, Customer Service Contact; Kenneth Solomon, Sales/Marketing Contact. **Alternate Name:** Birdie Jackets.

■ 5130 ■ **Letters N Logos Inc.**
3375 SW 182nd Ave.
Beaverton, OR 97006-3939
Phone: (503)642-1420
Products: Men's and boy's clothing, including sportswear, work clothing, and uniforms. **SIC:** 5136 (Men's/Boys' Clothing). **Officers:** Lisa Hilde, President.

■ 5131 ■ **Levi's Womenswear**
1411 Broadway
New York, NY 10018-3403
Phone: (212)354-5970 **Fax:** (212)704-3277
Products: Women's apparel. **SIC:** 5137 (Women's/Children's Clothing). **Emp:** 49.

■ 5132 ■ **Levoy's**
2511 S Temple W
Salt Lake City, UT 84115
Phone: (801)481-7300
Products: Women's white speciality dresses; Lingerie; Streetwear. **SIC:** 5137 (Women's/Children's Clothing). **Est:** 1960. **Sales:** $2,000,000 (2000). **Emp:** 80. **Officers:** J. Sorenson, CEO; J. Larson, CFO; Carol Browning, Dir. of Marketing.

■ 5133 ■ **Frank Levy Inc.**
Denver Merchandise Mart
451 E 58th Ave.
Denver, CO 80216
Phone: (303)295-2286 **Fax:** (303)649-9431
Products: Women's coats. **SIC:** 5137 (Women's/Children's Clothing). **Est:** 1967. **Emp:** 1.

■ 5134 ■ **Lewis Manufacturing Co.**
PO Box 190
Woodland, NC 27897
Phone: (919)587-5221 **Fax:** (919)587-2654
Products: Unisex sportswear. **SICs:** 5137 (Women's/Children's Clothing); 5136 (Men's/Boys' Clothing). **Sales:** $2,000,000 (2000). **Emp:** 60. **Officers:** Ed Lewis. **Former Name:** Daber Inc.

■ 5135 ■ **Livingston Apparel Inc.**
North Industrial Park
Livingston, AL 35470
Phone: (205)652-9566 **Fax:** (205)652-6119
Products: Apparel. **SICs:** 5136 (Men's/Boys' Clothing); 5137 (Women's/Children's Clothing). **Sales:** $1,600,000 (2000). **Emp:** 130. **Officers:** Alan Bolonkin; Bobby Young.

■ 5136 ■ **Liz and Co.**
1441 Broadway
New York, NY 10018
Phone: (212)354-4900
Products: Women's casual knit sportswear. **SIC:** 5137 (Women's/Children's Clothing). **Sales:** $84,000,000 (2000). **Emp:** 20. **Officers:** Kathryn L. White, VP & General Merchandising Mgr.

■ 5137 ■ **Loco Boutique**
150 Kaiulani Ave.
Honolulu, HI 96815-3247
Phone: (808)922-7160 **Fax:** (808)922-7160
Products: Women's swimsuits. **SIC:** 5137 (Women's/Children's Clothing). **Officers:** Michael Fieman, President.

■ 5138 ■ **Locoli Inc.**
9119 Wicker Ave.
PO Box 401
St. John, IN 46373-0401
Phone: (219)365-3125
Products: Men's and boys' clothing; Men's and boys' sportswear; Men's and boys' work clothing. **SIC:** 5136 (Men's/Boys' Clothing). **Officers:** John Collet, President.

■ 5139 ■ **Logo Apparel**
5301 Everhart Rd.
Corpus Christi, TX 78411
Phone: (512)855-7127
Products: Shirts. **SIC:** 5131 (Piece Goods & Notions).

■ 5140 ■ **Logo Designs**
5301 Everhart Rd.
Corpus Christi, TX 78411
Phone: (512)851-9560
Products: Shirts. **SIC:** 5131 (Piece Goods & Notions).

■ 5141 ■ **Logo-Wear Inc.**
717 W Freeport St.
Broken Arrow, OK 74012-2406
Phone: (918)251-2140 **Fax:** (918)258-0992
Products: Promotional products. **SICs:** 5136 (Men's/Boys' Clothing); 5199 (Nondurable Goods Nec). **Est:** 1983. **Emp:** 7. **Officers:** David Beinke, President.

■ 5142 ■ **Longwear Hosiery Mill**
PO Box 525
Hildebran, NC 28637-0525
Phone: (704)324-6430 **Fax:** (704)324-6430
Products: Socks. **SICs:** 5136 (Men's/Boys' Clothing); 5137 (Women's/Children's Clothing). **Sales:** $2,000,000 (2000). **Emp:** 30. **Officers:** Wayne Mosteller, President & Treasurer; Jeff Musteller, VP & Secty.

■ 5143 ■ **Loveline Industries Inc.**
385 Gerard Ave.
Bronx, NY 10451
Phone: (212)402-3500 **Fax:** (718)402-3408
Products: Raincoats and other waterproof outerwear; Vests; Prison clothing. **SICs:** 5136 (Men's/Boys' Clothing); 5137 (Women's/Children's Clothing). **Est:** 1933. **Sales:** $1,000,000 (2000). **Emp:** 35. **Officers:** M. Goldstein.

■ 5144 ■ **L.A. Loving**
409 W 78th St.
Bloomington, MN 55420
Phone: (612)888-8227
Free: (800)328-5927 **Fax:** (612)888-8706
Products: Imprintables. **SICs:** 5136 (Men's/Boys' Clothing); 5137 (Women's/Children's Clothing). **Officers:** Bryant S. Loving, CEO; Dick Ward, CFO; Dennis Loving, Vice President. **Former Name:** Loving & Associates Inc.

■ 5145 ■ **Lozars Total Screen Design**
PO Box 520
Polson, MT 59860-0239
Phone: (406)883-9218 **Fax:** (406)883-9253
E-mail: tsd@cyberport.net
Products: Men's, women's, and children's clothing, including sportswear, swimsuits, t-shirts, and sweatshirts; Embroidery. **SICs:** 5137 (Women's/Children's Clothing); 5136 (Men's/Boys' Clothing). **Est:** 1957. **Sales:** $500,000 (2000). **Emp:** 11. **Officers:** Stephen Lozar, President.

■ 5146 ■ **Lucia Inc.**
PO Box 12129
Winston-Salem, NC 27107-3500
Phone: (919)788-4901 **Fax:** (919)784-9148
Products: Ladies' sportswear. **SIC:** 5137 (Women's/Children's Clothing). **Sales:** $32,000,000 (2000). **Emp:** 600. **Officers:** Hans Pfohe.

■ 5147 ■ **LW Bristol Collection**
PO Box 3397
Bristol, TN 37620
Phone: (423)968-7777 **Fax:** (423)968-2177
Products: Embroidery for T-shirts and sweatshirts; Jewelry; Glassware; Ceramics; Table linens; Hats; Sterling silver pins and charms; Pendants and earrings. **SICs:** 5136 (Men's/Boys' Clothing); 5137 (Women's/Children's Clothing); 5094 (Jewelry & Precious Stones); 5023 (Homefurnishings). **Officers:** Verlin Smith, Manager.

■ 5148 ■ LWR Inc.
2323 Memorial Ave.
Lynchburg, VA 24501-2650
Phone: (804)528-2726 Fax: (804)847-2001
Products: Clothing. SIC: 5136 (Men's/Boys' Clothing).
Sales: $3,000,000 (2000). Emp: 12.

■ 5149 ■ M & M Wholesale
336 Willis St.
Batesburg, SC 29006
Phone: (803)532-3101
Products: Apparel and accessories. SICs: 5137
(Women's/Children's Clothing); 5136 (Men's/Boys'
Clothing). Officers: Marvin H. Aull.

■ 5150 ■ Mad Bomber Co.
134 Windy Hill Ln., W2-1
Winchester, VA 22602
Phone: (540)662-8840
Free: (800)662-8845 Fax: (540)667-2540
Products: Clothing. SIC: 5137 (Women's/Children's
Clothing).

■ 5151 ■ Madaris Hosiery Mill
1451 14th Ave. NE
Hickory, NC 28601-2729
Phone: (704)322-6841 Fax: (704)322-4041
Products: Underwear; Foot socks. SICs: 5137
(Women's/Children's Clothing); 5136 (Men's/Boys'
Clothing). Sales: $3,500,000 (2000). Emp: 55.
Officers: Bill Huffman; David Huffman.

■ 5152 ■ Mahan Western Industries, Inc.
11333 Rojas Dr.
El Paso, TX 79936
Free: (800)767-1024
Products: Western boots and apparel. SICs: 5136
(Men's/Boys' Clothing); 5139 (Footwear). Emp: 49.
Officers: Craig Schaffer, President.

■ 5153 ■ Ray Maier Sporting Goods Inc.
914 Main St.
PO Box 1027
Duncan, OK 73534-1027
Phone: (580)255-7412
Free: (800)252-7412 Fax: (580)255-5511
E-mail: maier@cottoninternet.net
URL: http://www.raymeier.com
Products: Industrial clothing; Safety boots; Luggage
and brief cases. SICs: 5137 (Women's/Children's
Clothing); 5136 (Men's/Boys' Clothing); 5139
(Footwear). Est: 1955. Sales: $1,000,000 (2000).
Emp: 6. Officers: Ray Maier, President, e-mail:
rmaier@cottoninternet.net.

■ 5154 ■ Majestic Glove Inc.
14660 NE N Woodinville Way, Ste. 100
Woodinville, WA 98072
Phone: (425)486-1606
Free: (800)FOR-GLOV Fax: (425)486-5080
E-mail: info@majglove.com
URL: http://www.majglove.com
Products: Work gloves; Welding clothing. SIC: 5136
(Men's/Boys' Clothing). Est: 1978. Sales: $8,000,000
(2000). Emp: 12. Officers: H. Kruiniger, President.

■ 5155 ■ Malco Modes Inc.
1596 Howard St.
San Francisco, CA 94103
Phone: (415)621-0840 Fax: (415)431-3699
Products: Women's clothing, including bridal
garments, square dance attire, and undergarments.
SIC: 5137 (Women's/Children's Clothing). Sales:
$4,000,000 (2000). Emp: 80. Officers: Albert C.
Malouf; James Baba, Sales/Marketing Contact.

■ 5156 ■ Manchester Manufacturing
Acquisitions Inc.
Gould St. Business Pk
Colebrook, NH 03576
Phone: (603)237-8383 Fax: (603)237-8386
Products: Women's, children's clothing and
accesories. SIC: 5137 (Women's/Children's Clothing).
Sales: $1,000,000 (1992). Emp: 10. Officers: Felix
Weingart Jr., VP of Finance.

■ 5157 ■ Manchester Manufacturing Inc.
8 Gould St.
Colebrook, NH 03576-0119
Phone: (603)237-8383
Products: Men's and boy's clothing. SIC: 5136
(Men's/Boys' Clothing). Officers: Felix Weingart,
President.

■ 5158 ■ Manhattan-Miami Corp.
5019 NW 165 St.
Hialeah, FL 33014
Phone: (305)628-3630 Fax: (305)628-3821
Products: Clothing. SIC: 5136 (Men's/Boys' Clothing).
Sales: $1,000,000 (2000). Emp: 99.

■ 5159 ■ Manhattan Shirt Company-Winnsboro
Distribution Center
321 By-pass
Winnsboro, SC 29180
Phone: (803)635-4671
Products: Men's and women's clothing. SICs: 5136
(Men's/Boys' Clothing); 5137 (Women's/Children's
Clothing). Officers: D.J. Weed, Manager.

■ 5160 ■ Manifatture Associate Cashmere USA
Inc.
745 5th Ave., Ste. 1225
New York, NY 10151
Phone: (212)753-7015 Fax: (212)753-7055
Products: Fine knitwear-made in Italy. SICs: 5136
(Men's/Boys' Clothing); 5137 (Women's/Children's
Clothing). Est: 1984. Sales: $15,000,000 (2000). Emp:
30. Officers: Luigi Leonardi, Exec. VP; Lawrence
Marchuck, Treasurer & CFO. Doing Business As:
MAC USA.

■ 5161 ■ Edward H. Manz, Jr.
2230 McCallie Ave.
Chattanooga, TN 37404-3203
Phone: (423)698-1081 Fax: (423)698-1650
Products: Pantyhose and socks. SIC: 5137
(Women's/Children's Clothing). Est: 1948. Emp: 7.
Officers: Edward Manz, Owner.

■ 5162 ■ Marco Polo Import & Export
2685 S Dayton Way, Ste. 82
Denver, CO 80231-3972
Phone: (303)695-8782 Fax: (303)695-6737
Products: Men's, women's, and children's clothing.
SICs: 5137 (Women's/Children's Clothing); 5136
(Men's/Boys' Clothing). Est: 1985. Sales: $800,000
(2000). Emp: 130. Officers: Eduardo Naude, Owner,
e-mail: enaude@uswest.net.

■ 5163 ■ R.B. Marco and Sons
609 W Flagler St.
Miami, FL 33130
Phone: (305)324-8308
Products: Hosiery. SIC: 5137 (Women's/Children's
Clothing).

■ 5164 ■ Marian Group Corp.
PO Box 51898
Lafayette, LA 70505-1898
Phone: (318)233-9996 Fax: (318)233-9990
Products: Men's and boys' clothing; Men's and boys'
sportswear. SIC: 5136 (Men's/Boys' Clothing).
Officers: Mike Mahtook, President.

■ 5165 ■ Marketing Success
PO Box 2182
Ketchum, ID 83340-2182
Phone: (208)726-9728 Fax: (208)726-9747
Products: Men's and boys' clothing; Men's and boys'
scarves; Men's and boys' gloves; Men's and boys' hats.
SIC: 5136 (Men's/Boys' Clothing). Officers: Mike
Thompson, Owner.

■ 5166 ■ Markos Wholesale Clothing
Distributors
127-129 S 3rd
La Crosse, WI 54601-3264
Phone: (608)784-8224 Fax: (608)784-8224
E-mail: shishmee@hotmail.com
Products: Men's and boys' clothing, including work
clothing, gloves, outerwear, underwear, sleepwear, and
uniforms; Footwear, including athletic footwear;
Blankets; Hunting equipment; Domestics;. SICs: 5136
(Men's/Boys' Clothing); 5023 (Homefurnishings); 5139

(Footwear). Est: 1901. Emp: 5. Officers: Richard E.
Markos; Gregory C. Markos.

■ 5167 ■ Marlboro Footworks Ltd.
60 Austin St.
Newton, MA 02460
Phone: (617)969-7070 Fax: (617)244-7463
Products: Shoes. SIC: 5139 (Footwear).

■ 5168 ■ Marlenes Inc.
669 Hogan Rd.
Bangor, ME 04401-3605
Phone: (207)945-9813
Free: (800)244-9813 Fax: (207)945-9813
Products: Women's and children's clothing, including
uniforms for restaurants, hotel, doctors, dentists,
nurses, and industrial wear. SIC: 5137
(Women's/Children's Clothing). Est: 1959. Sales:
$500,000 (2000). Emp: 7. Officers: Marlene D.
Thomas, President.

■ 5169 ■ Marlin Custom Embroidery
5230 Kostoryz Rd., No. 19
Corpus Christi, TX 78415
Phones: (512)854-0906 (361)854-0906
Products: Monogrammed clothing. SIC: 5131 (Piece
Goods & Notions). Est: 1991.

■ 5170 ■ Mary Fashion Manufacturing
Company Inc.
380 W Main St.
Bath, PA 18014
Phone: (610)837-6763 Fax: (215)837-6458
Products: Clothing, including women's and children's
sportswear. SIC: 5137 (Women's/Children's Clothing).
Sales: $5,000,000 (2000). Emp: 225. Officers:
Umberto Fantozzi.

■ 5171 ■ Maryland Industrial Inc.
28 Alco Pl.
Baltimore, MD 21227-2004
Phone: (410)247-9117 Fax: (410)247-3461
Products: Shoes. SIC: 5139 (Footwear). Sales:
$1,900,000 (2000). Emp: 8.

■ 5172 ■ Massachusetts Export Corp.
PO Box 823
Worcester, MA 01613-0823
Phone: (508)752-5496
Products: Men's and boys' clothing. SIC: 5136
(Men's/Boys' Clothing).

■ 5173 ■ Massive Graphic Screen Printing
2895 Broce Dr.
Norman, OK 73072-2405
Phone: (405)364-3594 Fax: (405)364-4162
Products: Men's and boy's clothing, sportswear, and
work clothing; Screenprinted garments. SIC: 5136
(Men's/Boys' Clothing). Officers: Kent Johnson,
President.

■ 5174 ■ Maui and Sons Corp.
PO Box 1251
Pacific Palisades, CA 90272-1251
Phone: (310)573-9499 Fax: (310)573-9477
E-mail: mauiandsons@earthlink.net
Products: Clothing; Sporting goods, including
skateboards, inline skates, and shoes. SIC: 5136
(Men's/Boys' Clothing). Est: 1980. Sales:
$100,000,000 (1999). Officers: Richard Harrington,
CEO & President.

■ 5175 ■ Mauney Hosiery Mills Inc.
PO Box 1279
Kings Mountain, NC 28086
Phone: (704)739-3621 Fax: (704)734-0608
Products: Foot socks; Hosiery. SICs: 5137
(Women's/Children's Clothing); 5136 (Men's/Boys'
Clothing). Est: 1939. Sales: $10,000,000 (1999). Emp:
200. Officers: W.K. Mauney Jr., Chairman of the
Board; Eddie Mauney, Treasurer; W.K. Mauney III,
President; David Faunce, VP of Sales; Debbie
Johnson, Customer Service Contact; Rita Lawing,
Human Resources Contact.

■ 5176 ■ Max Nitzberg Inc.
11800 NW 102nd Rd.
Medley, FL 33178
Phone: (305)883-8677 Fax: (305)888-1365
Products: Children's apparel. SIC: 5137
(Women's/Children's Clothing). Est: 1974. Sales:
$40,000,000 (2000). Emp: 50. Officers: Mark
Nitzberg, President; Maurice Aniel, CFO, e-mail:
maurice@topsville.com; Lori Nitzberg, Sales.

■ 5177 ■ McCubbin Hosiery Inc.
3B93 Apparel Mart
PO Box 585577
Dallas, TX 75258
Phone: (214)637-5224 Fax: (214)630-4078
Products: Children's hosiery. SIC: 5137
(Women's/Children's Clothing). Est: 1946. Sales:
$10,000,000 (2000). Emp: 53. Officers: Mark
McCubbin, Chairman of the Board; David McCubbin,
President.

■ 5178 ■ McCubbin Hosiery Inc.
PO Box 24047
Oklahoma City, OK 73124-0047
Phone: (405)236-8351
Free: (800)654-2301 Fax: (405)236-8389
Products: Women's and children's clothing and
hosiery, including infant's hosiery. SIC: 5137
(Women's/Children's Clothing). Est: 1952. Emp: 30.
Officers: Mark McCubbin, Chairman of the Board;
David McCubbin, President.

■ 5179 ■ McCullar Enterprises Inc.
1850 Gen. George Patton
Franklin, TN 37067
Phone: (615)371-1056
Free: (800)347-7463 Fax: (615)371-1059
Products: Shoes. SIC: 5139 (Footwear).

■ 5180 ■ Mary McFadden Inc.
240 W 35th St.
New York, NY 10001-2506
Phone: (212)736-4078 Fax: (212)239-7259
E-mail: mcfcouture@aol.com
URL: http://www.marymcfaddencouture.com
Products: Women's clothing. SIC: 5137
(Women's/Children's Clothing). Est: 1976. Sales:
$6,800,000 (1999). Emp: 29. Officers: Mary
McFadden, Chairman of the Board; Grant Nichols,
Sales Mgr. Alternate Name: Mary McFadden Couture.

■ 5181 ■ Danny McNutt Hosiery
Box 946
Ft. Payne, AL 35967
Phone: (205)845-4422 Fax: (205)845-4422
Products: Socks. SICs: 5137 (Women's/Children's
Clothing); 5136 (Men's/Boys' Clothing).

■ 5182 ■ Elizabeth Meade Hosiery
PO Box 1031
Burlington, NC 27216-1031
Phone: (919)226-7216 Fax: (919)226-0940
Products: Men's socks. SIC: 5136 (Men's/Boys'
Clothing). Sales: $2,500,000 (2000). Emp: 75.
Officers: Thomas J. Harper.

■ 5183 ■ Meca Sportswear Inc.
Lincoln St.
Ontario, WI 54651
Phone: (608)337-4436 Fax: (608)337-4436
Products: Men's sportswear; Women's sportswear.
SICs: 5136 (Men's/Boys' Clothing); 5137
(Women's/Children's Clothing). Emp: 80.

■ 5184 ■ Melody Gloves Inc.
171 Madison Ave.
New York, NY 10016-5110
Phone: (212)683-6878 Fax: (212)683-6862
E-mail: mgii@redconnect.net
Products: Bridal and dress gloves; Women's, men's,
and boys' gloves. SIC: 5137 (Women's/Children's
Clothing). Est: 1954. Emp: 4. Officers: M. Cohen,
President.

■ 5185 ■ Merit Marketing Inc.
5773 Arrowhead Dr., Ste. 204
Virginia Beach, VA 23462-3203
Phone: (757)490-9396 Fax: (757)473-3477
Products: Men's and boys' clothing; Women's

clothing; Food; Cameras; Stereo equipment. SICs:
5136 (Men's/Boys' Clothing); 5137
(Women's/Children's Clothing); 5141 (Groceries—
General Line); 5043 (Photographic Equipment &
Supplies); 5064 (Electrical Appliances—Television &
Radio). Est: 1976. Sales: $3,500,000 (2000). Emp: 7.
Officers: Jim Butler, President.

■ 5186 ■ Meshekow Brothers Inc.
527 W 7th St., No. 704
Los Angeles, CA 90014
Phone: (213)623-7177 Fax: (213)688-8734
Products: Dressed furs, garments and skins. SIC:
5137 (Women's/Children's Clothing). Est: 1937. Sales:
$2,000,000 (2000). Emp: 6. Officers: Alex Meshekow.

■ 5187 ■ Metro Export and Import Co.
1140 Broadway, Ste. 902
New York, NY 10001
Phone: (212)481-9077 Fax: (212)481-9126
Products: Men's and women's underwear; Bags,
including diaper and gym bags. SICs: 5137
(Women's/Children's Clothing); 5136 (Men's/Boys'
Clothing); 5199 (Nondurable Goods Nec).

■ 5188 ■ Metro Marketing Co.
PO Box 3031
Woburn, MA 01888
Phone: (781)933-3311 Fax: (781)933-3311
E-mail: srmarks@aol.com
URL: http://www.sexxy.com
Products: Women's and children's clothing, including
lingerie and undergarments. SIC: 5137
(Women's/Children's Clothing). Est: 1975. Sales:
$1,000,000 (2000). Emp: 15. Officers: Marcia
Hetman, Owner.

■ 5189 ■ Meystel Inc.
4666 S Halsted St.
Chicago, IL 60609
Free: (800)888-8999
Products: Sweatshirts; T-shirts. SICs: 5136
(Men's/Boys' Clothing); 5137 (Women's/Children's
Clothing). Est: 1925. Emp: 499. Officers: Isadore
Meystel.

■ 5190 ■ Miami Robes International
19401 W Dixie Hwy.
Miami, FL 33180-2214
Phone: (305)940-3377 Fax: (305)940-5028
Products: Robes and towels. SICs: 5136 (Men's/Boys'
Clothing); 5137 (Women's/Children's Clothing); 5023
(Homefurnishings). Sales: $3,000,000 (2000). Emp: 9.
Officers: Richard Rosenblum, President.

■ 5191 ■ Michigan Glove Company Inc.
12751 Capital St.
Oak Park, MI 48237-3113
Phone: (248)543-6191 Fax: (248)543-9632
Products: Gloves. SICs: 5136 (Men's/Boys' Clothing);
5137 (Women's/Children's Clothing). Officers: Timothy
Johns, President.

■ 5192 ■ Mid Atlantic Accessories
4809 Lindstrom Dr.
Charlotte, NC 28226-7905
Phone: (704)543-1828 Fax: (704)543-0132
Products: Women's clothing accessories. SIC: 5137
(Women's/Children's Clothing). Est: 1973. Officers:
Edward Schaefer, Owner.

■ 5193 ■ Mid-West Golf Inc.
PO Box 404
Westfield, IN 46074-0404
Phone: (317)896-3443
Free: (800)776-3443 Fax: (317)896-9094
Products: Men's and women's sportswear. SICs: 5137
(Women's/Children's Clothing); 5136 (Men's/Boys'
Clothing). Officers: J. Elliott, President.

■ 5194 ■ Midwest Athlete
402 Church St.
Ottumwa, IA 52501-4213
Phone: (515)682-2144
Products: Men's and boys' clothing; Men's and boys'
sportswear; Men's and boys' work clothing. SIC: 5136
(Men's/Boys' Clothing). Officers: Gary Smith, Owner.

■ 5195 ■ Miller Safety Products
1209 Orville Ave.
Kansas City, KS 66102-5114
Phone: (913)321-4955 Fax: (913)321-5661
Products: Shoes. SIC: 5139 (Footwear). Sales:
$95,000,000 (2000). Emp: 7.

■ 5196 ■ Milrank Knitwear Inc.
9731 Sinclair Cir.
Garden Grove, CA 92844-3247
Phone: (213)773-2588 Fax: (213)773-3223
Products: Sweaters. SIC: 5137 (Women's/Children's
Clothing). Est: 1949. Sales: $1,000,000 (2000). Emp:
35. Officers: Martin L. Wolf, President; David Wolf,
CFO; Donald A. Wolf, Dir. of Marketing.

■ 5197 ■ Miss Elliette Inc.
10829 Central Ave.
South El Monte, CA 91733-3309
Phone: (213)585-2222
Products: Mother-of-the-bride dresses. SIC: 5137
(Women's/Children's Clothing). Est: 1954. Sales:
$10,000,000 (2000). Emp: 85. Officers: Robert Ellis,
CEO & CFO.

■ 5198 ■ Mister Remo of California Inc.
1801 Flower Ave.
Duarte, CA 91010-2932
Phone: (626)357-3867 Fax: (626)358-3569
Products: Women's clothing. SIC: 5137
(Women's/Children's Clothing). Sales: $22,000,000
(2000). Emp: 70. Officers: Remo Ciarocchi; Walter
Sinfield; Bob Birkle.

■ 5199 ■ Mole Hole
7309 W 12th St.
Little Rock, AR 72204-2408
Phone: (501)663-4379 Fax: (501)663-4925
E-mail: mole@aristotle.net
Products: Women's clothing; Children's clothing and
accessories; Athletic uniforms; Ad specialities; Caps;
Jackets; Foam products. SICs: 5137
(Women's/Children's Clothing); 5136 (Men's/Boys'
Clothing); 5199 (Nondurable Goods Nec). Est: 1975.
Sales: $500,000 (2000). Emp: 5. Officers: Roy Burks,
Owner.

■ 5200 ■ Monarch Hosiery Mills Inc.
PO Box 1205
Burlington, NC 27216
Phone: (919)584-0361 Fax: (910)584-0366
Products: Mens' and boys' socks; Womens' sport
socks. SICs: 5136 (Men's/Boys' Clothing); 5137
(Women's/Children's Clothing). Officers: Richard
Keziah, President.

■ 5201 ■ Monarch Knit and Sportswear Inc.
122 E Washington Blvd.
Los Angeles, CA 90015
Phone: (213)746-5800 Fax: (213)742-6601
Products: Knit outerwear; Women's sportswear. SIC:
5137 (Women's/Children's Clothing). Est: 1935. Sales:
$25,000,000 (2000). Emp: 65. Officers: Sheldon N.
Goldman, President; Raymond F. Salim, VP &
Treasurer.

■ 5202 ■ Montgomery Hosiery Mill Inc.
PO Box 69
Star, NC 27356
Phone: (919)428-2191 Fax: (919)428-1620
Products: Men's hosiery; Children's hosiery; Women's
and misses' hosiery. SICs: 5137 (Women's/Children's
Clothing); 5136 (Men's/Boys' Clothing). Est: 1946.
Sales: $10,000,000 (2000). Emp: 150. Officers: H. R.
Russell.

■ 5203 ■ Moore Brothers Inc.
PO Box 1108
Cheraw, SC 29520
Phone: (803)537-5211
Products: Women's clothing; Men's and boys'
clothing. SICs: 5136 (Men's/Boys' Clothing); 5137
(Women's/Children's Clothing). Sales: $22,000,000
(2000). Emp: 50. Officers: J.C. Crawford Jr., President
& Chairman of the Board.

■ 5204 ■ **Moreland Hosiery**
PO Box 3245
Clearwater, FL 33767-8245
Phones: (813)585-9795   800-828-7025
Products: Socks and hosiery. **SICs:** 5137
(Women's/Children's Clothing); 5136 (Men's/Boys'
Clothing).

■ 5205 ■ **Morelle Products Ltd., Philippe
ADEC and Equipment**
209 W 38th St.
New York, NY 10018
Phone: (212)391-8070   **Fax:** (212)921-5321
E-mail: sales@morelleproducts.com
URL: http://www.equipmentstores.com
Products: Women's apparel. **SIC:** 5137
(Women's/Children's Clothing). **Est:** 1967. **Sales:**
$10,000,000 (2000). **Emp:** 35. **Officers:** Aby Saltiel,
President.

■ 5206 ■ **Jim Morris Environmental T-Shirts**
PO Box 18270
Boulder, CO 80308
Phone: (303)444-6430   **Fax:** (303)786-9095
Products: Unisex t-shirts. **SICs:** 5137
(Women's/Children's Clothing); 5136 (Men's/Boys'
Clothing). **Est:** 1977. **Officers:** James Morris, Owner.

■ 5207 ■ **Movie Star Inc.**
136 Madison Ave.
New York, NY 10016
Phone: (212)679-7260   **Fax:** (212)684-3295
Products: en's day wear, leisure wear, sleep wear,
and lingerie. **SIC:** 5137 (Women's/Children's Clothing).
Sales: $61,400,000 (2000). **Emp:** 732. **Officers:** Mark
M. David, CEO & Chairman of the Board; Saul
Pomerantz, CFO.

■ 5208 ■ **Mr. Logo Inc.**
302 Shelley St., Ste. 5
Springfield, OR 97477-5903
Phone: (541)744-1575   **Fax:** (541)744-1670
Products: Men's and boys' embroidered clothing. **SIC:**
5136 (Men's/Boys' Clothing). **Officers:** Ron Rohde,
President.

■ 5209 ■ **Multi-Line Industries Inc.**
124 Commerce St.
Bowdon, GA 30108-1505
Phone: (404)854-4049
Products: Men's suits and coats; Men's dress shirts;
Men's ties. **SIC:** 5136 (Men's/Boys' Clothing). **Est:**
1968. **Sales:** $1,000,000 (2000). **Emp:** 7. **Officers:**
James Jones, President; Rebecca Maishburn,
Treasurer & Secty.

■ 5210 ■ **Albert Naggar**
1407 Broadway
New York, NY 10018
Phone: (212)575-1851   **Fax:** (212)719-9514
Products: Sweaters and T-shirts. **SICs:** 5137
(Women's/Children's Clothing); 5136 (Men's/Boys'
Clothing). **Est:** 1970. **Sales:** $4,000,000 (2000). **Emp:**
5. **Officers:** Albert Naggar, President.

■ 5211 ■ **Name Game**
95 S Main St.
Memphis, TN 38103-2910
Phone: (901)527-3688   **Fax:** (901)527-3688
Products: Clothing; Customized sportswear. **SICs:**
5137 (Women's/Children's Clothing); 5136
(Men's/Boys' Clothing). **Est:** 1972. **Officers:** Danny
Howell, Partner.

■ 5212 ■ **Name Place**
5301 Everhart Rd.
Corpus Christi, TX 78411
Phone: (512)854-9923
Products: Shirts. **SIC:** 5131 (Piece Goods & Notions).

■ 5213 ■ **Nannette**
112 W 34th
New York, NY 10120-0093
Phone: (212)967-7800   **Fax:** (212)564-5201
Products: Children's dress clothes, including suits and
dresses. **SIC:** 5137 (Women's/Children's Clothing).
Est: 1992. **Sales:** $5,000,000 (2000). **Emp:** 20.
Officers: David Maleh, President.

■ 5214 ■ **Nantucket Inc.**
PO Drawer 429
Kinston, NC 28501
Phone: (919)523-7001   **Fax:** (919)523-2954
Products: Men's shirts; Men's ties; Shorts; Women's
clothing. **SICs:** 5136 (Men's/Boys' Clothing); 5137
(Women's/Children's Clothing). **Emp:** 23. **Officers:**
Fred A. Rouse, President.

■ 5215 ■ **National Dry Goods**
1200 Trumbull Ave.
Detroit, MI 48216-1941
Phone: (313)961-3656
Free: (800)783-3656   **Fax:** (313)961-8684
Products: Men's clothing. **SIC:** 5136 (Men's/Boys'
Clothing). **Est:** 1921. **Sales:** $3,000,000 (2000). **Emp:**
14. **Officers:** Katherine Richman, President.

■ 5216 ■ **National Rubber Footwear Inc.**
310 N Colvin St.
Baltimore, MD 21202-4808
Phone: (410)752-0910
Free: (800)966-7463   **Fax:** (410)332-8145
Products: Shoes. **SIC:** 5139 (Footwear). **Sales:**
$2,000,000 (2000). **Emp:** 6.

■ 5217 ■ **Nautica Enterprises Inc.**
40 West 57th St.
New York, NY 10019
Phone: (212)541-5757   **Fax:** (212)841-7228
Products: Men's brand name sportswear, outerwear,
robes, and loungewear; Chain store of men's brand
name sportswear, outerwear, robes, and loungewear.
SIC: 5136 (Men's/Boys' Clothing). **Sales:**
$552,700,000 (2000). **Emp:** 2,300. **Officers:** Harvey
Sanders, CEO, President & Chairman of the Board; W.
Donald Pennington, CFO.

■ 5218 ■ **Nautica International Inc.**
40 West 57th St., 7th Fl.
New York, NY 10019
Phone: (212)541-5990
Products: Men's brand name sportswear and
outerwear. **SIC:** 5136 (Men's/Boys' Clothing). **Officers:**
David Chu, President.

■ 5219 ■ **Charles Navasky & Company Inc.**
PO Box 728
Philipsburg, PA 16866
Phone: (814)342-1160
Products: Men's sportswear; Men's suits and coats.
SIC: 5136 (Men's/Boys' Clothing). **Est:** 1893. **Sales:**
$35,000,000 (2000). **Emp:** 600. **Officers:** Edward
Navasky, CEO; Charles Navasky, President.

■ 5220 ■ **Neff Athletic Lettering Co.**
645 Pine St.
Greenville, OH 45331
Phone: (513)548-3194   **Fax:** (513)548-3194
Products: Junior high and high school athletic wear,
including varsity jackets and varsity letters; Trophies.
SICs: 5136 (Men's/Boys' Clothing); 5137
(Women's/Children's Clothing). **Est:** 1949. **Sales:**
$29,000,000 (2000). **Emp:** 450. **Officers:** Lindley
Scarlett, President; Paul Reiss, CFO; Peter
Cannizzaro, VP of Marketing.

■ 5221 ■ **Neiman Marcus Co.**
1618 Main St.
Dallas, TX 75201
Phone: (214)741-6911   **Fax:** (214)573-6136
Products: Clothing. **SICs:** 5137 (Women's/Children's
Clothing); 5136 (Men's/Boys' Clothing).

■ 5222 ■ **Nelsons**
248-250 Main St.
Gloucester, MA 01930
Phone: (978)283-5675
Products: Men's and boys' clothing; Men's and boys'
sportswear; Men's and boys' work clothing. **SIC:** 5136
(Men's/Boys' Clothing). **Officers:** James Nelson,
Owner.

■ 5223 ■ **New American T-Shirt**
500 Alakawa St., No. 114
Honolulu, HI 96817-4576
Phone: (808)842-4466   **Fax:** (808)842-1911
Products: Unisex clothing. **SICs:** 5137
(Women's/Children's Clothing); 5136 (Men's/Boys'

Clothing). **Officers:** Charles Broder, President.
Alternate Name: Pax Pacifica Ltd.

■ 5224 ■ **New Era Cap Company Inc.**
8061 Erie Rd.
Derby, NY 14047
Phone: (716)549-0445   **Fax:** (716)549-5424
Products: Baseball caps. **SICs:** 5136 (Men's/Boys'
Clothing); 5137 (Women's/Children's Clothing). **Sales:**
$25,000,000 (2000). **Emp:** 499. **Officers:** David C.
Koch.

■ 5225 ■ **New Era Factory Outlet**
20 Orchard St.
New York, NY 10002
Phone: (212)966-4959   **Fax:** (212)941-6243
Products: Clothing, including infant's, men's, ladies',
and children's. **SICs:** 5137 (Women's/Children's
Clothing); 5136 (Men's/Boys' Clothing). **Est:** 1981.

■ 5226 ■ **New Fashion Inc.**
PO Box 148
Iva, SC 29655
Phone: (864)348-6151
Free: (800)845-6141   **Fax:** (864)348-6186
Products: Ladies' apparel. **SIC:** 5137
(Women's/Children's Clothing). **Est:** 1937. **Sales:**
$5,000,000 (2000). **Emp:** 30. **Officers:** G. Curtis
Wilson, President; Lindsey Funchess, VP of Finance.
Alternate Name: IVA Manufacturing Co.

■ 5227 ■ **New Hosiery**
PO Box 21176
Chattanooga, TN 37424-0176
Phone: (423)845-5101   **Fax:** (423)845-5101
Products: Foot socks; Hosiery. **SICs:** 5137
(Women's/Children's Clothing); 5136 (Men's/Boys'
Clothing). **Emp:** 30.

■ 5228 ■ **New York Enterprises**
32 W 30th
New York, NY 10001-4308
Phone: (212)725-5889   **Fax:** (212)725-5889
Products: Infant accessories, including diapers and
bibs. **SIC:** 5137 (Women's/Children's Clothing). **Emp:**
49.

■ 5229 ■ **Tony Newcomb Sportswear Inc.**
1824 Linwood Blvd.
Oklahoma City, OK 73106-2626
Phone: (405)232-0022   **Fax:** (405)232-0414
Products: Men's and boys' clothing, sportswear, and
work clothing. **SIC:** 5136 (Men's/Boys' Clothing).
Officers: Tony Newcomb, President.

■ 5230 ■ **Newsouth Athletic Co.**
PO Box 604
Dallas, NC 28034-0604
Phone: (704)922-1557   **Fax:** (704)922-5324
Products: Men's and boys' clothing; Men's and boys'
sportswear; Men's and boys' work clothing. **SIC:** 5136
(Men's/Boys' Clothing). **Officers:** Earl Groves,
President.

■ 5231 ■ **Ni-Co. Sales Company Inc.**
PO Box 578
Georgiana, AL 36033-0578
Phone: (205)376-2296   **Fax:** (205)376-2478
E-mail: nightingaleuniformpbcomputer@alaweb.com
Products: Nursing students' uniforms. **SICs:** 5137
(Women's/Children's Clothing); 5136 (Men's/Boys'
Clothing). **Est:** 1933. **Sales:** $2,000,000 (2000). **Emp:**
40. **Officers:** Patricia B. Compton, President.

■ 5232 ■ **Nitches Inc.**
10280 Camino Sante Fe.
San Diego, CA 92121
Phone: (619)625-2633
Products: Women's sportswear. **SIC:** 5137
(Women's/Children's Clothing). **Sales:** $48,400,000
(2000). **Emp:** 53. **Officers:** Steven P. Wyandt, CEO &
President; Thomas P. Baumann, VP & CFO.

■ 5233 ■ **Niver Western Wear Inc.**
1221 Hemphill St.
Ft. Worth, TX 76104
Phone: (817)336-2389   **Fax:** (817)332-1702
E-mail: gus@flash.net
Products: Men's and women's western-style clothing.

SICs: 5136 (Men's/Boys' Clothing); 5137 (Women's/Children's Clothing). **Est:** 1945. **Sales:** $5,000,000 (2000). **Emp:** 17. **Officers:** Robert H. Persons; Bert G. Niver.

■ **5234** ■ **Noe-Equal Hosiery Corporation**
207 S Payson St.
Baltimore, MD 21223
Phone: (410)945-0900
Free: (800)431-SOCK
Products: Hosiery; Foot socks; Pantyhose. **SIC:** 5137 (Women's/Children's Clothing). **Officers:** Arnold Bookoff, President.

■ **5235** ■ **Nolan Glove Company Inc.**
131 W 33rd St.
New York, NY 10001
Phone: (212)564-3266   **Fax:** (212)239-0426
Products: Children's gloves and hats. **SICs:** 5136 (Men's/Boys' Clothing); 5137 (Women's/Children's Clothing). **Est:** 1920. **Sales:** $6,000,000 (2000). **Emp:** 9. **Officers:** E.A. Nolan, President.

■ **5236** ■ **Nordic Wholesale Distributors Inc.**
1021 W Oak
Kissimmee, FL 34741
Phone: (407)859-8508
Free: (800)327-4516   **Fax:** (407)857-4689
Products: Children's clothing; Women's handbags; Collectors items. **SICs:** 5137 (Women's/Children's Clothing); 5199 (Nondurable Goods Nec).

■ **5237** ■ **Nordstrom Inc.**
1501 5th Ave.
Seattle, WA 98101-1603
Phone: (206)628-2111   **Fax:** (206)628-1795
Products: Shoes; Men's and boys' clothing; Girls' clothing; Women's clothing; Women's clothing accessories. **SICs:** 5137 (Women's/Children's Clothing); 5136 (Men's/Boys' Clothing); 5139 (Footwear).

■ **5238** ■ **North Shore Sportswear Company Inc.**
Dickson St.
Glen Cove, NY 11542
Phone: (516)671-4390
Products: Women's outerwear. **SIC:** 5137 (Women's/Children's Clothing). **Est:** 1953. **Sales:** $25,000,000 (2000). **Emp:** 25. **Officers:** Stephen Bass, President; Russell Windler, CFO.

■ **5239** ■ **North Star Glove Co.**
PO Box 1214
Tacoma, WA 98401
Phones: (253)627-7107   800-543-5101
Free: (800)423-1616   **Fax:** (253)627-0597
Products: Work gloves and mittens. **SIC:** 5136 (Men's/Boys' Clothing). **Est:** 1910. **Sales:** $6,000,000 (2000). **Emp:** 100. **Officers:** Rob Wekell, President; Tom Wekell.

■ **5240** ■ **North State Garment Company Inc.**
PO Box 215
Farmville, NC 27828
Phone: (919)753-3266   **Fax:** (919)753-4229
Products: Women's sportswear. **SIC:** 5137 (Women's/Children's Clothing). **Emp:** 110. **Officers:** Ed Jones.

■ **5241** ■ **North Warehouse Inc.**
6181 Taylor Dr.
Flint, MI 48507-4665
Phones: (810)767-5167   800-521-3373
Free: (800)428-1177   **Fax:** (810)767-7856
E-mail: awnwh@fruit.com
URL: http://www.northwarehouse.com
Products: Men's and boys' clothing, including sportswear; Work clothing, including uniforms. **SIC:** 5136 (Men's/Boys' Clothing). **Est:** 1984. **Officers:** Carmine Carbone, President.

■ **5242** ■ **Northwest Designs Ink Inc.**
12870 NE 15th Pl.
Bellevue, WA 98005-2212
Phone: (425)454-0707   **Fax:** (425)455-5778
Products: Unisex clothing, including T-shirts, sweatshirts, jogging pants, and jackets. **SICs:** 5136

(Men's/Boys' Clothing); 5137 (Women's/Children's Clothing). **Officers:** Ben Smith, President.

■ **5243** ■ **Nu-Look Fashions Inc.**
5080 Sinclair Rd.
Columbus, OH 43229
Phone: (614)885-4936   **Fax:** (614)885-4193
Products: Men's apparel. **SIC:** 5136 (Men's/Boys' Clothing). **Est:** 1964. **Sales:** $14,700,000 (2000). **Emp:** 121. **Officers:** L Fannin, President; James Merz, Controller.

■ **5244** ■ **NY Apparel**
350 5th Ave., Ste. 826
New York, NY 10118
Phone: (212)465-8053
Free: (800)332-5330   **Fax:** (212)465-8034
Products: Unisex apparel, including underwear. **SICs:** 5137 (Women's/Children's Clothing); 5136 (Men's/Boys' Clothing). **Est:** 1987. **Emp:** 3. **Officers:** Judy Forman, President; Steve Forman, Vice President.

■ **5245** ■ **Oakbrook Custom Embroidery**
960 Bacons Bridge Rd.
Summerville, SC 29485-4108
Phone: (803)875-0790
Products: Embroideries. **SICs:** 5136 (Men's/Boys' Clothing); 5137 (Women's/Children's Clothing). **Officers:** Vicki Gannon, President.

■ **5246** ■ **Ocean Originals**
3701 Wow Rd.
Corpus Christi, TX 78413
Phone: (512)852-0252
Products: Shirts. **SIC:** 5131 (Piece Goods & Notions).

■ **5247** ■ **Ocean Pacific Apparel Corp.**
3 Studebaker
Irvine, CA 92618-2013
Phone: (949)580-1888
Products: Men's and women's casual clothing. **SICs:** 5136 (Men's/Boys' Clothing); 5137 (Women's/Children's Clothing).

■ **5248** ■ **Ocean Pacific Sunwear Ltd.**
3 Studebaker
Irvine, CA 92602
Phone: (949)580-1888
Free: (800)899-6775   **Fax:** (949)580-1870
Products: Shorts; T-shirts. **SICs:** 5136 (Men's/Boys' Clothing); 5137 (Women's/Children's Clothing). **Est:** 1972. **Sales:** $68,000,000 (2000). **Emp:** 100. **Officers:** Jim Jenks, CEO & President; Jess Myers, CFO; John Patrick, Dir. of Sales; Jenny Ramirez, Dir. of Systems; Diane Miszcak, Dir of Human Resources.

■ **5249** ■ **Officers Equipment Co.**
PO Box 633
Stafford, VA 22554
Phone: (703)221-1912   **Fax:** (703)221-4115
Products: Military clothing and accessories. **SICs:** 5136 (Men's/Boys' Clothing); 5137 (Women's/Children's Clothing). **Officers:** Stephen Elms, President.

■ **5250** ■ **Kenneth P. Olson Inc.**
7600 W 27th St., Ste. 213
St. Louis Park, MN 55426-3163
Phone: (612)478-9854   **Fax:** (612)478-9856
Products: Men's and boy's clothing accessories. **SIC:** 5136 (Men's/Boys' Clothing). **Officers:** Kenneth Olson, President.

■ **5251** ■ **On the Beach, Inc.**
203 W M.L. King Jr. Blvd.
Los Angeles, CA 90037-1013
Phone: (213)234-9033   **Fax:** (213)232-2294
Products: Women's swimwear. **SIC:** 5137 (Women's/Children's Clothing). **Est:** 1976. **Sales:** $10,000,000 (2000). **Emp:** 49. **Officers:** Milt Bronson; Ralph Medina; Janet Wittenberg.

■ **5252** ■ **Only Hearts Ltd.**
15 E 32nd St.
New York, NY 10016
Phone: (212)689-7808   **Fax:** (212)685-0853
Products: Lingerie. **SIC:** 5137 (Women's/Children's

Clothing). **Est:** 1982. **Sales:** $1,300,000 (1999). **Emp:** 20. **Officers:** Jonathan Stuart, President.

■ **5253** ■ **Only Once Inc.**
266 Pine St.
Burlington, VT 05401-4751
Phone: (802)863-2302   **Fax:** (802)865-3114
E-mail: onlyonce@together.net
Products: Silk screened T-shirts. **SICs:** 5136 (Men's/Boys' Clothing); 5137 (Women's/Children's Clothing). **Est:** 1980. **Officers:** Ronald Baker, President.

■ **5254** ■ **Oogenesis Inc.**
66-249 Kam Hwy.
Haleiwa, HI 96712
Phone: (808)637-4580   **Fax:** (808)638-8776
E-mail: inga@hawaii.rr.com
URL: http://www.ingahomefurnishings.com
Products: Women's clothing, gifts, accessories, and jewelry. **SICs:** 5137 (Women's/Children's Clothing); 5094 (Jewelry & Precious Stones). **Est:** 1970. **Officers:** Inge Himmelmann, President.

■ **5255** ■ **Orbit Industries Inc. Clarkesville Garment Div.**
2320 Perimeter Park Dr., Ste. 101
Atlanta, GA 30341-1317
Phone: (706)754-2151
Products: Women's sportswear. **SIC:** 5137 (Women's/Children's Clothing). **Est:** 1966. **Sales:** $6,000,000 (2000). **Emp:** 100. **Officers:** R.L. Fowler, President.

■ **5256** ■ **Orchid Uniform Retail Sales**
501 N Meridian Ave., Ste. 104
Oklahoma City, OK 73107-5701
Phone: (405)947-2388   **Fax:** (405)949-2886
Products: Men's uniforms; Women's uniforms. **SICs:** 5137 (Women's/Children's Clothing); 5136 (Men's/Boys' Clothing). **Officers:** Gary Goeringer, Partner.

■ **5257** ■ **Don Overcast and Associates**
250 Spring St.
Atlanta, GA 30303
Phone: (404)523-4082
Free: (800)527-6234   **Fax:** (404)527-6668
E-mail: overcast01@aol.com
Products: Women's apparel. **SICs:** 5137 (Women's/Children's Clothing); 5136 (Men's/Boys' Clothing). **Est:** 1972. **Sales:** $10,000,000 (2000). **Emp:** 6. **Officers:** Don Overcast, President.

■ **5258** ■ **Owenby Co.**
5775 Murphy Hwy.
Blairsville, GA 30512
Phone: (706)745-5531   **Fax:** (706)745-3431
Products: Men's and boys' sportswear. **SIC:** 5136 (Men's/Boys' Clothing). **Est:** 1935. **Emp:** 140. **Officers:** Paul B. Owenby, President; Eb H. Eagar III, VP of Operations.

■ **5259** ■ **Oxford of Burgaw Co.**
PO Box 109
Columbia, SC 29202-0109
Products: Dresses; Women's sportswear. **SIC:** 5137 (Women's/Children's Clothing). **Sales:** $6,000,000 (2000). **Emp:** 140. **Officers:** George Arrington.

■ **5260** ■ **Oxford Industries Inc. Renny Div.**
1001 6th Ave.
New York, NY 10018
Phone: (212)556-5341   **Fax:** (212)556-2456
Products: Casual sportwear. **SICs:** 5137 (Women's/Children's Clothing); 5136 (Men's/Boys' Clothing). **Sales:** $17,000,000 (2000). **Emp:** 25. **Officers:** Debra Mabin, President; Mark Wolk, Exec. VP.

■ **5261** ■ **Oztex Inc.**
7717 SW Nimbus Ave.
Beaverton, OR 97008-6402
Phone: (503)644-2485   **Fax:** (503)644-2786
E-mail: diveskin@teleport.com
Products: Tropical wetsuits; Sportswear. **SICs:** 5136 (Men's/Boys' Clothing); 5137 (Women's/Children's Clothing). **Est:** 1985. **Emp:** 4. **Officers:** Robin Miller, President; Jose Rodriguez.

■ **5262** ■ **Pacasa**
PO Box 104
New Hampton, IA 50659-0104
Phone: (515)394-4686
Products: Women's clothing; Children's sportswear; Women's sportswear. **SIC:** 5137 (Women's/Children's Clothing). **Officers:** Sandra Claypool, President.

■ **5263** ■ **Pacific Trade Wind Inc.**
PO Box 42601
Portland, OR 97242-0601
Phone: (503)234-0355 **Fax:** (503)234-7294
E-mail: pactrader@hotmail.com
URL: http://www.pactrader.com
Products: Men's and boy's clothing; Textiles; Fabrics; Used clothing; Used shoes. **SICs:** 5136 (Men's/Boys' Clothing); 5131 (Piece Goods & Notions). **Sales:** $3,000,000 (2000). **Emp:** 13. **Officers:** Sunny Nmereole, President, e-mail: chidoenyi@aol.com.

■ **5264** ■ **Padre Island Screen Printing**
3728 Wow Rd.
Corpus Christi, TX 78413
Phone: (512)851-0700
Products: Shirts. **SIC:** 5131 (Piece Goods & Notions).

■ **5265** ■ **Paisano Publications**
PO Box 3000
Agoura Hills, CA 91376
Phone: (818)889-8740 **Fax:** (818)889-4726
Products: Publishes magazines on clothing; Novelties; Motorcycle accessories. **SICs:** 5136 (Men's/Boys' Clothing); 5137 (Women's/Children's Clothing). **Officers:** Brian Wood, President; Bob Davis, CFO.

■ **5266** ■ **Palisades Beach Club**
1936 Mateo
Los Angeles, CA 90021
Phone: (213)623-9233 **Fax:** (213)623-9377
Products: Swimwear; Women's sportswear; Men's sportswear; Children's sportswear. **SICs:** 5137 (Women's/Children's Clothing); 5136 (Men's/Boys' Clothing). **Sales:** $15,000,000 (2000). **Emp:** 60. **Officers:** Sandra Miller. **Former Name:** Beachville USA.

■ **5267** ■ **Panorama Casual**
605 E Main, Panora Plz.
Panora, IA 50216-0604
Phone: (515)755-3966
Free: (800)852-7922 **Fax:** (515)755-2031
Products: Clothing, including screen printed apparel. **SICs:** 5136 (Men's/Boys' Clothing); 5137 (Women's/Children's Clothing). **Officers:** Jason Clark, Owner.

■ **5268** ■ **Pappy's Customs Inc.**
244 E Main St.
Kingsport, TN 37660-4302
Phone: (615)246-9594
Free: (800)876-4789 **Fax:** (615)246-1987
Products: Leather clothing; Screen printing; Bike equipment; Motorcycle helmets; Stickers. **SICs:** 5136 (Men's/Boys' Clothing); 5091 (Sporting & Recreational Goods); 5137 (Women's/Children's Clothing). **Est:** 1973. **Emp:** 8. **Officers:** Fred Vineyard, President.

■ **5269** ■ **Paramount Manufacturing Co.**
42885 Swan Lake Dr.
Northville, MI 48167
Phone: (248)380-4927
Products: Clothing, including women's pants and shorts sets; Sportwear, including team hats; Fashion design T-shirts. **SICs:** 5137 (Women's/Children's Clothing); 5136 (Men's/Boys' Clothing).

■ **5270** ■ **Paramount Uniform Rental Inc.**
5421 Crestview Dr.
Memphis, TN 38134-6415
Phone: (901)382-4411 **Fax:** (901)382-5425
Products: Children's uniforms; Men's uniforms; Women's uniforms. **SICs:** 5137 (Women's/Children's Clothing); 5136 (Men's/Boys' Clothing). **Officers:** Charles Harlow, President.

■ **5271** ■ **Paris Vienna**
3912 S Broadway Pl.
Los Angeles, CA 90037
Phone: (213)231-0619 **Fax:** (213)231-0406
Products: Girl's clothing. **SIC:** 5137 (Women's/Children's Clothing). **Emp:** 49.

■ **5272** ■ **Park Manufacturing Co.**
PO Box 634
Jamestown, TN 38556-0634
Phone: (931)879-5894 **Fax:** (931)879-2596
Products: Men's casual wear clothing. **SIC:** 5136 (Men's/Boys' Clothing). **Sales:** $6,000,000 (2000). **Emp:** 100. **Officers:** Joe Williams.

■ **5273** ■ **Pence International, Inc.**
819 Cedar St.
Springfield, OH 45503
Phone: (937)325-1813
Products: Men's and boys' work clothing; Women's and misses' outerwear; Stationery products; Perfumes and cosmetics; Men's and boys' suits and coats. **SICs:** 5136 (Men's/Boys' Clothing); 5122 (Drugs, Proprietaries & Sundries); 5137 (Women's/Children's Clothing); 5112 (Stationery & Office Supplies). **Officers:** James W. Pence, President.

■ **5274** ■ **Penn Printed Shirts Corp.**
PO Box 516
Brooklyn, MI 49230-0516
Phone: (517)592-5642
Free: (800)772-2177 **Fax:** (517)592-2409
Products: Men's and boys' sportswear. **SIC:** 5136 (Men's/Boys' Clothing). **Officers:** Joseph Pennington, President.

■ **5275** ■ **Pincus Brothers Inc.**
Independence Mall E
Philadelphia, PA 19106
Phone: (215)922-4900
Free: (800)251-2323 **Fax:** (215)922-1140
Products: Suits and coats, tailored suits, including uniforms. **SICs:** 5136 (Men's/Boys' Clothing); 5137 (Women's/Children's Clothing). **Est:** 1911. **Emp:** 1,000.

■ **5276** ■ **Pine State Knitwear Co.**
PO Box 631
Mt. Airy, NC 27030
Phone: (919)789-9121 **Fax:** (919)789-5020
Products: Sweaters. **SICs:** 5136 (Men's/Boys' Clothing); 5137 (Women's/Children's Clothing). **Est:** 1929. **Sales:** $35,000,000 (2000). **Emp:** 500. **Officers:** Lindsay Holcomb Jr., President; Bill Murphy, Controller; Randy Menear, Dir. of Marketing.

■ **5277** ■ **Pioneer Industries Inc.**
11630 W 85th St.
Lenexa, KS 66214
Phone: (913)888-6760
Free: (800)255-0406 **Fax:** (913)888-6901
E-mail: dogdaze1@aol.com
Products: Headwear; Apparel. **SICs:** 5136 (Men's/Boys' Clothing); 5137 (Women's/Children's Clothing). **Est:** 1986. **Sales:** $8,000,000 (2000). **Emp:** 20. **Officers:** David Blackman, Chairman of the Board; Bruce Blackman, CEO & President; Steve Blackman, COO & VP.

■ **5278** ■ **Piramide Imports**
PO Box 246
Manitou Springs, CO 80829-0246
Phone: (719)685-5912
Products: Men's and boys' clothing; Women's clothing. **SICs:** 5136 (Men's/Boys' Clothing); 5137 (Women's/Children's Clothing). **Officers:** Thomas Fallon, Owner.

■ **5279** ■ **Pivot Rules Inc.**
42 W 39th St., Fl. 9
New York, NY 10018
Phone: (212)944-8000
Products: Golf lifestyle sportswear for men. **SIC:** 5136 (Men's/Boys' Clothing). **Sales:** $8,600,000 (2000). **Emp:** 11. **Officers:** E. Kenneth Seiff, CEO, President & Chairman of the Board; Meena N. Bhatia, CFO.

■ **5280** ■ **Plus Woman**
85 Laurel Haven Rd.
Fairview, NC 28730-9642
Phone: (704)628-3562 **Fax:** (704)628-2610
URL: http://www.pluswoman.com
Products: Women's large-sized clothing. **SIC:** 5137 (Women's/Children's Clothing). **Officers:** Laura Adams, President.

■ **5281** ■ **Podell Industries Inc.**
1930 E 65th St.
Los Angeles, CA 90001
Phone: (213)955-2550 **Fax:** (213)582-7950
Products: Women's clothing. **SIC:** 5137 (Women's/Children's Clothing). **Emp:** 130. **Officers:** Anthony Podell.

■ **5282** ■ **Polo Ralph Lauren Corp.**
650 Madison Ave.
New York, NY 10022
Phone: (212)318-7000
Products: Men's, women's and childrens apparel. **SICs:** 5136 (Men's/Boys' Clothing); 5137 (Women's/Children's Clothing). **Sales:** $909,700,000 (2000). **Emp:** 4,000. **Officers:** Ralph Lauren, CEO & Chairman of the Board; Nancy A. Platoni Poli, CFO.

■ **5283** ■ **Pope Distributing Co.**
PO Box 979
Coats, NC 27521
Phone: (919)897-6171
Products: Jackets; Dresses; Shirts; Slacks; Toys; Tools; Hammers; Screwdrivers. **SICs:** 5136 (Men's/Boys' Clothing); 5072 (Hardware); 5092 (Toys & Hobby Goods & Supplies); 5137 (Women's/Children's Clothing). **Est:** 1951. **Sales:** $3,000,000 (2000). **Emp:** 75. **Officers:** William R. Pope, President & Treasurer.

■ **5284** ■ **Portland Merchandise Corp.**
350 W 31st St., 4th Fl.
New York, NY 10001
Phone: (212)239-8650 **Fax:** (212)239-8841
E-mail: portland@portlandusa.com
URL: http://www.portlandusa.com
Products: Women's, men's, and children's clothing. **SICs:** 5137 (Women's/Children's Clothing); 5092 (Toys & Hobby Goods & Supplies); 5136 (Men's/Boys' Clothing); 5139 (Footwear). **Est:** 1979. **Sales:** $7,000,000 (2000). **Emp:** 10. **Officers:** Dan Melendez, Vice President, e-mail: dmelendez@portlandusa.com.

■ **5285** ■ **Portolano Products Inc.**
32 W 39th St.
New York, NY 10018
Phone: (212)719-4403 **Fax:** (212)302-6135
Products: Men's and women's gloves and accessories. **SICs:** 5136 (Men's/Boys' Clothing); 5137 (Women's/Children's Clothing). **Sales:** $6,000,000 (1999). **Emp:** 12. **Officers:** Aldo Portolano, President; James DiCicco, CFO; Francesca Portulano, Dir. of Marketing & Sales.

■ **5286** ■ **Prairie Belle Clothing Exports**
5243 Horton
Mission, KS 66202
Phone: (913)722-0732 **Fax:** (913)677-1536
Products: Women's clothing. **SIC:** 5137 (Women's/Children's Clothing). **Officers:** Jim Pond, Sales/Marketing Manager.

■ **5287** ■ **Pratt Medical Inc.**
404 N 4th
Olathe, CO 81425
Phone: (970)323-5616
Free: (800)233-3556 **Fax:** (970)323-5488
Products: Cloth diapers. **SIC:** 5137 (Women's/Children's Clothing). **Emp:** 7. **Officers:** Darin Pratt, President; Valdene Pratt, Treasurer & Secty.

■ **5288** ■ **Predot Company Inc.**
3923 Euphrosine
New Orleans, LA 70125-1308
Phone: (504)822-2952 **Fax:** (504)822-2952
Products: Jerseys. **SIC:** 5136 (Men's/Boys' Clothing). **Emp:** 20.

■ **5289** ■ **Prentiss Manufacturing Company Inc.**
PO Box 360
Booneville, MS 38829
Phone: (601)728-4446 **Fax:** (601)728-2128
Products: Men's shirts. **SIC:** 5136 (Men's/Boys' Clothing). **Sales:** $38,000,000 (2000). **Emp:** 900.
Officers: James H. Bethay.

■ **5290** ■ **Don Price Direct Sales**
PO Box 751
Elizabethton, TN 37644-0751
Phone: (423)283-0109 **Fax:** (423)283-0109
Products: Women's and children's clothing. **SIC:** 5137 (Women's/Children's Clothing). **Officers:** Don Price, Owner.

■ **5291** ■ **Psoul Company Inc.**
384 Kingston Ave.
Brooklyn, NY 11225
Phone: (718)756-9620 **Fax:** (718)953-1245
Products: Women's clothing. **SIC:** 5137 (Women's/Children's Clothing).

■ **5292** ■ **Pubco Corp.**
3830 Kelley Ave.
Cleveland, OH 44114
Phone: (216)881-5300 **Fax:** (216)881-8380
Products: Supplies for computer printers, and specialty construction products including hydraulic hammers; General apparel and related notions. **SICs:** 5136 (Men's/Boys' Clothing); 5137 (Women's/Children's Clothing). **Sales:** $68,700,000 (2000). **Emp:** 350. **Officers:** Robert H. Kanner, CEO & President; Maria Szubski, CFO.

■ **5293** ■ **Q-T Foundations Company Inc.**
385 Chestnut St.
Norwood, NJ 07648
Phone: (201)750-8100 **Fax:** (201)750-1819
E-mail: lkmk@cybernex.net
Products: Women's undergarments. **SIC:** 5137 (Women's/Children's Clothing). **Est:** 1945. **Sales:** $6,000,000 (2000). **Emp:** 100. **Officers:** M. Kutzin, President; Larry Kutzin, VP & Treasurer. **Former Name:** Q-T Intimates. **Former Name:** Sintrigue.

■ **5294** ■ **Q-T Foundations Company Inc.**
385 Chestnut St.
Norwood, NJ 07648
Phone: (201)750-8100 **Fax:** (201)750-1819
Products: Clothing. **SIC:** 5137 (Women's/Children's Clothing). **Sales:** $6,000,000 (2000). **Emp:** 100.

■ **5295** ■ **Queen Shebra Co.**
1421 62nd St.
Brooklyn, NY 11219
Phone: (718)837-2800
Free: (800)231-0303 **Fax:** (718)837-0052
Products: Lingerie. **SIC:** 5137 (Women's/Children's Clothing). **Est:** 1941. **Sales:** $6,000,000 (2000). **Emp:** 30. **Officers:** Ike Arnstein, President; Gita Arnstein, Vice President.

■ **5296** ■ **Quisenberrys Inc.**
PO Box 40
Vale, OR 97918-0040
Phone: (541)473-3932 **Fax:** (541)473-3946
Products: Men's clothing. **SIC:** 5136 (Men's/Boys' Clothing). **Officers:** Winston Quisenberry, President.

■ **5297** ■ **R & J Apparel Distributors**
130 Penn Am Dr.
Quakertown, PA 18951
Phone: (215)536-3633
Products: Women's clothing. **SIC:** 5137 (Women's/Children's Clothing).

■ **5298** ■ **Racewear Designs Inc.**
340 Coogan Way
El Cajon, CA 92020
Phone: (619)442-9651
Free: (800)824-0973 **Fax:** (619)442-6209
Products: Custom made jackets and team crew shirts. **SIC:** 5137 (Women's/Children's Clothing). **Est:** 1985. **Sales:** $2,500,000 (2000). **Emp:** 25. **Officers:** Terry Alden.

■ **5299** ■ **Rah Rah Sales Inc.**
Drawer 1170
Irmo, SC 29063-1170
Phone: (803)781-9729
Free: (800)845-6027 **Fax:** (803)781-8222
Products: Men's and boys' clothing; Men's and boys' sportswear. **SIC:** 5136 (Men's/Boys' Clothing).
Officers: Lanny Gunter, President.

■ **5300** ■ **Rainforest Inc.**
420 5th Ave. Fl 26
New York, NY 10018-2729
Phone: (212)695-3195 **Fax:** (212)967-2248
Products: Men's outerwear; Men's shirts; Sweaters. **SIC:** 5136 (Men's/Boys' Clothing). **Emp:** 9.

■ **5301** ■ **Raj India Trading Corp. Inc.**
PO Box 2644
Everett, WA 98203-0644
Phone: (425)257-0759
Free: (800)845-3665 **Fax:** (206)259-5244
E-mail: rajindia@juno.com
Products: Men's and women's imported clothing; Giftware, brassware, and general merchandise. **SICs:** 5136 (Men's/Boys' Clothing); 5137 (Women's/Children's Clothing); 5199 (Nondurable Goods Nec). **Est:** 1976. **Emp:** 7. **Officers:** Sukesh Chhabra; Nash Chhabra; Dinesh Chhabra.

■ **5302** ■ **Rally Products Inc.**
PO Box 702468
Tulsa, OK 74170-2468
Phone: (918)446-1006
Products: Men's sportswear; Women's sportswear. **SICs:** 5136 (Men's/Boys' Clothing); 5137 (Women's/Children's Clothing). **Officers:** Richard Blackburn, Chairman of the Board.

■ **5303** ■ **Ram Graphics Inc.**
PO Box 114
Alexandria, IN 46001
Phone: (765)724-7212
Free: (800)428-6444 **Fax:** (765)724-9767
Products: Imprinted and embroidered clothing. **SICs:** 5137 (Women's/Children's Clothing); 5136 (Men's/Boys' Clothing). **Est:** 1976. **Sales:** $10,000,000 (2000). **Emp:** 100. **Officers:** Larry Mercer, Partner; Dick Baker, Finance Officer; Ron Ruby, Partner; Patricia Mercer, Partner.

■ **5304** ■ **Harry J. Rashti and Company Inc.**
112 W 34th St., Ste. 921
New York, NY 10120-0101
Phone: (212)594-2939
Products: Infants' and children's clothing. **SIC:** 5137 (Women's/Children's Clothing). **Sales:** $34,000,000 (1994). **Emp:** 205. **Officers:** Michael Rashti, President; Lenny Walder, Controller.

■ **5305** ■ **Red Steer Glove Co.**
PO Box 7167
Salem, OR 97303-0034
Phone: (503)463-6227
Free: (800)727-1950 **Fax:** (503)463-6231
E-mail: redsteer@juno.com
URL: http://www.redsteer.com; http://www.redsteer.net
Products: Work gloves. **SICs:** 5136 (Men's/Boys' Clothing); 5137 (Women's/Children's Clothing). **Est:** 1983. **Sales:** $6,000,000 (1999). **Emp:** 15. **Officers:** R.W. Atwood II, President.

■ **5306** ■ **Mary Ann Reno**
9340-46 N May Ave.
Oklahoma City, OK 73120
Phone: (405)755-4033
Products: Men's and boys' clothing; Men's and boys' sportswear; Men's and boys' work clothing. **SIC:** 5136 (Men's/Boys' Clothing). **Est:** 1973. **Sales:** $500,000 (2000). **Emp:** 2. **Officers:** Mary Reno, Owner. **Former Name:** Richard H. & Mary Ann #Reno.

■ **5307** ■ **Reverse & Company**
745 Sunset Cliffs Blvd., Ste. 1001
San Diego, CA 92107
Phone: (619)223-5015 **Fax:** (619)523-1085
Products: Men's sportswear, including skiwear; Sporting goods, including skiing accessories; Toys; Sunglasses. **SICs:** 5136 (Men's/Boys' Clothing); 5091 (Sporting & Recreational Goods); 5092 (Toys & Hobby Goods & Supplies); 5048 (Ophthalmic Goods). **Officers:** Patrick D. Barker, President.

■ **5308** ■ **Reynolds Manufacturing Co.**
1 Paramount Dr.
PO Box 98
Bourbon, MO 65441
Phone: (573)732-4411 **Fax:** (573)732-5211
Products: Childrens' scarves; Men's scarves; Womens' scarves. **SICs:** 5136 (Men's/Boys' Clothing); 5137 (Women's/Children's Clothing). **Emp:** 49.

■ **5309** ■ **Rialto Inc.**
784 S San Pedro St.
Los Angeles, CA 90014
Phone: (213)689-9096
Products: Women's apparel. **SIC:** 5137 (Women's/Children's Clothing).

■ **5310** ■ **Ridgeview Inc.**
PO Box 8
Newton, NC 28658
Phone: (704)464-2972
Free: (800)438-9517 **Fax:** (704)464-2994
Products: Socks, including athletic socks. **SICs:** 5136 (Men's/Boys' Clothing); 5137 (Women's/Children's Clothing). **Est:** 1912. **Emp:** 300. **Officers:** Barry Tartarkin, VP of Marketing & Sales; Marc Swinnen, VP of International Sales; Ander Horne, Vice President.

■ **5311** ■ **Robela Knit Shop Ltd.**
250 N Main St.
Mt. Holly, NC 28120
Phone: (704)827-7246 **Fax:** (704)827-7248
Products: Women's sportswear; Children's sportswear; Men's sportswear. **SICs:** 5137 (Women's/Children's Clothing); 5136 (Men's/Boys' Clothing). **Sales:** $1,000,000 (2000). **Emp:** 10. **Officers:** Robert J. Freidl.

■ **5312** ■ **Robern Golfwear Inc.**
166 Whitney Ln.
Richboro, PA 18954-1080
Products: Sportswear, including golf and ski clothing. **SICs:** 5136 (Men's/Boys' Clothing); 5137 (Women's/Children's Clothing); 5139 (Footwear).

■ **5313** ■ **Robern Skiwear Inc.**
350 5th Ave.
New York, NY 10118
Phone: (212)563-7040
Products: Skiwear, including pants, jackets, and boots. **SICs:** 5136 (Men's/Boys' Clothing); 5091 (Sporting & Recreational Goods); 5137 (Women's/Children's Clothing); 5139 (Footwear).

■ **5314** ■ **Frank L. Robinson Co.**
1150 S Flower St.
Los Angeles, CA 90015
Phone: (213)748-8211
Free: (800)426-5280 **Fax:** (213)748-5808
Products: T-shirts and sweatpants. **SICs:** 5136 (Men's/Boys' Clothing); 5137 (Women's/Children's Clothing). **Est:** 1936. **Sales:** $32,000,000 (2000). **Emp:** 54. **Officers:** Harold Robinson, Partner; Jim Robinson, Partner; Jeff Robinson, Partner.

■ **5315** ■ **Robinson Manufacturing Company Inc.**
798 S Market St.
Dayton, TN 37321
Phone: (423)775-2212 **Fax:** (423)775-0489
Products: Clothes. **SIC:** 5136 (Men's/Boys' Clothing). **Est:** 1927. **Sales:** $80,000,000 (2000). **Emp:** 1,600. **Officers:** T. Jack Robinson.

■ **5316** ■ **Rock Candy Inc.**
1401 W 8th St.
Los Angeles, CA 90017-4302
Phone: (213)483-8570 **Fax:** (213)484-6220
Products: Women's apparel. **SIC:** 5137 (Women's/Children's Clothing). **Emp:** 10. **Officers:** Joyce Rothchild.

■ 5317 ■ **Rockmount of Arkansas**
17 N 2nd
Ft. Smith, AR 72901-1103
Phone: (501)782-4545 **Fax:** (501)782-4545
Products: Dresses; Blouses; Skirts and jackets;
Women's clothing accessories. **SIC:** 5137
(Women's/Children's Clothing). **Sales:** $1,000,000
(2000). **Emp:** 99. **Officers:** Jack A. Weil.

■ 5318 ■ **Rockmount Ranch Wear**
Manufacturing Co.
PO Box 481025
Denver, CO 80248
Phone: (303)629-7777 **Fax:** (303)629-5836
Products: Men's, women's and boy's western apparel
and accessories. **SIC:** 5136 (Men's/Boys' Clothing).
Sales: $13,000,000 (2000). **Emp:** 200.

■ 5319 ■ **Ronlee Apparel Co.**
165 Chubb Ave.
Lyndhurst, NJ 07071
Phone: (201)507-5300 **Fax:** (201)507-9790
Products: Fur and leather coats, jackets and skirts for
women. **SIC:** 5137 (Women's/Children's Clothing).
Sales: $43,000,000 (2000). **Emp:** 130. **Officers:** Y.W.
Lee, Sr. VP; Timmy Kim, Controller.

■ 5320 ■ **Rose's Stores Inc.**
PO Drawer 947
Henderson, NC 27536
Phone: (919)430-2100 **Fax:** (919)492-4226
Products: Department store merchandise, including
clothing, electronics, and household items. **SICs:** 5137
(Women's/Children's Clothing); 5136 (Men's/Boys'
Clothing); 5023 (Homefurnishings); 5064 (Electrical
Appliances—Television & Radio).

■ 5321 ■ **William Rosing**
4850 Diamond Dr.
Colorado Springs, CO 80918
Phone: (719)591-1606 **Free:** (800)458-1303
Products: T-shirts. **SICs:** 5136 (Men's/Boys' Clothing);
5137 (Women's/Children's Clothing). **Officers:** William
Rosing, Owner.

■ 5322 ■ **Royal Hawaiian Creations**
500 Alakawa St., No. 102-C
Honolulu, HI 96817-4576
Phone: (808)847-3663 **Fax:** (808)842-0516
Products: Women's clothing; Men's and boys'
clothing. **SICs:** 5137 (Women's/Children's Clothing);
5136 (Men's/Boys' Clothing). **Est:** 1987. **Sales:**
$6,500,000 (2000). **Emp:** 30. **Officers:** Bum Kang,
Owner.

■ 5323 ■ **Royal Textile Mills Inc.**
PO Box 250
Yanceyville, NC 27379-0250
Phone: (919)694-4121
Free: (800)334-9361 **Fax:** (919)694-9084
Products: Sporting and athletic goods; Children's
sportswear; Men's sportswear; Women's sportswear;
Body protective equipment of all types for baseball,
soccer, lacrosse, hockey, fencing, other sports. **SICs:**
5136 (Men's/Boys' Clothing); 5091 (Sporting &
Recreational Goods); 5137 (Women's/Children's
Clothing). **Sales:** $4,000,000 (2000). **Emp:** 99.
Officers: Mark V. Atwater.

■ 5324 ■ **Gene Roye**
756 S Spring St.
Los Angeles, CA 90014-2949
Phone: (213)629-9031 **Fax:** (213)623-1351
Products: Women's apparel. **SIC:** 5137
(Women's/Children's Clothing). **Est:** 1980. **Sales:**
$1,500,000 (2000). **Emp:** 25. **Officers:** Gene Roye,
President; Lisa Roye, Vice President.

■ 5325 ■ **Running Strong Inc.**
506 E Juanita Ave. 1
Mesa, AZ 85204-6544
Phone: (602)545-0068
Free: (800)736-1245 **Fax:** (602)545-7419
Products: Men's and boy's clothing, including t-shirts
and activewear. **SIC:** 5136 (Men's/Boys' Clothing). **Est:**
1987. **Sales:** $1,500,000 (2000). **Emp:** 15. **Officers:**
Randy Williams, President.

■ 5326 ■ **Russell Corp. Knit Apparel Div.**
PO Box 272
Alexander City, AL 35010
Phone: (256)329-4000 **Fax:** (256)329-4474
Products: Men's clothing and shirts, and women's
outwear. **SICs:** 5136 (Men's/Boys' Clothing); 5137
(Women's/Children's Clothing). **Sales:** $1,228,000,000
(2000). **Emp:** 18,000. **Officers:** John C. Adams, CEO,
President & Chairman of the Board; James D. Nabors,
Exec. VP & CFO.

■ 5327 ■ **S & L Monograms and Embroidery**
9808 Santa Fe Dr.
Overland Park, KS 66212-4564
Products: Women's and children's clothing. **SIC:** 5137
(Women's/Children's Clothing). **Officers:** Stanley
Brown, Chairman of the Board.

■ 5328 ■ **S & W Investments**
1600 Kentucky St. 2
Bellingham, WA 98226-4701
Phone: (206)676-0793
Free: (800)244-2530 **Fax:** 800-562-0414
Products: Printing on garments and apparel
accessories. **SICs:** 5136 (Men's/Boys' Clothing); 5137
(Women's/Children's Clothing). **Officers:** Wayne
Kanitz, Owner.

■ 5329 ■ **Safetywear**
1121 E Wallace
Ft. Wayne, IN 46803-2555
Phone: (219)456-3535 **Fax:** (219)744-9231
Products: Safety wear. **SICs:** 5136 (Men's/Boys'
Clothing); 5137 (Women's/Children's Clothing). **Emp:**
49. **Officers:** Dan Brough.

■ 5330 ■ **Samara Brothers, Inc.**
240 Mill Rd.
Edison, NJ 08817
Phone: (908)287-3939 **Fax:** (908)792-7320
Products: Children's clothing. **SIC:** 5137
(Women's/Children's Clothing). **Est:** 1953. **Sales:**
$20,000,000 (2000). **Emp:** 30. **Officers:** Donald F.
Gaffney, President; Jeff A. Meiskin, CFO; Gary
Goldman, Dir. of Marketing.

■ 5331 ■ **Joseph Sander Supply Co.**
3720 14th Ave.
Brooklyn, NY 11218-3608
Phone: (718)438-4223 **Fax:** (718)438-1496
Products: Sportswear. **SICs:** 5137
(Women's/Children's Clothing); 5136 (Men's/Boys'
Clothing). **Emp:** 50. **Officers:** Joseph Sander.

■ 5332 ■ **Sanford Shirt Co.**
529 W 29th St.
Baltimore, MD 21211-2916
Phone: (410)235-8338
Free: (800)541-9709 **Fax:** (410)235-6071
Products: Men's and boy's clothing, including
sportswear, work clothing, and uniforms. **SIC:** 5136
(Men's/Boys' Clothing). **Officers:** Sanford Panitz,
President.

■ 5333 ■ **Saxony Sportswear Co.**
2301 W Allegheny Ave.
Philadelphia, PA 19132
Phone: (215)227-0400 **Fax:** (215)227-6808
Products: Men's leather, sportswear, and golf clothing.
SIC: 5136 (Men's/Boys' Clothing). **Est:** 1957. **Sales:**
$10,000,000 (2000). **Emp:** 24. **Officers:** Harvey E.
Orman, Vice President; Neal Orman, President.

■ 5334 ■ **H. Schleifer and Son Inc.**
352 7th Ave.
New York, NY 10001
Phone: (212)564-5639
Products: Furs. **SIC:** 5137 (Women's/Children's
Clothing). **Sales:** $1,000,000 (2000). **Emp:** 2. **Officers:**
Michael Schleifer, President.

■ 5335 ■ **Schwartz and Benjamin Inc.**
PO Box 831
Lynn, MA 01903
Phone: (781)595-5600 **Fax:** (781)596-1475
Products: Ladies' leather shoes. **SIC:** 5139
(Footwear). **Sales:** $20,000,000 (2000). **Emp:** 30.
Officers: Danny Schwartz, President.

■ 5336 ■ **Jack Schwartz Shoes Inc.**
155 Avenue of the Americas
New York, NY 10013
Phone: (212)691-4700 **Fax:** (212)691-5350
Products: Footwear. **SIC:** 5139 (Footwear). **Sales:**
$170,000,000 (1999). **Emp:** 125. **Officers:** Bernard
Schwartz, Chairman of the Board; Jack Schwartz,
President.

■ 5337 ■ **Scope Imports Inc.**
8020 Blankenship Dr.
Houston, TX 77055
Phone: (713)688-0077 **Fax:** (713)688-8768
Products: Men's big and tall clothing. **SIC:** 5136
(Men's/Boys' Clothing). **Est:** 1967. **Sales:** $50,000,000
(2000). **Emp:** 55. **Officers:** Allan Finkelman, President;
Ray Brudno, CFO.

■ 5338 ■ **L.S. Scott Associates**
78-03 226th St., A
Flushing, NY 11364-3624
Phone: (212)695-2536
Products: Women's sportswear. **SIC:** 5137
(Women's/Children's Clothing). **Sales:** $1,000,000
(2000). **Emp:** 5. **Officers:** Margaret Scott, President.

■ 5339 ■ **Scottish Connection**
PO Box 94
Lincoln, NH 03251-0094
Phone: (603)745-3958 **Fax:** (603)745-8336
Products: Knit outerwear. **SICs:** 5136 (Men's/Boys'
Clothing); 5137 (Women's/Children's Clothing).
Officers: Callum Grant, Owner.

■ 5340 ■ **Scripts For All Reasons**
c/o Bill McDonnell
Silver Spring, MD 20902
Phone: (301)598-8584 **Fax:** (301)598-8584
Products: Offers script research and writing for video,
film, and audiovisual programs. Provides corporate
promotional, training and instructional media script
services. **SIC:** 5137 (Women's/Children's Clothing).
Emp: 1.

■ 5341 ■ **Segue Ltd.**
119 W 40th St., Fl 22
New York, NY 10018-2500
Phone: (212)869-8526 **Fax:** (212)869-0448
Products: Clothing, including sweaters, woven
blouses, and related separates. **SICs:** 5136
(Men's/Boys' Clothing); 5137 (Women's/Children's
Clothing). **Est:** 1980. **Sales:** $35,000,000 (2000). **Emp:**
18.

■ 5342 ■ **Seibel & Stern Corp.**
112 W 34th
New York, NY 10120-0093
Phone: (212)563-0326 **Fax:** (212)564-1434
Products: Girl's dresses. **SIC:** 5137
(Women's/Children's Clothing). **Sales:** $10,000,000
(2000). **Emp:** 499. **Officers:** Lawrence Davis.

■ 5343 ■ **William Self**
Statesboro Mall
Hwy. 80 E
Statesboro, GA 30458
Phone: (912)764-2226
Products: Men's and boy's clothing. **SIC:** 5136
(Men's/Boys' Clothing). **Officers:** William Self,
President.

■ 5344 ■ **Senor's Q Inc.**
11719 E Ashlan Ave.
Sanger, CA 93657-9326
Phone: (209)275-0780 **Fax:** (209)275-8663
Products: Baby blankets; Infant apparel. **SIC:** 5137
(Women's/Children's Clothing).

■ 5345 ■ **Shankles Hosiery Inc.**
804 Gault Ave. N
Ft. Payne, AL 35967-2725
Phone: (205)845-6161
Products: Foot socks. **SIC:** 5137 (Women's/Children's
Clothing). **Officers:** Gary Shankles, President.

■ 5346 ■ **Shawnee Garment Manufacturing Co.**
1 American Way
Shawnee, OK 74801
Phone: (405)273-0510 **Fax:** (405)273-0511
E-mail: roundhouse@mindspring.com
URL: http://www.round-house.com
Products: Bibs and overalls, including denim. **SIC:** 5136 (Men's/Boys' Clothing). **Est:** 1903. **Emp:** 50.
Officers: Jim Antosh, President; David Forgety, General Mgr.

■ 5347 ■ **Shelton Clothing Inc.**
2524 County Rd. 87
Moulton, AL 35650-5544
Phone: (205)974-9079 **Fax:** (205)974-9079
Products: Men's and boys' clothing; Men's and boys' suits and coats; Men's and boys' trousers; Women's clothing; Women's sportswear; Swimwear. **SICs:** 5136 (Men's/Boys' Clothing); 5137 (Women's/Children's Clothing). **Officers:** Bobby Shelton, President.

■ 5348 ■ **Shoe Corp. of Birmingham Inc.**
2320 1st Ave. N
Birmingham, AL 35203-4302
Phone: (205)326-2800 **Fax:** (205)326-2808
Products: Shoes. **SIC:** 5139 (Footwear). **Sales:** $2,000,000 (2000). **Emp:** 25.

■ 5349 ■ **Showroom Seven**
498 Swaitu Ave., 24th Fl.
New York, NY 10018
Phone: (212)643-4810 **Fax:** (212)971-6066
Products: Fashion designs; European and domestic womens' designer sportwear and accessories. **SIC:** 5137 (Women's/Children's Clothing). **Sales:** $10,000,000 (2000). **Emp:** 20. **Officers:** Jean-Marc Flack, President.

■ 5350 ■ **Showroom Seven**
498 Swaitu Ave., 24th Fl.
New York, NY 10018
Phone: (212)643-4810 **Fax:** (212)971-6066
Products: Clothing. **SIC:** 5137 (Women's/Children's Clothing). **Sales:** $10,000,000 (2000). **Emp:** 20.

■ 5351 ■ **Robert Sidney Furs Inc.**
150 W 30th St., Fl. 16
New York, NY 10001-4003
Phone: (212)279-4046
Products: Women's fur coats. **SIC:** 5137 (Women's/Children's Clothing). **Est:** 1969. **Sales:** $5,000,000 (2000). **Emp:** 9. **Officers:** Sidney Feldstein, President; Marissa Ash, Treasurer.

■ 5352 ■ **Sidneys Department Store & Uniforms, Inc.**
550-560 Broad St.
Augusta, GA 30901-1420
Phone: (706)722-3112
Free: (800)722-3112 **Fax:** (706)722-2262
Products: Men's and boys' clothing; Men's and boys' sportswear; Men's and boys' work clothing; Men's and boys' uniforms. **SIC:** 5136 (Men's/Boys' Clothing). **Est:** 1894. **Sales:** $1,000,000 (2000). **Emp:** 8. **Officers:** M. Steven Fishman, Chairman of the Board.

■ 5353 ■ **Siegels Inc.**
PO Box 984
Evansville, IN 47706-0984
Phone: (812)425-2268 **Fax:** (812)424-5961
Products: Uniforms and work clothing. **SICs:** 5136 (Men's/Boys' Clothing); 5137 (Women's/Children's Clothing).

■ 5354 ■ **Signature Apparel**
PO Box 3639
Brockton, MA 02304-3639
Phone: (508)587-2900
Free: (800)522-9004 **Fax:** (508)584-9338
URL: http://www.signatureapparel.com
Products: Custom-made uniforms; Embroidered and screen printed apparel; Promotional products. **SICs:** 5137 (Women's/Children's Clothing); 5136 (Men's/Boys' Clothing). **Est:** 1977. **Emp:** 35. **Officers:** William Pellegrini, President. **Former Name:** Aprons Unlimited Inc.

■ 5355 ■ **Silber Knitwear Corp.**
1635 Albany Ave.
Brooklyn, NY 11210-3513
Phone: (718)377-5252 **Fax:** (718)377-6883
Products: Women's apparel belts. **SIC:** 5137 (Women's/Children's Clothing). **Emp:** 49.

■ 5356 ■ **Silky's Sportswear**
RR 2 Box 1125
Mifflintown, PA 17059-9315
Phones: (717)567-6396 (717)567-7009
Fax: (717)567-7940
Products: Women's and children's apparel. **SIC:** 5137 (Women's/Children's Clothing). **Sales:** $1,400,000 (2000). **Emp:** 75. **Officers:** Richard E. Rhoads.

■ 5357 ■ **Simmons Hosiery Mill Inc.**
391 10th Ave. NE
Hickory, NC 28601-3833
Phone: (704)327-4890
Products: Men's and boys' clothing; Men's and boys' furnishings; Men's and boys' hosiery. **SIC:** 5136 (Men's/Boys' Clothing). **Officers:** Marion Roseman, President.

■ 5358 ■ **Simons Millinery Mart**
128 S 17th St.
Philadelphia, PA 19103
Phone: (215)569-9511 **Fax:** (215)963-0111
Products: Women's clothing, including jackets, blouses, pants, and dresses. **SIC:** 5137 (Women's/Children's Clothing). **Est:** 1965. **Sales:** $4,500,000 (2000). **Emp:** 46. **Officers:** Robert Brandt, President.

■ 5359 ■ **Singer Hosiery Mills Inc.**
PO Box 758
Thomasville, NC 27360
Phone: (919)475-2161 **Fax:** (919)475-6422
Products: Socks. **SICs:** 5137 (Women's/Children's Clothing); 5136 (Men's/Boys' Clothing). **Est:** 1945. **Sales:** $2,000,000 (2000). **Emp:** 50. **Officers:** Gerald Singer.

■ 5360 ■ **Howe K. Sipes Co.**
249 Mallory Ave. E
Memphis, TN 38109-2598
Phone: (901)948-0378 **Fax:** (901)774-4380
Products: Men's and boys' sportswear; Women's sportswear; Athletic uniforms. **SICs:** 5136 (Men's/Boys' Clothing); 5137 (Women's/Children's Clothing). **Est:** 1946. **Sales:** $6,000,000 (2000). **Emp:** 499. **Officers:** Howe K. Sipes Jr.

■ 5361 ■ **Skane Ltd.**
125 High St.
Farmington, ME 04938
Phone: (207)778-9508
Free: (800)848-0468 **Fax:** (207)778-5043
E-mail: skane@mainewest.com
Products: Ski wear. **SICs:** 5136 (Men's/Boys' Clothing); 5091 (Sporting & Recreational Goods); 5137 (Women's/Children's Clothing). **Est:** 1985. **Sales:** $2,000,000 (2000). **Emp:** 6. **Officers:** Leonard J. Widen, President; Kurt J. Widen, Vice President.

■ 5362 ■ **Skillers Workwear USA, Inc.**
601 Hansen Ave.
Butler, PA 16001-5664
Phone: (724)282-8581
Free: (800)325-8707 **Fax:** (724)282-7340
URL: http://www.skillers.com
Products: Professional tradesman and other workwear. **SICs:** 5136 (Men's/Boys' Clothing); 5137 (Women's/Children's Clothing). **Est:** 1997. **Sales:** $1,100,000 (2000). **Emp:** 5. **Officers:** James B. Rice, CEO & President; Johan Viio, Dir. of Mktg. & Sales; Steve Sloboda, Sec. & Treas.; Matti Viio, Chairman of the Board. **Former Name:** JDS Fashions Inc.

■ 5363 ■ **Slane Hosiery Mills Inc.**
PO Box 2486
High Point, NC 27261
Phone: (919)883-4136 **Fax:** (919)886-4543
Products: Men's and women's socks. **SICs:** 5136 (Men's/Boys' Clothing); 5137 (Women's/Children's Clothing).

■ 5364 ■ **Horace Small Apparel Co.**
350 28th Ave. N
Nashville, TN 37209
Phone: (615)320-1000 **Fax:** (615)327-1912
Products: Children's uniforms; Men's uniforms; Women's uniforms. **SICs:** 5137 (Women's/Children's Clothing); 5136 (Men's/Boys' Clothing). **Est:** 1937. **Sales:** $100,000,000 (2000). **Emp:** 1,400. **Officers:** Robert W. Gates, COO & President. **Former Name:** R & R Uniforms.

■ 5365 ■ **Sockyard Company Inc.**
366 5th Ave., No. 510
New York, NY 10001
Phone: (212)947-6295
Free: (800)223-7007 **Fax:** (212)564-0071
E-mail: sockyard@aol.com
Products: Socks. **SIC:** 5137 (Women's/Children's Clothing). **Est:** 1983. **Sales:** $20,000,000 (2000). **Emp:** 30. **Officers:** Stanley Kreinik, President; Gerry Cohen, VP of Finance; Gerry Cohen, Sales/Marketing Contact; R. Stanley Kreinik, Sales/Marketing Contact; Bob Estrich, Customer Service Contact.

■ 5366 ■ **Soft-As-A-Grape Inc.**
328 Marion Rd.
Wareham, MA 02571-1452
Phone: (508)548-6159
Free: (800)426-9525 **Fax:** (508)548-6263
Products: Men's, women's, and children's clothing and sportswear. **SICs:** 5136 (Men's/Boys' Clothing); 5137 (Women's/Children's Clothing). **Officers:** Allen Katzen, President.

■ 5367 ■ **Softouch Company Inc.**
1167 NW 159th Dr.
Miami, FL 33169-5807
Phone: (954)920-9117 **Fax:** (305)623-8717
Products: Sportswear. **SIC:** 5137 (Women's/Children's Clothing). **Sales:** $20,000,000 (2000). **Emp:** 120. **Officers:** N. Fixel.

■ 5368 ■ **South Carolina Tees Inc.**
PO Box 66
Columbia, SC 29202
Phone: (803)256-1393
Free: (800)829-5000 **Fax:** (803)771-7635
Products: Imprintable and embroidered sportswear. **SICs:** 5136 (Men's/Boys' Clothing); 5137 (Women's/Children's Clothing). **Emp:** 400. **Officers:** Bill Gregg.

■ 5369 ■ **South Wool**
PO Box 616
Stockbridge, MA 01262-0616
Phone: (413)298-4286 **Fax:** (413)298-4486
Products: Women's clothing, including sportswear and swimsuits. **SIC:** 5137 (Women's/Children's Clothing). **Officers:** Frederick Wallhausser, President.

■ 5370 ■ **Southern Apparel Corp.**
E 3rd Ext.
Robersonville, NC 27871
Phone: (919)795-3031 **Fax:** (919)795-4238
Products: Men's clothing; Children's clothing. **SICs:** 5136 (Men's/Boys' Clothing); 5137 (Women's/Children's Clothing). **Sales:** $5,000,000 (2000). **Emp:** 300. **Officers:** A. J. Mathews.

■ 5371 ■ **Southern Apparel Corp.**
12420 73rd Ct. W
Largo, FL 33773
Phone: (813)536-8672 **Fax:** (813)539-0752
Products: T-shirts. **SICs:** 5136 (Men's/Boys' Clothing); 5137 (Women's/Children's Clothing). **Est:** 1970. **Sales:** $12,000,000 (2000). **Emp:** 35. **Officers:** Robert W. Palmiero, CEO; Allen Fleeger, Treasurer & Secty.; Lynda L. Palmiero, VP of Marketing; Doug Chancey, Operations Mgr.

■ 5372 ■ **Southern California Tees**
5201 6th St.
Carpinteria, CA 93013
Phone: (805)684-0252
Free: (800)726-9001 **Fax:** (805)684-0554
Products: Imprintable and embroiderable sportswear. **SICs:** 5136 (Men's/Boys' Clothing); 5137 (Women's/Children's Clothing).

■ **5373** ■ **Southern Leather Co.**
PO Box 6
Memphis, TN 38101
Phone: (901)774-0400
Free: (800)844-6767   **Fax:** (901)946-1059
Products: Shoes and shoe findings. **SIC:** 5139 (Footwear). **Sales:** $177,000,000 (1999). **Emp:** 300. **Officers:** William I. Loewenberg, President; Joe Newsome, Controller.

■ **5374** ■ **Southwestern Wholesale Co. Inc.**
PO Box 18033
Shreveport, LA 71138-1033
Phone: (318)222-3184   **Fax:** (318)221-1810
Products: Men's and boys' clothing. **SIC:** 5136 (Men's/Boys' Clothing). **Officers:** Scott Lawrence, President.

■ **5375** ■ **Soyad Brothers Textile Corp.**
24011 Hoover Rd.
Warren, MI 48089
Phone: (810)755-5700
Free: (800)922-9923   **Fax:** (810)755-3790
E-mail: soyad@aol.comm
Products: Sport socks. **SICs:** 5137 (Women's/Children's Clothing); 5136 (Men's/Boys' Clothing). **Est:** 1977. **Sales:** $2,000,000 (2000). **Emp:** 49. **Officers:** Tom Soyad; Cecile Nuaman; George Soyad; Pierre Soyad; Joseph Soyad.

■ **5376** ■ **Spalding Holdings Corp.**
425 Meadow St.
Chicopee, MA 01021
Phone: (413)536-1200   **Fax:** (413)536-1404
Products: Athletic equipment maker. **SICs:** 5139 (Footwear); 5091 (Sporting & Recreational Goods). **Sales:** $800,000,000 (2000). **Emp:** 1,900. **Officers:** James Craigie, CEO & President; Wade Lewis, CFO.

■ **5377** ■ **Sparlon Hosiery Mills Inc.**
1600 SW 66th Ave.
Pembroke Pines, FL 33023
Phone: (954)966-2050
Free: (800)966-6636   **Fax:** (954)966-6428
Products: Children's clothing; Women's and men's hosiery; Men's underwear. **SICs:** 5137 (Women's/Children's Clothing); 5136 (Men's/Boys' Clothing). **Est:** 1967. **Sales:** $3,000,000 (1999). **Emp:** 8. **Officers:** Isaac Chocran; Miriam Abrams, Sales & Marketing Contact, e-mail: miriam2130@aol.com.

■ **5378** ■ **Specialty House Inc.**
411 5th Ave., No. 700
New York, NY 10016
Phone: (212)532-0700
Products: Silk and cotton scarves. **SIC:** 5137 (Women's/Children's Clothing). **Sales:** $13,000,000 (2000). **Emp:** 40. **Officers:** Kenneth Kures, CEO; Dennis Blaine, CFO.

■ **5379** ■ **Spectacular Modes Inc.**
2036-A NW 23rd Ave.
Miami, FL 33142-7354
Phone: (305)634-7575   **Fax:** (305)633-0751
Products: Clothes. **SICs:** 5137 (Women's/Children's Clothing); 5136 (Men's/Boys' Clothing). **Sales:** $1,056,500 (2000). **Emp:** 49. **Officers:** Manuel Coll.

■ **5380** ■ **I. Spiewalk & Sons, Inc.**
469 7th Ave., 10th Fl.
New York, NY 10018
Phone: (212)695-1620
Free: (800)223-6850   **Fax:** (212)629-4803
URL: http://www.spiewak.com
Products: Men's, women's, and children's outerwear and jackets. **SICs:** 5136 (Men's/Boys' Clothing); 5137 (Women's/Children's Clothing). **Est:** 1904. **Officers:** Gerald Spiewak; Michael Spiewak; Roy Spiewak; Sol Jacobs, Sales Mgr.; Doris Williams, Customer Service Mgr.; Jim Walsh, Human Resources; Roy Spiewak.

■ **5381** ■ **Spoiled Rotten USA Inc.**
305 E 140th St.
Bronx, NY 10454
Phone: (718)993-7006   **Fax:** (718)993-6314
Products: Women and children's clothing. **SIC:** 5137 (Women's/Children's Clothing).

■ **5382** ■ **Sport Palace Wholesale**
3808 Rosecrans, No. 215
San Diego, CA 92110
Phone: (619)299-5236   **Fax:** (619)299-5236
Products: Hats. **SICs:** 5136 (Men's/Boys' Clothing); 5137 (Women's/Children's Clothing). **Est:** 1974. **Sales:** $1,000,000 (2000). **Emp:** 8. **Officers:** Al Hammer; Bill Wilson.

■ **5383** ■ **Sport Spectrum**
4421 Highway 58
Chattanooga, TN 37416-3012
Phone: (423)899-9238   **Fax:** (423)892-9076
Products: High school and middle school team uniforms. **SICs:** 5136 (Men's/Boys' Clothing); 5137 (Women's/Children's Clothing). **Officers:** John Tindell, Owner.

■ **5384** ■ **Sportcap Inc.**
13401 S Main St.
Los Angeles, CA 90061-1813
Phone: (310)538-3312
Free: (800)421-5511   **Fax:** (310)324-3898
E-mail: sportcap@aol.com
URL: http://www.sportcap.com
Products: Baseball caps. **SICs:** 5136 (Men's/Boys' Clothing); 5137 (Women's/Children's Clothing). **Est:** 1978. **Sales:** $12,000,000 (2000). **Emp:** 60. **Officers:** Sam Meyerhoff, President; Susan Meyerhoff, Vice President.

■ **5385** ■ **Sportif USA Inc.**
1415 Greg St. No. 101
Sparks, NV 89431
Phone: (702)359-6400   **Fax:** (702)359-2098
URL: http://www.sportif.com
Products: Outdoor lifestyle clothing. **SICs:** 5136 (Men's/Boys' Clothing); 5137 (Women's/Children's Clothing). **Est:** 1965. **Sales:** $20,000,000 (2000). **Emp:** 42. **Officers:** John Kirsch, President; Doug Moir, Controller; Steven Kirsch, Dir. of Marketing & Sales.

■ **5386** ■ **Sporting Image Inc.**
1000 E Michigan Ave.
Paw Paw, MI 49079
Phone: (616)657-5646
Free: (800)818-5520   **Fax:** (616)657-2074
Products: Men's, women's, and children's sportswear. **SICs:** 5137 (Women's/Children's Clothing); 5136 (Men's/Boys' Clothing). **Est:** 1986. **Sales:** $500,000 (2000). **Emp:** 10. **Officers:** John Tapper, President.

■ **5387** ■ **Sports Specialties Corp.**
20001 Ellipse
Foothill Ranch, CA 92610
Phone: (949)768-4000
Free: (800)535-2222   **Fax:** 800-892-4607
Products: Professional sportswear, including headgear. **SICs:** 5136 (Men's/Boys' Clothing); 5091 (Sporting & Recreational Goods); 5137 (Women's/Children's Clothing). **Est:** 1970. **Sales:** $44,000,000 (2000). **Emp:** 85. **Officers:** Mark A, Hampton, General Mgr.; Steven Guizado, Finance Officer.

■ **5388** ■ **Sportsarama Inc.**
PO Box 596
Sturgis, MI 49091-0596
Phone: (616)651-4991   **Fax:** (616)659-4191
Products: Men's and boys' clothing; Men's and boys' sportswear. **SIC:** 5136 (Men's/Boys' Clothing). **Officers:** Gary Stewart, President.

■ **5389** ■ **Sportsprint Inc.**
6197 Bermuda Rd.
St. Louis, MO 63135
Phone: (314)521-9000
Free: (800)325-4858   **Fax:** (314)521-0395
E-mail: netsales@sportsprint.com
URL: http://www.sportsprint.com
Products: Team sportswear, including shirts, baseball uniforms, and jackets. **SICs:** 5136 (Men's/Boys' Clothing); 5137 (Women's/Children's Clothing). **Est:** 1973. **Sales:** $4,000,000 (2000). **Emp:** 61. **Officers:** Ralph Rockamann, e-mail: ralph@sportsprint.com.

■ **5390** ■ **Spyder Active Sports Inc.**
3600 Pearl St.
Boulder, CO 80301
Phone: (303)449-0611   **Fax:** (303)449-1404
URL: http://www.spyder.com
Products: Women's and children's ski apparel. **SICs:** 5137 (Women's/Children's Clothing); 5136 (Men's/Boys' Clothing). **Officers:** David Jacobs, President.

■ **5391** ■ **SST Sales Company Inc.**
1302 Stratton Ave.
Nashville, TN 37206
Phone: (615)262-7895   **Fax:** (615)333-0197
Products: Advertising specialty items; Embroidery and screen print sportswear. **SICs:** 5136 (Men's/Boys' Clothing); 5137 (Women's/Children's Clothing); 5199 (Nondurable Goods Nec). **Est:** 1982. **Emp:** 2. **Officers:** C. Ambrose, President.

■ **5392** ■ **Star of India Fashions**
1038 W Southern
Tempe, AZ 85282
Phone: (602)968-6195   **Fax:** (602)966-4552
Products: Women's clothing. **SIC:** 5137 (Women's/Children's Clothing). **Officers:** Satya Verma, President.

■ **5393** ■ **Starmac Group**
627 Vassar Rd.
Wenonah, NJ 08090
Phone: (856)582-4625   **Fax:** (856)582-1684
E-mail: mmmr@snip.net
Products: Men's jeans and casual wear; Leather goods; Medical equipment and supplies; Sporting goods; Sunglasses, handbags, watches, clothing, and clothing. **SICs:** 5136 (Men's/Boys' Clothing); 5199 (Nondurable Goods Nec); 5047 (Medical & Hospital Equipment); 5091 (Sporting & Recreational Goods). **Est:** 1985. **Sales:** $1,200,000 (2000). **Emp:** 6. **Officers:** Michael A. Colosi, President.

■ **5394** ■ **W. E. Stephens Manufacturing Company Inc.**
PO Box 190675
Nashville, TN 37219-0675
Phone: (615)255-1278   **Fax:** (615)256-3705
Products: Women's jeans; Men's pants. **SICs:** 5137 (Women's/Children's Clothing); 5136 (Men's/Boys' Clothing). **Sales:** $6,000,000 (2000). **Emp:** 499. **Officers:** Walter Marianelli.

■ **5395** ■ **Steven Hosiery Inc.**
997 13th St. SW
Hickory, NC 28602-4914
Phone: (704)328-1046   **Fax:** (704)327-7741
Products: Men's and boys' clothing; Men's and boys' furnishings; Men's and boys' hosiery. **SIC:** 5136 (Men's/Boys' Clothing). **Officers:** Kathleen Reese, President.

■ **5396** ■ **Robert Stock Ltd.**
1370 Broadway, 14th Fl.
New York, NY 10018-7302
Products: Men's, women's and boys clothing, men's and women's longwear. **SICs:** 5136 (Men's/Boys' Clothing); 5137 (Women's/Children's Clothing). **Sales:** $100,000,000 (2000). **Emp:** 25. **Officers:** Chuck Hellman, President; Robert Stock, CFO.

■ **5397** ■ **Stone Enterprises**
2570 Cloverdale Ave., No. C
Concord, CA 94518-2425
Phone: (510)582-4180   **Fax:** (510)582-2503
Products: Sportswear, exercisewear, lingerie, and swimsuits. **SIC:** 5137 (Women's/Children's Clothing).

■ **5398** ■ **C.P. Stone Island**
85 5th Ave., 11 Fl.
New York, NY 10003-3019
Phone: (212)366-9595
Products: Sportswear. **SIC:** 5136 (Men's/Boys' Clothing). **Est:** 1977. **Sales:** $3,000,000 (2000). **Emp:** 6. **Officers:** Martino Scabbia Guerrini, Vice President.

■ **5399** ■ **Stonehill Group Inc.**
PO Box 6488
Manchester, NH 03108-5033
Phone: (603)626-1677 **Fax:** (603)626-1660
Products: Health care uniforms. **SICs:** 5136 (Men's/Boys' Clothing); 5137 (Women's/Children's Clothing). **Officers:** Diann Steinberg, President.

■ **5400** ■ **Striker Products**
307 S Broadway
Pittsburg, KS 66762
Phone: (316)232-3111
Free: (800)669-4356 **Fax:** (316)232-3111
Products: Heat transfer T-shirts. **SICs:** 5137 (Women's/Children's Clothing); 5136 (Men's/Boys' Clothing).

■ **5401** ■ **Suave Noble Creations Inc.**
PO Box 8272
New York, NY 10116-4651
Phone: (212)563-3636 **Fax:** (212)563-4848
Products: Women's sportswear; Men's and boys' clothing; Children's outerwear; Leather and sheep-lined clothing; Personal leather goods; Jewelry. **SICs:** 5137 (Women's/Children's Clothing); 5094 (Jewelry & Precious Stones); 5136 (Men's/Boys' Clothing). **Sales:** $7,000,000 (2000). **Emp:** 9.

■ **5402** ■ **Suk Fashions**
747 Pittston
Allentown, PA 18103-3255
Phone: (215)435-4565 **Fax:** (215)435-2557
Products: Ladies' and men's clothing. **SICs:** 5137 (Women's/Children's Clothing); 5136 (Men's/Boys' Clothing). **Emp:** 49. **Officers:** Peter Cho.

■ **5403** ■ **Summit Hats**
1120 Roberts St.
Houston, TX 77003
Phone: (713)224-2683
Free: (888)741-5987 **Fax:** (713)224-2683
URL: http://www.summithatsinc.yahoo.com
Products: Clothing and hats. **SICs:** 5137 (Women's/Children's Clothing); 5136 (Men's/Boys' Clothing). **Est:** 1974. **Sales:** $500,000 (2000). **Emp:** 9.

■ **5404** ■ **Summit Hats**
1120 Roberts St.
Houston, TX 77003
Phone: (713)224-2683
Free: (888)741-5987 **Fax:** (713)224-2683
Products: Clothing. **SIC:** 5137 (Women's/Children's Clothing). **Sales:** $500,000 (2000). **Emp:** 9.

■ **5405** ■ **Sun Shader International, Inc.**
4601 10th Ave. N
Lake Worth, FL 33463-2203
Phone: (561)588-6887 **Fax:** (561)588-5930
E-mail: sunshader@eml.net
URL: http://www.sunshader.com
Products: Patented sun visors; Athletic headbands. **SICs:** 5136 (Men's/Boys' Clothing); 5137 (Women's/Children's Clothing); 5091 (Sporting & Recreational Goods). **Est:** 1976. **Emp:** 15. **Officers:** Jon Boswell; Helen Brown; Wayne Lisle.

■ **5406** ■ **Sundog Productions**
3809 Pickett Rd.
Fairfax, VA 22031-3605
Phone: (703)978-0041
Free: (800)338-0177 **Fax:** (703)978-0043
Products: Men's, women's, and children's clothing, specifically dyed garments. **SICs:** 5137 (Women's/Children's Clothing); 5136 (Men's/Boys' Clothing). **Officers:** Curtis Shiver, Owner.

■ **5407** ■ **Sunshine Cap Co.**
1142 W Main
Lakeland, FL 33815-4362
Phone: (941)688-8147
Free: (800)969-2050 **Fax:** (941)688-4930
E-mail: suncapco@aol.com
URL: http://www.sunshinecap.com
Products: Headwear, including caps. **SICs:** 5136 (Men's/Boys' Clothing); 5137 (Women's/Children's Clothing). **Sales:** $2,000,000 (2000). **Emp:** 56. **Officers:** Jordan Cokee; Matthew Cokee, Sales/Marketing Contact; Diana Todd, Customer Service Contact; Pat Kite, Human Resources Contact.

■ **5408** ■ **Superba Inc.**
350 5th Ave.
New York, NY 10118-0100
Phone: (212)594-2720 **Fax:** (212)629-5731
Products: Neck ties. **SIC:** 5136 (Men's/Boys' Clothing). **Emp:** 499. **Officers:** Mervyn Mandelbaum.

■ **5409** ■ **Surratt Hosiery Mill Inc.**
22872 NC Hwy. 8
Denton, NC 27239-8175
Phone: (336)859-4583 **Fax:** (336)859-4713
Products: Men's and women's socks. **SICs:** 5136 (Men's/Boys' Clothing); 5137 (Women's/Children's Clothing). **Est:** 1939. **Sales:** $3,000,000 (2000). **Emp:** 52. **Officers:** Martin Bundy, Plant Manager; Irving Surratt, President.

■ **5410** ■ **Sussex Company Inc.**
PO Box J
Milford, DE 19963
Phone: (302)422-8037 **Fax:** (302)422-8244
Products: Apparel and accessories. **SICs:** 5136 (Men's/Boys' Clothing); 5137 (Women's/Children's Clothing). **Sales:** $64,000,000 (2000). **Emp:** 93. **Officers:** Jerry Lear, President.

■ **5411** ■ **Frank Sussman Co.**
28 N 3rd St.
Philadelphia, PA 19106
Phone: (215)627-3221
Free: (800)541-3221 **Fax:** (215)627-7359
E-mail: sussman@ix.netcom.com
URL: http://www.franksussman.com
Products: Licensed sports apparel, including sweatshirts and hats. **SICs:** 5136 (Men's/Boys' Clothing); 5137 (Women's/Children's Clothing); 5091 (Sporting & Recreational Goods). **Est:** 1937. **Sales:** $12,000,000 (2000). **Emp:** 49. **Officers:** Lawrence Burstein.

■ **5412** ■ **Swany America Corp.**
PO Box 867
Gloversville, NY 12078
Phone: (518)725-3333 **Fax:** (518)725-2026
Products: Gloves. **SICs:** 5136 (Men's/Boys' Clothing); 5137 (Women's/Children's Clothing). **Sales:** $10,000,000 (2000). **Emp:** 25. **Officers:** Y.C. Son, Exec. VP; Yasu Kawakita, Treasurer; J.P. Kloser, Dir. of Marketing & Sales.

■ **5413** ■ **Sylvias Swimwear-Swim Shop**
14100 NE 20th St.
Bellevue, WA 98007-3727
Phone: (425)747-1131 **Fax:** (425)747-8924
Products: Men's, women's, children's, and infant's swimsuits. **SICs:** 5137 (Women's/Children's Clothing); 5136 (Men's/Boys' Clothing). **Officers:** Sylvia Powell, Partner.

■ **5414** ■ **Symphony Designs Inc.**
810 Shames Dr.
Westbury, NY 11590-1727
Phone: (212)695-2526
Products: Italian scarves. **SIC:** 5137 (Women's/Children's Clothing). **Est:** 1961. **Sales:** $3,000,000 (2000). **Emp:** 7. **Officers:** Lawrence Kogan, President.

■ **5415** ■ **T-J Knit Enterprises Inc.**
237 W 35th St., Ste. 806
New York, NY 10001-1905
Phone: (212)391-1700
Products: Sweaters and knit apparel. **SICs:** 5136 (Men's/Boys' Clothing); 5137 (Women's/Children's Clothing). **Est:** 1979. **Sales:** $15,000,000 (2000). **Emp:** 45. **Officers:** Mark Grebler, President; Robert Ezykowich, CFO.

■ **5416** ■ **T-Shirt City Inc.**
12080 Mosteller Rd.
Cincinnati, OH 45241-1529
Phone: (513)542-3500
Products: Plain T-shirts and sweatshirts. **SICs:** 5136 (Men's/Boys' Clothing); 5137 (Women's/Children's Clothing). **Est:** 1976. **Sales:** $55,000,000 (2000). **Emp:** 82. **Officers:** Mitch Shapiro, President; John Leopard, Controller; Mike Helscher, Dir. of Marketing & Sales; Shelby Davidson, Dir. of Data Processing; Nancy Helwig, Dir of Human Resources.

■ **5417** ■ **T-Shirt Factory & Odd Shop**
2630 1st Ave.
Hibbing, MN 55746-2245
Phone: (218)262-4224 **Fax:** (218)262-6380
Products: Men's and boys' clothing; Men's and boys' shirts; Men's and boys' sportswear; Unisex clothing. **SICs:** 5136 (Men's/Boys' Clothing); 5137 (Women's/Children's Clothing). **Officers:** John Fillman, Owner.

■ **5418** ■ **T-Shirt Gallery and Sports**
5815 Weber Rd.
Corpus Christi, TX 78413
Phone: (361)852-8992
Free: (877)852-8992 **Fax:** (361)852-0096
URL: http://www.jokaysports.com
Products: Shirts; Caps; Jackets; Sport uniforms and equipment. **SIC:** 5131 (Piece Goods & Notions). **Est:** 1978. **Sales:** $750,000 (2000). **Emp:** 7. **Officers:** Thomas J. Basile, President, e-mail: thmbasile@aol.com; Sharon K. Basile, Secretary.

■ **5419** ■ **Sergio Tacchini Apparel**
1055 W Victoria St.
Compton, CA 90220
Phone: (213)774-1746 **Fax:** (213)603-0588
Products: Children's clothing accessories; Women's clothing accessories; Men's and boys' clothing. **SICs:** 5136 (Men's/Boys' Clothing); 5137 (Women's/Children's Clothing). **Sales:** $25,000,000 (2000). **Emp:** 40.

■ **5420** ■ **Taj Inc.**
1050 Ala Moana Blvd., Ste. A7
Honolulu, HI 96814-4910
Phone: (808)592-1900 **Fax:** (808)592-1903
Products: Women's and children's clothing. **SIC:** 5137 (Women's/Children's Clothing). **Officers:** Teresa Ching-Wong, President.

■ **5421** ■ **Talbert Trading Corp.**
5 Quinsigamond Ave.
Worcester, MA 01610
Phone: (508)752-5496
Products: Clothing. **SICs:** 5136 (Men's/Boys' Clothing); 5137 (Women's/Children's Clothing). **Est:** 1967. **Sales:** $6,000,000 (2000). **Emp:** 200. **Officers:** S. Talbert, President.

■ **5422** ■ **Tamara Imports**
PO Box 47280
Dallas, TX 75247
Phone: (214)638-1889 **Fax:** (214)638-3436
Products: Dresses. **SIC:** 5137 (Women's/Children's Clothing). **Sales:** $15,000,000 (2000). **Emp:** 50. **Officers:** Jack Greenberg, President.

■ **5423** ■ **TBI**
6220 San Vivente Blvd.
Los Angeles, CA 90048
Phone: (213)965-9511 **Fax:** (213)965-9224
Products: Close-out clothing; Men's clothing; Women's clothing. **SICs:** 5136 (Men's/Boys' Clothing); 5137 (Women's/Children's Clothing). **Officers:** Toplyn Iyoha, President.

■ **5424** ■ **Tees Dyes**
114 Old Colony Dr.
Mashpee, MA 02649-2532
Phone: (781)643-8140 **Fax:** (781)648-8041
Products: Men's and boys' clothing; Women's clothing. **SICs:** 5136 (Men's/Boys' Clothing); 5137 (Women's/Children's Clothing). **Officers:** Timothy Putney, Owner.

■ **5425** ■ **Terramar Sports Worldwide Ltd.**
10 Midland Ave.
Port Chester, NY 10573
Phone: (914)934-8000
Free: (800)937-0600 **Fax:** (914)937-0600
E-mail: terramar25@aol.com
Products: Sports underwear products. **SICs:** 5136 (Men's/Boys' Clothing); 5137 (Women's/Children's Clothing). **Est:** 1971. **Sales:** $10,000,000 (2000). **Emp:** 15. **Officers:** Mel Shapiro, President; Russ Pitman, VP of Sales; Sheri Abalate, Customer Service Mgr.; Linda Shapiro, VP of Operations.

■ **5426** ■ **Terry Products Inc.**
Drawer 108
Kannapolis, NC 28082
Phone: (704)938-3191 **Fax:** (704)938-8830
Products: Infant apparel. **SIC:** 5137
(Women's/Children's Clothing). **Est:** 1961. **Sales:**
$30,000,000 (2000). **Emp:** 474. **Officers:** M.A. Kraft,
President; James Amweg, VP & CFO; Walter Lee
Troop, VP of Marketing & Sales.

■ **5427** ■ **TET Incorporated**
806 18th St.
Spirit Lake, IA 51360-1234
Phone: (712)338-6774 **Fax:** (712)338-0011
Products: Women's clothing accessories; Children's
clothing accessories. **SIC:** 5137 (Women's/Children's
Clothing). **Officers:** Tom Meinen, President.

■ **5428** ■ **Texas Tees**
3815-C Jarrett Way
Austin, TX 78728-1214
Phone: (512)388-3530
Free: (800)659-5060 **Fax:** (512)388-3935
E-mail: txtees@netzero.net
Products: Clothing, including t-shirts. **SICs:** 5136
(Men's/Boys' Clothing); 5137 (Women's/Children's
Clothing).

■ **5429** ■ **Frank R. Thomas Company Inc.**
PO Box 2587
Jackson, MS 39207-2587
Phone: (601)353-4793
Products: Men's and women's merchandise. **SICs:**
5136 (Men's/Boys' Clothing); 5137
(Women's/Children's Clothing). **Officers:** Elliot
Thomas, President.

■ **5430** ■ **Time Out For Sports**
8840 Orchard Tree Ln.
Baltimore, MD 21286-2143
Phone: (410)668-9160 **Fax:** (410)668-9217
Products: Women's sportswear; Swimwear;
Blankbooks and looseleaf binders. **SICs:** 5137
(Women's/Children's Clothing); 5112 (Stationery &
Office Supplies). **Officers:** Nancy Sommers, Owner.

■ **5431** ■ **Tinley Performancewear**
5111 Santa Fe St., Ste. F
San Diego, CA 92109-1614
Phone: (619)581-2800 **Fax:** (619)581-2860
Products: Children's sportswear; Men's sportswear;
Women's sportswear. **SICs:** 5136 (Men's/Boys'
Clothing); 5137 (Women's/Children's Clothing). **Est:**
1984. **Sales:** $10,000,000 (2000). **Emp:** 80. **Officers:**
Jeffrey Essakow; Jim Riley; Brad Shapiro.

■ **5432** ■ **Todd Uniform Inc.**
3668 S Geyer Rd.
St. Louis, MO 63127
Phone: (314)984-0365
Free: (800)325-9516 **Fax:** (314)984-5798
Products: Coveralls, overalls, and jumpsuits; Work
gloves and mittens; Jackets; Men's uniforms; Women's
uniforms. **SICs:** 5136 (Men's/Boys' Clothing); 5137
(Women's/Children's Clothing). **Est:** 1882.

■ **5433** ■ **Tom Thumb Glove Co.**
PO Box 640
Wilkesboro, NC 28697
Phone: (919)667-1281
Free: (800)334-8344 **Fax:** (919)667-3695
Products: Gloves. **SICs:** 5136 (Men's/Boys' Clothing);
5137 (Women's/Children's Clothing). **Sales:**
$15,000,000 (2000). **Emp:** 499. **Officers:** Harold
Plemmons.

■ **5434** ■ **Top Comfo Athletic Sox Inc.**
PO Box 10304
Lynchburg, VA 24506-0304
Phone: (804)237-2323 **Fax:** (804)846-3297
Products: Men's and women's athletic socks. **SICs:**
5136 (Men's/Boys' Clothing); 5137
(Women's/Children's Clothing). **Est:** 1971. **Emp:** 11.
Officers: T.C. Cochran, President; Jane R. Cochran,
Treasurer.

■ **5435** ■ **Topsville Inc.**
11800 NW 102nd Rd.
Medley, FL 33178
Phone: (305)883-8677 **Fax:** (305)888-1365
Products: Children's clothing. **SIC:** 5137
(Women's/Children's Clothing). **Est:** 1974. **Sales:**
$40,000,000 (2000). **Emp:** 50. **Officers:** Mark
Nitzberg, President; Maurice Aniel, CFO, e-mail:
maurice@topsville.com; Lori Nitzberg, Sales, e-mail:
lori@topsville.com.

■ **5436** ■ **Torres Hat Company**
216 Century Blvd.
Laredo, TX 78040
Phone: (956)724-1473 **Fax:** (956)723-3040
Products: Hats. **SICs:** 5136 (Men's/Boys' Clothing);
5137 (Women's/Children's Clothing).

■ **5437** ■ **Tots Wear Company Inc.**
235-239 Holliday St.
Baltimore, MD 21202
Phone: (410)752-0134 **Fax:** (410)576-8792
Products: Infants' and children's clothing, accessories,
and gift items. **SIC:** 5137 (Women's/Children's
Clothing). **Est:** 1947. **Emp:** 12. **Officers:** Mildred
Nochumowitz, President.

■ **5438** ■ **Town Talk Cap Manufacturing Co.**
PO Box 58157
Louisville, KY 40268-0157
Phone: (502)933-7575
Free: (800)626-2220 **Fax:** (502)933-7599
E-mail: custserv@ttcaps.com
URL: http://www.ttcaps.com
Products: Hats, including golf hats, women's visors,
straw hats, and caps. **SIC:** 5137 (Women's/Children's
Clothing). **Est:** 1919. **Sales:** $7,000,000 (2000). **Emp:**
90. **Officers:** Wayne O. Joplin; Rose M. Coomes.

■ **5439** ■ **Track 'N Trail**
4961-A Windplay Dr.
El Dorado Hills, CA 95762
Phone: (916)933-4525 **Fax:** (916)933-4521
Products: Full service specialty store focusing on a
broad range of high-quality branded casual, outdoor
and adventure footwear and apparel. **SICs:** 5136
(Men's/Boys' Clothing); 5137 (Women's/Children's
Clothing); 5139 (Footwear). **Sales:** $99,900,000
(2000). **Emp:** 1,560. **Officers:** Gregory M. Kilgore,
President & COO; Daniel J. Nahmens, Exec. VP &
CFO.

■ **5440** ■ **Trade Routes Ltd.**
39 New York Ave. NE
Washington, DC 20002-3327
Phone: (202)371-0090
Products: Women's and children's clothing, including
sportswear and swimsuits. **SIC:** 5137
(Women's/Children's Clothing). **Officers:** A Moss,
President.

■ **5441** ■ **Trophy Craft Source**
10001 3rd St., No. 7
Corpus Christi, TX 78404
Phone: (512)885-0500
Products: Shirts. **SIC:** 5131 (Piece Goods & Notions).

■ **5442** ■ **True Blue Inc.**
2601 W Commodore Way
Seattle, WA 98199-1231
Phone: (206)285-9480 **Fax:** (206)282-0032
Products: Women's western apparel. **SIC:** 5137
(Women's/Children's Clothing). **Officers:** Jeffery Hoch,
President.

■ **5443** ■ **TSF Sportswear**
4201 NE 12th Terrace
Oakland Park, FL 33334-4722
Phone: (954)564-4435
Free: (800)331-1067 **Fax:** (954)565-5542
E-mail: tshirtsfl@aol.com
URL: http://www.tsfsportswear.net
Products: Blank shirts, polo shirts, and women's
apparel. **SICs:** 5137 (Women's/Children's Clothing);
5136 (Men's/Boys' Clothing). **Est:** 1974. **Sales:**
$25,000,000 (2000). **Emp:** 85. **Officers:** B. Schulman;
Robert R. Randall, Sales/Marketing Contact. **Former
Name:** T-Shirts of Florida Inc.

■ **5444** ■ **Tuf-Nut Company Inc.**
715 E Austin
Nevada, MO 64772
Phone: (417)667-8151 **Fax:** (417)667-2008
Products: Work clothing. **SIC:** 5136 (Men's/Boys'
Clothing). **Sales:** $11,000,000 (1992). **Emp:** 30.
Officers: Leon Smith, President.

■ **5445** ■ **Turban Plus**
13692 Newhope St.
Garden Grove, CA 92843-3712
Phone: (714)530-9590
Free: (800)552-0589 **Fax:** (714)530-9671
Products: Hats. **SICs:** 5137 (Women's/Children's
Clothing); 5136 (Men's/Boys' Clothing). **Est:** 1961.
Emp: 88. **Officers:** Jorge A. Nunez.

■ **5446** ■ **Tuxedo Junction Inc.**
7105-7 Allentown Rd.
Ft. Washington, MD 20744
Phone: (301)449-4465
Products: Mens' and boys' tuxedos. **SIC:** 5136
(Men's/Boys' Clothing). **Officers:** Henry Becker,
President.

■ **5447** ■ **Twin City Manufacturing Co.**
PO Box 1797
Reidsville, NC 27323-1797
Phone: (912)763-2115 **Fax:** (912)763-2306
Products: Military shirts. **SICs:** 5136 (Men's/Boys'
Clothing); 5137 (Women's/Children's Clothing). **Sales:**
$6,000,000 (2000). **Emp:** 180. **Officers:** A. C. Cohen.

■ **5448** ■ **Uniform Center of Lansing Inc.**
425 N Clippert St.
Lansing, MI 48912
Phone: (517)332-2543
Free: (800)554-0234 **Fax:** (517)332-8999
Products: Mens'and women's clothing, including
uniforms. **SICs:** 5137 (Women's/Children's Clothing);
5136 (Men's/Boys' Clothing). **Officers:** Stephen Pratt,
President.

■ **5449** ■ **Uniform House Inc.**
1927 N Capitol Ave.
Indianapolis, IN 46202-1219
Phone: (317)926-4467
Free: (800)949-4467 **Fax:** (317)926-4460
Products: Men's and boys' uniforms. **SIC:** 5136
(Men's/Boys' Clothing). **Officers:** Leve Manuel,
Chairman of the Board.

■ **5450** ■ **United Sports Apparel Inc.**
6850 Central Park
Lincolnwood, IL 60712
Free: (800)843-0371
Products: Sports clothing, including running suits,
shorts, and jackets. **SICs:** 5136 (Men's/Boys' Clothing);
5137 (Women's/Children's Clothing). **Est:** 1982. **Sales:**
$5,000,000 (2000). **Emp:** 99. **Officers:** Frank Liebow,
President; Tim Cronin, VP of Sales; Don Kerstein,
Chairman of the Board & Finance Officer.

■ **5451** ■ **U.S. Marketing Services**
7127 E Becker Ln. 63
Scottsdale, AZ 85254-5206
Phone: (602)998-2859 **Fax:** (602)922-3606
Products: Women's and children's clothing; Sporting
goods; Hardware. **SICs:** 5137 (Women's/Children's
Clothing); 5091 (Sporting & Recreational Goods); 5072
(Hardware). **Officers:** Fred Young, President.

■ **5452** ■ **U.S. Products Inc.**
PO Box 1006
Orange, CT 06477-7006
Phone: (203)783-1468 **Fax:** (203)874-2830
Products: Protective clothing. **SICs:** 5136
(Men's/Boys' Clothing); 5137 (Women's/Children's
Clothing). **Officers:** John Pcolka, President.

■ **5453** ■ **United Uniforms Inc.**
15 Orange St.
New Haven, CT 06510-3300
Phone: (203)624-8931 **Fax:** (203)624-2548
Products: Men's uniforms; Women's uniforms; Shoes.
SICs: 5136 (Men's/Boys' Clothing); 5137
(Women's/Children's Clothing); 5139 (Footwear).
Officers: Sidney Wiesner, President.

■ **5454** ■ **Universal International Inc.**
5000 Winnetka Ave. N
New Hope, MN 55428
Phone: (612)533-1169 **Fax:** (612)533-1158
Products: Men's and women's clothing. **SICs:** 5136
(Men's/Boys' Clothing); 5137 (Women's/Children's
Clothing); 5023 (Homefurnishings). **Sales:** $87,600,000
(2000). **Emp:** 1,238. **Officers:** Richard Ennen,
President; Dennis A. Hill, CFO.

■ **5455** ■ **Unnex Industrial Corp.**
1141 Broadway, 9th Fl.
New York, NY 10001
Phone: (212)481-1900 **Fax:** (212)481-9173
Products: Women's hosiery; Men's underwear;
Women's underwear; Children's socks; Stationery;
Toys. **SICs:** 5137 (Women's/Children's Clothing); 5136
(Men's/Boys' Clothing); 5112 (Stationery & Office
Supplies); 5092 (Toys & Hobby Goods & Supplies).

■ **5456** ■ **Uranus Impex Co.**
5 Bank St.
Manchester, CT 06040-5701
Phone: (860)645-1029 **Fax:** (860)645-6008
E-mail: uranus.impex.co@prodigy.net
Products: Used clothing; Textiles; Imitation leather.
SICs: 5136 (Men's/Boys' Clothing); 5131 (Piece Goods
& Notions); 5137 (Women's/Children's Clothing). **Est:**
1988. **Officers:** Garo Kitischian, Owner.

■ **5457** ■ **Variety Hosiery Mills**
PO Box 446
Graham, NC 27253-2262
Phone: (919)226-6059
Free: (800)222-7937 **Fax:** (919)226-7441
Products: Hosiery. **SIC:** 5137 (Women's/Children's
Clothing). **Sales:** $3,000,000 (2000). **Emp:** 49.
Officers: F.T. Futrell.

■ **5458** ■ **Variety Sales, Inc.**
426 S Cross St.
PO Box 218
Youngsville, NC 27596-0218
Phone: (919)556-5630 **Fax:** (919)556-0580
E-mail: varietysales@pop.mindspring.com
URL: http://www.varietysalesinc.com
Products: Socks and hosiery. **SICs:** 5137
(Women's/Children's Clothing); 5136 (Men's/Boys'
Clothing). **Est:** 1971. **Sales:** $10,000,000 (2000). **Emp:**
40. **Officers:** Marshall Wiggins, President; Joan Tuton;
Sheryl Ritchie; Laurie McFarland, Sales/Marketing
Contact.

■ **5459** ■ **Joan Vass U.S.A.**
485 7th Ave., No. 301
New York, NY 10018
Phone: (212)947-3417 **Fax:** (212)563-0914
Products: Rlothing, including knit tops and bottoms.
SICs: 5137 (Women's/Children's Clothing); 5136
(Men's/Boys' Clothing). **Est:** 1984. **Sales:** $20,000,000
(2000). **Emp:** 15. **Officers:** Norman Weiss, Sr. VP.

■ **5460** ■ **Venture Trading**
PO Box 310
Nobleboro, ME 04555-0310
Free: (800)443-7970
Products: Women's clothing and outerwear. **SIC:** 5137
(Women's/Children's Clothing). **Officers:** John
Kennedy, Partner.

■ **5461** ■ **Vibrint Corp.**
4185 Heather Way
Cumming, GA 30041-8925
Phone: (404)887-4551
Products: Hand-knitted sweaters. **SICs:** 5137
(Women's/Children's Clothing); 5136 (Men's/Boys'
Clothing). **Officers:** Enrique Vizurraga, President.

■ **5462** ■ **Vickers International**
PO Box 6187
Kokomo, IN 46904
Phone: (765)453-2419 **Fax:** (765)453-1172
Products: Novelties, including t-shirts and tapestries.
SICs: 5136 (Men's/Boys' Clothing); 5137
(Women's/Children's Clothing); 5199 (Nondurable
Goods Nec).

■ **5463** ■ **Viking Technology Inc.**
115 Industrial Park Rd.
Lincolnton, NC 28092
Phone: (704)735-3754
Free: (888)454-6471 **Fax:** (704)732-6119
E-mail: vikingtech@abts.net
Products: Socks. **SICs:** 5131 (Piece Goods &
Notions); 5136 (Men's/Boys' Clothing). **Est:** 1995.
Sales: $4,000,000 (1999). **Emp:** 100. **Officers:** H.
Seely-Brown; Linda Harris. **Former Name:** Homespun
Hosiery.

■ **5464** ■ **George Vine Associates Inc.**
2380 Franklin Rd.
Bloomfield Hills, MI 48302-0332
Phone: (248)858-2440 **Fax:** (248)858-2511
Products: Women's plus-size apparel. **SIC:** 5137
(Women's/Children's Clothing). **Est:** 1956. **Officers:**
George Vine, President.

■ **5465** ■ **VIP Formal Wear Inc.**
3801 S Wilmington St.
Raleigh, NC 27603-3569
Phone: (919)772-7215 **Fax:** (919)662-8562
Products: Men's and boys' formal wear. **SIC:** 5136
(Men's/Boys' Clothing). **Officers:** Fred Miller,
President.

■ **5466** ■ **Virginia West Uniforms Inc.**
6601 Maccorkle Ave. SE
Charleston, WV 25304-2923
Phone: (304)925-0305
Products: Men's and boys' clothing; Men's and boys'
sportswear; Men's and boys' work clothing; Men's and
boys' uniforms. **SIC:** 5136 (Men's/Boys' Clothing).
Officers: Gary Heldman, President.

■ **5467** ■ **N. Wagman and Co.**
1450 Broadway, Ste. 3900
New York, NY 10018
Phone: (212)391-1700
Products: Men's and women's clothing. **SICs:** 5136
(Men's/Boys' Clothing); 5137 (Women's/Children's
Clothing). **Sales:** $15,000,000 (1993). **Emp:** 45.
Officers: Mark Grebler, President; Robert Ezykowich,
CFO.

■ **5468** ■ **Wagner Enterprises Inc.**
6015 Huntington Ct. NE
Cedar Rapids, IA 52402-1272
Phone: (319)393-3843
Free: (800)397-5224 **Fax:** (319)393-0917
Products: Men's and boys' clothing; Men's and boys'
sportswear. **SIC:** 5136 (Men's/Boys' Clothing).
Officers: James Wagner, President.

■ **5469** ■ **Wagners Formal Wear of
Washington**
PO Box 3851
Spokane, WA 99220-3851
Phone: (509)534-4481 **Fax:** (509)922-6477
Products: Men's and boy's clothing, including suits
and trousers. **SIC:** 5136 (Men's/Boys' Clothing).
Officers: Richard Wagner, President.

■ **5470** ■ **Waikiki Trader Corp.**
99-061 Koaha Way
Aiea, HI 96701
Phone: (808)487-3663
Products: Unisex clothing; Women's handbags and
purses; Children's handbags and purses; T-shirts.
SICs: 5099 (Durable Goods Nec); 5136 (Men's/Boys'
Clothing); 5199 (Nondurable Goods Nec).

■ **5471** ■ **Wallace Sportswear**
460 Veterans Dr.
Burlington, NJ 08016-3394
Phone: (609)387-3625 **Fax:** (609)387-2340
Products: Women's sportswear. **SIC:** 5137
(Women's/Children's Clothing). **Sales:** $2,000,000
(2000). **Emp:** 90. **Officers:** A. Wallace.

■ **5472** ■ **Wam Inc.**
565 Canyon Rd.
Wetumpka, AL 36093-1406
Phone: (205)262-8241 **Fax:** (205)262-1896
Products: Men's and boys' clothing; Hats; Scarves,
dickies, and other neckwear; Gloves and mittens;
Caps. **SICs:** 5136 (Men's/Boys' Clothing); 5137

(Women's/Children's Clothing). **Officers:** Wayne
Sanders, President.

■ **5473** ■ **Warnaco Inc.**
7915 Haskell Ave.
Van Nuys, CA 91409
Phone: (818)782-7568
Products: Women's underwear. **SIC:** 5137
(Women's/Children's Clothing). **Est:** 1941. **Sales:**
$70,000,000 (2000). **Emp:** 1,300. **Officers:** John B.
Semrad, CEO & President; Nicolette Sohl, VP of
Finance; Helen B. Lee, VP of Sales; Walter Callagy,
Dir. of Information Systems; Gene Kurai, Dir of Human
Resources.

■ **5474** ■ **Washington Shoe Company**
542 1st Ave. S
Seattle, WA 98104-2804
Phone: (206)622-8517
Free: (800)925-7463 **Fax:** (206)622-0201
Products: Shoes. **SIC:** 5139 (Footwear). **Sales:**
$11,000,000 (2000). **Emp:** 20.

■ **5475** ■ **Weekend Exercise Co., Inc.**
8960 Carroll Way, Ste. A
San Diego, CA 92121
Phone: (619)537-5300 **Fax:** (619)537-5400
Products: Bodywear. **SIC:** 5137 (Women's/Children's
Clothing). **Sales:** $35,000,000 (2000). **Emp:** 85.
Officers: Michael Levinson; Donald Schumacher.

■ **5476** ■ **Victoria Wells Designs Inc.**
2 Central St.
Framingham, MA 01701-4163
Phone: (508)877-6722
Products: Women's clothing, including sportswear and
swimsuits. **SIC:** 5137 (Women's/Children's Clothing).
Officers: Victoria Wells, President.

■ **5477** ■ **Wells Lamont Corp.**
299A W Beacon
Philadelphia, MS 39350-3151
Phone: (601)656-2772 **Fax:** (601)647-6943
Products: Work gloves. **SICs:** 5136 (Men's/Boys'
Clothing); 5137 (Women's/Children's Clothing). **Sales:**
$30,000,000 (2000). **Emp:** 999. **Officers:** Lamar
Fowler.

■ **5478** ■ **Wells Lamont Corp.**
6640 W Touhy Ave.
Niles, IL 60714
Phone: (847)647-8200
Free: (800)323-2830 **Fax:** (847)647-6943
URL: http://www.gloveshop.com
Products: Gloves. **SICs:** 5136 (Men's/Boys' Clothing);
5137 (Women's/Children's Clothing). **Est:** 1907.
Officers: Phillipe Milliet, CEO, e-mail: pmilliet@
wellslamont.com.

■ **5479** ■ **The Wermers Co.**
451 E 58th Ave., Ste. 3677
Denver, CO 80216
Phone: (303)295-1318
Free: (888)293-1318 **Fax:** (303)295-1318
Products: Women's clothing. **SIC:** 5137
(Women's/Children's Clothing). **Est:** 1976. **Sales:**
$1,000,000 (2000). **Emp:** 9. **Officers:** Thomas
Wermers; Rhona Wermers.

■ **5480** ■ **West Coast Liquidators Inc.**
2430 E Del Amo Blvd.
Compton, CA 90220-6306
Phone: (310)537-9220 **Fax:** (310)632-4477
Products: General close-out merchandise. **SICs:** 5136
(Men's/Boys' Clothing); 5137 (Women's/Children's
Clothing); 5131 (Piece Goods & Notions). **Sales:**
$180,000,000 (2000). **Emp:** 500. **Officers:** Mark Miller,
President.

■ **5481** ■ **West Coast Shoe Co.**
PO Box 607
Scappoose, OR 97056
Phone: (503)543-7114 **Fax:** (503)543-7110
Products: Shoes. **SIC:** 5139 (Footwear). **Sales:**
$5,000,000 (2000). **Emp:** 44.

■ 5482 ■ Westchester Marketing
100 Corridor Park Dr.
Monroe, OH 45050-1394
Free: (800)624-0381
Products: Work gloves. **SICs:** 5136 (Men's/Boys' Clothing); 5137 (Women's/Children's Clothing). **Sales:** $7,000,000 (2000). **Emp:** 150. **Officers:** Fred W. Stege, President.

■ 5483 ■ Whole Pie Company Ltd.
PO Box 130
Middleton, WI 53562
Phone: (608)836-4600 **Fax:** (608)836-4754
Products: Men's and women's clothing. **SICs:** 5137 (Women's/Children's Clothing); 5136 (Men's/Boys' Clothing). **Sales:** $30,000,000 (1994). **Emp:** 60. **Officers:** John Jeffery, President; Greg Hermus, Controller.

■ 5484 ■ Wholesale T-Shirt Supply
1352 N Illinois St.
Indianapolis, IN 46202
Phone: (317)634-4423
Free: (800)428-4606 **Fax:** (317)637-7670
Products: T-shirts, sweats, and baseball caps. **SICs:** 5136 (Men's/Boys' Clothing); 5137 (Women's/Children's Clothing).

■ 5485 ■ Wigwam Inc.
PO Box 288
Lake George, MN 56458-0228
Phone: (218)266-3978 **Fax:** (218)266-3978
Products: Shoes. **SIC:** 5139 (Footwear).

■ 5486 ■ Wild West Company Inc.
1400 N Rouse Ave.
Bozeman, MT 59715-2941
Phone: (406)587-5133
Products: Silk-screen clothing. **SICs:** 5136 (Men's/Boys' Clothing); 5137 (Women's/Children's Clothing). **Officers:** Don Cowles, President.

■ 5487 ■ Wilton Manufacturing Company Inc.
PO Box 329
Ware, MA 01082-0329
Phone: (413)967-5811 **Fax:** (413)967-6047
Products: Women's and children's clothing. **SIC:** 5137 (Women's/Children's Clothing). **Officers:** Robert Mc Lean, President.

■ 5488 ■ Winchester Hat Corp.
725 David Crockett
Winchester, TN 37398
Phone: (931)967-0686 **Fax:** (931)967-0686
Products: Hats. **SICs:** 5136 (Men's/Boys' Clothing); 5137 (Women's/Children's Clothing). **Sales:** $1,000,000 (2000). **Emp:** 49. **Officers:** Richard Bean.

■ 5489 ■ Windjammer Inc.
525 N Main
Bangor, PA 18013
Phone: (215)588-0626
Free: (800)441-6958 **Fax:** (215)588-2046
Products: Jackets; Tee shirts; Sweat suits. **SICs:** 5136 (Men's/Boys' Clothing); 5137 (Women's/Children's Clothing). **Est:** 1974. **Sales:** $3,500,000 (2000). **Emp:** 75. **Officers:** Anthony J. Capozzolo, CEO & President; Joseph H. Capozzolo, Vice President.

■ 5490 ■ Wise El Santo Company Inc.
PO Box 8360
St. Louis, MO 63132
Phone: (314)428-3100 **Fax:** (314)428-7017
Products: Work gloves; Safety equipment. **SICs:** 5136 (Men's/Boys' Clothing); 5199 (Nondurable Goods Nec). **Est:** 1892. **Sales:** $50,500,000 (2000). **Emp:** 100. **Officers:** Rudolph L. Wise, President; Michael Milne, Controller; John Kuntz, Dir. of Sales.

■ 5491 ■ Frank C. Wise & Son
RR 120
Hallowell, ME 04347-0120
Phone: (207)623-2363 **Fax:** (207)623-2743
Products: Men's and boy's clothing, including sportswear, work clothing, and uniforms; Police, fire,

and industrial equipment and clothing. **SIC:** 5136 (Men's/Boys' Clothing). **Officers:** George Cross, Chairman of the Board.

■ 5492 ■ Worldwide Distributors Inc.
PO Box 88607
Seattle, WA 98138-2607
Phone: (253)872-8746 **Fax:** (253)872-7603
Products: Clothing; Sporting goods; General merchandise. **SICs:** 5136 (Men's/Boys' Clothing); 5137 (Women's/Children's Clothing); 5199 (Nondurable Goods Nec). **Est:** 1955. **Sales:** $90,000,000 (1999). **Emp:** 50. **Officers:** Richard La Shance, President; Dean Sabey, VP of Finance; Gretchen Stewart, Sales & Marketing Contact.

■ 5493 ■ XNEX Inc.
900 N Lake Shore Dr., Ste. 1013
Chicago, IL 60611
Phone: (312)266-1808 **Fax:** (312)266-4999
Products: Men's and boys' socks and underwear; Women's hosiery; Groceries; Men's outerwear. **SICs:** 5136 (Men's/Boys' Clothing); 5137 (Women's/Children's Clothing); 5141 (Groceries—General Line). **Officers:** Len Sauer, President.

■ 5494 ■ Zanella Ltd.
681 5th Ave.
New York, NY 10022
Phone: (212)371-2121
Products: Men's and women's clothing. **SICs:** 5136 (Men's/Boys' Clothing); 5137 (Women's/Children's Clothing). **Est:** 1978. **Sales:** $7,000,000 (2000). **Emp:** 20. **Officers:** Armondo D'Natalie, President.

■ 5495 ■ Zimmerman Dry Goods
1656 Grand Ave.
St. Paul, MN 55105-1804
Phone: (612)699-4273 **Fax:** (612)699-5273
Products: Adult clothing. **SICs:** 5136 (Men's/Boys' Clothing); 5137 (Women's/Children's Clothing). **Officers:** Allen Brill, Owner.

(10) Communications Systems and Equipment

Entries in this section are arranged alphabetically by company name. When the company name is a personal name, the company name is alphabetized by the surname unless the first name or initial(s) are part of a trade name. See the User's Guide at the front of this directory for additional information.

■ 5496 ■ **2-Way Radio Communications Engineering**
309 Main St.
PO Box 209
Williamsburg, KY 40769-0209
Phone: (606)549-2250
Products: Commercial radios and satellite televisions. **SIC:** 5064 (Electrical Appliances—Television & Radio). **Officers:** James Sutton, President.

■ 5497 ■ **A and A Connections Inc.**
530 S Henderson Rd.
King of Prussia, PA 19406
Phone: (610)354-9070 **Fax:** (610)354-9030
Products: Used telephone systems. **SIC:** 5065 (Electronic Parts & Equipment Nec).

■ 5498 ■ **A & A Office Systems Inc.**
16 Old Forge Rd.
Rocky Hill, CT 06067-3729
Phone: (860)257-4646 **Fax:** (860)257-4615
Products: Communication systems and equipment; Fax machines; Photocopying equipment and supplies. **SICs:** 5065 (Electronic Parts & Equipment Nec); 5044 (Office Equipment). **Officers:** John Sullivan, President.

■ 5499 ■ **ABC Cellular Corp.**
16500 NW 52nd Ave.
Hialeah, FL 33014-6214
Phone: (305)621-6000 **Fax:** (305)625-3377
Products: Electronic equipment, including beepers and cellular phones. **SIC:** 5065 (Electronic Parts & Equipment Nec). **Est:** 1977. **Sales:** $27,000,000 (2000). **Emp:** 250. **Officers:** Randy Simon, President; Scott Rose, Controller.

■ 5500 ■ **ACT Teleconferencing Inc.**
1658 Cole Blvd., Ste. 130
Golden, CO 80401
Phone: (303)233-3500 **Free:** (800)228-2554
URL: http://www.acttel.com
Products: Teleconferencing services. **SIC:** 5065 (Electronic Parts & Equipment Nec). **Est:** 1989. **Sales:** $28,329,000 (1999). **Emp:** 300. **Officers:** Gerald D. Van Eeckhout, CEO; Gavin Thomson, CFO; Gene Warren, Managing Dir.; Thierry Bignet, Managing Dir.; Peter Eeles, Managing Dir.

■ 5501 ■ **Action Page Inc.**
PO Box 5338
Greeley, CO 80634
Phone: (303)292-1204 **Fax:** (303)292-1200
Products: Pagers. **SIC:** 5065 (Electronic Parts & Equipment Nec). **Sales:** $5,000,000 (2000). **Emp:** 30. **Officers:** Richard Redfern, President.

■ 5502 ■ **Advance Telecommunication Inc.**
2120 S Grape St.
Denver, CO 80222
Phone: (303)691-2220
Products: Telecommunications equipment. **SIC:** 5065 (Electronic Parts & Equipment Nec). **Sales:** $4,000,000 (1994). **Emp:** 15. **Officers:** Sue Bender, President.

■ 5503 ■ **AdvanTel Inc.**
2237 Paragon Dr.
San Jose, CA 95131
Phone: (408)435-5436
Products: Telecommunications equipment. **SIC:** 5065 (Electronic Parts & Equipment Nec).

■ 5504 ■ **Air Comm Corp.**
4614 E McDowell Rd.
Phoenix, AZ 85008-4508
Phone: (602)275-4505 **Fax:** (602)275-4555
Products: Two-way radios. **SIC:** 5065 (Electronic Parts & Equipment Nec). **Officers:** Sidney Cohen, President.

■ 5505 ■ **Air Mobile Systems**
14120 Alondra Blvd., Ste. G
Santa Fe Springs, CA 90670-5805
Phone: (562)921-6996 **Fax:** (562)802-0493
Products: Two-way radio communications system. **SIC:** 5065 (Electronic Parts & Equipment Nec). **Est:** 1977. **Emp:** 20. **Officers:** Harold Harris.

■ 5506 ■ **Allcomm of Wisconsin**
2045 W Mill Rd.
Glendale, WI 53209-3444
Phone: (414)228-4000 **Fax:** (414)352-0436
URL: http://www.allcom1.com
Products: Applied voice technology. **SIC:** 5065 (Electronic Parts & Equipment Nec). **Sales:** $20,000,000 (2000). **Emp:** 160. **Officers:** Harold Rosenzweig, CEO; Eric Martin, President.

■ 5507 ■ **ALLTEL Corp.**
1 Allied Dr.
Little Rock, AR 72202
Phone: (501)661-8000 **Fax:** (501)661-5444
Products: Telecommunications equipment and supplies. **SIC:** 5065 (Electronic Parts & Equipment Nec). **Est:** 1983. **Sales:** $1,747,700,000 (2000). **Emp:** 14,864. **Officers:** Joe T. Ford, CEO, President & Chairman of the Board; Dennis J. Ferra, Sr. VP & CFO; Ronald D. Payne, VP of Corp. Communications; John L. Comparin.

■ 5508 ■ **ALLTEL Supply Inc.**
6625 The Corners Pkwy.
Norcross, GA 30092
Phone: (404)448-5210
Free: (800)533-3161 **Fax:** (404)446-0420
Products: Communication systems and equipment. **SIC:** 5065 (Electronic Parts & Equipment Nec). **Sales:** $170,000,000 (2000). **Emp:** 250.

■ 5509 ■ **Alpha Communications Inc.**
951 N 1st St.
Albemarle, NC 28001-3353
Phone: (704)983-5252 **Fax:** (704)983-5250
Products: Two-way radios. **SIC:** 5065 (Electronic Parts & Equipment Nec). **Officers:** Raymond Miller, President.

■ 5510 ■ **Amateur Electronics Supply**
621 Commonwealth Ave.
Orlando, FL 32803
Phone: (407)894-3238
Free: (800)327-1917 **Fax:** (407)894-7553
E-mail: orlando@aesham.com
URL: http://www.aesham.com
Products: Ham-radio equipment; Electronics. **SIC:** 5065 (Electronic Parts & Equipment Nec).

■ 5511 ■ **Amcamex Electronics Corp.**
PO Box 50775
Amarillo, TX 79159
Phone: (806)354-2690
Free: (800)687-1111 **Fax:** (806)354-8800
E-mail: sbk@amcamexusa.com
URL: http://www.amcamexusa.com
Products: Cellular accessories; Consumer electronics; DC to AC power inverters; Telephone caller ID. **SIC:** 5065 (Electronic Parts & Equipment Nec). **Est:** 1992. **Sales:** $7,500,000 (2000). **Emp:** 31. **Officers:** Sam Kong, President; Chris Kong, Vice President.

■ 5512 ■ **American and International Telephone Inc.**
3612 Ventura Dr. E
Lakeland, FL 33811
Phone: (813)647-5885
Products: Telecommunications switching systems. **SIC:** 5065 (Electronic Parts & Equipment Nec).

■ 5513 ■ **American Telephone Systems**
5265 Edina Industrial Blvd.
Minneapolis, MN 55439-2910
Phone: (612)831-0888
Free: (800)323-3639 **Fax:** (612)832-3722
Products: Voiceprocessing, voice mail, interactive voice response, and video conferencing systems. **SIC:** 5065 (Electronic Parts & Equipment Nec). **Officers:** Robert Denman, President.

■ 5514 ■ **American Telephone Technology**
12668 Interurban Ave. S
Seattle, WA 98168-3314
Phone: (206)622-5199 **Fax:** (206)622-6894
Products: Telephone equipment. **SIC:** 5065 (Electronic Parts & Equipment Nec). **Officers:** Sheldon Allen, President.

■ 5515 ■ **Amtel Communications**
8503 Gulf Fwy.
Houston, TX 77017-5038
Phone: (713)223-5522 **Fax:** (713)223-4671
Products: Pagers and cellular phones. **SIC:** 5065 (Electronic Parts & Equipment Nec). **Est:** 1984. **Sales:** $500,000 (2000). **Emp:** 8. **Officers:** J.D. Smith, Payroll Mgr.; Joy L. Smith, Controller.

■ 5516 ■ **Applied Industrial Technologies**
291 Frontage Rd.
Burr Ridge, IL 60521
Phone: (630)325-7575 **Fax:** (630)325-7579
URL: http://www.applied_access.com
Products: Bearing, power transmission, rubber, fluid power, general mills, linear motion. **SIC:** 5065 (Electronic Parts & Equipment Nec). **Officers:** Carlton

Potts, Sales/Marketing Contact, e-mail: cpotts1911@aol.com. **Former Name:** Dodge Chicago/IBT.

■ 5517 ■ ASA Audiovox Specialized Applications
23319 Cooper Dr.
Elkhart, IN 46514
Phone: (219)264-3135 **Fax:** (219)264-3007
Products: Mobile electronic equipment. **SIC:** 5065 (Electronic Parts & Equipment Nec). **Est:** 1977. **Sales:** $50,000,000 (2000). **Emp:** 70. **Officers:** Thomas Irions, Chairman of the Board.

■ 5518 ■ Associated Industries
11347 Vanowen St.
North Hollywood, CA 91605
Phone: (818)760-1000 **Fax:** (818)760-2142
Products: Electronic equipment, including military communication devices. **SIC:** 5065 (Electronic Parts & Equipment Nec). **Est:** 1946. **Sales:** $10,000,000 (2000). **Emp:** 30. **Officers:** Arnold A. Semler, President; Karen Griffith, Controller; Ravi Achar, Dir. of Marketing.

■ 5519 ■ AT Products Inc.
PO Box 625
Harvard, IL 60033
Phone: (815)943-3590
Free: (800)848-2205 **Fax:** (815)943-3604
URL: http://www.atproducts.com
Products: Teleconference and audio equipment. **SICs:** 5064 (Electrical Appliances—Television & Radio); 5065 (Electronic Parts & Equipment Nec). **Est:** 1986. **Emp:** 15. **Officers:** Mike Rose, CEO & President.

■ 5520 ■ AT&T Business Markets Group Div.
831 Park Ave. SW
Norton, VA 24273-1927
Phone: (540)443-7000
Products: Telephones. **SIC:** 5065 (Electronic Parts & Equipment Nec). **Officers:** Jeff Weitzen, Exec. VP.

■ 5521 ■ ATCOM Inc.
PO Box 13476
Research Triangle Park, NC 27709
Phone: (919)314-1001 **Fax:** (919)314-1010
Products: Business telephone systems. **SIC:** 5065 (Electronic Parts & Equipment Nec). **Est:** 1979. **Sales:** $6,000,000 (2000). **Emp:** 60. **Officers:** James H. Watkins Jr., President; S. Yarborough, VP of Finance; D. Finch, VP of Marketing.

■ 5522 ■ ATI Communications
105 Broughton Rd.
Bethel Park, PA 15102-2801
Phone: (412)831-1300 **Fax:** (412)831-1323
URL: http://www.atiteam.com
Products: Cellular and business telephones; Satellite TV dishes. **SIC:** 5065 (Electronic Parts & Equipment Nec). **Est:** 1984. **Sales:** $33,000,000 (2000). **Emp:** 400. **Officers:** Scott Silverman; Mack Jackson.

■ 5523 ■ Audiovox Corp.
150 Marcus Blvd.
Hauppauge, NY 11788
Phone: (516)231-7750 **Fax:** (516)434-3995
Products: Alarms; Beepers; Radios. **SICs:** 5065 (Electronic Parts & Equipment Nec); 5064 (Electrical Appliances—Television & Radio); 5063 (Electrical Apparatus & Equipment). **Est:** 1965. **Sales:** $603,300,000 (2000). **Emp:** 1,018. **Officers:** John J. Shalam, CEO & President; Charles M. Stoehr, Sr. VP & CFO; Ann Boutcher, VP of Marketing; Richard Maddia, VP of Information Systems.

■ 5524 ■ Auto Comm Engineering Corp.
3014 Cameron
Lafayette, LA 70506-1519
Phone: (318)232-9610
Free: (800)284-1840 **Fax:** (318)237-8807
E-mail: sales@auto-comm.com
URL: http://www.auto-comm.com
Products: Communication and automation equipment and supplies. **SIC:** 5065 (Electronic Parts & Equipment Nec). **Est:** 1973. **Sales:** $7,500,000 (2000). **Emp:** 60. **Officers:** Ted Miller, President; Gene Callais, Vice President; Charles Kober, Sales.

■ 5525 ■ Baron Telecommunications
1204 Railroad Ave., No. 101
Bellingham, WA 98225-5008
Phone: (360)734-5082
Free: (800)327-0701 **Fax:** (360)734-1160
URL: http://www.barontele.com
Products: Communication systems and equipment; Telephone equipment. **SIC:** 5065 (Electronic Parts & Equipment Nec). **Est:** 1952. **Officers:** Phil Bratt, President. **Former Name:** BTC Corp.

■ 5526 ■ Bear Valley Communications Inc.
PO Box 27496
Denver, CO 80227-0496
Phone: (303)987-2680
Free: (877)987-2680 **Fax:** (303)985-2992
E-mail: csidenver@yahoo.com
URL: http://www.csidenver.bizland.com
Products: Communication equipment; System design and repair; Microwave radio service and repair; Ear protection devices. **SIC:** 5065 (Electronic Parts & Equipment Nec). **Est:** 1979. **Officers:** John Thomas, President.

■ 5527 ■ Bell Atlantic Meridian Systems Inc.
5 Greentree Ctr., No. 400
Marlton, NJ 08053
Phone: (609)988-5600
Products: Telephones. **SIC:** 5065 (Electronic Parts & Equipment Nec). **Sales:** $130,000,000 (2000). **Emp:** 800. **Officers:** Garry McGuire, President.

■ 5528 ■ Bell-Haun Systems Inc.
935 Eastwind Dr.
Westerville, OH 43081
Phone: (614)882-4040 **Fax:** (614)890-4970
Products: Cellular and business telephone systems. **SIC:** 5065 (Electronic Parts & Equipment Nec). **Est:** 1977. **Sales:** $2,500,000 (2000). **Emp:** 35. **Officers:** Tom Bell, CEO; Pat Freund, Vice President.

■ 5529 ■ Bellsonics
PO Box 1390
Lake Forest, CA 92630
Phone: (949)581-8101 **Fax:** (949)581-8112
E-mail: bellsonics@aol.com
Products: Computer peripheral equipment; Electronic testing equipment; Semiconductor test equipment; Probe reistivity test equipment; Safety and security products. **SICs:** 5065 (Electronic Parts & Equipment Nec); 5063 (Electrical Apparatus & Equipment); 5045 (Computers, Peripherals & Software); 5047 (Medical & Hospital Equipment). **Est:** 1983. **Emp:** 3. **Officers:** Richard T. Bellis, President; Lyliane Bellis, Vice President.

■ 5530 ■ BellSouth Communication Systems Inc.
1936 Blue Hills Dr. NE
Roanoke, VA 24012
Phone: (540)983-6000 **Fax:** (540)983-6006
Products: Telephone systems. **SIC:** 5065 (Electronic Parts & Equipment Nec). **Est:** 1969. **Sales:** $300,000,000 (2000). **Emp:** 1,300. **Officers:** Danny M. Helmly, President.

■ 5531 ■ Better Telephones and Technology Inc.
PO Box 15050
Cincinnati, OH 45215-0050
Phone: (513)821-8075
Products: Telephone equipment. **SIC:** 5065 (Electronic Parts & Equipment Nec). **Sales:** $3,000,000 (2000). **Emp:** 12. **Officers:** M. Verle Taulbee, President.

■ 5532 ■ Beyerdynamic
56 Central Ave.
Farmingdale, NY 11735
Phone: (631)293-3200
Free: (800)293-4463 **Fax:** (631)293-3288
E-mail: sales@beyerdynamic.com
URL: http://www.beyerdynamic.com
Products: Microphones and headphones. **SIC:** 5065 (Electronic Parts & Equipment Nec). **Est:** 1979. **Emp:** 15. **Officers:** Fred Beyer, President; Jerry Spriggs, Manager; Jeff Brownstien, Sales/Marketing Contact; Bob Lowing, Customer Service Contact; Bob Lowing, Customer Service Contact.

■ 5533 ■ Brightpoint, Inc.
6402 Corporate Dr.
Indianapolis, IN 46278
Phone: (317)297-6100
Free: (800)952-2355 **Fax:** (317)297-6114
Products: Wireless handsets and accessories. **SIC:** 5065 (Electronic Parts & Equipment Nec). **Est:** 1989.

■ 5534 ■ H.G. Brix Co.
565 Display Way
Sacramento, CA 95838
Phone: (916)646-9805 **Fax:** (916)646-9946
Products: Car audio equipment; Cellular phones. **SIC:** 5065 (Electronic Parts & Equipment Nec). **Est:** 1975. **Sales:** $13,000,000 (2000). **Emp:** 30. **Officers:** Harry G. Brix, President. **Alternate Name:** American Wireless.

■ 5535 ■ Broadcast Supply Worldwide
7012 27th St. W
Tacoma, WA 98466
Phone: (253)565-2301
Free: (800)426-8434 **Fax:** (253)565-8114
URL: http://www.bswusa
Products: Audio broadcast equipment. **SIC:** 5065 (Electronic Parts & Equipment Nec). **Est:** 1973. **Emp:** 30. **Officers:** Tim Schwieger; Kathy Thatcher; Tom Roalkvam, Sales/Marketing Contact, e-mail: tomr@bswusa.com. **Former Name:** Broadcast Supply West.

■ 5536 ■ Broadcasters General Store Inc.
2480 SE 52nd St.
Ocala, FL 34480
Phone: (352)622-7700 **Fax:** (352)629-7000
Products: Broadcast audio/video equipment. **SICs:** 5049 (Professional Equipment Nec); 5065 (Electronic Parts & Equipment Nec). **Est:** 1979. **Sales:** $12,000,000 (1999). **Emp:** 14. **Officers:** David Kerstin, President.

■ 5537 ■ Burk Electronics
35 N Kensington
La Grange, IL 60525
Phone: (708)482-9310
Products: Amateur radio equipment and supplies. **SIC:** 5065 (Electronic Parts & Equipment Nec). **Est:** 1982.

■ 5538 ■ Burroughs Communications Inc.
4701 Newbern Ave.
Raleigh, NC 27610
Phone: (919)212-7700
Free: (800)843-3595 **Fax:** (919)212-7703
Products: Telephones; Telephone answering machines; Alarm systems. **SICs:** 5065 (Electronic Parts & Equipment Nec); 5063 (Electrical Apparatus & Equipment). **Officers:** William Burroughs, President.

■ 5539 ■ Business Communications Inc.
7903 Thorndike Rd.
Greensboro, NC 27409
Phone: (336)668-4488 **Fax:** (336)665-7297
Products: Telecommunications equipment. **SIC:** 5065 (Electronic Parts & Equipment Nec). **Sales:** $23,000,000 (2000). **Emp:** 107. **Officers:** Linda Whitaker, President; Tom Lippard, Controller.

■ 5540 ■ C and L Communications Inc.
26254 Interstate Hwy. 10 W
Boerne, TX 78006
Phone: (210)698-3380 **Fax:** (210)698-0077
Products: Networking equipment for the communications industry. **SIC:** 5065 (Electronic Parts & Equipment Nec). **Est:** 1979. **Sales:** $25,000,000 (2000). **Emp:** 34. **Officers:** Lisa Chandler, President; John Stephenson, CFO; Roy Clark, Dir. of Marketing; Dee Benetti, Dir of Human Resources.

■ 5541 ■ CableLAN Express Inc.
PO Box 196
Norfolk, MA 02056
Phone: (508)384-7811
Free: (800)840-6655 **Fax:** (508)384-8554
Products: Fiber optics and data communications products. **SIC:** 5065 (Electronic Parts & Equipment Nec). **Est:** 1994. **Sales:** $3,000,000 (2000). **Emp:** 10. **Officers:** J. Pirrong, President.

■ 5542 ■ **Call Dynamics Inc.**
2020 N Central Ave., No. 1010
Phoenix, AZ 85016
Phone: (602)252-5800 **Fax:** (602)252-8580
E-mail: sales@calldynamics.com
Products: Voice processing technology. **SIC:** 5065
(Electronic Parts & Equipment Nec). **Est:** 1989. **Sales:**
$4,000,000 (2000). **Emp:** 15. **Officers:** Bruce
Andersen, President.

■ 5543 ■ **Cambridge Communication Inc.**
(Niles, Illinois)
1425 Busch Pkwy.
Buffalo Grove, IL 60089-4506
Phone: (847)647-8100
Products: Telephone headsets and
telecommunications equipment. **SIC:** 5065 (Electronic
Parts & Equipment Nec). **Sales:** $5,000,000 (2000).
Emp: 45. **Officers:** Richard H. Finn, President; J. Finn,
VP of Finance.

■ 5544 ■ **Cape Electronics**
19 Dupont Ave.
South Yarmouth, MA 02664-1203
Phone: (508)394-2405 **Fax:** (508)394-1535
Products: Mobile communications, including mobile
phones and two-way radios. **SIC:** 5065 (Electronic
Parts & Equipment Nec). **Est:** 1978. **Emp:** 12.
Alternate Name: RDC Communications Inc.

■ 5545 ■ **Capital GBS Communications Corp.**
1137 Hanley Indstl. Ct.
St. Louis, MO 63144
Phones: (314)961-0557 (314)961-5002
Fax: (314)961-4581
Products: Telephone equipment. **SIC:** 5065
(Electronic Parts & Equipment Nec). **Emp:** 70.
Officers: William McCormick.

■ 5546 ■ **Capital Telephone Co.**
6800 Willowwood Way
Sacramento, CA 95831-2131
Phone: (916)393-2700 **Fax:** (916)394-3260
Products: Business telephones. **SIC:** 5065 (Electronic
Parts & Equipment Nec). **Sales:** $3,000,000 (2000).
Emp: 27. **Officers:** Kin Shaw-Wong, President.

■ 5547 ■ **Capitol Electronics Inc.**
836 Prior Ave. N
St. Paul, MN 55104-1040
Phone: (651)646-2511
Free: (800)720-6981 **Fax:** (651)644-4598
E-mail: Capitolsales @Compuserve.com
Products: Electronic wireless parts; Wireless/mobile
communication equipment; Intercommunication
equipment. **SIC:** 5065 (Electronic Parts & Equipment
Nec). **Est:** 1959. **Emp:** 20. **Officers:** Alan Pahl,
President. **Alternate Name:** Capital 2-Way
Communications.

■ 5548 ■ **Carbone of America**
400 Myrtle Ave.
Boonton, NJ 07005
Phone: (973)334-0700 **Fax:** (973)334-6394
Products: Radio energy tacometers. **SIC:** 5064
(Electrical Appliances—Television & Radio). **Sales:**
$41,000,000 (2000). **Emp:** 350. **Officers:** Emilio
DeBarnardo, President; Gary Pavlosky, Controller.

■ 5549 ■ **Cartell Inc.**
34364 Goddard Rd.
Romulus, MI 48174
Phone: (313)941-5400
Products: Cellular telephones. **SIC:** 5065 (Electronic
Parts & Equipment Nec). **Sales:** $1,000,000 (2000).
Emp: 6. **Officers:** Joe Lewo, President; Gene Elliott,
Vice President.

■ 5550 ■ **Catalyst Telecom**
6 Logue Ct., Ste. G
Greenville, SC 29615
Phone: (864)288-2432
Products: Business telephone systems. **SIC:** 5065
(Electronic Parts & Equipment Nec). **Officers:** Andy
Heyman, President.

■ 5551 ■ **CBS Technologies LLC**
6900 Steger Dr.
Cincinnati, OH 45237
Phone: (513)361-9600
Free: (800)350-5735 **Fax:** (513)361-9663
URL: http://www.cbstech.net
Products: Telecommunications and computer
equipment. **SICs:** 5065 (Electronic Parts & Equipment
Nec); 5045 (Computers, Peripherals & Software). **Est:**
2000. **Officers:** Thomas Revely III, CEO & President.
Former Name: Cincinnati Bell Supply Co.

■ 5552 ■ **CBS WhitCom Technologies Corp.**
2990 Express Dr. S
Central Islip, NY 11722
Phone: (516)582-3200
Free: (800)338-3940 **Fax:** (516)582-6063
URL: http://www.cbswhit.com
Products: Telephone and voice mail systems; Data
networks, including local and long distance; Voice data
networks internet services. **SIC:** 5065 (Electronic Parts
& Equipment Nec). **Est:** 1971. **Sales:** $17,000,000
(1999). **Emp:** 98. **Officers:** Harry Whittelsey, Exec. VP,
e-mail: Hwhittelsey@CBSWhit.com; Bob Corvlan,
Exec. VP, e-mail: BCorvlan@CBSWhit.com; Joe
Nidzyn, President; B. Bednarik, e-mail: Bbednarik@
CBSWhit.com.

■ 5553 ■ **CCA Electronics**
360 Bohannon Rd.
Box 426
Fairburn, GA 30213
Phone: (404)964-3530 **Fax:** (404)964-2222
Products: Broadcast transmitters. **SIC:** 5065
(Electronic Parts & Equipment Nec). **Officers:** Ron
Baker, Pres.

■ 5554 ■ **Cel Tech Communications Inc.**
PO Box 430
Lakewood, CA 90714-0430
Phone: (562)421-2205 **Fax:** (562)421-1507
E-mail: radidar@aol.com
Products: Cellular phones. **SIC:** 5065 (Electronic Parts
& Equipment Nec). **Est:** 1985. **Officers:** Fuad Radi,
President.

■ 5555 ■ **CellStar Corp.**
1730 Briercroft Ct.
Carrollton, TX 75006
Phone: (972)323-0600 **Free:** (800)723-9010
Products: Cellular telephones. **SIC:** 5065 (Electronic
Parts & Equipment Nec). **Sales:** $1,482,800,000
(2000). **Emp:** 1,100. **Officers:** Alan H. Goldfield, CEO
& Chairman of the Board; Mark Q. Huggins, Sr. VP &
CFO.

■ 5556 ■ **CellStar Ltd.**
1730 Briercroft Ct.
Carrollton, TX 75006
Phone: (972)323-0600
Products: Cellular telephones and accessories;
Wireless data products. **SIC:** 5065 (Electronic Parts &
Equipment Nec). **Sales:** $510,000,000 (2000). **Emp:**
1,000. **Officers:** Alan H. Goldfield, CEO, President &
Chairman of the Board; Dick Grozia, Exec. VP & CFO.

■ 5557 ■ **Cellular Wholesales**
5151 Church St.
Skokie, IL 60076
Phone: (847)965-2300
Free: (800)395-0505 **Fax:** (847)676-8860
Products: Cellular products, including phones. **SIC:**
5065 (Electronic Parts & Equipment Nec).

■ 5558 ■ **Central States Electronics**
317 W 13th St.
Davenport, IA 52803-4901
Phone: (319)323-0180 **Fax:** (319)322-1242
Products: Commercial two-way radios. **SIC:** 5065
(Electronic Parts & Equipment Nec). **Officers:** William
Bolton, President.

■ 5559 ■ **Chase Com Corp.**
1604 State St.
Santa Barbara, CA 93101
Phone: (805)963-4864
Free: (800)288-9807 **Fax:** (805)962-0104
Products: Data communications hardware. **SIC:** 5045
(Computers, Peripherals & Software). **Sales:**

$1,000,000 (2000). **Emp:** 10. **Officers:** Herb Levitin,
President; Joanne Masotta, Bookkeeper.

■ 5560 ■ **Chicago Communications Service
Inc.**
200 Spangler Ave.
Elmhurst, IL 60126-1524
Phone: (312)585-4300
Products: Pagers; Car phones; Walkie talkies; Home
answering machines. **SIC:** 5065 (Electronic Parts &
Equipment Nec). **Sales:** $20,000,000 (2000). **Emp:**
185. **Officers:** Jerry Bear, President; Nick Pollman,
CFO.

■ 5561 ■ **Cincinnati Bell Long Distance Inc.**
36 E 7th St.
Cincinnati, OH 45202
Phone: (513)369-2100
Products: Telephone equipment. **SIC:** 5065
(Electronic Parts & Equipment Nec). **Sales:**
$50,000,000 (2000). **Emp:** 170. **Officers:** Barry L.
Nelson, CEO & President.

■ 5562 ■ **Clarion Corporation of America**
661 W Redondo Beach Blvd.
Gardena, CA 90247
Phone: (310)327-9100 **Fax:** (310)327-1999
Products: Cellular phones; Car stereos. **SIC:** 5065
(Electronic Parts & Equipment Nec). **Est:** 1963. **Sales:**
$140,000,000 (2000). **Emp:** 300. **Officers:** I. Ishitsubo,
CEO & President; Matt Matsuda, VP of Finance; Don
Cason, VP of Sales; Joe Lindsay, Dir. of Information
Systems; Richard Hendley, VP of Operations.

■ 5563 ■ **CMS Communications Inc.**
715 Goddard Ave.
Chesterfield, MO 63005-1106
Phone: (314)530-1320 **Fax:** (314)530-1316
Products: Used telecommunications equipment. **SIC:**
5099 (Durable Goods Nec). **Sales:** $25,000,000
(1994). **Emp:** 200. **Officers:** Tom Murphy, President;
Brent J. Bowman, CFO.

■ 5564 ■ **Coastal Electronics Inc.**
PO Box 12007
New Bern, NC 28561
Phone: (919)637-3167 **Fax:** (919)637-5110
E-mail: supportnbsc@coastalelectronics.com
URL: http://www.coastalelectronics.com
Products: Communications equipment, including
cellular phones and two-way radio systems. **SIC:** 5065
(Electronic Parts & Equipment Nec). **Est:** 1949. **Emp:**
49. **Officers:** Billy G. Haire.

■ 5565 ■ **Cobra Electronics Corp.**
6500 W Cortland St.
Chicago, IL 60707
Phone: (773)889-8870 **Fax:** (773)794-1930
URL: http://www.cobraelec.com
Products: Consumer electronics; Telecommunications
products. **SIC:** 5065 (Electronic Parts & Equipment
Nec). **Est:** 1961. **Sales:** $80,000,000 (2000). **Emp:**
150. **Officers:** James R. Bazet, CEO & President;
Gerald M. Laures, VP of Finance; Anthony Mirabelli, Sr.
VP of Marketing & Sales.

■ 5566 ■ **Coil Sales and Manufacturing Co.**
5600 Apollo Dr.
Rolling Meadows, IL 60008
Phone: (847)806-6300 **Fax:** (847)806-6231
Products: Telecommunications equipment. **SIC:** 5065
(Electronic Parts & Equipment Nec). **Est:** 1968. **Sales:**
$60,000,000 (2000). **Emp:** 900. **Officers:** Joseph
Charles, President; Robert Novak, CFO; J.A. Muntean,
VP of Marketing; M. Nichols, Manager; R. Palkoner.

■ 5567 ■ **Comlink Inc. (Marlborough,
Massachusetts)**
295 Donald Lynch Blvd.
Marlborough, MA 01752-4702
Phone: (508)460-7800 **Fax:** (508)832-3699
Products: Telephone, voice, and data communications
systems. **SIC:** 5065 (Electronic Parts & Equipment
Nec). **Sales:** $14,000,000 (1994). **Emp:** 110. **Officers:**
Peter Helwing, President; Robert Antcil, CFO.

■ 5568 ■ Commercial Telephone Systems Inc.
3531 Griffin Rd.
Ft. Lauderdale, FL 33312
Phone: (954)981-2586 **Fax:** (954)964-5956
Products: Commercial telephone systems. **SIC:** 5065 (Electronic Parts & Equipment Nec). **Sales:** $700,000 (2000). **Emp:** 10. **Officers:** Gail Smith, President.

■ 5569 ■ Communications Electronics Inc.
9494 Deereco Rd.
Timonium, MD 21093-2102
Phone: (410)252-1222
Free: (888)TALK-CEI **Fax:** (410)252-5231
URL: http://www.talkcei.com
Products: Cellular phones and accessories; Pagers; Radios, including two-way and mobile. **SIC:** 5065 (Electronic Parts & Equipment Nec). **Est:** 1976. **Sales:** $10,000,000 (2000). **Emp:** 80. **Officers:** Glenn D. Cassell.

■ 5570 ■ Communications Electronics Inc.
Emergency Operations Center
PO Box 2797
Ann Arbor, MI 48106-2797
Phone: (734)996-8888 **Fax:** (734)663-8888
Products: Radio parts and accessories; Citizens' band radios; Communication systems and equipment; Broadcast, studio, and related electronic equipment. **SIC:** 5065 (Electronic Parts & Equipment Nec). **Est:** 1869. **Sales:** $2,000,000 (2000). **Emp:** 38. **Officers:** Den Ascher, CEO & Chairman of the Board; Mike Bernson; Sam Ascher, VP of MIS.

■ 5571 ■ Communications Marketing S.E. Inc.
PO Box 823
Marietta, GA 30061
Phone: (404)424-9097 **Fax:** (404)428-2124
Products: Telecommunication equipment, including radios and antennas. **SIC:** 5065 (Electronic Parts & Equipment Nec). **Est:** 1977. **Sales:** $6,000,000 (2000). **Emp:** 3. **Officers:** Jerry Michael Bentley, President; Gayle B. Bentley, Treasurer & Secty.

■ 5572 ■ Communications Products Inc.
PO Box 509125
Indianapolis, IN 46250
Phone: (317)576-0332 **Fax:** (317)842-0278
Products: Electronic parts; Electric and electronic equipment; Intercommunication equipment; Communication systems and equipment. **SIC:** 5065 (Electronic Parts & Equipment Nec). **Officers:** Cliff Arellano, President.

■ 5573 ■ Communications Wholesale
17541 15th Ave. NE
Seattle, WA 98155
Phones: (206)364-6410 800-562-6539
Free: (800)233-2428 **Fax:** (206)364-0549
Products: Communications equipment, including radios. **SIC:** 5065 (Electronic Parts & Equipment Nec).

■ 5574 ■ Communications World of Costa Mesa
1278 Glenneyre St., Ste. 218
Laguna Beach, CA 92651
Phone: (714)491-1174
Products: Private telephone systems. **SIC:** 5065 (Electronic Parts & Equipment Nec).

■ 5575 ■ Communico Inc.
1710 N Hercules Ave., Ste. 111
Clearwater, FL 33764
Phone: (727)447-8145
Products: Telephone supplies. **SIC:** 5065 (Electronic Parts & Equipment Nec). **Sales:** $2,000,000 (2000). **Emp:** 9. **Officers:** John Lilla, President.

■ 5576 ■ Communico Inc. Communico Supply Div.
1710 N Hercules Ave.
Clearwater, FL 33765-1100
Phone: (813)442-8143 **Fax:** (813)443-7596
Products: Telecommunications equipment and supplies, including telephone parts. **SIC:** 5065 (Electronic Parts & Equipment Nec). **Sales:** $2,000,000 (2000). **Emp:** 12. **Officers:** John Lilla, President.

■ 5577 ■ Computer AC
721 Chaney
Collierville, TN 38017-2993
Phone: (901)854-5951
Free: (800)467-1099 **Fax:** (901)854-5851
E-mail: staff@computerac.com
URL: http://www.computerac.com
Products: Transformers; Uninterruptable power systems. **SIC:** 5065 (Electronic Parts & Equipment Nec). **Est:** 1975. **Officers:** William Yarbrough, President.

■ 5578 ■ ComTel Industries Inc.
6801 N 54th St.
Tampa, FL 33610
Phone: (813)623-3974 **Fax:** (813)664-1418
Products: Telephones. **SIC:** 5065 (Electronic Parts & Equipment Nec). **Est:** 1973. **Sales:** $13,000,000 (2000). **Emp:** 200. **Officers:** Richard G. Winslow, President; Richard W. Neal, VP of Finance; Michael A. Johnson, Dir. of Data Processing.

■ 5579 ■ Copier Supply Inc.
120 Amaral St.
PO Box 382
Seekonk, MA 02771
Phone: (508)431-9100 **Fax:** (978)438-5557
Products: Electronic parts and equipment, including communication and facsimile equipment. **SIC:** 5065 (Electronic Parts & Equipment Nec). **Officers:** Kenneth Pincins, President.

■ 5580 ■ D.F. Countryman Co.
480 N Pryor
St. Paul, MN 55104
Phones: (612)645-9153 800-832-6443
Free: (800)328-6820 **Fax:** (612)645-1298
Products: Coaxial communication supplies. **SIC:** 5065 (Electronic Parts & Equipment Nec). **Officers:** Don Countryman, Pres.; Joan Countryman, Treas.; Rick Countryman, Customer Service.

■ 5581 ■ CSSI Cellular
905 Palo Pinto St.
Weatherford, TX 76086-4135
Phone: (817)341-2337
Free: (800)588-2774 **Fax:** (817)598-1661
E-mail: chb890@aol.com
Products: Cellular phones. **SIC:** 5065 (Electronic Parts & Equipment Nec). **Est:** 1955. **Sales:** $3,500,000 (2000). **Emp:** 20. **Officers:** Charles Beard, President.

■ 5582 ■ Cumulous Communications Co.
6622 N Blackstone Ave.
Fresno, CA 93710
Phone: (209)431-1414
Products: Cellular telecommunications equipment. **SIC:** 5065 (Electronic Parts & Equipment Nec). **Sales:** $7,000,000 (2000). **Emp:** 18. **Officers:** Robert Mochizuki, Partner.

■ 5583 ■ Custom Phones Inc.
638 Virginia Ave.
Indianapolis, IN 46203
Phone: (317)638-6385
Free: (800)783-6385 **Fax:** (317)632-1407
URL: http://www.customphones.com
Products: Telephones; Telecommunications. **SIC:** 5065 (Electronic Parts & Equipment Nec). **Est:** 1988. **Officers:** Michael Irwin, President; Carin L. Irwin, Vice President, e-mail: carinirwin@aol.com.

■ 5584 ■ Dakota Communications Service
PO Box 2341
Bismarck, ND 58502-2341
Phone: (701)223-9581 **Fax:** (701)223-6651
Products: Cellular equipment. **SIC:** 5065 (Electronic Parts & Equipment Nec). **Officers:** Dwain Fick, President.

■ 5585 ■ H.L. Dalis, Inc.
35-35 24th St.
Long Island City, NY 11106
Phones: (718)361-1100 (718)361-1117
Free: (800)453-2547 **Fax:** (718)392-7654
Products: Car audio equipment; Cellular phones; Commercial electronic equipment; Wires; Beepers; Home audio equipment. **SICs:** 5065 (Electronic Parts & Equipment Nec); 5063 (Electrical Apparatus & Equipment); 5064 (Electrical Appliances—Television & Radio). **Est:** 1925. **Officers:** Jonathan Blumenfeld, President; Peter Blumenfeld, Sr. VP; Nick Deluca, Vice President; Daniel Oberman, Gen. Mgr.

■ 5586 ■ Lee Dan Communications Inc.
155 Adams Ave.
Hauppauge, NY 11788-3699
Phone: (631)231-1414
Free: (800)231-1414 **Fax:** (631)231-1498
E-mail: info@leedan.com
URL: http://www.leedan.com
Products: Intercoms; Mailboxes. **SICs:** 5065 (Electronic Parts & Equipment Nec); 5023 (Homefurnishings). **Est:** 1955. **Sales:** $2,500,000 (2000). **Emp:** 19. **Officers:** Lawrence J. Goldberg, President; David H. Goldberg, VP of Finance.

■ 5587 ■ Data Net Inc.
900 Huyler St.
Teterboro, NJ 07608
Phone: (201)288-9444
Products: Telecommunications equipment. **SIC:** 5065 (Electronic Parts & Equipment Nec). **Sales:** $30,000,000 (1993). **Emp:** 150. **Officers:** L. Rodger Loomis, President; Peter Smith, CFO.

■ 5588 ■ DATAVOX Inc.
5300 Memorial, 3rd Fl.
Houston, TX 77007
Phone: (713)741-6161
Products: Telecommunications equipment. **SIC:** 5065 (Electronic Parts & Equipment Nec).

■ 5589 ■ Datel Communications Corp.
145 Bodwell St.
Avon, MA 02322-1114
Phone: (508)580-2500 **Fax:** (508)583-8412
Products: Electronic systems and equipment; Electronic parts; Telephone equipment; Telegraph equipment. **SIC:** 5065 (Electronic Parts & Equipment Nec). **Officers:** Howard Davis, President.

■ 5590 ■ W.B. Davis Electric Supply Company Inc.
525 N Hollywood
Memphis, TN 38112-2544
Phone: (901)452-7363 **Fax:** (901)452-4931
Products: Intercom systems; Electrical wiring. **SICs:** 5065 (Electronic Parts & Equipment Nec); 5063 (Electrical Apparatus & Equipment). **Est:** 1920. **Emp:** 20.

■ 5591 ■ Dawn Co.
3340 S Lapeer Rd.
Orion, MI 48359
Phone: (248)391-9200 **Fax:** (248)391-9207
E-mail: sales@dawnco.com
URL: http://www.dawnco.com
Products: Commercial satellite and fiber optic communication equipment. **SIC:** 5065 (Electronic Parts & Equipment Nec). **Est:** 1987. **Sales:** $4,000,000 (2000). **Emp:** 11. **Officers:** Rosemarie L. Prete, CFO. **Former Name:** Dawn Satellite Inc.

■ 5592 ■ Denton Enterprises Inc.
PO Box 632
Harrisonburg, VA 22801-0632
Phone: (540)434-3193
Products: Pagers. **SIC:** 5065 (Electronic Parts & Equipment Nec). **Officers:** E. Denton, President.

■ 5593 ■ Diablo Cellular Phone Stores Inc.
1957 Arnold Industrial Way
Concord, CA 94520-5312
Phone: (510)674-9214 **Fax:** (510)674-9228
Products: Telephones. **SIC:** 5065 (Electronic Parts & Equipment Nec). **Est:** 1985. **Emp:** 49. **Officers:** Paula Shipley; Thomas Shipley; Timothy Westin.

■ 5594 ■ Dictaphone Corp.
340 N Sam Houston Pkwy. E, Ste. 180
Houston, TX 77060
Phone: (281)999-2323 **Fax:** (281)999-1010
Products: Voice messaging systems. **SIC:** 5065 (Electronic Parts & Equipment Nec). **Emp:** 39. **Officers:** Gary Hauser.

■ 5595 ■ **Digicorp Inc.**
2322 W Clybourn St.
Milwaukee, WI 53233
Phone: (414)343-1080
Free: (800)253-3978 **Fax:** (414)343-1099
Products: Telephone systems and cellular phones.
SIC: 5065 (Electronic Parts & Equipment Nec). **Sales:**
$2,900,000 (2000). **Emp:** 33. **Officers:** Stewart Clark,
President; Lisa Douglas, Controller.

■ 5596 ■ **Digitel Corp.**
2600 School Dr.
Atlanta, GA 30360
Phone: (770)451-1111 **Fax:** (770)452-5514
E-mail: bctate@digitelUSA.net
URL: http://www.digitelUSA.net
Products: Telephone equipment and business internet
services. **SIC:** 5065 (Electronic Parts & Equipment
Nec). **Est:** 1983. **Sales:** $20,600,000 (2000). **Emp:**
160. **Officers:** Bryan C. Tate, CEO & President;
Edward A. Locklin, CFO.

■ 5597 ■ **Dixie Electronics**
1900 Barnwell St.
Columbia, SC 29201-2604
Phone: (803)779-5332 **Fax:** (803)765-9275
Products: Electronic communications systems. **SIC:**
5065 (Electronic Parts & Equipment Nec). **Sales:**
$30,000,000 (2000). **Emp:** 150.

■ 5598 ■ **Dukes Car Stereo Inc.**
2833 S Dort Hwy.
Flint, MI 48507-5213
Phone: (810)744-2500 **Fax:** (810)744-0440
Products: Mobile electronics, including radar
detectors, phones, and radios. **SICs:** 5064 (Electrical
Appliances—Television & Radio); 5065 (Electronic
Parts & Equipment Nec). **Officers:** James Crary,
President.

■ 5599 ■ **Eagle Communications Technology**
2443 Fair Oaks Blvd., Ste. 102
Sacramento, CA 95825
Phone: (916)481-9210
Products: Commercial telephone equipment. **SIC:**
5065 (Electronic Parts & Equipment Nec).

■ 5600 ■ **EEV, Inc.**
80 Post Rd.
Buffalo, NY 14221
Phone: (716)626-9055
Free: (800)433-8269 **Fax:** (716)631-5117
Products: Broadcast equipment for television stations.
SIC: 5065 (Electronic Parts & Equipment Nec).
Officers: Rick Bossert.

■ 5601 ■ **Elcotel Inc.**
6428 Parkland Dr.
Sarasota, FL 34243
Phone: (941)758-0389
Free: (800)ELC-OTEL **Fax:** (941)755-1085
Products: Telecommunications equipment. **SIC:** 5065
(Electronic Parts & Equipment Nec). **Est:** 1985. **Sales:**
$25,000,000 (2000). **Emp:** 137. **Officers:** C. Shelton
James, CEO; Alvaro Quiros, Exec. VP; Tracey L. Gray,
COO; Ronald M. Tobin, CFO.

■ 5602 ■ **Electronic Tele-Communications Inc.**
3605 Clearview Place
Atlanta, GA 30340-2178
Phone: (404)457-5600 **Fax:** (404)455-3822
Products: Voice response equipment, including voice
mail; Intercept equipment. **SIC:** 5065 (Electronic Parts
& Equipment Nec). **Officers:** Dean W. Danner, Pres.;
James S. Fuller, V.P., Mktg.; Douglas R. Altman,
National Sales Mgr.; Phyllis McNeill, Advertising Mgr.

■ 5603 ■ **Eliza Corporation**
100 Cummings Ctr., Ste. 350C
Beverly, MA 01915-6138
Phone: (978)921-2700 **Fax:** (978)922-1528
Products: Integrated telecommunication systems. **SIC:**
5065 (Electronic Parts & Equipment Nec). **Officers:**
John Kroeker, President.

■ 5604 ■ **Encore Broadcast Equipment Sales Inc.**
2104 W Kennedy Blvd.
Tampa, FL 33606-1535
Phone: (813)253-2774
Free: (800)780-8857 **Fax:** (813)254-5907
Products: Video broadcasting equipment. **SIC:** 5065
(Electronic Parts & Equipment Nec). **Sales:** $2,000,000
(2000). **Emp:** 6. **Officers:** Susan Faiell, President;
Joseph N. Masotti, Treasurer & Secty.

■ 5605 ■ **Ernest Telecom Inc.**
6475 Jimmy Carter Blvd.
Norcross, GA 30071
Phone: (404)448-7788
Products: Coin operated telephones. **SIC:** 5065
(Electronic Parts & Equipment Nec). **Sales:** $2,000,000
(2000). **Emp:** 10. **Officers:** Joseph J. Ernest,
President; Pam Ernest, Vice President; Paul Masters,
Sales Mgr.

■ 5606 ■ **Executone of Fort Wayne Inc.**
3720 S Calhoun St.
Ft. Wayne, IN 46807
Phone: (219)744-3365 **Fax:** (219)745-1401
Products: Voice and data communications equipment
and supplies. **SIC:** 5065 (Electronic Parts & Equipment
Nec). **Est:** 1943. **Emp:** 12. **Officers:** Charles C.
Oberlin, CEO.

■ 5607 ■ **Executone Systems of St. Paul Inc.**
30 W Water St.
St. Paul, MN 55107
Phone: (612)292-0102 **Fax:** (612)292-0144
Products: Telephones. **SIC:** 5065 (Electronic Parts &
Equipment Nec). **Sales:** $5,000,000 (2000). **Emp:** 30.
Officers: Bob Brown, CEO.

■ 5608 ■ **Fairchild Communications Services Co.**
300 W Service Rd.
Chantilly, VA 20151
Phone: (703)478-5888 **Fax:** (703)478-5757
Products: Office building telecommunications
equipment including station equipment, data circuits
and voice mail. **SIC:** 5065 (Electronic Parts &
Equipment Nec). **Sales:** $68,100,000 (1993). **Emp:**
200. **Officers:** Mel Borer, President; Jon Peterson,
CFO.

■ 5609 ■ **Famous Telephone Supply Inc.**
PO Box 28577
Akron, OH 44319
Phone: (330)762-8811 **Fax:** (330)896-8844
Products: Telephones; Power wire and cable;
Telephone and telegraph wire and cable. **SIC:** 5065
(Electronic Parts & Equipment Nec). **Est:** 1974. **Sales:**
$14,000,000 (2000). **Emp:** 48. **Officers:** Jay Blaushild,
Owner.

■ 5610 ■ **Farmstead Telephone Group Inc.**
22 Prestige Park Circle
East Hartford, CT 06108
Phone: (860)282-0010
Free: (800)243-0234 **Fax:** (860)610-6001
URL: http://www.farmstead.com
Products: Telephone equipment. **SIC:** 5065
(Electronic Parts & Equipment Nec). **Est:** 1986. **Sales:**
$19,700,000 (2000). **Emp:** 99. **Officers:** George J.
Taylor Jr. Jr., CEO, President & Chairman of the Board;
Robert G. LaVigne, VP of Finance & Admin.; Alexander
E. Capo, VP of Sales; Neil R. Sullivan, VP of
Adminstration & Accounting; Joseaph A. Novak, VP of
Operations; Robert L. Saelens, VP of Marketing, e-
mail: rsaelens@farmstead.com.

■ 5611 ■ **Fast Track Communications Inc.**
1270 Techwood Dr. NW
Atlanta, GA 30318
Phone: (404)870-6690
Free: (800)876-1478 **Fax:** (404)875-1691
E-mail: fasttrack@mindspring.com
Products: Electrical appliances, including two-way
radios, intercom systems, and scanners. **SIC:** 5065
(Electronic Parts & Equipment Nec). **Est:** 1990. **Sales:**
$900,000 (2000). **Emp:** 3. **Officers:** Gwen Byrd,
President; Jason Wells, Sales/Marketing Contact, e-
mail: jrwells@mindspring.com.

■ 5612 ■ **Fiber Optic Center Inc.**
23 Center St.
New Bedford, MA 02740-6322
Phone: (508)992-6464
Free: (800)473-4237 **Fax:** (508)991-8876
Products: Fiber optic products. **SIC:** 5049
(Professional Equipment Nec). **Sales:** $12,000,000
(2000). **Emp:** 9. **Officers:** Neal H. Weiss, President;
Kathy Wing, Finance Officer.

■ 5613 ■ **Fibertron Corp.**
6400 Artesia Blvd.
Buena Park, CA 90620
Phone: (714)670-7711 **Fax:** (714)670-8811
Products: Fiber optics equipment. **SIC:** 5084
(Industrial Machinery & Equipment). **Sales:**
$84,000,000 (2000). **Emp:** 97. **Officers:** Marlene
Spiegel, President; Clint Willis, VP of Finance.

■ 5614 ■ **FM Systems, Inc.**
3877 S Main St.
Santa Ana, CA 92707
Phone: (714)979-3355
Free: (800)235-6960 **Fax:** (714)979-0913
URL: http://www.fmsystems-inc.com
Products: Audio transmission equipment. **SIC:** 5065
(Electronic Parts & Equipment Nec). **Est:** 1978.
Officers: Frank F. McClatchie, President; Don K.
McClatchie; Mike King, Sales/Marketing Contact; Terri
West, Customer Service Contact.

■ 5615 ■ **Fones West**
PO Box 6741
Denver, CO 80206
Phone: (303)393-7260
Products: Telecommunications equipment. **SIC:** 5065
(Electronic Parts & Equipment Nec). **Sales:** $7,000,000
(1993). **Emp:** 25. **Officers:** Mark Felsen, President.

■ 5616 ■ **Frontler Radio Inc.**
3401 Sirius Ave. 18
Las Vegas, NV 89102-8313
Phone: (702)871-6166 **Fax:** (702)367-0347
E-mail: frontler@tld.net
Products: Radio communication equipment and
systems, including two-way radios. **SIC:** 5065
(Electronic Parts & Equipment Nec). **Est:** 1953. **Sales:**
$1,000,000 (2000). **Emp:** 8. **Officers:** Roger Combs,
Manager.

■ 5617 ■ **Gately Communication Company Inc.**
501 Industry Dr.
Hampton, VA 23661-1314
Phone: (757)826-8210
Free: (800)428-3597 **Fax:** (757)826-7213
E-mail: gately@gately.com
URL: http://www.gately.com
Products: Card access; Telemetry; Vehicle warning
lights and sirens. **SIC:** 5065 (Electronic Parts &
Equipment Nec). **Est:** 1952. **Sales:** $4,500,000 (1999).
Emp: 48. **Officers:** Joseph R. Gately, President;
Cynthia Clemmons, Vice President; Ken Gately, Exec.
VP; Larry Gately, Sales/Marketing Contact, e-mail:
lgately@gately.com; Ed Allen, Customer Service
Contact, e-mail: eallen@gately.com; Cynthia
Clemmons, Human Resources Contact, e-mail:
cclemmons@gately.com.

■ 5618 ■ **General Communications**
2171 Ralph Ave.
Stockton, CA 95206-3625
Phone: (209)462-6059
Products: Two-way radios; Repeaters; Paging
equipment; Transmitter sites. **SIC:** 5065 (Electronic
Parts & Equipment Nec). **Emp:** 4. **Officers:** Robert
LaRue.

■ 5619 ■ **Genesis Telecom Inc.**
1235 North Loop W, Ste. 100
Houston, TX 77008
Phone: (713)868-5415
Products: Business communications equipment
including telephones, voice mail and video
conferencing systems. **SIC:** 5065 (Electronic Parts &
Equipment Nec). **Sales:** $6,000,000 (2000). **Emp:** 53.
Officers: Debra Schindler, President; Bradley
Petrasek, Exec. VP of Finance.

■ **5620** ■ **Global Telecommunications**
PO Box 2928
Winchester, VA 22604-2128
Phone: (540)667-6898 **Fax:** (540)665-8068
Products: Telephone and data transmission equipment. **SIC:** 5065 (Electronic Parts & Equipment Nec). **Officers:** Rudolf Bothe, President.

■ **5621** ■ **GMP**
3111 Old Lincoln Hwy.
Trevose, PA 19053-4996
Phone: (215)357-5500 **Fax:** (215)357-6216
E-mail: info@gmptools.com
URL: http://www.gmptools.com
Products: Telecommunications equipment; Cable television equipment; Outside plant specialty tools and equipment. **SICs:** 5065 (Electronic Parts & Equipment Nec); 5072 (Hardware). **Est:** 1936. **Emp:** 150. **Officers:** William N. Pfundt, President; Douglas H. Clemens, VP of Marketing & Sales, e-mail: dclemens@gmptools.com; David Lindsay, Customer Service Contact, e-mail: dlindsay@gmptools.com.

■ **5622** ■ **Gorton Communications Inc.**
190 London Dairy Tpke.
Hooksett, NH 03106
Phone: (603)622-9219
Products: Two-way radios. **SIC:** 5065 (Electronic Parts & Equipment Nec). **Officers:** William Gorton, President.

■ **5623** ■ **Government Electronic Systems Div.**
Marne Hwy.
Moorestown, NJ 08057
Phone: (609)722-4900
Products: Combat, battlefield, and intelligence systems equipment; Radars, including tracking systems. **SIC:** 5065 (Electronic Parts & Equipment Nec).

■ **5624** ■ **Granada Systems Design Inc.**
1886 Rte. 52
Hopewell Junction, NY 12533
Phone: (914)221-1617 **Fax:** (914)686-9181
Products: Telecommunications equipment. **SIC:** 5065 (Electronic Parts & Equipment Nec). **Sales:** $1,000,000 (2000). **Emp:** 12. **Officers:** Ashok Nagrath, President; Ruma Nagrath, Controller.

■ **5625** ■ **Graveline Electronics Inc.**
16415 NW 67th Ave.
Miami Lakes, FL 33014
Phone: (305)824-9000
Products: Cellular phones; Beepers. **SIC:** 5065 (Electronic Parts & Equipment Nec). **Sales:** $1,000,000 (2000). **Emp:** 6. **Officers:** Dave Graveline, President; Beth Graveline, Office Mgr.

■ **5626** ■ **GRE America Inc.**
425 Harbor Blvd.
Belmont, CA 94002
Phone: (415)591-1400
Free: (800)233-5973 **Fax:** (415)591-2001
Products: Phones and accessories for computer scanners. **SIC:** 5065 (Electronic Parts & Equipment Nec). **Sales:** $4,000,000 (2000). **Emp:** 40. **Officers:** T. Imazeki, President.

■ **5627** ■ **Group One Ltd.**
80 C Ln.
Farmingdale, NY 11735
Phone: (516)249-1399
Products: Microphones; Monitors. **SIC:** 5065 (Electronic Parts & Equipment Nec).

■ **5628** ■ **GTE Supply**
5615 Highpoint Dr.
Irving, TX 75038
Phone: (972)751-4100
Products: Telecommunications equipment. **SIC:** 5065 (Electronic Parts & Equipment Nec). **Est:** 1990. **Sales:** $840,000,000 (2000). **Emp:** 3,000. **Officers:** Larry Henry, VP & General Merchandising Mgr.; Chris McNabb, CFO.

■ **5629** ■ **Haddad Electronic Supply Inc.**
PO Box 2707
Fall River, MA 02722-2707
Phone: (508)679-2596 **Fax:** (508)677-6620
Products: Electronic supplies; Phone systems. **SIC:** 5065 (Electronic Parts & Equipment Nec). **Officers:** Solomon Haddad, President.

■ **5630** ■ **Harris Corp.**
4393 Digital Way
Mason, OH 45040
Phone: (513)459-3700 **Fax:** (513)701-5306
URL: http://www.harris.com
Products: Electronic equipment, including broadcast and studio. **SIC:** 5065 (Electronic Parts & Equipment Nec). **Sales:** $28,000,000 (2000). **Emp:** 115. **Officers:** Jim Woods, VP Product Lines.

■ **5631** ■ **Harris Corporation**
330 Twin Dolphin Dr.
Redwood City, CA 94065-1421
Phone: (650)594-3000
Free: (800)327-4666 **Fax:** (650)594-3110
E-mail: wireless@farinon.harris.com
URL: http://www.farinon.harris.com
Products: Telecommunication equipment. **SIC:** 5065 (Electronic Parts & Equipment Nec). **Officers:** Denis Cote, V.P.; Cliff Fields, Sales Mgr.

■ **5632** ■ **Hawk Electronics**
5718 Airport Fwy.
Ft. Worth, TX 76117
Phone: (817)429-0432
Products: Cellular phones. **SIC:** 5065 (Electronic Parts & Equipment Nec).

■ **5633** ■ **HB Distributors**
8741 Shirley Ave.
Northridge, CA 91324
Phone: (818)701-5100
Free: (800)266-3478 **Fax:** (818)700-1808
Products: Telecommunications equipment. **SIC:** 5065 (Electronic Parts & Equipment Nec). **Est:** 1976. **Sales:** $5,000,000 (1999). **Emp:** 12. **Officers:** Pam Branner; Howard Branner; Denise Derrico, Sales & Marketing Contact.

■ **5634** ■ **HD Communications Inc.**
15635 W McNichols Rd.
Detroit, MI 48235
Phone: (313)838-5860
Products: Public address systems; Cameras; Intercoms. **SICs:** 5065 (Electronic Parts & Equipment Nec); 5043 (Photographic Equipment & Supplies). **Sales:** $700,000 (2000). **Emp:** 3.

■ **5635** ■ **Hi Country Wire and Telephone Ltd.**
6275 Simms Ave.
Arvada, CO 80004
Phone: (303)467-9143
Products: Telephones; Telephone equipment. **SIC:** 5065 (Electronic Parts & Equipment Nec). **Sales:** $11,000,000 (2000). **Emp:** 40. **Officers:** Bob Whitfield Sr., President.

■ **5636** ■ **Hickory Tech-Enterprise Solutions**
2920 Centre Pointe Dr.
Roseville, MN 55113
Phone: (651)634-1800 **Fax:** (651)634-1566
URL: http://www.collins-com.com
Products: Telecommunications equipment. **SIC:** 5065 (Electronic Parts & Equipment Nec). **Est:** 1975. **Sales:** $20,000,000 (2000). **Emp:** 105. **Officers:** Jon L. Anderson, President. **Former Name:** Collins Communications Systems Co.

■ **5637** ■ **High Frequency Technology Company Inc.**
172-D Brook Ave.
Deer Park, NY 11729
Phone: (516)242-3020 **Fax:** (516)242-4823
Products: Radio frequency sealing equipment. **SIC:** 5065 (Electronic Parts & Equipment Nec). **Est:** 1975. **Sales:** $2,000,000 (2000). **Emp:** 10. **Officers:** Louis Amabile, President.

■ **5638** ■ **Holzberg Communications, Inc.**
Box 322
Totowa, NJ 07511
Phone: (973)389-9600
Free: (800)654-9550 **Fax:** (973)389-9696
E-mail: holzberg@juno.com
URL: http://www.holzberg.com
Products: Two-way radio products and accessories; General electronic components; Antennas; Batteries; Paging accessories; Cellular accessories. **SIC:** 5065 (Electronic Parts & Equipment Nec). **Est:** 1970. **Emp:** 5. **Officers:** Andy Holzberg. **Former Name:** Holzberg, Inc.

■ **5639** ■ **Home/Office Communications Supply**
430 Woodruff Rd., No. 300
Greenville, SC 29607
Phone: (803)297-6340 **Fax:** (803)458-9773
Products: Phones; Fax machines; Power systems; Paging systems. **SIC:** 5065 (Electronic Parts & Equipment Nec). **Est:** 1990. **Sales:** $4,000,000 (2000). **Emp:** 4. **Officers:** Bill Rogers, President; Don Boiter, Controller.

■ **5640** ■ **Howard Enterprises Inc.**
545 Calle San Pablo
Camarillo, CA 93012-8550
Phone: (805)383-7444 **Fax:** (805)383-7442
E-mail: stanh@howent.com
URL: http://www.howent.com
Products: Video conferencing equipment, computers, and software; Cameras. **SICs:** 5064 (Electrical Appliances—Television & Radio); 5045 (Computers, Peripherals & Software). **Est:** 1989. **Sales:** $1,000,000 (2000). **Emp:** 3. **Officers:** Stanley E. Howard Jr., CEO & President, e-mail: stanh@howent.com.

■ **5641** ■ **Hutton Communications Inc.**
2520 Marsh Ln.
Carrollton, TX 75006-2282
Phone: (972)417-0100 **Free:** (877)648-8866
E-mail: sales@huttoncom.com
URL: http://www.huttoncom.com
Products: Cellular land mobile communications equipment. **SIC:** 5065 (Electronic Parts & Equipment Nec). **Sales:** $72,000,000 (2000). **Emp:** 200. **Officers:** W.C. Mueller, President; Ron Ryan, VP of Sales.

■ **5642** ■ **ICS-Executone Telecom Inc.**
125 Highpower Rd.
Rochester, NY 14623
Phone: (716)427-7000 **Fax:** (716)427-0863
Products: Telecommunications systems; Voice mail. **SIC:** 5065 (Electronic Parts & Equipment Nec). **Est:** 1976. **Sales:** $7,000,000 (2000). **Emp:** 70. **Officers:** I.C. Shah, President; John Dobbertin, VP of Finance; Raj Shah, VP of Sales.

■ **5643** ■ **IDM Satellite Division Inc.**
311 F St.
ChuLa Vista, CA 91910
Phone: (619)422-1155 **Fax:** (619)422-1415
Products: Satellite communications equipment. **SIC:** 5065 (Electronic Parts & Equipment Nec). **Sales:** $4,000,000 (2000). **Emp:** 20. **Officers:** Jorge Valerdi, COO; John D. Caram, CFO.

■ **5644** ■ **Independent Telephone Network Inc.**
8741 Shirley Ave.
Northridge, CA 91324
Phone: (818)701-5100 **Fax:** (818)700-1808
Products: Telecommunication equipment and wire; Telephone headsets. **SIC:** 5065 (Electronic Parts & Equipment Nec). **Sales:** $3,000,000 (2000). **Emp:** 11. **Officers:** Pam Branner, CEO.

■ **5645** ■ **Industrial Communications Co.**
G 12157 N Saginaw
Clio, MI 48420-1036
Phone: (810)686-4990 **Fax:** (810)686-5980
Products: Communication systems. **SIC:** 5065 (Electronic Parts & Equipment Nec). **Emp:** 999.

■ **5646** ■ **Installation Telephone Services Inc.**
3920 Grape St.
Denver, CO 80207
Phone: (303)355-3330
Free: (800)544-3905 **Fax:** (303)355-3390
Products: Telecommunications equipment including

phone and voice mail systems and patch panels. **SIC:** 5065 (Electronic Parts & Equipment Nec). **Sales:** $3,000,000 (2000). **Emp:** 18. **Officers:** Robert Laureti, CEO & President; Howard Refsky, Finance General Manager.

■ **5647** ■ **Intelliphone Inc.**
191 Chandler Rd.
Andover, MA 01810
Phone: (978)688-4070 **Fax:** (978)688-3980
Products: Telecommunications equipment. **SIC:** 5065 (Electronic Parts & Equipment Nec). **Sales:** $3,000,000 (2000). **Emp:** 15. **Officers:** Charles P. Garabedian III, President; Debra M. Chesly, Controller.

■ **5648** ■ **Inter-Ocean Industries Inc.**
1140 Ave. of the Amer
New York, NY 10036
Phone: (212)921-1700
Products: Electronic equipment, including fax machines and telephones. **SIC:** 5065 (Electronic Parts & Equipment Nec). **Sales:** $30,000,000 (2000). **Emp:** 5. **Officers:** Benjamin Fishoff, President; Henry Shapiro, Vice President; Donald Fishoff, Secretary.

■ **5649** ■ **Inter-Tel Technologies, Inc.**
10160 Linn Station Rd.
Louisville, KY 40223
Phone: (502)426-2000
Free: (800)866-2000 **Fax:** (502)426-2029
Products: Telephone communication equipment; Health care paging equipment; Networks and applications; Video conferencing equipment; Computer telephone integration; Fiber optic cabling. **SIC:** 5065 (Electronic Parts & Equipment Nec). **Est:** 1946. **Sales:** $10,000,000 (2000). **Emp:** 85. **Officers:** Caldwell Willig. **Former Name:** ITS Corp.

■ **5650** ■ **International Telecom Systems Inc.**
8004 Split Oak Dr.
Bethesda, MD 20817-6953
Phone: (301)718-9800
Products: Pagers. **SIC:** 5065 (Electronic Parts & Equipment Nec). **Est:** 1991. **Sales:** $5,000,000 (2000). **Emp:** 20. **Officers:** Larry Harris, President; Mimi Harris, Dir. of Marketing.

■ **5651** ■ **ITBR, Inc.**
2 Cielo Center, 3rd Fl.
1250 Capital of Texas Hwy. S
Austin, TX 78746
Phone: (512)329-2170 **Fax:** (512)266-8832
Products: Telecommunications equipment and supplies; Medical and hospital equipment and supplies; Food products; Computer hardware and software. **SICs:** 5065 (Electronic Parts & Equipment Nec); 5141 (Groceries—General Line); 5047 (Medical & Hospital Equipment); 5045 (Computers, Peripherals & Software). **Est:** 1972. **Officers:** Ernesto Chavarria, President.

■ **5652** ■ **Ivanco Inc.**
218 Greenacres Rd.
Ft. Walton Beach, FL 32547
Phone: (850)862-9001 **Fax:** (850)864-2376
Products: Alarm systems; Communication systems and equipment; Intercommunication equipment; Telephone equipment; Electric and electronic equipment. **SICs:** 5065 (Electronic Parts & Equipment Nec); 5064 (Electrical Appliances—Television & Radio). **Emp:** 49.

■ **5653** ■ **Jenne Distributors**
33665 Chester Rd.
Avon, OH 44011-1307
Phone: (440)835-0040
Free: (800)835-2788 **Fax:** (440)835-2788
URL: http://www.jenne.com
Products: Fax machines; Telephones; Telephone equipment. **SIC:** 5065 (Electronic Parts & Equipment Nec). **Est:** 1986. **Sales:** $30,000,000 (1999). **Emp:** 33. **Officers:** Rosie Jenne, President, e-mail: rmj@jenne.com.

■ **5654** ■ **Jones Sales Group**
PO Box 270506
Flower Mound, TX 75027
Phone: (817)224-9000 **Fax:** (817)224-9030
E-mail: chris@jonessalesgroup.com
Products: Professional sound/audio equipment. **SIC:** 5065 (Electronic Parts & Equipment Nec). **Est:** 1987. **Emp:** 6. **Officers:** Christopher Jones, President, e-mail: chris@jonessalegroup.com; Charlie Cason, Customer Service Contact, e-mail: charlie@jonessdesgroup.com.

■ **5655** ■ **Just Phones**
15333 Culver Dr., Ste. 445
Irvine, CA 92604
Phone: (949)559-1844 **Fax:** (949)559-5941
Products: Telephone equipment. **SIC:** 5065 (Electronic Parts & Equipment Nec). **Sales:** $500,000 (2000). **Emp:** 3. **Officers:** Robert Gamer, President; G. Kraus, Controller.

■ **5656** ■ **Kansas Communications Inc.**
8206 Marshall Dr.
Lenexa, KS 66214
Phone: (913)752-9100 **Fax:** (913)888-6647
Products: Telecommunication products. **SIC:** 5065 (Electronic Parts & Equipment Nec). **Est:** 1974. **Sales:** $19,000,000 (2000). **Emp:** 100. **Officers:** Herb Sizemore, President; Mike Meurer, Controller.

■ **5657** ■ **Kash 'N Gold Ltd.**
1 Trade Zone Ct.
Ronkonkoma, NY 11779
Phone: (516)981-1600 **Fax:** (516)981-1702
Products: Novelty telephones; Electronics. **SICs:** 5064 (Electrical Appliances—Television & Radio); 5065 (Electronic Parts & Equipment Nec). **Est:** 1983. **Sales:** $21,000,000 (2000). **Emp:** 15. **Officers:** Kash Gobindram, President; Rama Krishnan, CFO; Stanley Reiff, Exec. VP.

■ **5658** ■ **KCG Communications Inc.**
7076 S Alton Way, Ste. E
Englewood, CO 80112
Phone: (303)773-1200
Products: Telecommunications equipment. **SIC:** 5065 (Electronic Parts & Equipment Nec). **Sales:** $2,100,000 (2000). **Emp:** 40. **Officers:** Charlie Beram, President; Jackie Beram, Vice President.

■ **5659** ■ **KTS Services Inc.**
5726 Corporate Ave.
Cypress, CA 90630
Phone: (714)827-2200
Products: Telephone systems. **SIC:** 5065 (Electronic Parts & Equipment Nec). **Sales:** $16,000,000 (2000). **Emp:** 40. **Officers:** Ken Treleani, President.

■ **5660** ■ **L-3 Communications Corp.**
600 3rd Ave.
New York, NY 10016
Phone: (212)697-1111 **Fax:** (212)682-9553
Products: Communications equipment for aerospace contactors and U.S. military and federal agencies. **SIC:** 5065 (Electronic Parts & Equipment Nec). **Officers:** Frank C. Lanza, CEO & Chairman of the Board; Robert V. LaPenta, President & CFO.

■ **5661** ■ **Larcan TTC**
1390 Overlook Dr., No.2
Lafayette, CO 80026
Phone: (303)665-8000 **Fax:** (303)673-9900
URL: http://www.larcan.com
Products: Radio and television transmitting equipment. **SIC:** 5065 (Electronic Parts & Equipment Nec). **Officers:** Tim Adamson, President; David Hale, Sales/Marketing Contact, e-mail: sales@earthnet.net; Don J. Massa, Dir., Mktg. & Sales. **Former Name:** Television Technology Corp.

■ **5662** ■ **LESCO Distributing**
51100 Bittersweet Rd.
Granger, IN 46530-9140
Phone: (219)277-8001
Free: (800)348-2888 **Fax:** (219)277-8018
URL: http://www.lescodistributing.com
Products: Electric and electronic equipment; Radio receivers; Citizens' band radios; car stereos. **SICs:** 5064 (Electrical Appliances—Television & Radio); 5065

(Electronic Parts & Equipment Nec). **Est:** 1980. **Emp:** 70. **Officers:** Karl L. Roesch.

■ **5663** ■ **Ludlow Telephone Company Inc.**
111 Main St.
Ludlow, VT 05149-1025
Phone: (802)485-6012 **Fax:** (802)228-5696
Products: Telephone and telegraphic equipment. **SIC:** 5065 (Electronic Parts & Equipment Nec). **Officers:** Robert Collins, President.

■ **5664** ■ **Magna Communications Inc.**
30680 Montpelier Dr.
Madison Heights, MI 48071-1800
Phone: (810)777-7999
Products: Telephones and telephone systems. **SIC:** 5064 (Electrical Appliances—Television & Radio). **Sales:** $1,000,000 (1994). **Emp:** 30. **Officers:** Ken Kargol, President.

■ **5665** ■ **Main Office Machine Co.**
613 Market St.
Kirkland, WA 98033-5422
Phone: (206)282-0302 **Free:** (800)558-5322
Products: Phone systems. **SIC:** 5065 (Electronic Parts & Equipment Nec). **Officers:** Philip Lavery, President.

■ **5666** ■ **Majestic Communications**
4091 Viscount
Memphis, TN 38118
Phone: (901)794-9494 **Fax:** (901)366-5736
Products: Electronic communication equipment. **SIC:** 5065 (Electronic Parts & Equipment Nec).

■ **5667** ■ **Marcom**
540 Hauer Apple Way
Aptos, CA 95003-9501
Phone: (831)768-8668 **Fax:** (831)768-7810
E-mail: info@mar-com.com
URL: http://www.mar-com.com
Products: Radio and broadcasting equipment. **SIC:** 5065 (Electronic Parts & Equipment Nec). **Est:** 1977. **Officers:** Martin Jackson, President; Shirley Jackson, Vice President.

■ **5668** ■ **Members Service Corp.**
1085 W Morse Blvd.
Winter Park, FL 32789
Phone: (407)647-6600
Products: Telephone equipment. **SIC:** 5065 (Electronic Parts & Equipment Nec). **Sales:** $2,500,000 (1992). **Emp:** 30. **Officers:** Arthur S. Feher Jr., CEO, President & Chairman of the Board; Irving J. Becker, Exec. VP & CFO.

■ **5669** ■ **Memphis Communications Corporation**
PO Box 41735
Memphis, TN 38174-1735
Phone: (901)725-9271
Products: Communications systems, including audio and visual equipment; Photocopiers and facsimile machines; Computers; Security systems; Mail handling/shipping systems. **SIC:** 5065 (Electronic Parts & Equipment Nec). **Est:** 1972. **Sales:** $11,000,000 (2000). **Emp:** 70. **Officers:** D.W. Berry Jr. Jr., Chairman of the Board.

■ **5670** ■ **Mer Communications Systems Inc.**
420 Fifth Ave.
New York, NY 10118-2702
Phone: (212)719-5959
Free: (800)933-8227 **Fax:** (212)719-4588
Products: Telecommunications equipment. **SIC:** 5065 (Electronic Parts & Equipment Nec). **Sales:** $2,000,000 (1993). **Emp:** 15. **Officers:** Roy Hess, President.

■ **5671** ■ **Mercury Communication Services, Inc.**
1263 Record Crossing
Dallas, TX 75235
Phone: (214)637-4900 **Fax:** (214)637-4905
E-mail: mercurycomm.com
Products: Business telephone and voice mail systems. **SIC:** 5065 (Electronic Parts & Equipment Nec). **Est:** 1980. **Sales:** $5,500,000 (2000). **Emp:** 25. **Officers:** Gregory F. Osler.

■ **5672** ■ **Mercury Communication Services, Inc.**
8711 Burnet Rd., Ste. E-56
Austin, TX 78758
Phone: (512)467-7227 **Fax:** (512)467-0455
E-mail: gosler@mercurycomm.com
URL: http://www.mercurycomm.com
Products: Business telephone and voice mail systems.
SIC: 5065 (Electronic Parts & Equipment Nec). **Est:** 1980.

■ **5673** ■ **MetaSystems Design Group Inc.**
2000 N 15th St., No. 103
Arlington, VA 22201
Phone: (703)243-6622 **Fax:** (703)841-9798
Products: Telecommunications networks. **SIC:** 5065 (Electronic Parts & Equipment Nec). **Est:** 1982. **Sales:** $600,000 (2000). **Emp:** 8. **Officers:** Lisa Kimball, CEO; Scott Burns, President; Frank Burns, Dir. of Marketing & Sales; Douglass Carmichael, Dir of Human Resources.

■ **5674** ■ **Micro Comm Inc.**
2612 Cameron
Mobile, AL 36607
Phone: (205)476-4872 **Fax:** (205)473-3522
Products: Telephones. **SIC:** 5065 (Electronic Parts & Equipment Nec). **Est:** 1983. **Sales:** $1,000,000 (2000). **Emp:** 49. **Officers:** David Sweatt.

■ **5675** ■ **Microtech-Tel Inc.**
4985 Ironton St.
Denver, CO 80239
Phone: (303)373-4444 **Fax:** (303)373-1077
Products: Telecommunications equipment. **SIC:** 5065 (Electronic Parts & Equipment Nec). **Sales:** $16,000,000 (2000). **Emp:** 140. **Officers:** Sam V. Kumar, President; Jim Harvey, VP of Finance.

■ **5676** ■ **Mid-Plains Communications Systems Inc.**
7520 Elmwood Ave.
Middleton, WI 53562
Phone: (608)836-1912 **Fax:** (608)828-5288
Products: Telephones; Sound systems. **SIC:** 5065 (Electronic Parts & Equipment Nec). **Emp:** 42. **Officers:** Daniel J. Stein.

■ **5677** ■ **Midwest Telephone Inc.**
883 S Lapeer Rd., Ste. 102
Lake Orion, MI 48362
Phone: (248)693-7775
Free: (800)860-7776 **Fax:** (248)693-9866
Products: Electronic parts and equipment, including telephone, telegraphic, and voice mail equipment. **SIC:** 5065 (Electronic Parts & Equipment Nec). **Est:** 1983. **Officers:** Darrel Maynard, President; Francis K. Rosebush, Vice President.

■ **5678** ■ **Millbrook Sales & Service Co.**
3060 Madison Ave. SE
Wyoming, MI 49548-1273
Phone: (616)241-0157
Products: Electronic parts and equipment, including audio and video communication equipment; Fire alarms. **SICs:** 5065 (Electronic Parts & Equipment Nec); 5063 (Electrical Apparatus & Equipment). **Officers:** Frederick Jeisy, President.

■ **5679** ■ **Miller-Jackson Co.**
PO Box 26226
Oklahoma City, OK 73126
Phone: (405)235-8426 **Free:** (800)749-6526
Products: Telephone equipment. **SIC:** 5065 (Electronic Parts & Equipment Nec). **Est:** 1905. **Sales:** $1,000,000 (2000). **Emp:** 4. **Officers:** Jeffrey S. Brown, President.

■ **5680** ■ **Mobile Communications of Gwinnett**
885 Cripple Creek Dr.
Lawrenceville, GA 30043-4402
Phone: (404)963-3748 **Fax:** (404)339-1325
Products: Electronic systems and equipment; Electronic parts; Telephone equipment; Telegraph equipment; Cellular telephones. **SIC:** 5065 (Electronic Parts & Equipment Nec). **Officers:** Wayne Powell, President.

■ **5681** ■ **Modemsplus Inc.**
3815 Presidential Pkwy.
Atlanta, GA 30340
Phone: (404)458-2232 **Fax:** (404)452-1641
Products: Electronic systems and equipment; Electronic parts; Communication systems and equipment; Intercommunication equipment. **SIC:** 5065 (Electronic Parts & Equipment Nec). **Officers:** H. Thorsen, President.

■ **5682** ■ **Motor Sound Corp.**
541 Division St.
Campbell, CA 95008
Phone: (408)374-7900 **Fax:** (408)374-3928
Products: Wireless communication equipment; Computer products. **SICs:** 5065 (Electronic Parts & Equipment Nec); 5045 (Computers, Peripherals & Software). **Sales:** $375,000,000 (2000). **Emp:** 320. **Officers:** William W. Topper, President; Dennis Pastinik, CFO.

■ **5683** ■ **Motorola Communications**
430 N George
York, PA 17404-2750
Phone: (717)843-6764 **Fax:** (717)854-3813
Products: Electronics, including communication equipment. **SIC:** 5065 (Electronic Parts & Equipment Nec). **Emp:** 49.

■ **5684** ■ **Motorola Inc. Communications and Electronics Div.**
8325 Lenexa Dr., Ste. 150
Lenexa, KS 66214-1695
Phone: (913)492-6060
Products: Communication systems equipment for public safety. for schools and cities. **SIC:** 5065 (Electronic Parts & Equipment Nec). **Sales:** $7,000,000 (1994). **Emp:** 25.

■ **5685** ■ **Mueller Telecommunications Inc.**
7334 S Alton Way, Bldg. 14, Ste. J
Englewood, CO 80112
Phone: (303)773-3575
Products: Telecommunications equipment. **SIC:** 5065 (Electronic Parts & Equipment Nec). **Sales:** $2,100,000 (1993). **Emp:** 8. **Officers:** W. John Mueller, President; Gary Mueller, Vice President.

■ **5686** ■ **Multimedia Pacific Inc.**
1725 Kalani St.
Honolulu, HI 96819
Phone: (808)842-0077
Products: Media equipment. **SICs:** 5049 (Professional Equipment Nec); 5065 (Electronic Parts & Equipment Nec).

■ **5687** ■ **NEC America Inc.**
14040 Park Center Rd.
Herndon, VA 20171
Phone: (703)834-4000
Free: (800)433-2745 **Fax:** (703)481-6904
URL: http://www.nec.com
Products: Telephones; Fax machines; Electric and electronic equipment; Computers. **SICs:** 5065 (Electronic Parts & Equipment Nec); 5045 (Computers, Peripherals & Software). **Est:** 1972. **Sales:** $240,000,000 (2000). **Emp:** 425. **Officers:** R. Maruta, Sr. VP; Larry Eagle, Vice President; Jim Eddy.

■ **5688** ■ **NEC Business Communication Systems East Inc.**
5890 Enterprise Pkwy.
East Syracuse, NY 13057-2924
Phone: (315)446-2400
Products: Business telephone systems. **SIC:** 5065 (Electronic Parts & Equipment Nec).

■ **5689** ■ **Network Access Corp. (Pittsburgh, Pennsylvania)**
7805 McKnight Rd., Ste. 206
Pittsburgh, PA 15237
Phone: (412)369-9790 **Fax:** (412)369-9610
Products: Data communication equipment. **SIC:** 5045 (Computers, Peripherals & Software). **Sales:** $1,400,000 (2000). **Emp:** 6. **Officers:** Jim Barnes, President; Rita Barnes, Mgr. of Finance.

■ **5690** ■ **Nokia Display Products Inc.**
123 Second St.
Sausalito, CA 94965
Phone: (415)331-4244
Free: (800)296-6542 **Fax:** (415)331-6211
URL: http://www.nokia.com
Products: Computer monitors. **SIC:** 5045 (Computers, Peripherals & Software). **Sales:** $16,000,000 (2000). **Emp:** 30. **Officers:** Jim Cookson, President; Dan Rush, Controller.

■ **5691** ■ **Norfolk Wire and Electronics Inc.**
5301 Cleveland St.
Virginia Beach, VA 23462
Phone: (757)499-1100
Products: Wire, cable, and fiber-optic products. **SIC:** 5063 (Electrical Apparatus & Equipment). **Sales:** $20,000,000 (2000). **Emp:** 95. **Officers:** Ron Hurley, CEO; Robert Jennings, President.

■ **5692** ■ **Norstan Inc.**
5101 Shady Oak Rd.
Minnetonka, MN 55343-5715
Phone: (612)352-4500 **Free:** (800)676-8893
URL: http://www.norstan.com
Products: Telephones. **SIC:** 5065 (Electronic Parts & Equipment Nec). **Est:** 1960. **Sales:** $483,000,000 (1999). **Emp:** 2,500. **Officers:** Robert J. Vold, Treasurer; Jerry Lehrman, VP & General Counsel; Paul Bazucki, CEO & Chairman of the Board; Richard Cohen, Vice Chairman of the Board & CFO.

■ **5693** ■ **Nortel Federal Systems**
2400 Lakeside Blvd.
Richardson, TX 75082
Phone: (972)301-7000
Products: Business phone systems. **SIC:** 5065 (Electronic Parts & Equipment Nec).

■ **5694** ■ **North Atlantic Communications Inc.**
48 South Mall
Plainview, NY 11803
Phone: (516)756-9000 **Fax:** (516)756-9128
URL: http://www.nactelsystems.com
Products: Telephone equipment. **SIC:** 5065 (Electronic Parts & Equipment Nec). **Est:** 1980. **Sales:** $2,000,000 (2000). **Emp:** 15. **Officers:** John Fries, Treasurer & Secty.; Jamie Buswell, Vice President.

■ **5695** ■ **North Pittsburgh Systems Inc.**
4008 Gibsonia Rd.
Gibsonia, PA 15044-9311
Phone: (724)443-9600
Free: (800)443-1550 **Fax:** (724)443-9663
Products: Telephone equipment. **SIC:** 5065 (Electronic Parts & Equipment Nec). **Sales:** $66,200,000 (2000). **Emp:** 276. **Officers:** Gerald A. Gorman, President; Allen P. Kimball, VP & Treasurer.

■ **5696** ■ **ORA Electronics**
9410 Owensmouth Ave.
PO Box 4029
Chatsworth, CA 91313
Phone: (818)772-4433 **Fax:** (818)718-8626
Products: Cellular telephone accessories. **SIC:** 5065 (Electronic Parts & Equipment Nec). **Est:** 1974. **Sales:** $25,000,000 (2000). **Emp:** 90. **Officers:** Gershon Cooper, President; Ruth Cooper, VP of Finance; Robert Schumacher, Dir. of Marketing & Sales; Madeline Bynder, Dir of Human Resources.

■ **5697** ■ **Pacific Dataport Inc.**
692 Mapunapuna St.
Honolulu, HI 96819-2031
Phone: (808)833-3135
Products: Telecommunications equipment for data transmission and servicing. **SICs:** 5065 (Electronic Parts & Equipment Nec); 5045 (Computers, Peripherals & Software). **Sales:** $400,000 (1994). **Emp:** 5. **Officers:** Jack Hughes, President.

■ **5698** ■ **Pacific Rim Telecommunications Inc.**
1153 E 72nd Ave.
Anchorage, AK 99518
Phone: (907)349-4933 **Fax:** (907)349-4388
Products: Electronic parts and equipment; Communication equipment; Intercommunication equipment. **SIC:** 5065 (Electronic Parts & Equipment Nec). **Officers:** Tammy Horton, President.

■ **5699** ■ **Paging Plus Co.**
PO Box 25019
Glendale, CA 91225
Phone: (818)242-6444 **Fax:** (818)242-0328
Products: Beepers. **SIC:** 5065 (Electronic Parts & Equipment Nec). **Sales:** $1,000,000 (2000). **Emp:** 12. **Officers:** Thomas W. Luczak, President.

■ **5700** ■ **Paging Products Group**
1500 Gateway Blvd.
Boynton Beach, FL 33426
Phone: (561)739-2000
Products: Pager and paging equipment. **SIC:** 5065 (Electronic Parts & Equipment Nec).

■ **5701** ■ **Paging Wholesalers**
1210 S Brand Blvd.
Glendale, CA 91204-2615
Phone: (818)240-5640
Free: (800)835-5758 **Fax:** (818)242-0328
Products: Pagers. **SIC:** 5065 (Electronic Parts & Equipment Nec). **Est:** 1982. **Emp:** 9. **Officers:** Tom Luczak.

■ **5702** ■ **Pana Pacific Corp.**
541 Division St.
Campbell, CA 95008
Phone: (408)374-7900 **Fax:** (408)379-3928
Products: Cellular telephones. **SIC:** 5065 (Electronic Parts & Equipment Nec). **Est:** 1972. **Sales:** $200,000,000 (2000). **Emp:** 272. **Officers:** Harry Brix, President.

■ **5703** ■ **PanAm Sat Corp.**
1 Pickwick Plz.
Greenwich, CT 06830
Phone: (203)622-6664 **Fax:** (203)622-9163
E-mail: webmaster@panamsat.com
URL: http://www.panamsat.com
Products: Satellite communications services. **SIC:** 5065 (Electronic Parts & Equipment Nec). **Est:** 1986. **Sales:** $6,000,000 (2000). **Emp:** 200. **Officers:** Frederick A. Landman, CEO & President; Lourdes Saralegui, Exec. VP; Daniel Marcus, Vice President.

■ **5704** ■ **Pavarini Business Communications Inc.**
10032 NW46th St.
Sunrise, FL 33351
Phone: (954)747-1298
Products: Telecommunications equipment. **SIC:** 5065 (Electronic Parts & Equipment Nec). **Sales:** $1,000,000 (2000). **Emp:** 10. **Officers:** William Muller, Partner.

■ **5705** ■ **Peacock Radio & Wilds Computer Services**
PO Box 2166
West Memphis, AR 72303-2166
Phone: (870)735-7715 **Free:** (800)232-7715
Products: Two-way radios; Cellular phones; Pagers. **SIC:** 5065 (Electronic Parts & Equipment Nec). **Officers:** John Peacock, Vice President.

■ **5706** ■ **Peninsula Engineering Group Inc.**
1150 Morse Ave.
Sunnyvale, CA 94089
Phone: (408)747-1900 **Fax:** (408)747-0376
Products: Communications equipment, including repeaters, cellular repeaters, and microwave microcells. **SIC:** 5065 (Electronic Parts & Equipment Nec). **Sales:** $5,600,000 (2000). **Emp:** 60. **Officers:** Barry Leff.

■ **5707** ■ **Penn Telecom Inc.**
2710 Rochester Rd., Ste. 1
Cranberry Twp, PA 16066-6546
Phone: (724)779-7700 **Fax:** (724)776-9199
Products: Telecommunications equipment including PBX, voice- mail products, key systems, and video conferencing. **SIC:** 5065 (Electronic Parts & Equipment Nec). **Officers:** Gerald A. Gorman, President & General Mgr.; N. William Barthlow, VP of Marketing.

■ **5708** ■ **PhoneAmerica Corp.**
70 W Lancaster Ave.
Malvern, PA 19355
Phone: (215)296-2850 **Fax:** (215)296-2863
Products: Business phone systems. **SIC:** 5065 (Electronic Parts & Equipment Nec). **Est:** 1981. **Sales:** $1,400,000 (2000). **Emp:** 19. **Officers:** Don Bailey, President; Charles T. Reimel, Exec. VP.

■ **5709** ■ **Phoneby**
2755 Bristol St., No. 100
Costa Mesa, CA 92626-5985
Phone: (714)754-4000
Products: Business phones; Voice mail systems. **SIC:** 5065 (Electronic Parts & Equipment Nec). **Est:** 1979. **Sales:** $15,000,000 (2000). **Emp:** 55. **Officers:** John Paul, President; Edward G. Danduran, CFO.

■ **5710** ■ **PHONEXPRESS Inc.**
14 Industrial Rd.
Fairfield, NJ 07004
Phone: (973)808-7000
Free: (800)774-6639 **Fax:** (973)227-3210
E-mail: info@phonextra.com
URL: http://www.phonextra.com
Products: Telephone systems; Voice messaging; Data networking. **SIC:** 5065 (Electronic Parts & Equipment Nec). **Est:** 1982. **Sales:** $18,000,000 (1999). **Emp:** 70. **Officers:** John Negri, President.

■ **5711** ■ **PicturePhone Direct**
200 Commerce Dr.
Rochester, NY 14623
Phone: (716)334-9040
Free: (800)521-5454 **Fax:** (716)359-4999
URL: http://www.picturephone.com
Products: Video conferencing equipment. **SIC:** 5065 (Electronic Parts & Equipment Nec). **Sales:** $2,000,000 (2000). **Emp:** 10. **Officers:** Jeremy Goldstein, Chairman of the Board; Mark Smith, Controller.

■ **5712** ■ **Power & Telephone Supply Company Inc.**
8017 Pinemont, Ste. 200
Houston, TX 77040-6519
Phone: (713)462-6447 **Fax:** (713)462-7074
URL: http://www.ptsupply.com
Products: Telephones; Cable television; Data and key equipment; Wire and cable; Hardware; Fiber optics. **SIC:** 5065 (Electronic Parts & Equipment Nec). **Est:** 1963.

■ **5713** ■ **Power and Telephone Supply Company Inc.**
2673 Yale Ave.
Memphis, TN 38112
Phone: (901)324-6116
Free: (800)238-7514 **Fax:** (901)320-3082
E-mail: ptsupply.com
Products: Power and telephone products; CATV products and hardware. **SICs:** 5065 (Electronic Parts & Equipment Nec); 5063 (Electrical Apparatus & Equipment). **Est:** 1963. **Emp:** 450. **Officers:** J. Miller Pentecost; Jim Pentecost; Laburn Dye; Sonny Dickinson; Mary Bowen, Marketing Contact, e-mail: mary.bowen@ptsupply.com; Judy Wakefield, Human Resources Contact, e-mail: judy.wakefield@ptsupply.com.

■ **5714** ■ **Power & Telephone Supply Company Inc.**
3107 SW 61st St.
Des Moines, IA 50321
Phone: (515)244-4375
Free: (800)247-0042 **Fax:** (515)244-4757
Products: Cable television and telephone systems products. **SIC:** 5065 (Electronic Parts & Equipment Nec).

■ **5715** ■ **Power & Telephone Supply Company, Inc.**
2950 Greensboro St. Extension
Lexington, NC 27292
Phone: (704)249-0256
Free: (800)438-2914 **Fax:** (704)249-7475
Products: Telecommunication and utility equipment and supplies. **SICs:** 5065 (Electronic Parts & Equipment Nec); 5063 (Electrical Apparatus & Equipment).

■ **5716** ■ **Power & Telephone Supply Company, Inc.**
3412 Ambrose Ave.
Nashville, TN 37207
Phone: (615)226-0321
Free: (800)251-1700 **Fax:** (615)227-0124
Products: Telephone equipment. **SIC:** 5065 (Electronic Parts & Equipment Nec).

■ **5717** ■ **Power & Telephone Supply Company, Inc.**
16666 SW 72nd, Bldg. 12
Portland, OR 97224
Phone: (503)620-4909 **Fax:** (503)620-9074
Products: Wire cables; Telephones. **SICs:** 5065 (Electronic Parts & Equipment Nec); 5063 (Electrical Apparatus & Equipment).

■ **5718** ■ **Power & Telephone Supply Company, Inc.**
Rte. 272
Reamstown, PA 17567
Phone: (717)336-4991 **Free:** (800)238-7514
Products: Telephone and cable television products and accessories. **SIC:** 5065 (Electronic Parts & Equipment Nec).

■ **5719** ■ **Prentke Romich Co.**
1022 Heyl Rd.
Wooster, OH 44691
Phone: (330)262-1984
Free: (800)262-1984 **Fax:** (330)263-4829
Products: Communications equipment for the physically challenged. **SIC:** 5065 (Electronic Parts & Equipment Nec).

■ **5720** ■ **Primus Electronics Corp.**
18424 S I-55 W Frontage Rd.
Joliet, IL 60435-9654
Phone: (815)436-8945
Free: (800)435-1636 **Fax:** 800-767-7605
Products: Communication systems and equipment; Radio and TV communication equipment; Speaker systems, microphones, home type electronic kits, and commercial sound equipment, including public address systems. **SIC:** 5065 (Electronic Parts & Equipment Nec). **Emp:** 7.

■ **5721** ■ **Professional Telecommunication Services Inc.**
2119 Beechmont Ave.
Cincinnati, OH 45230
Phone: (513)232-7700 **Fax:** (513)624-2144
Products: Telephone equipment. **SIC:** 5065 (Electronic Parts & Equipment Nec). **Sales:** $26,000,000 (2000). **Emp:** 93. **Officers:** Joe Hazenfield, President; Diane Hazenfield, Controller.

■ **5722** ■ **Progressive Concepts Inc.**
5718 Airport Fwy.
Ft. Worth, TX 76117
Phone: (817)429-0432
Free: (800)245-4411 **Fax:** (817)654-6970
E-mail: mbocchino@pcimktg.com
URL: http://www.pcimktg.com
Products: Cellular phones and accessories; Two way radios; Mobile entertainment; Car audio and security; Home theatre; Personal data devices. **SIC:** 5065 (Electronic Parts & Equipment Nec). **Est:** 1974. **Sales:** $120,000,000 (2000). **Emp:** 375. **Officers:** R. David Jones, CEO & Treasurer; Philip E. Kuntz, VP & Controller; Don Lenz, President.

■ **5723** ■ **ProNet Inc.**
6340 LBJ Frwy.
Dallas, TX 75240-6402
Phone: (972)687-2000 **Fax:** (972)774-0640
Products: Pagers; Tracking systems. **SIC:** 5065 (Electronic Parts & Equipment Nec). **Est:** 1982. **Sales:** $103,000,000 (2000). **Emp:** 831. **Officers:** David J. Vucina, President & COO; Jan E. Gaulding, Sr. VP & CFO.

■ **5724** ■ **Protech Communications**
3119 Lear Drv.
Burlington, NC 27215
Phone: (336)222-0000
Free: (800)283-3033 **Fax:** (336)222-9410
E-mail: info@pcitel.com
URL: http://www.pcitel.com
Products: Telephones. **SIC:** 5065 (Electronic Parts & Equipment Nec). **Est:** 1985. **Emp:** 55.

■ **5725** ■ **R & L Electronics**
1315 Maple Ave.
Hamilton, OH 45011
Phone: (513)868-6399 **Fax:** (513)868-6574
Products: Ham-radio equipment and electronics. **SIC:** 5065 (Electronic Parts & Equipment Nec).

■ **5726** ■ **Racom Products Inc.**
5504 State Rd.
Cleveland, OH 44134-2299
Phone: (216)351-1755
Free: (800)RACOM-OH **Fax:** (216)351-0392
E-mail: sales@racominc.com
URL: http://www.racominc.com
Products: Digital voice message repeaters; EMS emergency service equipment; Plug and play point-of-purchase products. **SIC:** 5065 (Electronic Parts & Equipment Nec). **Est:** 1963. **Sales:** $1,000,000 (2000). **Emp:** 49. **Officers:** Del Mintz; John M. Dukovich, e-mail: john@racominc.com; Leroy Ladyzhensky, e-mail: engineering@racominc.com; Ronald Lauber.

■ **5727** ■ **Radak Electronics**
1637 E Isaacs Ave.
WalLa Walla, WA 99362
Phone: (509)529-0090
Products: Radio equipment; Alarms. **SIC:** 5065 (Electronic Parts & Equipment Nec).

■ **5728** ■ **Radcom, Inc.**
12323 W Fairview Ave.
Milwaukee, WI 53226
Phone: (414)771-6900 **Fax:** (414)771-4980
URL: http://www.radcom2ay.com
Products: Mobile data systems; Radio equipment, including 2-way radios. **SIC:** 5065 (Electronic Parts & Equipment Nec). **Est:** 1946. **Emp:** 14.

■ **5729** ■ **Radio Communications Co.**
1282 Mountain Rd.
Glen Allen, VA 23060-4033
Phone: (804)266-8999 **Fax:** (804)262-6846
Products: Radio and TV communication equipment. **SIC:** 5065 (Electronic Parts & Equipment Nec). **Est:** 1954. **Emp:** 38. **Officers:** D. A. Hazelwood, President; J.H, Buttner, Vice President.

■ **5730** ■ **Radio Communications Co.**
2131 N Towne Ln. NE
Cedar Rapids, IA 52402-1913
Phone: (319)393-7150
Free: (800)833-3550 **Fax:** (319)393-9273
Products: Electronic systems and equipment; Electronic parts; Communication systems and equipment; Cellular telephones; CCTV; Two way radios; Lightbars. **SIC:** 5065 (Electronic Parts & Equipment Nec). **Est:** 1964. **Emp:** 12. **Officers:** Ronald Brainard, President.

■ **5731** ■ **Radio Communications Company Inc.**
PO Box 6630
Roanoke, VA 24017-0630
Phone: (540)342-8513
Free: (800)234-8513 **Fax:** (540)342-1250
Products: Electronic parts and equipment, including radio and television parts and equipment; Two-way radios. **SICs:** 5065 (Electronic Parts & Equipment Nec); 5064 (Electrical Appliances—Television & Radio). **Officers:** Barbara Cisco, President.

■ **5732** ■ **Radio Resources and Services Corp.**
814 A Light St
Baltimore, MD 21230
Phone: (410)783-0737
Free: (800)547-2346 **Fax:** (410)783-4635
E-mail: email@radioresources.com
URL: http://www.radioresources.com
Products: Radio broadcast equipment. **SIC:** 5065

(Electronic Parts & Equipment Nec). **Est:** 1990. **Sales:** $300,000 (1999). **Emp:** 2. **Officers:** Ashley Scarborough, President.

■ **5733** ■ **Rangel Distributing Co.**
PO Box 8192
Shawnee Mission, KS 66208
Phone: (913)262-4945
Products: Broadcast television equipment; Office supplies. **SICs:** 5064 (Electrical Appliances—Television & Radio); 5112 (Stationery & Office Supplies). **Est:** 1981. **Sales:** $2,000,000 (2000). **Emp:** 12. **Officers:** Josephine C. Rangel, President; Shirley Wolf, Finance Officer.

■ **5734** ■ **Ranger Communications Inc.**
401 W 35th St., No. B
National City, CA 91950-7909
Phone: (619)259-0287
Products: Radio communications equipment. **SIC:** 5065 (Electronic Parts & Equipment Nec).

■ **5735** ■ **Raycomm Telecommunications Inc.**
1230 S Parker Rd.
Denver, CO 80237
Phone: (303)755-6500
Products: Telecommunications equipment. **SIC:** 5065 (Electronic Parts & Equipment Nec). **Sales:** $3,600,000 (2000). **Emp:** 30. **Officers:** Joseph Williams, President; Cathy Secord, Accounting Manager.

■ **5736** ■ **RealCom Office Communications Inc.**
2030 Powers Ferry, No. 580
Atlanta, GA 30339
Phone: (404)859-1100 **Fax:** (404)859-9277
Products: Telephone systems. **SIC:** 5065 (Electronic Parts & Equipment Nec). **Est:** 1989. **Sales:** $50,000,000 (2000). **Emp:** 270. **Officers:** John Cunningham, President; Pat Delaney, CFO; Marshall Bauer, VP of Marketing; Steve Schilling, Dir. of Data Processing; Tom Thorsen, Dir of Human Resources.

■ **5737** ■ **ReCellular Inc.**
1580 E Elsworth Rd.
Ann Arbor, MI 48108-2417
Phone: (313)327-7200 **Free:** (800)441-1544
Products: Cellular phones. **SIC:** 5049 (Professional Equipment Nec). **Sales:** $25,000,000 (1994). **Emp:** 150. **Officers:** Charles Newman, President.

■ **5738** ■ **Regional Communications Inc.**
PO Box 144
Paramus, NJ 07653-0144
Phone: (201)261-6600
Free: (800)877-7234 **Fax:** (201)261-6304
Products: Communications equipment. **SIC:** 5065 (Electronic Parts & Equipment Nec). **Sales:** $5,000,000 (2000). **Emp:** 30. **Officers:** Anthony Sabino Jr., President; Bob Markson, CFO.

■ **5739** ■ **RELM Communications Inc.**
7707 Records St.
Indianapolis, IN 46226
Phone: (317)545-4281
Free: (800)874-4665 **Fax:** (317)545-2170
Products: Radio receivers; Citizens' band radios; Communications interface equipment. **SIC:** 5065 (Electronic Parts & Equipment Nec). **Emp:** 300.

■ **5740** ■ **Renault Telephone Supplies**
66-67 69th St.
Middle Village, NY 11379
Phone: (718)894-9404
Products: Pay telephone parts. **SIC:** 5065 (Electronic Parts & Equipment Nec). **Est:** 1961. **Sales:** $4,600,000 (2000). **Emp:** 25. **Officers:** David Ohayon, President.

■ **5741** ■ **RF Ltd. Inc.**
PO Box 1124
Issaquah, WA 98027-1124
Phone: (425)222-4295 **Fax:** (425)222-4294
Products: Communication systems and equipment. **SIC:** 5065 (Electronic Parts & Equipment Nec). **Officers:** Sam Lewis, President.

■ **5742** ■ **RF Technology, Inc.**
16 Testa Pl.
South Norwalk, CT 06854
Phone: (203)866-4283
Free: (800)762-4369 **Fax:** (203)853-3513
E-mail: sales@rftechnology.com
URL: http://www.rftechnology.com
Products: Microwave and satellite transmissions systems for the broadcast, service provision, and telecommunications industries. **SIC:** 5065 (Electronic Parts & Equipment Nec). **Officers:** Mal Wanduragala; Paul Brett; Paul Brett, Sales/Marketing Contact.

■ **5743** ■ **Rice Electronics LP**
PO Box 1481
Morgan City, LA 70381-1481
Phone: (504)385-5950
Free: (800)899-5950 **Fax:** (504)384-0992
Products: Communication and navigation electronics. **SIC:** 5065 (Electronic Parts & Equipment Nec). **Sales:** $10,000,000 (2000). **Emp:** 24. **Officers:** David Rice, COO & CFO. **Former Name:** Rice Electronics Inc.

■ **5744** ■ **Riverside Communications**
653 Commercial Rd., Ste. 8
Palm Springs, CA 92262-6264
Phone: (760)322-5556 **Fax:** (760)325-6170
Products: Two-way communication devices. **SIC:** 5065 (Electronic Parts & Equipment Nec). **Emp:** 49. **Officers:** Chuck Rich, Owner; Dave Laag, Owner.

■ **5745** ■ **RoData Inc.**
247 Fort Pitt Blvd., 4th Fl.
Pittsburgh, PA 15222
Phone: (412)316-6000
Free: (888)870-3282 **Fax:** (412)391-2588
Products: Video conferencing products. **SIC:** 5065 (Electronic Parts & Equipment Nec). **Sales:** $5,000,000 (2000). **Emp:** 30. **Officers:** John Rodella, President; Bari Weinberger, CFO.

■ **5746** ■ **Ronco Communications and Electronics Inc.**
595 Sheridan Dr.
Tonawanda, NY 14150
Phone: (716)873-0760
Free: (888)84-RONCO **Fax:** (716)879-8198
URL: http://www.ronconet.com
Products: Telecommunications equipment. **SIC:** 5065 (Electronic Parts & Equipment Nec). **Est:** 1965. **Sales:** $50,000,000 (2000). **Emp:** 316. **Officers:** Christopher P. Wasp, President; George J. Braun III, Dir. of Marketing, e-mail: gbraun@ronconet.com; Joseph Szczesniak, Customer Service Contact, e-mail: jszczesniak@ronco.com; Annette Spettazza, Human Resources Contact, e-mail: asperrazza@ronconet.com. **Alternate Name:** Ronco.

■ **5747** ■ **Rothenbuhler Engineering**
2191 Rhodes Rd.
PO Box 708
Sedro Woolley, WA 98284-0708
Phone: (360)856-0836 **Fax:** (360)856-2183
URL: http://www.rothenbuhlereng.com
Products: Alarm systems; Communication systems and equipment. **SICs:** 5065 (Electronic Parts & Equipment Nec); 5099 (Durable Goods Nec). **Est:** 1946. **Sales:** $2,000,000 (2000). **Emp:** 49. **Officers:** Neal Rothenbuhler, President; L. Dawson, Sales & Customer Service Contact.

■ **5748** ■ **St. Joe Communications Inc.**
PO Box 1007
Port St. Joe, FL 32456
Phone: (904)227-7272
Free: (800)441-4406 **Fax:** (850)227-7575
Products: Telephone systems. **SIC:** 5065 (Electronic Parts & Equipment Nec). **Est:** 1985. **Sales:** $45,000,000 (2000). **Emp:** 240. **Officers:** Milton Lewis, President; James B. Faison, VP & Controller; James B. Faison, VP & Controller; Bill Thomas, Dir. Products and Services.

■ 5749 ■ **Samson Technologies Inc.**
575 Underhill Blvd.
PO Box 9031
Syosset, NY 11791
Phone: (516)364-2244 **Fax:** (516)364-3888
E-mail: sales@samsontech.com
URL: http://www.samsontech.com
Products: Wireless microphones. **SIC:** 5065 (Electronic Parts & Equipment Nec). **Est:** 1979. **Sales:** $110,000,000 (2000). **Emp:** 40. **Officers:** Jerry Ash; Paul Ash; Scott Goodman, VP of Sales & Marketing.

■ 5750 ■ **Savannah Communications**
11 Minus Ave.
PO Box 7328
Savannah, GA 31418
Phone: (912)964-1479
Free: (800)634-0446 **Fax:** (912)966-5724
E-mail: sales@savannahcomm.com
URL: http://www.savannahcomm.com
Products: Two-way radio systems. **SIC:** 5065 (Electronic Parts & Equipment Nec). **Est:** 1960. **Sales:** $2,000,000 (1999). **Emp:** 43. **Officers:** Don Bigbie, President, e-mail: don@savannahcomm.com; Art Bryan, Sales/Marketing Contact, e-mail: art@savannahcomm.com; Lanell Ketchum, Customer Service Contact.

■ 5751 ■ **Schelle Cellular Group Inc.**
100 West Rd., Ste. 404
Baltimore, MD 21204-2331
Phone: (410)825-4211
Products: Corporate telecommunications systems. **SIC:** 5065 (Electronic Parts & Equipment Nec). **Sales:** $5,000,000 (1994). **Emp:** 20. **Officers:** Wayne N. Schelle, Chairman of the Board.

■ 5752 ■ **Arnold A. Semler Inc.**
11347 Vanowen St.
North Hollywood, CA 91605
Phone: (818)760-1000 **Fax:** (818)760-2142
E-mail: talk@associated-ind.com
URL: http://www.asssociated-ind.com
Products: Military and commercial communications equipment. **SIC:** 5065 (Electronic Parts & Equipment Nec). **Est:** 1946. **Sales:** $15,000,000 (2000). **Emp:** 50. **Officers:** Arnold A. Semler, CEO; Herbert B. Schlosberg, Vice President; Rosie Babic, Exec. Secty.; Ravi Achar, Contact; Caroline Intal, Customer Service Mgr.; Karen Griffith, Customer Service Mgr. **Doing Business As:** Associated Industries.

■ 5753 ■ **Shared Technologies Cellular Inc.**
1 International Pl.
Boston, MA 02110
Phone: (617)536-9152 **Fax:** (617)330-8788
Products: Telecommunications services. **SIC:** 5065 (Electronic Parts & Equipment Nec). **Sales:** $1,000,000 (2000). **Emp:** 15. **Officers:** Janis Wiley, President.

■ 5754 ■ **Sharp Communication**
3403 Governors Dr. SW
Huntsville, AL 35805-3635
Phone: (205)533-2484 **Fax:** (205)539-1663
Products: Two-way radios and cellular phones. **SIC:** 5065 (Electronic Parts & Equipment Nec). **Sales:** $4,000,000 (2000). **Emp:** 49. **Officers:** Tom Sharp.

■ 5755 ■ **Sigma Electronics Inc.**
5935 E Washington Blvd.
Los Angeles, CA 90040-2412
Phone: (213)721-2662 **Fax:** (213)225-5079
Products: Telephones, cassette recorders and television sets. **SIC:** 5064 (Electrical Appliances—Television & Radio). **Sales:** $10,000,000 (1994). **Emp:** 15. **Officers:** Henry S. Wong, President & Chairman of the Board; Peter Chen, VP & Controller.

■ 5756 ■ **Signalcom Systems Inc.**
1499 Bayshore Hwy., Ste. 134
Burlingame, CA 94010-1708
Phone: (650)692-1056 **Fax:** (707)598-1150
E-mail: sales@signalcom.net
URL: http://www.signalcom.net
Products: Non-verbal interoffice communication systems. **SIC:** 5065 (Electronic Parts & Equipment Nec). **Est:** 1972. **Sales:** $3,000,000 (2000). **Emp:** 25. **Officers:** Victor Lain, VP of Marketing.

■ 5757 ■ **Silke Communications Inc.**
680 Tyler St.
Eugene, OR 97402-4530
Phone: (541)687-1611 **Fax:** (541)687-1613
URL: http://www.silkecommunicationscom
Products: Two-way radios and systems. **SIC:** 5065 (Electronic Parts & Equipment Nec). **Est:** 1968. **Sales:** $1,000,000 (2000). **Emp:** 7. **Officers:** James Silke, President.

■ 5758 ■ **Single Point of Contact Inc.**
20914 Bake Pkwy., Ste. 110
Lake Forest, CA 92630-2174
Phone: (949)599-9037
Free: (800)472-5272 **Fax:** (949)599-9044
E-mail: spoc@deltanet.com
URL: http://www.spocusa.com
Products: Telephone equipment. **SIC:** 5065 (Electronic Parts & Equipment Nec). **Est:** 1985. **Sales:** $2,500,000 (1999). **Emp:** 6. **Officers:** Bruce Jensen, President, e-mail: bjensen@spocusa.com.

■ 5759 ■ **Smeed Sound Service Inc.**
PO Box 2099
Eugene, OR 97402-0036
Phone: (541)686-1654
Products: Communication systems and equipment. **SIC:** 5065 (Electronic Parts & Equipment Nec). **Officers:** Glenn Smeed, President.

■ 5760 ■ **Smith Two-Way Radio Inc.**
520 N College Ave.
Fayetteville, AR 72701-3401
Phone: (501)443-2222 **Fax:** (501)443-5677
Products: Two-way radio sales and service. **SIC:** 5065 (Electronic Parts & Equipment Nec). **Officers:** Michael B. Smith, President.

■ 5761 ■ **Sound Engineering**
12933 Farmington Rd.
Livonia, MI 48150-4202
Phone: (734)522-2910
Free: (800)686-8000 **Fax:** (734)522-1222
E-mail: sales@soundeng.com
URL: http://www.soundeng.com
Products: Telephone systems; Speakers; Satellite music; Sound and paging systems; intercommunication systems; Drive-thru systems; Healthcare systems; School systems; Integrated technology. **SIC:** 5065 (Electronic Parts & Equipment Nec). **Est:** 1973. **Emp:** 100.

■ 5762 ■ **Souris River Telephone Mutual Aid Cooperative**
PO Box 2027
Minot, ND 58702
Phone: (701)852-1151 **Fax:** (701)722-2290
Products: Telephones, including cellular phones; Satellite computers. **SICs:** 5045 (Computers, Peripherals & Software); 5065 (Electronic Parts & Equipment Nec). **Est:** 1951. **Sales:** $5,500,000 (2000). **Emp:** 100. **Officers:** Warren Hight, General Mgr.; Talmadge L. Smith, Marketing Mgr.; Barrie Campbell, Data Processing Mgr.

■ 5763 ■ **South West New Mexico Communications, Inc.**
665 Watson Ln.
Las Cruces, NM 88005
Phone: (505)524-0202 **Fax:** (505)524-0217
Products: Electronic parts and equipment; Business telephones. **SIC:** 5065 (Electronic Parts & Equipment Nec). **Est:** 1984. **Officers:** Barbara Hall, Mgr.

■ 5764 ■ **Space Page Inc.**
16 Ketchum St.
Westport, CT 06880-5908
Phone: (203)454-4150 **Fax:** (203)226-4827
Products: Communication systems and equipment; Electronic pagers; Electrical signaling equipment. **SIC:** 5063 (Electrical Apparatus & Equipment). **Officers:** Ben Pianka, President.

■ 5765 ■ **Spectrum Communications Corp.**
1055 W Germantown Pike
Norristown, PA 19403-3912
Phone: (215)631-1710
Free: (800)220-1710 **Fax:** (215)631-5017
Products: Communication systems and equipment.

SIC: 5065 (Electronic Parts & Equipment Nec). **Est:** 1974. **Sales:** $1,000,000 (2000). **Emp:** 30. **Officers:** Steve Bello, Sales Mgr.

■ 5766 ■ **SPOT Image Corp.**
1897 Preston White Dr.
Reston, VA 20191
Phone: (703)715-3100 **Fax:** (703)648-1813
Products: Satellite imagery equipment. **SIC:** 5065 (Electronic Parts & Equipment Nec). **Est:** 1986. **Emp:** 50. **Officers:** Theodore G. Nanz, President; Dan Carayiannis, VP of Sales; Ron Hodge, VP ofTechnical Operations; Neal Carney, VP of Finance & Admin.

■ 5767 ■ **Sprint North Supply**
600 New Century Pkwy.
New Century, KS 66031
Phone: (913)791-7000
Free: (800)755-3004 **Fax:** (913)791-7091
Products: Integrated solutions for voice, data and teleconferencing; Security and alarm systems; Cable television products. **SIC:** 5065 (Electronic Parts & Equipment Nec). **Est:** 1905. **Sales:** $1,000,000,000 (1999). **Emp:** 1,400. **Officers:** William Obermayer, President; Gerald Carson, VP of Finance; Brad Sumner, Information Systems Mgr.; Laird Simons, VP & General Mgr.; Phillip A. Harris, Exec. VP of Operations; Ted Hoagland, VP & General Merchandising Mgr.; Anita Roman-Garcia, Asst. VP.

■ 5768 ■ **ST and T Communications Inc.**
555 Iroquois St.
Chickasaw, AL 36611
Phone: (334)457-1404
Products: Telephone equipment. **SIC:** 5065 (Electronic Parts & Equipment Nec). **Est:** 1983. **Sales:** $6,500,000 (2000). **Emp:** 80. **Officers:** Joe Jefferson, President; Ralph Carter, Dir. of Marketing; Don Pearman, Dir. of Marketing & Sales.

■ 5769 ■ **Standard Telecommunications Systems Inc.**
175 Louis St.
South Hackensack, NJ 07606
Phone: (201)641-9700 **Fax:** (201)641-2523
Products: Telephones. **SIC:** 5065 (Electronic Parts & Equipment Nec). **Est:** 1972. **Sales:** $20,000,000 (2000). **Emp:** 500. **Officers:** M.F. Lagana, President; David Ross, VP of Finance.

■ 5770 ■ **Strata Inc.**
3501 Everett Ave.
Everett, WA 98201-3816
Phone: (425)259-6016 **Fax:** (425)339-2366
Products: Radio receivers; Telephones; Electronic pagers. **SIC:** 5065 (Electronic Parts & Equipment Nec). **Emp:** 20. **Officers:** Denise Beebe.

■ 5771 ■ **Sun Moon Star**
1941 Ringwood Ave.
San Jose, CA 95131
Phone: (408)452-7811
Products: Multimedia products. **SIC:** 5045 (Computers, Peripherals & Software). **Sales:** $3,000,000 (2000). **Emp:** 50. **Officers:** Donald Weng, President; Robert Yin, CFO.

■ 5772 ■ **Talk-A-Phone Co.**
5013 N Kedzie
Chicago, IL 60625-4988
Phone: (773)539-1100 **Fax:** (773)539-1241
E-mail: info@talkaphone.com
URL: http://www.talkaphone.com
Products: Communication systems and equipment; ADA compliant emergency phones; Intercom systems; Area of rescue systems. **SIC:** 5065 (Electronic Parts & Equipment Nec). **Est:** 1935. **Officers:** Abraham Shanes.

■ 5773 ■ **Talley Communications**
12866 Ann St., Bldg. 1
Santa Fe Springs, CA 90670
Phone: (562)906-8000
Free: (800)949-7079 **Fax:** (562)906-8080
E-mail: sales@talleycom.com
URL: http://www.talleycom.com
Products: Wireless communications infrastructure equipment and mobile products, including coaxial cable, antennas, connectors, solar solutions, and more.

SIC: 5065 (Electronic Parts & Equipment Nec). **Est:** 1983. **Emp:** 90. **Officers:** John R. Talley, President. **Former Name:** Talley Electronics.

■ 5774 ■ **Talley Electronics**
3137 Diablo Ave.
Hayward, CA 94545
Phones: (415)783-2111   800-223-4949
Free: (800)654-9616   **Fax:** (415)783-2118
Products: Two-way radios. **SIC:** 5065 (Electronic Parts & Equipment Nec).

■ 5775 ■ **TDK U.S.A. Corp.**
12 Harbor Park Dr.
Port Washington, NY 11050
Phone: (516)625-0100   **Fax:** (516)625-2923
Products: Audio and video tapes. **SIC:** 5065 (Electronic Parts & Equipment Nec). **Sales:** $1,260,000,000 (2000). **Emp:** 4,500. **Officers:** Kenjiro Kihira, President; Yoshimitsu Iwasaki, Exec. VP & Treasurer.

■ 5776 ■ **Techcom Systems Inc.**
2051 Palmer Ave.
Larchmont, NY 10538
Phone: (914)834-8007
Products: Telephone systems. **SIC:** 5065 (Electronic Parts & Equipment Nec). **Sales:** $3,000,000 (2000). **Emp:** 8. **Officers:** Bob Dowling, President.

■ 5777 ■ **Technical Telephone Systems Inc.**
18 Worldsfair Dr.
Somerset, NJ 08873
Phone: (732)560-9090
Products: Telephone equipment. **SIC:** 5065 (Electronic Parts & Equipment Nec). **Sales:** $31,000,000 (1993). **Emp:** 110. **Officers:** George Cruzado, CEO; Ray Pabon, President.

■ 5778 ■ **Technicom Corp.**
333 Cottonwood Dr.
Winchester, VA 22603-3229
Phone: (540)432-9282
Free: (800)296-9282   **Fax:** (540)432-9158
Products: Cellular telephones; Electronic pagers. **SIC:** 5065 (Electronic Parts & Equipment Nec). **Est:** 1993. **Sales:** $635,000 (2000). **Emp:** 7. **Officers:** Barbara A. Boughton.

■ 5779 ■ **Tel-Data Communications Inc.**
8980 Blue Ash Rd.
Cincinnati, OH 45242
Phone: (513)984-0749   **Fax:** (513)792-3371
Products: Telephone communication systems and auto attendant voice mail systems; Computer cables. **SIC:** 5065 (Electronic Parts & Equipment Nec). **Sales:** $6,000,000 (2000). **Emp:** 15. **Officers:** Doug Oppenheimer, President.

■ 5780 ■ **Tele Path Corp.**
49111 Milmont Dr.
Fremont, CA 94538-7347
Phone: (510)656-5600
Free: (800)292-1700   **Fax:** (510)656-2114
Products: Two-way radio equipment. **SIC:** 5065 (Electronic Parts & Equipment Nec). **Emp:** 12. **Officers:** Les Ettinger.

■ 5781 ■ **Teleco Inc.**
430 Woodruff Rd., No. 300
Greenville, SC 29607-3462
Phone: (803)297-4400
Free: (800)800-6159   **Fax:** (803)297-9983
E-mail: webmaster@teleco.com
URL: http://www.teleco.com
Products: Telephones and telephone equipment, including headsets, controls, voice mail, auto attendant and CTI Systems. **SIC:** 5065 (Electronic Parts & Equipment Nec). **Est:** 1981. **Sales:** $17,500,000 (2000). **Emp:** 125. **Officers:** William M. Rogers, CEO & President; Darrell Hensley, VP of Sales; G. Sarmento, VP of Marketing & Treasurer; Gerry Corn, Controller.

■ 5782 ■ **Telecom Engineering Consultants Inc.**
9400 NW 25th St.
Miami, FL 33172
Phone: (305)592-4328
Products: Telecommunications equipment. **SIC:** 5065

(Electronic Parts & Equipment Nec). **Sales:** $7,000,000 (2000). **Emp:** 130. **Officers:** Chris Sellati, President.

■ 5783 ■ **Telecommunications Bank Inc.**
302 Goodman St.
Rochester, NY 14607
Phone: (716)442-2040   **Fax:** (716)442-2941
Products: Telecommunications equipment; Office equipment. **SICs:** 5065 (Electronic Parts & Equipment Nec); 5044 (Office Equipment). **Est:** 1986. **Sales:** $600,000 (2000). **Emp:** 4. **Officers:** Perry Banks, President.

■ 5784 ■ **Telecommunications Concepts Inc.**
5554 Port Royal Rd.
Springfield, VA 22151
Phone: (703)321-3030
Free: (800)824-1001   **Fax:** (703)321-5046
Products: Telecommunications equipment. **SIC:** 5065 (Electronic Parts & Equipment Nec). **Sales:** $10,000,000 (2000). **Emp:** 99. **Officers:** Daniel M. Testa, President; Anna Barabasz, Controller.

■ 5785 ■ **Telelink Communications Co.**
7111 Governors Cir.
Sacramento, CA 95823
Phone: (916)424-5454
Products: Telephones. **SIC:** 5065 (Electronic Parts & Equipment Nec).

■ 5786 ■ **Telephony International Inc.**
2351 Merritt Dr.
Garland, TX 75041-6140
Phone: (972)423-6269
Free: (800)544-3758   **Fax:** (972)994-9038
Products: Telephone switching and switchboard equipment. **SIC:** 5065 (Electronic Parts & Equipment Nec). **Est:** 1989. **Sales:** $7,000,000 (2000). **Emp:** 28. **Officers:** G. Rick Holder.

■ 5787 ■ **Telesystems Inc.**
8626 I St.
Omaha, NE 68127-1618
Phone: (402)339-0600   **Fax:** (402)339-0600
Products: Communications systems, including telephone systems. **SIC:** 5065 (Electronic Parts & Equipment Nec). **Est:** 1967. **Sales:** $6,000,000 (2000). **Emp:** 40. **Officers:** Norm Vogel, President; Jim Kriegler.

■ 5788 ■ **Telewire Supply**
94 Inverness Terrace E
Englewood, CO 80112
Phone: (303)799-4343   **Fax:** (303)643-4797
URL: http://www.telewiresupply.com
Products: HFC broadband cable; Communications equipment. **SICs:** 5065 (Electronic Parts & Equipment Nec); 5063 (Electrical Apparatus & Equipment). **Est:** 1947. **Officers:** Gordy Halverson, CEO; Bob Puccini, President; Malcom Taylor, Exec. VP; Mark Howard, Dir. of Marketing; Ronnie Broadnax, Sales Support Manager; Catherine Gratton, Employee Services Manager.

■ 5789 ■ **Telrad Telecommunications Inc.**
135 Crossways Park Dr.
Woodbury, NY 11797
Phone: (516)921-8300
Free: (800)639-7466   **Fax:** (516)921-8064
Products: Telephone equipment. **SIC:** 5065 (Electronic Parts & Equipment Nec). **Sales:** $30,000,000 (2000). **Emp:** 100. **Officers:** Arnon Toussia-Cohen, President; Edith Friedmann, VP & CFO.

■ 5790 ■ **Terralink International**
67 Wall St., Ste. 2411
New York, NY 10005
Phone: (212)923-5280   **Fax:** (212)927-4662
Products: Telecommunications equipment; Electronic equipment; Pollution control equipment; Computers. **SICs:** 5065 (Electronic Parts & Equipment Nec); 5075 (Warm Air Heating & Air-Conditioning); 5045 (Computers, Peripherals & Software). **Officers:** Rudy N. Cuba, Mgr. Dir.

■ 5791 ■ **Tessco Technologies Inc.**
11126 McCormick Rd.
Hunt Valley, MD 21031-1494
Phone: (410)229-1000
Free: (800)505-5444   **Fax:** (410)527-0005
URL: http://www.tessco.com
Products: Cellular phone and paging system accessories. **SIC:** 5065 (Electronic Parts & Equipment Nec). **Est:** 1953. **Officers:** Robert C. Singer, CFO.

■ 5792 ■ **TESSCO Technologies Inc.**
11126 McCormick Rd.
Hunt Valley, MD 21031-1494
Phone: (410)229-1000   **Fax:** (410)527-0005
Products: Communications equipment. **SIC:** 5065 (Electronic Parts & Equipment Nec). **Sales:** $131,700,000 (2000). **Emp:** 290. **Officers:** Robert B. Barnhill Jr., CEO, President & Chairman of the Board; Gerald T. Garland, CFO & Treasurer.

■ 5793 ■ **Edwin L. Thompson & Son Inc.**
32 Billerica Rd.
Chelmsford, MA 01824-3152
Phone: (978)256-8825   **Fax:** (978)250-4042
Products: Two-way radios. **SIC:** 5065 (Electronic Parts & Equipment Nec). **Officers:** Michael Goguen, President.

■ 5794 ■ **TIE Systems Inc.**
10975 Grandview Dr., Bldg 27
Overland Park, KS 66210
Phone: (913)344-0400
Products: Telecommunications equipment. **SIC:** 5065 (Electronic Parts & Equipment Nec). **Sales:** $210,000,000 (2000). **Emp:** 550. **Officers:** Charlie McNane, President.

■ 5795 ■ **ToteVision**
969 Thomas St.
Seattle, WA 98109-5213
Phone: (206)623-6000   **Fax:** (206)623-6609
E-mail: totevision@accessone.com
URL: http://www.accessone.com/ntote
Products: CCTV cameras and monitors; DVD and VCP rental machines. **SICs:** 5064 (Electrical Appliances—Television & Radio); 5065 (Electronic Parts & Equipment Nec). **Est:** 1981. **Sales:** $43,000,000 (2000). **Emp:** 54. **Officers:** William S. Taraday, President; Roberta Farrington, Sales/Marketing Contact.

■ 5796 ■ **TRCA Electronic Division**
1429 Massaro Blvd.
Tampa, FL 33619-3519
Phone: (813)623-3545   **Fax:** (813)626-9610
Products: Pay phones. **SIC:** 5065 (Electronic Parts & Equipment Nec). **Emp:** 49. **Officers:** Paul Demirdjin.

■ 5797 ■ **Tri-Parish Communications Inc.**
7530 E Industrial Dr.
Baton Rouge, LA 70805-7517
Phone: (504)928-4151
Free: (800)694-4913   **Fax:** (504)928-4153
E-mail: tparish@bellsouth.net
Products: Two-way radios. **SIC:** 5065 (Electronic Parts & Equipment Nec). **Est:** 1980. **Sales:** $1,000,000 (2000). **Emp:** 5. **Officers:** Dyke Cloy, President.

■ 5798 ■ **TW Communication Corp.**
81 Executive Blvd.
Farmingdale, NY 11735
Phone: (516)753-0900
Products: Telephones; Wire and cable. **SICs:** 5063 (Electrical Apparatus & Equipment); 5065 (Electronic Parts & Equipment Nec). **Sales:** $42,000,000 (2000). **Emp:** 113. **Officers:** Ed Goodstein, President; Carl Palazzolo, CFO; Howard Griffith, VP of Sales; Mary Ann Boyle, Dir of Human Resources.

■ 5799 ■ **Uniden America Corp.**
4700 Amon Carter Blvd.
Ft. Worth, TX 76155
Phone: (817)858-3300   **Fax:** (817)858-3333
Products: Satellite dishes; CBs; Radar detectors; Cellular phones; Pagers. **SIC:** 5065 (Electronic Parts & Equipment Nec). **Est:** 1970. **Sales:** $760,000,000 (2000). **Emp:** 420. **Officers:** Al Silverberg, CEO & President; Doug Banister, VP of Admin.

■ **5800** ■ **Unique Communications Inc.**
3557 NW 53rd Ct.
Ft. Lauderdale, FL 33309
Phone: (954)735-4002
Products: Telecommunications equipment. **SIC:** 5065 (Electronic Parts & Equipment Nec). **Sales:** $4,000,000 (2000). **Emp:** 15. **Officers:** Patricia Parker, President; Dennis Parker, Vice President.

■ **5801** ■ **US TeleCenters**
745 Atlantic Ave., 9th Fl.
Boston, MA 02111
Phone: (617)439-9911
Products: Voicemail systems and video conferencing equipment. **SIC:** 5065 (Electronic Parts & Equipment Nec).

■ **5802** ■ **Valley Communications**
730 N 16th Ave. 1
Yakima, WA 98902-1897
Phone: (509)248-0314 **Fax:** (509)575-1159
Products: Commercial two-way radios; Mobile phones. **SIC:** 5065 (Electronic Parts & Equipment Nec). **Officers:** Randy Leffel, Owner.

■ **5803** ■ **Van Ran Communications Services Inc.**
3427 Oak Cliff Rd., No. 114
Doraville, GA 30340
Phone: (404)452-9929 **Fax:** (404)452-1213
Products: Telephone equipment. **SIC:** 5065 (Electronic Parts & Equipment Nec). **Sales:** $4,000,000 (2000). **Emp:** 15. **Officers:** Randy Satterlee, President.

■ **5804** ■ **Varilease Corp.**
8451 Boulder Ct.
Walled Lake, MI 48390
Phone: (248)366-5380
Free: (800)835-8847 **Fax:** (248)366-5332
URL: http://www.varilease.com
Products: Electronic parts and equipment, including telephone and telegraphic equipment. **SIC:** 5065 (Electronic Parts & Equipment Nec). **Officers:** Robert Van Hellemont, Chairman of the Board.

■ **5805** ■ **Veetronix Inc.**
1311 West Pacific
PO Box 480
Lexington, NE 68850
Phone: (308)324-6661
Free: (800)445-0007 **Fax:** (308)324-4985
URL: http://www.veetronix.com
Products: Reed switches. **SIC:** 5065 (Electronic Parts & Equipment Nec). **Sales:** $2,000,000 (2000). **Emp:** 50. **Officers:** Roger Teeters.

■ **5806** ■ **Visual Aids Electronics**
202 Perry Pkwy., Ste. 5
Gaithersburg, MD 20877-2172
Phone: (301)680-8400 **Fax:** (301)680-9245
Products: Audio-visual and simultaneous interpretation equipment. **SIC:** 5065 (Electronic Parts & Equipment Nec). **Emp:** 109. **Officers:** Jack Cassell.

■ **5807** ■ **VoiceWorld Inc.**
11201 N 70th St.
Scottsdale, AZ 85254
Phone: (480)922-5500
Free: (800)283-4759 **Fax:** (480)922-5572
E-mail: prospects@voiceworld.com
URL: http://www.voiceworld.com
Products: Voice and fax sytems software. **SIC:** 5045 (Computers, Peripherals & Software). **Est:** 1989. **Emp:** 5. **Officers:** Brian L. Berman, President.

■ **5808** ■ **Walker and Associates Inc. (Welcome, North Carolina)**
7129 Old Highway 52 N
Welcome, NC 27374
Phone: (336)731-6391
Free: (800)472-1746 **Fax:** (336)731-7253
Products: Telecommunications equipment. **SIC:** 5063 (Electrical Apparatus & Equipment). **Sales:** $170,000,000 (2000). **Emp:** 238. **Officers:** Mark Walker, President; Mark Whitley, CFO.

■ **5809** ■ **Wegener Communications Inc.**
11350 Technology Cir.
Duluth, GA 30026
Phone: (404)623-0096 **Fax:** (404)623-0698
Products: Satellite component parts. **SIC:** 5065 (Electronic Parts & Equipment Nec). **Officers:** Ned L. Mountain, V.P., Mktg.; Mickey Hudspeth, Sales Mgr.

■ **5810** ■ **West Tennessee Communications**
1295 US Hwy. 51, Bypass S
Dyersburg, TN 38024-9317
Phone: (901)286-6275
Free: (800)249-1250 **Fax:** (901)286-6438
Products: Communication systems and equipment. **SIC:** 5065 (Electronic Parts & Equipment Nec). **Est:** 1985. **Sales:** $2,800,000 (2000). **Emp:** 20. **Officers:** Chris Young, Partner.

■ **5811** ■ **Westcon Inc.**
150 Main St.
Eastchester, NY 10709
Phone: (914)779-4773 **Fax:** (914)779-4138
Products: Network communication devices. **SIC:** 5065 (Electronic Parts & Equipment Nec). **Sales:** $12,000,000 (2000). **Emp:** 50. **Officers:** Bo Michalowski, COO.

■ **5812** ■ **Westinghouse Electric Corp. Trading Co.**
11 Stanwix St.
Pittsburgh, PA 15222
Phone: (412)642-4141 **Fax:** (412)642-4123
Products: Communication systems and equipment; Broadcast, studio, and related electronic equipment; Electrical equipment and supplies. **SICs:** 5065 (Electronic Parts & Equipment Nec); 5063 (Electrical Apparatus & Equipment). **Est:** 1988. **Sales:** $11,000,000 (2000). **Emp:** 43. **Officers:** Ken Gallier, Director.

■ **5813** ■ **Bob White Associates**
PO Box 39104
Solon, OH 44139
Phone: (440)248-1317 **Fax:** (440)247-8892
E-mail: callbwa@aol.com
URL: http://www.enterlt.com
Products: Speaker systems, microphones, home type electronic kits, and commercial sound equipment, including public address systems; Broadcast, studio and related electronic equipment. **SIC:** 5065 (Electronic Parts & Equipment Nec). **Est:** 1965. **Emp:** 6. **Officers:** Bob White, President; Tod White, Vice President.

■ **5814** ■ **Williams Companies Inc.**
1 Williams Ctr.
Tulsa, OK 74172
Phone: (918)588-2000 **Fax:** (918)588-2296
Products: Data, voice, and video communications products. **SIC:** 5065 (Electronic Parts & Equipment Nec). **Sales:** $13,879,000,000 (2000). **Emp:** 15,000. **Officers:** Keith E. Bailey, CEO, President & Chairman of the Board; Jack D. McCarthy, Sr. VP & CFO.

■ **5815** ■ **Williams Investigation & SEC**
PO Box 1313
Garden City, KS 67846-1313
Phone: (316)275-1134
Free: (800)275-4816 **Fax:** (316)275-4299
Products: Electronic parts and equipment; Communication equipment; Paging and signaling equipment. **SICs:** 5065 (Electronic Parts & Equipment Nec); 5063 (Electrical Apparatus & Equipment). **Officers:** Dale Williams, President.

■ **5816** ■ **Wintenna Inc.**
911 Amity Rd.
Anderson, SC 29621
Phone: (864)261-3965
Free: (800)845-9724 **Fax:** (864)224-7920
E-mail: wintenna@carol.net
Products: Communication systems and equipment. **SIC:** 5065 (Electronic Parts & Equipment Nec). **Est:** 1975. **Emp:** 50. **Officers:** Jeff Wingard, President; Brenda Baughman, Sales/Marketing Contact.

■ **5817** ■ **Worad Inc.**
299 Brooks St.
Worcester, MA 01606-3308
Phone: (508)852-2693
Products: Two-way radios. **SIC:** 5065 (Electronic Parts & Equipment Nec). **Officers:** Stephen Breed, President.

■ **5818** ■ **World Access Inc.**
945 E Paces Ferry Rd., Ste. 2240
Atlanta, GA 30326
Phone: (404)231-2025 **Fax:** (404)262-2598
Products: Telephone switching and microwave point-to-point systems. **SIC:** 5065 (Electronic Parts & Equipment Nec). **Sales:** $152,100,000 (2000). **Emp:** 791. **Officers:** Steven A. Odom, CEO & Chairman of the Board; Mark A. Gergel, VP & CFO.

■ **5819** ■ **World Communications Inc.**
10405 Baur Blvd., Ste. E
St. Louis, MO 63132-1908
Phone: (314)993-0755
Products: Pay telephones. **SIC:** 5065 (Electronic Parts & Equipment Nec). **Est:** 1986. **Sales:** $7,000,000 (2000). **Emp:** 35. **Officers:** Stuart Hollander, CEO & Chairman of the Board; Robert Swift, Controller.

■ **5820** ■ **WorldCom Network Services Inc.**
PO Box 21348
Tulsa, OK 74121
Phone: (918)588-3210 **Fax:** (918)588-5611
Products: Telecommunications equipment, including fiber-optics. **SIC:** 5065 (Electronic Parts & Equipment Nec). **Est:** 1985. **Sales:** $340,000,000 (2000). **Emp:** 2,100. **Officers:** Roy A. Wilkins, CEO & President; Lawrence Littlefield, VP & CFO; Don Bolar, VP of Marketing; David Bishop, Exec. VP of Operations.

■ **5821** ■ **Zack Electronics**
1070 Hamilton Rd.
Duarte, CA 91010-2742
Phone: (626)303-0655
Free: (800)466-0449 **Fax:** (626)303-8694
URL: http://www.zackinc.com
Products: Test equipment; Broadcast supplies. **SIC:** 5065 (Electronic Parts & Equipment Nec). **Est:** 1931. **Sales:** $12,000,000 (2000). **Emp:** 38. **Officers:** Dennis J. Awad, President; Judi Lomas, Sales/Marketing Contact, e-mail: jlomas@zackinc.com.

(11) Compressors

Entries in this section are arranged alphabetically by company name. When the company name is a personal name, the company name is alphabetized by the surname unless the first name or initial(s) are part of a trade name. See the User's Guide at the front of this directory for additional information.

■ 5822 ■ **Accessorie Air Compressor Systems Inc.**
1858 N Case St.
Orange, CA 92865-4241
Phone: (714)634-2292 **Fax:** (714)974-3008
E-mail: aacser@pacbell.net
URL: http://www.accessorieair.com
Products: Air compressors. **SIC:** 5084 (Industrial Machinery & Equipment). **Est:** 1978. **Sales:** $3,000,000 (2000). **Emp:** 18. **Officers:** Leo Studer, President; Carl J. Sculteure, General Mgr.

■ 5823 ■ **Accurate Air Engineering Inc.**
PO Box 5526
Compton, CA 90224
Phone: (310)537-1350
Free: (800)438-5577 **Fax:** (310)537-1374
E-mail: accair@aol.com
Products: Air compressors; Air systems. **SIC:** 5084 (Industrial Machinery & Equipment). **Est:** 1941. **Sales:** $15,000,000 (2000). **Emp:** 60. **Officers:** John Lague, President; Mark Hana, Controller; John Fotch, Dir. of Operations.

■ 5824 ■ **Air Compressor Engineering Company Inc.**
17 Meadow St.
Westfield, MA 01085
Phone: (413)568-2884
Products: Air compressors. **SIC:** 5084 (Industrial Machinery & Equipment). **Est:** 1960. **Sales:** $10,000,000 (2000). **Emp:** 60. **Officers:** Jack H. Klaumbert, Chairman of the Board.

■ 5825 ■ **Air Power Equipment Corp.**
2400 N Washington Ave.
Minneapolis, MN 55411
Phone: (612)522-7000 **Fax:** (612)522-1553
E-mail: airpowerequip@ingerrand.com
URL: http://www.airpowerequip.com
Products: Air compressors and sand blasters. **SIC:** 5084 (Industrial Machinery & Equipment). **Est:** 1950. **Sales:** $8,000,000 (1999). **Emp:** 30. **Officers:** Tom Bierbrauer, CEO.

■ 5826 ■ **Air & Pump Co.**
585 S Padre Island Dr.
Corpus Christi, TX 78405
Phone: (512)289-7000
Products: Air compressors; Generators; Pumps. **SIC:** 5084 (Industrial Machinery & Equipment). **Est:** 1970. **Sales:** $6,000,000 (2000). **Emp:** 22. **Officers:** Ira Mendolsohn, President; Bruce Warren, CFO; Charles Willis, Dir. of Marketing & Sales.

■ 5827 ■ **Air Systems Inc.**
4512 Bishop Ln.
Louisville, KY 40218
Phone: (502)452-6312
Products: Air compressors. **SIC:** 5084 (Industrial Machinery & Equipment). **Est:** 1956. **Sales:** $9,000,000 (2000). **Emp:** 30. **Officers:** James A. Turner, President; Donna Dixon, Treasurer.

■ 5828 ■ **Air Technologies**
2501 Sandersville Rd.
Lexington, KY 40511
Phone: (606)254-2520 **Fax:** (606)255-0316
Products: Air compressors. **SIC:** 5084 (Industrial Machinery & Equipment).

■ 5829 ■ **Arnel Compressor Co.**
114 N Sunset Ave.
City of Industry, CA 91744
Phone: (626)968-3836 **Fax:** (626)961-6181
URL: http://www.arnelcompressor.com
Products: Compressors; Pumps. **SIC:** 5084 (Industrial Machinery & Equipment). **Est:** 1957. **Sales:** $6,500,000 (2000). **Emp:** 27. **Officers:** W.W. Hart, President; Retha Bradford, Controller; J.E. Carter, Dir. of Sales; Vickilynn Gline, Data Processing Mgr.

■ 5830 ■ **Benz Engineering Inc.**
PO Box 729
Montebello, CA 90640-6325
Phone: (213)722-6603 **Fax:** (213)725-1768
Products: Industrial air and gas compressors. **SIC:** 5084 (Industrial Machinery & Equipment). **Est:** 1926. **Sales:** $7,000,000 (2000). **Emp:** 33. **Officers:** Scott E. Smith, President; Vin Gupta, Controller; Said Mehdi, Dir. of Marketing & Sales.

■ 5831 ■ **Byrne Compressed Air Equipment Company, Inc.**
796 E 140th St.
Bronx, NY 10454
Phone: (718)292-7726
Free: (800)621-9397 **Fax:** (718)292-2812
Products: Air and gas compressors and vacuum pumps; Parts and attachments for air and gas compressors. **SICs:** 5085 (Industrial Supplies); 5084 (Industrial Machinery & Equipment). **Est:** 1949. **Emp:** 49.

■ 5832 ■ **C and B Sales and Service Inc.**
119 Nolan Rd.
Broussard, LA 70518
Phone: (318)837-2701
Free: (800)535-2834 **Fax:** (318)837-3250
E-mail: billco@candbsales.com
URL: http://www.candbsales.com
Products: Air compressors; Reciprocating pumps; Electric instrumentation; Pneumatic hand tools. **SICs:** 5084 (Industrial Machinery & Equipment); 5085 (Industrial Supplies). **Est:** 1965. **Sales:** $4,000,000 (2000). **Emp:** 12. **Officers:** William J. Cober, President; Troy Trahan, Sales/Marketing Contact, e-mail: sales@candbsales.com

■ 5833 ■ **Carlson and Beauloye**
PO Box 13622
San Diego, CA 92170
Phone: (619)234-2256 **Fax:** (619)234-2095
Products: Air compressors and parts. **SIC:** 5084 (Industrial Machinery & Equipment). **Est:** 1972. **Sales:** $2,000,000 (2000). **Emp:** 25. **Officers:** Ronald A. Beauloye Jr., President; Henry J. Beauloye Jr., Vice President.

■ 5834 ■ **Cascade Machinery and Electric Inc.**
PO Box 3575
Seattle, WA 98124
Phone: (206)762-0500 **Fax:** (206)767-5122
URL: http://www.cascade-machinery.com
Products: Compressors and water pumps. **SIC:** 5084 (Industrial Machinery & Equipment). **Est:** 1918. **Sales:** $14,000,000 (1999). **Emp:** 65. **Officers:** John Spring, President; Brian Hayward, VP of Service and Operations.

■ 5835 ■ **Central Air Compressor Co.**
28600 Lorna Ave.
Warren, MI 48092-3929
Phones: (810)558-9100 (810)558-9100
Fax: (810)558-9700
E-mail: sales@centralaircomp.com
URL: http://www.centralaircomp.com
Products: Air and gas compressors and vacuum pumps; Compressed air and gas dryers. **SIC:** 5084 (Industrial Machinery & Equipment). **Est:** 1956. **Sales:** $2,500,000 (2000). **Emp:** 18. **Officers:** Jacqueline Pifer, e-mail: Jackie@centralaircomp.com.

■ 5836 ■ **Clayhill**
141 S Lafayette Rd.
St. Paul, MN 55107
Phone: (651)290-0000
Free: (800)706-4779 **Fax:** (651)848-0205
URL: http://www.airus.com
Products: Air and gas compressors and vacuum pumps; Parts and attachments for air and gas compressors. **SICs:** 5084 (Industrial Machinery & Equipment); 5085 (Industrial Supplies). **Est:** 1964. **Sales:** $10,000,000 (2000). **Emp:** 21. **Officers:** Robert F. Simmer.

■ 5837 ■ **Cummins-Wagner Company Inc.**
10901 Pump House Rd.
Annapolis Junction, MD 20701
Phone: (410)792-4230 **Fax:** (301)490-7156
Products: Pumps, air compressors, boilers, and heat exchangers. **SIC:** 5084 (Industrial Machinery & Equipment). **Est:** 1960. **Sales:** $23,000,000 (2000). **Emp:** 85. **Officers:** Joseph D. Ford, President; Alan Wrobel, CFO; John Herder, Vice President.

■ 5838 ■ **Curtis Toledo Inc.**
1905 Kienlen Ave.
St. Louis, MO 63133
Phone: (314)383-1300 **Fax:** (314)381-1439
Products: Air and gas compressors and vacuum pumps. **SIC:** 5084 (Industrial Machinery & Equipment). **Sales:** $18,000,000 (2000). **Emp:** 175. **Officers:** Ken Carpenter.

■ 5839 ■ **Duo-Fast Carolinas Inc.**
PO Box 5564
Charlotte, NC 28225
Phone: (704)377-5721
Free: (800)438-4090 **Fax:** (704)333-9538
E-mail: duofast@worldnet.att.net
Products: Air compressors; Staples; Nails; Nail guns; Staple guns; Screws; Screw guns. **SICs:** 5084 (Industrial Machinery & Equipment); 5072 (Hardware).

Est: 1948. **Emp:** 50. **Officers:** Roy B. Cook III, President.

■ **5840** ■ **Fluid Engineering Inc.**
2227 S Mission Rd.
Tucson, AZ 85713
Phone: (520)623-9942 **Fax:** (520)624-4269
Products: Compressors; Hoses; Gas station supplies. **SICs:** 5084 (Industrial Machinery & Equipment); 5085 (Industrial Supplies). **Est:** 1947. **Sales:** $1,500,000 (2000). **Emp:** 9. **Officers:** James E. Byrne, President; C. Daniel Murr, Secretary.

■ **5841** ■ **Gale Force Compression Service**
PO Box 1187
Enid, OK 73702
Phone: (580)233-2667
Products: Natural gas compressing systems. **SIC:** 5082 (Construction & Mining Machinery).

■ **5842** ■ **General Machinery Company Inc.**
PO Box 606
Birmingham, AL 35201
Phone: (205)251-9243
Free: (800)821-5937 **Fax:** (205)252-9723
E-mail: genmach@snsnet.net
URL: http://www.generalmachinery.com
Products: Pumps and compressors, including industrial electric and automated. **SICs:** 5060 (Electrical Goods); 5063 (Electrical Apparatus & Equipment). **Est:** 1908. **Sales:** $22,000,000 (2000). **Emp:** 73. **Officers:** Francis H. Crockard, President; H.L. Bankson, Controller; Michael Balliet, Vice President; Paul Crockard, Mktg. and Quality Control Mgr.; John Zajic; Joel Walton; Frank Crockard, VP of Sales.

■ **5843** ■ **Jaytow International Inc.**
82 Lake Shore Dr., Ste. 211
Rockaway, NJ 07866
Phone: (973)625-1197 **Fax:** (201)725-4633
Products: Air compression equipment; Fishing flies and tackle; Essential oils; Flavorings. **SICs:** 5084 (Industrial Machinery & Equipment); 5149 (Groceries & Related Products Nec); 5169 (Chemicals & Allied Products Nec); 5091 (Sporting & Recreational Goods). **Officers:** Frank A. Campi, President.

■ **5844** ■ **Midwest Refrigeration Supply Inc.**
4717 F St.
Omaha, NE 68117
Phone: (402)733-4900 **Fax:** (402)731-0823
Products: Compressor parts. **SIC:** 5084 (Industrial Machinery & Equipment). **Est:** 1959. **Sales:** $400,000 (2000). **Emp:** 2. **Officers:** Don Erftmier, President.

■ **5845** ■ **Ohio Transmission Corp.**
666 Parsons Ave.
Columbus, OH 43206
Phone: (614)444-2172 **Fax:** (614)444-1235
URL: http://www.otpnet.com
Products: Power transmission equipment; Pumps and air compressors. **SIC:** 5084 (Industrial Machinery & Equipment). **Est:** 1949. **Sales:** $58,000,000 (2000). **Emp:** 200. **Officers:** Phillip Derrow, President; Alida Breen, VP of Finance; Jeff Pinney, Dir. of Data Processing.

■ **5846** ■ **Osterbauer Compressor Services**
5041 Santa Fe Ave.
Los Angeles, CA 90058
Phone: (323)583-4771
Free: (800)273-4771 **Fax:** (323)588-9072
E-mail: osterbauer@compuserve.com
URL: http://www.osterbauer.com
Products: Air compressors. **SIC:** 5084 (Industrial Machinery & Equipment). **Est:** 1934. **Sales:** $7,000,000 (2000). **Emp:** 32. **Officers:** R.F. Osterbauer, President; D. Michael, Vice President; H.J. Geerling, Dir. of Marketing.

■ **5847** ■ **Pattons Inc.**
3201 South Blvd.
Charlotte, NC 28209
Phone: (704)523-4122 **Fax:** (704)525-5148
E-mail: pattons-clt@mindspring.com
URL: http://www.pattonsinc.com
Products: Air and gas compressors and vacuum pumps. **SIC:** 5084 (Industrial Machinery & Equipment). **Est:** 1945. **Emp:** 130. **Officers:** J.C. Patton, President; J.D. Pool, Treasurer; M.S. Cranford, VP of Marketing & Sales.

■ **5848** ■ **Peterson Machinery Company Inc.**
309 7th Ave. S
Nashville, TN 37203
Phone: (615)255-8606 **Fax:** (615)255-1493
Products: Compressors; Mixers for industrial processes; Saws. **SIC:** 5084 (Industrial Machinery & Equipment). **Est:** 1929. **Sales:** $3,000,000 (2000). **Emp:** 16. **Officers:** Ronald R. Peterson, CEO & CFO; Eric Peterson, Partner.

■ **5849** ■ **Pioneer Equipment Inc.**
3738 E Miami St.
Phoenix, AZ 85040
Phone: (602)437-4312
Free: (800)523-9998 **Fax:** (602)437-0174
E-mail: general@pioneerequip.com
Products: Air compressors; Pumps; Vacuum pumps; Blowers; Dredges and mechanical seals. **SICs:** 5084 (Industrial Machinery & Equipment); 5085 (Industrial Supplies). **Est:** 1959. **Sales:** $5,000,000 (2000). **Emp:** 25. **Officers:** N.L. Thomas Jr., President; Rob Frye, Controller.

■ **5850** ■ **Rocket World Trade Enterprise**
118 W 137th St., Ste. 1b
New York, NY 10030
Phone: (212)281-6898
Products: Air compressors and motors; Vacuum pumps. **SIC:** 5084 (Industrial Machinery & Equipment).
Officers: A. Alam, President.

■ **5851** ■ **Scales Air Compressor Corp.**
110 Voice Rd.
Carle Place, NY 11514
Phone: (516)248-9096 **Fax:** (516)248-9639
Products: Air compressors. **SIC:** 5084 (Industrial Machinery & Equipment). **Est:** 1966. **Sales:** $10,000,000 (2000). **Emp:** 130. **Officers:** W. Scalchunes, President, Chairman of the Board & Treasurer; C. Denby, Controller; R. Ingrassia, Dir. of Marketing.

■ **5852** ■ **Symbol Inc.**
13030 S Kirkwood
Stafford, TX 77477
Phone: (281)240-7888
Products: Air compressors. **SIC:** 5075 (Warm Air Heating & Air-Conditioning).

■ **5853** ■ **Tate Engineering Systems, Inc.**
1560 Caton Center Dr.
Baltimore, MD 21227
Phone: (410)242-8800
Free: (800)800-TATE **Fax:** (410)242-7777
E-mail: emailus@tate.com
URL: http://www.tate.com
Products: Boilers; Compressors; Pumps; Filters. **SIC:** 5084 (Industrial Machinery & Equipment). **Est:** 1924. **Sales:** $27,000,000 (2000). **Emp:** 105. **Officers:** Robt Warfel, President; Jeff Moderacki, Treasurer & Secty.; Donald Peters, VP of Marketing; Brenda Taylor, Dir. of Data Processing; Carolynn Faidley, Dir of Human Resources.

■ **5854** ■ **Tri-Line Corp.**
250 Summit Point Dr.
Henrietta, NY 14467-9607
Phone: (716)874-2740
Products: Compressors. **SIC:** 5084 (Industrial Machinery & Equipment).

■ **5855** ■ **U.S. Equipment Company Inc.**
1810 W Venice Blvd.
Los Angeles, CA 90006
Phone: (213)733-4733 **Fax:** (213)733-1254
Products: Air compressors. **SIC:** 5084 (Industrial Machinery & Equipment). **Est:** 1923. **Sales:** $6,000,000 (2000). **Emp:** 25. **Officers:** Richard Colvin, President & Chairman of the Board; Cathy Fleming, Controller; David Dewees, General Mgr.

(12) Computers and Software

Entries in this section are arranged alphabetically by company name. When the company name is a personal name, the company name is alphabetized by the surname unless the first name or initial(s) are part of a trade name. See the User's Guide at the front of this directory for additional information.

■ 5856 ■ **A and A Technology Inc.**
45277 Fremont Blvd., Ste. 11
Fremont, CA 94538
Phone: (510)226-8650 **Fax:** (510)226-8652
E-mail: sales@aatechno.com
URL: http://www.aatechno.com
Products: Computer hardware and software. **SIC:** 5045 (Computers, Peripherals & Software). **Est:** 1992. **Sales:** $17,000,000 (2000). **Emp:** 36. **Officers:** Affif Siddique, President.

■ 5857 ■ **A C Systems**
3990 S Lipan St.
Englewood, CO 80110-4422
Phone: (303)771-5000 **Fax:** (303)789-1111
Products: Computer power systems. **SIC:** 5045 (Computers, Peripherals & Software). **Officers:** Joe Zuffoletto, President.

■ 5858 ■ **A/E MicroSystems Inc.**
4380 Malsbary Rd.
Cincinnati, OH 45242-5644
Phone: (513)772-6700 **Fax:** (513)672-7700
Products: Computer hardware and software. **SIC:** 5045 (Computers, Peripherals & Software). **Sales:** $16,000,000 (1994). **Emp:** 100. **Officers:** Jeff Holtmeir, President; Anne Wilkinson, CFO.

■ 5859 ■ **A Plus Sales & Service Inc.**
1114 Iberia St.
Franklin, LA 70538-4720
Phone: (318)828-4470 **Fax:** (318)828-0476
Products: Computers; Computer software; Peripheral computer equipment. **SIC:** 5045 (Computers, Peripherals & Software). **Officers:** Amar St. Germain, President.

■ 5860 ■ **AA Computech Inc.**
28170 Crocker Ave., Ste. 105
Valencia, CA 91355
Phone: (805)257-6801
Products: Computer hardware and peripherals. **SIC:** 5045 (Computers, Peripherals & Software). **Sales:** $900,000 (1993). **Emp:** 10. **Officers:** James Howard, President.

■ 5861 ■ **Abacus Data Systems Inc.**
6725 Mesa Ridge Rd., No. 204
San Diego, CA 92121
Phone: (619)452-4245
Free: (800)726-3339 **Fax:** (619)452-2073
Products: Software. **SIC:** 5045 (Computers, Peripherals & Software). **Est:** 1983. **Sales:** $1,000,000 (2000). **Emp:** 10. **Officers:** Judd Kessler, President.

■ 5862 ■ **ABC Systems and Development Inc.**
9 Bartlet St., Ste. 255
Andover, MA 01810
Phone: (978)463-8602
Products: Computer software. **SIC:** 5045 (Computers, Peripherals & Software). **Sales:** $10,000,000 (2000). **Emp:** 45. **Officers:** Simon A. Kniveton, President; Allan Kniveton, Vice President.

■ 5863 ■ **Aberdeen L.L.C.**
9728 Alburtis St.
Santa Fe Springs, CA 90670
Phone: (562)695-5570 **Fax:** (562)801-5629
Products: Computer peripheral equipment. **SIC:** 5045 (Computers, Peripherals & Software). **Sales:** $10,000,000 (2000). **Emp:** 27. **Officers:** Moshe Ovadya, President.

■ 5864 ■ **ACBEL Technologies Inc.**
472 Vista Way
Milpitas, CA 95035-5406
Phone: (408)452-7811 **Fax:** (408)452-1141
URL: http://www.sunmoonstar.com
Products: Computers; Phone systems. **SIC:** 5045 (Computers, Peripherals & Software).

■ 5865 ■ **Access Graphics**
1426 Pearl St.
Boulder, CO 80302
Phone: (303)938-9333 **Fax:** (303)442-7415
Products: High-end computer products. **SIC:** 5045 (Computers, Peripherals & Software). **Sales:** $1,032,000,000 (2000). **Emp:** 550. **Officers:** Perry Monych, President; Tom Carson, VP & CFO.

■ 5866 ■ **Access Graphics Technology Inc.**
1426 Pearl St.
Boulder, CO 80302
Phone: (303)938-9333
Free: (800)733-9333 **Fax:** (303)938-1708
Products: Computers; Peripheral computer equipment; Computer software. **SIC:** 5045 (Computers, Peripherals & Software). **Est:** 1984. **Sales:** $250,000,000 (2000). **Emp:** 150. **Officers:** John Ramsey, President; Tom Carson, VP & CFO; Don Paugh, VP of Operations; Judy Hamilton, Dir of Human Resources.

■ 5867 ■ **Access International Software**
432 Columbia St.
Cambridge, MA 02141-1000
Phone: (617)494-0066 **Fax:** (617)494-8404
Products: Computers, peripherals, and software. **SIC:** 5045 (Computers, Peripherals & Software). **Officers:** Mohammed Fotouhi, President.

■ 5868 ■ **Access Solutions Inc.**
11801 N Tatum Blvd., Ste. 108
Phoenix, AZ 85028
Phone: (602)953-7374
Products: Software. **SIC:** 5045 (Computers, Peripherals & Software).

■ 5869 ■ **Ace Technical Resources Inc.**
18 W State St., Ste. 42
Athens, OH 45701
Phone: (740)593-5993 **Fax:** (740)593-5993
Products: Computer software. **SIC:** 5045 (Computers, Peripherals & Software). **Est:** 1994.

■ 5870 ■ **ACMA Computers Inc.**
1505 Reliance Way
Fremont, CA 94539
Phones: (510)623-1212   800-786-8998
Free: (800)578-1888 **Fax:** (510)623-0818
URL: http://www.acma.com
Products: Computers. **SIC:** 5045 (Computers, Peripherals & Software). **Est:** 1989. **Sales:** $30,000,000 (1999). **Emp:** 41. **Officers:** Allen Lee, President, e-mail: allen_lee@acma.com; Rex Chu, VP of Sales, e-mail: rex_chu@acma.com.

■ 5871 ■ **Acom Computer Inc.**
2850 East 29th St.
Long Beach, CA 90806-2313
Phone: (562)424-7899
Free: (800)347-3638 **Fax:** (562)424-2699
Products: Micro-Laser printers. **SIC:** 5045 (Computers, Peripherals & Software). **Sales:** $10,000,000 (2000). **Emp:** 65. **Officers:** Edward Kennedy, President; Steve Snyder, CFO.

■ 5872 ■ **Action Business Systems**
151 E Olive St.
Newport, OR 97365-3052
Phone: (541)265-8226 **Fax:** (541)265-8946
Products: Computers; Computer software; Peripheral computer equipment. **SIC:** 5045 (Computers, Peripherals & Software). **Officers:** Doug Updenkelder, Owner.

■ 5873 ■ **ADA Computer Supplies Inc.**
PO Box 21704
Greensboro, NC 27420
Phone: (336)274-3441 **Fax:** (336)272-3041
E-mail: sales@adacomputersupplies.com
URL: http://www.adacomputersupplies.com
Products: Computers; Computer supplies, including paper, accessories, and printing ink; Computer printers. **SICs:** 5045 (Computers, Peripherals & Software); 5044 (Office Equipment). **Est:** 1979. **Sales:** $6,000,000 (2000). **Emp:** 15. **Officers:** Jerry Fox, President.

■ 5874 ■ **Adaptive Living**
403 N L St.
Lake Worth, FL 33460-3025
Phone: (561)235-7270 **Fax:** (561)235-0922
Products: Computers and software. **SIC:** 5045 (Computers, Peripherals & Software). **Sales:** $100,000 (2000). **Emp:** 2.

■ 5875 ■ **ADD Enterprises Inc.**
1552 Lost Hollow Dr.
Brentwood, TN 37027
Phone: (615)370-9646 **Fax:** (615)370-9644
Products: Training and education software for typing skills evaluation. **SIC:** 5045 (Computers, Peripherals & Software). **Sales:** $1,000,000 (2000). **Emp:** 1. **Officers:** Ann Dietrichson, Owner.

■ 5876 ■ **ADI Systems Inc.**
2115 Ringwood Ave.
San Jose, CA 95131
Phone: (408)944-0100
Free: (800)228-0530 **Fax:** (408)944-0300
Products: and wholesales computer peripheral CRT

devices. **SIC:** 5045 (Computers, Peripherals & Software). **Sales:** $1,000,000,000 (2000). **Emp:** 3,000. **Officers:** Steven Liu, CEO.

■ 5877 ■ **Admark Corp.**
2502 Mt. Moriah Rd., Ste. A-140
Memphis, TN 38115-1515
Phone: (901)795-8200
Free: (800)266-5678 **Fax:** (901)795-8469
E-mail: fms@admarkcorp.com
URL: http://www.admarkcorp.com
Products: Financial management software for advertising agencies and public relations firms. **SIC:** 5045 (Computers, Peripherals & Software). **Est:** 1995. **Sales:** $500,000 (1999). **Emp:** 6. **Officers:** Jr., Forrest S. May, CEO & President.

■ 5878 ■ **ADP Hollander Inc.**
PO Box 9405
Minneapolis, MN 55440
Phone: (612)553-0644
Free: (800)825-0644 **Fax:** (612)551-5720
Products: Computer systems and automobile parts books. **SIC:** 5045 (Computers, Peripherals & Software). **Sales:** $22,000,000 (2000). **Emp:** 120.

■ 5879 ■ **ADS Inc.**
355 Sinclair Frontage Rd.
Milpitas, CA 95035
Phone: (408)956-0800 **Fax:** (408)956-8668
Products: Personal computer systems. **SIC:** 5045 (Computers, Peripherals & Software).

■ 5880 ■ **Adtek Computer Systems Inc.**
4026 Devonshire Dr.
Marietta, GA 30066-2526
Phone: (404)565-0323
Products: Computers, peripherals, and software. **SIC:** 5045 (Computers, Peripherals & Software). **Officers:** Walter Kelley, President.

■ 5881 ■ **ADTRON. Corp**
3050 S Country Club Dr Ste 24
Mesa, AZ 85210
Phone: (480)926-9324 **Fax:** (480)926-9359
Products: Computer storage devices. **SIC:** 5045 (Computers, Peripherals & Software).

■ 5882 ■ **Advance Computer Systems**
39675 Cedar Blvd., Ste. 1004
Newark, CA 94560-5490
Phone: (408)732-6200
Products: Computers and software. **SIC:** 5045 (Computers, Peripherals & Software). **Sales:** $5,000,000 (1993). **Emp:** 26. **Officers:** Salim Mastan, Partner.

■ 5883 ■ **ADVANCED BusinessLink Corp.**
5808 Lake Washington Blvd. NE 100
Kirkland, WA 98033-7350
Phone: (425)602-4777
Free: (800)675-1855 **Fax:** (425)602-4789
URL: http://www.businesslink.com
Products: Software. **SIC:** 5045 (Computers, Peripherals & Software). **Est:** 1987. **Sales:** $10,000,000 (2000). **Emp:** 40. **Officers:** Chris Lategan, CEO.

■ 5884 ■ **Advanced Communication Design Inc.**
7901 12th Ave. S
Bloomington, MN 55425
Phone: (612)854-4000
Products: Computers; Peripheral equipment for electronic computers; Computer software; Communication systems and equipment. **SIC:** 5045 (Computers, Peripherals & Software). **Officers:** Marco Scibora, Chairman of the Board.

■ 5885 ■ **Advanced Computer Distributors Inc.**
2395 Pleasantdale Rd., Ste. 13
Atlanta, GA 30340
Phone: (770)453-9200
Free: (800)849-4223 **Fax:** (770)453-9288
E-mail: alcergiz@acd-usa.com
URL: http://www.acd-usa.com
Products: Computers and computer parts. **SIC:** 5045 (Computers, Peripherals & Software). **Est:** 1987.

Sales: $8,000,000 (2000). **Emp:** 18. **Officers:** Al Vural Cengiz, President; Trey Young, Vice President.

■ 5886 ■ **Advanced Concepts Inc.**
8875 N 55th St., No. 200
Milwaukee, WI 53223-2311
Phone: (414)362-9640 **Fax:** (414)362-9646
E-mail: info@advanced-concepts.com
URL: http://www.advanced-concepts.com
Products: Computer software; Sales force automation. **SIC:** 5045 (Computers, Peripherals & Software). **Est:** 1981. **Emp:** 10. **Officers:** Jeffrey W. Wohlfahrt, CEO, e-mail: jeffw@advanced-concepts.com.

■ 5887 ■ **Advanced Enterprise Solutions**
1805 E Dyer Rd., Ste. 212
Santa Ana, CA 92705
Phone: (949)756-0588 **Fax:** (949)756-0985
URL: http://www.aes4solutions.com
Products: Computers. **SIC:** 5045 (Computers, Peripherals & Software). **Est:** 1989. **Sales:** $120,000,000 (1999). **Emp:** 210. **Officers:** Nader Khoshniyati, President. **Former Name:** MicroCAD Technologies Inc.

■ 5888 ■ **Advanced Micro Solutions Inc.**
PO Box 830547
Richardson, TX 75083-0547
Phone: (972)480-8336
Products: Computer software. **SIC:** 5045 (Computers, Peripherals & Software). **Sales:** $2,000,000 (1993). **Emp:** 6. **Officers:** Keith Roberts, President.

■ 5889 ■ **Advanced Tech Distributors**
1571 Whitmore Ave.
Ceres, CA 95307
Phone: (209)541-1111 **Fax:** (209)541-1401
Products: Computers and computer hardware; Software. **SIC:** 5045 (Computers, Peripherals & Software). **Officers:** James Lawson, President.

■ 5890 ■ **Advanced Technology Center Inc.**
22982 Mill Creek Dr.
Laguna Hills, CA 92653-1214
Phone: (714)583-9119
Free: (800)999-5711 **Fax:** (714)583-9213
Products: Graphics software. **SIC:** 5045 (Computers, Peripherals & Software). **Est:** 1979. **Sales:** $1,000,000 (2000). **Emp:** 20. **Officers:** S.A. Dudani, President.

■ 5891 ■ **Advanced Technology Specialist**
116 Daten Dr.
Crossville, TN 38555-9809
Phone: (931)707-1662
Free: (800)548-5927 **Fax:** (931)456-9716
E-mail: atts@citlink.net
URL: http://www.AdvTechSpecialists.com
Products: Preventative maintenance supplies for computers. **SIC:** 5045 (Computers, Peripherals & Software). **Est:** 1986. **Emp:** 4. **Officers:** Brenda Ordway, Owner.

■ 5892 ■ **AeroSpace Computer Supplies, Inc.**
9270 Bryant Ave. S
Minneapolis, MN 55420
Phone: (612)884-4725
Free: (800)234-4725 **Fax:** (612)884-5561
Products: Specialty fasteners; Electronic components. **SICs:** 5045 (Computers, Peripherals & Software); 5063 (Electrical Apparatus & Equipment). **Emp:** 49. **Officers:** Steve Hanson.

■ 5893 ■ **Affinitec Corp.**
11737 Administration
St. Louis, MO 63146
Phone: (314)569-3450
Products: Computer software. **SIC:** 5045 (Computers, Peripherals & Software).

■ 5894 ■ **Aftec Inc.**
222 Columbia Tpke.
Florham Park, NJ 07932-1299
Phone: (908)789-3222
Products: Computer software. **SIC:** 5045 (Computers, Peripherals & Software). **Sales:** $3,000,000 (2000). **Emp:** 12. **Officers:** John Foss, President.

■ 5895 ■ **Agri-Logic Solution Systems**
State Rd. 59 S
Brazil, IN 47834
Phone: (812)448-8590
Free: (800)444-8214 **Fax:** (812)442-8214
Products: Computers; Peripheral computer equipment; Software. **SIC:** 5045 (Computers, Peripherals & Software). **Officers:** Dennis Bell, Owner.

■ 5896 ■ **AIS Computers**
165 Carnegie Pl.
Fayetteville, GA 30214
Phone: (770)461-2147
Products: Computers. **SIC:** 5045 (Computers, Peripherals & Software). **Sales:** $19,000,000 (2000). **Emp:** 40. **Officers:** Tommy Turner, CEO.

■ 5897 ■ **AITech International Corp.**
47971 Fremont Blvd.
Fremont, CA 94538-4508
Phone: (510)226-8960
Free: (800)882-8184 **Fax:** (510)226-8996
Products: Desktop video products; Overlay boards; Hardware. **SIC:** 5045 (Computers, Peripherals & Software). **Est:** 1991. **Sales:** $13,000,000 (2000). **Emp:** 80. **Officers:** Michael Chen, President; Jennifer Chen, Controller; Mark Wodyka, VP of Marketing.

■ 5898 ■ **Alacrity Systems Inc.**
43 Newburg Rd.
Hackettstown, NJ 07840
Phone: (908)813-2400
Products: Computer equipment and supplies, including desktop imaging systems, storing and retrieving equipment, and fan systems. **SIC:** 5045 (Computers, Peripherals & Software). **Est:** 1987. **Sales:** $2,000,000 (2000). **Emp:** 20. **Officers:** James R. Folts, CEO; John Reap, VP of Finance.

■ 5899 ■ **Alaska Micro Systems Inc.**
3211 Denali St.
Anchorage, AK 99503
Phone: (907)278-3900 **Fax:** (907)278-3410
Products: Computers; Peripheral computer equipment; Software. **SIC:** 5045 (Computers, Peripherals & Software). **Est:** 1980. **Officers:** Louis Picarella, President.

■ 5900 ■ **Algol Consultants Technology**
PO Box 1762
St. Johns, AZ 85936
Phone: (520)337-3694 **Fax:** (520)222-5896
Products: Software upgrades. **SIC:** 5045 (Computers, Peripherals & Software).

■ 5901 ■ **Alis-USA**
600 W Broadway
Glendale, CA 91214
Products: Delivery of advanced information processing solutions. **SIC:** 5045 (Computers, Peripherals & Software). **Officers:** V. Shafrazian, President.

■ 5902 ■ **All Computer Warehouse**
224 S 5th Ave.
City of Industry, CA 91746
Phone: (626)369-4181
Free: (800)775-1953 **Fax:** (626)961-7462
Products: Notebook computers and computer systems; Computers and peripherals. **SIC:** 5045 (Computers, Peripherals & Software). **Sales:** $4,000,000 (1999). **Emp:** 10. **Officers:** Diane Wang, President.

■ 5903 ■ **All Seas Exporting Inc.**
11630 Garfield St.
Denver, CO 80233-1618
Phone: (303)451-8313 **Fax:** (303)451-0331
Products: Computers; Computer software; Peripheral computer equipment. **SIC:** 5045 (Computers, Peripherals & Software). **Officers:** William Wirth, President.

■ 5904 ■ **Allanson Business Products**
10740 Lyndale Ave. S
Minneapolis, MN 55420-5615
Phone: (612)881-1151 **Fax:** (612)881-1698
Products: Office equipment, including computers, peripherals, and software. **SICs:** 5045 (Computers,

Peripherals & Software); 5044 (Office Equipment). **Officers:** Gloria Allanson, President.

■ **5905** ■ **Allen Systems Group Inc.**
750 11th St., S
Naples, FL 34102
Phone: (941)435-2200
Free: (800)932-5536 **Fax:** (941)263-3692
Products: Mainframe software. **SIC:** 5045 (Computers, Peripherals & Software). **Est:** 1986. **Sales:** $26,000,000 (2000). **Emp:** 180. **Officers:** Arthur L. Allen, CEO & President; Frederick Roberts, CFO; LeAnn Bridges, Dir. of Sales; Mac Davison, Dir. of Information Systems; Kimberly Fain.

■ **5906** ■ **Alligator Technologies**
2900 Bristol St., Ste. E-101
Costa Mesa, CA 92626-7906
Phone: (714)850-9984 **Fax:** (714)850-9987
Products: puters and software. **SIC:** 5045 (Computers, Peripherals & Software). **Sales:** $1,000,000 (2000). **Emp:** 12. **Officers:** Robert Galter, CEO & President; Crystal McDonald, Controller.

■ **5907** ■ **Allison-Erwin Co.**
2920 N Tryon St.
Charlotte, NC 28232
Phone: (704)334-8621
Free: (800)253-0370 **Fax:** (704)334-8381
E-mail: allison-erwin@mindspring.com
Products: Furniture, consumer electronics, appliances, computer products and peripherials. **SICs:** 5064 (Electrical Appliances—Television & Radio); 5021 (Furniture); 5063 (Electrical Apparatus & Equipment). **Est:** 1893. **Sales:** $25,000 (1999). **Emp:** 35. **Officers:** Bob Allison; Brennaan Giggey; Gary Watkins.

■ **5908** ■ **Allstar Systems Inc.**
6401 Southwest Frwy.
Houston, TX 77074
Phone: (713)795-2000 **Fax:** (713)795-2036
Products: Computer and telecommunications hardware and software products. Network applications design, LAN administration services, and computer/telephone integration software. **SICs:** 5045 (Computers, Peripherals & Software); 5065 (Electronic Parts & Equipment Nec). **Sales:** $167,200,000 (1999). **Emp:** 513. **Officers:** James H. Long, CEO, President & Chairman of the Board; Donald R. Chadwick, CFO.

■ **5909** ■ **Allview Services Inc.**
2215 S Castle Way
Lynnwood, WA 98036
Phone: (425)483-6103 **Fax:** (425)402-8334
Products: Computer systems and components, servers and storage solutions. **SIC:** 5045 (Computers, Peripherals & Software). **Officers:** Walter Schaplow, President.

■ **5910** ■ **Almaly Trading Corp.**
325 Alhambra Cir.
Coral Gables, FL 33134
Phone: (305)448-3033 **Fax:** (305)448-5707
Products: Computers, peripherals, and software. **SIC:** 5045 (Computers, Peripherals & Software). **Officers:** Alfred M. Menendez.

■ **5911** ■ **ALMO**
9815 Roosevelt Blvd.
Philadelphia, PA 19114
Phone: (215)698-4000
Free: (800)600-2566 **Fax:** (215)698-4037
Products: Computers; Computer software; Peripheral computer equipment; Electric and electronic equipment. **SICs:** 5045 (Computers, Peripherals & Software); 5063 (Electrical Apparatus & Equipment). **Est:** 1946. **Sales:** $200,000,000 (2000). **Emp:** 200. **Officers:** Gene Chaiken, President.

■ **5912** ■ **Almo Corp.**
9815 Roosevelt Blvd.
Philadelphia, PA 19114
Phone: (215)698-4080 **Fax:** (215)698-8831
Products: Computer hardware and software. **SIC:** 5045 (Computers, Peripherals & Software). **Sales:** $169,000,000 (2000). **Emp:** 270. **Officers:** Eugene B. Chaiken, CEO & Chairman of the Board; Matthew Elkes, Exec. VP & CFO.

■ **5913** ■ **Almo Distributing**
1349A Charwood Rd.
Hanover, MD 21076-3114
Phone: (301)459-2100
Free: (800)600-2566 **Fax:** (301)459-6416
Products: Peripheral computer equipment. **SIC:** 5045 (Computers, Peripherals & Software). **Est:** 1947. **Sales:** $200,000,000 (2000). **Emp:** 195. **Officers:** Gene Chaiken, President; Art Ross, Vice President; Dennis Bicodeau, VP of Purchasing.

■ **5914** ■ **AlphaNet Solutions Inc.**
7 Ridgedale Ave.
Cedar Knolls, NJ 07927
Phone: (973)267-0088 **Fax:** (973)267-8675
URL: http://www.alphanetcorp.com
Products: Computer hardware and software. **SIC:** 5045 (Computers, Peripherals & Software). **Est:** 1984. **Sales:** $136,500,000 (2000). **Emp:** 579. **Officers:** Stan Gang, CEO, President & Chairman of the Board; Robert G. Petoia, VP, CFO & Treasurer.

■ **5915** ■ **Alps Electric (USA) Inc.**
3553 N 1st St.
San Jose, CA 95134
Phone: (408)432-6000
Products: Computer printers; Peripheral computer equipment. **SIC:** 5045 (Computers, Peripherals & Software). **Sales:** $24,000,000 (2000). **Emp:** 50. **Officers:** Lalita Tademy, Sr. VP.

■ **5916** ■ **Alternative Computer Solutions Ltd.**
990 Washington Rd.
Washington, PA 15301-9633
Phone: (412)429-5370
Products: Computers. **SIC:** 5045 (Computers, Peripherals & Software). **Sales:** $8,000,000 (2000). **Emp:** 10. **Officers:** Russell Forrest, President.

■ **5917** ■ **Alternative Computer Technology Inc.**
7908 Cin-Day Rd.
West Chester, OH 45069
Phone: (513)755-1957 **Fax:** (513)755-1958
Products: Computers and anti-virus software. **SIC:** 5045 (Computers, Peripherals & Software). **Sales:** $12,000,000 (2000). **Emp:** 22. **Officers:** Tom Farrell, President.

■ **5918** ■ **Altura PC Systems Inc.**
2842A Janitell Rd.
Colorado Springs, CO 80909
Phone: (719)538-1014 **Fax:** (719)538-1017
Products: Computers and computer parts. **SIC:** 5045 (Computers, Peripherals & Software). **Officers:** Khalid Al-Abbasi, President.

■ **5919** ■ **Amemco**
697 North 700 East
Kaysville, UT 84037-0211
Phone: (801)544-9999
Products: Computers, peripherals, and software. **SIC:** 5045 (Computers, Peripherals & Software). **Officers:** Howard Cooper, Owner.

■ **5920** ■ **American Business Network and Associates Inc.**
2544 S 156th Cir.
Omaha, NE 68130
Phone: (402)691-8248
Products: Computer memory upgrades. **SIC:** 5045 (Computers, Peripherals & Software). **Sales:** $11,000,000 (1993). **Emp:** 17. **Officers:** Charles McDonald, CEO; Carol McDonald, President.

■ **5921** ■ **American Business Service and Computer Technologies Inc.**
9999 Rose Hills Rd.
Whittier, CA 90601-1701
Phone: (626)280-5150 **Fax:** (626)937-2322
Products: Microcomputers. **SIC:** 5045 (Computers, Peripherals & Software). **Sales:** $50,000,000 (2000). **Emp:** 70. **Officers:** Fred Chang, President.

■ **5922** ■ **American Business Systems Inc.**
315 Littleton Rd.
Chelmsford, MA 01824
Phone: (978)250-9600
Free: (800)356-4034 **Fax:** (978)250-8027
E-mail: sales@abs-software.com
URL: http://www.abs-software.com
Products: Software; Integrated accounting, order entry, inventory, point of sale, and multi-site remote processing products. **SIC:** 5045 (Computers, Peripherals & Software). **Est:** 1978. **Emp:** 16. **Officers:** James Hamilton, President; James Hanlon, Marketing Mgr. **Also Known by This Acronym:** ABS.

■ **5923** ■ **American Computer Hardware**
2205 S Wright St.
Santa Ana, CA 92705
Phone: (714)549-2688 **Fax:** (714)662-0491
Products: Computer printers. **SIC:** 5045 (Computers, Peripherals & Software).

■ **5924** ■ **American Custom Software**
1210 N Willow Ave.
Cookeville, TN 38501
Phone: (931)526-6100 **Fax:** (931)520-1960
Products: Developer of EDI Communications software. **SIC:** 5045 (Computers, Peripherals & Software). **Officers:** John Brady, President.

■ **5925** ■ **American Data Systems Marketing**
63 Independent Ave.
Stoughton, MA 02072-0065
Phone: (781)341-0171
Products: Computers; Computer software; Peripheral computer equipment. **SIC:** 5045 (Computers, Peripherals & Software). **Officers:** John Connolly, President.

■ **5926** ■ **American Digital Cartography Inc.**
115 W Washington St.
Appleton, WI 54911-4751
Phone: (920)733-6678
Free: (800)236-7973 **Fax:** (920)734-3375
E-mail: info@adci.com
URL: http://www.adci.com
Products: Maps in a digital format for computers. **SIC:** 5045 (Computers, Peripherals & Software). **Est:** 1988. **Sales:** $1,400,000 (2000). **Emp:** 15. **Officers:** Jim Reid, President; Michael Bauer, Chairman of the Board.

■ **5927** ■ **American Disc Corp.**
W 231 N 2811 Round Circle E Ste. 100
Pewaukee, WI 53072
Phone: (414)970-0500
Free: (800)840-3472 **Fax:** (414)970-0400
Products: Provider of media duplication services. **SIC:** 5045 (Computers, Peripherals & Software). **Officers:** Geoff Fox, CEO.

■ **5928** ■ **American Education Corp.**
7506 N Broadway
Oklahoma City, OK 73116-9016
Phone: (405)840-6031
Free: (800)222-2811 **Fax:** (405)848-3960
E-mail: christie@amered.com
URL: http://www.amered.com
Products: Educational software. **SIC:** 5045 (Computers, Peripherals & Software). **Est:** 1981. **Sales:** $8,560,000 (1999). **Emp:** 50. **Officers:** Jeffrey E. Butler, CEO & President; Thomas Shively, COO; Neil Johnson, CFO.

■ **5929** ■ **American ELTEC Inc.**
101 College Rd., E
Princeton, NJ 08540
Phone: (609)452-1555 **Fax:** (609)452-7374
Products: Computer hardware for industrial imaging and automation products. **SICs:** 5084 (Industrial Machinery & Equipment); 5065 (Electronic Parts & Equipment Nec). **Sales:** $1,000,000 (2000). **Emp:** 5. **Officers:** Axel Berghoff, General Mgr.; Janet R. Ferris, Finance Officer.

■ 5930 ■ **American Liquidators**
365 Canal St.
New York, NY 10013
Phone: (212)219-8521
Free: (800)219-8521 **Fax:** (212)219-3769
Products: Computers, including hardware and software; Music. **SIC:** 5045 (Computers, Peripherals & Software). **Est:** 1990. **Sales:** $5,000,000 (2000). **Emp:** 12.

■ 5931 ■ **American Netronic Inc.**
5212 Katella Ave., Ste. 104
Los Alamitos, CA 90720
Phone: (562)795-0147
Free: (800)447-2633 **Fax:** (562)795-0152
Products: Project management graphics software. **SIC:** 5045 (Computers, Peripherals & Software). **Sales:** $700,000 (2000). **Emp:** 4. **Officers:** Steven K. Mauss, CEO & President.

■ 5932 ■ **American Pennant Corp.**
PO Box 9627
Moscow, ID 83843-0178
Phone: (208)882-6323
E-mail: gunrunner@gunrunner.com
URL: http://www.gunrunner.com
Products: Firearms; Computer systems and software. **SIC:** 5045 (Computers, Peripherals & Software). **Est:** 1988. **Officers:** Lance Haserot, President.

■ 5933 ■ **American Software & Hardware Distributors, Inc.**
502 E Anthony Dr.
Urbana, IL 61801
Phone: (217)384-2050
Free: (800)225-7941 **Fax:** (217)384-2055
URL: http://www.ashd.com
Products: Computer software, hardware, and games. **SIC:** 5045 (Computers, Peripherals & Software). **Est:** 1986. **Sales:** $120,000,000 (2000). **Emp:** 50. **Officers:** Robert Washburn, President, e-mail: rob@cshd.com; Paul Deckard, VP of Maintenance; Dennis Carpenter, Chairman of the Board & Finance Officer.

■ 5934 ■ **AmeriData Inc.**
10200 51st Ave. N
Minneapolis, MN 55442
Phone: (612)557-2500
Products: Computers. **SIC:** 5045 (Computers, Peripherals & Software). **Sales:** $1,000,000,000 (2000). **Emp:** 1,800. **Officers:** James McCleary, President; Jared Sour, Dir. of Operations.

■ 5935 ■ **AmeriQuest Technologies Inc.**
2465 Maryland Rd.
Willow Grove, PA
Phone: (215)658-8900
Free: (800)223-7081 **Fax:** (215)658-8979
Products: Computer systems and related products. **SIC:** 5045 (Computers, Peripherals & Software). **Sales:** $216,000,000 (2000). **Emp:** 80. **Officers:** Alexander C. Kramer Jr., President; Jon D. Jensen, CFO.

■ 5936 ■ **Ames Sciences Inc.**
501 South St.
Easton, MD 21601-3845
Phone: (410)476-3200 **Fax:** (410)476-3396
Products: Computers; Computer software; Peripheral computer equipment. **SIC:** 5045 (Computers, Peripherals & Software). **Est:** 1979. **Officers:** William Ames, President.

■ 5937 ■ **Amex Inc.**
2724 Summer St. NE
Minneapolis, MN 55413
Phone: (612)331-3063 **Fax:** (612)331-3180
Products: Computers; Electronic equipment; Industrial machinery. **SICs:** 5045 (Computers, Peripherals & Software); 5065 (Electronic Parts & Equipment Nec); 5084 (Industrial Machinery & Equipment). **Officers:** Dale West, General Mgr.

■ 5938 ■ **AMOs Inc.**
2735 Harrison Ave. NW
Olympia, WA 98502-5240
Phone: (425)786-5112 **Fax:** (425)786-5127
Products: Computers, peripherals, and software. **SIC:**

5045 (Computers, Peripherals & Software). **Officers:** Scott Whitwam, President.

■ 5939 ■ **Amtron Corp.**
PO Box 2686
Kansas City, KS 66110-0686
Phone: (913)788-5000
Products: Computers; Peripheral computer equipment; Computer software. **SIC:** 5045 (Computers, Peripherals & Software). **Officers:** Owen Hawkins, President.

■ 5940 ■ **Analytcal Automation Specialists Inc.**
11723 Sun Belt Ct.
Baton Rouge, LA 70809-4211
Phone: (504)753-5467 **Fax:** (504)753-0916
Products: Computers; Computer software; Peripheral computer equipment. **SIC:** 5045 (Computers, Peripherals & Software). **Officers:** James Mc Dowell, President.

■ 5941 ■ **Analytic Associates**
4817 Browndeer Ln.
Rolling Hills Estates, CA 90275
Phone: (310)541-0418
Free: (800)959-3273 **Fax:** (310)541-1152
Products: Developer of software. **SIC:** 5045 (Computers, Peripherals & Software). **Officers:** Robert W. Feakins, President.

■ 5942 ■ **Andromeda Software Inc.**
123 Bucyrus Dr.
Amherst, NY 14228-1946
Phone: (716)691-4510
Products: Astronomy and science software. **SIC:** 5045 (Computers, Peripherals & Software). **Officers:** Robert Riberia, President.

■ 5943 ■ **Apex Data Systems Inc.**
6464 E Grant Rd.
Tucson, AZ 85715
Phone: (520)298-1991 **Fax:** (520)296-7948
Products: Insurance management, proposal, and claims processing software. **SIC:** 5045 (Computers, Peripherals & Software). **Officers:** Dwight Babcock, President.

■ 5944 ■ **APPIC Inc.**
623 S Main St.
Milpitas, CA 95035
Phone: (408)719-7575
Free: (800)872-7742 **Fax:** (408)719-7574
Products: Forms generation software. **SIC:** 5045 (Computers, Peripherals & Software). **Sales:** $2,500,000 (2000). **Emp:** 3. **Officers:** Paul Fuller, Payroll Mgr.; Verner Seele, Controller.

■ 5945 ■ **Apple Computer Inc. Federal Systems Group**
1892 Preston White Dr.
Reston, VA 20191-4359
Phone: (703)264-5155
Products: Computers. **SIC:** 5045 (Computers, Peripherals & Software).

■ 5946 ■ **Apple Pacific Div.**
20525 Mariani Ave.
Cupertino, CA 95014
Phone: (408)996-1010
Products: Computers, peripherals, and software. **SIC:** 5045 (Computers, Peripherals & Software).

■ 5947 ■ **Applied Business Computers Inc.**
R.R. Box 44A, Hwy. 321
Pineland, SC 29934
Phone: (843)726-6767
Products: Computers and software. **SIC:** 5045 (Computers, Peripherals & Software). **Sales:** $1,300,000 (2000). **Emp:** 4. **Officers:** David Bormen, President; Barbara Bormen, VP & Treasurer.

■ 5948 ■ **Applied Computer Solutions Inc. (New York, New York)**
1826 2nd Ave., Ste. 191
New York, NY 10016
Phone: (212)996-6609
Products: Software. **SIC:** 5045 (Computers, Peripherals & Software). **Sales:** $300,000 (1993). **Emp:** 2. **Officers:** Nick Toro, President.

■ 5949 ■ **Applied Computer Technology Inc.**
2573 Midpoint Dr.
Ft. Collins, CO 80525-4417
Phone: (970)490-1849
Free: (800)747-4228 **Fax:** (970)490-1439
Products: Computers; Computer software; Peripheral computer equipment. **SIC:** 5045 (Computers, Peripherals & Software). **Officers:** Bud Prentice, President.

■ 5950 ■ **Applied Educational Systems Inc.**
540 N Commercial St.
Manchester, NH 03101-1122
Phone: (603)225-5511
Free: (800)237-5530 **Fax:** (603)225-2311
Products: Educational software. **SIC:** 5045 (Computers, Peripherals & Software). **Est:** 1980. **Sales:** $1,000,000 (2000). **Emp:** 10. **Officers:** Robert C. Hamilton, President.

■ 5951 ■ **Applied Information Solutions Inc.**
1660 17th St. Ste. 400
Denver, CO 80202
Phone: (303)893-8936 **Fax:** (303)893-5046
Products: Partnership administration software. **SIC:** 5045 (Computers, Peripherals & Software). **Officers:** Ms. Ann C. Bennett, CEO & President.

■ 5952 ■ **Applied Microcomputer Solutions**
PO Box 47234
Plymouth, MN 55447-0234
Phone: (612)473-8167 **Fax:** (612)473-4726
Products: Computers; Peripheral computer equipment; Software. **SIC:** 5045 (Computers, Peripherals & Software). **Officers:** Dave Hargrove, President.

■ 5953 ■ **Applied Systems Technology and Resources**
2570 Route 900
Cornwall, NY 12518
Phone: (914)534-7100
Free: (800)929-3711 **Fax:** (914)534-8575
Products: Computer software. **SIC:** 5045 (Computers, Peripherals & Software).

■ 5954 ■ **Applied Technology Ventures Inc.**
4577 Hinkley Industrial Pkwy
Cleveland, OH 44109-6009
Phone: (216)459-0700
Free: (800)843-5010 **Fax:** (216)459-9168
URL: http://www.atvsi.com
Products: Computers and computer products. **SIC:** 5045 (Computers, Peripherals & Software). **Est:** 1980. **Sales:** $60,000,000 (2000). **Emp:** 88. **Officers:** Gary Regula, President; Jeff Dunlop, Controller; Brad Aten, VP of Sales; Kirsten Evans, VP of Marketing.

■ 5955 ■ **Appropriate Solutions**
PO Box 458
Peterborough, NH 03458
Phone: (603)924-6079 **Fax:** (603)924-8668
Products: Provdes of custom systems, software development services specializing in Macintosh, Windows, and Windows NT. **SIC:** 5045 (Computers, Peripherals & Software). **Officers:** Raymond Cote, President.

■ 5956 ■ **AR Industries Inc.**
3203 S Shannon St.
Santa Ana, CA 92704-6352
Phone: (714)434-8600 **Fax:** (714)434-8601
Products: Portable computer accessories; Computer repair and maintenance. **SIC:** 5045 (Computers, Peripherals & Software). **Sales:** $19,000,000 (2000). **Emp:** 30. **Officers:** Rod Hosilyk, President; Kevin Prince, Vice President.

■ 5957 ■ **Arch Associates Corp.**
PO Box 427
Fernwood, PA 19050
Phone: (215)626-2724
Products: Computers and peripheral equipment. **SIC:** 5045 (Computers, Peripherals & Software). **Sales:** $2,000,000 (2000). **Emp:** 10. **Officers:** Ralph Arch, President.

■ 5958 ■ Archway Systems Inc.
2130 Main St., #145
Huntington Beach, CA 92648
Phone: (714)374-0440   Fax: (714)374-0441
Products: Prepackaged CAD software. SIC: 5045
(Computers, Peripherals & Software). Sales:
$1,000,000 (2000). Emp: 5. Officers: Michael R.
Lazear, CEO & President; Sandy Lazear, CFO.

■ 5959 ■ AremisSoft Corp.
200 Central Park S
New York, NY 10019
Phone: (212)765-7383   Fax: (212)765-7385
Products: Develops software for midsized
organizations in health care. SIC: 5045 (Computers,
Peripherals & Software). Sales: $52,600,000 (2000).
Emp: 520. Officers: Lycourgos K. Kyprianon, CEO;
Michael Tymvios, CFO.

■ 5960 ■ Arista Enterprises Inc.
125 Commerce Dr.
Hauppauge, NY 11788
Phone: (516)435-0200
Products: Computers and telephone accessories,
including phone cords, mice, and pads. SICs: 5045
(Computers, Peripherals & Software); 5065 (Electronic
Parts & Equipment Nec). Est: 1962. Officers: Alan
Leifer, President.

■ 5961 ■ Aristo Computers Inc.
6700 SW 105th Ave., Ste. 300
Beaverton, OR 97008-5484
Phone: (503)626-6333
Free: (800)327-4786   Fax: (503)626-6492
E-mail: sales@memorytest.com
URL: http://www.memorytest.com
Products: Memory testers and accessories for testing
memory modules and chips. SIC: 5045 (Computers,
Peripherals & Software). Est: 1985. Sales: $2,000,000
(2000). Emp: 25. Officers: Ron Avni, President; David
Dublisky, Sales/Marketing Contact, e-mail: ddublisky@
memorytest.com.

■ 5962 ■ ARM Computer Inc.
998 Rock Ave.
San Jose, CA 95131-1615
Phone: (408)935-9800
Free: (800)765-1767   Fax: (408)935-9192
Products: Notebook computers. SIC: 5045
(Computers, Peripherals & Software). Sales:
$24,000,000 (2000). Emp: 35. Officers: Rocky Lee,
President.

■ 5963 ■ Arraid Inc.
PO Box 86249
Phoenix, AZ 85080
Phone: (623)582-4592   Fax: (623)582-4321
Products: Computer disk drive systems and tape drive
emulators. SIC: 5045 (Computers, Peripherals &
Software). Officers: Keith Blaich, CFO.

■ 5964 ■ Arrow Electronics Inc.
25 Hub Dr.
Melville, NY 11747
Phone: (516)391-1300   Fax: (516)391-1401
Products: Computers, parts, and accessories. SIC:
5045 (Computers, Peripherals & Software). Est: 1968.
Sales: $51,000,000 (2000). Emp: 150. Officers:
Robert McInerney, COO; Peter Ver-EEcke, Dir. of
Marketing.

■ 5965 ■ Arrow Electronics Inc. Almac/Arrow
Electronics Div.
3310 146th Pl. SE, Ste. B
Bellevue, WA 98007-6471
Phone: (425)643-9992   Fax: (425)643-9575
Products: Computers and parts. SIC: 5045
(Computers, Peripherals & Software). Est: 1946.
Sales: $50,000,000 (2000). Emp: 100. Officers: Fred
Warnock, President; Greg Hearn, Sales Mgr.; Eileen
Lutfi, Dir of Human Resources.

■ 5966 ■ A.R.T. Multimedia Systems, Inc.
56 S Abel St.
Milpitas, CA 95035
Phone: (408)946-7852   Fax: (408)946-7892
E-mail: artcom7853@aol.com
URL: http://www.artmul.com
Products: Computer peripherals. SIC: 5045

(Computers, Peripherals & Software). Est: 1997.
Sales: $4,000,000 (1999). Emp: 6. Officers: Jackie
Tran, Manager. Former Name: Art Computer Tech Inc.

■ 5967 ■ ARTiSan Software Tools
2 Lincoln Center Ste. 370
Portland, OR 97223
Phone: (503)245-6200
Free: (888)511-7975   Fax: (503)244-1443
Products: Provides services to acclerate your
development of technical systems and software. SIC:
5045 (Computers, Peripherals & Software). Officers:
Caine O'Brien, CEO.

■ 5968 ■ ARvee Systems Inc.
1461 Lakeland Ave., Ste. 19
Bohemia, NY 11716
Phone: (516)567-9409   Fax: (516)567-9608
Products: Computer hardware. SIC: 5045
(Computers, Peripherals & Software). Sales:
$2,000,000 (2000). Emp: 15. Officers: Michael
Gencarelli, President.

■ 5969 ■ ASAP Software Express Inc.
850 Asbury Dr.
Buffalo Grove, IL 60089
Phone: (847)465-3710
Products: Prepackaged software. SIC: 5045
(Computers, Peripherals & Software). Sales:
$48,800,000 (2000). Emp: 100. Officers: Scott Wald,
President; David Polster, VP & Controller.

■ 5970 ■ ASCII Group Inc.
7101 Wisconsin Ave., Ste. 1000
Bethesda, MD 20814-4805
Phone: (301)718-2600   Fax: (301)718-0435
Products: Computers. SIC: 5045 (Computers,
Peripherals & Software). Est: 1984. Sales:
$5,400,000,000 (2000). Emp: 15. Officers: Alan
Weinberger, Chairman of the Board; Jill Kerr, VP &
COO.

■ 5971 ■ Ashford International Inc.
2305 W Park Place Blvd ., No. N
Stone Mountain, GA 30087
Phone: (770)879-6266   Fax: (770)879-6265
URL: http://www.ashfordint.com
Products: Computers, peripherals, hardware, and
software. SIC: 5045 (Computers, Peripherals &
Software). Est: 1983. Sales: $13,900,000 (2000).
Emp: 28. Officers: Bernard Van Der Lande, President;
Betsy Jenkins, Finance Officer; Erin Joyner, Dir. of
Operations.

■ 5972 ■ Ashwood Computer Co.
10671 Techwoods Cir.,
Cincinnati, OH 45242
Phone: (513)563-2800   Fax: (513)554-6412
Products: Computer software. SIC: 5045 (Computers,
Peripherals & Software). Officers: Rod Owens,
President.

■ 5973 ■ ASNA Inc.
14855 Blanco Rd. Ste. 300
San Antonio, TX 78216
Phone: (210)408-0212
Free: (800)289-2762   Fax: (210)408-0211
Products: Developing visual programming and
systems software. SIC: 5045 (Computers, Peripherals
& Software).

■ 5974 ■ Aspen Data
345 Edgewood Dr.
Providence, UT 84332-9441
Phone: (435)863-5746   Fax: (435)753-5557
Products: Computers, peripherals, and software. SIC:
5045 (Computers, Peripherals & Software). Officers:
David Wilkes, Owner.

■ 5975 ■ Aspen Imaging International Inc.
3830 Kelley Ave.
Cleveland, OH 44114
Phone: (216)881-5300   Fax: (440)665-2972
Products: Computer printer supplies. SIC: 5045
(Computers, Peripherals & Software). Est: 1977.
Sales: $7,300,000 (2000). Emp: 28. Officers: Robert
H. Kanner, CEO & Chairman of the Board; Florine N.
Nath, VP of Finance & Admin.; Harry J. Fekkes, Sr. VP

of Marketing & Sales; Margaret Benton, Operations
Mgr.; Peg Bundgaard, Human Resources Mgr.

■ 5976 ■ Assi Computers Inc.
620 N Broadway
Pittsburg, KS 66762
Phone: (316)231-7833   Fax: (316)231-7133
Products: Computers; Computer software; Peripheral
computer equipment. SIC: 5045 (Computers,
Peripherals & Software). Officers: Mark Flood,
President.

■ 5977 ■ Associated Computers Services
PO Box 464057
Lawrenceville, GA 30042-4057
Phone: (404)962-7760
Products: Computers, peripherals, and software. SIC:
5045 (Computers, Peripherals & Software). Officers:
Patrick Rann, President.

■ 5978 ■ Associated Systems Inc.
1425 N Broadway
Wichita, KS 67214-1103
Phone: (316)263-1035
Free: (800)524-2327   Fax: (316)263-0961
Products: Computer software. SIC: 5045 (Computers,
Peripherals & Software). Officers: Francis Smith,
President.

■ 5979 ■ Associates in Software International
180 Crossen Ave.
Elk Grove Village, IL 60007
Phone: (847)763-5000   Fax: (847)982-9600
Products: Computer software and hardware. SIC:
5045 (Computers, Peripherals & Software). Est: 1984.
Sales: $4,000,000 (2000). Emp: 8. Officers: Henri
Ganancia, President.

■ 5980 ■ Atlantic Software
PO Box 299
Wenham, MA 01984
Phone: (508)922-4352
Products: Educational and scientific hardware. SIC:
5045 (Computers, Peripherals & Software). Est: 1986.
Sales: $1,000,000 (2000). Emp: 1. Officers: E.M.
Bellott, President.

■ 5981 ■ Atlantis Software
34740 Blackstone Way
Fremont, CA 94555
Phone: (510)796-2180   Fax: (510)796-8476
Products: Network and computer management tools.
SIC: 5045 (Computers, Peripherals & Software).
Officers: Rick Gordon, Owner.

■ 5982 ■ ATS Money Systems Inc.
25 Rockwood Pl.
Englewood, NJ 07631
Phone: (201)894-1700   Fax: (201)894-0958
Products: Currency counting systems, software
computer systems, computers and peripheral
equipment; Developer of customized software. SIC:
5045 (Computers, Peripherals & Software). Sales:
$14,447,000,000 (2000). Emp: 53. Officers: Gerard F.
Murphy, CEO & President; Joseph M. Burke, VP of
Finance.

■ 5983 ■ Attorney's Briefcase
519 17th St. FL. 7
Oakland, CA 94612-1527
Phone: (510)836-2743   Fax: (510)465-7348
Products: Computer software. SIC: 5045 (Computers,
Peripherals & Software). Officers: Carrett C. Dailey,
President.

■ 5984 ■ Authentica Security Technology
135 2nd Ave.
Waltham, MA 02451
Phone: (781)290-0418
Products: Computer software security. SIC: 5045
(Computers, Peripherals & Software). Officers: Brien
Wheeler, Manager.

■ 5985 ■ Auto-trol Technology Corp.
12500 N Washington St.
Denver, CO 80241-2400
Phone: (303)452-4919
Free: (800)233-2882   Fax: (303)252-2250
Products: Computers and software. SIC: 5045

(Computers, Peripherals & Software). **Sales:** $40,000,000 (1993). **Emp:** 435. **Officers:** Howard B. Hillman, CEO & President; Carl Maneri, VP & Treasurer.

■ 5986 ■ **Automated Data Systems Inc.**
PO Box 1076
Hickory, NC 28603-1076
Phone: (704)328-9365 **Fax:** (704)322-1218
Products: Computers; Computer software; Peripheral computer equipment. **SIC:** 5045 (Computers, Peripherals & Software). **Est:** 1974. **Sales:** $1,000,000 (2000). **Emp:** 8. **Officers:** Gene Miller, President.

■ 5987 ■ **Automated Office Systems of New England**
8 North St. R.
Plymouth, MA 02360
Phone: (508)747-0808 **Fax:** (508)747-5555
Products: Business systems and forms. **SIC:** 5045 (Computers, Peripherals & Software). **Est:** 1990. **Officers:** Norman Bryson, Owner.

■ 5988 ■ **Automated Register Systems, Inc.**
1437 S Jackson St.
Seattle, WA 98144-2022
Phone: (206)325-8922
Free: (800)544-8408 **Fax:** (206)325-9127
Products: Restaurant, grocery, and specialty retail point-of-sale scanning systems. **SIC:** 5045 (Computers, Peripherals & Software). **Est:** 1972. **Officers:** Michael Pollastro, President; Gary T. Pollastro, Vice President.

■ 5989 ■ **Automating Peripherals Inc.**
310 N Wilson Ave.
Hartford, WI 53027
Phone: (414)673-6815 **Fax:** (414)673-2650
Products: Time and attendence software. **SIC:** 5045 (Computers, Peripherals & Software). **Officers:** Luis Garcia, President.

■ 5990 ■ **Automation Image Inc.**
2650 Valley View Ln., Ste. 100
Dallas, TX 75234-6273
Phone: (972)247-8816 **Fax:** (972)243-2814
Products: Hardware and software. **SIC:** 5045 (Computers, Peripherals & Software). **Sales:** $12,000,000 (2000). **Emp:** 40. **Officers:** Indira Singla, President; Raghu Bellary, Controller.

■ 5991 ■ **Avant Computer Associates Inc.**
102 Powers Ferry Rd.
Marietta, GA 30067-7558
Phone: (404)977-7255
Products: Computers, peripherals, and software. **SIC:** 5045 (Computers, Peripherals & Software). **Officers:** William Gilmer, President.

■ 5992 ■ **Avanti 4 International Corp.**
42400 Garfield Rd., Ste. D
Clinton Township, MI 48038
Phone: (810)228-7090
Products: Computers, printers, and peripherals for corporate users. **SIC:** 5045 (Computers, Peripherals & Software). **Sales:** $10,000,000 (2000). **Emp:** 14. **Officers:** Joseph Romeo, President; Dave Cerrini, Vice President.

■ 5993 ■ **Avent Inc.**
80 Cutter Mill Rd.
Great Neck, NY 11021
Phone: (516)466-7000
Products: Electronic components and computer products. **SICs:** 5045 (Computers, Peripherals & Software); 5065 (Electronic Parts & Equipment Nec). **Sales:** $5,390,000,000 (2000). **Emp:** 9,400. **Officers:** Leon Machiz, CEO & Chairman of the Board; Raymond Sadowski, Sr. VP & CFO.

■ 5994 ■ **AVerMedia Technologies Inc.**
1161 Cadillac Ct.
Milpitas, CA 95035-3055
Phone: (510)770-9899 **Fax:** (510)770-9901
Products: Computer sound and graphics boards. **SIC:** 5045 (Computers, Peripherals & Software). **Sales:** $15,000,000 (2000). **Emp:** 20. **Officers:** Amy Wong, Vice President.

■ 5995 ■ **Avnet Computer Inc.**
3011 S 52nd St.
Tempe, AZ 85282
Phone: (602)414-6700 **Fax:** (602)280-3871
Products: Computers, micro computers, personal computers, and hard drives. **SIC:** 5045 (Computers, Peripherals & Software). **Est:** 1988. **Sales:** $800,000,000 (2000). **Emp:** 550. **Officers:** Rich Ward, Exec. VP.

■ 5996 ■ **Azerty Inc.**
13 Centre Dr.
Orchard Park, NY 14127
Phone: (716)662-0200
Free: (800)888-8080 **Fax:** (716)662-7616
E-mail: webmaster@azerty.com
URL: http://www.azerty.com
Products: Computer supplies, hardware, and accessories. **SIC:** 5045 (Computers, Peripherals & Software). **Est:** 1983. **Sales:** $750,000,000 (2000). **Emp:** 400. **Officers:** Rich Hediger, President; Jeff Willis, Dir. of Merchandising; Kevin Bowman, Dir. of Sales; Jeff Pease, Dir. of Marketing.

■ 5997 ■ **Baker & Taylor**
PO Box 6885
Bridgewater, NJ 08807-0885
Phone: (908)541-7305 **Fax:** (908)541-7853
Products: Computer software, including astronomy and air support. **SIC:** 5045 (Computers, Peripherals & Software). **Est:** 1983. **Emp:** 150. **Officers:** Jacqueline L. Cochran, President; Don Helfstein, VP of Marketing; David Nalley, VP of Sales; Katie Morgan, VP of Business Development; Frank Greico, VP of Finance; Tom Shields, VP of Operations; Barbara J. Gorkis, VP of Human Resources; Patricia Quimby, VP of Purchasing.

■ 5998 ■ **Balno Incorporated**
13506 W 72nd St.
Shawnee Mission, KS 66216-3721
Phone: (913)631-9979
Products: Computers, peripherals, and software. **SIC:** 5045 (Computers, Peripherals & Software). **Officers:** David Whitesel, President.

■ 5999 ■ **Banana Educational Software Distributors**
2501 W 84th St.
Bloomington, MN 55431
Phone: (612)944-0104
Products: Educational software. **SIC:** 5045 (Computers, Peripherals & Software). **Est:** 1982.

■ 6000 ■ **Bangert's Computer Systems**
506 Jefferson St.
Burlington, IA 52601-5426
Phone: (319)752-5484 **Free:** (800)458-7369
Products: Computers; Computer software; Peripheral computer equipment. **SIC:** 5045 (Computers, Peripherals & Software). **Officers:** Richard Bangert, President.

■ 6001 ■ **Baron Services, Inc.**
4930 Research Dr. NW
Huntsville, AL 35805
Phone: (256)881-8811 **Fax:** (256)881-8283
URL: http://www.baronservices.com
Products: Weather tracking software and hardware. **SIC:** 5045 (Computers, Peripherals & Software). **Est:** 1990. **Emp:** 40.

■ 6002 ■ **Bawamba Software Inc.**
150 E Olive Ave.
Burbank, CA 91502
Phone: (818)843-1627 **Fax:** (818)843-8364
Products: Software. **SIC:** 5045 (Computers, Peripherals & Software). **Sales:** $3,000,000 (2000). **Emp:** 23. **Officers:** Steve Greenfield, President.

■ 6003 ■ **Bay State Computer Group Inc.**
52 Roland St.
Boston, MA 02129
Phone: (617)623-3100
Products: Computer software, hardware, and computer parts. **SIC:** 5045 (Computers, Peripherals & Software). **Est:** 1984. **Sales:** $21,000,000 (2000). **Emp:** 75. **Officers:** James Claypoole, President;

Elizabeth Claypoole, Controller; George Troy, VP of Marketing & Sales.

■ 6004 ■ **Bay State Computer of New Jersey Inc.**
375 Raritan Ctr. Pkwy.
Edison, NJ 08837
Phone: (732)417-1122
Products: Computers and computer parts. **SIC:** 5045 (Computers, Peripherals & Software).

■ 6005 ■ **BCS*A**
385 Belmarin Keyes Blvd.
Novato, CA 94949
Phone: (415)883-7392
Products: Computer peripherals. **SIC:** 5045 (Computers, Peripherals & Software). **Sales:** $2,000,000 (2000). **Emp:** 10. **Officers:** David Zhao, President.

■ 6006 ■ **BCSR Inc.**
12015 115th Ave. NE, Ste. 130
Kirkland, WA 98034
Phone: (425)823-1188
Free: (800)759-2277 **Fax:** (425)821-8234
Products: Computer rental. **SIC:** 5045 (Computers, Peripherals & Software). **Sales:** $6,000,000 (2000). **Emp:** 8. **Officers:** Dan Hiatt, Owner.

■ 6007 ■ **BEAR Computers Inc.**
12727 Northup Way., Ste. 8
Bellevue, WA 98005-1917
Phone: (425)869-5900 **Fax:** (425)881-6367
Products: Computers. **SIC:** 5045 (Computers, Peripherals & Software).

■ 6008 ■ **BEK International Inc.**
2804 NW 72nd Ave.
Miami, FL 33122
Phone: (305)594-3756
Products: Computer components and motherboards. **SIC:** 5045 (Computers, Peripherals & Software).

■ 6009 ■ **Belmont Systems Inc.**
1555 Industrial Rd.
San Carlos, CA 94070
Phone: (650)598-9058
Products: Computer hardware and software. **SIC:** 5045 (Computers, Peripherals & Software). **Sales:** $4,000,000 (1993). **Emp:** 10. **Officers:** Andy Lin, President.

■ 6010 ■ **Benchmark Systems Inc. of Utah**
PO Box 782
Bountiful, UT 84011-0782
Phone: (801)298-8200 **Fax:** (801)298-8212
Products: Computers, peripherals, and software. **SIC:** 5045 (Computers, Peripherals & Software). **Officers:** Wayne Pillard, President.

■ 6011 ■ **Benton Ballard Co.**
PO Box 12375
Jackson, MS 39236-2375
Phone: (601)956-3560 **Fax:** (601)956-3885
Products: Computers; Computer software; Peripheral computer equipment. **SIC:** 5045 (Computers, Peripherals & Software). **Officers:** Benton Ballard, Owner.

■ 6012 ■ **Benton Electronics Inc.**
1191 Elmsford Dr.
Cupertino, CA 95014-4960
Phone: (408)996-1701
Products: Computers. **SIC:** 5045 (Computers, Peripherals & Software). **Sales:** $100,000 (1993). **Emp:** 2. **Officers:** Angela Liu, President & CFO.

■ 6013 ■ **Bernoulli Collection Inc.**
1821 West 4000 South
Roy, UT 84067
Phone: (801)524-2000
Products: Serial access storage units, such as magnetic tape storage units (magnetic tape drive). **SIC:** 5045 (Computers, Peripherals & Software). **Est:** 1988.

■ **6014** ■ **Best Data Products Inc.**
19748 Dearborn St.
Chatsworth, CA 91311
Phone: (818)773-9600
Free: (800)632-2378 **Fax:** (818)773-9619
URL: http://www.bestdata.com
Products: Computer modems. **SIC:** 5065 (Electronic Parts & Equipment Nec). **Est:** 1983. **Sales:** $16,000,000 (2000). **Emp:** 70. **Officers:** Bruce Zaman, President.

■ **6015** ■ **Bibliographical Center for Research Inc.**
14394 E Evans Ave.
Aurora, CO 80014-1478
Phone: (303)751-6277
Free: (800)397-1552 **Fax:** (303)751-9787
Products: Computers, peripherals, and software. **SIC:** 5045 (Computers, Peripherals & Software). **Est:** 1935. **Sales:** $7,000,000 (2000). **Emp:** 25. **Officers:** David H. Brunell, Director; Arleta Blades, Controller.

■ **6016** ■ **Big Blue Products Inc.**
386 Oakwood Rd.
Huntington Station, NY 11746-7223
Phone: (516)261-1000 **Fax:** (516)351-3607
E-mail: sales@bigblue-usa.com
URL: http://www.bigblue-usa.com
Products: Computer parts. **SIC:** 5045 (Computers, Peripherals & Software). **Est:** 1984. **Sales:** $3,500,000 (2000). **Emp:** 20. **Officers:** Jeffrey Alwick, President; Marie Alwick, Vice President.

■ **6017** ■ **BL Associates, Inc.**
145 Webster St.
Hanover, MA 02339
Phone: (781)982-9664 **Fax:** (781)871-4456
Products: Computer equipment. **SIC:** 5045 (Computers, Peripherals & Software). **Officers:** Paul Leeber, Owner.

■ **6018** ■ **BMS Inc. - Barcoded Management Systems, Inc.**
PO Box 49310
Dayton, OH 45449-0310
Phone: (937)643-2006
Free: (800)392-9660 **Fax:** (937)643-3290
URL: http://www.barcodems.com
Products: Bar code equipment; Printers; Labels and ribbons; Software design, installation, and service. **SIC:** 5045 (Computers, Peripherals & Software). **Sales:** $5,000,000 (1999). **Emp:** 24. **Officers:** Terry D. Carder, CEO & Chairman of the Board; Joyce Ashcraft, Finance Officer; Dennis Glidden, President.

■ **6019** ■ **Boston Computer Exchange Corp.**
100 Charlestown St.
Somerville, MA 02143
Phone: (617)625-7722
Free: (800)262-6399 **Fax:** (617)623-1133
URL: http://www.bocoex.com
Products: Computers, including laptops; Computer peripherals. **SIC:** 5045 (Computers, Peripherals & Software). **Est:** 1982. **Sales:** $500,000,000 (2000). **Emp:** 13. **Officers:** Barbara Geiger, President; e-mail: jmiller1@custom-edge.com

■ **6020** ■ **Boxlight Corp.**
19332 Powder Hill Pl.
Poulsbo, WA 98370
Phone: (360)779-7901
Free: (800)762-5757 **Fax:** 888-353-4242
Products: Computer-based presentation products, including liquid crystal display projection systems. **SIC:** 5045 (Computers, Peripherals & Software). **Sales:** $45,000,000 (2000). **Emp:** 100. **Officers:** Herb Myers, CEO & President; Stepanie White, Controller.

■ **6021** ■ **William K. Bradford Publishing Co.**
35 Forest Ridge Rd.
Concord, MA 01742-3834
Phone: (978)263-6996
Products: Educational software. **SIC:** 5045 (Computers, Peripherals & Software). **Sales:** $1,500,000 (2000). **Emp:** 13. **Officers:** Thomas Haver, President.

■ **6022** ■ **Brady Corp.**
PO Box 571
Milwaukee, WI 53202-0571
Phone: (414)358-6600
Free: (800)541-1686 **Fax:** (414)358-6798
Products: Identification safety, materials, and graphics solutions, with products ranging from high-performance labels, signs and tapes to software, printers and data-collection systems. **SIC:** 5045 (Computers, Peripherals & Software). **Sales:** $470,900,000 (1999). **Emp:** 2,700. **Officers:** Katherine M. Hudson, CEO & President; Frank M. Jaehnert, VP & CFO.

■ **6023** ■ **BrainTree Technology Inc.**
200 Cordwainer Dr.
Norwell, MA 02061-1619
Phone: (617)982-0200
Free: (800)232-5215 **Fax:** (617)982-8076
E-mail: info@bti.com
URL: http://www.bti.com
Products: Security management software. **SIC:** 5045 (Computers, Peripherals & Software). **Est:** 1989. **Sales:** $4,000,000 (2000). **Emp:** 25. **Officers:** R. Stephen Lilly, CEO & President; Gary Gallant, Vice President.

■ **6024** ■ **Bridge Technology Inc.**
45 Lyme Rd., Ste. 306
Hanover, NH 03755-1224
Phone: (603)643-6355
Products: Computer software. **SIC:** 5045 (Computers, Peripherals & Software). **Sales:** $2,000,000 (1993). **Emp:** 7. **Officers:** Gregory Ware, President.

■ **6025** ■ **Brigadoon.Com Inc.**
PO Box 53168
Bellevue, WA 98015
Phone: (206)652-9365
Products: Develops custom software for remote billing (cellular); Internet access wholesaler and service provider; Develops custom data communications/security equipment. **SIC:** 5045 (Computers, Peripherals & Software). **Officers:** John Hansen, CEO.

■ **6026** ■ **BRS Software Products**
5 Computer Dr. S
Albany, NY 12205-1608
Phone: (518)437-4000
Products: Software. **SIC:** 5045 (Computers, Peripherals & Software). **Est:** 1976. **Sales:** $9,000,000 (2000).

■ **6027** ■ **Business Computer Solutions**
1301 Fraser St., Ste. 11-A
Bellingham, WA 98226-5832
Phones: (360)671-9630 (360)671-9634
URL: http://www.officesystemsnow.com
Products: Computer peripherals and software; Document management; Fax services. **SIC:** 5045 (Computers, Peripherals & Software). **Est:** 1982. **Emp:** 25. **Officers:** Del Vande Kerk, President; Ron Taylor, Treasurer & Secty.

■ **6028** ■ **Business Integrators**
1240 Blalock
Houston, TX 77055
Phone: (713)973-8811 **Fax:** (713)973-8881
Products: Computer hardware, software, and related consultation services. **SIC:** 5045 (Computers, Peripherals & Software). **Sales:** $7,900,000 (2000). **Emp:** 16. **Officers:** Jon Bryan, President.

■ **6029** ■ **Business Machines Inc.**
549 Pylon Dr.
Raleigh, NC 27606-1414
Phone: (919)834-0100 **Fax:** (919)833-5866
Products: Computers; Computer software; Peripheral computer equipment. **SIC:** 5045 (Computers, Peripherals & Software). **Officers:** Michael Upchurch, President.

■ **6030** ■ **Business Management Software**
PO Box 228
Norfolk, NE 68702-0228
Phone: (402)371-1992 **Fax:** (402)371-1664
Products: Computers; Peripheral computer equipment; Computer software. **SIC:** 5045 (Computers,

Peripherals & Software). **Officers:** James Mc Kenzie, President.

■ **6031** ■ **Business Media Inc.**
300 Oak Creek Dr.
Lincoln, NE 68528
Phone: (402)476-6222
Products: Computer-presentation equipment and supplies. **SIC:** 5045 (Computers, Peripherals & Software). **Officers:** Karen Dunning, CFO.

■ **6032** ■ **Business Systems**
734 Forest St.
Marlborough, MA 01752-3002
Phone: (508)624-4600 **Fax:** (508)624-0100
Products: Computers; Computer software; Peripheral computer equipment. **SIC:** 5045 (Computers, Peripherals & Software). **Officers:** Marty Greenstein, Owner.

■ **6033** ■ **C Companies, Inc.**
10000 Flying Cloud Dr.
Eden Prairie, MN 55347
Phone: (612)942-6630
Free: (800)995-4111 **Fax:** (612)942-8980
URL: http://www.ccompanies.com
Products: Lucent technologies, new and used. **SIC:** 5045 (Computers, Peripherals & Software). **Est:** 1982. **Officers:** Loren Page, President.

■ **6034** ■ **C S & S Computer Systems Inc.**
1515 W University Dr., Ste. 103
Tempe, AZ 85281-3279
Phone: (602)968-8585 **Fax:** (602)968-9544
Products: Computers; Computer software; Peripheral computer equipment. **SIC:** 5045 (Computers, Peripherals & Software). **Officers:** Mike Kassab, President.

■ **6035** ■ **CableLink Inc.**
255 W 2950 S
Salt Lake City, UT 84115
Phone: (801)467-4511
Free: (800)858-3290 **Fax:** (801)467-2461
Products: Computer cables. **SIC:** 5199 (Nondurable Goods Nec). **Sales:** $4,100,000 (2000). **Emp:** 22. **Officers:** Ben Chase, CEO & President; Mike Berret, CFO.

■ **6036** ■ **Cables & Chips Inc.**
121 Fulton St., 4th Fl.
New York, NY 10038
Phone: (212)619-3132
Free: (800)843-4117 **Fax:** (212)619-3982
Products: Computer parts, including connectors. **SIC:** 5045 (Computers, Peripherals & Software). **Emp:** 49. **Officers:** Susan Feinstein.

■ **6037** ■ **CAD Store Inc.**
4494 W Peoria Ave., Ste. 105
Glendale, AZ 85302
Free: (800)576-6789
E-mail: sales@thecadstore.com
URL: http://www.thecadstore.com
Products: Computers; Printers. **SIC:** 5045 (Computers, Peripherals & Software). **Est:** 1985. **Sales:** $3,000,000 (2000). **Emp:** 8. **Officers:** Stephanie Kuammie, Owner; Russell Mickelson, Sales & Marketing Contact; Candace Hale, Customer Service Contact.

■ **6038** ■ **CADCentre Inc.**
10700 Richmond Ave., No. 300
Houston, TX 77042
Phone: (713)977-1225
Products: Computer software. **SIC:** 5045 (Computers, Peripherals & Software). **Est:** 1969. **Sales:** $3,000,000 (2000). **Emp:** 20. **Officers:** Robert Bishop, President; K.H. Reed, Controller; David Wheeldon, Marketing Mgr.

■ **6039** ■ **CADD Microsystems, Inc.**
6183 Grovedale Ct., Ste. 200
Alexandria, VA 22310
Phone: (703)719-0500 **Fax:** (703)719-0314
Products: Computers; Computer software; Peripheral computer equipment. **SIC:** 5045 (Computers, Peripherals & Software). **Officers:** Jeff Gravette, President.

■ 6040 ■ Cadec Corporation
8 E Perimeter Rd.
Londonderry, NH 03053
Phone: (603)668-1010   Fax: (603)623-0604
E-mail: info@cadec.com
URL: http://www.cadec.com
Products: On-board computers for the transportation and distribution industries. SIC: 5045 (Computers, Peripherals & Software). Sales: $9,000,000 (2000). Emp: 60. Officers: Les Dole, President.

■ 6041 ■ Call-A-Tech Inc.
2135 Market
Wheeling, WV 26003-2840
Phone: (304)233-1771   Fax: (304)233-1773
Products: Computers; Computer software; Peripheral computer equipment. SIC: 5045 (Computers, Peripherals & Software). Officers: Diane Higgs, President.

■ 6042 ■ Callback Software
265 Winn St.
Burlington, MA 01803
Phone: (781)273-3044
Free: (800)288-5383   Fax: (781)273-3053
Products: Sales automation software. SIC: 5045 (Computers, Peripherals & Software). Est: 1985. Sales: $2,000,000 (2000). Emp: 12.

■ 6043 ■ Cambridge Development Laboratory
86 West St.
Waltham, MA 02451-1110
Phone: (781)890-4640
Free: (800)637-0047   Fax: (781)890-2894
E-mail: marketing@coll-cambridge.com
URL: http://www.edumatch.com
Products: Software and hardware. SIC: 5045 (Computers, Peripherals & Software). Est: 1979. Emp: 20. Officers: Dominika Spetsmann, dspetsmann@cdl-cambridge.com.

■ 6044 ■ Cannon Technologies Inc.
505 Hwy. 169 N, Ste. 600
Minneapolis, MN 55441-6448
Phone: (612)544-7756   Fax: (612)544-6619
Products: Computers; Computer software; Peripheral computer equipment. SIC: 5045 (Computers, Peripherals & Software). Officers: Edward Cannon, President.

■ 6045 ■ Capital Business Systems Inc.
PO Box 2088
Napa, CA 94558
Phone: (707)252-9122   Fax: (707)252-6368
Products: Software. SIC: 5045 (Computers, Peripherals & Software). Sales: $1,000,000 (2000). Emp: 7. Officers: Edith Burch, CEO & President.

■ 6046 ■ Carolina Training Associates
PO Box 816
Sanford, NC 27331-0816
Phone: (919)776-8161   Fax: (919)774-6116
Products: Computers, peripherals, and software; Teaching aids. SIC: 5045 (Computers, Peripherals & Software). Officers: William Johnstone, President.

■ 6047 ■ Casey-Johnston Sales Inc.
4555 Las Positas Rd., Ste. B
Livermore, CA 94550-9615
Phone: (510)371-5900   Fax: (510)745-8669
Products: Computer-aided design equipment. SIC: 5045 (Computers, Peripherals & Software). Est: 1972. Sales: $10,000,000 (2000). Emp: 20. Officers: Donald Johnston Jr., President; Veronica Kyi, Controller.

■ 6048 ■ CCI Triad
3055 Triad Dr.
Livermore, CA 94550
Phone: (925)449-0606
Free: (888)463-4700   Fax: (925)449-1037
Products: Provides software for data processing, business information management solutions; Hardware for automotive aftermarket, hard lines and lumber industries. SIC: 5045 (Computers, Peripherals & Software).

■ 6049 ■ Cedar Co.
1502 North 150 West
Provo, UT 84604-2526
Phone: (801)375-3393
Products: Computers, peripherals, and software. SIC: 5045 (Computers, Peripherals & Software). Officers: Richard Thorpe, Owner.

■ 6050 ■ Cedar Group US Inc.
57 Wingate Street
Haverhill, MA 01832
Phone: (978)372-0770   Fax: (978)374-4382
Products: Software. SIC: 5045 (Computers, Peripherals & Software). Sales: $37,000,000 (1999). Emp: 400. Officers: Tom Rump, CEO; Ed Buscema, CFO.

■ 6051 ■ Centaurus Systems Inc.
4425 Cass St., Ste. A
San Diego, CA 92109
Phone: (858)270-4552
Products: Computer peripherals. SIC: 5045 (Computers, Peripherals & Software). Est: 1980. Sales: $2,100,000 (2000). Emp: 16. Officers: Robert D. Caldwell, CEO & President; Ruby M. Caldwell, CFO.

■ 6052 ■ Centel Information Systems Inc.
8725 Haggins Rd.
Chicago, IL 60631
Phone: (773)399-2735
Products: Computersoftware. SIC: 5045 (Computers, Peripherals & Software).

■ 6053 ■ Centenario Technologies, Inc.
14208 Atlanta Dr.
Laredo, TX 78041
Phone: (956)724-1887   Fax: (956)724-4123
Products: Computer hardware and software. SIC: 5045 (Computers, Peripherals & Software). Officers: Sergio Davila, President.

■ 6054 ■ Centerline Software Inc.
10 Fawcett St.
Cambridge, MA 02138-1110
Phone: (617)498-3000
Free: (800)922-3229   Fax: (617)868-5004
Products: Computer software. SIC: 5045 (Computers, Peripherals & Software). Est: 1987. Sales: $9,000,000 (2000). Emp: 60. Officers: Stephen Kaufer, President; Patricia Morton, VP of Finance & Admin.; Bob Cramer, VP of Marketing; Stephen Moran, Dir. of Data Processing; Betsey Rutnik, Dir of Human Resources.

■ 6055 ■ Centerspan Communications Corp.
7175 NW Evergreen Pkwy. Ste. 400
Hillsboro, OR 97124
Phone: (503)615-3200   Fax: (503)615-3300
Products: joysticks, PC game interface boards, other PC controllers and military simulation equipment. SIC: 5045 (Computers, Peripherals & Software). Sales: $19,400,000 (1999). Emp: 35. Officers: Frank G. Hausmann, CEO & President; Mark B. Conan, CFO.

■ 6056 ■ Central Computer Systems Inc.
3777 Stevens Creek Blvd.
Santa Clara, CA 95051
Phone: (408)248-5888   Fax: (408)241-0390
E-mail: central@centralcomputer.com
URL: http://www.centralcomputer.com
Products: Computers, peripherals, and software. SIC: 5045 (Computers, Peripherals & Software). Sales: $62,142,000 (2000). Emp: 66. Officers: Ann Lai, General Mgr.; Josephine Co, Accounting Manager.

■ 6057 ■ Central House Technologies
PO Box 1030
Plymouth, CA 95669
Phone: (209)245-5900   Fax: (209)245-5919
E-mail: info@centralhouse.com
URL: http://www.centralhouse.com
Products: Computer software for utilities. SIC: 5045 (Computers, Peripherals & Software). Est: 1994. Sales: $2,000,000 (2000). Emp: 6. Officers: Joseph Rohde, President & CFO.

■ 6058 ■ Certified Data Processing Inc.
1155 Main St.
South Weymouth, MA 02190-1514
Phone: (781)337-5495
Products: Computers, peripherals, and software. SIC: 5045 (Computers, Peripherals & Software). Officers: David Townson, President.

■ 6059 ■ Certified Ribbon Supply Inc.
335 Creekview Ter 100
Alpharetta, GA 30005-4697
Phone: (404)740-1600
Products: Computers, peripherals, and software. SIC: 5045 (Computers, Peripherals & Software). Officers: Peter Dukeman, President.

■ 6060 ■ Champion Computer Corp.
6421 Congress Ave.
Boca Raton, FL 33487
Phone: (561)997-2900
Free: (800)771-7000   Fax: (561)997-4043
Products: Computers Peripheral equipment; Software. SIC: 5045 (Computers, Peripherals & Software). Sales: $94,000,000 (2000). Emp: 125. Officers: Michael Baker, CEO; James Cullin, Controller.

■ 6061 ■ Chandler Enterprises
3925 Arroyo Seco
Schertz, TX 78154-2687
Products: Computers; Software; Peripheral computer equipment. SIC: 5045 (Computers, Peripherals & Software). Officers: Bill Chandler, Owner.

■ 6062 ■ Chester Technical Services Inc.
47 Clapboard Hill Rd.
Guilford, CT 06437-2200
Phone: (203)453-6209
Products: Computers, peripherals, and software. SIC: 5045 (Computers, Peripherals & Software). Officers: Douglas Rice, President.

■ 6063 ■ Chip Supply Inc.
7725 N Orange Blossom
Orlando, FL 32810
Phone: (407)298-7100   Fax: (407)290-0164
E-mail: eperrott@chipsupply.com
URL: http://www.chipsupply.com
Products: Computer chips; Silicon; Custom packaging; Die; Display Drivers. SIC: 5065 (Electronic Parts & Equipment Nec). Est: 1979. Sales: $25,000,000 (1999). Emp: 180. Officers: Edward J. Perrott, CEO & President; Dale Pullis, VP & CFO; Cynthia Hernandez, VP of Marketing & Sales, e-mail: chernandez@chipsupply.com; Debra Turner, e-mail: dturner@chipsupply.com.

■ 6064 ■ Choice Medical Distribution Inc.
9960 Corporate Campus Dr., Ste. 1000
Louisville, KY 40223
Phone: (502)357-6300
Free: (800)766-2464   Fax: (502)357-6400
E-mail: choice@choicesystemsinc.com
URL: http://www.choicesystemsinc.com
Products: Computer software for the medical field. SIC: 5045 (Computers, Peripherals & Software). Est: 1989. Emp: 65.

■ 6065 ■ Chrismann Computer Services Inc.
2601 W Dunlap Ave.
Phoenix, AZ 85021
Phone: (602)395-1500   Fax: (602)943-6663
E-mail: ccsdun@primenet.comm
URL: http://www.ccsaz.comm
Products: Computer cables. SIC: 5045 (Computers, Peripherals & Software). Est: 1986. Emp: 50. Officers: Robert Blanchard, Chairman of the Board.

■ 6066 ■ Chrismann Computer Services Inc.
2601 W Dunlap Ave. Ste 15
Phoenix, AZ 85021
Phone: (602)249-2385
Products: Sells, installs, repairs and networks computers, voice/date communication, and cables. SIC: 5045 (Computers, Peripherals & Software). Sales: $1,000,000 (2000). Emp: 17. Officers: R.W. Blanchard, President.

■ 6067 ■ CHS Electronics Inc.
2000 NW 84th Ave.
Miami, FL 33122
Phone: (305)908-7200 **Fax:** (305)908-7040
Products: Computers and accessories. **SIC:** 5045
(Computers, Peripherals & Software). **Sales:**
$4,756,400,000 (2000). **Emp:** 4,260. **Officers:** Claudio
E. Osorio, CEO, President & Chairman of the Board;
Craig S. Toll, CFO & Treasurer.

■ 6068 ■ CIC Systems Inc.
2425 Crown Pointe Executive Dr.
Charlotte, NC 28201-0000
Phone: (704)847-7800 **Free:** (800)274-1515
Products: Computers; Computer workstations and
related products. **SIC:** 5045 (Computers, Peripherals &
Software). **Sales:** $417,500,000 (2000). **Emp:** 400.
Officers: Frank Slovenec, President & COO; John
Chiste, CFO.

■ 6069 ■ Cirrus Technology Inc.
PO Box 1126
Nashua, NH 03061-1126
Phone: (603)882-2619 **Fax:** (603)882-9118
Products: Computers; Computer software; Peripheral
computer equipment. **SIC:** 5045 (Computers,
Peripherals & Software). **Officers:** David Zlotek,
President.

■ 6070 ■ CIS Corp.
6619 Joy Rd.
East Syracuse, NY 13057-1107
Phone: (315)432-1642
Products: Computer equipment. **SIC:** 5045
(Computers, Peripherals & Software).

■ 6071 ■ Citizen America Corp.
PO Box 4003
Santa Monica, CA 90411-4003
Phone: (310)453-0614
Free: (800)477-4683 **Fax:** (310)453-2814
URL: http://www.citizen-america.com
Products: Dot matrix printers, floppy disk drives, and
portable printers. **SIC:** 5045 (Computers, Peripherals &
Software). **Est:** 1984. **Sales:** $14,000,000 (2000).
Emp: 58. **Officers:** Hiroshi Takahashi, President;
Robert Thegze, Controller; Abderrahim Loh, Sr. VP of
Marketing & Sales; Phil Gurnee, Information Systems
Mgr.

■ 6072 ■ Clare Computer Solutions Inc.
2580 San Ramon Valley Blvd., Ste. B-107
San Ramon, CA 94583
Phone: (925)277-0690 **Fax:** (925)277-0694
Products: Computers. **SIC:** 5045 (Computers,
Peripherals & Software). **Sales:** $6,000,000 (2000).
Emp: 20. **Officers:** Anthony J. Barone, President;
Carol Eads, Controller.

■ 6073 ■ Frank Clark
202 Mustang Ct
Gambrills, MD 21054-1133
Phone: (410)551-9815 **Fax:** (410)551-5454
Products: Computers; Computer software; Peripheral
computer equipment. **SIC:** 5045 (Computers,
Peripherals & Software). **Officers:** Frank Clark, Owner.

■ 6074 ■ Classic Components Corp.
23605 Telo Ave.
Torrance, CA 90505-4028
Phone: (310)217-8020
Products: Intergrated circuits, passives and
peripherals. **SIC:** 5045 (Computers, Peripherals &
Software). **Sales:** $77,000,000 (2000). **Emp:** 250.
Officers: Jeff Klein, President; Nasser Schamsian,
CFO.

■ 6075 ■ CLG Inc.
3001 Spring Forest Rd.
Raleigh, NC 27604
Phone: (919)872-7920
Products: Computers. **SIC:** 5045 (Computers,
Peripherals & Software). **Sales:** $40,000,000 (2000).
Emp: 50. **Officers:** Dean Painter, CEO.

■ 6076 ■ Clinton Gas Marketing Inc.
4770 Indianola Ave.
Columbus, OH 43214
Phone: (614)888-9588
Products: Natural gas. **SIC:** 5171 (Petroleum Bulk
Stations & Terminals). **Sales:** $25,000,000 (1993).
Emp: 15. **Officers:** Jerry D. Jordan, CEO & Chairman
of the Board; Donald Nay, Exec. VP of Finance.

■ 6077 ■ CMOV, Inc.
100 S Marion Rd.
Sioux Falls, SD 57107
Phone: (605)338-6645
Free: (800)888-1649 **Fax:** (605)334-8521
E-mail: sales@cmov.com
URL: http://www.cmov.com
Products: Transportation computer software for
dispatch, billing, drivers log, financial accounting, and
shop maintenance. **SIC:** 5045 (Computers, Peripherals
& Software). **Est:** 1978. **Sales:** $1,000,000 (2000).
Emp: 15. **Officers:** Jay E. Mitchell. **Former Name:**
CMV Software Specialists Inc.

■ 6078 ■ Coaxis Inc. Insight Distribution
Systems
222 Schilling Cir., Ste. 275
Hunt Valley, MD 21031
Phone: (410)329-1158
Products: Computer hardware and software to
beverage distributors. **SIC:** 5045 (Computers,
Peripherals & Software).

■ 6079 ■ Color Group
6822 Del Monte Ave.
Richmond, CA 94805
Phone: (510)237-5577
Products: Computers and equipment and supplies.
SIC: 5045 (Computers, Peripherals & Software). **Est:**
1989. **Sales:** $1,500,000 (2000). **Emp:** 3. **Officers:**
Steve Shakrin, President.

■ 6080 ■ Comark Inc.
444 Scott Dr.
Bloomingdale, IL 60108
Phone: (630)351-9700 **Fax:** (630)351-7497
Products: Computers and software. **SIC:** 5045
(Computers, Peripherals & Software). **Est:** 1977.
Sales: $700,000,000 (2000). **Emp:** 600. **Officers:**
Charles S. Wolande, President; Dave Keilman, CFO;
Don Hoff, Dir. of Marketing; Chris Knox, Human
Resources Mgr.

■ 6081 ■ Comdisco Inc.
6111 N River Rd.
Rosemont, IL 60018-5159
Phone: (847)698-3000 **Fax:** (847)518-5440
Products: New and used computers and other high
technology equipment. **SIC:** 5045 (Computers,
Peripherals & Software). **Sales:** $3,243,000,000
(2000). **Emp:** 2,800. **Officers:** Jack Slevin, CEO &
Chairman of the Board; John J. Voskey, VP, CFO &
Treasurer.

■ 6082 ■ Comet Micro Systems Inc.
1301 Grandview Dr.
South San Francisco, CA 94080
Phone: (650)615-9123
Products: Computer peripherals. **SIC:** 5045
(Computers, Peripherals & Software). **Sales:** $300,000
(1993). **Emp:** 4.

■ 6083 ■ Comlink Inc.
1052 Melody Ln., No. 280
Roseville, CA 95678
Phone: (916)783-8885
Free: (800)433-3892 **Fax:** (916)783-2076
Products: Computers. **SIC:** 5065 (Electronic Parts &
Equipment Nec). **Est:** 1981. **Sales:** $15,000,000
(2000). **Emp:** 20. **Officers:** Wayne Stafford, President;
Shavnna Manner, CIO.

■ 6084 ■ Command Computer Maintenance
PO Box 3051
Springfield, MA 01101-3051
Phone: (413)782-9900
Products: Computers, peripherals, and software. **SIC:**
5045 (Computers, Peripherals & Software). **Officers:**
Larry Kardynal, Owner.

■ 6085 ■ Command Electronics Inc.
10100 Crosstown Cir.
Eden Prairie, MN 55344-3302
Phone: (612)943-1598 **Fax:** (612)943-1599
Products: Computer equipment, including hardware,
software, and supplies. **SIC:** 5045 (Computers,
Peripherals & Software). **Officers:** Richard Pomije,
President.

■ 6086 ■ Command Technology Inc.
404 Thames St.
Groton, CT 06340-3959
Phone: (860)445-0156 **Fax:** (860)446-2010
Products: Computers; Computer software; Peripheral
computer equipment. **SIC:** 5045 (Computers,
Peripherals & Software). **Officers:** Suzanne Boris,
President.

■ 6087 ■ Commercial and Industrial Design
Co. Inc.
1711 Langley Ave.
Irvine, CA 92614-5621
Phone: (949)261-5524 **Fax:** (949)261-6861
Products: Drive mounting hardware and enclosures.
SIC: 5045 (Computers, Peripherals & Software).
Sales: $400,000 (2000). **Emp:** 40. **Officers:** Jeff Wu,
President.

■ 6088 ■ Compar, Inc.
10301 Yellow Cir. Dr.
Minnetonka, MN 55343-9101
Phone: (612)945-0300
Free: (800)626-6727 **Fax:** (612)945-9611
URL: http://www.comparinc.com
Products: Computer hardware, software, and
peripherals. **SIC:** 5045 (Computers, Peripherals &
Software). **Est:** 1963.

■ 6089 ■ Compcom Enterprises Inc.
3185 Birchfield Trce
Marietta, GA 30068-3810
Phone: (404)971-6288 **Fax:** (404)971-3702
Products: Computers; Computer software; Peripheral
computer equipment; Communication systems and
equipment. **SICs:** 5045 (Computers, Peripherals &
Software); 5065 (Electronic Parts & Equipment Nec).
Officers: James Pounds, President.

■ 6090 ■ Competitive Edge
41806 Ford Rd.
Canton, MI 48187-3600
Phone: (734)981-8104 **Fax:** (734)981-8106
Products: Special purpose computers. **SIC:** 5045
(Computers, Peripherals & Software). **Est:** 1980. **Emp:**
7. **Officers:** Michael K. Sluder; Patricia Sluder.

■ 6091 ■ Compex Inc. (Anaheim, California)
4051 E La Palma Ave., Ste. A
Anaheim, CA 92807
Phone: (714)630-7302
Free: (800)279-8891 **Fax:** (714)237-7063
Products: Computer network hardware and software.
SIC: 5045 (Computers, Peripherals & Software).
Sales: $10,000,000 (2000). **Emp:** 15. **Officers:** Jason
Gu, President.

■ 6092 ■ Complete Computer Solutions of
New England
31 Syracuse Rd.
Nashua, NH 03060-1752
Phone: (603)880-0482
Products: Computers; Computer software; Peripheral
computer equipment. **SIC:** 5045 (Computers,
Peripherals & Software). **Officers:** Burton Janz,
Chairman of the Board.

■ 6093 ■ Comprehensive Systems Inc.
PO Box 760
Evergreen, CO 80439-0760
Phone: (303)697-9798
Free: (800)733-9798 **Fax:** (303)697-0209
Products: Computers; Peripheral computer
equipment. **SIC:** 5045 (Computers, Peripherals &
Software). **Officers:** Dick Johannsen, President.

■ 6094 ■ **CompuCom Systems Inc.**
7171 Forest Ln.
Dallas, TX 75230-2306
Phone: (972)856-3600
Free: (800)488-5266 **Fax:** (972)856-3200
Products: Microcomputer hardware, software, and peripheral products. **SIC:** 5045 (Computers, Peripherals & Software). **Sales:** $1,949,800,000 (2000). **Emp:** 4,300. **Officers:** Edward R. Anderson, CEO & President; M. Lazane Smith, Sr. VP & CFO.

■ 6095 ■ **Compucon Distributors Inc.**
701-1 Koehler Ave.
Ronkonkoma, NY 11779
Phone: (516)981-8810
Products: Interconnect devices. **SIC:** 5065 (Electronic Parts & Equipment Nec). **Officers:** William Miner, General Mgr.

■ 6096 ■ **CompuData Inc.**
10501 Drummond Rd.
Philadelphia, PA 19154
Phone: (215)824-3000 **Fax:** (215)824-4423
Products: Computers. **SIC:** 5045 (Computers, Peripherals & Software). **Sales:** $5,000,000 (2000). **Emp:** 50. **Officers:** Steven Ciarciello, CEO & President.

■ 6097 ■ **Compusol Inc.**
2832-C Walnut Ave.
Tustin, CA 92780
Phone: (714)734-1990
Free: (800)230-0314 **Fax:** (714)734-1980
Products: Computers. **SIC:** 5045 (Computers, Peripherals & Software). **Sales:** $2,500,000 (2000). **Emp:** 17. **Officers:** Joseph A. Traficante, President & Finance Officer.

■ 6098 ■ **Compusolve**
1135 Terminal Way, Ste. 108
Reno, NV 89502-2145
Phone: (702)324-6995 **Fax:** (702)324-4930
Products: Computers; Computer software; Peripheral computer equipment. **SIC:** 5045 (Computers, Peripherals & Software). **Officers:** Stan Bryant, Owner.

■ 6099 ■ **Compusystems Inc. South Carolina**
PO Box 4739
Rock Hill, SC 29732-6739
Phone: (803)366-8904 **Fax:** (803)366-8908
Products: Computers; Computer software; Peripheral computer equipment. **SIC:** 5045 (Computers, Peripherals & Software). **Officers:** C. Ray, President.

■ 6100 ■ **Computalabel International Ltd.**
29 Water St.
Newburyport, MA 01950-2763
Phone: (978)462-0993
Free: (800)284-0993 **Fax:** (978)468-9198
E-mail: info@computalabel.com
URL: http://www.computalabel.com
Products: Barcoding software for Macintosh systems. **SIC:** 5045 (Computers, Peripherals & Software). **Est:** 1995. **Sales:** $2,000,000 (2000). **Emp:** 6. **Officers:** Simon Virquhart, President. **Former Name:** Coastal International Inc.

■ 6101 ■ **Computer Banking Inc.**
4994 Waterport Way
Duluth, GA 30096-2927
Phone: (404)448-2990 **Fax:** (404)449-4808
Products: Computers; Computer software; Peripheral computer equipment. **SIC:** 5045 (Computers, Peripherals & Software). **Officers:** Charles Wall, President.

■ 6102 ■ **Computer Brokers of Kentucky**
2006 High Ridge Rd.
Louisville, KY 40207-1126
Phone: (502)897-1829
Products: Computers; Peripheral computer equipment. **SIC:** 5045 (Computers, Peripherals & Software). **Officers:** Joseph Lepping, President.

■ 6103 ■ **Computer Clearing House Inc.**
246 Commerce Dr.
Rochester, NY 14623
Phone: (716)334-0550 **Fax:** (716)334-2244
URL: http://www.computerclearinghouse.com
Products: Computer equipment and document management software. **SIC:** 5045 (Computers, Peripherals & Software). **Est:** 1983. **Sales:** $30,000,000 (2000). **Emp:** 50. **Officers:** Andy Wood, President; Greg Foley, CFO.

■ 6104 ■ **Computer Commodities Inc.**
7161 Shady Oak Rd.
Eden Prairie, MN 55344-3737
Phone: (612)942-0992 **Fax:** (612)942-8712
Products: Computers; Peripheral computer equipment. **SIC:** 5045 (Computers, Peripherals & Software). **Officers:** Robert Kern, President.

■ 6105 ■ **Computer Concepts Inc.**
PO Box 338
White River Junction, VT 05001-0338
Phone: (802)295-3089
Products: Computers, peripherals, and software. **SIC:** 5045 (Computers, Peripherals & Software). **Officers:** G. Kline, President.

■ 6106 ■ **Computer Corner Inc.**
4700 San Mateo Blvd. NE
Albuquerque, NM 87109-2422
Phone: (505)296-8424
Products: Computers; Computer software; Peripheral computer equipment. **SIC:** 5045 (Computers, Peripherals & Software). **Officers:** Carole Petranovich, President.

■ 6107 ■ **Computer Craft Co.**
119 North Rd.
Deerfield, NH 03037-1107
Phone: (603)463-5530
Products: Computers; Computer software; Peripheral computer equipment. **SIC:** 5045 (Computers, Peripherals & Software). **Officers:** Robert Berger, Owner.

■ 6108 ■ **Computer Data Systems, Inc.**
1 Curie Court
Rockville, MD 20850-4389
Phone: (301)921-7000 **Fax:** (301)948-9328
URL: http://www.cdsi.com
Products: Computer equipment and software. **SIC:** 5045 (Computers, Peripherals & Software). **Est:** 1968. **Sales:** $304,300,000 (2000). **Emp:** 3,900. **Officers:** Peter A. Bracken, CEO & President; Wyatt D. Tinsley, Exec. VP & CFO.

■ 6109 ■ **Computer Discounters**
5416 Veterans Blvd.
Metairie, LA 70003
Phone: (504)885-1635
Products: Computer hardware and peripherals. **SICs:** 5045 (Computers, Peripherals & Software); 5046 (Commercial Equipment Nec).

■ 6110 ■ **Computer Enterprises of Grand Rapids**
28 NW 4th St.
Grand Rapids, MN 55744-2714
Phone: (218)326-1897
Products: Computers, peripherals, and software. **SIC:** 5045 (Computers, Peripherals & Software). **Officers:** Tom Osborn, Owner.

■ 6111 ■ **Computer Equipment Warehouse Inc.**
7585 W 66th Ave.
Arvada, CO 80003-3909
Phone: (303)424-9710
Products: Computers and software. **SIC:** 5045 (Computers, Peripherals & Software). **Sales:** $12,000,000 (1994). **Emp:** 25. **Officers:** Joseph Calabria, President; Sharon Calabria, Accounting Manager.

■ 6112 ■ **Computer Graphics Distributing Co.**
620 E Diamond Ave.
Gaithersburg, MD 20877
Phone: (301)921-0011
Free: (800)548-5048 **Fax:** (301)990-1647
Products: Computer products, including hardware and software. **SIC:** 5045 (Computers, Peripherals & Software). **Est:** 1986. **Sales:** $15,000,000 (2000). **Emp:** 17. **Officers:** Lowell Nerenberg, President; Beverly Nerenberg, CFO.

■ 6113 ■ **Computer Hardware Maintenance Company Inc.**
PO Box 2025
Langhorne, PA 19047
Phone: (215)752-2221 **Fax:** (215)750-1510
Products: Computers and software. **SIC:** 5045 (Computers, Peripherals & Software). **Sales:** $105,000,000 (2000). **Emp:** 200. **Officers:** Jack Harding, President; Michael Jones, Controller.

■ 6114 ■ **Computer Lab International Inc.**
580 S Melrose St.
Placentia, CA 92870
Phone: (714)527-8000 **Fax:** (714)572-8008
URL: http://www.computerlab.com
Products: Computer peripherals for mid-range and mainframe systems. **SIC:** 5045 (Computers, Peripherals & Software). **Est:** 1988. **Sales:** $9,000,000 (2000). **Emp:** 35. **Officers:** Thomas Fei, President; T.C. Lin, Exec. VP; Mike Franke, Technical Dir.; Al Wilson, Dir. of Sales.

■ 6115 ■ **Computer Maintenance Service**
PO Box 17503
Nashville, TN 37217-0503
Phone: (615)831-0055 **Fax:** (615)931-9563
Products: Computers; Computer software; Peripheral computer equipment. **SIC:** 5045 (Computers, Peripherals & Software). **Officers:** Stephen Vire, President.

■ 6116 ■ **Computer Management Systems**
PO Box 407
Columbia City, IN 46725-1013
Phone: (219)248-2191
Free: (800)828-7218 **Fax:** (219)248-2801
E-mail: support@cmsmail.net
Products: Computers; Software; Peripheral computer equipment. **SIC:** 5045 (Computers, Peripherals & Software). **Est:** 1984. **Officers:** Rodney A. Reppen, President.

■ 6117 ■ **Computer and Networking Services Inc.**
14813 Morningside Dr.
Poway, CA 92064
Phone: (858)486-4707 **Fax:** (858)486-2461
Products: Industrial computer equipment. **SIC:** 5045 (Computers, Peripherals & Software). **Est:** 1993. **Sales:** $2,000,000 (2000). **Emp:** 9. **Officers:** Mathiew Vandenbergh, President.

■ 6118 ■ **Computer Parts and Services Inc.**
10205 51st Ave.
Plymouth, MN 55442
Phone: (612)553-1514
Products: Computers, parts, and components. **SIC:** 5045 (Computers, Peripherals & Software). **Sales:** $5,000,000 (2000). **Emp:** 50. **Officers:** Robert Kennedy, President.

■ 6119 ■ **Computer Plus, Inc.**
1101 Jefferson Rd.
Charleston, WV 25309-9780
Phone: (304)744-1832 **Fax:** (304)744-9300
E-mail: compplus3@newwave.net
URL: http://www.comppluswv.com
Products: Computers; Computer software; Peripheral computer equipment. **SIC:** 5045 (Computers, Peripherals & Software). **Est:** 1980. **Sales:** $2,000,000 (2000). **Emp:** 8. **Officers:** Jean Hall, President, e-mail: jeanhall@newwave.net.

■ 6120 ■ **Computer Products Center Inc.**
21 Morgan St.
Irvine, CA 92618
Phone: (949)588-9800 **Fax:** (949)588-5400
Products: Peripheral products including disk drives and CD-ROM. **SIC:** 5045 (Computers, Peripherals & Software). **Sales:** $50,000,000 (2000). **Emp:** 40. **Officers:** Winston Luu, President; Phyllis Luu, CFO.

■ **6121** ■ **Computer Products of Vermont Inc.**
14 Tracy Dr.
Shelburne, VT 05482
Phone: (802)862-1486 **Fax:** (802)985-3400
Products: Computer accessories. **SIC:** 5045
(Computers, Peripherals & Software). **Officers:** Joseph
St. George, President.

■ **6122** ■ **Computer Recyclers Inc.**
1005 N State St.
Orem, UT 84057-3153
Phone: (801)226-1892
Free: (800)635-2816 **Fax:** (801)226-2129
Products: Computers and software. **SIC:** 5045
(Computers, Peripherals & Software). **Sales:**
$10,000,000 (2000). **Emp:** 30. **Officers:** Tim Bird,
President; Steve Shaw, Controller.

■ **6123** ■ **Computer Research Inc.**
400 Southpoint Blvd., Ste. 300
Canonsburg, PA 15317
Phone: (724)745-0600 **Fax:** (724)745-8200
Products: Computerized accounting and record
keeping systems. **SIC:** 5045 (Computers, Peripherals &
Software). **Sales:** $6,800,000 (2000). **Emp:** 50.
Officers: James L. Schultz, CEO & Treasurer.

■ **6124** ■ **Computer Sales International Inc.**
10845 Olive Blvd., Ste. 300
St. Louis, MO 63141-7760
Phone: (314)997-7010
Free: (800)955-0960 **Fax:** (314)997-7844
URL: http://www.csileasing.com
Products: Computers. **SIC:** 5045 (Computers,
Peripherals & Software). **Est:** 1972. **Sales:**
$150,000,000 (2000). **Emp:** 200. **Officers:** Kenneth B.
Steinback, CEO & Chairman of the Board; E. William
Gillula, President & CFO.

■ **6125** ■ **Computer Service and Support**
PO Box 776
Rogers, AR 72757-0776
Phone: (501)631-0469 **Fax:** (501)631-9437
Products: Computers; Computer software; Peripheral
computer equipment. **SIC:** 5045 (Computers,
Peripherals & Software). **Officers:** James Deichman,
President.

■ **6126** ■ **Computer Source Inc.**
211 Broadway
Paducah, KY 42001-0711
Phone: (270)442-9726 **Fax:** (270)442-5058
URL: http://www.computer-source.com
Products: Computers; Computer software; Peripheral
computer equipment; Systems integration. **SIC:** 5045
(Computers, Peripherals & Software). **Est:** 1984. **Emp:**
10. **Officers:** Ed Rikel, President.

■ **6127** ■ **Computer Source Inc.**
3814 Williams Blvd.
Kenner, LA 70065
Phone: (504)443-4100
Products: Computer hardware and peripherals. **SIC:**
5045 (Computers, Peripherals & Software).

■ **6128** ■ **Computer Systems Inc.**
2819 S 125th Ave., Ste. 276
Omaha, NE 68144
Phone: (402)330-3600
Products: Computers and software. **SIC:** 5045
(Computers, Peripherals & Software). **Sales:**
$19,000,000 (2000). **Emp:** 40. **Officers:** Roger Able,
President.

■ **6129** ■ **Computer Systems Supply Corp.**
85 S Bragg St.
Alexandria, VA 22312-2731
Phone: (703)941-0336 **Fax:** (703)941-0355
E-mail: csscorp@csscorp.com
URL: http://www.csscorp.com/csscorp
Products: Computer hardware and software. **SIC:**
5045 (Computers, Peripherals & Software). **Est:** 1987.
Sales: $2,500,000 (2000). **Emp:** 4. **Officers:** Dennis
Akkor, President. **Alternate Name:** CSS Corp.

■ **6130** ■ **Computer Talk Inc.**
PO Box 148
Morrison, CO 80465
Phone: (303)697-5485
Products: Computer peripheral equipment; Develops
custom hardware, systems and software for special
robotic needs. **SIC:** 5045 (Computers, Peripherals &
Software). **Sales:** $500,000 (2000). **Emp:** 6. **Officers:**
William Barnes, President.

■ **6131** ■ **Computer Trading Co.**
2508 E 6th St.
Tucson, AZ 85716-4404
Phone: (520)323-3539
Free: (800)340-3539 **Fax:** (520)323-3184
E-mail: ctrading@flash.net
Products: Computers; Computer software; Peripheral
computer equipment. **SIC:** 5045 (Computers,
Peripherals & Software). **Est:** 1985. **Sales:** $3,000,000
(2000). **Emp:** 2. **Officers:** Luis Gomez, Owner.

■ **6132** ■ **Computer Trends**
PO Box 4757
Spartanburg, SC 29305-4757
Phone: (864)582-2021 **Fax:** (864)573-1185
E-mail: leasler@home.com
URL: http://www.ctrends.net
Products: Computer systems; components, repair
services. **SIC:** 5045 (Computers, Peripherals &
Software). **Est:** 1985. **Sales:** $800,000 (2000). **Emp:** 5.
Officers: Lawrence Easler, Owner; Jeff Easler,
Sales/Marketing Contact, e-mail: jeasler@ctrends.net.

■ **6133** ■ **Computers & Applications Inc.**
10623 NE 8th St.
Bellevue, WA 98004
Phone: (425)451-8077
URL: http://www.Betterguys.com
Products: Computers. **SIC:** 5045 (Computers,
Peripherals & Software). **Est:** 1981. **Sales:**
$19,000,000 (2000). **Emp:** 40. **Officers:** Telung
Chang, President.

■ **6134** ■ **Computers Unlimited Inc.**
2407 Montana Ave.
Billings, MT 59101-2336
Phone: (406)255-9500 **Fax:** (406)255-9595
E-mail: sales@cu.net
URL: http://www.cu.net
Products: Computers. **SIC:** 5045 (Computers,
Peripherals & Software). **Est:** 1978. **Sales:**
$20,000,000 (2000). **Emp:** 150. **Officers:** Michael
Schaer, President; Becky Madison, Accounting
Manager.

■ **6135** ■ **Computers of Willmar Inc.**
1401 1st St. S
Willmar, MN 56201-4221
Phone: (320)235-6425
Free: (800)262-6425 **Fax:** (320)231-1888
Products: Computers; Peripheral computer
equipment; Software. **SIC:** 5045 (Computers,
Peripherals & Software). **Officers:** Ted Olsen,
President.

■ **6136** ■ **ComputersAmerica Inc.**
PO Box 9127
San Rafael, CA 94912-9127
Phone: (415)257-1010
Free: (800)262-1010 **Fax:** 800-392-1010
Products: Computers. **SIC:** 5045 (Computers,
Peripherals & Software). **Est:** 1970. **Sales:**
$80,000,000 (2000). **Emp:** 152. **Officers:** John R.
Kalleen III, President; Michael Karl, Controller.

■ **6137** ■ **Computing Technology Inc.**
5314 S Yale Ave., Ste. 715
Tulsa, OK 74135-6274
Phone: (918)496-2570 **Fax:** (918)496-2578
Products: Computers; Computer software; Peripheral
computer equipment. **SIC:** 5045 (Computers,
Peripherals & Software). **Officers:** Randall Wohl,
President.

■ **6138** ■ **CompuTrend Systems Inc.**
938 Radecki Ct.
La Puente, CA 91748-1132
Phone: (818)333-5121 **Fax:** (818)369-6803
Products: Personal computers. **SIC:** 5065 (Electronic

Parts & Equipment Nec). **Est:** 1988. **Sales:**
$68,000,000 (2000). **Emp:** 200. **Officers:** Tom Tsao,
President; Crystal Wu, VP & Treasurer.

■ **6139** ■ **Comsel Corp.**
8453 N Tyco Rd.
Vienna, VA 22182
Phone: (703)734-3880 **Fax:** (703)734-3884
Products: Computer products, including hardware and
software. **SIC:** 5045 (Computers, Peripherals &
Software). **Est:** 1978. **Sales:** $2,500,000 (1999). **Emp:**
10. **Officers:** W. Douglas Ross, President.

■ **6140** ■ **Comstor**
14116 Newbrook Dr.
Chantilly, VA 20151
Phone: (703)802-0222 **Fax:** (703)802-1310
Products: Computers; Computer software; Peripheral
computer equipment. **SIC:** 5045 (Computers,
Peripherals & Software).

■ **6141** ■ **Comstor Technology Inc.**
3021 Hawkins Rd.
Warrenton, OR 97146-9758
Products: Data graphics equipment. **SIC:** 5045
(Computers, Peripherals & Software). **Sales:**
$43,000,000 (2000). **Emp:** 88. **Officers:** James Lewis,
President. **Former Name:** Comstor Productivity
Centers Inc.

■ **6142** ■ **Comtech Systems Brokers**
7860 NW 71st St.
Miami, FL 33166
Phone: (305)591-8248
Products: Computers. **SIC:** 5045 (Computers,
Peripherals & Software). **Sales:** $2,000,000 (1993).
Emp: 5. **Officers:** Jose Bernal, President.

■ **6143** ■ **Comtel Corp.**
PO Box 5034
Southfield, MI 48086
Phone: (313)358-2510 **Fax:** (313)352-2324
Products: Tapes audio and video recording;
Peripheral equipment for electronic computers. **SICs:**
5045 (Computers, Peripherals & Software); 5064
(Electrical Appliances—Television & Radio). **Est:** 1946.
Emp: 90. **Doing Business As:** Comtel Instruments
Co.

■ **6144** ■ **Comus Computer Corp.**
2502 Urbana Pke.
Ijamsville, MD 21754
Phone: (301)874-2900 **Fax:** (301)874-2994
E-mail: comus@comus.com
Products: Computers, peripherals, and software for
restaurants, bars, and clubs. **SIC:** 5045 (Computers,
Peripherals & Software). **Est:** 1976. **Emp:** 12. **Officers:**
Fred Ihrer, President, e-mail: fred@comus.com.

■ **6145** ■ **Comware Business Systems Inc.**
2440 E 88th Ave.
Anchorage, AK 99507-3812
Phone: (907)522-1188
Products: Computers, peripherals, and software. **SIC:**
5045 (Computers, Peripherals & Software). **Officers:**
Rod Stringer, President.

■ **6146** ■ **Concord Computing Corp.**
2525 Horizon Lake Dr.
Memphis, TN 38133
Phone: (901)371-8000
Products: Terminals and communications equipment
for transaction networks. **SIC:** 5045 (Computers,
Peripherals & Software). **Sales:** $44,600,000 (1991).
Emp: 350. **Officers:** Dan M. Palmer, CEO & President;
Thomas R. Renfro, CFO & Treasurer.

■ **6147** ■ **Concord Technologies Inc.**
600 Nickerson Rd.
Marlborough, MA 01752-4661
Phone: (508)460-9795
Products: Computer equipment, including scanners
and printers; Labels. **SICs:** 5045 (Computers,
Peripherals & Software); 5112 (Stationery & Office
Supplies). **Sales:** $3,800,000 (2000). **Emp:** 18.
Officers: Scott Arnold, President; Lisa Havens,
Controller.

■ **6148** ■ **Conductive Rubber Tech Inc.**
22125 17th Ave SE Ste. 117
Bothell, WA 98021
Phone: (425)486-8559 **Fax:** (425)487-0945
Products: Designs, and supplies silicone keypads, integrated assemblies and enclosures. **SICs:** 5045 (Computers, Peripherals & Software); 5065 (Electronic Parts & Equipment Nec).

■ **6149** ■ **Connecticut Micro Corp.**
PO Box 1067
Farmington, CT 06034-1067
Phone: (860)677-4344 **Fax:** (860)678-9331
Products: Computers; Computer software; Peripheral computer equipment. **SIC:** 5045 (Computers, Peripherals & Software). **Officers:** Leon Lemaire, Chairman of the Board.

■ **6150** ■ **Connections USA**
3404 Canton Rd.
Marietta, GA 30066-2615
Phone: (770)420-8990
Free: (888)878-2224 **Fax:** (770)420-8993
E-mail: support@connections-usa.com
URL: http://www.connections-usa.com
Products: Computers; Computer software; Peripheral computer equipment; Computer accessories. **SIC:** 5045 (Computers, Peripherals & Software). **Est:** 1988. **Sales:** $500,000 (2000). **Emp:** 8. **Officers:** Sidney Huff, President, e-mail: sid.huff@connections-usa.com. **Former Name:** Cable & Computer Connection.

■ **6151** ■ **Consan Inc.**
18750 Lake Dr., E
Chanhassen, MN 55317
Phone: (612)949-0053
Products: Tape drives and hard disk drives; Computer controllers. **SIC:** 5045 (Computers, Peripherals & Software). **Est:** 1992. **Sales:** $12,000,000 (2000). **Emp:** 60. **Officers:** Dennis Maetzold, President; Bob O'Callahah, Controller.

■ **6152** ■ **CONTEC Microelectronics USA**
744 S Hillview Dr.
Milpitas, CA 95035
Phone: (408)719-8200 **Fax:** (408)719-6750
Products: Data acquisition and control systems for PCs; Industrial PCs. **SIC:** 5045 (Computers, Peripherals & Software). **Officers:** Junichi Mizuno, President; Charles Lee, VP of Finance.

■ **6153** ■ **Contemporary Computer Wear**
201 Chester Ave.
San Francisco, CA 94132
Phone: (415)587-3002 **Fax:** (415)587-2229
Products: Protective dust covers for computers, typewriters; Computer keyboard skins. **SIC:** 5045 (Computers, Peripherals & Software). **Officers:** Joe D'Aura, President.

■ **6154** ■ **Continental Information Systems Corp.**
45 Broadway Atrium, Ste. 1105
New York, NY 10006-3007
Phone: (212)771-1000 **Fax:** (212)771-1100
Products: Computers; Telecommunications equipment; Aircraft. **SICs:** 5045 (Computers, Peripherals & Software); 5065 (Electronic Parts & Equipment Nec); 5088 (Transportation Equipment & Supplies). **Sales:** $18,400,000 (2000). **Emp:** 25. **Officers:** Michael L. Rosen, CEO & President; Jonah M. Meer, COO & CFO.

■ **6155** ■ **Continental Resources Inc. (Bedford, Massachusetts)**
PO Box 9137
Bedford, MA 01730
Phone: (781)275-0850
Free: (800)937-4688 **Fax:** (781)275-6563
Products: Computer peripheral equipment. **SICs:** 5045 (Computers, Peripherals & Software); 5065 (Electronic Parts & Equipment Nec). **Sales:** $251,000,000 (1999). **Emp:** 400. **Officers:** James McCann Jr., President; James Bunt, CFO.

■ **6156** ■ **CONVEX Computer Corp.**
PO Box 83351
Richardson, TX 75083-3851
Phone: (972)497-4000 **Fax:** (972)497-4441
Products: Super computers. **SIC:** 5045 (Computers, Peripherals & Software). **Est:** 1982. **Sales:** $198,100,000 (2000). **Emp:** 1,006. **Officers:** Robert J. Paluck, CEO, President & Chairman of the Board; William G. Bock, Sr. VP & CFO; James A. Balthazar, VP of Marketing; Terrence L. Rock, Sr. VP of Operations; John P. O'Loughlin.

■ **6157** ■ **Cony Computers Systems Inc.**
PO Box 712
Pine Brook, NJ 07058-0712
Phone: (973)276-0800
Products: Computers. **SIC:** 5045 (Computers, Peripherals & Software). **Sales:** $17,000,000 (2000). **Emp:** 10. **Officers:** Patrick Hegarty, President.

■ **6158** ■ **Cooper Industries Inc.**
67 Willowcrest Dr., Ste. 1441
Rochester, NY 14604
Phone: (716)256-0971 **Fax:** (716)244-6492
E-mail: cooperin@frontiernet.net
URL: http://www.frontiernet.net/cooperin
Products: Midrange computer hardware; Imaging and printing systems; Printing presses; Copiers; Network infrastructure equipment. **SICs:** 5045 (Computers, Peripherals & Software); 5065 (Electronic Parts & Equipment Nec). **Est:** 1976. **Officers:** Richard Cooper, President.

■ **6159** ■ **Copper Electronics**
3315 Gilmore Industrial Blvd.
Louisville, KY 40213
Phone: (502)968-8500 **Fax:** (502)968-0449
Products: CD-ROM products. **SIC:** 5045 (Computers, Peripherals & Software).

■ **6160** ■ **Coroant Inc.**
11400 Commerce Park Dr.
Reston, VA 20191
Phone: (703)758-7000
Products: Computer system integrators. **SIC:** 5045 (Computers, Peripherals & Software). **Sales:** $20,000,000 (2000). **Emp:** 220. **Officers:** Peter kusek, President; Michael Wiegold, CFO.

■ **6161** ■ **Corporate Computer Inc.**
11330 25th Ave. NE
Seattle, WA 98125
Phone: (206)365-3113 **Fax:** (206)365-2526
Products: Computers. **SIC:** 5045 (Computers, Peripherals & Software). **Est:** 1985. **Sales:** $1,000,000 (2000). **Emp:** 8. **Officers:** Fred Taucher, CEO & Chairman of the Board; Walt Taucher, President.

■ **6162** ■ **Corporate Computer Systems Inc.**
11925 Wentling Ave.
Baton Rouge, LA 70816-6057
Phone: (504)296-6800 **Fax:** (504)296-6839
Products: Computers; Computer software; Peripheral computer equipment. **SIC:** 5045 (Computers, Peripherals & Software). **Officers:** Gwynette Carley, President.

■ **6163** ■ **Corstar Business Computing Inc.**
50 Saw Mill River Rd.
Hawthorne, NY 10532
Phone: (914)347-2700 **Fax:** (914)347-5547
Products: Computers. **SIC:** 5045 (Computers, Peripherals & Software). **Est:** 1969. **Sales:** $15,000,000 (2000). **Emp:** 55. **Officers:** John Sitar, President; Thomas D. Duddy, VP of Marketing.

■ **6164** ■ **Cosmi Corp.**
2600 Homestead Pl.
Rancho Dominguez, CA 90220
Phone: (310)833-2000 **Fax:** (310)886-3500
Products: Prepackaged home office and games software; Home office and computer games software. **SIC:** 5045 (Computers, Peripherals & Software). **Sales:** $12,000,000 (1999). **Emp:** 80. **Officers:** George Johnson, President; Jeffrey Fryer, CFO.

■ **6165** ■ **COSMIC**
382 E Broad St.
Athens, GA 30602-4272
Phone: (706)542-3265 **Fax:** (706)542-4807
Products: NASA-developed software for engineering, graphics, manufacturing, networking, and design applications. **SIC:** 5045 (Computers, Peripherals & Software). **Emp:** 12.

■ **6166** ■ **CPS Technologies Inc.**
350 Rte. 46, Ste. 7
Rockaway, NJ 07866
Phone: (973)625-7900 **Fax:** (973)586-9478
E-mail: info@cpstech.net
URL: http://www.cpstech.net
Products: Personal computers and printers; Networks; Imagesetters. **SIC:** 5045 (Computers, Peripherals & Software). **Est:** 1991. **Sales:** $2,000,000 (2000). **Emp:** 7. **Officers:** John Attas, President; Brian Attas, Dir. of Information Systems; Brian Attas, Dir. of Information Systems.

■ **6167** ■ **Cranel Inc.**
8999 Gemini Pkwy.
Columbus, OH 43240-2010
Phone: (614)431-8000
Free: (800)288-3475 **Fax:** (614)431-8388
URL: http://www.cranel.com
Products: Computers, peripherals, and software. **SIC:** 5045 (Computers, Peripherals & Software). **Est:** 1985. **Sales:** $90,000,000 (2000). **Emp:** 175. **Officers:** Jim Wallace, President; John Lowden, VP of Finance; Mark Bramel, VP of Sales; Scott Slack, VP of Marketing, e-mail: sduckworthcontractornel.com;Bobbi Rhodebach, Customer Service Contact, e-mail: brhodebach@ cranel.com; Sandy Valvo, Human Resources Contact, e-mail: svalvocontractornel.com.

■ **6168** ■ **CSM International Corp.**
3545 Chain Bridge Rd., Ste. 210
Fairfax, VA 22030-2708
Phone: (703)591-2626 **Fax:** (703)591-1258
Products: Computer accessories, including workstations and equipment. **SIC:** 5045 (Computers, Peripherals & Software). **Officers:** William Cutler, President.

■ **6169** ■ **CTN Data Service Inc.**
PO Box 250
Hamilton, IN 46742-0250
Phone: (219)488-3388 **Fax:** (219)488-3737
Products: Computers; Computer software; Peripheral computer equipment. **SIC:** 5045 (Computers, Peripherals & Software). **Officers:** Norman Teegardin, President.

■ **6170** ■ **Cummins Electronics Company Inc.**
2851 State St.
Columbus, IN 47201
Phone: (812)377-8601
Products: On-board computers for the transportation and distribution industries. **SIC:** 5045 (Computers, Peripherals & Software). **Sales:** $320,000,000 (1994). **Emp:** 650. **Officers:** E.W. Booth, President.

■ **6171** ■ **Current Software**
3037 Dixie Hwy., Ste. 209
Covington, KY 41017-2364
Phone: (606)341-0702 **Fax:** (606)344-5644
Products: Computer software. **SIC:** 5045 (Computers, Peripherals & Software). **Officers:** Tom Wisenall, Owner.

■ **6172** ■ **Current Works Inc.**
1000 N Rand Rd Ste. 123
Wauconda, IL 60084
Phone: (847)526-1121 **Fax:** (847)526-1141
Products: cificdevices and educational software. **SIC:** 5045 (Computers, Peripherals & Software).

■ **6173** ■ **Cutting Edge Technology Inc.**
26071 Merit Circle, Ste. 108
Laguna Hills, CA 92653
Phone: (949)582-1946
Free: (800)722-7748 **Fax:** (949)582-3706
Products: Computer boards. **SIC:** 5045 (Computers, Peripherals & Software). **Sales:** $8,500,000 (2000). **Emp:** 7. **Officers:** Sonny Burkett, President; Angela Yee, CFO.

■ 6174 ■ CWC Group Inc.
290 Paseo Sonrisa
Walnut, CA 91789
Phone: (909)598-9366 Fax: (909)598-8046
Products: Computer peripherals. SIC: 5045
(Computers, Peripherals & Software). Sales:
$2,000,000 (2000). Emp: 6. Officers: Ken C. Chao,
CEO & President; Angleo Chao, CFO.

■ 6175 ■ D and H Distributing Co.
2525 N 7th St.
PO Box 5967
Harrisburg, PA 17110
Phone: (717)236-8001
Free: (800)877-1200 Fax: (717)255-7838
URL: http://www.dandh.com
Products: Computer hardware and software; Security
products; Home entertainment. SICs: 5045
(Computers, Peripherals & Software); 5063 (Electrical
Apparatus & Equipment). Est: 1918. Sales:
$600,000,000 (2000). Emp: 375. Officers: Izzy
Schwab, CEO; Robert J. Miller, CFO; Gary Brothers,
President.

■ 6176 ■ Daisytek Inc.
500 N Central Expwy.
Plano, TX 75074
Phone: (972)881-4700
Free: (800)527-4212 Fax: (972)881-1200
E-mail: info@daisytek.com
URL: http://www.daisytek.com
Products: Computer supplies and accessories. SICs:
5045 (Computers, Peripherals & Software); 5112
(Stationery & Office Supplies). Est: 1977. Sales:
$800,000,000 (2000). Emp: 1,120. Officers: David A.
Heap, CEO & Chairman of the Board; Mark C. Layton,
President & CFO.

■ 6177 ■ Dallas Digital Corp.
624 Krona Dr., No. 160
Plano, TX 75074
Phone: (214)424-2800
Free: (800)842-6333 Fax: (972)422-4842
E-mail: sales@daldig.com
URL: http://www.daldig.com
Products: Document imaging technologies; Storage
management solutions. SIC: 5045 (Computers,
Peripherals & Software). Est: 1981. Sales:
$30,000,000 (2000). Emp: 52. Officers: Roger Scott,
President; Carol Polasky, VP of Finance.

■ 6178 ■ Dalton Computer Services Inc.
PO Box 2469
Dalton, GA 30722-2469
Phone: (706)259-3327 Fax: (706)259-7944
Products: Computers; Computer software; Peripheral
computer equipment. SIC: 5045 (Computers,
Peripherals & Software). Officers: Gerald Merritt,
President.

■ 6179 ■ Danka E.B.S.
411 Waverly Oaks Rd., Bldg. 1
Waltham, MA 02454-8414
Phone: (617)894-6283 Fax: (617)894-1545
Products: Computers and software. SIC: 5045
(Computers, Peripherals & Software). Sales: $800,000
(2000). Emp: 18.

■ 6180 ■ Dartek Corp.
175 Ambassador Dr.
Naperville, IL 60540
Phone: (630)941-1000
Products: Computers; Monitors; Keyboards; Printers.
SIC: 5045 (Computers, Peripherals & Software).

■ 6181 ■ Dash Inc.
8226 Nieman Rd.
Lenexa, KS 66214
Phone: (913)888-6555
Free: (800)844-7620 Fax: (913)888-9559
URL: http://www.dashdist.com
Products: Computers. SIC: 5045 (Computers,
Peripherals & Software). Est: 1987. Sales:
$15,000,000 (2000). Emp: 35. Officers: David Allen,
CEO & President; Rick Temple, Controller.

■ 6182 ■ DATA COM
11205 S Main St., #109
Houston, TX 77025-5642
Phone: (713)665-5752 Fax: (713)665-5556
Products: Computer supplies. SIC: 5045 (Computers,
Peripherals & Software). Sales: $3,000,000 (2000).
Emp: 10. Officers: B.J. Selmon, President.

■ 6183 ■ Data Professionals
10716 N Westlakes Dr.
Ft. Wayne, IN 46804-8601
Products: Computers; Computer software; Peripheral
computer equipment. SIC: 5045 (Computers,
Peripherals & Software). Officers: Jon Alger,
President.

■ 6184 ■ Data Source Media Inc.
PO Box 4397
Lincoln, NE 68504
Phone: (402)466-3342 Fax: (402)466-0441
URL: http://www.dsmedia.com
Products: Computer supplies, including keyboards
and disk drives. SIC: 5045 (Computers, Peripherals &
Software). Est: 1973. Sales: $15,000,000 (2000).
Emp: 22. Officers: Mark H. Tallman, President; Linda
Clark, Bookkeeper; Lynn Frankowski, Manager.

■ 6185 ■ Data Tech Services Inc.
PO Box 82
Bryant, AR 72089-0082
Phone: (501)847-8998 Fax: (501)847-9010
E-mail: dts@ipa.net
URL: dts-computers.com
Products: Computers; Computer software; Peripheral
computer equipment. SIC: 5045 (Computers,
Peripherals & Software). Est: 1980. Officers: Robert
White, President.

■ 6186 ■ Database Computer Systems Inc.
RR 1, Box 228
Lynchburg, VA 24502-9701
Phone: (804)385-6020 Fax: (804)385-9098
Products: Computers; Computer software; Peripheral
computer equipment. SIC: 5045 (Computers,
Peripherals & Software). Officers: John Garner,
President.

■ 6187 ■ DataCal Corp.
531 E Elliot Rd.
Chandler, AZ 85225
Phone: (480)813-3100
Free: (800)223-0123 Fax: (480)545-7212
Products: Commercial printing; Computer and
software accessories and computer training materials.
SIC: 5045 (Computers, Peripherals & Software).
Sales: $3,000,000 (2000). Emp: 21. Officers: JimL
Lunt, CEO & President; Jim Lunt, Chairman of the
Board & Finance Officer.

■ 6188 ■ Datalink Corp.
7423 Washington Ave. S
Minneapolis, MN 55439-2410
Phone: (612)944-3462
Free: (800)448-6314 Fax: (612)944-7869
E-mail: info@datalink.com
URL: http://www.datalink.com
Products: Mass storage peripherals; Tape libraries;
Jukeboxes, including optical disk and CD-ROM;
Document imaging products, including scanners, high
resolution monitors, and image processing boards.
SIC: 5045 (Computers, Peripherals & Software).
Sales: $60,000,000 (2000). Emp: 65. Officers:
Stanley Clothier, Chairman of the Board; Greg Meland;
Bob Devere.

■ 6189 ■ Datamatics Management Services,
Inc.
330 New Brunswick Ave.
Fords, NJ 08863
Phone: (732)738-9600
Free: (800)673-0366 Fax: (732)738-9603
E-mail: info@Datamaticsinc.com
Products: Computer software for time and attendance.
SIC: 5045 (Computers, Peripherals & Software). Est:
1966. Sales: $2,500,000 (2000). Emp: 15. Officers: G.
Tollow, Vice President, e-mail: NCH40@Hotmail.com.

■ 6190 ■ Davis Associates Inc.
PO Box 803
Parker, CO 80134-0803
Phone: (303)841-8648 Fax: (303)841-9329
Products: Computers; Computer software; Peripheral
computer equipment. SIC: 5045 (Computers,
Peripherals & Software). Officers: Donald Davis,
President.

■ 6191 ■ DCE Corp.
5 Hillandale Ave.
Stamford, CT 06902-2843
Phone: (203)358-3940
Free: (800)326-3821 Fax: (203)358-3944
Products: Computer hardware, including fax servers.
SIC: 5065 (Electronic Parts & Equipment Nec). Est:
1969. Sales: $15,000,000 (2000). Emp: 90. Officers:
Eric Shepherd, CEO & President; Mike Greasby, CFO.

■ 6192 ■ Decision Data Service Inc.
PO Box 3004
Frazer, PA 19355-0704
Phone: (215)674-3300
Products: Computer equipment and parts. SIC: 5045
(Computers, Peripherals & Software). Est: 1969.
Sales: $195,000,000 (2000). Emp: 1,600. Officers:
Joseph J. Kroger, CEO & President; Anthony Bamber,
VP & CFO; Larry Scott, Dir. of Systems; Ernie Bock,
Vice President of Human Resources.

■ 6193 ■ Decision Support Systems Inc.
380 S State Rd., Ste. 1004-117
Altamonte Springs, FL 32714
Phone: (407)778-6447 Fax: (407)915-9500
Products: Hardware for computers, including monitors
and keyboards. SIC: 5045 (Computers, Peripherals &
Software). Est: 1982. Sales: $500,000 (2000). Emp: 8.
Officers: Robert E. Jackson, President; Robert Seville,
CFO; Paul Snyder, Dir. of Marketing.

■ 6194 ■ Deerfield Data Systems Inc.
267 Amherst Rd.
PO Box 471
Sunderland, MA 01375-0471
Phone: (413)665-3742
Free: (800)444-5049 Fax: (413)665-7360
E-mail: sales@deerfield-data.com
URL: http://www.deerfield-data.com
Products: Computers; Computer software; Peripheral
computer equipment. SIC: 5045 (Computers,
Peripherals & Software). Est: 1981. Sales:
$20,000,000 (2000). Emp: 30. Officers: Cynthia
Demers, VP of Marketing & Sales, e-mail: eerny@
deerfield-sata.com. Also Known by This Acronym:
DDS.

■ 6195 ■ Delker Electronics Inc.
PO Box 897
Smyrna, TN 37167-0897
Phone: (615)459-2636 Fax: (615)459-0038
Products: Computers; Computer software; Peripheral
computer equipment. SIC: 5045 (Computers,
Peripherals & Software). Officers: Thomas Delker,
President.

■ 6196 ■ Dell Computer Corp. Dell Marketing
L.P.
1 Dell Way
Round Rock, TX 78682-0001
Phone: (512)338-4400
Products: Computers. SIC: 5045 (Computers,
Peripherals & Software). Sales: $92,000,000 (2000).
Emp: 186. Officers: Rob Howe, Vice President.

■ 6197 ■ Delta Products Corp. (Nogales,
Arizona)
1650 W Calle Plata
Nogales, AZ 85621
Phone: (520)761-1111 Fax: (520)281-0776
Products: Electronic components, power supplies,
transformers and computer monitors. SICs: 5045
(Computers, Peripherals & Software); 5065 (Electronic
Parts & Equipment Nec).

■ 6198 ■ Dennis and Schwab Inc.
505 E 1st St., Ste. B
Tustin, CA 92780
Phone: (714)505-1270 Fax: (714)505-4557
Products: Computer peripheral equipment. SIC: 5045

(Computers, Peripherals & Software). **Sales:** $1,200,000 (2000). **Emp:** 6. **Officers:** Dennis Doi, President.

■ **6199** ■ **John J. Desfosses and Associates**
1728 Virginia Beach Blvd., Ste. 115
Virginia Beach, VA 23454-4536
Phone: (757)491-2882 **Fax:** (757)491-1547
Products: New and used peripherals and systems; Personal computers. **SIC:** 5045 (Computers, Peripherals & Software). **Officers:** John Desfosses, President.

■ **6200** ■ **Design Data Systems Corp.**
13830 58th St. N, Ste. 401
Clearwater, FL 33760-3720
Phone: (727)539-1077
Free: (800)655-6598 **Fax:** (727)539-8042
E-mail: info@designdatasystems.com
URL: http://www.designdatasystems.com
Products: Computer software. **SIC:** 5045 (Computers, Peripherals & Software). **Est:** 1988. **Sales:** $5,000,000 (2000). **Emp:** 50. **Officers:** Michael R. Meli, President.

■ **6201** ■ **Design Systems Inc.**
PO Box 25964
Oklahoma City, OK 73125-0964
Phone: (405)341-7353
Products: Computers, peripherals, and software. **SIC:** 5045 (Computers, Peripherals & Software). **Officers:** Patrick Young, President.

■ **6202** ■ **Deuteronomy Inc.**
224 S 5th Ave.
City of Industry, CA 91746
Phone: (626)369-4181
Free: (800)775-1953 **Fax:** (626)961-7462
Products: Computers and peripherals, including notebook computers and computer systems. **SIC:** 5045 (Computers, Peripherals & Software). **Sales:** $6,000,000 (2000). **Emp:** 15. **Officers:** Diane Wang, President.

■ **6203** ■ **Develcon Electronics Inc.**
1431 Bonnie Brae St.
Hermosa Beach, CA 90254-3207
Products: Computer networking communications products, including token rings, routers, and bridges. **SIC:** 5045 (Computers, Peripherals & Software). **Sales:** $13,000,000 (2000). **Emp:** 120. **Officers:** Geoffrey H. Bennett, CEO & President; Fran Sanda, Vice President.

■ **6204** ■ **Development Through Self-Reliance Inc.**
6679-P Santa Barbera Rd.
Elkridge, MD 21075
Phone: (410)579-4508 **Fax:** (410)579-8412
Products: Computers and software. **SIC:** 5045 (Computers, Peripherals & Software). **Sales:** $9,300,000 (2000). **Emp:** 20. **Officers:** Sally G. Smith, President; Donnie Orndoff, Dir. of Admin.

■ **6205** ■ **Deverger Systems Inc.**
7 1/2 Biltmore Ave.
Asheville, NC 28801-3603
Phone: (704)253-2255
Products: Computers, peripherals, and software. **SIC:** 5045 (Computers, Peripherals & Software). **Officers:** Derrick Deverger, President.

■ **6206** ■ **Diab Data Inc.**
323 Vintage Park Dr. Ste. C
Foster City, CA 94404
Phone: (650)571-1700 **Fax:** (650)571-9068
Products: Computer software. **SIC:** 5045 (Computers, Peripherals & Software). **Sales:** $16,000,000 (2000). **Emp:** 30. **Officers:** Sven Brehmer, President.

■ **6207** ■ **Diamond Flower Electric Instruments Company (USA) Inc.**
135 Main Ave.
Sacramento, CA 95838-2041
Phone: (916)568-1234 **Fax:** (916)568-1233
URL: http://www.dfiusa.com
Products: Computer hardware including printers, monitors, and computer boards. **SIC:** 5045 (Computers, Peripherals & Software). **Est:** 1981. **Sales:** $30,000,000 (1999). **Emp:** 150. **Officers:** David

Lu, President; Kent Greenough, VP of Marketing; Larry Armstrong, Information Systems Mgr.

■ **6208** ■ **Diamond Systems Corp.**
450 San Antonio Rd., Ste. 46
Palo Alto, CA 94306
Phone: (650)813-1100
Products: Computer peripheral circuit boards. **SIC:** 5045 (Computers, Peripherals & Software). **Sales:** $2,000,000 (2000). **Emp:** 9. **Officers:** Jonathan Miller, President; Melissa Ezzet, Finance Officer.

■ **6209** ■ **Dickens Data Systems Inc.**
1175 Northmeadow Pkwy., Ste. 150
Roswell, GA 30076-4922
Phone: (404)475-8860 **Fax:** (404)442-7525
Products: Computers. **SIC:** 5045 (Computers, Peripherals & Software). **Est:** 1981. **Sales:** $27,000,000 (2000). **Emp:** 120. **Officers:** Gordon Dickens, President; Norman Wickes, CFO; Barry Johnson, VP of Sales; Kathleen Elmore, Personnel Mgr.

■ **6210** ■ **Digital Storage Inc.**
7611 Green Meadows Dr.
Lewis Center, OH 43035-9445
Phone: (614)548-7179
Free: (800)232-3475 **Fax:** (614)548-7978
URL: http://www.digitalstorage.com
Products: Data storage. **SIC:** 5045 (Computers, Peripherals & Software). **Est:** 1986. **Sales:** $120,000,000 (2000). **Emp:** 85. **Officers:** George Babyak, President; Dave Burke, VP of Finance; Bill Damko, VP Marketing & Development; Jim Klebes, VP of Information Systems.

■ **6211** ■ **Dirt Cheap Drives Inc.**
3716 Timber Dr.
Dickinson, TX 77539
Phone: (281)534-4140
Products: Computer disk drives; Mail-order house. **SIC:** 5045 (Computers, Peripherals & Software). **Sales:** $24,000,000 (2000). **Emp:** 50. **Officers:** Albert Timme, Director.

■ **6212** ■ **Disc Distributing Corp.**
390 N Sepulveda Blvd., Ste. 3000
El Segundo, CA 90245
Phone: (310)322-6700
Free: (800)688-4545 **Fax:** (310)607-8079
Products: Computer supplies and accessories. **SICs:** 5045 (Computers, Peripherals & Software); 5112 (Stationery & Office Supplies). **Sales:** $115,000,000 (2000). **Emp:** 80. **Officers:** Carrie Pollare, President; Darin Salk, VP of Finance.

■ **6213** ■ **DistribuPro Inc.**
1288 McKay Dr.
San Jose, CA 95131
Phone: (408)922-2600 **Fax:** (408)922-2665
Products: Accounting and networking software. **SIC:** 5045 (Computers, Peripherals & Software). **Sales:** $8,000,000 (2000). **Emp:** 35. **Officers:** Mark Seidman, General Mgr.

■ **6214** ■ **Diversified Data Products Inc.**
1995 Highland Dr., Ste. D
Ann Arbor, MI 48108-2230
Phone: (734)761-7222
Products: Computer supplies. **SIC:** 5045 (Computers, Peripherals & Software).

■ **6215** ■ **DMACS International Corp.**
2 Perimeter Park S, 140 E Twr.
Birmingham, AL 35243
Phone: (205)967-2153
Products: Software and related products. **SIC:** 5045 (Computers, Peripherals & Software). **Sales:** $3,000,000 (2000). **Emp:** 25. **Officers:** Lester W. Piot Jr., President; Leslie P. Leath, CFO.

■ **6216** ■ **DMS Systems Corp.**
PO Box 8049
Rocky Mount, NC 27804-1049
Phone: (252)985-2500 **Fax:** (252)985-1900
E-mail: info@dms-systems.com
URL: http://www.dms-systems.com
Products: Computers; Computer software; Peripheral computer equipment. **SIC:** 5045 (Computers,

Peripherals & Software). **Est:** 1984. **Sales:** $4,000,000 (2000). **Emp:** 12. **Officers:** Grady Davis, President.

■ **6217** ■ **Doctor Computerized Systems**
100 Centerview Dr., Ste. 250
Birmingham, AL 35216-3749
Phone: (205)978-1088
Products: Computers, peripherals, and software. **SIC:** 5045 (Computers, Peripherals & Software). **Officers:** Richard Roberts, President.

■ **6218** ■ **Dollar Computer Corp.**
1809 E Dyer Rd., Ste. 304
Santa Ana, CA 92705
Phone: (949)975-0552
Free: (800)634-1415 **Fax:** (949)975-1560
E-mail: sales@dollarcomputer.com
URL: http://www.dollarcomputer.com
Products: Computers. **SIC:** 5045 (Computers, Peripherals & Software). **Est:** 1993. **Sales:** $10,000,000 (2000). **Emp:** 24.

■ **6219** ■ **Dopar Support Systems Inc.**
3011 W Grand Blvd., 322 Fisher Bldg.
Detroit, MI 48202-3011
Phone: (313)871-0990
Free: (800)752-6744 **Fax:** (313)871-9206
Products: Computers and peripherals. **SIC:** 5045 (Computers, Peripherals & Software). **Sales:** $7,000,000 (2000). **Emp:** 9. **Officers:** Douglas M. Doggett, President.

■ **6220** ■ **Douglas Stewart Co.**
2402 Advance Rd.
Madison, WI 53704
Phone: (608)221-1155
Free: (800)279-2795 **Fax:** (608)221-5217
Products: Computers and software. **SIC:** 5045 (Computers, Peripherals & Software). **Sales:** $40,300,000 (2000). **Emp:** 90.

■ **6221** ■ **DP Equipment Marketing Inc.**
7595 E Gray Rd., No. 1
Scottsdale, AZ 85260
Phone: (602)948-2720 **Fax:** (602)948-0615
URL: http://www.genesis-equipment.com
Products: Pre-press equipment. **SIC:** 5045 (Computers, Peripherals & Software). **Est:** 1979. **Sales:** $5,000,000 (2000). **Emp:** 15. **Officers:** John Wanner, President.

■ **6222** ■ **DS Design**
1157 Executive Cir., Ste. D
Cary, NC 27511
Phone: (919)319-1770
Free: (800)745-4037 **Fax:** (919)460-5983
Products: Software. **SIC:** 5045 (Computers, Peripherals & Software). **Sales:** $500,000 (2000). **Emp:** 1. **Officers:** Jane Scarano, President.

■ **6223** ■ **DsgnHaus, Inc.**
1375 Kings Hwy., Ste. E
Fairfield, CT 06430
Phone: (203)367-1993 **Fax:** (203)367-1860
E-mail: webmaster@dsgnhaus.com
URL: http://www.fordesigners.com
Products: Digital fonts; Clip art; Stock photography; Books. **SICs:** 5045 (Computers, Peripherals & Software); 5192 (Books, Periodicals & Newspapers). **Est:** 1990. **Emp:** 20. **Officers:** Mark Solsburg, President; Kevin Kiley, CFO. **Former Name:** FontHaus Inc.

■ **6224** ■ **DSi**
20A Oak Branch Dr.
Greensboro, NC 27407-2145
Phone: (336)294-0141 **Fax:** (336)294-4636
E-mail: nstella@netdsi.com
URL: http://www.netdsi.com
Products: Networking equipment sales, design, and service. **SIC:** 5045 (Computers, Peripherals & Software). **Est:** 1986. **Emp:** 38. **Officers:** T. Collins, President. **Former Name:** Datanet Services Inc.

■ **6225** ■ **DTK Computer Inc.**
770 Epperson Dr.
La Puente, CA 91748-1336
Phone: (626)810-0098 **Fax:** (626)810-0090
Products: Computers. **SIC:** 5045 (Computers,

Peripherals & Software). **Est:** 1981. **Sales:** $200,000,000 (2000). **Emp:** 300. **Officers:** Duke Liao, President; Dan Tsuei, CFO.

■ 6226 ■ **Dubl-Click Software Corp.**
20310 Empire Blvd., Ste. A102
Bend, OR 97701
Phone: (541)317-0355
E-mail: info@dublclick.com
Products: Computer software. **SIC:** 5045 (Computers, Peripherals & Software). **Est:** 1985. **Sales:** $1,000,000 (2000). **Emp:** 1. **Officers:** Cliff Joyce, President.

■ 6227 ■ **Durr and Partners**
57 Punkhorn Pl.
Mashpee, MA 02649
Phone: (508)477-5111
Products: Software. **SIC:** 5045 (Computers, Peripherals & Software). **Sales:** $300,000 (1993). **Emp:** 3. **Officers:** Bruno G. Durr, Mng. Partner.

■ 6228 ■ **Dyna Marketing**
10211 Foxrow, Ste. 101
Houston, TX 77064
Phone: (281)890-7107 **Fax:** (281)890-8051
Products: Computer software. **SIC:** 5045 (Computers, Peripherals & Software).

■ 6229 ■ **Dyna Marketing**
1425 W Pioneer Dr., Ste. 147
Irving, TX 75061
Phone: (972)259-2744 **Fax:** (972)251-1377
Products: Computer software. **SIC:** 5045 (Computers, Peripherals & Software).

■ 6230 ■ **Dynabit USA Inc.**
501 E Kennedy Blvd., Ste. 750
Tampa, FL 33602-5200
Phone: (813)222-2050
Products: Computer products, including mainframes and software. **SIC:** 5045 (Computers, Peripherals & Software). **Sales:** $4,000,000 (2000). **Emp:** 10. **Officers:** Daniel Aegerter, Partner; Sabina Aegerter, Partner.

■ 6231 ■ **Dynamic Computer Concepts**
8401 Corporate Dr., Ste. 460
Landover, MD 20785
Phone: (301)731-4393
Free: (800)346-0256 **Fax:** (301)731-3224
Products: Peripheral computer equipment; Computer software. **SIC:** 5045 (Computers, Peripherals & Software). **Est:** 1987. **Sales:** $2,000,000 (2000). **Emp:** 25. **Officers:** Rodney Drummond, President; John A. Laur, Vice President.

■ 6232 ■ **Eakins Associates Inc.**
67 E Evelyn Ave.
Mountain View, CA 94041
Phone: (415)969-5109
Free: (800)7EA-KINS **Fax:** (415)961-2130
E-mail: info@eos.com
URL: http://www.eos.com
Products: Computer equipment and supplies, including software and hardware. **SIC:** 5045 (Computers, Peripherals & Software). **Est:** 1972. **Sales:** $24,000,000 (1999). **Emp:** 40. **Officers:** Gil Eakins, President; Sandy Eakins, Vice President; David Phillips, Dir. of Mktg. & Sales.

■ 6233 ■ **E.A.P. Co.**
PO Box 14
Keller, TX 76248
Phone: (817)498-4242
Products: Business, educational, religious, financial, communications, and utility software. **SIC:** 5045 (Computers, Peripherals & Software). **Est:** 1976.

■ 6234 ■ **Eastes Distributing**
PO Box 534
Grabill, IN 46741-0534
Phone: (219)627-2905 **Fax:** (219)627-2905
Products: Computers; Computer software; Peripheral computer equipment. **SIC:** 5045 (Computers, Peripherals & Software). **Officers:** John Eastes, Owner.

■ 6235 ■ **ECW Enterprises Inc.**
740 N Mary Ave.
Sunnyvale, CA 94086
Phone: (408)245-5836
Free: (800)827-5836 **Fax:** (408)245-3108
Products: Computer systems. **SIC:** 5045 (Computers, Peripherals & Software). **Est:** 1986. **Sales:** $12,000,000 (2000). **Emp:** 40. **Officers:** Pei-Lin Tsai, President; Echo Tsai, Vice President; Echo Tsai, Vice President.

■ 6236 ■ **Educational Technology Inc.**
2224 Hewlett
Merrick, NY 11566-3692
Phone: (516)623-3200 **Fax:** (516)378-2672
Products: Educational products; Computers. **SICs:** 5045 (Computers, Peripherals & Software); 5099 (Durable Goods Nec). **Est:** 1963. **Sales:** $1,000,000 (2000). **Emp:** 10. **Officers:** Albert J. Nash, President.

■ 6237 ■ **Efficient Computer System**
PO Box 2524
Hickory, NC 28603-2524
Phone: (704)322-2263
Free: (800)833-3864 **Fax:** (704)308-8072
E-mail: ecs@w3link.com
URL: http://www.ecs.ibmbp.com
Products: Computers, peripherals, and software; Barcode equipment and supplies. **SIC:** 5045 (Computers, Peripherals & Software). **Est:** 1982. **Sales:** $1,000,000 (2000). **Emp:** 10. **Officers:** Jimmie Yoder, President.

■ 6238 ■ **EIZO Nanao Technologies Inc.**
5710 Warland Dr.
Cypress, CA 90630
Phone: (310)431-5011
Free: (800)800-5202 **Fax:** (310)530-1679
Products: Computer monitors. **SIC:** 5045 (Computers, Peripherals & Software). **Est:** 1985. **Sales:** $50,000,000 (2000). **Emp:** 28. **Officers:** Kurt Arata, Vice President.

■ 6239 ■ **EKD Computer Sales and Supplies Corp.**
PO Box 1300
Selden, NY 11784
Phone: (516)736-0500 **Fax:** (516)736-2209
Products: Computer equipment and supplies. **SIC:** 5045 (Computers, Peripherals & Software). **Est:** 1985. **Sales:** $2,000,000 (2000). **Emp:** 7. **Officers:** Dennis Raynoha, President; Thomas Green, CEO.

■ 6240 ■ **El Camino Resources International Inc.**
21051 Warner Center Ln.
Woodland Hills, CA 91367
Phone: (818)226-6600 **Fax:** (818)226-6794
Products: Computers. **SIC:** 5045 (Computers, Peripherals & Software). **Est:** 1979. **Sales:** $785,000,000 (1999). **Emp:** 1,000. **Officers:** David Harmon, President & COO; Mel Kleinman, Exec. VP of Sales; Rhett Mitchell, Dir. of Systems; J.J. Glascock, Personnel Mgr.

■ 6241 ■ **Electrograph Systems Inc.**
175 Commerce Dr.
Hauppauge, NY 11788
Phone: (631)436-5050 **Fax:** (631)436-5227
Products: Flat screen displays. **SIC:** 5045 (Computers, Peripherals & Software). **Est:** 1985. **Sales:** $100,000,000 (2000). **Emp:** 40. **Officers:** Samuel Taylor, President.

■ 6242 ■ **Electronic Arts Inc.**
1450 Fashion Island Blvd.
San Mateo, CA 94404
Phone: (650)571-7171
Free: (800)245-4525 **Fax:** (650)571-6375
Products: Software. **SIC:** 5045 (Computers, Peripherals & Software). **Sales:** $908,900,000 (2000). **Emp:** 2,100. **Officers:** Lawrence F. Probst III, CEO & Chairman of the Board; E. Stanton McKee Jr., Exec. VP & CFO.

■ 6243 ■ **Electronic Label Technology Inc.**
708 W Kenosha
Broken Arrow, OK 74012
Phone: (918)258-2121 **Fax:** (918)664-8207
Products: Computers and computer equipment, including printers. **SIC:** 5046 (Commercial Equipment Nec). **Est:** 1984. **Sales:** $30,000,000 (2000). **Emp:** 120. **Officers:** Tim Wright, CEO; Ted Morgan, CFO; Eric Green, Dir. of Marketing & Sales.

■ 6244 ■ **Electronics Discount World**
4935 Allison St.
Arvada, CO 80002
Phone: (303)426-7772
Products: Computers and software. **SIC:** 5045 (Computers, Peripherals & Software). **Sales:** $2,000,000 (2000). **Emp:** 4. **Officers:** Steve King, Partner.

■ 6245 ■ **Electronics and Information Systems**
PO Box 64525
St. Paul, MN 55164
Phone: (612)456-2222 **Fax:** (612)456-3098
Products: Computers. **SIC:** 5045 (Computers, Peripherals & Software). **Est:** 1946. **Sales:** $400,000,000 (2000). **Emp:** 4,500. **Officers:** A.F. Zettlemoyer, President; Dennis Harren, VP of Finance & Admin.; H.G. Jones Jr., Dir. of Marketing; Frank Gilligan, Dir. of Information Systems; Jennifer Smith, Dir of Human Resources.

■ 6246 ■ **E.L.F. Software Co.**
210 W 101 St.
New York, NY 10025
Free: (800)309-8669
Products: Computer software. **SIC:** 5045 (Computers, Peripherals & Software). **Est:** 1983. **Emp:** 5. **Officers:** Betty Erickson, President. **Former Name:** E.L.F. Software Distributors.

■ 6247 ■ **Elite Computers and Software Inc.**
PO Box 756
Cupertino, CA 95015-0756
Phone: (408)257-8000 **Fax:** (408)257-8001
Products: Computers and software. **SIC:** 5045 (Computers, Peripherals & Software). **Sales:** $3,000,000 (2000). **Emp:** 20. **Officers:** Thomas J. Armes, President.

■ 6248 ■ **Emulex Corp.**
3535 Harbor Blvd.
Costa Mesa, CA 92626
Phone: (714)662-5600
Free: (800)590-5773 **Fax:** (714)513-8266
Products: Computers. **SIC:** 5045 (Computers, Peripherals & Software). **Est:** 1978. **Sales:** $64,800,000 (2000). **Emp:** 332. **Officers:** Paul F. Folino, CEO & President; Michael J. Rockenbach, VP of Finance; Scott D. McVay, VP of Sales; Jim Hill, Dir. of Data Processing; Sadie Herrera, Dir of Human Resources.

■ 6249 ■ **En Pointe Technologies Inc.**
100 N Sepulveda Blvd., 19th Fl.
El Segundo, CA 90245
Phone: (310)725-5200 **Fax:** (310)725-5289
Products: Computers and computer-related products and services. **SIC:** 5045 (Computers, Peripherals & Software). **Sales:** $491,400,000 (2000). **Emp:** 434. **Officers:** Attiazaz Din, CEO, President & Chairman of the Board; Robert A. Mercer, CFO.

■ 6250 ■ **H.C. Engelhart Co.**
3811 N Pomona Rd.
Tucson, AZ 85705-2421
Phone: (520)887-2277 **Fax:** (520)887-3370
E-mail: hceco@flash.net
Products: New and used machine tools. **SIC:** 5045 (Computers, Peripherals & Software). **Est:** 1980. **Emp:** 2. **Officers:** Harry Engelhart, Owner.

■ 6251 ■ **Enterprise Computer Systems Inc.**
PO Box 2383
Greenville, SC 29602-2383
Phone: (864)234-7676 **Fax:** (864)281-3249
Products: Computers; Peripheral computer equipment; Computer software. **SIC:** 5045 (Computers, Peripherals & Software). **Officers:** James Sobeck, President.

■ 6252 ■ **Entre**
13400 Bishops Ln., No. 270
Brookfield, WI 53005
Phone: (414)821-1060
Free: (800)786-2933 **Fax:** (414)938-2155
E-mail: dschm@pcsentre.com
URL: http://www.pcsentre.com
Products: Computers; Computer hardware and software. **SIC:** 5045 (Computers, Peripherals & Software). **Est:** 1986. **Sales:** $60,000,000 (2000). **Emp:** 200. **Officers:** Robert Johansen, President; Diane Schmidt, Sales/Marketing Contact.

■ 6253 ■ **Eritech International**
4551 San Fernando Rd., Ste. 110
Glendale, CA 91204-1985
Phone: (818)244-6242
Products: Computer hardware and software. **SIC:** 5045 (Computers, Peripherals & Software). **Sales:** $4,000,000 (2000). **Emp:** 10. **Officers:** Andy Issagholian, President.

■ 6254 ■ **ERM Recycling Inc./Crazy Bob's**
50 New Salem St.
Wakefield, MA 01880-1906
Phone: (617)246-6767
Free: (800)776-5865 **Fax:** (617)246-6776
Products: Computers and software. **SIC:** 5045 (Computers, Peripherals & Software). **Sales:** $4,000,000 (2000). **Emp:** 20.

■ 6255 ■ **ESI Computing**
468 Westford Rd.
Carlisle, MA 01741
Phone: (978)369-8499 **Fax:** (978)369-7612
Products: Computer software. **SIC:** 5045 (Computers, Peripherals & Software).

■ 6256 ■ **ESI-Technologies Inc.**
The Rand Bldg., 7th Fl.
Buffalo, NY 14203-2702
Phone: (716)852-8000
Free: (800)873-3647 **Fax:** (716)845-5301
Products: Computer software. **SIC:** 5045 (Computers, Peripherals & Software). **Est:** 1964. **Sales:** $40,000,000 (2000). **Emp:** 25. **Officers:** John Davies, President; Greg Rosinksi, Controller.

■ 6257 ■ **Europa Consulting**
10905 Ashford Ct.
Upper Marlboro, MD 20772-2700
Phone: (301)627-8888 **Fax:** (301)627-7939
Products: Computers, hardware, and software. **SIC:** 5045 (Computers, Peripherals & Software). **Officers:** Marion Bishoff, Partner.

■ 6258 ■ **Executive Business Machines, Inc.**
2 Post Rd.
Fairfield, CT 06430-6216
Phone: (203)254-8500
Free: (800)535-5326 **Fax:** (203)254-8555
URL: http://www.entreebm.com
Products: Computer hardware; Software and networking services. **SIC:** 5045 (Computers, Peripherals & Software). **Est:** 1972. **Emp:** 35. **Officers:** Bryan Press, President; James M. Daly Sr., President, e-mail: jdalysr@entreebm.com; Bryan Press, Human Resources Contact.

■ 6259 ■ **Executive Productivity Systems**
PO Box 5539
Chesapeake, VA 23328
Phone: (757)547-0209 **Fax:** (757)547-5518
Products: Computer software and hardware. **SIC:** 5045 (Computers, Peripherals & Software).

■ 6260 ■ **Exodus Computers, Inc.**
70 East 3750 South
Salt Lake City, UT 84115
Phone: (801)265-8500
Free: (800)937-6772 **Fax:** (801)265-8580
URL: http://www.exoduscomp.com
Products: Computers, peripherals, software, hard drives, and network cards. Exodus pylon fileservers and workstations. **SIC:** 5045 (Computers, Peripherals & Software). **Officers:** Benito Rodriquez, President; Chris Parks, Customer Service Contact, e-mail: cparks@exoduscomp.com; Diane Fox, Human Resources Contact. **Former Name:** Network Center.

■ 6261 ■ **Exploration Resources Inc.**
394 S Milledge Ave.
Athens, GA 30605
Phone: (706)353-7983
Free: (800)231-3282 **Fax:** (706)546-8111
Products: Information management service assisting clients in acquiring, processing, interpreting, and communicating information, Lotus Notes, and environmental data management. Government, commercial, and industrial industries served. **SIC:** 5045 (Computers, Peripherals & Software). **Emp:** 85.

■ 6262 ■ **Export Services Inc.**
PO Box 814432
Dallas, TX 75381
Phone: (972)243-8588 **Fax:** (972)243-8589
Products: Computers; Computer software; Peripheral computer equipment; Mining machinery; Construction machinery. **SICs:** 5045 (Computers, Peripherals & Software); 5082 (Construction & Mining Machinery). **Officers:** Raul Caballero, President.

■ 6263 ■ **Facit Div.**
Ahearn & Soper Co. Inc.
59 Chenell Dr.
Concord, NH 03301-8541
Products: Computer peripherals. **SIC:** 5045 (Computers, Peripherals & Software). **Est:** 1938. **Sales:** $7,000,000 (2000). **Emp:** 20. **Officers:** Elizabeth Miller, President.

■ 6264 ■ **Fast Multimedia U.S. Inc.**
15029 Woodinville Redmond Rd. NE
Woodinville, WA 98072-6988
Phone: (425)354-2002
Free: (800)249-3278 **Fax:** (425)354-2005
Products: Computer peripheral equipment. **SIC:** 5045 (Computers, Peripherals & Software). **Sales:** $31,000,000 (2000). **Emp:** 40. **Officers:** Giuseppe Cavalli, President.

■ 6265 ■ **Fastlink Network Products**
90 S Spruce Ave., Ste. N
South San Francisco, CA 94080
Phone: (650)872-1376
Products: Computer network products. **SIC:** 5045 (Computers, Peripherals & Software). **Sales:** $2,000,000 (1993). **Emp:** 5. **Officers:** Patrick Yuen, Owner.

■ 6266 ■ **Federal Computer Corp.**
2745 Hartland Rd.
Falls Church, VA 22043
Phone: (703)698-7711
Products: Computers and software. **SIC:** 5045 (Computers, Peripherals & Software). **Sales:** $71,000,000 (2000). **Emp:** 50. **Officers:** William E. Hummel, President; Robert M. Ruiz, CFO.

■ 6267 ■ **Federal Systems Group Inc.**
7799 Leesburg Pike
Falls Church, VA 22043-2413
Phone: (703)848-4747
Free: (800)765-8374 **Fax:** (703)848-4758
Products: Computers; Computer software; Peripheral computer equipment. **SIC:** 5045 (Computers, Peripherals & Software). **Officers:** Daniel Retter, President.

■ 6268 ■ **FEI America Inc.**
PO Box 72
Tualatin, OR 97062
Phone: (503)620-8640 **Fax:** (503)620-8520
Products: Computer systems and components; Peripherals and prepackaged software; On-site consultation services. **SICs:** 5045 (Computers, Peripherals & Software); 5065 (Electronic Parts & Equipment Nec).

■ 6269 ■ **File TEC**
7480 Lemhi
Boise, ID 83709
Phone: (208)377-5522 **Fax:** (208)376-5121
Products: Computers; Computer software; Peripheral computer equipment; Office storage units, files, and tables, except wood. **SICs:** 5045 (Computers, Peripherals & Software); 5112 (Stationery & Office Supplies); 5044 (Office Equipment). **Officers:** H. Gebhardt, Owner.

■ 6270 ■ **Fireside Office Products Inc.**
PO Box 2116
Bismarck, ND 58502-2116
Phone: (701)258-8586 **Fax:** (701)223-9598
Products: Computers; Office machines. **SICs:** 5045 (Computers, Peripherals & Software); 5044 (Office Equipment). **Officers:** Bill Whalen, President.

■ 6271 ■ **First Class Business Systems Inc.**
PO Box 407
Seymour, IN 47274-2913
Phone: (812)522-3341
Products: Offers computer support services to businesses in Indiana. **SIC:** 5045 (Computers, Peripherals & Software). **Emp:** 5.

■ 6272 ■ **Fleet Distribution, Inc.**
2696 Briarlake Rd. NE
PO Box 98074
Atlanta, GA 30329
Phone: (404)325-9214 **Free:** (800)291-8565
Products: Computer software. **SIC:** 5045 (Computers, Peripherals & Software). **Est:** 1974. **Officers:** Sam B. Howard Jr., President.

■ 6273 ■ **Flytech Technology (USA) Inc.**
1931 Hartog Dr.
San Jose, CA 95131
Phone: (408)573-9113 **Fax:** (408)573-9509
E-mail: carry-1@flytech.com
URL: http://www.flytech.com.tw
Products: Small desktop computers. **SIC:** 5045 (Computers, Peripherals & Software). **Est:** 1984. **Sales:** $6,000,000 (2000). **Emp:** 6. **Officers:** Jenny Wang, President.

■ 6274 ■ **ForeFront Direct Inc.**
25400 U.S Hwy 19 N, Ste. 285
Clearwater, FL 33763
Phone: (813)724-8994
Free: (877)872-4646 **Fax:** (813)726-6922
E-mail: salesreps@smartcertify.com
URL: http://www.smartcertify.com
Products: Diagnostic software. **SIC:** 5045 (Computers, Peripherals & Software). **Sales:** $13,000,000 (2000). **Emp:** 130. **Officers:** Jerry Dias, General Mgr.; Jamie Sene, VP of Marketing; Ira Friedman, VP of Sales.

■ 6275 ■ **FORMation mg Inc.**
15540 Rockfield Blvd. Ste.A
Irvine, CA 92618
Phone: (949)598-8890
Free: (800)693-3933 **Fax:** (949)598-8899
Products: Software; Electronic document products; Laser printers; Laser printer toner. **SIC:** 5045 (Computers, Peripherals & Software). **Sales:** $2,000,000 (2000). **Emp:** 14. **Officers:** Daniel Forster, CEO; Konni Forster, VP.

■ 6276 ■ **Formtronix Inc.**
2516 McHenry Dr.
Silver Spring, MD 20904
Phone: (301)572-6902
Products: Computers.s. **SIC:** 5045 (Computers, Peripherals & Software).

■ 6277 ■ **Forsythe Technology Inc.**
7500 Frontage Rd.
Skokie, IL 60077
Phone: (847)675-8000 **Fax:** (847)675-2130
Products: Computer equipment. **SIC:** 5045 (Computers, Peripherals & Software). **Sales:** $357,000,000 (2000). **Emp:** 340. **Officers:** Rick Forsythe, CEO, President & Chairman of the Board; Gordon Decker, Sr. VP of Finance & Admin.

■ 6278 ■ **Four Wheeler Communications**
10 New Scotland Ave.
Albany, NY 12208
Phone: (518)465-4711 **Fax:** (518)465-2945
Products: Scanners. **SIC:** 5045 (Computers, Peripherals & Software).

■ 6279 ■ **FOX Systems Inc.**
3333 S Old U.S 23
Brighton, MI 48116
Phone: (810)227-4497
Products: Programmable logic controllers. **SIC:** 5045 (Computers, Peripherals & Software). **Sales:**

$11,000,000 (2000). **Emp:** 35. **Officers:** James A. Fox, CEO; Cherie DeLong, Dir. of Marketing.

■ **6280** ■ **Fran-TEC Computer**
PO Box 261
Somerset, MA 02726-0261
Phone: (508)675-3950 **Fax:** (508)675-3950
Products: Computers; Computer software; Peripheral computer equipment. **SIC:** 5045 (Computers, Peripherals & Software). **Officers:** Karen Benevides, Owner.

■ **6281** ■ **Franklin Quest Co.**
2200 W Parkway Blvd.
Salt Lake City, UT 84119
Phone: (801)975-1776 **Fax:** (801)975-9995
Products: Computers and software. **SIC:** 5045 (Computers, Peripherals & Software). **Est:** 1991. **Sales:** $2,000,000 (2000). **Emp:** 45. **Officers:** Todd Simons, Dir. of Marketing; Randy Linnell, Dir. of Production.

■ **6282** ■ **Fujitsu Computer Products of America Inc.**
2904 Orchard Pkwy.
San Jose, CA 95134-2009
Phone: (408)432-6333
Free: (800)626-4686 **Fax:** (408)894-1700
Products: Computer data storage and imaging products. **SIC:** 5045 (Computers, Peripherals & Software). **Sales:** $34,000,000 (2000). **Emp:** 700. **Officers:** Larry D. Sanders, CEO & President; Kevin T. Parker, VP of Finance.

■ **6283** ■ **Fujitsu Network Switching of America Inc.**
3055 Orchard Dr.
San Jose, CA 95134
Phone: (408)432-1300
Products: Computers, keyboards, and monitors. **SIC:** 5045 (Computers, Peripherals & Software).

■ **6284** ■ **Future Tech International Inc.**
7630 NW 25th St.
Miami, FL 33122-1314
Phone: (305)477-6406
Products: Computers, systems, and peripherals. **SIC:** 5045 (Computers, Peripherals & Software). **Sales:** $235,000,000 (2000). **Emp:** 125. **Officers:** Lou Leonardo, President.

■ **6285** ■ **FWB Inc.**
1555 Adams Dr.
Menlo Park, CA 94025
Phone: (415)325-4392 **Fax:** (415)833-4653
Products: Computer software. **SIC:** 5046 (Commercial Equipment Nec). **Est:** 1985. **Sales:** $40,000,000 (2000). **Emp:** 85. **Officers:** Norman Fong, President; Steve Gibbs, Controller.

■ **6286** ■ **Gagnons Reprographics Co.**
308 9th Ave. S
Great Falls, MT 59405-4034
Phone: (406)727-2278 **Fax:** (406)452-3297
Products: Computers; Peripheral computer equipment; Computer software. **SIC:** 5045 (Computers, Peripherals & Software). **Officers:** John Gagnon, President.

■ **6287** ■ **Galaxie Hardware Publishers Inc.**
5075 Nectar Way
Eugene, OR 97405
Phone: (541)345-1817 **Fax:** (541)345-3094
Products: Computer peripheral equipment. **SIC:** 5045 (Computers, Peripherals & Software). **Sales:** $700,000 (2000). **Emp:** 5. **Officers:** Ricki Shipway, President.

■ **6288** ■ **Gannsoft Publishing Co.**
806 A Gillette Rd.
Colville, WA 99114-9647
Phone: (509)684-7637 **Fax:** (509)684-7638
E-mail: gann@plix.com
Products: Computers, peripherals, and software. **SIC:** 5045 (Computers, Peripherals & Software). **Est:** 1983. **Sales:** $250,000 (2000). **Emp:** 2. **Officers:** Peter Pich, President.

■ **6289** ■ **Ganson Engineering Inc.**
18678 142nd Ave. NE
Woodinville, WA 98072
Phone: (425)489-2090
Free: (800)434-9011 **Fax:** (425)489-2088
Products: Printers. **SIC:** 5045 (Computers, Peripherals & Software). **Sales:** $2,000,000 (2000). **Emp:** 10. **Officers:** Glenn Ganson, President.

■ **6290** ■ **Gates/Arrow Distributing Inc.**
39 Pelham Ridge Dr.
Greenville, SC 29615
Free: (800)332-2222 **Fax:** (864)627-2182
E-mail: www.gatesarrow.com/feedback
URL: http://www.gatesarrow.com
Products: Computer systems, components, peripheral equipment, and software. **SIC:** 5045 (Computers, Peripherals & Software). **Est:** 1985. **Emp:** 354. **Officers:** Michael Long, President & CEO.

■ **6291** ■ **Gates/FA Distributing Inc.**
39 Pelham Ridge Dr.
Greenville, SC 29615
Phone: (803)234-0736 **Fax:** (803)234-6836
Products: Computers. **SIC:** 5045 (Computers, Peripherals & Software). **Est:** 1980. **Sales:** $307,300,000 (2000). **Emp:** 350. **Officers:** Philip D. Ellett, CEO & President; William T. Mauldin, VP & CFO; Jerry A. Lumpkin, VP of Marketing; Lee F. Nicholson, VP of Operations.

■ **6292** ■ **Gateswood Software Inc.**
222 S Rainbow, No. 111
Las Vegas, NV 89128
Phone: (702)363-7700 **Fax:** (702)363-0011
Products: Computers; Computer software; Peripheral computer equipment. **SIC:** 5045 (Computers, Peripherals & Software). **Officers:** Ronald Serandos, President.

■ **6293** ■ **Gateway Software Corp.**
PO Box 367
Fromberg, MT 59029
Phone: (406)668-7661
Free: (800)735-3637 **Fax:** (406)668-7665
Products: School administrative software for IBM AS/400 computers. **SIC:** 5045 (Computers, Peripherals & Software).

■ **6294** ■ **GBC Technologies Inc.**
6365 Carlson Dr., Ste. F
Eden Prairie, MN 55346
Phone: (612)947-1000
Products: Microcomputer products specializing in networking, connectivity and data communications hardware and software. **SIC:** 5045 (Computers, Peripherals & Software). **Sales:** $318,800,000 (1994). **Emp:** 371. **Officers:** Robert Zakheim, President; Richard C. Altus, VP of Finance & Treasurer.

■ **6295** ■ **GE Capital Information Technology Solutions**
220 Girard St.
Gaithersburg, MD 20884-6004
Phone: (301)258-2965 **Fax:** (301)258-9122
Products: Computers. **SIC:** 5045 (Computers, Peripherals & Software). **Est:** 1983. **Sales:** $100,000,000 (2000). **Emp:** 200. **Officers:** Jim Gorgei, President; Russell Harner, Accountant.

■ **6296** ■ **Gene Labs Inc.**
6638 Meadowlark Dr.
Indianapolis, IN 46226-3608
Phone: (317)547-3840
Products: Computers; Peripheral computer equipment; Software. **SIC:** 5045 (Computers, Peripherals & Software). **Officers:** Walter Larson, President.

■ **6297** ■ **General Automation Inc.**
17731 Mitchell N
Irvine, CA 92623
Phone: (949)250-4800
Free: (800)854-0140 **Fax:** (949)752-6772
Products: Software and hardware development for electronic commerce, data warehousing and databases. **SIC:** 5045 (Computers, Peripherals & Software). **Sales:** $28,900,000 (1999). **Emp:** 161.

Officers: Jane Christie, CEO & President; Richard H. Nance, VP, CFO & Treasurer.

■ **6298** ■ **General Microsystems Inc. (Bellevue, Washington)**
3220 118th Ave. SE, Ste. 100
Bellevue, WA 98005-4198
Phone: (425)644-2233
Products: Client server systems; Storage equipment; Network and network management products. **SIC:** 5045 (Computers, Peripherals & Software). **Sales:** $4,600,000 (2000). **Emp:** 6. **Officers:** Earl W. Overstreet II, President.

■ **6299** ■ **Generic Computer Products Inc.**
PO Box 790
Marquette, MI 49855
Phone: (906)226-7600
Products: Computer accessories; Peripheral computer equipment; Computer software. **SIC:** 5045 (Computers, Peripherals & Software). **Est:** 1981.

■ **6300** ■ **Georgia Business Solutions**
2010 Huntcliff Dr.
Lawrenceville, GA 30043-6357
Phone: (404)513-9280
Products: Computers, peripherals, and software. **SIC:** 5045 (Computers, Peripherals & Software). **Officers:** William Hudson, Owner.

■ **6301** ■ **Clark R. Gibb Co.**
5251 W 73rd St. J
Minneapolis, MN 55439-2206
Phone: (612)831-4890 **Fax:** (612)831-2736
Products: Computer electronics and software. **SIC:** 5045 (Computers, Peripherals & Software). **Officers:** Ronald Deharpporte, President.

■ **6302** ■ **Gigatec (U.S.A.) Inc.**
PO Box 4705
Portsmouth, NH 03802
Phone: (603)433-2227 **Fax:** (603)433-5552
Products: Computer peripheral equipment. **SIC:** 5045 (Computers, Peripherals & Software). **Sales:** $14,000,000 (1994). **Emp:** 30. **Officers:** Michel Barbini, CEO & President.

■ **6303** ■ **Global Computer Corp.**
11 Harbor Park Dr.
Port Washington, NY 11050
Phone: (516)625-6262
Products: Computers. **SIC:** 5045 (Computers, Peripherals & Software). **Sales:** $99,000,000 (1993). **Emp:** 200. **Officers:** Robert Leeds, President.

■ **6304** ■ **Golden Bear Services Inc.**
10511 E Tanglewood Rd.
Franktown, CO 80116-9439
Phone: (303)688-5655 **Fax:** (303)688-6618
Products: Computers; Computer software; Peripheral computer equipment. **SIC:** 5045 (Computers, Peripherals & Software). **Officers:** Joan Bond, President.

■ **6305** ■ **Government Micro Resources Inc.**
7203 Gateway Ct.
Manassas, VA 20109-7313
Phone: (703)330-1199 **Fax:** (703)263-9116
Products: Microcomputer equipment and supplies. **SIC:** 5045 (Computers, Peripherals & Software). **Est:** 1981. **Sales:** $85,000,000 (2000). **Emp:** 168. **Officers:** Humberto A. Pujals, COO; James Hoffmeyer, Dir. of Operations; Robert G. Slocum, Sr. VP of Marketing.

■ **6306** ■ **Government Technology Services Inc.**
4100 Lafayette Center Dr.
Chantilly, VA 20151
Phone: (703)502-2000 **Fax:** (703)222-5240
Products: Microcomputer hardware, software, networking products and work stations. **SIC:** 5045 (Computers, Peripherals & Software). **Sales:** $486,400,000 (2000). **Emp:** 519. **Officers:** M. Dendy Young, CEO & President; Stephen L. Waechter, Sr. VP & CFO.

■ **6307** ■ **Granite Microsystems, Inc.**
PO Box 579
Mequon, WI 53092
Phone: (414)242-8800
Free: (800)332-3475 **Fax:** (414)242-8825
E-mail: sales@granitemicrosystems.com
URL: http://www.granitemicrosystems.com
Products: Industrial computers and peripherals. **SIC:** 5045 (Computers, Peripherals & Software). **Est:** 1983. **Emp:** 75. **Former Name:** Softworks Development Corp.

■ **6308** ■ **Graphic Resources Corp.**
12311 Industry St.
Garden Grove, CA 92840
Phone: (714)891-1003
Products: Computer hardware and supplies. **SIC:** 5049 (Professional Equipment Nec). **Est:** 1971. **Sales:** $7,000,000 (2000). **Emp:** 25. **Officers:** Stephen Beko, President & Chairman of the Board.

■ **6309** ■ **Gray Sales Co. Inc.**
PO Box 38
Somerville, MA 02143-0001
Phone: (617)625-6200
Products: Computers, hardware, and software. **SIC:** 5045 (Computers, Peripherals & Software). **Officers:** John Wykoff, President.

■ **6310** ■ **Greenleaf Distribution Inc.**
PO Box 54959
Santa Clara, CA 95056
Phone: (408)653-0222 **Fax:** (408)653-0212
Products: Computers and supplies. **SIC:** 5045 (Computers, Peripherals & Software). **Officers:** James Lee, President; Dianne O'Brien, CFO.

■ **6311** ■ **Greenpages Inc.**
33 Badgers Island W
Kittery, ME 03904
Phone: (207)439-7310 **Fax:** (207)439-7334
Products: Computers and software. **SIC:** 5045 (Computers, Peripherals & Software). **Sales:** $82,000,000 (2000). **Emp:** 150. **Officers:** Kurt D. Bleicken, President.

■ **6312** ■ **Greenwich Instruments USA**
11925 Ramah Church Rd.
Huntersville, NC 28078
Phone: (704)875-1922
Free: (800)476-4070 **Fax:** (704)875-2801
Products: Computer equipment. **SIC:** 5045 (Computers, Peripherals & Software). **Sales:** $600,000 (2000). **Emp:** 9. **Officers:** Bruce Magruder, President.

■ **6313** ■ **Greystone Peripherals Inc.**
130-A Knowles Dr.
Los Gatos, CA 95030
Phone: (408)866-4739
Free: (800)600-5710 **Fax:** (408)866-8328
Products: Disk duplicating equipment. **SIC:** 5045 (Computers, Peripherals & Software). **Sales:** $6,500,000 (2000). **Emp:** 16. **Officers:** John Usher, President; Nancy Kurth, Accountant.

■ **6314** ■ **GT Interactive Software Corp.**
417 5th Ave., Rm. 789
New York, NY 10016-2204
Phone: (212)726-6500
Products: Consumer software. **SIC:** 5045 (Computers, Peripherals & Software). **Sales:** $530,700,000 (2000). **Emp:** 1,337. **Officers:** Ronald W. Chaimowitz, CEO & Chairman of the Board; Andrew Gregor, Sr. VP & CFO.

■ **6315** ■ **GT Interactive Software Corp. Value Products Div.**
2300 Berkshire Ln., N
Minneapolis, MN 55441-3606
Phone: (612)509-7600
Products: Software. **SIC:** 5045 (Computers, Peripherals & Software). **Sales:** $200,000,000 (2000). **Emp:** 100. **Officers:** Charles F. Bond, President; Gene Hamf, VP of Finance & Admin.

■ **6316** ■ **GTI**
7615 Golden Triangle Dr.
Eden Prairie, MN 55344
Phone: (480)820-7680 **Fax:** (480)820-8009
E-mail: sales@gtisales.com
URL: http://www.gtisales.com
Products: Computers; Computer software; Peripheral computer equipment. **SIC:** 5045 (Computers, Peripherals & Software). **Est:** 1986. **Sales:** $125,000,000 (2000). **Emp:** 40. **Officers:** Kevin Whitenack, Dir. of Marketing.

■ **6317** ■ **Guaranteed Business Services Inc.**
7 N Main St.
West Hartford, CT 06107-1918
Phone: (860)521-4949 **Fax:** (860)521-4906
Products: Computers, peripherals, and software. **SIC:** 5045 (Computers, Peripherals & Software). **Officers:** Sue Larson, President.

■ **6318** ■ **Gulf Coast Software & Systems**
549 E Pass Rd., Ste. M
Gulfport, MS 39507-3261
Phone: (228)896-8217 **Fax:** (228)897-2912
Products: Computers; Computer software; Peripheral computer equipment. **SIC:** 5045 (Computers, Peripherals & Software). **Officers:** Greg Robins, President.

■ **6319** ■ **H and H Computers**
3400 Bradshaw Rd., Ste. A2
Sacramento, CA 95827
Phone: (916)362-4884 **Fax:** (916)362-4886
Products: System integrators. **SIC:** 5045 (Computers, Peripherals & Software). **Sales:** $1,000,000 (2000). **Emp:** 20. **Officers:** Roger Hoss, Mng. Partner; Eve Dreyfuss-Holmes, CFO.

■ **6320** ■ **H & H Equipment Inc.**
611 Fairbanks St.
Anchorage, AK 99501-3744
Phone: (907)277-9432 **Fax:** (907)274-1221
Products: Computers; Peripheral computer equipment; Software. **SIC:** 5045 (Computers, Peripherals & Software). **Officers:** Jerry Harris, President.

■ **6321** ■ **Hagerman and Company Inc.**
PO Box 139
Mt Zion, IL 62549
Phone: (217)864-2326 **Fax:** (217)864-2281
Products: Computers, peripherals, and software. **SIC:** 5045 (Computers, Peripherals & Software). **Sales:** $2,000,000 (1994). **Emp:** 22. **Officers:** Dennis Hagerman, President; John Hagerman, Controller.

■ **6322** ■ **Hall Group Inc.**
215 S Highway Ave.
De Land, IL 61839
Phone: (217)664-3346 **Fax:** (217)664-3347
Products: Internet commerce software and automated payment systems. **SIC:** 5045 (Computers, Peripherals & Software).

■ **6323** ■ **Hall-Mark Electronics Corp.**
11333 Pagemill Rd.
Dallas, TX 75243
Phone: (214)343-5000 **Fax:** (214)343-5988
Products: Computers; Electronic components. **SICs:** 5045 (Computers, Peripherals & Software); 5065 (Electronic Parts & Equipment Nec). **Est:** 1962. **Sales:** $560,100,000 (2000). **Emp:** 1,491. **Officers:** Joseph W. Semmer, CEO & President; Bruce Evashevski, VP, CFO & Treasurer; Charles B. Smith, Sr. VP of Marketing; Bill B. Phillips, Sr. VP of Operations.

■ **6324** ■ **Hall Research Technologies**
3613 W Macarthur Blvd., Ste. 600
Santa Ana, CA 92704-6846
Phone: (714)641-6607
Products: Computer peripherals equipment. **SIC:** 5045 (Computers, Peripherals & Software). **Sales:** $4,000,000 (2000). **Emp:** 10. **Officers:** Ali Hall, President.

■ **6325** ■ **Hallogram Publishing**
14221 E 4th Ave.,
Aurora, CO 80011
Phone: (303)340-3404 **Fax:** (303)340-4404
Products: Programming software. **SIC:** 5045 (Computers, Peripherals & Software). **Sales:** $3,000,000 (1999). **Emp:** 12. **Officers:** Galen Hall, President.

■ **6326** ■ **Halted Specialties Co.**
3500 Ryder Ave.
Santa Clara, CA 95051
Phone: (408)732-1573 **Fax:** (408)732-6428
Products: Computer equipment; Electronics parts. **SICs:** 5065 (Electronic Parts & Equipment Nec); 5045 (Computers, Peripherals & Software). **Est:** 1963. **Sales:** $3,300,000 (2000). **Emp:** 30. **Officers:** Matt Dunstan, CEO; Robert Ellingson, President; Robert Ellington, CFO.

■ **6327** ■ **Hammond Computer Inc.**
70 E 3750 S
Salt Lake City, UT 84115
Phone: (801)265-8500 **Fax:** (801)265-8580
Products: Computer peripheral equipment; Prepackaged computer software. **SIC:** 5045 (Computers, Peripherals & Software). **Sales:** $11,000,000 (1993). **Emp:** 30. **Officers:** Walt Allan, President.

■ **6328** ■ **Hardware Knowledge Group Inc.**
448 E El Camino Real
Sunnyvale, CA 94087
Phone: (408)733-5454
Free: (800)308-0818 **Fax:** (408)733-5456
Products: Computer peripherals. **SIC:** 5045 (Computers, Peripherals & Software). **Sales:** $2,000,000 (2000). **Emp:** 7. **Officers:** Wayne Nip, President.

■ **6329** ■ **Harvard Associates Inc.**
10 Holworthy St.
Cambridge, MA 02138-4519
Phone: (617)492-0660
Free: (800)774-5646 **Fax:** (617)492-4610
E-mail: pclogo@harvassoc.com
URL: http://www.harvassoc.com
Products: Educational software. **SIC:** 5045 (Computers, Peripherals & Software). **Est:** 1983. **Sales:** $1,000,000 (2000). **Emp:** 5. **Officers:** William Glass, President.

■ **6330** ■ **Health Systems Technology Corp.**
11701 Yates Ford Rd.
Fairfax Station, VA 22039-1507
Phone: (703)978-2084 **Fax:** (703)978-2197
Products: Provides healthcare and case management services to businesses in the United States. **SIC:** 5045 (Computers, Peripherals & Software). **Emp:** 4.

■ **6331** ■ **Hewlett-Packard Co. International**
3495 Deer Creek Rd.
Palo Alto, CA 94304
Phone: (650)857-2032 **Fax:** (650)857-5837
Products: Computers; Peripheral computer equipment; Medical equipment; Laboratory and scientific equipment. **SICs:** 5045 (Computers, Peripherals & Software); 5047 (Medical & Hospital Equipment). **Est:** 1939. **Sales:** $42,900,000,000 (1999). **Emp:** 122,000. **Officers:** Lew Platt, CEO; Walt Reichert, Sales, e-mail: walt_reichart@hp.com.

■ **6332** ■ **Hickey and Associates**
3 Clarendon Ave.
Brockton, MA 02301
Phone: (508)559-5130 **Fax:** (508)559-2097
Products: Computer equipment. **SIC:** 5045 (Computers, Peripherals & Software). **Sales:** $28,000,000 (2000). **Emp:** 5. **Officers:** Robert Hickey, President; Dennis Hickey, Vice President.

■ **6333** ■ **Hitachi Data Systems Corp.**
PO Box 54996
Santa Clara, CA 95054
Phone: (408)970-1000 **Fax:** (408)982-0108
Products: Mainframe office computers. **SIC:** 5045 (Computers, Peripherals & Software). **Est:** 1989. **Sales:** $1,240,000,000 (2000). **Emp:** 2,500. **Officers:** John Staedke, CEO & President; Dave Roberson,

Treasurer; John Clark, VP of Marketing; Roger Kuhn, Dir of Human Resources.

■ 6334 ■ Hitachi Data Systems Corp.
750 Central Expy.
Santa Clara, CA 95050
Phone: (408)970-1000
Free: (800)227-1930 **Fax:** (408)727-8036
Products: Enterprise servers, storage subsystems and other computer peripherals. **SIC:** 5045 (Computers, Peripherals & Software). **Sales:** $2,000,000,000 (2000). **Emp:** 2,300. **Officers:** Steven M. West, CEO & President; Dave Roberson, Exec. VP & CFO.

■ 6335 ■ Hitachi Medical Systems America Inc.
1959 Summit Commerce Park
Twinsburg, OH 44087-2371
Phone: (330)425-1313 **Fax:** (330)425-1410
Products: Magnetic resonance imaging equipment. **SIC:** 5047 (Medical & Hospital Equipment). **Sales:** $85,000,000 (2000). **Emp:** 120. **Officers:** Richard Ernst, CEO & President; M. Yoshizawa, VP of Finance.

■ 6336 ■ Hitron Systems Inc.
3170 El Camino Real
Santa Clara, CA 95051
Phone: (408)261-2695
Products: Computer hardware and software. **SIC:** 5045 (Computers, Peripherals & Software). **Sales:** $2,000,000 (2000). **Emp:** 5. **Officers:** Dong Chao, President.

■ 6337 ■ HJV Inc.
742 S Division Ave.
Grand Rapids, MI 49503-5111
Phone: (616)241-1602 **Fax:** (616)241-2423
Products: Computers; Computer software; Peripheral computer equipment. **SIC:** 5045 (Computers, Peripherals & Software). **Officers:** Harold Verburg, President.

■ 6338 ■ HNSX Supercomputers Inc.
305 Foster St.
Littleton, MA 01460-2004
Phone: (978)742-4690 **Fax:** (978)742-4689
Products: Computers. **SIC:** 5045 (Computers, Peripherals & Software). **Est:** 1986. **Sales:** $11,000,000 (2000). **Emp:** 30. **Officers:** Akira Sekino, CEO & President; Samuel W. Adams, VP of Marketing & Sales.

■ 6339 ■ Hooleon Corp.
411 S 6th St Ste B
Cottonwood, AZ 86326
Phone: (520)634-7515
Free: (800)937-1337 **Fax:** (520)634-4620
Products: Custom key imprinting for computers; Computer keyboard accessories and enhancements. **SIC:** 5045 (Computers, Peripherals & Software). **Sales:** $282,000,000 (1999). **Emp:** 8. **Officers:** Robert Crozier, CEO; Ken Parrott, Controller.

■ 6340 ■ Horizon Business Systems
2 Townsend W
Nashua, NH 03063-1277
Phone: (603)882-8471 **Fax:** (603)882-6099
Products: Computers; Computer software; Peripheral computer equipment. **SIC:** 5045 (Computers, Peripherals & Software). **Officers:** John Monahan, Owner.

■ 6341 ■ Horizon Micro Distributors
7180 SW Sandburg St.
Portland, OR 97223
Phone: (503)684-5544 **Fax:** (503)684-0608
Products: Computer equipment. **SIC:** 5045 (Computers, Peripherals & Software).

■ 6342 ■ Horizon USA Data Supplies Inc.
4955 Energy Way
Reno, NV 89502-4105
Phone: (702)826-4392
Free: (800)325-1199 **Fax:** (702)826-4392
URL: http://www.horizonusa.com
Products: Computers and computer accessories. **SIC:** 5045 (Computers, Peripherals & Software). **Est:** 1991. **Officers:** Roger Woodward, President; Jim Schebler, Sales Mgr.

■ 6343 ■ House of Representatives Inc.
228 Willis Rd.
Sudbury, MA 01776
Phone: (978)443-4818
Products: Computer products. **SIC:** 5045 (Computers, Peripherals & Software).

■ 6344 ■ Howtek Inc.
21 Park Ave.
Hudson, NH 03051
Phone: (603)882-5200
Free: (800)444-6983 **Fax:** (603)880-3843
Products: Color scanners; Pre-press systems. **SIC:** 5045 (Computers, Peripherals & Software). **Est:** 1984. **Sales:** $11,300,000 (2000). **Emp:** 70. **Officers:** David R. Bothwell, CEO & President; Robert J. Lungo, VP & CFO; John L. Seguin, VP of Marketing & Sales; M. Russell Leonard, VP of Operations.

■ 6345 ■ HSB Computer Laboratories
34208 Aurora Rd., Ste. 207
Cleveland, OH 44139
Phone: (440)498-1356
Products: Computer hardware and software. **SIC:** 5045 (Computers, Peripherals & Software).

■ 6346 ■ Robert W. Hunt & Associates
2828 W Lake Sammamish Pkwy. SE
Bellevue, WA 98008-5645
Phone: (425)746-4186
Products: Computers; Computer software; Peripheral computer equipment. **SIC:** 5045 (Computers, Peripherals & Software). **Officers:** Robert Hunt, Owner.

■ 6347 ■ HVL Technical Services Inc.
PO Box 36266
Birmingham, AL 35236-6266
Phone: (205)822-2940 **Fax:** (205)979-0466
Products: Computers; Computer software; Peripheral computer equipment. **SIC:** 5045 (Computers, Peripherals & Software). **Officers:** Hubert Lindquist, President.

■ 6348 ■ HyperGlot Software Company Inc.
PO Box 10746
Knoxville, TN 37939-0746
Phone: (423)558-8270 **Fax:** (423)588-6569
Products: Software. **SIC:** 5045 (Computers, Peripherals & Software). **Est:** 1988. **Sales:** $12,400,000 (2000). **Emp:** 25. **Officers:** Phil M. Baggett, President & CFO.

■ 6349 ■ I-O Corp.
2256 South 3600 West
Salt Lake City, UT 84119-9965
Phone: (801)973-6767 **Free:** (800)871-9998
Products: Peripherals. **SIC:** 5045 (Computers, Peripherals & Software). **Est:** 1977. **Sales:** $22,000,000 (2000). **Emp:** 110. **Officers:** Doug Pack, President.

■ 6350 ■ ICG
30481 Whipple Rd.
Union City, CA 94587
Phone: (510)471-7000
Free: (800)659-4244 **Fax:** (510)471-7562
URL: http://www.icg.com
Products: Computers and peripherals. **SIC:** 5045 (Computers, Peripherals & Software). **Est:** 1984. **Sales:** $250,000,000 (1999). **Emp:** 110. **Officers:** Mike Ahmar, President; Feris Rifai, Vice President; Robbie Chikhani, Exec. VP.

■ 6351 ■ ICL Inc.
25902 Towne Centre Dr.
Foothill Ranch, CA 92610
Phone: (949)855-5505 **Fax:** (949)707-2566
Products: Computer hardware and software. **SIC:** 5045 (Computers, Peripherals & Software). **Sales:** $12,000,000 (1994). **Emp:** 25. **Officers:** Keith Todd, CEO & Chairman of the Board.

■ 6352 ■ Ideal Computer Services Inc.
113 Rickenbacker Cir.
Livermore, CA 94550
Phone: (925)447-4747
Products: Computer printers. **SIC:** 5045 (Computers,

Peripherals & Software). **Sales:** $3,500,000 (1993). **Emp:** 25. **Officers:** Paul H. Lawrence, President.

■ 6353 ■ IEEI
110 Agate Ave.
Newport Beach, CA 92662
Phone: (949)673-2943 **Fax:** (949)673-0249
E-mail: ieei@aol.com
URL: http://www.ieei.com
Products: Computer spare parts. **SIC:** 5045 (Computers, Peripherals & Software). **Est:** 1976. **Sales:** $900,000 (1999). **Emp:** 5. **Officers:** Dennis E. Bress Jr., President.

■ 6354 ■ Iiyama North America, Inc.
1 Ivy Brook Blvd., Ste. 120
Ivyland, PA 18974
Phone: (215)957-6543 **Fax:** (215)957-6551
URL: http://www.iiyama.com
Products: Color monitors; LCD panels. **SIC:** 5045 (Computers, Peripherals & Software). **Est:** 1991. **Sales:** $41,000,000 (2000). **Emp:** 30. **Officers:** Mike Omaru, President; Stephen Kocsi, VP & Gen. Mgr. **Former Name:** Idek North America.

■ 6355 ■ Image Processing Solutions
500 W Cummings Park
Woburn, MA 01801-6503
Phone: (781)932-9644 **Fax:** (781)932-3155
URL: http://www.imageprocsol.com
Products: Computers; Computer software; Peripheral computer equipment. **SIC:** 5045 (Computers, Peripherals & Software). **Est:** 1986. **Officers:** Eric Marino, President.

■ 6356 ■ Imagex Inc.
6845 Elm St., No. 305
McLean, VA 22101
Phone: (703)883-2500 **Fax:** (703)883-2537
E-mail: imagex@access.digex.net
URL: http://www.townwed.com/biz/imagex
Products: Computer graphics, micrographics, and supplies. **SIC:** 5045 (Computers, Peripherals & Software). **Est:** 1988. **Sales:** $4,000,000 (2000). **Emp:** 25. **Officers:** Nancy Gretzinger, President.

■ 6357 ■ Imge Guided Technologies, Inc.
5710 B Flatiron Pky.
Boulder, CO 80301
Phone: (303)447-0248 **Fax:** (303)447-3905
E-mail: info@imageguided.com
URL: http://www.imageguided.com
Products: Optical localizers. **SIC:** 5045 (Computers, Peripherals & Software). **Est:** 1989. **Emp:** 36. **Officers:** Paul Ray, CEO.

■ 6358 ■ Impression Technology Inc.
4270 Dow Rd., Ste. 213
Melbourne, FL 32934
Phone: (407)254-8700 **Fax:** (407)242-0258
Products: Printers for business applications. **SIC:** 5045 (Computers, Peripherals & Software). **Est:** 1985. **Sales:** $1,000,000 (2000). **Emp:** 4. **Officers:** Frank Price, President.

■ 6359 ■ Imrex Company Inc.
307 E Shore Rd.
Great Neck, NY 11023
Phone: (516)466-5210
Products: Computer equipment for military use. **SIC:** 5045 (Computers, Peripherals & Software).

■ 6360 ■ InaCom Corp.
10810 Farnam Dr.
Omaha, NE 68154
Phone: (402)392-3900 **Fax:** (402)392-3602
Products: Microcomputer systems and related products. **SIC:** 5045 (Computers, Peripherals & Software). **Sales:** $4,258,400,000 (2000). **Emp:** 12,000. **Officers:** Bill L. Fairfield, CEO & President; Dave Guenthner, Exec. VP & CFO.

■ 6361 ■ InaCom Information Systems
393 Inverness Dr. S
Englewood, CO 80112-5816
Phone: (303)754-5004 **Fax:** (303)759-6269
Products: Computers. **SIC:** 5045 (Computers, Peripherals & Software). **Sales:** $35,000,000 (2000). **Emp:** 125. **Officers:** Andrea Spronk, General Mgr.

■ **6362** ■ **InControl Solutions**
8285 SW Nimbus Ave Ste. 148
Beaverton, OR 97008
Phone: (541)574-4802 **Fax:** (541)574-4902
Products: Pointing devices used in multimedia controls
and games. **SIC:** 5045 (Computers, Peripherals &
Software). **Officers:** Chris Haverty, CEO, President &
Chairman of the Board.

■ **6363** ■ **Infinite Solutions Inc.**
3000 Miller Ct. W
Norcross, GA 30071
Phone: (770)449-4033 **Fax:** (770)449-8280
Products: Computer work stations. **SIC:** 5045
(Computers, Peripherals & Software). **Sales:**
$31,000,000 (2000). **Emp:** 50. **Officers:** Jay Rosovsky,
President & CFO.

■ **6364** ■ **Infinity Data Systems**
1801 Clearview Pkwy.
Metairie, LA 70001-2451
Phone: (504)455-8973
Products: Computer hardware and peripheral
equipment. **SIC:** 5045 (Computers, Peripherals &
Software).

■ **6365** ■ **Info-Mation Services Co.**
3035 Directors Row, Bldg. B, No. 12
Memphis, TN 38131-0416
Phone: (901)332-5770 **Fax:** (901)525-4373
Products: Computer hardware and software;
Computer printer paper. **SIC:** 5045 (Computers,
Peripherals & Software). **Est:** 1984. **Sales:** $2,000,000
(2000). **Emp:** 14. **Officers:** Raymond Henry, President;
Lloyd Henry Jr., Exec. VP; Sandra M. Henry, VP of
Marketing & Sales.

■ **6366** ■ **Info Systems Inc.**
590 Century Blvd.
Wilmington, DE 19808
Phone: (302)633-9800
Products: Computers and software. **SIC:** 5045
(Computers, Peripherals & Software).

■ **6367** ■ **Infomax Inc.**
5757 Ranchester Dr., No. 1900
Houston, TX 77036-1510
Phone: (713)776-1688
Products: Personal computers. **SIC:** 5045
(Computers, Peripherals & Software). **Est:** 1985.
Sales: $12,000,000 (1999). **Emp:** 25. **Officers:** Peggy
Sha, President; Ronica Lee, Dir of Personnel.

■ **6368** ■ **Information Analysis Inc.**
11240 Waples Mill Rd., Ste. 400
Fairfax, VA 22030
Phone: (703)383-3000
Free: (800)829-7614 **Fax:** (703)293-7979
Products: Software. **SIC:** 5045 (Computers,
Peripherals & Software). **Est:** 1979. **Sales:**
$15,600,000 (2000). **Emp:** 101. **Officers:** Sandor
Rosenberg, CEO; Brian R. Moore, Treasurer.

■ **6369** ■ **Information Management Inc.**
8110 E 32nd St. N, Ste. 150
Wichita, KS 67226-2616
Phone: (316)267-3163 **Fax:** (316)267-1544
Products: Computer hardware. **SIC:** 5045
(Computers, Peripherals & Software). **Officers:** Paul
Brunson, President.

■ **6370** ■ **InfoSource Inc.**
6947 University Blvd.
Winter Park, FL 32792
Phone: (407)677-0300
Free: (800)393-4636 **Fax:** (407)677-9226
URL: http://www.infosourcenet.com
Products: Computer software and training products.
SIC: 5045 (Computers, Peripherals & Software). **Est:**
1983. **Sales:** $12,000,000 (1999). **Emp:** 125. **Officers:**
Thomas Warrner, President; Elaine Pare, Dir. of
Marketing, e-mail: epare@isitraining.com.

■ **6371** ■ **Infotel**
6990 US Rte. 36 E
Fletcher, OH 45326
Phone: (937)368-2650 **Fax:** (937)368-2306
Products: Computers; Computer software; Peripheral

computer equipment. **SIC:** 5045 (Computers,
Peripherals & Software).

■ **6372** ■ **Ingram Industries Inc.**
PO Box 23049
Nashville, TN 37202
Phone: (615)298-8200 **Fax:** (615)298-8242
Products: Books; Videos; Software. **SICs:** 5045
(Computers, Peripherals & Software); 5192 (Books,
Periodicals & Newspapers). **Est:** 1978. **Sales:**
$5,500,000,000 (2000). **Emp:** 5,000. **Officers:** Martha
Ingram, CEO; Bob Mitchell, VP of Finance; Michael
Head, VP of Human Resources.

■ **6373** ■ **Ingram Micro Inc.**
1600 E St. Andrew Pl.
Santa Ana, CA 92704
Phone: (714)566-1000
Free: (800)456-8000 **Fax:** (714)566-7941
Products: Computers; Peripheral computer
equipment. **SIC:** 5045 (Computers, Peripherals &
Software). **Sales:** $940,000,000 (2000). **Emp:** 1,900.
Officers: Chip Lacy, CEO; Ron Hardaway, CFO; Mike
Kelly, Sr. VP of Information Systems; Andy Rich, VP of
Human Resources.

■ **6374** ■ **Ingram Micro Inc.**
1759 Wehrle Dr.
Williamsville, NY 14221
Phone: (716)633-3600
Free: (800)456-8000 **Fax:** (716)635-6498
Products: Computer hardware, software, and
peripherals. **SIC:** 5045 (Computers, Peripherals &
Software).

■ **6375** ■ **Inland Associates Inc.**
PO Box 940
Olathe, KS 66051
Phone: (913)764-7977
Free: (800)888-7800 **Fax:** (913)764-8721
URL: http://www.inlandassoc.com
Products: Computers and peripheral equipment. **SIC:**
5045 (Computers, Peripherals & Software). **Est:** 1971.
Sales: $20,000,000 (2000). **Emp:** 42. **Officers:** Peggy
Meader, President, e-mail: pmeader@
inlandassoc.com; Chuck Floyd, CFO, e-mail: cfloyd@
inlandassoc.com.

■ **6376** ■ **Insight Direct**
8123 S Hardy Dr.
Tempe, AZ 85284-1106
Phone: (520)333-3000 **Fax:** (602)902-1180
URL: http://www.insight.com
Products: Computers; Computer printers. **SIC:** 5045
(Computers, Peripherals & Software). **Est:** 1986.
Sales: $500,000,000 (2000). **Emp:** 800. **Officers:** Tim
Crown, President; Stan Laybourne, CFO; Valerie J.
Paxton-Maloney, Dir. of Marketing & Sales.

■ **6377** ■ **Intcomex**
2980 NW 108 Ave,
Miami, FL 33172
Phone: (305)477-6230 **Fax:** (305)477-5694
Products: Microcomputers and accessories. **SIC:**
5045 (Computers, Peripherals & Software). **Sales:**
$100,000,000 (2000). **Emp:** 60. **Officers:** Michael
Shalom, President.

■ **6378** ■ **Integral Systems Inc.**
2730 Shadelands Dr., No. 101
Walnut Creek, CA 94598-2515
Phone: (510)939-3900 **Fax:** (510)946-4891
Products: Software. **SIC:** 5045 (Computers,
Peripherals & Software). **Est:** 1972. **Sales:**
$48,000,000 (2000). **Emp:** 350. **Officers:** William R.
Leckonby, CEO & President; Chris Paul, VP & CFO; C.
David Snyder, Sr. VP of Marketing & Sales; James
Hardy, Dir. of Systems; Sandy Nakaji, Dir of Human
Resources.

■ **6379** ■ **Intel Corp.**
PO Box 58119
Santa Clara, CA 95052
Phone: (408)765-8080
Free: (800)628-8686 **Fax:** (408)765-6284
Products: Semiconductor devices, microcomputer
chips, chipsets, motherboards and flash memory. **SIC:**
5045 (Computers, Peripherals & Software). **Sales:**
$29,389,000,000 (1999). **Emp:** 64,500. **Officers:** Craig

Barrett, CEO, President & Chairman of the Board; Andy
D. Bryant, Sr. VP & CFO.

■ **6380** ■ **Intelligent Computer Networks**
613 Woodridge
Woodstock, GA 30188
Phone: (404)516-8445 **Free:** (800)546-7977
Products: Computers; Computer software; Peripheral
computer equipment. **SIC:** 5045 (Computers,
Peripherals & Software). **Officers:** Thomas Powell,
President.

■ **6381** ■ **Intelligent Electronics Inc.**
411 Eagleview Blvd.
Exton, PA 19341
Phone: (610)458-5500 **Fax:** (610)458-6702
Products: Computers and peripherals. **SIC:** 5045
(Computers, Peripherals & Software). **Est:** 1982.
Sales: $3,588,100,000 (2000). **Emp:** 2,569. **Officers:**
Richard D. Sanford, CEO, President & Chairman of the
Board; Thomas J. Coffey, Sr. VP & CFO.

■ **6382** ■ **Intelligent Electronics Inc. Advanced
Systems Div.**
411 Eagleview Blvd.
Exton, PA 19341
Phone: (215)458-5500
Products: Computer screens, keyboards, and
programs. **SIC:** 5045 (Computers, Peripherals &
Software).

■ **6383** ■ **Intelligent Systems Corp.**
4355 Shackleford Rd.
Norcross, GA 30093
Phone: (770)381-2900 **Fax:** (770)381-2808
Products: Computer monitors, graphics boards,
storage subsystems, network products, and electronic
design automation software. **SIC:** 5045 (Computers,
Peripherals & Software). **Sales:** $23,700,000 (2000).
Emp: 219. **Officers:** J. Leland Strange, CEO &
President; Henry Birdsong, CFO.

■ **6384** ■ **InterACT Systems Inc.**
PO Box 15084
Asheville, NC 28813
Phone: (828)254-9876 **Fax:** (828)254-0760
E-mail: interact@interactsys.com
URL: http://www.interactsys.com
Products: Computers, printers, and computer
supplies. **SIC:** 5045 (Computers, Peripherals &
Software). **Est:** 1978. **Sales:** $4,000,000 (2000). **Emp:**
25. **Officers:** William A. Rhodes III, President; Wvande
Groep, CFO. **Former Name:** Interact Computers
Systems Inc.

■ **6385** ■ **Interatech**
4455 Twain Ave., Ste. F
San Diego, CA 92120
Phone: (619)528-1984 **Fax:** (619)284-4711
Products: Computers; Electronic modems and
couplers; Air purifiers. **SICs:** 5045 (Computers,
Peripherals & Software); 5075 (Warm Air Heating & Air-
Conditioning); 5065 (Electronic Parts & Equipment
Nec). **Officers:** Frank Farsoudi, President.

■ **6386** ■ **Interface Data Inc.**
14 Heritage Rd.
Billerica, MA 01821-1108
Phone: (781)938-6333 **Free:** (800)370-3282
Products: Computer storage devices. **SIC:** 5045
(Computers, Peripherals & Software). **Sales:**
$2,100,000 (2000). **Emp:** 12. **Officers:** F. Scheuerle,
President.

■ **6387** ■ **Interface Systems Inc.**
5855 Interface Dr.
Ann Arbor, MI 48103
Phone: (734)769-5900
Free: (800)544-4072 **Fax:** (734)769-1047
Products: Plug-compatible printers and interfaces for
IBM mainframe and midrange computer systems. **SIC:**
5045 (Computers, Peripherals & Software). **Sales:**
$81,800,000 (2000). **Emp:** 220. **Officers:** Bob Nero,
CEO & President; John R. Ternes, VP & CFO.

■ **6388** ■ **International Business Machines Corp. EduQuest**
PO Box 2150
Atlanta, GA 30327
Phone: (404)238-3100
Products: Computers and software. **SIC:** 5045 (Computers, Peripherals & Software).

■ **6389** ■ **International Computer and Office Products Inc.**
108 E Ponce de Leon, No. 210
Decatur, GA 30030
Phone: (404)373-3683
Products: Computer parts and supplies; Office supplies. **SICs:** 5045 (Computers, Peripherals & Software); 5112 (Stationery & Office Supplies). **Est:** 1986. **Sales:** $1,000,000 (2000). **Emp:** 6. **Officers:** Eric Lucas, President.

■ **6390** ■ **International Data Acquisition and Control Inc.**
PO Box 397
Amherst, NH 03031
Phone: (603)673-0765   **Fax:** (603)673-0767
Products: Software systems for pathology labs. **SIC:** 5045 (Computers, Peripherals & Software). **Sales:** $2,000,000 (2000). **Emp:** 9. **Officers:** Gene Calvano, President; Gerry Klein, Vice President.

■ **6391** ■ **International Parts Inc.**
12677 Silicon Dr.
San Antonio, TX 78249-3412
Phone: (210)694-4313   **Fax:** (210)696-9736
Products: Computers, computer peripherals and software. **SIC:** 5045 (Computers, Peripherals & Software). **Sales:** $6,500,000 (2000). **Emp:** 35. **Officers:** Deb Walters, President; Kathy Fandel, CFO.

■ **6392** ■ **Internet Communication Corp.**
7100 E Belleview Ave.
Greenwood Village, CO 80111
Phone: (303)770-7600   **Fax:** (303)770-2706
Products: Computers; Computer software; Peripheral computer equipment. **SIC:** 5045 (Computers, Peripherals & Software). **Officers:** Thomas Galley, President.

■ **6393** ■ **Intrepid Systems Inc.**
16000 Sky Cliff Dr.
Brookfield, WI 53005-2870
Phone: (414)790-0080
Products: Computers and equipment and supplies. **SIC:** 5045 (Computers, Peripherals & Software). **Est:** 1988. **Sales:** $10,000,000 (2000). **Emp:** 8. **Officers:** Mike Kiefer, President.

■ **6394** ■ **Inventory Conversion Inc.**
102 Tide Mill Rd., Ste. 6
Hampton, NH 03842
Phone: (603)926-0300   **Fax:** (603)926-0301
Products: Computers. **SIC:** 5045 (Computers, Peripherals & Software). **Sales:** $6,000,000 (2000). **Emp:** 10. **Officers:** Donald Francoeur, President.

■ **6395** ■ **IOA Data Corp.**
383 Lafayette St.
New York, NY 10003
Phone: (212)673-9300   **Fax:** (212)460-0594
Products: Computers. **SIC:** 5045 (Computers, Peripherals & Software). **Est:** 1966. **Sales:** $4,000,000 (2000). **Emp:** 7. **Officers:** S. J. Rubenstein, President; Ron Reed, Controller; Annette Popowitz, Dir. of Marketing.

■ **6396** ■ **IOB Distributors**
PO Box 142307
Austin, TX 78714-2307
Phone: (512)835-9648
Products: Computer equipment. **SIC:** 5045 (Computers, Peripherals & Software).

■ **6397** ■ **IQ2000**
15402 Vantage Pky., No. 318
Houston, TX 77032
Phone: (281)447-1000
Products: Computers and peripheral equipment; Chairs. **SICs:** 5045 (Computers, Peripherals & Software); 5021 (Furniture). **Sales:** $1,000,000 (2000).

Emp: 37. **Officers:** Joseph W. Clapp, President; Noble Kidd, VP of Marketing & Sales.

■ **6398** ■ **ITEC Enterprises Inc.**
2955 Hartley Rd., Ste. 205
Jacksonville, FL 32257
Phone: (904)262-5066   **Fax:** (904)262-7139
Products: Computers, peripherals, and software; Tires and tubes. **SICs:** 5045 (Computers, Peripherals & Software); 5014 (Tires & Tubes). **Officers:** John Azzo, Vice President.

■ **6399** ■ **ITM**
6411 Lake Athabaska Place
San Diego, CA 92119
Phone: (619)697-3112   **Fax:** (619)697-3113
Products: Computer and office products. **SICs:** 5045 (Computers, Peripherals & Software); 5112 (Stationery & Office Supplies). **Officers:** Simon Meth, President. **Alternate Name:** International Trade Management.

■ **6400** ■ **Itron Inc.**
PO Box 15288
Spokane, WA 99215
Phone: (509)924-9900   **Fax:** (509)922-1897
Products: Designs and energy information and communication systems of hardware and software for utilities; provides implementation services, after-sale support, meter reading and meter shop service. **SIC:** 5045 (Computers, Peripherals & Software). **Sales:** $241,400,000 (2000). **Emp:** 1,137. **Officers:** Michael Chesser, CEO, President & Chairman of the Board; David G. Remington, CFO.

■ **6401** ■ **Iverson P.C. Warehouse Inc.**
1420 Spring Hill Rd., Ste. 570
McLean, VA 22102-3029
Phone: (703)749-1200
Products: Personal computers; Software. **SIC:** 5045 (Computers, Peripherals & Software). **Est:** 1990. **Sales:** $5,000,000 (2000). **Emp:** 12. **Officers:** Donald D. Iverson, President.

■ **6402** ■ **J & J Computer Resources**
6092 US Hwy. 49
Hattiesburg, MS 39401-6033
Phone: (601)544-6092   **Fax:** (601)544-6092
Products: Computers; Computer software; Peripheral computer equipment. **SIC:** 5045 (Computers, Peripherals & Software). **Officers:** Jerry King, President.

■ **6403** ■ **J & M Industries Inc.**
6803 W 64th St., Ste. 320
Shawnee Mission, KS 66202-4178
Phone: (913)362-8994
Products: Computers, peripherals, and software. **SIC:** 5045 (Computers, Peripherals & Software). **Officers:** Michael Mc Hugh, President.

■ **6404** ■ **Jacobson Computer Inc.**
5610 Monroe St.
Sylvania, OH 43560-2701
Phone: (419)885-0082   **Fax:** (419)885-2622
Products: Computers, peripheral equipment and software. **SIC:** 5045 (Computers, Peripherals & Software). **Sales:** $10,000,000 (2000). **Emp:** 49. **Officers:** Gary Jacobson, President; Lynn Jacobson, Vice President.

■ **6405** ■ **Jane Co.**
6901 Magda Dr.
Osseo, MN 55369-5639
Phone: (612)533-6040
Products: Computers, peripherals, and software. **SIC:** 5045 (Computers, Peripherals & Software). **Officers:** Jane Wampach, Owner.

■ **6406** ■ **JDL Technologies Inc.**
5555 West 78th St., Ste. E
Edina, MN 55439
Phone: (612)946-1810
Free: (800)535-3969   **Fax:** (612)946-1835
Products: Computer peripheral equipment for the education industry. **SIC:** 5045 (Computers, Peripherals & Software). **Sales:** $10,800,000 (2000). **Emp:** 25. **Officers:** Thomas J. Lapping, President; David Beck, CFO.

■ **6407** ■ **JDM Data Systems Inc.**
PO Box 4219
Fall River, MA 02723-0402
Phone: (508)678-4904   **Fax:** (508)678-6488
Products: Computers; Computer software; Peripheral computer equipment. **SIC:** 5045 (Computers, Peripherals & Software). **Officers:** Jose Medeiros, President.

■ **6408** ■ **JDR Microdevices Inc.**
1850 S 10th St.
San Jose, CA 95112-4108
Phone: (408)494-1400   **Fax:** (408)494-1420
Products: Personal computer products, including hard drives, modems, floppy drives, and mother boards. **SIC:** 5045 (Computers, Peripherals & Software). **Est:** 1979. **Sales:** $44,900,000 (2000). **Emp:** 150. **Officers:** Jeff Rose, President; Ruth Ann Hansen, Sales/Marketing Contact, e-mail: ruthannh@jdr.com.

■ **6409** ■ **Jones Business Systems Inc.**
13715 Murphy Rd., Ste. D
Stafford, TX 77477-4900
Phone: (281)403-8500
Free: (800)876-8649   **Fax:** (281)403-8591
E-mail: sales@jbsi.com
URL: http://www.jbsi.com
Products: Computers and software. **SIC:** 5045 (Computers, Peripherals & Software). **Est:** 1991. **Sales:** $80,000,000 (2000). **Emp:** 80. **Officers:** Bruce Parsons, President; Michael G. Colesante, CFO.

■ **6410** ■ **Joshua Distributing Co.**
9246 Trinity Dr.
Lake In The Hills, IL 60102
Phone: (708)697-5600
Free: (800)345-3603   **Fax:** (708)697-3200
Products: Computer software. **SIC:** 5045 (Computers, Peripherals & Software).

■ **6411** ■ **JRE Computing**
PO Box 762
Baldwinsville, NY 13027-0762
Phone: (315)635-5009   **Fax:** (315)638-8201
Products: Computer software. **SIC:** 5045 (Computers, Peripherals & Software).

■ **6412** ■ **JSB Software Technologies PLC**
108 Whispering Pine Dr.
Scotts Valley, CA 95066
Phone: (831)438-8300
Free: (800)359-3408   **Fax:** (831)438-8360
Products: Computer software. **SIC:** 5045 (Computers, Peripherals & Software). **Sales:** $10,216,000,000 (1999). **Emp:** 50. **Officers:** Nicholas Outteridge, Manager; Dave Bush, Controller.

■ **6413** ■ **JVLNET By Electrolarm**
1220 W Court St.
Janesville, WI 53545-3537
Phone: (608)758-8750   **Fax:** (608)754-0015
URL: http://www.jvlnet.com
Products: Internet services. **SICs:** 5087 (Service Establishment Equipment); 5045 (Computers, Peripherals & Software). **Est:** 1971. **Sales:** $1,500,000 (2000). **Emp:** 29. **Officers:** Robert Kerman, e-mail: rkerman@jvlnet.com. **Former Name:** Electrolarm Security Systems Inc.

■ **6414** ■ **JWS Corp.**
10000 W 75th St., Ste. 200A
Shawnee Mission, KS 66204-2241
Phone: (913)384-0880   **Fax:** (913)432-5242
URL: http://www.jwscorp.com
Products: Computer software. **SIC:** 5045 (Computers, Peripherals & Software). **Est:** 1983. **Officers:** James Wilson, President. **Former Name:** James William Scott Corp.

■ **6415** ■ **K Rep Sales**
2726 Shelter Island Dr., Ste. 237
San Diego, CA 92106
Phone: (619)457-9654   **Fax:** (619)457-1503
Products: Computer software. **SIC:** 5045 (Computers, Peripherals & Software).

■ **6416** ■ **Kalthoff International**
550 E 4th St., Apt. 7
Cincinnati, OH 45202-3333
Phone: (513)794-3367
Products: Computer conferencing hardware and software. **SIC:** 5045 (Computers, Peripherals & Software).

■ **6417** ■ **Kazette Enterprises Inc.**
5411 Coliseum Blvd., Ste. A
Alexandria, LA 71303-3521
Phone: (318)442-3593   **Fax:** (318)487-8401
URL: http://www.kazette.com
Products: Computers; Computer software; Peripheral computer equipment. **SIC:** 5045 (Computers, Peripherals & Software). **Officers:** Johnie Varnado, President.

■ **6418** ■ **Keep It Simple Technology Inc.**
PO Box 2981
Gaithersburg, MD 20886-2981
Products: Multimedia upgrade kits for personal computers, primarily CD-ROM drives, sound cards, and some software. **SIC:** 5045 (Computers, Peripherals & Software).

■ **6419** ■ **Kelly Computer Supplies**
3584 Hoffman Rd. E
St. Paul, MN 55110-5375
Phone: (651)773-1109
Free: (800)447-2929   **Fax:** (651)773-1381
E-mail: kellyrest@aol.com
URL: http://www.kellyrest.com
Products: Computer accessories; Ergonomic products; Wristrests (various sized and materials), copyholders, footrests, keyboard trays and drawers, monitor and keyboard solutions, and workstations, stocked nationally for quick and convenient service. **SICs:** 5045 (Computers, Peripherals & Software); 5044 (Office Equipment). **Est:** 1983. **Sales:** $1,600,000 (1999). **Emp:** 30. **Officers:** Robert Kelly, Owner.

■ **6420** ■ **Kenwood Data Systems Inc.**
918 10th St.
Greeley, CO 80631-1118
Phone: (970)353-4555   **Fax:** (970)353-3175
Products: Computers; Computer software; Peripheral computer equipment. **SIC:** 5045 (Computers, Peripherals & Software). **Officers:** Kristi Opp, Chairman of the Board.

■ **6421** ■ **Key Products Co.**
2659 Windmill Pkwy.
Henderson, NV 89014
Phone: (702)361-1220
Products: Computers. **SIC:** 5045 (Computers, Peripherals & Software).

■ **6422** ■ **KNB Computer Werx Inc.**
1717 Dell Ave.
Campbell, CA 95008-6904
Phone: (408)341-0570   **Fax:** (408)341-0581
Products: Computers and peripherals. **SIC:** 5045 (Computers, Peripherals & Software). **Sales:** $4,000,000 (1993). **Emp:** 10. **Officers:** Kelly Basoun, President.

■ **6423** ■ **Knox Computer Systems Inc.**
3860 Convoy St., Ste. 107
San Diego, CA 92111-3748
Phone: (619)502-1205   **Fax:** (619)535-0773
Products: Software. **SIC:** 5045 (Computers, Peripherals & Software). **Sales:** $2,000,000 (2000). **Emp:** 3. **Officers:** Sadaji Ohishi, CEO.

■ **6424** ■ **L and L Products**
2700 Conneticut Ave. NW
Washington, DC 20008-5330
Phone: (202)483-1510   **Fax:** (202)328-6681
Products: Educational software. **SIC:** 5045 (Computers, Peripherals & Software). **Sales:** $1,000,000 (2000). **Emp:** 2. **Officers:** Ronald Shapiro, Owner.

■ **6425** ■ **L.A. TRADE**
22825 Lockness Ave.
Torrance, CA 90501
Phone: (310)539-0019
Products: Computer memory chips. **SIC:** 5065 (Electronic Parts & Equipment Nec).

■ **6426** ■ **David Langer Inc.**
PO Box 2080
Beverly Hills, CA 90213
Phone: (213)466-2225   **Fax:** (213)466-7327
Products: Computer chips. **SIC:** 5045 (Computers, Peripherals & Software). **Est:** 1966. **Sales:** $21,000,000 (2000). **Emp:** 7. **Officers:** David Langer, President; Judy Meng, Exec. VP of Marketing.

■ **6427** ■ **Lansa USA Inc.**
1520 Kensinton Rd., Ste. 110
Oak Brook, IL 60523
Phone: (630)472-1234   **Fax:** (630)472-1004
E-mail: info@lansa.com
URL: http://www.lansa.com
Products: Computer software. **SIC:** 5045 (Computers, Peripherals & Software). **Est:** 1987. **Emp:** 110. **Officers:** John Smiscal, President; John Nannenhorn, VP of Finance; Bill Hood, Dir. of Marketing.

■ **6428** ■ **Lantec Inc.**
3549 N University Ave., Ste. 325
Provo, UT 84604
Phone: (801)375-7050
Products: Software. **SIC:** 5045 (Computers, Peripherals & Software). **Sales:** $2,000,000 (1994). **Emp:** 6. **Officers:** Marcelo Thiollier, President.

■ **6429** ■ **Laser-Scan Inc.**
45635 Willow Pond Plz.
Sterling, VA 20164
Phone: (703)709-9306
Products: Software. **SIC:** 5045 (Computers, Peripherals & Software). **Sales:** $3,000,000 (1994). **Emp:** 8. **Officers:** Wayne Colman, President.

■ **6430** ■ **LaserCard Systems Corp.**
2644 Bayshore Pkwy.
Mountain View, CA 94043
Phone: (650)969-4428   **Fax:** (650)967-6524
Products: Optical memory card systems. **SIC:** 5045 (Computers, Peripherals & Software). **Sales:** $4,000,000 (2000). **Emp:** 50. **Officers:** Jerome Drexler, CEO.

■ **6431** ■ **LaserTone Inc.**
8 Fairfield Dr.
North Little Rock, AR 72120-1816
Phone: (501)834-6557
Products: Recycled printers. **SIC:** 5045 (Computers, Peripherals & Software). **Est:** 1992. **Sales:** $1,000,000 (2000). **Emp:** 3. **Officers:** Guy V. Hooper, Owner.

■ **6432** ■ **Law Cypress Distributing**
5883 Eden Park Pl.
San Jose, CA 95138
Phone: (408)363-4700
Free: (800)344-3044   **Fax:** (408)363-8020
Products: Computer equipment, including monitors, scanners, and printers; Storage equipment. **SIC:** 5045 (Computers, Peripherals & Software). **Est:** 1983. **Sales:** $96,000,000 (2000). **Emp:** 95. **Officers:** David Law, CEO; Nick White, CFO; Suzanne Dodge, Dir of Human Resources.

■ **6433** ■ **Leader Technologies Inc.**
4590 MacArthur Blvd., Ste. 500
Newport Beach, CA 92660
Phone: (949)757-1787
Free: (800)922-1787   **Fax:** (949)757-1777
Products: Computers and related items. **SIC:** 5045 (Computers, Peripherals & Software). **Sales:** $4,000,000 (2000). **Emp:** 10. **Officers:** Nelson Greenwood, President.

■ **6434** ■ **Leading Edge Products Inc.**
10 Craig Rd.
Acton, MA 01720-5405
Phone: (978)562-3322   **Fax:** (978)568-3618
Products: Computers and peripheral equipment. **SIC:** 5045 (Computers, Peripherals & Software). **Sales:**

$22,000,000 (2000). **Emp:** 25. **Officers:** Y.S. Han, CEO & President; Miki Lee, CFO.

■ **6435** ■ **LeadingSpect Corp.**
1025 Segovia Cir.
Placentia, CA 92870
Phone: (714)632-3599
Free: (800)234-0688   **Fax:** (714)666-2900
URL: http://www.leadingspect.com
Products: Computer parts, including motherboards, microprocessors, RAM chips, and hard disks. **SIC:** 5045 (Computers, Peripherals & Software). **Sales:** $5,000,000 (2000). **Emp:** 20. **Officers:** Chung Lin, President; Jennie Huang, CFO.

■ **6436** ■ **Leecom Data Systems**
5952 Royal Ln., Ste. 166
Dallas, TX 75230
Phone: (214)750-8000   **Fax:** (214)750-8014
Products: Computers and computer components. **SIC:** 5045 (Computers, Peripherals & Software). **Emp:** 5.

■ **6437** ■ **Legend Computer Inc.**
542 Lakeside Dr., Ste. 1
Sunnyvale, CA 94085-4005
Phone: (408)720-0818   **Fax:** (408)720-0819
Products: Computer peripherals. **SIC:** 5045 (Computers, Peripherals & Software). **Sales:** $900,000 (2000). **Emp:** 10. **Officers:** H.C. Lyn, Manager.

■ **6438** ■ **Lex Computing and Management Corp.**
1 Elm St.
Keene, NH 03431
Phone: (603)357-3950
Products: Computer products, including disk drives and key boards. **SIC:** 5045 (Computers, Peripherals & Software).

■ **6439** ■ **Library Corp.**
Research Park
Inwood, WV 25428
Phone: (304)229-0100
Free: (800)624-0559   **Fax:** (304)229-0295
E-mail: info@tlcdelivers.com
URL: http://www.tlcdelivers.com
Products: Computers. **SIC:** 5045 (Computers, Peripherals & Software). **Est:** 1974. **Sales:** $14,000,000 (2000). **Emp:** 122. **Officers:** Annette H. Bakhtiar, President; Calvin Whittington, Controller; Gary Kirk, Dir. of Marketing & Sales; William Woodsmall, Dir. of Operations; Thomas W. Loy, Sales & Marketing Contact, e-mail: tloy@tlcdelivers.com.

■ **6440** ■ **Lite-On Inc.**
720 Hillview Dr.
Milpitas, CA 95035
Phone: (408)946-4873
Products: Keyboards; Monitors; Laser disc players. **SICs:** 5045 (Computers, Peripherals & Software); 5065 (Electronic Parts & Equipment Nec).

■ **6441** ■ **L.J. Technical Systems Inc.**
85 Corporate Dr.
Holtsville, NY 11742-2007
Phone: (516)234-2100   **Fax:** (516)234-2656
Products: Technical training systems. **SIC:** 5045 (Computers, Peripherals & Software). **Est:** 1961. **Sales:** $4,000,000 (2000). **Emp:** 20. **Officers:** Larry Rowe, President; Philip Berry, CFO; Christopher Rowe, Dir. of Marketing.

■ **6442** ■ **Logical Choice**
3118 Milton Rd.
Charlotte, NC 28204
Phone: (704)535-8451   **Fax:** (704)535-0847
Products: Computers; Computer software; Peripheral computer equipment. **SIC:** 5045 (Computers, Peripherals & Software). **Officers:** Mitch Pinion, President.

■ **6443** ■ **Logon Inc.**
611 U.S Hwy 46 W
Hasbrouck Heights, NJ 07604-3120
Phone: (201)393-7600
Products: Bar code machinery and parts; Printers and parts. **SIC:** 5045 (Computers, Peripherals & Software).

■ 6444 ■ London Litho Aluminum Company Inc.
7100 N Lawndale Ave.
Lincolnwood, IL 60645
Phone: (847)679-4600 **Fax:** (847)679-6453
Products: Photographic printing apparatus; Computers; Computer printers; Software. **SICs:** 5045 (Computers, Peripherals & Software); 5043 (Photographic Equipment & Supplies). **Est:** 1958. **Sales:** $60,000,000 (2000). **Emp:** 114. **Officers:** Mel London, Chairman & Treasurer; Eric London, President.

■ 6445 ■ Los Altos PC Inc.
PO Box 248
Los Altos, CA 94023-0248
Phone: (650)949-3451 **Fax:** (650)949-3567
Products: Computers, peripherals, and software. **SIC:** 5045 (Computers, Peripherals & Software). **Sales:** $2,000,000 (1993). **Emp:** 5. **Officers:** Ivy Yao, President.

■ 6446 ■ Lowry Computer Products Inc.
Lowry Technology Park
Brighton, MI 48116
Phone: (810)229-7200
Free: (800)556-7200 **Fax:** (810)229-5189
URL: http://www.lowrycomputer.com
Products: Peripheral computer equipment; Wireless, barcoding, and data collection solutions. **SIC:** 5045 (Computers, Peripherals & Software). **Est:** 1974. **Sales:** $60,000,000 (2000). **Emp:** 250. **Officers:** Michael R. Lowry, President; Steve Lowry, Exec. VP.

■ 6447 ■ Lucero Computer Products
1320 Lincoln Rd.
Idaho Falls, ID 83401
Phone: (208)524-0891
URL: http://www.lcsid.com
Products: Computers and software. **SIC:** 5045 (Computers, Peripherals & Software). **Est:** 1984. **Sales:** $8,000,000 (2000). **Emp:** 24. **Officers:** David Taylor, General Mgr.

■ 6448 ■ MA Laboratories Inc.
2075 N Capitol Ave.
San Jose, CA 95132
Phone: (408)954-8886
Products: Computer peripherals. **SIC:** 5045 (Computers, Peripherals & Software). **Sales:** $18,000,000 (2000). **Emp:** 200. **Officers:** Abraham Ma, Owner.

■ 6449 ■ Mac America
200 Continental Blvd.
El Segundo, CA 90245
Phone: (310)615-3080
Free: (800)462-5241 **Fax:** (408)434-1018
Products: Computer software. **SIC:** 5045 (Computers, Peripherals & Software).

■ 6450 ■ Dr. Macintosh Inc.
36 Peddlers Village Shop
Newark, DE 19702-1582
Phone: (302)738-0334 **Fax:** (302)738-0302
Products: Computers; Peripheral computer equipment; Computer software. **SIC:** 5045 (Computers, Peripherals & Software). **Officers:** Robert Greathouse, President.

■ 6451 ■ Maconomy NE Inc.
33 Boston Post Rd. W, Ste. 310
Marlborough, MA 01752
Phone: (508)460-8337 **Fax:** (508)303-8075
Products: Software for accounting, project management, and wholesale distributors. **SIC:** 5045 (Computers, Peripherals & Software). **Sales:** $69,000,000 (2000). **Emp:** 140. **Officers:** Poul Hebsgaard, President.

■ 6452 ■ Macro Computer Products Inc.
2523 Product Ct.
Rochester Hills, MI 48309
Phone: (248)853-5353
Free: (800)846-2276 **Fax:** (248)853-7140
Products: Computer supplies. **SIC:** 5045 (Computers, Peripherals & Software).

■ 6453 ■ MAG Innovision Inc.
2801 S Yale St.
Santa Ana, CA 92704-5850
Phone: (714)751-2008
Free: (800)827-3998 **Fax:** (714)751-5522
Products: Computer monitors; Video displays. **SIC:** 5045 (Computers, Peripherals & Software). **Est:** 1989. **Sales:** $600,000,000 (2000). **Emp:** 309. **Officers:** William Wang, President; Eunice Tseng, Controller.

■ 6454 ■ Mailers Equipment Co.
20 Squadron Blvd., Ste. 380
New City, NY 10956
Phone: (914)634-7676
Products: Microfilm equipment and supplies. **SIC:** 5044 (Office Equipment). **Sales:** $5,000,000 (1993). **Emp:** 6. **Officers:** Herbert Moelis, CEO.

■ 6455 ■ Majure Data Inc.
993 Mansell Rd.
Roswell, GA 30076-1505
Phone: (404)587-3054 **Fax:** (404)594-9224
Products: Computer software control products. **SIC:** 5045 (Computers, Peripherals & Software). **Officers:** James Majure, President.

■ 6456 ■ Management Computer Systems Inc.
7301 N Shadeland Ave., No. B
Indianapolis, IN 46250-2023
Phone: (317)842-9696
Products: Computer systems. **SIC:** 5045 (Computers, Peripherals & Software). **Est:** 1975. **Sales:** $5,000,000 (2000). **Emp:** 15. **Officers:** Richard H. Cruse, President.

■ 6457 ■ Management Techniques Inc.
760 Office Pkwy., Ste. 70
St. Louis, MO 63141
Phone: (314)994-9464 **Fax:** (314)994-9467
Products: Software with integrated accounting. **SIC:** 5045 (Computers, Peripherals & Software). **Sales:** $400,000 (2000). **Emp:** 4. **Officers:** William Molitoris, President.

■ 6458 ■ Manchester Equipment Company Inc.
160 Oser Ave.
Hauppauge, NY 11788
Phone: (516)435-1199
Free: (800)632-9880 **Fax:** (516)435-2113
E-mail: webmaster@mecnet.com
URL: http://www.manchesterequipment.com
Products: Computer hardware, software, and supplies. **SIC:** 5045 (Computers, Peripherals & Software). **Est:** 1973. **Sales:** $203,000,000 (2000). **Emp:** 340. **Officers:** Barry Steinberg, CEO & President; Joseph Looney, CFO; Joel Gilberts, VP of Marketing; Sharon M. Siegel, Human Resources Mgr.

■ 6459 ■ Manhattan Office Products Inc.
235 E 45th St.
New York, NY 10017
Phone: (212)557-0123 **Fax:** (212)557-0963
Products: Personal computers. **SIC:** 5045 (Computers, Peripherals & Software). **Sales:** $29,000,000 (2000). **Emp:** 60. **Officers:** Anthony Candido, President; Jeff Melnick, Controller.

■ 6460 ■ Manugistics Group Inc.
2115 E Jefferson St.
Rockville, MD 20852-4999
Phone: (301)984-5000 **Fax:** (301)984-5370
Products: Internet solutionss. **SIC:** 5045 (Computers, Peripherals & Software). **Officers:** Gregory J. Owens, CEO & President; Peter Q. Repetti, CFO.

■ 6461 ■ Maraj International
494 Walleyford Dr.
Berea, OH 44017
Phone: (440)891-3906 **Fax:** (440)891-4132
E-mail: maraj98@hotmail.com
Products: Computers and peripheral equipment; Food preparation machinery; Industrial abrasive products; Iron and steel forgings; Automotive parts. Paper; Metal scrap. **SICs:** 5045 (Computers, Peripherals & Software); 5085 (Industrial Supplies); 5051 (Metals Service Centers & Offices); 5013 (Motor Vehicle Supplies & New Parts). **Est:** 1994. **Sales:** $1,000,000 (2000). **Emp:** 3. **Officers:** P.K. Banerjee, President.

■ 6462 ■ Marathon Codestar
170 Knowles Dr., Ste. 212
Los Gatos, CA 95032
Phone: (408)366-9801
Free: (800)283-7354 **Fax:** (408)366-9815
E-mail: codestar@earthlink.net
URL: http://www.codestar.com
Products: Computer workstations; Barcode scanners; Networking hardware. **SIC:** 5045 (Computers, Peripherals & Software). **Est:** 1989. **Sales:** $14,500,000 (1999). **Emp:** 8. **Officers:** Gregory P. Hall, CEO. **Former Name:** Marathon International Group Inc.

■ 6463 ■ Marco Business Products Inc.
PO Box 250
St. Cloud, MN 56302
Phone: (320)259-3000
URL: http://www.marconet.com
Products: Computers; Furniture; Photocopiers. **SICs:** 5045 (Computers, Peripherals & Software); 5044 (Office Equipment); 5021 (Furniture). **Sales:** $28,000,000 (2000). **Emp:** 160. **Officers:** Gary Marsden, President.

■ 6464 ■ Marketex Computer Corp.
1601 Civic Center Dr., No. 206
Santa Clara, CA 95050
Phone: (408)241-3677 **Fax:** (408)248-3117
Products: Mainframe computers. **SIC:** 5045 (Computers, Peripherals & Software). **Est:** 1977. **Sales:** $6,000,000 (2000). **Emp:** 6. **Officers:** Russ Schneider, President.

■ 6465 ■ Marketware Corp.
101 Yesler Way, Ste. 101
Seattle, WA 98104-2595
Phone: (206)626-6100 **Fax:** (206)626-6102
Products: Computer software for space management. **SIC:** 5045 (Computers, Peripherals & Software).

■ 6466 ■ Martrex Alpha Corp.
PO Box 1709
Minnetonka, MN 55345
Phone: (612)933-5000 **Fax:** (612)933-1889
Products: Petroleum and chemical products. **SICs:** 5172 (Petroleum Products Nec); 5169 (Chemicals & Allied Products Nec). **Sales:** $40,000,000 (1993). **Emp:** 16. **Officers:** David Baugh, Controller.

■ 6467 ■ Marubeni Solutions USA, Corp.
790 Lucerne Dr.
Sunnyvale, CA 94086
Phone: (408)727-8447 **Fax:** (408)245-4525
Products: Computer graphics systems. **SIC:** 5045 (Computers, Peripherals & Software). **Sales:** $11,000,000 (2000). **Emp:** 18. **Officers:** Mr. Takashi Harnshiwa, President. **Former Name:** Marubeni International Electronics Corp.

■ 6468 ■ Mas-Tech International Inc.
29 Deer Run Dr.
Randolph, NJ 07869-4334
Phone: (973)895-2200 **Fax:** (973)895-4641
Products: Fiber optics. **SIC:** 5063 (Electrical Apparatus & Equipment). **Emp:** 6. **Officers:** Mas Oishi, President.

■ 6469 ■ Maverick.com Inc.
117 S Cook St., Ste. 335
Barrington, IL 60010
Free: (800)524-1773 **Fax:** (847)382-4298
Products: Softwaree. **SIC:** 5045 (Computers, Peripherals & Software). **Emp:** 2. **Officers:** William Schuze, CEO & CFO.

■ 6470 ■ Maxey System Inc.
5910 Youree Dr., Ste. D
Shreveport, LA 71105-4255
Phone: (318)868-5422
Products: Computers, peripherals, and software. **SIC:** 5045 (Computers, Peripherals & Software). **Officers:** J. Maxey, President.

■ 6471 ■ Maxi Switch Inc
2901 E Elvira Rd.
Tucson, AZ 85706
Phone: (520)294-5450 **Fax:** (520)294-6890
Products: Computer peripheral equipment,

specializing in computer input devices, electronic contract assembly manufacturing and surface mount technology. **SIC:** 5045 (Computers, Peripherals & Software). **Sales:** $42,000,000 (2000). **Emp:** 75.

■ 6472 ■ Maximum Performance
17551 E Tennessee Dr.
Aurora, CO 80017
Phone: (303)368-4124   **Fax:** (303)751-2683
Products: Semiconductors, computer products and memory devices. **SIC:** 5045 (Computers, Peripherals & Software). **Officers:** Philip Poremba, President.

■ 6473 ■ Maxwell Microsystems Inc.
552 S 14th Ct
Brighton, CO 80601
Phone: (303)252-4561   **Fax:** (303)452-6112
Products: Industrial, ruggedized transportable computers. **SIC:** 5045 (Computers, Peripherals & Software). **Officers:** Ken Maxwell, President.

■ 6474 ■ MBS/Net, Inc.
735 Beta Dr., Ste. C
Cleveland, OH 44143-2326
Phone: (440)461-7650
Free: (800)682-2479   **Fax:** (440)461-7038
Products: Computer software. **SIC:** 5045 (Computers, Peripherals & Software). **Est:** 1978. **Sales:** $3,000,000 (2000). **Emp:** 30. **Doing Business As:** Medical Business Systems Corp.

■ 6475 ■ McBride and Associates Inc.
PO Box 94090
Albuquerque, NM 87199-4090
Phone: (505)883-0600
Free: (800)353-8833   **Fax:** (505)837-7501
Products: Computer hardware and software. **SIC:** 5045 (Computers, Peripherals & Software). **Est:** 1986. **Sales:** $49,000,000 (2000). **Emp:** 100. **Officers:** Teresa McBride, President; Ray Garcia, Controller.

■ 6476 ■ McDATA Corp.
310 Interlocken Pkwy.
Broomfield, CO 80021
Phone: (303)460-9200
Free: (800)545-5773   **Fax:** (303)465-4996
Products: Designs and high band-width networking solutions and test equipment; Computer peripheral equipment. **SIC:** 5045 (Computers, Peripherals & Software). **Sales:** $190,000,000 (1999). **Emp:** 350. **Officers:** John McDonnell, President; Dee Perry, CFO.

■ 6477 ■ Thomas McGehee & Associates
PO Box 7331
Macon, GA 31209-7331
Phone: (912)471-0020
Products: Computers, peripherals, and software. **SIC:** 5045 (Computers, Peripherals & Software). **Officers:** J. McGehee, President.

■ 6478 ■ Medfax Corp.
1838 Gold Hill Rd.
Ft. Mill, SC 29715
Phone: (803)548-1502   **Fax:** (803)548-7534
E-mail: sales@medfax.com
Products: Computers, peripherals, and software for the medical profession. **SIC:** 5045 (Computers, Peripherals & Software). **Est:** 1980. **Emp:** 62. **Officers:** Robert Runde, President; Terry Corgan, Marketing & Sales Mgr.

■ 6479 ■ Media Recovery Inc.
PO Box 1407
Graham, TX 76450
Phone: (940)549-5462   **Fax:** (940)549-5728
Products: Computer related products and supplies. **SICs:** 5045 (Computers, Peripherals & Software); 5112 (Stationery & Office Supplies). **Sales:** $24,000,000 (2000). **Emp:** 180. **Officers:** Alan Myers, President; Tommy Dee Taylor, Vice President.

■ 6480 ■ Medical Manager Sales and Marketing Inc.
500 Clyde Ave.
Mountain View, CA 94043-2218
Phone: (415)969-7047
Free: (800)222-7701   **Fax:** (415)969-0118
Products: Software. **SIC:** 5045 (Computers, Peripherals & Software). **Est:** 1980. **Sales:**

$14,400,000 (2000). **Emp:** 40. **Officers:** Richard W. Mehrlich, CEO & President.

■ 6481 ■ MEGA HAUS Hard Drives
2201 Pine Dr.
Dickinson, TX 77539-4764
Phone: (281)534-3919
Free: (800)786-1153   **Fax:** (281)534-6452
E-mail: sales@megahaus.com
URL: http://www.megahaus.com
Products: Mass storage devices; Computers; Computer parts and equipment, including printers, monitors, video cards, and cpu/mtb/memory. **SIC:** 5045 (Computers, Peripherals & Software). **Est:** 1986. **Sales:** $58,000,000 (2000). **Emp:** 80. **Officers:** Robert Groover, e-mail: rgroover@megahaus.com.

■ 6482 ■ Memory Technologies Texas Inc.
PO Box 13166
Austin, TX 78711
Phone: (512)451-2600   **Fax:** (512)451-3323
Products: Computer memory chips. **SIC:** 5045 (Computers, Peripherals & Software). **Sales:** $15,000,000 (2000). **Emp:** 15. **Officers:** Roy Stocker, President; Shawn Welling, Dir. of Marketing.

■ 6483 ■ Mercury Computer Systems
2105 S Bascom Ave Ste. 130
Campbell, CA 95008
Phone: (408)371-2733   **Fax:** (408)371-2737
Products: Embedded multi-computer systems for government, medical and commercial markets; Prepackaged and custom software. **SIC:** 5045 (Computers, Peripherals & Software).

■ 6484 ■ Merisel Inc.
200 Continental Blvd.
El Segundo, CA 90245-0984
Phone: (310)615-3080
Free: (800)637-4735   **Fax:** (310)615-1263
Products: Micro-computers, equipment, and software. **SIC:** 5045 (Computers, Peripherals & Software).

■ 6485 ■ Merisel Inc. Macamerica Div.
631 River Oaks Pkwy.
San Jose, CA 95134
Phone: (408)434-0433
Free: (800)535-0900   **Fax:** (408)434-1186
Products: Computers. **SIC:** 5045 (Computers, Peripherals & Software). **Est:** 1984. **Sales:** $41,000,000 (2000). **Emp:** 45. **Officers:** Martin Fishman, General Mgr.; Kelly D. Conway, Dir. of Marketing.

■ 6486 ■ Merisel Inc. Merisel World Class Distribution
2010 NW 84th Ave.
Miami, FL 33122
Phone: (305)591-6800   **Fax:** (305)665-2327
Products: Computer equipment, including keyboards, pads, monitors, drives, and software. **SIC:** 5045 (Computers, Peripherals & Software). **Est:** 1982. **Sales:** $87,000,000 (2000). **Emp:** 80. **Officers:** Cliff Dyer, President; David Glait, Controller; Sam Atassi, Sales Mgr.

■ 6487 ■ MET International
212 Garret Ridge
Peachtree City, GA 30269
Phone: (770)487-6780   **Fax:** (770)487-6310
Products: Computer equipment. **SIC:** 5045 (Computers, Peripherals & Software). **Sales:** $400,000 (2000). **Emp:** 1. **Officers:** Klaus Schoeffler, President.

■ 6488 ■ Metal Commodities Inc.
721 Emerson, No. 695
St. Louis, MO 63141
Phone: (314)434-3600   **Fax:** (314)434-4475
Products: Mainframe computers. **SIC:** 5051 (Metals Service Centers & Offices). **Est:** 1986. **Sales:** $11,000,000 (2000). **Emp:** 15. **Officers:** Stan Shanker, President; Jerry Swehla, Controller.

■ 6489 ■ Michiana Micro Inc.
61045 US Hwy. 31
South Bend, IN 46614-5020
Phone: (219)291-1196   **Fax:** (219)291-1255
Products: Computers; Computer software; Peripheral computer equipment. **SIC:** 5045 (Computers,

Peripherals & Software). **Officers:** Robert Wilcox, President.

■ 6490 ■ Micro Central Inc.
8998 Route 18 N
Old Bridge, NJ 08857
Phone: (732)360-0300   **Fax:** (732)360-0303
E-mail: mcsalesmichiganrocentralcom
URL: http://www.microcentral.com
Products: Computers, printers, modems, software, and computer telephony. **SIC:** 5045 (Computers, Peripherals & Software). **Est:** 1984. **Sales:** $50,000 (2000). **Emp:** 60. **Officers:** Jay Lopatin, President; Richard Rugger, Controller; Jay Lopatin, Marketing Mgr.; Aneok Gomer, Technical Dir.

■ 6491 ■ Micro Computer Centre
11745 Bricksome Ave.
Baton Rouge, LA 70816-2369
Phone: (504)293-2733   **Fax:** (504)293-2735
Products: Personal computers, printers, networking equipment, and software. **SIC:** 5045 (Computers, Peripherals & Software). **Est:** 1983. **Officers:** Subhash Reddy, Owner.

■ 6492 ■ Micro Integrated Communications Corp.
3270 Scott Blvd.
Santa Clara, CA 95054
Phone: (408)980-9565
Products: Modems. **SIC:** 5065 (Electronic Parts & Equipment Nec). **Sales:** $4,000,000 (1994). **Emp:** 15. **Officers:** M.L. Lee, President; Maria Tung, Controller.

■ 6493 ■ Micro K Systems Inc.
15874 E Hamilton Pl.
Aurora, CO 80013
Phone: (303)693-3413
Products: Computer systems. **SIC:** 5045 (Computers, Peripherals & Software).

■ 6494 ■ Micro-Pace Computers Inc.
PO Box 6990
Champaign, IL 61826-6990
Phones: (217)356-1884   (217)356-1885
Free: (800)362-9653   **Fax:** (217)356-1881
E-mail: mpace@micropace.com
URL: http://www.micropace.com
Products: Computer hardware and software applications. **SIC:** 5045 (Computers, Peripherals & Software). **Est:** 1982. **Sales:** $24,000,000 (2000). **Emp:** 40. **Officers:** Robert Wolter, President.

■ 6495 ■ Micro Star
2245 Camino Vida Roble, No. 100
Carlsbad, CA 92009-1502
Phone: (760)931-4949   **Fax:** (760)931-4950
E-mail: sales@microstar-usa.com
URL: http://www.microstar-usa.com
Products: Software. **SIC:** 5045 (Computers, Peripherals & Software). **Est:** 1987. **Sales:** $10,000,000 (2000). **Emp:** 120. **Officers:** Stephen H. Benedict, President.

■ 6496 ■ Micro Symplex Corp.
2623 S 21st St.
Phoenix, AZ 85034
Phone: (602)244-0080
Free: (800)330-1349   **Fax:** (602)244-0344
Products: Computers and networks. **SIC:** 5045 (Computers, Peripherals & Software). **Sales:** $15,000,000 (1999). **Emp:** 29. **Officers:** Arun Patel, President; Minaxi Patel, CFO.

■ 6497 ■ Micro-Tron Inc.
2918 Bridgeford Rd.
Omaha, NE 68124-2515
Phone: (402)392-1856
Products: Computers, peripherals, and software. **SIC:** 5045 (Computers, Peripherals & Software). **Officers:** Richard Merten, President.

■ 6498 ■ Microage
219 1st Ave.
Jamestown, ND 58401
Phone: (701)252-1835   **Fax:** (701)252-1837
Products: Computers, peripherals, and software. **SIC:** 5045 (Computers, Peripherals & Software). **Officers:** Thomas Ashwell, Owner.

■ 6499 ■ MicroAge Inc.
PO Box 1920
Tempe, AZ 85282
Phone: (602)968-3168 **Fax:** (602)968-0177
Products: Computers; Computer software; Peripheral computer equipment. **SIC:** 5045 (Computers, Peripherals & Software).

■ 6500 ■ MicroCAD Technologies Inc.
1805 E Dyer Rd.
Santa Ana, CA 92705
Phone: (714)756-0588
Products: Computers and software. **SIC:** 5045 (Computers, Peripherals & Software). **Sales:** $100,000 (2000). **Emp:** 140.

■ 6501 ■ Microcomputer Company of Maryland Inc.
7668 Bel Air Rd.
Baltimore, MD 21236
Phone: (410)668-2600 **Fax:** (410)668-0194
Products: Microcomputers. **SIC:** 5045 (Computers, Peripherals & Software).

■ 6502 ■ Micrographics
PO Box 125
Waterloo, WI 53594-0125
Phone: (920)478-2889 **Fax:** (920)478-3689
Products: Computer software. **SIC:** 5045 (Computers, Peripherals & Software). **Est:** 1980.

■ 6503 ■ Microhelp Inc.
728 Thimble Shoals Blvd., No. E
Newport News, VA 23606-2574
Phone: (757)873-6707 **Fax:** (757)873-8895
Products: Computers; Computer software; Peripheral computer equipment. **SIC:** 5045 (Computers, Peripherals & Software). **Officers:** James Bird, President.

■ 6504 ■ Microlink Enterprises Inc.
13731 E Proctor Ave.
City of Industry, CA 91746
Phone: (626)330-9599 **Fax:** (626)330-4095
URL: http://www.microlinkinc.com
Products: Computers and computer accessories. **SIC:** 5045 (Computers, Peripherals & Software). **Est:** 1989. **Sales:** $21,000,000 (2000). **Emp:** 45. **Officers:** Don Liang, President.

■ 6505 ■ Micronetics Inc. Information Management Systems
14148 Magnolia Blvd.
Sherman Oaks, CA 91423
Phone: (818)784-6890 **Fax:** (818)784-6552
Products: Computers; Computer software. **SIC:** 5045 (Computers, Peripherals & Software). **Est:** 1981. **Sales:** $2,000,000 (2000). **Emp:** 32. **Officers:** Juan G. Ledo, President; Sam J. Boyer, CFO; Mike Brezner, General Mgr.

■ 6506 ■ Micros-to-Mainframes Inc.
614 Corporate Way
Valley Cottage, NY 10989
Phone: (914)268-5000
Free: (800)468-6782 **Fax:** (914)268-9695
Products: Computers and computer systems integration. **SIC:** 5045 (Computers, Peripherals & Software). **Sales:** $69,000,000 (1999). **Emp:** 181. **Officers:** Steven H. Rothman, CEO & President; Frank Wong, CFO.

■ 6507 ■ Microsearch Inc.
10515 Harwin Dr., Ste. 100
Houston, TX 77074
Phone: (713)988-2818 **Fax:** (713)995-4994
Products: Turnkey computer systems used in 3-D animation. **SIC:** 5045 (Computers, Peripherals & Software). **Sales:** $1,000,000 (2000). **Emp:** 15.

■ 6508 ■ Microsoft Corp.
1 Microsoft Way
Redmond, WA 98052-6399
Phone: (425)882-8080
Free: (800)426-9400 **Fax:** (425)936-7329
Products: Microcomputer software and hardware items; computer books and multimedia products. **SIC:** 5045 (Computers, Peripherals & Software). **Sales:** $19,747,000,000 (1999). **Emp:** 31,396. **Officers:**

Steven A. Ballmer, CEO & President; John Connors, VP & CFO.

■ 6509 ■ Microstar Computer Technology Inc.
13401 Brooks Dr.
Baldwin Park, CA 91706
Phone: (626)337-9770 **Fax:** (626)338-1375
Products: Computer monitors. **SIC:** 5045 (Computers, Peripherals & Software). **Est:** 1986. **Sales:** $25,000,000 (2000). **Emp:** 40. **Officers:** James Wang, CEO; Alvin Ho, Exec. VP; Tower Chang, General Mgr.; Matt Woo, VP of Operations.

■ 6510 ■ MicroTech Conversion Systems
2 Davis Dr.
Belmont, CA 94002
Phone: (650)596-1900
Free: (800)223-3693 **Fax:** (650)596-1915
Products: Software; R and D in conversion software, tape duplicating equipment and CD duplication. **SIC:** 5045 (Computers, Peripherals & Software). **Sales:** $1,508,000,000 (2000). **Emp:** 30. **Officers:** Corwin Nichols, President & Chairman of the Board.

■ 6511 ■ MICROTECH Systems Inc.
11940 SW Pacific Hwy., Ste. A
Tigard, OR 97223-6444
Phone: (503)620-9715
Products: Computers. **SIC:** 5045 (Computers, Peripherals & Software). **Sales:** $9,000,000 (2000). **Emp:** 20. **Officers:** Nick Park, Owner; Angie Beers, CFO.

■ 6512 ■ Microunited
2200 E Golf Rd.
Des Plaines, IL 60016
Phone: (847)699-5000 **Fax:** (847)699-0937
Products: Computers; Computer software; Peripheral computer equipment. **SIC:** 5045 (Computers, Peripherals & Software).

■ 6513 ■ Microware Inc.
PO Box 55068
Portland, OR 97238-5068
Phone: (503)644-1296
Products: Computer hardware. **SIC:** 5045 (Computers, Peripherals & Software). **Sales:** $200,000,000 (1994). **Emp:** 512. **Officers:** Rick Terrell, President.

■ 6514 ■ Mid-America Information Systems Inc.
908 Black Partridge
McHenry, IL 60050
Phone: (815)344-3564
Products: Accounting software for PICK operating systems and PC/MS-DOS. **SIC:** 5045 (Computers, Peripherals & Software). **Est:** 1980. **Sales:** $20,000 (2000).

■ 6515 ■ Mid America Ribbon & Supply Co.
5710 Northwood Dr.
Minneapolis, MN 55436-2054
Phone: (612)929-1656
Products: Computers; Computer software; Peripheral computer equipment. **SIC:** 5045 (Computers, Peripherals & Software). **Officers:** Clarence Anderson, President.

■ 6516 ■ Midland Computers
5699 W Howard St.
Niles, IL 60714-4011
Phone: (847)588-2130
Free: (800)407-0700 **Fax:** (847)588-2148
Products: Corporate computer hardware and software. **SIC:** 5045 (Computers, Peripherals & Software). **Sales:** $11,000,000 (2000). **Emp:** 22. **Officers:** Jay k. Overbye, Owner.

■ 6517 ■ MidWest Micro
6910 U.S Rte. 36 E
Fletcher, OH 45326
Phone: (937)368-2650
Free: (800)445-2015 **Fax:** 800-562-6622
Products: Notebook and desktop computers and other computer-related equipment. **SIC:** 5045 (Computers, Peripherals & Software). **Sales:** $308,000,000 (2000). **Emp:** 513. **Officers:** Kent Markley, President; Frank Urnick, Controller.

■ 6518 ■ Mikes Computerland
PO Box 1120
Lebanon, VA 24266-1120
Phone: (540)889-5738 **Fax:** (540)889-4334
E-mail: mcland@mounet.com
URL: http://www.mikeland.com
Products: Computers; Computer supplies and parts; Printers. **SIC:** 5045 (Computers, Peripherals & Software). **Est:** 1979. **Officers:** Michael Rhea, Owner, e-mail: miker@mounet.com.

■ 6519 ■ MIMICS Inc.
PO Drawer 606
Angel Fire, NM 87710
Phone: (505)377-3955 **Fax:** (505)377-6343
E-mail: finsoft@mimics.com
URL: http://www.mimics.com/finsoft
Products: Financial computer software programs. **SIC:** 5045 (Computers, Peripherals & Software). **Est:** 1976. **Sales:** $1,500,000 (2000). **Emp:** 13. **Officers:** Rich Wildgrube, President; Maggie Merten, CFO; Maggie Merten, Dir of Human Resources; Dave Wildgrube, Sales & Marketing Contact; Matt Batchelder, Customer Service Contact.

■ 6520 ■ MindWorks Corp.
PO Box 60325
Sunnyvale, CA 94088-0325
Phone: (408)730-2100
Free: (800)683-8005 **Fax:** (408)730-5202
Products: Computer software. **SIC:** 5045 (Computers, Peripherals & Software). **Sales:** $11,000,000 (2000). **Emp:** 30. **Officers:** Vish Mishra, President.

■ 6521 ■ Mini-Micro Supply Company Inc.
4900 Patrick Henry Dr.
Santa Clara, CA 95054
Phone: (408)327-0388
Free: (800)275-4642 **Fax:** (408)327-0389
Products: Computers. **SIC:** 5045 (Computers, Peripherals & Software). **Sales:** $155,000,000 (2000). **Emp:** 150. **Officers:** James Lee, President.

■ 6522 ■ Miracle Computers Inc.
780 Montague Expwy., Ste. 202
San Jose, CA 95131
Phone: (408)435-8177
Free: (877)377-2250 **Fax:** (408)435-8179
E-mail: charles@miraclecomputers.com
URL: http://www.miraclecomputers.com
Products: Computer hardware and software. **SIC:** 5045 (Computers, Peripherals & Software). **Est:** 1985. **Sales:** $8,000,000 (2000). **Emp:** 20. **Officers:** Mary Cheng, President, e-mail: mary@miraclecomputers.com.

■ 6523 ■ Mitsuba Corp.
1925 Wright Ave.
La Verne, CA 91750
Phone: (909)392-2000 **Fax:** (909)392-2021
Products: Computers and computer accessories. **SIC:** 5045 (Computers, Peripherals & Software). **Est:** 1982. **Sales:** $110,000,000 (2000). **Emp:** 51. **Officers:** James Chen, President; Monica Chen, Controller; Steve Daniels, Dir. of Marketing & Sales.

■ 6524 ■ Mitsui Comtek Corp.
12980 Saratoga Ave.
Saratoga, CA 95070
Phone: (408)725-8525
Products: Computers and computer software. **SIC:** 5045 (Computers, Peripherals & Software). **Sales:** $12,000,000 (1993). **Emp:** 25. **Officers:** T. Soejima, President; M. Ikushima, CFO.

■ 6525 ■ Mitsumi Electronics Corp.
5808 W Campus Cir. Dr.
Irving, TX 75063
Phone: (972)550-7300 **Fax:** (972)550-7424
Products: Computer components. **SIC:** 5045 (Computers, Peripherals & Software).

■ 6526 ■ MLH and Associates
1942 Mt. Shasta Dr.
San Pedro, CA 90732
Phone: (310)519-9158 **Fax:** (310)547-4693
Products: Computers. **SIC:** 5045 (Computers, Peripherals & Software). **Officers:** Michael Harris, President.

■ 6527 ■ Modular Mining Systems Inc.
3289 E Hemisphere Loop
Tucson, AZ 85706-5028
Phone: (520)746-9127 **Fax:** (520)889-5790
E-mail: products@mmsi.com
URL: http://www.mmsi.com
Products: Computer based mine management systems for open pit and underground mines and quarries. **SIC:** 5045 (Computers, Peripherals & Software). **Est:** 1979. **Sales:** $34,000,000 (1999). **Emp:** 259. **Officers:** James Wm. White, CEO & Chairman of the Board; Mark Baker, Exec. VP.

■ 6528 ■ Montero International, Inc.
11016 Myrtle St.
Downey, CA 90241
Phone: (562)862-0116 **Fax:** (562)862-7087
Products: Computer hardware and software; Electronic equipment, including televisions, radios, and motion picture equipment. **SICs:** 5045 (Computers, Peripherals & Software); 5064 (Electrical Appliances—Television & Radio). **Officers:** Jorge H. Montero, President.

■ 6529 ■ Moss Enterprises Inc.
137 Boyson Rd.
Hiawatha, IA 52233-1205
Phone: (319)393-4048 **Fax:** (319)393-4049
Products: Computer products, including peripherals, software, and self-training systems in educational markets. **SIC:** 5045 (Computers, Peripherals & Software). **Officers:** William Moss, President.

■ 6530 ■ Mountain High Technology Inc.
PO Box 5690
Steamboat Springs, CO 80477
Phone: (970)879-7063 **Fax:** (970)879-3594
Products: Computers; Computer software; Peripheral computer equipment. **SIC:** 5045 (Computers, Peripherals & Software). **Officers:** Martin Rosenzweig, President.

■ 6531 ■ Mountain Systems Inc.
966 W Main St., Ste. 8, Brooksfield Sq.
Abingdon, VA 24210
Phone: (540)676-2093 **Fax:** (540)676-4406
Products: Caller I.D. hardware. **SIC:** 5065 (Electronic Parts & Equipment Nec). **Sales:** $1,000,000 (2000). **Emp:** 7. **Officers:** Edward T. Dixon, President; Tina H. Dixon, CFO.

■ 6532 ■ Moustrak Inc.
503 N Division St., No. 2
Carson City, NV 89703-4104
Phone: (702)884-1925 **Fax:** (702)884-1827
Products: Computer mice and related peripherals. **SIC:** 5045 (Computers, Peripherals & Software). **Sales:** $9,000,000 (2000). **Emp:** 20. **Officers:** Bob McDermand, President.

■ 6533 ■ MPS Multimedia Inc.
451 Victory Ave., Ste. 1
South San Francisco, CA 94080
Phone: (650)872-7100 **Fax:** (650)583-0270
Products: Software. **SIC:** 5045 (Computers, Peripherals & Software). **Sales:** $14,000,000 (2000). **Emp:** 10. **Officers:** Steve Chen, President; Edgar S. Chen, CFO.

■ 6534 ■ MRK Technologies Ltd.
3 Summit Park Dr., No. 300
Independence, OH 44131
Phone: (216)520-4300
URL: http://www.mrktech.com
Products: Hardware; Software; Communications equipment. **SIC:** 5045 (Computers, Peripherals & Software). **Est:** 1994. **Sales:** $37,000,000 (2000). **Emp:** 80. **Officers:** Michael R. Kennedy, President & CEO; John Molchan, VP of Finance.

■ 6535 ■ J.B. Muncer and Associates Inc.
4041 Batton NE, Ste. 210
North Canton, OH 44720
Phone: (330)494-3355
Free: (800)837-3355 **Fax:** (330)494-4035
Products: Computer software. **SIC:** 5045 (Computers, Peripherals & Software). **Sales:** $1,000,000 (2000). **Emp:** 9. **Officers:** John B. Muncer II, President.

■ 6536 ■ MuTech Corp.
85 Rangeway Rd.
North Billerica, MA 01862-2105
Phone: (781)935-1770 **Fax:** (781)935-3054
Products: Imaging computer boards. **SIC:** 5045 (Computers, Peripherals & Software). **Sales:** $3,000,000 (2000). **Emp:** 15. **Officers:** John A. Morrissey, President.

■ 6537 ■ Vic Myers Associates Inc.
PO Box 3586
Albuquerque, NM 87190-3586
Phone: (505)884-6878 **Fax:** (505)883-4062
Products: Computer software. **SIC:** 5045 (Computers, Peripherals & Software). **Est:** 1980.

■ 6538 ■ Vic Myers Associates
7800 S Elati, Ste. 210
Littleton, CO 80120
Phone: (303)730-7313 **Fax:** (303)730-6961
Products: Computer software. **SIC:** 5045 (Computers, Peripherals & Software).

■ 6539 ■ Vic Myers Associates
4645 S Lakeshore Dr., Ste. 18
Tempe, AZ 85282
Phone: (602)345-6449 **Fax:** (602)345-6427
Products: Computer software. **SIC:** 5045 (Computers, Peripherals & Software).

■ 6540 ■ Vic Myers Associates
1935 S Main St., Ste. 539
Salt Lake City, UT 84115
Phone: (801)467-1795 **Fax:** (801)467-1745
Products: Computer software. **SIC:** 5045 (Computers, Peripherals & Software).

■ 6541 ■ Nanbren-Compsol Ltd.
1056 N Tustin Ave.
Anaheim, CA 92807
Phone: (714)632-5010
Products: Computers. **SIC:** 5045 (Computers, Peripherals & Software). **Sales:** $2,000,000 (1994). **Emp:** 10. **Officers:** Norm W. Hagelstrom, President.

■ 6542 ■ National Equipment Development Corp.
PO Box 244
Newtown Square, PA 19073
Phone: (215)353-7272 **Fax:** (215)353-6461
Products: Computers and computer equipment and supplies. **SIC:** 5045 (Computers, Peripherals & Software). **Est:** 1981. **Sales:** $3,000,000 (2000). **Officers:** Joseph A. Basile Sr., President; Daniel Delia, Controller.

■ 6543 ■ National Systems Corp.
414 N Orleans St., Ste. 501
Chicago, IL 60610
Phone: (312)855-1000
Products: Restaurant computer systems. **SIC:** 5045 (Computers, Peripherals & Software). **Sales:** $4,000,000 (2000). **Emp:** 45. **Officers:** James Kargman, President; Kimberly Hecker, Controller.

■ 6544 ■ Navarre Corp.
7400 49th Ave. N
New Hope, MN 55428
Phone: (612)535-8333 **Fax:** (612)533-2156
Products: Computer software; Audio products. **SIC:** 5045 (Computers, Peripherals & Software). **Est:** 1983. **Sales:** $200,700,000 (2000). **Emp:** 239. **Officers:** Eric H. Paulson, CEO, President & Chairman of the Board; Charles E. Cheney, Exec. VP & CFO; William L. Stocks III, VP of Marketing; Thomas R. Tuomela, VP of Operations; Marilyn K. Gabbert, Dir of Human Resources.

■ 6545 ■ NCD
6100 Hollywood Blvd.
Hollywood, FL 33024
Phone: (954)967-2397 **Fax:** (954)967-1132
Products: Computers; Computer software; Peripheral computer equipment. **SIC:** 5045 (Computers, Peripherals & Software).

■ 6546 ■ NCS Assessments
5605 Green Circle Dr.
Minnetonka, MN 55343
Phone: (612)939-5000
Products: Computer scoring systems. **SIC:** 5045 (Computers, Peripherals & Software). **Sales:** $22,000,000 (2000). **Emp:** 130. **Officers:** David Smith, President; Lee Koktan, Controller.

■ 6547 ■ NCUBE
1825 NW 167th Pl
Beaverton, OR 97006
Phone: (503)629-5088 **Fax:** (503)645-1737
Products: Super computer parallel systems. **SIC:** 5045 (Computers, Peripherals & Software).

■ 6548 ■ NEC America Inc. Data and Video Communications Systems Div.
110 Rio Robles
San Jose, CA 95134-1899
Phone: (408)433-1200 **Fax:** (408)433-1460
Products: Computers and printers; Electronic equipment, including telephones and mobile phones. **SICs:** 5045 (Computers, Peripherals & Software); 5065 (Electronic Parts & Equipment Nec). **Sales:** $30,000,000 (2000). **Emp:** 40. **Officers:** Maseo Hibino, General Mgr.; Dave L. Peters, Dir. of Marketing & Sales.

■ 6549 ■ NEC Technologies Inc.
1250 N Arlington Heights Rd., Ste. 500
Itasca, IL 60143-1248
Phone: (630)775-7900 **Fax:** (630)775-7901
Products: Computers, servers, disk drives and other computer peripherals. **SIC:** 5045 (Computers, Peripherals & Software). **Sales:** $26,200,000 (2000). **Emp:** 1,500. **Officers:** Toschiichi Ishii, CEO, President & Chairman of the Board; Sam Kawashima, Treasurer & Controller.

■ 6550 ■ Networks 2000
1201 Tourmaline St.
San Diego, CA 92109
Phone: (619)488-8753 **Fax:** (619)488-0673
Products: Firm specializes in installation and service of Windows NT and Novell Netware. Also provides network troubleshooting and technical support, LAN/WAN design, and user training. **SIC:** 5045 (Computers, Peripherals & Software). **Sales:** $300,000 (2000). **Emp:** 4.

■ 6551 ■ New Process Development
PO Box 462
Milltown, NJ 08850
Phone: (732)390-8893 **Fax:** (732)390-8898
Products: Computer software; Temperature pressured level controls. **SIC:** 5045 (Computers, Peripherals & Software). **Est:** 1911. **Officers:** Elliot S. Kuchinsky, President.

■ 6552 ■ NewSoft America Inc.
47470 Seabridge Dr.
Fremont, CA 94538
Phone: (510)445-8600
Free: (800)214-7059 **Fax:** (510)445-8601
Products: Consumer and business software. **SIC:** 5045 (Computers, Peripherals & Software). **Sales:** $3,000,000 (2000). **Emp:** 32. **Officers:** Andrew Wang, President.

■ 6553 ■ Nice Computer Inc.
4118 S 500 W
Salt Lake City, UT 84123
Phone: (801)261-3300 **Fax:** (801)261-0095
E-mail: jnice@rebeloffice.com
URL: http://www.rebeloffice.com
Products: Computers; Computer software; Peripheral computer equipment. **SICs:** 5045 (Computers, Peripherals & Software); 5112 (Stationery & Office Supplies). **Est:** 1985. **Emp:** 36. **Officers:** Joseph Nice, Owner, e-mail: joenice@email.com. **Former Name:** Nice Computer Designers.

■ 6554 ■ NIDI Northwest Inc.
15209 NE 95th St.
Redmond, WA 98052-2562
Phone: (425)861-6434 **Fax:** (425)861-8838
Products: Peripheral computer equipment; Parts for computers and peripheral equipment. **SIC:** 5045

(Computers, Peripherals & Software). **Officers:** John Showalter, President.

■ 6555 ■ NIDI Technologies Inc.
15209 NE 95th St.
Redmond, WA 98052-2562
Phone: (425)861-6434
Free: (800)367-6434 **Fax:** (425)861-8838
Products: Computer graphics and peripheral equipment. **SIC:** 5045 (Computers, Peripherals & Software). **Sales:** $6,000,000 (2000). **Emp:** 7.

■ 6556 ■ N.I.E. International Inc.
3000 E Chambers St.
Phoenix, AZ 85040
Phone: (602)470-1500
Free: (800)530-2684 **Fax:** (602)470-1540
Products: Computers and peripherals. **SIC:** 5045 (Computers, Peripherals & Software). **Sales:** $25,000,000 (2000). **Emp:** 200. **Officers:** Mike Mahmoodi, CEO & President; Rob Zack, VP of Finance.

■ 6557 ■ NIENEX Inc.
3000 E Chambers St.
Phoenix, AZ 85040
Phone: (602)470-1500
Products: Computers and peripherals. **SIC:** 5045 (Computers, Peripherals & Software). **Officers:** Mike Mahmoodi, CEO & President.

■ 6558 ■ Nimax Inc.
9275 Carroll Park Dr.
San Diego, CA 92121-3234
Phone: (619)452-2220
Free: (800)876-4629 **Fax:** (619)452-6669
Products: Computer peripheral equipment including bar code, point-of-sale and automatic identification systems. **SIC:** 5045 (Computers, Peripherals & Software). **Sales:** $70,000,000 (2000). **Emp:** 110. **Officers:** Steve Hsieh, CEO; Karen Harvey, CFO.

■ 6559 ■ Nokia Inc.
2300 Valley View Ln., Ste. 100
Irving, TX 75062
Phone: (817)355-9070
Products: Computer monitors; Mobile telephones. **SICs:** 5045 (Computers, Peripherals & Software); 5065 (Electronic Parts & Equipment Nec).

■ 6560 ■ Nordic Computers
5060 Commercial Cir Ste. A
Concord, CA 94520
Phone: (925)687-3050 **Fax:** (925)687-3173
Products: IBM-compatible computers. **SIC:** 5045 (Computers, Peripherals & Software). **Sales:** $3,000,000 (2000). **Emp:** 10. **Officers:** Andy Jacobson, President.

■ 6561 ■ Nova Technology Inc.
7135 Shady Oak Rd.
Eden Prairie, MN 55344-3516
Phone: (612)944-6785 **Fax:** (612)944-2815
Products: Networking equipment and supplies. **SIC:** 5045 (Computers, Peripherals & Software). **Officers:** Dennis Schuster, President.

■ 6562 ■ NovaQuest InfoSystems
19950 Mariner Ave.
Torrance, CA 90503
Phone: (310)214-4200 **Fax:** (310)214-4246
Products: Corporate microcomputers. **SIC:** 5045 (Computers, Peripherals & Software). **Sales:** $210,000,000 (2000). **Emp:** 350. **Officers:** Asif Hudani, President; Curtis Harward, CFO.

■ 6563 ■ NPA West Inc.
780 Chadbourne Rd., Ste. A
Suisun City, CA 94585
Phone: (707)421-1234
Free: (800)999-4NPA **Fax:** (707)427-1234
E-mail: sales@npa.com
Products: Computer systems, service, and maintenance. **SIC:** 5045 (Computers, Peripherals & Software). **Est:** 1985. **Sales:** $22,500,000 (2000). **Emp:** 38. **Officers:** Alan Rees, CEO & President; Bill Thomas, CFO; Ed Harper, VP of Marketing & Sales, e-mail: ed.harper@npawest.com; Brenda Sanders, Customer Service Contact, e-mail: brenda.sanders@

npawest.com; Bill Thomas, Human Resources Contact, e-mail: bill.thomas@npawest.com.

■ 6564 ■ Numeridex Inc.
241 Holbrook Dr.
Wheeling, IL 60090
Phone: (847)541-8840
Free: (800)323-7737 **Fax:** (847)541-8392
Products: Supplies and accessories for computer-aided-design and barcode products. **SIC:** 5045 (Computers, Peripherals & Software). **Sales:** $4,500,000 (2000). **Emp:** 16. **Officers:** William Gapp, President; Albert Hoyos, VP of Finance.

■ 6565 ■ NYMA Inc.
7501 Greenway Ctr. Dr., 1200
Greenbelt, MD 20770
Phone: (301)345-0832
Products: Computers, peripherals, and software. **SIC:** 5045 (Computers, Peripherals & Software). **Officers:** Azmat Ali, Chairman of the Board.

■ 6566 ■ O/E Automation Inc.
3290 W Big Beaver Rd.
Troy, MI 48084
Phone: (248)643-2035 **Fax:** (248)643-0728
Products: Computers. **SIC:** 5045 (Computers, Peripherals & Software). **Est:** 1979. **Sales:** $80,000,000 (2000). **Emp:** 500. **Officers:** Richard Austin, President.

■ 6567 ■ Ocean Interface Company Inc.
21221 Commerce Point Dr.
Walnut, CA 91789-3056
Phone: (909)595-1212 **Fax:** (909)595-9683
Products: Computer peripheral equipment and networking server workstations. **SIC:** 5045 (Computers, Peripherals & Software). **Sales:** $6,500,000 (2000). **Emp:** 20. **Officers:** Mei Chen, President.

■ 6568 ■ Office Manager, Inc.
143 Log Canoe Cir.
Stevensville, MD 21666
Phone: (410)643-8000 **Fax:** (410)643-8001
E-mail: omi@friend.ly.net
Products: Computers; Peripheral computer equipment; Computer software. **SIC:** 5045 (Computers, Peripherals & Software). **Est:** 1986. **Sales:** $750,000 (2000). **Emp:** 2. **Officers:** Marian Dipboye, President.

■ 6569 ■ Olicom USA Inc.
350 Park Pl.
Chagrin Falls, OH 44022-4456
Phone: (216)247-0024 **Free:** (800)265-4266
Products: Personal computer equipment, including token rings. **SIC:** 5045 (Computers, Peripherals & Software). **Est:** 1985. **Sales:** $238,200,000 (2000). **Emp:** 410. **Officers:** Michael Camp, CEO & President; David Burkey, CFO; Peter Haslam, VP of Marketing & Sales.

■ 6570 ■ Omicron Electronics
11240 E 9 Mile Rd.
Warren, MI 48089
Phone: (810)757-8192 **Fax:** (810)757-5262
Products: Computer electronics, including CAD systems. **SIC:** 5045 (Computers, Peripherals & Software). **Est:** 1973. **Sales:** $1,000,000 (2000). **Emp:** 8. **Officers:** Michael Tattan, President.

■ 6571 ■ Omnium Corp.
711 Keller Ave. S
Amery, WI 54001
Phone: (715)268-8500
Free: (800)328-0223 **Fax:** (715)268-8333
E-mail: unisource@win.bright.net
Products: Computer accessories; Ergonomic workstation improvements, including articulating wristrest mechanisms, foot rests, and caddies. **SICs:** 5045 (Computers, Peripherals & Software); 5044 (Office Equipment). **Est:** 1982. **Sales:** $600,000 (2000). **Emp:** 3. **Officers:** Dean G. Lubow, President; Tom Albrecht, Sales/Marketing Contact; Carol Wozniak, Customer Service Contact.

■ 6572 ■ Operator Interface Technology
650 Weaver Park Rd.
Longmont, CO 80501
Phone: (303)684-0094 **Fax:** (303)684-0062
Products: Custom keypads. **SIC:** 5045 (Computers, Peripherals & Software).

■ 6573 ■ Optical Advantage
8009 34th Ave. S, No. 125
Minneapolis, MN 55425
Phone: (612)854-6109
Products: Optical storage and retrieval systems. **SIC:** 5048 (Ophthalmic Goods). **Est:** 1990. **Sales:** $4,000,000 (2000). **Emp:** 330. **Officers:** Jim Leto, President; Jonge Forgues, CFO.

■ 6574 ■ Optical Laser Inc.
5702 Bolsa Ave.
Huntington Beach, CA 92649-1169
Phone: (714)379-4400
Free: (800)776-9215 **Fax:** (714)379-4413
Products: Optical disc drives and imaging software. **SIC:** 5045 (Computers, Peripherals & Software). **Sales:** $17,000,000 (2000). **Emp:** 30. **Officers:** Michael Raab, President; Karl Tao, CFO.

■ 6575 ■ Oracle Corp. USA Div.
500 Oracle Pkwy.
Redwood City, CA 94065
Phone: (650)506-7000
Products: Software. **SIC:** 5045 (Computers, Peripherals & Software).

■ 6576 ■ Oregon Educational Technology Consortium
707 13th St. SE, Ste. 260
Salem, OR 97301
Phone: (503)588-1343 **Fax:** (503)581-0468
E-mail: info@oetc.org
URL: http://www.oetc.org
Products: Educational software. **SIC:** 5045 (Computers, Peripherals & Software). **Est:** 1981. **Officers:** Thor Prichard, Executive Dir. **Former Name:** Oregon Educational Computing Consortium.

■ 6577 ■ Organization Systems Inc.
750 Old Main St.
Rocky Hill, CT 06067
Phone: (860)257-9322
Free: (800)969-4747 **Fax:** (860)257-8390
Products: Software. **SIC:** 5045 (Computers, Peripherals & Software). **Sales:** $500,000 (2000). **Emp:** 3. **Officers:** Frederick L. Bouchard, Chairman of the Board; Donna Pallone, President.

■ 6578 ■ P-80 Systems
3310 5th Ave.
Charleston, WV 25312
Phone: (304)744-7322 **Fax:** (304)744-7322
Products: Computer software, primarily for security industries. **SIC:** 5045 (Computers, Peripherals & Software). **Sales:** $100,000 (2000). **Emp:** 1. **Officers:** Larry Higginbotham, President.

■ 6579 ■ Pacific Coast Micro Inc.
P. O. Box 18265
Irvine, CA 92623
Phone: (714)993-0471
Products: Computer hardware and software. **SIC:** 5045 (Computers, Peripherals & Software).

■ 6580 ■ Pacific Interface
99-1285-B6 Hala Valley
Aiea, HI 96701
Phone: (808)488-3363 **Fax:** (808)488-2876
Products: Computers, peripherals, and software; Paper. **SICs:** 5045 (Computers, Peripherals & Software); 5112 (Stationery & Office Supplies). **Officers:** V. Grudgenski, CEO.

■ 6581 ■ Packaged Software Solutions Inc.
PO Box 87931
Canton, MI 48187
Phone: (734)453-6845 **Fax:** (734)453-4475
Products: Financial, manufacturing, and inventory management software for midrange IBM-compatible computer systems. **SIC:** 5045 (Computers, Peripherals & Software). **Sales:** $1,000,000 (2000). **Emp:** 5. **Officers:** Joseph H. Le Blanc, President.

■ 6582 ■ **Packet Engines**
11707 East Sprague #101
Spokane, WA 99206
Phone: (509)777-7000 **Fax:** (509)777-7001
Products: High-performance routing switches, hubs, network interface cards. **SIC:** 5045 (Computers, Peripherals & Software). **Sales:** $115,000,000 (2000). **Emp:** 178. **Officers:** Bernard Daines, CEO; Pete Price, CFO.

■ 6583 ■ **PAGG Corp.**
425 Fortune Blvd.
Milford, MA 01757
Phone: (508)478-8544
Products: Computer board turnkey assembly systems. **SIC:** 5084 (Industrial Machinery & Equipment).

■ 6584 ■ **Paige International**
3166 Tennyson St. NW
Washington, DC 20015-2360
Phone: (202)244-6406
Products: Computers, peripherals, and software. **SIC:** 5045 (Computers, Peripherals & Software). **Est:** 1988. **Officers:** Charles Paige, President.

■ 6585 ■ **Paoku International Company Ltd.**
1057 Shore Rd.
Naperville, IL 60563
Phone: (630)369-5199 **Fax:** (630)360-5935
Products: Electronic computers and computer products. **SIC:** 5045 (Computers, Peripherals & Software). **Sales:** $6,000,000 (2000). **Emp:** 20. **Officers:** Jennifer Chu, President; Sophia Tan, Accountant.

■ 6586 ■ **Paragram Sales Co. Inc.**
8455 -O Tyco Rd.
Vienna, VA 22182
Phone: (703)356-0808
Products: Computers, peripherals, and software. **SIC:** 5045 (Computers, Peripherals & Software). **Officers:** Stanley Drivas, President.

■ 6587 ■ **Parallel PCs Inc.**
1404 Durwood Dr.
Reading, PA 19609
Phone: (215)670-1710 **Fax:** (610)670-1710
Products: Software. **SIC:** 5045 (Computers, Peripherals & Software). **Sales:** $100,000 (1994). **Emp:** 3. **Officers:** Steven Rosenberry, President.

■ 6588 ■ **Paramount International**
92 Corporate Park, Ste. C-240
Irvine, CA 92606-5108
Phone: (949)252-8874 **Fax:** (949)252-1430
E-mail: webmaster@paramountinternationalcom
URL: http://www.paramountinternationalcom
Products: Computer equipment; Books. **SICs:** 5045 (Computers, Peripherals & Software); 5192 (Books, Periodicals & Newspapers). **Officers:** Alka Jobalia, Executive Director.

■ 6589 ■ **Paramount Technology**
1252 Diamond Way
Concord, CA 94520
Phone: (925)825-4046 **Fax:** (925)691-9386
E-mail: sales@paramounttechnology.com
URL: http://www.paramounttechnology.com
Products: Computer hardware and software. **SIC:** 5045 (Computers, Peripherals & Software). **Est:** 1993. **Sales:** $2,000,000 (2000). **Emp:** 6. **Officers:** Anton Luu, General Mgr., e-mail: anton@paramounttechnology.com. **Former Name:** Paramount Computer.

■ 6590 ■ **Parasoft Corp.**
27415 Trabuco Cir.
Mission Viejo, CA 92692
Phone: (714)380-9739
Products: Computers; Hard drives. **SIC:** 5045 (Computers, Peripherals & Software). **Est:** 1985. **Sales:** $600,000 (2000). **Emp:** 6. **Officers:** Larry Lesser, President.

■ 6591 ■ **B.A. Pargh Company Inc.**
PO Box 23770
Nashville, TN 37202
Phone: (615)254-2500
Free: (800)227-1000 **Fax:** (423)247-4329
Products: Computers and peripherals. **SICs:** 5045 (Computers, Peripherals & Software); 5065 (Electronic Parts & Equipment Nec). **Sales:** $62,000,000 (1993). **Emp:** 125. **Officers:** Bernard A. Pargh, President.

■ 6592 ■ **Parks Software Services Inc.**
PO Box 40763
Raleigh, NC 27629-0763
Phone: (919)872-9866 **Fax:** (919)981-0354
Products: Computers; Computer software; Peripheral computer equipment. **SIC:** 5045 (Computers, Peripherals & Software). **Officers:** Anthony Parks, President.

■ 6593 ■ **Parts Now! Inc.**
3517 W Beltline Hwy.
Madison, WI 53713
Phone: (608)276-8688 **Fax:** (608)276-9380
Products: Computer printers and parts. Computer printer repair. **SIC:** 5045 (Computers, Peripherals & Software). **Sales:** $88,000,000 (2000). **Emp:** 140. **Officers:** David Reinke, CEO.

■ 6594 ■ **PartsPort Ltd.**
1801 Walthall Creek Dr.
Colonial Heights, VA 23834
Phone: (804)530-1233 **Fax:** (804)530-1128
Products: Computer keypad overlays and parts for monitor repair. **SIC:** 5045 (Computers, Peripherals & Software). **Sales:** $1,000,000 (2000). **Emp:** 3. **Officers:** Cathy Sebastian, President.

■ 6595 ■ **Pathtrace Systems Inc.**
2143 Convention Center Way, Ste. 100
Ontario, CA 91764
Phone: (909)460-5522 **Fax:** (909)460-5529
Products: CAD/CAM computer software. **SIC:** 5045 (Computers, Peripherals & Software). **Sales:** $2,500,000 (2000). **Emp:** 15. **Officers:** Craig Perry, President; Lillian Flores, Controller.

■ 6596 ■ **PC Club Inc.**
18537 E Gale Ave.
City of Industry, CA 91748
Phone: (626)913-2582
Products: Computers. **SIC:** 5045 (Computers, Peripherals & Software). **Sales:** $61,400,000 (2000). **Emp:** 230. **Officers:** Jackson Lan, President.

■ 6597 ■ **PC L.P.**
500 Frank W Burr Blvd., Glenpointe Ctr.
Teaneck, NJ 07666
Phone: (201)928-1212 **Fax:** (201)928-1240
Products: Directory assistance database systems. **SIC:** 5045 (Computers, Peripherals & Software). **Sales:** $7,000,000 (2000). **Emp:** 15. **Officers:** Yusuf Bulan, President.

■ 6598 ■ **PC Professional Inc.**
1615 Webster St.
Oakland, CA 94612
Phone: (510)465-5700 **Fax:** (510)465-8327
Products: Computers. **SIC:** 5045 (Computers, Peripherals & Software). **Sales:** $18,000,000 (2000). **Emp:** 55. **Officers:** Daniel Sanguinetti, CEO; Jeff Klopstock, Controller.

■ 6599 ■ **PC Service Source Inc.**
2350 Valley View Ln.
Dallas, TX 75234
Phone: (214)406-8583 **Fax:** (214)406-9081
Products: Personal computer and laser printer components. **SIC:** 5045 (Computers, Peripherals & Software). **Est:** 1989. **Sales:** $110,100,000 (2000). **Emp:** 545. **Officers:** Mark T. Hilz, CEO & President; Avery More, Chairman of the Board & CFO.

■ 6600 ■ **P.C. Solutions Inc., Entre'**
13400 Bishops Ln., Ste. 270
Brookfield, WI 53005
Phone: (262)821-1060 **Fax:** (262)938-2155
URL: http://www.pcsentre.com
Products: Computers, peripherals, and software. **SIC:** 5045 (Computers, Peripherals & Software). **Est:** 1986.

Sales: $60,000,000 (1999). **Emp:** 200. **Officers:** Robert Johansen, President.

■ 6601 ■ **PC Wholesale Inc.**
444 Scott Dr.
Bloomingdale, IL 60108
Phone: (630)307-1700
Free: (800)525-4727 **Fax:** (630)307-2440
URL: http://www.pcwholesale.com
Products: Computers. **SIC:** 5045 (Computers, Peripherals & Software). **Est:** 1990. **Sales:** $440,000,000 (2000). **Emp:** 60.

■ 6602 ■ **PCC Group Inc.**
163 University Pkwy.
Pomona, CA 91768
Phone: (909)869-6133 **Fax:** (909)869-6128
Products: Computers. **SIC:** 5045 (Computers, Peripherals & Software). **Sales:** $63,600,000 (2000). **Emp:** 22. **Officers:** Jack Wen, CEO & President; J. Lauro Valdovinos, VP & CFO.

■ 6603 ■ **PCI Tech**
1103 Del Monte Ave.
Monterey, CA 93940
Phone: (831)375-7700 **Fax:** (831)375-1516
Products: Computers; Hardware and software. **SIC:** 5045 (Computers, Peripherals & Software).

■ 6604 ■ **PCs Compleat Inc.**
34 St. Martin Dr.
Marlborough, MA 01752
Phone: (508)480-8500 **Fax:** (508)480-8212
Products: Computer products, including disk drives and disks. **SIC:** 5045 (Computers, Peripherals & Software). **Est:** 1991. **Sales:** $100,000,000 (2000). **Emp:** 210. **Officers:** Gordon B. Hoffstein, CEO & Chairman of the Board; Steve Joseph, VP & CFO; John R. Poldoian, Dir. of Marketing; William Brown, VP of Operations.

■ 6605 ■ **PDP Systems**
2140 Bering Dr.
San Jose, CA 95131
Phone: (408)944-0301 **Fax:** (408)944-0811
Products: Peripherals; Memory upgrades for the PC industry. **SIC:** 5045 (Computers, Peripherals & Software). **Officers:** Douglas Diggs, CFO.

■ 6606 ■ **Peak Computer Solutions**
1426 Flower St.
Glendale, CA 91201-2422
Phone: (818)240-0036 **Fax:** (818)240-0652
Products: Computers and software. **SIC:** 5045 (Computers, Peripherals & Software). **Sales:** $2,500,000 (2000). **Emp:** 13. **Officers:** Vince Chiechi, CEO.

■ 6607 ■ **Peake Marketing Inc.**
18808 SE Mildred Ave.
Portland, OR 97267-6712
Phone: (503)653-1696
Products: Computers, peripherals, and software. **SIC:** 5045 (Computers, Peripherals & Software). **Officers:** Stephen Peake, President.

■ 6608 ■ **Perfect Solution Multimedia Inc.**
10032 San Pablo Ave.
El Cerrito, CA 94530
Phone: (510)527-6908
Products: Computer hardware and software. **SIC:** 5045 (Computers, Peripherals & Software).

■ 6609 ■ **Pericom Inc.**
2271 Hwy. 33
Hamilton, NJ 08690
Phone: (609)895-0404 **Fax:** (609)895-0408
Products: Computer software. **SIC:** 5045 (Computers, Peripherals & Software). **Sales:** $2,000,000 (2000). **Emp:** 10. **Officers:** Ron Cragg, President; Loraine Martin, CFO; Barry Brown, VP of Marketing & Sales.

■ 6610 ■ **Peripheral Land Inc.**
47421 Bayside Pkwy.
Fremont, CA 94538
Phone: (510)657-2211 **Fax:** (510)683-9713
Products: Peripheral computer equipment. **SIC:** 5045 (Computers, Peripherals & Software). **Est:** 1985. **Sales:** $36,000,000 (2000). **Emp:** 60. **Officers:** Leo

Berenguel, President; Daniel Loskt, VP of Marketing; Mark Menagh, Dir. of Information Systems; Elaine Skloot, Dir of Human Resources.

■ 6611 ■ Peripheral Resources Inc.
2721 La Cienega Blvd.
Los Angeles, CA 90034
Phone: (310)837-5888
Free: (800)533-2297 **Fax:** (310)837-0222
Products: Point-of-sale computer peripheral equipment. **SIC:** 5045 (Computers, Peripherals & Software). **Sales:** $8,000,000 (2000). **Emp:** 12. **Officers:** Paul Landazuri, CEO; Sue Cheng, CFO.

■ 6612 ■ Perisol Technology Inc.
1148 Sonora Ct.
Sunnyvale, CA 94086
Phone: (408)738-1311
Free: (800)447-8226 **Fax:** (408)738-0698
Products: Memory modules; CD-ROM service. **SIC:** 5045 (Computers, Peripherals & Software). **Sales:** $10,000,000 (2000). **Emp:** 8. **Officers:** Miten Marfatia, CEO & President.

■ 6613 ■ Peroni Business Systems Inc.
388 Concord Rd.
Billerica, MA 01821
Phone: (978)667-7200
Products: Computers and software. **SIC:** 5045 (Computers, Peripherals & Software).

■ 6614 ■ Pervone
790 Turnpike Ste. 202
North Andover, MA 01845
Phone: (508)725-5200
Products: Specializes in computer systems integration, hardware, and software design for general public worldwide. **SIC:** 5045 (Computers, Peripherals & Software). **Emp:** 3.

■ 6615 ■ PetrolSoft Corp.
12780 High Bluff Drive, Ste., 270
San Diego, CA 92130
Phone: (619)259-9724
Products: Computers and software. **SIC:** 5045 (Computers, Peripherals & Software). **Sales:** $2,800,000 (2000). **Emp:** 6. **Officers:** David Gamboa, CEO & President.

■ 6616 ■ Phoenix Computer Associates Inc.
10 Sasco Hill Rd.
Fairfield, CT 06430
Phone: (203)319-3060
Free: (800)432-1815 **Fax:** (203)319-3069
Products: Mainframe computers. **SIC:** 5045 (Computers, Peripherals & Software). **Est:** 1979. **Sales:** $5,000,000 (2000). **Emp:** 15. **Officers:** Lawrence Erdmann, President; Silvia Scarangella, Vice President.

■ 6617 ■ Phone Land Inc.
4380 Malsbary Rd.
Cincinnati, OH 45242-5644
Phone: (513)791-3000
Products: Computer hardware and software. **SIC:** 5045 (Computers, Peripherals & Software). **Sales:** $49,000,000 (1994). **Emp:** 100. **Officers:** Jeff Holtmeir, President.

■ 6618 ■ Pick Systems
1691 Browning
Irvine, CA 92606-4808
Phone: (949)261-7425
Free: (800)367-7425 **Fax:** (949)250-8187
URL: http://www.picksys.com
Products: Database management systems. **SIC:** 5045 (Computers, Peripherals & Software). **Est:** 1971. **Sales:** $20,000,000 (1999). **Emp:** 125. **Officers:** George Olenik, CEO; Steve Cobb, VP of Sales; Ted Ellison, VP of Marketing.

■ 6619 ■ Piedmont Technology Group Inc.
830 Tyvola Rd. Ste. 104
Charlotte, NC 28217
Phone: (704)523-2400 **Fax:** (704)523-7764
Products: Computers. **SIC:** 5045 (Computers, Peripherals & Software). **Sales:** $23,200,000 (2000). **Emp:** 65. **Officers:** Mitch Lemons, President; Mark Arnold, Vice President.

■ 6620 ■ Pinnacle Business Systems Inc.
100 S Baumann Ave.
Edmond, OK 73034-5610
Phone: (405)359-0121 **Fax:** (405)359-7490
Products: Computers; Computer software; Peripheral computer equipment. **SIC:** 5045 (Computers, Peripherals & Software). **Officers:** Martin McNeese, President.

■ 6621 ■ Pinnacle Business Systems, Inc.
810 S Cincinnati Ave.
Tulsa, OK 74119
Phone: (918)587-1500
Free: (800)369-6922 **Fax:** (918)587-1536
Products: Computers; Computer software; Peripheral computer equipment. **SIC:** 5045 (Computers, Peripherals & Software). **Officers:** Martin McNeese, President. **Former Name:** Mersch-Bacher Associates Inc.

■ 6622 ■ Pioneer Entertainment (USA) L.P.
2265 E 220th St.
Long Beach, CA 90810
Phone: (310)835-6177 **Fax:** (310)952-2142
Products: Laser disc software. **SIC:** 5045 (Computers, Peripherals & Software). **Sales:** $63,000,000 (2000). **Emp:** 70. **Officers:** James Kobayashi, President; Eiji Orii, Treasurer.

■ 6623 ■ Pioneer-Standard Electronics Inc.
9100 Gaither Rd.
Gaithersburg, MD 20877
Phone: (301)921-3800 **Fax:** (301)921-3852
Products: Computer hardware, systems, and components. **SIC:** 5065 (Electronic Parts & Equipment Nec.) **Est:** 1964. **Sales:** $365,000,000 (2000). **Emp:** 500. **Officers:** Bruce S. Tucker, President; Charles Rybos, CFO; John H. Wagner, Sr. VP of Marketing.

■ 6624 ■ Pixel U.S.A.
810 S Bascom Ave.
San Jose, CA 95128-2605
Phone: (408)929-7218
Products: Computer peripherals. **SIC:** 5045 (Computers, Peripherals & Software). **Sales:** $900,000 (1993). **Emp:** 10. **Officers:** Tony Nguyen, Owner.

■ 6625 ■ Plymouth Rock Associates
28 Kristin Rd.
Plymouth, MA 02360
Free: (800)350-7667 **Fax:** (508)746-1913
Products: Computer software titles to schools and libraries. **SIC:** 5045 (Computers, Peripherals & Software).

■ 6626 ■ Point of Sale System Services Inc.
40 Jytek Dr.
Leominster, MA 01453
Phone: (978)534-4445 **Fax:** (978)534-1335
URL: http://www.pss-pos.com
Products: Point of sale systems; Personal data collection devices; Customer retail software. **SIC:** 5045 (Computers, Peripherals & Software). **Est:** 1991. **Sales:** $7,000,000 (1999). **Emp:** 20. **Officers:** Donna M. Greene, President, e-mail: pssdmg@aol.com; Jeffry L. Swann, Vice President, e-mail: pssjeffs@aol.com.

■ 6627 ■ Poorman-Douglas Corp.
10300 SW Allen Blvd.
Beaverton, OR 97005
Phone: (503)350-5800 **Fax:** (503)350-5221
Products: Medical computer systems, including software. **SIC:** 5045 (Computers, Peripherals & Software). **Est:** 1968. **Sales:** $20,000,000 (2000). **Emp:** 225. **Officers:** Jeff Baker, President; Bruce Wakefield, Controller; J. Kelly, VP of Marketing; M. Ahlguist, Vice President; G. Miller, Dir of Human Resources.

■ 6628 ■ POS Systems Company Inc.
10027 S 51st St., Ste. 102
Phoenix, AZ 85044
Phone: (480)598-8000
Free: (800)628-8746 **Fax:** (480)598-8050
E-mail: sales@pos-systems.com
URL: http://www.pos-systems.com
Products: Debit and credit point-of-sale equipment. **SIC:** 5045 (Computers, Peripherals & Software). **Est:** 1982. **Emp:** 80. **Officers:** Kenneth MacDonald, CEO &

President; Sharon Denny, e-mail: dennys@pos-systems.com.

■ 6629 ■ POSitive Software Co.
2600 N Columbia Center Blvd.
Richland, WA 99352
Phone: (509)735-9194
Free: (800)735-6860 **Fax:** (509)781-2197
Products: Computer software. **SIC:** 5045 (Computers, Peripherals & Software).

■ 6630 ■ PowerData Corp.
500 108th Ave. NE
Bellevue, WA 98004
Phone: (425)637-9960
Free: (800)574-8588 **Fax:** (425)637-9971
Products: Computer software. **SIC:** 5045 (Computers, Peripherals & Software). **Officers:** Marck Robinson, CEO & President.

■ 6631 ■ PowerSolutions for Business
1920 S Broadway
St. Louis, MO 63104
Phone: (314)421-0670
Free: (800)955-4333 **Fax:** (314)421-0668
Products: Website promotion software provider. **SIC:** 5045 (Computers, Peripherals & Software). **Officers:** Thomas Carroll, CEO & President.

■ 6632 ■ Practical Computer Inc.
1200 Mohawk Blvd.
Springfield, OR 97477-3349
Phone: (541)726-7775 **Fax:** (541)726-7852
Products: Computers and peripherals. **SIC:** 5045 (Computers, Peripherals & Software). **Officers:** Peter Leung, President.

■ 6633 ■ L.F. Pratt & Co.
117 Huxley Rd. No. D
Knoxville, TN 37922-3113
Phone: (423)522-0100
URL: http://www.lfpratt.com
Products: Computers, peripherals, and software. **SIC:** 5045 (Computers, Peripherals & Software). **Est:** 1985. **Officers:** L. Pratt, President.

■ 6634 ■ Precision Type Inc.
47 Mall Dr.
Commack, NY 11725-5717
Phone: (516)864-0167
Free: (800)248-3668 **Fax:** (516)543-5721
Products: Postscript fonts for computers. **SIC:** 5045 (Computers, Peripherals & Software). **Sales:** $7,000,000 (2000). **Emp:** 16. **Officers:** Bruce Newman, President; Michael Polesky, CFO.

■ 6635 ■ Prima International
3350 Scott Blvd., #7
Santa Clara, CA 95054-3108
Phone: (408)727-2600
Free: (800)724-3000 **Fax:** (408)727-2435
Products: Computer peripheral equipment. **SIC:** 5045 (Computers, Peripherals & Software). **Sales:** $12,000,000 (2000). **Emp:** 10. **Officers:** Eugene E. Heller, CEO; Brena O'Maley, Accountant.

■ 6636 ■ Primary Image Inc.
PO Box 781207
Orlando, FL 32878-1207
Phone: (407)382-7100 **Fax:** (407)382-8004
Products: Computer security products and peripherals. **SIC:** 5045 (Computers, Peripherals & Software). **Sales:** $1,600,000 (2000). **Emp:** 3. **Officers:** Alan Davenport, President.

■ 6637 ■ Primax Inc.
10 Fox Hollow Rd.
Old Saybrook, CT 06475
Phone: (860)399-5293 **Fax:** (860)399-5293
Products: Computers and software. **SIC:** 5045 (Computers, Peripherals & Software). **Officers:** Andre Thouin, VP of Sales.

■ 6638 ■ Prime Systems
9888 Bissonet
Houston, TX 77036
Phone: (713)270-1586
Products: Computer hardware and software. **SIC:** 5045 (Computers, Peripherals & Software).

■ 6639 ■ Primeon
25 Burlington Mall Rd.
Burlington, MA 01803-4100
Phone: (781)685-2000 **Fax:** (781)359-9093
Products: Computer software. **SIC:** 5045 (Computers, Peripherals & Software). **Officers:** Andrew P. Kerr, CEO & President.

■ 6640 ■ The Print Machine Inc.
1003 Laurens Rd.
Greenville, SC 29607-1918
Phone: (864)271-4770 **Fax:** (864)271-0555
Products: Computers; Peripheral computer equipment; Computer software. **SIC:** 5045 (Computers, Peripherals & Software). **Officers:** Jerry Cooper, President.

■ 6641 ■ Pro Systems, Inc.
420 Lake Nepessing
Lapeer, MI 48446
Phone: (810)667-0749 **Fax:** (810)667-1961
Products: Accounting software. **SIC:** 5045 (Computers, Peripherals & Software). **Est:** 1978.

■ 6642 ■ Pro Systems Inc.
1020 Crews Rd., Ste. L
Matthews, NC 28105
Phone: (704)849-0400
Free: (800)849-0001 **Fax:** (704)849-0401
URL: http://www.prosystems.com
Products: Computers and software. **SIC:** 5045 (Computers, Peripherals & Software). **Sales:** $2,000,000 (2000). **Emp:** 17. **Officers:** Gary S. Hutchins, President.

■ 6643 ■ Pro-Tect Computer Products
PO Box 1002
Centerville, UT 84014-5002
Phone: (801)295-7739 **Fax:** (801)295-7786
Products: Computers, peripherals, and software. **SIC:** 5045 (Computers, Peripherals & Software). **Officers:** Gil Workman, President.

■ 6644 ■ Probe Technology Inc.
10159 J St.
Omaha, NE 68127
Phone: (402)593-9800 **Fax:** (402)593-8748
Products: Provides computer maintenance and repair, upgrades, network design, and Internet connectivity services Specializes in computer maintenance and consulting. Probe also offers customized computer system design, sales, and support. **SIC:** 5045 (Computers, Peripherals & Software). **Emp:** 4.

■ 6645 ■ Procise Corp.
PO Box 1011
Issaquah, WA 98027-1011
Phone: (425)392-0270 **Fax:** (425)392-7698
Products: Computers; Computer software; Peripheral computer equipment. **SIC:** 5045 (Computers, Peripherals & Software). **Officers:** Ronald Brooks, President.

■ 6646 ■ Prodata Computer Marketing Corp.
2333 Western Ave.
Seattle, WA 98121-1683
Phone: (206)441-4090 **Fax:** (206)441-6355
Products: Computers; Computer software; Peripheral computer equipment. **SIC:** 5045 (Computers, Peripherals & Software). **Officers:** Robert Foster, President.

■ 6647 ■ Prodata Systems Inc.
2333 Western Ave.
Seattle, WA 98121
Phone: (206)441-4090
Free: (800)422-7725 **Fax:** (206)441-6355
Products: Computer software. **SIC:** 5045 (Computers, Peripherals & Software). **Est:** 1958. **Sales:** $3,600,000 (2000). **Emp:** 47. **Officers:** Andrew W. Schellas, President; Rob Hills, VP of Operations; Andrew W. Schellhas, Exec. VP of Marketing; Rob Hills, VP of Operations.

■ 6648 ■ PRODUCT4
1 Insurance Center Plz.
St. Louis, MO 63141
Phone: (314)434-1999 **Fax:** (314)434-7172
Products: Computer software for the financial services industry. **SIC:** 5045 (Computers, Peripherals & Software). **Officers:** Dan Moskowitz, Chairman of the Board.

■ 6649 ■ Professional Computer Systems
849 E Greenville Ave
Winchester, IN 47394
Phone: (765)584-2288 **Fax:** (765)584-1283
URL: http://www.pcswin.com
Products: Computers, peripherals, and software. **SIC:** 5045 (Computers, Peripherals & Software). **Officers:** Mark Burkhardt, Partner.

■ 6650 ■ Professional Electronics Inc.
3855 Hughes Ave., 2nd Fl.
Culver City, CA 90232
Phone: (310)287-1400
Free: (800)432-4754 **Fax:** (310)287-0200
Products: Digital audio workstations. **SIC:** 5045 (Computers, Peripherals & Software). **Sales:** $18,000,000 (2000). **Emp:** 18. **Officers:** John Lancken, CEO; Randy Lewis, Controller.

■ 6651 ■ PROFITsystems Inc.
422 E Vermijo Ave., No. 100
Colorado Springs, CO 80903-3702
Phone: (719)471-3858 **Free:** (800)888-5565
Products: Computer software. **SIC:** 5045 (Computers, Peripherals & Software). **Sales:** $5,300,000 (2000). **Emp:** 42. **Officers:** Larry L. Stark, CEO; J.E. Stark, Chairman of the Board & CFO.

■ 6652 ■ Programart Corp.
124 Mount Auburn St.
Cambridge, MA 02138
Phone: (617)661-3020
Products: Application performance management software products. **SIC:** 5045 (Computers, Peripherals & Software). **Officers:** John Thron, President.

■ 6653 ■ Programma Incorporated
1697 Forestview Dr.
Bethel Park, PA 15102-1933
Products: Computers, peripherals, and software. **SIC:** 5045 (Computers, Peripherals & Software). **Officers:** Jeffrey Rankin, President.

■ 6654 ■ PSDI
1401 E Gartner
Naperville, IL 60540
Phone: (630)369-1680 **Fax:** (630)369-1264
Products: Computer software. **SIC:** 5045 (Computers, Peripherals & Software).

■ 6655 ■ PSDI
5215 N O'Connor Blvd., Ste. 1055
Irving, TX 75039
Phone: (972)402-8255 **Fax:** (972)402-8280
Products: Computer software. **SIC:** 5045 (Computers, Peripherals & Software).

■ 6656 ■ PSDI
19800 MacArthur Blvd., Ste. 1050
Irvine, CA 92612-2439
Products: Computer software. **SIC:** 5045 (Computers, Peripherals & Software).

■ 6657 ■ PSDI
100 Crosby Dr.
Bedford, MA 01730
Phone: (781)280-2000 **Fax:** (781)280-0207
E-mail: grace_ferry@psdi.com
URL: http://www.psdi.com
Products: Computer software. **SIC:** 5045 (Computers, Peripherals & Software). **Est:** 1968. **Sales:** $73,300,000 (2000). **Emp:** 480. **Officers:** David Sample, President & CEO; Chip Drapeau, Exec. VP of Sales, Marketing & Secty.; William Sawyer, Exec. VP of Operations; Paul Birch, Exec. VP of Finance & Admin.

■ 6658 ■ PSDI
151 W Passaic St.
Rochelle Park, NJ 07662
Phone: (201)909-3765 **Fax:** (201)587-1336
Products: Computer software. **SIC:** 5045 (Computers, Peripherals & Software).

■ 6659 ■ PSDI
300 Vanderbilt Motor Pky., Ste. 200
Hauppauge, NY 11788
Phone: (516)951-4113 **Fax:** (516)951-4116
Products: Computer software. **SIC:** 5045 (Computers, Peripherals & Software).

■ 6660 ■ PSDI
2014 Sierra Dr.
Fredericksburg, VA 22405-2786
Phone: (540)231-8660 **Fax:** (540)770-2144
Products: Computer software. **SIC:** 5045 (Computers, Peripherals & Software).

■ 6661 ■ PSDI
20 University Rd.
Cambridge, MA 02138
Phone: (617)661-1444 **Fax:** (617)661-1642
Products: Computers and software. **SIC:** 5045 (Computers, Peripherals & Software). **Sales:** $73,300,000 (2000). **Emp:** 480.

■ 6662 ■ Public Software Library
PO Box 35705
Houston, TX 77235
Phones: (713)665-7017 (713)524-6394
Products: Software. **SIC:** 5045 (Computers, Peripherals & Software). **Est:** 1982. **Sales:** $3,000,000 (2000). **Emp:** 12. **Officers:** Nelson Ford, Owner.

■ 6663 ■ Puget Sound Data Systems Inc.
10236 E Riverside Dr.
Bothell, WA 98011-3709
Phone: (425)488-0710 **Fax:** (425)488-6414
Products: Computers; Computer software; Peripheral computer equipment. **SIC:** 5045 (Computers, Peripherals & Software). **Officers:** Len Whitwer, President.

■ 6664 ■ Pulsar Data Systems Inc.
4500 Forbes Blvd., No. 400
Lanham, MD 20706
Phone: (301)459-2650
Free: (800)637-1926 **Fax:** (301)459-2654
Products: Computers. **SIC:** 5045 (Computers, Peripherals & Software). **Est:** 1983. **Sales:** $130,000,000 (2000). **Emp:** 150. **Officers:** William W. Davis Sr., CEO & President; Lillian Davis, Finance Officer; Rudy Menna, Dir. of Marketing; Lorian Lipton, Dir. of Data Processing; Patricia Burroughs, Dir of Human Resources.

■ 6665 ■ Purple Frog Software
PO Box 13928
Gainesville, FL 32604
Phone: (352)336-7208
Products: Specializes in World Wide Web development. Services include building networks, configuring machines, installing software, creating Web sites, and preparing database. **SIC:** 5045 (Computers, Peripherals & Software).

■ 6666 ■ PWI Technologies
3015 112th Ave. NE, Ste. 205
Bellevue, WA 98004
Phone: (425)828-4223 **Fax:** (425)827-5895
E-mail: info@pwi.com
URL: http://www.pwi.com
Products: Computer system integrators/consultants. **SIC:** 5045 (Computers, Peripherals & Software). **Est:** 1984. **Sales:** $40,000,000 (2000). **Emp:** 45. **Officers:** Barry Andersen, President, e-mail: barry.andersen@pwi.com. **Former Name:** Personal Workstations Inc.

■ 6667 ■ QA Technologies Inc.
222 S 72nd St., Ste. 301
Omaha, NE 68114
Phone: (402)391-9200 **Fax:** (402)391-1175
Products: Provides information systems consulting and software development and product services. Offers analysis, planning, implementation, and support of computer systems. Experienced in Client/server and Legacy Mainframe Systems. **SIC:** 5045 (Computers, Peripherals & Software). **Emp:** 15.

■ **6668** ■ **Q.I.V. Systems Inc.**
4242 Woodcock Dr., Ste. 101
San Antonio, TX 78228
Phone: (210)736-4126
Products: Computers. **SIC:** 5045 (Computers, Peripherals & Software). **Sales:** $7,000,000 (1994). **Emp:** 80. **Officers:** O.L. Trippe Jr., President; Barry Engelbrecht, Exec. VP of Finance.

■ **6669** ■ **Qualitas Trading Co.**
2029 Durant Ave.
Berkeley, CA 94704
Phone: (510)848-8080 **Fax:** (510)848-8009
Products: Word processing machines. **SIC:** 5045 (Computers, Peripherals & Software). **Est:** 1985. **Sales:** $1,600,000 (2000). **Emp:** 7. **Officers:** Kazue Osugi, President.

■ **6670** ■ **Quickshot Technology Inc.**
10423 Valley Blvd., No. N
El Monte, CA 91731
Phone: (626)444-3697 **Fax:** (626)442-1783
E-mail: qsmultimedia@aol.com
URL: http://www.quickshot.com
Products: Computer peripherals including joysticks, control pads, pointing devices, keyboards, microphones, and speakers. **SIC:** 5045 (Computers, Peripherals & Software). **Sales:** $12,000,000 (2000). **Emp:** 25. **Officers:** Phil Li, President; Chris Mak, Controller.

■ **6671** ■ **Qumax Corp.**
1746 Junction Ave., No. E
San Jose, CA 95112-1018
Phone: (408)954-8040 **Fax:** (408)954-8043
Products: Computer keyboards and peripherals. **SIC:** 5045 (Computers, Peripherals & Software). **Est:** 1989. **Sales:** $2,000,000 (2000). **Emp:** 6. **Officers:** Sam Chang, Vice President.

■ **6672** ■ **R-Computer**
30 Golf Club Rd.
Pleasant Hill, CA 94523
Phone: (925)798-4884
Products: Computer peripherals. **SIC:** 5045 (Computers, Peripherals & Software). **Sales:** $6,400,000 (2000). **Emp:** 32. **Officers:** Ed Roth, President.

■ **6673** ■ **R and D Industries Inc.**
1824 130th Ave. NE, No. 2
Bellevue, WA 98005
Phone: (425)881-8490
Free: (800)545-2305 **Fax:** (425)869-1515
Products: Computers; Network and internet integration. **SIC:** 5045 (Computers, Peripherals & Software). **Sales:** $50,000,000 (2000). **Emp:** 50. **Officers:** W.D. Dauenhauer, Owner.

■ **6674** ■ **R and D Industries Inc.**
10807 E Montgomery Dr., Ste. 7
Spokane, WA 99206
Phone: (509)924-9082 **Fax:** (509)927-5833
Products: Computer integrated system design; Computers and peripherals. **SIC:** 5045 (Computers, Peripherals & Software).

■ **6675** ■ **R & L Data Systems Inc.**
1616 E 17th St.
Idaho Falls, ID 83404-6366
Phone: (208)529-3785 **Fax:** (208)529-3793
Products: Computers; Peripheral computer equipment; Software. **SIC:** 5045 (Computers, Peripherals & Software). **Est:** 1979. **Officers:** Larry Brown, President.

■ **6676** ■ **R and W Technical Services Ltd.**
7324 Southwest Fwy., Ste. 1000, Arena Tower
Houston, TX 77074-2079
Phone: (713)995-4200 **Fax:** (713)995-4477
Products: Commodity trading software. **SIC:** 5045 (Computers, Peripherals & Software). **Sales:** $3,000,000 (2000). **Emp:** 19. **Officers:** Greg Reagan, CEO; Drawn Powler, Mgr. of Finance.

■ **6677** ■ **RACER Computer Corp.**
3000 E Chambers St.
Phoenix, AZ 85040
Phone: (602)304-2424
Free: (800)308-8767 **Fax:** (602)304-2506
Products: Computers and peripherals. **SIC:** 5045 (Computers, Peripherals & Software). **Officers:** Mike Mahmoodi, CEO & President.

■ **6678** ■ **RAD Graphics**
1427 Melody Ln.
Chattanooga, TN 37412-1119
Phone: (423)867-3542 **Fax:** (423)867-2068
Products: Computers, peripherals, and software. **SIC:** 5045 (Computers, Peripherals & Software). **Officers:** Robert Derryberry, Owner.

■ **6679** ■ **Rail Europe Group**
500 Mamaroneck Ave.
Harrison, NY 10528
Phone: (914)682-2999
Free: (800)438-7245 **Fax:** (914)682-2821
Products: Computerized reservation systems. **SIC:** 5045 (Computers, Peripherals & Software). **Sales:** $200,000,000 (2000). **Emp:** 300. **Officers:** Bernard Frelat, CEO & President; Patrice Sunsic, VP of Finance & Admin.

■ **6680** ■ **Rail Europe Holding**
500 Mamaroneck Ave.
Harrison, NY 10528
Phone: (914)682-2999
Free: (800)848-7245 **Fax:** (914)381-4219
Products: Computerized reservation systems. **SIC:** 5045 (Computers, Peripherals & Software). **Sales:** $191,000,000 (2000). **Emp:** 200. **Officers:** Bernard Frelat, CFO.

■ **6681** ■ **Rainbow Raster Graphics**
2212 Greenwich Ln.
Knoxville, TN 37932
Phone: (423)691-5080
Products: Computer graphics. **SIC:** 5045 (Computers, Peripherals & Software). **Officers:** Valarie Jones, Owner.

■ **6682** ■ **Ramacom Inc.**
PO Box E
Norman, OK 73070-7005
Phone: (405)360-2666 **Fax:** (405)360-5557
Products: Computers; Computer software; Peripheral computer equipment. **SIC:** 5045 (Computers, Peripherals & Software). **Officers:** Paul Wallace, President.

■ **6683** ■ **Raritan Computer Inc.**
400 Cottontail Ln.
Somerset, NJ 08873
Phone: (732)764-8886
Free: (800)724-8090 **Fax:** (732)764-8887
E-mail: sates@raritan.com
URL: http://www.raritan.com
Products: Computer equipment and supplies; KVM switches. **SIC:** 5045 (Computers, Peripherals & Software). **Est:** 1985. **Emp:** 100. **Officers:** Ching-I Hsu, President; Robert S. Pollack, VP of Sales/Marketing.

■ **6684** ■ **Raritan Computer Inc.**
400 Cottontail Ln.
Somerset, NJ 08873
Phone: (732)764-8886
Free: (800)724-8090 **Fax:** (732)764-8887
Products: Computers, peripherals, and software. **SIC:** 5045 (Computers, Peripherals & Software). **Est:** 1985. **Sales:** $28,000,000 (2000). **Emp:** 35. **Officers:** Ching-I Hsu, President.

■ **6685** ■ **Rave Computer Association Inc.**
36960 Metro Ct.
Sterling Heights, MI 48312
Phone: (810)939-8230
Free: (800)966-7283 **Fax:** (810)939-7431
Products: Computer work no space stations. **SIC:** 5046 (Commercial Equipment Nec). **Sales:** $28,000,000 (2000). **Emp:** 64. **Officers:** F. Darter, President; Dennis Asselin, Controller.

■ **6686** ■ **Redington USA Inc.**
65 Industrial Way
Wilmington, MA 01887
Phone: (978)988-7500 **Fax:** (978)988-7700
Products: Computers, computer parts, peripherals, and supplies. **SIC:** 5045 (Computers, Peripherals & Software). **Est:** 1986. **Sales:** $20,000,000 (2000). **Officers:** Sam Prasad, President.

■ **6687** ■ **Renick and Company Inc.**
1500 N Post Oak Dr., No. 180
Houston, TX 77055
Phone: (713)684-5930
Products: Data equipment, including ribbons, cartridges, and data cassettes. **SICs:** 5045 (Computers, Peripherals & Software); 5112 (Stationery & Office Supplies). **Est:** 1983. **Sales:** $1,500,000 (2000). **Emp:** 20. **Officers:** Torn W. Stinson, President.

■ **6688** ■ **ReproCAD Inc.**
1100 Kings Hwy. E
Fairfield, CT
Phone: (203)332-4700
Free: (800)873-7762 **Fax:** (203)332-4705
URL: http://www.reprocad.com
Products: CAD-plotting equipment. **SIC:** 5045 (Computers, Peripherals & Software). **Est:** 1984. **Sales:** $2,500,000 (2000). **Emp:** 8. **Officers:** Edward Severs, CEO & President; Kathy Cole, Manager.

■ **6689** ■ **The Reynolds and Reynolds Co.**
24800 Denso Dr., Ste. 140
Southfield, MI 48034
Phone: (248)353-8500 **Fax:** (248)351-4072
Products: Computers. **SIC:** 5045 (Computers, Peripherals & Software).

■ **6690** ■ **Ricom Electronics Ltd.**
PO Box 17882
Milwaukee, WI 53217-0882
Phone: (414)357-8181 **Fax:** (414)357-7814
Products: Computers, software, video equipment, and audio components. **SICs:** 5045 (Computers, Peripherals & Software); 5043 (Photographic Equipment & Supplies); 5064 (Electrical Appliances—Television & Radio). **Sales:** $45,000,000 (2000). **Emp:** 45. **Officers:** Marcia Rose, President.

■ **6691** ■ **Rodan Inc.**
5821 Citrus Blvd.
Harahan, LA 70123
Phone: (504)734-2640
Products: Computer hardware and peripheral equipment. **SIC:** 5045 (Computers, Peripherals & Software).

■ **6692** ■ **Roland Digital Group**
15271 Barranca
Irvine, CA 92618-2201
Phone: (714)975-0560
Free: (800)542-2307 **Fax:** (714)975-0569
URL: http://www.rolanddga.com
Products: Plotters; Computer peripherals. **SIC:** 5045 (Computers, Peripherals & Software). **Est:** 1983. **Sales:** $7,000,000 (2000). **Emp:** 30. **Officers:** Bob Curtis, President.

■ **6693** ■ **Rorke Data Inc.**
9700 W 76th St.
Eden Prairie, MN 55344-3714
Phone: (612)829-0300 **Fax:** (612)829-0988
Products: Computers; Computer software; Peripheral computer equipment. **SIC:** 5045 (Computers, Peripherals & Software). **Officers:** Herbert Rorke, President.

■ **6694** ■ **Rosas Computer Co.**
326 S Enterprise Pkwy.
Corpus Christi, TX 78405
Phone: (512)289-5991
Products: Computers. **SIC:** 5045 (Computers, Peripherals & Software). **Est:** 1981. **Sales:** $20,000,000 (2000). **Emp:** 80. **Officers:** Leo Rosas, President; Lee Polanco, CFO; Ray Hernandez, Dir. of Marketing & Sales.

■ **6695** ■ **Rovac Inc.**
3055 Old Hwy. 8
Minneapolis, MN 55418-2500
Phone: (612)779-9444 **Fax:** 800-428-5819
Products: Computers; Computer software; Peripheral computer equipment. **SIC:** 5045 (Computers, Peripherals & Software). **Officers:** Ronald Vagle, President.

■ **6696** ■ **RT Computers Inc.**
1673 Rogers Ave.
San Jose, CA 95112
Phone: (408)437-3063
Products: Computer peripherals. **SIC:** 5045 (Computers, Peripherals & Software). **Sales:** $2,400,000 (2000). **Emp:** 5. **Officers:** M. Yousuf Chaudhry, President; Oanh Do, CFO.

■ **6697** ■ **RTM Inc.**
13177 Ramona Blvd., Ste. F
Irwindale, CA 91706
Phone: (626)813-2630 **Fax:** (626)813-2638
Products: CD software and peripherals. **SIC:** 5045 (Computers, Peripherals & Software). **Est:** 1991. **Sales:** $1,500,000 (2000). **Emp:** 4. **Officers:** Christopher Chan, President; Rita Leung, Vice President.

■ **6698** ■ **Sabus Group**
1737 Aleutian St.
Anchorage, AK 99508-3276
Phone: (907)277-4232 **Fax:** (907)276-2839
Products: Computers, peripherals, and software. **SIC:** 5045 (Computers, Peripherals & Software). **Officers:** William Barnes, Owner.

■ **6699** ■ **SAFLINK Corp.**
2502 Rocky Point Dr.
Tampa, FL 33607
Phone: (813)636-0099 **Fax:** (813)636-0422
Products: Developer of data and network security software. **SIC:** 5045 (Computers, Peripherals & Software). **Sales:** $4,900,000 (1999). **Emp:** 22. **Officers:** Jeffrey P. Anthony, CEO, President & Chairman of the Board; James W. Sheppard, CFO.

■ **6700** ■ **Sager Midern Computer Inc.**
18005 Cortney Ct.
City of Industry, CA 91748
Phone: (626)964-8682
Free: (800)669-1624 **Fax:** (626)964-2381
E-mail: sales@sagernotebook.com
URL: http://www.sagernotebook.com
Products: Laptop computers. **SIC:** 5045 (Computers, Peripherals & Software). **Sales:** $44,000,000 (2000). **Emp:** 90. **Officers:** Tony Yuan, President.

■ **6701** ■ **SalePoint Inc.**
9909 Huennekens St.
San Diego, CA 92121-2929
Phone: (858)546-9400 **Fax:** (858)546-0725
E-mail: info@salepoint.com
URL: http://www.salepoint.com
Products: Computers. **SIC:** 5045 (Computers, Peripherals & Software). **Est:** 1987. **Emp:** 85. **Officers:** Larry Haworth, President; Cathy Christianson, VP of Finance; Marcia Thal, VP of Marketing; Eric Baez, VP of Sales; David Pieczynski, VP of Operations; Doug Whitehead, VP of Business Development.

■ **6702** ■ **Sampo Corporation of America**
5550 Peachtree Industrial Blvd.
Norcross, GA 30071
Phone: (770)449-6220
Products: Computers. **SIC:** 5045 (Computers, Peripherals & Software). **Sales:** $88,000,000 (2000). **Emp:** 40. **Officers:** Jung Ko, President; Victor Chen, Controller.

■ **6703** ■ **SAP America, Inc.**
3999 W Chester Pike
Newtown Square, PA 19073
Phone: (610)661-1000 **Fax:** (610)355-3106
URL: http://www.sap.com
Products: Management and finance software. **SIC:** 5045 (Computers, Peripherals & Software). **Est:** 1988. **Sales:** $479,000,000 (2000). **Emp:** 1,800. **Officers:** Paul Wahl, CEO; Kevin McKay, CFO; Jeremy Coote, President.

■ **6704** ■ **SARCOM Inc.**
8405 Pulsar Pl.
Columbus, OH 43240
Phone: (614)854-1000
Products: Computers. **SIC:** 5045 (Computers, Peripherals & Software). **Sales:** $240,000,000 (1993). **Emp:** 500. **Officers:** Randy Wilcox, President.

■ **6705** ■ **Satellite Information Systems Co.**
7464 Arapahoe Rd., Ste. B-17
Boulder, CO 80303
Phone: (303)449-0442 **Fax:** (303)449-0239
Products: Computer hardware. **SIC:** 5045 (Computers, Peripherals & Software). **Sales:** $838,200,000 (2000). **Emp:** 10. **Officers:** Michael J. Ellis, CEO, President & Chairman of the Board; Mark S. Boledovich, CFO.

■ **6706** ■ **Save On Software**
PO Box 1312
Wilkes Barre, PA 18703-1312
Phone: (717)822-9531
Products: Home entertainment computer software. **SIC:** 5045 (Computers, Peripherals & Software). **Sales:** $1,000,000 (1994). **Emp:** 3. **Officers:** Larry DeLaney, Mng. Partner; Al Komoreck, Partner.

■ **6707** ■ **Sawtooth Technologies Inc.**
1007 Church St., Ste. 402
Evanston, IL 60201
Phone: (847)866-0870 **Fax:** (847)866-0876
E-mail: info@sawtooth.com
URL: http://www.sawtooth.com
Products: Statistical analysis software. **SIC:** 5045 (Computers, Peripherals & Software). **Est:** 1983. **Sales:** $1,000,000 (2000). **Emp:** 8. **Officers:** Joseph Curry, President; Brett Jarvis, Dir. of Marketing & Sales.

■ **6708** ■ **Sayers Computer Source**
1150 Feehanville Dr.
Mt. Prospect, IL 60056
Phone: (708)391-4040
Products: Computers and peripheral equipment. **SIC:** 5045 (Computers, Peripherals & Software).

■ **6709** ■ **Scanning Technologies Inc.**
2314 Durwood
Little Rock, AR 72207
Phone: (501)663-6912 **Fax:** (501)663-0868
Products: Computers; Computer software; Peripheral computer equipment. **SIC:** 5045 (Computers, Peripherals & Software). **Officers:** Robert Bomar, President.

■ **6710** ■ **ScanSource Inc.**
6 Logue Court, Ste. G
Greenville, SC 29615
Phone: (864)288-2432
Free: (800)944-2432 **Fax:** (864)288-1165
URL: http://www.scansource.com
Products: Automatic identification and point-of-sale computer peripheral products; Business and computer telephone systems. **SIC:** 5045 (Computers, Peripherals & Software). **Est:** 1992. **Sales:** $470,000,000 (2000). **Emp:** 400. **Officers:** Steven H. Owings, Chairman of the Board; Jeffery A. Bryson, CFO & Treasurer; Michael L. Baur, President & CEO.

■ **6711** ■ **Schaeperkoetter Store Inc.**
PO Box 37
Mt. Sterling, MO 65062
Phone: (573)943-6321
Products: Petroleum bulk station. **SIC:** 5171 (Petroleum Bulk Stations & Terminals). **Sales:** $15,500,000 (1993). **Emp:** 37. **Officers:** Ivan R. Schaeperkoetter, President.

■ **6712** ■ **Scientific and Business Minicomputers Inc.**
7076 Peachtree Blvd., No. 200
Norcross, GA 30071
Phone: (770)446-0404
Products: Computers and software. **SIC:** 5045 (Computers, Peripherals & Software). **Est:** 1978. **Sales:** $27,000,000 (2000). **Emp:** 60. **Officers:** Jack Thornton, President; Eric Thornton, Mgr. of Finance; Carole L. Mazzei, Marketing Mgr.

■ **6713** ■ **Scruggs & Associates Inc.**
542 Central Ave.
Laurel, MS 39440-3955
Phone: (601)649-0383 **Fax:** (601)649-1885
E-mail: corporate@scruggsinc.com
URL: http://www.scruggsinc.com
Products: Computers; Computer software; Peripheral computer equipment. **SIC:** 5045 (Computers, Peripherals & Software). **Est:** 1985. **Emp:** 35. **Officers:** G. Bradley Ford, President; Robert Scruggs.

■ **6714** ■ **Seagull Software Systems Inc.**
2520 Northwinds Pkwy., Ste. 250
Alpharetta, GA 30004
Phone: (770)521-1445 **Fax:** (770)521-6770
Products: Software. **SIC:** 5045 (Computers, Peripherals & Software). **Sales:** $4,000,000 (2000). **Emp:** 35. **Officers:** Charles A. Brown, President; John A. Greenwood, Vice President.

■ **6715** ■ **Seattle Orthotics Group**
26296 Twelve Trees Ln NW
Poulsbo, WA 98370
Phone: (360)697-5656 **Fax:** (360)697-5876
Products: Designs and markets external leg prosthetic components; CAD/CAM equipment; Software for orthotics and prosthetics. **SICs:** 5045 (Computers, Peripherals & Software); 5047 (Medical & Hospital Equipment).

■ **6716** ■ **SEC International**
PO Box 32
Cambridge, MA 02139-0001
Phone: (617)354-9600 **Fax:** (617)754-6388
E-mail: galegroup@sec-international.com
URL: http://www.sec-international.com
Products: Computer software. **SIC:** 5045 (Computers, Peripherals & Software). **Est:** 1989. **Sales:** $5,000,000 (1999). **Emp:** 6. **Officers:** Michael Rooney, Chairman, e-mail: mrooney@sec-international.com. **Former Name:** Software Export Corporation.

■ **6717** ■ **SED International, Inc.**
4916 N Royal Atlanta Rd.
Tucker, GA 30085
Phone: (770)491-8962
URL: http://www.sed.online.com
Products: Computer and cellular products. **SICs:** 5045 (Computers, Peripherals & Software); 5065 (Electronic Parts & Equipment Nec). **Est:** 1980. **Sales:** $707,570,000 (1999). **Emp:** 314. **Officers:** Gerald Diamond, CEO & Chairman of the Board; Larry G. Ayers, VP, CFO & Treasurer; Mark Diamond, President & COO. **Former Name:** Southern Electronics Corp.

■ **6718** ■ **See First Technology Inc.**
18809 Cox Ave., Ste. 100
Saratoga, CA 95070
Phone: (408)866-8928 **Fax:** (408)866-8882
Products: Computers. **SIC:** 5045 (Computers, Peripherals & Software). **Sales:** $5,200,000 (2000). **Emp:** 4. **Officers:** James F. Martin, President; Elizabeth Herold, CFO.

■ **6719** ■ **Seikosha America Inc.**
111 Canfield Ave., No. Bld-A-14
Randolph, NJ 07869-1114
Phone: (201)327-7227 **Fax:** (201)818-9135
Products: Printers; Printer parts and supplies, including ribbon. **SIC:** 5045 (Computers, Peripherals & Software). **Est:** 1985. **Sales:** $5,000,000 (2000). **Emp:** 40. **Officers:** Takahide Kumayama, President; Wayne George, Dir. of Marketing.

■ **6720** ■ **Sejin America Inc.**
2004 Martin Ave.
Santa Clara, CA 95050
Phone: (408)980-7550
Free: (800)283-4080 **Fax:** (408)980-7562
Products: Computer peripheral equipment, including keyboards and mice. **SIC:** 5045 (Computers, Peripherals & Software). **Sales:** $80,000,000 (2000). **Emp:** 570. **Officers:** S.Y. Lee, President.

■ 6721 ■ Select Sales
7750 W 78th St.
Bloomington, MN 55439
Phone: (612)941-9388
Products: Computers. **SIC:** 5045 (Computers, Peripherals & Software).

■ 6722 ■ Select Sales Inc.
7750 W 78th St.
Bloomington, MN 55439
Phone: (612)941-9388 **Fax:** (612)941-7376
Products: Computer software. **SIC:** 5045 (Computers, Peripherals & Software). **Officers:** Christophe Conroy, President.

■ 6723 ■ Selectware Technologies, Inc.
PO Box G
Bridgeport, MI 48722-0617
Phone: (248)477-7340 **Fax:** (248)477-6488
Products: CD-ROM hardware and software. **SIC:** 5045 (Computers, Peripherals & Software). **Sales:** $2,000,000 (1994). **Emp:** 17. **Officers:** Jeffery J. Connors, CEO & President; Kathy Connors, CFO.

■ 6724 ■ Sherron Broom & Associates
1011 Hardy St.
PO Box 1308
Hattiesburg, MS 39403-1308
Phone: (601)544-0853 **Fax:** (601)582-8928
E-mail: sjbroom@ibm.net
Products: Computer software; Peripheral computer equipment. **SIC:** 5045 (Computers, Peripherals & Software). **Est:** 1976. **Emp:** 4. **Officers:** Sherron Broom, Owner.

■ 6725 ■ Shuttle Computer International
40760 Encyclopedia Cir
Fremont, CA 94538
Phone: (510)623-8816 **Fax:** (510)623-2823
Products: Computer motherboards; PC products. **SIC:** 5045 (Computers, Peripherals & Software).

■ 6726 ■ Siboney Learning Group
325 N Kirkwood Rd., Ste. 200
St. Louis, MO 63122
Phone: (314)909-1670
Free: (800)351-1404 **Fax:** (915)984-8063
URL: http://www.gamco.com
Products: Educational computer software; Teacher support software. **SIC:** 5045 (Computers, Peripherals & Software). **Est:** 1959. **Sales:** $5,000,000 (2000). **Emp:** 30. **Officers:** Bodie Marx, President; Joe Pruehl, Dir. of Operations; Mark Sweetnam, Dir. of Research & Development; Robin Tinker, Dir. of Sales & Marketing. **Former Name:** Gamco Education Materials.

■ 6727 ■ Sigma Data Inc.
26 Newport Rd.
New London, NH 03257-4565
Phone: (603)526-7100
Free: (800)446-4525 **Fax:** (603)526-6915
Products: Computer disk drives. **SIC:** 5045 (Computers, Peripherals & Software). **Sales:** $15,000,000 (2000). **Emp:** 25. **Officers:** J. Peter Kusinski, President; Helen Dutton, CFO.

■ 6728 ■ Silicon Valley Electronics International
7220 Trenton Pl.
Gilroy, CA 95020
Phone: (408)842-7731 **Fax:** (408)842-7731
Products: Computers and computer supplies and equipment. **SIC:** 5045 (Computers, Peripherals & Software). **Officers:** Nusret Yurutucu, Owner.

■ 6729 ■ Silicon Valley Technology Inc.
PO Box 1408
San Jose, CA 95109-1408
Phone: (408)934-8444
Products: Computers and software. **SIC:** 5045 (Computers, Peripherals & Software). **Sales:** $8,000,000 (2000). **Emp:** 18. **Officers:** Peter Boot, President; Chitra Jain, CFO.

■ 6730 ■ SilverPlatter Information Inc.
100 River Ridge Rd.
Norwood, MA 02062
Phone: (781)769-2599
Free: (800)343-0064 **Fax:** (781)769-8763
Products: CD-ROM publishing and proprietary search software and Internet distribution. **SIC:** 5045 (Computers, Peripherals & Software). **Sales:** $61,300,000 (2000). **Emp:** 230. **Officers:** Ronald Akie, President; Michael O'Donnell, CFO.

■ 6731 ■ Simsim Inc.
192 Worcester Rd.
Natick, MA 01760
Phone: (508)655-6415
Products: Computers. **SIC:** 5045 (Computers, Peripherals & Software).

■ 6732 ■ Sirsi Corp.
101 Washington St. SE
Huntsville, AL 35801-4827
Phone: (205)922-9820 **Fax:** (205)922-9818
Products: Software automation for library turnkey systems. **SIC:** 5045 (Computers, Peripherals & Software). **Est:** 1979. **Sales:** $12,000,000 (2000). **Emp:** 112. **Officers:** James J. Young, CEO; Jacqueline B. Young, COO.

■ 6733 ■ Sitek Inc.
30 Lowell Rd.
Hudson, NH 03051-2800
Phone: (603)889-0066 **Fax:** (603)889-3824
Products: Computers; Computer software; Peripheral computer equipment. **SIC:** 5045 (Computers, Peripherals & Software). **Officers:** David Tsai, President.

■ 6734 ■ Sky Knob Technologies LLC
53 W Main
Hancock, MD 21750-1630
Phone: (301)678-5129
Free: (800)755-5663 **Fax:** (301)678-7333
E-mail: steve@skyknob.com
URL: http://www.skyknob.com
Products: Computers; Computer software; Peripheral computer equipment. **SIC:** 5045 (Computers, Peripherals & Software). **Est:** 1991. **Sales:** $250,000 (2000). **Emp:** 4. **Officers:** Steve Hixon, Owner.

■ 6735 ■ Soft Solutions
6999 Dublin Blvd., Ste. B
Dublin, CA 94568
Phone: (925)803-1358 **Fax:** (925)803-1372
Products: Computer hardware and software. **SIC:** 5045 (Computers, Peripherals & Software). **Sales:** $1,300,000 (2000). **Emp:** 5. **Officers:** Harry Misfeldt, President.

■ 6736 ■ Softcell Inc.
307 Hempstead Ave.
Fairfield, IA 52556-2810
Phone: (515)693-4828
Products: Computers; Computer software; Peripheral computer equipment. **SIC:** 5045 (Computers, Peripherals & Software). **Officers:** Caroline Irwin, President.

■ 6737 ■ SoftKey International
500 Redwood Blvd.
Novato, CA 94947-6921
Free: (800)323-8088
Products: Computer software. **SIC:** 5045 (Computers, Peripherals & Software). **Former Name:** Spinnaker Software.

■ 6738 ■ SoftKlone Distributing Corp.
327 Office Plaza Dr., No. 100
Tallahassee, FL 32301
Phone: (904)878-8564
Free: (800)634-8670 **Fax:** (904)877-9763
Products: Computer software. **SIC:** 5045 (Computers, Peripherals & Software). **Est:** 1985. **Sales:** $1,500,000 (2000). **Emp:** 10. **Officers:** Bruce O. Justham, President; Doug Mintz, Information Systems Mgr.

■ 6739 ■ Software Associates Inc.
860 Broad St.
Emmaus, PA 18049
Phone: (215)967-1846 **Fax:** (215)965-3563
Products: Computer software and integration systems. **SIC:** 5045 (Computers, Peripherals & Software). **Est:** 1983. **Sales:** $15,000,000 (2000). **Emp:** 50. **Officers:** R. Keith Wolfe, President & Chairman of the Board; Michael Pavlo, Controller; Paul Cummings, VP of Marketing.

■ 6740 ■ Software and Electrical Engineering
248 Walnut St.
Willimantic, CT 06226-2322
Phone: (860)456-2022
Products: Computers; Computer software; Peripheral computer equipment. **SIC:** 5045 (Computers, Peripherals & Software). **Officers:** Victor Civie, Partner.

■ 6741 ■ Software Spectrum Inc.
PO Box 479501
Garland, TX 75047-9501
Phone: (214)840-6600
Free: (800)624-0503 **Fax:** (214)349-4862
Products: Disks; Hardware; Videos. **SIC:** 5045 (Computers, Peripherals & Software). **Est:** 1983. **Sales:** $796,300,000 (2000). **Emp:** 1,600. **Officers:** Judy O. Sims, CEO & President; Deborah A. Nugent, VP of Finance & Treasurer; Roger J. King, VP of Sales; Myra Canterbury, Chief Info. Officer; Judy Shoning, Human Resources Mgr.

■ 6742 ■ Software Technology Inc.
1621 Cushman Dr.
Lincoln, NE 68512
Phone: (402)423-1440 **Fax:** (402)423-2561
E-mail: sales@stilegal.com
URL: http://www.stilegal.com
Products: Software for the legal market. **SIC:** 5045 (Computers, Peripherals & Software). **Est:** 1979. **Emp:** 55. **Officers:** Dan Berlin, President; Ken Merkt, Dir. of Marketing, e-mail: kmerkt@stilegal.com; Jane Edgerton, Human Resources Contact, e-mail: jedgerton@stilegal.com. **Alternate Name:** STI.

■ 6743 ■ Softworks Development Corp.
PO Box 579
Mequon, WI 53092
Phone: (414)242-8800
Free: (800)332-3475 **Fax:** (414)242-8825
Products: Computers and software. **SIC:** 5045 (Computers, Peripherals & Software). **Sales:** $17,000,000 (2000). **Emp:** 35.

■ 6744 ■ Sokol Electronics Inc.
121 E Baltimore St.
Hagerstown, MD 21740-6103
Phone: (301)791-2562 **Fax:** (301)791-8146
Products: Computers; Computer software; Peripheral computer equipment. **SIC:** 5045 (Computers, Peripherals & Software). **Officers:** J. Sokol, President.

■ 6745 ■ Solutions
1330 Russ Ln.
McMinnville, OR 97128-5659
Phone: (503)472-9017 **Fax:** (503)472-3299
Products: Computers; Computer software; Peripheral computer equipment. **SIC:** 5045 (Computers, Peripherals & Software). **Officers:** Paul Durfee, Owner.

■ 6746 ■ Songtech International Inc.
46560 Fremont Blvd., #109
Fremont, CA 94538
Phone: (510)770-9051 **Fax:** (510)770-9060
Products: Computer hardware and software. **SIC:** 5045 (Computers, Peripherals & Software). **Sales:** $4,000,000 (2000). **Emp:** 10. **Officers:** Song Chen, President.

■ 6747 ■ Southern Business Communications Inc.
3175 Corners North Ct.
Norcross, GA 30071
Phone: (770)449-4088
Free: (800)849-4088 **Fax:** (770)449-0188
URL: http://www.sbcg.com
Products: Micrographics; Audio/visual. **SIC:** 5045 (Computers, Peripherals & Software). **Est:** 1980.

Sales: $500,000,000 (2000). **Emp:** 2,000. **Officers:** Scott Lloyd, President, e-mail: slloyd@sbcg.com.

■ 6748 ■ **Southern Contracts**
1608 Ridgeland Rd. W
Mobile, AL 36695-2720
Phone: (205)343-4777 **Fax:** (205)343-4777
Products: Computers; Computer software; Peripheral computer equipment; Computer accessories. **SIC:** 5045 (Computers, Peripherals & Software). **Officers:** Allen Clarke, Owner.

■ 6749 ■ **Southern Data Systems Inc.**
6758 Shiloh Rd. E
Alpharetta, GA 30005-8364
Products: Computers, peripherals, and software. **SIC:** 5045 (Computers, Peripherals & Software). **Officers:** Larry Tew, President.

■ 6750 ■ **Southwest CTI Inc.**
3625 W MacArthur Blvd., Ste. 311
Santa Ana, CA 92704-6849
Phone: (949)453-6200
Products: Computer telephone integrating. **SICs:** 5065 (Electronic Parts & Equipment Nec); 5045 (Computers, Peripherals & Software). **Sales:** $4,000,000 (2000). **Emp:** 10. **Officers:** John Lee, President; Anette LaMarche, Controller.

■ 6751 ■ **Southwest Modern Data Systems**
2816 NW 57th St., Ste. 101
Oklahoma City, OK 73112-7042
Phone: (405)842-6710 **Fax:** (405)842-7288
URL: http://www.swmds.com
Products: Computers; Computer software; Peripheral computer equipment. **SIC:** 5045 (Computers, Peripherals & Software). **Est:** 1980. **Sales:** $2,000,000 (2000). **Officers:** David Giles, President.

■ 6752 ■ **Vic Spainhower**
16680 S Beckman Rd.
Oregon City, OR 97045-9302
Phone: (503)631-2291
Products: Computers, peripherals, and software. **SIC:** 5045 (Computers, Peripherals & Software). **Officers:** Vic Spainhower, Owner.

■ 6753 ■ **Special Purpose Systems Inc.**
PO Box C-96078
Bellevue, WA 98009-9678
Phone: (425)451-8077 **Fax:** (425)454-5205
Products: Computers; Computer software; Peripheral computer equipment. **SIC:** 5045 (Computers, Peripherals & Software). **Officers:** Telung Chang, President.

■ 6754 ■ **Spectrum Computer & Business Supplies**
205 Windward Dr., Ste. B
Ocean City, MD 21842-4830
Phone: (410)524-0528
Products: Computers, peripherals, and software. **SIC:** 5045 (Computers, Peripherals & Software). **Officers:** William Grube, President.

■ 6755 ■ **Spectrum Data Systems Inc.**
1400 Lake Hearn Dr., Ste. 190
Atlanta, GA 30319-1464
Phone: (404)843-5560 **Fax:** (404)843-5377
Products: Computers; Computer software; Peripheral computer equipment; Multimedia kits. **SIC:** 5045 (Computers, Peripherals & Software). **Officers:** Daniel Knotts, President.

■ 6756 ■ **Squirrel Companies Inc.**
1550 Bryant St., No. 830
San Francisco, CA 94103
Phone: (415)255-0119
Products: Computer software. **SIC:** 5045 (Computers, Peripherals & Software). **Est:** 1989. **Sales:** $7,000,000 (2000). **Emp:** 67. **Officers:** Barry Logan, President; Richard Howie, CFO.

■ 6757 ■ **Stan Corporation of America**
447 Battery St., Ste. 300
San Francisco, CA 94111-3202
Phone: (415)677-0766
Products: Import/export software; Computer peripherals for the entertainment industry. **SIC:** 5045

(Computers, Peripherals & Software). **Sales:** $4,000,000 (1994). **Emp:** 2. **Officers:** Shinichiro Kondo, President; Shinichior Kondo, President.

■ 6758 ■ **Star Com Computers**
585 Cypress Dr.
Florence, AL 35630-1850
Phone: (205)766-7827 **Fax:** (205)766-0000
Products: Computers; Computer software; Peripheral computer equipment. **SIC:** 5045 (Computers, Peripherals & Software). **Officers:** Susan Norman, Owner.

■ 6759 ■ **Star Micronics America Inc.**
1150 King Georges Post Rd.
Edison, NJ 08837
Phone: (732)572-9512
Free: (800)782-7636 **Fax:** (732)572-5095
E-mail: sales@starus.com
Products: Receipt printers. **SIC:** 5045 (Computers, Peripherals & Software). **Est:** 1947. **Emp:** 4,000. **Officers:** Susumu Yamaguchi, President; Carmen Dancel, CFO.

■ 6760 ■ **StarTech International**
5575 Magnatron Blvd.
San Diego, CA 92111
Phone: (619)457-0781 **Fax:** (619)457-0199
Products: Computer hardware. **SIC:** 5045 (Computers, Peripherals & Software). **Est:** 1991. **Sales:** $2,000,000 (2000). **Emp:** 6. **Officers:** Henry Balagam, Partner.

■ 6761 ■ **Douglas Stewart Co.**
2402 Advance Rd.
Madison, WI 53718
Phone: (608)221-1155
Free: (800)279-2795 **Fax:** (608)221-5217
URL: http://www.dstewart.com
Products: Computer software; Writing instruments; School supplies; Office products; Computer accessories; Electronics. **SICs:** 5045 (Computers, Peripherals & Software); 5112 (Stationery & Office Supplies); 5044 (Office Equipment). **Est:** 1950. **Sales:** $120,000,000 (1999). **Emp:** 125. **Officers:** Scott Bukolt, President; John Thomson, VP of Operations; Jack Bahlman, VP of Marketing & Sales, e-mail: Jbahlman@dstewart.com; Bill Niebuhr, Dir. of Sales, e-mail: Bniehbuhr@dstewart.com; Jean Aden, Human Resources Contact, e-mail: jaden@dstewart.com; Cheryl Rosen Weston, CEO.

■ 6762 ■ **Stok Software Inc.**
373 Smithtown Byp., No. 287
Hauppauge, NY 11788-2516
Phone: (718)699-9393 **Fax:** (718)221-4404
Products: Computers, peripherals, and software. **SIC:** 5045 (Computers, Peripherals & Software). **Est:** 1982. **Sales:** $1,200,000 (2000). **Emp:** 15. **Officers:** Glenn Stok, President.

■ 6763 ■ **Storage Technology Corp.**
2270 S 88th St.
Louisville, CO 80028-4309
Phone: (303)673-5151
Free: (800)786-7835 **Fax:** (303)673-4444
Products: Information storage and retrieval subsystems, networking products, integrated software, disks and tapes. **SIC:** 5045 (Computers, Peripherals & Software). **Sales:** $2,368,200,000 (1999). **Emp:** 8,700. **Officers:** David E. Weiss, CEO & President; Victor M. Perez, Exec. VP, Chairman of the Board & CEO.

■ 6764 ■ **StorageTek**
10260 SW Greenburg Rd Ste. 400
Portland, OR 97223
Phone: (503)293-3589 **Fax:** (503)244-5822
Products: Provides information storage and retrieval solutions for mainframes, minis and distributed systems. **SIC:** 5045 (Computers, Peripherals & Software).

■ 6765 ■ **Strategic Products and Services Inc.**
10810 Farnam Dr.
Omaha, NE 68154
Phone: (402)392-3900
Products: Computers. **SIC:** 5045 (Computers, Peripherals & Software). **Sales:** $12,000,000 (2000). **Emp:** 50. **Officers:** Clay Sorensen, President.

■ 6766 ■ **Stream International Inc.**
275 Dan Rd.
Canton, MA 02021
Phone: (781)821-4500 **Fax:** (781)821-5688
Products: Computers and software. **SIC:** 5045 (Computers, Peripherals & Software). **Est:** 1983. **Sales:** $301,100,000 (2000). **Emp:** 600. **Officers:** Morton H. Rosenthal, CEO & Chairman of the Board; Douglass C. Greenlaw, VP & CFO; Joel M. Blenner, VP of Sales; Stephen D.R. Moore, President; Lianne Rasso, VP of Human Resources.

■ 6767 ■ **Strictly Business Computer Systems Inc.**
PO Box 2076
Huntington, WV 25720
Phone: (304)529-0401 **Fax:** (304)522-3254
Products: Computers and software in the Ada language. **SIC:** 5045 (Computers, Peripherals & Software). **Sales:** $1,000,000 (1994). **Emp:** 30. **Officers:** Michael G. Owens, President; Debra Smith, Operations Mgr.

■ 6768 ■ **STRO-WARE Inc.**
6035 Bristol Pkwy.
Culver City, CA 90230-6601
Phone: (310)575-1932 **Free:** (800)278-7876
Products: Multi-media based software. **SIC:** 5045 (Computers, Peripherals & Software). **Sales:** $1,000,000 (1994). **Emp:** 6. **Officers:** Neil Stromin, President.

■ 6769 ■ **Summation Legal Technologies Inc.**
100 Bush St., Ste. 2000
San Francisco, CA 94104
Phone: (415)442-0404
Free: (800)735-7866 **Fax:** (415)442-0403
URL: http://www.summation.com
Products: Computer software. **SIC:** 5045 (Computers, Peripherals & Software). **Est:** 1984. **Sales:** $2,000,000 (2000). **Emp:** 20. **Officers:** Jon Sigerman, President.

■ 6770 ■ **Sun Data Inc.**
PO Box 926020
Norcross, GA 30010
Phone: (770)449-6116
Free: (888)786-3282 **Fax:** (770)448-7726
Products: Computer peripheral equipment. **SIC:** 5045 (Computers, Peripherals & Software). **Sales:** $230,000,000 (2000). **Emp:** 300. **Officers:** Eric Prockow, CEO & Chairman of the Board; Bob Roddy, VP & CFO.

■ 6771 ■ **Sunbelt Data Systems Inc.**
2629 NW 39th, Ste. 200
Oklahoma City, OK 73112
Phone: (405)947-7617 **Fax:** (405)947-7629
E-mail: sunbelt@netplus.net
Products: Computers. **SIC:** 5045 (Computers, Peripherals & Software). **Est:** 1981. **Sales:** $25,000,000 (2000). **Emp:** 15. **Officers:** Victor Harris, President.

■ 6772 ■ **Sundog Technologies**
4505 Wasatch Blvd. Ste. 340
Salt Lake City, UT 84124-4709
Phone: (801)424-0044 **Fax:** (801)424-0033
Products: Computer software development. **SIC:** 5045 (Computers, Peripherals & Software). **Officers:** John Blumenthal, President.

■ 6773 ■ **Sunny Group Inc.**
2215 E Huntington Dr.
Duarte, CA 91010
Phone: (626)303-2050
Free: (888)786-6966 **Fax:** (626)305-1535
Products: Computer hardware including, multimedia speakers, keyboards, and mobile computing products. **SIC:** 5045 (Computers, Peripherals & Software). **Sales:** $20,000,000 (2000). **Emp:** 20. **Officers:** William Huang, CEO & President.

■ 6774 ■ **Sunnytech Inc.**
500 Hollister Rd.
Teterboro, NJ 07608
Phone: (201)288-8866
Products: Computer parts. **SIC:** 5045 (Computers, Peripherals & Software). **Est:** 1986. **Sales:**

$34,000,000 (2000). **Emp:** 70. **Officers:** Joe Niu, President; Phylia Wang, Controller.

■ **6775** ■ **SunRace Technology (USA) Corp.**
809 S Lemon Ave.
Walnut, CA 91789
Phone: (909)468-2933
Free: (800)786-3343 **Fax:** (909)468-2961
Products: Computer equipment. **SIC:** 5045 (Computers, Peripherals & Software). **Sales:** $5,000,000 (2000). **Emp:** 30. **Officers:** Toku Lee, President; Maggie Cao, Finance Officer.

■ **6776** ■ **Superscape Inc.**
3945 Freedom Cir.
Santa Clara, CA 95054
Phone: (408)969-0500 **Fax:** (408)969-0510
Products: 3-D virtual reality software. **SIC:** 5045 (Computers, Peripherals & Software). **Sales:** $2,000,000 (2000). **Emp:** 20. **Officers:** Robert Lowe, President.

■ **6777** ■ **Supplyline Inc.**
PO Box 915168
Longwood, FL 32791-5168
Phone: (407)843-5463 **Fax:** (407)843-8953
Products: Computer equipment. **SIC:** 5045 (Computers, Peripherals & Software). **Est:** 1982. **Sales:** $3,800,000 (2000). **Emp:** 25. **Officers:** Leonard E. Rodgers, President; Robert Seville, Controller; Joseph Noecker, Dir. of Sales.

■ **6778** ■ **Support Net Inc.**
4400 W 96 St.
Indianapolis, IN 46268
Phone: (317)735-0200
Free: (800)255-3390 **Fax:** (317)735-0201
Products: Computers and computer peripherals. **SIC:** 5045 (Computers, Peripherals & Software). **Sales:** $15,000,000 (2000). **Emp:** 240. **Officers:** Henry Camferdam Jr., President; Carol Trigillio, CFO.

■ **6779** ■ **Sutmyn America**
340 E Larkspur Ln.
Tempe, AZ 85281
Phone: (480)970-5401 **Fax:** (480)970-5089
Products: Provides enterprise network and storage solutions, integration and training. **SIC:** 5045 (Computers, Peripherals & Software).

■ **6780** ■ **Symantec Corp. Peter Norton Products Div.**
2500 Broadway St.
Santa Monica, CA 90404-3061
Phone: (310)453-4600 **Fax:** (310)453-0636
URL: http://www.symantec.com
Products: Computer software. **SIC:** 5045 (Computers, Peripherals & Software). **Est:** 1982. **Sales:** $100,000,000 (2000). **Emp:** 2,000. **Officers:** Gordon Eubanks, CEO & President; Enrique Salem.

■ **6781** ■ **Symco Group Inc.**
3073 McCall Dr., Ste. 1
Atlanta, GA 30340-2831
Phone: (404)451-8002
Products: Computers, peripherals, and software. **SIC:** 5045 (Computers, Peripherals & Software). **Officers:** Robert Williams, President.

■ **6782** ■ **Syslink Computer Corp.**
1025 S Placentia Ave.
Fullerton, CA 92831
Phone: (714)871-8000
Free: (888)979-5465 **Fax:** (714)871-8881
URL: http://www.syslinkcorp.com
Products: Computers. **SIC:** 5045 (Computers, Peripherals & Software). **Est:** 1990. **Sales:** $6,000,000 (2000). **Emp:** 13. **Officers:** Justin Chen, President, e-mail: justin@syslinkcorp.com.

■ **6783** ■ **System Solutions Technology Inc.**
14100 Laurel Park Dr.
Laurel, MD 20707
Phone: (301)725-6500 **Fax:** (301)725-7869
Products: Advanced technology industrial computers and peripheral equipment. **SIC:** 5045 (Computers, Peripherals & Software). **Sales:** $11,000,000 (2000). **Emp:** 25. **Officers:** Dale Foster, President.

■ **6784** ■ **Systems House Inc.**
1033 Rte. 46
Clifton, NJ 07013
Phone: (973)777-8050
Free: (800)MDS-5556 **Fax:** (973)777-3063
E-mail: sales@tshinc.com
URL: http://www.tshinc.com
Products: MDS distribution software; E-commerce software. **SIC:** 5045 (Computers, Peripherals & Software). **Est:** 1979. **Emp:** 40. **Officers:** Seymour Fertig, President.

■ **6785** ■ **Systems Solutions Inc.**
2108 E Thomas Rd.
Phoenix, AZ 85016-7758
Phone: (602)955-5566
Free: (800)232-0026 **Fax:** (602)955-0085
E-mail: tony@syspac.com
URL: http://www.syspac.com
Products: Computers; Computer software; Peripheral computer equipment. **SIC:** 5045 (Computers, Peripherals & Software). **Est:** 1982. **Sales:** $2,100,000 (2000). **Emp:** 26. **Officers:** Dr. Rajesh Kakar, President.

■ **6786** ■ **Tactical Business Services**
1260 W Northwest Hwy.
Palatine, IL 60067-1897
Phone: (708)358-1638
Products: Computer parts and equipment. **SIC:** 5065 (Electronic Parts & Equipment Nec). **Sales:** $3,000,000 (1993). **Emp:** 12. **Officers:** Larry Gatza, President.

■ **6787** ■ **Taft Development Group**
4605 Macky Way
Boulder, CO 80303-6743
Phone: (303)494-4575 **Fax:** (303)494-4575
Products: Computer software. **SIC:** 5045 (Computers, Peripherals & Software). **Officers:** James Taft, Owner.

■ **6788** ■ **Taneum Computer Products Inc.**
243 SW 41st St.
Renton, WA 98055
Phone: (425)251-0711
Free: (800)829-7768 **Fax:** (425)251-6332
Products: Computer peripheral equipment. **SIC:** 5045 (Computers, Peripherals & Software). **Sales:** $1,000,000 (2000). **Emp:** 5. **Officers:** Robert Meadows, President.

■ **6789** ■ **Tatung Company of America Inc.**
2850 El Presidio St.
Long Beach, CA 90810
Phone: (310)637-2105
Free: (800)827-2850 **Fax:** (310)637-8484
Products: Electronics, including monitors and computers. **SICs:** 5045 (Computers, Peripherals & Software); 5064 (Electrical Appliances—Television & Radio). **Est:** 1972. **Sales:** $45,000,000,000 (2000). **Emp:** 25,000. **Officers:** Hsin-Chin Liu, President; Michael Lai, CFO; Thomas Tsai, Dir. of Information Systems; C.C. Liu, Dir of Personnel.

■ **6790** ■ **TC Computers Inc.**
5005 Bloomfield St.
Jefferson, LA 70121
Phone: (504)733-0331
Products: Computers and related products. **SIC:** 5045 (Computers, Peripherals & Software). **Sales:** $49,000,000 (2000). **Emp:** 100. **Officers:** Darrin Davies, President; Don Halloran, Controller.

■ **6791** ■ **Teaching Aids Inc.**
711 W 17th St., No. E-2
Costa Mesa, CA 92627
Phone: (949)548-9321 **Fax:** (949)548-0936
Products: Multi-media materials, including video cassettes and computer software. **SIC:** 5045 (Computers, Peripherals & Software). **Est:** 1952.

■ **6792** ■ **Tech 101 Inc.**
16812 Milliken Ave.
Irvine, CA 92606
Phone: (949)261-5141 **Fax:** (949)622-6649
Products: Computer equipment. **SIC:** 5045 (Computers, Peripherals & Software). **Sales:** $22,000,000 (2000). **Emp:** 28. **Officers:** Grace Chiu, President & CFO.

■ **6793** ■ **Tech Arts**
829 E Molloy Rd.
Syracuse, NY 13211
Phone: (315)455-1003
Free: (800)455-9853 **Fax:** (315)455-5838
E-mail: sales@techarts.com
URL: http://www.techarts.com
Products: Computer products. **SIC:** 5045 (Computers, Peripherals & Software). **Est:** 1992. **Sales:** $1,000,000 (2000). **Emp:** 5. **Officers:** Steve Diederich, President.

■ **6794** ■ **Tech Data Corp.**
5350 Tech Data Dr.
Clearwater, FL 33760
Phone: (813)539-7429
Free: (800)237-8931 **Fax:** (813)538-7057
URL: http://www.techdata.com
Products: Technology products. **SIC:** 5045 (Computers, Peripherals & Software). **Est:** 1974. **Sales:** $20,000,000,000 (2000). **Emp:** 10,000. **Officers:** Steve A. Raymund, CEO & Chairman of the Board; Jeffery P. Howells, VP of Finance; Nestor Cano, President; Lawrence Hamilton, VP of Human Resources.

■ **6795** ■ **Techexport, Inc.**
1 North Ave.
Burlington, MA 01803
Phone: (781)229-6900 **Fax:** (781)229-7706
Products: Alphanumeric computer display terminals; Computer graphic displays. **SIC:** 5045 (Computers, Peripherals & Software). **Officers:** Donald F. Berman, President.

■ **6796** ■ **Techfarm Inc.**
200 W Evelyn Ave., No. 100
Mountain View, CA 94041-1365
Phone: (408)720-7080
Products: Computer systems and software for start-up companies. **SIC:** 5045 (Computers, Peripherals & Software).

■ **6797** ■ **Techlink Alaska**
1204 H St.
Anchorage, AK 99501-4359
Phone: (907)276-6862
E-mail: sales@techlinkalaska.com
URL: http://www.techlinkalaska.com
Products: Computers, peripherals, and software; Service, installations, repair, and warranty contracts. **SIC:** 5045 (Computers, Peripherals & Software). **Est:** 1988. **Emp:** 5. **Officers:** Waltraud Barron, President. **Former Name:** Brokerage Services International.

■ **6798** ■ **Techmedia Computer Systems Corp.**
37 Smith St.
Englewood, NJ 07631-4067
Phone: (201)567-1583
Products: Computer products. **SIC:** 5045 (Computers, Peripherals & Software). **Sales:** $300,000,000 (2000). **Emp:** 300. **Officers:** Andrew Park, CEO & Chairman of the Board.

■ **6799** ■ **Technical Business Specialists Inc.**
5720 E Washington St.
Los Angeles, CA 90040
Phone: (323)727-0039 **Fax:** (323)727-0083
Products: Printers, repairs and parts. **SICs:** 5045 (Computers, Peripherals & Software); 5044 (Office Equipment). **Est:** 1964. **Sales:** $2,000,000 (2000). **Emp:** 6. **Officers:** Dean Nelson, President; Joanna Nelson, Manager.

■ **6800** ■ **Technical and Scientific Application Inc.**
2040 W Sam Houston Parkway N
Houston, TX 77043
Phone: (713)935-1500 **Fax:** (713)935-1555
Products: Computers and peripheral devices. **SIC:** 5045 (Computers, Peripherals & Software). **Sales:** $26,000,000 (2000). **Emp:** 55. **Officers:** William C. Smith, President; Calvin Glover, Controller.

■ **6801** ■ **Technoland Inc.**
1050 Stewart Dr.
Sunnyvale, CA 94086
Phone: (408)992-0888
Free: (800)292-4500 **Fax:** (408)992-0808
Products: Computer systems integrator; Industrial

computers, computer peripherals and software. Industrial computers, computer peripherals and software. **SIC:** 5045 (Computers, Peripherals & Software). **Sales:** $15,000,000 (2000). **Emp:** 38. **Officers:** Jeff Hsu, Owner; Sabrina Lin, CFO.

■ 6802 ■ **Technology Specialists Inc.**
303 2nd St., Ste. E
Annapolis, MD 21403-2545
Phone: (410)268-2300
Products: Computer peripheral equipment. **SIC:** 5045 (Computers, Peripherals & Software). **Sales:** $2,000,000 (2000). **Emp:** 4. **Officers:** Christina Fisher, President.

■ 6803 ■ **TechQuest Inc.**
3816 Bagley Ave.
Culver City, CA 90232
Phone: (310)287-2444   **Fax:** (310)287-1817
Products: Computer services and sales. **SIC:** 5045 (Computers, Peripherals & Software). **Sales:** $500,000 (1999). **Emp:** 5. **Officers:** Marlene Chidiac, President; Sam Naddaf, CFO.

■ 6804 ■ **Tek-Gear LLC**
637 S Broadway St Ste. B347
Boulder, CO 80303
Phone: (303)494-1116
Products: Develops prepackaged software and hardware for scientific education programs. **SIC:** 5045 (Computers, Peripherals & Software). **Officers:** Dave Adamson, CFO.

■ 6805 ■ **Tektronix Inc.**
PO Box 500
Beaverton, OR 97077
Phone: (503)627-7111
Free: (800)835-9433   **Fax:** (503)627-2406
Products: Develops and X-terminals and video production, storage, editing and transmission systems—switchers, coders, network access platforms, server software and disk recorder/players. **SIC:** 5045 (Computers, Peripherals & Software). **Sales:** $1,861,100,000 (1999). **Emp:** 7,571. **Officers:** Richard H. Wills, CEO & President; Colin Slade, CFO.

■ 6806 ■ **Tektronix Inc. Logic Analyzer Div.**
26600 SW Parkway Ave.
Wilsonville, OR 97070
Phone: (503)627-7111
Free: (800)835-9433   **Fax:** (503)627-2406
Products: Develops and X-terminals and video production, storage, editing and transmission systems—switchers, coders, network access platforms, server software and disk recorder/players. **SIC:** 5045 (Computers, Peripherals & Software). **Officers:** Jerome Meyer, Chairman of the Board; William Walker, Vice Chairman of the Board.

■ 6807 ■ **Tekvisions Inc.**
2350 W Mission Ln.
Phoenix, AZ 85021
Phone: (602)943-6787   **Fax:** (602)943-2217
Products: Touch computer monitors; Computers and computer parts. **SIC:** 5045 (Computers, Peripherals & Software).

■ 6808 ■ **Tele-Vue Service Company Inc.**
947 Federal Blvd.
Denver, CO 80204
Phone: (303)623-3330
Products: Computers and software. **SIC:** 5045 (Computers, Peripherals & Software). **Sales:** $1,000,000 (2000). **Emp:** 15. **Officers:** Randy Prade, President.

■ 6809 ■ **Telecom Solutions Div.**
2300 Orchard Pkwy.
San Jose, CA 95131-1017
Phone: (408)433-0910   **Fax:** (408)428-7897
Products: System operator's transmission equipment. **SIC:** 5045 (Computers, Peripherals & Software). **Sales:** $23,000,000 (2000). **Emp:** 364. **Officers:** Dan Rascal, President; Jim Markham, Controller.

■ 6810 ■ **Telecomputer Inc.**
17481 Mount Cliffwood Cir
Fountain Valley, CA 92708
Phone: (714)438-3993   **Fax:** (714)438-3995
Products: Computer memory products; Intel CPUs. **SIC:** 5045 (Computers, Peripherals & Software). **Officers:** Joseph Nguyen, President.

■ 6811 ■ **Telmar Group Inc.**
148 Madison Ave.
New York, NY 10016
Phone: (212)460-9000
Products: Compute software. **SIC:** 5045 (Computers, Peripherals & Software). **Sales:** $10,000,000 (1994). **Emp:** 100. **Officers:** Stanley P. Federman, CEO & Chairman of the Board; Jennie E. Potter, President & COO.

■ 6812 ■ **Tenet Information Service Inc.**
4885 South 900 East, Ste. 107
Salt Lake City, UT 84117-5746
Phone: (801)268-3480   **Fax:** (801)268-1206
Products: Computers; Computer software; Peripheral computer equipment. **SIC:** 5045 (Computers, Peripherals & Software). **Officers:** Dennis Peterson, President.

■ 6813 ■ **Terco Computer Systems**
PO Box 1803
Lombard, IL 60148
Phone: (630)668-9999   **Fax:** (630)668-9999
Products: Software. **SIC:** 5045 (Computers, Peripherals & Software). **Sales:** $900,000 (2000). **Emp:** 3. **Officers:** Robert M. Grzyb, CEO.

■ 6814 ■ **Tesserax Information Systems**
18796 Academy Cir.
Huntington Beach, CA 92648
Phones: (714)841-0616   (714)841-0091
URL: http://www.tesserax.com
Products: Shareware software. **SIC:** 5045 (Computers, Peripherals & Software). **Est:** 1988. **Officers:** Peter Grigonis, Owner, e-mail: peterg@tesserax.com.

■ 6815 ■ **Textronix Inc. Semiconductor Test Div.**
PO Box 500
Beaverton, OR 97077
Phone: (503)627-7111
Products: Develops and X-terminals and video production, storage, editing and transmission systems—switchers, coders, network access platforms, server software and disk recorder/players. **SIC:** 5045 (Computers, Peripherals & Software).

■ 6816 ■ **Thinkware**
345 4th St.
San Francisco, CA 94107
Phone: (415)777-9876   **Fax:** (415)777-2972
Products: Multimedia computer hardware and software. **SIC:** 5045 (Computers, Peripherals & Software).

■ 6817 ■ **Johnny Thomas**
350 Avery Landing
Augusta, GA 30907-9749
Phone: (706)650-8613   **Fax:** (706)650-8613
Products: Computers; Computer software; Peripheral computer equipment. **SIC:** 5045 (Computers, Peripherals & Software). **Officers:** Johnny Thomas, Owner.

■ 6818 ■ **TimeSaving Services Inc.**
8601 Dunwoody Pl., Ste. 348
Atlanta, GA 30350
Phone: (770)649-9499   **Fax:** (770)649-9399
Products: A computer consulting firm specializing in client/server business automation. **SIC:** 5045 (Computers, Peripherals & Software). **Emp:** 10.

■ 6819 ■ **TMA Systems L.L.C.**
6846 S Canton Ave., Ste. 510
Tulsa, OK 74136
Phone: (918)494-2890
Free: (800)862-1130   **Fax:** (918)494-4892
Products: Computers. **SIC:** 5045 (Computers, Peripherals & Software). **Sales:** $5,000,000 (2000).

Emp: 24. **Officers:** Gary R. Schaecher, President; Dennis Phillips, Controller.

■ 6820 ■ **Tolman Computer Supply Group**
143 N 1200 E
Orem, UT 84097-5016
Phone: (801)576-1220
Products: Computers, peripherals, and software. **SIC:** 5045 (Computers, Peripherals & Software). **Officers:** Vincent Tolman, President.

■ 6821 ■ **Tomba Communications and Electronics Inc.**
718 Barataria Blvd.
Marrero, LA 70072
Phone: (504)340-2448
Products: Computer hardware and peripheral equipment. **SIC:** 5045 (Computers, Peripherals & Software).

■ 6822 ■ **Toshiba America Electronic Components Inc. Storage Device Div.**
35 Hammond
Irvine, CA 92618
Phone: (949)457-0777
URL: http://www.toshiba.com/taecsdd
Products: Hard drives; CD-ROM drives; DVD-ROM drives; DVD RAM drive; CD-RW/DVDROM drives. **SIC:** 5045 (Computers, Peripherals & Software).

■ 6823 ■ **Toshiba America Information Systems Inc. Network Products Div.**
PO Box 19724
Irvine, CA 92618-1697
Phone: (949)461-4840
Products: Computer network routers for small office or home office. **SIC:** 5045 (Computers, Peripherals & Software). **Officers:** Takao Sakamoto, Vice President.

■ 6824 ■ **Total Concepts Inc.**
501 W Glenoaks Blvd.
Glendale, CA 91202
Phone: (818)547-9476   **Fax:** (818)547-9473
URL: http://www.smartups.com
Products: Computer protection equipment, including UPS and battery packs. **SIC:** 5045 (Computers, Peripherals & Software). **Est:** 1989.

■ 6825 ■ **Tradequest International USA**
PO Box 2759
Bristol, CT 06010
Phone: (860)589-1508   **Fax:** (860)589-8293
Products: Computer supplies. **SIC:** 5045 (Computers, Peripherals & Software). **Officers:** Rebecca Starankewicz, Owner.

■ 6826 ■ **Tradewinds International Inc.**
8548 W River Rd.
Minneapolis, MN 55444-1311
Phone: (612)561-0009   **Fax:** (612)561-0260
Products: Computers; Computer software; Peripheral computer equipment. **SIC:** 5045 (Computers, Peripherals & Software). **Officers:** Leon Ulferts, President.

■ 6827 ■ **TransNet Corp.**
45 Columbia Rd.
Somerville, NJ 08876
Phone: (908)253-0500   **Fax:** (908)253-0600
Products: Computers. **SIC:** 5045 (Computers, Peripherals & Software). **Est:** 1969. **Sales:** $26,800,000 (2000). **Emp:** 100. **Officers:** Steven J. Wilk, CEO & President; John J. Wilk, Treasurer; Mark Stanoch, VP of Sales; Jay A. Smolyn, VP of Operations.

■ 6828 ■ **Transparent Technology Inc.**
520 Washington Blvd., No. 812
Marina Del Rey, CA 90292-5442
Phone: (310)215-8040
Free: (800)638-8486   **Fax:** (310)215-8070
Products: Technical software for UNIX and networking systems. **SIC:** 5045 (Computers, Peripherals & Software). **Sales:** $8,000,000 (2000). **Emp:** 17. **Officers:** Gary Hipsher, President; Juliet Mock, Accountant.

■ **6829** ■ **TransPro Marketing**
21408 50th Dr. SE
Woodinville, WA 98072-8378
Phone: (425)485-6098
Free: (800)222-1876 **Fax:** (425)485-6104
Products: Computer software used for vehicle maintenance. **SIC:** 5045 (Computers, Peripherals & Software). **Sales:** $500,000 (2000). **Emp:** 2. **Officers:** Glenn J. Douglas, Owner.

■ **6830** ■ **Triangle Computer Corp.**
50230 Pontiac Tr.
Wixom, MI 48393
Phone: (248)926-0330 **Fax:** (248)926-0199
Products: Computers. **SIC:** 5045 (Computers, Peripherals & Software). **Sales:** $1,000,000 (2000). **Emp:** 11. **Officers:** Thomas S. Tusan, President.

■ **6831** ■ **TriGem Corp.**
48400 Fremont Blvd.
Fremont, CA 94538-6505
Phone: (510)770-8787 **Fax:** (510)770-9866
Products: Personal computers. **SIC:** 5045 (Computers, Peripherals & Software). **Est:** 1989. **Sales:** $150,000,000 (2000). **Emp:** 70. **Officers:** Sam Muk, President; John Ham, VP of Finance; Terry J. Baker, VP of Marketing; Mark M. Ha, Dir of Human Resources.

■ **6832** ■ **TriTech Graphics Inc.**
3348 Commercial Ave.
Northbrook, IL 60062-1909
Phone: (847)564-7773
Free: (800)323-1950 **Fax:** (847)564-8042
URL: http://www.tritechgraphics.com
Products: Monitors; Digitizers; Scanners; Print servers. **SICs:** 5045 (Computers, Peripherals & Software); 5065 (Electronic Parts & Equipment Nec). **Est:** 1990. **Sales:** $10,000,000 (2000). **Emp:** 5. **Officers:** Roy A. Filinson, President, e-mail: rfilinson@tritechgraphics.com.

■ **6833** ■ **Triton Electronics**
4700 Loyola Ln.
Austin, TX 78723
Phone: (512)929-0073 **Fax:** (512)929-0115
Products: Computer monitors, peripherals, and printers. **SIC:** 5045 (Computers, Peripherals & Software). **Est:** 1985. **Sales:** $200,000 (2000). **Emp:** 4. **Officers:** Calvin G. Banks, President.

■ **6834** ■ **True Comp America Inc.**
1264 S Bascom Ave.
San Jose, CA 95128
Phone: (408)292-8889
Products: Computers and peripherals. **SIC:** 5045 (Computers, Peripherals & Software). **Sales:** $3,000,000 (2000). **Emp:** 7. **Officers:** Tim Nguyen, President; Cindy Phan, CFO.

■ **6835** ■ **Tucson Computer Products**
2850 W Camino De La Joya
Tucson, AZ 85741-9225
Phone: (520)297-6166 **Fax:** (520)297-6553
Products: Computers; Computer software; Peripheral computer equipment. **SIC:** 5045 (Computers, Peripherals & Software). **Officers:** William Hemmings, Owner.

■ **6836** ■ **TurningPoint Systems Inc.**
300 Rosewood Dr.
Danvers, MA 01923-4515
Phone: (978)777-9991
Free: (800)370-4500 **Fax:** (978)777-3335
Products: Computer hardware and software for remote order entry and executive information systems. **SIC:** 5045 (Computers, Peripherals & Software). **Sales:** $3,500,000 (2000). **Emp:** 24. **Officers:** Elery Le Blanc, President & Chairman of the Board; Stanley Gordon, VP of Finance.

■ **6837** ■ **TVM Professional Monitor Corp.**
4260 E Brickell St.
Ontario, CA 91761-1511
Phone: (909)390-8099 **Fax:** (909)390-8060
Products: Computer monitors and video cards. **SIC:** 5045 (Computers, Peripherals & Software). **Est:** 1986. **Sales:** $15,000,000 (2000). **Emp:** 15. **Officers:** Sjamsudin Ali, Vice President.

■ **6838** ■ **Ultima International Corp.**
38897 Cherry St.
Newark, CA 94560
Phone: (510)739-0800 **Fax:** (510)739-0500
Products: Computer peripherals. **SIC:** 5045 (Computers, Peripherals & Software). **Sales:** $97,000,000 (2000). **Emp:** 30. **Officers:** Shou Wang, President; Angela Wang, Controller.

■ **6839** ■ **UMAX Computer Corp.**
47470 Seabridge Dr.
Fremont, CA 94538
Phone: (510)226-6886
Free: (800)232-8629 **Fax:** (510)623-7350
Products: cificworkstations supporting Apple Macintosh operating systems. **SIC:** 5045 (Computers, Peripherals & Software). **Sales:** $34,000,000 (2000). **Emp:** 150. **Officers:** Vincent Tai, CEO & President; Julie Wu, VP of Finance.

■ **6840** ■ **Uniplex Software Inc.**
10606 Shady Trl. Ste. 107
Dallas, TX 75220-2528
Phone: (972)753-6544 **Free:** (800)356-8063
Products: Software. **SIC:** 5045 (Computers, Peripherals & Software). **Sales:** $25,000,000 (2000). **Emp:** 100. **Officers:** Tom Frederick, President.

■ **6841** ■ **U.S. AudioTex L.L.C.**
18 Crow Canyon Ct. Ste. 300
San Ramon, CA 94583
Phone: (925)838-7996
Free: (800)487-4567 **Fax:** (925)838-4395
Products: Installs interactive voice response systems; Over-the-phone credit card processing; Computer assembly and sales for government entities. **SIC:** 5045 (Computers, Peripherals & Software). **Sales:** $5,000,000 (2000). **Emp:** 19. **Officers:** Kenneth L. Stern, President; Debbie Soleta, VP of Finance.

■ **6842** ■ **U.S. Filter/Diversified Engineering**
8040 Villa Park Dr., Ste. 800
Richmond, VA 23228
Phone: (804)262-6600 **Fax:** (804)266-5462
Products: Turnkey instrumentation, computer and communication systems. **SIC:** 5045 (Computers, Peripherals & Software). **Sales:** $8,000,000 (2000). **Emp:** 60.

■ **6843** ■ **United Strategies Inc.**
10810 Guilford Rd., Ste. 103
Annapolis Junction, MD 20701-1102
Phone: (301)417-7319 **Fax:** (301)417-7381
Products: Advanced technology industrial computers and peripheral equipment. **SIC:** 5045 (Computers, Peripherals & Software). **Officers:** George Barstis, CEO; Brian Becker, CFO.

■ **6844** ■ **Unizone Inc.**
PO Box 27688
Tempe, AZ 85285-7688
Phone: (602)756-2806 **Fax:** (602)756-2035
Products: Computer systems. **SIC:** 5045 (Computers, Peripherals & Software). **Est:** 1989. **Sales:** $2,000,000 (2000). **Emp:** 5. **Officers:** James G. Manton, President; Harv Frost, General Mgr.

■ **6845** ■ **USAP**
2295 Paseo de las Americas, Ste. 19
San Diego, CA 92154
Phone: (619)671-2398 **Fax:** (619)671-2399
E-mail: sales@usap.net
URL: http://www.usap.net
Products: Computer peripherals, including modems, keyboards, and sound cards; Software. **SIC:** 5045 (Computers, Peripherals & Software).

■ **6846** ■ **User Friendly Software Hardware**
PO Box 2888
LaGrange, GA 30241-2888
Phone: (706)883-8734 **Fax:** (706)883-6004
Products: Computers; Computer software; Peripheral computer equipment. **SIC:** 5045 (Computers, Peripherals & Software). **Officers:** Jeffrey Cody, President.

■ **6847** ■ **V-Tek Associates**
2092 Wilshire Dr.
Marietta, GA 30064
Phone: (404)424-4043 **Fax:** (404)424-3220
Products: Computer software. **SIC:** 5045 (Computers, Peripherals & Software).

■ **6848** ■ **Jan Van Woerkom**
701 Tobacco St.
Lebanon, CT 06249-1633
Phone: (860)848-7535
Products: Computers, peripherals, and software. **SIC:** 5045 (Computers, Peripherals & Software). **Officers:** Jan Van Workon, Owner.

■ **6849** ■ **Vangard Technology, Inc.**
11211 E Arapahoe Rd.
Englewood, CO 80112
Phone: (303)790-6090 **Fax:** (303)799-9297
Products: Computers. **SIC:** 5045 (Computers, Peripherals & Software). **Est:** 1984. **Sales:** $50,000,000 (2000). **Emp:** 90. **Officers:** Cal Andre, President. **Former Name:** R Squared Inc.

■ **6850** ■ **Via West Interface Inc.**
1228 E Prince Rd.
Tucson, AZ 85719
Phone: (520)293-0771 **Fax:** (520)293-0036
Products: Interface converters, data switching equipment, printer-sharing switches and computer cable. **SIC:** 5045 (Computers, Peripherals & Software). **Officers:** Robert Bos, President.

■ **6851** ■ **ViaGrafix Corp.**
1 American Way
Pryor, OK 74361
Phone: (918)825-4844
Free: (800)233-3223 **Fax:** (918)825-6359
E-mail: sales@viagrafix.com
URL: http://www.viagrafix.com
Products: Software. **SIC:** 5045 (Computers, Peripherals & Software). **Est:** 1985. **Emp:** 150. **Officers:** Julianne Mooty, Sales & Marketing Contact, e-mail: jmooty@viagrafix.com. **Former Name:** American Small Business Computers, Inc.

■ **6852** ■ **Victs Computers Inc.**
1245 Spacepark Way
Mountain View, CA 94043
Phone: (650)960-6811 **Fax:** (650)960-6816
Products: Computers; Software. **SIC:** 5045 (Computers, Peripherals & Software). **Sales:** $4,000,000 (2000). **Emp:** 10. **Officers:** Gary Hon, President; Nichole Hon, VP & CFO.

■ **6853** ■ **Vine Trading Company**
PO Box 537
Canaan, NH 03741-0537
Phone: (603)844-9613 **Fax:** (603)273-0484
Products: Computer parts; Computers. **SIC:** 5045 (Computers, Peripherals & Software). **Officers:** David Walthour, President.

■ **6854** ■ **Vital Image Technology Inc.**
450 Portage Tr.
Cuyahoga Falls, OH 44221
Phone: (330)940-3200
Free: (800)860-4624 **Fax:** (330)940-3222
Products: Computer printers, monitors, hardware, software, and peripheral equipment used for video camera computer integration. **SIC:** 5045 (Computers, Peripherals & Software). **Sales:** $4,000,000 (2000). **Emp:** 11. **Officers:** Dennis DiPirro, President; James Yankovich, Treasurer.

■ **6855** ■ **Vitech America Inc.**
2190 Nw 89 Pl.
Miami, FL 33172-2419
Phone: (305)477-1161 **Fax:** (305)477-1379
URL: http://www.vitech.net
Products: Computers and peripheral equipment to Brazil. **SIC:** 5045 (Computers, Peripherals & Software). **Sales:** $117,500,000 (2000). **Emp:** 650. **Officers:** Georges C. St. Laurent III, CEO & Chairman of the Board; Edward A. Kelly, CFO.

■ **6856** ■ **Voice It Worldwide Inc.**
2643 Midpoint Dr.Ste. A
Ft. Collins, CO 80525
Phone: (970)221-1705 **Fax:** (970)221-2058
Products: Personal, consumer electronic notepads to verbalize reminders and short messages. **SIC:** 5045 (Computers, Peripherals & Software). **Sales:** $7,300,000 (2000). **Emp:** 19. **Officers:** Alex Kumar, President; John Ellerby, CFO.

■ **6857** ■ **VSS Inc.**
PO Box 2151
Manassas, VA 20108-0823
Products: Business computers; Business phone systems. **SICs:** 5045 (Computers, Peripherals & Software); 5065 (Electronic Parts & Equipment Nec). **Est:** 1987. **Sales:** $1,000,000 (2000). **Emp:** 11. **Officers:** Gary B. Nelson, President & Chairman of the Board.

■ **6858** ■ **The Wakanta Group**
PO Box 144
Still River, MA 01467-0144
Phone: (978)772-3432 **Fax:** (978)772-3432
Products: Computers, peripherals, and software. **SIC:** 5045 (Computers, Peripherals & Software). **Est:** 1982. **Sales:** $5,000,000 (2000). **Emp:** 14. **Officers:** R. Kitchin, Managing Partner.

■ **6859** ■ **Austin B. Wakely**
611 Broad St.
Altavista, VA 24517-1829
Phone: (804)369-4719 **Fax:** (804)369-4719
Products: Computers; Computer software; Peripheral computer equipment. **SIC:** 5045 (Computers, Peripherals & Software). **Officers:** B. Austin, Owner.

■ **6860** ■ **Steen Watkins & Associates**
390 Main St., No. 201
Woburn, MA 01801-4280
Phone: (781)932-6464 **Fax:** (781)932-9458
Products: Computers; Computer software; Peripheral computer equipment. **SIC:** 5045 (Computers, Peripherals & Software). **Officers:** Edward Steen, Partner.

■ **6861** ■ **WebAccess**
2573 Midpoint Dr.
Ft. Collins, CO 80525
Phone: (970)221-2555
Products: Computers and software; Computer repairs. **SIC:** 5045 (Computers, Peripherals & Software). **Sales:** $25,600,000 (2000). **Emp:** 66. **Officers:** Wiley E. Prentice, CEO & President; Daniel T. Radford, VP & CFO.

■ **6862** ■ **Wescorp International Ltd.**
PO Box 1816
Salem, NH 03079-1144
Phone: (603)893-6202 **Fax:** (603)894-6810
Products: Computers; Computer software; Peripheral computer equipment. **SIC:** 5045 (Computers, Peripherals & Software). **Officers:** Wesley Dolloff, President.

■ **6863** ■ **Westcon Inc.**
520 White Plains Rd.
Tarrytown, NY 10591
Phone: (914)768-7180
Free: (800)527-9516 **Fax:** (914)829-7184
Products: Computers and networking equipment. **SIC:** 5045 (Computers, Peripherals & Software). **Sales:** $148,000,000 (2000). **Emp:** 300. **Officers:** Roman Michalowski, President; Joe Renton, Controller.

■ **6864** ■ **Westech**
PO Box 376
Igo, CA 96047-0376
Phone: (408)997-3547 **Fax:** (408)997-7512
Products: Computer software. **SIC:** 5045 (Computers, Peripherals & Software). **Est:** 1982. **Sales:** $3,000,000 (2000). **Emp:** 2.

■ **6865** ■ **Western DataCom Company Inc.**
PO Box 45113
Westlake, OH 44145
Phone: (216)835-1510 **Fax:** (216)835-9146
E-mail: wdc@western-data.com
URL: http://www.western-data.com
Products: Computer modems. **SIC:** 5065 (Electronic Parts & Equipment Nec). **Est:** 1981. **Sales:** $4,000,000 (2000). **Emp:** 14. **Officers:** Phil Ardire, President; John G. Gross, Controller; Linda S. Naughton, Dir. of Sales.

■ **6866** ■ **Western Graphtec Inc.**
11 Vanderbilt
Irvine, CA 92618
Phone: (714)454-2800
Free: (800)854-8385 **Fax:** (714)855-0895
E-mail: cp-sales@graphtecusa.com
URL: http://www.graphtecusa.com
Products: Plotters; Cutters; Recorders. **SICs:** 5045 (Computers, Peripherals & Software); 5049 (Professional Equipment Nec). **Est:** 1971. **Sales:** $15,000,000 (2000). **Emp:** 40. **Officers:** Kunio Minejima, President; Kevin Nomura, VP of Finance.

■ **6867** ■ **Western Micro Technology Inc.**
6550 N Loop 1604 E
San Antonio, TX 78247-5004
Free: (800)338-1600
Products: Computer components and systems. **SICs:** 5065 (Electronic Parts & Equipment Nec); 5045 (Computers, Peripherals & Software). **Est:** 1977. **Sales:** $131,700,000 (2000). **Emp:** 103. **Officers:** P. Scott Munroe, CEO & President; James W. Dorst, CFO; Bryan C. Gannon, VP of Marketing & Sales; P. Scott Munro, Sr. VP of Systems.

■ **6868** ■ **Western Pacific Data Systems Inc.**
7590 Fay Ave.
La Jolla, CA 92037
Phone: (619)454-0028
Products: Software. **SIC:** 5045 (Computers, Peripherals & Software). **Est:** 1976. **Sales:** $16,000,000 (1999). **Emp:** 80. **Officers:** Margaret Jackson, President; Neil Hadfield, CFO; Terry Lubenow, Dir. of Marketing & Sales.

■ **6869** ■ **Whitebox Inc.**
3585 Habersham
Tucker, GA 30084
Phone: (404)414-0301 **Fax:** (404)414-0033
Products: Emulator cards. **SIC:** 5045 (Computers, Peripherals & Software). **Est:** 1990. **Sales:** $700,000 (2000). **Emp:** 3. **Officers:** Martin Huffham, President.

■ **6870** ■ **Whitlock Group**
3900 Gaskins Rd.
Richmond, VA 23233
Phone: (804)273-9100
Products: Computer hardware and software. **SIC:** 5045 (Computers, Peripherals & Software).

■ **6871** ■ **Windows Memory Corp.**
920 Kline St., Ste. 100
La Jolla, CA 92037
Phone: (619)454-9701
Products: Memory chips and computer peripheral equipment. **SICs:** 5065 (Electronic Parts & Equipment Nec); 5045 (Computers, Peripherals & Software).

■ **6872** ■ **Winners Circle Systems**
2618 Telegraph Ave.
Berkeley, CA 94704
Phone: (510)845-4823
Products: Computers and peripherals. **SIC:** 5045 (Computers, Peripherals & Software). **Sales:** $5,000,000 (1993). **Emp:** 12. **Officers:** Andy Jong, President.

■ **6873** ■ **Wireless Telecom Inc.**
3025 S Parker Rd., Ste. 1000
Aurora, CO 80014-2931
Phone: (303)338-4200
Products: Wireless computers. **SIC:** 5045 (Computers, Peripherals & Software).

■ **6874** ■ **Wiscomp Systems Inc.**
W266 N665 Eastmound Dr., Ste. 110
Waukesha, WI 53186
Phone: (414)544-5504 **Fax:** (414)544-5933
Products: Computers and software. **SIC:** 5045 (Computers, Peripherals & Software). **Sales:** $5,500,000 (2000). **Emp:** 40. **Officers:** Herb Harris, President; Bruce Comdohr, Controller.

■ **6875** ■ **Wong's Advanced Technologies Inc.**
3221 Danny Park
Metairie, LA 70002
Phone: (504)887-3333
Products: Computer hardware and peripheral equipment. **SIC:** 5045 (Computers, Peripherals & Software).

■ **6876** ■ **World Class Software Inc.**
415 U.S 1, Ste. F
Lake Park, FL 33403-3585
Phone: (561)585-7354
Products: Software. **SIC:** 5045 (Computers, Peripherals & Software). **Officers:** G. Darbyson, President.

■ **6877** ■ **World Computer Corp.**
PO Box 217006
Auburn Hills, MI 48326-2722
Phone: (313)377-4840
Products: Computer supplies. **SIC:** 5045 (Computers, Peripherals & Software).

■ **6878** ■ **World Computer Inc.**
3681 N Campbell Ave.
Tucson, AZ 85719
Phone: (520)327-2881 **Fax:** (520)327-2930
Products: Custom computers; Value-added reseller of computers and peripherals; Provides hardware, software and networking services. **SIC:** 5045 (Computers, Peripherals & Software). **Officers:** Deborah Hunter, CEO.

■ **6879** ■ **World Data Products Inc.**
121 Cheshire Ln.
Minnetonka, MN 55305
Phone: (612)476-9000 **Free:** (800)553-0592
Products: Computers; Peripheral computer equipment; Electronic computing equipment. **SIC:** 5045 (Computers, Peripherals & Software). **Est:** 1987. **Emp:** 40. **Officers:** Mark Ashton, President.

■ **6880** ■ **World Data Products Inc.**
121 Cheshire Ln.
Minnetonka, MN 55305-1063
Phone: (612)476-9000
Free: (800)553-0592 **Fax:** (612)476-1903
Products: Computer hardware. **SIC:** 5045 (Computers, Peripherals & Software). **Sales:** $24,000,000 (2000). **Emp:** 50. **Officers:** Mark Ashton, President; Tim Oster, CFO.

■ **6881** ■ **World-Net Microsystems Inc.**
PO Box 14010-513
Fremont, CA 94539-1410
Phone: (408)263-8088
Products: Computers, peripherals, and software. **SIC:** 5045 (Computers, Peripherals & Software). **Sales:** $3,000,000 (2000). **Emp:** 12. **Officers:** Chris Lin, President.

■ **6882** ■ **World Wen, Inc.**
580 Lincoln Park Blvd., Ste. 255
Dayton, OH 45429
Phone: (937)298-3383 **Fax:** (937)298-2550
E-mail: wtnet@infinet.com
Products: Motor oils; Lubricants and industrial food grade oils; Computers and peripheral equipment; Fitness and exercise equipment. **SICs:** 5045 (Computers, Peripherals & Software); 5091 (Sporting & Recreational Goods); 5172 (Petroleum Products Nec). **Emp:** 4. **Officers:** Michael J. Wenzler, President.

■ 6883 ■ WTI
75 Gilcrest Rd., Ste. 200
Londonderry, NH 30353
Phone: (603)425-1744
Free: (800)882-0007 **Fax:** (603)890-6720
E-mail: info@wrstech.com
URL: http://www.wrstech.com
Products: New and refurbished computer products, including software and hardware. **SIC:** 5045 (Computers, Peripherals & Software). **Est:** 1983. **Sales:** $12,000,000 (2000). **Emp:** 18. **Officers:** Michael J. Cavallaro, President; Jeanne Steele, Controller. **Former Name:** Workstation Technologies Inc.

■ 6884 ■ Wyle Systems
165 Technology
Irvine, CA 92618
Phone: (949)788-9953
Free: (800)318-9953 **Fax:** (949)753-9877
URL: http://www.wylesystems.com
Products: Computers; Hard drives; Tape drives; Modems; Servers; Networking equipment; Monitors; Enterprise systems; Maintenance service. **SICs:** 5045 (Computers, Peripherals & Software); 5065 (Electronic Parts & Equipment Nec). **Est:** 1949. **Sales:** $750,000,000 (1999). **Emp:** 400. **Officers:** William McMahon, CEO; Ken Bagley, VP of Marketing; Ron Pugh, VP of Sales; Bob Rose, VP of Operations; Rich Kain, VP of Strategic Planning. **Former Name:** Wyle Laboratories Electronics Marketing Group.

■ 6885 ■ XML Corp.
PO Box 164305
Austin, TX 78716
Phone: (512)442-2522 **Fax:** (512)445-5661
Products: Computers and computer peripherals. **SIC:** 5045 (Computers, Peripherals & Software). **Sales:** $2,000,000 (2000). **Emp:** 5. **Officers:** Jack Greyer, President; Marianne Greyer, Finance Officer.

■ 6886 ■ XYZ Electronics Inc.
4700 N 600 W
McCordsville, IN 46055-9508
Phone: (317)335-2128 **Fax:** (317)335-2128
Products: Computer equipment. **SIC:** 5045 (Computers, Peripherals & Software). **Officers:** Robert Frederick, President.

■ 6887 ■ Yosemite Technologies
2750 N Clovis Ave.
Fresno, CA 93727
Phone: (209)292-8888
Free: (800)228-9236 **Fax:** (209)292-8908
URL: http://www.tapeware.com
Products: Back up software. **SIC:** 5045 (Computers, Peripherals & Software). **Est:** 1996. **Sales:** $1,000,000 (2000). **Emp:** 10. **Officers:** Nick Cornacchia, President; Rod Christian, Vice President.

■ 6888 ■ Richard Young Journal Inc.
1096 E Newport Center Dr., Ste. 300
Deerfield Beach, FL 33442-7744
Phone: (954)426-8100 **Fax:** (954)421-4654
Products: Computer supplies and accessories, including ribbons, toner, and paper. **SICs:** 5045 (Computers, Peripherals & Software); 5112 (Stationery & Office Supplies). **Est:** 1979. **Sales:** $140,000,000 (2000). **Emp:** 275. **Officers:** Richard Young, Exec. VP of Sales; Tom Mizerak, VP of Finance; Brian Kaplan, Dir. of Marketing; Jim Barnwell, Dir. of Data Processing; Cathy Butler, Dir of Human Resources.

■ 6889 ■ Young Minds Inc.
1906 Orange Tree Ln., Ste. 220
Redlands, CA 92374-1350
Phone: (909)335-1350
Free: (800)964-4964 **Fax:** (909)798-0488
E-mail: info@ymi.com
URL: http://www.ymi.com
Products: Unix- and Windows-based software for CD and DVD mass storage devices. **SIC:** 5045 (Computers, Peripherals & Software). **Est:** 1989. **Sales:** $10,000,000 (2000). **Emp:** 25. **Officers:**

Matthew Hornbeck, President; Andrew Young, Chairman; David Cote, CEO.

■ 6890 ■ Zachary Software Inc.
1090 Kapp Dr.
Clearwater, FL 33755
Phone: (813)298-1181 **Fax:** (813)461-5808
Products: Software development tools. **SIC:** 5045 (Computers, Peripherals & Software). **Sales:** $5,600,000 (2000). **Emp:** 26. **Officers:** Scott Flynn, CEO; Mary Ann Kozmickas, CFO.

■ 6891 ■ Zortec International Inc.
1321 Murfressboro Rd.
Nashville, TN 37212
Phone: (615)361-7000
Free: (800)361-7005 **Fax:** (615)361-3800
Products: Computer hardware and software programs. **SIC:** 5045 (Computers, Peripherals & Software). **Est:** 1978. **Sales:** $4,000,000 (2000). **Emp:** 100. **Officers:** Jim H. Williams, CEO & President.

■ 6892 ■ Zytronix Inc.
1208 Apollo Way Ste. 504
Sunnyvale, CA 94086
Phone: (408)749-1326 **Fax:** (408)749-1329
Products: Computer equipment. **SIC:** 5045 (Computers, Peripherals & Software). **Officers:** Bill Byrne, President.

■ 6893 ■ Zzyzx Peripherals Inc.
5893 Oberlin Dr., Ste. 102
San Diego, CA 92121
Phone: (858)558-7800
Free: (800)876-7818 **Fax:** (858)558-8283
E-mail: info@zzyzx.com
URL: http://www.zzyzx.com
Products: Computer peripherals; Storage; Workstations and servers. **SICs:** 5044 (Office Equipment); 5045 (Computers, Peripherals & Software). **Sales:** $30,000,000 (2000). **Emp:** 50. **Officers:** Steve Rosoff, President; Michelle Lambert, CFO; Mary June Makoul, VP of Marketing; Steve Yamasaki, VP of Sales.

(13) Construction Materials and Machinery

Entries in this section are arranged alphabetically by company name. When the company name is a personal name, the company name is alphabetized by the surname unless the first name or initial(s) are part of a trade name. See the User's Guide at the front of this directory for additional information.

■ **6894** ■ **84 Lumber Co.**
Rte. 519, Box 8484
Eighty Four, PA 15330
Phone: (412)228-8820 **Fax:** (412)225-2530
URL: http://www.84lumber.com
Products: Lumber and building products. **SICs:** 5031 (Lumber, Plywood & Millwork); 5031 (Lumber, Plywood & Millwork); 5039 (Construction Materials Nec). **Est:** 1956. **Sales:** $1,600,000,000 (2000). **Emp:** 4,500. **Officers:** Joseph A. Hardy, President; Sid McAllister, Controller; Denny Brua, Exec. VP; Jim Allen, Dir of Human Resources; Margaret Hardy-Magerko, President.

■ **6895** ■ **A and H Building Materials Co.**
3361 E 36th St.
Tucson, AZ 85713
Phone: (520)622-4741
Free: (800)326-2962 **Fax:** (520)622-3178
Products: Drywall; Plaster; Roofing. **SICs:** 5033 (Roofing, Siding & Insulation); 5039 (Construction Materials Nec); 5032 (Brick, Stone & Related Materials). **Est:** 1963. **Sales:** $3,500,000 (2000). **Emp:** 12. **Officers:** David Havert, President; Dave Rung, General Mgr.

■ **6896** ■ **A and M Supply Inc.**
6701 90th Ave. N
Pinellas Park, FL 33782
Phone: (813)541-6631 **Fax:** (813)545-4685
Products: Plywood, particle board, and laminate. **SIC:** 5031 (Lumber, Plywood & Millwork). **Sales:** $26,000,000 (1992). **Emp:** 120. **Officers:** Charles A. Jackson, CEO; David M. Baccari, CFO.

■ **6897** ■ **A and R Lumber Sales Inc.**
PO Box 39
Junction City, OR 97448
Phone: (541)998-3700 **Fax:** (541)998-1445
Products: Lumber. **SIC:** 5031 (Lumber, Plywood & Millwork). **Est:** 1969. **Sales:** $12,000,000 (2000). **Emp:** 12. **Officers:** Daryl L. Richardson, President & Chairman of the Board; Diane Stanton, Treasurer & Secty.

■ **6898** ■ **A To Z Rental Center**
94-172 Leoole St.
Waipahu, HI 96797
Phone: (808)677-9181 **Fax:** (808)247-3842
Products: Chainsaws, wood trimmers, and jumping jacks. **SIC:** 5084 (Industrial Machinery & Equipment).

■ **6899** ■ **ABC Supply Co., Inc.**
21000 W 8 Mile Rd.
Southfield, MI 48075-5639
Phone: (248)542-2730 **Fax:** (248)542-6017
Products: Prepared asphalt and tar roofing and siding products; Siding; Door frames; Windows. **SICs:** 5033 (Roofing, Siding & Insulation); 5031 (Lumber, Plywood & Millwork); 5039 (Construction Materials Nec). **Officers:** Michael Bayer, Branch Mgr.

■ **6900** ■ **ABC Tile Distributors**
3105 18th St.
Metairie, LA 70010
Phone: (504)833-5543 **Fax:** (504)832-0932
Products: Floorcovering equipment and supplies. **SIC:** 5032 (Brick, Stone & Related Materials). **Sales:** $2,500,000 (2000). **Emp:** 10.

■ **6901** ■ **Abeita Glass Co.**
600 W Coal Ave.
Gallup, NM 87301
Phone: (505)722-7676
Products: Glass. **SIC:** 5039 (Construction Materials Nec).

■ **6902** ■ **Abilene Lumber Inc.**
2025 Industrial Blvd.
Abilene, TX 79604
Phone: (915)698-4465 **Fax:** (915)695-9957
Products: Lumber, including pine. **SIC:** 5031 (Lumber, Plywood & Millwork). **Est:** 1977. **Sales:** $12,000,000 (2000). **Emp:** 63. **Officers:** R.E. White, President.

■ **6903** ■ **Able Enterprises Inc.**
2205 Park St.
Ennis, TX 75119-1624
Phone: (972)875-8451 **Fax:** (972)875-2253
Products: Window glass; Windows. **SIC:** 5039 (Construction Materials Nec). **Est:** 1977. **Sales:** $5,000,000 (2000). **Emp:** 70. **Officers:** C. T. Abram, President.

■ **6904** ■ **Able Equipment Inc.**
5745 Angola Rd.
Toledo, OH 43615
Phone: (419)865-5539
Products: Construction equipment. **SIC:** 5082 (Construction & Mining Machinery). **Est:** 1972. **Sales:** $3,000,000 (2000). **Emp:** 23. **Officers:** N.J. Busch, President; C.F. Haas, Vice President.

■ **6905** ■ **ACI Distribution**
9010 S Norwalk Blvd.
Santa Fe Springs, CA 90670
Phone: (562)692-0395
Products: Glass construction materials. **SIC:** 5039 (Construction Materials Nec). **Sales:** $83,000,000 (2000). **Emp:** 250. **Officers:** Ted Zahairs, General Mgr.; Marvin Herriott, Controller.

■ **6906** ■ **Acmat Corp.**
PO Box 2350
New Britain, CT 06050-2350
Phone: (860)229-9000
Products: Construction materials. **SIC:** 5039 (Construction Materials Nec). **Est:** 1951. **Sales:** $37,000,000 (2000). **Emp:** 30. **Officers:** Henry W. Nozko Sr., CEO, President & Chairman of the Board; Henry W. Nozko Jr., Exec. VP & Treasurer.

■ **6907** ■ **Acme Brick Co.**
2510 Adie Rd.
Maryland Heights, MO 63043
Phone: (314)739-1810 **Fax:** (314)739-2465
URL: http://www.acmebrick.com
Products: Brick and tile supplies. **SIC:** 5032 (Brick, Stone & Related Materials). **Est:** 1891. **Emp:** 5. **Officers:** Charlie Miller.

■ **6908** ■ **Acme Brick, Tile and More**
Rte. 7, Box 337
Joplin, MO 64801
Phone: (417)781-1931 **Fax:** (417)781-0235
Products: Bricks, tile, and tile laying equipment; Address mounts. **SIC:** 5032 (Brick, Stone & Related Materials).

■ **6909** ■ **Acme Coal Co.**
Harvard Blvd.
Youngstown, OH 44514
Phone: (330)758-2313 **Free:** (800)441-2522
Products: Gypsum building materials; Road construction and mainenance machinery. **SICs:** 5039 (Construction Materials Nec); 5082 (Construction & Mining Machinery).

■ **6910** ■ **Acoustical Solutions, Inc.**
3603 Mayland Ct.
Richmond, VA 23233
Phone: (804)346-8350
Free: (800)782-5742 **Fax:** (804)346-8808
E-mail: info@acousticalsolutions.com
URL: http://www.acousticalsolutions.com
Products: Sound and noise control products. **SIC:** 5039 (Construction Materials Nec). **Officers:** Michael Binns, President; Don Strahle, Sales & Marketing Contact, e-mail: sales@acousticalsolutions.com.

■ **6911** ■ **Action Equipment Company Inc.**
PO Box 736
Candia, NH 03034
Phone: (603)483-2900
Free: (800)729-6780 **Fax:** (603)483-0299
Products: Compressors; Construction machinery and supplies; Builders' hardware; Industrial machinery and supplies; Generators; Hardware; Power handtools; Welding machinery and equipment; Concrete products. **SICs:** 5032 (Brick, Stone & Related Materials); 5072 (Hardware); 5039 (Construction Materials Nec); 5084 (Industrial Machinery & Equipment); 5082 (Construction & Mining Machinery). **Est:** 1980. **Sales:** $6,000,000 (2000). **Emp:** 50. **Officers:** Francis P. Rich Jr., President; Cliff Cormier, General Mgr.

■ **6912** ■ **Acutron Co.**
501 Sumner St., No. 601
Honolulu, HI 96817
Phone: (808)521-1151
Free: (800)227-6012 **Fax:** (808)521-9493
Products: Commercial and industrial insulation. **SIC:** 5033 (Roofing, Siding & Insulation).

■ **6913** ■ **Adam Wholesalers Inc.**
3005 Kemper E Rd.
Cincinnati, OH 45241
Phone: (513)772-9092 **Fax:** (513)772-0425
Products: Doors and windows. **SIC:** 5031 (Lumber, Plywood & Millwork). **Est:** 1940. **Sales:** $8,000,000 (2000). **Emp:** 30. **Officers:** George Thurner, President; Mike Hanrahan, CFO.

■ 6914 ■ Adams Wholesale Co. Inc.
PO Box 8
Greeneville, TN 37744
Phone: (423)638-4101
Products: Building supplies, including roofing and lumber. **SICs:** 5031 (Lumber, Plywood & Millwork); 5039 (Construction Materials Nec); 5033 (Roofing, Siding & Insulation). **Est:** 1956. **Sales:** $3,000,000 (2000). **Emp:** 12. **Officers:** W.C. Adams Jr., President.

■ 6915 ■ Addison Corp.
2575 Westside Pkwy., No. 800
Alpharetta, GA 30004
Phone: (404)551-8900   **Fax:** (404)551-8831
Products: Windows; Wood doors, interior and exterior. **SICs:** 5031 (Lumber, Plywood & Millwork); 5039 (Construction Materials Nec). **Est:** 1913. **Sales:** $87,000,000 (2000). **Emp:** 600. **Officers:** Benjamin Stevens, President; Emil Castanet, VP & CFO.

■ 6916 ■ Advance Scaffold of Alaska
2607 Barrow St.
Anchorage, AK 99503
Phone: (907)277-1803   **Fax:** (907)277-1803
Products: Scaffolding. **SIC:** 5082 (Construction & Mining Machinery).

■ 6917 ■ Advanced Ceramics Research Inc.
3292 E Hemisphere Loop
Tucson, AZ 85706
Phone: (520)573-6300   **Fax:** (520)573-2057
Products: High-temperature ceramic materials. **SIC:** 5032 (Brick, Stone & Related Materials). **Sales:** $5,200,000 (2000). **Emp:** 70.

■ 6918 ■ Advanced Equipment Inc.
PO Box 336720
North Las Vegas, NV 89033-0029
Phone: (702)644-4445
Products: Heavy equipment, including tractors and fork lifts. **SIC:** 5082 (Construction & Mining Machinery). **Est:** 1971. **Sales:** $1,000,000 (2000). **Emp:** 5. **Officers:** G. Fischer, President; Steve Fischer, Vice President.

■ 6919 ■ AFGD
3200 Austell Rd.
Marietta, GA 30060
Phone: (404)434-2041   **Fax:** (404)436-2654
Products: Glass. **SIC:** 5039 (Construction Materials Nec). **Officers:** Billy Blair.

■ 6920 ■ AFGD
3740 Pampas Dr.
Jacksonville, FL 32207
Phone: (904)398-8471   **Fax:** (904)398-5030
Products: Glass. **SIC:** 5039 (Construction Materials Nec). **Officers:** Darrell Everson.

■ 6921 ■ AFGD
575 Currant Rd.
Fall River, MA 02720
Phone: (508)675-9220   **Fax:** (508)677-3212
Products: Insulated glass. **SIC:** 5039 (Construction Materials Nec). **Officers:** Joe Lovett.

■ 6922 ■ AFGD
803 Prestige Pkwy.
Scotia, NY 12302
Phone: (518)374-3812   **Fax:** (518)372-2133
Products: Glass and glass products. **SIC:** 5039 (Construction Materials Nec). **Officers:** Greg Way.

■ 6923 ■ AFGD
6200 Gorman Rd.
Richmond, VA 23231
Phones: (804)222-0120   (804)226-1859
Fax: (804)226-1859
Products: Glass. **SIC:** 5039 (Construction Materials Nec). **Officers:** Al Abbott.

■ 6924 ■ AFGD
1419 Julia St.
Baton Rouge, LA 70802
Phone: (504)344-9401   **Fax:** (504)343-2318
Products: Glass and insulated glass. **SIC:** 5039 (Construction Materials Nec). **Officers:** Bill Currey.

■ 6925 ■ Agorra Building Supply Inc.
5965 Dougherty Rd.
Dublin, CA 94568
Phone: (925)829-2200
Products: Construction supplies. **SIC:** 5082 (Construction & Mining Machinery).

■ 6926 ■ Airtex Corp.
2900 N Western Ave.
Chicago, IL 60618
Phone: (312)463-2500   **Fax:** (312)463-0549
Products: Acoustical ceilings; Computer flooring. **SIC:** 5039 (Construction Materials Nec). **Est:** 1955. **Sales:** $20,000,000 (2000). **Emp:** 300. **Officers:** George Irving, President & Treasurer.

■ 6927 ■ AIS Construction Equipment Corp.
600 44th SW
Grand Rapids, MI 49548
Phone: (616)538-2400   **Fax:** (616)538-4554
URL: http://www.aisequip.com
Products: Construction equipment and parts; Toys, including tractors and trucks. **SICs:** 5039 (Construction Materials Nec); 5092 (Toys & Hobby Goods & Supplies). **Est:** 1961. **Sales:** $98,000,000 (2000). **Emp:** 450. **Officers:** Jim Behrenwald, President; Bob Allison, VP of Sales; Will Leistikow, VP of Marketing.

■ 6928 ■ Alaska Insulation Supply, Inc.
261 E 56th Ave., Bldg. B
Anchorage, AK 99518
Phone: (907)563-4125   **Fax:** (907)561-4698
E-mail: ais_ak@chugach.net
URL: www.alaskainsulation.com
Products: Insulation materials, including mechanical and industrial insulation. **SIC:** 5033 (Roofing, Siding & Insulation). **Est:** 1983. **Sales:** $3,000,000 (2000). **Emp:** 20. **Officers:** C.K. (Kelly) Key, President, e-mail: kelly@alaskainsulation.com.

■ 6929 ■ Albany Ladder Company Inc.
1586 Central Ave.
Albany, NY 12205
Phone: (518)869-5335   **Fax:** (518)869-0588
Products: Light construction equipment, ladders, personnel lifts and scaffolding. **SIC:** 5082 (Construction & Mining Machinery). **Emp:** 200. **Officers:** Anthony Groat, President; R. Zielinski, Controller.

■ 6930 ■ Alco Building Products Co.
4835 Para Dr.
Cincinnati, OH 45237-5008
Phone: (513)242-1100   **Fax:** (513)242-9336
Products: Doors; Bathroom supplies. **SICs:** 5031 (Lumber, Plywood & Millwork); 5023 (Homefurnishings). **Emp:** 40. **Officers:** Thomas Gaible.

■ 6931 ■ Alcoa Authorized Distributing
34 S Main St.
Butte, MT 59701
Phone: (406)782-6536
Products: Siding. **SIC:** 5033 (Roofing, Siding & Insulation).

■ 6932 ■ W.C. Alexander Wholesale Inc.
PO Box 727
2000 Forest St.
Mt. Vernon, IL 62864
Phone: (618)242-6515
Free: (800)642-3350   **Fax:** (618)242-6429
Products: Building materials, including insulation, roofing and siding. **SICs:** 5039 (Construction Materials Nec); 5033 (Roofing, Siding & Insulation). **Est:** 1949. **Sales:** $6,000,000 (2000). **Emp:** 13. **Officers:** R.C. Alexander, President; Mary Alexander, Treasurer.

■ 6933 ■ All Coast Forest Products Inc.
PO Box M
Chino, CA 91708
Phone: (909)627-8551
Products: Lumber and wood products. **SIC:** 5031 (Lumber, Plywood & Millwork). **Sales:** $16,000,000 (2000). **Emp:** 50. **Officers:** Daryl L. Bond, President; Jerry E. McDonald, CFO; Phil Dudson, Dir. of Marketing.

■ 6934 ■ All Coast Lumber Products Inc.
PO Box 9
Cloverdale, CA 95425
Phone: (707)894-4281
Products: Lumber. **SIC:** 5031 (Lumber, Plywood & Millwork). **Sales:** $16,000,000 (1990). **Emp:** 50. **Officers:** Daryl L. Bond, President; Jerry E. McDonald, CFO.

■ 6935 ■ All-Right
1500 Shelton Dr.
Hollister, CA 95023
Phone: (831)636-9566
Free: (800)642-9988   **Fax:** (831)636-9464
E-mail: sales@all-rite.com
URL: http://www.all-rite.com
Products: Siding; Metal roofing and roof drainage equipment; Prepared asphalt and tar roofing and siding products; Windows; Molding; Compartment doors; Entry doors. **SICs:** 5033 (Roofing, Siding & Insulation); 5031 (Lumber, Plywood & Millwork). **Est:** 1973. **Sales:** $4,000,000 (2000). **Emp:** 35. **Officers:** Ray Pelland, CFO; Ken Towsley, President; Kurt Pelland, Purchasing Dir. **Alternate Name:** Associated R.V. Ent., Inc.

■ 6936 ■ Allen and Allen Company Inc.
PO Box 5140
San Antonio, TX 78284
Phone: (210)733-9191
Free: (800)950-8579   **Fax:** (210)733-5043
URL: http://www.lumberhardware.com
Products: Lumber; Hardware, including sinks, faucets, tubs; Commercial hardware; Hollow metal doors and frames. **SICs:** 5031 (Lumber, Plywood & Millwork); 5072 (Hardware). **Est:** 1931. **Sales:** $20,000,000 (2000). **Emp:** 105. **Officers:** Buzz Miller, President, e-mail: buzzm@lumberhardware.com; Carlos Pena, Vice President; Kevin Canty, CFO.

■ 6937 ■ Allen Company Inc.
PO Box 537
Winchester, KY 40392-0537
Phone: (606)744-3361   **Fax:** (606)744-3961
Products: Construction goods, including limestone and asphalt. **SICs:** 5032 (Brick, Stone & Related Materials); 5039 (Construction Materials Nec). **Est:** 1939. **Sales:** $20,000,000 (2000). **Emp:** 155. **Officers:** J.B. Allen, CEO; James W. Lynch, Treasurer & Secty.; Richard Monokor, Vice President.

■ 6938 ■ Allen Millwork Inc.
PO Box 6480
Shreveport, LA 71136
Phone: (318)868-6541   **Fax:** (318)865-6102
Products: Lumber and construction materials. **SICs:** 5031 (Lumber, Plywood & Millwork); 5039 (Construction Materials Nec). **Sales:** $13,000,000 (1993). **Emp:** 65. **Officers:** Buzz Wheless Jr., President; Robert Shaw, Treasurer.

■ 6939 ■ Allied Building Products
622 E Grand River Ave.
Lansing, MI 48906-5338
Phone: (517)485-7121
Free: (800)968-0131   **Fax:** (517)485-4646
Products: Roofing supplies, including shingles, tar, and nails. **SIC:** 5033 (Roofing, Siding & Insulation). **Est:** 1945. **Sales:** $6,000,000 (2000). **Emp:** 20. **Former Name:** Lansing Wholesale.

■ 6940 ■ Allied Building Products Corp.
5252 Sherman St.
Denver, CO 80216
Phone: (303)296-2222   **Fax:** (303)296-3917
Products: Roofing supplies. **SIC:** 5033 (Roofing, Siding & Insulation). **Est:** 1971. **Sales:** $26,000,000 (2000). **Emp:** 80. **Officers:** Steve Neil, Regional Mgr. **Former Name:** Resco Inc.

■ 6941 ■ Allied Building Products Corp.
8207 Hartzell Rd.
Anchorage, AK 99507-3109
Phone: (907)349-6668   **Fax:** (907)349-6671
Products: Roofing supplies; Siding; Windows; Insulation. **SIC:** 5033 (Roofing, Siding & Insulation). **Est:** 1950.

■ 6942 ■ **Allied Building Products Corp.**
15 E Union Ave.
East Rutherford, NJ 07073
Phone: (201)507-8400
Free: (800)541-2198 **Fax:** (201)507-3855
Products: Construction materials. **SIC:** 5039 (Construction Materials Nec). **Sales:** $461,000,000 (2000). **Emp:** 1,800. **Officers:** Bob Feury, President; Jack Bickel, CFO.

■ 6943 ■ **Allied Construction Equipment Co.**
4015 Forest Park Ave.
St. Louis, MO 63108
Phone: (314)371-1818
Products: Road and commercial construction equipment. **SIC:** 5082 (Construction & Mining Machinery). **Est:** 1932. **Sales:** $6,000,000 (2000). **Emp:** 25. **Officers:** Tom Hill, President; Stan Novak, Treasurer.

■ 6944 ■ **Allied Distribution Systems**
11852 Alameda St.
Lynwood, CA 90262-4019
Products: Plywood and hardwood; Hardware. **SICs:** 5031 (Lumber, Plywood & Millwork); 5072 (Hardware). **Sales:** $96,000,000 (2000). **Emp:** 207. **Officers:** David A. Williams, President.

■ 6945 ■ **Allied Plywood Corp.**
6189 Grovedale Ct.
Alexandria, VA 22310
Phone: (703)922-2805 **Fax:** (703)922-3450
URL: http://www.alliedplywood.com
Products: Plywood; Lumber; Cabinets. **SIC:** 5031 (Lumber, Plywood & Millwork). **Est:** 1951. **Sales:** $67,000,000 (1999). **Emp:** 200. **Officers:** R.A. Shaw, President; K.C. Harris, CFO; G.C. Scales, Sec. & Treas.; Eric Baker, Customer Service Contact; Tom Simon, Human Resources Contact. **Alternate Name:** Alliance Products Company. **Alternate Name:** A2M Supply. **Alternate Name:** Allied Kitchen & Custom Cabinet.

■ 6946 ■ **Allied Plywood Corp.**
11852 Alameda St.
Lynwood, CA 90262-4019
Phone: (978)371-3399 **Fax:** (978)371-1644
Products: Lumber and plywood. **SIC:** 5031 (Lumber, Plywood & Millwork). **Sales:** $115,000,000 (2000). **Emp:** 230. **Officers:** Jerry Lavine, CEO & President; Richard A. Abbott, Comptroller.

■ 6947 ■ **Almond Brothers Lumber and Supply Inc.**
403 Ringgold
Coushatta, LA 71019
Phone: (318)932-4041
Products: Pine lumber, bark, and shavings. **SIC:** 5031 (Lumber, Plywood & Millwork). **Est:** 1946. **Sales:** $29,000,000 (2000). **Emp:** 105. **Officers:** Ardis V. Almond, President; William Almond, VP of Operations; Tiemmell Almond, Dir. of Sales.

■ 6948 ■ **Alpine Corp.**
250 W 57th St.
New York, NY 10019
Phone: (212)697-5167
Products: Aluminum doors and windows. **SIC:** 5031 (Lumber, Plywood & Millwork).

■ 6949 ■ **Aluma Systems USA Inc.**
6435 E 30th St.
Indianapolis, IN 46219
Phone: (317)543-4625 **Fax:** (317)549-0272
Products: Concrete equipment and supplies. **SICs:** 5032 (Brick, Stone & Related Materials); 5039 (Construction Materials Nec); 5084 (Industrial Machinery & Equipment). **Est:** 1926. **Sales:** $670,000,000 (2000). **Emp:** 3,000. **Officers:** Barry Thompson, President; Tom Bond, Vice President; Grant Drummond, Dir. of Marketing; Terry O'Toole, Dir. of Information Systems.

■ 6950 ■ **Aluminum Distributors Inc.**
706 E 2nd St.
Des Moines, IA 50309
Phone: (515)283-2383 **Fax:** (515)283-1325
Products: House siding, including steel, vinyl, and aluminum siding. **SICs:** 5033 (Roofing, Siding & Insulation); 5031 (Lumber, Plywood & Millwork). **Est:** 1959. **Sales:** $6,000,000 (2000). **Emp:** 15. **Officers:** George N. Van Patten, President; Jeff Graeve, Controller; Nick Van Patten, General Mgr.

■ 6951 ■ **Aluminum Products Co.**
3307 S Washington
Marion, IN 46953
Phone: (765)674-7759
Products: Building materials. **SICs:** 5039 (Construction Materials Nec); 5031 (Lumber, Plywood & Millwork); 5033 (Roofing, Siding & Insulation).

■ 6952 ■ **Alvin Equipment Company Inc.**
PO Box 1907
Alvin, TX 77512
Phone: (281)331-3177 **Fax:** (281)585-4012
Products: Trucks; Excavators. **SIC:** 5082 (Construction & Mining Machinery). **Est:** 1952. **Sales:** $7,000,000 (2000). **Emp:** 30. **Officers:** David C. Beaver, President.

■ 6953 ■ **Amarillo Building Products Inc.**
PO Box 9026
Amarillo, TX 79105
Phone: (806)373-4205 **Fax:** (806)373-4209
Products: Cement goods; Steel; Tools. **SICs:** 5032 (Brick, Stone & Related Materials); 5051 (Metals Service Centers & Offices); 5072 (Hardware). **Est:** 1981. **Sales:** $1,000,000 (2000). **Emp:** 5. **Officers:** Donald Rettenmaier, President.

■ 6954 ■ **AMC Tile Supply**
3905 Forest Park Blvd.
St. Louis, MO 63108
Phone: (314)371-2200
Free: (800)392-2181 **Fax:** (314)371-2214
URL: http://www.amctile.com
Products: Ceramic tile. **SIC:** 5032 (Brick, Stone & Related Materials). **Est:** 1947. **Emp:** 28. **Officers:** Stephen M. Arnold; Harold J. Sanger.

■ 6955 ■ **Amco Equipment and Steel Inc.**
PO Box 125
Midvale, UT 84047
Phone: (801)255-4257 **Fax:** (801)255-4277
Products: Mining and construction equipment, including drills, bits, and compressors. **SIC:** 5082 (Construction & Mining Machinery). **Sales:** $1,500,000 (2000). **Emp:** 8. **Officers:** James J. Keeney, President; LaVelle C. Tripp, Treasurer & Secty.; Ron Ross, Dir. of Marketing.

■ 6956 ■ **Amerhart Ltd.**
PO Box 10097
Green Bay, WI 54307-0097
Phone: (920)494-4744 **Fax:** (920)494-9410
Products: Lumber. **SIC:** 5031 (Lumber, Plywood & Millwork). **Sales:** $70,000,000 (1992). **Emp:** 150. **Officers:** Richard A. Kasper, CEO & President.

■ 6957 ■ **Ameri-Tech Equipment Co.**
PO Box 3075
Casper, WY 82602
Phone: (307)234-9921 **Fax:** (307)234-3432
Products: Truck equipment; Construction and mining machinery and equipment. **SIC:** 5082 (Construction & Mining Machinery). **Officers:** Larry Spence, President.

■ 6958 ■ **American Associated Roofing Distributor**
PO Box 4056
Atlanta, GA 30302
Phone: (404)522-7060
Free: (800)377-7060 **Fax:** (404)581-0116
Products: Roofing materials, including maps, tools, accessories, and safety equipment. **SICs:** 5033 (Roofing, Siding & Insulation); 5039 (Construction Materials Nec). **Est:** 1900. **Sales:** $7,000,000 (2000). **Emp:** 50. **Officers:** Roland T. Vann, President; Randy Parker, Sales Mgr.

■ 6959 ■ **American Builders and Contractors Supply Company Inc.**
One ABC Pkwy.
Beloit, WI 53511
Phone: (608)362-7777 **Fax:** (608)362-6529
Products: Building supplies. **SIC:** 5033 (Roofing, Siding & Insulation). **Est:** 1982. **Sales:** $1,416,000,000 (2000). **Emp:** 3,400. **Officers:** Kenneth Hendricks, President; Kender Story, Controller; Stan Wegrzyn, Dir. of Marketing & Sales; Kathy Murray, Dir. of Information Systems; Diane Hendricks, Vice President.

■ 6960 ■ **American Building Supply, Inc.**
4190 E Santa Ana
Ontario, CA 91761
Phone: (909)390-1700 **Fax:** (909)390-8773
Products: Doors; Windows. **SIC:** 5031 (Lumber, Plywood & Millwork). **Est:** 1985.

■ 6961 ■ **American Building Supply, Inc.**
8920 43rd Ave.
Sacramento, CA 95828
Phone: (916)387-4100 **Fax:** (916)387-4111
Products: Doors and windows. **SIC:** 5031 (Lumber, Plywood & Millwork). **Est:** 1987. **Sales:** $100,000,000 (2000).

■ 6962 ■ **American Distributing Co.**
PO Box 829
Modesto, CA 95353
Phone: (209)524-7425
Products: Building materials. **SICs:** 5031 (Lumber, Plywood & Millwork); 5039 (Construction Materials Nec). **Est:** 1953. **Sales:** $5,000,000 (2000). **Emp:** 17. **Officers:** Richard Morrison, President; John B. Mensinger, CFO; Tom Coffman, VP of Marketing; Gene Samuelson, Dir. of Systems.

■ 6963 ■ **American Equipment Company Inc.**
7001 Hawthorne Park Dr.
Indianapolis, IN 46220
Phone: (317)849-5400 **Fax:** (317)849-1195
Products: Floorcovering equipment and supplies. **SIC:** 5032 (Brick, Stone & Related Materials). **Sales:** $5,000,000 (2000). **Emp:** 20.

■ 6964 ■ **American Equipment Company Inc. (Greenville, South Carolina)**
2106 Anderson Dr.
Greenville, SC 29602
Phone: (864)295-7800 **Fax:** (864)295-7962
Products: New and used construction equipment. **SIC:** 5082 (Construction & Mining Machinery). **Sales:** $293,000,000 (2000). **Emp:** 2,500. **Officers:** Charles Snyder, President.

■ 6965 ■ **American Gulf Co.**
PO Box 721494
Houston, TX 77272
Phone: (281)561-6273 **Fax:** (281)495-9645
E-mail: amegu@aol.com
Products: Mining equipment; Laboratory equipment and supplies. **SICs:** 5082 (Construction & Mining Machinery); 5049 (Professional Equipment Nec). **Est:** 1984. **Sales:** $1,000,000 (2000). **Emp:** 5. **Officers:** Manuel Araya, President.

■ 6966 ■ **American Hardwood Co.**
15411 S Figueroa St.
Gardena, CA 90248-2122
Phone: (310)527-9066 **Fax:** (310)527-9074
Products: Lumber, including wood parts, custom mill parts, and wood window components. **SIC:** 5031 (Lumber, Plywood & Millwork). **Est:** 1914. **Sales:** $16,000,000 (2000). **Emp:** 135. **Officers:** W. Alexander Gray III, CEO; Brian Bibb, Controller; Phillip Sarris, Sales Mgr.

■ 6967 ■ **American Hydrotech Inc.**
541 N Fairbanks St.
Chicago, IL 60611
Phone: (312)337-4998
Products: Roofing and water proofing products. **SIC:** 5033 (Roofing, Siding & Insulation). **Sales:** $3,000,000 (2000). **Emp:** 11. **Officers:** David Spalding, President.

■ 6968 ■ **American International Forest Products Inc.**
5560 SW 107th Ave.
Beaverton, OR 97005
Phone: (503)641-1611 **Fax:** (503)641-2800
URL: http://www.lumber.com
Products: Lumber, plywood and millwork. **SIC:** 5031 (Lumber, Plywood & Millwork). **Est:** 1964. **Sales:** $150,000,000 (2000). **Emp:** 100. **Officers:** Craig Johnston, President; Georgia Hale, Controller.

■ 6969 ■ American Limestone Company Inc.
PO Box 2389
Knoxville, TN 37901
Phone: (423)573-4501
Products: Ready-mixed concrete, crushed, and agricultural limestone. **SIC:** 5032 (Brick, Stone & Related Materials). **Sales:** $45,000,000 (2000). **Emp:** 275. **Officers:** W. Hoyl Gill, President; Merle Westbrook, CFO.

■ 6970 ■ American Pecco Corp.
PO Box 670
Millwood, NY 10546
Phone: (914)762-0550　**Fax:** (914)262-0759
Products: Tower cranes; Construction elevators. **SIC:** 5082 (Construction & Mining Machinery). **Est:** 1957. **Sales:** $45,000,000 (2000). **Emp:** 150. **Officers:** Ronald A. Yakin, President.

■ 6971 ■ Ampco Products Inc.
11400 NW 36 Avenue
Miami, FL 33167-2907
Phone: (305)821-5700　**Fax:** (305)507-1414
E-mail: info@ampco.com
URL: http://www.ampco.com
Products: Restroom compartments; Door frame systems; Cabinetry. **SICs:** 5031 (Lumber, Plywood & Millwork); 5023 (Homefurnishings). **Est:** 1961. **Sales:** $14,000,000 (2000). **Emp:** 150. **Officers:** Stanley L. Krieger, President; Elyse Hurtado, Sales/Marketing Contact, e-mail: ehurtado@ampco.com.

■ 6972 ■ AMRE Inc.
3710 Rawlins St., Ste. 1220
Dallas, TX 75219-4276
Phone: (972)929-4088
Products: Kitchen cabinets and countertops. **SIC:** 5031 (Lumber, Plywood & Millwork). **Sales:** $271,300,000 (2000). **Emp:** 3,095. **Officers:** Robert M. Swartz, CEO & President; Larry H. Lattig, VP & Treasurer.

■ 6973 ■ Anchor Commerce Trading Corp.
PO Box 813
Hicksville, NY 11802
Phone: (516)822-1914　**Fax:** (516)931-4956
Products: Construction machinery and parts; Electronic components; Industrial inorganic chemicals; Air conditioning and refrigeration equipment. **SICs:** 5082 (Construction & Mining Machinery); 5065 (Electronic Parts & Equipment Nec); 5169 (Chemicals & Allied Products Nec); 5075 (Warm Air Heating & Air-Conditioning). **Officers:** Frank Williams, Vice President.

■ 6974 ■ Anderson Equipment Co.
PO Box 339
Bridgeville, PA 15017
Phone: (412)343-2300　**Fax:** (412)221-2087
Products: Heavy construction equipment. **SIC:** 5082 (Construction & Mining Machinery). **Est:** 1934. **Sales:** $70,000,000 (2000). **Emp:** 150. **Officers:** R.L. Anderson, President.

■ 6975 ■ Anderson & Jarvi Lumber
U.S 41
Chassell, MI 49916
Phone: (906)523-4265　**Fax:** (906)523-4783
Products: Lumber. **SIC:** 5031 (Lumber, Plywood & Millwork).

■ 6976 ■ Anderson Lumber Co.
PO Box 9459
Ogden, UT 84409
Phone: (801)479-3400　**Fax:** (801)476-1953
Products: Lumber, including pine and plywood; Paint; Insulation and shingles. **SICs:** 5031 (Lumber, Plywood & Millwork); 5033 (Roofing, Siding & Insulation); 5039 (Construction Materials Nec). **Est:** 1890. **Sales:** $285,000,000 (2000). **Emp:** 1,600. **Officers:** James C. Beardall, CEO & President; Dave Empey, VP of Finance; Robert Williams, Information Systems Mgr.; Lawrence Wright, Human Resources Mgr.

■ 6977 ■ Anderson Machinery Company Inc.
PO Box 4806
Corpus Christi, TX 78469
Phone: (512)289-6043　**Fax:** (512)289-6047
Products: Construction equipment, including cranes, back hoes, and excavators. **SIC:** 5082 (Construction & Mining Machinery). **Est:** 1957. **Sales:** $12,000,000 (2000). **Emp:** 90. **Officers:** Jim Anderson, CEO & President.

■ 6978 ■ Anderson Machinery San Antonio Inc.
PO Box 200380
San Antonio, TX 78220-0380
Phone: (210)661-2366　**Fax:** (210)661-4971
E-mail: amsaincmkt@aol.com
URL: http://www.andersonmachinerytexascom
Products: Construction machinery, including back hoes, cranes, wheel loaders, pavers, and compactors. **SIC:** 5082 (Construction & Mining Machinery). **Est:** 1957. **Sales:** $5,000,000 (2000). **Emp:** 25. **Officers:** Kirk Anderson, CEO; Tom Anderson, VP of Marketing.

■ 6979 ■ Anthony Forest Products Co.
PO Box 1877
El Dorado, AR 71730
Phone: (870)862-3414
Free: (800)856-2372　**Fax:** (870)862-4296
E-mail: info@anthonyforest.com
URL: http://www.anthonyforest.com
Products: Lumber; Engineered wood products and chips. **SIC:** 5031 (Lumber, Plywood & Millwork). **Est:** 1940. **Sales:** $100,000,000 (2000). **Emp:** 400. **Officers:** John L. Anthony, President & CEO.

■ 6980 ■ A.P.I. Inc.
2366 Rose Pl.
St. Paul, MN 55113
Phone: (612)636-4320　**Fax:** (612)636-0312
Products: Insulation. **SICs:** 5039 (Construction Materials Nec); 5039 (Construction Materials Nec). **Est:** 1932. **Sales:** $190,000,000 (2000). **Emp:** 500. **Officers:** Lee R. Anderson, CEO & Chairman of the Board; Loren Rachey, Treasurer; Robert Koth, President & COO.

■ 6981 ■ Applicator Sales & Service
PO Box 10109
Portland, ME 04104-0109
Phone: (207)797-7950　**Fax:** (207)797-8868
Products: Siding; Construction materials. **SIC:** 5033 (Roofing, Siding & Insulation). **Est:** 1958. **Officers:** Scott Koocher, President.

■ 6982 ■ Arch-I-Tech Doors Inc.
799 Allgood Rd.
Marietta, GA 30062
Phone: (404)426-0773　**Fax:** (404)426-9524
Products: Doors; Windows; Frames. **SIC:** 5031 (Lumber, Plywood & Millwork). **Est:** 1983. **Sales:** $5,000,000 (2000). **Emp:** 16. **Officers:** Greg Wood, President.

■ 6983 ■ Architectural Words Inc.
1201 Puyallup Ave.
Tacoma, WA 98421
Phone: (253)383-5484　**Fax:** (253)627-7546
E-mail: awi-wa@email.msn.com
URL: http://www.awi-wa.com
Products: Lumber and plywood; Moulding. **SIC:** 5031 (Lumber, Plywood & Millwork). **Est:** 1956. **Sales:** $25,000,000 (2000). **Emp:** 55. **Officers:** Michael Hathaway, CEO.

■ 6984 ■ Aring Equipment Company Inc.
13001 W Silver Spring Dr.
Butler, WI 53007
Phone: (414)781-3770
Products: Construction equipment. **SIC:** 5082 (Construction & Mining Machinery). **Est:** 1940. **Sales:** $20,000,000 (2000). **Emp:** 100. **Officers:** James Hock, President; Jeff Lemanczyk, Controller; George Mumau, Sales Mgr.

■ 6985 ■ Arling Lumber Inc.
PO Box 58359
Cincinnati, OH 45258-0359
Phone: (513)451-5700
Free: (800)543-7486　**Fax:** (513)451-5051
E-mail: sales@arlinglumber.com
URL: http://www.arlinglumber.com
Products: Lumber and plywood. **SIC:** 5031 (Lumber, Plywood & Millwork). **Est:** 1961. **Sales:** $70,000,000 (1999). **Emp:** 45. **Officers:** Rita L. Arling, VP & Secty.,

e-mail: rita@arlinglumber.com; P.J. Arling, President, e-mail: pj@arlinglumber.com.

■ 6986 ■ Armstrong and Dobbs Inc.
PO Box 8027
Athens, GA 30603-8027
Phone: (706)543-8271　**Fax:** (706)548-9367
Products: Lumber; Building materials. **SICs:** 5039 (Construction Materials Nec); 5031 (Lumber, Plywood & Millwork). **Est:** 1912. **Sales:** $6,000,000 (2000). **Emp:** 40. **Officers:** F.M. Williams, President.

■ 6987 ■ Arnold Lumber Company Inc.
Rte. 1
Bonifay, FL 32425
Phone: (850)547-5733　**Fax:** (850)547-5641
Products: Lumber. **SIC:** 5031 (Lumber, Plywood & Millwork). **Est:** 1962. **Sales:** $7,000,000 (2000). **Emp:** 14. **Officers:** Joe Jernigan, President; Carlton Treadwell, Secretary; Robert Payne, Dir. of Sales.

■ 6988 ■ Arnold Machinery Co.
PO Box 21005
Phoenix, AZ 85036
Phone: (602)237-3755　**Fax:** (602)237-4659
Products: Forklifts and mining equipment. **SIC:** 5082 (Construction & Mining Machinery). **Est:** 1929. **Sales:** $14,200,000 (2000). **Emp:** 71. **Officers:** Terry Cunningham, President.

■ 6989 ■ Arnold Machinery Co.
PO Box 30020
Salt Lake City, UT 84130
Phone: (801)972-4000　**Fax:** (801)237-4659
Products: Front end loaders; Excavators; Back hoes. **SIC:** 5082 (Construction & Mining Machinery). **Est:** 1929. **Sales:** $110,000,000 (2000). **Emp:** 330. **Officers:** Alvin Richer, President; Kayden W. Bell, Treasurer.

■ 6990 ■ Arnold Machinery Co.
6024 W Southern Ave.
Laveen, AZ 85339-9652
Phone: (602)237-3755　**Fax:** (602)237-4659
Products: Construction equipment. **SIC:** 5082 (Construction & Mining Machinery). **Sales:** $14,200,000 (2000). **Emp:** 71. **Officers:** Mike J. Coogan, General Mgr.

■ 6991 ■ Arnold Machinery Co.
PO Box 30020
Salt Lake City, UT 84130
Phone: (801)972-4000　**Fax:** (801)237-4659
Products: Construction materials and machinery. **SIC:** 5082 (Construction & Mining Machinery). **Sales:** $110,000,000 (2000). **Emp:** 330.

■ 6992 ■ Arrow-Master Inc.
1201 7th St.
East Moline, IL 61244-1465
Free: (800)325-4151　**Fax:** (309)752-1380
E-mail: amsales@emmetal.com
URL: http://www.arrowmaster.com
Products: Construction equipment, including concrete finishing equipment; Hydraulics, including mobile hydraulic-drop weight hammers; Industrial equipment, including riders, walk behinds, and vibrators. **SICs:** 5039 (Construction Materials Nec); 5082 (Construction & Mining Machinery). **Est:** 1986. **Sales:** $5,000,000 (1999). **Emp:** 30. **Officers:** J.M. Dowsett, President; C. Dowsett, Controller; Steven Ambrozi, Sales/Marketing Contact; Chad Walker, Customer Service Contact.

■ 6993 ■ Artesanos Imports Company Inc.
1414 Maclovia
PO Box G
Santa Fe, NM 87505
Phone: (505)471-8020
Free: (800)525-9525　**Fax:** (505)471-8108
URL: http://www.artesanos.com
Products: Tile; Light fixtures; Hand-forged iron hardware; Furniture. **SICs:** 5032 (Brick, Stone & Related Materials); 5072 (Hardware); 5021 (Furniture). **Est:** 1969. **Emp:** 14. **Officers:** Fernando Gomez, President, e-mail: service@artesanos.com. **Alternate Name:** Mexican Marketplace.

■ **6994** ■ **Arthur Lumber Trading Co.**
5550 SW Macadam Ave., No. 230
Portland, OR 97201-3771
Phone: (503)228-8160 **Fax:** (503)226-0284
Products: Lumber; Millwork. **SIC:** 5031 (Lumber, Plywood & Millwork). **Est:** 1963. **Sales:** $35,000,000 (2000). **Emp:** 9. **Officers:** Robert Borghorst, President; Tonnie Bailey, Controller; Larry Allison, VP of Marketing.

■ **6995** ■ **Arundel Corp.**
PO Box 5000
Sparks, MD 21152
Phone: (410)329-5000 **Fax:** (410)329-3499
Products: Aggregates, including stone. **SIC:** 5032 (Brick, Stone & Related Materials). **Est:** 1919. **Sales:** $100,000,000 (2000). **Emp:** 600. **Officers:** Daniel Williard, President; Marsh Himes, Controller; Mark Fitzgerald, Dir. of Mktg. & Sales; George Ross, VP of Data Processing; Anne Napoleone, Human Resources Contact.

■ **6996** ■ **ASA Builders Supply Inc.**
2040 Easy St.
Walled Lake, MI 48390
Phone: (248)624-7400 **Fax:** (248)624-1058
E-mail: twinpines@aol.com
Products: Doors; Trim; Cabinets. **SIC:** 5031 (Lumber, Plywood & Millwork). **Est:** 1953. **Sales:** $10,000,000 (2000). **Emp:** 44. **Officers:** Asa Shapiro, Chairman of the Board; Steven Shapiro, President.

■ **6997** ■ **Ashe Industries Inc.**
4505 Transport Dr.
Tampa, FL 33605
Phone: (813)247-2743
Products: Building materials. **SIC:** 5031 (Lumber, Plywood & Millwork).

■ **6998** ■ **Ashley Aluminum Inc.**
11651 Plano Rd.
Dallas, TX 75243
Phone: (214)860-5100
Products: Building materials. **SICs:** 5032 (Brick, Stone & Related Materials); 5033 (Roofing, Siding & Insulation); 5039 (Construction Materials Nec). **Officers:** Walter J. Muratori, President; Allan Potsic, CFO.

■ **6999** ■ **Associated Lumber Industries Inc.**
204 W Main St.
Fairfield, IL 62837
Phone: (618)842-3733 **Fax:** (618)842-7710
Products: Lumber; Millwork; Building materials. **SIC:** 5031 (Lumber, Plywood & Millwork). **Est:** 1940. **Sales:** $11,000,000 (2000). **Emp:** 50. **Officers:** Douglas F. Dickey, President.

■ **7000** ■ **Athens Building Supply**
120 Ben Burton Rd.
Bogart, GA 30622
Phone: (706)546-8318 **Fax:** (706)549-9609
Products: Lumber. **SIC:** 5031 (Lumber, Plywood & Millwork). **Emp:** 20. **Officers:** Andrew Sisk.

■ **7001** ■ **Atlantic Building Products**
PO Box 1287
Lakeville, MA 02347
Phone: (508)947-5000
Products: Building products, including fiberglass, cabinets, dry wall, shutters, and shingles. **SICs:** 5039 (Construction Materials Nec); 5031 (Lumber, Plywood & Millwork); 5033 (Roofing, Siding & Insulation). **Est:** 1932. **Sales:** $21,000,000 (2000). **Emp:** 40. **Officers:** Richard Malouf, CEO.

■ **7002** ■ **Atlantic Coast Fiberglass Co.**
510 Bullocks Point Ave.
Riverside, RI 02915
Phone: (401)433-2990
Products: Fiberglass. **SIC:** 5033 (Roofing, Siding & Insulation).

■ **7003** ■ **Atlantic Construction Fabrics Inc.**
1801-A Willis Rd.
Richmond, VA 23237
Phone: (804)271-2363
Free: (800)448-3636 **Fax:** (804)271-3074
Products: Steel concrete construction forms; Concrete

products. **SICs:** 5039 (Construction Materials Nec); 5032 (Brick, Stone & Related Materials). **Est:** 1984. **Sales:** $20,000,000 (2000). **Emp:** 60. **Officers:** R. J. DiLoreto Jr.

■ **7004** ■ **Atlantic Pre-Hung Doors Inc.**
143 W Concord
PO BOX 1258
West Concord, MA 01742
Phone: (978)369-5600 **Fax:** (978)369-8124
Products: Doors. **SIC:** 5031 (Lumber, Plywood & Millwork). **Est:** 1952. **Sales:** $12,000,000 (1999). **Emp:** 90. **Officers:** D.R. DeCiccio, President & Treasurer.

■ **7005** ■ **Averitt Lumber Company Inc.**
PO Box 2217
Clarksville, TN 37042-2217
Phone: (931)647-8394
Free: (800)647-8394 **Fax:** (931)645-3730
E-mail: sales@averitt.com
URL: http://www.averitt.com
Products: Hardwood lumber. **SIC:** 5031 (Lumber, Plywood & Millwork). **Est:** 1962. **Sales:** $35,000,000 (2000). **Emp:** 260. **Officers:** Dick Rossetti, President & CEO; Kenneth Averitt, Chairman of the Board; Larry Averitt, Exec. VP; Tim Treadway, CFO/VP.

■ **7006** ■ **Azcon Corp.**
13733 S Ave. O
Chicago, IL 60633-1547
Phone: (312)362-0066 **Fax:** (312)362-0094
Products: Scrap and semifinished metal products, transportation equipment. **SICs:** 5093 (Scrap & Waste Materials); 5051 (Metals Service Centers & Offices); 5088 (Transportation Equipment & Supplies). **Sales:** $140,000,000 (2000). **Emp:** 235. **Officers:** Jerrie Burtis, VP & CFO.

■ **7007** ■ **B & L Equipment**
PO Box 2278
Syracuse, NY 13220-2278
Phone: (315)458-9500
Products: Construction equipment. **SIC:** 5082 (Construction & Mining Machinery). **Est:** 1971. **Sales:** $3,000,000 (2000). **Emp:** 15. **Officers:** A.M. Breyton, President.

■ **7008** ■ **Henry Bacon Building Materials Inc.**
PO Box 7012
Issaquah, WA 98027-7012
Phone: (206)391-8000 **Fax:** (206)391-2060
Products: Lumber. **SIC:** 5031 (Lumber, Plywood & Millwork). **Est:** 1937. **Sales:** $44,000,000 (2000). **Emp:** 370. **Officers:** Richard Carroll, President.

■ **7009** ■ **Edward R. Bacon Company Inc.**
PO Box 21550
San Jose, CA 95151
Phone: (408)288-9500 **Fax:** (408)297-4686
Products: Construction materials. **SIC:** 5082 (Construction & Mining Machinery). **Est:** 1910. **Sales:** $5,500,000 (2000). **Emp:** 18. **Officers:** Harry N. How II, President.

■ **7010** ■ **Badger Corrugating Co.**
PO Box 1837
La Crosse, WI 54601
Phone: (608)788-0100 **Fax:** (608)788-1510
Products: Lumber and cabinets. **SICs:** 5031 (Lumber, Plywood & Millwork); 5032 (Brick, Stone & Related Materials); 5031 (Lumber, Plywood & Millwork). **Est:** 1903. **Sales:** $18,000,000 (1999). **Emp:** 90. **Officers:** Michael J. Sexauer, President & CFO; Bruce Nordeen, Dir. of Admin.; Arthur Sexauer, Vice President.

■ **7011** ■ **Bailey Lumber Co.**
5200 Christmas Pl.
Waldorf, MD 20601
Phone: (301)274-4116 **Fax:** (301)274-4124
Products: Rough, green, hard and railroad lumber. **SIC:** 5031 (Lumber, Plywood & Millwork). **Est:** 1959. **Sales:** $6,000,000 (2000). **Emp:** 4. **Officers:** Collins A. Bailey, President.

■ **7012** ■ **Baillie Lumber Co.**
4002 Legion Dr.
Hamburg, NY 14075
Phone: (716)649-2850
Free: (800)950-2850 **Fax:** (716)649-4741
E-mail: info@baillie.com
URL: http://www.baillie.com
Products: Hardwood lumber. **SIC:** 5031 (Lumber, Plywood & Millwork). **Est:** 1923. **Emp:** 350. **Officers:** D.L. Meyer, President; J. Dills, Vice President; J. Meyer, Vice President.

■ **7013** ■ **Baisley Lumber Corp.**
193 Horton Ave.
Lynbrook, NY 11563
Phone: (516)599-8100
Products: Lumber. **SIC:** 5031 (Lumber, Plywood & Millwork). **Est:** 1944. **Sales:** $3,000,000 (1999). **Emp:** 17. **Officers:** Sam Sperling, President; Robert Sperling, VP of Finance/Dir. of Marketing.

■ **7014** ■ **Baker Hardwood Lumber Co.**
3131 Hoover Ave.
National City, CA 91950-7221
Phone: (619)263-8102 **Fax:** (619)477-5690
Products: Lumber and custom milling. **SIC:** 5031 (Lumber, Plywood & Millwork). **Est:** 1921. **Sales:** $15,000,000 (2000). **Emp:** 43. **Officers:** Joe Bolton, President; Russell Hullinger, Vice President.

■ **7015** ■ **Bakersfield Sandstone Brick Co. Inc.**
PO Box 866
Bakersfield, CA 93302
Phone: (805)325-5722
Products: Building materials; Hardware; Roof trusses. **SICs:** 5031 (Lumber, Plywood & Millwork); 5072 (Hardware); 5039 (Construction Materials Nec). **Est:** 1886. **Sales:** $10,000,000 (2000). **Emp:** 140. **Officers:** Walter F. Heisey, President; Bill F. Steele, Treasurer; Gordon K. Foster, Dir. of Marketing & Sales.

■ **7016** ■ **J.C. Baldridge Lumber Co.**
PO Box 13537
Albuquerque, NM 87192
Phone: (505)298-5531
Products: Lumber, including pinewood; Hardware, including paints, faucets, and sinks. **SICs:** 5031 (Lumber, Plywood & Millwork); 5072 (Hardware); 5198 (Paints, Varnishes & Supplies). **Est:** 1881. **Sales:** $25,000,000 (2000). **Emp:** 140. **Officers:** W.C. Harley, CEO; George Harley, Exec. VP; Mahlon Elliott, VP of Marketing.

■ **7017** ■ **Gary Bale Ready-Mix Concrete**
16351 1/2 Construction Cir.
Irvine, CA 92614
Phone: (949)786-9441
Products: Ready-mix concrete. **SIC:** 5032 (Brick, Stone & Related Materials).

■ **7018** ■ **Balzer Pacific Equipment Co.**
2136 SE 8th St.
Portland, OR 97214
Phone: (503)232-5141 **Fax:** (503)232-9556
Products: Rock crushers. **SIC:** 5082 (Construction & Mining Machinery). **Est:** 1928. **Sales:** $16,000,000 (1999). **Emp:** 60. **Officers:** M.B. Allen, President; Jim Whitaker, CFO; Steve Schetky, Dir. of Marketing; Judy Curtis, Dir. of Systems.

■ **7019** ■ **Banks Lumber Company Inc.**
PO Box 2299
Elkhart, IN 46515
Phone: (219)294-5671
Free: (800)348-7405 **Fax:** (219)294-1032
Products: Lumber; Engineered wood; Trusses; Steel fabrication products. **SIC:** 5031 (Lumber, Plywood & Millwork). **Est:** 1927. **Sales:** $200,000,000 (2000). **Emp:** 1,100. **Officers:** William P. Banks, CEO; John K. Banks, COO.

■ **7020** ■ **Barber and Ross Co.**
PO Box 1294
Leesburg, VA 20177-1294
Phone: (703)478-1970 **Fax:** (703)777-5608
Products: Hardware; Windows, doors, and trim. **SICs:** 5031 (Lumber, Plywood & Millwork); 5072 (Hardware). **Est:** 1876. **Sales:** $26,000,000 (2000). **Emp:** 200.

Officers: David Joffe, President; Scott Joffe, Vice President; Thomas Dossenbach, General Mgr.

■ 7021 ■ **Bardon Trimount Inc.**
PO Box 39
Burlington, MA 01803
Phone: (617)221-8400   **Fax:** (617)221-8452
Products: Construction materials and machinery. SIC: 5032 (Brick, Stone & Related Materials). **Sales:** $200,000,000 (2000). **Emp:** 1,400.

■ 7022 ■ **Bark River Culvert and Equipment Co.**
PO Box 10947
Green Bay, WI 54307-0947
Phone: (414)435-6676   **Fax:** (414)435-5454
Products: Construction and highway repair equipment. **SIC:** 5082 (Construction & Mining Machinery). **Est:** 1906. **Sales:** $29,000,000 (2000). **Emp:** 140. **Officers:** Fred H. Lindner Jr., President.

■ 7023 ■ **Barker Steel Co. Inc. Lebanon Div.**
PO Box 436
Lebanon, NH 03766
Phone: (603)448-6030
Free: (800)757-7261   **Fax:** (603)448-5580
Products: Structural steel; Concrete accessories; Concrete sealers; Erosion control products; Flooring underlayment; Grouts and clements; Restoration cleaners; Vapor barrier; Concrete curing chemicals; Concrete specialties; Expansion joint materials; Foundation drainage; Masonry coatings; Rigid insulation; Waterproofing; Concrete forms and ties; Dampproofing materials; Filtration fabrics and mats; Geotextiles and silt fences; Reinforcing steel; Trench drains and grates; Welded wire mesh. **SICs:** 5032 (Brick, Stone & Related Materials); 5039 (Construction Materials Nec). **Est:** 1950. **Sales:** $9,000,000 (2000). **Emp:** 15. **Officers:** Sid Gold, Purchasing Mgr.; Michael Schwarz, Location Mgr., e-mail: mschwarz@barker.com.

■ 7024 ■ **Barnett Millworks Inc.**
PO Box 389
Theodore, AL 36590
Phone: (334)443-7710
Free: (800)443-3015   **Fax:** (334)443-6376
Products: Windows; Doors. **SIC:** 5039 (Construction Materials Nec). **Est:** 1945. **Sales:** $33,000,000 (2000). **Emp:** 240. **Officers:** C.E. Barnett, CEO & Chairman of the Board; Dan E. Barber, VP of Finance; William Rubley, VP of Sales; Paul Barnett, President.

■ 7025 ■ **E.J. Bartells Co.**
PO Box 4160
Renton, WA 98057-4160
Phone: (206)228-4111   **Fax:** (425)228-8807
E-mail: ejbartells.com
Products: Industrial insulation. **SIC:** 5033 (Roofing, Siding & Insulation). **Est:** 1923. **Sales:** $30,000,000 (2000). **Emp:** 425. **Officers:** E.A. Jensen, CEO; Harold Farnsworth, President.

■ 7026 ■ **Bartley Tile Concepts Inc.**
6931 Arlington Rd.
Bethesda, MD 20814
Phone: (301)913-9113
Products: Tile. **SIC:** 5032 (Brick, Stone & Related Materials).

■ 7027 ■ **E.C. Barton and Co.**
PO Box 4040
Jonesboro, AR 72403-4040
Phone: (501)932-6673   **Fax:** (501)972-1304
Products: Lumber, doors, and windows. **SICs:** 5039 (Construction Materials Nec); 5039 (Construction Materials Nec). **Est:** 1927. **Sales:** $71,000,000 (2000). **Emp:** 420. **Officers:** Niel Crowson, CEO & President; Tom Rainwater, Treasurer & Secty.; Bobby Rushing, VP of Marketing; David Cameron, Dir. of Data Processing.

■ 7028 ■ **Basins Inc.**
PO Box 845
Wheatland, WY 82201
Phone: (307)322-2479
Products: Crushed marble. **SIC:** 5032 (Brick, Stone & Related Materials). **Est:** 1958. **Sales:** $4,500,000 (2000). **Emp:** 30. **Officers:** Jerry Macarthur, CEO.

■ 7029 ■ **W.H. Basnight and Company Inc.**
PO Box 1365
Ahoskie, NC 27910
Phone: (919)332-3131
Free: (800)849-3365   **Fax:** (919)332-4573
Products: Building materials, including lumber, paneling, and siding. **SICs:** 5039 (Construction Materials Nec); 5033 (Roofing, Siding & Insulation). **Est:** 1927. **Sales:** $12,000,000 (2000). **Emp:** 40. **Officers:** Mike H. Basnight, President.

■ 7030 ■ **Bat Rentals**
2771 S Industrial Rd.
Las Vegas, NV 89109-1199
Phone: (702)731-1122   **Fax:** (702)731-6534
Products: Construction equipment, including pumps, fork lifts, and loaders, generators; Material handling equipment. **SIC:** 5082 (Construction & Mining Machinery). **Est:** 1962. **Sales:** $12,000,000 (1999). **Emp:** 50. **Officers:** Blake Jones, Asst. GM, e-mail: bjones@bat.N-E-S.com; James Sedeno, Equipment Sales Mgr., e-mail: jsedeno@bat.n-e-s.com; Kenny Yeoman, Service Mgr.; Joyce Hogg, Dir of Personnel, e-mail: jhogg@bat.n-e-s.com.

■ 7031 ■ **Baton Rouge Lumber Company LLC**
8675 S Choctaw
Baton Rouge, LA 70895
Phone: (225)927-2400   **Fax:** (225)929-9973
E-mail: brlumber@globalsurf.net
Products: Building materials, including lumber and plywood. **SIC:** 5031 (Lumber, Plywood & Millwork). **Est:** 1885. **Sales:** $7,000,000 (2000). **Emp:** 30. **Officers:** Thomas B. Hatfield. **Former Name:** Baton Rouge Lumber Company Inc.

■ 7032 ■ **J.H. Baxter Co.**
PO Box 5902
San Mateo, CA 94402-0902
Phone: (650)349-0201
Free: (800)780-7073   **Fax:** (650)570-6878
Products: Treated wood. **SIC:** 5031 (Lumber, Plywood & Millwork). **Est:** 1915. **Emp:** 230. **Officers:** Richard H. Baxter, CEO & President; John R. Sonsken, CFO; Sandra Lavino, VP of Marketing; Paul R. Boyle Jr., VP of Sales, e-mail: pboyle@jhbaxter.com.

■ 7033 ■ **Beal's Royal Glass and Mirror Inc.**
3350 Ali Baba Ln.
Las Vegas, NV 89118
Phone: (702)736-8788
Products: Commercial glass, including stained glass, heat mirrors, and window glass for high-rise buildings and shopping centers. **SIC:** 5039 (Construction Materials Nec). **Est:** 1971. **Sales:** $8,000,000 (2000). **Emp:** 20. **Officers:** Gloria Y. Beal, President; Buddy Rhodes, Dir. of Marketing.

■ 7034 ■ **Buddy Bean Lumber Co.**
3900 Malvern Ave.
Hot Springs National Park, AR 71901
Phone: (501)262-2820   **Fax:** (501)262-2840
Products: Lumber. **SIC:** 5031 (Lumber, Plywood & Millwork). **Est:** 1983. **Sales:** $20,000,000 (2000). **Emp:** 65. **Officers:** Buddy Bean, President.

■ 7035 ■ **Bear Cat Manufacturing Inc.**
3650 N Sabin Brown Rd.
Wickenburg, AZ 85390
Phone: (520)684-7851   **Fax:** (520)684-3241
Products: Road maintenance equipment. **SIC:** 5082 (Construction & Mining Machinery). **Officers:** Kenneth Hill, President.

■ 7036 ■ **Bear Paw Lumber Corp.**
PO Box 20
Fryeburg, ME 04037
Phone: (207)935-2951
Free: (877)400-5097   **Fax:** (207)935-3052
E-mail: bearpawlbr@landmarket.net
URL: http://www.bearpawlumber.com
Products: Lumber. **SIC:** 5031 (Lumber, Plywood & Millwork). **Est:** 1977. **Sales:** $8,000,000 (1999). **Emp:** 60. **Officers:** D.E. Keaten, President; G. Kellough, Vice President; Joe Newman, Sales Mgr.

■ 7037 ■ **E.N. Beard Hardwood Lumber Inc.**
PO Box 13608
Greensboro, NC 27415
Phone: (919)378-1265   **Fax:** (336)379-0863
E-mail: enbeard@aol.com
Products: Hardwood lumber, rough and dressed. **SIC:** 5031 (Lumber, Plywood & Millwork). **Est:** 1968. **Sales:** $34,000,000 (2000). **Emp:** 17. **Officers:** Thomas R. Beard, CEO; Charles F. Sievers, President & Treasurer.

■ 7038 ■ **Beaver Distributors**
1564 Northern Star Dr.
Traverse City, MI 49686
Phone: (231)929-9800
Free: (888)846-9800   **Fax:** (231)929-9889
URL: http://www.beavertile.com
Products: Marble and ceramic tiles; Stone products. **SIC:** 5032 (Brick, Stone & Related Materials). **Est:** 1997. **Emp:** 10. **Officers:** Jeff Seromik, Manager.

■ 7039 ■ **Becker Builders Supply Co.**
PO Box 1697
Wilmington, NC 28402
Phone: (910)791-7761
Products: Building supplies. **SICs:** 5031 (Lumber, Plywood & Millwork); 5033 (Roofing, Siding & Insulation). **Est:** 1918. **Sales:** $7,000,000 (2000). **Emp:** 100. **Officers:** Jere D. Freeman III, President.

■ 7040 ■ **Beco/Boyd Equipment Co.**
1896 National Ave.
Hayward, CA 94545-1708
Phone: (510)782-1500
Free: (800)559-2326   **Fax:** (510)782-0241
Products: Construction supplies and equipment. **SIC:** 5082 (Construction & Mining Machinery). **Est:** 1974. **Emp:** 10.

■ 7041 ■ **Bedrosians**
4285 N Golden State Blvd.
Fresno, CA 93722-6397
Phone: (209)275-5000
Free: (800)760-8453   **Fax:** (209)275-1753
Products: Floorcovering equipment and supplies. **SIC:** 5032 (Brick, Stone & Related Materials).

■ 7042 ■ **Bedrosians Tile and Marble**
4651 S Butterfield Dr.
Tucson, AZ 85714
Phone: (520)747-2000   **Fax:** (520)747-1982
Products: Floorcovering equipment and supplies. **SIC:** 5032 (Brick, Stone & Related Materials).

■ 7043 ■ **Gil Behling Building Products**
7101 E 8 Mile Rd.
Warren, MI 48091
Phone: (810)757-3500   **Fax:** (810)757-7576
Products: Prepared asphalt and tar roofing and siding products; Siding; Shingles; Nails. **SICs:** 5033 (Roofing, Siding & Insulation); 5031 (Lumber, Plywood & Millwork); 5072 (Hardware). **Est:** 1951. **Emp:** 40. **Officers:** Gil Behling, President; Robert Caillier, Vice President.

■ 7044 ■ **Belair Road Supply Company Inc.**
7750 Pulaski Hwy.
Baltimore, MD 21237
Phone: (410)687-4200   **Fax:** (410)687-2906
Products: Hardware; Building materials; Water and sewage supples. **SICs:** 5039 (Construction Materials Nec); 5072 (Hardware); 5032 (Brick, Stone & Related Materials); 5074 (Plumbing & Hydronic Heating Supplies). **Est:** 1917. **Sales:** $15,200,000 (2000). **Emp:** 47. **Officers:** T.R. Adams Jr., President; G. Adams, Treasurer & Secty.; George Russell, Dir. of Marketing & Sales.

■ 7045 ■ **James W. Bell Company Inc.**
1720 I Ave. NE
Cedar Rapids, IA 52406
Phone: (319)362-1151   **Fax:** (319)362-4876
Products: Construction equipment. **SIC:** 5082 (Construction & Mining Machinery). **Est:** 1923. **Sales:** $18,000,000 (1999). **Emp:** 60. **Officers:** David Bengford, President; Dennis J. McGivern, Treasurer & Secty.; W. John Bell, CEO.

■ 7046 ■ Bently Sand & Gravel
9220 Bennett Lake Rd.
Fenton, MI 48430
Phone: (810)629-6172
Products: Sand, gravel, topsoil, and peat. **SIC:** 5032 (Brick, Stone & Related Materials). **Est:** 1966. **Sales:** $200,000 (2000). **Emp:** 5. **Officers:** A. B. Bentley, Owner.

■ 7047 ■ Berg Equipment and Scaffolding Company Inc.
2130 E D St.
Tacoma, WA 98421
Phone: (253)383-2035
Products: Platforms and scaffolding. **SIC:** 5082 (Construction & Mining Machinery). **Est:** 1969. **Sales:** $3,000,000 (2000). **Emp:** 40. **Officers:** E. Berg, President.

■ 7048 ■ Berger Building Products Corp.
805 Pennsylvania Ave.
Feasterville, PA 19053
Phone: (215)355-1200
Free: (800)523-8852 **Fax:** (215)355-7738
E-mail: berger@bergerbros.com
URL: http://www.bergerbros.com
Products: Roof drainage products; Vinyl siding. **SIC:** 5033 (Roofing, Siding & Insulation). **Est:** 1874. **Sales:** $20,000,000 (2000). **Emp:** 75. **Officers:** Joseph Weiderman, President & CFO; William Collins, VP of Marketing & Sales.

■ 7049 ■ J.E. Berkowitz L.P.
PO Box 186
Westville, NJ 08093
Phone: (609)456-7800
Products: Flat glass; Mirrors. **SIC:** 5039 (Construction Materials Nec). **Est:** 1920. **Sales:** $20,000,000 (2000). **Emp:** 150. **Officers:** Arthur Berkowitz, President; David Byruch, Controller; Robert Price, Sales Mgr.

■ 7050 ■ Berks Products Corp.
PO Box 421
Reading, PA 19603
Phone: (610)374-5131 **Fax:** (610)375-1469
Products: Pre-hung doors; Building materials. **SIC:** 5031 (Lumber, Plywood & Millwork). **Est:** 1896. **Sales:** $35,000,000 (2000). **Emp:** 275. **Officers:** W.H. Fehr, CEO.

■ 7051 ■ Berry Companies Inc.
PO Box 829
Wichita, KS 67201
Phone: (316)832-0171 **Fax:** (316)832-1735
Products: Construction equipment. **SIC:** 5082 (Construction & Mining Machinery). **Est:** 1957. **Sales:** $70,000,000 (2000). **Emp:** 240. **Officers:** Walter Berry, President; Judy Worrell, Treasurer.

■ 7052 ■ Besse Forest Products Group
933 N 8th St.
PO Box 352
Gladstone, MI 49837-0352
Phone: (906)428-3113 **Fax:** (906)428-3310
E-mail: bessefp@up.net
URL: http://www.bessegroup.com
Products: Sliced hardwood veneer faces for decorative plywood. Rotary hardwood veneer for flooring. Curved plywood components, pin block and die board. Dyed veneers, clipped, bundled, and tied sliced veneer. Custom thickness cut on request. **SIC:** 5031 (Lumber, Plywood & Millwork). **Est:** 1965. **Emp:** 800. **Officers:** John D. Beese, President; Dean Karrigan, Sales Mgr.; John Noreus, Human Resources Contact. **Former Name:** Birds Eye Veneer Co.

■ 7053 ■ Best Glass Co.
1225 S Commerce
Las Vegas, NV 89102-2528
Phone: (702)382-7502 **Fax:** (702)384-5268
Products: Glass, including automobile and house. **SIC:** 5039 (Construction Materials Nec). **Est:** 1962. **Emp:** 16. **Officers:** Wiliam E. Krummel.

■ 7054 ■ BET Rentokil Plant Services
4067 Industrial Park Dr., No. 3A
Norcross, GA 30071-1638
Phone: (404)321-6067
Products: Construction equipment. **SICs:** 5082

(Construction & Mining Machinery); 5039 (Construction Materials Nec). **Sales:** $4,750,000,000 (2000). **Emp:** 12,500. **Officers:** Ralph A. Trallo, President.

■ 7055 ■ Better Buildings, Inc.
625 S Smallwood St.
Baltimore, MD 21223
Phone: (410)945-7733 **Fax:** (410)233-1844
Products: Used construction machinery; Used truck tractors; Hydraulic cement tank linings. **SICs:** 5082 (Construction & Mining Machinery); 5012 (Automobiles & Other Motor Vehicles). **Officers:** Edward L. Birtic, President.

■ 7056 ■ Bi-State Distributing Co.
3333 11th St.
Lewiston, ID 83501
Phone: (208)746-8295 **Fax:** (208)743-5341
Products: Prepared asphalt and tar roofing and siding products; Windows. **SICs:** 5033 (Roofing, Siding & Insulation); 5039 (Construction Materials Nec). **Officers:** Jerry Purington, Owner.

■ 7057 ■ Big River Industries Inc.
3700 Mansell Rd., No. 250
Alpharetta, GA 30022-8246
Phone: (678)461-2830 **Fax:** (678)461-2845
Products: Expanded clay lightweight aggregate. **SIC:** 5032 (Brick, Stone & Related Materials). **Est:** 1954. **Sales:** $35,000,000 (2000). **Emp:** 120. **Officers:** Timothy Friedel, President; Paul Barry, CFO; P.S. Stephens, VP of Sales.

■ 7058 ■ Bing Construction Company of Nevada
PO Box 487
Minden, NV 89423
Phone: (702)265-3641 **Fax:** (702)265-5475
Products: Concrete aggregates, including rock, sand, bricks, and whitesand blocks. **SIC:** 5032 (Brick, Stone & Related Materials). **Est:** 1967. **Sales:** $4,000,000 (2000). **Emp:** 25. **Officers:** D. Gerald Bing Jr., President; Chesley Wass, Vice President.

■ 7059 ■ Binswanger Glass Co.
PO Box 171173
Memphis, TN 38187
Phone: (901)767-7111
Free: (800)238-6057 **Fax:** (901)683-9351
Products: Glass products; Mirrors. **SIC:** 5039 (Construction Materials Nec). **Est:** 1872. **Sales:** $222,000,000 (2000). **Emp:** 2,143. **Officers:** Mark Burke, CEO & President; John Wagner, VP of Finance & Treasurer; Barry Williams, VP and General Mgr. — Dist. South; George Marshall, VP and General Mgr. — Dist. West.

■ 7060 ■ Bison Building Materials Inc.
PO Box 19849
Houston, TX 77224
Phone: (713)467-6700 **Fax:** (713)935-1223
Products: Lumber. **SIC:** 5031 (Lumber, Plywood & Millwork). **Sales:** $70,000,000 (2000). **Emp:** 350. **Officers:** Pat Bierschwale, President; Gary Turner, CFO.

■ 7061 ■ Black Forest Tile Distributors
1900 Hendersonville Rd.
Asheville, NC 28803
Phone: (828)681-9597
Products: Ceramic tile. **SIC:** 5032 (Brick, Stone & Related Materials).

■ 7062 ■ Blue Diamond Materials Co.
1245 Arrow Hwy.
Irwindale, CA 91706-6601
Phone: (626)303-2623
Products: Asphalt. **SIC:** 5032 (Brick, Stone & Related Materials). **Est:** 1991. **Sales:** $190,000,000 (2000). **Emp:** 490. **Officers:** Dave Hummel, President.

■ 7063 ■ BMI-France Inc.
27 Noblestown Rd.
Carnegie, PA 15106
Phone: (412)923-2525
Products: Insulation products. **SIC:** 5033 (Roofing, Siding & Insulation). **Est:** 1965. **Sales:** $113,700,000 (2000). **Emp:** 75. **Officers:** Willard Bellows, CEO.

■ 7064 ■ Boatwright Insulation Co.
PO Box 25516
Raleigh, NC 27611
Phone: (919)828-7102
Products: Insulation. **SIC:** 5033 (Roofing, Siding & Insulation). **Sales:** $2,000,000 (1993). **Emp:** 8. **Officers:** A.V. Stoycos, President.

■ 7065 ■ R.K. Bodden Lumber Company Inc.
PO Box 203
Mobile, AL 36601
Phone: (334)433-2736 **Fax:** (334)433-9035
Products: Lumber. **SIC:** 5031 (Lumber, Plywood & Millwork). **Est:** 1926. **Sales:** $5,000,000 (2000). **Emp:** 2. **Officers:** John T. Lutz, President; Laura Acker, Office Mgr.

■ 7066 ■ Boehm-Madisen Lumber Company Inc.
PO Box 906
Brookfield, WI 53008-0906
Phone: (262)544-4660
Free: (800)242-2069 **Fax:** (262)544-0795
Products: Lumber, including hardwood and softwood. **SICs:** 5031 (Lumber, Plywood & Millwork); 5072 (Hardware). **Est:** 1934. **Sales:** $18,000,000 (2000). **Emp:** 35. **Officers:** Thomas G. Kestly, President; John G. Kestly, Vice President.

■ 7067 ■ Boise Cascade
PO Box 130
Nutting Lake, MA 01865
Phone: (978)670-3800
Free: (800)THE-WOOD **Fax:** (978)673-3999
URL: http://www.bc.com
Products: Building products. **SIC:** 5031 (Lumber, Plywood & Millwork). **Est:** 1956. **Sales:** $675,000,000 (2000). **Emp:** 410. **Officers:** Barry L. Kronick, CEO & President; George Gray, Finance Officer; Richard Viola, Dir. of Marketing; William Perry, VP of Human Resources. **Former Name:** Furman Lumber Inc.

■ 7068 ■ Bonded Materials Co.
91-400 Komohana St.
Kapolei, HI 96707-1785
Phone: (808)832-1155
E-mail: bomat@bondedmaterials.com
Products: Concrete products. **SIC:** 5032 (Brick, Stone & Related Materials). **Est:** 1955.

■ 7069 ■ Bonnette Supply Inc.
PO Box 709
St. Albans, VT 05478-0709
Phone: (802)524-3806 **Fax:** (802)527-1374
Products: Prepared asphalt and tar roofing and siding products; Thermal insulation. **SIC:** 5033 (Roofing, Siding & Insulation). **Officers:** Maurice Bonnette, President.

■ 7070 ■ Booker and Company Inc.
4720 Oak Fair Blvd.
Tampa, FL 33610
Phone: (813)229-0931
Products: Building materials and supplies. **SICs:** 5031 (Lumber, Plywood & Millwork); 5039 (Construction Materials Nec). **Est:** 1920. **Sales:** $70,000,000 (1999). **Emp:** 100. **Officers:** Scott Henderson, General Mgr.

■ 7071 ■ F.D. Borkholder and Company Inc.
PO Box 32
Nappanee, IN 46550
Phone: (219)773-3144 **Fax:** (219)773-2897
Products: Trusses. **SIC:** 5031 (Lumber, Plywood & Millwork). **Est:** 1965. **Sales:** $6,000,000 (2000). **Emp:** 20. **Officers:** Freeman D. Borkholder, Chairman of the Board; Carl Bals, CFO; Larry Draper, Dir. of Marketing.

■ 7072 ■ Boston Metal Door Company Inc.
60 Lowell St.
Arlington, MA 02474
Phone: (781)648-6890
Products: Metal doors. **SIC:** 5039 (Construction Materials Nec). **Est:** 1952. **Sales:** $2,000,000 (2000). **Emp:** 12. **Officers:** H.E. Davidson Jr., President; Johnathan McClymont, Controller.

■ **7073** ■ **Bowie Industries Inc.**
PO Box 931
Bowie, TX 76230
Phone: (940)872-1106 **Fax:** (940)872-4792
Products: Landscaping equipment; Oil field equipment. **SICs:** 5082 (Construction & Mining Machinery); 5083 (Farm & Garden Machinery). **Est:** 1944. **Sales:** $5,000,000 (2000). **Emp:** 50. **Officers:** O. Meyer, President; H. Dean Myers, CFO; R.E. Jones, Dir. of Marketing.

■ **7074** ■ **C.L. Boyd Company Inc.**
PO Box 26427
Oklahoma City, OK 73126
Phone: (405)942-8000 **Fax:** (405)943-7260
Products: Tractors; Forklifts. **SIC:** 5082 (Construction & Mining Machinery). **Est:** 1913. **Sales:** $25,000,000 (2000). **Emp:** 65. **Officers:** Robert H. Crews, President.

■ **7075** ■ **R.W. Bradley Supply Company Inc.**
403 N 4th St.
Springfield, IL 62702
Phone: (217)528-8438
Products: Construction supplies, including drills and paints. **SICs:** 5039 (Construction Materials Nec); 5072 (Hardware); 5198 (Paints, Varnishes & Supplies). **Est:** 1955. **Sales:** $7,000,000 (2000). **Emp:** 30. **Officers:** Roger Reese, CEO.

■ **7076** ■ **Brands Inc.**
PO Box 90
Columbus, IN 47202
Phone: (812)379-9566 **Fax:** (812)372-9690
E-mail: brands@brandslumber.com
URL: http://www.brandslumber.com
Products: Lumber. **SIC:** 5031 (Lumber, Plywood & Millwork). **Est:** 1967. **Sales:** $7,000,000 (2000). **Emp:** 40. **Officers:** J.R. Brand, President, e-mail: jess@brandslumber.com.

■ **7077** ■ **Branton Industries Inc.**
PO Box 10536
New Orleans, LA 70181-0536
Phone: (504)733-7770 **Fax:** (504)734-7818
Products: Insulation materials; Glass and malite wall panels. **SICs:** 5033 (Roofing, Siding & Insulation); 5039 (Construction Materials Nec). **Est:** 1956. **Sales:** $15,000,000 (2000). **Emp:** 200. **Officers:** Harold T. Branton, CEO; Jack Biven, Controller; J. Malter, VP of Marketing.

■ **7078** ■ **Breckenridge Material**
2833 Breckenridge Rd.
St. Louis, MO 63144
Phone: (314)962-1234
Products: Concrete. **SIC:** 5032 (Brick, Stone & Related Materials). **Est:** 1925. **Sales:** $20,000,000 (2000). **Emp:** 100. **Officers:** G.R. McKean, President; A. Haskell, Controller; Roger Krechel, Dir. of Marketing; Carol Abeln, Dir. of Systems.

■ **7079** ■ **Brin-Northwestern Glass Co.**
2300 N 2nd St.
Minneapolis, MN 55411
Phone: (612)529-9671 **Fax:** (612)529-9670
Products: Glass; Mirrors; Aluminum doors and windows; Automatic doors. **SIC:** 5039 (Construction Materials Nec). **Est:** 1912. **Sales:** $15,000,000 (2000). **Emp:** 100. **Officers:** Douglas Nelson, CEO; P. Rone, President; Stan Mariska, Distribution Sales Manager; John Biehl, Contract Sales Manager.

■ **7080** ■ **Britton Explosive Supply Inc.**
125 Cronin Rd.
Queensbury, NY 12804
Phone: (518)793-4767
Products: Drilling and blasting equipment. **SICs:** 5082 (Construction & Mining Machinery); 5084 (Industrial Machinery & Equipment). **Sales:** $2,000,000 (2000). **Emp:** 4. **Officers:** Steve Britton, President.

■ **7081** ■ **Britton Lumber Company Inc.**
PO Box 38
Fairlee, VT 05045
Phones: (802)333-4388 800-343-5300
Free: (800)343-4300 **Fax:** (802)333-4295
E-mail: britton@together.net
Products: Lumber, including pine, spruce, and treated;
Roofing; Gypsum; Wood products; Building board. **SICs:** 5033 (Roofing, Siding & Insulation); 5031 (Lumber, Plywood & Millwork). **Est:** 1946. **Sales:** $18,000,000 (1999). **Emp:** 60. **Officers:** Douglas Britton, President; Sterling Golder, Sales/Marketing Contact; George Armstrong, Sales/Marketing Contact.

■ **7082** ■ **Brockway-Smith Co.**
146 Dascomb Rd.
Andover, MA 01810
Phone: (508)475-7100
Products: Wood doors, interior and exterior; Windows; Millwork products. **SIC:** 5031 (Lumber, Plywood & Millwork). **Sales:** $100,000,000 (2000). **Emp:** 497. **Officers:** Rodolph P. Gagnon, President; Paul J. Zocco, Controller.

■ **7083** ■ **Brookdale Lumber Inc.**
13602 Pacific Ave.
Tacoma, WA 98444
Phone: (253)537-8669
Products: Lumber; Hardware. **SICs:** 5031 (Lumber, Plywood & Millwork); 5072 (Hardware). **Est:** 1943. **Sales:** $7,000,000 (2000). **Emp:** 20. **Officers:** Ronald Torgeson, President.

■ **7084** ■ **Brookharts Inc.**
3105 N Stone Ave.
Colorado Springs, CO 80907-5305
Phone: (719)471-4500 **Fax:** (719)471-4505
Products: Lumber. **SIC:** 5031 (Lumber, Plywood & Millwork). **Est:** 1953. **Sales:** $96,000,000 (2000). **Emp:** 400. **Officers:** T.W. Watt, President; G.J. Wieder, Controller.

■ **7085** ■ **Herman M. Brown Co.**
PO Box 995
Des Moines, IA 50304
Phone: (515)282-0404
Products: Large construction equipment, including dump trucks and cranes. **SIC:** 5082 (Construction & Mining Machinery). **Est:** 1919. **Sales:** $29,000,000 (2000). **Emp:** 100. **Officers:** Dennis Roupe, Treasurer; Jim Miller, Dir. of Sales.

■ **7086** ■ **Brown-Graves Co.**
PO Box 869
Akron, OH 44309-0869
Phone: (330)434-7111 **Fax:** (330)434-6906
E-mail: beegraves@aol.com
Products: Lumber and wood products. **SIC:** 5031 (Lumber, Plywood & Millwork). **Est:** 1899. **Sales:** $35,000,000 (1999). **Emp:** 150. **Officers:** H.E. Graves Jr., CEO & President; D. Giannetti, CFO; Reed Kneale, Vice President; S. Keith Grave, VP of Construction; Reed Kneale, Sales/Marketing Contact.

■ **7087** ■ **Pat Brown Lumber Corp.**
PO Box 19065
Greensboro, NC 27419
Phone: (336)299-7755 **Fax:** (336)299-4050
Products: Lumber. **SIC:** 5031 (Lumber, Plywood & Millwork). **Est:** 1945. **Sales:** $8,000,000 (2000). **Emp:** 7. **Officers:** Paul D. Senior, President.

■ **7088** ■ **John V. Broz, Inc.**
PO Box 21345
Hilton Head Island, SC 29925
Phone: (803)689-9900 **Fax:** (803)689-6363
E-mail: jvbroz@aol.com
URL: http://www.brozexport@brozexport.com
Products: Building and plumbing supplies. **SICs:** 5039 (Construction Materials Nec); 5074 (Plumbing & Hydronic Heating Supplies). **Officers:** Chris Lindgren, President.

■ **7089** ■ **Brunner and Lay Inc.**
2425 E 37th St.
Los Angeles, CA 90058
Phone: (213)587-1233 **Fax:** (213)587-7513
Products: Rock drilling accessories; Paving breaker accessories. **SIC:** 5082 (Construction & Mining Machinery). **Est:** 1882. **Sales:** $4,000,000 (2000). **Emp:** 8. **Officers:** Gary Sublett, President.

■ **7090** ■ **BSH of Evansville**
2534 Locust Creek Dr
Evansville, IN 47720
Phone: (812)424-2901 **Fax:** (812)422-2665
E-mail: bshevv@evansville.net
URL: http://www.bsh1.com
Products: Components for stationary buildings, including wall, partition, floor, ceiling panels; Metal doors and frames; Wood doors, interior and exterior; Hardware. **SICs:** 5031 (Lumber, Plywood & Millwork); 5072 (Hardware). **Est:** 1984. **Sales:** $4,000,000 (2000). **Emp:** 20. **Officers:** Tim McAlpin, General Mgr.

■ **7091** ■ **BSTC Group Inc.**
75 Union Ave.
Rutherford, NJ 07070
Phone: (201)939-1200 **Fax:** (201)939-1720
Products: Building materials, includng nails, wire, wood, and fiberglass. **SICs:** 5031 (Lumber, Plywood & Millwork); 5051 (Metals Service Centers & Offices). **Est:** 1884. **Sales:** $35,000,000 (2000). **Emp:** 15. **Officers:** Andrew Berardinelli, President; John Schellberg, CFO.

■ **7092** ■ **Buckeye Ceramic Tile**
388 McClurg Rd., No. 5
Boardman, OH 44512
Phone: (330)758-5749 **Fax:** (330)758-5740
Products: Floorcovering equipment and supplies. **SIC:** 5032 (Brick, Stone & Related Materials). **Sales:** $1,500,000 (2000). **Emp:** 5.

■ **7093** ■ **Buckeye Pacific Corp.**
4380 S Macadam Ave.
Portland, OR 97207
Phone: (503)228-3330
Products: Lumber. **SIC:** 5031 (Lumber, Plywood & Millwork). **Est:** 1974. **Sales:** $21,000,000 (2000). **Emp:** 65. **Officers:** Steve Tennent, President & Treasurer; Carol Gilbert, Controller; Casey Keller, VP of Sales.

■ **7094** ■ **Budres Lumber Co.**
657 76th St. SW
Grand Rapids, MI 49509
Phone: (616)455-3510
Products: Lumber. **SIC:** 5031 (Lumber, Plywood & Millwork). **Est:** 1963. **Sales:** $10,000,000 (2000). **Emp:** 50. **Officers:** Edward Elderkin, President; Barbara Sexton, Personnel Mgr.

■ **7095** ■ **Buettner Brothers Lumber Co.**
PO Box 1087
Cullman, AL 35056-1087
Phone: (205)734-4221
Products: Lumber and building materials. **SIC:** 5031 (Lumber, Plywood & Millwork). **Est:** 1892. **Sales:** $9,000,000 (2000). **Emp:** 70. **Officers:** Jimmy Barnes, President & Treasurer; John McPhillps, VP & Secty.

■ **7096** ■ **Buffington Corp.**
PO Drawer 7420
Monroe, LA 71211
Phone: (318)387-0671
Products: Lumber and building materials. **SICs:** 5031 (Lumber, Plywood & Millwork); 5039 (Construction Materials Nec). **Est:** 1959. **Sales:** $14,000,000 (2000). **Emp:** 18. **Officers:** Lamar Buffington, President.

■ **7097** ■ **Buford White Lumber Company Inc.**
PO Box 1029
Shawnee, OK 74802-1029
Phone: (405)275-4900 **Fax:** (405)275-6425
Products: Lumber; Hardware. **SICs:** 5031 (Lumber, Plywood & Millwork); 5072 (Hardware). **Est:** 1964. **Sales:** $15,000,000 (1999). **Emp:** 100. **Officers:** Buford W. White, President; Janet Hodde, Controller; Jerry Austin, Dir. of Marketing & Sales.

■ **7098** ■ **Builder Marts of America Inc.**
PO Box 47
Greenville, SC 29602
Phone: (864)297-6101 **Fax:** (864)281-3381
Products: Building supplies, including brick and sand. **SIC:** 5032 (Brick, Stone & Related Materials). **Est:** 1966. **Sales:** $570,000,000 (2000). **Emp:** 175. **Officers:** David Clark, CEO; R. Steven Robins, Treasurer & Secty.; Duane H. Faulkner, President.

■ **7099** ■ **Builders Center Inc.**
12911 Florida Blvd.
Baton Rouge, LA 70815
Phone: (504)275-4125
Products: Building materials. **SICs:** 5031 (Lumber, Plywood & Millwork); 5039 (Construction Materials Nec). **Est:** 1957. **Sales:** $10,000,000 (2000). **Emp:** 30. **Officers:** Lamar N. Coxe Sr., President.

■ **7100** ■ **Builders General Supply Co.**
PO Box 95
Little Silver, NJ 07739
Phone: (732)747-0808 **Fax:** (732)741-1095
URL: http://www.buildersgeneral.com
Products: Building and construction materials. **SICs:** 5031 (Lumber, Plywood & Millwork); 5032 (Brick, Stone & Related Materials); 5033 (Roofing, Siding & Insulation); 5039 (Construction Materials Nec). **Est:** 1931. **Sales:** $72,000,000 (1999). **Emp:** 172. **Officers:** Timothy J. Shaheen, President; Philip Shaheen, Vice President.

■ **7101** ■ **Builders Specialties Co.**
PO Box 969
Pawtucket, RI 02862
Phone: (401)722-2988
Products: Building supplies, including siding, shutters, doors, and windows. **SICs:** 5033 (Roofing, Siding & Insulation); 5031 (Lumber, Plywood & Millwork). **Est:** 1940. **Sales:** $14,000,000 (2000). **Emp:** 50. **Officers:** Marvin G. Rumpler, President; Ron Rueter, Controller; Leonard Rumpler, Owner.

■ **7102** ■ **Builders Warehouse**
PO Box 1447
Grand Island, NE 68802
Phone: (308)382-9656 **Fax:** (308)382-9662
URL: http://www.builders-warehouse.com
Products: Lumber; Hardware; Varnish; Power tools; Kitchen cabinets. **SICs:** 5031 (Lumber, Plywood & Millwork); 5072 (Hardware); 5198 (Paints, Varnishes & Supplies). **Est:** 1975. **Sales:** $6,000,000 (2000). **Emp:** 40. **Officers:** Myron Anderson, President; Craig Bradshaw, General Mgr. **Former Name:** Spelts-Schultz Lumber Company of Grand Island.

■ **7103** ■ **Building and Industrial Wholesale Co.**
12 Davisville Rd.
PO Box 70
Davisville, WV 26142
Phone: (304)485-6500
Free: (800)955-0593 **Fax:** (304)485-6869
Products: Building materials; Vinyl fence and deck. **SICs:** 5031 (Lumber, Plywood & Millwork); 5033 (Roofing, Siding & Insulation); 5039 (Construction Materials Nec). **Est:** 1952. **Sales:** $3,000,000 (2000). **Emp:** 12. **Officers:** Revis Stephenson, President, e-mail: revisfifthst@msn.com. **Alternate Name:** B & I Wholesale.

■ **7104** ■ **Building Materials Distributors Inc.**
PO Box 606
Galt, CA 95632
Phone: (209)745-3001
Free: (800)356-3001 **Fax:** (209)745-0707
URL: http://www.bmdusa.com
Products: Construction materials. **SICs:** 5031 (Lumber, Plywood & Millwork); 5039 (Construction Materials Nec). **Est:** 1943. **Sales:** $92,000,000 (2000). **Emp:** 200. **Officers:** Steven Ellinwood, President; Randy Olsen, CFO; Garry Tabor, Vice President, e-mail: gtabor@bmdusa.com.

■ **7105** ■ **Building Materials Wholesale**
1571 W Sunnyside Rd.
Idaho Falls, ID 83402-4349
Phone: (208)529-8162 **Fax:** (208)529-8176
Products: Metal roofing and roof drainage equipment. **SIC:** 5033 (Roofing, Siding & Insulation). **Officers:** Jerry Tracy, President.

■ **7106** ■ **Building Products Inc.**
PO Box 1390
Watertown, SD 57201
Phone: (605)886-3495
Products: Lumber. **SICs:** 5031 (Lumber, Plywood & Millwork); 5033 (Roofing, Siding & Insulation). **Est:**

1957. **Sales:** $53,000,000 (2000). **Emp:** 100. **Officers:** Lee Schull, President; Earl Benson, Finance Officer.

■ **7107** ■ **Bun Patch Supply Corp.**
155 Tuckerton Rd.
Temple, PA 19560
Phone: (215)929-3668
Free: (800)828-5455 **Fax:** (215)929-5242
Products: Building supplies. **SICs:** 5031 (Lumber, Plywood & Millwork); 5032 (Brick, Stone & Related Materials); 5033 (Roofing, Siding & Insulation); 5039 (Construction Materials Nec).

■ **7108** ■ **Burke Equipment Co.**
PO Box 8010
Sterling Heights, MI 48311-8010
Phone: (810)939-4400
Free: (800)482-4952 **Fax:** (810)939-3112
Products: Construction equipment, including cranes. **SIC:** 5082 (Construction & Mining Machinery). **Est:** 1930. **Sales:** $12,000,000 (2000). **Emp:** 50. **Officers:** Michael C. Burke, President; Jennifer Kuczmarski, Controller; Brian Burke, Dir. of Marketing; John C. Burke, Dir. of Information Systems.

■ **7109** ■ **Burly Corporation of North America**
754 N Burleson Blvd.
Burleson, TX 76028
Phone: (817)295-1128
Free: (800)344-4755 **Fax:** (817)295-0000
Products: Fencing and agricultural equipment. **SIC:** 5039 (Construction Materials Nec). **Est:** 1959. **Sales:** $75,000,000 (2000). **Emp:** 250. **Officers:** David Davenport, President; John Jones, CFO; Bryan Davenport, Vice President.

■ **7110** ■ **Burnett Construction Co.**
PO Box 2707
Durango, CO 81302
Phone: (970)247-2172 **Fax:** (970)259-3631
Products: Concrete. **SIC:** 5032 (Brick, Stone & Related Materials). **Est:** 1969. **Sales:** $1,400,000 (2000). **Emp:** 40. **Officers:** Ronald W. Pettigrew, President; Gray Fields, Treasurer.

■ **7111** ■ **Burnett and Sons Mill and Lumber Co.**
PO Box 1646
Sacramento, CA 95812-1646
Phone: (916)442-0493 **Fax:** (916)442-0529
Products: Lumber. **SIC:** 5031 (Lumber, Plywood & Millwork). **Est:** 1869. **Sales:** $4,500,000 (2000). **Emp:** 45. **Officers:** R.B. Miller, President; Jim Miller, General Mgr.; Ken Oliver, Dir. of Sales.

■ **7112** ■ **Burns Industries Inc.**
PO Box 338
Line Lexington, PA 18932-0338
Phone: (215)699-5313
Products: Construction equipment; Medical equipment. **SICs:** 5039 (Construction Materials Nec); 5047 (Medical & Hospital Equipment). **Sales:** $13,000,000 (1994). **Emp:** 30. **Officers:** D.J. Burns, President; Jim Doherty, CFO.

■ **7113** ■ **Burt Millwork Corp.**
1010 Stanley Ave.
Brooklyn, NY 11208
Phone: (718)257-4601 **Fax:** (718)649-4398
Products: Wood moldings; Shelving; Wood window and door frames; Aluminum and vinyl windows; Steel and wood doors. **SIC:** 5031 (Lumber, Plywood & Millwork). **Est:** 1948. **Sales:** $3,000,000 (2000). **Emp:** 20. **Officers:** E. Gordon, President.

■ **7114** ■ **Burton Building Products Inc.**
9900 Maumelle Blvd.
North Little Rock, AR 72113-6610
Products: Siding; Gutters. **SIC:** 5033 (Roofing, Siding & Insulation). **Est:** 1934. **Sales:** $14,000,000 (2000). **Emp:** 60. **Officers:** Steven Burton, President; Alex Shelton, Treasurer; CArol Cunningham, Dir. of Marketing.

■ **7115** ■ **Burton Lumber Corp.**
835 Wilson Rd.
Chesapeake, VA 23324
Phone: (757)545-4613 **Fax:** (757)545-8852
E-mail: burton@bellatlantic.net
Products: Lumber; Windows; Doors; Building materials. **SICs:** 5031 (Lumber, Plywood & Millwork); 5039 (Construction Materials Nec). **Est:** 1945. **Sales:** $13,000,000 (2000). **Emp:** 55. **Officers:** George Burton Jr., President; George Burton III, Vice President.

■ **7116** ■ **Butler-Johnson Corp.**
PO Box 612110
San Jose, CA 95161-2110
Phone: (408)259-1800
Free: (800)776-2167 **Fax:** 800-736-0756
Products: Flooring and surfacing materials. **SIC:** 5039 (Construction Materials Nec). **Officers:** Ralphton Johnson, President.

■ **7117** ■ **Butterfield Building Supply**
375 N Main
Midvale, UT 84047-2486
Phone: (801)255-4201 **Fax:** (801)561-9259
Products: Lumber and wood products; Builders' hardware. **SICs:** 5031 (Lumber, Plywood & Millwork); 5039 (Construction Materials Nec). **Sales:** $26,000,000 (2000). **Emp:** 85. **Officers:** Ed Butterfield.

■ **7118** ■ **Byrne Co.**
200 Cabeza Negra Ct. SE
Rio Rancho, NM 87124-1344
Phone: (505)836-2600 **Fax:** (505)836-2600
Products: Roofing and roofing materials; Siding and siding materials; Insulation; Asphalt; Sheet metal. **SICs:** 5033 (Roofing, Siding & Insulation); 5032 (Brick, Stone & Related Materials); 5084 (Industrial Machinery & Equipment). **Officers:** Terry Byrne, Owner.

■ **7119** ■ **Byrne Plywood Co.**
2400 Cole Ave.
Birmingham, MI 48009
Phone: (248)642-8800 **Fax:** (248)642-0737
E-mail: byrne.plywood.inc.byrne@worldnet.att.net
Products: Plywood and lumber. **SIC:** 5031 (Lumber, Plywood & Millwork). **Est:** 1954. **Sales:** $3,000,000 (2000). **Emp:** 8. **Officers:** Mary E. Byrne, President; Keith Loruss, Vice President.

■ **7120** ■ **C & D Hardwoods**
PO Box 14, Hwy. 64 W
New Salisbury, IN 47161
Phone: (812)347-3278 **Fax:** (812)347-2047
Products: Building materials. **SIC:** 5031 (Lumber, Plywood & Millwork).

■ **7121** ■ **Cabinet & Cupboard Inc.**
PO Box 378
Seneca Tpke.
New Hartford, NY 13413
Phone: (315)735-4665
Free: (800)USA-WOOD **Fax:** (315)735-0775
Products: Kitchen cabinets. **SIC:** 5031 (Lumber, Plywood & Millwork). **Emp:** 25. **Officers:** Gail Ball, General Mgr.

■ **7122** ■ **Cache Valley Builders Supply**
PO Box 324
1488 N Zoowest
Logan, UT 84341
Phone: (435)752-6200 **Fax:** (435)752-6224
Products: Lumber; Drywall; Trusses; Insulation; Hardware; Tools; Fasteners. **SIC:** 5031 (Lumber, Plywood & Millwork). **Est:** 1946. **Sales:** $9,500,000 (2000). **Emp:** 65. **Officers:** C.R. Watts, President; J.E. Jeppesen, Office Mgr.; C.A. Watts, Vice President.

■ **7123** ■ **Cadillac Glass Co.**
11801 Commerce St.
Warren, MI 48089
Phone: (810)754-5277 **Fax:** (810)754-8390
Products: Glass. **SIC:** 5039 (Construction Materials Nec). **Est:** 1921. **Sales:** $4,500,000 (2000). **Emp:** 50. **Officers:** John L. Martin, President; Ronald Duleki, Treasurer & Secty.

■ 7124 ■ **Caffall Brothers Forest Products Inc.**
PO Box 725
Wilsonville, OR 97070
Phone: (503)682-1910
Free: (800)547-2011 **Fax:** (503)682-0505
Products: Cedar fencing, timbers, and tightknot. **SIC:** 5031 (Lumber, Plywood & Millwork). **Sales:** $45,000,000 (1992). **Emp:** 150. **Officers:** Douglas Caffall, President; H. Winters, CFO.

■ 7125 ■ **Calcasieu Lumber Co.**
PO Box 17097
Austin, TX 78760
Phone: (512)444-3172
Products: Lumber; Hardware. **SICs:** 5031 (Lumber, Plywood & Millwork); 5072 (Hardware). **Est:** 1883. **Sales:** $30,000,000 (2000). **Emp:** 170. **Officers:** Truman N. Morris, CEO & President.

■ 7126 ■ **California Glass Co.**
155 98th Ave.
Oakland, CA 94603
Phone: (510)635-7700
Products: Glass. **SIC:** 5039 (Construction Materials Nec). **Sales:** $12,000,000 (2000). **Emp:** 55. **Officers:** Marc Silbani, President; Doug Lacey, Controller.

■ 7127 ■ **California Panel and Veneer Co.**
PO Box 3250
Cerritos, CA 90703
Phone: (562)926-5834 **Fax:** (562)926-3139
Products: Wood products; Formica. **SICs:** 5031 (Lumber, Plywood & Millwork); 5039 (Construction Materials Nec). **Est:** 1923. **Sales:** $30,000,000 (2000). **Emp:** 47. **Officers:** J. Fahs, President; Carl Racovitch, Finance Officer; Gary Harker, Exec. VP.

■ 7128 ■ **Calotex Delaware, Inc.**
17 Wood St.
Middletown, DE 19709
Phone: (302)378-9568 **Fax:** (302)378-7389
Products: Construction materials. **SIC:** 5039 (Construction Materials Nec).

■ 7129 ■ **Calvert & Hoffman**
PO Box 20277
Louisville, KY 40250-0277
Phone: (502)459-0936 **Fax:** (502)458-1805
Products: Doors and door hardware; Entrance mats and grates. **SICs:** 5039 (Construction Materials Nec); 5031 (Lumber, Plywood & Millwork). **Est:** 1977. **Emp:** 4. **Officers:** Bob Calvert; Joe Calvert.

■ 7130 ■ **Cameron Ashley Building Products Inc.**
11651 Plano Rd., Ste. 100
Dallas, TX 75243
Phone: (214)860-5100
Products: Building materials. **SICs:** 5031 (Lumber, Plywood & Millwork); 5033 (Roofing, Siding & Insulation); 5039 (Construction Materials Nec). **Sales:** $762,000,000 (2000). **Emp:** 1,973. **Officers:** Walter J. Muratori, President; F. Dixon McElwee, VP & CFO.

■ 7131 ■ **Campbell-Payne Inc.**
PO Box 11255
Lynchburg, VA 24506
Phone: (804)847-8803 **Fax:** (804)846-4149
Products: Lumber. **SIC:** 5031 (Lumber, Plywood & Millwork). **Est:** 1932. **Sales:** $7,000,000 (2000). **Emp:** 60. **Officers:** K.L. White, President & Treasurer.

■ 7132 ■ **Canal Industries Inc.**
PO Box 260001
Conway, SC 29526-2601
Phone: (843)347-4251 **Fax:** (843)347-4141
URL: http://www.canalindustries.com
Products: Timber. **SIC:** 5031 (Lumber, Plywood & Millwork). **Sales:** $360,000,000 (2000). **Emp:** 425. **Officers:** Jeff Miller, CFO.

■ 7133 ■ **Cancos Tile Corp.**
1085 Portion Rd.
Farmingville, NY 11738
Phone: (516)736-0770
Free: (800)322-6267 **Fax:** (516)736-0371
Products: Marble, granite and ceramic tile; Custom granite and marble fabrications. **SIC:** 5032 (Brick,

Stone & Related Materials). **Sales:** $45,000,000 (1999). **Emp:** 100. **Officers:** Frank Valva, President.

■ 7134 ■ **C.L. Cannon and Sons Inc.**
PO Box 2404
Spartanburg, SC 29304
Phone: (864)503-3401
Free: (877)503-3400 **Fax:** (864)503-3401
Products: Building supplies, including bricks, drywall, and roofing shingles. **SICs:** 5033 (Roofing, Siding & Insulation); 5032 (Brick, Stone & Related Materials). **Est:** 1906. **Sales:** $6,000,000 (2000). **Emp:** 15. **Officers:** L.J. Cannon, President.

■ 7135 ■ **Cantwell Machinery Co.**
PO Box 44130
Columbus, OH 43204-0130
Phone: (614)276-5171
Free: (800)282-1604 **Fax:** (614)279-6287
E-mail: cantwelloh@aol.com
URL: http://www.cantwellmachinery.com
Products: Construction and large industrial machinery. **SICs:** 5082 (Construction & Mining Machinery); 5084 (Industrial Machinery & Equipment). **Est:** 1946. **Emp:** 70. **Officers:** Mark E. Cantwell, President; Edward P. Cantwell, Chairman of the Board; Christine Osterman, CFO; J. Thomas Cantwell, Vice President.

■ 7136 ■ **Capitol Concrete Products Co.**
PO Box 8159
Topeka, KS 66608
Phone: (785)233-3271
Products: Concrete blocks. **SIC:** 5032 (Brick, Stone & Related Materials). **Est:** 1924. **Sales:** $2,500,000 (2000). **Emp:** 19. **Officers:** Ray A. Browning, President; Jim Browning, Vice President; Jeff Preisner, Sales Mgr.

■ 7137 ■ **Capitol Plywood Inc.**
160 Commerce Cir.
Sacramento, CA 95815
Phone: (916)922-8861
Products: Plywood. **SIC:** 5031 (Lumber, Plywood & Millwork). **Est:** 1951. **Sales:** $24,000,000 (2000). **Emp:** 30. **Officers:** John Bozich, President.

■ 7138 ■ **The Car Place**
PO Box 13624
Florence, SC 29504
Phone: (803)665-2880 **Fax:** (803)669-2801
Products: Construction machinery. **SIC:** 5082 (Construction & Mining Machinery). **Officers:** Jerry Rasberry, Owner.

■ 7139 ■ **Carder Inc.**
PO Box 721
Lamar, CO 81052
Phone: (719)336-3479
Products: Gravel. **SIC:** 5032 (Brick, Stone & Related Materials). **Est:** 1961. **Sales:** $13,000,000 (2000). **Emp:** 50. **Officers:** John F. Carder, President & Treasurer.

■ 7140 ■ **Cardinal Glass Co.**
PO Box 707
Rockford, IL 61105-0707
Phone: (815)394-1400
Free: (800)728-3468 **Fax:** (815)397-1750
E-mail: cardinal65@aol.com
Products: Glass, including insulating glass. **SIC:** 5039 (Construction Materials Nec). **Est:** 1955. **Sales:** $10,000,000 (1999). **Emp:** 150. **Officers:** Walter H. Williams, CEO & Chairman of the Board; Linda Voss, Secretary; Angelo C. Bruscato, President. **Former Name:** Rhermaltite Insulating Glass.

■ 7141 ■ **Carlson Distributors Inc.**
2501 Charles St.
Rockford, IL 61108
Phone: (815)397-3101
Products: Siding; Shingles. **SIC:** 5033 (Roofing, Siding & Insulation). **Est:** 1947. **Sales:** $7,000,000 (2000). **Emp:** 15. **Officers:** William I. Carlson, President.

■ 7142 ■ **Carolina Building Co.**
1050 Berkley Ave. Ext.
Norfolk, VA 23523-1899
Phone: (757)543-6836 **Fax:** (757)545-6952
Products: Building supplies, including pre-hung doors

and windows. **SICs:** 5031 (Lumber, Plywood & Millwork); 5039 (Construction Materials Nec). **Est:** 1925. **Sales:** $30,000,000 (2000). **Emp:** 150. **Officers:** Noah H. Palmer, President.

■ 7143 ■ **Carolina Door Controls**
PO Box 15639
Durham, NC 27704
Phone: (919)381-0094 **Fax:** (919)381-4834
URL: http://www.carolinadoor.com
Products: Automatic doors. **SICs:** 5051 (Metals Service Centers & Offices); 5039 (Construction Materials Nec); 5051 (Metals Service Centers & Offices). **Est:** 1966. **Sales:** $50,000,000 (2000). **Emp:** 270. **Officers:** David McLeroy, President.

■ 7144 ■ **Carolina Tractor/CAT**
PO Box 1095
Charlotte, NC 28201-1095
Phone: (704)596-6700 **Fax:** (704)597-9875
Products: Construction equipment; Lift trucks; Truck engines; Generators. **SIC:** 5082 (Construction & Mining Machinery). **Est:** 1926. **Sales:** $97,000,000 (2000). **Emp:** 500. **Officers:** Edward I. Weisiger Jr., President; Kevin Franklin, VP of Finance; Bill Padula, VP of Sales; Ed Harris, Vice President; Mike Brown, Vice President.

■ 7145 ■ **Carolina Western Inc.**
PO Box 2524
Greenville, SC 29602
Phone: (803)246-0908 **Fax:** (803)294-0799
Products: Hardwood and softwood lumber; Hardwood logs; Textile machinery parts. **SICs:** 5031 (Lumber, Plywood & Millwork); 5099 (Durable Goods Nec); 5084 (Industrial Machinery & Equipment). **Officers:** Charles F. Travis, President.

■ 7146 ■ **Carroll Touch Inc.**
2800 Oakmont Dr.
Round Rock, TX 78664
Phone: (512)244-3500
Free: (800)386-8241 **Fax:** (512)244-7040
Products: Touch screen products. **SIC:** 5045 (Computers, Peripherals & Software). **Sales:** $74,100,000 (2000). **Emp:** 610. **Officers:** Chris Doggett, General Mgr.; Bob Pugh, Controller.

■ 7147 ■ **Carter-Lee Lumber Company Inc.**
1621 W Washington St.
Indianapolis, IN 46222
Phone: (317)639-5431
Products: Lumber and plywood. **SIC:** 5031 (Lumber, Plywood & Millwork). **Sales:** $32,000,000 (1994). **Emp:** 96. **Officers:** Lawrence N. Carter, President; Norm Duke, Controller.

■ 7148 ■ **Carter Lumber Co.**
601 Talmadge Rd.
Kent, OH 44240
Phone: (330)673-6100
Products: Lumber and building materials. **SIC:** 5031 (Lumber, Plywood & Millwork). **Sales:** $1,060,000,000 (2000). **Emp:** 4,000. **Officers:** Brian Carter, President; Ken Azar, CFO.

■ 7149 ■ **Carter-Waters Corp.**
PO Box 412676
Kansas City, MO 64141
Phone: (816)471-2570 **Fax:** (816)421-2946
Products: Construction materials, including steel and curing compounds. **SICs:** 5039 (Construction Materials Nec); 5031 (Lumber, Plywood & Millwork). **Est:** 1922. **Sales:** $24,000,000 (1999). **Emp:** 100. **Officers:** Jeff Hanes, CEO & President; Kim McDaniels, Marketing Contact, e-mail: kmcdaniels@carter-waters.com.

■ 7150 ■ **Cascade Pacific Lumber Co.**
1975 SW 5th Ave.
Portland, OR 97201
Phone: (503)223-2173 **Fax:** (503)223-4530
Products: Hardwood lumber and millwork; Decorative wood park benches; Playground equipment; Treated poles and pilings; Softwood, plywood, and lumber. **SICs:** 5031 (Lumber, Plywood & Millwork); 5099 (Durable Goods Nec); 5021 (Furniture); 5091 (Sporting & Recreational Goods). **Officers:** S. Kenneth Kirn, President.

■ **7151** ■ **Casco Industries Inc.**
540 W Division St.
South Elgin, IL 60177
Phone: (847)741-9595
Products: Aluminum window products. **SIC:** 5031 (Lumber, Plywood & Millwork). **Sales:** $4,000,000 (2000). **Emp:** 40. **Officers:** J.J. Castoro, Owner; John Schuman, Controller.

■ **7152** ■ **Castillo Ready-Mix Concrete**
304 Rosedale Cir.
Belen, NM 87002
Phone: (505)854-2492
Products: Concrete. **SIC:** 5032 (Brick, Stone & Related Materials).

■ **7153** ■ **Causeway Lumber Co.**
PO Box 21088
Ft. Lauderdale, FL 33335
Phone: (305)763-1224 **Fax:** (305)467-2389
Products: Lumber and building materials. **SIC:** 5031 (Lumber, Plywood & Millwork). **Est:** 1939. **Sales:** $50,000,000 (2000). **Emp:** 295. **Officers:** Michael S. Whiddon, CEO & President; David S. Newcombe, Vice President.

■ **7154** ■ **W.C. Caye and Company Inc.**
PO Box 4508
Atlanta, GA 30302
Phone: (404)688-2177
Products: Construction supplies, including plastic and wire. **SICs:** 5039 (Construction Materials Nec); 5051 (Metals Service Centers & Offices); 5162 (Plastics Materials & Basic Shapes). **Est:** 1946. **Sales:** $25,000,000 (2000). **Emp:** 100. **Officers:** Charles G. Caye, President; J.D. Nelson, Treasurer & Secty.; Charles Byrd, Dir. of Sales.

■ **7155** ■ **CBS Contractors Supply Co.**
3650 Hauck Rd.
Cincinnati, OH 45241
Phone: (513)769-6700
Products: Rainboots, small hydraulics, shovels, gloves, large hydraulics, and chain saws. **SICs:** 5082 (Construction & Mining Machinery); 5039 (Construction Materials Nec). **Est:** 1954. **Sales:** $5,000,000 (2000). **Emp:** 24. **Officers:** Stanley Kidd, President; John P. Gallagher, Vice President.

■ **7156** ■ **Cedarburg Lumber Company Inc.**
PO Box 999
Cedarburg, WI 53012
Phone: (262)377-2345 **Fax:** (262)377-4263
URL: http://www.cedarburglumber.com
Products: Lumber, cabinets, and hardwood. **SIC:** 5031 (Lumber, Plywood & Millwork). **Est:** 1913. **Sales:** $25,000,000 (2000). **Emp:** 120. **Officers:** William Wernecke, President; Greg Heberer, Treasurer; Patricia W. Juranitch, Vice President.

■ **7157** ■ **Cen-Cal Wallboard Supply Co.**
880 S River Rd.
West Sacramento, CA 95691
Phone: (916)372-2320
Products: Dry wall and plaster. **SIC:** 5032 (Brick, Stone & Related Materials). **Sales:** $18,000,000 (2000). **Emp:** 15. **Officers:** Dave Schlachton, Manager.

■ **7158** ■ **Central Door & Hardware**
656 RW Harris
Manton, MI 49663-9775
Phone: (616)824-3041 **Fax:** (616)824-6811
Products: Metal doors and frames; Wood window and door frames; Wood doors, interior and exterior; Windows. **SICs:** 5031 (Lumber, Plywood & Millwork); 5039 (Construction Materials Nec). **Emp:** 2. **Officers:** Janet Triplett.

■ **7159** ■ **Central Indiana Hardware Co.**
PO Box 6097
Fishers, IN 46038-6097
Phone: (317)253-6421 **Fax:** (317)254-2609
Products: Doors; Door hardware. **SICs:** 5072 (Hardware); 5031 (Lumber, Plywood & Millwork). **Est:** 1950. **Sales:** $18,500,000 (2000). **Emp:** 91. **Officers:** Norman L. Bristley, CEO & President; Javaid Majeed, Controller; William Hanley, Dir. of Marketing; James Stawick, Dir. of Systems.

■ **7160** ■ **Central Lumber Sales Inc.**
PO Box 22723
Lincoln, NE 68542-2723
Phone: (402)474-4441 **Fax:** (402)474-0595
Products: Lumber; Building supplies. **SICs:** 5031 (Lumber, Plywood & Millwork); 5033 (Roofing, Siding & Insulation). **Sales:** $8,000,000 (2000). **Emp:** 22. **Officers:** R.W. Welte, President; Barbara L. Welte, CFO.

■ **7161** ■ **Central Valley Builders Supply**
1100 Vintage Ave.
St. Helena, CA 94574
Phone: (707)963-3622 **Fax:** (707)963-8751
Products: Lumber; Hardware. **SICs:** 5031 (Lumber, Plywood & Millwork); 5072 (Hardware). **Sales:** $47,000,000 (2000). **Emp:** 220. **Officers:** Kathie Patterson, CEO; Robert Jessller, CFO.

■ **7162** ■ **Central Wholesale Supply Corp.**
1532 Ingleside Rd.
Norfolk, VA 23502
Phone: (804)855-3131 **Fax:** (804)855-4140
E-mail: cwscorp@erocs.com
Products: High pressure laminates; Cabinet hardware; Plywood; Lumber. **SICs:** 5039 (Construction Materials Nec); 5031 (Lumber, Plywood & Millwork). **Est:** 1958. **Sales:** $13,000,000 (2000). **Emp:** 50. **Officers:** E.L. Dominick Jr. Jr., Owner; Jim Evans, Controller; Steve W. Dominick, President.

■ **7163** ■ **Century Tile and Carpet**
5719 Diversey
Chicago, IL 60639
Phone: (773)622-6800 **Fax:** (773)735-0226
Products: Floorcovering equipment and supplies. **SIC:** 5032 (Brick, Stone & Related Materials). **Sales:** $37,000,000 (2000). **Emp:** 250.

■ **7164** ■ **Ceramic Tile Center**
4388 N Carson St.
Carson City, NV 89706
Phone: (775)883-0833
Products: Ceramic tile. **SIC:** 5032 (Brick, Stone & Related Materials).

■ **7165** ■ **Ceramic Tile International**
11525 Todd St.
Houston, TX 77055-1308
Phone: (713)686-8453 **Fax:** (713)462-2358
Products: Floorcovering equipment and supplies. **SIC:** 5032 (Brick, Stone & Related Materials). **Sales:** $13,000,000 (2000). **Emp:** 50.

■ **7166** ■ **Chadwick-BaRoss Inc.**
160 Warren Ave.
Westbrook, ME 04092
Phone: (207)854-8411
Free: (800)477-4963 **Fax:** (207)854-8237
E-mail: sysmgr@chadwick-baross.com
URL: http://www.chadwick-baross.com
Products: Vehicles for construction, forestry, and municipal uses, including back hoes, excavators, wheel loaders, skidders, feller bunchers, forwarders, and screens. **SIC:** 5082 (Construction & Mining Machinery). **Est:** 1929. **Sales:** $40,000,000 (1999). **Emp:** 117. **Officers:** George A. Corey, President & CEO; Stuart Welch, VP & Treasurer; Gary Thebarge, VP of Supply; Walt Hersey, Vice President; Dave Costanzo, Vice President; Mark Silva, Vice President; Dan Roti, General Mgr.

■ **7167** ■ **Challenger Ltd.**
PO Box 185
Nancy, KY 42544-9326
Phone: (606)636-6900 **Fax:** (606)636-6704
Products: Heavy equipment, including trucks. **SICs:** 5084 (Industrial Machinery & Equipment); 5082 (Construction & Mining Machinery). **Est:** 1975. **Sales:** $52,000,000 (2000). **Emp:** 142. **Officers:** Charles S. Hayes, President.

■ **7168** ■ **Charlotte Hardwood Center**
4250 Golf Acres Dr.
Charlotte, NC 28208
Phone: (704)394-9479 **Fax:** (704)398-2162
URL: http://www.hardwoodgroup.com
Products: Hardwood lumber, plywood, and flooring; Plastic laminate; Cabinet hardware. **SICs:** 5031

(Lumber, Plywood & Millwork); 5162 (Plastics Materials & Basic Shapes). **Est:** 1983. **Emp:** 200. **Officers:** Robert H. Stolz, President.

■ **7169** ■ **Chatfield Lumber Company Inc.**
25 W 3rd St.
Chatfield, MN 55923
Phone: (507)867-3300 **Fax:** (507)867-3319
Products: Lumber. **SIC:** 5031 (Lumber, Plywood & Millwork). **Est:** 1986. **Sales:** $3,000,000 (2000). **Emp:** 9. **Officers:** Andrew Danninger, Owner; Gary Shaw, Owner.

■ **7170** ■ **Christmas Lumber Company Inc.**
101 Roane St., PO Box 3
Harriman, TN 37748
Phone: (615)882-2362 **Fax:** (615)882-1973
Products: Building supplies, including lumber. **SIC:** 5031 (Lumber, Plywood & Millwork). **Est:** 1926. **Sales:** $15,500,000 (2000). **Emp:** 44. **Officers:** John H. Smith, Chairman of the Board.

■ **7171** ■ **Christy Refractories Co. L.L.C.**
4641 McRee Ave.
St. Louis, MO 63110
Phone: (314)773-7500 **Fax:** (314)773-8371
URL: http://www.christyco.com
Products: High temperature insulation. **SIC:** 5033 (Roofing, Siding & Insulation). **Est:** 1922. **Sales:** $17,500,000 (2000). **Emp:** 75. **Officers:** F.R. O'Brien, President; J.R. Biglin, VP & Secty.; Bill Ross, Sales/Marketing Contact, e-mail: wsross@christyco.com; Laura Bamvakais, Customer Service Contact, e-mail: llbamvakais@christyco.com.

■ **7172** ■ **Cimarron Lumber and Supply Co.**
4000 Main St.
Kansas City, MO 64111
Phone: (816)931-8700 **Fax:** (816)531-3344
Products: Building materials, including lumber; Home improvement materials. **SICs:** 5031 (Lumber, Plywood & Millwork); 5039 (Construction Materials Nec). **Emp:** 200. **Officers:** Steve Scott, Controller.

■ **7173** ■ **Cimarron Materials Inc.**
901 S 12th St.
Phoenix, AZ 85034-4124
Phone: (602)252-2525 **Fax:** (602)258-4650
Products: Dry wall; Metal studs; Acoustical ceilings and accessories. **SIC:** 5039 (Construction Materials Nec). **Emp:** 49. **Officers:** Everett Davis.

■ **7174** ■ **Circle Glass Co.**
8801 Fenkell
Detroit, MI 48238-1797
Phone: (313)931-5900
Free: (800)523-2111 **Fax:** (313)931-5776
Products: Glass, including plate, picture and window; Acrylic; Screenwire; Mirrors; Foam board; Glass supplies. **SIC:** 5039 (Construction Materials Nec). **Est:** 1967. **Emp:** 12. **Officers:** Seymour A. Wander, President.

■ **7175** ■ **C.L. Industries Inc.**
PO Box 593704
Orlando, FL 32854-3704
Phone: (407)851-2660
Free: (800)333-2660 **Fax:** (407)240-2743
Products: Specialty concrete items for pool interiors, decks, patios, and the building industry. **SIC:** 5032 (Brick, Stone & Related Materials). **Est:** 1975. **Emp:** 40. **Officers:** Mark A. Ayers, Sales Mgr.; Gordon Jones, Tech. Sales.

■ **7176** ■ **Clark-Schwebel Distribution Corp.**
PO Box 25
Arlington, WA 98223
Phone: (253)435-5501 **Fax:** (253)435-5503
Products: Fiberglass. **SIC:** 5033 (Roofing, Siding & Insulation). **Est:** 1960. **Sales:** $16,000,000 (2000). **Emp:** 80. **Officers:** R. Peterson, President.

■ **7177** ■ **Clay Classics Inc.**
763 Waverly St.
Framingham, MA 01702
Phone: (508)875-0055
Products: Tile. **SIC:** 5032 (Brick, Stone & Related Materials).

■ 7178 ■ **Clay Ingels Company Inc.**
PO Box 2120
Lexington, KY 40594-2120
Phone: (606)252-0836
Products: Bricks. **SICs:** 5032 (Brick, Stone & Related Materials); 5031 (Lumber, Plywood & Millwork). **Est:** 1920. **Sales:** $25,000,000 (2000). **Emp:** 40. **Officers:** W.S. Chapman Jr., President.

■ 7179 ■ **Cleasby Manufacturing Company Inc.**
1414 Bancroft Ave.
San Francisco, CA 94124
Phone: (415)822-6565
Free: (800)253-2729   **Fax:** (415)822-1843
E-mail: info@cleasby.com
URL: http://www.cleasby.com
Products: Roofing equipment; Dump trailers; Fastners (roofing); Safety equipment (personal fall arrest systems); Spray coating equipment. **SIC:** 5033 (Roofing, Siding & Insulation). **Est:** 1949. **Sales:** $4,000,000 (2000). **Emp:** 35. **Officers:** Lesley J. Cleasby Jr., President; John Cleasby, Vice President.

■ 7180 ■ **Clem Lumber Distributing Company Inc.**
16055 NE Waverly Ave.
Alliance, OH 44601
Phone: (216)821-2130   **Fax:** (216)821-6143
Products: Hardwood flooring; Molding; Red cedar shingles and shakes. **SIC:** 5031 (Lumber, Plywood & Millwork). **Est:** 1945. **Sales:** $24,000,000 (2000). **Emp:** 60. **Officers:** Don McAlister, President.

■ 7181 ■ **Clermont Lumber Co.**
105 Water St.
Milford, OH 45150
Phone: (513)831-2226
Products: Lumber. **SIC:** 5031 (Lumber, Plywood & Millwork). **Est:** 1933. **Sales:** $6,000,000 (2000). **Emp:** 38. **Officers:** Brian J. Critchell, President; Jerry L. Robinson, Vice President.

■ 7182 ■ **Cleveland Brothers Equipment Company Inc.**
PO Box 2535
Harrisburg, PA 17105
Phone: (717)564-2121   **Fax:** (717)564-6931
Products: Construction equipment, including bulldozers, tractors, and pulleys. **SIC:** 5082 (Construction & Mining Machinery). **Est:** 1948. **Sales:** $80,000,000 (2000). **Emp:** 285. **Officers:** Jay W. Cleveland, President; M. Ryan, CFO; Marty R. Kohr, Marketing Mgr.

■ 7183 ■ **Cleveland Plywood Co.**
5900 Harvard Ave.
Cleveland, OH 44105
Phone: (216)641-6600   **Fax:** (216)641-5241
Products: Lumber. **SIC:** 5031 (Lumber, Plywood & Millwork). **Est:** 1958. **Sales:** $10,000,000 (2000). **Emp:** 26. **Officers:** Darrell Morris, President; R. Cunningham, Controller; Tom McCombe, Dir. of Marketing.

■ 7184 ■ **Clipper Energy Supply Co.**
2900 Weslayan, Ste. 600
Houston, TX 77027
Phone: (713)965-0006
Free: (800)425-4737   **Fax:** (713)965-0209
E-mail: clipper1@flash.net
Products: Export oil field equipment and supplies; Industrial machinery, equipment, and supplies. **SICs:** 5039 (Construction Materials Nec); 5082 (Construction & Mining Machinery); 5084 (Industrial Machinery & Equipment). **Est:** 1985. **Sales:** $10,000,000 (2000). **Emp:** 16. **Officers:** Jeffrey J. Casey, President, e-mail: jcasey@clipperenergy.com; John Briscoe, Customer Service Contact, e-mail: j_briscoe@clipperenergy.com; Rose Mayfield, Human Resources Contact, e-mail: r_mayfield@clipperenergy.com. **Alternate Name:** Clipper International Trading Co.

■ 7185 ■ **Cloverdale Equipment Co.**
13133 Cloverdale
Oak Park, MI 48237-3272
Phone: (248)399-6600
Free: (800)822-7999   **Fax:** (248)399-7730
E-mail: tmcsc@aol.com
Products: Construction equipment, including cranes. **SIC:** 5082 (Construction & Mining Machinery). **Est:**

1963. **Sales:** $19,000,000 (1999). **Emp:** 50. **Officers:** Thomas A. Moilanen, President; Todd Moilanen, Vice President.

■ 7186 ■ **CMH Flooring Products Inc.**
Hwy. 74 E
Wadesboro, NC 28170
Phone: (704)694-6213
Free: (800)342-8523   **Fax:** (704)694-4806
Products: Floorcovering equipment and supplies. **SIC:** 5032 (Brick, Stone & Related Materials).

■ 7187 ■ **Coastal Equipment Inc.**
4871 Commerce Dr.
Trussville, AL 35173-2810
Phone: (205)849-5786
Products: Cranes. **SIC:** 5082 (Construction & Mining Machinery). **Sales:** $3,000,000 (2000). **Emp:** 12. **Officers:** Ritchie Lajaunte, Operations Mgr.

■ 7188 ■ **Cobb Rock Div.**
21305 SW Koehler Rd.
Beaverton, OR 97007
Phone: (503)649-5661
Products: Aggregate rock. **SIC:** 5032 (Brick, Stone & Related Materials). **Sales:** $12,000,000 (1993). **Emp:** 45.

■ 7189 ■ **Cobb Rock Inc.**
21305 SW Koehler
Beaverton, OR 97007
Phone: (503)649-5661
Products: Crushed rock. **SIC:** 5032 (Brick, Stone & Related Materials). **Est:** 1935. **Sales:** $11,000,000 (2000). **Emp:** 40. **Officers:** Phil Michelson, President; Clint Wilkins, Manager.

■ 7190 ■ **Cofer Brothers Inc.**
2300 Main St.
Tucker, GA 30084
Phone: (404)938-3200   **Fax:** (404)491-7583
Products: Building materials. **SIC:** 5039 (Construction Materials Nec). **Est:** 1919. **Sales:** $22,000,000 (2000). **Emp:** 55. **Officers:** Gene S. Cofer, CEO & President; Mildred Watson, Dir. of Data Processing.

■ 7191 ■ **Cofil Inc.**
PO Box 657
Naples, TX 75568
Phone: (903)897-5467   **Fax:** (903)897-2008
Products: Lumber and millwork; Timber products; Metal. **SICs:** 5031 (Lumber, Plywood & Millwork); 5051 (Metals Service Centers & Offices). **Officers:** C.M. Coker, President.

■ 7192 ■ **Colco Fine Woods and Tools Inc.**
PO Box 820449
Memphis, TN 38182-0449
Phone: (901)452-9663   **Fax:** (901)452-0277
E-mail: colco@colcofinewoods.com
URL: http://www.colcofinewoods.com
Products: Native and exotic hardwood plywood; Particleboard. **SIC:** 5031 (Lumber, Plywood & Millwork). **Est:** 1961. **Sales:** $2,000,000 (2000). **Emp:** 10. **Officers:** W.S. Cockroft, President.

■ 7193 ■ **Cole Hardwood Inc.**
PO Box 568
Logansport, IN 46947
Phone: (219)753-3151
Free: (800)536-3151   **Fax:** (219)753-2525
E-mail: colexx@colehardwood.com
Products: Hardwood. **SIC:** 5031 (Lumber, Plywood & Millwork). **Est:** 1919. **Sales:** $17,000,000 (2000). **Emp:** 70. **Officers:** William Cole, President; John Land, Controller; Dave Bramlage, VP of Marketing.

■ 7194 ■ **Coleman Equipment Inc.**
PO Box 456
Bonner Springs, KS 66012
Phone: (913)422-3040   **Fax:** (913)422-3044
Products: Construction equipment. **SIC:** 5082 (Construction & Mining Machinery). **Est:** 1941. **Sales:** $11,000,000 (2000). **Emp:** 25. **Officers:** Bruce A. Coleman, President; Del R. Coleman, Vice President.

■ 7195 ■ **Coleman Lumber Inc.**
4144 Bellamy 21
Rte. 1, Box 23
Livingston, AL 35470
Phone: (205)652-1132   **Fax:** (205)652-1131
Products: Lumber; Plywood. **SIC:** 5031 (Lumber, Plywood & Millwork). **Est:** 1970. **Sales:** $1,000,000 (2000). **Emp:** 3. **Officers:** Wallace Vaughan, President.

■ 7196 ■ **James Collins**
PO Box 478
Milton, VT 05468-0478
Phone: (802)893-4746
Products: Vinyl siding. **SIC:** 5033 (Roofing, Siding & Insulation). **Officers:** James Collins, Owner.

■ 7197 ■ **Colonial Brick Co.**
12844 Greenfield
Detroit, MI 48227
Phone: (313)272-2160   **Fax:** (313)272-7850
Products: Bricks; Masonry cement; Mason's materials. **SIC:** 5032 (Brick, Stone & Related Materials). **Est:** 1958. **Sales:** $8,000,000 (2000). **Emp:** 20. **Officers:** George Pearson, CEO & Chairman of the Board; Brian Pearson, President.

■ 7198 ■ **Colony Lumber Co.**
1083 Mentor Ave.
Painesville, OH 44077
Phone: (440)352-3351   **Fax:** (440)352-6515
Products: Lumber; Building materials. **SICs:** 5031 (Lumber, Plywood & Millwork); 5039 (Construction Materials Nec). **Est:** 1944. **Sales:** $5,000,000 (2000). **Emp:** 22. **Officers:** Arnold Sukenik, President; Lester Sukenik, Treasurer.

■ 7199 ■ **Comanche Lumber Company Inc.**
2 SW C Ave.
Lawton, OK 73501
Phone: (580)357-8630   **Fax:** (580)357-5402
Products: Lumber. **SIC:** 5031 (Lumber, Plywood & Millwork).

■ 7200 ■ **Compotite Corp.**
355 Glendale Blvd.
Los Angeles, CA 90026
Phone: (213)483-4444
Free: (800)221-1056   **Fax:** (213)483-4445
E-mail: compotite.la@mci2000.com
Products: Shower waterproofing membrane. **SIC:** 5039 (Construction Materials Nec). **Est:** 1938. **Sales:** $2,500,000 (1999). **Emp:** 6. **Officers:** Joan M. Hutchins, President; Elizabeth B. Galang, Treasurer; Patricia Draper, VP of Marketing.

■ 7201 ■ **Comtech**
PO Box 40408
Fayetteville, NC 28309-0408
Phone: (910)864-8787   **Fax:** (910)864-4444
Products: Roof and floor trusses; Lumber. **SICs:** 5031 (Lumber, Plywood & Millwork); 5039 (Construction Materials Nec). **Est:** 1926. **Sales:** $6,000,000 (2000). **Emp:** 65. **Officers:** V.E. Hollinshed Jr., President; Tom Hollinshead, VP, Treasurer & Secty.

■ 7202 ■ **Con-Mat Supply**
PO Box 1383
Glendive, MT 59330-1383
Phone: (406)365-6461
Free: (800)582-8449   **Fax:** (406)365-5150
Products: Roofing, siding, and insulation materials. **SIC:** 5033 (Roofing, Siding & Insulation). **Officers:** Roland Aldinger, Owner.

■ 7203 ■ **Concrete Products and Supply Co. Inc.**
PO Box 1388
Pascagoula, MS 39568
Phone: (228)762-8911   **Fax:** (228)762-4760
Products: Concrete. **SIC:** 5032 (Brick, Stone & Related Materials). **Est:** 1960. **Sales:** $6,700,000 (2000). **Emp:** 24. **Officers:** R. Huston Hollister, President; David P. Bosaige, VP & General Mgr.

■ **7204** ■ **Concrete Supply Co.**
3823 Raleigh St.
Charlotte, NC 28206
Phone: (704)372-2930
Products: Construction materials. **SIC:** 5039
(Construction Materials Nec). **Sales:** $75,000,000
(1999). **Emp:** 350. **Officers:** Raymond B. Ledford Jr.,
President.

■ **7205** ■ **Concrete Supply Corp.**
11700 Cherry Hill Rd.
Silver Spring, MD 20904
Phone: (301)622-2990
Products: Concrete. **SIC:** 5032 (Brick, Stone &
Related Materials). **Sales:** $9,000,000 (2000). **Emp:**
34. **Officers:** Lewis Davenport, President; Orlando
Docal, CFO.

■ **7206** ■ **Condeck Corp.**
3230 Matthew Ave. NE
Albuquerque, NM 87107-1927
Phone: (505)837-1112
Free: (800)338-6701 **Fax:** (505)837-1529
Products: Roofing, siding, and insulation materials,
except wood. **SIC:** 5033 (Roofing, Siding & Insulation).
Officers: Clay Wormington, President.

■ **7207** ■ **Conesco Industries Ltd.**
214 Gates Rd.
Little Ferry, NJ 07643
Phone: (201)641-6500
Free: (800)631-1978 **Fax:** (201)641-6254
E-mail: dest@conesco.com
URL: http://www.conesco.com
Products: Concrete forming equipment. **SIC:** 5082
(Construction & Mining Machinery). **Est:** 1969. **Sales:**
$30,000,000 (2000). **Emp:** 120. **Officers:** Charles J.
Trainor, President; Alan A. Pearson, Treasurer &
Secty.; James H.J. Hughes III, VP of Sales.

■ **7208** ■ **Construction Products of
Washington**
North 3515 Haven
Spokane, WA 99207
Phone: (509)489-0830 **Fax:** (509)489-0832
Products: Construction materials. **SIC:** 5039
(Construction Materials Nec).

■ **7209** ■ **Construction Specialties Inc.**
3 Werner Wy.
Lebanon, NJ 08833
Phone: (908)236-0800 **Fax:** (908)236-0801
Products: Architectural building products, including
louvers, sunscreens, handrails, and expansion joints.
SIC: 5049 (Professional Equipment Nec). **Sales:**
$160,000,000 (2000). **Emp:** 1,100. **Officers:** Ronald F.
Dadd, CEO & President; Edward J. Altieri, VP & CFO.

■ **7210** ■ **Continental Wood Preservers Inc.**
7500 E Davison Ave.
Detroit, MI 48212
Phone: (313)365-4200 **Fax:** (313)365-5039
E-mail: cwpi@mindspring.com
Products: Treated lumber. **SIC:** 5031 (Lumber,
Plywood & Millwork). **Est:** 1927. **Sales:** $10,000,000
(2000). **Emp:** 26. **Officers:** Dave Brandenburg,
President.

■ **7211** ■ **Contractors Machinery Co.**
13200 Northend Ave.
Oak Park, MI 48237
Phone: (248)543-4770
Free: (800)572-7479 **Fax:** (248)543-8582
Products: Heavy equipment, including loaders,
cranes, off-highway trucks, excavators, aggregate
processing equipment, concrete plants, trash
compactors, and street sweepers. **SIC:** 5082
(Construction & Mining Machinery). **Est:** 1933. **Sales:**
$28,000,000 (2000). **Emp:** 54. **Officers:** T. Steven
Stentz, President.

■ **7212** ■ **Convenience Products**
866 Horan Dr.
Fenton, MO 63026-2416
Phone: (636)349-5333
Free: (800)729-8220 **Fax:** (636)349-5335
E-mail: mrkting@convenienceproducts.com
URL: http://www.convenienceproducts.com
Products: Insulation and expanding foam. **SIC:** 5033

(Roofing, Siding & Insulation). **Est:** 1979. **Officers:**
Byron R. Lapin, President; Mary Ellen Mueller, Nat'l.
Sales Mgr.; Jeff Yoder; Dave Orf, Dir of Human
Resources.

■ **7213** ■ **Cook Concrete Products Inc.**
PO Box 720280
Redding, CA 96099
Phone: (530)243-2562 **Fax:** (530)243-6881
Products: Concrete products; Manhole covers;
Electrical boxes. **SICs:** 5032 (Brick, Stone & Related
Materials); 5065 (Electronic Parts & Equipment Nec).
Est: 1956. **Sales:** $1,500,000 (2000). **Emp:** 30.
Officers: Edward Shaw, CEO.

■ **7214** ■ **Cooke Sales and Service Company
Inc.**
PO Box 170
Chillicothe, MO 64601
Phone: (816)646-1166 **Fax:** (816)646-0381
E-mail: csales@greenhills.net
Products: Heavy and industrial construction sales,
parts and service. **SIC:** 5082 (Construction & Mining
Machinery). **Est:** 1943. **Sales:** $11,000,000 (2000).
Emp: 74. **Officers:** Oscar M. Cooke, President.

■ **7215** ■ **Cooley Forest Products**
PO Box 20188
Phoenix, AZ 85036-0188
Phones: (602)276-2402 (602)243-4288
Free: (800)223-5114 **Fax:** (602)276-2864
E-mail: cfp@cooleyforpro.com
URL: http://www.cooleyforpro.com
Products: Lumber products; Specialty millwork. **SIC:**
5031 (Lumber, Plywood & Millwork). **Est:** 1945. **Emp:**
70. **Officers:** Michael D. Cooley. **Alternate Name:**
Cooley Industries, Inc.

■ **7216** ■ **Cooley Industries Inc.**
PO Box 20188
Phoenix, AZ 85036
Phone: (602)243-4288 **Fax:** (602)276-2864
Products: Industrial and construction lumber, plywood,
and millwork. **SIC:** 5031 (Lumber, Plywood & Millwork).
Sales: $40,000,000 (2000). **Emp:** 90. **Officers:** Dean
L. Cooley, CEO & President; Samuel R. Martin, Sr. VP
& CFO.

■ **7217** ■ **Cooling Tower Resources, Inc.**
PO Box 159
Healdsburg, CA 95448
Phone: (707)433-3900 **Fax:** (707)431-8900
URL: http://www.cooltower.com
Products: Redwood lumber; Douglas Fir; Plywood.
SIC: 5031 (Lumber, Plywood & Millwork). **Est:** 1979.
Sales: $2,500,000 (2000). **Emp:** 18. **Officers:** G.
Martin, President; James Bucheister, Finance Officer;
James Betry, Vice President. **Former Name:** Martin
Forest Industries.

■ **7218** ■ **Cooperative Reserve Supply Inc.**
PO Box 39
Belmont, MA 02478
Phone: (617)864-1444 **Fax:** (617)868-6857
Products: Lumber. **SIC:** 5031 (Lumber, Plywood &
Millwork). **Est:** 1951. **Sales:** $25,000,000 (2000). **Emp:**
12. **Officers:** Richard Hosterman, General Mgr.

■ **7219** ■ **Cooperative Supply Inc.**
PO Box 278
Dodge, NE 68633
Phone: (402)693-2261
Products: Lumber; Pre-hung doors and cabinets. **SIC:**
5031 (Lumber, Plywood & Millwork). **Sales:** $7,000,000
(2000). **Emp:** 10. **Officers:** Charles Franzluebbers,
General Mgr.

■ **7220** ■ **Copeland Paving Inc.**
PO Box 608
Grants Pass, OR 97528-0261
Phone: (541)476-4441 **Fax:** (541)479-4881
Products: Asphalt, sand, and gravel. **SIC:** 5032 (Brick,
Stone & Related Materials). **Est:** 1947. **Sales:**
$10,000,000 (2000). **Emp:** 50. **Officers:** Robert
Copeland, President; Steven Ausland, Vice President.
Former Name: Copeland Fuel Inc.

■ **7221** ■ **Cornerstone Group**
2900 Patio Dr.
Houston, TX 77017
Phone: (713)946-9000
Products: Steel building products, including aluminum
sidings for houses, carports, and solariums. **SICs:** 5039
(Construction Materials Nec); 5033 (Roofing, Siding &
Insulation). **Sales:** $93,000,000 (2000). **Emp:** 275.
Officers: Michael E. Christopher, President; Ted
Thomas, Treasurer.

■ **7222** ■ **Corning-Donohue Inc.**
1407 Marshall Ave.
St. Paul, MN 55104
Phone: (612)646-8000 **Fax:** (612)646-5305
Products: Brick; Tile; Masonry supplies. **SICs:** 5032
(Brick, Stone & Related Materials); 5039 (Construction
Materials Nec). **Est:** 1916. **Sales:** $10,000,000 (2000).
Emp: 37. **Officers:** John H. Donohue IV, President;
Thomas Bartholomew, Controller.

■ **7223** ■ **Corriveau-Routhier, Inc.**
71 Broadway
Dover, NH 03820
Phone: (603)742-1901
Products: Ceramic wall and floor tile. **SIC:** 5032 (Brick,
Stone & Related Materials).

■ **7224** ■ **Corriveau-Routhier Inc.**
266 Clay St.
Manchester, NH 03103
Phone: (603)627-3805 **Fax:** (603)622-6798
Products: Ceramic tile, brick, stone, granite and
masonry supplies. **SIC:** 5032 (Brick, Stone & Related
Materials). **Sales:** $34,000,000 (2000). **Emp:** 75.
Officers: David J. Corriveau, President.

■ **7225** ■ **H.A. Cover and Son Wholesale
Lumber Inc.**
798 Front St.
Thayer, MO 65791
Phone: (417)264-7232
Free: (800)426-2490 **Fax:** (417)264-7234
E-mail: cover@wpcs.net
URL: http://www.CoverBuildingSupplies.com
Products: Construction materials, including lumber,
paint, and hardware. **SICs:** 5031 (Lumber, Plywood &
Millwork); 5072 (Hardware); 5198 (Paints, Varnishes &
Supplies). **Est:** 1949. **Sales:** $9,000,000 (2000). **Emp:**
25. **Officers:** Dan Cover, President; Judy Irby,
Bookkeeper; Doil Hickinbotham, Manager.

■ **7226** ■ **Cowin Equipment Company Inc.**
PO Box 10624
Birmingham, AL 35202
Phone: (205)841-6666 **Fax:** (205)849-0853
Products: Construction equipment. **SIC:** 5082
(Construction & Mining Machinery). **Est:** 1940. **Sales:**
$40,000,000 (2000). **Emp:** 177. **Officers:** Peter G.
Cowin, Chairman of the Board; D. Searcy, VP of
Finance; James P. Cowin, Dir. of Marketing & Sales.

■ **7227** ■ **Cox Industries, Inc.**
PO Drawer 1124
Orangeburg, SC 29116
Phone: (803)534-7467 **Fax:** (803)534-6328
Products: Pessure treated lumber and wood products.
SIC: 5031 (Lumber, Plywood & Millwork). **Est:** 1954.
Sales: $90,000,000 (2000). **Emp:** 225. **Officers:** W.B.
Cox Jr., President; Carl F. Mutch, CFO; Bruce R.
Palmer, VP of Marketing & Sales. **Former Name:** Cox
Wood Preserving Co.

■ **7228** ■ **Coyote Loader Sales Inc.**
6721 Chittenden Rd.
Hudson, OH 44236-4423
Phone: (330)650-5101 **Fax:** (330)650-5105
E-mail: info@coyoteloaders.com
URL: http://www.coyoteloaders.com
Products: Loaders and parts; Mini excavators and
dumpers. **SIC:** 5082 (Construction & Mining
Machinery). **Est:** 1984. **Sales:** $2,000,000 (2000).
Emp: 8. **Officers:** Steve Kabay, President.

■ **7229** ■ **Craftwood Lumber Co.**
1590 Old Deerfield Rd.
Highland Park, IL 60035
Phone: (847)831-2800 **Fax:** (847)831-2805
Products: Lumber and plywood. **SIC:** 5031 (Lumber,

Plywood & Millwork). **Est:** 1956. **Sales:** $5,000,000 (2000). **Emp:** 40. **Officers:** David Brunjes, President; Cynthia Brunjes, CFO.

■ **7230** ■ **Crane Co.**
100 1st Stamford Pl.
Stamford, CT 06902
Phone: (203)363-7300 **Fax:** (203)363-7295
Products: Doors, windows, moldings, and related building products. **SIC:** 5031 (Lumber, Plywood & Millwork). **Sales:** $2,036,800,000 (2000). **Emp:** 11,000. **Officers:** Robert S. Evans, CEO & Chairman of the Board; David S. Smith, VP & CFO.

■ **7231** ■ **E.F. Craven Co.**
PO Box 20807
Greensboro, NC 27420
Phone: (919)292-6921 **Fax:** (919)294-0599
Products: Heavy construction equipment. **SIC:** 5082 (Construction & Mining Machinery). **Est:** 1900. **Sales:** $25,000,000 (2000). **Emp:** 95. **Officers:** C.C. Carson, CEO & Chairman of the Board; W.D. Smith, Controller; Spencer Coble, Sr. VP of Operations; Judy Crook, Dir. of Data Processing; Thomas M. Reynolds, Vice President.

■ **7232** ■ **Crosslin Supply Company Inc.**
140 N Main St.
Eagleville, TN 37060
Phone: (615)274-6237 **Fax:** (615)274-3364
Products: Lumber; Doors; Roofing; Windows; Wallboard; Hardware; Tools; Insulation. **SIC:** 5031 (Lumber, Plywood & Millwork). **Est:** 1933. **Sales:** $33,000,000 (1999). **Emp:** 120. **Officers:** F.E. Crosslin Jr., President.

■ **7233** ■ **F.T. Crowe and Co.**
21229 84th Ave.
Kent, WA 98032
Phone: (253)872-9696 **Fax:** (253)872-3458
Products: Cranes and hoists. **SICs:** 5082 (Construction & Mining Machinery); 5084 (Industrial Machinery & Equipment). **Est:** 1907. **Sales:** $3,000,000 (2000). **Emp:** 22. **Officers:** Robert H. Grass, President; James Nazzal, Dir. of Marketing & Sales; Lois E. Almeda, Dir. of Data Processing; Mary Jo Landdeck, Dir of Human Resources.

■ **7234** ■ **Crystal Tile**
2011 Beech Ln.
Bensalem, PA 19020
Phone: (215)245-6739
Products: Tile. **SIC:** 5032 (Brick, Stone & Related Materials).

■ **7235** ■ **H.W. Culp Lumber Co.**
PO Box 235
New London, NC 28127
Phone: (704)463-7311 **Fax:** (704)463-4100
E-mail: culplbrsales@ctc.com
Products: Lumber. **SIC:** 5031 (Lumber, Plywood & Millwork). **Est:** 1929. **Sales:** $25,000,000 (2000). **Emp:** 75. **Officers:** Henry W. Culp Jr., President; Alena Burleson, Accounting Manager; Dan Smith, Sales Mgr.

■ **7236** ■ **Cummings, McGowan and West Inc.**
8668 Olive Blvd.
St. Louis, MO 63132
Phone: (314)993-1336
Free: (800)283-1336 **Fax:** (314)993-1467
E-mail: info@cmw-equip.com
URL: http://www.cmw-equip.com
Products: Concrete; Asphalt; Aggregate equipment. **SICs:** 5082 (Construction & Mining Machinery); 5032 (Brick, Stone & Related Materials). **Est:** 1956. **Sales:** $8,000,000 (1999). **Emp:** 20. **Officers:** Larry Glynn, President; Sherry Morse, Controller.

■ **7237** ■ **Curran Contracting Co.**
7502 S Main St.
Crystal Lake, IL 60014
Phone: (815)455-5100 **Fax:** (815)455-7894
Products: Asphalt. **SIC:** 5032 (Brick, Stone & Related Materials). **Est:** 1930. **Sales:** $75,000,000 (2000). **Emp:** 75. **Officers:** J.H. Curran, President; Jack Krejca, Controller; Mike Curran, Dir. of Systems.

■ **7238** ■ **Custom Bilt Cabinet and Supply Inc.**
PO Drawer 8969
Shreveport, LA 71148-8969
Phone: (318)865-1412
Products: Building supplies; Custom cabinets. **SIC:** 5031 (Lumber, Plywood & Millwork). **Est:** 1954. **Sales:** $25,000,000 (2000). **Emp:** 100. **Officers:** W.F. Lea, President; W.W. McCook, CFO.

■ **7239** ■ **CustomCraft**
40 Rte. 23
Riverdale, NJ 07457
Phone: (973)839-4286 **Fax:** (973)839-0523
Products: Kitchen and bath remodeling cabinetry. **SIC:** 5031 (Lumber, Plywood & Millwork).

■ **7240** ■ **D and B Tile Distributors**
14200 NW 4th St.
Sunrise, FL 33325
Phone: (954)846-2660
Free: (800)749-6280 **Fax:** (954)845-1112
Products: Floorcovering equipment and supplies. **SIC:** 5032 (Brick, Stone & Related Materials). **Sales:** $22,000,000 (2000). **Emp:** 116.

■ **7241** ■ **D & D Specialties Millwork**
3535 Princeton Dr. NE
Albuquerque, NM 87107
Phone: (505)888-4880
Products: Paneling and caulking. **SICs:** 5031 (Lumber, Plywood & Millwork); 5198 (Paints, Varnishes & Supplies).

■ **7242** ■ **D-J, Inc.**
PO Box 5240
Manchester, NH 03108-5240
Phone: (603)647-1301 **Fax:** (603)647-5302
Products: Wood window and door frames; Metal doors and frames; Window frames. **SIC:** 5031 (Lumber, Plywood & Millwork).

■ **7243** ■ **D & M Plywood, Inc.**
340 Seneca St.
Buffalo, NY 14204
Phone: (716)856-5656 **Fax:** (716)856-8809
Products: Softwood plywood specialities; Wood paneling. **SIC:** 5031 (Lumber, Plywood & Millwork). **Est:** 1968. **Officers:** George Driscoll Jr., President; Paul E. Maher, VP & Secty.

■ **7244** ■ **D.A. Distributors Inc.**
1128 Eureka
Wyandotte, MI 48192
Phone: (734)285-3350 **Fax:** (734)285-3371
Products: Wood, vinyl, and aluminum windows; Bath liners and wall surrounds. **SICs:** 5031 (Lumber, Plywood & Millwork); 5039 (Construction Materials Nec). **Est:** 1980. **Sales:** $6,000,000 (2000). **Emp:** 35. **Officers:** David S. Adamczyk, Dir. of Sales.

■ **7245** ■ **William E. Dailey Inc.**
PO Box 51
Shaftsbury, VT 05262
Phone: (802)442-9923 **Fax:** (802)442-9927
Products: Precast concrete, sand, and gravel. **SIC:** 5032 (Brick, Stone & Related Materials). **Est:** 1927. **Sales:** $7,000,000 (2000). **Emp:** 85. **Officers:** W. Dailey III, President; Jerry Keneally, Controller.

■ **7246** ■ **Dairyman's Supply Co.**
PO Box 528
Mayfield, KY 42066
Phone: (502)247-5642 **Fax:** (502)247-0327
Products: Building materials. **SIC:** 5039 (Construction Materials Nec). **Sales:** $94,000,000 (1993). **Emp:** 89. **Officers:** John E. Cook, President; Curtis Boyd, Treasurer & Secty.

■ **7247** ■ **Dal CAM Oil Co. Inc.**
PO Box 1761
Rapid City, SD 57709-1761
Phone: (605)341-5934
Free: (800)365-5934 **Fax:** (605)341-4241
Products: Roofing, siding, and insulation; Asphalt felts and coating. **SIC:** 5033 (Roofing, Siding & Insulation). **Officers:** Darrell Lich, President.

■ **7248** ■ **Daltile**
350 Dunksferry Rd.
Bensalem, PA 19020
Phone: (215)441-4977
Products: Tile. **SIC:** 5032 (Brick, Stone & Related Materials).

■ **7249** ■ **Damon Insulation Co.**
PO Box 1212
Auburn, ME 04211-1212
Phone: (207)783-4240
Products: Roofing; Siding; Thermal insulation and insulation materials. **SIC:** 5033 (Roofing, Siding & Insulation). **Officers:** Carl Damon, President.

■ **7250** ■ **Darr Equipment Company Inc.**
PO Box 540788
Dallas, TX 75354
Phone: (214)721-2000 **Fax:** (214)438-2481
Products: Heavy equipment, including forklifts. **SICs:** 5084 (Industrial Machinery & Equipment); 5082 (Construction & Mining Machinery). **Est:** 1954. **Sales:** $310,000,000 (2000). **Emp:** 1,000. **Officers:** Randall R. Engstrom, CEO; George Spencer, CFO; T.J. Blomberg, VP of Sales; Ric Scripps, Dir. of Information Systems.

■ **7251** ■ **Davidson Louisiana Inc.**
PO Box 1119
Lake Charles, LA 70602
Phone: (318)439-8393 **Fax:** (318)436-3089
Products: Windows; Wood doors, interior and exterior. **SICs:** 5031 (Lumber, Plywood & Millwork); 5039 (Construction Materials Nec). **Est:** 1919. **Sales:** $15,000,000 (2000). **Emp:** 100. **Officers:** Simon D. Davidson, Chairman of the Board.

■ **7252** ■ **Howard A. Davidson Lumber Co.**
PO Box 27066
Detroit, MI 48227
Phone: (313)834-6770 **Fax:** (313)834-0735
Products: Lumber. **SIC:** 5031 (Lumber, Plywood & Millwork). **Est:** 1923. **Sales:** $18,000,000 (2000). **Emp:** 50. **Officers:** J.H. Davidson, President.

■ **7253** ■ **Dayton Door Sales Inc.**
1112 Springfield St.
Dayton, OH 45403
Phone: (937)253-9181 **Fax:** (937)253-9222
Products: Garage doors. **SIC:** 5031 (Lumber, Plywood & Millwork). **Est:** 1958. **Sales:** $28,000,000 (2000). **Emp:** 100. **Officers:** Ken Monnin, President; Ralph Griggs, Controller; Ed Kemper, VP of Sales.

■ **7254** ■ **Dealers Supply Co.**
110 SE Washington St.
Portland, OR 97214
Phone: (503)236-1195 **Fax:** (503)236-4314
Products: Roofing materials. **SIC:** 5033 (Roofing, Siding & Insulation). **Est:** 1916. **Sales:** $15,000,000 (2000). **Emp:** 30. **Officers:** P. Francis, President; Diana Mack, Treasurer.

■ **7255** ■ **Dealers Supply Co.**
110 SE Washington St.
Portland, OR 97214
Phone: (503)236-1195 **Fax:** (503)236-4314
Products: Construction materials and machinery. **SIC:** 5033 (Roofing, Siding & Insulation). **Sales:** $15,000,000 (2000). **Emp:** 30.

■ **7256** ■ **Dealers Supply and Lumber Inc.**
PO Box 5025, Sta. B
Greenville, SC 29606
Phone: (803)242-6571 **Fax:** (803)242-0433
Products: Lumber and lumber supplies. **SIC:** 5031 (Lumber, Plywood & Millwork). **Est:** 1943. **Sales:** $16,000,000 (2000). **Emp:** 50. **Officers:** Knox Wherry, President; Kenny Edlin, CFO.

■ **7257** ■ **Dean's Materials Inc.**
PO Box 1547
Fresno, CA 93716
Phone: (209)268-9301
Free: (800)365-1849 **Fax:** (209)268-9389
Products: Residential steel framing. **SIC:** 5051 (Metals Service Centers & Offices). **Est:** 1967. **Sales:** $4,800,000 (2000). **Emp:** 20. **Officers:** Greg Shore,

President & CFO. **Doing Business As:** Construction Material Supplies.

■ **7258** ■ **Delaware Brick Co.**
1114 Centerville Rd.
Wilmington, DE 19804
Phone: (302)994-0949 **Fax:** (302)994-6359
Products: Cement, bricks, and sand. **SIC:** 5032 (Brick, Stone & Related Materials). **Est:** 1946. **Sales:** $4,000,000 (2000). **Emp:** 30. **Officers:** Eugene Callaghan, President.

■ **7259** ■ **Devine Brothers Inc.**
PO Box 189
Norwalk, CT 06852
Phone: (203)866-4421
Products: Concrete; Fuel oil. **SICs:** 5032 (Brick, Stone & Related Materials); 5172 (Petroleum Products Nec). **Est:** 1918. **Sales:** $4,000,000 (2000). **Emp:** 30. **Officers:** Maurice E. Devine, President & Treasurer.

■ **7260** ■ **Devlin Lumber and Supply Corp.**
PO Box 1306
Rockville, MD 20849
Phone: (301)881-1000 **Fax:** (301)468-0628
Products: Building supplies, including lumber. **SICs:** 5031 (Lumber, Plywood & Millwork); 5039 (Construction Materials Nec); 5072 (Hardware). **Sales:** $6,000,000 (2000). **Emp:** 99. **Officers:** Jonathan S. England.

■ **7261** ■ **Diamond Hill Plywood Co.**
600 E Broad St.
Darlington, SC 29532
Phone: (843)393-2803
Free: (800)737-7125 **Fax:** (843)393-2602
URL: http://www.dhpl995.com
Products: Plywood; Hardware; Drawer slides; Siding; Insulation. **SICs:** 5031 (Lumber, Plywood & Millwork); 5072 (Hardware). **Est:** 1945. **Sales:** $225,000,000 (2000). **Emp:** 245. **Officers:** John Ramsey, President; Kennedy Breeden, Treasurer & Secty.; Geary Sharber, VP of Marketing.

■ **7262** ■ **Diamond Hill Plywood Co.**
PO Box 3296
Jacksonville, FL 32206
Phone: (904)355-3592 **Fax:** (904)355-9228
Products: Building materials, including plywood. **SIC:** 5031 (Lumber, Plywood & Millwork).

■ **7263** ■ **D.W. Dickey and Son Inc.**
7896 Dickey Dr.
Lisbon, OH 44432
Phone: (216)424-1441 **Fax:** (216)424-1481
Products: Ready-mix concrete. **SIC:** 5032 (Brick, Stone & Related Materials). **Est:** 1948. **Sales:** $250,000,000 (2000). **Emp:** 180. **Officers:** G. Allen Dickey, President; Gary L. Neville, VP & Controller; Roger Kelch, Vice President; Steve Smith, Dir. of Data Processing.

■ **7264** ■ **Diener Brick Co.**
PO Box 130
Collingswood, NJ 08108
Phone: (856)858-2000 **Fax:** (856)858-6969
Products: Bricks; Glazed block; Mortar. **SIC:** 5032 (Brick, Stone & Related Materials). **Est:** 1933. **Sales:** $12,000,000 (2000). **Emp:** 12. **Officers:** Kevin Rutherford, President; Ed Makel, Controller.

■ **7265** ■ **Diesel Machinery Inc.**
4301 N Cliff Ave.
Sioux Falls, SD 57104
Phone: (605)336-0411
Free: (800)456-4005 **Fax:** (605)336-9503
E-mail: dmisf@dieselmachinery.com
URL: http://www.dieselmachinery.com
Products: Construction equipment. **SIC:** 5082 (Construction & Mining Machinery). **Est:** 1982. **Sales:** $29,000,000 (2000). **Emp:** 48. **Officers:** Pat Healy, President.

■ **7266** ■ **Diomede Enterprises, Inc.**
12790 Old Seward Hwy., Ste. B
Anchorage, AK 99515
Phone: (907)345-0043 **Fax:** (907)345-0247
Products: Metal roofing products; Prefabricated

building supplies. **SICs:** 5033 (Roofing, Siding & Insulation); 5039 (Construction Materials Nec).

■ **7267** ■ **Direct Distributors**
1933 Northern Star Dr.
Traverse City, MI 49686
Phone: (616)929-7031
Products: Ceiling materials. **SIC:** 5032 (Brick, Stone & Related Materials).

■ **7268** ■ **Discount Building Materials**
18 Old Volcano Rd.
PO Box 1539
Keaau, HI 96749
Phone: (808)966-7402 **Fax:** (808)966-8464
Products: Building materials, including windows, doors, lumber, and hardware. **SICs:** 5031 (Lumber, Plywood & Millwork); 5039 (Construction Materials Nec); 5072 (Hardware).

■ **7269** ■ **Ditch Witch of Illinois Inc.**
124 N Schmale Rd.
Carol Stream, IL 60188
Phone: (630)665-5600
Free: (800)243-1328 **Fax:** (630)665-6484
E-mail: dwimail@ditchwitchlwi.com
URL: http://www.ditchwitchlwi.com
Products: Underground construction equipment. **SIC:** 5082 (Construction & Mining Machinery). **Est:** 1970. **Sales:** $5,000,000 (1999). **Emp:** 25. **Officers:** Earl K. Harbaugh, President.

■ **7270** ■ **Ditch Witch Sales Inc.**
PO Box 429
Sullivan, MO 63080
Phone: (573)468-8012 **Fax:** (573)468-8016
Products: Ditch and trench digging machines. **SIC:** 5082 (Construction & Mining Machinery). **Est:** 1958. **Sales:** $10,000,000 (2000). **Emp:** 48. **Officers:** Grant Medlin, President.

■ **7271** ■ **Ditch Witch Trencher Incorporated of Florida**
PO Box 490667
Leesburg, FL 34749-0667
Phone: (904)787-7607 **Fax:** (904)787-7905
Products: Trenchers. **SIC:** 5082 (Construction & Mining Machinery). **Est:** 1964. **Sales:** $11,000,000 (2000). **Emp:** 60. **Officers:** Judy T. Bjorn, President.

■ **7272** ■ **Dixie Building Supplies Co.**
PO Box 31601
Tampa, FL 33631
Phone: (813)871-4811
Products: Building products. **SICs:** 5031 (Lumber, Plywood & Millwork); 5033 (Roofing, Siding & Insulation). **Est:** 1958. **Sales:** $10,000,000 (2000). **Emp:** 8. **Officers:** Robert W. Michael, President & COO; Kendall Baker, Treasurer.

■ **7273** ■ **Dixieline Lumber Co.**
3250 Sports Arena Blvd.
San Diego, CA 92110
Phone: (619)224-4120 **Fax:** (619)225-8192
URL: http://www.dixieline.com
Products: Lumber; Hardware. **SICs:** 5031 (Lumber, Plywood & Millwork); 5072 (Hardware). **Est:** 1913. **Sales:** $200,000,000 (1999). **Emp:** 800. **Officers:** William S. Cowling II, President; Hamid Daudani, CFO & Secty.; Bill Shadden, Dir. of Merchandising; Steve Solomon, Dir of Human Resources.

■ **7274** ■ **Dixon Lumber Company Inc.**
PO Box 907
Galax, VA 24333
Phone: (703)236-9963 **Fax:** (703)236-9490
Products: Lumber. **SIC:** 5031 (Lumber, Plywood & Millwork). **Sales:** $17,000,000 (2000). **Emp:** 350. **Officers:** Latham Wlliams, President; Donna Elliott, Treasurer & Secty.

■ **7275** ■ **Do It Best Corp.**
PO Box 868
Ft. Wayne, IN 46801
Phone: (219)748-5300 **Fax:** (219)493-1245
E-mail: mail@doitbest.com
Products: Hardware, including tools; Gifts; Appliances; Sporting goods; Automotive supplies; Office supplies; Lawn and garden supplies; Housewares; Building

supplies, including lumber, doors, windows, and adhesive. **SICs:** 5063 (Electrical Apparatus & Equipment); 5031 (Lumber, Plywood & Millwork); 5072 (Hardware); 5013 (Motor Vehicle Supplies & New Parts). **Est:** 1945. **Sales:** $2,450,000,000 (2000). **Emp:** 1,400. **Officers:** Michael McClelland, President; Dave Dietz, VP of Finance; Kay Williams, VP of I.T.; Nancy Harris, Dir of Human Resources. **Former Name:** Hardware Wholesalers Inc.

■ **7276** ■ **Doctor Ike's Home Center Inc.**
4200 Interstate 35 N
Laredo, TX 78040
Phone: (956)723-8266 **Fax:** (956)721-7316
Products: Lumber. **SIC:** 5031 (Lumber, Plywood & Millwork). **Sales:** $18,000,000 (2000). **Emp:** 125. **Officers:** Isaac Epstein, President; Larry Plotkin, Vice President.

■ **7277** ■ **Dodson Wholesale Lumber Company Inc.**
PO Box 1851
Roswell, NM 88201
Phone: (505)622-3278
Free: (800)545-7850 **Fax:** (505)624-1138
URL: http://www.dodsonlumber.com
Products: Lumber. **SIC:** 5031 (Lumber, Plywood & Millwork). **Est:** 1972. **Sales:** $13,000,000 (2000). **Emp:** 14. **Officers:** R.A. Dodson, President.

■ **7278** ■ **Dom-Ex Inc.**
109 Grant St.
PO Box 877
Hibbing, MN 55746
Phone: (218)262-6116 **Fax:** (218)263-8611
E-mail: info@dom-ex.com
URL: http://www.dom-ex.com
Products: Heavy, off-highway, mobile equipment and parts. **SIC:** 5082 (Construction & Mining Machinery). **Est:** 1982. **Sales:** $35,000,000 (2000). **Emp:** 55. **Officers:** David Ellefson, President; Daniel Motter, Vice President; Dana Ellefson, e-mail: danae@dom-ex.com; Tom Mantini, e-mail: tomm@dom-ex.com.

■ **7279** ■ **Donnybrook Building Supply Inc.**
PO Box 60509
Fairbanks, AK 99706
Phone: (907)479-2202 **Fax:** (907)479-3067
Products: Kitchen and bath cabinets; Countertops; Vanity tops; Windows; Doors. **SIC:** 5039 (Construction Materials Nec). **Est:** 1974. **Sales:** $1,000,000 (1999). **Emp:** 4. **Officers:** Lewis Bratcher, President.

■ **7280** ■ **Door Engineering Corp.**
PO Box 2378
Norfolk, VA 23501
Phone: (757)622-5355 **Fax:** (757)640-0312
E-mail: dooreng@aol.com
Products: Doors. **SIC:** 5031 (Lumber, Plywood & Millwork). **Est:** 1941. **Sales:** $8,000,000 (2000). **Officers:** W. Gordon Wilder Jr., CEO & President; Richard Clay, Sec. & Treas.

■ **7281** ■ **Doortown Inc.**
2200 Lauder Rd.
Houston, TX 77039-3112
Phone: (281)442-4200
Free: (800)745-3667 **Fax:** (281)442-2145
Products: Doors, including metal and wood; Frames, including metal and wood; Wood moldings. **SIC:** 5031 (Lumber, Plywood & Millwork). **Est:** 1965. **Sales:** $11,000,000 (2000). **Emp:** 56. **Officers:** Fred Thumann, President; Steve Thumann, Vice President, e-mail: sthumann@aol.com.

■ **7282** ■ **Double T Holding Co.**
4421 NE Columbia Blvd.
Portland, OR 97218
Phone: (503)288-6411
Products: Construction and logging equipment. **SIC:** 5082 (Construction & Mining Machinery). **Sales:** $90,000,000 (1994). **Emp:** 350. **Officers:** E.H. Halton Jr., President; Mark Fahey, CFO.

■ 7283 ■ Double-T Manufacturing Corp.
PO Box 1371
27139 CR-6
Elkhart, IN 46515
Phone: (219)262-1340 **Fax:** (219)262-2066
URL: http://www.double-t-usa.com
Products: Kitchen and bathroom countertops;
Cabinets. **SICs:** 5031 (Lumber, Plywood & Millwork);
5074 (Plumbing & Hydronic Heating Supplies). **Est:**
1974. **Sales:** $2,000,000 (1999). **Emp:** 26. **Officers:**
Gary E. Taska, Chairman and Co-owner; Howard
Carpenter, President & CEO; Dena Rozzi, Sales Mgr.

■ 7284 ■ Dougherty Hanna Resources Co.
6000 Harvard Ave.
Cleveland, OH 44105
Phone: (216)271-2400 **Fax:** (216)271-2405
Products: Lumber; Plywood; Plastic laminate; Solid
surface material; Particle board. **SICs:** 5031 (Lumber,
Plywood & Millwork); 5039 (Construction Materials
Nec). **Est:** 1982. **Sales:** $68,000,000 (2000). **Emp:**
130. **Officers:** Marcus Hanna, President; Ron
Cunningham, Controller; Donald R. Beun, Exec. VP.

■ 7285 ■ Dougherty Lumber Co.
6000 Harvard Ave.
Cleveland, OH 44105
Phone: (216)271-1200
Products: Lumber and building supplies. **SICs:** 5031
(Lumber, Plywood & Millwork); 5072 (Hardware).
Sales: $20,600,000 (2000). **Emp:** 45. **Officers:**
Marcus Hanna, President; Ron Cunningham,
Controller.

■ 7286 ■ J.H. Dowling Inc.
705 W Madison St.
PO Box 308
Tallahassee, FL 32302-0308
Phone: (850)222-2616 **Fax:** (850)222-2617
Products: Building materials, including lumber,
insulation, and hardware; Concrete and concrete
forming accessories; Waterproofing materials; Road
and bridge materials; Erosion control products; Rebar
fabrication. **SICs:** 5032 (Brick, Stone & Related
Materials); 5039 (Construction Materials Nec); 5033
(Roofing, Siding & Insulation); 5072 (Hardware); 5032
(Brick, Stone & Related Materials). **Est:** 1946. **Sales:**
$4,000,000 (2000). **Emp:** 19. **Officers:** J.H. Dowling
Jr., CEO; James A. Marlow, Controller; Rob Stefanick,
Sales Mgr.; J.H. Dowling III, Vice President.

■ 7287 ■ Doyle Equipment Co.
PO Box 1840
Cranberry Township, PA 16066-0840
Phone: (412)322-4500
Products: Heavy moving equipment. **SICs:** 5082
(Construction & Mining Machinery); 5084 (Industrial
Machinery & Equipment). **Sales:** $35,000,000 (2000).
Emp: 50. **Officers:** David M. Smail, President; Kathy
Winkelboss, Controller.

■ 7288 ■ DuBell Lumber Co.
Rte. 70 E
Medford, NJ 08055
Phone: (609)654-4143 **Fax:** (609)953-1783
Products: Lumber. **SIC:** 5031 (Lumber, Plywood &
Millwork). **Est:** 1922. **Sales:** $9,000,000 (2000). **Emp:**
90. **Officers:** A. Dimedio, President.

■ 7289 ■ Dunaway Supply Co.
211 Cherokee St.
Longview, TX 75604
Phone: (903)759-4481 **Fax:** (903)759-8730
Products: Millwork moldings; Pre-hung wood and
metal insulated doors; Windows; Hardware. **SICs:**
5031 (Lumber, Plywood & Millwork); 5039
(Construction Materials Nec); 5072 (Hardware). **Est:**
1945. **Sales:** $10,000,000 (1999). **Emp:** 50. **Officers:**
J. Dunaway, CEO; Charles Clark, VP & General Mgr.

■ 7290 ■ Dura Sales Inc.
RD 2, Box 81B
Tarentum, PA 15084
Phone: (724)224-7700
Products: Concrete blocks. **SIC:** 5032 (Brick, Stone &
Related Materials).

■ 7291 ■ Durand Equipment and Manufacturing Co.
5110 N Oak
Durand, MI 48429
Phones: (517)288-2626 800-338-9095
Free: (800)545-6342 **Fax:** (517)288-2128
Products: Masonry cement; Aluminum. **SIC:** 5032
(Brick, Stone & Related Materials). **Sales:** $4,000,000
(2000). **Emp:** 21. **Officers:** John Easton, President;
Harry Harden, Treasurer & Secty.

■ 7292 ■ Dutchess Quarry and Supply Company Inc.
PO Box 651
Pleasant Valley, NY 12569
Phone: (914)635-8151
Products: Stone; Concrete; Blacktop. **SICs:** 5039
(Construction Materials Nec); 5032 (Brick, Stone &
Related Materials). **Sales:** $15,000,000 (2000). **Emp:**
100. **Officers:** Joseph C. Arborio, President &
Treasurer.

■ 7293 ■ DW Distribution
PO Box 271023
Dallas, TX 75227
Phone: (214)381-2200
Free: (800)394-1992 **Fax:** (214)388-5079
Products: Building supplies, including moldings, doors,
and roofing. **SICs:** 5033 (Roofing, Siding & Insulation);
5031 (Lumber, Plywood & Millwork); 5039
(Construction Materials Nec). **Est:** 1955. **Sales:**
$64,000,000 (2000). **Emp:** 100. **Officers:** Byron Potter,
President; Mark Sattler, VP of Finance; Tim Dunlop,
VPGM & Building Maint.; Betty Evans, VP of Marketing;
Robert Harris, VP of Sales. **Former Name:** Dallas
Wholesale Builders Supply Inc.

■ 7294 ■ Dynamic Distributors
9621 S Dixie Hwy.
Miami, FL 33156
Phone: (305)665-5313 **Fax:** (305)666-3315
Products: Fireplaces; Barbecues; Kitchen range
hoods. **SICs:** 5074 (Plumbing & Hydronic Heating
Supplies); 5039 (Construction Materials Nec). **Est:**
1954. **Emp:** 30. **Officers:** David Zisman, President.

■ 7295 ■ Dynamic International Company Inc.
PO Box 640721
Kenner, LA 70064
Phone: (504)466-4703 **Fax:** (504)467-4752
E-mail: Dyngu51@aol.com
Products: Cement; Refined sugar. **SICs:** 5032 (Brick,
Stone & Related Materials); 5149 (Groceries & Related
Products Nec). **Est:** 1985. **Sales:** $1,450,000 (2000).
Emp: 5. **Officers:** Henry R. Guzman, Mgr. Dir.; Carlos
E. Guzman, President, e-mail: Cocoguzman@aol.com.

■ 7296 ■ Eagle Supply Inc.
PO Box 75305
Tampa, FL 33675
Phone: (813)248-4918 **Fax:** (813)247-4232
Products: Roofing supplies, including shingles. **SIC:**
5033 (Roofing, Siding & Insulation). **Est:** 1908. **Sales:**
$65,000,000 (2000). **Emp:** 165. **Officers:** Thomas
Havnes, President; Steven Skrotsky, Vice President;
Mark S. Gee, Dir. of Marketing; Ralph Anthony, Dir. of
Data Processing.

■ 7297 ■ Earthworm Inc.
495 Ashford Ave.
Ardsley, NY 10502
Phone: (914)693-0400
Products: Tractors and mining equipment. **SIC:** 5082
(Construction & Mining Machinery). **Est:** 1965. **Sales:**
$24,000,000 (2000). **Emp:** 7. **Officers:** Michael
Zinman, President; Lee Zinman, VP of Sales.

■ 7298 ■ East Alabama Lumber Co.
PO Box 110
Lafayette, AL 36862
Phone: (334)864-9800 **Fax:** (334)864-0600
Products: Pine lumber; Dimension; 5/4 prime; Export.
SIC: 5031 (Lumber, Plywood & Millwork). **Est:** 1952.
Sales: $30,000,000 (2000). **Emp:** 110. **Officers:**
Wayne Welch, President.

■ 7299 ■ East Coast Mill Sales Co.
PO Box 580
Charlestown, MA 02129
Phone: (617)241-0440 **Fax:** (617)241-7373
Products: Plywood; Hardboard; Veneer; Hardwood
logs. **SICs:** 5039 (Construction Materials Nec); 5031
(Lumber, Plywood & Millwork). **Est:** 1951. **Sales:**
$25,000,000 (2000). **Emp:** 16. **Officers:** M.S.
Waldfogel, Partner; Edward Gildea, Partner.

■ 7300 ■ East Coast Tile/Terrazzo
450 Old Dixie Hwy.
Vero Beach, FL 32960
Phone: (561)562-4164
Free: (877)328-8453 **Fax:** (561)778-5253
Products: Floorcovering equipment and supplies. **SIC:**
5032 (Brick, Stone & Related Materials). **Sales:**
$3,000,000 (2000). **Emp:** 24.

■ 7301 ■ Eastman-Cartwright Lumber Co.
Hwy. 61 N
Lancaster, WI 53813
Phone: (608)723-2177 **Fax:** (608)723-2178
Products: Lumber; Hardware supplies. **SICs:** 5031
(Lumber, Plywood & Millwork); 5072 (Hardware). **Est:**
1900. **Sales:** $3,000,000 (2000). **Emp:** 41. **Officers:**
Ted W. Schacht, President.

■ 7302 ■ Economy Builders Supply Inc.
3232 S 400 E
Salt Lake City, UT 84115-4102
Phone: (801)566-1500 **Fax:** (801)566-9591
Products: Building materials. **SICs:** 5039
(Construction Materials Nec); 5031 (Lumber, Plywood
& Millwork); 5032 (Brick, Stone & Related Materials).
Est: 1956. **Sales:** $20,000,000 (2000). **Emp:** 100.
Officers: Sheri Schauerhamer; Scott Schauerhamer.

■ 7303 ■ Frank A. Edmunds and Company Inc.
6111 S Sayre Ave.
Chicago, IL 60638
Phone: (773)586-2772 **Fax:** (773)586-2783
Products: Custom wood products. **SIC:** 5031 (Lumber,
Plywood & Millwork). **Est:** 1950. **Sales:** $2,000,000
(2000). **Emp:** 30. **Officers:** Dennis J. Clegg, President;
Frank Fry, CFO; Paul R. Stepuszek, Dir. of Marketing &
Sales; JoAnn Elrod, Customer Service Contact.

■ 7304 ■ Eikenhout and Sons Inc.
346 Wealthy St. SW
Grand Rapids, MI 49501-2862
Phone: (616)459-4523
Products: Roofing; Siding. **SIC:** 5033 (Roofing, Siding
& Insulation). **Est:** 1971. **Sales:** $16,000,000 (2000).
Emp: 40. **Officers:** Henry Schierbeek, President.

■ 7305 ■ El Rey Stucco Co.
4100 1/2 Broadway Blvd. SE
Albuquerque, NM 87105
Phone: (505)873-1180 **Fax:** (505)877-6670
Products: Stucco. **SIC:** 5032 (Brick, Stone & Related
Materials).

■ 7306 ■ Elk Supply Company Inc.
PO Box 1509
Clinton, OK 73601
Phone: (580)323-1250 **Fax:** (580)323-1639
Products: Lumber. **SIC:** 5031 (Lumber, Plywood &
Millwork). **Sales:** $18,000,000 (2000). **Emp:** 90.
Officers: Calvin D. Browning, President; Susan
Browning, Vice President; Deann Johnson, Dir. of
Marketing.

■ 7307 ■ Ellsworth Builders Supply Inc.
R.R. 4, Box 4
Ellsworth, ME 04605
Phone: (207)667-7134
Products: Building supplies. **SIC:** 5039 (Construction
Materials Nec). **Est:** 1959. **Sales:** $30,000,000 (2000).
Emp: 170. **Officers:** Austin Goodyear, President;
Barkley Van Vranken, CFO; Douglas G. Wentworth,
Dir. of Marketing; Daniel R. Garver, Data Processing
Mgr.

■ **7308** ■ **Elsinore Ready-Mix Co.**
PO Box 959
Lake Elsinore, CA 92530
Phone: (909)674-2127
Products: Concrete products. **SIC:** 5032 (Brick, Stone & Related Materials). **Est:** 1956. **Sales:** $15,000,000 (2000). **Emp:** 80. **Officers:** R.L. Cartier, President.

■ **7309** ■ **Emerson Hardwood Co.**
2279 NW Front Ave.
Portland, OR 97209
Phone: (503)227-4520   **Fax:** (503)227-0754
Products: Hardwood lumber. **SIC:** 5031 (Lumber, Plywood & Millwork). **Est:** 1907. **Sales:** $13,000,000 (2000). **Emp:** 60. **Officers:** Jim Price, President; Bob Coonrad, Controller; James T. Price, Exec. VP.

■ **7310** ■ **The Empire Company, Inc.**
8181 Logistic Dr.
Zeeland, MI 49464
Phone: (616)772-7272   **Fax:** (616)772-7020
URL: http://www.empireco.com
Products: Moulding, millwork and stairparts. **SIC:** 5031 (Lumber, Plywood & Millwork). **Est:** 1946. **Sales:** $100,000,000 (1999). **Emp:** 240. **Officers:** Thomas Highly, President; Steve Johandes, CFO; Steve Grossman, COO. **Former Name:** Empire Distributors Inc.

■ **7311** ■ **Empire Sand and Gravel Company Inc.**
PO Box 1215
Billings, MT 59103
Phone: (406)252-8465   **Fax:** (406)252-0506
E-mail: esg@wtp.net
Products: Asphalt, gravel, and sand. **SIC:** 5032 (Brick, Stone & Related Materials). **Est:** 1955. **Sales:** $30,000,000 (2000). **Emp:** 225. **Officers:** Meredith Reiter, President; Sandra Reiter, Treasurer & Secty.; Greg Reiter, Vice President.

■ **7312** ■ **Empire Southwest L.L.C.**
PO Box 2985
Phoenix, AZ 85062-2985
Phone: (480)633-4300
Free: (800)367-4731   **Fax:** (480)633-4489
URL: http://www.empire-cat.com
Products: Construction and mining equipment, farm and garden machinery, and equipment. **SICs:** 5082 (Construction & Mining Machinery); 5083 (Farm & Garden Machinery). **Est:** 1959. **Sales:** $545,000,000 (2000). **Emp:** 1,000. **Officers:** John O. Whiteman, CEO & Chairman of the Board; Richard C. Mente, VP of Finance.

■ **7313** ■ **Engineered Equipment Co.**
179 N Maple St.
Corona, CA 92880
Phone: (909)735-3326   **Fax:** (909)734-7085
Products: Sells mining equipment and components, steel plate. **SICs:** 5082 (Construction & Mining Machinery); 5051 (Metals Service Centers & Offices). **Sales:** $4,000,000 (2000). **Emp:** 11. **Officers:** Ted dobson, CEO; Patricia Contreras, Treasurer.

■ **7314** ■ **Equipment Corporation of America**
PO Box 306
Coraopolis, PA 15108
Phone: (412)264-4480   **Fax:** (412)264-1158
URL: http://www.ecanet.com
Products: Large construction equipment. **SIC:** 5082 (Construction & Mining Machinery). **Est:** 1918. **Sales:** $5,000,000 (2000). **Emp:** 30. **Officers:** A. Roy Kern Jr., President.

■ **7315** ■ **Erb Equipment Company Inc.**
200 Erb Industrial Dr.
Fenton, MO 63026
Phone: (636)349-0200   **Fax:** (636)349-4426
E-mail: erbgreg@jddealer.com
URL: http://www.erbequipment.com
Products: Construction equipment. **SIC:** 5082 (Construction & Mining Machinery). **Est:** 1944. **Sales:** $55,000,000 (2000). **Emp:** 160. **Officers:** R.S. Erb, President; Carrie Roider, Treasurer; Gregg Erb, Sales Mgr.

■ **7316** ■ **Erb Lumber Co. Materials Distributors Div.**
312 Mound St.
Dayton, OH 45407
Phone: (937)294-1297
Products: Lumber. **SIC:** 5031 (Lumber, Plywood & Millwork). **Sales:** $25,000,000 (1994). **Emp:** 60. **Officers:** Dan Pierce, General Mgr.; Kathy Sayer, Controller.

■ **7317** ■ **Erie Sand and Gravel Co.**
PO Box 179
Erie, PA 16512
Phone: (814)453-6721
Products: Limestone and sand. **SIC:** 5032 (Brick, Stone & Related Materials). **Est:** 1888. **Sales:** $14,000,000 (2000). **Emp:** 100. **Officers:** Sidney E. Smith Jr., President; Robert Boorum, Treasurer; Sidney E. Smith III, Dir. of Marketing.

■ **7318** ■ **Erie Stone Company Inc.**
500 Erie Stone Dr.
Huntington, IN 46750
Phone: (219)356-7214
Products: Limestone. **SIC:** 5032 (Brick, Stone & Related Materials). **Sales:** $5,000,000 (2000). **Emp:** 20. **Officers:** Pete Irving, President; Earl Brinker, CFO.

■ **7319** ■ **Escondido Lumber & True Value**
310 S Quince
Escondido, CA 92025-4047
Phone: (760)745-0881   **Fax:** (760)747-5367
Products: Lumber; Hardware. **SICs:** 5031 (Lumber, Plywood & Millwork); 5072 (Hardware). **Emp:** 7. **Officers:** James Gorman, Owner.

■ **7320** ■ **Espy Lumber Co.**
PO Box 5099
Hilton Head Island, SC 29938
Phone: (803)785-3821   **Fax:** (803)842-9053
Products: Lumber and lumber supplies. **SIC:** 5031 (Lumber, Plywood & Millwork). **Est:** 1958. **Sales:** $10,000,000 (2000). **Emp:** 33. **Officers:** R.A. McLeod, President; Michael W. Reeves, General Mgr.

■ **7321** ■ **ESSROC Corp.**
2 Oak Way
Berkeley Heights, NJ 07922
Phone: (908)771-0024   **Fax:** (908)771-9032
Products: Concrete. **SIC:** 5032 (Brick, Stone & Related Materials). **Est:** 1980. **Sales:** $850,000,000 (2000). **Emp:** 4,500. **Officers:** Philippe Milliet, President; Robert Rayner, VP & CFO; Richard Borway, VP & Treasurer.

■ **7322** ■ **ESSROC Corp.**
3251 Bath Pike Rd.
Nazareth, PA 18064
Phone: (610)837-6725   **Fax:** (610)837-9614
Products: Construction materials. **SIC:** 5063 (Electrical Apparatus & Equipment). **Sales:** $1,880,000,000 (2000). **Emp:** 10,000. **Officers:** Robert Rayner, President; Glenn Dalrymple, VP of Finance.

■ **7323** ■ **Ralph A. Esty and Sons Inc.**
441 Main St.
Groveland, MA 01834
Phone: (978)374-0333   **Fax:** (978)373-0383
E-mail: estylumber@mva.net
URL: http://www.estylumber.net
Products: Lumber; Building materials; Paints. **SICs:** 5031 (Lumber, Plywood & Millwork); 5039 (Construction Materials Nec); 5198 (Paints, Varnishes & Supplies). **Est:** 1917. **Sales:** $5,000,000 (2000). **Emp:** 44. **Officers:** Hobart B. Esty, President; Marjory S. Burke, Sales/Marketing Contact; Ken Monaco.

■ **7324** ■ **J.D. Evans Inc.**
4000 N Cliff Ave.
Sioux Falls, SD 57104
Phone: (605)336-2595   **Fax:** (605)338-1757
Products: Heavy road equipment. **SIC:** 5082 (Construction & Mining Machinery). **Est:** 1910. **Sales:** $5,000,000 (2000). **Emp:** 37. **Officers:** Jack Babb, President; Marvin Harr, Treasurer & Secty.

■ **7325** ■ **R.B. Everett and Co.**
PO Box 327
Houston, TX 77001
Phone: (713)224-8161   **Fax:** (713)225-5967
Products: Construction equipment. **SIC:** 5082 (Construction & Mining Machinery). **Est:** 1911. **Sales:** $13,000,000 (2000). **Emp:** 35. **Officers:** J. Farrel Henderson, President & Treasurer; Dean Henderson, Vice President.

■ **7326** ■ **Exchange Lumber and Manufacturing Div.**
15120 E Euclid Ave.
Spokane, WA 99216-1801
Products: Lumber, including redwood, cedar, plywood, and pine. **SIC:** 5031 (Lumber, Plywood & Millwork). **Est:** 1907. **Sales:** $19,500,000 (2000). **Emp:** 40. **Officers:** Glenn Hart, Chairman of the Board; Dick Bolka, Sales Mgr.; Frank Franciscovich, General Mgr.

■ **7327** ■ **Explosive Supply Company Inc.**
PO Box 217
Spruce Pine, NC 28777
Phone: (828)765-2762   **Fax:** (828)765-6044
Products: Crushed stone; Ready-mix concrete. **SICs:** 5032 (Brick, Stone & Related Materials); 5169 (Chemicals & Allied Products Nec). **Est:** 1940. **Sales:** $2,000,000 (2000). **Emp:** 50. **Officers:** C.E. Boone, President; Robert Boone, Vice President; Susan Gardin, Secretary.

■ **7328** ■ **Expo Industries Inc.**
PO Box 26370
San Diego, CA 92196
Phone: (619)566-4343   **Fax:** (619)566-0182
URL: http://www.expoindustries.com
Products: Stucco; Dry wall. **SICs:** 5039 (Construction Materials Nec); 5032 (Brick, Stone & Related Materials). **Est:** 1969. **Emp:** 65. **Officers:** Robert Papera, President; Ben Garcia, Sales/Marketing Contact, e-mail: bgarcia@expoindustries.com; Dave Crabtree, Customer Service Contact, e-mail: dcrabtree@expoindustries.com.

■ **7329** ■ **F & W Welding Service Inc.**
164 Boston Post Rd.
Orange, CT 06477
Phone: (203)795-0591   **Fax:** (203)795-0596
Products: Construction supplies. **SIC:** 5082 (Construction & Mining Machinery). **Est:** 1939. **Sales:** $2,000,000 (2000). **Emp:** 10. **Officers:** H. Roger Funk, Vice President.

■ **7330** ■ **John Fabick Tractor Co.**
1 Fabick Dr.
Fenton, MO 63026
Phone: (314)343-5900   **Fax:** (314)343-4910
Products: Construction machinery. **SICs:** 5082 (Construction & Mining Machinery); 5083 (Farm & Garden Machinery). **Sales:** $186,000,000 (2000). **Emp:** 500. **Officers:** Harry P. Fabick, President; J. Jansen, VP of Finance.

■ **7331** ■ **Faris Machinery Co.**
5770 E 77th Ave.
Commerce City, CO 80022
Phone: (303)289-5743   **Fax:** (303)287-9273
Products: Construction machinery. **SIC:** 5082 (Construction & Mining Machinery). **Est:** 1953. **Sales:** $9,000,000 (2000). **Emp:** 40. **Officers:** R.C. Poulson, President.

■ **7332** ■ **Federal Pipe and Supply Co.**
6464 E McNichols Rd.
Detroit, MI 48212
Phone: (313)366-3000   **Fax:** (313)366-6466
E-mail: federalpipe@hotmail.com
URL: http://www.federalpipe.com
Products: Construction materials and equipment; Pipes, valves, and fittings; Structural steel; Power tools; Paint; Aluminum shapes and sheets; Fencing, chain, and hardware. **SICs:** 5039 (Construction Materials Nec); 5051 (Metals Service Centers & Offices); 5039 (Construction Materials Nec); 5074 (Plumbing & Hydronic Heating Supplies). **Est:** 1930. **Sales:** $3,000,000 (2000). **Emp:** 25. **Officers:** Herbert Saperstein, President; Leon Saperstein, Treasurer; Carl Browning, Sales Mgr.; Jared Saperstein, Sales Contact.

■ 7333 ■ Federal Pipe and Supply Co.
6464 E McNichols Rd.
Detroit, MI 48212
Phone: (313)366-3000 **Fax:** (313)366-6466
Products: Construction materials and machinery. **SIC:**
5039 (Construction Materials Nec). **Sales:** $3,000,000
(2000). **Emp:** 25.

■ 7334 ■ Feenaughty Machinery Co.
PO Box 13279
Portland, OR 97213
Phone: (503)282-2566 **Fax:** (503)282-1755
Products: Hydraulic excavators and other excavating
machinery. **SIC:** 5082 (Construction & Mining
Machinery). **Est:** 1901. **Sales:** $18,000,000 (2000).
Emp: 24. **Officers:** D. Harris, President; William F.
Richardson, VP & Treasurer.

**■ 7335 ■ Ferguson Manufacturing and
    Equipment Co.**
4900 Harry Hines Blvd.
Dallas, TX 75235
Phone: (214)631-3000 **Fax:** (214)637-1530
E-mail: ferguson@unicomp.net
Products: Asphalt rollers. **SIC:** 5082 (Construction &
Mining Machinery). **Est:** 1933. **Officers:** D. Sheehan,
President; Evelyn Wilson, Controller, Human
Resources Contact; D. Zimmermann, VP of
Operations, Sales Contact; Jose Martinez, Customer
Service Contact.

■ 7336 ■ Ferrex International, Inc.
26 Broadway, 26th Fl.
New York, NY 10004
Phone: (212)509-7030 **Fax:** (212)344-4728
E-mail: ferrex@ferrex.com
URL: http://www.ferrex.com
Products: Construction pipeline equipment;
Construction and road building machinery; Electric
welding apparatus; Industrial exhaust and ventilation
fans; Agricultural equipment. **SICs:** 5084 (Industrial
Machinery & Equipment); 5082 (Construction & Mining
Machinery); 5083 (Farm & Garden Machinery). **Est:**
1914. **Emp:** 35. **Officers:** William J. Ferretti, President;
James T. Robinson, VP of Marketing & Sales.

■ 7337 ■ Fessenden Hall Inc.
1050 Sherman Ave.
Pennsauken, NJ 08110
Phone: (609)665-2210 **Fax:** (609)665-6518
Products: Hardwood; Plywood; Solid surface
materials; Laminates. **SIC:** 5031 (Lumber, Plywood &
Millwork). **Est:** 1890. **Sales:** $50,000,000 (2000). **Emp:**
120. **Officers:** R.H. Birdsall, Chairman of the Board;
Raymond A. Jungclaus Jr., VP of Finance; David S.
Emery, Sales Mgr.; Alfonse Minori, Data Processing
Mgr.

■ 7338 ■ Fiatallis North America Inc.
245 E North Ave.
Carol Stream, IL 60188
Phone: (630)260-4000
Products: Construction equipment. **SIC:** 5082
(Construction & Mining Machinery). **Sales:**
$40,000,000 (2000). **Emp:** 79. **Officers:** Lucio A.
Catone, CEO & Chairman of the Board; Bruce
Larrabee, Treasurer & Controller.

■ 7339 ■ Fiberlay Inc.
2419 NW Market St.
Seattle, WA 98107
Phone: (206)782-0660
Free: (800)942-0660 **Fax:** (206)782-0662
E-mail: fiberlay@aol.com
Products: Fiberglass; Polyester and epoxy resin; Vinyl
window repair kits; Vacuum bagging supplies; Molding
supplies. **SICs:** 5033 (Roofing, Siding & Insulation);
5039 (Construction Materials Nec). **Est:** 1952. **Sales:**
$600,000 (2000). **Emp:** 4. **Officers:** Dick MacIndoe,
President.

■ 7340 ■ J.D. Fields and Co.
PO Box 218424
Houston, TX 77218
Phone: (281)558-7199 **Fax:** (281)870-9918
Products: Steel products, including line pipe and sheet
piles. **SICs:** 5039 (Construction Materials Nec); 5074
(Plumbing & Hydronic Heating Supplies). **Est:** 1985.

Sales: $140,000,000 (1999). **Emp:** 37. **Officers:** Jerry
D. Field, President; Stanley N. Fisher, Exec. VP.

■ 7341 ■ Fingerle Lumber Co.
PO Box 1167
Ann Arbor, MI 48106
Phone: (734)663-0581 **Fax:** (734)663-2515
Products: Lumber and building materials. **SICs:** 5031
(Lumber, Plywood & Millwork); 5039 (Construction
Materials Nec). **Sales:** $32,000,000 (2000). **Emp:** 150.
Officers: John Fingerle; Mark Fingerle; Lawrence
Fingerle.

■ 7342 ■ Fircrest Pre-Fit Door Co.
3024 S Mullen St.
Tacoma, WA 98409
Phone: (253)564-6921
Products: Doors. **SIC:** 5031 (Lumber, Plywood &
Millwork). **Est:** 1958. **Sales:** $1,500,000 (2000). **Emp:**
7. **Officers:** Donald Klemme, President.

■ 7343 ■ Fire Brick Engineers Co.
PO Box 341278
Milwaukee, WI 53234-1278
Phone: (414)383-6000
Free: (800)657-0813 **Fax:** (414)383-6731
E-mail: fbemilw@aol.com
URL: http://www.firebrickengineers.com
Products: Refractory brick and cement. **SIC:** 5032
(Brick, Stone & Related Materials). **Est:** 1935. **Sales:**
$10,000,000 (2000). **Emp:** 40. **Officers:** James T.
Springer, President; Richard R. Powers, Controller;
Dennis Kranz, VP of Operations; Michael D. Skatter,
Sales Mgr.

■ 7344 ■ Firebird International, Inc.
PO Box 751299
Petaluma, CA 94975
Phone: (707)769-9410 **Fax:** (707)769-9483
Products: Pre-fabricated buildings, including houses.
SIC: 5039 (Construction Materials Nec). **Officers:**
Tammy Bransford, President.

■ 7345 ■ Firestone Plywood
210 Miller Pl.
Hicksville, NY 11801
Phone: (516)938-7007
Free: (800)366-4966 **Fax:** (516)938-7031
E-mail: AlanandSyb@aol.com
Products: Hardwood and softwood plywood type
products; High pressure plastic laminate; Veneers;
Contact cement; Curve ply moldings; Flakeboard. **SIC:**
5031 (Lumber, Plywood & Millwork). **Est:** 1969. **Emp:**
24. **Officers:** Alan Firestone.

■ 7346 ■ Fischer Lime and Cement Co.
PO Box 18383
Memphis, TN 38181-0383
Phone: (901)363-4986 **Fax:** (901)794-3569
Products: Building materials, including windows, steel,
and dirt. **SICs:** 5039 (Construction Materials Nec);
5051 (Metals Service Centers & Offices); 5031
(Lumber, Plywood & Millwork); 5032 (Brick, Stone &
Related Materials). **Est:** 1906. **Sales:** $45,000,000
(2000). **Emp:** 350. **Officers:** Thomas J. Sheppard,
President; Dayton P. Phillips, Treasurer; Bruce Wiltsey,
Marketing Mgr.; Joe Ramsey, Dir. of Information
Systems; David Swan, Dir of Human Resources.

■ 7347 ■ Fisher Sand and Gravel Co.
PO Box 1271
Midland, MI 48641-1271
Phone: (517)835-7187 **Fax:** (517)835-7882
Products: Concrete, stone, sand, and tile. **SIC:** 5032
(Brick, Stone & Related Materials). **Est:** 1926. **Sales:**
$9,000,000 (2000). **Emp:** 35. **Officers:** J.O. Fisher,
President.

■ 7348 ■ Fitzpatrick and Weller Inc.
PO Box 490
Ellicottville, NY 14731
Phone: (716)699-2393 **Fax:** (716)699-2893
E-mail: fwi@fitzweller.com
Products: Hardwood lumber, rough and dressed, and
components. **SIC:** 5031 (Lumber, Plywood & Millwork).
Est: 1895. **Sales:** $25,000,000 (2000). **Emp:** 205.
Officers: Dana G. Fitzpatrick, Exec. VP; Greg
Fitzpatrick, VP of Sales; Maureen Barlow, Customer

Service Contact; Michael Fitzpatrick, Human
Resources Contact.

■ 7349 ■ Flemington Block and Supply Inc.
Hwy. 31
Flemington, NJ 08822
Phone: (908)782-2021 **Fax:** (908)782-2378
Products: Ready-mixed concrete; Sand and gravel.
SIC: 5032 (Brick, Stone & Related Materials). **Sales:**
$10,000,000 (2000). **Emp:** 80. **Officers:** Frank Lentine,
President.

■ 7350 ■ Folcomer Equipment Corporation
PO Box 340
Aberdeen, MD 21001
Phone: (410)575-6580
Free: (800)737-0049 **Fax:** (410)575-7052
Products: Bull dozers and jack hammers; Loaders;
Excavators; Rollers; Forklifts. **SIC:** 5082 (Construction
& Mining Machinery). **Est:** 1994. **Sales:** $10,000,000
(2000). **Emp:** 23. **Officers:** David Folcomer, President.

■ 7351 ■ Fold-A-Way Corporation
307 New Venture Dr.
Louisville, KY 40214
Phone: (502)366-2927
Free: (800)443-8165 **Fax:** (502)361-1410
E-mail: foldaway@mindspring.com
URL: http://www.foldawaycorp.com
Products: Folding bumper steps. **SIC:** 5072
(Hardware). **Est:** 1986. **Sales:** $500,000 (1999). **Emp:**
13. **Officers:** Morris L. DeZern, President; Carolyn
DeZern, Vice President; Sherry McWilliams, General
Mgr.; Kenneth Wade, Sales & Marketing Contact.

■ 7352 ■ Foley Equipment Company Inc.
1550 S West St.
Wichita, KS 67213
Phone: (316)943-4211 **Fax:** (316)943-5658
Products: Construction and farm machinery. **SICs:**
5082 (Construction & Mining Machinery); 5083 (Farm &
Garden Machinery). **Est:** 1942. **Sales:** $45,000,000
(2000). **Emp:** 190. **Officers:** Ann Konecny, President;
Lewis Erickson, VP of Finance. **Former Name:** Foley
Tractor Company Inc.

■ 7353 ■ Fontaine Industries Inc.
1500 Urban Ctr. Dr., No. 400
Birmingham, AL 35242-2566
Phone: (205)969-1119
Products: Building materials; Office furniture;
Chemicals and biomedical products. **SIC:** 5039
(Construction Materials Nec). **Sales:** $255,000,000
(2000). **Emp:** 1,000. **Officers:** Kelly Dier, President.

■ 7354 ■ Foothills Mill & Supply Inc.
6455 E 56th Ave.
Commerce City, CO 80022
Phone: (303)287-2069 **Fax:** (303)287-9754
Products: Wood doors, interior and exterior; Metal
doors and frames. **SIC:** 5031 (Lumber, Plywood &
Millwork). **Est:** 1980. **Emp:** 15. **Officers:** Doug
Denman.

■ 7355 ■ For-Tek
1400 Ironhorse Pk.
North Billerica, MA 01862
Phone: (978)667-6011 **Fax:** (978)667-8978
E-mail: fortekinfo@aol.com
Products: Specialty treated wood products; Utility
poles and crossarms; Marine and highway products.
SIC: 5031 (Lumber, Plywood & Millwork). **Est:** 1968.
Sales: $15,000,000 (2000). **Emp:** 10. **Officers:** E.I.
Snider; Paul Snider, President. **Alternate Name:**
Massachusetts Lumber Co.

■ 7356 ■ Forderer Cornice Works Co.
269 Potrero Ave.
San Francisco, CA 94103
Phone: (415)431-4100 **Fax:** (415)431-6685
Products: Steel doors. **SIC:** 5039 (Construction
Materials Nec). **Est:** 1875. **Sales:** $2,000,000 (2000).
Emp: 37. **Officers:** Curt Forderer, President; A.E.
Forderer Jr., CFO.

■ 7357 ■ **Forest City-Babin Co.**
5111 Richmond Rd.
Cleveland, OH 44146
Phone: (216)292-2500 **Fax:** (216)292-2510
Products: Windows; Doors; Appliances; Hardware.
SICs: 5031 (Lumber, Plywood & Millwork); 5072
(Hardware). **Est:** 1916. **Sales:** $26,000,000 (2000).
Emp: 132. **Officers:** Joseph Babin, President; Jim
Wander, Finance Officer; Greg Bauchmoyer, Marketing
& Sales Mgr.

■ 7358 ■ **Forest City-North America Lumber**
26050 Richmond Rd.
Cleveland, OH 44146
Phone: (216)292-5660
Products: Lumber. **SIC:** 5031 (Lumber, Plywood &
Millwork). **Est:** 1983. **Sales:** $20,000,000 (2000). **Emp:**
60. **Officers:** J. Schleifer, President.

■ 7359 ■ **Forest City Trading Group Inc.**
PO Box 4209
Portland, OR 97208
Phone: (503)246-8500 **Fax:** (503)246-1116
Products: Lumber. **SIC:** 5031 (Lumber, Plywood &
Millwork). **Est:** 1976. **Sales:** $3,700,000,000 (1999).
Emp: 585. **Officers:** John W. Judy, President; Lois
Tonning, VP of Finance; Mark Donovan, VP of
Marketing & Sales; Charlotte Mires, Human Resources
Mgr.

■ 7360 ■ **Forest Lumber Co.**
PO Box 101063
Pittsburgh, PA 15237
Phone: (412)367-2004
Products: Lumber, including plywood, finished, and
rough wood. **SIC:** 5031 (Lumber, Plywood & Millwork).
Est: 1904. **Sales:** $6,000,000 (2000). **Emp:** 6.
Officers: Scott W. Prevost, President.

■ 7361 ■ **Forest Plywood Sales**
14711 Arteisa Blvd.
La Mirada, CA 90638
Phone: (310)523-1721 **Fax:** (213)523-7894
Products: Plywood. **SIC:** 5031 (Lumber, Plywood &
Millwork).

■ 7362 ■ **Ed Fountain Lumber Co.**
PO Box 904
Palos Verdes Estates, CA 90274-0904
Phone: (213)583-1381
Products: Lumber. **SIC:** 5031 (Lumber, Plywood &
Millwork). **Est:** 1938. **Sales:** $2,000,000 (2000). **Emp:**
6. **Officers:** Edward Fountain Jr., President.

■ 7363 ■ **Four States Industrial Distributors**
PO Box 2896
Farmington, NM 87499-2896
Phone: (505)326-0472 **Fax:** (505)326-0501
Products: Roofing, siding, and insulation. **SIC:** 5033
(Roofing, Siding & Insulation). **Officers:** Roy Fourr,
President.

■ 7364 ■ **R.W. Fowler and Associates Inc.**
4730 Prince Edward Rd.
Jacksonville, FL 32210-8118
Phone: (904)246-4886 **Fax:** (904)241-8056
Products: Fiberglass. **SIC:** 5033 (Roofing, Siding &
Insulation). **Est:** 1956. **Sales:** $8,000,000 (2000). **Emp:**
100. **Officers:** Robert W. Fowler, President; Robert
Woodruff, Controller; Carl M. Pope, Dir. of Marketing.

■ 7365 ■ **Fowler and Peth Inc.**
PO Box 16551
Denver, CO 80216
Phone: (303)388-6493
Free: (800)523-1241 **Fax:** 888-601-4583
URL: http://www.fowlerpeth.com
Products: Roofing. **SIC:** 5033 (Roofing, Siding &
Insulation). **Est:** 1948. **Sales:** $22,000,000 (2000).
Emp: 75. **Officers:** Eric W. Peth, President, e-mail:
ricpeth@worldnet.com; George Snyder, Controller.

■ 7366 ■ **Franciscan Glass Co.**
100 San Antonio Cir.
Mountain View, CA 94040
Phone: (650)948-6666
Free: (800)229-7728 **Fax:** (650)948-0736
Products: Stained glass products and supplies; Clear-
textured privacy and cast glass; Screens; Exotic

hardwood doors and flooring. **SICs:** 5039 (Construction
Materials Nec); 5031 (Lumber, Plywood & Millwork).
Est: 1960. **Emp:** 20.

■ 7367 ■ **Franklin Industries Inc.**
612 10th Ave. N
Nashville, TN 37203
Phone: (615)259-4222
Products: Brick and limestone. **SIC:** 5032 (Brick,
Stone & Related Materials). **Sales:** $40,000,000
(2000). **Emp:** 350. **Officers:** Nelson Sereringhaus Jr.,
President; M. Duncan, Treasurer; R.C. Freas, VP of
Marketing.

■ 7368 ■ **Frank's Supply Company Inc.**
3311 Stanford NE
Albuquerque, NM 87107
Phone: (505)884-0000 **Fax:** (505)884-1787
Products: Construction tools. **SIC:** 5082 (Construction
& Mining Machinery). **Est:** 1953. **Sales:** $11,000,000
(1994). **Emp:** 70. **Officers:** Dan F. Deaver, President;
Harvey L. Copass, CFO; Richard P. Crifasi, Dir. of
Marketing & Sales.

■ 7369 ■ **Frontier Lumber Co.**
1941 Elmwood Ave.
Buffalo, NY 14207
Phone: (716)873-8500 **Fax:** (716)873-8509
Products: Lumber; Custom millwork. **SIC:** 5031
(Lumber, Plywood & Millwork). **Est:** 1940. **Sales:**
$10,000,000 (2000). **Emp:** 70. **Officers:** Edward
McDermid, President.

■ 7370 ■ **Frontier Wholesale Co.**
PO Box 3928
Lubbock, TX 79452-3928
Phone: (806)744-1404 **Fax:** (806)744-1855
Products: Doors and windows. **SIC:** 5031 (Lumber,
Plywood & Millwork). **Est:** 1949. **Sales:** $4,500,000
(2000). **Emp:** 30. **Officers:** A.H. Faulkner Jr.,
President; H. Carrico, CFO; D.B. Thompson, Sales
Mgr.

■ 7371 ■ **Frost Hardwood Lumber Co.**
PO Box 919065
San Diego, CA 92191-9065
Phone: (619)455-9060 **Fax:** (619)455-0455
URL: http://www.frosthardwood.com
Products: Lumber. **SIC:** 5031 (Lumber, Plywood &
Millwork). **Est:** 1911. **Sales:** $10,000,000 (2000). **Emp:**
47. **Officers:** G.T. Frost Jr., President; Bruce Frost, VP
of Finance; Jim Frost, Treasurer.

■ 7372 ■ **FRP Supplies Inc.**
3 S Middlesex Ave., A
Cranbury, NJ 08512-3726
Phone: (201)288-7900
Products: Fiberglass. **SIC:** 5033 (Roofing, Siding &
Insulation). **Sales:** $7,000,000 (2000). **Emp:** 25.
Officers: Bob Keenan, General Mgr.

■ 7373 ■ **Futter Lumber Corp.**
PO Box 347
Rockville Centre, NY 11571
Phone: (516)764-4445
Free: (800)275-3888 **Fax:** (516)764-0579
Products: Lumber. **SIC:** 5031 (Lumber, Plywood &
Millwork). **Est:** 1945. **Sales:** $116,000,000 (2000).
Emp: 18. **Officers:** Bernard Futter, President; Kenneth
L. Futter, Treasurer & Secty.; James Futter, Vice
President.

■ 7374 ■ **W.T. Galliher and Brother Inc.**
PO Box 827
Springfield, VA 22150
Phone: (703)451-6500 **Fax:** (703)451-6601
E-mail: wtgbroinc@aol.com
URL: http://www.wtgalliher.com
Products: Lumber, including plywood and pine. **SIC:**
5031 (Lumber, Plywood & Millwork). **Est:** 1889. **Sales:**
$14,000,000 (1999). **Emp:** 55. **Officers:** John Lane Jr.,
President & Treasurer; Judy Griffin, Controller.

■ 7375 ■ **Ganahl Lumber Co.**
1220 E Ball Rd.
Anaheim, CA 92805
Phone: (714)772-5444 **Fax:** (714)772-0639
Products: Building supplies, including lumber. **SIC:**
5031 (Lumber, Plywood & Millwork). **Est:** 1884. **Sales:**

$61,000,000 (2000). **Emp:** 280. **Officers:** Peter
Ganahl, CEO; John Ganahl, CFO.

■ 7376 ■ **G.A.R. International Corp.**
3315 Commerce Parkway
Miramar, FL 33025
Phone: (954)704-9490
Free: (800)992-9140 **Fax:** (954)704-1959
E-mail: garmiami@aol.com
Products: Heavy equipment, including mining and
contracting supplies; Lattice; Crawler cranes. **SIC:**
5082 (Construction & Mining Machinery). **Est:** 1972.
Sales: $33,000,000 (2000). **Emp:** 52. **Officers:** N.F.
Gallinaro, CEO & Chairman of the Board; S.P.
Gallinaro, Treasurer; George McKinney, President.

■ 7377 ■ **Garden State Tile Distributors**
790 S Route 73
West Berlin, NJ 08091
Phone: (609)753-0300 **Fax:** (609)753-1835
Products: Floorcovering equipment and supplies. **SIC:**
5032 (Brick, Stone & Related Materials).

■ 7378 ■ **Gardner Hardware Co.**
515 Washington Ave. N
Minneapolis, MN 55401
Phone: (612)333-3393
Products: Doors and door hardware. **SICs:** 5072
(Hardware); 5031 (Lumber, Plywood & Millwork). **Est:**
1884. **Sales:** $6,000,000 (2000). **Emp:** 40. **Officers:**
Steven J. Healy, President & Treasurer.

■ 7379 ■ **E.L. Gardner Inc.**
1914 Forest Dr.
Annapolis, MD 21401-4343
Phone: (410)266-8239 **Fax:** (301)268-8641
Products: Ready-mixed concrete; Sand, gravel and
recycled materials. **SIC:** 5032 (Brick, Stone & Related
Materials). **Sales:** $77,000,000 (2000). **Emp:** 175.
Officers: E.L. Gardner Jr., President; Roland Hauser,
Controller.

■ 7380 ■ **Garka Mill Company Inc.**
60 State Ave.
Marysville, WA 98270
Phone: (206)659-8584 **Fax:** (206)653-4351
Products: Studs. **SICs:** 5031 (Lumber, Plywood &
Millwork); 5072 (Hardware). **Est:** 1956. **Sales:**
$1,000,000 (2000). **Emp:** 20. **Officers:** A.G. Garka,
President.

■ 7381 ■ **Geis Building Products Inc.**
PO Box 622
Brookfield, WI 53008-0622
Phone: (414)784-4250
Products: Garage doors; Openers; Shelving systems.
SIC: 5046 (Commercial Equipment Nec). **Emp:** 30.
Officers: Dan Hinkes, President.

■ 7382 ■ **Genalco Inc.**
333 Reservoir St.
Needham Heights, MA 02494
Phone: 877-436-2526 **Fax:** (781)449-6643
URL: http://www.genalco.com
Products: Construction supplies; Industrial supplies.
SICs: 5082 (Construction & Mining Machinery); 5085
(Industrial Supplies). **Est:** 1947. **Sales:** $8,500,000
(2000). **Emp:** 37. **Officers:** Joseph Mul Cahy,
President; Robert Bartley, Vice President.

■ 7383 ■ **General Equipment and Supplies Inc.**
PO Box 2145
Fargo, ND 58107
Phone: (701)282-2662 **Fax:** (701)281-9067
Products: Heavy construction equipment. **SIC:** 5082
(Construction & Mining Machinery). **Est:** 1984. **Sales:**
$13,000,000 (2000). **Emp:** 35. **Officers:** O. Stockstad,
President.

■ 7384 ■ **General Glass Company Inc.**
PO Box 3066
Charleston, WV 25331
Phone: (304)925-2171
Products: Glass windows and doors. **SIC:** 5039
(Construction Materials Nec). **Est:** 1944. **Sales:**
$4,500,000 (2000). **Emp:** 45. **Officers:** Rodney K.
Smith, President.

■ **7385** ■ **General Materials Inc.**
PO Box 824
Jackson, MI 49204
Phone: (517)784-3191
Products: Building materials, including lumber, roofing, siding, and insulation. **SICs:** 5031 (Lumber, Plywood & Millwork); 5033 (Roofing, Siding & Insulation). **Est:** 1952. **Sales:** $4,000,000 (2000). **Emp:** 15. **Officers:** F.E. Schmid, President & Treasurer; Dale Boyers, Controller; Andrew S. Woell, Dir. of Marketing & Sales.

■ **7386** ■ **Genesee Reserve Supply Inc.**
PO Box 20619
Rochester, NY 14602-0619
Phone: (716)292-7040 **Fax:** (716)292-7046
Products: Building supplies, including lumber, siding, windows, and doors. **SICs:** 5031 (Lumber, Plywood & Millwork); 5039 (Construction Materials Nec); 5033 (Roofing, Siding & Insulation). **Est:** 1952. **Sales:** $18,000,000 (2000). **Emp:** 20. **Officers:** Charles Frederick, CEO & President; Bill Bliss, Treasurer; John Fields, Chairman of the Board; Richard F. Buck, Exec. VP.

■ **7387** ■ **Geneva Corp.**
PO Box 21962
Greensboro, NC 27420
Phone: (910)275-9936 **Fax:** (910)274-4984
Products: Window and door products; Diesel engines. **SICs:** 5031 (Lumber, Plywood & Millwork); 5084 (Industrial Machinery & Equipment). **Est:** 1979. **Sales:** $128,000,000 (2000). **Emp:** 470. **Officers:** F. James Becher, President; Russell Myers, VP of Finance.

■ **7388** ■ **Gennett Lumber Co.**
PO Box 5088
Asheville, NC 28813-5088
Phone: (828)253-3626 **Fax:** (828)253-3628
Products: Lumber, including plywood and pine flooring. **SIC:** 5031 (Lumber, Plywood & Millwork). **Est:** 1901. **Sales:** $30,000,000 (2000). **Emp:** 11. **Officers:** P. Gennett, President.

■ **7389** ■ **Edward George Co.**
12650 Springfield S
Alsip, IL 60803
Phone: (708)371-0660 **Fax:** (708)385-0570
Products: Building materials; Closet shelving; Fireplaces and barbecues; Concrete and masonry products and supplies. **SICs:** 5031 (Lumber, Plywood & Millwork); 5032 (Brick, Stone & Related Materials); 5033 (Roofing, Siding & Insulation); 5039 (Construction Materials Nec); 5072 (Hardware). **Est:** 1945. **Sales:** $20,000,000 (2000). **Emp:** 85. **Officers:** E.G. Felsenthal, President & Treasurer.

■ **7390** ■ **Edward George Co.**
12650 S Springfield Ave.
Alsip, IL 60803
Phone: (708)371-0696 **Fax:** (708)385-0570
Products: Construction materials. **SIC:** 5039 (Construction Materials Nec). **Sales:** $18,000,000 (2000). **Emp:** 70. **Officers:** E.G. Felsenthal, President & Treasurer.

■ **7391** ■ **Georgetown Energy Inc.**
2104 N Austin Ave.
Georgetown, TX 78626
Phone: (512)863-8607
Products: Stones; Fireplaces. **SICs:** 5032 (Brick, Stone & Related Materials); 5074 (Plumbing & Hydronic Heating Supplies).

■ **7392** ■ **Georgia Flush Door Sales Inc.**
PO Box 43008
Atlanta, GA 30315-6008
Phone: (404)524-0223
Products: Wood doors, windows and shutters. **SIC:** 5031 (Lumber, Plywood & Millwork). **Sales:** $28,000,000 (1992). **Emp:** 100. **Officers:** Allen Bryan, Controller.

■ **7393** ■ **Georgia Marble Co.**
1201 Roberts Blvd.B, No. 100
Kennesaw, GA 30144-3619
Phone: (404)421-6500 **Fax:** (404)421-6507
Products: Marble. **SIC:** 5039 (Construction Materials Nec). **Est:** 1884. **Sales:** $97,000,000 (2000). **Emp:** 825. **Officers:** A.L. Gay Jr., President; Eugene Hartleb,

VP of Finance; Peter Landt, Dir. of Marketing & Sales; Jack Charlesworth, Dir. of Systems; Ray Barker, Dir of Human Resources.

■ **7394** ■ **Georgia-Pacific Corp. Distribution Div.**
PO Box 105605
Atlanta, GA 30348
Phone: (404)521-4000
Products: Lumber, including plywood; Paper; Paper towels and toilet paper. **SICs:** 5031 (Lumber, Plywood & Millwork); 5113 (Industrial & Personal Service Paper). **Sales:** $23,000,000 (2000). **Emp:** 100. **Officers:** George A. MacConnell, Vice President.

■ **7395** ■ **Gerrity Company Inc.**
90 Oak St.
Newton Upper Falls, MA 02464
Phone: (617)244-1400
Products: Marble and granite for building. **SIC:** 5032 (Brick, Stone & Related Materials). **Emp:** 60. **Officers:** James F. Gerrity III, President; Karen Moran, VP of Finance.

■ **7396** ■ **J. Gibson McIlvain Co.**
PO Box 222
White Marsh, MD 21162
Phone: (410)335-9600
Free: (800)638-9100 **Fax:** (410)335-3574
E-mail: info@mcilvain.com
URL: http://www.mcilvain.com
Products: Hard wood and soft wood, Importedd and Domestic millwork; Ipe decking; flooring, molding. **SIC:** 5031 (Lumber, Plywood & Millwork). **Sales:** $34,000,000 (2000). **Emp:** 130. **Officers:** J. Gibson McIlvain III, President; Scott A. McAllister, Controller; David C. Bell, VP of Sales, e-mail: info@mcilvain.com; Ada Swingler, Dir. of Data Processing.

■ **7397** ■ **GJ Sales Co.**
209 Nooseneck Hill Rd.
West Greenwich, RI 02817-2277
Phone: (401)397-6122 **Fax:** (401)397-4084
Products: Commercial and industrial construction specialty items. **SIC:** 5082 (Construction & Mining Machinery). **Officers:** Fred Jorgensen, President.

■ **7398** ■ **Glass Depot**
3235 Rosetta Place Dr., No. 2
South Bend, IN 46628-3448
Phone: (219)291-5150 **Fax:** (219)291-7981
Products: Glass; Windows. **SIC:** 5039 (Construction Materials Nec). **Est:** 1925. **Sales:** $20,000,000 (2000). **Emp:** 150. **Officers:** Jim Decrane, Vice President; Chuck Byers, Controller; Ray Murray, Sales Mgr.

■ **7399** ■ **Global Marketing Concepts**
PO Box 19444
Charlotte, NC 28219
Phone: (704)398-2352 **Fax:** (704)394-9255
Products: Lumber; Textile waste materials. **SICs:** 5031 (Lumber, Plywood & Millwork); 5093 (Scrap & Waste Materials). **Officers:** Thad Cloer, President.

■ **7400** ■ **GLS Corp.**
723 W Algonquin Rd.
Arlington Heights, IL 60006
Phone: (847)437-0200
Products: Fiberglass and plastics materials. **SICs:** 5033 (Roofing, Siding & Insulation); 5162 (Plastics Materials & Basic Shapes). **Sales:** $73,000,000 (2000). **Emp:** 200. **Officers:** Steven L. Dehmlow, President & Treasurer.

■ **7401** ■ **Vernon L. Goedecke Company Inc.**
4101 Clayton Ave.
St. Louis, MO 63110
Phone: (314)652-1810
Free: (800)392-1818 **Fax:** (314)652-9480
Products: Construction equipment, including lifts. **SIC:** 5082 (Construction & Mining Machinery). **Est:** 1946. **Sales:** $14,000,000 (2000). **Emp:** 100. **Officers:** Ronald A. Peterson, President & Chairman of the Board; Ralph H. Wagner, Exec. VP; Michael Braun, VP of Marketing.

■ **7402** ■ **Gold & Reiss Corp.**
254 Bay Ridge Ave.
Brooklyn, NY 11220-5801
Phone: (718)680-2600
Free: (800)843-5482 **Fax:** (718)680-2726
E-mail: goldnreiss@aol.com
Products: Cabinets, including kitchen and medicine. **SIC:** 5031 (Lumber, Plywood & Millwork). **Sales:** $10,000,000 (2000). **Emp:** 49. **Officers:** Shimon Eidlisz.

■ **7403** ■ **Gomoljak Block**
1841 McGuckian St.
Annapolis, MD 21401
Phone: (410)263-6744 **Fax:** (410)263-6460
Products: Cinder blocks and construction supplies. **SIC:** 5032 (Brick, Stone & Related Materials). **Est:** 1931. **Sales:** $3,000,000 (2000). **Emp:** 25. **Officers:** Kurt Pfaff, Operations Mgr.

■ **7404** ■ **Goodwin Machinery Co.**
3115 Central St. N
Knoxville, TN 37917-5192
Phone: (423)546-0841
Products: Construction machinery and equipment, including other construction machinery parts. **SIC:** 5082 (Construction & Mining Machinery). **Sales:** $6,000,000 (2000). **Emp:** 20. **Officers:** Curtis Goodwin, President.

■ **7405** ■ **Grabber Southeast**
3050 NW 60th St.
Ft. Lauderdale, FL 33309-2249
Phone: (954)971-4730 **Fax:** (954)977-3842
Products: Construction supplies. **SIC:** 5032 (Brick, Stone & Related Materials). **Emp:** 49. **Officers:** Bob Geyer.

■ **7406** ■ **Graebers Lumber Co.**
218 Lincoln Hwy.
Fairless Hills, PA 19030
Phone: (215)946-3000 **Fax:** (215)949-1133
Products: Lumber; Mill work; Kitchens. **SIC:** 5031 (Lumber, Plywood & Millwork). **Est:** 1951. **Sales:** $18,000,000 (2000). **Emp:** 55. **Officers:** Willard P. Graeber, President.

■ **7407** ■ **Grand Blanc Cement Products**
PO Box 585
Grand Blanc, MI 48439
Phone: (810)694-7500 **Fax:** (810)694-2995
Products: Concrete block and brick. **SIC:** 5032 (Brick, Stone & Related Materials). **Est:** 1926. **Sales:** $7,500,000 (2000). **Emp:** 53. **Officers:** Norman A. Nelson, President.

■ **7408** ■ **Grand Rapids Sash and Door**
PO Box E
Grand Rapids, MI 49501
Phone: (616)784-0101 **Fax:** (616)784-7830
Products: Windows, millwork, wood and steel doors. **SIC:** 5031 (Lumber, Plywood & Millwork). **Sales:** $70,000,000 (1994). **Emp:** 150. **Officers:** T.R. Hager, President; Paul Verbrugge, Controller.

■ **7409** ■ **Granger Lumber-Hardware, Inc.**
1180 Lane Ave. S
Jacksonville, FL 32205-6234
Phone: (904)781-4116 **Fax:** (904)783-3443
Products: Lumber; Hardware. **SICs:** 5031 (Lumber, Plywood & Millwork); 5072 (Hardware). **Est:** 1917. **Sales:** $10,000,000 (2000). **Emp:** 100. **Officers:** Sam Granger; Hugh Granger, General Mgr.; Joe McCollum, Marketing & Sales Mgr.

■ **7410** ■ **Granite City Ready Mix Inc.**
PO Box 1305
St. Cloud, MN 56302
Phone: (320)252-4324 **Fax:** (320)259-1792
Products: Concrete; Sand; Rock. **SIC:** 5032 (Brick, Stone & Related Materials). **Est:** 1959. **Sales:** $12,000,000 (2000). **Emp:** 105. **Officers:** Robert C. Bogard Sr., President.

■ **7411** ■ **Granite City Ready Mix Inc.**
PO Box 1305
St. Cloud, MN 56302
Phone: (320)252-4324 **Fax:** (320)259-1792
Products: Construction materials and machinery. **SIC:**

5032 (Brick, Stone & Related Materials). **Sales:** $12,000,000 (2000). **Emp:** 105.

■ **7412** ■ **Granite Rock Co.**
PO Box 50001
Watsonville, CA 95077
Phone: (831)768-2000 **Fax:** (831)768-2201
E-mail: info@graniterock.com
URL: http://www.graniterock.com
Products: Sand and rock; Concrete and asphalt. **SIC:** 5032 (Brick, Stone & Related Materials). **Est:** 1900. **Emp:** 700. **Officers:** Bruce W. Woolpert, CEO & President; Rita Alves, CFO; Keith Severson, Dir. of Marketing, e-mail: kseverson@graniterock.com; Sanjar Chakamian, Chief Investment Officer; Shirley Ow, Dir of Personnel.

■ **7413** ■ **Louis J. Grasmick Lumber Company Inc.**
6715 Quad Ave.
Baltimore, MD 21237
Phone: (410)325-9663 **Fax:** (410)325-6036
Products: Construction products, including lumber, plywood, and drywall accessories. **SIC:** 5031 (Lumber, Plywood & Millwork). **Est:** 1951. **Sales:** $48,000,000 (2000). **Emp:** 55. **Officers:** Louis J. Grasmick, CEO; Michael Hilditch, Controller; Dee-Dee Lancelotta, VP of Sales.

■ **7414** ■ **The Great Organization Inc.**
15125 N Hayden Rd., Ste. 120
Scottsdale, AZ 85260-2548
Phone: (480)998-1522 **Fax:** (480)998-3078
URL: http://www.greatorg.com
Products: Cabinets; Closets; Home offices. **SIC:** 5031 (Lumber, Plywood & Millwork). **Est:** 1987. **Sales:** $2,500,000 (1999). **Emp:** 38. **Officers:** Vern Mock, President.

■ **7415** ■ **Great Plains**
5445 27th St.
Moline, IL 61265
Phone: (309)764-8365 **Fax:** (309)764-9798
Products: Lumber and wood products. **SIC:** 5031 (Lumber, Plywood & Millwork). **Est:** 1868. **Sales:** $9,300,000 (2000). **Emp:** 70. **Officers:** William Mueller, Treasurer.

■ **7416** ■ **J.J. Gregory and Sons Inc.**
77 Highland Ave.
East Providence, RI 02914
Phone: (401)434-7700 **Fax:** (401)438-4643
Products: Construction equipment. **SIC:** 5082 (Construction & Mining Machinery). **Est:** 1950. **Sales:** $7,500,000 (2000). **Emp:** 40. **Officers:** Jack J. Gregory Jr., President; Richard Grogan, CFO; Jay Gregory, VP of Marketing.

■ **7417** ■ **R.C. Griffith Inc.**
1004 First Ave.
Council Bluffs, IA 51501
Phone: (712)322-7331 **Fax:** (712)322-7350
Products: Lumber and hardwood; Veneer logs. **SIC:** 5031 (Lumber, Plywood & Millwork). **Officers:** Robert C. Griffith, President.

■ **7418** ■ **Grinnell Door Inc. (GS & D)**
315 North Ave.
Mt. Clemens, MI 48043
Phone: (810)463-8667
Free: (800)451-4428 **Fax:** (810)463-4098
E-mail: grinelldr@aol.com
Products: Interior and exterior wood doors. **SICs:** 5031 (Lumber, Plywood & Millwork); 5039 (Construction Materials Nec). **Est:** 1930. **Emp:** 18. **Officers:** Mark Iannuzzi, President; Bryan Iannuzzi, Vice President; Keith Iannuzzi, Treasurer. **Former Name:** Grinnell Sash & Door Inc. (GS & D).

■ **7419** ■ **S.T. Griswold and Company Inc.**
PO Box 849
Williston, VT 05495
Phone: (802)658-0201 **Fax:** (802)658-6869
Products: Concrete blocks; Pipes; Manholes. **SICs:** 5032 (Brick, Stone & Related Materials); 5051 (Metals Service Centers & Offices). **Est:** 1957. **Sales:** $10,000,000 (2000). **Emp:** 90. **Officers:** Douglas H. Griswold, President; James B. Stillman Jr., VP of Finance.

■ **7420** ■ **Gross-Yowell and Company Inc.**
3720 Franklin Ave.
Waco, TX 76710
Phone: (254)754-5475
Products: Lumber and wood products; Paints and allied products; Hardware. **SICs:** 5031 (Lumber, Plywood & Millwork); 5072 (Hardware); 5198 (Paints, Varnishes & Supplies). **Est:** 1945. **Sales:** $9,000,000 (2000). **Emp:** 40. **Officers:** William O. Gross Jr., President; Harold Helpert, General Mgr.

■ **7421** ■ **GTH Holdings, Inc.**
PO Box 2617
Butler, PA 16003
Phone: (412)282-4528 **Fax:** (412)282-0558
Products: Construction materials; Industrial supplies; Sporting and recreational goods; Furniture; Carpet. **SICs:** 5039 (Construction Materials Nec); 5021 (Furniture); 5085 (Industrial Supplies); 5091 (Sporting & Recreational Goods); 5023 (Homefurnishings). **Officers:** G. Thomas Hammonds, President. **Former Name:** General Trading House.

■ **7422** ■ **Gino Guido Inc.**
PO Box 17207
San Antonio, TX 78217
Phone: (210)828-9911 **Fax:** (210)828-9194
Products: Lumber and supplies, including pine, whitewood, paper, insulation, and nails. **SICs:** 5031 (Lumber, Plywood & Millwork); 5033 (Roofing, Siding & Insulation). **Est:** 1971. **Sales:** $5,100,000 (2000). **Emp:** 25. **Officers:** G.C. Guido, President & Treasurer; M. Guido, Vice President.

■ **7423** ■ **Guido Lumber Company Inc.**
PO Box 790908
San Antonio, TX 78279-0908
Phone: (210)344-8321 **Fax:** (210)344-3469
Products: Lumber. **SIC:** 5031 (Lumber, Plywood & Millwork). **Est:** 1947. **Sales:** $6,000,000 (2000). **Emp:** 20. **Officers:** B.V. Guido, President.

■ **7424** ■ **Albert Gunther and Co.**
1201 Desoto Rd.
Baltimore, MD 21223
Phone: (410)644-0926 **Fax:** (410)644-0908
Products: Door frames; Door hardware; Handles; Builders' hardware. **SICs:** 5031 (Lumber, Plywood & Millwork); 5072 (Hardware). **Est:** 1936. **Sales:** $12,000,000 (2000). **Emp:** 85. **Officers:** Fernando Conepa, CEO.

■ **7425** ■ **Gunton Corp.**
26150 Richmond Rd.
Bedford Heights, OH 44146
Phone: (216)831-2420
Products: Windows and doors. **SIC:** 5031 (Lumber, Plywood & Millwork). **Est:** 1932. **Sales:** $85,000,000 (1999). **Emp:** 300. **Officers:** Mark Mead, President; Reggie Stacy, Treasurer; Kevin Gaffney, VP of Marketing & Sales; Joe Bobnar, VP of Operations.

■ **7426** ■ **Gypsum Wholesalers Inc.**
3334 Walters Rd.
Syracuse, NY 13209
Phone: (315)451-5322
Free: (800)782-3010 **Fax:** (315)457-4031
Products: Gypsum building materials. **SICs:** 5032 (Brick, Stone & Related Materials); 5039 (Construction Materials Nec); 5031 (Lumber, Plywood & Millwork). **Est:** 1977. **Sales:** $10,000,000 (2000). **Emp:** 49. **Officers:** Roy W. van Norstrand, Controller.

■ **7427** ■ **H & H Distributing Inc.**
550 E Amity Rd.
Boise, ID 83705-5206
Phone: (208)345-4086 **Fax:** (208)343-6571
Products: Fasteners; Hardware; Roofing, siding, and insulation. **SICs:** 5033 (Roofing, Siding & Insulation); 5072 (Hardware). **Officers:** Hal Hammaker, President.

■ **7428** ■ **T.W. Hager Lumber Company Inc.**
PO Box 912
Grand Rapids, MI 49509
Phone: (616)452-5151 **Fax:** (616)247-5100
Products: Lumber; Crating material; Particleboard; MDF. **SICs:** 5031 (Lumber, Plywood & Millwork); 5032 (Brick, Stone & Related Materials); 5039 (Construction Materials Nec). **Est:** 1927. **Sales:** $36,000,000 (1999).

Emp: 129. **Officers:** T. R. Hager, Co-Chairman; G. F. Vitale, President; D. F. Garver, Sec. & Treas.; J. Jager, General Mgr.

■ **7429** ■ **Haggerty Lumber**
PO Box 187
Walled Lake, MI 48390
Phone: (248)624-4551
Products: Lumber, windows, and doors. **SIC:** 5031 (Lumber, Plywood & Millwork). **Sales:** $19,000,000 (2000). **Emp:** 70. **Officers:** Ron Snyder, General Mgr.

■ **7430** ■ **Hahn Systems**
PO Box 42427
Indianapolis, IN 46242-0427
Phone: (317)243-3796 **Fax:** (317)244-9079
Products: Pneumatic stapling equipment and construction supplies. **SICs:** 5084 (Industrial Machinery & Equipment); 5082 (Construction & Mining Machinery). **Est:** 1938. **Sales:** $35,000,000 (1999). **Emp:** 156. **Officers:** George Hahn, President; Dave Hankins, VP of Admin.; Doug Hahn, COO; Ronald Leadmon; Leslie Whitlock, Customer Service Contact.

■ **7431** ■ **Hall & Reis, Inc.**
16 Short Hill Rd.
Forest Hills, NY 11375-6074
Phone: (718)458-2567 **Fax:** (718)458-9249
Products: Construction equipment; Electric welding apparatus; Electrical construction materials; Mining machinery and equipment; Oilfield machinery and equipment. **SICs:** 5082 (Construction & Mining Machinery); 5063 (Electrical Apparatus & Equipment); 5084 (Industrial Machinery & Equipment). **Officers:** Geoge Soukup, President.

■ **7432** ■ **Halliday Sand and Gravel Co.**
8340 Calkins Rd.
Houghton Lake, MI 48629
Phone: (517)422-3463
Products: Sand and gravel. **SIC:** 5032 (Brick, Stone & Related Materials).

■ **7433** ■ **Hallmark Building Supplies Inc.**
6060 N 77th St.
Milwaukee, WI 53218-1293
Phone: (414)464-9990
Free: (800)642-2246 **Fax:** (414)464-7928
Products: Kitchen and bathroom building supplies and other construction materials. **SIC:** 5039 (Construction Materials Nec). **Sales:** $17,000,000 (2000). **Emp:** 50. **Officers:** O. Joe Balthazor, President; Bonnie Jachowicz, VP of Finance.

■ **7434** ■ **Halton Co.**
4421 NE Columbia Blvd.
Portland, OR 97218
Phone: (503)288-6411 **Fax:** (503)281-9458
Products: Construction equipment. **SIC:** 5082 (Construction & Mining Machinery). **Est:** 1956. **Sales:** $80,000,000 (2000). **Emp:** 350. **Officers:** Edward H. Halton Jr., President; Mark Fahey, CFO; Rick Rentfro, Dir. of Sales.

■ **7435** ■ **Hammer-Johnson Supply Inc.**
12 S White St.
Athens, TN 37303
Phone: (423)745-2880
Products: Building supplies, including lumber, shingles, and paints. **SICs:** 5031 (Lumber, Plywood & Millwork); 5198 (Paints, Varnishes & Supplies). **Est:** 1917. **Sales:** $6,000,000 (2000). **Emp:** 23. **Officers:** Herbert E. Johnson, President.

■ **7436** ■ **Hammer Lumber Company Inc.**
PO Box 2550
Eugene, OR 97402
Phone: (541)687-1400 **Fax:** (541)485-4724
Products: Building materials; Lumber. **SICs:** 5031 (Lumber, Plywood & Millwork); 5039 (Construction Materials Nec). **Est:** 1950. **Sales:** $6,000,000 (2000). **Emp:** 20. **Officers:** Paul M. Hammer, President; Charles Darden, Dir. of Marketing & Sales.

■ **7437** ■ **Hampton Affiliates Inc.**
9600 SW Barnes Rd.
Ste. 200
Portland, OR 97225
Phone: (503)297-7691
Products: Lumber. **SIC:** 5031 (Lumber, Plywood & Millwork). **Officers:** Ron Parker, CEO.

■ **7438** ■ **Hampton Lumber Sales Co.**
9600 SW Barnes Rd., Ste. 200
Portland, OR 97225
Phone: (503)297-7691   **Fax:** (503)297-3188
Products: Lumber. **SIC:** 5031 (Lumber, Plywood & Millwork). **Est:** 1950. **Sales:** $650,000,000 (1999). **Emp:** 475. **Officers:** Michael Phillips, President; Steve Zika, VP of Finance; Carter Stinton, Dir. of Sales.

■ **7439** ■ **Hankins Lumber Company, Inc.**
PO Box 1397
Grenada, MS 38902-1397
Phone: (662)226-2961   **Fax:** (662)226-6404
E-mail: bhankins@ayrix.net
Products: Lumber; Treated lumber. **SIC:** 5031 (Lumber, Plywood & Millwork). **Est:** 1955. **Sales:** $75,000,000 (1999). **Emp:** 450. **Officers:** A.B. Hankins, CEO; Robert Lewis Smith, Controller; A.B. Hankins Jr., Vice President; Lee Joseph Hankins, Vice President.

■ **7440** ■ **Hanson Aggregates West, Inc.**
1900 W Garvy Ave. S, Ste. 200
West Covina, CA 91790
Phone: (626)856-6700
URL: http://www.hansonplc.com
Products: Concrete products; Asphalt. **SIC:** 5032 (Brick, Stone & Related Materials). **Est:** 1909. **Sales:** $70,000,000 (2000). **Emp:** 250. **Officers:** David Hummel, President; Carol Smith, CFO; William J. Pauro, VP of Marketing & Sales. **Former Name:** Livingston-Graham Inc.

■ **7441** ■ **Harbor Sales Company**
1000 Harbor Ct.
Sudlersville, MD 21668-1818
Free: (800)345-1712   **Fax:** 800-868-9257
Products: Plywood; Plastics. **SICs:** 5031 (Lumber, Plywood & Millwork); 5162 (Plastics Materials & Basic Shapes). **Est:** 1931. **Sales:** $6,000,000 (2000). **Emp:** 54. **Officers:** Don K. Covington Jr., Chairman of the Board; Duncan S. Covington, President.

■ **7442** ■ **James Hardie Export**
5931 E Marginal Way S
Seattle, WA 98134
Phone: (206)763-1550   **Fax:** (206)767-4309
Products: Metal studs; Fiberglass insulation; Electric lighting louvers; Solid wood paneling; Gypsum wallboard. **SICs:** 5031 (Lumber, Plywood & Millwork); 5051 (Metals Service Centers & Offices); 5033 (Roofing, Siding & Insulation); 5063 (Electrical Apparatus & Equipment); 5032 (Brick, Stone & Related Materials). **Officers:** Dick Aloworth, Manager/Intl. Export.

■ **7443** ■ **Harding and Lawler Inc.**
PO Box 580
Orange, TX 77630
Phone: (409)883-4371   **Fax:** (409)883-4375
Products: Lumber and wood products. **SIC:** 5031 (Lumber, Plywood & Millwork). **Est:** 1932. **Sales:** $6,500,000 (2000). **Emp:** 62. **Officers:** E. Maier, President & Treasurer.

■ **7444** ■ **Harding's Inc.**
PO Box 187
Lowell, IN 46356
Phone: (219)696-8911
Products: Heavy equipment parts; Used equipment parts. **SIC:** 5082 (Construction & Mining Machinery). **Est:** 1946. **Sales:** $4,500,000 (2000). **Emp:** 34. **Officers:** Clarence Harding Sr., President.

■ **7445** ■ **Hardware Imagination**
5329 W Crenshaw
Tampa, FL 33634
Phone: (813)882-0322
Free: (800)722-4409   **Fax:** (813)882-0264
Products: Raw materials for kitchen cabinets. **SIC:** 5031 (Lumber, Plywood & Millwork). **Officers:** Ed Vila.

■ **7446** ■ **Hardware Imagination**
603 Landstreet Rd.
Orlando, FL 32824
Phone: (407)855-2282
Free: (800)432-5433   **Fax:** (407)855-4453
Products: Cabinet supplies. **SIC:** 5031 (Lumber, Plywood & Millwork). **Officers:** Mike Raddick.

■ **7447** ■ **Hardwoods of Morganton Inc.**
PO Box 1099
Morganton, NC 28655-1099
Phone: (828)437-0761
Free: (800)438-7007   **Fax:** (828)438-5334
E-mail: sales@hwoods.com
Products: Hardwood lumber. **SIC:** 5031 (Lumber, Plywood & Millwork). **Est:** 1956. **Sales:** $30,000,000 (2000). **Emp:** 12. **Officers:** C. F. Hopkins, President; Wendell Sugg, Vice President; Chalres Kirksey, Sec. & Treas.

■ **7448** ■ **Hardy Corp.**
711 W 103rd St.
Chicago, IL 60628
Phone: (773)779-6600   **Fax:** (773)779-6618
Products: Windows. **SIC:** 5031 (Lumber, Plywood & Millwork). **Est:** 1933. **Sales:** $1,000,000 (2000). **Emp:** 12. **Officers:** William P. Hardy.

■ **7449** ■ **Joseph T. Hardy & Son**
425 Old Airport Rd.
New Castle, DE 19720
Phone: (302)328-9457   **Fax:** (302)328-0434
Products: Mechanical construction supplies. **SIC:** 5082 (Construction & Mining Machinery).

■ **7450** ■ **Harrison Supply Co.**
800 Passaic Ave.
East Newark, NJ 07029
Phone: (973)483-4494   **Fax:** (973)483-4411
Products: Concrete and masonry materials. **SIC:** 5032 (Brick, Stone & Related Materials). **Est:** 1885. **Sales:** $1,000,000 (2000). **Emp:** 10. **Officers:** Kenneth Phillips, President.

■ **7451** ■ **Harvey Industries Inc.**
43 Emerson Rd.
Waltham, MA 02454
Phone: (617)899-3500
Products: Doors, windows, roofing, and siding. **SICs:** 5033 (Roofing, Siding & Insulation); 5031 (Lumber, Plywood & Millwork). **Est:** 1961. **Sales:** $160,000,000 (2000). **Emp:** 1,100. **Officers:** Alan Marlow, President; Frank Martel, Exec. VP & Treasurer; Glen Frederick, Exec. VP of Marketing; Jeff Ribero, Dir. of Data Processing; Thomas Russell, Dir of Human Resources.

■ **7452** ■ **Harvey Lumber Company Inc.**
234 Primrose St.
Haverhill, MA 01830
Phone: (508)372-7727   **Fax:** (508)373-7443
Products: Lumber, including plywood. **SIC:** 5031 (Lumber, Plywood & Millwork). **Est:** 1959. **Sales:** $11,000,000 (2000). **Emp:** 32. **Officers:** Harvey L. Betournay, President & Treasurer.

■ **7453** ■ **Hatley Lumber Co. Inc.**
601 Emmonsville Rd.
PO Box 82
Hatley, WI 54440-0082
Phone: (715)446-3311   **Fax:** (715)446-3312
Products: Lumber and building materials. **SIC:** 5031 (Lumber, Plywood & Millwork). **Est:** 1938. **Sales:** $1,200,000 (2000). **Emp:** 6. **Officers:** Donald Pickering.

■ **7454** ■ **Hattenbach Co.**
1929 E 61st St.
Cleveland, OH 44103
Phone: (216)881-5200   **Fax:** (216)881-5425
Products: Custom cabinets, shelves, and platforms. **SICs:** 5031 (Lumber, Plywood & Millwork); 5039 (Construction Materials Nec). **Est:** 1940. **Sales:** $10,400,000 (2000). **Emp:** 55. **Officers:** H.A. Hattenbach, President; E.J. Klenotic, Controller.

■ **7455** ■ **Hauptly Construction and Equipment Company Inc.**
PO Box 225
Dunkerton, IA 50626-0225
Phone: (319)822-4205
Products: Construction installation equipment; Grain bins and elevators. **SICs:** 5082 (Construction & Mining Machinery); 5083 (Farm & Garden Machinery). **Est:** 1954. **Sales:** $7,000,000 (2000). **Emp:** 25. **Officers:** Carol Hauptly, President.

■ **7456** ■ **Hausman Corp.**
2842 Rand Rd.
Indianapolis, IN 46241
Phone: (317)844-6044
Products: Construction equipment. **SIC:** 5082 (Construction & Mining Machinery). **Sales:** $35,000,000 (1993). **Emp:** 400. **Officers:** Richard Raymond, President; J.R. Fowler, Treasurer.

■ **7457** ■ **Hawaii Modular Space Inc.**
91-252 Kauhi St.
Kapolei, HI 96707-1803
Phone: (808)682-5559
Products: Prefabricated modular offices. **SIC:** 5039 (Construction Materials Nec). **Sales:** $4,000,000 (2000). **Emp:** 17. **Officers:** Michael Fox, President.

■ **7458** ■ **Hawkeye Building Supply Co.**
PO Box 1343
Sioux City, IA 51102
Phone: (712)277-4001   **Fax:** (712)277-3316
Products: Building supplies, including lumber, steel, roofing, and insulation. **SICs:** 5031 (Lumber, Plywood & Millwork); 5033 (Roofing, Siding & Insulation). **Est:** 1953. **Sales:** $14,000,000 (2000). **Emp:** 28. **Officers:** William H. Engelen, President.

■ **7459** ■ **Hawkins Machinery Inc.**
1475-89 Thomas St.
Memphis, TN 38107
Phone: (901)525-5746
Products: Cranes; Front-end loaders; Road wideners. **SIC:** 5082 (Construction & Mining Machinery). **Est:** 1989. **Sales:** $3,000,000 (2000). **Emp:** 12. **Officers:** David Gully, President.

■ **7460** ■ **Hayden-Murphy Equipment Co.**
9301 E Bloomington Fwy.
Minneapolis, MN 55420
Phone: (612)884-2301
Free: (800)352-2757   **Fax:** (612)884-2293
Products: Heavy construction equipment. **SICs:** 5084 (Industrial Machinery & Equipment); 5082 (Construction & Mining Machinery). **Est:** 1962. **Sales:** $40,000,000 (1999). **Emp:** 46. **Officers:** Leonard Kirk, CEO; Don Knackstedt, Finance Officer; Greg Steege, Dir. of Sales.

■ **7461** ■ **Haywood Builders Supply Inc.**
PO Box 187
Waynesville, NC 28786
Phone: (704)456-6051   **Fax:** (704)456-7212
Products: Building supplies. **SIC:** 5039 (Construction Materials Nec). **Est:** 1948. **Sales:** $7,000,000 (2000). **Emp:** 30. **Officers:** VP and General Manager.

■ **7462** ■ **T.R. Hazlett Company Inc.**
11950 Baltimore Ave.
Beltsville, MD 20705
Phone: (301)419-0033
Free: (800)969-7220   **Fax:** (301)419-0041
Products: Floor finishers; Sanders; Edgers; Nailers; Abrasives; Moldings; Unfinished strip flooring. **SICs:** 5084 (Industrial Machinery & Equipment); 5072 (Hardware); 5085 (Industrial Supplies). **Est:** 1948. **Sales:** $2,800,000 (2000). **Emp:** 10. **Officers:** Karen Hazlett Keigher, President.

■ **7463** ■ **HC Supply**
PO Box 4748
Roanoke, VA 24015
Phone: (540)342-5327   **Fax:** (540)345-1762
Products: Ceiling tiles; Installation products. **SICs:** 5032 (Brick, Stone & Related Materials); 5039 (Construction Materials Nec). **Emp:** 5.

■ 7464 ■ Head and Engguist Equipment L.L.C.
PO Box 52945
Baton Rouge, LA 70892
Phone: (504)356-6113 Fax: (504)355-7734
Products: Construction equipment, including back hoes and bulldozers. SIC: 5082 (Construction & Mining Machinery). Est: 1962. Sales: $82,000,000 (2000). Emp: 230. Officers: John Engguist, CEO & President; Terence Eastman, CFO; Hubert Louque, Sr. VP; Richard Knight, Human Resources Mgr.

■ 7465 ■ Heap Lumber Sales Company Inc.
11136 Manchester Rd.
St. Louis, MO 63122
Phone: (314)966-3640
Products: Lumber and plywood. SIC: 5031 (Lumber, Plywood & Millwork). Sales: $22,000,000 (2000). Emp: 8. Officers: Lyle F. Heap, CEO; David Heap, Vice President.

■ 7466 ■ Heatilator Inc.
1915 W Saunders St.
Mt. Pleasant, IA 52641
Phone: (319)385-9211 Fax: (319)385-5805
Products: Fireplaces and accessories. SIC: 5074 (Plumbing & Hydronic Heating Supplies). Sales: $50,000,000 (2000). Emp: 400. Officers: Stan Askren, President; Thomas Dyer, CFO.

■ 7467 ■ E.P. Henry Corp.
PO Box 615
Woodbury, NJ 08096
Phone: (609)845-6200 Fax: (609)845-0023
Products: Customized block cement; Paving stones. SIC: 5032 (Brick, Stone & Related Materials). Est: 1913. Sales: $12,000,000 (2000). Emp: 100. Officers: J.C. Henry Jr., President.

■ 7468 ■ Hews Company Inc.
190 Rumery St.
South Portland, ME 04106
Phone: (207)767-2136 Fax: (207)767-5381
Products: Heavy vehicles, including dump trucks and truck cranes; Truck bodies and equipment. SICs: 5012 (Automobiles & Other Motor Vehicles); 5082 (Construction & Mining Machinery). Est: 1927. Sales: $4,500,000 (2000). Emp: 35. Officers: Robert E. Hews, President; Charles Hews, Dir. of Marketing & Sales; Corey Lathrop, Plant Mgr.

■ 7469 ■ Higginbotham-Bartlett Co.
PO Box 6880
Lubbock, TX 79493-6880
Phone: (806)793-8662 Fax: (806)792-8089
Products: Lumber and wood products. SIC: 5031 (Lumber, Plywood & Millwork). Est: 1912. Sales: $20,000,000 (2000). Emp: 130. Officers: J.L. Higginbotham Jr., President; C.S. Wood, Treasurer & Secty.

■ 7470 ■ J.E. Higgins Lumber Co.
6999 Southfront Rd.
Livermore, CA 94550
Phone: (925)245-4300
Free: (877)241-1883 Fax: (925)245-4343
URL: http://www.higlum.com
Products: Lumber. SIC: 5031 (Lumber, Plywood & Millwork). Est: 1883. Sales: $122,000,000 (2000). Emp: 450. Officers: Jonathan R. Long, President & CEO; Scott M. Watson, VP of Sales; Charles R. Robbins, VP of Purchasing; Randy Tunison, Dir. of Information Systems; Larry Knox, VP of Operations.

■ 7471 ■ J.E. Higgins Lumber Co.
4734 E Jensen Ave.
Fresno, CA 93725
Phone: (209)264-1771 Fax: (209)264-4413
Products: Lumber; Woodworking equipment and accessories. SIC: 5031 (Lumber, Plywood & Millwork).

■ 7472 ■ J.E. Higgins Lumber Co.
13290 Paxton St.
Pacoima, CA 91331
Phone: (818)890-2228 Fax: (818)896-6519
Products: Lumber. SIC: 5031 (Lumber, Plywood & Millwork).

■ 7473 ■ J.E. Higgins Lumber Co.
3612 Kurtz St.
San Diego, CA 92110-4432
Phone: (760)686-8690 Fax: (760)686-8699
Products: Lumber. SIC: 5031 (Lumber, Plywood & Millwork).

■ 7474 ■ J.E. Higgins Lumber Co.
939 W Boone
Santa Maria, CA 93454
Phone: (805)928-8325 Fax: (805)922-4254
Products: Lumber and lumber supplies. SIC: 5031 (Lumber, Plywood & Millwork).

■ 7475 ■ Hodgin Supply Company Inc.
PO Box 2160
Greensboro, NC 27402
Phone: (910)275-8561
Products: Aluminum and vinyl siding. SIC: 5033 (Roofing, Siding & Insulation). Est: 1946. Sales: $6,000,000 (2000). Emp: 23. Officers: J. Vernon Hodgin Jr., President.

■ 7476 ■ Hoffman International Inc.
300 S Randolphville Rd
Piscataway, NJ 08855
Phone: (732)752-3600
Free: (800)446-3362 Fax: (732)968-8371
E-mail: sales@hoffmanequip.com
URL: http://www.hoffmanequip.com
Products: Construction machinery and parts. SIC: 5082 (Construction & Mining Machinery). Est: 1920. Sales: $25,000,000 (2000). Emp: 50. Officers: W.A. Hoffman Jr., Chairman of the Board; J.F. Watters, President.

■ 7477 ■ Holland Southwest International Inc.
PO Box 330249
Houston, TX 77233
Phone: (713)644-1966
Free: (800)356-4144 Fax: (713)644-7223
URL: http://www.hollandsw.com
Products: Hardboard; Particleboard; MDF; Wall paneling; Tileboard; Lattice; Plywoods; Russian birch plywood; Cut-to-size and custom finishing. SIC: 5031 (Lumber, Plywood & Millwork). Est: 1953. Sales: $20,000,000 (1999). Emp: 21. Officers: B. Gillebaard, Chairman; JoAnn Gillebaard, President; Gary Hester, VP & Controller; Larry Svaton, Sales Mgr., e-mail: lsvaton@hollandsw.com.

■ 7478 ■ Holmes A-One Inc.
2105 Morrie Ave.
Cheyenne, WY 82001-3922
Phone: (307)632-6431 Fax: (307)778-8660
Products: Construction materials. SIC: 5039 (Construction Materials Nec). Officers: Duane Thomas, President.

■ 7479 ■ Holston Builders Supply Company Inc.
645 E Main St.
Kingsport, TN 37660
Phone: (615)247-8131
Products: Windows. SICs: 5031 (Lumber, Plywood & Millwork); 5039 (Construction Materials Nec). Est: 1958. Sales: $21,000,000 (2000). Emp: 60. Officers: Ed Roberts, CEO.

■ 7480 ■ Holt Company of Texas
PO Box 207916
San Antonio, TX 78220-7916
Phone: (210)648-1111
Free: (800)275-4658 Fax: (210)648-0079
E-mail: marketing@holttexas.com
URL: http://www.holttexas.com
Products: Construction equipment. SIC: 5082 (Construction & Mining Machinery). Est: 1933. Sales: $209,000,000 (2000). Emp: 800. Officers: Peter Holt, President & CEO. Former Name: Holt Cos.

■ 7481 ■ Home Lumber Company Inc.
PO Box 1037
Hazard, KY 41702
Phone: (606)436-3185
Free: (800)467-0185 Fax: (606)439-4299
E-mail: homelum@tgtel.com
Products: Lumber. SIC: 5031 (Lumber, Plywood & Millwork). Est: 1914. Sales: $7,000,000 (1999). Emp:

42. Officers: Peyton Morton, President; David Stanford, CFO.

■ 7482 ■ Homelite, Inc.
14401 Carowinds Blvd.
Charlotte, NC 28241
Phone: (704)588-3200 Fax: (704)587-2728
Products: Lawn and garden equipment; Construction machinery and equipment, including other construction machinery parts. SIC: 5082 (Construction & Mining Machinery). Officers: Martin Multer; Jan Boosman; Michael J. Hurst; Norman Giertz.

■ 7483 ■ J.H. Hommer Lumber Co.
Rte. 253
Glasgow, PA 16644
Phone: (814)687-4211 Fax: (814)687-3359
Products: Lumber and wood products. SIC: 5031 (Lumber, Plywood & Millwork). Est: 1954. Sales: $2,300,000 (2000). Emp: 23. Officers: Sandy Hommer, CEO & President; Gene Cree, Sales Mgr.; John Lloyd, Dir. of Data Processing.

■ 7484 ■ Honsador Inc.
91-151 Malakole Rd.
Ewa Beach, HI 96706
Phone: (808)682-2011 Fax: (808)682-5252
Products: Lumber; House packages, windows, doors, and building supplies. SIC: 5031 (Lumber, Plywood & Millwork). Est: 1935. Sales: $41,000,000 (2000). Emp: 100. Officers: J.J. Pappas, Chairman of the Board; Terris Inglett, President.

■ 7485 ■ Hoosier Company Inc.
PO Box 681064
Indianapolis, IN 46268
Phone: (317)872-8125 Fax: (317)926-2434
Products: Metal doors and frames; Metal partitions and fixtures. SIC: 5084 (Industrial Machinery & Equipment). Est: 1931. Sales: $3,000,000 (2000). Emp: 35. Officers: Cheryl P. Englehart, President; Robert E. Fisher, Vice President; Nelson S. Hart, Treasurer & Secty.

■ 7486 ■ Ora B. Hopper and Son Inc.
302 S 30th St.
Phoenix, AZ 85034
Phone: (602)273-1338
Products: Prefabricated interior wall systems. SIC: 5039 (Construction Materials Nec).

■ 7487 ■ Thomas R. Hopson Broker Inc.
PO Box 7295
Marietta, GA 30065
Phone: (404)578-2400 Fax: (404)565-9553
Products: Windows, roofing, and siding. SIC: 5031 (Lumber, Plywood & Millwork). Est: 1974. Sales: $94,000,000 (2000). Emp: 500. Officers: Steve Hopson, President; Jack Baker, CFO; Jim Stansbury, Dir. of Marketing; Jeff Arnold, Dir. of Data Processing; Pam Schulman, Dir of Human Resources.

■ 7488 ■ Horizon High Reach, Inc.
222 Bergen Tpk.
Ridgefield Park, NJ 07660
Phone: (201)440-6002 Fax: (201)440-4103
Products: Aerial platforms. SIC: 5082 (Construction & Mining Machinery). Est: 1947. Sales: $5,000,000 (2000). Emp: 18. Officers: Kevin Parr, Manager.

■ 7489 ■ Horizon High Reach Inc.
222 Bergen Tpk.
Ridgefield Park, NJ 07660
Phone: (201)440-6002 Fax: (201)440-4103
Products: Construction materials and machinery. SIC: 5082 (Construction & Mining Machinery). Sales: $5,000,000 (2000). Emp: 18.

■ 7490 ■ Houston Stained Glass Supply
2002 Brittmoore Rd.
Houston, TX 77043-2209
Phone: (713)690-8844
Free: (800)231-0148 Fax: (713)690-0009
E-mail: sales@hsgs.com
URL: http://www.hsgs.com
Products: Specialty glass products. SIC: 5039 (Construction Materials Nec). Est: 1976. Emp: 110. Officers: Neil Pickthall, Sales & Marketing Contact, e-mail: neil@hsgs.com.

■ **7491** ■ **Houston-Starr Co.**
300 Brushton Ave.
Pittsburgh, PA 15221
Phone: (412)242-6000 **Fax:** (412)242-4754
Products: Building supplies, including doors and cabinets. SIC: 5031 (Lumber, Plywood & Millwork). **Sales:** $9,800,000 (2000). **Emp:** 42. **Officers:** J.B. Starr, President.

■ **7492** ■ **HPG Industries Inc.**
PO Box 1001
Palm Beach, FL 33480-1001
Phone: (561)712-8842 **Fax:** (561)712-9736
E-mail: hpgind@mindspring.com
Products: Lumber, plywood, and millwork; Farm and garden machinery; Industrial machinery and equipment; Electronic parts and equipment; Computers, peripherals, and software, ups; Wood working machinery. **SICs:** 5031 (Lumber, Plywood & Millwork); 5045 (Computers, Peripherals & Software); 5083 (Farm & Garden Machinery); 5084 (Industrial Machinery & Equipment); 5065 (Electronic Parts & Equipment Nec). **Est:** 1968. **Sales:** $3,000,000 (2000). **Emp:** 10. **Officers:** H. Sharoubim, Contact.

■ **7493** ■ **Hudson Company**
PO Box 646
Winchester, KY 40392-0646
Phone: (606)744-7040 **Fax:** (606)745-1033
Products: Tires for earth moving equipment. SIC: 5082 (Construction & Mining Machinery). **Officers:** Steve Smith, Chairman, CEO.

■ **7494** ■ **Hudson Cos.**
89 Ship St.
Providence, RI 02903-4218
Phone: (401)274-2200 **Fax:** (401)274-2220
Products: Liquid asphalt. SIC: 5032 (Brick, Stone & Related Materials). **Est:** 1955. **Sales:** $70,000,000 (2000). **Emp:** 225. **Officers:** Thomas F. Hudson, CEO; Edward R. Lodge Jr., CFO; Francis J. O'Brien, Exec. VP of Marketing.

■ **7495** ■ **Hudson Glass Company Inc.**
219 N Division St.
Peekskill, NY 10566-2700
Phone: (914)737-2124
Free: (800)444-2748 **Fax:** (914)737-4447
E-mail: hudsonsg@aol.com
Products: Stained glass, tools, and supplies; Bent glass; Auto glass. SIC: 5039 (Construction Materials Nec). **Est:** 1966. **Sales:** $2,000,000 (2000). **Emp:** 20. **Officers:** Herb D. Lewis; Jeff Lewis, Vice President.

■ **7496** ■ **Hudson Liquid Asphalts, Inc.**
30 Shipyard St.
Providence, RI 02903
Phone: (401)781-8200 **Fax:** (401)781-6644
Products: Liquid asphalt. SIC: 5033 (Roofing, Siding & Insulation). **Officers:** Joseph Murphy, VP of Operations. **Former Name:** John J. Hudson, Inc.

■ **7497** ■ **Humac Engineering and Equipment Inc.**
PO Box 581519
Minneapolis, MN 55458
Phone: (612)541-0567 **Fax:** (612)541-0772
Products: Construction equipment; Fencing; Materials and handling equipment; Shelving-racking; Lockers; Work benches; Office and computer furniture. **SICs:** 5082 (Construction & Mining Machinery); 5112 (Stationery & Office Supplies); 5021 (Furniture); 5039 (Construction Materials Nec). **Est:** 1981. **Sales:** $1,800,000 (2000). **Emp:** 5. **Officers:** Tom McCoy, President; Gwendilyn A. Goodwin, CFO.

■ **7498** ■ **P.D. Humphrey Company Inc.**
590 Main Rd.
Tiverton, RI 02878
Phone: (401)624-8414 **Fax:** (401)625-6655
Products: Lumber and wood products; Tools. **SICs:** 5031 (Lumber, Plywood & Millwork); 5072 (Hardware). **Est:** 1885. **Sales:** $5,000,000 (2000). **Emp:** 83. **Officers:** William W. Humphrey, CEO & President; Scott Humphrey, Exec. VP & Controller.

■ **7499** ■ **Hundman Lumber Do-it Center Inc.**
1707 Hamilton Rd.
Bloomington, IL 61704
Phone: (309)662-0339
Products: Building materials. SIC: 5031 (Lumber, Plywood & Millwork).

■ **7500** ■ **Hurst Lumber Company Inc.**
104 E Hurst Blvd.
Hurst, TX 76053
Phone: (817)282-2519
Products: Lumber and plywood; Hardware including, nuts, screws, bolts. **SICs:** 5031 (Lumber, Plywood & Millwork); 5072 (Hardware). **Est:** 1947. **Emp:** 45. **Officers:** Richard D. Laxton, President; Allen Smith, CFO; Gene Fowler, VP of Operations.

■ **7501** ■ **Hurst Supply**
PO Box 580490
Tulsa, OK 74158
Phone: (918)835-4441 **Fax:** (918)835-2716
Products: Concrete mix and mortar. SIC: 5032 (Brick, Stone & Related Materials). **Est:** 1950. **Sales:** $5,000,000 (2000). **Emp:** 20. **Officers:** Jim L. Wagner, President; Irv Stemme, Controller; Micheal Braswell, Dir. of Sales.

■ **7502** ■ **Huttig Sash & Door Co.**
2059 Shawano Ave.
PO Box 10975
Green Bay, WI 54307-0975
Phone: (920)499-2117 **Fax:** (920)499-6708
Products: Wood window and door frames; Metal doors and frames; Window frames. SIC: 5031 (Lumber, Plywood & Millwork).

■ **7503** ■ **ICE Export Sales Corp.**
36 Maple Ave.
PO Box 11
Manhasset, NY 11030
Phone: (516)365-0011 **Fax:** (516)366-0017
Products: Road building, mining, crushing, and construction equipment and spare parts. **SICs:** 5082 (Construction & Mining Machinery); 5085 (Industrial Supplies). **Est:** 1974. **Sales:** $1,000,000 (2000). **Emp:** 3. **Officers:** Charles Cannam, President; Lisa Rizzo, Sales/Mktg.

■ **7504** ■ **IDA Inc.**
PO Box 13347
Memphis, TN 38113-0347
Phone: (901)757-8056 **Fax:** (901)757-8058
Products: Construction materials; Ceramic wall and floor tiles; Hardware; Lawn and garden equipment; Men's leather work gloves. **SICs:** 5039 (Construction Materials Nec); 5136 (Men's/Boys' Clothing); 5032 (Brick, Stone & Related Materials); 5072 (Hardware); 5083 (Farm & Garden Machinery). **Officers:** Michael Membreno, Sales Manager.

■ **7505** ■ **IHC Services Inc.**
1624-E Cross Beam Dr.
Charlotte, NC 28217
Phone: (704)357-1211 **Fax:** (704)357-1894
Products: Construction and oil field equipment. **SICs:** 5082 (Construction & Mining Machinery); 5084 (Industrial Machinery & Equipment). **Sales:** $30,000,000 (1994). **Emp:** 25. **Officers:** Robert B. Hall, President; Bruce D'Ambra, Vice President.

■ **7506** ■ **Imagination & Co.**
1575 Cattleman Rd.
Sarasota, FL 34232
Phone: (941)371-5238 **Fax:** (941)371-5846
Products: Cabinetry supplies. SIC: 5031 (Lumber, Plywood & Millwork).

■ **7507** ■ **Industrial Distributors**
PO Box 1061
Lewiston, ME 04243-1061
Phone: (207)782-4116 **Fax:** (207)782-9859
Products: Roofing; Siding; Insulation; Roofing and siding materials. SIC: 5033 (Roofing, Siding & Insulation). **Est:** 1961. **Emp:** 4. **Officers:** Oscar Hahnel, President; P.D. Sassano, Human Resources.

■ **7508** ■ **Industrial Management Systems Corp.**
PO Box 107
Worthington, CO 43085
Phone: (614)258-2580
Products: Manufactures, services and repairs hydraulic valves, pumps and related parts for the construction, agriculture and mining industries. **SICs:** 5082 (Construction & Mining Machinery); 5083 (Farm & Garden Machinery). **Sales:** $1,000,000 (2000). **Emp:** 5. **Officers:** Richard Lamprey, President; John Tysko, Partner, Finance.

■ **7509** ■ **Industrial Motor Supply Inc.**
PO Box 4128
Harrisburg, PA 17111-0128
Phone: (717)564-0550 **Fax:** (717)564-3502
Products: Construction supplies. **SICs:** 5039 (Construction Materials Nec); 5084 (Industrial Machinery & Equipment). **Est:** 1951. **Sales:** $3,100,000 (2000). **Emp:** 24. **Officers:** Michael S. Nelson Jr., President.

■ **7510** ■ **Industrial Products Co.**
105 Boswell St.
Mt. Pleasant, TN 38474
Phone: (931)379-3227 **Fax:** (931)379-0164
Products: Fiberglass insulation materials. SIC: 5033 (Roofing, Siding & Insulation). **Est:** 1942. **Sales:** $11,000,000 (2000). **Emp:** 32. **Officers:** Ruskin A. Vest, President & Treasurer.

■ **7511** ■ **Industrial and Wholesale Lumber Inc.**
4401 N 25th Ave.
Schiller Park, IL 60176
Phone: (847)678-0480 **Fax:** (847)678-3594
Products: Lumber and crates. SIC: 5031 (Lumber, Plywood & Millwork). **Est:** 1958. **Sales:** $5,000,000 (2000). **Emp:** 35. **Officers:** Jack Kathrein, President; Karna L. Schoedel, Controller; Richard Kouvacs, Sales Mgr.

■ **7512** ■ **Inland Plywood Co.**
375 Cass Ave.
Pontiac, MI 48342
Phone: (248)334-4706 **Fax:** (248)338-7407
Products: Plywood. SIC: 5031 (Lumber, Plywood & Millwork). **Est:** 1967. **Sales:** $12,000,000 (2000). **Emp:** 8. **Officers:** Timothy G. MacEachern, President & CFO.

■ **7513** ■ **Insular Lumber Sales Corp.**
280 Middlefield Rd.
Washington, MA 01223-9414
Phone: (413)623-6657 **Fax:** (413)684-4021
Products: Imported lumber and wood products. SIC: 5031 (Lumber, Plywood & Millwork). **Est:** 1927. **Sales:** $500,000 (2000). **Emp:** 2. **Officers:** Craig A. Walton, President, e-mail: craig@insularlumber.com.

■ **7514** ■ **Integral Kitchens**
6419 N McPhearson
Laredo, TX 78044
Phone: (956)724-4521 **Fax:** (956)727-0986
Products: Floorcovering equipment and supplies. SIC: 5032 (Brick, Stone & Related Materials). **Sales:** $3,000,000 (2000). **Emp:** 65.

■ **7515** ■ **Interior Supply Inc.**
481 E 11th Ave.
Columbus, OH 43211
Phone: (614)424-6611
Products: Paneling and acoustic tile. SIC: 5031 (Lumber, Plywood & Millwork).

■ **7516** ■ **Intermountain Lumber Co.**
PO Box 65970
Salt Lake City, UT 84165-0970
Phone: (801)486-5411 **Fax:** (801)485-6859
Products: Hardwood lumber. SIC: 5031 (Lumber, Plywood & Millwork). **Est:** 1931. **Sales:** $36,000,000 (2000). **Emp:** 50. **Officers:** Ben E. Banks, President; Scott Miles, Controller; Al Stosich, Dir. of Marketing.

■ **7517** ■ **International Consulting & Contracting Services**
PO Box 21202
Lansing, MI 48909
Phone: (517)393-3999 **Fax:** (517)393-3339
Products: Construction equipment; Automotive and truck spare parts; Boilers and water heaters; Plumbing supplies; Office and residential furniture. **SICs:** 5082 (Construction & Mining Machinery); 5021 (Furniture); 5013 (Motor Vehicle Supplies & New Parts); 5074 (Plumbing & Hydronic Heating Supplies). **Officers:** Joseph A. Badra, President.

■ **7518** ■ **International Industries Inc.**
PO Drawer D
Gilbert, WV 25621
Phone: (304)664-3227
Products: Lumber and plywood. **SIC:** 5031 (Lumber, Plywood & Millwork). **Sales:** $84,000,000 (1991). **Emp:** 300. **Officers:** James Harless, President; Ray McKinney, Controller.

■ **7519** ■ **International Paper Co. McEwen Lumber Co.**
PO Box 950
High Point, NC 27261
Phone: (919)472-1900 **Fax:** (919)472-1649
Products: Lumber. **SIC:** 5031 (Lumber, Plywood & Millwork). **Est:** 1899. **Sales:** $25,000,000 (2000). **Emp:** 200. **Officers:** Kenneth W. Shaw, General Mgr.; Lois K. Bohnsack, Manager.

■ **7520** ■ **International Procurement Services, Inc.**
300 Wildwood St.
Woburn, MA 01801
Phone: (781)932-0820 **Fax:** (781)932-0877
Products: Roofing materials; Plumbing supplies; Heating and air-conditioning equipment; Construction supplies; Construction materials, including brick and stone. **SICs:** 5032 (Brick, Stone & Related Materials); 5033 (Roofing, Siding & Insulation); 5074 (Plumbing & Hydronic Heating Supplies); 5075 (Warm Air Heating & Air-Conditioning); 5039 (Construction Materials Nec). **Officers:** Albert E. Pinard, President.

■ **7521** ■ **International Purchasers, Inc.**
PO Box 308
Reisterstown, MD 21136
Phone: (301)833-6400 **Fax:** (301)833-3429
Products: Clay, including acid-resistant cement, bricks, and blocks; Cast iron pressure pipes and fittings; Cast iron metal tanks, including acid coolers; High temperature, non-clay mortars. **SICs:** 5032 (Brick, Stone & Related Materials); 5051 (Metals Service Centers & Offices). **Officers:** William Gisiner Jr., President.

■ **7522** ■ **Interstate Equipment Co.**
1604 Salisbury Rd.
Statesville, NC 28677
Phone: (704)873-9048 **Fax:** (704)872-6071
Products: Trailers; Pumps; Front-end loaders. **SIC:** 5082 (Construction & Mining Machinery). **Est:** 1946. **Sales:** $12,000,000 (2000). **Emp:** 40. **Officers:** Franklin H. Eller, President; Mark Dillard, Treasurer & Secty.

■ **7523** ■ **Interstate Glass Distributors**
300 Unser Blvd. NW
Albuquerque, NM 87101
Phone: (505)836-2361
Products: Glass. **SIC:** 5039 (Construction Materials Nec).

■ **7524** ■ **Intile Designs Inc.**
PO Box 55645
Houston, TX 77255
Phone: (713)468-8400 **Fax:** (713)468-7116
Products: Bricks, lamps, wallpaper and related items. **SICs:** 5032 (Brick, Stone & Related Materials); 5023 (Homefurnishings). **Sales:** $13,000,000 (2000). **Emp:** 31. **Officers:** George Siller, Owner.

■ **7525** ■ **Intrepid Enterprises Inc.**
PO Box 1298
Harvey, LA 70059
Phone: (504)348-2870
Products: Marble and granite stone. **SIC:** 5032 (Brick, Stone & Related Materials).

■ **7526** ■ **Irex Corp.**
PO Box 1268
Lancaster, PA 17608
Phone: (717)397-3633
Products: Insulation and acoustical materials. **SIC:** 5033 (Roofing, Siding & Insulation). **Sales:** $244,400,000 (2000). **Emp:** 465. **Officers:** W. Kirk Liddell, CEO & President; T.L. Troupe, VP & CFO.

■ **7527** ■ **Irving Materials Inc.**
8032 N State Rd. 9
Greenfield, IN 46140
Phone: (317)326-3101 **Fax:** (317)326-8700
Products: Concrete; Aggregate supplies. **SICs:** 5039 (Construction Materials Nec); 5039 (Construction Materials Nec). **Est:** 1946. **Sales:** $120,000,000 (2000). **Emp:** 600. **Officers:** Fred R. Irving, President; Earl Brinker, CFO.

■ **7528** ■ **J & M Industries, Inc.**
1014 S Market St.
Wilmington, DE 19801
Phone: (302)995-2819
Products: Underground storage tank removers. **SICs:** 5082 (Construction & Mining Machinery); 5084 (Industrial Machinery & Equipment). **Former Name:** J & M Construction.

■ **7529** ■ **Jacobson & Company Inc.**
1079 E Grand St.
Elizabeth, NJ 07207-0511
Phone: (908)355-5200 **Fax:** (908)355-8680
URL: http://www.jacobsoncompany.com
Products: Acoustical ceiling and drywall installations. **SIC:** 5033 (Roofing, Siding & Insulation). **Est:** 1889. **Sales:** $25,000,000 (2000). **Emp:** 150. **Officers:** J. Jacobson, Chairman of the Board; A.A. Blattel, CFO; David P. Norgard, Dir. of Marketing; Thomas D. Jacobson, CEO & President.

■ **7530** ■ **J.A.H. Enterprises, Inc.**
PO Box 336
Livingston, LA 70754
Phone: (504)686-2252 **Fax:** (504)686-7658
URL: http://www.hendersonauctions.com
Products: Used construction equipment. **SIC:** 5082 (Construction & Mining Machinery). **Est:** 1992. **Sales:** $35,000,000 (2000). **Emp:** 25. **Officers:** Jeffrey A. Henderson, President, e-mail: jhenderson@hendersonauctions.com. **Doing Business As:** Henderson Auctions.

■ **7531** ■ **Jarvis Steel and Lumber Company Inc.**
1030 E Patapsco Ave.
Baltimore, MD 21225
Phone: (410)355-3000 **Fax:** (410)528-0405
Products: Steel; Lumber, timber, and wood siding. **SICs:** 5031 (Lumber, Plywood & Millwork); 5051 (Metals Service Centers & Offices). **Est:** 1959. **Sales:** $15,000,000 (2000). **Emp:** 75. **Officers:** Victor Frenkil Jr., President; Keith L. Straley, Treasurer; Patrick Dorn, Vice President.

■ **7532** ■ **Jay-K Independent Lumber Corp.**
PO Box 378
New Hartford, NY 13413
Phone: (315)735-4475
Products: Roofing supplies; Plumbing supplies; Wood. **SICs:** 5031 (Lumber, Plywood & Millwork); 5039 (Construction Materials Nec); 5074 (Plumbing & Hydronic Heating Supplies); 5033 (Roofing, Siding & Insulation). **Est:** 1937. **Sales:** $21,000,000 (2000). **Emp:** 125. **Officers:** Kevin M. Kelly, President; P.J. Bombardo, Comptroller; Dean Kelly, Sales Mgr.; Dan Zombek, Dir. of Data Processing; Pat Buckley, Dir of Human Resources.

■ **7533** ■ **Jemison Investment Company Inc.**
320 Park Place Twr.
Birmingham, AL 35203
Phone: (205)324-7681 **Fax:** (205)324-7684
Products: Lumber. **SIC:** 5051 (Metals Service Centers & Offices). **Sales:** $200,000,000 (2000). **Emp:** 250. **Officers:** James Davis, President; Edna Alderman, Controller.

■ **7534** ■ **JETT Supply Company Inc.**
PO Box 2400
Pueblo, CO 81005
Phone: (719)564-6791
Free: (800)367-3257 **Fax:** (719)564-6802
Products: Construction materials. **SIC:** 5039 (Construction Materials Nec). **Est:** 1953. **Emp:** 40.

■ **7535** ■ **Joffe Lumber and Supply Company Inc.**
18 Burns Ave.
Vineland, NJ 08360
Phone: (609)825-9550 **Fax:** (609)327-0798
Products: Lumber. **SIC:** 5031 (Lumber, Plywood & Millwork). **Sales:** $15,000,000 (1994). **Emp:** 80. **Officers:** Saul Joffe, President; Craig Wolf, Treasurer & Secty.

■ **7536** ■ **Johnson-Doppler Lumber Co.**
3320 Llewellyn Ave.
Cincinnati, OH 45223-2467
Phone: (513)541-0050 **Fax:** (513)853-3112
Products: Lumber. **SIC:** 5031 (Lumber, Plywood & Millwork). **Est:** 1920. **Sales:** $11,500,000 (1999). **Emp:** 23. **Officers:** D.E. Doppler, President.

■ **7537** ■ **Johnson Hardware Company Inc.**
1201 Pacific St.
Omaha, NE 68103
Phone: (402)444-1650 **Fax:** (402)444-1659
Products: Metal doors. **SIC:** 5039 (Construction Materials Nec). **Est:** 1855. **Sales:** $6,000,000 (2000). **Emp:** 41. **Officers:** Pat Nipp, President; Barbara Morris, CFO; David Sullivan, Operations Mgr.

■ **7538** ■ **Jordan Lumber and Supply Inc.**
PO Box 98
Mt. Gilead, NC 27306
Phone: (910)439-6121 **Fax:** (910)439-6105
Products: Lumber. **SIC:** 5031 (Lumber, Plywood & Millwork). **Est:** 1939. **Sales:** $60,000,000 (2000). **Emp:** 300. **Officers:** Robert B. Jordan III, President; Lewis H. Dorsett Jr., Controller; Ellen Thompson, Sales Mgr.

■ **7539** ■ **Judson Lumber Co.**
321 W Bigelow Ave.
Plain City, OH 43064
Phone: (614)873-3911
Free: (888)876-2058 **Fax:** (614)873-6920
Products: Lumber. **SIC:** 5031 (Lumber, Plywood & Millwork). **Est:** 1981. **Sales:** $13,500,000 (2000). **Emp:** 22. **Officers:** Judson E. Blaine, President; John R. Horne, Dir. of Marketing & Sales.

■ **7540** ■ **Kansas Brick and Tile Company Inc.**
PO Box 450
Hoisington, KS 67544
Phone: (316)653-2157
Free: (800)653-7609 **Fax:** (316)653-7609
E-mail: ksbrick@hoisington.com
URL: http://www.Kansasbrick.com
Products: Residential or commercial brick. **SIC:** 5032 (Brick, Stone & Related Materials). **Est:** 1954. **Sales:** $5,000,000 (2000). **Emp:** 50. **Officers:** L.R. Smith, President; Mel Wegele, Sales Mgr.

■ **7541** ■ **Kansas Brick and Tile Company Inc.**
PO Box 450
Hoisington, KS 67544
Phone: (316)653-2157
Free: (800)653-7609 **Fax:** (316)653-7609
Products: Construction materials and machinery. **SIC:** 5032 (Brick, Stone & Related Materials). **Sales:** $5,000,000 (2000). **Emp:** 50.

■ **7542** ■ **Kaplan Lumber Company Inc.**
PO Box 340
St. Peters, MO 63376
Phone: (314)397-4471 **Fax:** (314)278-4562
Products: Lumber, doors, and windows. **SIC:** 5031

(Lumber, Plywood & Millwork). **Est:** 1932. **Sales:** $16,000,000 (2000). **Emp:** 60. **Officers:** Paul M. Kaplan, President & Chairman of the Board.

■ **7543** ■ **Karpen Steel Custom Doors & Frames**
181 Reems Creek Rd.
Weaverville, NC 28787-8204
Phone: (828)645-4821 **Free:** (800)851-2131
E-mail: karpensteel@mindspring.com
URL: http://www.karpensteel.com
Products: Partitions, including free standing. **SIC:** 5031 (Lumber, Plywood & Millwork). **Est:** 1977. **Sales:** $2,000,000 (2000). **Emp:** 49. **Officers:** Harold Kardeman. **Former Name:** Karpen Steel Products Inc.

■ **7544** ■ **Kelley Manufacturing Corp.**
61501 Bremen Hwy.
Mishawaka, IN 46544
Phone: (219)255-4746 **Fax:** (219)255-6817
Products: Excavating machinery and equipment. **SIC:** 5082 (Construction & Mining Machinery). **Sales:** $4,000,000 (2000). **Emp:** 25. **Officers:** David Kelley, President; Tony Downing, Sales Mgr.

■ **7545** ■ **Kemlite Company, Inc.**
PO Box 2429
Joliet, IL 60434
Phone: (815)467-8600
Free: (800)435-0080 **Fax:** (815)435-0080
URL: http://www.kemlite.com
Products: Plastics (reinforced), fiberglass. **SIC:** 5162 (Plastics Materials & Basic Shapes). **Est:** 1954. **Emp:** 220. **Officers:** Rich W. Schueller, President; Jim K. Simmons, VP of Sales & Marketing.

■ **7546** ■ **Kentucky Indiana Lumber Company Inc.**
227 E Lee St.
Louisville, KY 40208
Phone: (502)637-1401
Products: Lumber. **SIC:** 5031 (Lumber, Plywood & Millwork). **Sales:** $50,000,000 (1993). **Emp:** 150. **Officers:** Walter Freeman, President; Dorris Matthis, Treasurer & Secty.

■ **7547** ■ **Kermit Nolan Lumber Sales**
1200 Rialto Rd.
PO Box 450
Yazoo City, MS 39194
Phone: (601)746-1661 **Fax:** (601)746-9817
Products: Lumber, including hardwoods and cypress. **SIC:** 5031 (Lumber, Plywood & Millwork). **Est:** 1998. **Emp:** 1. **Officers:** Kermit Nolan, Owner. **Former Name:** McGraw-Curran Lumber Co.

■ **7548** ■ **Kesseli Morse Company Inc.**
242 Canterbury St.
Worcester, MA 01603
Phone: (508)752-1901
Products: Construction materials, including bricks, blocks, and metals. **SICs:** 5039 (Construction Materials Nec); 5032 (Brick, Stone & Related Materials). **Est:** 1921. **Sales:** $15,000,000 (2000). **Emp:** 65. **Officers:** George P. Kustigian Jr., CEO & Treasurer.

■ **7549** ■ **Ketcham Lumber Company Inc.**
PO Box 22789
Seattle, WA 98122
Phone: (206)329-2700 **Fax:** (206)324-6301
Products: Lumber. **SIC:** 5031 (Lumber, Plywood & Millwork). **Est:** 1935. **Sales:** $7,000,000 (2000). **Emp:** 23. **Officers:** William Ketcham, President.

■ **7550** ■ **Key Wholesale Building Products Inc.**
PO Box 1256
Mason City, IA 50401
Phone: (515)423-0544
Products: Plywood and shingles. **SICs:** 5031 (Lumber, Plywood & Millwork); 5033 (Roofing, Siding & Insulation). **Est:** 1964. **Sales:** $10,000,000 (2000). **Emp:** 17. **Officers:** Marvin G. Willemsen, President.

■ **7551** ■ **Keystone Builders Supply Co.**
1075 Buffalo Rd.
Rochester, NY 14624-1814
Phone: (716)458-5442 **Fax:** (716)458-0149
URL: http://www.keystonebuilders.com
Products: Construction equipment and supplies. **SIC:** 5082 (Construction & Mining Machinery). **Sales:** $6,000,000 (2000). **Emp:** 44. **Officers:** John Odenbach, President.

■ **7552** ■ **Keystone Builders Supply Co.**
85 Palm St.
Rochester, NY 14615
Phone: (716)458-5442 **Fax:** (716)458-0149
Products: Construction materials and machinery. **SIC:** 5082 (Construction & Mining Machinery). **Sales:** $6,000,000 (2000). **Emp:** 44.

■ **7553** ■ **Keystone Cement Co.**
PO Box A
Bath, PA 18014
Phone: (610)837-1881
Products: Stone and cement. **SIC:** 5032 (Brick, Stone & Related Materials). **Sales:** $50,000,000 (2000). **Emp:** 175. **Officers:** Gary L. Pechota, President.

■ **7554** ■ **Keywest Wire Div.**
250 E Virginia St.
San Jose, CA 95112
Phone: (408)971-9473
Products: Fence, welded wire fabric, nails and other wire products. **SIC:** 5051 (Metals Service Centers & Offices). **Sales:** $3,000,000 (1993). **Emp:** 30. **Officers:** Jim Fiedler, Finance General Manager.

■ **7555** ■ **Kimbrell Ruffer Lumber**
PO Box 605
Meridian, MS 39302
Phone: (601)693-4331 **Fax:** (601)482-0979
Products: Plywood and lumber. **SIC:** 5031 (Lumber, Plywood & Millwork). **Est:** 1926. **Sales:** $4,000,000 (2000). **Emp:** 18. **Officers:** Bill Kimbrell, President.

■ **7556** ■ **E. Kinast Distributors Inc.**
9362 W Grand Ave.
Franklin Park, IL 60131
Phone: (708)451-9300
Products: Formica. **SIC:** 5039 (Construction Materials Nec). **Sales:** $28,000,000 (2000). **Emp:** 100. **Officers:** Nancy Schierer, President.

■ **7557** ■ **Kinetics Inc.**
PO Box 7426
Madison, WI 53707
Phone: (608)241-4118 **Fax:** (608)241-9590
E-mail: keeldivs.com
Products: Fiberglass products, including doors, ceilings, and siding. **SIC:** 5033 (Roofing, Siding & Insulation). **Est:** 1968. **Sales:** $2,500,000 (2000). **Emp:** 5. **Officers:** Ken Foss, President.

■ **7558** ■ **King Sash and Door Inc.**
PO Box 787
Clemmons, NC 27012
Phone: (910)768-4650 **Fax:** (919)768-4666
Products: Doors; Windows. **SIC:** 5031 (Lumber, Plywood & Millwork). **Est:** 1970. **Sales:** $15,000,000 (2000). **Emp:** 65. **Officers:** T. Bumgarner, President.

■ **7559** ■ **J. Kirby Forest Products**
15213 Louis Mill Dr.
Chantilly, VA 20151
Phone: (703)378-6930 **Fax:** (703)378-6930
Products: Rough timber; Lumber and millwork. **SICs:** 5031 (Lumber, Plywood & Millwork); 5099 (Durable Goods Nec). **Officers:** John D. Kirby, Owner/Agent.

■ **7560** ■ **Kiwi Fence Systems Inc.**
1145 E Roy Furman Hwy.
Waynesburg, PA 15370
Phone: (412)627-8159 **Fax:** (412)627-9791
E-mail: kiwiinfo@kiwifence.com
URL: http://www.kiwifence.com
Products: Components for smooth wire fences; Livestock fencing. **SIC:** 5039 (Construction Materials Nec). **Est:** 1978. **Sales:** $3,000,000 (2000). **Emp:** 18. **Officers:** Vanda L. Wall, President.

■ **7561** ■ **Klam International**
1234 Broadway
New York, NY 10001
Phone: (212)244-6990 **Fax:** (212)244-6814
Products: Construction equipment and parts; Toys; Homefurnishings; Electrical appliances; Textiles. **SICs:** 5082 (Construction & Mining Machinery); 5092 (Toys & Hobby Goods & Supplies); 5023 (Homefurnishings); 5064 (Electrical Appliances—Television & Radio); 5131 (Piece Goods & Notions). **Est:** 1987. **Emp:** 3. **Officers:** John Klam, Owner & Buyer.

■ **7562** ■ **Kleptz Aluminum Building Supply Co.**
1135 Poplar St.
Terre Haute, IN 47807
Phone: (812)238-2946 **Fax:** (812)238-1965
Products: Aluminum siding. **SIC:** 5033 (Roofing, Siding & Insulation). **Sales:** $1,000,000 (2000). **Emp:** 8. **Officers:** Frank Kleptz, Owner.

■ **7563** ■ **K.M.H. Equipment Co.**
12565 Emerson Dr.
Brighton, MI 48116-8562
Phone: (248)446-9002 **Fax:** (248)446-9003
E-mail: kmheq@ismi.net
Products: Trucks. **SIC:** 5082 (Construction & Mining Machinery). **Est:** 1967. **Sales:** $3,000,000 (2000). **Emp:** 5. **Officers:** David Kuhlman, CEO.

■ **7564** ■ **Knape and Vogt Manufacturing Co.**
2700 Oak Industrial Dr.
Grand Rapids, MI 49505-6083
Phone: (616)459-3311 **Fax:** (616)459-3290
URL: http://www.kv.com
Products: Drawer slides for kitchen cabinets and drawers. **SICs:** 5039 (Construction Materials Nec); 5099 (Durable Goods Nec). **Est:** 1898. **Emp:** 1,150. **Officers:** Allen E. Perry, CEO & President.

■ **7565** ■ **Knecht Home Lumber Center Inc.**
320 West Blvd.
Rapid City, SD 57701
Phone: (605)342-4840 **Fax:** (605)342-7079
Products: Lumber; Windows; Plumbing equipment and supplies; Power tools and nails. **SICs:** 5031 (Lumber, Plywood & Millwork); 5039 (Construction Materials Nec); 5072 (Hardware); 5074 (Plumbing & Hydronic Heating Supplies). **Est:** 1986. **Sales:** $16,000,000 (2000). **Emp:** 150. **Officers:** Peter Van Wingerden, CEO.

■ **7566** ■ **Kobelco Welding of America Inc.**
7478 Harwin Dr.
Houston, TX 77036-2008
Phone: (713)974-5774
Products: Excavators and earthmovers. **SIC:** 5039 (Construction Materials Nec). **Est:** 1990. **Sales:** $2,000,000 (2000). **Emp:** 8. **Officers:** Ted Nariai, President.

■ **7567** ■ **Kobrin Builders Supply Inc.**
1401 Atlanta Ave.
Orlando, FL 32806
Phone: (407)843-1000
Products: Building supplies. **SIC:** 5039 (Construction Materials Nec). **Sales:** $15,000,000 (1994). **Emp:** 50. **Officers:** Harvey Kobrin, President; Janet Winter, Controller.

■ **7568** ■ **Kohl Building Products**
1047 Old Bernville Rd.
Reading, PA 19605
Phone: (610)926-8800
Free: (800)578-5645 **Fax:** (610)926-0806
E-mail: Kbp01@ATTGlobal
URL: http://www.Kohlbp.com
Products: Building supplies, including roofing, windows, and siding materials. **SIC:** 5085 (Industrial Supplies). **Est:** 1806. **Emp:** 115. **Officers:** Joseph T. Kearse, President; Deb K. Ritter.

■ **7569** ■ **Don Koontz Equipment Co.**
6946 Lilac Rd.
Plymouth, IN 46563
Phone: (219)936-4847 **Fax:** (219)936-8911
Products: Construction cranes; Front-end loaders; Construction machinery and equipment, including other construction machinery parts; Used construction

equipment. **SICs:** 5082 (Construction & Mining Machinery); 5084 (Industrial Machinery & Equipment). **Est:** 1968. **Sales:** $10,000,000 (2000). **Emp:** 10. **Officers:** Don Koontz, Owner, e-mail: dkoontz@dnsonline.net.

■ **7570** ■ **Korte Brothers Inc.**
620 W Cook Rd.
Ft. Wayne, IN 46825-3324
Phone: (219)745-4941 **Fax:** (219)745-4945
Products: Excavating machinery and equipment; Tractor shovel loaders, excluding parts and attachments; Front-end loaders; Concrete products machinery; Air and gas compressors and vacuum pumps; Mixers, pavers, and related equipment, excluding parts. **SICs:** 5082 (Construction & Mining Machinery); 5084 (Industrial Machinery & Equipment). **Est:** 1924. **Sales:** $7,000,000 (2000). **Emp:** 26. **Officers:** W.L. Korte, President & Chairman of the Board; Beauford Mullins, Vice President.

■ **7571** ■ **R.E. Kramig Company Inc.**
323 S Wayne Ave.
Cincinnati, OH 45215
Phone: (513)761-4010
Products: Commercial and industrial insulation. **SIC:** 5033 (Roofing, Siding & Insulation). **Est:** 1896. **Sales:** $10,000,000 (2000). **Emp:** 100. **Officers:** George J. Kulesza, President.

■ **7572** ■ **Kuhlman Corp.**
PO Box 714
Toledo, OH 43697-0714
Phone: (419)897-6000
Free: (800)669-3309 **Fax:** (419)897-6061
E-mail: kuhlman-corp.com
URL: http://www.kuhlman-corp.com
Products: Building materials, including concrete and bricks. **SIC:** 5032 (Brick, Stone & Related Materials). **Est:** 1901. **Sales:** $22,000,000 (2000). **Emp:** 110. **Officers:** T.L. Goligoski, President; T.D. Schaefer, VP of Finance; J.D. Gilmore, Vice President.

■ **7573** ■ **L & L Insulation and Supply Co.**
PO Box 489
Ankeny, IA 50021-0489
Phone: (515)963-9170
Free: (800)747-5385 **Fax:** (515)963-9176
URL: http://www.llinsulation.com
Products: Insulation. **SIC:** 5033 (Roofing, Siding & Insulation). **Est:** 1988. **Sales:** $10,000,000 (2000). **Emp:** 85. **Officers:** R.E. Fligg, President; Joe Farnen, CFO; Kelly Reed.

■ **7574** ■ **L and W Supply Corp.**
125 S Franklin St.
Chicago, IL 60606
Phone: (312)606-5400 **Fax:** (312)606-5323
Products: Dry wall; Fasteners. **SIC:** 5039 (Construction Materials Nec). **Est:** 1971. **Sales:** $500,000,000 (2000). **Emp:** 1,700. **Officers:** Frank R. Wall, President.

■ **7575** ■ **Lafarge Concrete**
PO Box 726
San Marcos, TX 78667
Phone: (512)353-7733 **Fax:** (512)396-8750
Products: Concrete, cement, and steel reinforcement rods. **SICs:** 5032 (Brick, Stone & Related Materials); 5051 (Metals Service Centers & Offices); 5039 (Construction Materials Nec). **Est:** 1974. **Sales:** $8,000,000 (2000). **Emp:** 40. **Officers:** B.D. Moore, President.

■ **7576** ■ **Lafarge Corp.**
PO Box 4600
Reston, VA 22096
Phone: (703)264-3600 **Fax:** (703)264-0634
Products: Construction materials, including cement. **SIC:** 5032 (Brick, Stone & Related Materials). **Est:** 1983. **Sales:** $1,806,400,000 (2000). **Emp:** 7,300. **Officers:** John M. Piecuch, CEO & President; Larry J. Waisanen, Sr. VP & CFO; Thomas W. Tatum, Sr. VP of Human Resources.

■ **7577** ■ **Lake Erie Supply, Inc.**
2420 W 15th
Erie, PA 16505-4514
Phone: (814)453-6625 **Fax:** (814)453-2569
Products: Metal doors and door hardware, including specialty, overhead, and rolling steel doors; Electric operators; Dock equipment. **SICs:** 5031 (Lumber, Plywood & Millwork); 5072 (Hardware). **Emp:** 17. **Officers:** Nick Sanzo, President.

■ **7578** ■ **Lake States Lumber**
312 S Chester Street
PO Box 518
Sparta, WI 54656
Phone: (608)269-6714
Free: (800)362-5864 **Fax:** (608)269-7630
Products: Lumber and plywood. **SIC:** 5031 (Lumber, Plywood & Millwork).

■ **7579** ■ **Lake States Lumber**
2104 E 5th Street, Ste.
Superior, WI 54880
Phone: (715)398-2975
Free: (800)951-9899 **Fax:** (715)398-6294
Products: Lumber and plywood. **SIC:** 5031 (Lumber, Plywood & Millwork).

■ **7580** ■ **Lake States Lumber**
899 Grossman Road
PO Box 408
Schofield, WI 54476
Phone: (715)359-9111
Free: (800)472-0017 **Fax:** (715)359-8744
Products: Lumber and plywood. **SIC:** 5031 (Lumber, Plywood & Millwork).

■ **7581** ■ **Lake States Lumber inc.**
PO Box 310
Aitkin, MN 56431
Phone: (218)927-2125 **Fax:** (218)927-3513
Products: Lumber and plywood. **SIC:** 5031 (Lumber, Plywood & Millwork). **Est:** 1949. **Sales:** $85,000,000 (2000). **Emp:** 110. **Officers:** Roger D. Wilson, President; Keith A. Laugen, Treasurer & Secty.

■ **7582** ■ **Lakeside Harvestore Inc.**
2400 Plymouth St.
New Holstein, WI 53061
Phone: (920)898-5702 **Fax:** (920)898-5705
Products: Farm service type buildings. **SIC:** 5039 (Construction Materials Nec). **Est:** 1976. **Sales:** $5,500,000 (2000). **Emp:** 35. **Officers:** G. Lee, President; Jay Livingston, Controller; Dan Tongen, VP of Marketing; Nancy Hofschild, Dir of Personnel.

■ **7583** ■ **Lampert Yards Inc.**
1850 Como Ave.
St. Paul, MN 55108
Phone: (612)645-8155 **Fax:** (612)645-5814
Products: Lumber and wood products; Shingles; Fencing and fence gates. **SICs:** 5031 (Lumber, Plywood & Millwork); 5033 (Roofing, Siding & Insulation); 5039 (Construction Materials Nec). **Est:** 1887. **Sales:** $100,000,000 (2000). **Emp:** 450. **Officers:** Daniel L. Fesler, President.

■ **7584** ■ **Lance Construction Supplies Inc.**
4225 W Ogden Ave.
Chicago, IL 60623
Phone: (773)522-1900 **Fax:** (773)522-1618
Products: Mason's materials; Concrete supplies; Insulations; Caulking; Construction chemicals. **SIC:** 5032 (Brick, Stone & Related Materials). **Est:** 1945. **Sales:** $12,000,000 (2000). **Emp:** 30. **Officers:** Daniel Chodora, CEO; Marilyn Fors, Finance Officer.

■ **7585** ■ **Landvest Development Corp.**
2828 Emerson Ave. S
Minneapolis, MN 55408
Phone: (612)870-0801 **Fax:** (612)870-4407
Products: Housing lumber. **SIC:** 5031 (Lumber, Plywood & Millwork). **Est:** 1889. **Sales:** $11,700,000 (2000). **Emp:** 35. **Officers:** Bruce Nimmer, President; Robert Rudabaugh, Treasurer.

■ **7586** ■ **Ted Lansing Corp.**
8501 Sanford Dr.
Richmond, VA 23228
Phone: (804)266-8893
Products: Construction materials, including roofing, siding, windows, and guttering. **SICs:** 5039 (Construction Materials Nec); 5031 (Lumber, Plywood & Millwork); 5033 (Roofing, Siding & Insulation). **Est:** 1955. **Sales:** $50,000,000 (2000). **Emp:** 275. **Officers:** J. Christopher Lansing, President; Linda Keister, Controller; Glenda Miller, VP of Marketing.

■ **7587** ■ **Laurel Center**
PO Box 583
Laurel, MS 39441
Phone: (601)428-4364 **Fax:** (601)649-6089
Products: Bricks. **SIC:** 5032 (Brick, Stone & Related Materials). **Sales:** $2,000,000 (2000). **Emp:** 9. **Officers:** Rodney Mire, General Mgr.

■ **7588** ■ **Lawrence Plate Glass Co.**
PO Box 567
Lawrence, MA 01842
Phones: (978)683-7151 800-222-7923
Free: (800)766-6013 **Fax:** (978)685-7840
Products: Plate glass. **SIC:** 5039 (Construction Materials Nec). **Est:** 1918. **Sales:** $11,000,000 (2000). **Emp:** 70. **Officers:** Walter V. Demers Jr., President; David Berryan, Controller; Brooks O'Kane, Dir. of Marketing; Lillian Adams, Office Mgr.

■ **7589** ■ **L.B.I. Company**
3950 South 500 West
Salt Lake City, UT 84123
Phone: (801)262-9087
Free: (800)662-9087 **Fax:** (801)263-3404
Products: Floorcovering equipment and supplies. **SIC:** 5032 (Brick, Stone & Related Materials).

■ **7590** ■ **Lebanon Building Supply Co.**
225 N 10th St.
Lebanon, PA 17046
Phone: (717)272-4649 **Fax:** (717)272-1628
Products: Building supplies, including lumber, gravel, fence, shingles, and cement. **SICs:** 5031 (Lumber, Plywood & Millwork); 5051 (Metals Service Centers & Offices); 5032 (Brick, Stone & Related Materials). **Est:** 1943. **Sales:** $4,400,000 (2000). **Emp:** 17. **Officers:** Milan Lipensky, CEO & President; Henry Steckbeck, Manager; Donald Hoover, Dir. of Data Processing.

■ **7591** ■ **Lee Lumber and Building Materials Corp.**
633 W Pershing Rd.
Chicago, IL 60609
Phone: (773)927-8282 **Fax:** (773)890-6719
E-mail: http://www.leelumber.com
Products: Lumber and wood products; Hardware; Electrical equipment and supplies. **SICs:** 5031 (Lumber, Plywood & Millwork); 5072 (Hardware); 5063 (Electrical Apparatus & Equipment). **Est:** 1952. **Sales:** $32,000,000 (2000). **Emp:** 130. **Officers:** Lee A. Baumgarten, CEO; Major Eisman, Controller; Hugh Chardon, Human Resources Contact.

■ **7592** ■ **Lee Tractor Company Inc.**
PO Box 939
Kenner, LA 70063
Phone: (504)467-6794
Free: (800)486-2895 **Fax:** (504)467-6799
E-mail: lee_tractor@msn.com
Products: Construction tractors. **SIC:** 5082 (Construction & Mining Machinery). **Est:** 1947. **Sales:** $12,500,000 (2000). **Emp:** 38. **Officers:** R.K. Mathews, CEO & President; Robert Evangelista, Treasurer & Controller; Phil Fleming, Dir. of Marketing & Sales.

■ **7593** ■ **Lee Wholesale Supply Company Inc.**
PO Box 299
New Hudson, MI 48165-0299
Phone: (248)437-6044 **Fax:** (248)437-2124
Products: Roofing, siding, windows, and doors. **SICs:** 5033 (Roofing, Siding & Insulation); 5031 (Lumber, Plywood & Millwork). **Est:** 1972. **Sales:** $15,000,000 (2000). **Emp:** 45. **Officers:** John Wrobleski, President; Kathleen L. Wrobleski, Controller.

■ 7594 ■ Leingang Siding and Window
PO Box 579
Mandan, ND 58554-0579
Phone: (701)663-7966
Products: Insulation; Roofing and siding materials; Windows. **SICs:** 5033 (Roofing, Siding & Insulation); 5031 (Lumber, Plywood & Millwork). **Officers:** Alvin Leingang, President.

■ 7595 ■ Lensing Wholesale, Inc.
PO Box 965
Evansville, IN 47706
Phone: (812)423-6891 **Fax:** (812)421-3788
Products: Siding; Doors; Toilet paper dispensers. **SICs:** 5033 (Roofing, Siding & Insulation); 5031 (Lumber, Plywood & Millwork); 5023 (Homefurnishings).

■ 7596 ■ Leo Distributors Inc.
3721 E Dupont Rd.
Ft. Wayne, IN 46825
Phone: (219)484-0784 **Fax:** (219)484-0787
Products: Windows; Siding; Wood doors, interior and exterior. **SICs:** 5031 (Lumber, Plywood & Millwork); 5039 (Construction Materials Nec). **Est:** 1958. **Sales:** $4,000,000 (2000). **Emp:** 25. **Officers:** William Kurtz Jr., Owner; Ron Langley, Controller.

■ 7597 ■ Leppo Inc.
176 West Ave.
Tallmadge, OH 44278
Phone: (330)633-3978
Free: (800)453-7767 **Fax:** (330)633-3486
URL: http://www.leppos.com
Products: Loaders; Excavators; Forklifts; Trenchers; Saws. **SICs:** 5082 (Construction & Mining Machinery); 5084 (Industrial Machinery & Equipment). **Est:** 1945. **Sales:** $18,000,000 (1999). **Emp:** 49. **Officers:** Dale Leppo, Chairman of the Board; Sandra Geesaman, Treasurer; Glenn Lappo, President.

■ 7598 ■ Lewis Brothers Lumber Company Inc.
PO Box 334
Aliceville, AL 35442
Phone: (205)373-2496 **Fax:** (205)373-2122
E-mail: lewisbro@pickens.net
Products: Lumber, including oak and other hardwood. **SIC:** 5031 (Lumber, Plywood & Millwork). **Est:** 1948. **Sales:** $15,000,000 (2000). **Emp:** 70. **Officers:** A.B. Lewis, President; Joe B. Lewis, Treasurer & Secty.; Dean Lewis, Vice President.

■ 7599 ■ Dwight G. Lewis Company Inc.
PO Box A
Hillsgrove, PA 18619
Phone: (717)924-3507 **Fax:** (717)924-4233
Products: Lumber. **SIC:** 5031 (Lumber, Plywood & Millwork). **Est:** 1941. **Sales:** $6,000,000 (2000). **Emp:** 25. **Officers:** Dwight G. Lewis, President; Mark D. Lewis, Vice President.

■ 7600 ■ Lewisohn Sales Company Inc.
PO Box 192
4001 Dell Avenue
North Bergen, NJ 07047
Phone: (201)864-0300
Free: (800)631-3196 **Fax:** (201)864-1266
E-mail: lewisohn@.com
Products: Steel; Aluminum; Butcher block; Trailer and truck body parts. **SICs:** 5051 (Metals Service Centers & Offices); 5031 (Lumber, Plywood & Millwork); 5013 (Motor Vehicle Supplies & New Parts). **Est:** 1921. **Sales:** $8,000,000 (2000). **Emp:** 70. **Officers:** Rosette Standig, President; Micheal Sofer, Controller; Leon Krangle, Sales Mgr., e-mail: lewisohn@aol.com.

■ 7601 ■ LI Tinsmith Supply Corp.
76-11 88 St.
Glendale, NY 11385
Phone: (718)846-0400
Products: Building materials, including cement. **SICs:** 5039 (Construction Materials Nec); 5032 (Brick, Stone & Related Materials). **Est:** 1918. **Sales:** $10,000,000 (2000). **Emp:** 30. **Officers:** H.C. Lucks, CEO & President.

■ 7602 ■ Libbey Owens Ford Co.
500 E Louise Ave.
Lathrop, CA 95330-9606
Phone: (209)858-5151 **Fax:** (209)858-2024
Products: Glass. **SIC:** 5039 (Construction Materials Nec). **Sales:** $30,000,000 (2000). **Emp:** 500. **Officers:** C. A. Clark.

■ 7603 ■ Liberty Woods International, Inc.
1903 Wright Pl., Ste. 360
Carlsbad, CA 92008
Phone: (760)438-8030 **Fax:** (760)438-8018
E-mail: sales@libertywoods.com
Products: Plywood. **SIC:** 5031 (Lumber, Plywood & Millwork). **Est:** 1985. **Sales:** $8,000,000 (1999). **Emp:** 25. **Officers:** Roy Polatchek, President.

■ 7604 ■ Liebherr-America Inc.
PO Box Drawer O
Newport News, VA 23605
Phone: (757)245-5251 **Fax:** (757)928-8544
Products: Construction machinery, mining equipment. **SIC:** 5082 (Construction & Mining Machinery). **Sales:** $30,000,000 (2000). **Emp:** 80. **Officers:** Ron Jacobson, President; Sheri Cook, Controller.

■ 7605 ■ Liebherr Construction Equipment Co.
PO Box Drawer O
Newport News, VA 23605
Phone: (757)245-5251 **Fax:** (757)928-8700
Products: Construction machinery. **SIC:** 5082 (Construction & Mining Machinery). **Est:** 1970. **Emp:** 220. **Officers:** Edward Sprow, President.

■ 7606 ■ Liebherr Mining Equipment Co.
PO Box O
Newport News, VA 23605
Phone: (757)245-5251 **Fax:** (757)928-8701
Products: Importers of hydraulic excavators and backhoes; Hydrostatic crawler loaders and dozers; Mining trucks. **SIC:** 5082 (Construction & Mining Machinery). **Sales:** $69,000,000 (2000). **Emp:** 185.

■ 7607 ■ Lincoln-Kaltek
PO Box 88390
Atlanta, GA 30338
Phone: (404)457-9448
Products: Lumber, plywood, and millwork. **SIC:** 5031 (Lumber, Plywood & Millwork). **Officers:** Warwick Johnston, Director of Administrative Services.

■ 7608 ■ Locust Lumber Company Inc.
PO Box 130
Locust, NC 28097
Phone: (704)888-4412 **Fax:** (704)888-3419
Products: Lumber. **SIC:** 5031 (Lumber, Plywood & Millwork). **Est:** 1947. **Sales:** $5,000,000 (2000). **Emp:** 30. **Officers:** Joel Huneycutt, President.

■ 7609 ■ Lofland Co.
PO Box 35446
Dallas, TX 75235
Phone: (214)631-5250 **Fax:** (214)637-1110
Products: Steel; Concrete Accessories. **SICs:** 5032 (Brick, Stone & Related Materials); 5051 (Metals Service Centers & Offices). **Est:** 1934. **Sales:** $60,000,000 (1999). **Emp:** 500. **Officers:** Blake Irwin, CEO & President; Rick Teague, Sales/Marketing Contact.

■ 7610 ■ Long Machinery Inc.
PO Box 5508
Missoula, MT 59806
Phone: (406)721-4050
Products: Construction and farm equipment. **SICs:** 5084 (Industrial Machinery & Equipment); 5083 (Farm & Garden Machinery). **Sales:** $20,000,000 (1994). **Emp:** 140. **Officers:** T.E. Ritzheimer, Exec. VP & General Mgr.; C.J. Johnson, VP of Finance.

■ 7611 ■ Lore L. Ltd.
1631 S Nova Rd.
Daytona Beach, FL 32119-1729
Phone: (904)756-0500
Free: (800)395-0935 **Fax:** (904)756-8508
Products: Glass and mirror construction materials. **SIC:** 5039 (Construction Materials Nec). **Est:** 1983. **Sales:** $1,200,000 (2000). **Emp:** 20. **Officers:** Jeff Miller; Barbara Miller.

■ 7612 ■ Lott Builders Supply Co.
PO Box 269
Douglas, GA 31533
Phone: (912)384-1800 **Fax:** (912)384-1800
Products: Building supplies. **SIC:** 5031 (Lumber, Plywood & Millwork). **Est:** 1952. **Sales:** $14,000,000 (2000). **Emp:** 50. **Officers:** David S. Lott, President; Tony Wright, Controller.

■ 7613 ■ Louisville Plate Glass Company Inc.
1401 W Broadway
Louisville, KY 40203-2059
Phone: (502)584-6145 **Fax:** (502)584-2825
Products: Plate glass. **SIC:** 5039 (Construction Materials Nec). **Sales:** $7,000,000 (2000). **Emp:** 80. **Officers:** William Stone.

■ 7614 ■ Louisville Tile Distributors Inc.
4520 Bishop Ln.
Louisville, KY 40218-4508
Phone: (502)452-2037 **Fax:** (502)454-4114
Products: Tiles. **SIC:** 5032 (Brick, Stone & Related Materials). **Sales:** $12,000,000 (2000). **Emp:** 150. **Officers:** Jerry Short, President; John O'Mahoney, VP of Finance.

■ 7615 ■ Louisville Tile Distributors Inc.
1417 N Cullen Ave.
Evansville, IN 47715-2374
Phone: (812)473-0137 **Fax:** (812)477-7524
Products: Floorcovering equipment and supplies. **SIC:** 5032 (Brick, Stone & Related Materials).

■ 7616 ■ Lumber Exchange Terminal Inc.
171 West St.
Brooklyn, NY 11222
Phone: (718)383-5000
Products: Lumber. **SIC:** 5031 (Lumber, Plywood & Millwork). **Officers:** J. Stulman, President & Treasurer.

■ 7617 ■ Lumber Inc.
PO Box 26777
Albuquerque, NM 87125
Phone: (505)823-2700
Products: Lumber. **SIC:** 5031 (Lumber, Plywood & Millwork). **Est:** 1972. **Sales:** $25,000,000 (2000). **Emp:** 100. **Officers:** R.L. Wickens, President; Mary Stockavas, Controller.

■ 7618 ■ Lumberman of Indiana
849 Elston Dr.
Shelbyville, IN 46176-1817
Phone: (317)392-4145 **Fax:** (317)398-2462
Products: Building materials. **SIC:** 5039 (Construction Materials Nec). **Sales:** $15,000,000 (2000). **Emp:** 30. **Officers:** Randy Mertin, Manager.

■ 7619 ■ Lumbermen's Inc.
4433 Stafford St.
Grand Rapids, MI 49548
Phone: (616)538-5180
Products: Construction supplies, including laminates, windows, lumber, doors, and roofing. **SIC:** 5031 (Lumber, Plywood & Millwork). **Est:** 1955. **Sales:** $90,000,000 (1999). **Emp:** 200. **Officers:** Henry Bouma, CEO; Roger Vanderheide, President; Doug Rathbun, Dir. of Marketing & Sales; Steve Petersen, VP of Finance.

■ 7620 ■ Lumbermen's Merchandising Corp.
137 W Wayne Ave.
Wayne, PA 19087
Phone: (215)293-7000 **Fax:** (215)293-7098
URL: http://www.cyberyard.com
Products: Lumber and building materials. **SICs:** 5031 (Lumber, Plywood & Millwork); 5039 (Construction Materials Nec). **Est:** 1935. **Sales:** $1,700,000,000 (2000). **Emp:** 200. **Officers:** Anthony J. DeCarlo, President; David J. Gonze, Finance Officer.

■ 7621 ■ Lumbermens Millwork and Supply Co.
2211 Refinery Rd.
Ardmore, OK 73401-1666
Phone: (580)223-3080
Products: Millwork. **SIC:** 5031 (Lumber, Plywood & Millwork). **Est:** 1924. **Sales:** $3,000,000 (2000). **Emp:** 35. **Officers:** Charles Burnam, VP & General Merchandising Mgr.

■ 7622 ■ **Lumberyard Supply Co.**
5060 Manchester Ave.
St. Louis, MO 63110
Phone: (314)533-7557 **Fax:** (314)533-5730
E-mail: LmbrSupply@aol.com
Products: Wood paneling; Ceilings; Siding; Wood holding; Metal Connectors; Shutters; Composite trim; Drywall; Ventilation; Fireplaces. **SIC:** 5031 (Lumber, Plywood & Millwork). **Est:** 1937. **Sales:** $8,000,000 (2000). **Emp:** 20. **Officers:** Perry N. Sparks, Chairman of the Board; Robert Sparks, President.

■ 7623 ■ **Lyman Lumber Co.**
PO Box 40
Excelsior, MN 55331
Phone: (612)474-5991
Products: Lumber. **SIC:** 5031 (Lumber, Plywood & Millwork). **Est:** 1897. **Sales:** $65,000,000 (2000). **Emp:** 450. **Officers:** Thomas P. Lowe, President.

■ 7624 ■ **Lyman-Richey Corp.**
4315 Cuming St.
Omaha, NE 68131
Phone: (402)558-2727
Products: Construction materials. **SIC:** 5039 (Construction Materials Nec). **Sales:** $100,000,000 (1994). **Emp:** 400. **Officers:** Patrick Gorup, President & CEO.

■ 7625 ■ **Lynn Ladder and Scaffolding Company Inc.**
PO Box 346
West Lynn, MA 01905
Phone: (617)598-6010 **Fax:** (617)595-3980
Products: Ladders; Scaffolding. **SIC:** 5082 (Construction & Mining Machinery). **Est:** 1946. **Sales:** $29,000,000 (2000). **Emp:** 300. **Officers:** Bernard M. Kline, President.

■ 7626 ■ **Lyons Equipment Co.**
PO Box 107
Little Valley, NY 14755
Phone: (716)938-9175 **Fax:** (716)938-9227
Products: Logging and sawmill machinery. **SIC:** 5082 (Construction & Mining Machinery). **Sales:** $30,000,000 (2000). **Emp:** 70. **Officers:** John Lyons, President; Robert Tuyn, Mgr. of Finance.

■ 7627 ■ **M & N Supply Corp.**
30 Allen Blvd.
Farmingdale, NY 11735-5612
Phone: (516)694-2230
Free: (800)248-0362 **Fax:** (516)694-2265
Products: Cabinet hardware. **SIC:** 5031 (Lumber, Plywood & Millwork). **Est:** 1962. **Emp:** 49. **Officers:** Mel Silverman.

■ 7628 ■ **Mac Supply Co.**
16778 S Park Ave.
South Holland, IL 60473
Phone: (708)339-2666 **Fax:** (708)339-1991
Products: Gypsum building materials; Wallboard. **SIC:** 5039 (Construction Materials Nec). **Est:** 1925. **Sales:** $900,000 (2000). **Emp:** 7. **Officers:** Kevin Poffenbarger, Manager.

■ 7629 ■ **MacAllister Machinery Company Inc.**
PO Box 1941
Indianapolis, IN 46206
Phone: (317)545-2151 **Fax:** (317)543-0310
Products: Heavy construction equipment. **SIC:** 5082 (Construction & Mining Machinery). **Est:** 1945. **Sales:** $36,000,000 (2000). **Emp:** 200. **Officers:** Chris Macallister, President; Ron Roy, CFO; Cade Verner, Dir. of Marketing.

■ 7630 ■ **MacArthur Co.**
2400 Wycliff St.
St. Paul, MN 55114
Phone: (612)646-2773
Products: Insulation. **SIC:** 5033 (Roofing, Siding & Insulation). **Est:** 1913. **Sales:** $50,000,000 (2000). **Emp:** 325. **Officers:** Richard C. Lockwood, President.

■ 7631 ■ **MacDonald and Owen Lumber**
PO Box 238
Bangor, WI 54614
Phone: (608)486-2353
Free: (800)657-6990 **Fax:** (608)486-2764
Products: Hardwood lumber. **SIC:** 5031 (Lumber, Plywood & Millwork). **Est:** 1968. **Sales:** $10,000,000 (2000). **Emp:** 4. **Officers:** A. Macdonald, President; D. Twite, Dir. of Marketing.

■ 7632 ■ **Machine Maintenance Inc.**
2300 Cassens Dr.
Fenton, MO 63026-2591
Phone: (314)487-7100 **Fax:** (314)487-7100
Products: Construction equipment parts. **SIC:** 5039 (Construction Materials Nec). **Sales:** $1,000,000 (2000). **Emp:** 50. **Officers:** Bob Luby, President; Ted Rose, VP of Sales; Larry Valco, Dir. of Operations.

■ 7633 ■ **MacMillan Bloedel Building Materials**
5895 Windward Pkwy., Ste. 200
Alpharetta, GA 30022
Phone: (404)740-7516 **Fax:** (404)740-7513
Products: Plywood and lumber. **SIC:** 5031 (Lumber, Plywood & Millwork). **Officers:** Abbey L. Achs, Export Manager.

■ 7634 ■ **Ernest Maier Inc.**
4700 Annapolis Rd.
Bladensburg, MD 20710
Phone: (301)927-8300 **Fax:** (301)927-6923
Products: Cinder blocks; Building materials. **SIC:** 5032 (Brick, Stone & Related Materials). **Est:** 1926. **Sales:** $8,600,000 (2000). **Emp:** 56. **Officers:** Alvin Maier, President; Harvey McCombs, Treasurer & Secty.

■ 7635 ■ **Mallco Lumber and Building Materials Inc.**
PO Box 4397
Phoenix, AZ 85030
Phone: (602)252-4961 **Fax:** (602)258-7581
Products: Lumber. **SIC:** 5031 (Lumber, Plywood & Millwork). **Est:** 1947. **Sales:** $51,000,000 (2000). **Emp:** 50. **Officers:** Richard Bilby, President; Owen Pengelly, VP of Finance.

■ 7636 ■ **Mankato-Kasota Stone**
818 N Willow St.
PO Box 1358
Mankato, MN 56002
Phone: (507)625-2746 **Fax:** (507)625-2748
URL: http://www.mankato-kasota-stone.com
Products: Limestone. **SIC:** 5032 (Brick, Stone & Related Materials). **Est:** 1885. **Sales:** $5,000,000 (2000). **Emp:** 100. **Officers:** R.J. Coughlan, President; J.P. Coughlan, Exec. VP; Robert E. Schaffler, Business Sales Mgr. Contact.

■ 7637 ■ **Manufacturers Reserve Supply Inc.**
16 Woolsey St.
Irvington, NJ 07111-4089
Phone: (201)373-1881 **Fax:** (201)372-5659
URL: http://www.mrslumber.com
Products: Sawn lumber; Plywood. **SIC:** 5033 (Roofing, Siding & Insulation). **Est:** 1931. **Sales:** $16,000,000 (2000). **Emp:** 18. **Officers:** Stephen F. Boyd, President.

■ 7638 ■ **Manzo Contracting Co.**
PO Box 341
Matawan, NJ 07747
Phone: (732)721-6900
Products: Supplier of aggregates such as sand, gravel, and salt. **SIC:** 5032 (Brick, Stone & Related Materials). **Sales:** $5,500,000 (2000). **Emp:** 50. **Officers:** Roger Passarella, General Mgr.

■ 7639 ■ **Mar Vista Lumber Co.**
3860 Grandview Blvd.
Los Angeles, CA 90066
Phone: (213)870-7431 **Fax:** (310)397-4043
Products: Lumber. **SIC:** 5031 (Lumber, Plywood & Millwork). **Est:** 1955. **Sales:** $7,500,000 (2000). **Emp:** 35. **Officers:** George Swartz, President; Terry L. Laughlin, Vice President; Andrew McCuskey, Dir. of Marketing & Sales.

■ 7640 ■ **R.J. Marchand Contractors Specialties Inc.**
3515 Division St.
Metairie, LA 70002
Phone: (504)888-2922 **Fax:** (504)888-2936
Products: Tools and fasteners for construction. **SICs:** 5072 (Hardware); 5039 (Construction Materials Nec). **Est:** 1989. **Sales:** $5,000,000 (2000). **Emp:** 25. **Officers:** Frank Sibley, President.

■ 7641 ■ **Mariotti Building Products Inc.**
1 Louis Industrial Dr.
Old Forge, PA 18518
Phone: (717)457-6774
Products: Home building and remodeling supplies; Lumber. **SIC:** 5031 (Lumber, Plywood & Millwork). **Est:** 1962. **Sales:** $30,000,000 (2000). **Emp:** 90. **Officers:** Eugene Mariotti, CEO.

■ 7642 ■ **Marketor International Corp.**
PO Box 1721
Clackamas, OR 97015
Phone: (503)650-4788 **Fax:** (503)650-7221
E-mail: marketor@marketor.com
URL: http://www.marketor.com
Products: Lumber, plywood, and building materials. **SIC:** 5031 (Lumber, Plywood & Millwork). **Est:** 1978. **Emp:** 52. **Officers:** Gary Adams, President.

■ 7643 ■ **Marley Mouldings Inc.**
PO Box 610
Marion, VA 24354
Phone: (540)783-8161 **Fax:** (540)783-8169
Products: Plastic excursion molding. **SIC:** 5031 (Lumber, Plywood & Millwork). **Est:** 1973. **Sales:** $90,000,000 (2000). **Emp:** 700. **Officers:** Larry L. Davis, President; Robert Harris, VP & Controller; Art Ramey, Exec. VP of Marketing & Sales.

■ 7644 ■ **Marquart-Wolfe Lumber Company Inc.**
PO Box 9286
Newport Beach, CA 92658-9286
Phone: (714)966-0281
Products: Lumber and wood products. **SIC:** 5031 (Lumber, Plywood & Millwork). **Est:** 1953. **Sales:** $1,000,000 (2000). **Emp:** 5. **Officers:** Jonathan Wolfe, President.

■ 7645 ■ **Marquette Lumbermen's Warehouse Inc.**
PO Box 913
Grand Rapids, MI 49509-0913
Phone: (616)247-5100 **Fax:** (616)247-5198
Products: Lumber, plywood, laminated beams, and treated wood; Roofing; Siding; Insulation. **SIC:** 5031 (Lumber, Plywood & Millwork). **Est:** 1951. **Sales:** $12,000,000 (2000). **Emp:** 70. **Officers:** T.R. Hager, Co-Chairman; G.F. Vitale, President; D.F. Garver, Sec. & Treas.

■ 7646 ■ **Marr Scaffolding Company Inc.**
1 D St.
Boston, MA 02127
Phone: (617)269-7200 **Fax:** (617)269-8604
Products: Scaffolding. **SIC:** 5082 (Construction & Mining Machinery). **Est:** 1945. **Sales:** $12,000,000 (2000). **Emp:** 90. **Officers:** Robert L. Marr, President; Thomas J. McCabe, Controller; Daniel J. Marr III, Dir. of Marketing.

■ 7647 ■ **Marsh Kitchens Greensboro Inc.**
2503 Greengate Dr.
Greensboro, NC 27406-5242
Phone: (910)273-8196 **Fax:** (910)230-1957
Products: Kitchen and bathroom cabinets. **SIC:** 5031 (Lumber, Plywood & Millwork). **Officers:** Robert Jackson, President.

■ 7648 ■ **Marshall Building Specialties Company Inc.**
1001 E New York St.
Indianapolis, IN 46202
Phone: (317)635-3888 **Fax:** (317)638-4480
Products: Building materials. **SICs:** 5031 (Lumber, Plywood & Millwork); 5032 (Brick, Stone & Related Materials); 5039 (Construction Materials Nec). **Est:** 1965. **Sales:** $3,000,000 (2000). **Emp:** 8. **Officers:**

Robert T. Marshall, President; Jean Comer, Controller; Dan Gillin, Sales Mgr.

■ 7649 ■ **Marshall Building Supply**
4730 Wynn Rd.
Las Vegas, NV 89103-5422
Phone: (702)871-4166 **Fax:** (702)871-3862
Products: Roofing materials; Landscaping blocks.
SICs: 5033 (Roofing, Siding & Insulation); 5032 (Brick, Stone & Related Materials). **Officers:** Patrick Symons, General Mgr. **Former Name:** Southern Distributors Corp.

■ 7650 ■ **Marshalltown Trowel Co.**
PO Box 738
Marshalltown, IA 50158
Phone: (515)753-0127
Free: (800)888-0127 **Fax:** (515)753-9227
E-mail: marketing@marshalltown.com
URL: http://www.marshalltown.com
Products: Brick; Concrete; Drywall plastering and flooring tools. **SICs:** 5072 (Hardware); 5032 (Brick, Stone & Related Materials). **Est:** 1890. **Emp:** 305. **Officers:** G. Ward Miller, Exec. VP; Sue Blackford, Customer Service Mgr., e-mail: suebmarylandshalltown.com; Dick Hovey, Human Resources Contact, e-mail: dickh@marshalltown.com.

■ 7651 ■ **Martensen Enterprises Inc.**
1721 W Culver St.
Phoenix, AZ 85007
Phone: (602)271-9048 **Fax:** (602)253-5289
Products: Construction supplies, including wire, rope, and rigging. **SICs:** 5085 (Industrial Supplies); 5039 (Construction Materials Nec); 5063 (Electrical Apparatus & Equipment). **Est:** 1962. **Sales:** $3,000,000 (2000). **Emp:** 15. **Officers:** Glenn Evans, General Mgr.

■ 7652 ■ **E.A. Martin Co.**
2222 E Kearngy St.
PO Box 988
Springfield, MO 65803
Phone: (417)866-6651 **Fax:** (417)866-5476
Products: Earthmoving, construction, modern handling equipment; Truck engines and generators. **SICs:** 5082 (Construction & Mining Machinery); 5063 (Electrical Apparatus & Equipment). **Est:** 1915. **Sales:** $63,000,000 (2000). **Emp:** 252. **Officers:** Donald G. Martin Sr., Chairman of the Board; Johnny Mathis, CFO; Donald G. Martin Jr., President; Charles Martin, Exec. VP; Bill Mitchell, Marketing Mgr.; Steve Collins, Human Resources Mgr.

■ 7653 ■ **E.A. Martin Co.**
PO Box 988
Springfield, MO 65801-0988
Phone: (417)866-6651 **Fax:** (417)866-5476
E-mail: info@eamartinco.com
URL: http://www.eamartinco.com
Products: Construction and industrial machinery. **SICs:** 5082 (Construction & Mining Machinery); 5084 (Industrial Machinery & Equipment). **Est:** 1915. **Sales:** $63,000,000 (2000). **Emp:** 250. **Officers:** Donald G. Martin Sr., Chairman of the Board; Donald G. Martin Jr., President, e-mail: martin_don.jr@eamartinco.com; Charles Martin, Exec. VP of Sales, e-mail: martin_charles@eamartinco.com; Johnny Mathis, CFO, e-mail: mathis_john@eamartinco.com. **Former Name:** E.A. Martin Machinery Co.

■ 7654 ■ **Martin and MacArthur**
1815 Kahai St.
Honolulu, HI 96819
Phone: (808)845-6688
Free: (800)845-0099 **Fax:** (808)845-6680
URL: http://www.martinandmacarthur.com
Products: Lumber; Furniture; Picture framing supplies.
SICs: 5031 (Lumber, Plywood & Millwork); 5021 (Furniture). **Est:** 1963. **Sales:** $5,000,000 (1999). **Emp:** 50. **Officers:** Jon Martin, President; W.L. Jones, Vice President; Chris Grey, Sales/Marketing Contact, e-mail: chris@martinandmacarthur.com.

■ 7655 ■ **Martin Millwork Inc.**
PO Box 2859
Springfield, MA 01101
Phone: (413)788-9634 **Fax:** (413)746-2434
Products: Windows; Doors; Stairparts; Fiberglass;

Columns. **SIC:** 5031 (Lumber, Plywood & Millwork).
Est: 1917. **Emp:** 58. **Officers:** Carl B. Martin III III, President; Terry Chadboure, CFO; Brad Campbell, VP of Sales.

■ 7656 ■ **Martin Tractor Company Inc.**
1737 SW 42nd St.
Topeka, KS 66609
Phone: (785)266-5770 **Fax:** (785)267-3301
URL: http://www.martintractor.com
Products: Construction and farming equipment. **SICs:** 5082 (Construction & Mining Machinery); 5083 (Farm & Garden Machinery). **Est:** 1911. **Sales:** $79,000,000 (2000). **Emp:** 270. **Officers:** Harry Craig Jr., CEO & Chairman of the Board; Marcia Durkes, CFO.

■ 7657 ■ **Marvin Corp.**
2911 Slauson Ave.
Huntington Park, CA 90255
Phone: (213)585-5003 **Fax:** (213)582-6429
Products: Coatings, including roof, reflective, and white acrylic; Asphalt. **SICs:** 5033 (Roofing, Siding & Insulation); 5032 (Brick, Stone & Related Materials); 5169 (Chemicals & Allied Products Nec). **Est:** 1950. **Sales:** $3,000,000 (2000). **Emp:** 6. **Officers:** Bill Kern, General Mgr.

■ 7658 ■ **Maryland Clay Products**
7100 Muirkirk Rd.
Beltsville, MD 20705
Phone: (301)419-2214
Products: Brick. **SIC:** 5032 (Brick, Stone & Related Materials). **Est:** 1970. **Sales:** $6,000,000 (2000). **Emp:** 65. **Officers:** Paul R. Payne, President.

■ 7659 ■ **Maryland Clay Products**
7100 Muirkirk Rd.
Beltsville, MD 20705
Phone: (301)419-2214
Products: Construction materials and machinery. **SIC:** 5032 (Brick, Stone & Related Materials). **Sales:** $6,000,000 (2000). **Emp:** 65.

■ 7660 ■ **The Masonry Center**
1424 N Orchard
PO Box 7825
Boise, ID 83707
Phone: (208)375-1362 **Fax:** (208)327-1600
Products: Brick; Tile; Formica. **SIC:** 5032 (Brick, Stone & Related Materials).

■ 7661 ■ **Masonry Product Sales Inc.**
410 N Alexander St.
New Orleans, LA 70119
Phone: (504)486-4618 **Fax:** (504)488-2640
Products: Bricks. **SIC:** 5032 (Brick, Stone & Related Materials). **Sales:** $500,000 (2000). **Emp:** 20. **Officers:** Ron Foster, CEO.

■ 7662 ■ **Massachusetts Lumber Co.**
929 Massachusetts Ave.
Cambridge, MA 02139
Phone: (617)354-6000
Products: Lumber. **SIC:** 5031 (Lumber, Plywood & Millwork). **Est:** 1917. **Sales:** $58,000,000 (2000). **Emp:** 140. **Officers:** E.I. Snider, President & Treasurer.

■ 7663 ■ **Massey Builders Supply Corp.**
2303 Dabney Rd.
Richmond, VA 23230
Phone: (804)355-7891 **Fax:** (804)355-7898
Products: Framing and treated lumber; Power tools; Windows; Doors. **SICs:** 5039 (Construction Materials Nec); 5031 (Lumber, Plywood & Millwork); 5072 (Hardware). **Est:** 1925. **Sales:** $8,000,000 (2000). **Emp:** 50. **Officers:** Freeman Spencer Jr., President.

■ 7664 ■ **Master Building Supply and Lumber Co.**
10435 Reisterstown Rd.
Owings Mills, MD 21117
Phone: (410)363-0500
Products: Lumber. **SIC:** 5031 (Lumber, Plywood & Millwork). **Est:** 1943. **Sales:** $4,000,000 (2000). **Emp:** 14. **Officers:** Edwin Myerberg, President.

■ 7665 ■ **Material Service Corp.**
222 N La Salle St.
Chicago, IL 60601-1090
Phone: (312)372-3600 **Fax:** (312)782-1916
Products: Concrete and gravel. **SIC:** 5032 (Brick, Stone & Related Materials). **Est:** 1917. **Sales:** $130,000,000 (2000). **Emp:** 1,200. **Officers:** Walter Serwa, President; Jerry McMurtrey, VP of Finance; Al Nowak, VP of Sales; William Tomy, Dir. of Systems.

■ 7666 ■ **Material Supply Inc.**
255 Airport Rd.
New Castle, DE 19720
Phone: (302)633-5600
Products: Stone and stone dust. **SIC:** 5032 (Brick, Stone & Related Materials). **Sales:** $12,000,000 (1993). **Emp:** 100. **Officers:** Blaise Saienni, President; Quentin Saienni, Vice President.

■ 7667 ■ **Matheus Lumber Company Inc.**
15800 Woodinville Redmond Rd. NE
PO Box 2260
Woodinville, WA 98072-2260
Phone: (206)284-7500
Free: (800)284-7501 **Fax:** (206)822-4028
E-mail: matheus@ricochet.net
Products: Lumber, plywood, timbers, and treated wood. **SIC:** 5031 (Lumber, Plywood & Millwork). **Est:** 1933. **Sales:** $40,000,000 (2000). **Emp:** 40. **Officers:** Stuart M. Hagen, President; David Kahle, CFO; Gary Powell, President; Dan Powell, VP of Sales; Jim Reynolds, VP of Sales.

■ 7668 ■ **Manfred Mathews**
612 Civic Center Dr.
Augusta, ME 04330-9439
Phone: (207)622-9400 **Fax:** (207)622-9411
Products: Roofing; Siding; Insulation materials, including thermal insulation; Windows. **SIC:** 5033 (Roofing, Siding & Insulation). **Officers:** Manfred Mathews, Owner.

■ 7669 ■ **Mathie Supply Inc.**
4215 Portage St. NW
North Canton, OH 44720
Phone: (330)499-2575
Products: Bricks; Cement; Building stone. **SIC:** 5032 (Brick, Stone & Related Materials). **Est:** 1951. **Sales:** $4,000,000 (2000). **Emp:** 15. **Officers:** David H. Mathie, President; Robert J. Mathie, VP & Treasurer.

■ 7670 ■ **Matthews and Fields Lumber of Henrietta**
1230 Lehigh Station Rd.
Henrietta, NY 14467
Phone: (716)334-5500
Products: Lumber. **SIC:** 5031 (Lumber, Plywood & Millwork). **Est:** 1960. **Sales:** $10,000,000 (2000). **Emp:** 40. **Officers:** J.M. Fields, President; Scott M. Fields, Vice President; Douglas A. Fields, Treasurer & Secty.

■ 7671 ■ **Mayfield Building Supply Co.**
PO Box 398
Arlington, TX 76010
Phone: (817)640-1234
Products: Lumber; Building supplies, including hardware, locks, decorative bathroom fixtures, and door knobs. **SICs:** 5031 (Lumber, Plywood & Millwork); 5072 (Hardware). **Est:** 1953. **Sales:** $30,000,000 (2000). **Emp:** 150. **Officers:** Jack Lewis Jr., President; Rosemary Wright, Finance Officer.

■ 7672 ■ **McAllister Equipment Co.**
12500 S Cicero Ave.
Alsip, IL 60803
Phone: (708)389-7700 **Fax:** (708)389-2963
Products: Construction equipment. **SIC:** 5082 (Construction & Mining Machinery). **Est:** 1955. **Sales:** $26,000,000 (2000). **Emp:** 100. **Officers:** Craig Harris, President; Don Adamsitis, Treasurer; John Hovner, Exec. VP.

■ 7673 ■ **McBride Insulation Co.**
PO Box 358
Heyburn, ID 83336-0358
Phone: (208)678-9048 **Fax:** (208)678-8159
Products: Roofing; Siding; Thermal insulation and insulation materials. **SIC:** 5033 (Roofing, Siding & Insulation). **Officers:** Roger Mc Bride, President.

■ **7674** ■ **McCann Industries, Inc.**
543 Rohlwing Rd.
Addison, IL 60101
Phone: (630)627-0000 **Fax:** (630)627-8711
E-mail: mccanneq@aol.com
URL: http://www.mccannonline.com
Products: Construction supplies and equipment. **SIC:** 5082 (Construction & Mining Machinery). **Est:** 1967. **Sales:** $65,000,000 (2000). **Emp:** 160. **Officers:** D. Kruepke, President & CEO; S. Hilty, CFO; R. Howting, Inventory/Asset Manager. **Former Name:** McCann Construction Specialties Co.

■ **7675** ■ **McCausey Lumber Co.**
32205 Little Mack
Roseville, MI 48066
Phone: (810)294-9663
Free: (800)365-9663 **Fax:** (810)294-1505
URL: http://www.mccauseylumber.com
Products: Lumber and wood products. **SIC:** 5031 (Lumber, Plywood & Millwork). **Est:** 1935. **Emp:** 13. **Officers:** James R. Gilleran, President; Kenneth R. Roach, CEO; Heleen Roach-Heaton, Sales Mgr.; Mike Gilleran, General Mgr., e-mail: mikeg@ mccauseylumber.com; Don Hanney, Customer Service Contact, e-mail: donh@mccauseylumber.com.

■ **7676** ■ **Lawrence R. McCoy and Company Inc.**
100 Front St., Ste. 700
Worcester, MA 01608-1444
Phone: (508)368-7700
Free: (800)346-2269 **Fax:** (508)890-1199
E-mail: office1@lrmccoy.com
URL: http://www.lrmccoy.com
Products: Lumber; Fencing materials; Landscape materials. **SICs:** 5031 (Lumber, Plywood & Millwork); 5039 (Construction Materials Nec). **Est:** 1922. **Sales:** $88,000,000 (1999). **Emp:** 50. **Officers:** H.S. Poler, CEO & President; Richard K. Dale, VP & CFO; Beth J. Wojnar, Human Resources Contact, e-mail: bethj@ lrmccoy.com.

■ **7677** ■ **McCray Lumber Co.**
10741 Del Monte Ln.
Overland Park, KS 66211
Phone: (913)341-6900 **Fax:** (913)341-6994
Products: Lumber. **SIC:** 5031 (Lumber, Plywood & Millwork). **Est:** 1947. **Sales:** $100,000,000 (2000). **Emp:** 275. **Officers:** H.C. McCray Jr., Chairman of the Board; Jerry Tanner, Controller; Chandler McCray, President. **Former Name:** Daniels-McCray Lumber Co.

■ **7678** ■ **McDonald Industries Inc.**
PO Box 88000
Seattle, WA 98138
Phone: (206)872-3500 **Fax:** (206)872-3519
Products: Construction materials and machinery. **SIC:** 5082 (Construction & Mining Machinery). **Sales:** $72,000,000 (2000). **Emp:** 230.

■ **7679** ■ **McDonald Lumber Company Inc.**
126 Cedar Creek Rd.
Fayetteville, NC 28302
Phone: (910)483-0381
Products: Lumber and hardware. **SICs:** 5031 (Lumber, Plywood & Millwork); 5072 (Hardware). **Sales:** $17,000,000 (1994). **Emp:** 100. **Officers:** Kenneth McDonald, President; Robert McDonald, Treasurer & Secty.

■ **7680** ■ **John W. McDougall Company Inc.**
PO Box 90447
Nashville, TN 37209
Phone: (615)321-3900 **Fax:** (615)329-9069
Products: Construction materials. **SIC:** 5039 (Construction Materials Nec). **Sales:** $15,000,000 (1994). **Emp:** 150. **Officers:** J.W. McDougall Jr., Chairman of the Board; J. Robert Smith, Controller.

■ **7681** ■ **McGinnis Lumber Company Inc.**
PO Box 2049
Meridian, MS 39302
Phone: (601)483-3991 **Fax:** (601)483-2291
Products: Lumber, including plywood and millwork. **SIC:** 5031 (Lumber, Plywood & Millwork). **Est:** 1922. **Sales:** $15,000,000 (2000). **Emp:** 18. **Officers:** J.E. McGinnis Jr., President.

■ **7682** ■ **Alan McIlvain Co.**
5th & Market St.
Marcus Hook, PA 19061
Phone: (215)485-6240 **Fax:** (215)485-0471
Products: Lumber. **SIC:** 5031 (Lumber, Plywood & Millwork). **Sales:** $16,000,000 (2000). **Emp:** 70. **Officers:** Alan McIlvain Jr., President; Gordon McIlvain, Vice President.

■ **7683** ■ **T. Baird McIlvain Co.**
100 Filbert St.
Hanover, PA 17331-9045
Phone: (717)630-0025 **Fax:** (717)630-9706
E-mail: info@tbmlumber.com
URL: http://www.tbmlumber.com
Products: Lumber. **SIC:** 5031 (Lumber, Plywood & Millwork). **Est:** 1955. **Sales:** $25,000,000 (1999). **Emp:** 75. **Officers:** Thomas B. McIlvain Jr., CEO, e-mail: tomm@tbmlumber.com; Thomas Sandor, President, e-mail: toms@tbmlumber.com; John Gallatig, CFO/Treasurer, e-mail: johng@tbmlumber.com.

■ **7684** ■ **McKee Brothers Inc.**
PO Box 490
Saddle River, NJ 07458-0490
Phone: (201)327-0850
Products: Sand; Gravel. **SIC:** 5032 (Brick, Stone & Related Materials). **Est:** 1928. **Sales:** $3,500,000 (2000). **Emp:** 5. **Officers:** Bruce McKee, President.

■ **7685** ■ **C.D. McKenzie**
PO Box 1552
Fallon, NV 89407-1552
Phone: (702)423-1599 **Fax:** (702)423-2737
Products: Windows; Siding. **SICs:** 5033 (Roofing, Siding & Insulation); 5031 (Lumber, Plywood & Millwork). **Officers:** C.D. McKenzie, Owner.

■ **7686** ■ **J.E. McLaughlin Distributor**
155 Porter Pl.
Rutland, VT 05701
Phone: (802)773-6258
Free: (800)869-7514 **Fax:** (802)775-6450
Products: Insulation materials. **SIC:** 5033 (Roofing, Siding & Insulation).

■ **7687** ■ **Meadow Steel Products Div.**
5110 Santa Fe Rd.
Tampa, FL 33619
Phone: (813)248-1944 **Fax:** (813)248-0703
Products: Steel construction supports; Bar supports; Wall form accessories; Bridge overhanging brackets. **SIC:** 5039 (Construction Materials Nec). **Sales:** $29,000,000 (2000). **Emp:** 130. **Officers:** David Wilkes, Vice President.

■ **7688** ■ **Mechanics Building Materials Inc.**
82-40 73rd Ave.
Glendale, NY 11385
Phone: (718)381-6600
Products: Building materials, including laminate, marble, and hinges; Countertops. **SICs:** 5031 (Lumber, Plywood & Millwork); 5039 (Construction Materials Nec). **Est:** 1933. **Sales:** $10,000,000 (2000). **Emp:** 30. **Officers:** Michael Schwartz, President.

■ **7689** ■ **Mega Cabinets Inc.**
113 Albany Ave.
Amityville, NY 11701-2632
Phone: (516)789-4112 **Fax:** (516)789-8394
Products: Kitchen and bath cabinets. **SIC:** 5031 (Lumber, Plywood & Millwork). **Est:** 1978. **Sales:** $2,750,000 (2000). **Emp:** 35. **Officers:** Anthony Griffo; Arthur Griffo.

■ **7690** ■ **Mehrer Drywall Inc.**
2657 20th Ave. W
Seattle, WA 98199
Phone: (206)282-4288 **Fax:** (206)285-2092
Products: Dry wall products. **SIC:** 5031 (Lumber, Plywood & Millwork). **Emp:** 125. **Officers:** Morris B. Mehrer.

■ **7691** ■ **H.B. Mellott Estate Inc.**
100 Mellott Dr., Ste. 100
PO Box 25
Warfordsburg, PA 17267
Phone: (301)678-2000 **Fax:** (301)678-2001
Products: Limestone. **SIC:** 5032 (Brick, Stone & Related Materials). **Est:** 1952. **Sales:** $11,000,000 (2000). **Emp:** 120. **Officers:** Forrest Mellott, Chairman of the Board; Paul C. Mellott Jr., President & CEO.

■ **7692** ■ **Menominee Tribal Enterprises**
PO Box 10
Neopit, WI 54150
Phone: (715)756-2311 **Fax:** (715)756-2386
Products: Lumber. **SIC:** 5031 (Lumber, Plywood & Millwork). **Est:** 1908. **Sales:** $10,000,000 (2000). **Emp:** 160. **Officers:** Lawrence Waukau, President; Lawrence R. Johnson, Finance Officer; J. Kaquatosh, Sales Mgr., e-mail: jkaquatosh@mail.wiscnet.net; Al Quinney, Dir. of Data Processing; D. Leonard, e-mail: dleonard@ mail.wiscnet.net.

■ **7693** ■ **Menoni and Mocogni Inc.**
2160 Old Skokie Valley
Highland Park, IL 60035-0128
Phone: (847)432-0518
Products: Gravel, sand, and dirt; Bricks, cement, and concrete. **SICs:** 5032 (Brick, Stone & Related Materials); 5032 (Brick, Stone & Related Materials). **Est:** 1947. **Sales:** $1,000,000 (2000). **Emp:** 14. **Officers:** Mike Miotti, President.

■ **7694** ■ **Mentor Lumber and Supply Company Inc.**
7180 N Center St.
Mentor, OH 44060
Phone: (440)255-9145
Free: (800)216-WOOD **Fax:** (440)205-8288
E-mail: mentorlumber@ncweb.com
Products: Lumber; Plywood; Windows; Doors; Molding. **SICs:** 5031 (Lumber, Plywood & Millwork); 5039 (Construction Materials Nec). **Est:** 1922. **Sales:** $36,000,000 (1999). **Emp:** 150. **Officers:** Robert C. Sanderson, President; Reed H. Martin III, Treasurer & Secty.; Mac Stewart, VP of Marketing; Suzanne Matz, Human Resources Contact.

■ **7695** ■ **Mequon Distributors Inc.**
PO Box 366
Thiensville, WI 53092
Phone: (262)242-3600 **Fax:** (262)242-9654
Products: Lumber and wood products. **SIC:** 5031 (Lumber, Plywood & Millwork). **Est:** 1920. **Sales:** $17,500,000 (2000). **Emp:** 42. **Officers:** Neal E. Madisen, President.

■ **7696** ■ **Mercer's Dix Equipment**
21588 Dix-Toledo Rd.
Trenton, MI 48183
Phone: (734)676-9637 **Fax:** (734)676-8644
Products: Construction equipment. **SIC:** 5082 (Construction & Mining Machinery). **Est:** 1940. **Emp:** 20. **Officers:** Ron Mercer, President; Gary Mercer, Manager; Rick Mercer, Manager.

■ **7697** ■ **Merit Insulation Inc.**
PO Box 27500
Albuquerque, NM 87125-7500
Phone: (505)242-2681 **Fax:** (505)242-6499
Products: Insulation. **SIC:** 5033 (Roofing, Siding & Insulation). **Officers:** Rick Dunlap, President.

■ **7698** ■ **Merrimack Valley Wood Products Inc.**
1 B St.
Derry, NH 03038
Phone: (603)432-8845 **Fax:** (603)975-5549
Products: Windows; Pre-hung doors; Interior trim. **SIC:** 5031 (Lumber, Plywood & Millwork). **Est:** 1949. **Sales:** $11,000,000 (2000). **Emp:** 130. **Officers:** James Derderian Sr., President; James Derderian Jr., Vice President.

■ **7699** ■ **F.W. Mestre Equipment Co.**
5101 NW 79th Ave.
Miami, FL 33166
Phone: (305)592-2090 **Fax:** (305)591-9593
Products: Cranes; Construction machinery and equipment, including other construction machinery parts. **SIC:** 5082 (Construction & Mining Machinery). **Est:** 1963. **Sales:** $4,000,000 (2000). **Emp:** 7. **Officers:** Frank W. Mestre, President.

■ 7700 ■ Metal Industries Inc.
4314 State Route 209
Elizabethville, PA 17023-8438
Phone: (717)362-8196 **Fax:** (717)362-4012
Products: Windows, doors, and screen products. **SIC:** 5031 (Lumber, Plywood & Millwork).

■ 7701 ■ Michigan Industrial Hardwood Co.
PO Box 612
Whiting, IN 46394
Phone: (219)659-4255 **Fax:** (219)659-5821
Products: Hardwood lumber. **SIC:** 5031 (Lumber, Plywood & Millwork). **Est:** 1948. **Sales:** $5,000,000 (2000). **Emp:** 20. **Officers:** C.R. Morris, President.

■ 7702 ■ Michigan Lumber Co.
1919 Clifford St.
Flint, MI 48503
Phone: (810)232-4108 **Fax:** (810)232-7169
Products: Lumber and wood products. **SIC:** 5031 (Lumber, Plywood & Millwork). **Est:** 1915. **Sales:** $4,000,000 (2000). **Emp:** 33. **Officers:** Charles A. Olson, President; Jarold Haan, Vice President; Sharon Rouse, Dir. of Systems.

■ 7703 ■ Michigan Tractor and Machinery Co.
24800 Novi Rd.
Novi, MI 48375
Phone: (248)349-4800 **Fax:** (248)349-4800
Products: Tractors and heavy construction equipment. **SIC:** 5082 (Construction & Mining Machinery). **Est:** 1944. **Sales:** $230,000,000 (2000). **Emp:** 325. **Officers:** Gerald Jung, President; John O. McElroy, Treasurer; Joel E. House, Exec. VP of Admin.; Robert L. White, Exec. VP of Operations; Clair Ritchie, Dir of Human Resources.

■ 7704 ■ Mid-AM Building Supply Inc.
100 W Sparks
Moberly, MO 65270
Phone: (660)263-2140
Products: Building supplies, including doors, windows, roofing materials, siding, and insulation; Fireplaces; Kitchen cabinets. **SICs:** 5031 (Lumber, Plywood & Millwork); 5039 (Construction Materials Nec); 5033 (Roofing, Siding & Insulation). **Est:** 1967. **Sales:** $80,000,000 (2000). **Emp:** 200. **Officers:** J.F. Knaebel, President.

■ 7705 ■ Mid-South Building Supply of Maryland Inc.
5640 Sunnyside Ave.
Beltsville, MD 20705
Phone: (301)513-9000 **Fax:** (301)441-2481
Products: Building supplies, including siding, kitchen cabinets, windows, and doors. **SICs:** 5039 (Construction Materials Nec); 5033 (Roofing, Siding & Insulation); 5031 (Lumber, Plywood & Millwork). **Est:** 1966. **Sales:** $17,000,000 (2000). **Emp:** 40. **Officers:** J. Briggs, Partner; Harry Katz, Partner.

■ 7706 ■ Mid-State Industries Ltd.
1105 Catalyn St.
Schenectady, NY 12303
Phone: (518)374-1461 **Fax:** (518)381-6820
Products: Architectural sheet metal; Commerical roofing, including slate, copper, and tile; Flat painting; Masonry; Carpentry historical rehabilitation. **SIC:** 5033 (Roofing, Siding & Insulation). **Est:** 1970. **Sales:** $4,000,000 (2000). **Emp:** 20. **Officers:** Mike Lucey, President.

■ 7707 ■ Midpac Lumber Company Ltd.
1001 Ahua St.
Honolulu, HI 96819
Phone: (808)836-8111 **Fax:** (808)836-8297
Products: Lumber, plywood, millwork, wood panels, and construction materials. **SICs:** 5031 (Lumber, Plywood & Millwork); 5039 (Construction Materials Nec). **Sales:** $41,000,000 (1993). **Emp:** 180. **Officers:** Michael K. Yoshida, CEO & President; Dennis Hironaka, Exec. VP of Finance.

■ 7708 ■ Midwest Sales Company of Iowa Inc.
1700 W 29th St.
Kansas City, MO 64108
Phone: (816)753-0586
Products: Roofing supplies. **SIC:** 5033 (Roofing, Siding & Insulation). **Sales:** $35,000,000 (1993). **Emp:** 100. **Officers:** Barry Shepherd, President; Ray Borden, Treasurer.

■ 7709 ■ Midwest Veneer Company
21168 Pke. 136
Louisiana, MO 63353
Phone: (573)754-4072 **Fax:** (573)754-5015
Products: Veneer logs and lumber. **SIC:** 5031 (Lumber, Plywood & Millwork). **Est:** 1974. **Officers:** Karl Dewey, President.

■ 7710 ■ Milchap Products
PO Box 27286
Milwaukee, WI 53227
Phone: (414)321-3111 **Fax:** (414)321-3116
Products: Foundry and industry supplies, including clay, sand, and tiles. **SIC:** 5085 (Industrial Supplies). **Est:** 1926. **Sales:** $4,000,000 (2000). **Emp:** 11. **Officers:** Robert Rice, President; William Rice, CFO; David W. Letto, General Mgr.

■ 7711 ■ Mill Contractor and Industrial Supplies, Inc.
7522 Pendleton Pke.
Indianapolis, IN 46226
Phone: (317)545-6904
Free: (800)535-0680 **Fax:** (317)545-6940
Products: Construction supplies, including concrete. **SIC:** 5032 (Brick, Stone & Related Materials).

■ 7712 ■ Mill Creek Lumber and Supply Co.
6974 E 38th St.
Tulsa, OK 74145-3203
Products: Lumber, including treated and laminated lumber. **SIC:** 5031 (Lumber, Plywood & Millwork). **Est:** 1934. **Sales:** $30,000,000 (2000). **Emp:** 130. **Officers:** J.D. Dunn, President.

■ 7713 ■ Miller Bros. Lumber Company Inc.
4918 W Lawrence Ave.
Chicago, IL 60630-3883
Phone: (773)283-3460 **Fax:** (773)283-5361
Products: Lumber and wood products; Metal roofing and roof drainage equipment; Prepared asphalt and tar roofing and siding products. **SICs:** 5031 (Lumber, Plywood & Millwork); 5033 (Roofing, Siding & Insulation). **Est:** 1928. **Sales:** $5,000,000 (2000). **Emp:** 25. **Officers:** H.B. Miller, President.

■ 7714 ■ Miller and Company Inc.
500 Hooper Dr.
Selma, AL 36701
Phone: (205)874-8271 **Fax:** (205)875-9109
Products: Hardwood flooring; Lumber and wood products. **SIC:** 5031 (Lumber, Plywood & Millwork). **Est:** 1929. **Sales:** $130,000,000 (2000). **Emp:** 400. **Officers:** Bill Deramus, President; Cleve Hawkins, Treasurer; Mike Gurley, Dir. of Marketing.

■ 7715 ■ William T. Miller Lumber Inc.
PO Box 873
Camden, SC 29020
Phone: (803)432-6041 **Fax:** (803)432-6516
Products: Lumber; Doors; Windows; Shingles. **SICs:** 5031 (Lumber, Plywood & Millwork); 5033 (Roofing, Siding & Insulation). **Est:** 1940. **Sales:** $4,000,000 (2000). **Emp:** 32. **Officers:** J. Miller, CEO & President.

■ 7716 ■ Miller Lumber Industries Inc.
PO Box 207
Montross, VA 22520
Phone: (804)472-2040
Products: Building supplies, including windows, doors, lumber, and studs. **SIC:** 5031 (Lumber, Plywood & Millwork). **Est:** 1958. **Sales:** $1,000,000 (2000). **Emp:** 6. **Officers:** Patricia H. Miller, President; Jane Caylor, Vice President.

■ 7717 ■ Millman Lumber Co.
9264 Manchester Rd.
St. Louis, MO 63144
Phone: (314)968-1700 **Fax:** (314)968-0940
Products: Lumber; Millwork. **SIC:** 5031 (Lumber, Plywood & Millwork). **Est:** 1936. **Sales:** $84,000,000 (2000). **Emp:** 70. **Officers:** Richard G. Millman, CEO & President; John Ostermeyer, Treasurer.

■ 7718 ■ W.H. Milroy and Company Inc.
29 Washington Ave.
Hamden, CT 06518
Phone: (203)248-4451 **Fax:** (203)287-8516
Products: Sand, gravel, and stone; Industrial equipment and parts. **SICs:** 5032 (Brick, Stone & Related Materials); 5084 (Industrial Machinery & Equipment). **Est:** 1954. **Sales:** $1,000,000 (2000). **Emp:** 3. **Officers:** W.H. Milroy Jr., President.

■ 7719 ■ Minfelt Wholesale Company Inc.
PO Box 127
Syracuse, NY 13211
Phone: (315)455-5541
Products: Lumber; Building materials. **SICs:** 5031 (Lumber, Plywood & Millwork); 5039 (Construction Materials Nec). **Est:** 1949. **Sales:** $7,000,000 (2000). **Emp:** 40. **Officers:** Jim Wilton, President.

■ 7720 ■ Minneapolis Equipment Co.
520 2nd St., SE
Minneapolis, MN 55414
Phone: (612)378-0111
Products: Construction equipment, including cranes and tools. **SIC:** 5082 (Construction & Mining Machinery). **Est:** 1914. **Sales:** $6,000,000 (2000). **Emp:** 30. **Officers:** J.W. Griffith, President.

■ 7721 ■ Minneapolis Glass Co.
14600 28th Ave. N
Plymouth, MN 55447
Phone: (612)559-0635 **Fax:** (612)559-8816
Products: Glass. **SIC:** 5039 (Construction Materials Nec). **Est:** 1937. **Sales:** $10,000,000 (2000). **Emp:** 70. **Officers:** Michael Horovitz; Tom Stadler; Jennifer Lang.

■ 7722 ■ Minneapolis Rusco Inc.
9901 Smetana Rd.
Minnetonka, MN 55343-9003
Phone: (612)942-0641 **Fax:** (612)942-0644
Products: Gypsum building materials; Windows. **SIC:** 5031 (Lumber, Plywood & Millwork). **Est:** 1955. **Sales:** $2,000,000 (2000). **Emp:** 20. **Officers:** Mel Hazelwood, President.

■ 7723 ■ Minooka Grain Lumber and Supply Co.
PO Box 100
Minooka, IL 60447
Phone: (815)467-2232 **Fax:** (815)467-9220
E-mail: mingrain@cbcast.com
Products: Lumber; Hardware; Millwork; Plywood. **SICs:** 5031 (Lumber, Plywood & Millwork); 5072 (Hardware). **Est:** 1908. **Sales:** $10,800,000 (2000). **Emp:** 9. **Officers:** Bernard Bols, President.

■ 7724 ■ Minot Builders Supply Association
Hwy. 2 & 52 W
Minot, ND 58701
Phone: (701)852-1301 **Fax:** (701)852-8929
Products: Lumber, including cabinets and doors. **SIC:** 5031 (Lumber, Plywood & Millwork). **Est:** 1956. **Sales:** $35,000,000 (2000). **Emp:** 100. **Officers:** Robert M. Pope, President.

■ 7725 ■ Minton's Lumber and Supply Co.
455 W Evelyn Ave.
Mountain View, CA 94041
Phone: (650)968-9201 **Fax:** (650)966-8693
Products: Lumber and wood products; Tools. **SICs:** 5031 (Lumber, Plywood & Millwork); 5072 (Hardware). **Est:** 1911. **Sales:** $6,500,000 (2000). **Emp:** 79. **Officers:** Debra Schulz, President; Barbara Thomas, Controller.

■ 7726 ■ Mintzer Brothers Inc.
PO Box 955
Rutland, VT 05702
Phone: (802)775-0834
Products: Lumber and general building materials, including pre-hung doors and cabinets. **SICs:** 5031 (Lumber, Plywood & Millwork); 5039 (Construction Materials Nec). **Est:** 1923. **Sales:** $15,000,000 (2000). **Emp:** 45. **Officers:** Edward Gartner, President; Allen Gartner, VP & Treasurer.

■ 7727 ■ **Mission Lumber Co.**
2210 Kansas City Rd.
Olathe, KS 66061
Phone: (913)764-4243 **Fax:** (913)764-4531
Products: Lumber. **SIC:** 5031 (Lumber, Plywood & Millwork). **Est:** 1948. **Sales:** $7,000,000 (2000). **Emp:** 90. **Officers:** Jim Mahoney, President.

■ 7728 ■ **Mississippi Valley Equipment Co.**
1198 Pershall Rd.
St. Louis, MO 63137
Phone: (314)869-8600 **Fax:** (314)869-6862
URL: http://www.mktpile.com
Products: Drilling machines. **SIC:** 5082 (Construction & Mining Machinery). **Est:** 1933. **Sales:** $6,000,000 (2000). **Emp:** 11. **Officers:** Rick Henry, President; Mike Whisler, Vice President; Jack Gorzny; Karl Bogle.

■ 7729 ■ **Mitchell Distributing Co.**
PO Box 32156
Charlotte, NC 28232
Phone: (704)376-7554 **Fax:** (704)372-5923
Products: Earth moving vehicles, including bulldozers and excavators; Air compressors; Drills. **SIC:** 5082 (Construction & Mining Machinery). **Est:** 1967. **Sales:** $76,000,000 (2000). **Emp:** 280. **Officers:** Richard Arcilesi Sr., CEO.

■ 7730 ■ **E. Stewart Mitchell Inc.**
PO Box 2799
Baltimore, MD 21225
Phone: (410)354-0600
Products: Asphalt. **SIC:** 5032 (Brick, Stone & Related Materials). **Est:** 1941. **Sales:** $28,000,000 (2000). **Emp:** 100. **Officers:** Barton S. Mitchell, President; Robert Hankey, CFO.

■ 7731 ■ **MKS Industries Inc.**
5801 Court St. Rd.
PO Box 4948
Syracuse, NY 13221
Phone: (315)437-1511
Free: (877)465-7463 **Fax:** (315)437-8273
E-mail: mks@dreamscape.com
URL: http://www.modernkitchens.com
Products: Kitchen cabinets; Major appliances. **SICs:** 5031 (Lumber, Plywood & Millwork); 5064 (Electrical Appliances—Television & Radio). **Est:** 1953. **Sales:** $17,000,000 (2000). **Emp:** 70. **Officers:** Mark R. Martino, President; Beverly Martino, VP & Treasurer; Kirby Holekamp, Sales Mgr.; Dave Pappert, Controller.

■ 7732 ■ **Modern Door and Hardware Inc.**
PO Box 1930
Cordova, TN 38018-1930
Phone: (901)757-1300
Products: Light fixtures; Ceiling fans; Door hardware. **SICs:** 5063 (Electrical Apparatus & Equipment); 5031 (Lumber, Plywood & Millwork); 5023 (Homefurnishings). **Sales:** $3,000,000 (2000). **Emp:** 30. **Officers:** Brian Dunn, General Mgr.; Audrey Weaver, Finance Officer; Walt Star, Dir. of Sales.

■ 7733 ■ **Modern Equipment Sales and Rental Co.**
7667 Pulaski Hwy.
Baltimore, MD 21237-2669
Phone: (410)918-9770
Free: (800)841-3130 **Fax:** (410)918-9956
Products: Heavy equipment, including bulldozers, cranes, aerial lifts, and bucket trucks. **SICs:** 5084 (Industrial Machinery & Equipment); 5082 (Construction & Mining Machinery). **Est:** 1929. **Sales:** $12,000,000 (2000). **Emp:** 25. **Officers:** Dave Griffith, President; Al Funk, President of Sales; Steve Heyman, Sales Mgr., e-mail: heymans@moderngroup.com. **Former Name:** S.M. #Christhilf and Son Inc.

■ 7734 ■ **Modern Kitchen Center Inc.**
5050 County Rd. 154
Glenwood Springs, CO 81601-9320
Phone: (970)945-9194
Free: (800)875-0076 **Fax:** (970)945-9225
Products: Cabinetry; Countertops. **SICs:** 5039 (Construction Materials Nec); 5031 (Lumber, Plywood & Millwork). **Est:** 1977. **Emp:** 10. **Officers:** Robin Slattery, President.

■ 7735 ■ **Modern Methods Inc.**
PO Box 907
Owensboro, KY 42301
Phone: (502)685-5128
Products: Building bricks. **SIC:** 5032 (Brick, Stone & Related Materials). **Est:** 1972. **Sales:** $1,200,000 (2000). **Emp:** 2. **Officers:** William Richard, President & Treasurer; W.J. Richard, CFO.

■ 7736 ■ **Moderne Cabinet Shop**
2304 River Dr. N
Great Falls, MT 59401-1331
Phone: (406)453-4711 **Fax:** (406)453-1851
Products: Custom wood work. **SIC:** 5031 (Lumber, Plywood & Millwork). **Officers:** Layne Shanahan, President.

■ 7737 ■ **Modernfold of Florida, Inc.**
PO Box 451206
Ft. Lauderdale, FL 33345
Phone: (954)747-7400 **Fax:** (954)747-6600
E-mail: modernfoldfl@mindspring.com
URL: http://www.modernfold.com
Products: Building materials; Folding and moveable doors. **SIC:** 5031 (Lumber, Plywood & Millwork). **Est:** 1964. **Emp:** 10. **Officers:** Dan Watson; Sheryl Riggott.

■ 7738 ■ **Monje Forest Products Co.**
10800 SW Herman Rd., Ste. A
Tualatin, OR 97062-8033
Phone: (503)692-0758 **Fax:** (503)692-9669
Products: Building materials. **SIC:** 5039 (Construction Materials Nec). **Officers:** Henry Monje, President.

■ 7739 ■ **Monroe Insulation & Gutter Company Inc.**
100 Ontario St.
East Rochester, NY 14445-1340
Phone: (716)385-3030 **Fax:** (716)385-5959
URL: http://www.monroeinsulation.com
Products: Thermal insulation; Gutters; Security systems; Gas fireplaces; Central vacuum systems. **SICs:** 5033 (Roofing, Siding & Insulation); 5039 (Construction Materials Nec). **Est:** 1975. **Emp:** 75. **Officers:** Randy Williamson.

■ 7740 ■ **Montopolis Supply Co.**
255 Bastrop Hwy.
Austin, TX 78741-2399
Phone: (512)385-3270 **Fax:** (512)385-1160
Products: Steel roofing products. **SIC:** 5033 (Roofing, Siding & Insulation). **Est:** 1956. **Sales:** $6,000,000 (2000). **Emp:** 12. **Officers:** Ross R. Willhoite, Partner; David E. Willhoite, Dir. of Marketing.

■ 7741 ■ **Montrose Hardwood Company Inc.**
PO Box 278
Montross, VA 22520
Phone: (804)493-8021 **Fax:** (804)493-9444
Products: Lumber. **SIC:** 5031 (Lumber, Plywood & Millwork). **Est:** 1984. **Sales:** $3,000,000 (2000). **Emp:** 26. **Officers:** Ray Miller, President & CFO.

■ 7742 ■ **M.D. Moody and Sons Inc.**
4652 Phillips Hwy.
Jacksonville, FL 32207
Phone: (904)737-4401
Free: (800)869-4401 **Fax:** (904)636-2532
Products: Construction machinery, including cranes, barges, and tugs. **SIC:** 5082 (Construction & Mining Machinery). **Est:** 1946. **Sales:** $107,000,000 (2000). **Emp:** 150. **Officers:** Max D. Moody III, CEO; Jim Tompkins, Controller.

■ 7743 ■ **Morgan Distribution Inc.**
PO Box 2003
Mechanicsburg, PA 17055
Phone: (717)697-1151 **Fax:** (717)697-7409
Products: Doors and windows; Building supplies. **SICs:** 5031 (Lumber, Plywood & Millwork); 5039 (Construction Materials Nec). **Est:** 1986. **Officers:** David A. Braun.

■ 7744 ■ **Morgan Engineering Systems Inc.**
947 E Broadway
Alliance, OH 44601
Phone: (216)823-6130 **Fax:** (216)823-3050
Products: Overhead cranes. **SICs:** 5084 (Industrial Machinery & Equipment); 5082 (Construction & Mining Machinery). **Est:** 1868. **Sales:** $15,000,000 (2000). **Emp:** 30. **Officers:** Gary L. Smith, VP & General Merchandising Mgr.

■ 7745 ■ **Morgan Forest Products**
PO Box 20369
Columbus, OH 43220-0369
Phone: (614)457-3390 **Fax:** (614)457-0991
E-mail: sales@morganforest.com
URL: http://www.morganforest.com
Products: Wooden pallets; Plywood. **SIC:** 5031 (Lumber, Plywood & Millwork). **Est:** 1923. **Sales:** $50,000,000 (1999). **Emp:** 25. **Officers:** Harold W. Reinstetle, CEO; Dwight A. Reinstetle, CFO. **Former Name:** Morgan Lumber Sales Company Inc.

■ 7746 ■ **Morgan Lumber Company Inc.**
PO Box 309
Hwy. 74 West
Marshville, NC 28103
Phone: (704)624-2146 **Fax:** (704)624-6907
Products: Treated lumber. **SIC:** 5031 (Lumber, Plywood & Millwork). **Est:** 1945. **Sales:** $4,500,000 (2000). **Emp:** 17. **Officers:** J. Parks Morgan, President.

■ 7747 ■ **Morgan-Wightman Supply Company**
10199 Woodfield Ln.
St. Louis, MO 63132
Phone: (314)995-9990 **Fax:** (314)995-9781
Products: Millwork, including doors, windows, and cabinets. **SIC:** 5031 (Lumber, Plywood & Millwork). **Est:** 1950. **Sales:** $37,000,000 (1999). **Emp:** 160. **Officers:** Stuart P. Wells, CEO & President; George Kessel, CFO.

■ 7748 ■ **Morgan-Wightman Supply Inc.**
Indiana
3250 N Post Rd.
Indianapolis, IN 46226
Phone: (317)895-9595 **Fax:** (317)899-9759
Products: Wood window and door frames; Metal doors and frames; Locks and related materials; Metal doors, sash, and trim. **SICs:** 5031 (Lumber, Plywood & Millwork); 5072 (Hardware). **Est:** 1950. **Sales:** $10,000,000 (2000). **Emp:** 40. **Officers:** Robert L. Weber, Vice President.

■ 7749 ■ **Morgen Manufacturing Co.**
PO Box 160
Yankton, SD 57078
Phone: (605)665-9654 **Fax:** (605)665-7017
Products: Concrete construction equipment. **SIC:** 5082 (Construction & Mining Machinery). **Est:** 1950. **Sales:** $39,000,000 (2000). **Emp:** 120. **Officers:** Jim Cope, Chairman of the Board; Bill Cope, CFO.

■ 7750 ■ **Moser Lumber Inc.**
300 E 5th Ave., Ste. 430
Naperville, IL 60563-3182
Phone: (630)420-3000 **Fax:** (630)420-3023
Products: Hardware; Lumber and wood products; Electrical equipment and supplies. **SICs:** 5031 (Lumber, Plywood & Millwork); 5072 (Hardware); 5063 (Electrical Apparatus & Equipment). **Est:** 1941. **Sales:** $35,000,000 (2000). **Emp:** 200. **Officers:** James L. Moser, CEO.

■ 7751 ■ **Moshofsky Enterprises**
PO Box 2107
Lake Oswego, OR 97035-0034
Phone: (503)292-8861
Products: Lumber. **SIC:** 5031 (Lumber, Plywood & Millwork). **Est:** 1952. **Sales:** $600,000 (2000). **Emp:** 2. **Officers:** Arthur R. Moshofsky, Partner; Edward Moshofsky, Partner.

■ 7752 ■ **Roscoe Moss Co.**
PO Box 31064
Los Angeles, CA 90063
Phone: (213)261-4185 **Fax:** (213)263-4497
Products: Screens and casings for water wells. **SIC:** 5039 (Construction Materials Nec). **Est:** 1917. **Sales:** $19,000,000 (2000). **Emp:** 105. **Officers:** Bob Van Valer, President; Tony Creque, Controller; Bill Hyatt, VP of Marketing.

■ 7753 ■   Moynihan Lumber
PO Box 509
Beverly, MA 01915-4223
Phone: (978)927-0032   **Fax:** (978)927-8668
Products: Lumber and wood products; Prefabricated wood buildings and components; Hardware. **SICs:** 5031 (Lumber, Plywood & Millwork); 5072 (Hardware). **Emp:** 35. **Officers:** Michael Moynihan.

■ 7754 ■   MQ Power Corp.
18910 Wilmington Ave.
Carson, CA 90749
Phone: (310)537-3700   **Fax:** (310)632-2656
Products: Concrete; Construction equipment, including generators, water pumps, and mixers. **SICs:** 5082 (Construction & Mining Machinery); 5032 (Brick, Stone & Related Materials); 5084 (Industrial Machinery & Equipment). **Sales:** $20,000,000 (2000). **Emp:** 50. **Officers:** Hank Eisner, CFO; Jay Robinson, Exec. VP.

■ 7755 ■   Don Murphy Door Specialties Inc.
10390 Chester Rd.
Cincinnati, OH 45215
Phone: (513)771-6087   **Fax:** (513)771-6089
Products: Garage doors. **SICs:** 5063 (Electrical Apparatus & Equipment); 5039 (Construction Materials Nec). **Est:** 1963. **Sales:** $1,000,000 (2000). **Emp:** 12. **Officers:** Michael Murphy, President; Debbie Murphy, Vice President.

■ 7756 ■   M.W. Manufacturers Inc.
PO Box 136
Tupelo, MS 38802
Phone: (601)842-7311   **Fax:** (601)842-1242
Products: Windows; Doors; Moldings; Hardware. **SICs:** 5031 (Lumber, Plywood & Millwork); 5072 (Hardware). **Est:** 1957. **Sales:** $13,000,000 (2000). **Emp:** 68. **Officers:** David Colbert, General Mgr.

■ 7757 ■   John H. Myers and Son Inc.
1285 W King St.
York, PA 17405
Phone: (717)792-2500
Free: (800)637-0057   **Fax:** (717)792-8407
E-mail: sales2atsjhmson.com
URL: http://www.jhmson.com
Products: Plywood; Lumber; Builder's supplies; Millwork; Kitchen supplies; Flooring; Hardware. **SIC:** 5031 (Lumber, Plywood & Millwork). **Est:** 1916. **Sales:** $32,000,000 (2000). **Emp:** 90. **Officers:** Robert L. Myers III, President, e-mail: psubob@jhmson.com; Nick Gazanna, Controller.

■ 7758 ■   Myrmo and Sons Inc.
PO Box 3215
Eugene, OR 97403
Phone: (541)747-4565
Products: Heavy machinery. **SIC:** 5082 (Construction & Mining Machinery). **Est:** 1925. **Sales:** $6,500,000 (2000). **Emp:** 80. **Officers:** E.A. Myrmo, President; Vic Green, Manager; George Myrmo, Vice President.

■ 7759 ■   N & L Inc.
5525 Cameron St.
Las Vegas, NV 89118-2206
Phone: (702)362-4230   **Fax:** (702)876-6163
Products: Roofing, siding, and insulation materials. **SIC:** 5033 (Roofing, Siding & Insulation). **Officers:** Dennis Dean, President.

■ 7760 ■   Nailite International Inc.
1251 NW 165th St.
Miami, FL 33169
Phone: (305)620-6200   **Fax:** (305)623-8227
E-mail: sales@nailite.com
Products: Plastic siding. **SIC:** 5033 (Roofing, Siding & Insulation). **Est:** 1978. **Sales:** $18,000,000 (1999). **Emp:** 110. **Officers:** Howard Washington, CEO & President.

■ 7761 ■   Nally & Haydon Inc.
Springfield Rd.
Bardstown, KY 40004
Phone: (502)348-3926
Products: Surfacing materials, including crushed stone, blacktop, and asphalt. **SIC:** 5032 (Brick, Stone & Related Materials). **Est:** 1962. **Sales:** $20,000,000 (2000). **Emp:** 100. **Officers:** Albert Haydon, President; John Haydon, Treasurer.

■ 7762 ■   Naples Rent-All and Sales Company Inc.
2600 Davis Blvd.
Naples, FL 34104
Phone: (941)774-7117   **Fax:** (941)774-4218
E-mail: rentall@naplesnet.com
Products: Construction equipment. **SIC:** 5082 (Construction & Mining Machinery). **Est:** 1967. **Emp:** 30.

■ 7763 ■   Nashville Sash and Door Co.
PO Box 40780
Nashville, TN 37204-0780
Phone: (615)254-1371   **Fax:** (615)726-2704
Products: Windows; Metal doors and frames; Door frames. **SICs:** 5031 (Lumber, Plywood & Millwork); 5039 (Construction Materials Nec). **Est:** 1926. **Sales:** $17,000,000 (2000). **Emp:** 110. **Officers:** Syndey S. McAlister, President; Robert Chandler, Controller; Hill McAlister, Dir. of Marketing.

■ 7764 ■   National Industrial Lumber Co.
489 Rosemont Rd.
North Jackson, OH 44451
Phone: (330)538-3386   **Fax:** (330)538-2277
Products: Lumber. **SIC:** 5031 (Lumber, Plywood & Millwork). **Sales:** $12,000,000 (2000). **Emp:** 23. **Officers:** Michael Hoag, President.

■ 7765 ■   National Lumber Co.
24595 Groesbeck Hwy.
Warren, MI 48089
Phone: (313)775-8200   **Fax:** (810)775-4110
Products: Rough lumber. **SIC:** 5031 (Lumber, Plywood & Millwork). **Est:** 1946. **Sales:** $110,000,000 (2000). **Emp:** 220. **Officers:** James Rosenthal, President; Alan Strickstein, Vice President.

■ 7766 ■   National Manufacturing, Inc.
811 Atlantic
North Kansas City, MO 64116-3918
Phone: (816)221-8990
Free: (800)444-9978   **Fax:** (816)221-9454
Products: Siding; Wire screening. **SICs:** 5033 (Roofing, Siding & Insulation); 5051 (Metals Service Centers & Offices). **Est:** 1988. **Emp:** 40.

■ 7767 ■   National Mine Service Co. Mining Safety and Supply Div.
PO Box 310
Indiana, PA 15701
Phone: (412)349-7100
Free: (800)692-6672   **Fax:** (412)349-7352
URL: http://www.n-m-s.com
Products: Mining safety products, mining machinery parts, miner's cap lamps, gas detection monitors. **SICs:** 5082 (Construction & Mining Machinery); 5085 (Industrial Supplies). **Sales:** $20,000,000 (2000). **Emp:** 165. **Officers:** Herbert F. Gerhard, CEO & President.

■ 7768 ■   Nationwide Ladder & Equipment Company Inc.
180 Rockingham Rd.
Windham, NH 03087
Phone: (603)434-6911
Free: (800)228-2519   **Fax:** (603)434-0807
E-mail: natwidelad@aol.com
Products: Fiberglass, aluminum, and wood ladders; Steel scaffolding; Van shelving; Truck tool boxes; Safety equipment. **SICs:** 5084 (Industrial Machinery & Equipment); 5013 (Motor Vehicle Supplies & New Parts). **Est:** 1974. **Sales:** $5,000,000 (1999). **Emp:** 30. **Officers:** Dave Lyon, Human Resources Contact; Sean Cody, Customer Service Contact.

■ 7769 ■   Nattinger Materials Co.
PO Box 4007
Springfield, MO 65808
Phone: (417)869-2595   **Fax:** (417)869-6052
Products: Blocks for building. **SIC:** 5032 (Brick, Stone & Related Materials). **Est:** 1944. **Sales:** $8,000,000 (2000). **Emp:** 42. **Officers:** C.W. Nattinger, President & Chairman of the Board.

■ 7770 ■   Nebraska Machinery Co.
401 N 12th St.
Omaha, NE 68102
Phone: (402)346-6500   **Fax:** (402)346-3964
Products: Construction and farming tractors. **SIC:** 5082 (Construction & Mining Machinery). **Est:** 1938. **Sales:** $60,000,000 (2000). **Emp:** 300. **Officers:** Jerry L. Swanson, CEO; Robert E. Ulrich, Vice President; Robert F. Pospichal, Sales Mgr.; John R. Swanson, Dir. of Data Processing.

■ 7771 ■   Fred Netterville Lumber
PO Box 857
Woodville, MS 39669
Phone: (601)888-4343
Products: Lumber. **SIC:** 5031 (Lumber, Plywood & Millwork). **Sales:** $16,000,000 (1994). **Emp:** 152. **Officers:** Fred Netterville, President; Charlie Netterville, Treasurer & Secty.

■ 7772 ■   Neubert Millwork Co.
1901 Lee Blvd.
North Mankato, MN 56003
Phone: (507)387-1105   **Fax:** (507)387-1068
Products: Lumber; Doors; Windows. **SIC:** 5031 (Lumber, Plywood & Millwork). **Est:** 1926. **Sales:** $3,500,000 (2000). **Emp:** 18. **Officers:** C.J. Haefner, President; D.C. Rotchadl, Dir. of Marketing.

■ 7773 ■   New England Door Corp.
15 Campanelli Cir.
Canton, MA 02021-2480
Phone: (978)443-5131
Products: Pre-hung doors; Electronic garage doors. **SIC:** 5031 (Lumber, Plywood & Millwork). **Est:** 1952. **Sales:** $7,000,000 (2000). **Emp:** 30. **Officers:** Robert Frank, President; R. Frank, President.

■ 7774 ■   New England Sand and Gravel Co.
PO Box 3248
Framingham, MA 01701
Phone: (508)877-2460   **Fax:** (508)877-6970
Products: Sand and gravel. **SIC:** 5032 (Brick, Stone & Related Materials). **Est:** 1939. **Sales:** $2,000,000 (2000). **Emp:** 12. **Officers:** Frank Generazio Jr., President; Richard Generazio, Vice President.

■ 7775 ■   Newman Lumber Co.
PO Box 2580
Gulfport, MS 39505-2580
Phone: (601)832-1899
Products: Mahogany. **SIC:** 5031 (Lumber, Plywood & Millwork). **Est:** 1947. **Sales:** $20,000,000 (2000). **Emp:** 39. **Officers:** Roy Newman, CEO; Jannette Robbins, Finance Officer.

■ 7776 ■   Nezbeda Tile Inc.
2995 E Aukele St.
Lihue, HI 96766
Phone: (808)245-1765   **Fax:** (808)246-9395
Products: Floorcovering equipment and supplies. **SIC:** 5032 (Brick, Stone & Related Materials). **Sales:** $1,000,000 (2000). **Emp:** 7.

■ 7777 ■   Nickerson Lumber and Plywood Inc.
7875 Willis Ave.
Panorama City, CA 91402
Phone: (818)983-1127   **Fax:** (818)982-9257
URL: http://www.nickersonlbr.com
Products: Lumber; Plywood; Hardwood; Ash furniture parts. **SIC:** 5031 (Lumber, Plywood & Millwork). **Est:** 1962. **Sales:** $35,000,000 (1999). **Emp:** 62. **Officers:** Timothy P. Cheney, President, e-mail: tcheney@ nickersonlbr.com; Linda Hodges, Controller; Robert Lopez, Vice President.

■ 7778 ■   Niehaus Lumber Co.
PO Box 667
Vincennes, IN 47591
Phone: (812)882-2710
Products: Lumber. **SIC:** 5031 (Lumber, Plywood & Millwork). **Est:** 1933. **Sales:** $12,000,000 (2000). **Emp:** 85. **Officers:** Bernie Niehaus, CEO & President; Roger Brown, Controller.

■ 7779 ■   E.A. Nielsen Co. Inc.
1700 W 12th St.
Kansas City, MO 64101
Phone: (816)421-0633
Free: (800)821-2702   **Fax:** (816)421-0626
Products: Lumber. **SIC:** 5031 (Lumber, Plywood & Millwork). **Est:** 1963. **Sales:** $11,000,000 (2000). **Emp:** 15. **Officers:** James M. Nielsen, President; Karen Nielsen, Vice President.

■ 7780 ■ **Nippon Electric Glass America Inc.**
650 E Devon
Itasca, IL 60143
Phone: (630)285-8500 **Fax:** (630)285-8510
Products: Glass products. **SIC:** 5039 (Construction Materials Nec). **Est:** 1989. **Sales:** $10,800,000 (2000). **Emp:** 11.

■ 7781 ■ **Nissen and Company Inc.**
9508 Rush St.
South el Monte, CA 91733
Phone: (213)723-3636
Products: Fire resistant and non-fire resistant windows. **SIC:** 5051 (Metals Service Centers & Offices). **Est:** 1910. **Sales:** $2,000,000 (2000). **Emp:** 20. **Officers:** Erroll W. Murphy Sr., President; Erroll W. Murphy Jr., Vice President; Taki Roybal, Secretary; Debbie Rodriguez, Dir. of Systems.

■ 7782 ■ **Nitterhouse Concrete Product Inc.**
PO Box N
Chambersburg, PA 17201
Phone: (717)264-6154 **Fax:** (717)267-4518
Products: Concrete block; Concrete brick; Concrete reinforcing bars; Concrete products. **SIC:** 5032 (Brick, Stone & Related Materials). **Est:** 1923. **Sales:** $22,000,000 (2000). **Emp:** 250. **Officers:** William K. Nitterhouse, President; G.E. Meyers, Controller; R.G. Jones, VP of Marketing; Betty Shroeder, Dir. of Data Processing; William A. Martin, Dir of Human Resources.

■ 7783 ■ **Nitterhouse Masonry Products, LLC**
PO Box 692
Chambersburg, PA 17201
Phone: (717)267-4500 **Fax:** (717)267-4528
E-mail: nitmas@epix.net
URL: http://www.nitterhouse.com
Products: Concrete construction materials. **SIC:** 5039 (Construction Materials Nec). **Est:** 1923. **Sales:** $12,000,000 (2000). **Emp:** 100. **Officers:** William K. Nitterhouse, President; G.E. Meyers, Controller; Ronald G. Jones, Vice President.

■ 7784 ■ **Nolan Scott Chatard L.L.C.**
403 Allegheny Ave.
Towson, MD 21204
Phone: (410)296-7262
Products: Prefabricated buildings. **SIC:** 5039 (Construction Materials Nec). **Sales:** $14,000,000 (2000). **Emp:** 8. **Officers:** J. Albert Chatard III, President; Phylis N. Corby, Controller.

■ 7785 ■ **Norandex, Inc.**
1133 S Gordon
Wichita, KS 67213
Phone: (316)942-7417 **Fax:** (316)942-3689
Products: Wood doors, interior and exterior; Windows; Siding. **SICs:** 5031 (Lumber, Plywood & Millwork); 5033 (Roofing, Siding & Insulation).

■ 7786 ■ **Norandex, Inc.**
10 Adams Dr.
Williston, VT 05495
Phone: (802)864-0900 **Fax:** (802)864-5410
Products: Wood window and door frames; Metal doors and frames; Window frames. **SIC:** 5031 (Lumber, Plywood & Millwork).

■ 7787 ■ **Norandex Inc.**
8450 S Bedford Rd.
Macedonia, OH 44056
Phone: (330)468-2200 **Fax:** (330)468-8118
Products: Construction materials. **SIC:** 5039 (Construction Materials Nec). **Sales:** $650,000,000 (2000). **Emp:** 3,200. **Officers:** Daniel Dietzel, President; Lynn Kovalcheck, VP of Finance.

■ 7788 ■ **Norandex/Reynolds Distribution Co.**
8450 S Bedford Rd.
Macedonia, OH 44056
Phone: (330)468-2200 **Fax:** (330)468-8118
Products: Siding; Windows. **SICs:** 5039 (Construction Materials Nec); 5033 (Roofing, Siding & Insulation). **Est:** 1946. **Sales:** $610,000,000 (2000). **Emp:** 3,000. **Officers:** Daniel Dietzel; David Schreiner, VP of Operations; Raymond Valle, VP of Marketing.

■ 7789 ■ **Norandex Sales Co.**
2215 West 2200 South
Salt Lake City, UT 84119
Phone: (801)908-8747
Free: (800)344-5298 **Fax:** (801)975-0938
Products: Wood window and door framesl Siding; Windows. **SICs:** 5031 (Lumber, Plywood & Millwork); 5033 (Roofing, Siding & Insulation).

■ 7790 ■ **Norfield Industries**
PO Box 459
Chico, CA 95927-0459
Phone: (530)891-4214
Products: Cabinets; Pre-hung doors. **SIC:** 5031 (Lumber, Plywood & Millwork). **Est:** 1959. **Sales:** $6,000,000 (2000). **Emp:** 70. **Officers:** B. Norlie, President; Troy Wooten, Marketing & Sales Mgr.

■ 7791 ■ **North American Plywood Corp.**
351 Manhattan Ave.
Jersey City, NJ 07307-4441
Phone: (201)420-0440
Free: (800)759-6608 **Fax:** (201)420-4077
E-mail: njsales@northamply.com
URL: http://www.northamply.com
Products: Plywood. **SIC:** 5031 (Lumber, Plywood & Millwork). **Est:** 1948. **Sales:** $18,000,000 (2000). **Emp:** 22. **Officers:** Clifford Lowy, President.

■ 7792 ■ **North Brothers Co.**
3250 Woodstock Rd. SE
Atlanta, GA 30316
Phone: (404)627-1381 **Fax:** (404)622-9393
Products: Plastics foam products; Mineral wool for thermal and accoustical envelope insulation (for insulating homes, and commercial and industrial buildings). **SIC:** 5033 (Roofing, Siding & Insulation).

■ 7793 ■ **North Carolina Equipment**
PO Box 431
Raleigh, NC 27602
Phone: (919)833-4811 **Fax:** (919)828-6619
Products: Construction machinery. **SICs:** 5082 (Construction & Mining Machinery); 5084 (Industrial Machinery & Equipment). **Est:** 1931. **Sales:** $35,000,000 (2000). **Emp:** 300. **Officers:** R.J. Calton, President; Jr., C. Attardi, Treasurer & Secty.

■ 7794 ■ **North Pacific Group, Inc.**
PO Box 3915
Portland, OR 97208
Phone: (503)231-1166 **Fax:** (503)238-2641
URL: http://www.north_pacific.com
Products: Lumber; Building materials; Agricultural products, including grains and fertilizers. **SIC:** 5031 (Lumber, Plywood & Millwork); 5191 (Farm Supplies). **Est:** 1948. **Sales:** $1,100,000,000 (2000). **Emp:** 850. **Officers:** Thomas J. Tomjack, President; Jay Ross, COO; Irwin Rogers, COO; Karen Austin, Human Resources Contact. **Former Name:** North Pacific Lumber Co.

■ 7795 ■ **Northern Equipment Company Inc.**
1 Timber Trail Dr. SE
Ada, MI 49301-9300
Phone: (616)531-5000 **Fax:** (616)531-8269
Products: Heavy construction equipment. **SIC:** 5082 (Construction & Mining Machinery). **Est:** 1952. **Sales:** $9,000,000 (2000). **Emp:** 25. **Officers:** R.E. Hess, President.

■ 7796 ■ **Northern Jersey Reserve Supply Co.**
PO Box 440
Elmwood Park, NJ 07407
Phone: (201)796-3000
Products: Building material; Lumber; Shingles; Insulation. **SICs:** 5031 (Lumber, Plywood & Millwork); 5039 (Construction Materials Nec); 5033 (Roofing, Siding & Insulation). **Est:** 1936. **Sales:** $7,000,000 (2000). **Emp:** 10. **Officers:** Donald Rudbart, President; Chester R. Smalley Jr., General Mgr.

■ 7797 ■ **Northern Ohio Lumber and Timber Co.**
1895 Carter Rd.
Cleveland, OH 44113
Phone: (216)771-4080
Free: (800)771-4081 **Fax:** (216)771-4793
E-mail: northernohiolumber@msn.com
URL: http://www.northernohiolumber.com
Products: Lumber; Ceiling tile; Dry wall; Timbers; Metal studs; Fire tested lunber; wolmonized lumber; Hardwoods. **SICs:** 5031 (Lumber, Plywood & Millwork); 5051 (Metals Service Centers & Offices). **Est:** 1860. **Sales:** $5,000,000 (2000). **Emp:** 16. **Officers:** Virgel Zanick, President; Charles Bredt, Vice President.

■ 7798 ■ **Northland Corp.**
PO Box 265
La Grange, KY 40031
Phone: (502)222-2536
Free: (800)873-1444 **Fax:** (502)222-5355
URL: http://www.northlandcorp.com
Products: Lumber and wood products. **SIC:** 5031 (Lumber, Plywood & Millwork). **Est:** 1964. **Sales:** $40,000,000 (1999). **Emp:** 100. **Officers:** Orn Gudmundsson, President & CEO; Doug Atchinson, Accounting Manager; Joe Lesousky, Customer Service Mgr., e-mail: jlesousky@northlandcorp.com; Tim Girardi, Sales Mgr., e-mail: tgirardi@northlandcorp.com; Judy Splan-Larin, Human Resources Contact, e-mail: jsplanlarin@northlandcorp.com.

■ 7799 ■ **Northridge Lumber Company Inc.**
18537 Parthenia St.
Northridge, CA 91324
Phone: (818)349-6701
Products: Lumber; Hammers; Nails. **SICs:** 5031 (Lumber, Plywood & Millwork); 5072 (Hardware). **Est:** 1938. **Sales:** $7,000,000 (2000). **Emp:** 25. **Officers:** Richard E. Hawthorne, President; Tim Hawthorne, CFO.

■ 7800 ■ **Northwest Wood Products Inc.**
PO Box 377
Mill City, OR 97360
Phone: (503)897-2391 **Fax:** (503)879-3253
Products: Plywood; Lumber. **SIC:** 5031 (Lumber, Plywood & Millwork). **Est:** 1965. **Sales:** $4,000,000 (2000). **Emp:** 12. **Officers:** William R. Morgan, President; John Bishop, Sales Mgr.

■ 7801 ■ **Nu-Way Concrete Forms Inc.**
4190 Hofmeister Ave.
St. Louis, MO 63125
Phone: (314)544-1214
Products: Construction materials, concrete mixtures. **SICs:** 5039 (Construction Materials Nec); 5032 (Brick, Stone & Related Materials). **Sales:** $11,000,000 (1994). **Emp:** 67. **Officers:** Gerald Rhomberg, President; Paul Donovan, Controller.

■ 7802 ■ **John J. O'Connell Wholesale Lumber Co.**
PO Box 1250
Cedar Rapids, IA 52406
Phone: (319)366-5396 **Fax:** (319)366-8662
Products: Lumber, including spruce, oak, and pine boards. **SIC:** 5031 (Lumber, Plywood & Millwork). **Est:** 1939. **Sales:** $7,000,000 (2000). **Emp:** 20. **Officers:** John O'Connell, President & Treasurer.

■ 7803 ■ **Ocotillo Lumber Sales Inc.**
3121 N 28th Ave.
Phoenix, AZ 85017
Phone: (602)258-6951 **Fax:** (602)258-6172
Products: Steel fencing; Lumber. **SICs:** 5031 (Lumber, Plywood & Millwork); 5051 (Metals Service Centers & Offices). **Est:** 1961. **Sales:** $10,000,000 (2000). **Emp:** 17. **Officers:** Naidi Ivie, President; Robert J. Cordes, Vice President.

■ 7804 ■ **OCT Equipment Inc.**
7100 SW 3rd Ave.
Oklahoma City, OK 73128
Phone: (405)789-6812 **Fax:** (405)787-8649
URL: http://www.octequipement.com
Products: Heavy construction equipment. **SIC:** 5082 (Construction & Mining Machinery). **Est:** 1953. **Sales:** $30,000,000 (2000). **Emp:** 63. **Officers:** Robert H.

Vaughn, CEO & Chairman of the Board; R. Dale Vaughn, President.

■ **7805** ■ **Ohio Machinery Co.**
3993 E Royalton Rd.
Broadview Heights, OH 44147
Phone: (440)526-6200
Free: (800)837-6200 **Fax:** (440)526-9513
URL: http://www.ohiomachinery.com
Products: Earthmoving equipment; Engine dearlship. **SIC:** 5082 (Construction & Mining Machinery). **Est:** 1946. **Sales:** $100,000,000 (2000). **Emp:** 450. **Officers:** Ken Taylor, President; Dave Blocksom, Sec. & Treas.; Paul Liesem, VP of Sales; Kelly Love, VP of Product Support; Kelly Love, Dir of Human Resources.

■ **7806** ■ **Ohio Tile and Marble Co.**
3809 Spring Grove Ave.
Cincinnati, OH 45223
Phone: (513)541-4211 **Fax:** (513)541-2966
Products: Floorcovering equipment and supplies. **SIC:** 5032 (Brick, Stone & Related Materials).

■ **7807** ■ **Ohio Valley Supply Co.**
3512 Spring Grove Ave.
Cincinnati, OH 45223
Phone: (513)681-8300 **Fax:** (513)853-3307
Products: Corian. **SIC:** 5162 (Plastics Materials & Basic Shapes). **Est:** 1948. **Sales:** $24,000,000 (2000). **Emp:** 41. **Officers:** Thomas E. Butler, Chairman of the Board; Tom Ochs, Treasurer; Kenneth Shear, President.

■ **7808** ■ **Okaw Buildings Inc.**
PO Box 144A
Arthur, IL 61911
Phone: (217)543-3371
Products: Lumber. **SIC:** 5031 (Lumber, Plywood & Millwork). **Sales:** $15,000,000 (1993). **Emp:** 45. **Officers:** Chris Helmuth, President.

■ **7809** ■ **T. Oki Trading, Ltd.**
2722 Waiwai Loop
Honolulu, HI 96819
Phone: (808)834-2722 **Fax:** (808)839-1166
Products: Construction materials. **SIC:** 5039 (Construction Materials Nec).

■ **7810** ■ **Oliver Stores Inc.**
399 Lewiston Rd., Ste. 100
New Gloucester, ME 04260
Phone: (207)926-4123 **Fax:** (207)926-4009
Products: Logging equipment. **SIC:** 5082 (Construction & Mining Machinery). **Sales:** $15,000,000 (1994). **Emp:** 27. **Officers:** K. Scott Morrison, President & CFO.

■ **7811** ■ **Louis T. Ollesheimer & Son Inc.**
605 E 12 Mile Rd.
Madison Heights, MI 48071
Phone: (248)544-3900
Free: (800)572-5037 **Fax:** (248)545-6970
Products: Metal roofing and roof drainage equipment. **SIC:** 5033 (Roofing, Siding & Insulation). **Est:** 1916.

■ **7812** ■ **One Source Home and Building Centers**
PO Box 99
North Little Rock, AR 72115
Phone: (501)372-8100 **Fax:** (501)375-0941
Products: Building materials, including lumber, siding, and shingles. **SICs:** 5031 (Lumber, Plywood & Millwork); 5033 (Roofing, Siding & Insulation).

■ **7813** ■ **Ontario Stone Corp.**
34301 Chardon Rd., Ste. 5
Willoughby Hills, OH 44094
Phone: (216)631-3645 **Fax:** (216)943-9569
Products: Construction aggregates such as stone building materials. **SIC:** 5032 (Brick, Stone & Related Materials). **Sales:** $18,000,000 (2000). **Emp:** 50. **Officers:** Carl Barricelli, President; Matilda Barricelli, Treasurer & Secty.

■ **7814** ■ **OREPAC Millwork Products**
13971 Norton Ave.
Chino, CA 91710
Phone: (909)627-4043
Products: Molding; Windows. **SIC:** 5031 (Lumber,

Plywood & Millwork). **Est:** 1951. **Sales:** $18,000,000 (2000). **Emp:** 65. **Officers:** Gary Caster, VP & General Merchandising Mgr.

■ **7815** ■ **Oshtemo Hill Inc.**
2050 Turner NW
Grand Rapids, MI 49504-2046
Phone: (616)363-6854
Free: (800)821-8212 **Fax:** (616)363-6222
Products: Building supplies. **SIC:** 5039 (Construction Materials Nec). **Est:** 1971. **Sales:** $6,000,000 (2000). **Emp:** 22. **Officers:** Stan Jones, President.

■ **7816** ■ **A. Ottavino Corp.**
80-60 Pitkin Ave.
Ozone Park, NY 11417
Phone: (718)848-9404 **Fax:** (718)848-7156
Products: Stone. **SIC:** 5032 (Brick, Stone & Related Materials). **Est:** 1913. **Sales:** $3,000,000 (2000). **Emp:** 25. **Officers:** M. Elkordy, President; K. Ottavino, CFO.

■ **7817** ■ **Overhead Door Company Inc.**
34 N Lakewood
Tulsa, OK 74158
Phone: (918)838-9901
Free: (800)722-5935 **Fax:** (918)838-9647
URL: http://www.overheaddoortulsa.com
Products: Garage doors. **SIC:** 5031 (Lumber, Plywood & Millwork). **Est:** 1948. **Sales:** $6,000,000 (1999). **Emp:** 67. **Officers:** Frank D. Sanders, President.

■ **7818** ■ **Oxford Recycling Inc.**
2400 W Oxford Ave.
Englewood, CO 80110
Phone: (303)762-1160 **Fax:** (303)762-1746
E-mail: info@oxfordrecycling.com
URL: http://www.oxfordrecycling.com
Products: Concrete; Asphalt; Tires; Wood. **SICs:** 5032 (Brick, Stone & Related Materials); 5032 (Brick, Stone & Related Materials); 5014 (Tires & Tubes). **Est:** 1979. **Sales:** $4,000,000 (2000). **Emp:** 13. **Officers:** John F. Kent, President.

■ **7819** ■ **Pac-West Inc.**
2303 N Randolph St.
Portland, OR 97227
Phone: (503)288-0218
Products: Insulating glass. **SIC:** 5039 (Construction Materials Nec). **Sales:** $6,000,000 (2000). **Emp:** 50. **Officers:** Tom Tucker, President.

■ **7820** ■ **Pacific American Commercial Co.**
PO Box 3742
Seattle, WA 98124
Phone: (206)762-3550
Products: Construction equipment; Cranes; Air compressors. **SIC:** 5082 (Construction & Mining Machinery). **Est:** 1955. **Sales:** $13,000,000 (2000). **Emp:** 52. **Officers:** R. Paul Debruyn, President; Tom Gibbons, CFO.

■ **7821** ■ **Pacific Clay Brick Products Inc.**
14741 Lake St.
Lake Elsinore, CA 92530
Phone: (909)674-2131
Products: brick and structural clay products. **SIC:** 5032 (Brick, Stone & Related Materials). **Sales:** $17,000,000 (2000). **Emp:** 200. **Officers:** Dave Hollingsworth, President.

■ **7822** ■ **Pacific Coast Building Products Inc.**
PO Box 160488
Sacramento, CA 95816
Phone: (916)444-9304 **Fax:** (916)325-3697
Products: Building supplies and equipment, including paper, roofing, and doors. **SICs:** 5033 (Roofing, Siding & Insulation); 5031 (Lumber, Plywood & Millwork). **Est:** 1952. **Sales:** $350,000,000 (2000). **Emp:** 2,500. **Officers:** David Luccetti, CEO & President; Nick Kalanges, CFO; Jim Anderson, VP of Sales.

■ **7823** ■ **Pacific Coast Cement Corp.**
PO Box 4120
Ontario, CA 91761-1067
Phone: (909)390-7600 **Fax:** (818)568-9556
Products: Cement. **SIC:** 5032 (Brick, Stone & Related Materials). **Est:** 1980. **Sales:** $60,000,000 (2000). **Emp:** 24. **Officers:** Jon T. Pawley, President; Linda Robinson, Controller.

■ **7824** ■ **Pacific Machinery Inc.**
456 Kalanianole Ave.
Hilo, HI 96720
Phone: (808)961-3481 **Fax:** (808)961-2551
Products: Heavy construction equipment. **SIC:** 5082 (Construction & Mining Machinery).

■ **7825** ■ **Pacific Mutual Door Co.**
1525 W 31st St.
Kansas City, MO 64108
Phone: (816)531-0161 **Fax:** (816)531-2081
Products: Door moldings. **SIC:** 5031 (Lumber, Plywood & Millwork). **Est:** 1912. **Sales:** $60,000,000 (2000). **Emp:** 200. **Officers:** S.R. Lambert Jr., President.

■ **7826** ■ **Pacific North Equipment Co.**
PO Box 8000
Seattle, WA 98138
Phone: (253)872-3500 **Fax:** (253)872-3519
Products: Construction equipment, trailers and road machinery. **SIC:** 5082 (Construction & Mining Machinery). **Sales:** $42,000,000 (2000). **Emp:** 245. **Officers:** Wayne Leach, President.

■ **7827** ■ **Pacific Steel and Supply Corp.**
2062 W 140th
San Leandro, CA 94577
Phone: (510)357-0340
Products: Steel building materials. **SIC:** 5051 (Metals Service Centers & Offices). **Sales:** $89,000,000 (2000). **Emp:** 75. **Officers:** Ronald O'Connor, President; Robert Struch, Controller.

■ **7828** ■ **Pacific Supply**
4310 Westside Rd.
Redding, CA 96001-3747
Phone: (916)246-1191 **Fax:** (916)243-3127
Products: Building supplies, including roofing and drywall. **SICs:** 5032 (Brick, Stone & Related Materials); 5031 (Lumber, Plywood & Millwork); 5033 (Roofing, Siding & Insulation). **Est:** 1953. **Sales:** $6,000,000 (2000). **Emp:** 22. **Officers:** Dave Stockton, Manager; Nick Kalanges, CFO.

■ **7829** ■ **Packings & Insulations Corp.**
PO Box 6364
Providence, RI 02940-6364
Phone: (401)421-8090 **Fax:** (401)421-8942
Products: Roofing; Siding; Insulation and insulation materials. **SIC:** 5033 (Roofing, Siding & Insulation). **Officers:** Steven Gregson, Manager.

■ **7830** ■ **Pacor Inc.**
PO Box 29278
Philadelphia, PA 19125-0278
Phone: (215)978-7100 **Fax:** (215)978-7107
Products: Fiberglass plate covering. **SIC:** 5039 (Construction Materials Nec). **Est:** 1928. **Sales:** $26,000,000 (2000). **Emp:** 100. **Officers:** Paul T. Fraatz Jr., President; Michael Freda, Controller; James Brown, Vice President.

■ **7831** ■ **Palmer-Donovan Manufacturing**
312 Mound St.
Dayton, OH 45407
Phone: (937)461-1203 **Fax:** (937)461-9934
Products: Paneling; Siding. **SIC:** 5031 (Lumber, Plywood & Millwork). **Est:** 1957. **Sales:** $25,000,000 (2000). **Emp:** 60. **Officers:** Dan Pierce, General Mgr.; Kathy Sayer, Controller; John Bankowski, Sales Mgr.

■ **7832** ■ **Pamas and Company Inc.**
14 E Welsh Pool Rd.
Exton, PA 19341
Phone: (215)524-1980
Products: Carbon sidewall blocks. **SIC:** 5032 (Brick, Stone & Related Materials).

■ **7833** ■ **Pan Am Distributing Inc.**
2950 Thousand Oaks Dr., Ste. 23
San Antonio, TX 78247-3347
Phone: (210)225-3892
Products: Roofing materials, including shingles, nails, and tar. **SIC:** 5033 (Roofing, Siding & Insulation). **Sales:** $20,000,000 (2000). **Emp:** 75. **Officers:** Ken Hamill, President; Bill Warren, Controller.

■ 7834 ■ Pape Brothers Inc.
2300 Henderson Ave.
Eugene, OR 97403
Products: Heavy equipment, including truck engines and bulldozers. SIC: 5082 (Construction & Mining Machinery). Est: 1938. Sales: $94,000,000 (2000). Emp: 300. Officers: Randy Pape, President; Tom Saylor, Controller; Paul Meyerhoff, Marketing Mgr.

■ 7835 ■ Parr Lumber Co.
PO Box 989
Chino, CA 91708
Phone: (909)627-0953
Products: Lumber; Plywood; Hardwood. SIC: 5031 (Lumber, Plywood & Millwork). Est: 1976. Sales: $44,000,000 (2000). Emp: 20. Officers: Peter L. Parrella, President; Pamela A. Winters, Treasurer & Secty.

■ 7836 ■ Jack B. Parson Cos.
PO Box 3429
Ogden, UT 84409
Phone: (801)731-1111   Fax: (801)731-8800
Products: Ready-mixed concrete. SIC: 5032 (Brick, Stone & Related Materials). Est: 1946. Sales: $100,000,000 (2000). Emp: 900. Officers: John W. Parson, CEO & President; Doug Peterson, CFO.

■ 7837 ■ Parts Inc.
PO Box 394
Heber City, UT 84032
Phone: (801)972-5293   Fax: (801)972-0618
Products: Construction and mining machinery and equipment; signs-aluminum, wood and magnetic. SIC: 5082 (Construction & Mining Machinery). Officers: Steve White, CFO.

■ 7838 ■ Passaic Metal & Building Supplies Co.
5 Central Ave.
PO Box 1849
Clifton, NJ 07015
Phone: (973)546-9000
Free: (800)522-4575   Fax: (973)546-7179
Products: Roofing supplies; Siding; Sheet metal; Fireplaces. SICs: 5033 (Roofing, Siding & Insulation); 5051 (Metals Service Centers & Offices); 5074 (Plumbing & Hydronic Heating Supplies). Est: 1916. Officers: Frank Gurtman, President. Alternate Name: Passaic Metal Products.

■ 7839 ■ Patrick Industries Inc.
PO Box 638
Elkhart, IN 46515
Phone: (219)294-7511   Fax: (219)522-5213
URL: http://www.patrickind.com
Products: Building materials. SICs: 5031 (Lumber, Plywood & Millwork); 5033 (Roofing, Siding & Insulation); 5039 (Construction Materials Nec). Est: 1959. Sales: $460,000,000 (2000). Emp: 1,750. Officers: Mervin D. Lung, CEO & Chairman of the Board; Keith V. Kankel, VP of Finance & Treasurer; David Lung, COO & President.

■ 7840 ■ Patrick Lumber Company Inc.
828 SW 1st St.
Portland, OR 97204
Phone: (503)222-9671   Fax: (503)295-2611
Products: Lumber. SIC: 5031 (Lumber, Plywood & Millwork). Est: 1915. Sales: $52,000,000 (2000). Emp: 25. Officers: Robert D. McCracken, President; A. Leslie Oliver, CFO; Jim Rodway, VP of Marketing.

■ 7841 ■ Patten Industries Inc.
635 W Lake St.
Elmhurst, IL 60126
Phone: (708)279-4400   Fax: (708)279-7892
Products: Earth moving equipment; Generators. SIC: 5082 (Construction & Mining Machinery). Est: 1933. Sales: $150,000,000 (2000). Emp: 360. Officers: Byron C. Patten Jr., President; R.G. Nagode, CFO; J.B. Vukelich, Sales Mgr.; Art Baker, Dir. of Data Processing; Tom O'Neil, Dir of Human Resources.

■ 7842 ■ Pauls Tops & Knobs
7273 Old Pascagoula Rd.
Theodore, AL 36582
Phone: (205)653-6881   Fax: (205)653-0025
Products: Counter tops and supplies. SIC: 5031 (Lumber, Plywood & Millwork).

■ 7843 ■ Payne & Dolan Inc. Muskego Site
PO Box 708
Waukesha, WI 53187
Phone: (414)662-3366
Products: Sand and gravel. SIC: 5032 (Brick, Stone & Related Materials). Est: 1980. Sales: $500,000 (2000). Emp: 4. Officers: Edward Reesman, Vice President; John Jeffords, CFO. Former Name: Payne and Dolan Inc. State Sand and Gravel Co.

■ 7844 ■ Pella Windows and Doors Inc.
112 Alexandra Way
Carol Stream, IL 60188-2068
Phone: (630)682-4500
Free: (800)829-7034   Fax: (630)588-3880
Products: Windows; Doors. SIC: 5031 (Lumber, Plywood & Millwork). Est: 1925. Sales: $25,000,000 (2000). Emp: 150. Officers: Kevin Flannery, President.

■ 7845 ■ Penberthy Lumber Co.
2011 E Carson St.
Carson, CA 90810
Phone: (310)835-6222   Fax: (310)835-6823
E-mail: woodinfo@penberthy.com
URL: http://www.penberthy.com
Products: Lumber; Exotic woods and domestic hardwood; Moldings; Flooring; Imported wood specialist. SIC: 5031 (Lumber, Plywood & Millwork). Est: 1931. Sales: $11,000,000 (2000). Emp: 50. Officers: F. Penberthy, COO; Steve West, Sales Contact; Nancy Coulombe, Dir of Human Resources; Jeff Enright, Customer Service Contact; Gary Penberthy, Vice President.

■ 7846 ■ Peninsula Supply Company Inc.
PO Box 265
Newport News, VA 23607
Phone: (757)244-1496   Fax: (757)245-6801
Products: Lumber and wood products. SIC: 5031 (Lumber, Plywood & Millwork). Est: 1923. Sales: $2,000,000 (2000). Emp: 20. Officers: Raymond Hawthorne, President; Bernice Hawthorne, Treasurer.

■ 7847 ■ H.O. Penn Machinery Company Inc.
54 Noxon Rd.
Poughkeepsie, NY 12603
Phone: (914)452-1200   Fax: (914)452-3458
Products: Construction and industrial machinery. SICs: 5082 (Construction & Mining Machinery); 5084 (Industrial Machinery & Equipment). Est: 1923. Sales: $180,000,000 (2000). Emp: 325. Officers: C.E. Thomas Cleveland, President; Gerald Martin, CFO.

■ 7848 ■ Pennsylvania Plywood & Lumber
2590 Monroe St.
York, PA 17404
Phone: (717)792-0216
Free: (800)437-7789   Fax: (717)792-5028
Products: Plywood; Lumber and wood products; Glued laminated lumber. SIC: 5031 (Lumber, Plywood & Millwork).

■ 7849 ■ Pennville Custom Cabinetry for the Home
600 E Votaw
PO Box 1266
Portland, IN 47371
Phone: (219)726-9357   Fax: (219)726-7044
E-mail: pennville@jayco.net
Products: Cabinets. SIC: 5031 (Lumber, Plywood & Millwork). Est: 1926. Sales: $3,000,000 (1999). Emp: 42. Officers: Mark S. Goldman, President; Stanford C. Goldman, Chairman of the Board; Bonnie Goldman, Human Resources Contact.

■ 7850 ■ Penrod Co.
2809 S Lynnhaven Rd.,No. 350
Virginia Beach, VA 23454-6714
Phone: (757)498-0186   Fax: (757)489-1075
E-mail: penrod@thepenrodcompany.com
URL: http://www.thepenrodcompany.com
Products: Wood, lumber and plywood products. SIC:

5031 (Lumber, Plywood & Millwork). Est: 1888. Sales: $100,000,000 (1999). Emp: 150. Officers: E.A. Heidt Jr., President.

■ 7851 ■ Perry Supply Inc.
PO Box 1237
Birmingham, AL 35201
Phones: (205)252-3107   (205)943-7200
Free: (800)654-1935   Fax: (205)252-3227
E-mail: jeasterwood@perrysupply.com
Products: Industrial foundry supplies and equipment; Mining supplies and equipment. SICs: 5082 (Construction & Mining Machinery); 5085 (Industrial Supplies). Est: 1913. Sales: $14,500,000 (2000). Emp: 24. Officers: Gene Wilson, President, e-mail: genew@traveller.com; Bill Hicks, Sales Mgr.; Keith Parvin, Sales Contact.

■ 7852 ■ Perry Supply Inc.
PO Box 1237
Birmingham, AL 35201
Phone: (205)252-3107
Free: (800)233-9661   Fax: (205)252-3227
Products: Construction materials and machinery. SIC: 5082 (Construction & Mining Machinery). Sales: $12,300,000 (2000). Emp: 25.

■ 7853 ■ Peterson Tractor Co.
PO Box 5258
San Leandro, CA 94577
Phone: (510)357-6200   Fax: (510)352-5952
Products: Bulldozers; Tractors; Heavy earth moving equipment. SIC: 5082 (Construction & Mining Machinery). Est: 1936. Sales: $250,000,000 (2000). Emp: 360. Officers: William E. Doyle Jr., CEO & President; Walter Perry, CFO; Gerald Lopus, VP of Sales; Walter Perry, CFO; Michael Klapperich, Dir of Human Resources.

■ 7854 ■ Pfaff and Smith Builders Supply Co.
PO Box 2508
Charleston, WV 25329
Phone: (304)342-4171
Products: Building materials. SIC: 5039 (Construction Materials Nec). Est: 1902. Sales: $5,000,000 (2000). Emp: 35. Officers: Joseph B. Cook, President; Ronald Thompson, VP of Finance.

■ 7855 ■ PFT Of America Inc.
4857 W Van Buren St.
Phoenix, AZ 85043
Phone: (602)269-9311   Fax: (602)269-9566
Products: Construction machinery and equipment for mixing, pumping, spraying and conveying of dry pre-blended products; Precision metal fabrication. SIC: 5082 (Construction & Mining Machinery). Officers: Bernard Otremba, CEO & President.

■ 7856 ■ PGL Building Products
PO Box 1049
Auburn, WA 98071
Phone: (253)941-2600
Products: Building supplies, including cement. SICs: 5031 (Lumber, Plywood & Millwork); 5039 (Construction Materials Nec). Est: 1940. Sales: $190,000,000 (2000). Emp: 1,500. Officers: Carl Liliequist, General Mgr.; J.M. Cahir, Treasurer; Tom Turbeville, Dir. of Information Systems.

■ 7857 ■ Pharis Organization Inc.
111 Woodside Ave.
Ridgewood, NJ 07450
Phone: (201)447-4451   Fax: (201)447-0083
Products: Construction equipment and supplies. SIC: 5039 (Construction Materials Nec). Est: 1989. Sales: $400,000 (2000). Emp: 5. Officers: Vernon Pharis, President.

■ 7858 ■ Philadelphia Fire Retardant Company Inc.
PO Box 319
Haverford, PA 19041-0319
Phone: (610)527-1254   Fax: (610)527-4630
Products: Fire retardant doors, frames, and hardware. SICs: 5031 (Lumber, Plywood & Millwork); 5072 (Hardware). Est: 1915. Sales: $5,000,000 (2000). Emp: 15. Officers: James K. Young, Vice President.

■ 7859 ■ Philadelphia Reserve Supply Co.
400 Mack Dr.
Croydon, PA 19021
Phone: (215)785-3141
Free: (800)347-7726 **Fax:** (215)785-5806
URL: http://www.prsco.org
Products: Building materials, including lumber, windows, and doors. **SIC:** 5031 (Lumber, Plywood & Millwork). **Est:** 1930. **Sales:** $85,000,000 (2000). **Emp:** 35. **Officers:** Frank J. Dalinsky, President; Charles Gormley, Exec. VP; Sandra Spadaccino, VP of Sales.

■ 7860 ■ Victor L. Phillips Co.
PO Box 4915
Kansas City, MO 64120
Phone: (816)241-9290
Free: (800)878-9290 **Fax:** (816)241-9290
Products: Construction equipment; Construction equipment rental and repair. **SIC:** 5082 (Construction & Mining Machinery). **Sales:** $50,000,000 (2000). **Emp:** 100. **Officers:** James W. Foreman, President; David Leavitt, CFO.

■ 7861 ■ Phillips, Day and Maddock Inc.
1800 E 30th St.
Cleveland, OH 44114-4499
Phone: (216)861-5730
Products: Jack hammers, anchors, screws, and other construction equipment. **SIC:** 5082 (Construction & Mining Machinery). **Sales:** $50,000,000 (2000). **Emp:** 80. **Officers:** Bob Munson, President; Tom Munson, Treasurer.

■ 7862 ■ Phoenix Inc.
PO Box 676
Frederick, MD 21701-0676
Phone: (301)663-3151 **Fax:** (301)698-4057
Products: Construction material, including concrete blocks. **SIC:** 5032 (Brick, Stone & Related Materials). **Est:** 1970. **Sales:** $20,000,000 (2000). **Emp:** 200. **Officers:** Jr., A.W. Manning, CEO.

■ 7863 ■ Pikesville Lumber Co.
7104 Liberty Rd.
Baltimore, MD 21207
Phone: (410)484-3800 **Fax:** (410)484-3583
Products: Lumber; Plywood. **SIC:** 5031 (Lumber, Plywood & Millwork). **Est:** 1960. **Sales:** $1,500,000 (2000). **Emp:** 15. **Officers:** Howard A. Goldberg, President.

■ 7864 ■ Pine Cone Lumber Company Inc.
PO Box 61207
Sunnyvale, CA 94088
Phone: (408)736-5491
Products: Lumber; Doors; Windows; Power tools; Building supplies. **SICs:** 5031 (Lumber, Plywood & Millwork); 5039 (Construction Materials Nec); 5072 (Hardware). **Est:** 1959. **Sales:** $17,000,000 (2000). **Emp:** 55. **Officers:** George E. Cilker, President.

■ 7865 ■ Pine Tree Lumber Co.
707 N Andreason Dr.
Escondido, CA 92029
Phone: (760)745-0411
Products: Lumber and building materials. **SIC:** 5031 (Lumber, Plywood & Millwork). **Sales:** $15,000,000 (1993). **Emp:** 130. **Officers:** Warren S. Wexler, CEO; Mike Wexler, President.

■ 7866 ■ Pioneer Machinery
PO Box 9230
Richmond, VA 23227
Phone: (804)266-4911 **Fax:** (804)262-5726
Products: Wood and wood products. **SIC:** 5082 (Construction & Mining Machinery). **Sales:** $200,000,000 (2000). **Emp:** 550.

■ 7867 ■ Pittston Lumber and Manufacturing Co.
234 N Main St.
Pittston, PA 18640
Phone: (717)654-3329
Products: Lumber, roofing, plywood, and windows. **SICs:** 5031 (Lumber, Plywood & Millwork); 5033 (Roofing, Siding & Insulation). **Est:** 1956. **Sales:** $9,000,000 (2000). **Emp:** 28. **Officers:** Joseph Charge Jr., President; Roger Nocerini, Treasurer & Secty.

■ 7868 ■ Plant Insulation Co.
PO Box 8646
Emeryville, CA 94662
Phone: (510)654-7363 **Fax:** (510)654-4167
Products: Tank and pipe insulation; Fiberglass duct wrap. **SICs:** 5033 (Roofing, Siding & Insulation); 5039 (Construction Materials Nec). **Est:** 1937. **Sales:** $8,000,000 (2000). **Emp:** 79. **Officers:** D. Ralston, President; Robert Johnson, Treasurer & Secty.; J. Jones, Manager.

■ 7869 ■ Plaschem Supply & Consulting
1415 Spar Ave.
Anchorage, AK 99501
Phone: (907)274-5505 **Fax:** (907)274-9215
Products: Fiberglass. **SIC:** 5033 (Roofing, Siding & Insulation).

■ 7870 ■ Plaschem Supply & Consulting Inc.
1415 Spar Ave.
Anchorage, AK 99501
Phone: (907)274-5505
Free: (800)478-5505 **Fax:** (907)274-9215
Products: Wholesale, retail and custom fiberglass. **SIC:** 5033 (Roofing, Siding & Insulation). **Est:** 1980. **Emp:** 28. **Officers:** Floyd Apling, President; Randy Apling, Vice President; Sharon Apling, Sec. & Treas. **Former Name:** Fiberchem, Inc.

■ 7871 ■ Plunkett Webster Inc.
2 Clinton Pl.
New Rochelle, NY 10802-0251
Phone: (914)636-8770 **Fax:** (914)636-4477
URL: http://www.p-w.net
Products: Lumber, including plywood; Building materials. **SICs:** 5031 (Lumber, Plywood & Millwork); 5039 (Construction Materials Nec). **Est:** 1915. **Sales:** $130,000,000 (1999). **Emp:** 205. **Officers:** William E. Tufts, CEO; Jim Bryan, Controller; James A. Daniels, President; Joseph B. Croft, VP & Secty.

■ 7872 ■ Pluswood Distributors
PO Box 2248
Oshkosh, WI 54903
Phone: (920)235-0022 **Fax:** (920)235-7570
Products: Industrial boards for manufacturing. **SIC:** 5031 (Lumber, Plywood & Millwork). **Est:** 1957. **Sales:** $8,500,000 (2000). **Emp:** 10. **Officers:** DuWayne Bartel, Manager; Barbara Maloney; Barbara Maloney, Customer Service Contact. **Former Name:** Northern Wire & Cable.

■ 7873 ■ Plywood-Detroit Inc.
13250 Stephens Dr.
Warren, MI 48089
Phone: (810)755-4100 **Fax:** (810)755-9598
Products: Plywood; Particle board. **SIC:** 5031 (Lumber, Plywood & Millwork). **Est:** 1946. **Sales:** $10,000,000 (2000). **Emp:** 20. **Officers:** Craig Porter, President & Chairman of the Board.

■ 7874 ■ Plywood Discount Center
1021 Arbor Ln.
Glenview, IL 60025-3237
Phone: (773)478-2730 **Fax:** (773)478-9616
Products: Plywood and lumber. **SIC:** 5031 (Lumber, Plywood & Millwork).

■ 7875 ■ Plywood Supply Inc.
PO Box 82300
Kenmore, WA 98028
Phone: (206)485-8585
Products: Plywood; Lumber; Siding. **SICs:** 5031 (Lumber, Plywood & Millwork); 5033 (Roofing, Siding & Insulation). **Est:** 1953. **Sales:** $29,000,000 (2000). **Emp:** 67. **Officers:** Ralph Swanson, President; Kevin O'Keefe, Controller; Vaeth Hewitt Jr., Dir. of Marketing.

■ 7876 ■ Plywood Tropics USA Inc.
1 SW Columbia St.
Portland, OR 97258
Phone: (503)222-1622
Products: Paneling; Moldings. **SIC:** 5031 (Lumber, Plywood & Millwork). **Sales:** $900,000 (2000). **Emp:** 10. **Officers:** Richard C. Newman, President; Brian Tytler, Controller.

■ 7877 ■ Pneumatic and Electric Equipment Co.
501 Garfield Ave.
West Chester, PA 19380
Phone: (610)692-9270 **Fax:** (610)430-0778
Products: Construction equipment. **SIC:** 5082 (Construction & Mining Machinery). **Est:** 1930. **Sales:** $5,000,000 (2000). **Emp:** 20. **Officers:** P.C. Schramm, President; J. Bellis, Treasurer; D.J. Little, General Mgr.

■ 7878 ■ Polycoat Systems Inc.
5 Depot St.
Hudson Falls, NY 12839
Phone: (518)747-0654
Free: (800)547-4004 **Fax:** (518)747-5894
E-mail: fnestle/polycoat@global2000.net
URL: http://www.polycoat.com
Products: Insulation; Silicone; Polyurethane; Application equipment. **SICs:** 5033 (Roofing, Siding & Insulation); 5169 (Chemicals & Allied Products Nec). **Est:** 1978. **Sales:** $15,000,000 (2000). **Emp:** 22. **Officers:** George Carruthers, CEO & Finance Officer.

■ 7879 ■ Gregory Poole Equipment Co.
4807 Beryl Rd.
Raleigh, NC 27606
Phone: (919)828-0641 **Fax:** (919)890-4389
Products: Construction and industrial machinery and equipment. **SICs:** 5082 (Construction & Mining Machinery); 5084 (Industrial Machinery & Equipment). **Est:** 1951. **Sales:** $250,000,000 (2000). **Emp:** 800. **Officers:** Kathy Morris, Finance Officer; J. Gregory Poole III, President & COO.

■ 7880 ■ Powell Wholesale Lumber Co.
PO Box 65
Waynesville, NC 28786
Phone: (704)926-0848 **Fax:** (704)926-9117
Products: Lumber. **SIC:** 5031 (Lumber, Plywood & Millwork). **Est:** 1959. **Sales:** $3,500,000 (2000). **Emp:** 25. **Officers:** Carl Bruce Powell Sr., CEO; William Carrier, Controller; George E. Powell, Vice President.

■ 7881 ■ Power Equipment Co.
PO Box 2311
Knoxville, TN 37901
Phone: (615)577-5563 **Fax:** (615)579-7370
Products: Heavy construction equipment, including back hoes and bulldozers. **SICs:** 5082 (Construction & Mining Machinery); 5084 (Industrial Machinery & Equipment). **Est:** 1946. **Sales:** $38,300,000 (2000). **Emp:** 170. **Officers:** Roy Y. Gaylor, President; Jerry D. Hall, Treasurer; George G. Tibbs, Dir. of Marketing; Rodney B. Jones, Dir. of Data Processing; Amanda Williams, Dir of Human Resources.

■ 7882 ■ Powers Products Co.
1003 E Lincolnway St.
Cheyenne, WY 82001
Phone: (307)632-5521 **Fax:** (307)632-2335
Products: Doors; Hardware; Skylights; Operable partitions. **SICs:** 5039 (Construction Materials Nec); 5033 (Roofing, Siding & Insulation). **Est:** 1947. **Sales:** $1,500,000 (1999). **Emp:** 50. **Officers:** James M. Powers, President; Brent Powers, Exec. VP.

■ 7883 ■ Pozzolanic Northwest Inc.
7525 SE 24th St., Ste. 630
Mercer Island, WA 98040
Phone: (206)232-9320 **Fax:** (206)232-9501
E-mail: augustine@flyash.com
URL: http://www.flyash.com
Products: Fly ash. **SIC:** 5032 (Brick, Stone & Related Materials). **Est:** 1976. **Sales:** $20,000,000 (2000). **Emp:** 50. **Officers:** Gerald A. Peabody Jr., President.

■ 7884 ■ Prassel Lumber Company Inc.
PO Box 8549
Jackson, MS 39284
Phone: (601)922-0130 **Fax:** (601)922-0135
Products: Industrial supplies; Lumber. **SICs:** 5031 (Lumber, Plywood & Millwork); 5085 (Industrial Supplies). **Est:** 1959. **Sales:** $12,000,000 (2000). **Emp:** 75. **Officers:** Don Watkins, CEO; Jeanne Walters, Treasurer.

■ 7885 ■ **Pratt & Dudley Building Materials**
1002 University Pl.
Augusta, GA 30903
Phone: (706)724-7755 **Fax:** (706)724-1273
Products: Building materials. **SICs:** 5031 (Lumber, Plywood & Millwork); 5032 (Brick, Stone & Related Materials); 5033 (Roofing, Siding & Insulation); 5039 (Construction Materials Nec).

■ 7886 ■ **PrimeSource Inc.**
1881 Langley Ave.
Irvine, CA 92614-5623
Phone: (949)250-2002 **Fax:** (949)250-2099
Products: Building supplies, including wood and nails. **SICs:** 5031 (Lumber, Plywood & Millwork); 5039 (Construction Materials Nec); 5072 (Hardware). **Est:** 1990. **Sales:** $360,000,000 (2000). **Emp:** 830. **Officers:** Paul Hylbert, CEO & President; Gary Joslin, Sr. VP & CFO; Scott W. Klein, VP of Marketing; Michele Gamberutti, Dir. of Information Systems; James A. Carr, Dir of Human Resources.

■ 7887 ■ **Prudential Building Materials**
171 Milton St.
Dedham, MA 02026-0994
Phone: (617)329-3232
Products: Construction materials and machinery. **SIC:** 5039 (Construction Materials Nec). **Sales:** $65,500,000 (2000). **Emp:** 250.

■ 7888 ■ **Prudential Metal Supply Corp.**
171 Milton St.
Dedham, MA 02026
Phone: (781)329-3232 **Fax:** (781)326-0752
Products: Building materials. **SICs:** 5039 (Construction Materials Nec); 5031 (Lumber, Plywood & Millwork). **Sales:** $85,000,000 (2000). **Emp:** 250. **Officers:** Robert Kolikof, CEO; Jim Salerno, CFO.

■ 7889 ■ **Puckett Machinery Co.**
PO Box 3170
Jackson, MS 39207
Phone: (601)969-6000 **Fax:** (601)969-1339
Products: Heavy equipment, including tractors and loaders. **SIC:** 5082 (Construction & Mining Machinery). **Est:** 1982. **Sales:** $110,000,000 (2000). **Emp:** 230. **Officers:** Richard Puckett, President; Bill Farlow, Treasurer.

■ 7890 ■ **Puget Sound Manufacturing Co.**
1123 St. Paul Ave.
Tacoma, WA 98421-2404
Phone: (253)572-5666 **Fax:** (253)272-7516
Products: Wood doors. **SIC:** 5031 (Lumber, Plywood & Millwork). **Est:** 1919. **Sales:** $1,000,000 (2000). **Emp:** 2. **Officers:** J. Warnick, President.

■ 7891 ■ **Pumilite-Salem Inc.**
PO Box 5348
Salem, OR 97304-0348
Phone: (503)585-1323 **Fax:** (503)585-4545
Products: Masonry products; Drywall. **SIC:** 5032 (Brick, Stone & Related Materials). **Est:** 1947. **Sales:** $2,500,000 (2000). **Emp:** 10. **Officers:** Thomas S. Hammer, President; Paul Hammer, Vice President; Jerry Yarbrough, Sales Mgr.

■ 7892 ■ **Quality Window & Door**
27888 County Rd. 32 W
Elkhart, IN 46517
Phone: (219)674-0867
Free: (888)674-0867 **Fax:** (219)862-4090
Products: Windows; Doors. **SICs:** 5031 (Lumber, Plywood & Millwork); 5039 (Construction Materials Nec). **Est:** 1987. **Officers:** Dan King, Marketing & Sales Mgr.; Gloria King, Human Resources.

■ 7893 ■ **Quigley Sales and Marketing and Associates**
410 E 3rd St.
Royal Oak, MI 48067
Phone: (248)546-3220 **Fax:** (248)546-3288
Products: Specialty building materials. **SICs:** 5031 (Lumber, Plywood & Millwork); 5032 (Brick, Stone & Related Materials); 5033 (Roofing, Siding & Insulation); 5039 (Construction Materials Nec). **Est:** 1977. **Sales:** $7,000,000 (2000). **Emp:** 4. **Officers:** Kevin Quigley, Partner; Brian Quigley, Partner; Marianne Quigley,

Partner; Marianne Quigley, Partner. **Alternate Name:** Manufacturers Representatives.

■ 7894 ■ **R & R Sales Inc.**
944 Dorchester Ave.
Boston, MA 02125-1219
Phone: (617)265-0440 **Fax:** (617)282-4226
Products: Building materials. **SIC:** 5039 (Construction Materials Nec). **Officers:** Robert Raimondi, President.

■ 7895 ■ **R & R Scaffold Erectors, Inc.**
1150 E 68th Ave.
Anchorage, AK 99518
Phone: (907)344-5427 **Fax:** (907)349-3268
Products: Scaffolding products. **SICs:** 5082 (Construction & Mining Machinery); 5039 (Construction Materials Nec).

■ 7896 ■ **Fred Radandt Sons Inc.**
1800 Johnston Dr.
Manitowoc, WI 54220
Phone: (920)682-7758 **Fax:** (920)682-0169
Products: Gravel; Topsoil; Road gravel; Limestone; Excavating; Demolition; Trucking; Snowplowing; Rip rap. **SICs:** 5032 (Brick, Stone & Related Materials); 5082 (Construction & Mining Machinery). **Est:** 1913. **Sales:** $6,000,000 (2000). **Emp:** 65. **Officers:** George Radandt Jr., President; Bob Radandt, Vice President.

■ 7897 ■ **Radford Co.**
PO Box 2688
Oshkosh, WI 54903
Phone: (414)426-6200 **Fax:** (414)426-6215
Products: Windows. **SIC:** 5031 (Lumber, Plywood & Millwork). **Est:** 1871. **Sales:** $62,000,000 (2000). **Emp:** 205. **Officers:** Joe Dunn, President; Michael Walsh, VP & Treasurer; Peter Radford, Sr. VP of Marketing & Sales.

■ 7898 ■ **Rajala Lumber Co.**
PO Box 578
Deer River, MN 56636
Phone: (218)246-8277 **Fax:** (218)246-2822
Products: Stud mill. **SIC:** 5031 (Lumber, Plywood & Millwork). **Est:** 1969. **Sales:** $42,000,000 (2000). **Emp:** 150. **Officers:** Jack Rajala, President.

■ 7899 ■ **Randall Brothers Inc.**
PO Box 1678
Atlanta, GA 30371
Phone: (404)892-6666 **Fax:** (404)875-6102
Products: Lumber and building materials. **SIC:** 5031 (Lumber, Plywood & Millwork). **Sales:** $22,000,000 (2000). **Emp:** 135. **Officers:** Luther H. Randall III., President; Michael Reyland, CFO.

■ 7900 ■ **Randall's Lumber**
315 Paseo Del Pueblo Sur
Taos, NM 87571
Products: Lumber. **SIC:** 5031 (Lumber, Plywood & Millwork).

■ 7901 ■ **Rasmussen Equipment Co.**
3333 W 2100 S
Salt Lake City, UT 84119-1197
Phone: (801)972-5588 **Fax:** (801)972-2215
URL: http://www.rasmussenequipment.com
Products: Hydraulic excavators; Beakers; Wheel loaders; Compaction equipment; Cranes; Sweepers; Material separators and screening equipment. **SICs:** 5082 (Construction & Mining Machinery); 5085 (Industrial Supplies). **Est:** 1946. **Sales:** $26,000,000 (2000). **Emp:** 80. **Officers:** Richard F. Rasmussen, President & CEO.

■ 7902 ■ **Raymond Equipment Company Inc.**
3816 Bishop Ln.
Louisville, KY 40218-2906
Phone: (502)966-2118 **Fax:** (502)968-1823
Products: Earth moving equipment. **SIC:** 5082 (Construction & Mining Machinery). **Sales:** $39,500,000 (2000). **Emp:** 55. **Officers:** Oliver H. Raymond, CEO; James B. Lathrop, Treasurer & Secty.

■ 7903 ■ **RBC Tile and Stone**
1820 Berkshire Ln. N
Plymouth, MN 55441
Phone: (612)559-5531 **Fax:** (612)559-5520
Products: Floorcovering equipment and supplies. **SIC:** 5032 (Brick, Stone & Related Materials).

■ 7904 ■ **R.C.A. America**
25 E Front St., Ste. 700
Keyport, NJ 07735
Phone: (732)335-1474 **Fax:** (732)335-1666
Products: Heavy mining equipment; Mining bits and accessories; Boom trucks and cranes; Industrial carbide bits; Asphalt milling; Road construction equipment. **SICs:** 5082 (Construction & Mining Machinery); 5085 (Industrial Supplies). **Officers:** Richard Ayers, President.

■ 7905 ■ **R.C.P. Block and Brick Inc.**
PO Box 579
Lemon Grove, CA 91946
Phone: (619)460-7250 **Fax:** (619)460-3926
E-mail: sales@rcpblock.com
URL: http://www.rcpblock.com
Products: Concrete blocks; Keystone blocks; Brick. **SIC:** 5032 (Brick, Stone & Related Materials). **Est:** 1947. **Sales:** $19,000,000 (2000). **Emp:** 175. **Officers:** Mike Finch, President; Lawrence Como, CFO; Stan Stephens, Dir. of Systems; Mike Finch, Dir of Human Resources.

■ 7906 ■ **Reco Crane Inc.**
PO Box 10296
New Orleans, LA 70181
Phone: (504)733-6881 **Fax:** (504)733-4892
E-mail: reco@recoind.com
URL: http://www.recoind.com
Products: Link belt cranes. **SIC:** 5082 (Construction & Mining Machinery). **Est:** 1959. **Sales:** $11,000,000 (1999). **Emp:** 50. **Officers:** W. Crory, Chairman of the Board; R.L. Gravenhorst, Vice Chairman of the Board; Jack Pratt, Sales Mgr.; David Knerien, Vice President.

■ 7907 ■ **Redwood Empire Inc.**
PO Box 1300
Morgan Hill, CA 95038
Phones: (408)779-7354 (408)271-7900
Fax: (408)778-1076
Products: Lumber and plywood. **SIC:** 5031 (Lumber, Plywood & Millwork). **Est:** 1962. **Sales:** $130,000,000 (1999). **Emp:** 650. **Officers:** Rodger A. Burch, President & Treasurer; Austin Vanderhoof, CFO; Ed Paul, General Mgr.; Steve Hildreth, Sales & Marketing Contact.

■ 7908 ■ **Reeves Southeastern Corp.**
PO Box 1968
Tampa, FL 33601
Phone: (813)626-3191
Free: (800)669-9473 **Fax:** (813)623-3401
URL: http://www.reevesse.com
Products: Fences; Access control; Gate operators; Perimeter security products; Mechanical pipe and tubing. **SICs:** 5039 (Construction Materials Nec); 5031 (Lumber, Plywood & Millwork). **Est:** 1947. **Emp:** 350. **Officers:** Bill Everidge, Sales/Marketing Contact, e-mail: beveridge@reevesse.com; Ken Butler, Human Resources Contact, e-mail: kbutler@dhms.com. **Former Name:** Southeastern Access Control.

■ 7909 ■ **Reico Distributors Inc.**
6790 Commercial Dr.
Springfield, VA 22151
Phone: (703)256-6400 **Fax:** (703)642-9565
URL: http://www.reico.com
Products: Kitchen and medicine cabinets; Countertops; Adhesives; Faucets; Sinks; Shelving. **SIC:** 5031 (Lumber, Plywood & Millwork). **Est:** 1952. **Sales:** $50,000,000 (2000). **Emp:** 300. **Officers:** Richard Maresco, CEO.

■ 7910 ■ **Reisen Lumber and Millwork Co.**
1070 Morris Ave.
Union, NJ 07083
Phone: (908)354-1500
Products: Lumber. **SIC:** 5031 (Lumber, Plywood & Millwork). **Est:** 1922. **Sales:** $20,000,000 (2000). **Emp:** 100. **Officers:** Phillip Treppunti, President; Robert

Howard, CFO; Michael Catullo, Dir. of Marketing & Sales.

■ **7911** ■ **Reliable Architectural Metals Co.**
9751 Erwin
Detroit, MI 48213
Phone: (313)924-9750
Free: (800)334-8905 **Fax:** (313)924-8877
Products: Construction panels; Aluminum doors; Storefront metal. **SICs:** 5039 (Construction Materials Nec); 5051 (Metals Service Centers & Offices). **Est:** 1968. **Sales:** $5,000,000 (2000). **Emp:** 25. **Officers:** Doug Tarrance, President; Virgil Taylor, Vice President; Karen Havarilla, Secretary.

■ **7912** ■ **Reliable Glass Co.**
9751 Erwin
Detroit, MI 48213
Phone: (313)924-9750
Free: (800)445-0263 **Fax:** (313)924-8877
Products: Aluminum doors and frames; Storefront metal; Omega panels; Commercial glass. **SIC:** 5039 (Construction Materials Nec). **Est:** 1962. **Emp:** 24. **Officers:** Douglas F. Tarrence, President; Karen Havsille, Secretary. **Former Name:** Reliable Architectural Products.

■ **7913** ■ **Remixer Contracting Inc.**
PO Box 5090
Tyler, TX 75712
Phone: (512)258-8318
Products: Highway construction and maintenance supplies. **SIC:** 5082 (Construction & Mining Machinery).

■ **7914** ■ **Renaissance Drywall and Construction Supplies Inc.**
821 Sivert Dr.
Wood Dale, IL 60191
Phone: (708)766-1222 **Fax:** (708)766-1272
Products: Construction supplies, including drywall. **SIC:** 5039 (Construction Materials Nec). **Sales:** $5,000,000 (2000). **Emp:** 14. **Officers:** Carl Malone, President.

■ **7915** ■ **Renaissance Stoneworks**
8111 NW 2nd Ct.
Coral Springs, FL 33071
Phone: (954)971-9122 **Fax:** (954)971-8112
Products: Ceramic wall and floor tile. **SIC:** 5032 (Brick, Stone & Related Materials).

■ **7916** ■ **E.J. Renner & Associates**
1375 W Alameda Ave.
Denver, CO 80223
Phone: (303)744-3631
Free: (800)766-3631 **Fax:** (303)777-0706
Products: Tennis court and track construction supplies. **SICs:** 5039 (Construction Materials Nec); 5091 (Sporting & Recreational Goods). **Est:** 1968.

■ **7917** ■ **Replacement Hardware Manufacturing Inc.**
500 W 84th St.
Hialeah, FL 33014
Phone: (305)558-5051
Free: (800)780-5051 **Fax:** (305)557-5239
E-mail: info@rhmfg.com
URL: http://www.rhmfg.com
Products: Window and door hardware. **SICs:** 5031 (Lumber, Plywood & Millwork); 5039 (Construction Materials Nec). **Est:** 1982. **Emp:** 8. **Officers:** Mary E. Squires, President.

■ **7918** ■ **R.E.S. Associates**
PO Box 9520
Warwick, RI 02889
Phone: (401)738-0715 **Fax:** (401)738-0715
Products: Acoustical drywall and insulation; Pleasure boats; Seafood; Lumber and millwork; Gypsum building materials. **SICs:** 5032 (Brick, Stone & Related Materials); 5033 (Roofing, Siding & Insulation); 5091 (Sporting & Recreational Goods); 5146 (Fish & Seafoods); 5031 (Lumber, Plywood & Millwork). **Officers:** Bob Sweeney, President.

■ **7919** ■ **Reserve Industries Corp.**
20 1st Plz., No. 308
Albuquerque, NM 87102
Phone: (505)247-2384
Products: Bulk sands. **SIC:** 5039 (Construction Materials Nec). **Est:** 1957. **Sales:** $1,400,000 (2000). **Emp:** 19. **Officers:** Frank C. Melfi, CEO & President; William J. Melfi, VP of Finance & Admin.

■ **7920** ■ **Reserve Supply of Central New York Inc.**
PO Box 362
Syracuse, NY 13206
Phone: (315)463-4557 **Fax:** (315)463-7212
Products: Building supplies, including lumber, shingles, and insulation. **SICs:** 5033 (Roofing, Siding & Insulation); 5039 (Construction Materials Nec). **Est:** 1949. **Sales:** $12,000,000 (2000). **Emp:** 11. **Officers:** B. Edward Tracy, President; Herbert Edwards, Treasurer; David E. Brown, Sales Mgr.

■ **7921** ■ **Reuther Material Co.**
PO Box 106
North Bergen, NJ 07047
Phone: (201)863-3550 **Fax:** (201)863-0950
Products: Concrete blocks. **SIC:** 5032 (Brick, Stone & Related Materials). **Est:** 1927. **Sales:** $5,000,000 (1999). **Emp:** 20. **Officers:** Andrew Reuther, President; Marge Diehl, Finance Officer.

■ **7922** ■ **Revere Products**
4529 Industrial Pkwy.
Cleveland, OH 44135
Phone: (216)671-5500
Free: (800)321-1976 **Fax:** (216)671-5502
Products: Roofing; Floor coverings; Ice thawing materials. **SICs:** 5033 (Roofing, Siding & Insulation); 5032 (Brick, Stone & Related Materials). **Sales:** $26,000,000 (2000). **Emp:** 100. **Officers:** Jack Nesser, General Mgr.

■ **7923** ■ **Rew Material Inc.**
PO Box 3360
Kansas City, KS 66103
Phone: (913)236-4004 **Fax:** (913)236-4023
Products: Construction materials, including drywall, metal studs, insulation, and hardware. **SICs:** 5031 (Lumber, Plywood & Millwork); 5033 (Roofing, Siding & Insulation). **Est:** 1966. **Sales:** $11,000,000 (2000). **Emp:** 40. **Officers:** John Rew, President.

■ **7924** ■ **Rex Lumber Co. (Acton, Massachusetts)**
840 Main St.
Acton, MA 01720-5804
Phone: (978)263-0055 **Fax:** (978)263-9806
Products: Custom wood moldings, hardwood and softwood lumber. **SIC:** 5031 (Lumber, Plywood & Millwork). **Sales:** $60,000,000 (2000). **Emp:** 330. **Officers:** Benjamin Forester, CEO; William Clark, VP of Finance.

■ **7925** ■ **Reynolds Metals Co. Construction Products Div.**
PO Box 27003
Richmond, VA 23261
Phone: (804)281-2000
Products: Siding; Film; Food service products, including aluminum foil. **SICs:** 5033 (Roofing, Siding & Insulation); 5199 (Nondurable Goods Nec). **Est:** 1961. **Sales:** $250,000,000 (2000). **Emp:** 700. **Officers:** John Noonan, General Mgr.; John Shelhorse, Dir. of Marketing.

■ **7926** ■ **Reynolds Polymer Technology**
607 Hollingsworth St.
Grand Junction, CO 81505
Phone: (970)241-4700 **Fax:** (970)241-4747
Products: Acrylic viewing windows for aquariums. **SIC:** 5199 (Nondurable Goods Nec). **Sales:** $16,000,000 (1999). **Emp:** 165. **Officers:** Roger Reynolds, CEO; Scott Sullivan, VP of Finance.

■ **7927** ■ **Rhodes Supply Company Inc.**
Hwy. 303 S, Rte. 3
Mayfield, KY 42066-9725
Phone: (502)382-2185 **Fax:** (502)382-2184
Products: Building materials, including lumber. **SIC:** 5031 (Lumber, Plywood & Millwork). **Est:** 1954. **Sales:**

$34,000,000 (2000). **Emp:** 60. **Officers:** Gene Rhodes, President; T. Lynn Colley, Treasurer & Secty.; G. Rhodes, President.

■ **7928** ■ **RI Roof Truss Co. Inc.**
45 River Ave.
Johnston, RI 02919-6815
Phone: (401)942-7658
Products: Roofing. **SIC:** 5033 (Roofing, Siding & Insulation). **Officers:** George Mitola, President.

■ **7929** ■ **Richardson Dana Div.**
165 Presumpscot St.
Portland, ME 04103
Phone: (207)773-0227 **Fax:** (207)772-6053
Products: Lumber. **SIC:** 5031 (Lumber, Plywood & Millwork). **Est:** 1832. **Sales:** $12,000,000 (2000). **Emp:** 19. **Officers:** Richard Starrak, President; Eliot Snider, Treasurer; Irving E. Hibbard, Dir. of Marketing.

■ **7930** ■ **Richardson & Sons Distributors**
3631 Hwy. 231
Panama City, FL 32401
Phone: (850)785-6124 **Fax:** (850)785-0942
Products: Cabinet building materials. **SIC:** 5031 (Lumber, Plywood & Millwork). **Officers:** Mr. J. Richardson.

■ **7931** ■ **Richmond Machinery and Equipment Inc.**
PO Box 6588
Richmond, VA 23230
Phone: (804)359-4048 **Fax:** (804)359-4179
Products: Road construction equipment. **SIC:** 5082 (Construction & Mining Machinery). **Est:** 1919. **Sales:** $2,500,000 (2000). **Emp:** 19. **Officers:** Joseph B. Colley, CEO.

■ **7932** ■ **Ernie Rieke Equipment Co. Inc.**
3311 Merriam Ln.
Kansas City, KS 66106
Phone: (913)432-1600
Products: Heavy road equipment. **SIC:** 5082 (Construction & Mining Machinery). **Est:** 1958. **Sales:** $3,000,000 (2000). **Emp:** 8. **Officers:** Leo Rieke, President.

■ **7933** ■ **Riemeier Lumber Company Inc.**
1150 Tennessee Ave.
Cincinnati, OH 45229-1010
Phone: (513)242-3788 **Fax:** (513)242-7883
E-mail: riemeier@fuse.net
URL: http://www.riemeier.com
Products: Lumber, including hardwood, pallets, and crating. **SIC:** 5031 (Lumber, Plywood & Millwork). **Est:** 1925. **Sales:** $42,000,000 (2000). **Emp:** 112. **Officers:** Ken Franke, Exec. VP; Tom Franke, Exec. VP; Dave Hadden, President & CEO; John Murray, CFO; Jim Ruthemeyer, VP of O.S. Operations; Maurice Barker, VP of Purchasing; T.E. Franke, COO.

■ **7934** ■ **Riggs Wholesale Supply**
Hwy. 60 E
Poplar Bluff, MO 63901-9150
Phone: (573)785-5746 **Fax:** (573)785-3942
Products: Building materials, including lumber, plywood, and shingles. **SICs:** 5031 (Lumber, Plywood & Millwork); 5039 (Construction Materials Nec). **Emp:** 49. **Officers:** A. M. Riggs.

■ **7935** ■ **Riley-Stuart Supply Co.**
601 Western Dr.
Mobile, AL 36607
Phone: (205)471-4361
Products: Brick, sheet rock, and roofing. **SICs:** 5032 (Brick, Stone & Related Materials); 5039 (Construction Materials Nec); 5063 (Electrical Apparatus & Equipment). **Est:** 1945. **Sales:** $8,000,000 (2000). **Emp:** 32. **Officers:** K.T. Riley, Owner.

■ **7936** ■ **Rio Grande Co.**
PO Box 17227
Denver, CO 80217
Phone: (303)825-2211 **Fax:** (303)629-0417
Products: Rebar fabricating. **SIC:** 5032 (Brick, Stone & Related Materials). **Sales:** $43,000,000 (2000). **Emp:** 140. **Officers:** Donald Peterson, President; Dennis Sandusky, CFO.

■ **7937** ■ **Rish Equipment Co.**
PO Box 330
Bluefield, WV 24701
Phone: (304)327-5124 **Fax:** (304)327-8821
Products: Construction equipment. **SICs:** 5082 (Construction & Mining Machinery); 5084 (Industrial Machinery & Equipment). **Est:** 1935. **Sales:** $53,000,000 (2000). **Emp:** 176. **Officers:** Daniel T. Pochick, President; D. Steven Hamilton, Treasurer & Secty.; Jay W. Mullen, Dir. of Marketing & Sales; Warren Volk, Data Processing Mgr.

■ **7938** ■ **Rittner Products Inc.**
PO Box 301
Rochester, MI 48307
Phone: (248)651-1333
Free: (800)832-4773 **Fax:** (248)651-2650
E-mail: rfa4spec@aol.com
Products: Doors; Frames; Door hardware; Washroom accessories; Partitions. **SICs:** 5039 (Construction Materials Nec); 5072 (Hardware); 5031 (Lumber, Plywood & Millwork). **Est:** 1945. **Sales:** $20,000,000 (2000). **Emp:** 9. **Officers:** Ronald Rittner, President.

■ **7939** ■ **Rivard International Corp.**
10979 Reed Hartman Hwy., Ste. 200
Cincinnati, OH 45242-2855
Phone: (513)984-8821 **Fax:** (513)984-8944
E-mail: help@rivard-usa.com
URL: http://www.rivard-usa.com
Products: Health and beauty products; Pet-care and horse-care products; Specialty building materials; Consumer goods. **SICs:** 5039 (Construction Materials Nec); 5122 (Drugs, Proprietaries & Sundries); 5199 (Nondurable Goods Nec). **Est:** 1988. **Sales:** $2,000,000 (2000). **Emp:** 3. **Officers:** Steven Mark Rivard, President.

■ **7940** ■ **Riverside Group Inc.**
7800 Belfort Pkwy.
Jacksonville, FL 32256
Phone: (904)281-2200
Products: Lumber and wood-related building supplies. **SICs:** 5031 (Lumber, Plywood & Millwork); 5032 (Brick, Stone & Related Materials). **Sales:** $884,100,000 (2000). **Emp:** 39. **Officers:** J. Steven Wilson, CEO, President & Chairman of the Board; Catherine Gray, Sr. VP & Auditor.

■ **7941** ■ **Roberts and Dybdahl Inc.**
Box 1908
Des Moines, IA 50306
Phone: (515)283-7100 **Fax:** (515)283-7104
URL: http://www.robertsdybdahl.com
Products: Lumber. **SIC:** 5031 (Lumber, Plywood & Millwork). **Est:** 1955. **Sales:** $300,000,000 (2000). **Emp:** 326. **Officers:** Ted B. Roberts, President & Treasurer.

■ **7942** ■ **Roberts International, Inc.**
200 Office Park Dr., Ste. 215
Birmingham, AL 35223
Phone: (205)879-0033 **Fax:** (205)871-5661
Products: Lumber, including hardwood; Carpet; Gaskets; Roofing shingles. **SICs:** 5031 (Lumber, Plywood & Millwork); 5023 (Homefurnishings); 5085 (Industrial Supplies); 5033 (Roofing, Siding & Insulation). **Officers:** Daniel J. Roberts, President.

■ **7943** ■ **Frank Roberts and Sons Inc.**
R.R. 2, Box 81
Punxsutawney, PA 15767
Phone: (814)938-5000 **Fax:** (814)938-0880
E-mail: roberts@penn.com
Products: Building materials, including shingles, insulation, paints, and gutters; Construction materials; Polyethylene film and liners; Soil erosion control fabrics; Wire and plastic fencing; Silt fence. **SICs:** 5039 (Construction Materials Nec); 5072 (Hardware); 5033 (Roofing, Siding & Insulation); 5198 (Paints, Varnishes & Supplies). **Est:** 1959. **Sales:** $13,000,000 (2000). **Emp:** 40. **Officers:** Ralph Roberts, President & CFO; Fred Roberts, Treasurer; William M. Roberts, Secretary; Frank Roberts, Dir. of Systems; Robert Roberts, Sales/Marketing Contact; James Roberts, Customer Service Contact.

■ **7944** ■ **Robinson Brick Co.**
PO Box 5243
Denver, CO 80217
Phone: (303)783-3000 **Fax:** (303)781-1818
Products: Clay brick. **SIC:** 5032 (Brick, Stone & Related Materials). **Sales:** $12,500,000 (2000). **Emp:** 160. **Officers:** F Robinson, President.

■ **7945** ■ **Robinson Lumber Company Inc.**
4000 Tchoupitoulas St.
New Orleans, LA 70115
Phone: (504)895-6377 **Fax:** (504)897-0820
URL: http://www.roblumco.com
Products: Lumber. **SIC:** 5031 (Lumber, Plywood & Millwork). **Est:** 1893. **Sales:** $5,000,000 (2000). **Emp:** 70. **Officers:** Toto Robinson, President.

■ **7946** ■ **Rocco Building Supplies Inc.**
PO Box 1860
Harrisonburg, VA 22801-9500
Phone: (540)434-1371 **Fax:** (540)434-4593
Products: Building supplies. **SICs:** 5031 (Lumber, Plywood & Millwork); 5039 (Construction Materials Nec); 5032 (Brick, Stone & Related Materials); 5033 (Roofing, Siding & Insulation).

■ **7947** ■ **Glen Rock Lumber and Supply Co.**
PO Box 2545
Fair Lawn, NJ 07410
Phone: (201)796-4500
Free: (800)222-0423 **Fax:** (201)796-9323
Products: Lumber; Timber; Millwork products. **SIC:** 5031 (Lumber, Plywood & Millwork). **Est:** 1932. **Sales:** $12,000,000 (1999). **Emp:** 35. **Officers:** E.B. Leone, President.

■ **7948** ■ **Rockville Fuel and Feed Company Inc.**
14901 Southlawn Ln.
Rockville, MD 20850
Phone: (301)762-3988
Products: Pre-mixed concrete. **SIC:** 5032 (Brick, Stone & Related Materials). **Est:** 1926. **Sales:** $10,000,000 (2000). **Emp:** 100. **Officers:** James D. Ward, President.

■ **7949** ■ **Rockwell**
3323 Paterson Plank Rd.
North Bergen, NJ 07047
Phone: (201)865-2228 **Fax:** (201)865-2921
Products: Kitchen cabinets. **SIC:** 5031 (Lumber, Plywood & Millwork).

■ **7950** ■ **Rocky Mountain Machinery Co.**
PO Box 26737
Salt Lake City, UT 84126
Phone: (801)972-3660 **Fax:** (801)975-1354
Products: Heavy equipment. **SIC:** 5082 (Construction & Mining Machinery). **Est:** 1952. **Sales:** $55,000,000 (2000). **Emp:** 140. **Officers:** Edward Mullaney, President.

■ **7951** ■ **Roddis Lumber and Veneer Company Inc.**
PO Box 1446
San Antonio, TX 78295-1446
Phone: (210)226-1426 **Fax:** (210)226-1591
Products: Plywood. **SICs:** 5031 (Lumber, Plywood & Millwork); 5039 (Construction Materials Nec). **Est:** 1920. **Sales:** $9,000,000 (2000). **Emp:** 20. **Officers:** Thomas B. Weaver, President; James L. Falconnier, VP & Treasurer.

■ **7952** ■ **Roethele Building Materials Inc.**
3100 Wells St.
Ft. Wayne, IN 46808
Phone: (219)482-9591 **Fax:** (219)482-9596
URL: http://www.roethele.com
Products: Building materials, including pre-hung doors, windows, and steel studs. **SIC:** 5031 (Lumber, Plywood & Millwork). **Est:** 1928. **Sales:** $4,000,000 (1999). **Emp:** 25. **Officers:** Timothy J. Roethele, President.

■ **7953** ■ **Rogers Group Inc. Louisville**
12808 Townepark Way
Louisville, KY 40243-2312
Phone: (502)244-7060 **Fax:** (502)244-2573
Products: Construction materials. **SIC:** 5039

(Construction Materials Nec). **Sales:** $31,000,000 (2000). **Emp:** 92. **Officers:** Don Williamson, President; George Blankau, CFO.

■ **7954** ■ **Rogue Aggregates Inc.**
PO Box 4430
Medford, OR 97501
Phone: (541)664-4155 **Fax:** (541)664-8591
Products: Sand; Gravel; Crushed rock. **SIC:** 5032 (Brick, Stone & Related Materials). **Sales:** $8,000,000 (2000). **Emp:** 40. **Officers:** Bill Leavens, President; Michael Mills, Controller.

■ **7955** ■ **Roland Machinery Co.**
PO Box 2879
Springfield, IL 62708
Phone: (217)789-7711
Free: (800)252-2926 **Fax:** (217)744-7314
Products: Construction equipment. **SIC:** 5082 (Construction & Mining Machinery). **Est:** 1958. **Sales:** $100,000,000 (2000). **Emp:** 205. **Officers:** Raymond E. Roland, President; Mike Armstrong, Controller; Jim McKeever, Sales/Marketing Contact, e-mail: jmckeever@rolandmachinery.com; Jerry Eastburn, Customer Service Contact.

■ **7956** ■ **Roofers Supplies Inc.**
PO Box 126
Bergenfield, NJ 07621
Phone: (201)384-4224 **Fax:** (201)384-0436
URL: http://www.rooferssupplies.com
Products: Siding, including brick and wood; Roofing materials. **SIC:** 5033 (Roofing, Siding & Insulation). **Est:** 1910. **Sales:** $20,000,000 (2000). **Emp:** 50. **Officers:** Robert G. Austin, President; Philip A. Sommerfeld, Finance Officer.

■ **7957** ■ **Roofing Distributing Company Inc.**
4401 Appleton St.
Cincinnati, OH 45209
Phone: (513)871-4100
Products: Building materials. **SICs:** 5033 (Roofing, Siding & Insulation); 5039 (Construction Materials Nec). **Est:** 1937. **Sales:** $10,000,000 (2000). **Emp:** 25. **Officers:** D.L. Evans, President.

■ **7958** ■ **Roofing Supply Inc.**
PO Box 90100
Anchorage, AK 99509-0100
Phone: (907)349-3123 **Fax:** (907)349-3386
Products: Prepared asphalt and tar roofing and siding products; Mineral wool for thermal and accoustical envelope insulation (for insulating homes, and commercial and industrial buildings); Metal sheets. **SICs:** 5033 (Roofing, Siding & Insulation); 5032 (Brick, Stone & Related Materials). **Officers:** Patrick Reilly, President.

■ **7959** ■ **Roofing Wholesale Company Inc.**
1918 W Grant St.
Phoenix, AZ 85009
Phone: (602)258-3794 **Fax:** (602)254-9416
Products: Roofing; Stucco; Drywall; Insulation. **SIC:** 5033 (Roofing, Siding & Insulation). **Est:** 1957. **Sales:** $70,000,000 (2000). **Emp:** 200. **Officers:** Harley Lisherness, President; Steven K. Rold, VP & Controller; Bill Dykoff, VP of Sales; Michael O'Day, VP of Operations.

■ **7960** ■ **Ross Corp.**
PO Box 2577
Eugene, OR 97402
Phone: (541)689-5031 **Fax:** (541)689-4893
Products: Construction machinery and equipment; Recycling equipment. **SIC:** 5082 (Construction & Mining Machinery). **Officers:** Dennis Bottem, Treasurer.

■ **7961** ■ **Ross Island Sand and Gravel Co.**
PO Box 82249
Portland, OR 97282-0249
Phone: (503)239-5504 **Fax:** (503)235-1350
Products: Sand and gravel. **SIC:** 5039 (Construction Materials Nec). **Sales:** $22,000,000 (1994). **Emp:** 175. **Officers:** Robert B. Pamplin Jr., President; Michael Frazier, Controller.

■ 7962 ■ RPM Inc.
2628 Pearl Road
PO Box 777
Medina, OH 44258
Phone: (330)273-5090 **Fax:** (330)273-5061
Products: Roofing equipment. **SIC:** 5033 (Roofing, Siding & Insulation). **Est:** 1947. **Sales:** $500,300,000 (2000). **Emp:** 3,500. **Officers:** Thomas C. Sullivan, CEO & Chairman of the Board; Richard E. Klar, VP & Treasurer.

■ 7963 ■ RSB Tile Inc.
495 Route 208
Monroe, NY 10950
Phone: (914)783-6167 **Fax:** (914)783-1664
Products: Floorcovering equipment and supplies. **SIC:** 5032 (Brick, Stone & Related Materials). **Sales:** $1,000,000 (2000).

■ 7964 ■ Rudd Equipment Co.
PO Box 32427
Louisville, KY 40232-2427
Phone: (502)456-4050 **Fax:** (502)458-2515
URL: http://www.ruddequip.com
Products: Construction and mining machinery. **SIC:** 5082 (Construction & Mining Machinery). **Est:** 1952. **Emp:** 305. **Officers:** Steven F. Zagar, President; Robert Bramlett, VP of Finance & Admin.

■ 7965 ■ Ruffridge Johnson Equipment Company Inc.
3024 4th St. SE
Minneapolis, MN 55414
Phone: (612)378-9558 **Fax:** (612)378-9385
Products: Oil; Pavers; Rock crushers; Conveyors; Brooms; Brushes; Portable screens; Asphalt equipment. **SICs:** 5082 (Construction & Mining Machinery); 5172 (Petroleum Products Nec); 5085 (Industrial Supplies). **Est:** 1940.

■ 7966 ■ Rugby Building Products
2575 Westside Pky., No. 800
Alpharetta, GA 30004-3852
Phone: (770)625-1700
Products: Prepared asphalt and tar roofing and siding products. **SIC:** 5033 (Roofing, Siding & Insulation). **Officers:** Paul Lyle, Vice President. **Former Name:** DJ Wholesale Building Material Distributors.

■ 7967 ■ Rugby Building Products Inc.
1335 S Main
PO Box 728
Greensburg, PA 15601
Phone: (412)834-5706 **Fax:** (412)834-8560
Products: Doors; Roofing supplies, building materials. **SICs:** 5031 (Lumber, Plywood & Millwork); 5032 (Brick, Stone & Related Materials); 5033 (Roofing, Siding & Insulation). **Est:** 1964. **Sales:** $25,000,000 (2000). **Emp:** 40. **Officers:** Ben Rockwell, General Mgr.

■ 7968 ■ Rugby Building Products, Inc.
2829 Awaawaloa St.
Honolulu, HI 96819
Phone: (808)833-2731 **Fax:** (808)839-5412
Products: Building materials. **SICs:** 5039 (Construction Materials Nec); 5031 (Lumber, Plywood & Millwork); 5032 (Brick, Stone & Related Materials). **Est:** 1957. **Sales:** $6,000,000 (1999). **Emp:** 9. **Officers:** James Sharpe, General Mgr. **Former Name:** Aloha State Sales Company Inc.

■ 7969 ■ S and M Equipment Company Corp.
PO Box 9230
Richmond, VA 23227
Phone: (804)266-4911
Products: Construction and logging equipment. **SIC:** 5082 (Construction & Mining Machinery). **Sales:** $50,000,000 (1994). **Emp:** 130. **Officers:** Joseph E. Parker Jr., President.

■ 7970 ■ S & M Lumber Co.
424 W Main St.
Flushing, MI 48433
Phone: (810)659-5681 **Fax:** (810)659-7408
Products: Windows; Molding; Plywood; Wood treated products including plywood. **SIC:** 5031 (Lumber, Plywood & Millwork). **Est:** 1956. **Sales:** $10,000,000 (2000). **Emp:** 35. **Officers:** Lawrence Sharp, President; Scott Sharp, Secretary; William Sharp, Treasurer.

■ 7971 ■ Sagebrush Sales Inc.
PO Box 25606
Albuquerque, NM 87125
Phone: (505)877-7331 **Fax:** (505)873-4777
Products: Lumber and sheet goods. **SIC:** 5031 (Lumber, Plywood & Millwork). **Est:** 1966. **Sales:** $45,000 (1999). **Emp:** 50. **Officers:** Greg Trail, Manager; Randy Brown, Controller; Ted Ellis, Vice President.

■ 7972 ■ Sahuaro Petroleum-Asphalt Company Inc.
1935 W McDowell Rd.
Phoenix, AZ 85009
Phone: (602)252-3061 **Fax:** (602)257-8831
Products: Asphalt; Emulsified asphalt. **SIC:** 5032 (Brick, Stone & Related Materials). **Est:** 1960. **Sales:** $40,100,000 (2000). **Emp:** 100. **Officers:** Leland S. Brake, President; James R. Hird, CFO; Jeff Benedict, Dir. of Marketing.

■ 7973 ■ Saltillo Tile Co.
110 Este Es Rd.
Taos, NM 87571
Phone: (505)751-0977
Products: Tile. **SIC:** 5032 (Brick, Stone & Related Materials).

■ 7974 ■ Samsel Supply Co.
1285 Old River Rd.
Cleveland, OH 44113
Phone: (216)241-0333 **Fax:** (216)241-3426
Products: Heavy construction equipment. **SIC:** 5082 (Construction & Mining Machinery). **Est:** 1958. **Sales:** $7,000,000 (2000). **Emp:** 47. **Officers:** Kathleen A. Samsel, President; James J. Cooley, CFO; Tom Hodgkiss, Dir. of Operations.

■ 7975 ■ Samuels Glass Co.
PO Box 1769
San Antonio, TX 78296
Phone: (210)227-2481 **Fax:** (210)223-8640
Products: Glass and aluminum. **SICs:** 5039 (Construction Materials Nec); 5051 (Metals Service Centers & Offices). **Est:** 1914. **Sales:** $11,000,000 (2000). **Emp:** 100. **Officers:** Perry Samuels, CEO.

■ 7976 ■ San Joaquin Lumber Co.
PO Box 71
Stockton, CA 95201
Phone: (209)465-5651 **Fax:** (209)465-0552
Products: Lumber. **SIC:** 5031 (Lumber, Plywood & Millwork). **Est:** 1910. **Sales:** $12,000,000 (2000). **Emp:** 40. **Officers:** Carol Selleseth, Treasurer & Secty.; Don Woxberg, Merchandising Mgr.

■ 7977 ■ J.P. Sand and Gravel Co.
PO Box 2
Lockbourne, OH 43137
Phone: (614)497-0083
Products: Sand and gravel. **SIC:** 5032 (Brick, Stone & Related Materials). **Sales:** $5,000,000 (2000). **Emp:** 50. **Officers:** R.A. Roberts, CEO & President; Michael D. Craiglow, Vice President.

■ 7978 ■ Sanders Co.
PO Box 25758
Baltimore, MD 21224-0458
Phone: (410)288-6974 **Fax:** (410)282-9566
Products: Doors and windows. **SIC:** 5031 (Lumber, Plywood & Millwork). **Est:** 1954. **Sales:** $10,000,000 (2000). **Emp:** 32. **Officers:** J.W. Sanders Jr., President; Ted Sanders, Treasurer.

■ 7979 ■ M.L. Sandy Lumber Sales Company Inc.
PO Box 1535
Corinth, MS 38835-1535
Phone: (662)286-6087 **Fax:** (662)287-4187
Products: Lumber. **SIC:** 5031 (Lumber, Plywood & Millwork). **Est:** 1957. **Sales:** $12,000,000 (2000). **Emp:** 25. **Officers:** Milton L. Sandy Jr., President & CFO.

■ 7980 ■ Sashco Inc.
1232 Monte Vista Ave., Ste. 4
Upland, CA 91786-8213
Phone: (909)949-3082
Free: (800)600-3232 **Fax:** (909)949-3092
Products: Aluminum and steel windows; Storefront and curtain wall; Bullet resistant glazing; Detention screens; Fire rated steel windows; Wood windows and doors. **SIC:** 5031 (Lumber, Plywood & Millwork). **Est:** 1967. **Sales:** $3,000,000 (2000). **Emp:** 10. **Officers:** William R. Esken, President; Audrey Lozada, Controller.

■ 7981 ■ Sasser Lumber Company Inc.
PO Box 606
La Grange, NC 28551
Phone: (919)566-3121
Products: Lumber; Plywood. **SIC:** 5031 (Lumber, Plywood & Millwork). **Est:** 1933. **Sales:** $6,000,000 (2000). **Emp:** 8. **Officers:** Francis S. Salt, President; Steve Sasser, VP of Finance; Brian Rhodes, Dir. of Marketing.

■ 7982 ■ Saunders Oil Company Inc.
1200 W Marshall St.
Richmond, VA 23220
Phone: (804)358-7191 **Fax:** (804)257-5950
Products: Construction materials. **SIC:** 5039 (Construction Materials Nec). **Est:** 1946. **Sales:** $10,000,000 (2000). **Emp:** 42. **Officers:** Henry G. Beckstoffer Jr., President.

■ 7983 ■ Saunders Supply Company Inc.
PO Box 2278
Suffolk, VA 23432
Phone: (757)255-4531
Products: Residential lumber. **SIC:** 5031 (Lumber, Plywood & Millwork). **Est:** 1947. **Sales:** $4,000,000 (2000). **Emp:** 25. **Officers:** T.A. Saunders Jr., President.

■ 7984 ■ Saxonville USA
96 Springfield Rd.
Charlestown, NH 03603
Phone: (603)826-5719
Products: Plywood. **SIC:** 5031 (Lumber, Plywood & Millwork). **Sales:** $29,000,000 (2000). **Emp:** 45. **Officers:** D.P. Webb, President & Treasurer.

■ 7985 ■ Scharpfs Twin Oaks Builders Supply Co.
PO Box 887
Eugene, OR 97440
Phone: (541)342-1261
Products: Plasterboard. **SIC:** 5031 (Lumber, Plywood & Millwork). **Est:** 1924. **Sales:** $7,000,000 (2000). **Emp:** 23. **Officers:** Ted Scharpf, President.

■ 7986 ■ Scholl Forest Industries
502 N Water
Corpus Christi, TX 78471
Phone: (361)883-1144 **Fax:** (361)883-1468
Products: Lumber. **SIC:** 5031 (Lumber, Plywood & Millwork). **Est:** 1976. **Sales:** $100,000,000 (2000). **Emp:** 50. **Officers:** J.W. Scholl, President & CFO; Ward Scholl, Exec. VP; Anita Horton, Controller.

■ 7987 ■ Scholl Forest Products Inc.
PO Box 40458
Houston, TX 77240-0458
Phone: (713)329-5300
Products: Lumber, plywood, treated lumber and cedar fencing. **SIC:** 5031 (Lumber, Plywood & Millwork). **Sales:** $18,000,000 (1994). **Emp:** 31. **Officers:** Jack W. Scholl, President; C.D. Scholl, Treasurer & Secty.

■ 7988 ■ Norm Schorr Insulated Glass Inc.
6322 Easton Rd.
Pipersville, PA 18947
Phone: (215)766-2707 **Fax:** (215)766-2857
URL: http://www.normschorr.com
Products: Insulated glass; Custom screen and glass panels; Steel, vinyl, and wood windows and doors. **SICs:** 5039 (Construction Materials Nec); 5031 (Lumber, Plywood & Millwork); 5051 (Metals Service Centers & Offices). **Est:** 1982. **Sales:** $1,000,000 (2000). **Emp:** 6. **Officers:** Norm Schorr, President, e-mail: norm@normschorr.com; Howard Schorr, Vice President; Ro Schorr, Sec. & Treas.

■ 7989 ■ **Schultz Snyder Steele Lumber Co.**
2419 Science Pkwy.
Lansing, MI 48909
Phone: (517)349-8220 **Fax:** (517)349-8377
URL: http://www.ssslbr.com
Products: Building materials, including cedar, pine, lumber, and plywood; Vinyl siding; Deck supplies; Hardwood flooring and moldings. **SIC:** 5031 (Lumber, Plywood & Millwork). **Est:** 1948. **Sales:** $190,000,000 (1999). **Emp:** 210. **Officers:** Thomas G. LeVere, President.

■ 7990 ■ **Schutte Lumber Company Inc.**
3001 Southwest Blvd.
Kansas City, MO 64108
Phone: (816)753-6262 **Fax:** (816)753-7935
Products: Lumber. **SIC:** 5031 (Lumber, Plywood & Millwork). **Sales:** $11,000,000 (2000). **Emp:** 48. **Officers:** Clay Egner.

■ 7991 ■ **George Scofield Company Inc.**
3601 Taylor Way
Tacoma, WA 98421-4307
Phone: (253)272-8314
Products: Construction materials. **SIC:** 5032 (Brick, Stone & Related Materials). **Officers:** Ted Hutchinson, President; Patricia Normet, Controller.

■ 7992 ■ **Scott Lumber Co.**
253 N Lincoln Ave.
Bridgeport, OH 43912
Phone: (740)635-2345 **Fax:** (740)635-4816
Products: Lumber. **SIC:** 5031 (Lumber, Plywood & Millwork). **Est:** 1869. **Sales:** $14,000,000 (2000). **Emp:** 200. **Officers:** Dave Turner, General Mgr.; Frank Bonacci, Controller; Webster Wilson.

■ 7993 ■ **Scotty's Inc.**
5300 N Recker Hwy.
Winter Haven, FL 33882
Phone: (941)299-1111 **Fax:** (941)294-6840
Products: Wood kitchen cabinets; Treated lumber; Paints and allied products; Vitreous plumbing fixtures; Millwork products. **SICs:** 5031 (Lumber, Plywood & Millwork); 5074 (Plumbing & Hydronic Heating Supplies); 5198 (Paints, Varnishes & Supplies). **Officers:** Daniel Gonzalez, Export Sales Manager.

■ 7994 ■ **SCR Inc.**
PO Box 1607
Lake Oswego, OR 97035
Phone: (503)968-1300
Free: (800)735-5560 **Fax:** (503)968-1400
E-mail: scr@spiritone.com
Products: Plywood. **SIC:** 5031 (Lumber, Plywood & Millwork). **Est:** 1976. **Sales:** $32,000,000 (2000). **Emp:** 12. **Officers:** Terry Crabtree, President.

■ 7995 ■ **Scranton Equity Exchange Inc.**
PO Box 127
Scranton, ND 58653
Phone: (701)275-8221 **Fax:** (701)275-8281
Products: Lumber; Oil; Feed. **SICs:** 5031 (Lumber, Plywood & Millwork); 5191 (Farm Supplies); 5172 (Petroleum Products Nec). **Est:** 1914. **Sales:** $12,700,000 (2000). **Emp:** 20. **Officers:** Floyd C. Pierce, President.

■ 7996 ■ **C.A. Seaford and Sons Lumber**
127 Buck Seaford Rd.
Mocksville, NC 27028
Phone: (336)751-5148
Products: Lumber. **SIC:** 5031 (Lumber, Plywood & Millwork). **Est:** 1957. **Sales:** $1,000,000 (2000). **Emp:** 12. **Officers:** Glenn Seaford, President; Eloise Seaford, Vice President.

■ 7997 ■ **Seago Export**
PO Box 1894
Summerville, SC 29484
Phone: (843)875-2808 **Fax:** (843)871-1433
E-mail: ryan_glenn@seagoexport.com
URL: http://www.seagoexport.com
Products: Lumber and plywood; Poles and piling; Hardwood lumber, timber, and logs. **SIC:** 5031 (Lumber, Plywood & Millwork). **Est:** 1983. **Sales:** $4,000,000 (2000). **Officers:** George H. Seago Jr., President, e-mail: george_seago@seagoexport.com.

■ 7998 ■ **Louie Sedmak**
PO Box 51007
Casper, WY 82605-1007
Phone: (307)472-1904
Products: Roofing, siding, insulation, and insulation materials. **SIC:** 5033 (Roofing, Siding & Insulation). **Officers:** Louie Sedmak, Owner.

■ 7999 ■ **Seneca Supply and Equipment Co.**
Rte. 13 & Dryden Rd.
Ithaca, NY 14850
Phone: (607)347-4455 **Fax:** (607)347-4454
Products: Construction equipment, including compressors, generators, pumps, and snow plows. **SIC:** 5082 (Construction & Mining Machinery). **Est:** 1966. **Sales:** $4,500,000 (2000). **Emp:** 26. **Officers:** Don Bero II, President.

■ 8000 ■ **Sepia Interior Supply**
PO Box 82519
Kenmore, WA 98028
Phone: (425)486-3353 **Fax:** (425)486-3438
E-mail: sepiasply@aol.com
URL: http://www.sepiasupply.com
Products: Acoustical wall and ceiling tiles. **SIC:** 5039 (Construction Materials Nec). **Sales:** $10,000,000 (2000). **Emp:** 29. **Officers:** Wade Nash Prin.

■ 8001 ■ **Service Keystone Supply**
47 W Park Rd.
Roselle, IL 60172
Phone: (630)351-3838 **Fax:** (630)351-3840
Products: Retaining wall systems. **SIC:** 5039 (Construction Materials Nec). **Est:** 1995. **Emp:** 4.

■ 8002 ■ **SERVISTAR Corp.**
PO Box 1510
Butler, PA 16003-1510
Phone: (412)283-4567
Products: Lumber; Building supplies. **SICs:** 5072 (Hardware); 5039 (Construction Materials Nec); 5031 (Lumber, Plywood & Millwork). **Est:** 1910. **Sales:** $1,008,000,000 (2000). **Emp:** 1,400. **Officers:** Paul Pentz, CEO & President; Kenneth Drurett, VP & CFO; Donald C. Belt, Sr. VP of Marketing; Charlie Green, VP of Information Systems; Charles Rogner, Human Resources Mgr.

■ 8003 ■ **S.E.S. Inc.**
1400 Powis Rd.
West Chicago, IL 60185
Phone: (630)231-4840 **Fax:** (630)231-4945
Products: Large land moving equipment, including land hoes. **SIC:** 5082 (Construction & Mining Machinery). **Est:** 1968. **Sales:** $17,000,000 (2000). **Emp:** 60. **Officers:** S.L. Martines, President; Nancy Farina, Exec. VP; Richard Ripp, VP of Marketing.

■ 8004 ■ **Seven D Wholesale**
PO Box 67
Gallitzin, PA 16641-0067
Phone: (814)886-8151
Products: Lumber, including pine and plywood. **SIC:** 5031 (Lumber, Plywood & Millwork). **Est:** 1972. **Sales:** $67,000,000 (2000). **Emp:** 200. **Officers:** Donald A. DeGol Sr., CEO & CFO.

■ 8005 ■ **SG Wholesale Roofing Supply Inc.**
PO Box 1464
Santa Ana, CA 92702
Phone: (714)568-1900
Products: Roofing materials, including shingles, asphalt, rocks, and tiles. **SICs:** 5033 (Roofing, Siding & Insulation); 5032 (Brick, Stone & Related Materials). **Est:** 1960. **Sales:** $28,000,000 (2000). **Emp:** 75. **Officers:** Roger Glazer, President; Jamie Glazer, Dir. of Marketing & Sales; Brent Kroge, Dir. of Data Processing.

■ 8006 ■ **Shaw Lumber Co.**
217 Como Ave.
St. Paul, MN 55103
Phone: (612)488-2525
Products: Lumber; Windows; Doors. **SIC:** 5031 (Lumber, Plywood & Millwork). **Est:** 1886. **Sales:** $41,000,000 (2000). **Emp:** 180. **Officers:** M. Lindgren, President; William Winters, CFO; John Chenevert, VP of Marketing.

■ 8007 ■ **Shears Construction L.P.**
1600 N Lorraine St.
Hutchinson, KS 67501
Phone: (316)662-3307 **Fax:** (316)662-3181
Products: Sand, gravel and crushed stone. **SIC:** 5032 (Brick, Stone & Related Materials). **Sales:** $80,000,000 (2000). **Emp:** 475. **Officers:** William C. Girard, President; Cliff Craig, VP & CFO.

■ 8008 ■ **Shehan-Cary Lumber Co.**
PO Box 19770
St. Louis, MO 63144
Phone: (314)968-8600 **Fax:** (314)968-8644
Products: Lumber. **SIC:** 5031 (Lumber, Plywood & Millwork). **Est:** 1960. **Sales:** $4,000,000 (2000). **Emp:** 3. **Officers:** C.G. Cary Jr., President.

■ 8009 ■ **Shelley Tractor and Equipment Co.**
8015 NW 103rd St.
Hialeah, FL 33016-2201
Phone: (305)821-4040
Products: Parts and supplies for pit rock contractors and road builders. **SICs:** 5082 (Construction & Mining Machinery); 5083 (Farm & Garden Machinery). **Est:** 1939. **Sales:** $10,000,000 (2000). **Emp:** 27. **Officers:** Karlson Mitchell, President.

■ 8010 ■ **Shepherd Machinery Co.**
PO Box 6789
Los Angeles, CA 90022
Phone: (213)723-7191 **Fax:** (213)699-0491
Products: Heavy construction equipment. **SIC:** 5082 (Construction & Mining Machinery). **Est:** 1924. **Sales:** $210,000,000 (2000). **Emp:** 300. **Officers:** Willard Shepherd III, Partner; Bob Dean, Controller; Dale Hill, Dir. of Mktg. & Sales; Ben Blythe, Dir. of Systems; Tom Edwards, Dir of Human Resources.

■ 8011 ■ **Shepler International Inc.**
14206 Industry Rd.
Houston, TX 77053
Phone: (713)433-5938 **Fax:** (713)433-7363
Products: Lumber, plywood, and millwork; Construction materials, including brick and stone; Hardware; Furniture. **SICs:** 5039 (Construction Materials Nec); 5031 (Lumber, Plywood & Millwork); 5032 (Brick, Stone & Related Materials); 5021 (Furniture); 5072 (Hardware). **Officers:** Larry Phelps, Vice President.

■ 8012 ■ **Shepler's Equipment Company Inc.**
9103 E Almeda Rd.
Houston, TX 77054
Phone: (713)799-1150
Products: Concrete. **SIC:** 5072 (Hardware). **Sales:** $49,000,000 (2000). **Emp:** 150. **Officers:** John Richie, General Mgr.

■ 8013 ■ **Shook and Fletcher Supply of Alabama Inc.**
1041 11th Ct. W
Birmingham, AL 35204
Phone: (205)252-5157 **Fax:** (205)252-5163
Products: Drills; Bulldozers. **SIC:** 5082 (Construction & Mining Machinery). **Est:** 1908. **Sales:** $1,500,000 (2000). **Emp:** 6. **Officers:** Wayne Killion, CEO; David Jackson, President; Danylu Burnett, Assistant Gen. Mgr.; Tommy Hays, Service Manager.

■ 8014 ■ **Shorts Wholesale Supply Co.**
404 State Rte. 125
Brentwood, NH 03833
Phone: (603)772-6355 **Free:** (800)640-6355
Products: Building materials for residential use. **SICs:** 5033 (Roofing, Siding & Insulation); 5039 (Construction Materials Nec); 5032 (Brick, Stone & Related Materials).

■ 8015 ■ **Shuster's Builders Supply Co.**
2920 Clay Pike
Irwin, PA 15642
Phone: (412)351-0979
Products: Windows; Doors, including patio doors. **SIC:** 5031 (Lumber, Plywood & Millwork). **Est:** 1958. **Sales:** $44,000,000 (2000). **Emp:** 160. **Officers:** Anthony Shuster Jr., CEO.

■ 8016 ■ **Shutters Inc.**
12213 Illinois Rt. 173
Hebron, IL 60034
Phone: (815)648-2494   **Fax:** (815)648-2518
Products: Plastic shutters. **SIC:** 5031 (Lumber, Plywood & Millwork). **Sales:** $26,000,000 (2000). **Emp:** 80. **Officers:** Mike Ricard, President; Steve Schreiner, Controller.

■ 8017 ■ **Sierra Building Supply, Inc.**
PO Box 10
Soulsbyville, CA 95372
Phone: (209)532-3447   **Fax:** (209)532-0362
Products: Lumber. **SIC:** 5031 (Lumber, Plywood & Millwork).

■ 8018 ■ **Sierra Point Lumber and Plywood Co.**
601 Tunnel Ave.
San Francisco, CA 94134
Phone: (415)468-5620
Products: Lumber, including pine and plywood. **SIC:** 5031 (Lumber, Plywood & Millwork). **Sales:** $4,000,000 (2000). **Emp:** 25. **Officers:** Doug Galten, President.

■ 8019 ■ **Sierra Roofing Corp.**
PO Box 3041
Reno, NV 89505
Phone: (702)323-0747
Products: Shingles. **SIC:** 5033 (Roofing, Siding & Insulation). **Est:** 1963. **Sales:** $3,000,000 (2000). **Emp:** 8. **Officers:** David Hillerich, President.

■ 8020 ■ **Silo International Inc.**
60 E 42nd St.
New York, NY 10165
Phone: (212)682-4331   **Fax:** (212)983-7074
E-mail: siloint@aol.com
URL: http://www.siloint.com
Products: Construction equipment and parts; Mining equipment and parts; Motor vehicles; Electrical generators; Oil field equipment and parts. **SICs:** 5082 (Construction & Mining Machinery); 5084 (Industrial Machinery & Equipment); 5012 (Automobiles & Other Motor Vehicles); 5063 (Electrical Apparatus & Equipment). **Est:** 1969. **Sales:** $20,000,000 (2000). **Emp:** 36. **Officers:** George G. Varsa, President; John P. Allen, Vice President; Harold B. Nachitann, Treasurer.

■ 8021 ■ **Silver State Roofing Materials**
1434 Industrial Way
Gardnerville, NV 89410-5726
Phone: (702)782-7663   **Fax:** (702)782-3142
Products: Roofing, siding, and insulation materials. **SIC:** 5033 (Roofing, Siding & Insulation). **Officers:** Rudy Mc Tee, President.

■ 8022 ■ **Simmons Lumber Company Inc.**
PO Box 418
Booneville, AR 72927
Phone: (501)675-2430   **Fax:** (501)675-2433
Products: Lumber. **SIC:** 5031 (Lumber, Plywood & Millwork). **Est:** 1963. **Sales:** $3,500,000 (2000). **Emp:** 60. **Officers:** Howard Simmons, President; Linda Davis, Treasurer & Secty.; Don Roberts, Dir. of Sales.

■ 8023 ■ **Simpson Strong-Tie Company Inc.**
4637 Chabot Dr.
Pleasanton, CA 94588
Phone: (510)460-9912   **Fax:** (510)632-8925
Products: Connectors for construction. **SIC:** 5051 (Metals Service Centers & Offices). **Est:** 1914. **Sales:** $11,000,000 (2000). **Emp:** 433. **Officers:** T. Fitzmyers, President; E. Follet, VP of Marketing; S. Lamson, CFO; E. Johnson, Controller; V. Smith, Dir of Personnel.

■ 8024 ■ **Simpson's Inc.**
2 Dracut St.
Lawrence, MA 01843
Phone: (978)683-2417   **Fax:** (978)691-5120
Products: Heavy construction pads. **SIC:** 5082 (Construction & Mining Machinery).

■ 8025 ■ **Sinclair Lumber Co.**
PO Box 729
Laurinburg, NC 28352
Phone: (919)276-0371
Products: Lumber. **SIC:** 5031 (Lumber, Plywood &

Millwork). **Sales:** $26,000,000 (1990). **Emp:** 350. **Officers:** Duncan J. Sinclair, President; Kenneth Tuggell, COO.

■ 8026 ■ **Sioux Veneer Panel Co.**
PO Box 488
Payette, ID 83661-0488
Phone: (208)344-8358   **Fax:** (208)345-2759
Products: Veneer paneling. **SIC:** 5031 (Lumber, Plywood & Millwork). **Est:** 1966. **Sales:** $1,500,000 (2000). **Emp:** 30. **Officers:** George E. Betts, President; Mavis L. Betts, Dir. of Marketing & Sales.

■ 8027 ■ **Skelton and Skinner Lumber Inc.**
PO Box 810
Greencastle, IN 46135-0810
Phone: (765)653-9705   **Fax:** (765)653-3176
Products: Lumber; Hardware. **SICs:** 5031 (Lumber, Plywood & Millwork); 5072 (Hardware). **Est:** 1946. **Sales:** $600,000 (2000). **Emp:** 10. **Officers:** William Skinner, President; Phillip Skinner, Treasurer.

■ 8028 ■ **SKR Distributors**
195 Thatcher St.
Bangor, ME 04401
Phone: (207)945-9550
Products: Windows; Siding; Fencing. **SIC:** 5033 (Roofing, Siding & Insulation).

■ 8029 ■ **Sky-Reach Inc.**
53643 Grand River
PO Box 129
New Hudson, MI 48165
Phones: (248)437-1783   800-221-6006
Free: (800)221-6006   **Fax:** (248)437-7820
Products: Man lifts. **SICs:** 5082 (Construction & Mining Machinery); 5084 (Industrial Machinery & Equipment). **Est:** 1982. **Sales:** $3,500,000 (2000). **Emp:** 19. **Officers:** Frank Grech, Manager.

■ 8030 ■ **Slakey Brothers Inc.**
PO Box 15647
Sacramento, CA 95852
Phone: (916)329-3750   **Fax:** (916)443-2083
Products: Building supplies; Plumbing supplies; Electrical supplies. **SICs:** 5039 (Construction Materials Nec); 5075 (Warm Air Heating & Air-Conditioning); 5074 (Plumbing & Hydronic Heating Supplies). **Est:** 1939. **Sales:** $71,000,000 (2000). **Emp:** 300. **Officers:** Frank Nisonger, President; Karen Strand, CFO.

■ 8031 ■ **Slaughter Industries**
PO Box 551699
Dallas, TX 75355-1699
Phone: (214)342-4900   **Fax:** (214)342-4949
Products: Lumber. **SIC:** 5031 (Lumber, Plywood & Millwork). **Sales:** $42,000,000 (2000). **Emp:** 100. **Officers:** Greg Pray, General Mgr.; Irene Luo, Controller.

■ 8032 ■ **SM Building Supply Coompany, Inc.**
2140 Amnicola Hwy.
Chattanooga, TN 37406
Phone: (423)622-3333   **Fax:** (423)622-3013
Products: Lumber supplies. **SIC:** 5031 (Lumber, Plywood & Millwork). **Est:** 1958. **Sales:** $7,000,000 (2000). **Emp:** 32. **Officers:** John D. Martin, President; Thomas Cox, Controller.

■ 8033 ■ **SMA Equipment Inc.**
5230 Wilson St.
Riverside, CA 92509
Phone: (909)784-1444
Free: (800)762-4225   **Fax:** (909)782-6701
E-mail: robinsma1@aol.com
Products: Construction and mining equipment. **SIC:** 5082 (Construction & Mining Machinery). **Est:** 1989. **Sales:** $140,000,000 (2000). **Emp:** 175. **Officers:** Bob Ferguson, President.

■ 8034 ■ **G.W. Smith Lumber Co.**
720 W Center St.
Lexington, NC 27292
Phone: (336)249-4941
URL: http://www.smith.doitbest.com
Products: Lumber; Building supplies, including pre-hung doors and cabinets. **SIC:** 5031 (Lumber, Plywood & Millwork). **Est:** 1905. **Sales:** $8,000,000 (1999).

Emp: 28. **Officers:** Steve Smith, President; Thomas Smith, Controller.

■ 8035 ■ **Smith-Sheppard Concrete Company Inc.**
Tennille Rd.
PO Box 855
Sandersville, GA 31082
Phone: (912)552-2594   **Fax:** (912)552-6649
Products: Concrete; Building materials; Home decorating supplies. **SICs:** 5031 (Lumber, Plywood & Millwork); 5032 (Brick, Stone & Related Materials). **Est:** 1957. **Sales:** $5,000,000 (2000). **Emp:** 50. **Officers:** H. Sheppard, President.

■ 8036 ■ **Smith Tractor and Equipment Co.**
PO Box 2990
Tacoma, WA 98401-2990
Phone: (206)922-8718   **Fax:** (206)922-3562
Products: Tractors. **SICs:** 5082 (Construction & Mining Machinery); 5084 (Industrial Machinery & Equipment). **Est:** 1955. **Sales:** $60,000,000 (2000). **Emp:** 154. **Officers:** Scott Highland, President; John Harrison, Controller; Tim Hess, Vice President.

■ 8037 ■ **Snavely Forest Products Inc.**
PO Box 9808
Pittsburgh, PA 15227
Phone: (412)885-4000
Products: Lumber, including pine and engineered wood products; Screen doors. **SIC:** 5031 (Lumber, Plywood & Millwork). **Est:** 1902. **Sales:** $140,000,000 (2000). **Emp:** 130. **Officers:** S.V. Snavely, President; John Stockhausen, CFO; Susan Fitzsimmons, Dir. of Marketing.

■ 8038 ■ **Snowbelt Insulation Company Inc.**
664 County Rd.
East Fairfield, VT 05448-9725
Phone: (802)827-6171   **Fax:** (802)827-3985
Products: Roofing; Siding; Insulation and insulation materials. **SIC:** 5033 (Roofing, Siding & Insulation).

■ 8039 ■ **Sokkia Corp.**
PO Box 2934
Overland Park, KS 66211
Phone: (913)492-4900   **Fax:** (913)492-0188
Products: Surveying and mapping equipment and supplies for surveyors, engineers and construction. **SIC:** 5082 (Construction & Mining Machinery). **Sales:** $40,000,000 (1999). **Emp:** 120. **Officers:** Hitoshi Mitsuhashi, President; James Courtney, Vice President, Finance and Operations.

■ 8040 ■ **Somers Lumber and Manufacturing Inc.**
PO Box 87
Union Grove, NC 28689
Phone: (704)539-4751
Products: Yellow pine lumber. **SIC:** 5031 (Lumber, Plywood & Millwork). **Sales:** $3,000,000 (2000). **Emp:** 30. **Officers:** Dwight Somers, President; Keith Somers, Treasurer & Secty.

■ 8041 ■ **Soult Wholesale Co.**
PO Box 1112
Clearfield, PA 16830
Phone: (814)765-5591   **Fax:** (814)765-4204
Products: Building products, including roofing, windows, siding and doors. **SICs:** 5031 (Lumber, Plywood & Millwork); 5033 (Roofing, Siding & Insulation). **Est:** 1940. **Sales:** $24,000,000 (2000). **Emp:** 50. **Officers:** L.E. Soult Jr., President & Treasurer; William McBride, Controller; J.G. Soult, President & Secty.

■ 8042 ■ **South Texas Lumber Co.**
1308 Avenue E
Ozona, TX 76943
Phone: (915)392-2634   **Fax:** (915)392-2938
Products: Lumber. **SIC:** 5031 (Lumber, Plywood & Millwork). **Emp:** 13. **Officers:** W. M. Burk.

■ 8043 ■ Southeastern Access Control
PO Box 1968
Tampa, FL 33601
Phone: (813)626-3191
Free: (800)669-9473   Fax: (813)623-3401
Products: Construction materials and machinery. SIC: 5039 (Construction Materials Nec).

■ 8044 ■ Southeastern Construction Inc.
PO Box 203
Avon, MA 02322
Phone: (781)767-2202   Fax: (781)767-2991
Products: Concrete blocks. SIC: 5032 (Brick, Stone & Related Materials). Est: 1925. Sales: $3,000,000 (2000). Emp: 26. Officers: Albert Tiso, President & Treasurer.

■ 8045 ■ Southeastern Equipment Company Inc.
PO Box 536
Cambridge, OH 43725
Phone: (614)432-6131
Products: Construction equipment. SIC: 5082 (Construction & Mining Machinery). Est: 1956. Sales: $170,000,000 (2000). Emp: 250. Officers: W. Baker, President; Robert Nemitz, Treasurer & Secty.; C. Patterson, VP of Marketing.

■ 8046 ■ Southeastern Supply Company Inc.
PO Box 516
Indianapolis, IN 46206
Phone: (317)359-9551   Fax: (317)359-0176
Products: Lumber. SIC: 5031 (Lumber, Plywood & Millwork). Est: 1956. Sales: $10,000,000 (2000). Emp: 60. Officers: P.J. Wilhelm, President; V. Mckay, CFO; J. Moylan, Sales Mgr.

■ 8047 ■ Southern Architectural Systems, Inc.
10038 Talley Ln.
PO Box 40223
Houston, TX 77240-0223
Phone: (713)462-6379   Fax: (713)462-8506
Products: Metal doors and frames; Components for stationary buildings including wall, partition, floor, ceiling panels, etc.; Hardware. SICs: 5031 (Lumber, Plywood & Millwork); 5072 (Hardware); 5012 (Automobiles & Other Motor Vehicles). Sales: $8,000,000 (2000). Emp: 49.

■ 8048 ■ Southern California Pipe and Steel Co.
12711 E Imperial Hwy.
Santa Fe Springs, CA 90670
Phone: (562)868-1734   Fax: (562)868-1737
Products: Chain link fencing. SIC: 5039 (Construction Materials Nec). Est: 1947. Sales: $3,000,000 (2000). Emp: 10. Officers: C. Brown, President.

■ 8049 ■ Southern Cross and O'Fallon Building Products Co.
PO Box 907
O Fallon, MO 63366
Phone: (314)240-6226
Products: Building materials. SIC: 5039 (Construction Materials Nec). Sales: $18,000,000 (1994). Emp: 55. Officers: Dan McAteer, CFO.

■ 8050 ■ Southern Illinois Lumber Co.
204 W Main St.
Fairfield, IL 62837
Phone: (618)842-3733   Fax: (618)842-7710
Products: Lumber. SIC: 5031 (Lumber, Plywood & Millwork). Est: 1906. Sales: $6,000,000 (2000). Emp: 40. Officers: Jerry Reid, President.

■ 8051 ■ Southern Sash Sales and Supply Co.
PO Box 471
Sheffield, AL 35660
Phone: (205)383-3261
Products: Doors; Lumber; Hardware supplies. SICs: 5031 (Lumber, Plywood & Millwork); 5033 (Roofing, Siding & Insulation). Est: 1948. Sales: $24,000,000 (2000). Emp: 425. Officers: E.H. Darby, President; Elton Darby Jr., CFO.

■ 8052 ■ Southern Specialty Corp.
5334 Distributor Dr.
Richmond, VA 23225-6104
Phone: (804)232-5164   Fax: (804)232-1048
Products: Automatic door equipment; Door framing; Store front glass. SICs: 5031 (Lumber, Plywood & Millwork); 5039 (Construction Materials Nec). Emp: 15. Officers: Harvey E. Smith; M. B. Crenshaw.

■ 8053 ■ Southern States Lumber Company Inc.
PO Box 265
Laurens, SC 29360
Phone: (864)984-4531   Fax: (864)984-4533
Products: Lumber. SIC: 5031 (Lumber, Plywood & Millwork). Est: 1909. Sales: $4,000,000 (2000). Emp: 3. Officers: Bailey A. Crump, President & Treasurer.

■ 8054 ■ Southern Store Fixtures Inc.
275 Drexel Rd. SE
Bessemer, AL 35022
Phone: (205)428-4800   Fax: (205)428-2552
E-mail: sales@southernstorefixtures.com
URL: http://www.southernstorefixtures.com
Products: Custom wood fixtures and shelving. SIC: 5031 (Lumber, Plywood & Millwork). Est: 1981. Sales: $10,000,000 (2000). Emp: 80. Officers: William A. Cary Jr., President; Joe Moore, Controller.

■ 8055 ■ Southland Distributors
36 Sugar Loaf Rd. C.
Hendersonville, NC 28792
Phone: (828)696-3535
Products: Building materials; Siding; Windows. SICs: 5039 (Construction Materials Nec); 5033 (Roofing, Siding & Insulation).

■ 8056 ■ Southwest Plywood and Lumber Corp.
11852 Alameda St.
Lynwood, CA 90262-4019
Products: Hardwood lumber; Particle board. SIC: 5031 (Lumber, Plywood & Millwork). Est: 1945. Sales: $19,000,000 (2000). Emp: 38. Officers: Geoffrey M. Yates, CEO; Greg McWilliams, Controller.

■ 8057 ■ Spahn and Rose Lumber Co.
PO Box 149
Dubuque, IA 52004-0149
Phone: (319)582-3606   Fax: (319)582-3749
Products: Building materials. SICs: 5039 (Construction Materials Nec); 5031 (Lumber, Plywood & Millwork). Est: 1904. Sales: $56,000,000 (2000). Emp: 215. Officers: C.D. Spahn, CEO & President; R.K. Guthrie, Exec. VP; R.E. Gansen, Secretary; K.L. Funke, Treasurer.

■ 8058 ■ Spaulding Brick Company Inc.
120 Middlesex Ave.
Somerville, MA 02145
Phone: (617)666-3200   Fax: (617)625-8110
Products: Bricks; Restoration products. SICs: 5039 (Construction Materials Nec); 5032 (Brick, Stone & Related Materials). Est: 1933. Sales: $9,500,000 (1999). Emp: 36. Officers: Paul J. Farrington, President.

■ 8059 ■ Spaulding Brick Company Inc.
250 Station St.
Cranston, RI 02910
Phone: (401)467-2220   Fax: (401)467-2359
Products: Bricks; Tools. SICs: 5032 (Brick, Stone & Related Materials); 5072 (Hardware).

■ 8060 ■ Specialty Building Products Inc.
7505-C Veterans Pkwy.
Columbus, GA 31909-2501
Phone: (706)327-0668   Fax: (706)323-1840
Products: Floorcovering equipment and supplies. SIC: 5032 (Brick, Stone & Related Materials). Sales: $1,500,000 (2000). Emp: 5.

■ 8061 ■ Spellman Hardwoods Inc.
4645 N 43rd Ave.
Phoenix, AZ 85031
Phone: (602)272-2313   Fax: (602)272-2820
Products: Hardwood, lumber, and moldings. SICs: 5031 (Lumber, Plywood & Millwork); 5039 (Construction Materials Nec). Est: 1963. Sales:

$8,000,000 (2000). Emp: 25. Officers: J.W. Spellman, CEO; Paul D. Smith, President.

■ 8062 ■ SPH Crane and Hoist Div.
2920 National Ct.
Garland, TX 75041
Phone: (972)272-3599   Fax: (972)272-4719
Products: Construction cranes. SIC: 5082 (Construction & Mining Machinery). Sales: $9,000,000 (2000). Emp: 32. Officers: Mike Bunnell, General Mgr.; Rick Moreno, Controller.

■ 8063 ■ Spokane Machinery Company Inc.
E 3730 Trent Ave.
Spokane, WA 99202
Phone: (509)535-1576   Fax: (509)535-2509
Products: Crushing equipment and parts. SIC: 5082 (Construction & Mining Machinery). Est: 1946. Sales: $12,000,000 (1999). Emp: 28. Officers: J.L. Peplinski, President; W. Teter, Treasurer & Secty.

■ 8064 ■ Spreitzer Inc.
PO Box 1288
Cedar Rapids, IA 52406
Phone: (319)365-9155   Fax: (319)365-2525
E-mail: n93ka@aol.com
Products: Construction machinery. SIC: 5082 (Construction & Mining Machinery). Est: 1948. Sales: $15,000,000 (2000). Emp: 30. Officers: J.E. Spreitzer, President & Treasurer.

■ 8065 ■ Russell Stadelman and Co.
PO Box 381767
Germantown, TN 38183-1767
Phone: (901)755-1391   Fax: (901)754-4672
Products: Plywood. SIC: 5031 (Lumber, Plywood & Millwork). Est: 1968. Sales: $37,100,000 (2000). Emp: 15. Officers: Russell Stadelman II, President; Scott Vanderburg, Controller; Mike Heitzman, VP of Marketing.

■ 8066 ■ Stancorp Inc.
PO Box 500
Girard, OH 44420-0500
Phone: (330)747-5444
Products: Quarrying equipment and aggregation. SICs: 5082 (Construction & Mining Machinery); 5032 (Brick, Stone & Related Materials). Sales: $50,000,000 (2000). Emp: 900. Officers: R.T. Beeghly, President; R.I. Dillon, Treasurer & Secty.

■ 8067 ■ Standard Building Products
6550 Chase Rd.
Dearborn, MI 48126
Phone: (313)846-0600   Fax: (313)846-9903
Products: Metal roofing and roof drainage equipment; Prepared asphalt and tar roofing and siding products; Siding. SIC: 5033 (Roofing, Siding & Insulation).

■ 8068 ■ Standard Roofings Inc.
PO Box 1410
Tinton Falls, NJ 07724
Phone: (908)542-3300   Fax: (908)542-3807
Products: Roofing and siding supplies. SIC: 5033 (Roofing, Siding & Insulation). Est: 1933. Sales: $40,000,000 (2000). Emp: 150. Officers: William B. Higginson, President; John Askin, Exec. VP of Finance; Joe Licciardello, Exec. VP of Marketing.

■ 8069 ■ Standard Supplies Inc.
4 Meem Ave.
Gaithersburg, MD 20877
Phone: (301)948-2690   Fax: (301)590-1791
Products: Building materials; Fabricated steel. SIC: 5039 (Construction Materials Nec). Est: 1946. Sales: $22,000,000 (2000). Emp: 65. Officers: Deborah Murphy, CEO.

■ 8070 ■ Standard Supply Company Inc.
Hwy. 66
Neptune, NJ 07753
Phone: (732)922-1200
Products: Lumber. SIC: 5031 (Lumber, Plywood & Millwork). Est: 1940. Sales: $3,000,000 (2000). Emp: 14. Officers: Thomas R. Chapman, President & Treasurer.

■ 8071 ■ Stanford Lumber Company Inc.
2001 Rte. 286
Pittsburgh, PA 15239
Phone: (412)327-6800 **Fax:** (412)327-9302
Products: Lumber. **SIC:** 5031 (Lumber, Plywood & Millwork). **Est:** 1959. **Sales:** $40,000,000 (2000). **Emp:** 120. **Officers:** R.H. Piekarski, President; Daniel Duerring, Controller.

■ 8072 ■ Star Industries Inc.
130 Lakeside Ave.
Seattle, WA 98122-6538
Phone: (206)328-1600 **Fax:** (206)328-4036
Products: Construction equipment. **SIC:** 5082 (Construction & Mining Machinery). **Est:** 1900. **Sales:** $26,500,000 (2000). **Emp:** 181. **Officers:** L. W. Rabel, President.

■ 8073 ■ Star Sales and Distributing Co.
PO Box 4008
Woburn, MA 01888
Phone: (617)933-8830
Products: Builders' hardware; Fasteners; Construction tools and equipment. **SICs:** 5039 (Construction Materials Nec); 5072 (Hardware). **Est:** 1930. **Sales:** $20,000,000 (2000). **Emp:** 50. **Officers:** Robert F. Ryan, President.

■ 8074 ■ Stephenson Equipment Inc.
7201 Paxton St.
Harrisburg, PA 17111
Phone: (717)564-3434
Free: (800)325-6455 **Fax:** (717)564-7580
E-mail: www.seissc.com
Products: Cranes; Streetsweeping machine brooms; Chippers; Polishers, sanders, and grinders. **SICs:** 5082 (Construction & Mining Machinery); 5084 (Industrial Machinery & Equipment). **Est:** 1957. **Sales:** $25,000,000 (2000). **Emp:** 90. **Officers:** James A. Penman, CEO & President; Robert M. Crisk, VP & CFO.

■ 8075 ■ Stewart Lumber Co.
421 Johnson St. NE
Minneapolis, MN 55413
Phone: (612)378-1520 **Fax:** (612)378-1484
Products: Lumber and construction materials. **SICs:** 5031 (Lumber, Plywood & Millwork); 5039 (Construction Materials Nec). **Sales:** $12,000,000 (1994). **Emp:** 75. **Officers:** Mark Lindgren, President; William Winters, Finance Officer.

■ 8076 ■ Stottlemyer and Shoemaker Lumber Co.
2211 Fruitville Rd.
Sarasota, FL 34237
Phone: (813)366-8108 **Fax:** (813)366-1034
Products: Complete line of building products, including lumber, windows, doors, carpeting, and kitchen cabinets. **SICs:** 5031 (Lumber, Plywood & Millwork); 5039 (Construction Materials Nec). **Est:** 1960. **Sales:** $26,000,000 (2000). **Emp:** 200. **Officers:** Gregory A. Bell, General Mgr.

■ 8077 ■ Stowers Machinery Corp.
PO Box 14802
Knoxville, TN 37914
Phone: (615)546-1414 **Fax:** (615)546-1411
Products: Heavy equipment, including tractors and loaders. **SIC:** 5082 (Construction & Mining Machinery). **Est:** 1960. **Sales:** $50,000,000 (2000). **Emp:** 200. **Officers:** Harry W. Stowers Jr., President; Richard Perkey, CFO; David Waddilove, VP of Sales; Bill Hillhouse, Dir. of Data Processing.

■ 8078 ■ Stowers Manufacturing Inc.
PO Drawer A
Gadsden, AL 35904
Phone: (205)547-8647 **Fax:** (205)547-8649
Products: Siding. **SIC:** 5033 (Roofing, Siding & Insulation). **Est:** 1946. **Sales:** $3,000,000 (2000). **Emp:** 8. **Officers:** Danny J. Stowers, President; Debra Seals, Dir. of Data Processing.

■ 8079 ■ Strait and Lamp Lumber Company Inc.
PO Box 718
Hebron, OH 43025
Phone: (614)861-4620 **Fax:** (740)928-7220
Products: Lumber and building materials. **SIC:** 5031 (Lumber, Plywood & Millwork). **Sales:** $50,200,000 (1993). **Emp:** 150. **Officers:** Wilbur Strait, President.

■ 8080 ■ Strawn Merchandise Inc.
10966 Harry Hines Blvd.
Dallas, TX 75220
Phone: (214)352-4891
Products: Construction and lawn equipment, including back hoes, fork lifts, tractors, and trenchers. **SIC:** 5082 (Construction & Mining Machinery). **Est:** 1894. **Sales:** $13,000,000 (2000). **Emp:** 100. **Officers:** Bob E. Brothers, President; Bob Stewart, CFO; Gene Anderson, VP of Marketing.

■ 8081 ■ Stringfellow Lumber Co.
PO Box 1117
Birmingham, AL 35201
Phone: (205)731-9400 **Fax:** (205)731-9470
Products: Lumber. **SIC:** 5031 (Lumber, Plywood & Millwork). **Sales:** $110,000,000 (2000). **Emp:** 90. **Officers:** Donald R. Fisher, Chairman of the Board; J.R.J. Steverson, Controller.

■ 8082 ■ Stripling Blake Lumber Co.
PO Box 9008
Austin, TX 78766
Phone: (512)465-4200 **Fax:** (512)465-4222
Products: Lumber and plywood. **SIC:** 5031 (Lumber, Plywood & Millwork). **Est:** 1938. **Sales:** $50,000,000 (2000). **Emp:** 250. **Officers:** Kerry Merritt, CEO; Charles Bunker, VP of Finance.

■ 8083 ■ Strober Building Supply Center Inc.
695 Wyoming Ave.
Kingston, PA 18704
Phone: (717)287-5072
Products: Dry wall. **SIC:** 5039 (Construction Materials Nec). **Sales:** $800,000 (2000). **Emp:** 7. **Officers:** Robert Gates, President.

■ 8084 ■ Structural Materials Inc.
1401 NW 40th St.
Fargo, ND 58102
Phone: (701)282-7100
Products: Steel overhead doors. **SIC:** 5039 (Construction Materials Nec). **Est:** 1987. **Sales:** $7,000,000 (2000). **Emp:** 16. **Officers:** David P. Workin, President.

■ 8085 ■ Summit Brick and Tile Co.
PO Box 533
Pueblo, CO 81002-0533
Phone: (719)542-8278 **Fax:** (719)542-5243
Products: Ceramics; Brick; Ceramic tile. **SIC:** 5032 (Brick, Stone & Related Materials). **Est:** 1902. **Sales:** $10,000,000 (1999). **Emp:** 75. **Officers:** Joseph C. Welte, President; Thomas R. Welte, CFO; James Clemans, Dir. of Marketing & Sales; James Clemans, Sales/Marketing Contact; Butch Pacheco, Customer Service Contact.

■ 8086 ■ Sumter Wood Preserving Company Inc.
PO Box 637
Sumter, SC 29151
Phone: (803)775-5301 **Fax:** (803)773-1522
Products: Lumber. **SIC:** 5031 (Lumber, Plywood & Millwork). **Est:** 1962. **Sales:** $12,000,000 (2000). **Emp:** 37. **Officers:** Michael V. Mecionis, General Mgr.

■ 8087 ■ Sun Control Window Tinting and Shades
4700 Vestal Pky. E
Vestal, NY 13850
Phone: (607)723-3066 **Fax:** (607)766-9795
E-mail: suncontrol@juno.com
URL: http://www.webpan.com/windowquilt
Products: Window film and tinting; Window glass. **SICs:** 5031 (Lumber, Plywood & Millwork); 5039 (Construction Materials Nec). **Est:** 1995. **Emp:** 2. **Former Name:** N.Y. Sun Control.

■ 8088 ■ Sunnyvale Lumber Inc.
870 W Evelyn Ave.
Sunnyvale, CA 94086
Phone: (408)736-5411
Products: Lumber. **SIC:** 5031 (Lumber, Plywood & Millwork). **Est:** 1945. **Sales:** $13,500,000 (2000). **Emp:** 25. **Officers:** Robert L. Roberts, CEO & President; James L. Roberts, CFO.

■ 8089 ■ Sunrise Glass Distributors
916 4th St. SW
Albuquerque, NM 87101
Phone: (505)246-2997
Products: Glass. **SIC:** 5039 (Construction Materials Nec).

■ 8090 ■ Superior Block and Supply Co.
PO Box 57
Milldale, CT 06467-0057
Phone: (203)239-4216
Products: Concrete blocks and masonry equipment. **SIC:** 5032 (Brick, Stone & Related Materials). **Est:** 1922. **Sales:** $8,000,000 (2000). **Emp:** 57. **Officers:** Ralph Crispino Jr., CEO; Michael Picco, Treasurer; Joseph Rescigno, Vice President.

■ 8091 ■ Surface Sealing Inc.
235 E Dawson Rd.
Milford, MI 48381-3211
Phone: (248)685-7355 **Fax:** (248)685-7756
Products: Asphalt coatings. **SIC:** 5032 (Brick, Stone & Related Materials). **Est:** 1960. **Officers:** John E. Lieblich, Vice President.

■ 8092 ■ Swaner Hardwood Company Inc.
5 W Magnolia St.
Burbank, CA 91503
Phone: (213)849-6761
Products: Hardwood lumber. **SIC:** 5031 (Lumber, Plywood & Millwork). **Est:** 1967. **Sales:** $75,000,000 (2000). **Emp:** 370. **Officers:** Gary Swaner, President; Steve Haag, VP & Treasurer.

■ 8093 ■ R.E. Sweeney Company Inc.
PO Box 1921
Ft. Worth, TX 76101
Phone: (817)834-7191 **Fax:** (817)831-8914
Products: Lumber. **SIC:** 5031 (Lumber, Plywood & Millwork). **Sales:** $88,000,000 (2000). **Emp:** 140. **Officers:** R.E. Sweeney, President; Hal Hughes, Treasurer & Secty.

■ 8094 ■ Sweetman Construction Co.
1201 W Russell St.
Sioux Falls, SD 57104
Phone: (605)336-2928
Products: Concrete materials. **SIC:** 5039 (Construction Materials Nec). **Sales:** $27,000,000 (1994). **Emp:** 200. **Officers:** M. Davis, President; Gaylen Abels, CFO.

■ 8095 ■ Syracuse Supply Co.
PO Box 4814
Syracuse, NY 13221
Phone: (315)463-9511 **Fax:** (315)463-9831
Products: Construction machinery. **SIC:** 5082 (Construction & Mining Machinery). **Est:** 1885. **Sales:** $260,000,000 (2000). **Emp:** 370. **Officers:** Steven J. Suhowatsky, CEO & President; Addison Everett, CFO; Brian Murphy, Information Systems Mgr.; Sue LeRoy, Dir of Personnel.

■ 8096 ■ Tabor City Lumber Inc.
PO Box 37
Tabor City, NC 28463
Phone: (919)653-3162
Products: Lumber. **SIC:** 5031 (Lumber, Plywood & Millwork). **Est:** 1944. **Sales:** $8,000,000 (2000). **Emp:** 30. **Officers:** Ernest C. Sanders Jr., President & Treasurer.

■ 8097 ■ Tanner Forest Products Inc.
33 Vaughn Dr.
Natchez, MS 39120-2019
Phone: (601)445-8206 **Fax:** (601)442-7301
Products: Hardwood lumber. **SIC:** 5031 (Lumber, Plywood & Millwork). **Est:** 1973. **Sales:** $5,000,000 (1999). **Emp:** 54. **Officers:** Alan D. Tanner, President; Bonnie G. Pace, Sales Mgr.

■ 8098 ■ Tasco Insulations Inc.
PO Box 1167
Youngstown, OH 44501
Phone: (330)744-2146 **Fax:** (330)744-5243
Products: Industrial insulation. **SIC:** 5033 (Roofing, Siding & Insulation). **Est:** 1957. **Sales:** $5,000,000 (2000). **Emp:** 100. **Officers:** Donald Harrison, President; John R. Hartley Jr., Treasurer.

■ 8099 ■ Tate Builders Supply L.L.C.
PO Box 18817
Erlanger, KY 41018
Phone: (606)727-1212 **Fax:** (606)272-1588
Products: Building supplies, including brick, sand, gravel and steel; Fireplaces; Roofing. **SICs:** 5032 (Brick, Stone & Related Materials); 5033 (Roofing, Siding & Insulation); 5039 (Construction Materials Nec). **Est:** 1929. **Sales:** $6,000,000 (2000). **Emp:** 25. **Officers:** William Owens, Managing Member; Judy Kroger, Office Mgr.; Guy Riehemann, Dir. of Sales.

■ 8100 ■ Taylor Lumber and Treating Inc.
PO Box 158
Sheridan, OR 97378
Phone: (503)291-2550 **Fax:** (503)291-2574
Products: Lumber, including green douglas fir. **SIC:** 5031 (Lumber, Plywood & Millwork). **Est:** 1947. **Sales:** $34,500,000 (2000). **Emp:** 135. **Officers:** Walter H. Parks, President & COO; John Doss, CFO.

■ 8101 ■ Tayo's Tile Co.
12 Sunflower Ln.
Peralta, NM 87042
Phone: (505)865-7179
Products: Tiles. **SIC:** 5032 (Brick, Stone & Related Materials).

■ 8102 ■ TDA Industries Inc.
122 E 42nd St.
New York, NY 10168
Phone: (212)972-1510
Products: Roofing supplies, including shingles. **SIC:** 5039 (Construction Materials Nec). **Est:** 1968. **Sales:** $65,000,000 (2000). **Emp:** 400. **Officers:** Douglas P. Fields, President & Chairman of the Board; Fredrick M. Friedman, CFO.

■ 8103 ■ Tech-Aerofoam Products Inc.
3551 NW 116th St.
Miami, FL 33167
Phone: (305)685-5993
Products: Foam rubber, plywood, kitchen cabinets and hardware. **SICs:** 5085 (Industrial Supplies); 5031 (Lumber, Plywood & Millwork); 5023 (Homefurnishings); 5072 (Hardware). **Sales:** $5,000,000 (1994). **Emp:** 75. **Officers:** Dave Melin, President; Margaret Horvath, CFO.

■ 8104 ■ Tech Products, Inc.
5012 W Knollwood St.
Tampa, FL 33634
Phone: (813)884-2503
Free: (800)255-7296 **Fax:** (813)886-8944
Products: Materials for cabinet construction, including laminates and plywood. **SIC:** 5031 (Lumber, Plywood & Millwork).

■ 8105 ■ Temp Glass
291 M St.
Perrysburg, OH 43551
Phone: (419)666-2000
Free: (800)537-4064 **Fax:** 800-666-8367
Products: Glass. **SIC:** 5039 (Construction Materials Nec).

■ 8106 ■ Temp Glass Southern, Inc.
1101 Fountain Pkwy.
Grand Prairie, TX 75050
Phone: (972)647-4028 **Fax:** (972)647-2439
Products: Insulated and laminated units; Door openings; Stockwalls. **SICs:** 5031 (Lumber, Plywood & Millwork); 5039 (Construction Materials Nec).

■ 8107 ■ Tempco Contracting & Supply
PO Box 8305
Boise, ID 83707-2305
Phone: (208)376-0580 **Fax:** (208)376-0583
Products: Roofing; Siding; Insulation and insulation materials. **SIC:** 5033 (Roofing, Siding & Insulation). **Officers:** Robert Tallman, President.

■ 8108 ■ Tennessee Building Products Inc.
PO Box 40403
Nashville, TN 37204-0403
Phone: (615)259-4677 **Fax:** (615)242-6727
Products: Doors and windows. **SIC:** 5031 (Lumber, Plywood & Millwork). **Est:** 1913. **Sales:** $60,000,000 (2000). **Emp:** 180. **Officers:** James Fishel, President; Bob Durham, Comptroller.

■ 8109 ■ Tennessee-Carolina Lumber Company Inc.
PO Box 71855
Chattanooga, TN 37407-1855
Phone: (423)698-3381
Products: Lumber and plywood. **SIC:** 5031 (Lumber, Plywood & Millwork). **Est:** 1987. **Sales:** $7,000,000 (2000). **Emp:** 17. **Officers:** Robert L. Frederick, President.

■ 8110 ■ Tennison Brothers Inc.
PO Box 40126
Memphis, TN 38174-0126
Phone: (901)274-7773 **Fax:** (901)274-6093
Products: Gutter and roof supplies. **SIC:** 5033 (Roofing, Siding & Insulation). **Est:** 1891. **Sales:** $5,000,000 (2000). **Emp:** 50. **Officers:** G. Tennison, President; Bill Tennison, CFO; Andy Tennison, Dir. of Marketing & Sales.

■ 8111 ■ Terre Hill Concrete Products
PO Box 10
Terre Hill, PA 17581
Phone: (717)445-3100 **Fax:** (717)445-3108
Products: Concrete. **SIC:** 5032 (Brick, Stone & Related Materials). **Est:** 1928. **Sales:** $22,000,000 (2000). **Emp:** 180. **Officers:** Robert Lazarchick, CEO & President; Dale Wiest, Finance Officer; John Muntz, Sales Mgr.; Ron Bernas, Dir of Human Resources.

■ 8112 ■ Tews Co.
6200 W Center St.
Milwaukee, WI 53210
Phone: (414)442-8000 **Fax:** (414)442-3155
Products: Concrete. **SIC:** 5039 (Construction Materials Nec). **Est:** 1895. **Sales:** $40,000,000 (2000). **Emp:** 30. **Officers:** William Tews, CEO & President; Paul C. McDonald, CFO; Nick Rivecca, Sales Mgr.

■ 8113 ■ Tex-Mastic International Inc.
PO Box 210309
Dallas, TX 75211-0309
Phone: (214)330-4605 **Fax:** (214)331-5575
E-mail: txmastic@flash.net
Products: Construction materials. **SICs:** 5032 (Brick, Stone & Related Materials); 5039 (Construction Materials Nec). **Est:** 1946. **Sales:** $7,000,000 (2000). **Emp:** 10. **Officers:** R.A. Palmer, President; Michael Kirkpatrick, Controller; J.F. Plamer, Chairman of the Board.

■ 8114 ■ Texas Contractors Supply Co.
3221 Carpenter Fwy.
Irving, TX 75062
Phone: (214)438-3323 **Fax:** (214)438-2989
Products: Contractors' supplies, including nails, concrete, and tools. **SICs:** 5082 (Construction & Mining Machinery); 5072 (Hardware). **Est:** 1933. **Sales:** $30,000,000 (2000). **Emp:** 42. **Officers:** James L. Bilderback, President.

■ 8115 ■ Texas Mining Co.
PO Box 429
Brady, TX 76825-0429
Phone: (915)597-0721 **Fax:** (915)597-2645
Products: Industrial sand and oil field sands. **SICs:** 5032 (Brick, Stone & Related Materials); 5084 (Industrial Machinery & Equipment). **Sales:** $35,000,000 (2000). **Emp:** 80. **Officers:** Jeffrey Gray, President.

■ 8116 ■ Texas Plywood and Lumber Company Inc.
PO Box 531110
Grand Prairie, TX 75053
Phone: (972)263-1381 **Fax:** (972)262-1339
Products: Lumber. **SIC:** 5031 (Lumber, Plywood & Millwork).

■ 8117 ■ Texxon Enterprises Inc.
503 Bruce Ct.
Ovilla, TX 75154-3603
Phone: (972)230-1630
Products: Construction materials, including roofing and siding. **SIC:** 5033 (Roofing, Siding & Insulation).

■ 8118 ■ Thermal Tech, Inc.
2301 US Highway 2 E
Kalispell, MT 59901-2835
Phone: (406)755-3388 **Fax:** (406)752-4853
Products: Siding; Windows; Patio covers; Awnings. **SICs:** 5033 (Roofing, Siding & Insulation); 5031 (Lumber, Plywood & Millwork). **Est:** 1975. **Emp:** 10. **Officers:** Roy Nordwall, President.

■ 8119 ■ Thermax Insulation Inc.
3103 Stinson Ave.
Billings, MT 59102-1352
Phone: (406)656-1979 **Fax:** (406)245-3791
Products: Industrial and commercial insulation materials. **SIC:** 5033 (Roofing, Siding & Insulation). **Officers:** Denise Harmala, President.

■ 8120 ■ Thermwell Products Co. Inc.
150 E 7th St.
Paterson, NJ 07524
Phone: (973)684-5000 **Fax:** (973)278-2105
Products: Metal window and door screens and metal weather strip. **SIC:** 5039 (Construction Materials Nec).

■ 8121 ■ Thomas Kitchens, Inc.
560 S Poplar St.
Hazleton, PA 18201
Phone: (717)455-1546 **Fax:** (717)459-1956
Products: Kitchen cabinets. **SIC:** 5031 (Lumber, Plywood & Millwork).

■ 8122 ■ Thomas and Proetz Lumber Co.
3400 N Hall St.
St. Louis, MO 63147
Phone: (314)231-9343 **Fax:** (314)231-0313
Products: Lumber. **SIC:** 5031 (Lumber, Plywood & Millwork). **Sales:** $12,000,000 (2000). **Emp:** 39. **Officers:** Edwin R. Thomas Jr., President; Scott E. Thomas, Treasurer & Secty.

■ 8123 ■ Thompson Tractor Company Inc.
PO Box 10367
Birmingham, AL 35202
Phone: (205)841-8601 **Fax:** (205)841-5028
Products: Construction tractors. **SIC:** 5082 (Construction & Mining Machinery). **Est:** 1957. **Sales:** $500,000,000 (2000). **Emp:** 706. **Officers:** Michael Thompson, President; Tom McGough, Treasurer; Edward L. Cain, VP of Sales; William O. Mooney, Vice President; Frank Wright, Dir of Personnel.

■ 8124 ■ Thorpe Corp.
PO Box 330403
Houston, TX 77233
Phone: (713)644-1247 **Fax:** (713)649-6503
Products: Insulation; Refractory material. **SIC:** 5033 (Roofing, Siding & Insulation). **Sales:** $39,000,000 (1999). **Emp:** 140. **Officers:** Gerald Scott, President, e-mail: gws@thorpecorp.com; Richard A. Nowland, Exec. VP of Finance, e-mail: ran@thorpecorp.com.

■ 8125 ■ Thorpe Insulation Co.
2741 S Yates Ave.
Los Angeles, CA 90040
Phone: (323)726-7171 **Fax:** (323)728-6145
URL: http://www.thorpeinsulation.com
Products: Commercial and industrial fiberglass insulation and air-conditioning ducts. **SICs:** 5033 (Roofing, Siding & Insulation); 5075 (Warm Air Heating & Air-Conditioning). **Est:** 1948. **Sales:** $25,000,000 (2000). **Emp:** 200. **Officers:** H.M. Privette, President; P.C. Reynolds, CFO; S.C. Butler, Vice President; E.W. Fults, Exec. VP.

■ 8126 ■ **Thorpe Products Co.**
PO Box 330407
Houston, TX 77233-3361
Phone: (713)641-3361 **Fax:** (713)649-0368
E-mail: tphouston@thorpecorp.com
URL: http://www.thorpeproducts.com
Products: Insulation and insulating refractory materials; Specialty engineered refractory and high temperature textile materials. **SIC:** 5032 (Brick, Stone & Related Materials). **Est:** 1986. **Sales:** $26,000,000 (2000). **Emp:** 60. **Officers:** Gerald Scott, President; Mike Wilson, VP Div. Mgr.-Material Sales Div.; Mack Hounsel, VP Div. Mgr.-Engineered Prod. Div. **Alternate Name:** Thorpe Corp.

■ 8127 ■ **THP United Enterprises Inc.**
PO Box 1991
Milwaukee, WI 53201-1991
Phone: (262)523-6500
Free: (800)558-4772 **Fax:** (262)523-6595
E-mail: marketing@safway.com
URL: http://www.safway.com
Products: Concrete forming products; Scaffolding. **SIC:** 5169 (Chemicals & Allied Products Nec). **Est:** 1936. **Sales:** $170,000,000 (2000). **Emp:** 1,500. **Officers:** Marc Wilson, CEO & President; Bob Sukalich, CFO.

■ 8128 ■ **Three Rivers Aluminum Co.**
71 Progress Ave.
Cranberry Township, PA 16066
Phone: (724)776-7000 **Fax:** (724)776-7069
URL: http://www.traco.com
Products: Aluminum and vinyl windows. **SIC:** 5039 (Construction Materials Nec). **Est:** 1943. **Sales:** $200,000,000 (1999). **Emp:** 1,600. **Officers:** Robert Randall, President; W.R. Stevens, VP of Marketing & Sales; John Kalakos, Exec. VP of Marketing.

■ 8129 ■ **Thunander Corp.**
PO Box 1428
Elkhart, IN 46515
Phone: (219)295-4131
Products: Motor homes. **SIC:** 5039 (Construction Materials Nec). **Est:** 1981. **Sales:** $35,000,000 (2000). **Emp:** 300. **Officers:** Rick Heaton, President; Ken Horvath, Treasurer; Bill Milliner, Sales Mgr.

■ 8130 ■ **Thunderbird Steel Div.**
4300 2nd St. NW
Albuquerque, NM 87107
Phone: (505)345-7866
Products: Building material, including pre-hung doors and cabinets. **SICs:** 5039 (Construction Materials Nec); 5032 (Brick, Stone & Related Materials). **Est:** 1968. **Sales:** $11,000,000 (2000). **Emp:** 40. **Officers:** James R. Quillen II, Manager.

■ 8131 ■ **Tiger Machinery Co.**
1600 Walcutt Rd.
Columbus, OH 43228
Phone: (614)876-1141
Products: Construction and industrial machinery. **SICs:** 5082 (Construction & Mining Machinery); 5084 (Industrial Machinery & Equipment). **Sales:** $11,000,000 (1992). **Emp:** 30. **Officers:** Tom Langfelf, CEO.

■ 8132 ■ **Tilcon Tomasso Inc.**
909 Foxon Rd.
PO Box 67
North Branford, CT 06471
Phone: (203)484-2881 **Fax:** (203)484-4935
Products: Quarry trap rock; Concrete. **SIC:** 5032 (Brick, Stone & Related Materials). **Est:** 1980. **Sales:** $95,000,000 (2000). **Emp:** 800. **Officers:** Raymond Piscatelli, President.

■ 8133 ■ **Tile Club**
2122 W Mission Rd.
Escondido, CA 92029
Phone: (760)745-9123
Free: (800)700-TILE **Fax:** (760)480-9905
Products: Floorcovering equipment and supplies. **SIC:** 5032 (Brick, Stone & Related Materials). **Sales:** $6,000,000 (2000). **Emp:** 45.

■ 8134 ■ **Tile Distributor Company Inc.**
4421 Poplar Level Rd.
Louisville, KY 40213
Phone: (502)456-2410
Free: (800)274-8453 **Fax:** (502)456-2494
Products: Floorcovering equipment and supplies. **SIC:** 5032 (Brick, Stone & Related Materials). **Sales:** $2,500,000 (2000). **Emp:** 14.

■ 8135 ■ **Timber Products Co.**
PO Box 269
Springfield, OR 97477
Phone: (541)747-4577 **Fax:** (503)747-4577
Products: Lumber; Panels. **SIC:** 5031 (Lumber, Plywood & Millwork). **Est:** 1971. **Sales:** $360,000,000 (2000). **Emp:** 1,000. **Officers:** Joseph H. Gonyea, CEO; Al Emrick Jr. Jr., CFO; Donald G. Montgomery, COO.

■ 8136 ■ **Tink Inc.**
2361 Durham Dayton Hwy.
Durham, CA 95938
Phone: (530)895-0897 **Fax:** (530)895-0751
Products: Hydraulic lifts for loaders. **SIC:** 5082 (Construction & Mining Machinery). **Officers:** Robert DuBose, President.

■ 8137 ■ **T.J.T. Inc.**
PO Box 278
Emmett, ID 83617
Phone: (208)365-5321 **Fax:** (208)365-3983
Products: Vinyl and steel siding for the manufactured housing industry. **SIC:** 5033 (Roofing, Siding & Insulation). **Sales:** $34,100,000 (2000). **Emp:** 182. **Officers:** Terrence J. Sheldon, CEO, President & Chairman of the Board; Scott M. Beechie, Vice President.

■ 8138 ■ **TML Associates Inc.**
PO Box 2235
Spartanburg, SC 29304-2235
Phone: (864)583-2678
Free: (888)866-5962 **Fax:** (864)591-1225
Products: Forms, tags, and labels; Rubber; Plywood; Machine parts; Plating; New and rebuilt valves; Hoses; Building materials; Packaging supplies; Fasteners and maintenance hardware; Electronics assemblies and componenets; Insulated glass; Furniture. **SICs:** 5085 (Industrial Supplies); 5031 (Lumber, Plywood & Millwork); 5072 (Hardware); 5065 (Electronic Parts & Equipment Nec); 5021 (Furniture). **Est:** 1987. **Emp:** 4. **Officers:** Steve Wood, President.

■ 8139 ■ **Toolpushers Supply Co.**
PO Box 2360
Casper, WY 82602-2360
Phone: (307)266-0324 **Fax:** (307)266-0373
Products: Petroleum mining equipment; Oil field equipment. **SIC:** 5082 (Construction & Mining Machinery). **Est:** 1953. **Emp:** 27. **Officers:** Diemer True, President; H.A. True III, Vice President; David True, Vice President; Bob I. Selby, Manager.

■ 8140 ■ **Trade Corporation**
PO Box 30277
Raleigh, NC 27622
Phone: (919)571-8782
Products: Construction materials; Computer software and peripherals; Furniture; Jewelry. **SICs:** 5039 (Construction Materials Nec); 5094 (Jewelry & Precious Stones); 5045 (Computers, Peripherals & Software); 5021 (Furniture). **Officers:** Ali R. Gholizadeh, President.

■ 8141 ■ **Tradewinds International Inc.**
PO Box 9930
Savannah, GA 31412
Phone: (912)234-8050 **Fax:** (912)234-8046
Products: Lumber, including red and white oak, ash, poplar, and yellow pine. **SIC:** 5031 (Lumber, Plywood & Millwork). **Officers:** James H. Smith, VP of Sales.

■ 8142 ■ **Transit Mix Concrete Co.**
PO Box 1030
Colorado Springs, CO 80901
Phone: (719)475-0700 **Fax:** (719)475-0226
Products: Concrete products; Tools. **SICs:** 5032 (Brick, Stone & Related Materials); 5072 (Hardware).

Sales: $10,000,000 (2000). **Emp:** 150. **Officers:** Carl Herskind.

■ 8143 ■ **Trax Inc.**
1340 Perimeter Hwy. S
Atlanta, GA 30349
Phone: (770)996-6800
Free: (800)241-3057 **Fax:** (770)997-2167
URL: http://www.traxinc.com
Products: Construction equipment. **SIC:** 5082 (Construction & Mining Machinery). **Est:** 1962. **Sales:** $72,000,000 (2000). **Emp:** 325. **Officers:** Herb Humphrey, CEO; Richard F. Dundon, Exec. VP; Penny Rosser, VP of Human Resources; Paul Brenner, CFO.

■ 8144 ■ **Tri-State Brick and Tile Co.**
PO Box 31768
Jackson, MS 39286
Phone: (601)981-1410 **Fax:** (601)366-2205
Products: Brick. **SIC:** 5032 (Brick, Stone & Related Materials). **Sales:** $12,000,000 (2000). **Emp:** 109. **Officers:** R.D. Robinson, Chairman of the Board; Albert Baker, President; Jimmy Gallaher, Comptroller; Jimmy Gallagher, Comptroller.

■ 8145 ■ **Tri-State Insulation Co.**
PO Box 106
Miller, SD 57362
Phone: (605)853-2442
Free: (800)658-3531 **Fax:** (605)853-3022
Products: Roofing; Insulation; Siding, except wood; Replacement vinyl windows. **SIC:** 5033 (Roofing, Siding & Insulation). **Sales:** $1,050,000 (2000). **Emp:** 20. **Officers:** Vernon Joy, President.

■ 8146 ■ **Tri-State Truck and Equipment Inc.**
PO Box 1298
Billings, MT 59103
Phone: (406)245-3188 **Fax:** (406)238-1501
Products: Construction and mining equipment. **SIC:** 5082 (Construction & Mining Machinery). **Est:** 1963. **Sales:** $14,000,000 (2000). **Emp:** 60. **Officers:** T.W. Zimmer, President; Donna M. Timmerman, Treasurer & Secty.; Dewitt L. Boyd, VP of Marketing & Sales.

■ 8147 ■ **Triad Machinery Inc.**
PO Box 301099
Portland, OR 97230
Phone: (503)254-5100
Products: Construction equipment and accessories. **SIC:** 5082 (Construction & Mining Machinery). **Sales:** $49,000,000 (1999). **Emp:** 105. **Officers:** Michael Hildebrandt, President; Kristine Stubblefield, Vice President.

■ 8148 ■ **Triangle Pacific Corp. Beltsville Div.**
10500 Ewing Rd.
Beltsville, MD 20705
Phone: (301)937-5000 **Fax:** (301)937-6254
Products: Building products, including lumber and flooring. **SIC:** 5031 (Lumber, Plywood & Millwork). **Est:** 1943. **Sales:** $21,500,000 (2000). **Emp:** 121. **Officers:** Dave Weaver, General Mgr.; Greg Smith, Dir. of Marketing.

■ 8149 ■ **William S. Trimble Company Inc.**
PO Box 154
Knoxville, TN 37901
Phone: (615)573-1911
Products: Windows, mailboxes, and garage doors. **SICs:** 5031 (Lumber, Plywood & Millwork); 5039 (Construction Materials Nec). **Est:** 1936. **Sales:** $19,000,000 (2000). **Emp:** 85. **Officers:** William S. Trimble Jr., President; Belva King, Treasurer.

■ 8150 ■ **Troumbly Brothers Inc.**
PO Box 405
Taconite, MN 55786
Phone: (218)326-4815 **Fax:** (218)326-2072
Products: Concrete and aggregates. **SIC:** 5063 (Electrical Apparatus & Equipment). **Est:** 1951. **Sales:** $4,000,000 (2000). **Emp:** 25. **Officers:** Kenneth C. Troumbly, President.

■ 8151 ■ **Troy Top Soil Company Inc.**
748 Hudson River Rd.
Mechanicville, NY 12118-3802
Phone: (518)273-7665
Products: Gravel; Stone; Sandfill; Screens; Looms.

SICs: 5032 (Brick, Stone & Related Materials); 5039 (Construction Materials Nec). Est: 1949. Sales: $700,000 (2000). Emp: 11. Officers: Josephine Grande, President; Anthony Grande, Treasurer & Secty.

■ 8152 ■ Tulnoy Lumber Inc.
1620 Webster Ave.
Bronx, NY 10457
Phone: (718)901-1700   Fax: (718)901-2957
E-mail: info@tulnoylumber.com
URL: http://www.tulnoylumber.com
Products: Lumber; Plywood; Pine; Doors; Hardware. SICs: 5072 (Hardware); 5031 (Lumber, Plywood & Millwork). Est: 1930. Sales: $30,000,000 (2000). Emp: 78. Officers: H. Tulchin, President; A. Safenowitz, VP of Finance.

■ 8153 ■ Tumac Lumber Company Inc.
529 SW 3rd Ave., No. 600
Portland, OR 97204
Phone: (503)226-6661   Fax: (503)273-2650
Products: Lumber and plywood, including pine. SIC: 5031 (Lumber, Plywood & Millwork). Est: 1959. Sales: $318,000,000 (2000). Emp: 165. Officers: Michael Blanchat, President; Virgil Miller, Exec. VP of Finance.

■ 8154 ■ Tyler Equipment Corp.
PO Box 544
East Longmeadow, MA 01028
Phone: (413)525-6351   Fax: (413)525-6840
E-mail: tylerequipment@worldnet.att.net
Products: Construction equipment. SICs: 5082 (Construction & Mining Machinery); 5084 (Industrial Machinery & Equipment). Est: 1922. Sales: $20,000,000 (2000). Emp: 49. Officers: M.B. Tyler III III, President; P. Nossal, VP of Finance; William A. Tyler, VP of Marketing; Grant H. Tyler, VP of Sales.

■ 8155 ■ Underwood Builders Supply Co.
PO Box 1587
Mobile, AL 36633
Phone: (205)432-3581   Fax: (205)438-6913
Products: Concrete blocks. SIC: 5032 (Brick, Stone & Related Materials). Est: 1919. Sales: $5,000,000 (2000). Emp: 45. Officers: S.R. Milling, President; Michael K. Gurey, Dir. of Marketing & Sales.

■ 8156 ■ United Builders Supply of Jackson Inc.
PO Box 11367
Jackson, MS 39283-1367
Phone: (601)982-8421   Fax: (601)982-8536
Products: Building supplies, including steel foundations, lumber, roofing, and siding. SICs: 5031 (Lumber, Plywood & Millwork); 5039 (Construction Materials Nec); 5033 (Roofing, Siding & Insulation). Est: 1960. Sales: $8,000,000 (2000). Emp: 50. Officers: Richard Milne, President; Roger L. Clark, VP of Finance & Controller; Lyman E. Johnson Jr., VP of Operations.

■ 8157 ■ United Hardwood, L.L.C.
846 South EE Wallace Blvd.
PO Box 1795
Ferriday, LA 71334
Phone: (318)757-4508   Fax: (318)757-4763
E-mail: unitedhardwood@laribay.net
Products: Lumber. SIC: 5031 (Lumber, Plywood & Millwork). Est: 1997. Emp: 38. Officers: Judy Myles, President. Former Name: Rogers Lumber International.

■ 8158 ■ United International Inc.
PO Box 580
Charlestown, MA 02129
Phone: (617)241-0440   Fax: (617)241-7373
Products: Wood products, including plywood and hardboard; Logs and lumber. SICs: 5031 (Lumber, Plywood & Millwork); 5039 (Construction Materials Nec). Est: 1991. Sales: $35,000,000 (2000). Emp: 21. Officers: Morton S. Waldfogel, President; Peter D. Waldfogel, Vice President; Jane L. Waldfogel, Vice President; Jane Forbush, Controller.

■ 8159 ■ United Plywood and Lumber Inc.
PO Box 1088
Birmingham, AL 35201
Phone: (205)925-7601
Products: Plywood. SIC: 5031 (Lumber, Plywood & Millwork). Est: 1949. Sales: $24,000,000 (2000). Emp: 80. Officers: Mark Burdette, President; O.W. Norris, Treasurer & Secty.

■ 8160 ■ Universal Industries Inc.
325 E Stahl Rd.
Fremont, OH 43420
Phone: (419)334-9741
Products: specialty equipment and products. SIC: 5082 (Construction & Mining Machinery). Sales: $24,000,000 (2000). Emp: 30.

■ 8161 ■ Universal Marble and Granite Inc.
1954 Halethorpe Farms Rd., Ste. 500
Baltimore, MD 21227
Phone: (410)247-2442
Free: (800)828-5611   Fax: (410)247-8043
Products: Marble and granite. SIC: 5032 (Brick, Stone & Related Materials). Est: 1968. Sales: $5,000,000 (2000). Emp: 21. Officers: Adam Ganzermiller, President.

■ 8162 ■ Urban Ore Inc.
6082 Ralston Ave.
Richmond, CA 94805
Phone: (510)235-0172   Fax: (510)235-1098
Products: Construction materials, including doors and windows; Furniture, including desks and chairs. SICs: 5031 (Lumber, Plywood & Millwork); 5039 (Construction Materials Nec); 5021 (Furniture). Emp: 18.

■ 8163 ■ Urethane Contractors Supply
1425 Spar Ave.
Anchorage, AK 99501
Phone: (907)276-7932   Fax: (907)279-2749
Products: Foam insulation. SIC: 5033 (Roofing, Siding & Insulation).

■ 8164 ■ U.S.A. Woods International
PO Box 38507
Memphis, TN 38183
Phone: (901)753-7718   Fax: (901)753-7815
Products: Hardwood lumber. SIC: 5031 (Lumber, Plywood & Millwork). Officers: Ron Carlsson, President.

■ 8165 ■ Vaagen Brothers Lumber Inc.
565 W 5th St.
Colville, WA 99114
Phone: (509)684-5071   Fax: (509)684-2168
Products: Lumber. SIC: 5031 (Lumber, Plywood & Millwork). Est: 1955. Sales: $56,000,000 (2000). Emp: 430. Officers: Dwayne Vaagen, President; Robert Heater, VP of Finance.

■ 8166 ■ Valley Best-Way Building Supply
PO Box 14024
Spokane, WA 99214-0024
Phone: (509)924-1250   Fax: (509)928-0659
Products: Building materials, including framing, doors, and cabinets. SIC: 5031 (Lumber, Plywood & Millwork). Est: 1970. Sales: $5,000,000 (2000). Emp: 80. Officers: Gary Smith, Vice President.

■ 8167 ■ Valley Fir and Redwood Co.
903 Morris Rd.
Columbus, GA 31906
Phone: (706)687-9542
Products: Lumber. SIC: 5031 (Lumber, Plywood & Millwork). Sales: $2,000,000 (2000). Emp: 8. Officers: George Mitchell, Owner.

■ 8168 ■ Valley Hardwood Inc.
5004 Nancy Cir.
Huntsville, AL 35811
Phone: (205)852-6582   Fax: (205)851-7682
Products: Wood handle blanks and dowels; Plywood and lumber, including logs, softwood, and hardwood. SICs: 5031 (Lumber, Plywood & Millwork); 5099 (Durable Goods Nec). Officers: Howard Johnson, President.

■ 8169 ■ Van Arsdale-Harris Lumber
PO Box 34008
San Francisco, CA 94134
Phone: (415)467-8711   Fax: (415)467-8144
Products: Lumber, including pine, cedar, spruce, mahogany, oak, clear redwood, douglas fir, and hardwood plywood. SIC: 5031 (Lumber, Plywood & Millwork). Est: 1888. Sales: $3,600,000 (2000). Emp: 12. Officers: William J. Greggains, President.

■ 8170 ■ F.S. Van Hoose and Company Inc.
PO Box 1618
Paintsville, KY 41240
Phone: (606)789-5870
Products: Lumber supplies. SIC: 5031 (Lumber, Plywood & Millwork). Sales: $13,000,000 (2000). Emp: 47. Officers: Joe H. Van Hoose, President.

■ 8171 ■ G.W. Van Keppel Co.
PO Box 2923
Kansas City, KS 66110
Phone: (913)281-4800
Products: Heavy construction equipment. SICs: 5082 (Construction & Mining Machinery); 5084 (Industrial Machinery & Equipment). Est: 1926. Sales: $57,000,000 (1994). Emp: 80. Officers: T.E. Walker, CEO & Chairman of the Board; Marc Larson, Treasurer & Secty.

■ 8172 ■ Vansant Lumber
PO Box 50
Vansant, VA 24656
Phone: (540)935-4519   Fax: (540)935-5907
Products: Lumber, paneling, siding, and doors. SICs: 5031 (Lumber, Plywood & Millwork); 5033 (Roofing, Siding & Insulation); 5039 (Construction Materials Nec).

■ 8173 ■ Variform Inc.
PO Box 559
Kearney, MO 64060
Phone: (816)635-6400
Free: (800)800-2244   Fax: (816)635-6942
URL: http://www.variform.com
Products: Vinyl siding and accessories. SIC: 5033 (Roofing, Siding & Insulation). Est: 1964. Emp: 300. Officers: Lee Meyer, President; John Jurcak, Dir. of Marketing, e-mail: JurcakJ@variform.com; John Wayne, VP of Marketing & Sales; Larry Grace, Sales Administration Mgr., e-mail: GraceL@variform.com; Kurt Kuanke, Human Resources Contact, e-mail: KuankeK@variform.com.

■ 8174 ■ Vaughan and Sons Inc.
PO Box 17258
San Antonio, TX 78217
Phone: (210)352-1300   Fax: (210)590-1438
Products: Lumber. SIC: 5031 (Lumber, Plywood & Millwork). Est: 1893. Sales: $78,100,000 (2000). Emp: 250. Officers: Curtis Vaughan III III, President; Robert L. Vaughan, Exec. VP of Operations; George Vaughan, Exec. VP of Operations. Alternate Name: Alamo Forest Products, Inc.

■ 8175 ■ Emmet Vaughn Lumber Co.
PO Box 1747
Knoxville, TN 37901
Phone: (615)577-7577   Fax: (615)573-9319
Products: Lumber. SIC: 5031 (Lumber, Plywood & Millwork). Est: 1957. Sales: $18,000,000 (2000). Emp: 11. Officers: Emmet P. Vaughn Jr., President; Larry McClain, Sr. VP.

■ 8176 ■ Vaughn Materials Company Inc.
PO Box 679
Reno, NV 89504
Phone: (702)323-1381
Products: Doors; Hardware. SICs: 5031 (Lumber, Plywood & Millwork); 5072 (Hardware). Est: 1950. Sales: $6,000,000 (2000). Emp: 20. Officers: John Cavilia, President.

■ 8177 ■ Vector Industries Inc.
6701 90th Ave. N
Pinellas Park, FL 33782-4596
Phone: (813)541-6631   Fax: (813)545-4685
Products: Kitchen cabinets. SIC: 5031 (Lumber, Plywood & Millwork). Est: 1980. Sales: $98,000,000 (2000). Emp: 350. Officers: Charles Jackson, CEO; David Hughey, Controller.

■ 8178 ■ Venus Manufacturing Co.
707 E Curry Rd.
Tempe, AZ 85281-1912
Phone: (602)894-0444 **Fax:** (602)967-0443
E-mail: venusmfg@aol.com
Products: Shower doors; Mirrors; Chalk and marker boards; Marble. **SICs:** 5031 (Lumber, Plywood & Millwork); 5039 (Construction Materials Nec). **Est:** 1965. **Sales:** $1,500,000 (2000). **Emp:** 15. **Officers:** J.C. Gourley.

■ 8179 ■ H. Verby Company Inc.
186-14 Jamaica Ave.
Jamaica, NY 11423
Phone: (718)454-5522
Products: Roofing and siding materials, including shingles, aluminum siding, waterproofing, and masonry products; Interior design. **SIC:** 5033 (Roofing, Siding & Insulation). **Est:** 1924. **Sales:** $25,000,000 (2000). **Emp:** 45. **Officers:** Stanley M. Verby, President & Treasurer; Robert O. Brooks, Controller; Harry F. Verby, President.

■ 8180 ■ VerHalen Inc.
PO Box 11968
Green Bay, WI 54307
Phone: (920)435-3791 **Fax:** (920)435-0377
URL: http://www.verhaleninc.com
Products: Commercial and residential windows and doors. **SIC:** 5031 (Lumber, Plywood & Millwork). **Est:** 1911. **Sales:** $45,000,000 (1999). **Emp:** 200. **Officers:** John Calawerts, Mng. Partner; Chris Calawerts, Mng. Partner; Mike Calawerts, Mng. Partner.

■ 8181 ■ Vidalia Naval Stores Co.
PO Box 1659
Vidalia, GA 30474
Phone: (912)537-8964 **Fax:** (912)537-4839
Products: Lumber and millwork; Roofing equipment and supplies. **SICs:** 5031 (Lumber, Plywood & Millwork); 5033 (Roofing, Siding & Insulation). **Est:** 1947. **Sales:** $45,000,000 (2000). **Emp:** 200. **Officers:** Hugh Peterson Jr., President; Ray Blount, CFO; Gary Campbell, COO; Loyd Mobley, Sr. VP; Rodney Brooks, Exec. VP.

■ 8182 ■ Viking
295 E Industrial Park Dr.
Manchester, NH 03109
Phone: (603)668-4545 **Fax:** (603)666-3670
Products: Remodeling materials, including vinyl siding and roofing shingles. **SICs:** 5033 (Roofing, Siding & Insulation); 5031 (Lumber, Plywood & Millwork).

■ 8183 ■ Rene Ortiz Villafane Inc.
PO Box 2562
San Juan, PR 00902
Phone: (787)793-7141 **Fax:** (787)782-9542
Products: Lumber and plywood; Farm supplies, including nitrogenous fertilizer; Canned fruits, juices, and vegetables. **SICs:** 5031 (Lumber, Plywood & Millwork); 5191 (Farm Supplies); 5149 (Groceries & Related Products Nec). **Officers:** Rene Ortiz Villafane, President.

■ 8184 ■ Vimco Concrete Accessories Inc.
300 Hansen Access Rd.
King of Prussia, PA 19406
Phone: (215)768-0500
Products: Concrete products and accessories. **SIC:** 5032 (Brick, Stone & Related Materials). **Est:** 1960. **Sales:** $28,000,000 (2000). **Emp:** 100. **Officers:** Victor J. Maggitti Jr., President.

■ 8185 ■ Virginia Construction Supply Inc.
PO Box 20368
Roanoke, VA 24018
Phone: (540)776-0040 **Fax:** (540)776-0044
E-mail: vcsievev.net
Products: Commercial construction supplies, including wire mesh and pipes. **SIC:** 5039 (Construction Materials Nec). **Est:** 1985. **Sales:** $10,000,000 (1999). **Emp:** 40. **Officers:** Gerald McPeak, President.

■ 8186 ■ Virginia Hardwood Co.
PO Box 90
Monrovia, CA 91016
Phone: (626)358-4594
Products: Hardwood. **SIC:** 5031 (Lumber, Plywood &

Millwork). **Sales:** $19,000,000 (2000). **Emp:** 80. **Officers:** David V. Ferrari, President; Barry Silveus, VP of Marketing.

■ 8187 ■ Vivian Corp.
PO Box 1266
Kingston, PA 18704
Phone: (717)288-0492
Products: Windows; Wood doors, interior and exterior. **SIC:** 5031 (Lumber, Plywood & Millwork). **Est:** 1907. **Sales:** $1,000,000 (2000). **Emp:** 10. **Officers:** John R. Vivian, President; Leonard Dsmilka, Controller.

■ 8188 ■ VLP Holding Co.
PO Box 4915
Kansas City, MO 64120
Phone: (816)241-9290
Free: (800)878-9290 **Fax:** (816)241-1738
URL: http://www.vlpco.com
Products: Construction equipment. **SIC:** 5082 (Construction & Mining Machinery). **Est:** 1911. **Sales:** $50,000,000 (1999). **Emp:** 100. **Officers:** James W. Foreman, Chairman of the Board, e-mail: jforeman@vlpco.com; Robert W. Foreman, CEO, e-mail: bforeman@vlpco.com; Butch Teppe, President, e-mail: bteppe@vlpco.com.

■ 8189 ■ WACO Scaffolding and Equipment Co.
PO Box 318028
Cleveland, OH 44131-8028
Phone: (216)749-8900
Products: Scaffolding. **SIC:** 5082 (Construction & Mining Machinery). **Est:** 1945. **Sales:** $50,000,000 (2000). **Emp:** 375. **Officers:** George Mally, President; David Chorbenneau, CFO.

■ 8190 ■ Wade Distributors Inc.
1510 28th St.
Gulfport, MS 39501
Phone: (228)822-2550
Products: Brick, ceramic, and marble tile. **SIC:** 5032 (Brick, Stone & Related Materials).

■ 8191 ■ Waggener Lumber Co.
PO Box 430159
St. Louis, MO 63143-0259
Phone: (314)937-3618 **Fax:** (314)937-9495
Products: Construction lumber. **SICs:** 5039 (Construction Materials Nec); 5031 (Lumber, Plywood & Millwork). **Est:** 1880. **Sales:** $2,500,000 (2000). **Emp:** 12. **Officers:** John E. Scott Sr., President.

■ 8192 ■ Walczak Lumber Inc.
PO Box 340
Clifford, PA 18413
Phone: (717)222-9651
Products: Lumber; Mulch. **SIC:** 5031 (Lumber, Plywood & Millwork). **Est:** 1940. **Sales:** $6,000,000 (2000). **Emp:** 20. **Officers:** Leon Walczak, Owner; Ronald Walczak, Treasurer; Cindy Ross, Dir. of Data Processing.

■ 8193 ■ Waldo Brothers Co.
202 Southampton St.
Boston, MA 02118
Phone: (617)445-3000 **Fax:** (617)427-5691
Products: Masonry materials, including cement and brick. **SIC:** 5032 (Brick, Stone & Related Materials). **Est:** 1869. **Sales:** $12,000,000 (2000). **Emp:** 50. **Officers:** P.B. Colgan, CEO.

■ 8194 ■ William H. Walston Co.
8216 Grey Eagle Dr.
Upper Marlboro, MD 20772-2602
Phone: (301)967-3232 **Fax:** (301)568-7606
E-mail: whwco@prodigy.net
Products: Drywall; Acoustics; Plaster. **SIC:** 5031 (Lumber, Plywood & Millwork). **Est:** 1973. **Emp:** 50. **Officers:** Young S. Park, President; Richard Stuart; Stephen Lertura, Sales/Marketing Contact; Wanda Seymore, Human Resource Contact.

■ 8195 ■ Walton Lumber Company Inc.
Rte. 4
Mineral, VA 23117-9302
Phone: (540)894-5444
Products: Lumber. **SIC:** 5031 (Lumber, Plywood & Millwork). **Est:** 1939. **Sales:** $3,800,000 (2000). **Emp:**

14. **Officers:** H.H. Walton Jr., President; H.H. Walton III, Treasurer.

■ 8196 ■ Warrior Asphalt Refining Corp.
PO Box 40254
Tuscaloosa, AL 35404
Phone: (205)553-2060
Products: Asphalt. **SICs:** 5032 (Brick, Stone & Related Materials); 5033 (Roofing, Siding & Insulation). **Est:** 1949. **Sales:** $4,000,000 (2000). **Emp:** 15. **Officers:** Curtis Bale, CEO & President.

■ 8197 ■ Watson Lumber Co.
PO Box 1177
Liberty, KY 42539
Phone: (606)787-6221
Free: (800)682-0734 **Fax:** (606)787-5442
E-mail: howardbolt@kin.net
Products: Lumber; Furniture. **SICs:** 5031 (Lumber, Plywood & Millwork); 5021 (Furniture). **Est:** 1960. **Sales:** $4,000,000 (1999). **Emp:** 65. **Officers:** Gale Watson, President; Sheila Clark, Bookkeeper; Jennifer Denson, Dir. of Sales; Howard Bolt, Vice President; Bookkeeper.

■ 8198 ■ Wausau Supply Co.
PO Box 296
Wausau, WI 54402-0296
Phone: (715)359-2524 **Fax:** (715)359-4717
Products: Siding; Thermal insulation. **SIC:** 5033 (Roofing, Siding & Insulation).

■ 8199 ■ W.B.R. Inc.
PO Box 66001
Stockton, CA 95206
Phone: (209)983-0590
Products: Concrete. **SIC:** 5032 (Brick, Stone & Related Materials).

■ 8200 ■ WD Industries Inc.
PO Box 27100
Albuquerque, NM 87125-7100
Phone: (505)344-3441 **Fax:** (505)344-4030
Products: Insulating supplies; Thermal and other insulation materials. **SIC:** 5033 (Roofing, Siding & Insulation). **Officers:** Donald Duke, President.

■ 8201 ■ Weiler Wilhelm Window and Door Co.
16900 Bagley Rd.
Cleveland, OH 44130
Phone: (440)243-5000
Products: Windows and doors. **SIC:** 5031 (Lumber, Plywood & Millwork).

■ 8202 ■ Wesco Cedar Inc.
PO Box 40847
Eugene, OR 97404-0161
Phone: (503)688-5020 **Fax:** (503)688-5024
Products: Shake; Shingles. **SIC:** 5033 (Roofing, Siding & Insulation). **Est:** 1972. **Sales:** $30,000,000 (2000). **Emp:** 75. **Officers:** L.F. Plummer, President; John Roupe, Treasurer & Secty.

■ 8203 ■ William H. West Company
4509 Emerald St.
Boise, ID 83706-2042
Phone: (208)344-1449
Products: Siding. **SIC:** 5033 (Roofing, Siding & Insulation). **Officers:** William West, Owner.

■ 8204 ■ West Equipment Company Inc.
1545 E Broadway St.
Toledo, OH 43605
Phone: (419)698-1601 **Fax:** (419)698-2540
Products: Construction and industrial equipment. **SICs:** 5082 (Construction & Mining Machinery); 5084 (Industrial Machinery & Equipment). **Est:** 1952. **Sales:** $1,500,000 (2000). **Emp:** 13. **Officers:** Cecil Erdmann, President; Bernard Erdmann, Treasurer.

■ 8205 ■ West Virginia Tractor Co.
PO Box 473
Charleston, WV 25322
Phone: (304)346-5301 **Fax:** (304)346-5305
E-mail: wvtractor@msn.com
Products: Construction and municipal equipment. **SIC:** 5082 (Construction & Mining Machinery). **Est:** 1982.

Sales: $6,000,000 (2000). Emp: 6. Officers: Gary W. Grady, President.

■ 8206 ■ Western Door and Sash Co.
4601 Malat St.
Oakland, CA 94601
Phone: (510)535-2000 Fax: (510)261-3916
Products: Doors. SIC: 5031 (Lumber, Plywood & Millwork). Est: 1914. Sales: $6,900,000 (2000). Emp: 45. Officers: Joseeph Z. Todd III, President; S. Hamaguchi, Controller; Robert L. Smith, Dir. of Marketing & Sales.

■ 8207 ■ Western Home Center Inc.
7600 Colerain Ave.
Cincinnati, OH 45239
Phone: (513)931-6300 Fax: (513)931-1309
Products: Construction supplies, including lumber and millwork; Cabinets; Countertops; Windows; Doors. SICs: 5031 (Lumber, Plywood & Millwork); 5039 (Construction Materials Nec). Est: 1947. Sales: $59,000,000 (2000). Emp: 325. Officers: Edward A. Friesz, Chairman of the Board; Ken Eder, Treasurer; Larry Langdon, Dir. of Marketing; Terry Elliot, Dir of Human Resources.

■ 8208 ■ Western MacArthur Co.
2855 Mandela Pkwy.
Oakland, CA 94608
Phone: (510)251-2102
Products: Fiberglass pipe insulation; Products for heating and air conditioning, Adhesive; Duct products; Tape; Sheet metal. SICs: 5033 (Roofing, Siding & Insulation); 5075 (Warm Air Heating & Air-Conditioning); 5085 (Industrial Supplies); 5051 (Metals Service Centers & Offices). Est: 1913. Sales: $7,500,000 (2000). Emp: 25. Officers: Richard Lockwood, President; Richard Stahl, CFO.

■ 8209 ■ Western Materials Inc.
PO Box 430
Yakima, WA 98907
Phone: (509)575-3000 Fax: (509)453-3186
Products: Masonry, dry wall, and roofing materials. SICs: 5033 (Roofing, Siding & Insulation); 5032 (Brick, Stone & Related Materials). Est: 1922. Emp: 80. Officers: Stan Martinkus, President.

■ 8210 ■ Western Plains Machinery Co.
PO Box 30438
Billings, MT 59107
Phone: (406)259-5500 Fax: (406)259-8559
Products: Construction equipment. SIC: 5082 (Construction & Mining Machinery). Est: 1940. Sales: $10,000,000 (2000). Emp: 41. Officers: Mike G. Matz, President; Glenn Kudrna, CFO.

■ 8211 ■ Western Power and Equipment Corp.
4601 NE 77th Ave., Ste. 200
Vancouver, WA 98662
Phone: (360)253-2346
Free: (800)333-2346 Fax: (360)253-4830
URL: http://www.westernpower.com
Products: Construction equipment. SIC: 5082 (Construction & Mining Machinery). Sales: $163,650,000 (2000). Emp: 400. Officers: Dean McLain, CEO & President; Mark J. Wright, VP & CFO.

■ 8212 ■ Western Products Inc.
2001 1st Ave. N
Fargo, ND 58102-4120
Phone: (701)293-5310 Fax: (701)293-5370
Products: Steel siding. SIC: 5033 (Roofing, Siding & Insulation). Est: 1948. Sales: $15,000,000 (2000). Emp: 100. Officers: M. Bullinger, President.

■ 8213 ■ Western Shower Door Inc.
4140 Business Center
Fremont, CA 94538
Phone: (510)438-0340 Fax: (510)438-0346
Products: Doors; Dividers; Partitions; Mirrors. SICs: 5031 (Lumber, Plywood & Millwork); 5023 (Homefurnishings). Sales: $13,000,000 (2000). Emp: 99. Officers: David C. Geery.

■ 8214 ■ Western States Equipment
500 E Overland Rd.
Meridian, ID 83642
Phone: (208)888-2287 Fax: (208)884-2314
Products: Heavy construction equipment. SIC: 5082 (Construction & Mining Machinery). Est: 1957. Emp: 500. Officers: Wayne Denton, President; J. King, VP of Finance; Pete Edmunds, Dir. of Marketing; Tom Harris, Sales Contact; Fred Turner, Human Resources Contact.

■ 8215 ■ Westgate Building Materials
1908 Modoc
Madera, CA 93637
Phone: (209)673-9118
Products: Construction materials. SIC: 5031 (Lumber, Plywood & Millwork). Sales: $400,000 (2000). Emp: 4. Officers: D.L. Berry, President & CFO.

■ 8216 ■ Westshore Glass Corp.
PO Box 15216
Tampa, FL 33684-5216
Phone: (813)884-2561
Free: (800)284-5277 Fax: (813)885-9526
Products: Glass and mirrors; Storefront material. SIC: 5039 (Construction Materials Nec). Est: 1954. Sales: $25,000,000 (2000). Emp: 175. Officers: Ron Brock, CEO & President.

■ 8217 ■ Wheeler Consolidated Inc.
1100 Hoak Dr.
West Des Moines, IA 50265
Phone: (515)223-1584 Fax: (515)223-8899
Products: Building products. SIC: 5085 (Industrial Supplies).

■ 8218 ■ Brock White Co.
2575 Kasota Ave.
St. Paul, MN 55108
Phone: (612)647-0950 Fax: (612)647-0403
Products: Concrete and masonry equipment and supplies. SICs: 5082 (Construction & Mining Machinery); 5032 (Brick, Stone & Related Materials). Est: 1953. Sales: $28,000,000 (2000). Emp: 87. Officers: Richard Garland, President.

■ 8219 ■ White Star Machinery and Supply Company Inc.
PO Box 1180
Wichita, KS 67201
Phone: (316)838-3321 Fax: (316)832-1375
Products: Construction and machine equipment, including excavators, wheel loaders, cranes, and skid loaders. SIC: 5082 (Construction & Mining Machinery). Est: 1892. Sales: $20,000,000 (2000). Emp: 85. Officers: J. Engels, President; Walt Berry, CFO; Glenn Engels, Dir. of Marketing.

■ 8220 ■ Whiteman Industries
6850 Business Way
Boise, ID 83716-5522
Phone: (208)336-7650
Products: Cement finishing equipment. SIC: 5082 (Construction & Mining Machinery). Sales: $23,000,000 (2000). Emp: 75. Officers: Marv Whiteman, President.

■ 8221 ■ Whittier-Ruhle Millwork
80 N Main St.
Wharton, NJ 07885-1633
Phone: (973)347-6100
Products: Lumber and plywood. SIC: 5031 (Lumber, Plywood & Millwork). Sales: $37,000,000 (1993). Emp: 100. Officers: Skip Flinn, Manager.

■ 8222 ■ Wholesale Building Materials Co.
1701 Magoffin St.
El Paso, TX 79901
Phone: (915)533-9721
Products: Building materials, including plywood, lumber, windows, doors, and ceiling tiles. SICs: 5031 (Lumber, Plywood & Millwork); 5039 (Construction Materials Nec). Est: 1950. Sales: $3,000,000 (2000). Emp: 14. Officers: B. Byers, President.

■ 8223 ■ Wholesale Hardwood Interiors Inc.
1030 Campbellsville Bypass
PO Box 485
Campbellsville, KY 42719
Phone: (502)789-1323 Fax: (502)789-2321
Products: Interior moldings, stair parts, doors, and custom millwork. SICs: 5031 (Lumber, Plywood & Millwork); 5072 (Hardware). Est: 1985. Emp: 40. Officers: Don Gorin, President; Eugene Russell, Treasurer & Secty.; Michael G. Judd, VP of Operations.

■ 8224 ■ Wildish Land Co.
PO Box 7428
Eugene, OR 97401
Phone: (503)485-1700
Products: Building materials. SIC: 5032 (Brick, Stone & Related Materials). Sales: $37,000,000 (1991). Emp: 125. Officers: James A. Wildish, President.

■ 8225 ■ Wildish Sand and Gravel Co.
PO Box 7428
Eugene, OR 97401
Phone: (541)485-1700
Products: Construction materials, including sand, gravel, and concrete. SICs: 5032 (Brick, Stone & Related Materials); 5039 (Construction Materials Nec). Est: 1936. Sales: $56,000,000 (2000). Emp: 500. Officers: James Wildish, President; James Landen, Controller; Randy Hledik, Dir. of Marketing.

■ 8226 ■ Willamette Graystone Inc.
PO Box 7816
Eugene, OR 97401
Phone: (541)726-7666
Products: Masonry supplies. SIC: 5032 (Brick, Stone & Related Materials). Est: 1946. Sales: $7,000,000 (2000). Emp: 50. Officers: D.W. Jones, President.

■ 8227 ■ Williams Equipment and Supply Company Inc.
2425 S 3rd St.
Memphis, TN 38109
Phone: (901)366-9195
Free: (800)264-0195 Fax: (901)432-2071
E-mail: dthomason@williamsequipment.com
URL: http://www.williamsequipment.com
Products: Construction supplies; Generators; Pumps. SICs: 5039 (Construction Materials Nec); 5085 (Industrial Supplies). Est: 1961. Sales: $28,000,000 (1999). Emp: 100. Officers: James Williams, President & Chairman of the Board.

■ 8228 ■ Williams Industries Inc.
2849 Meadow View Rd.
Falls Church, VA 22042
Phone: (703)560-5196 Fax: (703)280-9082
Products: Erection equipment. SIC: 5082 (Construction & Mining Machinery). Est: 1970. Sales: $34,000,000 (1999). Emp: 420. Officers: Frank E. Williams III, CEO & President; Marianne V. Pastor, Dir. of Admin and VP.

■ 8229 ■ Wimsatt Brothers Inc.
PO Box 32488
Louisville, KY 40232
Phone: (502)458-3221
E-mail: sales@wimsatt.com
URL: http://www.wimsatt.com
Products: Roofing and building materials. SICs: 5033 (Roofing, Siding & Insulation); 5039 (Construction Materials Nec). Est: 1936. Sales: $40,000,000 (1999). Emp: 75. Officers: Raymond J. Paulin Jr., CEO & President; Robert H. Wimsatt, Exec. VP; J. Hays Wimsatt, Chairman of the Board; Nancy E. Smith, VP of Operations; Cheryl A. Bramer, VP of Marketing & Sales; David R. Muncy, CFO.

■ 8230 ■ Winco Distributors Inc.
PO Box 2401
Houston, TX 77252
Phone: (713)224-5361 Fax: (713)225-3294
Products: Lumber millwork. SIC: 5031 (Lumber, Plywood & Millwork). Sales: $60,000,000 (1993). Emp: 200. Officers: Joe Gehring, General Mgr.

■ **8231** ■ **Wind-Dorf (USA) Inc.**
11009 S Orange Blossom Trl
Orlando, FL 32837-9433
Phone: (407)438-3180 **Fax:** (407)438-3180
Products: Fencing and fence gates. **SIC:** 5039
(Construction Materials Nec). **Est:** 1990. **Sales:**
$1,000,000 (2000). **Emp:** 7. **Officers:** Rajul Patel,
President.

■ **8232** ■ **Window Components Manufacturing**
3443 NW 107th St.
Miami, FL 33167
Phone: (305)688-2521
Free: (800)382-9541 **Fax:** (305)688-7748
Products: Window hardware and parts. **SIC:** 5031
(Lumber, Plywood & Millwork). **Officers:** Dennis
Cooper, President; Dennis Knoll, Marketing & Sales
Mgr.

■ **8233** ■ **Window Headquarters Inc.**
1459 E 13th St.
Brooklyn, NY 11230-6603
Phone: (718)965-1200 **Fax:** (718)965-0215
Products: Windows. **SIC:** 5031 (Lumber, Plywood &
Millwork). **Est:** 1984. **Sales:** $8,300,000 (2000). **Emp:**
47. **Officers:** Donny Maleck, President.

■ **8234** ■ **Wisconsin Drywall Distributors**
1015 Femrite Dr.
Madison, WI 53701
Phone: (608)221-8636
Products: Drywall. **SIC:** 5031 (Lumber, Plywood &
Millwork).

■ **8235** ■ **Witch Equipment Company Inc.**
343 N Bowen Rd.
Arlington, TX 76012
Phone: (817)469-6096 **Fax:** (817)461-7961
URL: http://www.ditchwitch.com
Products: Trenchers. **SIC:** 5082 (Construction &
Mining Machinery). **Est:** 1960. **Sales:** $3,000,000
(2000). **Emp:** 20. **Officers:** Larry M. Glover, President,
e-mail: lglover@spisystems.com; A. Paul Knuckley,
Vice President.

■ **8236** ■ **Wizard Equipment Corp.**
920 Crooked Hill Rd.
Brentwood, NY 11717
Phone: (631)231-6200 **Fax:** (631)435-4343
Products: Construction equipment and supplies;
Rental and sales of skip steer ladder and rough terrain
forklifts. **SICs:** 5082 (Construction & Mining
Machinery); 5039 (Construction Materials Nec). **Est:**
1991. **Sales:** $250,000 (2000). **Emp:** 4. **Officers:** Todd
Bratone, Owner & General Mgr. **Former Name:**
Contractors Supply Corp.

■ **8237** ■ **W.N.C. Pallet & Forest Products
Company Inc.**
PO Box 38
Candler, NC 28715
Phone: (828)667-5426 **Fax:** (828)665-4759
Products: Pallets; Lumber. **SIC:** 5031 (Lumber,
Plywood & Millwork). **Est:** 1959. **Sales:** $10,000,000
(2000). **Emp:** 100. **Officers:** Thomas L. Thrash,
President; Tommy Orr, Vice President.

■ **8238** ■ **Wolohan Lumber Co.**
PO Box 3235
Saginaw, MI 48605
Phone: (517)793-4532 **Fax:** (517)793-5066
Products: Lumber and building materials. **SICs:** 5031
(Lumber, Plywood & Millwork); 5032 (Brick, Stone &
Related Materials); 5039 (Construction Materials Nec).
Sales: $404,000,000 (2000). **Emp:** 1,482. **Officers:**
James L. Wolohan, CEO, President & Chairman of the
Board; David G. Honaman, Vice President.

■ **8239** ■ **Wood Feathers Inc.**
PO Box 17566
Portland, OR 97217
Phone: (503)289-8813 **Free:** (800)874-8707
Products: Roofing materials, including shingles. **SIC:**

5033 (Roofing, Siding & Insulation). **Est:** 1955. **Sales:**
$21,000,000 (2000). **Emp:** 70. **Officers:** Lee Gotcher,
President; Virgil Stonecypher, Controller; Steve Clay,
Dir. of Marketing.

■ **8240** ■ **Wood & Plastics Industries**
2100 Universal Rd.
Pittsburgh, PA 15235
Phone: (412)793-7483
Products: Lamination products and supplies. **SICs:**
5031 (Lumber, Plywood & Millwork); 5162 (Plastics
Materials & Basic Shapes).

■ **8241** ■ **Woody's Big Sky Supply, Inc.**
1221 Round Butte Rd. W
Ronan, MT 59864
Phone: (406)676-5726 **Fax:** (406)676-5727
Products: Hardware; Building materials, including
lumber, plumbing, electrical equipment, windows, and
doors. **SICs:** 5039 (Construction Materials Nec); 5031
(Lumber, Plywood & Millwork); 5072 (Hardware). **Est:**
1975. **Emp:** 40.

■ **8242** ■ **Wyoming Machinery Co.**
PO Box 2335
Casper, WY 82602
Phone: (307)472-1000
Products: Heavy construction equipment. **SICs:** 5084
(Industrial Machinery & Equipment); 5082
(Construction & Mining Machinery). **Est:** 1969. **Sales:**
$93,000,000 (2000). **Emp:** 300. **Officers:** Richard
Wheeler, President; Robert Chynoweth, CFO; John
Thompson, Dir. of Sales; Ron Williams, Dir. of
Systems.

■ **8243** ■ **Wyoming Machinery Co.**
1700 Cutler Rd.
Cheyenne, WY 82003
Phone: (307)634-1561 **Fax:** (307)472-1002
Products: Heavy construction equipment. **SIC:** 5082
(Construction & Mining Machinery). **Est:** 1969. **Sales:**
$3,000,000 (2000). **Emp:** 30. **Officers:** Richard
Wheeler, President; Robert Schynoweth, Treasurer.

■ **8244** ■ **Yahara Materials Inc.**
PO Box 277
Waunakee, WI 53597
Phone: (608)849-4162
Products: Aggregates and crushed limestones. **SIC:**
5032 (Brick, Stone & Related Materials). **Sales:**
$15,500,000 (2000). **Emp:** 70. **Officers:** Larry
Burcalow, President.

■ **8245** ■ **Yardville Supply Co.**
PO Box 8427
Trenton, NJ 08650
Phone: (609)585-5000 **Fax:** (609)585-3769
Products: Building supplies, including lumber,
concrete, and hardware. **SICs:** 5039 (Construction
Materials Nec); 5031 (Lumber, Plywood & Millwork);
5032 (Brick, Stone & Related Materials); 5072
(Hardware). **Est:** 1946. **Sales:** $1,000 (1999). **Emp:**
50. **Officers:** George M. Smith, President; Diane
Flanigan, Office Mgr.; Edmund J. Smith, Exec. VP.

■ **8246** ■ **Yezbak Lumber Inc.**
108 N Beeson Blvd.
Uniontown, PA 15401
Phone: (412)438-5543 **Fax:** (412)483-1433
Products: Lumber; Weather-proofing products. **SICs:**
5031 (Lumber, Plywood & Millwork); 5039
(Construction Materials Nec). **Est:** 1966. **Sales:**
$3,000,000 (2000). **Emp:** 14. **Officers:** Thomas J.
Yezbak, Chairman of the Board & Treasurer; Van
Evans, Vice President; Rick Miller, President; Curtis
Henry, Manager; Mary Chomiak, Vice President.

■ **8247** ■ **Yorktowne Inc.**
PO Box 231
Red Lion, PA 17356
Phone: (215)739-7700
Free: (800)207-6720 **Fax:** (215)739-7792
Products: Kitchen cabinets. **SIC:** 5031 (Lumber,

Plywood & Millwork). **Est:** 1908. **Sales:** $10,000,000
(2000). **Emp:** 28. **Officers:** Fred Regnery.

■ **8248** ■ **Yorktowne Kitchens**
Distribution Center
3405 Board Rd.
York, PA 17402
Phone: (717)764-0699
Free: (800)999-1975 **Fax:** (717)764-0952
Products: Kitchen and vanity cabinets. **SIC:** 5031
(Lumber, Plywood & Millwork). **Sales:** $18,000,000
(2000). **Emp:** 60. **Officers:** Kim Powers; Jeff Grove.

■ **8249** ■ **Yorktowne Kitchens**
2070 Bennett Ave.
Lancaster, PA 17601
Phone: (717)291-1947 **Fax:** (717)291-1269
Products: Kitchen and vanity cabinets. **SIC:** 5031
(Lumber, Plywood & Millwork).

■ **8250** ■ **William M. Young Co.**
PO Box 10487
Wilmington, DE 19850
Phone: (302)654-4448 **Fax:** (302)654-3150
Products: Lumber.; Millwork and related products.
SIC: 5031 (Lumber, Plywood & Millwork). **Est:** 1963.
Sales: $50,000,000 (2000). **Emp:** 50. **Officers:** Tom
Shea Jr. Jr., President; John Gormely, Controller; John
Shortell, VP of Marketing; Joanne Pillinger.

■ **8251** ■ **Young Sales Corp.**
1054 Central Industrial
St. Louis, MO 63110
Phone: (314)771-3080
Products: Insulation. **SIC:** 5033 (Roofing, Siding &
Insulation). **Sales:** $60,000,000 (1994). **Emp:** 700.
Officers: W. Todd McCane, CEO & President; Donald
E. Amelung, CFO.

■ **8252** ■ **Yukon Equipment**
2020 E Third Ave.
Anchorage, AK 99501
Phone: (907)277-1541
Free: (800)478-1541 **Fax:** (907)258-0169
E-mail: sales@yukonequipment.com
URL: http://www.yukonequipment.com
Products: Case construction equipment. **SIC:** 5082
(Construction & Mining Machinery). **Est:** 1945. **Sales:**
$20,000,000 (2000). **Emp:** 30. **Officers:** Maurice
Hollowell, Vice President.

■ **8253** ■ **Zeeland Lumber and Supply Inc.**
146 E Washington Ave.
Zeeland, MI 49464
Phone: (616)772-2119 **Fax:** (616)772-6409
Products: Lumber; Finished wood; Paint; Hardware.
SICs: 5031 (Lumber, Plywood & Millwork); 5072
(Hardware); 5198 (Paints, Varnishes & Supplies). **Est:**
1943. **Sales:** $30,000,000 (2000). **Emp:** 47. **Officers:**
John Van Den Bosch, President.

■ **8254** ■ **Ziegler Steel Service Corp.**
7000 Van Dini Blvd.
Los Angeles, CA 90040
Phone: (213)726-7000
Products: Steel beams and other steel products. **SIC:**
5051 (Metals Service Centers & Offices). **Sales:**
$330,000,000 (1992). **Emp:** 450. **Officers:** G.H.
Ziegler, President; R.A. McDonald, VP of Finance.

■ **8255** ■ **Zumpano Enterprises Inc.**
6354 Warren Dr.
Norcross, GA 30093
Phone: (770)449-3528 **Fax:** (770)446-0294
Products: Floorcovering equipment and supplies. **SIC:**
5032 (Brick, Stone & Related Materials). **Sales:**
$13,000,000 (2000). **Emp:** 60.

(14) Electrical and Electronic Equipment and Supplies

Entries in this section are arranged alphabetically by company name. When the company name is a personal name, the company name is alphabetized by the surname unless the first name or initial(s) are part of a trade name. See the User's Guide at the front of this directory for additional information.

■ **8256** ■ **21st Century Telecom Group**
350 N Orleans St.
Chicago, IL 60654-1509
Phone: (312)955-2100
Free: (888)790-2121 **Fax:** (312)955-2111
Products: Cable television, Internet connection, and telephone service. **SIC:** 5065 (Electronic Parts & Equipment Nec). **Officers:** Robert Currey, CEO & President; Ronald Webster, CFO.

■ **8257** ■ **A and L Distributing Co.**
13970 SW 72nd Ave.
Portland, OR 97223
Phone: (503)684-9384 **Fax:** (503)684-5574
Products: Consumer electronics products. **SIC:** 5064 (Electrical Appliances—Television & Radio). **Sales:** $9,000,000 (2000). **Emp:** 21. **Officers:** W. James Cox, President & CFO.

■ **8258** ■ **AARP Inc.**
6019 Goshen Springs Rd.
Norcross, GA 30071-3502
Phone: (404)446-0400 **Fax:** (404)242-9295
Products: Electronic systems and equipment; Electronic parts; Refrigeration and air conditioning equipment; Heating equipment. **SICs:** 5065 (Electronic Parts & Equipment Nec); 5075 (Warm Air Heating & Air-Conditioning); 5064 (Electrical Appliances—Television & Radio). **Officers:** Donald Meyer, President.

■ **8259** ■ **Abacon Electronics Corp.**
PO Box 4565
Greensboro, NC 27404-4565
Phone: (910)275-5655 **Fax:** (910)376-1244
Products: Electronic parts and equipment; Telephone parts and equipment. **SIC:** 5065 (Electronic Parts & Equipment Nec). **Officers:** Harry Friedman, President.

■ **8260** ■ **ABB Pressure Systems Inc.**
501 Merritt 7, No. 5308
Norwalk, CT 06851-7000
Phone: (203)329-8771 **Fax:** (203)328-2263
Products: Electrical equipment and supplies. **SIC:** 5063 (Electrical Apparatus & Equipment). **Est:** 1949. **Sales:** $75,000,000 (2000). **Emp:** 1,400. **Officers:** J.J. Ohara.

■ **8261** ■ **Accu Tech Cable Inc.**
200 Hembree Park Dr.
Roswell, GA 30076-3868
Phone: (404)751-9473
Free: (800)221-4767 **Fax:** (404)475-4659
Products: Wire and cable. **SIC:** 5063 (Electrical Apparatus & Equipment). **Est:** 1983. **Sales:** $14,000,000 (2000). **Emp:** 53. **Officers:** Barry Heidt, President; Dan Delanie, Exec. VP; Randy Guhl, VP of Sales; Bill Lorey, VP of Operations; Bobby Dickson; Charles Goldgeier, CFO; Brian Henry.

■ **8262** ■ **Ace Electric Supply Co.**
5911 Phillips Hwy.
Jacksonville, FL 32216
Phone: (904)731-5900
Products: Electrical equipment and supplies. **SIC:** 5063 (Electrical Apparatus & Equipment). **Est:** 1931.

Sales: $58,000,000 (2000). **Emp:** 220. **Officers:** Barry Covington, Chairman of the Board; James Swindell, CFO.

■ **8263** ■ **ACF Components and Fasteners, Inc.**
31012 Huntwood Ave.
Hayward, CA 94544
Phone: (510)487-2100
Free: (800)227-2901 **Fax:** (510)471-7018
E-mail: acfcom@hotmail.com
URL: http://www.acfcom.com
Products: Fasteners and electronic components. **SICs:** 5072 (Hardware); 5065 (Electronic Parts & Equipment Nec). **Est:** 1976. **Sales:** $13,000,000 (2000). **Emp:** 62. **Officers:** Paul Rees, President & CEO; Wayne Jaton, VP/Chief Financial Officer/General Mgr.; Don Olander, Exec. VP. **Former Name:** AROW Components and Fasteners Inc.

■ **8264** ■ **Ack Electronics**
554 Deering Rd. NW
Atlanta, GA 30309-2267
Phone: (404)351-6340 **Free:** (800)282-7954
URL: http://www.acksupply.com
Products: Electronic parts; Electronic systems and equipment. **SIC:** 5065 (Electronic Parts & Equipment Nec). **Est:** 1946. **Emp:** 10. **Officers:** Steve Atkerson, President.

■ **8265** ■ **Ackerman Electrical Supply Co.**
131 Grand Trunk Ave.
Battle Creek, MI 49015
Phone: (616)459-8327 **Fax:** (616)963-5606
Products: Industrial switches; Computer systems; Flourescent lighting. **SICs:** 5063 (Electrical Apparatus & Equipment); 5065 (Electronic Parts & Equipment Nec). **Est:** 1973. **Sales:** $30,000,000 (2000). **Emp:** 80. **Officers:** Axel Johnson, President; James Treadwell, VP of Finance; Mike Rabe, Dir. of Marketing.

■ **8266** ■ **ACL Inc.**
2151 Bering Dr.
San Jose, CA 95131
Phone: (408)432-0270 **Fax:** (408)432-0273
Products: Computer components. **SIC:** 5065 (Electronic Parts & Equipment Nec). **Officers:** Larry Lo, President.

■ **8267** ■ **Acme Electric Supply Inc.**
2737 Central Ave.
Columbus, IN 47201
Phone: (812)372-8871 **Fax:** (812)372-0075
Products: Heating and cooling equipment and supplies. **SIC:** 5063 (Electrical Apparatus & Equipment). **Sales:** $3,000,000 (2000). **Emp:** 18.

■ **8268** ■ **Acro Electronics Corp.**
1101 W Chicago Ave.
East Chicago, IN 46312
Phone: (219)397-8681
Free: (800)288-2276 **Fax:** (219)397-2068
Products: Electronic parts and components. **SIC:** 5065 (Electronic Parts & Equipment Nec). **Sales:** $2,000,000 (2000). **Emp:** 6. **Officers:** J.A. Garcia, President.

■ **8269** ■ **ACT Services Inc.**
916 Pleasant St.
Norwood, MA 02062
Phone: (781)255-0978 **Fax:** (781)762-6580
Products: Wires, including water meter wire. **SIC:** 5063 (Electrical Apparatus & Equipment). **Est:** 1990. **Sales:** $2,000,000 (2000). **Emp:** 5. **Officers:** Ann C. Travis, President.

■ **8270** ■ **Action Communications Inc.**
2816 N Stone Ave.
Tucson, AZ 85705
Phone: (520)792-0326 **Fax:** (520)792-2709
Products: Two-way radio communications equipment; Repairs and rents radio equipment. **SIC:** 5065 (Electronic Parts & Equipment Nec).

■ **8271** ■ **Action Electric Sales Co.**
3900 N Rockwell St.
Chicago, IL 60618
Phone: (312)266-2600 **Fax:** (312)539-1800
Products: Wire and cable. **SIC:** 5063 (Electrical Apparatus & Equipment). **Est:** 1955. **Sales:** $10,000,000 (2000). **Emp:** 50. **Officers:** Philip Garoon, President.

■ **8272** ■ **Active Electrical Supply Co.**
4240 W Lawrence Ave.
Chicago, IL 60630
Phone: (312)282-6300 **Fax:** (312)282-5206
Products: Light fixtures. **SIC:** 5063 (Electrical Apparatus & Equipment). **Est:** 1953. **Sales:** $27,000,000 (2000). **Emp:** 80. **Officers:** H.C. Fox, President; Donald Huebner, Treasurer.

■ **8273** ■ **Adirondack Electronics Inc.**
PO Box 12759
Albany, NY 12212
Phone: (518)456-0203 **Fax:** (518)456-0887
E-mail: adelinc@logical.net
URL: http://www.AdirondackElectronics.com
Products: Computer wires; Terminal blocks; Cable ties; Networking accessories. **SIC:** 5063 (Electrical Apparatus & Equipment). **Est:** 1958. **Sales:** $3,000,000 (1999). **Emp:** 13. **Officers:** H. Douglas Hinkle, President; Margaret Hinkle, VP & Secty.; Kristin Hinkle, Sales/Marketing Contact, e-mail: khinkle@adelinc.com.

■ **8274** ■ **Advance Electrical Supply Co.**
263 N Oakley Blvd.
Chicago, IL 60612
Phone: (312)421-2300 **Fax:** (312)421-0926
E-mail: sales@advanceelectrical.com
URL: http://www.advanceelectrical.com
Products: Electrical supplies, including wire, conduit, and panel boards. **SIC:** 5063 (Electrical Apparatus & Equipment). **Est:** 1945. **Sales:** $20,000,000 (1999). **Emp:** 50. **Officers:** Steven Anixter, President; Kay Wolbrink, Controller; Dave Neubauer, Vice President; Scott Eubanks, MIS Mgr.

■ 8275 ■ Advent Electronics Inc.
2400 E Devon Ave., Ste. 205
Des Plaines, IL 60018
Phone: (847)297-6200 **Fax:** (847)297-6650
Products: Electronic components. **SIC:** 5065
(Electronic Parts & Equipment Nec). **Sales:**
$32,000,000 (2000). **Emp:** 110. **Officers:** Mark
Piepenbrink, President; Steve Starykovic, Controller.

■ 8276 ■ Adventure Lighting Supply Ltd.
90 Washington Ave.
Des Moines, IA 50314
Phone: (515)288-0444
Products: Lamps and lighting fixtures. **SIC:** 5063
(Electrical Apparatus & Equipment). **Sales:** $3,000,000
(2000). **Emp:** 8. **Officers:** Ed McCollom, President.

■ 8277 ■ AEI Electronic Parts
224 Washington Ave. N
Minneapolis, MN 55401
Phone: (612)338-4754
Free: (800)328-0270 **Fax:** (612)338-1102
URL: http://www.members.aol.com/aeimn
Products: Electronic parts and equipment. **SICs:** 5063
(Electrical Apparatus & Equipment); 5065 (Electronic
Parts & Equipment Nec); 5064 (Electrical Appliances—
Television & Radio). **Est:** 1950. **Emp:** 20. **Alternate
Name:** Acme Electronics, Inc.

■ 8278 ■ Aero-K.A.P. Inc.
PO Box 661240
Arcadia, CA 91066
Phone: (818)574-1704 **Fax:** (818)446-8630
Products: Wire and cable. **SIC:** 5063 (Electrical
Apparatus & Equipment). **Est:** 1969. **Sales:**
$1,000,000 (2000). **Emp:** 6. **Officers:** R.E. Stabler,
President & Treasurer.

■ 8279 ■ Aero-Motive Co.
PO Box 2678
Kalamazoo, MI 49003
Phone: (616)381-1242 **Fax:** (616)382-3086
Products: Electric cable and cords, slip rings,
conductor bars, festoon systems, hose reels, and tool
balancers. **SIC:** 5085 (Industrial Supplies). **Sales:**
$26,000,000 (2000). **Emp:** 200. **Officers:** Charles
Andersen, President; David Bastos, Controller.

■ 8280 ■ Aerospace Materials Corp.
1940 Petra Ln., No. D
Placentia, CA 92870-6750
Phone: (714)863-0811
Products: Interconnect materials, including wire and
cable. **SIC:** 5063 (Electrical Apparatus & Equipment).
Est: 1980. **Sales:** $1,000,000 (2000). **Emp:** 8.
Officers: Gerald Deland, President.

■ 8281 ■ Aerospace Southwest
21450 N 3rd Ave.
Phoenix, AZ 85027
Phone: (602)582-2779
Free: (800)289-2779 **Fax:** (602)582-2019
Products: Electrical hanging and fastening devices.
SIC: 5063 (Electrical Apparatus & Equipment).

■ 8282 ■ AGM Electronics Inc.
PO Box 32227
Tucson, AZ 85751
Phone: (520)722-1000 **Fax:** (520)722-1045
Products: Electronic components. **SIC:** 5065
(Electronic Parts & Equipment Nec).

■ 8283 ■ Air Electro Inc.
9452 De Soto Ave.
Chatsworth, CA 91311-2231
Phone: (818)407-5400 **Fax:** (818)407-5460
Products: Cylindrical connectors, contacts, and back
shelves. **SIC:** 5065 (Electronic Parts & Equipment
Nec). **Est:** 1953. **Sales:** $10,000,000 (2000). **Emp:** 38.
Officers: Steve Strull, President; William Strull, Vice
President; Todd Walk, Dir. of Marketing & Sales; Sara
Monsour, Dir. of Systems.

■ 8284 ■ Airtechnics Inc.
230 Ida
PO Box 3466
Wichita, KS 67201-3466
Phone: (316)267-2849
Free: (800)544-4070 **Fax:** (316)267-1482
E-mail: sales@airtechnics.com
URL: http://www.airtechnics.com
Products: Electronic parts and equipment, including
aviation, relays, switches, lamps, connectors, LEDs,
and remote control breakers. **SIC:** 5065 (Electronic
Parts & Equipment Nec). **Est:** 1957. **Sales:**
$56,000,000 (1999). **Emp:** 98. **Officers:** Ronald Mann,
President.

■ 8285 ■ Airtechnics Inc.
230 Ida
Wichita, KS 67201-3466
Phone: (316)267-2849
Free: (800)544-4070 **Fax:** (316)267-1482
Products: Electrical and electronic equipment and
supplies. **SIC:** 5065 (Electronic Parts & Equipment
Nec). **Sales:** $40,000,000 (2000). **Emp:** 53.

■ 8286 ■ Alaska General Alarm Inc.
405 W 27th Ave.
Anchorage, AK 99503-2612
Phone: (907)279-8511
Free: (800)770-8511 **Fax:** (907)279-9319
Products: Security and safety equipment. **SIC:** 5063
(Electrical Apparatus & Equipment). **Sales:** $3,000,000
(2000). **Emp:** 49.

■ 8287 ■ Alaska Quality Control Services
184 E 53rd Ave.
Anchorage, AK 99518-1222
Phone: (907)562-6439 **Fax:** (907)563-1318
Products: Electronic parts and equipment;
Communication equipment. **SIC:** 5065 (Electronic Parts
& Equipment Nec). **Officers:** Jim Taylor, President.

■ 8288 ■ Albertville Electric Motor
6621 U.S Hwy. 431
Albertville, AL 35950
Phone: (256)878-0491
Products: Electric motors, pumps, and generators.
SIC: 5063 (Electrical Apparatus & Equipment).

■ 8289 ■ Aleph International
1026 Griswold Ave.
San Fernando, CA 91340
Phone: (818)365-9856 **Fax:** (818)365-7274
Products: Relays, industrial controls and electronic
components; Security equipment. **SIC:** 5063 (Electrical
Apparatus & Equipment).

■ 8290 ■ Steve Alexander
124 2nd St. SE
Huron, SD 57350-2045
Phone: (605)352-6941
Free: (800)529-0053 **Fax:** (605)352-8059
E-mail: freddies@basec.net
Products: Electric motors. **SIC:** 5063 (Electrical
Apparatus & Equipment). **Est:** 1979. **Sales:** $170,000
(2000). **Emp:** 3. **Officers:** Steve Alexander, Owner.

■ 8291 ■ All American Semiconductor Inc.
16085 NW 52nd Ave.
Miami, FL 33014
Phone: (305)621-8282 **Fax:** (305)620-7831
Products: Semiconductors. **SIC:** 5065 (Electronic
Parts & Equipment Nec). **Est:** 1964. **Sales:**
$101,100,000 (2000). **Emp:** 340. **Officers:** Paul
Goldberg, CEO & Chairman of the Board; Howard L.
Flanders, VP & CFO; Rick Gordon, VP of Sales; Bob
Srdoch, Information Systems Mgr.; Denise Stolarik, Dir
of Human Resources.

■ 8292 ■ All Appliance Parts Inc.
40 Austin Blvd.
Commack, NY 11725
Phone: (516)543-4000 **Fax:** (516)864-6270
Products: Repair parts for major appliances. **SIC:**
5085 (Industrial Supplies). **Sales:** $12,000,000 (1994).
Emp: 100. **Officers:** Elliott Jonas, President; Rich
Kucera, Sr. VP & Finance Officer.

■ 8293 ■ All Phase Electric Supply
539 Union St.
Spartanburg, SC 29301-4469
Phone: (864)585-0103 **Fax:** (864)583-8366
Products: Electrical equipment and supplies. **SIC:**
5063 (Electrical Apparatus & Equipment). **Emp:** 10.
Officers: Ron Kinney, President; Vic Baldwin,
Manager.

■ 8294 ■ All Phase Electric Supply
731 N Market Blvd.
Sacramento, CA 95834-1211
Phone: (916)648-0134
Free: (800)535-7373 **Fax:** (916)923-9742
Products: Electrical supplies for new construction and
plant maintenance. **SIC:** 5063 (Electrical Apparatus &
Equipment). **Emp:** 20. **Officers:** Eric Schuller, Area
Mgr.; Don McKay, Area Operations Mgr.; Don Rainey,
Area Design Specialist.

■ 8295 ■ All Phase Electric Supply Co.
875 Riverview Dr.
Benton Harbor, MI 49022
Phone: (616)926-6194 **Fax:** (616)926-0077
Products: Electrical supplies, including light fixtures.
SIC: 5063 (Electrical Apparatus & Equipment). **Est:**
1959. **Sales:** $510,000,000 (2000). **Emp:** 1,850.
Officers: Ronald F. Kinney, President; William Vegter,
CFO; Frank Wimbush, VP of Marketing; Dick Lewis,
Dir. of Systems; Shaz Khan.

■ 8296 ■ All Spec Static Control Inc.
PO Box 1200
Wilmington, NC 28402-1200
Phone: (910)763-8111
Free: (800)537-0351 **Fax:** (910)763-5664
E-mail: agr@allspec.com
URL: http://www.allspec.com
Products: ESD and static control products. **SIC:** 5065
(Electronic Parts & Equipment Nec). **Est:** 1988. **Emp:**
28. **Officers:** Arthur G. Rice Sr., President.

■ 8297 ■ All Systems Inc.
3241 N 7th St. Trfy.
Kansas City, KS 66115-1105
Phone: (913)677-5333 **Fax:** (913)432-8400
Products: Electronic parts and equipment, including
communication equipment. **SIC:** 5065 (Electronic Parts
& Equipment Nec). **Officers:** Gary Venable, President.

■ 8298 ■ Allen Avionics, Inc.
224 E 2nd. St.
Box 350
Mineola, NY 11501
Phone: (516)248-8080 **Fax:** (516)747-6724
Products: Filters and delay lines. **SIC:** 5065
(Electronic Parts & Equipment Nec). **Officers:** A.K.
Allen, President; Richard Mintz, Vice President; James
Lyons.

■ 8299 ■ Allen Electric Supply Co.
31750 Plymouth Rd.
Livonia, MI 48151-1906
Phone: (734)421-9300 **Fax:** (734)421-0186
Products: Electrical supplies. **SIC:** 5063 (Electrical
Apparatus & Equipment). **Emp:** 49. **Officers:** Norman
Horowitz.

■ 8300 ■ Allied Electronics
7410 Pebble Dr.
Ft. Worth, TX 76118
Phone: (817)595-3500
Free: (800)433-5700 **Fax:** (817)595-6444
Products: Electronic components. **SICs:** 5065
(Electronic Parts & Equipment Nec); 5065 (Electronic
Parts & Equipment Nec). **Est:** 1920. **Emp:** 499.

■ 8301 ■ Allied Electronics
154 Technology Pkwy., Ste. 280
Norcross, GA 30092
Phone: (770)242-0699
Free: (800)433-5700 **Fax:** (770)242-0899
URL: http://www.alliedelec.com
Products: Electronic products and supplies, including
semi-conductors, head sets, batteries, fuses, relays,
power supplies, fans, wire cables, and motors. **SICs:**
5065 (Electronic Parts & Equipment Nec); 5064
(Electrical Appliances—Television & Radio); 5063
(Electrical Apparatus & Equipment). **Est:** 1989. **Sales:**

$120,000,000 (2000). Emp: 460. Officers: Brenda Moss, Branch Mgr., e-mail: brenda.moss@alliedelec.com.

■ 8302 ■ Allied Electronics
7134 Columbia Gateway Dr., Ste. 200
Columbia, MD 21046
Phone: (410)312-0810   Free: (800)433-5700
Products: Electronic equipment, including resistors, capacitors, transistors, fuses, relays, fans, headsets, semi-conductors, wire cables, batteries, transformers, and power supplies. SIC: 5065 (Electronic Parts & Equipment Nec). Officers: Pat Salerno, Sales Mgr.

■ 8303 ■ Allied Electronics
1580 S Milwaukee Ave., Ste 408
Libertyville, IL 60048
Phone: (847)918-0250
Free: (800)433-5700   Fax: (847)918-0247
Products: Electronic products, including fuses, relays, power supplies, fans, batteries, wire cables, motors, semi-conductors, and head sets. SIC: 5063 (Electrical Apparatus & Equipment). Officers: Toni Masella, Sales Mgr.

■ 8304 ■ Allied Electronics
260 Northland Blvd., Ste. 213
Cincinnati, OH 45246
Phone: (513)771-6990
Free: (800)433-5700   Fax: (513)771-7604
Products: Electronic products, including light item electric units, power supplies, and batteries. SIC: 5063 (Electrical Apparatus & Equipment).

■ 8305 ■ Allied Electronics
5755 Granger Rd., Ste. 756
Independence, OH 44131-1459
Phone: (216)831-4900
Free: (800)433-5700   Fax: (216)831-2339
Products: Electronic components. SIC: 5065 (Electronic Parts & Equipment Nec). Officers: Scott Cairns, Sales Mgr.

■ 8306 ■ Allied Electronics
659 Lakeview Plaza Blvd., Ste. A
Worthington, OH 43085-4775
Phone: (614)785-1270
Free: (800)433-5700   Fax: (614)785-1277
Products: Electronic supplies. SIC: 5065 (Electronic Parts & Equipment Nec). Officers: Cheri Gilroy, Sales Mgr.

■ 8307 ■ Allied Electronics
9550 Forest Ln., Ste. 511
Dallas, TX 75243
Phone: (214)553-4370
Free: (800)433-5700   Fax: (214)553-4383
Products: Electronic equipment and supplies, including wire, cable, tubing, and computer parts. SIC: 5063 (Electrical Apparatus & Equipment). Officers: Nancy Morrison, Sales Mgr.

■ 8308 ■ Allied Electronics
32180 Schoolcraft Rd.
Livonia, MI 48150
Phone: (734)266-0660
Free: (800)433-5700   Fax: (734)266-0670
URL: http://www.Alliedelec.com
Products: Electronic products. SIC: 5065 (Electronic Parts & Equipment Nec). Est: 1929. Sales: $120,000,000 (2000). Emp: 460. Officers: J.D. Flack, Sales Mgr., e-mail: jd.flack@alliedelec.com.

■ 8309 ■ Allied Electronics
7500 Viscount, Ste. 118
El Paso, TX 79925
Phone: (915)779-6294
Free: (800)433-5700   Fax: (915)778-6212
URL: http://www.alliedelec.com
Products: Electronic products. SIC: 5065 (Electronic Parts & Equipment Nec). Officers: Juan Galceran, Sales Mgr.; Alfredo R. Higuera, Branch Mgr., e-mail: alfredo.higuera@alliedelec.com.

■ 8310 ■ Allied Electronics
5500 Northland Dr. NE
Grand Rapids, MI 49505
Phone: (616)365-9960
Free: (800)433-5700   Fax: (616)365-9895
Products: Electronic products. SIC: 5065 (Electronic Parts & Equipment Nec). Officers: Greg Widey, Sales Mgr.

■ 8311 ■ Allied Electronics
2421 W 205 St., Ste. D-206B
Torrance, CA 90505
Phone: (310)783-0601   Fax: (310)783-0678
Products: Electronic components. SIC: 5065 (Electronic Parts & Equipment Nec). Officers: Davell Stewart, Sales Mgr.

■ 8312 ■ Allied Electronics
2448 S 102nd St., Ste. 150
West Allis, WI 53227
Phone: (414)543-3372
Free: (800)433-5700   Fax: (414)543-3272
URL: http://www.alliedelec.com
Products: Electronic products. SIC: 5065 (Electronic Parts & Equipment Nec). Est: 1932. Sales: $10,000,000 (2000). Emp: 400. Officers: Penny Scheel, Manager.

■ 8313 ■ Allied Electronics
6110 Blue Circle Dr., Ste. 220
Minnetonka, MN 55343
Phone: (612)938-5633
Free: (800)433-5700   Fax: (612)938-5992
Products: Electronic components. SIC: 5065 (Electronic Parts & Equipment Nec). Officers: Shirley Kippenhan, Sales Mgr.

■ 8314 ■ Allied Electronics
2970 Cottage Hill Rd.
Bell Air Park, Ste. 174
Mobile, AL 36606
Phone: (205)476-1875
Free: (800)433-5700   Fax: (205)473-4325
Products: Electronic components. SIC: 5065 (Electronic Parts & Equipment Nec). Officers: Brenda Strickland, Sales Mgr.

■ 8315 ■ Allied Electronics
860 U.S. Rte. 1, North
Edison, NJ 08817
Phone: (732)572-9600
Free: (800)433-5700   Fax: (732)572-9608
Products: Electronics. SIC: 5065 (Electronic Parts & Equipment Nec). Officers: Diana Lenz, Sales Mgr.

■ 8316 ■ Allied Electronics
10824 Old Mill Rd., Ste. 5
Omaha, NE 68154
Phone: (402)697-0038
Free: (800)433-5700   Fax: (402)697-0238
URL: http://www.allied.avnet.com
Products: Industrial electronics components. SIC: 5065 (Electronic Parts & Equipment Nec). Est: 1920. Officers: Cathy Olson, Sales Mgr.

■ 8317 ■ Allied Electronics
140 Technology, Ste. 400
Irvine, CA 92618-2426
Phone: (949)727-3010
Free: (800)433-5700   Fax: (949)727-2092
Products: Electronics. SIC: 5065 (Electronic Parts & Equipment Nec). Est: 1928. Sales: $120,000,000 (2000). Emp: 300. Officers: Chris Winfield, Sales Mgr.

■ 8318 ■ Allied Electronics
2111 E Baseball Rd., No. F3
Tempe, AZ 85283
Phone: (480)831-2002   Free: (800)433-5700
Products: Electronic equipment. SIC: 5065 (Electronic Parts & Equipment Nec). Officers: Vickie Burns, Sales Mgr.

■ 8319 ■ Allied Electronics
9750 SW Nimbus Ave.
Beaverton, OR 97005
Phone: (503)626-9921   Fax: (503)627-0404
Products: Electronic components. SIC: 5065 (Electronic Parts & Equipment Nec). Officers: Sandy Heup, Sales Mgr.

■ 8320 ■ Allied Electronics
22 Freedom Plains Rd., Ste. 138
Poughkeepsie, NY 12603-2670
Phone: (914)452-1470
Free: (800)433-5700   Fax: (914)452-1448
Products: Electronic equipment, including hardware. SIC: 5065 (Electronic Parts & Equipment Nec). Officers: Tina Hennes, Sales Mgr.

■ 8321 ■ Allied Electronics
5236 Greens Dairy Rd.
Raleigh, NC 27604
Phone: (919)876-5845
Free: (800)433-5700   Fax: (919)790-7647
Products: Electronic components; Broadline components. SIC: 5065 (Electronic Parts & Equipment Nec). Officers: Alan Brasof, Sales Mgr.

■ 8322 ■ Allied Electronics
580 Menlo Dr., Ste. 2
Rocklin, CA 95765
Phone: (916)632-3104   Fax: (916)632-0609
Products: Capacitors; Tools; Wires; Batteries; Computer products; Connectors. SICs: 5065 (Electronic Parts & Equipment Nec); 5063 (Electrical Apparatus & Equipment); 5072 (Hardware). Officers: Terry Carson, Sales Mgr.

■ 8323 ■ Allied Electronics
156 S Spruce, No. 204
South San Francisco, CA 94080
Phone: (650)952-9599   Fax: (650)952-4716
Products: Electronic components. SICs: 5065 (Electronic Parts & Equipment Nec); 5063 (Electrical Apparatus & Equipment). Officers: Harold Joseph, Sales Mgr.

■ 8324 ■ Allied Electronics
7406 Alban Station Ct., Ste. 211
Springfield, VA 22150
Phone: (703)644-9515
Free: (800)433-5700   Fax: (703)644-2294
URL: http://www.alliedelec.com
Products: Electronic components. SIC: 5065 (Electronic Parts & Equipment Nec). Officers: Virginia Moore, Sales Mgr.

■ 8325 ■ Allied Electronics
4525 E Honeygrove Rd., Ste. 201
Virginia Beach, VA 23455
Phone: (757)363-8662
Free: (800)433-5700   Fax: (757)363-9703
Products: Electronics equipment. SIC: 5065 (Electronic Parts & Equipment Nec). Officers: Lance Gardner, Sales Mgr.

■ 8326 ■ Allied Electronics
32180 Schoolcraft
Livonia, MI 48150
Free: (800)433-5700
Products: Electronic products. SIC: 5065 (Electronic Parts & Equipment Nec). Officers: Stephanie Bach, Sales Mgr.

■ 8327 ■ Allied Electronics Corp.
4530 McKnight Rd.
Pittsburgh, PA 15237-3162
Phone: (412)931-2774
Free: (800)433-5700   Fax: (412)367-0166
Products: Electronics, including resistors, conductors, and capacitors. SIC: 5065 (Electronic Parts & Equipment Nec). Officers: Joe Smonskey, Sales Mgr.

■ 8328 ■ Allied Electronics, Inc.
7410 Pebble Dr.
Ft. Worth, TX 76118
Phone: (817)595-3500
Free: (800)433-5700   Fax: (817)595-6444
URL: http://www.alliedelec.com
Products: Electronic parts; Electronic components. SIC: 5065 (Electronic Parts & Equipment Nec). Est: 1995. Officers: Sharon Miles, Sales Mgr.

■ 8329 ■ Allied-National Inc.
13270 Capital St.
Oak Park, MI 48237-3107
Phone: (248)543-1232   Fax: (248)543-9838
Products: Electronic parts; Electronic systems and

equipment. **SIC:** 5065 (Electronic Parts & Equipment Nec). **Officers:** Robert Zeman, President.

■ 8330 ■ Alpha-Omega Sales Corp.
325 Main St.
North Reading, MA 01864-1360
Phone: (978)664-1118 **Fax:** (978)664-3212
Products: Electronic systems and equipment; Electronic parts. **SIC:** 5065 (Electronic Parts & Equipment Nec). **Officers:** Vincent Sabella, President.

■ 8331 ■ Alpha Source Inc.
12104 West Carmen Ave.
Milwaukee, WI 53225
Phone: (414)760-2222
Free: (800)654-9845 **Fax:** (414)760-2070
E-mail: alphasource@worldnet.att.net
URL: http://www.alphasource.com
Products: Replacement bulbs, specialty lamps, and used micrographic and imaging equipment, batteries, and battery packs. **SICs:** 5063 (Electrical Apparatus & Equipment); 5065 (Electronic Parts & Equipment Nec); 5044 (Office Equipment). **Est:** 1986. **Sales:** $3,500,000 (2000). **Emp:** 16. **Officers:** Norine C. Weber, President.

■ 8332 ■ Alpha Wire Co.
711 Lidgerwood Ave.
Elizabeth, NJ 07207-0711
Phone: (908)925-8000
Free: (800)52A-LPHA **Fax:** (908)925-6923
E-mail: info@alphawire.com
URL: http://www.alphawire.com
Products: Wire; Cable; Tubing products. **SIC:** 5063 (Electrical Apparatus & Equipment). **Est:** 1922. **Emp:** 125. **Officers:** Paul M. Schlessman, General Mgr.; Allan Marconi, VP of Marketing & Sales.

■ 8333 ■ Altex-Mar Electronics Inc.
17201 Westfield Park Rd.
Westfield, IN 46074
Phone: (317)867-4000
Free: (800)783-2589 **Fax:** (317)867-2505
E-mail: customerservice@altex-mar.com
URL: http://www.altex-mar.com
Products: Passive and electro-mechanical electronic components; Cable and harness assemblies. **SIC:** 5065 (Electronic Parts & Equipment Nec). **Est:** 1981. **Sales:** $10,000,000 (2000). **Emp:** 40. **Officers:** Ben Weidberg, President, e-mail: ben@altex-mar.com.

■ 8334 ■ Amano Partners USA Inc.
140 Harrison Ave.
Roseland, NJ 07068
Phone: (973)227-8256
Products: Electrical apparatus. **SIC:** 5063 (Electrical Apparatus & Equipment). **Sales:** $72,000,000 (2000). **Emp:** 390. **Officers:** Ujnichi Minamoto, President.

■ 8335 ■ Amateur Electronics Supply
5710 W Good Hope Rd.
Milwaukee, WI 53223
Phone: (414)358-0333 **Fax:** (414)358-3337
Products: Electronic supplies. **SIC:** 5065 (Electronic Parts & Equipment Nec).

■ 8336 ■ America II Electronics
2600 118th Ave. N
St. Petersburg, FL 33716
Phone: (813)573-0900
Products: Integrated circuits and semiconductors. **SIC:** 5065 (Electronic Parts & Equipment Nec).

■ 8337 ■ American Communications Co.
180 Roberts St.
East Hartford, CT 06108
Phone: (860)289-3491 **Fax:** (860)289-7639
Products: Circuit boards. **SIC:** 5065 (Electronic Parts & Equipment Nec). **Est:** 1979. **Sales:** $15,000,000 (2000). **Emp:** 100. **Officers:** Stuart Sandler, President.

■ 8338 ■ American Contex Corp.
964 3rd Ave.
New York, NY 10155
Phone: (212)421-5430 **Fax:** (212)838-4615
Products: Electric motors and industrial roller chains. **SIC:** 5063 (Electrical Apparatus & Equipment). **Est:** 1965. **Sales:** $6,000,000 (2000). **Emp:** 70. **Officers:** Wolfgang A. Herz, President.

■ 8339 ■ American Electric Co.
911 S Stilwell
Pittsburg, KS 66762-5955
Phone: (316)231-3080 **Fax:** (316)232-9378
Products: Electrical components and supplies, including wires and cables. **SIC:** 5063 (Electrical Apparatus & Equipment). **Emp:** 8.

■ 8340 ■ American Electric Co.
302 N 3rd St.
PO Box 878
St. Joseph, MO 64502
Phone: (816)279-7405
Free: (800)289-7421 **Fax:** (816)364-2088
E-mail: aeco@americanelectric.com
URL: http://www.americanelectric.com
Products: Electrical supplies. **SIC:** 5063 (Electrical Apparatus & Equipment). **Est:** 1897. **Emp:** 49.

■ 8341 ■ American Electric Co.
115 SE Cholwell Ave.
Bartlesville, OK 74006-2302
Phone: (918)333-2596 **Fax:** (918)333-8460
Products: Electrical equipment and supplies. **SIC:** 5063 (Electrical Apparatus & Equipment). **Emp:** 7.

■ 8342 ■ American Electric Co.
PO Box 878
St. Joseph, MO 64502
Phone: (816)279-7405 **Fax:** (816)233-6338
URL: http://www.Americanelectric.com
Products: Electrical supplies. **SIC:** 5063 (Electrical Apparatus & Equipment). **Est:** 1897. **Emp:** 254. **Officers:** Louie DeLeon, Division Manager; Brad Haynes, Division Operations Manager.

■ 8343 ■ American Electric Supply
778 Albany St.
Schenectady, NY 12307-1324
Phone: (518)377-8509 **Fax:** (518)346-1327
Products: Electrical supplies. **SIC:** 5063 (Electrical Apparatus & Equipment). **Est:** 1955. **Emp:** 30. **Officers:** Dan Briskie.

■ 8344 ■ American Fluorescent Corp.
2345 Ernie Krueger Cir.
Waukegan, IL 60087
Phone: (847)249-5970 **Fax:** (847)249-2618
Products: Fluorescent light fixtures. **SIC:** 5063 (Electrical Apparatus & Equipment). **Est:** 1938. **Sales:** $35,000,000 (2000). **Emp:** 175. **Officers:** William Solomon, President; Tom Dicks, Dir. of Mktg. & Sales.

■ 8345 ■ Ametron
1546 N Argyle Ave.
Hollywood, CA 90028
Phones: (323)466-4321 (323)464-1144
  (323)462-1200 **Fax:** (323)871-0127
E-mail: info@ametron.com
URL: http://www.ametron.com
Products: Electronic parts. **SIC:** 5065 (Electronic Parts & Equipment Nec). **Est:** 1952. **Sales:** $2,000,000 (2000). **Emp:** 99. **Officers:** Maurice I. Rosenthal, President.

■ 8346 ■ Amherst Electrical Supply
1591 State Hwy. 38
Mt. Holly, NJ 08060-2751
Phone: (609)267-0900 **Fax:** (609)267-2932
Products: Lighting fixtures; Distribution panels; Wiring devices. **SIC:** 5063 (Electrical Apparatus & Equipment). **Emp:** 9. **Officers:** C. J. Nicodemus.

■ 8347 ■ Amidon Associates Inc.
PO Box 25867
Santa Ana, CA 92799
Phone: (714)850-4660 **Fax:** (714)850-1163
Products: Transformer cores and inductors. **SIC:** 5065 (Electronic Parts & Equipment Nec).

■ 8348 ■ Amkor Technology
1900 S Price Rd.
Chandler, AZ 85248
Phone: (480)821-5000 **Fax:** (480)821-2255
Products: Integrated circuit packaging for OEM semiconductors (sales and design). **SIC:** 5065 (Electronic Parts & Equipment Nec). **Officers:** John Boruch, President.

■ 8349 ■ AMP King Battery Company Inc.
10 Loomis St.
San Francisco, CA 94124
Phone: (415)648-7650 **Fax:** (415)648-0333
Products: Storage batteries. **SIC:** 5063 (Electrical Apparatus & Equipment). **Sales:** $5,000,000 (2000). **Emp:** 12. **Officers:** Brad Streelman, Owner; Kurt Streelman, CFO.

■ 8350 ■ Amway Corp.
7575 Fulton St. E
Ada, MI 49355-0001
Phone: (616)787-6000 **Fax:** (616)787-6177
Products: Consumer goods and electronics. **SICs:** 5149 (Groceries & Related Products Nec); 5064 (Electrical Appliances—Television & Radio). **Sales:** $5,700,000,000 (2000). **Emp:** 14,000. **Officers:** Richard M. DeVos, President; Lawrence Call, Sr. VP of Finance & Treasurer.

■ 8351 ■ Anderson and Associates Inc.
3007 N Slappey Blvd.
Albany, GA 31707
Phone: (912)436-4651
Products: Electronic parts and equipment; Mechanical constructions. **SIC:** 5065 (Electronic Parts & Equipment Nec). **Officers:** John Gay, President.

■ 8352 ■ S.W. Anderson Co.
2425 Wisconsin Ave.
PO Box 460
Downers Grove, IL 60515
Phone: (630)964-2600
Free: (800)323-8462 **Fax:** (630)964-2696
E-mail: sales@swaco.com
Products: Fasteners. **SIC:** 5063 (Electrical Apparatus & Equipment). **Est:** 1926. **Emp:** 50. **Officers:** Bill Taluc, Manager; Scott Muller, President; Richard Worcester, Vice President.

■ 8353 ■ SW Anderson Co.
7703 First Place, Unit E
Solon, OH 44139
Phone: (440)232-4415
Free: (800)351-0380 **Fax:** (440)232-4188
URL: http://www.swaco.com
Products: Slides; Fasteners; Rivets; Controls; Electronic hardware; Specialty hardware. **SICs:** 5063 (Electrical Apparatus & Equipment); 5049 (Professional Equipment Nec). **Est:** 1926. **Emp:** 50. **Officers:** Debbie Peters, Customer Service Contact; Greg Ferreri, Customer Service Contact.

■ 8354 ■ Angelo Brothers Co.
12401 McNulty Rd.
Philadelphia, PA 19154-3297
Phone: (215)671-2000 **Fax:** (215)464-4115
Products: Lighting and electrical supplies. **SIC:** 5063 (Electrical Apparatus & Equipment). **Est:** 1946. **Sales:** $72,000,000 (2000). **Emp:** 500. **Officers:** Stan Angelo Jr., President; Lou Di Lossi, CFO.

■ 8355 ■ Anicom
9299 Market Pl.
Broadview Heights, OH 44147
Phone: (440)546-2600
Free: (800)445-4630 **Fax:** (440)546-2616
Products: Wire and cable; Security and networking products. **SIC:** 5063 (Electrical Apparatus & Equipment). **Est:** 1976. **Emp:** 15. **Officers:** Scott Anixter, CEO; Carl Putnam, President.

■ 8356 ■ Anicom Inc.
6133 N River Rd., Ste. 410
Rosemont, IL 60018-5171
Phone: (847)518-8700
Free: (800)889-9473 **Fax:** (847)518-8791
Products: Wire, cable, fiber optics, computer network, and connectivity products. **SIC:** 5063 (Electrical Apparatus & Equipment). **Sales:** $243,700,000 (2000). **Emp:** 790. **Officers:** Scott C. Anixter, CEO; Donald C. Welchko, VP & CFO.

■ 8357 ■ **Anicom Multimedia Wiring Systems**
5475 S Wynn Rd., Ste. 100
Las Vegas, NV 89118
Phone: (702)739-9641
Free: (800)634-6051 **Fax:** (702)367-8644
URL: http://www.anicommm.com
Products: Electrical products; Electronic wire and cable; Fiber optics; Structured wiring; Security and fire alarm products. **SIC:** 5063 (Electrical Apparatus & Equipment). **Officers:** Matt Engle, Manager, e-mail: matte@anicommm.com.

■ 8358 ■ **Anixter Inc.**
10 Parkway View Dr., Bldg. O
Pittsburgh, PA 15205
Phone: (412)494-4320
Free: (800)743-2322 **Fax:** (412)494-4342
Products: Electronic wire and cable. **SIC:** 5063 (Electrical Apparatus & Equipment). **Emp:** 49. **Officers:** Francis C. Hynds, Senior Sales Specialist; Paul Aichele, Manager.

■ 8359 ■ **Anixter International Inc.**
4711 Golf Rd.
Skokie, IL 60076-1224
Phone: (847)677-2600 **Fax:** (847)677-8557
Products: Networking products for voice, data, video, and electrical power applications. **SIC:** 5063 (Electrical Apparatus & Equipment). **Sales:** $2,348,500,000 (2000). **Emp:** 6,000. **Officers:** Robert W. Grubbs, CEO & President; Dennis J. Letham, Sr. VP & CFO.

■ 8360 ■ **Antennas America Inc.**
4860 Robb St. Ste. 101
Wheat Ridge, CO 80033
Phone: (303)421-4063 **Fax:** (303)424-5085
Products: Various antennas for governmental, commercial and residential use. **SIC:** 5065 (Electronic Parts & Equipment Nec). **Sales:** $1,500,000 (2000). **Emp:** 40. **Officers:** Randy Marx, CEO; Julie Grimm, CFO.

■ 8361 ■ **Antex Incorporated**
PO Box 2570
Attleboro Falls, MA 02763
Phone: (508)699-6911 **Fax:** (508)695-8760
Products: Fiber optics for semiconductors; Electronic glass and metal seal packages; Electronic chip resistors; Electric semiconductor components and processing equipment. **SICs:** 5065 (Electronic Parts & Equipment Nec); 5063 (Electrical Apparatus & Equipment). **Officers:** John Antoine, President.

■ 8362 ■ **Antronnix Antenna Co. Inc.**
8800 Monard Dr.
Silver Spring, MD 20910-1815
Phone: (301)589-8857 **Fax:** (301)588-8105
E-mail: antronnix@erols.com
URL: http://www.erols.com/antronnix
Products: Electronic systems and equipment; Electronic parts. **SIC:** 5065 (Electronic Parts & Equipment Nec). **Est:** 1965. **Emp:** 18. **Officers:** Edwin Graves, President; Richard Dant, Sales/Marketing Contact.

■ 8363 ■ **Apem Components, Inc.**
134 Water St.
Wakefield, MA 01880
Phone: (781)246-1007
Free: (877)246-7890 **Fax:** (781)245-4531
URL: http://www.apem.com
Products: Switches and knobs. **SIC:** 5063 (Electrical Apparatus & Equipment). **Est:** 1991. **Sales:** $8,000,000 (2000). **Emp:** 60. **Officers:** Sidney F. Hooper.

■ 8364 ■ **Appliance Parts Center Inc.**
222 E 8th St.
National City, CA 91950
Phone: (619)474-6781
Free: (800)777-7909 **Fax:** (619)474-0463
Products: Household appliances. **SIC:** 5065 (Electronic Parts & Equipment Nec). **Sales:** $6,800,000 (2000). **Emp:** 50.

■ 8365 ■ **Applied Controls Inc.**
47 General Warren Blvd.
Malvern, PA 19355
Phone: (610)408-8000 **Fax:** (610)408-8048
Products: Timers and control equipment. **SICs:** 5063 (Electrical Apparatus & Equipment); 5084 (Industrial Machinery & Equipment). **Sales:** $12,000,000 (2000). **Emp:** 30. **Officers:** Rich Gehring, President; Jim Gehring, Controller.

■ 8366 ■ **APS Systems**
3535 W 5th St.
Oxnard, CA 93030
Phone: (805)984-0300 **Fax:** (805)984-2100
Products: Electric bus battery chargers; AC traction motors and controls. **SIC:** 5063 (Electrical Apparatus & Equipment). **Sales:** $3,000,000 (2000). **Emp:** 40. **Officers:** Edmond J. Atelian, CEO & President.

■ 8367 ■ **Aquatronics Inc.**
10706 Orchard St.
Fairfax, VA 22030
Phone: (703)273-3736
Products: Electrical transmission equipment. **SIC:** 5063 (Electrical Apparatus & Equipment).

■ 8368 ■ **Arcade Electronics Inc.**
5655 F. General Wash Dr.
Alexandria, VA 22312
Phone: (703)256-4610 **Fax:** (703)941-1325
E-mail: arcade@va.net
URL: http://www.arcade-electronics.com
Products: Electronic supplies. **SIC:** 5065 (Electronic Parts & Equipment Nec). **Est:** 1962. **Emp:** 19. **Officers:** Walter E. Smith, President.

■ 8369 ■ **Argraph Central**
111 Asia Pl.
Carlstadt, NJ 07072-2412
Free: (800)325-3988
Products: Electric and electronic equipment. **SIC:** 5065 (Electronic Parts & Equipment Nec).

■ 8370 ■ **Argraph Corp.**
111 Asia Pl.
Carlstadt, NJ 07072
Free: (800)526-6290 **Fax:** (201)939-7782
Products: Electric and electronic equipment. **SIC:** 5065 (Electronic Parts & Equipment Nec).

■ 8371 ■ **Argraph West**
2710 McCone Ave.
Hayward, CA 94545
Free: (800)323-9069 **Fax:** (510)293-0565
Products: Electric and electronic equipment. **SIC:** 5065 (Electronic Parts & Equipment Nec).

■ 8372 ■ **Arie Incorporated**
3405 Okeefe Dr.
El Paso, TX 79902-2023
Phone: (915)542-1848 **Fax:** (915)533-2362
Products: Electric street light fixtures; Parking meters. **SICs:** 5063 (Electrical Apparatus & Equipment); 5046 (Commercial Equipment Nec). **Officers:** M. Iwes Gonzalez, Manager.

■ 8373 ■ **Ariz Coin & Commercial Lndry Eq.**
740 W Grant
Phoenix, AZ 85007
Phone: (602)258-9274 **Fax:** (602)258-9297
E-mail: az258@wash.com
Products: Laundry equipment and related items. **SIC:** 5064 (Electrical Appliances—Television & Radio). **Est:** 1975. **Sales:** $2,000,000 (2000). **Emp:** 8. **Officers:** LeRoy Aman, Owner. **Former Name:** Washouse.

■ 8374 ■ **Arizona Commercial Lighting Co.**
4510 N 16th St.
Phoenix, AZ 85016
Phone: (602)230-8770
Products: Electrical equipment. **SIC:** 5063 (Electrical Apparatus & Equipment). **Est:** 1988. **Sales:** $500,000 (2000). **Emp:** 5. **Officers:** Clyde H. Kindred, Owner.

■ 8375 ■ **Arizona Electrical Prdts Inc.**
1867 E 3rd St.
Tempe, AZ 85281
Phone: (480)966-2167 **Fax:** (480)966-1085
Products: Cylindrical and rectangular electronic

connectors and contacts; Switches, relays and aircraft parts. **SICs:** 5065 (Electronic Parts & Equipment Nec); 5088 (Transportation Equipment & Supplies).

■ 8376 ■ **Array Microsystems Inc.**
987 University Ave. Ste. 6
Los Gatos, CA 95032
Phone: (408)399-1505
Products: Video conferencing equipment and video e-mail. **SIC:** 5065 (Electronic Parts & Equipment Nec). **Sales:** $8,000,000 (2000). **Emp:** 35. **Officers:** Paul Smith, CEO & President; E. Flint Seaton, VP & CFO.

■ 8377 ■ **Arrow Electronics Inc.**
25 Hub Dr.
Melville, NY 11747
Phone: (516)391-1300 **Fax:** (516)391-1640
Products: Electronic components, systems and computer products for industrial and commercial customers. **SICs:** 5065 (Electronic Parts & Equipment Nec); 5063 (Electrical Apparatus & Equipment). **Sales:** $8,260,000,000 (1999). **Emp:** 9,700. **Officers:** Stephen P. Kaufman, CEO & Chairman of the Board; Sam R. Leno, Sr. VP & CFO.

■ 8378 ■ **Arrow-Kierulff Electronics Group**
25 Hub Dr.
Melville, NY 11747
Phone: (516)391-1300 **Fax:** (516)391-1684
Products: Electronics equipment. **SIC:** 5065 (Electronic Parts & Equipment Nec). **Sales:** $360,000,000 (1994). **Emp:** 670. **Officers:** Steven W. Menefee, President; Sean Fernandez, VP of Finance & Admin.

■ 8379 ■ **Arthurs Enterprises Inc.**
PO Box 5654
Huntington, WV 25703
Phone: (304)523-7491 **Fax:** (304)525-8917
Products: Electrical products, including fixtures and wire. **SIC:** 5063 (Electrical Apparatus & Equipment). **Est:** 1986. **Sales:** $225,000,000 (2000). **Emp:** 800. **Officers:** Arthur Weisberg, CEO, President & Chairman of the Board; Clarence Martin, Exec. VP & CFO.

■ 8380 ■ **Artmark Associates Inc.**
11315 NW 36th Ter.
Miami, FL 33178
Phone: (305)715-9800 **Fax:** (305)715-9988
E-mail: sales@artmark.com
URL: http://www.artmark.com
Products: Electrical equipment, including wire, cable, fittings, outlet boxes, circuit breakers, and transformers. **SIC:** 5063 (Electrical Apparatus & Equipment). **Est:** 1945. **Sales:** $14,000,000 (2000). **Emp:** 18. **Officers:** Frank Kiernan, President; Ricardo Patterson, Vice President; Edmund Moore, Controller.

■ 8381 ■ **ASA Audiovox Specialized Applications**
23319 Cooper Dr.
Elkhart, IN 46514
Phone: (219)264-3135 **Fax:** (219)264-3007
Products: Communications systems and equipment. **SIC:** 5065 (Electronic Parts & Equipment Nec). **Sales:** $50,000,000 (2000). **Emp:** 70.

■ 8382 ■ **Ascom Timeplex Inc.**
7060 Koll Center Pkwy Ste. 340
Pleasanton, CA 94566
Phone: (925)461-2300 **Fax:** (925)462-3513
Products: Voice data multiplexer communication machines. **SIC:** 5065 (Electronic Parts & Equipment Nec).

■ 8383 ■ **Ashland Electric Company Inc.**
2430 Carter Ave.
Ashland, KY 41101-7828
Phone: (606)329-8544
Free: (800)926-0546 **Fax:** (606)329-9348
E-mail: rex@wwd.net
Products: Electric and electronic equipment; Electrical conduit and conduit fittings; Batteries; Electric motor controls; Electrical equipment and supplies. **SICs:** 5063 (Electrical Apparatus & Equipment); 5064 (Electrical Appliances—Television & Radio); 5065 (Electronic Parts & Equipment Nec). **Est:** 1929. **Sales:** $12,000,000 (2000). **Emp:** 49. **Officers:** Ralph Sturgill.

■ 8384 ■ **Ashland Electric Company Inc.**
2430 Carter Ave.
Ashland, KY 41101-7828
Phone: (606)329-8544
Free: (800)926-0546 **Fax:** (606)329-9348
Products: Electrical and electronic equipment and supplies. **SIC:** 5063 (Electrical Apparatus & Equipment). **Sales:** $12,000,000 (2000). **Emp:** 49.

■ 8385 ■ **Associated Industries**
11347 Van Owens St.
North Hollywood, CA 91605
Phone: (818)760-1000 **Fax:** (818)760-2142
Products: Distributor of military communication equipment. **SIC:** 5065 (Electronic Parts & Equipment Nec). **Sales:** $4,217,000,000 (2000). **Emp:** 30. **Officers:** Arnold A. Semler, President; Karen Griffith, Controller.

■ 8386 ■ **Associated of Los Angeles**
2585 E Olympic Blvd.
Los Angeles, CA 90023
Phone: (323)268-8411 **Fax:** (323)264-2244
Products: Electrical products and supplies, including wires and cables. **SIC:** 5063 (Electrical Apparatus & Equipment). **Est:** 1928. **Sales:** $20,000,000 (2000). **Emp:** 64. **Officers:** C.D. Russell Jr., President; Barry J. Ericksen, VP & Controller; Robert V. Mirolla, VP & General Merchandising Mgr.

■ 8387 ■ **Astrex Inc.**
205 Express St.
Plainview, NY 11803
Phone: (516)433-1700 **Fax:** (516)433-1796
Products: Connectors; Switches; Backshells; Contacts. **SICs:** 5065 (Electronic Parts & Equipment Nec); 5063 (Electrical Apparatus & Equipment). **Est:** 1960. **Sales:** $15,400,000 (2000). **Emp:** 75. **Officers:** Michael McGuire, CEO & President; Wayne Miller, Exec. VP.

■ 8388 ■ **Astro Industries Inc.**
4403 Dayton-Xenia Rd.
Dayton, OH 45432
Phone: (937)429-5900
Free: (800)543-5810 **Fax:** (937)429-4054
URL: http://www.astro-ind.com
Products: Electronic wire, cable, and tubing. **SIC:** 5063 (Electrical Apparatus & Equipment). **Est:** 1967. **Sales:** $7,500,000 (2000). **Emp:** 51. **Officers:** Don Tetmeyer; K. Joshi; Robert L. Scott, Marketing Mgr.

■ 8389 ■ **Astrokam**
9800 Rockside Rd.
Cleveland, OH 44125
Phone: (216)447-0404
Products: Consumer electronics. **SIC:** 5065 (Electronic Parts & Equipment Nec).

■ 8390 ■ **Atlantic-Pacific Technologies**
450 E 10th St.
Tracy, CA 95376
Phone: (209)836-4888 **Fax:** (209)836-9204
Products: Solar and telecommunications equipment—central office phones and systems. **SIC:** 5065 (Electronic Parts & Equipment Nec). **Officers:** Michael Clark, President.

■ 8391 ■ **Atlantic Solar Products Inc.**
9351-J Philadelphia Rd.
Baltimore, MD 21237
Phone: (410)686-2500 **Fax:** (410)686-6221
URL: http://www.atlanticsolar.com
Products: Solar electrical products. **SIC:** 5063 (Electrical Apparatus & Equipment). **Est:** 1983. **Sales:** $5,000,000 (2000). **Emp:** 11. **Officers:** Brent Atkins, President.

■ 8392 ■ **Atlas Energy Systems Inc.**
530 Baldwin Park Blvd.
La Puente, CA 91746
Phone: (626)855-0485 **Fax:** (626)855-0486
Products: Power converters and conditioners; Uninterruptible power supply systems. **SIC:** 5063 (Electrical Apparatus & Equipment). **Officers:** Sherry Arnold, VP of Finance.

■ 8393 ■ **Aucoin and Miller Electric Supply Inc.**
PO Box 53122
Houston, TX 77052
Phone: (713)224-2400 **Fax:** (713)547-9901
Products: Electrical supplies, including wire, fittings, and transformers. **SIC:** 5063 (Electrical Apparatus & Equipment). **Est:** 1966. **Sales:** $17,000,000 (2000). **Emp:** 40. **Officers:** Tim Reily, President; Brian Ahlquist, Controller; B. Thomas Miller, Exec. VP of Sales.

■ 8394 ■ **Audio-Technica U.S. Inc.**
1221 Commerce Dr.
Stow, OH 44224
Phone: (330)686-2600 **Fax:** (330)688-3572
Products: Phonograph cartridges, stereophones, microphones, headphones and audio accessories. **SIC:** 5065 (Electronic Parts & Equipment Nec). **Sales:** $13,000,000 (2000). **Emp:** 114. **Officers:** Phil Cajka, CEO & President.

■ 8395 ■ **Audiovox Specialized Applications LLC**
23319 Cooper Dr.
Elkhart, IN 46514
Phone: (219)264-3135
Free: (800)688-3135 **Fax:** (219)264-5886
URL: http://www.asa-avx.com
Products: Consumer mobile electronics. **SIC:** 5064 (Electrical Appliances—Television & Radio). **Est:** 1977. **Sales:** $867,000,000 (2000). **Emp:** 200. **Former Name:** Audiovox Specialty Markets Co.

■ 8396 ■ **AUDISSEY**
841 Pohukaina St., Ste. B
Honolulu, HI 96813-5332
Phone: (808)591-2791 **Fax:** (808)591-9497
E-mail: audissey808@aol.com
Products: Audio, visual, and control systems. **SICs:** 5065 (Electronic Parts & Equipment Nec); 5046 (Commercial Equipment Nec). **Sales:** $1,000,000 (2000). **Emp:** 6. **Officers:** Gerald Luke, President; Rick Parlee, Vice President.

■ 8397 ■ **Automatic Controls Co.**
50222 W Pontiac Tr.
Wixom, MI 48393-2023
Phone: (248)624-1990
Products: Recorders, monitors, and transformers. **SICs:** 5084 (Industrial Machinery & Equipment); 5045 (Computers, Peripherals & Software); 5065 (Electronic Parts & Equipment Nec). **Sales:** $4,000,000 (1994). **Emp:** 13. **Officers:** James Schembri, President.

■ 8398 ■ **Automatic Firing Inc.**
2100 Fillmore Ave.
Buffalo, NY 14214
Phone: (716)836-0300 **Fax:** (716)837-0561
Products: Combustion equipment and controls. **SIC:** 5063 (Electrical Apparatus & Equipment). **Sales:** $1,000,000 (1999). **Emp:** 8. **Officers:** James Pellegrino, President.

■ 8399 ■ **AV Associates Inc.**
1768 Storrs Rd.
Storrs Mansfield, CT 06268-1207
Phone: (860)487-1330
Free: (800)344-8033 **Fax:** (860)487-0893
URL: http://www.avai.com
Products: Electronic systems and equipment; Electronic parts. **SIC:** 5065 (Electronic Parts & Equipment Nec). **Emp:** 80. **Officers:** Norval Smith, President, e-mail: norval.smith@avai.com.

■ 8400 ■ **Avcom, Inc.**
20827 Lorain Rd.
Cleveland, OH 44126
Phone: (440)333-0111 **Fax:** (440)333-0818
Products: Electronic systems and equipment. **SIC:** 5065 (Electronic Parts & Equipment Nec).

■ 8401 ■ **Avec Electronics Corp.**
2002 Staples Mill Rd.
Richmond, VA 23230
Phone: (804)359-6071 **Fax:** (804)359-5609
Products: Electronic parts. **SIC:** 5065 (Electronic Parts & Equipment Nec). **Sales:** $2,000,000 (2000). **Emp:** 6. **Officers:** Craig Huizenga, President.

■ 8402 ■ **AVED Rocky Mountain Inc.**
4090 Youngfield St.
Wheat Ridge, CO 80033-3862
Phone: (303)422-1701 **Fax:** (303)442-2529
Products: Semiconductors and related devices. **SIC:** 5065 (Electronic Parts & Equipment Nec). **Officers:** Wayne Vannoy, President.

■ 8403 ■ **AVest Inc.**
205 Express St.
Plainview, NY 11803
Phone: (516)433-1700
Products: Connectors, relays, and switches. **SIC:** 5065 (Electronic Parts & Equipment Nec).

■ 8404 ■ **Avon Electrical Supplies, Inc.**
60 Hoffman Ave.
Hauppauge, NY 11788
Phones: (516)582-4770 (718)657-1600
Fax: (516)582-4237
E-mail: avongroup@msn.com
Products: Electrical products. **SIC:** 5063 (Electrical Apparatus & Equipment). **Est:** 1940. **Sales:** $125,000,000 (2000). **Emp:** 130. **Officers:** Kenneth Moskowitz; Leonard Moskowitz.

■ 8405 ■ **Axis Electronics Inc.**
22 Cessna Ct.
Gaithersburg, MD 20879-4145
Phone: (301)840-9640
Free: (800)368-2815 **Fax:** (301)840-9299
Products: Electronic parts; Electronic systems and equipment. **SIC:** 5065 (Electronic Parts & Equipment Nec). **Officers:** Robert Klink, President.

■ 8406 ■ **B & C Distributors**
143 Space Park S
Nashville, TN 37211
Phone: (615)831-7074
Products: Lighting fixtures. **SIC:** 5063 (Electrical Apparatus & Equipment).

■ 8407 ■ **Babco, Inc.**
60-10 Maurice Ave.
Maspeth, NY 11378
Free: (800)289-2943 **Fax:** (718)779-5709
URL: http://www.babcony.com
Products: Industrial electric blowers and fans; Electric motors and generators. **SICs:** 5063 (Electrical Apparatus & Equipment); 5084 (Industrial Machinery & Equipment). **Est:** 1915. **Sales:** $2,000,000 (2000). **Emp:** 12. **Officers:** Edith Barshov, President; David Barshov, Vice President; Jerry Barshov, Chairman of the Board.

■ 8408 ■ **Babsco Supply**
PO Box 1447
Elkhart, IN 46517
Phone: (219)293-0631
Free: (800)654-4849 **Fax:** (219)293-7207
Products: Electrical equipment. **SIC:** 5063 (Electrical Apparatus & Equipment). **Est:** 1988. **Officers:** Jan Farron, President. **Former Name:** Babsco.

■ 8409 ■ **L R Baggs Co.**
483 N Frontage Rd.
Nipomo, CA 93444
Phone: (805)929-3544 **Fax:** (805)929-2043
Products: Pick-ups for guitars and other string instruments. **SIC:** 5065 (Electronic Parts & Equipment Nec).

■ 8410 ■ **John P. Bagoy and Associates Inc.**
3210 Rampart Dr.
Anchorage, AK 99501-3133
Phone: (907)274-8531 **Fax:** (907)277-6966
Products: Electrical and electronic equipment and supplies. **SIC:** 5063 (Electrical Apparatus & Equipment). **Sales:** $1,400,000 (2000). **Emp:** 3.

■ 8411 ■ **BAI Distributors Inc.**
2312 NE 29 Ave.
Ocala, FL 34470
Phone: (352)732-7009 **Fax:** (352)732-1616
E-mail: Anita@baionline.com
URL: http://www.baionline.com
Products: Electronic systems and equipment; CCTV equipment. **SIC:** 5065 (Electronic Parts & Equipment Nec). **Est:** 1986. **Sales:** $3,000,000 (2000). **Emp:** 18.

Officers: Bill Bencsik; Janet Bencsik; Jim Ritchhart, Sales/Marketing Contact.

■ **8412** ■ **Ball Auto Tech Inc.**
2298 Young Ave.
Memphis, TN 38104-5755
Phone: (901)278-4922 **Fax:** (901)276-1248
Products: Car stereos. **SIC:** 5064 (Electrical Appliances—Television & Radio). **Officers:** Gerald Cook, President.

■ **8413** ■ **Baptist Electronics Supply Company Inc.**
419 S Mauvaisterre St.
Jacksonville, IL 62650
Phone: (217)245-6063
Products: Consumer electronics. **SIC:** 5064 (Electrical Appliances—Television & Radio). **Sales:** $7,000,000 (1994). **Emp:** 28. **Officers:** Don Fernandes, Owner.

■ **8414** ■ **Bar Code Applications Inc.**
816 Peace Portal Way, No. 113
Blaine, WA 98231
Phone: (604)451-7878 **Fax:** (604)451-9383
URL: http://www.barcode.bc.ca
Products: Bar coded labels and scanners; Time and stock tracker software. **SIC:** 5065 (Electronic Parts & Equipment Nec). **Est:** 1982. **Officers:** Mel J. Endelman, President, e-mail: melbca@barcode.bc.ca.

■ **8415** ■ **Barber-Nichols Inc.**
6325 W 55th Ave.
Arvada, CO 80002
Phone: (303)421-8111 **Fax:** (303)420-4679
Products: Geothermal, solar heat, and power system generators. **SIC:** 5063 (Electrical Apparatus & Equipment). **Sales:** $7,000,000 (2000). **Emp:** 49. **Officers:** Kenneth Nichols, CEO.

■ **8416** ■ **Barbey Electronics Corp.**
PO Box 2
Reading, PA 19603
Phone: (610)376-7451
Free: (800)822-2251 **Fax:** (610)372-8622
E-mail: info@barbeyele.com
URL: http://www.barbeyele.com
Products: Electric and electronic equipment. **SIC:** 5065 (Electronic Parts & Equipment Nec). **Est:** 1916. **Sales:** $9,000,000 (2000). **Emp:** 60. **Officers:** G.L. Gammell, President; K.D. Loudis, Dir. of Marketing; Nancy Nagle, Dir. of Data Processing.

■ **8417** ■ **Barno Electronics Corp.**
5403 W Smithfield St.
PO Box 93
Mc Keesport, PA 15135-1259
Phones: (412)751-5966 (412)751-5971
(412)751-5972 (412)751-5994
Fax: (412)751-6077
E-mail: barnoelect@aol.com
Products: Industrial electronics parts. **SIC:** 5065 (Electronic Parts & Equipment Nec). **Est:** 1923. **Sales:** $4,000,000 (1999). **Emp:** 9. **Officers:** Mary M. Frost, President; Samuel J. Frost, General Mgr.; Margaret Barno, AP/AR Office Mgr.; Michelle L. Sethman, Human Resources Contact; Bob Quinn, Sales. **Former Name:** Barno Radio Company.

■ **8418** ■ **Basic Wire & Cable Co.**
3900 N Rockwell
Chicago, IL 60618-3719
Phones: (773)266-2600 (773)539-1800
Fax: (773)539-3500
E-mail: basicwire@basicwire.com
URL: http://www.basicwire.com
Products: Electrical wire, including residential and commercial cable. **SIC:** 5063 (Electrical Apparatus & Equipment). **Emp:** 49.

■ **8419** ■ **Batteries Direct**
713 Gladstone St.
Parkersburg, WV 26101-5661
Phone: (304)428-2296
Free: (800)666-2296 **Fax:** (304)428-2297
E-mail: info@batteryking.com
URL: http://www.batteryking.com
Products: Replace batteries for the computer and wireless electronic industies; Power related items, including charging systems, car cords, AC adaptors for

portables. **SICs:** 5063 (Electrical Apparatus & Equipment); 5065 (Electronic Parts & Equipment Nec). **Est:** 1985. **Sales:** $1,000,000 (2000). **Emp:** 5. **Officers:** W. Lynn Fuller IV, CEO & CFO. **Former Name:** Fuller's Wholesale Electronics Inc.

■ **8420** ■ **Battery Products Inc.**
PO Box 589
Hartland, WI 53029-0589
Phone: (262)367-2411
Free: (800)456-2411 **Fax:** (262)367-8302
E-mail: info@batteryproducts.com
URL: http://www.batteryproducts.com
Products: Batteries for 2-way, cellular, medical equipment, exit lights, ups, alkaline, lithium, rechargeable, and lightsticks. **SIC:** 5063 (Electrical Apparatus & Equipment). **Est:** 1984. **Sales:** $1,000,000 (2000). **Emp:** 6. **Officers:** Michael Meyers, President.

■ **8421** ■ **Battery Specialties Inc.**
3530 Cadillac Ave.
Costa Mesa, CA 92626
Phone: (714)755-0888 **Fax:** (714)755-0889
Products: Custom battery packs—nickel cadmium, seal lead acid, alkaline, mercury and lithium. **SIC:** 5063 (Electrical Apparatus & Equipment). **Sales:** $9,000,000 (2000). **Emp:** 30. **Officers:** Gerald Kanen, President.

■ **8422** ■ **Battery Warehouse**
324 Martin St.
Dover, DE 19901
Phone: (302)674-4020 **Fax:** (302)674-4020
Products: Batteries, including automotive, aircraft, motorcycle, and marine batteries; Telephones; Camcorders; Toys. **SICs:** 5063 (Electrical Apparatus & Equipment); 5013 (Motor Vehicle Supplies & New Parts); 5092 (Toys & Hobby Goods & Supplies).

■ **8423** ■ **John Battin Power Service**
5004 SE Junction Creek Blvd.
Portland, OR 97222
Phone: (503)777-3065
Products: Electric generators. **SIC:** 5063 (Electrical Apparatus & Equipment).

■ **8424** ■ **BB & W Electronics**
2137 Euclid
Berwyn, IL 60402-1800
Phone: (708)749-1710
Free: (800)722-9684 **Fax:** (708)749-0325
Products: Electric and electronic equipment. **SICs:** 5065 (Electronic Parts & Equipment Nec); 5064 (Electrical Appliances—Television & Radio). **Est:** 1958. **Emp:** 49.

■ **8425** ■ **Beaver Creek Cooperative Telephone Co.**
PO Box 69
Beavercreek, OR 97004-0069
Phone: (503)632-3113 **Fax:** (503)632-4159
Products: Electronic parts and equipment; Telephone and telegraphic equipment. **SIC:** 5065 (Electronic Parts & Equipment Nec). **Officers:** Tom Linstrom, President.

■ **8426** ■ **J.A. Becker Co.**
1341 E 4th St.
Dayton, OH 45401
Phone: (513)226-1341
Products: Electrical equipment and supplies. **SIC:** 5063 (Electrical Apparatus & Equipment). **Est:** 1920. **Sales:** $39,000,000 (2000). **Emp:** 130. **Officers:** Tom Becker, CEO.

■ **8427** ■ **Becker Electric Supply**
11310 Mosteller Rd.
Cincinnati, OH 45241-1828
Phone: (513)771-2550 **Fax:** (513)771-6527
Products: Lighting fixtures. **SIC:** 5063 (Electrical Apparatus & Equipment). **Est:** 1920. **Emp:** 50. **Officers:** Jim Dichito.

■ **8428** ■ **Beeco Motors and Controls Inc.**
5630 Guhn Rd., No. 116
Houston, TX 77040
Phone: (713)690-0311
Free: (800)467-2332 **Fax:** (713)690-3328
Products: Electrical motors and controls. **SIC:** 5063 (Electrical Apparatus & Equipment). **Est:** 1966. **Sales:**

$6,000,000 (2000). **Emp:** 22. **Officers:** Gary H. Muslin, President; Eileen Novitt, Controller; Jim Hodge, Sales Mgr.; George Reynolds, Purchasing Manager.

■ **8429** ■ **Bell Microproducts Inc.**
1941 Ringwood Ave.
San Jose, CA 95131-1721
Phone: (408)451-9400 **Fax:** (408)451-1600
Products: Semiconductor and computer products. **SIC:** 5065 (Electronic Parts & Equipment Nec). **Sales:** $533,700,000 (2000). **Emp:** 650. **Officers:** W. Donald Bell, CEO & President; Remo E. Canessa, Sr. VP & CFO; Phil Roussey, Sr. VP of Marketing.

■ **8430** ■ **H.H. Benfield Electric Supply Co.**
25 Lafayette Ave.
White Plains, NY 10603
Phone: (914)948-6660 **Fax:** (914)993-0558
E-mail: mailbox@benfieldelectric.com
URL: http://www.benfieldelectric.com
Products: Electrical supplies; Data and communications products. **SIC:** 5063 (Electrical Apparatus & Equipment). **Est:** 1951. **Sales:** $75,000,000 (2000). **Emp:** 210. **Officers:** Roy C. Kohli, CEO & President; C.J. Peterson Jr., VP & CFO. **Alternate Name:** Benfield Control Systems. **Alternate Name:** Benfield Electric International, Ltd.

■ **8431** ■ **Benson Eyecare Corp.**
555 Theodore Fremd Ave.
Rye, NY 10580
Phone: (914)967-9400 **Fax:** (914)967-9405
Products: Specialty lighting products. **SIC:** 5063 (Electrical Apparatus & Equipment). **Sales:** $300,800,000 (2000). **Emp:** 2,468. **Officers:** Martin E. Franklin, Chairman of the Board; Ian Ashken, CFO.

■ **8432** ■ **Bergquist Co. Inc.**
5300 Edina Industrial Blvd.
Edina, MN 55439
Phone: (612)835-2322
Free: (800)347-4572 **Fax:** (612)835-0430
Products: Membrane switches; Termally conductive insulators; Electronic and electrical products. **SIC:** 5065 (Electronic Parts & Equipment Nec). **Est:** 1964. **Sales:** $76,000,000 (2000). **Emp:** 500. **Officers:** C. Bergquist Jr., President; L. Morgan, CFO; R. Savage, Vice President; D. Dungey, Vice President.

■ **8433** ■ **Besco Electic Supply Company of Florida Inc.**
711 S 14th St.
Leesburg, FL 34748
Phone: (352)787-4542
Free: (800)541-6618 **Fax:** (352)365-0554
Products: Electrical and lighting supplies. **SIC:** 5063 (Electrical Apparatus & Equipment). **Sales:** $5,000,000 (2000). **Emp:** 30. **Officers:** Douglas W. Braun, President.

■ **8434** ■ **Best Labs**
PO Box 20468
St. Petersburg, FL 33742
Phone: (813)525-0255 **Fax:** (813)527-8518
Products: Medical, dental, and optical equipment. **SIC:** 5063 (Electrical Apparatus & Equipment). **Sales:** $4,000,000 (2000). **Emp:** 44.

■ **8435** ■ **Bevan-Rabell Inc.**
1880 Airport Rd.
Wichita, KS 67209-1943
Phone: (316)946-4870 **Fax:** (316)946-4869
Products: Electronic parts; Electronic systems and equipment; Communication systems and equipment. **SIC:** 5065 (Electronic Parts & Equipment Nec). **Officers:** Robert Patterson, President.

■ **8436** ■ **Bext, Inc.**
1045 10th Ave.
San Diego, CA 92101-6961
Phone: (619)239-8462 **Fax:** (619)239-8474
E-mail: support@bext.com
URL: http://www.bext.com
Products: Electronic equipment and supplies. **SIC:** 5065 (Electronic Parts & Equipment Nec). **Est:** 1985. **Sales:** $1,000,000 (2000). **Emp:** 10. **Officers:** Anne De Fazio, President; Michelle De Fazio, Sales Coordinator; Dennis Pieri, Dir. of Marketing.

■ 8437 ■ BG Electronics Inc.
PO Box 810498
Dallas, TX 75381-0498
Phone: (972)492-7877 **Fax:** (972)492-8286
Products: Electronic components. **SIC:** 5065 (Electronic Parts & Equipment Nec). **Sales:** $5,000,000 (1994). **Emp:** 22.

■ 8438 ■ BGE and C Inc.
PO Box 810498
Dallas, TX 75381-0498
Phone: (972)492-7877
Products: Electronic components. **SIC:** 5065 (Electronic Parts & Equipment Nec). **Sales:** $17,000,000 (2000). **Emp:** 42. **Officers:** Bill Gonzalez, President.

■ 8439 ■ Billows Electric Supply Co.
9100 State Rd.
Philadelphia, PA 19136
Phone: (267)332-9700
Products: Electrical supplies, including light bulbs, wires, fuses and switches. **SIC:** 5063 (Electrical Apparatus & Equipment). **Sales:** $80,000,000 (2000). **Emp:** 260. **Officers:** Jeff Billow, President; Richard Alsdorf, CFO.

■ 8440 ■ Bird-X Inc.
300 N Elizabeth St.
Chicago, IL 60607
Phone: (312)226-2473
Free: (800)662-5021 **Fax:** (312)226-2480
Products: Bird control products and devices, ultrasonic pest repellers, plastic netting, vinyl inflatable predators and liquid repellents. **SICs:** 5063 (Electrical Apparatus & Equipment); 5065 (Electronic Parts & Equipment Nec). **Sales:** $2,000,000 (1999). **Emp:** 25.

■ 8441 ■ Biscayne Electric and Hardware Distributors Inc.
1140 NW 159th Dr.
Miami, FL 33169
Phone: (305)625-8526 **Fax:** (305)624-9251
URL: http://www.biscaynehardware.com
Products: Electrical equipment and supplies; Hardware. **SICs:** 5063 (Electrical Apparatus & Equipment); 5072 (Hardware). **Est:** 1952. **Sales:** $9,100,000 (2000). **Emp:** 39. **Officers:** Alan Troop, President, e-mail: atroop@biscaynehardware.com.

■ 8442 ■ Bisco Industries Inc.
704 W Southern Ave.
Orange, CA 92865
Phone: (714)283-7140
Free: (800)323-1232 **Fax:** (714)283-7180
E-mail: info@biscoind.com
URL: http://www.biscoind.com
Products: Electronic hardware, including latches, fuses, and connectors. **SIC:** 5065 (Electronic Parts & Equipment Nec). **Est:** 1973. **Sales:** $45,000,000 (2000). **Emp:** 160. **Officers:** Glen Ceiley, CEO & President; Steve Catanzaro, VP & CFO; William Means, Dir. of Information Systems.

■ 8443 ■ Don Blackburn and Co.
13335 Farmington Rd.
Livonia, MI 48150
Phone: (734)261-9100 **Fax:** (734)261-7173
Products: Electrical supplies. **SIC:** 5065 (Electronic Parts & Equipment Nec). **Est:** 1939. **Sales:** $30,000,000 (2000). **Emp:** 65. **Officers:** Keith J. Snider, CEO & Chairman of the Board.

■ 8444 ■ Blake Wire and Cable Corp.
16134 Runnymede St.
Van Nuys, CA 91406
Phone: (818)781-8300 **Fax:** (818)781-6534
Products: Wire and cable. **SIC:** 5063 (Electrical Apparatus & Equipment). **Sales:** $4,000,000 (2000). **Emp:** 21. **Officers:** Robert Weiner, President; Victor Weiner, VP of Finance.

■ 8445 ■ Blevins Inc.
421 Hart Ln.
Nashville, TN 37216
Phone: (615)227-7772 **Fax:** (615)228-1301
Products: Light bulbs for theaters. **SIC:** 5099 (Durable Goods Nec). **Sales:** $65,000,000 (1994). **Emp:** 150. **Officers:** James W. Blevins, CEO & President.

■ 8446 ■ Blue Ridge Electric Motor Repair
629 Emma Rd.
Asheville, NC 28806
Phone: (828)258-0800
Products: Electric motors. **SIC:** 5063 (Electrical Apparatus & Equipment).

■ 8447 ■ Bluff City Electronics
3339 Fontaine Rd.
Memphis, TN 38116
Phone: (901)345-9500
Products: Lighting supplies; Electrical outlets. **SIC:** 5063 (Electrical Apparatus & Equipment). **Est:** 1938. **Sales:** $25,000,000 (2000). **Emp:** 90. **Officers:** Alfred Cowles Jr., CEO & President; Alfred Cowles III, VP of Finance; Eddie Duncan, Marketing & Sales Mgr.

■ 8448 ■ Bob's Gard Duty
901 Market St.
Wheeling, WV 26003-2909
Phone: (304)234-7667 **Fax:** (304)234-7434
Products: Electrical equipment and supplies. **SIC:** 5063 (Electrical Apparatus & Equipment). **Emp:** 4. **Officers:** Rich Crumm, Manager.

■ 8449 ■ Bodine Electric of Decatur
1845 N 22nd St.
Decatur, IL 62526
Phone: (217)423-2593 **Fax:** (217)243-4658
Products: Electric motors. **SIC:** 5063 (Electrical Apparatus & Equipment). **Sales:** $25,000,000 (2000). **Emp:** 250. **Officers:** David Rathje, President; John Kileen, VP of Finance.

■ 8450 ■ Boettcher Supply Inc.
PO Box 486
Beloit, KS 67420
Phone: (785)738-5781
Products: Electrical and plumbing supplies; Lawnmowers. **SICs:** 5063 (Electrical Apparatus & Equipment); 5074 (Plumbing & Hydronic Heating Supplies); 5083 (Farm & Garden Machinery). **Sales:** $8,000,000 (2000). **Emp:** 27. **Officers:** Jarold W. Boettcher, Owner; Larry Golladay, CFO.

■ 8451 ■ Boggis-Johnson Electric Co.
2900 N 112th St.
Milwaukee, WI 53222
Phone: (414)475-6900 **Fax:** (414)475-6607
Products: Electrical supplies, including wires, circuit breakers, and panel boards. **SIC:** 5063 (Electrical Apparatus & Equipment). **Sales:** $13,000,000 (2000). **Emp:** 55. **Officers:** Ned Timarac, President.

■ 8452 ■ Boland Electric Supply Inc.
PO Box 3430
Decatur, IL 62524-3430
Phone: (217)423-3495 **Fax:** (217)423-1143
Products: Electronic equipment. **SIC:** 5063 (Electrical Apparatus & Equipment). **Est:** 1953. **Sales:** $4,200,000 (2000). **Emp:** 19. **Officers:** M.J. Boland, President & Treasurer.

■ 8453 ■ Bolts & Nuts Inc.
17407 Lorain Ave.
Cleveland, OH 44111-4022
Phone: (216)671-6670 **Fax:** (216)671-6222
Products: Electronic hardware components; Fasteners, including bolts and rivets. **SIC:** 5065 (Electronic Parts & Equipment Nec). **Emp:** 99. **Officers:** Tim Divis.

■ 8454 ■ Bondy Export Corp.
40 Canal St.
New York, NY 10002
Phone: (212)925-7785 **Fax:** (212)925-9270
Products: Electronic appliances and equipment. **SIC:** 5064 (Electrical Appliances—Television & Radio). **Est:** 1953. **Officers:** Bezalel Feigelstein, President.

■ 8455 ■ Border States Electric Supply
105 25th St., N
Fargo, ND 58102-4030
Phone: (701)293-5834 **Fax:** (701)237-9488
Products: Electrical supplies, including wire and panel boards. **SIC:** 5063 (Electrical Apparatus & Equipment). **Est:** 1952. **Sales:** $260,000,000 (2000). **Emp:** 600. **Officers:** Paul Madson, CEO; Tammy Miller, CFO;

Greg Hoffelt, VP of Marketing & Sales; J. Mark Weed, Dir of Human Resources.

■ 8456 ■ Border States Industries Inc.
PO Box 2767
Fargo, ND 58108-2767
Phone: (701)293-5834 **Fax:** (701)237-9811
Products: Electrical voice and data equipment and supplies. **SIC:** 5063 (Electrical Apparatus & Equipment). **Sales:** $240,000,000 (2000). **Emp:** 600. **Officers:** Paul Madson, CEO & President; Tammy Miller, VP of Finance.

■ 8457 ■ Boustead Electric and Manufacturing Co.
7135 Madison Ave. W
Minneapolis, MN 55427
Phone: (763)544-9131
Free: (800)742-0686 **Fax:** (763)544-8530
URL: http://www.bousteadelectric.com
Products: Industrial supplies, including motors, drives, and switches. **SICs:** 5063 (Electrical Apparatus & Equipment); 5085 (Industrial Supplies). **Est:** 1914. **Sales:** $11,000,000 (2000). **Emp:** 63. **Officers:** Steven Svendsen, President.

■ 8458 ■ Bowling Green Winlectric
1001A Shive Ln.
Bowling Green, KY 42101
Phone: (502)842-6153
Free: (800)264-1592 **Fax:** (502)842-6155
Products: Electric panels; Light fixtures. **SIC:** 5063 (Electrical Apparatus & Equipment). **Emp:** 5.

■ 8459 ■ Boyd Lighting Fixture Co
944 Folsom St.
San Francisco, CA 94107
Phone: (415)778-4300 **Fax:** (415)778-4319
Products: Custom lighting fixtures. **SIC:** 5063 (Electrical Apparatus & Equipment). **Sales:** $9,000,000 (1999). **Emp:** 60. **Officers:** Jay Sweet, CEO; Dorothy Boyd Sweet, CFO.

■ 8460 ■ W.H. Brady Co. Xymox Div.
PO Box 571
Milwaukee, WI 53223
Phone: (414)355-8300
Products: Membrane switches. **SICs:** 5065 (Electronic Parts & Equipment Nec); 5063 (Electrical Apparatus & Equipment). **Est:** 1977. **Sales:** $10,000,000 (2000). **Emp:** 160. **Officers:** J.D. Dick, General Mgr.; R.C. Rudolph, Controller; Francis P. Yorio, Dir. of Marketing.

■ 8461 ■ Braid Electric Company Inc.
PO Box 23710
Nashville, TN 37202
Phone: (615)242-6511 **Fax:** (615)242-9684
Products: Electrical supplies and lighting. **SICs:** 5063 (Electrical Apparatus & Equipment); 5065 (Electronic Parts & Equipment Nec). **Est:** 1879. **Sales:** $26,000,000 (2000). **Emp:** 110. **Officers:** Ben Gambell, President; Bill Fitts, Treasurer & Secty.; Charles West, VP of Marketing & Sales; Tom Gambell, VP of Operations.

■ 8462 ■ Branch Electric Supply Co.
1049 Prince Georges Blvd.
Upper Marlboro, MD 20774
Phone: (301)249-5005 **Fax:** (301)390-4134
E-mail: sales@branchelectric.com
URL: http://www.branchelectric.com
Products: Electric and electronic equipment; Electrical equipment for industrial use. **SICs:** 5063 (Electrical Apparatus & Equipment); 5063 (Electrical Apparatus & Equipment). **Est:** 1968. **Sales:** $200,000,000 (2000). **Emp:** 600. **Officers:** Adam Steiner, President, e-mail: adsteiner@branchelectric.com.

■ 8463 ■ Brand-Rex Co.
1600 W Main St.
Willimantic, CT 06226-1128
Phone: (860)456-8000 **Fax:** (860)423-8128
Products: Wiring and cable. **SIC:** 5065 (Electronic Parts & Equipment Nec). **Officers:** Ronald Filius, Pres.; Stephen J. Haas, Mgr., Mktg. Communications.

■ 8464 ■ Brandon and Clark Inc.
3623 Interstate 27
Lubbock, TX 79404
Phone: (806)747-3861 **Fax:** (806)747-2107
Products: Electrical motors. **SIC:** 5063 (Electrical Apparatus & Equipment). **Est:** 1950. **Sales:** $16,000,000 (2000). **Emp:** 165. **Officers:** Walt Clark, President; Roger Clark, VP of Finance; Bill Ross, Dir. of Marketing.

■ 8465 ■ Brantley Electrical Supply Inc.
2913 A Fort Bragg Rd.
Fayetteville, NC 28303
Phone: (910)485-2100
Free: (800)682-2560 **Fax:** (910)485-2328
E-mail: brantl@Fayetteville.net
Products: Electronic parts; Computer networking accessories; Tools and service aids. **SIC:** 5065 (Electronic Parts & Equipment Nec). **Est:** 1974. **Emp:** 9. **Officers:** Gene Brantley.

■ 8466 ■ Brauner Export Co.
1600 N Warson Rd.
St. Louis, MO 63132
Phone: (314)426-2600 **Fax:** (314)426-4300
E-mail: ebex@inlink.com
Products: Fabricated metal products; Photographic equipment; Electronic equipment; Printed circuit equipment. **SICs:** 5065 (Electronic Parts & Equipment Nec); 5051 (Metals Service Centers & Offices); 5043 (Photographic Equipment & Supplies). **Est:** 1945. **Emp:** 6. **Officers:** Paul Brauner, President.

■ 8467 ■ Brightpoint Inc.
6402 Corporate Dr.
Indianapolis, IN 46278
Phone: (317)297-6100
Free: (800)952-2355 **Fax:** (317)297-6114
Products: Cellular telephones and accessories. **SIC:** 5065 (Electronic Parts & Equipment Nec). **Sales:** $1,802,300,000 (1999). **Emp:** 1,500. **Officers:** Robert J. Laikin, CEO & Chairman of the Board; Phillip A. Bounsall, Exec. VP & CFO.

■ 8468 ■ Brinkmann Corp.
4215 McEwen Rd.
Dallas, TX 75244
Phone: (972)387-4939
Free: (800)527-0717 **Fax:** (972)490-7804
Products: Residential electric lighting fixtures; Flashlights. **SIC:** 5063 (Electrical Apparatus & Equipment).

■ 8469 ■ BroadBand Technologies Inc.
PO Box 13737
Research Triangle Park, NC 27709-3737
Phone: (919)544-0015 **Fax:** (919)544-3459
Products: Fiber optics equipment; Telecommunications equipment. **SIC:** 5065 (Electronic Parts & Equipment Nec). **Est:** 1988. **Sales:** $24,000,000 (2000). **Emp:** 162. **Officers:** Salim Bhatia, CEO & President.

■ 8470 ■ Brohl and Appell Inc.
PO Box 1419
Sandusky, OH 44871
Phone: (419)625-6761 **Fax:** (419)625-8103
E-mail: anyone@brohlandappell.com
URL: http://www.brohlandappell.com
Products: Electrical items. **SIC:** 5063 (Electrical Apparatus & Equipment). **Est:** 1889. **Sales:** $10,000,000 (2000). **Emp:** 43. **Officers:** Neal Ebert, President & CEO; Irene Lingenfelter, Sales/Marketing Contact, e-mail: irene@brohlandappell.com.

■ 8471 ■ Brownstown Electric Supply Inc.
690 E State Rd., No. 250
Brownstown, IN 47220
Phone: (812)358-4555
Products: High power line electrical equipment and supplies. **SIC:** 5063 (Electrical Apparatus & Equipment). **Est:** 1970. **Sales:** $22,000,000 (2000). **Emp:** 35. **Officers:** Earl Hobbs, President; Greg Deck, CFO.

■ 8472 ■ Bruce and Merrilee's Electric Co.
930 Cass St.
New Castle, PA 16101
Phone: (724)652-5566
Free: (800)652-5560 **Fax:** (724)652-8290
E-mail: bmcco@bruceandmerrillees.com
URL: http://www.bruceandmerrillees.com/
Products: Electrical supplies, including wire and lighting. **SIC:** 5063 (Electrical Apparatus & Equipment). **Emp:** 49. **Officers:** Gary Bruce.

■ 8473 ■ BTR Inc.
33 Commercial St., No. B5251
Foxboro, MA 02035-2530
Products: Electrical supplies. **SIC:** 5063 (Electrical Apparatus & Equipment). **Emp:** 135,133. **Officers:** John Thomas, CEO & President.

■ 8474 ■ Buckles-Smith Electric
801 Savaker Ave.
San Jose, CA 95126
Phone: (408)280-7777 **Fax:** (408)280-0720
Products: Automatic controls; Fuses and fuse equipment; Transformers; Switches; Motor vehicle lighting equipment (including parking light, dome light, and taillight fixtures). **SIC:** 5063 (Electrical Apparatus & Equipment). **Est:** 1939. **Emp:** 50.

■ 8475 ■ Bud Electronic Supply Co.
22 N Jackson St.
Danville, IL 61832
Phone: (217)446-0925 **Fax:** (217)446-0927
Products: Electronic components. **SIC:** 5065 (Electronic Parts & Equipment Nec). **Sales:** $2,500,000 (2000). **Emp:** 20. **Officers:** Marvin Ehrlich, President; Al Pontecore, Treasurer.

■ 8476 ■ Bulbman Inc.
PO Box 12280
Reno, NV 89510-2280
Free: (800)648-1163 **Fax:** 800-548-6216
E-mail: bulbman1@mindspring.com
URL: http://www.bulbman.com
Products: Lightbulbs. **SIC:** 5063 (Electrical Apparatus & Equipment). **Est:** 1975. **Sales:** $18,000,000 (2000). **Emp:** 60. **Officers:** Gerald Roth, President; Robert Roth, Vice President.

■ 8477 ■ Bulbtronics
45 Banfi Plz.
Farmingdale, NY 11735
Phone: (631)249-2272
Free: (800)654-8542 **Fax:** (631)249-6066
E-mail: bulbs@bultronics.com
URL: http://www.bulbtronics.com
Products: Electric light bulbs for medical, scientific, graphic, STTV, and energy efficient applications; Batteries; Lighting diffusion materials. **SIC:** 5063 (Electrical Apparatus & Equipment). **Est:** 1976. **Sales:** $25,000,000 (1999). **Emp:** 82. **Officers:** Bruce R. Thaw, CEO & President; Susan Winters, Exec. VP; Fran Brignoli, Human Resources.

■ 8478 ■ Bursma Electronic Distributing Inc.
2851 Buchanan Ave., SW
Grand Rapids, MI 49548-1025
Phone: (616)831-0080
Products: Electronic parts and equipment; Electrical appliances. **SICs:** 5065 (Electronic Parts & Equipment Nec); 5064 (Electrical Appliances—Television & Radio). **Sales:** $7,000,000 (2000). **Emp:** 50. **Officers:** D. Van Randwyk, President & Treasurer.

■ 8479 ■ Bush Supply Co.
1121 W Van Buren
Harlingen, TX 78550
Phone: (956)428-2425 **Fax:** (956)420-5094
URL: http://www.bushsupply.com
Products: Electrical and plumbing supplies. **SIC:** 5063 (Electrical Apparatus & Equipment). **Est:** 1926. **Sales:** $40,000,000 (2000). **Emp:** 130. **Officers:** Bob Burdette, President; Bill Collie, Vice President.

■ 8480 ■ C & G Electronics Co.
PO Box 1316
Tacoma, WA 98401
Phone: (253)272-3181
Free: (800)562-8458 **Fax:** (253)383-8037
Products: Electronic components, including

transformers, relays, and resistors. **SIC:** 5065 (Electronic Parts & Equipment Nec). **Est:** 1934. **Officers:** L. Norberg, President.

■ 8481 ■ Cable Converter Services Corp.
54 E Market St.
Box 407
Spencer, IN 47460
Phone: (812)829-4833 **Fax:** (812)829-4835
Products: Coaxial cable; Electronic wire and cable. **SIC:** 5063 (Electrical Apparatus & Equipment). **Officers:** John Wright, V.P., Engineering; Carlos Wright, Account Exec.

■ 8482 ■ Cain and Bultman Co.
4825 Fulton Industrial Blvd.
Atlanta, GA 30336
Phone: (404)691-0730
Products: Appliances; Heating equipment. **SICs:** 5064 (Electrical Appliances—Television & Radio); 5075 (Warm Air Heating & Air-Conditioning). **Sales:** $35,000,000 (2000). **Emp:** 68. **Officers:** V. Bauer, Manager.

■ 8483 ■ Cain Electrical Supply Corp.
PO Box 2158
Big Spring, TX 79720
Phone: (915)263-8421
Products: Electrical products, including wires. **SIC:** 5063 (Electrical Apparatus & Equipment). **Sales:** $18,000,000 (2000). **Emp:** 60. **Officers:** Tom R. Ross, President.

■ 8484 ■ California Eastern Laboratories Inc.
4590 Patrick Henry Dr.
Santa Clara, CA 95056
Phone: (408)988-3500 **Fax:** (408)988-0279
Products: Electronic parts and components. **SIC:** 5065 (Electronic Parts & Equipment Nec). **Sales:** $80,000,000 (2000). **Emp:** 180. **Officers:** Jerry A. Arden, CEO & President; R.W. Iles, CFO.

■ 8485 ■ California Electric Supply
1201 Callens Rd.
Ventura, CA 93003-5614
Phone: (805)642-2181 **Fax:** (805)642-8629
Products: Electrical equipment for industrial use. **SIC:** 5063 (Electrical Apparatus & Equipment). **Emp:** 23.

■ 8486 ■ California Micro Devices Inc.
2000 W 14th St.
Tempe, AZ 85281
Phone: (480)921-6000 **Fax:** (480)921-6598
Products: Integrated circuits and thin film passive components. **SIC:** 5065 (Electronic Parts & Equipment Nec).

■ 8487 ■ Call Management Products Inc.
510 Compton St. Ste. 102
Broomfield, CO 80020
Phone: (303)465-0651
Free: (800)245-9933 **Fax:** (303)465-0237
Products: Telephone interface equipment. **SIC:** 5065 (Electronic Parts & Equipment Nec). **Sales:** $800,000 (2000). **Emp:** 5. **Officers:** John O'Neill, President.

■ 8488 ■ Calrad Electronics
819 N Highland Ave.
Los Angeles, CA 90038
Phone: (323)465-2131 **Fax:** (323)465-3504
Products: Audio/video connectors, headphones and cable telephone accessories. **SIC:** 5065 (Electronic Parts & Equipment Nec). **Officers:** Robert Shupper, President.

■ 8489 ■ Caltemp Instrument Inc.
1871 Jeffrey Ave.
Escondido, CA 92027
Phone: (619)743-2800 **Fax:** (619)743-2801
Products: Electrical instruments. **SIC:** 5063 (Electrical Apparatus & Equipment). **Est:** 1973. **Sales:** $500,000 (2000). **Emp:** 3. **Officers:** William Loedel, CEO.

■ 8490 ■ Calvert Wire and Cable Corp.
5091 W 164th St.
Brook Park, OH 44142
Phone: (216)433-7600 **Fax:** (216)433-7614
Products: Electronic wire and cable; Electronic parts; Wire connectors for electrical circuitry; Power wire and

cable; Building wire and cable. **SIC:** 5063 (Electrical Apparatus & Equipment). **Est:** 1987. **Sales:** $20,000,000 (2000). **Emp:** 58. **Officers:** Brian Coughlin, President.

■ 8491 ■   Cambridge Engineering Inc.
233 Van Patten Hwy.
Burlington, VT 05401
Phone: (802)860-7228
Products: Electrical transmission equipment. **SIC:** 5063 (Electrical Apparatus & Equipment).

■ 8492 ■   Cameo Electronics Company Inc.
PO Box 724
Owings Mills, MD 21117
Phone: (410)363-6161   **Fax:** (410)363-2540
Products: Electronic components. **SIC:** 5065 (Electronic Parts & Equipment Nec). **Sales:** $10,000,000 (1994). **Emp:** 16. **Officers:** Marilyn M. Rawlings, President & CFO.

■ 8493 ■   Cameron & Barkley
PO Box 40519
Raleigh, NC 27629-0519
Phone: (919)834-6010   **Fax:** (919)834-1774
Products: Electronic and industrial supplies. **SICs:** 5065 (Electronic Parts & Equipment Nec); 5085 (Industrial Supplies).

■ 8494 ■   Canare
531 5th St., Unit A
San Fernando, CA 91340
Phone: (818)365-2446   **Fax:** (818)365-0479
E-mail: inf@canare.com
URL: http://www.canare.com
Products: Wire, wire connectors, and wire strippers; Cable reels. **SIC:** 5063 (Electrical Apparatus & Equipment). **Est:** 1983. **Officers:** Barry Brenner, COO.

■ 8495 ■   Capacitor Associates
486 Main St.
Eitzen, MN 55931-0486
Phone: (507)495-3306
Free: (800)328-0003   **Fax:** (507)495-3454
E-mail: capasc@means.net
Products: Capacitors; Resistors; Wire; Connectors; Inductors. **SICs:** 5065 (Electronic Parts & Equipment Nec); 5063 (Electrical Apparatus & Equipment). **Est:** 1984. **Emp:** 17. **Officers:** Roger Dunn, President; Steve Sand, Vice President.

■ 8496 ■   Capital Lighting & Supply - Baltimore/Lee Electric Div.
600 W Hamburg St.
Baltimore, MD 21230
Phone: (410)752-4080
Free: (800)533-1533   **Fax:** (410)332-1533
Products: Lamps and lighting fixtures. **SIC:** 5063 (Electrical Apparatus & Equipment). **Est:** 1908. **Sales:** $15,000,000 (2000). **Emp:** 50. **Officers:** David Pullias, President; Mark E. Coolahan, VP & General Mgr.
Former Name: Lee Electric Company of Baltimore City.

■ 8497 ■   Capital Lighting & Supply Inc.
3950 Wheeler Ave.
Alexandria, VA 22304-6429
Phone: (703)823-6000   **Fax:** (703)823-1766
Products: Electrical equipment and supplies. **SIC:** 5063 (Electrical Apparatus & Equipment). **Est:** 1958. **Sales:** $40,000,000 (2000). **Emp:** 62. **Officers:** John Hardy, President; Thomas J. Collins III, Exec. VP.

■ 8498 ■   Capitol Light and Supply Co.
270 Locust St.
Hartford, CT 06141-0179
Phone: (203)549-1230
Products: Electrical supplies, including lights and panel boards. **SIC:** 5063 (Electrical Apparatus & Equipment). **Est:** 1926. **Sales:** $55,000,000 (2000). **Emp:** 125. **Officers:** Mickey Cartin, CEO; Bob Compagna, President; Bob Capagna, General Mgr.; Greg Hushin, Dir. of Data Processing.

■ 8499 ■   Capp Inc.
201 Marple Ave.
Clifton Heights, PA 19018-2414
Phone: (215)472-7700
Products: Automatic controls. **SIC:** 5065 (Electronic

Parts & Equipment Nec). **Sales:** $20,000,000 (2000). **Emp:** 115. **Officers:** Chuck Caplan, President; Jim Caplan, Exec. VP of Finance.

■ 8500 ■   Captre Electrical Supply
2289 3rd Ave.
New York, NY 10035
Phone: (212)534-3546   **Fax:** (212)876-0837
Products: Electrical supplies, including light bulbs, circuit-breakers, and wire. **SIC:** 5063 (Electrical Apparatus & Equipment). **Emp:** 49.

■ 8501 ■   Cardello Electric Supply Co.
701 Chateau St.
Pittsburgh, PA 15233
Phone: (412)322-8031   **Fax:** (412)322-8060
Products: Electrical supplies. **SIC:** 5063 (Electrical Apparatus & Equipment). **Sales:** $20,000,000 (1992). **Emp:** 100. **Officers:** Nicholas Cardello, CEO; Robert Neeley, Treasurer.

■ 8502 ■   Carlberg Warren & Associates
181 W Orangethorpe, Ste. E
Placentia, CA 92870-6931
Phone: (714)961-7300   **Fax:** (714)961-7310
Products: Electronic systems and equipment. **SIC:** 5065 (Electronic Parts & Equipment Nec).

■ 8503 ■   Carlos Franco
311 S Broadway
McAllen, TX 78501
Phone: (956)687-4662   **Fax:** (956)682-3470
Products: Electrical and electronic equipment and supplies. **SIC:** 5065 (Electronic Parts & Equipment Nec).

■ 8504 ■   Carlton-Bates Co.
PO Box 192320
Little Rock, AR 72219
Phone: (501)562-9100   **Fax:** (501)562-4931
Products: Electronic parts. **SIC:** 5065 (Electronic Parts & Equipment Nec). **Sales:** $110,000,000 (2000). **Emp:** 370. **Officers:** Bill Carlton, President; Steve Allen, Treasurer & Secty.

■ 8505 ■   Carroll Electronics Inc.
PO Box 1513
Topeka, KS 66601-1513
Phone: (785)234-6677
Free: (800)926-7059   **Fax:** (785)234-6678
Products: Electronic parts and sound equipment. **SIC:** 5065 (Electronic Parts & Equipment Nec). **Officers:** Robert Radefeld, President.

■ 8506 ■   Casella Lighting Co.
111 Rhode Island St.
San Francisco, CA 94103
Phone: (415)626-9600   **Fax:** (415)626-4539
E-mail: info@casellalighting.com
URL: http://www.casellalighting.com
Products: Lighting and light fixtures. **SIC:** 5023 (Homefurnishings). **Est:** 1929. **Sales:** $4,900,000 (1999). **Emp:** 29. **Officers:** Georgine A. Casella, President; Georgine Casella, Dir. of Marketing; Tim Mulvenon, Controller.

■ 8507 ■   Cashway Electrical Supply Co.
275 Mariposa St.
Denver, CO 80223
Phone: (303)623-0151
Products: Electrical supplies, including panel boxes, breakers and switches. **SIC:** 5063 (Electrical Apparatus & Equipment). **Est:** 1918. **Sales:** $12,000,000 (2000). **Emp:** 53. **Officers:** Richard W. Allard, CEO.

■ 8508 ■   Cathay International
290 W Arrow Hwy.
San Dimas, CA 91773
Phone: (909)394-7806   **Fax:** (909)394-7813
Products: Electronics; Giftware; Cards. **SICs:** 5065 (Electronic Parts & Equipment Nec); 5112 (Stationery & Office Supplies); 5199 (Nondurable Goods Nec).

■ 8509 ■   Cayce Mill Supply Co.
PO Box 689
Hopkinsville, KY 42241-0689
Phone: (502)886-3335
Free: (800)462-8362   **Fax:** (502)886-5117
E-mail: sales@caymill.com
URL: http://www.caycemill.com
Products: Plumbing supplies; Electrical supplies; HVAC supplies; Industrial supplies. **SICs:** 5063 (Electrical Apparatus & Equipment); 5074 (Plumbing & Hydronic Heating Supplies); 5085 (Industrial Supplies). **Est:** 1919. **Sales:** $11,600,000 (1999). **Emp:** 58. **Officers:** Breck Cayce, President.

■ 8510 ■   CB Distributing
3297 Salem Ave. SE
Albany, OR 97321
Phone: (541)926-1027
Free: (800)553-1027   **Fax:** (541)926-7640
E-mail: sales@cbdistributing.com
URL: http://www.cbdistributing.com
Products: Electronics. **SIC:** 5065 (Electronic Parts & Equipment Nec).

■ 8511 ■   C.B. Electronic Marketing
6429 Iris Way
Arvada, CO 80004
Phone: (303)422-0561   **Fax:** (303)422-0668
Products: Electronic systems and equipment. **SIC:** 5065 (Electronic Parts & Equipment Nec).

■ 8512 ■   CBS WhitCom Technologies Corp.
2990 Express Dr. S
Islandia, NY 11749
Phone: (516)582-3200   **Fax:** (516)582-6063
Products: Communications Systems and Equipmentt. **SIC:** 5065 (Electronic Parts & Equipment Nec). **Sales:** $17,000,000 (2000). **Emp:** 98.

■ 8513 ■   CED Inc.
16 SE I Ave.
Lawton, OK 73501-2449
Phone: (580)355-5883   **Fax:** (580)355-5895
Products: Electrical products. **SIC:** 5063 (Electrical Apparatus & Equipment). **Emp:** 4.

■ 8514 ■   CED/Superior Electrical Supply Co.
PO Box 3156
Evansville, IN 47731
Phone: (812)423-7837   **Fax:** (812)429-1888
Products: Wires. **SIC:** 5063 (Electrical Apparatus & Equipment). **Est:** 1944. **Sales:** $4,000,000 (2000). **Emp:** 8. **Officers:** Brian C. Dunker, Manager.

■ 8515 ■   Cel Air Corp.
1605 Lakes Pkwy.
Lawrenceville, GA 30043
Phone: (770)339-1672
Products: Air alkaline batteries. **SIC:** 5063 (Electrical Apparatus & Equipment). **Sales:** $900,000 (1994). **Emp:** 3. **Officers:** Ivan Bilbao, President.

■ 8516 ■   Central California Electronics Inc.
139 E Belmont St.
Fresno, CA 93701
Phone: (209)485-1254
Products: Electronic parts and equipment. **SIC:** 5065 (Electronic Parts & Equipment Nec). **Sales:** $2,000,000 (2000). **Emp:** 30. **Officers:** Jay Johnson, CEO; John M. Peters, CFO.

■ 8517 ■   Central Electric Supply Co.
PO Box 1025
Worcester, MA 01613
Phone: (508)755-1271   **Fax:** (508)795-1638
Products: Electrical equipment. **SIC:** 5063 (Electrical Apparatus & Equipment). **Est:** 1923. **Emp:** 15. **Officers:** G.M. Freed, President; L. Freed, VP & Treasurer.

■ 8518 ■   Century Wheels Research
7800 Winn Rd.
Spring Grove, IL 60081-9687
Phone: (815)675-2366   **Fax:** (815)675-2509
Products: Telephone and telegraph wire and cable. **SIC:** 5065 (Electronic Parts & Equipment Nec). **Emp:** 20.

■ 8519 ■ CEO/United Electric Supply Co.
6910 Central Hwy.
Pennsauken, NJ 08109-4110
Products: Electrical equipment and supplies. **SIC:** 5063 (Electrical Apparatus & Equipment). **Sales:** $30,000,000 (2000). **Emp:** 100. **Officers:** Frank Carevelli, General Mgr.

■ 8520 ■ Cerprobe Corp.
1150 N Fiesta Blvd.
Gilbert, AZ 85233-2237
Phone: (480)333-1500 **Fax:** (480)333-1671
Products: Probe cards and interface devices for testing semiconductors. **SIC:** 5065 (Electronic Parts & Equipment Nec). **Sales:** $76,200,000 (2000). **Emp:** 590. **Officers:** C Zane Close, CEO & President; Randal L. Buness, Vice President, Finance & Administration.

■ 8521 ■ Certex Gulf Coast
PO Box 10367
New Orleans, LA 70181-0367
Phone: (504)734-5871 **Fax:** (504)733-1126
Products: Wire cable; Lifting products. **SIC:** 5063 (Electrical Apparatus & Equipment). **Est:** 1957. **Sales:** $14,000,000 (2000). **Emp:** 40. **Officers:** Darryll Porter, President; Chris Black, General Mgr.

■ 8522 ■ Channer Corp.
13720 Polo Trail Dr.
Lake Forest, IL 60045
Phone: (847)816-7000 **Fax:** (847)816-7077
Products: Insulated wire. **SIC:** 5063 (Electrical Apparatus & Equipment). **Sales:** $8,500,000 (2000). **Emp:** 65. **Officers:** J.W. Bauer, President; Dennis Mott, Treasurer.

■ 8523 ■ Chicago Electric Co.
901 S Route 53, No. H
Addison, IL 60101
Phone: (630)495-2900
Free: (800)777-2901 **Fax:** (630)495-2992
URL: http://www.chicagoelectric.com
Products: Electrical and industrial equipment. **SICs:** 5063 (Electrical Apparatus & Equipment); 5084 (Industrial Machinery & Equipment). **Est:** 1910. **Sales:** $5,000,000 (2000). **Emp:** 30. **Officers:** Robert E. Kaska, President.

■ 8524 ■ Christensen Electric Motor Inc.
2645 Lincoln Ave.
Ogden, UT 84401
Phone: (801)392-5309
Products: Electric motors. **SIC:** 5063 (Electrical Apparatus & Equipment).

■ 8525 ■ Cinemills Corp.
3500 W Magnolia Blvd.
Burbank, CA 91505
Phones: (818)843-4560 800-692-6700
Free: (800)325-7674 **Fax:** (818)843-7834
E-mail: slaes@cinemills.com
URL: http://www.cinemills.com
Products: Motion picture lighting; Lighting filters. **SIC:** 5063 (Electrical Apparatus & Equipment). **Est:** 1976. **Emp:** 35. **Officers:** Walter H. Mills, President; Sandra L. Mills, Vice President; Linda Roberts, Sales; Cathy Runyan, Sales & Marketing Contact, e-mail: cat@cinemills.com; Linda Roberts, Customer Service Contact, e-mail: linda@cinemills.com.

■ 8526 ■ Cisco Electrical Supply Co.
883 King Ave.
Columbus, OH 43212
Phone: (614)299-6606 **Fax:** (614)299-2378
Products: Electrical equipment and supplies. **SIC:** 5063 (Electrical Apparatus & Equipment). **Est:** 1978. **Sales:** $3,000,000 (2000). **Emp:** 10. **Officers:** Francisco Muguruza, President & Treasurer.

■ 8527 ■ City Electric Motor Co.
631 Kennedy Rd.
Lexington, KY 40511-1821
Phone: (859)254-5581
Free: (800)666-7707 **Fax:** (859)253-0121
Products: Electrical apparatus, including generators and motors. **SIC:** 5063 (Electrical Apparatus & Equipment). **Est:** 1947. **Emp:** 15.

■ 8528 ■ City Plumbing & Electrical Supply
206 College Ave. SE
Gainesville, GA 30501-4512
Phone: (404)532-4123 **Fax:** (404)534-8007
Products: Plumbing supplies; Electrical supplies. **SICs:** 5063 (Electrical Apparatus & Equipment); 5074 (Plumbing & Hydronic Heating Supplies). **Sales:** $7,000,000 (2000). **Emp:** 54. **Officers:** Ed Teaver.

■ 8529 ■ Claricom Inc.
850 Dubuque Ave.
South San Francisco, CA 94080
Phone: (650)952-2000 **Fax:** (650)244-6599
Products: Designs, and supports voice processing and digital business telephone systems. **SIC:** 5065 (Electronic Parts & Equipment Nec).

■ 8530 ■ Dick Clark Productions Inc.
3003 W Olive Ave.
Burbank, CA 91510-7811
Phone: (818)841-3003 **Fax:** (818)954-8609
Products: Movie and video production. **SIC:** 5043 (Photographic Equipment & Supplies). **Sales:** $73,200,000 (2000). **Emp:** 800. **Officers:** Richard W. Clark, CEO & Chairman of the Board; William S. Simon, VP, CFO & Treasurer; Francis L. LaMaina.

■ 8531 ■ Classic Components Supply Inc.
3336 Commercial Ave.
Northbrook, IL 60062
Phone: (708)272-9650 **Fax:** (708)272-9264
Products: Electronic components, including sockets, wire, capacitors, and resistors. **SIC:** 5063 (Electrical Apparatus & Equipment). **Est:** 1978. **Sales:** $4,000,000 (2000). **Emp:** 15. **Officers:** Robert J. Riley, President.

■ 8532 ■ Cleveland Electric Motors
2536 W Dixon Blvd.
Shelby, NC 28152
Phone: (704)484-0186
Products: Electric motors. **SIC:** 5063 (Electrical Apparatus & Equipment).

■ 8533 ■ Clifford of Vermont Inc.
Rte. 107, Box 51
Bethel, VT 05032
Phone: (802)234-9921
Free: (800)451-4381 **Fax:** (802)234-5006
E-mail: cablesales@cliffcom.com
URL: http://www.cliffordvt.com
Products: Wire, cable, and related supplies and equipment. **SIC:** 5063 (Electrical Apparatus & Equipment). **Est:** 1946. **Sales:** $28,000,000 (2000). **Emp:** 50. **Officers:** Maynard Nelson, President; Tyna Baird, Manufacturing Mgr.; Cyrus Parker, Sales Mgr.

■ 8534 ■ CLS
270 Locust St.
Hartford, CT 06141-0179
Phone: (860)549-1230 **Free:** (800)842-8078
URL: http://www.clsco.com
Products: Electrical equipment. **SIC:** 5063 (Electrical Apparatus & Equipment). **Est:** 1926. **Sales:** $105,000,000 (2000). **Emp:** 245. **Officers:** Mickey Cartin, CEO; Bob Compagna, President. **Alternate Name:** Capitol Light and Supply Inc. Co.

■ 8535 ■ CLS
270 Locust St.
Hartford, CT 06141-0179
Phone: (860)549-1230 **Free:** (800)842-8078
Products: Electrical and electronic equipment and supplies. **SIC:** 5063 (Electrical Apparatus & Equipment). **Sales:** $105,000,000 (2000). **Emp:** 245.

■ 8536 ■ Coast Wire and Plastic Tech Inc.
1510 W 135th St.
Gardena, CA 90249
Phone: (310)327-5260 **Fax:** (310)538-8997
Products: Wire and cable. **SIC:** 5063 (Electrical Apparatus & Equipment). **Est:** 1970. **Sales:** $3,000,000 (2000). **Emp:** 45. **Officers:** Terry McInnes, General Mgr.; Marie Ochoa, Controller; Gregg McAfee, Dir. of Marketing & Sales.

■ 8537 ■ Cobra Electronics Corp.
6500 W Cortland St.
Chicago, IL 60707
Phone: (773)889-8870 **Fax:** (773)889-4453
Products: Cordless telephones, answering systems, CB radios, safety and radar detection systems. **SIC:** 5065 (Electronic Parts & Equipment Nec). **Sales:** $103,400,000 (2000). **Emp:** 130. **Officers:** James R. Bazet, CEO & President.

■ 8538 ■ Codale Electric Supply Inc.
PO Box 651418
Salt Lake City, UT 84165
Phone: (801)263-3000
Products: Electrical supplies, including lamps, wires, cable, and switch boxes. **SIC:** 5063 (Electrical Apparatus & Equipment).

■ 8539 ■ Coleman Electric Company Inc.
222 Hamilton St
Allentown, PA 18101
Phone: (610)434-4881 **Fax:** (610)820-9020
Products: Electrical supplies, including lighting fixtures. **SIC:** 5063 (Electrical Apparatus & Equipment). **Est:** 1919. **Sales:** $600,000 (2000). **Emp:** 18. **Officers:** Harold McArdle, Manager.

■ 8540 ■ Coleman Powermate Inc.
PO Box 6001
Kearney, NE 68848-6001
Phone: (308)237-2181
Free: (800)445-1805 **Fax:** (308)234-4187
Products: Electrical generators. **SIC:** 5063 (Electrical Apparatus & Equipment).

■ 8541 ■ Colin Electric Motor Services
520 W O St.
Lincoln, NE 68528
Phone: (402)476-2121
Free: (800)233-5663 **Fax:** (402)476-8765
E-mail: cemsco@navix.net
URL: http://www.cemsco.com
Products: Electric motors. **SIC:** 5063 (Electrical Apparatus & Equipment). **Est:** 1912. **Sales:** $23,486,908 (1999). **Emp:** 54. **Officers:** Ron L. Colin, CEO; Sandra S. Love, Exec. VP; Shawn W. Traudt, VP of Operations.

■ 8542 ■ Paul Collins & Associates
1700 E Garry Ave., Ste. 101
Santa Ana, CA 92705-5828
Phone: (949)833-9949 **Fax:** (949)833-9945
Products: Electronic systems and equipment. **SIC:** 5065 (Electronic Parts & Equipment Nec).

■ 8543 ■ Collins Communications Inc.
1009 W Jackson St.
Demopolis, AL 36732-1617
Phone: (334)289-0439
Products: Communications equipment; Computers; Telephones. **SIC:** 5065 (Electronic Parts & Equipment Nec). **Est:** 1964. **Officers:** Woody Collins, President.

■ 8544 ■ Colombian Development Corp.
194 Melba St.
Staten Island, NY 10314-5335
Phone: (718)494-6034 **Fax:** (718)494-6139
Products: Electronic parts and equipment; Hardware; Construction and mining machinery; Industrial machinery and equipment; Electrical apparatus and equipment. **SICs:** 5063 (Electrical Apparatus & Equipment); 5065 (Electronic Parts & Equipment Nec); 5072 (Hardware); 5082 (Construction & Mining Machinery); 5084 (Industrial Machinery & Equipment). **Officers:** August Puca Jr., President.

■ 8545 ■ Colonial Electric Supply Company Inc.
485 S Henderson Rd.
King of Prussia, PA 19406
Phone: (610)312-8100 **Fax:** (610)312-8131
Products: Electrical supplies and equipment. **SIC:** 5063 (Electrical Apparatus & Equipment). **Sales:** $30,000,000 (2000). **Emp:** 100. **Officers:** Steve Bellwoar, President; Joseph W. Bellwoar, Chairman of the Board.

■ 8546 ■ Colorado Electronic Hardware Inc.
4975 Iris St.
Wheat Ridge, CO 80033
Phone: (303)431-4334
Free: (800)525-2129 **Fax:** (303)420-0479
Products: Electrical hanging and fastening devices.
SIC: 5063 (Electrical Apparatus & Equipment).

■ 8547 ■ Colorado Wire and Cable Company Inc.
485 Osage St.
Denver, CO 80204
Phone: (303)534-0114
Products: Electrical wire and cable. **SIC:** 5063
(Electrical Apparatus & Equipment). **Sales:** $3,000,000
(1993). **Emp:** 12. **Officers:** Bonnie Riley, President.

■ 8548 ■ Columbia Audio-Video Inc.
1741 2nd St.
Highland Park, IL 60035
Phone: (847)433-6010
Products: Consumer electronics. **SIC:** 5064 (Electrical
Appliances—Television & Radio). **Sales:** $56,000,000
(2000). **Emp:** 100. **Officers:** Norm Rozak, President.

■ 8549 ■ Com-Kyl
7939 SW Cirrus Dr.
Beaverton, OR 97005
Phone: (503)626-6633 **Fax:** (503)641-0504
Products: Electronic equipment; Hand tools. **SICs:**
5065 (Electronic Parts & Equipment Nec); 5072
(Hardware).

■ 8550 ■ Comlink Inc. (Roseville, California)
1052 Melody Ln., No. 280
Roseville, CA 95678
Phone: (916)783-8885
Free: (800)433-3892 **Fax:** (916)783-2076
Products: Multiplexes. **SIC:** 5065 (Electronic Parts &
Equipment Nec). **Est:** 1981. **Sales:** $5,000,000 (2000).
Emp: 20. **Officers:** Wayne Stafford, President; Cynthia
Zibull, Accounting Manager.

■ 8551 ■ Commercial Electric Products Corp.
1738 E 30th St.
Cleveland, OH 44114-4408
Phone: (216)241-2886 **Fax:** (216)241-1734
URL: http://www.commercialelectric.com
Products: Electric motors; Electric motor controls. **SIC:**
5063 (Electrical Apparatus & Equipment). **Est:** 1929.
Sales: $6,000,000 (2000). **Emp:** 65. **Officers:** R.W.
Meyer; R.F. Meyer.

■ 8552 ■ Communications Products and Services Inc.
1740 W Warren Ave.
Englewood, CO 80110
Phone: (303)922-4519
Free: (800)878-2771 **Fax:** (303)922-2722
E-mail: cpsinc@aol.com
Products: Conduit products; Fiber optic cable and
access; Outside plant materials. **SICs:** 5063 (Electrical
Apparatus & Equipment); 5193 (Flowers & Florists'
Supplies). **Est:** 1986. **Sales:** $10,000,000 (2000).
Emp: 9. **Officers:** Fred Briggs, President; Richard
Meierbachtol.

■ 8553 ■ Compass Technology of Burlington Massachusetts
111 S Bedford St.
Burlington, MA 01803
Phone: (781)272-9990
Products: Semiconductors. **SIC:** 5065 (Electronic
Parts & Equipment Nec).

■ 8554 ■ Component Resources Inc.
14525 SW Walker Rd.
Beaverton, OR 97006-5921
Phone: (503)641-8488
Free: (800)547-6523 **Fax:** (503)641-1298
E-mail: crior@compres.com
URL: http://www.compres.com
Products: Electromechanical components and
fasteners. **SICs:** 5063 (Electrical Apparatus &
Equipment); 5065 (Electronic Parts & Equipment Nec).
Est: 1978. **Emp:** 50. **Officers:** Paul A. Craig; Michael
W. Leiser.

■ 8555 ■ CompuLink Electronic Inc.
875 Ave. of the Amer., No. 2411
New York, NY 10001
Phone: (212)695-5465 **Fax:** (212)695-5560
URL: http://www.compu-link.com
Products: Networking equipment; Computers. **SICs:**
5065 (Electronic Parts & Equipment Nec); 5045
(Computers, Peripherals & Software). **Est:** 1980.
Sales: $2,500,000 (1999). **Emp:** 16. **Officers:** Rafael
Arboleda, President, e-mail: rafael@compu-link.com;
Shem Sargent, Sales/Marketing Contact, e-mail:
shem_sargent@compu-link.com; Lisa Badillo,
Customer Service Contact, e-mail: lisa@compu-
link.com; Denise Arboleda, Human Resource Contact,
e-mail: denise@compu-link.com.

■ 8556 ■ Computer Sports Systems Inc.
385 Western Ave.
Boston, MA 02135-1005
Phone: (617)492-6500 **Fax:** (617)492-7033
Products: Electronic parts and equipment;
Communication equipment; Modems and computers.
SICs: 5065 (Electronic Parts & Equipment Nec); 5045
(Computers, Peripherals & Software). **Officers:** Gene
Greystone, President.

■ 8557 ■ Computer Support Systems Inc.
PO Box 7738
Des Moines, IA 50322-0958
Phone: (515)276-8826 **Fax:** (515)276-8779
Products: Electrical and environmental systems. **SIC:**
5065 (Electronic Parts & Equipment Nec). **Officers:**
Ron Bieghler, President.

■ 8558 ■ Con Serve Electric Supply
3905 Crescent St.
Long Island City, NY 11101-3801
Phone: (718)937-6671 **Fax:** (718)937-4057
Products: Electrical and electronic equipment and
supplies. **SIC:** 5063 (Electrical Apparatus &
Equipment).

■ 8559 ■ Conformance Technology Inc.
PO Box 801207
Dallas, TX 75380
Phone: (972)233-0020
Products: Cables, connectors, and battery packs. **SIC:**
5063 (Electrical Apparatus & Equipment).

■ 8560 ■ Connectronics Corp.
PO Box 908
Southport, CT 06490-0908
Phone: (203)375-5577
Free: (800)322-2537 **Fax:** (203)375-5811
Products: Electronic wire and cable; Connectors for
electronic circuitry; Rack and panel connectors for
electronic circuitry; Electronic wire and cable. **SIC:**
5063 (Electrical Apparatus & Equipment). **Officers:**
Richard Chilvers, President.

■ 8561 ■ Conserve-A-Watt Lighting Inc.
PO Box 4279
Denver, CO 80204
Phone: (303)629-0066 **Fax:** (303)893-3315
Products: Electric light bulbs. **SIC:** 5063 (Electrical
Apparatus & Equipment). **Emp:** 33. **Officers:** Stephen
Koutavas.

■ 8562 ■ Conserve Electric
78 Myer St.
Hackensack, NJ 07601
Phone: (201)996-6090 **Fax:** (201)996-0012
E-mail: www.conserveelectric.com
Products: Electrical supplies. **SIC:** 5063 (Electrical
Apparatus & Equipment). **Est:** 1979. **Sales:**
$8,000,000 (2000). **Emp:** 25. **Officers:** L. Sullivan,
President; Stuart Cleary, Human Resources Contact;
Tony Buono, Sales & Marketing Contact; Charles
Danko, Customer Service Contact; Donna Hooper,
General Mgr.; Debbie Berrios, Controller. **Former
Name:** Con Serve Electric Supply.

■ 8563 ■ Consolidated Communications Corp.
6715 Cedar Springs Rd.
Charlotte, NC 28212
Phone: (704)536-8804 **Fax:** (704)537-6734
Products: Modems; Multiplex CRT monitors; Cables.
SIC: 5065 (Electronic Parts & Equipment Nec). **Est:**
1980. **Sales:** $500,000 (2000). **Emp:** 8. **Officers:**
James F. English, President; Bob Hunt, Controller.

■ 8564 ■ Consolidated Electrical Distributing
223 Sage St.
Carson City, NV 89706
Phone: (775)883-4508
Products: Electrical equipment. **SIC:** 5063 (Electrical
Apparatus & Equipment).

■ 8565 ■ Consolidated Electrical Distributor
330 19th Ave. N
Nashville, TN 37203
Phone: (615)340-7750
Products: Electrical equipment and supplies. **SIC:**
5063 (Electrical Apparatus & Equipment).

■ 8566 ■ Consolidated Electrical Distributor
343 Hilliard Ave.
Asheville, NC 28801
Phone: (828)252-5313
Products: Electrical equipment and supplies. **SIC:**
5063 (Electrical Apparatus & Equipment).

■ 8567 ■ Consolidated Electrical Distributors°
649 E 18th Pl.
Yuma, AZ 85365
Phone: (520)782-2586
Products: Electrical equipment and supplies. **SIC:**
5063 (Electrical Apparatus & Equipment).

■ 8568 ■ Consolidated Electrical Distributors
2611 Kimco Dr., No. 1
Lincoln, NE 68521
Phone: (402)465-5151
Products: Electrical equipment. **SIC:** 5063 (Electrical
Apparatus & Equipment).

■ 8569 ■ Consolidated Electrical Distributors Inc.
305 E University
Odessa, TX 79762-7664
Phone: (915)333-2812 **Fax:** (915)333-6536
Products: Motor controls; Conduit; Wire. **SIC:** 5063
(Electrical Apparatus & Equipment). **Emp:** 49.

■ 8570 ■ Consolidated Electrical Distributors Inc.
1807 Palma Dr.
Ventura, CA 93003
Phone: (805)642-0361 **Fax:** (805)654-0569
URL: http://www.cedis.com/ventura
Products: Electrical supplies. **SIC:** 5063 (Electrical
Apparatus & Equipment). **Est:** 1957. **Emp:** 24.
Officers: Frank Zych, Manager.

■ 8571 ■ Consolidated Electrical Distributors Inc.
31356 Via Colinas, Ste. 107
Westlake Village, CA 91362
Phone: (818)991-9000 **Fax:** (818)991-6858
Products: Electrical equipment and supplies. **SICs:**
5063 (Electrical Apparatus & Equipment); 5065
(Electronic Parts & Equipment Nec). **Sales:**
$640,000,000 (2000). **Emp:** 2,500. **Officers:** Keith W.
Colburn, CEO; Tom Lullo, CFO.

■ 8572 ■ Consolidated Electrical Distributors Inc. Perry-Mann Electrical
431 Williams St.
Columbia, SC 29201
Phone: (803)252-4373
Free: (800)467-2265 **Fax:** (803)254-5020
E-mail: ced1140@aol.com
Products: Electrical conduit and conduit fittings; Wiring
supplies; Panelboards; Switches; Electrical equipment
and supplies. **SIC:** 5063 (Electrical Apparatus &
Equipment). **Est:** 1899. **Sales:** $7,000,000 (1999).
Emp: 16. **Officers:** Gary Sibille, General Mgr.

■ 8573 ■ Consolidated Electronics Inc.
PO Box 20070
Dayton, OH 45420-0070
Phone: (937)252-5662
Free: (800)543-3568 **Fax:** (937)252-4066
E-mail: sales@ceitron.com
URL: http://www.ceitron.com
Products: Electronic components. **SIC:** 5063
(Electrical Apparatus & Equipment). **Est:** 1979. **Sales:**

$1,000,000 (2000). **Emp:** 4. **Officers:** Steven Coy, President.

■ **8574** ■ **Contech Instrumentation**
7 State Route 27, Ste. 103
Edison, NJ 08820-3965
Phone: (732)560-0702 **Fax:** (732)560-7389
Products: Electric and electronic equipment. **SIC:** 5065 (Electronic Parts & Equipment Nec). **Est:** 1993. **Sales:** $4,000,000 (2000). **Emp:** 5. **Officers:** Sam Simione, President.

■ **8575** ■ **Continental Marketing**
18175 SW 100th Ct.
Tualatin, OR 97062-9482
Phone: (503)692-8138 **Fax:** (503)692-8178
Products: Electronic systems and equipment. **SIC:** 5064 (Electrical Appliances—Television & Radio). **Officers:** Robert Budihas, President.

■ **8576** ■ **Control Switches International Inc.**
2405 Mira Mar Ave.
Long Beach, CA 90815
Phone: (562)498-3599
Free: (800)521-1677 **Fax:** (562)498-5894
E-mail: info@controlswitches.com
URL: http://www.controlswitches.com
Products: Electrical switches and components; Disconnects; Terminal blocks; Din rail; Wiring duct; Motor control; Pilot devices. **SIC:** 5063 (Electrical Apparatus & Equipment). **Est:** 1957. **Emp:** 35. **Officers:** D. Jack Armstrong, President; Susie A. Moore, Controller; Peggy A. Turner, Vice President; Jinny Elliott, Dir. of Data Processing; Vasile Boboaka, Engineering Mgr.

■ **8577** ■ **Controls-Instruments-Devices**
1810 Auger Dr., Ste. G
Tucker, GA 30084-6603
Phone: (404)491-3143 **Fax:** (404)934-1482
E-mail: dugroot@mindspring.com
URL: http://www.cidonline.com
Products: Electronic systems and equipment; Electronic parts. **SIC:** 5065 (Electronic Parts & Equipment Nec). **Est:** 1978. **Emp:** 10. **Officers:** Gary Root, President.

■ **8578** ■ **Cooper Electric Supply Co.**
70 Apple St.
Eatontown, NJ 07724
Phone: (908)747-2233 **Fax:** (908)576-8770
Products: Electrical supplies, including cable and wire. **SIC:** 5063 (Electrical Apparatus & Equipment). **Est:** 1961. **Sales:** $65,000,000 (2000). **Emp:** 210. **Officers:** Richard A. Cooper, President; Ralph Garrow, VP of Finance; Phil Leisure, Dir. of Marketing.

■ **8579** ■ **Copy Supply Concepts Inc.**
14998 W 6th Ave., Ste. E-550
Golden, CO 80401-5025
Phone: (303)271-1100 **Fax:** (303)271-1238
Products: Electronic parts and equipment, including facsimile equipment. **SIC:** 5065 (Electronic Parts & Equipment Nec). **Officers:** Tom Lutes, President.

■ **8580** ■ **Coral Sales Co.**
PO Box 22385
Milwaukie, OR 97269-2385
Phone: (503)655-6351 **Fax:** (503)657-9649
Products: Impact attenuators. **SIC:** 5065 (Electronic Parts & Equipment Nec). **Est:** 1979. **Sales:** $10,000,000 (2000). **Emp:** 5. **Officers:** Douglas P. Daniels, President; Brian Steenson, Secretary; Kathleen C. Johnson, Vice President.

■ **8581** ■ **Cordial/Riley Marketing**
5104 Bronco Dr.
Clarkston, MI 48346
Phone: (248)625-2420 **Fax:** (248)625-5959
Products: Electronic systems and equipment. **SIC:** 5065 (Electronic Parts & Equipment Nec).

■ **8582** ■ **Cornerstone Controls Inc.**
7251 E Kemper Rd.
Cincinnati, OH 45249
Phone: (513)489-2500 **Fax:** (513)489-3693
Products: Industrial electronic control systems; Control valves; Regulators and system integrators. **SICs:** 5085 (Industrial Supplies); 5085 (Industrial Supplies). **Est:**

1980. **Sales:** $24,000,000 (2000). **Emp:** 93. **Officers:** Lawrence B. Reams, President.

■ **8583** ■ **Cosmotec Inc.**
300 Long Beach Blvd.
Stratford, CT 06497-7153
Phone: (203)378-8388 **Fax:** (203)375-4423
Products: Electronic equipment and parts; Industrial, utility and aerospace equipment. **SICs:** 5065 (Electronic Parts & Equipment Nec); 5084 (Industrial Machinery & Equipment). **Officers:** Edward Matson, President.

■ **8584** ■ **Coyote Network Systems, Inc.**
1640 S Sepulveda Blvd.
Los Angeles, CA 90040
Phone: (818)735-7600 **Fax:** (818)735-7633
E-mail: asqueglia@cyoe.com
URL: http://www.cyoe.com
Products: Electronic equipment. Telecom equipment, international and domestic long distance services, network operations and communications support services. **SIC:** 5065 (Electronic Parts & Equipment Nec). **Est:** 1961. **Sales:** $43,318,000 (1999). **Emp:** 1. **Officers:** James J. Fielder, CEO; Brian A. Robson, VP & Controller. **Former Name:** Diana Corp.

■ **8585** ■ **Creative Stage Lighting Company Inc.**
149 Rte. 28 N
PO Box 567
North Creek, NY 12853-0567
Phone: (518)251-3302 **Fax:** (518)251-2908
E-mail: info@creativestagelighting.com
URL: http://www.creativestagelighting.com
Products: Stage lighting supplies. **SIC:** 5063 (Electrical Apparatus & Equipment). **Est:** 1977. **Sales:** $9,000,000 (1999). **Emp:** 32. **Officers:** George B. Studnicky III, President; Lily M. Studnicky, Secretary; Fred Mikeska, Sales/Marketing Contact, e-mail: fred@CreativeStageLighting.com; Laura Nevins, Customer Service Contact, e-mail: Laura@CreativeStageLighting.com; Lily Studnicky, Human Resources Contact, e-mail: Lily@CreativeStageLighting.com.

■ **8586** ■ **CREOS. Technologies LLC**
7388 S Revere Pkwy Ste. 1003
Englewood, CO 80112
Phone: (303)790-8888 **Fax:** (303)790-0808
Products: High voltage power supplies for medical equipment. **SIC:** 5065 (Electronic Parts & Equipment Nec).

■ **8587** ■ **Crescent Electric Supply Co.**
516 W Market St.
Anderson, SC 29624-1441
Phone: (864)225-4904 **Fax:** (864)226-5725
Products: Electrical supplies. **SIC:** 5063 (Electrical Apparatus & Equipment). **Emp:** 49. **Officers:** Joe A. Invester.

■ **8588** ■ **Crescent Electric Supply Co.**
2222 6th
Sioux City, IA 51101-1888
Phone: (712)277-1273 **Fax:** (712)277-0034
Products: Electrical parts. **SIC:** 5063 (Electrical Apparatus & Equipment). **Emp:** 13. **Officers:** Chris Jensen.

■ **8589** ■ **Crescent Electric Supply Co.**
PO Box 500
East Dubuque, IL 61025-4420
Phone: (815)747-3145 **Fax:** (815)747-7720
E-mail: dschmid@cesco.com
URL: http://www.cesco.com
Products: Electrical equipment and supplies. **SIC:** 5063 (Electrical Apparatus & Equipment). **Est:** 1919. **Emp:** 1,500. **Officers:** James A. Schmid.

■ **8590** ■ **Crescent Electric Supply Co.**
200 S Larkin Ave.
Joliet, IL 60436-1248
Phone: (815)725-3020 **Fax:** (815)725-3167
Products: Electrical equipment, including circuit breakers, and lighting. **SIC:** 5063 (Electrical Apparatus & Equipment). **Emp:** 21. **Officers:** John E. Smith.

■ **8591** ■ **Crescent Electric Supply Co.**
PO Box 1157
Appleton, WI 54912
Phone: (920)734-4517 **Fax:** (920)734-5393
Products: Electrical supplies, including wire and fittings. **SIC:** 5063 (Electrical Apparatus & Equipment). **Est:** 1949. **Sales:** $16,000,000 (2000). **Emp:** 49. **Officers:** Ron Buxman, General Mgr.; Donald J. Peterson, VP of Finance.

■ **8592** ■ **Crescent Electric Supply Co.**
PO Box 500
East Dubuque, IL 61025-4420
Phone: (815)747-3145 **Fax:** (815)747-7720
Products: Electrical equipment. **SIC:** 5063 (Electrical Apparatus & Equipment). **Sales:** $480,000,000 (2000). **Emp:** 1,500. **Officers:** James Schmid, CEO.

■ **8593** ■ **Crest Audio/Video/Electronics**
1662 Main St.
Buffalo, NY 14209
Phone: (716)885-5878
Free: (800)273-7828 **Fax:** (716)885-5882
Products: Audio and visual equipment; Sound equipment. **SIC:** 5065 (Electronic Parts & Equipment Nec). **Est:** 1960. **Sales:** $2,500,000 (1999). **Emp:** 12. **Officers:** John Stewart, President; Nelson Oldfield, Vice President; Chris Back, Customer Service Mgr.; Harold Worden, Customer Service Mgr.; Harold Warden, Building Department Manager.

■ **8594** ■ **Crest Industries Inc. (Alexandria, Louisiana)**
PO Box 6115
Alexandria, LA 71307-6115
Phone: (318)448-8287
Products: Electrical substations. **SIC:** 5063 (Electrical Apparatus & Equipment). **Sales:** $30,000,000 (1993). **Emp:** 200. **Officers:** J.T. Robison, President & Chairman of the Board; Robert Brinkerhoff, Treasurer.

■ **8595** ■ **Ralph Croy & Associates Inc.**
701 W Capitol Ave.
Little Rock, AR 72201-3203
Phone: (501)378-0109 **Fax:** (501)378-0164
Products: Electronic parts and equipment, including communication equipment and facsimile equipment. **SICs:** 5065 (Electronic Parts & Equipment Nec); 5044 (Office Equipment). **Officers:** Ralph Croy, Chairman of the Board.

■ **8596** ■ **Crum Electrical Supply Inc.**
1165 W English
Casper, WY 82601
Products: Lighting equipment. **SIC:** 5063 (Electrical Apparatus & Equipment). **Est:** 1975. **Sales:** $13,000,000 (2000). **Emp:** 45. **Officers:** Dave Crum, President; Jim Roden, Operations Mgr.

■ **8597** ■ **CUI Stack Inc.**
PO Box 609
Beaverton, OR 97075
Phone: (503)643-4899 **Fax:** (503)643-6129
Products: Electronic components, speakers and connectors; Power supplies. **SIC:** 5065 (Electronic Parts & Equipment Nec). **Officers:** James McKenzie, President.

■ **8598** ■ **T.F. Cushing Inc.**
PO Box 2049
Springfield, MA 01101
Phone: (413)788-7341
Free: (800)445-9763 **Fax:** (413)733-8160
E-mail: tfcushing@aol.com
Products: Connectors, relays, and switches; Valves. **SICs:** 5065 (Electronic Parts & Equipment Nec); 5063 (Electrical Apparatus & Equipment); 5085 (Industrial Supplies). **Est:** 1928. **Sales:** $1,800,000 (2000). **Emp:** 5. **Officers:** Charles Robinson, General Mgr.

■ **8599** ■ **Custom Cable Industries Inc.**
3221 Cherry Palm Dr.
Tampa, FL 33619
Phone: (813)623-2232
Free: (800)446-2232 **Fax:** (813)626-9630
Products: Telephone and telegraph wire and cable; Switches; Electronic components. **SIC:** 5063 (Electrical Apparatus & Equipment). **Est:** 1980. **Emp:** 90. **Officers:** Vejai Singh.

■ 8600 ■ **Custom Design and Manufacturing**
555 Alter St Ste. E
Broomfield, CO 80020
Phone: (303)465-2646   **Fax:** (303)465-2662
Products: Electronic components. **SIC:** 5065
(Electronic Parts & Equipment Nec).

■ 8601 ■ **Custom Supply Inc.**
2509 5th Ave. S
Birmingham, AL 35233-3303
Phone: (205)252-0141   **Fax:** (205)251-7118
Products: Electronic systems and equipment;
Electronic parts. **SIC:** 5065 (Electronic Parts &
Equipment Nec). **Officers:** Byron Purcell, President.

■ 8602 ■ **CW Magnet Wire Co.**
739 Roosevelt Rd., Ste. 301
Glen Ellyn, IL 60137
Phone: (630)469-8484   **Fax:** (630)469-1374
Products: Copper magnet wire. **SIC:** 5063 (Electrical
Apparatus & Equipment). **Emp:** 499.

■ 8603 ■ **Cyber-Tech Inc.**
PO Box 23801
Portland, OR 97281
Phone: (503)620-2285   **Fax:** (503)620-8580
Products: Handy-grips and joysticks. **SIC:** 5065
(Electronic Parts & Equipment Nec). **Officers:** Glenn
Dowers, President.

■ 8604 ■ **Cybernetic Micro Systems Inc.**
PO Box 3000
San Gregorio, CA 94074
Phone: (650)726-3000
Products: control integrated circuits. **SIC:** 5065
(Electronic Parts & Equipment Nec). **Sales:** $2,000,000
(2000). **Emp:** 25. **Officers:** E. Klingman, President.

■ 8605 ■ **Dakota Electric Supply Co.**
PO Box 2886
Fargo, ND 58108
Phone: (701)237-9440   **Fax:** (701)237-6504
Products: Telecommunications and electrical supplies;
Utility hardware. **SICs:** 5065 (Electronic Parts &
Equipment Nec); 5072 (Hardware). **Sales:** $30,000,000
(2000). **Emp:** 60. **Officers:** Ben Herr, CEO &
President; Todd Kumm, VP of Finance.

■ 8606 ■ **Dale Electronics Corp.**
7 E 20th St.
New York, NY 10003
Phone: (212)475-1124
Products: Electronics parts. **SIC:** 5065 (Electronic
Parts & Equipment Nec).

■ 8607 ■ **Dalis Electronic Supply Inc.**
2455 S 7th St., Bldg. 175
Phoenix, AZ 85034
Phone: (602)275-2626   **Fax:** (602)275-0578
E-mail: dalis1@aol.com
URL: http://www.daliselectronics.com
Products: Electronic parts and supplies. **SIC:** 5065
(Electronic Parts & Equipment Nec). **Est:** 1947. **Sales:**
$8,000,000 (2000). **Emp:** 12. **Officers:** Edward Bush,
President; John R. Keen, Exec. VP; Audrey Laliech,
Service Mgr. Contact.

■ 8608 ■ **D.A.S. Distributors, Inc.**
RR 2, Box 275K
Palmyra, PA 17078
Phone: (717)964-3642
Free: (800)233-7009   **Fax:** (717)964-3891
URL: http://www.dasroadpro.com
Products: Electronic systems and equipment;
Consumer high fidelity components; Motor vehicle
radios; 12 volt products. **SICs:** 5064 (Electrical
Appliances—Television & Radio); 5065 (Electronic
Parts & Equipment Nec). **Est:** 1978. **Officers:** David Z.
Abel, CEO; Michael Z. Abel, President; John Borst,
CFO; Blake Miller, VP of Sales.

■ 8609 ■ **Datalink Ready Inc.**
PO Box 2169
Melbourne, FL 32902-2169
Phone: (321)676-0500
Free: (800)233-5465   **Fax:** (321)676-0504
E-mail: dlr@datalinkready.com
URL: http://www.datalinkready.com
Products: Modems, multiplexers, and data
communication equipment. **SIC:** 5065 (Electronic Parts
& Equipment Nec). **Est:** 1982. **Sales:** $4,500,000
(2000). **Emp:** 15. **Officers:** James Deloatche,
President.

■ 8610 ■ **Datex Inc.**
320 Mears Blvd.
Oldsmar, FL 34677
Phone: (813)891-6464
Free: (800)933-2839   **Fax:** (813)891-6846
Products: Hand-held and pen-based portable
scanners and bar-code readers and maintenance and
repair service. **SIC:** 5065 (Electronic Parts &
Equipment Nec). **Sales:** $20,000,000 (2000). **Emp:** 50.
Officers: Samir Armanious, President; Tuan Phan, VP
of Finance.

■ 8611 ■ **Dauphin Electrical Supply Co.**
PO Box 2206
Harrisburg, PA 17105
Phone: (717)986-9300
Free: (800)932-0403   **Fax:** (717)986-9330
URL: http://www.dauphinelectric.com
Products: Electrical supplies. **SIC:** 5063 (Electrical
Apparatus & Equipment). **Est:** 1901. **Sales:**
$50,000,000 (2000). **Emp:** 140. **Officers:** Terry D.
Burkholder, President; J.D. Canfield, Exec. VP; Robert
Twomey, VP of Marketing & Sales; Laura Leese, Dir. of
Data Processing; Mim Hobbs, Dir of Human
Resources.

■ 8612 ■ **Davies Electric Supply Co.**
PO Drawer 759
North Little Rock, AR 72114
Phone: (501)375-3330
Products: Electrical supplies. **SIC:** 5065 (Electronic
Parts & Equipment Nec).

■ 8613 ■ **Kriz Davis Co.**
401 NW Norris
Topeka, KS 66608-1573
Phone: (785)354-9532   **Fax:** (785)354-1129
Products: Electrical supplies; Communications
supplies. **SIC:** 5065 (Electronic Parts & Equipment
Nec). **Est:** 1961. **Emp:** 22. **Officers:** Jerry Hopkins,
President; Jerry Hopkins, President.

■ 8614 ■ **Davis Electrical Supply Company
Inc.**
24 Anderson Rd.
Cheektowaga, NY 14225
Phone: (716)896-0100   **Fax:** (716)896-0138
E-mail: daviskorff@aol.com
Products: Panelboards and electrical supplies. **SIC:**
5063 (Electrical Apparatus & Equipment). **Est:** 1930.
Sales: $8,000,000 (2000). **Emp:** 50. **Officers:** Jim
DiVita, President.

■ 8615 ■ **De Sisti Lighting Corp.**
1109 Grand Ave.
North Bergen, NJ 07047-1628
Phone: (201)319-1100   **Fax:** (201)319-1104
E-mail: desisti@msn.com
URL: http://www.desisti.it
Products: Motion picture and studio lighting; Rigging
systems. **SIC:** 5063 (Electrical Apparatus &
Equipment). **Est:** 1982. **Emp:** 160. **Officers:** William J.
Liento Jr., President; Lowell Achziger, Gen. Mgr.

■ 8616 ■ **Dealers Electric Motor**
Brooklyn Navy Yard
Box 217
Brooklyn, NY 11205
Phone: (718)522-1110   **Fax:** (718)935-1927
Products: Electric motors. **SIC:** 5063 (Electrical
Apparatus & Equipment).

■ 8617 ■ **Deanco Inc.**
3230 Scott Blvd.
Santa Clara, CA 95054-3011
Phone: (408)654-9100   **Fax:** (408)257-5779
Products: Integrated circuits; High-powered
transistors; Fasteners; Nuts and bolts. **SICs:** 5065
(Electronic Parts & Equipment Nec); 5072 (Hardware).
Est: 1964. **Sales:** $110,000,000 (2000). **Emp:** 400.
Officers: Jerry Wamsley, CEO; Douglas Gillogly, VP of
Marketing & Sales; Wayne Castrovinci, Director; Robert
Wanner, Director.

■ 8618 ■ **Dearborn West L.P.**
5236 Bell Ct.
Chino, CA 91710-5701
Phone: (909)591-9393
Products: Electronic wire and cable. **SIC:** 5063
(Electrical Apparatus & Equipment). **Sales:** $4,000,000
(2000). **Emp:** 15. **Officers:** Roque Torrea, Vice
President.

■ 8619 ■ **Debenham Electric Supply Co.**
5333 Fairbanks St.
Anchorage, AK 99518-1258
Phone: (907)562-2800
Products: Electrical supplies, including motor starters,
conduits, switches, and transformers. **SIC:** 5063
(Electrical Apparatus & Equipment). **Est:** 1968. **Sales:**
$40,000,000 (2000). **Emp:** 150. **Officers:** Ray
Debenham, President; Dale Haynes, VP of Finance.

■ 8620 ■ **Defiance Inc.**
28271 Cedar Park Blvd.
Perrysburg, OH 43551
Phone: (419)661-1333   **Fax:** (419)661-1337
Products: Automotive tooling systems, cam follower
rollers, and axles and other precision machined metal
engine and drive-train components. **SIC:** 5013 (Motor
Vehicle Supplies & New Parts). **Sales:** $89,300,000
(2000). **Emp:** 691. **Officers:** Ralph Passino, President;
Mark Mueller, CFO.

■ 8621 ■ **Delta Materials Inc.**
3525 N Causeway, Ste. 620
Metairie, LA 70002
Phone: (504)219-9653   **Fax:** (504)219-9695
E-mail: deltam@bellsouth.net
Products: Electronic parts and equipment. **SIC:** 5065
(Electronic Parts & Equipment Nec). **Officers:** Timothy
H. Kelley, President.

■ 8622 ■ **Delta Star Inc.**
270 Industrial Rd.
San Carlos, CA 94070-6212
Phone: (650)508-2850   **Fax:** (650)593-0733
Products: Power Transformers; Mobile electrical
substations. **SIC:** 5063 (Electrical Apparatus &
Equipment). **Sales:** $73,000,000 (1999). **Emp:** 450.

■ 8623 ■ **Dencor Energy Cost Controls Inc.**
1450 W Evans Ave.
Denver, CO 80223
Phone: (303)922-1888
Free: (800)392-2690   **Fax:** (303)922-3903
Products: Energy control and demand control systems
for residential, commercial and utility applications. **SIC:**
5065 (Electronic Parts & Equipment Nec). **Sales:**
$300,000 (2000). **Emp:** 6. **Officers:** Maynard Moe,
President.

■ 8624 ■ **Leslie M. Devoe Co.**
4371 E 82nd St. D
Indianapolis, IN 46250-1678
Phone: (317)842-3245   **Fax:** (317)845-8440
Products: Electronic parts; Electric and electronic
equipment. **SIC:** 5065 (Electronic Parts & Equipment
Nec). **Officers:** Charles Devoe, Partner.

■ 8625 ■ **Dey Appliance Parts**
1401 Wolters Blvd.
Vadnais Heights, MN 55110
Phone: (612)490-9191   **Fax:** 800-728-3391
Products: Electrical parts; Appliance parts. **SIC:** 5063
(Electrical Apparatus & Equipment). **Officers:** Dennis
Dey.

■ 8626 ■ **DeYoung Mfg Inc.**
12920 NE 125th Way
Kirkland, WA 98034
Phone: (425)823-4798   **Fax:** (425)821-8633
Products: Custom electronic coils and transformers.
SIC: 5065 (Electronic Parts & Equipment Nec).

■ 8627 ■ **Diodes Inc.**
3050 E Hillcrest Dr.
Westlake Village, CA 91362
Phone: (805)446-4800   **Fax:** (805)446-4850
Products: Semiconductor rectifiers and associated
products. **SIC:** 5065 (Electronic Parts & Equipment
Nec). **Sales:** $79,300,000 (1999). **Emp:** 306. **Officers:**

Michael Rosenberg, CEO & President; Carl Wertz, CFO.

■ 8628 ■ Directed Energy Inc.
2401 Research Blvd Ste. 108
Ft. Collins, CO 80526
Phone: (970)493-1901   Fax: (970)493-1903
Products: Semiconductors and related solid-state devices; High voltage pulse generators and modulators, diode drivers current sources and transistors. SICs: 5063 (Electrical Apparatus & Equipment); 5065 (Electronic Parts & Equipment Nec).

■ 8629 ■ DIT-MCO International Corp.
5612 Brighton Ter.
Kansas City, MO 64130
Phone: (816)444-9700
Free: (800)821-3487   Fax: (816)444-9737
E-mail: infolink@ditmco.com
Products: High voltage wiring analyzers and cable testers. SIC: 5063 (Electrical Apparatus & Equipment). Est: 1948. Sales: $33,000,000 (2000). Emp: 260. Officers: F.L. Thompson, President; Jerry Meisenheimer, Controller.

■ 8630 ■ Dominion Electric Supply Co.
5053 Lee Hwy.
Arlington, VA 22207
Phone: (703)536-4400   Fax: (703)237-6713
Products: Electrical products, including pipewire and lighting fixtures. SIC: 5063 (Electrical Apparatus & Equipment). Est: 1808. Sales: $80,000,000 (2000). Emp: 149. Officers: Richard Sharlin, President; R.A. Williams, VP of Marketing & Strategic Planning; John Deil, VP of Sales.

■ 8631 ■ Double O Electronic Distributors
9440 NE Halsey St.
Portland, OR 97220-4580
Phone: (503)252-9500
Free: (888)452-7688   Fax: (503)252-4900
E-mail: sales@doubleo.com
URL: http://www.doubleo.com
Products: Electronic parts and equipment; Cable; Connectors. SIC: 5065 (Electronic Parts & Equipment Nec). Est: 1958. Emp: 8. Officers: Larry Ostrom, President.

■ 8632 ■ Dover Electric Supply Company Inc.
1631 S Du Pont Hwy.
Dover, DE 19901
Phone: (302)674-0115
Products: Electric supplies, including capacitors, resistors, wire, switches, breakers, and light bulbs. SIC: 5063 (Electrical Apparatus & Equipment). Est: 1948. Sales: $8,000,000 (2000). Emp: 36. Officers: Bernard Tudor, President.

■ 8633 ■ Dow Electronics Inc.
8603 Adamo Dr.
Tampa, FL 33619
Phone: (813)626-5195
Products: Electronics, including television parts. SIC: 5065 (Electronic Parts & Equipment Nec). Est: 1959. Sales: $35,000,000 (2000). Emp: 100. Officers: John Yodzis, President; Ed Kowalczyk, Controller; Greg Buffington, Sr. VP.

■ 8634 ■ Dreisilker Electric Motors Inc.
352 Roosevelt Rd.
Glen Ellyn, IL 60137
Phone: (630)469-7510
Free: (800)922-1882   Fax: (630)469-3474
URL: http://www.dreisilker.com
Products: Electric motors, drive systems, controls, and related products. SIC: 5063 (Electrical Apparatus & Equipment). Est: 1955. Sales: $15,000,000 (2000). Emp: 126. Officers: Leo Dreisilker, President, e-mail: dreisilk@dreisilker.com; Edward J. Horak, CFO.

■ 8635 ■ D.S.A. Materials Inc.
517 W Johnson St.
Jonesboro, AR 72403
Phones: (870)932-7461   (870)932-7461
Fax: (870)932-0489
E-mail: dsa@insolwwb.net
Products: Building, plumbing, and electrical materials. SICs: 5063 (Electrical Apparatus & Equipment); 5039 (Construction Materials Nec); 5074 (Plumbing &

Hydronic Heating Supplies). Est: 1950. Sales: $5,000,000 (1999). Emp: 30. Officers: William Latourette, President; Kathy Gustin, Vice President.

■ 8636 ■ R.C. Dudek & Company, Inc.
800 Del Norte Blvd.
Oxnard, CA 93030
Phone: (805)988-4882
Free: (800)488-1990   Fax: (805)988-1254
Products: Electronic hardware and fasteners. SIC: 5063 (Electrical Apparatus & Equipment).

■ 8637 ■ R.C. Dudek & Company, Inc.
2115 Old Oakland Rd.
San Jose, CA 95131
Phone: (408)321-9011   Fax: (408)321-0220
Products: Electrical hanging and fastening devices. SIC: 5063 (Electrical Apparatus & Equipment).

■ 8638 ■ Duellman Electric Co.
PO Box 771
Dayton, OH 45401
Phone: (937)461-8000   Fax: (937)222-0571
URL: http://www.rexelusa.com
Products: Electrical parts, including wires. SIC: 5063 (Electrical Apparatus & Equipment). Est: 1989. Sales: $16,000,000 (2000). Emp: 44. Officers: Lawson Nickol, General Mgr.; Tom Warner, Operations Mgr.

■ 8639 ■ Duraline
75 Hoffman Ln.
Central Islip, NY 11722-5007
Phone: (516)234-2002   Fax: (516)234-2360
Products: Electrical connectors and receptors. SIC: 5063 (Electrical Apparatus & Equipment). Sales: $5,000,000 (2000). Emp: 49. Officers: Paul C. Savoca.

■ 8640 ■ Dynamic Engineers Inc.
2000 Dairy Ashford, No. 128
Houston, TX 77077
Phone: (281)870-8822   Fax: (281)870-8218
URL: http://www.dynamiceng.com
Products: Electronic and microwave components; Communication parts and equipment. SIC: 5065 (Electronic Parts & Equipment Nec). Est: 1988. Sales: $5,000,000 (2000). Emp: 10. Officers: Roland Teoh, President, e-mail: troland@dynamiceng.com.

■ 8641 ■ E and B Electric Supply Co.
615 Strong Hwy.
El Dorado, AR 71730
Phone: (870)862-8101
Products: Electrical supply light fixtures. SIC: 5063 (Electrical Apparatus & Equipment). Sales: $2,000,000 (1994). Emp: 11. Officers: Gary Vogel, Manager.

■ 8642 ■ Eagle Electric Manufacturing Co.
112 Lake St S
Kirkland, WA 98033
Phone: (425)827-8401
Products: Electrical wiring devices. SIC: 5063 (Electrical Apparatus & Equipment).

■ 8643 ■ Eagle Sales Company Inc.
PO Box 22968
Memphis, TN 38122-0968
Phone: (901)458-6133
Free: (800)264-1180   Fax: (901)458-4144
Products: Electronic parts; Electronic systems and equipment. SIC: 5065 (Electronic Parts & Equipment Nec). Officers: William Kobeck, President.

■ 8644 ■ EASI (Electronic Applications Specialists Inc.)
1250 Holden Ave.
Milford, MI 48381
Phone: (248)685-8283   Fax: (248)684-6544
Products: Electronic design and fabrication instruments and systems. SIC: 5063 (Electrical Apparatus & Equipment). Est: 1968. Emp: 6. Officers: M. Dechape, President, e-mail: mdechape@aol.com.

■ 8645 ■ Easter-Owens Electric Co
6522 Fig St.
Arvada, CO 80004
Phone: (303)431-0111   Fax: (303)424-2040
Products: Industrial control systems; Electronic enclosures; Detention systems custom metal

enclosures. SICs: 5063 (Electrical Apparatus & Equipment); 5065 (Electronic Parts & Equipment Nec). Emp: 45. Officers: David Easter, President; Scott Easter, General Mgr.

■ 8646 ■ Eastern Bearings Inc.
158 Lexington St.
Waltham, MA 02454
Phone: (781)899-3952   Fax: (781)647-3227
Products: Power transmission equipment. SIC: 5063 (Electrical Apparatus & Equipment). Sales: $31,000,000 (2000). Emp: 100. Officers: Richard Gorsey, President; Seymour Schwartz, CFO.

■ 8647 ■ Eastern Electric Supply Co.
PO Box 1160
Rocky Mount, NC 27802
Phone: (252)442-5156   Fax: (252)442-1006
Products: Electrical apparatus and equipment. SIC: 5063 (Electrical Apparatus & Equipment). Sales: $7,000,000 (2000). Emp: 24. Officers: Charles E. Joyner, President.

■ 8648 ■ Eastern States Components Inc.
108 Pratts Junction Rd.
Sterling, MA 01564-2304
Phone: (978)422-7641   Fax: (978)422-6762
Products: Electronic parts; Electronic systems and equipment; Semiconductors and related devices. SIC: 5065 (Electronic Parts & Equipment Nec). Officers: Dwight Aubrey, President.

■ 8649 ■ Eck Supply Co.
PO Box 85618
Richmond, VA 23285
Phone: (804)359-5781   Fax: (804)358-1353
URL: http://www.ecksupply.com
Products: Electrical supplies, including wires and electrical outlets. SIC: 5063 (Electrical Apparatus & Equipment). Est: 1956. Sales: $100,000,000 (2000). Emp: 255. Officers: Edgar Eck Jr., President.

■ 8650 ■ Eckart Supply Company Inc.
426 Quarry Rd.
Corydon, IN 47112-8727
Phone: (812)738-3232   Fax: (812)949-2202
Products: Electrical supplies; Plumbing and heating supplies; Lighting supplies. SICs: 5063 (Electrical Apparatus & Equipment); 5074 (Plumbing & Hydronic Heating Supplies). Sales: $15,000,000 (2000). Emp: 69.

■ 8651 ■ Economy Electric Company Inc.
1158-1160 Hubbard
PO Box 299
Youngstown, OH 44501-0299
Phone: (330)744-4461   Fax: (330)744-1318
Products: Generators; Generator parts; Generator motors. SICs: 5063 (Electrical Apparatus & Equipment); 5084 (Industrial Machinery & Equipment). Est: 1916. Sales: $6,000,000 (2000). Emp: 15. Officers: Larry E. Justice, President.

■ 8652 ■ Economy Maintenance Supply Company Inc.
PO Box 349
Fairfax Station, VA 22039
Phone: (703)461-7700
Products: Electrical and plumbing maintenance supplies. SIC: 5065 (Electronic Parts & Equipment Nec).

■ 8653 ■ EDCO Electronics Inc.
2209 American Ave.
Hayward, CA 94545
Phone: (510)783-8900   Fax: (510)786-0187
Products: Home electronic supplies. SIC: 5063 (Electrical Apparatus & Equipment). Est: 1962. Emp: 49.

■ 8654 ■ Edcor Electronics
7130 National Parks Hwy.
Carlsbad, NM 88220
Phone: (505)887-6790
Free: (800)854-0259   Fax: (505)887-6880
URL: http://www.edcorusa.com
Products: Audio transformers. SIC: 5065 (Electronic Parts & Equipment Nec). Sales: $3,000,000 (2000). Emp: 49. Officers: Phyllis Weston.

■ 8655 ■ **EESCO, A Division of WESCO Distribution, Inc.**
3939 S Karlov Ave.
Chicago, IL 60632
Phone: (773)376-8750
Free: (800)333-0011 **Fax:** (773)376-8237
URL: http://www.eescodist.com
Products: Electrical and electronic supplies, including lighting switches, wiring, fuses, and factory automation equipment. **SIC:** 5063 (Electrical Apparatus & Equipment). **Est:** 1919. **Sales:** $340,000,000 (1999). **Emp:** 700. **Officers:** Ronald P. Van, VP & General Mgr., e-mail: rvan@eescodist.com; Ron Haley, President & CEO; Mike Dziewisz, Human Resources Contact, e-mail: mdziewisz@wescodist.com. **Alternate Name:** Englewood Electrical Supply/United Electric.

■ 8656 ■ **EESCO Inc. Farrell-Argast Div.**
PO Box 26066
Indianapolis, IN 46226
Phone: (317)546-4041 **Fax:** (317)543-3009
Products: Electrical equipment and supplies; Wiring supplies. **SIC:** 5063 (Electrical Apparatus & Equipment). **Est:** 1933. **Sales:** $8,000,000 (2000). **Emp:** 25. **Officers:** Wayne Rinker, President & CFO.

■ 8657 ■ **EH Engineering Ltd.**
3333 Cleveland Ave., No. 4
Lincoln, NE 68504
Phone: (402)466-6720
Products: Electrical transmissions. **SIC:** 5063 (Electrical Apparatus & Equipment).

■ 8658 ■ **EIS, Inc.**
3715 Northside Pkwy. Bldg. 100, Ste. 400
Atlanta, GA 30327
Phone: (404)355-1651 **Fax:** (404)355-1953
URL: http://www.eis-inc.com
Products: Electrical equipment and supplies. **SIC:** 5063 (Electrical Apparatus & Equipment). **Est:** 1949. **Sales:** $450,000,000 (1999). **Emp:** 1,200. **Officers:** Steve Kendall, CEO; Bob Watts, CFO; Jack Craig, Vice President; Dave Russell, MIS; Lou Ann Melton, Personnel Mgr.; Bob Gannon, Vice President; John Steel, Vice President. **Former Name:** Electrical Insulation Suppliers Inc.

■ 8659 ■ **Electrex Inc.**
108 E Sherman
Hutchinson, KS 67501
Phone: (316)669-9966
Free: (800)319-3676 **Fax:** (316)669-9988
Products: Electric wire harnesses; Panels and control boxes. **SIC:** 5063 (Electrical Apparatus & Equipment). **Est:** 1978. **Sales:** $5,000,000 (2000). **Emp:** 65. **Officers:** Robert T. Stancer, President, e-mail: bstancer@southwind.net; Buddy Aemstrong, Sales/Marketing Contact; Corrina Evans, Customer Service Contact.

■ 8660 ■ **Electric Fixture and Supply Co.**
PO Box 898
Omaha, NE 68101
Phone: (402)342-3050
Products: Electrical supplies, including fixtures, switches, capacitors, and resistors. **SIC:** 5063 (Electrical Apparatus & Equipment). **Est:** 1931. **Sales:** $18,000,000 (2000). **Emp:** 75. **Officers:** Gordon Gunderson, President.

■ 8661 ■ **Electric Motor and Control Corp.**
57 E Chestnut St.
Columbus, OH 43215
Phone: (614)228-6875 **Fax:** (614)228-0083
Products: Electrical supplies; Motors. **SIC:** 5063 (Electrical Apparatus & Equipment). **Est:** 1918. **Sales:** $22,000,000 (2000). **Emp:** 53. **Officers:** C.R. Guttadore, CEO & President; Greg A. Guttadore, CFO.

■ 8662 ■ **Electric Motor Repair & Sales**
1 Goodson St.
Bristol, VA 24201
Phone: (540)669-9428
Products: Electric motors. **SIC:** 5063 (Electrical Apparatus & Equipment).

■ 8663 ■ **Electric Motor Service**
2020 Division St.
PO Box 1224
St. Cloud, MN 56302
Phone: (320)251-8691 **Fax:** (320)251-7992
Products: Electric motors, power transmissions, and pumps. **SIC:** 5063 (Electrical Apparatus & Equipment).

■ 8664 ■ **Electric Motor and Supply Inc.**
PO Box 152
Altoona, PA 16603
Phone: (814)946-0401
Products: Electric motors. **SIC:** 5063 (Electrical Apparatus & Equipment). **Est:** 1956. **Sales:** $5,100,000 (2000). **Emp:** 54. **Officers:** R.E. Force, President.

■ 8665 ■ **Electric Motors Unlimited Inc.**
1000 Jonathon Dr.
Madison, WI 53701
Phone: (608)271-2311
Products: Electric motors. **SIC:** 5063 (Electrical Apparatus & Equipment).

■ 8666 ■ **Electric Supply Co.**
PO Box 6427
Raleigh, NC 27608
Phone: (919)834-7364 **Fax:** (919)833-3857
Products: Electrical supplies, including cable and wire. **SIC:** 5063 (Electrical Apparatus & Equipment). **Est:** 1945. **Sales:** $2,000,000 (2000). **Emp:** 10. **Officers:** Kenneth Kennedy Jr., President & Treasurer.

■ 8667 ■ **Electric Supply Co. (Asheville, North Carolina)**
PO Box 2389
Asheville, NC 28802-2389
Phone: (704)255-8899
Products: Electrical equipment. **SIC:** 5063 (Electrical Apparatus & Equipment). **Est:** 1903. **Sales:** $46,000,000 (2000). **Emp:** 151. **Officers:** Eugene M. Winner, President.

■ 8668 ■ **Electric Supply Company of Fayetteville Inc.**
PO Box 2158
Fayetteville, NC 28302
Phone: (919)323-4171
Products: Lighting equipment and supplies, including lamps, lightbulbs, and fluorescent lighting. **SIC:** 5063 (Electrical Apparatus & Equipment). **Sales:** $3,000,000 (2000). **Emp:** 12. **Officers:** K.D. Kennedy, President.

■ 8669 ■ **Electric Supply Co. (Raleigh, North Carolina)**
PO Box 6427
Raleigh, NC 27608
Phone: (919)834-7364 **Fax:** (919)833-3857
Products: Electrical supplies. **SIC:** 5063 (Electrical Apparatus & Equipment). **Sales:** $3,000,000 (1993). **Emp:** 10.

■ 8670 ■ **Electric Supply Co. (Wilson, North Carolina)**
PO Box 1968
Wilson, NC 27894
Phone: (919)237-0151
Products: Electrical supplies, including cable and wire. **SIC:** 5063 (Electrical Apparatus & Equipment). **Est:** 1945. **Sales:** $42,000,000 (2000). **Emp:** 140. **Officers:** Ken D. Kennedy Jr., President.

■ 8671 ■ **Electric Supply and Equipment Company Inc.**
1812 E Wendover Ave.
Greensboro, NC 27405
Phone: (336)272-4123
Free: (800)632-0268 **Fax:** (336)274-4632
URL: http://www.esc-co.com
Products: Electrical supplies and equipment. **SIC:** 5063 (Electrical Apparatus & Equipment). **Est:** 1935. **Emp:** 90. **Officers:** Dana Smith, President; Jim McCormick, Vice President.

■ 8672 ■ **Electric Switches Inc.**
PO Box 1868
Tehachapi, CA 93581
Phone: (661)823-7131
Free: (800)421-8855 **Fax:** 800-401-9499
E-mail: sales@electricswitches.com
URL: http://www.electricswitches.com
Products: Electric switches. **SIC:** 5063 (Electrical Apparatus & Equipment). **Est:** 1957. **Sales:** $9,000,000 (2000). **Emp:** 100. **Officers:** Mike Rockwood, President; Raul Guerra, Sales Mgr., e-mail: raulg@electricswitches.com.

■ 8673 ■ **Electrical Communications**
289 Scott
Memphis, TN 38112-3911
Phone: (901)324-8893 **Fax:** (901)324-6297
Products: Wire and wiring supplies. **SIC:** 5063 (Electrical Apparatus & Equipment). **Emp:** 1,000.

■ 8674 ■ **Electrical Construction Co.**
PO Box 10286
Portland, OR 97210
Phone: (503)224-3511 **Fax:** (503)224-0953
Products: Electrical equipment and supplies. **SIC:** 5063 (Electrical Apparatus & Equipment). **Est:** 1930. **Sales:** $35,000,000 (2000). **Emp:** 400. **Officers:** W.K. Deshler, President; J. Scroggy, Controller; Linda Woodall, Dir. of Marketing & Sales.

■ 8675 ■ **Electrical Controller Products Co.**
3225 McKinney St.
Houston, TX 77003
Phone: (713)222-9191
Free: (800)926-9029 **Fax:** (713)222-1457
URL: http://www.ecpsales.com
Products: Industrial replacement circuit breakers and motor controls. **SIC:** 5063 (Electrical Apparatus & Equipment). **Est:** 1957. **Sales:** $3,000,000 (1999). **Emp:** 10. **Officers:** John McLaughlin, Sales Mgr., e-mail: jmclaughlin@ecpsales.com.

■ 8676 ■ **Electrical Distributors Inc.**
74 Middlesex St.
PO Box 8547
Lowell, MA 01853-8547
Phone: (978)454-7719
Free: (800)696-3738 **Fax:** (978)459-2294
E-mail: edirab@msn.com
Products: Electrical products. **SIC:** 5063 (Electrical Apparatus & Equipment). **Est:** 1964. **Sales:** $2,500,000 (1999). **Emp:** 7. **Officers:** Robert A. Bourassa, President & Treasurer; Jason G. McManus, Sales & Customer Service Contact.

■ 8677 ■ **Electrical Engineering and Equipment Co.**
1201 Walnut St.
Des Moines, IA 50309
Phone: (515)282-0431
Free: (800)955-3633 **Fax:** (515)288-3810
Products: Electrical equipment and supplies, including light bulbs, lamps, conduits, wire, switches, and panels. **SICs:** 5063 (Electrical Apparatus & Equipment); 5084 (Industrial Machinery & Equipment). **Est:** 1920. **Sales:** $30,000,000 (2000). **Emp:** 185. **Officers:** Jeff Stroud, President & CEO.

■ 8678 ■ **Electrical Equipment Co.**
226 N Wilkonson Dr.
Laurinburg, NC 28352-1747
Phone: (919)276-2141 **Fax:** (919)276-7130
Products: Electrical supplies. **SIC:** 5063 (Electrical Apparatus & Equipment). **Emp:** 34. **Officers:** F. E. Ward.

■ 8679 ■ **Electrical Equipment Co.**
1440 Diggs Dr.
Raleigh, NC 27603
Phone: (919)828-5411
Products: Electrical equipment. **SIC:** 5063 (Electrical Apparatus & Equipment). **Est:** 1924. **Sales:** $61,000,000 (2000). **Emp:** 200. **Officers:** Jerry Walker, CEO; Tammy Wiles, Controller.

■ 8680 ■ **Electrical Materials Inc.**
796 San Antonio Rd.
Palo Alto, CA 94306
Phone: (650)494-0400 **Fax:** (650)857-1041
E-mail: electricalmaterials@msn.com
Products: Electrical equipment and supplies. **SICs:** 5063 (Electrical Apparatus & Equipment); 5065 (Electronic Parts & Equipment Nec). **Est:** 1959. **Emp:** 20. **Officers:** Craig Kelsey, President.

■ 8681 ■ **Electrical Power and Controls Inc.**
2405 Mira Mar Ave.
Long Beach, CA 90815
Phone: (310)498-6699
Free: (800)545-1569 **Fax:** (310)498-5894
E-mail: info@electricpwr.com
URL: http://www.electricpwr.com
Products: Electrical switches; Fuses; Motor control; Terminal blocks; Enclosures. **SIC:** 5065 (Electronic Parts & Equipment Nec). **Est:** 1974. **Sales:** $4,000,000 (2000). **Emp:** 30. **Officers:** K.A. Armstrong, President; Susan Moore, Controller; Judith A. Steward, Vice President; M. Howell, General Mgr.

■ 8682 ■ **Electrical Wholesale Supply Company Inc.**
PO Box 2147
Idaho Falls, ID 83403
Phone: (208)523-2800
Products: Wire; Electrical wire. **SIC:** 5063 (Electrical Apparatus & Equipment). **Est:** 1961. **Sales:** $15,000,000 (2000). **Emp:** 48. **Officers:** Reeve Norman, President; R. Norman, VP of Marketing.

■ 8683 ■ **Electro-Line Inc.**
PO Box 1688
Dayton, OH 45401
Phone: (513)461-5683 **Fax:** (513)461-0533
Products: Electrical components. **SIC:** 5065 (Electronic Parts & Equipment Nec). **Est:** 1958. **Sales:** $6,000,000 (2000). **Emp:** 6. **Officers:** Bruce A. Jump, President.

■ 8684 ■ **Electro-Matic Products Inc.**
23409 Industrial Park
Farmington Hills, MI 48335
Phone: (248)478-1182 **Fax:** (248)478-1472
Products: Industrial controls; Electrical industrial apparatus. **SIC:** 5063 (Electrical Apparatus & Equipment). **Sales:** $73,000,000 (2000). **Emp:** 160. **Officers:** Raymond Persia; Tom C. Moore; Robert Waldie.

■ 8685 ■ **Electro Media of Colorado**
5474 Marshall St.
Arvada, CO 80002-3802
Phone: (303)423-1050
Products: Electronic parts and equipment, including communication and electronic inter-communication equipment. **SIC:** 5065 (Electronic Parts & Equipment Nec). **Officers:** C. Hedlund, President.

■ 8686 ■ **Electro Rent Corp. Data Rentals/Sales Div.**
6060 Sepulveda Blvd.
Van Nuys, CA 91411-2501
Phone: (818)787-2100
Products: Electronic instrumentation. **SIC:** 5065 (Electronic Parts & Equipment Nec). **Est:** 1966. **Sales:** $16,000,000 (2000). **Emp:** 25. **Officers:** Rick Bilgrim, General Mgr.

■ 8687 ■ **Electroglas Inc.**
455 S 48th St Ste 102
Tempe, AZ 85281
Phone: (480)968-1110 **Fax:** (480)968-0975
Products: Automated wafer probing systems. **SIC:** 5065 (Electronic Parts & Equipment Nec).

■ 8688 ■ **Electronic Contracting Co.**
2630 N 27th St.
Lincoln, NE 68501
Phone: (402)466-8274 **Fax:** (402)466-0819
E-mail: ecco_ln@eccoinc.com
URL: http://www.eccoinc.com
Products: Electronic systems and equipment, including closed circuit television; Communication systems and equipment, including sound masking, access control, information systems, LAN's, nurse calls and telephones; Alarm systems, including fire alarms. **SICs:** 5065 (Electronic Parts & Equipment Nec); 5063 (Electrical Apparatus & Equipment); 5064 (Electrical Appliances—Television & Radio). **Est:** 1978. **Sales:** $15,000,000 (2000). **Emp:** 96. **Officers:** Adam Karavas.

■ 8689 ■ **Electronic Equipment Company Inc.**
4027 NW 24th St.
Miami, FL 33142-6715
Phone: (305)871-1500 **Fax:** (305)327-1526
Products: Electrical supplies. **SIC:** 5065 (Electronic Parts & Equipment Nec). **Est:** 1954. **Sales:** $27,000,000 (2000). **Emp:** 80. **Officers:** Phil Radell, CEO; Abe Jiminez, Dir. of Systems.

■ 8690 ■ **Electronic Hardware Ltd**
PO Box 15039
North Hollywood, CA 91615
Phone: (818)982-6100 **Fax:** (818)764-1889
Products: Electronic hardware and components; Screw machine parts. **SIC:** 5065 (Electronic Parts & Equipment Nec). **Officers:** Richard Degn, President.

■ 8691 ■ **Electronic Hook-up**
195 E Main St.
Milford, MA 01757
Phone: (508)478-3311 **Fax:** (508)296-7110
Products: Electronic supplies, including multimeters, batteries, and computer mice. **SIC:** 5065 (Electronic Parts & Equipment Nec). **Est:** 1929. **Sales:** $1,000,000 (2000). **Emp:** 7. **Officers:** Jeff Sequenzia, President.

■ 8692 ■ **Electronic Lighting Inc.**
37200 Central Ct
Newark, CA 94560
Phone: (510)795-8555 **Fax:** (510)795-0870
Products: Energy efficient light solutions and dimming ballasts. **SIC:** 5063 (Electrical Apparatus & Equipment).

■ 8693 ■ **Electronic Maintenance Supply Co.**
1230 W Central Blvd.
Orlando, FL 32805
Phone: (407)849-6362
Free: (800)432-4741 **Fax:** (305)843-0909
Products: General electronic parts. **SIC:** 5065 (Electronic Parts & Equipment Nec). **Emp:** 200. **Officers:** Grattan Hammond Jr., Chairman of the Board; John T. Hammond, President. **Also Known by This Acronym:** EMSCO.

■ 8694 ■ **Electronic Specialties Inc.**
PO Box 248
Algona, IA 50511-0248
Phone: (515)295-7752
Products: Electronic systems and equipment; Electronic parts; Communication systems and equipment. **SIC:** 5065 (Electronic Parts & Equipment Nec). **Officers:** Patricia Weber, President.

■ 8695 ■ **Electronic Surplus Services**
900 Candia Rd.
Manchester, NH 03109
Phone: (603)624-9600 **Fax:** (603)624-9700
E-mail: capbam4@aol.com
Products: Surplus electronics. **SIC:** 5065 (Electronic Parts & Equipment Nec). **Est:** 1982. **Emp:** 8. **Officers:** George Demarais, President; Bam DeMontigny, Sales/Marketing Contact.

■ 8696 ■ **Electronics Supply Co.**
4100 Main St.
Kansas City, MO 64111
Phone: (816)931-0250 **Fax:** (816)753-2595
URL: http://www.eskc.com
Products: Electronics repairing equipment, including wiring, connectors, ICS, and soldering equipment. **SIC:** 5065 (Electronic Parts & Equipment Nec). **Est:** 1952. **Sales:** $12,000,000 (2000). **Emp:** 37. **Officers:** Richard C. Labelle, President; Joanne Saviano, Finance Officer.

■ 8697 ■ **Electrorep Energy Products Inc.**
2121 Schuetz Rd.
St. Louis, MO 63146
Phone: (314)991-2600
Products: Electrical products, including batteries. **SIC:** 5063 (Electrical Apparatus & Equipment). **Sales:** $9,000,000 (2000). **Emp:** 40. **Officers:** Fred Herdlick, President.

■ 8698 ■ **Electrotex Inc.**
2300 Richmond Ave.
Houston, TX 77098
Phone: (713)526-3456
URL: http://www.electrotex.com
Products: Electronic parts, including capacitors, resistors, switches, conduits, and wires; Computers. **SIC:** 5065 (Electronic Parts & Equipment Nec). **Est:** 1954. **Sales:** $14,000,000 (2000). **Emp:** 90. **Officers:** Donald R. Simon, President; Chris Holmes, Controller; Charlie Dunn, Vice President, e-mail: cdunn@electrotex.com.

■ 8699 ■ **Elliot Electric Supply**
3804 South St.
PO Box 630610
Nacogdoches, TX 75963
Phone: (409)569-7941
Free: (800)288-3324 **Fax:** (409)560-4685
E-mail: nplumer@eesnet.com
URL: http://www.eesnet.com
Products: Electrical equipment and supplies. **SIC:** 5063 (Electrical Apparatus & Equipment). **Est:** 1972. **Sales:** $70,000,000 (2000). **Emp:** 230. **Officers:** W.M. Elliott.

■ 8700 ■ **Elmo Semiconductor Corp.**
7590 N Glenoaks Blvd.
Burbank, CA 91504-1052
Phone: (818)768-7400 **Fax:** (818)767-7038
Products: Semiconductor and memory modules. **SIC:** 5065 (Electronic Parts & Equipment Nec). **Est:** 1974. **Sales:** $42,000,000 (2000). **Emp:** 150. **Officers:** Elie J. Moreno, CEO; Larry Ellis, CFO; Larry Duncan, Dir. of Marketing; Clem Murdzak, Dir of Human Resources.

■ 8701 ■ **Emerson Radio Corp.**
PO Box 430
Parsippany, NJ 07054-0430
Phone: (973)884-5800
Products: Electronics, including radios and clocks. **SIC:** 5064 (Electrical Appliances—Television & Radio). **Est:** 1956. **Sales:** $178,700,000 (2000). **Emp:** 103. **Officers:** Geoffrey P. Jurick, CEO, President & Chairman of the Board; John P. Walker, Exec. VP & CFO; Gerald S. Calabrese, VP of Marketing; Toshinori Ishii, VP of Engineering.

■ 8702 ■ **Empire Generator Corp.**
PO Box 100
Thiensville, WI 53092-0100
Phone: (414)238-1311 **Fax:** (414)238-1312
Products: Generator parts. **SIC:** 5063 (Electrical Apparatus & Equipment). **Sales:** $100,000 (2000). **Emp:** 5.

■ 8703 ■ **Emporium Specialties Company Inc.**
PO Box 65
Austin, PA 16720
Phone: (814)647-8661 **Fax:** (814)647-5536
Products: Stamped electronic components, metal stamping, handtools, clutches and brakes. **SIC:** 5072 (Hardware). **Sales:** $5,000,000 (2000). **Emp:** 100. **Officers:** Marvin M. Deupree, President.

■ 8704 ■ **EMSCO Electric Supply Company Inc.**
1101 W Sheridan St.
Oklahoma City, OK 73106
Phone: (405)235-6331 **Fax:** (405)232-2733
Products: Electrical equipment. **SIC:** 5063 (Electrical Apparatus & Equipment). **Sales:** $10,000,000 (1993). **Emp:** 44. **Officers:** Larry Allen, President.

■ 8705 ■ **EMT Electronics Inc.**
1891 Grand Caillou Rd.
Houma, LA 70363-7076
Phone: (504)879-2084 **Fax:** (504)879-2144
Products: Industrial electrical controls, including radio and radar; Marine equipment supplies. **SIC:** 5064 (Electrical Appliances—Television & Radio). **Officers:** William Thibodeaux, President.

■ 8706 ■ **Emtel Electronics Inc.**
375 Vanderbilt Ave.
Norwood, MA 02062-5007
Phone: (781)769-9500
Products: Electronic parts and equipment. **SIC:** 5065 (Electronic Parts & Equipment Nec). **Officers:** Michael Tuminelli, President.

■ 8707 ■ **Engineered Components Inc.**
404 Dividend Dr.
Peachtree City, GA 30269
Phone: (404)487-7600
Free: (800)241-9300   **Fax:** (404)487-2730
Products: Electrical hanging and fastening devices. **SIC:** 5063 (Electrical Apparatus & Equipment).

■ 8708 ■ **Englewood Electric**
PO Box 2615
Kokomo, IN 46904-2615
Phone: (765)457-1136   **Fax:** (765)452-9683
Products: Electronic parts. **SIC:** 5065 (Electronic Parts & Equipment Nec). **Est:** 1928. **Sales:** $5,000,000 (2000). **Emp:** 26. **Officers:** Roger B. McClellan, President; Roger A. Wagner, Dir. of Marketing & Sales.

■ 8709 ■ **Englewood Electrical Supply**
3412 Boland Dr.
South Bend, IN 46628-4302
Phone: (219)233-8233
Free: (800)745-3372   **Fax:** (219)234-4918
Products: Electrical supplies and equipment. **SIC:** 5063 (Electrical Apparatus & Equipment). **Sales:** $1,000,000 (2000). **Emp:** 22.

■ 8710 ■ **Entrelec Inc.**
1950 Hurd Dr.
Irving, TX 75038-4312
Phone: (972)550-9025   **Fax:** (972)550-9215
E-mail: us@entrelec.com
URL: http://www.entrelec.com
Products: Electrical and electronic components. **SIC:** 5065 (Electronic Parts & Equipment Nec). **Sales:** $35,000,000 (1999). **Emp:** 95. **Officers:** Francis Leynaert, General Mgr.

■ 8711 ■ **Entronic Industries Inc.**
PO Box 1370
Kingston, NY 12401
Phone: (914)338-5300   **Free:** (800)433-4431
Products: Electronic parts. **SIC:** 5065 (Electronic Parts & Equipment Nec). **Est:** 1947. **Sales:** $700,000 (2000). **Emp:** 11. **Officers:** David Parkhurst Sr., President; Alice Parkhurst, CFO.

■ 8712 ■ **Eoff Electric Co.**
PO Box 709
Salem, OR 97308
Phone: (503)371-3633
Products: Electrical supplies. **SICs:** 5063 (Electrical Apparatus & Equipment); 5065 (Electronic Parts & Equipment Nec). **Est:** 1919. **Sales:** $56,000,000 (2000). **Emp:** 165. **Officers:** Joe I. Eoff, CEO; Vic Bartlett, CFO; Les Williamson, Vice President.

■ 8713 ■ **Esco Electric Supply Co.**
820 N 2nd St.
Philadelphia, PA 19123
Phone: (215)923-6050   **Fax:** (215)574-9817
E-mail: sales@escoelectric.com
URL: http://www.escoelectric.com
Products: Electronic apparatus and equipment; Electronic cables; Panel boards. **SIC:** 5063 (Electrical Apparatus & Equipment). **Est:** 1955. **Sales:** $3,000,000 (2000). **Emp:** 25. **Officers:** M. Hafter, CEO; Bernadette Kearney, VP of Finance; Robert Pressman, President.

■ 8714 ■ **ESD Co.**
7380 Convoy Ct.
San Diego, CA 92111
Phone: (619)636-4400
Products: Electrical equipment. **SIC:** 5063 (Electrical Apparatus & Equipment). **Sales:** $81,000,000 (1991). **Emp:** 200. **Officers:** Alan Rosenfeld, President.

■ 8715 ■ **Essex Electrical Supply Company Inc.**
762 Western Ave.
Lynn, MA 01905
Phone: (781)598-6200
Products: Electrical supplies. **SIC:** 5063 (Electrical Apparatus & Equipment). **Sales:** $12,000,000 (1994). **Emp:** 40. **Officers:** F. Scott Stephens, President & Treasurer.

■ 8716 ■ **Etchomatic Inc.**
179 Old Canal Dr.
Lowell, MA 01851-2736
Phone: (781)893-2020
Free: (800)634-3006   **Fax:** (781)899-1133
Products: Printed circuit and screen print supplies. **SIC:** 5065 (Electronic Parts & Equipment Nec). **Est:** 1957. **Sales:** $10,000,000 (2000). **Emp:** 18. **Officers:** Peter Loven, President.

■ 8717 ■ **ETMA**
6640 185th Ave. NE
Redmond, WA 98052
Phone: (425)885-0107   **Fax:** (425)867-5600
Products: Turnkey manufacturer of electronic products; Automated surface mount capability, in-house testing and final assembly; ISO 9002 certified. **SIC:** 5065 (Electronic Parts & Equipment Nec). **Sales:** $19,000,000 (2000). **Emp:** 125. **Officers:** Jerry Rise, President; Carolyn Quemuel, VP of Finance.

■ 8718 ■ **Evergreen Oak Electric Supply & Sales Co. Crest Lighting Studios Div.**
13400 S Cicero
Crestwood, IL 60445
Phone: (708)597-4220   **Fax:** (708)597-7333
E-mail: eocrest@evergreenoak.com
Products: Electrical supplies, including light fixtures. **SIC:** 5063 (Electrical Apparatus & Equipment). **Est:** 1964. **Sales:** $50,000,000 (2000). **Emp:** 180. **Officers:** Barton Kramer, President.

■ 8719 ■ **Evergreen Oak Electric Supply and Sales Co. Evergreen Oak Div.**
13400 S Cicero
Crestwood, IL 60445
Phone: (708)579-4220
Products: Electrical supplies and light fixtures. **SIC:** 5063 (Electrical Apparatus & Equipment).

■ 8720 ■ **Everpower Co.**
PO Box 2167 NMS
Niagara Falls, NY 14301-0167
Phone: (716)284-2809   **Fax:** (905)354-2764
Products: Operation specializing in industrial turnkey standby power systems for mobile or stationary laboratories and workshops, and the measuring instruments industry. It serves the export market in Canada and the Middle East. **SIC:** 5063 (Electrical Apparatus & Equipment). **Emp:** 3.

■ 8721 ■ **Ex-Eltronics Inc.**
137 Express St.
Plainview, NY 11803
Phone: (516)351-5900   **Fax:** (516)351-5912
E-mail: exel@exelgroup.com
URL: http://www.exelgroup.com
Products: Electronic transistors, diodes, and rectifiers; Electronic capacitors, resistors, semiconductors, and microcircuits. **SICs:** 5065 (Electronic Parts & Equipment Nec); 5063 (Electrical Apparatus & Equipment). **Est:** 1976. **Officers:** Charles S. Brackenridge, President.

■ 8722 ■ **Excel Electric Service Co.**
2415 W 19th St.
Chicago, IL 60608
Phone: (312)421-7220
Products: Breakers and wire. **SIC:** 5063 (Electrical Apparatus & Equipment). **Est:** 1927. **Sales:** $10,000,000 (2000). **Emp:** 55. **Officers:** William Floyd, General Mgr.

■ 8723 ■ **Excel Specialty Corp.**
6335 N Broadway
Chicago, IL 60660-1401
Phone: (773)262-4781   **Fax:** (773)262-1330
Products: Wire harnesses; Hot-stamped wire markers and insulators; Cable assemblies. **SIC:** 5063 (Electrical

Apparatus & Equipment). **Est:** 1949. **Sales:** $1,000,000 (2000). **Emp:** 49. **Officers:** Robert Kopf.

■ 8724 ■ **Excellence Marketing**
7024 Tartan Curve
Eden Prairie, MN 55346
Phone: (612)949-9011   **Fax:** (612)949-9012
Products: Electronic systems and equipment. **SIC:** 5065 (Electronic Parts & Equipment Nec).

■ 8725 ■ **Ezcony Interamerica Inc.**
7620 NW 25th St., Ste. 4
Miami, FL 33122-1719
Phone: (305)599-1352
Products: Electronic products, including stereos and televisions. **SIC:** 5064 (Electrical Appliances—Television & Radio).

■ 8726 ■ **F and B Marketing Inc.**
11920 W Silver Spring Dr.
Milwaukee, WI 53225
Phone: (414)466-4620   **Fax:** (414)466-4710
Products: Neon signs, menu systems and other sign products. **SICs:** 5046 (Commercial Equipment Nec); 5099 (Durable Goods Nec). **Sales:** $1,000,000 (2000). **Emp:** 4. **Officers:** Harry Dumville, President.

■ 8727 ■ **F & M Electric Supply Co.**
29 Federal Rd.
Danbury, CT 06810-5014
Phone: (203)744-7445   **Fax:** (203)744-3640
Products: Electrical supplies. **SIC:** 5065 (Electronic Parts & Equipment Nec). **Officers:** Fil Cerminara, President.

■ 8728 ■ **F & S Supply Company Inc.**
PO Box 373
Iola, KS 66749-0373
Phones: (316)365-3737   800-362-0760
Free: (800)835-0321   **Fax:** (316)365-2694
Products: Lighting equipment and supplies; Janitorial products. **SICs:** 5063 (Electrical Apparatus & Equipment); 5087 (Service Establishment Equipment); 5169 (Chemicals & Allied Products Nec). **Est:** 1978. **Emp:** 47. **Officers:** Frank Ball; Susie Ball; Stephen Douglas; Stanley Douglas, Sales/Marketing Contact; Ivan Collins, Customer Service Contact.

■ 8729 ■ **Fail-Safe Lighting Systems Inc.**
6721 W 73rd St.
Bedford Park, IL 60638-6006
Products: Ceiling lights. **SIC:** 5063 (Electrical Apparatus & Equipment). **Sales:** $30,000,000 (2000). **Emp:** 100. **Officers:** Peter Thornton, President.

■ 8730 ■ **Fairview-AFX Inc.**
4932 S 83rd East Ave.
Tulsa, OK 74145-6911
Phone: (918)664-8020   **Fax:** (918)664-0606
E-mail: info@fairview.galileo.net
URL: http://www.fairviewafx.com
Products: Electronic equipment, including video, audio, and computer equipment. **SICs:** 5065 (Electronic Parts & Equipment Nec); 5045 (Computers, Peripherals & Software). **Emp:** 60. **Officers:** Christopher T. Miller; Thomas J. Roberts.

■ 8731 ■ **Fargo Manufacturing Company Inc.**
PO Box 2900
Poughkeepsie, NY 12603
Phone: (914)471-0600   **Fax:** (914)471-8073
Products: Transmission fittings for telephones and electrical appliances. **SIC:** 5065 (Electronic Parts & Equipment Nec). **Est:** 1914. **Sales:** $23,000,000 (2000). **Emp:** 262. **Officers:** S.R. Wheaton, President; J.T. Fowler, CFO; C.B. Schmidt, Exec. VP of Marketing.

■ 8732 ■ **Fay Electric Wire Corp.**
752 N Larch Ave.
Elmhurst, IL 60126-1522
Phone: (630)530-7500   **Fax:** (630)530-7536
E-mail: Faywire@aol.com
Products: Wire; Lead wire; Magnet wire. **SIC:** 5063 (Electrical Apparatus & Equipment). **Est:** 1966. **Sales:** $13,000,000 (2000). **Emp:** 35. **Officers:** John J. O'Brien, President; Phillip Gnolfo, Treasurer.

■ 8733 ■ Fedco Electronics Inc.
PO Box 1403
Fond du Lac, WI 54936-1403
Phone: (920)922-6490
Free: (800)542-9761   **Fax:** (920)922-6750
Products: Computer batteries and battery packs. **SIC:** 5063 (Electrical Apparatus & Equipment). **Sales:** $16,000,000 (2000). **Emp:** 44. **Officers:** Carolyn A. Victor, CEO.

■ 8734 ■ Federal Signal Corp.
2645 Federal Signal Dr.
University Park, IL 60466-3195
Phone: (708)534-3400
Free: (800)972-9174   **Fax:** (708)534-4852
E-mail: elp@fedsig.com
Products: Industrial audio and visual signaling devices. **SICs:** 5063 (Electrical Apparatus & Equipment); 5085 (Industrial Supplies). **Est:** 1901. **Sales:** $1,000,000,000 (2000). **Emp:** 740. **Officers:** Tom Schonauer.

■ 8735 ■ Federated Purchaser Inc.
268 Cliffwood Ave.
Cliffwood, NJ 07721
Phone: (908)301-1333
Free: (877)679-2004   **Fax:** (908)301-0489
Products: Electronic components. **SIC:** 5065 (Electronic Parts & Equipment Nec). **Est:** 1928. **Sales:** $3,300,000 (2000). **Emp:** 17. **Officers:** Harry J. Fallon, CEO & President; Maria Santsira, Secretary.

■ 8736 ■ Fenton Brothers Electrical
235 Ray Ave. NE
PO Box 996
New Philadelphia, OH 44663
Phone: (330)343-8858
Free: (800)229-8858   **Fax:** (330)343-6874
E-mail: fenton@tusco.net
URL: http://www.fentonbros.com
Products: Electrical equipment; Light bulbs. **SIC:** 5063 (Electrical Apparatus & Equipment). **Est:** 1947. **Sales:** $2,000,000 (2000). **Emp:** 31. **Officers:** Thomas A. Fenton, President; Dennis L. Fenton, Vice President; Chris H. Fenton, Secretary; Brian K. Fenton, Treasurer.

■ 8737 ■ Ferguson Electric Construction Company Inc.
333 Ellicott St.
Buffalo, NY 14203
Phone: (716)852-2010
Products: Electrical construction supplies. **SICs:** 5063 (Electrical Apparatus & Equipment); 5039 (Construction Materials Nec). **Est:** 1935. **Sales:** $35,000,000 (2000). **Emp:** 250. **Officers:** Whitworth Ferguson Jr., President; Jon Neenos.

■ 8738 ■ Joseph T. Fewkes and Co.
6 Springdale Rd.
Cherry Hill, NJ 08003
Phone: (609)424-3932   **Fax:** (609)751-1118
Products: Electronic components. **SIC:** 5063 (Electrical Apparatus & Equipment). **Est:** 1903. **Sales:** $7,000,000 (2000). **Emp:** 30. **Officers:** R.E. Gillin, President; Suzanne M. Gibson, Accountant; A. Simeone, Dir. of Marketing; L.W. Gillin, Dir. of Systems.

■ 8739 ■ FIC Corp.
12216 Parklawn Dr.
Rockville, MD 20852
Phone: (301)881-8124
Free: (800)638-6594   **Fax:** (301)881-0530
Products: Fuses and fuse equipment; Electrical hanging and fastening devices. **SICs:** 5063 (Electrical Apparatus & Equipment); 5065 (Electronic Parts & Equipment Nec). **Est:** 1957. **Sales:** $2,000,000 (1999). **Emp:** 35. **Officers:** John C. Linton, President; Robert Frye, Vice President; Hermine Linton, Treasurer &

■ Fidus Instrument Corp.
itepine Rd.
VA 23237-2219
(804)275-1431
Electronic parts; Electric and electronic
C: 5065 (Electronic Parts & Equipment
William Nolley, President.

■ 8741 ■ Fife Electric Co.
42860 9 Mile Rd.
PO Box 8021
Novi, MI 48376-8021
Phone: (248)344-4100   **Fax:** (248)344-4159
Products: Electric supplies. **SICs:** 5063 (Electrical Apparatus & Equipment); 5065 (Electronic Parts & Equipment Nec). **Est:** 1928. **Emp:** 70.

■ 8742 ■ Fine Wire Coil Company
4130 E University Dr.
Phoenix, AZ 85034
Phone: (602)437-9194   **Fax:** (602)437-2956
Products: Coils and transformers for the electronics industry. **SIC:** 5065 (Electronic Parts & Equipment Nec). **Sales:** $1,000,000 (1999). **Emp:** 5. **Officers:** John Lapusan, Owner.

■ 8743 ■ Fitzpatrick Electric Supply Co.
PO Box 657
Muskegon, MI 49443-0657
Phone: (616)722-6621   **Fax:** (616)728-4487
Products: Electrical apparatus, parts and equipment. **SICs:** 5063 (Electrical Apparatus & Equipment); 5065 (Electronic Parts & Equipment Nec). **Sales:** $55,000,000 (1994). **Emp:** 210. **Officers:** L.P. Carlson, President.

■ 8744 ■ Flash Clinic Inc.
9 E 19th St., 10th Fl.
New York, NY 10003
Phone: (212)673-4030
Free: (800)752-7536   **Fax:** (212)505-8958
Products: Lighting and strobe equipment. **SIC:** 5063 (Electrical Apparatus & Equipment). **Emp:** 9.

■ 8745 ■ Flato Electric Supply Co.
PO Box 9317
Corpus Christi, TX 78469
Phone: (512)884-4555   **Fax:** (512)884-6077
Products: Wiring; Light fixtures; Breakers. **SIC:** 5063 (Electrical Apparatus & Equipment). **Est:** 1906. **Sales:** $6,000,000 (1999). **Emp:** 25. **Officers:** Edwin Flato, President; Terry Brogan, Controller; Bob Horny, General Mgr.

■ 8746 ■ FLEET Specialties Co.
PO Box 4575
Thousand Oaks, CA 91359
Phone: (818)340-8181   **Fax:** (818)889-3982
Products: Electronic tire-monitoring equipment. **SIC:** 5065 (Electronic Parts & Equipment Nec). **Est:** 1982.

■ 8747 ■ Florig Equipment
1611 Integrity Dr. E
Columbus, OH 43209
Phone: (614)443-5950
Free: (800)225-6788   **Fax:** (614)443-7546
Products: Commercial shearing equipment; Pumps; Motors; Valves. **SICs:** 5063 (Electrical Apparatus & Equipment); 5072 (Hardware); 5085 (Industrial Supplies).

■ 8748 ■ Forbes Distributing Co.
PO Box 1478
Birmingham, AL 35201
Phone: (205)251-4104
Free: (800)292-6004   **Fax:** (205)251-4115
E-mail: forbesdc@zebra.net
URL: www.forbes-elec.com
Products: Electronic parts. **SIC:** 5065 (Electronic Parts & Equipment Nec). **Est:** 1945. **Sales:** $4,000,000 (2000). **Emp:** 25. **Officers:** William K. Forbes Jr., President; Randy Ozley, General Mgr.

■ 8749 ■ Force Electronics Inc.
606 Hawaii St.
El Segundo, CA 90245
Phone: (213)772-1324
Products: Electronic components. **SIC:** 5065 (Electronic Parts & Equipment Nec). **Est:** 1960. **Sales:** $20,000,000 (2000). **Emp:** 100. **Officers:** Robert Clapp, President; David Murray, Controller.

■ 8750 ■ Force Electronics Inc.
606 Hawaii St.
El Segundo, CA 90245
Phone: (310)643-7676   **Fax:** (310)643-6735
Products: Electronic equipment. **SIC:** 5065 (Electronic

Parts & Equipment Nec). **Sales:** $198,000,000 (2000). **Emp:** 500. **Officers:** Robert Clapp, President; David Murray, Controller.

■ 8751 ■ Force Electronics Inc. Texas Div.
3218 Beltline Rd., Ste. 510
Farmers Branch, TX 75234
Phone: (972)247-9955   **Fax:** (214)247-0619
Products: Electrical and electronic equipment and supplies. **SIC:** 5065 (Electronic Parts & Equipment Nec). **Sales:** $3,000,000 (2000). **Emp:** 20.

■ 8752 ■ ForeSight Electronics Inc.
610 Palomar Ave.
Sunnyvale, CA 94086
Phone: (408)732-7777
Products: Power supplies and components. **SICs:** 5063 (Electrical Apparatus & Equipment); 5065 (Electronic Parts & Equipment Nec).

■ 8753 ■ Forest City Electric Supply
PO Box 297
Rockford, IL 61105-0297
Phone: (815)968-5781   **Fax:** (815)968-5079
Products: Wire, circuit breakers, and light fixtures; Light bulbs. **SIC:** 5063 (Electrical Apparatus & Equipment). **Est:** 1942. **Sales:** $10,000,000 (2000). **Emp:** 23. **Officers:** Tom Paulson, General Mgr.; Lee Roulson, Finance Officer. **Former Name:** Forest City Electric Supply.

■ 8754 ■ F.R. Industries Inc.
557 Long Rd.
Pittsburgh, PA 15235
Phone: (412)242-5903   **Fax:** (412)242-5908
Products: Relays and controls. **SIC:** 5063 (Electrical Apparatus & Equipment). **Sales:** $3,000,000 (2000). **Emp:** 11. **Officers:** Francois Reizine, President.

■ 8755 ■ Carlos Franco
311 S Broadway
McAllen, TX 78501
Phone: (956)687-4662   **Fax:** (956)682-3470
E-mail: carlosuno@aol.com
Products: Electronic parts, including transistors, integrated circuits, speaker parts, cables, antennae, belts, and needles for record players. **SIC:** 5065 (Electronic Parts & Equipment Nec). **Est:** 1966. **Emp:** 6.

■ 8756 ■ Lou Frankel & Company Inc.
68 Old Mill Rd.
Greenwich, CT 06831-3047
Phone: (203)661-2370
Products: Electronic parts and equipment. **SIC:** 5065 (Electronic Parts & Equipment Nec).

■ 8757 ■ Franki Sales Co.
10 Wentworth Dr.
Bedford, NH 03110
Phone: (603)472-6947   **Fax:** (603)472-6947
Products: Electronic systems and equipment. **SIC:** 5065 (Electronic Parts & Equipment Nec).

■ 8758 ■ Franklin Electric Company Inc. (Atlantic City, New Jersey)
1810 Baltic Ave.
Atlantic City, NJ 08401
Phone: (609)345-6154   **Fax:** (609)345-6958
Products: Electrical supplies. **SIC:** 5063 (Electrical Apparatus & Equipment). **Est:** 1919. **Sales:** $18,000,000 (2000). **Emp:** 62. **Officers:** E.R. Lowenstein, President; Melissa Ishee, Controller; Gary Lowenstein, Dir. of Marketing.

■ 8759 ■ Fravert Services Inc.
133 W Park Dr.
Birmingham, AL 35211
Phone: (205)940-7180
Free: (800)743-7191   **Fax:** (205)940-7190
Products: Lighting; Electrical work. **SIC:** 5063 (Electrical Apparatus & Equipment). **Est:** 1946. **Sales:** $3,000,000 (1999). **Emp:** 45. **Officers:** Craig Fravert, President.

■ 8760 ■ Fresno Distributing Co.
PO Box 6078
Fresno, CA 93703
Phone: (559)442-8800 **Fax:** (559)264-3809
Products: Electrical and plumbing supplies and fixtures. **SIC:** 5063 (Electrical Apparatus & Equipment). **Est:** 1946. **Sales:** $20,000,000 (2000). **Emp:** 60.
Officers: Jasmine Cloud, President; Sara Siroonian, Treasurer & Secty.; Steve Cloud, Vice President.

■ 8761 ■ Frezzolini Electronics Inc.
5 Valley St.
Hawthorne, NJ 07506-2084
Phone: (973)427-1160
Free: (800)345-1030 **Fax:** (973)427-0934
E-mail: frezzi@frezzi.com
URL: http://www.frezzi.com
Products: Electronic chargers; Lighting equipment; Power source integration equipment and supplies. **SIC:** 5065 (Electronic Parts & Equipment Nec). **Est:** 1968. **Emp:** 24. **Officers:** James Crawford, President; Ed Kuhn, VP of Sales; Kevin Crawford, VP of Engineering.

■ 8762 ■ Friedman Electric Supply
1321 Wyoming Ave.
Exeter, PA 18643-1425
Phone: (717)654-3371 **Fax:** (717)655-6194
Products: Breakers; Lighting fixtures and bulbs; Panels; PLCs and automation equipment. **SICs** 5063 (Electrical Apparatus & Equipment); 5085 (Industrial Supplies). **Emp:** 49. **Officers:** S. J. Friedman; R. Friedman.

■ 8763 ■ Frigid North Co.
3309 Spenard Rd.
Anchorage, AK 99503-4503
Phone: (907)561-4633
Free: (800)478-4633 **Fax:** (907)562-3219
E-mail: frigidn@alaska.net
URL: http://www.frigidn.com
Products: Electronic parts and equipment. **SIC:** 5065 (Electronic Parts & Equipment Nec). **Est:** 1979. **Sales:** $5,200,000 (1999). **Emp:** 32. **Officers:** Thomas McGrath, Owner.

■ 8764 ■ Fromm Electric Supply Corp.
PO Box 15147
Reading, PA 19612-5147
Phone: (215)374-4441 **Fax:** (215)374-8756
Products: Electrical products. **SIC:** 5063 (Electrical Apparatus & Equipment). **Est:** 1958. **Emp:** 80.

■ 8765 ■ Frontier Radio Inc.
3401 Sirius Ave. 18
Las Vegas, NV 89102-8313
Phone: (702)871-6166 **Fax:** (702)367-0347
Products: Communications Systems and Equipmentt. **SIC:** 5065 (Electronic Parts & Equipment Nec). **Sales:** $1,000,000 (2000). **Emp:** 8.

■ 8766 ■ Fujitsu Business Communication Systems Inc.
3190 E Miraloma Ave.
Anaheim, CA 92806
Phone: (714)630-7721 **Free:** (800)553-3263
Products: Private branch exchange manufacturing, distribution, R and D, sales and service. **SIC:** 5063 (Electrical Apparatus & Equipment). **Sales:** $199,000,000 (2000). **Emp:** 1,000. **Officers:** Glenda Davis, President; Richard Tracy, VP of Finance.

■ 8767 ■ Fulton Radio Supply Co.
PO Box 480
Jackson, MI 49204-0480
Phone: (517)784-6106
Free: (800)686-6106 **Fax:** (517)784-6665
Products: Electronic parts, microswitches, relays, wire, and cable. **SIC:** 5063 (Electrical Apparatus & Equipment). **Est:** 1930. **Emp:** 10. **Officers:** Leo M. Harley, President; Gordon Fulton, Chairman of the Board.

■ 8768 ■ Furbay Electric Supply Co.
PO Box 6268
Canton, OH 44706
Phone: (330)454-3033
Free: (800)438-7229 **Fax:** (330)454-6268
Products: Electrical supplies, including lighting fixtures and wiring. **SIC:** 5063 (Electrical Apparatus &

Equipment). **Est:** 1934. **Sales:** $18,000,000 (2000). **Emp:** 50. **Officers:** Tim A. Furbay, President; Paul Monaco, Vice President; Tim Furbay, Dir. of Marketing & Sales.

■ 8769 ■ Future Electronics Corporation
41 Main St.
Bolton, MA 01740
Phone: (978)779-3000
Free: (800)444-0050 **Fax:** (978)779-3050
URL: http://www.FutureElectronics.com
Products: Commercial and military electronic components. **SIC:** 5065 (Electronic Parts & Equipment Nec). **Est:** 1968. **Emp:** 5,600. **Officers:** Robert Miller, President; Robert Roop, CFO; Eddy Rosenberg, Exec. VP; Glen Brown, VP of Human Resources.

■ 8770 ■ Gaffney-Kroese Electrical Supply Corp.
1697 Elizabeth Ave.
Rahway, NJ 07065
Phone: (908)381-0500 **Fax:** (908)381-1996
Products: Electrical supplies. **SIC:** 5063 (Electrical Apparatus & Equipment). **Est:** 1929. **Sales:** $15,000,000 (2000). **Emp:** 25. **Officers:** Christopher C. Kroese, President.

■ 8771 ■ Gaines Electric Supply Co.
2501 Orange Ave.
Long Beach, CA 90801
Phone: (562)595-8321
Products: Electric supplies. **SIC:** 5063 (Electrical Apparatus & Equipment). **Sales:** $17,000,000 (2000). **Emp:** 55. **Officers:** Don Peters, President; Eric Peters, Treasurer & Secty.

■ 8772 ■ Galco Industrial Electronics
26010 Pinehurst Dr.
Madison Heights, MI 48071-4139
Phone: (248)542-9090
Free: (800)827-8902 **Fax:** (248)542-8031
E-mail: sales@galco.com
URL: http://www.galco.com
Products: Industrial electronic components and supplies, including drives, connectors, control products, fuses, panel meters, power quality products, power supplies, semi-conductors, test equipment, and transformers. **SICs:** 5065 (Electronic Parts & Equipment Nec); 5085 (Industrial Supplies). **Est:** 1975. **Emp:** 128. **Officers:** Daniel A. Galasso, CEO; Louis Molnar, President.

■ 8773 ■ Gately Communications Company Inc.
501 Industry Dr.
Hampton, VA 23661-1314
Phone: (757)826-8210
Free: (800)428-3597 **Fax:** (757)826-7213
Products: Communications systems and equipment. **SIC:** 5065 (Electronic Parts & Equipment Nec).

■ 8774 ■ Gates Arrow Distributing Inc.
39 Pleham Ridge Dr.
Greenville, SC 29615
Phone: (843)234-0736 **Free:** (800)332-2222
Products: Electronics. **SIC:** 5065 (Electronic Parts & Equipment Nec).

■ 8775 ■ Gaylon Distributing Inc.
10310 S Dolfield Rd.
Owings Mills, MD 21117-3510
Phone: (410)363-6600 **Fax:** (410)363-8749
Products: Electronic parts and equipment, including communication equipment. **SIC:** 5065 (Electronic Parts & Equipment Nec). **Officers:** Barbara Galonoy, President.

■ 8776 ■ Gaylord Manufacturing Co.
PO Box 547
Ceres, CA 95307
Phone: (209)538-3313 **Fax:** (209)538-8638
Products: Electrical enclosures; Metal stamping. **SICs** 5063 (Electrical Apparatus & Equipment); 5084 (Industrial Machinery & Equipment). **Sales:** $2,000,000 (2000). **Emp:** 22. **Officers:** Gaylord W. Lillemoen.

■ 8777 ■ GC Thorsen Inc.
1801 Morgan St.
Rockford, IL 61102-1209
Phone: (815)968-9661 **Fax:** (815)968-9731
Products: Electronic hook-up accessories for computers, audio, video and telephones. **SIC:** 5045 (Computers, Peripherals & Software). **Sales:** $43,800,000 (2000). **Emp:** 175. **Officers:** Roger Engle, CEO.

■ 8778 ■ G.D.E., Inc.
2715 E Saturn St.
Brea, CA 92821-6705
Phone: (714)528-6880 **Fax:** (714)528-2734
Products: Electronic components, including semiconductors. **SIC:** 5065 (Electronic Parts & Equipment Nec). **Officers:** M. Rodriguez, President.

■ 8779 ■ GE Supply
2 Corporate Dr.
PO Box 861
Shelton, CT 06484-0861
Phone: (203)944-3000 **Fax:** (203)944-3049
Products: Switches. **SIC:** 5063 (Electrical Apparatus & Equipment). **Est:** 1920. **Sales:** $1,100,000,000 (2000). **Emp:** 2,200. **Officers:** W.L. Meddaugh, CEO & President; Doug Seymour, CFO; J.H. Whitby, Marketing Mgr.; F.M. Billone, Dir. of Information Systems; R. Villani, Human Resources Mgr.

■ 8780 ■ GEC Alsthom Balteau, Inc.
300 W Antelope Rd.
Medford, OR 97503
Phone: (541)826-2113 **Fax:** (541)826-8847
Products: Transformers. **SIC:** 5063 (Electrical Apparatus & Equipment). **Est:** 1969. **Sales:** $23,000,000 (2000). **Emp:** 125. **Officers:** R. Sawyer, President; Bruce Deline, Controller; Thomas Steeber, Marketing Mgr.

■ 8781 ■ GEM Electronics
34 Hempstead Turnpike
Farmingdale, NY 11735
Phone: (516)249-6996 **Fax:** (516)694-6562
Products: Electronic parts. **SIC:** 5065 (Electronic Parts & Equipment Nec).

■ 8782 ■ Generac Corp.
PO Box 8
Waukesha, WI 53187
Phone: (414)544-4811 **Fax:** (414)544-4851
Products: RV trailers; Car washers; Portable generator sets. **SICs:** 5063 (Electrical Apparatus & Equipment); 5012 (Automobiles & Other Motor Vehicles); 5013 (Motor Vehicle Supplies & New Parts). **Officers:** Dorrance Noonan, Vice President of European Sales; Michael Sinai, Director of German Sales; Angela Philpott, European Sales Manager; Jose Fabregas, Director of Spanish Sales.

■ 8783 ■ General Electric Supply
684 Robbins Dr.
Troy, MI 48083-4563
Phone: (248)588-7300 **Fax:** (248)588-3169
Products: Electric supplies. **SIC:** 5063 (Electrical Apparatus & Equipment). **Emp:** 49. **Officers:** T. Roney.

■ 8784 ■ Generic Systems Inc.
PO Box 153
Perrysburg, OH 43552
Phone: (419)841-8460
Free: (888)488-8555 **Fax:** (419)841-1420
Products: Automated controls; Software developer for material handling applications. **SIC:** 5065 (Electronic Parts & Equipment Nec).

■ 8785 ■ Genesis Associates Inc.
128 Wheeler Rd.
Burlington, MA 01803-5170
Phone: (781)270-9540 **Fax:** (781)229-891
Products: Electronic systems and equipment Electronic parts; Semiconductors and related device **SIC:** 5065 (Electronic Parts & Equipment Ne
Officers: Daniel Fradkin, President.

■ **8786** ■ **Georgia Lighting Supply Co.**
530 14th St.
Atlanta, GA 30318
Phone: (404)875-4754
Free: (800)282-0220 **Fax:** (404)872-4679
Products: Lights and light fixtures, including chandeliers and ceiling fans. **SIC:** 5063 (Electrical Apparatus & Equipment). **Est:** 1960. **Sales:** $45,000,000 (2000). **Emp:** 220. **Officers:** Harry L. Gilham Jr., President; Ray M. Gardner, VP of Finance.

■ **8787** ■ **Gerber Radio Supply Co.**
128 Carnegie Row
Norwood, MA 02062
Phone: (781)329-2400 **Fax:** (781)762-8931
Products: Industrial electronic components. **SIC:** 5065 (Electronic Parts & Equipment Nec). **Officers:** Robert J. Gerber, President; Albert Gerber, Vice President.

■ **8788** ■ **Glaze Supply Company Inc.**
PO Box 1443
Dalton, GA 30720
Phone: (706)278-3663
Products: Electrical supplies, including wiring and cord; Plumbing supplies, including tubing and pipes. **SICs:** 5063 (Electrical Apparatus & Equipment); 5074 (Plumbing & Hydronic Heating Supplies). **Est:** 1950. **Sales:** $5,000,000 (2000). **Emp:** 25. **Officers:** Tom Lambert, President; Lisa Morgan, Treasurer.

■ **8789** ■ **Globe Electric Supply Company, Inc.**
33-70 10th St.
PO Box 6258
Long Island City, NY 11106
Phone: (718)932-1820
Free: (800)221-1500 **Fax:** (718)726-5008
E-mail: globework@aol.com
Products: Plugs and receptacles; Circuit breakers; Fuses and conduit fillings. **SIC:** 5063 (Electrical Apparatus & Equipment). **Est:** 1946. **Emp:** 22. **Officers:** J. Rosenzweig; Joel Mandel.

■ **8790** ■ **Globe-Hamburg, Import/Export**
3170 Durham Rd.
Hamburg, NY 14075
Phone: (716)627-3427 **Fax:** (716)648-2747
Products: Satellite disks. **SIC:** 5065 (Electronic Parts & Equipment Nec). **Est:** 1980. **Emp:** 3. **Officers:** Peter Steigert, Owner.

■ **8791** ■ **Globus Industries**
PO Box 173
Holmdel, NJ 07733
Phone: (732)671-8310 **Fax:** (732)957-0249
E-mail: globus@webspan.net
Products: Electronic equipment and supplies, including semiconductors, resistors, capacitors, and tubes; Electrical fuses and fuse holders; Computer disk drives and diskettes. **SICs:** 5065 (Electronic Parts & Equipment Nec); 5063 (Electrical Apparatus & Equipment); 5045 (Computers, Peripherals & Software). **Est:** 1962. **Sales:** $2,000,000 (2000). **Emp:** 3. **Officers:** James Zalayet, Partner; David Zalayet, Sales/Marketing Contact; Ezra Zalayet, Customer Service Contact.

■ **8792** ■ **GMP**
3111 Old Lincoln Hwy.
Trevose, PA 19053-4996
Phone: (215)357-5500 **Fax:** (215)357-6216
Products: Communications systems and equipment. **SIC:** 5065 (Electronic Parts & Equipment Nec).

■ **8793** ■ **Goforth Electric Supply Inc.**
PO Box 270
Gainesville, GA 30503
Phone: (404)536-3361
Products: Electrical supplies, including light fixtures, wiring, and light bulbs. **SIC:** 5063 (Electrical Apparatus & Equipment). **Est:** 1958. **Sales:** $4,000,000 (2000). **Emp:** 18. **Officers:** Charles R. Moore, President & CFO.

■ **8794** ■ **Gold Key Electronics Inc.**
PO Box 186
Goffstown, NH 03045
Phone: (603)625-8518 **Free:** (800)325-0150
Products: Electronic equipment for laser jets. **SIC:** 5065 (Electronic Parts & Equipment Nec). **Est:** 1983.

Sales: $3,000,000 (2000). **Emp:** 7. **Officers:** Green Adire, President.

■ **8795** ■ **Golden Electronics Inc.**
951 Aviation Pky.
Morrisville, NC 27560
Phone: (919)467-2466 **Free:** (800)234-5144
Products: Electronic parts. **SIC:** 5065 (Electronic Parts & Equipment Nec). **Est:** 1984. **Sales:** $2,300,000 (2000). **Emp:** 6. **Officers:** Ruby Bowden, President.

■ **8796** ■ **Goldfarb Electric Supply Company Inc.**
PO Box 3319
Charleston, WV 25333
Phone: (304)342-2153 **Fax:** (304)345-4321
Products: Electrical and lighting supplies, including light bulbs, lamps, wire, capacitors, and resistors. **SIC:** 5063 (Electrical Apparatus & Equipment). **Est:** 1933. **Sales:** $5,000,000 (2000). **Emp:** 35. **Officers:** Jack Goldfarb, President; Daniel Goldfarb, CFO.

■ **8797** ■ **Gopher Electronics Co.**
222 E Little Canada Rd.
St. Paul, MN 55117
Phone: (651)490-4900
Free: (800)592-9519 **Fax:** (651)490-4911
E-mail: info@gopherelectronics.com
URL: http://www.gopherelectronics.com
Products: Electronic products, including connectors, switches, sensors, LEDs, and relays for telecommunications, medical, and industrial control applications. **SIC:** 5065 (Electronic Parts & Equipment Nec). **Est:** 1952. **Sales:** $20,000,000 (1999). **Emp:** 49. **Officers:** Norris W. Carnes, CEO; John Reinke, President & General Mgr.

■ **8798** ■ **GPX Inc.**
108 Madison St.
St. Louis, MO 63102
Phone: (314)621-3314 **Fax:** (314)621-0869
Products: Electrical appliances, including radios, televisions, stereos, cd players, walkaround radios, and electronic toys. **SIC:** 5064 (Electrical Appliances—Television & Radio). **Est:** 1973. **Sales:** $200,000,000 (2000). **Emp:** 500. **Officers:** Ronald H. Richter, CEO; Fran Olsey, COO.

■ **8799** ■ **Graham/Davis, Inc.**
PO Box 941177
Houston, TX 77094-8177
Phone: (281)558-8662 **Fax:** (281)556-0052
Products: Electronic systems and equipment. **SIC:** 5065 (Electronic Parts & Equipment Nec).

■ **8800** ■ **Grainger, Inc.**
1938 Elm Tree Dr.
Nashville, TN 37210
Products: Electrical industrial equipment, including motors and transmissions. **SIC:** 5063 (Electrical Apparatus & Equipment).

■ **8801** ■ **Grainger Inc.**
834 Riverside Dr.
Asheville, NC 28806
Phone: (828)258-8986
Products: Electric motors. **SIC:** 5063 (Electrical Apparatus & Equipment).

■ **8802** ■ **W.W. Grainger Inc.**
100 Grainger Pkwy.
Lake Forest, IL 60045
Phone: (847)535-1000
Products: Hand tool motors. **SIC:** 5063 (Electrical Apparatus & Equipment). **Est:** 1927. **Sales:** $4,500,000,000 (1999). **Emp:** 16,000. **Officers:** Richard L. Keyser, Chairman of the Board; P. Ogden Loux, VP of Finance & CFO; Gary Goberville, VP of Human Resources.

■ **8803** ■ **Grainger Industrial Supply**
800 W Willard St.
Muncie, IN 47302
Phone: (765)741-8100
Products: Electric motors. **SIC:** 5063 (Electrical Apparatus & Equipment). **Former Name:** Grainger Inc.

■ **8804** ■ **Granada Electronics Corp.**
485 Kent Ave.
Brooklyn, NY 11211
Phone: (718)387-1157
Products: Electronics. **SIC:** 5065 (Electronic Parts & Equipment Nec). **Sales:** $6,000,000 (2000). **Emp:** 20. **Officers:** N Brach, CEO; Morris Hartman, VP of Marketing & Sales; Marla Dallal, Dir. of Data Processing.

■ **8805** ■ **Grand Light and Supply Co.**
PO Box 9402
New Haven, CT 06534
Phone: (203)777-5781 **Fax:** (203)785-1184
Products: Light bulbs, lamps, panels, plugs, and switches. **SIC:** 5063 (Electrical Apparatus & Equipment). **Est:** 1929. **Sales:** $25,000,000 (2000). **Emp:** 85. **Officers:** Steve Stockman, CEO & President; Dennis Macura, Vice Chairman of the Board; Brett Powers, Dir. of Sales; Lou Notarino, Information Systems Mgr.

■ **8806** ■ **Grand Transformers Inc.**
1500 Marion Ave.
Grand Haven, MI 49417
Phone: (616)842-5430
Products: Electric coil; Transformers. **SIC:** 5063 (Electrical Apparatus & Equipment).

■ **8807** ■ **Granite City Electric Supply Co.**
19 Quincy Ave.
Quincy, MA 02169
Phone: (617)472-6500 **Fax:** (617)773-8941
E-mail: granitecityelectric.com
URL: http://www.granitecityelectric.com
Products: Electrical supplies, including cable and wire. **SIC:** 5063 (Electrical Apparatus & Equipment). **Est:** 1923. **Sales:** $38,000,000 (1999). **Emp:** 120. **Officers:** Phyllis Godwin, CEO & Chairman of the Board; Peter Jacobson, CFO; Stephen Helle, CEO & President.

■ **8808** ■ **Graybar Electric Company Inc.**
1871 Old Okeechobee Rd.
West Palm Beach, FL 33409-4138
Phone: (561)683-3801 **Fax:** (561)683-5843
Products: Electrical products, including breakers. **SIC:** 5063 (Electrical Apparatus & Equipment). **Emp:** 30. **Officers:** Mark Thomas.

■ **8809** ■ **Graybar Electric Company Inc.**
220 Industrial Blvd.
Naples, FL 34104-3704
Phone: (941)643-4000 **Fax:** (941)643-3137
Products: Electrical supplies. **SIC:** 5063 (Electrical Apparatus & Equipment). **Emp:** 49. **Officers:** Dan Libby; Joseph Lakers.

■ **8810** ■ **Graybar Electric Company Inc.**
1740 Fortune Ct.
Lexington, KY 40509
Phone: (859)299-3787
Free: (800)666-3787 **Fax:** (859)299-7868
Products: Electrical supplies; Communication, voice, and data products. **SIC:** 5063 (Electrical Apparatus & Equipment). **Emp:** 30. **Officers:** Jim Tincher.

■ **8811** ■ **Graybar Electric Company Inc.**
717 S Good Latimer
Dallas, TX 75226-1815
Phone: (214)939-0844 **Fax:** (214)747-1429
Products: Electrical supplies, including bulbs, lights, and wiring. **SIC:** 5063 (Electrical Apparatus & Equipment). **Emp:** 49.

■ **8812** ■ **Graybar Electric Company Inc.**
655 S H St.
San Bernardino, CA 92410-3417
Phone: (714)889-1051 **Fax:** (714)889-1050
Products: Electrical equipment; Electronic wire and cable. **SIC:** 5063 (Electrical Apparatus & Equipment). **Emp:** 23.

■ **8813** ■ **Graybar Electric Company Inc.**
PO Box 970709
Quail Heights, FL 33197
Phone: (305)232-1530
Free: (800)395-1530 **Fax:** (305)238-5134
Products: Electric components and supplies, including wires and boxes. **SIC:** 5063 (Electrical Apparatus &

Equipment). **Emp:** 150. **Officers:** Homer Alexander, Branch Manager.

■ 8814 ■ Graybar Electric Company Inc.
PO Box 7231
St. Louis, MO 63177
Phone: (314)727-3900 **Fax:** (314)727-8218
Products: Power hand tools; Electric apparatus and equipment, including communication equipment. **SICs:** 5065 (Electronic Parts & Equipment Nec); 5072 (Hardware). **Officers:** W.R. Kuykendall, Intl. Sales Mgr.

■ 8815 ■ Great Lake Distributors
1717 W Beltline Hwy., Ste. 102
Madison, WI 53713
Phone: (608)274-3123
Free: (800)236-1717 **Fax:** (608)274-1108
Products: Laser products. **SIC:** 5065 (Electronic Parts & Equipment Nec). **Est:** 1972. **Sales:** $1,000,000 (2000). **Emp:** 4. **Officers:** Harold Palmer, Owner.

■ 8816 ■ Great Lakes Electronics Supply Div.
4560 W Dickman Rd.
Battle Creek, MI 49015
Phone: (616)963-6282
Free: (800)962-3144 **Fax:** (616)963-3432
E-mail: sales@glebc.com
URL: http://www.glebc.com
Products: Electronic parts and equipment, including controls and sensors. **SIC:** 5065 (Electronic Parts & Equipment Nec). **Est:** 1973. **Sales:** $11,000,000 (2000). **Emp:** 20. **Officers:** Robert D. Gammons, General Mgr.; James Tredwell, VP of Finance.

■ 8817 ■ Greenwood Supply Company Inc.
PO Box 3069
Greenwood, SC 29648-3069
Phone: (864)229-2501 **Fax:** (864)229-3201
E-mail: gws1@greenwood.net
URL: http://www.industry.net/mropgreenwood.supply
Products: Electrical supplies, including cable and wire; Industrial cutting tools. **SICs:** 5063 (Electrical Apparatus & Equipment); 5084 (Industrial Machinery & Equipment). **Est:** 1933. **Sales:** $10,000,000 (2000). **Emp:** 45. **Officers:** Joeseph Adams Jr., Chairman of the Board; Susan Dixon, Controller; Joe Adams III, President; Mike Adams, President.

■ 8818 ■ Greer Industries Inc.
PO Box 14249
Ft. Worth, TX 76117-0249
Phone: (817)222-1414 **Fax:** (817)222-1075
URL: http://www.greerindustriesinc.com
Products: Electrical supplies. **SIC:** 5063 (Electrical Apparatus & Equipment). **Est:** 1976. **Sales:** $3,000,000 (2000). **Emp:** 10. **Officers:** Robert J. Greer.

■ 8819 ■ Greylock Electronics Distributors
763 Ulster Ave. Mall
Kingston, NY 12401
Phone: (914)338-5300 **Free:** (800)433-4431
E-mail: xtalbay@aol.com
Products: Antennas, including wire and cable antennas. **SIC:** 5065 (Electronic Parts & Equipment Nec). **Est:** 1947. **Sales:** $700,000 (1999). **Emp:** 6. **Officers:** David Parkhurst Sr., President; James Parkhurst, Vice President; Alice Parkhurst, Dir. of Systems.

■ 8820 ■ Gross Electric Inc.
PO Box 352377
Toledo, OH 43635-2377
Phone: (419)537-1818 **Fax:** (419)537-6627
URL: http://www.grosselectric.com
Products: Electrical equipment and lighting fixture. **SIC:** 5063 (Electrical Apparatus & Equipment). **Est:** 1910. **Sales:** $6,000,000 (1999). **Emp:** 70. **Officers:** Laurie Gross, President; Hank Reinhard, Treasurer; Joe Gross, Vice President; Richard Gross, Chairman of the Board; Kristie Kraftchick, Human Resources Contact.

■ 8821 ■ Gulf Coast Electric Supply Company Inc.
PO Box 9588
Houston, TX 77261-9588
Phone: (713)222-9086
Free: (800)843-3195 **Fax:** (713)228-9732
Products: Incandescent and florescent electrical lamps; Electrical apparatus; Photographic projection lamps. **SICs:** 5063 (Electrical Apparatus & Equipment); 5043 (Photographic Equipment & Supplies). **Est:** 1938. **Sales:** $9,000,000 (2000). **Emp:** 32. **Officers:** Robert L. Snodgrass, Owner.

■ 8822 ■ Haig Lighting & Electric
34001 Groesbeck Hwy.
Clinton Township, MI 48035
Phone: (810)791-2380 **Fax:** (810)791-0970
Products: Electrical products, including light fixtures, table lamps, crystals, light bulbs, wire, and chandeliers. **SIC:** 5063 (Electrical Apparatus & Equipment). **Emp:** 9.

■ 8823 ■ Melville B. Hall Inc.
3001 Spruce
St. Louis, MO 63103
Phone: (314)371-7000 **Fax:** (314)371-7001
E-mail: mail@mbhall.com
URL: http://www.mbhall.com
Products: Electrical supplies, including wires and lighting; Automation and control products. **SIC:** 5063 (Electrical Apparatus & Equipment). **Est:** 1926. **Sales:** $4,000,000 (2000). **Emp:** 45. **Officers:** Clark S. Hall, President; Clinton McDanoll, CFO; David S. Kinsella, Dir. of Marketing & Sales.

■ 8824 ■ Hamilton Electric Works Inc.
3800 Airport Blvd.
Austin, TX 78722
Phone: (512)472-2428
Products: Electric motors. **SIC:** 5063 (Electrical Apparatus & Equipment). **Est:** 1946. **Sales:** $2,500,000 (2000). **Emp:** 25. **Officers:** Gary D. Hamilton, President; Dale Hamilton, Vice President.

■ 8825 ■ Hammond Electronics Inc.
1230 W Central Blvd.
Orlando, FL 32805
Phone: (407)849-6060 **Fax:** (407)872-0826
URL: http://www.hammondelec.com
Products: Electronic equipment. **SIC:** 5065 (Electronic Parts & Equipment Nec). **Est:** 1947. **Sales:** $55,000,000 (1999). **Emp:** 185. **Officers:** John T. Hammond, President; David T. Klein, VP of Finance; Doug Watson, VP of Operations; Pete Crescenti, Dir. of Mktg. & Sales.

■ 8826 ■ Hannan Supply Co.
PO Box 270
Paducah, KY 42002-0270
Phone: (502)442-5456 **Fax:** (502)442-9050
E-mail: info@hannansupply.com
Products: Electrical and industrial supplies. **SICs:** 5063 (Electrical Apparatus & Equipment); 5085 (Industrial Supplies). **Est:** 1935. **Sales:** $18,000,000 (2000). **Emp:** 61. **Officers:** James E. Nutty, President; Joseph Semeraro, Controller; Joe Semeraro, CFO; Bruce Brockenbrough, Operations Mgr.; Rich Eggemeyer, Sales Mgr.

■ 8827 ■ Hansen Electrical Supply
PO Box 604
Framingham, MA 01704-0604
Phone: (508)872-4353 **Fax:** (508)875-6544
Products: Lighting equipment; Electrical supplies; Lighting showrooms. **SIC:** 5063 (Electrical Apparatus & Equipment). **Est:** 1959. **Sales:** $6,000,000 (2000). **Emp:** 20. **Officers:** Wayne Hansen, CEO; Jeff Hansen, President.

■ 8828 ■ Hansful Trading Company Inc.
1 W 28th St.
New York, NY 10001
Phone: (212)696-1833 **Fax:** (212)213-9384
Products: Fashion watches; Musical alarm clockc; Calculators; General merchandise; Novelties. **SICs:** 5064 (Electrical Appliances—Television & Radio); 5094 (Jewelry & Precious Stones).

■ 8829 ■ Harco Electronics Inc.
PO Box 1136
Aberdeen, MD 21001
Phone: (410)575-6885 **Fax:** (410)734-7288
Products: Electronic parts for industrial use. **SIC:** 5065 (Electronic Parts & Equipment Nec). **Est:** 1959. **Sales:** $7,000,000 (2000). **Emp:** 24. **Officers:** Edward Schueler, President; Drew Devan, Vice President; Chuck Burgess, Dir. of Sales.

■ 8830 ■ Harris Electric Inc.
4020 23rd Ave. W
Seattle, WA 98199
Phone: (206)282-8080
Products: Electrical supplies, including panel boards, resistors, capacitors, and wire; Electronics. **SIC:** 5063 (Electrical Apparatus & Equipment). **Est:** 1928. **Sales:** $13,000,000 (2000). **Emp:** 85. **Officers:** R.A. Sundholm, President; Larry E. McDonald, CFO.

■ 8831 ■ Harris Semiconductor
3031 Tisch Way Ste. 800
San Jose, CA 95128
Phone: (408)985-7322 **Fax:** (408)985-7455
Products: discrete and intelligent-power semiconductors; Analog, digital and mixed-signal integrated (Western regional office). **SIC:** 5065 (Electronic Parts & Equipment Nec).

■ 8832 ■ Hartman-Spreng Co.
26 W 6th St.
Mansfield, OH 44901
Phone: (419)524-7211 **Fax:** (419)522-5659
Products: Electrical supplies, including wiring and light fixtures. **SIC:** 5063 (Electrical Apparatus & Equipment). **Est:** 1908. **Sales:** $10,000,000 (2000). **Emp:** 42. **Officers:** Tim Galliger, President.

■ 8833 ■ Hartmann of Florida
1774 Executive Rd.
Winter Haven, FL 33884
Phone: (863)325-8222
Free: (800)370-8222 **Fax:** (863)324-7933
Products: Ceiling fan pulls; Lamp finials; Vertical blind pulls; Key chains; Decorative plates. **SICs:** 5063 (Electrical Apparatus & Equipment); 5023 (Homefurnishings). **Est:** 1991. **Sales:** $500,000 (1999). **Emp:** 10. **Officers:** Glenn H. Ensminger; Mary K. Ensminger; Marenda Bragg, Customer Service Contact.

■ 8834 ■ Hawk Electronics Inc.
PO Box 1027F
Wheeling, IL 60090
Phone: (847)459-4030
Free: (800)843-4295 **Fax:** (847)459-4091
E-mail: sales@hawkusa.com
URL: http://www.hawksusa.com
Products: Electronic components. **SICs:** 5063 (Electrical Apparatus & Equipment); 5065 (Electronic Parts & Equipment Nec). **Est:** 1978. **Sales:** $19,000,000 (2000). **Emp:** 60. **Officers:** Charles D. Poncher, President.

■ 8835 ■ Hayes & Lunsford Motor Repair
226 Hilliard Ave.
Asheville, NC 28801
Phone: (828)252-4785
Products: Electric motors. **SIC:** 5063 (Electrical Apparatus & Equipment).

■ 8836 ■ HB Distributors
8741 Shirley Ave.
Northridge, CA 91324
Phone: (818)701-5100
Free: (800)266-3478 **Fax:** (818)700-1808
Products: Telephone systems and telecommunications equipment. **SIC:** 5065 (Electronic Parts & Equipment Nec). **Sales:** $4,000,000 (1999). **Emp:** 12. **Officers:** Pam Branner, President.

■ 8837 ■ Helsel-Jepperson Electric Inc.
197th & Halsted Sts.
Chicago Heights, IL 60411
Phone: (708)756-5600 **Fax:** (708)756-5673
Products: Electrical supplies, including transformers, capacitors, resistors, and wire. **SIC:** 5063 (Electrical Apparatus & Equipment). **Est:** 1946. **Sales:**

$7,500,000 (2000). **Emp:** 50. **Officers:** Delores Helsel, President.

■ 8838 ■ **Henry Radio Inc.**
2050 S Bundy Dr.
Los Angeles, CA 90025
Phone: (310)820-1234 **Free:** (800)877-7979
Products: Reamplifiers, generators. **SIC:** 5065 (Electronic Parts & Equipment Nec). **Sales:** $3,800,000 (1999). **Emp:** 15. **Officers:** James T. Henry, President; Meredith Henry, Treasurer.

■ 8839 ■ **Heyboer Transformers Inc.**
17382 Hayes St.
Grand Haven, MI 49417
Phone: (616)842-5830
Products: Electric coil; Transformers. **SIC:** 5063 (Electrical Apparatus & Equipment).

■ 8840 ■ **Hi-Line Electric Co.**
2121 Valley View Ln.
Dallas, TX 75234
Phone: (972)247-6200
Free: (800)944-5463 **Fax:** (972)247-5307
E-mail: hi-line@hi-line.com
URL: http://www.hi-line.com
Products: Electrical products; Electronic wire and cable. **SICs:** 5072 (Hardware); 5063 (Electrical Apparatus & Equipment). **Est:** 1959. **Sales:** $20,000,000 (2000). **Emp:** 166. **Officers:** Mike Sheaffer, President.

■ 8841 ■ **Hicks Equipment**
4444 W Bristol Rd.
Flint, MI 48507
Phone: (810)733-6191
Products: Electric transmissions. **SIC:** 5063 (Electrical Apparatus & Equipment).

■ 8842 ■ **K.C. Hilites**
Avenida De Luces
Williams, AZ 86046
Phone: (520)635-2607
Free: (800)528-0950 **Fax:** (520)635-2486
URL: http://www.kchilites.com
Products: Auxiliary lighting, including fog lights. **SIC:** 5063 (Electrical Apparatus & Equipment). **Est:** 1970. **Sales:** $5,000,000 (1999). **Emp:** 30. **Officers:** Peter K. Brown; Michael DeHaas, Sales/Marketing Contact.

■ 8843 ■ **Hisco**
488 Regal Row, Ste. 102
Brownsville, TX 78521
Phone: (956)542-0843 **Fax:** (956)548-1621
Products: Electrical products; Industrial products. **SICs:** 5063 (Electrical Apparatus & Equipment); 5084 (Industrial Machinery & Equipment).

■ 8844 ■ **Hisco**
10863 Rockwall Rd.
Dallas, TX 75238-1213
Phone: (214)343-8730
Free: (800)888-4472 **Fax:** (214)343-2044
URL: http://www.hiscoinc.com
Products: Electrical products; Industrial products; Packaging products, including adhesives and tapes; Silicones; Tools; Chemicals; Aerosol products. **SICs:** 5063 (Electrical Apparatus & Equipment); 5084 (Industrial Machinery & Equipment); 5169 (Chemicals & Allied Products Nec); 5072 (Hardware). **Est:** 1970. **Sales:** $110,000,000 (2000). **Emp:** 200. **Officers:** Paul M. Merriman, President; Merle O. Tanner, VP & General Mgr., e-mail: merletanner@hiscoinc.com.

■ 8845 ■ **Hisco**
6650 Concord Pk. Dr.
Houston, TX 77040
Phone: (713)934-1700
Free: (800)999-0984 **Fax:** (713)934-1645
URL: http://www.hiscoinc.com
Products: Electronic products; Industrial products; Packaging products. **SICs:** 5063 (Electrical Apparatus & Equipment); 5084 (Industrial Machinery & Equipment). **Est:** 1970. **Sales:** $122,000,000 (1999). **Emp:** 240. **Officers:** Bill Baird, President; Bob Dill, Exec. VP.

■ 8846 ■ **Hitachi America Ltd.**
200 Sierra Point Pkwy.
Brisbane, CA 94005
Phone: (650)244-7900
Free: (800)448-2244 **Fax:** (650)244-7920
Products: Electronic parts and equipment, computers, automobile parts and supplies. **SICs:** 5065 (Electronic Parts & Equipment Nec); 5045 (Computers, Peripherals & Software); 5013 (Motor Vehicle Supplies & New Parts). **Sales:** $3,500,000,000 (2000). **Emp:** 6,000. **Officers:** Tomoharu Shimayama, President; Katsumi Sakurai, VP of Finance.

■ 8847 ■ **Hitachi America Ltd. Electron Tube Div.**
3850 Holcomb Bridge Rd., Ste. 300
Norcross, GA 30092
Phone: (404)409-3000 **Fax:** (404)409-3028
Products: Electronic equipment, including tubes and flat panel displays. **SIC:** 5065 (Electronic Parts & Equipment Nec). **Sales:** $96,000,000 (2000). **Emp:** 42. **Officers:** James Aden, President.

■ 8848 ■ **Hitachi Inverter**
608 Mossycup Oak Dr.
Plano, TX 75025
Phone: (972)527-5313
Products: Electric motors. **SIC:** 5063 (Electrical Apparatus & Equipment).

■ 8849 ■ **Hite Co.**
1245 Benner Pike
State College, PA 16801-7324
Phone: (814)237-7649 **Fax:** (814)237-7935
Products: Electrical equipment and supplies. **SIC:** 5063 (Electrical Apparatus & Equipment). **Emp:** 499.

■ 8850 ■ **Hite Co.**
PO Box 1754
Altoona, PA 16603-1754
Phone: (814)944-6121
Free: (800)252-3598 **Fax:** (814)944-3052
URL: http://www.hiteco.com
Products: Electrical supplies; Lighting; Professional video and electronic equipment; Data com products; Automation products. **SICs:** 5063 (Electrical Apparatus & Equipment); 5065 (Electronic Parts & Equipment Nec); 5064 (Electrical Appliances—Television & Radio). **Est:** 1949. **Sales:** $61,000,000 (1999). **Emp:** 236. **Officers:** R. Lee Hite, CEO & President; Scott Cessna, Treasurer; John Hatch, Sr. VP of Marketing; Ronald Eberhart, VP of Operations; Angelo Perri, VP of Sales, e-mail: angeperri@hiteco.com; Denise Kelly, VP of Admin., e-mail: denkel@hiteco.com.

■ 8851 ■ **Hobgood Electric & Machinery Company, Inc.**
PO Box 3073
Columbia, SC 29203
Phone: (803)754-8700
Free: (800)922-1850 **Fax:** (803)786-2047
Products: Electric and electronic equipment. **SIC:** 5065 (Electronic Parts & Equipment Nec). **Est:** 1969. **Sales:** $4,000,000 (2000). **Emp:** 49. **Officers:** Herbert G. Hobgood, VP & General Mgr.; Lewis M. Hobgood, President; Perry Hobgood, Vice President; Pat Hobgood, Treasurer & Secty.

■ 8852 ■ **Holmes Distributors Inc.**
293 Target Industrial Cir.
Bangor, ME 04401
Phone: (207)942-7357 **Fax:** (207)941-2334
URL: http://www.holmesdist.com
Products: Electrical equipment and supplies. **SIC:** 5063 (Electrical Apparatus & Equipment). **Emp:** 18. **Officers:** Lyn Bragdon, Branch Mgr., e-mail: lynb@holmesdist.com.

■ 8853 ■ **Holt Electric Inc.**
1515 Walnut Ridge Dr.
Hartland, WI 53029
Phone: (262)369-7100 **Fax:** (262)369-7135
URL: http://www.holtelectric.com
Products: Electrical equipment and supplies. **SIC:** 5063 (Electrical Apparatus & Equipment). **Est:** 1892. **Sales:** $48,000,000 (2000). **Emp:** 100. **Officers:** William P. Cuff, President.

■ 8854 ■ **Holt Electric Motor Co.**
5225 W State St.
Milwaukee, WI 53208
Phone: (414)771-6600
Products: Electric motors and parts. **SIC:** 5063 (Electrical Apparatus & Equipment). **Est:** 1892. **Sales:** $35,000,000 (2000). **Emp:** 70. **Officers:** William P. Cuff, President.

■ 8855 ■ **Holzmueller Corp.**
1000 25th St.
San Francisco, CA 94107
Phone: (415)826-8383
Products: Stage lighting supplies and equipment. **SIC:** 5063 (Electrical Apparatus & Equipment). **Est:** 1902. **Sales:** $9,000,000 (2000). **Emp:** 30. **Officers:** Richard P. Gentschel, President; Nancy McLeod, CFO.

■ 8856 ■ **Honeywell Sensing and Control**
11 W Spring
Freeport, IL 61032-4353
Phone: (815)235-6847
Free: (800)537-6945 **Fax:** (815)235-6545
E-mail: info.sc@honeywell.com
URL: http://www.honeywell.com/sensing
Products: Switches, sensors, controls, fiber optics, and safety sensors. **SIC:** 5063 (Electrical Apparatus & Equipment). **Former Name:** Micro Switch/Honeywell.

■ 8857 ■ **Hooper Electronics Supply**
1917 6th St.
PO Box 1787
Meridian, MS 39301
Phones: (228)432-0584 (601)693-2668
Fax: (228)432-7651
Products: Electronic repair parts. **SIC:** 5065 (Electronic Parts & Equipment Nec).

■ 8858 ■ **House Of Batteries**
16512 Burke Ln.
Huntington Beach, CA 92647
Phone: (714)375-0222 **Fax:** (714)375-0235
Products: Electronic batteries; Value-added assembler. **SIC:** 5063 (Electrical Apparatus & Equipment). **Officers:** Maggie West, CEO.

■ 8859 ■ **Houston Wholesale Electronics Inc.**
5205 Telephone Rd.
Houston, TX 77087
Fax: (713)845-1412
E-mail: sales@houstoncommunications.com
URL: http://www.houstoncommunications.com
Products: Electronics, including 2-way radios, communications, cellular phones, CCTV, and sound equipment. **SICs:** 5065 (Electronic Parts & Equipment Nec); 5065 (Electronic Parts & Equipment Nec). **Est:** 1992. **Sales:** $3,000,000 (2000). **Emp:** 13. **Officers:** Duane J. Johnson, President; Duane J. Johnson, CFO.

■ 8860 ■ **Houston Wire and Cable Co.**
10201 N Loop E
Houston, TX 77028
Phone: (281)609-2200 **Fax:** (281)609-2205
Products: Wire; Cable. **SIC:** 5063 (Electrical Apparatus & Equipment). **Est:** 1975. **Sales:** $160,000,000 (2000). **Emp:** 287. **Officers:** Edward W. Holland III, President; Nic Graham, VP of Finance; Eric Blakenship, Exec. VP of Marketing & Sales.

■ 8861 ■ **Howard Electric Co.**
4801 Bellevue Ave.
Detroit, MI 48207-1394
Phone: (313)923-0430
Free: (800)248-1885 **Fax:** (313)923-0439
Products: Electric motors and controls; Pumps. **SIC:** 5063 (Electrical Apparatus & Equipment). **Est:** 1928. **Sales:** $600,000 (2000). **Emp:** 5. **Officers:** Eugene C. Howard, President & Treasurer.

■ 8862 ■ **Howland Electric Wholesale Co.**
PO Box 4338
El Monte, CA 91734
Phone: (818)444-0503 **Fax:** (818)401-9076
Products: Electrical equipment and supplies. **SIC:** 5063 (Electrical Apparatus & Equipment). **Est:** 1952. **Sales:** $6,000,000 (2000). **Emp:** 25. **Officers:** Kenneth D. Weed, President.

■ 8863 ■ **Hub Material Co.**
PO Box 526
Canton, MA 02021
Phone: (781)821-1870
Free: (800)482-4440 **Fax:** (781)821-4133
Products: Techical supplies to companies involved with the design, assembly, test and repair of electronic equipment and sub-assemblies. **SICs:** 5063 (Electrical Apparatus & Equipment); 5065 (Electronic Parts & Equipment Nec). **Sales:** $6,000,000 (1999). **Emp:** 20. **Officers:** Stanley Goldberg, President.

■ 8864 ■ **Hughes-Peters Inc.**
5030 Oaklawn Dr.
Cincinnati, OH 45227-1484
Phone: (513)351-2000
Free: (800)899-8228 **Fax:** (513)351-2365
E-mail: msmith@hughespeters.com
URL: http://www.hughes-peters.com
Products: Electronic components; Wire and cable; Test equipment. **SIC:** 5065 (Electronic Parts & Equipment Nec). **Est:** 1923. **Sales:** $15,000,000 (2000). **Emp:** 46. **Officers:** L. Richard Schieman, CEO; Jay Minser, Treasurer & Secty.; Angie Johnson, Operations Mgr.; Mike Okel, President.

■ 8865 ■ **Hunt Electric Supply Co.**
1600 Paramount Dr.
Waukesha, WI 53186
Phone: (262)513-0800
Free: (800)241-9090 **Fax:** (262)513-0808
URL: http://www.huntelectric.net
Products: Electrical equipment. **SIC:** 5063 (Electrical Apparatus & Equipment). **Est:** 1945. **Sales:** $2,000,000 (2000). **Emp:** 12. **Officers:** Keith Fisher, President. **Former Name:** Hunt Company Inc.

■ 8866 ■ **Hunzicker Brothers Inc.**
PO Box 25248
Oklahoma City, OK 73125
Phone: (405)239-7771
URL: http://www.hunzicker.com
Products: Electrical equipment. **SIC:** 5063 (Electrical Apparatus & Equipment). **Est:** 1920. **Sales:** $42,000,000 (2000). **Emp:** 140. **Officers:** Myers W. Lockard III, President; Jack Henderson, VP of Finance; J. Young, VP of Sales.

■ 8867 ■ **Hutch & Son Inc.**
300 N Main St.
Evansville, IN 47711-5416
Phone: (812)425-7201
Free: (800)457-3520 **Fax:** (812)421-4620
E-mail: sales@hutch-and-son.com
URL: http://www.hutch-and-son.com
Products: Electric and electronic equipment; Electronic parts. **SIC:** 5065 (Electronic Parts & Equipment Nec). **Est:** 1953. **Emp:** 10. **Officers:** John Taylor, President.

■ 8868 ■ **HWC Distribution Corp.**
10201 N Loop E
Houston, TX 77028
Phone: (713)609-2100
Products: Electrical wire and cables. **SIC:** 5063 (Electrical Apparatus & Equipment). **Sales:** $180,000,000 (2000). **Emp:** 260. **Officers:** Edward W. Holland, President; Jim Tessemer, Controller.

■ 8869 ■ **Ico Rally Corp.**
PO Box 51350
Palo Alto, CA 94303
Phone: (650)856-9900 **Fax:** (650)856-8378
Products: Electronic parts. **SIC:** 5065 (Electronic Parts & Equipment Nec). **Sales:** $3,100,000 (1993). **Emp:** 40. **Officers:** Robert C. Hamilton, President.

■ 8870 ■ **Idec**
1175 Elko Dr.
Sunnyvale, CA 94089
Phone: (408)747-0550 **Fax:** (408)744-9055
Products: Electronic components. **SIC:** 5065 (Electronic Parts & Equipment Nec).

■ 8871 ■ **iGo**
9393 Gateway Dr.
Reno, NV 89511-8910
Phone: (775)746-6140
Free: (800)228-8374 **Fax:** (775)746-6155
E-mail: sales@igo.com
URL: http://www.igo.com
Products: Mobile computing and communications products. **SIC:** 5063 (Electrical Apparatus & Equipment). **Est:** 1993. **Sales:** $23,400,000 (1999). **Emp:** 260. **Officers:** Ken Hawk, CEO; Mick Delargy, CFO; Tom de Jong, VP of Sales; Rod Hasilyk, VP of Operations. **Former Name:** 1-800-Batteries.

■ 8872 ■ **Inca Corp.**
1648 W 134th St.
Gardena, CA 90249
Phone: (310)808-0001 **Fax:** (310)808-9092
E-mail: inca1@msn.com
Products: Robotic devices for video and home entertainment industries. **SICs:** 5063 (Electrical Apparatus & Equipment); 5065 (Electronic Parts & Equipment Nec). **Est:** 1971. **Emp:** 30. **Officers:** George C. Roberts, President; Adriana Roberts, Vice President.

■ 8873 ■ **Ind-Co Cable TV Inc.**
PO Box 3799
Batesville, AR 72503-3799
Phone: (870)793-4174 **Fax:** (870)793-7439
Products: Electronic systems and equipment; Electronic parts. **SIC:** 5065 (Electronic Parts & Equipment Nec). **Officers:** J. Pierce, President.

■ 8874 ■ **Indus-Tool**
300 N Elizabeth St., 2N
Chicago, IL 60607
Phone: (312)226-2473
Free: (800)662-5021 **Fax:** (312)226-2480
E-mail: sales@indus-tool.com
URL: http://www.indus-tool.com
Products: Electric footwarmer mats; Battery backups and UPSs; Dock loading lights and vehicle warning lights; Backup alarms. **SICs:** 5063 (Electrical Apparatus & Equipment); 5065 (Electronic Parts & Equipment Nec). **Emp:** 20. **Officers:** Ronald I. Schwarcz, President; Mona G. Zemsky, Marketing Mgr., e-mail: mona@indust-tool.com; Maria Ramirez, Customer Service Cotact, e-mail: mramirez@indus-tool.com; Alison James, Human Resources Contact, e-mail: alison@indus-tool.com.

■ 8875 ■ **Indusco, Ltd.**
210 Midstream
Brick, NJ 08724
Phone: (732)899-2660 **Fax:** (732)899-8114
E-mail: induscol@bellatlantic.net
URL: http://www.indusco.com
Products: Locomotive parts; Motors; Gears; Mounted bearings; Off-highway truck parts; Circuit breakers. **SICs:** 5063 (Electrical Apparatus & Equipment); 5088 (Transportation Equipment & Supplies); 5084 (Industrial Machinery & Equipment); 5049 (Professional Equipment Nec). **Est:** 1984. **Sales:** $1,500,000 (2000). **Emp:** 5. **Officers:** Angelo C. Zappulla, Sales Manager.

■ 8876 ■ **Industrial Battery Engineering Inc.**
9121 De Garmo Ave.
Sun Valley, CA 91352
Phone: (818)767-7067 **Fax:** (818)767-7173
Products: Batteries and automatic control chargers for forklifts. **SIC:** 5063 (Electrical Apparatus & Equipment). **Emp:** 36. **Officers:** Birger Holmquist, President; Boyd Bailey, Treasurer.

■ 8877 ■ **Industrial Electrics Inc.**
1018 Arnold St.
Greensboro, NC 27405-7102
Phone: (919)275-9111 **Fax:** (919)370-0934
Products: Electrical parts. **SIC:** 5063 (Electrical Apparatus & Equipment). **Sales:** $1,000,000 (2000). **Emp:** 40. **Officers:** Robert Johannesen.

■ 8878 ■ **Industrial Electronic Supply Inc.**
2321 Texas Ave.
Shreveport, LA 71103
Phone: (318)222-9459 **Fax:** (318)227-3535
E-mail: iescorp@att.net
URL: http://www.goies.com
Products: Electronic and electrical/automation controls. **SICs:** 5063 (Electrical Apparatus & Equipment); 5065 (Electronic Parts & Equipment Nec). **Est:** 1963. **Emp:** 60. **Officers:** David Doyal, President.

■ 8879 ■ **George Ingraham Corp.**
4605 Stonegate Industrial Bldg.
Stone Mountain, GA 30083-1908
Phone: (404)296-0804
Free: (800)631-6283 **Fax:** (404)296-0952
Products: Electric and electronic equipment; Control and signal wire and cable; Cable conduit. **SIC:** 5063 (Electrical Apparatus & Equipment). **Emp:** 49. **Officers:** Betty Estes.

■ 8880 ■ **Inlite Corp.**
939 Grayson St.
Berkeley, CA 94710
Phone: (510)849-1067 **Fax:** (510)849-3230
Products: Track lighting. **SIC:** 5063 (Electrical Apparatus & Equipment). **Officers:** W Kent Runswick, President.

■ 8881 ■ **INOTEK Technologies Corp.**
11212 Indian Tr.
Dallas, TX 75229
Phone: (972)243-7000
Free: (800)492-6767 **Fax:** (972)243-2924
E-mail: info@inotek.com
URL: http://www.inotek.com
Products: Processing control equipment. **SIC:** 5065 (Electronic Parts & Equipment Nec). **Sales:** $24,800,000 (2000). **Emp:** 78. **Officers:** Neal E. Young, Chairman of the Board; Dennis W. Stone, CEO.

■ 8882 ■ **Inovonics Co**
2100 Central Ave.
Boulder, CO 80301
Phone: (303)939-9336 **Fax:** (303)939-8977
Products: Designs and wireless products; security and cordless headsets. **SIC:** 5065 (Electronic Parts & Equipment Nec).

■ 8883 ■ **Insight Electronics Inc.**
9980 Huennekens St.
San Diego, CA 92121
Phone: (619)677-3100
Products: Semiconductors and related devices. **SIC:** 5065 (Electronic Parts & Equipment Nec). **Est:** 1985. **Sales:** $29,000,000 (2000). **Emp:** 82. **Officers:** Mike Rohleder, President; Norma Samaniego, CFO.

■ 8884 ■ **Insulectro Corp.**
20362 Windrow Dr.
Lake Forest, CA 92630-8138
Phone: (949)587-3200
Products: Electronic parts for circuit boards. **SIC:** 5063 (Electrical Apparatus & Equipment). **Sales:** $61,000,000 (2000). **Emp:** 200. **Officers:** Don Redfern, President.

■ 8885 ■ **Intech EDM Electrotools**
2001 W 16th St.
Broadview, IL 60153
Phone: (708)681-6110
Products: Insulated wire. **SIC:** 5063 (Electrical Apparatus & Equipment). **Sales:** $5,000,000 (1993). **Emp:** 50. **Officers:** Mike Barry, Director.

■ 8886 ■ **Integral Marketing Inc.**
5000 Philadelphia Way, Ste. A
Lanham, MD 20706-4417
Phone: (301)731-4233
Products: Electronic equipment and supplies. **SIC:** 5065 (Electronic Parts & Equipment Nec). **Emp:** 3. **Officers:** Allen Schwitzer, President.

■ 8887 ■ **Intel Corp.**
5200 NE Elam Young Pkwy
Hillsboro, OR 97124
Phone: (503)696-8080
Products: Semiconductor devices, microcomputer

chips and related solid state devices. **SIC:** 5065 (Electronic Parts & Equipment Nec).

■ **8888** ■ **Intelligence Technology Corp.**
PO Box 671125
Dallas, TX 75367
Phone: (214)250-4277
Products: Modems. **SIC:** 5065 (Electronic Parts & Equipment Nec). **Est:** 1983. **Sales:** $10,000,000 (2000). **Emp:** 40. **Officers:** Walker Morris, President; Charles Ekurzel, CFO; Gary Bechtol, Dir. of Marketing & Sales.

■ **8889** ■ **Inter-Tel Integrated Systs Inc.**
7300 W Boston St.
Chandler, AZ 85226
Phone: (480)961-9000   **Fax:** (480)961-1370
Products: Research and development for integrated systems; Produces business telephone systems voice processing software, application software and services for small to medium size telephone communication systems. **SIC:** 5065 (Electronic Parts & Equipment Nec).

■ **8890** ■ **Inter-Tel Technologies Inc.**
4909 E McDowell Rd Ste 106
Phoenix, AZ 85008
Phone: (602)231-5151   **Fax:** (602)231-5172
Products: Provides solutions in telephone systems, voice processing software, video conferencing, long distance, leasing services, network products and applications software. **SIC:** 5065 (Electronic Parts & Equipment Nec). **Officers:** Craig Rauchle, President.

■ **8891** ■ **Intermetra Corp.**
10100 NW 116th Way, Ste. 14
Miami, FL 33178
Phone: (305)889-1194   **Fax:** (305)888-1190
Products: Electrical equipment. **SICs:** 5065 (Electronic Parts & Equipment Nec); 5065 (Electronic Parts & Equipment Nec); 5049 (Professional Equipment Nec); 5047 (Medical & Hospital Equipment). **Sales:** $12,000,000 (1993). **Emp:** 9. **Officers:** Ira Hartzman, President.

■ **8892** ■ **Internal Sound Communications**
10500 Chicago Dr., No. 80
Zeeland, MI 49464-9185
Phone: (616)772-4875
Products: Electronic parts and equipment, including telephones, business telephones, and voice mail systems. **SIC:** 5065 (Electronic Parts & Equipment Nec). **Officers:** Philip Walters, President.

■ **8893** ■ **International Components Corp.**
420 N May St.
Chicago, IL 60622-5888
Phone: (312)829-7101   **Fax:** (312)829-0422
Products: Battery and portable equipment chargers and systems. **SIC:** 5063 (Electrical Apparatus & Equipment). **Est:** 1967. **Sales:** $134,000,000 (2000). **Emp:** 700. **Officers:** Jim Gaza, President; Stuart B. kes, VP of Marketing.

■ **8894** ■ **International Importers Inc.**
1 S Millard Ave.
ago, IL 60632
ne: (773)581-5511   **Fax:** (773)581-5022
ucts: Electronic parts. **SIC:** 5065 (Electronic Parts uipment Nec). **Sales:** $12,000,000 (2000). **Emp:**
 fficers: Steve Davidson, President.

5 ■ **International Television Corp.**
DeSoto Ave.
worth, CA 91311
: (213)467-7148
cts: Electronic parts and accessories for
ons. **SIC:** 5065 (Electronic Parts & Equipment

■ **Interstate Battery System of Dallas**
Merit Dr., No. 400
TX 75251
(972)991-1444   **Fax:** (972)455-6560
p://www.interstatebatteries.com
: Batteries. **SIC:** 5063 (Electrical Apparatus & nt). **Est:** 1952. **Emp:** 350. **Officers:** R.T.

Miller, CEO & President; Carlos Sepulveda, Exec. VP & CFO.

■ **8897** ■ **Interstate Electric Supply**
1330 Courtland
Roanoke, VA 24012
Phone: (540)982-2500   **Fax:** (540)982-2567
Products: Lighting fixtures, including lamps, panels, and switches. **SIC:** 5063 (Electrical Apparatus & Equipment). **Emp:** 5.

■ **8898** ■ **Intrade, Inc.**
PO Box 10997
Southport, NC 28461-0997
Phone: (910)457-1935
Free: (800)243-5252   **Fax:** (910)456-6199
E-mail: Intrade@bcinet.net
Products: Tweezers; Precision equipment. **SIC:** 5065 (Electronic Parts & Equipment Nec). **Est:** 1963. **Officers:** Donald M. Cooley, Export Mgr.

■ **8899** ■ **IPC Information Systems Inc.**
350 Sansome St Ste. 640
San Francisco, CA 94104
Phone: (415)788-6500   **Fax:** (415)788-6499
Products: Telephone turret systems for stock brokers; Installs and services telephone systems. **SIC:** 5065 (Electronic Parts & Equipment Nec).

■ **8900** ■ **Stuart C. Irby Co.**
3418 Washington
Vicksburg, MS 39180-5060
Phone: (601)638-3262   **Fax:** (601)638-5137
Products: Electrical supplies. **SIC:** 5063 (Electrical Apparatus & Equipment). **Emp:** 49.

■ **8901** ■ **ITC Electronics**
2772 W Olympic Blvd.
Los Angeles, CA 90006-2631
Phone: (310)370-6211   **Fax:** (310)543-1222
Products: Electronics. **SIC:** 5065 (Electronic Parts & Equipment Nec). **Emp:** 49.

■ **8902** ■ **ITC International**
96 N 3rd St., Ste. 680
San Jose, CA 95112
Phone: (408)292-7000   **Fax:** (408)292-7050
Products: Electronic components; Consumer products. **SIC:** 5065 (Electronic Parts & Equipment Nec). **Est:** 1984. **Sales:** $5,000,000 (2000). **Emp:** 10. **Officers:** Marc S. Nehamkin, President.

■ **8903** ■ **Jaco Electronics Inc.**
145 Oser Ave.
Hauppauge, NY 11788
Phone: (516)273-5500
Free: (800)989-5226   **Fax:** (516)273-5640
E-mail: www.jacoelectronics.com
Products: Semiconductors, capacitors, and resistors. **SIC:** 5065 (Electronic Parts & Equipment Nec). **Est:** 1961. **Sales:** $155,100,000 (1999). **Emp:** 406. **Officers:** Joel H. Girsky, President, Chairman of the Board & Treasurer; Jeffrey D. Gash, VP of Finance.

■ **8904** ■ **Jademar Corp.**
10125 NW 116th Way, Ste. 10
Miami, FL 33178-1164
Phone: (305)488-5550
Products: Lamps and lamp fixtures. **SIC:** 5063 (Electrical Apparatus & Equipment). **Est:** 1950. **Sales:** $15,000,000 (2000). **Emp:** 17. **Officers:** Joseph Demartino Jr., President & Treasurer.

■ **8905** ■ **Jameco Electronics Inc.**
1355 Shoreway Rd.
Belmont, CA 94002
Phone: (650)592-8097
Free: (800)831-4242   **Fax:** (650)592-2503
Products: Markets integrated circuits, components and computer peripherals; Computer peripherals and test equipment. **SICs:** 5065 (Electronic Parts & Equipment Nec); 5045 (Computers, Peripherals & Software). **Sales:** $87,000,000 (2000). **Emp:** 115. **Officers:** Dennis Farrey, President; Steve Craig, CFO.

■ **8906** ■ **Jampro Antennas, Inc.**
6340 Sky Creek Rd.
Sacramento, CA 95828
Phone: (916)383-1177   **Fax:** (916)383-1182
Products: Broadcast, studio, and related electronic equipment. **SIC:** 5065 (Electronic Parts & Equipment Nec). **Officers:** James E. Olver, President; Alex Perchevitch, Vice President.

■ **8907** ■ **Janesway Electronic Corp.**
404 N Terrace Ave.
Mt. Vernon, NY 10552
Phone: (914)699-6710
Free: (800)431-1348   **Fax:** (914)699-6969
E-mail: sales@janesway.com
URL: http://www.janesway.com
Products: Semiconductor devices. **SIC:** 5065 (Electronic Parts & Equipment Nec). **Est:** 1980. **Sales:** $10,000,000 (2000). **Emp:** 14. **Officers:** Michael Cola, President.

■ **8908** ■ **Javatec Inc.**
State Rt. 684
Speedwell, VA 24374
Phone: (540)621-4572
Products: Electric transmission. **SIC:** 5063 (Electrical Apparatus & Equipment).

■ **8909** ■ **Jay Instrument and Specialty Co.**
555 N Wayne Ave.
Cincinnati, OH 45215
Phone: (513)733-5200   **Fax:** (513)733-5207
Products: Fluidic circuits, vapor heating controls, digital gauges, pneumatic relays, and chromatographs. **SIC:** 5084 (Industrial Machinery & Equipment). **Sales:** $14,000,000 (1994). **Emp:** 130. **Officers:** Dan Benton, CEO; Bill Wulf, Controller.

■ **8910** ■ **J.C. Supply**
10030 Talley Lane
Houston, TX 77041
Phone: (281)448-8682   **Fax:** (713)460-1141
Products: Electronic components. **SIC:** 5065 (Electronic Parts & Equipment Nec).

■ **8911** ■ **W.S. Jenks & Son**
1933 Montana Ave., NE
Washington, DC 20002
Phone: (202)529-6020   **Fax:** (202)832-3411
Products: Electronics; Woodworking tools. **SICs:** 5063 (Electrical Apparatus & Equipment); 5072 (Hardware). **Emp:** 99.

■ **8912** ■ **Jensen Tools Inc.**
7815 S 46th St.
Phoenix, AZ 85044
Phone: (602)453-3169
Free: (800)426-1194   **Fax:** (602)438-1690
E-mail: jensen@stanleyworks.com
URL: http://www.jensentools.com
Products: Tools and testing equipment for electronics and computers. **SIC:** 5065 (Electronic Parts & Equipment Nec). **Est:** 1954. **Emp:** 150. **Officers:** Gary Treiber, President; Norm Slone, VP of Finance; Rick Cowlin, VP of Operations; Rick Cowlin, VP of Operations.

■ **8913** ■ **J.H. Service Company Inc.**
PO Box 65
Bellaire, OH 43906-0218
Phone: (740)983-2525   **Fax:** (740)983-2569
Products: Power wire and cable. **SIC:** 5063 (Electrical Apparatus & Equipment). **Est:** 1959. **Sales:** $14,000,000 (2000). **Emp:** 100. **Officers:** R.T. Keller, President.

■ **8914** ■ **JH Service Company Inc.**
PO Box 65
Elberfeld, IN 47613
Phone: (812)983-2525   **Fax:** (812)983-2569
Products: High voltage electrical products. **SIC:** 5063 (Electrical Apparatus & Equipment). **Sales:** $8,000,000 (2000). **Emp:** 60. **Officers:** Ron Witt, President.

■ 8915 ■ Johnson Electric NA Inc.
3 Kent Pl.
Asheville, NC 28804
Phone: (828)285-0575
Products: Electric motors. **SIC:** 5063 (Electrical Apparatus & Equipment).

■ 8916 ■ Johnson Electric Supply Co.
1841 Eastern Ave.
Cincinnati, OH 45202
Phone: (513)421-3700
Free: (800)447-6506   **Fax:** (513)421-2469
E-mail: info@johnson-electric.com
URL: http://www.johnson-electric.com
Products: Electrical supplies. **SIC:** 5063 (Electrical Apparatus & Equipment). **Est:** 1907. **Sales:** $15,000,000 (2000). **Emp:** 49. **Officers:** Douglas Johnson, President; Robert White, Treasurer & Secty.; Robert D. Johnson, VP of Marketing & Sales; E. W. Mohr, Exec. VP; R. D. Johnson, VP of Sales.

■ 8917 ■ Johnson RDO Communications Co.
660 Transfer Rd.
St. Paul, MN 55114-1402
Phone: (612)645-6471
Products: Wireless communication; Two-way radios. **SICs:** 5065 (Electronic Parts & Equipment Nec); 5064 (Electrical Appliances—Television & Radio). **Officers:** Douglas Cole, President.

■ 8918 ■ Johnson Supply Controls Center
24 W Memicken Ave.
Cincinnati, OH 45210
Phone: (513)651-4328
Products: Electric equipment and supplies, including motors, tools, and refrigerators. **SIC:** 5063 (Electrical Apparatus & Equipment).

■ 8919 ■ Jones & Lee Supply Co.
1501 Linden Ave.
Knoxville, TN 37917-7817
Phone: (423)524-5566   **Fax:** (423)522-3003
Products: Electrical equipment and supplies. **SIC:** 5063 (Electrical Apparatus & Equipment). **Est:** 1948. **Sales:** $12,000,000 (2000). **Emp:** 31. **Officers:** Freeman Lee, Vice President; John E. Lee, President; Floyd E. Yarnell, Secretary.

■ 8920 ■ Edward Joy Co.
903 Canal St.
Syracuse, NY 13217
Phone: (315)474-3360   **Fax:** (315)474-2416
Products: Electrical equipment and supplies; Electronic wire and cable. **SIC:** 5063 (Electrical Apparatus & Equipment). **Est:** 1875. **Sales:** $21,000,000 (2000). **Emp:** 30. **Officers:** L.P. Markert III, CEO; William Stull, CFO; John Cutrone, Dir. of Sales; Elaine Trudell, Dir. of Information Systems; Carol Thomas, Dir of Human Resources.

■ 8921 ■ B. Frank Joy Company Inc.
5355 Kilmer Pl.
Bladensburg, MD 20710
Phone: (301)779-9400
Products: Conduit; Pipes. **SIC:** 5063 (Electrical Apparatus & Equipment). **Est:** 1917. **Sales:** $27,000,000 (2000). **Emp:** 450. **Officers:** T. Kenneth Joy, President; Mike Hone, CFO; Rod Wetherell, Dir. of Marketing; R. Shockley, Dir. of Data Processing; P. Beard, Dir of Human Resources.

■ 8922 ■ JR Electronics and Assembly Inc.
2125 S 48th St.
Tempe, AZ 85282
Phone: (602)438-2400   **Fax:** (602)438-2860
Products: Cable assemblies; electronic components. **SIC:** 5065 (Electronic Parts & Equipment Nec). **Sales:** $1,000,000 (1999). **Emp:** 6. **Officers:** Richard Saylor, President.

■ 8923 ■ Just Drop, Inc.
1950 NW 93rd Ave.
Miami, FL 33172
Phone: (305)594-2969
Free: (800)628-8281   **Fax:** (954)926-0155
Products: Cable television installation products. **SIC:** 5065 (Electronic Parts & Equipment Nec). **Officers:** Claud York, Mgr.; Scot Damroze, Sales.

■ 8924 ■ JVC Professional Products Co.
41 Slater Dr.
Elmwood Park, NJ 07407
Phone: (201)794-3900   **Fax:** (201)523-2077
Products: Electronic equipment. **SIC:** 5065 (Electronic Parts & Equipment Nec). **Est:** 1927. **Sales:** $19,000,000 (2000). **Emp:** 80. **Officers:** Mike Yoshida, President.

■ 8925 ■ Kahant Electrical Supply Co.
Rte. 10
Dover, NJ 07801
Phone: (201)366-2966   **Fax:** (201)366-1874
Products: Electrical supplies. **SIC:** 5063 (Electrical Apparatus & Equipment). **Est:** 1947. **Sales:** $4,000,000 (2000). **Emp:** 15. **Officers:** James Crummy, CEO; Charles J. Smith, President.

■ 8926 ■ Kaman Industrial Technologies
840 W 24th St.
Ogden, UT 84401
Products: Electric motors. **SIC:** 5063 (Electrical Apparatus & Equipment).

■ 8927 ■ Kansas Communications Inc.
8206 Marshall Dr.
Lenexa, KS 66214
Phone: (913)752-9100   **Fax:** (913)888-6647
Products: Communications systems and equipment. **SIC:** 5065 (Electronic Parts & Equipment Nec). **Sales:** $19,000,000 (2000). **Emp:** 100.

■ 8928 ■ Kansas Electric Supply Company Inc.
721 E 12th St.
Hays, KS 67601
Phone: (785)625-2516   **Fax:** (785)625-2517
Products: Electric and electronic equipment. **SIC:** 5063 (Electrical Apparatus & Equipment). **Est:** 1937. **Emp:** 3. **Officers:** Charles E. Greene, President; Arthur M. Burgess, Vice President; Edna M. Greene, Secretary; Charles E. Greene, Sales Mgr.

■ 8929 ■ Kass Electronics Distributors Inc.
2502 W Township Line Rd.
Havertown, PA 19083-5212
Phone: (215)449-2300
Products: Electronic components; Fuses; IC Chips; Shrink tubing; Connectors. **SIC:** 5065 (Electronic Parts & Equipment Nec). **Est:** 1959. **Sales:** $3,000,000 (2000). **Emp:** 20. **Officers:** Leonard Trames, President; Douglas Colston, VP of Finance; Jeff Scantling, Sales Mgr.

■ 8930 ■ Katolight Corp.
3201 3rd Ave
Mankato, MN 56001
Phone: (507)625-7973
Free: (800)325-5450   **Fax:** (507)625-2968
E-mail: kl@katolight.com
URL: http://www.katolight.com
Products: Generators. **SIC:** 5063 (Electrical Apparatus & Equipment). **Est:** 1952. **Sales:** $40,000,000 (2000). **Emp:** 155. **Officers:** L.G. Jacobson, CEO & President; T.L. Richards, C; Tom Ferris, Sales/Marketing Contact, e-mail: tomf@katolight.com; Tim Miller, Customer Service Contact, e-mail: timm@katolight.com; David Cole, Human Resources Contact, e-mail: davec@katolight.com.

■ 8931 ■ Katy Industries Inc.
6300 S Syracuse Way, Ste. 300
Englewood, CO 80111-6723
Phone: (303)290-9300
Products: Electronic components; Hand tools. **SICs:** 5065 (Electronic Parts & Equipment Nec); 5072 (Hardware). **Sales:** $171,300,000 (2000). **Emp:** 1,109. **Officers:** John R. Prann Jr., CEO & President; Stephen P. Nicholson, CFO & Treasurer.

■ 8932 ■ KEA Electronics
46759 Fremont Blvd.
Fremont, CA 94538
Phone: (510)651-2600   **Fax:** (510)651-2691
Products: Electronic component parts; Value-added services include cable assembly, kitting, switch assembly and bar coding. **SIC:** 5065 (Electronic Parts & Equipment Nec).

■ 8933 ■ Keathley-Patterson Electric Co.
4217 E 43rd St.
North Little Rock, AR 72117
Phone: (501)945-7143   **Fax:** (501)945-0882
Products: Electrical supplies. **SIC:** 5063 (Electrical Apparatus & Equipment). **Est:** 1960.

■ 8934 ■ Kenclaire Electrical Agencies Inc.
714 Old Country Rd.
Westbury, NY 11590
Phone: (516)333-7373
Free: (800)343-6126   **Fax:** (516)333-7755
E-mail: kenclaire@worldnet.att.net
Products: Electrical lighting fixtures and components. **SIC:** 5063 (Electrical Apparatus & Equipment). **Est:** 1960. **Sales:** $12,000,000 (2000). **Emp:** 12. **Officers:** A. Stuchbury, President.

■ 8935 ■ Kendall Electric Inc.
131 Grand Trunk Ave.
Battle Creek, MI 49015-2285
Phone: (616)963-5585
Free: (800)632-5422   **Fax:** (616)963-5606
Products: Electrical and telecommunications equipment. **SIC:** 5063 (Electrical Apparatus & Equipment). **Sales:** $150,000,000 (2000). **Emp:** 550. **Officers:** Axel Johnson, President; Jim Treadwell, VP of Finance.

■ 8936 ■ Kenkingdon & Associates
12813 Westbranch Ct.
Houston, TX 77072
Phone: (281)495-3071   **Fax:** (281)495-0389
Products: Electronic systems and equipment. **SIC:** 5065 (Electronic Parts & Equipment Nec).

■ 8937 ■ Kennewick Industrial and Electrical Supply Inc.
113 E Columbia Dr.
Kennewick, WA 99336
Phone: (509)582-5156   **Fax:** (509)582-5156
Products: Electrical, plumbing and turf irrigation equipment. **SICs:** 5063 (Electrical Apparatus & Equipment); 5074 (Plumbing & Hydronic Heating Supplies); 5083 (Farm & Garden Machinery). **Sales:** $8,000,000 (2000). **Emp:** 43. **Officers:** Augustan Kittson, General Mgr.

■ 8938 ■ Kennewick Industry & Electric Supply
113 E Columbia Dr.
Kennewick, WA 99336-3799
Phone: (509)582-5156
Free: (800)544-5156   **Fax:** (509)582-5156
E-mail: kie@webmail.bmi.net
URL: http://www.kiesupply.com
Products: Electrical supplies; Plumbing; Turf irrigation equipment. **SICs:** 5064 (Electrical Appliances—Television & Radio); 5074 (Plumbing & Hydronic Heating Supplies). **Est:** 1955. **Sales:** $10,000,000 (2000). **Emp:** 49. **Officers:** Augustan D. Kittson, Chairman of the Board, e-mail: augustan@aol.com; Patricia Morley, Human Resources Contact, e-mail: ricpatchel@aol.com. **Alternate Name:** KIE Supply Corp.

■ 8939 ■ Kern Special Tools Company Inc.
140 Glen St.
New Britain, CT 06051-2507
Phone: (860)223-0236   **Fax:** (860)223-9324
Products: Tools and dies; Electrical discharge machines (EDMs). **SICs:** 5065 (Electronic Parts & Equipment Nec); 5084 (Industrial Machinery & Equipment). **Officers:** Roger Kern, President.

■ 8940 ■ Key Distribution, Inc.
7611-K Rickenbacker Dr.
Gaithersburg, MD 20879
Phone: (301)258-8992   **Fax:** (301)840-0383
Products: Electronic systems and equipment. **SIC:** 5065 (Electronic Parts & Equipment Nec). **Est:** 1992. **Officers:** Kip Dellinger, e-mail: kipkey@erols.com. **Former Name:** Key Marketing Group.

■ 8941 ■ Key Electronics Inc.
46908 Liberty Dr.
Wixom, MI 48393-3600
Phone: (248)489-5455   **Fax:** (248)489-718
Products: Electronic parts; Electronic systems an

equipment. **SIC:** 5065 (Electronic Parts & Equipment Nec). **Officers:** Joseph Hodges, President.

■ 8942 ■ **Keystone Wire & Cable Company Inc.**
Northhampton Industrial Pk.
154 Railroad Dr.
Ivyland, PA 18974
Phone: (215)322-2390
Free: (800)223-7026 **Fax:** (215)322-1866
E-mail: sales@keystonewire.com
URL: http://www.keystonewire.com
Products: Wire; Cable. **SIC:** 5063 (Electrical Apparatus & Equipment). **Est:** 1983. **Emp:** 49.
Officers: Michael Schmittinger, Vice President.

■ 8943 ■ **Kiemle-Hankins Co.**
PO Box 507
Toledo, OH 43697-0507
Phone: (419)891-0262
Free: (800)695-0262 **Fax:** (419)893-8290
E-mail: info@kiemlehankins.com
URL: http://www.kiemlehankins.com
Products: Electrical equipment and supplies, including starters, controllers, and drives; Automation equipment; Motors. **SICs:** 5063 (Electrical Apparatus & Equipment); 5085 (Industrial Supplies). **Est:** 1928. **Sales:** $50,000,000 (2000). **Emp:** 190. **Officers:** A. Stephen Martindale, President; Judith A. Pokorny, Sales/Marketing Contact, e-mail: j.pokorny@kiemlehankins.com.

■ 8944 ■ **Kiesub Corp.**
3185 S Highland Dr., Ste. 10
Las Vegas, NV 89109
Phone: (702)733-0024 **Fax:** (702)733-0026
E-mail: kiesub@kiesub.com
URL: http://www.kiesub.com
Products: Electronic components, including communications equipment. **SICs:** 5065 (Electronic Parts & Equipment Nec); 5065 (Electronic Parts & Equipment Nec). **Sales:** $3,000,000 (2000). **Emp:** 15. **Officers:** Richard Farrah, General Mgr.; Eilene Hurley, Controller.

■ 8945 ■ **Kinder-Harris Inc.**
PO Box 1900
Stuttgart, AR 72160-1900
Phone: (501)673-1518 **Fax:** (501)673-4319
Products: Lamps. **SICs:** 5023 (Homefurnishings); 5063 (Electrical Apparatus & Equipment). **Est:** 1970. **Sales:** $10,000,000 (2000). **Emp:** 100. **Officers:** Joe Phillips, CEO; Kristina Lindsey, President; Bart Russo, Sales Mgr.

■ 8946 ■ **King Electronics Distributing**
1711 Southeastern Ave.
Indianapolis, IN 46201-3990
Phone: (317)639-1484 **Fax:** (317)639-4711
Products: Electric and electronic equipment; Switches; Audio cabinets, including radio, phonograph, stereo, and speaker cabinets; Bolts, nuts, rivets, screws, and washers; Batteries; Alarm systems; Electronic resistors; Transistors; Wiring supplies; Radio and TV communication equipment; Technical, scientific, and professional books. **SIC:** 5063 (Electrical Apparatus & Equipment). **Est:** 1961. **Sales:** $600,000 (2000). **Emp:** 8. **Officers:** Lawrence L. King, Owner.

■ 8947 ■ **King Wire and Cable Corp.**
PO Box 300
Jamaica, NY 11431
Phone: (718)657-4422 **Fax:** (718)739-7138
Products: Electrical equipment. **SICs:** 5063 (Electrical Apparatus & Equipment); 5063 (Electrical Apparatus & Equipment). **Est:** 1964. **Sales:** $32,000,000 (2000). **Emp:** 110. **Officers:** Robert Dorfman, CEO & President; Gordon Lewis, Controller.

■ 8948 ■ **King Wire Inc.**
1 Cable Pl.
North Chicago, IL 60064
Phone: (847)688-1100
Free: (800)453-5464 **Fax:** (847)688-0244
E-mail: sales@kingwireinc.com
URL: http://www.kingwire.com
Products: Electrical supplies, including wire and cable lines. **SIC:** 5063 (Electrical Apparatus & Equipment). **Est:** 1975. **Sales:** $32,000,000 (2000). **Emp:** 65.

Officers: Peter Leeb, President; Fay Goodwin, Sales/Marketing Contact.

■ 8949 ■ **Kirby Risk Electrical Supply**
PO Box 5089
Lafayette, IN 47903-5089
Phone: (317)448-4567 **Fax:** (765)448-1342
E-mail: info@kirbyrisk.com
URL: http://www.kirbyrisk.com
Products: Electrical supplies, including receptacles, wire, and electrical cable. **SIC:** 5063 (Electrical Apparatus & Equipment). **Est:** 1926. **Sales:** $270,000,000 (2000). **Emp:** 900. **Officers:** J.K. Risk III, President; Jason Bricker, VP & CFO.

■ 8950 ■ **K.J. Electric Inc.**
5894 E Molloy Rd.
Syracuse, NY 13211
Phone: (315)454-5535 **Fax:** (315)454-5564
E-mail: admin@kjelectric.com
URL: http://www.kjelectric.com
Products: Motors; Drives; Controls; Panels. **SIC:** 5063 (Electrical Apparatus & Equipment). **Est:** 1981. **Sales:** $25,000,000 (2000). **Emp:** 130. **Officers:** Ken Jacobs, President; Richard Maestri, CFO; George Eschenfelder, Marketing Mgr.; John Piedmonte.

■ 8951 ■ **KLH Industries Inc.**
703 Hwy. 80 W
Clinton, MS 39056
Phone: (601)924-3600
Products: Electronic transmission. **SIC:** 5063 (Electrical Apparatus & Equipment).

■ 8952 ■ **Knight Electronics Inc.**
10940 Alder Cir.
Dallas, TX 75238
Phone: (214)341-8631 **Fax:** (214)340-5870
URL: http://www.knightonline.com
Products: Electronic equipment. **SIC:** 5065 (Electronic Parts & Equipment Nec). **Est:** 1978. **Sales:** $5,000,000 (2000). **Emp:** 17. **Officers:** Robert P. Knight, President. **Former Name:** SW Marketing Associates Inc.

■ 8953 ■ **Knopp Inc.**
1307 66th St.
Emeryville, CA 94608
Phone: (510)653-1661
Free: (800)227-1848 **Fax:** (650)653-2220
E-mail: sales@knoppinc.com
URL: http://www.knoppinc.com
Products: Electrical testing equipment, including voltage testers. **SIC:** 5063 (Electrical Apparatus & Equipment). **Est:** 1928. **Sales:** $2,000,000 (2000). **Emp:** 20. **Officers:** Alex Finlay.

■ 8954 ■ **KOA Speer Electronics Inc.**
PO Box 547
Bradford, PA 16701
Phone: (814)362-5536
Free: (800)345-4562 **Fax:** (814)362-8883
Products: Resistors, capacitors, and inductors. **SIC:** 5065 (Electronic Parts & Equipment Nec). **Sales:** $150,000,000 (2000). **Emp:** 150. **Officers:** K. Kichiji, President; Lance Eastman, VP of Finance.

■ 8955 ■ **Konex Corp.**
270 N Smith Ave.
Corona, CA 92880
Phone: (909)371-1200 **Fax:** (909)735-1367
Products: Dip plugs and sockets; Electronics; Specializing in cable and harness assemblies. **SIC:** 5065 (Electronic Parts & Equipment Nec). **Officers:** Howard Wilkinson, President; Dennis Hill, Treasurer.

■ 8956 ■ **Koontz-Wagner Electric Company Inc.**
3801 Voorde Dr.
South Bend, IN 46628
Phone: (219)232-2051
Free: (800)345-2051 **Fax:** (219)288-8510
URL: http://www.koontz-wagner.com
Products: Electric motors; Electrical equipment; Electrical construction materials. **SIC:** 5063 (Electrical Apparatus & Equipment). **Est:** 1921. **Sales:** $56,000,000 (2000). **Emp:** 500. **Officers:** John Gish, President & Chairman of the Board; R.J. Pfeil, President & Chairman of the Board; Laura Pfeil, Dir. of

Marketing; Mitch Drechsler, Information Systems Mgr.; Larry E. Witek.

■ 8957 ■ **Kornfeld-Thorp Electric Co.**
PO Box 2904
Kansas City, KS 66110
Phone: (913)321-7070 **Fax:** (913)321-2657
Products: Electrical motors and supplies; Industrial motors. **SICs:** 5063 (Electrical Apparatus & Equipment); 5085 (Industrial Supplies). **Est:** 1938. **Sales:** $6,000,000 (2000). **Emp:** 40. **Officers:** Bruce Putman, President; Ellen Wyeth, CFO; Izzy Rowland, Dir. of Marketing; Dody Villarreal, Dir. of Systems.

■ 8958 ■ **Kovalsky-Carr Electric Supply Company Inc.**
208 St. Paul St.
Rochester, NY 14604-1188
Phone: (716)325-1950 **Fax:** (716)546-6904
E-mail: sales@kovalskycarr.com
URL: http://www.kovalskycarr.com
Products: Electrical and lighting equipment. **SIC:** 5063 (Electrical Apparatus & Equipment). **Est:** 1921. **Emp:** 30. **Officers:** Arnold Kovalsky, President; Laurence Kovalsky, Vice President; Donald Bausch, Vice President.

■ 8959 ■ **KS. Electronics L.L.C.**
16406 N Cave Creek Rd.
Phoenix, AZ 85032
Phone: (602)971-3301
Products: Electronic components—custom filters and oscillators. **SIC:** 5065 (Electronic Parts & Equipment Nec). **Officers:** Kirti Shah, Owner.

■ 8960 ■ **Kulwin Electric Supply**
PO Box 535001
Indianapolis, IN 46253-5001
Phone: (317)293-3363 **Fax:** (317)298-2888
Products: Electrical supplies, including lighting, wire, fixtures, receptacles, and baseboard heaters. **SIC:** 5063 (Electrical Apparatus & Equipment). **Est:** 1946. **Sales:** $28,000,000 (2000). **Emp:** 100. **Officers:** Bob Woods, President; Paul E. Nysewander, Controller; Paul Shinkle, Dir. of Marketing.

■ 8961 ■ **L-com Inc.**
45 Beechwood Dr.
North Andover, MA 01845
Phone: (978)682-6936
Free: (800)343-1455 **Fax:** (978)685-6467
Products: Electronic parts, including connectors and cable for computers. **SICs:** 5065 (Electronic Parts & Equipment Nec); 5063 (Electrical Apparatus & Equipment). **Sales:** $9,000,000 (2000). **Emp:** 57. **Officers:** Alfred F. Contarino Jr., President; Edward Caselden, CEO.

■ 8962 ■ **Labsphere**
Shaker St.
North Sutton, NH 03260
Phone: (603)927-4266 **Fax:** (603)927-4694
E-mail: labsphere@labsphere.com
URL: http://www.labsphere.com
Products: Electro-optic equipment. **SIC:** 5065 (Electronic Parts & Equipment Nec). **Est:** 1979. **Sales:** $15,000,000 (1999). **Emp:** 156. **Officers:** R. Claflin, President; KG Chitlim, VP of Marketing & Sales; Joan Beaulieu, Sales/Marketing Contact, e-mail: jbeaulieu@labsphere.com; Bonnie St. Lawrence, Human Resources Contact, e-mail: bstlawrence@labsphere.com.

■ 8963 ■ **Lacey-Harmer Co**
4320 NW Saint Helens Rd.
Portland, OR 97210
Phone: (503)222-9992 **Fax:** (503)222-0073
Products: Electrical machinery, equipment and supplies. **SIC:** 5063 (Electrical Apparatus & Equipment).

■ 8964 ■ **Lafayette Auto Electric**
102 Windsor Trl.
Pelham, AL 35124-2848
Phone: (205)347-2264
Products: Electronic parts and equipment; Radio and television equipment and parts; Automobile air-conditioning equipment. **SICs:** 5065 (Electronic Parts & Equipment Nec); 5064 (Electrical Appliances—

Television & Radio); 5013 (Motor Vehicle Supplies & New Parts). **Officers:** Bert Phillips, President.

■ 8965 ■ Lafayette Electronics Supply Inc.
PO Box 4549
Lafayette, IN 47903
Phone: (765)447-9660
Free: (800)842-1527 **Fax:** (765)447-6967
E-mail: lafelecsup@earthlink.net
URL: http://www.lafayetteelecsup.com
Products: Electronic components. **SIC:** 5065 (Electronic Parts & Equipment Nec). **Officers:** Ronald Hurst, President; Wayne King.

■ 8966 ■ Lakeland Engineer Equipment Co.
5735 Lindsay St.
Minneapolis, MN 55422
Phone: (612)544-0321 **Fax:** (612)544-5541
Products: Micro-switches; Controllers; Completers. **SIC:** 5063 (Electrical Apparatus & Equipment). **Est:** 1952. **Sales:** $8,000,000 (2000). **Emp:** 60. **Officers:** William C. Fox, President; Gene Fraley, Vice President.

■ 8967 ■ LAM Electrical Supply Company, Inc.
PO Box 429
Rte. 17M
Goshen, NY 10924-0429
Phones: (914)294-5469 (914)343-0221
(914)485-4202 **Fax:** (914)294-3705
Products: Residential electric lighting fixtures; Industrial electric lighting fixtures; Fluorescent lamp ballasts; Batteries; Circuit breakers; Electrical conduit and conduit fittings; Electric motor controls; Electrical boxes and fittings; Fuses and fuse equipment; Heating equipment; Lamps; Aluminum and aluminum-base alloy wire; Copper and copper-base alloy wire. **SIC:** 5063 (Electrical Apparatus & Equipment). **Emp:** 19.

■ 8968 ■ Lamar Wholesale and Supply Inc.
7135 N Lamar St.
Austin, TX 78752
Phone: (512)453-2852
Free: (800)282-2852 **Fax:** (512)453-0155
E-mail: sales@lightbulbshop.net
URL: http://www.lightbulbshop.net
Products: Light bulbs; Ballasts; Fixtures. **SIC:** 5063 (Electrical Apparatus & Equipment). **Est:** 1986. **Sales:** $1,200,000 (1999). **Emp:** 10. **Officers:** Edwin McGary, President; Charles Baker, Vice President; Greg Robbins, VP of Marketing; Chuck Lange, Vice President. **Doing Business As:** The Lightbulb Shop.

■ 8969 ■ Lamp Glow Industries Inc.
819 Pickens Industrial
Marietta, GA 30062
Phone: (404)514-1441
Products: Light bulbs; Transformers; Service lighting. **SIC:** 5063 (Electrical Apparatus & Equipment). **Sales:** $1,500,000 (2000). **Emp:** 6. **Officers:** Vern Haynes, President.

■ 8970 ■ Lang and Washburn Electric Inc.
185 Creekside Dr.
Amherst, NY 14228
Phone: (716)691-3333
Free: (888)786-6813 **Fax:** (716)691-8939
URL: http://www.langandwashburn.com
Products: Electrical supplies, including wire. **SIC:** 5063 (Electrical Apparatus & Equipment). **Est:** 1928. **Sales:** $7,000,000 (2000). **Emp:** 18. **Officers:** Keith Waldron, President; David Mislin, Vice President.

■ 8971 ■ Langstadt Electric Supply Co.
1524 W Civic St.
Appleton, WI 54911
Phone: (920)733-3791 **Fax:** (920)733-1701
Products: Motor starters and motor controls. **SIC:** 5065 (Electronic Parts & Equipment Nec). **Sales:** $9,000,000 (2000). **Emp:** 45. **Officers:** Stan Baehman, President.

■ 8972 ■ Larsen Associates Inc.
10855 W Potter Rd.
Wauwatosa, WI 53226
Phone: (414)258-0529 **Fax:** (414)258-9655
E-mail: larsenwi@execpc.com
Products: Electronic and electromechanical components. **SIC:** 5045 (Computers, Peripherals & Software). **Est:** 1970. **Sales:** $14,000,000 (1999).

Emp: 6. **Officers:** Jim Luther, President; Pete Auxier, Vice President; Steve Ehrmann, Vice President.

■ 8973 ■ J.H. Larson Co.
700 Colorado Ave. S
Minneapolis, MN 55416
Phone: (763)545-1717 **Fax:** (763)525-5884
URL: http://jhlarson.com
Products: Lighting fixtures; Electric motor controls; Panelboards; Switches for electrical circuitry; plumbing and HVAC products. **SIC:** 5063 (Electrical Apparatus & Equipment). **Est:** 1931. **Sales:** $80,000,000 (2000). **Emp:** 225. **Officers:** C.E. Pahl, CEO; Ed Chesen, VP & General Merchandising Mgr., e-mail: echesen@jhlarson.com. **Former Name:** J.H. #Larson Electrical Co.

■ 8974 ■ F.D. Lawrence Electric Co.
3450 Beekman St.
Cincinnati, OH 45223
Phone: (513)542-1100
Free: (800)582-4490 **Fax:** (513)542-2422
URL: http://www.sdlawrence.com
Products: Electrical equipment. **SIC:** 5063 (Electrical Apparatus & Equipment). **Est:** 1904. **Sales:** $75,300,000 (2000). **Emp:** 125. **Officers:** Dennis P. O'Leary, President; G.T. Menke, Treasurer; Richard G. Krueger, VP of Marketing; Patrick J. Retherford, Manager.

■ 8975 ■ L.B. Electric Supply Company Inc.
5202 New Utrecht Ave.
Brooklyn, NY 11219
Phone: (718)438-4700 **Fax:** (718)854-5183
Products: Electrical equipment and supplies; Lighting equipment. **SICs:** 5063 (Electrical Apparatus & Equipment); 5065 (Electronic Parts & Equipment Nec). **Est:** 1933. **Sales:** $10,000,000 (2000). **Emp:** 40. **Officers:** Harvey Lifton, President; Richard Lifton, Treasurer; Carol Lifton, VP of Marketing; Steve Andreala, Operations Mgr.

■ 8976 ■ LCD Systems Corp.
43150 Osgood Rd.
Fremont, CA 94539-5629
Phone: (510)353-1913 **Fax:** (510)353-0253
E-mail: info@lcdsystems.com
URL: http://www.lcdsystems.com
Products: Standard and custom liquid crystal displays and modules. **SIC:** 5065 (Electronic Parts & Equipment Nec). **Est:** 1986. **Sales:** $2,000,000 (2000). **Emp:** 5. **Officers:** Robert W. Haire, President; Lewis E. Chick III, Dir. of Mktg. & Sales, e-mail: lew@lcdsystems.com.

■ 8977 ■ Leader Instruments Corp.
380 Oser Ave.
Hauppauge, NY 11788
Phone: (631)231-6900
Free: (800)645-5104 **Fax:** (631)231-5295
E-mail: sales@leaderusa.com
URL: http://www.leaderusa.com
Products: Electric and electronic equipment. **SIC:** 5065 (Electronic Parts & Equipment Nec). **Est:** 1969. **Sales:** $10,000,000 (2000). **Emp:** 35. **Officers:** S. Nihei, President; G. Gonos, Dir. of Mktg. & Sales; J. Fiorni, e-mail: Human Resources Contact.

■ 8978 ■ Ledu Corp.
36 Midland Ave.
Port Chester, NY 10573
Phone: (914)937-4433 **Fax:** 800-648-2978
Products: Office lamps; Industrial lighting equipment. **SIC:** 5063 (Electrical Apparatus & Equipment). **Sales:** $10,000,000 (2000). **Emp:** 18. **Officers:** J. Stromberg, President; Tom Greer, Controller; P. Brady, VP of Marketing.

■ 8979 ■ H. Leff Electric Co.
1163 E 40th St.
Cleveland, OH 44114
Phone: (216)432-3000 **Fax:** (216)432-0051
Products: Electrical equipment. **SIC:** 5063 (Electrical Apparatus & Equipment). **Est:** 1921. **Sales:** $15,000,000 (2000). **Emp:** 70. **Officers:** Sanford Leff Sr., CEO; S.L. Leff Jr., Exec. VP & Treasurer; B.L. Leff, Dir. of Marketing & Sales; Larry Goldstein, Controller.

■ 8980 ■ Leff Electronics Inc.
225 Braddock Ave.
Braddock, PA 15104
Phone: (412)351-5000 **Fax:** (412)351-2227
E-mail: leff@nb.net
URL: http://www.leff.com
Products: Electronic parts, wire, and relays. **SIC:** 5065 (Electronic Parts & Equipment Nec). **Est:** 1946. **Emp:** 25. **Officers:** Jerry Leff, President; Nick Disaia, Secretary; Bob Cribbs, Sales/Marketing Contact; Terry Wilcox, Customer Service Contact; Norma McHirella, Human Resources Contact.

■ 8981 ■ Chester C. Lehmann Co. Inc.
1135 Auzerais St.
San Jose, CA 95126
Phone: (408)293-5818 **Fax:** (408)287-1152
Products: Electrical equipment and supplies. **SIC:** 5063 (Electrical Apparatus & Equipment). **Est:** 1948. **Sales:** $38,000,000 (2000). **Emp:** 90. **Officers:** Chet Lehman III, President; Jerry Potts, CFO; Scott Lehmann; Jack Westergren.

■ 8982 ■ Chester C. Lehmann Company Inc.
1135 Auzerais St.
San Jose, CA 95126
Phone: (408)293-5818 **Fax:** (408)287-1152
Products: Electrical equipment. **SIC:** 5063 (Electrical Apparatus & Equipment). **Emp:** 7. **Officers:** Chet Lehman III, President; Jerry Potts, CFO.

■ 8983 ■ Lemo USA, Inc.
PO Box 2408
Rohnert Park, CA 94927-2408
Phone: (707)578-8811
Free: (800)444-5366 **Fax:** (707)578-0869
E-mail: lemous@lemo.ch
Products: Electrical equipment and supplies. **SIC:** 5065 (Electronic Parts & Equipment Nec). **Officers:** Peter Mueller; Carol taylor, Sales/Marketing Contact; Hal Carroll, Customer Service Contact; Cheryll Powers, Human Resources Contact. **Alternate Name:** Redel.

■ 8984 ■ Lesco Distributing
1203 E Industrial Dr.
Orange City, FL 32763
Phone: (904)775-7244 **Fax:** (904)775-1146
Products: Electronics. **SIC:** 5065 (Electronic Parts & Equipment Nec).

■ 8985 ■ Lewis Electronics Co.
PO Box 100
Humboldt, TN 38343-0100
Phone: (901)784-2191 **Fax:** (901)784-2199
Products: Electronic parts; Electronic systems and equipment. **SIC:** 5065 (Electronic Parts & Equipment Nec). **Officers:** Austin Lewis, President.

■ 8986 ■ Light House Electrical Suppliers Inc.
609 Andrew Ave.
La Porte, IN 46350
Phone: (219)362-3171 **Fax:** (219)324-7837
Products: Electrical supplies, including light fixtures. **SIC:** 5063 (Electrical Apparatus & Equipment). **Est:** 1969. **Sales:** $4,000,000 (2000). **Emp:** 25. **Officers:** William Fullmer, President; David Fullmer, Vice President; Linda L. Northam, Office Mgr.

■ 8987 ■ Light Wave Systems
21029 Itasca St Ste. A-B
Chatsworth, CA 91311
Phone: (818)727-9900 **Fax:** (818)727-9930
Products: Audio equipment and accessories for microphones. **SIC:** 5065 (Electronic Parts & Equipment Nec). **Officers:** Leslie Drever, Owner.

■ 8988 ■ Lighting Parts Inc.
191 E Jefferson Blvd.
Los Angeles, CA 90011
Phone: (213)233-8111
Free: (800)826-0506 **Fax:** (213)232-1742
Products: Commercial lighting supplies. **SIC:** 5063 (Electrical Apparatus & Equipment). **Sales:** $6,000,000 (2000). **Emp:** 40. **Officers:** David Okun, CEO & President; Raymond Barin, Controller.

■ 8989 ■ **Lightolier Inc. Norwich Div.**
40 Wisconsin Ave.
Norwich, CT 06360
Phone: (860)886-2621 **Fax:** (860)886-9370
Products: Light fixtures. **SIC:** 5063 (Electrical Apparatus & Equipment). **Sales:** $5,000,000 (2000). **Emp:** 23. **Officers:** Cliff Jackson, General Mgr.

■ 8990 ■ **Lights Etc. Inc.**
4510 N 16th St.
Phoenix, AZ 85016
Phone: (602)230-8770 **Fax:** (602)230-0083
Products: Incandescent, fluorescent, and halogen lightbulbs. **SIC:** 5063 (Electrical Apparatus & Equipment). **Est:** 1988. **Sales:** $800,000 (2000). **Emp:** 7. **Officers:** Clyde H. Kindred, President.

■ 8991 ■ **Ligon Electric Supply Co.**
PO Box 5098
Winston-Salem, NC 27113
Phone: (919)723-9656 **Fax:** (919)777-0588
Products: Electrical supplies, including wire and cable. **SIC:** 5063 (Electrical Apparatus & Equipment). **Est:** 1951. **Sales:** $21,000,000 (2000). **Emp:** 60. **Officers:** Jim Latham, General Mgr.; Donny Boles, Vice President.

■ 8992 ■ **Lincoln Part Supply Inc.**
728 S 27th St.
Lincoln, NE 68510-3105
Phone: (402)476-6908 **Fax:** (402)476-6947
Products: Parts and attachments for small household appliances. **SIC:** 5064 (Electrical Appliances—Television & Radio). **Officers:** Harlan Zwiebel, President.

■ 8993 ■ **Linder Electric Motors Inc.**
308 Adrian St.
Wausau, WI 54401-6107
Phone: (715)842-3725 **Fax:** (715)845-5918
Products: Electric motors. **SIC:** 5063 (Electrical Apparatus & Equipment). **Est:** 1954. **Emp:** 5. **Officers:** Norm Randl, Vice President; Tom Hornung, President.

■ 8994 ■ **Lite Brite Distributors**
PO Box 142
475 E Broadway
Trenton, IL 62293
Phone: (618)224-7314
Products: Lighting equipment and supplies; Woodburning stoves and fireplaces. **SICs:** 5074 (Plumbing & Hydronic Heating Supplies); 5063 (Electrical Apparatus & Equipment).

■ 8995 ■ **Littelfuse Inc.**
800 E Northwest Hwy.
Des Plaines, IL 60016
Phone: (847)824-1188 **Fax:** (847)824-3024
Products: Fuses. **SICs:** 5063 (Electrical Apparatus & Equipment); 5065 (Electronic Parts & Equipment Nec). **Sales:** $200,000,000 (2000). **Emp:** 1,000. **Officers:** Howard B. Witt, President.

■ 8996 ■ **Liuski International Inc.**
6585 Crescent Dr.
Norcross, GA 30071
Phone: (770)447-9454 **Fax:** (770)441-0371
Products: Electronics equipment and parts; Computers and software. **SICs:** 5045 (Computers, Peripherals & Software); 5063 (Electrical Apparatus & Equipment). **Est:** 1984. **Sales:** $422,300,000 (2000). **Emp:** 526. **Officers:** Morries Liu, CEO & Chairman of the Board; Edward A. Williams, CFO; Shirley Lee, Sr. VP of Marketing & Sales; Manuel C. Tan, COO & Exec. VP; Diane Eckhoff, Dir of Personnel.

■ 8997 ■ **Living Systems Instrumentation**
156 Battery St.
Burlington, VT 05401
Phone: (802)863-5547
Products: Electrical equipment and supplies. **SIC:** 5063 (Electrical Apparatus & Equipment).

■ 8998 ■ **LKG Industries Inc.**
PO Box 6386
Rockford, IL 61125
Phone: (815)874-2301 **Fax:** (815)874-2896
E-mail: lkgindustries@compuserve.com
Products: Connectors; Electronic audio, video, and telephone accessories. **SIC:** 5065 (Electronic Parts & Equipment Nec). **Est:** 1921. **Sales:** $13,000,000 (2000). **Emp:** 45. **Officers:** Wayne Timpe, CEO; Judith Timpe, CFO; Kathryn Granath, Dir. of Data Processing.

■ 8999 ■ **Lodan West Inc.**
1050 Commercial St.
San Carlos, CA 94070
Phone: (650)592-4600 **Fax:** (650)592-4054
Products: Electronic connectors; Custom cable assemblies. **SIC:** 5065 (Electronic Parts & Equipment Nec).

■ 9000 ■ **Loeb Electric Co.**
915 Williams Ave.
Columbus, OH 43212
Phone: (614)294-6351
Free: (800)868-6351 **Fax:** (614)294-7640
URL: http://www.loeb-electric.com
Products: Electrical supplies, including circuit boxes, breakers, fuses, and wire. **SIC:** 5063 (Electrical Apparatus & Equipment). **Est:** 1916. **Sales:** $30,000,000 (2000). **Emp:** 80. **Officers:** Charles A. Loeb, President; Lon Smith, Controller; John Barney, Sales Mgr.

■ 9001 ■ **Loffler Business Systems Inc.**
5707 Excelsior Blvd.
Minneapolis, MN 55416
Phone: (612)925-6800 **Fax:** (612)925-5781
URL: http://www.loffler.com
Products: Copiers and fax machines; Voice products. **SICs:** 5065 (Electronic Parts & Equipment Nec); 5044 (Office Equipment). **Est:** 1986. **Sales:** $8,000,000 (2000). **Emp:** 55. **Officers:** James Loffler, President, e-mail: loffler@loffler.com; William Daly, Sales/Marketing Contact, e-mail: wdaly@loffler.com; Todd Wiles, Customer Service Contact, e-mail: twiles@loffler.com; Ron Bartel, Human Resources Contact, e-mail: rbartel@loffler.com.

■ 9002 ■ **Loppnow & Associates**
1420 NW Gilman Blvd., Ste. 2857
Issaquah, WA 98027
Phone: (425)392-3936 **Fax:** (425)392-3973
Products: Electronic systems and equipment. **SIC:** 5065 (Electronic Parts & Equipment Nec). **Emp:** 4. **Officers:** Jim Loppnow.

■ 9003 ■ **Loroman Co.**
95-25 149th St.
Jamaica, NY 11430
Phone: (718)291-0800
Products: Electrical equipment; Metals; Wood products. **SICs:** 5065 (Electronic Parts & Equipment Nec); 5051 (Metals Service Centers & Offices); 5031 (Lumber, Plywood & Millwork).

■ 9004 ■ **Loyd Armature Works Inc.**
4754 Center Park Blvd.
San Antonio, TX 78218-4426
Phone: (210)599-4515 **Fax:** (210)599-7351
Products: Electric motors, controls, and pumps. **SIC:** 5063 (Electrical Apparatus & Equipment). **Est:** 1930. **Sales:** $900,000 (2000). **Emp:** 8. **Officers:** Cory May, General Mgr.

■ 9005 ■ **Loyd's Electric Supply Co.**
117 E College St.
PO Box 1169
Branson, MO 65616
Phone: (417)334-2171 **Fax:** (417)334-6635
E-mail: loydselect@aol.com
Products: Electrical material for construction, including wiring. **SICs:** 5063 (Electrical Apparatus & Equipment); 5039 (Construction Materials Nec). **Est:** 1961. **Emp:** 75. **Officers:** Phillip Loyd.

■ 9006 ■ **L.S.I. Lectro Science Inc.**
380 Stewart Rd.
Wilkes Barre, PA 18706-1459
Phone: (570)825-1900
Free: (800)631-3814 **Fax:** (570)825-7108
E-mail: sales@kbs-inc.net
URL: http://www.lectro-sci.com; http://www.flashlight.com
Products: Hand-held spotlights; Rechargeable lanterns. **SIC:** 5063 (Electrical Apparatus & Equipment). **Est:** 1970. **Sales:** $6,000,000 (1999).

Emp: 102. **Officers:** Harry Kaplan, President; John Rilla, VP of Finance.

■ 9007 ■ **Lubbock Electric Co.**
1108 34th St.
Lubbock, TX 79405
Phone: (806)744-2336 **Fax:** (806)744-5690
Products: Electric motors. **SIC:** 5063 (Electrical Apparatus & Equipment). **Est:** 1944. **Sales:** $8,000,000 (2000). **Emp:** 79. **Officers:** Paul V. Bush, CEO; Jerry Bush, President.

■ 9008 ■ **Luckenbach and Johnson Inc.**
1828 Tilghman St.
Allentown, PA 18104
Phone: (610)434-6235
Products: Consumer electronics and major appliances. **SIC:** 5064 (Electrical Appliances—Television & Radio). **Sales:** $2,500,000 (2000). **Emp:** 7. **Officers:** Stephen Demchyk, President; Stephen J. Demchyk, Treasurer & Secty.

■ 9009 ■ **Lucky Electric Supply**
325 Calhoun Ave. E
Memphis, TN 38126-3219
Phone: (901)525-0264 **Fax:** (901)525-6990
Products: Electrical supplies. **SIC:** 5063 (Electrical Apparatus & Equipment). **Sales:** $7,000,000 (2000). **Emp:** 40. **Officers:** Don Herndon; Phil Jenkins.

■ 9010 ■ **Lucoral Company Inc.**
26 W 46th St.
New York, NY 10036
Phone: (212)575-9701
Products: Electrical process systems. **SIC:** 5063 (Electrical Apparatus & Equipment). **Sales:** $10,000,000 (2000). **Emp:** 18. **Officers:** Johnny Lu, President.

■ 9011 ■ **Lyncole XIT Grounding**
3547 Voyager St Ste. 104
Torrance, CA 90503
Phone: (310)214-4000 **Fax:** (310)214-1114
Products: Electrical grounding rods; Ground resistance test meters; Engineering design and technical services. **SIC:** 5063 (Electrical Apparatus & Equipment).

■ 9012 ■ **M & A Sales**
701 E Gude Dr.
Rockville, MD 20850
Phone: (301)424-2500 **Fax:** (301)424-5156
Products: Electronic components, including musical accessories and electric guitars. **SIC:** 5065 (Electronic Parts & Equipment Nec).

■ 9013 ■ **M & G Industries**
820 Greenleaf Ave.
Elk Grove Village, IL 60007
Phone: (847)437-6662
Free: (800)323-1592 **Fax:** (847)437-0468
Products: Marine and industrial cables and fittings. **SICs:** 5063 (Electrical Apparatus & Equipment); 5085 (Industrial Supplies).

■ 9014 ■ **M & G Industries Inc.**
85 Broadcommon Rd.
Bristol, RI 02809
Phone: (401)253-0096
Free: (800)323-0492 **Fax:** (401)434-1988
Products: Marine and industrial cables and fittings. **SICs:** 5063 (Electrical Apparatus & Equipment); 5085 (Industrial Supplies). **Officers:** Joan Rosenthal, President.

■ 9015 ■ **M/M Electronic Products Ltd.**
7 Corporate Dr., #117
North Haven, CT 06473-3258
Phone: (203)239-7099 **Fax:** (203)239-9343
E-mail: m.m.electronics@snet.net
Products: Electronic connectors. **SIC:** 5065 (Electronic Parts & Equipment Nec). **Est:** 1985. **Officers:** Frank Manzi, President.

■ 9016 ■ **M-Tron Components Inc.**
2110-1 Smithtown Ave.
Ronkonkoma, NY 11779
Phone: (516)467-5100 **Fax:** (516)467-5104
Products: Electronic components. **SICs:** 5063

(Electrical Apparatus & Equipment); 5065 (Electronic Parts & Equipment Nec). **Sales:** $3,800,000 (1993). **Emp:** 17. **Officers:** Mark H. Kealey, President; Michael D. Kealey, Vice President.

■ 9017 ■ **Maddux Supply Co.**
c/o Tommy Joyner
1512 Hooker Rd.
Greenville, NC 27834-6323
Phone: (919)756-5506 **Fax:** (919)756-0963
Products: Electrical supplies and wiring. **SIC:** 5063 (Electrical Apparatus & Equipment). **Emp:** 49. **Officers:** Joe Maddux.

■ 9018 ■ **MagneTek, Inc.**
26 Century Blvd.
Nashville, TN 37214
Phone: (615)316-5100 **Fax:** (615)316-5195
Products: Electrical power products and factory automation. **SIC:** 5064 (Electrical Appliances—Television & Radio). **Emp:** 14,900. **Officers:** R.N. Hoge, CEO & President; D.P. Reiland, Exec. VP & CFO; T.R. Kmak, VP & Controller; J.P. Colling Jr., VP & Treasurer.

■ 9019 ■ **Magnetic Technology**
290 W Madison St.
Wytheville, VA 24382
Phone: (540)228-7943
Products: Transformers. **SIC:** 5063 (Electrical Apparatus & Equipment).

■ 9020 ■ **Magtrol Inc. (Tucson, Arizona)**
PO Box 85099
Tucson, AZ 85726
Phone: (520)622-7802
Products: Electrical supplies. **SIC:** 5065 (Electronic Parts & Equipment Nec). **Est:** 1987. **Sales:** $1,000,000 (2000). **Emp:** 7. **Officers:** Jack Wissen, President.

■ 9021 ■ **Main Electric Supply Co.**
6700 S Main St.
Los Angeles, CA 90003-1541
Phone: (213)753-5131 **Fax:** (213)753-7750
Products: Electrical supplies. **SIC:** 5063 (Electrical Apparatus & Equipment). **Emp:** 46. **Officers:** Paul M. Vowels, President.

■ 9022 ■ **Main Line Equipment, Inc.**
20917 Higgins Ct.
Torrance, CA 90501-1723
Phone: (310)357-4450
Free: (800)444-2288 **Fax:** (310)357-4465
E-mail: sales@main-line-inc.com
URL: http://www.main-line-inc.com
Products: Cable television and broadband communication equipment. **SIC:** 5065 (Electronic Parts & Equipment Nec). **Est:** 1987. **Sales:** $20,000,000 (1999). **Emp:** 140. **Officers:** Mark Lipp, President & CEO; Mike DeSanto, Manufacturing Mgr.; Lou Kadison, Marketing & Sales Mgr.; David Neitzki, QA Mgr.; Norma Lipp, Human Resources Contact, e-mail: nlipp@main-line-inc.com.

■ 9023 ■ **Mallory Inc.**
550 Mallory Way
Carson City, NV 89701
Phone: (775)882-6600
Products: Electrical equipment, including engines and transformers. **SIC:** 5063 (Electrical Apparatus & Equipment).

■ 9024 ■ **Maltby Electric Supply Company Inc.**
336 7th St.
San Francisco, CA 94103
Phone: (415)863-5000 **Fax:** (415)863-5011
Products: Electrical components. **SIC:** 5063 (Electrical Apparatus & Equipment). **Est:** 1955. **Sales:** $28,000,000 (2000). **Emp:** 70. **Officers:** Susan Maltby, President.

■ 9025 ■ **Mania-Testerion**
1220 Village Way
Santa Ana, CA 92705
Phone: (714)564-9350 **Fax:** (714)564-9344
Products: Circuit testing equipment. **SIC:** 5063 (Electrical Apparatus & Equipment). **Sales:** $11,000,000 (2000). **Emp:** 100. **Officers:** Mike Winship, President; Jerry Troutman, Controller.

■ 9026 ■ **Mansfield Electric Supply Inc.**
2255 Stumbo Rd.
Mansfield, OH 44901
Phone: (419)529-2750 **Fax:** (419)529-2494
Products: General line of electrical equipment. **SIC:** 5063 (Electrical Apparatus & Equipment). **Sales:** $5,000,000 (1992). **Emp:** 13. **Officers:** Tim Furbay, President; Nick Gobora, Controller.

■ 9027 ■ **Mar Electronics Inc.**
17201 Westfield Park Dr.
Westfield, IN 46074-9537
Phone: (317)633-6699 **Fax:** (317)633-6687
Products: Electronic parts; Electric and electronic equipment. **SIC:** 5065 (Electronic Parts & Equipment Nec). **Officers:** Mark Ramser, President.

■ 9028 ■ **Marathon Electric Manufacturing Corp.**
417 Welshwood Dr., No. 201
Nashville, TN 37211
Phone: (615)834-3930
Products: Electric equipment and supplies. **SIC:** 5063 (Electrical Apparatus & Equipment).

■ 9029 ■ **Ken Marc Sales Corp.**
PO Box 188
Maspeth, NY 11378-0188
Phone: (718)386-4065 **Fax:** (718)386-1269
Products: Lighting, including lamps and fixtures. **SICs:** 5023 (Homefurnishings); 5063 (Electrical Apparatus & Equipment). **Emp:** 50. **Officers:** Ken Kramer.

■ 9030 ■ **Marinco-AFI**
2655 Napa Valley Corporate Dr.
Napa, CA 94558
Phone: (707)226-9600 **Fax:** (707)226-9670
E-mail: recreationalinfo@marinco.com
URL: http://www.marinco.com
Products: Electrical shore power systems; Horns, wiper systems, and ventilation systems; Teak accessories; Battery charges, switches and galvanic isolators. **SIC:** 5065 (Electronic Parts & Equipment Nec). **Est:** 1972. **Officers:** J. Marty O'Donohue, President.

■ 9031 ■ **Marsh Electronics Inc.**
1563 S 101st St.
Milwaukee, WI 53214
Phone: (414)475-6000 **Fax:** (414)771-2847
Products: Electric and electronic equipment; Semiconductors and related devices; Electronic capacitors; Electronic resistors. **SIC:** 5065 (Electronic Parts & Equipment Nec). **Est:** 1937. **Sales:** $39,000,000 (2000). **Emp:** 100. **Officers:** Jim Banovich, President.

■ 9032 ■ **Marshall Industries**
158 Gaither Rd.
Mt. Laurel, NJ 08054
Phone: (609)234-9100
Products: Electronic components. **SIC:** 5065 (Electronic Parts & Equipment Nec).

■ 9033 ■ **Marshall Industries**
155 Passaic Ave., Ste. 410
Fairfield, NJ 07004-3502
Phone: (201)273-1515
Products: Electronic equipment and supplies. **SIC:** 5065 (Electronic Parts & Equipment Nec).

■ 9034 ■ **Marshall Industries**
100 Marshall Dr.
Endicott, NY 13760
Phone: (607)785-2345 **Fax:** (607)785-5546
Products: Electronics. **SIC:** 5065 (Electronic Parts & Equipment Nec).

■ 9035 ■ **Marshall Industries**
30700 Bainbridge Rd., Unit A
Solon, OH 44139
Phone: (440)248-1788 **Fax:** (440)248-2312
Products: Electronic equipment and supplies. **SIC:** 5065 (Electronic Parts & Equipment Nec).

■ 9036 ■ **Marshall Industries**
15260 NW Greenbaier Pkwy.
Beaverton, OR 97006-5764
Phone: (503)644-5050 **Fax:** (503)646-8251
Products: Electronic parts and supplies. **SIC:** 5065 (Electronic Parts & Equipment Nec).

■ 9037 ■ **Marshall Industries**
8504 Cross Park Dr.
Austin, TX 78754
Phone: (512)837-1991 **Fax:** (512)832-9810
Products: Electronic components. **SIC:** 5065 (Electronic Parts & Equipment Nec).

■ 9038 ■ **Marshall Industries**
1551 N Glenville
Richardson, TX 75081
Phone: (972)705-0600 **Fax:** (972)705-0675
Products: Electronic components. **SIC:** 5065 (Electronic Parts & Equipment Nec).

■ 9039 ■ **Marshall Industries**
10681 Haddington, No. 160
Houston, TX 77043
Phone: (713)467-1666 **Fax:** (713)467-9805
Products: Electronic components. **SIC:** 5065 (Electronic Parts & Equipment Nec).

■ 9040 ■ **Marshall Industries**
2855 Cottonwood Pky., Ste. 220
Salt Lake City, UT 84121-7039
Phone: (801)973-2288 **Fax:** (801)973-2296
Products: Electronic components. **SIC:** 5065 (Electronic Parts & Equipment Nec).

■ 9041 ■ **Marshall Industries**
8214 154th Ave. NE
Redmond, WA 98052-3877
Phone: (425)486-5747 **Fax:** (425)486-6964
Products: Electronic components. **SIC:** 5065 (Electronic Parts & Equipment Nec).

■ 9042 ■ **Martindale Electric Co.**
PO Box 430
Cleveland, OH 44107-0430
Phone: (216)521-8567
Free: (800)344-9191 **Fax:** (216)521-9476
Products: Electrical maintenance equipment. **SIC:** 5065 (Electronic Parts & Equipment Nec). **Est:** 1913. **Sales:** $4,000,000 (2000). **Emp:** 60. **Officers:** J.C. Snyder, Vice President; A.J. Laco, Treasurer; R.J. Gamary, Sales Mgr.

■ 9043 ■ **Ronald A. Massa Associates**
164 C.J. Cushing Hwy.
Cohasset, MA 02025
Phone: (781)383-2100 **Fax:** (781)383-2727
Products: Vision image processing and graphics products. **SIC:** 5045 (Computers, Peripherals & Software). **Sales:** $5,000,000 (2000). **Emp:** 6. **Officers:** Ronald A. Massa, President.

■ 9044 ■ **Massachusetts Gas and Electric Lighting Supply Co.**
193 Friend St.
Boston, MA 02101-4022
Phone: (617)926-4700
Products: Electrical power equipment and supplies for the generation industry. **SIC:** 5063 (Electrical Apparatus & Equipment). **Sales:** $55,000,000 (1993). **Emp:** 195. **Officers:** Roger Weinreb, President.

■ 9045 ■ **Master International Corp.**
PO Box 25662
Los Angeles, CA 90025
Phone: (310)452-1229 **Fax:** (310)399-8600
URL: http://www.masterdistributors.com
Products: Relay switches, terminal blocks, and transformers. **SIC:** 5065 (Electronic Parts & Equipment Nec). **Est:** 1966. **Sales:** $52,600,000 (2000). **Emp:** 146. **Officers:** I.J. Nizam, President; S. New, CFO; Don Manssian, Dir. of Marketing.

■ 9046 ■ **Matthews Electric Supply Company Inc.**
3317 5th Ave. S
Birmingham, AL 35201
Phone: (205)254-3192 **Fax:** (205)254-0095
Products: Electrical equipment and supplies. **SIC:**

5063 (Electrical Apparatus & Equipment). **Est:** 1911. **Sales:** $25,000,000 (2000). **Emp:** 135. **Officers:** Hutch Cole Jr., President; Dave Stewart, VP of Sales; Arnetta Hartley, Vice President; Matthew H. Cole, Exec. VP; J.W. Jones, Dir of Human Resources.

■ **9047** ■ **Maverick Electric Supply Inc.**
9239 King Arthur
Dallas, TX 75247-3609
Phone: (214)630-8191 **Fax:** (214)630-4139
Products: Electrical supplies. **SIC:** 5063 (Electrical Apparatus & Equipment). **Est:** 1976. **Emp:** 39. **Officers:** Earl V. Davis, President; W.C. Nix Jr., Vice President; Robert A. Smart, Sec. & Treas.

■ **9048** ■ **Maxima Electrical Sales Company Inc.**
PO Box 398
Shawnee Mission, KS 66201
Phone: (913)722-1591
Products: Electrical equipment. **SIC:** 5063 (Electrical Apparatus & Equipment). **Est:** 1982. **Sales:** $20,000,000 (2000). **Emp:** 5. **Officers:** C.D. McCoullough, President.

■ **9049** ■ **Maxtec International Corp.**
175 Wall St.
Glendale Heights, IL 60139-1956
Phone: (773)889-1448 **Fax:** (773)794-9740
Products: Electronic systems and equipment. **SIC:** 5065 (Electronic Parts & Equipment Nec).

■ **9050** ■ **Mayer Electric Supply Co.**
3405 4th Ave. S
Birmingham, AL 35222-2300
Phone: (205)583-3500 **Fax:** (205)252-0315
E-mail: mayer@mayerelectric.com
URL: http://www.mayerelectric.com
Products: Electrical supplies, including wire, fittings, and conduit. **SIC:** 5063 (Electrical Apparatus & Equipment). **Est:** 1930. **Sales:** $327,000,000 (2000). **Emp:** 770. **Former Name:** Mayer Electric Co.

■ **9051** ■ **Mayer Electric Supply Co.**
PO Box 1328
Birmingham, AL 35201
Phone: (205)583-3500 **Fax:** (205)252-0315
URL: http://www.mayerelectric.com
Products: Electrical distribution equipment and supplies. **SIC:** 5063 (Electrical Apparatus & Equipment). **Est:** 1930. **Sales:** $327,000,000 (1999). **Emp:** 770. **Officers:** Charles A. Collat Sr., CEO & Chairman of the Board.

■ **9052** ■ **Mayer Electric Supply Company Inc.**
3405 4th Ave. S
PO Box 1328
Birmingham, AL 35222
Phone: (205)583-3500
Free: (800)444-8524 **Fax:** (205)252-0315
E-mail: mayer@mayerelectric.com
URL: http://www.mayerelectric.com
Products: Electrical equipment, including wiring and power distributing conduits. **SIC:** 5063 (Electrical Apparatus & Equipment). **Est:** 1930. **Sales:** $316,000,000 (2000). **Emp:** 750. **Officers:** Charles A. Collat, CEO; Jim Summerlin, COO & President; W. Joseph Lewellyn, Corporate Marketing Director.

■ **9053** ■ **Mayer-Hammant Equipment Inc.**
PO Box 733
Harvey, LA 70059
Phone: (504)368-4277 **Fax:** (504)368-4431
Products: Pumps; Lighting equipment; Parts and attachments for air and gas compressors; Compressors; Blowers and fans. **SICs:** 5063 (Electrical Apparatus & Equipment); 5084 (Industrial Machinery & Equipment). **Est:** 1971. **Sales:** $4,000,000 (2000). **Emp:** 32. **Officers:** Frank J. Hammant Jr., President.

■ **9054** ■ **McCullough Electric Co.**
419 Ft. Pitt Blvd.
Pittsburgh, PA 15219
Phone: (412)261-2420 **Fax:** (412)261-0862
E-mail: info@mcculloughelectric.com
URL: http://www.mcculloughelectric.com
Products: Motor control; Industrial and automation products. **SIC:** 5063 (Electrical Apparatus & Equipment). **Est:** 1904. **Sales:** $12,000,000 (2000).

Emp: 30. **Officers:** G.R. McCullough, President; G. Burleigh, Vice President; G.F. McCullough, Secretary.

■ **9055** ■ **McDiarmid Controls Inc.**
85579 Highway 99 S
Eugene, OR 97405
Phone: (541)726-1677 **Fax:** (541)747-9081
Products: Automated industrial controls; DC motors. **SIC:** 5063 (Electrical Apparatus & Equipment).

■ **9056** ■ **McDonald Equipment Co.**
37200 Vine St.
Willoughby, OH 44094-6346
Phone: (440)951-8222
Products: Electronic equipment. **SIC:** 5063 (Electrical Apparatus & Equipment). **Sales:** $5,000,000 (1994). **Emp:** 17. **Officers:** Scott McDonald, President.

■ **9057** ■ **McGowan Electric Supply Inc.**
PO Box 765
Jackson, MI 49204
Phone: (517)782-9301 **Fax:** (517)782-2511
Products: Electrical products, including wire and fittings. **SIC:** 5063 (Electrical Apparatus & Equipment). **Est:** 1962. **Sales:** $6,000,000 (2000). **Emp:** 20. **Officers:** Michael J. McGowan, President.

■ **9058** ■ **McJunkin Corp.**
U.S 460 E
Princeton, WV 24740
Phone: (304)425-7594
Free: (800)642-5819 **Fax:** (304)425-0981
Products: Steel pipes; Electrical items. **SICs:** 5063 (Electrical Apparatus & Equipment); 5085 (Industrial Supplies). **Emp:** 49.

■ **9059** ■ **McNaughton-McKay Electric Company**
1011 E 5th Ave.
Flint, MI 48501
Phone: (810)238-5611
Free: (800)388-0945 **Fax:** (810)767-4126
URL: http://www.mc-mc.com
Products: Electrical equipment and supplies. **SIC:** 5063 (Electrical Apparatus & Equipment). **Est:** 1910. **Sales:** $15,000,000 (2000). **Emp:** 40. **Officers:** Gregory Chun, General Mgr.; Bill Sarver, Sales Mgr. **Former Name:** Advance Electric Supply Company Inc.

■ **9060** ■ **McNaughton-McKay Electric Company Inc.**
1357 E Lincoln Ave.
Madison Heights, MI 48071
Phone: (810)399-7500 **Fax:** (810)399-6828
Products: Industrial controls. **SIC:** 5063 (Electrical Apparatus & Equipment). **Est:** 1910. **Sales:** $190,000,000 (2000). **Emp:** 310. **Officers:** William H. Bull, CEO & President; James Jackson, VP of Finance; David Beattie, VP of Marketing & Sales; Michael Jenkins, Data Processing Mgr.; Denise Bull, Personnel Mgr.

■ **9061** ■ **M.W. McWong International Inc.**
2544 Industrial Blvd.
West Sacramento, CA 95691
Phone: (916)371-8080 **Fax:** (916)371-6666
E-mail: mcwong@mcwonginc.com
Products: Electric industrial products, including ballasts. **SIC:** 5063 (Electrical Apparatus & Equipment). **Est:** 1984. **Emp:** 12. **Officers:** Margaret Wong, President.

■ **9062** ■ **Medler Electric Co.**
1313 Michigan Ave.
Alma, MI 48801
Phone: (517)463-1108 **Fax:** (517)463-4522
URL: http://www.medlerelectric.com
Products: Square D; Cutler hammer. **SIC:** 5063 (Electrical Apparatus & Equipment). **Est:** 1918. **Emp:** 140. **Officers:** Ronald S. Heine, President; Walter R. Lueth, CEO; Dave Simon, Human Resources Contact.

■ **9063** ■ **Meier Transmission Ltd.**
1845 E 40th St.
Cleveland, OH 44103
Phone: (216)881-0444
Free: (800)634-3764 **Fax:** (216)881-6093
E-mail: info@meiertransmission.com
URL: http://www.meiertransmission.com
Products: Power transmission products; Motion control products; Industrial safety products. **SIC:** 5063 (Electrical Apparatus & Equipment). **Est:** 1948. **Sales:** $15,000,000 (1999). **Emp:** 35. **Officers:** T.F. Bohardt, President; Richard Sisko, Vice President; Brian McMahon, Director, e-mail: bmcmahon@meiertransmission.com; Daryl Ryan, Customer Service Contact, e-mail: dryan@meiertransmission.com; Rick Sisko, e-mail: rsisko@meiertransmission.com.

■ **9064** ■ **Melan International Trading**
5943 Peacock Ridge Rd.
Rancho Palos Verdes, CA 90275-3406
Phone: (213)544-4109 **Fax:** (213)544-4109
Products: Medical equipment; Electric controllers; Electrical appliances. **SICs:** 5065 (Electronic Parts & Equipment Nec); 5063 (Electrical Apparatus & Equipment); 5064 (Electrical Appliances—Television & Radio); 5047 (Medical & Hospital Equipment). **Officers:** Paul Lan, President.

■ **9065** ■ **Menard Electronics Inc.**
6451 Choctaw Dr.
Baton Rouge, LA 70805
Phone: (504)355-0323 **Fax:** (504)351-6329
Products: Electronic parts and equipment. **SIC:** 5065 (Electronic Parts & Equipment Nec). **Officers:** William Menard, President.

■ **9066** ■ **Merchandise International**
2604 NE Industrial Dr., Ste. 230
North Kansas City, MO 64116
Phone: (816)842-6500
Products: Electronics equipment, including telephones and television sets. **SICs:** 5065 (Electronic Parts & Equipment Nec); 5064 (Electrical Appliances—Television & Radio). **Sales:** $4,000,000 (2000). **Emp:** 7. **Officers:** Gene Kane, Accountant.

■ **9067** ■ **Mesa Microwave Inc.**
2243 Verus St Ste. G
San Diego, CA 92154
Phone: (619)423-0705 **Fax:** (619)423-9006
Products: Radar communications equipment; Refurbishes waveguide and rotary couplers; Satellite communications components. **SIC:** 5063 (Electrical Apparatus & Equipment).

■ **9068** ■ **Metalink Corp.**
PO Box 1329
Chandler, AZ 85244
Phone: (480)926-0797 **Fax:** (480)926-1198
Products: In-circuit emulators for eight-bit and sixteen-bit microcontrollers. **SIC:** 5065 (Electronic Parts & Equipment Nec). **Officers:** Peter Secor, President.

■ **9069** ■ **Metro/North**
1199 Amboy Ave.
Edison, NJ 08837
Phone: (732)205-0088 **Fax:** (732)494-4550
Products: Electronic systems and equipment. **SIC:** 5065 (Electronic Parts & Equipment Nec).

■ **9070** ■ **Metrotek Industries Inc.**
12525 6th St. East
Treasure Island, FL 33706-2939
Phone: (727)547-8307 **Fax:** (727)547-0687
E-mail: fiberoptics@metrotek.com
URL: http://www.metrotek.com
Products: Fiberoptics. **SIC:** 5063 (Electrical Apparatus & Equipment). **Est:** 1989. **Sales:** $1,000,000 (2000). **Emp:** 3. **Officers:** Timothy C. Gressett, President; Thomas F. Tringall, Sales Mgr.

■ **9071** ■ **Meunier Electronics Supply Inc.**
3409 E Washington St.
Indianapolis, IN 46201
Phone: (317)635-3511
Free: (800)638-6437 **Fax:** (317)631-4707
E-mail: sales@meunierusa.com
URL: http://www.meunierusa.com
Products: Electronic parts, equipment, and tools. **SIC:**

5065 (Electronic Parts & Equipment Nec). **Est:** 1945. **Sales:** $4,000,000 (2000). **Emp:** 25. **Officers:** James F. Meunier, President; Mike Morone, Sales & Marketing Contact Contact; Rob Kerr, Customer Service Contact; Betty Jones, Human Resources Contact.

■ 9072 ■ Micro-Coax, Inc.
206 Jones Blvd.
Pottstown, PA 19464
Phone: (610)495-0110
Free: (800)223-2629   **Fax:** (610)495-6656
E-mail: sales@micro-coax.com
URL: http://www.micro-coax.com
Products: Coaxial cable; Delay lines; Microwave components. **SIC:** 5063 (Electrical Apparatus & Equipment). **Est:** 1985. **Sales:** $30,000,000 (2000). **Emp:** 200. **Officers:** Chris Kneizys, President. **Former Name:** Micro-Coax Communications Inc.

■ 9073 ■ Micro-Comp Industries Inc.
1271 Oakmead Pkwy.
Sunnyvale, CA 94086-4035
Phone: (408)733-2000   **Fax:** (408)970-0548
Products: Semi-conductors and parts. **SIC:** 5065 (Electronic Parts & Equipment Nec). **Est:** 1991. **Sales:** $4,000,000 (2000). **Emp:** 15. **Officers:** Tony Yu, President; Frank Yu, VP & CFO; Terry Snowdon, VP of Marketing & Sales.

■ 9074 ■ Microchip Technology Inc.
2355 W Chandler Blvd.
Chandler, AZ 85224-6199
Phone: (480)786-7200   **Fax:** (480)899-9210
URL: http://www.microchip.com
Products: Integrated circuits and development tools. **SIC:** 5065 (Electronic Parts & Equipment Nec). **Est:** 1989. **Sales:** $400,000,000 (2000). **Emp:** 2,600. **Officers:** Steve Sanghi, President & Chairman of the Board; G. Parnell, CFO.

■ 9075 ■ Microcomputer Cable Company Inc.
12200 Delta Dr.
Taylor, MI 48180
Phone: (734)946-9700
Products: Computer cable. **SIC:** 5045 (Computers, Peripherals & Software). **Sales:** $3,000,000 (1994). **Emp:** 19. **Officers:** Greg Danowski, President.

■ 9076 ■ Mid-Carolina Electric Supply Company, Inc.
1003 E Main
Rock Hill, SC 29730
Phone: (803)324-2944   **Fax:** (803)324-8643
Products: Electrical and lighting fixtures. **SIC:** 5063 (Electrical Apparatus & Equipment). **Emp:** 9. **Officers:** Steve Courtney.

■ 9077 ■ Mid-State Distributing
2600 Bell Ave.
Des Moines, IA 50321-1118
Phone: (515)244-7231   **Fax:** (515)244-3862
Products: Electronics equipment; Industrial supplies. **SICs:** 5063 (Electrical Apparatus & Equipment); 5085 (Industrial Supplies). **Sales:** $10,000,000 (2000). **Emp:** 49. **Officers:** Jim Hedden.

■ 9078 ■ Midland Suppliers Inc.
4804 Superior St.
Lincoln, NE 68504-1441
Phone: (402)466-4000
Free: (800)927-8728   **Fax:** (402)466-8728
E-mail: info@midlandsupplies.com
URL: http://www.midlandsupplies.com
Products: Electronic parts and equipment; Satellite parts. **SIC:** 5065 (Electronic Parts & Equipment Nec). **Est:** 1981. **Emp:** 15. **Officers:** Gary Willey, President, e-mail: gwilley@midlandsupplies.com

■ 9079 ■ Midtown Electric Supply
157 W 18th
New York, NY 10011-4101
Phone: (212)255-3388
Free: (888)255-3388   **Fax:** (212)255-3177
URL: http://www.midtownelectric.com
Products: Lighting tools and supplies; Communication and data equipment; Electrical supplies. **SIC:** 5063 (Electrical Apparatus & Equipment). **Est:** 1912. **Emp:** 55. **Officers:** Matthew Gold, President; Jonathan Gold, Vice President; Timothy Gold, Vice President.

■ 9080 ■ MIL-Pack Inc.
1380 Welsh Rd.
Montgomeryville, PA 18936
Phone: (215)628-8085
Products: Electrical and fiberoptical wire and cable. **SIC:** 5063 (Electrical Apparatus & Equipment). **Sales:** $3,000,000 (2000). **Emp:** 10.

■ 9081 ■ Mil-Spec Supply Inc.
21119 Superior St.
Chatsworth, CA 91311
Phone: (818)700-1001
Free: (800)266-9473   **Fax:** (818)700-1177
Products: Wire, cable, and tubing. **SIC:** 5063 (Electrical Apparatus & Equipment). **Est:** 1953. **Sales:** $1,900,000 (2000). **Emp:** 16. **Officers:** A.D. Lynn, President; Virginia Vitkowski, Controller; David Lynn, Sales Mgr.

■ 9082 ■ Milano Brothers International Corp.
378 SW 12th Ave.
Deerfield Beach, FL 33442-3106
Phone: (305)420-5000
Products: Electronics including capacitors and switches. **SICs:** 5065 (Electronic Parts & Equipment Nec); 5063 (Electrical Apparatus & Equipment). **Est:** 1941. **Sales:** $19,000,000 (2000). **Emp:** 68. **Officers:** Robert P. Milano, President.

■ 9083 ■ Milgray Electronics Inc.
220 Rabro Dr.
Hauppauge, NY 11788-4232
Phone: (516)420-9800
Free: (800)MIL-GRAY   **Fax:** (516)752-9870
Products: Batteries; Capacitors; Electronic coils; RF chokes; Semiconductors and related devices; Electric fans; Filters; Relays; Electronic wire and cable; Miscellaneous machinery products, including flexible metal hose and tubing, metal bellows, etc. **SIC:** 5065 (Electronic Parts & Equipment Nec). **Est:** 1951. **Sales:** $120,000,000 (2000). **Emp:** 375. **Officers:** Herbert S. Davidson, CEO & President; Richard Hyman, Exec. VP; John Tortorici, VP of Finance; Andy Epstien, VP of Operations.

■ 9084 ■ Miller Electric Co. (Omaha, Nebraska)
2501 St. Marys Ave.
Omaha, NE 68105
Phone: (402)341-6479   **Fax:** (402)341-1141
Products: Electrical apparatus and equipment, wiring supplies and fiber optics. **SIC:** 5063 (Electrical Apparatus & Equipment). **Sales:** $4,000,000 (1992). **Emp:** 100. **Officers:** Melvin N. Allen, President.

■ 9085 ■ Miller Wholesale Electric Supply Co., Inc.—Morristown Division
PO Box 337
Morristown, NJ 07963-0337
Phone: (973)538-1600
E-mail: sales@millerwholesale.com
URL: http://www.millerwholesale.com
Products: Electrical supplies, including wire, motor controls, panels, lamps, indoor and outdoor fixtures, circuit breakers, transformers, pipe, and batteries. **SIC:** 5063 (Electrical Apparatus & Equipment). **Est:** 1994. **Sales:** $6,000,000 (1999). **Emp:** 25. **Officers:** Robert Hirsch, President; J. Hess, CFO; Barry Miller, President. **Former Name:** Morristown Electrical Supply Co.

■ 9086 ■ Mills Communication Inc.
210 Pennsylvania Ave.
Westminster, MD 21157-4343
Phone: (410)876-8600   **Fax:** (410)857-1225
E-mail: millscom@cct.infi.net
URL: http://www.mills-wireless.com
Products: Commercial two-way radios. **SIC:** 5065 (Electronic Parts & Equipment Nec). **Est:** 1948. **Sales:** $2,000,000 (2000). **Emp:** 19. **Officers:** G. Mills, President; Fran Bosley; Kenneth Heinberger; Eugene Brewer, Sales/Marketing Contact; Candy Chapman, Customer Service Contact; G. Melvin Mills Jr., Human Resources Contact.

■ 9087 ■ Mills and Lupton Supply Co.
PO Box 1639
Chattanooga, TN 37401
Phone: (423)266-6171
Products: Industrial tools; Electrical components. **SICs:** 5063 (Electrical Apparatus & Equipment); 5085 (Industrial Supplies). **Est:** 1910. **Sales:** $11,000,000 (2000). **Emp:** 40. **Officers:** R. Richard Anderson, President; Harry H. Powell Jr., Exec. VP.

■ 9088 ■ Minnesota Electrical Supply Co.
PO Box 997
Willmar, MN 56201
Phone: (612)235-2255   **Fax:** (320)214-4242
URL: http://www.mnelectric.com
Products: Wire, fixtures, panels, and switches. **SIC:** 5063 (Electrical Apparatus & Equipment). **Est:** 1945. **Sales:** $17,000,000 (2000). **Emp:** 70. **Officers:** H.W. Linder, President; John Klaers, Controller.

■ 9089 ■ Missouri Valley Electric Co.
PO Box 419640
Kansas City, MO 64141
Phone: (816)471-5306
Products: Panel boards and strip gears. **SIC:** 5063 (Electrical Apparatus & Equipment). **Est:** 1914. **Sales:** $18,000,000 (2000). **Emp:** 75. **Officers:** C.R. Hopkins, President & Treasurer; Marc Horner, Exec. VP.

■ 9090 ■ R.W. Mitscher Company Inc.
9515 Main St.
Clarence, NY 14031
Phone: (716)759-2350   **Fax:** (716)759-6976
Products: Electrical equipment including wiring supplies and construction materials. **SIC:** 5063 (Electrical Apparatus & Equipment). **Sales:** $32,000,000 (2000). **Emp:** 33. **Officers:** R.L. Mitscher, President.

■ 9091 ■ MKM Electronic Components Inc.
997 Palmr Ave.
Mamaroneck, NY 10543-2409
Phone: (914)939-3940   **Fax:** (914)939-3973
Products: Electronic components. **SICs:** 5063 (Electrical Apparatus & Equipment); 5065 (Electronic Parts & Equipment Nec). **Sales:** $500,000 (1993). **Emp:** 6.

■ 9092 ■ Monarch Electric Company Inc.
PO Box CN40004
Fairfield, NJ 07004
Phone: (973)227-4151   **Fax:** (973)227-8455
Products: Electrical supplies, including pipe, wire, and fittings. **SIC:** 5063 (Electrical Apparatus & Equipment). **Est:** 1929. **Sales:** $34,900,000 (2000). **Emp:** 80. **Officers:** Max Pilger, President; S. Perlman, VP of Finance; B. Pilger, Dir. of Marketing.

■ 9093 ■ Monfort Electronic Marketing
6136 S Belmont St.
Indianapolis, IN 46217-9761
Phone: (317)872-8877   **Fax:** (317)876-2384
Products: Electronic systems and equipment. **SIC:** 5065 (Electronic Parts & Equipment Nec).

■ 9094 ■ Moniteq Research Labs Inc.
7640 Fulerton Rd.
Springfield, VA 22153-2814
Phone: (703)569-0195
Free: (800)989-9891   **Fax:** (703)569-0196
Products: Security and safety equipment. **SIC:** 5063 (Electrical Apparatus & Equipment). **Sales:** $1,000,000 (2000). **Emp:** 10.

■ 9095 ■ J.R. Morgan Agency
2540 E Thomas Rd.
Phoenix, AZ 85016
Phone: (602)912-9801   **Fax:** (602)912-9803
Products: Electronic systems and equipment. **SIC:** 5065 (Electronic Parts & Equipment Nec).

■ 9096 ■ Morley Murphy Co.
PO Box 19008
Green Bay, WI 54307-9008
Phone: (920)499-3171   **Fax:** (920)499-9409
Products: Electrical supplies, including light fixtures. **SIC:** 5063 (Electrical Apparatus & Equipment). **Est:** 1904. **Sales:** $20,000,000 (2000). **Emp:** 72. **Officers:** S.L. Stiles, President; R. Straebel, CFO; W. Edlbeck,

Dir. of Information Systems; J. Wigman, Dir of Human Resources.

■ 9097 ■ Morristown Electric Wholesalers Co.
1601 W Andrew Johnson
Morristown, TN 37814-3734
Phone: (423)586-5830 **Fax:** (423)586-2355
Products: Electrical parts, including wires, light bulbs, and light fixtures. **SIC:** 5063 (Electrical Apparatus & Equipment). **Emp:** 9.

■ 9098 ■ Morton Supply Inc.
1724 S 1st St.
Yakima, WA 98901
Phone: (509)248-3500 **Fax:** (509)248-3547
Products: Steel; Fabricated pipe and fittings; Electrical equipment and supplies. **SICs:** 5051 (Metals Service Centers & Offices); 5072 (Hardware); 5065 (Electronic Parts & Equipment Nec). **Est:** 1952. **Sales:** $2,700,000 (2000). **Emp:** 18. **Officers:** Arthur Berg, President; Gary McCauley, General Mgr.

■ 9099 ■ Mosebach Electric and Supply Co.
1315 Ridge Ave.
Pittsburgh, PA 15233-2102
Phone: (412)322-5000
Products: Electrical supplies. **SIC:** 5063 (Electrical Apparatus & Equipment). **Est:** 1924. **Sales:** $8,000,000 (2000). **Emp:** 29. **Officers:** George Bryant, General Mgr.

■ 9100 ■ Motloid Company
300 N Elizabeth St., 2N
Chicago, IL 60607
Phone: (312)226-2454
Free: (800)662-5021 **Fax:** (312)226-2480
Products: Medical, dental, and optical supplies. **SIC:** 5063 (Electrical Apparatus & Equipment).

■ 9101 ■ Motorola MIMS. VLSI Tech Center
4625 S Ash Ave Ste 12
Tempe, AZ 85282
Phone: (480)820-0885 **Fax:** (480)752-2759
Products: Designs modems and network management systems—very large scale integrated systems. **SIC:** 5063 (Electrical Apparatus & Equipment). **Officers:** Rashid Chaudhary, Director.

■ 9102 ■ Mountain Cable Industries Inc.
16026 W 5th Ave.
Golden, CO 80401-5518
Phone: (303)279-2825 **Fax:** (303)279-0285
Products: Electronic wire and cable; Peripheral computer equipment. **SICs:** 5063 (Electrical Apparatus & Equipment); 5045 (Computers, Peripherals & Software). **Officers:** Carol Meade, Chairman of the Board.

■ 9103 ■ Mouser Electronics
2401 Hwy. 287 N
Mansfield, TX 76063
Phone: (817)483-6828
Free: (800)346-6873 **Fax:** (817)483-6899
E-mail: sales@mouser.com
URL: http://www.mouser.com
Products: Electronic components, including resistors, diodes, capacitors, and connectors. **SIC:** 5065 (Electronic Parts & Equipment Nec). **Est:** 1964. **Sales:** $50,000,000 (2000). **Emp:** 350. **Officers:** Glenn Smith, President; Sharron Schmaltz.

■ 9104 ■ MRL Industries
19500 Nugget Blvd.
Sonora, CA 95370
Phone: (209)533-1990 **Fax:** (209)533-4079
Products: Electronic parts and systems for the computer chip and semiconductor industries. **SIC:** 5065 (Electronic Parts & Equipment Nec). **Officers:** Susie McEntire, VP of Finance.

■ 9105 ■ MSIS Semiconductor Inc.
2372 Qume Dr.Ste. B
San Jose, CA 95131
Phone: (408)944-6270 **Fax:** (408)944-6272
Products: Semiconductors and related solid-state devices. **SIC:** 5065 (Electronic Parts & Equipment Nec). **Sales:** $1,200,000 (2000). **Emp:** 5. **Officers:** Larry Matheny, President.

■ 9106 ■ Multi Communication Systems
30731 W 8 Mile Rd.
Livonia, MI 48152-1363
Phone: (248)478-5256 **Fax:** (248)478-5389
Products: Electric and electronic equipment; Electronic systems and equipment. **SIC:** 5065 (Electronic Parts & Equipment Nec). **Emp:** 49.
Officers: Lonnie Ervin.

■ 9107 ■ Jack H. Muntz Electrical Supply Co.
1211 23rd Ave.
Rockford, IL 61104
Phone: (815)968-8866
Products: Electrical supplies. **SIC:** 5063 (Electrical Apparatus & Equipment). **Sales:** $2,000,000 (2000). **Emp:** 13. **Officers:** Tom Eisner, President.

■ 9108 ■ Murata Erie North America Inc. State College Div.
1900 W College Ave.
State College, PA 16801
Phone: (814)237-1431 **Fax:** (814)238-0490
Products: Chip capacitors, filters, and oscillators. **SIC:** 5065 (Electronic Parts & Equipment Nec). **Est:** 1981. **Sales:** $87,000,000 (2000). **Emp:** 1,000. **Officers:** Fred Chanoki, President; Tony Tanabe, Controller; Jack Driscoll, VP of Marketing & Sales; Trieu Tran, Dir. of Information Systems.

■ 9109 ■ Murdock Companies Inc.
PO Box 2775
Wichita, KS 67201
Phone: (316)262-0401
Free: (800)876-6867 **Fax:** (316)262-4987
Products: Industrial distributor serving OEM and MRO customers with electric motors and controls, bearings, power transmission, hose, belting, hydraulic and pneumatic equipment and cutting tools. **SICs:** 5063 (Electrical Apparatus & Equipment); 5013 (Motor Vehicle Supplies & New Parts). **Sales:** $12,400,000 (1999). **Emp:** 43. **Officers:** Herb Coin, President; Brenda Blazer, CFO.

■ 9110 ■ Music People Inc.
PO Box 270648
West Hartford, CT 06127-0648
Phone: (860)236-7134
Free: (800)289-8889 **Fax:** (860)233-6888
Products: Audio equipment, microphones, music and audio stands. **SICs:** 5065 (Electronic Parts & Equipment Nec); 5099 (Durable Goods Nec). **Sales:** $10,000,000 (1999). **Emp:** 26. **Officers:** James R. Hennessey, Owner; John Gutowski, Accountant.

■ 9111 ■ Nappco Fastener Co.
11260 Hempstead Rd.
PO Box 55586
Houston, TX 77255-5586
Phone: (713)688-2521
Free: (800)580-2521 **Fax:** (713)957-4315
Products: Electrical hanging and fastening devices. **SIC:** 5063 (Electrical Apparatus & Equipment).

■ 9112 ■ Natchez Electric Supply
3051 Lynch
Jackson, MS 39209-7334
Phone: (601)352-5068 **Fax:** (601)352-7737
Products: Lamps; Alarm systems; Electric motors; Speed changers, drives, and gears. **SICs:** 5063 (Electrical Apparatus & Equipment); 5084 (Industrial Machinery & Equipment). **Emp:** 49. **Officers:** Dale McDonald, President; Kelly W. Durham, Branch Manager.

■ 9113 ■ National Barricade Co
6518 Ravenna Ave NE
Seattle, WA 98115
Phone: (206)523-4045 **Fax:** (206)525-2042
Products: Traffic control equipment and barricades; rental and sales. **SIC:** 5063 (Electrical Apparatus & Equipment). **Officers:** June Bryson, President.

■ 9114 ■ National Electrical Supply Corp.
1 Corporate Dr.
Holtsville, NY 11742-2006
Phone: (516)654-5533
Free: (800)678-9888 **Fax:** (516)654-1961
Products: Electrical supplies. **SIC:** 5063 (Electrical Apparatus & Equipment). **Est:** 1944. **Sales:**

$10,000,000 (1999). **Emp:** 100. **Officers:** Richard Berger, President; Genevieve Rossiello, Vice President.

■ 9115 ■ National Electro Sales Corp.
7110 Gerald Ave.
Van Nuys, CA 91406-3711
Phone: (818)781-0505 **Fax:** (818)786-2758
Products: Replacement batteries for consumer electronic products and AC & DC power adaptors. **SICs:** 5063 (Electrical Apparatus & Equipment); 5065 (Electronic Parts & Equipment Nec). **Sales:** $9,000,000 (2000). **Emp:** 30. **Officers:** K. J. Rothman, President & CFO.

■ 9116 ■ National Hardware and Supplies
5311 N Kedzie Ave.
Chicago, IL 60625
Phone: (773)463-1470 **Fax:** (773)583-5131
Products: Electrical supplies, including light bulbs. **SIC:** 5063 (Electrical Apparatus & Equipment). **Est:** 1949. **Sales:** $5,000,000 (2000). **Emp:** 35. **Officers:** R.W. Ramsden, President; J. Perell, General Mgr.

■ 9117 ■ National Plastics Corp.
4th & Gaskill Ave.
Jeannette, PA 15644
Phone: (412)523-5531 **Fax:** (412)523-5450
Products: Lighting fixtures. **SIC:** 5063 (Electrical Apparatus & Equipment). **Est:** 1945. **Sales:** $15,000,000 (2000). **Emp:** 25. **Officers:** Jack Millstein Jr., President; Fred Miller, Vice President; Gary Whitenight, Sales Mgr.

■ 9118 ■ National Switchgear Systems
649 Franklin St.
Lewisville, TX 75057
Phone: (972)420-0149
Free: (800)322-0149 **Fax:** (972)420-0938
URL: http://www.nationalswitchgear.com
Products: Switch gears and related products. **SIC:** 5063 (Electrical Apparatus & Equipment). **Est:** 1986. **Emp:** 25. **Officers:** Douglas Powell, President, e-mail: doug@nationalswitchgear.com; Robert Koren, VP of Sales, e-mail: robert@nationalswitchgear.com; Ross Smelley, VP of Production, e-mail: ross@ nationalswitchgear.com; Tammy Finn, Customer Service Contact, e-mail: tammy@ nationalswitchgear.com; Linda Klemme, Human Resources Contact, e-mail: linda@ nationalswitchgear.com.

■ 9119 ■ NECX Inc.
4 Technology Dr.
Peabody, MA 01960
Phone: (978)538-8000
Free: (800)922-6327 **Fax:** (978)538-8700
Products: Semiconductors, computer components, and peripherals. **SIC:** 5045 (Computers, Peripherals & Software). **Sales:** $501,000,000 (2000). **Emp:** 280. **Officers:** Henry Bertolon, CEO & President; Jeff Filmore, CFO.

■ 9120 ■ NEDCO Supply
4200 W Spring Mountain Rd.
Las Vegas, NV 89102-8748
Phone: (702)367-0400 **Fax:** (702)362-8365
Products: Electrical equipment and supplies. **SIC:** 5063 (Electrical Apparatus & Equipment). **Est:** 1982. **Sales:** $12,000,000 (2000). **Emp:** 30. **Officers:** Paul Winard; Marc Winard; Marshall E. Hunt.

■ 9121 ■ Nelson Electric Supply Co.
526 N Main St.
Tulsa, OK 74103
Phone: (918)583-1212
Products: Electrical equipment. **SIC:** 5063 (Electrical Apparatus & Equipment). **Sales:** $25,000,000 (1994). **Emp:** 58. **Officers:** Ken Mahl, General Mgr.; Rod Velasquez, Controller.

■ 9122 ■ Nelson Electric Supply Company Inc.
926 State St.
Racine, WI 53401
Phone: (414)637-7661 **Fax:** (414)637-2465
Products: Electrical supplies. **SIC:** 5063 (Electrical Apparatus & Equipment). **Est:** 1950. **Sales:** $14,000,000 (2000). **Emp:** 40. **Officers:** Richard Leuenberger, President.

■ 9123 ■ **Nesco Electrical Distributors Inc.**
PO Box 1484
Tupelo, MS 38802
Phone: (601)840-4750 **Fax:** (601)842-3139
Products: Electrical equipment and apparatus. **SIC:** 5063 (Electrical Apparatus & Equipment). **Est:** 1965. **Emp:** 30. **Officers:** Clarence E. Lomenick Jr., President; Joe C. Fowler, Dir. of Sales & Marketing.

■ 9124 ■ **Nevada Illumination Inc.**
2901 S Highland Dr. Bldg.3E
Las Vegas, NV 89109-1081
Phone: (702)735-8975
Products: Lighting systems. **SIC:** 5063 (Electrical Apparatus & Equipment). **Emp:** 12. **Officers:** Larry Cripe.

■ 9125 ■ **New American Electric Distributors, Inc.**
578 Perry St.
Trenton, NJ 08618
Phone: (609)394-1860 **Fax:** (609)394-0269
Products: Electrical apparatus and equipment. **SIC:** 5063 (Electrical Apparatus & Equipment). **Officers:** Thomas Phillips, President.

■ 9126 ■ **New DEST Corp.**
4180 Business Ctr. Dr.
Fremont, CA 94538
Phone: (510)249-0330 **Fax:** (510)249-0344
Products: Electronic scanners and optical character recognition software. **SIC:** 5045 (Computers, Peripherals & Software). **Sales:** $2,000,000 (1993). **Emp:** 6. **Officers:** Ting Wang, President; Twefun Chung, CFO.

■ 9127 ■ **New Jersey Semiconductor Products Inc.**
20 Stern Ave.
Springfield, NJ 07081
Phone: (201)376-2922 **Fax:** (201)376-8960
Products: Electronic parts; Diodes; Resistors. **SIC:** 5065 (Electronic Parts & Equipment Nec). **Est:** 1966. **Sales:** $4,000,000 (2000). **Emp:** 100. **Officers:** R. Hildebrandt, President; E. McGrath, CFO; J. De Falco, Dir. of Marketing; S. Pellegrino, Office Mgr.

■ 9128 ■ **New York Fastener Corp.**
599 Industrial Ave.
Paramus, NJ 07652
Phone: (201)265-8770
Free: (800)631-1993 **Fax:** (201)265-3765
Products: Electrical hanging and fastening devices. **SIC:** 5063 (Electrical Apparatus & Equipment).

■ 9129 ■ **Newark Electronics Corp.**
2021 E Hennepin Ave., Ste. 338
Minneapolis, MN 55413-2725
Phone: (612)331-6350 **Fax:** (612)331-1504
Products: Electronic parts. **SIC:** 5065 (Electronic Parts & Equipment Nec). **Emp:** 35. **Officers:** Anthony Schmid.

■ 9130 ■ **Nixon Power Services Co.**
297 Hill Ave.
Nashville, TN 37210
Phone: (615)244-0650
Products: Generators. **SIC:** 5063 (Electrical Apparatus & Equipment).

■ 9131 ■ **North Atlantic Communications Inc.**
207 Newtown Rd.
Plainview, NY 11803
Phone: (516)756-9000 **Fax:** (516)756-9128
Products: Communications Systems and Equipmentt. **SIC:** 5065 (Electronic Parts & Equipment Nec). **Sales:** $2,000,000 (2000). **Emp:** 15.

■ 9132 ■ **North Atlantic Engineering Co.**
15 Spencer St.
Newton, MA 02465
Phone: (617)964-6180
Free: (800)696-6180 **Fax:** (617)965-3829
Products: Warm air heating and cooling equipment; Alarm systems; Closed circuit television equipment. **SICs:** 5065 (Electronic Parts & Equipment Nec); 5075 (Warm Air Heating & Air-Conditioning); 5063 (Electrical Apparatus & Equipment). **Officers:** Brad Keyes, President.

■ 9133 ■ **North Coast Electric Co.**
110 110th NE, Ste. 616
Bellevue, WA 98004-5840
Phone: (425)454-1747 **Fax:** (425)454-7497
URL: http://www.ncelec.com
Products: Electrical equipment and supplies. **SIC:** 5063 (Electrical Apparatus & Equipment). **Est:** 1913. **Sales:** $229,000,000 (2000). **Emp:** 550. **Officers:** R.L. Lemman, Chairman of the Board; Peter R. Lemman, President; Dean M. Lemman, Exec. VP; Ronald G. Stewart, VP & CFO.

■ 9134 ■ **North Electric Supply Inc.**
1290 N Opdyke Rd.
Auburn Hills, MI 48326
Phone: (313)373-1070
Products: Electrical parts and supplies. **SIC:** 5063 (Electrical Apparatus & Equipment). **Est:** 1972. **Sales:** $10,000,000 (2000). **Emp:** 20. **Officers:** Harry Scarfe, President.

■ 9135 ■ **North Valley Distributing**
945 Merchant
PO Box 493789
Redding, CA 96049-3789
Phone: (530)222-1500
Free: (800)854-4555 **Fax:** (530)222-3543
E-mail: nvd@c-zone.net
Products: Electrical equipment; Electric and electronic equipment. **SICs:** 5063 (Electrical Apparatus & Equipment); 5065 (Electronic Parts & Equipment Nec). **Est:** 1983. **Emp:** 28. **Officers:** John Tetens, President; John Thomas, Vice President; Carl Kight, Human Resource Contact.

■ 9136 ■ **Northern Electronics Automation**
PO Box 4760
Manchester, NH 03108-4760
Phone: (603)669-6080 **Fax:** (603)669-7033
E-mail: sales@neainc.com
URL: http://www.neainc.com
Products: Circuit board assembly equipment. **SIC:** 5065 (Electronic Parts & Equipment Nec). **Est:** 1988. **Sales:** $10,000,000 (2000). **Emp:** 35. **Officers:** Steven Le Boeuf, President; Charles R. Morshead Jr., Vice President; Elizabeth Miller, Controller.

■ 9137 ■ **Northern Electronics Automation**
PO Box 4760
Manchester, NH 03108-4760
Phone: (603)669-6080 **Fax:** (603)669-7033
Products: Electrical and electronic equipment and supplies. **SIC:** 5065 (Electronic Parts & Equipment Nec). **Sales:** $10,000,000 (2000). **Emp:** 35.

■ 9138 ■ **Northern Power Technologies**
PO Box 2063
Rapid City, SD 57709
Phone: (605)342-2520 **Fax:** (605)343-9688
Products: Uninterruptible power systems and batteries. **SIC:** 5063 (Electrical Apparatus & Equipment). **Emp:** 2. **Officers:** Gary N. Johnson, e-mail: garyj@enetis.net.

■ 9139 ■ **Northern Telecom Inc.**
1771 E Flamingo Rd., Ste. B100
Las Vegas, NV 89119
Phone: (702)733-3800
Products: Telecommunications digital switching equipment. **SIC:** 5065 (Electronic Parts & Equipment Nec).

■ 9140 ■ **Northland Electric Supply Co.**
PO Box 1275
Minneapolis, MN 55440
Phone: (612)341-6100
Products: Electrical supplies, including motor controls. **SIC:** 5063 (Electrical Apparatus & Equipment). **Est:** 1920. **Sales:** $70,000,000 (2000). **Emp:** 155. **Officers:** Jack M. Vilett Jr., President; Marvin Spartz, VP of Finance; Fred Eiseman, General Mgr.; Julie Saari, Human Resources Mgr.

■ 9141 ■ **Northwest Electrical Supply**
30 S Main
Mt. Prospect, IL 60056-3224
Phones: (847)255-3706 (847)225-3700
(815)363-1800 **Fax:** (847)255-4321
Products: Electrical supplies. **SIC:** 5063 (Electrical

Apparatus & Equipment). **Emp:** 49. **Officers:** Thomas Reindl; Dennis Reindl; James Mill.

■ 9142 ■ **Norvac Electronics Inc.**
PO Box 277
Beaverton, OR 97075-0277
Phone: (503)644-1025
Free: (800)938-1025 **Fax:** (503)644-9298
Products: Electronic systems and equipment; Electronic parts. **SIC:** 5065 (Electronic Parts & Equipment Nec). **Est:** 1977. **Emp:** 30. **Officers:** Keith Dodd, President; Mona E. Anderson, Sec. & Treas.

■ 9143 ■ **Norvell Electronics Inc.**
2251 Chenault Dr.
Carrollton, TX 75006-5031
Phone: (214)233-0020
Products: Electronic components. **SICs:** 5063 (Electrical Apparatus & Equipment); 5065 (Electronic Parts & Equipment Nec). **Est:** 1955. **Sales:** $20,000,000 (2000). **Emp:** 70. **Officers:** A.W. Tvrdik, President; Carlotta Rhodes, VP & CFO; Bill Clem, VP of Sales.

■ 9144 ■ **Nova-Net Communications Inc.**
58 Inverness Dr. E
Englewood, CO 80112
Phone: (303)799-0990 **Fax:** (303)792-2813
URL: http://www.nova-netcomm.com
Products: Satellite communications equipment and network services. **SIC:** 5065 (Electronic Parts & Equipment Nec). **Est:** 1984. **Sales:** $10,000,000 (1999). **Emp:** 16. **Officers:** Dave Christenson, e-mail: david_christenson@nova-netcomm.com; Don Rowe, e-mail: don_rowe@nova-netcomm.com; Dana Scantland, e-mail: dana_scantland@nova-netcomm.com.

■ 9145 ■ **Nova Science Inc.**
9101 E Gelding Dr.
Scottsdale, AZ 85260
Phone: (480)860-4447 **Fax:** (480)860-1376
Products: Test burn-in sockets for semiconductors. **SIC:** 5065 (Electronic Parts & Equipment Nec). **Sales:** $1,000,000 (1999). **Emp:** 7. **Officers:** Vern Griffin, President.

■ 9146 ■ **Novellus Systems Inc.**
4000 N 1st St.
San Jose, CA 95134
Phone: (408)943-9700 **Fax:** (408)943-3422
Products: chemical vapor deposition systems. **SIC:** 5065 (Electronic Parts & Equipment Nec). **Sales:** $592,700,000 (1999). **Emp:** 1,524. **Officers:** Richard S. Hill, CEO & Chairman of the Board; Robert H. Smith, Exec. VP of Finance & Admin.

■ 9147 ■ **NTE Electronics Inc.**
44 Farrand St.
Bloomfield, NJ 07003
Phone: (973)748-5089
Free: (800)631-1250 **Fax:** (973)748-6224
E-mail: general@nteinc.com
URL: http://www.nteinc.com
Products: Replacement semiconductors; Relays; Capacitors; Resistors; Flyback transformers; Hook-Up wire; Potentiometers; Trimmers; Kester solder; Solder; Flux; Data networking products. **SIC:** 5065 (Electronic Parts & Equipment Nec). **Est:** 1974. **Emp:** 30. **Officers:** William Horstmann, VP & General Merchandising Mgr.; Judy Flaherty, Controller.

■ 9148 ■ **Nu Horizons Electronics Corp.**
70 Maxess Rd.
Melville, NY 11747
Phone: (516)226-6000 **Fax:** (516)396-5060
URL: http://www.nuhorizons.com
Products: Semiconductors; Microprocessors. **SIC:** 5065 (Electronic Parts & Equipment Nec). **Est:** 1982. **Sales:** $202,800,000 (2000). **Emp:** 400. **Officers:** Irving Lubman, CEO & Chairman of the Board; Paul Durano, VP of Finance; David Bowers, VP of Marketing; Mark Lamorte, Dir. of Information Systems; Robert Valone, Vice President.

■ 9149 ■ **Nunn Electric Supply Corp.**
105-19 Polk St.
Amarillo, TX 79189
Phone: (806)376-4581 **Fax:** (806)376-4154
Products: Electrical equipment and supplies; Plumbing equipment and supplies; Electronics and home appliances. **SICs:** 5063 (Electrical Apparatus & Equipment); 5064 (Electrical Appliances—Television & Radio). **Est:** 1910. **Sales:** $100,000,000 (2000). **Emp:** 375. **Officers:** Carl D. Hare, Chairman; Robert Burdette, President.

■ 9150 ■ **NWCS Inc.**
7006 27th St. W, No. E
Tacoma, WA 98466-5281
Phone: (253)566-8866 **Fax:** (253)566-4601
Products: Electronic systems and equipment; Electronic parts; Communication systems and equipment. **SIC:** 5065 (Electronic Parts & Equipment Nec). **Officers:** Martin Darrah, President.

■ 9151 ■ **Ohio Valley Sound Inc.**
20 E Sycamore St.
Evansville, IN 47713
Phone: (812)425-6173
Products: Electronic parts and equipment. **SIC:** 5065 (Electronic Parts & Equipment Nec). **Sales:** $3,000,000 (2000). **Emp:** 8. **Officers:** Ken Christian, General Mgr.

■ 9152 ■ **O.K. Electric Supply Co.**
PO Box 998
Perth Amboy, NJ 08862
Phone: (908)826-6100 **Fax:** (908)826-6540
Products: Electrical supplies, including wire, fuses, and connect switches. **SIC:** 5063 (Electrical Apparatus & Equipment). **Est:** 1919. **Sales:** $12,000,000 (2000). **Emp:** 30. **Officers:** John W. Nesti, President & CFO; Jerry Nesti, Dir. of Purchasing; Joan Messina, Human Resources.

■ 9153 ■ **OKI Semiconductor**
785 N Mary Ave.
Sunnyvale, CA 94086
Phone: (408)720-1900 **Fax:** (408)720-1918
Products: Semiconductors. **SIC:** 5065 (Electronic Parts & Equipment Nec). **Sales:** $40,000,000 (2000). **Emp:** 145. **Officers:** Hisao Baba, President; Graham Sangster, Accountant.

■ 9154 ■ **Olflex Wire and Cable Inc.**
30 Plymouth St.
Fairfield, NJ 07004-1697
Phone: (201)575-1101
Free: (888)789-FLEX **Fax:** (201)575-7178
E-mail: sales@olflex.com
URL: http://www.olflex.com
Products: Robotics cable; Cord grips; Flexible conduit; Custom cable; Cable track; Custom assemblies. **SIC:** 5063 (Electrical Apparatus & Equipment). **Est:** 1976. **Sales:** $40,000,000 (2000). **Emp:** 108. **Officers:** John Ciccone, President.

■ 9155 ■ **Onan Indiana**
5125 Beck Dr.
Elkhart, IN 46514
Phone: (219)262-4611 **Fax:** (219)295-8000
Products: Generators. **SIC:** 5084 (Industrial Machinery & Equipment). **Est:** 1993. **Emp:** 24. **Officers:** Mark Fortney, General Mgr.; Mark Fortney, Sales/Marketing Contact; Marrianne Vandygriff, Customer Service Contact; Jan Plummer, Human Resources Contact.

■ 9156 ■ **One Source Distributors**
6154 Nancy Ridge Dr.
San Diego, CA 92121-3223
Phone: (619)452-9001
Free: (800)350-9001 **Fax:** (619)597-1948
E-mail: mktngdpt@1sourcedist.com
URL: http://www.1sourcedist.com
Products: Electrical and electronic industrial automation products. **SICs:** 5063 (Electrical Apparatus & Equipment); 5085 (Industrial Supplies). **Est:** 1983. **Sales:** $60,000,000 (2000). **Emp:** 135. **Officers:** Robert S. Zamarripa, President; Paul S. Judge, Sr. VP of Sales; Lauren M. Reyno, Vice President; Carol Ulak, Sales/Marketing Contact; Stuart Builas, VP of Marketing; Eric Vielbig, Customer Service Contact; Rick Cobabe, Human Resources Contact.

■ 9157 ■ **Ontario Supply Corp.**
100 N Mohawk
Cohoes, NY 12047-1707
Phone: (518)237-4723 **Fax:** (518)237-9063
Products: Electrical equipment. **SIC:** 5063 (Electrical Apparatus & Equipment). **Emp:** 24. **Officers:** Ted Smith.

■ 9158 ■ **Operations Technology Inc.**
Lambert Rd.
PO Box 408
Blairstown, NJ 07825
Phone: (908)362-6200
Free: (800)869-5031 **Fax:** (908)362-5966
Products: Electronic equipment, including differential press laminators, automatic inspection equipment, measuring equipment, visual inspection equipment, video measurement equipment, and desktop measurement equipment. **SICs:** 5065 (Electronic Parts & Equipment Nec); 5049 (Professional Equipment Nec). **Officers:** Richard B. Amon, President.

■ 9159 ■ **Optical Cable Corp.**
PO Box 11967
Roanoke, VA 24022-1967
Phone: (540)265-0690
Free: (800)622-7711 **Fax:** (540)265-0724
URL: http://www.occfiber.com
Products: Fiber optic cables. **SIC:** 5063 (Electrical Apparatus & Equipment). **Est:** 1983. **Sales:** $50,700,000 (1999). **Emp:** 180. **Officers:** Bob Kopstein, CEO & President, e-mail: kopstein@occfiber.com; Susan S. Adams, Sales/Marketing Contact, e-mail: sadams@occfiber.com; Joyce Chevalier, Human Resources Contact, e-mail: jchevali@occfiber.com; Luke Huybrechts, Sr. VP of Sales, e-mail: lhuybrec@occfiber.com; Kenneth W. Harber, VP of Sales.

■ 9160 ■ **Optronics Inc.**
350 N Wheeler St.
Ft. Gibson, OK 74434-8965
Phone: (918)683-9514
Free: (800)FOG-LITE **Fax:** (918)683-9517
E-mail: sales@optronicsinc.com
URL: http://www.optronicsinc.com
Products: Electrical products and accessories for the automotive, OEM, recreation, hardware, emergency, and industrial markets. **SIC:** 5063 (Electrical Apparatus & Equipment). **Est:** 1972. **Sales:** $12,500,000 (2000). **Emp:** 41. **Officers:** Ralph Schrader, VP & CFO; Duncan M. Payne, President; Mark Corlee, COO; Marshall Ross, Recreation National Sales Mgr.; Brett Johnson, Automotive/Industrial National Sales Mgr. **Alternate Name:** Nightblaster.

■ 9161 ■ **Orton Industries Inc.**
PO Box 620130
Atlanta, GA 30362-2130
Phone: (404)986-9999
Free: (800)282-5685 **Fax:** (404)987-9990
Products: Electronic parts and equipment. **SIC:** 5065 (Electronic Parts & Equipment Nec). **Officers:** James Alexander, President.

■ 9162 ■ **Ottawa Electric Inc.**
1051 Jackson St.
Grand Haven, MI 49417
Phone: (616)733-2828
Products: Electric motors and equipment. **SIC:** 5063 (Electrical Apparatus & Equipment).

■ 9163 ■ **Ouzunoff & Associates**
74 E Rocks Rd.
Norwalk, CT 06851
Phone: (203)847-3285 **Fax:** (203)847-3526
Products: Electronic systems and equipment. **SIC:** 5065 (Electronic Parts & Equipment Nec).

■ 9164 ■ **Owens Electric Supply Companies Inc.**
PO Box 3427
Wilmington, NC 28406
Phone: (910)791-6058 **Fax:** (910)395-1376
Products: Conduit and conduit bodies; Lamps; Fixtures; Motor controls; Breakers, transformers, fuses, and switches; Wire and wiring devices; Cable. **SICs:** 5064 (Electrical Appliances—Television & Radio); 5065 (Electronic Parts & Equipment Nec). **Est:** 1970. **Sales:** $4,000,000 (2000). **Emp:** 13. **Officers:** John F. Owens Jr. Jr., President; Gregg Martin, VP of Marketing.

■ 9165 ■ **Owensboro Electric Supply**
1200 Moseley St.
PO Box 1628
Owensboro, KY 42303
Phone: (502)684-0606
Free: (800)537-6372 **Fax:** (502)683-6256
Products: Electrical conduit and conduit fittings; Power wire and cable; Electrical boxes and fittings; Switches; Lighting equipment; Sanitary ware, china or enameled iron. **SICs:** 5063 (Electrical Apparatus & Equipment); 5085 (Industrial Supplies). **Sales:** $10,000,000 (2000). **Emp:** 49. **Officers:** Mike Thompson.

■ 9166 ■ **Pabco Inc.**
PO Box 219
Perham, MN 56573-0219
Phone: (218)346-6660 **Fax:** (218)346-6664
Products: Electronic systems and equipment; Electronic parts. **SIC:** 5065 (Electronic Parts & Equipment Nec). **Officers:** William Donaldson, President.

■ 9167 ■ **Pac States Electric Wholesalers**
757 E Washington Blvd.
Los Angeles, CA 90021-3092
Phone: (213)749-7881
Free: (800)445-7739 **Fax:** (213)746-4914
Products: Electrical equipment and supplies; Building wire and cable; Tools. **SICs:** 5063 (Electrical Apparatus & Equipment); 5085 (Industrial Supplies). **Emp:** 16. **Officers:** Henry Haines.

■ 9168 ■ **Pace Electronics Inc.**
PO Box 6937
Rochester, MN 55903-6937
Phone: (507)288-1853
Free: (800)444-7223 **Fax:** (507)288-0831
E-mail: Kent@Pacemso.com
URL: http://www.pacemso.com
Products: Satellite parts; Electronic and satellite equipment. **SIC:** 5065 (Electronic Parts & Equipment Nec). **Est:** 1971. **Emp:** 30. **Officers:** Patrick J. Deutsch, President, e-mail: Pat@Pacemso.com.

■ 9169 ■ **Pacific Electrical Supply**
1906 Republic Ave.
San Leandro, CA 94577-4221
Phone: (510)483-0931 **Fax:** (510)352-9980
Products: Electrical products. **SIC:** 5063 (Electrical Apparatus & Equipment). **Emp:** 51. **Officers:** A. P. Russello.

■ 9170 ■ **Pacific Magtron Inc.**
1600 California Cir.
Milpitas, CA 95035
Phone: (408)956-8888 **Fax:** (408)956-8488
E-mail: sales@pacmag.com
URL: http://www.pacmag.com
Products: Storage; Multimedia peripheral. **SIC:** 5045 (Computers, Peripherals & Software). **Est:** 1989. **Sales:** $105,000,000 (1999). **Emp:** 100. **Officers:** Ted Li, President.

■ 9171 ■ **Pacific Radio Exchange Inc.**
969 N La Brea Ave.
Hollywood, CA 90038
Phone: (213)969-2035
Products: Electronic components. **SICs:** 5063 (Electrical Apparatus & Equipment); 5065 (Electronic Parts & Equipment Nec).

■ 9172 ■ **Pacific Southwest Sales Company Inc.**
4600 District Blvd.
Vernon, CA 90058
Phone: (213)582-6852 **Fax:** (213)582-2145
Products: Power struts; Steel channels; Extension cords; Conduit accessories. **SICs:** 5039 (Construction Materials Nec); 5084 (Industrial Machinery & Equipment). **Est:** 1960. **Sales:** $6,700,000 (2000). **Emp:** 20. **Officers:** Ervin H. Unvert, President; Donald V. Beisswanger, CFO; Curl Curtis, Dir. of Marketing & Sales.

■ 9173 ■ Paige Electric Company L.P.
PO Box 368
Union, NJ 07083-0368
Phone: (908)687-7810 **Fax:** (908)687-2722
Products: Wire cable. **SIC:** 5063 (Electrical Apparatus & Equipment). **Est:** 1958. **Sales:** $45,000,000 (2000). **Emp:** 70. **Officers:** L.W. Grotta, President; William Watkins, Controller.

■ 9174 ■ Pair Electronics Inc.
107 Trade St.
Greenville, NC 27834-6851
Phone: (919)756-2291 **Fax:** (919)756-2056
Products: Electronic systems and equipment; Electronic parts. **SIC:** 5065 (Electronic Parts & Equipment Nec). **Officers:** Percy Pair, President.

■ 9175 ■ PairGain Technologies Inc.
14402 Franklin Ave.
Tustin, CA 92780
Phone: (714)832-9922
Free: (800)370-9670 **Fax:** (714)832-9924
Products: Telephone transmission equipment based on high-speed digital subscriber line technology. **SIC:** 5065 (Electronic Parts & Equipment Nec). **Sales:** $274,000,000 (1999). **Emp:** 692. **Officers:** Charles S. Strauch, Chairman of the Board; Charles W. McBrayer, Sr. VP & CFO.

■ 9176 ■ Palco Electronics
18676 Eureka Rd.
Southgate, MI 48195-2925
Phone: (734)283-1313 **Fax:** (734)283-1855
Products: Electronic parts; Electric and electronic equipment; Motor vehicle radios. **SIC:** 5065 (Electronic Parts & Equipment Nec). **Officers:** Anthony Palmieri, Owner.

■ 9177 ■ Palmieri Associates
369 Passaic Ave., Ste. 116
Fairfield, NJ 07004
Phone: (973)882-1266 **Fax:** (973)882-1221
E-mail: jpalm6@aol.com
Products: Closed circuit televisions; Fiber optic wire and cable. **SICs:** 5064 (Electrical Appliances—Television & Radio); 5063 (Electrical Apparatus & Equipment). **Est:** 1984. **Emp:** 8.

■ 9178 ■ Panasonic Industrial Co.
2 Panasonic Way
Secaucus, NJ 07094
Phone: (201)348-7000
Products: Electronic parts and equipment. **SIC:** 5065 (Electronic Parts & Equipment Nec). **Sales:** $450,000,000 (2000). **Emp:** 1,050. **Officers:** Yoshinori Kobe, President; Ted Takahasi, VP of Finance.

■ 9179 ■ Park Corporation
PO Box 1488
Green Valley, AZ 85622
Phone: (520)648-1630 **Fax:** (520)647-0832
Products: Used machine tools; Used transformers and switchgears; Used electrical motors and generators; Used highway tractors and trailers; Used mining equipment. **SICs:** 5063 (Electrical Apparatus & Equipment); 5082 (Construction & Mining Machinery); 5065 (Electronic Parts & Equipment Nec); 5084 (Industrial Machinery & Equipment). **Officers:** Donald L. Cochrane, Sales & Purchasing.

■ 9180 ■ Patrick Electric Supply Co.
301 11th Ave. S
Nashville, TN 37203-4003
Phone: (615)242-1891 **Fax:** (615)726-2511
Products: Electronic systems and equipment; Electronic parts. **SIC:** 5065 (Electronic Parts & Equipment Nec). **Officers:** Roy Williams, President.

■ 9181 ■ PC Drilling Control Co.
4932 Highway 169 N
Minneapolis, MN 55428-4026
Phone: (612)535-8377 **Fax:** (612)535-8378
Products: Printed circuit boards. **SIC:** 5065 (Electronic Parts & Equipment Nec). **Officers:** Grant Hanson, President.

■ 9182 ■ PCE Inc.
468 Industrial Way W
Eatontown, NJ 07724
Phone: (732)542-7711
Products: Printed circuit boards. **SIC:** 5065 (Electronic Parts & Equipment Nec). **Sales:** $31,000,000 (2000). **Emp:** 76. **Officers:** Moshe Amit, President; Al Scipionie, Treasurer.

■ 9183 ■ PCI Rutherford Controls Intl. Corp.
2697 International Pkwy. 5, Ste. 100
Virginia Beach, VA 23452
Phone: (757)427-1230
Free: (800)899-5625 **Fax:** (757)427-9549
E-mail: sales@rutherfordusa.com
URL: http://www.rutherfordcontrols.com
Products: Electric locking hardware. **SIC:** 5065 (Electronic Parts & Equipment Nec). **Est:** 1990. **Emp:** 15. **Officers:** Tracy Rutherford, VP of Operations; David Halls, VP of Sales. **Former Name:** Rutherford Controls Inc.

■ 9184 ■ Pearson Electronics Inc.
1860 Embarcadero Rd.
Palo Alto, CA 94303
Phone: (650)494-6444 **Fax:** (650)494-6716
Products: Transformers; Current-monitoring, high-voltage pulse and capacitive voltage dividers. **SIC:** 5065 (Electronic Parts & Equipment Nec). **Sales:** $2,000,000 (1999). **Emp:** 18. **Officers:** Paul Pearson, CEO.

■ 9185 ■ Peer Light Inc.
301 Toland St.
San Francisco, CA 94124-1145
Phone: (415)543-8883 **Fax:** (415)957-1088
Products: Light fixtures; Electrical supplies. **SIC:** 5063 (Electrical Apparatus & Equipment). **Est:** 1930. **Sales:** $4,000,000 (2000). **Emp:** 10. **Officers:** Tony Leong, President.

■ 9186 ■ Peerless Electric Supply Co.
1401 Stadium Dr.
Indianapolis, IN 46202
Phone: (317)635-2361 **Fax:** (317)638-0019
Products: Electrical supplies, including wire, circuits, and fuses. **SIC:** 5063 (Electrical Apparatus & Equipment). **Est:** 1939. **Sales:** $30,000,000 (2000). **Emp:** 83. **Officers:** B.A. Butz, President; Ronald Fitzwater, CFO; John C. Gill, Dir. of Sales.

■ 9187 ■ PEI Genesis
2180 Hornig Rd.
Philadelphia, PA 19116
Phone: (215)673-0400
Free: (800)523-0727 **Fax:** (215)552-8022
Products: Electrical supplies including connectors, relays, wires, switches, lamps, and fixtures. **SICs:** 5065 (Electronic Parts & Equipment Nec); 5063 (Electrical Apparatus & Equipment). **Est:** 1959. **Sales:** $45,000,000 (2000). **Emp:** 190. **Officers:** Steve Fisher, President; Debbie Cader, Treasurer & Controller; Russ Dorwart, VP of Marketing.

■ 9188 ■ Peninsular Electric Distributors Inc.
PO Box 2887
West Palm Beach, FL 33402
Phone: (561)832-1626 **Fax:** (561)832-7267
Products: Electrical equipment for the construction industry. **SIC:** 5063 (Electrical Apparatus & Equipment). **Sales:** $28,000,000 (2000). **Emp:** 68. **Officers:** Pierre A. Larmoyeux Jr., President; Bethann Brock, Controller.

■ 9189 ■ Peninsular Electronic Distributors
PO Box 2887
West Palm Beach, FL 33402
Phone: (561)832-1626 **Fax:** (561)832-7267
Products: Electrical equipment, including wire, batteries, and light bulbs. **SIC:** 5063 (Electrical Apparatus & Equipment). **Sales:** $2,000,000 (2000). **Emp:** 49. **Officers:** Pierre Larmoyeux.

■ 9190 ■ Penstock
6321 San Ignacio Ave.
San Jose, CA 95119
Phone: (408)730-0300
Free: (800)736-7625 **Fax:** (408)730-4782
Products: Microwave chips. **SIC:** 5065 (Electronic

Parts & Equipment Nec). **Est:** 1975. **Sales:** $120,000,000 (2000). **Emp:** 150. **Officers:** Jerry Juinnell, CEO; Rob Hagen, CFO; Steve Ulett, Dir. of Marketing; Jerry Quinnell, Dir. of Data Processing; Lynn Arbrca, Dir of Human Resources.

■ 9191 ■ Persona Technologies Inc.
455 Valley Dr.
Brisbane, CA 94005-1209
Products: Cables; Audiovisual equipment. **SICs:** 5063 (Electrical Apparatus & Equipment); 5064 (Electrical Appliances—Television & Radio).

■ 9192 ■ PerTronix Inc.
440 E Arrow Hwy.
San Dimas, CA 91773-3340
Phone: (909)599-5955
Free: (800)827-3758 **Fax:** (909)599-6424
URL: http://www.pertronix.com
Products: Electronic ignition systems. **SIC:** 5065 (Electronic Parts & Equipment Nec). **Est:** 1962. **Emp:** 35. **Officers:** Rocky Sherer, Marketing & Sales Mgr.; Kim Hannah, Customer Service Mgr.; Tom Reh, President; John Gutheil, Sales Mgr.

■ 9193 ■ Peters-De Laet Inc.
340 Harbor Way
South San Francisco, CA 94080
Phone: (650)873-9595
Free: (800)735-7874 **Fax:** (650)873-1680
E-mail: delaet@aol.com
URL: http://www.pdel.com
Products: Electrical connectors; Fasteners; Wire harnessing products; Chemicals; Wire making systems. **SICs:** 5063 (Electrical Apparatus & Equipment); 5065 (Electronic Parts & Equipment Nec). **Est:** 1957. **Sales:** $7,000,000 (2000). **Emp:** 40. **Officers:** Steve De Laet, President.

■ 9194 ■ A.E. Petsche Company Inc.
2112 W Division St.
Arlington, TX 76012
Phone: (817)461-9473
Products: Electrical cable. **SIC:** 5063 (Electrical Apparatus & Equipment). **Sales:** $55,000,000 (2000). **Emp:** 84. **Officers:** Arnold E. Petsche, President; Ken Horst, CFO.

■ 9195 ■ Philips and Co.
PO Box 978
Columbia, MO 65205
Phone: (314)474-2800 **Fax:** (314)876-8076
Products: Electrical supplies. **SIC:** 5063 (Electrical Apparatus & Equipment). **Est:** 1934. **Officers:** Gary Bradley, Manager.

■ 9196 ■ Philips Key Modules
2001 Gateway Pl Ste. 650 W
San Jose, CA 95110
Phone: (408)453-7373
Products: Laser optics equipment. **SIC:** 5047 (Medical & Hospital Equipment).

■ 9197 ■ Photonics Management Corp.
360 Foothill Rd.
Bridgewater, NJ 08807
Phone: (908)231-1116 **Fax:** (908)231-0852
E-mail: usa@hamamatsu.com
URL: http://www.hamamatsu.com
Products: Electronic equipment. **SIC:** 5065 (Electronic Parts & Equipment Nec). **Est:** 1983. **Sales:** $70,000,000 (2000). **Emp:** 200. **Officers:** T. Hiruma, President; Keiji Ohashi, Controller.

■ 9198 ■ Phylon Communications Inc.
47436 Fremont Blvd.
Fremont, CA 94538
Phone: (510)656-2606 **Fax:** (510)656-0902
Products: Chip sets for modems. **SIC:** 5065 (Electronic Parts & Equipment Nec). **Sales:** $4,800,000 (2000). **Emp:** 24. **Officers:** Hamdi El-Sissi, President.

■ 9199 ■ Physimetrics Inc.
111205 Alpharetta Hwy., Unit C-4
Roswell, GA 30076
Phone: (770)751-6322
Products: Image processing equipment. **SIC:** 5045 (Computers, Peripherals & Software).

■ **9200** ■ **Picatti Brothers Inc.**
PO Box 9576
Yakima, WA 98909
Phone: (509)248-2540
Products: Industrial electronic equipment, including counters and timers. **SIC:** 5063 (Electrical Apparatus & Equipment). **Est:** 1928. **Sales:** $5,400,000 (2000). **Emp:** 30. **Officers:** Donald S. Picatti, President; Michael L. Picatti, CFO.

■ **9201** ■ **Pico Products, Inc.**
12500 Foothill Blvd.
Lake View Terrace, CA 91342
Phone: (818)897-0028
Free: (800)421-6511 **Fax:** (818)834-7185
URL: http://www.piconet.com
Products: Cable and wireless television equipment and components. **SIC:** 5065 (Electronic Parts & Equipment Nec). **Est:** 1969. **Sales:** $50,000,000 (1999). **Emp:** 63. **Officers:** Charles G. Emley Jr., CEO & Chairman of the Board; Mike Gavigan, CFO; Molly Coulter, Human Resources Contact; Mike Gavigan, Controller.

■ **9202** ■ **Piher International Corporation**
1640 Northwind Blvd.
Libertyville, IL 60048-9634
Phone: (847)390-6680 **Fax:** (847)390-9866
Products: Electronic modules; Ceramic dielectric capacitors; Metal and carbon film resistors; Electrical measuring potentiometers. **SICs:** 5065 (Electronic Parts & Equipment Nec); 5049 (Professional Equipment Nec); 5063 (Electrical Apparatus & Equipment). **Officers:** George DiMartino, President; Diane Jacobs, Sales/Marketing Contact, e-mail: diane@piherusa.com.

■ **9203** ■ **Ralph Pill Electric Supply Co.**
307 Dorchester Ave.
Boston, MA 02127
Phone: (617)269-8200 **Fax:** (617)269-7582
Products: Cable, wire, and electric supplies. **SIC:** 5063 (Electrical Apparatus & Equipment). **Est:** 1920. **Sales:** $30,000,000 (2000). **Emp:** 105. **Officers:** Alfred E. Pill, President; Selig Friedburg, Treasurer; Michael Dapkus, Marketing & Sales Mgr.; Robert Pill, Vice President.

■ **9204** ■ **Pinpoint Systems Inc.**
4505 S Broadway
Englewood, CO 80110
Phone: (303)761-5227 **Fax:** (303)781-5916
Products: Bar code equipment. **SIC:** 5045 (Computers, Peripherals & Software). **Sales:** $500,000 (2000). **Emp:** 5. **Officers:** Roy Warren, President; Jeff R. Warren, Vice President.

■ **9205** ■ **Pioneer**
5440 Naiman Pkwy.
Solon, OH 44139
Phone: (440)349-1300 **Fax:** (440)349-0754
Products: Electric products. **SIC:** 5063 (Electrical Apparatus & Equipment).

■ **9206** ■ **Pioneer Electric Inc.**
228 Mohonua Pl.
Honolulu, HI 96819
Phone: (808)841-0107 **Fax:** (808)847-7256
Products: Electrical equipment. **SIC:** 5063 (Electrical Apparatus & Equipment). **Est:** 1964. **Sales:** $5,000,000 (1999). **Emp:** 13. **Officers:** Hiura Colbert, President; Ben Petersen, VP & Secty.; Ron Higa, Treasurer.

■ **9207** ■ **Pioneer Electronics USA Inc.**
2265 E 220th St.
Long Beach, CA 90810
Phone: (310)835-6177 **Fax:** (310)816-0402
Products: Car and house electronics. **SIC:** 5065 (Electronic Parts & Equipment Nec). **Est:** 1982. **Sales:** $220,000,000 (2000). **Emp:** 900. **Officers:** Setsujiro Onami, President; Ronald N. Stone, CFO; Mike Fidler, Dir. of Marketing; Greg Peck, Dir. of Systems; Michael Solender, Human Resources Mgr.

■ **9208** ■ **Pioneer Music Company Inc.**
PO Box 646
Chanute, KS 66720-0646
Phone: (316)431-2710
Free: (800)362-0315 **Fax:** (316)431-2713
Products: Electrical entertainment appliances, including television sets and radios. **SIC:** 5064 (Electrical Appliances—Television & Radio). **Officers:** Jack Haight, President.

■ **9209** ■ **Pioneer-Standard Electronics Inc.**
4800 E 131st St.
Cleveland, OH 44105
Phone: (216)587-3600
Free: (800)362-9127 **Fax:** (216)587-3563
URL: http://www.pios.com
Products: Electronic components; Computer parts. **SICs:** 5065 (Electronic Parts & Equipment Nec); 5045 (Computers, Peripherals & Software). **Est:** 1963. **Sales:** $1,508,700,000 (2000). **Emp:** 2,066. **Officers:** James L. Bayman, CEO & Chairman of the Board; John V. Goodger, VP & Treasurer; Arthur Rhein, President; Robert E. Danielson, Sr. VP.

■ **9210** ■ **Piper Associates**
33 Marsh Rd.
Needham, MA 02492
Phone: (781)449-1144 **Fax:** (781)444-2304
Products: Electronic systems and equipment. **SIC:** 5065 (Electronic Parts & Equipment Nec).

■ **9211** ■ **PlastiCom Industries Inc.**
1011 W 45th Ave.
Denver, CO 80211
Phone: (303)433-2333 **Fax:** (303)433-7133
Products: Cable products; fabricates industrial plastics; Telecommunications supplies—wire, cable, PVC pipe and inner duct. **SIC:** 5063 (Electrical Apparatus & Equipment).

■ **9212** ■ **Platt Electric Supply Inc.**
10605 SW Allen Blvd.
Beaverton, OR 97005
Phone: (503)641-6121 **Fax:** (503)641-6155
Products: Electrical supplies. **SIC:** 5063 (Electrical Apparatus & Equipment). **Est:** 1953. **Sales:** $210,000,000 (2000). **Emp:** 800. **Officers:** Harvey J. Platt, President; Dave Dutton, VP & CFO; Jack Mumford, Sr. VP of Sales.

■ **9213** ■ **Platt Hardin Inc.**
7454 Harwin Dr.
Houston, TX 77036-2008
Phone: (713)784-0613 **Fax:** (713)784-1034
Products: Provides engineering manufacturing counsel, specializing in product development and patent/licensing needs to businesses worldwide. **SIC:** 5065 (Electronic Parts & Equipment Nec). **Emp:** 20.

■ **9214** ■ **PLX Technology Inc.**
390 Potrero Ave.
Sunnyvale, CA 94086
Phone: (408)774-9060
Free: (800)759-3735 **Fax:** (408)774-2169
Products: semiconductors and related solid-state devices. **SIC:** 5065 (Electronic Parts & Equipment Nec). **Emp:** 70. **Officers:** Mike Salameh, President.

■ **9215** ■ **PM Marketing**
109 Lake Ave., Ste. 18
Hilton, NY 14468-0613
Phone: (716)392-5110 **Fax:** (716)392-5204
Products: Electronic systems and equipment. **SIC:** 5065 (Electronic Parts & Equipment Nec).

■ **9216** ■ **H. Poll Electric Co.**
216 N Saint Clair St.
Toledo, OH 43603
Phone: (419)255-1660 **Fax:** (419)255-2915
URL: http://www.hpoll.com
Products: Electrical supplies. **SIC:** 5063 (Electrical Apparatus & Equipment). **Est:** 1919. **Sales:** $21,000,000 (2000). **Emp:** 55. **Officers:** Richard W. Poll, President; Michael C. King, Treasurer; Darrel Baker, Customer Service Contact; John Nelson, Dir. of Data Processing.

■ **9217** ■ **Polyconcept USA, Inc.**
69 Jefferson St.
Stamford, CT 06902-4506
Phone: (203)358-8100 **Fax:** (203)358-8366
Products: Novelty Radios; Electronic sound equipment. **SIC:** 5064 (Electrical Appliances—Television & Radio). **Officers:** Emile De Neree, President; Monica Noyes.

■ **9218** ■ **Ponto Associates**
12816 NE 125th Way
Kirkland, WA 98034
Phone: (425)821-2996 **Fax:** (425)823-9827
E-mail: info@ponto.com
Products: Audio and visual installation products. **SIC:** 5065 (Electronic Parts & Equipment Nec). **Est:** 1980. **Emp:** 6. **Officers:** Scott Ponto.

■ **9219** ■ **Port Electric Supply Corp.**
248-264 3rd St.
Elizabeth, NJ 07206
Phone: (908)355-1900 **Fax:** (908)355-0041
Products: Transportation equipment; Electrical equipment and supplies. **SICs:** 5063 (Electrical Apparatus & Equipment); 5088 (Transportation Equipment & Supplies). **Est:** 1955. **Sales:** $3,000,000 (2000). **Emp:** 16. **Officers:** Hank Barnes, President.

■ **9220** ■ **Port Huron Electric Motor**
321 Court St.
Port Huron, MI 48060
Phone: (810)985-7197
Products: Electric motors. **SIC:** 5063 (Electrical Apparatus & Equipment).

■ **9221** ■ **Powell Electronics Inc.**
PO Box 8765
Philadelphia, PA 19101
Phone: (215)365-1900 **Fax:** (215)245-3170
Products: Microswitches, including push buttons, rockers, paddles, indicators, and enunciators. **SIC:** 5065 (Electronic Parts & Equipment Nec). **Est:** 1946. **Sales:** $62,000,000 (2000). **Emp:** 330. **Officers:** Millard D. Brown II, President; Wayne Evans, CFO; John Lincavage, Dir. of Information Systems; Maryann Todd, Dir of Human Resources.

■ **9222** ■ **Power Equipment Corp.**
1005 E Marshall St.
Wytheville, VA 24382
Phone: (540)228-7371
Products: Electric equipment and supplies. **SIC:** 5063 (Electrical Apparatus & Equipment).

■ **9223** ■ **Power Machine Service**
44 Buck Shoals Rd., No. F3
Arden, NC 28704
Phone: (828)684-8044
Products: Electric motors. **SIC:** 5063 (Electrical Apparatus & Equipment).

■ **9224** ■ **Power/mation Inc.**
1310 Energy Ln.
St. Paul, MN 55108
Phone: (651)605-3312
Free: (800)843-9859 **Fax:** (651)605-4400
E-mail: info@powermation.com
URL: http://www.powermation.com
Products: Electrical equipment. **SIC:** 5063 (Electrical Apparatus & Equipment). **Est:** 1961. **Sales:** $45,000,000 (2000). **Emp:** 150. **Officers:** Chris Reed, President.

■ **9225** ■ **Power Solutions**
PO Box 877489
Wasilla, AK 99687
Phone: (907)229-0567 **Fax:** (907)373-1807
E-mail: powersol@alaska.net
URL: http://www.alaska.net/~powersol
Products: Electrical products. **SIC:** 5063 (Electrical Apparatus & Equipment). **Est:** 1999. **Sales:** $1,400,000 (2000). **Emp:** 1. **Officers:** Daniel Jacobson, Owner. **Former Name:** John P. #Bagoy & Associates, Inc.

■ 9226 ■ Power-Sonic Corp.
PO Box 5242
Redwood City, CA 94063
Phone: (650)364-5001 **Fax:** (650)366-3662
Products: Rechargeable batteries. **SIC:** 5063
(Electrical Apparatus & Equipment). **Sales:**
$50,000,000 (2000). **Emp:** 750. **Officers:** Guy Clum,
CEO; Jose Villanueva, CFO.

■ 9227 ■ Power Supply, Inc.
PO Box 1989
Houston, TX 77251
Phone: (713)674-3700
Free: (800)374-7697 **Fax:** (713)674-9522
Products: Electrical equipment and supplies. **SIC:**
5063 (Electrical Apparatus & Equipment). **Est:** 1979.
Sales: $23,000,000 (2000). **Emp:** 38. **Officers:** John L.
Sharman, CEO; Sally Sparks, Treasurer; John Myers,
Vice President; Ron Weiser, Vice President.

**■ 9228 ■ Power & Telephone Supply
Company, Inc.**
1645 North Pkwy.
Jackson, TN 38301
Phone: (901)423-0071
Free: (800)238-3979 **Fax:** (901)423-0073
Products: Power and utility equipment. **SIC:** 5065
(Electronic Parts & Equipment Nec).

**■ 9229 ■ Power & Telephone Supply
Company, Inc.**
3414 Henson Rd.
Knoxville, TN 37921
Phone: (423)588-7570
Free: (800)367-6047 **Fax:** (423)588-0659
Products: Power and utility products. **SIC:** 5065
(Electronic Parts & Equipment Nec).

**■ 9230 ■ Power & Telephone Supply
Company, Inc.**
987 Ehlers Rd.
Neenah, WI 54956
Phone: (920)725-5454
Free: (800)558-8448 **Fax:** (920)725-6162
Products: Electronic parts and equipment. **SIC:** 5065
(Electronic Parts & Equipment Nec).

■ 9231 ■ Powertronics Inc.
7171 Commorse Cir. W
PO Box 32065
Minneapolis, MN 55432-0065
Phone: (763)571-2325 **Fax:** (763)571-7315
E-mail: custserv@powertronicsinc.com
URL: http://www.powertronicsinc.com
Products: Electrical equipment. **SIC:** 5065 (Electronic
Parts & Equipment Nec). **Est:** 1974. **Sales:** $750,000
(2000). **Emp:** 3. **Officers:** Ralph Officer, President;
Mark Dahlin, Vice President. **Alternate Name:** Pinkney
& Associates Inc.

■ 9232 ■ Powr-Lite Electric Supplies
1333 Magnolia Ave.
Bowling Green, KY 42104-3050
Phone: (502)842-1694
Free: (800)869-1470 **Fax:** (502)781-8089
URL: http://www.braidelectric.com
Products: Electrical equipment and supplies. **SIC:**
5063 (Electrical Apparatus & Equipment). **Est:** 1950.
Sales: $7,000,000 (2000). **Emp:** 20. **Officers:** Bob
Hovious, VP & Mgr., e-mail: bhovious@blue.net; Billy
Fitts, Treasurer.

■ 9233 ■ Pratt Audio Visual and Video
200 3rd Ave., SW
Cedar Rapids, IA 52404-5717
Phone: (319)363-8144
Free: (800)332-5414 **Fax:** (319)363-2476
Products: Liquid crystal display (LCD) projectors for
electronic devices. **SIC:** 5065 (Electronic Parts &
Equipment Nec). **Est:** 1939. **Emp:** 78. **Officers:** Louise
Nordstrom, President.

■ 9234 ■ Premier Farnell Corp.
PO Box 94884
Cleveland, OH 44101-4884
Phone: (216)391-8300 **Fax:** (216)391-8327
URL: http://www.premierfarnell.com
Products: Electronic wiring supplies. **SIC:** 5065
(Electronic Parts & Equipment Nec). **Est:** 1966. **Sales:**

$1,170,300,000 (2000). **Emp:** 5,800. **Officers:** John
Hirst, CEO.

**■ 9235 ■ Preventive Electrical Maintenance
Co.**
PO Box 517
Marrero, LA 70073-0517
Phone: (504)341-3816
Products: Electric and electronic equipment;
Electronic parts. **SIC:** 5065 (Electronic Parts &
Equipment Nec). **Officers:** Richard Zelm, President.

■ 9236 ■ PRI Automation Inc.
1250 S Clearview Ave Ste 104
Mesa, AZ 85208
Phone: (480)807-4747 **Fax:** (480)807-4441
Products: Semiconductor automation systems. **SIC:**
5065 (Electronic Parts & Equipment Nec). **Officers:**
Theron Colvin, Director.

■ 9237 ■ Priester Supply Company Inc.
701 107th St.
Arlington, TX 76011
Phone: (817)640-6363
Products: Electrical equipment. **SIC:** 5063 (Electrical
Apparatus & Equipment). **Sales:** $30,000,000 (2000).
Emp: 100. **Officers:** Weldon Jaynes, President &
Treasurer.

■ 9238 ■ Producers Tape Service-All Media
395 E Elmwood
Troy, MI 48083
Phone: (248)585-8273
Free: (800)969-6909 **Fax:** (248)585-1270
Products: Video and audio supplies; Custom foil
stamping on video tapes. **SIC:** 5064 (Electrical
Appliances—Television & Radio). **Officers:** William
Guthrie, Owner; Scott Haines.

■ 9239 ■ Production Arts Lighting Inc.
7777 West Side Ave.
North Bergen, NJ 07047
Phone: (201)758-4000 **Fax:** (201)758-4312
E-mail: marketing@png.com
URL: http://www.prglighting.com
Products: Theatrical lighting. **SIC:** 5063 (Electrical
Apparatus & Equipment). **Est:** 1971. **Emp:** 125.
Officers: Steve Terry, President; Bill Callinghouse;
Anne Valentino, Sales/Marketing Contact, e-mail:
avelentino@prg.com.

■ 9240 ■ Progress Electrical Supply Co.
21750 Coolidge Hwy.
Oak Park, MI 48237
Phone: (248)541-8300
Free: (800)992-1555 **Fax:** (248)541-7843
E-mail: mazza@pe-co.com
URL: http://www.pe-co.com
Products: Electrical supplies. **SIC:** 5063 (Electrical
Apparatus & Equipment). **Est:** 1930. **Emp:** 35.
Officers: Wayne Stricher, CEO.

■ 9241 ■ Progressive Marketing
2980-A Enterprise St.
Brea, CA 92821
Phone: (714)528-2072
Free: (800)368-9700 **Fax:** (714)528-2062
E-mail: pmpi@pmpi.com
URL: http://www.pmpi.com/
Products: Projector; Plasma and TFT Screen Mounts;
Carts. **SIC:** 5065 (Electronic Parts & Equipment Nec).

■ 9242 ■ ProMark
7625 Hayvenhurst Ave., Unit 28
Van Nuys, CA 91406
Phone: (818)904-9390 **Fax:** (818)904-0692
Products: Electronic systems and equipment. **SIC:**
5065 (Electronic Parts & Equipment Nec).

■ 9243 ■ PSI Resources Inc.
1000 E Main St.
Plainfield, IN 46168
Phone: (317)839-9611 **Fax:** (317)838-2427
Products: Electric utility supplies. **SIC:** 5063 (Electrical
Apparatus & Equipment). **Est:** 1988. **Sales:**
$2,664,000,000 (2000). **Emp:** 4,248. **Officers:** James
E. Rogers, CEO, President & Chairman of the Board; J.
Wayne Leonard, Sr. VP & CFO.

■ 9244 ■ C.L. Pugh & Associates, Inc.
21510 Drake Rd.
Cleveland, OH 44136
Phone: (440)238-1777 **Fax:** (440)238-1776
E-mail: info@pugh.com
URL: http://www.pugh.com
Products: Electronic systems and equipment. **SIC:**
5065 (Electronic Parts & Equipment Nec). **Est:** 1943.

■ 9245 ■ C.L. Pugh & Associates, Inc.
2144 Riverside Dr.
Columbus, OH 43221
Phone: (614)486-9678 **Fax:** (614)486-0629
Products: Electronic systems and equipment; Speaker
systems, microphones, home type electronic kits, and
commercial sound equipment, including public address
systems. **SIC:** 5065 (Electronic Parts & Equipment
Nec).

■ 9246 ■ C.L. Pugh & Associates, Inc.
4838 Boomer Rd.
Cincinnati, OH 45247
Phone: (513)662-8373 **Fax:** (513)662-6168
Products: Electronic systems and equipment. **SIC:**
5065 (Electronic Parts & Equipment Nec).

■ 9247 ■ Purdy Electronics Corp.
720 Palomar Ave.
Sunnyvale, CA 94086
Phone: (408)523-8200 **Fax:** (408)733-1287
E-mail: email@purdyelectronics.com
URL: http://www.purdyelectronics.com
Products: Modems; Blowers and fans; Electronic wire
and cable; LEDs; LCDs; Flat-panel displays. **SICs:**
5065 (Electronic Parts & Equipment Nec); 5045
(Computers, Peripherals & Software). **Est:** 1930.
Sales: $9,000,000 (1999). **Emp:** 45. **Officers:** Bruce
Bastl, CEO, e-mail: bbastl@purdyelectronics.com.

■ 9248 ■ Pyramid Supply Inc.
PO Box 76239
Oklahoma City, OK 73147
Phone: (405)232-7628
Products: Electrical supplies and equipment. **SIC:**
5063 (Electrical Apparatus & Equipment). **Sales:**
$11,000,000 (1994). **Emp:** 25. **Officers:** Bob Marson,
Comptroller.

■ 9249 ■ QED
3560 S Valley View Blvd.
Las Vegas, NV 89103-1812
Phone: (702)871-4108 **Fax:** (702)871-0132
URL: http://www.qedelectric.com
Products: Electrical equipment and supplies. **SIC:**
5063 (Electrical Apparatus & Equipment). **Est:** 1986.
Emp: 30. **Officers:** Dean Stauffer; Steven LaTorra, e-
mail: SteveL@qedelectric.com. **Former Name:**
Statewide Electric Supply.

■ 9250 ■ Quement Electronics
1000 S Bascom Ave.
San Jose, CA 95150
Phone: (408)998-5900 **Fax:** (408)292-9920
Products: Electronics. **SIC:** 5065 (Electronic Parts &
Equipment Nec).

■ 9251 ■ Quest Electronic Hardware Inc.
6400 Congress Ave., Ste. 200
Boca Raton, FL 33487
Phone: (561)546-6200
Products: Electronic fasteners. **SIC:** 5072 (Hardware).
Sales: $6,900,000 (2000). **Emp:** 44. **Officers:** Milton
M. Adler, Treasurer.

■ 9252 ■ Quick Cable Corporation
3700 Quick Dr.
Franksville, WI 53126-0509
Phone: (262)824-3100
Free: (800)558-8667 **Fax:** (262)824-3199
URL: http://www.quickcable.com
Products: Battery connectors; Cable; Tools. **SICs:**
5063 (Electrical Apparatus & Equipment); 5072
(Hardware). **Est:** 1964. **Officers:** John Shannon Jr.

■ 9253 ■ **Quinn Electric Supply Co.**
2724 Keith St. NW
Cleveland, TN 37312
Phone: (423)472-4547 **Fax:** (423)479-1514
URL: http://www.quinnelectric.com
Products: Electrical equipment and supplies. **SIC:**
5063 (Electrical Apparatus & Equipment). **Est:** 1946.
Emp: 31. **Officers:** Charles Danner, President; Lamar
Anderson, Marketing & Sales Mgr.; Gary Suits,
Customer Service Contact, e-mail: quinngary@
aol.com.

■ 9254 ■ **R and R Electronic Supply Co.**
PO Box 1860
Lubbock, TX 79408
Phone: (806)765-7727 **Fax:** (806)763-6000
Products: Electronic components. **SICs:** 5065
(Electronic Parts & Equipment Nec); 5064 (Electrical
Appliances—Television & Radio). **Est:** 1936. **Emp:** 46.
Officers: R.N. Hewett, President; Ken Mitchell, VP &
Treasurer; J. Anderson, VP of Purchasing.

■ 9255 ■ **Radar Electric**
704 SE Washington
Portland, OR 97214
Phone: (503)232-3404 **Fax:** (503)235-0428
Products: Electronic parts. **SIC:** 5065 (Electronic Parts
& Equipment Nec).

■ 9256 ■ **Radar, Inc.**
168 Western Ave. W
Seattle, WA 98119
Phone: (206)282-2511 **Fax:** (206)282-1598
Products: Electronic products. **SIC:** 5065 (Electronic
Parts & Equipment Nec). **Former Name:** Radar
Electric.

■ 9257 ■ **Radio Research Instrument**
584 N Main St.
Waterbury, CT 06704-3506
Phone: (203)753-5840 **Fax:** (203)754-2567
E-mail: radiores@prodigy.net
URL: http://www.techexpo.com/WWW/radiores
Products: Electronic systems and equipment;
Electronic parts; Microwave components and devices.
SIC: 5065 (Electronic Parts & Equipment Nec). **Est:**
1953. **Sales:** $2,000,000 (1999). **Emp:** 15. **Officers:**
Paul Plishner, President.

■ 9258 ■ **Radio Resources and Services Corp.**
814 A Light St
Baltimore, MD 21230
Phone: (410)783-0737
Free: (800)547-2346 **Fax:** (410)783-4635
Products: Communications systems and equipment.
SIC: 5065 (Electronic Parts & Equipment Nec).

■ 9259 ■ **RadioShack Corp.**
100 Throckmorton St., Ste. 1800
Ft. Worth, TX 76102
Phone: (817)415-3700 **Fax:** (817)415-3500
URL: http://www.radioshack.com
Products: Electronics, including computers, radios,
and calculators. **SICs:** 5064 (Electrical Appliances—
Television & Radio); 5045 (Computers, Peripherals &
Software). **Est:** 1899. **Sales:** $4,126,200,000 (1999).
Emp: 41,000. **Officers:** Leonard Roberts, Chairman of
the Board, President & CEO; Dwain H. Hughes, Sr. VP
& CFO; George Burger, VP of Human Resources.
Former Name: Tandy Corp.

■ 9260 ■ **Radix Wire Co.**
26260 Lakeland Blvd.
Cleveland, OH 44132
Phone: (216)731-9191 **Fax:** (216)731-7082
URL: http://www.radix-wire.com
Products: High temperature insulated wire. **SIC:** 5063
(Electrical Apparatus & Equipment). **Est:** 1944. **Sales:**
$28,000,000 (2000). **Emp:** 124. **Officers:** R. C.
VerMerris, President.

■ 9261 ■ **Ram Meter Inc.**
1903 Barrett Rd.
Troy, MI 48084
Phone: (248)362-0990
Free: (800)446-4035 **Fax:** (248)362-1818
URL: http://www.rammeter.com
Products: Electrical and electronic equipment. **SICs:**
5065 (Electronic Parts & Equipment Nec); 5063

(Electrical Apparatus & Equipment). **Est:** 1936. **Sales:**
$2,800,000 (2000). **Emp:** 30. **Officers:** Richard L.
Troyanek, President; M.A. Smith, Treasurer; Jerry
Mattson, General Mgr.; Jerry Marsoupian, Sales Mgr.

■ 9262 ■ **Rancilio Associates**
PO Box 28869
St. Louis, MO 63123
Phone: (314)845-0202 **Fax:** (314)845-0330
Products: Electronic systems and equipment. **SIC:**
5065 (Electronic Parts & Equipment Nec).

■ 9263 ■ **Randolph, Hale & Matthews**
PO Box 828
Clarksville, TN 37041-0828
Phone: (931)647-2325
Free: (800)227-8652 **Fax:** (931)648-1701
E-mail: rhmatt@vsit.net
URL: http://www.rhmatt.com
Products: Electronic supplies. **SIC:** 5065 (Electronic
Parts & Equipment Nec). **Est:** 1958. **Emp:** 7. **Officers:**
Frank Matthews, President.

■ 9264 ■ **Randolph & Rice**
1213 McGavock St.
Nashville, TN 37203
Phone: (615)255-5601 **Fax:** (615)256-0634
E-mail: sales@randolbhandrice.com
URL: http://www.randolphandrice.com/
Products: Electronic components, including
capacitors, diodes and resistors; Chemicals; Control
automation; Connectors; Wire; Datacom; Relays;
Batteries. **SIC:** 5065 (Electronic Parts & Equipment
Nec). **Est:** 1946. **Emp:** 24.

■ 9265 ■ **Rasco Supply Company Ltd.**
PO Box 25
Lihue, HI 96766-0025
Phone: (808)245-5356 **Fax:** (808)245-1894
E-mail: rasco@hawaiian.net
Products: Electronic parts; Electronic systems and
equipment. **SIC:** 5065 (Electronic Parts & Equipment
Nec). **Est:** 1983. **Sales:** $4,000,000 (2000). **Emp:** 10.
Officers: Randy Rask, President.

■ 9266 ■ **Raybro Electric Supplies, Inc., Utility
Div.**
1012-1020 Ellamea Ave.
PO Box 1351
Tampa, FL 33601-4012
Phone: (813)227-9277
Free: (800)226-5391 **Fax:** (813)223-3112
Products: Electrical equipment for industrial use;
Electrical heating equipment for industrial use;
Electronic wire and cable. **SICs:** 5063 (Electrical
Apparatus & Equipment); 5065 (Electronic Parts &
Equipment Nec). **Est:** 1927. **Sales:** $100,000,000
(2000). **Emp:** 457. **Officers:** Paul DeWitt, General
Mgr.; Joe Roberts, Operations Mgr.; Gary Overstreet,
Contact.

■ 9267 ■ **Rayvern Lighting Supply Company
Inc.**
7901 Somerset Blvd., Ste. C
Paramount, CA 90723
Phone: (562)634-7020
Products: Various types of lighting. **SIC:** 5063
(Electrical Apparatus & Equipment).

■ 9268 ■ **Rea International Corp.**
1414 Randolph Ave.
Avenel, NJ 07001
Phone: (732)382-7100 **Fax:** (732)382-4996
Products: Power and electrical supplies, including
static inverted frequency converters. **SICs:** 5063
(Electrical Apparatus & Equipment); 5065 (Electronic
Parts & Equipment Nec). **Officers:** Mark Soltz,
Executive Vice President.

■ 9269 ■ **Red Wing Products Inc.**
PO Box 68
Kellyville, OK 74039-0068
Phone: (918)247-6162
Free: (800)331-2898 **Fax:** (918)247-3100
Products: Wire and harness cable. **SIC:** 5063
(Electrical Apparatus & Equipment). **Est:** 1975. **Sales:**
$2,000,000 (2000). **Emp:** 20. **Officers:** Katie Jones.

■ 9270 ■ **Redco Lighting & Maintenance**
145 Waterman Ave.
East Providence, RI 02914
Phone: (401)434-5511
Products: Lighting and lighting supplies, including
bulbs and fixtures; Cleaning chemicals and supplies.
SICs: 5063 (Electrical Apparatus & Equipment); 5087
(Service Establishment Equipment).

■ 9271 ■ **Reily Electrical Supply Inc.**
3011 Lausat St.
Metairie, LA 70001
Phone: (504)835-8888
Products: Electric supplies. **SIC:** 5063 (Electrical
Apparatus & Equipment).

■ 9272 ■ **Relay Specialties Inc.**
17 Raritan Rd.
Oakland, NJ 07436
Phone: (201)337-1000
Free: (800)526-5376 **Fax:** (201)337-1862
E-mail: sales@relayspec.com
URL: http://www.relayspec.com
Products: Relays; Switches; Connectors; Circuit
breakers; Terminal blocks; Sensors; Transformers;
Pilot lights and indicators; Monitors. **SIC:** 5065
(Electronic Parts & Equipment Nec). **Est:** 1963. **Sales:**
$15,000,000 (2000). **Emp:** 45. **Officers:** J.G. Sauer,
CEO; Barry Sauer, President; Steve Gershberg, Vice
President; Ken Cohen, Sales Mgr.

■ 9273 ■ **Reliable Battery Co.**
550 Springfield Rd.
San Antonio, TX 78219-1881
Phone: (512)737-2288
Products: Storage batteries, lead acid type. **SICs:**
5063 (Electrical Apparatus & Equipment); 5013 (Motor
Vehicle Supplies & New Parts). **Emp:** 25.

■ 9274 ■ **Reliance Electric Co.**
78 Crosby St.
Bangor, ME 04401-6838
Phone: (207)989-1634
Products: Electrical motors. **SIC:** 5063 (Electrical
Apparatus & Equipment).

■ 9275 ■ **REM Electronics Supply Company
Inc.**
PO Box 831
Warren, OH 44482
Phone: (330)373-1300 **Fax:** (330)392-1910
Products: Electronics and electrical parts, including
resistors, integrated circuits, and wires. **SIC:** 5065
(Electronic Parts & Equipment Nec). **Est:** 1955. **Sales:**
$15,000,000 (2000). **Emp:** 50. **Officers:** R.E. Miller,
President.

■ 9276 ■ **Reptron Electronics Inc.**
179 Witmer Rd.
Horsham, PA 19044
Phone: (215)855-0925 **Fax:** (215)672-4966
Products: Electric and electronic equipment;
Connectors for electronic circuitry; Electronic parts;
Connectors for electronic circuitry. **SICs:** 5063
(Electrical Apparatus & Equipment); 5065 (Electronic
Parts & Equipment Nec). **Est:** 1967. **Sales:**
$10,000,000 (2000). **Emp:** 55. **Officers:** H. Adams,
President.

■ 9277 ■ **Reptron Electronics Inc.**
14401 McCormick Dr.
Tampa, FL 33626-3046
Phone: (813)854-2351
Products: Electronic components, including
semiconductors. **SIC:** 5065 (Electronic Parts &
Equipment Nec). **Sales:** $223,300,000 (2000). **Emp:**
1,008. **Officers:** Michael L. Musto, CEO & Chairman of
the Board; Paul J. Plante, CFO.

■ 9278 ■ **The Republic Companies**
PO Box 3807
Davenport, IA 52805
Phone: (319)322-6204 **Fax:** (319)322-6194
Products: Electrical supplies and HVAC equipment
and supplies. **SIC:** 5063 (Electrical Apparatus &
Equipment). **Est:** 1916. **Sales:** $22,900,000 (2000).
Emp: 49. **Officers:** Mark Kilmer, President; Tom
Wagner, Controller; Ted Stephens, Vice President;

Roger Kelly, Vice President. **Former Name:** Republic Electric.

■ **9279** ■ **Republic Group**
5801 Lee Highway
Arlington, VA 22207
Phone: (703)533-8555 **Fax:** (703)533-2079
Products: Electrical wind shear warning equipment; Hydrometeorological equipment; Upper air sounding equipment; Environmental lidar equipment; Weather radar equipment. **SICs:** 5065 (Electronic Parts & Equipment Nec); 5049 (Professional Equipment Nec). **Officers:** Robert Rissland, Senior Vice President.

■ **9280** ■ **Rero Distribution Co., Inc.**
2005 Brighton Henrietta Townline Rd.
Rochester, NY 14623
Phone: (716)424-7376
Free: (800)724-4250 **Fax:** (716)272-0087
URL: http://www.Rero.com
Products: Electrical and industrial equipment and supplies; Safety products; Material handling products; Compressed air products. **SICs:** 5063 (Electrical Apparatus & Equipment); 5084 (Industrial Machinery & Equipment). **Est:** 1982. **Sales:** $80,000,000 (1999). **Emp:** 225. **Officers:** J. Richard Wilson, Chairman of the Board; Peter B. Roby, President; Michael C. Herrmann, Exec. VP; Donald E. Waltzer, VP of Operations & Secty.; Richard D. Castle, VP of Marketing & Sales, e-mail: rcastle@rero.com; Scott Wilson, Customer Service Contact, e-mail: rswilson@rero.com; Kathy Brink, Human Resources Contact, e-mail: kbrink@rero.com.

■ **9281** ■ **Resource Electronics, Inc.**
746 Vermont Ave.
Palatine, IL 60067
Phone: (847)359-5500 **Fax:** (847)359-9686
Products: Electronic devices. **SIC:** 5065 (Electronic Parts & Equipment Nec). **Emp:** 62. **Officers:** Michael Omansky. **Former Name:** OHM Electronics Inc.

■ **9282** ■ **Resource Electronics Inc.**
PO Box 408
Columbia, SC 29202
Phone: (803)779-5332 **Fax:** (803)765-9276
Products: Wiring; Cable; Electronic parts. **SICs:** 5063 (Electrical Apparatus & Equipment); 5065 (Electronic Parts & Equipment Nec). **Est:** 1929. **Sales:** $80,000,000 (2000). **Emp:** 240. **Officers:** Roy B. Reynolds, President; Lynwood Gibson, Controller; Lowry Plexico, Dir. of Marketing & Sales; Marilee Willis, Dir. of Information Systems.

■ **9283** ■ **Revere Electric Supply Co.**
2501 W Washington Blvd.
Chicago, IL 60612
Phone: (312)738-3636 **Fax:** (312)738-2725
E-mail: webmaster@revereelectric.com
URL: http://www.revereelectric.com
Products: Electrical supplies. **SIC:** 5063 (Electrical Apparatus & Equipment). **Est:** 1919. **Sales:** $75,000,000 (1999). **Emp:** 130. **Officers:** T.A. Eiseman, President; George Beeson, CFO; Greg Holst, VP of Sales; Roy Cpprio, VP of Operations.

■ **9284** ■ **Revere Electrical Supply Co.**
1211 23rd Ave.
Rockford, IL 61104
Phone: (815)968-8866 **Fax:** (815)968-5066
URL: http://www.reveleelectric.com
Products: Control products and techniques. **SIC:** 5063 (Electrical Apparatus & Equipment). **Emp:** 8. **Officers:** Tom Eiseman, President. **Former Name:** Jack W. #Muntz Electrical Supply Co.

■ **9285** ■ **Rexel Glasco**
712 E 18th St.
Kansas City, MO 64108-1705
Phone: (816)421-7020 **Fax:** (816)474-4085
Products: Conduits, wire, and transformers. **SIC:** 5063 (Electrical Apparatus & Equipment). **Emp:** 23. **Former Name:** Glasco Electric Co.

■ **9286** ■ **Rexel Inc.**
150 Alhambra Cir., Ste. 900
Coral Gables, FL 33134
Phone: (305)446-8000 **Fax:** (305)446-8128
URL: http://www.rexelusa.com
Products: Electrical equipment. **SIC:** 5065 (Electronic Parts & Equipment Nec). **Est:** 1866. **Sales:** $450,000,000 (2000). **Emp:** 3,300. **Officers:** Gilles Guinchard, President. **Former Name:** Summit Group.

■ **9287** ■ **Rexel Inc. (Coral Gables, Florida)**
150 Alhambra Circle, Ste. 900
Coral Gables, FL 33134
Phone: (305)446-8000 **Fax:** (305)446-8128
Products: Electronic supplies. **SIC:** 5065 (Electronic Parts & Equipment Nec). **Est:** 1866. **Sales:** $1,301,800,000 (2000). **Emp:** 3,200. **Officers:** Gilles Guinchard, President.

■ **9288** ■ **Rexel-Summers**
1424 Natchitoches St.
West Monroe, LA 71292-3751
Phone: (318)325-9696 **Fax:** (318)325-7747
E-mail: cross@rexelusa.com
URL: http://www.rexelusa.com
Products: Electrical and industrial supplies; Safety equipment. **SICs:** 5063 (Electrical Apparatus & Equipment); 5085 (Industrial Supplies). **Est:** 1908. **Sales:** $12,000,000 (2000). **Emp:** 25. **Officers:** M. Craig Ross, Regional Mgr. **Former Name:** Weaks Supply Co.

■ **9289** ■ **Rexel-Summers**
1424 Natchitoches St.
West Monroe, LA 71292-3751
Phone: (318)325-9696 **Fax:** (318)325-7747
Products: Electrical and electronic equipment and supplies. **SIC:** 5063 (Electrical Apparatus & Equipment).

■ **9290** ■ **Rexel-Taylor**
1709 SE 3rd Ave.
Portland, OR 97214
Phone: (503)233-5321 **Fax:** (503)233-1871
URL: http://www.rexelusa.com
Products: Full line electrical. **SIC:** 5063 (Electrical Apparatus & Equipment). **Est:** 1959. **Sales:** $40,000,000 (2000). **Emp:** 90. **Officers:** Rick Verhaeghe, Vice President. **Former Name:** Taylor Electric Supply Inc.

■ **9291** ■ **RF Power Products Inc.**
1007 Laurel Oak Rd.
Voorhees, NJ 08043
Phone: (609)627-6100 **Fax:** (609)627-7423
Products: RF power supplies and matching networks for the semiconductor industry. **SIC:** 5065 (Electronic Parts & Equipment Nec). **Sales:** $13,000,000 (2000). **Emp:** 173. **Officers:** Joseph Stach, CEO, President & Chairman of the Board; Christopher Ben, CFO & Treasurer.

■ **9292** ■ **Richard Electric Supply Company Inc.**
7281 NW 8th St.
Miami, FL 33126
Phone: (305)266-8000 **Fax:** (305)266-0579
Products: Electrical supplies. **SIC:** 5063 (Electrical Apparatus & Equipment). **Est:** 1961. **Sales:** $21,000,000 (2000). **Emp:** 69. **Officers:** J. Fernandez Jr., President; Jose M. Paz, VP & Controller.

■ **9293** ■ **Richardson Electronics, Ltd.**
40W267 Keslinger Rd.
Lafox, IL 60147-0393
Phone: (630)208-2787
Free: (800)222-2787 **Fax:** (630)208-2350
E-mail: dpg@rell.com
URL: http://www.crts.com/
Products: Electrical equipment and supplies. **SIC:** 5063 (Electrical Apparatus & Equipment).

■ **9294** ■ **Richardson Electronics, Ltd.**
40W267 Keslinger Rd.
PO BOX 393
Lafox, IL 60147-0393
Phone: (630)208-2200
Free: (800)348-5580 **Fax:** (630)208-2550
E-mail: info@rell.com
URL: http://www.rell.com
Products: Electronic components, including transistors, semiconductors, and vacuum tubes; Microwave components; Security equipment; Display products. **SIC:** 5065 (Electronic Parts & Equipment Nec). **Est:** 1947. **Sales:** $407,200,000 (2000). **Emp:** 900. **Officers:** Edward J. Richardson, CEO; Bruce W. Johnson, President & COO; Page Y. Chiang; Flint Cooper; William Garry; Joseph C. Grill; Kathleen M. McNally; Bart Petrini.

■ **9295** ■ **Richey Electronics Inc.**
7441 Lincoln Way
Garden Grove, CA 92841
Phone: (714)898-8288 **Fax:** (714)897-7887
E-mail: www.richeyelec.com
Products: Electronic components, including resistors and capacitors. **SIC:** 5065 (Electronic Parts & Equipment Nec). **Est:** 1947. **Sales:** $226,200,000 (2000). **Emp:** 1,080. **Officers:** William C. Cacciatore, CEO, President & Chairman of the Board; Richard N. Berger, VP & CFO; Bill Class, VP & Dir. of Sales; Norbert St. John, Executive VP of Marketing; Patti Tomaselli, Dir of Human Resources.

■ **9296** ■ **Richmond Electric Supply Co.**
PO Box 10
Richmond, IN 47374
Phone: (765)962-6543 **Fax:** (765)962-3365
Products: Electrical equipment. **SIC:** 5063 (Electrical Apparatus & Equipment). **Sales:** $4,000,000 (2000). **Emp:** 11. **Officers:** J.K. Risk, President.

■ **9297** ■ **Riley's Electrical Supply**
111435 Reiger Rd.
Baton Rouge, LA 70809
Phone: (504)755-0066 **Fax:** (504)755-0150
Products: Electrical supplies including wire, lights, and cords. **SIC:** 5063 (Electrical Apparatus & Equipment). **Est:** 1935. **Sales:** $21,000,000 (2000). **Emp:** 67. **Officers:** John V. Lapenas, President & Chairman of the Board. **Former Name:** Evans Electrical Supply Inc.

■ **9298** ■ **R.J. Marketing, Ltd.**
1010 Rockville Pike, Ste. 607
Rockville, MD 20852
Phone: (301)251-0330
Free: (800)938-0330 **Fax:** (301)424-2035
E-mail: rjmrktg@aol.com
Products: Electronic systems and equipment. **SIC:** 5065 (Electronic Parts & Equipment Nec). **Est:** 1980. **Emp:** 6. **Officers:** John Gallice; Ronald Wilson.

■ **9299** ■ **R.J. Marketing, Ltd.**
3523 W Crown Ave.
Philadelphia, PA 19114
Phone: (215)637-3429 **Fax:** (215)637-2883
Products: Electronic systems and equipment. **SIC:** 5065 (Electronic Parts & Equipment Nec).

■ **9300** ■ **RMT Engineering, Inc.**
9779 Business Park Dr., Ste. I
Sacramento, CA 95827-1715
Phone: (916)366-0261
Free: (800)228-0633 **Fax:** (916)366-3240
Products: Cable equipment and supplies. **SICs:** 5065 (Electronic Parts & Equipment Nec); 5063 (Electrical Apparatus & Equipment). **Officers:** Richard McLean, Pres.

■ **9301** ■ **D.B. Roberts Co.**
54 Jonspin Rd.
Wilmington, MA 01887
Phone: (978)658-7000
Free: (800)800-6887 **Fax:** (978)658-2900
Products: Electrical hanging and fastening devices. **SIC:** 5063 (Electrical Apparatus & Equipment).

■ 9302 ■ **D.B. Roberts Co.**
1100 Valwood Pkwy., Ste. 108
Carrollton, TX 75006
Phone: (972)466-3666
Free: (800)800-9991 **Fax:** (972)466-1646
E-mail: salestx@dbroberts.com
Products: Specialty fasteners. **SIC:** 5063 (Electrical Apparatus & Equipment). **Est:** 1976. **Sales:** $17,000,000 (2000). **Emp:** 150. **Officers:** Brian Chick, Division Manager; Bonnie Thompson, Customer Service Contact, e-mail: bthompson@dbroberts.com.

■ 9303 ■ **D.B. Roberts Co.**
3 Town Line Cir.
Rochester, NY 14623
Phone: (716)475-0070
Free: (800)788-4004 **Fax:** (716)475-0087
Products: Electrical hanging and fastening devices. **SIC:** 5063 (Electrical Apparatus & Equipment).

■ 9304 ■ **Robroy Industries**
Hwy. 49 E
Rte. 1, Box 1
Avinger, TX 75630
Phone: (903)562-1341 **Fax:** (903)562-1256
Products: Electrical fittings. **SIC:** 5063 (Electrical Apparatus & Equipment). **Sales:** $4,000,000 (1999). **Emp:** 49. **Officers:** Nelson Petzold.

■ 9305 ■ **Rochester Electronics Inc.**
10 Malcolm Hoyt Drive
Newburyport, MA 01950
Phone: (978)462-9332 **Fax:** (978)462-9512
Products: Obsolete semiconductors. **SIC:** 5065 (Electronic Parts & Equipment Nec). **Officers:** Curt Gerrish, President.

■ 9306 ■ **Rochester Instrument Systems Inc.**
255 N Union St.
Rochester, NY 14605-2699
Phone: (716)263-7700 **Fax:** (716)262-4777
Products: Electronic products, including recorders, alarms, and transistors. **SICs:** 5065 (Electronic Parts & Equipment Nec); 5063 (Electrical Apparatus & Equipment). **Est:** 1961. **Sales:** $45,000,000 (2000). **Emp:** 350. **Officers:** Ralph Foose, President; J. Brent Harl, CFO; Ross Sherwood, Dir of Human Resources.

■ 9307 ■ **Rockingham Electrical Supplies Inc.**
187 River Rd.
Newington, NH 03801
Phone: (603)436-2310
Products: Electrical supplies. **SIC:** 5063 (Electrical Apparatus & Equipment). **Est:** 1959. **Sales:** $30,000,000 (2000). **Emp:** 104. **Officers:** James E. Pender Sr., CEO.

■ 9308 ■ **Roden Electrical Supply Co.**
170 Mabry Hood Rd.
Knoxville, TN 37923
Phone: (615)546-8755
Free: (800)532-8742 **Fax:** (615)546-6076
E-mail: rodenelec@aol.com
URL: http://www.rodenelectric.com
Products: Electrical supplies. **SIC:** 5063 (Electrical Apparatus & Equipment). **Est:** 1936. **Sales:** $34,000,000 (2000). **Emp:** 110. **Officers:** S.C. McCamy, Chairman of the Board; Sam McCamy III, President; Jeff McCamy, Exec. VP of Sales, e-mail: jmccamy@rodenelectric.com; Logan Hill, VP of Marketing.

■ 9309 ■ **Roe-Comm Inc.**
1400 Ramona Ave.
Kalamazoo, MI 49002-3638
Phone: (616)327-1045
Free: (800)421-2621 **Fax:** (616)327-8784
E-mail: roecomm@roecomm.com
URL: http://www.roecomm.com
Products: Electronic parts and equipment; Communication, paging, and signaling equipment; Cellular products. **SIC:** 5065 (Electronic Parts & Equipment Nec). **Est:** 1950. **Sales:** $2,300,000 (2000). **Emp:** 15. **Officers:** John Carnago, President.

■ 9310 ■ **Chas. Rogers Electric Supply**
12745 Prospect
Dearborn, MI 48126-3653
Phone: (313)581-2611 **Fax:** (313)581-8365
Products: Electric supplies. **SIC:** 5063 (Electrical Apparatus & Equipment). **Est:** 1961. **Emp:** 14. **Former Name:** Charles #Rogers Electric.

■ 9311 ■ **Rogers Electric Supply Co.**
701 Jackson St.
Sioux City, IA 51102
Phone: (712)252-3251
Products: Electrical supplies. **SIC:** 5065 (Electronic Parts & Equipment Nec). **Est:** 1946. **Sales:** $4,000,000 (1999). **Emp:** 20. **Officers:** J. Pfeister, President.

■ 9312 ■ **Rohde and Schwarz Inc.**
4425 Nicole Dr.
Lanham Seabrook, MD 20706
Phone: (301)459-8800 **Fax:** (301)459-2810
Products: Electronic parts and equipment, including radio and television parts. **SIC:** 5065 (Electronic Parts & Equipment Nec). **Officers:** Erhard Thilo, President.

■ 9313 ■ **Romar Industries Inc.**
3149-B Haggerty Rd.
Walled Lake, MI 48390
Phone: (248)669-7080 **Fax:** (248)669-0465
Products: el sensors, timers, and controls; Panels, wire harnesses, pigtails, connectors, relays, and conduits. **SIC:** 5065 (Electronic Parts & Equipment Nec). **Emp:** 50. **Officers:** Ronald Rosen, President.

■ 9314 ■ **Rome Cable Corp.**
421 Ridge St.
Rome, NY 13440
Phone: (315)337-3000 **Fax:** (315)338-6700
Products: Electrical wiring and cable. **SIC:** 5063 (Electrical Apparatus & Equipment). **Sales:** $200,000,000 (2000). **Emp:** 475. **Officers:** David E. Harvey, CEO.

■ 9315 ■ **Ronco Communications and Electronics**
84 Grand Island Blvd.
Tonawanda, NY 14150
Phone: (716)873-0760
Free: (888)84R-ONCO **Fax:** (716)879-8150
Products: Telecommunication systems; Computer systems integration. **SIC:** 5065 (Electronic Parts & Equipment Nec). **Sales:** $68,000,000 (1999). **Emp:** 350. **Officers:** Chris Wasp, President; Tom Lippard, VP & Controller.

■ 9316 ■ **Ronco Power Systems Inc.**
84 Grand Island Blvd.
Tonawanda, NY 14150
Phone: (716)873-0760 **Fax:** (716)879-8156
Products: Generators. **SIC:** 5063 (Electrical Apparatus & Equipment). **Sales:** $3,000,000 (2000). **Emp:** 20. **Officers:** Robert W. Dutschman, President.

■ 9317 ■ **Ronco Specialized Systems Inc.**
84 Grand Island Blvd.
Tonawanda, NY 14150
Phone: (716)879-8136
Free: (888)84-RONCO **Fax:** (716)879-8189
URL: http://www.ronconet.com
Products: Care-giver products; Professional audio and paging products. **SIC:** 5065 (Electronic Parts & Equipment Nec). **Est:** 1965. **Sales:** $5,000,000 (2000). **Emp:** 20. **Officers:** Mark J. Deyle, President, e-mail: mdeyle@ronconet.com; George J. Braun III, Dir. of Marketing, e-mail: gbraun@ronconet.com; Mark Schmitkons, Customer Service Contact, e-mail: mschmitkons@ronconet.com; Annette Sperrazza, Human Resources Contact, e-mail: asperrazza@ronconet.com. **Alternate Name:** Ronco.

■ 9318 ■ **Root, Neal and Company Inc.**
PO Box 101
Buffalo, NY 14240
Phone: (716)824-6400 **Fax:** (716)824-6407
Products: Power transmission products and industrial pumps, scales and supplies. **SICs:** 5063 (Electrical Apparatus & Equipment); 5084 (Industrial Machinery & Equipment); 5085 (Industrial Supplies). **Sales:** $12,000,000 (1999). **Emp:** 40. **Officers:** Joseph F. Neal Sr., President; James C. Neal, VP of Finance.

■ 9319 ■ **Royalite Co.**
101 Burton St.
Flint, MI 48503
Phone: (810)238-4641
Free: (800)968-4641 **Fax:** (810)238-7329
E-mail: flint_branch@royaliteco.com
URL: http://www.royaliteco.com
Products: Electrical equipment for industrial. commercial and residential use. **SIC:** 5063 (Electrical Apparatus & Equipment). **Est:** 1930. **Sales:** $33,000,000 (1999). **Emp:** 100. **Officers:** Gilbert Gottlieb, President; Bob Workman, Industrial Sales Mgr.; Ken Moffitt, CFO; John Mydock, Commercial Sales Mgr.; Craig Adams, Operating Officer; Craig Adams, VP of Operations.

■ 9320 ■ **Royce Industries Inc.**
125 Rose Feiss Blvd.
Bronx, NY 10454
Phone: (718)292-2024
Products: Lighting fixtures. **SIC:** 5063 (Electrical Apparatus & Equipment).

■ 9321 ■ **RP Sales, Inc.**
23735 Research Dr.
Farmington Hills, MI 48335-2625
Phone: (313)937-3000
Free: (800)537-3221 **Fax:** (313)937-8090
Products: Electronic systems and equipment. **SIC:** 5065 (Electronic Parts & Equipment Nec).

■ 9322 ■ **RSC Electronics Inc.**
PO Box 1220
Wichita, KS 67201
Phone: (316)267-5213
Free: (800)456-1545 **Fax:** (316)267-8917
E-mail: rscict@earthlink.net
Products: Electronic equipment and supplies; Cable assembly and harnesses. **SIC:** 5065 (Electronic Parts & Equipment Nec). **Est:** 1939. **Sales:** $7,000,000 (1999). **Emp:** 39. **Officers:** Don Steiner, Sales/Marketing Contact; Todd Martin, Customer Service Contact.

■ 9323 ■ **R.S.R. Electronics Inc.**
365 Blair Rd.
Avenel, NJ 07001
Phone: (732)381-8777
Products: Electronic components. **SICs:** 5063 (Electrical Apparatus & Equipment); 5065 (Electronic Parts & Equipment Nec). **Sales:** $8,000,000 (1993). **Emp:** 30. **Officers:** Eli Rosenbaum, President & CFO.

■ 9324 ■ **Rueff Lighting Co.**
523 E Broadway
Louisville, KY 40202
Phone: (502)583-1617 **Fax:** (502)569-1616
Products: Lighting fixtures and supplies. **SIC:** 5063 (Electrical Apparatus & Equipment). **Est:** 1913. **Sales:** $18,000,000 (2000). **Emp:** 72. **Officers:** William P. Rueff, President.

■ 9325 ■ **RW Electronics Inc.**
206 Andover St.
Andover, MA 01810
Phone: (508)475-1303
Products: Electronic components for computers. **SICs:** 5063 (Electrical Apparatus & Equipment); 5065 (Electronic Parts & Equipment Nec). **Est:** 1979. **Sales:** $70,000,000 (2000). **Emp:** 45. **Officers:** P. Lesaffre, President; R.R. Benedict, CFO; John Lopes, Dir. of Marketing & Sales.

■ 9326 ■ **R.W. Sales, Inc.**
635 N Fairview Ave.
St. Paul, MN 55104-1785
Phone: (612)646-2710 **Fax:** (612)646-8970
URL: http://www.rwsales.com
Products: Electronic systems and equipment. **SIC:** 5065 (Electronic Parts & Equipment Nec). **Est:** 1984. **Emp:** 5. **Officers:** Russell Walde.

■ 9327 ■ **Ryall Electric Supply Co.**
2627 W 6th Ave.
Denver, CO 80204
Phone: (303)629-7721 **Fax:** (303)629-0133
URL: http://www.ryall.com
Products: Electrical equipment. **SIC:** 5063 (Electrical Apparatus & Equipment). **Est:** 1940. **Sales:**

$60,000,000 (2000). **Emp:** 150. **Officers:** George A. Wilson, CEO; Adelle Fontenot, Controller; Dick Stone, Vice President; Con Shillingburg, VP of Sales; Roxanne Harris, Human Resources Mgr.

■ 9328 ■ **S and J Chevrolet Inc.**
PO Box 186
Cerritos, CA 90703
Phone: (562)924-1676
Products: Retransmissions; Auto dealership. **SIC:** 5063 (Electrical Apparatus & Equipment). **Sales:** $49,000,000 (2000). **Emp:** 123. **Officers:** Douglas Corrigan, President.

■ 9329 ■ **Sacks Electrical Supply Co.**
711 Johnston St.
Akron, OH 44306
Phone: (330)253-2141
Products: Electrical supplies. **SIC:** 5063 (Electrical Apparatus & Equipment). **Sales:** $63,000,000 (2000). **Emp:** 200. **Officers:** Jules A. Altshuler, President; B.L. Laidman, VP of Marketing & Sales.

■ 9330 ■ **Safety Signals Systems Inc.**
PO Box 5098
Lynnwood, WA 98046
Phone: (425)775-1557
Products: Traffic control equipment. **SIC:** 5063 (Electrical Apparatus & Equipment).

■ 9331 ■ **Sager Electronics Inc.**
60 Research Rd.
Hingham, MA 02043
Phone: (617)749-6700   **Fax:** (617)749-3842
Products: Electronic equipment. **SIC:** 5063 (Electrical Apparatus & Equipment). **Est:** 1887. **Sales:** $150,000,000 (2000). **Emp:** 390. **Officers:** Raymond P. Norton III, CEO & President; Frank Flynn Jr., Exec. VP & CFO; P.J. Murphy, Vice President; Peter Morris, Vice President; Susan L. Hans, Vice President.

■ 9332 ■ **Sakata U.S.A. Corp.**
651 Bonnie Ln.
Elk Grove Village, IL 60009
Phone: (708)593-3211
Products: Electronic equipment. **SICs:** 5064 (Electrical Appliances—Television & Radio); 5065 (Electronic Parts & Equipment Nec).

■ 9333 ■ **Salinger Electric Co.**
1020 Livernois Rd.
Troy, MI 48083
Phone: (248)585-8330
Products: Electrical supplies. **SIC:** 5063 (Electrical Apparatus & Equipment). **Sales:** $3,400,000 (2000). **Emp:** 15. **Officers:** L.N. Cotsonika, President.

■ 9334 ■ **Sandusco Inc.**
11012 Aurora Hudson Rd.
Streetsboro, OH 44241
Phone: (330)528-0410   **Fax:** (330)528-0423
Products: Video cassettes and compact discs. **SIC:** 5065 (Electronic Parts & Equipment Nec). **Sales:** $54,000,000 (2000). **Emp:** 350. **Officers:** Edwin Singer, Chairman of the Board; Harry Singer, President.

■ 9335 ■ **Sandusky Electrical Inc.**
1516 Milan Rd.
Sandusky, OH 44870
Phone: (419)625-4915
Products: Electrical supplies. **SIC:** 5063 (Electrical Apparatus & Equipment). **Est:** 1939. **Sales:** $15,000,000 (2000). **Emp:** 66. **Officers:** Jerry Stevens, President.

■ 9336 ■ **Sat-Pak Inc.**
1492 N 6th St.
Redmond, OR 97756
Phone: (541)923-0467
Free: (800)922-0911   **Fax:** (541)923-5925
Products: Coaxial cable assemblies; Coaxial cable and connectors. **SIC:** 5065 (Electronic Parts & Equipment Nec). **Sales:** $1,000,000 (2000). **Emp:** 10. **Officers:** William Park, President.

■ 9337 ■ **Saturn Satellite System, Inc.**
DBA Saturn Distributing
1199 Main St.
Jackson, KY 41339
Phone: (606)666-8881   **Fax:** (606)666-8561
Products: Electronic equipment. **SIC:** 5065 (Electronic Parts & Equipment Nec). **Est:** 1982. **Emp:** 25.

■ 9338 ■ **Savannah Communications**
11 Minus Ave.
Savannah, GA 31418
Phone: (912)964-1479
Free: (800)634-0446   **Fax:** (912)966-5724
Products: Communications systems and equipment. **SIC:** 5065 (Electronic Parts & Equipment Nec). **Sales:** $2,000,000 (2000). **Emp:** 43.

■ 9339 ■ **Savoir Technology Group Inc.**
254 E Hacienda Ave.
Campbell, CA 95008
Phone: (408)379-0177   **Free:** (800)338-1600
URL: http://www.svtg.com
Products: Electrical equipment. **SICs:** 5065 (Electronic Parts & Equipment Nec); 5045 (Computers, Peripherals & Software). **Est:** 1977. **Sales:** $593,341,000 (2000). **Emp:** 557. **Officers:** P. Scott Munroe, CEO & President; James W. Dorst, CFO. **Alternate Name:** Western Micro Technology Inc.

■ 9340 ■ **SBM Industries Inc.**
1865 Palmer Ave.
Larchmont, NY 10538
Phone: (914)833-0649
Products: Watch batteries. **SIC:** 5063 (Electrical Apparatus & Equipment). **Sales:** $13,700,000 (2000). **Emp:** 70. **Officers:** Peter Nisselson, President; Kenneth Karlan, Vice President.

■ 9341 ■ **Schaedler/Yesco Distribution**
PO Box 2008
Harrisburg, PA 17105-2008
Phone: (717)233-1621
Free: (800)998-1621   **Fax:** (717)233-1626
URL: http://www.sydist.com
Products: Electrical supplies, including lighting fixtures, bulbs, lamps, transformers, conduit, and wire. Industrial automation supplies, data and telecommunication supplies. **SIC:** 5063 (Electrical Apparatus & Equipment). **Est:** 1924. **Sales:** $60,000,000 (2000). **Emp:** 150. **Officers:** James D. Schaedler, President; Henry Schaedler, VP Purchasing; James Hoffman, VP of Operations; Dean Krout, Dir. of Marketing; Dale Witmer, Vice President; Susan Fritz M.A., Dir of Human Resources. **Former Name:** Schaedler Brothers Inc.

■ 9342 ■ **Schillinger Associates Inc.**
2297 E Boulevard
Kokomo, IN 46902-2453
Phone: (765)457-7241   **Fax:** (765)457-7732
Products: Electronic systems and equipment; Electronic parts. **SIC:** 5065 (Electronic Parts & Equipment Nec). **Officers:** Donald Schillinger, President.

■ 9343 ■ **Schuster Electronics Inc.**
11320 Grooms Rd.
Cincinnati, OH 45242-1480
Phone: (513)489-1400
Free: (800)877-6875   **Fax:** (513)489-8686
E-mail: relay@schusterusa.com
URL: http://www.schusterusa.com
Products: Electrical components, including capacitors, connectors, semiconductors, wire, and cable. **SIC:** 5063 (Electrical Apparatus & Equipment). **Est:** 1904. **Sales:** $34,000,000 (2000). **Emp:** 110. **Officers:** Ted Ludeke, President; Bill Cassel, VP of Marketing; Mike McElhone, VP of Sales; Donna Rooney, Sr. VP of Operations.

■ 9344 ■ **Sci-Rep Inc.**
9512 Lee Hwy. A
Fairfax, VA 22031-2303
Phone: (703)385-0600   **Fax:** (703)385-0600
Products: Electronic systems and equipment; Electronic parts. **SIC:** 5065 (Electronic Parts & Equipment Nec). **Officers:** Donald George, President.

■ 9345 ■ **SCMS Inc.**
10201 Rodney St.
Pineville, NC 28134
Phone: (704)889-4508   **Fax:** (704)889-4540
Products: Electronic parts and equipment; Radio and television equipment and parts. **SICs:** 5065 (Electronic Parts & Equipment Nec); 5064 (Electrical Appliances—Television & Radio). **Officers:** Bob Cauthen, President.

■ 9346 ■ **Scott Electronics**
4040 Adams St.
Lincoln, NE 68504-1996
Phone: (402)466-8221
Free: (800)333-7952   **Fax:** 800-287-2688
E-mail: info@scottele.com
URL: http://www.scottele.com
Products: Electronic parts. **SIC:** 5065 (Electronic Parts & Equipment Nec). **Est:** 1953. **Officers:** Dave Porath, President.

■ 9347 ■ **SDI Technologies Inc.**
PO Box 2001
Rahway, NJ 07065-0901
Phone: (732)574-9000   **Fax:** (201)332-4993
Products: Consumer electronic equipment. **SIC:** 5065 (Electronic Parts & Equipment Nec). **Sales:** $35,000,000 (2000). **Emp:** 150. **Officers:** Morris Franco, President; C. Chraime, CFO.

■ 9348 ■ **SEA Wire & Cable Inc.**
451 Lanier Rd.
Madison, AL 35758
Phone: (205)772-9616
Free: (800)633-7210   **Fax:** (205)772-7402
URL: http://www.sea-wire.com
Products: Cable and wire; Aerospace; Mil spec; High temperature cable and wire; Heat shrink tubing; Molded shapes. **SIC:** 5063 (Electrical Apparatus & Equipment). **Est:** 1970. **Sales:** $22,000,000 (2000). **Emp:** 48. **Officers:** Bob Wills, President, e-mail: bobw@sea-wire.com; Jerry Sandlin, Sales & Marketing Contact, e-mail: jerry@sea-wire.com; Marty Clark, Human Resources Contact, e-mail: marty@sea-wire.com.

■ 9349 ■ **Seamans Supply Company Inc.**
PO Box 4540
Manchester, NH 03108-4540
Phone: (603)669-2700   **Fax:** (603)669-7920
Products: Electrical equipment. **SIC:** 5063 (Electrical Apparatus & Equipment). **Sales:** $12,000,000 (2000). **Emp:** 46. **Officers:** Donald March, President; Ronald Dunston, Treasurer.

■ 9350 ■ **Security Forces Inc.**
PO Box 36607
Charlotte, NC 28236-6607
Phone: (704)334-4751   **Fax:** (704)335-0446
Products: Electronic parts and equipment; Security control equipment and systems. **SICs:** 5065 (Electronic Parts & Equipment Nec); 5063 (Electrical Apparatus & Equipment). **Est:** 1949. **Sales:** $6,000,000 (2000). **Emp:** 2,800. **Officers:** Lawrence J. O'Brien Jr., President, PC; Donald W. Clark, VP, Treasurer & Secty.; Marshall T. Copeland, VP & General Mgr.

■ 9351 ■ **Sel-Tronics, Inc.**
9475 Lottsford Rd.
Landover, MD 20785
Phones: (301)341-2700   800-777-5481
Free: (800)899-5481   **Fax:** (301)341-3601
Products: Custom cable assembly equipment, including cable, wall outlets, suppressors, tools, and test equipment. **SIC:** 5063 (Electrical Apparatus & Equipment). **Officers:** Gary L. Brown, Pres.

■ 9352 ■ **Semispecialists of America Inc.**
226 Sherwood Ave.
Farmingdale, NY 11735
Phone: (516)293-2710
Products: Electrical equipment and supplies. **SIC:** 5065 (Electronic Parts & Equipment Nec). **Est:** 1973. **Sales:** $50,000,000 (2000). **Emp:** 95. **Officers:** Michael Kelly, President; Bernard Salter, Controller; Chris Conner, VP of Sales.

■ 9353 ■ **Semispecialists of America Inc.**
226 Sherwood Ave.
Farmingdale, NY 11735
Phone: (516)293-2710
Products: Electrical and electronic equipment and supplies. **SIC:** 5065 (Electronic Parts & Equipment Nec). **Sales:** $50,000,000 (2000). **Emp:** 95.

■ 9354 ■ **Sentex Corp.**
1920 Lafayette St., Ste. F
Santa Clara, CA 95050
Phone: (408)364-0112
Products: Electrical sensors. **SIC:** 5063 (Electrical Apparatus & Equipment). **Sales:** $600,000 (1994). **Emp:** 2. **Officers:** Jacques Franque, President.

■ 9355 ■ **Sentrol Inc.**
12345 SW Leveton Dr.
Tualatin, OR 97062
Phone: (503)691-4052
Free: (800)547-2556 **Fax:** (503)691-7566
Products: Security system components and smoke detectors. **SIC:** 5063 (Electrical Apparatus & Equipment). **Sales:** $108,000,000 (2000). **Emp:** 1,000. **Officers:** Brian McCarthy, CEO.

■ 9356 ■ **Server Technology Inc.**
521 E Weddell Dr., Ste. 120
Sunnyvale, CA 94089
Phone: (408)745-0300
Free: (800)835-1515 **Fax:** (408)745-0392
Products: Addressable remote power switches. **SIC:** 5045 (Computers, Peripherals & Software). **Sales:** $2,000,000 (2000). **Emp:** 20. **Officers:** Carrell Ewing, President.

■ 9357 ■ **Service Electric Supply Inc.**
15424 Oakwood Dr.
Romulus, MI 48174
Phone: (734)229-9100 **Fax:** (734)229-9101
Products: Electrical supplies, including wire, breakers, and fittings. **SIC:** 5063 (Electrical Apparatus & Equipment). **Est:** 1990. **Sales:** $24,000,000 (2000). **Emp:** 34. **Officers:** Dave Buszka, President; Robert Pauline, Vice Chairman of the Board & Treasurer.

■ 9358 ■ **Shealy Electrical Wholesalers Incorporated Co.**
PO Box 48
Greenville, SC 29602
Phone: (803)242-6880
Free: (800)868-7248 **Fax:** (864)235-6097
URL: http://www.shealyelectrical.com
Products: Electrical products, including wiring devices, connectors, and fuses. **SIC:** 5063 (Electrical Apparatus & Equipment). **Est:** 1945. **Sales:** $45,000,000 (2000). **Emp:** 110. **Officers:** John De Loache, President; David White, Exec. VP, e-mail: dwhite@shealyelectrical.com; Glenn Cockrell, VP of Marketing & Sales, e-mail: gcockrell@shealyelectrical.com.

■ 9359 ■ **Shelby Electric Company Inc.**
112 EH. Crump Blvd. E
Memphis, TN 38101
Phone: (901)948-1545
Free: (800)451-3548 **Fax:** (901)947-7310
E-mail: info@shelbyelectric.net
URL: http://www.shelbyelectric.net
Products: Electrical motors and equipment; Power transmission equipment and supplies. **SIC:** 5063 (Electrical Apparatus & Equipment). **Est:** 1919. **Sales:** $10,000,000 (1999). **Emp:** 80. **Officers:** Al Quarin, President.

■ 9360 ■ **Shelby Supply Company Inc.**
PO Box 9050
Shelby, NC 28151-9050
Phone: (704)482-6781 **Fax:** (704)481-0145
Products: Electrical equipment and supplies. **SIC:** 5063 (Electrical Apparatus & Equipment). **Est:** 1921. **Emp:** 99. **Officers:** M. C. Holloman.

■ 9361 ■ **Shelly Electric Inc.**
PO Box 5104
Potsdam, NY 13676
Phone: (315)265-3400 **Fax:** (315)265-8817
Products: Electrical supplies, including light bulbs, lamps, switches, transformers, and wire. **SIC:** 5063 (Electrical Apparatus & Equipment). **Est:** 1949. **Sales:**

$6,000,000 (2000). **Emp:** 40. **Officers:** R.F. Shelly, President & Treasurer; James Williams, Controller.

■ 9362 ■ **Shepherd Electric Company Inc.**
7401 Pulaski Hwy.
Baltimore, MD 21237
Phone: (410)866-6000
Free: (800)253-1777 **Fax:** (410)866-6001
URL: http://www.Sheperdelec.com
Products: Electrical supplies. **SIC:** 5063 (Electrical Apparatus & Equipment). **Est:** 1892. **Sales:** $49,000,000 (2000). **Emp:** 102. **Officers:** Stewart L. Vogel III, President.

■ 9363 ■ **Shepherd Electric Supply Company Inc.**
PO Box 27
Goldsboro, NC 27533
Phone: (919)735-1701
Free: (800)661-3210 **Fax:** (919)734-2461
Products: Electronic wire and cable; Electrical equipment and supplies. **SIC:** 5063 (Electrical Apparatus & Equipment). **Est:** 1947. **Sales:** $23,000,000 (2000). **Emp:** 94. **Officers:** Daniel B. Shepherd, CEO; Bobby Jordan, President.

■ 9364 ■ **Sherburn Electronics Corp.**
175 Commerce Dr.
Hauppauge, NY 11788
Phone: (631)231-4300
Free: (800)366-3066 **Fax:** (631)231-1587
E-mail: sales@sherburn.com
URL: http://www.sherburn.com
Products: Electronic components. **SICs:** 5063 (Electrical Apparatus & Equipment); 5065 (Electronic Parts & Equipment Nec). **Est:** 1981. **Sales:** $21,000,000 (2000). **Emp:** 35. **Officers:** James Burke, CFO, e-mail: jim_burke2atssherburn.com; James Burke, CFO.

■ 9365 ■ **Shokai Far East Ltd.**
9 Elena Ct.
Peekskill, NY 10566-6352
Phone: (914)736-5531
Products: Electronic components, including potentiometers and bulbs. **SIC:** 5063 (Electrical Apparatus & Equipment). **Est:** 1963. **Sales:** $20,000,000 (2000). **Emp:** 85. **Officers:** M.B. Rubin, President; Alan Weiss, VP of Finance; Lee Goldberg, Dir. of Marketing; Shirlee Serber, Dir. of Systems.

■ 9366 ■ **Si-Tex Marine Electronics Inc.**
11001 N Roosevelt Blvd., No. 800
St. Petersburg, FL 33716
Phone: (813)576-5995 **Fax:** (813)570-8646
URL: http://www.si-tek.com
Products: Marine electronic equipment. **SIC:** 5065 (Electronic Parts & Equipment Nec). **Est:** 1975. **Officers:** Ted L. Hansford, President; Chuck Nelson, VP of Finance; David Church, VP of Marketing; Daniel Garrido, Data Processing Mgr.

■ 9367 ■ **Sibley Industrial Tool Co.**
21938 John R
Hazel Park, MI 48030
Phone: (248)547-6942 **Fax:** (248)547-6954
Products: Electrical equipment for industrial use; Machine tools for home workshops, laboratories, garages; Electric-powered hand tools. **SICs:** 5063 (Electrical Apparatus & Equipment); 5084 (Industrial Machinery & Equipment); 5072 (Hardware). **Est:** 1985. **Sales:** $300,000 (2000). **Emp:** 2. **Officers:** Edward T. Leonard, President.

■ 9368 ■ **Siemens Energy and Automation Inc.**
3 Hutton Center Dr.
Santa Ana, CA 92707-5707
Phone: (714)979-6600 **Fax:** (714)755-1512
Products: Electrical products; Switchgear and switchboard apparatus; Panelboards; Computers. **SICs:** 5063 (Electrical Apparatus & Equipment); 5064 (Electrical Appliances—Television & Radio); 5045 (Computers, Peripherals & Software). **Emp:** 49. **Officers:** John M. McCarthy.

■ 9369 ■ **Siemens Energy and Automation Inc. Electrical Apparatus Div.**
3203 Woman'sClubDr. 202
Raleigh, NC 27612
Phone: (919)782-0904
Products: Electrical products, including motors; Computers; Hospital equipment. **SICs:** 5063 (Electrical Apparatus & Equipment); 5045 (Computers, Peripherals & Software); 5047 (Medical & Hospital Equipment).

■ 9370 ■ **Signal Electronic Supply**
589 New Park Ave.
West Hartford, CT 06110-1334
Phone: (860)233-8551
Free: (800)842-8240 **Fax:** (860)233-8554
E-mail: helpme@signalelectronics.com
URL: http://www.signalelectronics.com
Products: Electronic parts and equipment. **SIC:** 5065 (Electronic Parts & Equipment Nec). **Est:** 1954. **Sales:** $3,000,000 (2000). **Emp:** 15. **Officers:** Alexander Cohen, President; Bob Williamee, Vice President; Brian Dill, Sales/Marketing Contact; Michael McGuire, Customer Service Contact.

■ 9371 ■ **Signal Equipment Inc.**
PO Box 3866
Seattle, WA 98124
Phone: (206)324-8400
Products: Power generators and electrical equipment and supplies. **SIC:** 5063 (Electrical Apparatus & Equipment). **Sales:** $1,000,000 (2000). **Emp:** 8. **Officers:** Tony Hastings, President; Emely Mackey, Mgr. of Finance.

■ 9372 ■ **Signal Vision, Inc.**
27002 Vista Ter.
Lake Forest, CA 92630
Phone: (949)586-3196 **Fax:** (949)586-3952
E-mail: signalvis@aol.com
Products: Electronic cable parts. **SIC:** 5065 (Electronic Parts & Equipment Nec). **Est:** 1976. **Emp:** 15. **Officers:** Neil P. Phillips, President.

■ 9373 ■ **Sitler's Electric Supply Inc.**
PO Box 542
213-19 N Iowa
Washington, IA 52353
Phone: (319)653-2128 **Fax:** (319)653-2800
Products: Electrical equipment and supplies. **SIC:** 5063 (Electrical Apparatus & Equipment). **Emp:** 28.

■ 9374 ■ **SJS Products/Jamcor Corp.**
6261 Angelo Ct.
Loomis, CA 95650
Phone: (916)652-7713 **Fax:** (916)652-3293
E-mail: info@sjsproducts.com
URL: http://www.sjsproducts.com
Products: Electric components, including fasteners and screws. **SIC:** 5063 (Electrical Apparatus & Equipment). **Est:** 1932. **Sales:** $8,000,000 (2000). **Emp:** 35. **Officers:** William McGillivray, President.

■ 9375 ■ **SKC Communication Products Inc.**
8320 Hedge Lane Ter.
Shawnee Mission, KS 66227
Phone: (913)422-4222
Free: (800)882-7779 **Fax:** 800-454-4752
Products: Telephone headsets and volume control handsets and audio and video conferencing eqipment. **SIC:** 5065 (Electronic Parts & Equipment Nec). **Sales:** $27,000,000 (2000). **Emp:** 48. **Officers:** Paul Ammeen, CEO; Sondra Ammeen, President.

■ 9376 ■ **Sloan Electric Co**
1480 Simpson Way
Escondido, CA 92029
Phone: (760)745-5276 **Fax:** (760)745-2040
Products: Electric motors and generators. **SIC:** 5063 (Electrical Apparatus & Equipment).

■ 9377 ■ **Smarter Security Systems Inc.**
5825 Glenridge Dr.
Atlanta, GA 30328
Phone: (404)256-4244 **Fax:** (404)252-1340
Products: Industrial and commercial electronic security systems. **SIC:** 5063 (Electrical Apparatus & Equipment). **Sales:** $1,000,000 (1999). **Emp:** 10. **Officers:** John E. Forbat, President.

■ 9378 ■ SMARTEYE Corp.
2002, Ste.phenson Hwy.
Troy, MI 48083-2151
Phone: (248)589-3382 **Fax:** (248)589-1245
Products: Electronic routing and tracking equipment.
SIC: 5065 (Electronic Parts & Equipment Nec). **Est:**
1981. **Sales:** $5,000,000 (2000). **Emp:** 27. **Officers:**
Marty Peters, President; Jim DeLange, COO; Bob
Sattler, Dir. of Sales.

■ 9379 ■ SMC Electrical Products Inc.
PO Box 880
Barboursville, WV 25504
Phone: (304)736-8933
Products: Power distribution equipment. **SIC:** 5065
(Electronic Parts & Equipment Nec). **Officers:** Oliver
Fearing, President.

■ 9380 ■ Sommer Electric Corp.
818 3rd St., NE
Canton, OH 44704
Phone: (330)455-9454 **Fax:** (330)455-6561
Products: Electrical products, including lights and
wiring. **SIC:** 5063 (Electrical Apparatus & Equipment).
Emp: 35.

■ 9381 ■ SOR Inc.
14685 W 105th St.
Lenexa, KS 66215-5964
Phone: (913)888-2630 **Fax:** (913)888-0767
Products: Pressure switches, temperature switches,
and fluid control. **SICs:** 5063 (Electrical Apparatus &
Equipment); 5084 (Industrial Machinery & Equipment).
Sales: $15,000,000 (2000). **Emp:** 180. **Officers:** Roy
R. Dunlap.

■ 9382 ■ Sound Limited Inc.
1246 Blue Lakes Blvd. N
Twin Falls, ID 83301-3307
Phone: (208)733-2123 **Fax:** (208)734-2528
Products: Electronic parts and equipment. **SIC:** 5065
(Electronic Parts & Equipment Nec). **Officers:** Ronald
Victor, President.

■ 9383 ■ Sound Marketing Concepts
3854 S Peach Way
Denver, CO 80237-1256
Phone: (303)758-4303 **Fax:** (303)758-4032
Products: Electronic systems and equipment. **SIC:**
5065 (Electronic Parts & Equipment Nec).

■ 9384 ■ Southeastern Communications
3402 Oakcliff Rd., Ste. B-4
Atlanta, GA 30340
Phone: (404)455-0672 **Fax:** (404)451-6233
Products: Electronic systems and equipment. **SIC:**
5065 (Electronic Parts & Equipment Nec). **Also Known
by This Acronym:** SECOM.

**■ 9385 ■ Southern Electric Service Company,
Inc.**
2225 Freedom Dr.
Charlotte, NC 28208
Phone: (704)372-4832
Free: (800)487-3726 **Fax:** (704)358-1098
URL: http://www.southernelectricsvc.com
Products: Electrical motors; Variable speed drives;
Hoists and hoist parts. **SICs:** 5063 (Electrical
Apparatus & Equipment); 5039 (Construction Materials
Nec); 5082 (Construction & Mining Machinery). **Est:**
1913. **Sales:** $10,000,000 (2000). **Emp:** 50. **Officers:**
William H. Smith III, Chairman of the Board; Joan N.
Carrier, Treasurer; Kevin O. Henson, Vice President.

**■ 9386 ■ Southern Electric Supply Company
Inc.**
7401 W Ellis Rd.
Melbourne, FL 32904
Phone: (407)768-0223 **Fax:** (407)984-7916
Products: General electrical supplies, including wiring
and sockets. **SIC:** 5063 (Electrical Apparatus &
Equipment). **Emp:** 14. **Officers:** Ray Frelich.

**■ 9387 ■ Southern Electric Supply Company
Inc.**
301 46th Ct.
Meridian, MS 39301
Phone: (601)693-4141 **Fax:** (601)482-5770
Products: Electrical products, including wire,

lightbulbs, and feedings. **SIC:** 5063 (Electrical
Apparatus & Equipment). **Est:** 1945. **Sales:**
$110,000,000 (2000). **Emp:** 340. **Officers:** Timothy
Hogan, President; Judy McInnis, Treasurer & Secty.;
James M. Hopkins, VP of Marketing & Sales; Michael
Knost, Dir. of Data Processing; Guy Taylor, Exec. VP.

■ 9388 ■ Southern Electronics Supply, Inc.
1909 Tulane Ave.
New Orleans, LA 70112
Phone: (504)524-2345
Free: (800)447-0444 **Fax:** (504)523-1000
E-mail: email@southernele.com
URL: http://www.southernele.com
Products: Electronic components; Electrical supplies;
Voice and data products. **SICs:** 5065 (Electronic Parts
& Equipment Nec); 5063 (Electrical Apparatus &
Equipment); 5064 (Electrical Appliances—Television &
Radio). **Est:** 1932. **Sales:** $12,000,000 (2000). **Emp:**
54. **Officers:** Elmira S. Perrin, CEO; Iggie Perrin,
President; Ronald J. Schadler, VP of Operations; Johm
Lisotta, VP of Purchasing; Michelle Morris, Customer
Service Contact; Cheryl Belanger, Human Resources
Contact.

**■ 9389 ■ Southern Lighting and Supply
Company Inc.**
PO Box 16960
Memphis, TN 38116
Phone: (901)345-2871
Products: Lightbulbs. **SIC:** 5063 (Electrical Apparatus
& Equipment). **Est:** 1966. **Sales:** $3,000,000 (2000).
Emp: 12. **Officers:** Russel McCaslin, President.

■ 9390 ■ Southwest Electronics Inc.
12701 Royal Dr.
Stafford, TX 77477
Phone: (281)240-5672
Products: Electronic components. **SICs:** 5063
(Electrical Apparatus & Equipment); 5065 (Electronic
Parts & Equipment Nec).

■ 9391 ■ Spatron Inc.
2468 Mariondale Ave.
Los Angeles, CA 90032-3517
Phone: (323)227-6821 **Fax:** (323)227-5723
Products: Transformers. **SIC:** 5063 (Electrical
Apparatus & Equipment). **Est:** 1964. **Sales:**
$2,000,000 (2000). **Emp:** 99. **Officers:** F. W.
Schambeck.

■ 9392 ■ Special Mine Services Inc.
PO Box 188
West Frankfort, IL 62896
Phone: (618)932-2151 **Fax:** (618)937-2715
Products: Electrical mine connectors, mine cables,
and mine batteries. **SIC:** 5063 (Electrical Apparatus &
Equipment). **Est:** 1983. **Sales:** $9,000,000 (2000).
Emp: 55. **Officers:** Les Huntsman, CEO.

■ 9393 ■ Specialty Control Systems Inc.
100 E Nasa Rd. 1, Ste. 301
Webster, TX 77598
Phone: (281)332-0999
Free: (800)255-3121 **Fax:** (281)332-0990
E-mail: gmiller@specialtycontrol.com
URL: http://www.specialtycontrol.com
Products: Weidmuller terminal blocks. **SIC:** 5063
(Electrical Apparatus & Equipment). **Sales:** $1,200,000
(2000). **Emp:** 8. **Officers:** L. Jay Armstrong, President.

■ 9394 ■ Specialty Supply Co.
4364 Mangum St.
Flowood, MS 39208
Phone: (601)936-4900 **Fax:** (601)936-4909
Products: Bulbs, recepticle switches, and motor
conduit wiring. **SIC:** 5063 (Electrical Apparatus &
Equipment). **Sales:** $11,000,000 (2000). **Emp:** 36.
Officers: Julius M. Derryberry, Owner.

■ 9395 ■ Splane Electric Supply
8350 Haggerty Rd.
Belleville, MI 48111-1667
Phone: (734)957-5500 **Fax:** (734)957-5500
Products: Electrical supplies, including wiring devices,
fixtures, lamp bulbs, and wiring cable. **SIC:** 5063
(Electrical Apparatus & Equipment). **Emp:** 99.
Officers: A. Swartzenberg.

■ 9396 ■ Spring and Buckley Inc.
PO Box 1750
New Britain, CT 06050
Phone: (203)224-2451
Free: (800)382-0548 **Fax:** (203)827-0077
URL: http://www.springbuck.com
Products: Electrical supplies. **SIC:** 5063 (Electrical
Apparatus & Equipment). **Est:** 1910. **Sales:**
$9,000,000 (2000). **Emp:** 31. **Officers:** W.A. Hayden
Jr. Jr., CEO & President; Jim Adamson, CFO; B.D.
McAvay, VP & Treasurer; Kit Alexander, General Mgr.,
e-mail: kitallll@compsol.net; Tom Standin, Sales Mgr.,
e-mail: tstandin@erols.com.

■ 9397 ■ Springfield Electric Supply Co.
718 N 9th St.
Springfield, IL 62708
Phone: (217)788-2100
Products: Electrical supplies, including lighting fixtures
and panel boards. **SIC:** 5063 (Electrical Apparatus &
Equipment). **Est:** 1932. **Sales:** $49,000,000 (2000).
Emp: 160. **Officers:** William Schnirring Jr., CEO; Lee
Roulson, VP of Finance; J. Michael Barker, VP of
Marketing; Roger Steinbach, Data Processing Mgr.;
Eileen Higgs, Human Resources Mgr.

■ 9398 ■ SRS International
367 Orchard St.
Rochester, NY 14606-1040
Phone: (716)235-2040 **Fax:** (716)235-7827
Products: Electrical and electronic equipment and
supplies. **SIC:** 5065 (Electronic Parts & Equipment
Nec). **Sales:** $250,000,000 (2000). **Emp:** 5.

**■ 9399 ■ Staab Battery Manufacturing
Company Inc.**
931 S 11th St.
Springfield, IL 62703
Phone: (217)528-0421 **Fax:** (217)528-2030
Products: Starting, lighting, and ignition batteries. **SIC:**
5063 (Electrical Apparatus & Equipment). **Est:** 1930.
Sales: $3,000,000 (2000). **Emp:** 30. **Officers:** P.J.
Staab III, President.

■ 9400 ■ Stacoswitch Inc.
1139 W Baker St.
Costa Mesa, CA 92626-4114
Phone: (714)549-3041 **Fax:** (714)549-0930
E-mail: sales@stacoswitch.com
URL: http://www.stacoswitch.com
Products: Pushbutton switches; Keypads and
keyboards. **SIC:** 5063 (Electrical Apparatus &
Equipment). **Est:** 1956. **Sales:** $10,000,000 (1999).
Emp: 85. **Officers:** James F. Gust, President; Richard
Brown, VP of Marketing; Dan Sogg, VP of Sales; Bill
Swan, VP of Manufacturing; Pauline Cook, VP of
Admin.; Evelyn Hampton, Controller; Ron Shurring,
Quality Manager; Phil Hamidian, Engineering Mgr.

■ 9401 ■ Standard Electric Co.
PO Box 5289
Saginaw, MI 48603-0289
Phone: (517)497-2100
Free: (800)322-0215 **Fax:** (517)497-2101
URL: http://www.standardelectricco.com
Products: Electronic equipment and supplies. **SIC:**
5063 (Electrical Apparatus & Equipment). **Est:** 1929.
Sales: $100,000,000 (1999). **Emp:** 230. **Officers:**
Laverne N. Weber, President.

■ 9402 ■ Standard Electric Supply Co.
PO Box 651
Milwaukee, WI 53201-0651
Phone: (414)272-8100 **Fax:** (414)272-8111
Products: Electrical supplies. **SIC:** 5063 (Electrical
Apparatus & Equipment). **Est:** 1917. **Sales:**
$11,000,000 (2000). **Emp:** 50. **Officers:** Adolph Stern,
President; Larry Stern, CFO; Greg Dugan, VP of
Marketing; Cassie Konkol, Dir. of Data Processing.

■ 9403 ■ Standard Electronics
215 John Glenn Dr.
Amherst, NY 14228
Phone: (716)691-3061
Free: (800)333-1519 **Fax:** (716)691-3170
Products: Electronic equipment and supplies. **SIC:**
5065 (Electronic Parts & Equipment Nec). **Est:** 1946.
Emp: 50.

■ 9404 ■ Standard Motor Products Inc.
37-18 Northern Blvd.
Long Island City, NY 11101
Phone: (718)392-0200 **Fax:** (718)729-4549
Products: Insulated wire and cable, including automotive; Wiring supplies; Bolts, nuts, rivets, screws, and washers. **SIC:** 5063 (Electrical Apparatus & Equipment). **Sales:** $500,000,000 (2000). **Emp:** 3,500.
Officers: Bernard Fife; Nathaniel L. Sills; Lawrence I. Sills.

■ 9405 ■ Standard Wire & Cable Co.
1959 E Cashdan St.
Rancho Dominguez, CA 90220
Phone: (310)609-1811
Free: (800)326-0006 **Fax:** (310)609-1862
E-mail: sales@std-wire.com
URL: http://www.std-wire.com
Products: Wire; Cable. **SIC:** 5063 (Electrical Apparatus & Equipment). **Est:** 1947. **Sales:** $9,000,000 (1999). **Emp:** 40. **Officers:** R. Skrable, President; Joyce Lambdin, Controller; Bud Gardner, Vice President; Bruce Haft, Data Processing Mgr.

■ 9406 ■ Staneco Corp.
901 Sheehy Dr.
Horsham, PA 19044
Phone: (215)672-6500 **Fax:** (215)672-2065
Products: Electrical control panels and control system engineering. **SIC:** 5063 (Electrical Apparatus & Equipment).

■ 9407 ■ Stanion Wholesale Electric Company Inc.
PO Drawer F
Pratt, KS 67124
Phone: (316)672-5678 **Fax:** (316)672-6220
URL: http://www.stanion.com
Products: Electrical products. **SIC:** 5063 (Electrical Apparatus & Equipment). **Est:** 1961. **Sales:** $82,000,000 (2000). **Emp:** 300. **Officers:** Bill Keller, President; Bob Heitman, Vice President; Otto Buche, Vice President; Virgie Tiesing, Dir. of Data Processing.

■ 9408 ■ Star Beam/Nightray Div. Gralco Corp.
PO Box 471765
Tulsa, OK 74147
Phone: (918)664-2326 **Fax:** (918)622-4114
URL: http://www.starbeamusa.com
Products: Lighting equipment. **SIC:** 5063 (Electrical Apparatus & Equipment). **Est:** 1987. **Emp:** 10.
Officers: Gayle Lee, President. **Former Name:** Star Beam Inc.

■ 9409 ■ Star Electric Supply Company Inc.
PO Box 580640
Tulsa, OK 74158-0640
Phone: (918)835-7672 **Fax:** (918)835-0583
Products: Electrical supplies, including wire and lightbulbs. **SIC:** 5063 (Electrical Apparatus & Equipment). **Est:** 1946. **Sales:** $5,500,000 (2000). **Emp:** 16. **Officers:** Fred Mitchell, President; Lawrence E. Yelton, Treasurer.

■ 9410 ■ Starbuck Sprague Co.
PO Box 1111
Waterbury, CT 06721
Phone: (203)756-8184
Free: (800)992-0005 **Fax:** (203)757-9069
Products: Electrical supplies; Factory automation; Commercial lighting. **SICs:** 5063 (Electrical Apparatus & Equipment); 5064 (Electrical Appliances—Television & Radio). **Est:** 1927. **Sales:** $10,000,000 (2000). **Emp:** 30. **Officers:** H.W. Schultze, President.

■ 9411 ■ Stark Electronics Inc.
401 Royalston Ave. N
Minneapolis, MN 55405
Phone: (612)372-3161
Free: (888)372-3161 **Fax:** (612)332-1783
E-mail: sales@starkelectronics.com
URL: http://www.starkelectronics.com
Products: Electronic components. **SICs:** 5063 (Electrical Apparatus & Equipment); 5065 (Electronic Parts & Equipment Nec). **Est:** 1938. **Sales:** $7,900,000 (2000). **Emp:** 20. **Officers:** Duane L. Petersen, President & General Mgr.; Sandra Forberg, Treasurer.

■ 9412 ■ State Electric Supply
2700 Rydin Rd., Ste. D
Richmond, CA 94804-5800
Phone: (510)836-1717 **Fax:** (510)893-2575
Products: Lamps; Lighting fixtures; Power wire and cable; Electrical conduit and conduit fittings. **SIC:** 5063 (Electrical Apparatus & Equipment). **Est:** 1930. **Emp:** 16. **Officers:** Roger Stangier, Branch Manager; John Woffington, Operations Mgr.

■ 9413 ■ State Electric Supply Co.
PO Box 5397
Huntington, WV 25703
Phone: (304)523-7491 **Fax:** (304)525-8917
URL: http://www.stateelectric.com
Products: Electrical supplies. **SIC:** 5063 (Electrical Apparatus & Equipment). **Est:** 1952. **Sales:** $77,000,000 (2000). **Emp:** 500. **Officers:** Arthur Weisberg, Chairman of the Board; Clarence Martin, CEO & CFO; John T. Spoor, President; Arnold Moore, VP of Operations; Jeff Clark, Sales Mgr.; James Ware, Controller.

■ 9414 ■ State Electrical Supply Inc.
509 W Milwaukee St.
Janesville, WI 53545
Phone: (608)752-9451 **Fax:** (608)752-9485
Products: Electrical supplies. **SIC:** 5063 (Electrical Apparatus & Equipment). **Sales:** $3,000,000 (2000). **Emp:** 8. **Officers:** Ellen Ramberg, President; Dennis Ramberg, VP & Treasurer.

■ 9415 ■ Steiner Electric Co.
1250 Touhy Rd.
Elk Grove Village, IL 60007-5302
Phone: (708)228-0400 **Fax:** (708)228-1352
Products: Electrical supplies. **SIC:** 5063 (Electrical Apparatus & Equipment). **Est:** 1916. **Sales:** $130,000,000 (2000). **Emp:** 450. **Officers:** Harold M. Kerman, CEO & President; Barry Sanders, Controller; Richard A. Kerman, Exec. VP; Kay Fumarolo, Information Systems Mgr.; Carol Boling, Personnel Mgr.

■ 9416 ■ Sterett Supply Co.
4533 Baldwin
PO Box 5528
Corpus Christi, TX 78408-2709
Phone: (210)884-1661 **Fax:** (210)884-0644
Products: Electrical supplies, including wiring and sockets. **SIC:** 5063 (Electrical Apparatus & Equipment). **Est:** 1944. **Sales:** $10,000,000 (2000). **Emp:** 28. **Officers:** William G. Sterett III, President; Sally Davis, VP of Finance.

■ 9417 ■ Henry Stern & Company, Inc.
183 S Central Ave.
Hartsdale, NY 10530
Phone: (914)761-4800 **Fax:** (914)761-4933
Products: Electrical construction materials. **SIC:** 5063 (Electrical Apparatus & Equipment). **Officers:** Barton T. Guttag, Vice President.

■ 9418 ■ Stokes Electric Co.
1701 McCalla Ave.
Knoxville, TN 37915
Phone: (423)525-0351 **Fax:** (423)971-4149
URL: http://www.stokeselec.com
Products: Electrical supplies, including lighting products. **SIC:** 5063 (Electrical Apparatus & Equipment). **Est:** 1933. **Sales:** $28,000,000 (2000). **Emp:** 100. **Officers:** Brian G. LaLonde, President & CEO.

■ 9419 ■ Stone Electronic
2062 SW 4th Ave.
Ontario, OR 97914
Phone: (541)881-1338
Products: Electronics. **SIC:** 5065 (Electronic Parts & Equipment Nec).

■ 9420 ■ Stoneway Electric Supply Co.
N 402 Perry
Spokane, WA 99202
Phone: (509)535-2933 **Fax:** (509)535-9508
Products: Electrical equipment. **SIC:** 5063 (Electrical Apparatus & Equipment). **Emp:** 49. **Officers:** Ed Ralph.

■ 9421 ■ Stoneway Electric Supply Co.
3665 Stoneway Ave. N
Seattle, WA 98103
Phone: (206)634-2240
Free: (800)223-6513 **Fax:** (206)634-2528
URL: http://www.ieway.com
Products: Electrical supplies. **SIC:** 5063 (Electrical Apparatus & Equipment). **Sales:** $45,000,000 (2000). **Emp:** 170. **Officers:** Douglas Albright, President; Robert Headstrom, CFO.

■ 9422 ■ Storm Products Co.
116 Shore Dr.
Hinsdale, IL 60521-5819
Phone: (630)323-9121
Free: (800)247-8676 **Fax:** (630)323-9398
Products: Electronic components; Electronic wire and cable. **SICs:** 5065 (Electronic Parts & Equipment Nec); 5063 (Electrical Apparatus & Equipment). **Est:** 1978. **Sales:** $7,500,000 (2000). **Emp:** 70. **Officers:** Brian Holland.

■ 9423 ■ Storm Products Co.
3047 N 31st Ave.
Phoenix, AZ 85017
Phone: (602)269-3485 **Fax:** (602)278-8534
URL: http://www.stormproducts.com
Products: Electronic wire and cable; Wire harnesses and cable assemblies; Heat shrink sleeving. **SIC:** 5063 (Electrical Apparatus & Equipment). **Est:** 1969. **Sales:** $2,000,000 (2000). **Emp:** 20. **Officers:** J.A. Storm; Melanie Weingardt, Sales/Marketing Contact, e-mail: mkw@az.stormproducts.com.

■ 9424 ■ Storm Products Company Inc.
112 S Glasgow Ave.
Inglewood, CA 90301
Phone: (310)649-6141 **Fax:** (310)645-6701
Products: Cables. **SIC:** 5065 (Electronic Parts & Equipment Nec). **Est:** 1957. **Sales:** $8,000,000 (1999). **Emp:** 50. **Officers:** John A. Storm, President; John Redmond, General Mgr.; Allan Cube, Human Resources Contact.

■ 9425 ■ Stover Smith Electric Supplies Inc.
PO Box 446
Laurel, MS 39441
Phone: (601)425-4791 **Fax:** (601)428-8711
Products: Electrical supplies, including wires, switches, and feedings. **SIC:** 5063 (Electrical Apparatus & Equipment). **Est:** 1966. **Sales:** $4,000,000 (2000). **Emp:** 20. **Officers:** Gary Smith, CEO; Kimberly D. Chancellor, Sec. & Treas.

■ 9426 ■ Stratton Electronics Inc.
PO Box 4383
Missoula, MT 59806-4383
Phone: (406)728-8855 **Fax:** (406)728-8863
E-mail: strattonelectronics@hotmail.com
Products: Electronic parts. **SIC:** 5065 (Electronic Parts & Equipment Nec). **Est:** 1980. **Officers:** Vernon E. Stratton Jr., President; Cynthia A. Stratton.

■ 9427 ■ Stromberg Sales Company Inc.
PO Box 22487
Indianapolis, IN 46222-0487
Phone: (317)638-0772 **Fax:** (317)263-5243
Products: Electrical equipment and supplies. **SIC:** 5065 (Electronic Parts & Equipment Nec). **Officers:** George Stromberg, President.

■ 9428 ■ Stusser Electric Co.
660 S Andover St.
Seattle, WA 98108
Phone: (206)623-1501 **Fax:** (206)623-6234
Products: Electrical products. **SIC:** 5063 (Electrical Apparatus & Equipment). **Est:** 1919. **Sales:** $70,000,000 (2000). **Emp:** 250. **Officers:** Herbert C. Stusser, President; Leslie E. Stusser, Vice President.

■ 9429 ■ Stusser Electric Co.
1606 130th Ave. NE
Bellevue, WA 98005
Phone: (425)454-3339
Free: (800)877-8029 **Fax:** (425)453-4808
Products: Lamps; Lighting fixtures. **SIC:** 5063 (Electrical Apparatus & Equipment).

■ 9430 ■ **Stusser Electric Co.**
1815 Franklin St.
Bellingham, WA 98225
Phone: (206)734-5500
Free: (800)624-2999 **Fax:** (206)676-1759
Products: Electrical equipment and supplies. **SIC:** 5063 (Electrical Apparatus & Equipment).

■ 9431 ■ **Stusser Electric Co.**
917 N Wycoff Ave.
Bremerton, WA 98312-3808
Phone: (206)373-5018
Free: (800)652-5009 **Fax:** (206)479-5731
Products: Lamps; Fuses and fuse equipment; Circuit breakers; Electrical boxes and fittings. **SIC:** 5063 (Electrical Apparatus & Equipment).

■ 9432 ■ **Stusser Electric Co.**
1104 132nd St. SW
Everett, WA 98204
Phone: (425)745-9666
Free: (800)962-6773 **Fax:** (425)742-8300
Products: Electrical equipment and supplies. **SIC:** 5063 (Electrical Apparatus & Equipment).

■ 9433 ■ **Stusser Electric Co.**
310 E Olympia Ave.
Olympia, WA 98501
Phone: (206)943-1900
Free: (800)736-7218 **Fax:** (206)943-2052
Products: Circuit breakers; Lamps; Electrical receptacles; Electrical equipment and supplies. **SIC:** 5063 (Electrical Apparatus & Equipment).

■ 9434 ■ **Stusser Electric Co.**
21520 84th Place S
Kent, WA 98031
Phone: (253)395-3133 **Fax:** (253)395-3932
Products: Power wire and cable; Power circuit breakers, all voltages. **SIC:** 5063 (Electrical Apparatus & Equipment).

■ 9435 ■ **Stusser Electric Co.**
116 N 2nd Ave.
Yakima, WA 98902
Phone: (509)453-0378
Free: (800)572-6518 **Fax:** (509)452-3972
Products: Lamps; Circuit breakers; Electrical equipment and supplies. **SIC:** 5063 (Electrical Apparatus & Equipment).

■ 9436 ■ **Stusser Electric Co.**
27929 SW 95th Ave. Ste. 701
Wilsonville, OR 97070
Phone: (503)639-4993
Free: (800)570-8646 **Fax:** (503)570-8552
Products: Electrical products. **SIC:** 5063 (Electrical Apparatus & Equipment).

■ 9437 ■ **Stusser Electric Co.**
2290 Judson St., SE
Salem, OR 97302
Phone: (503)581-3711
Free: (800)366-6485 **Fax:** (503)363-2903
Products: Lighting fixtures. **SIC:** 5063 (Electrical Apparatus & Equipment).

■ 9438 ■ **Stusser Electric Company**
411 E 54th Ave.
Anchorage, AK 99518
Phone: (907)561-1061
Free: (800)478-1061 **Fax:** (907)561-0203
E-mail: stusser@alaska.net
Products: Lamps; Circuit breakers; Electrical equipment and supplies. **SIC:** 5063 (Electrical Apparatus & Equipment).

■ 9439 ■ **Summit Electric Supply Inc.**
PO Box 6409
Albuquerque, NM 87197-6409
Phone: (505)884-4400 **Fax:** (505)222-4981
Products: Load centers; Conduits; Resistors; Wire. **SIC:** 5063 (Electrical Apparatus & Equipment). **Est:** 1977. **Sales:** $91,000,000 (2000). **Emp:** 300. **Officers:** Victor Jury Jr., President.

■ 9440 ■ **Sun Supply Corp.**
PO Box 149
Abilene, TX 79604
Phone: (915)673-2505
Products: Electrical equipment; Floor covering. **SICs:** 5063 (Electrical Apparatus & Equipment); 5023 (Homefurnishings). **Est:** 1923. **Sales:** $5,500,000 (2000). **Emp:** 31. **Officers:** Robert Calk, President; John Self, General Mgr.

■ 9441 ■ **Sunbelt Transformer Inc.**
PO Box 1500
Temple, TX 76503-1500
Phone: (254)771-3777 **Fax:** (254)771-5719
Products: Power-distribution transformers. **SIC:** 5063 (Electrical Apparatus & Equipment). **Est:** 1981. **Sales:** $10,000,000 (2000). **Emp:** 50. **Officers:** R. Maddox, CEO; Kyle McQueen, Dir. of Marketing.

■ 9442 ■ **Sunray Electric Supply Co.**
PO Box 489
Mc Keesport, PA 15134
Phone: (412)678-8826 **Fax:** (412)678-8826
Products: Pipe; Wire; Fuses; Lamps; Lamp fixtures. **SIC:** 5063 (Electrical Apparatus & Equipment). **Est:** 1952. **Sales:** $8,000,000 (2000). **Emp:** 30. **Officers:** P.W. Latterman, President; I.J. Latterman, CFO; R. Weaver, Dir. of Marketing; Keith Latterman, Dir. of Data Processing.

■ 9443 ■ **Superior Electric Supply Co. (Elyria, Ohio)**
PO Box 509
Elyria, OH 44036
Phone: (216)323-5451 **Fax:** (216)323-5691
E-mail: sales@sescoelyria.com
URL: http://www.superiorelectricsupply.com
Products: Electrical supplies. **SIC:** 5063 (Electrical Apparatus & Equipment). **Est:** 1905. **Sales:** $10,000,000 (2000). **Emp:** 30. **Officers:** Timothy J. King, President.

■ 9444 ■ **Superior Insulated Wire Corp.**
40 Washburn Ln.
PO Box 658
Stony Point, NY 10980-0658
Phone: (845)942-1433
Free: (800)535-9473 **Fax:** (845)942-2007
E-mail: superiorwire@worldnet.att.net
Products: Electronic and electrical wire and cable; Insulated wire. **SICs:** 5065 (Electronic Parts & Equipment Nec); 5085 (Industrial Supplies). **Est:** 1945. **Sales:** $5,000,000 (1999). **Emp:** 30. **Officers:** Leonard M. Miller, CEO & President.

■ 9445 ■ **Superior Manufacturing Co. (Santa Ana, California)**
3133 W Harvard St.
Santa Ana, CA 92704
Phone: (714)540-4605 **Fax:** (714)540-4541
Products: Contract manufacturing of circuit board assemblies. **SIC:** 5065 (Electronic Parts & Equipment Nec). **Sales:** $24,000,000 (2000). **Emp:** 278.

■ 9446 ■ **Supertek**
2231 Colby Ave.
Los Angeles, CA 90064
Phone: (310)477-1481 **Fax:** (310)473-1691
Products: Electronic parts. **SIC:** 5065 (Electronic Parts & Equipment Nec). **Officers:** Sarah Kim, Contact.

■ 9447 ■ **Surel International, Inc.**
526 Garfield Ave., Ste. A
South Pasadena, CA 91030-2244
Products: Electronic modules and subsystems; Process control instruments; Electronic industrial controls; Telecommunication and electronic components. **SIC:** 5065 (Electronic Parts & Equipment Nec). **Officers:** Emil G. Surel, President.

■ 9448 ■ **Surge Components Inc.**
1016 Grand Blvd.
Deer Park, NY 11729
Phone: (631)595-1818 **Fax:** (631)595-1283
URL: http://www.surgecomponents.com
Products: Capacitors; Rectifiers; Transistors; Diodes. **SIC:** 5065 (Electronic Parts & Equipment Nec). **Est:** 1981. **Sales:** $12,300,000 (2000). **Emp:** 25. **Officers:** Ira Levy, President, e-mail: ira@ surgecomponents.com; Shana Spanier, Sales & Marketing Contact, e-mail: shana@ surgecomponents.com.

■ 9449 ■ **Swam Electric Company Inc.**
490 High
Hanover, PA 17331-2124
Phone: (717)637-3821 **Fax:** (717)637-8964
E-mail: swamelec@netrax.net
URL: http://www.swamelectric.com
Products: Control panels/power distributon; Electric motors; Electrical construction. **SIC:** 5063 (Electrical Apparatus & Equipment). **Est:** 1921. **Sales:** $4,000,000 (2000). **Emp:** 56. **Officers:** Glenn E. Bange.

■ 9450 ■ **Swanson-Nunn Electric Co.**
PO Box 508
Evansville, IN 47703-0508
Phone: (812)424-7931
Products: Electrical equipment, supplies and materials. **SIC:** 5063 (Electrical Apparatus & Equipment). **Sales:** $22,000,000 (1992). **Emp:** 300. **Officers:** Jack Buttrum, President; David A. Daniels, VP of Finance.

■ 9451 ■ **Swift Electric Supply Co.**
PO Box 4327
Union City, NJ 07087
Phone: (201)863-6457
Products: Wiring, bulbs, and electrical supplies. **SIC:** 5063 (Electrical Apparatus & Equipment). **Est:** 1943. **Sales:** $9,000,000 (2000). **Emp:** 40. **Officers:** August Sodora, President.

■ 9452 ■ **Sylvan Ginsbury Ltd.**
660 Kinderkamack Rd.
Oradell, NJ 07649
Phone: (201)261-3200 **Fax:** (201)261-2729
Products: Electronic components and accessories. **SIC:** 5065 (Electronic Parts & Equipment Nec). **Sales:** $24,000,000 (2000). **Emp:** 100. **Officers:** Mitchell A. Bacharach, Sales Administrator; William Munro, President.

■ 9453 ■ **T-Electra/TICA of Dallas Inc.**
1127 Airport Circle S
Euless, TX 76040-6805
Phone: (817)267-5678
Free: (800)553-2425 **Fax:** (817)283-6317
Products: Electrical equipment; Electronic components. **SICs:** 5063 (Electrical Apparatus & Equipment); 5065 (Electronic Parts & Equipment Nec). **Emp:** 9. **Officers:** T.L. Norris.

■ 9454 ■ **Tab Electric Supply Inc.**
PO Box 12510
New Bern, NC 28562
Phone: (919)633-4929
Products: Industrial electrical supplies. **SICs:** 5063 (Electrical Apparatus & Equipment); 5085 (Industrial Supplies). **Est:** 1983. **Sales:** $12,400,000 (2000). **Emp:** 31. **Officers:** Thomas A. Bayliss III, President.

■ 9455 ■ **Tab Electric Supply Inc.**
PO Box 12510
New Bern, NC 28562
Phone: (252)633-4929
Products: Electronic parts. **SIC:** 5065 (Electronic Parts & Equipment Nec). **Emp:** 50. **Officers:** Thomas A. Bayliss III, President.

■ 9456 ■ **Taitron Components Inc.**
25202 Anza Dr.
Santa Clarita, CA 91355
Phone: (805)257-6060
Free: (800)824-8766 **Fax:** (805)257-6415
E-mail: mikeadams@taitroncomponents.com
URL: http://www.taitroncomponents.com
Products: Transistors, diodes, and other discrete semiconductors and opto-electronic devices. **SIC:** 5065 (Electronic Parts & Equipment Nec). **Est:** 1990. **Sales:** $35,000,000 (2000). **Emp:** 60. **Officers:** Stewart Wang, CEO & President; Steven Dong, CFO.

■ 9457 ■ **Talays Inc.**
34443 Schoolcraft St.
Livonia, MI 48150
Phone: (313)525-1155   **Fax:** (313)525-1184
Products: Electronic equipment. **SICs:** 5065
(Electronic Parts & Equipment Nec); 5063 (Electrical
Apparatus & Equipment). **Est:** 1929. **Sales:**
$63,000,000 (2000). **Emp:** 180. **Officers:** Winston C.
Stalcup, CEO; Bruce Hoopes, CFO.

■ 9458 ■ **Talcup, Inc.**
34443 Schoolcraft
Livonia, MI 48150
Phone: (734)525-1155   **Fax:** (734)525-1184
URL: http://www.rselectronics.com
Products: Electronic components; Testing and
measurement products. **SICs:** 5065 (Electronic Parts &
Equipment Nec); 5063 (Electrical Apparatus &
Equipment). **Est:** 1929. **Sales:** $70,000,000 (2000).
Emp: 180. **Officers:** Winston C. Stalcup, CEO;
Howard   Taxe,   President;   Bill   Matravers,
Sales/Marketing Contact; Maureen Beaty, Human
Resources Contact. **Former Name:** Talays Inc.

■ 9459 ■ **Tapeswitch Corp.**
100 Schmitt Blvd.
Farmingdale, NY 11735
Phone: (631)630-0442
Free: (800)234-8273   **Fax:** (631)630-0454
E-mail: sales@tapeswitch.com
URL: http://www.tapeswitch.com
Products: Electrical equipment and supplies. **SIC:**
5063 (Electrical Apparatus & Equipment). **Sales:**
$12,000,000 (2000). **Emp:** 100. **Officers:** Ed Duhon,
President; Tom Polistina, VP of Sales.

■ 9460 ■ **Target Electronics Inc.**
16120 Caputo Dr.
Morgan Hill, CA 95037-5531
Phone: (408)778-0408
Free: (800)941-9242   **Fax:** (408)778-3807
E-mail: info@targetelectronics.com
Products: Electronic components. **SICs:** 5063
(Electrical Apparatus & Equipment); 5065 (Electronic
Parts & Equipment Nec). **Emp:** 25. **Officers:** Mike
Weseloh, President; Leo Adamski, Vice President.

■ 9461 ■ **TDK Corporation of America**
1600 Feehanville Dr.
Mt. Prospect, IL 60056
Phone: (847)803-6100   **Fax:** (847)803-6296
Products: Electronic components. **SICs:** 5065
(Electronic Parts & Equipment Nec); 5063 (Electrical
Apparatus & Equipment). **Est:** 1974. **Sales:**
$271,000,000 (2000). **Emp:** 235. **Officers:** Mitsikuni
Baba, CEO & President; Mitsuru Kurokawa, Treasurer;
Masaru Hirabayashi, Information Systems Mgr.; Steven
P. Callisher, Human Resources Mgr.

■ 9462 ■ **TDK Electronics Corp.**
12 Harbor Park Dr., Fl. 1
Port Washington, NY 11050
Phone: (516)625-0100
Free: (800)835-8273   **Fax:** (516)625-0171
Products: Blank audio and video tapes. **SIC:** 5065
(Electronic Parts & Equipment Nec). **Sales:**
$51,000,000 (2000). **Emp:** 125. **Officers:** Kuniyoshi
Matsui, President; Y. Magoshi, CFO.

■ 9463 ■ **TEAC America Inc.**
7733 Telegraph Rd.
Montebello, CA 90640
Phone: (213)726-0303
Free: (800)888-4923   **Fax:** (213)727-7672
Products: Electronics; Airborne cameras. **SIC:** 5065
(Electronic Parts & Equipment Nec). **Est:** 1967. **Sales:**
$380,000,000 (2000). **Emp:** 200. **Officers:** Hajime
Yamaguchi, President; Yoshihide Nomura, Controller;
Ted Oikawa, Dir. of Sales; Donald McCully, Data
Processing Mgr.; Christine Hunt, Human Resources
Mgr.

■ 9464 ■ **Teague Industries Inc.**
3445 County Rd. 154
McKinney, TX 75070
Phone: (972)516-0271
Products: Underground electrical cable. **SIC:** 5063
(Electrical Apparatus & Equipment).

■ 9465 ■ **Teal Electric Company Inc.**
PO Box 1189
Troy, MI 48099
Phone: (810)689-3000
Products: Electronic equipment and supplies. **SIC:**
5063 (Electrical Apparatus & Equipment). **Est:** 1891.
Sales: $5,000,000 (2000). **Emp:** 25. **Officers:** Vic L.
Kochajda, President & Treasurer.

■ 9466 ■ **Tech Electro Industries Inc.**
4300 Wiley Post Rd.
Dallas, TX 75244-2131
Phone: (972)239-7151   **Fax:** (972)661-3746
Products: Uninterruptable power supply batteries and
imported passive electronic components. **SIC:** 5063
(Electrical Apparatus & Equipment). **Sales:** $6,700,000
(2000). **Emp:** 33. **Officers:** William Kim Wah Tan,
CEO, President & Chairman of the Board; Sadasuki
Gomi, VP & Secty.

■ 9467 ■ **Teche Electric Supply Inc.**
PO Box 61640
Lafayette, LA 70596-1640
Phone: (318)234-7427
Products: Electrical appliances and equipment. **SIC:**
5063 (Electrical Apparatus & Equipment). **Sales:**
$12,000,000 (2000). **Emp:** 125. **Officers:** Peter B.
Hays, President; Tim Guidry, CFO.

■ 9468 ■ **Technical Advisory Service**
5115 S Valley View Blvd.
Las Vegas, NV 89118
Phone: (702)798-7926   **Fax:** (702)736-5899
Products: Electronic parts and equipment; Telephone
and data equipment. **SIC:** 5065 (Electronic Parts &
Equipment Nec). **Officers:** Ed Curry, President.

■ 9469 ■ **Technical Devices Co.**
PO Box 26655
Salt Lake City, UT 84126
Phone: (801)972-5935   **Fax:** (801)972-0646
Products: Electronic equipment, including hand tools.
SIC: 5065 (Electronic Parts & Equipment Nec).

■ 9470 ■ **Tecot Electrical Supply Company
Inc.**
PO Box 61
New Castle, DE 19720-0061
Phone: (302)421-3900
Products: Electrical supplies, including wires, tools,
and bulbs. **SIC:** 5063 (Electrical Apparatus &
Equipment). **Est:** 1955. **Sales:** $35,000,000 (2000).
Emp: 97. **Officers:** Vincent P. Sanzone, President;
Scott Cutler, CFO; Paul McKnight, Dir. of Marketing;
Mike Quirk, Dir. of Data Processing; Joe Cannan, VP of
Operations.

■ 9471 ■ **Teknis Corp.**
PO Box 3189
North Attleboro, MA 02761
Phone: (508)695-3591   **Fax:** (508)699-6059
E-mail: teknis@compuserve.com
URL: http://www.teknis.com
Products: UV curing equipment; Epoxies; Microwave
components; Metals; Air filters; Electronic parts and
equipment; Security protection devices. **SICs:** 5065
(Electronic Parts & Equipment Nec); 5075 (Warm Air
Heating & Air-Conditioning); 5063 (Electrical Apparatus
& Equipment); 5051 (Metals Service Centers &
Offices). **Est:** 1959. **Emp:** 4. **Officers:** Harold
Friedman, President.

■ 9472 ■ **Telebeep Wireless Inc.**
504 Prospect Ave.
Norfolk, NE 68701-4022
Phone: (402)371-2337   **Fax:** (402)371-4324
Products: Electronic parts; Electronic systems and
equipment; Telephone equipment; Telephone
equipment; Cellular telephones. **SIC:** 5065 (Electronic
Parts & Equipment Nec). **Officers:** Tom Schommer,
President.

■ 9473 ■ **Telecom Electric Supply Co.**
PO Box 860307
Plano, TX 75074
Phone: (214)422-0012   **Fax:** (214)422-0467
Products: Electrical supplies, including lamps,
switches, plates, conduits, tags, and labels. **SIC:** 5063
(Electrical Apparatus & Equipment). **Est:** 1985. **Sales:**

$3,000,000 (2000). **Emp:** 15. **Officers:** Fred Moses,
President.

■ 9474 ■ **Telectron Inc.**
3315 SW 11th Ave.
Ft. Lauderdale, FL 33315
Phone: (954)832-0046
Free: (800)366-8800   **Fax:** (954)832-9721
Products: Access control equipment, and gate
operators. **SIC:** 5065 (Electronic Parts & Equipment
Nec). **Sales:** $2,000,000 (2000). **Emp:** 12. **Officers:**
Karen J. Veltri, CEO; Jerry McSwain, Accountant.

■ 9475 ■ **Teledata Concepts Inc.**
4421 N Dixie Hwy.
Boca Raton, FL 33431
Phone: (561)367-1337   **Fax:** (561)367-1507
Products: Telecommunications   equipment;
Telecommunications   equipment   installation;
Telecommunications equipment repair. **SIC:** 5065
(Electronic Parts & Equipment Nec). **Sales:** $4,000,000
(2000). **Emp:** 33. **Officers:** Bob Chilton, General Mgr.;
Jeff Feinerman, CFO.

■ 9476 ■ **Telesensory Corp.**
520 Almanor Ave.
Sunnyvale, CA 94086
Phone: (408)616-8700   **Fax:** (408)616-8720
Products: Electronic and computer-based equipment
for the visually impaired and totally blind. **SIC:** 5065
(Electronic   Parts   &   Equipment   Nec).   **Sales:**
$35,000,000 (2000). **Emp:** 180. **Officers:** Larry Israel,
CEO & President; Ned Long, CFO.

■ 9477 ■ **Tennessee Electric Motor Co.**
PO Box 22839
Nashville, TN 37202
Phone: (615)255-7331
Free: (800)844-8362   **Fax:** (615)259-3264
Products: Motors and motor controls. **SIC:** 5063
(Electrical   Apparatus   &   Equipment).   **Sales:**
$12,000,000 (2000). **Emp:** 33. **Officers:** Edwin Grant,
President; William Grant, VP of Finance.

■ 9478 ■ **Tennessee Valley Electric Supply
Co.**
6210 Dividend St.
Little Rock, AR 72209
Phone: (501)568-3627   **Fax:** (501)568-0052
Products: Electrical supplies, including plugs, lights
and transformers. **SIC:** 5063 (Electrical Apparatus &
Equipment). **Emp:** 12.

■ 9479 ■ **Tepper Electrical Supply Inc.**
608 S Neil St.
Champaign, IL 61820
Phone: (217)356-3755
Products: Electrical supplies, including batteries, light
bulbs, and wire. **SIC:** 5063 (Electrical Apparatus &
Equipment). **Est:** 1951. **Sales:** $7,000,000 (2000).
Emp: 25. **Officers:** Fay Tepper, CEO & Chairman of
the Board; Edward Tepper, Exec. VP.

■ 9480 ■ **Terrile Export & Import Corp.**
20 E 46th St., Rm. 1003
New York, NY 10017-2417
Phone: (212)986-2930   **Fax:** (212)986-9390
Products: Industrial machinery and equipment;
Industrial supplies; Motor vehicle supplies and parts;
Commercial equipment; Electrical equipment; Textile
machinery parts; Major household applicances. **SICs:**
5063 (Electrical Apparatus & Equipment); 5084
(Industrial Machinery & Equipment); 5013 (Motor
Vehicle Supplies & New Parts); 5046 (Commercial
Equipment Nec). **Est:** 1942. **Officers:** Albert Terrile,
President.

■ 9481 ■ **Terry-Durin Company Inc.**
407 7th Ave. SE
Cedar Rapids, IA 52406
Phone: (319)364-4106
Products: Electrical supplies, including wire, panel
board, and conduits. **SIC:** 5063 (Electrical Apparatus &
Equipment). **Est:** 1907. **Sales:** $6,500,000 (2000).
Emp: 19. **Officers:** George W. Durin, President &
Chairman of the Board.

■ 9482 ■ Tescom
15527 Ranch Rd. 620 N
Austin, TX 78717-5299
Phone: (512)244-6689
Free: (800)550-1978   Fax: (512)244-6689
Products: Electronic components, batteries, telecommunications and data communications test equipment; Equipment repairs. SICs: 5065 (Electronic Parts & Equipment Nec); 5063 (Electrical Apparatus & Equipment). Sales: $7,500,000 (2000). Emp: 25. Officers: Fran Collmann, CEO & President.

■ 9483 ■ Test Systems Inc.
217 W Palmaire Ave.
Phoenix, AZ 85021
Phone: (602)861-1010
Products: Test equipment; Conducts training seminars and testing service. SIC: 5065 (Electronic Parts & Equipment Nec).

■ 9484 ■ Thalner Electronic Labs Inc.
7235 Jackson Rd.
Ann Arbor, MI 48103
Phone: (313)761-4506   Fax: (313)761-9776
Products: Electronic components and equipment. SIC: 5065 (Electronic Parts & Equipment Nec). Est: 1965. Sales: $12,000,000 (2000). Emp: 37. Officers: Karl Couyoumjian, President.

■ 9485 ■ Thermax Wire Corp.
3202 Linden Pl.
Flushing, NY 11354-2823
Phone: (718)939-8300   Fax: (718)886-3704
Products: Wire. SIC: 5063 (Electrical Apparatus & Equipment). Sales: $30,000,000 (2000). Emp: 200. Officers: M. Gold.

■ 9486 ■ Thomson-CSF Inc.
99 Canal Center Plz., No. 450
Alexandria, VA 22314-1588
Phone: (703)838-9685
Products: Defense electronics. SIC: 5065 (Electronic Parts & Equipment Nec). Est: 1958. Sales: $3,000,000 (2000). Emp: 10. Officers: James D. Bell, President; T. Weibel, VP of Finance; B. Duhov, VP of Business Development; Richard Keating, Dir. of Corp. Communications.

■ 9487 ■ Thor Electronics Corp.
321 Pennsylvania Ave.
Linden, NJ 07036
Phone: (908)486-3300
Free: (800)526-4052   Fax: (908)486-0923
E-mail: Thorelect@aol.com
URL: http://www.thorel.com
Products: Electronic components, including circuits, electron tubes, transistors, and transformers. SICs: 5065 (Electronic Parts & Equipment Nec); 5063 (Electrical Apparatus & Equipment). Est: 1961. Sales: $3,000,000 (2000). Emp: 15. Officers: A.C. Crudele, President; R. Gettis, CFO.

■ 9488 ■ Throttle Up Corp.
463 Turner Dr Ste. 104A
Durango, CO 81301
Phone: (970)259-0690   Fax: (970)259-0691
Products: Consumer electronics for model railroads. SIC: 5065 (Electronic Parts & Equipment Nec). Officers: Steven Dominguez, President.

■ 9489 ■ Time Systems Inc.
1434 Mishawaka Ave.
South Bend, IN 46615-1226
Phone: (219)289-5733
Free: (800)359-8463   Fax: (219)288-0681
Products: Electronic time and attendance equipment. SIC: 5064 (Electrical Appliances—Television & Radio). Officers: Jack Zimmer, President.

■ 9490 ■ The TK Group, Inc.
PO Box 867
Bountiful, UT 84011-0867
Phone: (801)298-8902   Fax: (801)298-8906
Products: Electronic systems and equipment. SIC: 5065 (Electronic Parts & Equipment Nec).

■ 9491 ■ TOA Electronics, Inc.
601 Gateway Blvd., Ste. 300
South San Francisco, CA 94080
Phone: (650)588-2538
Free: (800)733-4750   Fax: (650)588-3349
E-mail: info@toa.electronics.com
URL: http://www.toaelectronics.com
Products: Commerical, professional audio and communication equipment. SIC: 5065 (Electronic Parts & Equipment Nec). Est: 1973. Sales: $25,000,000 (2000). Emp: 45. Officers: Hiromi Fujita, President, e-mail: hiromi_fujita@toaelectronics.com; Jeff Pallin, Vice President, e-mail: jeff_pallin@toaelectronics.com.

■ 9492 ■ Tocos America Inc.
1177 E Tower Rd.
Schaumburg, IL 60173
Phone: (708)884-6664
Products: Electronic components. SIC: 5065 (Electronic Parts & Equipment Nec).

■ 9493 ■ Toppan Printronics (USA) Inc.
PO Box 655012
Dallas, TX 75265
Phone: (972)995-6575
Products: Semiconductor devices. SIC: 5065 (Electronic Parts & Equipment Nec).

■ 9494 ■ Topworx
PO Box 37290
Louisville, KY 40233
Phone: (502)969-8000   Fax: (502)969-5911
E-mail: info@topworx.com
URL: http://www.topworx.com
Products: Leverless limit switches; Valve position indicators; Integrated valve controllers and monitors. SIC: 5063 (Electrical Apparatus & Equipment). Est: 1950. Emp: 80. Officers: Charlie R. Marcum, President; Mark Peters, VP of Engineering; Chuck Russ, VP of Operations; Sue Shields, Dir. of Marketing, e-mail: sshields@topworx.com.

■ 9495 ■ Toshiba America Consumer Products Inc.
82 Totowa Rd.
Wayne, NJ 07470
Phone: (973)628-8000   Fax: (973)628-1875
Products: Consumer electronics. SIC: 5064 (Electrical Appliances—Television & Radio). Sales: $80,000,000 (2000). Emp: 170. Officers: Toshihide Yasui, President; Nobukiyo Ishikawa, CFO.

■ 9496 ■ Total Electric Distributors Inc.
388 South Ave.
Staten Island, NY 10303
Phone: (718)273-9300
Free: (800)616-9473   Fax: (718)273-9316
Products: Electrical supplies, including wire and cable. SIC: 5063 (Electrical Apparatus & Equipment). Est: 1989. Sales: $7,000,000 (2000). Emp: 14. Officers: Lenore Schwartz, President; Wendie Broker, Vice President; Diane Searles, VP of Sales.

■ 9497 ■ Tower Fasteners Company, Inc.
1690 N Ocean Ave.
Holtsville, NY 11742-1823
Phone: (516)289-8800
Free: (800)688-6937   Fax: (516)289-8810
Products: Electrical hanging and fastening devices. SIC: 5063 (Electrical Apparatus & Equipment).

■ 9498 ■ Townsend Supply Co.
120 Johnson St.
Jackson, TN 38301
Phone: (901)424-4300
Products: Electrical supplies; Hardware; Fasteners; Motor shop supplies. SICs: 5063 (Electrical Apparatus & Equipment); 5072 (Hardware); 5013 (Motor Vehicle Supplies & New Parts). Sales: $30,000,000 (2000). Emp: 140. Officers: Louie W. Hailey Jr., President; Charles Ferrell, CFO; James C. Wilson, VP of Sales; David Fesmire, Dir. of Data Processing.

■ 9499 ■ Tranex Inc.
2350 Executive Cir
Colorado Springs, CO 80906
Phone: (719)576-7994
Free: (800)580-8991   Fax: (719)576-1503
Products: Electronic coils, transformers and inductors.

SIC: 5065 (Electronic Parts & Equipment Nec). Sales: $7,800,000 (2000). Emp: 100. Officers: Troy Valdez, President.

■ 9500 ■ Trans West Communication Systems
PO Box 9069
Seattle, WA 98109-0069
Phone: (425)882-3140   Fax: (425)885-0747
Products: Electronic parts; Electronic systems and equipment; Telephone equipment; Telegraph equipment. SIC: 5065 (Electronic Parts & Equipment Nec). Officers: Bill Anderson, President.

■ 9501 ■ Transmission and Fluid Equipment Inc.
6912 Trafalgar Dr.
Ft. Wayne, IN 46803
Phone: (219)493-3223
Products: Power transmission equipment. SIC: 5063 (Electrical Apparatus & Equipment).

■ 9502 ■ Treadway Electric Co.
3300 W 65th St.
Little Rock, AR 72209
Phone: (501)562-2111
Products: Electrical supplies. SIC: 5063 (Electrical Apparatus & Equipment). Sales: $15,000,000 (2000). Emp: 35. Officers: Ted C. Treadway, President; Bob Knight, CFO.

■ 9503 ■ Tri City Electrical Supply Co.
1 E Hundred Rd.
Chester, VA 23831-2608
Phone: (804)530-1030   Fax: (804)530-1065
Products: Electrical supplies. SIC: 5063 (Electrical Apparatus & Equipment). Emp: 14.

■ 9504 ■ Tri-State Armature and Electrical Works Inc.
PO Box 466
Memphis, TN 38101
Phone: (901)527-8412
Products: Electrical supplies and apparatus. SIC: 5063 (Electrical Apparatus & Equipment). Sales: $20,500,000 (1993). Emp: 250. Officers: David Mayhall, President.

■ 9505 ■ Tri State Electric Company Inc.
PO Box 1107
Sioux Falls, SD 57101
Phone: (605)336-2870   Fax: (605)334-0798
Products: Electrical equipment, floor coverings and accessories. SICs: 5063 (Electrical Apparatus & Equipment); 5023 (Homefurnishings). Sales: $7,000,000 (1993). Emp: 35. Officers: Dolores Merges, Treasurer & Secty.

■ 9506 ■ Tri State Electrical Supply Inc.
PO Box 546
Michigan City, IN 46361-0546
Phone: (219)872-5551   Fax: (219)872-3233
Products: Electrical and electronic supplies. SIC: 5063 (Electrical Apparatus & Equipment). Est: 1948. Sales: $3,000,000 (1999). Emp: 15. Officers: Alan E. Hill, President.

■ 9507 ■ Tri-State Lighting and Supply Company Inc.
PO Box 327
Evansville, IN 47702-0327
Phone: (812)423-4257
Products: Wires; Lights; Receptacles. SIC: 5063 (Electrical Apparatus & Equipment). Est: 1976. Sales: $7,000,000 (2000). Emp: 34. Officers: Wayne Jeffers, President.

■ 9508 ■ Triangle Electric Supply Co.
3815 Durazno
El Paso, TX 79905
Phone: (915)533-5981
Products: Electrical supplies. SIC: 5063 (Electrical Apparatus & Equipment). Est: 1947. Sales: $17,000,000 (2000). Emp: 50. Officers: R. Acton, CEO; Y. Guillen, Dir. of Data Processing.

■ 9509 ■ Trillennium
8 Carter Dr.
Framingham, MA 01701-3003
Phone: (508)788-0330
Products: Electrical transmission equipment. SIC:
5063 (Electrical Apparatus & Equipment).

■ 9510 ■ Trinkle Sales Inc.
1010 Hadonfield Berlin Rd.
Cherry Hill, NJ 08034
Phone: (856)988-9900   Fax: (856)988-9909
E-mail: tsi@tsirep.com
URL: http://www.tsirep.com
Products: Electronic components. SIC: 5065
(Electronic Parts & Equipment Nec). Est: 1932. Sales:
$30,000,000 (1999). Emp: 14. Officers: Robert P.
Albert, Owner & Pres.

■ 9511 ■ Tristate Electrical & Electronics
Supply Company Inc./Uagemeyer N.V.
1741 Dual Hwy.
PO Box 469
Hagerstown, MD 21741
Phone: (301)733-1212
Free: (800)638-3552   Fax: (301)790-2423
E-mail: sales@tristate-electric.com
URL: http://www.tristate-electric.com
Products: Electrical and electronic supplies. SIC: 5063
(Electrical Apparatus & Equipment). Est: 1927. Sales:
$200,000,000 (1999). Emp: 540. Officers: G.W.
Oldfather, President; D.R. Oldfather, Exec. VP; Mel M.
Meienke, VP of Marketing. Former Name: Tristate
Electrical Supply Company Inc.

■ 9512 ■ Tristate Electrical Supply Company
Inc.
1741 Dual Hwy.
Hagerstown, MD 21741
Phone: (301)733-1212
Free: (800)638-3552   Fax: (301)790-2423
Products: Electrical and electronic equipment and
supplies. SIC: 5063 (Electrical Apparatus &
Equipment). Sales: $125,000,000 (2000). Emp: 400.

■ 9513 ■ Truex Associates
4864 S Orange Ave.
Orlando, FL 32806
Phone: (407)859-2160   Fax: (407)855-6439
Products: Electrical and electronic equipment and
supplies. SIC: 5065 (Electronic Parts & Equipment
Nec). Sales: $5,000,000 (2000). Emp: 2.

■ 9514 ■ TTI Inc.
2441 Northeast Pkwy.
Ft. Worth, TX 76106
Phone: (817)740-9000
Free: (800)CALL-TTI   Fax: (817)625-2661
URL: http://www.ttiinc.com
Products: Passive electronic equipment; Resistors,
capacitors, connectors, and diodes. SIC: 5065
(Electronic Parts & Equipment Nec). Est: 1971. Sales:
$555,000,000 (1999). Emp: 1,150. Officers: Paul
Andrews Jr., Chairman and CEO; Nick Kypreos, CFO;
Craig Concrad, Sr. VP of Sales; David Minter, Sr. VP of
Information Systems; Mike Morton, Sr. VP of Product
Marketing; John Davidson, Sr. VP of ILS & Value
Added Services.

■ 9515 ■ Tubelite Company, Inc.
4102 W Adams
Phoenix, AZ 85009
Phone: (602)484-0122
Free: (800)423-0669   Fax: 800-552-2341
Products: Screenprinting supplies; Lighting supplies.
SICs: 5063 (Electrical Apparatus & Equipment); 5199
(Nondurable Goods Nec).

■ 9516 ■ Tulare Pipe and Electric Supply Co.
800 W Inyo Ave.
Tulare, CA 93274
Phone: (209)686-8307
Products: Pipe and electric supplies. SICs: 5063
(Electrical Apparatus & Equipment); 5074 (Plumbing &
Hydronic Heating Supplies). Est: 1953. Sales:
$2,400,000 (2000). Emp: 14. Officers: Paul
Boghosian, President.

■ 9517 ■ Turtle and Hughes Inc.
1900 Lower Rd.
Linden, NJ 07036
Phone: (908)574-3600   Fax: (732)574-3723
URL: http://www.turtle.com
Products: Elecrical supplies; Industrial supplies. SICs:
5063 (Electrical Apparatus & Equipment); 5085
(Industrial Supplies). Est: 1923. Sales: $200,000,000
(2000). Emp: 420. Officers: Susan T. Millard,
President; Trevor Barnett, VP of Finance; J.G. Sinagra,
Sr. VP.

■ 9518 ■ Tuscaloosa Electrical Supply Inc.
1616 25th Ave.
Tuscaloosa, AL 35401
Phone: (205)759-5716   Fax: (205)345-2874
Products: Electrical supplies. SIC: 5065 (Electronic
Parts & Equipment Nec). Sales: $8,000,000 (2000).
Emp: 30. Officers: Eddy Mings, CEO; Jason Harless,
Controller.

■ 9519 ■ U and S Services Inc.
233 Fillmore Ave., No. 11
Tonawanda, NY 14150
Phone: (716)693-4490   Fax: (716)693-5280
Products: Control systems. SIC: 5065 (Electronic
Parts & Equipment Nec). Est: 1990. Sales: $1,900,000
(2000). Emp: 15. Officers: Russell J. Stuber,
President; Randy Urschel, Exec. VP.

■ 9520 ■ Unimark Inc.
9910 Widmer Rd.
Lenexa, KS 66215
Phone: (913)649-2424
Free: (800)255-6356   Fax: (913)649-5795
E-mail: barcode@unimark.com
URL: http://www.unimark.com
Products: Bar code printing, labels, and ribbon. SIC:
5065 (Electronic Parts & Equipment Nec). Est: 1976.
Emp: 100. Officers: Dean Lawrence, President.

■ 9521 ■ United Chemi-Con Inc.
9801 W Higgins Rd., Ste. 430
Rosemont, IL 60018-4725
Phone: (847)696-2000   Fax: (847)696-9278
Products: Electronic components. SIC: 5065
(Electronic Parts & Equipment Nec). Sales: $3,000,000
(2000). Emp: 400. Officers: A. Ishihara, President; T.
Tran, VP of Finance.

■ 9522 ■ United Electric Supply Co.
1530 Fairview
St. Louis, MO 63132-1344
Phone: (314)427-3333   Fax: (314)427-3618
Products: Electrical supplies. SIC: 5063 (Electrical
Apparatus & Equipment). Emp: 170.

■ 9523 ■ United Electric Supply Co. (Salt
Lake City, Utah)
117 W 400 S
Salt Lake City, UT 84110
Phone: (801)363-4431   Fax: (801)363-1101
Products: Electrical supplies, including cable and wire.
SIC: 5063 (Electrical Apparatus & Equipment). Est:
1919. Sales: $7,000,000 (2000). Emp: 35. Officers:
Richard Critchley, CEO & President; John Webb,
Treasurer & Secty.; John S. Critchley, VP/Dir. of
Marketing and Sales.

■ 9524 ■ United Electric Supply Inc.
PO Box 10287
Wilmington, DE 19850
Phone: (302)322-3333
Free: (800)324-3333   Fax: (302)322-3374
Products: Electrical supplies. SIC: 5063 (Electrical
Apparatus & Equipment). Sales: $53,600,000 (2000).
Emp: 193. Officers: Tom Cloud, President; Richard
Stagliano, CFO.

■ 9525 ■ United Light Co.
3959 Frankford Ave.
Philadelphia, PA 19124
Phone: (215)289-1453   Fax: (215)288-5830
Products: Electrical supplies, including light fixtures,
bulbs, and wires. SIC: 5063 (Electrical Apparatus &
Equipment). Est: 1919. Sales: $5,000,000 (2000).
Emp: 19. Officers: Lee Nitzky, President; David
Nitzky, President.

■ 9526 ■ United States Electric Co.
301 N 1st St.
Springfield, IL 62702
Phone: (217)522-3347
Free: (800)252-5101   Fax: (217)522-5026
Products: Electrical supplies; Refrigeration supplies.
SICs: 5063 (Electrical Apparatus & Equipment); 5078
(Refrigeration Equipment & Supplies). Est: 1923.
Sales: $8,000,000 (2000). Emp: 42. Officers: Paul
Branham, President.

■ 9527 ■ US Lighting & Electrical Supply
417 Jeff Davis Hwy.
Fredericksburg, VA 22401-3118
Phone: (703)373-8404   Fax: (540)371-2901
URL: http://www.uslighting.com
Products: Electrical supplies, including fixtures and
bulbs. SICs: 5063 (Electrical Apparatus & Equipment);
5065 (Electronic Parts & Equipment Nec). Est: 1976.
Emp: 10. Officers: Dale Treadway; Sandra Treadway,
Sales/Marketing Contact; Kim Greene, Customer
Service Contact; Sherry Caple, Human Resources
Contact. Alternate Name: United States Industrial
Supply, Inc. Former Name: Colonial Electric
Distributor.

■ 9528 ■ Uspar Enterprises Inc.
13404 S Monte Vista
Chino, CA 91710-5149
Phone: (909)591-7506
Free: (800)251-4612   Fax: (909)590-3220
E-mail: usparent@aol.com
URL: http://www.uspar.com
Products: Lighting fixtures. SIC: 5063 (Electrical
Apparatus & Equipment). Est: 1973. Sales:
$6,000,000 (2000). Emp: 50. Officers: Khalid Parekh,
Engineer; H.E. Parekh, President; Rizwan Parekh,
Engineer.

■ 9529 ■ UV Process Supply Inc.
1229 W Cortland St.
Chicago, IL 60614
Phone: (773)248-0099
Free: (800)621-1296   Fax: (773)880-6647
E-mail: info@uvps.com
URL: http://www.uvprocess.com
Products: Products for the ultraviolet industry. SIC:
5043 (Photographic Equipment & Supplies). Emp: 12.
Officers: Stephen B. Siggel, President.

■ 9530 ■ Val-Comm Inc.
249 Muriel St. NE
Albuquerque, NM 87123-2932
Phone: (505)292-7509   Fax: (505)299-4253
Products: Electronic parts; Electronic systems and
equipment; Communication systems and equipment.
SIC: 5065 (Electronic Parts & Equipment Nec).
Officers: Mel Pfeffer, President.

■ 9531 ■ Valhalla Scientific Inc.
9955 Mesa Rim Rd.
San Diego, CA 92121
Phone: (858)457-5576   Fax: (858)457-0127
Products: Energy testing equipment for government
and military. SIC: 5065 (Electronic Parts & Equipment
Nec). Officers: Joanne Clark, President.

■ 9532 ■ Valley Electric Company Inc.
PO Box 431
Manteca, CA 95337
Phone: (209)825-7000   Fax: (209)824-3187
URL: http://www.valleyelectric.com
Products: Electrical parts, including wiring, outlets, and
sockets; Lighting. SIC: 5063 (Electrical Apparatus &
Equipment). Est: 1921. Sales: $35,000,000 (2000).
Emp: 102. Officers: Tom Solari, Exec. VP, e-mail: t_
solar@valleyelectric.com; Doug Pringle, Dir. M.I.S.; Bill
Freize, Dir of Human Resources.

■ 9533 ■ Valley Electric Supply Corp.
PO Box 724
Vincennes, IN 47591
Phone: (812)882-7860
Free: (800)825-7877   Fax: (812)882-7893
E-mail: valley@vesupply.com
URL: http://www.vesupply.com
Products: Electrical parts and equipment. SIC: 5063
(Electrical Apparatus & Equipment). Est: 1959. Sales:
$21,000,000 (2000). Emp: 45. Officers: Donald C.

Hedstrom, President; John L. Curry, Treasurer; Richard J. Cannon, Secretary.

■ 9534 ■ **Valtronics Engineering and Mfg**
6602 N 58th Dr.
Glendale, AZ 85301
Phone: (623)937-0373 **Fax:** (623)931-6478
Products: Electronic assemblies; Electronic components. **SIC:** 5065 (Electronic Parts & Equipment Nec). **Officers:** Lorenzo Valenzuela, President.

■ 9535 ■ **Varta Batteries Inc.**
300 Executive Blvd.
Elmsford, NY 10523
Phone: (914)592-2500
Free: (800)GO-VARTA **Fax:** (914)592-2667
URL: http://www.varta.com
Products: Industrial equipment batteries and consumer batteries. **SIC:** 5063 (Electrical Apparatus & Equipment). **Sales:** $26,000,000 (2000). **Emp:** 40. **Officers:** Thomas Brodrick, President.

■ 9536 ■ **VID COM Distributing**
7622 Wornall
Kansas City, MO 64114
Phone: (816)363-3737
Free: (800)821-3636 **Fax:** (816)363-4466
E-mail: sales@vid-com.com
URL: http://www.vid-com.com
Products: Electronic merchandise; Security video systems. **SIC:** 5065 (Electronic Parts & Equipment Nec). **Est:** 1934. **Officers:** Joe Henshaw, e-mail: jhenshaw@vid-com.com.

■ 9537 ■ **VID COM Distributing**
7622 Wornall
Kansas City, MO 64114
Phone: (816)363-3737
Free: (800)821-3636 **Fax:** (816)363-4466
Products: Electrical and electronic equipment and supplies. **SIC:** 5065 (Electronic Parts & Equipment Nec).

■ 9538 ■ **Video Products Distributors**
5 Burlington Sq., Fl. 3
Burlington, VT 05401
Phone: (802)860-0040
Products: Videos. **SIC:** 5063 (Electrical Apparatus & Equipment).

■ 9539 ■ **Viking Supply Company Inc.**
6319 Northwest Hwy.
Chicago, IL 60631-1669
Phone: (773)775-5797 **Fax:** (773)775-3743
E-mail: viking-jt@att.net
URL: http://www.viking-supply.com
Products: Electrical supplies. **SIC:** 5063 (Electrical Apparatus & Equipment). **Est:** 1971. **Sales:** $1,000,000 (2000). **Emp:** 10. **Officers:** Jim Thompson. **Former Name:** Arntzen Electric Company Inc.

■ 9540 ■ **Villa Lighting Supply Company Inc.**
1218 S Vandeventer
St. Louis, MO 63110
Phone: (314)531-2600 **Fax:** (314)531-8720
Products: Light fixtures; Ceiling fans; Chandeliers. **SICs:** 5063 (Electrical Apparatus & Equipment); 5023 (Homefurnishings). **Est:** 1971. **Sales:** $45,000,000 (2000). **Emp:** 100. **Officers:** J.A. Villa, President; David D'Agrossa, Vice President; Mark Kaner, Vice President.

■ 9541 ■ **Villarreal Electric Company Inc.**
1400 Lincoln St.
PO Box 760
Laredo, TX 78040
Phone: (956)722-2471 **Fax:** (956)722-4175
Products: Electrical products. **SIC:** 5063 (Electrical Apparatus & Equipment). **Est:** 1930. **Sales:** $1,500,000 (1999). **Emp:** 14. **Officers:** Raul Villarreal, President; Lilia V. Vasquez, CFO; Mike A. Villarreal Sr., Dir. of Marketing.

■ 9542 ■ **Vineland Electric CED/Supply, Inc.**
301 Chestnut Ave.
Vineland, NJ 08360-9549
Phone: (609)691-1267 **Fax:** (609)691-0002
Products: Electrical equipment; Circuit breakers; Electrical conduit and conduit fittings; Power wire and cable. **SIC:** 5063 (Electrical Apparatus & Equipment). **Emp:** 14. **Officers:** Jack J. Tuso Jr., Branch Mgr.

■ 9543 ■ **Vista Manufacturing**
52864 Lillian St.
Elkhart, IN 46514
Phone: (219)264-0711 **Fax:** (219)264-4174
E-mail: nesales@vistamfg.com
URL: http://www.vistamfg.com
Products: Low-voltage tubular lighting. **SIC:** 5063 (Electrical Apparatus & Equipment). **Est:** 1980. **Sales:** $5,000,000 (2000). **Emp:** 35. **Officers:** James D. Tieszen, President; Dwayne E. Tieszen, Vice President; Wayne Hensley, Sales/Marketing Contact, e-mail: nesales@vistamfg.com; Lisa Dahlin, Customer Service Contact, e-mail: vistamfg1@sprynet.com; Kelly L. Daugherty, Human Resources Contact.

■ 9544 ■ **Vitramon Inc.**
PO Box 544
Bridgeport, CT 06601
Phone: (203)268-6261 **Fax:** (203)261-4446
Products: Ceramic capacitors; Electronic parts; Engines; Pacemakers. **SICs:** 5065 (Electronic Parts & Equipment Nec); 5063 (Electrical Apparatus & Equipment); 5047 (Medical & Hospital Equipment). **Est:** 1948. **Sales:** $38,400,000 (2000). **Emp:** 500. **Officers:** Robert H. Paquette, President; Everett Arndt, Controller; Gary F. Giordano, Dir. of Marketing; A.L. Fraser, Dir. of Data Processing; Gerald Sargent, Dir of Personnel.

■ 9545 ■ **Vitus Electric Supply Co.**
PO Box 2789
Eugene, OR 97402-0316
Phone: (541)484-6333
Products: Electrical products and supplies. **SIC:** 5063 (Electrical Apparatus & Equipment). **Est:** 1928. **Sales:** $2,900,000 (2000). **Emp:** 10. **Officers:** M.B. Vitus Jr., President; Felicia J. Vitus, VP & Treasurer; H.A. Huisel, Sales Mgr.; D.M. Vitus, Dir. of Systems.

■ 9546 ■ **Vodavi Technology Inc.**
8300 E Raintree Dr.
Scottsdale, AZ 85260
Phone: (480)443-6000 **Fax:** (480)998-2469
Products: Business communication systems. **SIC:** 5065 (Electronic Parts & Equipment Nec). **Officers:** Gregory Roeper, CEO & President; Tammy Powers, CFO.

■ 9547 ■ **Wabash Power Equipment Co.**
444 Carpenter St.
Wheeling, IL 60090
Phone: (847)541-5600
Free: (800)704-2002 **Fax:** (847)541-1279
Products: Boilers, generators, and power plant equipment. **SIC:** 5063 (Electrical Apparatus & Equipment). **Sales:** $15,000,000 (1999). **Emp:** 26. **Officers:** Richard Caitung, President; Arthur Winekoff, Controller.

■ 9548 ■ **W.A.C. Lighting**
615 South St.
Garden City, NY 11530
Free: (800)526-2588
E-mail: sales@waclighting.com
URL: http://www.waclighting.com
Products: Track and recessed lighting. **SIC:** 5063 (Electrical Apparatus & Equipment). **Est:** 1984. **Emp:** 213. **Officers:** Tony Wong, President; Leonard Schwartz; Pauline Tham.

■ 9549 ■ **Wacker Chemical Corp.**
460 McLaws Cir., Ste. 240
Williamsburg, VA 23185
Phone: (757)253-5663
Products: Electronic parts and equipment. **SIC:** 5065 (Electronic Parts & Equipment Nec). **Officers:** W Mastrolia, President.

■ 9550 ■ **Wagner-Electric of Fort Wayne Inc.**
3610 N Clinton St.
Ft. Wayne, IN 46805
Phone: (219)484-5532 **Fax:** (219)484-4485
Products: Electrical equipment, including drives, motors, and controls. **SIC:** 5063 (Electrical Apparatus & Equipment). **Est:** 1939. **Sales:** $4,000,000 (2000). **Emp:** 25. **Officers:** Marvin Bell, President; Margaret Williams, Operations Mgr.; Larry McComb, Sales/Marketing Contact; Andrew Bell, Sales/Marketing Contact; Jennifer Bell, Customer Service Contact; Don Bickford, Customer Service Contact; Margaret Williams, Human Resources Contact.

■ 9551 ■ **Walker and Associates Inc.**
PO Box 1029
Welcome, NC 27374
Phone: (704)731-6391
Products: Communications Systems and Equipmentt. **SIC:** 5065 (Electronic Parts & Equipment Nec). **Sales:** $200,000,000 (2000). **Emp:** 225.

■ 9552 ■ **Walker Component Group**
420 E 58th Ave.
Denver, CO 80216
Phone: (303)292-5537 **Fax:** (303)292-0114
URL: http://www.walkercomponent.com
Products: Semiconductors, connectors, electromechanical, passives. **SIC:** 5065 (Electronic Parts & Equipment Nec). **Est:** 1975. **Sales:** $40,000,000 (2000). **Emp:** 160. **Officers:** Craig J. Walker, CEO; Fritz E. Ieuter, VP of Finance; Bert McClung, VP of Sales; Doug Harris, Dir of Human Resources; Ken Morrison, VP of Marketing. **Former Name:** Integrated Electronics Corp.

■ 9553 ■ **Walker Group Inc.**
PO Box 1029
Welcome, NC 27374
Phone: (336)731-6391
Free: (800)472-1746 **Fax:** (336)731-7253
Products: Telecommunications equipment. **SIC:** 5063 (Electrical Apparatus & Equipment). **Sales:** $170,000,000 (1999). **Emp:** 238. **Officers:** Mark Walker, President; Mark Whitley, CFO.

■ 9554 ■ **Walters Wholesale Electric Co.**
2825 Temple Ave.
Long Beach, CA 90806
Phone: (562)988-3100 **Fax:** (562)988-3150
URL: http://www.walterswholesale.com
Products: Electrical materials; Transistors; Switches. **SICs:** 5063 (Electrical Apparatus & Equipment); 5065 (Electronic Parts & Equipment Nec). **Est:** 1960. **Sales:** $100,000,000 (2000). **Emp:** 290. **Officers:** John E. Walter, CEO; Bill Durkee, President; Nancy Nielsen, Secretary; James Johnson, Exec. VP; Richard Benbow, VP of Sales; Cheryl Thibauer, VP of Finance & Admin.; Denis Evert, VP ofCredit.

■ 9555 ■ **Warren Associates**
290 Rickenbacker Cir., Ste. 400
Livermore, CA 94550
Phone: (925)449-9000 **Fax:** (925)449-8648
E-mail: sales@warrenrep.com
URL: http://www.warrenrep.com
Products: Electronic systems and equipment. **SIC:** 5065 (Electronic Parts & Equipment Nec). **Est:** 1959. **Emp:** 10. **Officers:** Brad Warren, CEO, e-mail: sales@warrenrep.com; Allan F. Cravalho, e-mail: technical@warrenrep.com.

■ 9556 ■ **Warren Electric Co.**
303 Commerce
Clute, TX 77531-5605
Phone: (409)265-9371 **Fax:** (409)265-9379
Products: Electrical supplies, including wire and conduit. **SIC:** 5063 (Electrical Apparatus & Equipment). **Emp:** 49.

■ 9557 ■ **Warren Electric Group**
PO Box 67
Houston, TX 77001
Phone: (713)236-0971
Free: (800)232-0971 **Fax:** (713)236-2261
E-mail: wec@warrenelectric.com
URL: http://www.warrenelectric.com
Products: Electrical, automation, telecom, and utility supplies. **SIC:** 5065 (Electronic Parts & Equipment Nec). **Est:** 1919. **Sales:** $200,000,000 (1999). **Emp:** 600. **Officers:** Cheryl Thompson-Draper, President & CEO, e-mail: cheryltd@warrenelectric.com; John T. Draper, President & COO, e-mail: jtd@warrenelectric.com; Yvonne Oaks, Human Resources Contact, e-mail: yvonne@warrenelectric.com; Jack Barnes, Vice President; Phillip Thompson, VP of Marketing.

■ 9558 ■ Warren Supply Co.
300 E 50th St. N
Sioux Falls, SD 57104-0690
Phone: (605)336-1830
Free: (800)492-7736   **Fax:** 800-449-3042
E-mail: warren@direcpc.com
URL: http://www.warren-supply.com
Products: Satellites; TVs; Home automated living.
SICs: 5064 (Electrical Appliances—Television &
Radio); 5065 (Electronic Parts & Equipment Nec). **Est:**
1948. **Emp:** 25. **Officers:** Ronald Warren, President;
Michael Swiden, National Sales Mgr.

■ 9559 ■ Watmet Inc.
11 Montbleu Ct.
Getzville, NY 14068-1326
Phone: (716)568-1556
Products: Electronics. **SIC:** 5065 (Electronic Parts &
Equipment Nec). **Est:** 1961. **Sales:** $6,000,000 (2000).
Emp: 8. **Officers:** Greg Wiltrout, President.

■ 9560 ■ Watson Electric Supply Co.
1012 N Raguet
Lufkin, TX 75901-8212
Phone: (409)634-3373   **Fax:** (409)639-3244
Products: Electrical supplies, including wiring. **SIC:**
5063 (Electrical Apparatus & Equipment). **Emp:** 14.

■ 9561 ■ Watson Electric Supply Co.
PO Box 540297
Dallas, TX 75354-0297
Phone: (214)742-8441
Products: Fluorescent lights and lamps; Motor
controls; Starters; Fuses; Boxes; Wire. **SIC:** 5063
(Electrical Apparatus & Equipment). **Est:** 1947. **Sales:**
$46,000,000 (2000). **Emp:** 200. **Officers:** Malcolm L.
Watson, President; Tony Watson, Treasurer.

■ 9562 ■ Wayne Distributing Inc.
PO Box 68530
Indianapolis, IN 46268-0530
Phone: (317)875-5024   **Fax:** (317)871-6818
Products: Electrical items, including microwaves and
lighting systems. **SICs:** 5064 (Electrical Appliances—
Television & Radio); 5063 (Electrical Apparatus &
Equipment). **Est:** 1862. **Sales:** $20,000,000 (2000).
Emp: 11. **Officers:** Ted A. Barker, President; Arthur W.
Garringer, CFO; J. Phil Nolting, Dir. of Marketing.

■ 9563 ■ Waytek Inc.
PO Box 690
Chanhassen, MN 55317-0690
Phone: (612)949-0765
Free: (800)328-2724   **Fax:** (612)949-0965
URL: http://www.waytekwire.com
Products: Electrical supplies, including wire, terminals,
and connectors. **SIC:** 5063 (Electrical Apparatus &
Equipment). **Est:** 1973. **Emp:** 35.

■ 9564 ■ Webber Cable and Electronics
13477 12th St.
Chino, CA 91710
Phone: (909)464-1526   **Fax:** (909)464-1525
Products: Mil-spec manufacturer of custom cable,
cable assemblies, harnesses and harness assemblies;
Simple and complex electronic assemblies; Custom
molding cable heads and harness breakouts;
moldmaking. **SIC:** 5063 (Electrical Apparatus &
Equipment). **Sales:** $1,000,000 (1999). **Emp:** 4.
Officers: Nywood Wu, President; Roger Orton,
General Mgr.

■ 9565 ■ Wedco Inc.
PO Box 1131
Reno, NV 89504
Phone: (702)329-1131   **Fax:** (702)323-7339
Products: Electrical supplies. **SIC:** 5063 (Electrical
Apparatus & Equipment). **Est:** 1950. **Sales:**
$9,000,000 (2000). **Emp:** 32. **Officers:** R.J. Elmore,
General Mgr.; Alice DeRicco, Finance Officer; Brian
Elmore, Dir. of Marketing; Harry Caulk, Dir. of Data
Processing.

■ 9566 ■ Wedemeyer Electronic Supply Co.
2280 S Industrial Hwy.
Ann Arbor, MI 48104
Phone: (734)665-8611   **Fax:** (734)665-5896
Products: Electronics. **SIC:** 5065 (Electronic Parts &

Equipment Nec). **Est:** 1927. **Sales:** $5,100,000 (2000).
Emp: 35. **Officers:** G. William Wedemeyer, President.

■ 9567 ■ Wehle Electric Div.
475 Ellicott St.
Buffalo, NY 14203
Phone: (716)854-3270   **Fax:** (716)854-2987
URL: http://www.wehle.com
Products: Motor controls; Conduit; Light fixtures,
including lamps and light bulbs. **SIC:** 5063 (Electrical
Apparatus & Equipment). **Est:** 1923. **Sales:**
$50,000,000 (1999). **Emp:** 133. **Officers:** Ronald
Leffler, General Mgr.; Jeff Hazlett, Comptroller; Jim
Tallerico, Marketing Mgr.

■ 9568 ■ Weimer Bearing & Transmission Inc.
5368 Campbell Dr., No. W134
Menomonee Falls, WI 53052
Phone: (414)781-1992   **Fax:** (414)781-3034
Products: Small electrical and power transmissions.
SIC: 5063 (Electrical Apparatus & Equipment).

■ 9569 ■ WESCO Distribution Inc.
4 Station Sq.
Pittsburgh, PA 15219-1119
Phone: (412)454-2200   **Fax:** (412)454-2505
Products: Electrical and industrial equipment and
supplies. **SICs:** 5063 (Electrical Apparatus &
Equipment); 5084 (Industrial Machinery & Equipment);
5085 (Industrial Supplies). **Sales:** $2,500,000,000
(2000). **Emp:** 4,500. **Officers:** Roy W. Haley, CEO &
President; Dave McAnaly, CFO.

■ 9570 ■ West Philadelphia Electric Supply
Co.
5828 Market St.
Philadelphia, PA 19139
Phone: (215)474-9200
Products: Electrical supplies. **SIC:** 5063 (Electrical
Apparatus & Equipment). **Sales:** $16,000,000 (1992).
Emp: 40. **Officers:** H.J. Newman, President; Joseph
McGettigan, CFO.

■ 9571 ■ West Tennessee Communications
1295 US Hwy. 51, Bypass S
Dyersburg, TN 38024-9317
Phone: (901)286-6275
Free: (800)249-1250   **Fax:** (901)286-6438
Products: Communications Systems and Equipment.
SIC: 5065 (Electronic Parts & Equipment Nec). **Sales:**
$2,800,000 (2000). **Emp:** 20.

■ 9572 ■ Westburgh Electric Inc.
PO Box 1319
Jamestown, NY 14702-1319
Phone: (716)488-1172
Free: (800)828-8878   **Fax:** 888-488-1173
E-mail: sales@westburgh.com
URL: http://www.westburgh.com
Products: Electric motors and related products. **SIC:**
5063 (Electrical Apparatus & Equipment). **Est:** 1955.
Sales: $4,500,000 (2000). **Emp:** 23. **Officers:** Daniel
S. Blixt, President.

■ 9573 ■ Western Carolina Electrical Supply
Co.
PO Box 1530
Lenoir, NC 28645
Phone: (828)754-5311   **Fax:** (828)758-1280
E-mail: sales@wcesco.com
URL: http://www.wcesco.com
Products: Electrical supplies, including cable and wire.
SIC: 5063 (Electrical Apparatus & Equipment). **Est:**
1953. **Sales:** $4,000,000 (2000). **Emp:** 22. **Officers:**
Lyle Jensen, President, e-mail: lyle@wcesco.com; Don
Jensen, CEO; Brent Jensen, Vice President; Doris
Wallace, Sec. & Treas.

■ 9574 ■ Western Component Sales Div.
20953 Devonshire St., Ste. 5
Chatsworth, CA 91311
Phone: (818)882-6226
Products: Electro-mechanical components. **SIC:** 5084
(Industrial Machinery & Equipment).

■ 9575 ■ Western Extralite Co.
1470 Liberty St.
Kansas City, MO 64102
Phone: (816)421-8404
Products: Lighting systems. **SIC:** 5063 (Electrical
Apparatus & Equipment). **Sales:** $7,000,000 (1992).
Emp: 30. **Officers:** Thomas E. Isenberg, President;
Ken Keller, Controller.

■ 9576 ■ Western Radio Electronics Inc.
PO Box 790
San Diego, CA 92112-0790
Phone: (619)268-4400
Free: (800)777-4973   **Fax:** (619)279-7048
Products: Electronic equipment. **SIC:** 5065 (Electronic
Parts & Equipment Nec). **Sales:** $2,000,000 (2000).
Emp: 16. **Officers:** Jaime Brener, President.

■ 9577 ■ Western United Electric Supply
Corp.
1313 W 46th Ave.
Denver, CO 80211
Phone: (303)455-2725
Products: Electrical supplies and hardware. **SICs:**
5063 (Electrical Apparatus & Equipment); 5072
(Hardware). **Sales:** $4,000,000 (1993). **Emp:** 14.
Officers: William McClure, General Mgr.

■ 9578 ■ Westgate Enterprises Inc.
2118 Wilshire Blvd., No. 612
Santa Monica, CA 90403-5784
Phone: (310)477-5891   **Fax:** (310)478-1954
Products: Full spectrum lights. **SIC:** 5063 (Electrical
Apparatus & Equipment). **Est:** 1990. **Sales:** $100,000
(2000). **Emp:** 3. **Officers:** Christina Brady-Wokuluk,
Owner.

■ 9579 ■ Westinghouse Electical Supply
100 Oakley Ave.
Lynchburg, VA 24501-3237
Phone: (804)845-0948   **Fax:** (804)847-7292
Products: Circuit breakers; Electrical boxes and
fittings; Electrical conduit and conduit fittings; Power
wire and cable. **SIC:** 5063 (Electrical Apparatus &
Equipment). **Emp:** 499.

■ 9580 ■ Westland International Corp.
5000 Hwy. 80 E
Jackson, MS 39208
Phone: (601)932-7136
Products: Nuclear plant parts. **SIC:** 5084 (Industrial
Machinery & Equipment).

■ 9581 ■ Wheat International Communications
Corp.
1890 Preston White Drive
Reston, VA 20191
Phone: (703)262-9100
Products: Satellite Internet Connections; IP Internet
Telephony, PBXs, Voice Mail, and Call Centers; T-1
Connectivity with optional ISDN operations. **SIC:** 5065
(Electronic Parts & Equipment Nec). **Sales:**
$20,000,000 (2000). **Emp:** 55. **Officers:** Forrest C.
Wheat, Sr, CEO & President.

■ 9582 ■ William D. White Company Inc.
3427 Magnolia St.
Oakland, CA 94608
Phone: (510)658-8167
Products: Service entrance equipment. **SIC:** 5063
(Electrical Apparatus & Equipment). **Sales:** $2,000,000
(1992). **Emp:** 19. **Officers:** W.D. White Jr., President;
A. White, CFO.

■ 9583 ■ White Electric Supply Co.
427 S 10th St.
Lincoln, NE 68508
Phone: (402)476-7587
Free: (888)476-7598   **Fax:** (402)476-7589
E-mail: whiteelectric@navix.net
Products: Electrical lighting and supplies. **SIC:** 5063
(Electrical Apparatus & Equipment). **Est:** 1932. **Emp:**
12. **Officers:** Logan Ireland, Manager, e-mail:
loganireland@alltel.net; Jon Eicher, Sales Mgr., e-mail:
jeicher@alltel.net; Mike McAuliffe, Purchasing, e-mail:
mmcauliffe@alltel.net.

■ 9584 ■ **White Electric Supply Co. (Monroe City, Missouri)**
215 N Main St.
Monroe City, MO 63456
Phone: (314)735-4533 **Fax:** (314)735-2410
Products: Electrical supplies. **SIC:** 5063 (Electrical Apparatus & Equipment). **Est:** 1940. **Sales:** $2,000,000 (2000). **Emp:** 10. **Officers:** Keith Hays, President, e-mail: whiteele@nemonet.com.

■ 9585 ■ **Whitehill Lighting and Supply Inc.**
1524 N Atherton St.
State College, PA 16801
Phone: (814)238-2449 **Fax:** (814)238-1615
Products: Electrical supplies, including light bulbs, breakers, and panels. **SIC:** 5063 (Electrical Apparatus & Equipment). **Est:** 1962. **Sales:** $6,500,000 (2000). **Emp:** 29. **Officers:** Clyde Fuller, President.

■ 9586 ■ **Whitmor/Wirenetics**
27737 Hopkins Ave.
Valencia, CA 91355
Phone: (661)257-2400
Free: (800)822-9473 **Fax:** (661)257-2495
E-mail: sales@wirenetics.com
URL: http://www.wireandcable.com
Products: Wire; Cable; Heat shrink tubing. **SIC:** 5063 (Electrical Apparatus & Equipment). **Est:** 1959. **Sales:** $20,000,000 (2000). **Emp:** 58. **Officers:** H.R. Weiss, CEO; Michael Weiss, President; Mark Lee, VP of Sales, e-mail: m.lee@wirenetics.com. **Former Name:** Wirenetics Co.

■ 9587 ■ **Whitmor/Wirenetics**
27737 Hopkins Ave.
Valencia, CA 91355
Phone: (661)257-2400
Free: (800)822-WIRE **Fax:** (661)257-2495
E-mail: wirenetics@msn.com
URL: http://www.wireandcable.com
Products: Electrical equipment. **SIC:** 5063 (Electrical Apparatus & Equipment). **Est:** 1959. **Sales:** $20,000,000 (2000). **Emp:** 60. **Officers:** H.R. Weiss, CEO; Michael Weiss, President. **Former Name:** Wirenetics Co.

■ 9588 ■ **Whitson and Co.**
8107 Springdale Rd., Ste. 101
Austin, TX 78724-2437
Phone: (512)929-9600
Products: Instrumentation for the semiconductor industry, including tubing, valves, gages and fittings. **SIC:** 5065 (Electronic Parts & Equipment Nec). **Sales:** $10,000,000 (2000). **Emp:** 36. **Officers:** Kent Benton, President.

■ 9589 ■ **Wholesale Electric Supply Company of Houston Inc.**
PO Box 230197
Houston, TX 77223-0197
Phone: (713)748-6100 **Fax:** (713)749-8415
Products: Electric supplies, including starters for engines. **SIC:** 5063 (Electrical Apparatus & Equipment). **Est:** 1949. **Sales:** $110,000,000 (2000). **Emp:** 260. **Officers:** Clyde G. Rutland, President; Joe Jones Sr., VP of Operations; L.L. Elder, VP of Marketing; Jon Watkins, Dir. of Systems.

■ 9590 ■ **Wholesale Electric Supply Company Inc. (Bowling Green, Kentucky)**
PO Box 2500
Bowling Green, KY 42102-2500
Phone: (502)842-0156 **Fax:** (502)842-5055
Products: Electrical supplies. **SIC:** 5063 (Electrical Apparatus & Equipment). **Est:** 1946. **Sales:** $4,000,000 (2000). **Emp:** 15. **Officers:** John S. Bettersworth, President.

■ 9591 ■ **Wholesale Electric Supply Company Inc. (Texarkana, Texas)**
PO Box 1258
Texarkana, TX 75504
Phone: (903)794-3404
Products: Electrical supplies, including wires, cords, and light bulbs. **SIC:** 5063 (Electrical Apparatus & Equipment). **Est:** 1947. **Sales:** $21,000,000 (2000). **Emp:** 70. **Officers:** A. McCulloch Jr., President; M.J. Whitman, Controller; C. Shilling Jr., Dir. of Marketing.

■ 9592 ■ **Wholesale Electronic Supply Inc.**
2809 Ross Ave.
Dallas, TX 75201
Phone: (214)969-9400
Free: (800)880-9400 **Fax:** (214)969-0973
E-mail: wholesale@altinet.net
URL: http://www.wholesale-electronics.com
Products: Electronic components; Video equipment, including video conference; Calculators. **SICs:** 5065 (Electronic Parts & Equipment Nec); 5063 (Electrical Apparatus & Equipment); 5064 (Electrical Appliances—Television & Radio). **Est:** 1950. **Sales:** $17,000,000 (2000). **Emp:** 45. **Officers:** John Leedom, Chairman of the Board; Melinda Woodson, President; John M. Leedom JR., Exec. VP, e-mail: JLeedom@altinet.net; Anita Miller, CFO; Audra Hernandez, Customer Service Contact, e-mail: audra@altinet.net; Helen Johnson, Human Resources Contact.

■ 9593 ■ **Wholesale Electronics Inc.**
123 W 1st Ave.
PO Box 1011
Mitchell, SD 57301
Phone: (605)996-2233 **Fax:** (605)996-4300
E-mail: wei@weisd.com
URL: http://www.weisd.com
Products: Computer accessories; Test equipment for testing electrical, radio and communication circuits, and motors; Electronic resistors; Electronic parts. **SIC:** 5065 (Electronic Parts & Equipment Nec). **Est:** 1976. **Emp:** 9.

■ 9594 ■ **Wichita Falls Nunn Electrical Supply**
1300-14 Indiana
Wichita Falls, TX 76301
Phone: (940)766-4203
Products: Electrical apparatus and equipment. **SIC:** 5063 (Electrical Apparatus & Equipment). **Sales:** $8,000,000 (2000). **Emp:** 25. **Officers:** Coyal Francis Jr., President; Robert Francis, Treasurer.

■ 9595 ■ **Willcox and Gibbs Inc. Consolidated Electric Supply**
4561 34th St.
Orlando, FL 32811
Phone: (407)841-4860
Products: Electrical equipment. **SIC:** 5063 (Electrical Apparatus & Equipment). **Sales:** $360,000,000 (1993). **Emp:** 1,100. **Officers:** Pete Schiller, President; N. Taylor Carlson, VP of Finance & Admin.

■ 9596 ■ **Wille Electric Supply Co.**
101 S 7th St.
Modesto, CA 95354
Phone: (209)527-6800 **Fax:** (209)527-5872
URL: http://www.willeelectric.com
Products: Industrial electrical products. **SIC:** 5063 (Electrical Apparatus & Equipment). **Est:** 1922. **Sales:** $16,000,000 (2000). **Emp:** 40. **Officers:** L.R. Robinson III, President; Ron Lacher, Controller; Rob Robinson, Sales Mgr., e-mail: rob@willeelectric.com.

■ 9597 ■ **Williams Supply Inc.**
PO Box 2766
Roanoke, VA 24001
Phone: (540)343-9333 **Fax:** (540)342-3254
URL: http://www.williams-supply.com
Products: Electrical supplies, including wire, switches, and fixtures. **SIC:** 5063 (Electrical Apparatus & Equipment). **Est:** 1946. **Sales:** $26,000,000 (2000). **Emp:** 95. **Officers:** J. Arnold Jones, President; Billy Gamble, Vice President; Debbie Martin, Chairman of the Board & Finance Officer; Steve Hale; Tom Moody, Dir. of Operations.

■ 9598 ■ **H. Wilson Co.**
555 W Taft Dr.
South Holland, IL 60473
Phone: (708)339-5111
Free: (800)245-7224 **Fax:** 800-245-8224
E-mail: sales@hwilson.com
URL: http://www.hwilson.com
Products: Electric and electronic equipment. **SIC:** 5065 (Electronic Parts & Equipment Nec). **Est:** 1959. **Sales:** $10,000,000 (2000). **Emp:** 40. **Officers:** Matthew Glowiak, Dir. of Mktg. & Sales, e-mail: matt@hwilson.com.

■ 9599 ■ **Wilson Electric Supply Co.**
680 2nd St.
Macon, GA 31201-2848
Phone: (912)746-5656 **Fax:** (912)746-0064
URL: http://www.wilsonelectric.com
Products: Electrical products. **SIC:** 5063 (Electrical Apparatus & Equipment). **Est:** 1953. **Emp:** 29. **Officers:** Mike Wilson, e-mail: mike.w@att.net.

■ 9600 ■ **Windsor Distributors Co.**
19 Freeman St.
Newark, NJ 07105
Phone: (973)344-5700 **Fax:** (973)344-3282
Products: Electrical equipment and supplies; Electronic parts; Electronic wire and cable; Connectors for electronic circuitry. **SICs:** 5065 (Electronic Parts & Equipment Nec); 5063 (Electrical Apparatus & Equipment). **Officers:** Barry Erenburg, Purchasing Agent.

■ 9601 ■ **Wire Supplies Inc.**
PO Box 277
Beech Grove, IN 46107
Phone: (317)786-4485
Products: Electronic wire and cable; Terminals; Wire connectors for electrical circuitry. **SICs:** 5063 (Electrical Apparatus & Equipment); 5065 (Electronic Parts & Equipment Nec).

■ 9602 ■ **Wise Wholesale Electronics**
1001 Towson
Ft. Smith, AR 72901-4921
Phone: (501)783-8925
Free: (800)272-5011 **Fax:** (501)783-3380
Products: Electronics. **SIC:** 5065 (Electronic Parts & Equipment Nec). **Est:** 1930. **Sales:** $2,000,000 (2000). **Emp:** 18. **Officers:** Eddie Reichert, President.

■ 9603 ■ **Wolberg Electrical Supply Company Inc.**
35 Industrial Park Rd.
Albany, NY 12206
Phone: (518)489-8451
Products: Electrical equipment. **SIC:** 5063 (Electrical Apparatus & Equipment). **Sales:** $14,000,000 (1992). **Emp:** 75. **Officers:** Milton Bindell, Owner; Ralph F. Laporta, President.

■ 9604 ■ **L.A. Woolley Inc.**
620 Tifft St.
Buffalo, NY 14220
Phone: (716)821-1200 **Fax:** (716)821-1208
E-mail: office@lawoolley.com
URL: http://www.lawoolley.com
Products: Electrical parts, including wires, capacitors, resistors, and switches. **SIC:** 5063 (Electrical Apparatus & Equipment). **Est:** 1916. **Sales:** $5,000,000 (2000). **Emp:** 20. **Officers:** Dave A. Woolley, President.

■ 9605 ■ **World Buying Service Inc.**
PO Box 43369
Louisville, KY 40243
Phone: (502)245-1166 **Fax:** (502)245-7281
Products: Electronic components; Electrical supplies; Electrical household appliances; Motor vehicle parts; Aircraft parts. **SICs:** 5063 (Electrical Apparatus & Equipment); 5065 (Electronic Parts & Equipment Nec); 5088 (Transportation Equipment & Supplies); 5064 (Electrical Appliances—Television & Radio); 5013 (Motor Vehicle Supplies & New Parts). **Officers:** Robert L. Langford, President.

■ 9606 ■ **World Products Inc.**
19654 8th St. E
Sonoma, CA 95476
Phone: (707)996-5201 **Fax:** (707)996-3380
Products: Electronic components. **SIC:** 5065 (Electronic Parts & Equipment Nec). **Est:** 1969. **Sales:** $40,000,000 (2000). **Emp:** 43. **Officers:** Michael P. Stone, President; Patricia L. Grimmer, Treasurer & Secty.

■ 9607 ■ **World Traders (USA) Inc.**
98-05 67th Ave.
Rego Park, NY 11374
Phone: (718)896-9560 **Fax:** (718)896-9560
Products: Electronic parts and equipment; Stationery and office supplies; Jewelry and precious stones;

Furniture; Electrical apparatus and equipment. **SICs:** 5063 (Electrical Apparatus & Equipment); 5065 (Electronic Parts & Equipment Nec); 5112 (Stationery & Office Supplies); 5094 (Jewelry & Precious Stones); 5021 (Furniture). **Officers:** Denise Lanes, President.

■ **9608** ■ **Worldwide Exporters Inc.**
2600 Garden Rd., Ste. 202
Monterey, CA 93940
Phone: (408)648-8331
Products: Factory automation equipment. **SIC:** 5084 (Industrial Machinery & Equipment). **Sales:** $2,500,000 (2000). **Emp:** 3. **Officers:** Scott Manhard, President.

■ **9609** ■ **Worth Data**
623 Swift St.
Santa Cruz, CA 95060
Phone: (831)458-9938
Free: (800)345-4220   **Fax:** (831)458-9964
E-mail: wds@barcodehq.com
URL: http://www.barcodehq.com
Products: Bar coding equipment. **SIC:** 5065 (Electronic Parts & Equipment Nec). **Est:** 1985. **Sales:** $13,000,000 (2000). **Emp:** 30. **Officers:** Hall Worthington, President; Mary Reyes, CFO. **Former Name:** Worthington Data Solutions Inc.

■ **9610** ■ **Wren Electronics, Inc.**
1605 NW 82nd Ave.
Miami, FL 33122
Phone: (305)591-5888   **Fax:** (305)591-0660
Products: New and refurbished consumer electronics; Computers. **SICs:** 5064 (Electrical Appliances—Television & Radio); 5045 (Computers, Peripherals & Software). **Officers:** Jose Renteria. **Former Name:** Bosco Trading Corp.

■ **9611** ■ **Wyle Electronics**
15370 Barranca Pkwy.
Irvine, CA 92618-2215
Phone: (949)753-9953   **Fax:** (949)753-9909
Products: Electronic equipment, semiconductors, and computer products. **SICs:** 5065 (Electronic Parts & Equipment Nec); 5045 (Computers, Peripherals & Software). **Sales:** $1,450,000,000 (2000). **Emp:** 1,895. **Officers:** Mike Rohleder, President; R. Van Ness Holland Jr., Executive VP, Finance and Treasurer.

■ **9612** ■ **X-Ray Industries Inc.**
1961 Thunderbird St.
Troy, MI 48084
Phone: (248)362-2242   **Fax:** (248)362-4422
Products: Testing equipment and supplies. **SIC:** 5084 (Industrial Machinery & Equipment). **Sales:** $21,000,000 (2000). **Emp:** 180. **Officers:** Scott Thams, President; Kurt J. Andrews, CFO.

■ **9613** ■ **Xebec Corp.**
5612 Brighton Ter.
Kansas City, MO 64130
Phone: (816)444-9700
Products: Electronic parts and equipment. **SIC:** 5065 (Electronic Parts & Equipment Nec). **Sales:** $99,000,000 (1993). **Emp:** 400. **Officers:** Jerry Meisenheimer, Controller.

■ **9614** ■ **Xilinx Inc.**
2100 Logic Dr.
San Jose, CA 95124-3400
Phone: (408)559-7778   **Fax:** (408)559-7114
Products: Field programmable gate array and other semiconductor devices. **SIC:** 5065 (Electronic Parts & Equipment Nec). **Sales:** $568,100,000 (2000). **Emp:** 1,397. **Officers:** Willem P. Roelandts, CEO; Gordon M. Steel, Sr. VP & CFO.

■ **9615** ■ **Yale Electric Supply Company Inc.**
296 Freeport St.
Dorchester, MA 02122
Phone: (617)825-9253   **Fax:** (617)282-5002
Products: Lighting; Electric supplies. **SIC:** 5063 (Electrical Apparatus & Equipment). **Est:** 1923. **Sales:** $38,000,000 (2000). **Emp:** 50. **Officers:** W Sheinkopf, President.

■ **9616** ■ **Yamaha Systems Technology**
6600 Orangethorpe Ave.
Buena Park, CA 90620-1396
Phone: (408)437-3133
Free: (800)543-7457   **Fax:** (408)437-8791
Products: Electronic components. **SIC:** 5065 (Electronic Parts & Equipment Nec). **Est:** 1886. **Sales:** $56,000,000 (2000). **Emp:** 28. **Officers:** Ed Kishimune, President.

■ **9617** ■ **Yankee Electronics Inc.**
102 Maple St.
Manchester, NH 03103
Phone: (603)625-9746
Free: (800)365-9720   **Fax:** 800-947-8795
Products: Electrical and electronic equipment and supplies. **SIC:** 5065 (Electronic Parts & Equipment Nec). **Sales:** $10,000,000 (2000). **Emp:** 26.

■ **9618** ■ **Yates and Bird**
300 N Elizabeth St., 2N
Chicago, IL 60607
Phone: (312)226-2412
Free: (800)662-5021   **Fax:** (312)226-2480
Products: Medical, dental, and optical supplies. **SIC:** 5063 (Electrical Apparatus & Equipment).

■ **9619** ■ **York Electrical Supply Co.**
PO Box 2008
Harrisburg, PA 17105-2008
Phone: (717)843-9991   **Fax:** (717)843-7123
Products: Electrical supplies, including switches, controls, boxes, conduits, and wiring; Wrenches and hammers. **SIC:** 5063 (Electrical Apparatus & Equipment). **Est:** 1956. **Sales:** $18,000,000 (2000). **Emp:** 68. **Officers:** J. Livingston, President; Sue Fritz, Manager; Dale Witmer, Exec. VP; D. Deitz, Manager.

■ **9620** ■ **Zack Electronics Inc.**
309 E Brokaw Rd.
San Jose, CA 95112-4208
Phone: (408)324-0551   **Fax:** (408)324-1110
E-mail: info@zackinc.com
URL: http://www.zackinc.com
Products: Electronic parts and tools; Wire; Cable; Connectors. **SIC:** 5063 (Electrical Apparatus & Equipment). **Est:** 1931. **Sales:** $25,000,000 (2000). **Emp:** 80. **Officers:** Arthur Simpkins, CFO; Dennis J. Awad, President; Sandra Awad, Chairwoman.

■ **9621** ■ **Zapper Inc.**
3131 Western Ave., Ste. 330
Seattle, WA 98121-1034
Phone: (425)822-7800   **Fax:** (425)828-9498
Products: Electric fences and accessories. **SIC:** 5065 (Electronic Parts & Equipment Nec). **Officers:** Ulf Persson, CEO.

■ **9622** ■ **Zentao Corp.**
650 N Edgewood Ave.
Wood Dale, IL 60191-2615
Phone: (708)628-6780
Products: Continuous power supplies and accessoriess. **SIC:** 5063 (Electrical Apparatus & Equipment). **Est:** 1990. **Sales:** $2,000,000 (2000). **Emp:** 6. **Officers:** Wayne Bachar, VP of Operations.

■ **9623** ■ **Zero 88 Inc.**
PO Box 14982
North Palm Beach, FL 33408
Phone: (561)842-2263   **Fax:** (561)624-9691
Products: Electrical and electronic equipment and supplies. **SIC:** 5063 (Electrical Apparatus & Equipment). **Sales:** $1,000,000 (2000).

■ **9624** ■ **Zeta Associates Inc.**
10300 Eaton Pl., No. 500
Fairfax, VA 22030
Phone: (703)385-7050
Products: Electric transmissions. **SIC:** 5063 (Electrical Apparatus & Equipment).

■ **9625** ■ **Zetex Inc.**
47 Mall Dr., Ste. 4
Commack, NY 11725-5717
Phone: (516)543-7100   **Fax:** (516)864-7630
E-mail: usa.sales@zetex.com
URL: http://www.zetex.com
Products: Transistors; Diodes; Linear integrated circuits. **SIC:** 5065 (Electronic Parts & Equipment Nec). **Est:** 1989. **Sales:** $16,000,000 (2000). **Emp:** 9. **Officers:** John Lownds, Vice President.

■ **9626** ■ **Ziegenbein Associates Inc.**
200 Bishops Way
Brookfield, WI 53005
Phone: (414)785-1350
Products: Electro-mechanical components. **SIC:** 5065 (Electronic Parts & Equipment Nec). **Est:** 1944. **Sales:** $2,000,000 (2000). **Emp:** 9. **Officers:** Michael Stevens, President.

■ **9627** ■ **Zilkoski's Auto Electric**
200 N 39th
Springfield, OR 97478-5746
Phone: (541)747-9213
Free: (800)293-9213   **Fax:** (541)746-8641
Products: Engine electrical equipment; Parts for engine electrical equipment. **SIC:** 5013 (Motor Vehicle Supplies & New Parts). **Est:** 1953. **Emp:** 8. **Officers:** Arlen Kopperud.

■ **9628** ■ **Znyx Corp.**
48501 Warm Springs Blvd., Ste. 107
Fremont, CA 94539
Phone: (510)249-0800
Free: (800)724-0911   **Fax:** (510)656-2460
Products: Servers and multi-channel enhancement solutions including switches and adapters. **SIC:** 5063 (Electrical Apparatus & Equipment). **Sales:** $5,000,000 (2000). **Emp:** 40. **Officers:** Connie Austin, CEO & President.

■ **9629** ■ **Zytronics Inc.**
70 Tirrell Hill Rd.
Bedford, NH 03110
Phone: (603)623-8888   **Fax:** (603)623-4009
Products: Electrical equipment. **SIC:** 5063 (Electrical Apparatus & Equipment). **Est:** 1967. **Sales:** $5,000,000 (2000). **Emp:** 41. **Officers:** Van F. Gray, CEO; Henry Horner, Owner.

(15) Explosives

Entries in this section are arranged alphabetically by company name. When the company name is a personal name, the company name is alphabetized by the surname unless the first name or initial(s) are part of a trade name. See the User's Guide at the front of this directory for additional information.

■ **9630** ■ **B.J. Alan Co.**
555 Martin Luther King Jr. Blvd.
Youngstown, OH 44502-1102
Phone: (330)746-1064 **Fax:** (330)746-4410
Products: Fireworks; Novelties. **SIC:** 5092 (Toys & Hobby Goods & Supplies). **Est:** 1973. **Emp:** 250.
Officers: Bruce Zoldan, President.

■ **9631** ■ **American West Marketing Inc.**
2002 E McFadden Ave., No. 250
Santa Ana, CA 92705-4706
Phone: (714)550-6003 **Fax:** (714)550-7020
Products: Fireworks. **SIC:** 5092 (Toys & Hobby Goods & Supplies). **Est:** 1968. **Sales:** $23,000,000 (2000). **Emp:** 50. **Officers:** Terry Anderson, President; John Palme, Controller.

■ **9632** ■ **Burt Explosives Inc.**
294 North 500 West
Moab, UT 84532
Phone: (801)259-7181
Products: Explosives. **SIC:** 5169 (Chemicals & Allied Products Nec). **Est:** 1960. **Sales:** $8,000,000 (2000). **Emp:** 27. **Officers:** Ross Tabberer, President; Louann Adkison, Treasurer & Secty.

■ **9633** ■ **Celebrations Fireworks & Supply Co. Inc.**
5860 N Michigan Rd.
Indianapolis, IN 46208
Phone: (317)257-9446
Free: (800)762-8286 **Fax:** (317)257-9448
E-mail: joestanly@msn.com
Products: Fireworks; Halloween merchandise. **SIC:** 5092 (Toys & Hobby Goods & Supplies). **Est:** 1987. **Officers:** Joe Stanley. **Alternate Name:** Celebration Halloween. **Alternate Name:** Celebrations Creations.

■ **9634** ■ **Flying Phoenix Corp.**
PO Box 31
Riverton, WY 82501-0031
Phone: (307)856-0778 **Fax:** (307)856-3336
Products: Fireworks. **SIC:** 5092 (Toys & Hobby Goods & Supplies). **Est:** 1977. **Sales:** $2,000,000 (2000). **Emp:** 212. **Officers:** Jim Landis, President.

■ **9635** ■ **Garden State Fireworks Inc.**
383 Carlton Rd.
PO Box 403
Millington, NJ 07946
Phone: (908)647-1086 **Fax:** (908)647-6258
Products: Small and large fireworks. **SIC:** 5092 (Toys & Hobby Goods & Supplies). **Sales:** $2,000,000 (2000). **Emp:** 49. **Officers:** Nunzio Santore; August Santore.

■ **9636** ■ **Ladshaw Explosives Inc.**
393 Landa St.
New Braunfels, TX 78130
Phone: (830)625-4789 **Fax:** (830)620-6247
Products: Explosives. **SIC:** 5169 (Chemicals & Allied Products Nec). **Est:** 1963. **Sales:** $3,500,000 (2000). **Emp:** 30. **Officers:** John Ladshaw, President.

(16) Floorcovering Equipment and Supplies

Entries in this section are arranged alphabetically by company name. When the company name is a personal name, the company name is alphabetized by the surname unless the first name or initial(s) are part of a trade name. See the User's Guide at the front of this directory for additional information.

■ **9637** ■ **A & A Ceramic Tile, Inc.**
11908 Mariposa Rd.
Hesperia, CA 92345-1636
Phone: (760)948-3970
Products: Ceramic wall and floor tile. **SIC:** 5032 (Brick, Stone & Related Materials).

■ **9638** ■ **ABC Tile Distributors**
3105 18th St.
PO Box 7428
Metairie, LA 70010
Phone: (504)833-5543 **Fax:** (504)832-0932
Products: Ceramic and porcelain wall and floor tile; Natural stone products. **SIC:** 5032 (Brick, Stone & Related Materials). **Est:** 1965. **Sales:** $3,000,000 (1999). **Emp:** 10. **Officers:** S.E. Ebrahim, Contact; James F. Davision, Sales & Marketing Contact.

■ **9639** ■ **Accent On Tile**
3700 Liberty Ave.
Pittsburgh, PA 15201
Phone: (412)687-8453 **Fax:** (412)687-0460
Products: Ceramic tiles. **SIC:** 5032 (Brick, Stone & Related Materials). **Sales:** $1,000,000 (2000). **Emp:** 5.
Officers: Maryann Mahoney, President.

■ **9640** ■ **Accent Tile**
4801 Frankford Ave., Bldg. B-1
Lubbock, TX 79424
Phone: (806)796-2772
Products: Ceramic tile. **SIC:** 5032 (Brick, Stone & Related Materials).

■ **9641** ■ **Acme Brick Co.**
4747 Choctaw
Baton Rouge, LA 70805
Phone: (504)356-5281
Products: Ceramic wall and floor tile. **SIC:** 5032 (Brick, Stone & Related Materials).

■ **9642** ■ **Acme Brick Co.**
2325 W Battlefield
Springfield, MO 65807
Phone: (417)883-0502 **Fax:** (417)883-0269
Products: Ceramic wall and floor tile. **SIC:** 5032 (Brick, Stone & Related Materials). **Officers:** David Martin, Contact.

■ **9643** ■ **Acme Brick Co.**
2500 NW 10th
Oklahoma City, OK 73107
Phone: (405)525-7421 **Fax:** (405)525-7683
Products: Ceramic wall and floor tile. **SIC:** 5032 (Brick, Stone & Related Materials).

■ **9644** ■ **Acme Brick Co.**
307 W Santa Fe
Olathe, KS 66061
Phone: (913)782-9500 **Fax:** (913)782-1839
Products: Ceramic wall and floor tile. **SIC:** 5032 (Brick, Stone & Related Materials). **Officers:** Bob Long, Contact.

■ **9645** ■ **Acme Brick & Tile**
5690 Summer Ave.
Memphis, TN 38134
Phone: (901)387-4540
Products: Ceramic wall and floor tile; Dressed dimension marble and other stone; Glass products; Bricks. **SICs:** 5032 (Brick, Stone & Related Materials); 5039 (Construction Materials Nec).

■ **9646** ■ **Adleta Corp.**
1645 Diplomat Dr.
Carrollton, TX 75006
Phone: (972)620-5600 **Fax:** (972)620-5666
Products: Floorcoverings, including vinyl, laminate, and wood. **SICs:** 5023 (Homefurnishings); 5031 (Lumber, Plywood & Millwork). **Est:** 1922. **Sales:** $79,000,000 (2000). **Emp:** 101. **Officers:** Jack Adleta, CEO; John Snyder, President & COO, e-mail: jsnyder@adleta.com.

■ **9647** ■ **Admiralty Mills Inc.**
PO Box 745
639 Peeples Valley Rd.
Cartersville, GA 30120
Phone: (404)382-8244 **Fax:** (404)386-5891
Products: Carpets. **SIC:** 5023 (Homefurnishings). **Est:** 1970. **Sales:** $6,000,000 (2000). **Emp:** 49. **Officers:** J. D. LeMay Jr.

■ **9648** ■ **Adventure Group, Inc.**
1351F W 56 Hwy.
Olathe, KS 66061
Phone: (913)780-1195
Products: Ceramic wall and floor tile. **SIC:** 5032 (Brick, Stone & Related Materials). **Officers:** Evelyn Strong, Contact.

■ **9649** ■ **Charles Alan Inc.**
1942 Tigertail Blvd.
Dania, FL 33004-2105
Phone: (954)922-9663
Free: (800)741-3669 **Fax:** (954)925-7432
Products: Hardwood flooring. **SICs:** 5023 (Homefurnishings); 5031 (Lumber, Plywood & Millwork). **Est:** 1972. **Emp:** 49. **Officers:** Alan Weinger.

■ **9650** ■ **Albany Tile Supply**
452 N Pearl St.
Albany, NY 12204-1511
Phone: (518)434-0155
Products: Ceramic wall and floor tile. **SIC:** 5032 (Brick, Stone & Related Materials).

■ **9651** ■ **Alfredo's Tile Distributors**
Expy. 83
La Joya, TX 78560
Phone: (512)585-7200
Products: Ceramic tile. **SIC:** 5032 (Brick, Stone & Related Materials).

■ **9652** ■ **All Standard Tile Corp.**
21470 Jamaica Ave.
Queens Village, NY 11428
Phone: (718)389-2520 **Fax:** (718)383-7675
Products: Marble and tile. **SIC:** 5032 (Brick, Stone & Related Materials).

■ **9653** ■ **All Tile**
1201 Chase Ave.
Elk Grove Village, IL 60007
Phone: (847)364-9191 **Fax:** (847)364-9207
Products: Floor tile. **SIC:** 5032 (Brick, Stone & Related Materials).

■ **9654** ■ **Allegheny Inc.**
3600 William Flynn Hwy.
Allison Park, PA 15101
Phone: (412)486-5500
Free: (800)933-9336 **Fax:** (412)486-8950
E-mail: allinst@usaor.net
Products: Hard surface floor coverings. **SIC:** 5023 (Homefurnishings). **Est:** 1952. **Sales:** $2,000,000 (2000). **Emp:** 12. **Officers:** Michael Toole, President.

■ **9655** ■ **Allied Distributors Inc.**
555 State St.
Springfield, MA 01109
Phone: (413)781-7100 **Fax:** (413)737-7690
Products: Residential and commercial carpet; Sheet vinyl; Area rugs; Laminate flooring. **SIC:** 5023 (Homefurnishings). **Est:** 1967. **Emp:** 12. **Officers:** Jerome M. Kimball.

■ **9656** ■ **Allied-Eastern Distributors**
100 W Drullard Ave.
Lancaster, NY 14086
Phone: (716)684-0234 **Fax:** (716)684-3138
Products: Flooring supplies, including padding, vinyl, tile, and carpeting. **SICs:** 5023 (Homefurnishings); 5032 (Brick, Stone & Related Materials).

■ **9657** ■ **Allied-Eastern Distributors**
110 Baker St.
Syracuse, NY 13206
Phone: (315)437-2465 **Fax:** (315)433-1077
Products: Flooring supplies, including carpeting, tile, vinyl, and padding. **SICs:** 5023 (Homefurnishings); 5032 (Brick, Stone & Related Materials).

■ **9658** ■ **Allied Eastern Distributors**
1913 Commercial St.
Erie, PA 16503
Phone: (814)453-5648 **Fax:** (814)456-7138
Products: Carpeting; Rugs. **SIC:** 5023 (Homefurnishings).

■ **9659** ■ **Allied Flooring Supply**
PO Box 52005
Box 9
Knoxville, TN 37950-2005
Phone: (423)584-2386 **Fax:** (423)584-0265
Products: Ceramic wall and floor tile. **SIC:** 5032 (Brick, Stone & Related Materials). **Est:** 1985. **Emp:** 15. **Officers:** Bill Perkins, President.

■ **9660** ■ **Allied Floors, Inc.**
1815 S Kansas Ave.
PO Box 2453
Topeka, KS 66612
Phone: (785)232-0381 **Fax:** (785)232-5837
Products: Homefurnishings, including carpet, wallpaper, paint, tile, and blinds. **SIC:** 5023

(Homefurnishings). **Est:** 1984. **Emp:** 12. **Officers:** Charles Stearns; Kenneth Stearns.

■ 9661 ■ **Alpha Tile Distributors, Inc.**
10898 Metro Pkwy.
Ft. Myers, FL 33912
Phone: (941)275-8288
Free: (800)785-8288 **Fax:** (941)275-0116
URL: http://www.alphatile.com
Products: Ceramic and natural stone tile. **SIC:** 5032 (Brick, Stone & Related Materials).

■ 9662 ■ **Alpha Tile Distributors, Inc.**
2603 Ace Rd
Orlando, FL 32804-1910
Products: Ceramic tile. **SIC:** 5032 (Brick, Stone & Related Materials).

■ 9663 ■ **Alpha Tile Distributors, Inc.**
2443 Tampa East Blvd.
Tampa, FL 33619
Phone: (813)620-9000
Products: Ceramic tile. **SIC:** 5032 (Brick, Stone & Related Materials).

■ 9664 ■ **Alpha Tile Distributors, Inc.**
4301 31st St. N
St. Petersburg, FL 33714
Phone: (813)525-1213 **Fax:** (813)526-2436
Products: Ceramic wall and floor tile. **SIC:** 5032 (Brick, Stone & Related Materials).

■ 9665 ■ **Alpha Tile Distributors, Inc.**
12350 Automobile Blvd. Rd.
Clearwater, FL 33762-4425
Phone: (813)796-6569 **Fax:** (813)726-0053
Products: Ceramic wall and floor tile. **SIC:** 5032 (Brick, Stone & Related Materials). **Officers:** Cindy Sinclair, Contact.

■ 9666 ■ **Alpha Tile Distributors, Inc.**
1808 Whitfield Ave.
Sarasota, FL 34243-3919
Phone: (941)351-3484 **Fax:** (941)359-3103
Products: Ceramic wall and floor tile. **SIC:** 5032 (Brick, Stone & Related Materials). **Officers:** Kim Grinder, Contact.

■ 9667 ■ **American Ceramic Tile**
324 11th St.
Holly Hill, FL 32117
Phone: (904)672-1285 **Fax:** (904)238-3623
Products: Ceramic tile. **SIC:** 5032 (Brick, Stone & Related Materials).

■ 9668 ■ **American Equipment Marble & Tile, Inc.**
7001 Hawthorn Park Dr.
Indianapolis, IN 46220
Phone: (317)849-5400 **Fax:** (317)849-1195
URL: http://www.tileinfo.com
Products: Ceramic, granite, and marble tiles and related materials. **SICs:** 5032 (Brick, Stone & Related Materials); 5023 (Homefurnishings). **Est:** 1952. **Sales:** $4,000,000 (2000). **Emp:** 16. **Officers:** John A. Hill Jr., President; Carlin Chapman, CFO, e-mail: carlin@ indy.net. **Former Name:** American Equipment Company Inc.

■ 9669 ■ **American Floor Covering**
PO Box 10094
Green Bay, WI 54307
Phone: (920)337-0707 **Fax:** (920)337-0447
Products: Ceramic tile. **SIC:** 5032 (Brick, Stone & Related Materials).

■ 9670 ■ **American Import Tile**
7000 Wheeler Dr.
Orland Park, IL 60462
Phone: (708)614-8100 **Fax:** (708)614-8104
Products: Tile. **SIC:** 5032 (Brick, Stone & Related Materials). **Est:** 1979. **Emp:** 18. **Officers:** Martin Schultz; Gary Schultz.

■ 9671 ■ **American Marazzi Tile, Inc.**
Sales Service Ctr.
6313-A Airport Fwy.
Ft. Worth, TX 76117
Phone: (817)222-0510 **Fax:** (817)222-1510
Products: Ceramic wall and floor tile. **SIC:** 5032 (Brick, Stone & Related Materials).

■ 9672 ■ **American Tile Co. of Tucson**
2300 S Friebus, Ste. 103
Tucson, AZ 85713-4248
Phone: (520)323-9822 **Fax:** (520)323-9823
Products: Ceramic wall and floor tile. **SIC:** 5032 (Brick, Stone & Related Materials).

■ 9673 ■ **American Tile Distributors**
927 Bragg Blvd.
PO Box 58208
Fayetteville, NC 28305
Phone: (919)433-2757
Products: Ceramic wall and floor tile. **SIC:** 5032 (Brick, Stone & Related Materials). **Officers:** Cindy Smith, Contact.

■ 9674 ■ **American Tile Supply**
1701 Summit Ave.
Plano, TX 75074
Phone: (972)516-4926 **Fax:** (972)516-4925
Products: Ceramic wall and floor tile. **SIC:** 5032 (Brick, Stone & Related Materials). **Officers:** Sharon Moore, Contact.

■ 9675 ■ **American Tile Supply**
1707 Falcon Dr.
Desoto, TX 75115
Phone: (972)228-0066 **Fax:** (972)224-7707
Products: Ceramic wall and floor tile. **SIC:** 5032 (Brick, Stone & Related Materials). **Officers:** Jack Eastep, Contact.

■ 9676 ■ **American Tile Supply**
200 E Felix
Ft. Worth, TX 76115
Phone: (817)924-2231 **Fax:** (817)924-6367
Products: Ceramic wall and floor tile. **SIC:** 5032 (Brick, Stone & Related Materials). **Officers:** Fred Dean, Contact.

■ 9677 ■ **American Tile Supply**
2020-G Rutland Dr.
Austin, TX 78758
Phone: (512)837-2843 **Fax:** (512)834-1593
Products: Ceramic wall and floor tile. **SIC:** 5032 (Brick, Stone & Related Materials). **Officers:** Nancy Machu, Contact.

■ 9678 ■ **American Tile Supply Company, Inc.**
69 Main St.
Danbury, CT 06810-8011
Phone: (203)794-1191 **Fax:** (203)798-9983
Products: Ceramic wall and floor tile. **SIC:** 5032 (Brick, Stone & Related Materials).

■ 9679 ■ **American Tile Supply Inc.**
2839 Merrell
Dallas, TX 75229
Phone: (972)243-2377
E-mail: atsadmin@americantilesupply.com
URL: http://www.americantilesupply.com
Products: Ceramic and marble flooring; Wall tile; Porcelain tile; Engineered wood flooring. **SIC:** 5032 (Brick, Stone & Related Materials). **Est:** 1965. **Emp:** 230. **Officers:** Gregg Link, General Mgr., e-mail: g.link@americantilesupply.com.

■ 9680 ■ **AMS Enterprises**
1940 State Highway
Branson, MO 65616
Phone: (417)337-7640
Products: Carpets; Rugs. **SIC:** 5023 (Homefurnishings).

■ 9681 ■ **Anderson Tile Sales**
120 S Madison
San Angelo, TX 76903
Phone: (915)655-0646
Products: Ceramic tile. **SIC:** 5032 (Brick, Stone & Related Materials).

■ 9682 ■ **Anderson Tile Sales**
1801 Kermit Hwy.
Odessa, TX 79761
Phone: (915)337-0081 **Fax:** (915)337-0082
Products: Ceramic wall and floor tile. **SIC:** 5032 (Brick, Stone & Related Materials). **Officers:** Kim Alexander, Contact.

■ 9683 ■ **Anderson Tile Sales**
1703 S Midkiff
Midland, TX 79705
Phone: (915)683-5116 **Fax:** (915)683-5117
Products: Ceramic wall and floor tile. **SIC:** 5032 (Brick, Stone & Related Materials). **Officers:** Charlie Alexander, Contact.

■ 9684 ■ **Architectural Floor Systems, Inc.**
206 Campus Dr.
Arlington Heights, IL 60004-1402
Phone: (847)394-3944
Free: (800)323-6792 **Fax:** (847)394-3753
URL: http://www.techtonics.com
Products: Flooring, including sheet vinyl, linoleum and rubber. **SICs:** 5032 (Brick, Stone & Related Materials); 5023 (Homefurnishings). **Est:** 1984. **Emp:** 30. **Officers:** Dean W. Morgan, President, e-mail: dean@ techtonics.com.

■ 9685 ■ **Architectural Surfaces, Inc.**
3535 Princeton Dr. NE
Albuquerque, NM 87107-4213
Phone: (505)889-0124 **Fax:** (505)888-5012
Products: Ceramic wall and floor tile. **SIC:** 5032 (Brick, Stone & Related Materials).

■ 9686 ■ **Arley Wholesale Inc.**
700 N South Rd.
Scranton, PA 18504-1432
Phone: (717)451-8880 **Free:** (800)526-6205
Products: Commercial flooring. **SICs:** 5031 (Lumber, Plywood & Millwork); 5032 (Brick, Stone & Related Materials).

■ 9687 ■ **Armline**
2855 S Reservoir
Pomona, CA 91766
Phone: (714)591-0541
Products: Ceramic tile. **SIC:** 5032 (Brick, Stone & Related Materials).

■ 9688 ■ **Artistic Tile Co. Inc.**
661 E 48th Ave.
Anchorage, AK 99503-2929
Phone: (907)562-2122 **Fax:** (907)561-1805
Products: Ceramic wall and floor tile. **SIC:** 5032 (Brick, Stone & Related Materials).

■ 9689 ■ **Asmara Oriental Rugs**
451 D St.
Boston, MA 02210
Phone: (617)261-0222
Products: Oriental rugs. **SIC:** 5023 (Homefurnishings).

■ 9690 ■ **Associated Tile Sales**
9203 Broadway
San Antonio, TX 78218
Phone: (210)828-5761
Products: Ceramic tile. **SIC:** 5032 (Brick, Stone & Related Materials).

■ 9691 ■ **Atlanta Tile Supply, Inc.**
5845-C Oakbrook Pkwy.
Norcross, GA 30093
Phone: (770)409-8200 **Fax:** (770)409-1501
Products: Ceramic wall and floor tile. **SIC:** 5032 (Brick, Stone & Related Materials). **Est:** 1991. **Emp:** 10. **Officers:** James A. Estes, Contact.

■ 9692 ■ **Atlantic Ceramic Tile**
158-01 Crossbay Blvd.
Howard Beach, NY 11414-3137
Phone: (516)586-1080
Products: Ceramic wall and floor tile. **SIC:** 5032 (Brick, Stone & Related Materials). **Officers:** John Papa, Contact.

■ 9693 ■ Atlas Carpet Mills Inc.
2200 Saybrook Ave.
Los Angeles, CA 90040-1720
Phone: (323)724-9000 Fax: (323)724-4526
Products: Carpet. SIC: 5023 (Homefurnishings). Est: 1970. Sales: $75,000,000 (1999). Emp: 250. Officers: Peter Henschel.

■ 9694 ■ Owen M. Bastian Inc.
333 W Broad St.
Quakertown, PA 18951
Phone: (215)536-7939
Products: Carpeting; Rugs. SIC: 5023 (Homefurnishings).

■ 9695 ■ James B. Batts Distributing Co.
6616 Fleetwood Dr.
Raleigh, NC 27612-1837
Phone: (919)782-2982 Fax: (919)781-1124
Products: Ceramic wall and floor tile. SIC: 5032 (Brick, Stone & Related Materials).

■ 9696 ■ James B. Batts Distributing Co.
2146 Stantonsburg Rd.
Wilson, NC 27893-1000
Phone: (919)243-2134 Fax: (919)243-1481
Products: Ceramic wall and floor tile. SIC: 5032 (Brick, Stone & Related Materials). Est: 1957. Emp: 16. Officers: James B. Batts III, President.

■ 9697 ■ Beaver's Rugs
4745 Delight Rd.
Lawndale, NC 28090
Phone: (704)538-3141
Products: Rugs. SIC: 5023 (Homefurnishings).

■ 9698 ■ Bedrosian Building Supply
4055 Grass Valley Hwy. 110
Auburn, CA 95602
Phone: (530)888-1500
Products: Ceramic tile. SIC: 5032 (Brick, Stone & Related Materials).

■ 9699 ■ Bedrosian Building Supply
13405 Sherman Way
North Hollywood, CA 91605
Phone: (818)787-7310
Products: Ceramic tile. SIC: 5032 (Brick, Stone & Related Materials).

■ 9700 ■ Bedrosian Building Supply
426 Littlefield
South San Francisco, CA 94080
Phone: (650)876-0100
Products: Ceramic tile. SIC: 5032 (Brick, Stone & Related Materials).

■ 9701 ■ Bedrosian Tile & Marble Supply
798 E Glendale
Sparks, NV 89431
Phone: (775)331-4802 Fax: (775)331-0753
URL: http://www.bedrosians.com
Products: Ceramic, tile, marble, and setting equipment. SIC: 5032 (Brick, Stone & Related Materials).

■ 9702 ■ Bedrosian Tile Supply
1001 Shary Cir.
Concord, CA 94518
Phone: (510)676-4858 Fax: (510)676-8854
Products: Tile and setting materials. SIC: 5032 (Brick, Stone & Related Materials).

■ 9703 ■ Bedrosian Tile Supply
27695 Mission Blvd.
Hayward, CA 94544
Phone: (510)582-5000 Fax: (510)582-0270
Products: Floorcovering, including tile, marble, and granite. SIC: 5032 (Brick, Stone & Related Materials).

■ 9704 ■ Bedrosian Tile Supply
Canyon Industrial Center
9444 Chesapeake Dr.
San Diego, CA 92122
Phone: (619)565-1215 Fax: (619)565-0465
Products: Tile. SIC: 5032 (Brick, Stone & Related Materials).

■ 9705 ■ Bedrosian Tile Supply
2301 Junction Ave.
San Jose, CA 95131
Phone: (408)435-5544 Fax: (408)435-7390
URL: http://www.bedrosians.com
Products: Floor tile, including glass. SIC: 5032 (Brick, Stone & Related Materials).

■ 9706 ■ Bedrosian Tile Supply
2538 N West Ln., Bldg. A
Stockton, CA 95205
Phone: (209)463-5000 Fax: (209)463-3505
Products: Floor and wall tile; Marble. SIC: 5032 (Brick, Stone & Related Materials).

■ 9707 ■ Bedrosian Tile Supply
2045 E Main St.
Visalia, CA 93291
Phone: (209)734-4035 Fax: (209)734-1980
Products: Ceramic and marble tile. SIC: 5032 (Brick, Stone & Related Materials).

■ 9708 ■ Bedrosian Tile Supply
2701 Brundage Ln.
Bakersfield, CA 93304
Phone: (805)324-5000 Fax: (805)324-8000
Products: Ceramic wall and floor tile. SIC: 5032 (Brick, Stone & Related Materials).

■ 9709 ■ Bedrosian Tile Supply
1301 S State College Blvd., Ste. A
Anaheim, CA 92806
Phone: (714)778-8453 Fax: (714)778-4616
Products: Ceramic wall and floor tile. SIC: 5032 (Brick, Stone & Related Materials).

■ 9710 ■ Bedrosian Tile Supply
7319 Roseville Rd.
Sacramento, CA 95842
Phone: (916)348-4000 Fax: (916)348-4066
Products: Ceramic wall and floor tile. SIC: 5032 (Brick, Stone & Related Materials). Officers: David Mitchell, Contact.

■ 9711 ■ Bedrosian Tile Supply
500 N Carpenter Rd.
Modesto, CA 95351
Phone: (209)579-5000 Fax: (209)579-1619
Products: Ceramic wall and floor tile. SIC: 5032 (Brick, Stone & Related Materials).

■ 9712 ■ Bedrosian Tile Supply
11225 Trade Center Dr.
Rancho Cordova, CA 95742
Phone: (916)852-1000 Fax: (916)852-0992
Products: Ceramic wall and floor tile. SIC: 5032 (Brick, Stone & Related Materials). Officers: Jim Peters, Contact.

■ 9713 ■ Bedrosians
4285 N Golden State Blvd.
Fresno, CA 93722-6397
Phone: (209)275-5000
Free: (800)760-8453 Fax: (209)275-1753
E-mail: bedrosians@aol.com
URL: http://www.bedrosians.com
Products: Ceramic floor tile; Natural stone tile and slabs; Glass block; Setting materials and supplies. SICs: 5032 (Brick, Stone & Related Materials); 5039 (Construction Materials Nec). Est: 1948. Officers: Larry P. Bedrosian, CEO. Former Name: Bedrosian Tile and Marble.

■ 9714 ■ Bedrosians Tile & Marble
2946 E Broadway Rd.
Phoenix, AZ 85040-0700
Phone: (602)966-7800 Fax: (602)966-8900
Products: Ceramic wall and floor tile. SIC: 5032 (Brick, Stone & Related Materials).

■ 9715 ■ Bedrosians Tile & Marble
4651 S Butterfield Dr.
Tucson, AZ 85714
Phone: (520)747-2200 Fax: (520)747-1982
E-mail: bedrosians@aol.com
URL: http://www.bedrosians.com
Products: Ceramic and porcelain. SIC: 5032 (Brick, Stone & Related Materials). Est: 1948. Emp: 10.

■ 9716 ■ Bedrosians Tile & Marble
3646 Standish Ave.
Santa Rosa, CA 95407
Phone: (707)586-1800 Fax: (707)586-1860
Products: Ceramic wall and floor tile. SIC: 5032 (Brick, Stone & Related Materials).

■ 9717 ■ Bedrosians Tile & Marble
756 S Jason St., Unit 8-11
Denver, CO 80223
Phone: (303)722-2200 Fax: (303)722-2360
Products: Ceramic wall and floor tile. SIC: 5032 (Brick, Stone & Related Materials).

■ 9718 ■ Bedrosians Tile & Marble
6335 S Industrial Rd.
Las Vegas, NV 89103
Phone: (702)765-7400 Fax: (702)778-4616
Products: Ceramic wall and floor tile. SIC: 5032 (Brick, Stone & Related Materials).

■ 9719 ■ The Belknap White Group
111 Plymouth St.
Mansfield, MA 02048
Phones: (508)337-2700 (508)337-2727
Fax: 800-283-7500
Products: Ceramic wall and floor tile. SIC: 5032 (Brick, Stone & Related Materials). Est: 1981. Officers: R. Ciampi, President.

■ 9720 ■ The Bella Tile Company, Inc.
178 1st Ave.
New York, NY 10009-4508
Phone: (212)475-2909 Fax: (212)529-7667
Products: Ceramic wall and floor tile. SIC: 5032 (Brick, Stone & Related Materials).

■ 9721 ■ Bellini Co.
5550 Cameron St., Ste. A
Las Vegas, NV 89118-6221
Phone: (702)732-7275
Free: (888)288-1484 Fax: (702)732-3588
E-mail: info@jfbellini.com
URL: http://www.jfbellini.com
Products: Ceramic, porcelain, natural stone floor tiles; Turf carpet; Flooring installation tools and supplies. SIC: 5023 (Homefurnishings). Est: 1975. Sales: $5,000,000 (2000). Emp: 12. Officers: Warren Kirwin, Owner. Former Name: J.F. Bellini Co.

■ 9722 ■ Bentley Mills Inc.
451 D St., No. 919
Boston, MA 02210
Phone: (617)951-2575
Products: Carpeting; Rugs. SIC: 5023 (Homefurnishings).

■ 9723 ■ Best Tile Distributors of Albany, Inc.
2241 Central Ave.
Schenectady, NY 12304-4379
Phone: (518)869-0219
Products: Ceramic tile. SIC: 5032 (Brick, Stone & Related Materials).

■ 9724 ■ Best Tile Distributors of Syracuse, Inc.
5891 Firestone Dr.
Syracuse, NY 13206-1102
Phone: (315)437-1606 Fax: (315)437-1920
Products: Ceramic wall and floor tile. SIC: 5032 (Brick, Stone & Related Materials).

■ 9725 ■ Best Tile Distributors of Wexford, Inc.
11040 Perry Hwy.
Wexford, PA 15090-8331
Phone: (412)935-6965 Fax: (412)935-2409
Products: Ceramic wall and floor tile. SIC: 5032 (Brick, Stone & Related Materials).

■ 9726 ■ Bigelow-Sanford
300 Landrum Mill Rd.
Landrum, SC 29356
Phone: (864)457-3391
Products: Carpets and rugs. SIC: 5023 (Homefurnishings).

■ 9727 ■ William M. Bird and Company Inc.
PO Box 20040
Charleston, SC 29413
Phone: (803)722-5930 **Fax:** (803)723-5179
Products: Floor covering, including carpet and tile.
SICs: 5023 (Homefurnishings); 5032 (Brick, Stone &
Related Materials). **Est:** 1865. **Sales:** $35,000,000
(2000). **Emp:** 93. **Officers:** D. Maybank Hagood, CEO.

■ 9728 ■ Bishop Distributing Co.
5200 36th SE
Grand Rapids, MI 49508
Phone: (616)942-9734
Free: (800)748-0363 **Fax:** (616)942-6073
URL: http://www.bishopdistributing.com
Products: Flooring, including wood, carpet, vinyl,
ceramic, and laminate. **SICs:** 5023 (Homefurnishings);
5031 (Lumber, Plywood & Millwork); 5032 (Brick, Stone
& Related Materials). **Est:** 1959. **Sales:** $35,000,000
(1999). **Emp:** 100. **Officers:** Brian Bishop, President;
Dan Hocbert, CFO; Tom Boyle, VP of Sales.

**■ 9729 ■ B.J.'s Ceramic Tile Distributing
Company, Inc.**
512 Dexter Dr.
Jackson, MS 39208
Phone: (601)939-0111 **Fax:** (601)939-0114
Products: Ceramic wall and floor tile. **SIC:** 5032 (Brick,
Stone & Related Materials).

■ 9730 ■ Blackton Inc.
PO Bxo 536155
Orlando, FL 32853
Phone: (407)898-2661
Products: Floor coverings and carpets. **SIC:** 5023
(Homefurnishings).

■ 9731 ■ L. Bornstein and Company Inc.
PO Box 172
Somerville, MA 02143
Phone: (617)776-3555 **Fax:** (617)623-1913
Products: Floor coverings. **SIC:** 5023
(Homefurnishings). **Est:** 1961. **Sales:** $12,000,000
(2000). **Emp:** 30. **Officers:** Leslie Bornstein-Stacks,
President; George Minson, Comptroller.

■ 9732 ■ Boston Tile
632 White St.
Springfield, MA 01108-3221
Phone: (413)732-4191 **Fax:** (413)788-7190
E-mail: bostontilespfld@worldnet.att.net
Products: Ceramic wall and floor tile. **SIC:** 5032 (Brick,
Stone & Related Materials). **Est:** 1956. **Emp:** 9.
Officers: Walter Sawa, Store Mgr.; Karen Tesini,
Showroom Mgr. **Former Name:** Standard Tile
Distributors of Springfield, Inc.

**■ 9733 ■ Boston Tile Distributors of
Shrewsbury**
Rte. 9, 512 Turnpike Rd.
Shrewsbury, MA 01545-5970
Phone: (508)842-0178 **Fax:** (508)842-2610
E-mail: bostontile@worldnet.att.net.com
Products: Ceramic wall and floor tile. **SIC:** 5032 (Brick,
Stone & Related Materials).

■ 9734 ■ Boston Tile of Rhode Island
1112 Jefferson Blvd.
Warwick, RI 02886-2203
Phone: (401)738-2450 **Fax:** (401)738-7603
Products: Ceramic wall and floor tile. **SIC:** 5032 (Brick,
Stone & Related Materials).

■ 9735 ■ BPI
6001 Lindsey Rd.
Little Rock, AR 72206
Phone: (501)490-1924
Free: (800)766-1274 **Fax:** (501)490-1937
Products: Carpet, ceramic tile, and hardwood floor
coverings. **SICs:** 5023 (Homefurnishings); 5031
(Lumber, Plywood & Millwork); 5032 (Brick, Stone &
Related Materials). **Est:** 1973. **Sales:** $16,000,000
(2000). **Emp:** 27. **Officers:** Joe Newell.

■ 9736 ■ B.P.I.
3263 Sharpe Ave.
Memphis, TN 38111
Phone: (901)744-6414 **Fax:** (901)745-6380
Products: Ceramic wall and floor tile. **SIC:** 5032 (Brick,
Stone & Related Materials).

■ 9737 ■ BPI Inc.
2295 Bolling St.
Jackson, MS 39213
Phone: (601)981-6060 **Fax:** (601)982-2884
Products: Floor coverings, including tile, ceramic, and
carpet. **SICs:** 5023 (Homefurnishings); 5031 (Lumber,
Plywood & Millwork); 5032 (Brick, Stone & Related
Materials). **Est:** 1973. **Emp:** 18.

■ 9738 ■ BPI Inc.
507A Mapleleaf Dr.
Nashville, TN 37210
Phone: (615)391-3901 **Fax:** (615)889-3005
Products: Floor coverings, including tile, carpet, wood,
and vinyl. **SICs:** 5023 (Homefurnishings); 5032 (Brick,
Stone & Related Materials); 5031 (Lumber, Plywood &
Millwork).

■ 9739 ■ Bretlin Inc.
185 S Industrial Blvd.
Calhoun, GA 30701
Phone: (706)695-6734
Free: (800)831-7633 **Fax:** (706)695-6816
Products: Carpets; Wallcoverings, wallpaper; Carpets,
rugs, and mats; Commercial turf and grounds mowing
equipment; Scatter rugs, bathmats, and sets. **SICs:**
5023 (Homefurnishings); 5083 (Farm & Garden
Machinery). **Emp:** 49.

■ 9740 ■ LD Brinkman and Co.
1655 Waters Ridge Dr.
Lewisville, TX 75057
Phone: (972)353-3500 **Fax:** (214)579-3631
Products: Carpet; Flooring products. **SIC:** 5023
(Homefurnishings). **Est:** 1960. **Sales:** $270,000,000
(2000). **Emp:** 1,000. **Officers:** Levon Ezell, Chairman
of the Board; Jack Wulz, CFO; Jeff Sills, Dir. of
Marketing; Denny Rowe, VP of Information Systems.

■ 9741 ■ J. Brooks Designer Rugs
2928 Prosperity Ave.
Fairfax, VA 22031
Phone: (703)698-0790
Products: Rugs. **SIC:** 5023 (Homefurnishings).

■ 9742 ■ Brunt Tile & Marble
3036 De Siard St.
Monroe, LA 71211
Phone: (318)361-0100 **Fax:** (318)322-2466
Products: Ceramic; Adhesives; Marble. **SICs:** 5032
(Brick, Stone & Related Materials); 5169 (Chemicals &
Allied Products Nec).

■ 9743 ■ Buchanan Industries
3358 Carpet Capital Dr. SW
Dalton, GA 30720-4900
Phone: (404)277-3066 **Fax:** (404)277-3355
Products: Carpeting. **SIC:** 5023 (Homefurnishings).
Est: 1975. **Sales:** $16,000,000 (2000). **Emp:** 48.
Officers: G. Robert Buchanan, President; Ray Griffin,
Vice President; Glen Cheek, Manufacturing Mgr.;
Brenda Smith, Dir. of Marketing.

■ 9744 ■ Buckeye Ceramic Tile
388 McClurg Rd., No. 5
Boardman, OH 44512
Phone: (330)758-5749 **Fax:** (330)758-5740
Products: Ceramic tile. **SIC:** 5032 (Brick, Stone &
Related Materials). **Est:** 1983. **Sales:** $2,000,000
(2000). **Emp:** 5.

■ 9745 ■ Buena Tile Supply, Inc.
1717 Palma Dr.
Ventura, CA 93003
Phone: (805)650-1252 **Fax:** (805)650-1779
Products: Ceramic wall and floor tile. **SIC:** 5032 (Brick,
Stone & Related Materials).

■ 9746 ■ Building Plastics Inc.
3263 Sharpe Ave.
Memphis, TN 38111
Phone: (901)744-6414 **Fax:** (901)744-7622
Products: Carpet; Tile; Formica; Wood floor and vinyl
floor. **SICs:** 5023 (Homefurnishings); 5032 (Brick,
Stone & Related Materials). **Est:** 1963. **Sales:**
$125,000,000 (1999). **Emp:** 375. **Officers:** Wallace
McAlexander, VP & CFO; J.H. Frazier, Chairman of the
Board & President; Guy Helmers, Controller; Amanda
Daughtery, Dir of Human Resources.

■ 9747 ■ Butler-Johnson Corp.
5031 24th St.
Sacramento, CA 95822
Phone: (916)454-3512
Free: (800)776-2167 **Fax:** (916)457-7634
Products: Floor coverings, including vinyl, hardwood,
and ceramic tile. **SICs:** 5023 (Homefurnishings); 5031
(Lumber, Plywood & Millwork); 5032 (Brick, Stone &
Related Materials).

■ 9748 ■ Butler-Johnson Corp.
PO Box 612110
San Jose, CA 95161-2110
Phone: (408)259-1800 **Fax:** (408)251-9275
E-mail: cbrian.division@butler-johnson.com
Products: Floor coverings, including wood, vinyl, and
tile. **SICs:** 5023 (Homefurnishings); 5032 (Brick, Stone
& Related Materials); 5031 (Lumber, Plywood &
Millwork). **Est:** 1960. **Sales:** $55,000,000 (2000). **Emp:**
106. **Officers:** Rolston Johnson, President; Daniel J.
Ford, Vice President; Jack Mackall, Sales/Manager
Contact; Jennifer Patrick, Human Resource Contact.

■ 9749 ■ C & R Tile
1 Chabot St.
Westbrook, ME 04092
Phone: (207)854-2077 **Fax:** (207)856-6457
E-mail: crtilemasonry@webtv.net
Products: Tile; Tiling supplies and tools; Marble;
Granite. **SICs:** 5032 (Brick, Stone & Related Materials);
5072 (Hardware). **Est:** 1947. **Sales:** $5,000,000
(1999). **Emp:** 50.

■ 9750 ■ Cain & Bultman, Inc.
PO Box 2815
Jacksonville, FL 32203-2815
Phone: (305)625-0461
Products: Ceramic tile. **SIC:** 5032 (Brick, Stone &
Related Materials).

■ 9751 ■ California Tile Distributors
1306 W Magnolia Blvd.
Burbank, CA 91506
Phones: (213)849-1468 (818)846-5938
Products: Ceramic wall and floor tile. **SIC:** 5032 (Brick,
Stone & Related Materials).

■ 9752 ■ California Tile Supply
42704 10th St. W
Lancaster, CA 93534-7029
Phone: (661)942-2545 **Fax:** (661)942-8861
Products: Ceramic wall and floor tile. **SIC:** 5032 (Brick,
Stone & Related Materials). **Est:** 1971. **Sales:**
$5,000,000 (2000). **Emp:** 18. **Officers:** David Romar.

■ 9753 ■ Cancos Tile Corp.
1085 Portion Rd.
Farmingville, NY 11738
Phone: (516)736-0770
Products: Tile. **SIC:** 5032 (Brick, Stone & Related
Materials). **Sales:** $11,000,000 (2000). **Emp:** 42.
Officers: Frank Valva, President.

■ 9754 ■ Capel Rugs Inc.
6F6 Atlanta Merchandise Mart
240 Peachtree St.
Atlanta, GA 30303
Phone: (404)577-4320 **Fax:** (404)577-3615
Products: Rugs. **SIC:** 5023 (Homefurnishings). **Emp:**
49.

■ **9755** ■ **Capitol Ceramic Inc.**
4804 Thorton Rd.
PO Box 61174
Raleigh, NC 27661
Phone: (919)872-8263 **Fax:** (919)872-5011
Products: Ceramic tile. **SIC:** 5032 (Brick, Stone & Related Materials).

■ **9756** ■ **Capitol Distributors**
2801 Juniper St.
Fairfax, VA 22031
Phone: (703)560-8750 **Fax:** (703)560-1443
Products: Carpet; Floor covering installation supplies and accessories. **SIC:** 5087 (Service Establishment Equipment). **Est:** 1972. **Sales:** $380,000 (2000). **Emp:** 2. **Officers:** Arnold P. Casterline Jr.

■ **9757** ■ **Carabel Export & Import**
948 Roosevelt Ave.
San Juan, PR 00921
Phone: (787)781-2229
Products: Ceramic tile. **SIC:** 5032 (Brick, Stone & Related Materials).

■ **9758** ■ **Caravelle Distributing**
1615 Greenleaf Ave.
Elk Grove Village, IL 60007
Phone: (847)593-5240 **Fax:** (847)593-5249
Products: Floor coverings. **SIC:** 5023 (Homefurnishings). **Est:** 1969. **Sales:** $3,000,000 (2000). **Emp:** 6. **Officers:** Thomas E. Helbling, President. **Former Name:** Caravelle Distributors.

■ **9759** ■ **Caro-Tile Ltd.**
7 Task Industrial Ct.
Greenville, SC 29607
Phone: (864)297-1496 **Fax:** (864)288-4831
Products: Ceramic tile. **SIC:** 5032 (Brick, Stone & Related Materials).

■ **9760** ■ **Carolina Braided Rug**
622 Meswain Rd.
Shelby, NC 28150
Phone: (704)434-6483
Products: Rugs. **SIC:** 5023 (Homefurnishings).

■ **9761** ■ **Carpet Barn Inc.**
106 Pinehurst Rd.
Ellenboro, NC 28040
Phone: (828)245-2100
Products: Carpets and rugs; Tile; Non-ceramics. **SIC:** 5023 (Homefurnishings).

■ **9762** ■ **Carpet Basics**
101 Ambrogio Dr., Ste. L
Gurnee, IL 60031
Phone: (847)360-1303
Free: (800)886-4731 **Fax:** (847)360-1304
Products: Carpet installation equipment and supplies. **SICs:** 5046 (Commercial Equipment Nec); 5072 (Hardware).

■ **9763** ■ **Carpet Cushion Supply**
1001 Arthur Ave.
PO Box 653
Elk Grove Village, IL 60007
Phone: (847)364-6760
Free: (800)626-5572 **Fax:** (847)364-6785
Products: Carpet supplies and padding. **SIC:** 5023 (Homefurnishings). **Est:** 1979.

■ **9764** ■ **Carpet Cushion Supply**
4620 W 120th St.
Alsip, IL 60803-2317
Phone: (708)389-6460 **Fax:** (708)389-0971
Products: Carpeting installation materials. **SICs:** 5023 (Homefurnishings); 5072 (Hardware).

■ **9765** ■ **Carpet Cushion Supply**
1941 Woodlawn Ave.
Griffith, IN 46319
Phone: (219)838-9664
Free: (888)288-3141 **Fax:** (219)838-9770
Products: Carpet and tile supplies, including carpet binding; Pad recycling. **SICs:** 5023 (Homefurnishings); 5032 (Brick, Stone & Related Materials). **Officers:** Phil Davis, Customer Service Contact.

■ **9766** ■ **Carpet Cushion Supply**
543 S Vermont
Palatine, IL 60067
Phone: (847)991-4343
Products: Carpet padding and supplies. **SIC:** 5023 (Homefurnishings).

■ **9767** ■ **Carpet Cushion Supply**
5515 N Northwest Hwy.
Chicago, IL 60630
Phone: (773)631-0420 **Fax:** (773)631-3908
Products: Tools; Carpet flooring supplies. **SIC:** 5072 (Hardware). **Est:** 1979.

■ **9768** ■ **Carpet Factory Outlet**
2501 Broadway St.
Kansas City, MO 64108
Phone: (816)421-3170 **Fax:** (816)842-7650
Products: Carpeting and vinyl flooring. **SIC:** 5023 (Homefurnishings). **Est:** 1976. **Sales:** $20,000,000 (2000). **Emp:** 75. **Officers:** Sherman Johnson, President, e-mail: SJ@McIntyremann.com.

■ **9769** ■ **Carpet Isle Design Center**
741 Kanoelehua Ave.
Hilo, HI 96720
Phone: (808)935-0047 **Fax:** (808)935-0040
Products: Ceramic wall and floor tile. **SIC:** 5032 (Brick, Stone & Related Materials). **Officers:** Garret Sasaki, Contact.

■ **9770** ■ **Carpet Mart & Wallpaper**
1271 Manheim Pike
Lancaster, PA 17601-3121
Phone: (717)299-2381 **Fax:** (717)299-0316
Products: Carpet; Wallpaper; Tile. **SICs:** 5023 (Homefurnishings); 5198 (Paints, Varnishes & Supplies); 5032 (Brick, Stone & Related Materials).

■ **9771** ■ **Carpet Warehouse Connection**
1548 Ford Rd.
Bensalem, PA 19020
Phone: (215)633-9444 **Fax:** (215)633-9474
Products: Carpeting; Flooring; Window treatments. **SIC:** 5023 (Homefurnishings). **Est:** 1992. **Emp:** 2.

■ **9772** ■ **Carpetland U.S.A. Inc.**
8201 Calumet Ave.
Munster, IN 46321
Phone: (219)836-5555 **Fax:** (219)978-6555
Products: Carpet. **SIC:** 5023 (Homefurnishings). **Est:** 1960. **Sales:** $150,000,000 (2000). **Emp:** 550. **Officers:** David Cicchinelli, President; Paul Bomblauskas, VP of Finance.

■ **9773** ■ **Carroll Distribution Company, Inc.**
PO Box 2647
Davenport, IA 52809
Phone: (319)391-7500 **Fax:** (319)391-2345
Products: Floor coverings, including vinyl, tile, and carpet. **SICs:** 5023 (Homefurnishings); 5032 (Brick, Stone & Related Materials).

■ **9774** ■ **Casa Carpet Wholesale Distributors**
3737 Gateway Blvd. W
El Paso, TX 79903-4555
Phone: (915)562-9521
Free: (800)321-CASA **Fax:** (915)562-9533
Products: Carpets. **SIC:** 5023 (Homefurnishings). **Emp:** 49. **Officers:** Greg Coury.

■ **9775** ■ **Casa Mexicana**
Main St.
MesiLla Park, NM 88047
Phone: (505)523-2777
Products: Ceramic tile. **SIC:** 5032 (Brick, Stone & Related Materials).

■ **9776** ■ **Case Supply, Inc.**
507 N Montgall Ave.
Kansas City, MO 64120-1530
Phone: (816)231-2530 **Fax:** (816)231-7217
Products: Ceramic wall and floor tile. **SIC:** 5032 (Brick, Stone & Related Materials).

■ **9777** ■ **Case Supply, Inc.**
14851 101st Ter.
Overland Park, KS 66215
Phone: (913)492-6677 **Fax:** (913)492-5452
Products: Ceramic wall and floor tile. **SIC:** 5032 (Brick, Stone & Related Materials).

■ **9778** ■ **Case Supply, Inc.**
355 N Rock Island St.
Wichita, KS 67202-2725
Phone: (316)265-6653 **Fax:** (316)265-0138
Products: Ceramic wall and floor tile. **SIC:** 5032 (Brick, Stone & Related Materials).

■ **9779** ■ **Casey's Tile Supply Co.**
1402 S Clack
Abilene, TX 79605
Phone: (915)692-6621
Products: Ceramic mosaic tile; Clay or other ceramic tile. **SIC:** 5032 (Brick, Stone & Related Materials). **Emp:** 8.

■ **9780** ■ **Cathey Wholesale Co.**
202 36th St.
Lubbock, TX 79404-2414
Phone: (806)747-3121 **Fax:** (806)747-9011
Products: Vinyl flooring tile, adhesives, carpet, carpet padding, ceramic flooring, and wood flooring. **SICs:** 5023 (Homefurnishings); 5031 (Lumber, Plywood & Millwork); 5032 (Brick, Stone & Related Materials). **Emp:** 26. **Officers:** Bob Bevers.

■ **9781** ■ **CDC**
10511 Medallion Dr.
Cincinnati, OH 45241-3193
Phone: (513)771-3100
Free: (800)677-2321 **Fax:** (513)771-2920
Products: Flooring, including tile and carpeting; Cushions. **SICs:** 5023 (Homefurnishings); 5032 (Brick, Stone & Related Materials). **Est:** 1976. **Sales:** $30,000,000 (1999). **Emp:** 98. **Officers:** David J. Flaum, CEO & President; Tony Roberto, Vice President; Brenda Buchanon, Vice President, Credit; Alan Futschen, VP & CFO.

■ **9782** ■ **CDC**
5019 Trans-America Dr.
Columbus, OH 43228
Phone: (614)876-4057
Free: (800)666-2321 **Fax:** (614)876-5742
Products: Floor coverings, including tile and carpeting; Cushions. **SICs:** 5023 (Homefurnishings); 5032 (Brick, Stone & Related Materials).

■ **9783** ■ **Central Distributors Inc.**
117 College Ave.
Des Moines, IA 50314
Phone: (515)244-8103 **Fax:** (515)244-9536
Products: Carpeting; Vinyl; Plastic; Rubber; Tile, including ceramic tile; Tools; Metal. **SICs:** 5023 (Homefurnishings); 5032 (Brick, Stone & Related Materials); 5039 (Construction Materials Nec); 5051 (Metals Service Centers & Offices); 5162 (Plastics Materials & Basic Shapes). **Est:** 1956. **Sales:** $3,000,000 (2000). **Emp:** 12. **Officers:** G.L. Hendricks, President; Scott Hendricks, Dir. of Marketing.

■ **9784** ■ **Century Tile and Carpet**
747 E Roosevelt Rd.
Lombard, IL 60148
Phone: (630)495-2300 **Fax:** (630)495-8645
URL: http://www.century-tile.com
Products: Floorcoverings, including ceramic, wood, laminate, vinyl and carpeting. **SICs:** 5023 (Homefurnishings); 5032 (Brick, Stone & Related Materials). **Est:** 1948. **Sales:** $40,000,000 (2000). **Emp:** 250. **Officers:** Frederick M. Schmidt, President & CEO. **Former Name:** Century Tile and Supply Co.

■ **9785** ■ **Century Tile & Carpet**
200 Washington St.
Woodstock, IL 60098
Phone: (815)337-0400 **Fax:** (815)337-0400
Products: Ceramic wall and floor tile; Carpeting; Vanities. **SICs:** 5032 (Brick, Stone & Related Materials); 5023 (Homefurnishings). **Est:** 1948. **Sales:** $2,500,000 (2000). **Emp:** 10.

■ 9786 ■ Century Tile & Carpet
5719 Diversey
Chicago, IL 60639
Phone: (773)622-6800   Fax: (773)622-4539
E-mail: webmaster@century-tile.com
URL: http://www.century-tile.com
Products: Ceramic wall and floor tile; Vinyl tile; Floor setting materials; Pergo and laminate flooring. SIC: 5032 (Brick, Stone & Related Materials). Est: 1948. Sales: $40,000,000 (1999). Emp: 250. Officers: Fred Schmidt, President. Former Name: Centry Tile & Supply Co.

■ 9787 ■ Century Tile and Carpet
747 E Roosevelt Rd.
Lombard, IL 60148
Phone: (708)889-0800   Fax: (708)495-8645
URL: http://www.century-tile.com
Products: Floor coverings, including ceramic, wood, laminate, vinyl and carpeting. SIC: 5023 (Homefurnishings). Est: 1948. Sales: $40,000,000 (1999). Emp: 250. Officers: Frederick M. Schmidt, President. Former Name: Century Supply Corp.

■ 9788 ■ Century Tile and Supply
374 South Rt. 53
Bolingbrook, IL 60440
Phone: (630)972-1700   Fax: (630)972-1436
Products: Tile; Wood. SICs: 5032 (Brick, Stone & Related Materials); 5031 (Lumber, Plywood & Millwork).

■ 9789 ■ Century Tile and Supply Co.
1220 Norwood
Itasca, IL 60143
Phone: (708)250-8000   Fax: (708)250-8704
Products: Tile and tiling supplies. SIC: 5032 (Brick, Stone & Related Materials).

■ 9790 ■ Century Tile & Supply Co.
915 E Rand
Mt. Prospect, IL 60056
Phone: (847)392-4700   Fax: (847)392-4981
E-mail: webmaster@century-tile.com
URL: http://www.century-tile.com
Products: Ceramic wall and floor tile; Vinyl tile; Floor setting materials; Pergo and laminate flooring. SIC: 5032 (Brick, Stone & Related Materials). Est: 1948. Sales: $40,000,000 (1999). Emp: 250. Officers: Fred Schmidt, President.

■ 9791 ■ Ceramic Concept of Martin County
200 N Old Dixie Hwy.
Jupiter, FL 33458
Phone: (561)746-2230
Products: Ceramic tile. SIC: 5032 (Brick, Stone & Related Materials).

■ 9792 ■ Ceramic Tile Center Inc.
3945 Vernon St.
Long Beach, CA 90815-1727
Phone: (562)498-2336   Fax: (562)498-9387
E-mail: ctctile@ix.netcom.com
Products: Ceramic wall and floor tile. SIC: 5032 (Brick, Stone & Related Materials). Est: 1956. Emp: 28. Officers: Bob Mische, President; Vicki Holden, Chairman of the Board.

■ 9793 ■ Ceramic Tile Center Inc.
525 S Van Ness Ave.
Torrance, CA 90501-1424
Phone: (310)533-8231   Fax: (310)533-8189
Products: Ceramic wall and floor tile. SIC: 5032 (Brick, Stone & Related Materials).

■ 9794 ■ Ceramic Tile Center, Inc.
50 E Greg St., Ste. 114
Sparks, NV 89431-6595
Phone: (702)359-6770   Fax: (702)359-5423
Products: Ceramic wall and floor tile. SIC: 5032 (Brick, Stone & Related Materials).

■ 9795 ■ Ceramic Tile Distributors
PO Box 1107
Ft. Smith, AR 72902-1107
Phone: (501)646-7600   Fax: (501)646-2110
Products: Ceramic tile. SIC: 5032 (Brick, Stone & Related Materials).

■ 9796 ■ Ceramic Tile Distributors, Inc.
712 Fogg St.
Nashville, TN 37203
Phone: (615)255-6669
Products: Floorcoverings, including ceramic tile and marble. SIC: 5023 (Homefurnishings).

■ 9797 ■ Ceramic Tile International
2333 S Jupiter Rd.
Garland, TX 75041
Phone: (214)503-5500   Fax: (214)503-5555
URL: http://www.ceramictileintl.com
Products: Tile; Marble. SIC: 5032 (Brick, Stone & Related Materials). Est: 1984. Sales: $65,000,000 (1999). Emp: 200. Officers: Victor Almeida.

■ 9798 ■ Ceramic Tile International
2682 Forest Lane
Dallas, TX 75234
Phone: (972)243-4465   Fax: (972)243-7933
Products: Ceramic tile. SIC: 5032 (Brick, Stone & Related Materials).

■ 9799 ■ Ceramic Tile International
1458 Lee Trevino
El Paso, TX 79936
Phone: (915)593-7357   Fax: (915)594-7120
Products: Ceramic wall and floor tile and accessories. SIC: 5032 (Brick, Stone & Related Materials). Emp: 16. Officers: Rick Torres, Contact.

■ 9800 ■ Ceramic Tile Supply Co.
103 Green Bank Rd.
Wilmington, DE 19808-5963
Phone: (302)992-9212   Fax: (302)992-9207
Products: Ceramic wall and floor tile. SIC: 5032 (Brick, Stone & Related Materials).

■ 9801 ■ Ceramic Tile Supply, Inc.
1601 E 27th St.
Chattanooga, TN 37404-5722
Phone: (423)698-1512   Fax: (423)624-9043
Products: Ceramic wall and floor tile. SIC: 5032 (Brick, Stone & Related Materials).

■ 9802 ■ Charlotte Tile & Stone
1220 Commercial Ave.
Charlotte, NC 28205
Phone: (704)372-8180   Fax: (704)332-6527
Products: Ceramic wall and floor tile. SIC: 5032 (Brick, Stone & Related Materials). Officers: Chris Anderson, Contact.

■ 9803 ■ Charter Distributing
4054 Dolan Dr.
Flint, MI 48504
Phone: (810)789-5071
Products: Carpets and rugs. SIC: 5023 (Homefurnishings).

■ 9804 ■ Chicago Hardwood Flooring
509 S Vermont
Palatine, IL 60067
Phone: (847)991-9663
Products: Hardwood flooring. SICs: 5023 (Homefurnishings); 5031 (Lumber, Plywood & Millwork).

■ 9805 ■ Cinti Floor Co.
5162 Broerman Ave.
Cincinnati, OH 45217
Phone: (513)641-4500   Fax: (513)482-4204
Products: Flooring. SIC: 5023 (Homefurnishings). Est: 1894. Sales: $1,000,000 (2000). Emp: 49. Officers: D.J. Drenik, President.

■ 9806 ■ CISU of Dalton, Inc.
5102 Middlebrook Pl.
Knoxville, TN 37921-5908
Phone: (423)584-1854
Products: Ceramic wall and floor tile. SIC: 5032 (Brick, Stone & Related Materials).

■ 9807 ■ Citywide Floor Service
4011 E 138 St.
Grandview, MO 64030
Phone: (816)842-3151   Fax: (816)765-8585
Products: Floor coverings. SIC: 5023 (Homefurnishings).

■ 9808 ■ Clark and Mitchell Inc.
7820 Bluffton Rd.
Ft. Wayne, IN 46809
Phone: (219)747-7431
Products: Carpet; Furniture. SICs: 5023 (Homefurnishings); 5021 (Furniture). Est: 1962. Sales: $6,000,000 (2000). Emp: 40. Officers: C.W. Mitchell, President; Daniel Geary, Controller; Greg Mitchell, Dir. of Marketing & Sales.

■ 9809 ■ Clark's Carpet Connection
7450 Montgomery Rd.
Plain City, OH 43064
Phone: (614)873-6108
Products: Carpets. SIC: 5023 (Homefurnishings).

■ 9810 ■ Classic Flooring Distributors
PO Box 11706
Roanoke, VA 24022-1706
Phone: (804)329-4150   Fax: (804)329-5943
Products: Floor coverings, including carpet and tile. SICs: 5023 (Homefurnishings); 5032 (Brick, Stone & Related Materials).

■ 9811 ■ Classic Tile, Inc.
PO Box 6680
Elizabeth, NJ 07206-1999
Phone: (908)289-8400
Free: (800)352-2527   Fax: (908)289-6266
E-mail: classictile@worldnet.att.net
URL: http://www.classictile.com
Products: Tile, sheet wood, vinyl, rubber, laminate, cork, granite, marble, and ceramic flooring. SICs: 5023 (Homefurnishings); 5031 (Lumber, Plywood & Millwork); 5032 (Brick, Stone & Related Materials). Est: 1977. Emp: 65. Officers: Leah Teitel, Co-Owner; Jack Teitel, Co-Owner.

■ 9812 ■ Allen Clay Tile Products
7301 Georgetown Rd., Ste. 213
Indianapolis, IN 46268-4128
Phone: (317)872-5980
Free: (800)878-5980   Fax: (317)876-0732
Products: Ceramic tiles; Mirrors; Shower enclosures. SIC: 5032 (Brick, Stone & Related Materials). Est: 1957. Officers: Tom Langlois, Contact.

■ 9813 ■ Clayton Tile
PO Box 6151
Greenville, SC 29607
Phone: (864)288-6290
Products: Ceramic wall and floor tile. SIC: 5032 (Brick, Stone & Related Materials). Officers: Lonnie D. Clayton, Contact.

■ 9814 ■ CMH Flooring Products Inc.
Hwy. 74 E
Wadesboro, NC 28170
Phones: (704)694-6213   800-650-3060
Free: (800)342-8523   Fax: (704)694-4806
E-mail: cmh@vnet.net
URL: http://www.cmhflooring.com
Products: Hard surface floor coverings; Hardwood flooring. SICs: 5032 (Brick, Stone & Related Materials); 5031 (Lumber, Plywood & Millwork); 5023 (Homefurnishings). Est: 1989. Officers: Marsden Haigh; Hoy Lanning Jr.; John Capell; Kerry Capell.

■ 9815 ■ Coastal Tile & Roofing Co., Inc.
307 S Richardson
PO Box 638
Latta, SC 29565
Phone: (803)752-5851
Products: Tile; Roofing supplies. SICs: 5032 (Brick, Stone & Related Materials); 5033 (Roofing, Siding & Insulation).

■ 9816 ■ Cole Wholesale Flooring
1300 38th St. NW
PO Box 2967
Fargo, ND 58108-2967
Phone: (701)282-5311
Free: (800)800-8090   Fax: (701)282-0721
Products: Carpets. SIC: 5023 (Homefurnishings). Officers: Chuck Perkins.

■ 9817 ■ **Colonial Braided Rug Co.**
4345 W Dixon Blvd.
Mooresboro, NC 28114
Phone: (704)434-6922
Products: Rugs. **SIC:** 5023 (Homefurnishings).

■ 9818 ■ **Colonial Floors Inc.**
117 Waverly St.
Framingham, MA 01702-7127
Phone: (508)875-5521
Products: Floorcoverings. **SIC:** 5023 (Homefurnishings).

■ 9819 ■ **Commecial de Azulejos**
Ave. Hostos 131
Ponce, PR 00731
Phone: (787)844-0888
Products: Ceramic tile. **SIC:** 5032 (Brick, Stone & Related Materials).

■ 9820 ■ **Commercial Plamar**
1175 Ave. Emerito Estrada
San Sebastian, PR 00685
Phone: (787)896-2735
Products: Ceramic tile. **SIC:** 5032 (Brick, Stone & Related Materials).

■ 9821 ■ **Compass Concepts**
2220 E Artesia Blvd.
Long Beach, CA 90805
Phone: (562)422-6992
Free: (800)543-6033   **Fax:** (562)428-2361
Products: Hard surface floor coverings. **SIC:** 5032 (Brick, Stone & Related Materials).

■ 9822 ■ **Consolidated Tile and Carpet Co.**
15100 Ravinia Ave.
Orland Park, IL 60462-3745
Phone: (708)403-5000   **Fax:** (708)403-5030
Products: Flooring materials, including carpet, tiles, sheet vinyl, wood, marble, and related products. **SICs:** 5023 (Homefurnishings); 5032 (Brick, Stone & Related Materials); 5169 (Chemicals & Allied Products Nec). **Est:** 1947. **Sales:** $2,000,000 (2000). **Emp:** 25. **Officers:** Donald L. McGrath, CEO.

■ 9823 ■ **Contempo Ceramic Tile**
3732 S 330 W
Salt Lake City, UT 84115-9314
Phone: (801)262-1717   **Fax:** (801)268-3690
Products: Ceramic wall and floor tile. **SIC:** 5032 (Brick, Stone & Related Materials). **Officers:** Jan F. Kucera, Contact.

■ 9824 ■ **Continental Ceramic Tile**
2030 Grant Ave.
Philadelphia, PA 19115
Phone: (215)676-1119
Free: (800)497-1414   **Fax:** (215)676-1227
Products: Ceramic wall and floor tile. **SIC:** 5032 (Brick, Stone & Related Materials). **Officers:** Ernie Iacobucci, Contact.

■ 9825 ■ **Continental Flooring Inc.**
1446 39th St.
Brooklyn, NY 11218
Phone: (718)854-5800   **Fax:** (718)854-5142
E-mail: mdl1446@aol.com
Products: Flooring supplies, including tile, linoleum, and carpet. **SICs:** 5023 (Homefurnishings); 5032 (Brick, Stone & Related Materials). **Est:** 1990. **Sales:** $500,000 (2000). **Emp:** 3. **Officers:** David Leifer, President.

■ 9826 ■ **Contractors Floor Covering**
1440 Campbell Ln.
PO Box 20102
Bowling Green, KY 42104
Phone: (270)843-1542
Free: (800)843-8510   **Fax:** (270)781-0433
E-mail: contractorsfloor@aol.com
Products: Ceramic wall and floor tile. **SIC:** 5032 (Brick, Stone & Related Materials). **Est:** 1984. **Sales:** $3,000,000 (2000). **Emp:** 6. **Officers:** Bobby Wysong; Sally Wysong.

■ 9827 ■ **Corriveau-Routhier, Inc.**
375 N State
Concord, NH 03301
Phone: (603)228-0631   **Fax:** (603)226-0757
Products: Ceramic tile; Masonry products. **SIC:** 5032 (Brick, Stone & Related Materials).

■ 9828 ■ **Corriveau-Routhier Inc.**
266 Clay St.
PO Box 4127
Manchester, NH 03103
Phone: (603)627-3805   **Fax:** (603)622-6758
Products: Ceramic tile; Brick; Stone; Granite; Masonry. **SIC:** 5032 (Brick, Stone & Related Materials). **Est:** 1946. **Sales:** $21,000,000 (1992). **Emp:** 75. **Officers:** David Corriveau, President.

■ 9829 ■ **Corriveau-Routhier, Inc.**
159 Temple St.
Nashua, NH 03060
Phone: (603)889-2157
Products: Ceramic wall and floor tile. **SIC:** 5032 (Brick, Stone & Related Materials).

■ 9830 ■ **Craftsmen Supply, Inc.**
1170-A South Beltline
PO Box 16641
Mobile, AL 36609
Phone: (205)343-3398   **Fax:** (205)343-0150
Products: Ceramic tile. **SIC:** 5032 (Brick, Stone & Related Materials).

■ 9831 ■ **Craftsmen Supply, Inc.**
7457 Gunter Rd.
Pensacola, FL 32526-3843
Phone: (850)455-5429   **Fax:** (850)455-6481
Products: Bathroom and kitchen flooring, including tile and marble. **SICs:** 5023 (Homefurnishings); 5032 (Brick, Stone & Related Materials).

■ 9832 ■ **Crest Distributors**
1136 Longsdale Ave.
Central Falls, RI 02863
Phone: (401)723-9774
Products: Ceramic tile. **SIC:** 5032 (Brick, Stone & Related Materials).

■ 9833 ■ **The Cronin Co.**
2601 W 5th Ave.
Eugene, OR 97402
Phone: (541)485-6280
Products: Ceramic tile. **SIC:** 5032 (Brick, Stone & Related Materials).

■ 9834 ■ **The Cronin Co.**
1205 NW Marshall
Portland, OR 97209
Phone: (503)226-3508
Free: (800)683-5667   **Fax:** (503)226-3101
Products: Ceramic tile; Sheet vinyl; Vinyl tile; Laminate flooring; Plastic laminates; Wood flooring. **SICs:** 5032 (Brick, Stone & Related Materials); 5023 (Homefurnishings); 5031 (Lumber, Plywood & Millwork). **Est:** 1878. **Emp:** 130. **Officers:** Patrick M. Cronin, President.

■ 9835 ■ **Crown Tile & Marble**
4722 Sunrise Hwy.
Massapequa Park, NY 11762
Phone: (516)798-2457   **Fax:** (516)798-2371
Products: Ceramic wall and floor tile. **SIC:** 5032 (Brick, Stone & Related Materials). **Est:** 1940. **Sales:** $1,200,000 (2000). **Emp:** 10. **Officers:** Jeff Halpern, Contact; Peter Halpern, Contact.

■ 9836 ■ **Cubs Distributing Inc.**
3333 N 20th St.
Lincoln, NE 68521
Phone: (402)477-4411
Products: Carpets; Rugs. **SIC:** 5023 (Homefurnishings).

■ 9837 ■ **Custom Wholesale Flooring**
2020 NW 23rd St.
Miami, FL 33142
Phone: (305)635-6421   **Fax:** (305)635-6420
Products: Hardwood flooring. **SICs:** 5023 (Homefurnishings); 5031 (Lumber, Plywood & Millwork).

■ 9838 ■ **Custom Wholesale Flooring**
5910 D Breckenridge Pkwy.
Tampa, FL 33610
Phone: (813)626-8840
Free: (800)288-8840   **Fax:** (813)623-5605
Products: Wood flooring. **SIC:** 5031 (Lumber, Plywood & Millwork).

■ 9839 ■ **Custom Wholesale Flooring**
735 Park North Blvd.
Clarkston, GA 30021
Phone: (404)296-9663   **Fax:** (404)294-8109
Products: Hardwood flooring. **SICs:** 5031 (Lumber, Plywood & Millwork); 5023 (Homefurnishings).

■ 9840 ■ **D & B Tile**
781 S Congress Ave.
Delray Beach, FL 33445
Phone: (561)272-7022
Products: Ceramic tile. **SIC:** 5032 (Brick, Stone & Related Materials).

■ 9841 ■ **D & B Tile**
8550 SW 129th Ter.
Kendall, FL 33176
Phone: (305)238-1909
Products: Ceramic tile. **SIC:** 5032 (Brick, Stone & Related Materials).

■ 9842 ■ **D & B Tile**
4431 Corporate Sq.
Naples, FL 34104-4796
Phone: (941)643-7099
Products: Ceramic tile. **SIC:** 5032 (Brick, Stone & Related Materials).

■ 9843 ■ **D & B Tile**
4241 L.B. McLeod Dr.
Orlando, FL 32856
Phone: (407)849-6590
Products: Ceramic tile. **SIC:** 5032 (Brick, Stone & Related Materials).

■ 9844 ■ **D & B Tile**
1551 N Powerline Rd.
Pompano Beach, FL 33069
Phone: (954)979-2066
Products: Ceramic tile. **SIC:** 5032 (Brick, Stone & Related Materials).

■ 9845 ■ **D & B Tile**
3346 45th St.
West Palm Beach, FL 33407
Phone: (561)478-4242
Products: Ceramic tile. **SIC:** 5032 (Brick, Stone & Related Materials).

■ 9846 ■ **D & B Tile Distributors**
14200 NW 4th St.
Sunrise, FL 33325
Phone: (954)846-2660
Free: (800)749-6280   **Fax:** (954)845-1112
E-mail: dbtile@gate.net
URL: http://www.dbtile.com
Products: Ceramic tile and allied products. **SIC:** 5032 (Brick, Stone & Related Materials). **Est:** 1972. **Sales:** $22,000,000 (2000). **Emp:** 140. **Officers:** David A. Yarborough, President.

■ 9847 ■ **Dal Tile Corp.**
730 Dearborn Park Ln.
Worthington, OH 43085
Phone: (614)433-9181
Products: Tile. **SIC:** 5023 (Homefurnishings).

■ 9848 ■ **Davis Rug Co.**
3937 Barclay Rd.
Shelby, NC 28152
Phone: (704)434-7231
Products: Rugs. **SIC:** 5023 (Homefurnishings).

■ 9849 ■ **Dealers Supply Co.**
2100 Commerce Dr.
Cayce, SC 29033
Phone: (803)796-2495   **Fax:** (803)796-3574
Products: Floor coverings, including carpet, vinyl, and tile. **SICs:** 5023 (Homefurnishings); 5032 (Brick, Stone & Related Materials).

■ 9850 ■ Dealers Supply Co.
PO Box 2628
Durham, NC 27715-2628
Phone: (919)383-7451
Products: Floor coverings, including linoleum and carpets. **SIC:** 5023 (Homefurnishings). **Sales:** $28,000,000 (1992). **Emp:** 115. **Officers:** Russell N. Barringer Jr., CEO & President; Sunny Newcombe, Controller.

■ 9851 ■ Deaton's Carpet One
1000 Hwy. 45 Bypass
Jackson, TN 38301
Phone: (901)664-5200   **Fax:** (901)664-5203
Products: Carpets; Wallcoverings, wallpaper; Carpet tiles. **SICs:** 5023 (Homefurnishings); 5198 (Paints, Varnishes & Supplies). **Sales:** $1,800,000 (2000). **Emp:** 17. **Officers:** Gary Deaton, Owner.

■ 9852 ■ Decorative Products Group
128 Regional Park Dr.
Kingsport, TN 37660
Phone: (423)349-4129   **Fax:** (423)349-7794
Products: Vinyl, wood, and tile floorcoverings; Paints. **SICs:** 5023 (Homefurnishings); 5031 (Lumber, Plywood & Millwork); 5032 (Brick, Stone & Related Materials); 5198 (Paints, Varnishes & Supplies).

■ 9853 ■ Decorative Products Group
917 Dinwiddie
Knoxville, TN 37921
Phone: (423)525-0207   **Fax:** (423)525-0208
Products: Ceramic, vinyl, wood, and tile products. **SICs:** 5023 (Homefurnishings); 5031 (Lumber, Plywood & Millwork); 5032 (Brick, Stone & Related Materials).

■ 9854 ■ Del Sol Tile Co.
920 S 5th St.
Edinburg, TX 78539-4205
Phone: (956)381-4834
Free: (800)752-5861   **Fax:** (956)381-1308
E-mail: delsoltile@msn.com
Products: Clay floor and ceramic tile; Marble and clay pots. **SICs:** 5032 (Brick, Stone & Related Materials); 5023 (Homefurnishings). **Est:** 1988. **Sales:** $250,000 (2000). **Emp:** 4.

■ 9855 ■ Denver Hardwood Co.
4700B National Western Dr.
Denver, CO 80216
Phone: (303)296-1168
Free: (800)274-4144   **Fax:** (303)292-3118
Products: Hardwood flooring and supplies; Vinyl and formica high pressure laminate flooring. **SICs:** 5023 (Homefurnishings); 5031 (Lumber, Plywood & Millwork); 5072 (Hardware).

■ 9856 ■ Design Carpets
PO Box 15780
Richmond, VA 23227-5780
Phone: (804)550-2255
Free: (800)552-2898   **Fax:** (804)550-2260
Products: Hard surface floor coverings; Carpets. **SICs:** 5032 (Brick, Stone & Related Materials); 5023 (Homefurnishings).

■ 9857 ■ Design Distributing
1529 Seibel Dr. NE
Roanoke, VA 24012
Phone: (540)342-3471   **Fax:** (540)342-0620
Products: Wood floors; Carpets; Vinyl sheet goods. **SICs:** 5023 (Homefurnishings); 5031 (Lumber, Plywood & Millwork). **Sales:** $200,000 (2000). **Emp:** 6. **Officers:** Alan Harris Jr., President.

■ 9858 ■ Design Surfaces
24000 Sperry Dr.
Westlake, OH 44145
Phone: (440)899-9900   **Fax:** (440)899-3095
Products: Ceramic; Granite; Marble tile. **SIC:** 5032 (Brick, Stone & Related Materials).

■ 9859 ■ Design Surfaces
23225 Mercantile Rd.
Beachwood, OH 44122
Phone: (216)464-3430   **Fax:** (216)464-8144
Products: Clay or other ceramic tile; Dressed dimension marble and other stone; Granite products,

such as paving blocks and curbing. **SIC:** 5032 (Brick, Stone & Related Materials).

■ 9860 ■ Designed Flooring Distributors
3251 SW 13th Dr.
Deerfield Beach, FL 33442
Phone: (954)481-1900   **Fax:** (954)481-2001
Products: Hardwood floor supplies. **SIC:** 5031 (Lumber, Plywood & Millwork).

■ 9861 ■ Designer Tile Co. East
145 English Rd.
PO Box 7334
Rocky Mount, NC 27804-0334
Phone: (919)937-6090   **Fax:** (919)937-8205
Products: Ceramic tile. **SIC:** 5032 (Brick, Stone & Related Materials).

■ 9862 ■ Desso USA Inc.
387 Strathmore Rd.
Rosemont, PA 19010-1262
Phone: (215)526-9517   **Fax:** (215)525-4068
Products: Carpet. **SIC:** 5023 (Homefurnishings). **Emp:** 3.

■ 9863 ■ Diamond W Supply Co. Inc.
2017 N 23rd Ave.
Phoenix, AZ 85009
Phone: (602)252-5841
Free: (800)352-4584   **Fax:** (602)257-1059
Products: Floor coverings, including wood, vinyl, and ceramic. **SICs:** 5023 (Homefurnishings); 5032 (Brick, Stone & Related Materials); 5031 (Lumber, Plywood & Millwork).

■ 9864 ■ Diamond W Supply Co. Inc.
PO Box 2383
Los Angeles, CA 90051
Phones: (213)685-7400   (714)994-5920
Free: (800)523-6265   **Fax:** (213)889-6864
Products: Wood, plastic, vinyl, and hardwood floor coverings; Adhesives. **SICs:** 5023 (Homefurnishings); 5031 (Lumber, Plywood & Millwork); 5169 (Chemicals & Allied Products Nec).

■ 9865 ■ Diamond W Supply Co. Inc.
8410 Ajong Dr.
San Diego, CA 92126
Phone: (619)578-3260
Free: (800)548-2233   **Fax:** (619)578-3814
Products: Hardwood and ceramic floor coverings. **SICs:** 5023 (Homefurnishings); 5032 (Brick, Stone & Related Materials).

■ 9866 ■ Dimock, Gould and Co.
190 22nd St.
Moline, IL 61265
Phone: (309)797-0650   **Fax:** (309)764-9922
Products: Ceramic wall and floor tile. **SIC:** 5032 (Brick, Stone & Related Materials). **Officers:** Gordon Ainsworth, President; Daryl Nelson, Sec. & Treas.; Brad Scott, Vice President; Kim Kent, Vice President.

■ 9867 ■ DMI Tile & Marble
3012 5th Ave. S
Birmingham, AL 35233
Phone: (205)322-8473   **Fax:** (205)251-9647
Products: Ceramic wall and floor tile. **SIC:** 5032 (Brick, Stone & Related Materials). **Officers:** Terry Isaminger, Contact.

■ 9868 ■ W.W. Dobkin Company, Inc.
51 Benbro Dr.
Cheektowaga, NY 14225
Phone: (716)684-1200   **Fax:** (716)684-1294
E-mail: mzydel@aol.com
Products: Ceramic tile. **SIC:** 5032 (Brick, Stone & Related Materials).

■ 9869 ■ W.W. Dobkin Company, Inc.
801 E Hiawatha Rd.
Syracuse, NY 13208
Phone: (315)478-5769
Products: Ceramic wall and floor tile. **SIC:** 5032 (Brick, Stone & Related Materials). **Officers:** Lynn Plochko, Contact.

■ 9870 ■ Domestic Import Tile
3650 South 300 West
PO Box 65663
Salt Lake City, UT 84115
Phone: (801)262-3033
Free: (800)274-0383   **Fax:** (801)262-2234
Products: Ceramic and porcelain wall and floor tile. **SIC:** 5032 (Brick, Stone & Related Materials). **Est:** 1970. **Emp:** 11. **Officers:** David Elder, Owner; Mike Kelsch, General Mgr., e-mail: mike@domesticimport.com.

■ 9871 ■ Domus Corp.
9734 Hayne Blvd.
New Orleans, LA 70127-1202
Phone: (504)242-5480   **Fax:** (504)245-3849
Products: Ceramic wall and floor tile. **SIC:** 5032 (Brick, Stone & Related Materials). **Emp:** 5.

■ 9872 ■ Downs Supply Co.
PO Box 471010
Tulsa, OK 74147-1010
Phone: (918)252-5651   **Fax:** (918)252-7971
Products: Vinyl, wood, tile, carpet, and ceramic floor coverings. **SICs:** 5023 (Homefurnishings); 5032 (Brick, Stone & Related Materials); 5031 (Lumber, Plywood & Millwork).

■ 9873 ■ Duffy and Lee Co.
3351 SW 13th Ave.
Ft. Lauderdale, FL 33315
Phone: (954)467-1288
Products: Carpeting. **SIC:** 5023 (Homefurnishings). **Sales:** $5,500,000 (2000). **Emp:** 75. **Officers:** Charles J. Duffy Sr., President.

■ 9874 ■ Dunken Distributing Inc.
PO Box 1821
Twin Falls, ID 83303-1821
Phone: (208)733-3054
Products: Carpet installation tools and supplies. **SICs:** 5046 (Commercial Equipment Nec); 5072 (Hardware). **Officers:** Kenneth Dunken, President.

■ 9875 ■ East Coast Tile Imports—East
Ludlow Industrial Park, Gate 4, Bldg. 261
State St.
Ludlow, MA 01056
Phone: (413)589-0101   **Fax:** (413)583-5219
Products: Ceramic wall and floor tile. **SIC:** 5032 (Brick, Stone & Related Materials).

■ 9876 ■ East Coast Tile/Terrazzo
420 S Neiman Ave.
Melbourne, FL 32901
Phone: (407)723-4353
Products: Ceramic tile. **SIC:** 5032 (Brick, Stone & Related Materials).

■ 9877 ■ East Coast Tile/Terrazzo
450 Old Dixie Hwy.
Vero Beach, FL 32960
Phone: (561)562-4164
Free: (877)328-8453   **Fax:** (561)778-5253
E-mail: ectub@aol.com
Products: Ceramic tile. **SIC:** 5032 (Brick, Stone & Related Materials). **Est:** 1956. **Sales:** $3,000,000 (2000). **Emp:** 24.

■ 9878 ■ East Side Lumberyard Supply
1201 East University Ave.
Urbana, IL 61801
Phone: (217)367-7000   **Fax:** (217)367-9125
Products: Siding; Paneling; Rollers; Roofing. **SICs:** 5033 (Roofing, Siding & Insulation); 5031 (Lumber, Plywood & Millwork). **Est:** 1934. **Sales:** $4,500,000 (2000). **Emp:** 12. **Officers:** Brandon T. Pryor, Dir. of Marketing.

■ 9879 ■ Eastern Wood Products Company Inc.
PO Box 1056
Williamsport, PA 17703-1056
Phone: (570)326-1946   **Fax:** (570)327-1390
E-mail: ewp@mail.csrlink.net
URL: http://www.easternwood.com
Products: Wood products, including paneling and flooring; Kiln-dried hardwood; Specialty millwork. **SIC:** 5031 (Lumber, Plywood & Millwork). **Est:** 1939. **Sales:**

$3,000,000 (2000). **Emp:** 35. **Officers:** James M. Furey II, President; James M. Furey III, Vice President; Jamie Furey, Sales/Marketing Contact.

■ 9880 ■ **Eastside Wholesale Supply Co.**
6450 E 8 Mile Rd.
Detroit, MI 48234
Phone: (313)891-2900
Products: Vinyl flooring. **SIC:** 5023 (Homefurnishings).
Sales: $25,000,000 (2000). **Emp:** 86. **Officers:** Bob Paquette, President.

■ 9881 ■ **Ebling Distribution, Inc.**
711 E 14th St.
North Kansas City, MO 64116
Phone: (816)842-7095   **Fax:** (816)842-6972
Products: Floor coverings, including vinyl, carpet, padding, and ceramic. **SIC:** 5023 (Homefurnishings).

■ 9882 ■ **E.C.F. Supply**
7553 NW 50th St.
Miami, FL 33166
Phone: (305)477-5444
Free: (800)222-1004   **Fax:** (305)477-0085
E-mail: ecfsupply@aol.com
Products: Wood flooring and supplies. **SICs:** 5023 (Homefurnishings); 5031 (Lumber, Plywood & Millwork). **Est:** 1957. **Sales:** $2,000,000 (2000) **Emp:** 7. **Officers:** T. Worrell, President.

■ 9883 ■ **Empire State Marble Manufacturing Corp.**
207 E 110th St.
New York, NY 10029-3202
Phone: (212)534-2307
Products: Ceramic wall and floor tile. **SIC:** 5032 (Brick, Stone & Related Materials).

■ 9884 ■ **Empire Wholesale Supply**
5119 Irving St.
Boise, ID 83706-1207
Phone: (208)322-7889   **Fax:** (208)322-6634
Products: Ceramic tile; Carpet installation equipment. **SICs:** 5032 (Brick, Stone & Related Materials); 5046 (Commercial Equipment Nec). **Officers:** Ray Kelso, Owner.

■ 9885 ■ **Erickson's Flooring & Supply**
1013 Orchard St.
Ferndale, MI 48220
Phone: (248)543-9663   **Fax:** (248)543-7912
Products: Wood flooring. **SIC:** 5031 (Lumber, Plywood & Millwork).

■ 9886 ■ **Eskew, Smith & Cannon**
PO Box 1626
Charleston, WV 25326
Phone: (304)344-3414
Free: (800)223-2166   **Fax:** (304)344-3413
Products: Carpet, vinyl, and ceramic tile floor coverings; Tools; Grass. **SICs:** 5023 (Homefurnishings); 5032 (Brick, Stone & Related Materials); 5072 (Hardware); 5193 (Flowers & Florists' Supplies).

■ 9887 ■ **Esojon International, Inc.**
1871 Betmor Ln.
Anaheim, CA 92805
Phone: (714)937-1575   **Fax:** (714)937-1506
Products: Ceramic wall and floor tile; Electrical equipment and supplies; Fabricated pipe and fittings. **SICs:** 5032 (Brick, Stone & Related Materials); 5063 (Electrical Apparatus & Equipment); 5074 (Plumbing & Hydronic Heating Supplies). **Officers:** Rosemarie F. Lau, Contact.

■ 9888 ■ **Expert Tile, Inc.**
7795 Ellis Rd.
Melbourne, FL 32904
Phone: (407)723-4301   **Fax:** (407)723-4300
Products: Ceramic wall and floor tile. **SIC:** 5032 (Brick, Stone & Related Materials). **Officers:** Martha Thoma, Contact.

■ 9889 ■ **Fiorano Design Center**
1400 Hempstead Turnpike
Elmont, NY 11003
Phone: (516)354-8453   **Fax:** (516)352-0433
Products: Ceramic and marble tile. **SIC:** 5032 (Brick, Stone & Related Materials).

■ 9890 ■ **Albert F. Fitzgerald Inc.**
120 Commerce Way
Woburn, MA 01801
Phone: (781)935-7821
Free: (800)234-8453   **Fax:** (781)935-0841
E-mail: customerservice@fitzgeraldtile.com
URL: http://www.fitzgeraldtile.com
Products: Ceramic tile; Vinyl; Setting materials. **SICs:** 5032 (Brick, Stone & Related Materials); 5023 (Homefurnishings). **Est:** 1950. **Sales:** $12,000,000 (2000). **Emp:** 50. **Officers:** John Fitzgerald, President; Joseph P. Fitzgerald, Vice President; Mary E. Fitzgerald, Treasurer; Frank Dickhaut, Sales & Marketing Contact.

■ 9891 ■ **Fleischman Carpet Co.**
19655 Grand River
Detroit, MI 48223
Phone: (313)534-9300   **Fax:** (313)534-9300
Products: Hardwood flooring; Carpets, rugs, and mats. **SICs:** 5023 (Homefurnishings); 5031 (Lumber, Plywood & Millwork). **Est:** 1921. **Sales:** $300,000 (2000). **Emp:** 2. **Officers:** William P. Shanfield, President.

■ 9892 ■ **Floor Service Supply**
5860 88th St.
Sacramento, CA 95828
Phone: (916)381-5034   **Fax:** (916)381-0915
Products: Flooring; Flooring supplies. **SIC:** 5023 (Homefurnishings).

■ 9893 ■ **Floor Service Supply**
861 Auzerias Ave.
San Jose, CA 95126
Phone: (408)280-0222
Products: Hardwood flooring. **SIC:** 5031 (Lumber, Plywood & Millwork).

■ 9894 ■ **Floor Supply Co.**
1620 Spectrum Dr.
Lawrenceville, GA 30043-5742
Phone: (404)513-1132   **Fax:** (404)513-1134
Products: Floor covering materials and supplies. **SIC:** 5023 (Homefurnishings).

■ 9895 ■ **Floor Supply Distributing Inc.**
PO BOX 3005
Spokane, WA 99220
Phone: (509)535-9707   **Fax:** (509)535-0558
Products: Carpets and vinyl flooring. **SIC:** 5023 (Homefurnishings). **Sales:** $10,000,000 (2000). **Emp:** 45. **Officers:** Lynn L. Dilliner, President.

■ 9896 ■ **Flooring Distributors Inc.**
3209 6th Ave. SW
Huntsville, AL 35805-3641
Phone: (205)536-3384   **Fax:** (205)536-4711
Products: Hard surface floor coverings; Carpets. **SIC:** 5023 (Homefurnishings). **Emp:** 9. **Officers:** Ray C. Owen; Laverne Owen.

■ 9897 ■ **Flooring Distributors Inc.**
1100 Louisiana St., Ste. 5400
Houston, TX 77002-5218
Phone: (713)752-2200
Products: Ceramic tile. **SIC:** 5032 (Brick, Stone & Related Materials).

■ 9898 ■ **Floors, Inc.**
108 N 28th St.
Birmingham, AL 35203
Phone: (205)251-1733   **Fax:** (205)251-4690
Products: Hardwood flooring. **SIC:** 5031 (Lumber, Plywood & Millwork).

■ 9899 ■ **Floors, Inc.**
981 Corporate Dr., S
Mobile, AL 36607
Phone: (205)471-4677   **Fax:** (205)471-4669
Products: Hardwood flooring. **SIC:** 5031 (Lumber, Plywood & Millwork).

■ 9900 ■ **Floors Northwest Inc.**
5515 E River Rd., No. 414
Minneapolis, MN 55421
Phone: (763)586-7070
Free: (800)284-3595   **Fax:** (763)586-7074
E-mail: mary@floorsnw.com
URL: http://floorsnw.com
Products: Hardwood flooring products, prefinished, unfinished wood; Construction materials; Concrete coatings; Rubber and vinyl floor coverings. **SICs:** 5023 (Homefurnishings); 5031 (Lumber, Plywood & Millwork); 5032 (Brick, Stone & Related Materials). **Est:** 1979. **Emp:** 7. **Officers:** M.M. Sheehan, Owner & Pres.; Scott Groenke, Vice President, e-mail: scott@floorsnw.com. **Doing Business As:** Floors Northwest.

■ 9901 ■ **Florida Hardwood Floor Supply**
8506 Sunstate St.
Tampa, FL 33634
Phone: (813)887-3064   **Fax:** (813)885-6588
Products: Hardwood flooring and supplies. **SICs:** 5023 (Homefurnishings); 5031 (Lumber, Plywood & Millwork).

■ 9902 ■ **Florida Tile**
7029 Huntley Rd.
Columbus, OH 43085
Phone: (614)436-2511
Products: Tile. **SIC:** 5023 (Homefurnishings).

■ 9903 ■ **Focus Carpet Corp.**
PO Box 608
Chatsworth, GA 30705
Phone: (706)695-5942
Free: (800)533-4267   **Fax:** (706)695-3643
Products: Carpets; Carpet tiles. **SIC:** 5023 (Homefurnishings). **Est:** 1986. **Sales:** $10,000,000 (2000). **Emp:** 50. **Officers:** John Rearden, General Mgr.; Chuck Christiansen III, VP of Sales; Glenn Conway, VP of Marketing.

■ 9904 ■ **Forbex Corporation**
1167 Willis Ave.
Albertson, NY 11507-1233
Phone: (516)625-4700   **Fax:** (516)625-4710
Products: Residential and commercial carpet; Woven carpets; Synthetic grass; Moisture meters; Plastics polyvinyl film; Synthetic upholstery textiles; Outdoor aluminum furniture and fabrics; Woodworking glue. **SICs:** 5023 (Homefurnishings); 5063 (Electrical Apparatus & Equipment); 5162 (Plastics Materials & Basic Shapes); 5131 (Piece Goods & Notions); 5169 (Chemicals & Allied Products Nec). **Officers:** Ron Kauders, Vice President; H.P. Kauders, President.

■ 9905 ■ **Forbo Industries Inc.**
PO Box 667
Hazleton, PA 18201
Phone: (717)459-0771
Products: Floor coverings. **SIC:** 5023 (Homefurnishings). **Sales:** $26,000,000 (1994). **Emp:** 150. **Officers:** Richard Burkemper, CEO & President; Don Bilby, CFO.

■ 9906 ■ **Frank Brothers Flooring Distributors**
PO Box 4141
Albany, NY 12204
Phone: (518)462-5375   **Fax:** (518)462-1530
Products: Flooring supplies and coverings. **SIC:** 5023 (Homefurnishings).

■ 9907 ■ **Frey, Inc.**
3880 Fourteen Mile Dr.
Stockton, CA 95219-3809
Phone: (916)371-7914
Products: Ceramic wall and floor tile. **SIC:** 5032 (Brick, Stone & Related Materials).

■ 9908 ■ **Garden State Tile Design Center**
231 Rte. 73, RD. 3
Berlin, NJ 08009
Phone: (609)753-0300   **Fax:** (609)753-1835
Products: Ceramic wall and floor tile; Dressed dimension marble and other stone. **SIC:** 5032 (Brick, Stone & Related Materials).

■ **9909** ■ **Garden State Tile Distributors**
790 S Route 73
West Berlin, NJ 08091
Phone: (609)753-0300 **Fax:** (609)753-1835
E-mail: rfisc74818@aol.com
URL: http://www.gstile.com
Products: Tile and related products. **SIC:** 5032 (Brick, Stone & Related Materials). **Est:** 1957. **Officers:** Stephen A. Fisher, President; Robert A. Fisher.

■ **9910** ■ **Garden State Tile Distributors**
1290 Rte. 130
Dayton, NJ 08810
Phone: (732)329-0860 **Fax:** (732)329-4636
Products: Ceramic wall and floor tile. **SIC:** 5032 (Brick, Stone & Related Materials).

■ **9911** ■ **Garden State Tile Distributors**
5001 Industrial Rd., Rte. 34
Farmingdale, NJ 07727
Phone: (732)938-6663 **Fax:** (732)938-4558
URL: http://www.gstile.com
Products: Tile. **SIC:** 5032 (Brick, Stone & Related Materials). **Est:** 1957. **Officers:** Robert A. Fischer, e-mail: rfisc74818@aol.com; Stephen A. Fischer, President.

■ **9912** ■ **Garden State Tile Distributors, Inc.**
472 E Westfield Ave.
Roselle Park, NJ 07204
Phone: (908)241-4900 **Fax:** (908)241-5044
URL: http://www.gstile.com
Products: Tile. **SIC:** 5032 (Brick, Stone & Related Materials). **Est:** 1957. **Officers:** Robert A. Fischer, e-mail: rfisc74818@aol.com; Stephen A. Fischer, President.

■ **9913** ■ **Gateway Distributors Inc.**
3634 Village Ave.
Norfolk, VA 23502-5600
Phone: (757)857-5931 **Fax:** (757)857-5914
Products: Vinyl floor coverings. **SIC:** 5023 (Homefurnishings).

■ **9914** ■ **General Distributors Inc.**
PO Box 11343
800 E Indianapolis
Wichita, KS 67202
Phone: (316)267-2255 **Fax:** (316)267-0230
Products: Ceramic wall and floor tile. **SIC:** 5032 (Brick, Stone & Related Materials).

■ **9915** ■ **General Floor**
1720 Bayberry Rd.
Bensalem, PA 19020
Phone: (215)633-7373
Products: Floorcoverings. **SIC:** 5023 (Homefurnishings).

■ **9916** ■ **Genesee Ceramic Tile Distribution**
Michigan Design Ctr.
1700 Stuty Dr., Ste. 108
Troy, MI 48084
Phone: (248)637-3272 **Fax:** (248)637-3493
E-mail: bcokley@iflint.com
URL: http://www.geneseeceramictile.com
Products: Ceramic wall and floor tile; Natural stone. **SIC:** 5032 (Brick, Stone & Related Materials). **Est:** 1973.

■ **9917** ■ **Genesee Ceramic Tile Distributors**
1307 N Belsay Rd.
Burton, MI 48509
Phone: (810)743-2000 **Fax:** (810)742-6670
Products: Ceramic, porcelain, and natural stone tiles. **SIC:** 5032 (Brick, Stone & Related Materials). **Est:** 1975. **Emp:** 90.

■ **9918** ■ **Genesee Ceramic Tile Distributors**
24701 Telegraph Rd.
Southfield, MI 48034
Phone: (248)354-3550 **Fax:** (248)354-5671
Products: Ceramic, porcelain, and natural stone tiles. **SIC:** 5032 (Brick, Stone & Related Materials). **Officers:** J. C. Cokley; Bill Cokley.

■ **9919** ■ **Genesee Ceramic Tile Distributors**
43220 Merrill Rd.
Sterling Heights, MI 48314
Phone: (810)254-4744 **Fax:** (810)254-4023
Products: Ceramic, porcelain, and natural stone tiles. **SIC:** 5032 (Brick, Stone & Related Materials).

■ **9920** ■ **Genesee Ceramic Tile Distributors**
24260 Indoplex
Farmington Hills, MI 48335
Phone: (248)478-3958 **Fax:** (248)478-7067
Products: Flooring, including ceramic tile, marble, and granite. **SIC:** 5032 (Brick, Stone & Related Materials).

■ **9921** ■ **Genesee Ceramic Tile Distributors**
459 36th St. SE
Grand Rapids, MI 49548
Phone: (616)243-5811 **Fax:** (616)243-6106
Products: Ceramic tile. **SIC:** 5032 (Brick, Stone & Related Materials).

■ **9922** ■ **Global Tile**
9797 W 151st St.
Orland Park, IL 60462
Phone: (708)460-1600 **Fax:** (708)460-1605
Products: Ceramic tile; Porcelain products. **SICs:** 5032 (Brick, Stone & Related Materials); 5023 (Homefurnishings).

■ **9923** ■ **Golden State Flooring**
240 Littlefield Ave.
South San Francisco, CA 94080-6902
Phone: (650)872-0500 **Fax:** (650)872-0719
Products: Wood flooring and finishing products, tools, and equipment. **SICs:** 5023 (Homefurnishings); 5031 (Lumber, Plywood & Millwork); 5198 (Paints, Varnishes & Supplies). **Est:** 1925. **Emp:** 70. **Officers:** Rick P. Coates, Manager.

■ **9924** ■ **Golden State Flooring Sacramento**
1015 North Market Blvd., No. 2
Sacramento, CA 95834
Phone: (916)928-0400 **Fax:** (916)928-0177
Products: Hardwood flooring; Flooring supplies. **SIC:** 5031 (Lumber, Plywood & Millwork). **Est:** 1989. **Emp:** 11. **Former Name:** Golden State Flooring.

■ **9925** ■ **Great Lakes Sales, Inc.**
4203 Roger B. Chaffee
Grand Rapids, MI 49548
Phone: (616)538-3840 **Fax:** (616)538-9640
Products: Floor coverings, including vinyl, carpet, and ceramic. **SICs:** 5023 (Homefurnishings); 5032 (Brick, Stone & Related Materials).

■ **9926** ■ **Great Lakes Sales, Inc.**
11873 Belden
Livonia, MI 48150
Phone: (734)425-6227 **Fax:** (734)425-6304
Products: Floor coverings. **SICs:** 5023 (Homefurnishings); 5031 (Lumber, Plywood & Millwork); 5032 (Brick, Stone & Related Materials).

■ **9927** ■ **Greenville Tile Distributors**
5500 Augusta Rd.
Greenville, SC 29605
Phones: (803)277-3586 (864)277-3532
Fax: (803)277-1242
Products: Tile. **SIC:** 5032 (Brick, Stone & Related Materials). **Est:** 1930. **Emp:** 5. **Officers:** Ray Hawkins, Contact; J. Steve Morgan, Customer Service Mgr.

■ **9928** ■ **Gulf Enterprises**
4333 Washington Ave.
New Orleans, LA 70185
Phone: (504)822-0785 **Fax:** (504)822-7836
Products: Hard surface floor coverings. **SIC:** 5032 (Brick, Stone & Related Materials).

■ **9929** ■ **Gurley's Georgia Carpet**
15 Morrison Blvd.
Bristol, VA 24201
Phone: (540)466-2061
Products: Carpet. **SIC:** 5023 (Homefurnishings).

■ **9930** ■ **Guthrie-Linebaugh-Coffey, Inc.**
202 Oak Knoll Rd.
New Cumberland, PA 17070-2837
Phone: (717)767-6991 **Fax:** (717)764-9320
Products: Floor coverings, including carpeting, vinyl, wood, and tile. **SICs:** 5023 (Homefurnishings); 5031 (Lumber, Plywood & Millwork); 5032 (Brick, Stone & Related Materials).

■ **9931** ■ **J.J. Haines & Company, Inc.**
6950 Aviation Blvd.
Glen Burnie, MD 21061-2531
Phone: (410)760-4040
Free: (800)435-3216 **Fax:** 800-942-4637
URL: http://www.jjhaines.com
Products: Ceramic wall and floor tile. **SIC:** 5032 (Brick, Stone & Related Materials). **Est:** 1874. **Sales:** $200,000,000 (2000). **Emp:** 400. **Officers:** M. Lee Marston, Chairman of the Board, e-mail: lmarston@jjhaines.com; S. Mort Creech Jr., CEO, e-mail: mcreech@jjhaines.com; Robert Thompson, COO & President, e-mail: rthompson@jjhaines.com; Ed Curtis, CFO, e-mail: ecurtis@jjhaines.com; Neal Smith, VP of Sales, e-mail: nsmith@jjhaines.com; Greg Johnson, VP of Sales F/P, e-mail: gjohnson@jjhaines.com.

■ **9932** ■ **J.J. Haines & Company, Inc.**
422 Business Ctr. Bldg. Z2630
Montgomery Ave.
Oaks, PA 19456-0410
Phone: (215)666-1007 **Fax:** (215)666-0994
Products: Ceramic wall and floor tile. **SIC:** 5032 (Brick, Stone & Related Materials).

■ **9933** ■ **J.J. Haines & Co.**
3283 Hwy. 70 W
Goldsboro, NC 27530-9567
Free: (800)447-9498
Products: Ceramic tile. **SIC:** 5032 (Brick, Stone & Related Materials).

■ **9934** ■ **Michael Halebian**
557 Washington Ave.
Carlstadt, NJ 07072
Phone: (201)935-3535
Free: (800)631-4115 **Fax:** (201)460-1138
Products: Hard surface floor coverings. **SIC:** 5032 (Brick, Stone & Related Materials).

■ **9935** ■ **Hamilton-Parker, Co.**
1865 Leonard Ave.
PO Box 15217
Columbus, OH 43219
Phone: (614)358-7800
Free: (800)341-2314 **Fax:** (614)358-2315
URL: http://www.hamiltonparker.com
Products: Ceramic wall and floor tile; Fireplaces; Gas logs and accessories; Garage doors and openers. **SIC:** 5032 (Brick, Stone & Related Materials). **Est:** 1934. **Emp:** 70. **Officers:** Milton Lewin, President; Adam Lewin, Exec. VP; Connie Tuckerman, Vice President.

■ **9936** ■ **Hardco, Inc.**
3305 S Hwy. 79
Rapid City, SD 57701
Phone: (605)342-7860 **Fax:** (605)342-2790
Products: Ceramic wall and floor tile. **SIC:** 5032 (Brick, Stone & Related Materials). **Est:** 1950. **Emp:** 11. **Officers:** Jim Tobin.

■ **9937** ■ **Hardwood Flooring & Finishes**
6831 Keating
Lincolnwood, IL 60646
Phone: (847)982-0665 **Fax:** (847)982-9054
Products: Hardwood floors and finishes. **SICs:** 5023 (Homefurnishings); 5198 (Paints, Varnishes & Supplies).

■ **9938** ■ **Edward R. Hart Co. Inc.**
437 McGregor NW
Canton, OH 44706
Phone: (330)452-4055 **Fax:** (330)453-3190
Products: Floorcoverings; Carpets; Ceramic wall and floor tile. **SICs:** 5032 (Brick, Stone & Related Materials); 5023 (Homefurnishings). **Est:** 1920. **Sales:** $10,000,000 (2000). **Emp:** 36. **Officers:** Michael A. McAndrew, President.

■ **9939** ■ **Hawaiian Ceramic Tile**
703 Lower Main St.
Wailuku, HI 96793
Phone: (808)242-1511 **Fax:** (808)242-4196
Products: Ceramic wall and floor tile. **SIC:** 5032 (Brick,

Stone & Related Materials). **Officers:** Susan Hiramatsu, Contact.

■ **9940** ■ **Hawkinson**
149 Seegers
Elk Grove Village, IL 60007
Phone: (847)228-6222 **Fax:** (847)228-6222
Products: Ceramic and marble tile. **SIC:** 5032 (Brick, Stone & Related Materials). **Est:** 1982. **Officers:** Thomas R. Hawkinson, VP, Treasurer & Secty.; Richard Hawkinson, President.

■ **9941** ■ **Robert F. Henry Tile Co.**
119 45th Pl. N
PO Box 11329
Birmingham, AL 35222
Phone: (205)592-8615 **Fax:** (205)592-8625
Products: Floorcoverings, including tile, ceramics, and marble. **SICs:** 5032 (Brick, Stone & Related Materials); 5032 (Brick, Stone & Related Materials). **Officers:** Earl Norman, Contact.

■ **9942** ■ **Robert F. Henry Tile Co.**
919 Bell St.
PO Box 2230
Montgomery, AL 36102-2230
Phone: (334)269-2518 **Fax:** (334)269-4678
E-mail: henrytile@mindspring.com
Products: Ceramic wall and floor tile. **SIC:** 5032 (Brick, Stone & Related Materials). **Est:** 1933. **Sales:** $15,000,000 (2000). **Emp:** 70. **Officers:** Bob Henry, Contact.

■ **9943** ■ **Herregan Distributors Inc.**
2128 NE Broadway
Des Moines, IA 50313
Phone: (515)265-9807 **Fax:** (515)265-7706
Products: Floor coverings, including sheet vinyl and carpet. **SIC:** 5023 (Homefurnishings).

■ **9944** ■ **Herregan Distributors, Inc.**
3695 Kennebec
Eagan, MN 55122
Phone: (612)452-7200
Free: (800)325-2625 **Fax:** (612)452-7683
Products: Floor coverings, including tile, wood, and carpet. **SICs:** 5023 (Homefurnishings); 5031 (Lumber, Plywood & Millwork); 5032 (Brick, Stone & Related Materials).

■ **9945** ■ **Herregan Distributors Inc.**
1446 Taney
North Kansas City, MO 64116
Phone: (816)221-3355 **Fax:** (816)221-3359
Products: Floor coverings, including vinyl, wood, carpet, tile, and ceramic. **SICs:** 5023 (Homefurnishings); 5032 (Brick, Stone & Related Materials); 5031 (Lumber, Plywood & Millwork).

■ **9946** ■ **Herregan Distributors, Inc.**
13412 Industrial Rd.
Omaha, NE 68137
Phone: (402)330-4445 **Fax:** (402)330-3415
Products: Floor coverings, including vinyl, hardwood, tile, and ceramic. **SICs:** 5023 (Homefurnishings); 5031 (Lumber, Plywood & Millwork).

■ **9947** ■ **Herregan Distributors Inc.**
9340 N 107 St.
Milwaukee, WI 53224
Phone: (414)354-1810 **Fax:** (414)354-0364
Products: Flooring supplies, including carpet, vinyl, and tile. **SICs:** 5023 (Homefurnishings); 5032 (Brick, Stone & Related Materials).

■ **9948** ■ **Hoboken Wood Flooring Corp.**
Adirondack Div.
22 Kairnes St.
Albany, NY 12205
Phone: (518)459-0277 **Fax:** (518)459-4262
Products: Ceramic tile; Wood flooring. **SIC:** 5032 (Brick, Stone & Related Materials). **Emp:** 30. **Officers:** Bud Kolbe, General Mgr.

■ **9949** ■ **Hoboken Wood Floors**
70 Dermerast Dr.
Wayne, NJ 07470
Phone: (973)694-2888 **Fax:** (973)694-6885
Products: Hard surface flooring. **SICs:** 5023

(Homefurnishings); 5031 (Lumber, Plywood & Millwork).

■ **9950** ■ **Hoboken Wood Floors**
181 Campanelli Pkwy.
Stoughton, MA 02072
Phone: (781)341-2881
Free: (800)462-1181 **Fax:** (781)341-4189
E-mail: hoboken@ma.ultranet.com
URL: http://www.hobokenfloors.com
Products: Hardwood flooring; Ceramic wall and floor tile; Linoleum. **SICs:** 5023 (Homefurnishings); 5031 (Lumber, Plywood & Millwork); 5032 (Brick, Stone & Related Materials).

■ **9951** ■ **David Hockstein Inc.**
8600 Ashwood Dr.
Capitol Heights, MD 20743-3720
Phones: (301)336-6600 (301)792-0135
Fax: (301)336-6978
Products: Carpets; Floorcoverings. **SIC:** 5023 (Homefurnishings). **Est:** 1967. **Emp:** 18. **Officers:** David Hockstein.

■ **9952** ■ **Holt and Bugbee Co.**
PO Box 37
Tewksbury, MA 01876
Phone: (508)851-7201
Products: Hardwood flooring. **SIC:** 5031 (Lumber, Plywood & Millwork). **Est:** 1825. **Sales:** $20,000,000 (2000). **Emp:** 100. **Officers:** Mary T. Pierce, President, Chairman of the Board & Treasurer; William Collins, Controller; Roger Pierce Jr., Dir. of Sales.

■ **9953** ■ **Horner Flooring Company Inc.**
S Maple Ave.
PO Box 380
Dollar Bay, MI 49922
Phone: (906)482-1180
Free: (800)380-0119 **Fax:** (906)482-6115
E-mail: info@hornerflooring.com
URL: http://www.hornerflooring.com
Products: Hardwood flooring. **SIC:** 5031 (Lumber, Plywood & Millwork). **Est:** 1891. **Emp:** 75. **Officers:** Douglas Hamar, President & CEO; Lewis Bosco, Sales Mgr., e-mail: lbosco@hornerflooring.com.

■ **9954** ■ **House of Carpets, Inc.**
3737 Gateway W
El Paso, TX 79932
Phone: (915)562-9521
Free: (800)321-2272 **Fax:** (915)562-9533
Products: Ceramic tile. **SIC:** 5032 (Brick, Stone & Related Materials). **Est:** 1975. **Emp:** 60.

■ **9955** ■ **Hudson Valley Tile Co.**
470 Central Ave.
Albany, NY 12206-2213
Phone: (518)489-8989 **Fax:** (518)489-8988
Products: Ceramic wall and floor tile. **SIC:** 5032 (Brick, Stone & Related Materials). **Officers:** Frank Orciuoli Jr., Contact.

■ **9956** ■ **Iberia Tile**
4221 Ponce De Leon Blvd.
Coral Gables, FL 33146
Phone: (305)446-0222 **Fax:** (305)446-3134
Products: Marble and ceramic tile. **SIC:** 5032 (Brick, Stone & Related Materials).

■ **9957** ■ **Iberia Tile**
1711 N Powerline Rd.
Pompano Beach, FL 33069
Phone: (954)978-8453 **Fax:** (954)978-2129
Products: Tiles. **SIC:** 5032 (Brick, Stone & Related Materials).

■ **9958** ■ **Iberia Tiles Inc.**
2975 NW 77th Ave.
Miami, FL 33122
Phone: (305)591-3880
Free: (877)71T-ILES **Fax:** (305)591-4341
URL: http://www.iberiatiles.com
Products: Tile; Natural stones; Porcelane and fabrication services. **SIC:** 5032 (Brick, Stone & Related Materials). **Est:** 1979. **Sales:** $28,000,000 (2000). **Emp:** 120. **Officers:** Fernando Rodriguez-Vila, President; Rosa Sugranes, Chairman of the Board.

■ **9959** ■ **Ideal Tile Co.**
Mt. Laurel, Inc,
1316 Rte. 73
Mt. Laurel, NJ 08054
Phone: (609)722-9393 **Fax:** (609)722-9306
Products: Tile and related products. **SIC:** 5032 (Brick, Stone & Related Materials).

■ **9960** ■ **ImpoGlaztile**
2852 W 167th St.
PO Box 220
Markham, IL 60426-0220
Phone: (708)333-1800 **Fax:** (708)333-2190
Products: Ceramic wall and floor tile. **SIC:** 5032 (Brick, Stone & Related Materials). **Officers:** Ron Fox, Contact.

■ **9961** ■ **Import Tile Co.**
611 Hearst Ave.
Berkeley, CA 94710
Phone: (510)843-5744
Products: Ceramic wall and floor tile; Dressed dimension marble and other stone; Building stone. **SICs:** 5032 (Brick, Stone & Related Materials); 5039 (Construction Materials Nec). **Emp:** 15.

■ **9962** ■ **Inland Northwest Distributors Inc.**
5327 Southgate Dr.
Billings, MT 59101
Phone: (406)248-2125 **Fax:** (406)248-2182
Products: Floor coverings, including vinyl and ceramic; Flooring tools and glue. **SICs:** 5023 (Homefurnishings); 5072 (Hardware).

■ **9963** ■ **Integral Kitchens**
6419 N McPhearson
Laredo, TX 78044
Phone: (956)724-4521 **Fax:** (956)727-0986
Products: Ceramic tile. **SIC:** 5032 (Brick, Stone & Related Materials). **Est:** 1977. **Sales:** $3,000,000 (2000). **Emp:** 65.

■ **9964** ■ **Interceramic Inc.**
2333 S Jupiter Rd.
Garland, TX 75041
Phone: (214)503-5500
Products: Tile. **SIC:** 5032 (Brick, Stone & Related Materials). **Officers:** Dave Hyland, President; Rick Alexader, Finance General Manager.

■ **9965** ■ **Intercoastal Tile**
5189 NW 15th St.
Margate, FL 33063-3714
Phone: (954)971-5294
Products: Ceramic wall and floor tile. **SIC:** 5032 (Brick, Stone & Related Materials). **Officers:** John Boyd, Contact.

■ **9966** ■ **Interior Specialties of the Ozarks**
1314 N Nias
Springfield, MO 65808
Phone: (417)865-5447 **Fax:** (417)865-0368
Products: Ceramic wall and floor tile. **SIC:** 5032 (Brick, Stone & Related Materials).

■ **9967** ■ **International Tile & Marble, Ltd.**
828 Principal
Chesapeake, VA 23320
Phone: (757)549-0055 **Fax:** (757)549-0035
Products: Tile wallcoverings; Floor coverings, including marble, granite, and stone. **SICs:** 5023 (Homefurnishings); 5032 (Brick, Stone & Related Materials).

■ **9968** ■ **International Tile & Marble Ltd.**
11761 Rock Landing Dr.
Newport News, VA 23606
Phone: (757)873-1343 **Fax:** (757)873-1696
Products: Ceramic wall and floor tile. **SIC:** 5032 (Brick, Stone & Related Materials). **Officers:** Kevin Smith, Contact.

■ **9969** ■ **Interstate Supply**
9258 Bond St.
Overland Park, KS 66214
Phone: (913)894-2663 **Fax:** (913)894-2663
Products: Ceramic wall and floor tile; Vinyl and hardwood flooring; Adhesive sundries; Carpet and padding; Area rugs. **SICs:** 5032 (Brick, Stone &

Related Materials); 5023 (Homefurnishings); 5031 (Lumber, Plywood & Millwork); 5169 (Chemicals & Allied Products Nec). **Est:** 1946. **Emp:** 90. **Officers:** Gary Morrow, President.

■ **9970** ■ **Interstate Supply Co.**
2330 NW 10th
Oklahoma City, OK 73107-5616
Phone: (405)525-0041   **Fax:** (405)525-0041
Products: Carpets; Floorcoverings; Ceramic wall and floor tile; Linoleum. **SICs:** 5023 (Homefurnishings); 5032 (Brick, Stone & Related Materials). **Emp:** 18. **Officers:** Kim Kessler.

■ **9971** ■ **Interstate Supply Co.**
4445 Gustine Ave.
St. Louis, MO 63116
Phone: (314)481-2222   **Fax:** (314)481-8435
Products: Floor coverings, including carpet, wood, ceramic and vinyl flooring. **SICs:** 5023 (Homefurnishings); 5031 (Lumber, Plywood & Millwork); 5032 (Brick, Stone & Related Materials). **Est:** 1951. **Sales:** $28,400,000 (2000). **Emp:** 79. **Officers:** Gary K. Morrow, President; B. Vaught, Controller; J. Lindenschmidt, VP of Marketing & Sales; C.J. Kuldell, VP of Marketing & Sales.

■ **9972** ■ **Intertile Distributors, Inc.**
3651 Park Rd.
Benicia, CA 94510
Phone: (707)745-4300
Products: Ceramic tile. **SIC:** 5032 (Brick, Stone & Related Materials).

■ **9973** ■ **Intertile Distributors, Inc.**
2021 N Fine Ave.
Fresno, CA 93727
Phone: (209)454-5000
Products: Ceramic tile. **SIC:** 5032 (Brick, Stone & Related Materials).

■ **9974** ■ **Intertile Distributors, Inc.**
PO Box 2106
Oakland, CA 94621-0006
Phone: (510)351-4600   **Fax:** (510)351-0202
E-mail: intertileinfo@intertile.com
URL: http://www.intertile.com
Products: Marble, granite and all natural stone. **SIC:** 5032 (Brick, Stone & Related Materials). **Est:** 1976. **Emp:** 100.

■ **9975** ■ **Intile Designs, Inc.**
3750 Wow Rd.
Corpus Christi, TX 78413
Phone: (512)855-9848   **Fax:** (512)992-9311
Products: Ceramic wall and floor tile. **SIC:** 5032 (Brick, Stone & Related Materials). **Officers:** Flora Thornsbury, Contact.

■ **9976** ■ **Island-Northwest Distributing, Inc.**
N 2003 Waterworks
Spokane, WA 99212
Phone: (509)535-1601   **Fax:** (509)535-4128
Products: Ceramic wall and floor tile. **SIC:** 5032 (Brick, Stone & Related Materials).

■ **9977** ■ **Jaeckle Distributors**
3171 Rider Trl S
Bridgeton, MO 63045-1519
Phone: (314)344-9905   **Fax:** (314)344-9945
Products: Floor covering, including linoleum, carpet, and vinyl; Ceramic countertops; Pionite decorative laminate; Cabinet hardware. **SIC:** 5023 (Homefurnishings). **Est:** 1995. **Sales:** $1,000,000 (2000). **Emp:** 5. **Officers:** Fred Jaeckle, President.

■ **9978** ■ **Jaeckle Wholesale Inc.**
2310 Daniels St.
Madison, WI 53704-6706
Phones: (608)221-8400   800-362-7225
Free: (800)236-7225   **Fax:** (608)221-8593
URL: http://www.jaecklewholesale.com
Products: Floorcoverings; Glazed and unglazed floor and wall tile; Hardwood flooring; Asphalt and vinyl composition floor tile; Ceramic wall and ****oor tile; Decorative plastic laminate; Cabinet hardware. **SICs:** 5023 (Homefurnishings); 5031 (Lumber, Plywood & Millwork); 5032 (Brick, Stone & Related Materials). **Est:**

1958. **Sales:** $48,000,000 (2000). **Emp:** 131. **Officers:** Fred W. Jaeckle, President.

■ **9979** ■ **Jasco Tile Company, Inc.**
2345 Rte. 22, Center Island
Union, NJ 07083
Phone: (908)688-4900   **Fax:** (908)688-7266
Products: Ceramic wall and floor tile, including marble, granite, carpet, porcelain, vinyl, linoleum, and wood. **SIC:** 5032 (Brick, Stone & Related Materials). **Est:** 1949. **Sales:** $2,000,000 (2000). **Emp:** 10. **Officers:** Larry Kreinberg, Contact.

■ **9980** ■ **JB Tile Co.**
PO Box 65217
Salt Lake City, UT 84165
Phone: (801)972-4444   **Fax:** (801)973-0164
Products: Plastic tile, including laminated tile. **SIC:** 5023 (Homefurnishings). **Est:** 1935. **Sales:** $5,000,000 (2000). **Emp:** 17. **Officers:** Jerry Blackburn, President.

■ **9981** ■ **JTM Tile Distributing, Inc.**
112 N Layfair Dr.
Jackson, MS 39208
Phone: (601)932-8689   **Fax:** (601)932-8496
Products: Ceramic tile and marble. **SIC:** 5032 (Brick, Stone & Related Materials). **Est:** 1977. **Emp:** 9.

■ **9982** ■ **Irvin Kahn & Son, Inc.**
6555 Guion Rd.
Indianapolis, IN 46268
Phone: (317)328-8989
Free: (800)759-4414   **Fax:** (317)328-8181
Products: Floor coverings, including vinyl and ceramic tile. **SICs:** 5023 (Homefurnishings); 5032 (Brick, Stone & Related Materials).

■ **9983** ■ **Irvin Kahn & Son, Inc.**
1205 E Washington
PO Box 6093
Louisville, KY 40206
Phone: (502)584-2306   **Fax:** (502)589-3183
Products: Vinyl composition floor covering. **SIC:** 5023 (Homefurnishings).

■ **9984** ■ **Kaough Distributing Company, Inc.**
2601 Brocklyn Ave.
PO Box 10087
Ft. Wayne, IN 46850
Phone: (219)432-5556   **Fax:** (219)432-5559
Products: Floor coverings, including ceramic, vinyl, and carpet. **SICs:** 5023 (Homefurnishings); 5032 (Brick, Stone & Related Materials).

■ **9985** ■ **Kate-Lo Div.**
701 N Berkshire Ln.
Plymouth, MN 55441
Phone: (612)545-5455   **Fax:** (612)542-9830
E-mail: kate-lo@mn.uswest.net
URL: http://www.katelotile.com
Products: Ceramic tile; Marble; Stone. **SIC:** 5032 (Brick, Stone & Related Materials). **Est:** 1964. **Sales:** $10,000,000 (2000). **Emp:** 39. **Officers:** Tim Beaupre.

■ **9986** ■ **Kelaty International Inc.**
8020 Lefferts Blvd.
Kew Gardens, NY 11415-1724
Phone: (917)617-8282   **Fax:** (917)617-8282
Products: Carpets. **SIC:** 5023 (Homefurnishings). **Est:** 1988. **Sales:** $3,000,000 (2000). **Emp:** 12. **Officers:** Joel Ebrahimoff, President.

■ **9987** ■ **Kenco Distributors, Inc.**
436 Atlas Dr.
Nashville, TN 37211
Phone: (615)244-3180
Products: Drywall equipment and supplies; Floor materials. **SIC:** 5023 (Homefurnishings).

■ **9988** ■ **Kepcor Inc.**
215 Bridge St.
PO Box 119
Minerva, OH 44657
Phone: (330)868-6434   **Fax:** (330)868-6497
Products: Tiles and ceramic pavers; Ceramic floor and wall tile; Countertop and backsplash shapes; Ceramic moldings. **SIC:** 5032 (Brick, Stone & Related Materials). **Est:** 1989. **Sales:** $300,000 (1999). **Emp:** 8.

Officers: Robert B. Keplinger Jr., President; Connie Keplinger, VP & Secty.

■ **9989** ■ **Knox Tile & Marble**
3032 Commerce St.
Dallas, TX 75226-2581
Phone: (972)243-6100
Products: Ceramic tile. **SIC:** 5032 (Brick, Stone & Related Materials).

■ **9990** ■ **Lanham Hardwood Flooring Co.**
4704 Pinewood Rd.
Louisville, KY 40218
Phone: (502)969-1345   **Fax:** (502)966-4533
Products: Hardwood flooring and supplies. **SICs:** 5023 (Homefurnishings); 5031 (Lumber, Plywood & Millwork).

■ **9991** ■ **Larson Distributing Company Inc.**
PO Box 16189
Denver, CO 80216
Phone: (303)296-7253
Products: Tiles, including linoleum and ceramic. **SICs:** 5023 (Homefurnishings); 5032 (Brick, Stone & Related Materials). **Est:** 1922. **Sales:** $25,000,000 (2000). **Emp:** 70. **Officers:** John L. Larson, President; Allen Kliewer, Treasurer; Roger Hill, Controller.

■ **9992** ■ **Laufen International Inc.**
PO Box 570
Tulsa, OK 74101-0570
Phone: (918)428-3851
Free: (800)331-3651   **Fax:** (918)428-0695
URL: http://www.usa.laufen.com
Products: Ceramic wall and floor tile; Stones. **SIC:** 5032 (Brick, Stone & Related Materials). **Est:** 1980. **Officers:** Bruce DePasquale, VP of Marketing & Sales.

■ **9993** ■ **L.B.I. Company**
3950 South 500 West
Salt Lake City, UT 84123
Phone: (801)262-9087
Free: (800)662-9087   **Fax:** (801)263-3404
E-mail: lbi@xmission.com
Products: Hard surface floor coverings. **SIC:** 5032 (Brick, Stone & Related Materials). **Est:** 1957. **Emp:** 15.

■ **9994** ■ **Leese Flooring Supply**
63 San Rico Dr.
Manchester, CT 06040
Phone: (860)649-7627
Products: Floor finishes. **SICs:** 5023 (Homefurnishings); 5198 (Paints, Varnishes & Supplies).

■ **9995** ■ **Lexco Tile**
1616 S 108th St.
West Allis, WI 53214
Phone: (414)771-2900
Free: (800)242-2249   **Fax:** (414)771-9153
URL: http://www.lexcotile.com
Products: Tile. **SIC:** 5032 (Brick, Stone & Related Materials). **Est:** 1970. **Emp:** 25. **Officers:** Neal Wallner, Sales/Marketing Contact; Steve Spieker, Customer Service Contact.

■ **9996** ■ **Loboflor Bonar Flotex**
14286 Gillis Rd.
Dallas, TX 75244
Phone: (972)788-2233
Free: (800)334-7331   **Fax:** (972)490-7144
Products: Carpet. **SIC:** 5023 (Homefurnishings). **Emp:** 49.

■ **9997** ■ **Longust Distributing Inc.**
5333 S Kyrene Rd.
Tempe, AZ 85283
Phone: (602)820-6244   **Fax:** (602)345-0324
Products: Floor coverings. **SIC:** 5023 (Homefurnishings).

■ **9998** ■ **Louisville Tile Distributors**
650 Melrose Ave.
Nashville, TN 37211-2161
Phone: (615)333-3196   **Fax:** (615)331-7820
Products: Tile. **SIC:** 5032 (Brick, Stone & Related Materials).

■ 9999 ■ **Louisville Tile Distributors, Inc.**
2495 Palumbo Dr.
Lexington, KY 40509-1116
Phone: (606)268-8373 **Fax:** (606)268-1601
Products: Ceramic wall and floor tile. **SIC:** 5032 (Brick, Stone & Related Materials).

■ 10000 ■ **Louisville Tile Distributors Inc.**
4520 Bishop Ln.
Louisville, KY 40218
Phone: (502)452-2037 **Fax:** (502)454-4114
Products: Ceramic wall and floor tile. **SIC:** 5032 (Brick, Stone & Related Materials).

■ 10001 ■ **Louisville Tile Distributors, Inc.**
1417 N Cullen Ave.
Evansville, IN 47715-2374
Phone: (812)473-0137 **Fax:** (812)477-7524
E-mail: ltd@sigecom.net
Products: Ceramic wall and floor tile. **SIC:** 5032 (Brick, Stone & Related Materials).

■ 10002 ■ **Lowy Group Inc.**
4001 N Kingshighway Blvd.
St. Louis, MO 63115
Phone: (314)383-2055
Free: (800)325-8686 **Fax:** (314)383-7135
Products: Flooring products. **SIC:** 5023 (Homefurnishings). **Est:** 1939. **Sales:** $75,000,000 (2000). **Emp:** 450. **Officers:** Mike Hart, President; Frank Klaus, CFO; Kenneth Sleet, Dir. of Information Systems; Ethel Maas, Dir of Human Resources.

■ 10003 ■ **Magic Touch Enterprises, Inc.**
836 Sox St.
West Columbia, SC 29169-5028
Phone: (803)791-8516
Free: (800)226-4975 **Fax:** (803)791-8564
Products: Floor coverings, including carpet, vinyl, and hardwood; Tools and machinery; Countertops. **SICs:** 5023 (Homefurnishings); 5031 (Lumber, Plywood & Millwork); 5072 (Hardware); 5084 (Industrial Machinery & Equipment). **Est:** 1985. **Sales:** $2,000,000 (2000). **Emp:** 8. **Officers:** Adrian Gardner.

■ 10004 ■ **Mainline Supply Corp.**
2 Gaines St.
Binghamton, NY 13905
Phone: (607)772-1212 **Fax:** (607)772-0917
Products: Flooring supplies, including tile and padding. **SICs:** 5023 (Homefurnishings); 5032 (Brick, Stone & Related Materials).

■ 10005 ■ **Malisani, Inc.**
PO Box 1195
Great Falls, MT 59403
Phone: (406)761-0108
Products: Ceramic wall and floor tile. **SIC:** 5032 (Brick, Stone & Related Materials). **Officers:** Art Malisani Sr., Contact.

■ 10006 ■ **Maly**
711 Windsor St.
Sun Prairie, WI 53590
Phone: (608)837-6927 **Fax:** (608)837-6927
Products: Ceramic wall and floor tile. **SIC:** 5032 (Brick, Stone & Related Materials). **Officers:** Leonard Maly, Contact.

■ 10007 ■ **Maneto Wholesale Flooring, Inc.**
2509 Commercial NE
Albuquerque, NM 87102
Phone: (505)766-5161 **Fax:** (505)247-8303
Products: Flooring supplies, including padding. **SIC:** 5023 (Homefurnishings).

■ 10008 ■ **Mannington Wood Floors**
1327 Lincoln Dr.
High Point, NC 27260-9945
Phone: (336)884-5600 **Fax:** (336)812-4981
URL: http://www.mannington.com
Products: Engineered hardwood floors; Laminate flooring. **SIC:** 5023 (Homefurnishings). **Est:** 1988. **Officers:** Douglas Brown, VP of Operations; John Patterson.

■ 10009 ■ **Marino Marble & Tile**
444 Graham Ave.
Brooklyn, NY 11211
Phone: (718)389-2191 **Fax:** (718)383-7675
Products: Marble and ceramic tile. **SIC:** 5032 (Brick, Stone & Related Materials).

■ 10010 ■ **Marshall's Tile Co.**
1970 N Holmes Ave.
Idaho Falls, ID 83402
Phone: (208)523-4800 **Fax:** (208)523-3456
Products: Ceramic wall and floor tile. **SIC:** 5032 (Brick, Stone & Related Materials). **Est:** 1993. **Sales:** $1,500,000 (1999). **Emp:** 10. **Officers:** Marshall H. Riggs, Contact.

■ 10011 ■ **Maryland Tile Distributors**
5621 Old Frederick Rd.
Baltimore, MD 21228
Phone: (410)747-1416 **Fax:** (410)747-8163
Products: Ceramic wall and floor tile. **SIC:** 5032 (Brick, Stone & Related Materials). **Est:** 1952. **Emp:** 15. **Officers:** John Mianulli, Contact.

■ 10012 ■ **Master Tile**
7170 W 43rd St., Ste. 150
Houston, TX 77092
Phone: (713)331-3800
Free: (800)392-3725 **Fax:** (713)331-3879
URL: http://www.mastertile.net
Products: Ceramic tile, marble, stone, porcelain, and related products. **SIC:** 5032 (Brick, Stone & Related Materials). **Est:** 1948. **Sales:** $50,000,000 (2000). **Emp:** 225. **Officers:** Tom Cosky, e-mail: tom@ mastertile.net.

■ 10013 ■ **McCartney Carpet**
110 E Pioneer Park Rd.
Westfield, WI 53964
Phone: (608)296-4444
Products: Carpets. **SIC:** 5023 (Homefurnishings).

■ 10014 ■ **McCullough Ceramic**
4801 Kellywood Dr.
Glen Allen, VA 23060-3642
Phone: (804)747-8300 **Fax:** (804)747-6752
Products: Ceramic tile. **SIC:** 5032 (Brick, Stone & Related Materials).

■ 10015 ■ **McEllin Company, Inc.**
17 Water St.
Waltham, MA 02454
Phone: (781)647-9322 **Fax:** (781)674-4740
Products: Hardwood floors. **SICs:** 5023 (Homefurnishings); 5031 (Lumber, Plywood & Millwork).

■ 10016 ■ **McKee Enterprises Inc.**
1425 41st St. NW
Fargo, ND 58102-2822
Phone: (701)281-1600 **Fax:** (701)281-3090
Products: Floor coverings, including carpeting, vinyl, linoleum, and tile. **SIC:** 5023 (Homefurnishings). **Emp:** 49. **Officers:** Randy Vaagen.

■ 10017 ■ **McKee Enterprises Inc.**
2785 Hwy. 55
St. Paul, MN 55121
Phone: (612)454-1700 **Free:** (800)747-4307
Products: Floor coverings. **SIC:** 5023 (Homefurnishings). **Sales:** $25,000,000 (1994). **Emp:** 100.

■ 10018 ■ **Medallion Carpets**
2434 Polvorosa Ave.
San Leandro, CA 94577
Phone: (510)351-8104
Products: Ceramic tile. **SIC:** 5032 (Brick, Stone & Related Materials).

■ 10019 ■ **Medallion Carpets**
1583 Enterprise Blvd.
West Sacramento, CA 95691
Phone: (916)372-8500
Products: Ceramic tile. **SIC:** 5032 (Brick, Stone & Related Materials).

■ 10020 ■ **Mees Distributors**
645 S Broadway
Lexington, KY 40508
Phone: (606)252-4545 **Fax:** (606)252-4535
Products: Ceramic tile. **SIC:** 5032 (Brick, Stone & Related Materials).

■ 10021 ■ **Mees Distributors**
1541 West Fork Rd.
Cincinnati, OH 45223
Phone: (513)541-2311 **Fax:** (513)541-4831
Products: Clay or other ceramic tile; Dressed dimension marble and other stone; Granite products, such as paving blocks and curbing. **SIC:** 5032 (Brick, Stone & Related Materials).

■ 10022 ■ **Mees Distributors**
5193 Sinclair Rd.
Columbus, OH 43229
Phone: (614)844-5830 **Fax:** (614)844-5833
Products: Ceramic tile, tools, supplies, marble, and granite. **SICs:** 5023 (Homefurnishings); 5032 (Brick, Stone & Related Materials).

■ 10023 ■ **Mees Distributors**
2425 Stanley
Dayton, OH 45404
Phone: (937)224-1506 **Fax:** (937)224-5267
Products: Ceramic tile; Marble. **SIC:** 5032 (Brick, Stone & Related Materials).

■ 10024 ■ **Mees Tile and Marble Inc.**
4536 Poplar Level Rd.
Louisville, KY 40213
Phone: (502)969-5858
Free: (800)264-1858 **Fax:** (502)969-3838
Products: Tile and marble; Setting materials, including glue. **SICs:** 5032 (Brick, Stone & Related Materials); 5169 (Chemicals & Allied Products Nec).

■ 10025 ■ **Menchaca Brick & Tile Co.**
3613 W Hwy. 83
Harlingen, TX 78552
Phone: (956)428-6956
Products: Ceramic tile. **SIC:** 5032 (Brick, Stone & Related Materials).

■ 10026 ■ **Merit Industries**
PO Box 1448
Dalton, GA 30722-1448
Phone: (706)695-7581
Free: (800)241-4032 **Fax:** (706)695-0548
Products: Floorcoverings; Carpets; Tufted carpets and rugs. **SIC:** 5023 (Homefurnishings).

■ 10027 ■ **Metro Tile & Marble, Inc.**
5455 Shirley St.
Naples, FL 34109-1848
Phone: (941)598-4060
Products: Ceramic wall and floor tile. **SIC:** 5032 (Brick, Stone & Related Materials).

■ 10028 ■ **Michigan Hardwood Distributors**
30691 Wixom Rd.
Wixom, MI 48393
Phone: (248)669-0790 **Fax:** (248)669-4426
Products: Hardwood floors. **SICs:** 5023 (Homefurnishings); 5031 (Lumber, Plywood & Millwork).

■ 10029 ■ **Mid-America Tile**
1650 Howard St.
Elk Grove Village, IL 60007
Phone: (847)439-3110 **Fax:** (847)439-5889
Products: Tiles; Stone; Setting materials and related products. **SIC:** 5032 (Brick, Stone & Related Materials). **Est:** 1961. **Emp:** 55. **Officers:** Thomas J. Kotel, President.

■ 10030 ■ **Mid-America Tile**
1412 Joliet Rd.
Romeoville, IL 60446
Phone: (630)972-1500 **Fax:** (630)972-1566
URL: http://www.midamericatile.com
Products: Ceramic and porcelain tile; Marble; Granite; Vinyl; Rubber; Setting materials. **SICs:** 5032 (Brick, Stone & Related Materials); 5023 (Homefurnishings). **Est:** 1961. **Emp:** 6.

■ **10031** ■ **Mid-America Tile, Inc.**
108 Terrace Dr.
Mundelein, IL 60060
Phone: (847)566-5566 **Fax:** (847)566-7242
URL: http://www.MidAmericaTile.com
Products: Ceramic tile; Marble; Granite; Quarry; Porcelain. **SIC:** 5032 (Brick, Stone & Related Materials). **Emp:** 7. **Officers:** Heidi Kuhl, Branch Manager.

■ **10032** ■ **Mid-America Tile L.P.**
4809 W 128th Pl.
Alsip, IL 60803
Phone: (708)388-4344 **Fax:** (708)388-6988
Products: Ceramic tile, marble, and vinyl; Rubber; Setting materials; Chrome and ceramic fixtures. **SICs:** 5032 (Brick, Stone & Related Materials); 5023 (Homefurnishings). **Est:** 1961. **Emp:** 12. **Officers:** Ed Hommelsen. **Alternate Name:** Ed Hommelsen.

■ **10033** ■ **Midwest Floors**
2714 Breckenridge Indct.
St. Louis, MO 63144
Phone: (314)647-6060 **Fax:** (314)647-9189
Products: Floor coverings; Wall coverings. **SICs:** 5023 (Homefurnishings); 5198 (Paints, Varnishes & Supplies).

■ **10034** ■ **Midwest Tile**
200W Industrial Lake Dr.
Lincoln, NE 68528
Phone: (402)476-2542 **Fax:** (402)476-7891
Products: Ceramic tile. **SIC:** 5032 (Brick, Stone & Related Materials).

■ **10035** ■ **Midwest Tile**
1421 Locust St.
Des Moines, IA 50309
Phone: (515)283-1242 **Fax:** (515)284-0957
Products: Ceramic wall and floor tile. **SIC:** 5032 (Brick, Stone & Related Materials). **Officers:** Patrick Fisher, Contact.

■ **10036** ■ **Midwest Tile Supply Co.**
4515 S 90th St.
Omaha, NE 68127-1313
Phone: (402)331-3800 **Fax:** (402)593-7529
Products: Ceramic wall and floor tile. **SIC:** 5032 (Brick, Stone & Related Materials).

■ **10037** ■ **Milford Enterprises, Inc.**
950 Glenmore Ave.
Brooklyn, NY 11208
Phone: (718)277-6913 **Fax:** (718)277-4811
Products: Ceramic tile. **SIC:** 5032 (Brick, Stone & Related Materials).

■ **10038** ■ **Miller's Interiors Inc.**
PO Box 1116
Lynnwood, WA 98046
Phone: (425)743-3213 **Fax:** (206)363-4788
Products: Floorcoverings. **SIC:** 5023 (Homefurnishings). **Est:** 1936. **Emp:** 125. **Officers:** William W. Miller, CEO & Chairman of the Board; Gary M. Miller, President; Joe Miller, VP of Sales.

■ **10039** ■ **Milliken & Co.**
419 Skyline Dr.
Elkhorn, NE 68022
Phone: (402)289-1029
Products: Carpeting; Rugs. **SIC:** 5023 (Homefurnishings).

■ **10040** ■ **Aladin Mills, Inc.**
1320 NW 163rd St.
Miami, FL 33169
Phone: (305)624-8787 **Fax:** (305)620-7341
Products: Floor covering, including carpet, carpet cushion, and ceramic tile. **SICs:** 5023 (Homefurnishings); 5032 (Brick, Stone & Related Materials).

■ **10041** ■ **Mirage Rug Imports**
18924 S Laurel Park Rd.
Rancho Dominguez, CA 90220
Phone: (310)669-8533 **Fax:** (310)669-8533
Products: Rugs. **SIC:** 5023 (Homefurnishings). **Sales:** $20,000,000 (1994). **Emp:** 85. **Officers:** Saleh Shalomi, CEO.

■ **10042** ■ **Misco Shawnee Inc.**
2200 Forte Ct.
Maryland Heights, MO 63043
Phone: (314)739-3337
Free: (800)999-3363 **Fax:** (314)739-8163
E-mail: inquiry@misconet.com
URL: http://www.misconet.com
Products: Carpeting; Vinyl flooring; Wood flooring. **SICs:** 5023 (Homefurnishings); 5031 (Lumber, Plywood & Millwork). **Est:** 1912. **Sales:** $80,000,000 (2000). **Emp:** 200. **Officers:** Courtney A. Gould, Chairman of the Board; James Gould, Vice Chairman of the Board; Paul Mursin, President; Rob Olsen, Sales/Marketing Contact, e-mail: robolsen@misconet.com; Melanie Jordan, Customer Service Contact, e-mail: mjordan@misconet.com.

■ **10043** ■ **Modern Builders Supply**
3684 Community Rd.
Brunswick, GA 31520
Phone: (912)265-5885 **Fax:** (912)265-4663
Products: Ceramic tile; Marble; Stone. **SIC:** 5032 (Brick, Stone & Related Materials). **Emp:** 17. **Officers:** Angela K. Rowe, President.

■ **10044** ■ **Modern Builders Supply**
116 Central Junction Dr.
Savannah, GA 31405
Phone: (912)234-8224 **Fax:** (912)234-1409
Products: Ceramic tile; Marble; Stone. **SIC:** 5032 (Brick, Stone & Related Materials). **Emp:** 17. **Officers:** Angela K. Rowe, President.

■ **10045** ■ **Mohr Vinyl & Carpet Supplier**
1510 Rockwell Dr.
Midland, MI 48642
Phone: (517)837-6647
Products: Carpeting; Rugs. **SIC:** 5023 (Homefurnishings).

■ **10046** ■ **Momeni Inc.**
36 E 31st St.
New York, NY 10016
Phone: (212)532-9577 **Fax:** (212)413-2154
Products: Wool carpeting and rugs. **SIC:** 5023 (Homefurnishings). **Est:** 1975. **Sales:** $15,000,000 (2000). **Emp:** 35. **Officers:** Reza Momeni, Vice President; Arya Momeni, Vice President.

■ **10047** ■ **Monarch Ceramic Tile**
3361 Columbia NE
Albuquerque, NM 87107
Phone: (505)881-0971
Products: Ceramic tile. **SIC:** 5032 (Brick, Stone & Related Materials).

■ **10048** ■ **Monarch Ceramic Tile**
3635 N 124th St.
Milwaukee, WI 53205
Phone: (262)781-3110
Free: (800)843-1550 **Fax:** (262)781-5079
Products: Ceramic wall and floor tile. **SICs:** 5032 (Brick, Stone & Related Materials); 5072 (Hardware); 5169 (Chemicals & Allied Products Nec).

■ **10049** ■ **Monarch Ceramic Tile Inc.**
PO Box 853058
Mesquite, TX 75185
Free: (800)BUY-TILE
URL: http://www.monarchceramic.com
Products: Wall and floor tile. **SIC:** 5023 (Homefurnishings). **Est:** 1946. **Sales:** $55,000,000 (2000). **Emp:** 565. **Officers:** Thomas S. White III, CEO & President; David Guthrie, Vice President. **Former Name:** Monarch Tile Inc.

■ **10050** ■ **Monarch Cermaic Tile, Inc.**
5545 W Latham, Ste. 1
Phoenix, AZ 85043
Phone: (602)352-0301 **Fax:** (602)352-1952
Products: Ceramic tile. **SIC:** 5032 (Brick, Stone & Related Materials). **Emp:** 7.

■ **10051** ■ **Monarch Tile**
15000 N Hayden Rd., No. 400
Scottsdale, AZ 85260
Phone: (602)991-2626
Products: Ceramic tile. **SIC:** 5032 (Brick, Stone & Related Materials).

■ **10052** ■ **Monarch Tile**
5225 Phillips Hwy.
Jacksonville, FL 32207
Phone: (904)733-0727
Products: Ceramic tile. **SIC:** 5032 (Brick, Stone & Related Materials).

■ **10053** ■ **Monarch Tile**
93 Weldon Pkwy.
Maryland Heights, MO 63043
Phone: (314)569-5956
Products: Ceramic tile. **SIC:** 5032 (Brick, Stone & Related Materials).

■ **10054** ■ **Monarch Tile**
4375 S Valley View, Ste. A
Las Vegas, NV 89103
Phone: (702)252-0999 **Fax:** (702)252-8595
Products: Ceramic tile. **SIC:** 5032 (Brick, Stone & Related Materials).

■ **10055** ■ **Monarch Tile**
143 W Rhapsody
San Antonio, TX 78216
Phone: (210)341-2521
Products: Ceramic tile. **SIC:** 5032 (Brick, Stone & Related Materials).

■ **10056** ■ **Montgomery Building Materials**
919 Bell St.
Montgomery, AL 36104-3003
Phone: (205)269-2518 **Fax:** (205)269-4678
Products: Ceramic wall and floor tile. **SIC:** 5032 (Brick, Stone & Related Materials).

■ **10057** ■ **Moreira Tile**
1297 Kaumualii St.
Honolulu, HI 96817
Phone: (808)845-6461 **Fax:** 800-845-7461
Products: Ceramic tile. **SIC:** 5032 (Brick, Stone & Related Materials).

■ **10058** ■ **Morris Tile Distributors**
9132 Gaither Rd.
Gaithersburg, MD 20877
Phone: (301)670-4222
Products: Ceramic tile. **SIC:** 5032 (Brick, Stone & Related Materials).

■ **10059** ■ **Morris Tile Distributors**
2525 Kenilworth Ave.
Tuxedo, MD 20781
Phone: (301)773-7000
Products: Ceramic tile. **SIC:** 5032 (Brick, Stone & Related Materials).

■ **10060** ■ **Morris Tile Distributors Inc.**
2525 Kenilworth Ave.
Hyattsville, MD 20781
Phone: (301)772-2820
Products: Ceramic tile. **SIC:** 5032 (Brick, Stone & Related Materials). **Sales:** $4,500,000 (2000). **Emp:** 50. **Officers:** Ed Condolon, President; Joseph Hogan, Treasurer.

■ **10061** ■ **Morris Tile Distributors Inc.**
1890 Woodhaven
Philadelphia, PA 19116
Phone: (215)969-3400
Free: (800)347-6677 **Fax:** (215)673-3131
Products: Vinyl, wood, tile, carpet, and ceramic floor coverings. **SICs:** 5023 (Homefurnishings); 5031 (Lumber, Plywood & Millwork); 5032 (Brick, Stone & Related Materials).

■ **10062** ■ **Morris Tile Distributors of Norfolk, Inc.**
1339 Ingleside Rd.
Norfolk, VA 23502-1914
Phone: (757)855-8017 **Fax:** (757)857-4374
Products: Ceramic wall and floor tile. **SIC:** 5032 (Brick, Stone & Related Materials).

■ **10063** ■ **Morris Tile Distributors of Richmond**
2280 Dabney Rd.
Richmond, VA 23230-3344
Phone: (804)353-4427 **Fax:** (804)353-7923
Products: Ceramic wall and floor tile. **SIC:** 5032 (Brick, Stone & Related Materials).

■ **10064** ■ **Morris Tile Distributors of Roanoke, Inc.**
3610 Aerial Way Dr. SW
Roanoke, VA 24018-1508
Phone: (540)343-4100 **Fax:** (540)343-9673
Products: Ceramic wall and floor tile. **SIC:** 5032 (Brick, Stone & Related Materials).

■ **10065** ■ **Mosaic Tile**
10911 Trade Rd.
Richmond, VA 23236
Products: Ceramic wall and floor tile. **SIC:** 5032 (Brick, Stone & Related Materials). **Officers:** Shawn Shaffer, Contact.

■ **10066** ■ **Mosaic Tile Co.**
7890 Backlick Rd.
Springfield, VA 22150
Phone: (703)451-8805 **Fax:** (703)451-8151
URL: http://www.mosaictileco.com
Products: Ceranic tile. **SIC:** 5032 (Brick, Stone & Related Materials). **Est:** 1972. **Officers:** James Igoe, Sales/Marketing Contact, e-mail: jigoe@ mosaictileco.com; Sean Schaefer, Customer Service Contact, e-mail: sscheafer@mosaictileco.com.

■ **10067** ■ **Mountain Tile**
585 West Maple
PO Box 465
Pocatello, ID 83204-0465
Phone: (208)232-6696 **Fax:** (208)232-6694
Products: Ceramic and marble tile; Bricks. **SIC:** 5032 (Brick, Stone & Related Materials). **Est:** 1990. **Sales:** $1,000,000 (2000). **Emp:** 10. **Officers:** Chris J. Schut.

■ **10068** ■ **Mr. Hardwoods, Inc.**
210 Commerce Way
Jupiter, FL 33458
Phone: (561)746-9663
Free: (800)226-9664 **Fax:** (561)743-0447
E-mail: sales@mrhardwoods.com
URL: http://www.mrhardwoods.com
Products: Hardwood floor supplies; Sanding equipment; Coatings; Abrasives; Installation equipment. **SICs:** 5023 (Homefurnishings); 5031 (Lumber, Plywood & Millwork); 5039 (Construction Materials Nec); 5169 (Chemicals & Allied Products Nec). **Est:** 1986. **Emp:** 6. **Officers:** Dick Johnson, President, e-mail: dicj@mrhardwoods.com; Larabee Johnson, Human Resources Contact; Ron Eddy, Sales & Marketing Contact, e-mail: rone@mrhardwoods.com; Larabee Johnson, Customer Service Contact, e-mail: larabeej@mrhardwoods.com. **Former Name:** Mr. Hardwood Distributors.

■ **10069** ■ **Murphy's Tile & Marble**
4208 Henry S Grace Fwy.
Wichita Falls, TX 76302
Phone: (940)767-1861 **Fax:** (940)767-8648
Products: Ceramic wall and floor tile. **SIC:** 5032 (Brick, Stone & Related Materials). **Officers:** Jerry Murphy, Contact.

■ **10070** ■ **Lon Musolf Distributing Inc.**
985 Berwood Ave.
St. Paul, MN 55110-5144
Phone: (612)631-8586 **Fax:** (612)631-0999
Products: Hardwood flooring. **SIC:** 5031 (Lumber, Plywood & Millwork).

■ **10071** ■ **Lon Musolf Distributing Inc.**
7452 Washington Ave.
Eden Prairie, MN 55344
Phone: (612)946-1332 **Fax:** (612)946-1355
Products: Hardwood flooring. **SICs:** 5023 (Homefurnishings); 5031 (Lumber, Plywood & Millwork).

■ **10072** ■ **Musson Rubber Co.**
PO Box 7038
Akron, OH 44306-0038
Phone: (330)773-7651
Free: (800)321-2381 **Fax:** (330)773-3254
E-mail: musson@ezo.net
URL: http://www.mussonrubber.com
Products: Floor coverings. **SIC:** 5023 (Homefurnishings). **Est:** 1945. **Sales:** $9,000,000 (2000). **Emp:** 45. **Officers:** B. D. Segers, President.

■ **10073** ■ **Nemo Tile Company, Inc.**
177-02 Jamaica Ave.
Jamaica, NY 11432
Phone: (718)291-5969 **Fax:** (718)291-5992
Products: Ceramic and vinyl tile. **SIC:** 5032 (Brick, Stone & Related Materials).

■ **10074** ■ **Nemo Tile Company, Inc.**
277 Old Country Rd. E
Hicksville, NY 11801
Phone: (516)935-5300 **Fax:** (516)935-5322
URL: http://www.Nemotile.com
Products: Ceramic tile. **SIC:** 5032 (Brick, Stone & Related Materials).

■ **10075** ■ **Nemo Tile Company, Inc.**
48 E 21st St.
New York, NY 10010
Phone: (212)505-0009 **Fax:** (718)291-5992
E-mail: nemotile@aol.com
URL: http://www.nemotile.com
Products: Ceramic tile. **SIC:** 5032 (Brick, Stone & Related Materials). **Est:** 1921. **Emp:** 65. **Officers:** Bert P. Karlin, President; Martin Kriegel, General Mgr.

■ **10076** ■ **New Hampshire Tile Distributors**
Sheep Davis Rd., Rte. 106
Pembroke, NH 03275
Phone: (603)225-4075
Products: Ceramic wall and floor tile. **SIC:** 5032 (Brick, Stone & Related Materials). **Officers:** Bill Smethurst, Contact.

■ **10077** ■ **C.A. Newell Company Inc.**
9877 40th S
Seattle, WA 98118
Phone: (206)722-0800
Free: (800)288-9877 **Fax:** (206)721-5213
URL: http://www.canewell.com
Products: Floorings, including linoleum, vinyl, laminate, and carpet; Ceramic and wood countertops. **SICs:** 5023 (Homefurnishings); 5031 (Lumber, Plywood & Millwork); 5039 (Construction Materials Nec). **Est:** 1947. **Emp:** 70. **Officers:** Dennis Gullickson, President; Monte Asken, Exec. VP; Chris Newell, Vice President, e-mail: cnewell@sprynet.com.

■ **10078** ■ **Nezbeda Tile, Inc.**
2995 E Aukele St.
Lihue, HI 96766
Phone: (808)245-1765 **Fax:** (808)246-9395
Products: Ceramic wall and floor tile. **SIC:** 5032 (Brick, Stone & Related Materials). **Est:** 1974. **Sales:** $1,000,000 (2000). **Emp:** 7. **Officers:** Milan Nezbeda, Contact.

■ **10079** ■ **Rafael J. Nido, Inc.**
PO Box 11978
Carparra Heights
San Juan, PR 00922
Phone: (787)251-1000
Free: (800)981-6565 **Fax:** (787)251-1011
E-mail: ranido@ranido.com
URL: http://www.ranido.com
Products: Ceramic wall and floor tile; Galvanized steel wire products; Fencing products; Galvanized steel tubular products; Plumbing products; Tools; Electrical supplies. **SIC:** 5032 (Brick, Stone & Related Materials). **Est:** 1953. **Sales:** $50,000,000 (2000). **Emp:** 200. **Officers:** R.J. Nido Jr.; A. Galinanes; C.R. White; L. Vallecillo; J. Merioyo; H. Cuebas.

■ **10080** ■ **North Branch Flooring**
2415 W Barry Ave.
Chicago, IL 60618
Phone: (312)935-3400
Free: (800)688-0144 **Fax:** (312)935-7301
Products: Hardwood flooring; Fionishes; Tools and machines. **SICs:** 5023 (Homefurnishings); 5031 (Lumber, Plywood & Millwork); 5072 (Hardware). **Est:** 1906. **Emp:** 11. **Officers:** Donna Edwards, President; Jim Duffek, Vice President; Robert Edwards, Vice President.

■ **10081** ■ **N.R.F. Distributors, Inc.**
PO Box 2467
Augusta, ME 04338-2467
Phones: (207)622-4744 800-452-1918
Free: (800)777-2037 **Fax:** (207)622-4847
Products: Floor coverings, including carpet, vinyl and ceramic tiles, and wood. **SICs:** 5023 (Homefurnishings); 5031 (Lumber, Plywood & Millwork); 5032 (Brick, Stone & Related Materials). **Est:** 1973.

■ **10082** ■ **Nueces Tile Sales**
4516 S Padre Island Dr.
Corpus Christi, TX 78411
Phone: (361)854-3166 **Fax:** (361)854-6677
Products: Ceramic tile. **SIC:** 5032 (Brick, Stone & Related Materials). **Est:** 1969. **Emp:** 4. **Officers:** Russell L. Hudler, Manager.

■ **10083** ■ **Ohio Tile & Marble Co.**
3809 Spring Grove Ave.
Cincinnati, OH 45223
Phone: (513)541-4211 **Fax:** (513)541-2966
E-mail: ohiotile@choice.net
URL: http://www.ohiotile.com
Products: Ceramic wall and floor tile; Custom fabrication on natural stones. **SIC:** 5032 (Brick, Stone & Related Materials). **Est:** 1937. **Emp:** 20.

■ **10084** ■ **Ohio Valley Flooring**
5555 Murray Rd.
Cincinnati, OH 45227
Phone: (513)561-3399
Products: Ceramic tile. **SIC:** 5032 (Brick, Stone & Related Materials).

■ **10085** ■ **Old Masters Products Inc.**
3791 2nd Ave.
Los Angeles, CA 90018
Phone: (323)291-0677 **Fax:** (323)291-2567
URL: http://www.omp-inc.com
Products: Hardwood flooring and finishing products. **SICs:** 5023 (Homefurnishings); 5031 (Lumber, Plywood & Millwork). **Est:** 1950. **Sales:** $11,000,000 (1999). **Emp:** 30. **Officers:** Jack Schoen, President; Jim Hilaski, Vice President; Angela Schoen, Human Resources Contact.

■ **10086** ■ **Old Masters Products Inc.**
7023 Valjean Avenue
Van Nuys, CA 91406
Phone: (818)785-8886 **Fax:** (818)785-8883
URL: www.omp-inc.com
Products: Hardwood flooring and finishing products. **SICs:** 5023 (Homefurnishings); 5031 (Lumber, Plywood & Millwork). **Officers:** Jack Schoen, President; Jim Hilaski; Angela Schoen, Human Resources Contact.

■ **10087** ■ **Olympic Flooring Distributors Inc.**
1000 Kieley
Cincinnati, OH 45217
Phone: (513)242-6500
Free: (800)635-0400 **Fax:** (513)242-6507
Products: Floor coverings, including vinyl, carpet, tile, and wood. **SICs:** 5023 (Homefurnishings); 5031 (Lumber, Plywood & Millwork); 5032 (Brick, Stone & Related Materials).

■ **10088** ■ **Orders Distributing Company Inc.**
PO Box 17189
Greenville, SC 29606
Phone: (803)288-4220 **Fax:** (803)458-7348
Products: Ceramic tiles; Wood flooring; Carpeting; Sheet vinyl. **SICs:** 5023 (Homefurnishings); 5031 (Lumber, Plywood & Millwork). **Est:** 1955. **Sales:** $34,000,000 (2000). **Emp:** 185. **Officers:** C. Micheal Smith, President; David Williams, VP of Finance.

■ **10089** ■ **Orian Rugs Inc.**
Hwy. 81 N
Anderson, SC 29621
Phone: (864)224-0271 **Fax:** (864)225-6344
E-mail: orian-rugs@worldnet.att.net
URL: http://www.orianrugs.com
Products: Rugs. **SIC:** 5023 (Homefurnishings). **Est:** 1979. **Emp:** 250. **Officers:** Jean Baptiste Santens; Tony Saad.

■ 10090 ■ **Ornamental Tile and Design Center**
11450 Overseas Hwy.
Marathon, FL 33050
Phone: (305)743-6336
Products: Brick and structural clay tile; Ceramic mosaic tile; Carpets; Cement. **SICs:** 5032 (Brick, Stone & Related Materials); 5023 (Homefurnishings). **Emp:** 50.

■ 10091 ■ **Pacific Flooring Supply**
965 Detroit Ave., Ste. C
Concord, CA 94518
Phone: (925)682-5697 **Fax:** (925)682-5697
Products: Flooring tools and supplies. **SIC:** 5072 (Hardware).

■ 10092 ■ **Pacific Flooring Supply**
4220 Hubbard St.
Emeryville, CA 94608
Phone: (510)654-0485 **Fax:** (510)654-2813
Products: Floor covering, including hardwood patches and finishes. **SICs:** 5023 (Homefurnishings); 5198 (Paints, Varnishes & Supplies). **Est:** 1948.

■ 10093 ■ **Pacific Flooring Supply**
1308 Kansas Ave.
Modesto, CA 95351
Phone: (209)522-5937 **Fax:** (209)522-1935
Products: Floor covering and carpet supplies. **SIC:** 5023 (Homefurnishings).

■ 10094 ■ **Pacific Flooring Supply**
5042 Westside Rd.
Redding, CA 96001
Phone: (530)244-3832
Products: Hardwood flooring. **SIC:** 5031 (Lumber, Plywood & Millwork).

■ 10095 ■ **Pacific Flooring Supply**
1527 North C St.
Sacramento, CA 95814
Phone: (916)442-0491 **Fax:** (916)447-3809
Products: Floor covering and flooring supplies. **SICs:** 5023 (Homefurnishings); 5039 (Construction Materials Nec).

■ 10096 ■ **Pacific Flooring Supply**
770 Tennessee St.
San Francisco, CA 94107
Phone: (415)826-4375 **Fax:** (415)826-4353
Products: Flooring and flooring supplies. **SIC:** 5023 (Homefurnishings).

■ 10097 ■ **Pacific Flooring Supply**
2754 Teepee Dr., Ste E
Stockton, CA 95205
Phone: (209)463-6842
Products: Carpeting. **SIC:** 5023 (Homefurnishings).

■ 10098 ■ **Palmetto Tile Distributor**
316 Huger St.
PO Box 42
Columbia, SC 29201
Phone: (803)771-4001 **Fax:** (803)252-6071
Products: Ceramic wall and floor tile. **SIC:** 5032 (Brick, Stone & Related Materials). **Est:** 1982. **Emp:** 17. **Officers:** Henry Goldberg, Contact.

■ 10099 ■ **Peter Paracca & Sons**
20254 Rte. 19
Evans City, PA 16033
Products: Ceramic wall and floor tile. **SIC:** 5032 (Brick, Stone & Related Materials).

■ 10100 ■ **Paradise Ceramics**
Deviso Sur, No. 16
Aguada, PR 00602
Phone: (787)868-4981
Products: Ceramic tile. **SIC:** 5032 (Brick, Stone & Related Materials).

■ 10101 ■ **Parma Tile Mosaic & Marble**
29-10 14th St.
Astoria, NY 11102-4119
Phone: (718)278-3060 **Fax:** (718)278-1096
Products: Ceramic wall and floor tile. **SIC:** 5032 (Brick, Stone & Related Materials).

■ 10102 ■ **Billy D. Pearson Rug Manufacturing Co.**
2240 Flint Hill Church Rd.
Shelby, NC 28152
Phone: (704)434-9331
Products: Rugs. **SIC:** 5023 (Homefurnishings).

■ 10103 ■ **Peeler's Rug Co.**
1224 Champion Ferry Rd.
Gaffney, SC 29341
Phone: (864)489-3010
Products: Rugs. **SIC:** 5023 (Homefurnishings).

■ 10104 ■ **Pennsylvania Floor Coverings**
250 Seco Rd.
Monroeville, PA 15146
Phone: (412)373-1700
Products: Ceramic tile. **SIC:** 5032 (Brick, Stone & Related Materials).

■ 10105 ■ **Pink Business Interiors Inc.**
5825 Excelsior Blvd.
St. Louis Pk., MN 55416
Phone: (612)915-3100 **Fax:** (612)915-3121
Products: Contract furniture, contract carpet, and residential carpet. **SICs:** 5021 (Furniture); 5023 (Homefurnishings). **Sales:** $22,000,000 (2000). **Emp:** 75. **Officers:** Bye Barsness, President; Jane Petron, CFO.

■ 10106 ■ **Preferred Carpets**
2600 Lakeland Rd.
Dalton, GA 30721-4907
Phone: (706)277-2732 **Fax:** (706)277-1549
Products: Carpets. **SIC:** 5023 (Homefurnishings). **Emp:** 12. **Officers:** George Wiggin.

■ 10107 ■ **Prestige Marble & Tile Co.**
22 E Merrick Rd.
Freeport, NY 11520
Phone: (516)223-4100
Products: Ceramic wall and floor tile. **SIC:** 5032 (Brick, Stone & Related Materials).

■ 10108 ■ **Primavera Distributing**
3401 Ambrose Ave.
Nashville, TN 37222
Phone: (423)899-2997
Free: (800)255-9370 **Fax:** (423)899-7793
Products: Asphalt and vinyl asbestos floor tile; Ceramic wall and floor tile. **SICs:** 5023 (Homefurnishings); 5032 (Brick, Stone & Related Materials). **Emp:** 24. **Former Name:** Ervin Supply Corp. (Chattanooga, Tennessee).

■ 10109 ■ **Primavera Distributing**
1312 Chilhowee Ave.
Knoxville, TN 37917
Phone: (423)899-2997
Free: (800)255-9370 **Fax:** (423)899-7793
Products: Asphalt and vinyl asbestos floor tile; Ceramic wall and floor tile. **SICs:** 5023 (Homefurnishings); 5032 (Brick, Stone & Related Materials). **Alternate Name:** Ervin Supply Corp. (Chattanooga, Tennessee).

■ 10110 ■ **Prince Street Technologies Ltd.**
1450 W Ave.
PO Drawer 2530
Cartersville, GA 30120
Phone: (770)606-0507 **Free:** (800)221-3684
Products: Carpets. **SIC:** 5023 (Homefurnishings). **Emp:** 185. **Officers:** Robert Weiner.

■ 10111 ■ **Quality Tile Corp.**
2541 Boston Rd.
Bronx, NY 10467
Phone: (718)653-0830 **Fax:** (718)515-1968
Products: Ceramic wall and floor tile. **SIC:** 5032 (Brick, Stone & Related Materials). **Officers:** Perry Coscia, Contact.

■ 10112 ■ **R & R Hardwood Floors**
5125 W Gage St.
Boise, ID 83706
Phone: (208)377-5563 **Fax:** (208)377-0318
Products: Hardwood floors. **SIC:** 5023 (Homefurnishings).

■ 10113 ■ **Rainbow Rug Inc.**
74 Old Airport Rd.
Sanford, ME 04073
Phone: (207)324-6600
Products: Rugs. **SIC:** 5023 (Homefurnishings).

■ 10114 ■ **Randall Tile Company, Inc.**
PO Box 69
Phenix City, AL 36868-0069
Phone: (205)298-0327 **Fax:** (205)298-0357
Products: Ceramic tile. **SIC:** 5032 (Brick, Stone & Related Materials).

■ 10115 ■ **RBC Tile & Stone**
1820 Berkshire Ln. N
Plymouth, MN 55441
Phone: (612)559-5531 **Fax:** (612)559-5520
E-mail: sales@rbctile.com
URL: http://www.rbctile.com
Products: Ceramic tile; Stone. **SIC:** 5032 (Brick, Stone & Related Materials). **Est:** 1959. **Emp:** 70. **Officers:** Brian Mark.

■ 10116 ■ **Readers Wholesale Distributors Inc.**
PO Box 2407
Houston, TX 77252-2407
Phone: (713)224-8300
Products: Floorcoverings, including carpet and tile. **SICs:** 5023 (Homefurnishings); 5032 (Brick, Stone & Related Materials). **Est:** 1952. **Sales:** $23,000,000 (2000). **Emp:** 90. **Officers:** Lucky Burke, President; Edward Mahler, Controller.

■ 10117 ■ **Charles H. Reed Export, Inc.**
894 Main St
PO Box 596
Norwell, MA 02061
Phone: (781)659-1555 **Fax:** (781)659-1357
Products: Wood flooring, including hard maple; Signs, including electric scoreboards; Food processing machinery, including potato slicers; Stadium and gymnasium seating. **SICs:** 5023 (Homefurnishings); 5031 (Lumber, Plywood & Millwork); 5046 (Commercial Equipment Nec). **Officers:** Damon P. Reed, President.

■ 10118 ■ **Cynthia Rees Ceramic Tile**
454 E Jericho Tpke.
Huntington Station, NY 11746
Phone: (516)673-8453
Products: Ceramic tile. **SIC:** 5032 (Brick, Stone & Related Materials).

■ 10119 ■ **Renaissance Ceramic Tile**
1250 Easton Rd.
Horsham, PA 19044
Phone: (215)674-4848 **Fax:** (215)674-4399
Products: Ceramic wall and floor tile. **SIC:** 5032 (Brick, Stone & Related Materials). **Officers:** Danny Goodwin, Contact.

■ 10120 ■ **Renfrow Tile Distributing Company, Inc.**
PO Box 9388
Charlotte, NC 28204
Phones: (910)275-7607 (704)334-6811
Fax: (910)272-6741
Products: Ceramic wall and floor tile. **SIC:** 5032 (Brick, Stone & Related Materials). **Sales:** $3,000,000 (2000). **Emp:** 10. **Officers:** James R. Harkey, President.

■ 10121 ■ **Rhode Island Tile/G & M Co.**
55 Industrial Rd.
Cranston, RI 02920
Phone: (401)942-6700
Free: (800)866-8453 **Fax:** (401)946-2877
Products: Ceramic wall and floor tile; Sheet vinyl and vinyl tile. **SICs:** 5032 (Brick, Stone & Related Materials); 5023 (Homefurnishings). **Est:** 1944. **Emp:** 50. **Officers:** Jim Galli, President; Joe Galli, Vice President; Thomas Laviano, Sales Mgr.

■ 10122 ■ **Riviera Tile Inc.**
4515 North Expy.
Brownsville, TX 78520
Phone: (956)350-4545
Free: (800)835-9892 **Fax:** (956)350-9892
Products: Ceramic wall and floor tile. **SIC:** 5032 (Brick, Stone & Related Materials). **Est:** 1972. **Emp:** 12.

Officers: Joe Rivera, President; Joe Ray Rivera, Manager; Jose Becerra, Estimator.

■ **10123** ■ **The Roane Co.**
14141 Arbor Pl.
Cerritos, CA 90703
Phone: (562)404-3464
Free: (800)223-6499 **Fax:** (562)404-8028
URL: http://www.theroaneco.com
Products: Hardwood and formica flooring; Eurostyle ceramic and porcelain tile; Fastile peel and stick; Unfinished plank and strip. **SIC:** 5031 (Lumber, Plywood & Millwork). **Est:** 1947. **Sales:** $15,000,000 (2000). **Emp:** 45. **Officers:** Jack Wilcox, President; Brent Wilcox, Vice President; Allen Smith, General Mgr., e-mail: allen@theroaneco.com; Cozette Livingston, Marketing Mgr., e-mail: lcozette@theroaneco.com; Janelle Henderson, Customer Service Contact, e-mail: janelle@theroane.com.

■ **10124** ■ **The Roane Co.**
6160 Marindustry Dr.
San Diego, CA 92121-9663
Phone: (619)455-9663 **Fax:** (619)455-8477
URL: http://www.theroaneco.com
Products: Hardwood and formica flooring. **SIC:** 5023 (Homefurnishings). **Est:** 1947. **Officers:** John DeLoa, Operations Mgr.

■ **10125** ■ **The Roane Co.**
3537 E Corona Ave.
Phoenix, AZ 85040-2841
Phone: (602)268-1441 **Fax:** (602)243-3840
URL: http://www.theroaneco.com
Products: Hardwood and formica flooring. **SIC:** 5023 (Homefurnishings). **Est:** 1947. **Officers:** Kay Chute, Operations Mgr.

■ **10126** ■ **The Roane Co.**
3955 W Mesa Vista Ave., No. A8
Las Vegas, NV 89118-2339
Phone: (702)736-1811 **Fax:** (702)736-2320
URL: http://www.theroaneco.com
Products: Hardwood and formica flooring. **SIC:** 5023 (Homefurnishings). **Est:** 1947. **Officers:** Angelo Morrero, Operations Mgr.

■ **10127** ■ **Robison Distributors Co.**
PO Box 2309
Salt Lake City, UT 84110
Phone: (801)486-3511 **Fax:** (801)486-3544
Products: Floorcoverings, including vinyl. **SIC:** 5023 (Homefurnishings).

■ **10128** ■ **Roma Tile Co., Inc.**
306 Wolf St.
Syracuse, NY 13208
Phone: (315)471-7856 **Fax:** (315)471-7331
Products: Ceramic wall and floor tile. **SIC:** 5032 (Brick, Stone & Related Materials). **Officers:** Nick Romanagla, Contact.

■ **10129** ■ **Royal Carpet Distribution, Inc.**
20750 Hoover Rd.
Warren, MI 48089
Phone: (810)756-2400 **Fax:** (810)756-5077
Products: Floor coverings, including tile, carpet, and wood. **SICs:** 5023 (Homefurnishings); 5031 (Lumber, Plywood & Millwork); 5032 (Brick, Stone & Related Materials).

■ **10130** ■ **Royal Floor Mats**
5951 E Firestone Blvd.
South Gate, CA 90280
Phone: (562)928-3381
Free: (800)237-8628 **Fax:** (562)776-4482
Products: Rubber floor mats. **SIC:** 5023 (Homefurnishings). **Former Name:** Royal Rubber and Manufacturing Co.

■ **10131** ■ **Royalty Carpet Mills Inc.**
17111 Red Hill Ave.
Irvine, CA 92614-5877
Phone: (714)474-4000
Products: Carpeting and supplies. **SIC:** 5023 (Homefurnishings). **Emp:** 499. **Officers:** Mike Derderian.

■ **10132** ■ **RSB Tile, Inc.**
495 Route 208
Monroe, NY 10950
Phone: (914)783-6167 **Fax:** (914)783-1664
Products: Ceramic wall and floor tile; Adhesives; Grout; Custom decorated ceramics. **SICs:** 5032 (Brick, Stone & Related Materials); 5169 (Chemicals & Allied Products Nec); 5023 (Homefurnishings). **Est:** 1979. **Sales:** $1,000,000 (2000). **Officers:** Donna Baruffaldi, Contact.

■ **10133** ■ **Rubin Brothers Company Inc.**
5600 Bucknell Dr. SW
Atlanta, GA 30336
Phone: (404)349-6900 **Fax:** (404)349-4584
Products: Floor coverings, including tile and carpet. **SICs:** 5023 (Homefurnishings); 5032 (Brick, Stone & Related Materials). **Est:** 1951. **Sales:** $31,000,000 (2000). **Emp:** 100. **Officers:** Ralph Kahn, President; Michael Kahn, Vice President.

■ **10134** ■ **Salinas Tile Sales Co.**
1 Spring St.
Salinas, CA 93901-3616
Phone: (408)424-8046 **Fax:** (408)424-9836
Products: Ceramic wall and floor tile. **SIC:** 5032 (Brick, Stone & Related Materials).

■ **10135** ■ **Salinas Tile Sales, Inc.**
1830 California St.
Sand City, CA 93955
Phone: (408)899-5377
Products: Ceramic wall and floor tile. **SIC:** 5032 (Brick, Stone & Related Materials).

■ **10136** ■ **Samuels Tile**
223 Nepperhan Ave.
Yonkers, NY 10701
Phone: (914)423-0880
Products: Ceramic wall and floor tile. **SIC:** 5032 (Brick, Stone & Related Materials).

■ **10137** ■ **Sanford Tile Co.**
5506 Wares Ferry Rd.
Montgomery, AL 36117
Phone: (334)272-4498 **Fax:** (334)272-5244
Products: Ceramic tile. **SIC:** 5032 (Brick, Stone & Related Materials).

■ **10138** ■ **Santa Clara Tile Supply**
1129 Richard Ave.
Santa Clara, CA 95050
Phone: (408)727-9050 **Fax:** (408)727-2064
Products: Italian marble and granite. **SIC:** 5032 (Brick, Stone & Related Materials).

■ **10139** ■ **Sawtooth Builders**
312 4th St.
Ithaca, NY 14850
Products: Ceramic wall and floor tile. **SIC:** 5032 (Brick, Stone & Related Materials). **Officers:** Randolph C. Murphy, Contact.

■ **10140** ■ **Sea-Pac Sales Co.**
PO Box 3846
Seattle, WA 98124-3846
Phone: (206)223-5353
Products: Flooring, including vinyl and wood. **SICs:** 5023 (Homefurnishings); 5031 (Lumber, Plywood & Millwork). **Sales:** $50,000,000 (2000). **Emp:** 100. **Officers:** Dale R. Griffiths, President.

■ **10141** ■ **Seatile Distributors**
4311 N Monroe St.
Tallahassee, FL 32303
Phone: (850)562-2888 **Fax:** (850)562-2887
Products: Ceramic tile; Marble. **SIC:** 5032 (Brick, Stone & Related Materials).

■ **10142** ■ **Self's, Inc.**
721 E Mount Vernon
Wichita, KS 67211
Phone: (316)267-1295
Products: Ceramic tile. **SIC:** 5032 (Brick, Stone & Related Materials).

■ **10143** ■ **Self's, Inc.**
2720 S Austin
Springfield, MO 65807
Phone: (417)886-3332
Products: Ceramic tile. **SIC:** 5032 (Brick, Stone & Related Materials).

■ **10144** ■ **Sellers Tile Distributors**
109 Booker Ave.
Albany, GA 31701-2541
Phone: (912)435-7474
Products: Ceramic wall and floor tile. **SIC:** 5032 (Brick, Stone & Related Materials). **Officers:** Kay C. Fickel, Contact.

■ **10145** ■ **Shaheen Carpet Mills**
PO Box 167
Resaca, GA 30735-0167
Phone: (706)629-9544
Free: (800)241-4352 **Fax:** (706)625-5341
E-mail: smcpt@aol.com
Products: Carpet. **SIC:** 5023 (Homefurnishings). **Est:** 1964. **Sales:** $10,000,000 (2000). **Emp:** 49. **Officers:** Said Shaheen.

■ **10146** ■ **Shannon Brothers Tile**
1309 Putnam Dr.
Huntsville, AL 35816
Phone: (205)837-6520
Products: Ceramic wall and floor tile. **SIC:** 5032 (Brick, Stone & Related Materials). **Emp:** 35.

■ **10147** ■ **William G. Sharp Co.**
414 NE 11th
PO Box 10106
Amarillo, TX 79116-1106
Phone: (806)376-4440
Free: (800)843-0388 **Fax:** (806)371-0052
E-mail: sharpco1@aol.com
Products: Ceramic wall and floor tile; Carpet and floor coverings. **SICs:** 5032 (Brick, Stone & Related Materials); 5023 (Homefurnishings). **Est:** 1984. **Sales:** $3,500,000 (2000). **Emp:** 15. **Officers:** Bill Sharp, Contact.

■ **10148** ■ **Silver Loom Associates**
271-80 Grand Central Pky., No. 80
Floral Park, NY 11005-1209
Phone: (212)684-2350 **Fax:** (212)889-2177
Products: Rugs. **SIC:** 5023 (Homefurnishings). **Sales:** $6,000,000 (2000). **Emp:** 49.

■ **10149** ■ **Simmons Yarn & Rug Co.**
835 Poplar Springs Church Rd.
Shelby, NC 28152
Phone: (704)484-8691
Products: Rugs. **SIC:** 5023 (Homefurnishings).

■ **10150** ■ **Sita Tile Distributors, Inc.**
523 Dunmore Pl.
Capitol Heights, MD 20743
Phone: (301)336-0450 **Fax:** (301)336-1526
Products: Ceramic wall and floor tile. **SIC:** 5032 (Brick, Stone & Related Materials). **Officers:** Jim Sita Sr., Contact.

■ **10151** ■ **William Smethurst & Sons**
344 Eastern Ave.
Malden, MA 02148
Phone: (781)322-3210
Free: (800)323-8453 **Fax:** (781)397-8084
Products: Ceramic tile. **SIC:** 5032 (Brick, Stone & Related Materials).

■ **10152** ■ **Smith Floor Covering**
3106 Essex Path
Hendersonville, NC 28791-1869
Phone: (704)252-1038
Products: Ceramic wall and floor tile. **SIC:** 5032 (Brick, Stone & Related Materials). **Officers:** George Orr, Contact.

■ **10153** ■ **Smith Floor Covering Distributors**
1118 Smith St.
PO Box 2826
Charleston, WV 25330
Phone: (304)344-2493
Free: (800)927-7323 **Fax:** (304)344-2475
Products: Floor covering. **SIC:** 5032 (Brick, Stone &

Related Materials). **Est:** 1963. **Sales:** $6,000,000 (2000). **Emp:** 17. **Officers:** W.E. Smith, President; C.L. Smith, Vice President.

■ 10154 ■ Smith Hardwood Floors
1115 S 10th
Ft. Smith, AR 72901
Phone: (501)783-2850 **Fax:** (501)783-2850
Products: Hardwood flooring. **SICs:** 5023 (Homefurnishings); 5031 (Lumber, Plywood & Millwork). **Est:** 1951. **Sales:** $1,000,000 (2000). **Emp:** 13. **Officers:** Raymond Smith, President; Raymond E. Smith Jr., Vice President.

■ 10155 ■ Merle B. Smith
161 Tower Dr., Unit I
Burr Ridge, IL 60521
Phone: (630)325-0770
Free: (800)244-0770 **Fax:** (630)325-0784
Products: Hardwood flooring; Sanding equipment; Finishes. **SICs:** 5023 (Homefurnishings); 5031 (Lumber, Plywood & Millwork); 5072 (Hardware); 5198 (Paints, Varnishes & Supplies). **Est:** 1971. **Emp:** 15. **Officers:** Merle B. Smith, President.

■ 10156 ■ Sorce, Inc.
2495 Walden Ave.
Cheektowaga, NY 14225-4717
Phone: (716)681-3780
Free: (800)283-RUGS **Fax:** (716)681-9371
Products: Floorcoverings; Carpets. **SIC:** 5023 (Homefurnishings). **Emp:** 20.

■ 10157 ■ Sound Floor Coverings Inc.
18375 Olympic Ave. S
Tukwila, WA 98188
Phone: (206)575-1181 **Fax:** (206)251-0581
Products: Ceramic floorcoverings and carpet. **SICs:** 5023 (Homefurnishings); 5032 (Brick, Stone & Related Materials). **Est:** 1947. **Sales:** $29,000,000 (2000). **Emp:** 84. **Officers:** Peter H. Chick, President; Kurt Kentfield, Controller; Dave Wakely, Dir. of Marketing & Sales; Alan Larson, Dir. of Information Systems.

■ 10158 ■ South Alabama Brick
230 Ross Clark Cir. NE
Dothan, AL 36303-5843
Phone: (334)794-4173
Free: (800)239-3368 **Fax:** (334)794-9725
Products: Ceramic wall and floor tile; Glass block and related materials. **SIC:** 5032 (Brick, Stone & Related Materials). **Est:** 1990. **Emp:** 100. **Doing Business As:** Whatley Supply Co.

■ 10159 ■ Southampton Brick & Tile, Inc.
1540 North Hwy.
Southampton, NY 11968
Phone: (516)283-8088 **Fax:** (516)283-8349
Products: Ceramic wall and floor tile. **SIC:** 5032 (Brick, Stone & Related Materials).

■ 10160 ■ Southern Flooring Distributors
PO Box 30337
Charlotte, NC 28230-0337
Products: Floor coverings, including vinyl, wood, ceramics, and carpet. **SICs:** 5023 (Homefurnishings); 5032 (Brick, Stone & Related Materials); 5031 (Lumber, Plywood & Millwork).

■ 10161 ■ Southern Flooring Distributors
2008 Brengle Ave.
Orlando, FL 32808
Phone: (407)578-7448
Free: (800)763-7308 **Fax:** (407)578-7819
Products: Floor coverings, including vinyl, carpeting, and ceramic. **SICs:** 5023 (Homefurnishings); 5032 (Brick, Stone & Related Materials).

■ 10162 ■ Southern Flooring Distributors
6675 Jimmy Carter Blvd.
Norcross, GA 30071
Phone: (404)237-9276 **Fax:** (404)699-0540
Products: Floor covering, including vinyl and wood. **SICs:** 5023 (Homefurnishings); 5031 (Lumber, Plywood & Millwork).

■ 10163 ■ Southern Flooring Distributors
727 Lakeside Dr.
Mobile, AL 36693
Phone: (205)666-1587
Products: Flooring and supplies. **SIC:** 5023 (Homefurnishings).

■ 10164 ■ Southern Flooring Distributors
1001 S Dupre St.
New Orleans, LA 70125
Phone: (504)821-2211 **Fax:** (504)821-2333
Products: Tile, ceramic, and wood flooring. **SICs:** 5023 (Homefurnishings); 5032 (Brick, Stone & Related Materials); 5031 (Lumber, Plywood & Millwork).

■ 10165 ■ Southern Tile Distributors Inc.
1328 Canton Rd.
Marietta, GA 30066
Phone: (404)423-0858 **Fax:** (404)423-0704
Products: Ceramic tile. **SIC:** 5032 (Brick, Stone & Related Materials).

■ 10166 ■ Southern Tile Distributors Inc.
1814 Mt. Zion Rd.
Morrow, GA 30260
Phone: (404)961-6179 **Fax:** (404)961-4133
Products: Ceramic tile. **SIC:** 5032 (Brick, Stone & Related Materials).

■ 10167 ■ Southland Carpet Supplies
1450 N Wood Dale Rd.
Wood Dale, IL 60191-1096
Products: Carpeting supplies. **SIC:** 5023 (Homefurnishings).

■ 10168 ■ Southland Flooring Supplies Inc.
1450 N Wood Dale Rd.
Wood Dale, IL 60191-1096
Phone: (630)227-1600 **Fax:** (630)227-1600
Products: Flooring supplies. **SIC:** 5023 (Homefurnishings). **Est:** 1987. **Emp:** 7. **Officers:** Wm. N. Lockwood, Vice President. **Former Name:** Southland Carpet Supplies.

■ 10169 ■ Southland Flooring Supply
6019 E 30th St.
Indianapolis, IN 46219
Phone: (317)541-3333 **Fax:** (317)541-3327
Products: Flooring supplies. **SIC:** 5023 (Homefurnishings). **Sales:** $2,500,000 (2000). **Emp:** 10.

■ 10170 ■ Southland Floors, Inc.
2701 NW 17th Ln.
Pompano Beach, FL 33064-1561
Phone: (954)974-4700
Free: (800)432-4520 **Fax:** (305)973-6333
Products: Residential and commercial floor covering, including carpet, sheet vinyl, ceramic tile, and wood. **SICs:** 5023 (Homefurnishings); 5031 (Lumber, Plywood & Millwork); 5032 (Brick, Stone & Related Materials). **Est:** 1974. **Emp:** 60. **Officers:** Gary Henick, President.

■ 10171 ■ Southwestern Ceramic, Tile & Marble Co.
999 Racheros Dr., No. A
San Marcos, CA 92069-3028
Phone: (619)298-3511 **Fax:** (619)298-7089
Products: Ceramic wall and floor tile. **SIC:** 5032 (Brick, Stone & Related Materials).

■ 10172 ■ Southwestern Ceramic, Tile & Marble Co.
999 Rancheros Dr.
San Marcos, CA 92069-3028
Phone: (760)741-2033
Products: Ceramic wall and floor tile. **SIC:** 5032 (Brick, Stone & Related Materials).

■ 10173 ■ Sovereign Distributors, Inc.
3157 Fire Rd.
Pleasantville, NJ 08232
Phone: (609)641-2770
Products: Ceramic tile. **SIC:** 5032 (Brick, Stone & Related Materials).

■ 10174 ■ Specialty Building Products, Inc.
7505-C Veterans Pkwy.
Columbus, GA 31909-2501
Phone: (706)327-0668 **Fax:** (706)323-1840
Products: Ceramic wall and floor tile. **SIC:** 5032 (Brick, Stone & Related Materials). **Est:** 1984. **Sales:** $1,500,000 (2000). **Emp:** 5. **Doing Business As:** The Tile Shop.

■ 10175 ■ Specialty Distribution
402 Staats Ave.
PO Box 305
Maupin, OR 97037
Phone: (541)395-2553
Products: Paint; Floor coverings. **SICs:** 5023 (Homefurnishings); 5198 (Paints, Varnishes & Supplies). **Officers:** Jack M. McLeod, Owner.

■ 10176 ■ Stanline Inc.
2855 S Reservoir
Pomona, CA 91766
Phone: (909)591-0541 **Fax:** (909)591-7062
Products: Floor coverings, including vinyl and tile; Countertops. **SICs:** 5023 (Homefurnishings); 5031 (Lumber, Plywood & Millwork). **Est:** 1961. **Sales:** $64,000,000 (2000). **Emp:** 168. **Officers:** Stanley Frahm, CEO & President; Roger S. Johnson, VP & CFO.

■ 10177 ■ Star International Ltd.
3343 Dug Gap Rd.
Dalton, GA 30720
Phone: (706)277-4410 **Fax:** (706)277-9578
Products: Tufted carpet made of manmade fibers, nylon, and polyamides. **SIC:** 5023 (Homefurnishings). **Officers:** Richard Butler, President.

■ 10178 ■ Stark Carpet Corp.
979 3rd Ave.
New York, NY 10022
Phone: (212)752-9000 **Fax:** (212)758-4342
Products: Commercial and residential carpet. **SIC:** 5023 (Homefurnishings). **Emp:** 99.

■ 10179 ■ State Ceramic Tile, Inc.
23700 Aurora Rd.
Bedford Heights, OH 44146
Phone: (440)439-3131 **Fax:** (440)439-3225
Products: Ceramic wall and floor tile. **SIC:** 5032 (Brick, Stone & Related Materials).

■ 10180 ■ States Distributing
100 E 5th St.
PO Box 638
Brookport, IL 62910
Phone: (618)564-3377
Products: Ceramic wall and floor tile. **SIC:** 5032 (Brick, Stone & Related Materials). **Officers:** Bob Farlee, Contact.

■ 10181 ■ Stanley Stephens
2565 Pearl Buck Rd.
PO Box 2205
Bristol, PA 19007
Phone: (215)788-1515
Free: (800)523-5200 **Fax:** (215)788-8535
Products: Hard surface floor coverings. **SIC:** 5032 (Brick, Stone & Related Materials).

■ 10182 ■ Stiller Distributors Inc.
833 Dyer
Cranston, RI 02920
Phone: (401)946-6600
Free: (800)634-2183 **Fax:** (401)943-8243
Products: Floor coverings, including vinyl, tile, wood, and carpet. **SICs:** 5023 (Homefurnishings); 5032 (Brick, Stone & Related Materials); 5031 (Lumber, Plywood & Millwork).

■ 10183 ■ Stockdale Ceramic Tile Center, Inc.
6301 District Blvd.
Bakersfield, CA 93313-2143
Phone: (805)398-6000 **Fax:** (805)398-0749
Products: Ceramic wall and floor tile. **SIC:** 5032 (Brick, Stone & Related Materials).

■ **10184** ■ **Stroud Braided Rug Co.**
2627 Rockford Rd.
Shelby, NC 28152
Phone: (704)434-5098
Products: Rugs. **SIC:** 5023 (Homefurnishings).

■ **10185** ■ **Sullivan Tile Distributors**
10 Railroad Ave.
PO Box 485
West Haven, CT 06516
Phones: (203)934-2600   (203)934-2609
Fax: (203)933-0510
Products: Tile. **SIC:** 5032 (Brick, Stone & Related
Materials). **Est:** 1953. **Sales:** $2,000,000 (2000). **Emp:**
12. **Officers:** Arnold Agnoli, President; Ann Piscitelli,
Manager; Tracy Rapetski, Head Buyer.

■ **10186** ■ **Summitville Atlanta**
8607 Roswell Rd.
Atlanta, GA 30350
Phone: (404)587-1744   **Fax:** (404)998-4704
Products: Ceramic tile; Marble; Granite; Rugs. **SICs:**
5023 (Homefurnishings); 5032 (Brick, Stone & Related
Materials).

■ **10187** ■ **Summitville Baltimore**
8 W Aylesbury Rd.
Timonium, MD 21093
Phone: (410)252-0112   **Fax:** (410)252-2321
Products: Commercial and residential ceramic tile;
Marble, granite, carpet, vinyl, and wood floor coverings.
SICs: 5023 (Homefurnishings); 5031 (Lumber,
Plywood & Millwork); 5032 (Brick, Stone & Related
Materials). **Est:** 1966. **Emp:** 10. **Officers:** K. Kevin
Gahan.

■ **10188** ■ **Summitville Boardman**
631 Boardman Canfield Rd.
Boardman, OH 44512
Phone: (330)758-0835   **Fax:** (330)758-4650
Products: Clay or other ceramic tile; Dressed
dimension marble and other stone; Mason's materials.
SIC: 5032 (Brick, Stone & Related Materials).

■ **10189** ■ **Summitville Charlotte**
4618 South Blvd.
Charlotte, NC 28209
Phone: (704)525-8453   **Fax:** (704)525-1508
Products: Ceramic tile; Marble. **SIC:** 5032 (Brick,
Stone & Related Materials).

■ **10190** ■ **Summitville Fairfax**
6464 A General Green Way
Alexandria, VA 22312
Phone: (703)750-2660   **Fax:** (703)750-0119
Products: Ceramic tile; Setting products, including
glue. **SICs:** 5032 (Brick, Stone & Related Materials);
5169 (Chemicals & Allied Products Nec).

■ **10191** ■ **Summitville Orlando**
4210 L.B. McLeod, Ste. 101
Orlando, FL 32811
Phone: (407)849-5193   **Fax:** (407)849-5196
Products: Ceramic tile. **SIC:** 5032 (Brick, Stone &
Related Materials).

■ **10192** ■ **Summitville Pompano**
1330 S Andrews Ave.
Pompano Beach, FL 33069
Phone: (954)782-3522   **Fax:** (954)943-6981
Products: Porcelain tile. **SIC:** 5032 (Brick, Stone &
Related Materials).

■ **10193** ■ **Summitville, USA**
1101 Lunt Ave.
Elk Grove Village, IL 60007
Phone: (847)439-8820   **Fax:** (847)439-9421
Products: Tiles. **SIC:** 5032 (Brick, Stone & Related
Materials).

■ **10194** ■ **Sun Coast Tile Distributors Inc.**
2457 Fowler St.
Ft. Myers, FL 33901
Phone: (941)334-3461   **Fax:** (941)334-1341
E-mail: suncoasttile@juno.com
Products: Ceramic wall and floor tile. **SICs:** 5032
(Brick, Stone & Related Materials); 5023
(Homefurnishings). **Est:** 1960. **Emp:** 7.

■ **10195** ■ **Superior Products, Inc.**
7575 Washington Blvd.
Baltimore, MD 21227
Phone: (410)799-1000   **Fax:** (410)799-1515
Products: Floor coverings, including carpet, vinyl, tile,
and wood. **SICs:** 5023 (Homefurnishings); 5031
(Lumber, Plywood & Millwork); 5032 (Brick, Stone &
Related Materials).

■ **10196** ■ **Swiff-Train Co.**
2500 Agnes St.
PO Box 9095
Corpus Christi, TX 78405
Phone: (361)883-1707   **Fax:** (361)883-9653
E-mail: sales@swiff-train.com
URL: http://www.swiff-train.com
Products: Floor coverings, including vinyl and ceramic
tile, vinyl sheet goods, carpet and padding, and
hardwood; Plastic laminate and solid surface
countertops; Accessory products. **SICs:** 5023
(Homefurnishings); 5031 (Lumber, Plywood &
Millwork); 5032 (Brick, Stone & Related Materials). **Est:**
1935. **Emp:** 150. **Officers:** L.A. Train, President;
Kenneth Train, Exec. VP of Marketing & Sales; Don
Evans, VP of Sales; Jeffrey Train, VP of Operations &
Secty.; Jonathan Train, Asst. Secty.

■ **10197** ■ **Swiff-Train Co.**
405 N "T" St.
Harlingen, TX 78550
Phone: (956)428-6751   **Fax:** (956)428-6757
Products: Floor coverings, including wood, tile, and
carpeting. **SICs:** 5023 (Homefurnishings); 5031
(Lumber, Plywood & Millwork).

■ **10198** ■ **Swiff-Train Co.**
4650 S Pinemont, Ste. 100
Houston, TX 77047
Phone: (713)690-4472
Free: (800)275-7943   **Fax:** (713)460-3804
E-mail: sales@swiff-train.com
URL: http://www.swiff-train.com
Products: Tile and carpet; Wood; Ceramic; Laminate.
SICs: 5023 (Homefurnishings); 5031 (Lumber,
Plywood & Millwork); 5032 (Brick, Stone & Related
Materials). **Est:** 1937. **Emp:** 140. **Officers:** L.A. Train;
Kenny Train; Jeff Train; Don Evans.

■ **10199** ■ **Swiff-Train Co.**
3318 North Pan-Am Expressway
San Antonio, TX 78219
Phone: (210)227-2406   **Fax:** (210)227-4027
Products: Floor coverings. **SIC:** 5023
(Homefurnishings).

■ **10200** ■ **Swiff-Train Co.**
1304 E Rio Grande, Ste. 1
Victoria, TX 77901
Phone: (512)578-0286   **Fax:** (512)578-0290
Products: Floor coverings. **SIC:** 5023
(Homefurnishings).

■ **10201** ■ **Syverson Tile, Inc.**
4015 S Western Ave.
Sioux Falls, SD 57105-6540
Phone: (605)336-1175   **Fax:** (605)336-1179
Products: Building materials, including ceramic tile,
brick, granite, and marble. **SIC:** 5032 (Brick, Stone &
Related Materials). **Est:** 1932. **Emp:** 44.

■ **10202** ■ **T & A Supply Co.**
757 Highland Dr.
Seattle, WA 98109-3550
Phone: (206)282-3770
Free: (800)562-2857   **Fax:** (206)284-0591
Products: Floor and counter top coverings, including
sheet vinyl, carpet, wood, and tile. **SICs:** 5023
(Homefurnishings); 5031 (Lumber, Plywood &
Millwork). **Sales:** $60,000,000 (2000). **Emp:** 140.
Officers: Owen Strecker; Mark Strecker. **Alternate
Name:** Pacific Mat. **Alternate Name:** T & A Trym-Tox.

■ **10203** ■ **T & L Distributors Company Inc.**
451 W 61st
Shreveport, LA 71106
Phone: (318)865-8072   **Fax:** (318)865-6399
Products: Floor coverings, including tile, vinyl, and
carpet. **SICs:** 5023 (Homefurnishings); 5032 (Brick,
Stone & Related Materials).

■ **10204** ■ **T & L Distributors Company Inc.**
3201 Long Horn Blvd., Ste. 117
Austin, TX 78759
Phone: (512)832-0711
Free: (800)252-3566   **Fax:** (512)832-6404
Products: Floor coverings, including tile, wood, and
carpet. **SICs:** 5023 (Homefurnishings); 5032 (Brick,
Stone & Related Materials); 5031 (Lumber, Plywood &
Millwork).

■ **10205** ■ **T & L Distributors Company Inc.**
4051 La Reunion Pkwy., Ste. 180
Dallas, TX 75212
Phone: (214)630-6101   **Fax:** (214)630-4607
Products: Vinyl floor coverings. **SIC:** 5023
(Homefurnishings).

■ **10206** ■ **T & L Distributors Company Inc.**
PO Box 431709
Houston, TX 77243
Phone: (713)461-7802
Free: (800)888-0601   **Fax:** (713)932-6790
Products: Floor coverings, including tile, carpet, wood,
and vinyl. **SICs:** 5023 (Homefurnishings); 5032 (Brick,
Stone & Related Materials); 5031 (Lumber, Plywood &
Millwork).

■ **10207** ■ **T & L Distributors Company Inc.**
3453 N Panam Expy., Ste. 417
San Antonio, TX 78219-2340
Phone: (210)662-8200
Free: (800)888-0604   **Fax:** (210)662-0827
Products: Floor coverings, including wood tile and
carpeting. **SICs:** 5023 (Homefurnishings); 5031
(Lumber, Plywood & Millwork).

■ **10208** ■ **T & T Tile Distribution Inc.**
PO Box 5075
Winter Park, FL 32793-5075
Products: Ceramic wall and floor tile. **SIC:** 5032 (Brick,
Stone & Related Materials). **Officers:** Timothy C.
Dodgens, Contact.

■ **10209** ■ **Tampa Tile Center**
13670 Roosevelt Blvd.
Clearwater, FL 33762
Phone: (813)573-5386
Products: Ceramic tile. **SIC:** 5032 (Brick, Stone &
Related Materials).

■ **10210** ■ **Taylor Distributors**
1651 S Rio Grande Ave.
Orlando, FL 32805
Phone: (407)425-4145
Free: (800)432-3481   **Fax:** (407)423-5364
Products: Hard surface floor coverings. **SIC:** 5032
(Brick, Stone & Related Materials).

■ **10211** ■ **Tee Tile Distributors, Inc.**
2140 Jonathan Dr.
PO Box 461
Huntsville, AL 35804
Phone: (205)852-0025   **Fax:** (205)852-0026
Products: Ceramic wall and floor tile. **SIC:** 5032 (Brick,
Stone & Related Materials). **Officers:** Jerry Tomlin,
Contact.

■ **10212** ■ **Thomas Tile & Carpet Supply Co.
Inc.**
645 W Lake St.
Addison, IL 60101
Phone: (630)543-9694   **Fax:** (630)543-9705
Products: Tile and flooring products, including
ceramic, vinyl, carpet, marble, and hardwood. **SICs:**
5032 (Brick, Stone & Related Materials); 5023
(Homefurnishings); 5031 (Lumber, Plywood &
Millwork). **Emp:** 20. **Former Name:** Thomas Tile.

■ **10213** ■ **Thompson Tile Co., Inc.**
E 3900 Alki
PO Box 2944
Spokane, WA 99220
Phone: (509)535-2925   **Fax:** (509)534-5218
Products: Ceramic wall and floor tile. **SIC:** 5032 (Brick,
Stone & Related Materials). **Officers:** Jim Lammers,
Contact.

■ **10214** ■ **Thompson Tile Co., Inc.**
6700 Riverside Dr.
Tukwila, WA 98188
Phone: (425)251-0575 **Fax:** (425)251-0365
Products: Ceramic wall and floor tile. **SIC:** 5032 (Brick, Stone & Related Materials). **Officers:** Bill Mockli, Contact.

■ **10215** ■ **Thompson Tile Co., Inc.**
4456 NW Yeon Ave.
Portland, OR 97210-1430
Phone: (503)225-1273
Free: (800)827-4092 **Fax:** (503)222-0731
Products: Ceramic tile. **SIC:** 5032 (Brick, Stone & Related Materials). **Officers:** Nic Hawken, Manager.

■ **10216** ■ **Tile America**
487 Federal Rd.
Brookfield, CT 06804
Phone: (203)740-8858
Free: (800)360-TILE **Fax:** (203)740-1405
E-mail: tileamerica@worldnet.att.net
URL: http://www.tileamerica.com
Products: Ceramic wall and floor tile. **SIC:** 5032 (Brick, Stone & Related Materials). **Emp:** 8. **Former Name:** Ceramic Tile Outlet.

■ **10217** ■ **The Tile Barn**
1271 Rte. 22 E
Lebanon, NJ 08833
Phone: (908)236-9200
Products: Ceramic wall and floor tile. **SIC:** 5032 (Brick, Stone & Related Materials). **Officers:** Frank E. Scaccio, Contact.

■ **10218** ■ **The Tile Center, Inc.**
1221 Reynolds St.
Augusta, GA 30901-1050
Phone: (404)722-6804
Products: Ceramic wall and floor tile. **SIC:** 5032 (Brick, Stone & Related Materials).

■ **10219** ■ **Tile City**
c/o M & M Floor Covering, Inc.
359 E Park Ave.
Chico, CA 95928-7125
Phone: (530)895-3455
Free: (800)947-3455 **Fax:** (530)342-7416
Products: Ceramic wall and floor tile. **SIC:** 5032 (Brick, Stone & Related Materials). **Est:** 1966. **Emp:** 40. **Officers:** Eric Murray, President.

■ **10220** ■ **Tile City**
c/o M & M Floor Covering, Inc.
2560 Creater Lake Hwy., Unit C
Medford, OR 97504-4167
Phone: (541)779-8453
Products: Ceramic wall and floor tile. **SIC:** 5032 (Brick, Stone & Related Materials).

■ **10221** ■ **Tile City**
1355 Hartnell Ave.
Redding, CA 96002
Phone: (530)221-0826
Free: (800)834-0826 **Fax:** (530)221-6952
E-mail: tcrdg@aol.com
URL: http://www.tilecity.net
Products: Ceramic wall and floor tile. **SIC:** 5032 (Brick, Stone & Related Materials). **Est:** 1966. **Emp:** 6. **Officers:** Jeff Davis, Manager.

■ **10222** ■ **Tile Club**
1655 Broadway St., Ste. 21
Chula Vista, CA 91911
Phone: (619)420-8801
Products: Ceramic wall and floor tile. **SIC:** 5032 (Brick, Stone & Related Materials).

■ **10223** ■ **Tile Club**
2122 W Mission Rd.
Escondido, CA 92029
Phone: (760)745-9123
Free: (800)700-TILE **Fax:** (760)480-9905
Products: Ceramic wall and floor tile; Marble. **SIC:** 5032 (Brick, Stone & Related Materials). **Est:** 1979. **Sales:** $6,000,000 (2000). **Emp:** 45.

■ **10224** ■ **Tile Club**
1833 State College
Anaheim, CA 92806
Phone: (714)385-1717 **Fax:** (714)939-7545
Products: Ceramic wall and floor tile. **SIC:** 5032 (Brick, Stone & Related Materials). **Officers:** Oliver Migneco, Contact.

■ **10225** ■ **Tile Club**
1022 W Morena Blvd.
San Diego, CA 92110
Phone: (619)276-0271
Products: Ceramic wall and floor tile. **SIC:** 5032 (Brick, Stone & Related Materials).

■ **10226** ■ **Tile Club**
7129 Reseda Blvd.
Reseda, CA 91335-4211
Phone: (818)345-2276 **Fax:** (818)776-0907
URL: http://www.tileclub.com
Products: Ceramic wall, floor, and pool tile, including marble, granite, slate, and travertine. **SIC:** 5032 (Brick, Stone & Related Materials). **Est:** 1982. **Sales:** $1,000,000 (1999). **Emp:** 4. **Officers:** Oliver Mignano, Owner & Pres.

■ **10227** ■ **Tile Collection**
4420 Edna Rd.
San Luis Obispo, CA 93401
Phone: (805)549-0606 **Fax:** (805)549-0190
Products: Ceramic wall and floor tile. **SIC:** 5032 (Brick, Stone & Related Materials). **Doing Business As:** Tile Collections.

■ **10228** ■ **The Tile Collection, Inc.**
518 E Haley St.
Santa Barbara, CA 93103-3108
Phone: (805)963-8638 **Fax:** (805)965-6158
Products: Ceramic wall and floor tile. **SIC:** 5032 (Brick, Stone & Related Materials).

■ **10229** ■ **Tile Country Inc.**
265 Rt. 22E
Green Brook, NJ 08812
Phone: (732)752-6622 **Fax:** (732)752-1483
Products: Tile and related products. **SIC:** 5032 (Brick, Stone & Related Materials).

■ **10230** ■ **Tile Creations**
200 Bustleton Pke.
Feasterville, PA 19053
Phone: (215)357-2400 **Fax:** (215)364-4560
URL: http://www.tile-creations.com
Products: Ceramic, marble, and granite tile. **SIC:** 5032 (Brick, Stone & Related Materials). **Officers:** Kenneth Sonabend.

■ **10231** ■ **Tile Distributor Company Inc.**
4421 Poplar Level Rd.
Louisville, KY 40213
Phone: (502)456-2410
Free: (800)274-8453 **Fax:** (502)456-2494
URL: http://www.tiledistributor.com
Products: Ceramic tile; Setting material and tools. **SICs:** 5032 (Brick, Stone & Related Materials); 5169 (Chemicals & Allied Products Nec). **Est:** 1989. **Sales:** $2,500,000 (1999). **Emp:** 14. **Officers:** Gene Roberts, Sales & Marketing Contact; David E. King, President; Susan Samples, Customer Service Contact.

■ **10232** ■ **Tile Distributors Inc.**
3002 N Nuygant
Portland, OR 97217
Phone: (503)286-6613 **Fax:** (503)286-8201
Products: Floor coverings, including wood, vinyl, carpet, and ceramic tile. **SICs:** 5023 (Homefurnishings); 5032 (Brick, Stone & Related Materials); 5031 (Lumber, Plywood & Millwork).

■ **10233** ■ **Tile Distributors, Inc.**
333 East College St.
Florence, AL 35630
Phone: (256)766-1110
Products: Ceramic wall and floor tile. **SIC:** 5032 (Brick, Stone & Related Materials). **Est:** 1968. **Emp:** 4. **Officers:** Dossey O'Steen, Contact.

■ **10234** ■ **Tile Expressions**
1420 Granite Ln.
Modesto, CA 95351
Phone: (209)525-9337
Products: Ceramic wall and floor tile. **SIC:** 5032 (Brick, Stone & Related Materials). **Emp:** 3.

■ **10235** ■ **Tile For Less**
1640 Abilene
Aurora, CO 80012
Products: Ceramic wall and floor tile. **SIC:** 5032 (Brick, Stone & Related Materials).

■ **10236** ■ **Tile Gallery Inc.**
Rte. 130 at Brooklawn Circle
Brooklawn, NJ 08030
Phone: (609)456-4777 **Fax:** (609)456-4819
Products: Ceramic tile and related products. **SIC:** 5032 (Brick, Stone & Related Materials).

■ **10237** ■ **Tile Gallery Inc.**
1500 Woodhaven Dr.
Bensalem, PA 19020
Phone: (215)638-4130 **Fax:** (215)639-4626
Products: Ceramic wall and floor tile. **SIC:** 5032 (Brick, Stone & Related Materials). **Officers:** Kevin Maier, Contact.

■ **10238** ■ **Tile Helper Inc.**
3110 N River Rd.
River Grove, IL 60171
Phone: (708)453-6900 **Fax:** (708)453-6903
Products: Tile floor; Wall products and sundries. **SICs:** 5032 (Brick, Stone & Related Materials); 5023 (Homefurnishings).

■ **10239** ■ **Tile Inc. of Fayetteville**
646 Winslow St.
Fayetteville, NC 28306-1536
Phone: (919)484-2119 **Fax:** (919)484-4381
Products: Ceramic wall and floor tile. **SIC:** 5032 (Brick, Stone & Related Materials).

■ **10240** ■ **Tile International**
319 Waverly Oaks Rd.
Waltham, MA 02454
Phone: (781)899-8286 **Fax:** (781)893-8159
Products: Marble, granite, and ceramic tile. **SIC:** 5032 (Brick, Stone & Related Materials).

■ **10241** ■ **Tile Mart, Inc.**
1020 SE 14th St.
Hialeah, FL 33010
Phone: (305)885-9804 **Fax:** (305)885-1652
Products: Ceramic wall and floor tile. **SIC:** 5032 (Brick, Stone & Related Materials). **Officers:** Thomas E. Mayo, Contact.

■ **10242** ■ **The Tile Place**
1604 Hwy. 35
Oakhurst, NJ 07755
Phone: (732)531-0500
Products: Ceramic tile. **SIC:** 5032 (Brick, Stone & Related Materials).

■ **10243** ■ **The Tile Place**
27 Englishtown Rd.
Old Bridge, NJ 08857
Phone: (732)251-7711
Products: Ceramic tile. **SIC:** 5032 (Brick, Stone & Related Materials).

■ **10244** ■ **The Tile Place**
720 Rte. 70
Brick, NJ 08723
Phone: (732)477-4141 **Fax:** (732)477-3290
Products: Ceramic wall and floor tile. **SIC:** 5032 (Brick, Stone & Related Materials).

■ **10245** ■ **Tile Warehouse**
74-5602D Alapa St.
Kailua Kona, HI 96740
Phone: (808)329-8855
Products: Ceramic wall and floor tile. **SIC:** 5032 (Brick, Stone & Related Materials). **Officers:** Scott B. Giles, Contact.

■ 10246 ■ Tile Wholesalers of Rochester
470 Hollenbeck St.
Rochester, NY 14621
Phone: (716)544-3200 **Fax:** (716)544-0766
Products: Ceramic tiles. **SIC:** 5032 (Brick, Stone & Related Materials). **Est:** 1972.

■ 10247 ■ J.R. Tilers—Pergo Shop
11125 S Leamington Ave.
Alsip, IL 60803-6026
Phone: (708)425-2145 **Fax:** (708)425-2146
E-mail: rollerg999@aol.com
URL: http://www.angelfire.com/il/pergo/index.html
Products: Floor and wall coverings, including ceramic tile and wood. **SICs:** 5023 (Homefurnishings); 5032 (Brick, Stone & Related Materials); 5198 (Paints, Varnishes & Supplies); 5031 (Lumber, Plywood & Millwork). **Est:** 1953. **Sales:** $140,000 (2000). **Emp:** 2.
Alternate Name: J.R. #Tilers.

■ 10248 ■ Tiles For Less
1718 NE 122nd St.
Portland, OR 97230
Phone: (503)252-4127
Products: Ceramic wall and floor tile. **SIC:** 5032 (Brick, Stone & Related Materials). **Officers:** Don Benchik, Contact.

■ 10249 ■ Tiles International
6140 W Quaker St.
Orchard Park, NY 14127-2639
Phone: (716)662-4441 **Fax:** (716)662-0417
E-mail: tilesintl@aol.com
URL: http://www.tiles-international.com
Products: Ceramic wall and floor tile. **SIC:** 5032 (Brick, Stone & Related Materials). **Est:** 1954. **Emp:** 12.
Former Name: GCM International.

■ 10250 ■ Tiles Plus
139-8 Westgate Parkway
Dothan, AL 36303
Phone: (205)671-4292 **Fax:** (205)671-4292
Products: Ceramic tile, carpet, and marble flooring; Vertical and mini blinds; Architectural moldings. **SICs:** 5023 (Homefurnishings); 5031 (Lumber, Plywood & Millwork); 5032 (Brick, Stone & Related Materials).

■ 10251 ■ Tileworks
8481 Bash St., 1100
Indianapolis, IN 46250
Phone: (317)842-6641
Free: (800)473-8453 **Fax:** (317)842-6642
Products: Ceramic wall and floor tile. **SIC:** 5032 (Brick, Stone & Related Materials). **Est:** 1985. **Officers:** Marj Sparks, Manager, e-mail: msparks@netdirect.net.

■ 10252 ■ Toland Enterprises Inc.
1751 South Ln.
Mandeville, LA 70471
Phone: (504)893-9503 **Fax:** (504)893-4492
URL: http://www.tolandnet.com
Products: Floormats; Flags; Gifts and decor; Wind chimes. **SIC:** 5023 (Homefurnishings). **Emp:** 275.
Officers: David T. Sands.

■ 10253 ■ Toledo Tile
2121 N Reynolds Rd.
Toledo, OH 43615
Phone: (419)536-9321
Products: Ceramic wall and floor tile. **SIC:** 5032 (Brick, Stone & Related Materials).

■ 10254 ■ Torosian Brothers
492 Main St.
Ft. Lee, NJ 07024
Phone: (201)944-5119 **Fax:** (201)944-5131
Products: Floor coverings, including carpeting and linoleum. **SIC:** 5023 (Homefurnishings).

■ 10255 ■ Townzen Tile & Laminates
13455 Puppy Creek
Springdale, AR 72762
Phone: (501)751-4043 **Fax:** (501)751-5395
Products: Ceramic wall and floor tile. **SIC:** 5032 (Brick, Stone & Related Materials). **Officers:** Johnny Townzen, Contact.

■ 10256 ■ Trade Am International Inc.
6580 Jimmy Carter Blvd.
Norcross, GA 30071
Phone: (770)263-6144 **Fax:** (770)263-1734
Products: Rugs, carpets, textiles, and other home furnishings. **SICs:** 5023 (Homefurnishings); 5131 (Piece Goods & Notions). **Sales:** $30,600,000 (2000). **Emp:** 120. **Officers:** Ashu Ladha, President; Nick Howard, CFO.

■ 10257 ■ Travis Tile Sales
3811 Airport Rd.
Austin, TX 78722-1335
Phone: (512)478-8705 **Fax:** (512)478-8373
Products: Ceramic wall and floor tile. **SIC:** 5032 (Brick, Stone & Related Materials).

■ 10258 ■ Travis Tile Sales
10542 Sentinel Dr.
San Antonio, TX 78217-3822
Phone: (210)653-8372 **Fax:** (210)653-0805
Products: Ceramic wall and floor tile. **SIC:** 5032 (Brick, Stone & Related Materials).

■ 10259 ■ Trym-Tex, Inc.
6032 N Cutter Cir., Ste. 400
Portland, OR 97217-3900
Phone: (503)233-1181 **Fax:** (503)233-3862
Products: Floor coverings, including tile, carpets, and vinyl; Aluminum siding. **SICs:** 5023 (Homefurnishings); 5032 (Brick, Stone & Related Materials); 5033 (Roofing, Siding & Insulation).

■ 10260 ■ Twin City Marble
333 E 9th St.
Texarkana, AR 71854
Phone: (870)772-3769
Products: Ceramic tile; Custom made cultured marble. **SIC:** 5032 (Brick, Stone & Related Materials).

■ 10261 ■ Twin City Tile
34 State St.
Brewer, ME 04412
Phone: (207)989-8060 **Fax:** (207)989-6574
Products: Tile. **SIC:** 5023 (Homefurnishings). **Est:** 1995. **Sales:** $500,000 (2000). **Emp:** 2.

■ 10262 ■ Uniq Distributing Corp.
909 N Nelson St., Ste. 60
Spokane, WA 99202-3729
Phone: (509)922-1000 **Fax:** (509)682-9679
Products: Ceramic wall and floor tile; Hardwood. **SIC:** 5032 (Brick, Stone & Related Materials).

■ 10263 ■ Uniq Distributing Group
2020 Auiki St.
Honolulu, HI 96819
Phone: (808)847-6767
Products: Ceramic tile. **SIC:** 5032 (Brick, Stone & Related Materials).

■ 10264 ■ United Distributors, Inc.
20 Terry Ave.
Burlington, MA 01803-2516
Phone: (781)272-6540 **Fax:** (781)272-8630
E-mail: united@tiac.net
Products: Ceramic wall and floor tile. **SIC:** 5032 (Brick, Stone & Related Materials). **Est:** 1950. **Emp:** 26.
Officers: Donald Rober; Gregory Rober; Doug Maynes, Marketing & Sales Mgr.; Charles Randall, Human Resources Mgr.

■ 10265 ■ United Flooring Distributors Inc.
6201 Material Ave.
Loves Park, IL 61111
Phone: (815)654-8383 **Fax:** (815)654-8398
Products: Floor coverings, including ceramic tile and carpets. **SICs:** 5023 (Homefurnishings); 5032 (Brick, Stone & Related Materials).

■ 10266 ■ United Tile Company, Inc.
2350 Levy St.
Shreveport, LA 71103-3656
Phone: (318)222-5150 **Fax:** (318)222-1575
Products: Ceramic tile. **SIC:** 5032 (Brick, Stone & Related Materials).

■ 10267 ■ United Tile of LaFayette, LLC
1505 Eraste Landry Rd.
Lafayette, LA 70506
Phones: (318)234-2310 (318)234-2319
Fax: (318)232-2014
Products: Ceramic wall and floor tile. **SIC:** 5032 (Brick, Stone & Related Materials). **Officers:** Stan F. Mesinger, Contact. **Former Name:** United Tile Company, Inc.

■ 10268 ■ Valley Tile Distributors
1510 Southside Dr.
PO Box 187
Salem, VA 24153
Phone: (540)387-0300 **Fax:** (540)389-1816
Products: Ceramic tile. **SIC:** 5032 (Brick, Stone & Related Materials).

■ 10269 ■ Valley Tile & Marble
1618 S San Gabriel Blvd.
San Gabriel, CA 91776-3926
Phone: (626)572-0881 **Fax:** (626)573-0136
Products: Tile and marble. **SIC:** 5032 (Brick, Stone & Related Materials).

■ 10270 ■ Valley-Western Distributors, Inc.
9666 Telstar Ave.
El Monte, CA 91731
Phone: (626)443-1777
Free: (800)800-4577 **Fax:** (626)444-4631
Products: Carpet; Ceramic and vinyl tile; Rubber flooring; Sheet vinyl; Hardwood and laminate flooring. **SICs:** 5023 (Homefurnishings); 5031 (Lumber, Plywood & Millwork); 5032 (Brick, Stone & Related Materials). **Est:** 1951. **Officers:** Steve Carroll, President; Rob Carroll, VP of Marketing & Sales.

■ 10271 ■ Valley-Western Distributors, Inc.
4763 S Procyon
Las Vegas, NV 89103
Phone: (702)795-8284
Free: (800)800-3566 **Fax:** (702)795-4662
Products: Carpet; Ceramic and vinyl tile; Flooring including rubber, hardwood, and laminate. **SICs:** 5023 (Homefurnishings); 5031 (Lumber, Plywood & Millwork); 5032 (Brick, Stone & Related Materials). **Officers:** Steve Carroll, President; Rob Carroll, VP of Marketing & Sales.

■ 10272 ■ Valley-Western, Inc.
401 S Jay St.
San Bernardino, CA 92410
Phone: (714)885-0286
Free: (800)800-3566 **Fax:** (714)889-8515
Products: Floor coverings, including vinyl, tile, wood, and carpet. **SICs:** 5023 (Homefurnishings); 5031 (Lumber, Plywood & Millwork); 5032 (Brick, Stone & Related Materials).

■ 10273 ■ Valley-Western, Inc.
8060 Ajong Dr.
San Diego, CA 92126
Phone: (619)578-6801
Free: (800)800-6802 **Fax:** (619)578-0363
Products: Floor coverings including vinyl, tile, wood, and carpet. **SICs:** 5023 (Homefurnishings); 5031 (Lumber, Plywood & Millwork); 5032 (Brick, Stone & Related Materials).

■ 10274 ■ Vantage Industries Inc.
PO Box 43944
Atlanta, GA 30336
Phone: (404)691-9500
Free: (800)221-4329 **Fax:** (404)691-9149
Products: Non-skid industrial padding. **SIC:** 5085 (Industrial Supplies). **Est:** 1983. **Sales:** $40,000,000 (2000). **Emp:** 125. **Officers:** Robert F. Weber, President; Susan Keim, Customer Service Contact; Melisia Kidd, Dir of Human Resources.

■ 10275 ■ VC Glass Carpet Co.
801 Logan St.
Louisville, KY 40204
Phone: (502)584-5324 **Fax:** (502)583-5540
Products: Carpet. **SIC:** 5023 (Homefurnishings). **Sales:** $2,000,000 (2000). **Emp:** 12. **Officers:** Ray Glass, CEO & President.

■ **10276** ■ **Viking Distributors Inc.**
1508 28th St.
Gulfport, MS 39501
Phone: (228)868-1896
Products: Carpeting; Rugs. **SIC:** 5023
(Homefurnishings).

■ **10277** ■ **Virginia Hardwood Co.**
818 E Hammond Ln.
Phoenix, AZ 85034
Phone: (602)252-6818 **Fax:** (602)252-5463
Products: Hardwood flooring; Maple countertops.
SICs: 5023 (Homefurnishings); 5039 (Construction
Materials Nec).

■ **10278** ■ **Virginia Hardwood Co.**
241 Lombard
Oxnard, CA 93030
Phone: (805)988-6017 **Fax:** (805)988-6019
Products: Hardwood flooring. **SIC:** 5031 (Lumber,
Plywood & Millwork).

■ **10279** ■ **Virginia Hardwood Co.**
8533 Production Ave.
San Diego, CA 92121
Phone: (619)271-6890
Free: (800)326-6890 **Fax:** (619)271-5215
Products: Hardwood flooring. **SICs:** 5023
(Homefurnishings); 5031 (Lumber, Plywood &
Millwork).

■ **10280** ■ **Virginia Hardwood Co.**
1000 W Foothill Blvd.
Azusa, CA 91702
Phone: (626)815-0540 **Fax:** (626)969-5697
Products: Hardwood flooring. **SIC:** 5031 (Lumber,
Plywood & Millwork). **Sales:** $26,800,000 (2000). **Emp:**
80. **Officers:** David V. Ferrari, President; Steve Gores,
Vice President.

■ **10281** ■ **Virginia Tile Co.**
24404 Indoplex Cir.
Farmington Hills, MI 48335-2526
Phone: (248)476-7850 **Fax:** (248)476-7854
Products: Ceramic wall and floor tile. **SIC:** 5032 (Brick,
Stone & Related Materials).

■ **10282** ■ **Virginia Tile Co.**
6575 19 Mile Rd.
Sterling Heights, MI 48314-2116
Fax: (810)254-9631
Products: Ceramic wall and floor tile. **SIC:** 5032 (Brick,
Stone & Related Materials).

■ **10283** ■ **Wade Distributors, Inc.**
1150 N Beltline Hwy.
Mobile, AL 36617-1504
Phone: (205)476-1140 **Fax:** (205)479-3716
Products: Ceramic wall and floor tile. **SIC:** 5032 (Brick,
Stone & Related Materials).

■ **10284** ■ **Walton Wholesale Corp.**
PO Box 38-1983
Miami, FL 33138
Phone: (305)757-0348 **Fax:** (305)751-0586
Products: Floor coverings, including vinyl, carpet,
wood, and tile. **SICs:** 5023 (Homefurnishings); 5031
(Lumber, Plywood & Millwork); 5032 (Brick, Stone &
Related Materials).

■ **10285** ■ **Wanke Cascade**
1030 West 2610 South
Salt Lake City, UT 84119-2434
Phone: (801)972-1391
Products: Ceramic wall and floor tile. **SIC:** 5032 (Brick,
Stone & Related Materials).

■ **10286** ■ **Wanke Cascade**
6330 N Cutter Cir.
Portland, OR 97217
Phone: (503)289-8609 **Fax:** (503)285-5640
Products: Floor coverings. **SIC:** 5023
(Homefurnishings). **Sales:** $37,000,000 (1994). **Emp:**
130. **Officers:** Brian Radditz, President; Art Conner,
VP of Finance.

■ **10287** ■ **Wayne Tile Co.**
Rt. 23 N
Hamburg, NJ 07419
Phone: (973)875-7400 **Fax:** (973)875-1439
Products: Ceramic tile. **SIC:** 5032 (Brick, Stone &
Related Materials).

■ **10288** ■ **Wayne Tile Co.**
333 Rt. 46 W
Rockaway, NJ 07866
Phone: (973)625-3209 **Fax:** (973)625-2084
Products: Tile and related products. **SIC:** 5032 (Brick,
Stone & Related Materials).

■ **10289** ■ **Wayne Tile Co.**
1459 Rte. 23 S
Wayne, NJ 07470
Phone: (973)694-5480
Free: (800)739-8453 **Fax:** (973)694-5455
Products: Ceramic wall and floor tile. **SIC:** 5032 (Brick,
Stone & Related Materials). **Est:** 1953. **Emp:** 20.
Officers: Mike Westra, Contact; Tim Westra, Contact.

■ **10290** ■ **H.J. Weber Co.**
3140 W 25th St.
Cleveland, OH 44109
Phone: (216)351-1200
Free: (800)362-2270 **Fax:** (216)351-4084
Products: Floor covering. **SIC:** 5023
(Homefurnishings). **Est:** 1969. **Officers:** Henry L.
Weber.

■ **10291** ■ **Westcott Worldwide**
11708 S Mayfield Ave.
Worth, IL 60482
Phone: (708)389-7300
Products: Ceramic tile. **SIC:** 5032 (Brick, Stone &
Related Materials).

■ **10292** ■ **Western Design Tile**
9926 Horn Rd., Ste. I
Sacramento, CA 95827-1960
Phone: (916)366-8453 **Fax:** (916)366-8480
Products: Ceramic wall and floor tile. **SIC:** 5032 (Brick,
Stone & Related Materials).

■ **10293** ■ **Western Pacific Interior**
73-5564 Olowalu St.
Kailua Kona, HI 96740
Phone: (808)329-6602 **Fax:** (808)329-6605
Products: Carpet and area rugs; Ceramic tile; Paint;
Tools; Sheet vinyl. **SICs:** 5023 (Homefurnishings);
5032 (Brick, Stone & Related Materials); 5072
(Hardware); 5198 (Paints, Varnishes & Supplies).

■ **10294** ■ **Western Tile Design Center**
1290 Diamond Way
Concord, CA 94520
Phone: (925)671-0145 **Fax:** (925)671-7313
URL: http://www.westerntiledesign.com
Products: Ceramic wall and floor tile. **SIC:** 5032 (Brick,
Stone & Related Materials). **Est:** 1940. **Emp:** 8.
Officers: David Miller, President. **Former Name:**
Western Tile Distributors.

■ **10295** ■ **Western Tile Design Center (Dublin)**
11825 Dublin Blvd.
Dublin, CA 94568
Phone: (925)829-5544 **Fax:** (925)829-5592
URL: http://www.westerntiledesign.com
Products: Ceramic wall and floor tile including,
ceramica catalina, cepac, american universal,
eurowest, jasba, latco, pan american, porcelanosa,
santa fe, tau, westminster. **SIC:** 5032 (Brick, Stone &
Related Materials). **Est:** 1940. **Emp:** 3. **Officers:** David
Miller, President.

■ **10296** ■ **Western Tile Santa Rosa, Inc.**
3780 Santa Rosa Ave.
Santa Rosa, CA 95407-8287
Phone: (707)585-1501 **Fax:** (707)584-1237
Products: Ceramic wall and floor tile; Natural stone
and cabinets. **SIC:** 5032 (Brick, Stone & Related
Materials). **Est:** 1940. **Sales:** $4,000,000 (2000). **Emp:**
20. **Officers:** Jess Flores, President. **Former Name:**
Western Tile Distributors. **Doing Business As:**
Western Tile & Kitchen Design.

■ **10297** ■ **Westside Tile Co.**
6408 Depot Dr.
Waco, TX 76712
Phone: (254)776-1122
Products: Ceramic wall and floor tile. **SIC:** 5032 (Brick,
Stone & Related Materials). **Officers:** Frank Hulke,
Contact.

■ **10298** ■ **Wholesale Ceramic Tile**
2885 Immanuel Rd.
Greensboro, NC 27407
Phone: (910)292-0130 **Fax:** (910)292-0131
Products: Ceramic and marble tile. **SIC:** 5032 (Brick,
Stone & Related Materials).

■ **10299** ■ **Wiggins Concrete Products, Inc.**
100 River St.
Springfield, VT 05156-2909
Phone: (802)886-8326 **Fax:** (802)886-8313
Products: Ceramic wall and floor tile. **SIC:** 5032 (Brick,
Stone & Related Materials).

■ **10300** ■ **Elias Wilf Corp.**
10234 S Dolfield Rd.
Owings Mills, MD 21117
Phone: (410)363-2400
Free: (800)727-9453 **Fax:** (410)363-2409
Products: Floor coverings, including vinyl, ceramic,
carpets, and wood. **SICs:** 5023 (Homefurnishings);
5031 (Lumber, Plywood & Millwork); 5032 (Brick, Stone
& Related Materials).

■ **10301** ■ **Elias Wilf Corp.**
12700 Townsend Rd.
Philadelphia, PA 19154
Phone: (215)673-9161
Free: (800)627-9453 **Fax:** (215)673-9096
Products: Carpet. **SIC:** 5023 (Homefurnishings).

■ **10302** ■ **Winburn Tile**
1709 E 9th St.
Little Rock, AR 72202
Phone: (501)375-7251 **Fax:** (501)372-4325
E-mail: customerservice@winburntile.com
URL: http://www.winburntile.com
Products: Clay and ceramic tile. **SIC:** 5032 (Brick,
Stone & Related Materials). **Est:** 1947. **Sales:**
$10,000,000 (1999). **Emp:** 125. **Former Name:**
Winburn Tile Supply.

■ **10303** ■ **Wisconsin Brick & Block Corp.**
6399 Nesbitt Rd.
Madison, Oahu, 53719-1817
Phone: (608)845-8636 **Fax:** (608)845-8630
Products: Ceramic wall and floor tile. **SIC:** 5032 (Brick,
Stone & Related Materials).

■ **10304** ■ **W.N.C. Tile Distributors**
508 Swannanoa River Rd.
Asheville, NC 28805
Phone: (704)298-3251 **Fax:** (704)298-9343
Products: Ceramic tile. **SIC:** 5032 (Brick, Stone &
Related Materials).

■ **10305** ■ **Wood Floor Wholesalers**
5151 Convoy, Ste. B
San Diego, CA 92111
Phone: (619)467-9663 **Fax:** (619)467-9665
Products: Hardwood flooring and related products.
SIC: 5031 (Lumber, Plywood & Millwork).

■ **10306** ■ **Wood Floor Wholesalers**
1541 S Ritchey
Santa Ana, CA 92705
Phone: (714)542-9900 **Fax:** (714)542-8514
Products: Hardwood flooring and related products.
SIC: 5031 (Lumber, Plywood & Millwork).

■ **10307** ■ **Wood Flooring Distributors**
2341 Industrial Pkwy. W
Hayward, CA 94545
Phone: (510)293-3939 **Fax:** (510)293-2055
Products: Hardwood flooring. **SIC:** 5031 (Lumber,
Plywood & Millwork).

■ **10308** ■ **World Carpets Inc.**
PO Box 1448
Dalton, GA 30722
Phone: (706)278-8000 **Fax:** (706)278-9454
Products: Carpets. **SIC:** 5023 (Homefurnishings).

Sales: $275,000,000 (2000). **Emp:** 2,000. **Officers:** Shaheen Shaheen.

■ **10309** ■ **Yeager Hardware**
1610 E Main St.
Van Buren, AR 72956
Phone: (501)474-5278
Products: Ceramic wall and floor tile. **SIC:** 5032 (Brick, Stone & Related Materials). **Officers:** Bill Glass, Contact.

■ **10310** ■ **Zumpano Enterprises, Inc.**
764 Miami Cir., NE, Ste. 100
Atlanta, GA 30324-5909
Phone: (404)233-2943
Products: Ceramic tile. **SIC:** 5032 (Brick, Stone & Related Materials).

■ **10311** ■ **Zumpano Enterprises, Inc.**
119 Ben Burton Rd.
Bogart, GA 30622
Phone: (404)549-5455
Products: Ceramic tile. **SIC:** 5032 (Brick, Stone & Related Materials).

■ **10312** ■ **Zumpano Enterprises, Inc.**
7411 Tara Blvd.
Jonesboro, GA 30236
Phone: (404)471-0666
Products: Ceramic tile. **SIC:** 5032 (Brick, Stone & Related Materials).

■ **10313** ■ **Zumpano Enterprises, Inc.**
6354 Warren Dr.
Norcross, GA 30093
Phone: (770)449-3528   **Fax:** (770)446-0294
Products: Ceramic tile; Stone. **SIC:** 5032 (Brick, Stone & Related Materials). **Est:** 1971. **Sales:** $13,000,000 (2000). **Emp:** 60. **Officers:** James J. Zumpano, CEO.

(17) Food

Entries in this section are arranged alphabetically by company name. When the company name is a personal name, the company name is alphabetized by the surname unless the first name or initial(s) are part of a trade name. See the User's Guide at the front of this directory for additional information.

■ **10314** ■ **3 Springs Water Co.**
1800 Pine Run Rd.
Wilkes Barre, PA 18702-9419
Phone: (717)823-7019 **Fax:** (717)822-6177
Products: Soft drinks. **SIC:** 5149 (Groceries & Related Products Nec).

■ **10315** ■ **A-1 International Foods**
5560 E Slauson Ave.
City of Commerce, CA 90040
Phone: (213)722-2100 **Fax:** (213)722-0100
Products: Food. **SIC:** 5141 (Groceries—General Line).

■ **10316** ■ **A. Camacho Inc.**
2502 Walden Woods Dr.
Plant City, FL 33566
Phone: (813)305-4534
Free: (800)881-4534 **Fax:** (813)305-4545
Products: Spanish olives, olive oil and fresh grated cheeses; Preserves. **SICs:** 5149 (Groceries & Related Products Nec); 5143 (Dairy Products Except Dried or Canned). **Sales:** $20,000,000 (2000). **Emp:** 40. **Officers:** Merle Hanneken, President; Bob Fiddelke, VP of Distribution and Procurement.

■ **10317** ■ **Abbaco Inc.**
230 5th Ave., Ste. 1409
New York, NY 10001
Phone: (212)679-4550 **Fax:** (212)679-5395
Products: French foods; Soaps; Tarnish remover. **SICs:** 5141 (Groceries—General Line); 5122 (Drugs, Proprietaries & Sundries); 5169 (Chemicals & Allied Products Nec). **Sales:** $500,000 (2000). **Emp:** 3. **Officers:** Allan I. Adell, President.

■ **10318** ■ **Abbott's Premium Ice Cream Inc.**
PO Box 411
Conway, NH 03818
Phone: (603)356-2344
Products: Ice cream. **SIC:** 5143 (Dairy Products Except Dried or Canned). **Est:** 1950. **Sales:** $18,000,000 (2000). **Emp:** 13. **Officers:** Charles S. Marshall, CEO.

■ **10319** ■ **ABC Coffee Co.**
24691 Telegraph Rd.
Southfield, MI 48034
Phone: (248)352-1222 **Fax:** (248)352-4869
Products: Coffee; Juice; Snacks; Chocolate; Sugar; Soup cups; Paper products; Spoons and forks. **SICs:** 5149 (Groceries & Related Products Nec); 5113 (Industrial & Personal Service Paper). **Est:** 1966. **Sales:** $1,500,000 (2000). **Emp:** 10. **Officers:** Tony Nicolaides, President.

■ **10320** ■ **Acme Food Sales Inc.**
5940 1st Ave. S
Seattle, WA 98108-3248
Phone: (206)762-5150 **Fax:** (206)762-8629
Products: Canned foods, including mushrooms and tuna. **SIC:** 5149 (Groceries & Related Products Nec). **Emp:** 49.

■ **10321** ■ **Acosta-PMI St. Louis Div.**
3171 Riverport Tech. Ct. Dr.
Maryland Heights, MO 63043
Phone: (314)991-3992 **Fax:** (314)991-1504
URL: http://www.acosta-pmi.com
Products: Food. **SIC:** 5141 (Groceries—General Line). **Est:** 1974. **Emp:** 125. **Officers:** Doug Eisenhart, VP & General Mgr. **Alternate Name:** PMI-Eisenhart St. Louis Div.

■ **10322** ■ **Acosta Sales Co.**
6850 Belfort Oaks Pl.
Jacksonville, FL 32216
Phone: (904)281-9800 **Fax:** (904)281-9966
Products: Food broker. **SICs:** 5141 (Groceries—General Line); 5142 (Packaged Frozen Foods). **Sales:** $70,000,000 (1999). **Emp:** 110. **Officers:** Gary Schartrand, CEO; Mike Diaz, CFO.

■ **10323** ■ **Adams Brothers Produce Company Inc.**
PO Box 2682
Birmingham, AL 35202
Phone: (205)323-2455
Products: Fresh produce. **SIC:** 5148 (Fresh Fruits & Vegetables). **Est:** 1903. **Sales:** $21,000,000 (2000). **Emp:** 90. **Officers:** Carl Adams Jr., Chairman of the Board.

■ **10324** ■ **Adams Brothers Produce Company of Tuscaloosa Inc.**
PO Box 2474
Tuscaloosa, AL 35403
Phone: (205)758-2891
Products: Fruits; Vegetables. **SIC:** 5148 (Fresh Fruits & Vegetables). **Est:** 1981. **Sales:** $2,000,000 (2000). **Emp:** 12. **Officers:** Gray Cayton, General Mgr.; Curtis Diffy, Dir. of Marketing & Sales; Eva Patton, Dir. of Data Processing.

■ **10325** ■ **Adderton Brokerage Co.**
140 Weldon Pkwy.
Maryland Heights, MO 63043-3102
Phone: (314)298-7000
Products: Food. **SIC:** 5141 (Groceries—General Line). **Sales:** $7,000,000 (2000). **Emp:** 15. **Officers:** Chris Adderton, President.

■ **10326** ■ **ADM-Growmark Inc.**
PO Box 1470
Decatur, IL 62525
Phone: (217)424-5900 **Fax:** (217)424-5990
Products: Grain; River freight transportation of grain. **SIC:** 5153 (Grain & Field Beans). **Sales:** $584,000,000 (2000). **Emp:** 650. **Officers:** Burnell Kraft, President.

■ **10327** ■ **Admiral Exchange Company Inc.**
1443 Union St.
San Diego, CA 92101
Phone: (619)239-2165 **Fax:** (619)239-1843
Products: Semi-perishable food products. **SIC:** 5141 (Groceries—General Line). **Sales:** $6,000,000 (2000). **Emp:** 20. **Officers:** Dean L. Edwards, President; Douglas A. Edwards, VP & General Mgr.

■ **10328** ■ **Adohr Farms Inc.**
PO Box 1945
Santa Ana, CA 92702
Phone: (714)775-7600 **Fax:** (714)265-0401
Products: Dairy products, including ice cream, milk, and cheese. **SIC:** 5143 (Dairy Products Except Dried or Canned). **Est:** 1990. **Sales:** $120,000,000 (2000). **Emp:** 600. **Officers:** Louis Stremick, President; Michael Malone, Controller; Michael Greenwald, Dir. of Marketing; Tayna Rosenblum, Dir. of Data Processing; Francine Cronin, Dir of Human Resources.

■ **10329** ■ **Advanced Specialties**
974 E 650 Rd.
Lawrence, KS 66047
Phone: (785)748-9847 **Fax:** (785)748-9847
Products: Food preparations; Dried and dehydrated products; Potatoes; Egg noodle products; Health foods; Spices; Produce. **SICs:** 5149 (Groceries & Related Products Nec); 5148 (Fresh Fruits & Vegetables). **Est:** 1982. **Emp:** 4. **Officers:** Mike Fangman, Owner.

■ **10330** ■ **Advantage Crown**
11875 Dublin Blvd., Ste. C 258
Dublin, CA 94568-2834
Phone: (510)828-0126 **Fax:** (510)828-6935
Products: Groceries. **SICs:** 5141 (Groceries—General Line); 5149 (Groceries & Related Products Nec). **Est:** 1972. **Emp:** 75. **Officers:** Scott Presnall, President; Thomas H. Rickard Sr.

■ **10331** ■ **Advantage Food Marketing Corp.**
PO Box 367
Roslyn Heights, NY 11577
Phone: (516)625-2600
Free: (800)645-6367 **Fax:** (516)625-2612
Products: Food. **SICs:** 5141 (Groceries—General Line); 5142 (Packaged Frozen Foods). **Sales:** $35,000,000 (2000). **Emp:** 40. **Officers:** Jerome B. Rounds, President; David Kalman, Exec. VP of Finance.

■ **10332** ■ **Advantage Sales and Marketing**
18851 Bardeen Ave.
Irvine, CA 92612-1520
Phone: (949)833-1200
Products: Food broker. **SICs:** 5141 (Groceries—General Line); 5142 (Packaged Frozen Foods). **Sales:** $18,000,000,000 (2000). **Emp:** 12,000. **Officers:** Sonny King, President.

■ **10333** ■ **Affiliated Food Stores Inc.**
PO Box 2938
Abilene, OK 79604-2938
Products: Groceries. **SIC:** 5141 (Groceries—General Line). **Sales:** $260,000,000 (2000). **Emp:** 280. **Officers:** Robert Rippley, President & CEO; Bruce Hutto, Exec. VP; J. Robert Jones, Sales/Marketing Contact; Jane Brewer, Human Resources Contact.

■ **10334** ■ **Affiliated Food Stores Inc. (Tulsa, Oklahoma)**
PO Box 629
Tulsa, OK 74101
Phone: (918)446-5531 **Fax:** (918)445-9135
Products: General line of groceries. **SIC:** 5141

(Groceries—General Line). **Sales:** $260,000,000 (2000). **Emp:** 300. **Officers:** Robert Rippley, CEO & President; Karl Wolfenberger, Controller.

■ **10335** ■ **Affiliated Foods Cooperative Inc.**
PO Box 1067
Norfolk, NE 68702-1067
Phone: (402)371-0555 **Fax:** (402)371-1884
URL: http://www.afnorfolk.com
Products: General line groceries, fresh fruits and vegetables and meat. **SICs:** 5141 (Groceries—General Line); 5148 (Fresh Fruits & Vegetables); 5147 (Meats & Meat Products). **Sales:** $700,000,000 (2000). **Emp:** 700. **Officers:** Virgil Froehlich, President; Duane Severson, VP & Controller.

■ **10336** ■ **Affiliated Foods Inc.**
PO Box 30300
Amarillo, TX 79120
Phone: (806)372-1404 **Fax:** (806)374-2655
Products: Groceries, including meats, produce, dairy products, and bakery products. **SICs:** 5141 (Groceries—General Line); 5122 (Drugs, Proprietaries & Sundries). **Est:** 1946. **Sales:** $600,000,000 (2000). **Emp:** 900. **Officers:** Benny Cooper, President; George Lankford, Exec. VP; Wayne Smith, CFO; Mark Griffin, Dir. of Marketing; Merle Voigt, Dir of Human Resources.

■ **10337** ■ **Affiliated Foods Inc.**
PO Box 30300
Amarillo, TX 79120
Phone: (806)372-1404 **Fax:** (806)374-2655
Products: Food. **SIC:** 5141 (Groceries—General Line). **Sales:** $600,000,000 (2000). **Emp:** 900.

■ **10338** ■ **Affiliated Foods Midwest**
PO Box 1067
Norfolk, NE 68701
Phone: (402)371-0555 **Fax:** (402)371-1884
Products: Food; General line groceries. **SICs:** 5149 (Groceries & Related Products Nec); 5141 (Groceries—General Line). **Former Name:** Affiliated Foods Inc.

■ **10339** ■ **Affiliated Foods Southwest Inc.**
PO Box 3627
Little Rock, AR 72203
Phone: (501)455-3590 **Fax:** (501)455-6575
Products: Groceries. **SIC:** 5141 (Groceries—General Line). **Est:** 1957. **Sales:** $441,000,000 (2000). **Emp:** 925. **Officers:** Jerry Davis, President & COO; John Mills, CFO; Al Miller, VP of Marketing; Ron Rivers, Dir. of Systems; Robert Southern, Dir of Personnel.

■ **10340** ■ **Affy Tapple Inc.**
7110 N Clark St.
Chicago, IL 60626
Phone: (773)338-1100
Products: Candy; Food preparations; Fresh fruits. **SICs:** 5145 (Confectionery); 5148 (Fresh Fruits & Vegetables); 5149 (Groceries & Related Products Nec). **Sales:** $2,000,000 (2000). **Emp:** 49. **Officers:** Edna Kastrup.

■ **10341** ■ **AFI Food Service Distributors Inc.**
PO Box 6070
Elizabeth, NJ 07207-6070
Phone: (908)629-1800 **Fax:** (908)629-0500
URL: http://www.afifoods.com
Products: Food for restaurants, hospitals, and schools. **SIC:** 5141 (Groceries—General Line). **Est:** 1955. **Emp:** 300. **Officers:** Steven Spinner, President.

■ **10342** ■ **Ag Partners Co. Cannon Falls Div.**
PO Box 308
Cannon Falls, MN 55009
Phone: (507)263-4651
Products: Livestock and farm products. **SIC:** 5153 (Grain & Field Beans). **Sales:** $17,000,000 (2000). **Emp:** 10.

■ **10343** ■ **Agar Supply Company Inc.**
1100 Massachusetts Ave.
Boston, MA 02125
Phone: (617)442-8989 **Fax:** (617)442-3277
Products: Beef, pork, lamb, veal, sausage, poultry, fish, and produce. **SICs:** 5147 (Meats & Meat Products); 5144 (Poultry & Poultry Products); 5146 (Fish & Seafoods). **Sales:** $400,000,000 (2000). **Emp:** 350. **Officers:** Alan Bressler, President; Norman Chamberlin, VP of Finance.

■ **10344** ■ **Agco Inc.**
PO Box 668
Russell, KS 67665
Phone: (785)483-2128 **Fax:** (785)483-4872
Products: Grain, field beans, feeds, fertilizers and agricultural chemicals. Gasoline service station. **SICs:** 5153 (Grain & Field Beans); 5191 (Farm Supplies). **Sales:** $15,000,000 (2000). **Emp:** 25. **Officers:** Bill Burton, General Mgr.

■ **10345** ■ **Agri-Empire**
PO Box 490
San Jacinto, CA 92581
Phone: (909)654-7311 **Fax:** (909)654-7639
Products: Potatoes. **SIC:** 5148 (Fresh Fruits & Vegetables). **Est:** 1970. **Sales:** $75,000,000 (2000). **Emp:** 200. **Officers:** Larry Minor, President; Wayne Minor, Vice President; Mike Haddad, Dir. of Marketing; Jeff Burke, Controller.

■ **10346** ■ **Agricultural Survey Development Associates**
380 Tomkins Ct.
Gilroy, CA 95020
Phone: (408)848-1090
Products: Nuts; Dried fruits and vegetables. **SICs:** 5148 (Fresh Fruits & Vegetables); 5159 (Farm-Product Raw Materials Nec); 5145 (Confectionery). **Officers:** Steven R. Muir, Associate.

■ **10347** ■ **Agrimor**
5861 SW 99th Lane
Ft. Lauderdale, FL 33328
Phone: (954)434-9848 **Fax:** (954)680-6974
Products: Fresh citrus fruits; Fresh strawberries; Dried fruits; Nuts, including almonds; Fresh tropical fruits and melons. **SICs:** 5148 (Fresh Fruits & Vegetables); 5149 (Groceries & Related Products Nec); 5159 (Farm-Product Raw Materials Nec). **Officers:** Bernardo Levinstein, Mgr. Dir.

■ **10348** ■ **Aimonetto and Sons, Inc.**
5950 6th Ave. S, Ste. 204
Seattle, WA 98108-3305
Phone: (206)767-2777 **Fax:** (206)762-6792
Products: Dairy products. **SIC:** 5143 (Dairy Products Except Dried or Canned). **Est:** 1977. **Emp:** 15. **Officers:** James Aimonetto, President & CEO, e-mail: jaimonetto@aimonetto.com. **Former Name:** JLA Distributors Inc.

■ **10349** ■ **AIPC**
1000 Italian Way
Excelsior Springs, MO 64024
Phone: (816)637-6400 **Fax:** (816)637-6416
Products: Pasta. **SIC:** 5149 (Groceries & Related Products Nec). **Sales:** $75,000,000 (2000). **Emp:** 499. **Officers:** Richard Thompson; Tim Webster.

■ **10350** ■ **Ajinomoto U.S.A. Inc.**
Country Club Plz.
115 W Century Rd.
Paramus, NJ 07652-1432
Phone: (201)261-1789
Free: (800)456-4666 **Fax:** (201)261-6871
URL: http://www.ajinomoto-usa.com
Products: Food. **SIC:** 5141 (Groceries—General Line). **Est:** 1956. **Sales:** $150,000,000 (2000). **Emp:** 264. **Officers:** Yoichi Kobayashi, President; Koji Fujitani, Sr. VP; Tom Atwood, Group VP.

■ **10351** ■ **Alabama Food Group Inc.**
P.O. Drawer 1207
Alexander City, AL 35011-1207
Phone: (256)234-5071
Free: (800)634-8668 **Fax:** (256)329-2812
Products: Groceries including frozen and fresh produce. **SICs:** 5142 (Packaged Frozen Foods); 5148 (Fresh Fruits & Vegetables); 5141 (Groceries—General Line). **Sales:** $18,000,000 (2000). **Emp:** 55. **Officers:** Hugh A. Neighbors III, President.

■ **10352** ■ **Alabama Institutional Foods Inc.**
1801 39th St.
PO Box 1420
Tuscaloosa, AL 35403
Phone: (205)345-0474 **Fax:** (205)345-1475
Products: Meat; Vegetables; Seafood; Paper products. **SICs:** 5147 (Meats & Meat Products); 5113 (Industrial & Personal Service Paper); 5146 (Fish & Seafoods); 5148 (Fresh Fruits & Vegetables). **Emp:** 50.

■ **10353** ■ **Alakef Coffee Roasters Inc.**
1600 London Rd.
Duluth, MN 55812
Phone: (218)724-6849
Products: Specialty roasted coffee beans. **SIC:** 5149 (Groceries & Related Products Nec).

■ **10354** ■ **Alaskan Glacier Seafoods**
PO Box 209
Petersburg, AK 99833
Phone: (907)772-3333
Products: Seafood including pink shrimp, salmon, and crab. **SIC:** 5142 (Packaged Frozen Foods).

■ **10355** ■ **Alaskan Gold Seafood Inc.**
PO Box 806
Soldotna, AK 99669
Phone: (907)262-5797 **Fax:** (907)262-6860
Products: Canned, cured, and smoked seafood; Fresh and frozen seafoods. **SICs:** 5146 (Fish & Seafoods); 5142 (Packaged Frozen Foods). **Officers:** Steven D. Ellis, General Mgr.

■ **10356** ■ **Albaco Foods Inc.**
Rte. 1, Box 744
Alma, GA 31510-9801
Phone: (912)632-7213 **Fax:** (912)632-7215
Products: Bakery products. **SIC:** 5149 (Groceries & Related Products Nec). **Sales:** $10,000,000 (2000). **Emp:** 49. **Officers:** Loyce Sherrow.

■ **10357** ■ **Albert Poultry Co. Inc.**
318 10th Ave.
Columbus, GA 31901-3310
Phone: (706)323-6096 **Fax:** (706)322-5115
Products: Foods. **SICs:** 5141 (Groceries—General Line); 5147 (Meats & Meat Products); 5144 (Poultry & Poultry Products). **Emp:** 8.

■ **10358** ■ **Albert W. Sisk and Son Inc.**
3601 Choptawk Rd.
PO Box 70
Preston, MD 21655
Phone: (410)673-7111 **Fax:** (410)673-7360
Products: Food products; Dry commodities. **SIC:** 5149 (Groceries & Related Products Nec). **Est:** 1891. **Sales:** $8,000,000 (2000). **Emp:** 9. **Officers:** Al Turner, President & Treasurer, e-mail: alturn@awsisk.com.

■ **10359** ■ **Albert's Organics Inc.**
3268 E Vernon Ave.
Vernon, CA 90058
Phone: (323)587-6367 **Fax:** (323)587-6567
Products: Organic produce, nuts and dairy products. **SICs:** 5148 (Fresh Fruits & Vegetables); 5145 (Confectionery); 5149 (Groceries & Related Products Nec). **Sales:** $50,000,000 (2000). **Emp:** 73. **Officers:** Albert Lusk, President; Bob Paradise, Controller.

■ **10360** ■ **Alderfer, Inc.**
PO Box 2
382 Main St.
Harleysville, PA 19438
Phone: (215)256-8818
Free: (800)341-1121 **Fax:** (215)256-6120
URL: http://www.alderfermeats.com
Products: Natural wood smoked meats; Beef, pork, and turkey products. **SIC:** 5147 (Meats & Meat Products). **Est:** 1922. **Emp:** 65. **Officers:** John U. Young, President; Scott W. Moyer, Sales Mgr. **Former Name:** Alderfer Bologna Inc.

■ **10361** ■ **Alex City Provision Inc.**
PO Box 1207
Alexander City, AL 35011
Phone: (256)234-5071
E-mail: acprn@lakemartin.net
Products: Food, including produce, canned goods, and frozen foods. **SICs:** 5141 (Groceries—General

Line); 5148 (Fresh Fruits & Vegetables); 5149 (Groceries & Related Products Nec); 5142 (Packaged Frozen Foods). **Est:** 1946. **Sales:** $30,000,000 (2000). **Emp:** 45. **Officers:** Hugh A. Neighbors III, President.

■ **10362** ■ **Alex Lee Inc.**
PO Box 800
Hickory, NC 28603
Phone: (828)323-4424   **Fax:** (828)323-4435
Products: General groceries. **SIC:** 5141 (Groceries—General Line). **Sales:** $1,516,000,000 (2000). **Emp:** 7,432. **Officers:** Boyd L. George, CEO & Chairman of the Board; Ronald W. Knedlik, Sr. VP of Finance & Admin.

■ **10363** ■ **Alexander Koetting Poole and Buehrle Inc.**
737 Goddard Ave.
Chesterfield, MO 63005
Phone: (314)537-5200   **Fax:** (314)537-1232
Products: Food. **SIC:** 5141 (Groceries—General Line). **Sales:** $24,000,000 (2000). **Emp:** 20. **Officers:** James Alexander, President; David Poole, Vice President.

■ **10364** ■ **Alimenta (USA) Inc.**
100 N Point Cir., No. 450
Alpharetta, GA 30022-8230
Phone: (404)255-5050   **Fax:** (404)250-9471
Products: Peanut cake and meal; Peanut oil. **SICs:** 5149 (Groceries & Related Products Nec); 5199 (Nondurable Goods Nec). **Officers:** Larry J. Lemley, Vice President.

■ **10365** ■ **All Kitchens Inc.**
209 W Main St.
Boise, ID 83702
Phone: (208)336-7003   **Fax:** (208)338-7180
Products: Food. **SIC:** 5141 (Groceries—General Line). **Sales:** $20,000,000 (2000). **Emp:** 40. **Officers:** Harry Reifschneider, President.

■ **10366** ■ **All Seas Wholesale Inc.**
2414 San Bruno Ave.
San Francisco, CA 94134-1503
Phone: (415)468-4800   **Fax:** (415)468-5570
Products: Seafood. **SIC:** 5146 (Fish & Seafoods). **Est:** 1985. **Sales:** $9,000,000 (2000). **Emp:** 23. **Officers:** Richard Howse, President.

■ **10367** ■ **All Season's Kitchen L.L.C.**
PO Box 64887
Burlington, VT 05406-4887
Phone: (802)865-0412
Products: Flavored cream cheese, bagel spreads, salsa, and tortilla chips. **SICs:** 5149 (Groceries & Related Products Nec); 5145 (Confectionery). **Sales:** $1,000,000 (2000). **Emp:** 3. **Officers:** Bill Davis, President.

■ **10368** ■ **Allegiance Brokerage Co.**
PO Drawer 410529
Charlotte, NC 28241-0529
Phone: (704)529-1176
Products: Food. **SICs:** 5141 (Groceries—General Line); 5142 (Packaged Frozen Foods). **Sales:** $110,000,000 (2000). **Emp:** 210. **Officers:** Terry Pietsch, CEO & President.

■ **10369** ■ **Allegro Coffee Co.**
1930 Central Ave.
Boulder, CO 80301
Phone: (303)444-4844
Free: (800)666-4869   **Fax:** (303)449-5259
E-mail: prodinfo@allegro-coffee.com
URL: http://www.allegro-coffee.com
Products: Coffee. **SIC:** 5149 (Groceries & Related Products Nec). **Est:** 1977. **Sales:** $13,000,000 (2000). **Emp:** 75. **Officers:** Terry Tierney, President; Richard Kessler, VP of Sales.

■ **10370** ■ **Allen Foods Inc.**
8543 Page Ave.
St. Louis, MO 63114
Phone: (314)426-4100   **Fax:** (314)426-0391
Products: Meat; Dairy products; Produce; Cleaning products. **SICs:** 5147 (Meats & Meat Products); 5143 (Dairy Products Except Dried or Canned); 5148 (Fresh Fruits & Vegetables); 5169 (Chemicals & Allied Products Nec). **Est:** 1901. **Sales:** $120,000,000

(2000). **Emp:** 540. **Officers:** Stanley Allen, President; Angelo Nebuloni, CFO; Michael May, Dir. of Marketing.

■ **10371** ■ **Alliance Foods Inc.**
PO Box 339
Coldwater, MI 49036
Phone: (517)278-2396   **Fax:** (517)278-7936
Products: Food broker. **SIC:** 5141 (Groceries—General Line). **Sales:** $105,200,000 (2000). **Emp:** 200. **Officers:** James Erickson, President; Craig Lynch, Controller.

■ **10372** ■ **Alliant Foodservice, Inc.**
7598 NW 6th Ave.
Boca Raton, FL 33487
Phone: (561)994-8500
Free: (800)331-6569   **Fax:** (561)995-4440
Products: Frozen foods; Seafood; Beverages. **SICs:** 5143 (Dairy Products Except Dried or Canned); 5146 (Fish & Seafoods); 5149 (Groceries & Related Products Nec). **Sales:** $140,000,000 (2000). **Emp:** 237. **Officers:** Pete Chiappetta, President; George Baldino, VP of Operations; Steve Humphreys, VP of Sales; Allison Key, VP of Finance; Marilou Lotito, Human Resources Mgr.; Tim Marten, VP Procurement; Barry Rubin, Marketing Mgr.

■ **10373** ■ **Alliant Foodservice Inc.**
12000 Crown Pt. Dr., Ste. 125
San Antonio, TX 78233
Phone: (210)657-6901   **Fax:** (210)657-0238
Products: Groceries, including produce and frozen goods. **SIC:** 5141 (Groceries—General Line).

■ **10374** ■ **Alliant Foodservice Inc.**
7598 NW 6th Ave.
Boca Raton, FL 33487
Phone: (561)994-8500
Free: (800)331-6569   **Fax:** (561)995-4440
Products: Food. **SIC:** 5143 (Dairy Products Except Dried or Canned). **Sales:** $140,000,000 (2000). **Emp:** 237.

■ **10375** ■ **Alliant Foodservice Indianapolis**
12301 Cumberland Rd.
Fishers, IN 46038
Phone: (317)585-6600   **Fax:** (317)842-9625
Products: Food and supplies for hotels and restaurants. **SIC:** 5141 (Groceries—General Line). **Emp:** 280. **Officers:** Stuart Schuette.

■ **10376** ■ **Allied Grocers Cooperative Inc.**
1 Market Cir.
Windsor, CT 06095
Phone: (860)688-8341   **Fax:** (860)688-8052
Products: Groceries. **SIC:** 5141 (Groceries—General Line). **Est:** 1928. **Sales:** $240,000,000 (2000). **Emp:** 225. **Officers:** Calvin J. Miller, CEO & President; Bernard Larose, VP of Finance; Edward Stalmann, Dir. of Sales; James Brown, Dir. of Systems; William Hettrick.

■ **10377** ■ **Alpena Wholesale Grocery Co.**
170 N Industrial Hwy.
Alpena, MI 49707
Phone: (517)356-2281   **Fax:** (517)356-2510
URL: http://www.greatnorthfoods.com
Products: Groceries, including dairy products and frozen foods; Cigarettes. **SICs:** 5141 (Groceries—General Line); 5194 (Tobacco & Tobacco Products). **Est:** 1930. **Sales:** $62,000,000 (1999). **Emp:** 100. **Officers:** Ronald P. Baxter, Exec. VP & COO; Stephen L. Chapman, Controller; Pete Bilitzke, Dir. of Mktg. & Sales; Liz Downing, Dir. of Data Processing.

■ **10378** ■ **Morris Alper Inc.**
130 Lizotte Dr.
Marlborough, MA 01752-3080
Phone: (508)875-5600   **Fax:** (508)875-1145
Products: General line groceries; Restaurant food. **SIC:** 5141 (Groceries—General Line). **Est:** 1932. **Sales:** $240,000,000 (2000). **Emp:** 475. **Officers:** Victor Del Regno, President; Alan Doyon, Sr. VP of Finance & Admin.; Patricia Nicolino, Sr. VP of Marketing & Sales; Susan Berner, Dir of Human Resources.

■ **10379** ■ **Alpha Distributors Ltd.**
20W151 101st St.
Lemont, IL 60439-8876
Products: Food. **SICs:** 5149 (Groceries & Related Products Nec); 5141 (Groceries—General Line).

■ **10380** ■ **Alpha Star International Inc.**
550 Pharr Rd.
Atlanta, GA 30305
Phone: (404)237-7175   **Fax:** (404)237-7462
Products: Frozen poultry and meat. **SIC:** 5142 (Packaged Frozen Foods). **Officers:** Peter Landskroener, Executive Director.

■ **10381** ■ **Alphin Brothers Inc.**
Rte. 8, Box 40
Dunn, NC 28334
Phone: (910)892-8751   **Fax:** (910)892-2709
Products: Deli meats; Seafood. **SICs:** 5142 (Packaged Frozen Foods); 5146 (Fish & Seafoods). **Est:** 1949. **Sales:** $13,100,000 (2000). **Emp:** 65. **Officers:** J.C. Alphin Jr., President; E. Alphin, VP of Finance.

■ **10382** ■ **Alpine Distribution Services**
16956 S Harlan Rd.
Lathrop, CA 95330-8737
Phone: (510)795-4100   **Fax:** (510)796-3894
Products: Frozen foods; Ice cream. **SICs:** 5143 (Dairy Products Except Dried or Canned); 5142 (Packaged Frozen Foods). **Est:** 1962. **Sales:** $15,000,000 (2000). **Emp:** 48. **Officers:** Michael Gafney, President.

■ **10383** ■ **Alpine Packing Co.**
9900 Lower Sacramento Rd.
Stockton, CA 95210
Phone: (209)477-2691   **Fax:** (209)477-1994
Products: Meat products. **SIC:** 5147 (Meats & Meat Products). **Sales:** $41,000,000 (2000). **Emp:** 105. **Officers:** Jerry Singer, CEO & President.

■ **10384** ■ **Alshefski Enterprise**
Rte. 93, Box 330B
West Hazleton, PA 18201
Phone: (717)455-1577   **Fax:** (717)455-4856
Products: Bakery products. **SIC:** 5149 (Groceries & Related Products Nec). **Sales:** $7,000,000 (2000). **Emp:** 49. **Officers:** Jerry Alshefski Sr.; Jerry Alshefski Jr.

■ **10385** ■ **Alsum Produce Inc.**
N9083 Highway EF
PO Box 188
Friesland, WI 53935-0188
Phone: (920)348-5127   **Fax:** (920)348-5174
E-mail: alsum@alsum.com
URL: http://www.alsum.com
Products: Fruits and vegetables, including potatoes and onions. **SIC:** 5148 (Fresh Fruits & Vegetables). **Est:** 1973. **Sales:** $18,000,000 (2000). **Emp:** 80. **Officers:** Larry Alsum, President & Treasurer, e-mail: larry.alsum@alsum.com; Paula Alsum, VP & Secty.; Dave Katsma, Sales/Marketing Contact, e-mail: dave.katsma@alsum.com; Corey Gerritsen, Customer Service Contact, e-mail: corey.gerritsen@alsum.com; Darlene Schultz, Human Resource Contact; John Scheuers, VP of Marketing & Sales.

■ **10386** ■ **Alta Dena Certified Dairy**
17637 E Valley Blvd.
City of Industry, CA 91744
Phone: (626)964-6401
Free: (800)535-1369   **Fax:** (626)965-1960
URL: http://www.altadenadairy.com
Products: Milk; Ice cream; Cultured products. **SIC:** 5143 (Dairy Products Except Dried or Canned). **Est:** 1945. **Sales:** $235,000,000 (1999). **Emp:** 550.

■ **10387** ■ **Altitude Wholesale Co. Inc.**
6334 S Racine Cir 200
Englewood, CO 80111-6426
Products: Food. **SIC:** 5141 (Groceries—General Line). **Sales:** $12,000,000 (2000). **Emp:** 35. **Officers:** Neil Rose, President; Ed Barbara, Treasurer & Secty.; Warren Schencker, Sales Mgr.

■ 10388 ■ Altitude Wholesale Company Inc.
6334 S Racine Cir., No. 200
Englewood, CO 80111-6426
Phone: (303)779-1141
Products: Groceries. SIC: 5141 (Groceries—General Line). **Sales:** $25,000,000 (2000). **Emp:** 50. **Officers:** Steven Gollob, President.

■ 10389 ■ Amato International Inc.
11 Broadway
New York, NY 10004
Phone: (212)943-4974 **Fax:** (212)425-0203
E-mail: amatocy@aol.com
Products: Vegetable oils; glycerine. **SICs:** 5147 (Meats & Meat Products); 5149 (Groceries & Related Products Nec). **Est:** 1948. **Sales:** $15,000,000 (2000). **Emp:** 4. **Officers:** Claudette Touzard, President; Armand W. Schnabel, Treasurer; Anthony Touzard, Secretary.

■ 10390 ■ Amberstar International Inc.
105 E Laurel
San Antonio, TX 78212
Phone: (210)227-7289 **Fax:** (210)227-7296
Products: Foods, including powdered milk, picante sauce, and candy; Cigarettes; Auto parts. **SICs:** 5149 (Groceries & Related Products Nec); 5012 (Automobiles & Other Motor Vehicles). **Sales:** $100,000 (1994). **Emp:** 2. **Officers:** Theresa Sotooden, President; Larry S. Sotooden, Vice President.

■ 10391 ■ Ambriola Co. Inc.
2 Burma Rd.
Jersey City, NJ 07305
Phone: (201)434-6289
Free: (800)962-8224 **Fax:** (201)434-5505
Products: Cheese. SIC: 5143 (Dairy Products Except Dried or Canned). **Est:** 1922. **Sales:** $8,000,000 (2000). **Emp:** 11. **Officers:** Mary Anna Ajemian, President.

■ 10392 ■ AMCON Distributing Co.
PO Box 241230
Omaha, NE 68124
Phone: (402)331-3727 **Fax:** (402)331-4834
Products: Food; Tobacco; Cigarettes; Beverages; Toiletries and cosmetics; General line groceries. **SICs:** 5141 (Groceries—General Line); 5194 (Tobacco & Tobacco Products); 5149 (Groceries & Related Products Nec); 5122 (Drugs, Proprietaries & Sundries). **Est:** 1981. **Sales:** $250,000,000 (2000). **Emp:** 400. **Officers:** Kathleen Evans, President.

■ 10393 ■ AME Food Service Inc.
PO Box 3105
Scottsdale, AZ 85271-3105
Phone: (602)947-8021
Products: Foods, including fresh meats, fresh and frozen vegetables, canned soups and vegetables, and produce. **SICs:** 5141 (Groceries—General Line); 5142 (Packaged Frozen Foods); 5149 (Groceries & Related Products Nec); 5147 (Meats & Meat Products); 5148 (Fresh Fruits & Vegetables). **Est:** 1965. **Sales:** $8,000,000 (2000). **Emp:** 45. **Officers:** Frank Machin, Chairman of the Board; Penni Traylor, President.

■ 10394 ■ Amende and Schultz
PO Box 788
South Pasadena, CA 91030
Phone: (213)682-3806 **Fax:** (213)799-7572
Products: Frozen shrimp. SIC: 5146 (Fish & Seafoods). **Est:** 1955. **Sales:** $20,000,000 (2000). **Emp:** 6. **Officers:** Neal F. Rosser, President.

■ 10395 ■ American Cheeseman Inc.
PO Box 261
Clear Lake, IA 50428
Phone: (515)357-7176 **Fax:** (515)357-7177
Products: Cheese products; Bulk ingredients. **SICs:** 5143 (Dairy Products Except Dried or Canned); 5149 (Groceries & Related Products Nec). **Est:** 1975. **Sales:** $8,000,000 (2000). **Emp:** 9. **Officers:** Paul F. Austin, President.

■ 10396 ■ American Food Export Co.
1290-D Maunakea St. No. 238
Honolulu, HI 96817
Phone: (808)523-3500 **Fax:** (808)524-8116
Products: Fruits and vegetables. SIC: 5148 (Fresh Fruits & Vegetables). **Officers:** Kenneth Chan, Vice President.

■ 10397 ■ American Foods
131 New Jersey St.
Mobile, AL 36603
Phone: (334)433-2528
Products: General line of institutional food. SIC: 5141 (Groceries—General Line). **Sales:** $9,000,000 (2000). **Emp:** 20.

■ 10398 ■ American FoodService
4721 Simonton Rd.
Dallas, TX 75244
Phone: (972)385-5800
Free: (800)268-7875 **Fax:** (972)385-5809
URL: http://www.freshpoint.com
Products: Frozen, canned, dry, and refrigerated food; Fresh produce; Deli meats; Poultry; Full-line non-food grocery items. **SICs:** 5141 (Groceries—General Line); 5142 (Packaged Frozen Foods); 5144 (Poultry & Poultry Products); 5148 (Fresh Fruits & Vegetables); 5149 (Groceries & Related Products Nec). **Est:** 1917. **Sales:** $60,000,000 (2000). **Emp:** 170. **Officers:** Lucian M. La Barba, President; Hant Weinstein, Sales/Marketing Contact; Giselle Minojosa, Customer Service Contact; Connie Southwood, Human Resources Contact. **Former Name:** American Produce & Vegetable Co.

■ 10399 ■ American Key Food Products Inc.
1 Reuten Dr.
Closter, NJ 07624-2115
Phone: (201)767-8022
Free: (877)263-7539 **Fax:** (201)767-9124
E-mail: akpnewyork@aol.com
Products: Potato starch; Corn starch; Sago; Tapioca starch; Arrow root. SIC: 5149 (Groceries & Related Products Nec). **Est:** 1946. **Sales:** $12,000,000 (2000). **Emp:** 15. **Officers:** Murray Feinblatt, President; Motilal Sarda, Exec. VP; Philip Benyair, VP of Marketing; Ivan Sarda.

■ 10400 ■ American Management Group
PO Box 701809
Dallas, TX 75370
Phone: (972)349-1100
Products: Frozen meat and groceries. **SICs:** 5147 (Meats & Meat Products); 5149 (Groceries & Related Products Nec). **Officers:** Austin Bell, President.

■ 10401 ■ American Poultry International Ltd.
PO Box 16805
Jackson, MS 39236
Phone: (601)956-1715
Free: (888)392-4832 **Fax:** (601)956-1755
E-mail: apiltd@aol.com
URL: http://www.membersaol.com/apiltd/page
Products: Catfish; Poultry; Beef; Pork. **SICs:** 5144 (Poultry & Poultry Products); 5146 (Fish & Seafoods). **Est:** 1970. **Sales:** $6,000,000 (1999). **Emp:** 5. **Officers:** Donald Ford, President; Carolyn Hust, Sec. & Treas.; Bob Anthony, Chairman of the Board; Karla A. Ford, Sales/Marketing Contact, e-mail: apiltd@aol.com.

■ 10402 ■ American Products Company Inc.
10741 Miller Rd.
Dallas, TX 75238-1303
Phone: (214)357-3961 **Fax:** (214)387-8842
Products: Bakery products. SIC: 5149 (Groceries & Related Products Nec). **Est:** 1926. **Sales:** $36,000,000 (2000). **Emp:** 139. **Officers:** Jerry Haugen, General Mgr.

■ 10403 ■ American Provisions Co.
103 19th
Rock Island, IL 61201
Phone: (309)786-7757 **Fax:** (309)788-8111
Products: Meat. SIC: 5147 (Meats & Meat Products). **Emp:** 49. **Alternate Name:** United Steaks of America.

■ 10404 ■ American Seaway Foods Inc.
5300 Richmond Rd.
Bedford Heights, OH 44146
Phone: (216)641-2360 **Fax:** (216)591-2640
Products: Groceries. SIC: 5141 (Groceries—General Line). **Est:** 1957. **Sales:** $310,000,000 (2000). **Emp:** 700. **Officers:** Anthony C. Rego, CEO & Chairman of the Board; Ronald W. Ocasek, Sr. VP & Auditor; John Koscielski, Dir. of Marketing & Sales; Al Van Luvender, VP of Information Systems; Glen A. Garson.

■ 10405 ■ American Sweeteners Inc.
11 Lee Blvd.
Frazer, PA 19355
Phone: (610)647-2905
Products: Corn syrup and other food sweeteners. SIC: 5149 (Groceries & Related Products Nec). **Sales:** $5,000,000 (2000). **Emp:** 28. **Officers:** Raymond McCormick Jr., CEO; Joe Koletty, CFO.

■ 10406 ■ AmeriQual Foods Inc.
PO Box 4597
Evansville, IN 47724-0597
Phone: (812)867-1444
Products: Canned foods. SIC: 5149 (Groceries & Related Products Nec). **Est:** 1988. **Sales:** $15,000,000 (2000). **Emp:** 100. **Officers:** Ronald C. Coleman, CEO & President; Timothy Brauer, CFO.

■ 10407 ■ AmeriServe Food Distribution Inc.
17975 W Sarah Ln., Ste. 100
Brookfield, WI 53045
Phone: (414)792-9300 **Fax:** (414)650-3434
Products: Food. SIC: 5141 (Groceries—General Line). **Sales:** $1,519,000,000 (2000). **Emp:** 1,700.

■ 10408 ■ L.D. Amory and Company Inc.
101 S King St.
Hampton, VA 23669
Phone: (804)722-1915 **Fax:** (804)723-1184
Products: Fish. SIC: 5146 (Fish & Seafoods). **Est:** 1935. **Sales:** $6,000,000 (2000). **Emp:** 25. **Officers:** C.R. Amory, President, Chairman of the Board & Treasurer; William E. Reynolds, Comptroller.

■ 10409 ■ Amsing International Inc.
PO Box 1467
San Pedro, CA 90733-1467
Phone: (310)834-3514 **Fax:** (310)834-3127
Products: Seafood. SIC: 5146 (Fish & Seafoods). **Sales:** $2,000,000 (2000). **Emp:** 5.

■ 10410 ■ Ancona Midwest Foodservices
PO Box 27787
9320 J St.
Omaha, NE 68127-0787
Phone: (402)331-6262 **Fax:** (402)331-3913
E-mail: midwest.foods@mci.com
Products: Frozen and canned, refrigerated, dry-non food supplies and equipment. **SICs:** 5142 (Packaged Frozen Foods); 5149 (Groceries & Related Products Nec). **Est:** 1915. **Sales:** $70,000,000 (2000). **Emp:** 150. **Officers:** Mike Ancona, President; Don Martens, Sales/Marketing Contact; Pat Avolio, Customer Service Contact; Pat Avolio, Human Resources Contact. **Former Name:** Ancona Brothers Co.

■ 10411 ■ Ancona/Midwest Inc.
PO Box 27787
Omaha, NE 68127-0787
Phone: (402)331-6262 **Fax:** (402)331-3913
Products: General groceries and frozen foods; Non-foods. **SICs:** 5141 (Groceries—General Line); 5142 (Packaged Frozen Foods). **Est:** 1915. **Sales:** $70,000,000 (2000). **Emp:** 145. **Officers:** Mike Ancona, COO & President; Sid Abraham, Chairman of the Board.

■ 10412 ■ Anderson-DuBose Co.
6575 Davis Industrial Pkwy.
Solon, OH 44139
Phone: (440)248-8800 **Fax:** (440)248-6208
Products: Restaurant supplies, including food. SIC: 5141 (Groceries—General Line). **Est:** 1991. **Sales:** $131,000,000 (2000). **Emp:** 95. **Officers:** Warren E. Anderson, Owner.

■ **10413** ■ **Anderson Erickson Dairy Co.**
2229 Hubbell
Des Moines, IA 50317-2599
Phone: (515)265-2521 **Fax:** (515)263-6301
Products: Dairy products, including milk, cheese, cottage cheese, and ice cream. **SIC:** 5143 (Dairy Products Except Dried or Canned). **Sales:** $100,000,000 (2000). **Emp:** 435. **Officers:** James W. Erickson.

■ **10414** ■ **Andersons Candy Company**
1010 State
Baden, PA 15005-1338
Phone: (724)869-3018 **Fax:** (724)869-7240
Products: Candy. **SIC:** 5145 (Confectionery). **Est:** 1916. **Emp:** 75. **Officers:** Mary Candace Anderson Cardwell; Goldie Anderson.

■ **10415** ■ **Anderson's Peanuts**
PO Drawer 420
Opp, AL 36467-0420
Phone: (205)493-4591 **Fax:** (205)493-7767
Products: Peanuts. **SIC:** 5159 (Farm-Product Raw Materials Nec). **Est:** 1935. **Sales:** $50,000,000 (2000). **Emp:** 250. **Officers:** John Fryer, General Mgr.; John Reed, Dir. of Marketing & Sales; Mike Gilmer, Dir. of Data Processing.

■ **10416** ■ **Andrew and Williamson Sales Co.**
9940 Marconi Dr.
San Diego, CA 92173
Phone: (619)661-6000 **Fax:** (619)661-6007
Products: Fruits and vegetables. **SIC:** 5148 (Fresh Fruits & Vegetables). **Sales:** $9,000,000 (2000). **Emp:** 30. **Officers:** Fred L. Williamson, President.

■ **10417** ■ **Andrews Produce Inc.**
100 S Main
PO Box 1027
Pueblo, CO 81002
Phone: (719)543-3846
Free: (800)289-8810 **Fax:** (719)543-3021
E-mail: gandrews@andrewsfoodservice.com
URL: http://www.andrewsfoodservice.com
Products: Fresh fruits and vegetables; Canned goods; Frozen items; Paper products; Equipment and smallwares; Box beef; Refrigerated dairy and cheese products. **SICs:** 5148 (Fresh Fruits & Vegetables); 5149 (Groceries & Related Products Nec). **Est:** 1926. **Sales:** $30,000,000 (2000). **Emp:** 80. **Officers:** George Andrews III, President; Debbie Bassetti, Vice President.

■ **10418** ■ **Angel Food Ice Cream**
368 Industrial Dr. S
Madison, MS 39110
Phone: (601)898-0081
Products: Ice cream. **SIC:** 5143 (Dairy Products Except Dried or Canned).

■ **10419** ■ **Annabelle Candy Company Inc.**
27211 Industrial Blvd.
Hayward, CA 94545-3347
Phone: (510)783-2900 **Fax:** (510)785-7675
Products: Candy bars, including chocolate and nougat with peanuts and taffy. **SIC:** 5145 (Confectionery). **Est:** 1950. **Sales:** $10,000,000 (2000). **Emp:** 51. **Officers:** Susan Gamson Karl, CEO & President.

■ **10420** ■ **Ann's House of Nuts, Inc.**
8375 Patuxent Range Rd.
Jessup, MD 20794
Phone: (301)317-0900 **Fax:** (301)317-6248
Products: Nuts and seeds(salted, roasted, cooked, or blanched); Dried and dehydrated fruits; Trail mixes. **SICs:** 5149 (Groceries & Related Products Nec); 5145 (Confectionery). **Est:** 1973. **Emp:** 150. **Officers:** Ed Zinke; Ann Zinke.

■ **10421** ■ **Anthony Farms Inc.**
PO Box 4
Scandinavia, WI 54977
Phone: (715)467-2212 **Fax:** (715)467-2626
Products: Fresh potatoes. **SIC:** 5148 (Fresh Fruits & Vegetables). **Est:** 1966. **Sales:** $4,000,000 (2000). **Emp:** 60. **Officers:** Victor Anthony Jr., President.

■ **10422** ■ **Joseph Antognoli and Co.**
1800 N Pulaski Rd.
Chicago, IL 60639-4916
Phone: (312)772-1800 **Fax:** (312)772-0031
Products: Italian food products. **SIC:** 5141 (Groceries—General Line). **Est:** 1909. **Sales:** $4,000,000 (2000). **Emp:** 25. **Officers:** J.H. Antognoli, President; Vincent T. Candice, VP of Finance; Mitchell J. Formato, Dir. of Marketing & Sales.

■ **10423** ■ **Appert Foods**
809 SE Hwy. 10
St. Cloud, MN 56304-1808
Phone: (320)251-3200
Free: (800)225-3883 **Fax:** (320)259-0747
Products: Seafood; Fresh meat; Frozen meat; Frozen vegetables; Fresh fruits; Frozen fruits. **SICs:** 5146 (Fish & Seafoods); 5147 (Meats & Meat Products); 5148 (Fresh Fruits & Vegetables). **Sales:** $6,000,000 (2000). **Emp:** 55. **Officers:** Timothy J. Appert.

■ **10424** ■ **Apple Food Sales Company Inc.**
117 Fort Lee Rd.
Leonia, NJ 07605
Phone: (201)592-0277
Products: Pastas, olive oil, bottled artichokes, and other gourmet foods. **SICs:** 5141 (Groceries—General Line); 5149 (Groceries & Related Products Nec).

■ **10425** ■ **Applewood Farms Inc.**
PO Box 445
Lansing, IL 60438-0445
Products: Food, including dairy and meat products. **SICs:** 5141 (Groceries—General Line); 5149 (Groceries & Related Products Nec); 5143 (Dairy Products Except Dried or Canned); 5147 (Meats & Meat Products). **Est:** 1953. **Sales:** $30,000,000 (2000). **Emp:** 125. **Officers:** Joseph A. Mulligan, Comptroller; William J. Mulligan, CFO.

■ **10426** ■ **APW/Wyott Food Service Equipment Co.**
729 3rd Ave.
Dallas, TX 75226
Phone: (214)421-7366 **Fax:** (214)565-0976
Products: Food service equipment. **SIC:** 5046 (Commercial Equipment Nec). **Sales:** $28,000,000 (2000). **Emp:** 300. **Officers:** Hylton Jonas, Principal; Don Wall, VP of Finance.

■ **10427** ■ **Aqua Gourmet Foods, Inc.**
Hwy. 694
Abbeville, LA 70510
Phone: (318)893-9494 **Fax:** (318)893-9499
Products: Shellfish and alligator. **SIC:** 5146 (Fish & Seafoods). **Sales:** $2,000,000 (2000). **Emp:** 60. **Officers:** Ted Noel.

■ **10428** ■ **Aqua Star Inc.**
2025 1st Ave.
Seattle, WA 98121
Phone: (206)448-5400
Products: Seafood. **SIC:** 5146 (Fish & Seafoods). **Sales:** $10,000,000 (2000). **Emp:** 40. **Officers:** Mike Girton, President.

■ **10429** ■ **Araban Coffee Co. Inc.**
2 Keith Way
Hingham, MA 02043-4204
Phone: (617)439-3900 **Fax:** (617)439-3091
Products: Coffee. **SIC:** 5149 (Groceries & Related Products Nec). **Est:** 1929. **Sales:** $15,000,000 (2000). **Emp:** 55. **Officers:** H.J. Perry, President; Joseph Leary, Controller.

■ **10430** ■ **Archway Cookie Co.**
2419 Industrial Park Rd.
Boone, IA 50036
Phone: (515)432-4084 **Fax:** (515)432-2770
Products: Cookies. **SIC:** 5149 (Groceries & Related Products Nec). **Emp:** 499.

■ **10431** ■ **Arco Coffee Co.**
2206 Winter
Superior, WI 54880-1437
Phone: (715)392-4771
Products: Coffee. **SIC:** 5149 (Groceries & Related Products Nec). **Est:** 1916. **Emp:** 39. **Officers:** Donald Andersen, Secretary.

■ **10432** ■ **Arctic Ice Co.**
Industrial Park W
Gallup, NM 87301
Phone: (505)722-9470
Products: Ice. **SIC:** 5141 (Groceries—General Line).

■ **10433** ■ **Arkansas Valley Wholesale Grocers Co.**
PO Box 380
Morrilton, AR 72110
Phone: (501)354-3451 **Fax:** (501)354-1388
Products: Groceries, including canned vetgetables, soups, fruits, and packaged meats. **SIC:** 5141 (Groceries—General Line). **Est:** 1932. **Sales:** $6,000,000 (2000). **Emp:** 18. **Officers:** Larry Gordon, CEO & President.

■ **10434** ■ **Armour Food Ingredients Co.**
223 Progress Rd.
Springfield, KY 40069
Phone: (606)336-3922
Free: (800)777-1945 **Fax:** (606)336-7542
URL: http://www.armourfoods.com
Products: Dry dairy products; Dairy flavors, including spray dried and paste; Dairy blends; Dairy, fruit, savory, non-dairy creamers and shortenings. **SIC:** 5149 (Groceries & Related Products Nec). **Est:** 1920. **Sales:** $60,000,000 (2000). **Emp:** 135. **Officers:** Jon Hedlund, General Mgr., e-mail: jhedlund@armourfoods.com; Dathel Nimmons, Mgr. of Business Development, e-mail: dnimmons@armourfoods.com. **Former Name:** Armour Food Co.

■ **10435** ■ **Armstrong Produce Ltd.**
651 Ilalo Bldg. 1
Honolulu, HI 96813-5525
Phone: (808)538-7051 **Fax:** (808)538-1401
Products: Groceries, including head lettuce. **SICs:** 5149 (Groceries & Related Products Nec); 5148 (Fresh Fruits & Vegetables). **Sales:** $15,000,000 (2000). **Emp:** 70.

■ **10436** ■ **Robert Arranaga and Co.**
216 S Alameda St.
Los Angeles, CA 90012
Phone: (213)622-7249 **Fax:** (213)895-4372
Products: Food; Restaurant supplies. **SICs:** 5141 (Groceries—General Line); 5046 (Commercial Equipment Nec). **Est:** 1957. **Sales:** $12,000,000 (2000). **Emp:** 35. **Officers:** Robert Arranaga Sr., President; Jr.

■ **10437** ■ **Arrow-SYSCO**
1451 River Oaks W
Harahan, LA 70123
Phone: (504)734-1015
Free: (800)786-3001 **Fax:** (504)731-3378
Products: Prepared and institutional foods. **SIC:** 5149 (Groceries & Related Products Nec).

■ **10438** ■ **Arrow-Sysco Food Services Inc.**
PO Box 10038
New Orleans, LA 70181
Phone: (504)837-1015
Products: Food products. **SIC:** 5141 (Groceries—General Line). **Officers:** Bruce L. Soltis, President.

■ **10439** ■ **Arrowhead Mills Inc.**
PO Box 2059
Hereford, TX 79045-2059
Phone: (806)364-0730 **Fax:** (806)364-8242
Products: Health foods; Breakfast cereals; Flour and other grain mill products; Nuts and seeds (salted, roasted, cooked, or blanched). **SICs:** 5141 (Groceries—General Line); 5149 (Groceries & Related Products Nec); 5145 (Confectionery). **Est:** 1960. **Sales:** $30,000,000 (2000). **Emp:** 145. **Officers:** Boyd Foster; Mark Novak; John Goodman.

■ **10440** ■ **Artemia of Utah Inc.**
PO Box 978
Farmington, UT 84025
Phone: (801)532-5426 **Fax:** (801)359-4748
E-mail: artemia@prodigy.net
Products: Shrimp eggs. **SIC:** 5146 (Fish & Seafoods). **Est:** 1983. **Sales:** $2,000,000 (2000). **Emp:** 8. **Officers:** Craig Tilley, President.

■ 10441 ■ Artesia Water Co.
PO Box 790210
San Antonio, TX 78279-0210
Phone: (210)654-0293 **Fax:** (210)654-3027
Products: Bottled water. **SIC:** 5149 (Groceries & Related Products Nec). **Est:** 1980. **Sales:** $5,000,000 (2000). **Emp:** 35. **Officers:** Margaret Shodrock; Casey Jones.

■ 10442 ■ Artusos Pastry Shop
670 E 187th
Bronx, NY 10458-6802
Phones: (718)367-2515 (718)367-2553
Fax: (718)367-2553
E-mail: nycannoli@aol.com
URL: http://www.artusopastry.com
Products: Cakes and Italian pastry. **SIC:** 5149 (Groceries & Related Products Nec). **Est:** 1946. **Sales:** $1,000,000 (2000). **Emp:** 49. **Officers:** Anthony Artuso Sr., President.

■ 10443 ■ Associated Brokers Inc.
PO Box 26328
Raleigh, NC 27611
Phone: (919)833-2651
Products: Food. **SICs:** 5141 (Groceries—General Line); 5142 (Packaged Frozen Foods). **Sales:** $110,000,000 (2000). **Emp:** 225. **Officers:** Pete Troutman, President; David W. Dewar, VP of Finance.

■ 10444 ■ Associated Buyers
PO Box 399
Barrington, NH 03825
Phone: (603)664-5656
Free: (800)639-2081 **Fax:** (603)664-2299
Products: Bulk whole foods. **SIC:** 5141 (Groceries—General Line). **Est:** 1974. **Emp:** 30.

■ 10445 ■ Associated Food Stores Inc.
305 W Quinn Rd.
Pocatello, ID 83202-1932
Phone: (208)237-4511
Products: Food. **SICs:** 5141 (Groceries—General Line); 5149 (Groceries & Related Products Nec). **Emp:** 130. **Officers:** Gary Angell.

■ 10446 ■ Associated Food Stores Inc.
122-20 Merrick Blvd.
Jamaica, NY 11433
Phone: (718)341-2100
Products: Food. **SIC:** 5141 (Groceries—General Line). **Est:** 1951. **Sales:** $19,000,000 (2000). **Emp:** 54. **Officers:** Harry Laufer, Partner; Ira Gober, Partner; Adam Laufer, VP of Marketing.

■ 10447 ■ Associated Food Stores Inc.
PO Box 30430
Salt Lake City, UT 84130
Phone: (801)973-4400 **Fax:** (801)973-2158
Products: Groceries. **SIC:** 5141 (Groceries—General Line). **Est:** 1940. **Sales:** $745,800,000 (2000). **Emp:** 1,300. **Officers:** Gill Warner, President; Neal Berube, Controller; Dean Payne, Dir. of Marketing; Stanley Brewer, VP & Secty.; Larry Rowe.

■ 10448 ■ Associated Food Stores Inc. (Salt Lake City, Utah)
PO Box 30430
Salt Lake City, UT 84130
Phone: (801)973-4400
Products: General line of groceries and produce. **SICs:** 5141 (Groceries—General Line); 5148 (Fresh Fruits & Vegetables). **Sales:** $842,000,000 (2000). **Emp:** 1,300. **Officers:** Richard A. Parkinson, CEO & President; S. Neal Berube, Sr. VP & CFO.

■ 10449 ■ Associated Grocers of Florida Inc.
7000 NW 32nd Ave.
Miami, FL 33147
Phone: (305)696-0080 **Fax:** (305)835-8041
Products: Groceries; Health and beauty aids. **SICs:** 5141 (Groceries—General Line); 5122 (Drugs, Proprietaries & Sundries). **Est:** 1947. **Sales:** $210,000,000 (2000). **Emp:** 400. **Officers:** Calvin J. Miller, President; Lewis Thomas, Sr. VP & Finance Officer; Robert Beaudette, VP of Sales; Louis Barroso, Dir. of Systems; Buford Cochran, Dir of Personnel.

■ 10450 ■ Associated Grocers, Inc.
3301 S Norfolk
Seattle, WA 98118
Phone: (206)762-2100 **Fax:** (206)764-7731
Products: Groceries. **SIC:** 5141 (Groceries—General Line). **Est:** 1934. **Sales:** $1,200,000,000 (2000). **Emp:** 1,300. **Officers:** Donald W. Benson, CEO; Tom Sterken, CFO; Harold Ravenscraft, Human Resources Contact.

■ 10451 ■ Associated Grocers of Maine Inc.
PO Box 1000
Gardiner, ME 04345
Phone: (207)582-6500 **Fax:** (207)582-3461
Products: Groceries. **SIC:** 5141 (Groceries—General Line). **Est:** 1953. **Sales:** $140,000,000 (2000). **Emp:** 200. **Officers:** Alan Decker, President; Tom Kelley, CFO; Arthur Heathcote, VP of Marketing; Ronald Cain, Operations Mgr.; Katherine Harrington, Dir of Human Resources.

■ 10452 ■ Associated Grocers of New England Inc.
PO Box 5200
Manchester, NH 03108
Phone: (603)669-3250 **Fax:** (603)669-5423
Products: Groceries, including meat, produce, HBA, and general merchandise. **SIC:** 5141 (Groceries—General Line). **Est:** 1945. **Sales:** $226,000,000 (1999). **Emp:** 300. **Officers:** Norman J. Turcotte, President; Richard A. Ennis, Exec. VP & Treasurer; Michael Violette; Arthur Heathcote; Steven N. Murphy, Sr. VP of Finance & Admin.; Michael Violette, VP of Sales & Support Services; Ron Cain Sr., VP of Operations; Arthur Heathcote, Dir. of IS & Customer Service.

■ 10453 ■ Associated Milk Producers Inc. North Central Region
PO Box 455
New Ulm, MN 56073
Phone: (507)354-8295 **Fax:** (507)359-8695
Products: Dairy products, including milk, cheese, and butter. **SIC:** 5143 (Dairy Products Except Dried or Canned). **Est:** 1969. **Sales:** $1,300,000,000 (2000). **Emp:** 1,900. **Officers:** Mark Furth, Manager; Ken Spoon, Controller; Pat Mathiowetz, Dir. of Marketing.

■ 10454 ■ Associated Milk Producers Inc. Southern Region
3500 William D. Tate Ave., No. 100
Grapevine, TX 76051-8734
Phone: (817)461-2674 **Fax:** (817)548-5201
Products: Milk. **SIC:** 5143 (Dairy Products Except Dried or Canned). **Est:** 1969. **Sales:** $1,060,000,000 (2000). **Emp:** 1,700. **Officers:** Nobel Anderson, Manager; Ernest Terry, CFO.

■ 10455 ■ Associated Milk Producers Inc. Sulphur Springs Div.
PO Box 939
Sulphur Springs, TX 75482
Phone: (903)885-6518
Products: Dairy products. **SIC:** 5143 (Dairy Products Except Dried or Canned). **Officers:** Ken Burtch, Manager.

■ 10456 ■ Associated Potato Growers Inc.
2001 North 6th Street
Grand Forks, ND 58203
Phone: (701)775-4614
Free: (800)437-4685 **Fax:** (701)746-5767
E-mail: apgi@gfherald.infi.net
Products: Potatoes. **SIC:** 5148 (Fresh Fruits & Vegetables). **Est:** 1948. **Sales:** $10,000,000 (1999). **Emp:** 105. **Officers:** Paul Dolan, General Mgr.; Greg Holtman, Sales/Marketing Contact, e-mail: apgspud@gfherald.infi.net; Steve Johnson, Sales.

■ 10457 ■ Associated Wholesale Grocers Inc.
5000 Kansas Ave.
Kansas City, KS 66106
Phone: (913)321-1313 **Fax:** (913)573-1508
Products: Food. **SIC:** 5141 (Groceries—General Line). **Sales:** $2,000,000 (2000). **Emp:** 1,000.

■ 10458 ■ Associated Wholesalers Inc.
PO Box 67
Robesonia, PA 19551
Phone: (610)693-3161 **Fax:** (215)693-3171
Products: Meat; Produce. **SICs:** 5147 (Meats & Meat Products); 5148 (Fresh Fruits & Vegetables). **Est:** 1928. **Sales:** $700,000,000 (2000). **Emp:** 1,050. **Officers:** J. Christopher Michael, CEO & President; Thomas Teeter, CFO; Donald Tiesenga, Dir. of Marketing; P. William Diener III, Dir. of Systems; George Connolly, Dir of Human Resources.

■ 10459 ■ Assumption Cooperative Grain Co.
104 W North St.
Assumption, IL 62510
Phone: (217)226-3213
Free: (800)252-6542 **Fax:** (217)226-3244
Products: Grain and farm supplies. **SICs:** 5153 (Grain & Field Beans); 5191 (Farm Supplies). **Sales:** $21,000,000 (2000). **Emp:** 25. **Officers:** Robert Adcock, President; Thomas Bressner, Controller.

■ 10460 ■ Astor Foods Inc.
4000 Highlands Pkwy.
Smyrna, GA 30082
Phone: (770)436-0411
Products: Food. **SIC:** 5141 (Groceries—General Line).

■ 10461 ■ Atalanta Corp.
1 Atalanta Plz.
Elizabeth, NJ 07206
Phone: (908)351-8000 **Fax:** (908)351-1844
Products: Cheese products; Tuna; Processed, frozen, or cooked meats. **SICs:** 5141 (Groceries—General Line); 5142 (Packaged Frozen Foods); 5143 (Dairy Products Except Dried or Canned); 5146 (Fish & Seafoods); 5147 (Meats & Meat Products). **Sales:** $300,000,000 (2000). **Emp:** 200. **Officers:** George G. Gellert.

■ 10462 ■ Atherton Grain Co.
PO Box 366
Walnut, IL 61376
Phone: (815)379-2177 **Fax:** (815)379-2424
Products: Grain, field beans, feeds and fertilizers. **SICs:** 5153 (Grain & Field Beans); 5191 (Farm Supplies). **Sales:** $14,000,000 (2000). **Emp:** 16. **Officers:** Roy A. Atherton, President & CFO.

■ 10463 ■ Atlanta Ice Inc.
1587 E Taylor Ave.
East Point, GA 30344
Phone: (404)762-0139 **Fax:** (404)766-4380
Products: Ice. **SIC:** 5143 (Dairy Products Except Dried or Canned). **Est:** 1980. **Sales:** $1,000,000 (1999). **Emp:** 4. **Officers:** Charles Sinagra, President; Susan Sinagra, Treasurer.

■ 10464 ■ Atlantic Premium Brands Ltd.
650 Dundee Rd., Ste. 370
Northbrook, IL 60062
Phone: (847)480-4000
Products: Sausage and meat; Beverage products. **SICs:** 5147 (Meats & Meat Products); 5149 (Groceries & Related Products Nec). **Sales:** $172,200,000 (2000). **Emp:** 465. **Officers:** Alan F. Sussna, CEO & President.

■ 10465 ■ Atlas Distributing Inc.
44 Southbridge St.
Auburn, MA 01501
Phone: (508)791-6221 **Fax:** (508)791-0812
Products: Soft drinks. **SIC:** 5149 (Groceries & Related Products Nec). **Sales:** $35,000,000 (2000). **Emp:** 105.

■ 10466 ■ Atlas Marketing Co. Inc.
PO Box 29100
Charlotte, NC 28229-9100
Phone: (704)847-8600 **Fax:** (704)847-2592
Products: Food. **SIC:** 5141 (Groceries—General Line). **Est:** 1969. **Sales:** $240,000,000 (2000). **Emp:** 600. **Officers:** Gynn Eller, CEO; Luther Pitts, Exec. VP; Scott Ranson, Information Systems Mgr.

■ 10467 ■ Atlas Vegetable Exchange
PO Box 36A88
Los Angeles, CA 90036-1135
Phone: (213)749-4347 **Fax:** (213)749-7253
Products: Fresh vegetables, including potatos, onions,

and lettuce. **SIC:** 5148 (Fresh Fruits & Vegetables). **Emp:** 49. **Officers:** Tok Ishizawa.

■ **10468** ■ **Auburn Merchandise Distributors Inc.**
355 Main St.
Whitinsville, MA 01588-1860
Phone: (508)234-9000 **Fax:** (508)234-9900
Products: Groceries; Tobacco; Candy; Paper; Beverages. **SICs:** 5141 (Groceries—General Line); 5145 (Confectionery); 5194 (Tobacco & Tobacco Products). **Sales:** $200,000,000 (1999). **Emp:** 150. **Officers:** Bill Potvin, President; Tom Dion, CFO; Ken Updike, Exec. VP; Robert Pontes, VP of Purchasing.

■ **10469** ■ **Auddino's Italian Bakery Inc.**
1490 Clara St.
Columbus, OH 43211
Phone: (614)294-2577
Free: (800)294-2558 **Fax:** (614)294-0080
Products: Bread products, including rolls and sandwich buns; Breadsticks;Pizza crust. **SIC:** 5149 (Groceries & Related Products Nec). **Est:** 1968. **Sales:** $2,500,000 (2000). **Emp:** 49. **Officers:** Michael Auddino, President.

■ **10470** ■ **Aunt Mid Produce Co.**
7939 W Lafayette
Detroit, MI 48209
Phones: (313)841-1420 (313)841-6220
(313)841-7911
Products: Produce. **SIC:** 5148 (Fresh Fruits & Vegetables).

■ **10471** ■ **Aurora Packing Company Inc.**
PO Box 209
North Aurora, IL 60542
Phone: (630)897-0551 **Fax:** (630)897-0647
Products: Meats and meat products. **SIC:** 5147 (Meats & Meat Products). **Sales:** $68,000,000 (2000). **Emp:** 200. **Officers:** Marvin Fagel, President.

■ **10472** ■ **The Auster Co. Inc.**
51 S Water Market
Chicago, IL 60608-2209
Phone: (312)829-6550
Free: (800)621-4296 **Fax:** (312)666-0095
Products: Fresh fruits and vegetables. **SIC:** 5148 (Fresh Fruits & Vegetables). **Est:** 1947. **Sales:** $30,000,000 (2000). **Emp:** 49.

■ **10473** ■ **Austin Quality Foods, Inc.**
1 Quality Ln.
Cary, NC 27513-2004
Phone: (919)677-3400 **Fax:** (919)677-0017
Products: Snack foods, including crackers and cookies. **SIC:** 5149 (Groceries & Related Products Nec). **Est:** 1949. **Sales:** $197,000,000 (1999). **Emp:** 1,200. **Officers:** Mark Bernel, Bakery Dir.; Boyd Gilley, Plant Mgr. **Former Name:** Bahlsen, Inc.

■ **10474** ■ **Avalon Distributing Inc.**
1 Avalon Dr.
PO Box 536
Canal Fulton, OH 44614-0536
Phone: (330)854-4551
Free: (800)362-0622 **Fax:** (330)854-4556
Products: Frozen foods; Canned vegetables; Canned fruits. **SICs:** 5141 (Groceries—General Line); 5142 (Packaged Frozen Foods); 5149 (Groceries & Related Products Nec). **Est:** 1957. **Sales:** $18,000,000 (2000). **Emp:** 53. **Officers:** Dave Lee, Warehouse Mgr.

■ **10475** ■ **Avico Distributing Inc.**
729 Broad
Utica, NY 13501-1313
Phone: (315)724-8243 **Fax:** (315)724-7697
Products: Institutional food; Paper products; Cleaning supplies. **SICs:** 5141 (Groceries—General Line); 5113 (Industrial & Personal Service Paper); 5169 (Chemicals & Allied Products Nec). **Emp:** 21. **Officers:** John S. Zumpano; Robert Zumpano.

■ **10476** ■ **Axelrod Distributors**
4646 King Graves Rd.
Vienna, OH 44473-9700
Phone: (216)721-6010 **Fax:** (216)721-5448
Products: Specialty foods, including smoked fish.

SICs: 5149 (Groceries & Related Products Nec); 5146 (Fish & Seafoods).

■ **10477** ■ **Axelrod Foods Inc.**
PO Box 795
Paterson, NJ 07533
Phone: (973)684-0600 **Fax:** (973)684-0943
Products: Cheese. **SIC:** 5143 (Dairy Products Except Dried or Canned). **Est:** 1955. **Sales:** $14,000,000 (2000). **Emp:** 40. **Officers:** Mitch Tisch, General Mgr.

■ **10478** ■ **Azure Standard**
79709 Dufur Valley Rd.
Dufur, OR 97021
Phone: (541)467-2230 **Fax:** (541)467-2210
Products: Food preparations; Dried and dehydrated food products; Head rice not packaged with other ingredients; Potatoes; Egg noodle products; Health foods. **SIC:** 5149 (Groceries & Related Products Nec).

■ **10479** ■ **B and B Fisheries Inc.**
715 E International
Daytona Beach, FL 32118
Phone: (904)252-6542 **Free:** (800)553-9047
Products: Fish; Shrimp; Oysters; Scallops. **SIC:** 5146 (Fish & Seafoods). **Est:** 1932. **Sales:** $1,000,000 (2000). **Emp:** 20. **Officers:** Ralph Flippo, President; Stuart Flippo, Vice President.

■ **10480** ■ **B and B Produce Inc.**
PO Box 415
Johnson City, TN 37605
Phone: (423)926-2191 **Fax:** (423)926-7458
Products: Fresh produce. **SIC:** 5148 (Fresh Fruits & Vegetables). **Est:** 1943. **Sales:** $3,000,000 (2000). **Emp:** 20. **Officers:** Michael B. Dennis, Owner & Pres.

■ **10481** ■ **B & B Specialty Foods**
4050 Stoneleigh Rd.
Bloomfield Hills, MI 48302
Phone: (248)645-2096 **Fax:** (248)645-6725
Products: Gourmet foods. **SIC:** 5149 (Groceries & Related Products Nec).

■ **10482** ■ **B-G Lobster and Shrimp Corp.**
95 South St.
New York, NY 10038
Phone: (212)732-3060 **Fax:** (212)392-0068
URL: http://www.seatogo.com
Products: Seafood, including shrimp, lobster, lobster tails, clams, squid, fillet, scallops, and crab. **SIC:** 5146 (Fish & Seafoods). **Est:** 1957.

■ **10483** ■ **B & M Provision Co.**
1040 N Graham
Allentown, PA 18103
Phone: (215)434-9611 **Fax:** (215)434-9988
Products: Meats and frozen foods. **SICs:** 5147 (Meats & Meat Products); 5142 (Packaged Frozen Foods). **Emp:** 49. **Officers:** Richard Oravec.

■ **10484** ■ **Badalament Inc.**
515 10th St.
Detroit, MI 48216
Phone: (313)963-0746 **Fax:** (313)963-5877
Products: Produce; Packaging supplies. **SICs:** 5148 (Fresh Fruits & Vegetables); 5113 (Industrial & Personal Service Paper). **Est:** 1903. **Sales:** $5,000,000 (2000). **Emp:** 20. **Officers:** Louis T. Badalament, President; Michael L. Badalament, Finance Officer; Mark A. Badalament, VP of Marketing.

■ **10485** ■ **Badalament Inc.**
515 10th St.
Detroit, MI 48216
Phone: (313)963-0746 **Fax:** (313)963-5877
Products: Fresh fruits and vegetables. **SIC:** 5148 (Fresh Fruits & Vegetables). **Sales:** $15,000,000 (1999). **Emp:** 44. **Officers:** Mark Badalament, President; Michael L. Badalament, Finance Officer.

■ **10486** ■ **Badger Farmers Cooperative**
PO Box 97
Badger, SD 57214
Phone: (605)983-3241 **Fax:** (605)983-5831
Products: Agricultural equipment and supplies. **SIC:** 5153 (Grain & Field Beans). **Sales:** $5,000,000 (2000). **Emp:** 6.

■ **10487** ■ **Badger Popcorn Co.**
2914 Latham Dr.
Madison, WI 53701
Phone: (608)274-5058
Products: Popcorn. **SIC:** 5141 (Groceries—General Line).

■ **10488** ■ **Bagatelle**
1425 N Pershing
Wichita, KS 67208-2211
Phone: (316)684-5662 **Fax:** (316)684-1781
Products: Bread, cake, and related products; Pastries. **SIC:** 5149 (Groceries & Related Products Nec). **Emp:** 30. **Officers:** Antoine Toubia, Owner.

■ **10489** ■ **Bakalars Brothers Sausage Co.**
2219 South Ave.
La Crosse, WI 54601
Phone: (608)784-0384 **Fax:** (608)784-8361
Products: Meats, fish, and cheese. **SICs:** 5147 (Meats & Meat Products); 5146 (Fish & Seafoods); 5143 (Dairy Products Except Dried or Canned). **Sales:** $10,000,000 (2000). **Emp:** 49. **Officers:** Glen Bakalars.

■ **10490** ■ **Baker Candy Co. Inc.**
12534 Lake City Way N
Seattle, WA 98125
Phone: (206)363-5227 **Fax:** (206)361-7009
Products: Candy. **SIC:** 5145 (Confectionery). **Sales:** $1,500,000 (2000). **Emp:** 45. **Officers:** Nancy L. Prevele, President; Ron R. Prevele, Vice President; Richard L. Prevele, Treasurer & Secty.

■ **10491** ■ **Bakers Chocolate and Coconut**
PO Box 398
Memphis, TN 38101
Phone: (901)766-2100
Products: Shortening; Cheese powders. **SIC:** 5149 (Groceries & Related Products Nec).

■ **10492** ■ **Bakers Choice**
21400 Telegraph Rd.
Southfield, MI 48034
Phone: (248)827-7500 **Fax:** (248)827-7505
Products: Cookies and snack cakes. **SIC:** 5149 (Groceries & Related Products Nec). **Est:** 1979. **Emp:** 99. **Officers:** Wayne E. Sonkin.

■ **10493** ■ **Bakery Management Corp.**
15625 NW 15th Ave.
Miami, FL 33169
Phone: (305)623-3838 **Fax:** (305)626-9189
URL: http://www.Bakerycorp.com
Products: Bakery products. **SIC:** 5149 (Groceries & Related Products Nec). **Est:** 1986. **Sales:** $1,600,000 (2000). **Emp:** 16. **Officers:** Luis A. Lacal, President; Juan Carlos Lacal, Vice President.

■ **10494** ■ **Balfour Maclaine Corp.**
61 Broadway, Ste. 2700
New York, NY 10006-2704
Phone: (212)269-0800 **Fax:** (212)269-1041
Products: Groceries; Grain; Paraffin wax products. **SICs:** 5141 (Groceries—General Line); 5153 (Grain & Field Beans); 5172 (Petroleum Products Nec). **Est:** 1953. **Sales:** $1,312,000,000 (1990). **Emp:** 800. **Officers:** Anthonie C. Van Ekris, CEO, President & Chairman of the Board; Russell E. Diaz, Sr. VP & CFO.

■ **10495** ■ **Bama Companies Inc.**
PO Box 4829
Tulsa, OK 74159
Phone: (918)592-0778 **Fax:** (918)732-2811
URL: http://bamapie.com
Products: Fried turnovers; Pie shells; Biscuits; Frozen dough. **SICs:** 5149 (Groceries & Related Products Nec); 5142 (Packaged Frozen Foods). **Est:** 1937. **Sales:** $100,000,000 (2000). **Emp:** 700. **Officers:** Paula Marshall-Chapman, President & CEO.

■ **10496** ■ **Banana Supply Company Inc.**
3030 NE 2nd Ave.
Miami, FL 33137
Phone: (305)573-7610 **Fax:** (305)576-2563
Products: Bananas and plantains. **SIC:** 5148 (Fresh Fruits & Vegetables). **Sales:** $62,000,000 (2000). **Emp:** 200. **Officers:** Thomas R. Nest, President; William Jordan, Treasurer.

■ **10497** ■ **Banner Wholesale Grocers Inc.**
115 S Water Market St.
Chicago, IL 60608
Phone: (312)421-2650 **Fax:** (312)421-1257
Products: Groceries. **SIC:** 5141 (Groceries—General Line). **Est:** 1921. **Sales:** $45,000,000 (2000). **Emp:** 70. **Officers:** A.S. Friedman, President; Irving Saltzman, Treasurer; Richard Saltzman, VP of Marketing.

■ **10498** ■ **Banner Wholesale Grocers Inc.**
115 S Water Market St.
Chicago, IL 60608
Phone: (312)421-2650 **Fax:** (312)421-5175
Products: Groceries. **SIC:** 5141 (Groceries—General Line). **Sales:** $38,000,000 (2000). **Emp:** 60. **Officers:** A.S. Friedman, President; Irving Saltzman, Treasurer.

■ **10499** ■ **Banta Foods Inc.**
PO Box 8246
Springfield, MO 65801
Phone: (417)862-6644 **Fax:** (417)865-7223
URL: http://www.Bantafoods.com
Products: Food. **SIC:** 5141 (Groceries—GeneralLine). **Est:** 1895. **Sales:** $78,900,000 (2000). **Emp:** 150. **Officers:** Chuck Banta Jr., President; David Toft, Controller.

■ **10500** ■ **Bar Harbor Lobster Co.**
2000 Premier Row
Orlando, FL 32809
Phone: (407)851-4001 **Fax:** (407)857-5300
Products: Lobster, oysters, clams, mussels, fresh fish, and frozen seafood. **SIC:** 5146 (Fish & Seafoods). **Emp:** 49. **Officers:** Jeff P. Hazel.

■ **10501** ■ **Bar-S Foods Co.**
PO Box 29049
Phoenix, AZ 85038
Phone: (602)264-7272 **Fax:** (602)285-5252
Products: Processes and smokes meats; Natural and processed cheese. **SIC:** 5143 (Dairy Products Except Dried or Canned). **Sales:** $300,000,000 (2000). **Emp:** 1,100. **Officers:** Timothy Day, Chairman of the Board.

■ **10502** ■ **Baraboo-Sysco Food Services Inc.**
910 South Blvd.
Baraboo, WI 53913
Phone: (608)356-8711
Products: Food products. **SIC:** 5141 (Groceries—General Line). **Officers:** Eugene M. Bohlmeyer, President; Robert A. Jauch, Exec. VP of Finance.

■ **10503** ■ **Barbara's Bakery Inc.**
3900 Cypress Dr.
Petaluma, CA 94954
Phone: (707)765-2273 **Fax:** (707)765-2927
E-mail: info@barbarasbakery.com
URL: http://www.barbarasbakery.com
Products: Cereals; Bakery products and snack foods. **SIC:** 5149 (Groceries & Related Products Nec). **Emp:** 125. **Officers:** Gil Pritchard, President; David Weber, Controller; Rod Stringer, Dir. of Manufacturing.

■ **10504** ■ **Barbero Bakery Inc.**
51-61 Conrad
Trenton, NJ 08611-1011
Phone: (609)394-5122 **Fax:** (609)394-5567
Products: Bread and cake. **SIC:** 5149 (Groceries & Related Products Nec). **Sales:** $3,000,000 (2000). **Emp:** 70. **Officers:** Gerard A. Barbero, President; Angelo Barbero, Chairman of the Board.

■ **10505** ■ **Barber's Poultry Inc.**
PO Box 363
Broomfield, CO 80038
Phone: (303)466-7338 **Fax:** (303)466-6960
Products: Poultry products. **SIC:** 5144 (Poultry & Poultry Products). **Sales:** $5,500,000 (2000). **Emp:** 12. **Officers:** David R. Barber, President; Michael W. Barber, Treasurer & Secty.

■ **10506** ■ **Barentsen Candy Co.**
PO Box 686
Benton Harbor, MI 49023-0686
Phone: (616)927-3171 **Fax:** (616)925-4570
Products: Candy. **SIC:** 5145 (Confectionery). **Sales:** $11,000,000 (2000). **Emp:** 25. **Officers:** Grant Derfelt, CEO.

■ **10507** ■ **Barkett Fruit Co. Inc.**
205 Deeds Dr.
Dover, OH 44622-9652
Phone: (330)364-6645
Free: (800)824-8399 **Fax:** (330)364-7683
E-mail: barkett@tusco.net
Products: Fruits and vegetables; Dairy products; Dry preparations. **SICs:** 5148 (Fresh Fruits & Vegetables); 5143 (Dairy Products Except Dried or Canned); 5141 (Groceries—General Line). **Est:** 1924. **Emp:** 40. **Officers:** William M. Barkett; Ronald W. Barkett; Thomas R. Barkett; James L. Barkett.

■ **10508** ■ **Barnacle Seafood**
5301 NW 35th Ave.
Ft. Lauderdale, FL 33309-6315
Phone: (954)486-8000
Free: (800)647-2857 **Fax:** (954)486-8092
Products: Fresh and frozen smoked domestic and imported seafood. **SIC:** 5146 (Fish & Seafoods). **Emp:** 49. **Officers:** Mark Reed, COO & President.

■ **10509** ■ **Barnett Brothers Brokerage Co. Inc.**
2509 74th St.
Lubbock, TX 79423
Phone: (806)745-7575
Products: Cheeses; Hard candy; Deodorizers. **SICs:** 5143 (Dairy Products Except Dried or Canned); 5145 (Confectionery); 5169 (Chemicals & Allied Products Nec). **Est:** 1965. **Sales:** $95,000,000 (2000). **Emp:** 55. **Officers:** Tom Barnett, President; Earl Barnett, Treasurer & Secty.; Wayne Jones, VP of Marketing; Neil Burrus, Dir. of Systems.

■ **10510** ■ **Barnie's Coffee and Tea Company Inc.**
340 N Primrose Dr.
Orlando, FL 32803
Phone: (407)894-1416
Free: (800)284-1416 **Fax:** (407)898-5341
URL: http://www.barniescoffee.com
Products: Coffee, tea, and accessories. **SIC:** 5149 (Groceries & Related Products Nec). **Est:** 1980. **Sales:** $35,000,000 (2000). **Emp:** 850. **Officers:** Richard Ungaro, COO & President; Joe Russell, CFO.

■ **10511** ■ **Baronet Coffee Inc.**
PO Box 987
Hartford, CT 06143-0987
Phone: (860)527-7253
Free: (800)227-6638 **Fax:** (860)524-9130
E-mail: baronet98@aol.com
URL: http://www.baronetcoffee.com
Products: Roasted coffee beans. **SIC:** 5149 (Groceries & Related Products Nec). **Est:** 1930. **Emp:** 10. **Officers:** Bruce Goldsmith, President, e-mail: bhgoldsmith@aol.com. **Former Name:** Baronet Gourmet Coffee Inc.

■ **10512** ■ **Base Inc.**
5307 E Pine St.
Tulsa, OK 74115-5329
Phone: (918)732-2540
Free: (800)364-3702 **Fax:** (918)732-2888
Products: Bakery mixes, starches, and sweeteners. **SIC:** 5149 (Groceries & Related Products Nec). **Sales:** $2,500,000 (2000). **Emp:** 14. **Officers:** Paula Marshall-Chapman, CEO.

■ **10513** ■ **Baskin-Robbins USA Co.**
1918 S Texas Ave.
Bryan, TX 77802-1831
Phone: (409)779-0091 **Fax:** (409)775-0459
Products: Ice cream. **SIC:** 5143 (Dairy Products Except Dried or Canned). **Sales:** $6,000,000 (2000). **Emp:** 52. **Officers:** Teresa Gallihet.

■ **10514** ■ **Bassett Dairy Products Inc.**
2197 S Byron Butler Pkwy.
Perry, FL 32347
Phone: (850)584-5149 **Fax:** (850)584-8162
Products: Dairy products. **SICs:** 5143 (Dairy Products Except Dried or Canned); 5149 (Groceries & Related Products Nec). **Est:** 1969. **Sales:** $3,000,000 (2000). **Emp:** 15. **Officers:** James C. Bassett, President; James Bassett Jr., Treasurer & Secty.

■ **10515** ■ **Bay State Lobster Company Inc.**
PO Box 347
Lynn, MA 01905-0647
Phone: (617)523-4588 **Fax:** (617)523-0216
Products: Seafood. **SIC:** 5146 (Fish & Seafoods). **Sales:** $15,000,000 (2000). **Emp:** 60. **Officers:** Richard Faro, President; Joseph Faro, Treasurer.

■ **10516** ■ **Bay View Food Products Co.**
2606 N Huron Rd.
Pinconning, MI 48650
Phone: (517)879-3555 **Fax:** (517)879-2659
Products: Cucumbers. **SIC:** 5148 (Fresh Fruits & Vegetables). **Est:** 1946. **Sales:** $4,000,000 (2000). **Emp:** 12. **Officers:** Joseph Janicke, President; Francis Janicke, Chairman of the Board.

■ **10517** ■ **Baye & Rhodes**
181 Joaquin Circle
Danville, CA 94526-3014
Phone: (510)837-9147 **Fax:** (510)837-2119
Products: Groceries. **SIC:** 5141 (Groceries—General Line).

■ **10518** ■ **Bayou Caddy Fisheries Inc.**
PO Box 44
Lakeshore, MS 39558
Phone: (228)467-4332
Products: Seafood. **SIC:** 5146 (Fish & Seafoods). **Sales:** $1,500,000 (1993). **Emp:** 10. **Officers:** Joseph Cure, President.

■ **10519** ■ **Bayou Land Seafood**
1008 Vincent Berard Rd.
Breaux Bridge, LA 70517
Phone: (318)667-6118
Free: (800)737-6868 **Fax:** (318)667-6059
Products: Seafood. **SIC:** 5146 (Fish & Seafoods). **Est:** 1973. **Sales:** $3,600,000 (2000). **Emp:** 50. **Officers:** Roy J. Robin, Owner; Anna Robin, VP of Sales.

■ **10520** ■ **Bays Corp.**
PO Box 1455
Chicago, IL 60690-1455
Phone: (312)346-5757 **Fax:** (312)346-8990
Products: Bakery products. **SIC:** 5149 (Groceries & Related Products Nec). **Sales:** $58,000,000 (2000). **Emp:** 122. **Officers:** James N. Bay, President; James N. Bay Jr., VP & CFO.

■ **10521** ■ **Beaver Street Fisheries, Inc.**
1741 W Beaver St.
Jacksonville, FL 32209
Phone: (904)354-8533
Free: (800)874-6426 **Fax:** (904)633-7271
URL: http://www.beaverfish.com
Products: Seafood; Lamb; Meat; Breaded food products. **SICs:** 5146 (Fish & Seafoods); 5142 (Packaged Frozen Foods); 5141 (Groceries—General Line). **Est:** 1955. **Sales:** $200,000,000 (1999). **Emp:** 200. **Officers:** Fred Frisch; Hans Frisch; Karl Frisch; Charles R. Trager, Sales/Marketing Contact, e-mail: ctrager@Beaverfish.com; Shauneen Murphy, Customer Service Contact, e-mail: smurphy@beaverfish.com; Nick Malie, Human Resources Contact, e-mail: nmalie@Beaverfish.com; Shauneen Murphy, Customer Service Contact, e-mail: smuphy@beaverfish.com.

■ **10522** ■ **Beaverton Foods Inc.**
4220 SW Cedar Hills Blvd.
Beaverton, OR 97005-2029
Phone: (503)646-8138
Free: (800)223-8076 **Fax:** (503)644-9204
E-mail: sales@beavertonfoods.com
Products: Sauces and condiments, including mustards, horseradish, and garlic. **SIC:** 5149 (Groceries & Related Products Nec). **Est:** 1929. **Sales:** $15,000,000 (2000). **Emp:** 85. **Officers:** Gene Biggi, President; Bill Small, CEO; Domonic Biggi, Vice President.

■ **10523** ■ **Becker Food Company Inc.**
4160 N Port Washington Rd.
Milwaukee, WI 53212
Phone: (414)964-5353
Products: Meat. **SIC:** 5147 (Meats & Meat Products). **Est:** 1923. **Emp:** 75. **Officers:** Stephen S. Becker, CEO & President.

■ **10524** ■ **Beckman Produce Inc.**
415 Grove St.
St. Paul, MN 55101
Phone: (612)222-1212 **Fax:** (612)222-4191
Products: Fresh fruits and vegetables. **SIC:** 5148
(Fresh Fruits & Vegetables). **Est:** 1974. **Sales:**
$180,000,000 (2000). **Emp:** 675. **Officers:** Kathy
Lalibete, President.

■ **10525** ■ **Bedford Food Products Inc.**
1320 Avenue N
Brooklyn, NY 11230-5906
Phone: (718)237-9595 **Fax:** (718)237-9861
Products: Bakery supplies, including cocoa and nuts.
SIC: 5149 (Groceries & Related Products Nec). **Est:**
1945. **Sales:** $1,750,000 (2000). **Emp:** 5.

■ **10526** ■ **Katharine Beecher Candies**
PO Box 3411
Camp Hill, PA 17011-3411
Phone: (717)266-3641
Free: (800)708-3641 **Fax:** (717)266-4227
Products: Candy. **SIC:** 5145 (Confectionery). **Sales:**
$6,000,000 (2000). **Emp:** 49. **Officers:** L.A. Warrell,
CEO; R.P. Billman, President; Logan Jones, Vice
President; A.W. Strom, Sr. VP of Marketing.

■ **10527** ■ **Bel Canto Fancy Foods Ltd.**
57-01 49th Pl.
Maspeth, NY 11378
Phone: (718)497-3888
Free: (800)597-2151 **Fax:** (718)497-3799
E-mail: belcantofd@cs.com
URL: http://www.belcanto-fancy-food.com
Products: Specialty foods from Europe. **SIC:** 5149
(Groceries & Related Products Nec). **Est:** 1977. **Sales:**
$10,000,000 (2000). **Emp:** 25. **Officers:** Luciano
Todaro, President; Angela Zambelli, Customer Service
Contact; Mary Todaro, Human Resources Contact.

■ **10528** ■ **Bel-Pak Foods Inc.**
1411 W Chicago Ave.
Chicago, IL 60622
Phone: (312)421-2440
Products: Food, including pizzeria supplies. **SIC:** 5149
(Groceries & Related Products Nec). **Est:** 1962. **Sales:**
$4,000,000 (2000). **Emp:** 8. **Officers:** Vitto Frettilio,
President; Rich Komperda, Treasurer.

■ **10529** ■ **Bell-Carter Foods Inc.**
3742 Mt Diablo Blvd.
Lafayette, CA 94549
Phone: (925)284-5933
Products: Ripe olive canning. **SIC:** 5148 (Fresh Fruits
& Vegetables). **Sales:** $100,000,000 (2000). **Emp:**
450. **Officers:** Tim Carter, CEO; Mike Hoversen, CFO.

■ **10530** ■ **A.P. Bell Fish Company, Inc.**
4600 124th St. W
PO Box 276
Cortez, FL 34215
Phone: (941)794-1249 **Fax:** (941)795-4637
URL: http://www.bellfish.com
Products: Fish, including frozen and fresh; Seafood,
including shrimp. **SIC:** 5146 (Fish & Seafoods). **Est:**
1940. **Emp:** 29. **Officers:** Walter Bell.

■ **10531** ■ **Belle Island International Inc.**
3 Mary Austin Pl.
Norwalk, CT 06850
Phone: (203)840-8890 **Fax:** (203)840-8898
Products: Beef products. **SIC:** 5147 (Meats & Meat
Products). **Est:** 1989. **Sales:** $40,000,000 (2000).
Emp: 3. **Officers:** Paul Krause, Treasurer.

■ **10532** ■ **Belli-Childs Wholesale Produce**
512 W Cowles
Long Beach, CA 90813
Phone: (562)437-7441 **Fax:** (562)436-3151
Products: Frozen foods; Fresh vegetables. **SICs:**
5148 (Fresh Fruits & Vegetables); 5142 (Packaged
Frozen Foods). **Emp:** 49. **Officers:** Tony Belli, Sales
Rep.

■ **10533** ■ **Bell's Produce, Inc.**
3401 Michigan Ave.
Flint, MI 48505
Phone: (810)235-6668 **Fax:** (810)235-5721
Products: Produce. **SIC:** 5148 (Fresh Fruits &
Vegetables).

■ **10534** ■ **Belmont Wholesale Co. Inc.**
4432 Ardmore Ave.
Ft. Wayne, IN 46809
Phone: (219)747-7582 **Fax:** (219)747-4884
Products: Food; Clothing. **SICs:** 5149 (Groceries &
Related Products Nec); 5136 (Men's/Boys' Clothing);
5137 (Women's/Children's Clothing). **Sales:**
$10,000,000 (2000). **Emp:** 200. **Officers:** David A.
Johnson, President; Eugene Johnson, Treasurer &
Secty.

■ **10535** ■ **Benham and Company Inc.**
PO Box 29
Mineola, TX 75773
Phone: (903)569-2636 **Fax:** (903)569-2120
Products: Beans, rice, popcorn, and household
aluminum foil. **SICs:** 5153 (Grain & Field Beans); 5145
(Confectionery); 5149 (Groceries & Related Products
Nec). **Sales:** $20,000,000 (2000). **Emp:** 66. **Officers:**
Raymond Curbow, Finance General Manager.

■ **10536** ■ **Bennett Vending**
2032 S St. Aubin
Sioux City, IA 51106
Phone: (712)276-0173
Products: Food products, including candy and snacks
for vending machines. **SIC:** 5149 (Groceries & Related
Products Nec).

■ **10537** ■ **Bensinger's**
8543 Page Ave.
St. Louis, MO 63114
Phone: (314)426-5100
Products: Food; Fresh meat; Dairy products; Fruits
and vegetables. **SICs:** 5046 (Commercial Equipment
Nec); 5147 (Meats & Meat Products); 5143 (Dairy
Products Except Dried or Canned); 5148 (Fresh Fruits
& Vegetables). **Est:** 1970. **Sales:** $6,000,000 (2000).
Emp: 35. **Officers:** Rick Allen, Vice President.

■ **10538** ■ **Bensons Backery**
PO Box 429
Bogart, GA 30622
Phone: (770)725-5711 **Fax:** (770)725-5888
Products: Baked goods. **SIC:** 5149 (Groceries &
Related Products Nec). **Emp:** 65. **Officers:** Larry
Benson, President; C.B. Clark, President Bakery
Division.

■ **10539** ■ **Berelson Export Corp.**
291 Geary St., Ste. 407
San Francisco, CA 94102
Phone: (415)956-6600 **Fax:** (415)956-7439
Products: Frozen, canned, and dehydrated foods.
SICs: 5142 (Packaged Frozen Foods); 5149
(Groceries & Related Products Nec). **Est:** 1974. **Sales:**
$12,000,000 (2000). **Emp:** 5. **Officers:** Herb Wiltsek,
President, e-mail: herbberex@aol.com; Jeff Wartell,
Dir. of Sales, e-mail: dbbeo@aol.com. **Alternate
Name:** Sun Down Foods, U.S.A.

■ **10540** ■ **Berelson Export Corp.**
291 Geary St., Ste. 407
San Francisco, CA 94102
Phone: (415)956-6600 **Fax:** (415)956-7439
Products: Food. **SIC:** 5142 (Packaged Frozen Foods).
Sales: $12,000,000 (2000). **Emp:** 5.

■ **10541** ■ **H.J. Bergeron Pecan Shelling Plant,
Inc.**
10003 False River Rd.
New Roads, LA 70760
Phone: (504)638-7667
Free: (800)256-4675 **Fax:** (504)638-4721
Products: Pecans. **SIC:** 5145 (Confectionery). **Sales:**
$2,000,000 (2000). **Emp:** 49. **Officers:** Lester
Bergeron Jr.

■ **10542** ■ **William Bernstein Company Inc.**
155 W 72nd St.
New York, NY 10023
Phone: (212)799-3200 **Fax:** (212)799-3209
Products: Gum olbanum, myrrh, and benzoin;
Botanical crude drugs; Spices; Apricot kernels. **SIC:**
5149 (Groceries & Related Products Nec). **Est:** 1939.
Sales: $3,000,000 (2000). **Emp:** 6. **Officers:** William
Bernstein, President.

■ **10543** ■ **Berthold Farmers Elevator Co.**
PO Box 38
Berthold, ND 58718
Phone: (701)453-3431 **Fax:** (701)453-3424
Products: Grain. **SIC:** 5153 (Grain & Field Beans).
Sales: $17,000,000 (2000). **Emp:** 18. **Officers:** Alan
Lee, President.

■ **10544** ■ **Bertolli U.S.A. Inc.**
300 Harmon Meadow Blvd.
Secaucus, NJ 07094
Phone: (201)863-2088
Products: Olive oil. **SIC:** 5149 (Groceries & Related
Products Nec). **Sales:** $13,000,000 (2000). **Emp:** 28.
Officers: William Monroe, President.

■ **10545** ■ **Teddy Bertuca Co.**
PO Box 217
McAllen, TX 78502
Phone: (956)631-7123 **Fax:** (956)682-5765
Products: Cabbage. **SIC:** 5148 (Fresh Fruits &
Vegetables). **Sales:** $90,000,000 (2000). **Emp:** 250.
Officers: Teddy Bertuca, President.

■ **10546** ■ **Best Brands Inc.**
6307 N 53rd St.
Tampa, FL 33610
Phone: (813)621-7802 **Fax:** (813)626-7897
Products: Baked goods. **SIC:** 5149 (Groceries &
Related Products Nec). **Emp:** 49. **Officers:** Dennis
Kneip.

■ **10547** ■ **Best Foods**
2816 S Kilbourn
Chicago, IL 60623-4299
Phone: (773)247-5800 **Fax:** (773)247-6146
Products: Mayonnaise. **SIC:** 5149 (Groceries &
Related Products Nec). **Sales:** $200,000,000 (2000).
Emp: 499. **Officers:** J. W. Warner.

■ **10548** ■ **Best Sausage Inc.**
805 E Kemper Rd.
Cincinnati, OH 45246-2515
Products: Sausage and pork. **SIC:** 5147 (Meats &
Meat Products). **Emp:** 24. **Officers:** Robert Best,
President.

■ **10549** ■ **Beyer Farms Inc.**
265 Malta St.
Brooklyn, NY 11207
Phone: (718)272-4500
Products: Milk. **SIC:** 5143 (Dairy Products Except
Dried or Canned).

■ **10550** ■ **Allen Beyer Livestock**
N942 State Rd. 13
PO Box 1
Stetsonville, WI 54480
Phone: (715)678-2711
Products: Meat; Livestock. **SICs:** 5147 (Meats & Meat
Products); 5154 (Livestock).

■ **10551** ■ **Bi Rite Foodservice Distributors**
PO Box 410417
San Francisco, CA 94141-0417
Phone: (415)656-0254 **Fax:** (415)394-7808
Products: Food and related products. **SIC:** 5149
(Groceries & Related Products Nec). **Sales:**
$56,000,000 (1993). **Emp:** 140. **Officers:** William P.
Barulich, President; Albert Lee, Controller.

■ **10552** ■ **Bianchi and Sons Packing Co.**
PO Box 190
Merced, CA 95341-0190
Phone: (209)722-8134 **Fax:** (209)722-4013
Products: Tomatoes. **SIC:** 5148 (Fresh Fruits &
Vegetables). **Est:** 1948. **Sales:** $10,000,000 (2000).
Emp: 250. **Officers:** Larry Bianchi, President; John
Bianchi, Secretary.

■ 10553 ■ Bickford Flavors Inc.
19007 St. Clair Ave.
Cleveland, OH 44117
Phone: (216)531-6006 **Fax:** (216)531-2006
Products: Vanilla and flavorings. **SIC:** 5149 (Groceries & Related Products Nec). **Officers:** Barbara Sofer.

■ 10554 ■ Big Banana Fruit Market
Bute Rd.
Uniontown, PA 15401
Phone: (412)438-4980 **Fax:** (412)438-6386
Products: Produce. **SIC:** 5148 (Fresh Fruits & Vegetables). **Emp:** 15.

■ 10555 ■ Big Boy Ice Cream
602 E Lohman Ave.
Las Cruces, NM 88001
Phone: (505)541-0413
Products: Ice cream. **SIC:** 5143 (Dairy Products Except Dried or Canned).

■ 10556 ■ Big Sandy Wholesale Co.
PO Box 249
Harold, KY 41635
Phone: (606)478-9591 **Fax:** (606)478-9578
Products: Dried and dehydrated food products. **SIC:** 5149 (Groceries & Related Products Nec). **Sales:** $32,000,000 (2000). **Emp:** 100. **Officers:** P. Justice, President.

■ 10557 ■ Birdsong Corp.
612 Madison Ave.
Suffolk, VA 23434
Phone: (804)539-3456 **Fax:** (804)539-7360
Products: Peanuts. **SIC:** 5159 (Farm-Product Raw Materials Nec). **Est:** 1947. **Sales:** $180,000,000 (2000). **Emp:** 500. **Officers:** William J. Spain Jr., CEO; Frank R. Johns, Controller; Everett Birdsong, Information Systems Mgr.

■ 10558 ■ BiRite Foodservice
201 Alabama St.
San Francisco, CA 94103
Phone: (415)621-6909 **Fax:** (415)394-7808
Products: General line groceries. **SIC:** 5141 (Groceries—General Line).

■ 10559 ■ Bishop Baking Co.
PO Box 3720
Cleveland, TN 37320
Phone: (423)472-1561 **Fax:** (423)478-3320
Products: Snack cakes. **SIC:** 5149 (Groceries & Related Products Nec). **Est:** 1955. **Sales:** $35,000,000 (2000). **Emp:** 350. **Officers:** A. E. Veazey.

■ 10560 ■ Bishop-Epicure Foods Company Inc.
PO Box 48426
Atlanta, GA 30362-1428
Phone: (404)441-2227
Products: General line of groceries. **SIC:** 5141 (Groceries—General Line).

■ 10561 ■ Bison Products Co. Inc.
81 Dingens St.
Buffalo, NY 14206
Phone: (716)826-2700 **Fax:** (716)826-0603
Products: Deli meats. **SIC:** 5147 (Meats & Meat Products). **Sales:** $12,500,000 (2000). **Emp:** 55. **Officers:** Alvino Battistoni.

■ 10562 ■ Bivins Barbecue Sauce
6129 N Dort Hwy.
Flint, MI 48505
Phone: (810)789-5444
Products: Food, including barbecue sauce. **SIC:** 5141 (Groceries—General Line).

■ 10563 ■ Black Hills Milk Producers
PO Box 2084
Rapid City, SD 57709
Phone: (605)342-3780
Products: Milk. **SIC:** 5143 (Dairy Products Except Dried or Canned). **Est:** 1950. **Sales:** $11,000,000 (2000). **Emp:** 4. **Officers:** Mel Pittman, President; Mike Paulsen, General Mgr.

■ 10564 ■ Blackburn-Russell Company Inc.
PO Box 157
Bedford, PA 15522-0157
Phone: (814)623-5181
Free: (800)325-2815 **Fax:** (814)623-1216
E-mail: Blackbur@Bedford.net
Products: Food, including frozen and fresh. **SICs:** 5141 (Groceries—General Line); 5142 (Packaged Frozen Foods). **Est:** 1904. **Sales:** $19,000,000 (1999). **Emp:** 44. **Officers:** Robert B. Blackburn, President; Jeffrey R. Blackburn, VP & CFO.

■ 10565 ■ Blackmore Master Distributor
7100 Jackson St.
Paramount, CA 90723
Phone: (562)634-5600 **Fax:** (562)634-5609
Products: Frozen foods. **SIC:** 5142 (Packaged Frozen Foods). **Emp:** 20.

■ 10566 ■ Blackwell Stevenson Co.
3270 Sunnyside Rd.
Bethel Park, PA 15102-1247
Phone: (412)257-1470
Products: Food. **SIC:** 5141 (Groceries—General Line).

■ 10567 ■ Bland Farms Inc.
PO Box 506
Glennville, GA 30427
Phone: (912)654-1426 **Fax:** (912)654-1330
Products: Onions. **SIC:** 5148 (Fresh Fruits & Vegetables). **Sales:** $8,000,000 (2000). **Emp:** 65. **Officers:** Delbert Bland, President; Sandra Bland, Secretary.

■ 10568 ■ Bob Blanke Sales Inc.
1549 Helton Dr.
Florence, AL 35631
Phone: (205)764-5983
Products: Frozen vegetables; Frozen meats. **SICs:** 5142 (Packaged Frozen Foods); 5147 (Meats & Meat Products); 5148 (Fresh Fruits & Vegetables). **Est:** 1952. **Sales:** $6,000,000 (2000). **Emp:** 24. **Officers:** Henry T. Blanke, President.

■ 10569 ■ Bloemer Food Service Co.
925 S 7th St.
Louisville, KY 40203
Phone: (502)584-8338 **Fax:** (502)584-8844
Products: Food and food service supplies. **SICs:** 5141 (Groceries—General Line); 5145 (Confectionery); 5142 (Packaged Frozen Foods); 5143 (Dairy Products Except Dried or Canned); 5149 (Groceries & Related Products Nec). **Est:** 1919. **Sales:** $12,000,000 (2000). **Emp:** 50. **Officers:** Larry Bloemer; Brent Haire; Shawn Kemper.

■ 10570 ■ Blooming Prairie Cooperative Warehouse
2340 Heinz Rd.
Iowa City, IA 52240
Phone: (319)337-6448 **Fax:** (319)337-4592
URL: http://www.bpco-op.com
Products: Natural foods; Nutritional supplements. **SIC:** 5141 (Groceries—General Line). **Est:** 1974. **Emp:** 200. **Officers:** K. Jesse Singerman, President & CEO; Sue Futrell, Dir. of Mktg. & Sales; Cathy Hirsch, Director of Human Resources. **Former Name:** Blooming Prairie. **Also Known by This Acronym:** BP.

■ 10571 ■ Blooming Prairie Natural Foods
510 Kasota Ave. SE
Minneapolis, MN 55414
Phone: (612)378-9774 **Fax:** (612)378-9780
URL: http://www.bpco-op.com
Products: Health and organic foods, including packaged groceries; Bulk, frozen, and refrigerated foods; Nutritional supplements; Health and beauty products. **SICs:** 5149 (Groceries & Related Products Nec); 5122 (Drugs, Proprietaries & Sundries). **Est:** 1974. **Emp:** 200.

■ 10572 ■ Blount Seafood Corp.
PO Box 327
Warren, RI 02885
Phone: (401)245-8800
Free: (800)274-2526 **Fax:** (401)247-2391
E-mail: sales@blountseafood.com
URL: http://www.blountseafood.com
Products: Frozen seafood. **SIC:** 5146 (Fish & Seafoods). **Est:** 1946. **Sales:** $25,000,000 (2000). **Emp:** 150. **Officers:** Frederick N. Blount, Chairman of the Board; George Richardson, President; Bob Sewal, VP of Sales; Julie Rencurrer, Customer Service Contact; Shelley Swallow, Human Resources Contact; F. Nelson Blount, Vice President.

■ 10573 ■ Blue Anchor Inc.
301 North G St.
Exeter, CA 93221-1123
Phone: (916)929-3050
Products: Fruits and vegetables. **SIC:** 5148 (Fresh Fruits & Vegetables). **Sales:** $68,000,000 (2000). **Emp:** 100. **Officers:** Pat Sanguinetti, President.

■ 10574 ■ Blue Grass Quality Meats
PO Box 17658
Crescent Springs, KY 41017
Phone: (606)331-7100
Products: Smoked meat products. **SIC:** 5147 (Meats & Meat Products). **Est:** 1867. **Sales:** $22,000,000 (2000). **Emp:** 90. **Officers:** Sam Finch, President.

■ 10575 ■ Blue Line Distributing
24120 Haggerty Rd.
Farmington Hills, MI 48335
Phone: (248)478-6200 **Fax:** (248)478-1412
Products: Food supplies for pizza chains. **SIC:** 5149 (Groceries & Related Products Nec).

■ 10576 ■ Blue Mountain Growers Inc.
PO Box 156
Milton-Freewater, OR 97862
Phone: (541)938-3391 **Fax:** (541)938-5304
E-mail: bluemtn@bmi.net
Products: Apples; Cherries; Prunes; and Plums. **SIC:** 5148 (Fresh Fruits & Vegetables). **Est:** 1927. **Sales:** $6,000,000 (2000). **Emp:** 200. **Officers:** John D. Wilcox, President & General Mgr.

■ 10577 ■ Blue Ribbon Foods
PO Box 1805
Wenatchee, WA 98801
Phone: (509)662-2181 **Fax:** (509)663-2930
Products: Meat, including beef and pork; Fish. **SICs:** 5147 (Meats & Meat Products); 5146 (Fish & Seafoods). **Est:** 1975. **Sales:** $2,500,000 (2000). **Emp:** 12. **Officers:** J. Sanchez, President; Sharon Wong, Vice President; Naomi Sanchez, Sales/Marketing Contact; Nora Williams, Customer Service Contact.

■ 10578 ■ Blue Ribbon Meat Co.
PO Box 633
Sparks, NV 89431
Phone: (702)358-8116 **Fax:** (702)358-0992
Products: Meat. **SIC:** 5147 (Meats & Meat Products). **Est:** 1947. **Sales:** $7,000,000 (2000). **Emp:** 24. **Officers:** Scott Taylor, President; Helen Kennedy, Controller.

■ 10579 ■ Blue Ribbon Meat Company Inc.
PO Box 1805
Wenatchee, WA 98801
Phone: (509)662-2181 **Fax:** (509)663-2930
Products: Meat. **SICs:** 5147 (Meats & Meat Products); 5149 (Groceries & Related Products Nec). **Est:** 1975. **Sales:** $2,500,000 (1999). **Emp:** 10. **Officers:** George L. Dosser, President.

■ 10580 ■ Blue Ridge Beef Plant Inc.
PO Box 397
Belton, SC 29627
Phone: (803)338-5544
Products: Beef. **SIC:** 5147 (Meats & Meat Products). **Est:** 1965. **Sales:** $6,000,000 (2000). **Emp:** 5. **Officers:** Harry C. Mullinax, President; Linda Mullinax, Treasurer.

■ 10581 ■ Blue Star Growers Inc.
PO Box I
Cashmere, WA 98815
Phone: (509)782-2922 **Fax:** (509)782-3646
Products: Fresh fruits. **SIC:** 5148 (Fresh Fruits & Vegetables). **Sales:** $20,000,000 (2000). **Emp:** 250. **Officers:** Jerry Kenoyer, Dir. of Marketing; Tom Griffith, Chairman of the Board.

■ 10582 ■ **Bluefin Seafoods Corp.**
141 N Spring St.
Louisville, KY 40206
Phone: (502)587-1505
Products: Seafood. **SICs:** 5146 (Fish & Seafoods);
5142 (Packaged Frozen Foods).

■ 10583 ■ **BMT Commodity Corp.**
750 Lexington Ave.
New York, NY 10022
Phone: (212)759-4505
Products: Food, including fruit and vegetable powders,
and tomato paste. **SIC:** 5085 (Industrial Supplies). **Est:**
1922. **Sales:** $42,000,000 (2000). **Emp:** 25. **Officers:**
Peter Ganz, CEO; Robert Ganz, President & CFO.

■ 10584 ■ **Bob's Candies Inc.**
PO Box 3170
Albany, GA 31707
Phone: (912)430-8300
Free: (800)841-3602 **Fax:** (912)430-8331
URL: http://www.bobscandies.com
Products: Candies. **SIC:** 5145 (Confectionery). **Est:**
1919. **Sales:** $30,000,000 (2000). **Emp:** 550. **Officers:**
Greg McCormack.

■ 10585 ■ **Bob's Fruit Market & Deli**
12418 Dix-Toledo
Southgate, MI 48195
Phone: (810)282-1057
Products: Fruits and vegetables; Deli foods; Bedding
plants. **SICs:** 5148 (Fresh Fruits & Vegetables); 5149
(Groceries & Related Products Nec). **Sales:**
$2,100,000 (1999). **Emp:** 22. **Officers:** Robert Wood.

■ 10586 ■ **A. Bohrer Inc.**
50 Knickerbocker Rd.
Moonachie, NJ 07074
Phone: (201)935-1600 **Fax:** (201)935-3579
Products: Produce; Frozen food. **SICs:** 5148 (Fresh
Fruits & Vegetables); 5142 (Packaged Frozen Foods).
Est: 1895. **Sales:** $60,000,000 (2000). **Emp:** 175.
Officers: Arthur Bohrer, President; Vincent Piscopo,
Controller; Leonard Nash, General Mgr.

■ 10587 ■ **Bomadi Inc.**
28 E Jackson Blvd., Ste. 1109
Chicago, IL 60604
Phone: (312)663-3880 **Fax:** (312)663-9079
Products: Sugar; Rice, corn, and wheat. **SICs:** 5149
(Groceries & Related Products Nec); 5153 (Grain &
Field Beans). **Officers:** Victor Ogbebor, Marketing
Manager.

■ 10588 ■ **Bon Secour Fisheries Inc.**
PO Box 60
Bon Secour, AL 36511
Phone: (334)949-7411
Free: (800)633-6854 **Fax:** (334)949-6478
E-mail: bonsec@gulftel.com
Products: Shrimp, oysters, and fish. **SIC:** 5146 (Fish &
Seafoods). **Est:** 1896. **Sales:** $24,000,000 (2000).
Emp: 180. **Officers:** John R. Nelson, President; Frank
Bailey, Controller; David Nelson, VP of Marketing;
Melani Parker, Dir. of Data Processing.

■ 10589 ■ **Bon Ton Foods Inc.**
1120 Zinns Quarry Rd.
York, PA 17404
Phone: (717)843-0738
Free: (800)233-1933 **Fax:** (717)843-5192
Products: Potato chips. **SIC:** 5145 (Confectionery).
Sales: $15,000,000 (2000). **Emp:** 78. **Officers:**
Edward J. Tessier; Donald J. Long.

■ 10590 ■ **Borden Inc.**
103 W 11th
Lake Charles, LA 70601-6034
Phone: (318)494-3830 **Fax:** (318)436-2022
Products: Dairy products. **SIC:** 5143 (Dairy Products
Except Dried or Canned). **Sales:** $10,000,000 (2000).
Emp: 33. **Officers:** H. R. LaFleur.

■ 10591 ■ **Borden Inc.**
500 N Jackson
Sulphur Springs, TX 75482-2846
Phone: (903)885-7573 **Fax:** (903)885-6236
Products: Cultured dairy products, including cottage
cheese, yogurt, sour cream, and fresh juices. **SIC:**
5143 (Dairy Products Except Dried or Canned). **Sales:**
$6,000,000 (2000). **Emp:** 99. **Officers:** Tom Blake.

■ 10592 ■ **Borden Inc.**
805 W Front
Tyler, TX 75702-7953
Phone: (903)595-4461 **Fax:** (903)595-6874
Products: Milk. **SIC:** 5143 (Dairy Products Except
Dried or Canned). **Sales:** $17,000,000 (2000). **Emp:**
99. **Officers:** Bill Holder.

■ 10593 ■ **Borden Milk Products LLP**
PO Box 7651
Waco, TX 76714-7651
Phone: (254)420-3374
Free: (800)826-6455 **Fax:** (254)420-3544
Products: Milk. **SIC:** 5143 (Dairy Products Except
Dried or Canned). **Emp:** 10. **Officers:** Rick Perkins,
Branch Sales Mgr. **Former Name:** Borden Inc.

■ 10594 ■ **Borstein Seafood Inc.**
PO Box 188
Bellingham, WA 98227
Phone: (360)734-7990 **Fax:** (360)734-5732
Products: Fish. **SIC:** 5146 (Fish & Seafoods). **Est:**
1930. **Sales:** $19,000,000 (2000). **Emp:** 250. **Officers:**
Jay Bornstein, CEO; Bev Seager, Accountant; Jim
Humphrey, Dir. of Marketing & Sales.

■ 10595 ■ **Borton Brokerage Co.**
PO Box 410167
St. Louis, MO 63141
Phone: (314)991-3355
Products: Food. **SIC:** 5141 (Groceries—General Line).

■ 10596 ■ **Bosco Products Inc.**
441 Main Rd.
Towaco, NJ 07082
Phone: (973)334-7777
Products: Chocolate syrup. **SIC:** 5149 (Groceries &
Related Products Nec). **Sales:** $2,000,000 (2000).
Emp: 5. **Officers:** Steve Sanders, President.

■ 10597 ■ **Boston Brands**
8 Faneuil Hall Market Pl.
Boston, MA 02109
Phone: (617)973-9100
Products: Frozen desserts, including ice cream. **SIC:**
5143 (Dairy Products Except Dried or Canned).

■ 10598 ■ **Boston Sea Foods Inc.**
982 Main
Springfield, MA 01103-2120
Phone: (413)732-3663 **Fax:** (413)732-3663
Products: Seafood. **SIC:** 5146 (Fish & Seafoods). **Est:**
1923. **Emp:** 11. **Officers:** Allan A. Ardito.

■ 10599 ■ **Bounty Trading Co.**
PO Box 5
Winthrop, ME 04364
Phone: (207)377-6900 **Fax:** (207)377-6699
E-mail: calra@aol.com
Products: Food; General merchandise. **SICs:** 5141
(Groceries—General Line); 5199 (Nondurable Goods
Nec). **Est:** 1991. **Officers:** Ralph Calcagni, President.
Former Name: Bounty Food Co.

■ 10600 ■ **Boyajian Inc.**
349 Lenox St.
Norwood, MA 02062-3417
Phone: (617)965-5800
Products: Caviar, vegetable oils, and other gourmet
food products. **SICs:** 5146 (Fish & Seafoods); 5149
(Groceries & Related Products Nec).

■ 10601 ■ **E. Boyd & Associates, Inc.**
7009 Harps Mill Rd.
PO Box 99189
Raleigh, NC 27624-9189
Phone: (919)846-8000 **Fax:** (919)846-8197
E-mail: eboyd@att.net
Products: Food. **SIC:** 5141 (Groceries—General Line).
Est: 1979. **Officers:** Elbert M. Boyd Jr., CEO, e-mail:
eboyd@worldnet.att.net; T.Y. Baker III, President.

■ 10602 ■ **Boyd-Bluford Co. Inc.**
PO Box 12240
Norfolk, VA 23541-0240
Phone: (757)855-6036
Products: Restaurant supplies, including candy, pop

syrup, and paper supplies. **SICs:** 5145 (Confectionery);
5046 (Commercial Equipment Nec); 5113 (Industrial &
Personal Service Paper); 5149 (Groceries & Related
Products Nec). **Est:** 1941. **Sales:** $8,000,000 (1999).
Emp: 20. **Officers:** Bruce Melchor, President.

■ 10603 ■ **Boyd Coffee Co.**
PO Box 20547
Portland, OR 97294
Phone: (503)666-4545
Free: (800)545-4077 **Fax:** (503)669-2223
URL: http://www.boyds.com
Products: Coffee; Juices; Soups; Sauces; Coffee and
espresso brewing equipment. **SICs:** 5149 (Groceries &
Related Products Nec); 5099 (Durable Goods Nec).
Est: 1900. **Emp:** 475. **Officers:** David D. Boyd, Exec.
VP, e-mail: davidb@boyds.com.

■ 10604 ■ **Boyle Meat Co.**
1638 St. Louis Ave.
Kansas City, MO 64101
Phone: (816)842-5852
Free: (800)821-3626 **Fax:** (816)221-3888
URL: http://www.boylesteaks.com
Products: Beef. **SIC:** 5147 (Meats & Meat Products).
Est: 1932. **Sales:** $6,000,000 (2000). **Emp:** 20.
Officers: Christy Chester, President; e-mail:
christysteaks@worldnet.att.net

■ 10605 ■ **Bozzuto's Inc.**
275 Schoolhouse Rd.
Cheshire, CT 06410-0340
Phone: (203)272-3511 **Fax:** (203)250-8005
Products: Groceries. **SIC:** 5141 (Groceries—General
Line). **Est:** 1945. **Sales:** $378,400,000 (2000). **Emp:**
1,000. **Officers:** Michael A. Bozzuto, CEO, President &
Treasurer; Robert H. Wood, VP of Finance; Patricia S.
Houle, Secretary.

■ 10606 ■ **BPC Foodservice Inc.**
PO Box 301
Bloomington, IL 61702
Phone: (309)828-6271 **Fax:** (309)827-4682
Products: Food, including meat, milk, and cheese.
SICs: 5141 (Groceries—General Line); 5147 (Meats &
Meat Products); 5143 (Dairy Products Except Dried or
Canned). **Est:** 1944. **Sales:** $5,000,000 (2000). **Emp:**
24. **Officers:** James R. Stevens, President.

■ 10607 ■ **Branch Cheese Co.**
PO Box 198
Lena, WI 54139-0198
Phone: (920)684-0121
Products: Cheese, including mozzarella and
provolone. **SIC:** 5143 (Dairy Products Except Dried or
Canned). **Est:** 1964. **Sales:** $15,000,000 (2000). **Emp:**
65. **Officers:** Evan D. Metropoulos, CEO; Alfred
LeBlanc, VP of Finance; John Sottile, VP of Marketing.

■ 10608 ■ **Brans Nut Co. Inc.**
581 Bonner Rd.
Wauconda, IL 60084-1103
Phone: (847)526-0700
Free: (800)238-0400 **Fax:** (847)526-4093
Products: Nuts and seeds (salted, roasted, cooked, or
blanched); Candy. **SIC:** 5145 (Confectionery). **Est:**
1976. **Emp:** 49. **Officers:** Bill Collins; Gary Olson,
Warehouse Mgr.

■ 10609 ■ **Bratt-Foster Inc.**
PO Box 3650
Syracuse, NY 13220
Phone: (315)488-3840 **Fax:** (315)488-9079
Products: Grocery items, including frozen foods, dairy
products, deli items, and general merchandise. **SICs:**
5141 (Groceries—General Line); 5143 (Dairy Products
Except Dried or Canned); 5149 (Groceries & Related
Products Nec); 5146 (Fish & Seafoods); 5142
(Packaged Frozen Foods). **Est:** 1978. **Emp:** 30.
Officers: John L. Foster, President, e-mail:
fosterjohn@aol.com; David Lesko, VP of Marketing;
Stephen Barone, VP of Sales. **Doing Business As:**
Advantage Sales and Marketing.

■ 10610 ■ **J.F. Braun and Sons**
265 Post Ave.
Westbury, NY 11590
Phone: (516)997-2200 **Fax:** (516)997-2478
Products: Dried fruit; Shelled nuts; Cocoa powder.

SIC: 5149 (Groceries & Related Products Nec). **Est:** 1945. **Sales:** $85,000,000 (2000). **Emp:** 25. **Officers:** Gerald Vogel, President, e-mail: jvogel@jfbny.com; Gilbert Coffin, Controller, e-mail: gcoffin@jfbny.com; Ed Howard, Exec. VP, e-mail: ehoward@jfbny.com; Ben Benigno, Vice President, e-mail: abenigno@jfbny.com.

■ **10611** ■ **Otto Brehm Inc.**
75 Tuckahoe Rd.
Yonkers, NY 10710-5321
Phone: (914)968-6100 **Fax:** (914)968-8926
Products: Flour and other grain mill products; Sugar cane mill products and byproducts. **SIC:** 5149 (Groceries & Related Products Nec). **Emp:** 90.

■ **10612** ■ **Bremner Biscuit Co.**
4600 Joliet St.
Denver, CO 80239
Phone: (303)371-8180
Products: Crackers. **SIC:** 5149 (Groceries & Related Products Nec). **Sales:** $3,100,000 (2000). **Emp:** 20. **Officers:** Edward Bremner, President.

■ **10613** ■ **Brenham Wholesale Grocery Company Inc.**
PO Box 584
Brenham, TX 77834
Phone: (409)836-7925 **Fax:** (409)830-0346
Products: Groceries. **SIC:** 5141 (Groceries—General Line). **Est:** 1905. **Sales:** $130,000,000 (2000). **Emp:** 217. **Officers:** Luther Utesch, President; Stephen Miller, CFO; Robert Kolkhorst Jr., VP of Marketing; Glenwood Hertel, Dir. of Systems; Bill Allard, Personnel Mgr.

■ **10614** ■ **J.C. Brock Corp.**
River Ranch Northeast
1156 Abbott St.
Salinas, CA 93901-4503
Products: Fruits and vegetables. **SIC:** 5148 (Fresh Fruits & Vegetables). **Officers:** Joseph Brock, President.

■ **10615** ■ **Bromar Inc.**
744 N Eckhoff St.
Orange, CA 92868-1020
Phone: (714)640-6221
Products: Food. **SIC:** 5141 (Groceries—General Line). **Sales:** $680,000,000 (2000). **Emp:** 1,300. **Officers:** Clifford Mayotte, CFO.

■ **10616** ■ **Bromar Inc. Bromar Hawaii**
2770 Waiwai Loop
Honolulu, HI 96819
Phone: (808)836-3553 **Fax:** (808)836-3032
Products: General line of groceries. **SICs:** 5141 (Groceries—General Line); 5142 (Packaged Frozen Foods). **Sales:** $22,000,000 (2000). **Emp:** 35. **Officers:** Darryl Sato, General Mgr.

■ **10617** ■ **Bromar Montana/Wyoming**
PO Box 22599
Billings, MT 59102
Phone: (406)245-5134 **Fax:** (406)245-0483
Products: Groceries. **SIC:** 5141 (Groceries—General Line). **Est:** 1945. **Sales:** $42,000,000 (2000). **Emp:** 23. **Officers:** Wendell R. Wardell, President.

■ **10618** ■ **Bromar Utah**
1279 W 2200 S, Ste. C
West Valley City, UT 84119
Phone: (801)973-8669
Products: Food. **SIC:** 5141 (Groceries—General Line). **Sales:** $15,000,000 (2000). **Emp:** 30. **Officers:** James Batestas, President; Colleen Aird, Comptroller.

■ **10619** ■ **Bronson Syrup Company Inc.**
1650 Locust Ave.
Bohemia, NY 11716
Phone: (516)563-1177
Products: Popcorn, soda, fruit juices, bar supply items and beverage dispensing equipment. **SICs:** 5145 (Confectionery); 5046 (Commercial Equipment Nec). **Sales:** $1,000,000 (1994). **Emp:** 8. **Officers:** Steven Goldstein, President.

■ **10620** ■ **Brooklyn Bagels Inc.**
7412 Bustleton Ave.
Philadelphia, PA 19152-4312
Phone: (215)342-1661
Products: Bakery products. **SIC:** 5149 (Groceries & Related Products Nec). **Emp:** 49.

■ **10621** ■ **H. Brooks and Co.**
2521 E Hennepin Ave.
Minneapolis, MN 55413
Phone: (612)331-8413
Products: Produce. **SIC:** 5148 (Fresh Fruits & Vegetables). **Est:** 1926. **Sales:** $25,000,000 (2000). **Emp:** 70. **Officers:** Irving Brooks, CEO; Ray Ralston, Controller.

■ **10622** ■ **Broughton Foods LLC**
PO Box 656
Marietta, OH 45750
Phone: (740)373-4121
Free: (800)283-2479 **Fax:** (740)373-2861
Products: Dairy products, including ice cream and milk. **SIC:** 5143 (Dairy Products Except Dried or Canned). **Est:** 1933. **Sales:** $75,000,000 (2000). **Emp:** 345. **Officers:** Jeff Monroe, General Mgr.; David Broughton, Controller. **Former Name:** Broughton Foods Co.

■ **10623** ■ **Lewis A. Brown and Co.**
PO Box 9336
Metairie, LA 70055
Phone: (504)835-4201
Products: Lumber. **SICs:** 5141 (Groceries—General Line); 5143 (Dairy Products Except Dried or Canned); 5147 (Meats & Meat Products); 5148 (Fresh Fruits & Vegetables). **Est:** 1959. **Sales:** $300,000 (1999). **Emp:** 1. **Officers:** Lewis A. Brown Jr., Owner.

■ **10624** ■ **Lewis A. Brown and Co.**
PO Box 9336
Metairie, LA 70055
Phone: (504)835-4201
Products: Food. **SIC:** 5141 (Groceries—General Line). **Sales:** $300,000 (2000). **Emp:** 1.

■ **10625** ■ **Brown Food Service**
PO Box 690
Louisa, KY 41230
Phone: (606)638-1139
Free: (800)422-1058 **Fax:** (606)638-1130
E-mail: brownfoodservice@brownfoodservice.com
URL: http://www.brownfoodservice.com
Products: Full line food service distributor. **SIC:** 5141 (Groceries—General Line). **Est:** 1942. **Sales:** $40,000,000 (1999). **Emp:** 125. **Officers:** Wayne L. Brown, VP & General Mgr.; John Brown, VP & CFO.

■ **10626** ■ **Brown & Haley**
PO Box 1596
Tacoma, WA 98401-1596
Phone: (253)620-3000
Free: (800)426-8400 **Fax:** (253)272-6742
E-mail: sweets@brown-haley.com
URL: http://www.brown-haly.com
Products: Confectionery products. **SIC:** 5145 (Confectionery). **Est:** 1912. **Emp:** 300. **Officers:** Mark T. Haley, CEO & Chairman of the Board; Pierson B. Clare, President & COO; Don Richardson, Dir. of Sales, e-mail: donr@ibm.net; Richard Nicks, Customer Service Mgr., e-mail: rnicks@aol.com.

■ **10627** ■ **Brown Moore and Flint Inc.**
1920 Westridge
Irving, TX 75038-2901
Phone: (972)518-1442
Products: Food. **SICs:** 5141 (Groceries—General Line); 5142 (Packaged Frozen Foods). **Sales:** $110,000,000 (2000). **Emp:** 211. **Officers:** Tom Garrison, President; Linda Briley, Chairman of the Board.

■ **10628** ■ **Brown Packing Co. Inc.**
PO Box 2378
Little Rock, AR 72203
Phone: (501)565-2351 **Fax:** (501)565-2356
Products: Processed, frozen, or cooked meats; Processed or cured pork. **SICs:** 5147 (Meats & Meat Products); 5142 (Packaged Frozen Foods). **Emp:** 250.

■ **10629** ■ **Brown Swiss/Gillette Quality Checkered Dairy**
PO Box 2553
Rapid City, SD 57701-4177
Phone: (605)348-1500
Products: Dairy products, including ice cream. **SIC:** 5143 (Dairy Products Except Dried or Canned). **Emp:** 99.

■ **10630** ■ **Browns Bakery Inc.**
PO Box 1040
Defiance, OH 43512
Phone: (419)784-3330 **Fax:** (419)784-5346
Products: Bread. **SIC:** 5149 (Groceries & Related Products Nec). **Est:** 1873. **Sales:** $10,000,000 (1999). **Emp:** 110. **Officers:** David B. Graham, COO & President; Margaret B. Graham, Chairman of the Board; Richard Z. Graham, CEO.

■ **10631** ■ **Brown's Ice Cream Co.**
2929 University Ave. SE
Minneapolis, MN 55414
Phone: (612)378-1075 **Fax:** (612)331-9273
Products: Ice cream; Frozen pizza. **SICs:** 5143 (Dairy Products Except Dried or Canned); 5142 (Packaged Frozen Foods). **Sales:** $11,000,000 (2000). **Emp:** 20. **Officers:** Tim Nelson, President.

■ **10632** ■ **Bruno's Inc.**
PO Box 2486
Birmingham, AL 35201-2486
Phones: (205)940-9400 (205)940-9400
Fax: (205)940-9568
Products: Grocery items, including produce, frozen foods, health and beauty aids, and meats. **SIC:** 5141 (Groceries—General Line).

■ **10633** ■ **Bruss Co.**
3548 N Kostner Ave.
Chicago, IL 60641
Phone: (773)282-2900 **Fax:** (773)282-6966
Products: Specialty foods. **SIC:** 5149 (Groceries & Related Products Nec). **Sales:** $80,000,000 (1993). **Emp:** 240. **Officers:** Dan Timm, President & COO; Ellard Afaelzer Jr., CFO.

■ **10634** ■ **Bubbles Baking Co.**
15215 Keswick St.
Van Nuys, CA 91405
Phone: (818)786-1700
Free: (800)777-4970 **Fax:** (818)786-3617
Products: Bakery products. **SIC:** 5149 (Groceries & Related Products Nec). **Emp:** 99.

■ **10635** ■ **Buchanan Farmers Elevator Co.**
PO Box 100
Buchanan, ND 58420
Phone: (701)252-6622 **Fax:** (701)252-6655
Products: Livestock and farm products. **SIC:** 5153 (Grain & Field Beans). **Sales:** $6,100,000 (2000). **Emp:** 4.

■ **10636** ■ **Buchy Food Products**
195 N Broadway
PO Box 899
Greenville, OH 45331-2251
Phone: (937)548-2128
Free: (800)762-1060 **Fax:** (937)548-6880
E-mail: bchyfood@bright.net
Products: Restaurant supplies; Food. **SIC:** 5141 (Groceries—General Line). **Est:** 1878. **Emp:** 30. **Officers:** G. James Buchy, President; John Buchy, Purchasing Manager.

■ **10637** ■ **Buckeye Cooperative Elevator Co.**
PO Box 2037
Buckeye, IA 50043
Phone: (515)855-4141 **Fax:** (515)855-4278
Products: Grain and feed mixing and blending. **SICs:** 5153 (Grain & Field Beans); 5191 (Farm Supplies); 5172 (Petroleum Products Nec). **Sales:** $14,000,000 (2000). **Emp:** 15.

■ **10638** ■ **Bucks County Distributors**
1724 Eagen Ct.
Bensalem, PA 19020
Phone: (215)638-2687 **Fax:** (215)638-2027
URL: http://www.buckscountydistributors.com
Products: Candy; Snack foods. **SIC:** 5145

(Confectionery). **Est:** 1996. **Sales:** $300,000 (2000). **Emp:** 4. **Officers:** Monica Richards, President; Harry N. Richards, Dir. of Operations, e-mail: hnriii@aol.com.

■ 10639 ■ **Bucky Bairdo's Inc.**
103 E Silverspring Dr.
Whitefish Bay, WI 53217
Phone: (414)332-9007
Products: Candy. **SIC:** 5145 (Confectionery).

■ 10640 ■ **Buikema Produce Co.**
2150 Bernice Rd.
Lansing, IL 60438
Phone: (708)474-5750 **Fax:** (708)474-5844
Products: Vegetables. **SIC:** 5148 (Fresh Fruits & Vegetables).

■ 10641 ■ **Bumble Bee Seafoods Inc.**
PO Box 85362
San Diego, CA 92186-5362
Phone: (619)550-4000 **Fax:** (619)560-6595
Products: Canned tuna, salmon, and oysters. **SICs:** 5146 (Fish & Seafoods); 5149 (Groceries & Related Products Nec). **Sales:** $400,000,000 (2000). **Emp:** 2,000. **Officers:** Mark Koob.

■ 10642 ■ **Bunker Hill Foods**
PO Box 1048
Bedford, VA 24523-1048
Phone: (540)586-8274 **Fax:** (540)586-6106
E-mail: bunkhillfd@aol.com
Products: Canned meats and meat entrees; Sauces, soups, and gravies. **SICs:** 5147 (Meats & Meat Products); 5149 (Groceries & Related Products Nec). **Est:** 1934. **Sales:** $25,000,000 (2000). **Emp:** 200. **Officers:** L.H. Peterson; J.F. Vaeth.

■ 10643 ■ **Bunn Capitol Co.**
PO Box 4227
Springfield, IL 62708
Phone: (217)529-5401
Products: Groceries; Paper products, including cups, plates, and napkins. **SICs:** 5141 (Groceries—General Line); 5113 (Industrial & Personal Service Paper). **Est:** 1840. **Sales:** $95,000,000 (2000). **Emp:** 250. **Officers:** B. Bunn, President; Doug Meyer, CFO.

■ 10644 ■ **Bur-Bee Co. Inc.**
PO Box 797
WalLa Walla, WA 99362-0252
Phone: (509)525-5040 **Fax:** (509)525-5253
Products: Tobacco; Candy; Foods. **SICs:** 5141 (Groceries—General Line); 5145 (Confectionery); 5194 (Tobacco & Tobacco Products). **Est:** 1937. **Sales:** $30,000,000 (2000). **Emp:** 90. **Officers:** W.E. Pribilsky, CEO; Kevin Pribilsky, President; Robert Randle, Dir. of Data Processing.

■ 10645 ■ **Burklund Distributors Inc.**
2500 N Main St., Ste. 3
East Peoria, IL 61611-1789
Phone: (309)694-1900
E-mail: jon@burklund.com
Products: Candy; Tobacco; Groceries; Automotive and related items. **SICs:** 5141 (Groceries—General Line); 5013 (Motor Vehicle Supplies & New Parts); 5145 (Confectionery); 5194 (Tobacco & Tobacco Products). **Est:** 1939. **Emp:** 100. **Officers:** Dale E. Burklund, CEO; Daniel E. Meyer, VP of Operations; Jon D. Burklund, President & COO; James L. Centers Jr., Sales Mgr., e-mail: jim@burklund.com; Frank J. Reid, VP of Marketing, e-mail: frank@burkland.com.

■ 10646 ■ **Burris Foods Inc.**
PO Box 219
Milford, DE 19963
Phone: (302)422-4531 **Fax:** (302)422-7588
Products: Frozen foods. **SICs:** 5142 (Packaged Frozen Foods); 5143 (Dairy Products Except Dried or Canned). **Est:** 1925. **Sales:** $190,000,000 (2000). **Emp:** 450. **Officers:** Robert D. Burris, CEO; John M. Cross, CFO; Elliott Friedman, Dir. of Marketing; Edward Krupka, Dir. of Data Processing; Marie Isenberg, Dir of Human Resources.

■ 10647 ■ **John H. Burrows Inc.**
PO Box 604
Sparks, NV 89431
Phone: (702)358-2442
Products: Fresh fruit and vegetables. **SIC:** 5148 (Fresh Fruits & Vegetables). **Sales:** $47,000,000 (2000). **Emp:** 150. **Officers:** John H. Burrows, President; Tammy Price, Controller.

■ 10648 ■ **Butler Beef Inc.**
4700 N 132nd
Butler, WI 53007-1603
Phone: (414)781-4545
Products: Beef. **SIC:** 5147 (Meats & Meat Products). **Emp:** 25. **Officers:** Thomas F. Tobin, General Mgr.

■ 10649 ■ **Butler National Corp.**
19920 W 161st St.
Olathe, KS 66062-2700
Phone: (913)780-9595
Products: Food. **SIC:** 5141 (Groceries—General Line). **Sales:** $21,500,000 (2000). **Emp:** 65. **Officers:** Clark D. Stewart, CEO & President; Stephanie S. Ruskey, VP & CFO.

■ 10650 ■ **Butte Produce Co.**
605 Utah Ave.
Butte, MT 59701-2607
Phone: (406)782-2369
Free: (800)823-7763 **Fax:** (406)782-3929
Products: Spices; Natural and process cheese; Produce; Meat; Dry grocery; Frozen food; Small wares; Janitorial equipment and specialties. **SICs:** 5143 (Dairy Products Except Dried or Canned); 5149 (Groceries & Related Products Nec). **Est:** 1966. **Sales:** $4,500,000 (2000). **Emp:** 20.

■ 10651 ■ **Butterfield and Company Inc.**
6930 Atrium Boardwalk S, Ste. 300
Indianapolis, IN 46250
Phone: (317)841-6500 **Fax:** (317)849-9826
Products: Food broker. **SIC:** 5141 (Groceries—General Line). **Sales:** $6,000,000 (2000). **Emp:** 10. **Officers:** George Butterfield, President.

■ 10652 ■ **Buurma Farms Inc.**
3909 Kok Rd.
Willard, OH 44890
Phone: (419)935-6411 **Fax:** (419)935-1918
Products: Produce. **SIC:** 5148 (Fresh Fruits & Vegetables).

■ 10653 ■ **Buy for Less Inc.**
730 E Charles Page Blvd.
Sand Springs, OK 74063-8507
Phone: (918)742-2456
Products: Grocery items; Fish; Spaghetti; Bread. **SICs:** 5149 (Groceries & Related Products Nec); 5146 (Fish & Seafoods). **Emp:** 350.

■ 10654 ■ **Byrnes and Kiefer Company Inc.**
131 Kline Ave.
Callery, PA 16024
Phone: (412)321-1900 **Fax:** (724)538-9200
Products: Confectionery. **SIC:** 5145 (Confectionery). **Sales:** $11,000,000 (1994). **Emp:** 45. **Officers:** E.G. Byrnes Jr., President; J.J. Their, VP of Finance.

■ 10655 ■ **C-Corp.**
30 Beaver Pond Rd.
Beverly, MA 01915-1203
Phone: (978)281-6490 **Fax:** (978)283-6735
Products: Frozen seafood. **SICs:** 5146 (Fish & Seafoods); 5142 (Packaged Frozen Foods). **Est:** 1971. **Sales:** $14,000,000 (2000). **Emp:** 6. **Officers:** Sydney H. Cohen, CEO.

■ 10656 ■ **C & R Distributors**
1615 Tomlinson
Mason, MI 48854-9257
Phone: (517)694-7218
E-mail: crj@acd.net
Products: Nutritional products. **SIC:** 5141 (Groceries—General Line). **Est:** 1977. **Officers:** Chuck Loveless, Owner; Roz Loveless, Owner.

■ 10657 ■ **C and S Wholesale Grocers Inc.**
PO Box 821
Brattleboro, VT 05302
Phone: (802)257-4371 **Fax:** (802)257-6715
Products: Groceries. **SIC:** 5141 (Groceries—General Line). **Officers:** Richard Cohen, Chairman of the Board.

■ 10658 ■ **C and W Food Service Inc.**
PO Box 5346
Tallahassee, FL 32314-5346
Phone: (850)877-5853 **Fax:** (850)877-4682
E-mail: cwfood@cwfood.com
URL: http://www.cwfood.com
Products: Food service products. **SIC:** 5141 (Groceries—General Line). **Est:** 1985. **Sales:** $22,500,000 (1999). **Emp:** 57. **Officers:** Roger Champion, President; Johnny Gallion, Sales & Marketing Contact; Donna Champion, Customer Service Contact; Craig Fletcher, Human Resources Contact; Nat Galldn, Vice President; Frank Soggins, Vice President.

■ 10659 ■ **Cade Grayson Co.**
2445 Cade's Way
Vista, CA 92083-7831
Phone: (760)727-1000 **Fax:** (760)727-1188
Products: Dried and dehydrated vegetables. **SIC:** 5149 (Groceries & Related Products Nec). **Est:** 1963. **Sales:** $20,000,000 (2000). **Emp:** 99. **Officers:** Steven Cade, President; Lynn Lockyer, VP of Marketing; Dan Stouder, Sales Mgr.

■ 10660 ■ **Caffe Latte**
6254 Wilshire Blvd.
Los Angeles, CA 90048
Phone: (213)936-5213 **Fax:** (213)936-4756
Products: Coffee beans and teas. **SIC:** 5149 (Groceries & Related Products Nec). **Est:** 1988. **Emp:** 23.

■ 10661 ■ **Cagle's Inc.**
2000 Hills Ave. NW
Atlanta, GA 30318
Phone: (404)355-2820 **Fax:** (404)355-9326
Products: Poultry. **SIC:** 5144 (Poultry & Poultry Products). **Est:** 1945. **Sales:** $345,000,000 (2000). **Emp:** 3,100. **Officers:** J. Douglas Cagle, CEO & Chairman of the Board; Kenneth R. Barkley, Sr. VP & CFO; John Bruno, Sr. VP of Marketing & Sales; Mark M. Ham IV, VP of Information Systems; Jerry Gahis, President & COO.

■ 10662 ■ **Cahokia Flour Co.**
2701 Hereford St.
St. Louis, MO 63139-1021
Phone: (314)781-1211 **Fax:** (314)781-6151
Products: Bakery supplies. **SIC:** 5149 (Groceries & Related Products Nec). **Est:** 1912. **Sales:** $88,000,000 (2000). **Emp:** 110. **Officers:** Carl Zimmerman, President; Charles Nuttman, VP & CFO; Jim Zimmerman, President.

■ 10663 ■ **Cains Foods, L.P.**
E Main St.
Ayer, MA 01432-1832
Phone: (978)772-0300 **Fax:** (978)772-9254
Products: Condiments. **SIC:** 5149 (Groceries & Related Products Nec). **Est:** 1914. **Emp:** 200. **Officers:** Denis J. Keaveny, President. **Former Name:** Cains Foods, Inc.

■ 10664 ■ **Caito Foods Service, Inc.**
3120 N Post Rd.
Indianapolis, IN 46226
Phone: (317)897-2009 **Fax:** (317)899-1174
Products: Produce. **SIC:** 5148 (Fresh Fruits & Vegetables).

■ 10665 ■ **Cal Compack Foods Inc.**
4906 W 1st St.
Santa Ana, CA 92703
Phone: (714)775-7757 **Fax:** (714)531-4848
Products: Spices. **SIC:** 5149 (Groceries & Related Products Nec). **Sales:** $75,000,000 (2000). **Emp:** 499. **Officers:** R. Tognazzini, President.

■ **10666** ■ **Cal Fruit**
14310 Gannet
La Mirada, CA 90638-5221
Phone: (562)941-8794 **Fax:** (714)523-2480
Products: Tomatoes. **SIC:** 5148 (Fresh Fruits & Vegetables). **Emp:** 49.

■ **10667** ■ **Cal-Growers Corp.**
447 N 1st St.
San Jose, CA 95112-4018
Phone: (408)573-1000 **Fax:** (408)573-0591
Products: Private label food products. **SIC:** 5141 (Groceries—General Line). **Sales:** $416,700,000 (2000). **Emp:** 125. **Officers:** Clem Perrucci, CEO & Chairman of the Board; Ed Sacks, President & COO.

■ **10668** ■ **Cal-West Foodservice Inc.**
12015 Slauson Ave., Ste. F
Santa Fe Springs, CA 90670
Phone: (562)945-1355
Products: Food. **SICs:** 5142 (Packaged Frozen Foods); 5141 (Groceries—General Line). **Sales:** $4,000,000 (1993). **Emp:** 10. **Officers:** Norman P. Weaver, President.

■ **10669** ■ **Calco of Minneapolis Inc.**
2751 Minnehaha Ave. S
Minneapolis, MN 55406
Phone: (612)724-0067 **Fax:** (612)724-1377
Products: Fruits and vegetables. **SIC:** 5148 (Fresh Fruits & Vegetables). **Emp:** 49. **Officers:** Jimmy Yang.

■ **10670** ■ **Caldwell Milling Company Inc.**
PO Box 179
Rose Bud, AR 72137-0179
Phone: (501)556-5121
Products: Eggs. **SIC:** 5191 (Farm Supplies). **Est:** 1969. **Sales:** $13,000,000 (2000). **Emp:** 65. **Officers:** W.H. Caldwell, President & Treasurer.

■ **10671** ■ **Calhoun Enterprises**
810 S West Blvd.
Montgomery, AL 36105
Phone: (205)272-4400 **Fax:** (205)286-8066
Products: Groceries. **SIC:** 5141 (Groceries—General Line). **Est:** 1984. **Sales:** $30,000,000 (2000). **Emp:** 400. **Officers:** Greg Calhoun, President; Edwin Lewis, Finance Officer; Arthur Jackson, Dir. of Marketing & Sales; Angala Towels, Dir. of Information Systems.

■ **10672** ■ **California Milk Producers**
11709 E Artesia Blvd.
Artesia, CA 90701
Phone: (562)865-1291
Products: Milk; Dried milk; Condensed and evaporated milk; Natural cheese. **SIC:** 5143 (Dairy Products Except Dried or Canned). **Est:** 1974. **Sales:** $83,000,000 (2000). **Emp:** 230. **Officers:** Gary Korsmeier, CEO; Fred Erdtsieck, Controller; Rafael Munoz, Dir. of Data Processing.

■ **10673** ■ **California Naturals**
2054 S Garfield Ave.
City of Commerce, CA 90040
Phone: (213)889-6889 **Fax:** (213)889-8269
Products: Dried fruits; Nuts, seeds, and trail mix. **SICs:** 5149 (Groceries & Related Products Nec); 5145 (Confectionery). **Emp:** 49. **Officers:** Semyon Kantor; Boris M. Tonoff; Geoffrey Cox, Sales/Mktg.; Liz Morales, Customer Service.

■ **10674** ■ **California Pacific Fruit Co.**
2001 Main St.
San Diego, CA 92113-2216
Phone: (619)236-9100 **Fax:** (619)236-1364
Products: Fresh fruits. **SIC:** 5148 (Fresh Fruits & Vegetables). **Officers:** Frederick M. Olivo, General Mgr.

■ **10675** ■ **California Shellfish Co.**
2601 5th
Sacramento, CA 95818
Phone: (916)446-0251 **Fax:** (916)446-1917
Products: Fresh fish, including salmon, halibut, and swordfish. **SIC:** 5146 (Fish & Seafoods). **Emp:** 110.

■ **10676** ■ **California Shellfish Company Inc.**
505 Beach Court, Ste. 200
San Francisco, CA 94133-1321
Phone: (415)923-7400
Products: Prepared fresh, frozen and canned fish and seafood. **SICs:** 5146 (Fish & Seafoods); 5142 (Packaged Frozen Foods); 5149 (Groceries & Related Products Nec). **Sales:** $140,000,000 (2000). **Emp:** 500. **Officers:** Eugene Bugatto, President; David Zeller, CFO.

■ **10677** ■ **Calihan Pork Processors**
One South St.
Peoria, IL 61602
Phone: (309)674-9175 **Fax:** (309)674-3003
E-mail: Deadhog@aol.com
Products: Pre-Rigor pork. **SIC:** 5147 (Meats & Meat Products). **Est:** 1937. **Sales:** $3,500,000 (1999). **Emp:** 49. **Officers:** Louis M. Landon, President; Jim Forbes, General Mgr. **Alternate Name:** Calihan and Co.

■ **10678** ■ **Calihan Pork Processors**
PO Box 1155
Peoria, IL 61653
Phone: (309)674-9175 **Fax:** (309)674-3003
E-mail: calpork@prodigy.net
Products: Pre-rigor pork, boneless ham cuts, loins, tenderloins, back ribs, spare ribs, and pork offal. **SIC:** 5147 (Meats & Meat Products). **Est:** 1937. **Sales:** $20,000,000 (2000). **Emp:** 40. **Officers:** Louis M. Landon, President, e-mail: deadhog@aol.com. **Former Name:** Calihan and Co.

■ **10679** ■ **Callahan Grocery Co. Inc.**
528 N Broad St.
Bainbridge, GA 31717
Phone: (912)246-0844
Products: Canned food; Tobacco; Paper products, including cups and plates. **SICs:** 5149 (Groceries & Related Products Nec); 5194 (Tobacco & Tobacco Products); 5113 (Industrial & Personal Service Paper). **Est:** 1906. **Sales:** $13,000,000 (2000). **Emp:** 25. **Officers:** David T. Bryan Sr., CEO; William D. Bryan, Vice President.

■ **10680** ■ **Callif Co.**
4561 E 5th Ave.
Columbus, OH 43219
Phone: (614)238-7300
Products: Produce. **SIC:** 5148 (Fresh Fruits & Vegetables). **Sales:** $5,000,000 (2000). **Emp:** 16. **Officers:** Michael L. Callif, CEO.

■ **10681** ■ **Calvada Sales Co.**
950 Southern Way
Sparks, NV 89431-6120
Phone: (702)359-4740 **Fax:** (702)359-1743
Products: Meat; Poultry; Beef; Seafood; Deli items. **SICs:** 5144 (Poultry & Poultry Products); 5147 (Meats & Meat Products); 5146 (Fish & Seafoods); 5149 (Groceries & Related Products Nec). **Emp:** 49. **Officers:** Tom MacKey.

■ **10682** ■ **James Calvetti Meats Inc.**
4240 S Morgan St.
Chicago, IL 60609
Phone: (773)927-9242 **Fax:** (773)927-8256
Products: Hand-cut steaks. **SIC:** 5147 (Meats & Meat Products). **Est:** 1972. **Sales:** $20,000,000 (2000). **Emp:** 65. **Officers:** James C. Calvetti, President; Veronica Calvetti, Treasurer.

■ **10683** ■ **Camellia Food Stores Inc.**
PO Box 2320
Norfolk, VA 23501
Phone: (757)855-3371
Products: Groceries. **SIC:** 5141 (Groceries—General Line). **Sales:** $250,000,000 (1994). **Emp:** 1,600. **Officers:** Walter L. Grant, CEO & President; Jay P. Bhatt, VP & CFO.

■ **10684** ■ **Camerican International**
45 Eisenhower Dr.
Paramus, NJ 07652
Phone: (201)587-0101 **Fax:** (201)587-2040
E-mail: cii@camerican-foods.com
Products: Canned fruit and vegetables; Tuna; Olives; Canned Meat. **SIC:** 5149 (Groceries & Related Products Nec). **Est:** 1916. **Sales:** $100,000,000

(2000). **Emp:** 30. **Officers:** Lawrence Abramson, President; Jay Breslow, CFO.

■ **10685** ■ **Campbell Supply Company Inc.**
1526 N Industrial Ave.
Sioux Falls, SD 57104
Phone: (605)331-5470 **Fax:** (605)331-4161
Products: Farm, home, and auto. **SIC:** 5141 (Groceries—General Line). **Est:** 1954. **Sales:** $20,000,000 (1999). **Emp:** 100. **Officers:** David Campbell, President; Mike Will, Controller.

■ **10686** ■ **Campbell's Fresh Inc.**
1501 62nd St.
Fennville, MI 49408
Phone: (616)236-5024 **Fax:** (616)236-6354
Products: Fresh mushrooms. **SIC:** 5148 (Fresh Fruits & Vegetables). **Emp:** 299.

■ **10687** ■ **Campbell's Fresh Inc.**
PO Box 169
Blandon, PA 19510
Phone: (610)926-4101
Free: (800)221-3126 **Fax:** (610)926-7025
Products: Fresh mushrooms. **SIC:** 5148 (Fresh Fruits & Vegetables). **Est:** 1938. **Sales:** $150,000,000 (2000). **Emp:** 2,000. **Officers:** Mark I. McCallum, Manager; Jerome Nachlis, Controller; Jack Reitnauer, Dir. of Marketing; Doug Nelson, Dir. of Information Systems.

■ **10688** ■ **Candy by Bletas**
PO Box 57
Abilene, TX 79604
Phone: (915)673-2505
Products: Candy. **SIC:** 5145 (Confectionery).

■ **10689** ■ **Cannizzaro's Distributors**
4373 Michoud Blvd.
New Orleans, LA 70129
Phone: (504)254-4000 **Fax:** (504)254-5406
Products: Foods, including gourmet. **SIC:** 5149 (Groceries & Related Products Nec).

■ **10690** ■ **Cape Dairy Products Inc.**
44 Bodick Rd.
Hyannis, MA 02601
Phone: (508)771-4700
Products: Dairy products. **SIC:** 5143 (Dairy Products Except Dried or Canned).

■ **10691** ■ **Cape Oceanic Corp.**
41 Rosary Ln.
Hyannis, MA 02601-2024
Phone: (508)775-8693 **Fax:** (508)775-2318
Products: Scallops. **SIC:** 5146 (Fish & Seafoods). **Emp:** 20. **Officers:** Jimmy Spalt.

■ **10692** ■ **Capitol City Produce**
12509 S Choctaw Dr.
Baton Rouge, LA 70815-2195
Phone: (504)272-8153 **Fax:** (504)272-8152
Products: Fruits and vegetables. **SIC:** 5148 (Fresh Fruits & Vegetables). **Est:** 1947. **Emp:** 49. **Officers:** Vince A. Ferachi; Paul Ferachi.

■ **10693** ■ **Capitol Foods Inc.**
555 Beale St.
Memphis, TN 38103
Phone: (901)526-9300 **Fax:** (901)525-2357
Products: Gifts and novelties. **SIC:** 5149 (Groceries & Related Products Nec). **Sales:** $1,500,000 (2000). **Emp:** 7.

■ **10694** ■ **Capricorn Coffees Inc.**
353 10th St.
San Francisco, CA 94103
Phone: (415)621-8500 **Free:** (800)541-0758
Products: Coffee, tea, coffee filters, and coffee cups. **SIC:** 5149 (Groceries & Related Products Nec). **Est:** 1963. **Sales:** $4,000,000 (2000). **Emp:** 15. **Officers:** Craig Edwards, President.

■ **10695** ■ **Capricorn Foods**
2540 Shader Rd.
Orlando, FL 32804
Phone: (407)291-9035 **Fax:** (407)290-1083
Products: Meat, including beef. **SIC:** 5147 (Meats & Meat Products).

■ 10696 ■ **Cara Donna Provision Co.**
55 Food Mart Rd.
Boston, MA 02118
Phone: (617)268-0346
Products: Food, including cheese and meat. **SICs:** 5143 (Dairy Products Except Dried or Canned); 5147 (Meats & Meat Products).

■ 10697 ■ **Cardinal Frozen Distributors Co.**
617 E Washington St.
Louisville, KY 40202
Phone: (502)589-0378
Products: Ice cream. **SIC:** 5143 (Dairy Products Except Dried or Canned). **Sales:** $5,000,000 (2000). **Emp:** 14. **Officers:** Tom Korb, President.

■ 10698 ■ **Cardinal Ice Cream Corp.**
617 E Washington St.
Louisville, KY 40202
Phone: (502)589-0378
Products: Ice cream. **SIC:** 5143 (Dairy Products Except Dried or Canned). **Sales:** $12,000,000 (2000). **Emp:** 22. **Officers:** David E. Trauth, President.

■ 10699 ■ **Cargill Peanut Products**
PO Box 272
Dawson, GA 31742
Phone: (912)995-2111 **Fax:** (912)995-3268
Products: Shelled peanuts. **SIC:** 5159 (Farm-Product Raw Materials Nec). **Sales:** $140,000,000 (2000). **Emp:** 280. **Officers:** Simon Oosterman, General Mgr.; Andy Workman, Controller.

■ 10700 ■ **Cariba International Corp.**
1020 Harbor Lake Dr.
Safety Harbor, FL 34695
Phone: (813)725-2517 **Fax:** (813)726-7832
Products: Canned food specialties; Flour and grain mill products; Industrial service paper; Insecticides; Toilet articles and cosmetics. **SICs:** 5149 (Groceries & Related Products Nec); 5122 (Drugs, Proprietaries & Sundries); 5191 (Farm Supplies); 5113 (Industrial & Personal Service Paper); 5153 (Grain & Field Beans). **Officers:** Stephen Hopwood, President.

■ 10701 ■ **Caro Foods Inc.**
2324 Bayou Blue Rd.
Houma, LA 70364
Phone: (504)872-1483 **Fax:** (504)876-0825
Products: Commercial food. **SIC:** 5141 (Groceries—General Line). **Est:** 1964. **Sales:** $1,500,000 (2000). **Emp:** 250. **Officers:** Ricky Thibodaux, President; Brian McNamara, VP of Sales; Jerry Adams, VP of Merchandising. **Former Name:** Caro Produce and Institutional Foods Inc.

■ 10702 ■ **Caro Produce and Institutional Foods Inc.**
2324 Bayou Blue Rd.
Houma, LA 70364
Phone: (504)872-1483 **Fax:** (504)876-0825
Products: General line of groceries and fresh vegetables. **SICs:** 5141 (Groceries—General Line); 5148 (Fresh Fruits & Vegetables). **Sales:** $71,000,000 (2000). **Emp:** 400. **Officers:** Ricky Thibodaux, President; Louis Taylor, VP of Finance.

■ 10703 ■ **Carolyn Candies, Inc.**
PO Box 7689
Winter Haven, FL 33883-7689
Phone: (352)394-8555 **Fax:** (352)394-3452
Products: Candy; Coconut, sweetened, creamed, and toasted. **SICs:** 5145 (Confectionery); 5149 (Groceries & Related Products Nec). **Emp:** 25. **Officers:** R. Norman; G. Norman; D. James, General Mgr.

■ 10704 ■ **Carrollton Farmers Elevator Co.**
PO Box 264
Carrollton, IL 62016
Phone: (217)942-6922
Products: Feed grinding. **SICs:** 5153 (Grain & Field Beans); 5191 (Farm Supplies). **Sales:** $9,000,000 (2000). **Emp:** 10.

■ 10705 ■ **Casa Italia**
2080 Constitution Blvd.
Sarasota, FL 34231
Phone: (941)924-9293
Products: General line groceries; Wine. **SICs:** 5141 (Groceries—General Line); 5182 (Wines & Distilled Beverages).

■ 10706 ■ **Casani Candy Co.**
145 N 2nd St.
Philadelphia, PA 19106
Phone: (215)627-2570 **Fax:** (215)627-5429
Products: Candies. **SIC:** 5145 (Confectionery). **Est:** 1865. **Emp:** 20. **Officers:** John J. Lees, President; Larry Laiken, Dir. of Sales; Joseph D. Lees, Vice President.

■ 10707 ■ **Cascadian Fruit Shippers Inc.**
2701 Euclid Ave.
Wenatchee, WA 98801-5913
Phone: (509)662-8131
Products: Fresh fruits and vegetables. **SIC:** 5148 (Fresh Fruits & Vegetables). **Sales:** $12,500,000 (2000). **Emp:** 155. **Officers:** David Smeltzer, General Mgr.; Lisa Clymens, Accountant.

■ 10708 ■ **Case Farms of North Carolina Inc.**
PO Box 308
Morganton, NC 28655
Phone: (704)438-6900 **Fax:** (704)437-8566
Products: Chicken. **SIC:** 5144 (Poultry & Poultry Products). **Est:** 1955. **Sales:** $130,000,000 (2000). **Emp:** 650. **Officers:** Thomas Shelton, President; Ralph Johnson, Controller; George Anderson, Dir. of Marketing.

■ 10709 ■ **Casey's General Stores Inc.**
1 Convenience Blvd.
Ankeny, IA 50021
Phone: (515)965-6280 **Fax:** (515)965-6292
E-mail: billbrauer@casey's.com
Products: General line groceries; Paper supplies; Toiletries. **SICs:** 5141 (Groceries—General Line); 5113 (Industrial & Personal Service Paper); 5122 (Drugs, Proprietaries & Sundries). **Est:** 1982. **Emp:** 120.

■ 10710 ■ **Cash and Carry Stores Inc.**
PO Box 308
Elkin, NC 28621
Phone: (919)835-4405 **Fax:** (919)835-4938
Products: Groceries. **SIC:** 5141 (Groceries—General Line). **Emp:** 49. **Officers:** David W. Myers; Charles C. Myers.

■ 10711 ■ **Cash Way Distributors**
PO Box 309
Kearney, NE 68848
Phone: (308)237-3151 **Fax:** (308)234-6010
E-mail: tjamesh@aol.com
URL: http://www.cashwa.com
Products: Food. **SIC:** 5141 (Groceries—General Line). **Est:** 1934. **Sales:** $140,000,000 (2000). **Emp:** 320.

■ 10712 ■ **Cash Wholesale Candy Co.**
PO Box 53
Cody, WY 82414-0053
Phone: (307)587-6226 **Fax:** (307)587-6227
Products: Cigarettes and tobacco; Snack foods; Paper and allied products; Chips; Candy. **SICs:** 5145 (Confectionery); 5194 (Tobacco & Tobacco Products); 5113 (Industrial & Personal Service Paper). **Est:** 1987. **Sales:** $1,500,000 (2000). **Emp:** 10. **Officers:** Theola M. Caddy, Owner.

■ 10713 ■ **Casing Associates Inc.**
1120 Close Ave.
Bronx, NY 10472
Phone: (212)842-7151
Products: Sausage casings. **SIC:** 5147 (Meats & Meat Products). **Est:** 1955. **Sales:** $10,000,000 (2000). **Emp:** 30. **Officers:** Louis Schwartz, President; Phillip Schwartz, Treasurer.

■ 10714 ■ **Frank Catanzaro Sons and Daughters Inc.**
535 Shepherd Ave.
Cincinnati, OH 45215-3115
Phone: (513)421-9184
Free: (800)338-2377 **Fax:** (513)421-0284
Products: Fresh, frozen, and canned foods. **SICs:** 5141 (Groceries—General Line); 5142 (Packaged Frozen Foods); 5149 (Groceries & Related Products Nec). **Est:** 1940. **Sales:** $30,000,000 (2000). **Emp:** 95. **Officers:** Frank Cantanzaro Jr., President.

■ 10715 ■ **Cattleman's Inc.**
1825 Scott St.
Detroit, MI 48207
Phone: (313)833-2700 **Fax:** (313)833-7164
Products: Beef, including hamburger. **SIC:** 5147 (Meats & Meat Products). **Est:** 1972. **Sales:** $124,385,423 (2000). **Emp:** 250. **Officers:** David S. Rohtbart, CEO & President.

■ 10716 ■ **Cattleman's Meat Co.**
1825 Scott St.
Detroit, MI 48207
Phone: (313)833-2700 **Fax:** (313)833-7164
Products: Beef. **SIC:** 5147 (Meats & Meat Products). **Sales:** $105,000,000 (1999). **Emp:** 275. **Officers:** David S. Rohtbart, CEO & President.

■ 10717 ■ **Cavalier, Gulling, and Wilson Inc.**
3800 Orange Ave.
Cleveland, OH 44115
Phone: (216)431-2117 **Fax:** (216)431-6815
Products: Fruits and vegetables. **SIC:** 5148 (Fresh Fruits & Vegetables). **Est:** 1931. **Sales:** $6,300,000 (2000). **Emp:** 20. **Officers:** Joseph Cavalier, President.

■ 10718 ■ **Central Carolina Grocers Inc.**
829 Graves St.
Kernersville, NC 27284
Phone: (919)996-2501
Products: Groceries. **SIC:** 5141 (Groceries—General Line). **Est:** 1965. **Sales:** $36,000,000 (2000). **Emp:** 100. **Officers:** Dean Hartgrove, President.

■ 10719 ■ **Central City Produce Inc.**
E 2nd, Box 227
Central City, KY 42330-1227
Phone: (502)754-1991 **Fax:** (502)754-4831
Products: Fruits and vegetables. **SIC:** 5148 (Fresh Fruits & Vegetables). **Est:** 1947. **Sales:** $6,000,000 (2000). **Emp:** 44. **Officers:** Phil Roscoe; Don Adams.

■ 10720 ■ **Central Farmers Cooperative**
Box 330
O' Neill, NE 68763-0330
Phone: (402)843-2223
Products: Agricultural equipment and supplies. **SIC:** 5153 (Grain & Field Beans). **Sales:** $12,000,000 (2000). **Emp:** 30.

■ 10721 ■ **Central Grocers Co-op Inc.**
3701 N Centralia St.
Franklin Park, IL 60131
Phone: (708)678-0660 **Fax:** (708)678-1606
Products: Non-perishable groceries. **SIC:** 5141 (Groceries—General Line). **Est:** 1913. **Sales:** $380,000,000 (2000). **Emp:** 250. **Officers:** John Cortesi, President; Jane Hidalgo, Controller; Jim Denges, VP of Marketing; Mark Brandes, Dir. of Information Systems.

■ 10722 ■ **Central Meat Packing**
1120 Kempsville Rd.
Chesapeake, VA 23320-8127
Phone: (757)547-2161
Free: (800)552-6651 **Fax:** (757)547-0114
Products: Processed, frozen, or cooked meats. **SIC:** 5147 (Meats & Meat Products). **Sales:** $2,000,000 (2000). **Emp:** 49. **Officers:** Earl L. Edmondson.

■ 10723 ■ **Central Seaway Co.**
1845 Oak St., Ste. 1
Northfield, IL 60093
Phone: (847)446-3720
Free: (800)323-1815 **Fax:** (847)446-9410
URL: http://www.censea.com
Products: Frozen fish and seafood, including shellfish. **SICs:** 5146 (Fish & Seafoods); 5142 (Packaged Frozen Foods). **Est:** 1950. **Sales:** $200,000,000 (1999). **Officers:** Daniel Kaplan, President.

■ 10724 ■ **Central Snacks**
1700 N Pearl St.
Carthage, MS 39051
Phones: (601)267-3023 (601)267-3112
Fax: (601)267-3025
Products: Pork skins. **SIC:** 5149 (Groceries & Related Products Nec). **Officers:** N. L. Carson.

■ 10725 ■ Century Acres Eggs Inc.
3420 Hwy. W
Port Washington, WI 53074
Phone: (414)284-0568
Products: Eggs. **SIC:** 5144 (Poultry & Poultry Products). **Sales:** $1,000,000 (1994). **Emp:** 8. **Officers:** Paul Brunnguell, President; John Brunnguell, Treasurer & Secty.

■ 10726 ■ Cereal Food Processors, Inc.
Foot of N Lombard
Portland, OR 97217
Phone: (503)286-1656   **Fax:** (503)286-2483
Products: Flour and wheat germ. **SIC:** 5149 (Groceries & Related Products Nec). **Sales:** $20,000,000 (1999). **Emp:** 30. **Officers:** Mark R. Smith, Sales & Marketing Contact.

■ 10727 ■ Cerenzia Foods Inc.
8707 Utica
Rancho Cucamonga, CA 91730
Phone: (909)989-4000
Products: Italian food, including spaghetti. **SIC:** 5149 (Groceries & Related Products Nec). **Sales:** $7,000,000 (2000). **Emp:** 15.

■ 10728 ■ Certified Grocers of California Ltd.
PO Box 3396, Terminal Annex
Los Angeles, CA 90051
Phone: (213)726-2601   **Fax:** (213)724-7667
Products: General line groceries. **SICs:** 5149 (Groceries & Related Products Nec); 5142 (Packaged Frozen Foods). **Est:** 1925. **Sales:** $2,307,000,000 (2000). **Emp:** 2,400. **Officers:** Alfred Plamann, CEO & President; Daniel T. Bane, Sr. VP of Finance & Admin.; Gerald Friedler, Sr. VP of Marketing; Jerry Lauer, VP of Information Systems; Don Grose, Sr. VP of Human Resources.

■ 10729 ■ Certified Grocers Midwest Inc.
1 Certified Dr.
Hodgkins, IL 60525
Phone: (708)579-2100   **Fax:** (708)579-9874
Products: Groceries, including frozen food, canned food, and meats. **SICs:** 5141 (Groceries—General Line); 5142 (Packaged Frozen Foods); 5147 (Meats & Meat Products). **Est:** 1940. **Sales:** $700,000,000 (2000). **Emp:** 700. **Officers:** James E. Bradley, President; Michael P. O'Neill, VP of Marketing & Merchandising; Theodore J. Clinnin, VP of Operations.

■ 10730 ■ Cervena Co.
780 3rd. Ave., Ste. 1904
New York, NY 10017
Phone: (212)832-7964   **Fax:** (212)832-7602
Products: Venison. **SIC:** 5142 (Packaged Frozen Foods). **Sales:** $3,000,000 (1993). **Emp:** 8. **Officers:** Richard Janes, President.

■ 10731 ■ CGF Cash & Carry
455 Toland
San Francisco, CA 94124-1624
Phone: (415)285-9333   **Fax:** (415)285-9346
Products: Grocers' bags and sacks; Food. **SICs:** 5141 (Groceries—General Line); 5113 (Industrial & Personal Service Paper). **Emp:** 25.

■ 10732 ■ C.H. Robinson Company Inc.
8100 Mitchell Rd.
Eden Prairie, MN 55344
Phone: (612)937-8500
Free: (800)219-2202   **Fax:** (612)937-7809
Products: Fresh fruit and vegetable. **SIC:** 5148 (Fresh Fruits & Vegetables). **Sales:** $2,038,100,000 (2000). **Emp:** 2,205. **Officers:** Daryl R. Verdoorn, CEO, President & Chairman of the Board; John P. Wiehoff, Sr. VP & CFO.

■ 10733 ■ Chandler Foods Inc.
2727 Immanuel Rd.
Greensboro, NC 27407-2515
Phone: (336)299-1934
Free: (800)537-6219   **Fax:** (336)854-4649
URL: http://www.carolinabarbecue.com
Products: Barbecue meats, including pork, beef, and chicken barbecue; Chili. **SICs:** 5149 (Groceries & Related Products Nec); 5147 (Meats & Meat Products). **Est:** 1955. **Sales:** $7,500,000 (2000). **Emp:** 30. **Officers:** Jerry C. Hendrix, e-mail: jch@ chandlerfoodsinc.com; Jeffery Chandler, Exec. VP, e-mail: jec@chandlerfoodsinc.com.

■ 10734 ■ Chapin's Supreme Foods
4190 Garfield
Denver, CO 80216
Phone: (303)321-1985   **Fax:** (303)321-6393
Products: Prepared sauces; Salad dressings. **SIC:** 5149 (Groceries & Related Products Nec).

■ 10735 ■ Chappells Cheese Co.
922 W Hwy. 24
Loa, UT 84747-0307
Phone: (435)836-2821
Free: (800)552-3641   **Fax:** (435)836-2836
E-mail: ccheese@color-country.net
Products: Cheese. **SIC:** 5143 (Dairy Products Except Dried or Canned). **Est:** 1984. **Sales:** $50,000,000 (2000). **Emp:** 20. **Officers:** M. Chappell, President.

■ 10736 ■ Chazy Orchards Inc.
9486 Rte. 9
Chazy, NY 12921
Phone: (518)846-7171   **Fax:** (518)846-8171
E-mail: chazyapples@westelcom.com
URL: http://www.chazy.com
Products: Apples. **SIC:** 5148 (Fresh Fruits & Vegetables). **Est:** 1927. **Sales:** $2,000,000 (1999). **Emp:** 45. **Officers:** Donald F. Green III, President; Betty A. Green, Treasurer & Secty.

■ 10737 ■ Cheese Importers Warehouse
PO Box 1717
Longmont, CO 80501
Phone: (303)443-4444
Free: (800)443-2166   **Fax:** (303)443-4492
E-mail: customerservice@cheeseimporters.com
URL: http://www.cheeseimporters.com
Products: Cheese; Gourmet specialty foods. **SIC:** 5143 (Dairy Products Except Dried or Canned). **Est:** 1925.

■ 10738 ■ Chermak Sausage Co.
2915 Calumet Ave.
PO Box
Manitowoc, WI 54221-1267
Phone: (920)683-5980   **Fax:** (920)682-2588
URL: http://www.cher-make.com
Products: Sausage; Meat snacks. **SIC:** 5147 (Meats & Meat Products). **Est:** 1928. **Sales:** $13,000,000 (2000). **Emp:** 100. **Officers:** Arthur T. Chermak, Chairman of the Board; Tom Chermak, President; Jim Grosser, Dir. of Sales; Larry Franke, Dir. of Finance; Rick Balzon, Human Resources; Chuck Hoefner, Plant Mgr.

■ 10739 ■ Cherry Central, Inc.
PO Box 988
Traverse City, MI 49685-0988
Phone: (231)946-1860   **Fax:** (231)941-4167
E-mail: fruitbiz@cherrycentral.com
URL: http://www.cherrycentral.com
Products: Various fruits, including tart cherries, sweet cherries, blueberries, apples, cranberries, and strawberries available as frozen, dried, puree, concentrate, and canned; Asparagus, apple sauce, apple juice. **SICs:** 5148 (Fresh Fruits & Vegetables); 5149 (Groceries & Related Products Nec). **Est:** 1973. **Sales:** $150,000,000 (2000). **Emp:** 50. **Officers:** Richard Bogard, President & General Mgr.; James Giannestras, VP of Sales; Steve Eiseler, VP of Operations; Chris Olsen, Sales/Marketing Contact, e-mail: colsen@cherrycentral.com; Jim Palmer, Sales/Marketing Contact, e-mail: retsales@ cherrycentral.com. **Former Name:** Cherry Central Cooperative Inc.

■ 10740 ■ Chesapeake Fish Company Inc.
535 Harbor Ln.
San Diego, CA 92101
Phone: (619)238-0526   **Fax:** (619)238-0566
Products: Fresh and frozen seafood. **SICs:** 5146 (Fish & Seafoods); 5142 (Packaged Frozen Foods). **Est:** 1915. **Sales:** $25,000,000 (2000). **Emp:** 76. **Officers:** Nick Vitalich, Owner; Mark Bailey, CFO.

■ 10741 ■ Chestnut Hill Farms Inc.
1500 Port Blvd.
Miami, FL 33132
Phone: (305)530-4700   **Fax:** (305)374-4481
Products: Produce. **SIC:** 5148 (Fresh Fruits & Vegetables). **Emp:** 49. **Officers:** Jack Neuhaus, General Mgr.

■ 10742 ■ Chicago Fish House Inc.
1455 W Willow St.
Chicago, IL 60622-1525
Phone: (773)227-7000
Products: Fresh and frozen seafood. **SIC:** 5146 (Fish & Seafoods). **Sales:** $50,000,000 (1993). **Emp:** 140. **Officers:** Jack Mitsakopoulos, Owner; Sean O'Scannlain, CFO.

■ 10743 ■ Chico Produce, Inc.
PO Box 1069
Durham, CA 95938
Phone: (530)893-0596   **Fax:** (530)893-0255
Products: Fruits and vegetables. **SIC:** 5148 (Fresh Fruits & Vegetables). **Emp:** 68. **Officers:** Bruce Parks; Rich Stewart; Jim Duggan.

■ 10744 ■ Chief Tonasket Growers
437 S Railroad Ave.
Tonasket, WA 98855-0545
Phones: (509)486-2914   (509)486-1626
Fax: (509)486-1815
Products: Fresh fruits. **SIC:** 5148 (Fresh Fruits & Vegetables). **Est:** 1928. **Sales:** $20,000,000 (2000). **Emp:** 150. **Officers:** Robert L. Green, General Mgr.

■ 10745 ■ Chief Wenatchee
PO Box 1091
Wenatchee, WA 98807-1091
Phone: (509)662-5197   **Fax:** (509)662-9415
Products: Fruit, including apples and pears. **SIC:** 5148 (Fresh Fruits & Vegetables). **Est:** 1945. **Sales:** $27,000,000 (2000). **Emp:** 300. **Officers:** Brian Birdsall, President; Ron Ward, Controller; Bill Knight, Dir. of Sales.

■ 10746 ■ Chihade International Inc.
PO Box 451329
Atlanta, GA 31145
Phone: (404)292-5033   **Fax:** (404)297-8920
Products: Groceries, including frozen foods, canned foods, and meats. **SICs:** 5142 (Packaged Frozen Foods); 5147 (Meats & Meat Products); 5149 (Groceries & Related Products Nec). **Est:** 1979. **Officers:** Tawfig Chihade, President.

■ 10747 ■ Chikara Products Inc.
99-1245 Halawa Valley St.
Aiea, HI 96701-3281
Phone: (808)486-3000   **Fax:** (808)488-0661
Products: Bakery products, including pita bread, bagels, and muffins; Tofu; Japanese foods; Salad; Candy; Beef jerky. **SICs:** 5149 (Groceries & Related Products Nec); 5145 (Confectionery). **Est:** 1950. **Emp:** 30.

■ 10748 ■ Chilay Corp.
12881 166th St.
Cerritos, CA 90703-2103
Phone: (714)632-9332
Products: Meat and deli items. **SICs:** 5141 (Groceries—General Line); 5147 (Meats & Meat Products). **Sales:** $100,000,000 (2000). **Emp:** 200. **Officers:** Jerry Murdock, President.

■ 10749 ■ Chilli-O Frozen Foods Inc.
1251 Shermer Rd.
Northbrook, IL 60062
Phone: (847)562-1991   **Fax:** (847)562-1882
Products: Frozen food, including meat; Food preparations. **SICs:** 5142 (Packaged Frozen Foods); 5147 (Meats & Meat Products); 5149 (Groceries & Related Products Nec). **Est:** 1945. **Sales:** $6,000,000 (2000). **Emp:** 49. **Officers:** Jeffrey L. Rothschild.

■ 10750 ■ China First Merchandising Co.
101 Fair Oaks Lane
Atherton, CA 94027
Phone: (650)327-7850
Products: Ingredients for ice cream. **SICs:** 5149

(Groceries & Related Products Nec); 5143 (Dairy Products Except Dried or Canned).

■ 10751 ■ Chin's Import Export Co. Inc.
2035 NW Overton St.
Portland, OR 97209
Phone: (503)224-4082
Products: Canned foods, including rice and shrimp. **SICs:** 5149 (Groceries & Related Products Nec); 5146 (Fish & Seafoods).

■ 10752 ■ Chipwich Inc.
PO Box 346
Piermont, NY 10968-0346
Products: Ice cream. **SIC:** 5143 (Dairy Products Except Dried or Canned). **Former Name:** Best of the Best.

■ 10753 ■ Chock Full o'Nuts
1455 E Chestnut Expy.
Springfield, MO 65802
Phone: (417)869-5523
Free: (800)641-4025 **Fax:** (417)869-1201
Products: Food service products; Flavored and regular coffee; Spices. **SIC:** 5149 (Groceries & Related Products Nec). **Est:** 1984. **Sales:** $14,000,000 (2000). **Emp:** 30. **Officers:** Sephen H. Flowers, Regional Mgr. **Doing Business As:** Cain's Coffee Co.

■ 10754 ■ Chocolate Shoppe Ice Cream
2221 Daniels St.
Madison, WI 53701
Phone: (608)221-8640
Products: Ice cream. **SIC:** 5143 (Dairy Products Except Dried or Canned).

■ 10755 ■ Chocolate Specialty Corp.
10308 Metcalf, Ste. 215
Overland Park, KS 66202
Phone: (913)941-3088 **Fax:** (913)941-4004
Products: Chocolate products. **SIC:** 5145 (Confectionery). **Emp:** 49. **Officers:** B.A. Nelson, President.

■ 10756 ■ Choe Meat Co.
2637 E Vernon Ave.
Los Angeles, CA 90058
Phone: (213)589-5271 **Fax:** (213)589-4874
Products: Fresh pork. **SIC:** 5147 (Meats & Meat Products). **Est:** 1961. **Sales:** $32,000,000 (2000). **Emp:** 47. **Officers:** Harold Choe, CEO; Collin Choe, General Mgr.

■ 10757 ■ Church Point Wholesale Groceries Inc.
Hwy. 35 S
Church Point, LA 70525
Phone: (318)684-5413
Free: (800)960-1106 **Fax:** (318)684-6666
Products: Groceries; Meat. **SICs:** 5141 (Groceries—General Line); 5182 (Wines & Distilled Beverages); 5142 (Packaged Frozen Foods). **Est:** 1890. **Sales:** $40,000,000 (1999). **Emp:** 95. **Officers:** Jack Casanova, General Mgr.

■ 10758 ■ Churny Company Inc.
2215 Sanders Rd., No. 550
Northbrook, IL 60062
Phone: (847)480-5500 **Fax:** (847)480-5590
Products: Cheese. **SIC:** 5143 (Dairy Products Except Dried or Canned). **Sales:** $150,000,000 (2000). **Emp:** 220. **Officers:** Mark Magnesen, President.

■ 10759 ■ Circle Food Products Inc.
3959 Lockridge St.
San Diego, CA 92102-4507
Phone: (619)263-8000 **Fax:** (619)263-8088
E-mail: enriquez@tortillaland.com
Products: Mexican food specialties; Corn and flour tortillas. **SIC:** 5149 (Groceries & Related Products Nec). **Est:** 1983. **Emp:** 150.

■ 10760 ■ Circle Produce Co.
2360 M. L. King Ave.
Calexico, CA 92231-1737
Phone: (760)357-5454 **Fax:** (760)357-5444
E-mail: circlepro@aol.com
Products: Fresh vegetables. **SIC:** 5148 (Fresh Fruits & Vegetables). **Emp:** 49.

■ 10761 ■ City Market Inc.
PO Box 729
Grand Junction, CO 81502
Phone: (970)241-0750 **Fax:** (970)244-1052
Products: Groceries, including meat, fruits, and vegetables. **SICs:** 5141 (Groceries—General Line); 5147 (Meats & Meat Products); 5148 (Fresh Fruits & Vegetables). **Est:** 1924. **Emp:** 5,200. **Officers:** Anthony Prinster, President & CEO; Phyllis Norris, Vice President.

■ 10762 ■ City Meat & Provisions Company, Inc.
2721 W Willetta
Phoenix, AZ 85009-3501
Phone: (602)269-7717 **Fax:** (602)269-0044
Products: Frozen meats. **SIC:** 5142 (Packaged Frozen Foods). **Emp:** 200. **Officers:** Michael S. Brown; Robert McMahon.

■ 10763 ■ City Provisioners Inc.
PO Box 2246
Daytona Beach, FL 32115
Phone: (904)673-2443
Products: Fresh fish, pork, and beef; Potatoes; Onions; Tomatoes; Apples and oranges. **SICs:** 5148 (Fresh Fruits & Vegetables); 5146 (Fish & Seafoods); 5147 (Meats & Meat Products).

■ 10764 ■ Clark Food Service Inc.
950 Arthur Ave.
Elk Grove Village, IL 60007
Phone: (708)956-1730 **Fax:** (708)956-0199
Products: Groceries. **SIC:** 5141 (Groceries—General Line). **Est:** 1912. **Sales:** $325,000,000 (2000). **Emp:** 780. **Officers:** Donald J. Hindman, CEO & President; Gerald E. Dematteo, VP of Finance.

■ 10765 ■ Clark Seafood Company Inc.
4401 Clark St.
Pascagoula, MS 39567
Phone: (601)762-4511 **Fax:** (601)769-5108
Products: Seafood, including lobster, crab legs, scallops, and squid. **SIC:** 5146 (Fish & Seafoods). **Est:** 1956. **Sales:** $10,000,000 (2000). **Emp:** 100. **Officers:** R. Horn, President.

■ 10766 ■ Clay Cass Creamery
200 N 20th
Fargo, ND 58102
Phone: (701)293-6455 **Fax:** (701)241-9154
URL: http://www.cassclay.com
Products: Dairy products, including milk and ice cream. **SIC:** 5143 (Dairy Products Except Dried or Canned). **Est:** 1934. **Sales:** $100,000,000 (2000). **Emp:** 375. **Officers:** Keith Pagel, e-mail: Keith@cassclay.com.

■ 10767 ■ Clear Eye
302 Route 89 S
Savannah, NY 13146
Phone: (315)365-2816
Free: (800)724-2233 **Fax:** (315)365-2819
Products: Food products, including canned vegetables and fruits; Dried fruits; Beauty aids, including soaps, shampoo, and lotion. **SICs:** 5149 (Groceries & Related Products Nec); 5122 (Drugs, Proprietaries & Sundries). **Est:** 1974.

■ 10768 ■ Clear Springs Foods Inc.
1500 E 4424 N
Buhl, ID 83316
Phone: (208)543-4316
Free: (800)635-8211 **Fax:** (208)543-5608
E-mail: csf@clearsprings.com
URL: http://www.clearsprings.com
Products: Trout. **SIC:** 5146 (Fish & Seafoods). **Est:** 1966. **Sales:** $40,000,000 (1999). **Emp:** 420. **Officers:** L. Cope, CEO & President; K. Quigley, VP & CFO; T. Hanifen, VP of Operations; R. MacMillan, VP Reasearch and Environmental Affairs.

■ 10769 ■ Clegg Seafood International
PO Drawer C
Port Lavaca, TX 77979
Phone: (512)552-3761 **Fax:** (512)552-3985
Products: Seafood. **SIC:** 5146 (Fish & Seafoods). **Est:** 1947. **Sales:** $22,000,000 (2000). **Emp:** 100. **Officers:**

S. Clegg, President; M. Clegg, Treasurer; Jeanne Grove, Dir. of Marketing.

■ 10770 ■ Clem Wholesale Grocer Co. Inc.
PO Box 666
Malvern, AR 72104
Phone: (501)332-5406
Products: General line groceries. **SIC:** 5141 (Groceries—General Line). **Est:** 1948. **Sales:** $7,000,000 (2000). **Emp:** 29. **Officers:** Darryl Massey, President; John Jones, Treasurer & Secty.

■ 10771 ■ Clipper Quality Seafood, Inc.
3502 Gulfview Ave.
Marathon, FL 33050-2341
Phone: (305)743-3637 **Fax:** (305)743-2783
Products: Fresh fish; Seafood. **SIC:** 5146 (Fish & Seafoods). **Sales:** $5,000,000 (2000). **Emp:** 49. **Officers:** Robert J. Trafford, President.

■ 10772 ■ Clofine Dairy and Food Products Inc.
PO Box 335
Linwood, NJ 08221
Phone: (609)653-1000
Free: (800)441-1001 **Fax:** (609)653-0127
Products: Dairy products. **SIC:** 5143 (Dairy Products Except Dried or Canned). **Est:** 1937. **Sales:** $42,000,000 (2000). **Emp:** 17. **Officers:** H.L. Clofine, President; Marie Losco, Controller; Richard Eluk, Dir. of Marketing.

■ 10773 ■ Clougherty Packing Co.
PO Box 58870
Los Angeles, CA 90058
Phone: (213)583-4621 **Fax:** (213)584-1699
Products: Meat packing plant; Fresh pork products. **SIC:** 5147 (Meats & Meat Products). **Sales:** $350,000,000 (2000). **Emp:** 1,100. **Officers:** Joseph Clougherty, President & Chairman of the Board; Jim Stephenson, CFO.

■ 10774 ■ Clover Leaf Ice Cream
16 E 11th
Newport, KY 41071-2110
Phone: (606)431-7550 **Fax:** (606)431-0349
Products: Milk products. **SIC:** 5143 (Dairy Products Except Dried or Canned). **Emp:** 49.

■ 10775 ■ Cloverdale Foods Company Inc.
PO Box 667
Mandan, ND 58554
Phone: (701)663-9511
Free: (800)669-9511 **Fax:** (701)663-0690
URL: http://www.cloverdalefoods.com
Products: Processed meats. **SIC:** 5147 (Meats & Meat Products). **Est:** 1915. **Sales:** $59,000,000 (2000). **Emp:** 250. **Officers:** Don Russell, CEO; Steven Russell, President.

■ 10776 ■ Cloverhill Pastry-Vending Inc.
2020 N Parkside Ave.
Chicago, IL 60639-2991
Phone: (312)745-9800 **Fax:** (312)745-1647
Products: Frozen danishes. **SIC:** 5142 (Packaged Frozen Foods). **Est:** 1961. **Sales:** $6,500,000 (2000). **Emp:** 80. **Officers:** William Gee III, President; Edward Gee, VP & CFO.

■ 10777 ■ Cloverleaf Farms Distributors Inc.
13835 S Kostner Ave.
Crestwood, IL 60445
Phone: (708)597-2200
Products: Milk. **SIC:** 5149 (Groceries & Related Products Nec). **Sales:** $9,000,000 (1994). **Emp:** 20. **Officers:** Michael Bailey, President.

■ 10778 ■ Club Chef
800 Bank St.
Cincinnati, OH 45214
Phone: (513)562-4200 **Fax:** (513)562-4245
URL: http://www.clubchef.com
Products: Fruits and vegetables. **SIC:** 5148 (Fresh Fruits & Vegetables). **Est:** 1975. **Sales:** $45,000,000 (1999). **Emp:** 500. **Officers:** John O'Brian, Exec. VP; William E. Petty, Controller; Jeff Klare, VP of Sales; Tom Duggan, Dir. of Operations.

■ 10779 ■ CMA Incorporated
904 Kohou St., Ste. 308
Honolulu, HI 96817
Phone: (808)841-8011 **Fax:** (808)845-7277
Products: Frozen seafood products; Stuffed sheepskin toys; Scrap copper and aluminum; Construction materials, including marble and granite; Fishing equipment; Housewares. **SICs:** 5091 (Sporting & Recreational Goods); 5142 (Packaged Frozen Foods); 5092 (Toys & Hobby Goods & Supplies); 5093 (Scrap & Waste Materials); 5039 (Construction Materials Nec). **Officers:** Henry J.S. Choi, President.

■ 10780 ■ Co-op Country Farmers Elevator
PO Box 604
Renville, MN 56284
Phone: (320)329-8377 **Fax:** (320)329-3446
Products: Fertilizer and grain mixing and blending. **SICs:** 5153 (Grain & Field Beans); 5191 (Farm Supplies). **Sales:** $37,000,000 (2000). **Emp:** 41.

■ 10781 ■ Co-Sales Co.
PO Box 551
Phoenix, AZ 85001
Phone: (602)254-5555
Products: Canned fruits and vegetables; Ice cream novelties. **SICs:** 5149 (Groceries & Related Products Nec); 5143 (Dairy Products Except Dried or Canned). **Est:** 1905. **Sales:** $30,000,000 (2000). **Emp:** 110. **Officers:** Don Cox, CEO & President; Judy Lawson, CFO; Mike Richards, Dir. of Marketing.

■ 10782 ■ Coastal Berry Company
480 W Beach St.
Watsonville, CA 95076-4510
Phone: (408)724-1366 **Fax:** (408)722-1407
E-mail: info@coastalberry.com
URL: http://www.coastalberry.com
Products: Strawberries; Blackberries; Raspberries. **SIC:** 5148 (Fresh Fruits & Vegetables). **Emp:** 40. **Officers:** Vince Lopes, Dir. of Sales, e-mail: vinnielopes@coastalberry.com. **Alternate Name:** N.T. #Garialo.

■ 10783 ■ Cochran Brothers Cash & Carry
PO Box 370
Dublin, GA 31040
Phone: (912)272-5144 **Fax:** (912)272-4400
Products: Groceries. **SIC:** 5141 (Groceries—General Line). **Emp:** 2. **Officers:** Adam Hodges.

■ 10784 ■ Cocoa Barry U.S.
1500 Suckle Hwy.
Pennsauken, NJ 08110-1432
Phone: (609)663-2260
Free: (800)836-2626 **Fax:** (609)665-0474
Products: Chocolate and cocoa products. **SIC:** 5149 (Groceries & Related Products Nec). **Sales:** $6,000,000 (2000). **Emp:** 49. **Officers:** R. S. McNeil, President; E. A. Smith Sr., Vice President.

■ 10785 ■ Coeur d'Alene Cash & Carry
1114 N 4th St.
Coeur D Alene, ID 83814-3217
Phone: (208)765-4924
Products: Paper products; Bulk food items. **SICs:** 5141 (Groceries—General Line); 5113 (Industrial & Personal Service Paper). **Officers:** Tom Dorsey, Owner.

■ 10786 ■ Coffee Bean International Inc.
2181 NW Nicolai St.
Portland, OR 97210
Phone: (503)227-4490
Free: (800)877-0474 **Fax:** (503)225-9604
E-mail: products@coffeebeanintl.com
Products: Coffees, teas, cocoas, and blender mixes. **SICs:** 5149 (Groceries & Related Products Nec); 5145 (Confectionery). **Est:** 1972. **Sales:** $25,000,000 (1999). **Emp:** 50. **Officers:** Bob Sharp, President; Jim Keller, CFO; Karen Hunt, Dir. of Marketing & Sales; Hazel Philbrook, Dir. of Data Processing; Michael Smith, Purchasing Mgr., e-mail: msmith@coffeebeanintl.com.

■ 10787 ■ Coffee Mill Roastery
161 E Franklin St.
Chapel Hill, NC 27514
Phone: (919)929-1727
Free: (800)729-1727 **Fax:** (919)929-5899
Products: Coffee roasting. **SIC:** 5199 (Nondurable Goods Nec). **Sales:** $3,000,000 (1999). **Emp:** 24. **Officers:** Jan Lawrence, Owner; Richard Lawrence, Owner.

■ 10788 ■ Coleman Natural Products Inc.
5140 Race Ct. Ste. 4
Denver, CO 80216
Phone: (303)297-9393 **Fax:** (303)297-0426
Products: Packs hormone-free and antibiotic-free beef. **SIC:** 5147 (Meats & Meat Products). **Sales:** $50,000,000 (2000). **Emp:** 145. **Officers:** Lee Arst, CEO & President; Rick Dutkiewicz, CFO.

■ 10789 ■ Coleman's Ice Cream
2195 Old Philadelphia Pke.
Lancaster, PA 17601
Phone: (717)394-8815
Products: Ice cream. **SIC:** 5143 (Dairy Products Except Dried or Canned).

■ 10790 ■ Colombo Baking Co.
1329 Fee Dr.
Sacramento, CA 95815
Phone: (916)648-1011 **Fax:** (916)649-2534
Products: Sourdough and French bakery products. **SIC:** 5149 (Groceries & Related Products Nec).

■ 10791 ■ Colombo, Inc.
PO Box 1113
Minneapolis, MN 55440-1113
Phone: (612)797-8866 **Fax:** (612)797-0458
Products: Frozen yogurt. **SIC:** 5143 (Dairy Products Except Dried or Canned). **Sales:** $6,000,000 (2000). **Emp:** 49. **Officers:** R. A. Kinnear.

■ 10792 ■ Colonial Baking Co.
3310 Panthersville
Decatur, GA 30034
Phone: (404)284-7477 **Fax:** (404)244-4469
Products: Bakery products, including bread and buns. **SIC:** 5149 (Groceries & Related Products Nec). **Emp:** 53. **Officers:** Zellie Carter.

■ 10793 ■ Colonial Beef Co.
3333 S 3rd St.
Philadelphia, PA 19148
Phone: (215)467-0900 **Fax:** (215)336-6025
Products: Philly steaks; Beef; Chicken. **SIC:** 5147 (Meats & Meat Products). **Sales:** $30,000,000 (2000). **Emp:** 150. **Officers:** H. Ota, President; J.P. O'Donnell, National Sales Manager.

■ 10794 ■ Colorado Potato Growers Exchange
2401 Larimer St.
Denver, CO 80205
Phone: (303)292-0159 **Fax:** (303)298-8445
Products: Potatoes and onions. **SIC:** 5148 (Fresh Fruits & Vegetables). **Est:** 1923. **Sales:** $10,000,000 (2000). **Emp:** 4. **Officers:** Byron Kunugi, President; Becky Derry, Mgr. of Finance; Tonya Bennetts, Dir. of Marketing.

■ 10795 ■ Columbia Bean & Produce Co., Inc.
2705 Rd. O
PO Box 122
Moses Lake, WA 98837
Phone: (509)765-8893 **Fax:** (509)766-1255
Products: Beans; Rice; Popcorn. **SICs:** 5145 (Confectionery); 5149 (Groceries & Related Products Nec). **Est:** 1952. **Emp:** 38.

■ 10796 ■ Columbia Packing Co. Inc.
2807 E 11th St.
Dallas, TX 75203-2010
Phone: (214)946-8171
Products: Meat. **SIC:** 5147 (Meats & Meat Products). **Est:** 1931. **Sales:** $20,000,000 (2000). **Emp:** 49. **Officers:** Joseph C. Ondrusek; Bob Ondrusek.

■ 10797 ■ Comer Packing Company Inc.
PO Box 33
Aberdeen, MS 39730
Phone: (601)369-9325
Free: (800)748-8916 **Fax:** (601)369-9375
Products: Meat packing. **SICs:** 5147 (Meats & Meat Products); 5144 (Poultry & Poultry Products). **Sales:** $12,000,000 (2000). **Emp:** 36. **Officers:** Jimmy Comer, Owner.

■ 10798 ■ Common Health Warehouse Cooperative Association
1505 N 8th St.
Superior, WI 54880-6610
Phone: (715)392-9862 **Fax:** (715)392-4517
Products: Health foods. **SIC:** 5149 (Groceries & Related Products Nec). **Est:** 1976. **Sales:** $5,000,000 (2000). **Emp:** 35. **Officers:** Bruce Mork. **Doing Business As:** Common Health Foods.

■ 10799 ■ Community Coffee Company Inc.
PO Box 791
Baton Rouge, LA 70821
Phone: (504)291-3900 **Fax:** (504)295-4584
E-mail: http://www.communitycoffee.com
Products: Coffee. **SIC:** 5149 (Groceries & Related Products Nec). **Est:** 1919. **Sales:** $78,000,000 (2000). **Emp:** 300. **Officers:** L. Patrick Pettijohn, President; Stephen J. Smith, CFO; Ralph J. Henn, Vice President; Kevin Stevenson, VP of Marketing.

■ 10800 ■ Community Coffee Company LLC
PO Box 791
Baton Rouge, LA 70821
Phone: (504)291-3900
URL: http://www.communitycoffee.com
Products: Coffee. **SIC:** 5149 (Groceries & Related Products Nec). **Est:** 1919. **Sales:** $78,000,000 (2000). **Emp:** 600. **Officers:** L. Patrick Pettijohn, President. **Alternate Name:** Community Coffee Company Inc.

■ 10801 ■ Community Suffolk Inc.
304 2nd St.
Everett, MA 02149
Phone: (617)389-5200 **Fax:** (617)389-6680
Products: Fresh produce. **SIC:** 5148 (Fresh Fruits & Vegetables). **Est:** 1946. **Sales:** $50,000,000 (2000). **Emp:** 40. **Officers:** Joe Piazza, President.

■ 10802 ■ Compass Foods Eight O'Clock Coffee
2 Paragon Dr.
Montvale, NJ 07645
Phone: (201)573-9700
Products: Groceries; Cigarettes; Health and beauty aids. **SICs:** 5149 (Groceries & Related Products Nec); 5122 (Drugs, Proprietaries & Sundries); 5141 (Groceries—General Line). **Sales:** $14,000,000 (2000). **Emp:** 40. **Officers:** R. Paul Gallant, CEO.

■ 10803 ■ ComSource Independent Foodservice Companies Inc.
2500 Cumberland Pky.
Atlanta, GA 30339
Phone: (770)952-0871 **Fax:** (770)952-0872
URL: http://www.uniprofoodservice.com
Products: Groceries, including beef, dairy, and poultry products; Food service supplies and equipment; Paper products; Chemicals. **SICs:** 5141 (Groceries—General Line); 5113 (Industrial & Personal Service Paper); 5143 (Dairy Products Except Dried or Canned); 5147 (Meats & Meat Products); 5169 (Chemicals & Allied Products Nec). **Est:** 1988. **Sales:** $200,000,000 (2000). **Emp:** 126. **Officers:** Alan Plassche, President; David Joss, Exec. VP & CFO; Dan Woodside, COO; Chris Kurek, Sr. VP of Sales & Marketing. **Former Name:** ComSource Independent Foodservice Companies Inc.

■ 10804 ■ Comstock Distributing
1897 N Edmonds Dr.
Carson City, NV 89701
Phone: (775)882-7067
Products: Beverages. **SIC:** 5141 (Groceries—General Line).

■ **10805** ■ **ConAgra Grain Co.**
730 2nd Ave. S 14th Fl.
Minneapolis, MN 55402
Phone: (612)370-7500 **Fax:** (612)370-7522
Products: Grain. **SIC:** 5153 (Grain & Field Beans).
Sales: $1,080,000,000 (2000). **Emp:** 1,260. **Officers:**
Fred Page, President; Mike McCord, VP & Controller.

■ **10806** ■ **ConAgra Poultry Co. (Duluth, Georgia)**
2475 Meadow Brook Pkwy.
Duluth, GA 30096
Phone: (770)232-4200
Products: Poultry. **SIC:** 5144 (Poultry & Poultry Products). **Sales:** $45,000,000 (2000). **Emp:** 120.
Officers: Russ Bragg, CEO.

■ **10807** ■ **ConAgra Trading Cos.**
PO Box 2910
Minneapolis, MN 55402
Phone: (612)370-7500
Products: Grain. **SIC:** 5153 (Grain & Field Beans).
Sales: $1,800,000,000 (2000). **Emp:** 2,000. **Officers:**
Fred Page, President; Michael McCord, CFO.

■ **10808** ■ **Conco Food Service**
PO Box 61028
New Orleans, LA 70161
Phone: (504)733-5200
Free: (800)488-3988 **Fax:** (504)734-7156
Products: Food. **SIC:** 5141 (Groceries—General Line).
Est: 1904. **Sales:** $100,000,000 (1999). **Emp:** 200.
Officers: J. Kurzweg, CEO; Pete Alegro, CFO;
Winslow Chadwick, President.

■ **10809** ■ **Conco Food Service Inc.**
524 W 61st
Shreveport, LA 71106
Phone: (318)869-3061 **Fax:** (318)869-0074
Products: Institutional foods. **SIC:** 5141 (Groceries—General Line). **Emp:** 160. **Officers:** Joseph A.
Salpietra.

■ **10810** ■ **Congdon Orchards Inc.**
302 W Superior St., No. 510
Duluth, MN 55802
Phone: (218)722-4757
Products: Fruit. **SIC:** 5148 (Fresh Fruits & Vegetables). **Est:** 1932. **Sales:** $4,000,000 (1999).
Emp: 100. **Officers:** Gene R. Woodin, President; Ken
Maine, Treasurer.

■ **10811** ■ **Connell Co.**
45 Cardinal Dr.
Westfield, NJ 07090
Phone: (908)233-0700 **Fax:** (908)233-1070
Products: Rice; Dairy. **SICs:** 5149 (Groceries & Related Products Nec); 5143 (Dairy Products Except Dried or Canned). **Est:** 1926. **Sales:** $975,000,000 (2000). **Emp:** 160. **Officers:** Grover Connell, President & Chairman of the Board; Vince Krzywocz, Controller; Rosalie Fleming, Exec. VP; Terry Connell, Dir. of Information Systems.

■ **10812** ■ **Steve Connolly Seafood**
34 Newmarket Sq.
Roxbury, MA 02118-2601
Phone: (617)427-7700
Free: (800)225-5595 **Fax:** (617)427-7697
Products: Seafood, including fresh, frozen, and smoked; Live lobsters. **SIC:** 5146 (Fish & Seafoods).
Est: 1981. **Emp:** 70. **Officers:** Steve Connolly Sr.;
Steve Connolly Jr.; Walter Perry; Jack Curley; David
Coombs; Michael Petrie.

■ **10813** ■ **Connors Brothers Inc.**
PO Box 308
Calais, ME 04619-0308
Phone: (207)941-6900 **Fax:** (207)941-6995
Products: Frozen seafood; Prepared fresh fish and seafood. **SIC:** 5146 (Fish & Seafoods). **Est:** 1980.
Sales: $100,000,000 (2000). **Emp:** 24. **Officers:** Jerry
Ward, President; M. Johnson, VP of Sales; D. Augello,
Vice President of Corporate Accounts.

■ **10814** ■ **Conrad Sales Company, Inc.**
81 McKinley Way
PO Box 5087
Poland, OH 44514-1953
Phone: (330)757-0711
Free: (800)888-0711 **Fax:** (330)757-0714
Products: Food preparations; Cheese, natural and processed; Vegetable oils. **SICs:** 5141 (Groceries—General Line); 5149 (Groceries & Related Products Nec).

■ **10815** ■ **Consolidated Companies Inc.**
PO Box 6096
Metairie, LA 70009
Phone: (504)834-4082 **Fax:** (504)834-2572
Products: Groceries. **SIC:** 5141 (Groceries—General Line). **Est:** 1896. **Sales:** $260,000,000 (2000). **Emp:**
500. **Officers:** Victor J. Kurzweg, CEO; Tony
McMahon, VP of Finance.

■ **10816** ■ **Consolidated Factors, Inc.**
140 Olivier St.
Monterey, CA 93940
Phone: (408)375-5121 **Fax:** (408)375-0754
Products: Produce; Seafood products. **SICs:** 5148 (Fresh Fruits & Vegetables); 5146 (Fish & Seafoods).
Est: 1945. **Sales:** $75,000,000 (2000). **Emp:** 250.
Officers: Alan Nobusada, VP of Production; Warren
Nobusada, CEO & President; Max Boland, VP of
Sales, e-mail: maddmaxb@aol.com.

■ **10817** ■ **Consolidated Foodservice Companies L.P.**
PO Box 8790
Virginia Beach, VA 23450
Phone: (757)463-5000 **Fax:** (757)463-6898
Products: Food. **SIC:** 5141 (Groceries—General Line).
Est: 1989. **Sales:** $540,000,000 (2000). **Emp:** 1,200.
Officers: Arthur Sandler, President; Steve Sandler,
CFO; Dawson Mills, Dir of Human Resources.

■ **10818** ■ **Consolidated Pet Foods Inc.**
1840 14th St.
Santa Monica, CA 90404
Phone: (310)393-9393
Products: fresh and frozen beef pet foods, baked pet loaf and dry foods. **SIC:** 5149 (Groceries & Related Products Nec). **Sales:** $3,000,000 (2000). **Emp:** 20.
Officers: H Brahms, President; V Souerwine,
Treasurer.

■ **10819** ■ **Consolidated Poultry and Egg Co.**
426 St. Paul Ave.
Memphis, TN 38126
Phone: (901)526-7392 **Fax:** (901)324-7283
Products: Poultry; Beef; Pork; Frozen food; Frozen vegetables; Canned goods. **SICs:** 5144 (Poultry & Poultry Products); 5142 (Packaged Frozen Foods); 5147 (Meats & Meat Products); 5149 (Groceries & Related Products Nec). **Est:** 1954. **Sales:** $4,500,000 (2000). **Emp:** 10. **Officers:** James J. Skefos,
President.

■ **10820** ■ **Consumers Choice Coffee Inc.**
4271 Produce Rd.
Louisville, KY 40218
Phone: (502)968-4151
Products: Coffee and tea. **SIC:** 5149 (Groceries & Related Products Nec).

■ **10821** ■ **Consumers Produce Co.**
1 21st St.
Pittsburgh, PA 15222
Phone: (412)281-0722 **Fax:** (412)281-6541
Products: Fresh fruits and vegetables. **SIC:** 5148 (Fresh Fruits & Vegetables). **Est:** 1952. **Sales:**
$45,000,000 (2000). **Emp:** 75. **Officers:** Alan Siger,
President.

■ **10822** ■ **Consumers Supply Cooperative Co.**
PO Box 868
Canyon, TX 79015
Phone: (806)655-2134 **Fax:** (806)655-8787
Products: Grain and petroleum bulk station. **SICs:**
5153 (Grain & Field Beans); 5171 (Petroleum Bulk Stations & Terminals). **Sales:** $3,800,000 (2000). **Emp:**
8. **Officers:** Louis Schenk, General Mgr.

■ **10823** ■ **Consumers Vinegar and Spice Co.**
4723 S Washtenaw Ave.
Chicago, IL 60632
Phone: (773)376-4100
Products: Spices; Seasonings. **SIC:** 5149 (Groceries & Related Products Nec). **Est:** 1950. **Sales:**
$1,500,000 (2000). **Emp:** 10. **Officers:** Stanley J.
Zarnowiecki Jr., President.

■ **10824** ■ **Contadina Foods**
PO Box 29059
Glendale, CA 91209
Phone: (818)549-6000
Products: Food and beverage products, candy, chocolate and confectionery products; Pet care products. **SICs:** 5141 (Groceries—General Line); 5149 (Groceries & Related Products Nec). **Sales:**
$20,000,000 (2000). **Emp:** 500.

■ **10825** ■ **Continental Baking Co.**
3645 W Henrietta Rd.
Rochester, NY 14623-3529
Phone: (716)334-2340
Products: Bread, cake, and related products. **SIC:**
5149 (Groceries & Related Products Nec). **Emp:** 66.
Officers: Richard P. Majewicz.

■ **10826** ■ **Continental Baking Co.**
1525 Bryant
San Francisco, CA 94103-4889
Phone: (415)552-0950 **Fax:** (415)255-0718
Products: Bakery products; Bread, cake, and related products. **SIC:** 5149 (Groceries & Related Products Nec). **Sales:** $30,000,000 (2000). **Emp:** 499. **Officers:**
Marv Reyburn.

■ **10827** ■ **Continental Commodities L.P.**
2750 Jewel Ave.
Vernon, CA 90058
Phone: (213)588-2274
Products: Shortening. **SIC:** 5149 (Groceries & Related Products Nec). **Est:** 1961. **Sales:** $9,000,000 (2000).
Emp: 50. **Officers:** Edmond J. Dugas, VP of
Operations; Linda Houston, Sales Mgr.

■ **10828** ■ **Continental Foods Corp.**
1701 E 123rd Ave.
Olathe, KS 66061
Phone: (913)829-2293
Products: Pastries and chocolate items. **SIC:** 5149 (Groceries & Related Products Nec). **Sales:**
$3,000,000 (2000). **Emp:** 14. **Officers:** Norman Haas,
President; Jack Tobie, VP & General Merchandising
Mgr.

■ **10829** ■ **Continental Foods Inc.**
2730 Wilmarco Ave.
Baltimore, MD 21223-3306
Phone: (410)233-5500
Free: (800)288-5500 **Fax:** (410)566-2130
Products: Food. **SICs:** 5141 (Groceries—General Line); 5149 (Groceries & Related Products Nec). **Est:**
1932. **Emp:** 155.

■ **10830** ■ **Convenience Store Distributing Company L.L.C.**
PO Box 1799
Richmond, IN 47374
Phone: (317)962-8521
Free: (800)428-6513 **Fax:** (317)966-3974
URL: http://www.csdist.com
Products: Groceries, frozen foods, and candy; Tobacco products. **SICs:** 5141 (Groceries—General Line); 5142 (Packaged Frozen Foods); 5145 (Confectionery). **Est:** 1973. **Sales:** $462,000,000 (2000). **Emp:** 320. **Officers:** Ted Varner, President & COO, e-mail: trvarner@marsh.net.

■ **10831** ■ **Conway Import Co. Inc.**
5 Warehouse Ln.
Elmsford, NY 10523
Phone: (914)592-1310
Free: (800)283-5808 **Fax:** (914)592-1104
Products: Mayonnaise, salad dressings, and sandwich spreads. **SIC:** 5149 (Groceries & Related Products Nec). **Est:** 1912. **Emp:** 100. **Officers:** Nicholas
Heineman.

■ 10832 ■ Cook Chocolate Co.
4801 S Lawndale Ave.
Chicago, IL 60632-3062
Phone: (773)847-4600
Free: (800)366-2462 **Fax:** (773)847-4006
Products: Chocolate products. **SIC:** 5149 (Groceries & Related Products Nec). **Sales:** $30,000,000 (2000).
Emp: 499. **Officers:** Ed Opler Jr.

■ 10833 ■ Cook's Gourmet
5821 Wilderness Ave.
Riverside, CA 92504
Phone: (909)352-5700 **Fax:** (909)352-5711
Products: Salad dressings. **SIC:** 5149 (Groceries & Related Products Nec). **Est:** 1983. **Sales:** $2,000,000 (2000). **Emp:** 2. **Officers:** Sheila Cook, President.

■ 10834 ■ Cooperative Elevator Co.
7211 E Michigan Ave.
Pigeon, MI 48755
Phone: (517)453-4500
Free: (800)968-0601 **Fax:** (517)453-3942
Products: Agricultural equipment and supplies. **SIC:** 5153 (Grain & Field Beans). **Sales:** $92,000,000 (2000). **Emp:** 160.

■ 10835 ■ Cooperative Grain and Supply
PO Box 8
Bazine, KS 67516
Phone: (785)398-2271
Free: (877)294-4427 **Fax:** (785)398-2273
Products: Livestock and farm products. **SIC:** 5153 (Grain & Field Beans). **Sales:** $9,000,000 (2000). **Emp:** 12.

■ 10836 ■ Coors Brewing Co.
PO Box 4030
Golden, CO 80401
Phone: (303)279-6565 **Fax:** (303)277-6246
Products: Beer and malt-based beverages; Glass bottles and aluminum cans. **SIC:** 5149 (Groceries & Related Products Nec). **Sales:** $1,889,500,000 (2000). **Emp:** 5,800. **Officers:** Peter H. Coors, CEO; Timothy V. Wolf, Sr. VP & CFO.

■ 10837 ■ Coors Brothers Co.
4354 Boomer Rd.
Cincinnati, OH 45247-7947
Phone: (513)541-3271
Products: Fluid milk, canned juices. **SICs:** 5143 (Dairy Products Except Dried or Canned); 5149 (Groceries & Related Products Nec). **Sales:** $4,000,000 (1994). **Emp:** 27. **Officers:** Clifford Coors, Treasurer.

■ 10838 ■ Copps Corp.
2828 Wayne St.
Stevens Point, WI 54481
Phone: (715)344-5900 **Fax:** (715)344-7378
Products: General line groceries. **SIC:** 5141 (Groceries—General Line). **Est:** 1892. **Sales:** $452,100,000 (2000). **Emp:** 3,500. **Officers:** Michael Copps, CEO; J. Thomas Sievwright, CFO; Don Copps, VP of Marketing & Sales; Rolland Schroeder, VP of Information Systems; Walter Geis.

■ 10839 ■ Copps Distributing Co.
2828 Wayne St.
Stevens Point, WI 54481
Phone: (715)344-5900 **Fax:** (715)344-7378
Products: Food products. **SIC:** 5141 (Groceries—General Line). **Sales:** $150,000,000 (2000). **Emp:** 300. **Officers:** Michael Copps, CEO & Chairman of the Board; Tom Sievwright, CFO.

■ 10840 ■ Core-Mark International Inc.
395 Oyster Point Blvd., No. 415
South San Francisco, CA 94080
Phone: (650)589-9445 **Fax:** (650)952-4284
Products: Food. **SICs:** 5194 (Tobacco & Tobacco Products); 5145 (Confectionery); 5141 (Groceries—General Line); 5122 (Drugs, Proprietaries & Sundries). **Est:** 1882. **Sales:** $220,000,000 (2000). **Emp:** 2,200. **Officers:** Gary L. Walsh, CEO & Chairman of the Board; Leo F. Korman, VP & CFO; Ronald L. Bane, Sr. VP of Marketing & Sales; Gerald J. Bolduc, VP of Information Systems; Hank Hautau, VP of Employee Relations.

■ 10841 ■ Core-Mark International Inc. Core-Mark International Incorporated Div.
3650 Fraser St.
Aurora, CO 80011
Phone: (303)373-2300 **Fax:** (303)371-8803
Products: Groceries, confectionary products, tobacco products. **SICs:** 5141 (Groceries—General Line); 5145 (Confectionery); 5194 (Tobacco & Tobacco Products). **Sales:** $44,000,000 (2000). **Emp:** 100. **Officers:** Bill Murray, General Mgr.

■ 10842 ■ Alex D. Corids & Son Inc.
212 Shaw Rd.
South San Francisco, CA 94080-6604
Phone: (650)873-1900 **Fax:** (650)952-4470
Products: Fresh produce. **SIC:** 5148 (Fresh Fruits & Vegetables). **Emp:** 10. **Officers:** D. G. Corids.

■ 10843 ■ George J. Cornille and Sons Inc.
60 S Water Mkt. W
Chicago, IL 60608
Phone: (312)226-1015
Products: Root vegetables, including radishes and parsnips. **SIC:** 5148 (Fresh Fruits & Vegetables).

■ 10844 ■ J. Cosentino Company Inc.
88 S Water Market
Chicago, IL 60608
Phone: (312)421-2000 **Fax:** (312)421-6003
Products: Produce. **SIC:** 5148 (Fresh Fruits & Vegetables). **Est:** 1946. **Sales:** $5,000,000 (2000). **Emp:** 14. **Officers:** P.A. Cosentino, President.

■ 10845 ■ Cosgrove Distributors Inc.
120 S Greenwood St.
Spring Valley, IL 61362
Phone: (815)664-4121 **Fax:** (815)663-1433
E-mail: cosgrove@ivnet.com
Products: Food service. **SIC:** 5141 (Groceries—General Line). **Est:** 1958. **Sales:** $3,000,000 (1999). **Emp:** 18. **Officers:** Nora Cosgrove, President, e-mail: cosgrove@ivnet.com.

■ 10846 ■ Cosmos Import Export Inc.
PO Box 2797
Fall River, MA 02722
Phone: (508)674-8451 **Fax:** (508)673-6464
Products: Frozen fish. **SIC:** 5146 (Fish & Seafoods). **Sales:** $2,000,000 (2000). **Emp:** 6. **Officers:** John Moniz, President.

■ 10847 ■ Cost-U-Less
12410 SE 32nd St.
Bellevue, WA 98005
Phone: (425)644-4241
Products: Groceries. **SICs:** 5141 (Groceries—General Line); 5182 (Wines & Distilled Beverages); 5122 (Drugs, Proprietaries & Sundries).

■ 10848 ■ Costa Fruit and Produce Co.
414 Rutherford Ave.
Charlestown, MA 02129
Phone: (617)241-8007 **Fax:** (617)241-8718
Products: Fruit and produce. **SICs:** 5141 (Groceries—General Line); 5149 (Groceries & Related Products Nec); 5148 (Fresh Fruits & Vegetables). **Est:** 1950. **Sales:** $48,000,000 (2000). **Emp:** 250. **Officers:** Manuel R. Costa.

■ 10849 ■ Costas Provisions Corp.
255 S Hampton St.
Boston, MA 02119
Phone: (617)427-0900
Products: Meat and poultry. **SICs:** 5147 (Meats & Meat Products); 5144 (Poultry & Poultry Products).

■ 10850 ■ Costco Companies, Inc.
999 Lake Dr.
Issaquah, WA 98027
Phone: (425)313-8100 **Fax:** (425)313-8103
URL: http://www.costco.com
Products: Groceries; Alcoholic beverages; Computer hardware and software; Pharmaceuticals; Tires. **SICs:** 5141 (Groceries—General Line); 5014 (Tires & Tubes); 5045 (Computers, Peripherals & Software); 5122 (Drugs, Proprietaries & Sundries); 5182 (Wines & Distilled Beverages). **Est:** 1976. **Sales:** $27,000,000,000 (1999). **Emp:** 65,000. **Officers:** James D. Sinegal, CEO; Richard A. Galanti, CFO; John

Matthews, Human Resources Contact; Court Newberry, Marketing Contact.

■ 10851 ■ Costco Wholesale
999 Lake Dr.
Issaquah, WA 98027
Phone: (425)313-8100
Products: Food; Major appliances; Electronics equipment. **SICs:** 5141 (Groceries—General Line); 5064 (Electrical Appliances—Television & Radio). **Est:** 1976. **Sales:** $24,000,000,000 (1999). **Emp:** 65,000. **Officers:** James D. Sinegal, CEO & President; Richard A. Galanti, Exec. VP & CFO; Court Newberry, Sr. VP of Marketing; Paul Moulton, E-commerce Membership/Marketing; John Matthews, Dir of Human Resources. **Former Name:** Price/Costco Inc.

■ 10852 ■ Couch's Inc.
U.S. 30
Latrobe, PA 15650
Phone: (412)539-2238
Products: Fresh meat; Chicken; Fresh and frozen seafood. **SICs:** 5147 (Meats & Meat Products); 5146 (Fish & Seafoods); 5144 (Poultry & Poultry Products). **Est:** 1948. **Sales:** $1,700,000 (2000). **Emp:** 12. **Officers:** A.C. Couch, Owner.

■ 10853 ■ Cougle Commission Co.
345 N Aberdeen
Chicago, IL 60607
Phone: (312)666-7861 **Fax:** (312)666-6434
Products: Beef, pork, and poultry; Spices; Paper products, including towels, napkins, and cups. **SICs:** 5147 (Meats & Meat Products); 5149 (Groceries & Related Products Nec); 5113 (Industrial & Personal Service Paper). **Est:** 1873. **Sales:** $20,000,000 (2000). **Emp:** 50. **Officers:** Edgar Freidheim, Chairman of the Board; Louis E. Freidheim, President; John Freidheim, Dir. of Marketing.

■ 10854 ■ Country Classic Dairies Inc.
1001 N 7th Ave.
Bozeman, MT 59715
Phone: (406)586-5425
Free: (800)321-4563 **Fax:** (406)586-5110
URL: http://www.darigold-mt.com
Products: Dairy products, including milk, ice cream, sour cream, butter, and cheese. **SIC:** 5143 (Dairy Products Except Dried or Canned). **Est:** 1932. **Sales:** $40,000,000 (2000). **Emp:** 55. **Officers:** Keith Nye, CEO.

■ 10855 ■ Country Club Foods Inc.
PO Box 228
Kaysville, UT 84037
Phone: (801)546-1201 **Fax:** (801)547-2245
Products: Potato chips, tortilla chips, and popcorn. **SICs:** 5145 (Confectionery); 5149 (Groceries & Related Products Nec). **Est:** 1938. **Sales:** $50,000,000 (2000). **Emp:** 450. **Officers:** Jordan Clements, Chairman of the Board; John Bowman, President; Scott Tanner, CFO; Spencer Hill, Vice President.

■ 10856 ■ Country Fresh Inc.
2555 Buchanan SW
Grand Rapids, MI 49508-1006
Phone: (616)243-0173 **Fax:** (616)243-5926
Products: Dairy products, including milk and cheese. **SIC:** 5143 (Dairy Products Except Dried or Canned). **Sales:** $250,000,000 (2000). **Emp:** 800. **Officers:** Delton Parks.

■ 10857 ■ Country Oven Bakery
2840 Pioneer Dr.
Bowling Green, KY 42102
Phone: (502)782-3200
Products: Baked goods. **SIC:** 5149 (Groceries & Related Products Nec).

■ 10858 ■ Country Smoked Meats Inc.
PO Box 46
Bowling Green, OH 43402
Phone: (419)353-0783
Free: (800)321-4766 **Fax:** (419)352-7330
Products: Smoked and processed meats, including beef jerky, Canadian bacon, and hams. **SIC:** 5147 (Meats & Meat Products). **Est:** 1977. **Sales:** $6,000,000 (2000). **Emp:** 49. **Officers:** Don Contris.

■ **10859** ■ **Country Springs Farmers**
8419 N State Rte. 19
Green Springs, OH 44836
Phone: (419)639-2242 **Fax:** (419)639-2990
Products: Grain and farm supplies. **SICs:** 5153 (Grain & Field Beans); 5191 (Farm Supplies). **Sales:** $71,000,000 (2000). **Emp:** 78. **Officers:** George Secord, President; Jim Rolf, Dir. of Operations.

■ **10860** ■ **Country Wide Transport Services Inc.**
119 Despatch Dr.
East Rochester, NY 14445
Phone: (716)381-5470
Products: Produce. **SIC:** 5148 (Fresh Fruits & Vegetables). **Sales:** $34,000,000 (2000). **Emp:** 37. **Officers:** Timothy Lepper, CEO, President & Chairman of the Board.

■ **10861** ■ **Dale Cox Distributing**
2210 Pineview
Petaluma, CA 94954
Phone: (707)778-7793
Products: Cookies, condiments, and potato chips. **SICs:** 5149 (Groceries & Related Products Nec); 5145 (Confectionery).

■ **10862** ■ **L. Craelius and Company Inc.**
1100 W Fulton St.
Chicago, IL 60607
Phone: (312)666-7100
Products: Poultry. **SIC:** 5144 (Poultry & Poultry Products). **Est:** 1939. **Sales:** $47,000,000 (2000). **Emp:** 30. **Officers:** Larry A. Craelius, President; Larry J. Craelius, Vice President.

■ **10863** ■ **Craig & Hamilton Meat Co.**
721 N Union
Stockton, CA 95205-4150
Phone: (209)465-5838
Free: (800)925-5838 **Fax:** (209)464-8135
Products: Fresh meat; Cured or smoked meat; Frozen meat; Seafood; Fresh pork. **SICs:** 5147 (Meats & Meat Products); 5146 (Fish & Seafoods); 5142 (Packaged Frozen Foods). **Emp:** 60. **Officers:** Pat Craig.

■ **10864** ■ **Cream O' Weber**
4282 W 1730 South
Salt Lake City, UT 84104
Phone: (801)973-9922 **Fax:** (801)977-5053
Products: Dairy products. **SIC:** 5143 (Dairy Products Except Dried or Canned). **Emp:** 225.

■ **10865** ■ **Creme Curls Bakery Inc.**
5292 Lawndale
POB 276
Hudsonville, MI 49426
Phone: (616)669-6230
Free: (800)466-1219 **Fax:** (616)669-2468
Products: Baked goods, including cream curls, eclairs, cream puffs, turnovers, and strudels. **SIC:** 5149 (Groceries & Related Products Nec). **Est:** 1966. **Sales:** $5,000,000 (1999). **Emp:** 150. **Officers:** Henry F. Bierling, President; Tom Bierling Jr., Vice President.

■ **10866** ■ **Crest Fruit Co. Inc.**
100 N Tower Rd.
Alamo, TX 78516
Phone: (956)787-9971
Products: Fruit and vegetables, including citrus fruit, cantaloupe, and onions. **SIC:** 5148 (Fresh Fruits & Vegetables). **Est:** 1966. **Sales:** $17,000,000 (2000). **Emp:** 200. **Officers:** Harry D. Goodwin, President; Marianne Seal, Controller; Richard B. Hamilton, VP of Marketing; Keith Sanders, Dir. of Systems.

■ **10867** ■ **Crestar Food Products Inc.**
750 Old Hickory Blvd.
Burns, TN 37029
Phone: (615)377-4400
Free: (800)733-2990 **Fax:** (615)377-4411
Products: Pizza products. **SICs:** 5149 (Groceries & Related Products Nec); 5143 (Dairy Products Except Dried or Canned). **Est:** 1968. **Sales:** $85,000,000 (2000). **Emp:** 200. **Officers:** Donald J. Kerr, CEO & President; Rex King, Finance Officer; Jim DiLorio, VP of Marketing.

■ **10868** ■ **Crispy's Inc.**
544 E 24th St.
Tucson, AZ 85713
Phone: (520)623-3403 **Fax:** (520)623-3404
Products: Potato chips; Cookies; Crackers; Snack foods. **SICs:** 5145 (Confectionery); 5149 (Groceries & Related Products Nec). **Sales:** $6,000,000 (2000). **Emp:** 55. **Officers:** E. E. Maseeh.

■ **10869** ■ **Cross and Company Inc.**
PO Box 920628
Houston, TX 77058-2504
Phone: (713)673-3100
Products: Food for ships. **SIC:** 5141 (Groceries—General Line). **Est:** 1921. **Sales:** $17,000,000 (2000). **Emp:** 33. **Officers:** Robert Kimbrough, President; Ada Lam, Controller; Gary Lacy, General Mgr.

■ **10870** ■ **Cross Mark Southern California**
12131 Telegraph Rd.
Santa Fe Springs, CA 90670
Phone: (562)946-7333
Products: Food brokerage firm. **SIC:** 5141 (Groceries—General Line). **Sales:** $194,000,000 (2000). **Emp:** 450. **Officers:** Rick Mitchell, President.

■ **10871** ■ **Crossmark Sales and Marketing**
444 W 21st St., Ste. 101
Tempe, AZ 85282
Phone: (602)437-0616 **Fax:** (602)829-7078
Products: Frozen meats and general line groceries. **SICs:** 5147 (Meats & Meat Products); 5149 (Groceries & Related Products Nec). **Sales:** $6,000,000 (2000). **Emp:** 120. **Officers:** Allan Viles, President.

■ **10872** ■ **Crown Distributing Inc.**
3401 Bridgeland Dr.
Bridgeton, MO 63045
Phone: (314)291-5545 **Fax:** (314)291-2467
Products: Dairy products; Meats. **SICs:** 5143 (Dairy Products Except Dried or Canned); 5147 (Meats & Meat Products). **Est:** 1980. **Sales:** $3,500,000 (2000). **Emp:** 12. **Officers:** R.F. Crowe, President.

■ **10873** ■ **Crown Foods Inc.**
5243 Manchester Rd.
St. Louis, MO 63110
Phone: (314)645-5300
Products: Fresh meat, including poultry, beef, and pork. **SICs:** 5147 (Meats & Meat Products); 5144 (Poultry & Poultry Products). **Est:** 1975. **Sales:** $72,000,000 (2000). **Emp:** 200. **Officers:** Larry Stein, President; Don Kohl, Controller; Rick Stein, VP of Marketing & Sales.

■ **10874** ■ **Crown Inc. (Cerritos, California)**
12881 166th St.
Cerritos, CA 90703
Phone: (562)926-3939
Products: Food. **SIC:** 5141 (Groceries—General Line).

■ **10875** ■ **Crown Products Inc.**
3500 North Causeway Blvd., Ste. 1548
Metairie, LA 70002
Phone: (504)837-5342 **Fax:** (504)831-1219
Products: Breakfast cereals; Peanut butter; Hot sauce; Popcorn. **SICs:** 5149 (Groceries & Related Products Nec); 5145 (Confectionery). **Officers:** Jeffrey L. Teague, Vice President.

■ **10876** ■ **Crystal City Bakers**
25 Riverside Dr.
Corning, NY 14830-2237
Phone: (607)937-5331
Products: Bakery products. **SIC:** 5149 (Groceries & Related Products Nec). **Est:** 1937. **Sales:** $2,000,000 (2000). **Emp:** 50. **Officers:** Harold S. Berge.

■ **10877** ■ **Crystal Farms Refrigerated Distribution Co.**
6465 Wayzata Blvd., Ste. 200
Minneapolis, MN 55426
Phone: (612)544-8101 **Fax:** (612)544-8069
Products: Eggs, dairy products and general food products. **SICs:** 5144 (Poultry & Poultry Products); 5143 (Dairy Products Except Dried or Canned); 5149 (Groceries & Related Products Nec); 5141 (Groceries—General Line). **Sales:** $155,800,000 (2000). **Emp:** 425. **Officers:** Norman A. Rodriquez, President; James Grosh, CFO.

■ **10878** ■ **Crystal Food Import Corp.**
245 Sumner St. E
Boston, MA 02128-2121
Phone: (617)569-7500
Free: (800)225-3573 **Fax:** (617)561-0397
E-mail: crystalfoods@earthlink.net
Products: Natural and process cheese and related products; Vegetables; Crackers; Sun dried meat; Olives. **SIC:** 5143 (Dairy Products Except Dried or Canned). **Est:** 1969. **Sales:** $15,000,000 (2000). **Emp:** 30. **Officers:** John A. Ciano; Stephanie Ciano, Sales Contact; William Martin, CFO.

■ **10879** ■ **Crystal Products Corp.**
50 Knickerbocker Rd.
Moonachie, NJ 07074-1613
Phone: (908)249-6602 **Fax:** (908)214-1785
Products: Frozen meats, beef, shrimp, cod, and halibut; Canned vegetables and soups. **SICs:** 5142 (Packaged Frozen Foods); 5146 (Fish & Seafoods); 5149 (Groceries & Related Products Nec). **Est:** 1946. **Sales:** $12,000,000 (2000). **Emp:** 35. **Officers:** Elizabeth Szegeski, President; Micheal Szegeski, Vice President.

■ **10880** ■ **Cub Foods**
421 S 3rd St.
PO Box 9
Stillwater, MN 55082-0009
Phone: (612)439-7200 **Fax:** (612)779-2057
Products: Groceries. **SIC:** 5141 (Groceries—General Line). **Est:** 1959. **Sales:** $1,600,000,000 (2000). **Emp:** 4,000. **Officers:** Michael W. Wright, CEO & President; Laurence L. Anderson, Sr. VP; Arnold R. Weber, President; Carole F. St. Mark, President.

■ **10881** ■ **Cuetara America Co.**
15925 NW 52nd Ave.
Miami Lakes, FL 33014
Phone: (305)625-8888 **Fax:** (305)625-4001
E-mail: cuetara@usa.com
URL: http://www.goldenbake.com
Products: Miniature chocolate chip gourmet cookies, crackers and snacks. **SIC:** 5149 (Groceries & Related Products Nec). **Est:** 1981. **Sales:** $1,000,000 (2000). **Emp:** 49. **Officers:** Isaac Gomez, President. **Former Name:** Southern Gourmet Products Inc.

■ **10882** ■ **Culver Dairy Inc.**
868 Bridle Ln.
Webster, NY 14580-2606
Phone: (716)671-6709
Products: Dairy products; Milk; Fresh fruit juices and nectars; Sour cream unflavored; Natural and process cheese and related products. **SICs:** 5143 (Dairy Products Except Dried or Canned); 5149 (Groceries & Related Products Nec). **Est:** 1980. **Emp:** 5.

■ **10883** ■ **Curtis Packing Co. Inc.**
2416 Randolph Ave.
Greensboro, NC 27406
Phone: (910)275-7684 **Fax:** (910)230-0057
Products: Hot dogs and bologna. **SIC:** 5147 (Meats & Meat Products). **Officers:** D. B. Curtis.

■ **10884** ■ **Curtis Packing Co. Inc.**
115 Sycamore St.
Tifton, GA 31794-9511
Phone: (912)382-4014 **Fax:** (912)382-9540
Products: Sausage, hamburger, beef, and pork. **SIC:** 5147 (Meats & Meat Products). **Sales:** $10,000,000 (2000). **Emp:** 49. **Officers:** D. Earl Branch.

■ **10885** ■ **Penny Curtiss Bakery**
PO Box 486
Syracuse, NY 13211-0486
Phone: (315)454-3241 **Fax:** (315)455-1934
Products: Bread; Doughnuts and other sweet yeast goods; Cookies. **SIC:** 5149 (Groceries & Related Products Nec). **Est:** 1963. **Sales:** $45,000,000 (2000). **Emp:** 299. **Officers:** David A. Adamsen, President; Robert Shannor Sr., Vice President; David Pawlowski, Sales/Mktg.; Michael Lawler, Human Resources.

■ 10886 ■ Cusack Wholesale Meat Co.
PO Box 25111
Oklahoma City, OK 73125
Phone: (405)232-2115 **Free:** (800)241-6328
Products: Beef; Lamb; Veal. **SIC:** 5147 (Meats & Meat Products). **Est:** 1933. **Sales:** $4,000,000 (2000). **Emp:** 20. **Officers:** Francis L. Cusack, President; Terry Gray, CFO.

■ 10887 ■ Cutie Pie Corp.
443 W 400 N
Salt Lake City, UT 84103
Phone: (801)533-9550
Free: (800)453-4575 **Fax:** (801)355-8021
Products: Fruit turnover pies. **SIC:** 5142 (Packaged Frozen Foods). **Sales:** $8,800,000 (2000). **Emp:** 75. **Officers:** Bill Reynolds, President; Craig Shiner, CFO.

■ 10888 ■ Cutrufellos Creamery Inc.
1390 Barnum Ave.
Stratford, CT 06497
Phone: (203)378-2651
Products: Cheese. **SIC:** 5143 (Dairy Products Except Dried or Canned). **Sales:** $2,000,000 (2000). **Emp:** 14. **Officers:** Trent D'Eramo, President.

■ 10889 ■ CWT International Inc.
PO Box 1396
Gainesville, GA 30501
Phone: (404)532-3181
Products: Eggs. **SIC:** 5144 (Poultry & Poultry Products). **Est:** 1989. **Sales:** $20,000,000 (2000). **Emp:** 100. **Officers:** Dave Neff, CEO; Michael Hulsey, Treasurer & Secty.; Michael C. Steffen, Dir. of Marketing; Kay Renner, Dir. of Data Processing.

■ 10890 ■ D E B Industries, Inc.
2918 S Poplar Ave.
Chicago, IL 60608
Phone: (312)225-3600 **Fax:** (312)225-4444
E-mail: allidebindinc@juno.com
Products: Snack foods, including potato sticks and nuts; Motor vehicle parts and supplies. **SICs:** 5145 (Confectionery); 5013 (Motor Vehicle Supplies & New Parts). **Sales:** $2,000,000 (1999). **Emp:** 9. **Officers:** David Brost, President; Elayne Brost, Vice President. **Alternate Name:** Brost International Trading Co.

■ 10891 ■ Dadco Food Products Inc.
PO Box 1107
Eau Claire, WI 54702-1107
Phone: (715)834-3418
Free: (800)279-3663 **Fax:** (715)834-0151
Products: Frozen pizza. **SIC:** 5142 (Packaged Frozen Foods). **Sales:** $13,000,000 (2000). **Emp:** 150.

■ 10892 ■ Daily Bread Company Inc.
PO Box 1091
Portsmouth, NH 03802
Phone: (603)436-2722
Free: (800)635-5668 **Fax:** (603)436-0282
Products: Bread and bagel mixes. **SIC:** 5149 (Groceries & Related Products Nec). **Sales:** $3,000,000 (2000). **Emp:** 6. **Officers:** Robert Lynch, President.

■ 10893 ■ Dairy Export Co. Inc.
635 Elliott W
Seattle, WA 98119
Phone: (206)284-7220 **Fax:** (206)281-3456
Products: Dairy products. **SIC:** 5143 (Dairy Products Except Dried or Canned). **Sales:** $43,000,000 (2000). **Emp:** 140. **Officers:** John Mueller; Phil Difliese.

■ 10894 ■ Dairy Fresh Corp.
PO Box 159
Greensboro, AL 36744
Phone: (334)624-3041
Products: Dairy products. **SIC:** 5143 (Dairy Products Except Dried or Canned). **Est:** 1951. **Sales:** $180,000,000 (2000). **Emp:** 750. **Officers:** Betty Gist, President.

■ 10895 ■ Dairy Fresh Products Co.
601 Rockefeller Ave.
Ontario, CA 91761
Phone: (909)975-1019
Products: Food. **SICs:** 5149 (Groceries & Related Products Nec); 5143 (Dairy Products Except Dried or Canned). **Sales:** $175,000,000 (2000). **Emp:** 470. **Officers:** Jim DeKeyser, President; Bill Barrett, CFO.

■ 10896 ■ Dairy Gold Foods Co.
909 E 21st St.
Cheyenne, WY 82001
Phone: (307)634-4433
Products: Ice cream. **SIC:** 5143 (Dairy Products Except Dried or Canned). **Est:** 1926. **Sales:** $4,000,000 (2000). **Emp:** 27. **Officers:** Robert McClusky, President; Wayne Brown, General Mgr.

■ 10897 ■ Dairy Maid Dairy Inc.
706 Vernon Ave.
Frederick, MD 21701
Phone: (301)663-5114
Products: Dairy products. **SIC:** 5143 (Dairy Products Except Dried or Canned). **Sales:** $30,000,000 (2000). **Emp:** 95. **Officers:** Joseph Vona, President; J. H. Vona, VP of Sales; J. A. Vona, VP of Operations.

■ 10898 ■ Dairy Maid Foods Inc.
2434 E Pecan St.
Phoenix, AZ 85040
Phone: (602)243-3090
Products: Ice cream. **SIC:** 5141 (Groceries—General Line). **Sales:** $86,000,000 (2000). **Emp:** 165. **Officers:** Norman McClelland, President; Jim Coakley, VP & General Mgr.

■ 10899 ■ Dairy-Mix Inc.
3020 46th Ave. N
St. Petersburg, FL 33714
Phone: (813)525-6101
Products: Ice milk mix; Ice cream mix. **SIC:** 5143 (Dairy Products Except Dried or Canned). **Sales:** $12,000,000 (2000). **Emp:** 18. **Officers:** Edward J. Coryn, President.

■ 10900 ■ Dairy-Mix Inc.
3020 46th Ave. N
St. Petersburg, FL 33714
Phone: (727)525-6101 **Fax:** (727)522-0769
Products: Dairy products. **SIC:** 5143 (Dairy Products Except Dried or Canned). **Sales:** $8,000,000 (2000). **Emp:** 15. **Officers:** Edward J. Coryn, President; John Coryn, Vice President.

■ 10901 ■ Dairy Valley
1201 S 1st St.
Mt. Vernon, WA 98273
Phone: (360)424-7091
Products: Dairy products. **SIC:** 5143 (Dairy Products Except Dried or Canned).

■ 10902 ■ Dairylea Cooperative Inc.
PO Box 4844
Syracuse, NY 13221
Phone: (315)433-0100 **Fax:** (315)433-2345
URL: http://www.dairylea.com
Products: Raw milk. **SIC:** 5143 (Dairy Products Except Dried or Canned). **Est:** 1988. **Sales:** $550,000,000 (2000). **Emp:** 80. **Officers:** Gregory Wickham, COO; Richard P. Smith, CEO; Clyde E. Rutherford, President.

■ 10903 ■ Dallas City Packing Inc.
3049 Morrell St.
Dallas, TX 75203
Phone: (214)948-3901 **Fax:** (214)942-2039
Products: Beef. **SIC:** 5147 (Meats & Meat Products). **Emp:** 100. **Officers:** Milton Rubin.

■ 10904 ■ Dallas Market Center Company Ltd.
2100 Stemmons Fwy.
Dallas, TX 75207
Phone: (214)655-6100
Products: Food. **SIC:** 5141 (Groceries—General Line). **Sales:** $200,000,000 (2000). **Emp:** 400. **Officers:** Bill Winsor, President; Dan Fitzgerald, CFO.

■ 10905 ■ Damore's Wholesale Produce
2206 Delaware Blvd.
Saginaw, MI 48602-5226
Phone: (517)793-1511
Products: Produce. **SIC:** 5148 (Fresh Fruits & Vegetables).

■ 10906 ■ Dan Valley Foods, Inc.
PO Box 441
Danville, VA 24543
Phone: (804)792-4311
Free: (800)873-9928 **Fax:** (804)791-3067
Products: Frozen foods, canned foods, and produce. **SICs:** 5148 (Fresh Fruits & Vegetables); 5142 (Packaged Frozen Foods); 5149 (Groceries & Related Products Nec). **Emp:** 26. **Former Name:** Canada Produce and Plants, Inc.

■ 10907 ■ Danvers Farmers Elevator Co.
200 S W St.
Danvers, IL 61732
Phone: (309)963-4305 **Fax:** (309)963-5524
Products: Grain and farm supplies. **SICs:** 5153 (Grain & Field Beans); 5191 (Farm Supplies). **Sales:** $11,000,000 (2000). **Emp:** 10. **Officers:** Jim Vierling, CEO & Chairman of the Board; Dan Deal, Treasurer & Secty.

■ 10908 ■ Darigold
520 E Albany
Caldwell, ID 83605-3539
Phone: (208)459-3687 **Fax:** (208)459-9135
Products: Cheese; Powdered milk. **SICs:** 5143 (Dairy Products Except Dried or Canned); 5149 (Groceries & Related Products Nec). **Sales:** $139,000,000 (2000). **Emp:** 325. **Officers:** Frank W. Krone.

■ 10909 ■ Darisil, Inc.
PO Box 457
Suffern, NY 10901
Phones: (914)357-2740 (914)347-5555
Fax: (914)357-1966
E-mail: rksilv@aol.com
Products: Packaged foods, including dairy products, potatoes, and rice, grain, and beans; Vegetable salad oils. **SICs:** 5149 (Groceries & Related Products Nec); 5143 (Dairy Products Except Dried or Canned). **Est:** 1976. **Sales:** $5,000,000 (2000). **Officers:** J.S. Silver, President; R.K. Silver, Vice President; Josephine Silver, Vice President.

■ 10910 ■ Darlington Farms
PO Box 390
Springboro, OH 45066-0390
Free: (800)882-7076
Products: Institutional cookies; Food products for fundraisers. **SICs:** 5149 (Groceries & Related Products Nec); 5145 (Confectionery). **Emp:** 49. **Officers:** Brian Ellis.

■ 10911 ■ D'Arrigo Brothers of Massachusetts Inc.
105 New England Produce Ctr.
Chelsea, MA 02150
Phone: (617)884-0316
Products: Fruits and vegetables. **SIC:** 5148 (Fresh Fruits & Vegetables). **Est:** 1946. **Sales:** $30,000,000 (2000). **Emp:** 22. **Officers:** Peter D'Arrigo, President.

■ 10912 ■ D'Artagnan Inc.
280 Wilson Ave.
Newark, NJ 07105
Phone: (973)344-0565
Free: (800)327-8246 **Fax:** (973)465-1870
Products: Fresh game; Fine foods. **SICs:** 5147 (Meats & Meat Products); 5149 (Groceries & Related Products Nec). **Est:** 1985. **Sales:** $16,000,000 (2000). **Emp:** 70. **Officers:** George Faison, President; Steve Johnson, Controller.

■ 10913 ■ J.T. Davenport and Sons Inc.
PO Box 1105
Sanford, NC 27330
Phone: (919)774-9444
Free: (800)868-7550 **Fax:** (919)774-4282
URL: http://www.jtdavenport.com
Products: Convenience store items. **SICs:** 5141 (Groceries—General Line); 5194 (Tobacco & Tobacco Products); 5145 (Confectionery). **Est:** 1917. **Sales:** $290,000,000 (2000). **Emp:** 370. **Officers:** John T. Davenport Jr., CEO & Chairman of the Board; Mark Davenport, Co-President.

■ **10914** ■ **Davenport-Webb Inc.**
1190 Harlem Rd.
Buffalo, NY 14216
Phone: (716)834-9443
Products: Food. **SICs:** 5141 (Groceries—General Line); 5142 (Packaged Frozen Foods).

■ **10915** ■ **Davis Bakery Inc.**
13940 Cedar Rd.
Cleveland, OH 44118
Phone: (216)932-7788
Products: Bread; Pastry products, including pies and cakes. **SIC:** 5149 (Groceries & Related Products Nec). **Est:** 1939. **Emp:** 100.

■ **10916** ■ **H.C. Davis Company Inc.**
PO Box 346
Bridgeville, DE 19933
Phone: (302)337-7001
Products: Deli and pizza supplies, including lunchmeat, cheese, sauce, and dough. **SICs:** 5149 (Groceries & Related Products Nec); 5143 (Dairy Products Except Dried or Canned); 5147 (Meats & Meat Products). **Est:** 1919. **Sales:** $3,500,000 (2000). **Emp:** 8. **Officers:** H.C. Davis, President; J. Davis, Treasurer; M. Davis, VP of Marketing.

■ **10917** ■ **John Davis Produce, Inc.**
State Farmers Mkt. Bldg. C
PO Box 713
Forest Park, GA 30298
Phone: (404)366-0150   **Fax:** (404)366-5921
Products: Produce, including sweet potatoes, green vegetables, and peanuts. **SIC:** 5148 (Fresh Fruits & Vegetables).

■ **10918** ■ **William E. Davis & Sons**
5333 G. S Mingo
Tulsa, OK 74145
Phone: (918)665-3737   **Fax:** (918)665-3757
Products: Institutional food. **SIC:** 5141 (Groceries—General Line).

■ **10919** ■ **Daymon Associates Inc.**
700 Fairfield Ave.
Stamford, CT 06902
Phone: (203)352-7500
Products: Groceries. **SIC:** 5141 (Groceries—General Line).

■ **10920** ■ **Daystar-Robinson Inc.**
1979 Marcus Ave., #234
Lake Success, NY 11042
Phone: (516)328-3900   **Fax:** (516)358-0508
Products: Fruit juice concentrates, natural colors and related fruit products. **SIC:** 5141 (Groceries—General Line). **Sales:** $28,000,000 (2000). **Emp:** 12. **Officers:** Mark Prizer, President; Carol Simpson, Controller.

■ **10921** ■ **Daytona Beach Cold Storage Inc.**
PO Box 1752
Daytona Beach, FL 32115-1752
Phone: (904)252-3746
Products: Fresh fish, chicken, beef, pork; Cereals; Canned vegetables; Soups; Cakes; Pies. **SICs:** 5141 (Groceries—General Line); 5144 (Poultry & Poultry Products); 5146 (Fish & Seafoods); 5147 (Meats & Meat Products).

■ **10922** ■ **D.B. Brown Inc.**
400 Port Carteret Dr.
Carteret, NJ 07008
Phone: (732)541-0200   **Fax:** (732)969-6042
Products: Meat, meat products and seafood. **SICs:** 5147 (Meats & Meat Products); 5146 (Fish & Seafoods). **Sales:** $340,000,000 (2000). **Emp:** 240. **Officers:** Jeffrey Stavitsky, President; Stuart Lipkin, VP of Finance.

■ **10923** ■ **DBB Marketing Co.**
155 Sansome St., Ste. 810
San Francisco, CA 94104
Phone: (415)956-7860   **Fax:** (415)356-3120
Products: General line groceries and frozen vegetables. **SICs:** 5141 (Groceries—General Line); 5142 (Packaged Frozen Foods). **Sales:** $6,000,000 (2000). **Emp:** 9. **Officers:** Douglas Clendenning, President.

■ **10924** ■ **De Bruyn Produce Company Inc.**
PO Box 76
Zeeland, MI 49464
Phone: (616)772-2102
Products: Onions; Mixed vegetables. **SIC:** 5148 (Fresh Fruits & Vegetables). **Sales:** $50,000,000 (2000). **Emp:** 300. **Officers:** Robert D. De Bruyn, President; Rick B. LaHuis, Treasurer; Dennis Van Dreumel, Dir of Human Resources.

■ **10925** ■ **De Vries Imports & Distributors**
16700 Schoenborn St.
North Hills, CA 91343
Phone: (818)893-6906   **Fax:** (818)893-9446
Products: Gourmet food items; Candy and chocolate; Gift baskets. **SICs:** 5149 (Groceries & Related Products Nec); 5145 (Confectionery). **Emp:** 19. **Officers:** Hugh J. De Vries; Louise De Vries.

■ **10926** ■ **Deaktor/Sysco Food Services Co.**
PO Box 1000
Harmony, PA 16037
Phone: (724)452-2100   **Fax:** (724)452-1033
Products: Resturant food and supplies. **SIC:** 5141 (Groceries—GeneralLine). **Sales:** $96,000,000 (2000). **Emp:** 300. **Officers:** Barry Friends, President; Thomas Riccobelli, Sr. VP; Jean Doro-Wagner, VP of Sales; Raymond Wimple, Dir of Human Resources.

■ **10927** ■ **Dealers Food Products Co.**
23800 Commerce Park Rd., Ste. D
Cleveland, OH 44122-5828
Phone: (216)292-6666   **Fax:** (216)292-4600
E-mail: dealersfoods@msn.com
Products: Candy; Seasonings; Dairy products. **SICs:** 5143 (Dairy Products Except Dried or Canned); 5149 (Groceries & Related Products Nec); 5145 (Confectionery). **Est:** 1927. **Sales:** $5,000,000 (2000). **Emp:** 5. **Officers:** Donald Glaser, Vice President.
Former Name: Dealers Dairy Products Co.

■ **10928** ■ **Dealers Food Products Co.**
23800 Commerce Park Rd., Ste. D
Cleveland, OH 44122-5828
Phone: (216)292-6666   **Fax:** (216)292-4600
Products: Foodd. **SIC:** 5143 (Dairy Products Except Dried or Canned). **Sales:** $5,000,000 (2000). **Emp:** 5.

■ **10929** ■ **Dean Foods Co.**
3600 N River Rd.
Franklin Park, IL 60131
Products: Ice cream. **SIC:** 5143 (Dairy Products Except Dried or Canned). **Est:** 1925. **Sales:** $10,000,000 (1999). **Emp:** 99. **Officers:** Gordon Willis.

■ **10930** ■ **Dearborn Wholesale Grocers L.P.**
2801 S Western Ave.
Chicago, IL 60608
Phone: (773)254-4300   **Fax:** (312)847-3838
Products: General line groceries. **SIC:** 5141 (Groceries—General Line). **Est:** 1974. **Sales:** $230,000,000 (2000). **Emp:** 450. **Officers:** Sherwin Friedman, President; Peter Westerberg, Finance Officer; Keith Scott, Dir. of Marketing; Jean Bishop, Dir. of Information Systems.

■ **10931** ■ **DeBragga and Spitler Inc.**
826-D Washington St.
New York, NY 10014
Phone: (212)924-1311
Products: Meat. **SIC:** 5147 (Meats & Meat Products).

■ **10932** ■ **Decatur Coca-Cola Bottling Co.**
PO Box 1687
Decatur, AL 35602
Phone: (205)353-9211
Products: Beverages. **SIC:** 5149 (Groceries & Related Products Nec). **Est:** 1928. **Sales:** $6,000,000 (2000). **Emp:** 40. **Officers:** Randy Troup, President; Greg Clemons, VP & CFO.

■ **10933** ■ **DeConna Ice Cream Inc.**
PO Box 39
Orange Lake, FL 32681
Phone: (904)591-1530
Free: (800)824-8254   **Fax:** (352)591-4418
E-mail: customerservice@deconna.com
URL: http://www.deconna.com
Products: Ice cream. **SIC:** 5143 (Dairy Products

Except Dried or Canned). **Est:** 1947. **Sales:** $10,000,000 (1999). **Emp:** 75. **Officers:** Vince DeConna, President.

■ **10934** ■ **Decoster Egg Farms**
PO Box 216
Turner, ME 04282
Phone: (207)224-8222
Products: Brown chicken eggs. **SIC:** 5144 (Poultry & Poultry Products).

■ **10935** ■ **Deen Meat Co., Inc.**
PO Box 4155
Ft. Worth, TX 76164
Phone: (817)335-2257   **Fax:** (817)338-9256
URL: http://www.deenmeat.com
Products: Meat products, including chili; Food products. **SIC:** 5147 (Meats & Meat Products). **Est:** 1946. **Sales:** $17,000,000 (2000). **Emp:** 50. **Officers:** Danny Deen, President; Craig Deen, VP of Sales; Mike Pritchard, Customer Service Contact.

■ **10936** ■ **Deen Wholesale Meat Co.**
PO Box 4155
Ft. Worth, TX 76164
Phone: (817)335-2257   **Fax:** (817)338-9256
Products: Fresh beef, pork, chicken, and catfish. **SICs:** 5147 (Meats & Meat Products); 5144 (Poultry & Poultry Products); 5146 (Fish & Seafoods). **Est:** 1946. **Sales:** $17,000,000 (2000). **Emp:** 50. **Officers:** Danny Deen, President.

■ **10937** ■ **Deerwood Rice Grain Produce**
21926 County Rd. 10
Deerwood, MN 56444
Phone: (218)534-3762   **Fax:** (218)534-3802
Products: Wild rice; Animal feed. **SICs:** 5149 (Groceries & Related Products Nec); 5191 (Farm Supplies). **Sales:** $10,000,000 (2000). **Emp:** 49. **Officers:** Harold Kosbau; Dan Mohs.

■ **10938** ■ **D. DeFranco and Sons Inc.**
1000 Lawrence St.
Los Angeles, CA 90021
Phone: (213)627-8575   **Fax:** (213)627-9837
Products: Tomatoes; Mixed nuts. **SICs:** 5148 (Fresh Fruits & Vegetables); 5145 (Confectionery). **Est:** 1916. **Sales:** $14,000,000 (2000). **Emp:** 50. **Officers:** Victor R. DeFranco, CEO; Dennis Mejiah, Bookkeeper; Richard DeFranco, General Mgr.; Paul DeFranco, Manager; Gerald DeFranco, Manager.

■ **10939** ■ **Delaware Foods Inc.**
313 E Centennial Ave.
Muncie, IN 47303
Phone: (765)284-1406   **Fax:** (765)284-1561
Products: Food, including meat. **SIC:** 5147 (Meats & Meat Products). **Est:** 1946. **Sales:** $150,000,000 (2000). **Emp:** 18. **Officers:** Shirley L. Shaw, President; David Rahe, Dir. of Operations; Kevin Mitchell, Plant Manager.

■ **10940** ■ **Deli USA**
PO Box 106
Mayville, WI 53050
Phone: (920)387-5740   **Fax:** (920)387-2194
Products: Cheese. **SIC:** 5143 (Dairy Products Except Dried or Canned). **Sales:** $20,000,000 (1999). **Emp:** 18. **Officers:** Daniel Carter, CEO, e-mail: dcarter@ dcarter.com; Tim Omer, President.

■ **10941** ■ **Demakes Enterprises and Co. Inc.**
37 Waterhill St.
Lynn, MA 01905
Phone: (781)595-1557   **Fax:** (781)595-7523
E-mail: demakes@thinntrim.com
URL: http://www.thinntrim.com
Products: Fresh meat; Sausage and other prepared meats; Cooked deli meats. **SIC:** 5147 (Meats & Meat Products). **Est:** 1914. **Sales:** $33,000,000 (2000). **Emp:** 200. **Officers:** Thomas Demakes, President.

■ **10942** ■ **Demase and Manna Co.**
110 19th St.
Pittsburgh, PA 15222
Phone: (412)281-8880   **Fax:** (412)281-8892
Products: Fresh produce. **SIC:** 5148 (Fresh Fruits & Vegetables). **Est:** 1919. **Sales:** $6,000,000 (2000). **Emp:** 10. **Officers:** William Padrick, CEO.

■ 10943 ■ Demerico Corp.
6605 E 14th St.
Brownsville, TX 78521
Phone: (956)838-1290 **Fax:** (956)838-1289
Products: Frozen seafood. **SIC:** 5146 (Fish & Seafoods). **Emp:** 1. **Officers:** Michael Pashos.

■ 10944 ■ Dennis Sales Ltd.
PO Box 4056
Salisbury, MD 21803-4056
Phone: (410)742-1585 **Fax:** (410)742-3789
Products: Frozen fruits and vegetables; Frozen foods; Dehydrated fruits and vegetables. **SICs:** 5142 (Packaged Frozen Foods); 5149 (Groceries & Related Products Nec). **Officers:** P. Long, Contact.

■ 10945 ■ Dependable Food Corp.
593 McDonald Ave.
Brooklyn, NY 11218
Phone: (718)435-4880 **Fax:** (718)435-5538
Products: Frozen and dry foods; Eggs. **SICs:** 5141 (Groceries—General Line); 5142 (Packaged Frozen Foods); 5144 (Poultry & Poultry Products); 5149 (Groceries & Related Products Nec). **Est:** 1993. **Sales:** $14,000,000 (2000). **Emp:** 26. **Officers:** Samuel Blau, President; Anatea Faitel, Sales/Marketing Contact.

■ 10946 ■ Depoe Bay Fish Co.
617 SW Bay Blvd.
Newport, OR 97365-4718
Phone: (541)265-8833 **Fax:** (541)265-2145
Products: Fresh fish. **SIC:** 5146 (Fish & Seafoods). **Sales:** $11,000,000 (2000). **Emp:** 149. **Officers:** Jerry Bates.

■ 10947 ■ Des Moines Marketing Associates
2231 NW 108th St.
Des Moines, IA 50322-3714
Phone: (515)270-9595 **Fax:** (515)270-1031
Products: Garbage bags; Frozen foods; Taco sauce. **SICs:** 5142 (Packaged Frozen Foods); 5113 (Industrial & Personal Service Paper); 5149 (Groceries & Related Products Nec). **Emp:** 49. **Officers:** Robert E. Buising.

■ 10948 ■ DeSantis Distributors
3179 W 21st
Lorain, OH 44053-1115
Phone: (440)282-9742
Products: Snack foods. **SIC:** 5145 (Confectionery). **Emp:** 19. **Officers:** Peter DeSantis.

■ 10949 ■ Desert Delights Wholesale Ice
2305 E Palo Verde St.
Yuma, AZ 85365
Phone: (520)344-2311
Products: Ice cream; Frozen desserts. **SIC:** 5143 (Dairy Products Except Dried or Canned).

■ 10950 ■ Desert Mesquite of Arizona
3458 E Illini St.
Phoenix, AZ 85040-1839
Phone: (602)437-3135 **Fax:** (602)437-1354
E-mail: koehler@godnet.com
URL: http://www.virtual-showcase.com/llc/desert_mesquite/mesquite.html
Products: Mesquite wood chips and sawdust; Mesquite liquid smoke flavoring. **SICs:** 5149 (Groceries & Related Products Nec); 5099 (Durable Goods Nec). **Est:** 1980. **Sales:** $500,000 (2000). **Emp:** 3. **Officers:** John Koehler, President.

■ 10951 ■ Detail Fresh Sandwich Co.
414 W Isabella Rd.
Midland, MI 48640
Phone: (517)631-6240
Products: Food. **SIC:** 5149 (Groceries & Related Products Nec).

■ 10952 ■ Detroit City Dairy Inc.
15004 3rd Ave.
Highland Park, MI 48203
Phone: (313)868-5511 **Fax:** (313)868-4304
Products: Dairy products; Meats. **SICs:** 5143 (Dairy Products Except Dried or Canned); 5147 (Meats & Meat Products). **Sales:** $80,000,000 (2000). **Emp:** 180. **Officers:** M. Must, Chairman of the Board.

■ 10953 ■ John Dewar & Company Inc.
136 Newmarket Sq.
Boston, MA 02118-2603
Phone: (617)442-4292 **Fax:** (617)442-9743
E-mail: jdewar07@aol.com
Products: Beef; Lamb; Veal, not canned or made into sausage; Pork; Poultry. **SICs:** 5147 (Meats & Meat Products); 5144 (Poultry & Poultry Products); 5149 (Groceries & Related Products Nec). **Est:** 1978. **Sales:** $10,000,000 (1999). **Emp:** 40. **Officers:** John Dewar, e-mail: jdewar07@aol.com; Bonita Welch; Susan Scheller, Customer Service Mgr.; Ross Archer, Customer Service Mgr.; Chris Radley, Sales Mgr.; Scott Brueggeman, Operations Mgr.

■ 10954 ■ Dewied International Inc.
5010 E I-Hwy 10
San Antonio, TX 78219
Phone: (210)661-6161
Free: (800)992-5600 **Fax:** (210)662-6112
E-mail: sales@dewiedint.com
URL: http://www.dewied.com
Products: Sausage casings. **SICs:** 5149 (Groceries & Related Products Nec); 5147 (Meats & Meat Products). **Est:** 1932. **Emp:** 64. **Officers:** Howard de Wied, President; Bill Holden, Controller; Fred Opper, Vice President.

■ 10955 ■ Di Paolo Baking Company, Inc.
598 Plymouth Ave. N
Rochester, NY 14608-1629
Phone: (716)232-3510 **Fax:** (716)423-5975
Products: Bread, cake, and related products. **SIC:** 5149 (Groceries & Related Products Nec). **Sales:** $3,000,000 (2000). **Emp:** 65. **Officers:** D. Massa; S. Woerner.

■ 10956 ■ Diamond Bakery Co. Ltd.
PO Box 17760
Honolulu, HI 96817
Phone: (808)847-3551 **Fax:** (808)847-7482
Products: Crackers and cookies. **SICs:** 5145 (Confectionery); 5149 (Groceries & Related Products Nec). **Est:** 1921. **Sales:** $6,000,000 (2000). **Emp:** 57. **Officers:** P. Ishii, President; Eddie Yu, Controller; Stephen Sasaki, Marketing & Sales Mgr.

■ 10957 ■ Diamond Foods Inc.
4916 Ohara Dr.
Evansville, IN 47711-2474
Phone: (812)425-2685 **Fax:** (812)425-4821
Products: Foods, including canned and frozen foods. **SICs:** 5149 (Groceries & Related Products Nec); 5142 (Packaged Frozen Foods). **Emp:** 49.

■ 10958 ■ Diamond Fruit Growers
PO Box 180
Hood River, OR 97031
Phone: (541)354-5300 **Fax:** (541)354-2123
Products: Pears, apples, and cherries. **SIC:** 5148 (Fresh Fruits & Vegetables). **Est:** 1913. **Sales:** $31,772,000 (2000). **Emp:** 499. **Officers:** Gene Evwer, Chairman of the Board; Ron Girardelli, CEO.

■ 10959 ■ Diamond Fruit Growers
PO Box 180
Hood River, OR 97031
Phone: (541)354-5300 **Fax:** (541)354-2123
Products: Fresh fruits. **SIC:** 5148 (Fresh Fruits & Vegetables). **Sales:** $20,000,000 (2000). **Emp:** 200. **Officers:** Ronald K. Girardelli, President; David Garcia, Controller.

■ 10960 ■ Diamond Nut Company of California
16500 W 103rd St.
Lemont, IL 60439
Phone: (630)739-3000 **Fax:** (630)739-1446
Products: Inshell nuts. **SIC:** 5148 (Fresh Fruits & Vegetables). **Est:** 1932. **Sales:** $20,000,000 (2000). **Emp:** 25. **Officers:** Larry Rehmann, General Mgr.; John Czukiewski, Controller; Mike Cicero, Produce/Distribution Mgr. **Alternate Name:** Sun Diamond Growers of California Mixed Nut Div.

■ 10961 ■ Diamond Tager Co.
28th St.
PO Box 310085
Tampa, FL 33680
Phone: (813)238-3111 **Fax:** (813)238-3114
Products: Fresh produce. **SIC:** 5148 (Fresh Fruits & Vegetables). **Est:** 1934. **Sales:** $3,000,000 (2000). **Emp:** 18. **Officers:** Spencer Dimond.

■ 10962 ■ Diaz Foods Inc.
5500 Bucknell Dr. SW
Atlanta, GA 30336-2531
Phone: (404)344-5421 **Fax:** (404)344-3003
URL: http://www.diazfoods.com
Products: Mexican foods, including cheeses, spices, tortillas, and cleaners. **SIC:** 5149 (Groceries & Related Products Nec). **Est:** 1980. **Sales:** $45,000,000 (1999). **Emp:** 100. **Officers:** Rene Diaz, President; Lourdes winklemann, Treasurer; Carmen Saldana, VP Sales/Food Service; Rosa Arce, VP Sales/Retail.

■ 10963 ■ Diaz Wholesale and Manufacturing Company Inc.
5500 Bucknell Dr. SW
Atlanta, GA 30336-2531
Phone: (404)344-5421
Free: (800)394-4639 **Fax:** (404)344-3003
Products: Groceries. **SIC:** 5141 (Groceries—General Line). **Sales:** $34,100,000 (2000). **Emp:** 65. **Officers:** Rene M. Diaz, CEO.

■ 10964 ■ Dierks Foods Inc.
PO Box 2579
Rockford, IL 61103-2579
Phone: (815)877-7031
Products: Groceries. **SICs:** 5149 (Groceries & Related Products Nec); 5148 (Fresh Fruits & Vegetables); 5142 (Packaged Frozen Foods). **Sales:** $21,000,000 (2000). **Emp:** 80. **Officers:** Ron Dierks, President; Rich Jones, VP of Finance.

■ 10965 ■ DiMare Brothers Inc.
84 New England Produce Ctr.
Chelsea, MA 02150
Phone: (617)889-3800
Products: Vegetables. **SIC:** 5148 (Fresh Fruits & Vegetables). **Est:** 1970. **Sales:** $31,000,000 (2000). **Emp:** 100. **Officers:** Charles Dolan, General Mgr.

■ 10966 ■ DiMare Homestead Inc.
PO Box 900460
Homestead, FL 33090-0460
Phone: (305)245-4211
Products: Tomatoes. **SIC:** 5148 (Fresh Fruits & Vegetables).

■ 10967 ■ Distribution Plus Inc.
825 Green Bay Rd., Ste. 200
Wilmette, IL 60091
Phone: (847)256-8289 **Fax:** (847)256-8299
Products: Specialty food items, including perishable foodstuffs, canned dry items. **SIC:** 5149 (Groceries & Related Products Nec). **Est:** 1990. **Sales:** $600,000,000 (2000). **Emp:** 1,250. **Officers:** Dan O'Connell, President; Patrick Langan, CFO.

■ 10968 ■ Dixie Produce and Packaging Inc.
PO Box 23647
New Orleans, LA 70183-0647
Phone: (504)733-7500
Free: (800)952-5637 **Fax:** (504)733-1545
Products: Vegetables, including tomatoes, potatoes, and onions; Fruit. **SIC:** 5148 (Fresh Fruits & Vegetables). **Est:** 1962. **Sales:** $50,000,000 (2000). **Emp:** 300. **Officers:** Sal J. Peraino, CEO; Judy Druery, Controller.

■ 10969 ■ Dixon Tom-A-Toe Cos.
1640 Power Ferry Rd.
Marietta, GA 30067
Phone: (404)955-0947
Products: Fresh produce. **SIC:** 5148 (Fresh Fruits & Vegetables). **Sales:** $150,000,000 (2000). **Emp:** 500. **Officers:** Jimmy Smith, President.

■ 10970 ■ DMV USA Inc.
1285 Rudy St.
Onalaska, WI 54650-8580
Phone: (608)781-2345
Free: (800)359-2345   Fax: (608)781-3299
E-mail: information@dmvusa.com
Products: Milk proteins. SIC: 5143 (Dairy Products Except Dried or Canned). Sales: $25,000,000 (2000). Emp: 7. Officers: David Lee, e-mail: leed@dmvusa.com.

■ 10971 ■ DNE World Fruit Sales Inc.
1900 Old Dixie Hwy.
Ft. Pierce, FL 34946
Phone: (407)465-1110   Fax: (407)465-1181
Products: Citrus fruit. SIC: 5148 (Fresh Fruits & Vegetables). Est: 1914. Sales: $14,000,000 (2000). Emp: 48. Officers: Bernard Egan, President; Glen W. Reed, Controller.

■ 10972 ■ Dr. Pepper/Seven Up, Inc.
5301 Legacy Dr.
Plano, TX 75024
Phone: (972)673-7000   Fax: (972)673-7980
Products: Beverages. SIC: 5149 (Groceries & Related Products Nec). Sales: $255,000,000 (2000). Emp: 425.

■ 10973 ■ Doerle Food Services Inc.
PO Box 9230
New Iberia, LA 70562
Phone: (318)367-8551
Free: (800)256-1631   Fax: (318)365-7181
Products: Food, including canned vegetables and soups, fresh and frozen meats, fruits, cheese, milk, ice cream, and bread; Chemicals; Paper goods. SICs: 5141 (Groceries—General Line); 5147 (Meats & Meat Products); 5143 (Dairy Products Except Dried or Canned); 5148 (Fresh Fruits & Vegetables); 5149 (Groceries & Related Products Nec). Est: 1950. Sales: $69,000,000 (2000). Emp: 192. Officers: Carolyn Doerle, President.

■ 10974 ■ Dole and Bailey Inc.
PO Box 2405
Woburn, MA 01888
Phone: (781)935-1234
Free: (800)777-2648   Fax: (781)935-9085
E-mail: iluvcab@ix.netcom.com
URL: http://www.doleandbailey.com
Products: Gourmet food, including certified beef, lamb, pork, veal, and seafood; Produce; Groceries. SICs: 5147 (Meats & Meat Products); 5146 (Fish & Seafoods); 5149 (Groceries & Related Products Nec). Est: 1868. Sales: $45,000,000 (1999). Emp: 150. Officers: D.M. Matheson, Chairman of the Board; N. Matheson-Burns, President & CEO.

■ 10975 ■ Dole Bakersfield Inc.
6001 Snow Rd.
Bakersfield, CA 93308-9546
Phone: (805)664-6100   Fax: (805)664-6339
Products: Fresh fruit. SIC: 5148 (Fresh Fruits & Vegetables). Emp: 175. Officers: Greg Costley, President; Rick Ybarra, VP of Finance.

■ 10976 ■ Dole Fresh Vegetables Co.
PO Box 1759
Salinas, CA 93902
Phone: (408)422-8871
Products: Produce; Canned fruits and vegetables. SICs: 5148 (Fresh Fruits & Vegetables); 5149 (Groceries & Related Products Nec).

■ 10977 ■ Dole Nut Co. Inc.
PO Box 845
Orland, CA 95963
Phone: (530)865-5511   Fax: (530)865-7864
Products: Almond products. SIC: 5145 (Confectionery). Est: 1987. Officers: Greg Costley, President; Tim Gray, Controller; Steve Spellman, Sales/Marketing Contact.

■ 10978 ■ Dolgencorp
427 Beech St.
Scottsville, KY 42164
Phone: (502)237-5444   Fax: (502)237-3213
Products: Clothes; Groceries; Home furnishings. SICs: 5141 (Groceries—General Line); 5137 (Women's/Children's Clothing); 5136 (Men's/Boys' Clothing); 5023 (Homefurnishings).

■ 10979 ■ Dolly Madison Bakery
10343-A Julian Dr.
Woodlawn, OH 45215
Phone: (513)771-0077
Products: Baked goods, including snack cakes. SIC: 5149 (Groceries & Related Products Nec). Emp: 49.

■ 10980 ■ Dolly Madison Cake Co.
4400 Dodds Ave.
Chattanooga, TN 37407-3033
Phone: (423)867-9041
Products: Snack foods; Soft cakes, except frozen; Pies. SICs: 5149 (Groceries & Related Products Nec); 5145 (Confectionery). Emp: 13,741. Officers: Dan Adkins, Sales Mgr.

■ 10981 ■ Doneli Foods, Inc.
3104 Nebraska Ave.
Fremont, NE 68025-2070
Phones: (402)986-1372   (402)693-2249
Products: Dairy products. SIC: 5143 (Dairy Products Except Dried or Canned). Emp: 99. Officers: Don Wadzinski.

■ 10982 ■ Dot Foods Inc.
PO Box 192
Mt. Sterling, IL 62353
Phone: (217)773-4411   Fax: (217)773-2286
Products: Dry, frozen, packaged, and canned foods. SICs: 5141 (Groceries—General Line); 5142 (Packaged Frozen Foods); 5149 (Groceries & Related Products Nec). Est: 1960. Sales: $260,000,000 (2000). Emp: 500. Officers: Robert Tracy, CEO; Tom Tracy, CFO; Mike Buckley, Dir. of Marketing; Jim Tracy, Vice President; Keith Truelove, Dir of Human Resources.

■ 10983 ■ Double A Provisions Inc.
64 Main St.
Queensbury, NY 12804
Phone: (518)792-2494   Fax: (518)792-0963
Products: Meat; Food service provisions. SICs: 5147 (Meats & Meat Products); 5046 (Commercial Equipment Nec); 5149 (Groceries & Related Products Nec). Est: 1932. Sales: $16,000,000 (2000). Emp: 28. Officers: Ben Aronson, President & CEO.

■ 10984 ■ Doughtie's Foods Inc.
2410 Wesley St.
Portsmouth, VA 23707
Phone: (804)393-6007
Products: Fresh foods, including meat; Tables, chairs, and utensils. SICs: 5147 (Meats & Meat Products); 5113 (Industrial & Personal Service Paper); 5021 (Furniture). Est: 1952. Sales: $73,400,000 (2000). Emp: 250. Officers: Vernon W. Mules, CEO & Chairman of the Board; H. Glenn Gray, Treasurer & Secty.; Levis E. Cothran, Sales Mgr.; Dewey A. Rodgerson, Dir. of Information Systems.

■ 10985 ■ Douglas Brothers Produce Co.
648 Cowles St.
Long Beach, CA 90813
Phone: (562)436-2213   Fax: (562)435-4321
Products: Fresh and frozen fruits and vegetables. SICs: 5148 (Fresh Fruits & Vegetables); 5142 (Packaged Frozen Foods). Sales: $4,000,000 (2000). Emp: 18. Officers: N.P. Douglas, President.

■ 10986 ■ Douglas Northeast Inc.
2507 E 9th St.
Texarkana, AR 71854
Phone: (870)773-3633
Products: Grocery items; Tobacco and cigarettes; Candy. SICs: 5141 (Groceries—General Line); 5145 (Confectionery); 5194 (Tobacco & Tobacco Products). Est: 1940. Sales: $20,000,000 (2000). Emp: 55. Officers: Bob Douglas, CEO; Bill Selles, Dir. of Marketing & Sales; Helen Heflin, Dir. of Admin.

■ 10987 ■ Tony Downs Foods Co.
PO Box 28
St. James, MN 56081
Phone: (507)375-3111   Fax: (507)375-3048
Products: Frozen food; Canned boned chicken. SICs: 5149 (Groceries & Related Products Nec); 5142 (Packaged Frozen Foods). Sales: $30,000,000 (2000). Emp: 450. Officers: Dick Downs; Dave Sawyer; Terry Mace; Patricia Johnson.

■ 10988 ■ DPI-Epicurean Fine Foods
PO Box 5940
Mesa, AZ 85211-5940
Phone: (480)969-9333   Fax: (480)461-3645
Products: Groceries. SIC: 5141 (Groceries—General Line). Est: 1948. Sales: $35,000,000 (2000). Emp: 82. Officers: Chip Forster, President; Zen Miller, Controller. Former Name: Taylor Brothers Wholesale Distributors Inc. Former Name: DPI-Taylor Brothers.

■ 10989 ■ DPI Food Products Co.
8125 E 88th Ave.
Henderson, CO 80640-8121
Phone: (303)301-1226
Products: Dried and dehydrated food products; Egg noodle products; Dry food and produce, including pet and animal food, specialty meats and cheeses. SICs: 5141 (Groceries—General Line); 5148 (Fresh Fruits & Vegetables); 5149 (Groceries & Related Products Nec). Former Name: Food Products.

■ 10990 ■ DPI Southwest Distributing Inc.
PO Box 25025
Albuquerque, NM 87125
Phone: (505)345-4488   Fax: (505)345-4494
E-mail: info@dpisouthwest.com
URL: http://www.dpisouthwest.com
Products: Dry, fresh, and frozen food; Kitchenware; Janitorial supplies. SICs: 5142 (Packaged Frozen Foods); 5087 (Service Establishment Equipment); 5141 (Groceries—General Line). Est: 1946. Sales: $30,000,000 (2000). Emp: 170. Officers: Tom Boyden, President; Don O'Connell, CFO; Richard Burch, Sales Mgr.; Melissa Hallada, Sales/Marketing Contact, e-mail: mhallada@dpisouthwest.com; Carlos Arias, Customer Service Contact, e-mail: info@dpisouthwest.com; Sheila Snyder, Human Resources Contact, e-mail: ssnyder@dpisouthwest.com. Former Name: Southwest Distributing Inc.

■ 10991 ■ DPI Southwest Distributing Inc.
PO Box 25025
Albuquerque, NM 87125
Phone: (505)345-4488   Fax: (505)345-4494
Products: Food. SIC: 5142 (Packaged Frozen Foods). Sales: $30,000,000 (2000). Emp: 170.

■ 10992 ■ DPI-Taylor Brothers
PO Box 5940
Mesa, AZ 85211-5940
Phone: (602)834-6081   Fax: (602)461-3645
Products: Food. SIC: 5141 (Groceries—General Line). Sales: $35,000,000 (2000). Emp: 82.

■ 10993 ■ DPM of Arkansas
400 Mario Del Pero St.
Booneville, AR 72927-0200
Phone: (501)675-4555   Fax: (501)675-4588
Products: Beef. SIC: 5147 (Meats & Meat Products). Sales: $52,000,000 (2000). Emp: 300. Officers: Ken Moore.

■ 10994 ■ Draper Valley Farms Inc.
PO Box 838
Mt. Vernon, WA 98273
Phone: (360)424-7947   Fax: (360)424-1666
Products: Integrated poultry company; Egg hatching, chick processing and packaging. SIC: 5144 (Poultry & Poultry Products). Sales: $32,000,000 (2000). Emp: 350. Officers: James Koplowitz, President.

■ 10995 ■ P. Drescher Company Inc.
200 Monarch Ln.
Liverpool, NY 13088
Phone: (315)457-4911   Fax: (315)457-2898
Products: Bakery supplies, including flour and spices. SIC: 5149 (Groceries & Related Products Nec). Sales: $35,000,000 (2000). Emp: 99. Officers: Peter H. Drescher; W.V. Brutzman Jr.; Paul A. Drescher; John Drescher.

■ 10996 ■ **Driscoll Grain Cooperative Inc.**
PO Box 208
Driscoll, TX 78351
Phone: (512)387-6242 **Fax:** (512)387-6242
Products: Livestock and farm products. SIC: 5153
(Grain & Field Beans). **Sales:** $4,000,000 (2000). **Emp:**
12.

■ 10997 ■ **Dublin Yogurt Co.**
9129 Haddington Ct.
Dublin, OH 43017
Phone: (614)761-3415
Products: Yogurt. SIC: 5143 (Dairy Products Except
Dried or Canned).

■ 10998 ■ **Duffco**
PO Box 1513
Conway, NH 03818-1513
Phone: (603)356-7940
Products: Candy and fudge. SIC: 5145
(Confectionery). **Officers:** George Bisson, Partner.

■ 10999 ■ **Dundee Citrus Growers Association**
PO Box 1739
Dundee, FL 33838
Phone: (941)439-1574
Free: (877)438-4350 **Fax:** (941)439-1535
URL: http://www.dun-d.com
Products: Fruit, including oranges and grapefruit. SIC:
5148 (Fresh Fruits & Vegetables). **Est:** 1924. **Sales:**
$25,000,000 (1999). **Emp:** 250. **Officers:** Frank
Dunnahoe, President; Jon Marone, CFO.

■ 11000 ■ **Durham Meat Co.**
160 Sunol St.
San Jose, CA 95126
Phone: (408)291-3600
Products: Beef; Pork; Lamb; Veal. SIC: 5147 (Meats &
Meat Products). **Est:** 1880. **Sales:** $65,000,000 (2000).
Emp: 100. **Officers:** Bud Flocchini, CEO; Richard J.
Flocchini, Dir. of Marketing & Sales.

■ 11001 ■ **Durst Brokerage Inc.**
135 E Algonquin Rd.
Arlington Heights, IL 60005
Phone: (847)981-8880 **Fax:** (847)981-8886
Products: Institutional food service. SIC: 5141
(Groceries—General Line). **Sales:** $16,000,000 (2000).
Emp: 32. **Officers:** William E. Salisbury, President;
Thomas Kabat, Finance Officer.

■ 11002 ■ **Duso Food Distributors**
Rte. 52
Ellenville, NY 12428
Phone: (914)647-4600
Free: (800)582-4770 **Fax:** (914)647-1047
Products: Perishable frozen foods. SIC: 5142
(Packaged Frozen Foods). **Emp:** 49. **Officers:**
Nachman Kanovsky.

■ 11003 ■ **Dutch Gold Honey Inc.**
2220 Dutch Gold Dr.
Lancaster, PA 17601-1941
Phone: (717)393-1716 **Fax:** (717)393-8687
URL: http://www.dutchgoldhoney.com
Products: Honey. SIC: 5149 (Groceries & Related
Products Nec). **Emp:** 49. **Officers:** Nancy Gamber
Olcott; William R. Gamber II; Jill Clark, Sales/Marketing
Contact, e-mail: jill@dutchgoldhoney.com.

■ 11004 ■ **Dutt and Wagner of Virginia Inc.**
PO Box 518
Abingdon, VA 24212-0518
Phone: (703)628-2116
Products: Eggs. SIC: 5144 (Poultry & Poultry
Products). **Est:** 1926. **Sales:** $35,000,000 (2000).
Emp: 100. **Officers:** Peggy Wagner, President; Kenny
Hobbs, CFO; Lori Hagga, Dir. of Marketing.

■ 11005 ■ **B.W. Dyer and Co.**
106 Mine Brook Rd.
Bernardsville, NJ 07924-2432
Phone: (908)204-9800
Products: Sweeteners and food ingredients. SICs:
5149 (Groceries & Related Products Nec); 5141
(Groceries—General Line). **Sales:** $2,000,000 (2000).
Emp: 6. **Officers:** Chip Dyer, Mng. Partner; Suzanne
Dyer, Controller.

■ 11006 ■ **Dykstra Food Service**
498 7 Mile Rd. NW
Comstock Park, MI 49321-9545
Phone: (616)784-1300 **Fax:** (616)754-0017
Products: Food. SIC: 5141 (Groceries—General Line).
Est: 1934. **Sales:** $32,000,000 (2000). **Emp:** 75.
Officers: H. D. Dykstra; Dick Elenbaas.

■ 11007 ■ **E & M Ice Cream Distributors**
61 Hungerford Ter.
Burlington, VT 05401
Phone: (802)862-6746
Products: Ice cream. SIC: 5143 (Dairy Products
Except Dried or Canned).

■ 11008 ■ **E-Z Mart Stores Inc.**
PO Box 1426
Texarkana, TX 75504
Phone: (903)838-0558 **Fax:** (903)832-7903
Products: Convenience foods. SIC: 5149 (Groceries &
Related Products Nec).

■ 11009 ■ **Eagle Food Centers Inc.**
Rte. 67 & Knoxville Rd.
Milan, IL 61264
Phone: 800-322-3143 **Fax:** (309)787-7895
Products: General line groceries. SIC: 5141
(Groceries—General Line).

■ 11010 ■ **Eagle Foods Co.**
3547 E 14th St., Ste. D
Brownsville, TX 78521-3242
Phones: (512)544-7721 (512)544-7361
Fax: (512)544-1367
Products: Mexican food specialties. SIC: 5149
(Groceries & Related Products Nec). **Emp:** 7.

■ 11011 ■ **Eagle Wholesale L.P.**
PO Box 742
Tyler, TX 75710
Phone: (903)592-4321 **Fax:** (903)592-2044
Products: General line groceries, candy, and tobacco.
SICs: 5141 (Groceries—General Line); 5145
(Confectionery); 5194 (Tobacco & Tobacco Products).
Sales: $5,000,000 (2000). **Emp:** 18. **Officers:** Gordon
Atkins, President.

■ 11012 ■ **Earp Meat Company Inc.**
6550 Kansas Ave.
Kansas City, KS 66111
Phone: (913)287-3311
Products: Fast food products. SIC: 5147 (Meats &
Meat Products). **Est:** 1960. **Sales:** $190,000,000
(2000). **Emp:** 150. **Officers:** Donald C. Earp,
President; Willard A. Small, General Mgr.

■ 11013 ■ **Earth Brothers Ltd.**
PO Box 188
Proctorsville, VT 05153
Phone: (802)226-7480
Products: Produce. SIC: 5148 (Fresh Fruits &
Vegetables). **Sales:** $21,000,000 (2000). **Emp:** 70.
Officers: Steve Birge, President.

■ 11014 ■ **Earth Grains Company of
Sacramento**
3211 6th Ave.
Sacramento, CA 95817-0387
Phone: (916)456-3863 **Fax:** (916)456-3093
Products: Bread, buns, and rolls. SIC: 5149
(Groceries & Related Products Nec). **Emp:** 750.

■ 11015 ■ **Earthgrains/Waldensian Bakerie**
320 E Main St.
Valdese, NC 28690
Phone: (704)874-2130 **Fax:** (704)874-4910
Products: Breads; Cakes. SIC: 5149 (Groceries &
Related Products Nec). **Est:** 1914. **Sales:** $75,000,000
(2000). **Emp:** 900. **Officers:** Steven Cooper, Plant
Mgr.; Bob Kern, Zone VP of Sales.

■ 11016 ■ **East Central Iowa Cooperative**
PO Box 300
Hudson, IA 50643
Phone: (319)988-3257 **Fax:** (319)988-3371
Products: Grain and farm supplies. SICs: 5153 (Grain
& Field Beans); 5191 (Farm Supplies). **Sales:**
$45,000,000 (2000). **Emp:** 50. **Officers:** George Rude,
General Mgr.; Steve Potter, Controller.

■ 11017 ■ **Eastern Shore Seafood**
PO Box 38
Mappsville, VA 23407
Phone: (804)824-5651 **Fax:** (804)824-4135
Products: Seafood, including shrimp, lobster, and fish.
SIC: 5142 (Packaged Frozen Foods). **Sales:**
$8,000,000 (2000). **Emp:** 300. **Officers:** Rick Myers,
President; Mary Myers, Treasurer & Secty.; Scott
James, Dir. of Marketing.

■ 11018 ■ **Fred C. Ebel Company Inc.**
3101 N Causeway Blvd., Ste. D
Metairie, LA 70002-4831
Phone: (504)832-5000 **Fax:** (504)836-6802
Products: Produce. SIC: 5148 (Fresh Fruits &
Vegetables). **Emp:** 9.

■ 11019 ■ **C. Eberle Sons Co.**
3222 Beekman St.
Cincinnati, OH 45223
Phone: (513)542-7200
Products: Institutional products, including toilet paper
and milk. SICs: 5113 (Industrial & Personal Service
Paper); 5143 (Dairy Products Except Dried or Canned).
Est: 1864. **Sales:** $15,000,000 (2000). **Emp:** 45.
Officers: Walter F. Eberle III, President.

■ 11020 ■ **Echo Spring Dairy Inc.**
1750 W 8th Ave.
Eugene, OR 97402
Phone: (541)342-1291 **Fax:** (541)342-8379
Products: Dairy products. SIC: 5143 (Dairy Products
Except Dried or Canned). **Est:** 1960. **Sales:**
$21,000,000 (2000). **Emp:** 100. **Officers:** Jack Bruni,
President; David Brooks, Controller.

■ 11021 ■ **Echter Ornaments Inc.**
225 Beach 142nd St.
Neponsit, NY 11694-1253
Phones: (718)639-3194 (718)639-2828
Products: Bakery supplies. SIC: 5149 (Groceries &
Related Products Nec). **Emp:** 49.

■ 11022 ■ **Economy Cash and Carry Inc.**
1000 E Overland
El Paso, TX 79901
Phone: (915)532-2660 **Fax:** (915)534-7673
Products: Food. SICs: 5141 (Groceries—General
Line); 5122 (Drugs, Proprietaries & Sundries). **Est:**
1958. **Sales:** $75,000,000 (2000). **Emp:** 75. **Officers:**
Michael J. Dipp Jr., Chairman; Paul Dipp, President &
Treasurer.

■ 11023 ■ **Economy Foods**
333 7th Ave.
Huntington, WV 25701-1927
Phone: (304)697-5280 **Free:** (800)422-5280
Products: Frozen foods; Food; Paper and allied
products; Specialty cleaning and sanitation products;
Miscellaneous plastic products. SICs: 5141
(Groceries—General Line); 5142 (Packaged Frozen
Foods); 5113 (Industrial & Personal Service Paper);
5169 (Chemicals & Allied Products Nec); 5199
(Nondurable Goods Nec). **Sales:** $3,000,000 (2000).
Emp: 16.

■ 11024 ■ **Economy Wholesalers**
4765 Bellevue St.
Detroit, MI 48207
Phone: (313)922-0001
Products: Food products. SIC: 5141 (Groceries—
General Line).

■ 11025 ■ **E.D. Packing Co.**
Rte. 3, Box 79
Lake City, SC 29560-9336
Phone: (803)389-7241 **Fax:** (803)389-7240
Products: Vegetables, including string beans, butter
beans, and peas. SIC: 5148 (Fresh Fruits &
Vegetables). **Sales:** $10,000,000 (2000). **Emp:** 49.
Officers: James Eaddy.

■ 11026 ■ **Eden Valley Growers Inc.**
7502 N Gowanda State
Eden, NY 14057
Phone: (716)992-9721 **Fax:** (716)992-3882
Products: Fruits and vegetables. SIC: 5148 (Fresh
Fruits & Vegetables). **Emp:** 12.

■ 11027 ■ **Edgerton Cooperative Farm Service Center**
PO Box 126
Edgerton, MN 56128
Phone: (507)442-4571
Products: Fluid milk. **SIC:** 5143 (Dairy Products Except Dried or Canned). **Est:** 1943. **Sales:** $7,000,000 (2000). **Emp:** 4. **Officers:** Loran Vandertop, CEO.

■ 11028 ■ **Edmiston Brothers Inc.**
PO Box 371
Crockett, TX 75835
Phone: (409)544-2118
Products: Full line of groceries, tobacco and candy products. **SICs:** 5141 (Groceries—General Line); 5194 (Tobacco & Tobacco Products); 5145 (Confectionery). **Sales:** $9,000,000 (1993). **Emp:** 25. **Officers:** Charles L. Edmiston Jr., CEO & President.

■ 11029 ■ **Edsung Foodservice Co.**
1337 Mookaula
Honolulu, HI 96817-4308
Phone: (808)845-3931   **Fax:** (808)842-4702
Products: General line groceries. **SICs:** 5141 (Groceries—General Line); 5149 (Groceries & Related Products Nec). **Est:** 1946. **Sales:** $12,000,000 (2000). **Emp:** 36. **Officers:** E. Choi.

■ 11030 ■ **Edwards Fruit Co.**
PO Box 1687
Lakeland, FL 33802-1687
Phone: (813)682-8196   **Fax:** (813)682-5249
Products: Fruit, including bananas and oranges. **SIC:** 5148 (Fresh Fruits & Vegetables). **Est:** 1977. **Sales:** $5,000,000 (2000). **Emp:** 50. **Officers:** David L. Edwards, President; Louise E. Hudgins, Controller.

■ 11031 ■ **M and B Edwards Produce Co.**
PO Box 661688
Miami Springs, FL 33266-1688
Phone: (305)324-6143   **Fax:** (305)324-0192
Products: Produce. **SIC:** 5148 (Fresh Fruits & Vegetables). **Est:** 1941. **Sales:** $12,000,000 (2000). **Emp:** 45. **Officers:** Luther M. Edwards, President; Clifton C. Edwards, Vice President.

■ 11032 ■ **Bernard Egan and Co.**
1900 Old Dixie Hwy.
Ft. Pierce, FL 34946
Phone: (561)465-7555   **Fax:** (561)465-1181
Products: Fruit. **SIC:** 5148 (Fresh Fruits & Vegetables). **Sales:** $14,000,000 (2000). **Emp:** 48. **Officers:** Bernard Egan, President; Glen W. Reed, Controller.

■ 11033 ■ **Egerstrom Inc.**
10012 E 64th St.
Kansas City, MO 64133
Phone: (816)358-3025
Free: (800)821-8570   **Fax:** (816)737-0042
E-mail: pegerstrom@msn.com
Products: Food. **SIC:** 5141 (Groceries—General Line). **Est:** 1978. **Sales:** $240,000 (1999). **Emp:** 8. **Officers:** Tom Egerstrom, Vice President. **Former Name:** Egerstrom-Kramer Inc.

■ 11034 ■ **Karl Ehmer Inc.**
63-35 Fresh Pond Rd.
Ridgewood, NY 11385
Phone: (718)456-8100
Free: (800)487-5295   **Fax:** (718)456-2270
E-mail: info@karlehmer.com
URL: http://www.karlehmer.com
Products: Meat products. **SIC:** 5147 (Meats & Meat Products). **Est:** 1932. **Sales:** $10,000,000 (2000). **Emp:** 70. **Officers:** Mark Hanssler, President; Stephanie Oken, Accountant.

■ 11035 ■ **El Charro Mexican Foods**
1707 SE Main St.
Roswell, NM 88201
Phone: (505)622-8590
Products: Mexican food. **SIC:** 5141 (Groceries—General Line).

■ 11036 ■ **El Encanto Inc.**
PO Box 293
Albuquerque, NM 87103
Phone: (505)243-2722
Free: (800)888-7336   **Fax:** (505)242-1680
URL: http://www.buenofoods.com
Products: Frozen green chili peppers; Spices; Mexican prepared entree. **SICs:** 5142 (Packaged Frozen Foods); 5149 (Groceries & Related Products Nec). **Est:** 1951. **Sales:** $24,000,000 (2000). **Emp:** 200. **Officers:** Jacqueline Baca, President; Chris Mensay, Controller; Mike Brunich, Marketing Mgr.; Jim Tilesson, Human Resources Mgr.; Mike Dunivan, VP of Marketing & Sales.

■ 11037 ■ **El Galindo Inc.**
1601 E 6th St.
Austin, TX 78702
Phone: (512)478-5756   **Fax:** (512)478-5839
Products: Corn products, including tortillas and chips. **SIC:** 5149 (Groceries & Related Products Nec). **Sales:** $10,000,000 (2000). **Emp:** 110. **Officers:** Ernestine Galindo.

■ 11038 ■ **El Indio Shop**
3695 India
San Diego, CA 92103-4749
Phone: (619)299-0333   **Fax:** (619)299-5071
Products: Mexican food. **SIC:** 5149 (Groceries & Related Products Nec). **Emp:** 99.

■ 11039 ■ **Eldorado Artesian Springs Inc.**
PO Box 445
Eldorado Springs, CO 80025-0445
Phone: (303)499-1316   **Fax:** (303)499-1339
Products: Soft drinks. **SIC:** 5149 (Groceries & Related Products Nec). **Sales:** $4,000,000 (2000). **Emp:** 47.

■ 11040 ■ **Elkhart Cooperative Equity Exchange**
PO Box G
Elkhart, KS 67950
Phone: (316)697-2135   **Fax:** (316)697-2910
Products: Grain and farm supplies; Farm products warehouse. **SICs:** 5153 (Grain & Field Beans); 5191 (Farm Supplies). **Sales:** $49,800,000 (2000). **Emp:** 60. **Officers:** Larry E. Dunn, General Manager, Finance.

■ 11041 ■ **Elki Corp.**
2215 Merrill Creek Pkwy.
Everett, WA 98203
Phone: (425)261-1002   **Fax:** (425)261-1001
E-mail: elie@elki.com
URL: http://www.elki.com
Products: Gourmet foods. **SIC:** 5149 (Groceries & Related Products Nec). **Est:** 1984.

■ 11042 ■ **Elm Hill Meats Inc.**
PO Box 429
Lenoir City, TN 37771
Phone: (423)986-8005   **Fax:** (423)986-7171
Products: Meat products. **SIC:** 5147 (Meats & Meat Products). **Sales:** $25,000,000 (2000). **Emp:** 110. **Officers:** Harry Wampler.

■ 11043 ■ **Elmore & Stahl Inc.**
11 N Birch
Pharr, TX 78577
Phone: (956)787-2714   **Fax:** (956)787-1897
Products: Honeydew melons; Cantaloupe; Onions. **SIC:** 5148 (Fresh Fruits & Vegetables). **Est:** 1929. **Emp:** 180. **Officers:** Bobby Bell.

■ 11044 ■ **Empire Beef Company Inc.**
171 Weidner Rd.
Rochester, NY 14624
Phone: (716)235-7350
Free: (800)235-1776   **Fax:** (716)462-6804
Products: Meat products. **SIC:** 5147 (Meats & Meat Products). **Sales:** $542,000,000 (2000). **Emp:** 234. **Officers:** Steve Levine, CEO; Michael Quinn, Controller.

■ 11045 ■ **Empire Fish Co.**
11200 Watertown Plank Rd.
Milwaukee, WI 53226
Phone: (414)259-1120   **Free:** (800)236-4900
Products: Fresh fish; Frozen fish. **SICs:** 5146 (Fish & Seafoods); 5142 (Packaged Frozen Foods). **Emp:** 40. **Officers:** Thomas G. Kutchera; G.E. Kutchera.

■ 11046 ■ **Empire Seafood**
1116 2nd Ave. N
Birmingham, AL 35203
Phone: (205)252-0344   **Fax:** (205)252-3432
Products: Seafood, including crab meat and oysters. **SIC:** 5146 (Fish & Seafoods). **Est:** 1935. **Sales:** $10,000,000 (2000). **Emp:** 60. **Officers:** George A. Drakos, President; George C. Sarris, Vice President. **Former Name:** Empire Sea Food Co. Inc.

■ 11047 ■ **Empress International Ltd.**
10 Harbor Park Dr.
Port Washington, NY 11050
Phone: (516)621-5900
Free: (800)645-6244   **Fax:** (516)621-8318
E-mail: info@empfish.com
URL: http://www.empfish.com
Products: Seafood, including lobster and shrimp. **SIC:** 5146 (Fish & Seafoods). **Est:** 1953. **Sales:** $170,000,000 (2000). **Emp:** 30. **Officers:** Joel Kolen, President; Kevin Kent, Controller; Joseph Klaus, Dir. of Marketing & Sales, e-mail: joe@empfish.com; Burt Faure, Chairman of the Board; Ernie Wayland, Exec. VP of Marketing & Sales.

■ 11048 ■ **Enrico Food Products Co. Inc.**
6050 Court St. Rd.
Syracuse, NY 13206
Phone: (315)463-2384   **Fax:** (315)463-5897
E-mail: ventre/enricos.com
Products: Sauces, including ketchup, pizza and spaghetti sauce; Dips; Salsa. **SIC:** 5149 (Groceries & Related Products Nec). **Est:** 1938. **Sales:** $10,000,000 (2000). **Emp:** 49. **Officers:** John Ventre Jr., CEO.

■ 11049 ■ **Enstrom Candies Inc.**
PO Box 1088
Grand Junction, CO 81502
Phone: (970)242-1655   **Fax:** (970)245-7727
Products: Candy and confectionery products. **SIC:** 5145 (Confectionery).

■ 11050 ■ **Entree Corp.**
8200 W Brown Deer Rd.
Milwaukee, WI 53223
Phone: (414)355-0037
Products: Meats, seafood, and other products. **SICs:** 5146 (Fish & Seafoods); 5147 (Meats & Meat Products); 5144 (Poultry & Poultry Products). **Sales:** $219,000,000 (2000). **Emp:** 269.

■ 11051 ■ **Epco-JKD Food Brokers Inc.**
925 Pennsylvania Blvd.
Feasterville, PA 19053
Phone: (215)322-9200
Products: Food. **SIC:** 5141 (Groceries—General Line).

■ 11052 ■ **Epicure Foods Inc.**
2760 Bakers Industrial Dr.
Atlanta, GA 30360-1230
Phone: (404)441-2227   **Fax:** (404)441-3739
Products: Restaurant foods, including meat and seafood. **SICs:** 5141 (Groceries—General Line); 5147 (Meats & Meat Products); 5146 (Fish & Seafoods). **Emp:** 35. **Officers:** John Albano.

■ 11053 ■ **Essex Grain Products Inc.**
9 Lee Blvd.
Frazer, PA 19355
Phone: (610)647-3800
Free: (800)441-1017   **Fax:** (610)647-4990
URL: http://www.essexgrain.com
Products: Food staples, including salt, sugar, soy protein, food starches, and dextrose. **SIC:** 5149 (Groceries & Related Products Nec). **Est:** 1972. **Sales:** $65,000,000 (2000). **Emp:** 35. **Officers:** Alice Bierer, CEO; Luke Pallante, President.

■ 11054 ■ **Estrella Tortilla Factory & Deli Store**
1004 S Central Ave.
Phoenix, AZ 85004-2732
Phone: (602)253-5947   **Fax:** (602)253-3911
Products: Mexican grocery products, including tortillas. **SIC:** 5149 (Groceries & Related Products Nec). **Est:**

1940. **Sales:** $6,000,000 (2000). **Emp:** 52. **Officers:** Ruben Parra Sr.

■ **11055** ■ **Ethel M. Chocolates, Inc.**
1 Sunset Way
Henderson, NV 89014
Phone: (702)458-8864
Free: (800)438-4356 **Fax:** (702)451-8379
Products: Chocolates. **SIC:** 5145 (Confectionery).
Emp: 49.

■ **11056** ■ **Etheridge Produce**
3001 Barnsley Tr.
Raleigh, NC 27604
Phone: (919)231-7546 **Fax:** (919)231-7645
Products: Watermelons. **SIC:** 5148 (Fresh Fruits & Vegetables). **Est:** 1953. **Sales:** $4,000,000 (2000).
Emp: 2. **Officers:** Gordon S. Etheridge, Owner.

■ **11057** ■ **Eureka Fisheries**
151 Starfish Way
Crescent City, CA 95531-4447
Phone: (707)464-3149 **Fax:** (707)465-1015
Products: Fish, including dover sole, channel rock, and black cod. **SIC:** 5146 (Fish & Seafoods). **Sales:** $10,000,000 (2000). **Emp:** 49. **Officers:** Chris Moulton.

■ **11058** ■ **Euro American Trading-Merchants Inc.**
37 Centennial St.
Collegeville, PA 19426-1847
Phone: (610)454-0854 **Fax:** (610)454-0854
Products: Snack foods. **SIC:** 5145 (Confectionery).
Sales: $400,000 (2000). **Emp:** 4. **Officers:** Robert D. Moyer, CEO & President.

■ **11059** ■ **EuroAmerican Brands LLC**
15 Prospect St.
Paramus, NJ 07652
Phone: (201)368-2624 **Fax:** (201)368-2512
Products: Cookies; Candies; Chocolates; Novelties; Confections; Coffee; Breads; Preserves. **SIC:** 5149 (Groceries & Related Products Nec). **Est:** 1989. **Sales:** $30,000,000 (1999). **Emp:** 20. **Officers:** Dite W. Van Clief, President; Tami Targovnik, Controller; Peter Leiennectiel, Exec. VP; Beth Forman, Sales/Marketing Contact, e-mail: BForman@euroamericanbrands.com; Robin Schirmer, Customer Service Contact; Debbie Higgins, Human Resources Contact; Deb Hughes.

■ **11060** ■ **European Kosher Provision**
21231 E Baltimore St.
Baltimore, MD 21231-1403
Phone: (410)342-2002 **Fax:** (410)558-1228
Products: Deli products. **SIC:** 5147 (Meats & Meat Products). **Sales:** $2,000,000 (2000). **Emp:** 49.
Officers: Mutty Abramson.

■ **11061** ■ **EVCO Wholesale Foods Co.**
309 Merchant
Emporia, KS 66801
Phone: (316)343-7000
Products: Food, including frozen and canned foods, meats, vegetables, eggs, cottage cheese, and sour cream. **SICs:** 5141 (Groceries—General Line); 5142 (Packaged Frozen Foods); 5147 (Meats & Meat Products); 5148 (Fresh Fruits & Vegetables); 5143 (Dairy Products Except Dried or Canned). **Est:** 1900. **Sales:** $25,000,000 (2000). **Emp:** 109. **Officers:** C.C. Evans, President; Jerry Swift, Dir. of Information Systems.

■ **11062** ■ **Everson Distributing Company, Inc.**
280 New Ludlow Rd.
Chicopee, MA 01020-4468
Phone: (413)533-9261 **Fax:** (413)536-4564
E-mail: everson@mbusa.net
Products: Candy. **SIC:** 5145 (Confectionery). **Est:** 1960. **Sales:** $5,000,000 (2000). **Emp:** 49. **Officers:** Robert Everson.

■ **11063** ■ **Excel Corp.**
4800 S Central
Chicago, IL 60638
Phone: (708)594-8887 **Fax:** (708)594-8982
Products: Beef. **SIC:** 5147 (Meats & Meat Products).
Emp: 49.

■ **11064** ■ **Excel Corp. DPM Foods Div.**
1109 Chestnut St.
Marysville, CA 95901
Phone: (530)742-2311 **Fax:** (530)634-8020
Products: Beef. **SIC:** 5147 (Meats & Meat Products).
Est: 1953. **Sales:** $80,000,000 (2000). **Emp:** 250.
Officers: Mike Middleton, President; Karen Nugen, Controller; Joe Del Pero, VP of Marketing.

■ **11065** ■ **Ezell-Key Grain Company Inc.**
PO Box 1062
Snyder, TX 79550
Phone: (915)573-9373
Free: (800)299-4496 **Fax:** (915)573-9374
Products: Livestock feed blending. **SIC:** 5153 (Grain & Field Beans). **Sales:** $4,200,000 (2000). **Emp:** 25.
Officers: Weldon Key, President.

■ **11066** ■ **F & A Dairy California**
691 Inyo
Newman, CA 95360-9707
Phone: (209)862-1732 **Fax:** (209)862-1043
Products: Cheese. **SIC:** 5143 (Dairy Products Except Dried or Canned). **Emp:** 100. **Officers:** Frank Terranova Jr.

■ **11067** ■ **F & A Food Sales Inc.**
2221 Lincoln
PO Box 651
Concordia, KS 66901
Phone: (785)243-2301 **Fax:** (785)243-3331
Products: Groceries; Produce; Meat; Frozen foods; Juices; Paper products. **SICs:** 5148 (Fresh Fruits & Vegetables); 5142 (Packaged Frozen Foods); 5149 (Groceries & Related Products Nec); 5113 (Industrial & Personal Service Paper); 5147 (Meats & Meat Products). **Est:** 1970. **Emp:** 90. **Officers:** Danny R. Farha, Owner and President; Shari Johnson, Asst. VP.

■ **11068** ■ **F and E Wholesale Food Service Inc.**
PO Box 2080
Wichita, KS 67201
Phone: (316)838-2400 **Fax:** (316)838-5942
URL: http://www.fefs.com
Products: Food products, including frozen meats and vegetables, and canned vegetables; Cleaning products; Small wares; Restaurant supplies. **SICs:** 5149 (Groceries & Related Products Nec); 5142 (Packaged Frozen Foods); 5148 (Fresh Fruits & Vegetables). **Est:** 1913. **Sales:** $30,000,000 (2000).
Emp: 100. **Officers:** Norman S. Farha, Chairman of the Board; Keith Hill, President; Farris S. Farha, VP of Sales; H.R. Barkett, VP of Operations.

■ **11069** ■ **Fadler Company Inc.**
PO Box 472306
Tulsa, OK 74147-2306
Phone: (918)627-0770 **Fax:** (918)627-4763
Products: Food. **SIC:** 5141 (Groceries—General Line).

■ **11070** ■ **Fairbank Reconstruction Corp.**
PO Box 170
Ashville, NY 14710
Phone: (716)782-2000 **Fax:** (716)782-2900
Products: Meats, including ground beef. **SIC:** 5147 (Meats & Meat Products). **Est:** 1872. **Sales:** $30,000,000 (2000). **Emp:** 60. **Officers:** Rickey G. Fahle, President; A. Joseph Fairbank, Vice President; Bartt Hollingshead, Controller; Luella Sard, Sales Contact.

■ **11071** ■ **Fairco, Inc.**
518 Gravier St.
New Orleans, LA 70130
Phone: (504)524-0467 **Fax:** (504)524-6931
Products: Canned vegetables; Hot sauce; Salt; Honey; Popcorn and marshmallows. **SIC:** 5141 (Groceries—General Line). **Officers:** Ted Van Norman, Sales Development.

■ **11072** ■ **Fairview Dairy Inc. & Valley Dairy**
3200 Graham Ave.
Windber, PA 15963-2539
Phone: (814)467-5537
Products: Ice cream. **SIC:** 5143 (Dairy Products Except Dried or Canned). **Est:** 1938. **Sales:** $6,000,000 (2000). **Emp:** 275. **Officers:** Joseph E. Greubel.

■ **11073** ■ **Fairway Foods Inc.**
PO Box 1224
Minneapolis, MN 55440
Phone: (612)830-1601 **Fax:** (612)830-1663
URL: http://www.fairwayfoods.com
Products: Dry, canned, and frozen food; Meat, milk, and produce; General merchandise. **SICs:** 5149 (Groceries & Related Products Nec); 5142 (Packaged Frozen Foods); 5147 (Meats & Meat Products); 5143 (Dairy Products Except Dried or Canned). **Est:** 1914.
Sales: $700,000,000 (2000). **Emp:** 425. **Officers:** James H. Lukens, President; Mark Webster, Controller; Patrick Lee, VP of Marketing; Bob Michalek, VP of Sales.

■ **11074** ■ **Fairway Foods Inc.**
PO Box 1224
Minneapolis, MN 55440
Phone: (612)830-1601 **Fax:** (612)830-8864
Products: General groceries. **SIC:** 5141 (Groceries— General Line). **Sales:** $750,000,000 (2000). **Emp:** 425.
Officers: Jim Lukens, President; Mark Webster, Controller.

■ **11075** ■ **Fairway Foods of Michigan Inc.**
1230 48th Ave.
Menominee, MI 49858
Phone: (906)863-5503
Products: Groceries. **SIC:** 5141 (Groceries—General Line). **Est:** 1891. **Sales:** $120,000,000 (2000). **Emp:** 130. **Officers:** J. Vandelaarschot, President; Strohl Shrol, VP of Finance; Gene Mylener, VP of Marketing.

■ **11076** ■ **Falcon Trading Co.**
1055 17th Ave.
Santa Cruz, CA 95062-3033
Phone: (831)462-1280 **Fax:** (831)462-9431
E-mail: sunridge@cruzio.com
URL: http://www.sunridgefarms.com
Products: Bulk food, including organic and natural nuts and seeds, dried fruits, coffees and teas, grains and beans, herbs, snack foods, candy, juice, and pasta.
SICs: 5149 (Groceries & Related Products Nec); 5145 (Confectionery). **Est:** 1979. **Emp:** 125. **Officers:** Morty Cohen, President; Gregg Armstrong, Sales Mgr. **Doing Business As:** Sunridge Farms.

■ **11077** ■ **Falcone and Italia Foods**
1361 NW 155th Dr.
Miami, FL 33169
Phone: (954)467-8910
Products: Italian food ingredients. **SICs:** 5149 (Groceries & Related Products Nec); 5143 (Dairy Products Except Dried or Canned). **Sales:** $14,000,000 (1993). **Emp:** 30. **Officers:** Sal Falcone, President.

■ **11078** ■ **Family Sweets Candy Co. Inc.**
1010 Reed St.
Winston-Salem, NC 27107-5446
Phone: (910)788-5068
Free: (800)334-1607 **Fax:** (910)784-6708
Products: Candy. **SIC:** 5145 (Confectionery). **Est:** 1970. **Sales:** $5,000,000 (2000). **Emp:** 55. **Officers:** Eugene Fields, CEO; Leroy B. Mansson, President; Gregory Fetty, Vice President; Ray Strader, VP of Sales.

■ **11079** ■ **Fancy Fare Distributors**
19-4 Freedom Park, Ste. 3
Bangor, ME 04401
Phone: (207)529-5879
Free: (800)736-3692 **Fax:** (207)529-5813
E-mail: ffd@mint.net
URL: http://www.fancyfare.com
Products: Gourmet specialty food products. **SIC:** 5149 (Groceries & Related Products Nec). **Sales:** $250,000 (1999). **Emp:** 9. **Officers:** Sarah A. Johnson, Co-owner; Jeffrey S. Johnson, Co-owner.

■ **11080** ■ **Fantastic Foods Inc.**
1250 N McDowell Blvd.
Petaluma, CA 94954
Phone: (707)778-7801 **Fax:** (707)778-7607
Products: Food preparations; Dried and dehydrated food products; Head rice not packaged with other ingredients; Potatoes; Egg noodle products; Health foods. **SICs:** 5149 (Groceries & Related Products Nec); 5148 (Fresh Fruits & Vegetables). **Emp:** 49. **Officers:** Barbara Chapman, Sales Mgr.

■ 11081 ■ Fareway Wholesale
PO Box 70
Boone, IA 50036
Phone: (515)432-2623   Fax: (515)432-2623
Products: General line groceries. SIC: 5141
(Groceries—General Line).

■ 11082 ■ Fargo-Moorhead Jobbing Co.
1017 4th Ave. N
Fargo, ND 58107
Phone: (701)293-1521
Free: (800)453-2742   Fax: (701)293-1528
Products: General line groceries; Manufactured
tobacco products; Candy; Paper and allied products.
SICs: 5141 (Groceries—General Line); 5145
(Confectionery); 5194 (Tobacco & Tobacco Products);
5113 (Industrial & Personal Service Paper). Est: 1962.
Officers: Joe Cummings, Chairman of the Board; Jim
Cummings, President.

■ 11083 ■ Farm Boy Meats Inc.
PO Box 996
Evansville, IN 47706
Phone: (812)425-5231   Free: (800)852-3976
Products: Meat and poultry; Foodservice supplies.
SICs: 5141 (Groceries—General Line); 5046
(Commercial Equipment Nec); 5144 (Poultry & Poultry
Products); 5147 (Meats & Meat Products). Est: 1952.
Sales: $25,000,000 (2000). Emp: 80. Officers: Bob
Bonenberger, President.

■ 11084 ■ Farm Fresh Catfish Co.
1616 Rice-Mill Rd.
PO Box 85
Hollandale, MS 38748
Phone: (601)827-2204
Free: (800)862-2824   Fax: (601)827-7348
Products: Catfish. SIC: 5146 (Fish & Seafoods). Est:
1971. Sales: $60,000,000 (1999). Emp: 499. Officers:
Jim Hoffman, President & COO; Steve Osso,
Controller; Charlotte Porter, Human Resources Mgr.;
Kelly Framer, CEO; Virginia Garnett, Customer Service
Contact.

■ 11085 ■ Farm Fresh Foods Inc.
6534 Clara St.
Bell Gardens, CA 90201
Phone: (562)927-2586   Fax: (562)928-5538
Products: Refrigerated potato products. SICs: 5148
(Fresh Fruits & Vegetables); 5149 (Groceries & Related
Products Nec). Emp: 48. Officers: Bryan Studemann,
General Mgr.

■ 11086 ■ Farm Fresh Inc.
7255 Sheridan Blvd.
Arvada, CO 80003
Phone: (303)429-1536
Products: Food. SIC: 5143 (Dairy Products Except
Dried or Canned). Sales: $3,500,000 (2000). Emp: 16.

■ 11087 ■ Farmer Johns Packing Co.
222 S 9th Ave.
Phoenix, AZ 85007-3103
Phone: (602)254-6685   Fax: (602)254-4336
Products: Processed or cured pork. SIC: 5147 (Meats
& Meat Products). Sales: $10,000,000 (2000). Emp:
49. Officers: Anthony Clougherty.

■ 11088 ■ Farmers Cooperative Association
PO Box 196
Meno, OK 73760
Phone: (580)776-2241   Fax: (580)776-2242
Products: Agricultural equipment and supplies. SIC:
5153 (Grain & Field Beans). Sales: $3,000,000 (2000).
Emp: 11.

■ 11089 ■ Farmers Cooperative Association
Main St.
Lindsay, NE 68644
Phone: (402)428-2305   Fax: (402)428-2108
Products: Livestock and farm products. SIC: 5153
(Grain & Field Beans). Sales: $12,000,000 (2000).
Emp: 10.

■ 11090 ■ Farmers Cooperative Association
(Brule, Nebraska)
PO Box 127
Brule, NE 69127
Phone: (308)287-2304   Fax: (308)287-2238
Products: Grain. SIC: 5153 (Grain & Field Beans).
Sales: $30,000,000 (2000). Emp: 34. Officers: Tom
Struckman, President.

■ 11091 ■ Farmers Cooperative Co.
PO Box 186
Clear Lake, IA 50428
Phone: (515)357-5274   Fax: (515)397-5275
Products: Agricultural equipment and supplies. SIC:
5153 (Grain & Field Beans). Sales: $5,000,000 (2000).
Emp: 15.

■ 11092 ■ Farmers Cooperative Co.
PO Box 127
Brookings, SD 57006
Phone: (605)692-6216
Products: Agricultural equipment and supplies. SIC:
5153 (Grain & Field Beans). Sales: $15,000,000
(2000). Emp: 22.

■ 11093 ■ Farmers Cooperative Co.
PO Box 192
Mondamin, IA 51557
Phone: (712)646-2411
Products: Agricultural equipment and supplies. SIC:
5153 (Grain & Field Beans). Sales: $10,400,000
(2000). Emp: 16.

■ 11094 ■ Farmers Cooperative Co.
304 Ellsworth St.
Dows, IA 50071
Phone: (515)852-4136   Fax: (515)852-4139
Products: Livestock and farm products. SIC: 5153
(Grain & Field Beans). Sales: $30,000,000 (2000).
Emp: 25.

■ 11095 ■ Farmers Cooperative Co.
PO Box 399
Alton, IA 51003
Phone: (712)756-4121
Free: (800)732-9655   Fax: (712)756-4199
Products: Agricultural equipment and supplies. SIC:
5153 (Grain & Field Beans). Sales: $26,000,000
(2000). Emp: 100.

■ 11096 ■ Farmers Cooperative Co. (Britt,
Iowa)
368 Main Ave. N
Britt, IA 50423
Phone: (515)843-3878
Products: Animal feed. SICs: 5153 (Grain & Field
Beans); 5191 (Farm Supplies). Sales: $18,000,000
(2000). Emp: 20. Officers: Ron Eisenman, President.

■ 11097 ■ Farmers Cooperative Dairy Inc.
PO Box 685
Blakeslee, PA 18610
Phone: (570)454-0821
Free: (800)548-8787   Fax: (570)643-5390
Products: Milk products including fluid, skim and
flavoredmilk, lemonade. SICs: 5143 (Dairy Products
Except Dried or Canned); 5149 (Groceries & Related
Products Nec). Sales: $6,000,000 (2000). Emp: 14.
Officers: John Moisey, General Mgr.

■ 11098 ■ Farmers Cooperative Elevator
Association
1016 2nd Ave.
Sheldon, IA 51201
Phone: (712)324-2548   Fax: (712)324-5297
Products: Agricultural equipment and supplies. SIC:
5153 (Grain & Field Beans). Sales: $30,000,000
(2000). Emp: 60.

■ 11099 ■ Farmers Cooperative Elevator Co.
(Buffalo Lake, Minnesota)
PO Box 98
Ireton, IA 51027
Phone: (320)833-5981
Products: Feed, seed, fertilizer and chemicals. SIC:
5153 (Grain & Field Beans). Sales: $48,000,000
(2000). Emp: 60.

■ 11100 ■ Farmers Cooperative Exchange
109 South St.
Pella, IA 50219
Phone: (515)628-4167   Fax: (515)628-8195
Products: Agricultural equipment and supplies. SIC:
5153 (Grain & Field Beans). Sales: $12,000,000
(2000). Emp: 22.

■ 11101 ■ Farmers Cooperative Exchange
(Elgin, Nebraska)
PO Box 159
Elgin, NE 68636
Phone: (402)843-2223
Products: Grain, farm supplies, lumber and hardware.
SICs: 5153 (Grain & Field Beans); 5191 (Farm
Supplies); 5031 (Lumber, Plywood & Millwork); 5072
(Hardware). Sales: $138,000,000 (2000). Emp: 150.
Officers: Doug Derscheid, CEO; Sheldon Kangas,
General Manager, Finance.

■ 11102 ■ Farmers Cooperative Grain and
Supply Co.
815 N Brown St.
Minden, NE 68959
Phone: (308)832-2380   Fax: (308)832-2442
Products: Agricultural equipment and supplies. SIC:
5153 (Grain & Field Beans). Sales: $25,000,000
(2000). Emp: 25.

■ 11103 ■ Farmers Elevator Co.
201 E Campbell
Ransom, IL 60470
Phone: (815)586-4221   Fax: (815)586-4248
Products: Livestock and farm products. SIC: 5153
(Grain & Field Beans). Sales: $15,000,000 (2000).
Emp: 10.

■ 11104 ■ Farmers Union Co-op
600 W Broad St.
Blue Springs, NE 68318-0008
Phone: (402)645-3356   Fax: (402)645-8114
Products: Livestock and farm products. SIC: 5153
(Grain & Field Beans). Sales: $4,000,000 (2000). Emp:
7.

■ 11105 ■ Farmers Union Cooperative
(Harvard, Nebraska)
PO Box 147
Harvard, NE 68944
Phone: (402)762-3239
Products: Grain and beans. SICs: 5153 (Grain & Field
Beans); 5191 (Farm Supplies). Officers: Wilbur
Pauley, CEO.

■ 11106 ■ Farmland Foods
20 Carando Dr.
Springfield, MA 01104
Phone: (413)781-5620   Fax: (413)737-7314
Products: Deli meats. SIC: 5147 (Meats & Meat
Products). Sales: $71,000,000 (1999). Emp: 300.
Officers: Todd Gerken, Plant Mgr. Former Name:
Carando Inc.

■ 11107 ■ Farner Bocken Co.
PO Box 716
Sioux City, IA 51102
Phone: (712)258-5555   Fax: (712)255-6144
Products: Cigarettes; Candy; Institutional-sized food.
SICs: 5149 (Groceries & Related Products Nec); 5194
(Tobacco & Tobacco Products); 5145 (Confectionery).

■ 11108 ■ Farner & Co.
600 E Norfolk Ave.
Norfolk, NE 68701
Phone: (402)371-2662   Fax: (402)371-8610
Products: Candy; Tobacco. SICs: 5145
(Confectionery); 5194 (Tobacco & Tobacco Products).

■ 11109 ■ Asael Farr & Sons Co.
274 21st St.
Ogden, UT 84401
Phone: (801)393-8629
Products: Ice cream. SIC: 5143 (Dairy Products
Except Dried or Canned).

■ 11110 ■ FDL Marketing Inc.
2040 Kerper Blvd.
Dubuque, IA 52004
Phone: (319)588-5400   **Fax:** (319)588-5446
Products: Pork. **SIC:** 5147 (Meats & Meat Products).
Sales: $90,000,000 (2000). **Emp:** 250. **Officers:** Al
Byers, President & COO; Kurt Mueller, Dir. of
Marketing.

■ 11111 ■ Feaster Foods Co.
11808 W Center Rd.
Omaha, NE 68144-4397
Phone: (402)691-8800
Free: (800)228-6098   **Fax:** (402)691-7921
Products: Seasonings, including pure and imitation
bacon bits. **SIC:** 5149 (Groceries & Related Products
Nec). **Est:** 1950. **Sales:** $5,000,000 (2000). **Emp:** 49.
Officers: Richard S. Westin, Chairman of the Board;
Scott M. Bailey, President.

■ 11112 ■ Feather Crest Farms Inc.
14374 E SH 21
Bryan, TX 77808
Phone: (979)589-2576   **Fax:** (979)589-3052
Products: Eggs. **SIC:** 5144 (Poultry & Poultry
Products). **Est:** 1968. **Sales:** $14,000,000 (2000).
Emp: 90. **Officers:** D.R. Barrett, CEO; Brian D. Barrett,
President; Glenn Barrett, Exec. VP.

■ 11113 ■ Federal Fruit and Produce Co.
1890 E 58th Ave.
Denver, CO 80216
Phone: (303)292-1303   **Fax:** (303)292-0019
Products: Fruit. **SIC:** 5148 (Fresh Fruits &
Vegetables). **Est:** 1937. **Sales:** $23,000,000 (2000).
Emp: 75. **Officers:** Stan Kouba, President; John
Domenico, Treasurer & Secty.

■ 11114 ■ Federated Foods Inc.
3025 W Salt Creek Ln.
Arlington Heights, IL 60005
Phone: (847)577-1200   **Fax:** (847)632-8204
URL: http://www.fedgroup.com
Products: Food, including meats and deli products.
SICs: 5141 (Groceries—General Line); 5147 (Meats &
Meat Products). **Est:** 1945. **Emp:** 338. **Officers:** David
Dougherty, CEO & President; Rodger Soeldner, VP &
CFO; Vincent Wilson; Stephen Freskos, VP Mgt.
Information Systems; William Bolton, Vice President.

■ 11115 ■ Federated Group, Inc.
3025 W Salt Creek Ln.
Arlington Heights, IL 60005
Phone: (847)577-1200
Free: (800)234-0011   **Fax:** (847)632-8306
URL: http://www.fedgroup.com
Products: Food. **SIC:** 5141 (Groceries—General Line).
Emp: 325. **Officers:** David Dougherty, CEO &
President; Vincent Wilson, Vice President; Roger
Soeldner, VP of Finance.

■ 11116 ■ Federation of Ohio River Co-ops
320 Outerbelt St., Ste. E
Columbus, OH 43213
Phone: (614)861-2446   **Fax:** (614)861-7638
URL: http://www.forcwarehouse.com
Products: Natural food products. **SIC:** 5149 (Groceries
& Related Products Nec). **Est:** 1976.

■ 11117 ■ Feesers Inc.
PO Box 4055
Harrisburg, PA 17111
Phone: (717)564-4636
Free: (800)326-2828   **Fax:** (717)558-7440
E-mail: sales@Feeser.com
URL: http://www.Feeser.com
Products: Canned and frozen foods; Cleaning
chemicals; Paper; Produce; Seafood; Small-wares.
SICs: 5149 (Groceries & Related Products Nec); 5142
(Packaged Frozen Foods); 5169 (Chemicals & Allied
Products Nec). **Est:** 1901. **Sales:** $200,000,000
(2000). **Emp:** 335. **Officers:** Lester Miller, President;
Terry Kaufman, VP of Operations; John Tighe, CEO.

■ 11118 ■ Ference Cheese Inc.
174 Weaverville Rd., No. A
Asheville, NC 28804
Phone: (828)658-3101
Products: Food, including cheese. **SIC:** 5143 (Dairy
Products Except Dried or Canned).

■ 11119 ■ Ferrara Food and Confections Inc.
195 Grand St.
New York, NY 10013
Phone: (212)226-6150   **Fax:** (212)226-0667
E-mail: fer1892@aol.com
URL: http://www.ferraracafe.com
Products: Cakes; Pastries. **SICs:** 5149 (Groceries &
Related Products Nec); 5145 (Confectionery). **Est:**
1892. **Sales:** $5,000,000 (2000). **Emp:** 100. **Officers:**
Alfred Lepore, President.

■ 11120 ■ Ferrara Pan Candy Co.
7301 W Harrison St.
Forest Park, IL 60130
Phone: (708)366-0500   **Fax:** (708)366-5921
Products: Candy. **SIC:** 5145 (Confectionery).
Officers: Salvatore Ferrara II.

■ 11121 ■ James Ferrera and Sons Inc.
135 Will Dr.
Canton, MA 02021
Phone: (617)828-6150   **Fax:** (617)821-2682
Products: Groceries. **SIC:** 5141 (Groceries—General
Line). **Est:** 1946. **Sales:** $150,000,000 (2000). **Emp:**
300. **Officers:** Kenneth Ferrera, President; James J.
Ferrera, Treasurer; C. Lee Gibson Sr., VP of Marketing;
George Pereira, Dir. of Systems; Diane Ferrera, Dir of
Human Resources.

■ 11122 ■ Ferro Foods Corp.
25 53rd St.
Brooklyn, NY 11232
Phone: (718)492-0793   **Fax:** (718)492-3482
Products: Olive oil; Pasta; Mozzarella cheese. **SICs:**
5149 (Groceries & Related Products Nec); 5143 (Dairy
Products Except Dried or Canned). **Est:** 1975. **Sales:**
$18,000,000 (2000). **Emp:** 40. **Officers:** F. Ferro,
President.

■ 11123 ■ Fieldbrook Farms Inc.
1 Ice Cream Dr.
Dunkirk, NY 14048
Phone: (716)366-5400
Free: (800)333-0805   **Fax:** (716)366-3588
URL: http://fieldbrookfarms.com
Products: Frozen desserts. **SIC:** 5143 (Dairy Products
Except Dried or Canned). **Sales:** $100,000,000 (2000).
Emp: 600. **Officers:** James J. Greco, CEO; Ken
Johnson, Vice President; Tony Magine, Customer
Service Contact; Rosemary Olow, Human Resources
Contact. **Former Name:** Dunkirk Ice Cream Company,
Inc.

■ 11124 ■ Fiesta Foods
2570 Kiel Way
North Las Vegas, NV 89030-4153
Phone: (702)735-2198   **Fax:** (702)735-4686
Products: Groceries. **SIC:** 5141 (Groceries—General
Line). **Est:** 1965. **Sales:** $14,000,000 (2000). **Emp:** 49.

■ 11125 ■ Figueroa International Inc.
239 N Causeway Blvd.
Metairie, LA 70001-5452
Phone: (504)831-0037   **Fax:** (504)524-8941
Products: Sauces, including hot and barbecue sauce;
Salsa. **SIC:** 5149 (Groceries & Related Products Nec).
Est: 1988. **Sales:** $4,000,000 (2000). **Emp:** 20.
Officers: Gregory P. Figueroa, President; David O.
Figueroa Jr., Exec. VP.

■ 11126 ■ Fine Distributing Inc.
3225 Meridian Pkwy.
Ft. Lauderdale, FL 33331-3503
Phone: (954)384-8005
Products: Specialty foods. **SIC:** 5141 (Groceries—
General Line). **Sales:** $102,000,000 (2000). **Emp:** 200.
Officers: Dick Trimarche, President; Jerry Coeppicus,
Controller.

■ 11127 ■ Fines Distributing Inc.
4000 Highlands Pkwy.
Smyrna, GA 30082
Phone: (770)436-0411
Products: Food. **SIC:** 5141 (Groceries—General Line).

■ 11128 ■ Fink Baking Corp.
5-35 54th Ave.
Long Island City, NY 11101
Phone: (718)392-8300   **Fax:** (718)729-1303
Products: Bread. **SIC:** 5149 (Groceries & Related
Products Nec). **Sales:** $30,000,000 (2000). **Emp:** 499.
Officers: Stephan A. Fink.

■ 11129 ■ Fiorucci Foods USA Inc.
1800 Ruffin Mill Rd.
Colonial Heights, VA 23834-5936
Phone: (804)520-7775
Free: (800)524-7775   **Fax:** (804)520-7180
E-mail: roni@msn.com
Products: Fresh meat; Processed, frozen, or cooked
meats. **SIC:** 5147 (Meats & Meat Products). **Est:** 1985.
Emp: 90. **Officers:** Jack Kelly, Exec. VP; John Jack,
Vice President; Kim Wilson, Customer Service.

■ 11130 ■ First Choice Food Distributors Inc.
6800 Snowden Rd.
Ft. Worth, TX 76140
Phone: (817)551-5704
Products: Milk, ice cream, and frozen french fries.
SICs: 5147 (Meats & Meat Products); 5142 (Packaged
Frozen Foods); 5143 (Dairy Products Except Dried or
Canned). **Est:** 1976. **Sales:** $26,000,000 (2000). **Emp:**
40. **Officers:** William Burgess, President; Calvin
Prowell, Vice President.

■ 11131 ■ First Choice Ingredients
4208 San Saba Ct.
Plano, TX 75074
Phone: (972)881-2794
Products: Food. **SIC:** 5141 (Groceries—General Line).

■ 11132 ■ First Cooperative Association
5057 Hwy. 3 W
Cherokee, IA 51012
Phone: (712)225-5400   **Fax:** (712)225-5493
Products: Grain; Farm supplies. **SICs:** 5153 (Grain &
Field Beans); 5191 (Farm Supplies). **Sales:**
$130,000,000 (2000). **Emp:** 150. **Officers:** Dennis
Larson, President; Ted Wall, Bookkeeper.

■ 11133 ■ Fisher Central Coast
5949 S Eastern Ave.
Los Angeles, CA 90040-4003
Phone: (805)962-5551
Products: Produce. **SIC:** 5141 (Groceries—General
Line). **Sales:** $8,000,000 (2000). **Emp:** 33. **Officers:**
Mark E. Spear, General Mgr.; Mariann G. Bottiani,
Controller.

■ 11134 ■ Fisher Mills Inc.
PO Box C-3765
Seattle, WA 98124
Phone: (206)622-4430   **Fax:** (206)682-3676
Products: Cereals, feeds and flour. **SIC:** 5149
(Groceries & Related Products Nec).

■ 11135 ■ Fishery Products International
18 Electronics Ave.
Danvers, MA 01923
Phone: (978)777-2660   **Fax:** (978)777-7458
Products: Fish, seafood, and vegetable products.
SICs: 5146 (Fish & Seafoods); 5148 (Fresh Fruits &
Vegetables). **Sales:** $127,400,000 (2000). **Emp:** 484.
Officers: John Cummings, President; Peter Colbourne,
VP of Finance & Admin.

■ 11136 ■ Fishery Products International USA
18 Electronics Ave.
Danvers, MA 01923
Phone: (978)777-2660   **Fax:** (978)777-2660
Products: Prepared fresh fish and seafood. **SIC:** 5146
(Fish & Seafoods). **Emp:** 499. **Officers:** Donald J.
Short.

■ 11137 ■ **Clifford D. Fite Co.**
PO Box 616
Cedartown, GA 30125
Phone: (770)748-5315   **Fax:** (770)748-4332
Products: Groceries. **SIC:** 5141 (Groceries—General Line). **Est:** 1937. **Sales:** $20,000,000 (2000). **Emp:** 45. **Officers:** Tom Steel, President & CFO.

■ 11138 ■ **Fitness Plus II**
PO Box 3641
Bozeman, MT 59772
Phone: (406)585-9204   **Fax:** (406)585-9204
Products: Health foods. **SIC:** 5149 (Groceries & Related Products Nec). **Est:** 1982. **Emp:** 3.

■ 11139 ■ **Five H Island Foods Inc.**
PO Box 19160
Honolulu, HI 96817
Phone: (808)848-2067
Products: Confectionery products. **SIC:** 5145 (Confectionery). **Sales:** $4,000,000 (1993). **Emp:** 50. **Officers:** Tom Horiuchi, President.

■ 11140 ■ **Flanigan Farms**
PO Box 347
Culver City, CA 90232
Phone: (310)836-8437   **Fax:** (310)838-0743
E-mail: nuts@flaniganfarms.com
URL: http://www.flaniganfarms.com
Products: Nuts and seeds(unsalted, dry roasted, or blanched); Nut mixes. **SICs:** 5149 (Groceries & Related Products Nec); 5145 (Confectionery). **Est:** 1970. **Emp:** 14. **Officers:** Patsy Flanigan.

■ 11141 ■ **Flav-O-Rich Inc.**
316 North 4th St.
Campbellsville, KY 42718
Phone: (502)465-8119   **Fax:** (502)423-6794
Products: Dairy products, including milk, cheese, cottage cheese, and buttermilk. **SIC:** 5143 (Dairy Products Except Dried or Canned). **Est:** 1972. **Sales:** $530,000,000 (2000). **Emp:** 2,500. **Officers:** Steve G. Conerly, CEO; James E. Mueller, CFO; Dave Lardner, Information Systems Mgr.; Jerry Roadcap, VP of Human Resources.

■ 11142 ■ **Flavtek Inc.**
1960 Hawkins Cir.
Los Angeles, CA 90001
Phone: (323)588-5880
Free: (800)562-5880   **Fax:** (323)588-0178
E-mail: support@flavtek.com
URL: http://www.flavtek.com
Products: Flavorings for food, including ice cream, juices, and cakes. **SIC:** 5149 (Groceries & Related Products Nec). **Est:** 1977. **Sales:** $3,500,000 (2000). **Emp:** 25. **Officers:** Richard J. Nikola Jr., President; Pam Wilson, Controller; David W. Ames, Dir. of Marketing & Sales; Sylvia Arelano, Customer Service Contact.

■ 11143 ■ **Flay-O-Rich Inc.**
2537 Catherine St.
Bristol, VA 24201
Phone: (540)669-5161
Products: Milk and ice cream. **SIC:** 5143 (Dairy Products Except Dried or Canned).

■ 11144 ■ **Fleet Wholesale**
PO Box 971
Brainerd, MN 56401
Phone: (218)829-3521   **Fax:** (218)829-1636
Products: Food; Clothing; Sporting goods; Lawn supplies; Household goods. **SICs:** 5141 (Groceries—General Line); 5137 (Women's/Children's Clothing); 5091 (Sporting & Recreational Goods); 5023 (Homefurnishings); 5136 (Men's/Boys' Clothing).

■ 11145 ■ **Fleming**
91-315 Hanua St.
Kapolei, HI 96707-1799
Phone: (808)682-7300   **Fax:** (808)682-5670
Products: Wholesale food. **SICs:** 5141 (Groceries—General Line); 5143 (Dairy Products Except Dried or Canned); 5149 (Groceries & Related Products Nec); 5182 (Wines & Distilled Beverages); 5194 (Tobacco & Tobacco Products). **Emp:** 200. **Officers:** Ralph Stussi.

■ 11146 ■ **Fleming Companies, Inc.**
1700 South Laemie Ave.
PO Box 490
Marshfield, WI 54449
Phone: (715)384-3191   **Fax:** (715)387-6930
Products: General line groceries. **SIC:** 5141 (Groceries—General Line). **Est:** 1934. **Emp:** 350. **Officers:** Gus Ferracane, President; Dwayne Maroszek, Controller; Steve Coy, Dir. of Sales; Dan Peterson, Dir. of Materials; Bill Krohn, Dir. of Information Systems; Randy Schwartz; Scott Godfroy.

■ 11147 ■ **Fleming Companies, Inc.**
PO Box 1149
Superior, WI 54880
Phone: (715)392-8880   **Fax:** (715)394-1665
URL: http://www.fleming.com
Products: Groceries. **SIC:** 5141 (Groceries—General Line). **Est:** 1930. **Sales:** $110,000,000 (2000). **Emp:** 400. **Officers:** Perry Fleming, President; Ken Taylor, Controller; John Sorci, Dir. of Sales; Roy Tollefson, Dir. of Data Processing; Mark Pentleton, Dir of Human Resources. **Former Name:** Gateway Foods of Twin Ports Inc.

■ 11148 ■ **Fleming Companies Inc.**
PO Box 26647
Oklahoma City, OK 73126-0647
Phone: (405)840-7200   **Fax:** (405)841-8003
Products: Dried food; Canned food; Meats; Dairy products. **SICs:** 5141 (Groceries—General Line); 5143 (Dairy Products Except Dried or Canned); 5147 (Meats & Meat Products). **Est:** 1916. **Sales:** $16,487,000,000 (2000). **Emp:** 41,200. **Officers:** Robert E. Stauth, CEO & Chairman of the Board; Harry L. Winn Jr., Exec. VP & CFO; Derreld E. Easter, Sr. VP of Marketing; Robert G. Dolan Jr., Sr. VP of Information Systems; Larry A. Wagner, Sr. VP of Human Resources.

■ 11149 ■ **Fleming Companies Inc. Garland Div.**
PO Box 469012
Garland, TX 75046-9012
Phone: (972)840-4400
Products: General line of groceries. **SIC:** 5141 (Groceries—General Line). **Sales:** $280,000,000 (1993). **Emp:** 400. **Officers:** Jim Griffin, President; Steve Eckles, Controller.

■ 11150 ■ **Fleming Companies Inc. Heartland Div.**
PO Box 419796
Kansas City, MO 64141
Phone: (816)221-9200
Products: General line groceries. **SIC:** 5141 (Groceries—General Line). **Est:** 1921. **Sales:** $140,000,000 (2000). **Emp:** 250. **Officers:** Lou Degginger, President; Wilber Auernheimer, Controller; Shannon Bennett, Contact.

■ 11151 ■ **Fleming Companies Inc. Oklahoma City Div.**
10 E Memorial Rd.
Oklahoma City, OK 73114
Phone: (405)755-2420
Products: General line groceries. **SIC:** 5141 (Groceries—General Line).

■ 11152 ■ **Fleming Companies Inc. Philadelphia Div.**
PO Box 935
Oaks, PA 19456
Phone: (215)935-5000   **Fax:** (215)935-5023
Products: Canned and dry grocery goods. **SICs:** 5141 (Groceries—General Line); 5149 (Groceries & Related Products Nec). **Sales:** $330,000,000 (2000). **Emp:** 792. **Officers:** Mark Batenick, President; Cathy Gold, Controller; Robert Yannerall, Sales Mgr.; Roy Powell, Data Processing Mgr.; Morris Taormina, Human Resources Mgr.

■ 11153 ■ **Fleming Foods**
1015 W Magnolia
Geneva, AL 36340
Phone: (205)684-3631
Free: (800)635-6389   **Fax:** (205)684-5392
Products: General line groceries. **SIC:** 5141 (Groceries—General Line). **Sales:** $100,000,000

(2000). **Emp:** 450. **Officers:** Ivan Mulen, President; Greg Ross, Controller; Donald Furrer, Dir. of Marketing.

■ 11154 ■ **Fleming Foods of Alabama Inc.**
PO Box 398
Geneva, AL 36340
Phone: (334)684-3631   **Fax:** (334)684-5233
Products: Groceries. **SIC:** 5141 (Groceries—General Line). **Sales:** $170,000,000 (2000). **Emp:** 450. **Officers:** Greg Ross, General Mgr.; Martin Walden, Accountant.

■ 11155 ■ **Fleming Foods of Ohio Inc.**
PO Box 207
Massillon, OH 44648
Phone: (216)879-5681   **Fax:** (216)879-5196
Products: Groceries. **SIC:** 5141 (Groceries—General Line). **Est:** 1884. **Sales:** $519,000,000 (2000). **Emp:** 450. **Officers:** Mark Grossett, President; John Huron, Controller; Bill Brock, Sales Mgr.; Barb Baxter, Dir. of Data Processing; Richard Florio, Dir of Human Resources.

■ 11156 ■ **Fleming Foods of Tennessee Inc.**
PO Box 448
Goodlettsville, TN 37070-0448
Products: General line groceries. **SIC:** 5141 (Groceries—General Line). **Est:** 1940. **Sales:** $110,000,000 (2000). **Emp:** 200. **Officers:** Tom Krieger, President; Frank Hutchens, Controller; Brad Dalton, Sales Mgr.; Bob Berquist, Information Systems Mgr.; Carol Cross, Human Resources Mgr.

■ 11157 ■ **Fleming Foodservice**
PO Box 66
Cornelia, GA 30531
Phone: (706)778-2256   **Fax:** (706)776-2101
Products: Fish; Poultry. **SICs:** 5146 (Fish & Seafoods); 5144 (Poultry & Poultry Products). **Est:** 1953. **Sales:** $18,000,000 (2000). **Emp:** 50. **Officers:** Richard Gauger, General Mgr.; Matt Coloma, Controller.

■ 11158 ■ **Fleming/Gateway**
3501 Marshall St. NE
Minneapolis, MN 55418
Phone: (612)781-8051
Products: Groceries. **SIC:** 5141 (Groceries—General Line). **Sales:** $900,000,000 (2000). **Emp:** 630. **Officers:** Carey Mike, Director; John Kline, Accounting Manager.

■ 11159 ■ **Tom Flemming and Associates Inc.**
10273 Yellow Circle Dr.
Minnetonka, MN 55343
Phone: (612)933-2263   **Fax:** (612)933-0179
Products: Food. **SIC:** 5141 (Groceries—General Line). **Sales:** $52,000,000 (2000). **Emp:** 100. **Officers:** Jim McLellan.

■ 11160 ■ **Flite Service**
9655 E 25th Ave., Unit 107
Aurora, CO 80010-1056
Phone: (303)363-6336   **Fax:** (303)830-0234
Products: Airline food. **SIC:** 5149 (Groceries & Related Products Nec). **Emp:** 49. **Officers:** Richard Scarbeary.

■ 11161 ■ **Floribbean Wholesale Inc.**
5151 NW 17th St.
Margate, FL 33063
Phone: (954)968-4091
Products: Fish. **SIC:** 5146 (Fish & Seafoods). **Sales:** $5,000,000 (2000). **Emp:** 12. **Officers:** Mike Black, President.

■ 11162 ■ **Florimex Inc.**
PO Box 260277
Tampa, FL 33685
Phone: (813)886-0470
Products: General line of Spanish groceries. **SIC:** 5141 (Groceries—General Line). **Sales:** $4,300,000 (2000). **Emp:** 25. **Officers:** Matias Milla, President.

■ 11163 ■ **Flowers Industries Inc.**
PO Box 1338
Thomasville, GA 31799-1338
Phone: (912)226-9110   **Fax:** (912)225-3808
Products: Bakery products; Frozen vegetables. **SIC:**

5142 (Packaged Frozen Foods). **Sales:** $738,000,000 (2000). **Emp:** 9,000.

■ 11164 ■ Flower's Shellfish Distributors
5 Carr Pl.
Bayville, NY 11709
Phone: (516)628-1263 **Fax:** (516)628-1651
Products: Fresh oysters and clams. **SIC:** 5146 (Fish & Seafoods). **Emp:** 6. **Officers:** Jerry Flower Sr., President; Jerry Flower Jr., Vice President.

■ 11165 ■ Fmali Inc.
831 Almar Ave.
Santa Cruz, CA 95060
E-mail: sales@goodearthteas.com
URL: http://www.goodearth.com
Products: Tea; Bulk herbs. **SIC:** 5122 (Drugs, Proprietaries & Sundries). **Est:** 1972. **Sales:** $14,000,000 (2000). **Emp:** 80. **Officers:** Ben Zaricor, CEO; Garth Gregson, CFO.

■ 11166 ■ Louis Foehrkolb Inc.
7901 Oceano Ave.
Jessup, MD 20794
Phone: (410)799-4260
Products: Fresh and frozen seafood. **SICs:** 5146 (Fish & Seafoods); 5142 (Packaged Frozen Foods).

■ 11167 ■ Foell Packing Co.
3117 W 47th St.
Chicago, IL 60632
Phone: (773)523-5220 **Fax:** (773)523-2142
URL: http://www.foellpacking.com
Products: Canned processed meats. **SIC:** 5147 (Meats & Meat Products). **Est:** 1905. **Sales:** $5,000,000 (2000). **Emp:** 40. **Officers:** D. Johnson, e-mail: www.djohnson@foellpacking.com.

■ 11168 ■ M.F. Foley Company Inc.
PO Box 3093
New Bedford, MA 02740
Phone: (508)997-0773
Products: Seafood. **SIC:** 5146 (Fish & Seafoods). **Sales:** $10,300,000 (2000). **Emp:** 40. **Officers:** M.F. Foley, President & Treasurer.

■ 11169 ■ Folloder Co.
PO Box 19975
Houston, TX 77224-1975
Phone: (713)932-7171
Products: Frozen foods. **SICs:** 5141 (Groceries—General Line); 5142 (Packaged Frozen Foods). **Sales:** $5,000,000 (2000). **Emp:** 220. **Officers:** Steven Blake, President; Brian Folloder, Exec. VP & CFO.

■ 11170 ■ Food Country USA
Deadmore
Abingdon, VA 24210
Phone: (540)628-2562 **Fax:** (540)628-2562
Products: Groceries. **SIC:** 5141 (Groceries—General Line). **Emp:** 49. **Officers:** Charlie Henderson.

■ 11171 ■ Food For Life Baking Co.
PO Box 1434
Corona, CA 92878
Phone: (909)279-5090 **Fax:** (909)279-1784
Products: Wholesale bakery, sprouted grain breads, natural muffins and cakes. **SIC:** 5149 (Groceries & Related Products Nec). **Sales:** $3,000,000 (2000). **Emp:** 32. **Officers:** Jim Torres, President.

■ 11172 ■ Food Gems Ltd.
84 23 Rockaway Blvd.
Ozone Park, NY 11417
Phone: (718)296-7788
Products: Bakery products; Pies; Bread, cake, and related products. **SIC:** 5149 (Groceries & Related Products Nec). **Emp:** 49. **Officers:** Bradley Stroll.

■ 11173 ■ Food Lion Inc.
PO Box 1330
Salisbury, NC 28145-1330
Phone: (704)633-8250 **Fax:** (704)637-2581
Products: Milk; Canned specialties. **SICs:** 5143 (Dairy Products Except Dried or Canned); 5149 (Groceries & Related Products Nec). **Sales:** $5,584,410 (2000). **Emp:** 50,000. **Officers:** Tom E. Smith, Chairman, President, & CEO.

■ 11174 ■ Food Marketing Corp.
4815 Executive Blvd.
Ft. Wayne, IN 46808-1150
Phone: (219)483-2146 **Fax:** (219)482-6434
Products: Grocery store supplies; Food; Cleaning supplies; Beauty aids. **SICs:** 5141 (Groceries—General Line); 5122 (Drugs, Proprietaries & Sundries); 5169 (Chemicals & Allied Products Nec); 5149 (Groceries & Related Products Nec). **Sales:** $550,000 (2000). **Emp:** 1,125.

■ 11175 ■ Food Masters Inc.
300 W Broad St.
PO Box 1565
Griffin, GA 30224
Phone: (404)521-0780 **Fax:** (404)228-4281
Products: Salad dressings. **SIC:** 5149 (Groceries & Related Products Nec). **Emp:** 25. **Officers:** Pradeep Kumarhia; Ruchi Kumarhia.

■ 11176 ■ Food Match, Inc.
180 Duane St.
New York, NY 10013
Phone: (212)334-5044 **Fax:** (212)334-5042
Products: Olives; Olive oil; Roasted peppers; Capers; Pasta; Roasted tomatoes; Mustard; Vinegars. **SICs:** 5149 (Groceries & Related Products Nec); 5149 (Groceries & Related Products Nec); 5148 (Fresh Fruits & Vegetables); 5145 (Confectionery); 5144 (Poultry & Poultry Products). **Est:** 1996. **Emp:** 9. **Officers:** Phil Meldrum, President, e-mail: phil@foodmatch.com.

■ 11177 ■ Food Service Action Inc.
675 Village Square Dr.
Stone Mountain, GA 30083
Phone: (404)296-2700 **Fax:** (404)292-5916
URL: http://www.fsaction.com
Products: Food. **SIC:** 5141 (Groceries—General Line). **Est:** 1972. **Sales:** $9,000,000 (2000). **Emp:** 22. **Officers:** Randy Reid, President.

■ 11178 ■ Food Services of America
4101 15th Ave. NW
Fargo, ND 58102-2830
Phone: (701)282-8200 **Fax:** (701)282-3546
Products: Food; Restaurant supplies; Household cooking equipment. **SICs:** 5141 (Groceries—General Line); 5046 (Commercial Equipment Nec); 5113 (Industrial & Personal Service Paper). **Officers:** Richard Knapp.

■ 11179 ■ Food Services of America
802 Parkway Ln.
Billings, MT 59101
Phone: (406)245-4181 **Fax:** (406)245-3942
Products: Food; Beverages. **SICs:** 5141 (Groceries—General Line); 5149 (Groceries & Related Products Nec). **Emp:** 100. **Officers:** Tom Jacobson.

■ 11180 ■ Food Services of America Inc.
4025 Delridge Way SW
Seattle, WA 98106
Phone: (206)933-5000 **Fax:** (206)933-5279
Products: Meat, produce, and dairy products. **SICs:** 5141 (Groceries—General Line); 5148 (Fresh Fruits & Vegetables). **Est:** 1890. **Sales:** $862,500,000 (2000). **Emp:** 2,300. **Officers:** Tom Staley, President; Dennis Specht, CFO; Roger Toomey, VP Marketing & Development; Ellnie Snyder, VP of Operations; Carol Sidell, Dir of Personnel.

■ 11181 ■ Foodsales Inc.
14 Spring Mill Dr.
Malvern, PA 19355
Phone: (215)644-8900
Products: Food. **SIC:** 5141 (Groceries—General Line).

■ 11182 ■ FoodSalesWest Inc.
235 Baker St.
Costa Mesa, CA 92626
Phone: (714)966-2900
Products: General groceries and frozen food products. **SICs:** 5141 (Groceries—General Line); 5142 (Packaged Frozen Foods). **Sales:** $43,000,000 (1994). **Emp:** 75. **Officers:** Joseph C. Myers, President; Bonnie Crawford, Controller.

■ 11183 ■ FoodScience Corp.
20 New England Dr., Ste. C-1504
Essex Junction, VT 05452
Phone: (802)863-1111
Free: (800)451-4590 **Fax:** (802)878-0549
Products: Nutritional food supplements. **SIC:** 5149 (Groceries & Related Products Nec). **Sales:** $10,000,000 (2000). **Emp:** 47. **Officers:** Lou R. Drudi, President; Patricia Wunsch, Controller.

■ 11184 ■ FoodSource, Inc.
PO Box 217
Smyrna, TN 37167
Phone: (615)459-2519 **Fax:** (615)355-0637
E-mail: foodsourcetn@aol.com
Products: Fresh meats; Frozen foods; Dairy; Canned and groceries; Non-foods and chemicals. **SICs:** 5147 (Meats & Meat Products); 5142 (Packaged Frozen Foods); 5149 (Groceries & Related Products Nec); 5169 (Chemicals & Allied Products Nec). **Est:** 1971. **Sales:** $20,000,000 (2000). **Emp:** 60. **Officers:** Gus Pantazopoulos, President; Arlou Moss, Sales Mgr. **Former Name:** Imperial Foods, Inc.

■ 11185 ■ Ford Brothers Wholesale Meats Inc.
9129 Rte. 219
West Valley, NY 14171
Phone: (716)592-9126
Free: (800)836-4221 **Fax:** (716)942-3775
Products: Beef and pork. **SIC:** 5147 (Meats & Meat Products). **Est:** 1970. **Sales:** $25,000,000 (2000). **Emp:** 50. **Officers:** R.D. Ford, CEO; R.A. Ford, President; Richard Ford, Sales/Marketing Contact; George Burgard, Human Resources Contact.

■ 11186 ■ Foreign Candy Company Inc.
1 Foreign Candy Dr.
Hull, IA 51239
Phone: (712)439-1496
Free: (800)831-8541 **Fax:** (712)439-1434
E-mail: customer.service@foreigncandy.com
URL: http://www.megawarheads.com
Products: Imported candy, including gummies, sour candy, suckers, lollipops, coffee candy, seasonal candies and toffee; Kids novelties. **SIC:** 5145 (Confectionery). **Est:** 1978. **Emp:** 170. **Officers:** Peter W. De Yager, Chairman of the Board; Mike Fisher, President & Chairman of the Board; Mike Fisher, Sr. VP of Sales & Marketing.

■ 11187 ■ Foreign Trade Marketing
1279 Starboard Ln.
Sarasota, FL 34242
Phone: (941)346-9900 **Fax:** (941)349-8181
E-mail: FTM5@hotmail.com
URL: http://www.foreigntrademarketing.com
Products: General merchandise; Food; Diapers; Picnic packs. **SICs:** 5141 (Groceries—General Line); 5199 (Nondurable Goods Nec); 5122 (Drugs, Proprietaries & Sundries). **Est:** 1976. **Sales:** $100,000,000 (1999). **Emp:** 16. **Officers:** David Tobocman, Vice President; Karen Bailey, President; Irv Tobocman, Chairman of the Board.

■ 11188 ■ Foresight Partners, LLC
209 W Main St.
Boise, ID 83702
Phone: (208)336-7003 **Fax:** (208)338-7186
URL: http://www.foresightpartners.com
Products: Full line groceries, non-food, frozen, center of the plate, refrigerated. **SIC:** 5141 (Groceries—General Line). **Est:** 1971. **Sales:** $14,000,000,000 (1999). **Emp:** 49. **Officers:** Harry Reifschneider, CEO; Dave Dougherty, Co-Chairman; Patrick Haas, President; Pam Bly, Vice President of Marketing; Leigh Lotspeich, Vice President Sales Administration; Michael Mangum, VP & General Mgr.; Mike Mattlin, National Director, Distributor Marketing; Steve Lipari, Director, Distributor Development; Eileen Thuesen, Comptroller; Gayle Nay, Brands Manager. **Former Name:** All Kitchens Inc.

■ 11189 ■ Forlizzi Brothers
114 New England Providence Center
Chelsea, MA 02150
Phone: (617)884-1858
Products: Vegetables. **SIC:** 5148 (Fresh Fruits & Vegetables).

■ 11190 ■ **Fornaca Inc.**
2400 National City Blvd.
National City, CA 91950
Phone: (619)474-5573 **Fax:** (619)474-7754
Products: Breads. **SIC:** 5141 (Groceries—General
Line). **Est:** 1959. **Sales:** $180,000,000 (2000). **Emp:**
500. **Officers:** Frank Fornaca, President; Jim Fornaca,
VP & CFO; Sandy Owens, Dir of Personnel.

■ 11191 ■ **Forsythe Ice Cream**
689 Cross Trail
Piqua, OH 45356
Phone: (937)773-6322
Products: Ice cream. **SIC:** 5143 (Dairy Products
Except Dried or Canned).

■ 11192 ■ **Fort Pitt Brand Meat Co.**
PO Box F
Evans City, PA 16033
Phone: (724)538-3160
Products: Sausages and prepared meats. **SIC:** 5147
(Meats & Meat Products). **Sales:** $5,200,000 (2000).
Emp: 3. **Officers:** J.H. Deily, CEO & President.

■ 11193 ■ **Foster's Good Service Dairy**
PO Box 129
Westerville, OH 43081
Phone: (614)891-6407
Products: Milk; Cheese; Eggs; Ice cream; Juices;
Bread; Lunch meats; Sweet rolls; Soft drinks. **SICs:**
5143 (Dairy Products Except Dried or Canned); 5149
(Groceries & Related Products Nec). **Sales:**
$3,000,000 (2000). **Emp:** 6. **Officers:** Steve Foster,
Owner.

■ 11194 ■ **R. Fournier & Sons Seafoods**
9391 Fournier Ave.
Biloxi, MS 39532-5419
Phone: (228)392-4293 **Fax:** (228)392-7130
Products: Oysters and shrimp; Crab meat. **SIC:** 5146
(Fish & Seafoods). **Est:** 1928. **Emp:** 99.

■ 11195 ■ **Fowler Brothers**
110 Gary Pl.
San Rafael, CA 94912
Phone: (415)459-3406 **Fax:** (415)459-0658
Products: Organic and natural foods. **SIC:** 5149
(Groceries & Related Products Nec). **Est:** 1974.

■ 11196 ■ **Fowler Equity Exchange Inc.**
Hwy. 54 and Main St.
Fowler, KS 67844
Phone: (316)646-5262 **Fax:** (316)646-5372
Products: Livestock and farm products. **SIC:** 5153
(Grain & Field Beans). **Sales:** $8,800,000 (2000). **Emp:**
12.

■ 11197 ■ **Fox River Foods Inc.**
5030 Baseline Rd.
Montgomery, IL 60538
Phone: (630)896-1991 **Fax:** (630)896-0157
Products: Groceries for restaurants and hospitals,
including canned goods and frozen vegetables; Meat,
including beef, pork, and chicken. **SICs:** 5149
(Groceries & Related Products Nec); 5142 (Packaged
Frozen Foods); 5147 (Meats & Meat Products); 5144
(Poultry & Poultry Products). **Est:** 1956. **Sales:**
$85,000,000 (2000). **Emp:** 220. **Officers:** Kenneth
Nagel, President; Mary Kay Pilmer, Controller; Mary
Kay Pilmer, Controller.

■ 11198 ■ **FPC Foodservices**
321 E 5th St.
Frederick, MD 21701
Phone: (301)663-3171 **Fax:** (301)662-8397
URL: http://www.fpcfoodservices.com
Products: Fruits and vegetables; Frozen poultry and
food; Canned grocery; Disposables; Chemicals. **SICs:**
5148 (Fresh Fruits & Vegetables); 5144 (Poultry &
Poultry Products). **Est:** 1935. **Sales:** $45,000,000
(2000). **Emp:** 100. **Officers:** J.D. Brunk, President; E.
Blumenauer, Treasurer & Secty.; Richard Walther, VP
of Marketing, e-mail: richw@fpcfoodservices.com.
Former Name: Frederick Produce Company Inc.

■ 11199 ■ **Francisco Distributing**
5301 N Robin Ave.
Livingston, CA 95334
Phone: (209)394-8001 **Fax:** (209)394-7911
Products: Sweet potatoes. **SIC:** 5148 (Fresh Fruits &
Vegetables). **Sales:** $30,000,000 (2000). **Emp:** 499.
Officers: Lilian Comorosky.

■ 11200 ■ **Frankferd Farms**
318 Love Rd., No. 1
Valencia, PA 16059
Phone: (412)898-2242 **Fax:** (412)898-2968
Products: Food preparations; Dried and dehydrated
food products; Head rice not packaged with other
ingredients; Potatoes; Egg noodle products; Health
foods. **SICs:** 5149 (Groceries & Related Products Nec);
5148 (Fresh Fruits & Vegetables).

■ 11201 ■ **M.E. Franks Inc.**
175 Strafford Ave., Ste. 230
Wayne, PA 19087
Phone: (610)989-9688
Free: (800)635-3726 **Fax:** (610)989-8989
URL: http://www.mefranks.com
Products: Dairy products; Dry milk. **SIC:** 5143 (Dairy
Products Except Dried or Canned). **Est:** 1948. **Sales:**
$100,000,000 (1999). **Emp:** 15. **Officers:** Donald W.
Street, CEO & President, e-mail: dstreet@melfran.com;
Bart Van Belleghem, Sales/Marketing Contact, e-mail:
bvanbell@melfran.com; Page Simpson, Customer
Service Contact, e-mail: psimpson@melfran.com.

■ 11202 ■ **Fredonia Cooperative Association**
PO Box 538
Fredonia, KS 66736
Phone: (316)378-2191
Products: Livestock and farm products. **SIC:** 5153
(Grain & Field Beans). **Sales:** $7,000,000 (2000). **Emp:**
9.

■ 11203 ■ **Julian Freirich Food**
46-01 5th St.
Long Island City, NY 11101
Phone: (718)361-9111
Free: (800)221-1315 **Fax:** (718)392-0396
E-mail: jfreirich@aol.com
URL: http://www.freirich.com
Products: Processed meats, including roast beef,
pastrami, and corned beef. **SIC:** 5147 (Meats & Meat
Products). **Est:** 1921. **Sales:** $20,000,000 (2000).
Emp: 99. **Officers:** Jerry Freirich, Chairman of the
Board; Jeff Freirich, President.

■ 11204 ■ **French Gourmet Inc.**
500 Kuwili St.
Honolulu, HI 96817
Phone: (808)524-4000 **Fax:** (808)528-0329
E-mail: chef@frenchgourmet.com
URL: http://www.frenchgourmet.com
Products: Frozen bakery products. **SIC:** 5142
(Packaged Frozen Foods). **Est:** 1984. **Sales:**
$21,500,000 (2000). **Emp:** 85. **Officers:** Patrick Novak,
President; Kristie Novak, Secretary; Linda Coffman,
Vice President.

■ 11205 ■ **Fresh Advantage**
5051 Speaker Rd.
Kansas City, KS 66106-1043
Phone: (913)321-0691 **Fax:** (913)321-7518
Products: Fruits and vegetables. **SIC:** 5148 (Fresh
Fruits & Vegetables). **Emp:** 160. **Officers:** Walt Armijo,
General Mgr.; Bruce Helmich, Sales/Marketing
Contact; Ladanious Johnson, Human Resources
Contact. **Former Name:** Dixon Tom-a-Toe Co.

■ 11206 ■ **Fresh America Corp.**
6600 LBJ Freeway, Ste. 180
Dallas, TX 75240
Phone: (972)774-0575 **Fax:** (972)774-0515
Products: Produce. **SIC:** 5148 (Fresh Fruits &
Vegetables). **Sales:** $349,300,000 (2000). **Emp:** 1,202.
Officers: David I. Sheinfeld, CEO & Chairman of the
Board; Robert C. Kiehnle, Exec. VP & CFO.

■ 11207 ■ **Fresh Express**
PO Box 298
Greencastle, PA 17225-1424
Phone: (717)597-1804 **Fax:** (717)597-4302
Products: Produce. **SIC:** 5148 (Fresh Fruits &

Vegetables). **Sales:** $18,000,000 (2000). **Emp:** 200.
Officers: George A. Stewart.

■ 11208 ■ **Fresh Fish Company Inc.**
8501 Page Blvd.
St. Louis, MO 63114
Phone: (314)428-7777
Free: (800)294-3474 **Fax:** (314)428-0781
Products: Fresh and frozen seafood. **SICs:** 5146 (Fish
& Seafoods); 5142 (Packaged Frozen Foods). **Sales:**
$13,000,000 (2000). **Emp:** 42. **Officers:** Thomas J.
Hillman, CEO; Kevin Sullivan, CFO.

■ 11209 ■ **Fresh Fish Inc.**
1116 2nd Ave. N
Birmingham, AL 35203
Phone: (205)252-0344 **Fax:** (205)252-3432
Products: Fish and seafood. **SIC:** 5146 (Fish &
Seafoods). **Sales:** $5,000,000 (2000). **Emp:** 20.
Officers: George Drakos, President.

■ 11210 ■ **Fresh Freeze Supply Inc.**
2841 E St.
Eureka, CA 95501
Phone: (707)442-8488 **Fax:** (707)442-0864
Products: Groceries. **SIC:** 5141 (Groceries—General
Line). **Sales:** $96,000,000 (2000). **Emp:** 150. **Officers:**
Steven Dolfini, President; Susan Rigge, Controller.

■ 11211 ■ **Fresh Start Produce Sales, Inc.**
5353 West Atlantic Ave.
Delray Beach, FL 33484-8166
Phone: (561)496-7250 **Fax:** (561)496-7670
Products: Produce. **SIC:** 5148 (Fresh Fruits &
Vegetables).

■ 11212 ■ **FreshPoint Inc.**
15305 Dallas Pkwy.
Dallas, TX 75248
Phone: (972)392-8100 **Fax:** (972)392-8130
Products: Foods and fresh produce. **SIC:** 5148 (Fresh
Fruits & Vegetables). **Officers:** Mitt Parker, CEO &
President; Bernadette Kruk, CFO.

■ 11213 ■ **FreshWorld Farms Inc.**
6701 San Pablo Ave.
Emeryville, CA 94608
Phone: (510)547-2395
Products: Vegetables, including peppers, carrots, and
tomatoes. **SIC:** 5148 (Fresh Fruits & Vegetables). **Est:**
1989. **Sales:** $8,000,000 (2000). **Emp:** 25. **Officers:**
Robert Serenbetz, President; Jennifer Rubis,
Treasurer.

■ 11214 ■ **Frieda's Inc.**
4465 Corporate Center Dr.
Los Alamitos, CA 90720
Phone: (714)826-6100 **Fax:** (714)816-0277
URL: http://www.friedas.com
Products: Specialty produce. **SIC:** 5140 (Groceries &
Related Products). **Est:** 1962. **Sales:** $32,000,000
(2000). **Emp:** 115. **Officers:** Karen B. Caplan, CEO &
President.

■ 11215 ■ **Frito-Lay Co.**
7701 Legacy Dr.
Plano, TX 75024
Phone: (972)334-7000 **Fax:** (972)334-2045
Products: Snack foods. **SICs:** 5145 (Confectionery);
5149 (Groceries & Related Products Nec).

■ 11216 ■ **Frito-Lay Inc.**
35855 Stanley
Sterling Heights, MI 48312
Phone: (810)978-8770 **Fax:** (810)978-8846
Products: Potato chips. **SIC:** 5145 (Confectionery).
Emp: 78. **Officers:** Rod Singer.

■ 11217 ■ **Frito-Lay Inc.**
7491 Clyde Park Ave. SW
Wyoming, MI 49509-9708
Phone: (616)878-9579 **Fax:** (616)878-4374
Products: Snack foods. **SIC:** 5149 (Groceries &
Related Products Nec). **Emp:** 49. **Officers:** Chris
Halfmann.

■ 11218 ■ **Fritz Company Inc.**
1912 Hastings Ave.
Newport, MN 55055
Phone: (612)459-9751
Products: Confectionery and tobacco products. **SICs:** 5145 (Confectionery); 5194 (Tobacco & Tobacco Products). **Sales:** $40,000,000 (2000). **Emp:** 100. **Officers:** Ed Lindborg, President.

■ 11219 ■ **L.H. Frohman & Sons Inc.**
1580 N Northwest Hwy.
Park Ridge, IL 60068-1444
Phone: (847)635-6520 **Fax:** (847)635-7595
Products: Food. SIC: 5141 (Groceries—General Line).
Emp: 49. **Officers:** Eugene Marre; Stephen J. Diebold; George B. Marczewski.

■ 11220 ■ **Frontier Co-op Herbs**
Box 299
Norway, IA 52318
Phone: (319)227-7996
Free: (800)669-3275 **Fax:** (319)227-7966
Products: Spices; Coffee; Medicinals and botanicals.
SICs: 5149 (Groceries & Related Products Nec); 5122 (Drugs, Proprietaries & Sundries). **Est:** 1976. **Emp:** 250.

■ 11221 ■ **Fruit Distributors Inc.**
129 S Central Ave.
Lima, OH 45801
Phone: (419)223-8105
Products: Food, including fruit. **SIC:** 5141 (Groceries—General Line).

■ 11222 ■ **Fruit a Freeze**
12919 Leyva St.
Norwalk, CA 90650
Phone: (562)407-2881 **Fax:** (562)407-2889
Products: Frozen fruit bars. **SIC:** 5142 (Packaged Frozen Foods). **Est:** 1977. **Sales:** $15,000,000 (2000). **Emp:** 49. **Officers:** Phillip Zobrist, CEO, e-mail: phillip@fruitafreeze.com; Carmelita Soto, Sec. & Treas., e-mail: carmelita@fruitafreeze.com; Roger Soto, President, e-mail: roger@fruitafreeze.com; Kevan Farrer, Corp. Controller, e-mail: kevan@fruitafreeze.com.

■ 11223 ■ **Fuji Natural Food Co.**
515 S 1st St.
Phoenix, AZ 85004-2503
Phone: (602)254-3890 **Fax:** (602)255-0764
Products: Ethnic food. **SIC:** 5149 (Groceries & Related Products Nec). **Est:** 1980. **Sales:** $7,000,000 (1999). **Emp:** 999. **Officers:** Shozo Takahashi; Kent Callister; Sherry Callister.

■ 11224 ■ **G.A. Funderburk Company Inc.**
PO Box 338
Jefferson, SC 29718-0338
Phone: (843)658-3405 **Fax:** (843)658-3313
Products: Watermelon. **SICs:** 5148 (Fresh Fruits & Vegetables); 5153 (Grain & Field Beans). **Est:** 1967. **Sales:** $600,000 (1993). **Emp:** 7. **Officers:** Gerald A. Funderburk, President.

■ 11225 ■ **G and G Produce Company Inc.**
5949 S Eastern Ave.
City of Commerce, CA 90040
Phone: (213)727-1212 **Fax:** (213)252-9116
Products: Produce. **SIC:** 5148 (Fresh Fruits & Vegetables). **Est:** 1921. **Sales:** $80,000,000 (2000). **Emp:** 270. **Officers:** L.D. Ligier, President; Len Ronan, CFO; Robert E. Hana Jr., VP of Sales.

■ 11226 ■ **Gachot & Gachot, Inc.**
440 W 14th St.
New York, NY 10014-1004
Phone: (212)675-2868 **Fax:** (212)929-5772
E-mail: gachot@ix.netcom.com
Products: Fresh meat, including cured and smoked; Poultry and small game; Food preparations. **SICs:** 5147 (Meats & Meat Products); 5144 (Poultry & Poultry Products). **Est:** 1903. **Emp:** 25. **Officers:** Charles Gachot, Chairman of the Board; Chistopher Gachot, President.

■ 11227 ■ **Gaetano Food Distributor**
940 Forrester Way
Eugene, OR 97401
Phone: (541)344-6758
Products: Food. SIC: 5141 (Groceries—General Line).

■ 11228 ■ **Gage Food Products Co.**
1501 N 31st Ave.
Melrose Park, IL 60160
Phone: (708)338-1501 **Fax:** (708)343-0454
Products: General line groceries. **SIC:** 5141 (Groceries—General Line). **Est:** 1955. **Emp:** 50. **Officers:** James J. Piccione, President; Roy T. Thiel, Vice President.

■ 11229 ■ **Gai's Northwest Bakeries Inc.**
PO Box 24327
Seattle, WA 98124
Phone: (206)322-0931 **Fax:** (206)726-7555
Products: Breads, rolls, buns, pastries and donuts. **SIC:** 5149 (Groceries & Related Products Nec). **Sales:** $200,000,000 (2000). **Emp:** 1,200. **Officers:** George Gagliardi, Director.

■ 11230 ■ **L.H. Gamble Co.**
3615 Harding Ave., Ste. 502
Honolulu, HI 96816-3735
Phone: (808)735-8199 **Fax:** (808)737-2835
Products: Ham, pork, and bacon; Canned spam and other canned goods. **SICs:** 5147 (Meats & Meat Products); 5149 (Groceries & Related Products Nec). **Emp:** 3.

■ 11231 ■ **Gant Food Distributors Inc.**
1200 Carter Rd.
Owensboro, KY 42301
Phone: (502)684-2382
Products: Meat, poultry, fish, and eggs. **SICs:** 5147 (Meats & Meat Products); 5144 (Poultry & Poultry Products); 5146 (Fish & Seafoods). **Est:** 1958. **Sales:** $10,000,000 (2000). **Emp:** 25. **Officers:** James Gant, President; Robert Gant, VP of Finance.

■ 11232 ■ **Garber Brothers Inc.**
PO Box 296
Randolph, MA 02368
Phone: (617)341-0800
Products: Groceries; Cigarettes and tobacco products; Candy; Health and beauty aids. **SICs:** 5141 (Groceries—General Line); 5122 (Drugs, Proprietaries & Sundries); 5145 (Confectionery); 5194 (Tobacco & Tobacco Products).

■ 11233 ■ **Garbo Lobster Company Inc.**
PO Box 906
Stonington, CT 06378
Phone: (203)535-1590 **Fax:** (203)535-2149
Products: Lobster. **SIC:** 5146 (Fish & Seafoods). **Sales:** $4,000,000 (2000). **Emp:** 15. **Officers:** David Garbo, Owner.

■ 11234 ■ **Garden Foods Products**
4844 Butterfield Rd.
Hillside, IL 60162
Phone: (708)449-0171 **Fax:** (708)449-0172
Products: Health foods. **SIC:** 5149 (Groceries & Related Products Nec).

■ 11235 ■ **Garden Spot Distributors**
438 White Oak Rd.
New Holland, PA 17557
Phone: (717)354-4936
Free: (800)829-5100 **Fax:** (717)354-4934
E-mail: grdnspot@ptd.net
Products: Breads and pastas; Snack foods; Flours and grains; Nuts. **SICs:** 5149 (Groceries & Related Products Nec); 5145 (Confectionery). **Est:** 1982. **Emp:** 26.

■ 11236 ■ **Gardenview Eggs**
PO Box 494
Reedsville, PA 17084
Phone: (717)667-2711
Free: (800)488-3447 **Fax:** (717)667-9583
Products: Eggs; Cheese; Butter; Meat. **SICs:** 5141 (Groceries—General Line); 5147 (Meats & Meat Products); 5144 (Poultry & Poultry Products); 5143 (Dairy Products Except Dried or Canned). **Emp:** 19. **Officers:** Orland Bethel; Jerry Zeiders.

■ 11237 ■ **Gardners Good Foods Inc.**
250 North St.
White Plains, NY 10625
Phone: (914)335-2500
Products: Cereal; Rice; Cheese; Coffee; Beverages; Dressings. **SIC:** 5141 (Groceries—General Line).

■ 11238 ■ **John Garner Meats Inc.**
PO Box 625
Van Buren, AR 72957
Phone: (501)474-6894 **Fax:** (501)474-6897
Products: Ground beef; Fresh and frozen cuts of beef; Frozen pork and chicken. Fresh and frozen Food Dist. **SICs:** 5147 (Meats & Meat Products); 5142 (Packaged Frozen Foods); 5144 (Poultry & Poultry Products). **Est:** 1947. **Sales:** $7,500,000 (2000). **Emp:** 45. **Officers:** John Garner, CEO; DeWayne Garner, President.

■ 11239 ■ **Gary's Everfresh Products Inc.**
1614 Dolwick Rd.
Erlanger, KY 41018
Phone: (606)525-8228
Products: Peanuts. **SIC:** 5145 (Confectionery). **Sales:** $10,000,000 (2000). **Emp:** 16. **Officers:** Robert Thomas, President.

■ 11240 ■ **Gate Petroleum Co.**
PO Box 23627
Jacksonville, FL 32241
Phone: (904)737-7220 **Fax:** (904)739-0769
Products: Snack foods, including potato chips, crackers, and soft drinks. **SICs:** 5145 (Confectionery); 5149 (Groceries & Related Products Nec). **Est:** 1960. **Sales:** $220,000,000 (2000). **Emp:** 2,000. **Officers:** Herbert Peyton, CEO; Louis Zemanek, Treasurer; Wayne Levitt, Vice President; Ron Kalapp, Dir. of Information Systems; Marlene Gise, Manager.

■ 11241 ■ **Gateway Distributing Co.**
120 26th St.
Ogden, UT 84401
Phone: (801)394-8839
Products: Food and beverages, including candy and beer. **SIC:** 5141 (Groceries—General Line).

■ 11242 ■ **Gateway Foods Inc.**
1637 St. James St.
La Crosse, WI 54602
Phone: (608)785-1330 **Fax:** (608)779-3940
Products: Health and beauty care items; Groceries, including baked goods, dairy products, and frozen foods. **SICs:** 5141 (Groceries—General Line); 5122 (Drugs, Proprietaries & Sundries). **Est:** 1922. **Sales:** $1,620,000,000 (1999). **Emp:** 4,500. **Officers:** Mike Carey, COO; Greg Kyle, Controller; Rich Kelly, Dir. of Data Processing; Lyell Montgomery, Dir of Personnel.

■ 11243 ■ **Gateway Foods of Pennsylvania Inc.**
PO Box 478
Huntingdon, PA 16652
Phone: (814)643-2300 **Fax:** (814)643-3040
Products: Food, including frozen, canned, dry, meat, milk, and produce. **SICs:** 5141 (Groceries—General Line); 5142 (Packaged Frozen Foods); 5143 (Dairy Products Except Dried or Canned); 5148 (Fresh Fruits & Vegetables); 5149 (Groceries & Related Products Nec). **Sales:** $190,000,000 (2000). **Emp:** 325. **Officers:** Jack Martin, General Mgr.; Dale Hoffman, Controller; Roy Szak, Dir. of Sales; Gail Leiby-Heath, Dir of Human Resources.

■ 11244 ■ **Gatzke Farms Inc.**
Hwy. 22, PO Box 247
Montello, WI 53949-0247
Phone: (608)297-2193 **Fax:** (608)297-7378
Products: Mints; Carrots; Onions; Potatoes. **SICs:** 5148 (Fresh Fruits & Vegetables); 5145 (Confectionery). **Sales:** $2,000,000 (2000). **Emp:** 25. **Officers:** Don Gatzke.

■ 11245 ■ **Gaucho Foods Inc.**
PO Box 307
Westmont, IL 60559
Phone: (630)241-3663 **Fax:** (630)241-3917
E-mail: mscinc@aol.com
Products: Frozen beef and gravy; Barbecued beef; Turkey and gravy. **SICs:** 5142 (Packaged Frozen Foods); 5147 (Meats & Meat Products). **Est:** 1947.

Sales: $2,400,000 (1999). Emp: 15. Officers: Mark D. Smith, President; Richard J. Cobb, Exec. VP; Tom Naumcheff, VP of Sales; Kelly Cheop, Office Mgr.

■ 11246 ■ Gaylord Cash & Carry
860 N Center Ave.
Gaylord, MI 49735-1510
Phones: (517)732-8200   (517)732-8756
Fax: (517)732-8804
Products: General line groceries; Poultry and livestock feed; Pet food; Pet supplies. SICs: 5141 (Groceries—General Line); 5149 (Groceries & Related Products Nec); 5199 (Nondurable Goods Nec); 5153 (Grain & Field Beans). Emp: 3. Officers: Bart Lambram, Sales; Gary Trelfa, Personnel.

■ 11247 ■ Gemmex Intertrade America Inc.
PO Box 3274
West McLean, VA 22103-3274
Phone: (703)893-9601   Fax: (703)893-7737
E-mail: gia@clark.net
URL: http://www.gemmex.com
Products: Food and beverages; Medical equipment; Toiletries and cosmetics; Footwear. SICs: 5199 (Nondurable Goods Nec); 5122 (Drugs, Proprietaries & Sundries); 5047 (Medical & Hospital Equipment); 5023 (Homefurnishings); 5139 (Footwear). Est: 1994. Sales: $500,000 (2000). Emp: 2. Officers: Ned Vidakovic, President; Tatiana Maria, Vice President. Also Known by This Acronym: GIA.

■ 11248 ■ General Brokerage Co.
600-604 E 9th
Los Angeles, CA 90015-1820
Phone: (213)627-9032   Fax: (213)627-9561
Products: Polynesian foods. SIC: 5149 (Groceries & Related Products Nec). Emp: 49. Officers: Richard K. Stone.

■ 11249 ■ General Mills Operations
500 W Walnut St.
Johnson City, TN 37604
Phone: (423)928-3137   Fax: (423)928-3821
Products: Flour and other grain mill products. SIC: 5149 (Groceries & Related Products Nec). Emp: 41. Officers: Fran Churchill, Plant Mgr.; Tim Vossberg, Distribution Mgr. Former Name: General Mills Inc.

■ 11250 ■ General Potato and Onion Inc.
PO Box 630
Stockton, CA 95201
Phone: (209)464-4621   Fax: (209)464-2170
Products: Potatoes and onions. SIC: 5148 (Fresh Fruits & Vegetables). Est: 1931. Sales: $2,000,000 (2000). Emp: 21. Officers: T. Cumberlege, President; Henry Ebstein, Treasurer & Secty.

■ 11251 ■ General Produce Company Ltd.
PO Box 308
Sacramento, CA 95812-0308
Phone: (916)441-6431
Free: (800)366-4985   Fax: (916)441-2483
Products: Fresh fruits and vegetables. SIC: 5148 (Fresh Fruits & Vegetables). Sales: $26,000,000 (2000). Emp: 200. Officers: T. Chan, President; D. Chan, VP of Finance.

■ 11252 ■ General Trading Company Inc.
455 16th St.
Carlstadt, NJ 07072
Phone: (201)935-7717   Fax: (201)438-6353
E-mail: gentrad@worldnet.att.net
URL: http://www.generaltradingcoinc.com
Products: General line groceries, including dairy and deli products; Cigarettes; Health and beauty aids. SICs: 5141 (Groceries—General Line); 5122 (Drugs, Proprietaries & Sundries); 5194 (Tobacco & Tobacco Products). Est: 1935. Sales: $300,000,000 (2000). Emp: 400. Officers: George Abad, President; Jerry Goetting, Controller; Cora Koch, Human Resources Mgr.; Mary Leonard; Phil Roland, Sales/Marketing Contact; Kim Lipscomb, Customer Service Contact; Carole Tirella, Human Resources Contact. Alternate Name: Jonathan Abad.

■ 11253 ■ Genesee Natural Foods
Rd. 2, Box 105
Genesee, PA 16923
Phone: (814)228-3200
Free: (800)445-0094   Fax: (814)228-3638
Products: Health foods. SIC: 5149 (Groceries & Related Products Nec). Est: 1979.

■ 11254 ■ William George Co., Inc.
1002 Mize Ave.
Lufkin, TX 75901-0102
Phone: (409)634-7738   Fax: (409)634-9148
Products: Food service supplies. SICs: 5149 (Groceries & Related Products Nec); 5113 (Industrial & Personal Service Paper); 5148 (Fresh Fruits & Vegetables). Est: 1932. Emp: 99. Officers: Randy George.

■ 11255 ■ Gerber Agri-Export Inc.
1640 Powers Ferry Rd., Bldg. 29, Ste. 200
Marietta, GA 30067
Phone: (404)952-4187   Fax: (404)952-3290
Products: Fresh vegetables; Meats. SICs: 5147 (Meats & Meat Products); 5148 (Fresh Fruits & Vegetables). Officers: D. Threatte, Vice President.

■ 11256 ■ Gerber Cheese Company Inc.
175 Clearbrook Rd.
Elmsford, NY 10523-1109
Products: Specialty cheeses and foods, including swiss and processed cheeses. SICs: 5143 (Dairy Products Except Dried or Canned); 5149 (Groceries & Related Products Nec). Est: 1920. Sales: $1,000,000 (2000). Emp: 4. Officers: Martin P. Whalen, President; Rudolf W. Kern, CFO; James DeLaurentis, Dir. of Marketing & Sales; Kathleen O'Farrell, Dir. of Information Systems.

■ 11257 ■ Gerlach Beef Inc.
841 Washington
New York, NY 10014-1307
Phone: (212)255-4750   Fax: (212)645-2515
Products: Meat, including provision, poultry and game. SIC: 5147 (Meats & Meat Products). Est: 1977. Emp: 6.

■ 11258 ■ Getchell Brothers Inc.
1 Union St.
Brewer, ME 04412
Phone: (207)989-7335
Products: Ice cream and frozen desserts. SIC: 5143 (Dairy Products Except Dried or Canned).

■ 11259 ■ GFG Foodservice Inc.
PO Box 14489
Grand Forks, ND 58208-4489
Phone: (701)795-5900   Free: (800)434-9950
Products: General line of groceries. SIC: 5141 (Groceries—General Line). Sales: $100,000,000 (2000). Emp: 290. Officers: James D. Kennelly, CEO.

■ 11260 ■ GFI America Inc.
2815 Blaisdell Ave. S
Minneapolis, MN 55408
Phone: (612)872-6262   Fax: (612)870-4955
Products: Beef. SIC: 5147 (Meats & Meat Products). Sales: $400,000,000 (2000). Emp: 499. Officers: Bob Goldberg. Former Name: Foldberger Foods Inc.

■ 11261 ■ Ghiselli Brothers
625 Du Bois St., No. A-B
San Rafael, CA 94901-3944
Phone: (415)282-7303   Fax: (415)282-0103
Products: Fresh fruits and vegetables. SIC: 5148 (Fresh Fruits & Vegetables). Officers: Mark Hansen, Export Sales.

■ 11262 ■ J.T. Gibbons Inc.
649 Papworth Ave.
Metairie, LA 70005
Phone: (504)831-9907   Fax: (504)837-5516
E-mail: gibbons@gibbonsinc.com
URL: http://www.gibbonsinc.com
Products: Groceries; Paper bags and liners; Aluminum foil; Cosmetic and toilet preparations; Agricultural chemicals, including rodenticides; Health and beauty aids. SICs: 5149 (Groceries & Related Products Nec); 5113 (Industrial & Personal Service Paper); 5122 (Drugs, Proprietaries & Sundries); 5169 (Chemicals & Allied Products Nec). Est: 1862. Emp: 10. Officers: Richard M. Keeney, President, e-mail: rkeeney@gibbonsinc.com; Blanca Solorzano, Sales/Marketing Contact, e-mail: bsolorzano@gibbonsinc.com; Art Schott, Human Resources Contact, e-mail: aschott@gibbonsinc.com.

■ 11263 ■ Gilbert Foods Inc.
7251 Standard Dr.
Hanover, MD 21076
Phone: (410)712-6000   Fax: (410)712-6058
Products: Bulk and precut fruit, vegetables, meat, seafood and dairy. SICs: 5148 (Fresh Fruits & Vegetables); 5147 (Meats & Meat Products); 5146 (Fish & Seafoods). Est: 1946. Sales: $30,000,000 (1999). Emp: 150. Officers: Charles Gilbert, President; Peter Gilbert, CEO; Trish McCawley, Vice President.

■ 11264 ■ Gilco Meats Inc.
1111 Greenwood Rd.
Baltimore, MD 21208
Phone: (410)484-3900
Products: Meat for hotels and restaurants. SIC: 5147 (Meats & Meat Products). Est: 1966. Sales: $3,000,000 (2000). Emp: 16. Officers: Peter Gilbert, CEO; Charles Gilbert, President.

■ 11265 ■ Gillies Coffee Co.
PO Box 320206
Brooklyn, NY 11232-1005
Phone: (718)499-7766
Free: (800)344-5526   Fax: (718)499-7771
E-mail: Gilliescoffee@mindspring.com
Products: Coffee. SIC: 5149 (Groceries & Related Products Nec). Est: 1840. Sales: $5,000,000 (2000). Emp: 25. Officers: Donald N. Schoenholt, CEO & President; Hy Chabbott, VP & CFO.

■ 11266 ■ Ginsbergs Institutional Food Service Supplies Inc.
Rte. 66
PO Box 17
Hudson, NY 12534
Phone: (518)828-4004
Free: (800)999-6006   Fax: (518)828-2630
E-mail: ginsbergs@taconic.net
URL: http://www.ginsbergs.com
Products: Food service supplies. SIC: 5141 (Groceries—General Line). Est: 1905. Sales: $60,000,000 (2000). Emp: 180. Officers: David M. Ginsberg, President; Ira M. Ginsberg, Exec. VP; Suzanne Rajczi, VP of Merchandising; Greg Grazian, VP of Operations.

■ 11267 ■ Giumarra Brothers Fruit Company, Inc.
PO Box 21218
Los Angeles, CA 90021-1218
Phone: (213)627-2900   Fax: (213)628-4878
Products: Fruits and vegetables. SIC: 5148 (Fresh Fruits & Vegetables). Est: 1950. Sales: $70,000,000 (2000). Emp: 40. Officers: Donald J. Corsaro, President; Ted Nakamura, Vice President; Tom Uchizono, Vice President; William E. Clausen, Exec. VP.

■ 11268 ■ Glacier Seafoods
7930 King St.
Anchorage, AK 99518-3058
Phone: (907)258-1234   Fax: (907)258-4949
Products: Food. SIC: 5146 (Fish & Seafoods).

■ 11269 ■ Glen Rose Meat Services Inc.
PO Box 58146
Vernon, CA 90058
Phone: (213)589-3393   Fax: (213)589-3712
Products: Ham, bacon and other smoked pork products, beef and poultry. SIC: 5147 (Meats & Meat Products). Sales: $30,000,000 (2000). Emp: 26. Officers: Glen Rose, President; Peter Waxler, Vice President.

■ 11270 ■ Glencourt Inc.
2800 Ygnacio Valley Rd.
Walnut Creek, CA 94598
Phone: (925)944-4444   Fax: (925)944-4009
Products: Grocery and beverage products. SIC: 5141 (Groceries—General Line). Sales: $460,000,000

(2000). **Emp:** 2,100. **Officers:** Lawrence Jackson, President.

■ **11271** ■ **Gliers Meats Inc.**
533 W 11th St.
PO Box 1052
Covington, KY 41011
Phone: (606)291-1800 **Fax:** (606)291-1846
E-mail: sales@goetta.com
URL: http://www.goetta.com
Products: Lunch meats; Hot dogs; Specialty sausages. **SIC:** 5147 (Meats & Meat Products). **Est:** 1946. **Sales:** $2,500,000 (2000). **Emp:** 19. **Officers:** Dan Glier, President. **Alternate Name:** Gliers Specialty Hams.

■ **11272** ■ **Global Bakeries, Inc.**
13336 Paxton St.
Pacoima, CA 91331-2339
Phone: (818)896-0525 **Fax:** (818)896-3237
Products: Bread, bagels, croissants, and related products. **SIC:** 5149 (Groceries & Related Products Nec). **Est:** 1984. **Sales:** $16,000,000 (2000). **Emp:** 130. **Officers:** Albert Boyajian, President; Onnig Hamalian, General Mgr.; Ray Rubio, Sales Mgr.; Rose Bagdasaryan, Customer Service Mgr.; Mimi Haddad, Human Resources Contact.

■ **11273** ■ **Global Tropical**
91 Brooklyn Terminal Market
Brooklyn, NY 11236
Phone: (718)763-4603 **Fax:** (718)531-7467
Products: Bananas. **SIC:** 5148 (Fresh Fruits & Vegetables). **Emp:** 65. **Officers:** Emil Serafino.

■ **11274** ■ **Globe Trends Inc.**
PO Box 461
Chatham, NJ 07928
Phone: (973)984-7444
Free: (800)416-8327 **Fax:** (973)984-7422
E-mail: taylorstea@aol.com
Products: Gourmet foods; Tea. **SIC:** 5149 (Groceries & Related Products Nec). **Est:** 1990. **Sales:** $1,200,000 (1999). **Emp:** 8. **Officers:** Al Sharif, Director; Ellen Hall, Sales/Marketing Contact.

■ **11275** ■ **Glorybee Foods Inc.**
PO Box 2744
Eugene, OR 97402
Phone: (541)689-0913 **Fax:** (541)689-9692
Products: Processes and packages honey, molasses, maple syrup and sorghum; distributes food ingredients; flavored honey sticks, bee pollen and royal jelly. **SIC:** 5149 (Groceries & Related Products Nec).

■ **11276** ■ **Gloucester County Packing Co.**
Evergreen & Glassboro
Woodbury, NJ 08096-7178
Phone: (609)845-0195
Products: Potatoes; Onions. **SIC:** 5148 (Fresh Fruits & Vegetables). **Est:** 1950. **Sales:** $9,000,000 (2000). **Emp:** 25. **Officers:** David L. Budd, President.

■ **11277** ■ **Glover Wholesale Inc.**
PO Box 484
Columbus, GA 31902
Phone: (706)324-3647 **Fax:** (706)324-0607
Products: Beef; Corn; Paper goods, including toilet paper and napkins. **SICs:** 5141 (Groceries—General Line); 5113 (Industrial & Personal Service Paper); 5148 (Fresh Fruits & Vegetables). **Est:** 1892. **Sales:** $25,000,000 (2000). **Emp:** 91. **Officers:** Wally S. Summers, President; William S. Harris Jr., Exec. VP; Mark Barrett, Manager; Brenda Law, Dir. of Data Processing.

■ **11278** ■ **GNS Foods Inc.**
2109 E Division St.
Arlington, TX 76011
Phone: (817)795-4671
Products: Nuts and dried fruit products. **SICs:** 5145 (Confectionery); 5148 (Fresh Fruits & Vegetables); 5149 (Groceries & Related Products Nec).

■ **11279** ■ **Gold Medal Bakery Inc.**
21 Penn St.
Fall River, MA 02724
Phone: (508)674-5766
Products: Bakery products. **SIC:** 5149 (Groceries &

Related Products Nec). **Sales:** $8,000,000 (2000). **Emp:** 275. **Officers:** John LeCompe, Owner.

■ **11280** ■ **Gold Star Dairy**
6901 I-30
Little Rock, AR 72209
Phone: (501)568-6237 **Fax:** (501)568-5245
Products: Dairy products. **SIC:** 5143 (Dairy Products Except Dried or Canned). **Sales:** $50,000,000 (2000). **Emp:** 99. **Officers:** Walt Coleman, General Mgr.; David Peters, Sales Mgr.

■ **11281** ■ **Goldberg and Solovy Food Inc.**
5925 S Alcoa Ave.
Vernon, CA 90058
Phone: (213)581-6161 **Fax:** (213)583-8629
E-mail: gsfoods@aol.com
Products: Meat; Poultry; Seafood; Frozen and canned foods. **SICs:** 5149 (Groceries & Related Products Nec); 5142 (Packaged Frozen Foods); 5144 (Poultry & Poultry Products); 5146 (Fish & Seafoods). **Est:** 1978. **Sales:** $60,000,000 (2000). **Emp:** 275. **Officers:** Michael Solovy, President; Essy Fisher, Controller; Dennis Hajjar, General Mgr.; Kyle Koestner, Dir. of Sales; Lori Zavala, Customer Service Mgr.; Ed Garidia, Dir of Human Resources.

■ **11282** ■ **Golden Boy Pies Inc.**
4945 Hadley St.
Overland Park, KS 66203-1329
Phone: (913)384-6460
Free: (800)634-7284 **Fax:** (913)384-3352
E-mail: gbp@birch.net
Products: Bakery products, including bread, cake, and pies. **SIC:** 5149 (Groceries & Related Products Nec). **Est:** 1973. **Sales:** $2,500,000 (2000). **Emp:** 32. **Officers:** Terry D. Hunt, President; Nancy J. Williams, Exec. VP; Connie Campbell, Sales Mgr.; Pat Hamilton, Customer Service Mgr.

■ **11283** ■ **Golden Capital Distributors**
6610 Cabot Dr.
Baltimore, MD 21226
Phone: (410)360-1300 **Fax:** (410)360-1019
Products: Groceries; Cleaning supplies. **SICs:** 5141 (Groceries—General Line); 5169 (Chemicals & Allied Products Nec). **Sales:** $1,000,000,000 (2000). **Emp:** 1,100. **Officers:** Dennis Lowry, President.

■ **11284** ■ **Golden Peanut Co. De Leon Div.**
PO Box 226
De Leon, TX 76444
Phone: (254)893-2071
Products: Peanuts. **SIC:** 5145 (Confectionery). **Est:** 1912. **Sales:** $6,000,000 (2000). **Emp:** 20. **Officers:** Milton Smith, General Mgr.

■ **11285** ■ **Golden Poultry Company Inc.**
PO Box 2210
Atlanta, GA 30301
Phone: (404)393-5000 **Fax:** (404)393-5347
Products: Frozen poultry, including chicken and ducks. **SIC:** 5144 (Poultry & Poultry Products). **Est:** 1982. **Sales:** $600,200,000 (2000). **Emp:** 5,658. **Officers:** Kenneth N. Whitmire, CEO; Langley C. Thomas Jr., CFO & Treasurer; Mike Thrailkill, VP of Information Systems; Andy Epperson, VP of Human Resources.

■ **11286** ■ **Golden Pride International**
PO Box 21109
West Palm Beach, FL 33416-1109
Phone: (561)640-5700
Products: Food supplements, skin care products, cosmetics, herbs and household items. **SIC:** 5122 (Drugs, Proprietaries & Sundries). **Sales:** $30,900,000 (2000). **Emp:** 45. **Officers:** Harry W. Hersey, Owner; Betsy Stockdill, Exec. VP of Finance.

■ **11287** ■ **Golden State Foods Corp.**
1391 Progress Rd.
Suffolk, VA 23434-2154
Phone: (757)538-8068
Products: Food for McDonald's restaurants. **SIC:** 5141 (Groceries—General Line). **Emp:** 99. **Officers:** Joe Michel.

■ **11288** ■ **Morris J. Golombeck Inc.**
960 Franklin Ave.
Brooklyn, NY 11225
Phone: (718)284-3505 **Fax:** (718)693-1941
E-mail: golspice@aol.com
Products: Spices. **SIC:** 5149 (Groceries & Related Products Nec). **Est:** 1931. **Sales:** $10,000,000 (2000). **Emp:** 18. **Officers:** H.P. Golombeck, President & Treasurer.

■ **11289** ■ **Good Food Inc.**
4960 Horseshoe Pke.
Box 160
Honey Brook, PA 19344
Phone: (610)273-3776
Free: (800)327-4406 **Fax:** (610)273-2087
E-mail: goodfood@goldenbarrel.com
Products: Syrups; Molasses; Cooking oils; Sugars. **SIC:** 5149 (Groceries & Related Products Nec). **Est:** 1980. **Sales:** $25,000,000 (2000). **Emp:** 49. **Officers:** Larry Martin, President.

■ **11290** ■ **Good Health Natural Foods Inc.**
81 Scudder Ave.
Northport, NY 11768
Phone: (631)261-2111 **Fax:** (631)261-2147
E-mail: frank@e-goodhealth.com
URL: http://www.e-goodhealth.com
Products: Snack foods, including apple chips, flavored popcorn, peanut butter pretzels, potato chips, veggie sticks, and crackers; Candy. **SICs:** 5149 (Groceries & Related Products Nec); 5145 (Confectionery). **Est:** 1993. **Emp:** 5.

■ **11291** ■ **Goodson Farms Inc.**
PO Box 246
Balm, FL 33503
Phone: (813)634-6679
Products: Vegetables, including peppers and cauliflower. **SIC:** 5148 (Fresh Fruits & Vegetables). **Est:** 1988. **Sales:** $6,000,000 (2000). **Emp:** 20. **Officers:** Don Goodson, President.

■ **11292** ■ **Gordon Food Company Inc.**
PO Box 41534
Memphis, TN 38174
Phone: (901)523-0077
Products: Deli meats; Cheeses; Specialty items. **SICs:** 5143 (Dairy Products Except Dried or Canned); 5147 (Meats & Meat Products). **Est:** 1981. **Sales:** $4,000,000 (2000). **Emp:** 8. **Officers:** Michael J. Gordon, President.

■ **11293** ■ **Gordon Food Service Inc.**
PO Box 1787
Grand Rapids, MI 49501
Phone: (616)530-7000 **Fax:** (616)249-4165
Products: Full line food service. **SICs:** 5141 (Groceries—General Line); 5046 (Commercial Equipment Nec). **Est:** 1942. **Sales:** $1,970,400,000 (1999). **Emp:** 4,200. **Officers:** Daniel Gordon, President; Steve Plakmeyer, Exec. VP of Finance I/T, Stores; Dave Dow, Exec VP of Sales Procurement, H/R, e-mail: ddow@gfs.com; David Vickery, Human Resources Contact, e-mail: dvickery@gfs.com.

■ **11294** ■ **Slade Gorton & Co., Inc.**
225 Southampton St.
Boston, MA 02118
Phone: (617)442-5800
Free: (800)225-1573 **Fax:** (617)541-3189
E-mail: info@sladegorton.com
URL: http://www.sladegorton.com
Products: Seafood. **SIC:** 5146 (Fish & Seafoods). **Est:** 1929. **Officers:** Slade Gorton Jr., Founder.

■ **11295** ■ **Slade Gorton and Company Inc.**
225 Southampton St.
Boston, MA 02118
Phone: (617)442-5800
Free: (800)225-1573 **Fax:** (617)442-9090
Products: Fresh and frozen seafood. **SIC:** 5146 (Fish & Seafoods). **Sales:** $34,000,000 (1999). **Emp:** 150. **Officers:** Michael C. Gorton, CEO & Chairman of the Board; James W. Stauffer, CFO.

■ 11296 ■ **Gourmet Award Foods**
PO Box 12579
Albany, NY 12212-2579
Phone: (518)456-1888
Free: (800)669-1880 **Fax:** (518)456-1429
Products: Food. **SIC:** 5141 (Groceries—General Line).

■ 11297 ■ **Gourmet Award Foods Tree of Life Inc.**
2050 Elm St. SE
Minneapolis, MN 55414-2531
Products: Specialty foods. **SIC:** 5149 (Groceries & Related Products Nec). **Est:** 1960. **Sales:** $60,000,000 (2000). **Emp:** 250. **Officers:** Douglas M. Rotchadl, President.

■ 11298 ■ **Gourmet Regency Coffee Inc.**
5500 Cottonwood Lane
Prior Lake, MN 55372
Phone: (612)226-4100 **Fax:** (612)226-4106
Products: Coffee. **SIC:** 5149 (Groceries & Related Products Nec). **Sales:** $3,000,000 (2000). **Emp:** 20. **Officers:** William Kirkpatrick, President.

■ 11299 ■ **Gourmet Specialties**
21001 Cabot Blvd.
Hayward, CA 94545
Phone: (510)887-7322
Free: (800)824-8948 **Fax:** (510)887-4203
Products: Gourmet food, including noodles, nuts, and candy. **SICs:** 5141 (Groceries—General Line); 5145 (Confectionery). **Emp:** 125.

■ 11300 ■ **GPOD of Idaho**
PO Box 514
Shelley, ID 83274
Phone: (208)357-7646
Products: Fresh potatoes. **SIC:** 5148 (Fresh Fruits & Vegetables). **Est:** 1957. **Sales:** $54,000,000 (2000). **Emp:** 150. **Officers:** Bob Wilkins, General Mgr.

■ 11301 ■ **Gracewood Fruit Co.**
PO Box 370
Vero Beach, FL 32961
Phone: (561)567-1151 **Fax:** (561)567-2719
Products: Fresh fruit. **SIC:** 5148 (Fresh Fruits & Vegetables). **Sales:** $16,000,000 (2000). **Emp:** 350. **Officers:** John M. Luther, CEO; Gary M. Rust, CFO.

■ 11302 ■ **Graf Creamery Co.**
N 4051 Creamery St.
PO Box 49
Zachow, WI 54182-0049
Phone: (715)758-2137 **Fax:** (715)758-8020
Products: Butter and cheese. **SIC:** 5143 (Dairy Products Except Dried or Canned). **Sales:** $20,000,000 (2000). **Emp:** 35. **Officers:** James Bleick, President; Margery Bleick, Vice President; Ruth Suski, Sec. & Treas.

■ 11303 ■ **Gragnon Wholesale**
625 Weeks
New Iberia, LA 70560-5544
Phone: (318)364-6611 **Fax:** (318)364-6645
Products: General line groceries; Candy; Tobacco. **SICs:** 5141 (Groceries—General Line); 5145 (Confectionery); 5194 (Tobacco & Tobacco Products). **Est:** 1935. **Sales:** $14,500,000 (2000). **Emp:** 29. **Officers:** Paul G. Landry.

■ 11304 ■ **Grainland**
Rte. 1, Box 860
Eureka, IL 61530
Phone: (309)467-2355 **Fax:** (309)467-2357
Products: Grain elevator. **SIC:** 5153 (Grain & Field Beans). **Sales:** $15,800,000 (2000). **Emp:** 15. **Officers:** Ed Wyss, President; Jeff Brook, CFO.

■ 11305 ■ **Grand River Meat Center**
8428 Grand River
Detroit, MI 48204-2234
Phone: (313)898-6743 **Fax:** (313)858-2714
Products: Processed, frozen, and cooked meats; Milk; Bread. **SICs:** 5147 (Meats & Meat Products); 5143 (Dairy Products Except Dried or Canned); 5149 (Groceries & Related Products Nec). **Est:** 1957. **Sales:** $2,000,000 (2000). **Emp:** 49. **Officers:** L. N. Radden.

■ 11306 ■ **Grandma Brown's Beans Inc.**
PO Box 230
Mexico, NY 13114-0230
Phone: (315)963-7221 **Fax:** (315)963-4072
Products: Canned baked beans and canned soups. **SIC:** 5149 (Groceries & Related Products Nec). **Est:** 1938. **Sales:** $5,000,000 (2000). **Emp:** 20. **Officers:** Sandra L. Brown, President & CEO.

■ 11307 ■ **Grandma's Bake Shoppe**
201 S 5th St.
PO Box 457
Beatrice, NE 68310
Phone: (402)223-2358
Free: (800)228-4030 **Fax:** (402)223-4465
E-mail: rony@metzbaking.com
URL: http://www.grandmasbakeshoppe.com
Products: Fruit and dessert cakes. **SIC:** 5149 (Groceries & Related Products Nec). **Est:** 1964. **Emp:** 50. **Officers:** Greg Leech, General Mgr.; Ron Young, Marketing & Sales Mgr., e-mail: ryoung@metzbaking.com; Connie Warnsing, Sales Assistant; Merle Renner, General Mgr.

■ 11308 ■ **Granger Farmers Cooperative Creamery Association**
PO Box 67
Granger, MN 55939
Phone: (507)772-4433 **SIC:** 5143 (Dairy Products Except Dried or Canned). **Sales:** $1,000,000 (2000). **Emp:** 4. **Officers:** Benjamin Phillips, President.

■ 11309 ■ **Grapevine**
59 Maxwell Ct.
Santa Rosa, CA 95401
Phone: (707)576-3950 **Fax:** (707)576-3945
Products: Dried specialty foods, including vegetables, fruits, and nuts. **SIC:** 5149 (Groceries & Related Products Nec).

■ 11310 ■ **Grassland Dairy Products Inc.**
PO Box 160
Greenwood, WI 54437
Phone: (715)267-6182 **Fax:** (715)267-6044
Products: Butter; Butter oil. **SIC:** 5143 (Dairy Products Except Dried or Canned). **Est:** 1904. **Sales:** $120,000,000 (2000). **Emp:** 150. **Officers:** Dallas L. Wuethrich, President; Tayt Wuethrich, Treasurer & Secty.; Trevor Wuethrich, VP of Marketing; Darryl B. Maresch, Dir. of Systems; K. Steiger, Dir of Human Resources.

■ 11311 ■ **Great Health**
2663 Saturn St.
Brea, CA 92821-6703
Phone: (714)996-8600 **Fax:** (714)996-7494
Products: Health food. **SIC:** 5149 (Groceries & Related Products Nec).

■ 11312 ■ **Great Lakes Marketing Inc.**
2236G Bluemound Rd.
Waukesha, WI 53186-2919
Phone: (414)798-6800
Products: Food. **SIC:** 5141 (Groceries—General Line). **Sales:** $9,000,000 (2000). **Emp:** 25. **Officers:** Bruce Magolan, President; Ron Drought, CFO.

■ 11313 ■ **Great Northern Products Ltd.**
PO Box 7622
Warwick, RI 02887
Phone: (401)821-2400 **Fax:** (401)821-2419
E-mail: domestic@northernproducts.com
URL: http://www.northernproducts.com
Products: Food, including fruit, nuts, vegetables, and seafood. **SIC:** 5146 (Fish & Seafoods). **Est:** 1988. **Sales:** $50,000,000 (2000). **Emp:** 15. **Officers:** George Nolan; Tom Lucia, Sales/Marketing Contact, e-mail: tl@northernproducts.com.

■ 11314 ■ **Great Southwest Sales**
3311 81st St.
Lubbock, TX 79423
Phone: (806)792-9981 **Fax:** (806)792-9983
Products: Groceries and general merchandise, including gloves, soap, rice, and chili and picante sauces. **SICs:** 5141 (Groceries—General Line); 5149 (Groceries & Related Products Nec). **Emp:** 34. **Officers:** Robert McIntyre.

■ 11315 ■ **Great Western Meats**
437 W Kaley St.
Orlando, FL 32806
Phone: (407)841-4270 **Fax:** (407)841-4307
Products: Meats, including pork; Specialty food, including egg rolls and crab rengoon. **SICs:** 5147 (Meats & Meat Products); 5142 (Packaged Frozen Foods); 5149 (Groceries & Related Products Nec). **Emp:** 99. **Officers:** Richard Harris; Gregory P. Voorhees, President.

■ 11316 ■ **Great Western Meats Inc.**
PO Box 568366
Orlando, FL 32856
Phone: (407)841-4270
Products: Food and meat. **SICs:** 5141 (Groceries—General Line); 5147 (Meats & Meat Products). **Sales:** $34,000,000 (2000). **Emp:** 65. **Officers:** Richard Harris, CFO.

■ 11317 ■ **Great Western Products Inc.**
PO Box 466
Hollywood, AL 35752
Phone: (256)259-1079
Free: (800)239-2143 **Fax:** (256)574-2116
E-mail: info@gwproducts.com
URL: http://www.gwproducts.com
Products: Popcorn and popcorn oils; Concession supplies and equipment. **SICs:** 5145 (Confectionery); 5149 (Groceries & Related Products Nec). **Est:** 1977. **Sales:** $27,000,000 (2000). **Emp:** 128. **Officers:** Scott Martin, President.

■ 11318 ■ **Green Acre Farms Inc.**
PO Box 319
Sebastopol, MS 39359
Phone: (601)625-7432 **Fax:** (601)625-8880
Products: Chicken. **SIC:** 5144 (Poultry & Poultry Products). **Sales:** $67,200,000 (2000). **Emp:** 700. **Officers:** Howard Kerr, CEO; Kirk Wardlow, Controller; Sue Eddins, Dir. of Sales.

■ 11319 ■ **A.A. Green and Company Inc.**
3330 NW 125th St.
Miami, FL 33167
Phone: (305)685-7751
Products: Ice cream; Garbage bags; Frozen fish sticks; Cheese. **SICs:** 5141 (Groceries—General Line); 5143 (Dairy Products Except Dried or Canned).

■ 11320 ■ **M.H. Greenebaum Inc.**
PO Box 6192
Parsippany, NJ 07054
Phone: (973)538-9200 **Fax:** (973)538-3599
Products: Imported ham and cheese. **SICs:** 5143 (Dairy Products Except Dried or Canned); 5147 (Meats & Meat Products). **Est:** 1894. **Sales:** $21,000,000 (2000). **Emp:** 7. **Officers:** Ole Nielsen, President; Debra Sayer, CFO.

■ 11321 ■ **Greenleaf Produce**
1955 Jerrold Ave.
San Francisco, CA 94124-1603
Phone: (415)647-2991 **Fax:** (415)647-2996
Products: Fruits and vegetables. **SIC:** 5148 (Fresh Fruits & Vegetables). **Est:** 1955. **Officers:** Jameson Patton.

■ 11322 ■ **Greg Orchards & Produce Inc.**
4949 N Branch Rd.
Benton Harbor, MI 49022-0000
Phone: (616)944-1414 **Fax:** (616)944-5754
Products: Fresh fruits. **SIC:** 5148 (Fresh Fruits & Vegetables). **Sales:** $6,000,000 (2000). **Emp:** 49. **Officers:** Barry L. Winkel.

■ 11323 ■ **Greg's Cookies Inc.**
4500 1st Ave. N
Birmingham, AL 35222
Phone: (205)595-4627 **Fax:** (205)545-4629
Products: Cookies. **SIC:** 5149 (Groceries & Related Products Nec). **Sales:** $18,000,000 (2000). **Emp:** 171. **Officers:** Kevin R. Mooi.

■ **11324** ■ **Griffin and Brand Produce Sales Agency Inc.**
PO Box 833
Hereford, TX 79045
Phone: (806)364-1610 **Fax:** (806)364-7811
Products: Fresh fruits and vegetables. **SIC:** 5148 (Fresh Fruits & Vegetables). **Sales:** $15,000,000 (2000). **Emp:** 100. **Officers:** A.T. Griffin, President.

■ **11325** ■ **Griffin & Brand Sales Agency, Inc.**
PO Box 833
Hereford, TX 79045
Phone: (806)364-1610 **Fax:** (806)364-7811
Products: Potatoes and onions. **SIC:** 5148 (Fresh Fruits & Vegetables). **Emp:** 49. **Officers:** A. T. Griffin.

■ **11326** ■ **Griffin-Holder Co.**
PO Box 511
Rocky Ford, CO 81067
Phone: (719)254-3363
Products: Onions. **SIC:** 5148 (Fresh Fruits & Vegetables). **Est:** 1960. **Sales:** $4,000,000 (2000). **Emp:** 20. **Officers:** Hal Holder, President; Dallas Geist, Controller.

■ **11327** ■ **Griffin Manufacturing**
Box 1928
Muskogee, OK 74402
Phone: (918)687-6311
Free: (800)866-6311 **Fax:** (918)687-3579
E-mail: griffin@ok.azalea.net
URL: http://www.griffinfoods.com
Products: Groceries. **SIC:** 5141 (Groceries—General Line). **Est:** 1908. **Sales:** $13,000,000 (1999). **Emp:** 60. **Officers:** John Griffin, President & CEO; D.C. Smith, Sales Mgr., e-mail: griffin@ok.azalea.net; Melinda Horton, Order Entry/Customer Service, e-mail: mhorton@muskogeeok.com; Carol Winn, Human Resources Contact, e-mail: griffin@ok.azalea.net; John W. Griffin, President & CEO; Marti Killingsworth, Chairman of the Board & Finance Officer; Jim Heidenriech, Production Mgr.; D.C. Smith, Sales Mgr.

■ **11328** ■ **Grist Mill Co.**
21340 Hayes Ave.
PO Box 430
Lakeville, MN 55044
Phone: (612)469-4981 **Fax:** (612)469-5550
Products: Cereal and cereal bars; Pie crusts; Fruit snacks. **SICs:** 5149 (Groceries & Related Products Nec); 5145 (Confectionery). **Sales:** $98,400,000 (2000). **Emp:** 600. **Officers:** Ronald K. Zuckerman, Chairman & CEO; Glen S. Bolander, President & COO.

■ **11329** ■ **Grocers Specialty Co.**
5200 Shelia St.
Commerce, CA 90040
Phone: (213)726-2601
Products: General-line of groceries including specialty ethnic foods, candy,frozen foods and tobacco. **SICs:** 5141 (Groceries—General Line); 5145 (Confectionery); 5142 (Packaged Frozen Foods); 5194 (Tobacco & Tobacco Products). **Sales:** $110,000,000 (2000). **Emp:** 60. **Officers:** Alfred Plamann, CEO & President; Richard Martin, VP & CFO.

■ **11330** ■ **Grocers Supply Co.**
4310 Stout Field N Dr.
Indianapolis, IN 46241-4002
Phone: (317)243-6000 **Fax:** (317)244-8423
Products: Frozen and canned food. **SICs:** 5149 (Groceries & Related Products Nec); 5142 (Packaged Frozen Foods). **Est:** 1938. **Sales:** $80,000,000 (2000). **Emp:** 99. **Officers:** Ron Perkins, CEO; Sidney Sakowitz, Exec. VP.

■ **11331** ■ **Grocers Supply Company Inc.**
PO Box 14200
Houston, TX 77221
Phone: (713)747-5000 **Fax:** (713)749-9320
URL: http://www.grocerybiz.com; www.grocersupply.com
Products: Groceries and General merchandise. **SIC:** 5141 (Groceries—General Line). **Est:** 1926. **Sales:** $1,500,000,000 (1999). **Emp:** 1,800. **Officers:** Milton Levit, CEO; Jerry Levit, Vice President; Dave Hoffman Sr., VP of Sales; Jill Levit-Talisman, Sec. & Treas.; Tom Becker, Sr. VP of Buying; Bob Hart, Sr. VP of Warehouse & Transportation; Mike Castleberry, Sr. VP of Accounting.

■ **11332** ■ **Grocers Wholesale Co.**
105 Embarcadero
Oakland, CA 94606-5138
Phone: (415)826-1235 **Fax:** (415)285-4118
Products: Food preparations; Fruits and vegetables; Processed, frozen, or cooked meats; Canned specialties. **SICs:** 5141 (Groceries—General Line); 5149 (Groceries & Related Products Nec); 5142 (Packaged Frozen Foods); 5148 (Fresh Fruits & Vegetables). **Emp:** 19. **Officers:** Jauw Tan.

■ **11333** ■ **Grocery Supply Co.**
PO Box 638
Sulphur Springs, TX 75483-0638
Phone: (903)885-7621
Free: (800)231-1938 **Fax:** (903)439-3249
E-mail: jgillem@grocerysupply.com
URL: http://www.grocerysupply.com
Products: Groceries, tobacco, candy, deli, and health and beauty aids. **SICs:** 5141 (Groceries—General Line); 5194 (Tobacco & Tobacco Products); 5145 (Confectionery). **Est:** 1949. **Sales:** $450,000,000 (1999). **Emp:** 500. **Officers:** Jerry Gillem, Division Mgr.; Jerry Jackson, Controller, e-mail: jjackson@grocerysupply.com.

■ **11334** ■ **Grocery Supply Co., Inc.**
2330 Roosevelt Ave.
San Antonio, TX 78210
Phone: (210)533-1281 **Fax:** (210)533-3006
Products: Groceries, including canned vegetables, soups, cereals, powdered juices, frozen vegetables, and meats. **SIC:** 5141 (Groceries—General Line). **Est:** 1922. **Sales:** $200,000,000 (2000). **Emp:** 400. **Officers:** David E. Spencer, President; Robert B. Cody, Controller; Jerry Donaho, Dir. of Systems. **Former Name:** Sweeney & Co.

■ **11335** ■ **Grocery Supply Company - Southeast**
PO Box 17209
Pensacola, FL 32522
Phone: (850)438-9651 **Fax:** (850)469-8691
URL: http://www.grocerysupply.com
Products: Groceries. **SIC:** 5141 (Groceries—General Line). **Est:** 1972. **Sales:** $350,000,000 (1999). **Emp:** 350. **Officers:** Henry H. Huelsbeck, Division President; Roger D. Noble, Division VP & Controller; Pat Johnson, Sales/Marketing Contact; Claire Alger, Customer Service Contact; Bill Scallan, Human Resources Contact.

■ **11336** ■ **Groff Meats Inc.**
33 N Market St.
Elizabethtown, PA 17022-2039
Phone: (717)367-1246
Products: Processed, frozen, or cooked meats, including bologna and mincemeat. **SIC:** 5147 (Meats & Meat Products). **Est:** 1875. **Sales:** $6,000,000 (2000). **Emp:** 40. **Officers:** Joseph G. Groff.

■ **11337** ■ **Grower Shipper Potato Co.**
PO Box 432
Monte Vista, CO 81144-0432
Phone: (719)852-3569
Products: Potatoes. **SIC:** 5148 (Fresh Fruits & Vegetables). **Est:** 1941. **Sales:** $5,000,000 (2000). **Emp:** 55. **Officers:** Bill Riggenbach, President; Ken Shepherd, General Mgr.

■ **11338** ■ **Growers Marketing Service Inc.**
PO Box 2595
Lakeland, FL 33806
Phone: (941)644-2414
Free: (800)476-2037 **Fax:** (941)647-1086
Products: Watermelons. **SIC:** 5148 (Fresh Fruits & Vegetables). **Est:** 1938. **Sales:** $4,000,000 (2000). **Emp:** 10. **Officers:** W.R. Ward Jr., President & Treasurer.

■ **11339** ■ **Growers Precooler Inc.**
2880 Lust Rd.
Apopka, FL 32703
Phone: (407)889-4000 **Fax:** (407)889-2552
Products: Carrots. **SIC:** 5148 (Fresh Fruits & Vegetables). **Emp:** 99. **Officers:** Rex Clonts, President; Kent Crakes, Vice President; Scott Stroup, Treasurer & Secty.; Claire Wright.

■ **11340** ■ **Grower's Produce Corp.**
380 3rd St.
Oakland, CA 94607
Phone: (510)834-5280
Products: Fruits and vegetables. **SIC:** 5148 (Fresh Fruits & Vegetables). **Sales:** $23,000,000 (1993). **Emp:** 75. **Officers:** Hideo Uchiyama, CEO; Anthony Marr, Controller.

■ **11341** ■ **GSC Enterprises Inc.**
PO Box 638
Sulphur Springs, TX 75483-0638
Phone: (903)885-7621 **Fax:** (903)885-6928
URL: http://www.grocerysupply.com
Products: General line groceries. **SIC:** 5141 (Groceries—General Line). **Est:** 1947. **Sales:** $1,110,000,000 (1999). **Emp:** 1,300. **Officers:** Michael K. McKenzie, CEO & Chairman of the Board; Kerry Law, CFO; Larry Kerns, COO & President.

■ **11342** ■ **GSC Enterprises Inc.**
PO Box 638
Sulphur Springs, TX 75483-0638
Phone: (903)885-0829 **Fax:** (903)885-6928
Products: Groceries and tobacco products. **SICs:** 5141 (Groceries—General Line); 5194 (Tobacco & Tobacco Products). **Sales:** $1,000,000,000 (2000). **Emp:** 2,000. **Officers:** Michael K. McKenzie, CEO & Chairman of the Board; Kerry Law, VP & CFO.

■ **11343** ■ **Guernsey Farms Dairy**
21300 Novi Rd.
Northville, MI 48167-9701
Phone: (248)349-1466 **Fax:** (248)349-1975
Products: Dairy products, including milk, ice cream, butter, eggs, and cheese. **SIC:** 5143 (Dairy Products Except Dried or Canned). **Sales:** $6,000,000 (2000). **Emp:** 49. **Officers:** John McGuire.

■ **11344** ■ **Gulf Central Seafoods Inc.**
155 5th St.
Biloxi, MS 39530
Phone: (228)436-6346 **Fax:** (228)374-1207
Products: Frozen and canned shrimp. **SIC:** 5146 (Fish & Seafoods). **Sales:** $6,000,000 (2000). **Emp:** 49. **Officers:** Rock Sekul.

■ **11345** ■ **Gulf Go-Fers Inc.**
2136 Corporation Blvd.
Naples, FL 34109-2053
Phone: (941)591-1353
Products: Sandwiches, including ham and cheese, turkey, and roast beef. **SIC:** 5149 (Groceries & Related Products Nec).

■ **11346** ■ **Gulf Marine and Industrial Supplies**
401 St. Joseph St.
New Orleans, LA 70130
Phone: (504)525-6252 **Fax:** (504)525-4761
Products: Food; Medicinal products; Transportation equipment hardware; Rope. **SICs:** 5141 (Groceries—General Line); 5149 (Groceries & Related Products Nec); 5072 (Hardware); 5122 (Drugs, Proprietaries & Sundries). **Est:** 1952. **Sales:** $20,000,000 (2000). **Emp:** 60. **Officers:** S.J. Cotsoradis; Clyde Merritt.

■ **11347** ■ **Gulf Pacific Rice Company Inc.**
12010 Taylor Rd.
Houston, TX 77041-1222
Phone: (713)464-0606
Products: Rice. **SIC:** 5153 (Grain & Field Beans). **Sales:** $11,000,000 (2000). **Emp:** 13. **Officers:** Fred Brenchman, President.

■ **11348** ■ **H and F Food Products Inc.**
321 Ramsdell Ave.
Buffalo, NY 14216
Phone: (716)876-4345 **Fax:** (716)876-7455
Products: Olives and peppers. **SIC:** 5144 (Poultry & Poultry Products). **Sales:** $1,300,000 (2000). **Emp:** 4. **Officers:** Thomas Amabile, President.

■ 11349 ■ **H & H Foodservice**
304 S Vine
PO Box 494
West Union, IA 52175-0494
Phone: (319)422-3846
Free: (800)747-5915 **Fax:** (319)422-3296
E-mail: h&hfoodservice@hhfoodservice.com
URL: http://www.hhfoodservice.com
Products: Institutional canned, frozen, and fresh foods;
Food preparation equipment. **SICs:** 5141 (Groceries—
General Line); 5046 (Commercial Equipment Nec).
Est: 1946. **Sales:** $32,000,000 (2000). **Emp:** 96.
Officers: Ruth L. Hansen; Sandra K. Baldwin, e-mail:
sbaldwin@hhfoodservice.com.

■ 11350 ■ **H and H Meat Products Company Inc.**
PO Box 358
Mercedes, TX 78570
Phone: (210)565-6363 **Fax:** (210)565-4108
Products: Meats; Poultry; Seafood. **SICs:** 5149
(Groceries & Related Products Nec); 5144 (Poultry &
Poultry Products); 5146 (Fish & Seafoods). **Est:** 1947.
Sales: $67,000,000 (2000). **Emp:** 320. **Officers:**
Liborio Hinojosa, CEO & Chairman of the Board;
Ruben E. Hinojosa, President; Rene Hinojosa Sr., VP &
Treasurer; Cliferd Menezes, Director; Erlinda Cavazos,
Dir of Personnel.

■ 11351 ■ **H and N Fish Co.**
2390 Jerrold Ave.
San Francisco, CA 94124
Phone: (415)821-6637
Products: Fish. **SIC:** 5146 (Fish & Seafoods).

■ 11352 ■ **H n' M Associates Inc.**
4520 E West Hwy., Ste. 300
Bethesda, MD 20814-3347
Phone: (301)776-9222
Products: Food. **SICs:** 5141 (Groceries—General
Line); 5142 (Packaged Frozen Foods). **Sales:**
$6,000,000 (1993). **Emp:** 12. **Officers:** Hans
Rosenfeld, President; John LaHart, Exec. VP of
Finance.

■ 11353 ■ **Habbersett Sausage Inc.**
PO Box 146
Folcroft, PA 19032
Phone: (610)532-9973 **Fax:** (610)586-2396
Products: Sausages and other prepared meat
products. **SIC:** 5147 (Meats & Meat Products). **Sales:**
$9,000,000 (2000). **Emp:** 12. **Officers:** Walt Crouse,
General Mgr.

■ 11354 ■ **Habys Sales Candy Co.**
PO Box 1612
Castroville, TX 78009-9402
Phone: (512)538-3164
Products: Cigarettes; Candy; Canned goods;
Beverages. **SICs:** 5145 (Confectionery); 5149
(Groceries & Related Products Nec); 5194 (Tobacco &
Tobacco Products). **Emp:** 3.

■ 11355 ■ **H.T. Hackney Co.**
PO Box 238
Knoxville, TN 37901
Phone: (423)546-1291 **Fax:** (615)546-1501
Products: General line groceries. **SIC:** 5141
(Groceries—General Line). **Est:** 1891. **Sales:**
$800,000,000 (2000). **Emp:** 1,900. **Officers:** William
Sansom, CEO & Chairman of the Board; Michael
Morton, Finance Officer; Dean Ballinger, VP of
Operations; Leonard Robinette, VP of Information
Systems.

■ 11356 ■ **Haddon House Food Products Inc.**
PO Box 907
Medford, NJ 08055
Phone: (609)654-7901 **Fax:** (609)654-0412
Products: Non-perishable gourmet foods. **SIC:** 5149
(Groceries & Related Products Nec).

■ 11357 ■ **Hadley Braithwait Co.**
2519 11th St.
Columbus, NE 68601-5723
Phone: (402)564-7279
Products: Paper goods or products, including book
mailers; Candy; Tobacco; Cigarettes; Canned
vegetables. **SICs:** 5145 (Confectionery); 5194
(Tobacco & Tobacco Products); 5113 (Industrial &
Personal Service Paper); 5149 (Groceries & Related
Products Nec). **Emp:** 13.

■ 11358 ■ **Raymond Hadley Corp.**
89 Tompkins St.
Spencer, NY 14883
Phone: (607)589-4415
Free: (800)252-5220 **Fax:** (607)589-6442
E-mail: hadnew@lightlink.com
Products: Dried beans and peas; Hot cereals;
Specialty foods. **SICs:** 5153 (Grain & Field Beans);
5149 (Groceries & Related Products Nec). **Est:** 1892.
Emp: 20. **Officers:** Lori E. Maratea, President; Tracy
McLutcheon, Sales; Elliot Dutra, Co-Mgr.,
Sales/Purchasing; Christine Baglivio, Treas., Ofc. Mgr.

■ 11359 ■ **Hahn Bros. Inc.**
PO Box 407
Westminster, MD 21158
Phone: (410)848-4200 **Fax:** (410)848-1247
E-mail: pigs@qis.net
Products: Meat, including bacon, pork, hot dogs,
turkey, roast beef, corned beef, and sausage. **SIC:**
5147 (Meats & Meat Products). **Est:** 1918. **Sales:**
$7,000,000 (2000). **Emp:** 40. **Officers:** William H.
Redmer, President; Barbara J. Brown, VP & Treasurer;
Bruce W. Redmer, Secretary.

■ 11360 ■ **Hahns of Westminster**
440 Hahn Rd.
Westminster, MD 21157
Phone: (410)848-4200
Free: (800)227-7675 **Fax:** (410)848-1247
Products: Processed, frozen, or cooked meats. **SIC:**
5147 (Meats & Meat Products). **Est:** 1918. **Emp:** 38.
Officers: William H. Redmer, President; Bruce
Redmer, Vice President; Barbara Brown, Asst. VP.

■ 11361 ■ **Haitai America Inc.**
7227 Telegraph Rd.
Montebello, CA 90640
Phone: (562)923-3945 **Fax:** (213)724-7373
Products: Korean groceries. **SIC:** 5149 (Groceries &
Related Products Nec). **Sales:** $39,000,000 (2000).
Emp: 85. **Officers:** Taeki Min, President; Soon Seok
Cha, CFO.

■ 11362 ■ **Hale Brothers Inc.**
530 E Main St.
Morristown, TN 37814
Phone: (615)586-6231
Products: General-line groceries. **SIC:** 5141
(Groceries—General Line). **Officers:** W.T. Hale,
President.

■ 11363 ■ **Hale-Halsell Co.**
PO Box 582898
Tulsa, OK 74158
Phone: (918)835-4484 **Fax:** (918)835-7834
Products: Groceries. **SIC:** 5141 (Groceries—General
Line). **Est:** 1901. **Sales:** $384,000,000 (2000). **Emp:**
1,500. **Officers:** Robert D. Hawk, President; Jim Lewis,
CFO; Paul Stephens, Dir. of Marketing; Mark Long, Dir.
of Information Systems; Paul Bradley, Dir of Human
Resources.

■ 11364 ■ **Caleb Haley and Company Inc.**
14 Fulton Fish Market
New York, NY 10038
Phone: (212)732-7474 **Fax:** (212)349-2991
Products: Seafood. **SIC:** 5146 (Fish & Seafoods). **Est:**
1859. **Sales:** $40,000,000 (2000). **Emp:** 48. **Officers:**
Neil Smith, President; Michael Driansky, Vice
President.

■ 11365 ■ **Hallock Cooperative Elevator Co.**
310 S Atlantic St.
Hallock, MN 56728
Phone: (218)843-2624
Products: Grain elevator. **SIC:** 5153 (Grain & Field
Beans). **Sales:** $15,000,000 (2000). **Emp:** 3. **Officers:**
Ken Turner, General Manager, Finance.

■ 11366 ■ **Hallsmith-Sysco Food Services**
380 S Worcester St.
Norton, MA 02766
Phone: (508)285-6361 **Fax:** (508)285-5067
Products: Groceries. **SICs:** 5141 (Groceries—General
Line); 5141 (Groceries—General Line); 5046
(Commercial Equipment Nec); 5087 (Service
Establishment Equipment). **Sales:** $450,000,000
(2000). **Emp:** 1,100. **Officers:** William Holden,
President; Bruce Horton, VP of Finance.

■ 11367 ■ **W.L. Halsey Company Inc.**
PO Box 6485
Huntsville, AL 35824
Phone: (256)772-9691 **Fax:** (256)461-8386
Products: Groceries, industrial supplies, and paper
products. **SICs:** 5141 (Groceries—General Line); 5085
(Industrial Supplies); 5113 (Industrial & Personal
Service Paper). **Est:** 1879. **Sales:** $28,600,000 (2000).
Emp: 100. **Officers:** Cecilia Halsey, President &
Treasurer.

■ 11368 ■ **Hammond Candy Co**
2530 W 29th Ave.
Denver, CO 80211
Phone: (303)455-2320 **Fax:** (303)455-2993
Products: Chocolates and traditional hard candy and
confectionery products. **SIC:** 5145 (Confectionery).
Officers: Robert List, President.

■ 11369 ■ **Hammons Products Co.**
PO Box H
Stockton, MO 65785
Phone: (417)276-5181 **Fax:** (417)276-5187
URL: http://www.black-walnuts.com
Products: Nuts and seeds (salted, roasted, cooked, or
blanched); Black walnuts. **SIC:** 5145 (Confectionery).
Est: 1946. **Sales:** $10,000,000 (2000). **Emp:** 100.
Officers: Brian K. Hammons, President; Dave
Steinmuller, VP of Sales.

■ 11370 ■ **John T. Handy Company Inc.**
PO Box 309
Crisfield, MD 21817
Phone: (410)968-1772
Products: Crabs. **SIC:** 5146 (Fish & Seafoods). **Sales:**
$54,000,000 (2000). **Emp:** 200. **Officers:** Carol
Haltaman, President.

■ 11371 ■ **Hanks Seafood Company Inc.**
PO Box 70
Easton, MD 21601
Phone: (410)822-4141
Products: Frozen clams. **SIC:** 5146 (Fish & Seafoods).
Est: 1956. **Sales:** $5,000,000 (2000). **Emp:** 5.
Officers: Arthur R. Myers, President & Chairman of the
Board; Mary J. Myers, Treasurer & Secty.

■ 11372 ■ **Hanover Sales Co.**
1550 York Ct.
Hanover, PA 17331-9803
Phone: (717)632-6000 **Fax:** (717)632-6681
Products: Canned vegetables; Frozen vegetables;
Frozen foods. **SICs:** 5149 (Groceries & Related
Products Nec); 5142 (Packaged Frozen Foods). **Emp:**
49.

■ 11373 ■ **Hanover Warehousing**
Box 888
Winston-Salem, NC 27102
Phone: (919)723-1615
Products: Frozen food storage; Dry goods storage.
SICs: 5149 (Groceries & Related Products Nec); 5142
(Packaged Frozen Foods). **Est:** 1989. **Emp:** 7.
Officers: H. Richard Joyce Jr.

■ 11374 ■ **Hansen Caviar Co.**
93 D S Railroad Ave.
Bergenfield, NJ 07621
Phone: (201)385-6221
Free: (800)735-0441 **Fax:** (201)385-9882
Products: Caviar, smoked fish, goose liver, and other
specialty food products. **SIC:** 5149 (Groceries &
Related Products Nec). **Sales:** $5,000,000 (1999).
Emp: 5. **Officers:** Arnold H. Hansen-Sturm, CEO,
President & Treasurer; Andrea Drayfus, Accountant.

■ 11375 ■ **Happy Refrigerated Services**
900 Turk Hill Rd.
Fairport, NY 14450
Phone: (716)388-0300
Products: Bottled spring water. **SIC:** 5149 (Groceries
& Related Products Nec). **Sales:** $5,000,000 (1994).

Emp: 70. Officers: Kerry Chamberlain, President; Joanne Palmer, Controller.

■ 11376 ■ T. Hara and Company Ltd.
51 Makaala St.
Hilo, HI 96720
Phone: (808)935-5425
Products: Canned goods. SIC: 5149 (Groceries & Related Products Nec). Est: 1952. Sales: $5,000,000 (2000). Emp: 15. Officers: George K. Hara, President.

■ 11377 ■ Hardin's-Sysco Food Services Inc.
4359 B.F. Goodrich Blvd.
Memphis, TN 38118
Phone: (901)795-2300 Fax: (901)365-1576
Products: Food and supplies for restaurants, hospitals, and schools. SIC: 5141 (Groceries—General Line). Est: 1939. Sales: $260,000,000 (2000). Emp: 500. Officers: Bill Bowden, President; Jerry Earhart, VP of Finance; Nick Taras, Sr. VP of Marketing & Sales; David Pritchett, Information Systems Mgr.

■ 11378 ■ Hardy Cooperative Elevator Co.
PO Box 8
Hardy, IA 50545
Phone: (515)824-3221 Fax: (515)824-3222
Products: Grain and farm supplies. SICs: 5153 (Grain & Field Beans); 5191 (Farm Supplies). Sales: $16,000,000 (2000). Emp: 18. Officers: Virgil Davis, President; Dean Reichter, Mgr. of Finance.

■ 11379 ■ Harker's Distribution Inc.
801 6th St., SW
Le Mars, IA 51031
Phone: (712)546-8171 Fax: (712)546-3159
Products: Frozen beef, pork, poultry and seafood. SICs: 5142 (Packaged Frozen Foods); 5144 (Poultry & Poultry Products). Sales: $160,000,000 (2000). Emp: 475. Officers: Ron Geiger, CEO & President; James Ryan, Treasurer & Controller.

■ 11380 ■ Harrington Produce
1207 S Harwood
Dallas, TX 75201-6190
Phone: (214)747-8701 Fax: (214)748-9200
Products: Fruits and vegetables. SIC: 5148 (Fresh Fruits & Vegetables). Emp: 26. Officers: S. M. Harrington.

■ 11381 ■ Harrison Company Inc.
PO Box 72179
Bossier City, LA 71172-2179
Phone: (318)747-0700
Products: General line of groceries. SIC: 5141 (Groceries—General Line). Sales: $200,000,000 (1999). Emp: 165. Officers: Hal Martin, CEO.

■ 11382 ■ Harrison Poultry Inc.
PO Box 550
Bethlehem, GA 30620
Phone: (404)867-7511 Fax: (404)867-0999
Products: Frozen broiler chickens and chicken parts. SIC: 5142 (Packaged Frozen Foods). Sales: $50,000,000 (1993). Emp: 450. Officers: Harold Harrison, Owner.

■ 11383 ■ Hartford Provision Co.
159 Main St.
Stamford, CT 06904
Phone: (203)324-6194 Fax: (203)357-8357
Products: Equipment; Chemicals; Food, including fresh meats, produce, and frozen vegetables. SICs: 5141 (Groceries—General Line); 5147 (Meats & Meat Products); 5169 (Chemicals & Allied Products Nec); 5142 (Packaged Frozen Foods); 5148 (Fresh Fruits & Vegetables). Est: 1898. Sales: $76,000,000 (2000). Emp: 500. Officers: Ralph Lotstein, President; Jonathan Gates, Controller; Joel Retner, Sales Mgr.

■ 11384 ■ Hartford Provision Co.
159 Main St.
Stamford, CT 06904
Phone: (203)324-6194
Free: (800)883-7500 Fax: (203)357-8357
Products: General line of groceries, meat and other meat products. SICs: 5141 (Groceries—General Line); 5147 (Meats & Meat Products). Sales: $50,000,000 (2000). Emp: 100. Officers: Barry Pearson, President; Herbert Berman, CFO.

■ 11385 ■ The C.D. Hartnett Co.
300 N Main
Weatherford, TX 76086-3245
Phone: (817)594-3813 Fax: (817)594-9714
Products: Groceries. SIC: 5141 (Groceries—General Line). Emp: 150. Officers: Charles Milliken, Chairman of the Board; Steve Milliken, President.

■ 11386 ■ C.D. Hartnett Co. Food Service Div.
4151 Blue Mound Rd.
Ft. Worth, TX 76106
Phone: (817)625-8921 Fax: (817)626-2507
Products: General line groceries. SIC: 5141 (Groceries—General Line). Emp: 60. Officers: Charles Milliken, Owner and General Manager.

■ 11387 ■ Hartog Foods Inc.
529 5th Ave.
New York, NY 10017
Phone: (212)687-2000 Fax: (212)687-2659
E-mail: info@hartogfoods.com
Products: Juice concentrates. SIC: 5149 (Groceries & Related Products Nec). Est: 1957. Sales: $18,000,000 (2000). Emp: 30. Officers: Jack Hartog Jr., President; Chris Daly, Exec. VP & CFO; Emad Hosh, Vice President; Randy Lewis, Vice President; Kelly Good; Gaye Tomlinson.

■ 11388 ■ Harvin Choice Meats Inc.
PO Box 939
Sumter, SC 29150
Phone: (803)775-9367
Free: (800)849-6328 Fax: (803)775-9369
Products: Bologna and sausage. SIC: 5147 (Meats & Meat Products). Sales: $5,000,000 (2000). Emp: 60. Officers: S. A. Harvin Jr.

■ 11389 ■ Harvin Foods Inc.
620 A St.
Wilmington, DE 19801
Phone: (302)984-9500
Free: (800)355-1950 Fax: (302)984-9585
Products: Fruits; Vegetables; Grocery. SICs: 5148 (Fresh Fruits & Vegetables); 5143 (Dairy Products Except Dried or Canned); 5147 (Meats & Meat Products); 5141 (Groceries—General Line); 5113 (Industrial & Personal Service Paper). Emp: 40. Officers: Keith Harvin, President of Purchasing Dir.

■ 11390 ■ Hatfield Quality Meats Inc.
PO Box 902
Hatfield, PA 19440
Phone: (215)368-2500
Free: (800)523-5291 Fax: (215)362-1750
Products: Pork products. SIC: 5147 (Meats & Meat Products). Est: 1895. Sales: $200,000,000 (2000). Emp: 1,200. Officers: Douglas Clemens, President; Paul J. Emery Jr., Sr. VP of Sales & Marketing.

■ 11391 ■ Hattiesburg Grocery Co.
PO Box 350
Hattiesburg, MS 39403-0350
Phone: (601)584-7544
Free: (800)748-9689 Fax: (601)584-7546
Products: Bulk food; Dog feed; Candies; Cigarettes. SICs: 5141 (Groceries—General Line); 5145 (Confectionery); 5149 (Groceries & Related Products Nec); 5194 (Tobacco & Tobacco Products). Est: 1905. Sales: $10,000,000 (2000). Emp: 55. Officers: William T. Russell Jr., President.

■ 11392 ■ Hautly Cheese Company Inc.
5130 Northrup Ave.
St. Louis, MO 63110
Phone: (314)772-9339
Products: Cheese. SIC: 5143 (Dairy Products Except Dried or Canned). Est: 1934. Sales: $5,000,000 (2000). Emp: 13. Officers: Alan C. Hautly, President & Treasurer.

■ 11393 ■ Hawaiian Distributor Ltd.
96-1282 Waihona St.
Pearl City, HI 96782
Phone: (808)456-3334 Fax: (808)456-5043
Products: Dog food; Canned specialties; Milk; Paper goods or products, including book mailers. SICs: 5141 (Groceries—General Line); 5143 (Dairy Products Except Dried or Canned); 5149 (Groceries & Related Products Nec); 5113 (Industrial & Personal Service Paper). Emp: 37. Officers: Christopher Wilks.

■ 11394 ■ Hawaiian Grocery Stores Ltd.
80 Sand Island Excess Rd.
Honolulu, HI 96819
Phone: (808)839-5121 Fax: (808)833-5025
Products: General line of groceries, packaged frozen foods and dairy products. SICs: 5141 (Groceries—General Line); 5142 (Packaged Frozen Foods); 5143 (Dairy Products Except Dried or Canned). Sales: $70,000,000 (2000). Emp: 108. Officers: Richard H. Loeffler, CEO & President; Bruce Barber, CFO.

■ 11395 ■ Hawk Flour Mills Inc.
639 Grammes Ln.
Allentown, PA 18104
Phone: (215)435-8068 Fax: (215)366-1039
Products: Flour, sugar, and donut and pie filling. SIC: 5149 (Groceries & Related Products Nec). Emp: 35. Officers: Edward W. Zuber; Marcus R. Hilbert Jr.; Cynthia F. Zuber; Jessica J. Hilbert.

■ 11396 ■ Hay-A-Bar Dry Ice Wholesaler
3207 S Grand Traverse St.
Flint, MI 48507
Phone: (810)234-4155
Products: Ice cream and frozen desserts; Dry ice. SIC: 5143 (Dairy Products Except Dried or Canned).

■ 11397 ■ Marvin Hayes Associates
PO Box 10
Samburg, TN 38254
Phone: (901)538-2166 Fax: (901)538-9432
Products: Fish, including fresh and frozen. SIC: 5146 (Fish & Seafoods). Est: 1947. Sales: $6,000,000 (2000). Emp: 40. Officers: Jill White, CEO.

■ 11398 ■ John Hayes and Sons
PO Box 6184
Wolcott, CT 06716
Phone: (203)879-4616
Free: (800)322-8363 Fax: (203)879-1324
Products: Candy. SIC: 5145 (Confectionery). Sales: $5,000,000 (2000). Emp: 20. Officers: John F. Hayes III, President.

■ 11399 ■ Hazle Park Packing Co.
260 Washington Ave.
West Hazleton, PA 18201
Phone: (570)455-7571
Free: (800)238-4331 Fax: (570)455-6030
E-mail: hazlepk@epix.net
URL: http://www.hazlepark.com
Products: Meat. SIC: 5147 (Meats & Meat Products). Est: 1964. Sales: $8,000,000 (2000). Emp: 49. Officers: Henry Kreisl; Gary Kreisl.

■ 11400 ■ H.E. Butt Grocery Co. San Antonio Distribution/Manufacturing Center
4710 N Pan Am Expwy.
San Antonio, TX 78218
Phone: (210)662-5000
Products: Groceries. SIC: 5141 (Groceries—General Line).

■ 11401 ■ HealthComm Inc.
5800 Soundview Dr.
Gig Harbor, WA 98335
Phone: (253)851-3943
Free: (800)843-9660 Fax: (253)851-9749
Products: Soft drinks. SIC: 5149 (Groceries & Related Products Nec).

■ 11402 ■ Hearn Kirkwood
7251 Standard Dr.
Hanover, MD 21076
Phone: (410)712-6000 Fax: (410)379-6058
Products: Fresh produce, meats, seafood, frozen and dairy products. SICs: 5148 (Fresh Fruits & Vegetables); 5142 (Packaged Frozen Foods); 5147 (Meats & Meat Products); 5146 (Fish & Seafoods). Sales: $36,000,000 (2000). Emp: 170. Officers: Charles Gilbert, President; Patricia McCawley, Exec. VP of Finance.

■ **11403** ■ **William P. Hearne Produce Co.**
PO Box 1975
Salisbury, MD 21802
Phone: (410)742-1552
Products: Fruits and vegetables. **SIC:** 5148 (Fresh Fruits & Vegetables). **Sales:** $1,500,000 (2000). **Emp:** 21. **Officers:** Susan Smith, Finance Officer.

■ **11404** ■ **Heart of Iowa Coop.**
229 E Ash St.
Roland, IA 50236
Phone: (515)388-4341
Free: (800)662-4642   **Fax:** (515)388-4657
Products: Grain and farm supplies. **SICs:** 5153 (Grain & Field Beans); 5191 (Farm Supplies). **Sales:** $56,000,000 (2000). **Emp:** 70. **Officers:** James Penney, General Mgr.; Mike Thomas, Controller.

■ **11405** ■ **Heddinger Brokerage Inc.**
PO Box 65037
West Des Moines, IA 50265
Phone: (515)222-4458   **Fax:** (515)222-5699
Products: Food broker. **SIC:** 5141 (Groceries—General Line). **Sales:** $7,000,000 (2000). **Emp:** 15. **Officers:** George Heddinger, President.

■ **11406** ■ **Heeren Brothers, Inc.**
1020 Hall St. SW
Grand Rapids, MI 49503
Phone: (616)452-8641   **Fax:** (616)452-8725
Products: Fruits and vegetables. **SIC:** 5148 (Fresh Fruits & Vegetables).

■ **11407** ■ **Helena Wholesale Inc.**
202 York St.
Helena, AR 72342-3333
Phone: (501)338-3421   **Fax:** (501)338-3424
Products: General line groceries. **SICs:** 5141 (Groceries—General Line); 5191 (Farm Supplies). **Est:** 1910. **Sales:** $11,000,000 (2000). **Emp:** 25. **Officers:** Don Archibald, General Mgr.

■ **11408** ■ **J. Hellman Produce Inc.**
1601 E Olympic Blvd., No. 200
Los Angeles, CA 90021-1942
Phone: (213)627-1093   **Fax:** (213)243-9281
Products: Vegetables, including potatoes, onions, and tomatoes. **SIC:** 5148 (Fresh Fruits & Vegetables). **Est:** 1956. **Sales:** $23,000,000 (2000). **Emp:** 40. **Officers:** Bryce Hellman, President; Charles Johnson, Sales Mgr.

■ **11409** ■ **Fritz Helmbold Inc.**
12 Industrial Park Rd.
Troy, NY 12180-6197
Phone: (518)273-0810   **Fax:** (518)273-5735
Products: Meat products, including hot dogs. **SIC:** 5147 (Meats & Meat Products). **Est:** 1909. **Emp:** 20. **Officers:** Denise Widmer, President; Marilyn Widmer; Heidi Widmer Yetto; Roland Widmer.

■ **11410** ■ **Helms Candy Company Inc.**
3001 Lee Hwy.
Bristol, VA 24201-8315
Phone: (540)669-2612   **Fax:** (540)669-0150
Products: Sugar stick candy. **SIC:** 5145 (Confectionery). **Sales:** $1,000,000 (2000). **Emp:** 15. **Officers:** George F. Helms.

■ **11411** ■ **Hemmelgran and Sons Inc.**
PO Box 169
Coldwater, OH 45828
Phone: (419)678-2351   **Fax:** (419)678-4922
Products: Eggs. **SIC:** 5144 (Poultry & Poultry Products). **Est:** 1930. **Sales:** $30,000,000 (2000). **Emp:** 100. **Officers:** Ronald L. Gross, CEO.

■ **11412** ■ **Ron Hennessy Ingredients**
1709 Pennsylvania Ave.
Augusta, GA 30904
Phone: (706)736-7104
Free: (800)872-0674   **Fax:** (706)738-7174
Products: Nuts and seeds (salted, roasted, cooked, or blanched); Dried and dehydrated fruits. **SICs:** 5145 (Confectionery); 5149 (Groceries & Related Products Nec). **Est:** 1984. **Officers:** Paul Hennessy, President.

■ **11413** ■ **Henry J. Easy Pak Meats**
4460 W Armitage Ave.
Chicago, IL 60639
Phone: (773)227-5400   **Fax:** (773)227-0414
Products: Rolled pak corned beef hash; Uncooked and cooked corned beef; Sliced corned beef and roast beef. **SIC:** 5147 (Meats & Meat Products). **Est:** 1945. **Emp:** 15. **Officers:** Henry J. Juracic, President. **Alternate Name:** Henry J. Meat Specialties. **Former Name:** Bar-B-Que Industries Inc.

■ **11414** ■ **Henry's Foods Inc.**
PO Box 1057
Alexandria, MN 56308
Phone: (320)763-3194   **Fax:** (320)763-6250
E-mail: henrys@henrysfoods.com
URL: http://www.henrysfoods.com
Products: Groceries; Disposables; Candy; Tobacco; Automotive supplies; Health and beauty care; Hardware. **SICs:** 5149 (Groceries & Related Products Nec); 5145 (Confectionery); 5194 (Tobacco & Tobacco Products). **Est:** 1929. **Emp:** 150. **Officers:** Thomas Eidsvold, President; Jim Eidsvold, Vice President; Dale Erickson, General Mgr.; Terry Loeffler, Sales Manager and Food Service Director; Pauline Rortvedt, Customer Service Contact; Bev Clansen-Kieffer, Human Resources Contact.

■ **11415** ■ **Henry's Hickory House Inc.**
PO Box 2823
Jacksonville, FL 32203
Phone: (904)354-6839
Free: (800)637-4555   **Fax:** (904)354-1946
URL: http://www.henryshickoryhouse.com
Products: Bacon and bacon by-products. **SIC:** 5147 (Meats & Meat Products). **Sales:** $26,000,000 (2000). **Emp:** 100. **Officers:** William H. Morris; Ted Sheldon, e-mail: tsheldons@mindspring.com; Tom Lewis.

■ **11416** ■ **Henry's Homemade Ice Cream**
2909 W 15th St.
Plano, TX 75075
Phone: (972)612-9949
Products: Ice cream. **SIC:** 5143 (Dairy Products Except Dried or Canned).

■ **11417** ■ **Herb's Seafood**
112 School House Rd.
Mt. Holly, NJ 08060-9601
Phone: (609)267-0276   **Fax:** (609)261-1949
Products: Breaded and unbreaded seafood. **SIC:** 5146 (Fish & Seafoods). **Emp:** 49. **Officers:** Nash Cohen.

■ **11418** ■ **Heritage Marketing Inc.**
PO Box 225
Commack, NY 11725-0225
Phone: (516)499-9380
Products: Food. **SIC:** 5141 (Groceries—General Line). **Sales:** $4,000,000 (2000). **Emp:** 8. **Officers:** David Johnson, President.

■ **11419** ■ **Heritage Wafers Ltd.**
850 Vermont
Ripon, WI 54971
Phone: (920)748-7716
Free: (800)325-6830   **Fax:** (920)748-7210
Products: Produce; Wafers. **SICs:** 5149 (Groceries & Related Products Nec); 5148 (Fresh Fruits & Vegetables). **Est:** 1978. **Sales:** $10,000,000 (2000). **Emp:** 499. **Officers:** Ed Bumby.

■ **11420** ■ **T.L. Herring & Co.**
PO Box 3186
Wilson, NC 27895-3186
Phone: (919)291-1141   **Fax:** (919)291-1142
Products: Fresh meat. **SIC:** 5147 (Meats & Meat Products). **Sales:** $3,000,000 (2000). **Emp:** 17. **Officers:** T. L. Herring Jr.; Mike Herring; Mark Herring; Jean Herring.

■ **11421** ■ **Hershey Foods Corp.**
PO Box 810
Hershey, PA 17033-0810
Phone: (717)534-6799
URL: http://www.hersheys.com
Products: Chocolate; Confectionery. **SICs:** 5145 (Confectionery); 5149 (Groceries & Related Products Nec). **Est:** 1894. **Sales:** $4,300,000,000 (2000). **Emp:** 14,900. **Officers:** Kenneth L. Wolfe, Chairman & CEO; Joseph P. Viviano, Vice Chairman of the Board.

■ **11422** ■ **Hester Industries Inc. Pierce Foods Div.**
PO Box 2140
Winchester, VA 22604
Phone: (703)667-7878
Products: Food. **SIC:** 5141 (Groceries—General Line).

■ **11423** ■ **HFM Foodservice**
PO Box 855
Honolulu, HI 96808
Phone: (808)545-2111   **Fax:** (808)527-3252
E-mail: hfmadm@aol.com
Products: Food. **SIC:** 5141 (Groceries—General Line). **Est:** 1964. **Sales:** $88,000,000 (2000). **Emp:** 130. **Officers:** Barry O'Connell, President. **Former Name:** Hawaiian Flour Mills Inc.

■ **11424** ■ **Hi Grade Meats Inc.**
2160 SW Temple
Salt Lake City, UT 84115-2530
Phone: (801)487-5818   **Fax:** (801)487-4343
Products: Meats, including hot dogs and sausages. **SIC:** 5147 (Meats & Meat Products). **Sales:** $11,000,000 (1999). **Emp:** 80. **Officers:** Randall Maxfield, Vice President; Kenneth Lippman, President; Richard Conde, Sales & Marketing Contact.

■ **11425** ■ **HI-Pac Ltd.**
PO Box 25038
Honolulu, HI 96825-0038
Phone: (808)395-0388   **Fax:** (808)395-0322
Products: Food. **SIC:** 5141 (Groceries—General Line). **Officers:** Jean Pestel, General Partner.

■ **11426** ■ **Hickenbottom and Sons Inc.**
301 Warehouse Ave.
Sunnyside, WA 98944
Phone: (509)837-4100   **Fax:** (509)837-5130
Products: Rhubarb and asparagus. **SIC:** 5148 (Fresh Fruits & Vegetables). **Est:** 1939. **Sales:** $4,800,000 (2000). **Emp:** 20. **Officers:** Jerry Hickenbottom, President.

■ **11427** ■ **Hickory Farms Inc.**
PO Box 219
Maumee, OH 43537
Phone: (419)893-7611   **Fax:** (419)893-0164
Products: Specialty foods including smoked meats and cheeses. **SICs:** 5147 (Meats & Meat Products); 5143 (Dairy Products Except Dried or Canned). **Sales:** $160,000,000 (2000). **Emp:** 2,300. **Officers:** Ike Herb, COO; John Brenholt, Vice President.

■ **11428** ■ **HIE Holdings, Inc.**
2839 Mokumoa St.
Honolulu, HI 96819
Phone: (808)833-2244
Free: (800)657-7716   **Fax:** (808)833-6328
E-mail: hikcc@hawaii-coffee.com
URL: http://www.hawaiianisles.com
Products: Coffee; bottled water; tobacco; vending. **SICs:** 5149 (Groceries & Related Products Nec); 5194 (Tobacco & Tobacco Products); 5046 (Commercial Equipment Nec). **Emp:** 225. **Officers:** Michael Bouleware, CEO; Sidney Bouleware, COO; Merwyn Manago, CEO & Finance Officer; Lance Lee, Sales/Marketing Contact, e-mail: lance_lee@hawaiianisles.com; Dion Yasui, Customer Service Contact, e-mail: dion_yasui@hawaiianisles.com. **Former Name:** Hawaiian Iles Distributors.

■ **11429** ■ **Ira Higdon Grocery Company Inc.**
E Industrial Area
Cairo, GA 31728
Phone: (912)377-1272   **Fax:** (912)377-8756
Products: Groceries. **SIC:** 5149 (Groceries & Related Products Nec). **Est:** 1909. **Sales:** $65,000,000 (2000). **Emp:** 82. **Officers:** I. Higdon Jr. Jr., President & Treasurer.

■ **11430** ■ **High Grade Beverage**
PO Box 7092
North Brunswick, NJ 08902
Phone: (732)821-7600   **Fax:** (732)821-5953
Products: Soft drinks, fruit drinks, spring water and beer. **SICs:** 5149 (Groceries & Related Products Nec);

5181 (Beer & Ale). **Sales:** $192,000,000 (2000). **Emp:** 400. **Officers:** Joe De Marco, CEO; Herbert Schloss, CFO.

■ **11431** ■ **Highland Exchange Service Co-op**
PO Box K
Waverly, FL 33877
Phone: (813)439-3661
Products: Citrus products. **SIC:** 5148 (Fresh Fruits & Vegetables). **Sales:** $18,000,000 (2000). **Emp:** 42. **Officers:** Perry Hanson, President; Wally Houk, Treasurer.

■ **11432** ■ **Hillandale Farms Inc. of Pennsylvania**
12481 Rte. 6
Corry, PA 16407-9537
Phone: (814)664-9681
Free: (800)836-7460 **Fax:** (814)664-3693
Products: Eggs. **SIC:** 5144 (Poultry & Poultry Products). **Emp:** 12. **Officers:** Orland Bethel.

■ **11433** ■ **Hillcrest Foods Inc.**
2300 Louisiana St.
Lawrence, KS 66046
Phone: (785)843-0023 **Fax:** (785)843-7247
Products: General line groceries. **SIC:** 5141 (Groceries—General Line). **Est:** 1982. **Sales:** $13,000,000 (2000). **Emp:** 100. **Officers:** J.F. Lewis, President.

■ **11434** ■ **Hillside Coffee of California Holding Co.**
PO Box 223200
Carmel, CA 93922
Phone: (408)633-6300
Products: Gourmet coffee. **SIC:** 5149 (Groceries & Related Products Nec).

■ **11435** ■ **Hillside Dairy Inc.**
2600 W 11th
Pueblo, CO 81003
Phone: (719)544-7898
Products: Milk; Ice cream. **SIC:** 5143 (Dairy Products Except Dried or Canned). **Est:** 1919. **Sales:** $2,000,000 (2000). **Emp:** 8. **Officers:** Larry Maes, Manager.

■ **11436** ■ **Hilmar Cheese Company Inc.**
PO Box 910
Hilmar, CA 95324
Phone: (209)667-6076 **Fax:** (209)634-1408
URL: http://www.hilmarcheese.com
Products: Cheese; Whey; Lactose. **SIC:** 5143 (Dairy Products Except Dried or Canned). **Est:** 1985. **Sales:** $400,000,000 (1999). **Emp:** 400.

■ **11437** ■ **Hilton, Gibson, and Miller Inc.**
PO Box 1237
Newburgh, NY 12551
Phone: (914)562-0353 **Fax:** (914)562-0506
Products: Groceries. **SIC:** 5141 (Groceries—General Line). **Est:** 1904. **Sales:** $12,000,000 (2000). **Emp:** 35.

■ **11438** ■ **Hinckley and Schmitt Bottled Water Group**
6055 S Harlem Ave.
Chicago, IL 60638
Phone: (773)586-8600
Products: Bottled water. **SIC:** 5149 (Groceries & Related Products Nec). **Sales:** $79,000,000 (2000). **Emp:** 1,000. **Officers:** Harry Hersh, President; Chester E. Matykiewicz, CFO.

■ **11439** ■ **Hines Nut Co.**
2404 Canton
Dallas, TX 75226-1803
Phone: (214)939-0253 **Fax:** (214)761-0720
Products: Nuts. **SIC:** 5145 (Confectionery). **Sales:** $16,000,000 (2000). **Emp:** 50. **Officers:** Howard C. Hines.

■ **11440** ■ **Hipp Wholesale Foods Inc.**
PO Box 1145
North Platte, NE 69103
Phone: (308)532-0791 **Fax:** (308)532-0799
Products: Food. **SIC:** 5141 (Groceries—General Line). **Sales:** $7,000,000 (2000). **Emp:** 32.

■ **11441** ■ **R. Hirt Jr., Co.**
3000 N Chrysler Dr.
Detroit, MI 48207
Phone: (313)831-2020 **Fax:** (313)831-2024
Products: Specialty foods. **SIC:** 5149 (Groceries & Related Products Nec).

■ **11442** ■ **HMA/International Business Development Ltd.**
P.O Box 38602
Greensboro, NC 27438
Phone: (336)282-4773 **Fax:** (336)282-4773
E-mail: 103631.3613@compuserve.com
Products: Food processing machinery; Food sauces. **SICs:** 5149 (Groceries & Related Products Nec); 5064 (Electrical Appliances—Television & Radio). **Est:** 1971. **Sales:** $6,000,000 (1999). **Emp:** 68. **Officers:** Dr. Michael K. Jones, President, e-mail: 103637.3413@compuserve.com.

■ **11443** ■ **Hoban Foods Inc.**
1599 E Warren Ave.
Detroit, MI 48207
Phone: (313)831-7900 **Fax:** (313)833-0629
Products: Frozen foods, dairy products and dry goods. **SICs:** 5142 (Packaged Frozen Foods); 5143 (Dairy Products Except Dried or Canned); 5149 (Groceries & Related Products Nec). **Sales:** $16,000,000 (2000). **Emp:** 130. **Officers:** Donald VanTiem, President.

■ **11444** ■ **Hoegemeyer Hybrids Inc.**
1755 Hoegemeyer Rd.
Hooper, NE 68031
Phone: (402)654-3399
Free: (800)245-4631 **Fax:** (402)654-3342
Products: Livestock and farm products. **SIC:** 5153 (Grain & Field Beans). **Sales:** $10,000,000 (2000). **Emp:** 35.

■ **11445** ■ **Holberg Industries Inc.**
545 Steamboat Rd.
Greenwich, CT 06830
Phone: (203)661-2500 **Fax:** (203)661-5756
Products: Frozen foods; Dairy products; Meats; Vegetables. **SICs:** 5142 (Packaged Frozen Foods); 5143 (Dairy Products Except Dried or Canned); 5144 (Poultry & Poultry Products); 5146 (Fish & Seafoods); 5147 (Meats & Meat Products). **Sales:** $10,100,000,000 (2000). **Emp:** 19,800. **Officers:** John V. Holten, CEO & Chairman of the Board; A. Peter Ostberg, CFO.

■ **11446** ■ **Holiday Cos.**
PO Box 1224
Minneapolis, MN 55440
Phone: (612)830-8700
Products: Groceries; Gasoline. **SICs:** 5141 (Groceries—General Line); 5172 (Petroleum Products Nec). **Est:** 1928. **Emp:** 6,000. **Officers:** Ron Erickson, CEO & President; Arnold Mickelson, Vice President. **Doing Business As:** Fairway Foods, Inc. **Doing Business As:** Erickson Petroleum Corp. **Doing Business As:** World Wide, Inc.

■ **11447** ■ **Holiday Stores Inc.**
4567 W 80th St.
Bloomington, MN 55437
Phone: (612)830-8700
Products: Groceries, including canned vegetables, soups, meats, powdered drinks, and cereal; Gasoline. **SICs:** 5141 (Groceries—General Line); 5172 (Petroleum Products Nec). **Sales:** $650,000,000 (2000). **Emp:** 5,000. **Officers:** Ronald Erickson, President.

■ **11448** ■ **Hollandale Marketing Association**
PO Box 70
Hollandale, MN 56045
Phone: (507)889-4421 **Fax:** (507)889-3351
Products: Produce. **SIC:** 5148 (Fresh Fruits & Vegetables). **Est:** 1926. **Sales:** $3,500,000 (1999). **Emp:** 45. **Officers:** Peter Van Erkel, President; Miles Haug, Sales & Marketing Contact.

■ **11449** ■ **Hollar and Greene Produce**
PO Box 3500
Boone, NC 28607
Phone: (828)264-2177 **Fax:** (828)264-4413
Products: Fruits and vegetables. **SIC:** 5148 (Fresh Fruits & Vegetables). **Sales:** $40,000,000 (2000). **Emp:** 85. **Officers:** D.L. Greene, President; J.M. Payne, Treasurer & Secty.

■ **11450** ■ **Hollar and Greene Produce Co., Inc.**
PO Box 3500
230 Cabbage Row
Boone, NC 28607-3500
Phone: (704)264-2177
Free: (800)222-1077 **Fax:** (704)264-4413
E-mail: cabbage@boone.net
Products: Produce. **SIC:** 5148 (Fresh Fruits & Vegetables). **Est:** 1963. **Sales:** $35,000,000 (2000). **Emp:** 83. **Officers:** Dale Greene, President; John Payne, Treasurer & Secty.

■ **11451** ■ **Holly Sea Food Inc.**
414 Towne Ave.
Los Angeles, CA 90013-2125
Phone: (213)625-2513 **Fax:** (213)620-9693
Products: Seafood. **SIC:** 5146 (Fish & Seafoods). **Emp:** 19. **Officers:** Richard Merry; Rick Merry; Jim Merry; Robert Merry.

■ **11452** ■ **S and D Holmes Smokehouse Inc.**
PO Box 1166
Rosenberg, TX 77471
Phone: (281)342-3749
Products: Smoked and fresh meats, including smoked sausages. **SIC:** 5147 (Meats & Meat Products). **Est:** 1985. **Sales:** $1,500,000 (2000). **Emp:** 26. **Officers:** Luvine Holmes, President.

■ **11453** ■ **Holten Meat Inc.**
1682 Sauget Business Blvd.
East St. Louis, IL 62206
Phone: (618)423-8400
Products: Beef and pork. **SIC:** 5147 (Meats & Meat Products). **Sales:** $52,000,000 (2000). **Emp:** 153. **Officers:** Jim Holten, CEO.

■ **11454** ■ **Holthouse Brothers**
4373 State
Rte. 103
Willard, OH 44890
Phone: (419)935-0151 **Fax:** (419)933-2178
Products: Vegetables. **SIC:** 5148 (Fresh Fruits & Vegetables).

■ **11455** ■ **Homa Co.**
PO Box 5425
Parsippany, NJ 07054
Phone: (201)887-6500 **Fax:** (201)887-6971
Products: Nuts; Dry fruits. **SICs:** 5145 (Confectionery); 5149 (Groceries & Related Products Nec). **Est:** 1975. **Sales:** $26,000,000 (2000). **Emp:** 110. **Officers:** Ali Amin, Owner; Ron Schaefer, VP & Treasurer; Danny Thomas, Dir. of Marketing.

■ **11456** ■ **Honor Snack Inc.**
6846 S Canton Ave., Ste. 110
Tulsa, OK 74136
Phone: (918)496-2666
Products: Snack trays which include candy bars and chips. **SIC:** 5145 (Confectionery).

■ **11457** ■ **Hoopers Candies**
4632 Telegraph Ave., No. 4632
Oakland, CA 94609-2022
Phone: (510)654-3373 **Fax:** (510)654-3376
Products: Chocolates and candies. **SIC:** 5145 (Confectionery). **Est:** 1939. **Sales:** $2,000,000 (2000). **Emp:** 49. **Officers:** Robin Hooper.

■ **11458** ■ **Hope Cooperative Creamery**
PO Box 117
Hope, MN 56046
Phone: (507)451-2029
Products: Butter. **SIC:** 5143 (Dairy Products Except Dried or Canned). **Est:** 1912. **Sales:** $1,000,000 (2000). **Emp:** 2. **Officers:** Eugene Kruckeberg, General Mgr.

■ **11459** ■ **Hopewell Valley Specialties**
1360 Clifton Ave., No. 331
Clifton, NJ 07012-1343
Phone: (609)275-7426 **Fax:** (609)299-8654
Products: General line groceries; Bakers' equipment

and supplies. **SICs:** 5141 (Groceries—General Line); 5046 (Commercial Equipment Nec). **Officers:** John Samu, Director/Special Proj.

■ **11460** ■ **Hopkinsville Elevator Co.**
PO Box 767
Hopkinsville, KY 42241
Phone: (502)886-5191 **Fax:** (502)887-1608
Products: Grain and farm supplies. **SICs:** 5153 (Grain & Field Beans); 5191 (Farm Supplies). **Sales:** $30,000,000 (1999). **Emp:** 40. **Officers:** Ronald Berry, President; Jay Doss, CFO.

■ **11461** ■ **Hopkinsville Milling Company Inc.**
PO Box 669
Hopkinsville, KY 42241-0669
Phone: (502)886-1231 **Fax:** (502)886-6407
Products: Wheat flour and corn meal. **SIC:** 5149 (Groceries & Related Products Nec). **Est:** 1874. **Sales:** $14,000,000 (2000). **Emp:** 50. **Officers:** Frank A. Yost, Chairman of the Board; Robert Y. Harper, President.

■ **11462** ■ **Hormel Foods International Corp.**
1 Hormel Pl.
Austin, MN 55912
Phone: (507)437-5478 **Fax:** (507)437-5113
Products: Spam, beef stew, and children's microwavable meals. **SICs:** 5147 (Meats & Meat Products); 5149 (Groceries & Related Products Nec). **Est:** 1967. **Emp:** 20. **Officers:** Ronald W. Fielding, President.

■ **11463** ■ **Horton's Smoked Seafoods**
PO Box 430
Waterboro, ME 04087
Phone: (207)247-6900
Free: (800)346-6066 **Fax:** (207)247-6902
URL: http://www.hortons.com
Products: Smoked seafood. **SIC:** 5146 (Fish & Seafoods). **Sales:** $1,900,000 (2000). **Emp:** 27. **Officers:** Glen Cooke, e-mail: gcooke@truenorthsalmon.com. **Former Name:** Horton's Downeast Foods Inc.

■ **11464** ■ **Clarence H. Houk Co. Inc.**
1650 E Main St.
Rochester, NY 14609
Phone: (716)482-5880 **Fax:** (716)482-9946
Products: Frozen foods. **SIC:** 5142 (Packaged Frozen Foods). **Est:** 1983. **Emp:** 14. **Officers:** Clarence H. Houk.

■ **11465** ■ **House of Raeford Farms**
405 W Burr Oak
Athens, MI 49011
Phone: (616)729-5411 **Fax:** (616)729-5076
Products: Turkeys (including frozen, whole or parts); Young chickens. **SIC:** 5144 (Poultry & Poultry Products). **Sales:** $13,000,000 (2000). **Emp:** 150. **Officers:** Raymond Pontoni, CEO; Donald Canfield, VP of Marketing & Sales.

■ **11466** ■ **Houston Harvest Gift Products LLC**
3501 Mount Prospect Rd.
Franklin Park, IL 60131
Phone: (847)957-9191
Products: Popcorn and novelty tins; Food, candy, licensed and pet gifts. **SICs:** 5145 (Confectionery); 5143 (Dairy Products Except Dried or Canned); 5149 (Groceries & Related Products Nec). **Est:** 1955. **Emp:** 150. **Officers:** Robert P. Pesch, President; Brent Messick, Exec. VP & CFO; Brett Glass, Exec. VP of Marketing & Sales; Jim Wisniewski, Exec. VP of Operations; Victor Baez, VP of Project Development; Chuck Kukla, VP of Purchasing. **Former Name:** Houston Foods Co.

■ **11467** ■ **George J. Howe Company Inc.**
PO Box 269
Grove City, PA 16127
Phone: (724)458-9410 **Fax:** (724)458-1134
Products: Confectionery. **SICs:** 5145 (Confectionery); 5149 (Groceries & Related Products Nec). **Est:** 1927. **Sales:** $16,000,000 (2000). **Emp:** 110. **Officers:** Ernie May, President; Joe Trinch, Treasurer; Dan Phillips, VP & General Mgr.; Dick Beech, Vice President.

■ **11468** ■ **HRD International**
148 Clarkson Executive Park
Ballwin, MO 63011
Phone: (314)230-5004 **Fax:** (314)230-5005
Products: Snack foods. **SIC:** 5145 (Confectionery). **Officers:** Robert Lemon, President.

■ **11469** ■ **Hsu's Ginseng Enterprises Inc.**
T6819 Hwy. W
PO Box 509
Wausau, WI 54402-0509
Phone: (715)675-2325
Free: (800)826-1577 **Fax:** (715)675-3175
E-mail: info@hsuginseng.com
URL: http://www.hsuginseng.com
Products: Ginseng; Flavoring extracts and herbal powder; Herbal preparations. **SICs:** 5149 (Groceries & Related Products Nec); 5122 (Drugs, Proprietaries & Sundries). **Est:** 1974. **Emp:** 49. **Officers:** Paul C. Hsu, President; Ron Rambadt, Sales/Marketing Contact.

■ **11470** ■ **Hub City Foods Inc.**
PO Box 490
Marshfield, WI 54449
Phone: (715)384-3191 **Fax:** (715)387-6930
Products: Groceries. **SIC:** 5141 (Groceries—General Line). **Sales:** $180,000,000 (1994). **Emp:** 211. **Officers:** James Douglas Schneeberger, President; R.D. Wuethrich, Controller.

■ **11471** ■ **Hubbard Peanut Company Inc.**
PO Box 94
Sedley, VA 23878
Phone: (757)562-4081
Products: Nuts. **SIC:** 5145 (Confectionery).

■ **11472** ■ **Hubert Co.**
9555 Dry Fork Rd.
Harrison, OH 45030-1906
Phone: (513)367-8600
Free: (800)543-7374 **Fax:** (513)367-8603
E-mail: sales@hubert.com
URL: http://www.hubert.com
Products: Equipment and supplies. **SIC:** 5146 (Fish & Seafoods). **Est:** 1946. **Emp:** 300. **Officers:** Bart Kohler, CEO & President; G. Ollinger, VP of Finance; Andy Hallock, VP of Marketing; Carlin Stamm, VP of Sales.

■ **11473** ■ **Huckleberry People Inc.**
1021 Waverly St.
Missoula, MT 59802
Phone: (406)721-6024 **Fax:** (406)721-6024
Products: Candy, jams, jellies, syrups and honey; Gift products including candles and jewelry. **SIC:** 5199 (Nondurable Goods Nec).

■ **11474** ■ **Mike Hudson Distributing Inc.**
PO Box 808033
Petaluma, CA 94975-8033
Phone: (707)763-7388
Products: Meats and cheeses for delicatessens. **SICs:** 5147 (Meats & Meat Products); 5143 (Dairy Products Except Dried or Canned). **Sales:** $18,000,000 (2000). **Emp:** 50. **Officers:** Barbara Hudson, President; George Parisi, Controller.

■ **11475** ■ **Hull Cooperative Association**
PO Box 811
Hull, IA 51239
Phone: (712)439-2831 **Fax:** (712)439-1752
Products: Prepared feeds. **SICs:** 5153 (Grain & Field Beans); 5191 (Farm Supplies). **Sales:** $27,000,000 (2000). **Emp:** 30. **Officers:** Don Hoksbergen, Chairman of the Board.

■ **11476** ■ **Humpty Dumpty Potato Chip Co.**
PO Box 2247
Portland, ME 04116-2247
Phone: (207)883-8422
Free: (800)274-2447 **Fax:** (207)885-0773
Products: Snacks. **SIC:** 5145 (Confectionery). **Sales:** $15,000,000 (2000). **Emp:** 150. **Officers:** Whitney Smith, President; Turk Thatcher, Vice President.

■ **11477** ■ **Hundley Brokerage Company Inc.**
613 River Dr.
PO Box 838
Marion, IN 46952-0838
Phone: (765)662-0027 **Fax:** (765)662-0028
Products: Food brokerage. **SICs:** 5149 (Groceries & Related Products Nec); 5141 (Groceries—General Line). **Est:** 1940. **Officers:** David M. Hundley, President.

■ **11478** ■ **Hunt Wesson Inc.**
1351 Williams Ave.
Memphis, TN 38104
Phone: (901)726-6929
Products: Cooking oils. **SIC:** 5149 (Groceries & Related Products Nec). **Sales:** $75,000,000 (2000). **Emp:** 499. **Officers:** Ray Carroll, Plant Mgr.; Greg Martin.

■ **11479** ■ **Hunter Farms**
7303 Orr Rd.
Charlotte, NC 28213
Phone: (704)596-3001 **Fax:** (704)597-9578
Products: Milk; Ice cream. **SIC:** 5143 (Dairy Products Except Dried or Canned). **Sales:** $2,000,000 (2000). **Emp:** 20. **Officers:** Tony Morris.

■ **11480** ■ **Hunter, Walton and Company Inc.**
PO Box 525
South Plainfield, NJ 07080
Phone: (908)769-0099 **Fax:** (908)769-0445
E-mail: hunterwalton@earthlink.net
URL: http://www.hunterwalton.com
Products: Cheese, margarine, and butter; Dry milk products. **SICs:** 5143 (Dairy Products Except Dried or Canned); 5149 (Groceries & Related Products Nec). **Est:** 1827. **Sales:** $25,000,000 (2000). **Emp:** 10. **Officers:** Glenn Grimshaw Sr., President; Peter W. Love, CFO.

■ **11481** ■ **Huskers Coop.**
PO Box 1129
Columbus, NE 68601
Phone: (402)563-3636 **Fax:** (402)564-3162
Products: Grain, farm supplies, feed, ferilizer and chemicals. **SICs:** 5153 (Grain & Field Beans); 5191 (Farm Supplies). **Sales:** $92,000,000 (2000). **Emp:** 100. **Officers:** Greg Melliger, President; Paul Torey, CFO.

■ **11482** ■ **Husky Food Products of Anchorage**
6361 Nielson Way, Ste. 116
Anchorage, AK 99518-1715
Phone: (907)563-1836 **Fax:** (907)563-5574
Products: Snack foods; Bar and restaurant supplies. **SICs:** 5141 (Groceries—General Line); 5046 (Commercial Equipment Nec); 5145 (Confectionery). **Est:** 1978. **Emp:** 17. **Officers:** Wayne Wilken, President; Sherry Wilken, Treasurer & Secty.

■ **11483** ■ **Hutchings Brokerage Co.**
PO Box 11487
Mobile, AL 36671
Phone: (205)457-7641 **Fax:** (205)457-4569
Products: Frozen foods and dry groceries. **SIC:** 5141 (Groceries—General Line). **Sales:** $4,000,000 (1994). **Emp:** 8. **Officers:** Gerald Baggett, President.

■ **11484** ■ **Hybco USA**
333 S Mission Rd.
Los Angeles, CA 90033-3718
Phone: (213)269-3111 **Fax:** (213)269-3130
Products: Oils; Shortenings; Rice and rice flour; Custom packaging. **SIC:** 5149 (Groceries & Related Products Nec). **Est:** 1981. **Emp:** 49. **Officers:** David Kashani.

■ **11485** ■ **Hygrade Food Products**
8400 Executive Ave.
Philadelphia, PA 19153-3806
Phone: (215)365-8700 **Fax:** (215)937-4565
Products: Hot dogs. **SIC:** 5147 (Meats & Meat Products). **Emp:** 499. **Officers:** William Sweeny.

■ **11486** ■ **I. Wanna Distribution Company Inc.**
2540 Shader Rd.
Orlando, FL 32804
Phone: (407)292-0299 **Fax:** (407)292-0322
Products: Gourmet foods. **SIC:** 5149 (Groceries &

Related Products Nec). **Sales:** $3,000,000 (2000). **Emp:** 10. **Officers:** William Sullivan, President; Susan B. Sullivan, Vice President.

■ **11487** ■ **Icicle Seafoods Inc. Port Chatham Div.**
4019 21st Ave. W
Seattle, WA 98107
Phone: (206)783-8200
Products: Gourmet smoked seafood. **SIC:** 5142 (Packaged Frozen Foods). **Sales:** $30,000,000 (1994). **Emp:** 70. **Officers:** Lori Kaiser, General Mgr.; Fred Anderson, Controller.

■ **11488** ■ **I.D. Foods, Inc.**
1121 S Claiborne Ave.
New Orleans, LA 70125
Phone: (504)523-6882 **Fax:** (504)592-2784
Products: Food, including general line groceries, gourmet food, and institutional food. **SICs:** 5141 (Groceries—General Line); 5149 (Groceries & Related Products Nec). **Est:** 1968. **Emp:** 22. **Officers:** Mike Menard, Contact.

■ **11489** ■ **Idaho Supreme Potatoes Inc.**
PO Box 246
Firth, ID 83236-0246
Phones: (208)346-6841 (208)745-7717
Fax: (208)346-4104
E-mail: spuds@idahosupreme.com
URL: http://www.idahosupreme.com
Products: Potatoes. **SIC:** 5148 (Fresh Fruits & Vegetables). **Est:** 1966. **Sales:** $40,000,000 (2000). **Emp:** 300. **Officers:** Wilford Chapman, President; Steve Prescott, CFO; Wayne Allen, Dir. of Marketing; Paul Byington, CFO.

■ **11490** ■ **Ideal American Dairy**
PO Box 4038
Evansville, IN 47711
Phone: (812)424-3351 **Fax:** (812)423-9809
Products: Dairy products. **SIC:** 5143 (Dairy Products Except Dried or Canned). **Est:** 1978. **Sales:** $21,000,000 (2000). **Emp:** 85. **Officers:** Henry Shearer, President.

■ **11491** ■ **IGA Inc.**
8725 W Higgins Rd.
Chicago, IL 60631
Phone: (312)693-4520 **Fax:** (312)693-1271
Products: Food; Frozen dinners; Breakfast cereals; Milk; Canned fruit juices, nectars, and concentrates; Canned vegetables; Soups. **SICs:** 5141 (Groceries— General Line); 5142 (Packaged Frozen Foods); 5143 (Dairy Products Except Dried or Canned). **Sales:** $26,000,000 (2000). **Emp:** 35. **Officers:** Tom Haggai, CEO & Chairman of the Board; John Baloun, Controller.

■ **11492** ■ **IJ Co.**
PO Box 51890
Knoxville, TN 37950-1890
Phone: (423)970-3200
Free: (800)251-9516 **Fax:** (423)970-9442
URL: http://www.ijcompany.com
Products: Foods, including frozen, dried, and canned. **SICs:** 5141 (Groceries—General Line); 5142 (Packaged Frozen Foods); 5149 (Groceries & Related Products Nec). **Est:** 1946. **Sales:** $400,000,000 (2000). **Emp:** 600. **Officers:** Tim Keller, CEO; Mike Akers, CFO; L.J. Cirina, President; Mick Simpson, VP of Sales, e-mail: msampson@ijcompany.com; David North, Dir. of Information Systems. **Alternate Name:** Institutional Jobbers. **Alternate Name:** Joseph Foodservice.

■ **11493** ■ **IJ Co. Tri-Cities Div.**
2722 S Roan St.
Johnson City, TN 37601-7588
Products: Institutional food. **SICs:** 5141 (Groceries— General Line); 5046 (Commercial Equipment Nec). **Est:** 1946. **Sales:** $52,000,000 (2000). **Emp:** 100. **Officers:** Tim Keller, CEO; Larry Cirina, President; Bill Wampler, Sales Mgr.

■ **11494** ■ **I.J. Cos.**
PO Box 51890
Knoxville, TN 37950-1890
Phone: (423)970-7800
Products: Groceries. **SIC:** 5141 (Groceries—General Line). **Sales:** $240,000,000 (2000). **Emp:** 350. **Officers:** Larry Cirina, President.

■ **11495** ■ **ILHWA**
91 Terry St.
Belleville, NJ 07109
Phone: (973)759-1996
Free: (800)446-7364 **Fax:** (973)450-0562
Products: Ginseng concentrates and teas. **SIC:** 5149 (Groceries & Related Products Nec). **Est:** 1974. **Officers:** Mr. Han.

■ **11496** ■ **Illinois Fruit and Produce Corp.**
1 Quality Ln.
Streator, IL 61364
Phone: (815)673-3311 **Fax:** (815)672-3717
Products: Food. **SIC:** 5141 (Groceries—General Line). **Est:** 1929. **Sales:** $170,000,000 (2000). **Emp:** 360. **Officers:** Bruce A. Kleinlein, General Mgr.; John Sinotto, Controller; Bob Capponi, Sales Mgr.; Terry Flahaven, Data Processing Mgr.; Tammy Sarnes, Dir of Human Resources.

■ **11497** ■ **Illycaffe Espresso USA Inc.**
15455 N Greenway Hayden Loop, Ste. 7
Scottsdale, AZ 85260-1611
Phone: (602)951-0468 **Fax:** (602)951-8299
Products: Espresso coffee. **SIC:** 5149 (Groceries & Related Products Nec). **Sales:** $15,000,000 (2000). **Emp:** 33. **Officers:** Stefano Ripanmonti, President; Kathy Overland, Controller.

■ **11498** ■ **Imlers Poultry**
3421 Beale Ave.
Altoona, PA 16601-1311
Phone: (814)943-5563 **Fax:** (814)943-2837
Products: Chicken, beef, pork, cheese, lunch meats, and salads. **SICs:** 5147 (Meats & Meat Products); 5144 (Poultry & Poultry Products); 5143 (Dairy Products Except Dried or Canned); 5148 (Fresh Fruits & Vegetables). **Emp:** 115. **Officers:** Fred Imler Sr., President; Marshall Detwiler, Sales Mgr.; Clyde Monahan.

■ **11499** ■ **Imperia Foods Inc.**
234 St. Nicholas Ave.
South Plainfield, NJ 07080
Phone: (908)756-7333 **Fax:** (908)756-6076
Products: Bread, cake, and related products; Natural and process cheese and related products. **SICs:** 5143 (Dairy Products Except Dried or Canned); 5149 (Groceries & Related Products Nec). **Est:** 1955. **Sales:** $8,000,000 (2000). **Emp:** 38. **Officers:** Ira J. Weissman, President & Treasurer.

■ **11500** ■ **Imperial Commodities Corp.**
17 Battery Pl.
New York, NY 10004-1102
Phone: (212)837-9400 **Fax:** (212)269-9878
Products: Coffee and tea; Canned meats; Rubber products. **SICs:** 5149 (Groceries & Related Products Nec); 5199 (Nondurable Goods Nec). **Est:** 1941. **Sales:** $140,000,000 (2000). **Emp:** 35. **Officers:** Lee J. Muenzen, CEO; John Morley, CFO.

■ **11501** ■ **Imperial Frozen Foods Company Inc.**
45 N Station Plz.
Great Neck, NY 11022
Phone: (516)487-0670
Products: Frozen foods. **SIC:** 5142 (Packaged Frozen Foods). **Est:** 1958. **Sales:** $3,000,000 (2000). **Emp:** 7. **Officers:** Tom Garbo, Vice President.

■ **11502** ■ **Independent Bakers' Cooperative**
300 Washington St.
Chicago, IL 60606
Phone: (312)726-4606
Products: Bread, including buns and rolls. **SIC:** 5149 (Groceries & Related Products Nec). **Sales:** $37,000,000 (2000). **Emp:** 45. **Officers:** Bernard Forrest, President.

■ **11503** ■ **Indiana Botanic Gardens**
3401 W 37th Ave.
Hobart, IN 46342
Phone: (219)947-2912
Free: (888)315-3077 **Fax:** (219)947-4148
E-mail: wholesale@botanichealth.com
URL: http://www.botanichealth.com
Products: Herbal products, including supplements, teas, and oils; Vitamins and minerals. **SICs:** 5149 (Groceries & Related Products Nec); 5122 (Drugs, Proprietaries & Sundries). **Est:** 1910. **Emp:** 190.

■ **11504** ■ **Indiana Concession Supply Inc.**
2402 Shadeland Ave.
Indianapolis, IN 46219
Phone: (317)353-1667
Products: Food, including popcorn, catsup, mustard, and nachos; Paper products; Janitorial supplies. **SICs:** 5141 (Groceries—General Line); 5113 (Industrial & Personal Service Paper); 5087 (Service Establishment Equipment). **Est:** 1980. **Sales:** $2,000,000 (2000). **Emp:** 5. **Officers:** Dave Battas, President.

■ **11505** ■ **Indianapolis Fruit Company, Inc.**
4501 Massachusetts Ave.
Indianapolis, IN 46218
Phone: (317)546-2425 **Fax:** (317)543-0521
Products: Fresh produce; Floral items. **SICs:** 5148 (Fresh Fruits & Vegetables); 5193 (Flowers & Florists' Supplies). **Est:** 1947. **Emp:** 175. **Officers:** Mike Mascari, President; Pete Piazza, Vice President; Chris Mascari, Vice President; Joe Corsaro, Vice President; Dan Corsaro, Vice President; Greg Corsaro, Secretary.

■ **11506** ■ **Ingardia Brothers Inc.**
2120 Placentia Ave.
Costa Mesa, CA 92627
Phone: (714)645-1365
Products: Produce; Seafood. **SICs:** 5148 (Fresh Fruits & Vegetables); 5146 (Fish & Seafoods). **Est:** 1973. **Officers:** Joseph Ingardia, President; Sam Ingardia, Vice President.

■ **11507** ■ **Inland Fruit and Produce Company Inc.**
PO Box 158
Wapato, WA 98951
Phone: (509)877-2126 **Fax:** (509)877-3121
Products: Apples, pears, cherries, potatoes, and onions. **SIC:** 5148 (Fresh Fruits & Vegetables). **Est:** 1952. **Sales:** $37,000,000 (2000). **Emp:** 250. **Officers:** Jeannine Buntain, President.

■ **11508** ■ **Inland Seafood Corp.**
1222 Menlo Dr.
Atlanta, GA 30318
Phone: (404)350-5850
Free: (800)883-3474 **Fax:** (404)350-5855
E-mail: inlandsfd@aol.com
URL: http://www.inlandseafood.com
Products: Seafood. **SIC:** 5146 (Fish & Seafoods). **Est:** 1978. **Sales:** $66,000,000 (2000). **Emp:** 250. **Officers:** Joel Knox, President; Eric Sussman, Controller; Bill Demmond, Vice President; Chris Rosenberger, General Mgr.

■ **11509** ■ **Paul Inman Associates Inc.**
PO Box 1600
Farmington Hills, MI 48333
Phone: (248)626-8300 **Fax:** (248)626-6893
Products: Food broker. **SIC:** 5141 (Groceries— General Line). **Sales:** $900,000,000 (1999). **Emp:** 350. **Officers:** Jerry Inman, CEO; Malcolm York, Exec. VP of Finance.

■ **11510** ■ **Institution Food House Inc.**
PO Drawer 2947
Hickory, NC 28603-2947
Phone: (828)323-4500 **Fax:** (828)323-4577
URL: http://www.ifh.com
Products: Foodservice. **SIC:** 5141 (Groceries— General Line). **Sales:** $240,000,000 (2000). **Emp:** 505. **Officers:** David A. Stansfield, President; Gerald C. Burke, Director of Finance; Mike O'Brien, Vice President; William C. Speed, Vice President; Tom Dooley, Human Resources Contact.

■ 11511 ■ **Institution Food House Inc.**
PO Box 1368
Hickory, NC 28603-1368
Phone: (828)328-5301 **Fax:** (828)323-4435
Products: Groceries. **SIC:** 5141 (Groceries—General
Line). **Sales:** $140,000,000 (1999). **Emp:** 600.
Officers: Dennis Hatchell, President; Craig Keenan,
Finance Officer.

■ 11512 ■ **Institutional Distributors Inc.**
2742 Hwy. 25 N
PO Box 520
East Bernstadt, KY 40729
Phone: (606)843-2100
Free: (800)442-7885 **Fax:** (606)843-2108
URL: http://www.idifoods.com
Products: Food products. **SIC:** 5141 (Groceries—
General Line). **Est:** 1969. **Sales:** $300,000,000 (2000).
Emp: 657. **Officers:** Randal Durham, President, e-
mail: rdurham@idifoods.com; Brady Brummett,
Controller, e-mail: bbrummett@idifoods.com.

■ 11513 ■ **Institutional Distributors, Inc.**
417 Welshwood Dr.
Nashville, TN 37211
Phone: (615)832-9198
Products: Food. **SIC:** 5141 (Groceries—General Line).

■ 11514 ■ **Institutional Sales Associates**
PO Box 8938
Houston, TX 77249
Phone: (713)692-7213
Products: Food. **SICs:** 5141 (Groceries—General
Line); 5142 (Packaged Frozen Foods).

■ 11515 ■ **Institutional Wholesale Co.**
25 S Whitney Ave.
Cookeville, TN 38501
Phone: (615)526-9588 **Fax:** (615)520-1660
Products: Food, including dried and frozen goods,
seafood, and produce; Chemicals. **SICs:** 5141
(Groceries—General Line); 5169 (Chemicals & Allied
Products Nec). **Est:** 1958. **Sales:** $37,000,000 (2000).
Emp: 108. **Officers:** Jimmy W. Mackie, President;
John Mackie, Treasurer & Secty.; Bob Mackie, VP of
Business Development; Larry Welte, Dir. of Systems;
Gena Muncey, General Mgr.

■ 11516 ■ **Inter-County Bakers**
1110 Rte. 109
Lindenhurst, NY 11757
Phone: (516)957-1350 **Fax:** (516)957-1013
Products: Baking products. **SICs:** 5145
(Confectionery); 5149 (Groceries & Related Products
Nec). **Est:** 1950. **Sales:** $30,000,000 (2000). **Emp:** 53.
Officers: Theodore P. Heim Sr., President; Theodore
P. Heim Jr., Vice President.

■ 11517 ■ **Intermountain Trading Company
Ltd.**
1455 5th St.
Berkeley, CA 94710-1337
Phone: (510)526-3623 **Fax:** (510)524-0372
Products: Food products, including pemmican meal
packs and high-energy food bars. **SIC:** 5149 (Groceries
& Related Products Nec). **Est:** 1972. **Officers:** Robert
Kelso, President; Leisa Rossman, General Mgr.

■ 11518 ■ **International Baking Co.**
737 N Great SW Pkwy.
Arlington, TX 76011-5426
Phone: (817)640-5284 **Fax:** (817)633-4212
Products: Pita bread. **SIC:** 5149 (Groceries & Related
Products Nec). **Sales:** $6,000,000 (2000). **Emp:** 50.
Officers: Ara Baliozian.

■ 11519 ■ **International Baking Co.**
5200 S Alameda St.
Vernon, CA 90058
Phone: (213)583-9841
Products: Bagels. **SIC:** 5149 (Groceries & Related
Products Nec). **Sales:** $140,000,000 (2000). **Emp:**
300. **Officers:** Simon Mani, President; Monte Keene,
VP of Finance; Ken Tusup, VP of Sales.

■ 11520 ■ **International Components Corp.**
175 Marcus Blvd.
Hauppauge, NY 11788
Phone: (631)952-9595
Free: (800)645-9154 **Fax:** (631)952-9597
E-mail: oemsales@icc107.com
URL: http://www.icc107.com
Products: Electronic components, including buzzers,
piezos, transducers, sirens, speakers, microphones,
capacitors, connectors, cables, and accessories. **SICs:**
5060 (Electrical Goods); 5136 (Men's/Boys' Clothing);
5137 (Women's/Children's Clothing). **Est:** 1949. **Sales:**
$10,000,000 (2000). **Emp:** 25. **Officers:** Irwin
Friedman, President; Harvey Grossman, CFO; Fred
Grossman, Dir. of Marketing.

■ 11521 ■ **International Food and Beverage
Inc.**
8635 W Sahara Ave., No. 433
Las Vegas, NV 89117-5859
Phone: (702)858-8800
Products: Bread, cake, and related products; Frozen
foods. **SICs:** 5142 (Packaged Frozen Foods); 5149
(Groceries & Related Products Nec). **Sales:**
$12,000,000 (2000). **Emp:** 75. **Officers:** Michael W.
Hogarty, CEO & President; Ann M. Gooch, VP of
Finance.

■ 11522 ■ **International Industries Corporation**
880 E Main St.
Spartanburg, SC 29302-2000
Phone: (864)597-1414 **Fax:** (864)542-0001
Products: Bakery products; Snack foods;
Confectionery products. **SICs:** 5149 (Groceries &
Related Products Nec); 5145 (Confectionery). **Est:**
1974. **Emp:** 5. **Officers:** David Cloer, President.

■ 11523 ■ **International Pizza Co.**
801 Dye Mill Rd.
Troy, OH 45373
Phone: (937)335-2115 **Fax:** (937)492-5121
Products: Pizza. **SIC:** 5149 (Groceries & Related
Products Nec). **Est:** 1958. **Sales:** $15,000,000 (2000).
Emp: 200. **Officers:** Mike Gillardi, President; Jan
Spornhauer, VP of Finance; Chris Meinerding, Dir. of
Marketing.

■ 11524 ■ **International Trading Co.**
3100 Canal St.
Houston, TX 77003
Phone: (713)224-5901 **Fax:** (713)923-9448
Products: Specialty foods. **SIC:** 5149 (Groceries &
Related Products Nec).

■ 11525 ■ **Interstate Brands Corp.**
6301 N Broadway
St. Louis, MO 63147-2802
Phone: (314)385-1600 **Fax:** (314)385-4034
Products: Bread and cakes. **SIC:** 5149 (Groceries &
Related Products Nec). **Emp:** 999. **Former Name:**
Continental Baking Co.

■ 11526 ■ **Interstate Brands Corp. Cotton
Brothers Baking Co.**
3400 Macarthur Dr.
Alexandria, LA 71302
Phone: (318)448-6600 **Fax:** (318)448-6655
Products: Breads, including hamburger and hot dogs
buns. **SIC:** 5149 (Groceries & Related Products Nec).
Est: 1923. **Sales:** $65,000,000 (2000). **Emp:** 869.
Officers: Steve Cooper, General Mgr.; Jon Cook,
Controller; Marshall Haney, General Sales Mgr.;
Michael Jouban, HR Manager.

■ 11527 ■ **Interstate Brands Corp. Dolly
Madison Cakes Div.**
PO Box 419627
Kansas City, MO 64141-6627
Phone: (816)561-6600 **Fax:** (816)561-6600
Products: Cakes and butternut bread. **SIC:** 5149
(Groceries & Related Products Nec). **Sales:**
$325,000,000 (2000). **Emp:** 4,650. **Officers:** Frank A.
Fiorini, Exec. VP; Steven Gibb, CFO; Robert Morgan,
Dir. of Sales; Russ Baker, Dir of Human Resources.

■ 11528 ■ **Intexco Inc.**
7270 NW 12th St., Ste. 555
Miami, FL 33126-1927
Phone: (305)592-7063 **Fax:** (305)599-0308
Products: Food; Food preparations. **SIC:** 5141
(Groceries—General Line). **Est:** 1987. **Sales:**
$2,900,000 (2000). **Emp:** 1. **Officers:** Frank X.
Barrera, Mgr. Dir.

■ 11529 ■ **Ireland Coffee and Tea Inc.**
PO Box 1103
Pleasantville, NJ 08232
Phone: (609)646-7200
Products: Coffee; Tea. **SIC:** 5149 (Groceries &
Related Products Nec).

■ 11530 ■ **Thomas Iseri Produce Co.**
PO Box 250
Ontario, OR 97914-0250
Phone: (541)889-5337 **Fax:** (541)889-6008
Products: Fruits and vegetables. **SIC:** 5148 (Fresh
Fruits & Vegetables). **Est:** 1962. **Sales:** $6,000,000
(2000). **Emp:** 99. **Officers:** Tom Anderson, Sales Mgr.

■ 11531 ■ **Italian Sausage Inc.**
8 Brightwater Dr.
Savannah, GA 31410-3301
Phone: (912)354-8884
Products: Seafood; Sausage; Onions; Pasta. **SICs:**
5149 (Groceries & Related Products Nec); 5146 (Fish
& Seafoods); 5147 (Meats & Meat Products); 5148
(Fresh Fruits & Vegetables).

■ 11532 ■ **ITOCHU International Inc.**
335 Madison Ave.
New York, NY 10017
Phone: (212)818-8000 **Fax:** (212)818-8361
Products: General line groceries; Primary metal
products. **SIC:** 5141 (Groceries—General Line). **Est:**
1952. **Emp:** 400. **Officers:** Jay W. Chai, CEO &
Chairman of the Board; Tadayuki Seki, Treasurer.

■ 11533 ■ **It's Coffee Lovers Time, Inc.**
6601 Lyons Rd., Ste. C-12
Coconut Creek, FL 33073
Phone: (954)420-0882 **Fax:** (954)420-0811
Products: Roasted and flavored coffees. **SIC:** 5149
(Groceries & Related Products Nec). **Est:** 1997. **Sales:**
$900,000 (2000). **Emp:** 7. **Officers:** Herbert
Glaubman, CEO & President; Francis Glaubman,
Secretary. **Former Name:** Food Concepts Inc.

■ 11534 ■ **J and B Meats Corp.**
PO Box 69
Coal Valley, IL 61240
Phone: (309)799-7341 **Fax:** (309)799-7633
Products: Beef and pork. **SIC:** 5147 (Meats & Meat
Products). **Est:** 1970. **Sales:** $16,000,000 (2000).
Emp: 50. **Officers:** Jeff Tube, President; James
Simmer, VP of Operations; Greg Peikos, VP of Sales.

■ 11535 ■ **J and B Meats Corp.**
PO Box 69
Coal Valley, IL 61240
Phone: (309)799-7341
Products: Meat processing and packing. **SIC:** 5147
(Meats & Meat Products). **Sales:** $30,000,000 (2000).
Emp: 50. **Officers:** Jeff Jobe, President.

■ 11536 ■ **J and B Wholesale Distribution**
PO Box 212
St. Michael, MN 55376
Phone: (612)497-3913
Products: Meat, deli, and cheese. **SIC:** 5147 (Meats &
Meat Products). **Sales:** $117,000,000 (2000). **Emp:**
350. **Officers:** Bob Hageman, Chairman of the Board;
Mike Hageman, President.

■ 11537 ■ **J and J Food Service Inc.**
PO Box 1370
Meadville, PA 16335
Phone: (814)336-4435 **Fax:** (814)336-5890
Products: Canned vegetables and fruit. **SIC:** 5149
(Groceries & Related Products Nec). **Sales:**
$17,000,000 (2000). **Emp:** 57. **Officers:** A. Ronald
Miller, President.

■ 11538 ■ J and R Bottling and Distribution Co.
820 S Vail Ave.
Montebello, CA 90640
Phone: (213)685-8387 **Fax:** (213)724-0338
Products: bottled beverages and soft drinks. **SIC:** 5149 (Groceries & Related Products Nec). **Sales:** $7,000,000 (2000). **Emp:** 25. **Officers:** Ralph Santora, President.

■ 11539 ■ JaCiva's Chocolate and Pastries
4733 SE Hawthorne
Portland, OR 97215
Phone: (503)234-8115 **Fax:** (503)234-0681
Products: Tortes; Chocolates; Pastries. **SICs:** 5145 (Confectionery); 5149 (Groceries & Related Products Nec). **Sales:** $1,000,000 (2000). **Emp:** 35. **Officers:** Jack Elmer, Owner; Iva Elmer, Owner; Karen Hickey, Manager.

■ 11540 ■ Jack and Jill Ice Cream
3100 Marwin Ave.
Bensalem, PA 19020
Phone: (215)639-2300
Products: Ice cream. **SIC:** 5143 (Dairy Products Except Dried or Canned).

■ 11541 ■ Jack's Bean Co.
PO Box 327
Holyoke, CO 80734
Phone: (970)854-3702 **Fax:** (970)854-3707
Products: Dry beans; Popcorn; Canned dry beans. **SICs:** 5153 (Grain & Field Beans); 5145 (Confectionery). **Est:** 1938. **Sales:** $30,100,000 (2000). **Emp:** 64. **Officers:** Steve Brown, Manager; Mark Gurk, Controller.

■ 11542 ■ Jacks Original Pizza
401 W North Ave.
Little Chute, WI 54140
Phone: (920)788-7320 **Fax:** (920)788-7327
Products: Food. **SIC:** 5149 (Groceries & Related Products Nec). **Est:** 1973. **Sales:** $50,000,000 (2000). **Emp:** 275. **Officers:** James E. Geerts.

■ 11543 ■ Jackson Produce Co.
3226 McKelvey Rd.
Bridgeton, MO 63044
Phone: (314)291-1080
Products: Produce. **SIC:** 5148 (Fresh Fruits & Vegetables). **Sales:** $3,100,000 (2000). **Emp:** 12. **Officers:** Gerald Jackson, President.

■ 11544 ■ Jackson Wholesale Co.
PO Box 634
Jackson, KY 41339
Phone: (606)666-2495
Products: Food. **SIC:** 5141 (Groceries—General Line). **Est:** 1956. **Sales:** $18,000,000 (2000). **Emp:** 40. **Officers:** Dan C. McIntyre, CEO.

■ 11545 ■ Paul Jackson Wholesale Company Inc.
PO Box 1020
Roseburg, OR 97470
Phone: (541)672-7771 **Fax:** (541)440-3732
URL: http://www.pjwholesale.com
Products: Groceries; Frozen food; General merchandise; Health and beauty products; Candy; Tobacco; Deli products. **SIC:** 5141 (Groceries—General Line). **Est:** 1954. **Sales:** $24,000,000 (2000). **Emp:** 65. **Officers:** Jacob T. Notenboom, President & CEO; Pat Florence, Controller.

■ 11546 ■ Jacksonville Candy Company Inc.
218 Woodrow St.
Jacksonville, TX 75766
Phone: (903)586-8334 **Fax:** (903)586-8334
Products: Candy, including peanut brittle and candy bars. **SIC:** 5145 (Confectionery). **Est:** 1924. **Sales:** $2,000,000 (2000). **Emp:** 20. **Officers:** Lewis N. Holcomb, President; Lisha Holcomb, Vice President; Neal Holcomb.

■ 11547 ■ Java City Inc.
717 W Del Paso Rd.
Sacramento, CA 95834
Phone: (916)565-5500
Free: (800)528-2289 **Fax:** (916)565-5519
Products: Coffee. **SIC:** 5149 (Groceries & Related Products Nec). **Est:** 1985. **Sales:** $50,000,000 (1999). **Emp:** 589. **Officers:** Tom Weborg, CEO & President; John Kelleher, CFO.

■ 11548 ■ Java Dave's Executive Coffee Service
6239 E 15th St.
Tulsa, OK 74112
Phone: (918)836-5570
Free: (800)725-7315 **Fax:** (918)835-4348
E-mail: davebeans.com
URL: http://www.javedavescoffee.com
Products: Coffee; tea; instant cocoa; cappuccio. **SIC:** 5149 (Groceries & Related Products Nec). **Sales:** $8,000,000 (2000). **Emp:** 65. **Officers:** David Neighbors, President; Stan Neighbors, Vice President; Mike Blair, Sales/Marketing Contact. **Former Name:** Executive Coffee Service.

■ 11549 ■ Javi Farm Inc.
425 E Moore Dr.
Pharr, TX 78577-6309
Phone: (956)783-1112
Products: Fruits and vegetables. **SIC:** 5148 (Fresh Fruits & Vegetables). **Est:** 1989. **Sales:** $6,000,000 (1999). **Emp:** 12. **Officers:** David Seal, Vice President; J. Zerlejcs, President.

■ 11550 ■ Jawd Associates Inc.
47-49 Little W 12th St.
New York, NY 10014
Phone: (212)989-2000 **Fax:** (212)727-0234
Products: Poultry and poultry products. **SIC:** 5144 (Poultry & Poultry Products). **Sales:** $11,000,000 (2000). **Emp:** 30. **Officers:** Robert Dee, President.

■ 11551 ■ JC Produce Inc.
PO Box 1027
West Sacramento, CA 95691
Phone: (916)372-4050
Free: (800)400-1990 **Fax:** (916)372-5560
URL: http://www.jcproduce.com
Products: Fresh fruits and vegetables. **SIC:** 5148 (Fresh Fruits & Vegetables). **Est:** 1982. **Emp:** 250. **Officers:** Jim Lennane, President; John Tedesco, CFO.

■ 11552 ■ Jetfreeze Distributing
2501 30th Ave.
Gulfport, MS 39501
Phone: (228)864-1434
Products: Frozen desserts, including ice cream. **SIC:** 5143 (Dairy Products Except Dried or Canned).

■ 11553 ■ Jetro Cash and Carry Enterprises Inc.
1506 132nd St.
College Point, NY 11356
Phone: (718)649-8000
Products: Frozen food, fresh produce, dairy and deli products, and meat; Food service supplies. **SIC:** 5141 (Groceries—General Line). **Sales:** $520,000,000 (2000). **Emp:** 1,000. **Officers:** Stanley Fleishman, President; Richard Kirschner, VP of Finance.

■ 11554 ■ JFC International Inc.
540 Forbes Blvd.
South San Francisco, CA 94080
Phone: (415)873-8400 **Fax:** (415)952-3272
Products: Rice and noodles. **SIC:** 5149 (Groceries & Related Products Nec). **Est:** 1958. **Sales:** $193,000,000 (2000). **Emp:** 430. **Officers:** N. Enokido, President; Naohiro Hara, Treasurer; M. Ogihara, VP of Marketing.

■ 11555 ■ Jimmy's Seaside Co.
1 Boston Fish Pier
Boston, MA 02110
Phone: (978)256-2062 **Fax:** (617)426-3096
Products: Seafood. **SIC:** 5146 (Fish & Seafoods). **Est:** 1972. **Sales:** $3,500,000 (2000). **Emp:** 26. **Officers:** James M. Iodice, President, Secretary & Treasurer.

■ 11556 ■ J.O. Spice Company Inc.
3721 Old Georgetown Rd.
Baltimore, MD 21227
Phone: (410)247-5205
Products: Spices. **SIC:** 5149 (Groceries & Related Products Nec).

■ 11557 ■ Jogue Corp.
6349 E Palmer St.
Detroit, MI 48211
Phone: (313)921-4802
Products: Flavoring extracts and syrups. **SIC:** 5145 (Confectionery).

■ 11558 ■ Johnson Dairy Co.
PO Box 28
Bloomington, IN 47402
Phone: (812)332-2126
Products: Milk and ice cream. **SIC:** 5143 (Dairy Products Except Dried or Canned). **Sales:** $4,000,000 (2000). **Emp:** 19. **Officers:** Phil Tinkle, CEO.

■ 11559 ■ Joiner Foodservice Inc.
PO Drawer 2547
Harlingen, TX 78550-0589
Phone: (956)423-2003 **Fax:** (956)421-2025
Products: Institutional food. **SIC:** 5149 (Groceries & Related Products Nec). **Sales:** $12,000,000 (2000). **Emp:** 34. **Officers:** Andy Joiner, President.

■ 11560 ■ J.M. Jones Co.
2611 N Lincoln Ave.
Urbana, IL 61801
Phone: (217)384-2800 **Fax:** (217)384-2663
Products: General line groceries. **SIC:** 5141 (Groceries—General Line). **Sales:** $340,000,000 (2000). **Emp:** 950. **Officers:** Richard R. Hensley, President; Dick Hemsley, CEO; Don Ritten, Controller; Gary Gionette, Dir. of Merchandising; Jim Kouzmanoff, Dir. of Systems.

■ 11561 ■ Jones Dairy Farm Distributors
N2195 Jones Ave.
Ft. Atkinson, WI 53538
Phone: (920)563-2486
Products: Dairy products. **SIC:** 5143 (Dairy Products Except Dried or Canned).

■ 11562 ■ Rolland Jones Potatoes Inc.
PO Box 475
Rupert, ID 83350
Phone: (208)436-9606 **Fax:** (208)436-5685
Products: Fresh packed potatoes. **SIC:** 5148 (Fresh Fruits & Vegetables). **Est:** 1951. **Sales:** $16,000,000 (2000). **Emp:** 80. **Officers:** Roger L. Jones, President; Bill Schow, VP of Finance; Steve Trevino, Dir. of Marketing.

■ 11563 ■ Jonesboro Grocer Co.
PO Box 1873
Jonesboro, AR 72403
Phone: (501)932-3080 **Fax:** (501)935-2759
Products: Dried and canned foods. **SIC:** 5149 (Groceries & Related Products Nec). **Est:** 1916. **Sales:** $18,000,000 (2000). **Emp:** 35. **Officers:** Bob Pope, President.

■ 11564 ■ Jordan Meat and Livestock Company Inc.
1225 W 3300 S
Salt Lake City, UT 84119
Phone: (801)972-8770 **Fax:** (801)972-4136
Products: Fresh meat; Turkeys (including frozen, whole or parts). **SICs:** 5142 (Packaged Frozen Foods); 5147 (Meats & Meat Products); 5144 (Poultry & Poultry Products). **Est:** 1940. **Sales:** $15,000,000 (2000). **Emp:** 40. **Officers:** Irvin Guss, President; Nadine Guss, Controller.

■ 11565 ■ Jordanos Inc.
550 S Patterson Ave.
Santa Barbara, CA 93111
Phone: (805)964-0611
Free: (800)325-2278 **Fax:** (805)967-0306
URL: http://www.jordanos.com
Products: Institutional food for restaurants, schools, and prisons. **SICs:** 5141 (Groceries—General Line); 5149 (Groceries & Related Products Nec). **Est:** 1915. **Sales:** $120,000,000 (2000). **Emp:** 410. **Officers:**

Peter Jordano, President; M. Sieckowski, CFO; Jeff Jordan, Vice President; Tina Hammond, Dir of Human Resources.

■ 11566 ■ Jordan's Foods
PO Box 4657
Portland, ME 04112-4657
Phone: (207)871-0700   Fax: (207)871-0339
Products: Food. SICs: 5141 (Groceries—General Line); 5142 (Packaged Frozen Foods). Sales: $101,000,000 (2000). Emp: 160. Officers: Richard Giles, President; Terry Plourde, Treasurer.

■ 11567 ■ Jordan's Meats Inc.
PO Box 588
Portland, ME 04112
Phone: (207)772-5411
Products: Sausage and meat processing. SICs: 5141 (Groceries—General Line); 5142 (Packaged Frozen Foods). Sales: $271,000,000 (2000). Emp: 750. Officers: Jim VanStone, CEO & President.

■ 11568 ■ Joyce Brothers Inc.
PO Box 888
Winston-Salem, NC 27102
Phone: (910)765-6927   Fax: (910)765-0462
Products: General line groceries. SIC: 5141 (Groceries—General Line). Est: 1909. Sales: $17,500,000 (2000). Emp: 62. Officers: Harry Joyce, President; H. Richard Joyce Jr., Vice President.

■ 11569 ■ JP Foodservice Inc.
9830 Patuxent Woods Dr.
Columbia, MD 21046
Phone: (410)312-7100   Fax: (410)712-4598
Products: General foods, including canned, boxed, and produce. SIC: 5141 (Groceries—General Line). Est: 1989. Sales: $1,691,900,000 (2000). Emp: 3,700. Officers: James L. Miller, CEO, President & Chairman of the Board; Lewis Hay III, Sr. VP & CFO; Mark Kaiser, VP of Marketing; Carl Wilbert, Dir. of Information Systems.

■ 11570 ■ JP Foodservice Inc.
9830 Patuxent Woods Dr.
Columbia, MD 21046
Phone: (410)312-7100   Fax: (410)712-4598
Products: Food. SIC: 5141 (Groceries—General Line). Sales: $1,691,900,000 (2000). Emp: 3,700.

■ 11571 ■ JR Distributors
3041 Marwin Rd.
Bensalem, PA 19020
Phone: (215)639-1455
Products: Dairy products. SIC: 5143 (Dairy Products Except Dried or Canned).

■ 11572 ■ Juno Chefs Inc.
230 49th St.
Brooklyn, NY 11220-1708
Phone: (718)492-1300   Fax: (718)492-1334
E-mail: junochef@aol.com
Products: Food, including frozen and breakfast foods. SIC: 5142 (Packaged Frozen Foods). Est: 1969. Emp: 65. Officers: Julius Spessot, President; Onofrio Demattia, Customer Service Contact.

■ 11573 ■ Just Desserts Inc.
1970 Carroll Ave.
San Francisco, CA 94124
Phone: (415)330-3600   Fax: (415)468-4811
Products: Bakery products. SIC: 5149 (Groceries & Related Products Nec). Sales: $14,000,000 (2000). Emp: 360. Officers: Elliott Hoffman, President; Shyam Kataruka, Controller.

■ 11574 ■ K & L Associates, Inc.
1710 Clavinia Ave.
Deerfield, IL 60015
Phone: (847)948-9438   Fax: (847)948-5527
Products: Confectionery products, including chocolate; Soft drinks. SICs: 5145 (Confectionery); 5149 (Groceries & Related Products Nec). Officers: Kenneth J. Goldstein, President.

■ 11575 ■ K and N Meats
PO Box 897
Renton, WA 98057
Phone: (425)226-7300   Fax: (425)204-8122
Products: Meat processing; food. SIC: 5149 (Groceries & Related Products Nec). Officers: Wayne Keener, CEO; Gene Orrico, Treasurer.

■ 11576 ■ Kaelbel Wholesale Inc.
2501 SW 31st. St.
Ft. Lauderdale, FL 33312
Phone: (305)797-7789
Products: Fresh seafood. SICs: 5142 (Packaged Frozen Foods); 5146 (Fish & Seafoods).

■ 11577 ■ Kahn's Bakery Inc.
4130 Rio Bravo St., No. B100
El Paso, TX 79902-1002
Phone: (915)533-8433   Fax: (915)534-0043
Products: Bread and bakery products. SIC: 5149 (Groceries & Related Products Nec). Officers: Seymore Wallace, Vice President.

■ 11578 ■ Kamaaina Distribution
99-1305 Koaha Pl.
Aiea, HI 96701
Phone: (808)488-8758   Fax: (808)488-8525
E-mail: kamaain@aol.com
Products: Candies; Snacks; Cigarette and tobacco accessories; Groceries. SICs: 5149 (Groceries & Related Products Nec); 5072 (Hardware); 5122 (Drugs, Proprietaries & Sundries); 5148 (Fresh Fruits & Vegetables); 5194 (Tobacco & Tobacco Products). Est: 1945. Officers: Von Petrossian, Contact.

■ 11579 ■ Kane International Corp.
411 Theodore Fremd Ave.
Rye, NY 10580
Phone: (914)921-3100   Fax: (914)921-3180
Products: Dried and dehydrated fruits. SIC: 5149 (Groceries & Related Products Nec). Est: 1931. Sales: $25,000,000 (2000). Emp: 8. Officers: Thomas E. Kohlberg, CEO & President; Thomas Neeves, Controller.

■ 11580 ■ Kangaroo Brand Inc.
7620 N 81st St.
Milwaukee, WI 53223
Phone: (414)355-9696   Fax: (414)355-4295
Products: Bread. SIC: 5149 (Groceries & Related Products Nec). Sales: $2,000,000 (2000). Emp: 99. Officers: John Kashou.

■ 11581 ■ Kansas City Salad Company Inc.
5252 Speaker Rd.
Kansas City, KS 66106
Phone: (913)371-4466
Products: Vegatables. SIC: 5148 (Fresh Fruits & Vegetables). Sales: $9,000,000 (1993). Emp: 125. Officers: John Guarino, President.

■ 11582 ■ Karn Meats Inc.
922 Taylor Ave.
Columbus, OH 43219
Phone: (614)252-3712
Free: (800)221-9585   Fax: (614)252-8273
E-mail: karnmeats@worldnet.att.net
URL: http://www.karnmeats.com
Products: Meat products, including ground meat patties, cooked meats; Deli items. SICs: 5147 (Meats & Meat Products); 5149 (Groceries & Related Products Nec). Sales: $20,000,000 (1999). Emp: 20. Officers: Richard Karn, President; Lori Richmond, Comptroller.

■ 11583 ■ Karp's BakeMark
9401 Le Saint Dr.
Fairfield, OH 45014
Phone: (513)870-0880
Free: (800)383-5277   Fax: (513)870-0997
URL: http://www.bakemarkeast.com
Products: Bakery ingredients and products. SIC: 5149 (Groceries & Related Products Nec). Est: 1974. Emp: 51. Officers: Doug Townsend, Sales/Mktg., e-mail: dtownsend@bakemarkeast.com; Teri Gallisdorfer, Human Resources. Former Name: L. Karp and Sons.

■ 11584 ■ Kaw Valley Company Inc.
116 - 30 S Kansas Ave.
Topeka, KS 66603
Phone: (785)233-3201
Products: Full-line groceries. SIC: 5141 (Groceries—General Line). Sales: $6,300,000 (2000). Emp: 12. Officers: Ralph Cohen, President & CFO.

■ 11585 ■ Kay Distributing Co.
1063 W Lincoln
Ionia, MI 48846-1457
Phone: (616)527-0120   Fax: (616)527-4677
Products: Bulk and packaged deli products. SIC: 5149 (Groceries & Related Products Nec). Est: 1951. Sales: $2,000,000 (2000). Emp: 49. Officers: Catherine Gallagher.

■ 11586 ■ Kaye Brothers Inc.
590 NE 185th St.
North Miami Beach, FL 33179
Phone: (305)653-2880   Free: (800)432-2880
Products: Meats. SIC: 5147 (Meats & Meat Products). Sales: $5,000,000 (2000). Emp: 43. Officers: Allan Kaye, President.

■ 11587 ■ Keebler Co.
3875 Bay Center Pl
Hayward, CA 94545
Phone: (510)783-5754   Fax: (510)783-9165
Products: crackers, cookies and bakery products. SIC: 5149 (Groceries & Related Products Nec).

■ 11588 ■ Kehe Food Distributors Inc.
333 S Swift Rd.
Addison, IL 60101
Phone: (630)953-2829
Free: (800)323-0137   Fax: (630)953-2298
Products: Specialty foods. SIC: 5149 (Groceries & Related Products Nec). Sales: $120,000,000 (2000). Emp: 350. Officers: Jerry Kehe, President.

■ 11589 ■ Kehe Food Distributors Inc.
900 Schmidt Rd.
Romeoville, IL 60446
Phone: (815)886-0700   Fax: (815)886-1111
Products: Specialty foods and groceries. SICs: 5141 (Groceries—General Line); 5149 (Groceries & Related Products Nec). Sales: $154,000,000 (2000). Emp: 300. Officers: Jerry Kehe, President; Scott Kimball, Controller.

■ 11590 ■ Ben E. Keith Co.
PO Box 2628
Ft. Worth, TX 76113
Phone: (817)877-5700   Fax: (254)388-1701
Products: Groceries and beer. SICs: 5141 (Groceries—General Line); 5181 (Beer & Ale). Sales: $725,900,000 (2000). Emp: 1,400. Officers: Howard P. Hallam, President; Mel Cockrell, CFO.

■ 11591 ■ Ben E. Keith Foods
3205 Broadway Blvd. SE
Albuquerque, NM 87101
Phone: (505)843-7766
Products: Food. SIC: 5141 (Groceries—General Line).

■ 11592 ■ Kelley and Abide Company Inc.
PO Box 13516
New Orleans, LA 70185
Phone: (504)822-2700   Fax: (504)822-2761
Products: Dry goods. SIC: 5149 (Groceries & Related Products Nec). Est: 1910. Sales: $6,000,000 (2000). Emp: 25. Officers: A.J. Abide, Chairman of the Board & CFO.

■ 11593 ■ Kelley Bean Co., Inc.
PO Box 2488
Scottsbluff, NE 69363-2488
Phone: (308)635-2438   Fax: (308)635-7345
URL: http://www.kelleybean.com
Products: Dry beans, peas, and lentils. SIC: 5149 (Groceries & Related Products Nec). Est: 1927. Sales: $50,000,000 (2000). Emp: 200. Officers: Gary L. Kelley, Chairman of the Board; Robert L. Kelley Jr., President; G. Lee Glenn, VP & CFO.

■ 11594 ■ Kelley-Clarke
4845 Oakland St.
Denver, CO 80239-2721
Phone: (303)371-1112
Free: (800)541-8649 **Fax:** (303)371-2008
Products: Tuna; Soaps and detergents; Household type utensils. **SICs:** 5149 (Groceries & Related Products Nec); 5122 (Drugs, Proprietaries & Sundries). **Emp:** 148. **Officers:** Edward P. Rumpf, President; Gary Van Doorn, Vice President; Rod Schmidt, Vice President. **Former Name:** Highland Stone Hall.

■ 11595 ■ Kelley-Clarke Inc.
PO Box 5326
Culver City, CA 90231-5326
Phone: (310)641-0672 **Fax:** (310)216-0594
Products: Food. **SIC:** 5141 (Groceries—General Line). **Est:** 1884. **Sales:** $1,500,000,000 (2000). **Emp:** 850. **Officers:** John F. Blazin, CEO & President; Donald Busse, Controller.

■ 11596 ■ M.J. Kellner Co., Inc.
4880 Industrial Dr.
Springfield, IL 62704
Phone: (217)787-4070 **Fax:** (217)787-4136
Products: Groceries. **SIC:** 5141 (Groceries—General Line). **Officers:** W.P. Ryan, Vice President.

■ 11597 ■ Kellogg Co.
PO Box 14756
Memphis, TN 38114-0756
Phone: (901)743-0250 **Fax:** (901)745-9842
Products: Cereal; Croutons. **SIC:** 5149 (Groceries & Related Products Nec). **Sales:** $200,000,000 (2000). **Emp:** 999. **Officers:** Artie Byrd.

■ 11598 ■ Kemps Dairy Products Distributors
825 Woodside Ave.
Ripon, WI 54971
Phone: (920)748-2353
Products: Dairy products. **SIC:** 5143 (Dairy Products Except Dried or Canned).

■ 11599 ■ Ken-Son Inc.
PO Box 25487
Salt Lake City, UT 84125
Phone: (801)972-5585
Products: Food. **SIC:** 5141 (Groceries—General Line). **Sales:** $1,000,000 (1994). **Emp:** 16. **Officers:** Sam Pew, President.

■ 11600 ■ Kenan Oil Co.
100 Europa Dr., No. 450
Chapel Hill, NC 27514
Phone: (919)929-9979 **Fax:** (919)929-9979
Products: Convenience products, including cigarettes, beer, sodas, chips, and snacks; Petroleum products. **SICs:** 5172 (Petroleum Products Nec); 5149 (Groceries & Related Products Nec); 5194 (Tobacco & Tobacco Products); 5181 (Beer & Ale). **Est:** 1936. **Sales:** $27,000,000 (2000). **Emp:** 65. **Officers:** Owen Kenan, President; Rodney Reade, Sr. VP & Finance Officer.

■ 11601 ■ Kennedy Wholesale Inc.
205 W Harvard St.
Glendale, CA 91204
Phone: (818)241-9977
Products: Candy; Tobacco. **SICs:** 5145 (Confectionery); 5194 (Tobacco & Tobacco Products). **Est:** 1935. **Sales:** $5,000,000 (2000). **Emp:** 18. **Officers:** Robert Kennedy, President; Jeff Tanker, General Mgr.

■ 11602 ■ Kennesaw Fruit Juice Co.
1300 SW 1st Ct.
Pompano Beach, FL 33065
Phone: (954)782-9800
Free: (800)949-0371 **Fax:** (954)784-1222
Products: Fresh fruits; Juices. **SICs:** 5148 (Fresh Fruits & Vegetables); 5141 (Groceries—General Line). **Sales:** $42,000,000 (2000). **Emp:** 45. **Officers:** Len Roseberg, President.

■ 11603 ■ Lowell C. Kenyon Packing Co.
PO Box 328
Tulelake, CA 96134
Phone: (916)667-2225 **Fax:** (916)667-5693
Products: Potatoes. **SIC:** 5148 (Fresh Fruits &

Vegetables). **Est:** 1961. **Sales:** $4,000,000 (2000). **Emp:** 40. **Officers:** Lowell C. Kenyon, President.

■ 11604 ■ Jacob Kern & Sons
Nicholas St.
Lockport, NY 14094
Phone: (716)434-3577
Free: (800)248-8408 **Fax:** (716)434-0821
Products: Candy; Cookies; Snacks; School supplies; Tobacco; Cigarettes; Novelty items; Fund raising. **SICs:** 5145 (Confectionery); 5194 (Tobacco & Tobacco Products); 5149 (Groceries & Related Products Nec); 5112 (Stationery & Office Supplies). **Est:** 1931. **Emp:** 15. **Officers:** Paul Kern, Vice President.

■ 11605 ■ Kerr Pacific Corp.
811 SW Front St., No. 620
Portland, OR 97204
Phone: (503)221-1301
Products: Food. **SIC:** 5141 (Groceries—General Line). **Sales:** $31,000,000 (2000). **Emp:** 200. **Officers:** E. Randolf Labbe, President.

■ 11606 ■ Kettle Foods
PO Box 664
Salem, OR 97308
Phone: (503)364-0399 **Fax:** (503)371-1447
Products: Processes and distributes snack foods and chips. **SIC:** 5149 (Groceries & Related Products Nec).

■ 11607 ■ Key Food Stores Cooperative Inc.
8925 Avenue D
Brooklyn, NY 11236
Phone: (718)451-1000 **Fax:** (718)451-1202
Products: Food. **SIC:** 5141 (Groceries—General Line). **Est:** 1937. **Sales:** $490,000,000 (2000). **Emp:** 352. **Officers:** Richard Palitto, CEO; Ronald D. Phillips, Controller; Ken Nastro, Dir. of Advertising; Jerry Cesaro, Vice President.

■ 11608 ■ Kido Brothers Exports, Inc.
1028 Heartland Dr.
Nampa, ID 83686-8158
Phone: (208)372-3827
Products: Dried beans, peas, lentils, and onions; Frozen corn, peas, and mixed vegetables; Canned corn, peas, and beans; Rice and rice bran flour; Fresh onions. **SICs:** 5149 (Groceries & Related Products Nec); 5148 (Fresh Fruits & Vegetables); 5142 (Packaged Frozen Foods). **Officers:** Hiro Kido, President.

■ 11609 ■ Kim's Processing Plant
417 3rd St.
Clarksdale, MS 38614-4425
Phone: (601)627-2389 **Fax:** (601)627-2389
Products: Snack foods; Processed or cured pork. **SIC:** 5149 (Groceries & Related Products Nec). **Est:** 1985. **Sales:** $770,000 (2000). **Emp:** 19. **Officers:** Kim Wong, Warehouse Mgr.

■ 11610 ■ King Arthur Flour Co.
Box 1010
Norwich, VT 05055
Phone: (802)649-3881
Free: (877)523-5687 **Fax:** (802)649-3323
URL: http://www.kingarthurflour.com
Products: Flour. **SIC:** 5149 (Groceries & Related Products Nec). **Sales:** $25,000,000 (1999). **Emp:** 115. **Officers:** Steve Voigt, President; Frank Sands, Chairman of the Board. **Former Name:** Sands, Taylor and Wood Co.

■ 11611 ■ King Cotton Foods
8000 Centerview Pkwy., Ste. 500
Cordova, TN 38018
Phone: (901)942-3221
Products: Meats. **SIC:** 5147 (Meats & Meat Products). **Sales:** $39,000,000 (1994). **Emp:** 40. **Officers:** Rick Lowry, President.

■ 11612 ■ King Fish Inc.
414 S Lake St.
Burbank, CA 91502-2114
Phone: (213)849-1226 **Fax:** (213)849-3474
Products: Fish and seafood. **SIC:** 5146 (Fish & Seafoods). **Emp:** 49. **Officers:** Henry Kagawa.

■ 11613 ■ King Food Service
4215 Exchange Ave.
Los Angeles, CA 90058-2604
Phone: (213)582-7401 **Fax:** (213)582-1813
Products: Frozen foods. **SIC:** 5142 (Packaged Frozen Foods). **Est:** 1975. **Sales:** $20,000,000 (2000). **Emp:** 25.

■ 11614 ■ King Lobster Connection
7403 Princess View Dr., Ste. A
San Diego, CA 92102
Phone: (619)286-3617 **Fax:** (619)229-8717
Products: Seafood. **SIC:** 5146 (Fish & Seafoods). **Officers:** Virgil Marcus, Contact.

■ 11615 ■ King Milling Co.
PO Box 99
Lowell, MI 49331
Phone: (616)897-9264
Products: Flour and other grain mill products. **SIC:** 5149 (Groceries & Related Products Nec). **Sales:** $10,000,000 (2000). **Emp:** 49. **Officers:** K. Doyle.

■ 11616 ■ King Provision Corp.
9009 Regency Square Blvd.
Jacksonville, FL 32211
Phone: (904)725-4122 **Fax:** (904)723-3498
Products: Fast food restaurant equipment. **SICs:** 5142 (Packaged Frozen Foods); 5149 (Groceries & Related Products Nec). **Sales:** $120,000,000 (2000). **Emp:** 350. **Officers:** Edward F. Hicks, President; Marc A. Carlson, VP of Finance.

■ 11617 ■ King Salmon Inc.
4163 S Lowe
Chicago, IL 60609-2627
Phone: (773)927-3366 **Fax:** (773)927-3570
Products: Smoked fish. **SIC:** 5146 (Fish & Seafoods). **Emp:** 99. **Officers:** Robert Kahan.

■ 11618 ■ J. Kings Food Service Professionals Inc.
700 Furrows Rd.
Holtsville, NY 11742
Phone: (631)289-8401 **Fax:** (631)563-2925
Products: Groceries, including soups, nuts, and poultry; Cleaners; Paper towels; Fresh produce; Fresh seafood; Frozen food. **SICs:** 5142 (Packaged Frozen Foods); 5113 (Industrial & Personal Service Paper); 5143 (Dairy Products Except Dried or Canned); 5144 (Poultry & Poultry Products); 5169 (Chemicals & Allied Products Nec). **Est:** 1974. **Sales:** $74,000,000 (2000). **Emp:** 195. **Officers:** John King, President; Bob DeLuca, CFO.

■ 11619 ■ Kings Foodservice
404 Arlington Ave.
Nashville, TN 37210
Phone: (615)244-4626
SIC: 5141 (Groceries—General Line).

■ 11620 ■ King's Foodservice Inc.
2333 Old Frankfort Rd.
Lexington, KY 40510-9615
Phone: (606)254-6475 **Fax:** (606)231-9794
Products: Foods, including frozen, dried, and canned foods. **SICs:** 5149 (Groceries & Related Products Nec); 5142 (Packaged Frozen Foods). **Est:** 1936. **Sales:** $16,000,000 (2000). **Emp:** 38. **Officers:** Steve Potaniec, President; Emely Gibson, CFO.

■ 11621 ■ T.F. Kinnealey & Co.
1000 Massachusetts Ave.
Boston, MA 02118-2621
Phone: (617)442-1200 **Fax:** (617)427-4657
Products: Beef, lamb, veal, pork, and poultry. **SICs:** 5147 (Meats & Meat Products); 5144 (Poultry & Poultry Products). **Emp:** 99. **Officers:** T. F. Kinnealey.

■ 11622 ■ Kirchhoff Distributing Co.
2000 15th Ave. S
PO Box 1686
Clinton, IA 52733-1686
Phone: (319)242-3919 **Fax:** (319)242-9142
Products: Snack foods. **SIC:** 5149 (Groceries & Related Products Nec). **Emp:** 49. **Officers:** Ronald J. Kirchhoff, President; Steven Perrin, General Mgr.

■ 11623 ■ **Kitchens of the Oceans Inc.**
104 SE 5th Ct.
Deerfield Beach, FL 33441
Phone: (954)421-2192
Free: (800)327-0132 **Fax:** (954)421-5207
Products: Seafood, including shrimp, lobster, and scallops. **SICs:** 5146 (Fish & Seafoods); 5142 (Packaged Frozen Foods). **Sales:** $70,000,000 (2000). **Emp:** 350. **Officers:** A. F. Margus; B. A. Margus. **Alternate Name:** Margus.

■ 11624 ■ **KLF, Inc.**
359 E Park Dr.
Harrisburg, PA 17111-2727
Phone: (717)564-4040 **Fax:** (717)564-7695
Products: General food and goods; Powdered juices; Canned vegatables; Dog and cat foods. **SICs:** 5141 (Groceries—General Line); 5149 (Groceries & Related Products Nec). **Emp:** 49. **Officers:** John C Byrnes Jr. **Former Name:** Leaman Co.

■ 11625 ■ **Klosterman Bakery Outlet**
2655 Courtright
Columbus, OH 43232
Phone: (614)338-8111
Free: (888)900-8111 **Fax:** (614)338-8114
Products: Breads, rolls, and buns. **SIC:** 5149 (Groceries & Related Products Nec). **Emp:** 4. **Officers:** Kenny Klosterman. **Doing Business As:** Designer Vertical Blind.

■ 11626 ■ **Klosterman Baking Co. Inc.**
4760 Paddock Rd.
Cincinnati, OH 45229-1004
Phone: (513)242-1004 **Fax:** (513)242-3151
Products: Bakery products. **SIC:** 5149 (Groceries & Related Products Nec). **Sales:** $62,000,000 (2000). **Emp:** 810. **Officers:** Kenneth Klosterman Jr.

■ 11627 ■ **Kluge, Finkelstein & Co.**
6325 Woodside Ct.
Columbia, MD 21046
Phone: (410)720-5300 **Fax:** (301)381-1490
Products: Groceries; Health and beauty supplies. **SICs:** 5141 (Groceries—General Line); 5122 (Drugs, Proprietaries & Sundries).

■ 11628 ■ **Knaubs Bakery**
218 Dew Drop Rd.
York, PA 17402-4610
Phone: (717)741-0861 **Fax:** (717)741-2881
Products: Frozen cakes. **SIC:** 5142 (Packaged Frozen Foods). **Sales:** $5,000,000 (2000). **Emp:** 50. **Officers:** Ronald L. Knaub.

■ 11629 ■ **E.W. Knauss and Son Inc.**
625 E Broad St.
Quakertown, PA 18951
Phone: (215)536-4220
Free: (800)648-4220 **Fax:** (215)536-1129
Products: Cured or smoked meat. **SIC:** 5147 (Meats & Meat Products). **Est:** 1902. **Sales:** $32,000,000 (1999). **Emp:** 89. **Officers:** E. William Knauss, CEO; Brian T. Fleming, President; Richard K. Harlan, VP of Sales.

■ 11630 ■ **Knott's Wholesale Foods Inc.**
125 N Blakemore
Paris, TN 38242-4283
Phone: (901)642-1961 **Fax:** (901)644-1962
Products: Foods. **SIC:** 5141 (Groceries—General Line). **Sales:** $7,000,000 (1993). **Emp:** 71. **Officers:** Jerry Knott, President.

■ 11631 ■ **Koa Trading Co.**
2975 Aukele St.
Lihue, HI 96766
Phone: (808)245-1866 **Fax:** (808)245-8036
Products: General groceries. **SIC:** 5141 (Groceries—General Line). **Sales:** $18,000,000 (2000). **Emp:** 39. **Officers:** Peter Yukimura, President; Richard Fujii, Controller.

■ 11632 ■ **John E. Koerner and Company Inc.**
PO Box 10218
New Orleans, LA 70181
Phone: (504)734-1100 **Fax:** (504)734-0630
Products: Food, including meats, frozen items, and produce. **SICs:** 5149 (Groceries & Related Products Nec); 5142 (Packaged Frozen Foods). **Est:** 1907.

Sales: $16,000,000 (2000). **Emp:** 50. **Officers:** Tim Koerner, President; Earl P. Koerner, CFO.

■ 11633 ■ **N. Kohl Grocer Company Inc.**
PO Box 729
Quincy, IL 62306
Phone: (217)222-5000
Products: Foods; Canned soups and vegetables; Frozen and fresh meat; Beef; Pork; Fish. **SICs:** 5141 (Groceries—General Line); 5147 (Meats & Meat Products); 5146 (Fish & Seafoods). **Est:** 1873. **Sales:** $18,000,000 (2000). **Emp:** 70. **Officers:** Richard Ehrhart, President.

■ 11634 ■ **Kolb-Lena Cheese Co.**
3990 N Sunnyside Rd.
Lena, IL 61048
Phone: (815)369-4577 **Fax:** (815)369-4914
Products: Natural cheese. **SIC:** 5143 (Dairy Products Except Dried or Canned). **Est:** 1925. **Sales:** $10,000,000 (2000). **Emp:** 78. **Officers:** Jim Williams, CEO; Rene Weber, Plant Mgr.

■ 11635 ■ **Kona Farmers Coop**
PO Box 309
Captain Cook, HI 96704-0309
Phone: (808)328-2411 **Fax:** (808)328-2414
Products: Nuts and seeds (salted, roasted, cooked, or blanched); Coffee. **SICs:** 5149 (Groceries & Related Products Nec); 5145 (Confectionery). **Sales:** $6,000,000 (2000). **Emp:** 49. **Officers:** Walter Kimura.

■ 11636 ■ **Koolies Ice Cream**
3324 W Pierson Rd.
Flint, MI 48504
Phone: (810)787-2140
Products: Ice cream. **SIC:** 5143 (Dairy Products Except Dried or Canned).

■ 11637 ■ **William H. Kopke Jr. Inc.**
3000 Marcus Ave.
New Hyde Park, NY 11040
Phone: (516)328-6800
Products: Fruit. **SIC:** 5148 (Fresh Fruits & Vegetables). **Est:** 1943. **Sales:** $20,000,000 (2000). **Emp:** 40. **Officers:** P. Kopke, President.

■ 11638 ■ **Kowalski Sausage Company Inc.**
2270 Holbrook Ave.
Hamtramck, MI 48212
Phone: (313)873-8200
Products: Sausage. **SIC:** 5147 (Meats & Meat Products). **Est:** 1920. **Sales:** $20,000,000 (2000). **Emp:** 250. **Officers:** L. Kowalski, Controller.

■ 11639 ■ **K.R. International**
14106 W 69th St.
Shawnee, KS 66216
Phone: (913)268-6112 **Fax:** (913)268-5139
Products: Unprocessed or shelled nuts; Nuts and seeds (salted, roasted, cooked, or blanched); Raw cane sugar and byproducts; Milled rice and byproducts; Wheat; Wheat flour, except flour mixes. **SICs:** 5149 (Groceries & Related Products Nec); 5145 (Confectionery); 5159 (Farm-Product Raw Materials Nec); 5153 (Grain & Field Beans). **Officers:** R.R. Sharma, Partner.

■ 11640 ■ **Kraft Food Ingredients**
8000 Horizon Center Blvd.
Memphis, TN 38133-5197
Phone: (901)381-6500
Free: (800)323-1092 **Fax:** (901)381-6524
Products: Food ingredients, including cheese, cheese powder, flavors and bakers coconut. **SICs:** 5149 (Groceries & Related Products Nec); 5143 (Dairy Products Except Dried or Canned). **Officers:** Mike Taylor, VP & General Mgr.; Andreas Schauffler, Controller.

■ 11641 ■ **Kraft Foods Inc. Distribution, Sales, Service Div.**
1601 Ogletown Rd.
Newark, DE 19711-5425
Phone: (302)453-7000 **Fax:** (302)453-7089
Products: Grocery items. **SIC:** 5141 (Groceries—General Line). **Sales:** $75,000,000 (2000). **Emp:** 37. **Officers:** Sam Speakman, Mgr. of Admin.

■ 11642 ■ **Kraft Foodservice Inc.**
800 Supreme Dr.
Bensenville, IL 60106-1107
Phone: (708)595-1200 **Fax:** (708)250-4202
Products: Foods, including mayonnaise, salad dressing, and cheese. **SICs:** 5149 (Groceries & Related Products Nec); 5143 (Dairy Products Except Dried or Canned). **Sales:** $1,500,000,000 (2000). **Emp:** 350.

■ 11643 ■ **Kraft General Foods Group. Kraft Food Service**
PO Box 324
Deerfield, IL 60015
Phone: (847)405-8500
Products: Cheese; Dried food products. **SICs:** 5141 (Groceries—General Line); 5143 (Dairy Products Except Dried or Canned).

■ 11644 ■ **Kraft-Holleb**
800 Supreme Dr.
Bensenville, IL 60106
Phone: (708)595-1200 **Fax:** (708)250-4202
Products: Groceries and restaurant supplies. **SICs:** 5141 (Groceries—General Line); 5149 (Groceries & Related Products Nec). **Officers:** Robert J. Holleb, President.

■ 11645 ■ **Kraft USA**
3692 West 2100 South
Salt Lake City, UT 84120-1202
Phone: (801)972-5904 **Fax:** (801)973-0731
Products: Macaroni and cheese. **SIC:** 5149 (Groceries & Related Products Nec). **Emp:** 49. **Officers:** Tracy A. Van Bibber.

■ 11646 ■ **Krantor Corp.**
120 E Industry Ct.
Deer Park, NY 11729
Phone: (516)935-7007
Products: Grocery items; Health and beauty aids. **SICs:** 5141 (Groceries—General Line); 5122 (Drugs, Proprietaries & Sundries).

■ 11647 ■ **Krasdale Foods Inc.**
65 W Red Oak Ln.
White Plains, NY 10604
Phone: (914)694-6400
Products: Food. **SIC:** 5141 (Groceries—General Line). **Sales:** $300,000,000 (2000). **Emp:** 499.

■ 11648 ■ **Krasdale Foods Inc.**
65 W Red Oak Ln.
White Plains, NY 10604
Phone: (914)694-6400 **Fax:** (914)697-5225
Products: General line groceries. **SIC:** 5141 (Groceries—General Line). **Sales:** $459,000,000 (2000). **Emp:** 600. **Officers:** Charles A. Krasne, President; R. Brian Cassidy, VP of Finance.

■ 11649 ■ **Krema Nut Co.**
1000 W Goodale Blvd.
Columbus, OH 43212
Phone: (614)299-4131
Products: Nuts. **SIC:** 5145 (Confectionery). **Sales:** $1,000,000 (2000). **Emp:** 6. **Officers:** M. Giunta, President.

■ 11650 ■ **Kroger Co.**
PO Box 305103
Nashville, TN 37230-5103
Phone: (615)871-2400 **Fax:** (615)871-2736
Products: General line groceries. **SIC:** 5141 (Groceries—General Line).

■ 11651 ■ **Kroger Co. Dairy-Bakery Div.**
1783 Ohio Pike
Amelia, OH 45102
Phone: (513)797-4900
Products: Canned fruits; Fresh fruits; Canned specialties; Processed, frozen, or cooked meats. **SICs:** 5149 (Groceries & Related Products Nec); 5148 (Fresh Fruits & Vegetables); 5147 (Meats & Meat Products).

■ 11652 ■ **KT Distributors**
10 Bridge St.
Benton, ME 04901-3404
Phone: (207)453-2239 **Fax:** (207)453-2239
Products: Candy and chocolates. **SIC:** 5145

(Confectionery). **Officers:** Kelley Warren, Owner; Tamara Sheaff, Owner.

■ **11653** ■ **Kuehl's Distributors**
3401 S 7th St.
Lincoln, NE 68502
Phone: (402)423-2596 **Fax:** (402)423-3130
Products: Vegetarian and meatless soy products. **SICs:** 5149 (Groceries & Related Products Nec); 5148 (Fresh Fruits & Vegetables).

■ **11654** ■ **Otto L. Kuehn Company Inc.**
160 Bishops Way
Brookfield, WI 53005
Phone: (414)784-1600 **Fax:** (414)784-5327
Products: Groceries, general line. **SIC:** 5141 (Groceries—General Line). **Est:** 1883. **Sales:** $39,000,000 (2000). **Emp:** 100. **Officers:** Kenneth L. Kuehn, CEO; Donald J. Horen, Sr. VP.

■ **11655** ■ **Lee Kum Kee (USA) Inc.**
304 S Date Ave.
Alhambra, CA 91803
Phone: (626)282-0337
Free: (800)654-5082 **Fax:** (626)282-3425
URL: http://www.lkk.com
Products: Oriental cooking sauces and oils. **SIC:** 5149 (Groceries & Related Products Nec). **Est:** 1984. **Officers:** Betty Tsang, Marketing Mgr.; Grace Chow, Marketing Executive; Gary Cheung, Food Service Sales Mgr.; Clarence Carr, Retail Sales Mgr.

■ **11656** ■ **Kunzler and Company Inc.**
PO Box 4747
Lancaster, PA 17604
Phone: (717)390-2100
Free: (800)233-0203 **Fax:** (717)390-2170
Products: Meat. **SIC:** 5147 (Meats & Meat Products). **Est:** 1901. **Sales:** $100,000,000 (2000). **Emp:** 250. **Officers:** Christian C. Kunzler Jr., President; Betty Loht, Sales Mgr.

■ **11657** ■ **Kwik-Way Corp.**
PO Box 340
Gratz, PA 17030-0340
Phone: (903)572-3435
Products: General line of groceries. **SIC:** 5141 (Groceries—GeneralLine). **Sales:** $31,000,000 (1992). **Emp:** 170. **Officers:** Cliff Snedeker, President.

■ **11658** ■ **L and L Concession Co.**
1307 Maple Rd.
Troy, MI 48084
Phone: (810)689-3850 **Fax:** (313)689-4653
Products: Concession supplies, including hot dogs, soda pop, and cups. **SICs:** 5149 (Groceries & Related Products Nec); 5113 (Industrial & Personal Service Paper). **Sales:** $121,500,000 (2000). **Emp:** 500. **Officers:** Jerome B. Levy, CEO.

■ **11659** ■ **La Madeleine Inc.**
6060 N Central Expy.
Dallas, TX 75206
Phone: (214)696-6962 **Fax:** (214)696-0584
URL: http://www.lamadeleine.com
Products: Bread, soup, and sauces. **SIC:** 5149 (Groceries & Related Products Nec). **Est:** 1982. **Sales:** $6,000,000 (2000). **Emp:** 50. **Officers:** John G. Corcoran, CEO & Chairman of the Board; Brant Wood, CFO.

■ **11660** ■ **La Piccolina and Co. Inc.**
2834 Franklin St.
Avondale Estates, GA 30002
Phone: (404)296-1624 **Fax:** (404)296-2008
URL: http://www.lapiccolina.com
Products: Gourmet food. **SIC:** 5149 (Groceries & Related Products Nec). **Est:** 1986. **Sales:** $300,000 (2000). **Emp:** 7. **Officers:** Olympia Manning, Owner.

■ **11661** ■ **La Reina Inc.**
316 N Ford Blvd.
Los Angeles, CA 90022
Phone: (213)268-2791 **Fax:** (213)265-4295
Products: Flour tortillas. **SIC:** 5149 (Groceries & Related Products Nec). **Sales:** $15,000,000 (2000). **Emp:** 260. **Officers:** Mauro Robles.

■ **11662** ■ **La Vencedora Products**
3322 Fowler
Los Angeles, CA 90063-2510
Phone: (213)269-7273
Free: (800)32S-ALSA **Fax:** (213)269-8775
Products: Bean chips; Tortilla chips; Fresh salsa. **SIC:** 5149 (Groceries & Related Products Nec). **Emp:** 19. **Officers:** Morris E. Victor.

■ **11663** ■ **Labatt Food Service**
PO Box 2140
San Antonio, TX 78297
Phone: (210)661-4216
Products: Institutional food and supplies. **SIC:** 5141 (Groceries—General Line).

■ **11664** ■ **Labatt Institutional Supply Company Inc.**
PO Box 2140
San Antonio, TX 78297
Phone: (210)661-4216 **Fax:** (210)661-0973
Products: General line of groceries. **SIC:** 5141 (Groceries—General Line). **Sales:** $202,000,000 (2000). **Emp:** 500. **Officers:** Blair P. Labatt Jr., CEO; Al Silva, CFO.

■ **11665** ■ **Lady Baltimore Foods Inc.**
1601 Fairfax Trafficway
Kansas City, KS 66115
Phone: (913)371-8300
Products: Institutional food and non-food products; Industrial chemicals. **SICs:** 5149 (Groceries & Related Products Nec); 5169 (Chemicals & Allied Products Nec). **Est:** 1946. **Sales:** $185,000,000 (2000). **Emp:** 650. **Officers:** Melvin Cosner, President; Alan Cosner, Vice President; Tom Miller, VP of Sales; Clifford A. Cohen, Assistant Secretary; Jim Driskell, VP of Finance.

■ **11666** ■ **Lake Andes Farmers Cooperative Co.**
PO Box 217
Lake Andes, SD 57356
Phone: (605)487-7681
Products: Agricultural equipment and supplies. **SIC:** 5153 (Grain & Field Beans). **Sales:** $6,000,000 (2000). **Emp:** 9.

■ **11667** ■ **Lake Region Pack Association**
Box 1047
Tavares, FL 32778
Phone: (352)343-3111 **Fax:** (352)343-1616
URL: http://www.lakeregionpacking.com
Products: Citrus fruits. **SIC:** 5148 (Fresh Fruits & Vegetables). **Est:** 1909. **Sales:** $10,000,000 (2000). **Emp:** 250. **Officers:** B.B. Osgood, President & Chairman of the Board; Joseph M. Souza, CFO; Kevin Martin, Dir. of Sales; John F. Ueldhuis, Exec. VP & General Mgr.

■ **11668** ■ **Lakeland Wholesale Grocery**
1292 S Crystal
Benton Harbor, MI 49022-1808
Phone: (616)926-6644
Products: Food. **SIC:** 5141 (Groceries—GeneralLine).
Emp: 49.

■ **11669** ■ **Lakeside Mills Inc.**
716 W Main St.
Spindale, NC 28160
Phone: (704)286-4866 **Fax:** (704)287-3361
Products: Flour and other grain mill products. **SIC:** 5149 (Groceries & Related Products Nec). **Sales:** $6,000,000 (2000). **Emp:** 49. **Officers:** A. H. King, President; Kim King, Vice President; Bryan King, Vice President; Charles Wethrington, Plant Mgr.; Aaron King, Vice President.

■ **11670** ■ **Lamanuzzi and Pantaleo**
PO Box 296
Clovis, CA 93613
Phone: (209)299-7258
Products: Grapes. **SIC:** 5148 (Fresh Fruits & Vegetables). **Sales:** $16,500,000 (2000). **Emp:** 125. **Officers:** Frank Pantaleo, Partner.

■ **11671** ■ **Lambert's Coffee Services**
PO Box 181252-125
Memphis, TN 38181-1252
Phone: (901)365-7626
Products: Coffee. **SIC:** 5149 (Groceries & Related Products Nec). **Sales:** $4,300,000 (2000). **Emp:** 40. **Officers:** Bill Lambert, CEO; David Lambert, President.

■ **11672** ■ **Land O Lakes Inc.**
2001 Mogadore Rd.
Kent, OH 44240-7274
Phone: (330)678-1578 **Fax:** (330)678-2950
Products: Butter, margarine, and spreads. **SIC:** 5143 (Dairy Products Except Dried or Canned). **Sales:** $200,000,000 (2000). **Emp:** 144. **Officers:** Elliot Culp.

■ **11673** ■ **Land O Lakes Inc.**
W Hwy. 4
Luverne, MN 56156-0189
Phone: (507)283-4421 **Fax:** (507)283-9076
Products: Dairy products; Dried milk products. **SICs:** 5149 (Groceries & Related Products Nec); 5143 (Dairy Products Except Dried or Canned). **Est:** 1921. **Sales:** $10,000,000 (2000). **Emp:** 17. **Officers:** Cliff Hansen; Bernie Heikes.

■ **11674** ■ **Carl Landman Co. Inc.**
200 Arlington Way
Menlo Park, CA 94025
Phones: (415)821-6710 800-821-8184
Free: (800)821-8184 **Fax:** (415)641-7424
E-mail: landmark90@aol.com
URL: http://www.landmarkcoffee.com
Products: Roasted gourmet coffee, whole bean or ground. **SIC:** 5149 (Groceries & Related Products Nec). **Est:** 1958. **Sales:** $700,000 (2000). **Emp:** 2. **Officers:** Jim Landman; Doris Landman.

■ **11675** ■ **Landsman International Inc.**
18071 Biscayne Blvd.
North Miami Beach, FL 33160
Phone: (305)931-1090 **Fax:** (305)931-1091
Products: Fresh fruits. **SIC:** 5148 (Fresh Fruits & Vegetables). **Est:** 1957. **Sales:** $10,000,000 (2000). **Emp:** 30. **Officers:** S. Landsman, President & CFO.

■ **11676** ■ **Tom Lange Co.**
2031 Penn Ave.
Pittsburgh, PA 15222-4417
Phone: (412)566-1700 **Fax:** (412)566-1219
Products: Fruits and vegetables. **SIC:** 5148 (Fresh Fruits & Vegetables). **Emp:** 49.

■ **11677** ■ **Lankford-Sysco Food Services Inc.**
PO Box 477
Pocomoke City, MD 21851
Phone: (410)632-3271
Products: General line of groceries. **SIC:** 5141 (Groceries—General Line). **Sales:** $377,000,000 (2000). **Emp:** 600. **Officers:** C. Frederick Lankford, President; John A. Hall, Exec. VP of Finance.

■ **11678** ■ **Lantev**
460 Kent Ave.
Brooklyn, NY 11211
Phone: (718)599-1900 **Fax:** (718)599-6307
Products: Health foods; Natural foods; Kosher foods. **SIC:** 5149 (Groceries & Related Products Nec). **Est:** 1979. **Officers:** Hyman Landau, President.

■ **11679** ■ **Lascco Fish Products**
778 Kohler
Los Angeles, CA 90021
Phone: (213)622-0724
Products: Canned seafood; Fresh packaged fish; Packaged frozen seafood. **SIC:** 5146 (Fish & Seafoods).

■ **11680** ■ **Latina Niagara Importing Co.**
2299 Millitary Rd.
Tonawanda, NY 14150
Phone: (716)693-9999 **Fax:** (716)693-0303
Products: Pizza supply items including cheese and olives. **SICs:** 5143 (Dairy Products Except Dried or Canned); 5148 (Fresh Fruits & Vegetables); 5149 (Groceries & Related Products Nec). **Emp:** 20. **Officers:** Chuck Marazzo.

■ **11681** ■ **Latina Trading Corp.**
226 Cannon Blvd.
Staten Island, NY 10306-4256
Phone: (718)351-1400 **Fax:** (718)351-1044
Products: Vegetable oil. **SIC:** 5149 (Groceries & Related Products Nec). **Sales:** $1,000,000 (2000).
Emp: 3. **Officers:** Fred Kolb, President.

■ **11682** ■ **Latona's Food Importing Corp.**
PO Box 10
Wood Ridge, NJ 07075-0010
Phone: (973)916-5646 **Fax:** (973)916-5648
Products: Italian foods. **SIC:** 5149 (Groceries & Related Products Nec). **Sales:** $45,000,000 (2000).
Emp: 8. **Officers:** Vincent Latona, Treasurer.

■ **11683** ■ **Laurel Farms**
PO Box 7405
Studio City, CA 91614
Phone: (213)650-1060
Products: Mushrooms. **SIC:** 5148 (Fresh Fruits & Vegetables).

■ **11684** ■ **Laurel Grocery Company Inc.**
PO Box 4100
London, KY 40741
Phone: (606)843-9700 **Fax:** (606)843-9515
Products: Groceries. **SIC:** 5141 (Groceries—General Line). **Sales:** $170,000,000 (2000). **Emp:** 305.
Officers: Bruce Chestnut, CEO; George Griffin, President.

■ **11685** ■ **Lavin Candy Company Inc.**
4989 S Catherine St.
Plattsburgh, NY 12901
Phone: (518)563-4630 **Fax:** (518)563-4778
Products: Candy, tobacco, and cigarettes. **SICs:** 5145 (Confectionery); 5194 (Tobacco & Tobacco Products).
Sales: $14,000,000 (2000). **Emp:** 35. **Officers:** Irvin C. Reid, President.

■ **11686** ■ **Lawson Seafood Company Inc.**
15 Rudds Ln.
Hampton, VA 23669
Phone: (804)722-6211 **Fax:** (804)728-9687
Products: Seafood. **SIC:** 5146 (Fish & Seafoods). **Est:** 1956. **Sales:** $15,000,000 (2000). **Emp:** 125. **Officers:** Jerry L. Olson, President.

■ **11687** ■ **Laymon Candy Company Inc.**
276 East Commercial Rd.
San Bernardino, CA 92408
Phone: (909)825-4408 **Fax:** (909)825-4693
Products: Candy; Chocolate and chocolate-type confectionery products; Candy novelties. **SIC:** 5145 (Confectionery). **Est:** 1927. **Sales:** $2,800,000 (2000).
Emp: 23. **Officers:** Lon L. Laymon, President.

■ **11688** ■ **Lays Fine Foods**
400 E Jackson Ave.
Knoxville, TN 37901
Phone: (423)546-2511 **Fax:** (423)546-2130
Products: Meats. **SIC:** 5147 (Meats & Meat Products). **Est:** 1921. **Sales:** $48,000,000 (2000). **Emp:** 225.
Officers: Joe L. Lay Jr., President; Ferril Maddox, Sales/Marketing Contact. **Alternate Name:** Lay Packing Co.

■ **11689** ■ **LBM Sales Inc.**
304 Walnut St.
PO Box 488
Fayetteville, NY 13066
Phone: (315)637-5147 **Fax:** (315)637-0024
E-mail: lbmsyr@mindspring.com
Products: Confectionery; Snacks; Beverages. **SICs:** 5145 (Confectionery); 5149 (Groceries & Related Products Nec). **Est:** 1972. **Emp:** 49. **Officers:** Nick Bellanca, President; Kevin Weiner, Exec. VP; Paul Weiler, Vice President.

■ **11690** ■ **LBM Sales Inc.**
1307 Military Rd.
Buffalo, NY 14217
Phone: (716)873-7251 **Fax:** (716)874-4043
E-mail: lbmbuf@mindspring.com
Products: Candy; Snacks; Beverages; Health and beauty supplies. **SICs:** 5145 (Confectionery); 5122 (Drugs, Proprietaries & Sundries). **Est:** 1972. **Emp:** 24.
Officers: Nick Bellanca, President.

■ **11691** ■ **Lee Cash & Carry**
PO Box 630
Everett, WA 98206-0630
Phone: (425)259-6155 **Fax:** (425)259-6156
Products: Dry goods; Juice; Cereal; Cigarrettes; Candy. **SICs:** 5141 (Groceries—General Line); 5145 (Confectionery); 5149 (Groceries & Related Products Nec); 5194 (Tobacco & Tobacco Products). **Emp:** 99.
Officers: Dan Rochon.

■ **11692** ■ **Henry Lee Co.**
3301 NW 125th St.
Miami, FL 33167
Phone: (305)685-5851
Free: (800)284-4533 **Fax:** (305)685-1794
E-mail: julieb3@ix.netcom.com
Products: Food. **SIC:** 5141 (Groceries—General Line). **Est:** 1946. **Sales:** $175,000,000 (2000). **Emp:** 500.
Officers: Ed Sternlieb, President; Mike Primrose, COO; Mickey Biggs, Vice President; Terry Otero, Supervisor; Crystal Duxbury, Vice President; Maria Vidal, Exec. VP.

■ **11693** ■ **W.S. Lee and Sons Inc.**
PO Box 1631
Altoona, PA 16603
Phone: (814)696-3535
Free: (800)452-7507 **Fax:** (814)695-9217
URL: http://www.wslee.com
Products: Full line groceries, including frozen foods, meats, seafood, produce, chicken, canned goods, coffee, and beverages; Restaurant supplies and equipment; Paper goods; Chemicals. **SICs:** 5141 (Groceries—General Line); 5142 (Packaged Frozen Foods); 5147 (Meats & Meat Products); 5146 (Fish & Seafoods); 5149 (Groceries & Related Products Nec).
Est: 1872. **Sales:** $60,000,000 (2000). **Emp:** 158.
Officers: Walter J. Lee Jr., Board Chairman; Robert E. Lee, President & CEO; W. James Lee, Exec. VP & COO; John T. Bandzuh, Dir. of Purchasing and Marketing; Asher Sky, Dir. of Sales; James PLummer, VP of Finance; Ann D. Price, Dir. of Information Systems; Stephen J. Pustay, Dir. of Operations; Renee Kyle, Multi-Unit Account Manager.

■ **11694** ■ **Lee Tomato Co.**
140 Timberlawn Rd.
Jackson, MS 39212-2329
Phone: (601)352-0821
Products: Fruits and vegetables. **SIC:** 5148 (Fresh Fruits & Vegetables). **Emp:** 10.

■ **11695** ■ **L.E.G. Inc.**
501 S 9th St.
Reading, PA 19602-2503
Phone: (610)374-4148 **Fax:** (610)374-7439
E-mail: perfectmfg@aol.com
Products: Candy. **SIC:** 5145 (Confectionery). **Est:** 1984. **Emp:** 49. **Officers:** Robert Erkes.

■ **11696** ■ **Charles Lehman Co.**
14611 S Carmenita Rd.
Norwalk, CA 90650-5228
Phone: (562)921-4424 **Fax:** (562)921-1077
Products: Food. **SIC:** 5141 (Groceries—General Line).
Emp: 49.

■ **11697** ■ **Leidy's Inc.**
266 W Cherry Ln.
PO Box 257
Souderton, PA 18964
Phone: (215)723-4606
Free: (800)222-2319 **Fax:** (215)721-2003
Products: Pork products. **SIC:** 5147 (Meats & Meat Products). **Est:** 1968. **Sales:** $49,000,000 (2000).
Emp: 225. **Officers:** Thomas K. Leidy, President & CFO.

■ **11698** ■ **Lemke Cheese and Packaging Company Inc.**
PO Box 688
Wausau, WI 54402
Phone: (715)842-3214 **Fax:** (715)842-4452
Products: Natural and processed cheese. **SIC:** 5143 (Dairy Products Except Dried or Canned). **Sales:** $14,000,000 (2000). **Emp:** 70. **Officers:** Randall J. Lewis, President; Daniel Zagzebski, Treasurer.

■ **11699** ■ **Leon Supply Company, Inc.**
PO Box 1437
Ogunquit, ME 03907-1437
E-mail: leonsup2atsleonsupply.com
URL: http://www.leonsupply.com
Products: Food; Paper products. **SICs:** 5141 (Groceries—General Line); 5113 (Industrial & Personal Service Paper). **Est:** 1946. **Sales:** $5,700,000 (1999).
Emp: 22. **Officers:** Ed Williams, President.

■ **11700** ■ **Leon Supply Company Inc.**
160 Goddard Memorial Dr.
Worcester, MA 01603-1260
Phone: (508)756-8768 **Fax:** (508)797-9605
Products: Food. **SIC:** 5141 (Groceries—General Line).

■ **11701** ■ **Leonard and Harral Packing Company Inc.**
PO Box 14514
San Antonio, TX 78214
Phone: (210)924-4403 **Fax:** (210)927-9339
Products: Meat. **SIC:** 5147 (Meats & Meat Products).
Est: 1963. **Sales:** $160,000,000 (2000). **Emp:** 600.
Officers: Kenneth Leonard, President; Terry Black, CFO; Neal Leonard, Sales Mgr.; Mark Myers, VP of Operations; Mary Cheddie, Dir of Human Resources.

■ **11702** ■ **Leone Food Service Corp.**
30660 Plymouth Rd.
Livonia, MI 48150
Phone: (313)427-7650 **Fax:** (313)427-7473
Products: Frozen foods; Dry goods; Paper; Fresh fruits and vegetables. **SICs:** 5149 (Groceries & Related Products Nec); 5113 (Industrial & Personal Service Paper); 5142 (Packaged Frozen Foods); 5148 (Fresh Fruits & Vegetables). **Est:** 1922. **Sales:** $60,000,000 (2000). **Emp:** 130. **Officers:** Bob Greene, President.

■ **11703** ■ **Level Valley Creamery, Inc.**
807 Pleasant Valley Rd.
West Bend, WI 53095-9781
Phone: (414)675-6533 **Fax:** (414)675-2827
Products: Dairy products. **SIC:** 5143 (Dairy Products Except Dried or Canned). **Est:** 1935. **Emp:** 210.
Officers: A.J. Costigan; R. Rosenbalm; W. Koch Jr.; Joni Crivello, Customer Service Contact. **Former Name:** Level Valley.

■ **11704** ■ **M. Levin and Company Inc.**
326 Pattison Ave.
Philadelphia, PA 19148
Phone: (215)336-2900
Products: Fresh fruit and vegetables, including bananas. **SIC:** 5148 (Fresh Fruits & Vegetables). **Est:** 1906. **Sales:** $24,000,000 (2000). **Emp:** 120. **Officers:** Leon Levin, President; Michael Levin, Treasurer.

■ **11705** ■ **Levonian Brothers Inc.**
PO Box 629
Troy, NY 12180
Phone: (518)274-3610 **Fax:** (518)274-0098
Products: Meat. **SIC:** 5147 (Meats & Meat Products).
Est: 1947. **Sales:** $40,000,000 (2000). **Emp:** 70.
Officers: R. Dariah, President; T. Haggarty, Chairman of the Board & Finance Officer; R. Nazarian, Dir. of Data Processing.

■ **11706** ■ **Lewis Brothers Bakeries Inc.**
500 N Fulton Ave.
Evansville, IN 47710
Phone: (812)425-4642 **Fax:** (812)425-7609
Products: Bread. **SIC:** 5149 (Groceries & Related Products Nec). **Est:** 1925. **Sales:** $150,000,000 (2000). **Emp:** 1,562. **Officers:** R.J. Lewis Jr., President; R.L. Lesh, VP of Finance; Jim McRae, Sr. VP of Sales; Chris Frano, Dir. of Information Systems; Ann Greeenfield, VP of Human Resources.

■ **11707** ■ **Lewis Grocer Co.**
Hwy. 49 S
Indianola, MS 38751
Phone: (601)887-3211 **Fax:** (601)887-8424
Products: Groceries. **SIC:** 5141 (Groceries—General Line). **Officers:** Ted L. Crouse, President.

■ **11708** ■ **Liberty Gold Fruit Co.**
PO Box 2187
South San Francisco, CA 94083
Phone: (650)583-4700 **Fax:** (650)583-4770
Products: General line groceries. **SIC:** 5141
(Groceries—General Line). **Est:** 1932. **Sales:**
$1,000,000 (2000). **Emp:** 5. **Officers:** Harry Battat,
President.

■ **11709** ■ **Liberty Richter Inc.**
1 Park 80 Olz. West
Saddle Brook, NJ 07663-5808
Phone: (201)843-8900 **Fax:** (201)935-2993
Products: Food preparations; Dried and dehydrated
food products; Head rice not packaged with other
ingredients; Potatoes; Egg noodle products; Health
foods. **SICs:** 5149 (Groceries & Related Products Nec);
5148 (Fresh Fruits & Vegetables). **Sales:**
$150,000,000 (2000). **Emp:** 75. **Officers:** Richard
Blasczak, President.

■ **11710** ■ **Lifeline Food Company Inc.**
426 Orange St.
Sand City, CA 93955
Phone: (831)899-5040 **Fax:** (831)899-0285
E-mail: lifetimefatfree@aol.com
Products: Low-fat and fat-free cheeses. **SIC:** 5143
(Dairy Products Except Dried or Canned). **Est:** 1983.
Emp: 20. **Officers:** Jone Chappell, President; Cynde
Brown, Vice President.

■ **11711** ■ **Lil Brave Distributors Inc./Division
of Plee-Zing Inc.**
1640 Pleasant Rd.
Glenview, IL 60025
Phone: (847)998-0200 **Fax:** (847)998-8059
Products: Private labeled food, disposables and paper
products. **SICs:** 5141 (Groceries—General Line); 5142
(Packaged Frozen Foods). **Est:** 1968. **Officers:**
William Stickney III, Secretary.

■ **11712** ■ **Lincoln Packing Co.**
137 Newmarket Sq.
Boston, MA 02118-2603
Phone: (617)427-2836 **Fax:** (617)427-8160
Products: Sausage. **SIC:** 5147 (Meats & Meat
Products). **Emp:** 16. **Officers:** Muriel Gold.

■ **11713** ■ **Lincoln Poultry and Egg Co.**
2005 M St.
Lincoln, NE 68510
Phone: (402)477-3757 **Fax:** (402)477-1800
Products: Food; Specialty cleaning and sanitation
products. **SICs:** 5141 (Groceries—General Line); 5169
(Chemicals & Allied Products Nec). **Est:** 1957. **Sales:**
$25,000,000 (2000). **Emp:** 80. **Officers:** Richard
Evnen.

■ **11714** ■ **Lindemann Produce Inc.**
923 E Pacheco Blvd.
Los Banos, CA 93635
Phone: (209)826-2442 **Fax:** (209)826-0295
Products: Fresh fruits. **SIC:** 5148 (Fresh Fruits &
Vegetables). **Est:** 1928. **Sales:** $32,000,000 (2000).
Emp: 200. **Officers:** George Lindemann, President;
Rhett Salha, CFO; David B. Goforth, Sales Mgr.

■ **11715** ■ **Lindemann Produce Inc.**
300 E 2nd St., Ste. 1200
Reno, NV 89501
Phone: (775)323-2442 **Fax:** (775)826-0295
Products: Fresh fruits and vegetables. **SIC:** 5148
(Fresh Fruits & Vegetables). **Sales:** $80,000,000
(2000). **Emp:** 200. **Officers:** Garry Davenport, CFO.

■ **11716** ■ **Lindsay Foods Inc.**
PO Box 04403
Milwaukee, WI 53204
Phone: (414)649-2500
Products: Meat. **SIC:** 5147 (Meats & Meat Products).

■ **11717** ■ **Lionel Lavallee Company Inc.**
PO Box 229
Haverhill, MA 01830
Phone: (978)374-6391
Products: Meat including ground beef for the food
service industry. **SIC:** 5147 (Meats & Meat Products).
Sales: $15,000,000 (1994). **Emp:** 45. **Officers:**
Leonard Lavallee, CEO.

■ **11718** ■ **John Livacich Produce Inc.**
PO Box 70209
Riverside, CA 92513
Phone: (909)734-6060 **Fax:** (909)734-3778
E-mail: jljsales@aol.com
Products: Fruit and vegetables. **SIC:** 5148 (Fresh
Fruits & Vegetables). **Est:** 1960. **Sales:** $25,000,000
(2000). **Emp:** 22. **Officers:** John Livacich, President;
Lori C. Livacich, Secretary.

■ **11719** ■ **Lo-An Foods Inc.**
6002 Benjamin Rd.
Tampa, FL 33634
Phone: (813)886-3590 **Fax:** (813)888-8604
Products: Egg rolls. **SIC:** 5149 (Groceries & Related
Products Nec). **Est:** 1971. **Sales:** $15,000,000 (2000).
Emp: 80. **Officers:** Lo-An Nguyen, President; George
Hammil, Controller; John R. Bottomley, Sales Mgr.;
Sumati Villaman, Dir of Human Resources.

■ **11720** ■ **Lockney Cooperative Gin**
PO Box 128
Lockney, TX 79241
Phone: (806)652-3377
Products: Grain and beans. **SIC:** 5153 (Grain & Field
Beans). **Sales:** $20,000,000 (1992). **Emp:** 20.
Officers: John Carthel, President; Fern Hartsell,
Comptroller.

■ **11721** ■ **Loda Poultry Company Inc.**
551 E 400 North Rd.
Loda, IL 60948
Phone: (217)386-2381
Products: Poultry; Beef; Pork; Deli items. **SICs:** 5144
(Poultry & Poultry Products); 5147 (Meats & Meat
Products); 5149 (Groceries & Related Products Nec).
Sales: $15,000,000 (2000). **Emp:** 40. **Officers:** Beth
Bauman, President.

■ **11722** ■ **Logan Inc.**
653 Evans City Rd.
Butler, PA 16001-8759
Phone: (724)482-4715 **Fax:** (724)482-4498
Products: Candy; Tobacco; Cigars; Cigarettes; Food
service products; Paper products. **SICs:** 5145
(Confectionery); 5113 (Industrial & Personal Service
Paper); 5046 (Commercial Equipment Nec); 5141
(Groceries—General Line); 5149 (Groceries & Related
Products Nec). **Est:** 1930. **Sales:** $15,000,000 (2000).
Emp: 27. **Officers:** W. Allen Ward, VP & General Mgr.;
W. Ward, CFO.

■ **11723** ■ **Logan International Ltd.**
PO Box 1000
Boardman, OR 97818
Phone: (541)481-3070
Free: (800)883-5832 **Fax:** (541)481-3079
Products: Frozen french fries. **SIC:** 5142 (Packaged
Frozen Foods). **Sales:** $7,900,000 (2000). **Emp:** 96.
Officers: Dennis Logan, President.

■ **11724** ■ **Lomar Foods**
PO Box 180
Des Moines, IA 50301
Phone: (515)244-3105 **Fax:** (515)244-0515
Products: Groceries, Specialty foods. **SICs:** 5149
(Groceries & Related Products Nec); 5148 (Fresh
Fruits & Vegetables). **Est:** 1960. **Sales:** $50,000,000
(2000). **Emp:** 60. **Officers:** Louis G. Hurwitz,
President.

■ **11725** ■ **London's Farm Dairy, Inc.**
2136 Pine Grove Ave.
Port Huron, MI 48060
Phone: (810)984-5111 **Fax:** (810)984-3139
Products: Ice cream. **SIC:** 5143 (Dairy Products
Except Dried or Canned). **Est:** 1936. **Sales:**
$6,000,000 (2000). **Emp:** 49. **Officers:** Doug Mowat.

■ **11726** ■ **Lone Elm Sales Inc.**
9695 N Van Dyne Rd.
Van Dyne, WI 54979
Phone: (920)688-2338
Free: (800)950-8275 **Fax:** (920)688-5233
Products: Pizza supplies; Cheese; Cooking supplies.
SICs: 5143 (Dairy Products Except Dried or Canned);
5046 (Commercial Equipment Nec). **Est:** 1949. **Sales:**
$7,000,000 (2000). **Emp:** 11. **Officers:** Glen Dedow,
President.

■ **11727** ■ **Lone Star Food Service Co.**
PO Box 2005
Austin, TX 78768-2005
Phone: (512)478-3161 **Fax:** (512)478-3938
Products: Foods, including meats, seafood, frozen
vegetables, cookies, and muffins. **SICs:** 5147 (Meats &
Meat Products); 5142 (Packaged Frozen Foods); 5146
(Fish & Seafoods); 5149 (Groceries & Related Products
Nec). **Sales:** $9,000,000 (2000). **Emp:** 45. **Officers:** F.
E. Hall.

■ **11728** ■ **Lone Star Institutional Grocers**
PO Box 28928
Dallas, TX 75228-0928
Phone: (214)357-1871
Products: Groceries. **SIC:** 5141 (Groceries—General
Line). **Est:** 1930. **Sales:** $38,000,000 (2000). **Emp:**
140. **Officers:** Don Stahl, President; Cathy Cloud,
Comptroller; Jerry Martin, Sales Mgr.; Tom Kahle, Dir.
of Systems; Rita Harwell, Dir of Human Resources.

■ **11729** ■ **Lone Star Produce Inc.**
12450 Cutten Rd.
Houston, TX 77066
Phone: (281)444-8596
Products: Produce. **SIC:** 5148 (Fresh Fruits &
Vegetables).

■ **11730** ■ **Long Wholesale Distributors Inc.**
201 N Fulton Dr.
Corinth, MS 38834-4621
Phone: (662)287-2421 **Free:** (800)822-LONG
Products: Groceries. **SIC:** 5141 (Groceries—General
Line). **Emp:** 49.

■ **11731** ■ **Long Wholesale Inc.**
PO Box 70
Meridian, MS 39301-0070
Phone: (601)482-3144
Products: Groceries. **SIC:** 5141 (Groceries—General
Line). **Est:** 1918. **Sales:** $81,000,000 (2000). **Emp:**
155. **Officers:** Erst Long Jr., President; Sam Long,
Vice President.

■ **11732** ■ **O.W. and B.S. Look Company Inc.**
PO Box 504
Jonesport, ME 04649
Phone: (207)497-2353 **Fax:** (207)497-8554
Products: Lobsters. **SIC:** 5146 (Fish & Seafoods). **Est:**
1910. **Sales:** $6,000,000 (2000). **Emp:** 20. **Officers:** B.
Sid Look, President; Priscilla Look, Vice President.

■ **11733** ■ **Lords Sausage**
411 Harvey St.
Dexter, GA 31019
Phone: (912)875-3101
Free: (800)342-6002 **Fax:** (912)875-3039
Products: Pork products. **SIC:** 5147 (Meats & Meat
Products). **Emp:** 24.

■ **11734** ■ **Los Amigos Tortilla Manufacturing
Inc.**
251 Armour Dr. NE
Atlanta, GA 30324-3979
Phone: (404)876-8153
Free: (800)969-TACO **Fax:** (404)876-8102
Products: Mexican food specialties. **SIC:** 5149
(Groceries & Related Products Nec). **Est:** 1969. **Emp:**
49.

■ **11735** ■ **Los Angeles Nut House**
1601 E Olympic Blvd., Ste. 200
Los Angeles, CA 90021
Phone: (213)623-2541
Free: (800)526-8846 **Fax:** (213)624-9168
Products: Salted nuts. **SIC:** 5145 (Confectionery).
Sales: $66,700,000 (2000). **Emp:** 40. **Officers:**
Michael Booker, CEO & President; Kevin Strecker,
CFO.

■ **11736** ■ **Louis Rich Co.**
3704 Louis Rich Dr.
Newberry, SC 29108
Phone: (803)276-5015 **Fax:** (803)321-1502
Products: Turkey. **SIC:** 5144 (Poultry & Poultry
Products). **Sales:** $208,000,000 (2000). **Emp:** 2,050.
Officers: Lyle Olson.

■ **11737** ■ **Lov-It Creamery Inc.**
443 N Henry St.
Green Bay, WI 54302-1838
Phone: (920)432-4383 **Fax:** (920)432-1290
Products: Butter and butter blends. **SIC:** 5143 (Dairy Products Except Dried or Canned). **Est:** 1942. **Sales:** $50,000,000 (2000). **Emp:** 65. **Officers:** William Wangerin.

■ **11738** ■ **Lowell Packing Co.**
PO Box 220
Fitzgerald, GA 31750
Phone: (912)423-2051 **Fax:** (912)423-6601
Products: Pork, including wieners and bologna. **SIC:** 5147 (Meats & Meat Products). **Est:** 1970. **Sales:** $17,000,000 (2000). **Emp:** 100. **Officers:** L.M. Downing Jr., Vice President.

■ **11739** ■ **L.T. Plant, Inc.**
PO Box 609
Montville, NJ 07045
Phone: (973)882-9190 **Fax:** (973)263-2287
E-mail: baratfound@aol.com
Products: Vegetarian food entrees and canned goods. **SIC:** 5149 (Groceries & Related Products Nec). **Est:** 1981. **Sales:** $800,000 (2000). **Emp:** 2. **Officers:** Chandri Barat, President & Treasurer.

■ **11740** ■ **Luanka Seafood Co.**
814 E Harrison St.
PO Box 1086
Harlingen, TX 78551
Phone: (956)428-1862
Free: (800)553-6114 **Fax:** (956)428-3356
Products: Frozen seafood; Shrimp; Fresh fish; Frozen fish; Prepared fresh fish and seafood. **SICs:** 5146 (Fish & Seafoods); 5142 (Packaged Frozen Foods). **Emp:** 5.

■ **11741** ■ **Luberski Inc.**
PO Box 34001
Fullerton, CA 92834
Phone: (714)680-3447 **Fax:** (714)680-3080
URL: http://www.hiddenvilla.com
Products: Eggs; Cheese; Milk; Poultry. **SICs:** 5143 (Dairy Products Except Dried or Canned); 5144 (Poultry & Poultry Products). **Est:** 1977. **Sales:** $70,000,000 (2000). **Emp:** 110. **Officers:** Tim Luberski, President; Michael Sencer, Exec. VP. **Doing Business As:** Hidden Villa Ranch.

■ **11742** ■ **Luce Candy Co.**
3304 W Oceanfront
Newport Beach, CA 92663-3026
Phone: (213)221-4646
Products: Candy. **SIC:** 5145 (Confectionery). **Est:** 1897. **Sales:** $800,000 (2000). **Emp:** 12. **Officers:** Angie Luce, President; Joe Apodaca, Dir. of Production.

■ **11743** ■ **Lucky Fruit and Produce Company Inc.**
7735 Hill Rd.
Granite Bay, CA 95746-6953
Phone: (916)446-7621
Products: Fruit and produce. **SIC:** 5148 (Fresh Fruits & Vegetables). **Est:** 1960. **Sales:** $19,000,000 (2000). **Emp:** 16. **Officers:** Emery Mitchell, President.

■ **11744** ■ **Lumen Foods**
409 Scott St.
Lake Charles, LA 70601
Phone: (318)436-6748
Free: (800)256-2253 **Fax:** (318)436-1769
E-mail: lumenfoods@aol.com
URL: http://www.lumenfds.com
Products: Meat replacement products and imitation jerky snacks. **SICs:** 5147 (Meats & Meat Products); 5149 (Groceries & Related Products Nec). **Est:** 1986. **Sales:** $2,800,000 (2000). **Emp:** 15. **Officers:** Cathryn Caton, President; Katy Herr, Customer Service; Jeannette Nelson, General Mgr.

■ **11745** ■ **Lun Fat Produce Inc.**
227 Harrison Ave.
Boston, MA 02111
Phone: (617)426-4045
Products: Fresh fruit and vegetables. **SIC:** 5148 (Fresh Fruits & Vegetables). **Sales:** $2,000,000 (2000). **Emp:** 6. **Officers:** Peter Tham, President.

■ **11746** ■ **Luter Packing Company Inc.**
PO Box 929
Laurinburg, NC 28353
Phone: (910)844-5201
Products: Beef and pork. **SIC:** 5147 (Meats & Meat Products). **Est:** 1947. **Sales:** $2,000,000 (2000). **Emp:** 6. **Officers:** J.C. Burnette, President.

■ **11747** ■ **Luxor California Export Corp.**
3659 India St., Ste. 200
San Diego, CA 92103
Phone: (619)692-9330
Free: (800)500-5896 **Fax:** (619)692-4292
URL: http://www.luxorexports.com
Products: Dairy products. **SIC:** 5143 (Dairy Products Except Dried or Canned). **Est:** 1986. **Sales:** $50,000,000 (2000). **Emp:** 11. **Officers:** Ray Kafaji, General Mgr.; Holland Clem, Sales/Marketing Contact.

■ **11748** ■ **Lykes Bros. Inc.**
PO Box 1690
Tampa, FL 33601
Phone: (813)223-3981 **Fax:** (813)273-5421
Products: Lunch meats; Hot dogs; Bacon; Sausage. **SIC:** 5147 (Meats & Meat Products). **Emp:** 1,000.

■ **11749** ■ **M & B Distributors, Inc.**
3896 Virginia Ave.
Cincinnati, OH 45227
Phone: (513)561-0060
Products: Sandwiches. **SIC:** 5141 (Groceries—General Line).

■ **11750** ■ **M & F Foods**
PO Box 5317
East Orange, NJ 07019-5317
Phone: (973)344-6700 **Fax:** (973)344-2957
Products: Frozen food, including meat, vegetables, and fruit. **SIC:** 5142 (Packaged Frozen Foods).

■ **11751** ■ **M & L Trading Company, Inc.**
PO Box 263
Bothell, WA 98041
Phone: (425)481-3014 **Fax:** (425)485-5087
E-mail: mltrding_engineering@msn.com
Products: Fresh fruit and vegetables; Wastewater treatment equipment; Pumps; Packaged frozen food. **SICs:** 5148 (Fresh Fruits & Vegetables); 5074 (Plumbing & Hydronic Heating Supplies); 5084 (Industrial Machinery & Equipment); 5142 (Packaged Frozen Foods). **Officers:** Terry Losh, Vice President.

■ **11752** ■ **M & V Provision Company Inc.**
146 N 6th St.
Brooklyn, NY 11211-3201
Phones: (718)388-3440 (718)388-6209
Fax: (718)388-1744
E-mail: tciuffo@aol.com
Products: Processed, frozen, and cooked meats; Natural and processed cheese, and related products. **SICs:** 5147 (Meats & Meat Products); 5142 (Packaged Frozen Foods); 5143 (Dairy Products Except Dried or Canned). **Est:** 1949. **Emp:** 35. **Officers:** Paul Vallario; Tony Ciuffo; Mike Ciuffo, Sales/Marketing Contact; Tony Ciuffo, Sales/Marketing Contact, e-mail: tciuffo@aol.com.

■ **11753** ■ **Mac Nuts of Hawaii**
PO Box 833
Kealakekua, HI 96750
Phone: (808)328-7234 **Fax:** (808)328-9601
Products: Bulk macadamia nuts. **SIC:** 5145 (Confectionery). **Est:** 1997. **Emp:** 20. **Officers:** William L. Goulding, Partner.

■ **11754** ■ **Made in Nature Inc.**
1448 Industrial Ave.
Sebastopol, CA 95472-4848
Phone: (707)535-4000
Free: (800)906-7426 **Fax:** (707)535-4039
URL: http://www.madeinnature.com
Products: Dried fruit and vegetables. **SIC:** 5148 (Fresh Fruits & Vegetables). **Est:** 1989. **Sales:** $10,000,000 (1999). **Emp:** 15. **Officers:** William C. Burgess, President.

■ **11755** ■ **Made Rite Potato Chip Company Inc.**
PO Box 1100
Bay City, MI 48706
Phone: (517)684-6271 **Fax:** (517)684-3950
Products: Potato chips. **SIC:** 5149 (Groceries & Related Products Nec). **Est:** 1932. **Sales:** $7,000,000 (2000). **Emp:** 100. **Officers:** Russ Ruhland, Controller.

■ **11756** ■ **Madison Dairy Produce Company Inc.**
PO Box 389
Madison, WI 53701
Phone: (608)256-5561 **Fax:** (608)256-5561
Products: Butter. **SIC:** 5143 (Dairy Products Except Dried or Canned). **Est:** 1906. **Sales:** $13,000,000 (2000). **Emp:** 65. **Officers:** Frederick C. Steinhauer, President; Linda Wiedenfeld, CFO; Gary Steinhauer, Dir. of Marketing.

■ **11757** ■ **Madison Grocery Company Inc.**
PO Box 580
Richmond, KY 40476-0580
Phone: (606)623-2416
Products: General line groceries. **SIC:** 5141 (Groceries—General Line). **Est:** 1934. **Sales:** $20,000,000 (2000). **Emp:** 60. **Officers:** Maurice Baker, CEO.

■ **11758** ■ **Magi Inc.**
Hwy. 97
Brewster, WA 98812
Phone: (509)689-2511
Products: Fruit. **SIC:** 5148 (Fresh Fruits & Vegetables). **Sales:** $25,000,000 (1994). **Emp:** 300. **Officers:** George Chapman, General Mgr.; Edward A. Meyers, Comptroller.

■ **11759** ■ **Main Street Produce Inc.**
2165 W Main St.
Santa Maria, CA 93454
Phone: (805)349-7170 **Fax:** (805)349-7174
Products: Produce. **SIC:** 5148 (Fresh Fruits & Vegetables). **Sales:** $12,000,000 (2000). **Emp:** 26. **Officers:** Paul Allen, President.

■ **11760** ■ **Maine Potato Growers Inc.**
PO Box 271
Presque Isle, ME 04769
Phone: (207)764-3131 **Fax:** (207)764-8450
URL: http://www.mpgco-op.com
Products: Potatoes. **SIC:** 5148 (Fresh Fruits & Vegetables). **Est:** 1932. **Sales:** $54,000,000 (2000). **Emp:** 140. **Officers:** J.G. Lallande III, CEO.

■ **11761** ■ **Maines Paper and Food Service Inc.**
12 Terrace Dr.
PO Box 450
Conklin, NY 13748
Phone: (607)772-1936
Free: (800)366-3669 **Fax:** (607)723-8526
URL: http://www.maines.net
Products: General line groceries and foodservice products. **SIC:** 5141 (Groceries—General Line). **Sales:** $260,000,000 (2000). **Emp:** 500. **Officers:** Floyd Maines, President; Mary Broderick, Controller; Phil Campolo, VP of Sales; Dennis Wysocki, VP of Information Systems; Bill Maines, Exec. VP; David Maines, Exec. VP.

■ **11762** ■ **Majji Produce, Inc.**
6170 Toledo
Detroit, MI 48209
Phone: (313)843-0660 **Fax:** (313)843-6969
Products: Produce. **SIC:** 5148 (Fresh Fruits & Vegetables).

■ **11763** ■ **Major-Sysco Food Services Inc.**
136 Mariposa Rd.
Modesto, CA 95354
Phone: (209)527-7700
Products: General line groceries. **SIC:** 5141 (Groceries—General Line). **Est:** 1938. **Sales:** $98,000,000 (2000). **Emp:** 250. **Officers:** Richard L. Friedlen, President; Doug Schultz, VP of Finance.

■ **11764** ■ **Malin Potato Cooperative Inc.**
E 4th
Merrill, OR 97633
Phone: (541)798-5665   **Fax:** (541)798-1049
Products: Potatoes. **SIC:** 5148 (Fresh Fruits &
Vegetables). **Emp:** 49. **Officers:** Don Micka, Manager.

■ **11765** ■ **Mallor Brokerage Co.**
147-17 105th Ave.
Jamaica, NY 11435-4917
Phone: (718)291-9300   **Fax:** (718)523-4259
Products: Canned and frozen foods. **SIC:** 5142
(Packaged Frozen Foods). **Est:** 1942. **Emp:** 4.
Officers: Joseph Mallor.

■ **11766** ■ **Malone and Hyde Inc.**
1991 Corporate Ave.
Memphis, TN 38132
Phone: (901)367-8200   **Fax:** (901)395-8543
Products: General line groceries. **SIC:** 5141
(Groceries—General Line). **Est:** 1907. **Sales:**
$3,119,000,000 (2000). **Emp:** 4,000. **Officers:** Bob
Harris, President; Ruth Ann Ray, VP & Controller;
Robert Sandifer, VP of Information Systems; Christian
Goddard, Dir of Human Resources.

■ **11767** ■ **Malone and Hyde Inc. Lafayette
Div.**
PO Box 91910
Lafayette, LA 70509
Phone: (318)236-3800
Products: Groceries, frozen foods, and meats. **SICs:**
5141 (Groceries—General Line); 5142 (Packaged
Frozen Foods); 5147 (Meats & Meat Products).
Officers: Nolan Milam, President.

■ **11768** ■ **Malone Products Inc.**
3050 Classen Blvd.
Norman, OK 73071
Phone: (405)321-5310
Products: Frozen and dried foods; Paper products.
SICs: 5142 (Packaged Frozen Foods); 5149
(Groceries & Related Products Nec); 5113 (Industrial &
Personal Service Paper). **Emp:** 40.

■ **11769** ■ **Maloney, Cunningham & Devic**
1114 W Fulton St.
Chicago, IL 60607
Phone: (312)666-4452   **Fax:** (312)666-6789
Products: Food. **SICs:** 5149 (Groceries & Related
Products Nec); 5141 (Groceries—General Line).

■ **11770** ■ **Mama Rosa's Slice of Italy**
616 N Rampart
New Orleans, LA 70112-3538
Phone: (504)523-5546
Products: Italian food specialties. **SIC:** 5149
(Groceries & Related Products Nec). **Emp:** 21.
Officers: A. Gerald Pelayo; James S. Storer.

■ **11771** ■ **Manassas Ice and Fuel Company
Inc.**
9009 Center St.
Manassas, VA 20110-5486
Phone: (703)368-3121
Free: (888)368-3121   **Fax:** (703)368-1476
URL: http://www.mifco-fuel.com
Products: Frozen food and meat products; Fuel and
petroleum products; Ice. **SICs:** 5142 (Packaged Frozen
Foods); 5147 (Meats & Meat Products); 5172
(Petroleum Products Nec). **Est:** 1922. **Sales:**
$15,871,565 (2000). **Emp:** 41. **Officers:** Harry J.
Parrish II, President; John W. Fraber III, Controller.

■ **11772** ■ **Manchester Wholesale Distributors**
64 Old Granite St.
Manchester, NH 03101
Phone: (603)625-5461   **Fax:** (603)625-5148
URL: http://www.manchesterwholesale.com
Products: General line groceries; Candy; Tobacco.
SIC: 5141 (Groceries—General Line). **Est:** 1939.
Sales: $50,000,000 (1999). **Officers:** Emile Tetu,
CEO; Raymond Tetu, Vice President; Gerard Gregoire,
Sales Mgr.; Christine Letares, Exec. Administrator;
Thomis Fillingim, President.

■ **11773** ■ **Mancini & Groesbeck, Inc.**
164 East 3900 South
PO Box 57218
Salt Lake City, UT 84157-0218
Phone: (801)266-4453   **Fax:** (801)265-9487
E-mail: mancini@mancini-slc.com
Products: Food; Grocery; HBC; Confection;
Frozen/refrigerated. **SIC:** 5141 (Groceries—General
Line). **Est:** 1962. **Emp:** 72. **Officers:** Tad Mancini.

■ **11774** ■ **Manhattan Coffee Co.**
PO Box 14583
St. Louis, MO 63178
Phone: (314)731-2500
Products: Coffee. **SIC:** 5149 (Groceries & Related
Products Nec). **Est:** 1934. **Sales:** $10,000,000 (2000).
Emp: 45. **Officers:** Tom Allen, Manager.

■ **11775** ■ **Manhattan Wholesale Meat
Company Inc.**
209 Yuma St.
Manhattan, KS 66502
Phone: (913)776-9203
Free: (800)432-2706   **Fax:** (785)776-5940
Products: Meats; Frozen vegetables; Canned fruits
and vegetables; Entrees. **SIC:** 5147 (Meats & Meat
Products). **Est:** 1952. **Sales:** $7,000,000 (2000). **Emp:**
20. **Officers:** Donald E. Ince, President.

■ **11776** ■ **Manildra Milling Corp.**
4210 Shawnee Mission
Shawnee Mission, KS 66205
Phone: (913)362-0777
Free: (800)323-8435   **Fax:** (913)362-0674
E-mail: sales@manildrausa.com
Products: Baking supplies, including wheat gluten and
starch. **SIC:** 5149 (Groceries & Related Products Nec).
Est: 1926. **Sales:** $75,000,000 (2000). **Emp:** 65.
Officers: William T. McCurry, President; Thomas S.
McCurry, Sales & Marketing Contact.

■ **11777** ■ **Maple Valley Cooperative**
PO Box 68
Leigh, NE 68643
Phone: (402)487-2295   **Fax:** (402)487-3365
Products: Small engine repair, agricultural and
industrial machinery repair. **SICs:** 5153 (Grain & Field
Beans); 5191 (Farm Supplies). **Sales:** $10,000,000
(2000). **Emp:** 20. **Officers:** Mike Malena, President.

■ **11778** ■ **Maranatha**
710 Jefferson St.
Ashland, OR 97520
Phone: (541)488-2747   **Fax:** (541)488-3369
Products: Food preparations; Dried and dehydrated
food products; Head rice not packaged with other
ingredients; Potatoes; Egg noodle products; Health
foods; Snack foods. **SIC:** 5149 (Groceries & Related
Products Nec).

■ **11779** ■ **Mariani Packing Company Inc.**
320 Jackson St.
San Jose, CA 95112
Phone: (408)288-8300   **Fax:** (408)280-5219
Products: Dried fruit; Processed fruit. **SIC:** 5149
(Groceries & Related Products Nec). **Sales:**
$61,000,000 (2000). **Emp:** 280. **Officers:** Mark
Mariani, Chairman of the Board.

■ **11780** ■ **Marie's Quality Foods**
1244 E Beamer
Woodland, CA 95776
Phone: (530)662-9638
Free: (800)544-9516   **Fax:** (530)662-9084
E-mail: mariesfood@aol.com
Products: Salad dressings. **SIC:** 5149 (Groceries &
Related Products Nec). **Est:** 1960. **Sales:** $18,000,000
(1999). **Emp:** 30. **Officers:** Richard Orr,
Sales/Marketing Contact, e-mail: richardorr@aol.com.

■ **11781** ■ **Market Share International Inc.**
1230 S Main St.
Gainesville, FL 32601
Phone: (352)372-9186
Products: Nutritional drinks, tablets, and power bars.
SIC: 5149 (Groceries & Related Products Nec). **Sales:**
$500,000 (2000). **Emp:** 2. **Officers:** John Hoce,
President.

■ **11782** ■ **Market Specialties**
536 Mariposa Rd.
Modesto, CA 95352
Phone: (209)526-8511
Free: (800)753-4432   **Fax:** (209)526-9153
Products: General line groceries. **SIC:** 5141
(Groceries—General Line).

■ **11783** ■ **Marketing Performance Inc.**
2147 Riverchase Office Rd.
Birmingham, AL 35244
Phone: (205)982-1121   **Fax:** (205)982-1156
Products: Food broker. **SIC:** 5141 (Groceries—
General Line). **Sales:** $125,000,000 (2000). **Emp:** 76.
Officers: Fred Brown, President; Ann Howlett, Exec.
VP of Finance.

■ **11784** ■ **Marketing Specialist Corp.**
17855 Dallas Pkwy., Ste. 200
Dallas, TX 75287-6852
Phone: (972)349-6200   **Fax:** (972)349-6400
URL: http://www.mssc.com
Products: Food. **SIC:** 5141 (Groceries—General Line).
Sales: $450,000,000 (2000). **Emp:** 6,500. **Officers:**
Ron Pedersen, Chairman of the Board, e-mail:
ronpedersen@mssc.com; Jerry Leonard, President &
CEO, e-mail: jerryleonard@mssc.com. **Former Name:**
Marketing Specialist Inc.

■ **11785** ■ **Marketing Specialista**
2848 Coheatland Dr.
Fargo, ND 58103
Phone: (701)235-8964   **Fax:** (701)235-8986
Products: Food. **SIC:** 5141 (Groceries—General Line).
Emp: 13. **Former Name:** Sales Force of Fargo.

■ **11786** ■ **Marketing Specialists - Southern
California Div.**
744 N Eckhuff St.
Orange, CA 92868-1020
Phone: (714)939-6275
Products: Food. **SIC:** 5149 (Groceries & Related
Products Nec). **Former Name:** Bromar Inc. Southern
California Div.

■ **11787** ■ **Mark's Quality Meats**
6800 Dix St.
Detroit, MI 48209-1269
Phone: (313)554-2500   **Fax:** (313)554-2504
Products: Meats. **SIC:** 5147 (Meats & Meat Products).
Est: 1973. **Emp:** 25. **Officers:** Mark Garrison.

■ **11788** ■ **Marmelstein and Associates Inc.**
PO Box 1268
Jackson, NJ 08527
Phone: (908)363-5626   **Fax:** (908)905-6570
Products: Grocery and dairy products. **SICs:** 5141
(Groceries—General Line); 5143 (Dairy Products
Except Dried or Canned). **Est:** 1981. **Sales:**
$5,500,000 (2000). **Emp:** 8. **Officers:** Saul
Marmelstein, President.

■ **11789** ■ **A.W. Marshall Co.**
PO Box 16127
Salt Lake City, UT 84116
Phone: (801)328-4713
Free: (800)273-4713   **Fax:** (801)328-9600
Products: Candy; Health and beauty aids; Groceries.
SICs: 5141 (Groceries—General Line); 5122 (Drugs,
Proprietaries & Sundries); 5145 (Confectionery); 5122
(Drugs, Proprietaries & Sundries). **Est:** 1948. **Sales:**
$17,000,000 (2000). **Emp:** 28. **Officers:** A.W.
Marshall, President; Dennis R. Eaton, Treasurer; D.W
DeHaan, Dir. of Marketing.

■ **11790** ■ **Marshall Distributing Co.**
2625 W 1100 S Directors Row
Salt Lake City, UT 84104
Phone: (801)973-8855
Free: (800)453-7405   **Fax:** (801)973-8881
Products: Health foods. **SIC:** 5149 (Groceries &
Related Products Nec).

■ **11791** ■ **Marshmallow Products Inc.**
9 W Mitchell Ave.
Cincinnati, OH 45217-1525
Phone: (513)641-2345
Free: (800)641-8551 **Fax:** (513)641-2557
Products: Food. **SIC:** 5149 (Groceries & Related Products Nec). **Sales:** $2,000,000 (2000). **Emp:** 30.

■ **11792** ■ **MarshmallowCone Co.**
5141 Fischer Ave.
Cincinnati, OH 45217-1157
Phone: (513)641-2345
Free: (800)641-8551 **Fax:** (513)641-2557
E-mail: customerserv@marshmallowcone.com
URL: http://www.marshmallowcone.com
Products: Marshmallow filled ice cream cones. **SICs:** 5149 (Groceries & Related Products Nec); 5145 (Confectionery). **Est:** 1936. **Sales:** $2,000,000 (2000). **Emp:** 30. **Officers:** William W. Ward, Partner; William M. Clark, Partner. **Former Name:** Marshmallow Products Inc.

■ **11793** ■ **Martin Bros. Distributing Co., Inc.**
406 Viking Rd.
PO Box 69
Cedar Falls, IA 50613-0069
Phone: (319)266-1775 **Fax:** (319)277-1238
URL: http://www.martinsnet.com
Products: Groceries; Medical supplies; Janitorial supplies. **SICs:** 5141 (Groceries—General Line); 5113 (Industrial & Personal Service Paper). **Est:** 1940. **Sales:** $112,000,000 (1999). **Emp:** 316. **Officers:** John Martin, President; Doug Coen, Dir. of Mktg. & Sales; Brooks Martin, Finance Mgr.

■ **11794** ■ **Martin-Brower Co.**
333 E Butterfield Rd.
Lombard, IL 60148
Phone: (630)271-8300
Products: Food and paper products for the food service industry. **SICs:** 5141 (Groceries—General Line); 5113 (Industrial & Personal Service Paper). **Sales:** $1,570,000,000 (1993). **Emp:** 3,000. **Officers:** Herbert Heller, President; John Winton, VP of Finance.

■ **11795** ■ **John Martinelli Inc.**
105 Avocado St.
PO Box 3211
Springfield, MA 01101-3211
Phone: (413)732-4193 **Fax:** (413)736-3480
Products: Nuts and seeds (salted, roasted, cooked, or blanched); Unprocessed, unshelled peanuts. **SIC:** 5145 (Confectionery). **Est:** 1934. **Sales:** $5,250,000 (2000). **Emp:** 10. **Officers:** Aaron M. Sanofsky, President; Mike Bigda, General Mgr.

■ **11796** ■ **Marvin Hayes Fish Co.**
PO Box 187
Samburg, TN 38254
Phone: (901)538-2166 **Fax:** (901)538-2166
Products: Fish and seafood. **SIC:** 5146 (Fish & Seafoods). **Sales:** $1,000,000 (2000). **Emp:** 4. **Officers:** Jan Dyer, President.

■ **11797** ■ **Mary Ann's Baking Co.**
324 Alhambra Blvd.
Sacramento, CA 95816
Phone: (916)441-4741 **Fax:** (916)441-5448
Products: Doughnuts and other sweet yeast goods. **SIC:** 5149 (Groceries & Related Products Nec). **Est:** 1963. **Sales:** $10,000,000 (2000). **Emp:** 70. **Officers:** J Demas, President; Robert Burzinski, Controller; Will Camp, Dir. of Marketing.

■ **11798** ■ **Maryland Hotel Supply Co.**
701 W Hamburg St.
Baltimore, MD 21230
Phone: (410)539-7055
Free: (800)369-2579 **Fax:** (410)685-6720
Products: Meat, including beef, lamb, and veal; Poultry. **SICs:** 5147 (Meats & Meat Products); 5142 (Packaged Frozen Foods); 5143 (Dairy Products Except Dried or Canned). **Est:** 1927. **Sales:** $53,000,000 (2000). **Emp:** 150. **Officers:** R.D. Niller III, President; Patricia Rowan, VP of Finance; Dennis Steele, VP of Sales.

■ **11799** ■ **Maryland and Virginia Milk Producers Cooperative Association Inc.**
1985 Isaac Newton Sq. W
Reston, VA 20190-5094
Phone: (703)742-6800
Free: (800)552-1976 **Fax:** (703)742-7459
URL: http://www.mdvamilk.com
Products: Milk. **SIC:** 5143 (Dairy Products Except Dried or Canned). **Est:** 1920. **Sales:** $620,709,686 (1999). **Emp:** 400. **Officers:** John D. Hardesty, President; Robert L. Shore, Secretary and General Mgr.

■ **11800** ■ **Charles Mascari & Associations**
32823 W 12 Mile Rd.
Farmington Hills, MI 48334-3304
Phone: (248)399-0950 **Fax:** (248)399-2533
Products: Food. **SIC:** 5141 (Groceries—General Line). **Emp:** 49.

■ **11801** ■ **Master Purveyors**
PO Box 10063
Tampa, FL 33679-0063
Phone: (813)253-0865
Free: (800)741-4632 **Fax:** (813)253-0996
Products: Beef; Fresh pork; Lamb and mutton; Veal, not canned or made into sausage; Poultry and small game; Natural and process cheese and related products. **SICs:** 5147 (Meats & Meat Products); 5144 (Poultry & Poultry Products); 5143 (Dairy Products Except Dried or Canned). **Emp:** 20. **Officers:** Michael P. McCranie.

■ **11802** ■ **Matanuska Maid Dairy**
814 Northern Lights
Anchorage, AK 99503
Phone: (907)561-5223 **Fax:** (907)563-7492
Products: Milk; Cottage cheese; Yogurt; Sour cream; Orange juice; Water; Soft serve ice cream mix. **SIC:** 5143 (Dairy Products Except Dried or Canned). **Sales:** $14,500,000 (2000). **Emp:** 44. **Officers:** Joseph Van Treeck, General Mgr.; Delene Bartel, Dir. of Sales.

■ **11803** ■ **Matarazzo Brothers Company Inc.**
290 4th St.
Chelsea, MA 02150
Phone: (617)889-0516 **Fax:** (617)884-0602
Products: Fresh tomatoes, green peppers, and watermelon. **SIC:** 5148 (Fresh Fruits & Vegetables). **Emp:** 30.

■ **11804** ■ **G.D. Mathews and Sons Inc.**
521 Medford St.
Boston, MA 02129
Phone: (617)242-1770
Free: (800)447-4005 **Fax:** (617)242-1989
Products: Prepared salads; Chicken pies, and other kosher products. **SICs:** 5149 (Groceries & Related Products Nec); 5148 (Fresh Fruits & Vegetables); 5147 (Meats & Meat Products). **Est:** 1927. **Sales:** $10,000,000 (1999). **Emp:** 20. **Officers:** Leo Mathews, President; L. Mathews, President; David Mathews, Sales/Marketing Contact; Joanne Savinen, Customer Service Contact and HRCT.

■ **11805** ■ **Mathias and Company Inc.**
PO Box 67
Petersburg, WV 26847
Phone: (304)257-1611
Products: Canned fruits and vegetables. **SIC:** 5148 (Fresh Fruits & Vegetables). **Sales:** $3,000,000 (2000). **Emp:** 15. **Officers:** V. Mathias, President.

■ **11806** ■ **Matthes and Associates**
PO Box 50
Maryland Heights, MO 63043-9050
Phone: (314)569-3030 **Fax:** (314)569-0149
Products: Food. **SIC:** 5141 (Groceries—General Line). **Sales:** $23,000,000 (2000). **Emp:** 45. **Officers:** Gary Matthes, President.

■ **11807** ■ **Mattingly Foods Inc.**
PO Box 2668
Zanesville, OH 43702-2668
Phone: (740)454-0136
Free: (800)777-6288 **Fax:** (740)454-2649
URL: http://www.mattinglyfoods.com
Products: Frozen, cooler, and dried meats for chain restaurants. **SICs:** 5147 (Meats & Meat Products); 5142 (Packaged Frozen Foods). **Est:** 1947. **Sales:** $200,000,000 (2000). **Emp:** 200. **Officers:** Robert K. Mattingly, Chairman of the Board; Barbara Callahan, President.

■ **11808** ■ **Mattingly Foods Inc.**
PO Box 2668
Zanesville, OH 43702-2668
Phone: (740)454-0136
Free: (800)777-6288 **Fax:** (740)454-2649
Products: Food. **SIC:** 5147 (Meats & Meat Products). **Sales:** $200,000,000 (2000). **Emp:** 200.

■ **11809** ■ **Maui Potato Chip Factory**
295 Lalo Pl.
Kahului, HI 96732-2915
Phone: (808)877-3652
Products: Potato chips. **SIC:** 5145 (Confectionery). **Est:** 1956. **Emp:** 12. **Officers:** Mark Kobayashi.

■ **11810** ■ **Maverick Ranch Lite Beef Inc.**
5360 N Franklin St.
Denver, CO 80216
Phone: (303)294-0146 **Fax:** (303)294-0623
Products: Meats, including beef, buffalo, lamb, pork, and ostrich. **SIC:** 5147 (Meats & Meat Products). **Est:** 1986. **Sales:** $25,000,000 (2000). **Emp:** 110. **Officers:** Roy Moore, President; Rex Moore, Vice President.

■ **11811** ■ **Maxim's Import Corp.**
2719 NW 24th St.
Miami, FL 33142
Phone: (305)633-2167 **Fax:** (305)638-1348
Products: Seafood; Beef; Poultry. **SICs:** 5147 (Meats & Meat Products); 5146 (Fish & Seafoods). **Est:** 1974. **Sales:** $35,000,000 (2000). **Emp:** 55. **Officers:** Luis Chi; Joe L. Chi.

■ **11812** ■ **Mayco Fish Company Ltd.**
2535 Jefferson Ave.
Tacoma, WA 98402-1303
Phone: (253)572-3070 **Fax:** (253)572-2437
Products: Salmon; Caviar. **SIC:** 5146 (Fish & Seafoods). **Est:** 1987. **Sales:** $10,000,000 (1999). **Emp:** 99. **Officers:** Katsukichi Chikamatsu.

■ **11813** ■ **Budd Mayer Co.**
4429 Shores Dr.
Metairie, LA 70006-2329
Phone: (504)885-6870 **Fax:** (504)885-6882
Products: General line groceries. **SIC:** 5141 (Groceries—General Line). **Emp:** 43. **Officers:** Bill Chadwell.

■ **11814** ■ **Mazon Farmers Elevator**
604 South St.
Mazon, IL 60444
Phone: (815)448-2113 **Fax:** (815)448-2609
Products: Agricultural equipment and supplies. **SIC:** 5153 (Grain & Field Beans). **Sales:** $42,000,000 (2000). **Emp:** 20.

■ **11815** ■ **Mazzetta Co.**
1990 St. Johns Ave.
Highland Park, IL 60035
Products: Frozen seafood. **SIC:** 5146 (Fish & Seafoods). **Est:** 1987. **Sales:** $70,000,000 (2000). **Emp:** 11. **Officers:** Tom Mazzetta, President.

■ **11816** ■ **M.B.M. Corp.**
PO Box 800
Rocky Mount, NC 27802
Phone: (919)985-7200
Products: Frozen foods; Fresh produce. **SICs:** 5142 (Packaged Frozen Foods); 5148 (Fresh Fruits & Vegetables). **Est:** 1970. **Sales:** $700,000,000 (2000). **Emp:** 400. **Officers:** Jerry Wordsworth, President; Ernest Avert, Controller; J. Sabiston, Dir. of Marketing.

■ **11817** ■ **McCabe's Quality Foods Inc.**
17600 NE San Rafael St.
Portland, OR 97230-5924
Phone: (503)256-4770 **Fax:** (503)256-1263
Products: Groceries, including meat, frozen foods, beverages, dairy products, and produce; Paper products. **SICs:** 5141 (Groceries—General Line); 5147 (Meats & Meat Products); 5143 (Dairy Products Except Dried or Canned); 5148 (Fresh Fruits & Vegetables).

Est: 1964. **Sales:** $100,000,000 (2000). **Emp:** 90. **Officers:** Jan McCabe, President.

■ **11818** ■ **McCarty-Holman Company Inc.**
PO Box 3409
Jackson, MS 39207
Phone: (601)948-0361 **Fax:** (601)352-0483
Products: Groceries. **SIC:** 5141 (Groceries—General Line). **Est:** 1912. **Sales:** $1,040,000,000 (2000). **Emp:** 10,000. **Officers:** William H. Holman Jr., CEO & Chairman of the Board; Roger P. Friou, CFO; William H. Holman III, Sr. VP of Marketing; Roger Parks, Sr. VP of Information Systems; Jerry Jones, Sr. VP of Human Resources.

■ **11819** ■ **McClesky Mills Inc.**
Rhodes St.
Smithville, GA 31787
Phone: (912)846-2003 **Fax:** (912)846-4805
Products: Peanuts. **SIC:** 5145 (Confectionery). **Est:** 1984. **Sales:** $53,000,000 (2000). **Emp:** 100. **Officers:** Jerry M. Chandler, President.

■ **11820** ■ **F. McConnell and Sons Inc.**
PO Box 417
New Haven, IN 46774
Phone: (219)493-6607
Free: (800)552-0835 **Fax:** (219)949-6116
URL: http://www.fmcconnell.com
Products: Convenience store and restaurant supplies. **SICs:** 5141 (Groceries—General Line); 5149 (Groceries & Related Products Nec); 5113 (Industrial & Personal Service Paper). **Est:** 1914. **Sales:** $65,000,000 (2000). **Emp:** 80. **Officers:** K.J. McConnell, Chairman of the Board; James K. McConnell, President & Chairman of the Board, e-mail: jmcconnell@fmcconnell.com.

■ **11821** ■ **S.J. McCullagh Inc.**
245 Swan St.
Buffalo, NY 14204
Phone: (716)856-3473 **Fax:** (716)856-3486
E-mail: sjmccullagh@compuserve.com
Products: Coffee; Fresh fruit juices and nectars. **SIC:** 5149 (Groceries & Related Products Nec). **Est:** 1867. **Officers:** Warren Emblidge Jr., President; Daniel Phillips, CFO.

■ **11822** ■ **McDermott Food Brokers Inc.**
PO Box 13300
Albany, NY 12212
Phone: (518)783-8844 **Fax:** (518)785-5991
Products: Food. **SIC:** 5141 (Groceries—General Line). **Sales:** $69,000,000 (2000). **Emp:** 130. **Officers:** Edward J. Evers, President; Deborah Tozier, Comptroller.

■ **11823** ■ **McDonald Candy Company Inc.**
2350 W Broadway St.
Eugene, OR 97402
Phone: (541)345-8421 **Fax:** (541)345-7146
Products: Candy; Institutional foods; Frozen foods; Non foods; Disposables; Tobacco; Chemicals; Dairy products; Produce; Ice creams; Small wares. **SIC:** 5145 (Confectionery). **Est:** 1928. **Sales:** $50,000,000 (2000). **Emp:** 275. **Officers:** Rod Hvey, President; Gary Thomsen, Treasurer & Secty.; Steven R. Hayes, General Mgr.; Greg Smith, Dir. of Systems.

■ **11824** ■ **McDonald Farms, Inc.**
2313 Middle Rd.
Winchester, VA 22601-2755
Phone: (540)662-1057 **Fax:** (540)667-2142
Products: Fruits and vegetables. **SIC:** 5148 (Fresh Fruits & Vegetables). **Est:** 1970. **Emp:** 20. **Officers:** J. Kenneth McDonald Jr.; Kimberly G. McDonald; Joan D. McDonald.

■ **11825** ■ **McDonough Brothers**
PO Box 249
Fairmont, WV 26555
Phone: (304)366-3279
Products: Snack foods. **SICs:** 5149 (Groceries & Related Products Nec); 5145 (Confectionery). **Emp:** 49.

■ **11826** ■ **McFarling Foods Inc.**
333 W 14th St.
Indianapolis, IN 46202
Phone: (317)635-2633 **Fax:** (317)636-2951
Products: Dry, fresh, frozen and canned foods. **SICs:** 5141 (Groceries—General Line); 5149 (Groceries & Related Products Nec). **Est:** 1948. **Sales:** $68,000,000 (2000). **Emp:** 200. **Officers:** Don McFarling, President; Greg Clay, Sales/Marketing Contact; Natali Chia, Human Resources Contact.

■ **11827** ■ **McGee's Packing Co.**
Rte. J
Mexico, MO 65265
Phone: (573)581-4145 **Fax:** (573)581-6145
Products: Beef. **SIC:** 5147 (Meats & Meat Products). **Sales:** $7,000,000 (2000). **Emp:** 25. **Officers:** Bob McGee.

■ **11828** ■ **P. McGill & Co.**
416 N Glendale Ave.
Glendale, CA 91206-3398
Phone: (818)247-2552 **Fax:** (818)546-8828
Products: Frozen foods; Canned fruit juices, nectars, and concentrates; Spices; Cooking oils; Candy; Peanut butter; Confectionery products; Food. **SICs:** 5141 (Groceries—General Line); 5149 (Groceries & Related Products Nec); 5145 (Confectionery). **Est:** 1966. **Emp:** 49. **Officers:** Tim McGill, President.

■ **11829** ■ **McInerney-Miller Brothers Inc.**
2001 Brewster St.
Detroit, MI 48207
Phone: (313)833-4800
Products: Meat, poultry, and fish. **SICs:** 5144 (Poultry & Poultry Products); 5146 (Fish & Seafoods). **Est:** 1886. **Sales:** $47,000,000 (2000). **Emp:** 125. **Officers:** D.I. Miller, President; Richard Miller, VP of Finance; Robert Raine, Dir. of Marketing.

■ **11830** ■ **McIntosh Cooperative Creamery**
245 State St.
McIntosh, MN 56556
Phone: (218)563-2555
Products: Dairy products and farm supplies. **SICs:** 5143 (Dairy Products Except Dried or Canned); 5191 (Farm Supplies). **Sales:** $1,000,000 (2000). **Emp:** 6. **Officers:** Phillip Quam, President.

■ **11831** ■ **McLane Company Inc.**
PO Box 6115
Temple, TX 76503-6115
Phone: (254)771-7500 **Fax:** (254)771-7449
Products: General groceries. **SIC:** 5141 (Groceries—General Line). **Sales:** $5,252,000,000 (2000). **Emp:** 10,000. **Officers:** Grady Rosier, President; Bud Harger, VP of Finance.

■ **11832** ■ **McLane Company Inc. High Plains**
PO Box 5550
Lubbock, TX 79408-5550
Phone: (806)766-2966 **Fax:** (806)766-2936
Products: Restaurant food supplies. **SIC:** 5141 (Groceries—General Line). **Est:** 1894. **Sales:** $650,000,000 (2000). **Emp:** 400. **Officers:** Stuart Clark, President; Dennis Hruby, Controller; Wayne Wood, VP of Sales; Brandi Fernandez, Human Resources Mgr.

■ **11833** ■ **McLane Group Interntional L.P.**
455 Market St., Ste. #210
San Francisco, CA 94105
Phone: (415)543-1455 **Fax:** (415)986-5525
Products: Groceries, drugs and electrical appliances. **SICs:** 5141 (Groceries—General Line); 5122 (Drugs, Proprietaries & Sundries); 5063 (Electrical Apparatus & Equipment). **Sales:** $57,000,000 (2000). **Emp:** 100. **Officers:** Ron Messner, CEO & President; Richard Mosher, Controller.

■ **11834** ■ **McLane Southwest, Inc.**
PO Box 6116
Temple, TX 76503-6116
Phone: (254)770-2800 **Fax:** (254)770-2834
Products: Groceries. **SIC:** 5141 (Groceries—General Line).

■ **11835** ■ **McLane Western, Inc.**
2100 E Highway 119
Longmont, CO 80504
Phones: (303)682-7500 (303)682-7500
Fax: (303)678-9831
Products: General line groceries; General merchandise, including school supplies. **SICs:** 5141 (Groceries—General Line); 5112 (Stationery & Office Supplies).

■ **11836** ■ **McLemore Wholesale and Retail Inc.**
PO Box 3409
Jackson, MS 39207
Phone: (601)948-0361 **Fax:** (228)435-3008
Products: Food. **SIC:** 5141 (Groceries—General Line). **Est:** 1932. **Sales:** $42,000,000 (2000). **Emp:** 459. **Officers:** W.H. Holman Jr. Jr., President; Roger Friou, VP & CFO.

■ **11837** ■ **McLendon Co.**
1200 Dallas Trade Mart
Dallas, TX 75207
Phone: (214)748-1555 **Fax:** (214)747-4934
E-mail: bob@mclendon.com
Products: Specialty foods and related products, including spices, chocolate, and coffee; Kitchenwares; Cookbooks; Giftwares; Store fixtures and equipment. **SICs:** 5149 (Groceries & Related Products Nec); 5023 (Homefurnishings). **Est:** 1954. **Sales:** $3,000,000 (2000). **Emp:** 12. **Officers:** William J. McLendon, CEO, e-mail: joel@mclendon.com.

■ **11838** ■ **McMahon Foodservice Outlet**
2835 Madison Ave.
Indianapolis, IN 46225-2405
Products: Food products. **SIC:** 5141 (Groceries—General Line).

■ **11839** ■ **McNabb Grain Co.**
PO Box 128
McNabb, IL 61335
Phone: (815)882-2131
Products: Corn. **SIC:** 5148 (Fresh Fruits & Vegetables). **Est:** 1913. **Sales:** $5,000,000 (2000). **Emp:** 5. **Officers:** Ben Day, President; Roger Dixon, Manager.

■ **11840** ■ **M.E. Carter of Jonesboro Inc.**
PO Box 217
Jonesboro, AR 72403
Phone: (870)932-6668
Products: Produce and frozen foods. **SICs:** 5148 (Fresh Fruits & Vegetables); 5142 (Packaged Frozen Foods). **Sales:** $5,000,000 (2000). **Emp:** 30. **Officers:** Warren Gray, President; George Kalughirou, Mgr. of Finance.

■ **11841** ■ **Meadow Gold Dairies**
420 Nora
Missoula, MT 59801-8057
Phone: (406)543-3173 **Fax:** (406)721-4504
Products: Dairy products. **SIC:** 5143 (Dairy Products Except Dried or Canned). **Sales:** $2,000,000 (2000). **Emp:** 23. **Officers:** Leroy Scott.

■ **11842** ■ **Meadow Gold Dairy**
4820 Forge Rd.
Colorado Springs, CO 80907-3523
Phone: (719)599-8844 **Fax:** (719)599-7365
Products: Milk, cheese, and ice cream. **SIC:** 5143 (Dairy Products Except Dried or Canned). **Sales:** $30,000,000 (2000). **Emp:** 24. **Officers:** Bob Dickerson.

■ **11843** ■ **Meat Processors Inc.**
2210 Hutson Rd.
Green Bay, WI 54307-1327
Phone: (920)499-4841
Products: Processed, frozen, or cooked meats. **SICs:** 5147 (Meats & Meat Products); 5142 (Packaged Frozen Foods). **Emp:** 49. **Officers:** Doug F. Farah.

■ **11844** ■ **Walter Meier Inc.**
12555 W Wirth St.
Brookfield, WI 53005
Phone: (414)783-7100 **Fax:** (414)783-5094
Products: Frozen seafoods, including shrimp, crab, and lobsters. **SIC:** 5146 (Fish & Seafoods). **Est:** 1948.

Sales: $2,000,000 (2000). Emp: 10. Officers: Steven W. Meier, President & General Mgr.

■ 11845 ■ Meijer Inc.
2929 Walker NW
Grand Rapids, MI 49504
Phone: (616)453-6711 Fax: (616)791-2572
Products: Food; Toiletries and cosmetics; Hardware. SICs: 5141 (Groceries—General Line); 5122 (Drugs, Proprietaries & Sundries); 5072 (Hardware). Est: 1934. Sales: $5,390,000,000 (2000). Emp: 53,000. Officers: Earl D. Holton, President; Fritz Kolk, VP & CFO; Bill Smith, VP of Marketing; Dave Paasche, VP of Information Systems; Wendy Ray, Contact.

■ 11846 ■ Melchs Food Products Inc.
PO Box 278
Medina, OH 44258-0278
Phone: (330)253-8612 Fax: (330)253-1005
Products: Prepared salads. SIC: 5148 (Fresh Fruits & Vegetables). Sales: $5,000,000 (1993). Emp: 50. Officers: Mark Sandridge, CEO; Bill Frantz, Vice President.

■ 11847 ■ Mellobuttercup Ice Cream Co.
400 S Douglas St.
PO Box 324
Wilson, NC 27894
Phone: (919)243-6161 Fax: (919)243-7687
Products: Ice cream; Yogurt. SIC: 5143 (Dairy Products Except Dried or Canned). Est: 1946. Sales: $16,500,000 (2000). Emp: 125. Officers: R.J. Barnes, Chairman of the Board; T.E. Beaman, President; R.J. Barnes Jr., Vice President.

■ 11848 ■ Melody Farms Inc.
31111 Industrial Rd.
Livonia, MI 48150
Phone: (734)525-4000 Fax: (734)525-7601
Products: Dairy products and fresh fruit juices. SICs: 5143 (Dairy Products Except Dried or Canned); 5149 (Groceries & Related Products Nec). Sales: $100,000,000 (2000). Emp: 470. Officers: Rodney George, President; Thomas A. George, Treasurer & Secty.

■ 11849 ■ Melster Candies Inc.
Madison St.
PO Box 47
Cambridge, WI 53523
Phone: (608)423-3221
Free: (800)535-4401 Fax: (608)423-3195
E-mail: melster@melster.com
Products: Candy. SIC: 5145 (Confectionery). Est: 1919. Emp: 150. Officers: L.A. Warrell, CEO & President; R.P. Billman, Exec. VP; A.W. Strom, Sr. VP of Sales & Marketing; Leo Halpin, VP of Operations; Robin Salley, Customer Service Contact, e-mail: robin@melster.com; Diane Flores, Human Resources Contact; Diane Flores, Human Resources Contact.

■ 11850 ■ Mendocino Coast Produce, Inc.
543 N Franklin St.
Ft. Bragg, CA 95437-3211
Phone: (707)964-3539 Fax: (707)964-4877
Products: Fruits; Vegetables. SIC: 5148 (Fresh Fruits & Vegetables). Est: 1965. Sales: $691,000 (2000). Emp: 4. Officers: Samuel J. Ware, President; Brenda L. Ware, Vice President.

■ 11851 ■ Mendocino Sea Vegetable Co.
PO Box 1265
Mendocino, CA 95460
Phone: (707)937-2050
E-mail: mail@seaweed.net
URL: http://www.seaweed.net
Products: Seaweed. SIC: 5146 (Fish & Seafoods). Est: 1980. Sales: $100,000 (2000). Emp: 2. Officers: John Lewallen, Owner; Eleanor Lewallen, Owner.

■ 11852 ■ Merchants Coffee Co.
PO Box 50654
New Orleans, LA 70150
Phone: (504)581-7515 Fax: (504)581-7518
Products: Coffee. SIC: 5149 (Groceries & Related Products Nec). Est: 1901. Sales: $5,000,000 (2000). Emp: 33. Officers: Peter W. Dodge, Treasurer & Secty.

■ 11853 ■ Merchants Co.
PO Box 1351
Hattiesburg, MS 39403-1351
Phone: (601)583-4351 Fax: (601)582-5333
Products: Food and foodservice. SICs: 5141 (Groceries—General Line); 5142 (Packaged Frozen Foods). Est: 1904. Sales: $115,000,000 (2000). Emp: 325. Officers: Donald B. Suber, President; Andy Mercier, Exec. VP; Ken Moore, Montgomery Operations; Lee Walker, Data Processing Mgr.; Patti Wigly, Dir of Human Resources.

■ 11854 ■ Merchants Distributors Inc.
PO Box 2148
Hickory, NC 28603
Phone: (704)323-4100 Fax: (704)213-8104
Products: Groceries. SIC: 5141 (Groceries—General Line). Est: 1931. Sales: $870,000,000 (2000). Emp: 1,200. Officers: Gerald Davis, President; Ronald Knedlik, Sr. VP & Finance Officer; Allen Bolick, Dir. of Marketing; Calvin Sihilling, VP of Information Systems; Glen DeBiasi, VP of Human Resources.

■ 11855 ■ Merchants Grocery Co.
PO Box 1268
Culpeper, VA 22701
Phone: (540)825-0786 Fax: (540)825-9016
URL: http://www.merchants-grocery.com
Products: General line groceries; Candy; Tobacco; Canned and frozen food; Produce. SICs: 5141 (Groceries—General Line); 5148 (Fresh Fruits & Vegetables); 5142 (Packaged Frozen Foods). Est: 1917. Sales: $106,000,000 (2000). Emp: 180. Officers: E.V. Smythers, President; David G. Cooper, Vice President; Michael Hicks, Treasurer; Robert Jenkins Jr., Dir. of Sales & Marketing; Steve Hicks, Human Resources.

■ 11856 ■ Meredith and Meredith Inc.
2343 Farm Creek Rd.
Toddville, MD 21672
Phone: (410)397-8151
Products: Blue crab meat. SIC: 5146 (Fish & Seafoods). Est: 1920. Sales: $2,000,000 (2000). Emp: 55. Officers: Jennings C. Tolley, CEO & President.

■ 11857 ■ Merkert Enterprises Inc.
500 Turnpike St.
Canton, MA 02021
Phone: (781)828-4800
Free: (800)637-5378 Fax: (781)828-8274
Products: Food and beverages. SICs: 5141 (Groceries—General Line); 5149 (Groceries & Related Products Nec). Est: 1950. Sales: $130,000,000 (2000). Emp: 1,800. Officers: Gerald Leonard, President; Sidney Rogers, CFO; Robert Carrell, Dir. of Data Processing; Steven Loffredo, Dir of Personnel.

■ 11858 ■ Merrill Distributing, Inc.
PO Box 707
Merrill, WI 54452-0707
Phone: (715)536-4551 Fax: (715)536-5757
Products: Food service and convenience store products. SICs: 5145 (Confectionery); 5141 (Groceries—General Line); 5149 (Groceries & Related Products Nec). Est: 1912. Sales: $20,000,000 (2000). Emp: 48. Officers: Ralph A. Schewe; John Schewe.

■ 11859 ■ Metro Foods Inc.
PO Box 688
Olive Branch, MS 38654-0688
Phone: (601)895-8880 Fax: (601)895-7141
Products: Meat. SICs: 5147 (Meats & Meat Products); 5141 (Groceries—General Line). Est: 1980. Sales: $52,000,000 (2000). Emp: 155. Officers: T. J. Mattingly, President; Keenan Dodson, Sales/Marketing Contact; David Mattingly, Human Resources Contact.

■ 11860 ■ Metropolitan Marketing Inc.
3890 W Northwest Hwy., Ste. 500
Dallas, TX 75220-5167
Phone: (214)330-5088
Products: Food. SICs: 5141 (Groceries—General Line); 5142 (Packaged Frozen Foods).

■ 11861 ■ Metropolitan Poultry and Seafood Co.
1920 Stanford Ct.
Landover, MD 20785-3219
Phone: (301)772-0060
Free: (800)522-0060 Fax: (301)772-1013
E-mail: metropsc@aol.com
URL: http://www.metropoultry.com
Products: Poultry; Seafood; Meat; Dairy; Specialty frozen. SICs: 5144 (Poultry & Poultry Products); 5146 (Fish & Seafoods); 5147 (Meats & Meat Products). Est: 1944. Sales: $90,000,000 (2000). Emp: 165. Officers: Brian C. Willard, CEO & President; Melvin Willard, VP of Operations; Barry G. Kohan, VP of Marketing & Sales; B. J. Willard, Sales Mgr.; Tracy Brassel, CFO.

■ 11862 ■ Metz Baking Co.
981 Division St.
Sharon, PA 16146-2884
Phone: (724)346-3103
Products: Bakery products, including pies and cookies. SIC: 5149 (Groceries & Related Products Nec). Est: 1951. Sales: $500,000 (2000). Emp: 18. Officers: George Metz Jr.; Lucille Metz.

■ 11863 ■ Metz Baking Co.
PO Box 1475
Watertown, SD 57201
Phone: (605)886-5832 Fax: (605)886-5833
Products: Pastries; Bread, cake, and related products. SIC: 5149 (Groceries & Related Products Nec). Emp: 103. Officers: Roger Best, General Mgr.

■ 11864 ■ Metz Baking Co.
PO Box 448
Sioux City, IA 51102
Phone: (712)255-7611 Fax: (712)255-2285
Products: Buns, rolls, and bread. SIC: 5149 (Groceries & Related Products Nec). Est: 1926. Sales: $472,000,000 (2000). Emp: 7,000. Officers: William H. Metz, CEO & Chairman of the Board; William K. Stoneburg, Sr. VP & Finance Officer; Frank D. Gruenzner, Sr. VP of Sales; Larry Hames, VP of Information Systems; Paula S. Burwell, VP of Human Resources.

■ 11865 ■ Meyer Tomatoes
PO Box 606
King City, CA 93930
Phone: (408)385-4047 Fax: (408)385-3883
Products: Tomatoes. SIC: 5148 (Fresh Fruits & Vegetables). Est: 1955. Sales: $18,000,000 (2000). Emp: 500. Officers: R.L. Meyer, Owner; J. Scott Wharton, Controller; B. La Velle, Dir. of Marketing.

■ 11866 ■ Meyer Vegetables
PO Box 1117
Nogales, AZ 85628-1117
Phone: (520)761-4119 Fax: (520)761-4202
Products: Vegetables, including bell peppers, cucumbers, and squash. SIC: 5148 (Fresh Fruits & Vegetables). Est: 1988. Sales: $300,000 (2000). Emp: 10. Officers: Robert L. Meyer, President; Balta Valencia, Sales Mgr.

■ 11867 ■ Michael Foods Inc.
5353 Wayzata Blvd., Ste. 324
Minneapolis, MN 55416
Phone: (612)546-1500 Fax: (612)540-9100
Products: Grocery products including cheese, butter, milk, potato products, juice, bagels, muffins, and ice cream mix. SICs: 5143 (Dairy Products Except Dried or Canned); 5149 (Groceries & Related Products Nec). Sales: $1,020,500,000 (2000). Emp: 4,160. Officers: Gregg A. Ostrander, CEO & President; John D. Reedy, VP, CFO & Treasurer.

■ 11868 ■ Michael Foods Refrigerated Distribution Cos.
5353 Wayzata Blvd. No. 324
Minneapolis, MN 55416
Phone: (612)546-1500
Products: Dairy products. SIC: 5143 (Dairy Products Except Dried or Canned).

■ **11869** ■ **Michaud Distributors**
92 Perry Rd.
Bangor, ME 04401
Phone: (207)989-0747
Products: Food; Snacks, including potato chips. **SIC:** 5145 (Confectionery).

■ **11870** ■ **Michaud Distributors**
5 Lincoln Ave.
Scarborough, ME 04074
Phone: (207)885-9473
Products: Potato chips. **SIC:** 5145 (Confectionery).

■ **11871** ■ **Michelle's Family Bakery**
4321 41st St.
Brentwood, MD 20722-1513
Phone: (301)985-6050   **Fax:** (301)985-6055
Products: Cakes; Pies; Doughnuts; Bagels; Muffins. **SICs** 5149 (Groceries & Related Products Nec); 5145 (Confectionery). **Est:** 1946. **Sales:** $14,000,000 (2000). **Emp:** 40. **Officers:** Jon Liss, CEO & President; John Marshal, CFO; Bill Lenick, Sales Mgr.

■ **11872** ■ **Michigan Sugar Co.**
PO Box 1348
Saginaw, MI 48605
Phone: (517)799-7300   **Fax:** (517)799-7310
URL: http://www.michigansugar.com
Products: Sugar. **SIC:** 5149 (Groceries & Related Products Nec). **Est:** 1906. **Sales:** $200,000,000 (2000). **Emp:** 1,000. **Officers:** Mark Flegenheimer, President & CEO; Barry Brown, VP of Marketing; John Curry, Sales Mgr.; Glenn Peacock.

■ **11873** ■ **Micro Chef Inc.**
2200 Huntington Dr.
Plano, TX 75075
Phone: (972)985-4757
Products: Food. **SIC:** 5141 (Groceries—General Line).

■ **11874** ■ **Mid-America Dairymen Inc. Brown Swiss**
PO Box 2553
Rapid City, SD 57709-2553
Products: Dairy products, including milk and cheese. **SIC:** 5143 (Dairy Products Except Dried or Canned). **Est:** 1983. **Sales:** $1,000,000 (2000). **Emp:** 5. **Officers:** C. Vanderbush, Dir. of Sales.

■ **11875** ■ **Mid-America Dairymen Inc. Southern Div.**
3253 E Chestnut Expwy.
Springfield, MO 65802
Phone: (417)865-7100   **Fax:** (417)865-0962
Products: Dairy products, including ice cream and yogurt. **SIC:** 5143 (Dairy Products Except Dried or Canned). **Est:** 1950. **Sales:** $575,000,000 (2000). **Emp:** 150. **Officers:** Gary Hanman, President; Jerry Bos, VP & CFO; Lonnie Spurgeon, VP of Marketing; Leroy Robertson, Dir. of Systems.

■ **11876** ■ **Mid Atlantic Foods Inc.**
1842 Broad St.
PO Box 367
Pocomoke City, MD 21851-9647
Phone: (410)957-4100   **Fax:** (410)957-4500
Products: Seafood. **SIC:** 5146 (Fish & Seafoods). **Est:** 1982. **Emp:** 55.

■ **11877** ■ **Mid-Atlantic Snacks Inc.**
PO Box 232
York, PA 17405
Phone: (717)792-3454   **Fax:** (717)792-2670
Products: Cookies; Chips. **SICs** 5149 (Groceries & Related Products Nec); 5145 (Confectionery). **Sales:** $3,000,000 (2000). **Emp:** 7. **Officers:** Pressley Pullen, President.

■ **11878** ■ **Mid-Central/Sysco Food Services Inc.**
PO Box 820
Olathe, KS 66061
Phone: (913)829-5555
Products: General line of groceries. **SIC:** 5141 (Groceries—General Line). **Officers:** James C. Graham, President.

■ **11879** ■ **Mid-Mountain Foods Inc.**
PO Box 129
Abingdon, VA 24210
Phone: (540)628-3105   **Fax:** (540)628-6321
Products: General line groceries. **SIC:** 5141 (Groceries—General Line). **Est:** 1976. **Sales:** $260,000,000 (2000). **Emp:** 500. **Officers:** Harold Harwood, President; Donald Lay, Treasurer; Ralph McCready, Dir. of Systems; John Dollar, Dir of Human Resources.

■ **11880** ■ **Mid-State Potato Distributors Inc.**
4302 W Airport Rd.
Plant City, FL 33567-2489
Phone: (813)752-8866   **Fax:** (813)752-5044
Products: Potatoes and onions. **SIC:** 5148 (Fresh Fruits & Vegetables). **Est:** 1974. **Sales:** $21,000,000 (2000). **Emp:** 70. **Officers:** Ken R. Wyles, President.

■ **11881** ■ **Mid States Concession Supply**
1026 S Burlington Dr.
Muncie, IN 47302
Phone: (765)289-5505
Products: Candy; Chips; Popcorn. **SIC:** 5145 (Confectionery).

■ **11882** ■ **Midamar Corp.**
PO Box 218
Cedar Rapids, IA 52406
Phone: (319)362-3711   **Fax:** (319)362-4111
Products: Industrial equipment and parts; Meat products, including beef and poultry; Restaurant equipment; Food, including dry goods. **SICs** 5149 (Groceries & Related Products Nec); 5046 (Commercial Equipment Nec); 5085 (Industrial Supplies); 5147 (Meats & Meat Products). **Est:** 1972. **Emp:** 20. **Officers:** Bill Aossey, President; Doug Robinson, Sales/Marketing Contact.

■ **11883** ■ **Midland Cooperative Inc.**
101 Main St.
Axtell, NE 68924
Phone: (308)743-2424
Products: Agricultural equipment and supplies. **SIC:** 5153 (Grain & Field Beans). **Sales:** $55,000,000 (2000). **Emp:** 65.

■ **11884** ■ **Midland Groceries Michigan Inc.**
PO Box 570
Muskegon, MI 49443
Phone: (616)722-3151
Products: General line groceries. **SIC:** 5141 (Groceries—General Line). **Emp:** 150. **Officers:** Elroy Buckner.

■ **11885** ■ **Midland Grocery Co.**
PO Box 125
Westville, IN 46391
Phone: (219)785-4671   **Fax:** (219)785-4774
Products: General line groceries. **SICs** 5141 (Groceries—General Line); 5049 (Professional Equipment Nec); 5112 (Stationery & Office Supplies).

■ **11886** ■ **Midstate Mills Inc.**
PO Box 349
Newton, NC 28658
Phone: (704)464-1611   **Fax:** (704)465-5139
Products: Flour mixes; Animal feeds. **SICs** 5149 (Groceries & Related Products Nec); 5191 (Farm Supplies). **Est:** 1935. **Emp:** 140. **Officers:** Boyd H. Drum.

■ **11887** ■ **Midtown Packing Company Inc.**
2276 12th Ave.
New York, NY 10027
Phone: (212)866-9150
Products: Beef, pork, and lamb. **SIC:** 5147 (Meats & Meat Products). **Est:** 1940. **Sales:** $3,000,000 (2000). **Emp:** 11. **Officers:** Julius Lowenstein, President.

■ **11888** ■ **Midwest Coop.**
PO Box 366
Quinter, KS 67752
Phone: (785)754-3348   **Fax:** (785)754-3826
Products: Grain, field beans, feeds, fertilizers, agricultural chemicals and fuel oil; Gasoline service stations. **SICs** 5153 (Grain & Field Beans); 5191 (Farm Supplies); 5172 (Petroleum Products Nec). **Sales:** $45,000,000 (2000). **Emp:** 80. **Officers:** Ross Bone, President; Ron Koehn, General Manager, Finance.

■ **11889** ■ **Midwest Farmers Cooperative**
PO Box 65
Hospers, IA 51238
Phone: (712)752-8421   **Fax:** (712)752-8457
Products: Agricultural equipment and supplies. **SIC:** 5153 (Grain & Field Beans). **Sales:** $100,000,000 (2000). **Emp:** 6.

■ **11890** ■ **Miedema Produce, Inc.**
5005 40th Ave.
Hudsonville, MI 49426
Phone: (616)669-9420   **Fax:** (616)669-2524
Products: Fresh fruits and vegetables. **SIC:** 5148 (Fresh Fruits & Vegetables).

■ **11891** ■ **Mike-Sell's Inc.**
333 Leo St.
Dayton, OH 45404
Phone: (937)228-9400
Products: Potato chips, corn chips and other snacks. **SIC:** 5145 (Confectionery). **Sales:** $70,000,000 (2000). **Emp:** 290. **Officers:** Leslie C. Mapp, CEO, President & Treasurer.

■ **11892** ■ **Mike Sell's Indiana Inc.**
5767 Dividend Rd.
Indianapolis, IN 46277
Phone: (317)241-7422
Products: Pretzels, corn chips, and other snacks. **SIC:** 5145 (Confectionery). **Sales:** $8,000,000 (1993). **Emp:** 35. **Officers:** Norman Johnson, Exec. VP; Thomas Kendall, Exec. VP of Finance.

■ **11893** ■ **Mike-Sell's Potato Chip Co.**
333 Leo St.
Dayton, OH 45404
Phone: (513)228-9400
Products: Potato chips. **SIC:** 5145 (Confectionery). **Est:** 1910. **Sales:** $60,000,000 (2000). **Emp:** 250. **Officers:** Leslie C. Mapp, CEO & President; Thomas Kendall, Exec. VP.

■ **11894** ■ **Milan Farmers Elevator**
PO Box 32
Milan, MN 56262
Phone: (320)734-4435   **Fax:** (320)734-4437
Products: Livestock and farm products. **SIC:** 5153 (Grain & Field Beans). **Sales:** $5,000,000 (2000). **Emp:** 6.

■ **11895** ■ **Mile Hi Frozen Food Co.**
4770 E 51st
Denver, CO 80216
Phone: (303)399-6066   **Fax:** (303)355-0238
Products: Frozen foods. **SIC:** 5142 (Packaged Frozen Foods). **Est:** 1980. **Sales:** $60,000,000 (2000). **Emp:** 170. **Officers:** Michael Desmarais, Vice President, e-mail: mdesmarais@mhff.net.

■ **11896** ■ **Milk Marketing Inc.**
PO Box 5530
Akron, OH 44334-0530
Phone: (216)826-4730   **Fax:** (216)826-1971
Products: Milk; Dairy products. **SIC:** 5143 (Dairy Products Except Dried or Canned). **Est:** 1979. **Sales:** $650,000,000 (2000). **Emp:** 700. **Officers:** Donald H. Schriver, CEO; Rod Carlson, Dir. of Marketing; Cecil B. Parker, Information Systems Mgr.; John P. Fisher, Human Resources Mgr.

■ **11897** ■ **Milk Products Holdings Inc.**
3645 Westwind Blvd.
Santa Rosa, CA 95403
Phone: (707)524-6700   **Fax:** (707)524-6719
Products: Milk proteins. **SIC:** 5143 (Dairy Products Except Dried or Canned). **Est:** 1986. **Sales:** $31,000,000 (2000). **Emp:** 120. **Officers:** James Hepburn, CEO; Gwen Poargetzi, Communications Mgr.; Lynda Brinn, VP of Human Resources.

■ **11898** ■ **Miller and Hartman Inc.**
PO Box 81784
Lancaster, PA 17608
Phone: (717)397-8261   **Fax:** (717)295-9008
Products: Groceries. **SIC:** 5141 (Groceries—General Line). **Est:** 1868. **Sales:** $600,000,000 (2000). **Emp:**

500. **Officers:** John H. Brown III, President; George Dvoryak, Controller; Nevin Glatfelter, Dir of Human Resources; Robert W. Shangraw, Chairman of the Board & CFO.

■ **11899** ■ **Miller and Hartman South Inc.**
PO Box 218
Leitchfield, KY 42755-0218
Phones: (502)444-7246   (502)259-9341
Fax: (502)444-9424
Products: Groceries; Cigarettes. **SICs:** 5141 (Groceries—General Line); 5194 (Tobacco & Tobacco Products). **Emp:** 125. **Officers:** Wayne Jones, General Mgr.; Rebecca Tucker, Controller; Eddie Bullock, Sales Mgr.; Randall Farris; Gary Beauchamp.

■ **11900** ■ **Miller's Bakery Inc.**
1415 N 5th St.
Milwaukee, WI 53212
Phone: (414)347-2300
Products: Baked food products. **SIC:** 5149 (Groceries & Related Products Nec). **Sales:** $16,000,000 (1993). **Emp:** 36. **Officers:** Richard Miller, President.

■ **11901** ■ **Millstone Service Div.**
20320 80th Ave. S
Kent, WA 98032
Phone: (206)575-1243
Products: Gourmet coffee; Brewing equipment. **SICs:** 5149 (Groceries & Related Products Nec); 5046 (Commercial Equipment Nec); 5064 (Electrical Appliances—Television & Radio).

■ **11902** ■ **Milton's Institutional Foods**
Old Oakwood Rd.
Oakwood, GA 30566-2802
Phone: (404)532-7779   **Fax:** (404)531-1960
Products: Food. **SIC:** 5141 (Groceries—General Line). **Sales:** $40,000,000 (2000). **Emp:** 160. **Officers:** Milton Robson.

■ **11903** ■ **Milwaukee Biscuit**
6200 N Baker Rd.
Milwaukee, WI 53209
Phone: (414)228-8585   **Fax:** (414)351-8796
Products: Food. **SIC:** 5149 (Groceries & Related Products Nec).

■ **11904** ■ **Mims Meat Company Inc.**
PO Box 24776
Houston, TX 77015
Phone: (713)453-0151
Free: (800)396-3860   **Fax:** (713)453-6714
Products: Beef; Pork; Poultry. **SICs:** 5147 (Meats & Meat Products); 5144 (Poultry & Poultry Products). **Est:** 1951. **Sales:** $35,000,000 (2000). **Emp:** 110. **Officers:** A.D. Mims, President.

■ **11905** ■ **Ed Miniat Inc.**
945 W 38th St.
Chicago, IL 60609
Phone: (773)927-9200   **Fax:** (773)927-8839
Products: Processed, frozen, or cooked meats; Vegetable oils. **SICs:** 5147 (Meats & Meat Products); 5149 (Groceries & Related Products Nec). **Est:** 1958. **Sales:** $97,200,000 (2000). **Emp:** 150. **Officers:** Ronald Miniat, CEO & President; Ed Miniat, Treasurer & Secty.; Mike Miniat, VP of Marketing; Mike Broderick, Personnel Mgr.

■ **11906** ■ **Minnesota Cultivated Wild Rice Council**
1306 W County Rd. F, Ste. 109
St. Paul, MN 55112
Phone: (612)638-1955   **Fax:** (612)638-0756
Products: Wild rice. **SIC:** 5149 (Groceries & Related Products Nec). **Officers:** Beth C.W. Nelson.

■ **11907** ■ **Minnesota Produce Inc.**
2801 Wayzata Blvd.
Minneapolis, MN 55405
Phone: (612)377-6790   **Fax:** (612)377-3768
Products: Produce, including onions, potatoes, apples, and oranges. **SIC:** 5148 (Fresh Fruits & Vegetables). **Est:** 1961. **Sales:** $6,000,000 (2000). **Emp:** 4. **Officers:** R.G. Stillman, President; Paul Piazza, Manager.

■ **11908** ■ **Minter-Weisman Co.**
1035 Nathan Ln. W
Plymouth, MN 55441-5081
Phone: (612)545-3706
Products: Candy; Tobacco. **SICs:** 5145 (Confectionery); 5194 (Tobacco & Tobacco Products).

■ **11909** ■ **Minyard Food Stores Inc.**
777 Freeport Pkwy.
Coppell, TX 75019
Phone: (972)393-8700   **Fax:** (972)393-8550
Products: Groceries. **SIC:** 5141 (Groceries—General Line). **Sales:** $850,000,000 (2000). **Emp:** 7,000. **Officers:** J.L. Williams, President; Mario Laforte, Vice President.

■ **11910** ■ **Minyard Food Stores Inc. Carnival Food Stores**
PO Box 518
Coppell, TX 75019
Phone: (972)393-8700   **Fax:** (972)393-8714
Products: General line groceries. **SIC:** 5141 (Groceries—General Line). **Est:** 1932. **Sales:** $550,000,000 (2000). **Emp:** 6,100. **Officers:** J.L. Williams, President; John Bennett, Sr. VP & Finance Officer; Joe Tarver, Vice President; Rick Frost, Dir. of Information Systems; Alan Zaughan, Dir of Human Resources.

■ **11911** ■ **Miss Kings Kitchen Inc, The Original Yahoo! Baking Co.**
5302 Texoma Pkwy.
Sherman, TX 75090-2112
Phone: (903)893-8151
Free: (800)575-9573   **Fax:** (903)893-5030
E-mail: wholesale@yahoocake.com
URL: http://www.yahoocake/wholesale
Products: Dessert cakes; Seasonal cakes; Cookies; Fillings; Prepared doughs; Custom formulations. **SICs:** 5149 (Groceries & Related Products Nec); 5142 (Packaged Frozen Foods). **Sales:** $6,000,000 (2000). **Emp:** 100. **Officers:** Geoffrey Crowley.

■ **11912** ■ **Mission Produce Inc.**
PO Box 5267
Oxnard, CA 93031-5267
Phone: (805)981-3650   **Fax:** (805)981-3660
Products: Avocados, mangos, lemons and limes. **SIC:** 5148 (Fresh Fruits & Vegetables). **Sales:** $28,000,000 (2000). **Emp:** 100. **Officers:** Steve Barnard, President; Tim Albers, CFO.

■ **11913** ■ **Allen Mitchell Products**
1155 Industrial Ave.
Oxnard, CA 93030-7407
Phone: (805)487-8595   **Fax:** (805)487-8596
Products: Food and snack products, including gelatin and potato chips. **SICs:** 5145 (Confectionery); 5149 (Groceries & Related Products Nec). **Est:** 1968. **Emp:** 5. **Officers:** Allen Mitchell.

■ **11914** ■ **Mitsubishi Intl Corp./Foods Div**
333 S Hope St Ste. 2500
Los Angeles, CA 90071
Phone: (213)687-2800   **Fax:** (213)687-2946
Products: Cans tuna; Processed food products. **SIC:** 5146 (Fish & Seafoods).

■ **11915** ■ **Mitsui Foods, Inc.**
35 Maple St.
Norwood, NJ 07648-0409
Phone: (201)750-0500
Products: Tuna. **SIC:** 5149 (Groceries & Related Products Nec). **Est:** 1970. **Sales:** $30,000,000 (2000). **Emp:** 100. **Officers:** David D. DeMartini, President; Gary Dairs, Controller; Murray Lurka, Dir. of Marketing & Sales; Phil De Mierest, Dir. of Data Processing; Jane McGriger, Dir. of Human Resources.

■ **11916** ■ **Mixon Fruit Farms Inc.**
PO Box 25200
Bradenton, FL 34206
Phone: (941)748-5829   **Fax:** (941)748-1085
Products: Fruit. **SIC:** 5148 (Fresh Fruits & Vegetables). **Est:** 1939. **Sales:** $6,300,000 (2000). **Emp:** 125. **Officers:** W.P. Mixon Jr., President; William D. Mixon, CFO.

■ **11917** ■ **Mohawk Dairy**
260 Forest Ave.
Amsterdam, NY 12010
Phone: (518)842-4940   **Fax:** (518)842-4942
Products: Milk. **SIC:** 5143 (Dairy Products Dried or Canned). **Emp:** 49. **Officers:** Richard Rzeszotarski.

■ **11918** ■ **Mohawk Farms Inc.**
112 Holmes Rd.
Newington, CT 06111
Phone: (860)666-3361
Products: Fluid milk. **SIC:** 5143 (Dairy Products Except Dried or Canned). **Sales:** $1,000,000 (2000). **Emp:** 15. **Officers:** Robert Spring, President.

■ **11919** ■ **Mom's Food Co.**
1308 Potrero Ave.
South El Monte, CA 91733-3013
Phone: (626)444-4115   **Fax:** (626)444-2793
Products: Biscuits; Cobblers. **SIC:** 5149 (Groceries & Related Products Nec). **Est:** 1979. **Emp:** 16. **Officers:** Sam Keith.

■ **11920** ■ **Monel Distributors**
2770 NW 24th St.
Miami, FL 33142
Phone: (305)635-7331   **Fax:** (305)638-8636
Products: Confections; Food. **SICs:** 5149 (Groceries & Related Products Nec); 5145 (Confectionery). **Est:** 1955. **Sales:** $10,000,000 (2000). **Emp:** 50. **Officers:** Robert Walsky.

■ **11921** ■ **Monfort Inc.**
PO Box G
Greeley, CO 80632
Phone: (970)353-2311   **Fax:** (970)395-8903
Products: Beef, pork, and lamb. **SIC:** 5147 (Meats & Meat Products). **Sales:** $7,093,000,000 (2000). **Emp:** 19,000. **Officers:** Tom Manuel, President; George Reiswig, CFO.

■ **11922** ■ **Monfort International Sales Corp.**
PO Box G
Greeley, CO 80632
Phone: (303)353-2311
Products: Fresh beef, pork, and lamb. **SIC:** 5147 (Meats & Meat Products). **Est:** 1988. **Sales:** $2,472,700,000 (2000). **Emp:** 100. **Officers:** Charles Monfort, President; Thomas Smerud, CFO; Joe H. Meilinger, VP of Marketing.

■ **11923** ■ **Monfort-Swift Support Centers**
PO Box G
Greeley, CO 80632
Phone: (970)353-2311   **Fax:** (970)351-0096
Products: Beef, pork, and lamb. **SIC:** 5147 (Meats & Meat Products). **Est:** 1970. **Sales:** $450,000,000 (2000). **Emp:** 295. **Officers:** John DeMoney, VP & General Mgr.; Les Scott, Controller.

■ **11924** ■ **Monroe and Associates Inc.**
1870 W Bitters
San Antonio, TX 78248
Phone: (210)493-5700   **Fax:** (210)493-4620
Products: General line food broker. **SIC:** 5141 (Groceries—General Line). **Sales:** $35,000,000 (2000). **Emp:** 30. **Officers:** John Monroe, CEO.

■ **11925** ■ **Monroe Foods**
102 E Grove St.
Monroe, MI 48162
Phone: (734)243-5660
Products: Food. **SIC:** 5141 (Groceries—General Line).

■ **11926** ■ **Monsour's Inc.**
112 N Elm St.
Pittsburg, KS 66762
Phone: (316)231-6363   **Fax:** (316)231-6479
Products: Food, including dried and canned; Cleaning supplies; Restaurant equipment and supplies, including coffee makers and paper products. **SICs:** 5141 (Groceries—General Line); 5149 (Groceries & Related Products Nec); 5087 (Service Establishment Equipment); 5169 (Chemicals & Allied Products Nec); 5113 (Industrial & Personal Service Paper). **Emp:** 71. **Officers:** Mark D. Monsour, President.

■ 11927 ■ **Montage Foods Inc.**
885 Providence Rd.
Scranton, PA 18508
Phone: (717)347-2400
Free: (800)521-8325 **Fax:** (717)347-4123
Products: Veal; Lamb. **SIC:** 5147 (Meats & Meat Products). **Est:** 1985. **Sales:** $24,000,000 (2000). **Emp:** 175.

■ 11928 ■ **Montana Naturals Int'l. Inc.**
19994 U.S Highway 93 N
Arlee, MT 59821
Phone: (406)726-3214
Free: (800)872-7218 **Fax:** (406)726-3287
Products: Food preparations; Honey. **SIC:** 5149 (Groceries & Related Products Nec). **Est:** 1982. **Sales:** $6,000,000 (2000). **Emp:** 69. **Officers:** Charles Walgreen, President. **Former Name:** Big Sky Trading Co. **Former Name:** Montana Pollen & Herb.

■ 11929 ■ **Moody Creek Produce Inc.**
PO Box 329
Sugar City, ID 83448
Phone: (208)356-9447
Free: (800)657-5553 **Fax:** (208)356-4373
Products: Potatoes. **SIC:** 5148 (Fresh Fruits & Vegetables). **Est:** 1986. **Sales:** $17,000,000 (2000). **Emp:** 55. **Officers:** Roland Blaser, President; Phil Rassmusson, General Mgr.

■ 11930 ■ **Moore Food Distributors Inc.**
9910 Page Blvd.
St. Louis, MO 63132
Phone: (314)426-1300 **Fax:** (314)426-6692
Products: Meat; Produce; Dairy products; Canned and frozen foods. **SICs:** 5148 (Fresh Fruits & Vegetables); 5142 (Packaged Frozen Foods); 5149 (Groceries & Related Products Nec); 5147 (Meats & Meat Products). **Est:** 1986. **Sales:** $15,000,000 (2000). **Emp:** 47. **Officers:** Alwal B. Moore, President; Bill Schultz, Sr. VP; Scott Bekker; James Gambrel, Controller; Joe Mowry, Dir. of Purchasing.

■ 11931 ■ **Moore-Handley Inc.**
3140 Pelham Pkwy.
Pelham, AL 35124
Phone: (205)663-8011 **Fax:** (205)663-8315
URL: http://www.moorehandley.com
Products: Plumbing products; Electrical products; Fencing; Paints; Lawn and garden supplies; Building materials; Housewares; Lumber; Locksets; Wires; Chains; Farm Products; Automotive products; Heating and cooling products; Tools, including fastening tools; Fasteners; Cordage. **SICs:** 5074 (Plumbing & Hydronic Heating Supplies); 5065 (Electronic Parts & Equipment Nec); 5083 (Farm & Garden Machinery); 5072 (Hardware). **Est:** 1882. **Sales:** $170,000,000 (1999). **Emp:** 404. **Officers:** William Riley, CEO & Chairman of the Board; Michael J. Gaines, President & COO, e-mail: mgaines@moorehandley.com; Robert Tolbert, Director-Marketing and advertising; Drew Reid, VP of Sales; Evelyn Stephens, Customer Service Contact.

■ 11932 ■ **Moore's Quality Snack Foods Div.**
PO Box 1909
Bristol, VA 24203
Phone: (540)669-6194
Free: (800)289-7622 **Fax:** (540)645-2138
Products: Corn chips; Pretzels; Potato chips. **SICs:** 5145 (Confectionery); 5149 (Groceries & Related Products Nec). **Est:** 1924. **Sales:** $65,000,000 (2000). **Emp:** 425. **Officers:** C. Stephen Gregg.

■ 11933 ■ **Moorhead and Company Inc.**
PO Box 8092
Van Nuys, CA 91409-8092
Phone: (818)873-6640
Free: (877)290-2427 **Fax:** (818)787-2010
E-mail: mail@moorhead-agar.com
URL: http://www.moorhead-agar.com
Products: Agar and agar products. **SIC:** 5149 (Groceries & Related Products Nec). **Est:** 1933. **Officers:** Brenda Franklin, Marketing & Sales.

■ 11934 ■ **Mor-Rad Foodservice**
315 Hoohana St.
Kahului, HI 96732
Phone: (808)877-2017 **Fax:** (808)877-8034
Products: Dry goods; Frozen foods; Meat and fish; Produce; Canned goods. **SICs:** 5149 (Groceries & Related Products Nec); 5142 (Packaged Frozen Foods); 5147 (Meats & Meat Products); 5146 (Fish & Seafoods); 5148 (Fresh Fruits & Vegetables).

■ 11935 ■ **Moreland Wholesale Co., Inc.**
1812 Snyder Ave.
Cheyenne, WY 82001
Phone: (307)638-8592
Free: (800)252-8592 **Fax:** (307)637-7144
Products: Candy; Tobacco; Snack food; Cleaning products. **SICs:** 5145 (Confectionery); 5194 (Tobacco & Tobacco Products); 5169 (Chemicals & Allied Products Nec); 5087 (Service Establishment Equipment). **Est:** 1956. **Emp:** 25. **Officers:** Del Peterson, President, e-mail: delpeterson@juno.com.

■ 11936 ■ **Morley Sales Company Inc.**
809 W Madison St.
Chicago, IL 60607
Phone: (312)829-1125 **Fax:** (312)829-3680
Products: Fresh fish; Frozen fish; Seafood. **SIC:** 5146 (Fish & Seafoods). **Est:** 1932. **Sales:** $20,000,000 (2000). **Emp:** 6. **Officers:** Robert G. Slavik, President; Jerome Slavik Jr., VP of Finance; Gary R. Slavik, Treasurer & Secty.

■ 11937 ■ **Mosey's Inc.**
4 Mosey Dr.
Bloomfield, CT 06002
Phone: (203)243-1725
Products: Frozen and non-frozen meat and meat products. **SICs:** 5147 (Meats & Meat Products); 5142 (Packaged Frozen Foods). **Sales:** $51,000,000 (1994). **Emp:** 150. **Officers:** Russel Pouliot, VP & General Mgr.

■ 11938 ■ **Motivatit Seafoods Inc.**
PO Box 3916
Houma, LA 70361-3916
Phones: (504)868-7191 (504)872-4825
E-mail: msi1@cajunnet.com
URL: http://www.motivatit.com
Products: Seafood. **SIC:** 5146 (Fish & Seafoods). **Est:** 1971. **Sales:** $10,000,000 (2000). **Emp:** 50. **Officers:** Mike Voisin; Steve Voisin; Ernie Voisin.

■ 11939 ■ **Mott Meat Company, Inc.**
HWY B
PO Box 19
Rockville, MO 64780
Phone: (660)598-2365
Products: Beef; Sausage and other prepared meats. **SIC:** 5147 (Meats & Meat Products). **Est:** 1948. **Sales:** $30,000,000 (2000). **Emp:** 99. **Officers:** Bernard Mott.

■ 11940 ■ **Mound City Industries Inc.**
1315 Cherokee St.
St. Louis, MO 63118-3206
Phone: (314)773-5200
Free: (800)727-1548 **Fax:** (314)773-7453
Products: Candy; Tobacco; Toiletries; Paper. **SICs:** 5145 (Confectionery); 5194 (Tobacco & Tobacco Products); 5122 (Drugs, Proprietaries & Sundries); 5113 (Industrial & Personal Service Paper). **Est:** 1956. **Sales:** $82,000,000 (2000). **Emp:** 75. **Officers:** Robert L. Krekeler, President; Thomas P. Wilde, Sales Mgr.; Jeffery L. Plunkett.

■ 11941 ■ **Mt. Horeb Farmers Coop.**
501 W Main
Mt. Horeb, WI 53572
Phone: (608)437-5536 **Fax:** (608)437-5700
Products: Grain, feed, fertilizers and agricultural chemicals; Gasoline; Lumber; Auto towing and repair. **SICs:** 5153 (Grain & Field Beans); 5191 (Farm Supplies). **Sales:** $15,300,000 (2000). **Emp:** 73. **Officers:** Mark Farrell, President; Jack Mlsna, General Manager, Finance.

■ 11942 ■ **Mount Pleasant Seafood Co.**
1 Seafood Dr.
Mt. Pleasant, SC 29464
Phone: (843)884-4122
Products: Seafood. **SIC:** 5146 (Fish & Seafoods). **Sales:** $3,000,000 (2000). **Emp:** 10. **Officers:** Rial Fitch, President.

■ 11943 ■ **Mt. Union Cooperative Elevator**
PO Box 57
Mt. Union, IA 52644
Phone: (319)865-1450 **Fax:** (319)865-1452
Products: Livestock and farm products. **SIC:** 5153 (Grain & Field Beans). **Sales:** $16,000,000 (2000). **Emp:** 18.

■ 11944 ■ **Mountain Ark Trading Co.**
1601 Pump Station Rd.
Fayetteville, AR 72701
Phone: (501)442-7191 **Fax:** (501)442-7199
Products: Microbiotic foods; Cookware; Literature. **SICs:** 5149 (Groceries & Related Products Nec); 5046 (Commercial Equipment Nec).

■ 11945 ■ **Mountain Food Products**
570 Brevard Rd.
Asheville, NC 28806
Phone: (828)255-7630
Products: Fruits and vegetables. **SIC:** 5148 (Fresh Fruits & Vegetables).

■ 11946 ■ **Mountain People's Warehouse**
12745 Earhart Ave.
Auburn, CA 95602
Phone: (530)889-9531
Free: (800)679-6733 **Fax:** (530)889-9544
Products: Health foods. **SIC:** 5149 (Groceries & Related Products Nec).

■ 11947 ■ **Mountain People's Warehouse Inc.**
12745 Earhart Ave.
Auburn, CA 95602
Phone: (530)889-9531
Products: Natural foods. **SIC:** 5141 (Groceries—General Line). **Sales:** $200,000,000 (2000). **Emp:** 500. **Officers:** Michael Funk, President; Kevin Michel, CFO.

■ 11948 ■ **Mountain Sun Organic Juices**
18390 Highway 145
Dolores, CO 81323
Phone: (970)882-2283 **Fax:** (970)882-2270
Products: Natural and organic juices; Grows organic apples. **SIC:** 5149 (Groceries & Related Products Nec). **Officers:** William Russell, CEO; Denise Russell, Treasurer.

■ 11949 ■ **Movsovitz and Sons of Florida Inc.**
PO Box 41565
Jacksonville, FL 32203
Phone: (904)764-7681 **Fax:** (904)765-5508
Products: Fruits and vegetables. **SIC:** 5148 (Fresh Fruits & Vegetables). **Sales:** $65,000,000 (2000). **Emp:** 180. **Officers:** Larry Movsovitz, President.

■ 11950 ■ **Mr. Dell Foods, Inc.**
300 W Major St.
PO Box 494
Kearney, MO 64060
Phone: (816)903-4644 **Fax:** (816)903-4633
E-mail: mrdell@qni.com
Products: Potatoes. **SIC:** 5148 (Fresh Fruits & Vegetables). **Est:** 1970. **Sales:** $5,000,000 (1999). **Emp:** 49. **Officers:** Kurt D. Johnsen, Vice President; Rich Wilkins, Operations Mgr.

■ 11951 ■ **Mrs. Leeper's Pasta, Inc.**
12455 Kerran St., Ste. 200
Poway, CA 92064-6855
Phone: (858)486-1101 **Fax:** (858)486-1770
E-mail: mlpinc@pacbell.net
URL: http://www.mrsleeperspasta.com
Products: Dry pasta. **SIC:** 5149 (Groceries & Related Products Nec). **Est:** 1927. **Sales:** $4,741,000 (1999). **Emp:** 35. **Officers:** Michelle Muscat, President. **Former Name:** Gaston Dupre Inc.

■ 11952 ■ **MSM Solutions**
9427 F St.
Omaha, NE 68127
Phone: (402)592-4300 **Fax:** (402)592-1535
E-mail: rssm@compuserve.com
Products: Food. **SIC:** 5141 (Groceries—General Line). **Est:** 1982. **Sales:** $28,000,000 (2000). **Emp:** 32. **Officers:** Reynold Smith, President; Lynette Ward, Finance Officer. **Former Name:** Reynold S. Smith Marketing Inc.

■ **11953** ■ **Mueller Bean Co.**
254 Main St.
Sunfield, MI 48890
Phone: (517)566-8031 **Fax:** (517)566-8995
Products: Grain and dry beans. **SIC:** 5153 (Grain & Field Beans). **Sales:** $6,000,000 (1994). **Emp:** 20.
Officers: Mark H. Mueller, Director.

■ **11954** ■ **Muffin Town Inc.**
17 Walden
Winthrop, MA 02152-2708
Phone: (617)846-1565 **Fax:** (617)539-0364
Products: Muffins, brownies, and cakes. **SIC:** 5149 (Groceries & Related Products Nec). **Emp:** 49.
Officers: John Anderson.

■ **11955** ■ **Muir-Roberts Company Inc.**
PO Box 328
Salt Lake City, UT 84110
Phone: (801)363-7695
Products: Fruits and vegetables. **SIC:** 5148 (Fresh Fruits & Vegetables). **Sales:** $20,000,000 (2000).
Emp: 200. **Officers:** Phillip R. Muir, President; Chuck Madsen, Treasurer.

■ **11956** ■ **Mulligan Sales Inc.**
PO Box 90008
City of Industry, CA 91714
Phone: (818)968-9621 **Fax:** (626)369-8452
Products: Nonfat and dry milk; Cheese powders; Spices; Vegetables; Preservatives; Phosphates; Sweeteners; Gums; Colors; Creamers. **SICs:** 5143 (Dairy Products Except Dried or Canned); 5149 (Groceries & Related Products Nec). **Est:** 1951. **Sales:** $60,000,000 (1999). **Emp:** 20. **Officers:** James Mulligan, CEO & President; Hank Duguid, Treasurer.

■ **11957** ■ **Multifoods Specialty Distribution**
PO Box 173773
Denver, CO 80217-3774
Free: (800)880-9900 **Fax:** (303)662-7500
Products: Food for restaurants, including Italian and Mexican food. **SICs:** 5149 (Groceries & Related Products Nec); 5143 (Dairy Products Except Dried or Canned). **Est:** 1978. **Sales:** $850,000,000 (2000).
Emp: 1,200. **Officers:** Jeff Boies, President; Patrick Hagerty, VP of Purchasing; Jim Peach, Dir. of Data Processing; Mary Jacobs, Dir of Human Resources.

■ **11958** ■ **Murray Biscuit Co., LLC (Division of Keebler Co.)**
933 Louise Ave.
Charlotte, NC 28204
Phone: (704)334-7611
Free: (800)438-5932 **Fax:** (704)375-6448
Products: Cookies. **SIC:** 5149 (Groceries & Related Products Nec). **Emp:** 300. **Officers:** Guy Ball. **Former Name:** President Baking Co., Inc.

■ **11959** ■ **Murry's Inc.**
8300 Pennsylvania Ave.
Upper Marlboro, MD 20772-2673
Phone: (301)420-6400
Free: (800)638-8280 **Fax:** (301)967-4816
Products: Frozen meat; Frozen poultry; Seafood; Frozen specialties. **SICs:** 5147 (Meats & Meat Products); 5144 (Poultry & Poultry Products); 5146 (Fish & Seafoods); 5142 (Packaged Frozen Foods).
Est: 1952. **Sales:** $100,000,000 (2000). **Emp:** 1,000.
Officers: Ira Mendelson, President & CEO; Stuart A. Mendelson, Sr. VP.

■ **11960** ■ **Musco Olive Products Inc.**
17950 Via Nicolo
Tracy, CA 95376
Phone: (209)836-4600
Free: (800)523-9828 **Fax:** (209)836-0518
E-mail: sales@muscoolive.com
Products: Black ripe olives, green sicilian style olives, and imported spanish green olives; Onions; Peppers; Capers. **SICs:** 5149 (Groceries & Related Products Nec); 5148 (Fresh Fruits & Vegetables). **Est:** 1940.
Sales: $25,000,000 (2000). **Emp:** 100. **Officers:** Yauna Throne, Sales/Marketing Contact, e-mail: yauna@muscoolive.com; Loren York, Customer Service Contact, e-mail: loren@muscoolive.com; Janet Mitchell, Human Resources Contact, e-mail: janet@muscoolive.com.

■ **11961** ■ **Mutual Distributors Inc.**
PO Box 330
Lakeland, FL 33802
Phone: (941)688-0042 **Fax:** (813)687-1926
Products: Confectionery. **SICs:** 5113 (Industrial & Personal Service Paper); 5145 (Confectionery). **Sales:** $110,000,000 (1993). **Emp:** 355. **Officers:** William D. Mills, President; Angel Musalen, Controller.

■ **11962** ■ **Mutual Trading Co. Inc.**
431 Crocker St.
Los Angeles, CA 90013
Phone: (213)626-9458
Products: Japanese food. **SICs:** 5141 (Groceries—General Line); 5087 (Service Establishment Equipment). **Est:** 1926. **Sales:** $3,000,000 (2000).
Emp: 100. **Officers:** N. Kanai, President; Hiro Kodama, CFO.

■ **11963** ■ **Mutual Wholesale Co.**
2800 N Andrews Ave. Ext.
Pompano Beach, FL 33069
Phone: (954)973-4300 **Fax:** (954)974-5461
Products: Institutional foods; Paper; Janitorial supplies; USDA meat processing. **SICs:** 5141 (Groceries—General Line); 5113 (Industrial & Personal Service Paper); 5087 (Service Establishment Equipment). **Emp:** 499. **Officers:** Barbara Andrews; Paul Boerstler.

■ **11964** ■ **Mutual Wholesale Co.**
PO Box 330
Lakeland, FL 33802
Phone: (863)688-0042 **Fax:** (863)687-1926
URL: http://www.mutualwholesale.com
Products: Paper; Food; Janitorial supplies. **SICs:** 5141 (Groceries—General Line); 5087 (Service Establishment Equipment); 5113 (Industrial & Personal Service Paper). **Sales:** $303,000,000 (2000). **Emp:** 550. **Officers:** Steve Buck, President; Barbara Andrews, President.

■ **11965** ■ **Nabisco Foods. Phoenix Confections Div.**
170 34th St.
Brooklyn, NY 11232-2304
Phone: (718)768-7900 **Fax:** (718)768-9546
Products: Hard taffy. **SIC:** 5145 (Confectionery).
Sales: $34,000,000 (2000). **Emp:** 220. **Officers:** Joe Stein.

■ **11966** ■ **Napoli Foodservices Inc.**
13623 Barrett Office Dr.
Ballwin, MO 63021-7802
Phone: (314)821-3553
Products: Food. **SIC:** 5141 (Groceries—General Line).
Sales: $9,000,000 (2000). **Emp:** 18. **Officers:** Bob Lenzen, President; Tom Mullen, Vice President.

■ **11967** ■ **Nardone Bakery Pizza Co.**
420 New Commerce Blvd.
Wilkes Barre, PA 18706-1445
Phone: (717)825-3421 **Fax:** (717)826-0874
Products: Bakery products. **SIC:** 5149 (Groceries & Related Products Nec). **Sales:** $500,000 (2000). **Emp:** 49. **Officers:** Tom Nardone.

■ **11968** ■ **Nash Finch/Bluefield**
PO Box 949
Bluefield, VA 24605
Phone: (540)326-2654
Products: Meat, including fresh and frozen beef, chicken, and seafood; Fresh and frozen vegetables; Canned food. **SICs:** 5147 (Meats & Meat Products); 5144 (Poultry & Poultry Products); 5142 (Packaged Frozen Foods); 5148 (Fresh Fruits & Vegetables); 5146 (Fish & Seafoods). **Est:** 1945. **Sales:** $105,000,000 (2000). **Emp:** 130. **Officers:** J.F. Russell, CEO.

■ **11969** ■ **Nash Finch Co.**
Hwy. 72 W
Lumberton, NC 28358
Phone: (919)739-4161 **Fax:** (919)739-0679
Products: Food. **SIC:** 5141 (Groceries—General Line).
Sales: $150,000,000 (2000). **Emp:** 300.

■ **11970** ■ **Nash Finch Co.**
PO Box 1418
St. Cloud, MN 56302
Phone: (320)251-3961 **Fax:** (320)251-0519
Products: General line groceries. **SIC:** 5141 (Groceries—General Line). **Emp:** 205. **Officers:** Ray Hampton, General Mgr.; Roger Nelson; Mark Mortimore; Del Wittenhager.

■ **11971** ■ **Nash Finch Co.**
1425 Burdick Expwy. W
Minot, ND 58701-4255
Phone: (701)852-0365 **Fax:** (701)852-3594
Products: Groceries. **SIC:** 5141 (Groceries—General Line). **Emp:** 98.

■ **11972** ■ **Nash Finch Co.**
1402 W 2nd St.
Liberal, KS 67901
Phone: (316)624-5655 **Fax:** (316)624-0744
Products: General line groceries. **SIC:** 5141 (Groceries—General Line). **Est:** 1977. **Sales:** $85,000,000 (2000). **Emp:** 100. **Officers:** Ron Riebe, General Mgr.; D. Zanghi, Controller.

■ **11973** ■ **Nash Finch Co.**
PO Box 355
Minneapolis, MN 55440-0355
Phone: (612)832-0534 **Fax:** (612)844-1237
URL: http://www.nashfinch.com
Products: Groceries. **SIC:** 5141 (Groceries—General Line). **Est:** 1921. **Sales:** $4,123,000 (1999). **Emp:** 14,000. **Officers:** Ron Marshall, President & CEO; Christopher Brown, VP of Marketing; Bruce Cross, Sr VP Business Transformation.

■ **11974** ■ **Natco Food Service Merchants**
PO Box 52209
New Orleans, LA 70152-2209
Phone: (504)525-7224 **Fax:** (504)525-4499
Products: Beef. **SIC:** 5147 (Meats & Meat Products).
Est: 1925. **Sales:** $10,000,000 (2000). **Emp:** 57.
Officers: Leonard D. Lalla.

■ **11975** ■ **National Candy**
15925 NW 52 Ave.
Miami, FL 33014
Phone: (305)625-8888 **Fax:** (305)625-4001
E-mail: cuetara@usa.com
URL: http://www.nationalbiscuit.com
Products: Candies; Chocolates; Gum; Snacks, including cookies and crackers. **SIC:** 5145 (Confectionery). **Est:** 1981. **Sales:** $2,000,000 (2000).
Emp: 8. **Officers:** Isaac Gomez, President.

■ **11976** ■ **National Enzyme Co.**
PO Box 128
Forsyth, MO 65653
Phone: 800-825-8545 **Fax:** (417)546-6433
Products: Health food supplements. **SIC:** 5149 (Groceries & Related Products Nec).

■ **11977** ■ **National Foods**
600 Food Center Dr.
Bronx, NY 10474-7037
Phone: (718)842-5000 **Fax:** (718)842-5664
URL: http://www.hebrewnational.com
Products: Kosher provisions; Sausage products.
SICs: 5149 (Groceries & Related Products Nec); 5147 (Meats & Meat Products). **Sales:** $120,000,000 (2000).
Emp: 200. **Officers:** Martin Silver, Exec. VP & General Mgr.; Mark Kleinman, VP of Marketing; Leigh Platte, Dir. of Marketing. **Alternate Name:** Swift-Eckrich, Inc.

■ **11978** ■ **National Heritage Sales Corp.**
PO Box 1956
Cleburne, TX 76033-1956
Phone: (817)477-5324 **Fax:** (817)641-3683
Products: Fresh beef products. **SIC:** 5147 (Meats & Meat Products). **Sales:** $9,000,000 (2000). **Emp:** 12.
Officers: Walter Mize, President.

■ **11979** ■ **National Supermarkets**
PO Box 23528
New Orleans, LA 70183
Phone: (504)733-6610 **Fax:** (504)734-9050
Products: General line groceries. **SIC:** 5141 (Groceries—General Line).

■ 11980 ■ Nationwide Beef Inc.
219 N Green St.
Chicago, IL 60607
Phone: (312)829-4900
Products: Fresh pork; Frozen pork; Processed or cured pork. **SICs:** 5147 (Meats & Meat Products); 5142 (Packaged Frozen Foods). **Est:** 1969. **Sales:** $45,000,000 (2000). **Emp:** 135. **Officers:** Frank Swan, President; E. Rabin, CFO.

■ 11981 ■ Nat's Garden Produce, Inc.
7200 S Kimbark Ave.
PO Box 19176
Chicago, IL 60619
Phone: (773)643-3121 **Fax:** (773)643-8273
Products: Produce. **SIC:** 5148 (Fresh Fruits & Vegetables).

■ 11982 ■ Natural Energy Unlimited Inc.
108 Royal St.
New Orleans, LA 70130
Phone: (504)525-6887
Products: Natural snack foods. **SICs:** 5148 (Fresh Fruits & Vegetables); 5149 (Groceries & Related Products Nec). **Sales:** $10,000,000 (2000). **Emp:** 250. **Officers:** Ruthann Menutis, President; Jerry Bargoon, CFO; Julie Blue, Dir. of Marketing & Sales; Debra Smith, Dir. of Data Processing.

■ 11983 ■ Natural Meat Specialties
6331 Brightstar Dr.
Colorado Springs, CO 80918
Phone: (719)548-1735
Products: Meat. **SIC:** 5147 (Meats & Meat Products).

■ 11984 ■ Natural Ovens of Manitowoc Inc.
PO Box 730
Manitowoc, WI 54221-0730
Phone: (920)758-2500 **Fax:** (920)758-2594
Products: Whole grain breads and rolls; Muffins; Granolas. **SIC:** 5149 (Groceries & Related Products Nec). **Emp:** 186.

■ 11985 ■ Natural Resources
6680 Harvard Dr.
Sebastopol, CA 95472
Phone: (707)823-4340 **Fax:** (707)823-4340
E-mail: natres@sonic.net
Products: Herbs; Natural foods. **SIC:** 5149 (Groceries & Related Products Nec). **Est:** 1988. **Sales:** $250,000 (2000). **Emp:** 1.

■ 11986 ■ Natural Sales Network, Inc.
19290 S Harbor Dr.
Ft. Bragg, CA 95437-5722
Phone: (707)964-1261 **Fax:** (707)964-1281
Products: Seafood. **SIC:** 5146 (Fish & Seafoods). **Emp:** 99. **Officers:** David Showalter.

■ 11987 ■ Nature's Best
PO Box 2248
Brea, CA 92822-2248
Phone: (714)441-2378 **Fax:** (714)441-2330
Products: Natural health products. **SICs:** 5149 (Groceries & Related Products Nec); 5122 (Drugs, Proprietaries & Sundries).

■ 11988 ■ Naturipe Berry Growers
PO Box 1630
Watsonville, CA 95077-1630
Phone: (408)722-2430 **Fax:** (408)728-9398
URL: http://www.naturipe.com
Products: Strawberries. **SIC:** 5148 (Fresh Fruits & Vegetables). **Est:** 1917. **Sales:** $75,000,000 (2000). **Emp:** 250. **Officers:** Larry Shikuma, CEO & President; Jeff Mink, CFO; Nick Pasculli, VP of Marketing & Business Development, e-mail: pasculli@ix.netcom.com; Craig Moriyama, VP of Fresh Sales; Tetsuo Fujimoto, VP of Freezer Sales.

■ 11989 ■ Ne-Mo's Bakery Inc.
416 N Hale Ave.
Escondido, CA 92029
Phone: (760)741-5725 **Fax:** (760)741-0659
E-mail: salenemo@aol.com
URL: http://www.nemosbakery.com
Products: Frozen baked goods. **SIC:** 5142 (Packaged Frozen Foods). **Est:** 1975. **Emp:** 210. **Officers:** Ed Smith, President; Edward Carson, Controller; Samuel

J. DeLucca Jr., Sr. VP of Marketing & Sales; Nancy Calegari, Dir. of Mktg. & Sales, e-mail: salenemo@aol.com.

■ 11990 ■ Nebraska Popcorn, Inc.
RR 1, Box 50A
Clearwater, NE 68726-9720
Phones: (402)887-5335 (402)887-5421
Free: (800)253-6502 **Fax:** (402)887-4709
E-mail: Morrison@Bloomnet.com
Products: Popcorn; Poly-bags. **SIC:** 5145 (Confectionery). **Emp:** 25. **Officers:** Frank Morrison; Nancy A. Dietz, Sales Mgr.; Michele Steskal, Custom Support. **Former Name:** Morrison Farms Popcorn.

■ 11991 ■ Nehawka Farmers Coop.
PO Box 159
Nehawka, NE 68413
Phone: (402)227-2715 **Fax:** (402)227-2062
Products: Grain, feed and fertilizers; Grain storage; Gas service station. **SICs:** 5153 (Grain & Field Beans); 5191 (Farm Supplies). **Sales:** $20,000,000 (2000). **Emp:** 40. **Officers:** Dale Piper, General Manager, Finance.

■ 11992 ■ Neiman Brothers Company Inc.
3322 W Newport Ave.
Chicago, IL 60618
Phone: (312)463-3000 **Fax:** (312)463-3181
Products: Bakery supplies; Flour and other grain mill products; Refined sugar. **SIC:** 5149 (Groceries & Related Products Nec). **Est:** 1920. **Sales:** $12,000,000 (2000). **Emp:** 75. **Officers:** W.J. Neiman, President; S.W. Neiman, Finance Officer.

■ 11993 ■ Neithart Meats Inc.
12301 Gladstone Ave.
Sylmar, CA 91342-5319
Phone: (818)361-7141
Free: (800)266-7141 **Fax:** (818)361-7143
Products: Seafood; Poultry products; Beef; Fresh pork; Frozen pork. **SICs:** 5147 (Meats & Meat Products); 5144 (Poultry & Poultry Products); 5146 (Fish & Seafoods). **Emp:** 24. **Officers:** Robert A. Neithart.

■ 11994 ■ Nelson-Ricks Creamery Co.
314 W 3rd S
Salt Lake City, UT 84101
Phone: (801)364-3607 **Fax:** (801)364-3600
Products: Cheese. **SIC:** 5143 (Dairy Products Except Dried or Canned). **Est:** 1907. **Sales:** $18,500,000 (2000). **Emp:** 75. **Officers:** Calvin L. Nelson, President; Dean Barker, Vice President; J.R. Lundgren, Sales Mgr.

■ 11995 ■ Neshaminy Valley Natural Foods Distributor, Ltd.
5 Louise Dr.
Ivyland, PA 18974-1525
Phone: (215)443-5545 **Fax:** (215)443-7087
Products: Health foods; Gourmet foods. **SIC:** 5149 (Groceries & Related Products Nec). **Est:** 1977. **Sales:** $10,000,000 (2000). **Emp:** 40. **Officers:** Philip Margolis, President; Eugene S. Margolls, Vice President; John Bacon, Sales/Marketing Contact.

■ 11996 ■ Nesson Meat Sales
PO Box 11207
Norfolk, VA 23517
Phone: (804)622-6625
Free: (800)622-6487 **Fax:** (757)623-2595
Products: Fresh meat; Frozen meat. **SIC:** 5147 (Meats & Meat Products). **Est:** 1928. **Sales:** $14,000,000 (2000). **Emp:** 60. **Officers:** Bobby Goldwasser, Owner; Renee' Hill, Controller; Bob Unterbrink, Dir. of Marketing.

■ 11997 ■ Nestle Carnation Food Service Co.
800 N Brand Blvd.
Glendale, CA 91203
Phone: (818)549-6000
Products: Food. **SIC:** 5141 (Groceries—General Line).

■ 11998 ■ Neuman Distributors
903 Moralis
San Antonio, TX 78207
Phone: (210)225-4123 **Fax:** (210)225-5810
Products: Ham; Turkey; Brie. **SICs:** 5147 (Meats &

Meat Products); 5144 (Poultry & Poultry Products); 5143 (Dairy Products Except Dried or Canned).

■ 11999 ■ Nevada Food Service
3550 S Procyon Ave.
Las Vegas, NV 89103
Phone: (702)876-3606 **Fax:** (702)876-1085
Products: Ham, bacon, sausage, roast beef, and pastrami. **SIC:** 5147 (Meats & Meat Products). **Est:** 1953. **Sales:** $2,000,000 (2000). **Emp:** 7. **Officers:** Richard Parmenter, President.

■ 12000 ■ New Cooperative Company Inc.
PO Box 607
Dillonvale, OH 43917
Phone: (614)769-2331
Products: Grocery products; Frozen foods; Canned foods; Produce; Milk; Meat. **SICs:** 5099 (Durable Goods Nec); 5149 (Groceries & Related Products Nec); 5143 (Dairy Products Except Dried or Canned); 5147 (Meats & Meat Products); 5142 (Packaged Frozen Foods). **Est:** 1908. **Sales:** $9,000,000 (2000). **Emp:** 110. **Officers:** John Pastre, General. Mgr.

■ 12001 ■ New England Frozen Foods Inc.
1 Harvest Ln.
Southborough, MA 01772
Phone: (508)481-0300
Products: Frozen foods and dairy products. **SICs:** 5142 (Packaged Frozen Foods); 5143 (Dairy Products Except Dried or Canned). **Sales:** $200,000,000 (1994). **Emp:** 400. **Officers:** Walter Stella, Exec. VP of Finance.

■ 12002 ■ New England Variety Distributors
PO Box 804
Niantic, CT 06357
Phone: (860)739-6291 **Fax:** (860)739-2119
Products: Vending machine operators; Candy, cigarettes, and tobacco. **SICs:** 5145 (Confectionery); 5194 (Tobacco & Tobacco Products). **Emp:** 3. **Officers:** Bruce Engelman, CEO.

■ 12003 ■ New Horizons Meats and Dist., L.L.C.
2842 Massachusetts Ave.
Cincinnati, OH 45225
Phone: (513)681-2850 **Fax:** (513)853-6545
Products: Beef; Honey-glazed ham. **SIC:** 5147 (Meats & Meat Products). **Est:** 1997. **Sales:** $10,000,000 (2000). **Emp:** 40. **Officers:** Terry Carmack, Partner; Michael G. Kluener, Partner; Joseph Rettig, Partner.

■ 12004 ■ Niagara Foods Inc.
PO Box 177
Middleport, NY 14105
Phone: (716)735-7722
Products: Frozen fruit. **SIC:** 5142 (Packaged Frozen Foods). **Est:** 1984. **Sales:** $43,000,000 (2000). **Emp:** 100. **Officers:** B. Schneider, President.

■ 12005 ■ Nicholas and Co.
PO Box 45005
Salt Lake City, UT 84145-5005
Phone: (801)531-1100
Products: Perishable and non-perishable food, including meat and dairy products. **SICs:** 5141 (Groceries—General Line); 5143 (Dairy Products Except Dried or Canned); 5147 (Meats & Meat Products). **Sales:** $78,000,000 (2000). **Emp:** 150. **Officers:** Bill Mouskondis, President.

■ 12006 ■ Nichols Companies of South Carolina
PO Box 827
Florence, SC 29503
Phone: (803)667-0096 **Fax:** (803)669-0951
Products: Poultry further processor. **SIC:** 5144 (Poultry & Poultry Products). **Est:** 2000. **Sales:** $25,000,000 (2000). **Emp:** 80. **Officers:** J.L. Nichols III, President; Steve McAlister, VP & General Mgr. **Former Name:** Carolina Poultry Sales. **Former Name:** Columbia Farms.

■ 12007 ■ **Nichols Foodservice Inc.**
PO Box 729
Wallace, NC 28466
Phone: (910)285-3197 **Fax:** (910)285-3596
E-mail: nicfoods@mail.duplin.net
URL: http://www.nicholsfoods.com
Products: Food and food supplies for foodservice operators. **SIC:** 5141 (Groceries—General Line). **Est:** 1946. **Sales:** $30,000,000 (2000). **Emp:** 95. **Officers:** J.L. Nichols III, CEO & President.

■ 12008 ■ **Niser Ice Cream**
16 E 11th
Newport, KY 41071-2137
Phone: (606)431-7556 **Fax:** (606)431-7556
Products: Milk and ice cream. **SIC:** 5143 (Dairy Products Except Dried or Canned). **Emp:** 49.

■ 12009 ■ **John J. Nissen Baking Co.**
75 Quinsigamond Ave.
Worcester, MA 01610-1893
Phone: (508)791-5571 **Fax:** (508)791-5571
Products: Bread. **SIC:** 5149 (Groceries & Related Products Nec). **Est:** 1925. **Sales:** $50,000,000 (2000). **Emp:** 499. **Officers:** J. R. Nissen.

■ 12010 ■ **NM Bakery Service Co.**
310 San Pedro Dr. SE
Albuquerque, NM 87108-3033
Phone: (505)255-5225
Free: (800)284-5225 **Fax:** (505)265-3413
E-mail: nmbakery@aol.com
Products: Bakery products; Chocolate; Bakery supplies; Packaging; Novelties; Ribbons; Cutlery. **SICs:** 5149 (Groceries & Related Products Nec); 5072 (Hardware); 5113 (Industrial & Personal Service Paper); 5145 (Confectionery); 5140 (Groceries & Related Products). **Est:** 1973. **Emp:** 12. **Officers:** Harriet V. Mozley, President; Norman Mozley, Vice President.

■ 12011 ■ **Nobel/Sysco Food Services Co.**
PO Box 5566
Denver, CO 80217
Phone: (303)458-4000
Products: Fresh fish; Fresh produce. **SICs:** 5146 (Fish & Seafoods); 5148 (Fresh Fruits & Vegetables). **Est:** 1938. **Sales:** $400,000,000 (2000). **Emp:** 900. **Officers:** Michael L. Kauffman, President; Tom Culbertson, VP of Finance; Jay Miller, Dir. of Systems; Cindy Trost, Dir of Personnel.

■ 12012 ■ **Noerenberg's Wholesale Meats Inc.**
PO Box 23241
Milwaukee, WI 53223
Phone: (414)365-3553
Free: (800)833-6090 **Fax:** (414)365-3733
Products: Meats; Poultry; Fish. **SICs:** 5147 (Meats & Meat Products); 5146 (Fish & Seafoods); 5144 (Poultry & Poultry Products). **Est:** 1940. **Sales:** $10,000,000 (2000). **Emp:** 65. **Officers:** V. Noerenberg.

■ 12013 ■ **Nonesuch Foods**
197 Rte. 1
Scarborough, ME 04074
Phone: (207)883-1440
Products: Food. **SIC:** 5141 (Groceries—General Line).

■ 12014 ■ **Noon Hour Food Products Inc.**
660 W Randolph
Chicago, IL 60661
Phone: (312)782-1177
Free: (800)621-6636 **Fax:** (312)236-0420
Products: Fish; Cheese; Flour mixes. **SIC:** 5146 (Fish & Seafoods). **Est:** 1876. **Sales:** $7,000,000 (2000). **Emp:** 25. **Officers:** Paul A. Buhl, President; Pat Freeman, Controller.

■ 12015 ■ **Nor-Cal Beverage Company Inc.**
PO Box 1823
West Sacramento, CA 95691
Phone: (916)372-0600
Products: Bbeverages; Beer. **SICs:** 5149 (Groceries & Related Products Nec); 5181 (Beer & Ale). **Sales:** $120,000,000 (2000). **Emp:** 400. **Officers:** Grant Deary, President; Pete Ruhkala, Treasurer.

■ 12016 ■ **Nor-Cal Produce Inc.**
PO Box 980188
West Sacramento, CA 95798-0188
Phone: (916)373-0830
Products: Produce. **SIC:** 5148 (Fresh Fruits & Vegetables).

■ 12017 ■ **Nor-Joe Cheese Importing**
505 Frisco Ave.
Metairie, LA 70005
Phones: (504)833-9240 (504)833-9275
Fax: (504)833-9240
Products: Natural cheese; Cured or smoked meat; Oils; Candy; Cookies. **SICs:** 5143 (Dairy Products Except Dried or Canned); 5147 (Meats & Meat Products); 5145 (Confectionery); 5149 (Groceries & Related Products Nec).

■ 12018 ■ **Norbest Inc.**
PO Box 1000
Midvale, UT 84047
Phone: (801)566-5656
Free: (800)453-5327 **Fax:** (801)255-2309
E-mail: norbest@norbest.com
URL: http://www.norbest.com
Products: Turkey, including parts and processed products. **SIC:** 5144 (Poultry & Poultry Products). **Est:** 1930. **Sales:** $140,000,000 (2000). **Emp:** 1,200. **Officers:** Steven Jensen, President; Ronald Attebury, Treasurer; John Hall, Sr. VP of Operations; Rick Hauert, Controller; Jack Sandridge, Sales/Marketing Contact; Steven G. Johnson, Human Resources Contact.

■ 12019 ■ **Nordic Delights Foods Inc.**
72 Water St.
Lubec, ME 04652
Phone: (207)733-5556 **Fax:** (207)733-2034
Products: Fresh fish. **SIC:** 5146 (Fish & Seafoods). **Sales:** $16,000,000 (2000). **Emp:** 60. **Officers:** Robert Hood, Finance General Manager.

■ 12020 ■ **Normans Inc.**
86 S Division St.
Battle Creek, MI 49017
Phone: (616)968-6136
Products: Produce and frozen foods. **SICs:** 5141 (Groceries—General Line); 5148 (Fresh Fruits & Vegetables). **Est:** 1946. **Sales:** $19,000,000 (2000). **Emp:** 58. **Officers:** Wayne L. Norman, President; Dennis Elmer, Treasurer & Secty.

■ 12021 ■ **Norpac Fisheries, Inc.**
3140 Ualena St., Ste. 205
Honolulu, HI 96819
Phone: (808)528-3474 **Fax:** (808)537-6880
Products: Fresh and frozen live seafood, including salmon, black cod, king crab, snow crab, lobster, shrimp, octopus, clams, and oysters. **SICs:** 5146 (Fish & Seafoods); 5142 (Packaged Frozen Foods). **Est:** 1987. **Sales:** $10,000,000 (1999). **Emp:** 11. **Officers:** Michael Budke, CEO.

■ 12022 ■ **Norpac Fisheries Inc.**
3140 Valena St., Ste. 205
Honolulu, HI 96819
Phone: (808)528-3474 **Fax:** (808)537-6880
Products: Food. **SIC:** 5146 (Fish & Seafoods). **Sales:** $10,000,000 (1999). **Emp:** 8.

■ 12023 ■ **Norpac Food Sales Inc.**
4350 SW Galewood St.
Lake Oswego, OR 97035
Phone: (503)635-9311
URL: http://www.norpac.com
Products: Frozen and canned fruits, juices, and vegetables. **SICs:** 5142 (Packaged Frozen Foods); 5149 (Groceries & Related Products Nec). **Sales:** $400,000,000 (2000). **Emp:** 70. **Officers:** Michael J. Wood, CEO & President; Craig Yamasaki, Treasurer; Jerry E. Peacock, Exec. VP; Roy M. Flaherty, Exec. VP.

■ 12024 ■ **Norseland Inc.**
1290 E Main St.
Stamford, CT 06902
Phone: (203)324-5620
Products: Cheese. **SIC:** 5143 (Dairy Products Except Dried or Canned). **Sales:** $9,000,000 (2000). **Emp:** 16.

Officers: David Brohel, President; Michael Albano, Controller.

■ 12025 ■ **North Castle Produce Inc.**
911 N Broadway
North White Plains, NY 10603
Phone: (914)683-5771
Products: Produce. **SIC:** 5148 (Fresh Fruits & Vegetables).

■ 12026 ■ **North Central Grain Coop.**
PO Box 8
Bisbee, ND 58317
Phone: (701)656-3263 **Fax:** (701)656-3371
Products: Grain elevator with storage. **SIC:** 5153 (Grain & Field Beans). **Sales:** $30,000,000 (2000). **Emp:** 25. **Officers:** Dwayne Kaleva, President; Steve Oakland, President.

■ 12027 ■ **North Coast Sea Foods Inc.**
12-14 Fargo
Boston, MA 02210-1915
Phone: (617)345-4400 **Fax:** (617)345-4415
Products: North Atlantic fish. **SIC:** 5146 (Fish & Seafoods). **Emp:** 99.

■ 12028 ■ **North Farm Cooperative**
204 Regas Rd.
Madison, WI 53714
Phone: (608)241-2667
Free: (800)236-5880 **Fax:** (608)241-0688
E-mail: nfcoop@northfarm.com
URL: http://www.northfarm.com
Products: Natural and organic food; Cleaning products; Bulk goods; Natural supplements; Homeopathic remedies; Vegetarian and soy foods; Allergy-free products; Cheese. **SIC:** 5149 (Groceries & Related Products Nec). **Est:** 1971. **Sales:** $30,000,000 (2000). **Emp:** 130. **Officers:** Bill Lathrop, General Mgr., e-mail: wlathrop@northfarm.com; Rebecca Sonstrom, Sales Mgr., e-mail: rsonstrom@northfarm.com.

■ 12029 ■ **North Star Distributors**
2210 Hewitt Ave.
Everett, WA 98201
Phone: (425)252-9600 **Fax:** (425)252-7598
Products: Soft Drinkss. **SIC:** 5149 (Groceries & Related Products Nec).

■ 12030 ■ **NorthCenter Foodservice Corp.**
PO Box 2628
Augusta, ME 04338-2628
Phone: (207)623-8451 **Fax:** (207)623-2197
Products: Food. **SIC:** 5141 (Groceries—General Line). **Est:** 1982. **Sales:** $112,000,000 (1999). **Emp:** 250. **Officers:** H. Allen Ryan, Chairman of the Board; David Crowell, Exec. VP; Greg Piper, President; Larry Davis, VP of Human Resources.

■ 12031 ■ **Northeast Cooperatives**
PO Box 8188
Brattleboro, VT 05304-8188
Phone: (802)257-5856
Free: (800)334-9939 **Fax:** (802)451-1444
E-mail: info@northeastcoop.com
URL: http://www.northeastcoop.com
Products: Organic produce; Natural and organic foods; Natural personal care; Vitamins and supplements; Bulk; Herbs; Frozen and refrigerated natural foods. **SICs:** 5149 (Groceries & Related Products Nec); 5122 (Drugs, Proprietaries & Sundries). **Est:** 1984. **Sales:** $110,000,000 (2000). **Emp:** 350. **Officers:** George Southworth, General Mgr.; Mary Carol Skinner, Dir. of Mktg. & Sales; Valerie Dahl, CFO; Pamela Sopczyk, Human Resources Mgr.; Mark Novak, COO.

■ 12032 ■ **Northern Wind, Inc.**
PO Box M40144
New Bedford, MA 02740
Phone: (508)997-0727 **Fax:** (508)990-8792
E-mail: nwind@northernwind.com
URL: http://www.northernwind.com
Products: Fresh and frozen seafood. **SIC:** 5146 (Fish & Seafoods). **Est:** 1986. **Emp:** 80. **Officers:** Kenneth Melanson; Michael T. Fernandes; Doreen Wotton, Human Resources Contact.

■ 12033 ■ **Northland Cranberries Inc.**
PO Box 8020
Wisconsin Rapids, WI 54495-8020
Phone: (715)424-4444 **Fax:** (715)422-6897
E-mail: dlang@northlandcran.com
URL: http://www.northlandcran.com
Products: Cranberries, including juices and concentrates. **SICs:** 5148 (Fresh Fruits & Vegetables); 5149 (Groceries & Related Products Nec). **Est:** 1987. **Sales:** $50,000,000 (2000). **Emp:** 206. **Officers:** John Swendrowski, CEO & Chairman of the Board; Robert E. Hawk, Exec. VP; Scott Corriveau, President, Branded Division.

■ 12034 ■ **Northland Hub Inc.**
PO Box 73800
Fairbanks, AK 99707
Phone: (907)456-4425
Products: Groceries, including canned, frozen, and fresh foods; Produce; Milk. **SICs:** 5141 (Groceries—General Line); 5149 (Groceries & Related Products Nec); 5148 (Fresh Fruits & Vegetables); 5143 (Dairy Products Except Dried or Canned).

■ 12035 ■ **Northland Marketing, Inc.**
1131 Westrac Dr., Ste. 107
PO Box 9948
Fargo, ND 58106-9948
Phone: (701)232-7220 **Fax:** (701)280-1640
Products: Dry beans. **SIC:** 5153 (Grain & Field Beans). **Est:** 1985. **Officers:** Patrick King, President.

■ 12036 ■ **Northwest Farm Food Cooperative**
1370 S Anacortes St.
Burlington, WA 98233-3038
Phone: (360)757-4225 **Fax:** (360)757-8206
Products: Veterinary products. **SIC:** 5149 (Groceries & Related Products Nec). **Sales:** $3,200,000 (2000). **Emp:** 25.

■ 12037 ■ **Northwest Foods**
1311 Lowe Ave.
Bellingham, WA 98226
Phone: (206)647-2195 **Fax:** (206)733-2460
Products: Fresh fruits and vegetables; Fish and seafood. **SICs:** 5146 (Fish & Seafoods); 5148 (Fresh Fruits & Vegetables). **Officers:** David Pollack, International Sales.

■ 12038 ■ **Northwest Meats Inc.**
2615 E N St.
Tacoma, WA 98421-2203
Phone: (253)383-3688
Free: (800)562-9841 **Fax:** (253)383-5339
Products: Portion cut meat products, including beef, pork, lamb, and veal. **SIC:** 5147 (Meats & Meat Products). **Emp:** 49. **Officers:** Bruno I. Nicoli.

■ 12039 ■ **Northwood Meats Inc.**
Hwy. 65 N
Northwood, IA 50459
Phone: (515)324-2483 **Fax:** (515)324-2488
Products: Pork and Beef. **SIC:** 5147 (Meats & Meat Products). **Emp:** 49.

■ 12040 ■ **John Notari Sales Co.**
6715 Masonic Dr.
Alexandria, LA 71301-2114
Phone: (318)442-0004 **Fax:** (318)448-0989
Products: Candy; Snacks, including corn chips, potato chips, nuts, seeds, and crackers; Cookies. **SIC:** 5145 (Confectionery). **Est:** 1960. **Emp:** 10. **Officers:** John Notari, President.

■ 12041 ■ **Novartis Nutrition Corp.**
PO Box 370
Minneapolis, MN 55440
Phone: (612)925-2100
Free: (800)999-9978 **Fax:** (612)593-2087
Products: Medical Foods. **SIC:** 5149 (Groceries & Related Products Nec).

■ 12042 ■ **J.C. Noyes and Son Inc.**
PO Box 17382
Covington, KY 41017-0382
Phone: (606)431-4743 **Fax:** (606)655-4100
Products: General line groceries; Tobacco; Candy. **SICs:** 5141 (Groceries—General Line); 5145 (Confectionery); 5194 (Tobacco & Tobacco Products).

Est: 1941. **Sales:** $19,000,000 (2000). **Emp:** 36.
Officers: Tim Noyes, President.

■ 12043 ■ **Nueske Hillcrest Farm Meats**
RR 2
PO Box D
Wittenberg, WI 54499-0904
Phone: (715)253-2226
Free: (800)382-2266 **Fax:** (715)253-2021
E-mail: nueske@nueske.com
URL: http://www.nueske.com
Products: Applewood smoked specialties. **SIC:** 5147 (Meats & Meat Products). **Est:** 1933. **Sales:** $12,500,000 (2000). **Emp:** 85. **Officers:** Robert D. Nueske, President; James A. Nueske, Vice President; Gilbert Thompson, National Sales Dir.

■ 12044 ■ **Nugget Distributors Inc.**
PO Box 8309
Stockton, CA 95208
Phone: (209)948-8122 **Fax:** (209)943-7529
E-mail: webmaster@nugget.com
URL: http://www.nugget.com
Products: Food; Food preparation equipment. **SICs:** 5141 (Groceries—General Line); 5087 (Service Establishment Equipment). **Est:** 1966. **Sales:** $32,000,000 (2000). **Emp:** 65. **Officers:** Ted D. Peralta, President; Phil Bishop, Vice President; Richard D. Rasmussen, Exec. VP; James Lay, VP of Information Systems.

■ 12045 ■ **Nulaid Foods Inc.**
200 W 5th St.
Ripon, CA 95366
Phone: (209)599-2121
Free: (800)788-8871 **Fax:** (209)599-4822
Products: Eggs and egg products. **SICs:** 5144 (Poultry & Poultry Products); 5149 (Groceries & Related Products Nec). **Est:** 1916. **Sales:** $7,000,000 (2000). **Emp:** 75. **Officers:** David Crockett, CEO & President; Stan Andre, Sr. VP of Sales & Marketing; Dawn Shakeshaft, Controller.

■ 12046 ■ **Nunez Seafood**
PO Box 126
Lafitte, LA 70067
Phones: (504)689-2389 (504)689-2250
Products: Seafood. **SIC:** 5146 (Fish & Seafoods). **Emp:** 6.

■ 12047 ■ **NutraSource Inc.**
PO Box 1856
Auburn, WA 98071-1856
Phone: (206)467-7190
Products: Natural foods. **SIC:** 5149 (Groceries & Related Products Nec).

■ 12048 ■ **NutriCology Inc.**
PO Box 55907
Hayward, CA 94544
Phone: (510)487-8526
Free: (800)545-9960 **Fax:** (510)487-8682
Products: Food supplements and vitamins. **SICs:** 5149 (Groceries & Related Products Nec); 5122 (Drugs, Proprietaries & Sundries). **Sales:** $14,000,000 (2000). **Emp:** 75. **Officers:** Marian Sum, President; Edward Lau, CFO.

■ 12049 ■ **O'Brien and Co.**
3302 Harlan Lewis Rd.
Bellevue, NE 68005
Phone: (402)291-3600
Free: (800)433-7567 **Fax:** (402)291-0237
URL: http://www.obrienmeatsnacks.com
Products: Meat snacks. **SIC:** 5147 (Meats & Meat Products). **Est:** 1946. **Sales:** $6,400,000 (2000). **Emp:** 30. **Officers:** John O'Brien, President; Tom O'Brien, Vice President.

■ 12050 ■ **Ocean Crest Seafoods Inc.**
PO Box 1183
Gloucester, MA 01930
Phone: (978)281-0232 **Fax:** (978)283-3211
Products: Fresh fish. **SIC:** 5146 (Fish & Seafoods). **Sales:** $2,000,000 (2000). **Emp:** 16. **Officers:** Anthony P. Parco, President.

■ 12051 ■ **Ocean Floor Abalone**
1075 Reed Ave.
San Diego, CA 92109
Phones: (858)271-5676 (858)271-5676
Products: Frozen shellfish; Seafood; Abalone-wavalone. **SIC:** 5146 (Fish & Seafoods). **Est:** 1967. **Sales:** $1,500,000 (2000). **Emp:** 6. **Officers:** Dave Qnade, Manager.

■ 12052 ■ **Ocean Mist Farms**
10855 Cara Mia Pkwy.
Castroville, CA 95012
Phones: (831)633-2144 (831)633-5420
Fax: (831)633-0561
E-mail: maggi@oceanmist.com
URL: http://www.oceanmist.com
Products: Vegetables, including artichokes. **SIC:** 5148 (Fresh Fruits & Vegetables). **Est:** 1924. **Sales:** $90,000,000 (2000). **Emp:** 180. **Alternate Name:** California Artichoke and Vegetable Growers Corp.

■ 12053 ■ **Odessa Trading Company Inc.**
PO Box 277
Odessa, WA 99159
Phone: (509)982-2661 **Fax:** (509)982-2540
Products: Grain, farm machinery and equipment including combines, weeders and tractors. **SICs:** 5153 (Grain & Field Beans); 5083 (Farm & Garden Machinery). **Sales:** $16,500,000 (2000). **Emp:** 25. **Officers:** Mark Cronrath, General Mgr.

■ 12054 ■ **Off the Dock Seafood Inc.**
2224 Southern St.
Memphis, TN 38104
Phone: (901)276-8784 **Fax:** (901)276-8792
Products: Seafood. **SIC:** 5146 (Fish & Seafoods). **Sales:** $500,000 (2000). **Emp:** 4. **Officers:** David Feinstone, Owner.

■ 12055 ■ **Ohio Farmers Inc.**
2700 E 55th
Cleveland, OH 44104
Phone: (216)391-9733 **Fax:** (216)391-4023
Products: Produce. **SIC:** 5148 (Fresh Fruits & Vegetables). **Est:** 1952. **Sales:** $25,000,000 (2000). **Emp:** 52. **Officers:** Bernard Gelb, CEO; Eliot Gelb, President; Thomas Burdette, General Mgr.

■ 12056 ■ **Ohio Steak and Barbecue Co.**
3880 Lockbourne Rd.
Columbus, OH 43207-4215
Phone: (614)491-3245
Free: (800)229-6446 **Fax:** (614)491-4611
Products: Restaurant food. **SIC:** 5141 (Groceries—General Line). **Est:** 1937. **Sales:** $5,000,000 (2000). **Emp:** 30. **Officers:** William Greer, CEO.

■ 12057 ■ **Oilseeds International Ltd.**
855 Sansome, Ste. 100
San Francisco, CA 94111-1507
Phone: (415)956-7251 **Fax:** (415)394-9023
E-mail: info@oilseedssf.com
URL: http://www.oilseedssf.com
Products: Vegetable cooking oil. **SIC:** 5149 (Groceries & Related Products Nec). **Est:** 1981. **Emp:** 36.

■ 12058 ■ **Okleelanta Corp.**
PO Box 86
South Bay, FL 33493
Phone: (407)996-9072
Products: Sugar. **SIC:** 5159 (Farm-Product Raw Materials Nec). **Sales:** $200,000,000 (2000). **Emp:** 5,000. **Officers:** Alfonso Fanjul Jr., President.

■ 12059 ■ **Olbro Wholesalers**
45 Park Ln.
Rochester, NY 14625
Phone: (716)381-9521 **Fax:** (716)248-8292
E-mail: webmaster@olbro.com
Products: Hot pepper sauces; Marinades. **SIC:** 5149 (Groceries & Related Products Nec). **Est:** 1990. **Officers:** Bill Olsan, Owner; John Olsan, Owner.

■ 12060 ■ **Old Dominion Export-Import Co. Inc.**
2409 Garnett Ct.
Vienna, VA 22180-6908
Phone: (703)204-2918 **Fax:** (703)560-9762
Products: Spices, including saffron and paprika; Guar

gum and splits; Ice cream ingredients. **SICs:** 5149 (Groceries & Related Products Nec); 5143 (Dairy Products Except Dried or Canned). **Est:** 1988. **Sales:** $3,000,000 (2000). **Emp:** 3. **Officers:** V.S. Alsi, General Mgr., e-mail: vijayalsi@juno.com. **Alternate Name:** Old Dominion.

■ **12061** ■ **Old Dutch Bakery Inc.**
PO Box 319
Blandon, PA 19510
Phone: (215)926-1311 **Fax:** (215)926-0984
Products: Bread, cake, and related products. **SIC:** 5149 (Groceries & Related Products Nec). **Est:** 1980. **Sales:** $3,000,000 (2000). **Emp:** 49. **Officers:** Sam Chudnovsky, CEO & Chairman of the Board; Werner Ammann, President; Edward Kapsa, Vice President.

■ **12062** ■ **Old Dutch Foods Inc.**
2375 Terminal Rd.
Roseville, MN 55113-2577
Phone: (612)633-8810
Products: Potato chips. **SIC:** 5145 (Confectionery). **Sales:** $62,000,000 (2000). **Emp:** 425. **Officers:** Vernon O. Aanenson, President; Trace Benson, CFO.

■ **12063** ■ **Old Home Foods Inc.**
370 University Ave.
St. Paul, MN 55103
Phone: (651)228-9035
Free: (800)309-9035 **Fax:** (651)228-1820
Products: Dairy products. **SIC:** 5143 (Dairy Products Except Dried or Canned). **Est:** 1925. **Sales:** $45,000,000 (2000). **Emp:** 100. **Officers:** Richard Hanson, President & Chairman of the Board.

■ **12064** ■ **Old World Bakery**
6210 Eastern Ave.
Baltimore, MD 21224
Phone: (410)633-6690
URL: http://www.oldworld-bakery.com
Products: Natural breads and rolls. **SIC:** 5149 (Groceries & Related Products Nec). **Est:** 1980. **Sales:** $4,000,000 (2000). **Emp:** 13. **Officers:** Maria Lackey, CEO.

■ **12065** ■ **Olean Wholesale Grocery Cooperative Inc.**
PO Box 1070
Olean, NY 14760
Phone: (716)372-2020
Products: General line groceries. **SIC:** 5141 (Groceries—General Line). **Sales:** $110,000,000 (2000). **Emp:** 220. **Officers:** Jim Robinson, President; Andy Lindquist, Finance Officer.

■ **12066** ■ **P. Olender and Company Inc.**
27000 Wick Rd.
Taylor, MI 48180-3015
Phone: (313)921-3310 **Fax:** (313)921-0555
Products: Bakery supplies. **SIC:** 5149 (Groceries & Related Products Nec). **Est:** 1921. **Sales:** $46,000,000 (2000). **Emp:** 100. **Officers:** Marvin Olender, President; Jeff Olender, Vice President.

■ **12067** ■ **Olson-Kessler Meat Company Inc.**
PO Box 9175
Corpus Christi, TX 78469
Phone: (512)853-6291
Products: Processed meat, frozen food including seafood and vegetables. **SICs:** 5147 (Meats & Meat Products); 5146 (Fish & Seafoods); 5142 (Packaged Frozen Foods). **Sales:** $11,000,000 (2000). **Emp:** 62. **Officers:** Donald P. Olson, President; Bernice Johnston, Treasurer & Secty.

■ **12068** ■ **Omaha Steaks Foodservice**
11030 O St.
Omaha, NE 68137-2346
Phone: (402)597-8106
Free: (800)228-9521 **Fax:** (402)597-8222
E-mail: foodservice@omahasteaks.com
URL: http://www.omahasteaks.com/foodservice
Products: Meat, including beef, pork, veal, and lamb. **SIC:** 5147 (Meats & Meat Products). **Est:** 1917. **Emp:** 22. **Officers:** Stephen H. Simon, Vice President & General Manager, e-mail: ssimon@omahasteaks.com. **Former Name:** Omaha Steaks International.

■ **12069** ■ **Omaha Steaks International**
PO Box 3300
Omaha, NE 68103
Phone: (402)331-1010 **Fax:** (402)391-1628
Products: Direct marketing and distributing of food to service institutions. **SIC:** 5147 (Meats & Meat Products). **Sales:** $196,000,000 (2000). **Emp:** 1,200. **Officers:** Alan Simon, CEO & Chairman of the Board; Curt Todd, CFO.

■ **12070** ■ **Omega Produce Company Inc.**
PO Box 277
Nogales, AZ 85628
Phone: (602)281-0410
Products: Fruits and vegetables. **SIC:** 5148 (Fresh Fruits & Vegetables). **Sales:** $3,000,000 (1993). **Emp:** 12. **Officers:** George Gotsis, President.

■ **12071** ■ **Omnitrition**
PO Box 111640
Carrollton, TX 75011-1640
Phones: (972)417-9200 (972)417-9321
Free: (800)446-1025 **Fax:** (972)417-9240
E-mail: omlife@aol.com
URL: http://www.omnitron.com
Products: Health foods; Natural products, including shampoos. **SICs:** 5122 (Drugs, Proprietaries & Sundries); 5149 (Groceries & Related Products Nec). **Est:** 1989. **Sales:** $25,000,000 (2000). **Emp:** 60. **Officers:** Barbara Daley, President, e-mail: jarrett@omnilife.com; William A. McDonald, CFO. **Alternate Name:** Omnitron International, Inc.

■ **12072** ■ **Oneonta Trading Corp.**
PO Box 549
Wenatchee, WA 98801
Phone: (509)663-2631 **Fax:** (509)663-6333
Products: Fresh produce. **SIC:** 5148 (Fresh Fruits & Vegetables). **Est:** 1936. **Sales:** $8,000,000 (2000). **Emp:** 28. **Officers:** Dalton Thomas, Owner; Herb Thomas, Owner.

■ **12073** ■ **Oppenheimer Corp. Golbon**
877 W Main St.
Boise, ID 83702
Phone: (208)342-7771 **Fax:** (208)336-9212
Products: Food for institutions. **SIC:** 5141 (Groceries—General Line).

■ **12074** ■ **Orange Bakery Inc.**
17751 Cowan Ave.
Irvine, CA 92614
Phone: (949)863-1377 **Fax:** (949)863-1932
Products: Frozen pastries. **SICs:** 5149 (Groceries & Related Products Nec); 5142 (Packaged Frozen Foods). **Emp:** 120. **Officers:** Shigeo Ueki, President; Takashi Numao, VP of Sales & Marketing.

■ **12075** ■ **Ore-Cal Corp.**
634 S Crocker St.
Los Angeles, CA 90021-1002
Phone: (213)680-9540
Free: (800)827-7474 **Fax:** (213)629-3326
Products: Seafood. **SIC:** 5146 (Fish & Seafoods). **Est:** 1961. **Sales:** $6,000,000 (1999). **Emp:** 150. **Officers:** William Shinbane.

■ **12076** ■ **Original Chili Bowl Inc.**
PO Box 470125
Tulsa, OK 74147
Phone: (918)628-0225 **Fax:** (918)663-0539
Products: Chili; Seasonings; Beans; Barbecue baskets. **SICs:** 5141 (Groceries—General Line); 5149 (Groceries & Related Products Nec). **Sales:** $17,000,000 (2000). **Emp:** 125. **Officers:** Bob Berryhill, President.

■ **12077** ■ **Orion Food Systems**
PO Box 780
Sioux Falls, SD 57101
Phone: (605)336-6961
Products: Food. **SIC:** 5141 (Groceries—General Line).

■ **12078** ■ **Orrell's Food Service Inc.**
9827 S NC Hwy. 150
Linwood, NC 27299-9461
Phone: (336)752-2114 **Fax:** (336)752-2060
Products: Food. **SIC:** 5141 (Groceries—General Line). **Est:** 1954. **Sales:** $35,500,000 (2000). **Emp:** 70.

Officers: Tony R. Orrell, President; Judy M. Orrell, Treasurer & Secty.

■ **12079** ■ **Osage Cooperative Elevator**
PO Box 358
Osage, IA 50461
Phone: (515)732-3768 **Fax:** (515)732-3250
Products: Animal feed and grain. **SICs:** 5153 (Grain & Field Beans); 5191 (Farm Supplies); 5172 (Petroleum Products Nec). **Sales:** $14,000,000 (2000). **Emp:** 16.

■ **12080** ■ **O'San Products Inc.**
PO Box 468
Camilla, GA 31730
Phone: (912)336-0387
Free: (800)673-6433 **Fax:** (912)336-0390
Products: Institutional products, including poultry and seafood. **SICs:** 5144 (Poultry & Poultry Products); 5141 (Groceries—General Line); 5146 (Fish & Seafoods); 5149 (Groceries & Related Products Nec). **Est:** 1973. **Sales:** $10,000,000 (2000). **Emp:** 40. **Officers:** Howard Truitt, President; Don Gilliard, Buyer.

■ **12081** ■ **Osborn Brothers Inc.**
PO Box 649
Gadsden, AL 35907
Phone: (205)547-8601 **Fax:** (205)546-1634
Products: Food for restaurants. **SIC:** 5141 (Groceries—General Line). **Est:** 1955. **Sales:** $30,000,000 (2000). **Emp:** 85. **Officers:** Joel Osborn, CEO.

■ **12082** ■ **Oscars Wholesale Meats Company Inc.**
250 W 31st
Ogden, UT 84401-3836
Phone: (801)394-6472 **Fax:** (801)394-8113
Products: Meat products. **SIC:** 5147 (Meats & Meat Products). **Emp:** 20.

■ **12083** ■ **Ottenbergs Bakery**
655 Taylor NE
Washington, DC 20017-2063
Phones: (202)529-5800 (202)529-2751
Free: (800)334-7264 **Fax:** (202)529-3121
Products: Bakery products. **SIC:** 5149 (Groceries & Related Products Nec). **Emp:** 250.

■ **12084** ■ **Overhill Farms**
PO Box 6017
Inglewood, CA 90312-6017
Phone: (310)641-3680 **Fax:** (310)645-3914
Products: Frozen foods, including entrees, soups, sauces, and processed chicken. **SIC:** 5142 (Packaged Frozen Foods). **Est:** 1964. **Sales:** $100,000,000 (2000). **Emp:** 900. **Officers:** James Rudis, President.

■ **12085** ■ **Ozark Co-op Warehouse**
PO Box 1528
Fayetteville, AR 72702
Phone: (501)521-4920 **Fax:** (501)521-9100
Products: Food preparations; Dried and dehydrated food products; Head rice not packaged with other ingredients; Potatoes; Egg noodle products; Health foods. **SICs:** 5149 (Groceries & Related Products Nec); 5148 (Fresh Fruits & Vegetables).

■ **12086** ■ **Pace Fish Company Inc.**
PO Box 3365
Brownsville, TX 78523
Phone: (210)546-5536
Products: Fish. **SIC:** 5146 (Fish & Seafoods). **Est:** 1959. **Sales:** $7,000,000 (2000). **Emp:** 50. **Officers:** Pat L. Pace, President.

■ **12087** ■ **James A. Pacheco**
648 S St.
Raynham, MA 02767
Phone: (508)822-4792 **Fax:** (508)823-5670
Products: Eggs. **SIC:** 5144 (Poultry & Poultry Products). **Sales:** $5,000,000 (2000). **Emp:** 100. **Officers:** J.A. Pacheco, Owner.

■ **12088** ■ **Pacific Coast Fruit Co.**
201 NE 2nd Ave.
Portland, OR 97232-2984
Phones: (503)234-6411 (503)234-2470
Fax: (503)234-0072
Products: Fruits and vegetables. **SIC:** 5148 (Fresh

Fruits & Vegetables). **Emp:** 147. **Officers:** Emil Nemarnik.

■ 12089 ■ **Pacific Commerce Company Inc.**
PO Box 3110
Wilsonville, OR 97070
Phone: (503)570-0200
Products: Groceries. **SIC:** 5141 (Groceries—General Line). **Sales:** $15,000,000 (2000). **Emp:** 4. **Officers:** Han Peng Chen, President; Gary Roberts, Vice President.

■ 12090 ■ **Pacific Fruit Processors Inc.**
12128 Center St.
South Gate, CA 90280-8048
Phones: (213)774-6000   (213)531-1770
Fax: (213)310-8392
Products: Fruit; Processed fruit for yogurt. **SICs:** 5143 (Dairy Products Except Dried or Canned); 5148 (Fresh Fruits & Vegetables). **Sales:** $10,000,000 (2000). **Emp:** 49.

■ 12091 ■ **Pacific Grain Products, Inc.**
PO Box 2060
Woodland, CA 95776
Phone: (530)662-5056
Free: (800)333-0110   **Fax:** (530)662-6074
E-mail: pgp@pacgrain.com
URL: http://www.pacgrain.com
Products: Grains; Rice-based specialty ingredients; Rice cereal; Crisped rice. **SIC:** 5149 (Groceries & Related Products Nec). **Est:** 1983. **Emp:** 100. **Officers:** Zach Wochok, CEO & President; Rose Donohue, VP of Sales.

■ 12092 ■ **Pacific PreCut Produce Inc.**
PO Box 26428
San Jose, CA 95159
Phone: (408)998-0773
Products: Fresh produce. **SIC:** 5148 (Fresh Fruits & Vegetables).

■ 12093 ■ **Pacific Salmon Company Inc.**
3407 E Marginal Way S
Seattle, WA 98134
Phone: (206)682-6501   **Fax:** (206)682-6441
Products: Seafood, including salmon, halibut, and black cod. **SIC:** 5146 (Fish & Seafoods). **Est:** 1975. **Emp:** 20. **Officers:** John A. McCallum, President; John W. McCallum, Vice President.

■ 12094 ■ **Pacific Sea Food Company Inc.**
15501 SE Piazza
Clackamas, OR 97015-9145
Phone: (503)657-1101   **Fax:** (503)655-8166
Products: Seafood. **SIC:** 5146 (Fish & Seafoods). **Est:** 1941. **Emp:** 125. **Officers:** Dominic Dulcich; Frank Dulcich; Joe Ohlallorum.

■ 12095 ■ **Packaging Concepts Corp.**
12910 Woodburn Dr.
Hagerstown, MD 21742
Phone: (301)733-5771
Products: Produce. **SIC:** 5148 (Fresh Fruits & Vegetables). **Est:** 1989. **Sales:** $6,000,000 (2000). **Emp:** 4. **Officers:** David Bradley, President.

■ 12096 ■ **Packers Distributing Co.**
1301 E Commercial
Springfield, MO 65803
Phone: (417)866-7230   **Fax:** (417)863-9511
Products: Fresh meat; Frozen meat; Seafood. **SICs:** 5147 (Meats & Meat Products); 5142 (Packaged Frozen Foods); 5146 (Fish & Seafoods). **Est:** 1975. **Sales:** $19,000,000 (2000). **Emp:** 33. **Officers:** J.D. Melton, President.

■ 12097 ■ **Palacios Processors**
9 8th St.
Palacios, TX 77465
Phone: (512)972-3932   **Fax:** (512)972-6616
Products: Processed shrimp. **SIC:** 5146 (Fish & Seafoods). **Est:** 1980. **Emp:** 49. **Officers:** John M. Stephens, President; Bruce A. Sundberg, Vice President. **Doing Business As:** Bama Shrimp Co.

■ 12098 ■ **Palagonia Italian Bread**
508 Junius St.
Brooklyn, NY 11212-7126
Phone: (718)272-5400   **Fax:** (718)272-5427
Products: Bread. **SIC:** 5149 (Groceries & Related Products Nec). **Sales:** $6,000,000 (2000). **Emp:** 499. **Officers:** Joseph P. Palagonia; Chris Palagonia.

■ 12099 ■ **Palermo's Frozen Pizza**
800 W Maple
Milwaukee, WI 53204-3524
Phone: (414)643-0919   **Fax:** (414)643-1696
Products: Frozen pizzas. **SIC:** 5142 (Packaged Frozen Foods). **Emp:** 49. **Officers:** Jack Fallucca.

■ 12100 ■ **Palmer Candy Co.**
PO Box 326
Sioux City, IA 51102
Phone: (712)258-5543
Free: (800)831-0828   **Fax:** (712)258-3224
URL: http://www.palmercandy.com
Products: Confectionery and snack products. **SIC:** 5145 (Confectionery). **Est:** 1878. **Emp:** 100. **Officers:** Martin B. Palmer; Jerry Christensen, Sales & Marketing Contact; Christy Miller, Customer Service Contact; Vicki Sabasta, Human Resources Contact.

■ 12101 ■ **Pamida Inc.**
8800 F St.
Omaha, NE 68127
Phone: (402)339-2400   **Fax:** (402)393-3230
Products: General line groceries. **SIC:** 5141 (Groceries—General Line).

■ 12102 ■ **Pan American Frozen Food Inc.**
1496 NW 23rd St.
PO Box 420592
Miami, FL 33142-7625
Phone: (305)633-3344   **Fax:** (305)633-1023
Products: Frozen foods, including frozen french fries. **SIC:** 5142 (Packaged Frozen Foods). **Est:** 1972. **Emp:** 9. **Officers:** Lazaro Munarriz, President.

■ 12103 ■ **Pancho's Mexican Foods Inc.**
2881 Lamar Ave.
Memphis, TN 38114
Phone: (901)744-3900   **Fax:** (901)744-0514
Products: Ethnic foods. **SIC:** 5141 (Groceries—General Line). **Sales:** $10,000,000 (2000). **Emp:** 500. **Officers:** Brenda O'Brien, CEO & President.

■ 12104 ■ **Papetti's Hygrade Egg Products Inc.**
1 Papetti Plaza
Elizabeth, NJ 07206
Phone: (908)354-4844   **Fax:** (903)351-7528
Products: Frozen liquid egg products. **SIC:** 5144 (Poultry & Poultry Products). **Est:** 1908. **Sales:** $275,000,000 (2000). **Emp:** 1,200. **Officers:** Arthur N. Papetti, President; Stephen Papetti, Dir. of Marketing; Joe Vagnuolo, VP & Controller.

■ 12105 ■ **Paradise Products Corp.**
1080 Leggett Ave.
Bronx, NY 10470-5605
Phone: (718)423-2601
Products: Onions; Olives; Cherries; Condiments. **SICs:** 5149 (Groceries & Related Products Nec); 5148 (Fresh Fruits & Vegetables). **Est:** 1946. **Sales:** $15,000,000 (2000). **Emp:** 40. **Officers:** David Lax, President; Morry Strauss, VP of Sales; Andrew Lax, VP of Operations.

■ 12106 ■ **Paragon/Monteverde Food Service**
55 36th St.
Pittsburgh, PA 15201
Phone: (412)621-2626   **Fax:** (412)621-3660
Products: General line groceries; Fruits and vegetables. **SICs:** 5141 (Groceries—General Line); 5148 (Fresh Fruits & Vegetables). **Est:** 1962. **Emp:** 95. **Officers:** Elaine Bellin; Mark Balukin, Sales/Marketing Contact; Gloria Garofalo, Customer Service Contact.

■ 12107 ■ **Paramount Export Co.**
280 17th St.
Oakland, CA 94612
Phone: (510)839-0150   **Fax:** (510)839-1002
Products: Fruits and vegetables. **SICs:** 5148 (Fresh Fruits & Vegetables); 5149 (Groceries & Related

Products Nec). **Est:** 1939. **Sales:** $100,000,000 (2000). **Emp:** 82. **Officers:** Nick Kukulan, President; Andrew Wasserman, CFO.

■ 12108 ■ **Parco Foods LLC**
2200 W 138th St.
Blue Island, IL 60406
Phone: (708)371-9200
Free: (888)77P-ARCO   **Fax:** (708)371-4190
URL: http://www.parcofoods.com
Products: Cookies; Frozen bakery products; Soft cakes, except frozen; Bakery products. **SIC:** 5149 (Groceries & Related Products Nec). **Est:** 1963. **Emp:** 300. **Officers:** Charles A. Hoch, Chairman of the Board, e-mail: chochsr@parcofoods.com; Richard A. Kent, President, e-mail: rakent@parcfoods.com.

■ 12109 ■ **Paris Food Corp.**
1632 Carman St.
Camden, NJ 08105
Phone: (609)964-0915   **Fax:** (609)964-9719
Products: Frozen foods, including vegetables and french fries. **SIC:** 5142 (Packaged Frozen Foods). **Est:** 1969. **Sales:** $12,000,000 (2000). **Emp:** 47. **Officers:** S. Rudderow, President.

■ 12110 ■ **Park Farms Inc.**
1925 30th NE
Canton, OH 44705
Phone: (330)455-0241   **Fax:** (330)455-5820
Products: Processed poultry and small game. **SIC:** 5144 (Poultry & Poultry Products). **Est:** 1946. **Sales:** $50,400,000 (2000). **Emp:** 410. **Officers:** Anthony M. Pastore, President; Richard Leggett, VP of Sales; Steve Daniels, Dir. of Information Systems; Craig Haueter, Dir of Human Resources.

■ 12111 ■ **Park Orchards Inc.**
4428 Broadview Rd.
Richfield, OH 44286
Phone: (216)659-6134   **Fax:** (216)659-9218
Products: Groceries. **SIC:** 5141 (Groceries—General Line). **Est:** 1948. **Sales:** $80,000,000 (2000). **Emp:** 550. **Officers:** David A. Vaughn, President & CFO; John Foss, Dir. of Advertising.

■ 12112 ■ **Parker Banana Company Inc.**
1801 E Sahlman Dr.
Tampa, FL 33605
Phone: (813)248-5448   **Fax:** (813)248-3790
Products: Bananas. **SIC:** 5148 (Fresh Fruits & Vegetables). **Sales:** $21,000,000 (2000). **Emp:** 5. **Officers:** Fred Hirons, CEO & CFO.

■ 12113 ■ **Mitt Parker Co.**
PO Box 1565
Forest Park, GA 30298-1565
Phone: (404)361-8600
Free: (800)241-0656   **Fax:** (404)363-1778
Products: Fruits and vegetables. **SIC:** 5148 (Fresh Fruits & Vegetables). **Est:** 1975. **Emp:** 99. **Officers:** Mitt Parker.

■ 12114 ■ **Parker-Tilton Inc.**
PO Box 840
Scarborough, ME 04070
Phone: (207)883-3417
Products: Food. **SICs:** 5141 (Groceries—General Line); 5142 (Packaged Frozen Foods). **Sales:** $8,000,000 (1993). **Emp:** 16. **Officers:** David Parker, President.

■ 12115 ■ **Charles C. Parks Company Inc.**
PO Box 119
Gallatin, TN 37066
Phone: (615)452-2406
Free: (800)873-2406   **Fax:** (615)451-4212
E-mail: info@charlescparks.com
URL: http://www.charlescparks.com
Products: Groceries. **SIC:** 5141 (Groceries—General Line). **Est:** 1934. **Sales:** $170,000,000 (2000). **Emp:** 150. **Officers:** Charles C. Parks, President; Allen Hanks, Vice President.

■ 12116 ■ **Parkside Candy Co.**
3208 Main St.
Buffalo, NY 14214
Phone: (716)833-7540   **Fax:** (716)833-7560
Products: Candy stores. Lollipops, taffy and chocolate.

SIC: 5145 (Confectionery). **Est:** 1927. **Sales:** $1,000,000 (2000). **Emp:** 25. **Officers:** Phillip Buffamonte, President; Phillip Buffamonte, President.

■ 12117 ■ **Parkway Food Service Inc.**
PO Box 86
Greensburg, PA 15601
Phone: (412)837-6580
Free: (800)833-1530 **Fax:** (412)837-1530
Products: Groceries, including meat, milk, seafood, and frozen products; Paper and janitorial products. **SICs:** 5147 (Meats & Meat Products); 5113 (Industrial & Personal Service Paper); 5149 (Groceries & Related Products Nec). **Est:** 1966. **Sales:** $173,000,000 (2000). **Emp:** 275. **Officers:** David Reese, President; Ken Campbell, CFO; Edwin E. Beckel, Dir. of Marketing; Vincent Fredo, Dir. of Information Systems.

■ 12118 ■ **Parmalat USA**
520 Main Ave.
Wallington, NJ 07057
Phone: (973)777-2500
Free: (888)PAR-MALAT **Fax:** (973)777-7648
URL: http://www.parmalatusa.com
Products: Dairy products. **SIC:** 5143 (Dairy Products Except Dried or Canned). **Est:** 1982. **Sales:** $575,000,000 (1999). **Emp:** 600. **Officers:** Aldo Uva, President & CEO. **Former Name:** Farmland Dairies Inc.

■ 12119 ■ **Paskesz Candies & Confectionery**
4473 1st Ave.
Brooklyn, NY 11232
Phone: (718)832-2400 **Fax:** (718)832-3492
Products: Candy. **SIC:** 5145 (Confectionery). **Est:** 1959. **Emp:** 49. **Officers:** Henri Schmidt.

■ 12120 ■ **Pastorelli Food Products Inc.**
162 N Sangamon St.
Chicago, IL 60607
Phone: (312)666-2041
Free: (800)767-2829 **Fax:** (312)666-2415
E-mail: sosavcy@ixnet.com.com
URL: http://www.pastorelli.com
Products: Food products, including pizza sauces, spaghetti sauces, oils, vinegars, peppers, pasta, tomato products, cheese, and spices. **SIC:** 5141 (Groceries—General Line). **Est:** 1931. **Sales:** $7,000,000 (2000). **Emp:** 25. **Officers:** Robert Pastorelli, Chairman of the Board; Richard Pastorelli, Vice President; Angela Pastorelli, Treasurer; Jim Paglim, Sales/Marketing Contact; Linda Fraid, Customer Service Contact.

■ 12121 ■ **Patterson Brothers Meat Co.**
PO Box 710505
Dallas, TX 75371-0505
Phone: (214)821-3300 **Fax:** (214)821-3039
Products: Meat and meat products. **SIC:** 5147 (Meats & Meat Products). **Sales:** $8,000,000 (2000). **Emp:** 53. **Officers:** Dennis Schirato, President; Dorsha Compton, Treasurer & Secty.

■ 12122 ■ **H.B. Paulk Grocery**
PO Box 637
Opp, AL 36467
Phone: (334)493-3255 **Fax:** (334)493-7966
E-mail: hbpaulk@hbpaulk.com
Products: Groceries, including dry and frozen foods; Candy; Health and beauty aids; Tobacco. **SICs:** 5141 (Groceries—General Line); 5122 (Drugs, Proprietaries & Sundries); 5142 (Packaged Frozen Foods). **Est:** 1929. **Sales:** $106,000,000 (2000). **Emp:** 155. **Officers:** Ferris P. Youmans, President; Jeff Gwynne, Exec. VP.

■ 12123 ■ **H.B. Paulk Grocery Inc.**
PO Box 637
Opp, AL 36467
Phone: (334)493-3255
Free: (800)467-2855 **Fax:** (334)493-7966
Products: Groceries. **SIC:** 5141 (Groceries—General Line). **Sales:** $79,000,000 (2000). **Emp:** 150. **Officers:** Ferris P. Youmans, President; Renee Anderson, Treasurer & Secty.

■ 12124 ■ **Pay Cash Grocery Co.**
PO Box 469016
Garland, TX 75046-9016
Phone: (713)637-3550 **Fax:** (713)637-3550
Products: Groceries. **SIC:** 5141 (Groceries—General Line). **Est:** 1927. **Sales:** $100,000,000 (2000). **Emp:** 165. **Officers:** Ron Coleman, President; Michael Kuczmarski, Controller; Jan Harbort, Dir. of Sales; Bob Hermacinski, Dir. of Operations.

■ 12125 ■ **A.J. Peachey and Sons Inc.**
RD 1, Box 101
Belleville, PA 17004
Phone: (717)667-2185 **Free:** (800)982-9755
Products: Food. **SICs:** 5141 (Groceries—General Line); 5147 (Meats & Meat Products). **Sales:** $1,000,000 (2000). **Emp:** 99.

■ 12126 ■ **Peak Distributing Co.**
3636 South 300 West
Salt Lake City, UT 84115-4312
Phone: (801)261-3597
Free: (800)472-7006 **Fax:** (801)261-3772
Products: Food, including bakery products, chips, and pretzels. **SICs:** 5149 (Groceries & Related Products Nec); 5145 (Confectionery). **Est:** 1958. **Emp:** 49. **Officers:** Kay Peacock.

■ 12127 ■ **Peanut Processors Inc.**
PO Box 160
Dublin, NC 28332
Phone: (910)862-2136
Free: (800)334-8383 **Fax:** (910)862-8076
E-mail: pnutoutlet@aol.com
URL: http://www.peanutprocessors.com
Products: Peanut butter; Peanuts, including raw shelled and unshelled, oil roasted, dry roasted, granulated, salted and roasted in shell. **SICs:** 5145 (Confectionery); 5149 (Groceries & Related Products Nec). **Est:** 1961. **Sales:** $15,000,000 (2000). **Emp:** 50. **Officers:** Houston Brisson, President; Dennis Cedzo, Controller; Gene Brisson, Plant Mgr.

■ 12128 ■ **The Pearl Coffee Co.**
675 S Broadway
Akron, OH 44311-1099
Phone: (330)253-7184
Free: (800)822-5282 **Fax:** (330)253-7185
Products: Coffee. **SIC:** 5149 (Groceries & Related Products Nec). **Est:** 1919. **Emp:** 14. **Officers:** John N. Economou, President.

■ 12129 ■ **Peco Foods Inc.**
3701 Kauloosa Ave.
Tuscaloosa, AL 35405
Phone: (205)345-3955 **Fax:** (205)345-4173
Products: Poultry and small game. **SIC:** 5142 (Packaged Frozen Foods). **Est:** 1969. **Sales:** $50,000,000 (2000). **Emp:** 700. **Officers:** Denny Hickman, President.

■ 12130 ■ **Peerless Coffee Co.**
260 Oak St.
Oakland, CA 94607
Phone: (510)763-1763
Free: (800)235-3237 **Fax:** (510)763-5026
E-mail: peerlesscoffee@pacbell.net
URL: http://www.peerlesscoffee.com
Products: Regular and flavored coffee. **SIC:** 5149 (Groceries & Related Products Nec). **Est:** 1924. **Sales:** $16,000,000 (2000). **Emp:** 80. **Officers:** George Vukasin, President; Mike Pine, CFO.

■ 12131 ■ **Peets Coffee and Tea Inc.**
PO Box 12509
Berkeley, CA 94712
Phone: (510)594-2100 **Fax:** (510)594-2180
Products: Roasted coffee; Assorted prepackaged teas. **SIC:** 5149 (Groceries & Related Products Nec). **Officers:** Chris Mottern, President.

■ 12132 ■ **Pegler-Sysco Food Services Co.**
1700 Center Park Rd.
Lincoln, NE 68512
Phone: (402)423-1031
Products: Food and medical equipment for restaurants, hospitals, and nursing homes. **SICs:** 5141 (Groceries—General Line); 5046 (Commercial Equipment Nec); 5047 (Medical & Hospital Equipment).

Est: 1895. **Sales:** $150,000,000 (2000). **Emp:** 420. **Officers:** Donald H. Pegler III, President.

■ 12133 ■ **Peirone Produce Co.**
E 524 Trent Ave.
Spokane, WA 99202
Phone: (509)838-3515
Products: Fruits and vegetables. **SIC:** 5148 (Fresh Fruits & Vegetables). **Est:** 1945. **Sales:** $30,000,000 (2000). **Emp:** 135. **Officers:** P.A. Davidson, CEO & President; Ken Owen, Controller; Dale Arneson, Dir. of Marketing.

■ 12134 ■ **Pellman Foods Inc.**
122 S Shirk Rd.
PO Box 337
New Holland, PA 17557
Phone: (717)354-8070 **Fax:** (717)355-9944
Products: Frozen baked goods, including cheesecakes, cakes, and pies. **SIC:** 5149 (Groceries & Related Products Nec). **Est:** 1973. **Sales:** $5,000,000 (2000). **Emp:** 45. **Officers:** Michael Pellman, President & Treasurer; Scott Pellman, VP & Secty.; Ron Hostetter, Sales/Marketing Contact.

■ 12135 ■ **Nick Penachio Company Inc.**
240 Food Center Dr.
Bronx, NY 10474
Phone: (718)842-0630
Products: Produce; Frozen and canned foods; Paper products; Janitorial supplies. **SICs:** 5148 (Fresh Fruits & Vegetables); 5113 (Industrial & Personal Service Paper); 5142 (Packaged Frozen Foods). **Est:** 1920. **Sales:** $75,000,000 (2000). **Emp:** 200. **Officers:** Nick A. Penachio, President; Anthony Penachio, CFO.

■ 12136 ■ **W.J. Pence Company Inc.**
W 227 N880 Westmound Dr.
Waukesha, WI 53186
Phone: (262)524-6300 **Fax:** (262)782-6693
E-mail: sales@wjpence.com
Products: Food. **SIC:** 5141 (Groceries—General Line). **Est:** 1953. **Sales:** $49,000,000 (2000). **Emp:** 25. **Officers:** John Pence, CEO & President.

■ 12137 ■ **Penguin Point Systems Inc.**
PO Box 975
Warsaw, IN 46581-0975
Phone: (219)267-3107
Products: Restaurant equipment. **SIC:** 5046 (Commercial Equipment Nec). **Sales:** $5,000,000 (1993). **Emp:** 20. **Officers:** W.E. Stouder, CEO & President.

■ 12138 ■ **Peninsula Bottling Company Inc.**
311 S Valley St.
Port Angeles, WA 98362
Phone: (360)457-3383 **Fax:** (360)457-3384
Products: Soft drinks. **SIC:** 5149 (Groceries & Related Products Nec). **Sales:** $12,000,000 (2000). **Emp:** 24. **Officers:** Jeffrey Hinds, President; Jeffrey Hinds, CFO.

■ 12139 ■ **Penn Traffic Co.**
PO Box 4737
Syracuse, NY 13221-4737
Phone: (315)453-7284
Products: General line of groceries. **SIC:** 5141 (Groceries—General Line). **Sales:** $3,010,100,000 (2000). **Emp:** 20,500. **Officers:** Phillip E. Hawkins, CEO & President; Robert J. Davis, Sr. VP & CFO.

■ 12140 ■ **Penn Traffic Co. Riverside Div.**
Rte. 255 & Shaffer Rd.
PO Box 607
Du Bois, PA 15801
Phone: (814)375-3663 **Fax:** (814)375-2922
Products: Food and supermarket supplies. **SIC:** 5141 (Groceries—General Line). **Sales:** $240,000,000 (2000). **Emp:** 4,000. **Officers:** Larry Ammons, President; Frederick R. Beck, Vice President; Tom Korthaus, VP of Sales & Merchandising; Robert Good, Vice President; Mark Kerswell, Dir of Human Resources.

■ **12141** ■ **Penna Dutch Co.**
408 N Baltimore Ave.
Mt. Holly Springs, PA 17065-1603
Phone: (717)486-3496
Free: (800)233-7082 **Fax:** (717)486-4678
Products: Food. **SIC:** 5145 (Confectionery). **Sales:**
$30,000,000 (2000). **Emp:** 150.

■ **12142** ■ **Pennfield Corp. Pennfield Farms-Poultry Meat Div.**
Rte. 22
Fredericksburg, PA 17026
Phone: (717)865-2153
Products: Processed poultry. **SIC:** 5144 (Poultry &
Poultry Products). **Est:** 1949. **Sales:** $40,000,000
(2000). **Emp:** 400. **Officers:** Anthony D. Chivinski, Vice
President; Tom O'Connor, Dir. of Marketing; Pam
Wolfe, Controller; Don Horn Jr., Dir of Human
Resources.

■ **12143** ■ **Penny Curtiss Bakery**
PO Box 486
Syracuse, NY 13211-0486
Phone: (315)454-3241 **Fax:** (315)455-1934
Products: Food. **SIC:** 5149 (Groceries & Related
Products Nec). **Sales:** $45,000,000 (2000). **Emp:** 299.

■ **12144** ■ **Pepper Products**
3750 N IH 35
San Antonio, TX 78219-2222
Phone: (210)661-0940 **Fax:** (210)666-8415
Products: Diced jalapenos and onions. **SIC:** 5149
(Groceries & Related Products Nec). **Emp:** 49.

■ **12145** ■ **Pepsi-Cola General Bottlers of South Bend**
PO Box 1596
South Bend, IN 46634
Phone: (219)234-1311 **Fax:** (219)234-0270
Products: Soft drinks. **SIC:** 5149 (Groceries & Related
Products Nec). **Sales:** $46,000,000 (2000). **Emp:** 96.
Officers: Richard Rahal, VP & General Merchandising
Mgr.; Jim Raa, Mgr. of Finance.

■ **12146** ■ **Pepsi-Cola Northwest**
2300 26th Ave. S
Seattle, WA 98144
Phone: (206)323-2932 **Fax:** (206)326-7496
Products: Soft drinks and carbonated waters. **SIC:**
5149 (Groceries & Related Products Nec). **Sales:**
$90,000,000 (2000). **Emp:** 1,500. **Officers:** Bill
Flahrety, Finance Officer.

■ **12147** ■ **Pepsi-Cola Pittsfield**
1 Pepsi Cola Dr.
Latham, NY 12110-2306
Phone: (518)445-4579
Products: Soft drinks. **SIC:** 5149 (Groceries & Related
Products Nec). **Sales:** $4,000,000 (2000). **Emp:** 25.

■ **12148** ■ **Perez Farms Inc.**
22001 E St.
Crows Landing, CA 95313
Phone: (209)837-4701 **Fax:** (209)837-4224
Products: Fruits and vegetables for canning. **SIC:**
5148 (Fresh Fruits & Vegetables). **Emp:** 50. **Officers:**
Mark Perez.

■ **12149** ■ **Perfection Bakeries Inc.**
350 Pearl St.
Ft. Wayne, IN 46802
Phone: (219)424-8245
Products: Bread, buns, rolls, bagels and doughnuts.
SIC: 5149 (Groceries & Related Products Nec). **Sales:**
$696,000,000 (2000). **Emp:** 1,500. **Officers:** John F.
Popp, President; Jay Miller, CFO.

■ **12150** ■ **Performance Food Group Co.**
6800 Paragon Pl., Ste. 500
Richmond, VA 23230
Phone: (804)285-7340 **Fax:** (804)285-5360
URL: http://www.pfgc.com
Products: Food, including meats, dairy products, and
produce. **SICs:** 5141 (Groceries—General Line); 5143
(Dairy Products Except Dried or Canned); 5147 (Meats
& Meat Products); 5148 (Fresh Fruits & Vegetables).
Est: 1987. **Sales:** $2,400,000,000 (2000). **Emp:** 4,500.
Officers: Robert C. Sledd, CEO & Chairman of the

Board; Roger L. Boeve, Exec. VP & CFO; Nathan Duet,
Dir of Human Resources.

■ **12151** ■ **Performance Northwest Inc.**
PO Box 23139
Portland, OR 97224
Phone: (503)624-0624 **Fax:** (503)620-6101
Products: Food. **SIC:** 5141 (Groceries—General Line).
Est: 1964. **Sales:** $78,000,000 (2000). **Emp:** 150.
Officers: Jack Wynne, CEO; Dwayne Horne,
Controller.

■ **12152** ■ **Perishable Distributors of Iowa Ltd.**
2741 PDI Pl.
Ankeny, IA 50021
Phone: (515)965-6300 **Fax:** (515)965-1105
Products: Bakery products; Meat products, including
beef, poultry, and pork. **SICs:** 5147 (Meats & Meat
Products); 5149 (Groceries & Related Products Nec).
Est: 1982. **Sales:** $300,000,000 (2000). **Emp:** 480.
Officers: Ken Waller, President; Dick Smith, Sr. VP &
Treasurer.

■ **12153** ■ **Perugina Brands of America**
299 Market St.
Saddle Brook, NJ 07663
Phone: (201)587-8080
Free: (800)223-0039 **Fax:** (201)587-9636
URL: http://www.baciperugina.com
Products: Imported chocolate, cookies, and hard
candy. **SICs:** 5145 (Confectionery); 5149 (Groceries &
Related Products Nec). **Est:** 1942. **Sales:** $50,000,000
(2000). **Emp:** 30. **Officers:** J. Dattoli, General Mgr.

■ **12154** ■ **Pet Food Wholesale Inc.**
3160B Enterprise St.
Brea, CA 92821
Phone: (714)254-1200 **Fax:** (714)572-8265
Products: Veterinary products. **SIC:** 5149 (Groceries &
Related Products Nec).

■ **12155** ■ **Petaluma Poultry Processors Inc.**
PO Box 7368
Petaluma, CA 94955
Phone: (707)763-1907 **Fax:** (707)763-3924
Products: Raises, slaughters and processes poultry.
SIC: 5144 (Poultry & Poultry Products). **Sales:**
$76,000,000 (2000). **Emp:** 200. **Officers:** Allen
Shainsky, President.

■ **12156** ■ **Peter Pan of Hollywood Inc.**
5430 Satsuma Ave.
North Hollywood, CA 91601-2837
Phones: (213)877-9939 (818)761-2892
Fax: (213)877-9930
Products: Bread, cake, and related products. **SICs:**
5149 (Groceries & Related Products Nec); 5181 (Beer
& Ale). **Emp:** 49.

■ **12157** ■ **Petri Baking Products**
18 Main
Silver Creek, NY 14136-1433
Phone: (716)934-2661
Free: (800)346-1981 **Fax:** (716)934-3054
E-mail: petri@cecomet.net
Products: Cookies; Bakery products. **SIC:** 5149
(Groceries & Related Products Nec). **Est:** 1935. **Emp:**
99. **Officers:** Richard L. Cattau.

■ **12158** ■ **Peyton Meats Inc.**
PO Box 9066
El Paso, TX 79982
Phone: (915)858-6632
Products: Fresh and frozen meats. **SICs:** 5147 (Meats
& Meat Products); 5142 (Packaged Frozen Foods).
Sales: $13,000,000 (1993). **Emp:** 35. **Officers:** Keith
Veale, General Mgr.

■ **12159** ■ **Pez Candy Inc.**
35 Prindle Hill Rd.
Orange, CT 06477
Phone: (203)795-0531 **Fax:** (203)799-1679
Products: Candy. **SIC:** 5145 (Confectionery). **Emp:**
170. **Officers:** Scott McWhinnie, CEO & President;
Louis P. Falango, VP of Finance & Admin.; Bill Walsh,
VP of Sales; C. Balay, Data Processing Mgr.; Kathy
Testa, Customer Service Contact.

■ **12160** ■ **Pezrow Food Brokers Inc.**
535 E Crescent Ave.
Ramsey, NJ 07446
Phone: (201)825-9400
Products: Food. **SIC:** 5141 (Groceries—General Line).

■ **12161** ■ **PFG Lester**
PO Box 340
Lebanon, TN 37087
Phone: (615)444-2963
Products: Food service equipment and supplies.
SICs: 5046 (Commercial Equipment Nec); 5141
(Groceries—General Line). **Est:** 1931. **Sales:**
$98,000,000 (2000). **Emp:** 180. **Officers:** Thomas
Hoffman, President; Steve Neely, Dir. of Systems;
Kevin Lester, Dir of Human Resources.

■ **12162** ■ **PFG Milton's**
3501 Old Oakwood Rd.
Oakwood, GA 30566
Phone: (404)532-7779
Products: Food. **SIC:** 5141 (Groceries—General Line).
Officers: Danny Berry, President. **Former Name:**
Milton's Foodservice Inc.

■ **12163** ■ **PFS**
PO Box 230765
Houston, TX 77223-0765
Phone: (713)923-6060 **Fax:** (713)923-5890
Products: Beef, pork, poultry, seafood, and cheese.
SICs: 5147 (Meats & Meat Products); 5146 (Fish &
Seafoods); 5143 (Dairy Products Except Dried or
Canned); 5144 (Poultry & Poultry Products).

■ **12164** ■ **Phillips Mushroom Farms**
PO Box 190
Kennett Square, PA 19348
Phone: (610)444-4492 **Fax:** (610)444-4751
Products: Mushrooms. **SIC:** 5148 (Fresh Fruits &
Vegetables). **Est:** 1958. **Sales:** $11,000,000 (2000).
Emp: 100. **Officers:** R.M. Phillips, President.

■ **12165** ■ **Pick'n Save Warehouse Foods Inc.**
11500 W Burleigh St.
Wauwatosa, WI 53222
Phone: (414)453-7081
Products: Full line groceries. **SIC:** 5141 (Groceries—
General Line). **Sales:** $530,000,000 (2000). **Emp:**
2,000. **Officers:** Don Twist, President; Mike Selenka,
VP of Marketing; Jane Yockey, Dir of Human
Resources.

■ **12166** ■ **Piedmont Candy Co.**
PO Box 1722
Lexington, NC 27292
Phone: (704)246-2477
Free: (800)360-5394 **Fax:** (704)246-5841
Products: Candy. **SIC:** 5145 (Confectionery). **Est:**
1890. **Sales:** $1,000,000 (2000). **Emp:** 14. **Officers:**
Doug Reid.

■ **12167** ■ **Pierre's French Ice Cream Distributing Company of Akron**
1350 Kelly Ave.
Akron, OH 44306
Phone: (216)724-5858
Products: Ice cream; Sherbet; Yogurt; Lemon sorbet.
SIC: 5143 (Dairy Products Except Dried or Canned).
Est: 1979. **Sales:** $1,000,000 (2000). **Emp:** 3.
Officers: Bill Myers, Owner.

■ **12168** ■ **Piggly Wiggly Alabama Distributing Company Inc.**
2400 J.T. Wooten Dr.
Bessemer, AL 35020
Phone: (205)481-2300 **Fax:** (205)426-2400
Products: General line groceries. **SIC:** 5141
(Groceries—General Line).

■ **12169** ■ **Pinahs Company Inc.**
N8W22100 Johnson Dr.
Waukesha, WI 53186
Phone: (262)547-2447
Free: (800)967-2447 **Fax:** (262)547-2047
E-mail: info@pinahs.com
URL: http://www.pinahs.com
Products: Bagel chips, rye chips, snack chips, and
fried pasta rotini. **SIC:** 5149 (Groceries & Related
Products Nec). **Est:** 1917. **Emp:** 120. **Officers:** Chris

Pinahs, Owner & Pres.; Jeff Handrich, VP of Sales/Marketing, e-mail: jeffhandrich@worldnet.com; John Tucker, VP of Operations; Bill Bruggink, VP of Admin.

■ 12170 ■ **Pint Size Corp.**
991287 Waiua Pl.
Aiea, HI 96701
Phone: (808)487-0030 **Fax:** (808)488-0123
Products: Ice cream and other food products. **SIC:** 5143 (Dairy Products Except Dried or Canned). **Sales:** $20,000,000 (2000). **Officers:** Clayton Fim, President.

■ 12171 ■ **Pioneer Dairy Inc.**
214 Feeding Hills Rd.
Southwick, MA 01077-9522
Phone: (413)569-6132 **Fax:** (413)569-3762
Products: Milk; Cream; Ice cream; Ice cream mix and related products; Fresh fruit juices and nectars; Fruit drinks, cocktails, and ades. **SICs:** 5143 (Dairy Products Except Dried or Canned); 5149 (Groceries & Related Products Nec). **Est:** 1919. **Sales:** $6,000,000 (1999). **Emp:** 30. **Officers:** Anne Colson; Brett Colson; Paul Colson.

■ 12172 ■ **Pioneer French Baking Company Inc.**
512 Rose Ave.
Venice, CA 90291
Phone: (310)392-4128 **Fax:** (310)392-7845
Products: Bread and bakery products. **SIC:** 5149 (Groceries & Related Products Nec).

■ 12173 ■ **Pioneer Growers Co-Op**
PO Box 490
Belle Glade, FL 33430
Phone: (407)996-5561
Products: Produce, including celery, radishes, corn, and salad items. **SIC:** 5159 (Farm-Product Raw Materials Nec). **Est:** 1950. **Sales:** $29,000,000 (2000). **Emp:** 150. **Officers:** Gene Duff, President.

■ 12174 ■ **Pioneer Snacks Inc.**
30777 Northwestern Hwy. Ste. 300
Farmington Hills, MI 48334
Phone: (248)862-1990
Free: (800)837-6225 **Fax:** (248)862-1991
E-mail: info@PioneerSnacks.com
URL: http://www.PioneerSnacks.com
Products: Snack foods; Meat snacks, including beef jerky, kippered beef steak and meat sticks. **SIC:** 5147 (Meats & Meat Products). **Est:** 1986. **Sales:** $37,000,000 (2000). **Emp:** 125. **Officers:** Robert George, CEO & President, e-mail: robertg@PioneerSnacks.com.

■ 12175 ■ **Pioneer Wholesale Meat**
1000 W Carroll Ave.
Chicago, IL 60607-1208
Phone: (312)243-6180 **Fax:** (312)243-9175
Products: Veal, not canned or made into sausage. **SIC:** 5147 (Meats & Meat Products). **Est:** 1970. **Emp:** 20. **Officers:** W.C. Milligan.

■ 12176 ■ **Mike Pirrone Produce, Inc.**
56825 Romeo Plank Rd.
Macomb, MI 48042
Phone: (810)781-3303 **Fax:** (810)781-6207
Products: Produce. **SIC:** 5148 (Fresh Fruits & Vegetables).

■ 12177 ■ **Pittsburgh Oakland Enterprises Inc.**
377 McKee Pl.
Pittsburgh, PA 15213
Phone: (412)683-9006
Products: Meat. **SIC:** 5147 (Meats & Meat Products).

■ 12178 ■ **Pizza Commissary Inc.**
W226N767 Eastmound Dr., Ste. B2
Waukesha, WI 53186-1694
Phone: (414)781-6177 **Fax:** (414)781-2605
Products: Food preparations. **SICs:** 5141 (Groceries—General Line); 5149 (Groceries & Related Products Nec). **Est:** 1972. **Emp:** 35. **Doing Business As:** PCI Foodservice.

■ 12179 ■ **Pizza Needs of Memphis Inc.**
49 S Walnut Bend Rd.
Cordova, TN 38018-7206
Phone: (901)372-4588 **Free:** (800)633-2286
Products: Food preparations; Paper and allied products. **SICs:** 5149 (Groceries & Related Products Nec); 5113 (Industrial & Personal Service Paper). **Est:** 1982. **Emp:** 49.

■ 12180 ■ **Plains Dairy Products**
300 N Taylor
Amarillo, TX 79107
Phone: (806)374-0385 **Fax:** (806)374-0396
E-mail: afidairy@arn.net
Products: Beverages, including orange juice, fruit drinks, and water; Dairy products, including sour cream and cottage cheese. **SICs:** 5143 (Dairy Products Except Dried or Canned); 5149 (Groceries & Related Products Nec). **Est:** 1934. **Sales:** $40,000,000 (2000). **Emp:** 99. **Officers:** Dub Garlington, President; Frank Jones, Sales Mgr.

■ 12181 ■ **Plee-Zing Inc.**
1640 Pleasant Rd.
Glenview, IL 60025
Phone: (847)998-0200 **Fax:** (847)998-8059
Products: Food broker for a general line of groceries and frozen foods. **SICs:** 5141 (Groceries—General Line); 5142 (Packaged Frozen Foods). **Sales:** $8,000,000 (2000). **Emp:** 12. **Officers:** William Stickney, CEO & Chairman of the Board; Don Donakowski, President.

■ 12182 ■ **Plus Distributors Inc.**
210 Airport Rd.
Fletcher, NC 28732
Phone: (828)684-1992
Products: Groceries; Food. **SIC:** 5141 (Groceries—General Line).

■ 12183 ■ **PMI-Eisenhart**
500 Waters Edge
Lombard, IL 60148
Phone: (630)620-7600
Products: General groceries. **SIC:** 5141 (Groceries—General Line). **Sales:** $440,000,000 (2000). **Emp:** 850. **Officers:** James Eisenhart Sr., CEO; Robert McCarthy Jr., President.

■ 12184 ■ **PMI-Eisenhart, St. Louis Div.**
10430 Baur Blvd.
St. Louis, MO 63132
Phone: (314)991-3992
Products: Groceries. **SIC:** 5141 (Groceries—General Line). **Est:** 1974. **Sales:** $57,000,000 (2000). **Emp:** 110. **Officers:** Doug Eisenhart, President.

■ 12185 ■ **PMI-Eisenhart Wisconsin Div.**
PO Box 0948
Waukesha, WI 53187
Phone: (414)523-0300 **Fax:** (414)523-0400
Products: Food; Health and beauty aids. **SICs:** 5141 (Groceries—General Line); 5122 (Drugs, Proprietaries & Sundries). **Est:** 1957. **Sales:** $84,000,000 (2000). **Emp:** 160. **Officers:** Tom Meehan, General Mgr.

■ 12186 ■ **Pocahontas Foods USA Inc.**
PO Box 9729
Richmond, VA 23228
Phone: (804)262-8614
URL: http://www.pocahontasfoods.com
Products: Groceries; Nonfood products. **SIC:** 5141 (Groceries—General Line). **Est:** 1970. **Sales:** $26,600,000 (2000). **Emp:** 115. **Officers:** Michael Jochim, President.

■ 12187 ■ **Pola Foods Inc.**
2303 W Cermak
Chicago, IL 60608-3896
Phone: (773)254-1700 **Fax:** (773)254-9782
Products: Perishable prepared foods sold in bulk or packages. **SIC:** 5141 (Groceries—General Line). **Sales:** $2,000,000 (2000). **Emp:** 24. **Officers:** Henry E. Szadziewicz; Peter M. Szadziewicz.

■ 12188 ■ **Ralph Pollock**
12310 W Stark St.
Portland, OR 97229
Phone: (503)644-8954
Products: Popcorn. **SIC:** 5145 (Confectionery).

■ 12189 ■ **Polly-O Dairy**
856 64th St.
Brooklyn, NY 11220
Phone: (718)361-9420 **Fax:** (718)833-9160
Products: Dairy products. **SIC:** 5143 (Dairy Products Except Dried or Canned). **Sales:** $1,000,000 (2000). **Emp:** 3. **Officers:** Pat Haas, General Mgr.

■ 12190 ■ **Pompeian Inc.**
4201 Pulaski Hwy.
Baltimore, MD 21224
Phone: (410)276-6900
Free: (800)638-1224 **Fax:** (410)276-3764
URL: http://www.pompeian.com
Products: Olive oil; Red wine and balsamic vinegars; Olives and artichokes. **SIC:** 5149 (Groceries & Related Products Nec). **Est:** 1917. **Sales:** $35,000,000 (2000). **Emp:** 45. **Officers:** Frank Patton, President.

■ 12191 ■ **Pond Brothers Peanut Company Inc.**
PO Box 1370
Suffolk, VA 23439-1370
Phone: (757)539-2356 **Fax:** (757)539-3995
Products: Unprocessed or shelled nuts; Unprocessed, unshelled peanuts. **SIC:** 5145 (Confectionery). **Est:** 1915. **Sales:** $53,000,000 (2000). **Emp:** 100. **Officers:** Richard L. Pond Sr., CEO.

■ 12192 ■ **Poore Brothers Distributing Inc.**
3500 S Lacometa
Goodyear, AZ 85338
Phone: (602)925-0731
Free: (800)279-2250 **Fax:** (623)525-2363
Products: Salty snack foods. **SIC:** 5145 (Confectionery). **Sales:** $16,000,000 (1999). **Emp:** 75. **Officers:** Eric Kufel, CEO & President; Tom Freeze, CFO.

■ 12193 ■ **Poore Brothers Inc.**
3500 S Lacometa
Goodyear, AZ 85338
Phone: (602)925-0731
Free: (800)279-2250 **Fax:** (623)925-2363
URL: http://www.poorebrothers.com
Products: Snack foods. **SIC:** 5145 (Confectionery). **Est:** 1995. **Sales:** $36,000,000 (2000). **Emp:** 200. **Officers:** Eric J. Kufel; Thomas W. Freeze.

■ 12194 ■ **Poppers Supply Co.**
340 SE 7th Ave.
Portland, OR 97214
Phone: (503)239-3792 **Fax:** (503)235-6221
E-mail: poppers@poppers.com
Products: Popcorn; Popcorn poppers; Popcorn concession supplies. **SICs:** 5149 (Groceries & Related Products Nec); 5046 (Commercial Equipment Nec). **Est:** 1945. **Sales:** $5,000,000 (2000). **Emp:** 11. **Officers:** Roxanne Jordan, COO; Brad Weaver, CFO; Karren Bjelland, Marketing & Sales Mgr.

■ 12195 ■ **Poritzky's Wholesale Meats and Food Services**
6 John Walsh Blvd.
Peekskill, NY 10566
Phone: (914)737-2154 **Fax:** (914)737-5026
Products: Groceries, including meats, frozen foods, and produce; Paper products; Chemicals. **SICs:** 5147 (Meats & Meat Products); 5113 (Industrial & Personal Service Paper); 5141 (Groceries—General Line); 5142 (Packaged Frozen Foods); 5169 (Chemicals & Allied Products Nec). **Sales:** $11,000,000 (2000). **Emp:** 30. **Officers:** Sandy Poritzky.

■ 12196 ■ **Pork Packers International**
PO Box 158
Downs, KS 67437
Phone: (785)454-3396 **Fax:** (785)454-3552
Products: Pork. **SIC:** 5147 (Meats & Meat Products). **Est:** 1969. **Sales:** $30,000,000 (2000). **Emp:** 65. **Officers:** Lance C. Kennedy.

■ 12197 ■ Port Cargo Service Inc.
5200 Coffee Dr.
New Orleans, LA 70115
Phone: (504)891-9494 **Fax:** (504)897-3951
Products: Coffee grains. **SIC:** 5149 (Groceries & Related Products Nec). **Est:** 1983. **Sales:** $7,000,000 (2000). **Emp:** 100. **Officers:** Kevin Kelly, President.

■ 12198 ■ Portland Bottling Co.
1321 NE Couch St.
Portland, OR 97232
Phone: (503)230-7777 **Fax:** (503)239-8710
Products: Bottled and canned soft drinks. **SIC:** 5149 (Groceries & Related Products Nec). **Sales:** $47,000,000 (2000). **Emp:** 200. **Officers:** Robert Cole, President.

■ 12199 ■ Poultry Specialties Inc.
PO Box 2061
Russellville, AR 72811
Phone: (501)968-1777 **Fax:** (501)967-1111
Products: Chicken. **SIC:** 5144 (Poultry & Poultry Products). **Est:** 1980. **Sales:** $30,000,000 (2000). **Emp:** 7. **Officers:** Phil Carruth, President; Hugh Davis, CFO; C. Carruth, Dir. of Marketing; Nancy Canerday, Dir. of Data Processing.

■ 12200 ■ W.J. Powell Company Inc.
PO Box 1308
Thomasville, GA 31799
Phone: (912)226-4331
Products: Groceries, including meat, beef, fish, chicken, cereal, and cheese; Paper towels. **SICs:** 5148 (Fresh Fruits & Vegetables); 5149 (Groceries & Related Products Nec); 5142 (Packaged Frozen Foods); 5113 (Industrial & Personal Service Paper). **Est:** 1931. **Sales:** $30,000,000 (2000). **Emp:** 140. **Officers:** Johnny Gay, General Mgr.

■ 12201 ■ Powers Candy Company Inc.
PO Box 4338
Pocatello, ID 83205-4338
Phone: (208)237-3311 **Fax:** (208)237-3325
Products: Cigarettes and tobacco; Candy; Groceries; Paper products; Bar supplies; Juices. **SICs:** 5145 (Confectionery); 5141 (Groceries—General Line); 5149 (Groceries & Related Products Nec); 5194 (Tobacco & Tobacco Products). **Est:** 1963. **Emp:** 25. **Officers:** David Powers, President; Joanne Powers, Sec. & Treas.; Steve Kenison, General Mgr.; Bart Rankin, Sales Mgr.

■ 12202 ■ Powers Candy & Nut Co.
6061 N Freya
Spokane, WA 99207-4910
Phone: (509)489-1955 **Fax:** (509)489-8609
Products: Candy and nut products. **SIC:** 5145 (Confectionery). **Sales:** $5,000,000 (2000). **Emp:** 25. **Officers:** Gilbert L. Cooley.

■ 12203 ■ PPI Del Monte Tropical Fruit Co.
800 Douglas Rd.
Coral Gables, FL 33134
Phone: (305)520-8400 **Fax:** (305)520-8495
Products: Fresh fruits. **SIC:** 5148 (Fresh Fruits & Vegetables). **Emp:** 180. **Officers:** Brian Haycox.

■ 12204 ■ Prairie Farms Dairy Inc. Fort Wayne Div.
PO Box 10419
Ft. Wayne, IN 46852
Phone: (219)483-6436
Products: Milk; Sour cream; Cottage cheese. **SIC:** 5143 (Dairy Products Except Dried or Canned). **Est:** 1939. **Sales:** $35,000,000 (2000). **Emp:** 130. **Officers:** Charles Allen, General Mgr.; Ward Krause, Controller; Jerry Widenhofer, Dir. of Marketing.

■ 12205 ■ Prairie Farms Dairy Inc. Ice Cream Specialties Div.
PO Box 19766
St. Louis, MO 63144
Phone: (314)631-8171
Products: Ice cream. **SIC:** 5143 (Dairy Products Except Dried or Canned). **Est:** 1930. **Sales:** $14,000,000 (2000). **Emp:** 25. **Officers:** Wes Lopez, General Mgr.

■ 12206 ■ Prasek's Hillje Smokehouse
Rte. 3
Box 18
El Campo, TX 77437
Phone: (409)543-8312 **Fax:** (409)543-4106
Products: Meat products, including sausage and jerky; Cheese. **SICs:** 5147 (Meats & Meat Products); 5143 (Dairy Products Except Dried or Canned).

■ 12207 ■ Prawn Seafoods Inc.
6851 NW 32nd Ave.
Miami, FL 33147-6656
Phone: (305)691-2435 **Fax:** (305)693-6348
Products: Frozen fish; Vegetables; Seafood. **SICs:** 5146 (Fish & Seafoods); 5148 (Fresh Fruits & Vegetables); 5142 (Packaged Frozen Foods). **Est:** 1968. **Emp:** 15.

■ 12208 ■ Preferred Brokerage Co.
3627 Mattox, No. 4
El Paso, TX 79925-3629
Phone: (915)772-8559 **Fax:** (915)779-8871
Products: Food. **SIC:** 5141 (Groceries—General Line). **Emp:** 1. **Officers:** Virginia Braden.

■ 12209 ■ Preferred Brokerage Co.
1131 University Blvd. NE, Ste. H
Albuquerque, NM 87102-1701
Phone: (505)842-5996 **Fax:** (505)843-1449
Products: Canned goods. **SIC:** 5149 (Groceries & Related Products Nec). **Emp:** 49. **Officers:** Virginia Schroeder.

■ 12210 ■ Preferred Meats Inc.
PO Box 565854
Dallas, TX 75356
Phone: (214)565-0243
Free: (800)397-7333 **Fax:** (214)428-2748
Products: Meat, including veal, pork, beef, lamb, and game birds. **SIC:** 5147 (Meats & Meat Products). **Est:** 1977. **Sales:** $17,000,000 (2000). **Emp:** 35. **Officers:** Steve Robbins, President.

■ 12211 ■ Preferred Products Inc.
PO Box 59294
Minneapolis, MN 55459-0294
Phone: (612)448-5252 **Fax:** (612)448-4084
Products: Peanut butter and coconut; Packaged candies. **SICs:** 5141 (Groceries—General Line); 5145 (Confectionery). **Officers:** R. F. Zettell, President.

■ 12212 ■ Preferred Products Inc.
11095 Viking Dr.
Eden Prairie, MN 55344-7223
Phone: (612)996-7400
Products: Peanut butter, packaged baking and eating nuts and candies. **SIC:** 5145 (Confectionery). **Sales:** $36,000,000 (2000). **Emp:** 150. **Officers:** Glenn Fischer, President; Brad Willems, Controller.

■ 12213 ■ Premier Food Marketing Inc.
6 Way Rd.
Middlefield, CT 06455
Phone: (860)349-7040 **Fax:** (860)349-7041
E-mail: premfood@aol.com
Products: Instore bakery. **SIC:** 5141 (Groceries—General Line). **Est:** 1989. **Sales:** $1,000,000 (2000). **Emp:** 10. **Officers:** Robert W. Goodman, President; Joseph Holovach Jr., Vice President; Wanda Davis, Personnel Mgr. **Former Name:** Premier Food Brokerage Inc.

■ 12214 ■ PrePeeled Potato Co.
1585 S Union
Stockton, CA 95206-2269
Phone: (209)469-6911 **Fax:** (209)469-6914
Products: Potatoes, including frozen and fresh. **SICs:** 5148 (Fresh Fruits & Vegetables); 5142 (Packaged Frozen Foods). **Est:** 1964. **Emp:** 19. **Officers:** Jack Vogel.

■ 12215 ■ President Baking Co., Inc.
PO Box 218
North Little Rock, AR 72115
Phone: (501)372-2123 **Fax:** (501)372-3793
Products: Cookies. **SIC:** 5149 (Groceries & Related Products Nec). **Sales:** $10,000,000 (2000). **Emp:** 105. **Officers:** Wendell Horner; Jerry Cavitt.

■ 12216 ■ President Global Corp.
6965 Aragon Cir.
Buena Park, CA 90620
Phone: (714)994-2990 **Fax:** (714)523-3142
Products: Groceries. **SIC:** 5141 (Groceries—General Line). **Sales:** $19,000,000 (2000). **Emp:** 125. **Officers:** P.C. Wu, President; Richard T. Wu, CFO.

■ 12217 ■ Pricing Dynamics
21 Dale St.
Methuen, MA 01844
Phone: (978)685-5655
Products: Canned food. **SIC:** 5149 (Groceries & Related Products Nec).

■ 12218 ■ Prime Poultry Corp.
24 Chesterton St.
Boston, MA 02119
Phone: (617)442-0707
Products: Poultry. **SIC:** 5144 (Poultry & Poultry Products).

■ 12219 ■ Prince of Peace Enterprises Inc.
3536 Arden Rd.
Hayward, CA 94545
Phone: (510)887-1899
Free: (800)732-2328 **Fax:** (510)887-1999
E-mail: popsf@popus.com
URL: http://www.popus.com
Products: Bottled and canned iced coffee drinks; Energy drinks; Teas; Chocolate; Gourmet cookies and confections; Natural health products; Herbal products. **SICs:** 5149 (Groceries & Related Products Nec); 5145 (Confectionery). **Est:** 1983. **Sales:** $21,000,000 (2000). **Emp:** 75. **Officers:** Kenneth Yeung, President; Jeannie Chen, Vice President.

■ 12220 ■ Pringle Meats Inc.
216 7th St.
Oakland, CA 94607-4493
Phone: (510)893-7400 **Fax:** (510)893-2272
Products: Fresh meat; Beef; Fresh pork; Lamb; Veal; Poultry. **SICs:** 5147 (Meats & Meat Products); 5144 (Poultry & Poultry Products). **Emp:** 25.

■ 12221 ■ Priscilla Gold Seal Corp.
25 Charlotte Ave.
Hicksville, NY 11801
Phone: (718)852-2500 **Fax:** (718)852-0183
Products: Ice cream. **SIC:** 5143 (Dairy Products Except Dried or Canned). **Sales:** $13,000,000 (2000). **Emp:** 90. **Officers:** Allen Newman, President.

■ 12222 ■ Pro-Fac Cooperative Inc.
PO Box 682
Rochester, NY 14603-0682
Phone: (716)383-1850 **Fax:** (716)383-1281
Products: Canned vegetables; Chips; Snack foods; Salad dressings. **SICs:** 5149 (Groceries & Related Products Nec); 5142 (Packaged Frozen Foods); 5141 (Groceries—General Line). **Est:** 1960. **Sales:** $730,800,000 (2000). **Emp:** 3,363. **Officers:** Roy A. Myers, CEO & President; William D. Rice, Sr. VP & CFO.

■ 12223 ■ PROACT
2600 Garden Rd., No. 410
Monterey, CA 93940
Phone: (831)656-1470 **Fax:** (831)656-1477
URL: http://www.proactusa.com
Products: Produce. **SIC:** 5148 (Fresh Fruits & Vegetables). **Est:** 1991. **Sales:** $1,000,000,000 (2000). **Emp:** 3,000. **Officers:** James Catchot, COO, e-mail: jcatchot@proactusa.com; Manuel Costa, Sales/Marketing Contact, e-mail: mrcosta@proactusa.com.

■ 12224 ■ Produce Distributors Co.
1918 Wilson St.
Jackson, MS 39202
Phone: (601)969-3133
Products: Fruits and vegetables. **SIC:** 5148 (Fresh Fruits & Vegetables).

■ 12225 ■ **Producers Rice Mill Inc.**
PO Box 461
Stuttgart, AR 72160
Phone: (870)673-4444 **Fax:** (870)673-8131
URL: http://www.producersrice.com
Products: Rice. **SIC:** 5149 (Groceries & Related Products Nec). **Est:** 1943. **Sales:** $242,790,000 (1999). **Emp:** 500. **Officers:** Keith Glover, President.

■ 12226 ■ **Products Corp. of North America, Inc.**
6726 SW Burlingname Ave.
Portland, OR 97219-2126
Phone: (503)244-0701 **Fax:** (503)244-0589
E-mail: askfred@productscorp.com
URL: http://www.productscorp.com
Products: Food; Feed; Wood and metal products; Pulp, paper, and plastics; Chemicals and fertilizer; General commodities and merchandise; Machinery and equipment; Marine cargo. **SICs:** 5031 (Lumber, Plywood & Millwork); 5191 (Farm Supplies); 5169 (Chemicals & Allied Products Nec); 5113 (Industrial & Personal Service Paper); 5084 (Industrial Machinery & Equipment). **Est:** 1983. **Officers:** Fred Pfaffle, President.

■ 12227 ■ **Proferas Pizza Bakery Inc.**
1130 Moosic St.
Scranton, PA 18505
Phone: (717)342-4181 **Fax:** (717)342-4853
Products: Pizza. **SIC:** 5149 (Groceries & Related Products Nec). **Est:** 1920. **Sales:** $8,300,000 (2000). **Emp:** 60. **Officers:** Tom Basta, President.

■ 12228 ■ **Professional Marketers Inc.**
500 Waters Edge
Lombard, IL 60148
Phone: (630)620-7600
Products: Groceries; Paper goods. **SICs:** 5141 (Groceries—General Line); 5113 (Industrial & Personal Service Paper). **Est:** 1970. **Sales:** $95,000,000 (2000). **Emp:** 263. **Officers:** Robert McCarty Jr., CEO; Jim Moore, General Mgr.; Richard Hurst, Exec. VP.

■ 12229 ■ **Progressive Companies Inc.**
PO Box B
Spirit Lake, IA 51360
Phone: (712)336-1750
Free: (800)831-5174 **Fax:** (712)336-4681
E-mail: stolfish@rconnect.com
URL: http://www.sfish.com
Products: Fish. **SIC:** 5146 (Fish & Seafoods). **Est:** 1932. **Sales:** $2,500,000 (2000). **Emp:** 50. **Officers:** Larry Stoller, President; Jed Banas, Treasurer.

■ 12230 ■ **Progressive Marketing**
8026 Vantage
San Antonio, TX 78230-4733
Phone: (210)525-9171 **Fax:** (210)525-9910
Products: General line groceries. **SIC:** 5141 (Groceries—General Line). **Emp:** 99.

■ 12231 ■ **Progressive Produce Co.**
PO Box 911231
Los Angeles, CA 90091-1231
Phone: (323)890-8100
Free: (800)900-0757 **Fax:** (323)890-8191
E-mail: sales@progressiveproduce.com
Products: Potatoes, onions, rice and beans. **SIC:** 5148 (Fresh Fruits & Vegetables). **Est:** 1967. **Sales:** $50,000,000 (2000). **Emp:** 100. **Officers:** James K. Leimkuhler, President; Bruce MacCallum, CFO.

■ 12232 ■ **Protein Foods Inc.**
PO Box 1545
Gainesville, GA 30503
Phone: (404)534-3514
Products: Food. **SIC:** 5144 (Poultry & Poultry Products). **Sales:** $30,000,000 (2000). **Emp:** 80.

■ 12233 ■ **Pruden Packing Company Inc.**
1201 N Main St.
Suffolk, VA 23434
Phone: (757)539-6261 **Fax:** (757)925-4971
Products: Processed, frozen, or cooked meats. **SICs:** 5147 (Meats & Meat Products); 5142 (Packaged Frozen Foods). **Est:** 1917. **Sales:** $3,000,000 (2000). **Emp:** 12. **Officers:** Peter D. Pruden III, President.

■ 12234 ■ **Pueblo Fruits Inc.**
5821-G Midway Park Blvd. NE
Albuquerque, NM 87109-5823
Phone: (505)344-2554 **Fax:** (505)344-2786
Products: Bananas. **SIC:** 5148 (Fresh Fruits & Vegetables). **Est:** 1988. **Emp:** 6. **Officers:** Pat DeVenzeio.

■ 12235 ■ **Purcell & Associates**
7 Crow Canyon Ct., Ste. 200
San Ramon, CA 94583
Phone: (510)855-9910 **Fax:** (510)855-1147
E-mail: purcell510@aol.com
Products: Canned fruits; Frozen fruits and juice concentrates; Dehydrated fruits and vegetables; Tomato and fruit paste; Fire roasted tomatoes. **SICs:** 5142 (Packaged Frozen Foods); 5149 (Groceries & Related Products Nec). **Est:** 1956. **Sales:** $100,000,000 (2000). **Officers:** Carlos Steffens, VP of Marketing; T.J. Purcell, President; Jason Bellingham; Luke Brassinga; Sherry Heacox; Eleanore Rewerts.

■ 12236 ■ **Pure Sealed Dairy**
5031 Bass Rd.
Ft. Wayne, IN 46808
Phone: (219)432-3575
Free: (800)862-6455 **Fax:** (219)432-7844
Products: Milk. **SIC:** 5143 (Dairy Products Except Dried or Canned). **Est:** 1984. **Sales:** $7,000,000 (2000). **Emp:** 22. **Officers:** Thomas Schenkel, President; W. Kent Schenkel, Treasurer & Secty.; Robert Cashdollar, General Mgr.

■ 12237 ■ **Purity Dairies, Inc.**
PO Box 100957
Nashville, TN 37224-0957
Products: Ice cream and frozen desserts. **SIC:** 5143 (Dairy Products Except Dried or Canned).

■ 12238 ■ **Purity Minonk Baking Co.**
447 Oak
Minonk, IL 61760-1309
Phone: (309)432-2612 **Fax:** (309)432-2705
Products: Breads. **SIC:** 5149 (Groceries & Related Products Nec). **Emp:** 49. **Officers:** Nicholas Butera.

■ 12239 ■ **Purity Wholesale Grocers Inc.**
5400 Broken Sound Blvd. Ste. 100
Boca Raton, FL 33487-3594
Phone: (561)994-9360
Products: General line of groceries. **SIC:** 5149 (Groceries & Related Products Nec). **Sales:** $1,200,000,000 (2000). **Emp:** 600. **Officers:** Jeff Levitetz, CEO & Chairman of the Board; Alan Rutner, Sr. VP & Finance Officer.

■ 12240 ■ **PYA/Monarch Chain Distribution**
PO Box 1004
Greenville, SC 29602
Phone: (864)295-8199
Products: Food. **SIC:** 5141 (Groceries—General Line). **Est:** 1984. **Sales:** $600,000,000 (2000). **Emp:** 300. **Officers:** John R. Millard, President; Richard Hall, VP of Finance. **Alternate Name:** Specialty Distribution.

■ 12241 ■ **PYA/Monarch Inc.**
PO Box 1328
Greenville, SC 29602
Phone: (803)676-8600 **Fax:** (803)676-8701
Products: General line groceries. **SIC:** 5141 (Groceries—General Line). **Est:** 1900. **Sales:** $1,400,000,000 (2000). **Emp:** 2,500. **Officers:** James Carlson, CEO & President; Steve Stolz, CFO; Bill Loe, CIO; Cliff Cole, Contact.

■ 12242 ■ **Pyrenees French Bakery Inc.**
PO Box 3626
Bakersfield, CA 93385
Phone: (661)322-7159 **Fax:** (661)322-6713
Products: Bread and bakery products. **SIC:** 5149 (Groceries & Related Products Nec). **Sales:** $3,000,000 (1999). **Emp:** 36. **Officers:** Mike George, President.

■ 12243 ■ **Q.A. Products Inc.**
1301 Mark St.
Elk Grove Village, IL 60007
Phone: (708)595-2390 **Fax:** (708)595-1960
Products: Food toppings and decorations. **SIC:** 5149

(Groceries & Related Products Nec). **Est:** 1987. **Sales:** $18,000,000 (2000). **Emp:** 98. **Officers:** John R. Tritt.

■ 12244 ■ **Q.E.D. Exports**
PO Box 15005
Riverside, RI 02915
Phone: (401)433-4045 **Fax:** (401)433-4022
Products: Olive oil; Candy and chocolate; Cosmetics and skin care products; Live lobster; Pasta. **SICs:** 5149 (Groceries & Related Products Nec); 5145 (Confectionery); 5122 (Drugs, Proprietaries & Sundries); 5146 (Fish & Seafoods). **Officers:** Charles Didonato, President.

■ 12245 ■ **Quaker Oats Co. International Foods Div.**
PO Box 9001
Chicago, IL 60604-9001
Phone: (312)222-7111 **Fax:** (312)222-8392
Products: Sports beverages and cereal. **SIC:** 5149 (Groceries & Related Products Nec). **Sales:** $1,741,000,000 (2000). **Emp:** 9,000. **Officers:** Barbara Allen, President.

■ 12246 ■ **Quality Bakery Co.**
1105 Schrock Rd., No. 300
Columbus, OH 43085
Phone: (614)846-2232
Products: Baked goods. **SIC:** 5141 (Groceries—General Line).

■ 12247 ■ **Quality Bakery Products Inc.**
888 Las Olas Blvd., Ste. 700
Ft. Lauderdale, FL 33301-2272
Phone: (954)779-3663
Free: (800)590-3663 **Fax:** (954)779-7837
Products: Pan style, cube style, and crumb style stuffing. **SICs:** 5141 (Groceries—General Line); 5149 (Groceries & Related Products Nec). **Sales:** $23,000,000 (2000). **Emp:** 300. **Officers:** Harold Hink, President; Ronald Hink, Treasurer & Secty.

■ 12248 ■ **Quality Banana Inc.**
3196 Produce Row
Houston, TX 77023-5814
Phone: (713)921-4161 **Fax:** (713)921-7859
Products: Bananas. **SIC:** 5148 (Fresh Fruits & Vegetables). **Emp:** 49. **Officers:** Paul B. Zubowski, General Mgr.

■ 12249 ■ **Quality Croutons Inc.**
825 W 37th Pl.
Chicago, IL 60609
Phone: (773)927-8200
Free: (800)334-2796 **Fax:** (773)927-8228
E-mail: croutons@interaccess.com
URL: http://www.qualitycroutons.com
Products: Croutons; Stuffings. **SIC:** 5149 (Groceries & Related Products Nec). **Emp:** 50. **Officers:** David M. Moore; Vicki Scurlock, Sales/Marketing Contact; e-mail: dfm@ameritech.net; Deadra Ashford, Customer Service Contact; Diane Simmons, Human Resources Contact.

■ 12250 ■ **Quality Foods Inc.**
PO Box 4908
Little Rock, AR 72214
Phone: (501)568-3141 **Fax:** (501)565-8821
Products: Food; Paper and allied products; Commercial cooking and food warming equipment. **SICs:** 5149 (Groceries & Related Products Nec); 5113 (Industrial & Personal Service Paper); 5046 (Commercial Equipment Nec). **Sales:** $105,000,000 (2000). **Emp:** 499. **Officers:** Philip Tappan; Don Kirkpatrick; Homer Feltner; Gene May.

■ 12251 ■ **Quality Foods Inc.**
PO Box 4908
Little Rock, AR 72214
Phone: (501)568-3141 **Fax:** (501)565-8821
Products: Complete line of groceries and food service equipment. **SICs:** 5141 (Groceries—General Line); 5149 (Groceries & Related Products Nec); 5046 (Commercial Equipment Nec). **Sales:** $280,000,000 (2000). **Emp:** 800. **Officers:** Don Kirkpatrick, President; Debbie Clement, Controller.

■ 12252 ■ Quality Meat Company Inc.
340 North Ave.
Grand Junction, CO 81501
Phone: (970)242-1872
Free: (800)447-5764 **Fax:** (970)241-2985
Products: Frozen foods; Fresh meat; Frozen meat;
Canned specialties; Produce. **SICs:** 5147 (Meats &
Meat Products); 5149 (Groceries & Related Products
Nec); 5142 (Packaged Frozen Foods). **Est:** 1959.
Emp: 12. **Officers:** Philip Emerson, Manager.

■ 12253 ■ Quality Meats and Seafood Inc.
PO Box 337
West Fargo, ND 58078
Phone: (701)282-0202
Free: (800)353-4250 **Fax:** (701)282-0583
Products: Pork, beef, poulty, and seafood. **SICs:** 5146
(Fish & Seafoods); 5144 (Poultry & Poultry Products);
5147 (Meats & Meat Products). **Est:** 1967. **Sales:**
$25,000,000 (2000). **Emp:** 100. **Officers:** R. Rieth,
President; K. Scherber, CFO; S. Wetzstein, Dir. of
Marketing.

■ 12254 ■ Quarex Industries Inc.
47-05 Metropolitan Ave.
Ridgewood, NY 11385
Phone: (718)821-0011 **Fax:** (718)497-4462
Products: Processed, frozen, or cooked meats. **SIC:**
5147 (Meats & Meat Products). **Est:** 1963. **Sales:**
$225,000,000 (2000). **Emp:** 500. **Officers:** Frank
Castellana, President.

■ 12255 ■ Queen City Wholesale Inc.
PO Box 1083
Sioux Falls, SD 57101
Phone: (605)336-3215
Free: (800)479-3215 **Fax:** (605)336-2423
Products: Tobacco; Candy; Vending machines; Paper
products; Institutional food; Juice; Bar supplies;
Convenience store supplies. **SICs:** 5145
(Confectionery); 5194 (Tobacco & Tobacco Products);
5046 (Commercial Equipment Nec). **Est:** 1946. **Emp:**
43.

■ 12256 ■ Queen City Wholesale Inc.
PO Box 1083
Sioux Falls, SD 57101
Phone: (605)336-3215 **Fax:** (605)336-2423
Products: Candy and tobacco. **SICs:** 5145
(Confectionery); 5194 (Tobacco & Tobacco Products).
Sales: $16,000,000 (2000). **Emp:** 40. **Officers:** Pat
Wehrkamp, President & CFO.

■ 12257 ■ Quinn Coffee Co.
1455 E Chestnut Expwy.
Springfield, MO 65802
Phone: (417)869-5523 **Fax:** (417)869-1201
Products: Spices; Flavored and regular coffee. **SIC:**
5149 (Groceries & Related Products Nec). **Est:** 1984.
Sales: $14,000,000 (2000). **Emp:** 30. **Officers:** Jerry
Ward, General Mgr. **Former Name:** Quinn Coffee Co.

■ 12258 ■ R and R Provision Co.
PO Box 889
Easton, PA 18042
Phone: (215)258-5366 **Fax:** (215)252-4583
Products: Meat packing plant products; Canned
specialties; Frozen foods. **SICs:** 5147 (Meats & Meat
Products); 5142 (Packaged Frozen Foods); 5149
(Groceries & Related Products Nec). **Est:** 1934. **Sales:**
$22,000,000 (2000). **Emp:** 75. **Officers:** James Evely,
President; R.W. Rogers, VP of Finance; Michael Hieter,
Dir. of Marketing; Michael Dacorn, Dir. of Data
Processing; Daniel Bennett, Dir of Human Resources.

■ 12259 ■ R.A.B. Holdings Inc.
444 Madison Ave.
New York, NY 10022
Phone: (212)688-4500 **Fax:** (212)888-5025
Products: Kosher foods and health foods to retail
grocery stores. **SIC:** 5149 (Groceries & Related
Products Nec). **Sales:** $511,000,000 (2000). **Emp:**
2,120. **Officers:** Richard Bernstein, CEO & President;
Steven Grossman, CFO.

■ 12260 ■ Race Street Foods Inc.
PO Box 28385
San Jose, CA 95159-8385
Phone: (408)294-6161
Free: (800)394-5179 **Fax:** (408)294-2080
Products: Meat, fish, and poultry. **SICs:** 5146 (Fish &
Seafoods); 5144 (Poultry & Poultry Products); 5147
(Meats & Meat Products). **Est:** 1947. **Sales:**
$12,500,000 (2000). **Emp:** 100. **Officers:** G. Barsanti,
CEO; D. Barsanti, CFO; D. Daly, Dir. of Marketing; A.
McClelland, Dir. of Systems; Bob Maguire, Dir of
Human Resources.

■ 12261 ■ Radium Cooperative Co.
Rte. 2
Radium, KS 67550
Phone: (316)982-4364
Products: Livestock and farm products. **SIC:** 5153
(Grain & Field Beans). **Sales:** $5,000,000 (2000). **Emp:**
22.

■ 12262 ■ Radways Dairy
29 Jefferson Ave.
New London, CT 06320
Phone: (203)443-8921
Products: Dairy products, including eggs, cheese, and
milk. **SIC:** 5143 (Dairy Products Except Dried or
Canned). **Est:** 1890. **Sales:** $12,000,000 (2000). **Emp:**
38. **Officers:** Alexander Guida III, CEO.

■ 12263 ■ C.B. Ragland Co.
PO Box 40587
Nashville, TN 37204
Phone: (615)259-4622 **Fax:** (615)254-5867
Products: General line groceries. **SIC:** 5141
(Groceries—General Line). **Est:** 1919. **Sales:**
$200,000,000 (2000). **Emp:** 250. **Officers:** Buddy
Best, President; Baker Walker, Controller; Bill Townes,
President; Robert Agee, Dir. of Systems.

■ 12264 ■ Ragu Foods Co.
1135 E Artesia Blvd.
Carson, CA 90746-1602
Phone: (818)760-0800 **Fax:** (818)980-5542
Products: Marinades and tenderizers. **SIC:** 5149
(Groceries & Related Products Nec). **Sales:**
$6,000,000 (2000). **Emp:** 50. **Officers:** Jim DeRose,
Plant Manager.

■ 12265 ■ Rainbo Baking Co.
1916 N Broadway, Box 16
Oklahoma City, OK 73103
Phone: (405)524-8454 **Fax:** (405)556-2153
Products: Bread. **SIC:** 5149 (Groceries & Related
Products Nec). **Sales:** $30,000,000 (2000). **Emp:** 325.
Officers: J. Michael Krafft.

■ 12266 ■ Rainbo Baking Co.
4104 Leeland
Houston, TX 77023-3014
Phone: (713)237-0001
Products: Bread. **SIC:** 5149 (Groceries & Related
Products Nec). **Sales:** $10,000,000 (2000). **Emp:** 499.
Officers: Richard Wyche.

■ 12267 ■ Rainbo Baking Co.
303 E 4th
Pueblo, CO 81003-3313
Phone: (719)543-3725 **Fax:** (719)545-5863
Products: Bread. **SIC:** 5149 (Groceries & Related
Products Nec). **Sales:** $13,000,000 (2000). **Emp:** 135.
Officers: Mike George.

■ 12268 ■ Rainbow Inc. (Pearl City, Hawaii)
98-715 Kuahao Pl.
Pearl City, HI 96782
Phone: (808)487-6455 **Fax:** (808)487-0888
Products: Frozen foods. **SICs:** 5142 (Packaged
Frozen Foods); 5141 (Groceries—General Line).
Sales: $8,000,000 (2000). **Emp:** 15. **Officers:** William
Prideaux, CEO & President; Larry Kimata, Controller.

■ 12269 ■ Rainbow Natural Foods
15965 E 32nd Ave.
Aurora, CO 80011
Phones: (303)373-1144 (303)373-1111
Free: (800)522-7633 **Fax:** (303)373-1859
Products: Health and gourmet foods. **SIC:** 5149

(Groceries & Related Products Nec). **Officers:** Pattie
Siwa, Sales Mgr.

■ 12270 ■ Rainsweet
PO Box 6109
Salem, OR 97304
Phone: (503)363-4293 **Fax:** (503)585-4657
Products: Processes frozen onions, berries,
mushrooms and peppers. **SIC:** 5142 (Packaged Frozen
Foods). **Emp:** 170. **Officers:** George Crispin, CEO &
President; David Gati, Controller.

■ 12271 ■ Ralston Purina/Pet Products
4555 York St.
Denver, CO 80216
Phone: (303)295-0818 **Fax:** (303)295-7442
Products: Formulas for dog and cat foods. **SIC:** 5149
(Groceries & Related Products Nec).

■ 12272 ■ RAMM Global
50 Abele Rd., Ste. 1005
Bridgeville, PA 15017
Phone: (412)221-3700 **Fax:** (412)221-7470
Products: Chemicals; Chinaware; Beverages,
including water; Food and grocery products; Household
products. **SIC:** 5141 (Groceries—General Line). **Est:**
1981. **Sales:** $7,000,000 (1999). **Emp:** 10. **Officers:**
Michael Pierce, CEO; Marc Pierce, President, e-mail:
marcpierce@earthlink.net. **Alternate Name:** RAMM
Metals Inc.

■ 12273 ■ RAMM Metals Inc.
50 Abele Rd., Ste. 1005
Bridgeville, PA 15017
Phone: (412)221-3700 **Fax:** (412)221-7470
Products: Food. **SIC:** 5141 (Groceries—General Line).
Sales: $7,000,000 (2000). **Emp:** 10.

■ 12274 ■ Randall Foods Inc.
PO Box 2669
Huntington Park, CA 90255
Phone: (213)587-2383 **Fax:** (213)586-1587
Products: Chicken, beef, and pork. **SICs:** 5144
(Poultry & Poultry Products); 5147 (Meats & Meat
Products). **Est:** 1952. **Sales:** $168,000,000 (1999).
Emp: 500. **Officers:** Stan M. Bloom, President; Jack
Broker, Controller; Ronald Totin, VP of Marketing &
Sales; Ranbir Samry, Dir. of Data Processing; Geroge
Oalivaren, Dir of Human Resources.

■ 12275 ■ Randazzo's Fruit Market #2
49800 Hayes Rd.
Macomb, MI 48044
Phone: (810)566-8700 **Fax:** (810)566-0208
Products: Fruits and vegetables. **SIC:** 5148 (Fresh
Fruits & Vegetables).

■ 12276 ■ Randolph Slaughter Co.
PO Box 556
Laredo, TX 78042
Phone: (956)722-2252 **Fax:** (956)722-8675
Products: Dried chilis; Garlic. **SIC:** 5149 (Groceries &
Related Products Nec). **Emp:** 49. **Officers:** Randolph
Slaughter.

■ 12277 ■ Randy's Frozen Meats
1910 NW 5th St.
Faribault, MN 55021-4606
Phone: (507)334-7177
Free: (800)354-7177 **Fax:** (507)334-9210
Products: Frozen meat; Frozen foods; Sandwiches;
Frozen specialties. **SICs:** 5142 (Packaged Frozen
Foods); 5147 (Meats & Meat Products); 5149
(Groceries & Related Products Nec). **Est:** 1955. **Emp:**
49. **Officers:** Neal Gragg; Randy Creasman; Oean
Manz; Jon Welborn.

■ 12278 ■ Rangen Inc.
PO Box 706
Buhl, ID 83316
Phone: (208)543-6421 **Fax:** (208)543-6090
Products: Feeds, dry edible beans and seeds and
commercial grains. **SIC:** 5153 (Grain & Field Beans).
Sales: $31,000,000 (2000). **Emp:** 145. **Officers:**
Christopher Rangen, President.

■ 12279 ■ **Isadore A. Rapasadi Sons**
N Peterboro
Canastota, NY 13032
Phone: (315)697-2216 **Fax:** (315)697-3300
Products: Onions and potatoes. **SIC:** 5148 (Fresh Fruits & Vegetables). **Emp:** 49.

■ 12280 ■ **Rappahannock Seafood Company Inc.**
PO Box 816
Kilmarnock, VA 22482-0816
Phone: (804)435-1605 **Fax:** (804)435-0616
Products: Seafood. **SIC:** 5146 (Fish & Seafoods). **Est:** 1947. **Sales:** $10,000,000 (2000). **Emp:** 99. **Officers:** Charles C. Chase II, Owner; Martha Chase McLaughlin, Owner.

■ 12281 ■ **Ray's Wholesale Meat**
2113 S 3rd Ave.
Yakima, WA 98903-1413
Phone: (509)575-0729
Free: (800)572-7350 **Fax:** (509)457-3804
Products: Meat. **SIC:** 5147 (Meats & Meat Products). **Est:** 1958. **Sales:** $12,000,000 (1999). **Emp:** 52. **Officers:** Jack Bixler, Controller; Ray Shuel, President.

■ 12282 ■ **Red Apple Food Marts Inc.**
5218 Milford Rd.
East Stroudsburg, PA 18301
Phone: (717)588-9391
Products: Fruit; Produce. **SIC:** 5148 (Fresh Fruits & Vegetables). **Est:** 1954. **Sales:** $1,000,000 (2000). **Emp:** 4. **Officers:** James Coco, Owner.

■ 12283 ■ **Red Apple Supermarkets**
823 11th Ave. (57th)
New York, NY 10019
Phone: (212)956-5770 **Fax:** (212)333-7418
Products: Groceries; Produce; Meat. **SICs:** 5149 (Groceries & Related Products Nec); 5148 (Fresh Fruits & Vegetables); 5147 (Meats & Meat Products).

■ 12284 ■ **Red Diamond Inc.**
PO Box 2168
Birmingham, AL 35201
Phone: (205)254-3138
Free: (800)292-4651 **Fax:** (205)254-6062
Products: Roasted coffee and tea. **SIC:** 5149 (Groceries & Related Products Nec). **Est:** 1906. **Emp:** 180. **Officers:** William A. Bowron Jr., President.

■ 12285 ■ **Red Mill Farms Inc.**
290 S 5th St.
Brooklyn, NY 11211-6214
Phones: (718)384-4887 (718)384-2150
Free: (800)344-2253 **Fax:** (718)384-2988
E-mail: redmill@aol.com
URL: http://www.redmillfarms.com
Products: Individually packaged sliced cake, macaroons, and canned macaroons. **SICs:** 5145 (Confectionery); 5149 (Groceries & Related Products Nec). **Est:** 1919. **Sales:** $2,000,000 (2000). **Emp:** 49. **Officers:** Arnold Badner; Lenny Brauner, VP of Marketing & Sales.

■ 12286 ■ **Red River Barbeque and Grille**
PO Box 1342
Wexford, PA 15090-1342
Phone: (412)366-9200 **Fax:** (412)366-9200
Products: Meats,including beef, chicken, pork, ribs; Seafood; Salad; Barbeque sauce; Beer. **SICs:** 5149 (Groceries & Related Products Nec); 5144 (Poultry & Poultry Products). **Est:** 1987. **Sales:** $4,000,000 (2000). **Emp:** 90. **Officers:** Ronald Sofranko, CEO & President; Connie Eckstein, Accountant.

■ 12287 ■ **Red Star Yeast and Products, A Division of Universal Foods Corp.**
433 E Michigan St.
Milwaukee, WI 53202
Phone: (414)221-6333
Free: (877)677-7000 **Fax:** (414)347-4789
URL: http://redstaryeast.com
Products: Yeast; Baking powder; Malt products; Yeast foods; Dough conditioners; Mold inhibitors. **SIC:** 5149 (Groceries & Related Products Nec). **Est:** 1882. **Sales:** $164,000,000 (1999). **Emp:** 350. **Officers:** Jack Koberstine, President, e-mail: jack.koberstine@universalfoods.com; Paul J. Ernster, Controller, e-mail: paul.ernster@universalfoods.com; Roderick Sowders, VP of Marketing & Sales, e-mail: roderick.sowders@universalfoods.com. **Former Name:** Red Star Bio Products.

■ 12288 ■ **Red Trolley Co.**
1643 10th St.
Santa Monica, CA 90404
Phone: (310)450-0400
Products: Dry groceries and paper goods. **SIC:** 5141 (Groceries—General Line). **Sales:** $1,300,000 (2000). **Emp:** 5. **Officers:** Andy Brand, Partner.

■ 12289 ■ **Reddi-Made Foods Inc.**
5302 E Diana St.
Tampa, FL 33610
Phone: (813)623-3333
Products: Chilled citrus fruit. **SIC:** 5149 (Groceries & Related Products Nec). **Sales:** $23,000,000 (1994). **Emp:** 50. **Officers:** David Morris, General Mgr.

■ 12290 ■ **Reddy Ice Company Inc.**
4444 Vine St.
Riverside, CA 92507
Phone: (909)683-1730 **Fax:** (909)683-1615
Products: Packaged ice. **SIC:** 5149 (Groceries & Related Products Nec). **Est:** 1924. **Sales:** $3,000,000 (2000). **Emp:** 20. **Officers:** Jim Weaver, President.

■ 12291 ■ **REDI-FROZ**
6500 S US Hwy. 421
Westville, IN 46391-9420
Phone: (219)237-5111 **Fax:** (219)234-4162
Products: Frozen food. **SIC:** 5142 (Packaged Frozen Foods). **Est:** 1958. **Sales:** $64,000,000 (2000). **Emp:** 90. **Officers:** Ernie Lehman, President; John Wicker, Controller; Terry Tchoukaleff, VP of Marketing; Mark Millen, Dir. of Data Processing.

■ 12292 ■ **Red's/Fisher Inc.**
8801 Exchange Dr.
Orlando, FL 32809-7970
Phone: (407)857-3930 **Fax:** (407)859-2305
Products: Produce for grocery stores and restaurants. **SIC:** 5148 (Fresh Fruits & Vegetables). **Est:** 1948. **Sales:** $48,000,000 (2000). **Emp:** 288. **Officers:** Kent Shoemaker; Wanda Evans.

■ 12293 ■ **Red's Market Inc.**
8801 Exchange Dr.
Orlando, FL 32809-7970
Phone: (407)857-3930 **Fax:** (407)859-1125
Products: Fresh fruits and vegetables. **SIC:** 5148 (Fresh Fruits & Vegetables). **Sales:** $70,000,000 (1993). **Emp:** 350. **Officers:** Kent Shoemaker, President; Wanda Evans, Controller.

■ 12294 ■ **Reeves Peanut Company Inc.**
PO Box 565
Eufaula, AL 36027
Phone: (205)687-2756 **Fax:** (205)687-9126
Products: Peanuts. **SIC:** 5145 (Confectionery). **Est:** 1946. **Sales:** $5,000,000 (2000). **Emp:** 15. **Officers:** B.C. Reeves, President.

■ 12295 ■ **Regal Fruit Co.**
215 W 4th
PO Box 428
Tonasket, WA 98855
Phone: (509)486-2158 **Fax:** (509)486-4786
Products: Apples and pears. **SIC:** 5148 (Fresh Fruits & Vegetables). **Est:** 1948. **Sales:** $8,000,000 (1999). **Emp:** 105. **Officers:** Tom Call, General Mgr.; Jack Arbuckle, Chairman of the Board.

■ 12296 ■ **Reilly Dairy and Food Co.**
PO Box 19217
Tampa, FL 33686
Phone: (813)839-8458
Free: (800)282-8787 **Fax:** (813)839-0394
E-mail: reilly@gte.net
URL: http://www.reillydairy.com
Products: Dairy and other perishable refrigerated products. **SICs:** 5143 (Dairy Products Except Dried or Canned); 5149 (Groceries & Related Products Nec). **Est:** 1951. **Sales:** $76,000,000 (2000). **Emp:** 55. **Officers:** Gerald Reilly, President.

■ 12297 ■ **Reinhart Food Service Inc.**
PO Box 2859
La Crosse, WI 54602-2859
Phone: (608)782-2660
Products: Groceries. **SIC:** 5141 (Groceries—General Line). **Est:** 1972. **Sales:** $600,000,000 (2000). **Emp:** 1,100. **Officers:** Mark Drazkowski, President; Linda Brueggen, Controller; Greg Parish, Dir. of Information Systems. **Alternate Name:** Reinhart Institutional Foods Inc.

■ 12298 ■ **Reinhart Institutional Foods Inc. Milwaukee Div.**
PO Box 395
Oak Creek, WI 53154-0395
Phone: (414)761-5000 **Fax:** (414)761-4780
Products: Dairy products, meats, vegetables, fruits, and convenience foods. **SICs:** 5141 (Groceries—General Line); 5147 (Meats & Meat Products); 5143 (Dairy Products Except Dried or Canned); 5148 (Fresh Fruits & Vegetables). **Est:** 1972. **Sales:** $20,000,000 (2000). **Emp:** 80. **Officers:** Boyd Jordan, General Mgr.

■ 12299 ■ **Reiter Dairy**
10456 S State Rte. 224
Findlay, OH 45839
Phone: (419)423-2341
Products: Dairy products. **SIC:** 5143 (Dairy Products Except Dried or Canned).

■ 12300 ■ **Reliv' World Corp.**
PO Box 405
Chesterfield, MO 63005
Phone: (314)537-9715
Products: Food products, including granola bars; Nutritional supplements, diet management products, functional foods, and skin care products; Sports drink mixes. **SICs:** 5149 (Groceries & Related Products Nec); 5122 (Drugs, Proprietaries & Sundries).

■ 12301 ■ **Renzi Brothers Inc.**
948 Bradley
Watertown, NY 13601-1209
Phone: (315)788-5610
Free: (800)633-4311 **Fax:** (315)788-9097
URL: http://www.renzibros.com
Products: Full line of groceries. **SIC:** 5141 (Groceries—General Line). **Emp:** 75. **Officers:** Mike Renzi.

■ 12302 ■ **Resaca Inc.**
PO Box 3691
Brownsville, TX 78520
Phone: (956)546-5525
Products: Fish and seafood. **SIC:** 5146 (Fish & Seafoods). **Sales:** $8,500,000 (1992). **Emp:** 3. **Officers:** Michael Pashos, President.

■ 12303 ■ **Reser's Fine Foods Inc.**
PO Box 8
Beaverton, OR 97075
Phone: (503)643-6431
Products: Salads. **SIC:** 5141 (Groceries—General Line). **Est:** 1950. **Sales:** $180,000,000 (2000). **Emp:** 900. **Officers:** Al Reser, President; Gary Wills, CFO; Ron Leeper, VP of Marketing; Darrell G. Vandehey, VP of Production; Mary Jo Pralin, Human Resources Mgr.

■ 12304 ■ **Resource Trading Co.**
PO Box 1698
Portland, ME 04104
Phone: (207)772-2299
Free: (800)373-6339 **Fax:** (207)772-4709
E-mail: rtcl@worldnet.att.net
Products: Seafood, including lobster, shrimp, crawfish. **SIC:** 5146 (Fish & Seafoods). **Est:** 1984. **Sales:** $18,000,000 (2000). **Emp:** 50. **Officers:** Spencer Fuller, President; Janine Cary, Vice President.

■ 12305 ■ **Rhee Bros. Inc.**
9505 Berger Rd.
Columbia, MD 21046
Phone: (410)381-9000 **Fax:** (410)381-4989
Products: Oriental products, including rice, candy, and noodles. **SIC:** 5149 (Groceries & Related Products Nec). **Sales:** $30,000,000 (2000). **Emp:** 70. **Officers:** Jae Do Koh, General Mgr.; Ha Dyo Jang, Accountant; David Lee, Dir. of Marketing & Sales; Victor Ahn, Secretary.

■ 12306 ■ **P.J. Rhodes Corp.**
1016 Railroad Ave.
Novato, CA 94945-2510
Phone: (415)892-0022   **Fax:** (415)892-0022
E-mail: sales@pjrhodes.com
Products: Groceries; Confectionery and candy, including chocolate. **SICs:** 5145 (Confectionery); 5149 (Groceries & Related Products Nec); 5141 (Groceries—General Line). **Est:** 1946. **Officers:** Philip T. Rhodes, President.

■ 12307 ■ **Ribbons Pasta Co.**
823 Yale Ave., Ste. C
Seattle, WA 98109
Phone: (206)623-7552   **Fax:** (206)623-7554
Products: Pasta and filled products, including noodles, ravioli and tortellini. **SIC:** 5149 (Groceries & Related Products Nec). **Emp:** 9. **Officers:** Diane Symms.

■ 12308 ■ **Rice Growers Association of California**
1620 E Kentucky Ave
Woodland, CA 95776
Phone: (530)662-3235   **Fax:** (530)662-0674
Products: Milled and packaged rice. **SIC:** 5149 (Groceries & Related Products Nec). **Est:** 1921. **Emp:** 60. **Officers:** William J. Ludwig.

■ 12309 ■ **Riceland Foods Inc.**
PO Box 927
Stuttgart, AR 72160
Phone: (870)673-5500
Free: (888)664-RICE   **Fax:** (870)673-3366
URL: http://www.riceland.com
Products: Rice, including long and medium grain, brown, quickcooking, instant, and flavored mixes. **SIC:** 5149 (Groceries & Related Products Nec). **Sales:** $643,900,000 (1999). **Emp:** 1,800. **Officers:** Richard E. Bell, President & CEO; Terry Trice, Vice President.

■ 12310 ■ **RiceTec Inc.**
PO Box 1305
Alvin, TX 77512
Phone: (281)331-5655   **Fax:** (281)393-3532
Products: Rice. **SIC:** 5149 (Groceries & Related Products Nec). **Emp:** 41.

■ 12311 ■ **Rich Planned Foods**
1821 Ivystone Dr.
Richmond, VA 23233-4215
Phone: (804)266-7468   **Fax:** (804)266-2362
Products: Beef products. **SIC:** 5147 (Meats & Meat Products).

■ 12312 ■ **Rich Products Corp. Food Service Div.**
PO Box 245
Buffalo, NY 14240
Phone: (716)878-8000
Products: Non-dairy frozen foods, including toppings, creamers, baked products, and doughs. **SIC:** 5142 (Packaged Frozen Foods). **Est:** 1945. **Sales:** $1,600,000,000 (2000). **Emp:** 6,000. **Officers:** Robert E. Rich, President; Charles Trego, CFO; Kevin R. Malchoff, Exec. VP; William Gisel, President; Mike Bigham, Exec. VP.

■ 12313 ■ **Richard's American Food Service**
14323 W College Ave.
Muskego, WI 53150
Phone: (262)679-1617   **Fax:** (262)679-5066
Products: Meats. **SIC:** 5147 (Meats & Meat Products). **Sales:** $5,000,000 (2000). **Emp:** 15. **Officers:** Darrell Skrove, President.

■ 12314 ■ **Richardson Brands Co.**
6330 Manor Ln.
Miami, FL 33143
Phone: (305)667-3291   **Fax:** (305)666-0079
Products: Candy. **SIC:** 5145 (Confectionery). **Sales:** $13,000,000 (2000). **Emp:** 100. **Officers:** Jorge Carulla, President; Pietro Fenu, COO; Paul Navarro, VP of Sales.

■ 12315 ■ **Richfood Holdings Inc.**
PO Box 26967
Richmond, VA 23261-6967
Phone: (804)746-6000   **Fax:** (804)746-6179
Products: Groceries. **SIC:** 5141 (Groceries—General Line). **Sales:** $3,411,600,000 (2000). **Emp:** 5,151. **Officers:** John E. Stokely, President & COO; David W. Hoover, VP of Finance.

■ 12316 ■ **Richfood Inc.**
PO Box 26967
Richmond, VA 23261-6967
Phone: (804)746-6000   **Fax:** (804)746-6057
Products: Perishable foods; Grocery wholesaler. **SIC:** 5141 (Groceries—General Line). **Est:** 1935. **Sales:** $4,500,000,000 (1999). **Emp:** 5,900. **Officers:** Alec C. Covington, President & CEO; Michael Rotelle III, VP of Human Resources; William C. Stocker, Sr. VP of Marketing; Larry King, Exec. VP.

■ 12317 ■ **Richman's Ice Cream Div.**
Rte. 40 and Kings Hwy.
Woodstown, NJ 08098
Phone: (609)769-0350   **Fax:** (609)769-0397
Products: Ice cream. **SIC:** 5143 (Dairy Products Except Dried or Canned). **Sales:** $3,000,000 (1994). **Emp:** 40. **Officers:** Mario Calbi, CEO.

■ 12318 ■ **Rimfire Imports, Inc.**
831-106 Eha St.
Wailuku, HI 96793
Phone: (808)242-6888   **Fax:** (808)242-9217
Products: Specialty gourmet products for foodservice. **SICs:** 5147 (Meats & Meat Products); 5146 (Fish & Seafoods); 5143 (Dairy Products Except Dried or Canned). **Est:** 1914. **Sales:** $5,000,000 (2000). **Emp:** 9. **Officers:** Sam Stephens, President; Ron Neal, Vice President.

■ 12319 ■ **A.J. Rinella and Company Inc.**
Broadway Menands Regional Market
Albany, NY 12204
Phone: (518)465-4581
Products: Fresh produce, including lettuce, tomatoes, and onions. **SIC:** 5148 (Fresh Fruits & Vegetables). **Est:** 1950. **Sales:** $10,000,000 (2000). **Emp:** 20. **Officers:** Peter Rinella, President; A.J. Rinella, CFO.

■ 12320 ■ **Ritchie Grocer Co.**
PO Box 71
El Dorado, AR 71730
Phones: (870)863-8191   (870)863-8192
Fax: (870)863-8193
Products: General line groceries. **SIC:** 5141 (Groceries—General Line). **Est:** 1886. **Sales:** $12,000,000 (2000). **Emp:** 50. **Officers:** J.S. Benson, President; J. S. Benson Jr., VP, CFO & Secty.

■ 12321 ■ **Ritter Sysco Food Services Inc.**
640 Dowd Ave.
Elizabeth, NJ 07207
Phone: (908)558-2700   **Fax:** (908)558-2791
Products: Food for restaurants and schools; Commercial cooking equipment. **SICs:** 5141 (Groceries—General Line); 5142 (Packaged Frozen Foods); 5149 (Groceries & Related Products Nec). **Est:** 1922. **Sales:** $170,000,000 (2000). **Emp:** 400. **Officers:** Martin Ritter, President; Karen Casey, VP & CFO; Peter Floerscheimer, Dir. of Marketing; John Linden, Exec. VP; Joan Schluter, Dir of Human Resources.

■ 12322 ■ **Riverside Foods**
2520 Wilson
Two Rivers, WI 54241
Phone: (920)793-4511   **Fax:** (920)793-5923
URL: http://www.riversidefoods.com
Products: Food. **SIC:** 5146 (Fish & Seafoods). **Est:** 1956. **Sales:** $12,000,000 (2000). **Emp:** 100. **Officers:** Mark A. Kornely, President. **Former Name:** Riverside Seafoods Inc.

■ 12323 ■ **Riverside Homemade Ice Cream**
409 Marion Cardington Rd. W
Marion, OH 43301
Phone: (740)389-1013
Products: Ice cream. **SIC:** 5143 (Dairy Products Except Dried or Canned).

■ 12324 ■ **Riverside Potatoes Inc.**
23611 Adams Point Rd.
PO Box 535
Merrill, OR 97633
Phone: (541)798-5184   **Fax:** (541)798-0160
Products: Potatoes. **SIC:** 5148 (Fresh Fruits & Vegetables). **Est:** 1984. **Emp:** 30. **Officers:** Terry Guthrie, President.

■ 12325 ■ **Riviana Foods Inc.**
PO Box 2636
Houston, TX 77252-2141
Phone: (713)529-3251   **Fax:** (713)529-1866
Products: Rice; Crackers and cookies, processed fruits and vegetables. **SICs:** 5149 (Groceries & Related Products Nec); 5148 (Fresh Fruits & Vegetables). **Est:** 1911. **Sales:** $463,000,000 (2000). **Emp:** 2,751. **Officers:** Joseph A. Hafner Jr., CEO & President; E. Wayne Ray Jr., VP, CFO & Treasurer.

■ 12326 ■ **RLB Food Distributors L.P.**
2 Dedrick Pl.
West Caldwell, NJ 07007
Phone: (973)575-9526   **Fax:** (973)575-1019
Products: Produce and deli products. **SIC:** 5148 (Fresh Fruits & Vegetables). **Sales:** $5,000,000 (2000). **Emp:** 125. **Officers:** Robert L. Bildner, President; Barbara Bear, Controller; Floyd Avillo, Dir. of Operations.

■ 12327 ■ **RMC Foods, Inc.**
PO Box 338
St. George, UT 84771
Phone: (435)673-3583   **Fax:** (435)628-4985
Products: Fresh produce. **SIC:** 5148 (Fresh Fruits & Vegetables). **Est:** 1941. **Sales:** $55,000,000 (2000). **Emp:** 170. **Officers:** B. Stucki, President; E.W. Stucki, Controller.

■ 12328 ■ **Roberts Dairy Co.**
PO Box 1435
Omaha, NE 68101
Phone: (402)344-4321   **Fax:** (402)345-1987
Products: Dairy products, including milk, sour cream, cottage cheese, ice cream, and butter. **SIC:** 5143 (Dairy Products Except Dried or Canned). **Est:** 1906. **Emp:** 49. **Officers:** Ron Richardson.

■ 12329 ■ **Roberts Dairy Co.**
3805 Van Brunt Blvd.
Kansas City, MO 64128
Phone: (816)921-7370   **Fax:** (816)921-3437
Products: Dairy products including, ice cream and milk; Juice; Cultured products. **SICs:** 5143 (Dairy Products Except Dried or Canned); 5149 (Groceries & Related Products Nec). **Est:** 1913. **Sales:** $92,000,000 (1999). **Emp:** 247. **Officers:** Jeff Powell, General Mgr.; Robert Bixler, Asst. General Mgr.; Don Fisher, Dir. of Data Processing & Controller; Larry Boudeman, Marketing & Sales Mgr. **Former Name:** Fairmont Roberts Dairy Co.

■ 12330 ■ **Roberts Foods Inc.**
1615 W Jefferson St.
Springfield, IL 62702
Phone: (217)793-2633   **Fax:** (217)793-3054
Products: Fresh produce. **SIC:** 5148 (Fresh Fruits & Vegetables). **Est:** 1912. **Sales:** $25,000,000 (2000). **Emp:** 80. **Officers:** Dean Robert Jr., President; Steve LaRocca, CFO; Jerry Kalteux, Dir. of Marketing & Sales; Gregg Haack, Dir. of Data Processing.

■ 12331 ■ **Robins Brokerage Co.**
PO Box 1506
Salt Lake City, UT 84110
Phone: (801)974-0500   **Fax:** (801)972-0429
E-mail: rbc@utah-inter.net
Products: Canned fruits; Canned vegetables; Crackers; Potato chips; Cured or smoked meat; Foot; Cleaning products; Sugar; Cereal. **SICs:** 5141 (Groceries—General Line); 5145 (Confectionery); 5147 (Meats & Meat Products); 5149 (Groceries & Related Products Nec). **Est:** 1882. **Sales:** $2,500,000 (1999). **Emp:** 40. **Officers:** John H. Robins, CEO; Richard Robins, President; Roger Player, Chairman of the Board & Finance Officer.

■ 12332 ■ **Robin's Food Distribution Inc.**
PO Box 617637
Chicago, IL 60661
Phone: (312)243-8800 **Fax:** (312)243-9495
Products: Food; Fresh meats, including fish, beef, chicken, and pork; Cereal; Ice cream; Milk; Produce. **SICs:** 5141 (Groceries—General Line); 5143 (Dairy Products Except Dried or Canned); 5148 (Fresh Fruits & Vegetables). **Est:** 1981. **Sales:** $14,900,000 (2000). **Emp:** 22. **Officers:** Robin Wold, President; Ilene Quinn, Controller.

■ 12333 ■ **Robinson Barbecue Sauce Company Inc.**
942 Madison St.
Oak Park, IL 60302
Phone: (708)383-1333
Free: (800)836-6750 **Fax:** (708)383-9486
Products: Prepared sauces. **SIC:** 5149 (Groceries & Related Products Nec). **Est:** 1982. **Sales:** $800,000 (2000). **Emp:** 49. **Officers:** Charlie Robinson.

■ 12334 ■ **Robzens Inc.**
240 River St.
Scranton, PA 18505-1182
Phone: (717)344-1141 **Fax:** (717)961-5798
Products: Beef. **SIC:** 5147 (Meats & Meat Products). **Sales:** $43,000,000 (2000). **Emp:** 140. **Officers:** Sidney Robzen, CEO.

■ 12335 ■ **Rock Island North**
38 Hamilton Dr.
Ignacio, CA 94949
Phone: (415)883-2375 **Fax:** (415)883-9550
Products: Ice cream. **SIC:** 5143 (Dairy Products Except Dried or Canned). **Est:** 1972.

■ 12336 ■ **Rock River Provision Company Inc.**
3309 W Rock Falls Rd.
Rock Falls, IL 61071
Phone: (815)625-1195
E-mail: butcher@cin.net
Products: Beef and pork; Seafood; Poultry; Produce; Frozen foods, including vegetables, potato products, and fruits; Dairy products; Dry goods, including bakery products and canned foods; Chemicals. **SICs:** 5147 (Meats & Meat Products); 5143 (Dairy Products Except Dried or Canned); 5146 (Fish & Seafoods); 5169 (Chemicals & Allied Products Nec). **Est:** 1954. **Sales:** $10,000,000 (2000). **Emp:** 40. **Officers:** David Hoffman, President.

■ 12337 ■ **Rockview Farms Inc.**
PO Box 668
Downey, CA 90241
Phone: (562)927-5511 **Fax:** (562)928-9866
Products: Dairy products. **SIC:** 5143 (Dairy Products Except Dried or Canned). **Est:** 1967. **Sales:** $100,000,000 (2000). **Emp:** 200. **Officers:** E.J. Degroot, President & Chairman of the Board; F. Medearis, Controller.

■ 12338 ■ **Rocky Mountain Food Factory Inc.**
2825 S Raritan St.
Englewood, CO 80110
Phone: (303)761-3330 **Fax:** (303)761-0447
Products: Mexican canned specialties and frozen foods. **SICs:** 5142 (Packaged Frozen Foods); 5149 (Groceries & Related Products Nec). **Sales:** $2,000,000 (2000). **Emp:** 20. **Officers:** Mercedes Huang, President; Whittak Huang, Treasurer.

■ 12339 ■ **Rocky Mountain Marketing Services Inc.**
10885 E 51st Ave.
Denver, CO 80239
Phone: (303)371-9770 **Fax:** (303)371-2349
Products: Food. **SIC:** 5141 (Groceries—General Line). **Sales:** $44,000,000 (1993). **Emp:** 85. **Officers:** Rick C. Gervasini, President.

■ 12340 ■ **Rocky Mountain Natural Meats Inc.**
2351 E 70th Ave.
Denver, CO 80229
Phone: (303)287-7100
Free: (800)327-2706 **Fax:** (303)287-7272
Products: Buffalo meat; Cervena venison; Game birds; Wild boar; Ostrich/emu. **SIC:** 5147 (Meats &

Meat Products). **Est:** 1986. **Sales:** $3,800,000 (1999). **Emp:** 9. **Officers:** Bob Dineen, President.

■ 12341 ■ **Rodgers International Trading Inc.**
16716 Wanda Ct. SE, No. 1
Yelm, WA 98597
Phone: (206)458-2203
Products: Packaged frozen foods; Poultry and poultry products; Fresh fruit and vegetables; Irrigation equipment. **SICs:** 5148 (Fresh Fruits & Vegetables); 5142 (Packaged Frozen Foods); 5144 (Poultry & Poultry Products); 5083 (Farm & Garden Machinery). **Officers:** Raymond F. Rodgers, President.

■ 12342 ■ **Rodon Foods**
1333 West 7900 South
West Jordan, UT 84088-9438
Phone: (801)566-0616 **Fax:** (801)566-6931
Products: Food. **SIC:** 5141 (Groceries—General Line). **Emp:** 49. **Officers:** Cory Rasmussen; Scott Rasmussen.

■ 12343 ■ **Rodriguez Festive Foods Inc.**
PO Box 4369
Ft. Worth, TX 76164-0369
Phone: (817)624-2123
Free: (800)486-0361 **Fax:** (817)624-9955
URL: http://www.rodriguezfoods.com
Products: Mexican food. **SIC:** 5149 (Groceries & Related Products Nec). **Est:** 1965. **Sales:** $30,000,000 (2000). **Emp:** 499. **Officers:** Rudy Rodriguez, e-mail: rudy@rodriguezfoods.com; David Sheehan, Controller, e-mail: dsheehan@rodriguezfoods.com.

■ 12344 ■ **Rogers Brothers Wholesale Inc.**
470 E Brooks St.
Galesburg, IL 61401
Phone: (309)342-2127
Products: Fresh fruits and vegetables, frozen foods, canned goods, meat and dairy products. **SICs:** 5148 (Fresh Fruits & Vegetables); 5142 (Packaged Frozen Foods); 5149 (Groceries & Related Products Nec); 5147 (Meats & Meat Products). **Sales:** $11,000,000 (2000). **Emp:** 35. **Officers:** George Rogers, CEO.

■ 12345 ■ **Rohtstein Corp.**
PO Box 2129
Woburn, MA 01888
Phone: (781)935-8300 **Fax:** (781)932-3917
Products: General groceries. **SIC:** 5141 (Groceries—General Line). **Sales:** $45,000,000 (2000). **Emp:** 90. **Officers:** Steven Rohtstein, President; Misha Santoso, Controller.

■ 12346 ■ **Roland Foods**
2421 Schuster Dr.
Cheverly, MD 20781
Phone: (301)322-5444 **Fax:** (301)322-5460
Products: Specialty foods; Gourmet foods. **SIC:** 5149 (Groceries & Related Products Nec).

■ 12347 ■ **Rolet Food Products Co.**
70 Scott Ave.
Brooklyn, NY 11237
Phone: (718)497-0476
Free: (800)229-0476 **Fax:** (718)497-0137
Products: Pork rinds, potato sticks, and beef sticks. **SICs:** 5145 (Confectionery); 5147 (Meats & Meat Products); 5149 (Groceries & Related Products Nec). **Emp:** 49. **Officers:** Charles E. Littman, Vice President.

■ 12348 ■ **Roma Food Enterprises Inc.**
45 Stanford Rd.
Piscataway, NJ 08854
Phone: (908)463-7662 **Fax:** (908)356-4852
Products: Italian specialty goods, including mozzarella cheese and canned tomatoes. **SICs:** 5149 (Groceries & Related Products Nec); 5147 (Meats & Meat Products). **Est:** 1955. **Sales:** $210,000,000 (2000). **Emp:** 450. **Officers:** Louis Piancone, CEO & President; Joe Meola, CFO.

■ 12349 ■ **Romeo & Sons**
100 Romeo Ln.
Uniontown, PA 15401-2337
Phone: (724)438-5561 **Fax:** (724)438-1149
Products: Food; Paper and allied products. **SICs:** 5141 (Groceries—General Line); 5149 (Groceries &

Related Products Nec). **Est:** 1936. **Emp:** 49. **Officers:** Frank A. Romeo; Ronald J. Romeo; Frank S. Romeo.

■ 12350 ■ **Ron's Produce Company Inc.**
4504 S Country Club Rd.
Tucson, AZ 85714-2046
Phone: (520)294-3796 **Fax:** (520)294-6904
Products: Fruits and vegetables. **SIC:** 5148 (Fresh Fruits & Vegetables). **Emp:** 15.

■ 12351 ■ **Roots & Fruits Cooperative Produce**
451E Industrial Blvd. NE
Minneapolis, MN 55413-2930
Phone: (612)722-3030 **Fax:** (612)722-0882
Products: Produce. **SIC:** 5148 (Fresh Fruits & Vegetables).

■ 12352 ■ **Rose Hill Distribution Inc.**
81 Rose Hill Rd.
Branford, CT 06405
Phone: (203)488-7231 **Fax:** (203)488-2100
Products: Poultry. **SIC:** 5144 (Poultry & Poultry Products). **Est:** 1945. **Sales:** $13,000,000 (2000). **Emp:** 29. **Officers:** Frank Vastola, President; David Schebell, Vice President; Matt Oliver, Dir. of Sales.

■ 12353 ■ **Roselli's Wholesale Foods Inc.**
33069 Groesbeck Hwy.
Fraser, MI 48026
Phone: (810)296-9780
Products: Meats; Cheese; Food containers. **SICs:** 5141 (Groceries—General Line); 5147 (Meats & Meat Products); 5143 (Dairy Products Except Dried or Canned); 5113 (Industrial & Personal Service Paper). **Est:** 1971. **Sales:** $10,000,000 (2000). **Emp:** 35. **Officers:** Antonio Roselli, President.

■ 12354 ■ **Mark Ross and Company International**
PO Box 410506
San Francisco, CA 94141-0506
Phone: (415)285-5500 **Fax:** (415)285-8836
URL: http://www.globalexporter.com
Products: Food; Clothing; Construction materials; Industrial equipment and parts; Peas and beans. **SICs:** 5141 (Groceries—General Line); 5146 (Fish & Seafoods). **Est:** 1946. **Sales:** $26,000,000 (2000). **Emp:** 14. **Officers:** Mina Vitlin, President; James J. Connell, VP & General Merchandising Mgr.

■ 12355 ■ **Rotelle Inc.**
PO Box 370
West Point, PA 19486
Phone: (215)699-5300 **Fax:** (215)699-4401
Products: Fresh produce. **SIC:** 5148 (Fresh Fruits & Vegetables). **Est:** 1926. **Emp:** 350. **Officers:** John Rotelle, President; Joe Pugliese, Finance Officer; Frank Mastrangelo, Sales Mgr.; George Marin, VP of Operations; Michael Rotelle III, Dir of Human Resources.

■ 12356 ■ **Roundy's Foods**
4501 Peters Rd.
Evansville, IN 47711
Phone: (812)423-8034 **Fax:** (812)422-4035
Products: Food. **SIC:** 5141 (Groceries—General Line). **Sales:** $30,000,000 (2000). **Emp:** 70. **Officers:** Fred Cox, President; Don Totten, CFO.

■ 12357 ■ **Roundy's, Inc.**
23000 Roundy Dr.
Pewaukee, WI 53072-4095
Phone: (262)953-7999 **Fax:** (262)953-7989
URL: http://www.roundys.com
Products: Groceries. **SIC:** 5141 (Groceries—General Line). **Est:** 1872. **Sales:** $2,700,000,000 (1999). **Emp:** 8,000. **Officers:** Jerry Lestina, CEO & President; Robert D. Ranus, VP & CFO; Marion Sullivan, VP of Marketing; Charles Kosmaler, VP of Information Systems.

■ 12358 ■ **Roundy's Inc.**
1100 Prosperity Rd.
Lima, OH 45801
Phone: (419)228-3141 **Fax:** (419)998-2579
Products: Groceries. **SIC:** 5141 (Groceries—General Line). **Est:** 1962. **Sales:** $580,000,000 (2000). **Emp:** 675. **Officers:** Stan Alexander, President; John

Zachary, VP of Sales; Michael Christy; Mike Parish, Dir. of Systems.

■ 12359 ■ Roundy's Inc. Eldorado Div.
PO Box 411
Eldorado, IL 62930
Phone: (618)273-2671
Products: Groceries. **SIC:** 5141 (Groceries—General Line). **Sales:** $17,000,000 (2000). **Emp:** 325. **Officers:** W. Swart, President; A. Vogel, Controller.

■ 12360 ■ Roundy's Inc. Lima Div.
1100 Prosperity Rd.
Lima, OH 45801
Phone: (419)228-3141 **Fax:** (419)998-2579
Products: General line of groceries. **SICs:** 5141 (Groceries—General Line); 5142 (Packaged Frozen Foods). **Sales:** $420,000,000 (2000). **Emp:** 600. **Officers:** Stan Alexander, President; Robert Henry, VP of Finance.

■ 12361 ■ Roundy's Westville Div.
PO Box 125
Westville, IN 46391
Phone: (219)785-4671 **Fax:** (219)785-4774
Products: Groceries. **SIC:** 5141 (Groceries—General Line). **Sales:** $280,000,000 (2000). **Emp:** 375. **Officers:** Gregg Claassen, President; Steve Davis, VP of Finance.

■ 12362 ■ R.J. Rous Inc.
4366 W Ogden Ave.
Chicago, IL 60623
Phone: (773)521-3663
Products: Milk and cream. **SIC:** 5143 (Dairy Products Except Dried or Canned). **Est:** 1918. **Sales:** $5,000,000 (2000). **Emp:** 3. **Officers:** Rudolph J. Rous, President; Joseph Rous, Treasurer & Secty.

■ 12363 ■ Royal Cup Inc.
PO Box 170971
Birmingham, AL 35217-0971
Phone: (205)849-5836
Free: (800)366-5636 **Fax:** (205)841-8210
Products: Food products. **SIC:** 5142 (Packaged Frozen Foods). **Sales:** $130,000,000 (2000). **Emp:** 500. **Officers:** Hatton Smith, President; Lamar Bagby, VP of Finance.

■ 12364 ■ Royal Foods Distributors Inc.
215 Blair Rd.
Woodbridge, NJ 07095
Phone: (732)636-0900 **Fax:** (732)855-6341
Products: Perishable foods. **SICs:** 5141 (Groceries—General Line); 5149 (Groceries & Related Products Nec). **Sales:** $220,000,000 (2000). **Emp:** 400. **Officers:** Jack Zumba, President; Pat McGrath, Controller; Mitchell Klein, Dir. of Marketing; Lynn Volpe, Dir. of Data Processing; Mike Tait, Dir of Human Resources.

■ 12365 ■ Royal Seafoods Inc.
PO Box 1347
Wharf 2
Monterey, CA 93942
Phone: (408)373-7920 **Fax:** (408)373-8336
Products: Seafood. **SIC:** 5146 (Fish & Seafoods). **Sales:** $6,000,000 (2000). **Emp:** 49. **Officers:** Giuseppi Pennisi, President; Elaine Pennisi, Vice President.

■ 12366 ■ Rudis Bakery
3640 Walnut
Boulder, CO 80301-2500
Phone: (303)447-0495 **Fax:** (303)447-0516
Products: Breads, rolls, and related products. **SIC:** 5149 (Groceries & Related Products Nec). **Est:** 1976. **Sales:** $5,000,000 (1999). **Emp:** 60. **Officers:** Sheldon Romer, President; John D. Hay, CEO.

■ 12367 ■ Russell Stover Candies
4900 Oak Street
Kansas City, MO 64112
Phone: (816)842-9240 **Fax:** (816)842-5593
Products: Candy; Chocolate and chocolate-type confectionery products. **SIC:** 5145 (Confectionery). **Est:** 1923. **Emp:** 225. **Officers:** Scott H. Ward, Co-President; Thomas S. Ward, Co-President; Bob Love,

Sr. VP of Sales; Robinn Wiber, VP of Human Resources.

■ 12368 ■ Russell Stover Candies
4900 Oaks St.
Kansas City, MO 64112
Phone: (816)842-9240 **Fax:** (816)842-5593
Products: Candy; Chocolate and chocolate-type confectionery products. **SIC:** 5145 (Confectionery).

■ 12369 ■ Russells Ice Cream
2575 South 300 West
Salt Lake City, UT 84115-2908
Phone: (801)484-8724 **Fax:** (801)484-8768
Products: Ice cream. **SIC:** 5143 (Dairy Products Except Dried or Canned). **Sales:** $8,000,000 (2000). **Emp:** 35. **Officers:** Howard J. Russell; Richard J. Russell; David L. Russell; Doug L. Russell; Lynn H. Russell.

■ 12370 ■ Russo Farms Inc.
1962 S East Ave.
Vineland, NJ 08360
Phone: (609)692-5942
Products: Produce. **SIC:** 5148 (Fresh Fruits & Vegetables). **Est:** 1972. **Sales:** $8,000,000 (2000). **Emp:** 100. **Officers:** Damian Russo, Partner; Thomas Russo, Partner.

■ 12371 ■ Rust Wholesale Company Inc.
PO Box 230
Greensburg, IN 47240
Phone: (812)663-7394 **Fax:** (812)663-3005
E-mail: rustsales@voyager.net
URL: http://www.rustwholesale.com
Products: Candy; Children's clothing; Toys; Crafts; Housewares; Party supplies; Stationary; Seasonal products; Fabrics, sewing notions and yarns; Ready-to-wear. **SICs:** 5199 (Nondurable Goods Nec); 5092 (Toys & Hobby Goods & Supplies); 5137 (Women's/Children's Clothing); 5141 (Groceries—General Line). **Est:** 1937. **Sales:** $32,000,000 (2000). **Emp:** 90. **Officers:** Joseph F. Rust, President & Treasurer; Susan A. Rust, Secretary; Darwin Lytle, Dir. of Sales; Richard C. Rust, Dir of Personnel.

■ 12372 ■ W.E. Ryan Company Inc.
2325 N American
Philadelphia, PA 19133-3308
Phone: (215)427-3030 **Fax:** (215)427-0903
Products: Frozen poultry; Eggs; Butter; Cheese, natural and processed; Frozen foods. **SICs:** 5143 (Dairy Products Except Dried or Canned); 5144 (Poultry & Poultry Products); 5142 (Packaged Frozen Foods). **Emp:** 26. **Officers:** L. C. Campanale, President.

■ 12373 ■ Ryan's Wholesale Food Distributors
PO Box 30838
Billings, MT 59107
Phone: (406)657-1400 **Fax:** (406)657-1532
Products: Groceries; Hair care products; House cleaning products. **SICs:** 5149 (Groceries & Related Products Nec); 5122 (Drugs, Proprietaries & Sundries); 5169 (Chemicals & Allied Products Nec). **Sales:** $110,000,000 (2000). **Emp:** 350. **Officers:** Bill Benzing, CEO; Tom Morris, Controller.

■ 12374 ■ S.E. Rykoff & Co.
PO Box 13489
Phoenix, AZ 85002
Phone: (602)352-3300
Products: Food; Restaurant supplies. **SICs:** 5141 (Groceries—General Line); 5113 (Industrial & Personal Service Paper).

■ 12375 ■ Rykoff-Sexton Distribution Div.
9755 Patuxent Woods Dr.
Columbia, MD 21046-2286
Products: Groceries; Meats; Canned fruit; Dairy products. **SICs:** 5141 (Groceries—General Line); 5147 (Meats & Meat Products); 5149 (Groceries & Related Products Nec); 5143 (Dairy Products Except Dried or Canned). **Est:** 1883. **Sales:** $1,433,200,000 (2000). **Emp:** 2,500. **Officers:** Gary Cooper, President & COO; Jim Couch, CFO; George Collins, Dir. of Marketing & Sales; Gene Karczewski, Dir. of Data Processing; Fred Gillette, Dir of Human Resources.

■ 12376 ■ Rykoff-Sexton Inc.
9755 Patuxent Woods Dr.
Columbia, MD 21046-2286
Products: Groceries and related products. **SIC:** 5141 (Groceries—General Line). **Est:** 1911. **Sales:** $1,789,500,000 (2000). **Emp:** 5,400. **Officers:** Mark Van Stekelenburg, CEO & Chairman of the Board; Richard J. Martin, Sr. VP & CFO; Thomas O. Brant, VP of Information Systems; Robert Harter Jr., Sr. VP of Human Resources.

■ 12377 ■ Rykoff-Sexton Manufacturing L.L.C.
737 Terminal St.
Los Angeles, CA 90021
Phone: (213)622-4131 **Fax:** (213)689-9766
Products: Food items and restaurant supplies. **SICs:** 5141 (Groceries—General Line); 5142 (Packaged Frozen Foods); 5149 (Groceries & Related Products Nec); 5199 (Nondurable Goods Nec). **Sales:** $152,000,000 (2000). **Emp:** 250. **Officers:** Jerry Reich, President; David F. McAnally, Sr. VP & CFO.

■ 12378 ■ Rymer Foods Inc.
4600 S Packers Ave.
Chicago, IL 60609
Phone: (773)927-7777 **Fax:** (773)650-0500
E-mail: info@rymerfoods.com
URL: http://www.rymerfoods.com
Products: Meat, including beef, chicken, and seafood. **SICs:** 5146 (Fish & Seafoods); 5147 (Meats & Meat Products). **Est:** 1893. **Sales:** $33,900,000 (2000). **Emp:** 228. **Officers:** P. Edward Schenk, CEO, President & Chairman of the Board; Edward M. Hebert, Sr. VP of Finance & Treasurer.

■ 12379 ■ S and D Coffee Inc.
300 Concord Pky. S
Concord, NC 28027
Phone: (704)782-3121 **Free:** (800)933-2210
URL: http://www.sndcoffee.com
Products: Coffee; Tea; Juice. **SICs:** 5141 (Groceries—General Line); 5149 (Groceries & Related Products Nec). **Est:** 1927. **Emp:** 475. **Officers:** J.R. Davis Jr., CEO & President; Steven Cole, Exec. VP of Finance; Ron Hinson, Exec. VP of Marketing & Sales.

■ 12380 ■ S and M Food Service Inc.
12935 Lake Charles Hwy.
Leesville, LA 71446
Phone: (318)537-3588
Products: Fresh, canned, and frozen fruits and vegetables. **SICs:** 5148 (Fresh Fruits & Vegetables); 5141 (Groceries—General Line). **Est:** 1956. **Sales:** $5,000,000 (2000). **Emp:** 17. **Officers:** Warren Smith, President; Vicki Rashal, Treasurer & Secty.

■ 12381 ■ S & M Produce
42 S Water Mark
Chicago, IL 60608
Phone: (312)829-0155 **Fax:** (312)829-5442
Products: Fresh produce. **SIC:** 5148 (Fresh Fruits & Vegetables).

■ 12382 ■ S & N Sales
13 West Ln.
Dearborn, MI 48124
Phone: (734)425-8277 **Fax:** (734)427-6065
Products: Polish and Yugoslavian meats. **SIC:** 5147 (Meats & Meat Products). **Est:** 1947. **Sales:** $2,000,000 (2000). **Emp:** 4. **Officers:** Stanley R. Nycek, President.

■ 12383 ■ S and S Meat Company Inc.
637 Prospect Ave.
Kansas City, MO 64124
Phone: (816)241-4700
Products: Beef, pork, lamb and veal. **SIC:** 5147 (Meats & Meat Products). **Sales:** $17,000,000 (1994). **Emp:** 35. **Officers:** John Scavuzzo, President; Don Askey, Finance Office Manager.

■ 12384 ■ Saag's Products Inc.
PO Box 2078
San Leandro, CA 94577
Phone: (510)352-8000
Free: (800)352-SAAG **Fax:** (510)352-4100
Products: Processed meats. **SIC:** 5147 (Meats & Meat Products). **Sales:** $20,000,000 (2000). **Emp:** 85. **Officers:** Jim Mosle; Tim Dam.

■ 12385 ■ Sabrett Food Products
50 Colden St.
Jersey City, NJ 07302
Phone: (201)434-7062
Products: Food. **SIC:** 5149 (Groceries & Related Products Nec). **Officers:** B Adelman, President; M Katz, Treasurer & Secty.

■ 12386 ■ Safa Enterprises Co., Inc.
6803 S Western Ave., No. 409
Oklahoma City, OK 73139
Phone: (405)631-0453 **Fax:** (405)631-0454
Products: Hot sauce; Canned vegetables and juices; Popcorn; Corn oil; Honey. **SICs:** 5149 (Groceries & Related Products Nec); 5145 (Confectionery). **Officers:** Mostafa Radmard, President.

■ 12387 ■ Safier's Inc.
8700 Harvard Ave.
Cleveland, OH 44105
Phone: (216)341-8700
Products: Canned, frozen, and dry foods. **SICs:** 5194 (Tobacco & Tobacco Products); 5145 (Confectionery). **Est:** 1914. **Sales:** $45,000,000 (2000). **Emp:** 65. **Officers:** S.J. Safier, President & Treasurer.

■ 12388 ■ St. Angsar Mills Inc.
PO Box 370
St. Ansgar, IA 50472-0370
Phone: (515)736-4520
Products: Livestock and farm products. **SIC:** 5153 (Grain & Field Beans). **Sales:** $12,000,000 (2000). **Emp:** 14.

■ 12389 ■ St. John's Food Service, Inc.
4 Louise St.
St. Augustine, FL 32095
Phone: (904)824-0493 **Fax:** (904)824-6527
Products: Food, including dairy products, frozen products, meats, seafood, and produce. **SICs:** 5147 (Meats & Meat Products); 5142 (Packaged Frozen Foods); 5148 (Fresh Fruits & Vegetables); 5146 (Fish & Seafoods). **Est:** 1949. **Sales:** $6,000,000 (2000). **Emp:** 20. **Officers:** Melvin McQuaig; Steven McQuaig; Bonnie Andreu.

■ 12390 ■ Saint Louis Restaurant Steaks Inc.
9216 Clayton Rd.
St. Louis, MO 63124
Phone: (314)993-6600 **Fax:** (314)993-6630
Products: Steaks. **SIC:** 5147 (Meats & Meat Products). **Officers:** Jerome M. Mertens, President.

■ 12391 ■ Salasnek Fisheries Inc.
12301 Conant St.
Detroit, MI 48212
Phone: (313)368-2500 **Fax:** (313)368-9657
Products: Fresh fish and seafood. **SIC:** 5146 (Fish & Seafoods). **Sales:** $55,000,000 (2000). **Emp:** 100. **Officers:** Jordan Salasnek, President; Michael Pickens, Treasurer.

■ 12392 ■ Richard Saleff & Son New York Pastry
807 Rennard Cir.
Philadelphia, PA 19116-2921
Phone: (215)698-0525
Products: Pastries. **SIC:** 5149 (Groceries & Related Products Nec). **Est:** 1975. **Sales:** $535,000 (2000). **Emp:** 4. **Officers:** Richard Saleff; Scott Saleff.

■ 12393 ■ Sales Corporation of Alaska
355 E 76th Ave., Ste. 104
Anchorage, AK 99518
Phone: (907)522-3057 **Fax:** (907)344-7932
E-mail: scoa@micronet.net
Products: Groceries; HBA; GM; Giftwares; Outdoor goods; Recreational; Food service; C-stores and distributors. **SIC:** 5141 (Groceries—General Line). **Sales:** $1,000,000 (2000). **Emp:** 12. **Officers:** Mark Cohen, President; Phil Cohen, Treasurer & Secty.; Ron Henderson, Vice President.

■ 12394 ■ Sales Force Companies Inc.
180 Hansen Ct.
Wood Dale, IL 60191-1114
Phone: (630)787-2600 **Fax:** (630)787-1045
Products: General line groceries. **SIC:** 5141 (Groceries—General Line). **Sales:** $490,000,000

(2000). **Emp:** 765. **Officers:** William F. Lee, CEO & President; Thomas Gallagher, CFO & Treasurer.

■ 12395 ■ Sales Force of Omaha
8642 F St.
Omaha, NE 68127
Phone: (402)331-1666 **Fax:** (402)331-1282
Products: Food, including jelly and fish. **SICs:** 5141 (Groceries—General Line); 5149 (Groceries & Related Products Nec); 5146 (Fish & Seafoods). **Sales:** $10,000,000 (2000). **Emp:** 24. **Officers:** Jim Murray, President.

■ 12396 ■ Sales Mark Alpha One Inc.
6400 International Pkwy.
Plano, TX 75093
Phone: (972)349-1100
Products: Food. **SIC:** 5141 (Groceries—General Line). **Sales:** $1,571,000,000 (2000). **Emp:** 3,000. **Officers:** O.R. Smith Jr., President; Jim Morgan, CFO.

■ 12397 ■ Sales Results
1192 Clubview Blvd. S
Columbus, OH 43235
Phone: (614)885-4127 **Fax:** (614)885-2621
Products: Snack foods; Disposables. **SICs:** 5141 (Groceries—General Line); 5149 (Groceries & Related Products Nec). **Est:** 1979. **Emp:** 5. **Officers:** Scot Malenky, Vice President.

■ 12398 ■ A. Sam Farm Inc.
PO Box 591
Dunkirk, NY 14048
Phone: (716)366-6666
Free: (800)344-5496 **Fax:** (716)366-8912
URL: http://www.cabbage.net
Products: Cabbage. **SIC:** 5148 (Fresh Fruits & Vegetables). **Est:** 1943. **Sales:** $30,000,000 (1999). **Emp:** 97. **Officers:** Charles Sam, President.

■ 12399 ■ Sam's Gourmet
1577 N Laurel Ave.
Upland, CA 91786-2216
Phone: (714)986-1908
Products: Sandwiches. **SIC:** 5149 (Groceries & Related Products Nec). **Emp:** 49.

■ 12400 ■ Sam's Ice Cream Inc.
2912 Broadway Blvd. SE
Albuquerque, NM 87101
Phone: (505)764-9524
Products: Ice cream. **SIC:** 5143 (Dairy Products Except Dried or Canned).

■ 12401 ■ San Jacinto Foods
314 S Fannin
Amarillo, TX 79106-6799
Phone: (806)374-4202
Free: (800)530-4994 **Fax:** (806)374-9814
Products: Frozen meat; Fresh meat; Seafood; Frozen juices, ades, drinks, and cocktails; Frozen fruits; Frozen vegetables. **SICs:** 5141 (Groceries—General Line); 5142 (Packaged Frozen Foods); 5147 (Meats & Meat Products); 5149 (Groceries & Related Products Nec); 5146 (Fish & Seafoods). **Emp:** 29. **Officers:** Henry Vogeler, General Mgr.

■ 12402 ■ San Luis Sourdough
3580 Sueldo St.
San Luis Obispo, CA 93401
Phone: (805)544-7687
Free: (800)266-7687 **Fax:** (805)543-1279
Products: Sourdough and french breads. **SIC:** 5149 (Groceries & Related Products Nec). **Est:** 1983. **Sales:** $7,000,000 (2000). **Emp:** 90. **Officers:** Linda West, President.

■ 12403 ■ San Saba Pecan, Inc.
2803 W Wallace
San Saba, TX 76877
Phone: (915)372-5727
Free: (800)683-2101 **Fax:** (915)372-5729
Products: Pecans. **SIC:** 5145 (Confectionery). **Est:** 1973. **Sales:** $10,000,000 (2000). **Emp:** 70. **Officers:** R. D. Adams.

■ 12404 ■ Sanborn Farmers Elevator
PO Box 67
Sanborn, MN 56083
Phone: (507)648-3851 **Fax:** (507)648-3826
Products: Livestock and farm products. **SIC:** 5153 (Grain & Field Beans). **Sales:** $17,000,000 (2000). **Emp:** 13.

■ 12405 ■ Sandridge Foods Corp.
133 Commerce Dr.
Medina, OH 44256
Phone: (330)725-2348
Products: Salads and refrigerated foods. **SIC:** 5148 (Fresh Fruits & Vegetables). **Sales:** $38,000,000 (2000). **Emp:** 350. **Officers:** Mark D. Sandridge, President; William G. Frantz, CFO.

■ 12406 ■ Sandridge Gourmet Salads
133 Commerce Dr.
Medina, OH 44256
Phone: (330)725-2348 **Fax:** (330)722-3998
Products: Salads. **SIC:** 5148 (Fresh Fruits & Vegetables). **Sales:** $10,000,000 (2000). **Emp:** 499. **Officers:** Mark Sandridge.

■ 12407 ■ John B. Sanfilippo Co.
16435 I-Hwy., 35 N
Selma, TX 78154-1200
Phone: (210)651-5300 **Fax:** (210)651-6244
Products: Nuts and dried fruits. **SICs:** 5145 (Confectionery); 5149 (Groceries & Related Products Nec). **Sales:** $198,000,000 (1999). **Emp:** 500. **Officers:** John B. Sanfilippo, President; Bill Pokrajac, Controller.

■ 12408 ■ Gene Sanford and Associates Inc.
PO Box 37589
Phoenix, AZ 85069-7589
Phone: (602)997-6886 **Fax:** (602)997-7590
Products: Prepackaged frozen foods. **SICs:** 5142 (Packaged Frozen Foods); 5141 (Groceries—General Line). **Sales:** $26,000,000 (2000). **Emp:** 50. **Officers:** Gene Sanford, President; Beverly Sanford, Treasurer.

■ 12409 ■ Sanson Co.
4000 Orange Ave.
Cleveland, OH 44115
Phone: (216)431-8560
Products: Produce. **SIC:** 5148 (Fresh Fruits & Vegetables). **Est:** 1929. **Sales:** $20,000,000 (2000). **Emp:** 65. **Officers:** Sam Singalli, Controller.

■ 12410 ■ Santanna Banana Co.
12th & Kelker
Harrisburg, PA 17105
Phone: (717)238-8321 **Fax:** (717)238-4480
Products: Bananas. **SIC:** 5148 (Fresh Fruits & Vegetables). **Emp:** 49. **Officers:** Dave Santana.

■ 12411 ■ Santucci-Trigg Sales Co.
1195 NW 119th St.
Miami, FL 33168
Phone: (305)685-7781
Products: Frozen foods; Processed, frozen, or cooked meats; Dried and dehydrated vegetables. **SICs:** 5141 (Groceries—General Line); 5142 (Packaged Frozen Foods); 5147 (Meats & Meat Products).

■ 12412 ■ Sara Lee Corp.
3 1st National Plz.
Chicago, IL 60602-4260
Phone: (312)726-2600 **Fax:** (312)558-8567
Products: Baked goods; Shoes; Leather products. **SICs:** 5149 (Groceries & Related Products Nec); 5139 (Footwear); 5199 (Nondurable Goods Nec). **Est:** 1939. **Sales:** $12,381,000,000 (2000). **Emp:** 138,000. **Officers:** John H. Bryan Jr., CEO & Chairman of the Board; Michael E. Murphy, Exec. VP & CFO; Rebecca Folds, Dir. of Marketing; Vincent H. Swoyers, VP of Information Systems; Gary C. Grom.

■ 12413 ■ Saratoga Specialties
200 Wrightwood
Elmhurst, IL 60126-1113
Phone: (708)833-3810 **Fax:** (708)833-1932
Products: Spices, including pepper and oregano; Industrial cleaning chemicals. **SICs:** 5149 (Groceries & Related Products Nec); 5169 (Chemicals & Allied

Products Nec). **Sales:** $17,000,000 (2000). **Emp:** 62. **Officers:** J. Chiarugi; Carlton Staten.

■ 12414 ■ **Sargento Foods Inc.**
1 Persnickety Pl.
Plymouth, WI 53073
Phone: (920)893-8484
Free: (800)558-5802   **Fax:** (920)893-8399
URL: http://www.sargento.com
Products: Cheese and cheese related products. **SIC:** 5141 (Groceries—General Line). **Est:** 1953. **Emp:** 1,000. **Officers:** Lou Gentine, CEO & Chairman of the Board. **Former Name:** Sargento Specialty Foods Inc.

■ 12415 ■ **Sargento Foods Inc.**
1 Persnickety Pl
Plymouth, WI 53073
Phone: (920)893-8484   ,   **Free:** (800)558-5802
Products: Cheese packaging. **SIC:** 5143 (Dairy Products Except Dried or Canned).

■ 12416 ■ **Sam Saroff & Company Inc.**
223 Yuma
Manhattan, KS 66502-6235
Phone: (785)776-4846
Products: Fruits and vegetables. **SIC:** 5148 (Fresh Fruits & Vegetables). **Est:** 1943. **Sales:** $4,000,000 (2000). **Emp:** 11. **Officers:** Frank Burns, President.

■ 12417 ■ **Sartori Food Corp.**
107 Pleasant View Rd.
PO Box 258
Plymouth, WI 53073
Phone: (920)893-6061
Free: (800)558-5888   **Fax:** (920)892-2732
E-mail: custserv@sartorifoods.com/
URL: http://www.sartorifoods.com
Products: Italian cheeses. **SIC:** 5143 (Dairy Products Except Dried or Canned). **Est:** 1939. **Emp:** 125. **Officers:** J.C. Sartori, CEO & President; Fred Bowes, Exec. VP of Finance & Admin.; Wayne Casper, Sr. VP of Business Development; Bill Michel, VP of Sales; Ken Sampson, Exec. VP of Operations; Phillis Camilli, Customer Service Contact; Lou Sartori, Human Resources. **Former Name:** Sartori Foods.

■ 12418 ■ **Sathers Inc.**
PO Box 28
Round Lake, MN 56167
Phone: (507)945-8181   **Fax:** (507)945-8343
Products: Candies; Baked goods, including cookies. **SICs:** 5145 (Confectionery); 5149 (Groceries & Related Products Nec). **Est:** 1946. **Sales:** $360,000,000 (2000). **Emp:** 1,500. **Officers:** Bill Bradfield, President; Jim F. Schuller, VP of Finance; Mike Halverson, Dir. of Marketing; Tom Warrant, Information Systems Mgr.

■ 12419 ■ **Satori Herbal-Business Development Labs**
825 W Market
Salinas, CA 93901
Phone: (408)475-6154
Free: (800)444-7286   **Fax:** (408)475-6192
Products: Tea. **SIC:** 5149 (Groceries & Related Products Nec). **Sales:** $3,000,000 (2000). **Emp:** 67. **Officers:** Steven Steigman.

■ 12420 ■ **Keifer Saunders & Associates**
785 S Commerce St.
Jackson, MS 39201-5618
Phone: (601)352-0737   **Fax:** (601)355-1745
Products: Food. **SIC:** 5141 (Groceries—General Line). **Emp:** 49.

■ 12421 ■ **Saval Foods**
6740 Dorsey Rd.
Elkridge, MD 21075
Phone: (410)379-5100
Free: (800)52S-AVAL   **Fax:** (410)379-5109
Products: Deli meats; Condiments; Salads; Fresh produce; Bakery products; Chemicals; Canned goods; smoked fish. **SICs:** 5147 (Meats & Meat Products); 5141 (Groceries—General Line); 5148 (Fresh Fruits & Vegetables); 5169 (Chemicals & Allied Products Nec). **Est:** 1932. **Sales:** $43,000,000 (2000). **Emp:** 143. **Officers:** Paul Saval, President; Albert E. Saval, CEO; Rick Hatcher, VP of Marketing, e-mail: rickhatcher@savalfoods.com; Linda Sevison, Inside Sales Mgr.; Paula Motsay, Human Resources Contact, e-mail:

paulamotsay@savalfoods.com; Jeffrey Saval, VP of Production; Mike Sapperstein, D.S.M.'s; Brian Hopper, D.S.M.'s; Robin Volpe, National Sales Mgr.; Howard Saval, VP of Purchasing. **Alternate Name:** Jud Bacastow.

■ 12422 ■ **Scariano Brothers Inc.**
PO Box 26009
New Orleans, LA 70186
Phone: (504)733-5033
Products: Meat. **SIC:** 5147 (Meats & Meat Products).

■ 12423 ■ **Schaefer's Cold Storage**
9820 D St.
Oakland, CA 94603
Phone: (510)632-5064   **Fax:** (510)632-2754
E-mail: schaefmeat@aol.com
URL: http://www.schaefersmeats.com
Products: Pork; Beef; Lamb; Poultry; Cold storage. **SIC:** 5147 (Meats & Meat Products). **Est:** 1945. **Sales:** $13,000,000 (2000). **Emp:** 13. **Officers:** Otto Schaefer, President; Nelson McAfee, Controller; Warren Cho, VP of Marketing. **Former Name:** Schaefer's Meats Inc.

■ 12424 ■ **Scheidelman Inc.**
1201 Thorn St.
Utica, NY 13502
Phone: (315)732-6186
Free: (800)621-6186   **Fax:** (315)732-6219
Products: Groceries. **SIC:** 5141 (Groceries—General Line). **Est:** 1896. **Sales:** $50,000,000 (2000). **Emp:** 40. **Officers:** Dean Willis, President; Reed F. Willis, CFO; Gary Lenard, Dir. of Systems.

■ 12425 ■ **Bruno Scheidt Inc.**
71 W 23rd St.
New York, NY 10010
Phone: (212)741-8290
Free: (800)221-4030   **Fax:** (212)741-6572
E-mail: sales@rolandfood.com
URL: http://www.rolandfood.com
Products: Gourmet and specialty foods, including caviar, sardines, and truffles. **SIC:** 5149 (Groceries & Related Products Nec). **Est:** 1939. **Emp:** 49. **Officers:** Joanne Scheidt, e-mail: joannescheidt@rolandfood.com

■ 12426 ■ **Schenck Foods Company Inc.**
PO Box 2298
Winchester, VA 22604
Phone: (703)869-1870   **Fax:** (703)869-4273
URL: http://www.schenckfoods.com
Products: Food. **SIC:** 5141 (Groceries—General Line). **Est:** 1928. **Sales:** $36,000,000 (1999). **Emp:** 120. **Officers:** David C. Huntsberry, President.

■ 12427 ■ **Edward J. Schlachter Co. Inc.**
9930 Commerce Park Dr.
Cincinnati, OH 45246
Phone: (513)860-0700   **Fax:** (513)860-0938
Products: Meats; Frozen foods; Soups; Yogurt; Chicken. **SICs:** 5147 (Meats & Meat Products); 5142 (Packaged Frozen Foods); 5143 (Dairy Products Except Dried or Canned); 5144 (Poultry & Poultry Products); 5149 (Groceries & Related Products Nec). **Emp:** 49. **Officers:** Ray Schlachter; Mary Packard; Edward J. Schlachter.

■ 12428 ■ **Schneider Dairy**
726 Frank
Pittsburgh, PA 15227-1210
Phone: (412)881-3525
Free: (800)222-3525   **Fax:** (412)881-7722
Products: Dairy products; Juices. **SICs:** 5143 (Dairy Products Except Dried or Canned); 5149 (Groceries & Related Products Nec). **Est:** 1935. **Sales:** $35,000,000 (2000). **Emp:** 199. **Officers:** William J. Schneider, President.

■ 12429 ■ **Schnieber Fine Food Inc.**
2510 S 64th Ave.
Omaha, NE 68106
Phone: (402)558-5728   **Fax:** (402)466-7352
Products: Seafood. **SIC:** 5146 (Fish & Seafoods). **Sales:** $15,000,000 (2000). **Emp:** 49. **Officers:** Jim Jessen; Mike Sortivo; Richard Westin.

■ 12430 ■ **Schnieber Fine Food Inc.**
2500 State Fair Park Dr.
Lincoln, NE 68504
Phone: (402)466-3663
Products: Groceries, including milk, fresh vegetables, meat, and baked goods. **SICs:** 5141 (Groceries—General Line); 5143 (Dairy Products Except Dried or Canned); 5148 (Fresh Fruits & Vegetables); 5147 (Meats & Meat Products); 5149 (Groceries & Related Products Nec). **Est:** 1991. **Sales:** $30,000,000 (2000). **Emp:** 75. **Officers:** Louis Sortino Jr., General Mgr.; Richard Westin Jr., President; Larry Reigert, Dir. of Marketing & Sales; Steve Schnieber, Controller; Randy Schnieber, Dir of Human Resources.

■ 12431 ■ **Schultz Sav-O Stores Inc.**
PO Box 419
Sheboygan, WI 53082-0419
Phone: (920)457-4433   **Fax:** (920)457-6295
Products: General line groceries. **SIC:** 5141 (Groceries—General Line). **Est:** 1912. **Sales:** $473,000,000 (2000). **Emp:** 1,680. **Officers:** James H. Dickelman, CEO, President & Chairman of the Board; John H. Dahly, Exec. VP & CFO; Michael Houser, Sr. VP of Marketing; Robert A. Hobart, VP of Information Systems; D. Weigel, Dir of Human Resources.

■ 12432 ■ **Schumacher Wholesale Meats Inc.**
1114 Zane Ave. N
Golden Valley, MN 55422
Phone: (612)546-3291   **Fax:** (612)546-0053
Products: Beef; Processed or cured pork. **SIC:** 5147 (Meats & Meat Products). **Emp:** 49. **Officers:** J. F. Schumacher.

■ 12433 ■ **Schwan Wholesale Co.**
221 S 3rd St.
PO Box 710
Devils Lake, ND 58301-0710
Phone: (701)662-4981   **Fax:** (701)662-7399
Products: Groceries. **SIC:** 5149 (Groceries & Related Products Nec). **Est:** 1958. **Emp:** 48. **Officers:** David Schwan; Wade Schwan; Jeff Schwan.

■ 12434 ■ **Sconza Candy Co.**
919 81st Ave.
Oakland, CA 94621-2511
Phone: (510)568-8137
Free: (877)568-8137   **Fax:** (510)638-5792
Products: Candy. **SIC:** 5145 (Confectionery). **Est:** 1939. **Emp:** 49. **Officers:** James Sconza, President; Greg Cater, VP of Sales.

■ 12435 ■ **Scotty's Foods Inc.**
5037 SE Powell Blvd.
Portland, OR 97206
Phone: (503)777-5484
Free: (800)777-5710   **Fax:** (503)777-1174
Products: Sandwiches. **SIC:** 5149 (Groceries & Related Products Nec). **Sales:** $3,000,000 (2000). **Emp:** 35. **Officers:** Jim Worthylake, General Mgr.

■ 12436 ■ **Scrivner Inc.**
PO Box 26030
Oklahoma City, OK 73126
Phone: (405)841-5500   **Fax:** (405)841-5793
Products: Grocery products, including canned and dried foods, dairy products, and meats. **SICs:** 5141 (Groceries—General Line); 5147 (Meats & Meat Products); 5143 (Dairy Products Except Dried or Canned); 5149 (Groceries & Related Products Nec). **Est:** 1918. **Sales:** $3,980,000,000 (2000). **Emp:** 11,000. **Officers:** Jerry D. Metcalf, CEO & Chairman of the Board; Larry K. Kordisch, Exec. VP of Finance; Craig Hoff, VP Marketing & Development; Arlyn Larson, Information Systems Mgr.

■ 12437 ■ **Scrivner Inc. Buffalo Div.**
1 Scrivner St.
Cheektowaga, NY 14227-2721
Phone: (716)668-7200   **Fax:** (716)668-7379
Products: General line groceries. **SIC:** 5141 (Groceries—General Line). **Sales:** $520,000,000 (1993). **Emp:** 1,000. **Officers:** Jerry D. Metcalf, President; Larry Kordisch, CFO.

■ 12438 ■ Scrivner of New York
1 Scrivner Dr.
Cheektowaga, NY 14227
Phone: (716)668-7200 **Fax:** (716)668-7379
Products: Fresh produce; Dried groceries. **SICs:** 5149 (Groceries & Related Products Nec); 5148 (Fresh Fruits & Vegetables); 5149 (Groceries & Related Products Nec). **Est:** 1930. **Sales:** $450,000,000 (2000). **Emp:** 400. **Officers:** Clark Ogle, Sr. VP; Mark Flint, VP of Admin.; Gerald Lindsner, Vice President; Paul Lasley, Dir. of Data Processing; Jack Mitchell, Dir of Human Resources.

■ 12439 ■ Scrivner of North Carolina Inc.
PO Box 565
Warsaw, NC 28398
Phone: (919)293-7821 **Fax:** (919)293-3899
Products: General line groceries; Paper goods or products, including book mailers; Paper towels; Canned vegetables; Fresh meat; Frozen meat; Fresh fish; Frozen fish; Seafood. **SICs:** 5141 (Groceries—General Line); 5113 (Industrial & Personal Service Paper); 5147 (Meats & Meat Products); 5146 (Fish & Seafoods). **Est:** 1943. **Sales:** $360,000,000 (2000). **Emp:** 500. **Officers:** William C. Garner, CEO; Doug Sennglor, Controller; Benny K. Wilson, VP of Sales; Donny Ezzell, Dir. of Systems; Ron Padgett, Dir of Human Resources.

■ 12440 ■ Scrivner of Pennsylvania Inc.
1100 N Sherman St.
York, PA 17402-2131
Phone: (717)755-1976 **Fax:** (717)755-2020
Products: General line groceries. **SIC:** 5141 (Groceries—General Line). **Est:** 1809. **Sales:** $370,000,000 (2000). **Emp:** 1,100. **Officers:** Gerald Totoritis, President; Terry Bush, Controller; Gary Lauer, Dir. of Marketing; Gary Swanson, Dir. of Data Processing; Delores Remlinger, Human Resources Mgr.

■ 12441 ■ Sculli Brothers Inc.
1114-18 S Front St.
Philadelphia, PA 19147
Phone: (215)336-1223
Products: Prepared meat products and cheese. **SICs:** 5147 (Meats & Meat Products); 5143 (Dairy Products Except Dried or Canned). **Sales:** $2,000,000 (2000). **Emp:** 3. **Officers:** Robert Sculli, President.

■ 12442 ■ Sea Harvest Packing Co.
PO Box 818
Brunswick, GA 31521
Phone: (912)264-3212
Free: (800)627-4300 **Fax:** (912)264-2749
E-mail: cwells@technonet.com
URL: http://www.seaharvest.com
Products: Shrimp, scallops, tilapia. **SIC:** 5146 (Fish & Seafoods). **Est:** 1966. **Sales:** $6,000,000 (2000). **Emp:** 85. **Officers:** Charles Wells, President; G.W. Wells, VP & Treasurer; Dick Bobb, Dir. of Marketing.

■ 12443 ■ Sea K. Fish Company Inc.
PO Box 2040
Blaine, WA 98230
Phone: (360)332-5121 **Fax:** (360)332-8785
Products: Fish. **SIC:** 5146 (Fish & Seafoods). **Est:** 1958. **Sales:** $12,000,000 (2000). **Emp:** 100. **Officers:** Martin Kuljis, President; Steve Kulvis, Treasurer.

■ 12444 ■ Sea View Fillet Company Inc.
16 Hassey St.
New Bedford, MA 02740
Phone: (508)994-1233 **Fax:** (508)990-7280
Products: Fish. **SIC:** 5146 (Fish & Seafoods). **Est:** 1969. **Sales:** $28,000,000 (2000). **Emp:** 50. **Officers:** C.L. Nunes, President; E.C. Nunes, CFO; Curtis Nunes, Dir. of Marketing.

■ 12445 ■ Seaboard Corp.
200 Boylston St.
Chestnut Hill, MA 02467
Phone: (617)332-8492
Products: Poultry. **SIC:** 5153 (Grain & Field Beans). **Est:** 1916. **Sales:** $1,053,700,000 (2000). **Emp:** 12,873. **Officers:** H.H. Bresky, President; Joe E. Rodrigues, Exec. VP & CFO; Jack S. Miller, VP of Operations; Tom Martin, Dir of Human Resources.

■ 12446 ■ Seafood Express
248 Chunns Cove Rd.
Asheville, NC 28805
Phone: (704)252-1779
Products: Fresh seafood, including shrimp, halibut, cod, and crab. **SIC:** 5146 (Fish & Seafoods).

■ 12447 ■ Seafood Marketing
814 E Harrison
PO Box 1086
Harlingen, TX 78551
Phone: (956)440-8840
Free: (800)449-8840 **Fax:** (956)440-8845
Products: Seafood. **SIC:** 5146 (Fish & Seafoods).

■ 12448 ■ Seafood Producers Cooperative
2875 Roeder Ave.
Bellingham, WA 98225
Phone: (206)733-0120 **Fax:** (206)733-0513
E-mail: spc@spcsales.com
URL: http://www.spcsales.com
Products: Salmon; Black cod; Halibut. **SIC:** 5146 (Fish & Seafoods). **Est:** 1944. **Sales:** $24,000,000 (2000). **Emp:** 120. **Officers:** Barry S. Lester, CEO; Gerald Smith, CFO; Jeff Reynolds, Dir. of Marketing.

■ 12449 ■ Seafood Wholesalers Inc.
4746 Dodge
San Antonio, TX 78217
Phone: (210)655-4746
Free: (800)209-4746 **Fax:** (210)655-0252
Products: Frozen seafood; Prepared fresh fish and seafood. **SICs:** 5146 (Fish & Seafoods); 5142 (Packaged Frozen Foods). **Est:** 1986. **Sales:** $8,500,000 (2000). **Emp:** 32. **Officers:** James R. Leininger; Wesley Gibson; John P. Starnes. **Former Name:** North Atlantic Seafood Inc.

■ 12450 ■ J.M. Sealts Co.
PO Box 300
Lima, OH 45802
Phone: (419)224-8075 **Fax:** (419)224-8095
Products: Groceries. **SICs:** 5141 (Groceries—General Line); 5142 (Packaged Frozen Foods). **Est:** 1877. **Sales:** $16,500,000 (2000). **Emp:** 26. **Officers:** Monty R. Stubbs Sr., President; Larry Easterday, CFO.

■ 12451 ■ Seashore Food Distributors
1 Satt Bl Railroad Ave.
Rio Grande, NJ 08242-1652
Phone: (609)886-3100 **Fax:** (609)886-7262
E-mail: seashore@jerseycape
Products: Food. **SIC:** 5141 (Groceries—General Line). **Est:** 1920. **Sales:** $7,000,000 (2000). **Emp:** 30. **Officers:** Henry Satt; Ken Cramer; Randy Weist, Sales & Marketing Contact; Lisa Bunch, Customer Service Contact; Mary Anne Satt, Human Resources Contact.

■ 12452 ■ Seasia
4601 6th Ave. S
Seattle, WA 98108-1716
Phone: (206)624-6380 **Fax:** (206)624-0377
Products: Asian food. **SIC:** 5149 (Groceries & Related Products Nec). **Est:** 1966. **Emp:** 50.

■ 12453 ■ Seattle Fish Co.
6211 E 42nd Ave.
Denver, CO 80216
Phone: (303)329-9595 **Fax:** (303)329-4157
E-mail: info@seattlefish.com
URL: http://www.seattlefish.com
Products: Fresh and frozen fish. **SIC:** 5146 (Fish & Seafoods). **Est:** 1917. **Sales:** $45,000,000 (2000). **Emp:** 123. **Officers:** E. Iacino, President.

■ 12454 ■ Seaway Distributors
Rte. 12, Box 128
Alexandria Bay, NY 13607
Phone: (315)482-9903 **Fax:** (315)482-4504
Products: Fish; Tackle. **SICs:** 5146 (Fish & Seafoods); 5091 (Sporting & Recreational Goods).

■ 12455 ■ Seaway Foods Co.
2223 Velp Ave.
Green Bay, WI 54303-6529
Phone: (920)434-1636
Products: Frozen seafood; Prepared fresh fish and seafood. **SICs:** 5146 (Fish & Seafoods); 5142

(Packaged Frozen Foods). **Emp:** 15. **Officers:** Dave Anderson; Dan Tonnon; Jeff Tonnon.

■ 12456 ■ Seawind International
5375 Avenida Encinas, Ste. A
Carlsbad, CA 92008
Phone: (760)438-5600 **Fax:** (760)438-5677
Products: Dried fruit, spices and vegetables. **SIC:** 5149 (Groceries & Related Products Nec). **Est:** 1989. **Officers:** Stephen Ward; Rick Rosenquist.

■ 12457 ■ Secor Elevator Company Inc.
PO Box 79
Secor, IL 61771
Phone: (309)744-2218 **Fax:** (309)744-2416
Products: Livestock and farm products. **SIC:** 5153 (Grain & Field Beans). **Sales:** $14,000,000 (2000). **Emp:** 6.

■ 12458 ■ Select Foods Inc.
PO Box 3097
Hayward, CA 94540
Phone: (510)785-1000 **Free:** ((51))785-5827
Products: Frozen foods. **SIC:** 5142 (Packaged Frozen Foods). **Est:** 1950. **Emp:** 20. **Officers:** Edmond R. Rasnick, CEO; William Rasnick, CFO; Dave Moederman, Dir. of Sales; Mary Hovingh, Dir. of Information Systems.

■ 12459 ■ Self Service Grocery
PO Box 277
Collinsville, VA 24078
Phone: (540)647-3452 **Fax:** (540)647-3452
Products: Groceries, including frozen foods and dry foods. **SICs:** 5141 (Groceries—General Line); 5142 (Packaged Frozen Foods). **Est:** 1978. **Emp:** 4. **Officers:** Hank DeMart, Business Manager.

■ 12460 ■ Senex Harvest States
PO Box 387
Mcville, ND 58254
Phone: (701)322-4317 **Fax:** (701)322-4785
Products: Grain and field beans, agricultural chemicals, fertilizers and other farm supplies. **SICs:** 5153 (Grain & Field Beans); 5191 (Farm Supplies). **Sales:** $14,000,000 (2000). **Emp:** 15. **Officers:** John Jonson, CFO.

■ 12461 ■ Service Brokerage Inc.
PO Box 18316
Shreveport, LA 71138
Phone: (318)688-1400 **Fax:** (318)687-7931
Products: Frozen foods; Health and beauty aids. **SICs:** 5142 (Packaged Frozen Foods); 5122 (Drugs, Proprietaries & Sundries). **Emp:** 49.

■ 12462 ■ Service Supply
2400 N Walnut Rd.
PO Drawer 2090
Turlock, CA 95380
Phone: (209)667-1072 **Fax:** (209)667-6938
Products: Groceries. **SIC:** 5141 (Groceries—General Line).

■ 12463 ■ Services Group of America Inc.
4025 Delridge Way SW, Ste. 500
Seattle, WA 98106
Phone: (206)933-5000 **Fax:** (206)933-5248
Products: General line of groceries. **SIC:** 5141 (Groceries—General Line). **Sales:** $1,412,000,000 (2000). **Emp:** 2,700. **Officers:** Thomas J. Stewart, CEO & Chairman of the Board; Dennis Specht, CFO.

■ 12464 ■ Sessions Company Inc.
PO Box 311310
Enterprise, AL 36331
Phone: (334)393-0200 **Fax:** (334)393-0240
Products: Peanuts. **SIC:** 5159 (Farm-Product Raw Materials Nec). **Sales:** $50,000,000 (2000). **Emp:** 75. **Officers:** Bill Venterss, President; H.M. Sessions Jr., CFO.

■ 12465 ■ Setton's International Foods Inc.
85 Austin Blvd.
Commack, NY 11725
Phone: (516)543-8090
Free: (800)227-4397 **Fax:** (516)543-8070
Products: Unprocessed or shelled nuts. **SIC:** 5145 (Confectionery). **Est:** 1971. **Sales:** $55,000,000 (2000).

Emp: 150. **Officers:** Josh Setton, President; Morris Setton, Vice President.

■ **12466** ■ **Severn Peanut Company Inc.**
PO Box 710
Severn, NC 27877
Phone: (919)585-0838 **Fax:** (919)585-1718
Products: Peanuts. **SIC:** 5159 (Farm-Product Raw Materials Nec). **Est:** 1948. **Sales:** $25,000,000 (2000). **Emp:** 100. **Officers:** Dallas Barnes, President; Keith Ricks, Controller.

■ **12467** ■ **SGA Sales and Marketing Inc.**
155 White Plains Rd
Tarrytown, NY 10591
Phone: (914)694-4090 **Fax:** (914)694-4319
Products: Food. **SIC:** 5141 (Groceries—General Line). **Emp:** 50. **Officers:** Donald Shaevitz, President.

■ **12468** ■ **Shaheen Brothers Inc.**
PO Box 897
Amesbury, MA 01913
Phone: (978)688-1844 **Fax:** (978)388-6617
E-mail: shaheen@seacoast.com
Products: Food, including dried, canned, and frozen; Paper; Chemicals; Produce. **SICs:** 5141 (Groceries—General Line); 5113 (Industrial & Personal Service Paper); 5169 (Chemicals & Allied Products Nec). **Est:** 1940. **Sales:** $25,000,000 (2000). **Emp:** 70. **Officers:** Donald Shaheen, President; Fred Shaheen, VP & Treasurer; Mary A. Janes, Dir. of Marketing.

■ **12469** ■ **Shaklee Distributor**
3440 Lynngate Cir.
Birmingham, AL 35216
Phone: (205)823-2340
Products: Vitamins and health foods. **SICs:** 5149 (Groceries & Related Products Nec); 5122 (Drugs, Proprietaries & Sundries).

■ **12470** ■ **Shaklee Distributor**
15123 Woodland Dr.
Monroe, MI 48161
Phone: (734)242-0712
Products: Health and diet foods. **SIC:** 5149 (Groceries & Related Products Nec).

■ **12471** ■ **Shamrock Farms Creamery**
2434 E Pecan Rd Fl 2
Phoenix, AZ 85040
Phone: (602)243-3244 **Fax:** (602)243-9150
Products: Fresh and frozen dairy products, ice-cream and frozen deserts; Food and related products. **SICs:** 5141 (Groceries—General Line); 5149 (Groceries & Related Products Nec).

■ **12472** ■ **Shamrock Foods Co.**
2228 N Black Canyon Hwy.
Phoenix, AZ 85009
Phone: (602)272-6721 **Fax:** (602)233-2791
Products: Dairy products, including milk, yogurt, and ice cream. **SIC:** 5143 (Dairy Products Except Dried or Canned). **Est:** 1922. **Sales:** $1,052,000,000 (2000). **Emp:** 2,000. **Officers:** Kent McClelland, President; Phil Giltner, CFO; Richard Brooks, VP of Marketing; Wiley Burns, Dir. of Systems; Charlie Roberts, Dir of Human Resources.

■ **12473** ■ **L.P. Shanks Co.**
PO Box 1068
Crossville, TN 38557-1068
Phone: (931)484-5155
Products: Groceries. **SIC:** 5141 (Groceries—General Line). **Sales:** $23,000,000 (1994). **Emp:** 45. **Officers:** Scott Shanks, President; Naomi Noland, Bookkeeper.

■ **12474** ■ **Shari Candies Inc.**
1804 N 2nd St.
Mankato, MN 56001
Phone: (507)387-1181
Free: (800)658-7059 **Fax:** (507)387-4463
Products: Confectionary and related products. **SIC:** 5145 (Confectionery). **Est:** 1944. **Sales:** $22,000,000 (2000). **Emp:** 150. **Officers:** Arlen T. Kitsis, President; Susan Caven, Controller.

■ **12475** ■ **Ted Shear Associates Inc.**
1 West Ave.
Larchmont, NY 10538
Phone: (914)833-0017 **Fax:** (914)833-0233
Products: Specialty foods. **SIC:** 5149 (Groceries & Related Products Nec).

■ **12476** ■ **Shelmar Food**
PO Box 277
Montrose, CA 91021-0277
Phone: (213)585-0972
Products: Fresh meat; Frozen meat; Poultry equipment; Fresh fish; Frozen fish. **SICs:** 5147 (Meats & Meat Products); 5046 (Commercial Equipment Nec); 5142 (Packaged Frozen Foods); 5146 (Fish & Seafoods). **Emp:** 4.

■ **12477** ■ **Shenandoah Foods, Inc.**
4048 Valley Pike
Winchester, VA 22604
Phone: (540)869-6300
Free: (800)888-3287 **Fax:** (540)869-6658
E-mail: jjvsfi@visuallink.com
URL: http://www.ShenandoahFoods.com
Products: Food. **SIC:** 5141 (Groceries—General Line). **Est:** 1967. **Sales:** $12,000,000 (2000). **Emp:** 49. **Officers:** Alson H. Smith, Chairman of the Board; John Good, Vice President.

■ **12478** ■ **Sherwood Food Distributors**
16625 Granite Rd.
Maple Heights, OH 44137
Phone: (216)662-8000 **Fax:** (216)662-1884
Products: Beef; Lamb; Chicken. **SICs:** 5147 (Meats & Meat Products); 5144 (Poultry & Poultry Products). **Sales:** $800,000,000 (1999). **Emp:** 350. **Former Name:** A and W Foods Inc.

■ **12479** ■ **Shimaya Shoten Ltd.**
710 Kohou St.
Honolulu, HI 96817
Phone: (808)845-6691 **Fax:** (808)847-2791
Products: Dry foods, canned goods, and cereal. **SICs:** 5141 (Groceries—General Line); 5149 (Groceries & Related Products Nec). **Est:** 1917. **Sales:** $9,000,000 (2000). **Emp:** 25. **Officers:** Ichiro Onoye, President.

■ **12480** ■ **Shoemakers Candies Inc.**
PO Box 3345
Santa Fe Springs, CA 90670
Phone: (562)944-8811 **Fax:** (562)944-1308
Products: Candy. **SIC:** 5145 (Confectionery). **Sales:** $3,000,000 (2000). **Emp:** 35. **Officers:** Nancy Shoemaker, President.

■ **12481** ■ **Shojin Natural Foods**
PO Box 247
Kealakekua, HI 96750-0247
Phone: (808)322-3651 **Fax:** (808)322-6636
Products: Food. **SIC:** 5141 (Groceries—General Line). **Est:** 1978. **Sales:** $2,000,000 (2000). **Emp:** 15. **Officers:** Franz Weber, General Mgr.

■ **12482** ■ **ShopKo Stores Inc.**
PO Box 19060
Green Bay, WI 54307-9060
Phone: (920)429-2211
URL: http://www.shopko.com
Products: General merchandise. **SIC:** 5141 (Groceries—General Line). **Est:** 1962. **Sales:** $4,000,000,000 (2000). **Officers:** William J. Podany, Chairman of the Board, President & CEO.

■ **12483** ■ **Shopper's Food Warehouse Corp.**
4600 Forbes Blvd.
Lanham, MD 20706
Phone: (301)306-8600
Products: Fruit, meat, and canned goods. **SICs:** 5148 (Fresh Fruits & Vegetables); 5147 (Meats & Meat Products); 5149 (Groceries & Related Products Nec). **Sales:** $540,400,000 (2000). **Emp:** 3,500. **Officers:** Kenneth Herman, President.

■ **12484** ■ **Shurfine International Inc.**
2100 N Mannheim Rd.
Northlake, IL 60164
Phone: (708)236-7100 **Fax:** (708)236-6127
URL: http://shurfine.com
Products: Food, including produce, meat, and non-perishable items. **SICs:** 5141 (Groceries—General Line); 5147 (Meats & Meat Products); 5148 (Fresh Fruits & Vegetables). **Est:** 1948. **Sales:** $1,000,000,000 (2000). **Emp:** 100. **Officers:** James R. Barth, CEO & President; John Stanhaus, Treasurer; Dennis Dangerfield, Sr. VP of Procurement; Jonas Rupkalvis, VP of MIS; Carol Lemmer, Personnel Mgr.

■ **12485** ■ **Shurfine International Inc.**
2100 N Mannheim Rd.
Northlake, IL 60164
Phone: (708)681-2000 **Fax:** (708)681-2067
Products: Groceries; Grocery bags. **SIC:** 5141 (Groceries—General Line). **Sales:** $933,000,000 (2000). **Emp:** 120. **Officers:** James R. Barth, CEO & President; John Stanhaus, CFO.

■ **12486** ■ **Sierra**
PO Box 899
Brisbane, CA 94005
Phone: (650)871-8775
Products: Food preparations; Dried and dehydrated food products; Head rice not packaged with other ingredients; Potatoes; Egg noodle products; Health foods. **SICs:** 5149 (Groceries & Related Products Nec); 5148 (Fresh Fruits & Vegetables).

■ **12487** ■ **Sierra Meat Company Inc.**
PO Box 2456
Reno, NV 89505
Phone: (702)322-4073
Products: Meat, including pork and beef. **SIC:** 5147 (Meats & Meat Products). **Est:** 1966. **Sales:** $21,000,000 (2000). **Emp:** 42. **Officers:** Armando Flocchini, CEO; Steve Rucker, Dir. of Marketing & Sales.

■ **12488** ■ **Sierra Seafood Co.**
PO Box 235
Oakhurst, CA 93644
Phone: (209)683-3479
Products: Seafood. **SIC:** 5146 (Fish & Seafoods).

■ **12489** ■ **Sigma Food Distributing**
25523 Seaboard Lane
Hayward, CA 94545-3209
Phone: (510)785-1492 **Fax:** (510)785-4750
Products: Bakery goods. **SIC:** 5149 (Groceries & Related Products Nec). **Emp:** 49.

■ **12490** ■ **Sigma International Inc.**
333 16th Ave. S
St. Petersburg, FL 33701
Phone: (727)822-1288 **Fax:** (727)822-6782
E-mail: sigma@sigmacorp.com
Products: Prepared fresh fish and seafood, including shrimp. **SIC:** 5146 (Fish & Seafoods). **Est:** 1978. **Sales:** $25,000,000 (2000). **Emp:** 49. **Officers:** Tony Huang; Andy Walton; Anita Layton.

■ **12491** ■ **Silver Foods Corp.**
2935 St. Xavier
Louisville, KY 40212-1936
Phone: (502)778-1649 **Fax:** (502)778-0435
Products: Salad dressings. **SIC:** 5149 (Groceries & Related Products Nec). **Est:** 1945. **Sales:** $6,000,000 (2000). **Emp:** 49. **Officers:** James R. Smith, President.

■ **12492** ■ **Silver Lake Cookie Co.**
141 Freeman Ave.
Islip, NY 11751-1420
Phone: (516)581-4000 **Fax:** (516)581-4510
Products: Cookies. **SIC:** 5149 (Groceries & Related Products Nec). **Est:** 1963. **Sales:** $15,000,000 (1999). **Emp:** 499.

■ **12493** ■ **Silver Springs Farm Inc.**
640 Meeting House Rd.
Harleysville, PA 19438-2247
Phone: (215)256-4321 **Fax:** (215)256-6295
Products: Frozen processed meats. **SIC:** 5147 (Meats & Meat Products). **Emp:** 35. **Officers:** Dan Fillippo.

■ **12494** ■ **Simco Sales Service of Pennsylvania**
3100 Marwin Ave.
Bensalem, PA 19020
Phone: (215)639-2300
Products: Ice cream and frozen desserts. **SIC:** 5143

(Dairy Products Except Dried or Canned). **Est:** 1929. **Sales:** $10,000,000 (2000). **Emp:** 200. **Officers:** Jay Schwartz, President; Mary Fox, CFO; Maria Smith, Dir. of Marketing; Robert Van De Rijn, Dir. of Information Systems.

■ **12495** ■ **Sinbad Sweets Inc.**
2585 N Larkin Ave.
Fresno, CA 93727
Phone: (209)298-3700
Free: (800)350-7932 **Fax:** (209)298-9194
Products: Phyllo dough; Pastries, including baklava, strudel, rugelach, and nut tarts. **SIC:** 5149 (Groceries & Related Products Nec). **Est:** 1978. **Sales:** $5,000,000 (2000). **Emp:** 57. **Officers:** Edwina Sedel, President; Jim Mueller, Marketing & Sales Mgr.; Donna Hardin, Customer Service.

■ **12496** ■ **Sinton Dairy Foods Co. Inc.**
PO Box 578
Colorado Springs, CO 80901
Phone: (719)633-3821
Free: (800)666-4597 **Fax:** (303)294-9215
Products: Milk; Ice cream. **SIC:** 5143 (Dairy Products Except Dried or Canned). **Est:** 1880. **Emp:** 300. **Officers:** John Haberkorn, CEO.

■ **12497** ■ **Sioux Honey Association**
PO Box 388
Sioux City, IA 51102-0388
Phone: (712)258-0638 **Fax:** (712)258-1332
Products: Honey. **SIC:** 5149 (Groceries & Related Products Nec). **Est:** 1921. **Sales:** $60,000,000 (2000). **Emp:** 100. **Officers:** Gary Evans, President.

■ **12498** ■ **Sioux Preme Packing Co.**
PO Box 255
Sioux Center, IA 51250-0255
Phone: (712)722-2555 **Fax:** (712)722-2666
Products: Meat packing plant products; Processed, frozen, or cooked meats; Processed or cured pork. **SICs:** 5147 (Meats & Meat Products); 5142 (Packaged Frozen Foods). **Sales:** $60,000,000 (2000). **Emp:** 99. **Officers:** Stanley G. Lammers.

■ **12499** ■ **SK Food International, Inc.**
PO Box 1236
Wahpeton, ND 58074
Phone: (701)642-3929 **Fax:** (701)642-4102
URL: http://www.skfood.com
Products: Snack foods, including cookies, crackers, and licorice candies; Beverages, including beer; Soybeans; Seeds; Grains. **SICs:** 5149 (Groceries & Related Products Nec); 5145 (Confectionery). **Est:** 1989. **Officers:** David Skyberg, President; Jennifer Tesch, Marketing & Sales Mgr.

■ **12500** ■ **S.K.H. Management Co.**
PO Box 1500
Lititz, PA 17543-7025
Phone: (717)626-4771 **Fax:** (717)626-0499
URL: http://www.skh.com
Products: Groceries. **SIC:** 5141 (Groceries—General Line). **Est:** 1932. **Sales:** $64,000,000 (2000). **Emp:** 950. **Officers:** Paul W. Stauffer, President; Donovan S. Oberholtzer, VP of Information Systems.

■ **12501** ■ **Skidmore Sales & Distributing Company, Inc.**
9889 Cincinnati Dayton Rd.
West Chester, OH 45069
Phone: (513)772-4200
Free: (800)468-SKID **Fax:** (513)772-4931
Products: Industrial food ingredients; Chemicals; Bailers; Bale wire. **SICs:** 5141 (Groceries—General Line); 5149 (Groceries & Related Products Nec); 5169 (Chemicals & Allied Products Nec). **Emp:** 34. **Officers:** Doug Skidmore; Steve Jackson, VP of Sales.

■ **12502** ■ **James Skinner Baking Co.**
4657 G St.
Omaha, NE 68117-1410
Phone: (402)558-7428 **Fax:** (402)588-7817
Products: Frozen baked goods. **SIC:** 5142 (Packaged Frozen Foods). **Est:** 1985. **Sales:** $8,000,000 (2000). **Emp:** 100. **Officers:** Jim Skinner, James Skinner, Owner; Lyn Juric, President.

■ **12503** ■ **Sky Brothers Inc.**
PO Box 632
Altoona, PA 16603
Phone: (814)946-1201 **Fax:** (814)949-8398
Products: Groceries; Paper products, including napkins, towels, and cups. **SICs:** 5142 (Packaged Frozen Foods); 5141 (Groceries—General Line); 5149 (Groceries & Related Products Nec). **Est:** 1946. **Sales:** $180,000,000 (2000). **Emp:** 400. **Officers:** Rocco Alianiello, President; Donna Lakner, Controller; Tony Chwatek, VP of Sales; Terry Green, Dir. of Data Processing.

■ **12504** ■ **M. Slavin and Sons Ltd.**
31 Belmont Ave.
Brooklyn, NY 11212
Phone: (718)495-2800 **Fax:** (718)485-6769
E-mail: info@mslavin.com
URL: http://www.mslavin.com
Products: Fish and seafood, including fresh, frozen, and live; Caviar; Salads; Specialty items. **SIC:** 5146 (Fish & Seafoods). **Est:** 1919. **Sales:** $85,000,000 (2000). **Emp:** 210. **Officers:** Stanley Slavin, President.

■ **12505** ■ **Smart & Final Foodservice**
PO Box 30
Stockton, CA 95201
Phone: (209)948-1814
Products: Food; Restaurant supplies and equipment. **SICs:** 5141 (Groceries—General Line); 5113 (Industrial & Personal Service Paper). **Emp:** 800. **Former Name:** Port Stockton Food Distributors Inc.

■ **12506** ■ **Smith Bros. Food Service Inc.**
PO Box 410
Port Washington, WI 53074-0410
Phone: (414)284-5577
Products: Fresh and frozen fish. **SIC:** 5146 (Fish & Seafoods). **Sales:** $6,000,000 (1994). **Emp:** 35. **Officers:** Ned Huwatschek, President; Chris Gagnon, Mgr. of Finance.

■ **12507** ■ **Smith Brothers Farms Inc.**
27441 68th Ave. S
Kent, WA 98032
Phone: (206)852-1000
Products: Milk. **SIC:** 5143 (Dairy Products Except Dried or Canned). **Est:** 1922. **Sales:** $60,000,000 (2000). **Emp:** 250. **Officers:** Alexis Koester, President; Earl Davenport, Treasurer; Earl Keller, Sales Mgr.

■ **12508** ■ **Smith Brothers Food Service Inc.**
815 Sunset Rd.
PO Box 410
Port Washington, WI 53074-0410
Phone: (414)284-5577
Free: (800)236-FISH **Fax:** (414)284-5504
E-mail: sbrosfish@aol.com
Products: Food service products; Fish and seafood. **SICs:** 5146 (Fish & Seafoods); 5142 (Packaged Frozen Foods); 5149 (Groceries & Related Products Nec). **Est:** 1848. **Emp:** 34. **Officers:** Ned Huwatschek; Jeffrey S. Smith; Grant O. Smith.

■ **12509** ■ **The Miles Smith Family Corp.**
2705 5th St., Ste. 5
Sacramento, CA 95818
Phone: (916)442-1292
Free: (800)400-5543 **Fax:** (916)442-0557
E-mail: calfresh@pacbell.net
Products: Produce. **SIC:** 5148 (Fresh Fruits & Vegetables). **Sales:** $24,000,000 (1999). **Emp:** 60. **Officers:** Miles Smith; Sue Smith. **Doing Business As:** Cal Fresh Products.

■ **12510** ■ **Del Cher Smith Inc.**
8440 Ashland Ave.
Pensacola, FL 32534
Phone: (850)474-0119
Products: Bakery products; Bakery supplies. **SIC:** 5149 (Groceries & Related Products Nec). **Est:** 1984. **Emp:** 4. **Officers:** L. Delores Smith; Dan Smith.

■ **12511** ■ **Smith Packing Company Inc.**
PO Box 446
Utica, NY 13503-0446
Phone: (315)732-5125
Free: (800)832-5125 **Fax:** (315)732-1166
E-mail: sales@smithfoods.com
Products: Meat. **SIC:** 5147 (Meats & Meat Products). **Est:** 1911. **Sales:** $17,000,000 (2000). **Emp:** 50. **Officers:** Wesley Smith, President; Alan Williamson, Controller.

■ **12512** ■ **H. Smith Packing Corp.**
PO Box 189
Blaine, ME 04734
Phone: (207)425-3421 **Fax:** (207)429-8026
Products: Fresh fruits and vegetables. **SIC:** 5148 (Fresh Fruits & Vegetables). **Sales:** $10,000,000 (2000). **Emp:** 45. **Officers:** Herschel Smith, President; Jason Barnes, Controller.

■ **12513** ■ **Smith Potato Inc.**
Farm Rd. 145 E
PO Box 467
Hart, TX 79043
Phone: (806)938-2166
Free: (800)933-7783 **Fax:** (806)938-2209
Products: Fruits and vegetables. **SIC:** 5148 (Fresh Fruits & Vegetables). **Est:** 1977. **Sales:** $2,500,000 (2000). **Emp:** 50. **Officers:** Earl Smith, General Mgr.; Harold Smith; Patty Smith.

■ **12514** ■ **Smith Provision Company Inc.**
2251 W 23rd St.
Erie, PA 16506
Phone: (814)459-4974 **Fax:** (814)452-3142
Products: Hot dogs, ham, and smoked sausages. **SIC:** 5147 (Meats & Meat Products). **Est:** 1927. **Sales:** $7,500,000 (2000). **Emp:** 36. **Officers:** Michael Weber, President.

■ **12515** ■ **Luther Smith & Son Fish**
1023 S Sea Shore Dr.
Atlantic, NC 28511-9702
Phone: (919)225-3341 **Fax:** (919)225-6391
Products: Seafood. **SIC:** 5146 (Fish & Seafoods). **Sales:** $6,000,000 (2000). **Emp:** 99. **Officers:** William E. Smith.

■ **12516** ■ **Dale T. Smith & Sons Co.**
12450 S State
Draper, UT 84020-9510
Phone: (801)571-3611 **Fax:** (801)571-3685
Products: Meat; Packaging supplies. **SICs:** 5147 (Meats & Meat Products); 5113 (Industrial & Personal Service Paper). **Sales:** $20,000,000 (2000). **Emp:** 55. **Officers:** Dale E. Smith.

■ **12517** ■ **Smith and Sons Foods Inc.**
PO Box 4688
Macon, GA 31213-5799
Phone: (912)745-4759
Free: (800)841-5385 **Fax:** (912)746-8233
URL: http://www.sandscafeterias.com
Products: Cafeteria foods. **SICs:** 5141 (Groceries—General Line); 5149 (Groceries & Related Products Nec). **Est:** 1936. **Sales:** $50,000,000 (1999). **Emp:** 1,100. **Officers:** James A. Smith III, President; D.R. Johnson, Controller; Angelia Freeman, Dir. of Data Processing; Melissa Wilkins, Human Resources.

■ **12518** ■ **Smithfield Companies Inc.**
311 County St., No. 203
Portsmouth, VA 23704
Phone: (804)399-3100 **Fax:** (804)399-0916
URL: http://www.smithfield-companies.com
Products: Branded foods. **SIC:** 5147 (Meats & Meat Products). **Est:** 1981. **Sales:** $21,200,000 (2000). **Emp:** 212. **Officers:** Richard S. Fuller, CEO & President; Mark D. Bedard, CFO.

■ **12519** ■ **Smithfield Ham Products Co. Inc.**
401 N Church St.
PO Box 487
Smithfield, VA 23430-0487
Phone: (757)357-2121 **Fax:** (757)357-5407
E-mail: smithfield_Inc@seva.net
URL: http://www.smithfield-companies.com
Products: Barbeques; Chilies; Barbeque sauces. SIC:

5147 (Meats & Meat Products). **Emp:** 72. **Officers:** Peter D. Pruden III, President; Donald Burke, Exec. VP.

■ 12520 ■ **Leroy E. Smith's Sons Inc.**
4776 Old Dixie Hwy.
Vero Beach, FL 32967
Phone: (407)567-3421 **Fax:** (407)567-8428
Products: Citrus fruits. **SIC:** 5148 (Fresh Fruits & Vegetables). **Est:** 1947. **Sales:** $31,000,000 (2000). **Emp:** 100. **Officers:** E.R. Smith Jr., President; Lucille Goff, Controller.

■ 12521 ■ **SNACC Distributing Co.**
2105 Central Ave.
Cincinnati, OH 45214
Phone: (513)723-1777
Free: (800)568-3135 **Fax:** (513)723-1556
E-mail: candyman@isol.com
Products: Food, including nuts and candy. **SIC:** 5145 (Confectionery). **Est:** 1986. **Sales:** $2,000,000 (1999). **Emp:** 17. **Officers:** Gary Krummen, President; Nina Krummen, Vice President.

■ 12522 ■ **Snak King Corp.**
16150 E Stephens St.
City of Industry, CA 91745
Phone: (626)336-7711 **Fax:** (626)336-3777
E-mail: info@snakking.com
URL: http://www.snakking.com
Products: Snack foods, including tortilla chips, corn chips, cheese puffs, pretzels, cheese curls, popcorn, trail mix, caramel corn, and pork rinds; Nuts; Candy. **SICs:** 5145 (Confectionery); 5149 (Groceries & Related Products Nec). **Est:** 1978. **Emp:** 350. **Officers:** Barry Levin; Joe Papiri, Sales/Marketing Contact.

■ 12523 ■ **Snokist Growers**
PO Box 1587
Yakima, WA 98907
Phone: (509)453-5631
Free: (800)377-2857 **Fax:** (509)453-9577
URL: http://www.snokist.com
Products: Fresh and processed fruit. **SIC:** 5148 (Fresh Fruits & Vegetables). **Est:** 1903. **Sales:** $90,000,000 (2000). **Emp:** 750. **Officers:** Dave Long, President; Brados Simpson, CFO; F. McCarthy, Sr. VP of Marketing & Sales; L. Frymier, Dir. of Data Processing.

■ 12524 ■ **Snyder Wholesale Inc.**
1107 David Ln.
PO Box 869
Blytheville, AR 72316-0869
Phone: (870)763-7341 **Fax:** (870)763-1234
Products: Paper and allied products; Specialty cleaning and sanitation products; Frozen foods; Tobacco; Candy. **SICs:** 5142 (Packaged Frozen Foods); 5145 (Confectionery); 5113 (Industrial & Personal Service Paper); 5169 (Chemicals & Allied Products Nec); 5194 (Tobacco & Tobacco Products). **Est:** 1958. **Emp:** 49.

■ 12525 ■ **Sofco-Mead Inc.**
PO Box 2023
Scotia, NY 12302
Phone: (518)374-7810 **Fax:** (518)374-8437
Products: Food service, janitorial and office nondurable goods. **SIC:** 5113 (Industrial & Personal Service Paper). **Sales:** $429,000,000 (2000). **Emp:** 625. **Officers:** Jim Gargiulo, CEO & President; William Sweeney, CFO.

■ 12526 ■ **Sommer Advantage Food Brokers**
2056 Central Ave.
Albany, NY 12205
Phone: (518)452-1834 **Fax:** (518)452-7762
Products: General line groceries, including deli, meat, and bakery products. **SIC:** 5141 (Groceries—General Line). **Emp:** 49. **Officers:** Donald Sommer.

■ 12527 ■ **John Sommer Inc.**
31 Pamaran Way
Novato, CA 94949
Phone: (415)884-2091 **Fax:** (415)884-2092
Products: Frozen foods; Dry food and produce, including pet and animal food. **SICs:** 5142 (Packaged Frozen Foods); 5149 (Groceries & Related Products Nec); 5148 (Fresh Fruits & Vegetables). **Est:** 1969. **Emp:** 6.

■ 12528 ■ **Sona & Hollen Foods Inc.**
3712 Cerritos Ave.
Los Alamitos, CA 90720-2481
Phone: (562)431-1379
Free: (800)200-7662 **Fax:** (562)598-6207
E-mail: sona@flash.net
Products: Condiments. **SIC:** 5149 (Groceries & Related Products Nec). **Est:** 1985. **Sales:** $10,500,000 (1999). **Emp:** 50. **Officers:** John E. Kidde, CEO; Ronald R. Cramer, CFO; Wes Stroben, VP of Sales; Tammie Hagadorn, Sales Assistant; Susan Scott, Human Resource Contact.

■ 12529 ■ **L.S. Sorem and Associates**
7825 Telegraph Rd.
Bloomington, MN 55438-1133
Phone: (612)934-0996
Products: Food. **SIC:** 5141 (Groceries—General Line).

■ 12530 ■ **J. Sosnick and Son**
258 Littlefield Ave.
South San Francisco, CA 94080
Phone: (650)952-2226
Free: (800)443-6737 **Fax:** (650)952-2439
E-mail: jhsosnick@worldnet.att.net
Products: Deli meats; Gourmet food; Candy. **SICs:** 5145 (Confectionery); 5147 (Meats & Meat Products); 5149 (Groceries & Related Products Nec). **Est:** 1906. **Sales:** $30,000,000 (2000). **Emp:** 100. **Officers:** Martin Sosnick, CEO; Robert Sosnick, CFO; Jeffrey Sosnick, General Mgr.

■ 12531 ■ **South Bay Growers Inc.**
PO Box 1207
Clewiston, FL 33440-1207
Phone: (561)996-2085 **Fax:** (561)996-2095
Products: Fruits and vegetables. **SIC:** 5148 (Fresh Fruits & Vegetables). **Sales:** $60,000,000 (2000). **Emp:** 500. **Officers:** Frank Teets, General Mgr.; Charles Wilson.

■ 12532 ■ **South Lake Apopka Citrus Growers Association**
PO Box 8
Oakland, FL 34760
Phone: (954)656-2881
Products: Oranges and grapefruit. **SIC:** 5148 (Fresh Fruits & Vegetables). **Est:** 1909. **Sales:** $5,000,000 (2000). **Emp:** 17. **Officers:** William S. Arrington, General Mgr.

■ 12533 ■ **South Pier Fish Co.**
PO Box 5310
Wakefield, RI 02880
Phone: (401)783-6611 **Fax:** (401)782-8690
Products: Seafood, including whole fish and fillets. **SIC:** 5146 (Fish & Seafoods). **Est:** 1982. **Sales:** $10,000,000 (2000). **Emp:** 30. **Officers:** L. Paul Barbera, President; Terri Cram, Accountant.

■ 12534 ■ **South Shore Produce Co.**
216 Riviera Dr. W
Massapequa, NY 11758-8523
Phone: (516)799-2223 **Fax:** (516)798-5944
Products: Produce. **SIC:** 5148 (Fresh Fruits & Vegetables). **Emp:** 49.

■ 12535 ■ **Southeast Dairy Products**
3803 Columbus Dr. E
PO Box 5088
Tampa, FL 33675-5088
Phone: (813)621-3233
Free: (800)633-1824 **Fax:** (813)626-1516
Products: Coffee creamers; Sour cream; Whipping cream. **SIC:** 5143 (Dairy Products Except Dried or Canned). **Est:** 1934. **Emp:** 49. **Officers:** William B. Tiller, President; Donald H. Tiller, Vice President; Steve Buckley, VP of Marketing & Sales.

■ 12536 ■ **Southeast Frozen Food Co.**
18770 NE 6th Ave.
Miami, FL 33179
Phone: (305)652-4622
Products: Frozen foods. **SIC:** 5142 (Packaged Frozen Foods). **Sales:** $350,000,000 (2000). **Emp:** 520. **Officers:** John Robinson, President; Doug Myers, CFO.

■ 12537 ■ **Southeastern Colorado Coop.**
408 S 1st St.
Holly, CO 81047
Phone: (719)537-6514
Products: Grain, farm supplies. **SICs:** 5153 (Grain & Field Beans); 5191 (Farm Supplies). **Sales:** $17,000,000 (2000). **Emp:** 33. **Officers:** Douglas Wilson, General Mgr.

■ 12538 ■ **Southeastern Mills Inc.**
PO Box 908
Rome, GA 30161
Phone: (706)291-6528
Products: Flour, cornmeal, grits, and mixes. **SIC:** 5153 (Grain & Field Beans). **Est:** 1942. **Sales:** $34,000,000 (2000). **Emp:** 150. **Officers:** V. Grizzard Jr., President.

■ 12539 ■ **Southern Foods Inc.**
117 Mitch McConnell Way
PO Box 1657
Bowling Green, KY 42102-1657
Phone: (270)843-1121
Free: (800)264-4862 **Fax:** (270)782-8031
URL: http://www.southernfoodsinc.com
Products: Foodservice, including frozen and dry grocery; Fresh meat, produce, beverages; Equipment and smallwares; Chemicals. **SIC:** 5141 (Groceries—General Line). **Est:** 1958. **Emp:** 85. **Officers:** Joe Natcher, President.

■ 12540 ■ **Southern Produce Inc.**
1100 Pleasantville Dr.
Houston, TX 77029-3232
Phone: (713)678-9000
Products: Fresh fruits and vegetables. **SIC:** 5148 (Fresh Fruits & Vegetables). **Sales:** $28,000,000 (2000). **Emp:** 86. **Officers:** Ron Frump, President; Kathy Halthom, Controller.

■ 12541 ■ **Southern Seafood Co.**
7901 Oceano Ave.
Jessup, MD 20794
Phone: (410)799-5641 **Fax:** (410)799-8763
Products: Frozen seafood. **SICs:** 5146 (Fish & Seafoods); 5142 (Packaged Frozen Foods). **Est:** 1922. **Sales:** $19,500,000 (2000). **Emp:** 22. **Officers:** Robert Millhauser, President.

■ 12542 ■ **A Southern Season**
Eastgate Shopping Center
Chapel Hill, NC 27514
Phone: (919)929-7133
Free: (800)253-3663 **Fax:** (919)942-9274
E-mail: customerservice@southernseason.com
URL: http://www.southernseason.com
Products: Specialty foods, including baked goods, wines, coffee, cheese, and chocolates. **SICs:** 5149 (Groceries & Related Products Nec); 5182 (Wines & Distilled Beverages); 5145 (Confectionery); 5143 (Dairy Products Except Dried or Canned). **Est:** 1975. **Emp:** 200. **Officers:** Michael Barefoot, President.

■ 12543 ■ **Southern Tea Co.**
1267 Cobb Industrial Dr.
Marietta, GA 30066
Phone: (770)428-5555
Products: Tea. **SIC:** 5149 (Groceries & Related Products Nec). **Est:** 1959. **Sales:** $50,000,000 (2000). **Emp:** 450. **Officers:** Daniel T. Reed, VP of Operations; Jeff Fabian, Controller; John L. Dinos, VP of Sales; Susan Partus, Personnel Mgr.

■ 12544 ■ **Southtowns Seafood & Meats**
PO Box 1956
Blasdell, NY 14219-0156
Phone: (716)824-4900 **Fax:** (716)822-8216
Products: Fresh seafood. **SIC:** 5146 (Fish & Seafoods). **Est:** 1984. **Emp:** 49. **Officers:** David J. Norton, President; David E. Norton, Treasurer & Secty.

■ 12545 ■ **Southwest Specialties**
PO Box 5407
San Clemente, CA 92674-5407
Phone: (949)492-3070 **Fax:** (949)492-0107
Products: Snack foods. **SIC:** 5149 (Groceries & Related Products Nec). **Est:** 1984. **Sales:** $750,000 (2000). **Emp:** 3.

■ **12546** ■ **SPADA Enterprises Ltd.**
2711 SE Woodward St.
Portland, OR 97202-1357
Phone: (503)234-9215 **Fax:** (503)232-7807
E-mail: spadent@aol.com
Products: Fresh fruits, vegetables, grass, alfalfa hay, and alcoholic beverages. **SICs:** 5148 (Fresh Fruits & Vegetables); 5191 (Farm Supplies); 5181 (Beer & Ale); 5182 (Wines & Distilled Beverages). **Est:** 1977. **Sales:** $8,000,000 (2000). **Emp:** 5. **Officers:** George Spada, President.

■ **12547** ■ **Spartan Stores Inc.**
PO Box 8700
Grand Rapids, MI 49518
Phone: (616)878-2000
Products: General line groceries. **SIC:** 5141 (Groceries—General Line). **Est:** 1917. **Sales:** $2,000,000,000 (2000). **Emp:** 2,100. **Officers:** James Meyer, CEO.

■ **12548** ■ **Spartan Stores Inc.**
PO Box 8700
Grand Rapids, MI 49518
Phone: (616)878-2000 **Fax:** (616)878-8802
Products: General line of groceries. **SIC:** 5141 (Groceries—General Line). **Sales:** $2,489,200,000 (2000). **Emp:** 2,900. **Officers:** James D. Meyer, President; Charles B. Fosnaugh, CFO.

■ **12549** ■ **Specialized Marketing**
PO Box 809
Marshall, CA 94940
Phone: (510)420-1134
Free: (800)344-1114 **Fax:** (510)420-1196
Products: Baking powder, shortening, and cooking oils. **SIC:** 5149 (Groceries & Related Products Nec). **Sales:** $16,000,000 (2000). **Emp:** 9.

■ **12550** ■ **Specialty Distribution**
PO Box 1328
Greenville, SC 29602
Phone: (864)676-8600
Products: Institutional food. **SIC:** 5141 (Groceries—General Line). **Est:** 1968. **Sales:** $300,000,000 (2000). **Emp:** 536. **Officers:** John R. Millard, President; Eric Hartis, Finance Officer.

■ **12551** ■ **Specialty Food Distributors, Inc.**
4006 Airport Rd.
Plant City, FL 33567-1124
Phone: (813)752-8558 **Fax:** (813)754-7971
Products: Imported specialty foods. **SIC:** 5149 (Groceries & Related Products Nec). **Est:** 1965. **Emp:** 500.

■ **12552** ■ **Specialty Grain Products Co.**
PO Box 3100
Omaha, NE 68103
Phone: (402)595-4000
Products: Frozen dinners. **SIC:** 5142 (Packaged Frozen Foods).

■ **12553** ■ **Specialty World Foods Inc.**
84 Montgomery St.
Albany, NY 12207
Phone: (518)436-7603
Free: (800)233-0913 **Fax:** (518)436-9035
Products: Gourmet food, including game and mushrooms. **SIC:** 5149 (Groceries & Related Products Nec). **Est:** 1980. **Sales:** $2,000,000 (2000). **Emp:** 6. **Officers:** Joseph R. Messina, President; Jan Peno, Office Mgr.; Eric Guenther, Office Mgr.; James Kelly, Sales/Marketing Contact.

■ **12554** ■ **Spencer Fruit Co.**
1500 W Manning Ave.
Reedley, CA 93654
Phone: (209)659-2055 **Fax:** (209)659-2371
Products: Fruits and vegetables. **SIC:** 5148 (Fresh Fruits & Vegetables). **Sales:** $88,000,000 (2000). **Emp:** 200. **Officers:** Bill Spencer, President; Ken Engelman, CFO.

■ **12555** ■ **Spindler Co.**
4430 Portage Rd.
North Canton, OH 44720-7397
Phone: (330)499-2560
Free: (800)269-2560 **Fax:** (216)499-2562
Products: Baking ingredients. **SIC:** 5149 (Groceries & Related Products Nec). **Est:** 1945. **Sales:** $10,600,000 (2000). **Emp:** 20. **Officers:** George E. Kittoe, CEO; Dave C. Kittoe, President.

■ **12556** ■ **Spokane Seed Co.**
PO Box 11007
Spokane, WA 99211-1007
Phone: (509)535-3671 **Fax:** (509)535-0874
Products: Grain, peas and lentils. **SIC:** 5153 (Grain & Field Beans). **Sales:** $46,000,000 (1999). **Emp:** 50. **Officers:** Jeff White, Treasurer.

■ **12557** ■ **Spring Tree Corp.**
28 Vernon St., No. 412
Brattleboro, VT 05301-3623
Phone: (802)254-8784 **Fax:** (802)254-8648
Products: Maple syrup; Margarine. **SIC:** 5149 (Groceries & Related Products Nec). **Est:** 1976. **Officers:** Myron Golden.

■ **12558** ■ **Springfield Grocer Company Inc.**
PO Box 8500
Springfield, MO 65801
Phone: (417)883-4230
Products: General line of groceries. **SIC:** 5141 (Groceries—General Line). **Sales:** $37,000,000 (2000). **Emp:** 100. **Officers:** William M. Tynes, President; David Smith, Controller.

■ **12559** ■ **Springfield Sugar and Products Co.**
PO Box 385
Windsor Locks, CT 06096
Phone: (860)623-1681 **Fax:** (860)627-5076
Products: Groceries and grocery supplies. **SICs:** 5149 (Groceries & Related Products Nec); 5141 (Groceries—General Line). **Est:** 1916. **Sales:** $300,000,000 (2000). **Emp:** 650. **Officers:** J.J. Leavitt, CEO; Joe Fusco, President; Peter Leavitt, VP of Marketing; Ed Hammett, Dir of Human Resources.

■ **12560** ■ **Squeri FoodService**
PO Box 14180
Cincinnati, OH 45250-0180
Phone: (513)381-1106
Products: General line food service. **SIC:** 5141 (Groceries—General Line). **Est:** 1952. **Sales:** $86,500,000 (2000). **Emp:** 225. **Officers:** John Squeri, President; Mark Foegler, CFO.

■ **12561** ■ **Stacyville Cooperative Creamery Association**
206 N Lawrence St.
Stacyville, IA 50476
Phone: (515)737-2101 **Fax:** (515)737-2655
Products: Milk, cheese and other dairy products. **SIC:** 5143 (Dairy Products Except Dried or Canned). **Est:** 1937. **Sales:** $21,000,000 (2000). **Emp:** 6. **Officers:** Gene Myhre, President; Frederick Brumm, Treasurer; Randy Stephenson, Dir. of Marketing.

■ **12562** ■ **Stahl's Bakery**
51021 Washington St.
New Baltimore, MI 48047
Phone: (810)725-6990
Products: ed goods. **SIC:** 5149 (Groceries & Related Products Nec). **Sales:** $1,500,000 (1994). **Emp:** 45. **Officers:** Max Plant, President.

■ **12563** ■ **Standard Fruit and Vegetable Company Inc.**
PO Box 225027
Dallas, TX 75222-5027
Phone: (214)428-3600
Free: (800)428-3600 **Fax:** (214)428-8834
Products: Fruits; Vegetables. **SIC:** 5148 (Fresh Fruits & Vegetables). **Est:** 1933. **Sales:** $150,000,000 (2000). **Emp:** 350. **Officers:** Martin H. Rutchik, CEO; Steve Gray, CFO; Dave Russell, Sales & Marketing Contact; Mike Kissner, Human Resources Contact.

■ **12564** ■ **Standard Meat Co.**
700 Van Dorn
Lincoln, NE 68502-3342
Phone: (402)475-6328 **Fax:** (402)475-3045
Products: Meat, including beef and pork. **SIC:** 5147 (Meats & Meat Products). **Sales:** $16,000,000 (2000). **Emp:** 49. **Officers:** Stanley Sands.

■ **12565** ■ **Stanley Brothers Inc.**
237 7th Ave.
Huntington, WV 25701
Phone: (304)529-7114 **Fax:** (304)529-7117
Products: Produce. **SIC:** 5148 (Fresh Fruits & Vegetables). **Est:** 1937. **Sales:** $4,500,000 (2000). **Emp:** 11. **Officers:** Edd Stanley, President.

■ **12566** ■ **Stan's Frozen Foods**
2101 Columbia Dr. SE
Albuquerque, NM 87101
Phone: (505)247-3707
Products: Frozen foods. **SIC:** 5141 (Groceries—General Line).

■ **12567** ■ **Stan's Smokehouse Inc.**
3533 E Jensen Rd.
El Reno, OK 73036
Phone: (405)422-5375 **Fax:** (405)262-6959
E-mail: stan@stanssmokehouse.com
URL: http://www.stanssmokehouse.com
Products: Meat snacks and cured and smoked meats; Candy. **SIC:** 5147 (Meats & Meat Products). **Est:** 1970. **Emp:** 15. **Officers:** Stan Brooks, President. **Former Name:** Stan's Inc.

■ **12568** ■ **Stanz Cheese Company Inc.**
PO Box 24
South Bend, IN 46624
Phone: (219)232-6666
Products: Groceries; Paper products; Flatware; Hot dog machines. **SICs:** 5141 (Groceries—General Line); 5199 (Nondurable Goods Nec); 5113 (Industrial & Personal Service Paper). **Est:** 1923. **Sales:** $40,000,000 (2000). **Emp:** 150. **Officers:** Clyde J. Geraghty, President.

■ **12569** ■ **Starboard Inc.**
1714 E Blvd.
Charlotte, NC 28203
Phone: (704)334-1677
Free: (800)777-0575 **Fax:** (704)332-9352
URL: http://www.Starboard-inc.com
Products: Fish, including flounder, whiting, and sea trout; Shrimp and crab. **SIC:** 5146 (Fish & Seafoods). **Est:** 1982. **Sales:** $50,000,000 (2000). **Emp:** 9. **Officers:** Ronald Wrenn, President, e-mail: ronnie@starboard-inc.com.

■ **12570** ■ **Starbuck Creamery Co.**
101 E 5th St.
Starbuck, MN 56381
Phone: (612)239-2226
Products: Blend fertilizers; Feed, grain and agronomy. **SICs:** 5153 (Grain & Field Beans); 5191 (Farm Supplies). **Sales:** $9,000,000 (2000). **Emp:** 20. **Officers:** Rod Leinen, General Mgr.

■ **12571** ■ **Starbucks Corp.**
PO Box 34067
Seattle, WA 98124-1067
Phone: (206)447-1575
Products: fee. **SIC:** 5149 (Groceries & Related Products Nec). **Sales:** $1,308,000,000 (2000). **Emp:** 26,000. **Officers:** Howard Schultz, CEO & Chairman of the Board; Michael Casey, Sr. VP & CFO.

■ **12572** ■ **Stark Candy Co., Division of New England Confectionery Co.**
700 Hickory St.
PO Box 65
Pewaukee, WI 53072
Phone: (414)691-0600
Free: (800)558-2300 **Fax:** (414)691-2947
Products: Candy. **SIC:** 5145 (Confectionery). **Est:** 1939. **Emp:** 499. **Officers:** Domenic M. Antonellis, President; Walter J. Marshall, VP of Mktg.; Hans Becher, CEO & VP of Sales & Marketing.

■ **12573** ■ **Stark & Company Inc.**
30301 Northwestern Hwy.
Farmington Hills, MI 48334
Phone: (248)851-5700 **Fax:** (248)851-1760
Products: Food. **SIC:** 5141 (Groceries—General Line).
Sales: $360,000,000 (2000). **Emp:** 265. **Officers:**
Randall D. Odom, Sr. Exec. VP; Larry H. Stark,
President.

■ **12574** ■ **Stark and Company Inc.**
30301 Northwestern Hwy.
Farmington Hills, MI 48334
Phone: (248)851-5700 **Fax:** (248)851-1760
Products: Food. **SIC:** 5141 (Groceries—General Line).
Sales: $360,000,000 (2000). **Emp:** 265.

■ **12575** ■ **StarKist Seafood/Heinz Pet Prd**
1054 Ways St.
San Pedro, CA 90731
Phone: (310)519-2200 **Fax:** (310)519-2269
Products: Pet food. **SIC:** 5149 (Groceries & Related
Products Nec).

■ **12576** ■ **Stash Tea Co.**
PO Box 910
Portland, OR 97207
Phone: (503)684-4482
Free: (800)547-1514 **Fax:** (503)684-4424
E-mail: stash@stashtea.com
URL: http://www.stashtea.com
Products: Teas. **SIC:** 5149 (Groceries & Related
Products Nec). **Est:** 1972. **Sales:** $20,000,000 (1999).
Emp: 50. **Officers:** Tom Lisicki, CEO; Dick Larsen,
Controller. **Former Name:** Universal Tea Co.

■ **12577** ■ **State Fish Company Inc.**
2194 Signal Pl.
San Pedro, CA 90731
Phone: (310)832-2633 **Fax:** (310)831-2402
E-mail: calsquid@aol.com
Products: Fish. **SIC:** 5146 (Fish & Seafoods). **Est:**
1932. **Emp:** 200.

■ **12578** ■ **State Line Potato Chip Co.**
PO Box 218
Wilbraham, MA 01095-0218
Phone: (413)596-8331
Products: Potato chips. **SIC:** 5145 (Confectionery).
Est: 1919. **Sales:** $20,000,000 (2000). **Emp:** 250.
Officers: William J. Salmon, President; William A.
Fontes, CFO; Christine Halpin, Dir. of Marketing.

■ **12579** ■ **Staunton Food Inc.**
PO Box 569
Staunton, VA 24402
Phone: (540)885-1214
Free: (800)932-2228 **Fax:** (540)885-0021
Products: Food, including frozen and canned
vegetables, dressings, and meats; Cleaning products.
SICs: 5149 (Groceries & Related Products Nec); 5113
(Industrial & Personal Service Paper); 5142 (Packaged
Frozen Foods); 5169 (Chemicals & Allied Products
Nec). **Est:** 1960. **Sales:** $5,300,000 (2000). **Emp:** 35.
Officers: James C. Coffey, President & Treasurer.

■ **12580** ■ **Stavis Seafoods Inc.**
7 Channel St.
Boston, MA 02210
Phone: (617)482-6349 **Fax:** (617)482-1340
E-mail: fish@stavis.com
URL: http://www.stavis.com
Products: Frozen and fresh seafood. **SIC:** 5146 (Fish
& Seafoods). **Est:** 1929. **Sales:** $100,000,000 (2000).
Emp: 65. **Officers:** Ed Stavis, President; Richard
Stavis, CEO; Mary Stavis Fleming, Sales Mgr.

■ **12581** ■ **Staz Food Services**
101 Alan Dr.
Newark, DE 19711
Phone: (302)366-8990 **Fax:** (302)366-8925
Products: Coffee. **SIC:** 5149 (Groceries & Related
Products Nec).

■ **12582** ■ **Steel City Milling Inc.**
120 Victoria Rd.
Youngstown, OH 44515
Phone: (216)793-3925 **Fax:** (216)793-1643
Products: Baking goods, including flour and sugar.
SIC: 5149 (Groceries & Related Products Nec). **Est:**

1936. **Sales:** $11,000,000 (2000). **Emp:** 20. **Officers:**
G. Timothy Dove, General Mgr.

■ **12583** ■ **Stella D'Oro Biscuit Company Inc.**
184 W 237th St.
Bronx, NY 10463
Phone: (718)601-9200 **Fax:** (718)884-6494
Products: Cookies; Breadsticks. **SIC:** 5149 (Groceries
& Related Products Nec). **Est:** 1930. **Sales:**
$53,000,000 (2000). **Emp:** 300. **Officers:** Don Rogers,
President; Bill Ilariz, Dir. of Marketing; Rosa Toledo,
Dir. of Information Systems; Margaret Campos, Dir of
Human Resources.

■ **12584** ■ **Sterzing Food Co.**
1819 Charles St.
Burlington, IA 52601-2201
Phone: (319)754-8467 **Fax:** (319)752-7195
E-mail: Sterzing@lisco.com
URL: http://www.sterzingchips.com
Products: Potato chips. **SIC:** 5145 (Confectionery).
Sales: $6,000,000 (2000). **Emp:** 30. **Officers:** Warren
E. Duttweiler.

■ **12585** ■ **Steuart Investment Co.**
4646 40th NW
Washington, DC 20016
Phone: (202)537-8940
Products: Fish and seafood. **SIC:** 5146 (Fish &
Seafoods). **Sales:** $50,000,000 (1993). **Emp:** 400.
Officers: Guy Steuart, President; Michael B. Goheen,
Treasurer.

■ **12586** ■ **Stokes Canning Co.**
5590 High St.
Denver, CO 80216
Phone: (303)292-4018
Products: Canned specialties. **SIC:** 5149 (Groceries &
Related Products Nec). **Sales:** $17,000,000 (2000).
Emp: 118. **Officers:** G Robert Page, President.

■ **12587** ■ **Stokes-Shaheen Produce Inc.**
477 Hawthorn St.
Macon, GA 31201
Phone: (912)742-4517
Products: Produce. **SIC:** 5148 (Fresh Fruits &
Vegetables). **Sales:** $10,000,000 (2000). **Emp:** 30.
Officers: Preston P. Tucker, CEO.

■ **12588** ■ **Joseph H. Stomel & Sons**
1 Stomel Plz.
33 Suffolk Rd.
West Berlin, NJ 08091
Phone: (609)768-9770 **Fax:** (609)768-0104
Products: Tobacco; Candy; Groceries; Health and
beauty products. **SICs:** 5141 (Groceries—General
Line); 5122 (Drugs, Proprietaries & Sundries); 5145
(Confectionery); 5194 (Tobacco & Tobacco Products).
Est: 1929. **Sales:** $441,000,000 (1999). **Emp:** 385.
Officers: Steve Stomel, President; Leo Pound, CFO.

■ **12589** ■ **Joseph H. Stomel and Sons**
55 Corporate Dr.
Hauppauge, NY 11788
Phone: (516)231-1852 **Fax:** (516)231-1549
Products: General line groceries, including frozen
foods, snacks, candy, and beverages; Paper products;
Cleaning supplies; Tobacco products; General
merchandise, including pet products, automotive
products, and seasonal items. **SICs:** 5141 (Groceries—
General Line); 5113 (Industrial & Personal Service
Paper); 5169 (Chemicals & Allied Products Nec); 5194
(Tobacco & Tobacco Products); 5199 (Nondurable
Goods Nec). **Emp:** 110. **Officers:** Mike Maslen, Dir. of
Information Systems; Mark Tosti, Sales Mgr.; Jayne
Hickerson, Executive Administrator.

■ **12590** ■ **Stone Commodities Corp.**
30 S Wacker Dr., Ste. 1300
Chicago, IL 60606
Phone: (312)454-3000
Products: Meat, livestock and raw materials. **SICs:**
5147 (Meats & Meat Products); 5154 (Livestock); 5159
(Farm-Product Raw Materials Nec). **Sales:**
$54,000,000 (2000). **Emp:** 100. **Officers:** William C.
Bachman, President; Robert Pagliuco, CFO.

■ **12591** ■ **Stouffer Foods Corp.**
PO Box 87008
22800 Saui Ranch Pkwy.
Yorba Linda, CA 92885
Phone: (714)282-4270 **Fax:** (714)282-0198
Products: Frozen foods. **SIC:** 5142 (Packaged Frozen
Foods). **Emp:** 40. **Officers:** Greg Neff.

■ **12592** ■ **Stow Mills**
PO Box 301
Chesterfield, NH 03443
Phone: (603)256-3000 **Fax:** (603)256-8106
Products: Natural foods; Vitamins. **SICs:** 5149
(Groceries & Related Products Nec); 5122 (Drugs,
Proprietaries & Sundries); 5148 (Fresh Fruits &
Vegetables). **Officers:** Jay Jacobowitz, Sales Mgr.

■ **12593** ■ **Mrs. Stratton's Salads**
380 Industrial Ln.
PO Box 190187
Birmingham, AL 35219-0187
Phone: (205)940-9640 **Fax:** (205)940-9650
E-mail: mssalad@aol.com
Products: Prepared salads, pizzas, sausages, and
luncheon meats. **SICs:** 5149 (Groceries & Related
Products Nec); 5147 (Meats & Meat Products). **Est:**
1973. **Sales:** $26,000,000 (2000). **Emp:** 130. **Officers:**
R. Vance Fulkerson, President; George Bradford,
Exec. VP; Patricia Azlin, Human Resources Mgr.

■ **12594** ■ **W.F. Straub and Co.**
5520 Northwest Hwy.
Chicago, IL 60630
Phone: (773)763-5520 **Fax:** (773)763-0141
Products: Molasses. **SIC:** 5149 (Groceries & Related
Products Nec). **Sales:** $600,000 (2000). **Emp:** 4.
Officers: John Straub, President & Chairman of the
Board; Sam Tang, Vice President.

■ **12595** ■ **Strohmeyer and Arpe Co.**
636 Morris Tpke.
Short Hills, NJ 07078
Phone: (201)379-6600
Products: Fruits and vegetables; Natural wax. **SIC:**
5148 (Fresh Fruits & Vegetables). **Est:** 1881. **Sales:**
$4,000,000 (2000). **Emp:** 10. **Officers:** Guy Peronard,
President.

■ **12596** ■ **Stutz Candy Co., Inc.**
400 S Warminster Rd.
Hatboro, PA 19040-4015
Phone: (215)675-2630 **Fax:** (215)675-1438
Products: Candy; Chocolate and chocolate-type
confectionery products. **SICs:** 5145 (Confectionery);
5149 (Groceries & Related Products Nec). **Sales:**
$2,000,000 (2000). **Emp:** 49. **Officers:** John E. Glaser,
President.

■ **12597** ■ **V. Suarez and Co.**
Rexco Industrial Park
PO Box 364588
Guaynabo
San Juan, PR 00901
Phone: (787)792-1212
Products: Food and beverages. **SICs:** 5141
(Groceries—General Line); 5149 (Groceries & Related
Products Nec).

■ **12598** ■ **C.G. Suarez Food Distribution Co.**
355 N C.R. 427
Longwood, FL 32750-5440
Phone: (407)834-1300 **Fax:** (407)834-5293
Products: Dry food, including pet and animal food.
SICs: 5141 (Groceries—General Line); 5149
(Groceries & Related Products Nec). **Est:** 1923. **Emp:**
56. **Officers:** A.R. Lewis, e-mail: ALLewis@IAG.net.

■ **12599** ■ **Sugar Foods Corp.**
950 3rd Ave., 21st Fl.
New York, NY 10022-2705
Phone: (212)753-6900 **Fax:** (212)753-6988
Products: Coffee sweetener. **SIC:** 5149 (Groceries &
Related Products Nec). **Est:** 1963. **Sales:** $50,000,000
(2000). **Emp:** 300. **Officers:** Stephen Odell, President;
Jack Vivinetto, CFO; Rich Tickma, VP of Marketing;
Doug Josephson, Dir. of Operations; George Rieckel,
Treasurer.

■ **12600** ■ **Barney Summers Sales Company Inc.**
6226 Prospect Ave.
Kansas City, MO 64130
Phone: (816)444-3474
Products: Seafood and fish. **SIC:** 5146 (Fish & Seafoods). **Est:** 1920. **Sales:** $5,000,000 (1991). **Emp:** 28. **Officers:** Barney Summers, President.

■ **12601** ■ **Summertime Potato Co.**
2001 E Grand
Des Moines, IA 50317-5235
Phone: (515)265-9865   **Fax:** (515)265-9871
Products: Produce. **SIC:** 5148 (Fresh Fruits & Vegetables). **Emp:** 26.

■ **12602** ■ **Summit Import Corp.**
415 Greenwich St.
New York, NY 10013-2099
Phone: (212)226-1662
Free: (800)888-8288   **Fax:** (212)925-0559
E-mail: info@summitimport.com
URL: http://www.summitimport.com
Products: Oriental groceries, including frozen. **SICs:** 5149 (Groceries & Related Products Nec); 5142 (Packaged Frozen Foods). **Est:** 1955. **Sales:** $43,000,000 (1999). **Emp:** 100. **Officers:** Whiting Wu, CEO & President.

■ **12603** ■ **Sun-Diamond Growers of California. Mixed Nut Div.**
16500 W 103rd St.
Lemont, IL 60439
Phone: (630)739-3000   **Fax:** (630)739-1446
Products: Fruits and vegetables. **SIC:** 5148 (Fresh Fruits & Vegetables). **Est:** 1932. **Sales:** $20,000,000 (2000). **Emp:** 25. **Officers:** Gary Ford, General Mgr.; Mary Langner, Accounting Manager.

■ **12604** ■ **Sun Glo of Idaho Inc.**
PO Box 98
Rexburg, ID 83440
Phone: (208)356-7346   **Fax:** (208)356-7351
Products: Fresh and frozen potatoes. **SICs:** 5148 (Fresh Fruits & Vegetables); 5142 (Packaged Frozen Foods). **Sales:** $25,000,000 (2000). **Emp:** 200. **Officers:** Jerry Hastings.

■ **12605** ■ **Sun-Ni Cheese Co.**
8738 W Chester Pike
Upper Darby, PA 19082-2618
Phone: (215)789-4340   **Fax:** (215)789-4436
Products: Natural and process cheese and related products. **SIC:** 5143 (Dairy Products Except Dried or Canned). **Est:** 1974. **Sales:** $2,500,000 (2000). **Emp:** 20. **Officers:** Pete Seropian.

■ **12606** ■ **Sun Office Service**
PO Box 19523
Austin, TX 78760
Phone: (512)444-3809   **Fax:** (512)444-8338
Products: Coffee. **SIC:** 5149 (Groceries & Related Products Nec).

■ **12607** ■ **Sunbelt Distributors Inc.**
4494 Campbell Rd.
Houston, TX 77041
Phone: (713)329-9988
Products: Icecream. **SIC:** 5143 (Dairy Products Except Dried or Canned). **Sales:** $50,000,000 (2000). **Emp:** 200. **Officers:** Mike Stamper, CEO & Chairman of the Board; Steve Ginsburg, Controller.

■ **12608** ■ **Sunbelt Food Sales**
1425 S 21st St., Ste. 102
Birmingham, AL 35205
Phone: (205)933-6833   **Fax:** (205)933-6834
Products: Food products. **SICs:** 5141 (Groceries—General Line); 5149 (Groceries & Related Products Nec). **Emp:** 4. **Officers:** R.W. Handrahan.

■ **12609** ■ **Sunburst Foods Inc.**
1002 Sunburst Dr.
Goldsboro, NC 27534
Phone: (919)778-2151   **Fax:** (919)778-9203
Products: Prepackaged sandwiches. **SIC:** 5149 (Groceries & Related Products Nec). **Est:** 1947. **Sales:** $15,000,000 (2000). **Emp:** 100. **Officers:** Bob Darden, President.

■ **12610** ■ **Sunfire Corporation**
150 Algerita Dr.
San Antonio, TX 78230-4613
Phone: (210)340-9609   **Fax:** (210)340-9609
Products: Groceries; Food products; Men's and boys' clothing; Industrial products; Books and periodicals. **SICs:** 5149 (Groceries & Related Products Nec); 5194 (Tobacco & Tobacco Products); 5136 (Men's/Boys' Clothing); 5113 (Industrial & Personal Service Paper); 5192 (Books, Periodicals & Newspapers). **Est:** 1983. **Emp:** 5. **Officers:** Carlos Freymann, President.

■ **12611** ■ **Sunflower Restaurant Supply**
PO Box 1277
Salina, KS 67402-1277
Phone: (785)823-6394   **Fax:** (785)823-5512
Products: Coffee; Restaurant equipment and supplies. **SICs:** 5149 (Groceries & Related Products Nec); 5113 (Industrial & Personal Service Paper). **Est:** 1947. **Sales:** $3,000,000 (2000). **Emp:** 28. **Officers:** Leroy Baumberger, President; Wanda Baumberger, Treasurer & Secty. **Former Name:** Salina Coffee House Inc.

■ **12612** ■ **Sunflower Restaurant Supply Inc.**
PO Box 1277
Salina, KS 67402-1277
Phone: (785)823-6394   **Fax:** (785)823-5512
Products: Grocery products, commercial equipment. **SICs:** 5149 (Groceries & Related Products Nec); 5046 (Commercial Equipment Nec). **Sales:** $7,000,000 (2000). **Emp:** 27. **Officers:** Leroy A. Baumberger, President; Wanda Baumberger, Treasurer & Secty.

■ **12613** ■ **Sunfresh Inc.**
PO Box 400
Royal City, WA 99357
Phone: (509)346-9223
Free: (800)255-9009   **Fax:** (509)346-2286
E-mail: sunfresh@atnet.net
Products: Vegetables, including potatoes, onions, asparagus, and beans; Fruit, including cherries and apples. **SIC:** 5148 (Fresh Fruits & Vegetables). **Est:** 1971. **Sales:** $36,000,000 (2000). **Emp:** 100. **Officers:** Randy Niessner, President; Debra Hellewell, Treasurer & Secty.; Larry D. Sieg, Dir. of Marketing & Sales.

■ **12614** ■ **Sunkist Growers Inc.**
14130 Riverside Dr.
Sherman Oaks, CA 91423
Phone: (818)986-4800   **Fax:** (818)379-7142
Products: Fruit, including oranges, grapefruits, tangerines, and lemons. **SIC:** 5148 (Fresh Fruits & Vegetables). **Sales:** $430,000,000 (2000). **Emp:** 750. **Officers:** R. L. Hanlin.

■ **12615** ■ **Sunkist Growers Inc.**
PO Box 7888
Van Nuys, CA 91409-7888
Phone: (818)986-4800   **Fax:** (818)379-7511
Products: Citrus fruits. **SIC:** 5148 (Fresh Fruits & Vegetables). **Est:** 1893. **Sales:** $1,100,000,000 (2000). **Emp:** 1,000. **Officers:** Russell L. Hanlin, CEO & President; H.B. Flach, VP of Finance; R.J. Mead, VP of Marketing; C.C. Marshall, VP of Finance & Admin.; J.R. McGovern, VP of Finance & Admin.

■ **12616** ■ **Sunlight Foods Inc.**
3550 NW 112th St.
PO Box 680670
Miami, FL 33167
Phone: (305)688-5400
Free: (800)325-8201   **Fax:** (305)688-9903
Products: Dry food and produce, including pet and animal food; Salad dressings; Dried and dehydrated fruits; Dried and dehydrated vegetables. **SIC:** 5149 (Groceries & Related Products Nec). **Sales:** $60,000,000 (1999). **Emp:** 151. **Officers:** Arthur Green, President; Robert Contento, CFO; Tom Girdner, Vice President; William N Green, VP of Sales.

■ **12617** ■ **Sunnyland Farms, Inc.**
PO Box 1275
Albany, GA 31702
Phone: (912)436-5654
Free: (800)999-2488   **Fax:** (912)888-8332
E-mail: sunyland@aol.com
Products: Nuts and seeds (salted, roasted, cooked, or blanched) including pecans, and walnuts. **SIC:** 5145

(Confectionery). **Est:** 1948. **Sales:** $20,000,000 (2000). **Emp:** 60. **Officers:** W.H. Willson, Chairman of the Board; Jane S. Willson, President.

■ **12618** ■ **Sunset Ice Cream Offices and Sales**
1849 Lycoming Creek Rd.
Williamsport, PA 17701
Phone: (570)326-7475
Products: Ice cream. **SIC:** 5143 (Dairy Products Except Dried or Canned).

■ **12619** ■ **Sunshine Dairy Foods Inc.**
584 Coleman Rd.
Middletown, CT 06457
Phone: (860)346-6644
Products: Dairy products. **SIC:** 5143 (Dairy Products Except Dried or Canned). **Est:** 1963. **Sales:** $5,000,000 (2000). **Emp:** 16. **Officers:** Nancy A. Guida, President.

■ **12620** ■ **Sunshine Dairy Foods Inc.**
801 NE 21st Ave.
Portland, OR 97232
Phone: (503)234-7526
Products: Dairy products. **SIC:** 5143 (Dairy Products Except Dried or Canned). **Est:** 1937. **Sales:** $27,000,000 (2000). **Emp:** 122. **Officers:** Paul Arbuthnot, CEO & President; Leon Easley, Controller.

■ **12621** ■ **Sunshine Market Inc.**
1492 Hwy. 315
Wilkes Barre, PA 18702
Phone: (570)829-1392
Products: Grocery stores. **SIC:** 5141 (Groceries—General Line). **Sales:** $50,000,000 (2000). **Emp:** 240. **Officers:** Elizabeth Colonna, President.

■ **12622** ■ **Sunsweet Growers Inc.**
901 N Walton Ave.
Yuba City, CA 95993
Phone: (530)751-5203   **Fax:** (530)751-5395
Products: Dried fruit processing and marketing—prunes, peaches, apricots and pears. **SIC:** 5149 (Groceries & Related Products Nec). **Sales:** $37,000,000 (2000). **Emp:** 350. **Officers:** Bill Haase, President.

■ **12623** ■ **Super Food Services Inc.**
Kettering Box 2323
Dayton, OH 45429
Phone: (513)439-7500   **Fax:** (513)439-7514
Products: Groceries. **SIC:** 5141 (Groceries—General Line). **Est:** 1957. **Sales:** $1,155,000,000 (2000). **Emp:** 1,670. **Officers:** Jack Twyman, CEO & Chairman of the Board; Robert F. Koogler, Sr. VP of Finance & Treasurer; Lewis Beynon, Manager; Robert McCarthy, Sr. VP of Information Systems.

■ **12624** ■ **Super Rite Foods Inc.**
PO Box 2261
Harrisburg, PA 17110
Phone: (717)232-6821   **Fax:** (717)257-4527
Products: Food. **SIC:** 5141 (Groceries—General Line). **Sales:** $1,000,000,000 (2000). **Emp:** 2,500.

■ **12625** ■ **Super Store Industries/Fairfield Dairy Division**
PO Box 2898
Fairfield, CA 94533
Phone: (707)864-0502
Free: (800)678-7331   **Fax:** (707)864-8203
Products: Dairy products. **SIC:** 5143 (Dairy Products Except Dried or Canned). **Est:** 1985. **Sales:** $160,000,000 (2000). **Emp:** 115. **Officers:** Dennis Winter, President; Julie Marchman, Dir of Human Resources. **Former Name:** Mid Valley Dairy Inc.

■ **12626** ■ **Super Stores Industries**
PO Box 549
Lathrop, CA 95330
Phone: (209)858-2010
Products: Groceries; Frozen food. **SICs:** 5141 (Groceries—General Line); 5142 (Packaged Frozen Foods). **Est:** 1991. **Sales:** $900,000,000 (2000). **Emp:** 500. **Officers:** Dennis Winter, CEO. **Former Name:** Super Valu Stores Inc., Westpac Pacific Foods Div.

■ 12627 ■ Super Stores Industries
PO Box 549
Lathrop, CA 95330
Phone: (209)858-2010
Products: Food. **SIC:** 5141 (Groceries—General Line).
Sales: $900,000,000 (2000). **Emp:** 500.

■ 12628 ■ Super Valu Inc. - Midwest Region
7400 95th St.
PO Box 581908
Pleasant Prairie, WI 53158
Phone: (262)947-7290   **Fax:** (262)947-9210
Products: Grocery items; Beauty aids. **SICs:** 5141
(Groceries—General Line); 5122 (Drugs, Proprietaries
& Sundries). **Officers:** James Campbell, President.

■ 12629 ■ Super Valu Stores Inc.
Industrial Park
Roberts Dr.
Anniston, AL 36201
Phone: (205)831-1840   **Fax:** (205)235-3437
Products: Groceries. **SIC:** 5141 (Groceries—General
Line). **Officers:** Charles H. Ping, President.

■ 12630 ■ Super Valu Stores Inc.
600 Selig Dr. SW
Atlanta, GA 30336
Phone: (404)699-3600   **Fax:** (404)691-4054
Products: Groceries. **SIC:** 5141 (Groceries—General
Line). **Officers:** Joel W. Raffenbeul, President.

■ 12631 ■ Super Valu Stores Inc.
1983 Tower Rd.
Aurora, CO 80011
Phone: (303)361-0386   **Fax:** (303)361-0376
Products: Groceries. **SIC:** 5141 (Groceries—General
Line). **Officers:** Kenneth M. Kegerreis, President.

■ 12632 ■ Super Valu Stores Inc.
3900 NW 106th St.
Des Moines, IA 50322
Phone: (515)278-0211   **Fax:** (515)270-4454
Products: Groceries. **SIC:** 5141 (Groceries—General
Line). **Officers:** Gene R. Foltz, President.

■ 12633 ■ Super Valu Stores Inc.
101 S Jefferson Ave.
Hopkins, MN 55343
Phone: (612)932-4300   **Fax:** (612)932-4615
Products: General line groceries; Personal goods;
Frozen foods. **SICs:** 5141 (Groceries—General Line);
5142 (Packaged Frozen Foods). **Officers:** Gary G.
Zimmerman.

■ 12634 ■ Super Valu Stores Inc.
11016 E Montgomery Ave.
Spokane, WA 99206
Phone: (509)928-7700   **Fax:** (509)922-9617
Products: Groceries; General merchandise. **SICs:**
5141 (Groceries—General Line); 5199 (Nondurable
Goods Nec). **Officers:** Ronald D. Skeels, President.

■ 12635 ■ Super Valu Stores Inc.
1525 East D. St.
Tacoma, WA 98421
Phone: (253)593-3200   **Fax:** (253)593-8544
Products: Groceries; General merchandise. **SICs:**
5141 (Groceries—General Line); 5199 (Nondurable
Goods Nec). **Officers:** Herbert M. Engdahl, President.

■ 12636 ■ Super Valu Stores Inc.
3900 106th St.
Urbandale, IA 50322
Phone: (515)278-0211
Products: Frozen food; Meats; Dairy products;
Produce. **SICs:** 5147 (Meats & Meat Products); 5142
(Packaged Frozen Foods); 5143 (Dairy Products
Except Dried or Canned); 5148 (Fresh Fruits &
Vegetables).

■ 12637 ■ Super Valu Stores Inc. Ohio Valley
1003 Belbrook Ave.
Xenia, OH 45385
Phone: (937)374-7611   **Fax:** (937)374-7535
Products: Groceries. **SIC:** 5141 (Groceries—General
Line). **Officers:** Nick Connavino, Regional Pres.

■ 12638 ■ Superior Confections
501 Industry Rd.
Staten Island, NY 10314-3607
Phone: (718)698-3300   **Fax:** (718)494-4576
E-mail: Superior@Earthlink.com
URL: http://www.superiorchocolatier.com
Products: Chocolate and chocolate-type confectionary
products. **SICs:** 5145 (Confectionery); 5149 (Groceries
& Related Products Nec). **Est:** 1911. **Sales:**
$10,000,000 (2000). **Emp:** 99. **Officers:** Peter Kaye;
George Kaye.

■ 12639 ■ Superior Foods
275 Westgate Dr.
Watsonville, CA 95076
Phone: (408)728-3691
Products: Food. **SICs:** 5141 (Groceries—General
Line); 5142 (Packaged Frozen Foods). **Sales:**
$14,000,000 (1993). **Emp:** 28. **Officers:** Mateo
Lettunich, President; Robert Scully, CFO.

■ 12640 ■ Superior Nut Company Inc.
225 Monsignor O'Brien Hwy.
Cambridge, MA 02141
Phone: (617)876-3808
Products: Nuts. **SIC:** 5145 (Confectionery). **Est:** 1933.
Sales: $5,000,000 (2000). **Emp:** 35. **Officers:** Harry
Hintlian, President.

■ 12641 ■ Superior Trading Co.
837 Washington St.
San Francisco, CA 94108
Phone: (415)982-8722   **Fax:** (415)982-7786
E-mail: super837@aol.com
Products: Ginseng tea and related products. **SIC:**
5149 (Groceries & Related Products Nec). **Est:** 1957.
Emp: 12. **Officers:** Michael Chung, President.

■ 12642 ■ SUPERVALU
3501 12th Ave. N
Fargo, ND 58102
Phone: (701)293-2100   **Fax:** (701)293-2124
Products: General line groceries. **SIC:** 5141
(Groceries—General Line). **Officers:** Jack C. Toy,
President.

**■ 12643 ■ SUPERVALU Champaign
    Distribution Center**
PO Box 9008
Champaign, IL 61826-9008
Phone: (217)384-2800   **Fax:** (217)384-2663
Products: Groceries and general merchandise. **SICs:**
5141 (Groceries—General Line); 5099 (Durable Goods
Nec). **Sales:** $1,000,000,000 (2000). **Emp:** 850.
Officers: Jerry Salfrank, Finance Officer.

■ 12644 ■ SuperValu Inc.
PO Box 58506
Bismarck, ND 58502
Phone: (701)222-5600   **Fax:** (701)222-5667
Products: Groceries, including canned and frozen
products. **SICs:** 5149 (Groceries & Related Products
Nec); 5141 (Groceries—General Line); 5142
(Packaged Frozen Foods). **Officers:** Roger Olhauser,
Contact. **Former Name:** Super Valu Stores Inc.

■ 12645 ■ SUPERVALU Inc.
PO Box 990
Minneapolis, MN 55440
Phone: (612)828-4000   **Fax:** (612)828-8998
Products: Food and non-food products. **SIC:** 5141
(Groceries—General Line). **Est:** 1942. **Sales:**
$23,000,000,000 (1999). **Emp:** 60,000. **Officers:**
Michael W. Wright, CEO, President & Chairman of the
Board; Pamela K. Knous, Exec. VP & CFO; Jeffrey
Noddle, Exec. VP; Ronald C. Tortelli, Sr. VP of Human
Resources; William Bolton, Exec. VP & COO; David L.
Boehnen, Exec. VP.

**■ 12646 ■ SUPERVALU Inc. Charley Brothers
    Div.**
PO Box 1000
New Stanton, PA 15672
Phone: (412)925-6600   **Fax:** (412)925-5385
Products: General line groceries. **SIC:** 5141
(Groceries—General Line). **Est:** 1903. **Sales:**
$1,000,000,000 (2000). **Emp:** 1,000. **Officers:** Conrad
Stephanites, President; Ron Eberhardt, Controller; Bill

Shaner, Dir. of Marketing; Lynn Steuart, Dir. of
Systems; Fran Lynch, Dir of Human Resources.

**■ 12647 ■ SUPERVALU Inc. Food Marketing
    Div.**
PO Box 1198
Ft. Wayne, IN 46801-1198
Phone: (219)483-2146   **Fax:** (219)483-4984
Products: Groceries, drugs, and meats. **SICs:** 5141
(Groceries—General Line); 5122 (Drugs, Proprietaries
& Sundries); 5147 (Meats & Meat Products). **Sales:**
$556,000,000 (2000). **Emp:** 500. **Officers:** John
Gerber, General Mgr.; Don Kyng, Accounting Manager.

■ 12648 ■ SuperValu International
495 E 19th St.
Tacoma, WA 98421
Phone: (253)593-3198   **Fax:** (253)593-7828
Products: Confectionery; Packaged frozen foods;
Dairy products; General line groceries; Fresh fruits and
vegetables. **SICs:** 5141 (Groceries—General Line);
5145 (Confectionery); 5142 (Packaged Frozen Foods);
5143 (Dairy Products Except Dried or Canned); 5148
(Fresh Fruits & Vegetables). **Officers:** Charles K.
Witzleben, President.

■ 12649 ■ Supervalu - Milton Div.
PO Box 386
Milton, WV 25541
Phone: (304)743-9087   **Fax:** (304)743-6206
Products: Groceries, including fresh beef, pork,
chicken, canned vegetables, fruit, soups, cereals,
frozen, produce, deli, bakery, and general
merchandise. **SICs:** 5141 (Groceries—General Line);
5147 (Meats & Meat Products); 5144 (Poultry & Poultry
Products). **Est:** 1940. **Sales:** $120,000,000 (2000).
Emp: 330. **Officers:** Ted Terek, President; Mike
Harper, Controller; Jamie Fincke, Dir. of Operations;
Stewart Varney, Information Systems Mgr.; Carolyn
Mount, Dir of Human Resources. **Former Name:**
Wetterau Inc. West Virginia Div.

■ 12650 ■ SuperValu—New England
2700 Plainfield Rd.
Cranston, RI 02921
Phone: (401)942-4000
Products: Perishable goods, including meat, seafood,
poultry, frozen food, dairy items, deli, ice cream, and
bakery items. **SICs:** 5147 (Meats & Meat Products);
5146 (Fish & Seafoods); 5144 (Poultry & Poultry
Products); 5142 (Packaged Frozen Foods); 5143
(Dairy Products Except Dried or Canned). **Former
Name:** Wetterau Inc. Providence Div.

■ 12651 ■ SuperValu Quincy Div.
PO Box 1021
Quincy, FL 32353
Phone: (850)875-2600   **Fax:** (850)875-5316
Products: Groceries; Meat; Frozen foods; Dairy. **SICs:**
5141 (Groceries—General Line); 5142 (Packaged
Frozen Foods); 5143 (Dairy Products Except Dried or
Canned); 5147 (Meats & Meat Products). **Est:** 1920.
Sales: $300,000,000 (2000). **Emp:** 400. **Officers:** Jim
Dunni, President. **Former Name:** Supervalu.

■ 12652 ■ Sutherland Foodservice Inc.
PO Box 786
Forest Park, GA 30298
Phone: (404)366-8550   **Fax:** (404)366-8599
Products: Fresh produce. **SIC:** 5144 (Poultry & Poultry
Products). **Est:** 1947. **Sales:** $63,000,000 (2000).
Emp: 200. **Officers:** J.E. Sutherland, President &
Chairman of the Board.

■ 12653 ■ Swanton Packing, Inc.
PO Box 704
Swanton, VT 05488
Phone: (802)868-4469
Products: Meat, including beef and veal. **SIC:** 5147
(Meats & Meat Products).

■ 12654 ■ Sweet Life Foods Inc.
PO Box 385
Windsor Locks, CT 06096
Phone: (860)623-1681   **Fax:** (860)627-5076
Products: Groceries. **SIC:** 5141 (Groceries—General
Line). **Est:** 1924. **Sales:** $300,000,000 (2000). **Emp:**
650. **Officers:** J.J. Leavitt, CEO; Joe Fusco, President;

Peter Leavitt, VP of Marketing; Ed Hammett, Dir of Human Resources.

■ 12655 ■ **A.J. Sweet of Madison, Inc.**
PO Box 8608
Madison, WI 53718
Phone: (608)222-8222 **Fax:** (608)222-1488
Products: Groceries, including fruits and vegetables.
SIC: 5148 (Fresh Fruits & Vegetables). **Est:** 1917.
Sales: $20,000,000 (2000). **Emp:** 53. **Officers:** Gary
Sweet, President; John Linder, CFO; Don Malotke,
Sales Mgr.; Al Scavon, Food Service Sales Dir.; Marc
Nordstrom, Operations Mgr.

■ 12656 ■ **Sweet Street Desserts**
722 Hiesters Ln.
Reading, PA 19605
Phone: (215)921-8113
Free: (800)Swe-et97 **Fax:** (215)921-0915
E-mail: mailbox@sweetstreet.com
URL: http://www.sweetstreet.com
Products: Desserts, including cakes, pies, gourmet
dessert bars, brownies, coffee cakes, cheesecakes,
and bundt cakes. **SIC:** 5149 (Groceries & Related
Products Nec). **Est:** 1979. **Emp:** 450. **Officers:** Sandy
Solmon, President & CEO.

■ 12657 ■ **Sweet Sue Kitchens**
106 Sweet Sue Dr.
Athens, AL 35611
Phone: (205)232-4201 **Fax:** (205)232-9631
Products: Poultry products. **SIC:** 5144 (Poultry &
Poultry Products). **Est:** 1961. **Sales:** $50,000,000
(2000). **Emp:** 275. **Officers:** Gary Piearson, VP of
Operations; David Zimmerman, Director.

■ 12658 ■ **Sweet Things Bakery**
1 Blackfield Dr.
Tiburon, CA 94920
Phone: (415)388-8583 **Fax:** (415)388-8581
E-mail: sweets@sweetthings.com
URL: http://www.sweetthings.com
Products: American homestyle desserts. **SIC:** 5149
(Groceries & Related Products Nec). **Est:** 1977. **Emp:**
35. **Officers:** Marsha Lasky, President; Sharon Leach,
Vice President.

■ 12659 ■ **Swensen's Inc.**
200 Bullfinch Dr., No. 1000
Andover, MA 01810
Phone: (978)975-1283 **Fax:** (978)686-2390
Products: Ice cream. **SIC:** 5143 (Dairy Products
Except Dried or Canned). **Est:** 1983. **Sales:**
$12,000,000 (2000). **Emp:** 225. **Officers:** John R.
Welty, President; Richard Anderthak, VP & Treasurer.

■ 12660 ■ **Swire Coca-Cola USA**
PO Box 794
Walla Walla, WA 99362
Phone: (509)529-0753
Products: Soft drinks and carbonated waters. **SIC:**
5149 (Groceries & Related Products Nec). **Sales:**
$27,000,000 (2000). **Emp:** 1,300.

■ 12661 ■ **Switzers Inc.**
575 N 20th St.
East St. Louis, IL 62205
Phone: (618)271-6336 **Fax:** (618)271-6339
Products: Canned goods, including green beans and
corn. **SICs:** 5141 (Groceries—General Line); 5149
(Groceries & Related Products Nec). **Est:** 1933. **Sales:**
$7,000,000 (2000). **Emp:** 35. **Officers:** Joe Switzer,
President; Carolyn Hundley, Controller.

■ 12662 ■ **Sygma Network**
660 Detroit St.
Monroe, MI 48162
Phone: (734)241-2890
Products: Groceries. **SIC:** 5141 (Groceries—General
Line).

■ 12663 ■ **SYGMA Network of Ohio Inc.**
4265 Diplomacy Dr.
Columbus, OH 43228
Phone: (614)876-2500 **Fax:** (614)771-5821
Products: Food. **SIC:** 5141 (Groceries—General Line).
Est: 1979. **Sales:** $2,000,000,000 (2000). **Emp:** 1,600.
Officers: Steve Deasey, President; Ron Epple, VP of
Finance; Mike Grey, Vice President; Lowell Rickards,

VP of Information Systems; Pat Clayton, Dir of Human
Resources.

■ 12664 ■ **SYGMA Network of Pennsylvania
Inc.**
4000 Industrial Rd.
Harrisburg, PA 17110
Phone: (717)232-3111 **Fax:** (717)697-6850
Products: Fast food products. **SIC:** 5141 (Groceries—
General Line). **Est:** 1976. **Sales:** $160,000,000 (2000).
Emp: 220. **Officers:** Gregory K. Marshall, President;
David Cleck, Vice President; David Crawford, Dir. of
Sales; David Myers, Dir. of Information Systems; Cary
Patrick, Dir. of Personnel.

■ 12665 ■ **Syracuse Banana Co.**
2100 Park
Syracuse, NY 13208-1041
Phone: (315)471-2251 **Fax:** (315)471-5247
Products: Fresh fruits; Fruits and vegetables. **SIC:**
5148 (Fresh Fruits & Vegetables). **Emp:** 49. **Officers:**
Frank Inserra.

■ 12666 ■ **Syracuse Cooperative Exchange**
PO Box 946
Syracuse, KS 67878
Phone: (316)384-5751
Products: Livestock and farm products. **SIC:** 5153
(Grain & Field Beans). **Sales:** $8,000,000 (2000). **Emp:**
17.

■ 12667 ■ **SYSCO/Alamo Food Services, Inc.**
PO Box 18364
San Antonio, TX 78218
Phone: (210)661-4581 **Fax:** (210)661-3217
Products: Institutional food. **SIC:** 5141 (Groceries—
General Line).

■ 12668 ■ **Sysco Corp.**
1390 Enclave Pkwy.
Houston, TX 77077-2099
Phone: (281)584-1390 **Fax:** (281)584-2524
Products: Food service supplies. **SIC:** 5149
(Groceries & Related Products Nec).

■ 12669 ■ **Sysco Food Service of Cincinnati
Inc.**
10510 Evendale Dr.
Cincinnati, OH 45241
Phone: (513)563-6300
Products: Food. **SIC:** 5141 (Groceries—General Line).
Officers: Jeffrey E. Boies, President; Gail E. Allen,
Exec. VP of Finance.

■ 12670 ■ **SYSCO Food Service, Inc.**
4753 S Union
Tulsa, OK 74107
Phone: (918)445-7772
Free: (800)441-0206 **Fax:** (918)445-3164
Products: Food; Cleaning supplies; Paper goods.
SICs: 5141 (Groceries—General Line); 5113 (Industrial
& Personal Service Paper); 5169 (Chemicals & Allied
Products Nec).

■ 12671 ■ **Sysco Food Service of Jamestown**
PO Box 160
Jamestown, NY 14702-0160
Phone: (716)665-5620
Products: Food service and restaurant supplies;
Beverages and food; Utensils. **SICs:** 5141
(Groceries—General Line); 5149 (Groceries & Related
Products Nec). **Sales:** $140,000,000 (2000). **Emp:**
325. **Officers:** Vernon E. Wetmore Jr., President.

■ 12672 ■ **Sysco Food Service of Seattle Inc.**
PO Box 97054
Kent, WA 98064-9754
Phone: (206)622-2261 **Fax:** (206)721-2787
Products: Groceries including canned, frozen, dry, and
fresh food; Produce. **SICs:** 5141 (Groceries—General
Line); 5142 (Packaged Frozen Foods); 5148 (Fresh
Fruits & Vegetables); 5149 (Groceries & Related
Products Nec). **Est:** 1953. **Sales:** $280,000,000
(2000). **Emp:** 650. **Officers:** Robert M. Jenson,
President; David Valentine, VP of Finance; Jim Bayne,
Dir. of Marketing; Fred LaCroix, Dir. of Information
Systems; Barbara Startz, Dir of Human Resources.

■ 12673 ■ **SYSCO Food Services**
PO Box 26004
Beaumont, TX 77720-6004
Phone: (409)892-3330 **Fax:** (409)892-0554
Products: Food; Small wares; Paper goods;
Chemicals. **SICs:** 5141 (Groceries—General Line);
5149 (Groceries & Related Products Nec); 5113
(Industrial & Personal Service Paper); 5169 (Chemicals
& Allied Products Nec).

■ 12674 ■ **Sysco Food Services of Atlanta
Inc.**
2225 Riverdale Rd.
College Park, GA 30349
Phone: (404)765-9900 **Fax:** (404)765-0708
Products: Food; Restaurant equipment and supplies,
including silverware. **SICs:** 5141 (Groceries—General
Line); 5046 (Commercial Equipment Nec). **Est:** 1969.
Sales: $180,000,000 (2000). **Emp:** 655. **Officers:**
Larry Accardi, President; Kirk Drummond, VP of
Finance; Jim Laonberger, VP of Marketing; Thom
Petty, Data Processing Mgr.; Bob Mitchell, Human
Resources Mgr.

■ 12675 ■ **SYSCO Food Services of Atlantic
City Inc.**
100 Century Dr.
Pleasantville, NJ 08232
Phone: (609)646-5300 **Fax:** (609)383-2111
Products: Meat; Soup; Peanuts. **SIC:** 5141
(Groceries—General Line). **Est:** 1935. **Sales:**
$60,000,000 (2000). **Emp:** 120. **Officers:** Tom
Lankford, President; Steven R. Burnette, Exec. VP;
Edward Custer, Dir. of Marketing & Sales.

■ 12676 ■ **Sysco Food Services of Austin Inc.**
PO Box 149024
Austin, TX 78714
Phone: (512)388-8000
Products: Groceries. **SIC:** 5141 (Groceries—General
Line). **Sales:** $184,100,000 (2000). **Emp:** 350.
Officers: Gary L. Ross, President; Lynn Gustafson,
CFO.

■ 12677 ■ **Sysco Food Services of Beaumont
Inc.**
PO Box 26004
Beaumont, TX 77720-6004
Phone: (409)892-3330 **Fax:** (409)892-0554
Products: General line of groceries. **SIC:** 5141
(Groceries—General Line). **Sales:** $70,000,000 (2000).
Emp: 180. **Officers:** James E. White, President;
William Hodgkins, CFO.

■ 12678 ■ **Sysco Food Services-Chicago Inc.**
250 Wieboldt Dr.
Des Plaines, IL 60016
Phone: (847)699-5400
Products: Fresh and frozen food. **SICs:** 5141
(Groceries—General Line); 5142 (Packaged Frozen
Foods). **Est:** 1925. **Sales:** $250,000,000 (2000). **Emp:**
700. **Officers:** Charles W. Staes, President; Greg
Neely, CFO; Maurice Woll, VP of Marketing; Bill
O'Mara, VP of Operations.

■ 12679 ■ **SYSCO Food Services of Detroit,
LLC**
PO Box 33579
Detroit, MI 48232-5579
Phone: (734)397-7990 **Fax:** (734)397-7474
Products: Frozen and dry food. **SICs:** 5149 (Groceries
& Related Products Nec); 5142 (Packaged Frozen
Foods). **Est:** 1934. **Emp:** 700. **Officers:** Michael W.
Green, President; Tom Barnes, Exec. VP. **Former
Name:** Miesel/SYSCO Food Service Co.

■ 12680 ■ **SYSCO Food Services of Grand
Rapids**
3700 Sysco Ct. SE
Grand Rapids, MI 49512
Phone: (616)949-3700 **Fax:** (616)977-4528
Products: Groceries, including fresh produce and
canned goods. **SICs:** 5141 (Groceries—General Line);
5148 (Fresh Fruits & Vegetables). **Est:** 1941. **Emp:**
630. **Officers:** David L. De Kock, President; Michael L.
Pattison, Sr. VP Finance and Operations; Richard A.
Johnston, Exec. VP; Randall L. Rutter, Sr. VP of
Merchandising; Eva Weber, Dir of Human Resources.
Former Name: SYSCO/Frost-Pack Food Services Inc.

■ 12681 ■ Sysco Food Services of Houston Inc.
PO Box 15316
Houston, TX 77220
Phone: (713)672-8080
Products: General line of groceries. **SIC:** 5141 (Groceries—General Line). **Sales:** $280,000,000 (2000). **Emp:** 650. **Officers:** Kenneth Spitler, President; Leonard Bryan, VP of Finance.

■ 12682 ■ SYSCO Food Services of Indianapolis Inc.
P.O .Box 248
Indianapolis, IN 46206
Phone: (317)291-2020
Products: General line of groceries. **SIC:** 5141 (Groceries—General Line). **Sales:** $170,000,000 (2000). **Emp:** 400. **Officers:** Walter C. Mills, President.

■ 12683 ■ SYSCO Food Services Los Angeles Inc.
20701 E Currier Rd.
Walnut, CA 91789-2904
Phone: (909)595-9595   **Fax:** (909)598-6383
Products: Food and food-related products for the hospitality industry. **SIC:** 5141 (Groceries—General Line). **Est:** 1930. **Sales:** $500,000,000 (2000). **Emp:** 1,000. **Officers:** Bruce J. Schwartz, President; John Kao, Sr. VP of Finance & Admin.; Verne Lusby, VP of Marketing; Mary Brumbugh, Dir. of Data Processing; Jim Gagnon, Dir of Human Resources.

■ 12684 ■ SYSCO Food Services of Minnesota Inc.
2400 County Rd. J
Mounds View, MN 55112
Phone: (612)785-9000   **Fax:** (612)785-7385
Products: Food, including frozen and canned; Produce; Meat; Cleaning supplies; Health supplies, including shampoo and deodorant; Medical supplies, including mattresses, bandages, and stethoscopes; Restaurant equipment and supplies, including booths. **SICs:** 5141 (Groceries—General Line); 5149 (Groceries & Related Products Nec); 5047 (Medical & Hospital Equipment); 5147 (Meats & Meat Products); 5148 (Fresh Fruits & Vegetables). **Est:** 1882. **Sales:** $228,000,000 (2000). **Emp:** 600. **Officers:** Philip J. Seipp, CEO & President; Debra Hamernick, Sr. VP.

■ 12685 ■ Sysco Food Services of Philadelphia Inc.
PO Box 6499
Philadelphia, PA 19145
Phone: (215)218-1600   **Fax:** (215)218-1617
Products: General line groceries; Restaurant equipment. **SICs:** 5141 (Groceries—General Line); 5046 (Commercial Equipment Nec). **Est:** 1969. **Sales:** $175,000,000 (2000). **Emp:** 450. **Officers:** James E. Lankford, CEO & President; William Mastrosimone, VP & CFO; Stewart Sapnas, Dir. of Marketing; Tom Gruppo, VP of Information Systems.

■ 12686 ■ SYSCO Food Services of Portland
PO Box 527
Wilsonville, OR 97070
Phone: (503)682-8700   **Fax:** (503)682-6699
Products: Food; Frozen foods; Milk; Fresh meat; Dried and dehydrated food products; Fruits and vegetables. **SICs:** 5141 (Groceries—General Line); 5142 (Packaged Frozen Foods); 5143 (Dairy Products Except Dried or Canned); 5148 (Fresh Fruits & Vegetables); 5149 (Groceries & Related Products Nec). **Est:** 1951. **Sales:** $195,000,000 (2000). **Emp:** 425. **Officers:** John P. Lampros, President; Curt Charon, VP of Finance; Dennis Lee, VP of Marketing; Cathy LaTourette, Dir of Human Resources.

■ 12687 ■ Sysco Food Services of San Francisco, Inc.
5900 Stewart Ave.
Fremont, CA 94538-3134
Phone: (510)226-3000
Products: Food for hospitals, schools, restaurants, and all food service establishments. **SIC:** 5141 (Groceries—General Line). **Sales:** $625,000,000 (2000). **Emp:** 1,150. **Officers:** Jack Schaefer, CEO & President; Zillah B. Fossum, Controller; Jim Simmons, VP of

Sales; Sidney Johnson, Information Systems Mgr.
Former Name: Sysco Food Service.

■ 12688 ■ SYSCO Food Services of South Florida
555 NE 185 St.
Miami, FL 33179
Phone: (305)651-5421   **Fax:** (305)770-1436
Products: Restaurant supplies, including detergent and cleaner; Food, including frozen fries, seafood, meats, vegetables, and fruits. **SICs:** 5141 (Groceries—General Line); 5046 (Commercial Equipment Nec); 5169 (Chemicals & Allied Products Nec); 5142 (Packaged Frozen Foods); 5146 (Fish & Seafoods). **Est:** 1948. **Sales:** $200,000,000 (2000). **Emp:** 600. **Officers:** Joseph M. Sciortino, CEO; Doug Schultz, VP of Finance; Tim Brown, VP of Sales; Denny Mirabella, Dir. of Data Processing; Dominic D'Angelo, Dir of Human Resources.

■ 12689 ■ Sysco Food Services of South Florida Inc.
555 NE 185th St.
Miami, FL 33179
Phone: (305)651-5421   **Fax:** (305)770-1436
Products: General line groceries. **SIC:** 5141 (Groceries—General Line). **Sales:** $200,000,000 (2000). **Emp:** 600. **Officers:** Joseph M. Sciortino, Chairman of the Board; Michael Headrick, Sr. VP & Finance Officer.

■ 12690 ■ Sysco Intermountain Food Services Inc.
PO Box 27638
Salt Lake City, UT 84127-0638
Phone: (801)972-5484   **Fax:** (801)977-2326
Products: General-line of groceries. **SIC:** 5141 (Groceries—General Line). **Sales:** $273,500,000 (2000). **Emp:** 520. **Officers:** Thomas M. Kesteloot, President; Pete Winder, CFO.

■ 12691 ■ SYSCO of Louisville
PO Box 32470
Louisville, KY 40232
Phone: (502)364-4300   **Fax:** (502)364-4344
Products: Grocery products and equipment for restaurants. **SICs:** 5141 (Groceries—General Line); 5046 (Commercial Equipment Nec). **Emp:** 2.

■ 12692 ■ Taiyo Inc.
PO Box 31087
Honolulu, HI 96820-1087
Phone: (808)537-4951   **Fax:** (808)851-1030
E-mail: taiyo@gte.net
Products: Food preparations; Dried and dehydrated food products; Head rice not packaged with other ingredients; Potatoes; Egg noodle products; Health foods. **SICs:** 5149 (Groceries & Related Products Nec); 5148 (Fresh Fruits & Vegetables). **Est:** 1946. **Sales:** $3,500,000 (2000). **Emp:** 20. **Officers:** Eric Tagashira.

■ 12693 ■ Tam Produce Inc.
PO Box 6986
Fullerton, CA 92834-6986
Phone: (213)620-0650
Products: Tomatoes. **SIC:** 5148 (Fresh Fruits & Vegetables). **Emp:** 120. **Officers:** Samuel J. Licato; Arthur Nigorizawa; Douglas Tambara.

■ 12694 ■ Tamarkin Company Inc.
375 Victoria Rd.
Youngstown, OH 44515
Phone: (330)792-3811   **Fax:** (330)792-8914
Products: Frozen foods; Dairy products; Produce. **SICs:** 5142 (Packaged Frozen Foods); 5148 (Fresh Fruits & Vegetables); 5143 (Dairy Products Except Dried or Canned). **Est:** 1923. **Sales:** $150,000,000 (2000). **Emp:** 250. **Officers:** Ray Burgo, President; Mark Minnaugh, VP & CFO; Joe Faccenda, Sr. VP of Marketing & Sales; Bill Lowery, Dir. of Distribution.

■ 12695 ■ Tamashiro Market Inc.
802 N King
Honolulu, HI 96817-4513
Phone: (808)841-8047
Products: Seafood; Fruits and vegetables. **SICs:** 5146 (Fish & Seafoods); 5148 (Fresh Fruits & Vegetables). **Emp:** 45. **Officers:** Walter H. Tamashiro, CEO & Chairman of the Board; Cyrus K. Tamashiro, President;

Guy K. Tamashiro, Vice President; Louise Tamashiro, Sec. & Treas.

■ 12696 ■ Tanner Enterprises, Inc.
PO Box 292638
Columbus, OH 43229-2638
Phone: (614)433-7020   **Fax:** (614)433-7533
E-mail: tannent@cs@com
Products: Institutional canned foods. **SIC:** 5149 (Groceries & Related Products Nec). **Est:** 1996. **Sales:** $4,000,000 (2000). **Emp:** 1. **Officers:** Martha M. Tanner, President & Treasurer. **Former Name:** English Tanner Enterprises.

■ 12697 ■ C.M. Tanner Grocery Company Inc.
PO Box 487
Carrollton, GA 30117
Phone: (404)832-6381
Products: Groceries. **SIC:** 5141 (Groceries—General Line). **Est:** 1893. **Sales:** $4,000,000 (2000). **Emp:** 25. **Officers:** John W. Tanner III, CEO; Karen Buchanan, Treasurer.

■ 12698 ■ Lee Ray Tarantino Company Inc.
PO Box 2408
South San Francisco, CA 94083
Phone: (650)871-4323   **Fax:** (650)873-5550
E-mail: Tarantino@freshpoint.com
URL: http://www.freshpoint.com
Products: Produce. **SIC:** 5148 (Fresh Fruits & Vegetables). **Est:** 1948. **Sales:** $60,000,000 (2000). **Emp:** 125. **Officers:** Joe Tarantino, CEO; Michael Lai, CFO; Mark Majewski, Sales Mgr.

■ 12699 ■ Tastee Apple Inc.
60810 County Rd. 9
Newcomerstown, OH 43832
Phone: (740)498-8316   **Fax:** (740)498-6108
Products: Dried and dehydrated fruits; Vinegar and cider. **SICs:** 5149 (Groceries & Related Products Nec); 5145 (Confectionery). **Est:** 1974. **Sales:** $7,000,000 (2000). **Emp:** 60. **Officers:** Greg Hackenbracht.

■ 12700 ■ Tasty Mix Quality Foods Inc.
88-90 Walworth St.
Brooklyn, NY 11205
Phone: (718)855-7680   **Fax:** (718)855-7681
E-mail: tastymx@aol.com
URL: http://www.tastymix.com
Products: Dough conditioners and stabilizers for the pasta and bakery industries. **SIC:** 5149 (Groceries & Related Products Nec). **Est:** 1991. **Sales:** $500,000 (1999). **Emp:** 8. **Officers:** Salvatore Ballarino Jr., Sec. & Treas. **Alternate Name:** Tasty Mix Products.

■ 12701 ■ Taylor and Sledd Inc.
PO Box 9729
Richmond, VA 23228
Phone: (804)262-8614
Products: Food, including frozen, dry, and canned foods. **SICs:** 5141 (Groceries—General Line); 5142 (Packaged Frozen Foods); 5149 (Groceries & Related Products Nec). **Est:** 1918. **Sales:** $31,500,000 (2000). **Emp:** 90. **Officers:** James R. Sledd, President & Treasurer.

■ 12702 ■ Tayters Inc.
738 Main St., No. 250
Waltham, MA 02454
Phone: (781)893-2065   **Fax:** (781)893-9015
Products: Snacks, including potato chips, nacho chips, and pretzels. **SIC:** 5145 (Confectionery). **Est:** 1946. **Emp:** 49. **Officers:** Bruce Whitmore; Keith Whitmore. **Alternate Name:** Tayters Inc. **Alternate Name:** Tayters Distributing.

■ 12703 ■ T.B.I. Corp.
700 E Industrial Park Dr.
Manchester, NH 03109
Phone: (603)668-6223   **Fax:** (603)668-6384
Products: General line groceries; Tobacco. **SICs:** 5141 (Groceries—General Line); 5194 (Tobacco & Tobacco Products).

■ 12704 ■ T.E.I./Texaco Bulk Services
53 County Rd. 2AB
Cody, WY 82414
Phone: (307)527-7575   **Fax:** (307)587-8039
Products: Snack foods. **SIC:** 5145 (Confectionery).

■ **12705** ■ **Tennessee Dressed Beef Company Inc.**
PO Box 23031
Nashville, TN 37202
Phone: (615)742-5800 **Fax:** (615)742-5814
Products: Beef, lamb, pork and veal. **SIC:** 5147 (Meats & Meat Products). **Sales:** $64,000,000 (2000). **Emp:** 24. **Officers:** R.N. Hall, President; Vicki Dark, Dir. of Admin.

■ **12706** ■ **Tennessee Shell Company, Inc.**
PO Box 609
Camden, TN 38320
Phone: (901)584-7747
Free: (800)835-0964 **Fax:** (901)584-8043
Products: Freshwater mussel shells. **SIC:** 5146 (Fish & Seafoods). **Est:** 1962. **Emp:** 28. **Officers:** Tadashi Konishi, President; William Jarnagin, Chairman of the Board.

■ **12707** ■ **Tenneva Food and Supplies Inc.**
PO Box 1719
Bristol, VA 24201
Phone: (540)669-7126 **Fax:** (540)669-8932
Products: Meat, including fresh beef, chicken, fish, and shrimp; Canned vegetables and soups; Frozen vegetables and fruits. **SICs:** 5147 (Meats & Meat Products); 5142 (Packaged Frozen Foods); 5146 (Fish & Seafoods); 5149 (Groceries & Related Products Nec). **Est:** 1945. **Sales:** $7,500,000 (2000). **Emp:** 30. **Officers:** Frank Grove, CEO; Steve Whiteside, Dir. of Sales.

■ **12708** ■ **Terry Bros. Inc.**
PO Box 87
Willis Wharf, VA 23486
Phone: (757)442-6251 **Fax:** (757)442-4134
Products: Fresh oysters and clams. **SIC:** 5146 (Fish & Seafoods). **Est:** 1903. **Sales:** $1,000,000 (2000). **Emp:** 9. **Officers:** N. Wec Terry Jr., Vice President, e-mail: wec@visi.net; K. S. Pete Terry, President. **Former Name:** H.M. Terry Company Inc.

■ **12709** ■ **Texas Health Distributors**
840 Interchange Blvd.
Austin, TX 78721
Phone: (512)385-3853 **Fax:** (512)385-2399
Products: Health food, including canned goods; Vitamins. **SICs:** 5149 (Groceries & Related Products Nec); 5122 (Drugs, Proprietaries & Sundries).

■ **12710** ■ **Thayer Food Products Inc.**
962 87th Ave.
Oakland, CA 94621
Phone: (510)569-7943 **Fax:** (510)569-0352
Products: Eggs, egg products, and butter. **SICs:** 5144 (Poultry & Poultry Products); 5143 (Dairy Products Except Dried or Canned). **Est:** 1921. **Sales:** $14,000,000 (2000). **Emp:** 40. **Officers:** R.W. Thayer Sr., President; Jr.; Jill Benson, VP Sales & Marketing.

■ **12711** ■ **Thibodeau's Farms**
419 Buxton Rd.
Saco, ME 04072
Phone: (207)283-3761
Products: Ice cream/frozen desserts. **SIC:** 5143 (Dairy Products Except Dried or Canned).

■ **12712** ■ **Thiel Cheese Inc.**
N 7630 County Hwy. BB
Hilbert, WI 54129
Phone: (920)989-1440
Free: (800)232-2928 **Fax:** (920)989-1288
URL: http://www.thielcheese.com
Products: Cheese products, including pasteurized processed cheese, foods, spreads, imitation cheese, club cheese and cold pack cheese. **SIC:** 5143 (Dairy Products Except Dried or Canned). **Est:** 1952. **Sales:** $10,000,000 (2000). **Emp:** 45. **Officers:** Stephen A. Thiel, President; Michael J. Ritchie, Sales Mgr., e-mail: mritchie@thielcheese.com.

■ **12713** ■ **Thomas Brothers Ham Co.**
1852 Gold Hill Rd.
Asheboro, NC 27203
Phone: (910)672-0337 **Fax:** (910)672-1782
Products: Country ham. **SIC:** 5147 (Meats & Meat Products). **Est:** 1959. **Sales:** $13,000,000 (2000). **Emp:** 43. **Officers:** Howard M. Thomas, President.

■ **12714** ■ **Thomas and Howard Company Inc.**
PO Box 23659
Columbia, SC 29224
Phone: (803)788-5520 **Fax:** (803)699-9097
Products: Groceries, including produce, meat, and canned products. **SICs:** 5141 (Groceries—General Line); 5147 (Meats & Meat Products); 5149 (Groceries & Related Products Nec); 5148 (Fresh Fruits & Vegetables). **Est:** 1897. **Sales:** $220,000,000 (2000). **Emp:** 440. **Officers:** David R. Clark, President; Thomas Perkins, Treasurer & Secty.; John White, Division President; Wilson Frayer, VP of Information Systems; Diane Jackson, Office Mgr.

■ **12715** ■ **Thomas Meat Co.**
2055 Nelson Miller Pky.
Louisville, KY 40223-2185
Phone: (502)587-6947
Products: Meat. **SIC:** 5147 (Meats & Meat Products). **Sales:** $52,000,000 (2000). **Emp:** 100. **Officers:** Anthony J. Thomas, President; Tom George, Controller.

■ **12716** ■ **Thomas-Walker-Lacey Inc.**
PO Box 1625
Canton, MS 39046
Phone: (601)859-1421 **Fax:** (601)859-8642
Products: Food; General merchandise. **SICs:** 5141 (Groceries—General Line); 5099 (Durable Goods Nec); 5199 (Nondurable Goods Nec). **Officers:** Toxey Hall, President.

■ **12717** ■ **Thompson-Clark-Gerritsen Co.**
2120 Pewaukee Rd.
Waukesha, WI 53188
Phone: (414)521-4300
Products: Food. **SIC:** 5141 (Groceries—General Line). **Sales:** $68,000,000 (1993). **Emp:** 130. **Officers:** Harlan J. Gerritsen, President.

■ **12718** ■ **Thompson Company Inc.**
1219 W North Front
Box 1466
Grand Island, NE 68802
Phone: (308)382-6581 **Fax:** (308)382-1813
Products: Cigarettes; Tobacco; Candy; Chewing gum; Dairy products; Frozen foods. **SICs:** 5145 (Confectionery); 5143 (Dairy Products Except Dried or Canned); 5194 (Tobacco & Tobacco Products); 5142 (Packaged Frozen Foods). **Est:** 1936. **Sales:** $18,000,000 (2000). **Emp:** 70. **Officers:** Tony Wald; Barbara Wald.

■ **12719** ■ **Thrift Products Company Inc.**
41 44th St. SE
Grand Rapids, MI 49548
Phone: (616)538-0930
Free: (800)538-6887 **Fax:** (616)538-7797
Products: Nuts and candy. **SIC:** 5145 (Confectionery). **Est:** 1940. **Sales:** $3,000,000 (2000). **Emp:** 25. **Officers:** Dan Lemmink.

■ **12720** ■ **Thruway Produce Inc.**
99 West Ave.
Lyndonville, NY 14098-9744
Phone: (716)765-2277 **Fax:** (716)765-9710
Products: Apples. **SIC:** 5148 (Fresh Fruits & Vegetables). **Emp:** 49. **Officers:** Howard H. Dobbin.

■ **12721** ■ **Tichon Seafood Corp.**
PO Box 948
New Bedford, MA 02741
Phone: (508)999-5607 **Fax:** (508)990-8271
Products: Seafood. **SIC:** 5146 (Fish & Seafoods). **Est:** 1943. **Sales:** $25,000,000 (2000). **Emp:** 100. **Officers:** D.E. Tichon, President; R.D. Tichon, CFO; P. Mello, Sales Mgr.

■ **12722** ■ **Timber Crest Farms**
4791 Dry Creek Rd.
Healdsburg, CA 95448
Phone: (707)433-8251 **Fax:** (707)433-8255
E-mail: tcf@timbercrest.com
URL: http://www.timbercrest.com
Products: Dried and dehydrated fruits; Dried and dehydrated vegetables. **SICs:** 5149 (Groceries & Related Products Nec); 5145 (Confectionery). **Est:** 1957. **Sales:** $7,000,000 (1999). **Emp:** 50. **Officers:** Ruth W. Waltenspiel, Sales/Marketing Contact, e-mail: Ruth@timbercrest.com; Ronald Waltenspiel.

■ **12723** ■ **Tims Cascade Style Chips**
1502 Pike St. NW
Auburn, WA 98001
Phone: (253)833-0255 **Fax:** (253)939-9411
URL: http://www.timschips.com
Products: Snack foods. **SIC:** 5149 (Groceries & Related Products Nec). **Est:** 1986. **Sales:** $15,000,000 (2000). **Emp:** 65. **Officers:** Tim Kennedy.

■ **12724** ■ **TLC Beatrice International Holdings Inc.**
9 W 57th St., No. 3910
New York, NY 10019
Phone: (212)756-8900 **Fax:** (212)888-3093
Products: Groceries. **SIC:** 5141 (Groceries—General Line). **Est:** 1987. **Sales:** $1,400,000,000 (2000). **Emp:** 1,800. **Officers:** Loida Nicolas, CEO & Chairman of the Board; Peter Offermann, Exec. VP & CFO; Dennis Jones, Sr. VP of Business Development.

■ **12725** ■ **To Market Two Markets Inc.**
107 Lakemont Park Blvd.
Altoona, PA 16602
Phone: (814)941-3090 **Fax:** (814)941-3094
Products: Specialty foods. **SIC:** 5149 (Groceries & Related Products Nec). **Sales:** $1,000,000 (2000). **Officers:** e-mail: philsky@aasdcat.com

■ **12726** ■ **Tom Cat Bakery**
43-05 10th St.
Long Island City, NY 11101-6829
Phone: (718)786-4224
Products: Bread; Rolls. **SIC:** 5149 (Groceries & Related Products Nec). **Est:** 1988. **Sales:** $4,000,000 (2000). **Emp:** 75. **Officers:** Noel Comess, President; Aman Khan, Controller.

■ **12727** ■ **Tomahawk Farms Inc.**
603 S Wilson
Dunn, NC 28334
Phone: (919)892-6174
Products: Ham. **SIC:** 5147 (Meats & Meat Products). **Est:** 1957. **Sales:** $10,000,000 (2000). **Emp:** 50. **Officers:** Lewis Fetterman Jr., President; Charles N. Gancer, Dir. of Marketing.

■ **12728** ■ **Tomfoolery Serious Chocolate, Inc.**
5362 Oceanus Dr., Ste. C
Huntington Beach, CA 92649
Phone: (714)903-6800 **Fax:** (714)892-4345
URL: http://www.tomfooleryinc.com
Products: Chocolate products. **SIC:** 5145 (Confectionery). **Est:** 1979. **Sales:** $200,000 (2000). **Emp:** 12. **Officers:** Millie Sweesy.

■ **12729** ■ **Tom's Foods Inc.**
2648 Byington Sloway Rd.
Knoxville, TN 37931-3213
Phone: (423)690-8170 **Fax:** 800-742-0290
Products: Snack foods, including chips, peanuts, and candy. **SICs:** 5141 (Groceries—General Line); 5149 (Groceries & Related Products Nec). **Sales:** $30,000,000 (2000). **Emp:** 300. **Officers:** Wyatt Hearp.

■ **12730** ■ **Tom's Toasted Peanuts**
824 N Gloster
Tupelo, MS 38801-1949
Phone: (601)842-7537
Products: Nuts and seeds (salted, roasted, cooked, or blanched); Candy; Potato chips; Corn chips. **SIC:** 5145 (Confectionery). **Emp:** 49. **Officers:** William W. Timbes.

■ **12731** ■ **Tony's Fine Foods**
PO Box 1501
West Sacramento, CA 95605-1501
Phone: (916)374-4000 **Fax:** (916)372-0727
URL: http://www.tonysfinefoods.com
Products: Deli, bakery and related products. **SICs:** 5147 (Meats & Meat Products); 5143 (Dairy Products Except Dried or Canned); 5149 (Groceries & Related Products Nec). **Est:** 1934. **Sales:** $150,000,000 (1999). **Emp:** 500. **Officers:** Karl Berger, President, e-mail: karl@tonysfinefoods.com; Scott Berger, CEO, e-mail: scott@tonysfinefoods.com; James DeSalles, CFO, e-mail: desalles@tonysfinefoods.com; Karl

Berger, Sales/Marketing Contact; Mike Smith, Human Resources Contact. **Former Name:** Tony Ingoglia Salami and Cheese Company Inc.

■ 12732 ■ Too Goo Doo Farms Inc.
4693 Too Goo Doo Farm Rd.
Yonges Island, SC 29449
Phone: (843)889-6468 **Fax:** (843)889-2762
E-mail: tgdfarms@mindspring.com
Products: Fresh, precut vegetables. **SIC:** 5148 (Fresh Fruits & Vegetables). **Est:** 1957. **Sales:** $1,500,000 (1999). **Emp:** 35. **Officers:** J.A. Smoak, Chairman of the Board; Josefa Smoak, President.

■ 12733 ■ Top Taste Bakery Inc.
PO Box 297
Finley, ND 58230-0297
Phone: (701)524-1380
Products: Dry bakery products. **SIC:** 5149 (Groceries & Related Products Nec). **Sales:** $1,500,000 (2000). **Emp:** 49. **Officers:** Harold Fetting.

■ 12734 ■ Topco Associates Inc.
7711 Gross Point Rd.
Skokie, IL 60077
Phone: (847)676-3030 **Fax:** (847)676-4949
Products: Groceries. **SIC:** 5141 (Groceries—General Line). **Est:** 1944. **Sales:** $3,500,000 (1999). **Emp:** 360. **Officers:** Steven K. Lauer, CEO & President; Kenneth H. Guy, Member Development.

■ 12735 ■ Torn and Glasser Inc.
PO Box 21823
Los Angeles, CA 90021
Phone: (213)627-6496
Free: (800)282-6887 **Fax:** (213)688-0941
E-mail: sales@tornandglasser.com
Products: Groceries, including rice, beans, dried fruits, and nuts. **SICs:** 5141 (Groceries—General Line); 5145 (Confectionery); 5153 (Grain & Field Beans); 5149 (Groceries & Related Products Nec). **Est:** 1928. **Sales:** $30,000,000 (2000). **Emp:** 60. **Officers:** Robert Glasser, President; Rick Bode, CFO; Brian Franklin, Dir. of Marketing.

■ 12736 ■ Totem Food Products Co.
6203 S 194th
Kent, WA 98032-2127
Phone: (253)872-9200
Free: (800)347-6330 **Fax:** (253)872-9366
Products: Snack foods, including potato chips, corn chips, and popcorn; Processed, frozen, and cooked meats. **SICs:** 5145 (Confectionery); 5149 (Groceries & Related Products Nec); 5147 (Meats & Meat Products). **Est:** 1961. **Sales:** $4,250,000 (2000). **Emp:** 24. **Officers:** D. E. McKeen, President; K. H. Autry, VP & Secty.; D.E. Mckeen Jr., Vice President.

■ 12737 ■ Toudouze Inc.
PO Box 7449
San Antonio, TX 78207-0449
Phone: (210)224-1891 **Fax:** (210)224-5752
Products: Groceries. **SIC:** 5149 (Groceries & Related Products Nec). **Sales:** $9,000,000 (1994). **Emp:** 29. **Officers:** Charles Toudouze Jr., President.

■ 12738 ■ TownTalk/Hostess
1700 Island Ave.
Pittsburgh, PA 15233
Phone: (412)231-2000 **Fax:** (412)231-7242
Products: Bread and cakes. **SICs:** 5149 (Groceries & Related Products Nec); 5145 (Confectionery). **Est:** 1889. **Sales:** $40,000,000 (2000). **Emp:** 350. **Officers:** Jeffrey A. Keeton, General Sales Mgr.

■ 12739 ■ T.R. Distributing
7228 NW 79th Terr.
Miami, FL 33166
Phone: (305)883-0697 **Fax:** (305)883-0521
Products: Dried and dehydrated fruits; Nuts and seeds (salted, roasted, cooked, or blanched); Candy. **SICs:** 5149 (Groceries & Related Products Nec); 5145 (Confectionery).

■ 12740 ■ Trader Vic's Food Products
PO Box 8603
Emeryville, CA 94662
Phone: (510)658-9722
Free: (800)200-5355 **Fax:** (510)658-8110
E-mail: fthittell@tradervics.com
URL: http://www.tradervics.com
Products: Salad dressing; Non-alcoholic drink mixes; Drink syrups; Sauces. **SIC:** 5149 (Groceries & Related Products Nec). **Est:** 1946. **Sales:** $10,000,000 (1999). **Emp:** 9. **Officers:** Ted Hittell, Vice President.

■ 12741 ■ Traditional Quality Corp.
4498 Main St.
Buffalo, NY 14226
Phone: (716)839-1018
Products: Sugar. **SIC:** 5149 (Groceries & Related Products Nec). **Est:** 1987. **Sales:** $1,000,000 (2000). **Emp:** 4. **Officers:** Daniel Irwin Jr., President.

■ 12742 ■ Trailblazer Foods
PO Box 441
Fairview, OR 97024
Phone: (503)666-5800 **Fax:** (503)666-6800
Products: Preserves and pie fillings. **SIC:** 5149 (Groceries & Related Products Nec).

■ 12743 ■ Trans World Company of Miami Inc.
2090 NW 13th Ave.
Miami, FL 33142-7702
Phone: (305)545-5639 **Fax:** (305)545-7727
Products: Fruits and vegetables. **SIC:** 5148 (Fresh Fruits & Vegetables). **Sales:** $2,000,000 (2000). **Emp:** 3. **Officers:** Anthony Vitale; Dulce A. Vitale.

■ 12744 ■ Transmudo Company Inc.
999 Brickell Ave., No. 1001
Miami, FL 33131-9044
Phone: (305)539-1205 **Fax:** (305)539-0022
E-mail: transmundo@aol.com
Products: Canned corned beef; Frozen cooked beef; Candy and confectionery. **SICs:** 5142 (Packaged Frozen Foods); 5147 (Meats & Meat Products). **Est:** 1953. **Sales:** $7,000,000 (1999). **Emp:** 5. **Officers:** Alberto J. Senosiain, President; Esther G. Gomez, CFO.

■ 12745 ■ Trax Farms Inc.
RD 1, Box 68A
Rte. 88
Finleyville, PA 15332-9801
Phone: (412)835-3246 **Fax:** (412)835-7286
Products: Vegetables and fruits, including apples, lettuce, onions, and potatoes; Baked goods, including bread and rolls; Deli meats. **SICs:** 5148 (Fresh Fruits & Vegetables); 5149 (Groceries & Related Products Nec); 5147 (Meats & Meat Products). **Est:** 1868. **Emp:** 60. **Officers:** John Trax, General Mgr.

■ 12746 ■ Tree of Life/Gourmet Award Foods
12601 SE Highway 212
PO Box 919
Clackamas, OR 97015
Phone: (503)655-1177 **Fax:** (503)650-5550
Products: Food preparations; Dried and dehydrated food products; Head rice not packaged with other ingredients; Potatoes; Egg noodle products; Health foods; Milk. **SICs:** 5149 (Groceries & Related Products Nec); 5143 (Dairy Products Except Dried or Canned). **Former Name:** Ray's Food Service.

■ 12747 ■ Tree of Life Inc.
PO Box 410
St. Augustine, FL 32085
Phone: (904)824-8181
Products: Full-line health food groceries. **SIC:** 5141 (Groceries—General Line). **Sales:** $84,000,000 (1993). **Emp:** 600. **Officers:** Richard A. Thorne, CEO; Henry Puente, CFO.

■ 12748 ■ Tree of Life Inc. Midwest
PO Box 2629
Bloomington, IN 47402
Phone: (812)333-1511
Free: (800)999-4200 **Fax:** 800-395-0384
Products: Pet supplies; Food; Beverages; Vitamins. **SICs:** 5141 (Groceries—General Line); 5149 (Groceries & Related Products Nec); 5122 (Drugs, Proprietaries & Sundries); 5199 (Nondurable Goods Nec).

■ 12749 ■ Tree of Life Inc. Northeast
2501 71st St.
Box 852
North Bergen, NJ 07047
Phone: (201)662-7200 **Fax:** (201)854-8769
Products: Food preparations; Dried and dehydrated food products; Head rice not packaged with other ingredients; Potatoes; Egg noodle products; Health foods. **SICs:** 5149 (Groceries & Related Products Nec); 5148 (Fresh Fruits & Vegetables).

■ 12750 ■ Tree of Life Inc. Northwest
PO Box 88830
Seattle, WA 98188
Phone: (425)251-5220 **Fax:** (425)251-6381
Products: Natural health foods and supplements. **SICs:** 5149 (Groceries & Related Products Nec); 5122 (Drugs, Proprietaries & Sundries).

■ 12751 ■ Tree of Life Inc. Southwest
105 Bluebonnet Dr.
Cleburne, TX 76031
Phone: (817)641-6678 **Fax:** (817)556-4956
Products: Food preparations; Dried and dehydrated food products; Head rice not packaged with other ingredients; Potatoes; Egg noodle products; Health foods. **SIC:** 5149 (Groceries & Related Products Nec).

■ 12752 ■ Tri Marine International
150 W 7th
San Pedro, CA 90731-3336
Phone: (310)548-6245 **Fax:** (310)548-0452
Products: Seafood. **SIC:** 5146 (Fish & Seafoods). **Emp:** 49. **Officers:** Renato Curto, President; Mike Walsh, Vice President.

■ 12753 ■ Tri River Foods Inc.
PO Box 545
Bethel Park, PA 15102
Phone: (412)831-9090
Products: Groceries. **SIC:** 5141 (Groceries—General Line).

■ 12754 ■ Tri-State Wholesale Associated Grocers Inc.
PO Box 971970
El Paso, TX 79997-1970
Phone: (915)774-6400 **Fax:** (915)774-6443
Products: General line groceries; Tobacco. **SICs:** 5141 (Groceries—General Line); 5194 (Tobacco & Tobacco Products).

■ 12755 ■ Triarc Companies Inc.
280 Park Ave.
New York, NY 10017
Phone: (212)451-3000 **Fax:** (212)451-3023
URL: http://www.triarc.com
Products: Beverages and restaurant franchising. **SIC:** 5149 (Groceries & Related Products Nec). **Est:** 1929. **Sales:** $854,000,000 (1999). **Emp:** 1,194. **Officers:** Nelson Peltz, CEO & Chairman of the Board; John L. Barnes Jr., Exec. VP & CFO; Peter W. May, President & COO.

■ 12756 ■ Trinidad/Benham
PO Box 29
Mineola, TX 75773
Phone: (903)569-2636 **Fax:** (903)569-2120
Products: Groceries, including dry beans, rice, and popcorn; Aluminum foil. **SIC:** 5141 (Groceries—General Line). **Sales:** $17,000,000 (2000). **Emp:** 65. **Officers:** Carl Hartman.

■ 12757 ■ Tripifoods Inc.
PO Box 1107
Buffalo, NY 14240
Phone: (716)853-7400
Free: (800)851-7400 **Fax:** (716)852-7400
Products: General line groceries, Cigarettes; Candy. **SICs:** 5141 (Groceries—General Line); 5148 (Fresh Fruits & Vegetables). **Est:** 1917. **Sales:** $200,000,000 (2000). **Emp:** 275. **Officers:** Gregory G. Tripi, President; Joseph C. Tripi II, Sr. VP.

■ 12758 ■ **Triton Marketing Inc.**
8255 Dunwoody Pl.
Atlanta, GA 30350
Phone: (404)992-7088 **Fax:** (404)992-8537
Products: Convenience store items. **SIC:** 5141
(Groceries—General Line). **Est:** 1954. **Sales:**
$40,000,000 (2000). **Emp:** 160. **Officers:** James L.
Richardson, President; Weldon Tollison, Controller;
Leslie E. Blubaugh II, VP of Marketing; Anthony P.
Phillips, Dir. of Information Systems; Melvin Seligman,
VP of Admin.

■ 12759 ■ **Trophy Nut Company**
PO Box 199
Tipp City, OH 45371
Phone: (937)667-8478
Free: (800)729-6887 **Fax:** (937)667-4656
Products: Nuts and candies. **SIC:** 5145
(Confectionery). **Sales:** $20,000,000 (2000). **Emp:** 99.
Officers: G.J. Allen; R.J. Bollinger; Joe R. Joity, Sales
Mgr.

■ 12760 ■ **Tropical Hawaiian Products**
PO Box 210
Keaau, HI 96749
Phone: (808)966-7435 **Fax:** (808)966-7367
Products: Fresh papaya; Pureed food products. **SIC:**
5148 (Fresh Fruits & Vegetables). **Officers:** Lee Cole,
Dir. of Sales.

■ 12761 ■ **Tropical Nut and Fruit**
11517-A Cordage St.
Charlotte, NC 28273
Phone: (704)588-0400
Products: Nuts, dried fruit, grain, seeds, candy, and
other dried foods. **SICs:** 5159 (Farm-Product Raw
Materials Nec); 5149 (Groceries & Related Products
Nec); 5153 (Grain & Field Beans); 5145
(Confectionery).

■ 12762 ■ **Trout-Blue Chelan, Inc.**
PO Box 669
Chelan, WA 98816
Phones: (509)682-2591 (509)682-2539
Products: Fresh apples and pears. **SIC:** 5148 (Fresh
Fruits & Vegetables). **Est:** 1921. **Sales:** $30,000,000
(2000). **Emp:** 150. **Officers:** Richard Easley, Sales
Mgr.; Margo Thorndike, Controller. **Alternate Name:**
Trout Inc.

■ 12763 ■ **Troyer Foods Inc.**
17141 State Rd., No. 4
PO Box 608
Goshen, IN 46526
Phone: (219)533-0302
Free: (800)876-9377 **Fax:** (219)533-3851
URL: http://www.troyers.com
Products: Meats; Deli and bakery products. **SICs:**
5147 (Meats & Meat Products); 5149 (Groceries &
Related Products Nec). **Est:** 1948. **Sales:**
$150,000,000 (1999). **Emp:** 185. **Officers:** Paris Ball-
Miller, President, e-mail: paris@troyers.com; J.
Christopher Ulmer, Treasurer; B. Eldridge, Dir. of
Information Systems; Dave Trick, Dir of Human
Resources.

■ 12764 ■ **True World Foods, Inc. of Alabama**
PO Box 767
Bayou la Batre, AL 36509
Phone: (334)824-4193
Free: (800)816-1832 **Fax:** (334)824-7687
Products: Shrimp, scallops, snapper, and whitting.
SIC: 5146 (Fish & Seafoods). **Est:** 1979. **Sales:**
$27,000,000 (2000). **Emp:** 100. **Officers:** Clinton
Jones, VP & General Merchandising Mgr.; Robert J.
Finamore, VP of Sales. **Doing Business As:**
International Oceanic Enterprises Inc. of Alabama.

■ 12765 ■ **Trundle and Company Inc.**
155 E 55th St.
New York, NY 10022
Phone: (212)486-1011 **Fax:** (212)486-1304
Products: Fresh fruit juices, canned vegetables and
concentrates. **SIC:** 5149 (Groceries & Related
Products Nec). **Sales:** $1,000,000 (2000). **Emp:** 4.
Officers: Edward Trundle, President.

■ 12766 ■ **Tucson Co-op Wholesale**
350 S Toole Ave.
Tucson, AZ 85701
Phone: (520)884-9951
Free: (800)350-2667 **Fax:** (520)792-3258
Products: Organic and natural foods and products,
including vitamins. **SIC:** 5149 (Groceries & Related
Products Nec). **Est:** 1974. **Emp:** 70.

■ 12767 ■ **Tufts Ranch Packing Shed**
27260 State, Hwy. 128
Winters, CA 95694-9701
Phone: (530)795-4144 **Fax:** (530)795-3844
Products: Produce. **SIC:** 5148 (Fresh Fruits &
Vegetables). **Sales:** $2,000,000 (2000). **Emp:** 50.

■ 12768 ■ **Tumbleweed Distributors**
6315 Doyle St.
Emeryville, CA 94608
Phone: (650)428-9242 **Fax:** (650)428-1532
Products: Food preparations; Dried and dehydrated
food products; Head rice not packaged with other
ingredients; Potatoes; Egg noodle products; Health
foods. **SICs:** 5149 (Groceries & Related Products Nec);
5148 (Fresh Fruits & Vegetables).

■ 12769 ■ **Tung Pec Inc.**
6965 Aragon Cir.
Buena Park, CA 90620
Phone: (714)562-0848 **Fax:** (714)562-0849
Products: Frozen foods, beverages, and dry groceries.
SICs: 5142 (Packaged Frozen Foods); 5182 (Wines &
Distilled Beverages); 5141 (Groceries—General Line).
Est: 1994. **Sales:** $600,000 (2000). **Emp:** 5. **Officers:**
Frank C. Liu, President.

■ 12770 ■ **Dam Tuong**
76 N Pauati St.
Honolulu, HI 96817-5128
Phone: (808)531-6132 **Fax:** (808)524-4989
Products: Candy; Seeds. **SIC:** 5145 (Confectionery).
Officers: Tuong Dam, Owner.

■ 12771 ■ **Tupman Thurlow Company Inc.**
40 Tower Ln.
Avon, CT 06001-4222
Phone: (860)677-8933
Free: (800)296-1412 **Fax:** (860)678-0601
Products: Canned meats. **SIC:** 5149 (Groceries &
Related Products Nec). **Sales:** $33,000,000 (2000).
Emp: 8. **Officers:** Paul Blakeley, President.

■ 12772 ■ **Turbana Corp.**
550 Biltmore Way, Ste. 730
Coral Gables, FL 33134-5730
Phone: (305)445-1542
Free: (800)BAN-ANAS **Fax:** (305)443-8908
E-mail: info@turbana.com
URL: http://www.turbana.com
Products: Bananas and plantains. **SIC:** 5148 (Fresh
Fruits & Vegetables). **Est:** 1970. **Sales:** $110,000,000
(2000). **Emp:** 29. **Officers:** Jorge H. Pineda, CEO;
Herb Garritt, VP of Sales; Elkin J. Escobar, Chairman
of the Board & Finance Officer.

■ 12773 ■ **Turner Dairy**
PO Box 337
Paragould, AR 72450
Phone: (870)239-2143 **Fax:** (870)239-2891
Products: Milk; Natural and process cheese and
related products. **SIC:** 5143 (Dairy Products Except
Dried or Canned). **Sales:** $14,000,000 (2000). **Emp:**
59.

■ 12774 ■ **Turner Shellfish New Zealand Inc.**
PO Box 8919
Newport Beach, CA 92658
Phone: (949)622-6181 **Fax:** (949)622-6182
E-mail: info@turner.co.nz
URL: http://www.turnernewzealand.com
Products: Seafood; Shellfish; Meat; Sparkling water;
Fish; Venison; Lamb. **SICs:** 5142 (Packaged Frozen
Foods); 5146 (Fish & Seafoods). **Sales:** $5,000,000
(2000). **Emp:** 15. **Officers:** Noel Turner, President &
Chairman of the Board; Kathrin Turner, Vice President.

■ 12775 ■ **Tuscan Dairy Farms Inc.**
750 Union Ave.
Union, NJ 07083
Phone: (908)686-1500 **Fax:** (908)687-5130
Products: Dairy products, including milk. **SIC:** 5143
(Dairy Products Except Dried or Canned). **Est:** 1906.
Sales: $770,000,000 (2000). **Emp:** 1,400. **Officers:**
Robert W. Allen, President; Tim Natole, VP & CFO;
Peter Stigi, Sr. VP of Sales & Marketing. **Former
Name:** Tuscan Dairy Farms Inc.

■ 12776 ■ **Tuscan/Lehigh Dairies L.P.**
750 Union Ave.
Union, NJ 07083
Phone: (908)851-5180 **Fax:** (908)686-3145
Products: Dairy products. **SIC:** 5143 (Dairy Products
Except Dried or Canned). **Sales:** $800,000,000 (2000).
Emp: 1,350. **Officers:** Robert W. Allen, CEO &
President; Tim Natole, Exec. VP & CFO.

■ 12777 ■ **Tusco Grocers Inc.**
30 S Fourth St.
PO Box 240
Dennison, OH 44621-0240
Phone: (740)922-2223
Free: (800)545-4084 **Fax:** (740)922-4443
Products: Groceries, including dairy products, frozen
foods, meat products, deli items, and baked goods.
SICs: 5141 (Groceries—General Line); 5147 (Meats &
Meat Products); 5142 (Packaged Frozen Foods); 5143
(Dairy Products Except Dried or Canned). **Est:** 1990.
Sales: $30,500,000 (2000). **Emp:** 70. **Officers:**
Gregory Kimble, President; David Weaver, Dir. of
Sales; James Weaver, Dir. of Information Systems;
Mike Angelozzi, Distribution Mgr.; Mike Angelozzi,
Director of Retail Operations.

■ 12778 ■ **Twin County Grocers Inc.**
145 Talmadge Rd.
Edison, NJ 08818
Phone: (732)287-4600 **Fax:** (732)248-8099
Products: General line groceries; Frozen foods; Dairy
products; Fruits and vegetables. **SICs:** 5141
(Groceries—General Line); 5148 (Fresh Fruits &
Vegetables); 5143 (Dairy Products Except Dried or
Canned); 5142 (Packaged Frozen Foods). **Est:** 1944.
Sales: $1,000,000,000 (2000). **Emp:** 980. **Officers:**
James A. Burke, CEO; Victor Bonini, CFO; Mike
Stolarz, Dir. of Marketing; Bob Helmer, Dir. of Data
Processing; Joe Cassamento, Dir of Human
Resources.

■ 12779 ■ **Twin Valley Farmers Exchange Inc.**
845 E Main St.
Hegins, PA 17938
Phone: (717)682-3171
Products: Eggs. **SIC:** 5144 (Poultry & Poultry
Products). **Est:** 1943. **Sales:** $7,000,000 (2000). **Emp:**
20. **Officers:** Gary Eshelman, President.

■ 12780 ■ **Tyson Seafood Group**
PO Box 79021
Seattle, WA 98119
Phone: (206)282-3445 **Fax:** (206)281-8052
Products: frozen seafood processed aboard vessels.
SIC: 5142 (Packaged Frozen Foods). **Officers:** Roy
Brown, President.

■ 12781 ■ **Tzetzo Brothers Inc.**
1100 Military Rd.
Buffalo, NY 14217
Phone: (716)877-0800
Products: Food; T-shirts; Candy. **SICs:** 5141
(Groceries—General Line); 5145 (Confectionery); 5136
(Men's/Boys' Clothing); 5137 (Women's/Children's
Clothing). **Est:** 1926. **Sales:** $54,000,000 (2000). **Emp:**
120. **Officers:** Perry Tzetzo, President & Chairman of
the Board.

■ 12782 ■ **Umpqua Dairy Products Co.**
PO Box 1306
Roseburg, OR 97470
Phone: (541)672-2638 **Fax:** (541)673-0256
Products: Dairy products. **SIC:** 5143 (Dairy Products
Except Dried or Canned). **Sales:** $20,000,000 (2000).
Emp: 120. **Officers:** Douglas B. Feldkamp, President;
Steven D. Feldkamp, Vice President.

■ **12783** ■ **Uncle Bens Inc.**
5721 Harvey Wilson
Houston, TX 77020-8025
Phone: (713)674-9484 **Fax:** (713)670-2227
Products: Rice. **SIC:** 5149 (Groceries & Related Products Nec). **Officers:** James R. Webb, President.

■ **12784** ■ **Uni-Marts Inc.**
477 E Beaver Ave.
State College, PA 16801-5690
Phone: (814)234-6000 **Fax:** (814)234-3277
URL: http://www.uni-mart.com
Products: Gas; Groceries. **SICs:** 5141 (Groceries—General Line); 5172 (Petroleum Products Nec). **Est:** 1972. **Sales:** $252,000,000 (1999). **Emp:** 2,100. **Officers:** Henry D. Sahakian, Chairman & CEO; N. Gregory Petrick, Sr. VP & CFO.

■ **12785** ■ **UniMark Group Inc.**
PO Box 229
Argyle, TX 76226
Phone: (817)491-2992 **Fax:** (817)491-1272
URL: http://www.sunfreshfruit.com
Products: Fruit. **SIC:** 5148 (Fresh Fruits & Vegetables). **Emp:** 3,300. **Officers:** Soren Bjorn, CEO & President; Charles Horne, CFO.

■ **12786** ■ **Union Grocery Company Inc.**
PO Box 327
New Albany, MS 38652
Phone: (601)534-5089 **Fax:** (601)534-8085
Products: Groceries. **SIC:** 5141 (Groceries—General Line). **Est:** 1951. **Sales:** $10,000,000 (2000). **Emp:** 20. **Officers:** William T. Shannon, President; Ray Tune, CFO.

■ **12787** ■ **Union Incorporated**
14522 Myford Rd.
Irvine, CA 92606
Phone: (714)734-2200
Free: (888)767-2636 **Fax:** (714)734-2222
E-mail: unionfoods.com
Products: Oriental ramen noodle soups. **SIC:** 5149 (Groceries & Related Products Nec). **Est:** 1974. **Emp:** 150. **Officers:** Kyung L. Choi, Gen. Mgr. of Intl. Trade; Gary Munro, Sales/Marketing Contact, e-mail: gary@unionfoods.com; Mary Lawler, Customer Service Contact, e-mail: mary@unionfoods.com; KC Kwak, Human Resources Contact, e-mail: kckwak@unionfoods.com.

■ **12788** ■ **UNIPRO Foodservice, Inc.**
2500 Cumberland Pkwy. , No. 600
Atlanta, GA 30339
Phone: (770)952-0871 **Fax:** (770)952-0872
URL: http://www.uniprofoodservice.com
Products: Groceries. **SIC:** 5141 (Groceries—General Line). **Est:** 1988. **Sales:** $300,000,000 (2000). **Emp:** 200. **Officers:** Alan Plassche, CEO; David Joss, CFO. **Former Name:** ComSource Independent Foodservice Companies Inc.

■ **12789** ■ **United-A.G. Cooperative Inc.**
PO Box 24887
Omaha, NE 68124-0887
Phone: (402)339-7300 **Fax:** (402)734-0650
Products: General line groceries. **SIC:** 5141 (Groceries—General Line). **Est:** 1933. **Sales:** $270,000,000 (2000). **Emp:** 315. **Officers:** Terrence W. Olsen, President; Janet Larson, Treasurer & Secty.; Glen Tylutki, VP of Marketing; Dale Williamsen, Dir. of Systems.

■ **12790** ■ **United Beverage Inc.**
2307 E Blanding Ave.
Alameda, CA 94501
Phone: (510)748-0595 **Fax:** (510)748-0599
Products: Soft drinks. **SICs:** 5149 (Groceries & Related Products Nec); 5182 (Wines & Distilled Beverages); 5149 (Groceries & Related Products Nec). **Est:** 1933. **Sales:** $150,000 (1999). **Emp:** 2. **Officers:** John G. Roveda, CEO & President.

■ **12791** ■ **United Dairymen of Arizona**
PO Box 26877
Tempe, AZ 85285-6877
Phone: (480)966-7211 **Fax:** (480)829-7491
Products: Dairy products, including milk, butter, and lactose. **SIC:** 5143 (Dairy Products Except Dried or Canned). **Est:** 1960. **Sales:** $112,000,000 (1999). **Emp:** 196. **Officers:** Jim Boyle, President; Scott H. Benson, Finance Officer; Dermot Carey, Editor.

■ **12792** ■ **United Farmers Cooperative**
PO Box 4
Lafayette, MN 56054
Phone: (507)228-8224 **Fax:** (507)228-8766
Products: Agricultural equipment and supplies. **SIC:** 5153 (Grain & Field Beans). **Sales:** $44,000,000 (2000). **Emp:** 80.

■ **12793** ■ **United Food Service Inc.**
1047 Broadway
Albany, NY 12204
Phone: (518)436-4401
Free: (800)274-7276 **Fax:** (518)463-1607
Products: Restaurant food supplies. **SIC:** 5141 (Groceries—General Line). **Est:** 1946. **Sales:** $41,500,000 (2000). **Emp:** 110. **Officers:** Robert T. Quenneville, President; Frank J. Quenneville, Treasurer & Secty.; Robert Quenneville, VP of Sales; Thomas Connally, Dir. of Data Processing; Toni M. Dowd, Human Resources Mgr.

■ **12794** ■ **United Foods Inc.**
10 Pictsweet Dr.
Bells, TN 38006
Phone: (901)422-7600 **Fax:** 800-235-3203
Products: Fresh and frozen vegetables. **SICs:** 5148 (Fresh Fruits & Vegetables); 5142 (Packaged Frozen Foods). **Est:** 1956. **Officers:** James I. Tankersley, CEO & Chairman of the Board; C.W. Gruenewald II, Sr. VP & CFO; Donald Dresser, Exec. VP, Admin./Sec.; B.M Ennis, President.

■ **12795** ■ **United Fruit and Produce Company Inc.**
55 Produce Row
St. Louis, MO 63102
Phone: (314)621-9440 **Fax:** (314)621-1873
Products: Produce. **SIC:** 5148 (Fresh Fruits & Vegetables).

■ **12796** ■ **United Grocers, Inc.**
PO Box 22187
Milwaukie, OR 97269
Phone: (503)833-1000 **Fax:** (503)833-1974
Products: General merchandise; Groceries, including deli foods. **SIC:** 5141 (Groceries—General Line). **Est:** 1915.

■ **12797** ■ **United Heritage Corp.**
PO Box 1956
Cleburne, TX 76033-1956
Phone: (817)641-3681 **Fax:** (817)641-3683
Products: Beef. **SIC:** 5147 (Meats & Meat Products). **Est:** 1981. **Sales:** $7,800,000 (2000). **Emp:** 7. **Officers:** Walter G. Mize, CEO & President; Harold L. Gilliam, CFO.

■ **12798** ■ **United Meat Company Inc.**
1040 Bryant St.
San Francisco, CA 94103
Phone: (415)864-2118
Products: Meats, including beef, veal, lamb, pork, and chicken. **SICs:** 5147 (Meats & Meat Products); 5144 (Poultry & Poultry Products). **Est:** 1925. **Sales:** $13,000,000 (2000). **Emp:** 50. **Officers:** Douglas Gee, President; Philip Gee Jr., Controller.

■ **12799** ■ **United Natural Foods, Inc.**
PO Box 999
Dayville, CT 06241
Phone: (860)779-2800
Free: (800)877-8898 **Fax:** (860)779-2811
URL: http:/www.unfi.com
Products: Meat substitutes; Natural foods; Oils; Soy products; Canned vegetables and fruits; Cat and dog food; Health supplies. **SICs:** 5149 (Groceries & Related Products Nec); 5122 (Drugs, Proprietaries & Sundries). **Sales:** $915,000,000 (2000). **Emp:** 2,700. **Officers:** Michael Funk, CEO; Kevin Michel, CFO; Thomas Simone, Chairman of the Board. **Former Name:** Cornucopia Natural Foods Inc.

■ **12800** ■ **United Noodles Inc.**
2015 E 24th St.
Minneapolis, MN 55404
Phone: (612)721-6677 **Fax:** (612)721-4255
Products: Groceries, including dry foods, canned foods, and noodles. **SIC:** 5149 (Groceries & Related Products Nec). **Est:** 1972. **Sales:** $3,000,000 (2000). **Emp:** 20. **Officers:** Ted Wong, President; Ramon Tan, Treasurer & Secty.; Joseph Lee, Dir. of Marketing; Cora Santos, Dir. of Data Processing.

■ **12801** ■ **U.S. Food Service**
2800 NE 410, No. 105
San Antonio, TX 78218
Phone: (210)590-1322 **Fax:** (210)590-2377
Products: General line groceries. **SICs:** 5141 (Groceries—General Line); 5149 (Groceries & Related Products Nec).

■ **12802** ■ **U.S. Foodservice - RRS Div.**
PO Box 40
Salem, VA 24153
Phone: (540)387-1151 **Fax:** (540)387-1143
Products: Food; Food service equipment. **SICs:** 5141 (Groceries—General Line); 5087 (Service Establishment Equipment). **Est:** 1954. **Emp:** 350. **Officers:** Dale Brown, President; Doug Taylor, CFO; Rob Lee, Controller; Nina Edwards, Dir of Human Resources. **Former Name:** RRS Div.

■ **12803** ■ **U.S. Import Export Corp.**
830 7th St.
San Francisco, CA 94107
Phone: (415)863-7886 **Fax:** (415)863-2768
Products: Oriental foods. **SIC:** 5149 (Groceries & Related Products Nec). **Est:** 1964. **Sales:** $10,000,000 (2000). **Emp:** 14. **Officers:** Arthur Chan, President; Amphorn Chan, Vice President; Angela Chan, Secretary.

■ **12804** ■ **U.S. Sugar Company Inc.**
PO Box 549
Buffalo, NY 14240
Phone: (716)828-1170 **Fax:** (716)828-1509
Products: Packaged sugar. **SIC:** 5149 (Groceries & Related Products Nec). **Est:** 1961. **Sales:** $20,000,000 (2000). **Emp:** 50. **Officers:** William K. McDaniel Jr., CEO & President; Tom Ferlito, Sr. VP of Sales.

■ **12805** ■ **U.R.M. Cash & Carry**
902 E Springfield
Spokane, WA 99202-2075
Phone: (509)489-4555
Free: (800)541-0335 **Fax:** (509)484-1206
Products: General line groceries. **SIC:** 5141 (Groceries—General Line). **Emp:** 12.

■ **12806** ■ **U.R.M. Stores Inc.**
PO Box 3365
Spokane, WA 99220-3365
Phone: (509)467-2620 **Fax:** (509)468-1334
Products: General full-line groceries, including produce, general merchandise, meat, and dairy. **SIC:** 5141 (Groceries—General Line). **Est:** 1921. **Sales:** $500,000,000 (2000). **Emp:** 650. **Officers:** Greg Tarr, President & CEO; Laurie Bigej, CFO.

■ **12807** ■ **US Food Service-Pittston Division**
13 Rutledge Dr.
Pittston, PA 18640
Phone: (717)654-3374 **Fax:** (717)654-2510
Products: Groceries; Food service equipment. **SICs:** 5141 (Groceries—General Line); 5046 (Commercial Equipment Nec). **Est:** 1977. **Sales:** $125,000,000 (2000). **Emp:** 250.

■ **12808** ■ **US FoodService Inc. Carolina Div.**
125 Fort Mill Pkwy.
Ft. Mill, SC 29715
Phone: (803)802-6000
Free: (800)453-3314 **Fax:** (803)802-2443
Products: Groceries. **SIC:** 5141 (Groceries—General Line). **Sales:** $452,300,000 (2000). **Emp:** 1,050. **Officers:** Steve Potaniec, President; Emily Gibson, CFO.

■ 12809 ■ **Albert Uster Imports, Inc.**
9211 Gaither Rd.
Gaithersburg, MD 20877-1419
Phone: (301)258-7350
Free: (800)231-8154 **Fax:** (301)948-2601
Products: Specialty foods. **SIC:** 5141 (Groceries—General Line). **Est:** 1980. **Emp:** 50. **Officers:** Albert Uster, President; Joanna Peschin, Sales/Mktg.; Marc Bitbol, Sales/Mktg.; Chance Ashman, Customer Service.

■ 12810 ■ **Utica Cooperative Grain Company Inc.**
PO Box 216
Utica, NE 68456
Phone: (402)527-5511
Free: (800)742-7813 **Fax:** (402)527-5515
Products: Grain, feed, fertilizers and agricultural chemicals. **SICs:** 5153 (Grain & Field Beans); 5191 (Farm Supplies). **Sales:** $59,000,000 (2000). **Emp:** 65. **Officers:** Gerald Johnson, President; Ron Golka, General Manager, Finance.

■ 12811 ■ **Uvalde Meat Processing**
508 S Wood
Uvalde, TX 78801
Phone: (512)278-6247
Products: Processed, frozen, or cooked meats. **SIC:** 5147 (Meats & Meat Products). **Emp:** 49.

■ 12812 ■ **U.W. Provision Co.**
2315 Evergreen Rd.
Middleton, WI 53562-4244
Phone: (608)836-7421 **Fax:** (608)836-6328
Products: Meat. **SIC:** 5147 (Meats & Meat Products). **Sales:** $100,000,000 (2000). **Emp:** 120. **Officers:** James Kalscheur; Steve Kalscheur; Ron Krantz.

■ 12813 ■ **V-Labs Inc.**
423 N Theard St.
Covington, LA 70433
Phone: (504)893-0533 **Fax:** (504)893-0517
Products: Offers analytical service for carbohydrates and polysaccharides; performs contract research and consulting for pharmaceutical, chemical, and food companies. **SIC:** 5149 (Groceries & Related Products Nec).

■ 12814 ■ **J.C. Valenti Company Inc.**
PO Box 11128
Tampa, FL 33680
Phone: (813)238-7981 **Fax:** (813)239-2583
Products: Tomatoes. **SIC:** 5148 (Fresh Fruits & Vegetables). **Est:** 1952. **Sales:** $26,000,000 (2000). **Emp:** 140. **Officers:** Paul Dimare, President; Kip Rabin, CFO; Charles Bruno, VP of Marketing.

■ 12815 ■ **Vallet Food Service Inc.**
1230 E 12th St.
Dubuque, IA 52001
Phone: (319)588-2347 **Fax:** 800-553-0516
Products: Food. **SIC:** 5141 (Groceries—General Line). **Est:** 1949. **Sales:** $9,000,000 (2000). **Emp:** 35. **Officers:** Edward G. White, President; Kelvin Buss, Treasurer & Secty.

■ 12816 ■ **Valley Farm Dairy Co.**
PO Box 78039
St. Louis, MO 63178-8039
Phone: (314)535-4004
Free: (800)883-4004 **Fax:** (314)241-7061
E-mail: vfd@vfdco.com
URL: http://www.vfdco.com
Products: Dairy products; Produce; Poultry; Bread. **SICs:** 5143 (Dairy Products Except Dried or Canned); 5148 (Fresh Fruits & Vegetables); 5144 (Poultry & Poultry Products); 5149 (Groceries & Related Products Nec). **Est:** 1908. **Sales:** $24,000,000 (2000). **Emp:** 70. **Officers:** R.T. Winkler, President, e-mail: rtw@vfdco.com; R.W. Winkler, VP of Marketing.

■ 12817 ■ **Valley Foods**
PO Box 50048
Santa Barbara, CA 93150
Phone: (805)565-1621 **Fax:** (805)565-1584
Products: Non-perishable foods. **SIC:** 5149 (Groceries & Related Products Nec). **Sales:** $26,000,000 (2000). **Emp:** 7. **Officers:** Donald Sherwin, Mng. Partner.

■ 12818 ■ **Valley Fruit**
12 Hoffer Rd.
Wapato, WA 98951
Phone: (509)877-4188 **Fax:** (509)877-2533
Products: Apples; Pears. **SIC:** 5148 (Fresh Fruits & Vegetables). **Est:** 1982. **Sales:** $20,000,000 (2000). **Emp:** 125. **Officers:** Martin Verbrugge; Peter Verbrugge; Andy Black, Sales/Marketing Contact; Joe Cozzetto, Sales/Marketing Contact.

■ 12819 ■ **Valley Isle Produce Inc.**
PO Box 517
Kahului, HI 96732
Phone: (808)877-5055 **Fax:** (808)877-4960
Products: Food, including produce, frozen foods, seafood, boxed beef, and groceries; Paper and chemicals. **SIC:** 5148 (Fresh Fruits & Vegetables). **Est:** 1950. **Sales:** $50,000,000 (1999). **Emp:** 120. **Officers:** Roy H. Okumura, President; Alton Nakagawa, VP of Finance; Nelson Okumura, President; Stephen Smith, VP of Purchasing; Brian Tokesai, VP of Operations; Lorraine Okumura, Treasurer.

■ 12820 ■ **Valley Packing Service**
310 Walker St.
Watsonville, CA 95076
Phone: (408)724-7551
Products: Food. **SICs:** 5141 (Groceries—General Line); 5142 (Packaged Frozen Foods). **Sales:** $10,000,000 (1993). **Emp:** 20. **Officers:** Jack Randle, President.

■ 12821 ■ **Val's Homemade Bagels Inc.**
PO Box 671
Clackamas, OR 97015
Phone: (503)656-2777
Products: Bakery products. **SIC:** 5149 (Groceries & Related Products Nec). **Sales:** $1,000,000 (2000). **Emp:** 22. **Officers:** Valerie Schaffroth, President.

■ 12822 ■ **Van Dam Brothers Co.**
9753 East Ave.
Lancaster, CA 93535
Phone: (805)946-1630
Products: Milk. **SIC:** 5143 (Dairy Products Except Dried or Canned). **Est:** 1965. **Sales:** $1,000,000 (2000). **Emp:** 10. **Officers:** Delmar Van Dam, CEO; Dean Van Dam, CFO.

■ 12823 ■ **Van Eerden Distribution Co.**
PO Box 3110
Grand Rapids, MI 49501-3110
Phone: (616)452-1426 **Fax:** (616)452-5954
URL: http://www.vaneerden.com
Products: Food. **SIC:** 5141 (Groceries—General Line). **Est:** 1920. **Emp:** 250. **Officers:** Daniel Van Eerden; Harold Van Eerden; Andy Van Eerden.

■ 12824 ■ **Van Roy Coffee Co.**
2900 Detroit Ave.
Cleveland, OH 44113
Phone: (216)771-1220
Free: (877)VAN-ROOY **Fax:** (216)771-2622
E-mail: coffee1@npk.net
URL: http://www.vanroycoffee.com
Products: Coffee. **SIC:** 5149 (Groceries & Related Products Nec). **Est:** 1930. **Sales:** $1,300,000 (2000). **Emp:** 14. **Officers:** J.M. Schanz Jr., Chairman of the Board; Jeffrey S. Miller, CEO & President; John M. Schanz III, Vice President; Leslie Cory, Controller.

■ 12825 ■ **Van Solkema Produce Inc.**
PO Box 308
Byron Center, MI 49315
Phone: (616)878-1508 **Fax:** (616)878-1432
Products: Vegetables. **SIC:** 5148 (Fresh Fruits & Vegetables).

■ 12826 ■ **Vancol Industries Inc.**
2460 W 26th Ave., No. 180C
Denver, CO 80211-0037
Phone: (303)455-6112 **Fax:** (303)455-6270
Products: Food products. **SIC:** 5149 (Groceries & Related Products Nec). **Est:** 1988. **Sales:** $4,700,000 (2000). **Emp:** 15. **Officers:** Robert Yates, President.

■ 12827 ■ **Jac Vandenberg Inc.**
100 Corporate Blvd.
Yonkers, NY 10701-0811
Phone: (914)964-5900 **Fax:** (914)964-5901
Products: Fresh fruit, including oranges, cherries, and apples. **SIC:** 5148 (Fresh Fruits & Vegetables). **Est:** 1947. **Sales:** $56,000,000 (2000). **Emp:** 25. **Officers:** David Schiro, President; Eduard Paap, Controller; Fred Vandenberg, VP of Marketing.

■ 12828 ■ **Vanee Foods Co.**
5418 W McDermott Dr.
Berkeley, IL 60163
Phone: (708)449-7300 **Fax:** (708)449-2558
Products: Food preparations; Prepared sauces. **SIC:** 5149 (Groceries & Related Products Nec). **Sales:** $6,000,000 (2000). **Emp:** 99. **Officers:** Al Vaneekeren.

■ 12829 ■ **Vanguard Trading Services Inc.**
22605 SE 56th St., No. 200
Issaquah, WA 98029-5289
Phone: (425)557-8250 **Fax:** (425)557-8260
Products: Fruits and vegetables. **SIC:** 5148 (Fresh Fruits & Vegetables). **Est:** 1990. **Sales:** $24,000,000 (2000). **Emp:** 6. **Officers:** Craig W. Stauffer, CEO & President, e-mail: craig-stauffer@vangd.com; Guy A. Kisling, Exec. VP & CFO.

■ 12830 ■ **Van's Candy & Tobacco Service**
PO Box 1105
Laramie, WY 82070
Phone: (307)745-4665
Products: Candy; Tobacco; Cleaning products. **SICs:** 5145 (Confectionery); 5169 (Chemicals & Allied Products Nec); 5194 (Tobacco & Tobacco Products).

■ 12831 ■ **J.A. Vassilaros and Sons Inc.**
29-05 120th St.
Flushing, NY 11354
Phone: (718)886-4140 **Fax:** (718)463-5037
URL: http://www.vassilaroscoffee.com
Products: Coffee; Tea; Chocolate and cocoa products. **SICs:** 5149 (Groceries & Related Products Nec); 5145 (Confectionery). **Est:** 1919. **Sales:** $13,000,000 (2000). **Emp:** 40. **Officers:** John Vassilaros, President.

■ 12832 ■ **Vaughn Meat Packing Company Inc.**
2117 Country Club Rd.
PO Box 568
Greer, SC 29652
Phone: (803)877-0926
Products: Fresh beef, pork, and sausage; Fresh and frozen chicken; Frozen seafood; Cheese; Canned goods; Condiments; Cured hams. **SICs:** 5147 (Meats & Meat Products); 5146 (Fish & Seafoods); 5144 (Poultry & Poultry Products); 5143 (Dairy Products Except Dried or Canned). **Est:** 1955. **Sales:** $2,000,000 (2000). **Emp:** 25. **Officers:** E. D. Vaughn.

■ 12833 ■ **VEC Inc.**
PO Box 3110
Grand Rapids, MI 49501-3110
Phone: (616)452-1426 **Fax:** (616)452-5954
Products: General line groceries. **SIC:** 5141 (Groceries—General Line). **Sales:** $90,000,000 (2000). **Emp:** 250. **Officers:** Dan Van Eerden, President; Barry Waters, CFO.

■ 12834 ■ **Velda Farms**
5200 S Manhattan Ave.
Tampa, FL 33611
Phone: (813)837-8555
Free: (800)867-8555 **Fax:** (813)837-3831
Products: Dairy products; Ice cream; Butter; Milk. **SIC:** 5143 (Dairy Products Except Dried or Canned). **Sales:** $16,000,000 (2000). **Emp:** 40. **Officers:** Michelle Mora.

■ 12835 ■ **John Vena Inc.**
3301 S Galloway St., Unit 77
Philadelphia, PA 19148
Phone: (215)336-0766 **Fax:** (215)336-2812
Products: Fresh produce. **SIC:** 5148 (Fresh Fruits & Vegetables). **Est:** 1919. **Emp:** 10.

■ 12836 ■ Vendor Supply of America Inc.
PO Box 17387
Denver, CO 80217
Phone: (303)634-1400 **Fax:** (303)721-1918
Products: Potato chips; Candy; Chewing gum. **SIC:**
5145 (Confectionery). **Sales:** $360,000,000 (2000).
Emp: 1,500. **Officers:** Devendra Mishra, President;
Richard Halterman, CFO; Ron Roth, Sr. VP of
Marketing.

■ 12837 ■ Veri-Best Bakers
PO Box 426
La Porte, IN 46352-0426
Phone: (219)398-4200
Products: Breads; Sweets; Cakes; Coffee Cakes. **SIC:**
5149 (Groceries & Related Products Nec).

■ 12838 ■ Vermont Whey Co.
PO Box 2129
Milton, VT 05468
Phone: (802)527-7737 **Fax:** (802)524-5331
Products: Whey; Powder and colidesed. **SIC:** 5143
(Dairy Products Except Dried or Canned). **Est:** 1980.
Sales: $1,800,000 (2000). **Emp:** 32. **Officers:** Carl
Rosenquist, President.

■ 12839 ■ Vermont Whey Co.
PO Box 2129
Georgia, VT 05468-2129
Phone: (802)527-7737 **Fax:** (802)524-5331
Products: Whey. **SIC:** 5149 (Groceries & Related
Products Nec). **Sales:** $45,000,000 (2000). **Emp:** 88.
Officers: Carl Rosenquist, President; Chuck Wolf,
Controller.

■ 12840 ■ W.R. Vernon Produce Co.
PO Box 4054
Winston-Salem, NC 27115-4054
Phone: (919)725-9741
Products: Produce. **SIC:** 5148 (Fresh Fruits &
Vegetables). **Est:** 1950. **Sales:** $36,000,000 (2000).
Emp: 70. **Officers:** Arlis E. Vernon, President.

■ 12841 ■ Veronica Foods Co.
PO Box 2225
Oakland, CA 94621
Phone: (510)535-6833 **Fax:** (510)532-2837
Products: Salvaged food. **SIC:** 5149 (Groceries &
Related Products Nec). **Est:** 1914. **Sales:** $25,000,000
(2000). **Emp:** 55. **Officers:** M. Bradley, CEO; Don
Mankins, CFO; B. Miller, Dir. of Marketing.

■ 12842 ■ Very Fine Resources Inc.
128 Parkville Ave.
Brooklyn, NY 11230
Phone: (718)438-3191 **Fax:** (718)435-8543
Products: Groceries, including canned goods. **SIC:**
5149 (Groceries & Related Products Nec). **Emp:** 49.

■ 12843 ■ Victory Seafood Processors Inc.
208 W Elina St.
Abbeville, LA 70510
Phone: (318)893-9029 **Fax:** (318)898-0614
Products: Crab meat. **SIC:** 5146 (Fish & Seafoods).
Est: 1984. **Sales:** $3,000,000 (2000). **Emp:** 100.
Officers: Jason G. Guidry, President.

■ 12844 ■ Viles and Associates Inc.
444 W 21st St.
Tempe, AZ 85282
Phone: (602)437-0616 **Fax:** (602)829-7078
Products: Foods, including canned and
nonperishables. **SICs:** 5141 (Groceries—General
Line); 5149 (Groceries & Related Products Nec). **Emp:**
99. **Officers:** Allan J. Viles.

■ 12845 ■ Vilrore Foods Company Inc.
8220 San Lorenzo St.
Laredo, TX 78041
Phone: (956)726-3633 **Fax:** (952)727-1499
E-mail: vilore@icsi.net
Products: Jalapeno peppers; Canned nectars. **SIC:**
5148 (Fresh Fruits & Vegetables). **Est:** 1983. **Sales:**
$12,000,000 (2000). **Emp:** 23. **Officers:** Marco Mena,
President; Glen Leonard, National Sales Director, e-
mail: glen@vilore.com.

■ 12846 ■ Vina & Son Meat Distributors
2020 NW 22nd St.
Miami, FL 33142-7334
Phone: (305)545-6500 **Fax:** (305)324-8547
Products: Meat. **SIC:** 5147 (Meats & Meat Products).
Emp: 49. **Officers:** Medardo Vina.

■ 12847 ■ VIP Sales Company Inc.
6116 S Memorial Dr.
Tulsa, OK 74133
Phone: (918)252-5791 **Fax:** (918)254-1667
URL: http://www.vipfoods.com
Products: Frozen vegetables; Entrees; Vegetables
with sauces and proteins. **SIC:** 5142 (Packaged Frozen
Foods). **Est:** 1967. **Sales:** $80,000,000 (2000). **Emp:**
62. **Officers:** G. W. Lewis, President; Michael Lewis,
Controller, e-mail: mlewis@vipfoods.com; Steve Beck,
VP of Marketing & Sales.

■ 12848 ■ Virginia Food Service Group
PO Box 28010
Richmond, VA 23228
Phone: (804)266-0300
Products: Institutional food and kitchen supplies. **SIC:**
5141 (Groceries—General Line). **Est:** 1930. **Sales:**
$55,000,000 (2000). **Emp:** 145. **Officers:** Jim Cremins,
President; Bruce Kennedy, Controller.

■ 12849 ■ Virginia Wholesale Co.
70 Commonwealth Ave.
Bristol, VA 24201-3802
Phone: (540)669-4181
Free: (800)228-4181 **Fax:** (540)669-1160
E-mail: vawholesale@prodigy.net
Products: Groceries; Tobacco; Health and beauty
aids; Candy and gum. **SICs:** 5141 (Groceries—General
Line); 5122 (Drugs, Proprietaries & Sundries); 5194
(Tobacco & Tobacco Products). **Est:** 1901. **Sales:**
$48,000,000 (1999). **Emp:** 49. **Officers:** Howard H.
Moser, Chairman of the Board; Edith P. Moser,
President; Charles D. White, Data Processing Mgr.;
Randall Childress, Customer Service Contact.

■ 12850 ■ Vista Bakery, Inc.
PO Box 888
Burlington, IA 52601
Phone: (319)754-6551
Free: (800)553-2343 **Fax:** (319)752-0063
URL: http://www.vistabakery.com
Products: Cookies and crackers. **SIC:** 5149 (Groceries
& Related Products Nec). **Sales:** $70,000,000 (2000).
Emp: 399. **Officers:** Dean Fields, President; Bill
Hayman, VP of Marketing; Darren Crandall,
Sales/Marketing Contact, e-mail: dcrandall@
vistabakery.com; Monita Gonterman, Customer Service
Contact, e-mail: mgonterman@vistabakery.com.

■ 12851 ■ Vitex Foods Inc.
1821 E 48th Pl.
Los Angeles, CA 90058
Phone: (213)234-4400 **Fax:** (213)234-3947
Products: Dry food. **SIC:** 5149 (Groceries & Related
Products Nec). **Sales:** $30,000,000 (2000). **Emp:** 125.
Officers: R. Orkand; N. Lovett, Marketing & Sales Mgr.

■ 12852 ■ C.J. Vitner Company Inc.
4202 W 45th St.
Chicago, IL 60632
Phone: (312)523-7900 **Fax:** (773)523-9143
Products: Potato chips. **SIC:** 5145 (Confectionery).
Est: 1926. **Sales:** $48,000,000 (2000). **Emp:** 440.
Officers: William A. Vitner, President; Pat Hudgin,
Controller; Phil Bremser, VP of Sales.

■ 12853 ■ Tony Vitrano Co.
Maryland Wholesale Product Market
Jessup, MD 20794
Phone: (410)799-7444
Products: Vegetables and fruits. **SIC:** 5148 (Fresh
Fruits & Vegetables). **Est:** 1932. **Sales:** $32,000,000
(2000). **Emp:** 90. **Officers:** J.A. Vitrano, President; A.
Vitrano, CFO.

■ 12854 ■ Vogue Cuisine Inc.
3710 Grandview Blvd.
Los Angeles, CA 90066-3110
Phone: (310)391-1053 **Fax:** (310)390-0883
URL: http://www.freeyellow.com/members2/
voguewest
Products: Dehydrated soup products. **SIC:** 5149
(Groceries & Related Products Nec). **Est:** 1938. **Sales:**
$200,000 (2000). **Emp:** 4. **Officers:** Clinton Helvey,
President, e-mail: helvey@mediaone.net; Carol
Helvey, Vice President; Minnie Schlanger, Vice
President; David Helvey, Vice President.

■ 12855 ■ Volunteer Produce Co.
2015 Grand Ave.
Knoxville, TN 37916-1207
Phone: (423)525-7078 **Fax:** (423)637-3354
Products: Fruits and vegetables. **SIC:** 5148 (Fresh
Fruits & Vegetables). **Sales:** $6,000,000 (2000). **Emp:**
49. **Officers:** Tony Neely; Ed Neely; Lori Neely Mason.

■ 12856 ■ Volunteer Sales Co.
PO Box 22087
Chattanooga, TN 37422-2087
Phone: (615)821-3575
Products: Food. **SICs:** 5141 (Groceries—General
Line); 5142 (Packaged Frozen Foods).

■ 12857 ■ Vowles Farm Fresh Foods
PO Box 2868
El Cajon, CA 92021
Phone: (619)448-2101 **Fax:** (619)448-4671
Products: Food. **SICs:** 5141 (Groceries—General
Line); 5147 (Meats & Meat Products). **Sales:**
$70,000,000 (2000). **Emp:** 110. **Officers:** Bill Vowles,
General Mgr.; Frank Parker, Controller.

■ 12858 ■ Waco Meat Service Inc.
PO Box 7249
Waco, TX 76714-7249
Phone: (817)772-5644
Free: (800)460-6370 **Fax:** (817)254-1599
Products: Beef, pork, catfish, and cheese. **SICs:** 5147
(Meats & Meat Products); 5143 (Dairy Products Except
Dried or Canned); 5146 (Fish & Seafoods). **Est:** 1940.
Sales: $16,000,000 (2000). **Emp:** 30. **Officers:** Dana
Dee Harrell, President; Richard Spitzer, Treasurer; Bill
Bell, Sales Mgr.

■ 12859 ■ Waddington Dairy
PO Box 550
Alloway, NJ 08001-0550
Phone: (609)935-2333
Free: (800)526-2706 **Fax:** (609)935-3533
Products: Dairy products. **SIC:** 5143 (Dairy Products
Except Dried or Canned). **Est:** 1952. **Emp:** 49.
Officers: James Waddington.

■ 12860 ■ Waddington/Richman Inc.
PO Box 229
Woodstown, NJ 08098-0229
Phone: (609)769-0350 **Fax:** (609)769-0397
Products: Ice cream. **SIC:** 5143 (Dairy Products
Except Dried or Canned). **Sales:** $6,000,000 (2000).
Emp: 499.

■ 12861 ■ Wades Dairy Inc.
1316 Barnum Ave.
Bridgeport, CT 06610-2825
Phone: (203)579-9233
Free: (800)247-9233 **Fax:** (203)696-6121
E-mail: doug@wadesdairy.com
URL: http://www.wadesdairy.com
Products: Dairy products; Desserts; Pastas; Soups;
Juices. **SICs:** 5143 (Dairy Products Except Dried or
Canned); 5149 (Groceries & Related Products Nec).
Est: 1893. **Sales:** $8,500,000 (2000). **Emp:** 34.
Officers: David L. Wade, COO; Susan Warner, CFO;
D.H. Wade Jr., CEO.

■ 12862 ■ Wagner Candy Co.
118 Joe Clifton Dr.
Paducah, KY 42002
Phone: (502)442-6301
Products: Candy and groceries; Tobacco. **SICs:** 5145
(Confectionery); 5141 (Groceries—General Line); 5194
(Tobacco & Tobacco Products).

■ **12863** ■ **Wagner Mills Inc.**
PO Box 545
Schuyler, NE 68661
Phone: (402)352-2471
Products: Livestock and farm products. **SIC:** 5153 (Grain & Field Beans). **Sales:** $9,000,000 (2000). **Emp:** 18.

■ **12864** ■ **John Wagner and Sons Inc.**
900 Jacksonville Rd.
Ivyland, PA 18974-1778
Phone: (215)674-5000
Free: (800)832-9017 **Fax:** (215)674-0398
Products: Homemade jellies and preserves; Gourmet teas. **SIC:** 5149 (Groceries & Related Products Nec). **Sales:** $6,000,000 (2000). **Emp:** 99. **Officers:** Ralph T. Starr.

■ **12865** ■ **Wakefern Food Corp.**
600 York St.
Elizabeth, NJ 07207
Phone: (908)527-3300
Products: Food, including peanut butter and jelly. **SIC:** 5149 (Groceries & Related Products Nec). **Est:** 1954. **Sales:** $3,500,000,000 (2000). **Emp:** 3,000. **Officers:** Thomas Infusino, CEO & Chairman of the Board; Jerome Yaguda, President; Dean Janeway, Sr. VP of Marketing; Marty Glass.

■ **12866** ■ **Wakefern Food Corp.**
600 York St.
Elizabeth, NJ 07207
Phone: (908)527-3300 **Fax:** (908)527-3397
Products: General-line of groceries. **SIC:** 5141 (Groceries—General Line). **Sales:** $5,000,000,000 (2000). **Emp:** 3,000. **Officers:** Thomas Infusino, CEO & Chairman of the Board; Ken Jasinkiewicz, CFO.

■ **12867** ■ **J.F. Walker Company, Inc.**
1180 58th Street
Wyoming, MI 49509
Phone: (616)261-6600 **Fax:** (616)261-6677
Products: Convenience store products and supplies. **SIC:** 5141 (Groceries—General Line). **Est:** 1978. **Sales:** $400,000 (2000). **Emp:** 375. **Officers:** Joseph R. White, VP of Operations.

■ **12868** ■ **Walker Distributors Inc.**
413 W Chatham St.
Cary, NC 27511
Phone: (919)467-1673
Products: Snack food, including potato chips, popcorn, and candy. **SICs:** 5149 (Groceries & Related Products Nec); 5145 (Confectionery). **Sales:** $3,000,000 (2000). **Emp:** 7. **Officers:** Norwood Walker, President.

■ **12869** ■ **Joe Walker Distributors Inc.**
3522 SW 42nd Ave.
Gainesville, FL 32608
Phone: (352)376-6524 **Fax:** (352)373-4810
Products: Snack foods. **SICs:** 5145 (Confectionery); 5149 (Groceries & Related Products Nec). **Est:** 1969. **Sales:** $1,300,000 (2000). **Emp:** 13. **Officers:** J.K. Walker, President.

■ **12870** ■ **Wallace's Old Fashion Skins Inc.**
1512 McCurdy Rd.
Florence, SC 29506
Phone: (803)665-5607
Products: Snack foods; Popcorn. **SICs:** 5149 (Groceries & Related Products Nec); 5145 (Confectionery). **Est:** 1977. **Sales:** $6,000,000 (2000). **Emp:** 99. **Officers:** James T. Wallace.

■ **12871** ■ **Wallach's Poultry Farms**
PO Box 144
Toms River, NJ 08754
Phone: (732)349-1694
Free: (800)344-1694 **Fax:** (732)349-5046
Products: Groceries, including eggs, cheese, produce, and deli products. **SICs:** 5144 (Poultry & Poultry Products); 5143 (Dairy Products Except Dried or Canned); 5149 (Groceries & Related Products Nec); 5148 (Fresh Fruits & Vegetables). **Est:** 1928. **Sales:** $3,400,000 (2000). **Emp:** 32. **Officers:** Stanley Wallach, President.

■ **12872** ■ **Walter's Meat Co.**
8901 Wattsburg Rd.
Erie, PA 16509
Phone: (814)825-4857
Products: Fish; Meats, including pork, beef, ham, bacon, and sausage. **SICs:** 5147 (Meats & Meat Products); 5146 (Fish & Seafoods). **Est:** 1940. **Sales:** $1,500,000 (2000). **Emp:** 9. **Officers:** H. Wagner, President.

■ **12873** ■ **Walton & Post**
8105 NW 77 St.
Miami, FL 33166
Phones: (305)591-1111 (305)593-7070
URL: http://www.waltonpost.com
Products: General line groceries; Candies and chocolates; Produce; Housewares; Hardware; Health and beauty aids; Paper products. **SICs:** 5141 (Groceries—General Line); 5122 (Drugs, Proprietaries & Sundries); 5023 (Homefurnishings); 5148 (Fresh Fruits & Vegetables); 5072 (Hardware).

■ **12874** ■ **Wamplers Farm Sausage**
781 Hwy 70 W
Lenoir City, TN 37771-9808
Phone: (423)986-2056 **Fax:** (423)988-3280
Products: Sausage. **SIC:** 5147 (Meats & Meat Products). **Sales:** $30,000,000 (1999). **Emp:** 102. **Officers:** Tod L. Wampler Jr.

■ **12875** ■ **Wapsie Valley Creamery Inc.**
Box 391
Independence, IA 50644
Phone: (319)334-7193 **Fax:** (319)334-4914
Products: Natural and process cheese and related products. **SIC:** 5143 (Dairy Products Except Dried or Canned). **Est:** 1906. **Sales:** $35,000,000 (2000). **Emp:** 49. **Officers:** W. C. Nielsen; Mark Nielsen.

■ **12876** ■ **Ward Egg Ranch Corp.**
2900 Harmony Grove Rd.
Escondido, CA 92029
Phone: (619)745-5689 **Fax:** (760)745-5865
Products: Eggs. **SIC:** 5144 (Poultry & Poultry Products). **Est:** 1966. **Sales:** $7,000,000 (2000). **Emp:** 70. **Officers:** Edward Wilgenburg, President; Arie Wilgenburg, Vice President; Arie Wilgenburg, Sec. & Treas.

■ **12877** ■ **Wards Cove Packing Co.**
PO Box C-5030
Seattle, WA 98105
Phone: (206)323-3200 **Fax:** (206)323-8759
Products: Salmon, including canned, fresh or frozen; Halibut; Cod; Surimi; Salmon caviar. **SIC:** 5146 (Fish & Seafoods). **Est:** 1928. **Sales:** $100,000,000 (2000). **Emp:** 210. **Officers:** Alec W. Brindle, President; Gordon Williams, CFO; Robert Nickinovich, VP of Marketing & Administration; Brian Peterman, Dir. of Data Processing.

■ **12878** ■ **Warner Candy Company Inc.**
10507 Delta Pkwy.
Schiller Park, IL 60176
Phone: (708)928-7200 **Fax:** (708)928-2115
Products: Candy; Nuts. **SIC:** 5145 (Confectionery). **Est:** 1927. **Sales:** $20,000,000 (2000). **Emp:** 180. **Officers:** Phillip Kesler, President, e-mail: Phil.Kesler@warnercandy.com; Wylie B. Douglass, VP & Controller; Nick Kaup, Sales Mgr.; Robert Douglass, Dir of Human Resources.

■ **12879** ■ **Warrell Corp.**
PO Box 3411
Shiremanstown, PA 17011-3411
Phone: (717)761-5440
Free: (800)233-7082 **Fax:** (717)761-5702
E-mail: kevins@warrellcorp.com
URL: http://www.padutchcandies.com
Products: Candy; Snack foods. **SIC:** 5145 (Confectionery). **Est:** 1965. **Sales:** $30,000,000 (1999). **Emp:** 150. **Officers:** Lincoln A. Warrell, Chairman of the Board; Richard P. Billman, President; Tom Yantis, Controller. **Doing Business As:** Pennsylvania Duth Candies.

■ **12880** ■ **Warren Cheese Plants**
415 Jefferson St.
Warren, IL 61087-9768
Phone: (815)745-2627 **Fax:** (815)745-2843
Products: Natural cheese. **SIC:** 5143 (Dairy Products Except Dried or Canned). **Sales:** $10,000,000 (2000). **Emp:** 35. **Officers:** John F. Bussman.

■ **12881** ■ **Washington Natural Foods and Co.**
2421 Schuster Ave.
Cheverly, MD 20781
Phone: (301)595-3500
Products: Natural food, including organically grown vegetables. **SIC:** 5148 (Fresh Fruits & Vegetables).

■ **12882** ■ **J.C. Watson Company Inc.**
PO Box 300
Parma, ID 83660
Phone: (208)722-5141 **Fax:** (208)722-6646
Products: Potatoes, onions and apples. **SIC:** 5148 (Fresh Fruits & Vegetables). **Est:** 1912. **Sales:** $10,000,000 (2000). **Emp:** 100. **Officers:** Jon C. Watson, President; Doug Siron, Controller; Nancy Carter, Dir. of Marketing.

■ **12883** ■ **Watson Foodservice Inc.**
PO Box 5910
Lubbock, TX 79408
Phone: (806)747-2678 **Fax:** (806)762-5112
Products: Frozen food; Produce; Bakery products. **SICs:** 5149 (Groceries & Related Products Nec); 5148 (Fresh Fruits & Vegetables); 5142 (Packaged Frozen Foods). **Est:** 1946. **Sales:** $75,000,000 (2000). **Emp:** 140. **Officers:** Mike Davis, President; Crystal Overton, CFO; Billy Watson, Exec. VP; Fred Steck; Rob Knight, Dir of Human Resources.

■ **12884** ■ **Waukesha Wholesale Foods Inc.**
900 Gale St.
Waukesha, WI 53186
Phone: (414)542-8841 **Fax:** (414)542-4356
Products: General line groceries, including frozen entrees, produce, and baking supplies. **SICs:** 5141 (Groceries—General Line); 5149 (Groceries & Related Products Nec). **Est:** 1955. **Sales:** $50,000,000 (2000). **Emp:** 150. **Officers:** Eric J. Muehl, Chairman of the Board; Kevin Musser, VP & CFO; Thomas Muehl, Dir. of Marketing; Clarine Hermersmann, Dir. of Data Processing.

■ **12885** ■ **Waverly Growers Cooperative**
PO Box 287
Waverly, FL 33877
Phone: (941)439-3602
Products: Fresh citrus fruit. **SIC:** 5148 (Fresh Fruits & Vegetables). **Est:** 1914. **Sales:** $55,000,000 (2000). **Emp:** 500. **Officers:** N.P. Hansen, General Mgr.; Edgar Clark, Controller.

■ **12886** ■ **Waxler Co.**
565 Lakeview Pkwy.
Vernon Hills, IL 60061
Phone: (847)816-0100
Products: Frozen chicken, pork, and beef. **SIC:** 5142 (Packaged Frozen Foods). **Sales:** $19,000,000 (2000). **Emp:** 37. **Officers:** George Goldberg, President.

■ **12887** ■ **Waymouth Farms Inc.**
5300 Boone Ave. N
New Hope, MN 55428
Phone: (612)553-5300 **Free:** (800)527-0094
Products: Candy; Nuts and seeds (salted, roasted, cooked, or blanched); Snack foods. **SICs:** 5149 (Groceries & Related Products Nec); 5145 (Confectionery). **Est:** 1976. **Emp:** 49. **Officers:** Jerry Knight.

■ **12888** ■ **W.D. Trading Company Inc.**
250 Beacham St.
Everett, MA 02149
Phone: (617)389-5100 **Fax:** (617)389-9915
Products: Grocery products. **SIC:** 5141 (Groceries—General Line). **Sales:** $92,000,000 (1991). **Emp:** 175. **Officers:** Timothy Wilkins, General Mgr.

■ **12889** ■ **We Market Success Inc.**
255 Colraid Ave., S W
Grand Rapids, MI 49548
Phone: (616)241-3476 **Fax:** (616)241-2415
Products: Groceries, including cereal, frozen foods, canned vegetables, and soups. **SIC:** 5141 (Groceries—General Line). **Sales:** $10,000,000 (2000). **Emp:** 33. **Officers:** Jack Greenwald, President; Jay Fox, Controller; Gary A. Sobkowiak, Dir. of Marketing; Cheryl Foland, Dir. of Information Systems.

■ **12890** ■ **James A. Weaver Co.**
PO Box 11268
Lancaster, PA 17605-1268
Phone: (717)393-0474 **Fax:** (717)392-7419
Products: Soft drinks; General merchandise; Groceries; Candy. **SICs:** 5141 (Groceries—General Line); 5149 (Groceries & Related Products Nec); 5145 (Confectionery).

■ **12891** ■ **Joseph Webb Foods Inc.**
PO Box 1749
Vista, CA 92085
Phone: (760)599-6200
Products: Food. **SIC:** 5141 (Groceries—General Line). **Sales:** $181,000,000 (2000). **Emp:** 292. **Officers:** Alan Motter, President; Dean Janke, VP of Finance.

■ **12892** ■ **Wechsler Coffee Corp.**
10 Empire Blvd.
Moonachie, NJ 07074
Phone: (201)440-1700
Products: Gourmet coffee. **SIC:** 5149 (Groceries & Related Products Nec). **Sales:** $79,000,000 (2000). **Emp:** 485. **Officers:** Michael Slater, President; Frank Osusky, CFO; Evan De Martin, Dir. of Marketing & Sales; Frank Serino, Dir. of Data Processing; Rita Weisblatt, Dir of Human Resources.

■ **12893** ■ **Wedemeyers Bakery**
314 Harbor Way
South San Francisco, CA 94080
Phone: (650)873-1000 **Fax:** (650)873-3170
Products: Bakery goods, including bread, bagels, and rolls. **SIC:** 5149 (Groceries & Related Products Nec). **Est:** 1936. **Sales:** $3,500,000 (1999). **Emp:** 35. **Officers:** Ben Aubrecht, Owner.

■ **12894** ■ **Weeks Div.**
330 N State St.
Concord, NH 03301
Phone: (603)225-3379 **Fax:** (603)228-9015
Products: Dairy products, including ice cream. **SIC:** 5143 (Dairy Products Except Dried or Canned). **Est:** 1930. **Sales:** $60,000,000 (2000). **Emp:** 150. **Officers:** David A. French, Manager; Ernest R. Wilcox, Controller; Mark A. Reil, Dir. of Marketing & Sales; Donna M. Brochu, Personnel Mgr.

■ **12895** ■ **Weeks Div.**
330 N State St.
Concord, NH 03301
Phone: (603)225-3379 **Fax:** (603)228-9015
Products: Food. **SIC:** 5143 (Dairy Products Except Dried or Canned). **Sales:** $60,000,000 (2000). **Emp:** 150.

■ **12896** ■ **Weems Brothers Seafood Co.**
320 E Bayview Ave.
Biloxi, MS 39530
Phone: (228)432-5422
Products: Frozen seafood. **SICs:** 5142 (Packaged Frozen Foods); 5146 (Fish & Seafoods). **Est:** 1942. **Sales:** $43,000,000 (2000). **Emp:** 100. **Officers:** L. Weems, President.

■ **12897** ■ **J. Weil and Co.**
5907 Clinton St.
Boise, ID 83704
Phone: (208)377-0590
Free: (800)755-3885 **Fax:** (208)378-1682
E-mail: gbassjweil@aol.com
Products: Groceries, including canned foods, frozen chicken, and meat; Paper products; Dairy, Chemicals; Beverages. **SICs:** 5149 (Groceries & Related Products Nec); 5142 (Packaged Frozen Foods); 5144 (Poultry & Poultry Products); 5147 (Meats & Meat Products); 5113 (Industrial & Personal Service Paper). **Est:** 1946.

Sales: $9,000,000 (1999). **Emp:** 36. **Officers:** Cecil Grow, President; Craig Grow, General Mgr.

■ **12898** ■ **Weiland Associates**
1131 Rte. 31 S
Lebanon, NJ 08833
Phone: (908)735-9115 **Fax:** (908)735-6678
Products: Food. **SIC:** 5141 (Groceries—General Line). **Emp:** 49. **Officers:** Doug Wieland.

■ **12899** ■ **Weinstein International Seafood Inc.**
5738 Olson Hwy.
Minneapolis, MN 55422
Phone: (612)546-4471
Products: Shrimp. **SIC:** 5146 (Fish & Seafoods). **Est:** 1953. **Sales:** $20,000,000 (2000). **Emp:** 12. **Officers:** Louis Lipschultz, President; Doug Hagen, Treasurer.

■ **12900** ■ **Wells International**
PO Box 189
Pearblossom, CA 93553
Phone: (805)944-2146
Products: Skin lotions, cremes, and moisturizers; Fresh fruits and vegetables; Prepared mustards. **SICs:** 5149 (Groceries & Related Products Nec); 5148 (Fresh Fruits & Vegetables); 5122 (Drugs, Proprietaries & Sundries). **Officers:** Karin B. Wells, President.

■ **12901** ■ **Wenatchee-Okanogan Cooperative Federation**
PO Box 658
Wenatchee, WA 98807
Phone: (509)663-8585
Products: Fruit, including apples and peaches. **SIC:** 5148 (Fresh Fruits & Vegetables). **Est:** 1921. **Sales:** $52,000,000 (2000). **Emp:** 16. **Officers:** Jerry Kenyoer, President; William G. Kuest, Treasurer; Gerald M. Jessup, General Mgr.

■ **12902** ■ **Wenzel Farm Sausage**
E 29th
Marshfield, WI 54449-5313
Phone: (715)387-1218 **Fax:** (715)384-4292
Products: Sausage. **SIC:** 5147 (Meats & Meat Products). **Sales:** $4,000,000 (2000). **Emp:** 25. **Officers:** Russell R. Wenzel.

■ **12903** ■ **Max Werner & Son**
1750 2nd Ave.
New York, NY 10128-5361
Phone: (212)744-7373 **Fax:** (212)427-8822
Products: Fruits and vegetables; Eggs; Cooking oils; Mayonaise; Soup. **SICs:** 5148 (Fresh Fruits & Vegetables); 5144 (Poultry & Poultry Products); 5149 (Groceries & Related Products Nec); 5142 (Packaged Frozen Foods). **Est:** 1921. **Emp:** 9. **Officers:** Charles Werner, Owner.

■ **12904** ■ **Allen Wertz Candies**
PO Box 1168
Chino, CA 91708
Phone: (909)613-0030 **Fax:** (909)613-0321
Products: Candy, chocolates and popcorn. **SIC:** 5145 (Confectionery). **Sales:** $31,000,000 (2000). **Emp:** 250. **Officers:** Gino Marinelli, CEO; Marlei Dai, CFO.

■ **12905** ■ **Wesley Ice Cream**
3717 King Hwy.
Kalamazoo, MI 49001
Phone: (616)343-1291
Products: Ice cream. **SIC:** 5143 (Dairy Products Except Dried or Canned). **Sales:** $1,000,000 (1993). **Emp:** 3. **Officers:** Robert Cooley, General Mgr.

■ **12906** ■ **Westby Cooperative Creamery**
401 S Main St.
Westby, WI 54667
Phone: (608)634-3181
Free: (800)492-9282 **Fax:** (608)634-3194
E-mail: cheese@mwt.net
URL: http://www.westbycreamery.com
Products: Dairy products, including cheddar cheese, cottage cheese, butter, sour cream, and cheese curds. **SIC:** 5143 (Dairy Products Except Dried or Canned). **Est:** 1903. **Sales:** $15,000,000 (2000). **Emp:** 44. **Officers:** Tom Gronemus, General Mgr.; Curt Geier, Office Mgr.; David Barnette, Sales Mgr.

■ **12907** ■ **Westco-BakeMark Las Vegas**
2570 Kiel Way
North Las Vegas, NV 89030
Phone: (702)642-4500 **Fax:** (702)642-0009
Products: Dairy products, including butter, cheese, and eggs; Canned goods; Frozen food; Deli items. **SICs:** 5143 (Dairy Products Except Dried or Canned); 5142 (Packaged Frozen Foods); 5149 (Groceries & Related Products Nec). **Est:** 1957. **Sales:** $43,000,000 (2000). **Emp:** 50. **Officers:** Dave Bensten, Controller; Jim Moody, President.

■ **12908** ■ **Westco Food Service Co.**
2570 Kiel Way
North Las Vegas, NV 89030
Phone: (702)642-4500
Products: Groceries. **SICs:** 5142 (Packaged Frozen Foods); 5149 (Groceries & Related Products Nec); 5141 (Groceries—General Line). **Est:** 1957. **Sales:** $10,000,000 (2000). **Emp:** 29. **Officers:** Rick Ruc, President; Glen Benitze, Controller.

■ **12909** ■ **Western Beef Inc.**
47-05 Metropolitan Ave.
Ridgewood, NY 11385
Phone: (718)417-3770 **Fax:** (718)366-6148
Products: Poultry, beef and pork. **SICs:** 5144 (Poultry & Poultry Products); 5147 (Meats & Meat Products). **Sales:** $301,000,000 (2000). **Emp:** 1,800. **Officers:** Peter Castellana Jr., CEO & President; Robert C. Ludlow, Sr. VP & CFO.

■ **12910** ■ **Western Cold Storage**
1505 W Lee Rd.
Othello, WA 99344
Phone: (509)488-6677
Products: Potatoes. **SIC:** 5148 (Fresh Fruits & Vegetables). **Sales:** $3,000,000 (2000). **Emp:** 60. **Officers:** Jack L. Krumm, President.

■ **12911** ■ **Western Dairy Products Inc.**
3625 Westwind Blvd.
Santa Rosa, CA 95403
Phone: (707)524-6770 **Fax:** (707)524-6777
Products: Processed dairy products. **SIC:** 5143 (Dairy Products Except Dried or Canned). **Est:** 1980. **Sales:** $90,000,000 (2000). **Emp:** 14. **Officers:** Graeme Honeyfield, President.

■ **12912** ■ **Western Dairymen Cooperative Inc.**
1140 South 3200 West
Salt Lake City, UT 84104
Phone: (801)977-3000 **Fax:** (801)322-2325
Products: Milk. **SIC:** 5143 (Dairy Products Except Dried or Canned). **Sales:** $450,000,000 (2000). **Emp:** 900.

■ **12913** ■ **Western Export Services, Inc.**
Export Management Center
140 E 19th Ave., Ste. 201
Denver, CO 80203-1011
Phone: (303)302-5899 **Fax:** (303)302-5882
E-mail: wesdenver@aol.com
URL: http://www.wesdenver.com
Products: Food; Beverages; Licensed merchandise. **SICs:** 5149 (Groceries & Related Products Nec); 5091 (Sporting & Recreational Goods). **Est:** 1989. **Emp:** 7. **Officers:** Steven P. Meier, Manager; David Cisneros.

■ **12914** ■ **Western Family Foods Inc.**
PO Box 4057
Portland, OR 97208
Phone: (503)639-6300
Products: Food. **SIC:** 5141 (Groceries—General Line). **Sales:** $600,000,000 (2000). **Emp:** 67. **Officers:** Ronald King, CEO & President; Philip Juckeland, Sr. VP & CFO.

■ **12915** ■ **Western North Carolina Apple Growers**
Rte. 9
PO Box 699
Hendersonville, NC 28792
Phone: (704)685-3232
Products: Groceries, including apples. **SICs:** 5148 (Fresh Fruits & Vegetables); 5141 (Groceries—General Line). **Emp:** 49.

■ **12916** ■ **Westside Distributors**
PO Box 649
South Gate, CA 90280
Phone: (213)566-5181
Products: Snacks; Beer; Non-alcoholic beverages.
SIC: 5149 (Groceries & Related Products Nec).

■ **12917** ■ **Westway Trading Corp.**
7901 Xerxes Ave. S, Ste. 320
Minneapolis, MN 55431
Phone: (612)885-0233   **Fax:** (612)885-0226
Products: Molasses and molasses products. **SIC:**
5149 (Groceries & Related Products Nec). **Est:** 1961.
Officers: Phillip Coyle.

■ **12918** ■ **Westway Trading Corp.**
365 Canal Pl., No. 2200
New Orleans, LA 70130
Phone: (504)525-9741   **Fax:** (504)522-1638
Products: Molasses. **SIC:** 5149 (Groceries & Related
Products Nec). **Est:** 1970. **Sales:** $300,000,000
(2000). **Emp:** 200. **Officers:** Arthur W. Huguley IV,
President; Bryan Shoemaker, Exec. VP; Arthur
Haguley IV, VP of Sales; James Lacy, VP of
Operations.

■ **12919** ■ **Wetterau Inc.**
Greene Dr.
PO Box 427
Greenville, KY 42345
Phone: (502)338-2833
Products: Canned specialties; Frozen foods; Milk.
SICs: 5149 (Groceries & Related Products Nec); 5142
(Packaged Frozen Foods); 5143 (Dairy Products
Except Dried or Canned). **Emp:** 499. **Officers:** David
Israel.

■ **12920** ■ **Wetterau Inc.**
600 Daugherty St.
Scott City, MO 63780-0999
Phone: (573)264-3811   **Fax:** (573)264-2406
Products: Dairy products; Frozen foods; Fresh meat;
Frozen meat. **SICs:** 5141 (Groceries—General Line);
5143 (Dairy Products Except Dried or Canned); 5142
(Packaged Frozen Foods); 5147 (Meats & Meat
Products). **Est:** 1961. **Sales:** $156,000,000 (2000).
Emp: 240. **Officers:** Darrell L. Long; Bob Irlbeck,
Warehouse Mgr.

■ **12921** ■ **Wetterau Inc. Northeast**
56 Milliken St.
Portland, ME 04104
Phone: (207)797-5490   **Fax:** (207)797-3283
Products: Groceries, including produce, dairy, and
frozen products. **SICs:** 5141 (Groceries—General
Line); 5148 (Fresh Fruits & Vegetables); 5143 (Dairy
Products Except Dried or Canned); 5142 (Packaged
Frozen Foods). **Est:** 1856. **Sales:** $100,000,000
(2000). **Emp:** 200. **Officers:** Bruce Brandfon,
President; Michael Westort, Controller; Michael
Violette, Dir. of Sales; James Glover, VP of Operations;
Sally Semmes, Personnel Mgr.

■ **12922** ■ **Wexler Meat Co.**
963 W 37th St.
Chicago, IL 60609-1436
Phone: (773)927-5656   **Fax:** (773)927-1853
Products: Meat products. **SIC:** 5147 (Meats & Meat
Products). **Sales:** $140,000 (1999). **Emp:** 185.
Officers: Mike Gitelman, President; Barry S. Chudnow,
Exec. VP; Anne Kiernan, Vice President; John
Alexander, Vice President.

■ **12923** ■ **Whaley Pecan Company Inc.**
PO Drawer 609
Troy, AL 36081
Phone: (205)566-3504   **Fax:** (205)566-9336
Products: Pecans. **SIC:** 5145 (Confectionery). **Est:**
1937. **Sales:** $6,000,000 (2000). **Emp:** 65. **Officers:** R.
L. Whaley.

■ **12924** ■ **Wheeler Brothers**
420 Santa Fe
Alva, OK 73717
Phone: (580)327-0141   **Fax:** (580)327-1802
Products: Livestock and farm products. **SIC:** 5153
(Grain & Field Beans). **Sales:** $5,500,000 (2000). **Emp:**
7.

■ **12925** ■ **White Coffee Corp.**
18-35 38th St.
Long Island City, NY 11105
Phone: (718)204-7900
Free: (800)221-0140   **Fax:** (718)956-8504
URL: http://www.whitecoffee.com
Products: Coffee; Tea. **SIC:** 5149 (Groceries &
Related Products Nec).

■ **12926** ■ **White Commercial Corp.**
1101 E Ocean Blvd.
Stuart, FL 34996
Phone: (561)283-2420
Free: (800)327-7000   **Fax:** (561)288-1685
Products: Grain merchandising consultants. **SIC:** 5153
(Grain & Field Beans).

■ **12927** ■ **John R. White Company Inc.**
PO Box 10043
Birmingham, AL 35202
Phone: (205)595-8381
Products: Food. **SIC:** 5141 (Groceries—General Line).
Est: 1946. **Sales:** $9,000,000 (2000). **Emp:** 13.
Officers: Donald Patton, President; A. L. Inzinnia, Vice
President.

■ **12928** ■ **L.N. White and Company Inc.**
225 W 34th St.
New York, NY 10122
Phone: (212)239-7474   **Fax:** (212)563-5389
E-mail: jwhite@interactive.net
Products: Frozen seafood. **SICs:** 5146 (Fish &
Seafoods); 5142 (Packaged Frozen Foods). **Est:** 1923.
Sales: $20,000,000 (2000). **Emp:** 4. **Officers:** D.
White, President.

■ **12929** ■ **White Feather Farms Inc.**
800 W 17th St.
Muncie, IN 47302
Phone: (765)288-6636
Products: Food. **SIC:** 5141 (Groceries—General Line).

■ **12930** ■ **White Swan, Inc.**
915 E 50th
Lubbock, TX 79404
Phone: (806)747-5204   **Fax:** (806)747-6388
Products: Groceries; Produce; Paper items. **SICs:**
5141 (Groceries—General Line); 5148 (Fresh Fruits &
Vegetables); 5113 (Industrial & Personal Service
Paper). **Emp:** 178.

■ **12931** ■ **White Swan, Inc.**
5330 Fleming Ct.
Austin, TX 78744-1122
Phone: (512)447-4121
Free: (800)369-9022   **Fax:** (512)440-4233
Products: Food for restaurants, schools, and colleges.
SIC: 5141 (Groceries—General Line).

■ **12932** ■ **White Swan, Inc.**
PO Box 948
Houston, TX 77001
Phone: (713)672-2279   **Fax:** (713)670-3627
Products: Food for restaurants, schools, and colleges.
SIC: 5141 (Groceries—General Line).

■ **12933** ■ **Delavan E. Whitenight**
Rd. 6
Danville, PA 17821-9806
Phone: (717)275-5698   **Fax:** (717)275-0513
Products: Produce. **SIC:** 5148 (Fresh Fruits &
Vegetables). **Emp:** 26. **Officers:** Shirley Whitenight.

■ **12934** ■ **Whole Herb Co.**
19800 8th St. E
PO Box 1203
Sonoma, CA 95476
Phone: (707)935-1077   **Fax:** (707)935-3447
E-mail: sales@wholeherbcompany.com
URL: http://www.wholeherbcompany.com
Products: Botanicals; Herbs and spices. **SICs:** 5149
(Groceries & Related Products Nec); 5122 (Drugs,
Proprietaries & Sundries). **Est:** 1975. **Sales:**
$10,000,000 (2000). **Emp:** 30. **Officers:** Jim Thrower,
President; George Blasiola, General Mgr., e-mail:
George@wholeherbcompany.com; Stanley Ball,
Sales/Marketing Contact; Jessie Mendosa, Customer
Service Contact.

■ **12935** ■ **Wholesale Produce Supply**
Company Inc.
752 Kasota Cir.
Minneapolis, MN 55414
Phone: (612)378-2025   **Fax:** (612)378-9547
Products: Fruits and vegetables. **SIC:** 5148 (Fresh
Fruits & Vegetables). **Est:** 1950. **Sales:** $36,000,000
(2000). **Emp:** 100. **Officers:** Max Berc Sr., CEO; Ted
Shabert, President.

■ **12936** ■ **Robert Wholey and Company Inc.**
1501 Penn Ave.
Pittsburgh, PA 15222
Phone: (412)261-3693
Products: Fish; Meat; Poultry. **SICs:** 5146 (Fish &
Seafoods); 5147 (Meats & Meat Products); 5144
(Poultry & Poultry Products). **Sales:** $64,500,000
(2000). **Emp:** 175. **Officers:** Robert L. Wholey,
President.

■ **12937** ■ **Wiers Farm Inc.**
PO Box 385
Willard, OH 44890
Phone: (419)935-0131   **Fax:** (419)933-2117
Products: Vegetables. **SIC:** 5148 (Fresh Fruits &
Vegetables).

■ **12938** ■ **Wilbur Chocolate Company Inc.**
517 Clearview Pky.
Metairie, LA 70001-4626
Phone: (504)454-0124   **Fax:** (504)454-0125
Products: Chocolate and cocoa products. **SIC:** 5145
(Confectionery). **Est:** 1921. **Sales:** $300,000 (2000).
Emp: 19. **Officers:** Frank Carriere, General Mgr.;
Catherine Capozza, Customer Service Mgr.

■ **12939** ■ **Wilcox Frozen Foods Inc.**
2200 Oakdale Ave.
San Francisco, CA 94124
Phone: (415)282-4116
Free: (800)4WI-LCOX   **Fax:** (415)282-3044
Products: Institutional frozen food. **SIC:** 5142
(Packaged Frozen Foods). **Est:** 1947. **Sales:**
$15,000,000 (2000). **Emp:** 30. **Officers:** Robert C.
Smith, CEO; Rodney Smith, President.

■ **12940** ■ **Wild Craft Herb**
831 Almar Ave.
Santa Cruz, CA 95060
Phone: (831)423-7913   **Fax:** (831)429-5173
E-mail: sales@goodearthteas.com
URL: http://www.goodearth.com
Products: Bulk herbs. **SIC:** 5122 (Drugs, Proprietaries
& Sundries). **Est:** 1972. **Sales:** $8,000,000 (2000).
Emp: 80. **Officers:** Ben Zaricor, CEO.

■ **12941** ■ **Wild Game Inc.**
2475 N Elston Ave.
Chicago, IL 60647-2033
Phone: (773)278-1661
Products: Wild game, including venison, caribou,
buffalo, and pheasant. **SIC:** 5147 (Meats & Meat
Products). **Est:** 1982. **Sales:** $5,000,000 (2000). **Emp:**
16. **Officers:** Kaye Zubow, President.

■ **12942** ■ **Wildwood Natural Foods**
135 Bolinas Rd.
Fairfax, CA 94930
Phone: (415)459-3919   **Fax:** (415)485-3966
Products: Tofu and related products. **SIC:** 5149
(Groceries & Related Products Nec). **Est:** 1980. **Emp:**
99. **Officers:** Paul Orbuch, President & CEO; Dave
Knepler, Sales Mgr.

■ **12943** ■ **Rudie Wilhelm Warehouse**
Company Inc.
2400 SE Mailwell Dr.
Milwaukie, OR 97222
Phone: (503)653-1501   **Fax:** (503)652-2145
Products: Canned and dry foods. **SIC:** 5149
(Groceries & Related Products Nec). **Est:** 1925. **Sales:**
$30,000,000 (2000). **Emp:** 187. **Officers:** R.J. Wilhelm
Sr., President; Rudie Wilhelm Jr., CEO; Keith Bell, VP
of Marketing.

■ 12944 ■ **Wilke International Inc.**
15036 W 106th St.
Lenexa, KS 66215-2052
Phone: (913)438-5544
Products: Food. **SIC:** 5141 (Groceries—General Line).
Sales: $4,000,000 (2000). **Emp:** 7. **Officers:** Wayne
Wilke, President.

■ 12945 ■ **Wilkersons Pecans**
304 Eldridge St.
Sylvester, GA 31791-1310
Phone: (912)776-3505
Free: (800)523-3505 **Fax:** (912)776-6712
Products: Pecans. **SIC:** 5145 (Confectionery). **Est:**
1960. **Sales:** $2,000,000 (2000). **Emp:** 30. **Officers:** H.
Leroy Wilkerson.

■ 12946 ■ **Will Poultry Co.**
1075 William St.
Buffalo, NY 14206
Phone: (716)853-2000
Products: Fresh beef, chicken, and pork; Frozen
shrimp, crab, halibut, and cod. **SICs:** 5144 (Poultry &
Poultry Products); 5142 (Packaged Frozen Foods);
5146 (Fish & Seafoods); 5147 (Meats & Meat
Products). **Est:** 1926. **Sales:** $54,000,000 (2000).
Emp: 150. **Officers:** Donald E. Will, CEO; Karl
Kaminsky, Manager.

■ 12947 ■ **M.R. Williams Inc.**
235 Raleigh Rd.
Henderson, NC 27536
Phone: (919)438-8104 **Fax:** (919)438-2117
Products: General line groceries. **SIC:** 5141
(Groceries—General Line). **Emp:** 99. **Officers:** M. R.
Williams.

■ 12948 ■ **T.O. Williams Inc.**
300 Wythe St.
Portsmouth, VA 23704-5208
Phone: (757)397-0771
Free: (888)343-0771 **Fax:** (757)397-5702
E-mail: towi@Bellatlantic.net
Products: Sausage. **SIC:** 5147 (Meats & Meat
Products). **Est:** 1917. **Sales:** $2,000,000 (2000). **Emp:**
39. **Officers:** Hyun J. Chay, CEO & President; Peter J.
Chay, Vice President.

■ 12949 ■ **Ron Williams Produce**
76 N Trenton
Tulsa, OK 74120-1602
Phone: (918)582-3908 **Fax:** (918)583-6837
Products: Fruits and vegetables. **SIC:** 5148 (Fresh
Fruits & Vegetables). **Emp:** 9.

■ 12950 ■ **Willmar Poultry Company Inc.**
PO Box 753
Willmar, MN 56201
Phone: (612)235-3113 **Fax:** (612)235-8073
Products: Poultry products; Feeding machinery for
swine. **SICs:** 5144 (Poultry & Poultry Products); 5191
(Farm Supplies). **Est:** 1945. **Sales:** $56,000,000
(2000). **Emp:** 360. **Officers:** Ray Norling, President;
Ronald Hansen, Controller; Jerry Isley, Dir. of
Marketing & Sales.

■ 12951 ■ **Willow Hill Grain Inc.**
PO Box 213
Willow Hill, IL 62480
Phone: (618)455-3201
Products: Livestock and farm products. **SIC:** 5153
(Grain & Field Beans). **Sales:** $5,000,000 (2000). **Emp:**
8.

■ 12952 ■ **Willow Run Foods Inc.**
PO Box 1350
Binghamton, NY 13902
Phone: (607)729-5221
Products: Food; Fresh meats; Fish; Beef; Pork;
Canned vegetables. **SICs:** 5141 (Groceries—General
Line); 5147 (Meats & Meat Products); 5146 (Fish &
Seafoods).

■ 12953 ■ **Wilson Foods Company L.L.C.**
1811 W 1700 S
Salt Lake City, UT 84104
Phone: (801)972-5633 **Fax:** (801)977-9526
Products: Frozen Mexican food specialties. **SIC:** 5142

(Packaged Frozen Foods). **Sales:** $11,000,000 (1999).
Emp: 160. **Officers:** Robert Lovejoy, CEO & President.

■ 12954 ■ **Wilson Marketing & Sales**
202 Union St.
PO Box 487
Westfield, MA 01086
Phone: (413)568-8181 **Fax:** (413)562-8462
Products: Fresh potatoes; Maple syrup and candy;
Fresh blueberries; Fresh seaweed. **SICs:** 5148 (Fresh
Fruits & Vegetables); 5145 (Confectionery). **Officers:**
Grant Wilson, Owner.

■ 12955 ■ **Wilson Products Company Inc.**
1811 W 1700 S
Salt Lake City, UT 84104
Phone: (801)972-5633
Free: (800)950-8226 **Fax:** (801)977-9526
URL: http://www.lynnwilson.com
Products: Mexican food specialties. **SIC:** 5149
(Groceries & Related Products Nec). **Est:** 1938. **Sales:**
$12,500,000 (2000). **Emp:** 175.

■ 12956 ■ **Wilton Industries Inc.**
2240 W 75th St.
Woodridge, IL 60517
Phone: (630)963-7100
Products: Cake decorating supplies. **SIC:** 5149
(Groceries & Related Products Nec). **Est:** 1981. **Sales:**
$104,000,000 (2000). **Emp:** 500. **Officers:** V.A.
Naccarato, President; Stew Witkov, Exec. VP; John
Knepper, Dir. of Information Systems; R.A. Miller, Dir of
Personnel.

■ 12957 ■ **Winchell's Donut Houses Operating
Company L.P.**
1800 E 16th St.
Santa Ana, CA 92701
Phone: (714)565-1800
Free: (800)347-9347 **Fax:** (714)565-1801
Products: Donuts. **SIC:** 5149 (Groceries & Related
Products Nec). **Sales:** $94,000,000 (2000). **Emp:**
2,000. **Officers:** Thomas Dowolig, President; Janet
Pirus, VP of Finance.

■ 12958 ■ **Winkler Inc.**
PO Box 68
Dale, IN 47523
Phone: (812)937-4421 **Fax:** (812)937-2044
Products: Dry groceries. **SIC:** 5141 (Groceries—
General Line). **Est:** 1932. **Sales:** $110,000,000 (2000).
Emp: 490. **Officers:** Tom Winkler, President; Lynn
Howell, VP & Treasurer; Ron Carey, Dir. of Sales.

■ 12959 ■ **Winrock Bakery Inc.**
3320 2nd St. NW
Albuquerque, NM 87107
Phone: (505)345-7773 **Fax:** (505)345-2088
E-mail: pastian's@aol.com
Products: Baked goods, including breads, cakes, rolls,
donuts, and pies. **SIC:** 5149 (Groceries & Related
Products Nec). **Est:** 1961. **Sales:** $1,350,000 (1999).
Emp: 39. **Officers:** Harry Pastian, President. **Doing
Business As:** Pastian's Bakery.

■ 12960 ■ **Winter Gardens Quality Foods**
304 Commerce St.
New Oxford, PA 17350
Phone: (717)624-4911
Free: (800)242-7637 **Fax:** (717)624-7729
URL: http://www.wintergardens.com
Products: Fresh prepared foods. **SIC:** 5149 (Groceries
& Related Products Nec). **Est:** 1966. **Emp:** 160.
Officers: Tom Bross III, CEO; Jason Bross, Vice
President; Kim Wehland, Dir. of Sales & Marketing.
Former Name: Winter Gardens Salad Co.

■ 12961 ■ **Winter Harbor Fisheries**
HC 1 Box 41c
East Jewett, NY 12424-9707
Phone: (516)477-1170 **Fax:** (516)477-0543
Products: Seafood. **SIC:** 5146 (Fish & Seafoods).
Sales: $3,000,000 (2000). **Emp:** 20. **Officers:** Mark S.
Middleton.

■ 12962 ■ **Winter Haven Citrus Grower
Association**
PO Box 1874
Dundee, FL 33838-1874
Phone: (941)294-2959
Products: Citrus fruits. **SIC:** 5148 (Fresh Fruits &
Vegetables). **Est:** 1909. **Sales:** $10,000,000 (2000).
Emp: 150. **Officers:** Richard L. Ruis, CEO; Kenneth
Sikes, Treasurer & Secty.

■ 12963 ■ **Adam Winters**
Southard Ave.
Peekskill, NY 10566-1830
Phone: (914)737-6464 **Fax:** (914)737-6464
Products: Cigarettes; Candy; Groceries. **SICs:** 5141
(Groceries—General Line); 5194 (Tobacco & Tobacco
Products); 5145 (Confectionery). **Emp:** 49.

■ 12964 ■ **Winward Trading Company.**
PO Box 9833
San Rafael, CA 94912
Phone: (415)457-2411
Free: (800)858-8119 **Fax:** (415)457-4916
Products: Coffee; Tea and accessories. **SIC:** 5149
(Groceries & Related Products Nec). **Est:** 1967.
Officers: Rena Rein, President.

■ 12965 ■ **Wisco Farm Cooperative**
PO Box 753
Lake Mills, WI 53551
Phone: (920)648-3466
Products: Cheese and eggs. **SICs:** 5144 (Poultry &
Poultry Products); 5143 (Dairy Products Except Dried
or Canned).

■ 12966 ■ **Wisconsin Packing Company Inc.**
PO Box 913
Butler, WI 53007-0913
Phone: (414)781-2400 **Fax:** (414)781-3538
Products: Hamburgers. **SIC:** 5147 (Meats & Meat
Products). **Est:** 1926. **Sales:** $63,600,000 (2000).
Emp: 175. **Officers:** G. Woodrow Adkins, President;
George Lange, Controller; Greg Stephenson, Dir. of
Marketing.

■ 12967 ■ **Wise Snacks Bryden Distributors**
100 W Lincoln Ave.
Williamsport, PA 17701
Phone: (570)323-5150
Products: Snacks, including potato chips. **SIC:** 5145
(Confectionery).

■ 12968 ■ **A.B. Wise & Sons**
4544 Muhlhauser Rd.
Hamilton, OH 45011
Phone: (513)874-9642 **Fax:** (513)874-1229
Products: Groceries. **SIC:** 5141 (Groceries—General
Line).

■ 12969 ■ **Witmer Foods Inc.**
PO Box 3307
Lavale, MD 21502
Phone: (301)724-5950 **Fax:** (301)724-6936
Products: Frozen, canned, and fresh foods. **SICs:**
5141 (Groceries—General Line); 5142 (Packaged
Frozen Foods). **Est:** 1964. **Sales:** $6,000,000 (2000).
Emp: 24. **Officers:** Kenneth Witmer, President; Jerri L.
Witmer, Vice President.

■ 12970 ■ **The Eli Witt Co.**
PO Box 1510
8305 SE 58th Ave.
Ocala, FL 34480
Phone: (352)245-5151 **Fax:** (352)347-6086
Products: Food. **SIC:** 5141 (Groceries—General Line).
Est: 1947. **Sales:** $482,000,000 (2000). **Emp:** 888.
Officers: Tony DeMarco, VP of Distribution Center.
Former Name: Certified Grocers of Florida Inc.

■ 12971 ■ **Wolcott and Lincoln Inc.**
4800 Main St.
Kansas City, MO 64112
Phone: (816)753-6750 **Fax:** (816)531-6876
Products: Grain; Farm product storage. **SIC:** 5153
(Grain & Field Beans). **Sales:** $37,000,000 (1999).
Emp: 40. **Officers:** Ira Polk, General Mgr.

■ 12972 ■ D.E. Wolfgang Candy Co. Inc.
50 E 4th Ave.
PO Box 226
York, PA 17405
Phone: (717)843-5536
Free: (800)248-4273 **Fax:** (717)845-2881
Products: Candy. **SIC:** 5145 (Confectionery). **Sales:** $8,500,000 (2000). **Emp:** 99. **Officers:** Robert L. Wolfgang II, President.

■ 12973 ■ Wolfstein International, Inc.
900 Wilshire Blvd., Ste 1530
Los Angeles, CA 90017
Phone: (213)689-9514 **Fax:** (213)689-1069
E-mail: wolfintl@earthlink.net
URL: http://www.wolfsteinintl.com
Products: Fresh and frozen beef, pork, veal, and poultry; Frozen meat by-products; Fresh, live, and frozen fish and seafood products. **SICs:** 5147 (Meats & Meat Products); 5144 (Poultry & Poultry Products); 5142 (Packaged Frozen Foods); 5146 (Fish & Seafoods); 5149 (Groceries & Related Products Nec). **Est:** 1977. **Sales:** $5,000,000 (2000). **Emp:** 3. **Officers:** Philip Wolfstein, President.

■ 12974 ■ Wolverine Packing Co.
1340 Winder St.
Detroit, MI 48207
Phone: (313)259-7500 **Fax:** (313)568-1909
Products: Veal, lamb, and beef. **SIC:** 5147 (Meats & Meat Products). **Sales:** $160,000,000 (2000). **Emp:** 155. **Officers:** Jim Bonahour.

■ 12975 ■ Wonder Bread Thrift Store Inc.
5923 S 350 W
Murray, UT 84107
Phone: (801)268-8774
Products: Bread. **SIC:** 5149 (Groceries & Related Products Nec). **Est:** 1977. **Sales:** $5,000,000 (2000). **Emp:** 100. **Officers:** Bob Johansen, General Mgr.; Dennis McDonald, CFO; Paul McKennan, Manager.

■ 12976 ■ Wood-Fruitticher Grocery
PO Box 610130
Birmingham, AL 35261-0130
Phone: (205)836-9663
Products: General line groceries. **SIC:** 5141 (Groceries—General Line). **Est:** 1913. **Sales:** $76,000,000 (2000). **Emp:** 150. **Officers:** D. Wood, Owner.

■ 12977 ■ J.R. Wood Inc.
PO Box 545
Atwater, CA 95301
Phone: (209)358-5643 **Fax:** (209)358-6351
E-mail: jwidick@jsrwood.com
URL: http://www.jrwood.com
Products: Frozen fruits and vegetables, control packaging. **SIC:** 5142 (Packaged Frozen Foods). **Est:** 1919. **Sales:** $120,000,000 (2000). **Emp:** 1,000. **Officers:** Jim Wood.

■ 12978 ■ Woodhaven Foods Inc.
1101 Market St.
Philadelphia, PA 19107
Phone: (215)698-1200
Products: Food. **SIC:** 5141 (Groceries—General Line).

■ 12979 ■ Casey Woodwyk Inc.
PO Box 9
Hudsonville, MI 49426-0009
Phone: (616)669-1700
Products: Onions. **SIC:** 5148 (Fresh Fruits & Vegetables). **Est:** 1945. **Sales:** $11,000,000 (2000). **Emp:** 38. **Officers:** Jim Woodwyk, President; Jim Woodwyk, Dir. of Marketing.

■ 12980 ■ World Candies Inc.
185 30th St.
Brooklyn, NY 11232-1705
Phone: (718)768-8100
Free: (800)252-2639 **Fax:** (718)499-4918
Products: Candy sticks. **SIC:** 5145 (Confectionery). **Emp:** 49. **Officers:** Samuel Cohen.

■ 12981 ■ World Finer Foods Inc.
300 Broadacres Dr.
Bloomfield, NJ 07003
Phone: (973)338-0300
Products: Gourmet foods. **SIC:** 5149 (Groceries & Related Products Nec). **Est:** 1932. **Sales:** $90,000,000 (2000). **Emp:** 25. **Officers:** John Beers, President; Barry J. O'Brien, VP & Treasurer; Frank Muchel, Dir. of Sales; Neal Kaskel, VP & Controller.

■ 12982 ■ World Food Tech Services
153 Cherry St.
Malden, MA 02148
Phone: (781)321-3750 **Fax:** (781)321-3750
Products: Frozen shrimp and fish; Cake decorations and ice cream toppings; Maple syrup; Maple sugar chocolate products; Smoked salmon; Sesame paste and oil; Frozen vegetables and tropical fruits. **SICs:** 5149 (Groceries & Related Products Nec); 5142 (Packaged Frozen Foods); 5145 (Confectionery); 5146 (Fish & Seafoods). **Officers:** Daniel Casper, President.

■ 12983 ■ World Variety Produce Inc.
5325 S Soto St.
PO Box 21127
Los Angeles, CA 90058-3624
Phone: (213)588-0151 **Fax:** (213)588-7841
Products: Fruits and vegetables. **SIC:** 5148 (Fresh Fruits & Vegetables). **Est:** 1984. **Sales:** $35,000,000 (2000). **Emp:** 175. **Officers:** Joe Hernandez, President; Lee A. Zeller, CFO.

■ 12984 ■ Worldwide Wonders
PO Box 82086
Portland, OR 97282
Phone: (503)239-7004
Products: Herbs. **SIC:** 5149 (Groceries & Related Products Nec). **Emp:** 5. **Officers:** Jean C. Vanderflute, General Mgr.

■ 12985 ■ Wricley Nut Products Co.
110 Tasker St.
Philadelphia, PA 19147-0095
Phone: (215)467-1106
Products: Edible nuts and dried fruits. **SICs:** 5159 (Farm-Product Raw Materials Nec); 5149 (Groceries & Related Products Nec).

■ 12986 ■ Wricley Nut Products Co. Edwards-Freeman Div.
441 E Hector St.
Conshohocken, PA 19428
Phone: (215)828-7440 **Fax:** (215)832-0126
Products: Nuts and seeds (salted, roasted, cooked, or blanched); Dried and dehydrated fruits; Snack foods; Candy. **SICs:** 5145 (Confectionery); 5149 (Groceries & Related Products Nec). **Sales:** $12,000,000 (2000). **Emp:** 35. **Officers:** Edward A. Comer, President.

■ 12987 ■ Wright Brokerage Inc.
1815 Erle Rd.
Mechanicsville, VA 23111-1505
Phone: (804)746-5294 **Fax:** (804)746-3676
Products: Groceries, including frozen food. **SICs:** 5141 (Groceries—General Line); 5142 (Packaged Frozen Foods); 5149 (Groceries & Related Products Nec). **Emp:** 42.

■ 12988 ■ William S. Wright Co.
PO Box 1729
Nogales, AZ 85628-1729
Phone: (520)281-0951 **Fax:** (520)281-0214
Products: Fruits and vegetables. **SIC:** 5148 (Fresh Fruits & Vegetables). **Sales:** $5,000,000 (2000). **Emp:** 25. **Officers:** J. Ruiz, Partner.

■ 12989 ■ Xcell International Corp.
644 Blackhawk Dr.
Westmont, IL 60559
Phone: (630)323-0107
Free: (800)722-7751 **Fax:** (630)323-0217
E-mail: xcellint@aol.com
Products: Coffee makers; Coffee flavorings; Seasonings and spices, including peppercorns; Confectionery toppings. **SICs:** 5149 (Groceries & Related Products Nec); 5023 (Homefurnishings); 5149 (Groceries & Related Products Nec). **Est:** 1987. **Sales:** $5,000,000 (2000). **Emp:** 6. **Officers:** Raymond Henning, CEO & Chairman of the Board; Dean Henning, President; David B. Elsner, Sales/Marketing Contact; Barb Soenke, Customer Service Contact.

■ 12990 ■ Yankee Marketers Inc.
PO Box 370
Middleton, MA 01949
Phone: (978)777-9181
Free: (800)343-8272 **Fax:** (978)777-5823
E-mail: headquarters@yankeemarketers.com
URL: http://www.yankeemarketers.com
Products: Food. **SIC:** 5141 (Groceries—General Line). **Est:** 1971. **Sales:** $50,000,000 (2000). **Emp:** 18. **Officers:** Robert Johnson, President; Brad Johnson, VP of Sales; Amy Fay, Sr. VP; Sandra Johnson, VP of Customer Services.

■ 12991 ■ YAO Industries
535 5th Ave., 33rd Fl.
New York, NY 10017
Phone: (212)697-8686
Products: Groceries; Pharmaceuticals and sundries; Chemicals and allied products; Transportation equipment and supplies. **SICs:** 5141 (Groceries—General Line); 5088 (Transportation Equipment & Supplies); 5122 (Drugs, Proprietaries & Sundries); 5169 (Chemicals & Allied Products Nec). **Est:** 1965. **Sales:** $22,000,000 (2000). **Emp:** 20. **Officers:** Fred Yao, President. **Alternate Name:** Yao Shih-Chin Corp.

■ 12992 ■ Yarnell Ice Cream Company Inc.
205 S Spring
Searcy, AR 72143-6730
Phone: (501)268-2414 **Fax:** (501)268-2414
Products: Ice cream; Frozen desserts. **SIC:** 5143 (Dairy Products Except Dried or Canned). **Sales:** $12,000,000 (2000). **Emp:** 99. **Officers:** A. Roger Yarnell.

■ 12993 ■ Yell-O-Glow Corp.
PO Box 6265
Chelsea, MA 02150-0007
Phone: 800-767-3225 **Fax:** (617)394-0470
Products: Tropical produce, including bananas. **SIC:** 5148 (Fresh Fruits & Vegetables). **Emp:** 49. **Officers:** Louis Markos.

■ 12994 ■ Yoders Inc.
PO Box 249
Grantsville, MD 21536-0249
Phone: (301)895-5121 **Fax:** (301)895-3158
Products: Meats and processed pork. **SIC:** 5147 (Meats & Meat Products). **Est:** 1947. **Sales:** $10,000,000 (2000). **Emp:** 99. **Officers:** Eli Yodes, Vice President; Lowell Bender, President.

■ 12995 ■ York River Seafood Company Inc.
PO Box 239
Hayes, VA 23072-9802
Phone: (804)642-2151 **Fax:** (804)642-3474
E-mail: crab@inna.net
Products: Seafood, fish, crabmeat, and conch. **SIC:** 5146 (Fish & Seafoods). **Est:** 1945. **Sales:** $6,000,000 (2000). **Emp:** 70. **Officers:** J.M. Shackelford, President.

■ 12996 ■ Yorkshire Food Sales Corp.
2000 Plaza Ave.
PO Box 148
New Hyde Park, NY 11040-0136
Phone: (516)328-1500 **Fax:** (516)326-6838
Products: Snacks, including potato chips, pretzels, popcorn, nuts, tortilla chips, plantain chips, and corn chips. **SICs:** 5149 (Groceries & Related Products Nec); 5145 (Confectionery). **Emp:** 49. **Officers:** Bruce D. Brown, CEO; Anthony Gerbino, President; William M. Timlen, Dir. of Merchandising.

■ 12997 ■ Young Pecan Shelling Company Inc.
PO Box 5779
Florence, SC 29502
Phone: (843)664-2330
Free: (800)829-6864 **Fax:** (843)664-2344
E-mail: sales@youngpecan.com
URL: http://www.youngpecan.com
Products: Pecans. **SIC:** 5159 (Farm-Product Raw Materials Nec). **Est:** 1945. **Sales:** $80,000,000 (2000). **Emp:** 235. **Officers:** James W. Swink, President; Murray Garber, VP of Finance; Helen Watts,

Sales/Marketing Contact, e-mail: hwatts@youngpecan.com; Stephanie Faidley, Customer Service Contact, e-mail: sfaidley@youngpecan.com.

■ **12998** ■ **Yum Yum Donut Shops, Inc.**
18830 E San Jose Ave.
City of Industry, CA 91748
Phone: (626)964-1478 **Fax:** (626)912-2779
Products: Bakery products. **SIC:** 5149 (Groceries & Related Products Nec). **Est:** 1971. **Sales:** $16,000,000 (2000). **Emp:** 500. **Officers:** Lincoln Watase, President.

■ **12999** ■ **Zacky Foods Co.**
2000 N Tyler Ave.
South el Monte, CA 91733
Phone: (818)443-9351 **Fax:** (818)401-4291
Products: Poultry. **SICs:** 5144 (Poultry & Poultry Products); 5142 (Packaged Frozen Foods). **Est:** 1935. **Sales:** $600,000,000 (2000). **Emp:** 3,000. **Officers:** Robert Zacky, President; Hank Frederick, Exec. VP; Richard Sorensen, General Mgr.; Royce Peterson, Dir of Human Resources.

■ **13000** ■ **Zanders Creamery Inc.**
1214 Main
Cross Plains, WI 53528-9647
Phone: (608)798-3261 **Fax:** (608)798-4988
Products: Butter. **SIC:** 5143 (Dairy Products Except Dried or Canned). **Sales:** $31,000,000 (2000). **Emp:** 49. **Officers:** Paul H. Zander.

■ **13001** ■ **Zanios Foods**
221 Airport Dr. NW
Albuquerque, NM 87101
Phone: (505)831-1411
Products: Foods. **SIC:** 5141 (Groceries—General Line).

■ **13002** ■ **Zanios Foods Inc.**
PO Box 27730
Albuquerque, NM 87125-7730
Phone: (505)831-1411 **Fax:** (505)831-4022
E-mail: zaniosfood@aol.com
Products: Dry goods; Paper. **SICs:** 5147 (Meats & Meat Products); 5146 (Fish & Seafoods); 5144 (Poultry & Poultry Products); 5143 (Dairy Products Except Dried or Canned). **Est:** 1956. **Sales:** $60,000,000 (2000). **Emp:** 150. **Officers:** Jim Zanios, CEO; John Gonau, President.

■ **13003** ■ **Zatarain's**
PO Box 347
Gretna, LA 70054
Phone: (504)367-2950 **Fax:** (504)362-2004
E-mail: inquires@zatarain.com
URL: http://www.zatarain.com
Products: Food products and grocery items. **SIC:** 5141 (Groceries—General Line). **Est:** 1889.

■ **13004** ■ **Zenobia Co.**
3632 Kingsbridge Ave.
Bronx, NY 10463-2339
Phone: (718)796-7700 **Fax:** (718)548-2313
E-mail: mail@zenobianut.com
URL: http://www.zenobianut.com
Products: Edible nuts and seeds. **SIC:** 5145 (Confectionery). **Est:** 1926. **Sales:** $8,000,000 (2000). **Emp:** 49. **Officers:** Ira Agress; Jack Bobker; Ken Bobker; John Agress.

■ **13005** ■ **Zephyr Egg Co.**
PO Box 9005
Zephyrhills, FL 33539-9005
Phone: (813)782-1521 **Fax:** (813)782-7070
Products: Eggs. **SIC:** 5144 (Poultry & Poultry Products). **Est:** 1961. **Sales:** $30,000,000 (2000). **Emp:** 200. **Officers:** Lois Linville, President; Terry Linville, Secretary; Danny Linville, Dir. of Marketing.

■ **13006** ■ **Ziegler's Bakers Supply and Equipment Corp.**
6890 Kinne St.
East Syracuse, NY 13057
Phones: (315)463-0060 (315)463-0060
Free: (800)252-2225 **Fax:** (315)437-6666
Products: Baking powder and yeast; Flour and other grain mill products; Soft or brown sugar; Refined cane sugar and byproducts. **SICs:** 5149 (Groceries & Related Products Nec); 5159 (Farm-Product Raw Materials Nec). **Sales:** $18,000,000 (2000). **Emp:** 37. **Officers:** Michael A. Berger, Warehouse Manager.

(18) Furniture and Fixtures

Entries in this section are arranged alphabetically by company name. When the company name is a personal name, the company name is alphabetized by the surname unless the first name or initial(s) are part of a trade name. See the User's Guide at the front of this directory for additional information.

■ 13007 ■ **A-Dec Inc.**
PO Box 111
Newberg, OR 97132
Phone: (503)538-9471
Products: Dental chairs, stools, and cabinetry; Pneumatic valves; Support arm systems. **SICs:** 5021 (Furniture); 5047 (Medical & Hospital Equipment). **Sales:** $130,000,000 (2000). **Emp:** 920. **Officers:** George Austin, President.

■ 13008 ■ **A Pickle House/Judy Blair's Rustic Collectibles**
1401 E Van Buren St.
Phoenix, AZ 85006-3523
Phone: (602)257-1915 **Fax:** (602)257-9224
Products: Furniture made from pickle vats and metal bands. **SIC:** 5021 (Furniture). **Est:** 1905. **Sales:** $250,000 (1999). **Emp:** 9. **Officers:** Philip Arnold Blair D.V.M.; Judy C. Blair. **Former Name:** A Pickle House.

■ 13009 ■ **A.A. Importing Co. Inc.**
7700 Hall St.
St. Louis, MO 63147
Phone: (314)383-8800 **Fax:** (314)383-2608
Products: Antique reproductions, including merchandise and furniture. **SICs:** 5023 (Homefurnishings); 5021 (Furniture). **Est:** 1934. **Sales:** $6,000,000 (2000). **Emp:** 50. **Officers:** R.B. Tallin, President & Treasurer.

■ 13010 ■ **Accurate Partitions Corp.**
PO Box 287
Lyons, IL 60534
Phone: (708)442-6800 **Fax:** (708)442-7439
Products: Toilet components. **SIC:** 5046 (Commercial Equipment Nec). **Est:** 1957. **Sales:** $10,000,000 (2000). **Emp:** 80. **Officers:** Carl Liggett, General Mgr.; Roy White, Chicago Marketing & Sales Mgr.; Guy Bagger, National Sales & Marketing Mgr.; John Stewack, Purchasing Agent.

■ 13011 ■ **Adirondack Chair Company Inc.**
31-01 Vernon Blvd.
Long Island City, NY 11106
Fax: 800-477-1330
Products: Office equipment and supplies. **SIC:** 5021 (Furniture). **Sales:** $20,000,000 (2000). **Emp:** 100.

■ 13012 ■ **Airmo Div.**
950 Mason St.
San Francisco, CA 94106
Phone: (415)772-5336 **Fax:** (415)772-5012
Products: Furniture, silverware, linen and other related items for The Fairmont hotels. **SICs:** 5021 (Furniture); 5094 (Jewelry & Precious Stones); 5023 (Homefurnishings). **Sales:** $9,000,000 (2000). **Emp:** 3. **Officers:** Edward Mace, CEO & President; Chuck Bond, Finance Officer.

■ 13013 ■ **Alden Comfort Mills**
1708 14th
Plano, TX 75074-6404
Phone: (972)423-4000 **Free:** (800)822-5336
Products: Mattresses; Bedsprings; Bedspreads and bedsets. **SICs:** 5021 (Furniture); 5023 (Homefurnishings). **Emp:** 7. **Officers:** Richard Pool.

■ 13014 ■ **Allied Sales Co.**
509 N Saint Andrews St.
Dothan, AL 36303-4557
Phone: (334)792-1627 **Fax:** (334)793-8271
Products: Furniture. **SIC:** 5021 (Furniture). **Est:** 1975. **Sales:** $350,000 (2000). **Emp:** 4. **Officers:** Wes Moss, President.

■ 13015 ■ **Alpha Fine Computer Furniture**
2241 N Main St.
Walnut Creek, CA 94596
Phone: (925)930-0277
Products: Computer furniture including desks, organizers, and file cabinets. **SIC:** 5021 (Furniture).

■ 13016 ■ **Alumacast Inc.**
3112 S Highland Dr.
Las Vegas, NV 89109
Phone: (702)871-7944 **Fax:** (702)871-7892
Products: Lawn furniture. **SIC:** 5021 (Furniture). **Officers:** Donald Williams, President.

■ 13017 ■ **American Locker Security Systems Inc.**
608 Allen St.
Jamestown, NY 14701-3966
Phone: (716)664-9600
Free: (800)828-9118 **Fax:** (716)664-2949
Products: Distributor of coin, key, and electronic security lockers. **SIC:** 5046 (Commercial Equipment Nec). **Sales:** $23,000,000 (2000). **Emp:** 88. **Officers:** Roy J. Glosser, President & COO.

■ 13018 ■ **American Seating Co.**
401 American Seating Ctr.
Grand Rapids, MI 49504
Phone: (616)732-6600
Free: (800)748-0268 **Fax:** (616)732-6401
URL: http://www.americanseating.com
Products: Seating, including transportation and public seating; Office furniture. **SIC:** 5021 (Furniture). **Est:** 1886. **Sales:** $160,000,000 (2000). **Emp:** 900. **Officers:** Edward J. Clark, President & COO.

■ 13019 ■ **Ampco/Rosedale Fabricators**
PO Box 608
Rosedale, MS 38769
Phone: (601)759-3521
Free: (800)289-2672 **Fax:** (601)759-3721
Products: Cabinets for the kitchen and office; Institutional furniture. **SICs:** 5021 (Furniture); 5031 (Lumber, Plywood & Millwork). **Est:** 1946. **Sales:** $3,000,000 (2000). **Emp:** 100. **Officers:** R.L. Kanary, CEO; Lewis Merrell, CFO.

■ 13020 ■ **Amtec International Inc.**
1200 Woodruff Rd., No. A-2
Greenville, SC 29607-5730
Phone: (864)288-5064 **Fax:** (864)288-9476
Products: Furniture, including wood and upholstered; Disposable medical supplies. **SICs:** 5021 (Furniture); 5047 (Medical & Hospital Equipment). **Est:** 1980. **Sales:** $11,000,000 (2000). **Emp:** 7. **Officers:** Mohammad R. Oweis, President; Deeb R. Oweis, Treasurer; Samar R. Oweis, Secretary.

■ 13021 ■ **Anderson's Woodwork Inc.**
3220 Anderson Way
Strawberry Plains, TN 37871
Phone: (423)933-8662
Products: Wood household furniture; Wood office furniture. **SIC:** 5021 (Furniture). **Sales:** $1,000,000 (2000). **Emp:** 25. **Officers:** Mary Sue Anderson, Vice President; Robert F. Anderson, President.

■ 13022 ■ **Arcadia Chair Co.**
5692 Fresca Dr.
La Palma, CA 90623
Phone: (714)562-8200
Free: (800)585-5957 **Fax:** (714)562-8202
E-mail: sales@arcadiachair.com
Products: Furniture. **SIC:** 5021 (Furniture). **Est:** 1979. **Emp:** 125. **Officers:** Casey Journigan, President; Randolph A. Kemp, VP of Mktg. & Sales.

■ 13023 ■ **Art Metal Products**
115 S Wilke Rd.
Arlington Heights, IL 60006
Phone: (708)577-0330
Products: Metal lockers. **SIC:** 5046 (Commercial Equipment Nec). **Sales:** $300,000 (1994). **Emp:** 3. **Officers:** Ted Shiakalli, Sales Mgr.

■ 13024 ■ **Artlite Office Supply and Furniture Co.**
1851 Piedmont Rd.
Atlanta, GA 30324
Phone: (404)875-7271
Products: Office furniture. **SIC:** 5021 (Furniture).

■ 13025 ■ **Aspen Furniture Inc.**
2929 Grand Ave.
Phoenix, AZ 85017-4933
Phone: (602)233-0224 **Fax:** (602)269-1277
Products: Marketing of oak furniture. **SIC:** 5021 (Furniture). **Sales:** $114,000,000 (2000). **Emp:** 300. **Officers:** Stan Sapp, President; Mike Rigsbee, Controller.

■ 13026 ■ **Associated Building Specialties**
20 Frankford Ave.
Blackwood, NJ 08012-2850
Phone: (609)227-3900 **Fax:** (609)227-9307
Products: Toilet partitions and accessories; Metal doors, frames, and hardware; Office partitions; Folding doors and walls; Lockers; Fire extinguishers. **SICs:** 5046 (Commercial Equipment Nec); 5031 (Lumber, Plywood & Millwork). **Est:** 1957. **Sales:** $4,500,000 (2000). **Emp:** 40. **Officers:** Edwin H. Janka.

■ 13027 ■ **A.W. Industries**
8415 Ardmore Rd.
Landover, MD 20785
Phone: (301)322-1000
Free: (800)638-0520 **Fax:** (301)341-4639
Products: Furniture and fixtures. **SIC:** 5021 (Furniture). **Sales:** $30,000,000 (2000). **Emp:** 225.

■ 13028 ■ AWD International Inc.
410 Oakmears Cres, Ste. 202
Virginia Beach, VA 23462-4235
Phone: (757)625-0883   Fax: (757)625-5564
Products: Household furniture; Sail boats; Mining equipment; Motor vehicles. SICs: 5021 (Furniture); 5012 (Automobiles & Other Motor Vehicles); 5091 (Sporting & Recreational Goods); 5082 (Construction & Mining Machinery). Officers: Ashton W. Davis, President.

■ 13029 ■ B J's Wholesale Club Inc.
PO Box 9601
Natick, MA 01760
Phone: (508)651-7400   Fax: (508)651-6114
Products: Furniture; Appliances; Food and other products. SICs: 5021 (Furniture); 5064 (Electrical Appliances—Television & Radio); 5141 (Groceries—General Line); 5137 (Women's/Children's Clothing). Sales: $3,552,200,000 (2000). Emp: 12,500. Officers: John J. Nugent, CEO & President; Frank D. Forward, Exec. VP & CFO.

■ 13030 ■ Bank and Office Interiors
5601 6th Ave. S
Seattle, WA 98108
Phone: (206)768-8000
Products: Office furniture. SIC: 5021 (Furniture).

■ 13031 ■ Barber Cabinet Co. Inc.
2957 Collier St.
Indianapolis, IN 46241-5903
Phone: (317)247-4747   Fax: (317)247-4748
Products: Custom cabinets for kitchen and bath. SIC: 5031 (Lumber, Plywood & Millwork). Officers: John Barber, President.

■ 13032 ■ Barclay Dean Interiors
1917 120th Ave. NE
Bellevue, WA 98005
Phone: (425)451-8940
Products: Office furniture. SIC: 5021 (Furniture). Sales: $20,000,000 (1994). Emp: 90. Officers: Harlan B. Dean, CEO & President; Valarie Schmidt, CFO.

■ 13033 ■ Russ Bassett Co.
8189 Byron Rd.
Whittier, CA 90606
Phones: (562)945-2445   (310)350-2445
Free: (800)350-2445   Fax: (562)698-8972
E-mail: mail@russbassett.com
URL: http://www.russbassett.com
Products: Steel filing, visuflex and promedia cabinets; Shelving product lines, including Gemtrac pullout, slidetrac slide to slide, carousels and stationery. SICs: 5021 (Furniture); 5021 (Furniture). Est: 1960. Officers: Mike Dressendorfer.

■ 13034 ■ Philip M. Bell
118 Northeast Dr.
Loveland, OH 45140
Phone: (513)683-6300
Products: Home furniture. SIC: 5021 (Furniture).

■ 13035 ■ BenchCraft
PO Box 86
Blue Mountain, MS 38610
Phone: (662)685-4711   Fax: (662)685-4784
URL: http://www.benchcraft.com
Products: Upholstered furniture. SIC: 5021 (Furniture). Est: 1976. Sales: $200,000,000 (2000). Emp: 1,900. Officers: Tom Cunningham, CEO & President; Jim Owen, Sr. VP & Finance Officer, e-mail: jowen@benchcraft.com; Ron Spivey, Sr. VP of Sales.

■ 13036 ■ BFI/Specmark
133 Rahway Ave.
Elizabeth, NJ 07202
Phone: (908)355-3400
Products: Office furniture. SIC: 5021 (Furniture).

■ 13037 ■ B.G. Office Products
3236 Auburn Blvd.
Sacramento, CA 95821
Phone: (916)484-7300
Products: Office furniture and supplies. SICs: 5021 (Furniture); 5112 (Stationery & Office Supplies).

■ 13038 ■ Big Reds Antiques
PO Box 160
Forney, TX 75126
Phone: (214)552-2949
Products: Furniture; Bronze statues; Cut glass; Paintings. SIC: 5021 (Furniture). Est: 1954. Sales: $2,000,000 (2000). Emp: 4. Officers: G.R. Whaley, President.

■ 13039 ■ Bleecker Furniture Inc.
PO Box 5084
Missoula, MT 59806-5084
Phone: (406)543-8593   Fax: (406)542-1567
Products: Household furniture. SIC: 5021 (Furniture). Est: 1980. Officers: Michael Bleecker, President.

■ 13040 ■ Bodine Inc.
2141 14th Ave. S
Birmingham, AL 35205
Phone: (205)933-9100   Fax: (205)933-8607
Products: Office furniture. SIC: 5021 (Furniture). Sales: $19,000,000 (2000). Emp: 52. Officers: Eddie Miller, President.

■ 13041 ■ Booker-Price Co.
1318 McHenry St.
Louisville, KY 40217
Phone: (502)637-2531   Fax: (502)637-1535
Products: Furniture. SIC: 5021 (Furniture). Sales: $4,000,000 (2000). Emp: 30. Officers: B. Booker Jr., CEO.

■ 13042 ■ Bowlus School Supply Inc.
PO Box 1349
Pittsburg, KS 66762
Phone: (316)231-3450
Free: (800)362-0573   Fax: (316)231-7351
Products: School furniture; Lead pencils, crayons, and artists' materials. SICs: 5021 (Furniture); 5112 (Stationery & Office Supplies). Est: 1927. Emp: 70. Officers: Rudy Simoncic, Owner and President.

■ 13043 ■ Braden's Wholesale Furniture Company Inc.
1335 Western Ave.
Knoxville, TN 37921
Phone: (423)549-5000
Products: Furniture. SIC: 5021 (Furniture). Est: 1956. Sales: $7,000,000 (2000). Emp: 40. Officers: Gary M. Braden, President; David Pesterfield, CFO.

■ 13044 ■ Bradshaw International Inc.
9409 Buffalo Ave.
Rancho Cucamonga, CA 91730-6012
Phone: (310)946-7466
Products: Homefurnishings. SIC: 5023 (Homefurnishings). Sales: $84,000,000 (2000). Emp: 65. Officers: Mike Rodrigue, President; Jerry Vitliotti, VP of Finance.

■ 13045 ■ Brennans Ltd.
2770 E Flamingo Rd.
Las Vegas, NV 89121-5210
Phone: (702)731-2001   Fax: (702)794-0104
E-mail: jendsignerswksp@usa.net
Products: Furniture. SIC: 5021 (Furniture). Est: 1969. Emp: 8.

■ 13046 ■ Brown Distributing Co. Inc.
6085 Lagrange Blvd. SW
Atlanta, GA 30336-2817
Phone: (404)753-6136   Fax: (404)753-6130
Products: Household furniture; Household appliances; Electronic systems and equipment. SICs: 5021 (Furniture); 5064 (Electrical Appliances—Television & Radio). Est: 1929. Sales: $3,000,000 (2000). Emp: 15. Officers: Robert Brown, CEO; F. Harvey Mayes, Treasurer & Secty.

■ 13047 ■ Brueton Industries Inc.
145-68 228th St.
Springfield Gardens, NY 11413
Phone: (718)527-3000
Free: (800)221-6783   Fax: (718)712-6783
E-mail: Brueton@aol.com
URL: http://www.brueton.com
Products: Furniture. SIC: 5021 (Furniture). Est: 1970. Sales: $10,000,000 (1999). Emp: 100. Officers: R. Somma, President; Deborah Cvirko, Dir. of Marketing & Sales; Judy Sabatino, Customer Service Contact; Bobbi Scibelli, Human Resources Contact.

■ 13048 ■ Builders Wholesale Supply Company, Inc.
Forbes Industrial Park
7215 S Topeka Blvd., No. 9C
PO Box 19286
Topeka, KS 66619-1423
Phone: (913)642-4334
Free: (800)224-9996   Fax: (913)648-5598
Products: Custom cabinets. SIC: 5031 (Lumber, Plywood & Millwork). Est: 1977. Sales: $2,000,000 (2000). Emp: 20. Officers: Byron W. Whetstone, President; Sandra Kelly, Controller; Byron W. Whatstone, President; T.M.R. Jones, General Mgr. Doing Business As: American Millwork.

■ 13049 ■ Burcham and McCune Inc.
5300 District Blvd.
Bakersfield, CA 93313
Phone: (805)397-5300
Products: Office furniture and supplies. SICs: 5021 (Furniture); 5112 (Stationery & Office Supplies).

■ 13050 ■ Burgess, Anderson and Tate Inc.
1455 S Lakeside Dr.
Waukegan, IL 60085-8314
Phone: (847)872-4543   Fax: (847)872-1847
Products: Office furniture and supplies. SICs: 5021 (Furniture); 5112 (Stationery & Office Supplies). Sales: $20,000,000 (2000). Emp: 70. Officers: John K. Burgess, President; Tim Rush, CFO.

■ 13051 ■ Burkett's Office Supply Inc.
8520 Younger Creek Dr.
Sacramento, CA 95828
Phone: (916)387-8900
Products: Office furniture; Office supplies and equipment. SICs: 5021 (Furniture); 5112 (Stationery & Office Supplies); 5044 (Office Equipment).

■ 13052 ■ Burlington House Inc.
1250 Shelburne Rd.
South Burlington, VT 05403-7707
Phone: (802)863-7902
Products: Bedding furniture. SIC: 5021 (Furniture). Officers: Nathaniel Lash, President.

■ 13053 ■ Business Concepts Inc.
PO Box 261400
Littleton, CO 80163-1400
Phone: (303)755-4988
Products: Office furniture. SIC: 5021 (Furniture). Sales: $1,300,000 (1993). Emp: 2. Officers: Ross Goscha, President.

■ 13054 ■ Business Environments Inc.
4121 Prospect Ave. NE
Albuquerque, NM 87110-3817
Phone: (505)888-4400   Fax: (505)889-9146
E-mail: busenviro@aol.com
URL: http://www.businessenvironments.com
Products: Office and public building furniture. SIC: 5021 (Furniture). Est: 1973. Sales: $15,000,000 (2000). Emp: 65. Officers: B. Hoover, Chairman of the Board.

■ 13055 ■ Business Furnishings Co.
10801 Kempwood Dr., Ste. 8
Houston, TX 77043
Phone: (713)462-5742
Products: Office furniture. SIC: 5021 (Furniture).

■ 13056 ■ Business Interiors Inc. (Denver, Colorado)
4141 Colorado Blvd.
Denver, CO 80216
Phone: (303)321-6671   Fax: (303)321-1913
Products: Office furniture; Interior design. SIC: 5021 (Furniture). Sales: $28,000,000 (1999). Emp: 72. Officers: James Walters, President; Nancy Paddack, Controller.

■ 13057 ■ **Business Interiors Northwest Inc.**
710 Pacific Ave.
Tacoma, WA 98402
Phone: (253)627-1000 **Fax:** (253)627-1032
E-mail: info@binw.com
URL: http://www.binw.com
Products: Office furniture. **SIC:** 5021 (Furniture). **Est:** 1982. **Sales:** $42,000,000 (2000). **Emp:** 150. **Officers:** Rich Lacher, President, e-mail: rlacher@binw.com; Sean O'Brien, Vice President, e-mail: sobrien@binw.com.

■ 13058 ■ **Business Resource Group**
2150 N 1st St., Ste. 101
San Jose, CA 95131
Phone: (408)325-3200
Products: Office furniture. **SIC:** 5021 (Furniture). **Sales:** $72,700,000 (2000). **Emp:** 248. **Officers:** John W. Peth, CEO, President & Finance Officer; Brian D. McNay, Exec. VP of Sales.

■ 13059 ■ **California School Furnishing Company Inc.**
4450 N Brawley St., No. 125
Fresno, CA 93722
Phone: (559)276-0561 **Fax:** (559)276-0963
Products: Church and business furniture. **SIC:** 5021 (Furniture). **Est:** 1985. **Sales:** $19,000,000 (2000). **Emp:** 57. **Officers:** Robyn Davidian, President.

■ 13060 ■ **Cameo Kitchens Inc.**
PO Box 191
Mifflintown, PA 17059-0191
Phone: (717)436-9598 **Fax:** (717)436-9649
Products: Custom wood kitchen cabinets and cabinetwork. **SIC:** 5031 (Lumber, Plywood & Millwork). **Est:** 1983. **Sales:** $2,300,000 (2000). **Emp:** 25. **Officers:** John Shellenberger; Roy Knepp.

■ 13061 ■ **Camilo Office Furniture Inc.**
4110 Laguna St.
Coral Gables, FL 33146
Phone: (305)445-3505 **Fax:** (305)447-8566
Products: Office equipment and supplies. **SIC:** 5021 (Furniture). **Sales:** $7,500,000 (2000). **Emp:** 105.

■ 13062 ■ **Cardinal Office Systems**
101 Bradley Dr.
Nicholasville, KY 40356
Phone: (606)885-6161
Free: (800)766-0963 **Fax:** (606)885-9610
Products: Office equipment and supplies. **SIC:** 5021 (Furniture). **Sales:** $6,000,000 (2000). **Emp:** 49.

■ 13063 ■ **Carithers-Wallace-Courtenay Inc.**
4343 Northeast Expwy.
Atlanta, GA 30301
Phone: (770)493-8200 **Fax:** (770)491-6374
Products: Furniture, including home and office. **SIC:** 5021 (Furniture). **Est:** 1929. **Sales:** $39,700,000 (2000). **Emp:** 100. **Officers:** G.M. Brandon, President; Louis Benton, Treasurer; Wayne Langley, VP of Sales.

■ 13064 ■ **Carroll Seating Company Inc.**
1835 W Armitage Ave.
Chicago, IL 60622
Phone: (773)772-0160 **Fax:** (773)772-3777
E-mail: seating@aol.com
URL: http://www.carrollseating.com
Products: Bleachers; Auditorium seating; Laboratory and library casework; Athletic equipment; Operable partitions; Metal library shelving. **SIC:** 5021 (Furniture). **Est:** 1954. **Sales:** $15,000,000 (2000). **Emp:** 15. **Officers:** Patrick J. Carroll, President; Anita Frazier, Customer Service Contact; Sharon J. Wilkes, Human Resources Contact.

■ 13065 ■ **Carroll's Discount Office Furniture Co.**
5615 S Rice Ave.
Houston, TX 77081
Phone: (713)667-6668
Products: Office furniture. **SIC:** 5021 (Furniture).

■ 13066 ■ **Castleberry Office Interiors Inc.**
3600 American Dr.
Atlanta, GA 30341
Phone: (404)452-6600
Products: Office furniture. **SIC:** 5021 (Furniture).

■ 13067 ■ **Chair King Furniture Co.**
4701 Blalock Dr.
Houston, TX 77041-9240
Phone: (713)690-1919 **Fax:** (713)781-0498
Products: Wood porch, lawn, beach, and similar furniture, including gliders, swings, folding cots, tables, and picnic table sets; Metal dining, dinette, and breakfast furniture. **SIC:** 5021 (Furniture). **Est:** 1950. **Emp:** 49. **Officers:** Marvin Barish, President; David Barish, Exec. VP; Jackie Herzstein, Vice President.

■ 13068 ■ **Chair Place**
2623 J St.
Sacramento, CA 95816
Phone: (916)446-1771
Products: Office furniture. **SIC:** 5021 (Furniture).

■ 13069 ■ **Clapper's Building Materials Inc.**
PO Box 335
Meyersdale, PA 15552
Phone: (814)634-5931 **Fax:** (814)634-0111
Products: Table tops. **SIC:** 5031 (Lumber, Plywood & Millwork). **Est:** 1925. **Sales:** $1,900,000 (2000). **Emp:** 22. **Officers:** David B. Clapper, President; Jon C. Clapper, Treasurer.

■ 13070 ■ **Classic Designs**
35 Angell Rd.
Lincoln, RI 02865-4708
Phone: (401)725-8083
Products: Household furniture. **SIC:** 5021 (Furniture). **Officers:** Adele Beck, Owner.

■ 13071 ■ **Coaster Company of America**
12928 Sandoval St.
Santa Fe Springs, CA 90670-4061
Phone: (562)944-7899
Free: (800)221-9699 **Fax:** 800-221-9813
Products: Household furniture, including tables, bars, entertainment centers, book cases, recliners, futons, desks, vanities, mirrors, plant stands, chairs, wall units, and beds(including bunk beds); Etageres; Lamps; Art; Screens. **SIC:** 5021 (Furniture). **Est:** 1977. **Sales:** $100,000,000 (2000). **Emp:** 350. **Officers:** Norman Dinner, CEO.

■ 13072 ■ **Colton Piano and Organ**
1405 W Valley Blvd.
Colton, CA 92324
Phone: (909)825-5537 **Fax:** (909)825-2114
Products: Pianos and organs; Antiques; Office furniture. **SIC:** 5021 (Furniture). **Emp:** 3. **Officers:** Vern Schaefer, Owner; George Heys, CFO.

■ 13073 ■ **Comex International**
PO Box 545
Driggs, ID 83422-0545
Phone: (208)354-8801 **Fax:** (208)354-2281
Products: Household furniture. **SIC:** 5021 (Furniture). **Officers:** Peter Estay, Owner.

■ 13074 ■ **Commercial Furniture Services Inc.**
PO Box 24220
Houston, TX 77029-4220
Phone: (713)673-2100 **Fax:** (713)673-0825
Products: Furniture. **SIC:** 5021 (Furniture). **Sales:** $22,000,000 (2000). **Emp:** 84.

■ 13075 ■ **Commercial Laminations**
2801 Murfreesboro Rd.
Antioch, TN 37013
Phone: (615)361-0000 **Fax:** (615)366-4324
Products: Restaurant furniture. **SIC:** 5021 (Furniture). **Sales:** $6,000,000 (2000). **Emp:** 99. **Officers:** George Cone.

■ 13076 ■ **Commercial Office Interiors Inc.**
2601 4th Ave., Ste. 100
Seattle, WA 98121
Phone: (206)448-7333
Products: Office furniture. **SIC:** 5021 (Furniture).

■ 13077 ■ **Complete Office Solutions Inc.**
600 Meridian Ave.
San Jose, CA 95126
Phone: (408)275-9700
Products: Office furniture. **SIC:** 5021 (Furniture).

■ 13078 ■ **Barrie Connolly & Associates**
2188 Bluestem Ln.
Boise, ID 83706-6116
Phone: (208)345-6225 **Fax:** (208)345-6233
Products: Furniture. **SIC:** 5021 (Furniture). **Officers:** Barrie Connolly, Owner.

■ 13079 ■ **Conso Products Co.**
PO Box 326
Union, SC 29379
Phone: (864)427-9004
Products: Brassware and home furnishings accessories. **SIC:** 5023 (Homefurnishings). **Sales:** $125,500,000 (2000). **Emp:** 1,478. **Officers:** S. Duane Southerland Jr., CEO & President; Gilbert G. Bartell, CFO & Treasurer.

■ 13080 ■ **Continental Office Furniture and Supply Corp.**
2061 Silver Dr.
Columbus, OH 43211
Phone: (614)262-8088 **Fax:** (614)261-1183
Products: Furniture and office supplies. **SICs:** 5021 (Furniture); 5112 (Stationery & Office Supplies). **Sales:** $45,000,000 (1992). **Emp:** 300. **Officers:** John Lucks, President; David Maul, CFO.

■ 13081 ■ **Contract Interiors**
950 Laidlaw Ave.
Cincinnati, OH 45237
Phone: (513)641-3700 **Fax:** (513)641-0744
Products: Home and business furniture. **SIC:** 5021 (Furniture). **Sales:** $10,000,000 (2000). **Emp:** 55. **Officers:** Ed Robbe, President; Judy Helmes, Dir of Personnel.

■ 13082 ■ **Contracted Associates Office Interiors Inc.**
3111 Fite Cir., Ste. 101
Sacramento, CA 95827
Phone: (916)366-7878
Products: Office furniture. **SIC:** 5021 (Furniture).

■ 13083 ■ **Corporate Design Group**
2150 Douglas Blvd., Ste. 225
Roseville, CA 95661
Phone: (916)781-6543
Products: Office furniture. **SIC:** 5021 (Furniture).

■ 13084 ■ **D & J Cabinet Co. Inc.**
285 Industrial Way
Fayetteville, GA 30214-6816
Phone: (404)461-1260 **Fax:** (404)461-0916
Products: Custom wood kitchen cabinets and cabinetwork. **SIC:** 5031 (Lumber, Plywood & Millwork). **Officers:** Dean Turner, President.

■ 13085 ■ **Davison Inc.**
1 Design Ctr. Pl., No. 410
Boston, MA 02210
Phone: (617)348-2870 **Fax:** (617)737-2006
E-mail: davison1@idt.net
Products: Furniture; Carpeting; Upholstery fabrics. **SIC:** 5021 (Furniture). **Est:** 1959. **Emp:** 17. **Officers:** Frances S. Davison, President & Treasurer.

■ 13086 ■ **Decorative Crafts Inc.**
50 Chestnut St.
Greenwich, CT 06830
Phone: (203)531-1500
Free: (800)431-4455 **Fax:** (203)531-1590
URL: http://www.decorativecrafts.com
Products: Furniture and accessories. **SICs:** 5099 (Durable Goods Nec); 5023 (Homefurnishings). **Est:** 1928. **Sales:** $15,000,000 (1999). **Emp:** 50. **Officers:** J. Cohn, President.

■ 13087 ■ **Design Finishes Inc.**
PO Box E
Americus, GA 31709
Phone: (912)924-0341 **Fax:** (912)924-8664
Products: Furniture; Varnishes. **SICs:** 5021 (Furniture); 5198 (Paints, Varnishes & Supplies). **Sales:** $2,000,000 (2000). **Emp:** 20. **Officers:** Roy Frost; Bill Forehand. **Former Name:** Turner Enterprises Inc.

■ 13088 ■ **Design Marketing Associates**
329 East 300 South
Salt Lake City, UT 84111
Phone: (801)531-9903   **Fax:** (801)531-9903
Products: Systems furniture, including lounge seating and hospitality; Lighting fixtures. **SICs:** 5021 (Furniture); 5063 (Electrical Apparatus & Equipment); 5021 (Furniture); 5198 (Paints, Varnishes & Supplies). **Est:** 1981. **Officers:** Mark K. O'Neill, e-mail: moneill1@uswest.net.

■ 13089 ■ **Design Toscano Inc.**
17 E Campbell St.
Arlington Heights, IL 60004
Phone: (847)255-6799   **Free:** (800)525-0733
Products: Garden statues. **SIC:** 5021 (Furniture). **Sales:** $13,000,000 (2000). **Emp:** 94. **Officers:** Michale Stopka, President.

■ 13090 ■ **Desks Inc. (Denver, Colorado)**
1385 S Santa Fe Dr.
Denver, CO 80223
Phone: (303)777-8880
Products: Furniture. **SIC:** 5021 (Furniture). **Sales:** $24,500,000 (1994). **Emp:** 101. **Officers:** Marshall A. Abrahams, Chairman of the Board; Robert Capstick, Sr. VP & Finance Officer.

■ 13091 ■ **Discount Desk Etc. Inc.**
955 S McCarrah
Sparks, NV 89431-5815
Phone: (702)359-4440   **Fax:** (702)359-3378
Products: Office equipment and supplies. **SIC:** 5021 (Furniture). **Sales:** $1,000,000 (2000). **Emp:** 4.

■ 13092 ■ **Discount Office Equipment Inc.**
1991 Coolidge Hwy.
Berkley, MI 48072
Phone: (248)548-6900   **Fax:** (248)548-6905
Products: Office equipment and supplies. **SIC:** 5021 (Furniture). **Sales:** $2,500,000 (2000). **Emp:** 15.

■ 13093 ■ **Donie Chair Co.**
2380 N Indiana
Brownsville, TX 78521
Phone: (956)838-0005   **Fax:** (956)838-0006
E-mail: doniecha@aol.com
URL: http://www.doniechair.com
Products: Chairs, rockers, and barstools, adult and juvenile lines. **SIC:** 5021 (Furniture). **Est:** 1902. **Sales:** $6,000,000 (2000). **Emp:** 82. **Officers:** Joe R. Hutchens; Sharon A. Hutchens.

■ 13094 ■ **Douron Incorporated Corporate Furniture**
30 New Plant Ct.
Owings Mills, MD 21117
Phone: (410)363-2600
Free: (800)533-1296   **Fax:** (410)363-1659
Products: Wood and metal office and educational furniture and office products. **SICs:** 5021 (Furniture); 5046 (Commercial Equipment Nec). **Sales:** $28,000,000 (2000). **Emp:** 110. **Officers:** Eugene L. Hux, CEO; Ronlad W. Hux, President.

■ 13095 ■ **Eads Brothers Wholesale Furniture Co.**
PO Box 1546
Ft. Smith, AR 72902
Phone: (501)646-6617
Free: (800)624-9370   **Fax:** (501)646-6815
Products: Home furniture. **SIC:** 5021 (Furniture). **Est:** 1901. **Sales:** $6,000,000 (2000). **Emp:** 35. **Officers:** William M. Eads Jr., President; William M. Eads III, Vice President.

■ 13096 ■ **Eastern Butcher Block Corp.**
25 Eagle St.
Providence, RI 02908-5622
Phone: (401)273-6330
Free: (800)666-4322   **Fax:** (401)274-1811
E-mail: factory@great-woods.com
URL: http://www.butcherblock.com
Products: Hardwood furniture, including tables, chairs, and stools; Countertops; Cutting boards. **SIC:** 5021 (Furniture). **Est:** 1976. **Sales:** $6,000,000 (2000). **Emp:** 80. **Officers:** Joel Scanlon, President; Rebecca Squier, Human Resources Contact; Mary Ann Fisher, Customer Service Contact; Rebecca Squire, Human Resources Contact. **Former Name:** Great Woods Fine Furniture.

■ 13097 ■ **Eastern Butcher Block Corp.**
25 Eagle St.
Providence, RI 02908-5622
Phone: (401)273-6330
Free: (800)666-4322   **Fax:** (401)274-1811
Products: Furniture and fixtures. **SIC:** 5021 (Furniture). **Sales:** $6,000,000 (2000). **Emp:** 80.

■ 13098 ■ **Eastern Furniture Distributors**
2424 State Rd.
Bensalem, PA 19020
Phone: (215)633-8484
Products: Furniture. **SIC:** 5021 (Furniture).

■ 13099 ■ **Eastern Moulding, Inc.**
2370 Brentwood Rd.
Columbus, OH 43209
Phone: (614)258-0207   **Fax:** (614)258-9498
E-mail: bm@beol.net
Products: Millwork; Furniture parts; Prefinished moulding. **SICs:** 5021 (Furniture); 5031 (Lumber, Plywood & Millwork). **Est:** 1971. **Sales:** $2,500,000 (2000). **Emp:** 4. **Officers:** Henry Gruesen, President; Gene Blankenship, Vice President.

■ 13100 ■ **Eastman Sign Co.**
701 E Main St.
Lewistown, MT 59457-1966
Phone: (406)538-2500
Products: Commercial equipment, including store fixtures, display equipment, neon and vinyl signs, and window quilt insulating shades. **SIC:** 5046 (Commercial Equipment Nec). **Est:** 1974. **Officers:** Kirk Eastman, Owner.

■ 13101 ■ **Edelsteins Better Furniture Inc.**
PO Box 3369
Brownsville, TX 78523
Phone: (956)542-5605
E-mail: ebfurn@worldnet.att.net
Products: Furniture. **SIC:** 5021 (Furniture). **Est:** 1906. **Sales:** $17,000,000 (2000). **Emp:** 250. **Officers:** Ruben Edelstein, President; Ben Edelstein, VP of Finance; Julie E. Best, Manager; George Fuchs, Dir. of Systems; Mary-Jane Garcia, Dir of Human Resources.

■ 13102 ■ **Educational Distributors of America**
PO Box 1579
Appleton, WI 54913-1579
Phone: (920)734-5712
Products: School furniture; Educational supplies and equipment. **SICs:** 5021 (Furniture); 5044 (Office Equipment).

■ 13103 ■ **El Dorado Furniture Co.**
1260 NW 72nd Ave.
Miami, FL 33126
Phone: (305)592-5470   **Fax:** (305)592-6419
Products: Furniture and fixtures. **SIC:** 5021 (Furniture). **Sales:** $30,000,000 (2000). **Emp:** 240. **Officers:** Manuel Capo; Luis Capo; Pedro Capo; Carlos Capo; Julio Capo.

■ 13104 ■ **Elberfeld Company Inc.**
PO Box 788
Logan, OH 43138
Phone: (740)385-5656   **Fax:** (740)385-0319
Products: Furniture; Appliances. **SICs:** 5021 (Furniture); 5064 (Electrical Appliances—Television & Radio). **Est:** 1926. **Sales:** $1,000,000 (2000). **Emp:** 7. **Officers:** Harrold T. Elberfeld, Vice President.

■ 13105 ■ **Enfield Industries Inc.**
PO Box 2530
Conway, NH 03818
Phone: (603)447-8500
Free: (800)843-6341   **Fax:** (603)447-1717
Products: Wood furniture and accessories. **SIC:** 5021 (Furniture). **Est:** 1946. **Officers:** Brenda A. Bailey, Vice President.

■ 13106 ■ **Environment Ltd.**
10865 Seaboard Loop
Houston, TX 77099
Phone: (281)983-0100
Products: Office furniture. **SIC:** 5021 (Furniture).

■ 13107 ■ **Ergonomic Specialties Ltd.**
954 N Du Page Ave.
Lombard, IL 60148-1243
Phone: (630)268-1809
Free: (800)707-7060   **Fax:** (630)268-1810
Products: Ergonomic office and industrial consulting services, worksite evaluations, review, assessmentand training. Ergonomic office and industrial product distribution. **SIC:** 5021 (Furniture).

■ 13108 ■ **Facility Resource Inc. (Seattle, Washington)**
Seattle Design Ctr. 5701 6th Ave. S
Seattle, WA 98108
Phone: (206)764-7000
Products: Office furniture. **SIC:** 5021 (Furniture).

■ 13109 ■ **Falcon Products Inc.**
9387 Dielman Industrial Dr.
St. Louis, MO 63132
Phone: (314)991-9200   **Fax:** (314)991-9295
URL: http://www.falconproducts.com
Products: Furniture for the foodservice hospitality, contract, and healthcare industries. **SIC:** 5021 (Furniture). **Est:** 1959. **Sales:** $113,010,000 (2000). **Emp:** 2,000. **Officers:** Franklin A. Jacobs.

■ 13110 ■ **Farmers Furniture Company Inc.**
1851 Telefair
Dublin, GA 31021
Phone: (912)275-3150   **Fax:** (912)275-6133
Products: Household furniture. **SIC:** 5021 (Furniture). **Sales:** $120,000,000 (2000). **Emp:** 200. **Officers:** Greg Glass, President; Phillip D. Faircloth, Sr. VP & CFO.

■ 13111 ■ **Fashion Bed Group**
5950 W 51st St.
Chicago, IL 60638
Phone: (708)458-1800
Free: (800)825-5233   **Fax:** (708)458-5109
Products: Brass and brass-plated beds; Daybeds; Futons; Bedding. **SICs:** 5021 (Furniture); 5023 (Homefurnishings). **Sales:** $39,300,000 (2000). **Emp:** 100. **Officers:** Joe Geiger, CEO & President; Roger Filizetti, VP of Finance & Admin.

■ 13112 ■ **Finger Office Furniture**
4001 Gulf Fwy.
Houston, TX 77003
Phone: (713)225-1371
Products: Office furniture. **SIC:** 5021 (Furniture).

■ 13113 ■ **Fixture Hardware Co.**
4711 N Lamon
Chicago, IL 60630-3896
Phone: (773)777-6100   **Fax:** (773)777-6118
URL: http://www.fhcfixture.com
Products: Store fixtures and point of purchase displays. **SIC:** 5046 (Commercial Equipment Nec). **Est:** 1920. **Sales:** $8,000,000 (2000). **Emp:** 49. **Officers:** Ray Wolf; Roger Wolf; Todd Carmichael. **Also Known by This Acronym:** FHC.

■ 13114 ■ **Flowers School Equipment Company Inc.**
PO Box 70039
Richmond, VA 23255-0039
Phone: (804)288-8291
Products: Bleachers, including basketball; Auditorium seating. **SIC:** 5021 (Furniture). **Est:** 1927. **Sales:** $2,000,000 (2000). **Emp:** 10. **Officers:** Cloyd D. Flowers Jr., President.

■ 13115 ■ **Fraenkel Wholesale Furniture Company Inc.**
PO Box 15385
Baton Rouge, LA 70895
Phone: (504)275-8111
Free: (800)847-2580   **Fax:** (504)272-7319
Products: Upholstery; Furniture; Mattresses. **SIC:** 5021 (Furniture). **Sales:** $41,000,000 (2000). **Emp:** 225. **Officers:** Harvey Hoffman, President; Susan Pourciau, Treasurer.

■ 13116 ■ Furniture on Consignment Inc.
4911 S 72nd St.
Omaha, NE 68127
Phone: (402)339-7848
Products: Furniture. **SIC:** 5021 (Furniture).

■ 13117 ■ Furniture Distributors Inc.
PO Box 11117
Charlotte, NC 28220
Phone: (704)523-3424
Products: Book cases, couches, sofas, and coffee tables. **SIC:** 5021 (Furniture). **Est:** 1915. **Sales:** $50,000,000 (2000). **Emp:** 600. **Officers:** Henry L. Johnson, President; Russell Thorne, Secretary.

■ 13118 ■ Gamma Inc.
3289 Mill Branch Rd.
Memphis, TN 38116
Phone: (901)332-2944 **Fax:** (901)332-6460
Products: Fireplace mantles. **SIC:** 5023 (Homefurnishings). **Sales:** $2,000,000 (2000). **Emp:** 10. **Officers:** Jim Pearl, President.

■ 13119 ■ Gem Furniture Co. Inc.
711 Westminster St.
Providence, RI 02903-4016
Phone: (401)831-9737
Products: Household furniture. **SIC:** 5021 (Furniture). **Est:** 1979. **Sales:** $260,000 (2000). **Emp:** 3. **Officers:** George White, President.

■ 13120 ■ General Office Interiors
1071 Springfield Rd.
Union, NJ 07083
Phone: (908)688-9400 **Fax:** (908)688-6894
E-mail: furniture@genoffint.com
Products: Commercial decoration items; Furniture. **SIC:** 5021 (Furniture). **Est:** 1922. **Sales:** $18,000,000 (1999). **Emp:** 48. **Officers:** Kurt Meyer, President & Chairman of the Board; Kirk Lippincott, CFO; Peter Debase, VP of Sales.

■ 13121 ■ Georgia Impression Products Inc.
4215 Wendell Dr., Ste. H
Atlanta, GA 30336
Phone: (404)691-1230
Products: Office furniture. **SIC:** 5021 (Furniture).

■ 13122 ■ Globe Business Resources Inc.
1925 Greenwood Ave.
Cincinnati, OH 45246
Phone: (513)771-4242 **Fax:** (513)771-3577
URL: http://www.glbe.com
Products: Office and residential furniture. **SIC:** 5021 (Furniture). **Sales:** $103,900,000 (2000). **Emp:** 669. **Officers:** David D. Hoguet, CEO & Chairman of the Board; Sharon G. Kebe, Sr. VP of Finance & Treasurer.

■ 13123 ■ Globe Industrial Supply Inc.
PO Box 50826
Indianapolis, IN 46250
Phone: (317)841-9322
Free: (800)428-4782 **Fax:** (317)577-7368
URL: http://www.globeind.com
Products: Steel shelving; Work gloves; Racking; Filing Systems; High density storage; Rotary files. **SICs:** 5021 (Furniture); 5046 (Commercial Equipment Nec); 5136 (Men's/Boys' Clothing). **Est:** 1946. **Sales:** $4,000,000 (2000). **Emp:** 14. **Officers:** Don Kincaid, Owner; Dana D. Kincaid, Dir. of Marketing & Sales; Randy Kincaid, Dir. of Data Processing, e-mail: rkincaid@iquest.net. **Former Name:** Globe Business Products.

■ 13124 ■ Glover Equipment Inc.
PO Box 405
Cockeysville, MD 21030
Phone: (410)771-8000
Free: (800)966-9016 **Fax:** (410)771-8010
E-mail: glover@smarty.smart.net
URL: http://www.smart.net/˜GLOVER
Products: Office and institutional furniture, including desks and chairs. **SIC:** 5021 (Furniture). **Est:** 1962. **Sales:** $7,000,000 (2000). **Emp:** 25. **Officers:** Paul H. Glover, CEO; G. Stephen Glover, President; Roger Mueller; Lois Calzone, Dir. of Systems.

■ 13125 ■ Goldsmiths Inc.
151 N Main St.
Wichita, KS 67202
Phone: (316)263-0131 **Fax:** (316)262-0691
Products: Furniture. **SIC:** 5021 (Furniture). **Sales:** $42,000,000 (1999). **Emp:** 110. **Officers:** R.M. Arst, CEO.

■ 13126 ■ Hampton House
100 Furniture Pkwy.
Norwalk, OH 44857
Phone: (419)668-4461
Products: Upholstered household furniture. **SIC:** 5021 (Furniture). **Sales:** $4,000,000 (1993). **Emp:** 25.

■ 13127 ■ Harris Marcus Group
3757 S Ashland
Chicago, IL 60609-2130
Phone: (773)247-7500 **Fax:** (773)247-7865
Products: Furniture and home accessories; Portable and home lighting. **SICs:** 5021 (Furniture); 5063 (Electrical Apparatus & Equipment). **Est:** 1972. **Sales:** $35,000,000 (2000). **Emp:** 450. **Officers:** David Harris; David Marcus; Ronald Harris; Aaron Harris, Sales/Marketing Contact. **Alternate Name:** Harris Lamps. **Alternate Name:** Rembrandt Lamps. **Alternate Name:** Harris Marcus Furniture. **Alternate Name:** Cameo. **Alternate Name:** Harris Marcus Furniture.

■ 13128 ■ Hart Furniture Company Inc. (Siler City, North Carolina)
Hwy. 64 E
Siler City, NC 27344
Phone: (919)742-4141 **Fax:** (919)742-4323
Products: Furniture, including tables, chairs, file cabinets, sofas, and couches. **SIC:** 5021 (Furniture). **Est:** 1969. **Sales:** $12,000,000 (2000). **Emp:** 21. **Officers:** H.K. Hart, President.

■ 13129 ■ Hartzell Acquisition Corp.
13405 15th Ave. N
Plymouth, MN 55441
Phone: (612)553-8200
Products: Contract furniture. **SIC:** 5021 (Furniture).

■ 13130 ■ Hi Lo Table Manufacturing Inc.
915 W Cherry
PO Box 945
Chanute, KS 66720
Phone: (316)431-7140 **Fax:** (316)431-0848
Products: Mattresses; Cabinets; Furniture and fixtures. **SICs:** 5021 (Furniture); 5023 (Homefurnishings); 5031 (Lumber, Plywood & Millwork). **Est:** 1976. **Sales:** $9,000,000 (2000). **Emp:** 175. **Officers:** James M. Caldwell, President.

■ 13131 ■ Higgins Purchasing Group
625 Market St.
San Francisco, CA 94105
Phone: (415)908-0700 **Fax:** (415)908-0710
E-mail: info@higginspurchasing.com
Products: Furniture; Light fixtures; China; Wall coverings. **SICs:** 5021 (Furniture); 5023 (Homefurnishings); 5063 (Electrical Apparatus & Equipment). **Est:** 1989. **Sales:** $1,500,000,000 (2000). **Emp:** 11. **Officers:** Steve Higgins, CEO; Cary Schirmer, President; Debbie Higgins, Partner; Tom Sikes, Partner.

■ 13132 ■ Highsmith Inc.
W5527 Hwy. 106
Ft. Atkinson, WI 53538-0800
Phone: (920)563-9571 **Fax:** (920)563-7395
Products: School and library supplies, furniture and equipment via direct mail catalogs. School and library supplies, furniture and equipment via direct mail catalogs. **SIC:** 5099 (Durable Goods Nec). **Sales:** $50,000,000 (1999). **Emp:** 250. **Officers:** Duncan Highsmith, CEO & President; Steve Hudson, VP of Finance.

■ 13133 ■ Fred Hill and Son Co.
2101 Hornig Rd.
Philadelphia, PA 19116
Phone: (215)698-2200 **Fax:** (215)698-4539
Products: Ladders; Panel and modular systems furniture and all other nonwood office furniture; Wood office furniture; Storage equipment. **SICs:** 5021

(Furniture); 5046 (Commercial Equipment Nec). **Est:** 1894. **Sales:** $20,000,000 (1994). **Emp:** 65. **Officers:** Kenneth Shaw Jr., President; James Hartey, VP of Marketing.

■ 13134 ■ Hilton Equipment Corp.
9336 Civic Center Dr.
Beverly Hills, CA 90210
Phone: (310)278-4321 **Fax:** (310)205-4305
Products: Furniture and commercial equipment. **SICs:** 5021 (Furniture); 5046 (Commercial Equipment Nec). **Sales:** $88,000,000 (2000). **Emp:** 45. **Officers:** Tony Nieves, VP & General Merchandising Mgr.; Edwina Burtt, Controller.

■ 13135 ■ Himark Enterprises Inc.
497 Pinehurst Ct.
Roslyn, NY 11576-3070
Phone: (516)273-3300
Free: (800)645-5296 **Fax:** (516)435-0558
E-mail: azuskin@hi-mark.com
Products: Wood and ceramic products; Housewares; Planters; Decorative giftware and accessories; Furniture. **SICs:** 5021 (Furniture); 5023 (Homefurnishings). **Est:** 1968. **Sales:** $30,000,000 (2000). **Emp:** 205. **Officers:** Arnold Holtzman, President; Elliott Thau, CFO.

■ 13136 ■ Horizon Trading Company
1510 H St. NW, 5th Fl.
Washington, DC 20005
Phone: (202)783-4455 **Fax:** (202)783-4465
Products: Panel and modular systems furniture and all other nonwood office furniture; Computers. **SICs:** 5021 (Furniture); 5045 (Computers, Peripherals & Software). **Est:** 1980. **Emp:** 20. **Officers:** Browning Rockwell, President.

■ 13137 ■ Huntington Wholesale Furniture Company Inc.
740 8th Ave.
Huntington, WV 25715
Phone: (304)523-9415
Products: Furniture. **SIC:** 5021 (Furniture). **Est:** 1918. **Sales:** $5,000,000 (2000). **Emp:** 21. **Officers:** Frank Hanshaw Jr., President; C. W. Hanshaw, General Mgr.; Margot H. Pliml, Corp. Secty.

■ 13138 ■ ICF Gropu Showroom
920 Broadway
New York, NY 10010
Free: (800)237-1625 **Fax:** 888-784-8209
E-mail: info@icfgroup.com
URL: http://www.icfgroup.com
Products: Furniture; Fabric. **SICs:** 5021 (Furniture); 5023 (Homefurnishings). **Est:** 1962. **Sales:** $28,000,000 (2000). **Emp:** 60. **Officers:** Janes Kasschaw, President; Dan Fogelson, VP of Marketing. **Former Name:** International Contract Furnishings Inc.

■ 13139 ■ Imports International
3670 Rosalinda Dr.
Reno, NV 89503-1813
Phone: (702)786-5820 **Fax:** (702)786-8044
Products: Custom ordered furniture. **SIC:** 5021 (Furniture). **Officers:** Orlando Cellucci, Owner.

■ 13140 ■ Incorporated Business Interiors Inc.
2271 W 205th St., Ste. 101
Torrance, CA 90501
Phone: (310)257-0200 **Fax:** (310)257-0202
E-mail: ibimaas@aol.com
Products: Office furnishings; Rotary filing systems. **SIC:** 5021 (Furniture). **Est:** 1985. **Sales:** $2,500,000 (2000). **Emp:** 10.

■ 13141 ■ Inside Source
100 Industrial Rd.
San Carlos, CA 94070-
Phone: (415)508-9101
Products: Office furniture. **SIC:** 5021 (Furniture). **Sales:** $9,900,000 (2000). **Emp:** 32. **Officers:** Dave Denny, President; Ed Doody, CFO.

■ 13142 ■ Institutional Contract Sales
PO Box 4092
Manchester, NH 03108-4092
Phone: (603)432-2129 **Fax:** (603)434-4455
Products: Furniture, including institutional furniture.

SIC: 5021 (Furniture). **Officers:** Michael Garrity, Vice President.

■ **13143** ■ **Interior Services Inc.**
1360 Kemper Meadow Dr.
Cincinnati, OH 45240
Phone: (513)851-0933 **Fax:** (513)742-6415
Products: Office equipment and supplies. **SIC:** 5021 (Furniture). **Sales:** $6,000,000 (2000). **Emp:** 18.

■ **13144** ■ **Interior Systems Contract Group Inc.**
28000 Woodward
Royal Oak, MI 48067-1051
Phone: (248)399-1600 **Fax:** (248)399-1601
Products: Office furniture. **SIC:** 5021 (Furniture). **Sales:** $16,400,000 (2000). **Emp:** 28. **Officers:** Billie Wanink, President; Maryann Lievois, Finance Officer.

■ **13145** ■ **Interior Systems and Installation Inc.**
15534 W Hardy, Ste. 100
Houston, TX 77060
Phone: (281)820-2600
Products: Office furniture. **SIC:** 5021 (Furniture).

■ **13146** ■ **International Trading & Investment**
5159 Tilly Mill Rd.
Atlanta, GA 30338
Phone: (404)451-1396 **Fax:** (404)451-1397
Products: Furniture for offices, libraries, and schools; Construction equipment; Industrial materials handling equipment, including cranes and hoists. **SICs:** 5021 (Furniture); 5082 (Construction & Mining Machinery); 5084 (Industrial Machinery & Equipment). **Officers:** Steve C. Sinno, Managing Director.

■ **13147** ■ **Intertrade, Inc.**
29444 Northwestern Hwy., Ste. 600
Southfield, MI 48034
Phone: (248)356-1800 **Fax:** (248)356-1978
E-mail: intertradeusa@msn.com
Products: Furniture, including indoor, steel, and folding furniture; Charcoal grills; Automotive body hardware; Garden sheds; Plastic pet products; Bird food. **SICs:** 5021 (Furniture); 5064 (Electrical Appliances—Television & Radio); 5013 (Motor Vehicle Supplies & New Parts); 5099 (Durable Goods Nec). **Est:** 1984. **Sales:** $15,000,000 (1999). **Emp:** 6. **Officers:** Martin Katz.

■ **13148** ■ **Bill Jackson Associates Inc.**
PO Box 801867
Dallas, TX 75380-1867
Phone: (972)233-8954
Products: Commercial and residential furniture. **SIC:** 5021 (Furniture). **Est:** 1967. **Sales:** $5,400,000 (2000). **Emp:** 23. **Officers:** William R. Jackson, President.

■ **13149** ■ **Walter Jacobi and Sons Inc.**
PO Box 471
Belmont, CA 94002
Phone: (650)593-6815 **Fax:** (650)592-2434
Products: Pews and pew chairs; Courtroom benches and chairs. **SIC:** 5021 (Furniture). **Est:** 1921. **Sales:** $700,000 (2000). **Emp:** 16. **Officers:** Leo Jacoby, President; Frank Jacoby, CFO; A.M. Jacobi, Dir. of Marketing.

■ **13150** ■ **Walter Jacobi and Sons Inc.**
PO Box 471
Belmont, CA 94002
Phone: (650)593-6815 **Fax:** (650)592-2434
Products: Furniture and fixtures. **SIC:** 5021 (Furniture). **Sales:** $700,000 (2000). **Emp:** 16.

■ **13151** ■ **Jamesville Office Furnishing**
11309 Folsom Blvd., Ste. B
Rancho Cordova, CA 95742
Phone: (916)638-4050 **Fax:** (916)638-4049
Products: Office furniture and systems furniture. **SIC:** 5021 (Furniture). **Est:** 1992.

■ **13152** ■ **Johnson and Associates Business Interiors Inc.**
223 W Erie St.
Chicago, IL 60610
Phone: (312)649-0074 **Fax:** (312)649-0342
E-mail: info@johnsonasssoc.net
Products: Commercial furniture, including files, cabinets, desks, chairs, panels, tables; Interior design; Space planning; Asset management; Floor and wall covering sales and installation. **SIC:** 5021 (Furniture). **Est:** 1978. **Sales:** $12,300,000 (1999). **Emp:** 20. **Officers:** Cynthia J. Johnson, President; Sean Bowler, CFO; John Johnson, VP of Operations.

■ **13153** ■ **Jones-Campbell Co.**
3766 Bradview Dr.
Sacramento, CA 95827
Phone: (916)362-0123
Products: Office furniture. **SIC:** 5021 (Furniture).

■ **13154** ■ **KBM Workspace**
320 S 1st St.
San Jose, CA 95113-2803
Phone: (408)938-2200 **Fax:** (408)938-0699
URL: http://www.kbmworkspace.com
Products: Furniture. **SIC:** 5021 (Furniture). **Est:** 1946. **Sales:** $38,000,000 (1999). **Emp:** 90. **Officers:** Steve Caplan, President, e-mail: stevec@kbmonline.com; John Halter, COO; Stan Vuokovich, VP of Sales. **Alternate Name:** KBM Office Equipment Inc.

■ **13155** ■ **Keller Group**
3041 65th St. Ste. 3
Sacramento, CA 95820-2021
Products: Office furniture. **SIC:** 5021 (Furniture). **Sales:** $1,200,000 (2000). **Emp:** 6. **Officers:** Paul Keller, Owner.

■ **13156** ■ **F.S. Kelly Furniture Co.**
204 Beal Bldg.
Duluth, MN 55802
Phone: (218)722-6301 **Fax:** (218)722-6302
Products: Furniture, including recliners, mattresses, and sofas. **SIC:** 5021 (Furniture). **Est:** 1886. **Sales:** $3,000,000 (2000). **Emp:** 8. **Officers:** Richard Kelly, President.

■ **13157** ■ **J.A. Kindel Co.**
605 N Wayne Ave.
Cincinnati, OH 45215
Phone: (513)733-9600
Products: Office furniture. **SIC:** 5021 (Furniture). **Sales:** $50,000,000 (1993). **Emp:** 120. **Officers:** John Berning, President.

■ **13158** ■ **R.H. Kyle Furniture Co.**
PO Box 793
Charleston, WV 25323
Phone: (304)346-0671 **Fax:** (304)346-0674
Products: Furniture. **SIC:** 5021 (Furniture). **Est:** 1923. **Sales:** $8,000,000 (2000). **Emp:** 28. **Officers:** J.M. Wells Sr., President & Chairman of the Board.

■ **13159** ■ **L. Powell Co./Generations for the 21st Century**
PO Box 1408
Culver City, CA 90232-1408
Phone: (310)204-2224
Free: (800)622-4456 **Fax:** (310)837-6223
Products: Furniture and fixtures. **SIC:** 5021 (Furniture). **Sales:** $135,000,000 (2000). **Emp:** 100.

■ **13160** ■ **La Belle Provence Ltd.**
185 W Maple Rd.
Birmingham, MI 48009
Phone: (248)540-3876 **Fax:** (248)540-6881
Products: Furniture; Decorative items for the home; Interior design. **SICs:** 5021 (Furniture); 5023 (Homefurnishings).**Est:** 1989. **Sales:** $500,000 (2000). **Emp:** 2. **Officers:** Leslie Benser Luciani, President.

■ **13161** ■ **La Plante Gallery Inc.**
529 Adams St. NE
Albuquerque, NM 87108-1228
Phone: (505)265-2977 **Fax:** (505)265-2977
Products: Spanish colonial furniture; Mexican lighting. **SICs:** 5021 (Furniture); 5063 (Electrical Apparatus & Equipment). **Sales:** $350,000 (2000). **Emp:** 2. **Officers:** Robert La Plante, President.

■ **13162** ■ **Laboratory Design and Equipment**
2615 Hwy. 160 W
Ft. Mill, SC 29715-8488
Phone: (803)548-0067 **Fax:** (803)548-3043
Products: Laboratory furniture. **SIC:** 5021 (Furniture). **Officers:** Cynthia Jentz, Chairman of the Board.

■ **13163** ■ **Lee Company Inc.**
PO Box 567
Terre Haute, IN 47807
Phone: (812)235-8156
Products: School furniture. **SIC:** 5021 (Furniture). **Est:** 1952. **Sales:** $3,000,000 (2000). **Emp:** 22. **Officers:** D. Sensement, President; Blanche Lau, Secretary.

■ **13164** ■ **Lindsay-Ferrari**
1057 Montague Expwy.
Milpitas, CA 95035
Phone: (408)435-1300 **Fax:** (408)263-3322
Products: Office furniture. **SIC:** 5021 (Furniture). **Sales:** $60,000,000 (2000). **Emp:** 350. **Officers:** David Ferrari, President; Debra Robinson, CFO.

■ **13165** ■ **Lite Source Inc.**
4401 Eucalyptus Ave.
Chino, CA 91710-9703
Phone: (909)597-8892 **Fax:** (909)598-7815
Products: Lamps. **SIC:** 5064 (Electrical Appliances—Television & Radio). **Sales:** $16,000,000 (2000). **Emp:** 28. **Officers:** David Lu, President; Celia Lu, Controller.

■ **13166** ■ **F.W. Lombard Co.**
34 S Pleasant St.
Ashburnham, MA 01430-0539
Phone: (978)827-5333 **Fax:** (978)827-6553
Products: Wood tables and chairs. **SIC:** 5021 (Furniture). **Est:** 1898. **Sales:** $2,000,000 (2000). **Emp:** 45. **Officers:** Carl F. Mellin Jr., President; Robert Joyal, Vice President.

■ **13167** ■ **Macke Business Products**
55 Railroad St.
Rochester, NY 14609
Phone: (716)325-4120
Products: Office furniture. **SIC:** 5021 (Furniture).

■ **13168** ■ **Main Auction**
2912 Main St.
Boise, ID 83702-4635
Phone: (208)344-8314
Products: Household furniture; Building materials. **SICs:** 5021 (Furniture); 5039 (Construction Materials Nec). **Officers:** Danny Wesely, Owner.

■ **13169** ■ **Maine Cottage Furniture Inc.**
PO Box 935
Yarmouth, ME 04096-1935
Phone: (207)846-1430 **Fax:** (207)846-0602
Products: Furniture. **SIC:** 5021 (Furniture). **Est:** 1988. **Sales:** $2,000,000 (2000). **Emp:** 12. **Officers:** Peter Bass, President.

■ **13170** ■ **Man-I-Can Store Fixtures, Inc.**
2519 Comanche Rd. NE
Albuquerque, NM 87107-4720
Phone: (505)881-2712
Free: (800)753-5337 **Fax:** (505)884-3372
Products: Store fixtures and displays. **SIC:** 5046 (Commercial Equipment Nec). **Est:** 1981. **Officers:** Cheryl Smith, President.

■ **13171** ■ **Mantua Manufacturing Co.**
7900 Northfield Rd.
Walton Hills, OH 44146-5525
Phone: (440)232-8865 **Fax:** (440)232-5622
E-mail: mantua@bedframes.com
URL: http://www.bedframes.com
Products: Bed frames. **SIC:** 5021 (Furniture). **Est:** 1952. **Sales:** $30,000,000 (2000). **Emp:** 135. **Officers:** H. L. Weintraub; Edward Weintraub; Fran Lasky; Neil Dwyer, Sales/Marketing Contact.

■ **13172** ■ **Martin Universal Design Inc.**
4444 Lawton St.
Detroit, MI 48208-2162
Phone: (313)895-0700 **Fax:** (313)895-0709
E-mail: mudmfwdet@aol.com
Products: Chairs, drafting tables, easels, and computer furniture. **SIC:** 5021 (Furniture). **Sales:**

$5,000,000 (2000). **Emp:** 35. **Officers:** Dennis Kapp, CEO; Daran K. Bair, President.

■ **13173** ■ **Masco Corp. Beacon Hill Showroom**
1 Design Center Pl.
Boston, MA 02210
Phone: (617)482-6600
Products: Panel and modular systems furniture and all other nonwood office furniture; Wood office furniture. **SIC:** 5021 (Furniture). **Sales:** $3,000,000 (2000). **Emp:** 20. **Officers:** David Kaplan, President.

■ **13174** ■ **Mastercraft Inc.**
PO Box 326
Shipshewana, IN 46565
Phone: (219)768-4101 **Fax:** (219)768-7353
Products: Furniture. **SIC:** 5021 (Furniture). **Est:** 1971. **Sales:** $11,100,000 (2000). **Emp:** 150. **Officers:** C. Reynolds, President.

■ **13175** ■ **McCall Woodworks Inc.**
861 Timber Ridge
Mc Call, ID 83638-5133
Phone: (208)634-2378
Free: (800)322-5542 **Fax:** (208)634-2592
Products: Interior and exterior Western log furniture. **SICs:** 5021 (Furniture); 5031 (Lumber, Plywood & Millwork). **Officers:** Steven Wurster, President.

■ **13176** ■ **McGuire Furniture Co.**
151 Vermont St.
San Francisco, CA 94103-5020
Phone: (415)986-0812 **Fax:** (415)621-4903
URL: http://www.mcguirefurniture.com
Products: Rattan, teak, and bamboo furniture; Lighting. **SICs:** 5021 (Furniture); 5063 (Electrical Apparatus & Equipment). **Est:** 1948. **Emp:** 100. **Officers:** Sarah Garcia, President; Don Miller, VP of Sales.

■ **13177** ■ **McKenzie Galleries and Commercial**
3200 W Dallas Ave.
Houston, TX 77019-3803
Phone: (713)528-1561 **Fax:** (713)528-1562
Products: Wood office furniture; Household furniture. **SIC:** 5021 (Furniture). **Est:** 1955. **Sales:** $700,000 (2000). **Emp:** 6.

■ **13178** ■ **Meridian Mattress Factory Inc.**
PO Box 5127
Meridian, MS 39301
Phone: (601)693-3875 **Fax:** (601)693-5462
Products: Mattresses and box springs. **SIC:** 5021 (Furniture). **Sales:** $7,000,000 (2000). **Emp:** 55. **Officers:** Gerald T. Crudup, President; H. G. Brown, Vice President; Mike Ellmo, Vice President.

■ **13179** ■ **M.G. West**
180 Hubbell St.
San Francisco, CA 94107
Phone: (415)861-4800
Products: Office furniture. **SIC:** 5021 (Furniture).

■ **13180** ■ **Miles Treaster and Associates**
3480 Industrial Blvd.
West Sacramento, CA 95691
Phone: (916)373-1800
Products: Office furniture. **SIC:** 5021 (Furniture).

■ **13181** ■ **Herman Miller Inc.**
2525 Arizona Biltmore Circle, No. 142
Phoenix, AZ 85016-2146
Phone: (602)955-3779 **Fax:** (602)956-7502
Products: Furniture. **SIC:** 5021 (Furniture). **Emp:** 12.

■ **13182** ■ **Minton-Jones Co.**
1859-I Beaver Ridge Cir.
Norcross, GA 30071
Phone: (770)449-4787
Free: (888)817-7907 **Fax:** (770)446-0609
E-mail: minjo@mindspring.com
URL: http://www.mintonjones.com
Products: Office furniture. **SIC:** 5021 (Furniture). **Est:** 1946. **Emp:** 50.

■ **13183** ■ **Missco Corporation of Jackson**
2510 Lakeland Ter., #100
Jackson, MS 39216
Phone: (601)948-8600
Free: (800)647-5333 **Fax:** (601)987-3038
Products: School furniture and equipment, laboratory equipment. **SICs:** 5021 (Furniture); 5049 (Professional Equipment Nec). **Sales:** $47,000,000 (2000). **Emp:** 125. **Officers:** Victor L. Smith, President; Adrienne Brantley, CFO.

■ **13184** ■ **Monarch Toilet Partition**
200 Buffalo Ave.
Freeport, NY 11520-4732
Phone: (516)379-2700 **Fax:** (516)867-4675
Products: Toilet partitions. **SIC:** 5046 (Commercial Equipment Nec). **Emp:** 49.

■ **13185** ■ **National Business Furniture Inc.**
PO Box 514052
Milwaukee, WI 53203-3452
Phone: (414)276-8511 **Fax:** (414)276-2025
URL: http://www.nationalbusinessfurniturecom
Products: Office furniture. **SIC:** 5021 (Furniture). **Sales:** $150,000,000 (2000). **Emp:** 145. **Officers:** George Mosher, President; Kent Anderson, COO.

■ **13186** ■ **National Equipment Co.**
3401 E Truman Rd.
Kansas City, MO 64127
Phone: (816)262-8200 **Fax:** (816)920-5155
Products: Store fixtures for retail stores. **SIC:** 5046 (Commercial Equipment Nec). **Sales:** $2,500,000 (2000). **Emp:** 17. **Officers:** Ron Parker, President; Russell Fuchs, CFO.

■ **13187** ■ **New Mexico Mattress Co. Inc.**
4015 Menaul Blvd. NE
Albuquerque, NM 87110-2935
Phone: (505)888-3533 **Fax:** (505)889-9065
Products: Beds and bedding; Mattresses. **SIC:** 5021 (Furniture). **Officers:** Robert Medina, Vice President.

■ **13188** ■ **Northeast Interior Systems Inc.**
PO Box 809
Clifton Park, NY 12065
Phone: (518)371-4080 **Fax:** (518)371-0394
Products: Cabinetry for schools and health care facilities. **SIC:** 5021 (Furniture). **Est:** 1977. **Sales:** $10,000,000 (2000). **Emp:** 27. **Officers:** Robert Bowden, President.

■ **13189** ■ **Northwest Futon Co.**
PO Box 14952
Portland, OR 97214
Phone: (503)224-3199 **Fax:** (503)231-9489
Products: Futons. **SIC:** 5021 (Furniture). **Est:** 1978. **Sales:** $300,000 (2000). **Emp:** 40. **Officers:** Valko Sichel, President; Karen McKnight, Vice President; Tracy Waidely-Craig, Dir. of Marketing; Mark Harris, Dir. of Data Processing.

■ **13190** ■ **Nova International Inc.**
3401 K St. NW, Ste. 201
Washington, DC 20007
Phone: (202)338-4009 **Fax:** (202)338-4138
Products: Furniture. **SIC:** 5021 (Furniture). **Officers:** Tim H. Rose, Chairman.

■ **13191** ■ **Office Furniture Warehouse Inc.**
1625 Cobb Pkwy. SE
Marietta, GA 30062
Phone: (404)988-0091
Products: Office furniture. **SIC:** 5021 (Furniture).

■ **13192** ■ **Office Pavillion**
9850 16th St. N
St. Petersburg, FL 33716-4210
Phone: (813)577-2300 **Fax:** (813)577-4200
Products: Office equipment and supplies. **SIC:** 5021 (Furniture). **Sales:** $10,000,000 (2000). **Emp:** 49.

■ **13193** ■ **Office Planning Group Inc.**
11330 Sunrise Park Dr., Ste. B
Rancho Cordova, CA 95742
Phone: (916)638-2999
Products: Office furniture. **SIC:** 5021 (Furniture).

■ **13194** ■ **Omnirax**
PO Box 1792
Sausalito, CA 94966
Phone: (415)332-3392
Free: (800)332-3393 **Fax:** (415)332-2607
E-mail: info@omnirax.com
URL: http://www.omnirax.com
Products: Studio furniture. **SIC:** 5021 (Furniture).

■ **13195** ■ **One Workplace L. Ferrari LLC**
1057 Montague Expressway
Milpitas, CA 95035
Phone: (408)263-1001
Free: (800)899-4324 **Fax:** (408)263-3322
URL: http://www.oneworkplace.com
Products: Office furniture and related services. **SIC:** 5021 (Furniture). **Est:** 1999. **Sales:** $210,000,000 (2000). **Emp:** 450. **Officers:** David Ferrari, President; Jean Pedelty, CFO; Mark Ferrari, CEO; John Schultz, COO; Kristina Hansen, VP of Human Resources. **Former Name:** Rucker Fuller Co.

■ **13196** ■ **Oriental Furniture Warehouse**
9030 W Sahara Ave., Ste. 132
Las Vegas, NV 89117-5826
Phone: (702)255-4056 **Fax:** (702)255-4056
Products: Furniture. **SIC:** 5021 (Furniture). **Officers:** Lydia Hawkins, Contact.

■ **13197** ■ **Owen Distributors Inc.**
295 S Eastern Ave.
PO Box 2445
Idaho Falls, ID 83403-2445
Phone: (208)524-1880 **Fax:** (208)524-4301
Products: Furniture; Floor covering; Window covering. **SICs:** 5021 (Furniture); 5023 (Homefurnishings). **Est:** 1972. **Sales:** $1,000,000 (2000). **Emp:** 3. **Officers:** Sharon Ward, President; Michael L. Ward, CEO; Brad L. Thompson, Vice President.

■ **13198** ■ **Oxford Metal Products**
2629 Belgrade
Philadelphia, PA 19125-3899
Phone: (215)739-5000
Free: (800)524-5000 **Fax:** (215)739-5109
Products: Metal bed frames. **SIC:** 5021 (Furniture). **Officers:** A. T. Feldman, President; J. Hoban, Vice President.

■ **13199** ■ **Pacific Design Center**
8687 Melrose Ave.
West Hollywood, CA 90069
Phone: (310)657-0800
Products: Home and office furniture, including desks, chairs, tables, and file cabinets. **SIC:** 5021 (Furniture). **Sales:** $8,000,000 (2000). **Emp:** 45. **Officers:** Richard Norfolk, President; Cinnia Curran, Dir. of Marketing.

■ **13200** ■ **Paddock Seating Co.**
1527 Madison Rd.
Cincinnati, OH 45206
Phone: (513)961-1821 **Fax:** (513)961-5548
Products: Lawn furniture. **SIC:** 5021 (Furniture). **Est:** 1963. **Sales:** $400,000 (2000). **Emp:** 6. **Officers:** Edie Guida, President; Nancy Baker.

■ **13201** ■ **Page Foam Cushion Products Inc.**
850 Eisenhower Blvd.
Johnstown, PA 15904
Phone: (814)266-6969
Free: (800)422-0669 **Fax:** (814)266-7500
Products: Mattresses; Bedsprings. **SIC:** 5021 (Furniture). **Est:** 1966. **Sales:** $3,200,000 (2000). **Emp:** 60. **Officers:** Walter F. Page, President & Treasurer; Ronald Baywood, Vice President; Robert Trotz, Secretary.

■ **13202** ■ **Palay Display Industries Inc.**
2307 S Washington St.
Grand Forks, ND 58201-6347
Phone: (701)775-0606
Free: (800)437-5377 **Fax:** (701)746-5693
E-mail: pdind@aaol.com
URL: http://www.palaydisplay.com
Products: Commercial equipment, including store fixtures and display equipment, except refrigerated. **SIC:** 5046 (Commercial Equipment Nec). **Est:** 1945. **Emp:** 18. **Officers:** Howard Palay, President, e-mail: howard.palay@aol.com.

■ 13203 ■ **Palay Display Industries Inc.**
5250 W 73rd St.
Minneapolis, MN 55439
Phone: (612)835-7171
Free: (800)446-6106 **Fax:** (612)835-7590
Products: Commercial equipment, including store fixtures and display equipment. **SIC:** 5046 (Commercial Equipment Nec).

■ 13204 ■ **Palmer/Snyder Furniture Co.**
400 N Executive Dr., Ste. 200
Brookfield, WI 53005
Phone: (414)351-2693
Free: (800)762-0415 **Fax:** (414)351-2698
E-mail: palmersnyder@compuserv.com
URL: http://www.palmersnyder.com
Products: Tables, including plywood, laminate, and mobile folding cafeteria tables. **SIC:** 5021 (Furniture). **Est:** 1919. **Sales:** $18,000,000 (2000). **Emp:** 200. **Officers:** Kenneth Hootnick; Roger A. Clark, Marketing & Sales Mgr.; Stacey Brennan, Customer Service Contact; Susan Zietlow, Customer Service Contact.

■ 13205 ■ **Passport Furniture**
PO Box 4750
Roanoke, VA 24015
Phone: (540)342-7800
Products: Ornamental furniture. **SIC:** 5021 (Furniture).

■ 13206 ■ **Patio Production Inc.**
4716 2nd St. NW
Albuquerque, NM 87107-4005
Phone: (505)344-5864
Products: Furniture. **SIC:** 5021 (Furniture). **Officers:** Beverly Turner, President.

■ 13207 ■ **David Peysen Inc.**
1401 Oak Lawn Ave.
Dallas, TX 75207-3613
Phone: (214)748-8181 **Fax:** (214)748-8244
Products: Furniture and fixtures. **SIC:** 5021 (Furniture). **Emp:** 5. **Officers:** David Peysen.

■ 13208 ■ **Phifer Wire Products Inc.**
PO Box 1700
Tuscaloosa, AL 35403-1700
Phone: (205)345-2120
Free: (800)633-5955 **Fax:** (205)759-4450
E-mail: phiferad@dbtech.net
URL: http://www.phifer.com
Products: Wire screening; Outdoor furniture covers. **SIC:** 5021 (Furniture). **Est:** 1952.

■ 13209 ■ **Pivot Interiors**
2740 Zanker Rd., Ste. 100
San Jose, CA 95134-2116
Phone: (408)432-5600
URL: http://www.pivotinteriors.com
Products: Office furniture. **SIC:** 5021 (Furniture). **Est:** 1999. **Sales:** $150,000,000 (2000). **Emp:** 225. **Officers:** Ken Baugh, President. **Former Name:** Space Designs Inc.

■ 13210 ■ **Plywood Oshkosh Inc.**
PO Box 2248
Oshkosh, WI 54903
Phone: (920)235-0022 **Fax:** (920)235-7570
Products: Kitchen cabinets, counter tops, thermofused and laminated particleboard. **SIC:** 5031 (Lumber, Plywood & Millwork). **Sales:** $10,000,000 (2000). **Emp:** 10. **Officers:** Bill Donnelly, CEO.

■ 13211 ■ **L. Powell Co./Generations for the 21st Century**
PO Box 1408
Culver City, CA 90232-1408
Phone: (310)204-2224
Free: (800)622-4456 **Fax:** (310)837-6223
E-mail: powell@powellcompany.com
URL: http://www.powellcompany.com
Products: Furniture. **SIC:** 5021 (Furniture). **Est:** 1968. **Sales:** $150,000,000 (2000). **Emp:** 100. **Officers:** Richard Powell, President & CEO; Andrew Cohen, Exec. VP.

■ 13212 ■ **Price Modern Inc.**
2604 Sisson St.
Baltimore, MD 21211
Phone: (410)366-5500
Free: (800)366-5501 **Fax:** (410)662-6892
Products: Office furniture; Office supplies and stationary. **SICs:** 5021 (Furniture); 5112 (Stationery & Office Supplies). **Sales:** $65,000,000 (2000). **Emp:** 240. **Officers:** Milford H. Marchant, President; Thomas Morton, CFO.

■ 13213 ■ **Richard Pruitt**
1212 S Rainbow Blvd.
Las Vegas, NV 89102-9009
Phone: (702)870-8995 **Fax:** (702)870-0996
Products: Furniture; Outdoor and lawn furniture; Barbecues; Fireplaces. **SICs:** 5021 (Furniture); 5099 (Durable Goods Nec). **Officers:** Richard Pruitt, Owner.

■ 13214 ■ **R & R Wood Products**
601 E Karcher Rd.
Nampa, ID 83687-8281
Phone: (208)467-2406 **Fax:** (208)467-2406
Products: Furniture, including beds and bedding; Mobile home supplies. **SIC:** 5021 (Furniture). **Officers:** Bob Brizendine, Owner.

■ 13215 ■ **Rainbow Trading Company Inc.**
5-05 48th Ave.
Long Island City, NY 11101
Phone: (718)784-3700
Free: (800)666-7826 **Fax:** (718)784-3709
Products: Wood furniture parts. **SIC:** 5122 (Drugs, Proprietaries & Sundries). **Est:** 1929. **Sales:** $15,000,000 (2000). **Emp:** 20. **Officers:** Myrna Gilbert, President; Stuart Gilbert, Secretary.

■ 13216 ■ **Randolph Distributing Corp.**
31399 Farimount Blvd.
Cleveland, OH 44124-4810
Phone: (216)883-0360
Products: Home furniture. **SIC:** 5021 (Furniture). **Est:** 1965. **Sales:** $2,500,000 (2000). **Emp:** 10. **Officers:** L.R. Weiss, President.

■ 13217 ■ **Refrigeration Supply Inc.**
8110 Eager Rd.
St. Louis, MO 63144
Phone: (314)644-5500
Free: (800)627-4774 **Fax:** (314)645-9227
Products: Wooden kitchen cabinets and appliances. **SICs:** 5031 (Lumber, Plywood & Millwork); 5064 (Electrical Appliances—Television & Radio). **Est:** 1947. **Sales:** $13,000,000 (2000). **Emp:** 49. **Officers:** A.F. Piazza, General Mgr.; Chuck Meyer, Vice President; Chris Piazza.

■ 13218 ■ **Reliance Bedding Corp.**
3437 D St.
Philadelphia, PA 19134-2540
Phone: (215)739-9900 **Fax:** (215)739-9906
Products: Mattresses. **SIC:** 5021 (Furniture). **Est:** 1946. **Sales:** $2,900,000 (2000). **Emp:** 25.

■ 13219 ■ **Restonic Carolina Inc.**
3100 Camden Rd.
Fayetteville, NC 28306-3260
Phone: (919)425-0131 **Fax:** (919)425-1602
Products: Mattresses and box springs. **SIC:** 5021 (Furniture). **Emp:** 99. **Officers:** Mary J. Giersch.

■ 13220 ■ **Retail Service Company Inc.**
PO Box 1216
Portland, ME 04104
Phones: (207)839-2516 (207)772-8888
Fax: (207)871-1836
Products: Commercial equipment, including store fixtures and display equipment. **SIC:** 5046 (Commercial Equipment Nec). **Officers:** Timothy Fitzpatrick, President.

■ 13221 ■ **Rex Mid-South Service**
PO Box 30169
Memphis, TN 38130-0169
Phone: (901)332-2229
URL: http://www.babytimememphis.com
Products: Infants' and children's furniture. **SIC:** 5021 (Furniture). **Est:** 1966. **Sales:** $2,000,000 (2000). **Officers:** Thomas Herriman, Owner.

■ 13222 ■ **Richards Quality Bedding**
702 Hall SW
Grand Rapids, MI 49503-4899
Phone: (616)241-2481
Free: (800)632-9625 **Fax:** (616)241-2790
Products: Bedsprings; Mattresses. **SIC:** 5021 (Furniture). **Sales:** $2,400,000 (2000). **Emp:** 24. **Officers:** Carl H. Richards Jr.; Carl H. Richards III; Bruce H. Richards.

■ 13223 ■ **Roberts Manufacturing Inc.**
120 West 300 South
American Fork, UT 84003-2646
Phone: (801)756-6016 **Fax:** (801)756-5758
Products: Sewing machine cabinets. **SIC:** 5021 (Furniture). **Est:** 1972. **Emp:** 30. **Officers:** Fred Roberts.

■ 13224 ■ **Rogers Kitchens Inc.**
130 Chestnut St.
Norwich, CT 06360-4552
Phone: (860)886-0505 **Fax:** (860)886-0505
Products: Wood kitchen cabinets; Medicine cabinets. **SIC:** 5031 (Lumber, Plywood & Millwork). **Officers:** Jerome Rogers, President.

■ 13225 ■ **Thomas W. Ruff and Co. Business Furniture Div.**
911 S Orlando
Maitland, FL 32751
Phone: (407)628-2400 **Fax:** (407)628-8941
Products: Furniture, commercial and residential including desks, file cabinets, chairs, and tables. **SIC:** 5021 (Furniture). **Est:** 1936. **Sales:** $16,000,000 (2000). **Emp:** 60. **Officers:** Mike Gorman, President; John Crane, CFO; Thomas W. Davis, Sr. VP of Marketing & Sales.

■ 13226 ■ **Ruland's Used Office Furnishings**
215 North 16th St.
Sacramento, CA 95814
Phone: (916)441-0706
Products: Used office furniture. **SIC:** 5021 (Furniture).

■ 13227 ■ **Rustic Creations**
118 Main St.
PO Box 174
Streetman, TX 75859
Phone: (903)599-3181 **Free:** (800)410-3200
Products: Mirror and picture frames; Wood household furniture. **SIC:** 5021 (Furniture). **Est:** 1992. **Sales:** $250,000 (2000). **Emp:** 3. **Officers:** Kurt Lupo, Owner.

■ 13228 ■ **S.A.K. Industries**
PO Box 725
148 E Olive Ave.
Monrovia, CA 91016
Phone: (626)359-5351 **Fax:** (626)359-3155
Products: Cast and wrought iron porch, lawn, and outdoor furniture. **SIC:** 5021 (Furniture). **Sales:** $1,000,000 (2000). **Emp:** 49. **Officers:** S. L. Kreizel, President; Jose Garcia, Dir. of Sales; Larry Evans, General Mgr.

■ 13229 ■ **Salman**
2425 W Commonwealth
Fullerton, CA 92833
Phone: (714)994-0990 **Fax:** (714)680-6710
Products: Furniture. **SIC:** 5021 (Furniture). **Sales:** $10,000,000 (2000). **Emp:** 100. **Officers:** Mike Parkinson. **Alternate Name:** Salman Inc.

■ 13230 ■ **L.L. Sams Inc.**
1201 Industrial Blvd.
Cameron, TX 76520
Phone: (254)752-9751
Free: (800)537-4723 **Fax:** (254)697-4900
Products: Church pews. **SIC:** 5021 (Furniture). **Est:** 1898. **Emp:** 150. **Officers:** David Petty, President; Deborah Moon, CFO.

■ 13231 ■ **San Francisco Mart**
1355 Market St.
San Francisco, CA 94103
Phone: (415)552-2311 **Fax:** (415)558-9589
Products: Furniture, including sofas and chairs. **SIC:** 5021 (Furniture). **Est:** 1915. **Sales:** $14,000,000 (2000). **Emp:** 40. **Officers:** Michael Gennet, President; Ray Babcock, CFO; Valerie Pollock, Dir. of Marketing.

■ 13232 ■ **Sarreid Ltd.**
PO Box 3548
Wilson, NC 27895-3548
Phone: (919)291-1414 **Fax:** (919)237-1592
Products: Furniture, including chairs and dining tables;
Lighting accessories, desk top accessories, bookends,
and brass shelves. **SICs:** 5021 (Furniture); 5023
(Homefurnishings); 5063 (Electrical Apparatus &
Equipment). **Est:** 1967. **Sales:** $7,000,000 (2000).
Emp: 43. **Officers:** Alex R. Sarratt III, Partner; Charles
W. Mauze Jr., Partner; Charles A. Hoffman Jr., Partner.

■ 13233 ■ **School Specialties Inc.**
1000 N Bluemound Dr.
Appleton, WI 54914
Phone: (920)734-5712
Products: School furniture and supplies. **SICs:** 5021
(Furniture); 5112 (Stationery & Office Supplies). **Sales:**
$310,500,000 (2000). **Emp:** 1,220. **Officers:** Daniel P.
Spalding, CEO & Chairman of the Board; Donald J.
Noskowiak, Sr. VP & CFO.

■ 13234 ■ **Louis J. Schwartz Co.**
17 Wellington Pl.
Amityville, NY 11701
Phone: (631)691-8889 **Fax:** (631)691-1579
Products: Lamps. **SIC:** 5023 (Homefurnishings).
Sales: $12,000,000 (2000). **Emp:** 48. **Officers:** Steven
Schwartz, President.

■ 13235 ■ **Sealy Mattress Georgia**
1705 Rockdale Industrial Blvd.
Conyers, GA 30012-3937
Phone: (404)483-3810 **Fax:** (404)922-2667
Products: Mattresses. **SIC:** 5021 (Furniture). **Sales:**
$6,000,000 (2000). **Emp:** 99. **Officers:** Jack Wallace.

■ 13236 ■ **Seattle Kitchen Design Inc.**
10002 Holman Rd. NW
Seattle, WA 98177-4921
Phone: (206)782-4900 **Fax:** (206)782-4345
Products: Wood kitchen cabinets and cabinetwork,
stock line. **SIC:** 5031 (Lumber, Plywood & Millwork).
Est: 1966. **Sales:** $1,000,000 (2000). **Emp:** 10.
Officers: James Rados, President.

■ 13237 ■ **Seret & Sons Inc.**
149 E Alameda St.
Santa Fe, NM 87501-2117
Phone: (505)988-9151 **Fax:** (505)982-3027
Products: Household furniture; Rugs. **SICs:** 5021
(Furniture); 5023 (Homefurnishings). **Officers:** Ira
Seret, President.

■ 13238 ■ **S.G. & B. Inc.**
8075 Reading Rd., Ste. 408
Cincinnati, OH 45237-1417
Phone: (513)761-2600 **Fax:** (513)761-2681
Products: Household furniture; Household appliances.
SICs: 5021 (Furniture); 5064 (Electrical Appliances—
Television & Radio). **Est:** 1939. **Sales:** $5,000,000
(2000). **Emp:** 65. **Officers:** Stanley A. Schwart,
President. **Doing Business As:** Ball Furniture &
Appliances.

■ 13239 ■ **Cliff Sharpe**
PO Box 1282
Londonderry, NH 03053-1282
Phone: (603)432-7394 **Fax:** (603)432-1580
Products: School furniture; Public building furniture.
SIC: 5021 (Furniture). **Officers:** Cliff Sharpe, Owner.

■ 13240 ■ **Sharut Furniture Co.**
220 Passaic St.
Passaic, NJ 07055
Phone: (973)473-1000 **Fax:** (973)473-4416
Products: Bedroom furniture; Dining room wall units.
SIC: 5021 (Furniture). **Est:** 1977. **Sales:** $2,000,000
(2000). **Emp:** 130. **Officers:** Elliot Bissu, President.

■ 13241 ■ **Sheffield Furniture Corp.**
2100 E 38th St.
Los Angeles, CA 90058
Phone: (323)232-4161 **Fax:** (323)233-8020
E-mail: sheffurn@concentric.net
Products: Residential furniture. **SIC:** 5021 (Furniture).
Est: 1970. **Sales:** $15,000,000 (2000). **Emp:** 120.
Officers: Ernest E. Warsaw, Chairman of the Board;

Charles W. Koch, President; Patsy A. Garrett, Sec. &
Treas.

■ 13242 ■ **Silvers Inc.**
151 W Fort St.
Detroit, MI 48232
Phone: (313)963-0000 **Fax:** (313)963-0814
Products: Furniture. **SICs:** 5021 (Furniture); 5112
(Stationery & Office Supplies). **Sales:** $52,000,000
(1992). **Emp:** 300. **Officers:** Ira Silver, CEO; Damian
Zikakis, Controller.

■ 13243 ■ **W. Simmons Mattress Factory Inc.**
11030 E Artesia Blvd.
Cerritos, CA 90701
Phone: (562)865-0294
Products: Beds. **SIC:** 5021 (Furniture). **Sales:**
$18,000,000 (2000). **Emp:** 100. **Officers:** Robert
Woods, President.

■ 13244 ■ **SIS Human Factor Technologies Inc.**
55C Harvey Rd.
Londonderry, NH 03053-7414
Phone: (603)432-4495 **Fax:** (603)434-8456
Products: Furniture. **SIC:** 5021 (Furniture). **Est:** 1984.
Sales: $6,000,000 (2000). **Emp:** 10. **Officers:** Alan
Morse, President.

■ 13245 ■ **Skinner Corp.**
1009 N Lanier Ave.
Lanett, AL 36863
Phone: (205)644-2136 **Fax:** (205)644-6895
Products: Furniture. **SIC:** 5021 (Furniture). **Est:** 1946.
Sales: $25,000,000 (2000). **Emp:** 400. **Officers:**
Robert E. Culbreth, Treasurer & Secty.

■ 13246 ■ **Skyline Designs**
1090 John Stark Hwy.
Newport, NH 03773
Phone: (603)542-6649
Free: (800)775-1478 **Fax:** (603)542-8854
E-mail: admin@skyline.com
URL: http://www.skylinedesigns.com
Products: Signs and advertising displays; Furniture
and fixtures; Tables. **SICs:** 5046 (Commercial
Equipment Nec); 5021 (Furniture). **Est:** 1986. **Sales:**
$1,000,000 (2000). **Emp:** 14. **Officers:** Mark Overman;
Richard Bean, Human Resources Contact; Andy
Lafreniere, Marketing & Sales Mgr.; Bill Stone, Fixture
Design Mgr.; Andy Lafreniere, Sales/Marketing
Contact; Andy Lafienere, Customer Service Contact.

■ 13247 ■ **Sloan Miyasato**
2 Henry Adams St.
San Francisco, CA 94103-5016
Phone: (415)431-1465
Free: (800)783-1398 **Fax:** (415)431-1397
Products: Furniture; Fabric; Lighting; Antiques; Wall
coverings. **SICs:** 5021 (Furniture); 5023
(Homefurnishings); 5063 (Electrical Apparatus &
Equipment). **Emp:** 49.

■ 13248 ■ **Southwest Business Furniture**
3110 McKinney
Houston, TX 77003
Phone: (713)227-4141 **Fax:** (713)227-7755
E-mail: swb7inc@aol.com
URL: http://www.southwestbusinessfurniturecom
Products: Office furniture. **SIC:** 5021 (Furniture). **Est:**
1985. **Officers:** Gene Duncan.

■ 13249 ■ **Specialized Marketing**
138 West St.
Annapolis, MD 21401-2802
Phone: (410)267-0545 **Fax:** (410)267-7576
Products: Office equipment and supplies. **SIC:** 5021
(Furniture). **Sales:** $6,000,000 (2000). **Emp:** 8.

■ 13250 ■ **Spivack's Antiques**
54 Washington
Wellesley, MA 02481
Phone: (781)235-1700 **Fax:** (781)239-0210
Products: Antiques. **SIC:** 5021 (Furniture). **Emp:** 5.

■ 13251 ■ **Stein World Inc.**
PO Box 9491
Memphis, TN 38109
Phone: (901)942-2441
Products: Furniture. **SIC:** 5021 (Furniture).

■ 13252 ■ **Gloria Sundin Rand**
PO Box 133
Kennebunkport, ME 04046-0133
Phone: (207)967-4887 **Fax:** (207)967-2846
Products: Furniture; Gifts; Home appliances. **SICs:**
5021 (Furniture); 5064 (Electrical Appliances—
Television & Radio). **Officers:** Gloria Sundin, Owner.

■ 13253 ■ **Swindal-Powell Co.**
PO Box 24428
Jacksonville, FL 32241-4428
Phone: (904)739-0100 **Fax:** (904)737-2330
Products: Furniture. **SIC:** 5021 (Furniture). **Est:** 1923.
Sales: $15,000,000 (2000). **Emp:** 70. **Officers:** Mike
Swindal, President; David Cook, Controller; R.P.
Wainwright Jr., VP of Sales.

■ 13254 ■ **TAB Products Co.**
1400 Page Mill Rd.
Palo Alto, CA 94304-1179
Phone: (650)852-2400
Free: (800)676-3109 **Fax:** (650)852-2687
Products: Furniture; Office supplies. **SICs:** 5021
(Furniture); 5112 (Stationery & Office Supplies). **Est:**
1949. **Sales:** $154,500,000 (2000). **Emp:** 1,075.
Officers: Philip C. Kantz, CEO & President; John M.
Palmer, VP & CFO; Kenneth L. Disselkoen, Sr. VP of
Marketing & Sales.

■ 13255 ■ **Tailor-Made Signs**
PO Box 5421
Pawtucket, RI 02862-5421
Phone: (401)331-0400 **Fax:** (401)331-0400
Products: Commercial equipment; Store fixtures and
display equipment; Electrical signs. **SICs:** 5046
(Commercial Equipment Nec); 5063 (Electrical
Apparatus & Equipment). **Est:** 1976. **Officers:** Manny
Pasquale, Partner.

■ 13256 ■ **TBT Industries Inc.**
838 Granada St.
Socorro, NM 87801-4308
Phone: (505)835-3348
Products: Furniture, including beds, bedding, and
mattresses. **SIC:** 5021 (Furniture). **Officers:** Tim
Gleeson, President.

■ 13257 ■ **Teaneck Graphics Inc.**
197 Washington Ave.
Carlstadt, NJ 07072
Phone: (201)438-2500
Products: Light tables; Sinks; Vacuum frames. **SIC:**
5021 (Furniture). **Sales:** $9,000,000 (2000). **Emp:** 22.
Officers: J. Labokey, President.

■ 13258 ■ **Techline Studio Inc.**
11225 Trade Center Dr., Ste. 150
Rancho Cordova, CA 95742
Phone: (916)638-1991
Products: Office furniture. **SIC:** 5021 (Furniture).

■ 13259 ■ **Term City Furniture & Appliance**
2255 Lamar
PO Box 14665
Memphis, TN 38114-0665
Phone: (901)452-6558
Products: Furniture. **SIC:** 5021 (Furniture). **Officers:**
Robert Holmes, President.

■ 13260 ■ **Tradeways Inc.**
8 Music Fair Rd., No. A
Owings Mills, MD 21117
Phone: (410)664-7000
Free: (800)882-8258 **Fax:** (410)466-1806
Products: Furniture; Cabinetry. **SICs:** 5021
(Furniture); 5031 (Lumber, Plywood & Millwork). **Est:**
1965. **Emp:** 10. **Officers:** T. Elliot Leban, President.

■ **13261** ■ **Tri-Dee Distributors**
215 S 1st St.
Mt. Vernon, WA 98273
Phone: (360)336-6131
Products: Antiques; Collectibles. **SIC:** 5023 (Homefurnishings).

■ **13262** ■ **Tri E Distributors**
PO Box 163
Nampa, ID 83653-0163
Phone: (208)466-7889 **Fax:** (208)466-2291
Products: Furniture, including beds and bedding. **SIC:** 5021 (Furniture). **Officers:** Wendell Everton, Partner.

■ **13263** ■ **Tucker Library Interiors LLC**
155 Dow St., Ste. 402
Manchester, NH 03101
Phone: (603)666-7030 **Fax:** (603)666-7032
E-mail: tclibint@aol.com
URL: http://www.tuckerlibraryinteriorscom
Products: Furniture, including office, library, and public building furniture; Shelving. **SICs:** 5021 (Furniture); 5046 (Commercial Equipment Nec). **Est:** 1978. **Emp:** 5. **Officers:** Richard Tucker; Cori McGrath. **Former Name:** Richard Tucker.

■ **13264** ■ **Unicorn International Inc.**
7079 Depot St.
Olive Branch, MS 38654-1603
Phone: (601)895-2921
Products: Motel furnishings. **SIC:** 5021 (Furniture). **Sales:** $4,000,000 (1994). **Emp:** 13. **Officers:** Bill Cruthirds, President.

■ **13265** ■ **United Corporate Furnishings Inc.**
1332 N Market Blvd.
Sacramento, CA 95834
Phone: (916)553-5900
Products: Office furniture. **SIC:** 5021 (Furniture).

■ **13266** ■ **University Publishing Co.**
PO Box 80298
Lincoln, NE 68501
Phone: (402)476-2761 **Fax:** (402)476-3727
Products: School and office furniture and equipment. **SIC:** 5021 (Furniture). **Est:** 1902. **Sales:** $3,000,000 (2000). **Emp:** 7. **Officers:** Joseph E. Wachter, President; John M. Gill, VP & General Merchandising Mgr.

■ **13267** ■ **Value City Furniture Div.**
1800 Moler Rd.
Columbus, OH 43207
Phone: (614)221-9200 **Fax:** (614)449-4389
Products: Furniture. **SIC:** 5021 (Furniture). **Est:** 1951. **Sales:** $425,000,000 (1999). **Emp:** 4,000. **Officers:** David Thompson, President; Mark Lang, Controller; Gary Tittle, Sr. VP of Operations; Ed Helmuth, VP of Information Systems; Herbert Minkin, VP of Human Resources.

■ **13268** ■ **VersaTec**
PO Box 2095
Tampa, FL 33601-2095
Phone: (813)251-2431 **Fax:** (813)251-3567
Products: Furniture. **SIC:** 5021 (Furniture). **Est:** 1923. **Sales:** $1,500,000 (2000). **Emp:** 49. **Officers:** Ted T. Fielland, President; Dan Keenan, VP of Marketing.

■ **13269** ■ **Virginia City Furniture Inc.**
3333 N Carson St.
Carson City, NV 89706-0155
Phone: (702)883-3333 **Fax:** (702)883-4214
Products: Furniture. **SIC:** 5021 (Furniture). **Officers:** Charles Herman, President.

■ **13270** ■ **Vogue Bedding Co.**
8937 National Blvd.
Los Angeles, CA 90034
Phones: (213)870-5800 (213)839-2188
Products: Beds. **SIC:** 5021 (Furniture). **Emp:** 49.

■ **13271** ■ **Walker and Zanger Inc.**
31 Warren Pl.
Mt. Vernon, NY 10550-4527
Phone: (914)667-1600 **Fax:** (914)667-6244
E-mail: wzny@marblestone.com
URL: http://www.marblestone.com
Products: Stone, including marble, limestone, soapstone, granite, slate. **SICs:** 5032 (Brick, Stone & Related Materials); 5021 (Furniture). **Est:** 1952. **Sales:** $100,000,000 (1999). **Emp:** 370. **Officers:** Leon Zanger, President; Pat Petrocelli, COO; Jonathan A. Zanger, Vice President; Jeff Lupica, General Mgr., e-mail: jlupica@marblestone.com; Steve Marchese, Customer Service Contact, e-mail: smarchese@marblestone.com; Bill Brown, Vice President; Mike Bastone, Vice President; Don Bastone, Vice President; Jamie Maskel, Asst. VP.

■ **13272** ■ **Walton Manufacturing Co.**
1912 Nancita Cir.
Placentia, CA 92870-6737
Phone: (714)996-4111
Free: (800)792-5866 **Fax:** (714)996-3930
Products: Wood household furniture. **SIC:** 5021 (Furniture). **Sales:** $4,000,000 (2000). **Emp:** 70. **Officers:** Dale Walton.

■ **13273** ■ **Walton Manufacturing Co.**
1912 Nancita Cir.
Placentia, CA 92870-6737
Phone: (714)996-4111
Free: (800)792-5866 **Fax:** (714)996-3930
Products: Furniture and fixtures. **SIC:** 5021 (Furniture). **Sales:** $4,000,000 (2000). **Emp:** 70.

■ **13274** ■ **Warehouse Home Furnishing Distributors Inc.**
1851 Telfair St.
PO Box 1140
Dublin, GA 31040
Phone: (912)275-3150 **Fax:** (912)275-6133
Products: Furniture; Appliances; Electronics. **SICs:** 5021 (Furniture); 5064 (Electrical Appliances—Television & Radio); 5065 (Electronic Parts & Equipment Nec). **Est:** 1949. **Sales:** $110,000,000 (2000). **Emp:** 1,300. **Officers:** Sherwin Glass, President & CEO; Phillip Faircloth, Sr. VP & CFO; Robert Garrett, Sr. VP of Sales & Marketing; Craig Lasting, Dir. of Information Systems.

■ **13275** ■ **Vivian Watson Associates Inc.**
316 Oak Lawn Design Plaza
1444 Oak Lawn Ave.
Dallas, TX 75207-3613
Phone: (214)651-0211 **Fax:** (214)748-6774
Products: Furniture and fixtures. **SIC:** 5021 (Furniture). **Est:** 1968. **Emp:** 4. **Officers:** David Olenzek, President.

■ **13276** ■ **Wells and Kimich Inc.**
PO Box 19216
Houston, TX 77224
Phone: (713)984-9993
Products: Office furniture. **SIC:** 5021 (Furniture).

■ **13277** ■ **West Coast Industries Inc.**
3150 18th St.
San Francisco, CA 94110
Phone: (415)621-6656
Free: (800)243-3150 **Fax:** (415)552-5368
Products: Commercial furniture. **SIC:** 5021 (Furniture). **Sales:** $6,000,000 (2000). **Emp:** 100. **Officers:** Harry Liss.

■ **13278** ■ **Western Office Interiors**
5809 E Telegraph Rd.
City of Commerce, CA 90040
Phone: (213)721-8833 **Fax:** (213)724-1949
Products: Office and commercial furniture. **SIC:** 5021 (Furniture). **Est:** 1918. **Sales:** $15,000,000 (2000). **Emp:** 25. **Officers:** Paul Miller, CEO; B.E. Doney, CFO; J. Silverman, Dir. of Marketing.

■ **13279** ■ **Wholesale Furniture Distributors**
7015 Grand Blvd.
Houston, TX 77054-2205
Phone: (713)747-1167 **Fax:** (713)747-0346
Products: Furniture and fixtures. **SIC:** 5021 (Furniture). **Emp:** 99. **Officers:** Richard Dickson; James Dickson. **Alternate Name:** Dickson Furniture Industries. **Alternate Name:** Star Products.

■ **13280** ■ **Wholesale and Home Supply Company Inc.**
4829 W Pico Blvd.
Los Angeles, CA 90019
Phone: (213)263-2127 **Fax:** (213)263-0090
Products: Furniture, including chairs, sofas, tables, and bedroom sets. **SIC:** 5021 (Furniture). **Sales:** $2,000,000 (2000). **Emp:** 10. **Officers:** Camron Gabay, Owner; Dorothy K. Garner, Treasurer; Robert A. Garner, General Mgr.

■ **13281** ■ **Winkler Store Fixtures Co.**
1611 Westminster St.
Providence, RI 02909-1808
Phone: (401)351-2124
Products: Fixtures for stores, banks, offices. **SIC:** 5046 (Commercial Equipment Nec). **Officers:** Milton Winkler, Owner.

■ **13282** ■ **Wittigs Office Interiors**
2013 Broadway
San Antonio, TX 78215-1117
Phone: (512)270-0100 **Fax:** (210)270-0126
Products: Office equipment and supplies. **SIC:** 5021 (Furniture). **Sales:** $15,000,000 (2000). **Emp:** 75.

■ **13283** ■ **Woodworks**
108 S State St.
Nampa, ID 83686-2630
Phone: (208)466-8823
Products: Furniture, including beds, waterbeds, and bedding. **SIC:** 5021 (Furniture). **Officers:** Noman Oliva, Owner.

■ **13284** ■ **Worden Co.**
199 E 17th St.
Holland, MI 49423
Phone: (616)392-1848
Free: (800)748-0561 **Fax:** (616)392-2542
Products: Library furniture. **SIC:** 5021 (Furniture). **Est:** 1949. **Sales:** $21,000,000 (2000). **Emp:** 200. **Officers:** William B. Hendrick, Owner; Donald G. Wassink, President; Kenneth Peirce, Exec. VP; Daniel Linscott, Controller.

■ **13285** ■ **A.D. Wynne Company Inc.**
710 Baronne St.
New Orleans, LA 70113
Phone: (504)522-9558
Products: Office furniture. **SIC:** 5021 (Furniture).

■ **13286** ■ **Young's**
55 Cherry Ln.
Souderton, PA 18964
Phone: (215)723-4400
Free: (800)523-5454 **Fax:** 800-544-3239
E-mail: custrep@youngscatalog.com
Products: Furniture replacement parts, including casters and glides. **SIC:** 5021 (Furniture). **Est:** 1945. **Sales:** $5,000,000 (2000). **Emp:** 30. **Officers:** P.O. Young, President.

■ **13287** ■ **Zip Dee Inc.**
96 Crossen Ave.
Elk Grove Village, IL 60007
Phone: (847)437-0980
Free: (800)338-2378 **Fax:** (847)437-7064
URL: http://www.zipdeeinc.com
Products: Awnings; Metal chairs and stools. **SIC:** 5021 (Furniture). **Est:** 1967. **Emp:** 30. **Officers:** Judith D. Miller, Vice President; Robert H. Miller, President.

(19) Gifts and Novelties

Entries in this section are arranged alphabetically by company name. When the company name is a personal name, the company name is alphabetized by the surname unless the first name or initial(s) are part of a trade name. See the User's Guide at the front of this directory for additional information.

■ **13288** ■ **Accessories Palace**
Gaslight Business Park
1953 10th Ave. N
Lake Worth, FL 33461
Phone: (561)582-1812 **Fax:** (561)582-1435
Products: Novelties; Hair accessories; Jewelry. **SICs:** 5199 (Nondurable Goods Nec); 5094 (Jewelry & Precious Stones).

■ **13289** ■ **Achievement Products Inc.**
PO Box 388
294 Rt. 10 W
East Hanover, NJ 07936
Phone: (973)887-5090 **Fax:** (973)515-0171
E-mail: achievement_inc@prodigy.com
URL: http://www.pages.prodigy.com/achieveprod
Products: Plaques; Trophies; Awards. **SIC:** 5199 (Nondurable Goods Nec). **Est:** 1958. **Sales:** $2,000,000 (2000). **Emp:** 15. **Officers:** Edward Van Rooyen, President.

■ **13290** ■ **Ad House Inc.**
1801 Shelby Oaks Dr.
Memphis, TN 38104
Phone: (901)387-5555 **Fax:** (901)276-0911
Products: Promotional goods. **SIC:** 5199 (Nondurable Goods Nec). **Est:** 1976. **Sales:** $4,000,000 (2000). **Emp:** 15. **Officers:** David Tate, President; Neil Arnold, Operations Mgr.; Elizabeth B. Tate, VP of Sales.

■ **13291** ■ **Adams Apple Distributing L.P.**
5100 N Ravenswood
Chicago, IL 60640
Phone: (312)275-7800
Products: Removable tattoos. **SIC:** 5199 (Nondurable Goods Nec). **Sales:** $7,800,000 (2000). **Emp:** 30. **Officers:** Ellis Levin, President; Allan Kandelman, CFO; Richard Steele, Exec. VP of Sales; Jim Kelly, Dir. of Information Systems; Gene Pytlewicz, Dir of Human Resources.

■ **13292** ■ **Kurt S. Adler Inc.**
1107 Broadway
New York, NY 10010
Phone: (212)924-0900
Free: (800)243-9627 **Fax:** (212)807-0575
Products: Christmas decorations, including ornaments, stockings, lights, and trees. **SIC:** 5199 (Nondurable Goods Nec). **Est:** 1950. **Sales:** $80,000,000 (1999). **Emp:** 200. **Officers:** Kurt S. Adler, Chairman of the Board; Clifford Adler, President.

■ **13293** ■ **Advertising Gifts Inc.**
39 W 19th St.
New York, NY 10011
Phone: (212)255-4300
Free: (800)555-1212 **Fax:** (212)255-4331
Products: Advertising specialties; Business gifts; Premium imprinted give-a-ways. **SIC:** 5199 (Nondurable Goods Nec). **Est:** 1904. **Sales:** $1,000,000 (2000). **Emp:** 10. **Officers:** Stan Weintraub, President.

■ **13294** ■ **Advertising Products Company Inc.**
10670 E Bathany Dr.
Aurora, CO 80014
Phone: (303)751-4300 **Fax:** (303)750-3730
Products: Promotional pens, cups, bags, and t-shirts. **SIC:** 5199 (Nondurable Goods Nec). **Est:** 1971. **Sales:** $2,000,000 (2000). **Emp:** 8. **Officers:** Richard H. Bowman, President.

■ **13295** ■ **A/E Supplies**
3695 Springer St.
Anchorage, AK 99503-5810
Phone: (907)277-2506 **Fax:** (907)274-5741
Products: Art supplies; Engineering supplies. **SICs:** 5199 (Nondurable Goods Nec); 5049 (Professional Equipment Nec).

■ **13296** ■ **A.K. International**
1116 Marshall Ave.
Lancaster, PA 17601
Phone: (717)394-0202 **Fax:** (717)392-4232
Products: Mugs; Dolls; Picture frames; Ornaments. **SIC:** 5199 (Nondurable Goods Nec). **Est:** 1972. **Sales:** $12,000,000 (2000). **Emp:** 40. **Officers:** O.A. Akinciler, President; Trish Akinciler, Controller; Barry Spector, Dir. of Sales.

■ **13297** ■ **A.L. Investors Inc.**
5601 Logan
Denver, CO 80216
Phone: (303)295-0196 **Fax:** (303)296-3912
Products: Souvenirs, including caps, toys, mugs, T-shirts, and sweatshirts. **SICs:** 5199 (Nondurable Goods Nec); 5137 (Women's/Children's Clothing). **Est:** 1952. **Sales:** $11,000,000 (2000). **Emp:** 55. **Officers:** Doran E. Carrell, President.

■ **13298** ■ **Allstar Enterprises Inc.**
51 Stouts Ln., Ste. 1
Monmouth Junction, NJ 08852
Phone: (732)329-6095
Free: (800)777-2535 **Fax:** (732)329-6238
Products: Gift items; Martial arts supplies; Phone batteries. **SIC:** 5199 (Nondurable Goods Nec).

■ **13299** ■ **Almar Industries**
Rte. 10 E, Bldg. 2
Succasunna, NJ 07876
Phone: (973)927-3050 **Fax:** (973)927-3334
Products: Seasonal products including lawn, garden, stove, and fireplace accessories. **SIC:** 5199 (Nondurable Goods Nec).

■ **13300** ■ **A.M. Associates Inc.**
21 Hampden Dr. 9
South Easton, MA 02375-1183
Phone: (508)230-2401 **Fax:** (508)230-8176
Products: Souvenirs. **SIC:** 5199 (Nondurable Goods Nec). **Officers:** Monte Gross, President.

■ **13301** ■ **American Gift Corp.**
6600 NW 74th Ave.
Miami, FL 33166
Phone: (305)884-6800
Free: (800)262-4438 **Fax:** (305)375-0790
URL: http://www.agiftcorp.com
Products: Gifts and novelties. **SIC:** 5199 (Nondurable Goods Nec). **Est:** 1935. **Sales:** $5,000,000 (2000). **Emp:** 49. **Officers:** Hal Kluger.

■ **13302** ■ **American Sandpainting**
2421 NW 16th Ln., No. 3
Pompano Beach, FL 33064
Phone: (954)971-0021
Free: (800)258-0483 **Fax:** (954)974-2666
E-mail: sandpix@aol.com
URL: http://www.sandpix.com
Products: Background pictures; Glow-in-the-dark pictures; Window boxes; Sand picures; Custom pictures. **SIC:** 5199 (Nondurable Goods Nec). **Est:** 1991. **Emp:** 3.

■ **13303** ■ **AMG Corp.**
PO Box 130
Madison, NJ 07940
Phone: (973)377-4300 **Fax:** (973)377-5370
Products: Decorative tins. **SIC:** 5199 (Nondurable Goods Nec). **Officers:** Andrew Gole, Sales/Marketing Contact; Lara Willis, Customer Service Contact.

■ **13304** ■ **Angel Gifts and Noah's Art**
PO Box 530
Fairfield, IA 52556
Phone: (515)472-5481
Free: (800)354-8362 **Fax:** (515)472-7353
Products: Posters and art prints; Framed art and displays. Inspirational gift products. **SIC:** 5199 (Nondurable Goods Nec). **Est:** 1981. **Emp:** 20. **Officers:** Donald Schmit, President; Bruce Hoium, Sales/Marketing Contact. **Former Name:** Angel Graphics and Signature Series.

■ **13305** ■ **Another Dancing Bear Productions**
220 Montgomery St., No. 975
San Francisco, CA 94104
Phone: (415)291-8200
Products: Crystal; Gift items; Pens. **SIC:** 5199 (Nondurable Goods Nec). **Est:** 1988. **Sales:** $600,000 (2000). **Emp:** 2. **Officers:** Jonathan Stone, President.

■ **13306** ■ **Around the Corner**
618 N Doheny Dr.
Los Angeles, CA 90069-5506
Phone: (310)276-8635
Free: (800)376-8635 **Fax:** (310)276-1740
Products: Ribbon; Beeswax candles. **SICs:** 5199 (Nondurable Goods Nec); 5131 (Piece Goods & Notions). **Est:** 1978. **Emp:** 49.

■ **13307** ■ **Artistic Stone of America**
33757 Groesbeck Hwy.
Fraser, MI 48026
Phone: (810)293-2120
Products: Statues. **SIC:** 5199 (Nondurable Goods Nec).

■ 13308 ■ ArtSource Inc.
5515 S Westridge Dr.
New Berlin, WI 53151
Phone: (414)860-4260
Free: (800)553-0081 **Fax:** (414)860-4278
E-mail: sales@artsourceonline.com
URL: http://www.artsourceonline.com
Products: Framed art. **SIC:** 5099 (Durable Goods Nec). **Est:** 1977. **Sales:** $2,500,000 (1999). **Emp:** 30. **Officers:** Maggie Smith, President; Bonnie Eckhart, Controller; Kelly Megonigle, Customer Service Contact.

■ 13309 ■ Astra International
1140 Broadway
New York, NY 10001
Phone: (212)251-0120 **Fax:** (212)251-0129
Products: Seasonal items; Novelties; Gifts. **SIC:** 5199 (Nondurable Goods Nec). **Est:** 1939. **Emp:** 8. **Officers:** David Gluckman, CEO. **Former Name:** Astra Trading Corp.

■ 13310 ■ John Barbuscak and Associates
3856 W 12 Mile Rd.
Berkley, MI 48072-1111
Phone: (248)544-2800 **Fax:** (248)544-3921
Products: Promotional products. **SIC:** 5199 (Nondurable Goods Nec). **Est:** 1975. **Sales:** $500,000 (2000). **Emp:** 5. **Officers:** John Barbuscak, President; Jan Barbuscak, Customer Service Contact.

■ 13311 ■ L.W. Barrett Company Inc.
PO Box 19430
Denver, CO 80219
Phone: (303)934-5755 **Fax:** (303)935-8814
Products: Advertising specialties, including pens, pencils, cups, mugs, and caps. **SIC:** 5199 (Nondurable Goods Nec). **Est:** 1953. **Sales:** $9,500,000 (2000). **Emp:** 18. **Officers:** Dennis Vick, CEO; Tina Montgomery, Vice President.

■ 13312 ■ Basketville Inc.
PO Box 710
Putney, VT 05346
Phone: (802)387-5509
Free: (800)258-4553 **Fax:** (802)387-5235
Products: Baskets. **SIC:** 5199 (Nondurable Goods Nec). **Est:** 1842. **Emp:** 100. **Officers:** Greg Wilson, President; Betty J. McGinn, Sales Mgr.

■ 13313 ■ Beachcombers International Inc.
PO Box 250
Ft. Myers, FL 33902
Phone: (941)731-2111
Free: (800)237-7080 **Fax:** (941)731-1100
Products: Souvenir and gift items; Beach items. **SIC:** 5199 (Nondurable Goods Nec). **Est:** 1946. **Sales:** $5,000,000 (2000). **Emp:** 35. **Officers:** Harry Chernin, President; Irwin Chernin, CFO; Joseph Romstadt, Dir. of Data Processing; Leslie Morreale, Dir of Human Resources.

■ 13314 ■ Beistle Co.
PO Box 10
Shippensburg, PA 17257
Phone: (717)532-2131 **Fax:** (717)532-7789
E-mail: beistle@cvn.net
URL: http://www.beistle.com
Products: Paper novelties. **SIC:** 5199 (Nondurable Goods Nec). **Est:** 1900. **Sales:** $14,000,000 (2000). **Emp:** 350. **Officers:** H. Ric Luhrs, President.

■ 13315 ■ Ben Wa Novelty Corp.
4731 W Jefferson Blvd.
Los Angeles, CA 90016
Phone: (323)731-2424
Free: (800)252-3692 **Fax:** (323)731-4306
URL: http://www.ben-wa.com
Products: Adult novelties. **SIC:** 5199 (Nondurable Goods Nec). **Est:** 1946. **Sales:** $7,000,000 (2000). **Emp:** 45. **Officers:** Fred Malorrus, President; Colleen Mott, Dir. of Data Processing; Farley Malorrus, General Mgr.; Ron Rovin, Operations Mgr.; Julie Kelly, Sales. **Doing Business As:** United Sales.

■ 13316 ■ Best Regards Inc.
344 7th Ave.
San Diego, CA 92101
Phone: (619)685-5840
Free: (800)544-6234 **Fax:** (619)685-5845
Products: Personalized labels for wines and gifts. **SIC:** 5182 (Wines & Distilled Beverages). **Est:** 1988. **Sales:** $500,000 (2000). **Emp:** 2. **Officers:** Dennis Miller, Owner.

■ 13317 ■ Big Apple Enterprises
230 5th Ave.
New York, NY 10010
Phone: (212)685-6755 **Fax:** (212)779-1669
Products: Tattoos; Stuffed animals; T-shirts; Souvenirs. **SIC:** 5199 (Nondurable Goods Nec). **Est:** 1973. **Sales:** $18,000,000 (2000). **Emp:** 12. **Officers:** Kenneth Bookbinder.

■ 13318 ■ Mel Blackman Associates, Inc.
PO Box 284
Canton, MA 02021
Phone: (781)828-9020 **Fax:** (781)828-1101
Products: High end giftware; Tabletop and gourmet serveware; Glassware. **SIC:** 5199 (Nondurable Goods Nec). **Est:** 1962. **Emp:** 3. **Officers:** Mel Blackman, President & Treasurer.

■ 13319 ■ Blaine's Art & Graphic Supply
2803 Spenard Rd.
Anchorage, AK 99503
Phone: (907)561-5344 **Fax:** (907)562-5988
Products: Art supplies, including framing equipment. **SIC:** 5199 (Nondurable Goods Nec).

■ 13320 ■ Blue Ridge Mountain Woodcrafts Inc.
PO Box 566
Ellijay, GA 30540
Phone: (706)276-2222
Free: (800)348-0748 **Fax:** (706)276-1297
Products: Trophies. **SIC:** 5199 (Nondurable Goods Nec). **Est:** 1974. **Emp:** 200.

■ 13321 ■ Bouquet Enterprises Inc.
233 Glasgow Ave.
Kellogg, MN 55945
Phone: (507)767-4994
Free: (800)328-5598 **Fax:** (507)767-4766
Products: Gifts and novelties. **SIC:** 5199 (Nondurable Goods Nec). **Est:** 1979. **Sales:** $5,400,000 (2000). **Emp:** 93. **Officers:** Tom Bouquet, President.

■ 13322 ■ Robert W. Boyd & Associates
PO Box 7442
Reno, NV 89510-7442
Phone: (702)847-9399 **Free:** (800)641-1100
Products: Novelties. **SIC:** 5199 (Nondurable Goods Nec). **Officers:** Robert Boyd, Owner.

■ 13323 ■ Brighter Image Publishing
2040 Amber Creek
Buford, GA 30518
Phone: (404)339-1361
Products: Fine art prints. **SIC:** 5199 (Nondurable Goods Nec).

■ 13324 ■ Buckler's Inc.
225 5th Ave.
New York, NY 10010
Phone: (212)684-1534 **Fax:** (212)447-7015
Products: Mirror and picture frames; Women's handbags and purses. **SICs:** 5137 (Women's/Children's Clothing); 5199 (Nondurable Goods Nec). **Est:** 1951. **Sales:** $19,000,000 (2000). **Emp:** 60. **Officers:** Bruce Buckler, President & Treasurer; Jerry Parent, Dir. of Marketing & Sales.

■ 13325 ■ Caliendo-Savio Enterprises Inc.
16800 W Cleveland Ave.
New Berlin, WI 53151
Phone: (262)786-8400 **Fax:** (262)796-2089
URL: http://www.csepromo.com
Products: Promotional products. **SIC:** 5199 (Nondurable Goods Nec). **Est:** 1979. **Sales:** $27,500,000 (2000). **Emp:** 110. **Officers:** Charles Caliendo, Co-Chairman & Owner; Gerard Sabio, Co-Chairman & Owner.

■ 13326 ■ Cardona Inc.
PO Box 81
Fremont, CA 94537
Phone: (510)786-0159 **Fax:** (510)786-0756
Products: Gift items, including wind chimes. **SIC:** 5199 (Nondurable Goods Nec).

■ 13327 ■ Carlson Dolls Co.
210 W 1st St.
PO Box 279
Maple Lake, MN 55358
Phone: (320)963-3713 **Fax:** (320)963-5166
Products: Souvenir dolls. **SIC:** 5199 (Nondurable Goods Nec). **Sales:** $6,000,000 (2000). **Emp:** 99. **Officers:** Lowell Carlson.

■ 13328 ■ CCL Creative Ltd
354 N Main St.
Freeport, NY 11520
Phone: (516)223-9800 **Fax:** (516)223-9826
Products: Gifts and novelties. **SIC:** 5199 (Nondurable Goods Nec). **Est:** 1990. **Sales:** $1,000,000 (2000). **Emp:** 3. **Officers:** Teresa Cheng. **Former Name:** CCL Products Ent. Inc.

■ 13329 ■ Noel R. Chapin Co.
1201 S Ervay St.
Dallas, TX 75215
Phone: (214)565-1883
Products: Picture frame moldings and supplies. **SIC:** 5199 (Nondurable Goods Nec). **Sales:** $26,000,000 (1994). **Emp:** 60. **Officers:** Noel R. Chapin, President; Anita Chapin, Treasurer.

■ 13330 ■ Charles Products Inc.
12118 Nebel St.
Rockville, MD 20852
Phone: (301)881-1966 **Fax:** (301)468-6340
Products: Gifts, souvenirs, and novelty items. **SIC:** 5199 (Nondurable Goods Nec). **Est:** 1952. **Sales:** $2,000,000 (2000). **Emp:** 15. **Officers:** Frank Stopak, President; Marshall Cannon, CFO.

■ 13331 ■ Chicago Import Inc.
3311 W Montrose Ave.
Chicago, IL 60618-1205
Phone: (773)588-3399
Free: (800)854-0881 **Fax:** (773)588-3285
Products: General merchandise. **SIC:** 5199 (Nondurable Goods Nec).

■ 13332 ■ Comer Packing Company Inc.
PO Box 33
Aberdeen, MS 39730
Phone: (601)369-9325
Products: Pre-packaged products. **SIC:** 5199 (Nondurable Goods Nec). **Sales:** $9,000,000 (2000). **Emp:** 27. **Officers:** Jimmie Comer, President.

■ 13333 ■ Connor and Associates Inc.
3595 Almaden Rd.
San Jose, CA 95118-1503
Phone: (408)445-0911
Products: Promotional premiums and incentives, including electric and electronic appliances and jewelry. **SICs:** 5064 (Electrical Appliances—Television & Radio); 5065 (Electronic Parts & Equipment Nec); 5094 (Jewelry & Precious Stones). **Est:** 1965. **Sales:** $1,000,000 (2000). **Emp:** 5. **Officers:** Connie Connor, President; Kim Connor, General Mgr.

■ 13334 ■ Consolidated International
300 Phillipi Rd.
Columbus, OH 43228
Phone: (614)278-3700
Free: (800)877-1254 **Fax:** (614)278-3701
Products: General merchandise. **SIC:** 5199 (Nondurable Goods Nec).

■ 13335 ■ Cooper and Associates
333 West North Ave.
Chicago, IL 60610
Phone: (312)988-7766
Free: (800)388-9270 **Fax:** (312)988-9050
Products: Unique quality products. **SIC:** 5099 (Durable Goods Nec). **Officers:** Ed Cooper, CEO.

■ **13336** ■ **Country Originals Inc.**
3844 W Northside Dr.
Jackson, MS 39209
Phone: (601)366-4229
Products: Gift items, including candles, candle stands, novelties, rugs, birdhouses, and jars. **SIC:** 5199 (Nondurable Goods Nec). **Sales:** $6,000,000 (2000). **Emp:** 25. **Officers:** Doug Williams, President; Kathy Leraue, CFO.

■ **13337** ■ **Cowan Costume, Inc.**
108 S Caddo
Cleburne, TX 76031
Phone: (817)641-3126   **Fax:** (817)641-3149
E-mail: cowan@airmail.net
Products: Mascot costumes. **SIC:** 5199 (Nondurable Goods Nec). **Est:** 1986. **Emp:** 13. **Officers:** Karen Cowan, President; Carole Wheeler, Sales/Marketing Contact, e-mail: carole5@airmail.net; Jackie Sexton, General Mgr., e-mail: jackie22@airmail.net.

■ **13338** ■ **Craft-Tex/Phase IV Inc.**
2637 E Green Dr.
High Point, NC 27260-7112
Phone: (919)861-2009   **Fax:** (919)861-2010
Products: Figurines. **SIC:** 5199 (Nondurable Goods Nec). **Est:** 1982. **Sales:** $4,000,000 (2000). **Emp:** 101. **Officers:** Paul Saperstein.

■ **13339** ■ **Creative Merchandising Inc.**
9917 Glenwood St.
Overland Park, KS 66212
Phone: (913)642-3816   **Fax:** (913)642-3816
Products: Crystal bells. **SIC:** 5199 (Nondurable Goods Nec). **Est:** 1972. **Sales:** $400,000 (2000). **Emp:** 3. **Officers:** Susan Jones-Gronquist, President; Glen Jones, VP & Treasurer.

■ **13340** ■ **Cresc Corp.**
3550 Broad St., Ste. H-1
Chamblee, GA 30341
Phone: (404)452-1155   **Fax:** (404)451-0281
Products: Gifts and novelties. **SIC:** 5199 (Nondurable Goods Nec). **Est:** 1977. **Emp:** 49.

■ **13341** ■ **Crown Imports**
11311 Harry Hines, No. 302
PO Box 59872
Dallas, TX 75229
Phone: (972)241-0401
Free: (800)955-4443   **Fax:** (972)241-9758
E-mail: amjadmitha@aol.com
Products: Gifts and novelties. **SIC:** 5199 (Nondurable Goods Nec).

■ **13342** ■ **Customline of North America, Inc.**
438 W 37th St., Ste. 3B
New York, NY 10018-4095
Phone: (212)967-6266   **Fax:** (212)967-8042
Products: Gifts and novelties. **SIC:** 5199 (Nondurable Goods Nec). **Est:** 1985. **Sales:** $1,000,000 (2000). **Emp:** 5. **Officers:** David Fiderer, President; Alice Slater, Dir. of Sales.

■ **13343** ■ **D & J Manufacturing Inc.**
4758 Angola Rd.
Toledo, OH 43615
Phone: (419)382-1327
Free: (800)634-5982   **Fax:** (419)382-0505
E-mail: Dandjmfg@mindspring.com
Products: Car and household air fresheners. **SIC:** 5199 (Nondurable Goods Nec). **Est:** 1984. **Emp:** 120. **Officers:** John Elassir, President; Danny Elassir, Vice President; Sean Alekhtiar, Human Resources Contact; Cress Miano, Marketing & Customer Service.

■ **13344** ■ **Dawg Luvers & Co.**
2600 Lanes Bridge Rd.
Jesup, GA 31545
Phones: (912)427-6178   (912)427-4130
Fax: (912)427-6130
Products: Gifts and novelties; Men's and boys' sportswear. **SICs:** 5199 (Nondurable Goods Nec); 5136 (Men's/Boys' Clothing). **Emp:** 10. **Officers:** Carolyn Kendrick.

■ **13345** ■ **The Depot Ltd.**
1015 W Jackson St.
Sullivan, IL 61951
Phone: (217)728-2567
Free: (800)223-3768   **Fax:** (217)728-8480
Products: Art goods; Gifts and novelties. **SIC:** 5199 (Nondurable Goods Nec). **Est:** 1969. **Emp:** 50. **Officers:** Burnett Harshman, President; Vesta Harshman, Secretary.

■ **13346** ■ **Dessau Brass Inc.**
39 Graphic Pl.
Moonachie, NJ 07074
Phone: (201)440-5150   **Fax:** (201)440-7627
Products: Brass items. **SIC:** 5199 (Nondurable Goods Nec). **Sales:** $7,000,000 (2000). **Emp:** 52. **Officers:** Robert Dessau, President; Howard Dessau, Vice President.

■ **13347** ■ **Gloria Duchin Inc.**
PO Box 4860
Rumford, RI 02916-0860
Phone: (401)438-5400   **Fax:** (401)438-5490
Products: Christmas tree ornaments; Bookmarks; Engraved brass items. **SICs:** 5199 (Nondurable Goods Nec); 5023 (Homefurnishings). **Officers:** Gloria Duchin, CEO.

■ **13348** ■ **Durand International**
PO Box 5001
Millville, NJ 08332
Phone: (609)825-5620
Products: Crystal gifts and tableware. **SIC:** 5023 (Homefurnishings). **Sales:** $24,000,000 (1994). **Emp:** 180. **Officers:** Jean-Rene Gougelet, CEO.

■ **13349** ■ **Dyna Group International Inc.**
1661 S Sequin Ave.
New Braunfels, TX 78130-3856
Phone: (830)620-4400
Free: (800)341-4436   **Fax:** (830)620-8430
URL: http://www.gap1.com
Products: Pewter giftware, including buckles, keychains, and sports collectibles. **SICs:** 5091 (Sporting & Recreational Goods); 5091 (Sporting & Recreational Goods). **Est:** 1971. **Sales:** $10,000,000 (2000). **Emp:** 221. **Officers:** Roger R. Tuttle, CEO & Chairman of the Board; William M. Sandstrom, Treasurer & Controller; Jeff Smith, Vice President.

■ **13350** ■ **E & R Sales Inc.**
4800 Market Square Ln.
Midlothian, VA 23112
Phone: (804)744-8000
Free: (800)234-7474   **Fax:** (804)744-5125
URL: http://www.ersales.com
Products: Mylar balloons. **SIC:** 5099 (Durable Goods Nec). **Est:** 1986. **Emp:** 20. **Officers:** Harry Gellis, President; Elissa Mast, VP of Operations & Secty.

■ **13351** ■ **Ebeling & Reuss Co.**
6500 Chapmans Rd.
Allentown, PA 18106-9280
Phone: (215)776-7100   **Fax:** (215)366-8307
Products: Collectible porcelain and china products. **SIC:** 5199 (Nondurable Goods Nec). **Est:** 1886. **Sales:** $10,000,000 (2000). **Emp:** 32. **Officers:** Ron Rapelje, President.

■ **13352** ■ **El Paso Onyx Co. Inc.**
1414 Common Dr.
El Paso, TX 79936
Phone: (915)591-6699
Free: (800)872-8411   **Fax:** (915)591-0929
E-mail: eponyx@ix.netcom.com
Products: Souvenir novelties, including license plates and key chains; Mexican imports; Indian goods. **SIC:** 5199 (Nondurable Goods Nec).

■ **13353** ■ **Espana General Importers**
1615 SW 8th St.
Miami, FL 33135-3310
Phone: (305)856-4844   **Fax:** (305)856-1221
Products: Religious statues; Flamenco dancer dolls; Folding fans; Guitars; Ceramic wall plates; Hand carved shields and swords. **SICs:** 5199 (Nondurable Goods Nec); 5099 (Durable Goods Nec). **Est:** 1963. **Sales:** $140,000 (2000). **Emp:** 2.

■ **13354** ■ **Fallah Enterprises**
11601 Seaboard Cir.
Stanton, CA 90680-3427
Phone: (562)799-6642   **Fax:** (562)799-6640
Products: Household appliances; Gifts and novelties. **SICs:** 5199 (Nondurable Goods Nec); 5064 (Electrical Appliances—Television & Radio).

■ **13355** ■ **Far Corners Importers Ltd.**
1006 Benstein, Ste. 105
Walled Lake, MI 48390
Phone: (248)669-7492
Free: (800)346-7676   **Fax:** (248)669-7494
Products: Cultural gifts. **SIC:** 5199 (Nondurable Goods Nec). **Est:** 1956. **Sales:** $300,000 (2000). **Emp:** 2. **Officers:** Terry Dryer, President.

■ **13356** ■ **Feldstein and Associates Inc.**
6500 Weatherfield Ct.
Maumee, OH 43537
Phone: (419)867-9500
Free: (800)755-6504   **Fax:** (419)867-9210
E-mail: mfasales@markfeldstein.com
URL: http://www.markfeldstein.com
Products: Gifts and novelties. **SIC:** 5199 (Nondurable Goods Nec). **Est:** 1985. **Emp:** 12. **Officers:** Mark Feldstein, President; Harley Kripke, Vice President.

■ **13357** ■ **Fetco International Corp.**
PO Box 165
Randolph, MA 02368-0165
Phone: (617)871-2000
Free: (800)225-0468   **Fax:** (781)871-0829
Products: Picture frames, photo albums, and photo accessories. **SIC:** 5023 (Homefurnishings). **Est:** 1974. **Sales:** $35,000,000 (2000). **Emp:** 80. **Officers:** John Whoriskey, President; John Calhoun, Dir. of Information Systems.

■ **13358** ■ **Flury & Co. Ltd.**
322 1st Ave. S
Seattle, WA 98104-2506
Phone: (206)587-0260   **Fax:** (206)382-3519
E-mail: curtis@fluryco.com
URL: http://www.fluryco.com
Products: Vintage photography of Edward S. Curtis; Fine antique native american art objects from the Northwest Coast and Alaska, the Great Plains, and the Southwest. **SIC:** 5199 (Nondurable Goods Nec). **Est:** 1971. **Emp:** 5. **Officers:** Lois Flury, Owner; Jane Davis, Human Resources Contact.

■ **13359** ■ **Franco-American Novelty Company Inc.**
8400 73rd Ave.
Glendale, NY 11385
Phone: (718)821-3100   **Fax:** (718)821-1307
Products: Halloween costumes; Novelty items. **SICs:** 5092 (Toys & Hobby Goods & Supplies); 5199 (Nondurable Goods Nec). **Est:** 1910. **Sales:** $5,000,000 (2000). **Emp:** 30. **Officers:** Robert Oumano, President.

■ **13360** ■ **C.R. Gibson Co.**
32 Knight St.
Norwalk, CT 06856
Phone: (203)847-4543   **Fax:** (203)847-7613
Products: Gift cards; Photo albums. **SICs:** 5199 (Nondurable Goods Nec); 5113 (Industrial & Personal Service Paper).

■ **13361** ■ **Glass Crafters Stain Glass Supply**
398 Interstate Ct.
Sarasota, FL 34240
Free: (800)422-4552
URL: http://www.glasscrafters.com
Products: Stained glass. **SIC:** 5199 (Nondurable Goods Nec). **Est:** 1975. **Former Name:** Glass Crafters of Manhasset, Inc.

■ **13362** ■ **Glaze Inc.**
11-B Jane Pl.
Edison, NJ 08820
Phone: (908)755-2233   **Fax:** (908)755-2213
E-mail: glazeinc@hotmail.com
Products: Gifts and novelties. **SIC:** 5199 (Nondurable Goods Nec). **Est:** 1985. **Emp:** 14. **Officers:** Bihari Lund; Vijay Lund; Sylvon Heatai, Sales/Marketing Contact; Sean Ferris, Customer Service Contact.

■ 13363 ■ Golden State Trading Co.
888 Brannan, Ste. 278
San Francisco, CA 94103-4928
Phone: (415)621-4653 **Fax:** (415)621-0415
Products: Brass, bronze, and silver giftware and accessories. **SIC:** 5199 (Nondurable Goods Nec). **Est:** 1977. **Emp:** 49. **Officers:** Bettie Lum, Owner.

■ 13364 ■ Goldman Associates Inc.
10515 Liberty Ave.
St. Louis, MO 63132
Phone: (314)428-3000
Products: Imprinted goods, including pens, shirts, and caps. **SIC:** 5199 (Nondurable Goods Nec). **Est:** 1960. **Sales:** $6,500,000 (2000). **Emp:** 12. **Officers:** Kenneth Goldman, President; Don Goldman, Exec. VP.

■ 13365 ■ Hanford's Inc.
PO Box 32666
Charlotte, NC 28232-2666
Phone: (704)375-2528 **Fax:** (704)376-7081
Products: Silk flowers, christmas ornaments and gifts. **SICs:** 5193 (Flowers & Florists' Supplies); 5099 (Durable Goods Nec). **Sales:** $12,500,000 (1992). **Emp:** 100. **Officers:** Paul Norman, CEO; H. Berry Petty, Controller.

■ 13366 ■ HHS USA Inc.
1733 H St., No. 330-705
Blaine, WA 98230-5107
Phones: (360)354-6515 (360)533-0727
Fax: (360)530-4413
Products: Gifts and novelties. **SIC:** 5199 (Nondurable Goods Nec).

■ 13367 ■ Edna Hibel Studio
PO Box 9967
Riviera Beach, FL 33419
Phone: (561)848-9633
Free: (800)275-3426 **Fax:** (561)848-9640
E-mail: hibel@worldnet.att.net
URL: http://www.hibel.com
Products: Gifts; Fine art collectibles; Original and reproduction art; Decorative accessories. **SIC:** 5199 (Nondurable Goods Nec). **Est:** 1960. **Emp:** 45. **Officers:** Andy Plotkin, Vice President; Theodore Plotkin, President; Cheryll Plotkin, Human Resources Contact; Randy Matthews, Sales & Marketing Contact; Pamela Stewart, Customer Service Contact.

■ 13368 ■ William J. Hirten Company Inc.
6100 17th Ave.
Brooklyn, NY 11204
Phone: (718)256-4801
Free: (888)WHI-RTEN **Fax:** (718)236-0825
E-mail: sales@wjhirten.com
Products: Religious articles. **SIC:** 5199 (Nondurable Goods Nec). **Est:** 1922. **Sales:** $4,000,000 (2000). **Emp:** 30. **Officers:** Dolores King, President; Maria Bruno, Treasurer; Ronald Bloom, VP of Sales.

■ 13369 ■ J. Hofert Co.
PO Box 51330
Sparks, NV 89435
Phone: (775)331-4000 **Fax:** (775)352-7474
E-mail: christmas@hofertholly.com
URL: http://www.ropelites.com
Products: Christmas merchandise; Glass Christmas ornaments. **SICs:** 5199 (Nondurable Goods Nec); 5099 (Durable Goods Nec). **Est:** 1880. **Emp:** 250. **Officers:** Edward Scott, Chairman; Dan Webb, Controller; Bart H. Scott, President.

■ 13370 ■ Horns Inc.
8101 Grand Ave.
Billings, MT 59106-1901
Phone: (406)652-0550 **Free:** (800)652-0550
Products: Horns. **SIC:** 5199 (Nondurable Goods Nec).
Officers: Rick Alkire, President.

■ 13371 ■ House of Ceramics Inc.
1011 N Hollywood St.
Memphis, TN 38108
Phone: (901)324-3851
Products: Ceramics. **SIC:** 5199 (Nondurable Goods Nec). **Sales:** $8,000,000 (2000). **Emp:** 31. **Officers:** Bond Sandoe, President; Bob Willoughby, Vice President.

■ 13372 ■ House of Lloyd Inc.
11901 Grandview Rd.
Grandview, MO 64030
Phone: (816)966-2222 **Fax:** (816)767-2177
Products: Christmas ornaments; Cooking related items. **SIC:** 5099 (Durable Goods Nec). **Sales:** $110,000,000 (2000). **Emp:** 650. **Officers:** Verny Lloyd, CEO; Kevin Murphy, VP of Finance.

■ 13373 ■ Idaho Souvenir
8004 Woodlark
Boise, ID 83709
Phone: (208)362-9300
Free: (800)456-5157 **Fax:** (208)362-9114
Products: Gifts and novelties; Cards, including picture postcards, souvenir cards, etc. **SIC:** 5199 (Nondurable Goods Nec). **Est:** 1976. **Officers:** Leslie Gill, President; Mark Shirrod, VP, Treasurer & Secty.

■ 13374 ■ Import Warehouse Inc.
PO Box 29102
Dallas, TX 75229-0102
Phone: (972)241-4818 **Fax:** (972)241-2139
Products: Gift items; Homefurnishings; Toys; Cleaning supplies; Candy. **SICs:** 5199 (Nondurable Goods Nec); 5023 (Homefurnishings); 5092 (Toys & Hobby Goods & Supplies); 5149 (Groceries & Related Products Nec); 5169 (Chemicals & Allied Products Nec). **Est:** 1983. **Sales:** $7,000,000 (2000). **Emp:** 11.

■ 13375 ■ Importmex
4 Harness Ct., Ste. 101
Baltimore, MD 21208-1352
Phone: (410)484-9996 **Fax:** (410)484-4106
Products: Gifts and novelties. **SIC:** 5199 (Nondurable Goods Nec). **Est:** 1991. **Sales:** $700,000 (2000). **Emp:** 15. **Officers:** Paulino Garcia, President.

■ 13376 ■ Industrial Trade and Development Co.
620 San Francisco Ave.
Long Beach, CA 90802
Phone: (562)432-4583 **Fax:** (562)432-2968
Products: Brass novelty items. **SIC:** 5199 (Nondurable Goods Nec). **Est:** 1964. **Sales:** $2,000,000 (2000). **Emp:** 12. **Officers:** Suresh C. Bhatti, CEO & President.

■ 13377 ■ International Advertising Gifts
710 E San Ysidro Blvd., Ste B
San Ysidro, CA 92173
Phone: (619)428-5475 **Fax:** (619)690-1942
Products: Promotional materials. **SIC:** 5199 (Nondurable Goods Nec).

■ 13378 ■ JanWay Co.
11 Academy Rd.
Cogan Station, PA 17728
Phone: (570)494-1239
Free: (800)877-5242 **Fax:** (570)494-1350
E-mail: janway@janway.com
URL: http://www.janway.com
Products: Canvas and nylon bags; Custom printed advertising specialty and fund raising items. **SIC:** 5199 (Nondurable Goods Nec). **Est:** 1981. **Sales:** $2,000,000 (1999). **Emp:** 20. **Officers:** Janice M. Stebbins; Gary Stebbins, e-mail: garys@janway.com; Linda Shelmire, e-mail: lindas@janway.com; Janice M. Stebbins.

■ 13379 ■ Jimson Novelties Inc.
28 E 18th St.
New York, NY 10003
Phones: (212)477-3386 (212)477-3692
Fax: (212)228-3394
Products: Adult novelties, including gag gifts and inflatable dolls. **SIC:** 5199 (Nondurable Goods Nec).

■ 13380 ■ Karla's Kreations Inc.
1561 N 158th Ave.
Omaha, NE 68118-2310
Products: Wood and fabric art and crafts, including pictures and animals. **SIC:** 5199 (Nondurable Goods Nec). **Sales:** $2,000,000 (2000). **Emp:** 20. **Officers:** Karla Blevins, President.

■ 13381 ■ Knobler International Ltd.
225 5th Ave.
New York, NY 10010-1101
Phone: (212)679-5577 **Fax:** (212)545-8599
E-mail: showroom@knoblerinternational.com
Products: Gifts; Housewares. **SICs:** 5199 (Nondurable Goods Nec); 5023 (Homefurnishings). **Est:** 1949. **Emp:** 49. **Officers:** Alfred Knobler, CEO; Al Reiner, President.

■ 13382 ■ KoolaBrew Inc.
271 Calabash Rd. NW
Calabash, NC 28467
Phone: (919)579-6711
Free: (800)332-7399 **Fax:** (919)579-6335
Products: Foam rubber beverage holders. **SIC:** 5199 (Nondurable Goods Nec). **Est:** 1979. **Emp:** 49. **Officers:** Genny Lassiter.

■ 13383 ■ Mal La Francis Associates
59 Middlesex Tpke., No. 310
Bedford, MA 01730-1415
Phone: (781)275-2438 **Fax:** (978)461-2021
E-mail: info@lafrancis.com
URL: http://www.lafrancis.com
Products: Gifts and novelties. **SICs:** 5199 (Nondurable Goods Nec); 5092 (Toys & Hobby Goods & Supplies). **Est:** 1968. **Emp:** 5. **Officers:** Tim La Francis, Sales & Marketing Contact, e-mail: tim@lafrancis.com.

■ 13384 ■ LaBelle Time Inc.
65 NW 166 St.
North Miami, FL 33169
Phone: (305)940-1507 **Fax:** (305)940-0621
E-mail: info@labelletime.com
URL: http://www.labelletime.com
Products: Watches; Calculators; Clocks; Portfolios; Wood and brass pens; Pen boxes; Small electronics; Key chains; Promotional items. **SICs:** 5199 (Nondurable Goods Nec); 5112 (Stationery & Office Supplies). **Est:** 1986. **Officers:** Alan Tabasky; Heidi Tabasky; Mr. Laufer.

■ 13385 ■ LamRite West Inc.
13000 Danice Pkwy.
Strongsville, OH 44136
Phone: (440)238-7318
Products: Art and crafts materials. **SIC:** 5092 (Toys & Hobby Goods and Supplies).

■ 13386 ■ Larriva Corp.
75 N Terrace Ave.
Nogales, AZ 85621-3298
Phone: (602)287-5815 **Fax:** (602)287-5816
Products: General merchandise. **SIC:** 5199 (Nondurable Goods Nec). **Est:** 1937. **Sales:** $3,500,000 (2000). **Emp:** 15. **Officers:** Richard Larriva, President; Leonilo Larriva IV IV, CFO; Ken Larriva, Dir. of Marketing.

■ 13387 ■ Bill Larsen and Associates Inc.
PO Box 1194
Tacoma, WA 98401
Phone: (253)383-4444
Free: (800)326-2684 **Fax:** (253)383-1217
E-mail: associates@bill-larsen.com
URL: http://promo-web.com/billlarsen
Products: Imprinted promotional products and incentive premium programs. **SIC:** 5199 (Nondurable Goods Nec). **Est:** 1985. **Sales:** $2,000,000 (1999). **Emp:** 5. **Officers:** Tina Montgomery, President; Dennis Vick, VP & Treasurer; Scott A. Larsen, VP of Sales.

■ 13388 ■ LBK Marketing Corp.
7800 Bayberry Rd.
Jacksonville, FL 32256-6818
Phone: (904)737-8500 **Fax:** (904)737-9526
Products: Pottery, gifts items, and silk flowers. **SICs:** 5199 (Nondurable Goods Nec); 5193 (Flowers & Florists' Supplies). **Sales:** $20,000,000 (1994). **Emp:** 50. **Officers:** David M. Bailys, President; Gary Stutzman, CFO.

■ 13389 ■ Leeber Ltd. USA
115 Pencader Dr.
Newark, DE 19702-3322
Phone: (302)733-0998
Free: (800)533-2372 **Fax:** (302)656-7375
Products: Silver plated gift items. **SIC:** 5199

(Nondurable Goods Nec). **Est:** 1981. **Emp:** 11. **Officers:** Alice Ho.

■ **13390** ■ **Lib-Com Ltd.**
1150 Motor Pkwy.
Central Islip, NY 11722
Phone: (516)582-8800 **Fax:** (516)582-8366
Products: Novelty glassware; Gifts and novelties; Christmas trees; Lawn furniture. **SICs:** 5099 (Durable Goods Nec); 5021 (Furniture). **Est:** 1932. **Sales:** $80,000,000 (2000). **Emp:** 60. **Officers:** Joel Margolin, President; Dan Smith, Controller; Vito Badalamenti, Dir. of Marketing & Sales; Jim Lysaght, Dir. of Data Processing.

■ **13391** ■ **Little Brass Shack Imports**
2708 N Armistead Ave.
Hampton, VA 23666-1628
Phone: (757)766-1011
Free: (800)439-7496 **Fax:** (757)766-0433
Products: Giftware. **SIC:** 5199 (Nondurable Goods Nec). **Est:** 1972. **Emp:** 18. **Officers:** Thomas E. Grasso, Owner.

■ **13392** ■ **Loui Michel Cie.**
1927 W 139th St., Fl. 2
Gardena, CA 90249
Phone: (310)323-4567
Products: Picture frames. **SIC:** 5199 (Nondurable Goods Nec). **Sales:** $89,000,000 (1993). **Emp:** 200. **Officers:** Michael Block, Vice President.

■ **13393** ■ **Lynnwood Co.**
8840 Elder Creek Rd., Unit B
Sacramento, CA 95828
Phone: (916)381-0293
Free: (800)382-7484 **Fax:** (916)689-4249
Products: Windchimes. **SIC:** 5199 (Nondurable Goods Nec).

■ **13394** ■ **Harold Mangelsen and Sons Inc.**
8200 J. St.
Omaha, NE 68127
Phone: (402)339-3922 **Fax:** (402)339-3296
Products: Arts and crafts. **SIC:** 5099 (Durable Goods Nec). **Sales:** $8,100,000 (2000). **Emp:** 70.

■ **13395** ■ **Manneco, Inc.**
600 S Cottage Ave.
Independence, MO 64050
Phone: (816)833-3325
Free: (800)397-9627 **Fax:** (816)833-3327
E-mail: hoho@manneco.com
URL: http://www.manneco.com
Products: Christmas decorations, including bulbs, wreaths, and lights. **SIC:** 5199 (Nondurable Goods Nec). **Est:** 1946. **Sales:** $500,000 (2000). **Emp:** 8. **Officers:** Hoot Mann, President.

■ **13396** ■ **R. Marlin Manufacturing & Distribution Inc.**
302 N Townsend
Santa Ana, CA 92703-3543
Phone: (714)547-3220 **Fax:** (714)541-0570
Products: Ceramic, stoneware, and clay products, including planters and vases. **SIC:** 5032 (Brick, Stone & Related Materials). **Est:** 1975. **Emp:** 99. **Officers:** Rick Marlin; Brad Davidson.

■ **13397** ■ **Martek Ltd.**
Dept. LH
PO Box 15160
Charlotte, NC 28211
Phone: (704)364-7213 **Fax:** (704)364-7253
E-mail: martekltd@aol.com
URL: http://www.martekltd.com
Products: Clocks; Gifts and novelties. **SICs:** 5199 (Nondurable Goods Nec); 5094 (Jewelry & Precious Stones). **Est:** 1980. **Emp:** 2. **Officers:** Paul Muckler.

■ **13398** ■ **Martha Weems Ltd.**
8351 Leesburg Pike
Vienna, VA 22182
Phone: (703)827-9510 **Fax:** (703)827-3456
Products: Advertising specialty products for corporations including mugs and T-Shirts with logos. **SIC:** 5199 (Nondurable Goods Nec). **Sales:** $2,000,000 (2000). **Emp:** 4. **Officers:** Deborah Dunn, President; Dottie Travers, Bookkeeper.

■ **13399** ■ **Maruri USA Corp.**
21510 Gledhill St.
Chatsworth, CA 91311
Phone: (818)717-9900
Free: (800)562-7874 **Fax:** (818)717-9901
Products: Porcelain figurines. **SIC:** 5199 (Nondurable Goods Nec). **Emp:** 49.

■ **13400** ■ **Mello Smello**
5100 Hwy. 169 N
Minneapolis, MN 55428-4028
Phone: (612)504-5400 **Fax:** (612)504-5493
URL: http://www.mellosmello.com
Products: Licensed stickers and activities (Power Puff Girls, Digimon, and Barney); Seasonal decorations (Clings, Bags, and Stickers). **SIC:** 5199 (Nondurable Goods Nec). **Est:** 1980. **Emp:** 138. **Officers:** Jeff Murphy, Exec. VP.

■ **13401** ■ **F.O. Merz and Company Inc.**
PO Box 430
Cowpens, SC 29330
Phone: (864)463-4200 **Fax:** (864)463-4210
E-mail: fomerz@mindspring.com
URL: http://www.fomerzco.com
Products: Bamboo, rattan, willow, and chip, basketwork; wicker work; Teak furniture; nautical items. **SIC:** 5199 (Nondurable Goods Nec). **Est:** 1931. **Sales:** $10,000,000 (2000). **Emp:** 50. **Officers:** F.O. Merz, President; Steve McCollough, Office Mgr.; Eric Hallbach-Merz, Vice President.

■ **13402** ■ **Mexican Art Imports**
3103 E Van Buren
Phoenix, AZ 85008
Phone: (602)275-9552 **Fax:** (602)220-9855
Products: Ironwood figurines; Buckles; Mexican imports, including leather and textiles. **SICs:** 5199 (Nondurable Goods Nec); 5131 (Piece Goods & Notions).

■ **13403** ■ **Frances Meyer Inc.**
104 Coleman Blvd.
Savannah, GA 31408-9540
Phone: (912)748-5252 **Fax:** 800-545-8378
Products: Party goods, including napkins, streamers and key chains; Stationery. **SICs:** 5199 (Nondurable Goods Nec); 5112 (Stationery & Office Supplies). **Emp:** 87. **Officers:** Frances Meyer.

■ **13404** ■ **Minami International Corp.**
4 Executive Plz.
Yonkers, NY 10701
Phone: (914)969-7555
Products: Christmas lights. **SIC:** 5063 (Electrical Apparatus & Equipment). **Sales:** $3,000,000 (2000). **Emp:** 13. **Officers:** Hisashi Juba, President & Chairman of the Board; Marvin Press, VP of Finance.

■ **13405** ■ **Mirror Lite Co.**
PO Box 358
Rockwood, MI 48173-0358
Phone: (734)379-9828 **Fax:** (734)379-4985
Products: Mirrors for school buses and trucks. **SIC:** 5023 (Homefurnishings). **Emp:** 40. **Officers:** William Schmidt, President; Karen Botkin, Vice President.

■ **13406** ■ **Mitchell Mogal Inc.**
25 Hempstead Gardens Dr.
West Hempstead, NY 11552
Phone: (516)564-1894
Free: (800)221-8272 **Fax:** (516)489-4022
Products: Knives; Watches; Flashlights; Lighters; Pocketwatches. **SIC:** 5199 (Nondurable Goods Nec).

■ **13407** ■ **National Capital Flag Co. Inc.**
100 S Quaker Ln.
Alexandria, VA 22314-4526
Phone: (703)751-2411
Free: (800)368-3524 **Fax:** (703)751-4874
URL: http://www.natlcapflag.com
Products: Flags and flag poles; Banners. **SIC:** 5199 (Nondurable Goods Nec). **Est:** 1962. **Sales:** $2,000,000 (1999). **Emp:** 30. **Officers:** Claude L. Haynes Jr., CEO; A.E. Ulmer Jr., President.

■ **13408** ■ **National Potteries Corp.**
7800 Bayberry Rd.
Jacksonville, FL 32256
Phone: (904)737-8500
Products: Gift items, including silk flowers, potteries, and baskets. **SICs:** 5023 (Homefurnishings); 5099 (Durable Goods Nec); 5199 (Nondurable Goods Nec). **Est:** 1954. **Sales:** $10,000,000 (2000). **Emp:** 60. **Officers:** David M. Bailys, President; R.C. Fullerton, CFO; Tom Stewart, Dir. of Marketing.

■ **13409** ■ **Nationwide Advertising Specialty Inc.**
PO Box 928
Arlington, TX 76004-0928
Phone: (817)275-2678 **Fax:** (817)274-4301
Products: Promotional goods, including pens, pencils, and calendars. **SIC:** 5199 (Nondurable Goods Nec). **Est:** 1937. **Sales:** $22,300,000 (2000). **Emp:** 50. **Officers:** John Newbern, President; Floyd Dale, Controller.

■ **13410** ■ **New England Pottery Co.**
1000 Washington St., Rte. 1
Foxboro, MA 02035
Phone: (508)543-7700 **Fax:** (508)543-9861
Products: Pottery; Plant containers and accessories; Christmas specialty lightings. **SICs:** 5193 (Flowers & Florists' Supplies); 5199 (Nondurable Goods Nec). **Sales:** $16,000,000 (2000). **Emp:** 100. **Officers:** Lawrence D. Gitlitz, CEO; Alan Antokal, President.

■ **13411** ■ **Newton Manufacturing Co.**
1123 1st Ave. E
Newton, IA 50208
Phone: (515)792-4121 **Fax:** (515)792-6261
URL: http://www.newtonmfg.com
Products: Calendars; Gifts; Clothing; Writing instruments; Glassware. **SIC:** 5199 (Nondurable Goods Nec). **Est:** 1909. **Sales:** $52,000,000 (2000). **Emp:** 175. **Officers:** Clayton C. Case, President; Lee Cochran, Treasurer; Jerome Hoxton, VP of Marketing.

■ **13412** ■ **Northern Sun**
2916 E Lake St.
Minneapolis, MN 55406-2065
Phone: (612)729-2001
Free: (800)258-8579 **Fax:** (612)729-0149
E-mail: nsm@scc.net
URL: http://www.northernsun.com
Products: T-shirts; Buttons; Miscellaneous publications, including posters, and calendars. **SIC:** 5199 (Nondurable Goods Nec). **Est:** 1979. **Emp:** 15.

■ **13413** ■ **Northwest Blueprint and Supply**
13450 Farmington Rd.
Livonia, MI 48150
Phone: (734)525-1990
Products: Art, drafting and office supplies. **SICs:** 5199 (Nondurable Goods Nec); 5112 (Stationery & Office Supplies). **Sales:** $22,000,000 (1994). **Emp:** 88. **Officers:** Mary Ann Lewis, CEO; Joe Kapp, President.

■ **13414** ■ **Novelty Poster Co.**
26 Clinton Ave.
Valley Stream, NY 11580
Phone: (516)561-1378 **Fax:** (516)561-3605
E-mail: novelty@juno.com
URL: http://www.noveltytoys.com
Products: Novelty items, including posters, buttons, and stickers; Action figures; Licensed items for the entertainment industry. **SIC:** 5199 (Nondurable Goods Nec).

■ **13415** ■ **Novelty Poster Co.**
26 Clinton Ave.
Valley Stream, NY 11580
Phone: (516)561-1378 **Fax:** (516)561-3605
Products: Gifts and novelties. **SIC:** 5199 (Nondurable Goods Nec).

■ **13416** ■ **Now Products**
1141 Mt. Zion Rd.
Bucyrus, OH 44820
Phone: (419)562-9118 **Fax:** (419)562-2943
E-mail: nowproducts@bright.net
Products: Clocks; Mirror and picture frames; Gifts and novelties. **SICs:** 5199 (Nondurable Goods Nec); 5094 (Jewelry & Precious Stones). **Est:** 1993. **Emp:** 15.

Officers: Dodie Koge, President; Sandy Sweitzer, Treasurer. Former Name: Good Time Clock Shop.

■ 13417 ■ Pacific Group International
2633 S Dupont, Ste. A
Anaheim, CA 92806
Phone: (714)634-4171   Fax: (714)634-4581
Products: Flags and flag poles; Windsocks; Toys. SICs: 5199 (Nondurable Goods Nec); 5092 (Toys & Hobby Goods & Supplies).

■ 13418 ■ Patriotic Fireworks Inc.
1314 S High School Rd.
Indianapolis, IN 46241-3129
Phone: (317)243-7469   Fax: (317)484-9148
Products: Party supplies; Wedding supplies; Holiday supplies; Halloween supplies; Fireworks. SICs: 5199 (Nondurable Goods Nec); 5092 (Toys & Hobby Goods & Supplies). Officers: Ron Surenkamp, President.

■ 13419 ■ Peenware International
7171 Harwin Dr., Stes. 208-210
Houston, TX 77036
Phone: (713)266-0137   Fax: (713)266-0006
Products: Gifts and novelties; Flags, banners, and similar emblems. SIC: 5199 (Nondurable Goods Nec).

■ 13420 ■ Pepline/Wincraft
1124 W 5th St.
Winona, MN 55987
Phone: (507)454-5510
Free: (800)533-8006   Fax: (507)454-6403
Products: Gifts and novelties; Cards, including picture postcards, souvenir cards, etc. SIC: 5199 (Nondurable Goods Nec). Sales: $18,000,000 (2000). Emp: 499. Officers: Dick Pope.

■ 13421 ■ Pioneer Photo Albums Inc.
9801 Deering Ave.
Chatsworth, CA 91311-4304
Phone: (818)882-2161   Fax: (818)882-6239
E-mail: pioneer@pioneerphotoalbums.com
Products: Photo albums and scrapbooks. SIC: 5112 (Stationery & Office Supplies). Est: 1952. Sales: $70,000,000 (1999). Emp: 270. Officers: Shell Plutsky; D. D. Plutsky.

■ 13422 ■ PK Imports Inc.
1225 Broadway, Ste. 609
New York, NY 10001
Phone: (212)683-9350   Fax: (212)532-1468
Products: Brass handcrafted gift items. SIC: 5199 (Nondurable Goods Nec).

■ 13423 ■ Plastic Dress-Up Co.
11077 E Rush St.
South El Monte, CA 91733
Phone: (626)442-7711
Products: Plastic trophy components. SIC: 5162 (Plastics Materials & Basic Shapes). Officers: David P. Bates, Sales Mgr.

■ 13424 ■ Posters Please Inc.
37 Riverside Dr.
New York, NY 10023
Phone: (212)787-4000
Products: Antique advertising posters. SIC: 5199 (Nondurable Goods Nec).

■ 13425 ■ Pottery Manufacturing and Distributing Inc.
18881 S Hoover St.
Gardena, CA 90248-4284
Phone: (310)323-7754
Free: (800)991-9914   Fax: (310)323-6613
E-mail: potterymfg@earthlink.net
URL: http://www.potterymfg.com
Products: Imported Italian, Mexican, Chinese, and Malaysian terra cotta pottery. SIC: 5023 (Homefurnishings). Est: 1973. Emp: 49. Officers: Carol Jones.

■ 13426 ■ Albert E. Price Inc.
PO Box 607
Bellmawr, NJ 08031
Phone: (609)933-1111   Fax: (609)933-0303
Products: Picture frames; Music boxes; Ceramic and porcelain trinket boxes. SIC: 5199 (Nondurable Goods Nec). Est: 1929. Sales: $13,000,000 (2000). Emp:

100. Officers: J. Price, President; E. Cummings, Treasurer; B. Price, Dir. of Marketing.

■ 13427 ■ Prime Resources Corp.
1100 Boston Ave.
Bridgeport, CT 06610
Phone: (203)331-9100   Fax: (203)330-0123
Products: Key tags. SIC: 5199 (Nondurable Goods Nec). Est: 1978. Sales: $8,000,000 (2000). Emp: 90. Officers: R. Lederer, President; Jerry Russo, CFO; Herb Levy, Vice President.

■ 13428 ■ Print Gallery Inc.
29203 Northwestern Hwy.
Southfield, MI 48034
Phone: (248)356-5454   Fax: (248)356-5421
Products: Posters. SIC: 5199 (Nondurable Goods Nec). Sales: $2,000,000 (2000). Emp: 5. Officers: Diane Shipley.

■ 13429 ■ Promotions Plus
112 N University Dr., Ste. L-126
Fargo, ND 58102
Phone: (701)236-7774   Fax: (701)236-5253
Products: Advertising specialties; Gifts and novelties. SIC: 5199 (Nondurable Goods Nec). Est: 1982. Emp: 5. Officers: Nona Martens, Owner.

■ 13430 ■ Pryor Novelty Co., Inc.
1991 Hwy. 52
PO Box 4
Tuscumbia, MO 65082-0004
Phone: (573)369-2354
Free: (800)325-0270   Fax: (573)369-2356
E-mail: pncgifts@pncgifts.com
URL: http://www.pncgifts.com
Products: Gifts; Small boxes; Desk accessories. SICs: 5199 (Nondurable Goods Nec); 5099 (Durable Goods Nec). Est: 1937. Sales: $800,000 (2000). Emp: 35. Officers: Tim Pryor, President.

■ 13431 ■ QCU Inc.
3056 Palm Ave.
Warehouses 2 & 3
Ft. Myers, FL 33901
Phone: (941)332-2205
Free: (800)729-2205   Fax: (941)332-2093
URL: http://www.qcu.com
Products: Gift and gourmet products, including baskets, boxes, mugs, shrink wrap, ribbons, balloons, teacups, trays, wine glasses, bath and fragrance products, baby gifts, romantic gifts, books, golf gifts, fishing gifts, seasonal gifts, cello wrap and basket bags, shredded fillers, gormet foods, beverages, and candy. SICs: 5199 (Nondurable Goods Nec); 5149 (Groceries & Related Products Nec); 5193 (Flowers & Florists' Supplies). Est: 1989. Sales: $500,000 (2000). Emp: 4. Officers: Jeanne Gates, President, e-mail: Jeanne@qcu.com; Donald Morley, VP & General Merchandising Mgr., e-mail: Don@qcu.com. Former Name: QCU Inc.

■ 13432 ■ Rainbow Sales Distributing
1637 S 83rd St.
West Allis, WI 53214
Phone: (414)774-4949   Fax: (414)774-6965
Products: Gifts and novelties. SIC: 5199 (Nondurable Goods Nec). Est: 1985. Sales: $2,000,000 (2000). Emp: 10. Officers: David Gray, President. Former Name: Distributing Inc.

■ 13433 ■ Ramson's Imports
5159 Sinclair Rd.
Columbus, OH 43229
Phone: (614)846-4447
Free: (800)669-0874   Fax: (614)846-4809
E-mail: ramsonsinc@aol.com
URL: http://www.ramsoninc.com
Products: Novelties; General merchandise; Toys; Flags, Lighters; Jewelry; Clocks; Masks; Artificial flowers; Professional sport products. SICs: 5199 (Nondurable Goods Nec); 5092 (Toys & Hobby Goods & Supplies); 5094 (Jewelry & Precious Stones). Est: 1972. Emp: 15. Officers: Mahesh Chabria, Sales/Marketing Contact, e-mail: RamsonsInc@aol.com; Nita Chabria, Customer Service Contact, e-mail: RamsonsInc@aol.com.

■ 13434 ■ Ray's Beaver Bag
727 Las Vegas Blvd. S
Las Vegas, NV 89101
Phone: (702)386-8746
Products: Gift items, including antiques. SIC: 5199 (Nondurable Goods Nec).

■ 13435 ■ RCF Inc.
Altlanta Gift Mart
230 Spring St. NW, Ste. 1127
Atlanta, GA 30303
Phone: (404)688-0304   Fax: (404)577-0550
Products: Gift items, including candles, crystal, and linens. SIC: 5199 (Nondurable Goods Nec). Est: 1982. Emp: 4. Officers: Fred Wright; Steve Akins; Jane Oliver.

■ 13436 ■ Ri-Mat Enterprises Inc.
PO Box 606
San Gabriel, CA 91776
Phone: (626)287-9793   Fax: (213)283-1155
Products: Wall accessories and wall paintings. SIC: 5199 (Nondurable Goods Nec). Est: 1962. Sales: $2,000,000 (2000). Emp: 10. Officers: Richard T. Matsuura, President & Chairman of the Board; Lorena Beas, Controller.

■ 13437 ■ RNM Specialty Co.
PO Box 542
Bethpage, NY 11714
Phone: (516)933-1940
E-mail: suncatch@optonline.net
URL: http://www.wholesalecentral.com/suncatchers
Products: Stained glass like Suncatchers; Night lights-bases/bulbs; 3D magnetic photo frames; Puff magnetic photo frames; 3D photo night lights. SIC: 5199 (Nondurable Goods Nec). Est: 1989. Sales: $5,000,000 (2000). Emp: 16. Officers: Richard Gallo.

■ 13438 ■ Rock Mirrors Inc.
130 Ferry Ave.
Oaklyn, NJ 08107
Phones: (609)962-6720   (609)962-6726
Fax: (609)962-6667
Products: Mirror and picture frames. SIC: 5199 (Nondurable Goods Nec). Est: 1976. Sales: $3,500,000 (2000). Emp: 36. Officers: Robert Neiman.

■ 13439 ■ Roman Inc.
555 Lawrence Ave.
Roselle, IL 60172
Phone: (630)529-3000
Free: (800)540-4754   Fax: (630)529-1121
Products: Giftware and religious items. SIC: 5199 (Nondurable Goods Nec). Sales: $117,000,000 (2000). Emp: 350. Officers: Ronald Jedlinski, CEO & President; Lee Hanson, COO.

■ 13440 ■ Sangamon Co.
PO Box 410
Taylorville, IL 62568
Phone: (217)824-2261
Products: Greeting cards. SIC: 5113 (Industrial & Personal Service Paper). Est: 1931. Sales: $45,000,000 (2000). Emp: 300. Officers: G.A. Westrick, President; E. Buss, Treasurer; T. Tisdale, VP of Marketing.

■ 13441 ■ Sangray Corporation
2318 Lakeview Ave.
PO Box 2388
Pueblo, CO 81004
Phone: (719)564-3408
Free: (800)525-5660   Fax: (719)564-0956
E-mail: sangray@rmi.net
URL: http://www.sangray.com
Products: Ceramic tiles; Refrigerator magnets; Wood and gift items. SIC: 5199 (Nondurable Goods Nec). Est: 1971. Emp: 30. Officers: James Stuart, President; Darin Stuart, Vice President; Christine Stewart, Sec. & Treas.; Barbara Straw, Sales & Marketing Contact.

■ 13442 ■ Sanrio Inc.
570 Eccles Ave.
South San Francisco, CA 94080
Phone: (650)952-2880   Fax: (650)872-2730
Products: Gifts. SICs: 5092 (Toys & Hobby Goods & Supplies); 5112 (Stationery & Office Supplies). Est:

1976. **Sales:** $150,000,000 (2000). **Emp:** 500. **Officers:** K. Tsuji, President; Katsumi Murakami, CFO; Peter Gastaldi, Exec. VP; Randall C. Patterson, VP of Sales.

■ **13443** ■ **Sarah's Attic Inc.**
PO Box 448
Chesaning, MI 48616
Phone: (517)845-3990
Free: (800)437-4363 **Fax:** (517)845-3477
E-mail: info@sarahsattic.com
URL: http://www.sarahsattic.com
Products: Painted figurines. **SIC:** 5199 (Nondurable Goods Nec). **Est:** 1983. **Emp:** 20. **Officers:** Sally A. Schultz, CEO; Timothy J. Shultz, VP of Finance.

■ **13444** ■ **Nathan Schecter and Sons, Inc.**
B & Lippincott St.
Philadelphia, PA 19134
Phone: (215)634-2400
Free: (800)342-9444 **Fax:** (215)739-8840
E-mail: mschecter@aol.com
Products: Christmas decorations. **SIC:** 5199 (Nondurable Goods Nec). **Est:** 1913. **Sales:** $4,000,000 (2000). **Emp:** 8. **Officers:** Martin Schecter, President.

■ **13445** ■ **Shell's Bags Hats**
PO Box 1701
Lahaina, HI 96761
Phone: (808)669-8349 **Fax:** (808)667-2706
Products: Novelty items, including shells, bags, and hats. **SIC:** 5199 (Nondurable Goods Nec). **Emp:** 3. **Officers:** Agneta Falk-Hansson, Purchaser.

■ **13446** ■ **Shiau's Trading Co.**
67-21 Fresh Meadow Ln.
Flushing, NY 11365
Phone: (718)539-8276 **Fax:** (718)463-2795
Products: Handcrafted wood carvings. **SIC:** 5199 (Nondurable Goods Nec).

■ **13447** ■ **S.N.S. International Trading**
9910 Harwin Dr.
Houston, TX 77036
Phone: (713)789-9847
Free: (800)667-3524 **Fax:** (713)789-8282
Products: Flags and banners, including military, college, sports teams, seasonal, decorative, historical, car racing, rock groups, and confederate flags. **SIC:** 5199 (Nondurable Goods Nec). **Est:** 1985. **Sales:** $1,000,000 (2000). **Emp:** 5. **Officers:** Sharif Kesbeh; Fawzi Kesbeh.

■ **13448** ■ **Southern California Trophy Co.**
2515 S Broadway
Los Angeles, CA 90007-2729
Phone: (213)623-3166 **Fax:** (213)746-9180
E-mail: sctc@pacbell.net
URL: http://www.socaltrophy.com
Products: Trophies and plaques; Desk accessories. **SIC:** 5199 (Nondurable Goods Nec). **Est:** 1927. **Sales:** $2,000,000 (2000). **Emp:** 19. **Officers:** Karl Bathke.

■ **13449** ■ **Southwest Import Co.**
7047 Casa Loma
Dallas, TX 75214
Phone: (214)327-8006
Free: (800)521-8091 **Fax:** (214)321-1208
Products: Novelty flags and license plates. **SIC:** 5199 (Nondurable Goods Nec).

■ **13450** ■ **Specially Yours Inc.**
3651 Joppa Ave. S
Minneapolis, MN 55416-4815
Phone: (612)927-4246 **Fax:** (612)927-4281
Products: Gifts and novelties. **SIC:** 5199 (Nondurable Goods Nec). **Officers:** Joanne Glotter, President.

■ **13451** ■ **Specialty Merchandise Corp.**
9401 De Soto Ave.
Chatsworth, CA 91311-4991
Phone: (818)998-3300 **Fax:** (818)998-2635
Products: Gift items. **SIC:** 5199 (Nondurable Goods Nec). **Est:** 1955. **Sales:** $30,000,000 (2000). **Emp:** 200. **Officers:** Mark Schwartz, President; J.P. Wolk, Controller.

■ **13452** ■ **Sports Impressions Corp.**
225 Windsor Dr.
Itasca, IL 60143
Phone: (708)875-5300
Free: (800)436-3726 **Fax:** (708)875-5352
Products: Figurines and plates imprinted with sports designs. **SIC:** 5199 (Nondurable Goods Nec). **Emp:** 600. **Officers:** Eugene Freedman, President.

■ **13453** ■ **Star Creation Inc.**
1934 Westminster St.
Providence, RI 02909
Phone: (401)421-9454 **Fax:** (401)274-1788
Products: Victorian reproductions. **SIC:** 5199 (Nondurable Goods Nec).

■ **13454** ■ **Style Asia Inc.**
450 Barell Ave.
Carlstadt, NJ 07072-2810
Phone: (201)532-5720 **Fax:** (201)532-6476
Products: Novelties and general gift items; Clocks; Calculators; Stationery. **SICs:** 5199 (Nondurable Goods Nec); 5094 (Jewelry & Precious Stones); 5044 (Office Equipment); 5112 (Stationery & Office Supplies).

■ **13455** ■ **Sullivan's**
PO Box 5361
Sioux Falls, SD 57117-5361
Phone: (605)339-4274
URL: http://www.sullivangift.com
Products: Giftware. **SIC:** 5199 (Nondurable Goods Nec). **Est:** 1968. **Sales:** $30,000,000 (2000). **Emp:** 80. **Officers:** Marian Sullivan, President; William Sullivan, Vice President, e-mail: wsullivan2@aol.com.

■ **13456** ■ **Sun/Day Distributor Corp.**
1940 Railroad Dr.
Sacramento, CA 95815-3514
Phone: (916)922-4370
Free: (800)235-1419 **Fax:** (916)921-5504
Products: Arts and crafts supplies. **SIC:** 5199 (Nondurable Goods Nec).

■ **13457** ■ **Sun & Fun Specialties Inc.**
PO Box 1406
Las Cruces, NM 88004-1406
Phone: (505)526-8906 **Fax:** (505)526-8906
Products: Sunglasses; Hats; Novelty items. **SICs:** 5199 (Nondurable Goods Nec); 5136 (Men's/Boys' Clothing); 5137 (Women's/Children's Clothing). **Officers:** Randy Lancaster, President.

■ **13458** ■ **Sun Hing Trading Company Inc.**
16816 Johnson Dr.
City of Industry, CA 91745
Phone: (626)330-0667 **Fax:** (818)330-0937
Products: Oriental furniture, arts, and crafts. **SICs:** 5199 (Nondurable Goods Nec); 5021 (Furniture). **Est:** 1991. **Emp:** 10. **Officers:** Lee Yee Soon, President, e-mail: sunhinginc@hotmail.com.

■ **13459** ■ **Sunset Supply**
2411 S Hwy. 79
PO Box 2248
Rapid City, SD 57701
Phone: (605)342-5220
Free: (800)456-1179 **Fax:** (605)342-7166
Products: T-shirts; Gifts and novelties; Cards, including picture postcards, souvenir cards, etc. **SICs:** 5199 (Nondurable Goods Nec); 5136 (Men's/Boys' Clothing); 5137 (Women's/Children's Clothing). **Emp:** 6. **Officers:** Bill Petersen.

■ **13460** ■ **T & E Wholesale Outlet**
1019 S Craig Ave.
Covington, VA 24426-2248
Phone: (540)962-0454 **Fax:** (540)962-0477
Products: Automotive accessories; Dolls; Gifts and novelties. **SICs:** 5199 (Nondurable Goods Nec); 5013 (Motor Vehicle Supplies & New Parts); 5092 (Toys & Hobby Goods & Supplies). **Officers:** George Clemons, Owner.

■ **13461** ■ **TCC Industries Inc.**
PO Box 684925
Austin, TX 78768
Phone: (512)708-5000 **Fax:** (512)494-0416
Products: Souvenir, novelty, and gift items. **SIC:** 5199

(Nondurable Goods Nec). **Sales:** $7,100,000 (2000). **Emp:** 70. **Officers:** Robert Thomajan, President.

■ **13462** ■ **TEM Inc.**
302 York
Gettysburg, PA 17325-1930
Phone: (717)334-6251 **Fax:** (717)334-9174
Products: Gifts and novelties; Cards, including picture postcards, souvenir cards, etc. **SIC:** 5199 (Nondurable Goods Nec). **Sales:** $8,000,000 (2000). **Emp:** 50.

■ **13463** ■ **Thomas Nelson Inc.**
501 Nelson Pl.
Nashville, TN 37214-1000
Phone: (615)889-9000
Products: Gifts, stationery, and music products. **SICs:** 5112 (Stationery & Office Supplies); 5065 (Electronic Parts & Equipment Nec). **Sales:** $253,000,000 (2000). **Emp:** 1,250. **Officers:** Sam Moore, CEO & President; Vance Lawson, VP of Finance.

■ **13464** ■ **Tobe Turpen's Indian Trading Co.**
1710 S 2nd St.
Gallup, NM 87301
Phone: (505)722-3806
Products: Arts and crafts products. **SIC:** 5094 (Jewelry & Precious Stones). **Est:** 1939. **Sales:** $11,000,000 (2000). **Emp:** 20. **Officers:** Tobe Turpen Jr. Jr., President; Joyce Kozeliski, Treasurer & Secty.

■ **13465** ■ **Unique Crafters Co.**
10702 Trenton Ave.
St. Louis, MO 63132
Phone: (314)427-5310
Free: (800)747-4926 **Fax:** (314)427-5312
E-mail: info@uniquecrafterscompany.com
URL: http://www.uniquecrafterscompany.com
Products: Gifts and novelties; Toys; Educational products. **SICs:** 5199 (Nondurable Goods Nec); 5092 (Toys & Hobby Goods & Supplies); 5099 (Durable Goods Nec). **Est:** 1962. **Emp:** 6. **Officers:** Alan Zarkowsky, Vice President, e-mail: alan@ uniquecrafterscompany.com.

■ **13466** ■ **Unique Industries Inc. (Philadelphia, PA)**
2400 S Weccacoe Ave.
Philadelphia, PA 19148
Phone: (215)336-4300 **Fax:** (215)334-7869
Products: Party supplies. **SIC:** 5092 (Toys & Hobby Goods & Supplies). **Sales:** $45,000,000 (2000). **Emp:** 150. **Officers:** Everett Novak, President; Patricia Karpinski, VP of Finance.

■ **13467** ■ **Vicki Lane Design**
303 S 5th
Springfield, OR 97477-7507
Phone: (541)726-0397 **Fax:** (541)747-1957
Products: Gifts and novelties. **SIC:** 5199 (Nondurable Goods Nec). **Est:** 1983. **Emp:** 40. **Officers:** Vicki Anderson; Ron Anderson.

■ **13468** ■ **Wagners**
601 W Cook St.
Wendell, NC 27591
Phone: (919)365-6669
Free: (800)551-0247 **Fax:** (919)365-4804
Products: Party favors. **SIC:** 5099 (Durable Goods Nec). **Est:** 1970.

■ **13469** ■ **Warrior Inc.**
825 S Dickerson Rd., Apt. 175
Goodlettsville, TN 37072-1738
Phone: (615)859-0026 **Fax:** (615)859-0204
Products: T-shirts; Novelties. **SIC:** 5199 (Nondurable Goods Nec).

■ **13470** ■ **Fannie Watson Inc.**
2714 Riopelle St.
Detroit, MI 48207
Phone: (313)831-4438
Free: (800)203-6744 **Fax:** (313)831-0746
Products: Gift baskets; Packaging services. **SICs:** 5199 (Nondurable Goods Nec); 5113 (Industrial & Personal Service Paper). **Est:** 1983. **Sales:** $300,000 (2000). **Emp:** 8. **Officers:** Fannie Watson, President.

■ **13471** ■ **WB Stores Inc.**
35 Temple Pl.
Boston, MA 02111
Phone: (617)426-8549 **Fax:** (617)330-1977
Products: Handcrafted items. **SIC:** 5131 (Piece Goods
& Notions). **Est:** 1936. **Sales:** $4,000,000 (2000). **Emp:**
50. **Officers:** Stephen Rittenburg, President.

■ **13472** ■ **Wildlife Lithographs, Inc.**
PO Box 403
Dixon, IL 61021
Phone: (815)284-3871
Free: (800)523-1443 **Fax:** (815)284-8493
Products: Lithograph prints; Clock parts. **SICs:** 5199
(Nondurable Goods Nec); 5094 (Jewelry & Precious
Stones). **Officers:** John F. King.

■ **13473** ■ **William's Umbrella Co.**
1255 Post Rd.
Scarsdale, NY 10583
Phone: (914)472-2098
Products: Umbrellas; Parasols; Canes. **SIC:** 5199
(Nondurable Goods Nec). **Est:** 1949. **Officers:** William
M. Schwartzenberg, Owner.

■ **13474** ■ **Wills Co.**
301 4th Ave. SE
Waseca, MN 56093-3067
Phone: (507)835-2670 **Fax:** (507)835-2686
Products: Ribbons for gifts; Seasonal cards; Gifts and
novelties; Dolls. **SICs:** 5199 (Nondurable Goods Nec);
5092 (Toys & Hobby Goods & Supplies); 5112
(Stationery & Office Supplies); 5113 (Industrial &

Personal Service Paper). **Emp:** 49. **Officers:** Richard
Will.

■ **13475** ■ **Sam Zukerman and Sons Inc.**
1650 Smallman St.
Pittsburgh, PA 15222
Phone: (412)261-0818
Free: (800)375-0818 **Fax:** (412)261-5890
Products: Imported wicker baskets; Seasonal wreaths;
Centerpieces; Cemetery vases; Gift baskets;
Packaging supplies. **SIC:** 5199 (Nondurable Goods
Nec). **Est:** 1952. **Sales:** $900,000 (2000). **Emp:** 4.
Officers: Ron Geistman, President; Linda Geistman,
Vice President.

(20) Guns and Weapons

Entries in this section are arranged alphabetically by company name. When the company name is a personal name, the company name is alphabetized by the surname unless the first name or initial(s) are part of a trade name. See the User's Guide at the front of this directory for additional information.

■ 13476 ■ **Arizona Sportsman, Inc.**
5146 E Pima St.
Tucson, AZ 85712
Phone: (520)321-3878 **Fax:** (520)321-3864
URL: http://www.arizona-sportsman.com
Products: Firearms. **SIC:** 5099 (Durable Goods Nec).
Est: 1992. **Sales:** $20,000,000 (2000). **Emp:** 150.
Officers: Glenn Links, CEO. **Former Name:** Lathrop's
Shooters Supply Inc.

■ 13477 ■ **Brownells Inc.**
200 S Front St.
Montezuma, IA 50171
Phone: (515)623-5401 **Fax:** (515)623-3896
Products: Gun parts and related items, including
screwdriver kits; Books. **SICs:** 5091 (Sporting &
Recreational Goods); 5192 (Books, Periodicals &
Newspapers). **Est:** 1939. **Sales:** $10,000,000 (2000).
Emp: 95. **Officers:** F. Brownell III, President.

■ 13478 ■ **Browning**
1 Browning Pl.
Morgan, UT 84050-9326
Phone: (801)876-2711 **Fax:** (801)876-3331
URL: http://www.browning.com
Products: Firearms; Safes; Outdoor apparel and
accessories. **SIC:** 5091 (Sporting & Recreational
Goods). **Est:** 1927. **Sales:** $200,000,000 (1999).
Officers: Charles Gueuremont, President, e-mail:
charlesg@browning.com; Bertrand Devilliers, VP of
Finance; Roger Koenig, Information Systems Mgr.;
Dave Rich, Human Resources Mgr.

■ 13479 ■ **Bumble Bee Wholesale**
12521 Oxnard St.
North Hollywood, CA 91606
Phone: (818)985-2329 **Fax:** (818)985-6914
Products: Firearms and accessories. **SIC:** 5091
(Sporting & Recreational Goods). **Est:** 1968. **Sales:**
$13,000,000 (2000). **Emp:** 25. **Officers:** Robert Kahn,
CEO.

■ 13480 ■ **Camel Outdoor Products Inc.**
PO Box 7225
Norcross, GA 30091
Phone: (404)449-4687
Products: Black powder guns; Tents and camp
accessories. **SIC:** 5199 (Nondurable Goods Nec). **Est:**
1919. **Sales:** $6,000,000 (2000). **Emp:** 40. **Officers:**
Robert Hickey, President.

■ 13481 ■ **Clark's Gun Shop**
1006 James Madison Hwy.
Warrenton, VA 20186-7820
Phone: (703)439-8988 **Fax:** (703)439-2825
Products: Firearms and hunting accessories;
Fireworks; Souvenirs; Fishing tackle; Canoes. **SICs:**
5091 (Sporting & Recreational Goods); 5099 (Durable
Goods Nec). **Est:** 1957. **Sales:** $3,000,000 (2000).
Emp: 19. **Officers:** John M. Clark; Stephen L. Clark.
Alternate Name: Clark Brothers. **Alternate Name:** The
Red Shed.

■ 13482 ■ **Cogdells Westview Inc.**
615 N Valley Mills
Waco, TX 76710
Phone: (254)772-8224
Products: Used collectible firearms. **SIC:** 5091
(Sporting & Recreational Goods). **Est:** 1932. **Sales:**
$500,000 (2000). **Emp:** 1. **Officers:** Leo H. Bradshaw
Jr., President.

■ 13483 ■ **Connecticut Valley Arms Inc.**
5988 Peachtree Corners E
Norcross, GA 30071
Phone: (404)449-4687 **Fax:** (404)242-8546
Products: Black powder guns. **SIC:** 5091 (Sporting &
Recreational Goods). **Est:** 1971. **Sales:** $15,000,000
(2000). **Emp:** 49. **Officers:** R.R. Hickey, President.

■ 13484 ■ **CR Specialty Co.**
1701 Baltimore
Kansas City, MO 64108
Phone: (816)221-3550 **Fax:** (816)421-3036
Products: Archery equipment; Guns and ammunition;
Clothing. **SICs:** 5091 (Sporting & Recreational Goods);
5099 (Durable Goods Nec); 5136 (Men's/Boys'
Clothing); 5137 (Women's/Children's Clothing).

■ 13485 ■ **Crosman Corporation**
Rtes. 5 & 20
East Bloomfield, NY 14443
Phone: (716)657-6161 **Fax:** (716)657-5405
E-mail: info@crosman.com
URL: http://www.crosman.com; www.sheridanusa.
com
Products: Air guns and accessories; Paintball makers
and accessories. **SIC:** 5091 (Sporting & Recreational
Goods). **Est:** 1923. **Emp:** 350. **Officers:** Leonard
Pickett, President; Mary Pickett, VP of Operations;
Lloyd Heise, VP of Marketing & Sales. **Former Name:**
Crosman Seed Corp.

■ 13486 ■ **Davidson's**
6100 Wilkinson Dr.
Prescott, AZ 86301
Phone: (520)776-8055
Products: Firearms. **SIC:** 5091 (Sporting &
Recreational Goods).

■ 13487 ■ **DayMark Corp.**
PO Box 350
Delmar, NY 12054
Phone: (518)439-9985 **Fax:** (518)439-9602
E-mail: daymarkco@aol.com
Products: Ammunition and firearms. **SIC:** 5099
(Durable Goods Nec). **Emp:** 13. **Officers:** Bradley M.
Day, President, e-mail: bradleymd@aol.com. **Former
Name:** Levin-Liston and Associates Inc.

■ 13488 ■ **Deans Firearms, Ltd.**
7024 W Colfax
Lakewood, CO 80215
Phone: (303)234-1111 **Fax:** (303)234-5678
Products: Shooting accessories; Firearms. **SICs:** 5091
(Sporting & Recreational Goods); 5099 (Durable Goods
Nec).

■ 13489 ■ **Dixon Muzzleloading Shop**
9952 Kunkels Mill Rd.
Kempton, PA 19529
Phone: (610)756-6271 **Fax:** (610)756-4201
Products: Antiques, including guns. **SIC:** 5091
(Sporting & Recreational Goods). **Est:** 1975.

■ 13490 ■ **Ellett Brothers Inc.**
PO Box 128
Chapin, SC 29036
Phone: (803)345-3751
Free: (800)845-3711 **Fax:** (803)345-1820
URL: http://www.ellettbrothers.com
Products: Hunting, shooting,archery,camping, and
marine. **SIC:** 5091 (Sporting & Recreational Goods).
Est: 1933. **Sales:** $150,000,000 (2000). **Emp:** 445.
Officers: Joseph F. Murray Jr., CEO & President;
George Loney, VP & CFO; Doug McMillan, Exec. VP;
Donna Matthews, Director of Sales, e-mail:
DonnaMatthews@ellett.com.

■ 13491 ■ **F.B.F. Inc.**
1925 N McArthur Blvd.
Oklahoma City, OK 73127
Phone: (405)789-0651
Free: (800)323-4867 **Fax:** (405)789-5810
E-mail: info@fbfguns.com
URL: http://www.fbfguns.com
Products: Firearms. **SICs:** 5091 (Sporting &
Recreational Goods); 5099 (Durable Goods Nec). **Est:**
1967. **Emp:** 32. **Former Name:** Fred Baker Firearms.

■ 13492 ■ **GSI, Inc.**
PO Box 129
Trussville, AL 35173
Phone: (205)655-8299 **Fax:** (205)655-7078
E-mail: info@gsifirearms.com
URL: http://www.gsifirearms.com
Products: Firearms. **SICs:** 5091 (Sporting &
Recreational Goods); 5099 (Durable Goods Nec). **Est:**
1983. **Sales:** $6,000,000 (1999). **Emp:** 25. **Officers:**
Donald Wood, President. **Former Name:** Gun South
Inc.

■ 13493 ■ **Guns Of Yesteryear**
3936 Chattanooga Rd.
Tunnel Hill, GA 30755
Phone: (706)673-2506
Products: Guns, including antique guns and
accessories. **SIC:** 5091 (Sporting & Recreational
Goods).

■ 13494 ■ **Heckler and Koch Inc.**
21480 Pacific Blvd.
Sterling, VA 20166-8903
Phone: (703)450-1900
Products: Firearms. **SICs:** 5099 (Durable Goods Nec);
5091 (Sporting & Recreational Goods).

■ 13495 ■ **Heritage Manufacturing Inc.**
4530 NW 135th St.
Opa Locka, FL 33054
Phone: (305)685-5966 **Fax:** (305)687-6721
Products: Handguns. **SICs:** 5091 (Sporting &
Recreational Goods); 5099 (Durable Goods Nec). **Est:**
1966. **Sales:** $1,000,000 (2000). **Emp:** 11. **Officers:**

Jay Bernkront, President; James Sprague, VP of Marketing.

■ 13496 ■ John Jovino Company, Inc.
5 Center Market Pl.
New York, NY 10013
Phone: (212)925-4881   **Fax:** (212)966-4986
Products: Small firearms(including combination rifle-shotguns). **SICs:** 5091 (Sporting & Recreational Goods); 5099 (Durable Goods Nec). **Est:** 1911. **Sales:** $500,000 (2000). **Emp:** 5. **Officers:** Anthony Imperato, Sales Mgr.

■ 13497 ■ Ledford's Trading Post
1833 12th Ave. NE
Hickory, NC 28601
Phone: (704)327-0055
Products: Guns. **SICs:** 5091 (Sporting & Recreational Goods); 5099 (Durable Goods Nec).

■ 13498 ■ Lipsey's Inc.
PO Box 83280
Baton Rouge, LA 70884
Phone: (225)755-1333
Free: (800)666-1333   **Fax:** (225)755-3333
E-mail: firearms@lipseys.com
URL: http://www.lipseys.com
Products: Firearms. **SICs:** 5091 (Sporting & Recreational Goods); 5099 (Durable Goods Nec). **Est:** 1953. **Emp:** 25. **Officers:** Richard Lipsey, President.

■ 13499 ■ Log Cabin Sport Shop
8010 Lafayette Rd.
Lodi, OH 44254
Phone: (330)948-1082   **Fax:** (330)948-4307
Products: Black powder firearms and accessories. **SIC:** 5091 (Sporting & Recreational Goods).

■ 13500 ■ LSI (Legacy Sports International LLC)
10 Prince St.
Alexandria, VA 22314
Phone: (703)739-1560   **Fax:** (703)549-7826
URL: http://www.legacysports.com
Products: Howa sporting rifles. **SICs:** 5091 (Sporting & Recreational Goods); 5099 (Durable Goods Nec). **Est:** 1999. **Sales:** $3,000,000 (2000). **Emp:** 6. **Officers:** David L. MacGillivray, President. **Former Name:** International Armament Corp.

■ 13501 ■ Marksman Products Inc.
5482 Argosy Ave.
Huntington Beach, CA 92649-1039
Phone: (714)898-7535   **Fax:** (714)891-0782
Products: Air pistols, air rifles, slingshots. **SIC:** 5091 (Sporting & Recreational Goods). **Sales:** $2,000,000 (2000). **Emp:** 99. **Officers:** Robert A. Eck.

■ 13502 ■ Bob Moates Sport Shop Inc.
10418 Hull St.
Midlothian, VA 23112
Phone: (804)276-2293   **Fax:** (804)276-2332
URL: http://www.shopva/bobmoates.com
Products: Sporting firearms; Fishing tackle and equipment; Archery equipment. **SIC:** 5091 (Sporting & Recreational Goods). **Est:** 1960. **Sales:** $500,000 (2000). **Emp:** 11. **Officers:** Bob Moates.

■ 13503 ■ Mountain State Muzzleloading Supplies, Inc.
RR 2, Box 154-1
Williamstown, WV 26187
Phone: (304)375-7842
Free: (800)445-1776   **Fax:** (304)375-3737
E-mail: orders@mtnstatemuzzleloading.com
URL: http://www.mtnstatemuzzleloading.com
Products: Muzzleloading guns and accessories. **SICs:** 5091 (Sporting & Recreational Goods); 5099 (Durable Goods Nec). **Est:** 1971. **Sales:** $1,900,000 (2000). **Emp:** 8. **Officers:** Fred Lambert; Terry Lambert,

Sales/Marketing Contact; Mike Lambert, Customer Service Contact.

■ 13504 ■ Numrich Gunparts Corp.
226 Williams Ln.
West Hurley, NY 12491
Phone: (914)679-2417   **Fax:** 877-486-7278
E-mail: info@gunpartscorp.com
URL: http://www.gunpartscorp.com
Products: Guns; Gun parts. **SICs:** 5099 (Durable Goods Nec); 5091 (Sporting & Recreational Goods). **Est:** 1986. **Sales:** $18,000,000 (2000). **Emp:** 85. **Officers:** Gregory M. Jenks, President; Linda Munro, Sales/Marketing Contact, e-mail: linda@ gunpartscorp.com; Cassandra Hamed, Customer Service Contact, e-mail: cass@gunpartscorp.com; Diane Gulnick, Human Resources Contact. **Former Name:** Gun Parts Corp.

■ 13505 ■ RSR Group Florida, Inc.
4405 Metric Dr.
Winter Park, FL 32792
Phone: (407)677-1000
Free: (800)541-4867   **Fax:** (407)677-4489
E-mail: salesfl@rsrwholesale.com
URL: http://www.rsrwholesale.com
Products: Sporting firearms and accessories. **SIC:** 5091 (Sporting & Recreational Goods). **Est:** 1977. **Emp:** 150. **Former Name:** RSR Wholesale Guns South Inc.

■ 13506 ■ RSR Group Texas, Inc.
1450 Post & Paddock Rd.
Grand Prairie, TX 75053
Phone: (972)602-3131
Free: (800)752-4867   **Fax:** (972)602-0727
URL: http://www.rsrwholesale.com
Products: Guns and Ammunition. **SIC:** 5091 (Sporting & Recreational Goods). **Est:** 1977. **Emp:** 150. **Officers:** Jarrod VanBrocklin, Sales Mgr.; Beatiz Atorresagasti, Marketing Mgr. **Former Name:** RSR Wholesale Guns Texas, Inc.

■ 13507 ■ RSR Wholesale Guns Inc.
21 Trolley Cir.
PO Box 60679
Rochester, NY 14606
Phone: (716)426-4380
Free: (800)458-4867   **Fax:** (716)426-3814
URL: http://www.salesny@rsrwholesale.com
Products: Sporting firearms. **SIC:** 5091 (Sporting & Recreational Goods). **Est:** 1977.

■ 13508 ■ RSR Wholesale Guns Inc.
4405 Metric Dr.
Winter Park, FL 32792
Phone: (407)677-4342
Products: Firearms. **SIC:** 5091 (Sporting & Recreational Goods). **Sales:** $49,000,000 (1992). **Emp:** 200.

■ 13509 ■ RSR Wholesale Guns Midwest, Inc.
8817 W Lynx Ave.
Milwaukee, WI 53225
Phone: (414)461-1111
Free: (800)832-4867   **Fax:** (414)461-9836
E-mail: saleswi@rsrwholesale.com
URL: http://rsrwholesale.com
Products: Guns and ammunition. **SIC:** 5091 (Sporting & Recreational Goods). **Est:** 1977. **Emp:** 150. **Officers:** Ken Schiedemeyer, Sales Mgr.

■ 13510 ■ RSR Wholesale Guns West, Inc.
4700 Aircenter Cir.
PO Box 71540
Reno, NV 89502
Phone: (702)827-2111
Free: (800)634-4867   **Fax:** (702)827-2380
Products: Sporting firearms. **SIC:** 5091 (Sporting & Recreational Goods).

■ 13511 ■ RSR Wholesale South Inc.
4405 Metric Dr.
Winter Park, FL 32792
Phone: (407)677-1000
Free: (800)541-4867   **Fax:** (407)677-4489
Products: Guns and weapons. **SIC:** 5099 (Durable Goods Nec).

■ 13512 ■ S & S Firearms
74-11 Myrtle Ave.
Glendale, NY 11385
Phone: (718)497-1100   **Fax:** (718)497-1105
E-mail: info@ssfirearms.com
URL: http://www.ssfirearms.com
Products: Antique U.S. military gun parts; U.S. military insignia and belt buckles. **SICs:** 5091 (Sporting & Recreational Goods); 5099 (Durable Goods Nec); 5136 (Men's/Boys' Clothing). **Est:** 1957. **Emp:** 3. **Officers:** E. Siess.

■ 13513 ■ Sile Distributors Inc.
7 Centre Market Pl.
New York, NY 10013
Phone: (212)925-4111   **Fax:** (212)925-3149
Products: Firearms and ammunition; Security equipment; Wood stocks and equipment. **SICs:** 5099 (Durable Goods Nec); 5091 (Sporting & Recreational Goods); 5063 (Electrical Apparatus & Equipment). **Est:** 1960. **Sales:** $10,000,000 (2000). **Emp:** 21. **Officers:** Dominic Derobertis, President; Charles Ursitti, Dir. of Marketing & Sales.

■ 13514 ■ Simmons Gun Specialty Inc.
20241 W 207th
Spring Hill, KS 66083
Phone: (913)686-3939   **Fax:** (913)686-3299
Products: Guns; Ammunition. **SICs:** 5091 (Sporting & Recreational Goods); 5099 (Durable Goods Nec). **Sales:** $25,000,000 (2000). **Emp:** 60. **Officers:** Terre Tanney, General Mgr.; Art Huffman, Sales Mgr.

■ 13515 ■ Tamiami Range and Gun Distributors Inc.
2925 SW 8th St.
Miami, FL 33135
Phone: (305)642-1941
Products: Guns. **SICs:** 5099 (Durable Goods Nec); 5091 (Sporting & Recreational Goods). **Sales:** $15,000,000 (2000). **Emp:** 30. **Officers:** John Kanton, President.

■ 13516 ■ Valley Gun of Baltimore
7719 Hartford Rd.
Baltimore, MD 21234
Phone: (410)668-2171   **Fax:** (410)668-6693
E-mail: abrmum@aol.com
URL: http://www.valleygunofbaltimore.com
Products: Firearms. **SIC:** 5091 (Sporting & Recreational Goods). **Est:** 1954. **Sales:** $1,250,000 (1999). **Emp:** 10. **Officers:** Sanford Abrams, President.

■ 13517 ■ Ye Old Black Powder Shop
994 W Midland Rd.
Auburn, MI 48611
Phone: (517)662-2271   **Fax:** (517)662-2666
Products: Guns, including muzzle loaders. **SIC:** 5091 (Sporting & Recreational Goods).

■ 13518 ■ Yeck Antique Firearms
579 Tecumseh St.
Dundee, MI 48131
Phone: (734)529-3456
Products: Antique firearms and supplies. **SIC:** 5091 (Sporting & Recreational Goods).

(21) Hardware

Entries in this section are arranged alphabetically by company name. When the company name is a personal name, the company name is alphabetized by the surname unless the first name or initial(s) are part of a trade name. See the User's Guide at the front of this directory for additional information.

■ 13519 ■ **A & H Turf & Specialties Inc.**
468 S Moore Ln.
Billings, MT 59101-4729
Phone: (406)245-8466 **Fax:** (406)245-0108
Products: Hardware. **SIC:** 5072 (Hardware). **Officers:** Mona Anderson, President.

■ 13520 ■ **AAA Supply Corp.**
608 Rte. 41
Schererville, IN 46375
Phone: (219)865-8500 **Fax:** (219)865-4244
Products: Steel; Contruction equipment, including ladders and anchor bolts. **SIC:** 5072 (Hardware). **Est:** 1965. **Sales:** $10,000,000 (2000). **Emp:** 25. **Officers:** M. Kikkert, President; Eleanor Kikkert, Treasurer & Secty.

■ 13521 ■ **AB Wholesale Co.**
710 S College Ave.
Bluefield, VA 24605-1639
Phone: (703)322-4686
Products: Hardware; Electrical appliances; General merchandise. **SICs:** 5072 (Hardware); 5064 (Electrical Appliances—Television & Radio); 5099 (Durable Goods Nec). **Sales:** $70,000,000 (1994). **Emp:** 110. **Officers:** Kaleel A. Ammar Jr., President & Chairman of the Board.

■ 13522 ■ **Ababa - QA**
1466 Pioneer Way No. 1
El Cajon, CA 92020
Phone: (619)440-1781 **Fax:** (619)440-5371
E-mail: sales@ababaqa.com
URL: http://www.ababaqa.com
Products: Hardware fasteners. **SICs:** 5072 (Hardware); 5085 (Industrial Supplies). **Est:** 1975. **Emp:** 31. **Officers:** Cathleen J. Law.

■ 13523 ■ **Abrasive-Tool Corp.**
1555 Emerson St.
Rochester, NY 14606
Phone: (716)254-4500 **Fax:** (716)254-2247
E-mail: InsideSales@atcsales.com
URL: http://www.atcsales.com
Products: Bonder and coated abrasive products; Tools, including cutting, carbide and precision tools. **SIC:** 5072 (Hardware). **Est:** 1968. **Sales:** $30,000,000 (2000). **Emp:** 45. **Officers:** M. Hanna.

■ 13524 ■ **Access International Marketing Inc.**
330 S Decatur, Ste. 322
Las Vegas, NV 89107
Phone: (702)870-3906 **Fax:** (702)870-3906
Products: Power hand tools; Industrial machinery; Cutlery; Farm machinery and equipment; Hand and edge tools. **SICs:** 5072 (Hardware); 5084 (Industrial Machinery & Equipment); 5023 (Homefurnishings); 5083 (Farm & Garden Machinery). **Officers:** David Mule, Vice President.

■ 13525 ■ **Ace Hardware Corp.**
8338 Oak St.
New Orleans, LA 70118
Phone: (504)861-4502 **Fax:** (504)861-4501
Products: Hardware, including fasteners, handtools, and power handtools; Household chemicals; Plumbing supplies; Electrical supplies. **SICs:** 5072 (Hardware); 5169 (Chemicals & Allied Products Nec); 5074 (Plumbing & Hydronic Heating Supplies); 5063 (Electrical Apparatus & Equipment). **Est:** 1929. **Sales:** $800,000 (2000). **Emp:** 7. **Officers:** Bruce Foret, Vice President.

■ 13526 ■ **Ace Hardware Corp.**
2200 Kensington Court
Oak Brook, IL 60523-2100
Phone: (630)990-6600 **Fax:** (630)990-6856
URL: http://www.acehardware.com
Products: Hardware. **SIC:** 5072 (Hardware). **Est:** 1924. **Sales:** $3,120,000,000 (1999). **Emp:** 4,900. **Officers:** David F. Hodnik, CEO & President, e-mail: hodnik@memo.acehardware.com; Rita Kahle, Sr. VP of Wholesale Sales, e-mail: kahle@memo.acehardware.com; Paul M. Ingevaldson, Sr. VP, International and Technology, e-mail: inge@memo.acehardware.com; Michael C. Bodzewski, VP, Marketing, Advertising & Retail Oper, e-mail: mbodz@memo.acehardware.com; Lori L. Bossmann, VP of Finance, e-mail: schoo@memo.acehardware.com; Ray A. Griffith, VP of Merchandising, e-mail: rgriff@memo.acehardware.com; David W. League, VP, General Counsel & Secty., e-mail: league@memo.acehardware.com; David F. Myer, VP, Retail Support, e-mail: dmyer@memo.acehardware.com; Fred J. Neer, VP of Human Resources, e-mail: fneer@memo.acehardware.com; Ken Nichols, VP, Retail Operations West, e-mail: knich@memo.acehardware.com.

■ 13527 ■ **Ace Tool Co.**
PO Box 1650
Pinellas Park, FL 33780
Phone: (813)544-4331 **Fax:** (813)544-6211
Products: Hand tools, pneumatic tools, hydraulic equipment. **SICs:** 5072 (Hardware); 5084 (Industrial Machinery & Equipment). **Sales:** $35,000,000 (1994). **Emp:** 120. **Officers:** Brian Nestor, President; Bill Brown, Controller.

■ 13528 ■ **Action Threaded Products Inc.**
6955 S Harlem Ave.
Bedford Park, IL 60638
Phone: (708)496-0100 **Fax:** (708)496-8086
Products: Fasteners. **SIC:** 5072 (Hardware). **Sales:** $10,000,000 (2000). **Emp:** 60. **Officers:** Gerald Ablan, President & Chairman of the Board; Mark Novak, Sales Mgr.

■ 13529 ■ **Action Tool Company Inc.**
1959 Tigertail Blvd.
Dania, FL 33004
Phone: (954)920-2700
Free: (800)233-0220 **Fax:** (954)920-8780
E-mail: acttool@aol.com
URL: http://www.acttool.com
Products: Tools and hardware. **SIC:** 5072 (Hardware). **Est:** 1981. **Sales:** $1,600,000 (2000). **Emp:** 4. **Officers:** Joel Lazar.

■ 13530 ■ **Active Screw and Fastener**
1065 Chase Ave.
Elk Grove Village, IL 60007-4827
Phone: (847)427-0500 **Fax:** (847)427-0550
Products: Screws and fasteners. **SICs:** 5072 (Hardware); 5085 (Industrial Supplies). **Est:** 1933. **Sales:** $10,000,000 (2000). **Emp:** 30. **Officers:** A. Granat, Chairman of the Board; Ken Granat, President; Marc Kaplan, General Mgr.

■ 13531 ■ **Adams Industries Inc.**
PO Box 291
Windsor Locks, CT 06096
Phone: (860)668-1201 **Fax:** (860)668-4139
Products: Hardware. **SIC:** 5088 (Transportation Equipment & Supplies). **Sales:** $9,000,000 (2000). **Emp:** 30. **Officers:** David Morgenstein, President.

■ 13532 ■ **Adams Supply Co.**
PO Box 2938
Torrance, CA 90501
Phone: (310)533-8088 **Fax:** (310)212-7939
Products: Military nuts, bolts, fasteners. **SICs:** 5072 (Hardware); 5085 (Industrial Supplies). **Est:** 1952. **Sales:** $3,000,000 (2000). **Emp:** 19. **Officers:** B.E. Wright, President; Ron Vandiver, Treasurer & Secty.; Dan Van Meeteren, VP of Marketing.

■ 13533 ■ **Addkison Hardware Co. Inc.**
126 E Amite St.
PO Box 102
Jackson, MS 39205-0102
Phone: (601)354-3756
Free: (800)821-2750 **Fax:** (601)354-1916
URL: http://www.addkisson.com
Products: Tools, including power hand tools; General industrial machinery; Hardware. **SICs:** 5072 (Hardware); 5084 (Industrial Machinery & Equipment). **Est:** 1925. **Emp:** 10. **Officers:** H. M. Addkison.

■ 13534 ■ **Adelman Sales Corp.**
4153 Roswell Rd. NE
Atlanta, GA 30342-3715
Phone: (404)255-8096 **Fax:** (404)255-5458
Products: Hardware. **SIC:** 5072 (Hardware). **Officers:** Nelson Adelman, CEO.

■ 13535 ■ **Adjustable Clamp Co.**
225 Riverview Ave.
Waltham, MA 02454
Phone: (781)647-5560 **Fax:** (781)891-8375
Products: Hardware. **SIC:** 5072 (Hardware). **Officers:** Joaquim Pires; Clinton McKim; Dan Holman.

■ 13536 ■ **Advanced Affiliates Inc.**
9612 43rd Ave.
Flushing, NY 11368-2143
Phone: (718)335-3566
Free: (800)367-4393 **Fax:** (718)565-1444
Products: Handles; Locks and related materials; Hardware. **SICs:** 5072 (Hardware); 5099 (Durable Goods Nec). **Emp:** 49.

■ 13537 ■ Ahlander Wholesale Hardware Co.
490 S University Ave.
Provo, UT 84601
Phone: (801)373-6463
Products: Hardware supplies, including cords, nails, and hammers. **SIC:** 5072 (Hardware). **Est:** 1894. **Sales:** $2,000,000 (2000). **Emp:** 11. **Officers:** Michael B. Ahlander, President; Michael Markham, Controller; Steve Ahlander, Vice President.

■ 13538 ■ Aimsco Inc.
PO Box 80304
Seattle, WA 98108-0304
Phone: (206)762-8014
Free: (800)426-0244   **Fax:** (206)762-8394
E-mail: aimscoinc@aol.com
Products: Fasteners, imported and exported. **SICs:** 5072 (Hardware); 5085 (Industrial Supplies). **Est:** 1916. **Sales:** $4,000,000 (2000). **Emp:** 125. **Officers:** Chad Ernst, President; Bea J. Winn, Treasurer & Secty.; Carl Teichman, Marketing & Sales Mgr.; Charles R. Rogers, Data Processing Mgr.; Jayson R. Stevens, Mgr. of Insustrial Relations.

■ 13539 ■ Airmatic Inc.
7317 State Rd.
Philadelphia, PA 19136-4292
Phone: (215)333-5600
Free: (800)332-9770   **Fax:** 888-964-3866
E-mail: excel@airmatic.com
URL: http://www.airmatic.com
Products: Industrial supplies and equipment; bulk materials handling equipment; pneumatic, gasoline, electric and hydraulic toll and equipment repair service. **SICs:** 5072 (Hardware); 5084 (Industrial Machinery & Equipment); 5085 (Industrial Supplies). **Est:** 1944. **Sales:** $10,000,000 (2000). **Emp:** 30. **Officers:** Wm. J. Dougherty Jr., Vice President.

■ 13540 ■ Ajax Tool Works Inc.
10801 Franklin
Franklin Park, IL 60131
Phone: (847)455-5420
Free: (800)323-9129   **Fax:** (847)455-9242
Products: Hardware. **SIC:** 5072 (Hardware). **Est:** 1946. **Officers:** Robert Benedict, President; Lynn Collins, VP of Sales; Frank Baxpehler, International Sales.

■ 13541 ■ Alaska Nut & Bolt
3041 Cottonwood
Anchorage, AK 99508-4316
Phone: (907)276-3885   **Fax:** (907)276-7549
Products: Fasteners, including nuts, bolts, and screws. **SICs:** 5072 (Hardware); 5085 (Industrial Supplies). **Emp:** 2. **Officers:** Pierre E. Giliam.

■ 13542 ■ Alatec Products
21123 Nordoff St.
Chatsworth, CA 91311
Phone: (818)727-7800
Free: (800)554-4449   **Fax:** (818)727-9636
Products: Fasteners and component hardware for the aerospace and electronics industries. **SIC:** 5072 (Hardware). **Sales:** $81,000,000 (2000). **Emp:** 290. **Officers:** Don List, President; Joanne Caputo, Controller.

■ 13543 ■ Albany Steel & Brass Corp.
1900 W Grand
Chicago, IL 60622-6286
Phone: (312)733-1900   **Fax:** (312)733-9887
URL: http://www.albanysteel.com
Products: Fasteners; Tools; Contractor's equipment. **SICs:** 5072 (Hardware); 5075 (Warm Air Heating & Air-Conditioning). **Est:** 1918. **Emp:** 40. **Officers:** David Lebovitz, e-mail: davidl@albanysteel.com.

■ 13544 ■ Albuquerque Bolt & Fastener
2926 2nd St. NW
Albuquerque, NM 87107-1416
Phone: (505)345-5869
Products: Bolts, nuts, rivets, screws, and washers; Hardware fasteners. **SIC:** 5072 (Hardware). **Emp:** 499. **Officers:** Pete Tabet.

■ 13545 ■ Alco Tool Supply Inc.
54847 County Rd. 17
Elkhart, IN 46516-9792
Phone: (219)295-5535
Free: (800)437-2911   **Fax:** (219)293-2254
Products: Drill bits; Paint; Adhesives; Sandpaper; Small hand tools; Large power tools. **SICs:** 5072 (Hardware); 5084 (Industrial Machinery & Equipment); 5169 (Chemicals & Allied Products Nec). **Est:** 1972. **Sales:** $10,000,000 (2000). **Emp:** 30. **Officers:** Joe Kinneman, President; Curt Heeg, Treasurer & Secty.

■ 13546 ■ All Fasteners Inc.
2620 4 Mile Rd.
PO Box 427
Racine, WI 53401-0427
Phone: (414)639-4200
Free: (800)472-3362   **Fax:** (414)639-4285
Products: Hardware fasteners. **SICs:** 5072 (Hardware); 5085 (Industrial Supplies). **Emp:** 40. **Officers:** George Ruetz, Chairman of the Board; James Ruetz, President & General Mgr.; Richard Ruetz, Vice President; Ginni Guendel, Business Mgr.

■ 13547 ■ All-Pro Fasteners, Inc.
1916 Peyco Dr. N
PO Box 151227
Arlington, TX 76015
Phone: (817)467-5700
Free: (800)361-6277   **Fax:** (817)467-5365
E-mail: AllProFastenersInc@worldnet.att.net
Products: Nuts and bolts. **SIC:** 5072 (Hardware). **Est:** 1976. **Sales:** $32,000,000 (1999). **Emp:** 125. **Officers:** Jerry Dunsmore, Vice President; Tom Shelton, President; Jennifer Neal, Sales/Marketing Contact; Liz Craig, Customer Service Contact; Ruth Stiver, Human Resources Contact.

■ 13548 ■ All Stainless Inc.
992 Temple St., Ste. 2
Whitman, MA 02382-1066
Phone: (781)749-7100   **Fax:** (781)749-2935
E-mail: njr@ici.net
URL: http://www.allstainless.com
Products: Stainless steel products, including fasteners, pipes, and fittings. **SIC:** 5072 (Hardware). **Est:** 1952. **Sales:** $3,000,000 (2000). **Emp:** 17. **Officers:** Phillip Roundtree, President; Nicholas J. Roundtree, Dir. of Marketing.

■ 13549 ■ All State Fastener Corp.
PO Box 356
Eastpointe, MI 48021
Phone: (810)773-5400   **Fax:** (810)773-7244
Products: Bolts, nuts, rivets, screws, and washers; Hard fiber rope and cable. **SIC:** 5072 (Hardware). **Est:** 1963. **Emp:** 49.

■ 13550 ■ All Tool Sales Inc.
PO Box 517
Racine, WI 53401
Phone: (414)637-7447   **Fax:** (414)637-5611
E-mail: ats@toolsales.com
URL: http://www.alltoolsales.com
Products: Cutting and air tools; Machine tools. **SIC:** 5072 (Hardware). **Est:** 1962. **Sales:** $6,000,000 (2000). **Emp:** 35. **Officers:** G.J. Ruetz, CEO; R.G. Ruetz, President; Bruce Haertel, Customer Service Contact. **Alternate Name:** R Ruetz.

■ 13551 ■ Allied Bolt Co.
PO Box 80604
Seattle, WA 98108
Phone: (206)763-2275
Products: Nuts, bolts, screws, and anchor products. **SIC:** 5072 (Hardware). **Est:** 1970. **Sales:** $3,000,000 (2000). **Emp:** 25. **Officers:** Dave Melin, President.

■ 13552 ■ Allied Wholesale Inc.
13207 Bradley Ave.
Sylmar, CA 91342
Phone: (818)364-2333   **Fax:** (818)362-9066
Products: Tool kits that include jacks, hammers, hydraulic tools, and wrenches. **SICs:** 5072 (Hardware); 5084 (Industrial Machinery & Equipment). **Est:** 1962. **Sales:** $70,300,000 (2000). **Emp:** 60. **Officers:** Timothy Florian, CEO & President; Norton Medina, CFO; Dave Waters, Marketing Mgr.

■ 13553 ■ Alpine Supply
2841 W Parkway Blvd.
Salt Lake City, UT 84119
Phone: (801)972-0477
Free: (800)284-3350   **Fax:** (801)972-0526
Products: Hardware. **SICs:** 5072 (Hardware); 5065 (Electronic Parts & Equipment Nec); 5085 (Industrial Supplies). **Est:** 1976. **Emp:** 20. **Officers:** Mike Ellsworth; Butch Ellsworth; Shawn Meeks.

■ 13554 ■ Alsdorf International Ltd.
209 E Lake Shore Rd., No. 15W
Chicago, IL 60611-1307
Phone: (847)501-3335   **Fax:** (847)501-3920
Products: Hardware, including hand operated sanders; Automotive switches; Hand lanterns; Electric coffee grinders; Mechanical pencils. **SICs:** 5072 (Hardware); 5046 (Commercial Equipment Nec); 5112 (Stationery & Office Supplies); 5013 (Motor Vehicle Supplies & New Parts); 5063 (Electrical Apparatus & Equipment). **Officers:** James W. Alsdorf, Chairman and CEO.

■ 13555 ■ Amarillo Hardware Co.
PO Box 1891
Amarillo, TX 79172
Phone: (806)376-4722   **Fax:** (806)374-5520
Products: Hardware supplies, including sinks, faucets, tubs, drills, and saws. **SICs:** 5072 (Hardware); 5074 (Plumbing & Hydronic Heating Supplies); 5021 (Furniture); 5064 (Electrical Appliances—Television & Radio). **Est:** 1904. **Sales:** $35,000,000 (2000). **Emp:** 155. **Officers:** Joe Wildman, President; Wayne Smith, CFO; C.B. Streeter, VP of Marketing & Sales; Cindy Kile, VP & Controller.

■ 13556 ■ AMB Tools & Equipment
608 W Nob Hill Blvd.
Yakima, WA 98902-5559
Phone: (509)452-7123
Products: Tools; Steel products. **SICs:** 5072 (Hardware); 5051 (Metals Service Centers & Offices). **Emp:** 49.

■ 13557 ■ American Fastener Specialty Company
5900 Park Ave.
Cleveland, OH 44105-4993
Phone: (216)883-1550   **Fax:** (216)883-2746
Products: Hardware fasteners. **SIC:** 5072 (Hardware). **Sales:** $2,000,000 (2000). **Emp:** 49. **Officers:** Robin Bauer.

■ 13558 ■ American Global Co.
4305 35th
Long Island City, NY 11101-1205
Phone: (718)729-7500   **Fax:** (718)784-4847
Products: Bolts, nuts, rivets, screws, and washers. **SICs:** 5072 (Hardware); 5099 (Durable Goods Nec). **Emp:** 49.

■ 13559 ■ American Kal Enterprises Inc.
4265 Puenta Ave.
Baldwin Park, CA 91706-3420
Phone: (626)961-9471
Products: Hardware. **SIC:** 5072 (Hardware). **Est:** 1965. **Sales:** $32,000,000 (1993). **Emp:** 100. **Officers:** John Toshima, President; Robert Mandeville, VP of Finance.

■ 13560 ■ American Millwork & Hardware, Inc.
4505 W Woolworth Ave.
Milwaukee, WI 53218-1414
Phone: (414)353-1234   **Fax:** (414)358-3649
Products: Commercial and residential doors, frames, millwork, hardware, bath accessories, postal,and lighting. **SICs:** 5072 (Hardware); 5063 (Electrical Apparatus & Equipment); 5031 (Lumber, Plywood & Millwork). **Est:** 1985. **Sales:** $8,000,000 (1999). **Emp:** 31. **Officers:** Gary Rattner.

■ **13561** ■ **American Saw & Manufacturing Co.**
301 Chestnut St.
East Longmeadow, MA 01028
Phone: (413)525-3961
Free: (800)628-3030 **Fax:** (413)525-2336
E-mail: info@lenoxsaw.com
URL: http://www.lenoxsaw.com
Products: Saw blades; Hardware. **SIC:** 5072 (Hardware). **Est:** 1915. **Emp:** 650.

■ **13562** ■ **American Tool Companies Inc.**
701 Woodlands Pky.
Vernon Hills, IL 60061
Phone: 800-838-7845 **Fax:** (847)478-1091
URL: http://www.americantool.com
Products: Hand tools; Power tool accessories. **SIC:** 5072 (Hardware).

■ **13563** ■ **Architects Hardware & Specialty Company Inc.**
Railroad & Dott Aves.
Albany, NY 12205
Phone: (518)489-4478
Free: (800)924-9247 **Fax:** (518)489-6856
Products: Door hardware; Caulking compounds and sealants; Tarpaulins and other covers; Cabinet hardware. **SICs:** 5072 (Hardware); 5169 (Chemicals & Allied Products Nec). **Est:** 1954. **Emp:** 16. **Officers:** Richard M. Englander.

■ **13564** ■ **Architectural Building Supply**
2965 S Main St.
Salt Lake City, UT 84115
Phone: (801)486-3481
Products: Hardware, including locks; Doors. **SICs:** 5072 (Hardware); 5031 (Lumber, Plywood & Millwork). **Est:** 1967. **Sales:** $9,000,000 (2000). **Emp:** 55. **Officers:** Craig Tolboe, President; Roy Smith, Vice President.

■ **13565** ■ **Arizona Sash and Door Co.**
1265 S Pima
Mesa, AZ 85210-5347
Phone: (602)253-3151
Products: Hardware; Doors. **SICs:** 5072 (Hardware); 5031 (Lumber, Plywood & Millwork). **Est:** 1925. **Sales:** $10,000,000 (2000). **Emp:** 50. **Officers:** H.S. Galbraith, President.

■ **13566** ■ **Assembly Component Systems**
240 W 83rd St.
Burr Ridge, IL 60521
Phone: (630)654-1113 **Fax:** (630)654-0763
Products: Fasteners. **SIC:** 5072 (Hardware). **Est:** 1917. **Sales:** $10,000,000 (2000). **Emp:** 20. **Officers:** Stanley Belsky, President; Thomas E. Shem, Manager.

■ **13567** ■ **Assembly Components Systems Co.**
PO Box 22536
Memphis, TN 38122
Phone: (901)274-0050 **Fax:** (901)272-9832
Products: Bolts; Nuts; Washers. **SIC:** 5072 (Hardware). **Est:** 1969. **Sales:** $7,000,000 (2000). **Emp:** 47. **Officers:** James H. Allen, President.

■ **13568** ■ **Assembly Components Systems Inc.**
PO Box 1608
Decatur, AL 35602
Phone: (256)353-1931 **Fax:** (256)355-3612
Products: Metal fasteners. **SIC:** 5072 (Hardware). **Sales:** $18,000,000 (2000). **Emp:** 65. **Officers:** Stanley Belsky, President.

■ **13569** ■ **Associated Springs**
100 Underwood Rd.
Arden, NC 28704
Phone: (828)684-7836
Products: Springs. **SIC:** 5072 (Hardware).

■ **13570** ■ **Athens Hardware Co.**
PO Box 552
Athens, GA 30603-0552
Phone: (706)543-4391 **Fax:** (706)353-2028
Products: Hardware supplies. **SIC:** 5072 (Hardware). **Est:** 1865. **Sales:** $4,000,000 (1999). **Emp:** 27. **Officers:** Nick Nickerson, President; Steve McCannon, CFO.

■ **13571** ■ **Atlantic Hardware and Supply Corp.**
601 W 26th St.
New York, NY 10001
Phone: (212)924-0700
Products: Hardware supplies, including nuts and bolts; Building materials. **SICs:** 5072 (Hardware); 5039 (Construction Materials Nec). **Est:** 1944. **Sales:** $13,700,000 (2000). **Emp:** 63. **Officers:** Paul R. Selden, President; Donald Gensinger, Controller.

■ **13572** ■ **Atlantic Pacific Industries**
4223 W Jefferson Blvd.
Los Angeles, CA 90016
Phone: (213)766-9075
Free: (800)766-9076 **Fax:** (213)766-8866
Products: Builders and cabinet hardware. **SIC:** 5072 (Hardware). **Est:** 1967. **Emp:** 49.

■ **13573** ■ **Atlas Copco North America Inc.**
1211 Hamburg Tpk.
Wayne, NJ 07470
Phone: (973)439-3400 **Fax:** (973)435-9188
Products: Construction equipment, including air compressors, hand tools, and power tools. **SICs:** 5072 (Hardware); 5084 (Industrial Machinery & Equipment). **Est:** 1950. **Sales:** $2,500,000,000 (2000). **Emp:** 10,000. **Officers:** Mark Cohen, President; William Garofalo, VP of Finance.

■ **13574** ■ **Atlas Copco Tools Inc.**
37735 Enterprise Ct. Ste.300
Farmington Hills, MI 48331-3480
Phone: (248)489-1260 **Fax:** (248)489-0130
Products: Power tools and equipment. **SIC:** 5072 (Hardware). **Est:** 1960. **Sales:** $17,000,000 (2000). **Emp:** 50. **Officers:** Charles Robison, President; Ted Mazur, CFO; Daniel Grippo, Product Manager.

■ **13575** ■ **L.P. Atlas Screw and Specialty Co.**
PO Box 41389
New Bedford, MA 02744-1389
Phone: (508)990-2054 **Fax:** (508)993-3687
Products: Fasteners, including screws, bolts, and washers. **SICs:** 5072 (Hardware); 5085 (Industrial Supplies). **Est:** 1935. **Sales:** $6,500,000 (2000). **Emp:** 35. **Officers:** David Hirsh, President; Vik Shah, CFO; Ed Sierman, VP of Sales.

■ **13576** ■ **W.E. Aubuchon Company Inc.**
95 Aubuchon Dr.
Westminster, MA 01473
Phone: (508)874-0521 **Fax:** (508)874-2096
Products: Hardware. **SIC:** 5072 (Hardware). **Est:** 1908. **Sales:** $80,000,000 (2000). **Emp:** 835. **Officers:** William E. Aubuchon Jr., President; M. Marcus Moran Jr., CFO; William E. Aubuchon III, Dir. of Marketing; Peter J. Aubuchon Jr., Dir. of Systems; Daniel P. Aubuchon, Dir of Human Resources.

■ **13577** ■ **Auto Bolt & Nut Co.**
4619 Perkins Ave.
Cleveland, OH 44103-3595
Phone: (216)881-3913
Free: (800)988-2658 **Fax:** (216)881-3918
E-mail: autobolt@lightstream.net
Products: Long and heavy fasteners; Carriage, standard, special, and plow bolts. **SIC:** 5072 (Hardware). **Est:** 1948. **Sales:** $5,000,000 (2000). **Emp:** 25. **Officers:** Cliff Kocian, President; Andrew J. Viktor, Vice President; Rob Kocian, General Mgr.; Rick Maurer, Sales/Marketing Contact, e-mail: r.maurer@yahoo.com; Debbie Luzius, Human Resources Contact.

■ **13578** ■ **B & N Industries**
111 Albany Ave.
Freeport, NY 11520-4715
Phone: (516)623-1440
Products: Hardware; Automotive parts and supplies, New. **SICs:** 5072 (Hardware); 5013 (Motor Vehicle Supplies & New Parts). **Emp:** 49.

■ **13579** ■ **B & S Bolts Corp.**
2610 Arkansas Ave.
Norfolk, VA 23513-4402
Phone: (757)855-2000 **Fax:** (757)858-3923
Products: Bolts, nuts, rivets, screws, and washers; Hardware fasteners. **SICs:** 5072 (Hardware); 5085

(Industrial Supplies). **Est:** 1979. **Emp:** 9. **Officers:** M. L. Chesire III.

■ **13580** ■ **B and T Wholesale Distributors Inc.**
846 Lind SW
Renton, WA 98055
Phone: (206)235-3592 **Fax:** (206)235-3599
Products: Hardware. **SIC:** 5072 (Hardware). **Est:** 1952. **Sales:** $25,000,000 (2000). **Emp:** 30. **Officers:** T.G. McLendon, President; R.W. McLendon, CFO; M.L. Easton, Dir. of Marketing.

■ **13581** ■ **Baer Supply Co.**
909 Forest Edge Dr.
Vernon Hills, IL 60061
Phone: (847)913-2237
Free: (800)913-2237 **Fax:** (847)913-2230
Products: Hardware and fittings; Shop supplies; Machine tools; Laminate products. **SIC:** 5072 (Hardware). **Est:** 1950. **Sales:** $75,000,000 (2000). **Emp:** 300. **Officers:** Peter Zinni, Vice President; Gary Sickles, Dir. of Sales; Stanley J. Rzasa, Dir. of Marketing.

■ **13582** ■ **Bamal Fastener Corp.**
23240 Industrial Park Dr.
Farmington Hills, MI 48335
Phone: (248)477-8101 **Fax:** (248)477-8107
Products: Hardware. **SIC:** 5072 (Hardware). **Sales:** $45,000,000 (1994). **Emp:** 105. **Officers:** Douglas V. Miller, Chairman of the Board; John Ancona, CFO.

■ **13583** ■ **Barco Industries Inc.**
1020 MacArthur Rd.
Reading, PA 19605-9404
Free: (800)234-TOOL **Fax:** (610)374-6320
E-mail: service@barcotools.com
URL: http://www.barcotools.com
Products: Hammers; Axes, adzes, and hatchets; Axes, picks, hammers, etc.; Mason's materials; Knives. **SICs:** 5072 (Hardware); 5032 (Brick, Stone & Related Materials). **Sales:** $2,000,000 (2000). **Emp:** 49. **Officers:** Owen W. Blum.

■ **13584** ■ **Barker-Jennings Corp.**
PO Box 11289
Lynchburg, VA 24506
Phone: (804)846-8471
Free: (800)289-2520 **Fax:** (804)846-8169
Products: Hardware, industrial supplies and automotive parts. **SICs:** 5072 (Hardware); 5085 (Industrial Supplies); 5015 (Motor Vehicle Parts—Used). **Sales:** $13,000,000 (2000). **Emp:** 82. **Officers:** Frank Blankenship, President & Treasurer.

■ **13585** ■ **Barrett Hardware and Industrial Supply Co.**
324 Henderson Ave.
Joliet, IL 60432
Phone: (815)726-4341
Free: (800)892-4011 **Fax:** (815)726-5607
Products: Hardware. **SICs:** 5072 (Hardware); 5085 (Industrial Supplies). **Est:** 1850. **Sales:** $6,000,000 (2000). **Emp:** 99.

■ **13586** ■ **S.H. Basnight & Sons**
PO Drawer 249
Carrboro, NC 27510-0249
Phone: (919)942-3158 **Fax:** (919)933-5461
Products: Architectural hardware. **SIC:** 5072 (Hardware). **Est:** 1924. **Sales:** $3,000,000 (2000). **Emp:** 21. **Officers:** W. D. Basnight; Jesse S. Basnight Sr.

■ **13587** ■ **Baxter International Representations Inc.**
303 W Sunset Rd., Ste. 100B
San Antonio, TX 78209
Phone: (210)829-7793 **Fax:** (210)828-5405
E-mail: baxrep@stic.net
Products: Tools and hardware, including pipes, screwdrivers, and hammers. **SIC:** 5072 (Hardware). **Est:** 1990. **Sales:** $2,500,000 (2000). **Emp:** 2. **Officers:** James E. Baxter, President.

■ **13588** ■ **BBC Fasteners Inc.**
4210 Shirley Ln.
Alsip, IL 60803
Phone: (708)597-9100
Free: (800)323-1347 **Fax:** (708)597-0423
Products: Hot forged specialty fasteners; CNC machined specialty components. **SIC:** 5072 (Hardware). **Est:** 1958. **Sales:** $3,500,000 (2000). **Emp:** 60. **Officers:** Eugene R. Sullivan, President; James L. Dion, VP of Sales.

■ **13589** ■ **Becknell Wholesale Co.**
PO Box 2008
Lubbock, TX 79408
Phone: (806)747-3201
Products: Hardware and farm equipment, including knives, U-joints, sweeps, hydraulic hoses, and couples. **SICs:** 5072 (Hardware); 5083 (Farm & Garden Machinery). **Est:** 1952. **Sales:** $12,000,000 (2000). **Emp:** 65. **Officers:** Eugene Becknell, President; Ron Chandler, Vice President; Don Walker, Dir. of Marketing.

■ **13590** ■ **Beeson Hardware Industrial Sales Co.**
1114 Dorris Ave.
PO Box 1390
High Point, NC 27260-1390
Phone: (336)821-2145
Free: (800)967-0394 **Fax:** (336)883-2410
E-mail: sandpaper4@aol.com
URL: http://www.beeson@infoave.net
Products: Hardware; Adhesives; Fasteners; Coated abrasives; Abrasive belt recycling. **SICs:** 5072 (Hardware); 5169 (Chemicals & Allied Products Nec). **Est:** 1875. **Sales:** $4,500,000 (2000). **Emp:** 12. **Officers:** Ed Spivey, President; Jim Kinney, Vice President; Bubba Judy, Sales/Marketing Contact; Cyndi Claggett, Customer Service Contact.

■ **13591** ■ **H. Belmer Co.**
555 Carr St.
Cincinnati, OH 45203
Phone: (513)241-4341 **Fax:** (513)241-0493
Products: Construction tools; Hardware; Fireplaces; Safety compressors and generator; Pneumatic air tools; Fasteners, nails, and wire products. **SICs:** 5072 (Hardware); 5074 (Plumbing & Hydronic Heating Supplies); 5082 (Construction & Mining Machinery). **Est:** 1866. **Sales:** $7,000,000 (2000). **Emp:** 29. **Officers:** John Duncan, President & Treasurer; John Scheidler, CFO.

■ **13592** ■ **Howard Berger and Company Inc.**
808 Georgia Ave.
Brooklyn, NY 11207
Phone: (718)272-1540
Products: Hardware. **SIC:** 5072 (Hardware). **Sales:** $66,000,000 (2000). **Emp:** 325. **Officers:** Howard Berger, President; Jerrold Blatt, Controller; Robert Winterstein, VP of Marketing & Sales.

■ **13593** ■ **Berint Trading, Ltd.**
12 Westchester Ave.
White Plains, NY 10601
Phone: (914)948-0030
Products: Paints; Hardware and hand tools; Industrial equipment and machinery; Service establishment equipment and supplies; Automotive supplies. **SICs:** 5072 (Hardware); 5198 (Paints, Varnishes & Supplies); 5013 (Motor Vehicle Supplies & New Parts); 5084 (Industrial Machinery & Equipment); 5087 (Service Establishment Equipment). **Officers:** Bert Rosenstock, President.

■ **13594** ■ **Tom Berube Municipal Supply**
421 Worcester Rd.
Barre, MA 01005-9006
Phone: (978)355-2366 **Fax:** (978)355-6371
Products: Street signs; Shovels; Rakes; Tools; Footwear. **SICs:** 5082 (Construction & Mining Machinery); 5139 (Footwear); 5072 (Hardware). **Officers:** Thomas Berube, Owner.

■ **13595** ■ **Best Electric Supply**
6201 Regency West Dr.
Racine, WI 53406-4947
Phone: (414)554-0600 **Fax:** (414)554-0777
Products: Tools. **SIC:** 5063 (Electrical Apparatus & Equipment). **Emp:** 49. **Officers:** Ben Cook.

■ **13596** ■ **Best Way Tools**
171 Brook Ave.
Deer Park, NY 11729
Phone: (516)586-4702 **Fax:** (516)586-4126
Products: Screwdrivers. **SIC:** 5072 (Hardware).

■ **13597** ■ **Big Blue Store**
149 South Blvd.
Clinton, NC 28328-4617
Phone: (910)592-6707
Free: (800)682-3563 **Fax:** (910)592-1289
E-mail: bblue@intrstar.net
Products: Hardware; Plumbing and heating valves and specialties. **SICs:** 5072 (Hardware); 5074 (Plumbing & Hydronic Heating Supplies). **Emp:** 49. **Officers:** Delmar Pollert.

■ **13598** ■ **Big D Bolt & Screw Co.**
11112 Grader St.
Dallas, TX 75238-2403
Phone: (214)349-8162
Free: (800)344-2443 **Fax:** (214)349-7144
Products: Contractor and industrial supplies. **SICs:** 5072 (Hardware); 5085 (Industrial Supplies). **Est:** 1979. **Emp:** 15.

■ **13599** ■ **Bild Industries Inc.**
800 Clear Water Loop
Post Falls, ID 83854
Phone: (208)773-0630 **Fax:** (208)773-0902
Products: Fasteners including nuts, bolts, and washers. **SIC:** 5072 (Hardware). **Est:** 1961. **Sales:** $4,000,000 (2000). **Emp:** 16. **Officers:** Stephen Bild, President; Betty Summerville, CFO.

■ **13600** ■ **Blaine Window Hardware Inc.**
17319 Blaine Dr.
Hagerstown, MD 21740
Phone: (301)797-6500 **Fax:** (301)797-2510
Products: Window hardware. **SIC:** 5072 (Hardware). **Est:** 1953. **Sales:** $4,500,000 (2000). **Emp:** 125. **Officers:** E.A. Blaine, President & Chairman of the Board; William A. Pasquerette, Controller; Edward Blaine, Dir. of Marketing & Sales.

■ **13601** ■ **Blish-Mize Co.**
223 S 5th St.
Atchison, KS 66002
Phone: (913)367-1250 **Fax:** (913)367-0667
Products: Hardware. **SIC:** 5072 (Hardware). **Sales:** $40,000,000 (1992). **Emp:** 200. **Officers:** J.H. Mize Jr., CEO & President; L.H. Boknecht, VP of Finance.

■ **13602** ■ **Bon Tool Co.**
4430 Gibsonia Rd.
Gibsonia, PA 15044
Phone: (724)443-7080 **Fax:** (724)443-7090
E-mail: sales@bontool.com
URL: http://www.bontool.com
Products: Tools. **SICs:** 5072 (Hardware); 5085 (Industrial Supplies). **Est:** 1958. **Emp:** 49. **Officers:** Carl Bongiovanni; John Wight, Sales & Marketing Contact.

■ **13603** ■ **Bonanza Nut and Bolt Inc.**
1890 Purina Way
Sparks, NV 89431
Phone: (702)358-2638
Free: (800)648-1110 **Fax:** (702)358-3653
Products: Nuts and bolts. **SIC:** 5072 (Hardware). **Est:** 1975. **Sales:** $4,500,000 (2000). **Emp:** 30. **Officers:** Dick Sawtell, President; Brandon Liebhard, VP of Marketing; Brandon Liebhard, Sales/Marketing Contact; Glenda Newby, Customer Service Contact.

■ **13604** ■ **Bostwick-Braun Co.**
PO Box 912
Toledo, OH 43697
Phone: (419)259-3600 **Fax:** (419)259-3959
Products: Hardware. **SIC:** 5072 (Hardware).

■ **13605** ■ **E.B. Bradley Co.**
5080 S Alameda St.
Los Angeles, CA 90058-2810
Phone: (323)585-9201 **Fax:** (323)585-5414
URL: http://www.ebbradley.com
Products: Cabinets, hardware, and surfacing products. **SICs:** 5072 (Hardware); 5031 (Lumber, Plywood & Millwork). **Est:** 1929. **Sales:** $15,000,000 (2000). **Emp:** 200. **Officers:** Robert B. Bradley Jr., President & CEO; Don Lorey, National Sales Mgr.

■ **13606** ■ **Brighton-Best Socket Screw Manufacturing Inc.**
3105 Medlock Bridge Rd.
Norcross, GA 30071
Phone: (770)368-2300 **Fax:** (770)836-1734
URL: http://www.brightonbest.com
Products: Socket cap screws; Hexagon cap screws; Nuts and washers. **SIC:** 5072 (Hardware). **Est:** 1925. **Sales:** $50,000,000 (1999). **Emp:** 200. **Officers:** Perry Rosenstein, President.

■ **13607** ■ **Brownell & Associates, Inc.**
14731-E Franklin Ave.
Tustin, CA 92780
Phone: (714)544-8003 **Fax:** (714)544-9301
E-mail: brnlassoc@aol.com
Products: Hardware and electronic hardware; Building supplies; Specialty doors and frames. **SICs:** 5072 (Hardware); 5031 (Lumber, Plywood & Millwork). **Est:** 1976. **Sales:** $10,000,000 (1999). **Emp:** 7. **Officers:** Mike Brownell.

■ **13608** ■ **Bruckner Machine**
36 Harbor Park Dr.
Port Washington, NY 11050
Phone: (516)484-6070
Products: Hand tools. **SIC:** 5072 (Hardware).

■ **13609** ■ **Buhrman-Pharr Hardware Co.**
PO Box 1818
Texarkana, AR 71854
Phone: (501)773-3122 **Fax:** (501)772-7974
Products: Hardware supplies. **SIC:** 5072 (Hardware). **Est:** 1879. **Sales:** $15,000,000 (2000). **Emp:** 100. **Officers:** S.H. Jones, President; Les Smith, Finance Officer.

■ **13610** ■ **Builders Brass Works Corp.**
3528 Emery St.
Los Angeles, CA 90023
Phone: (213)269-8111 **Fax:** (213)269-1872
Products: Door handles; Exit devices. **SIC:** 5072 (Hardware). **Sales:** $6,000,000 (2000). **Emp:** 99. **Officers:** Peter Mantarakis.

■ **13611** ■ **Builders Hardware & Specialties**
2002 W 16th St.
Erie, PA 16505-4816
Phone: (814)453-4736
Free: (800)284-5386 **Fax:** (814)454-0275
Products: Commercial doors, frames, and hardware; Keying systems; Architectural aluminum railings. **SICs:** 5072 (Hardware); 5031 (Lumber, Plywood & Millwork); 5039 (Construction Materials Nec). **Est:** 1956. **Emp:** 49. **Officers:** Dennis Coughlin, General Mgr.

■ **13612** ■ **Builders Hardware and Supply Co. Inc.**
1516 15th Ave. W
Box C79005
Seattle, WA 98119-3185
Phone: (206)281-3700
Free: (800)999-5158 **Fax:** (206)281-3747
Products: Hardware. **SICs:** 5072 (Hardware); 5031 (Lumber, Plywood & Millwork); 5198 (Paints, Varnishes & Supplies); 5169 (Chemicals & Allied Products Nec). **Sales:** $20,000,000 (2000). **Emp:** 116. **Officers:** Shirley Henry.

■ **13613** ■ **Buttery Hardware Company Inc.**
201 W Main
Llano, TX 78643
Phone: (915)247-4141 **Fax:** (915)247-3090
Products: Hardware; Plumbing and electrical supplies. **SIC:** 5072 (Hardware). **Est:** 1900. **Sales:** $40,000,000 (2000). **Emp:** 150. **Officers:** H. Buttery, CEO; Juo Buttery, President; W.M. Buttery, Exec. VP.

■ **13614** ■ **C & J Fasteners**
25136 5 Mile Rd.
Redford, MI 48239-3717
Phone: (313)535-8835 **Fax:** (313)535-9711
Products: Fasteners and bolts. **SIC:** 5072 (Hardware).
Emp: 25. **Officers:** Cheryl Williams, President; Joseph Willis, CEO.

■ **13615** ■ **California Fasteners Inc.**
PO Box 18328
Anaheim, CA 92817
Phone: (714)970-9090 **Fax:** (714)970-8185
Products: Fasteners. **SIC:** 5072 (Hardware). **Est:** 1946. **Sales:** $6,000,000 (2000). **Emp:** 20. **Officers:** D.E. Bastian, President.

■ **13616** ■ **California Hardware Co.**
PO Box 3640
Ontario, CA 91764
Phone: (909)390-6100 **Fax:** (909)390-8799
Products: Hardware supplies. **SIC:** 5072 (Hardware). **Est:** 1880. **Sales:** $79,000,000 (2000). **Emp:** 191. **Officers:** Hardy Soberholm, COO; Cindy Kile, CFO; C.C. Snyder, VP of Marketing; Wes L. Fitzpatrick, VP of Information Systems; Rhonda Mata, Dir. of Admin.

■ **13617** ■ **D.E. Calotex Inc.**
24 W Main St.
Middletown, DE 19709-1039
Phone: (302)378-2461 **Fax:** (302)378-9568
Products: Hardware. **SIC:** 5072 (Hardware). **Sales:** $5,000,000 (2000). **Emp:** 100.

■ **13618** ■ **Camper's Trade Emporium**
PO Box 131097
San Diego, CA 92170-1097
Phone: (619)264-5578 **Fax:** (619)264-5593
Products: Bolts, nuts, screws, and rivets; Plumbing fixtures and fittings; Manual and power hand tools; Orthopedic surgical shoes; Hardware. **SICs:** 5072 (Hardware); 5074 (Plumbing & Hydronic Heating Supplies); 5047 (Medical & Hospital Equipment). **Officers:** Maitland E. Camper, President/Owner.

■ **13619** ■ **Carapace Corp.**
8705 Bollman Pl., Ste. C
Savage, MD 20763-9775
Phone: (301)403-2900
Products: Hardware. **SIC:** 5072 (Hardware).

■ **13620** ■ **Carlson Systems Corp.**
8990 F St.
Omaha, NE 68127
Phone: (402)593-5300 **Fax:** (402)593-5966
URL: http://www.csystems.com
Products: Tools and nails; Packaging. **SICs:** 5072 (Hardware); 5113 (Industrial & Personal Service Paper). **Est:** 1947. **Sales:** $105,000,000 (2000). **Emp:** 365. **Officers:** Donald W. Carlson, President; Mike Carlson, CFO; Todd Carlson, VP of Sales.

■ **13621** ■ **Carroll Building Specialties**
PO Box 61928
Lafayette, LA 70596
Phone: (318)233-6311 **Fax:** (318)235-1780
Products: Building materials; Hardware; Cabinets; Specialty items. **SICs:** 5072 (Hardware); 5031 (Lumber, Plywood & Millwork). **Est:** 1968. **Sales:** $500,000 (1999). **Emp:** 10. **Officers:** Carroll LeBlanc.

■ **13622** ■ **Cascade Wholesale Hardware, Inc.**
PO Box 1659
Hillsboro, OR 97123
Phone: (503)614-2600
Free: (800)877-9987 **Fax:** (503)614-2685
URL: http://www.cascade.com
Products: Hand tools, power tools, and builders hardware. **SIC:** 5072 (Hardware). **Est:** 1990. **Emp:** 50. **Officers:** Michael Parr, General Mgr.; Dan Peterson, Asst. General Mgr.

■ **13623** ■ **Cash Supply Co.**
PO Box 2311
Spartanburg, SC 29304-2311
Phone: (864)585-9326 **Fax:** (864)585-1113
Products: Abrasive products; Saws; Hand saws and saw blades; Brushes; Bolts, nuts, rivets, screws, and washers; Polishers, sanders, and grinders; Wrenches; Power hand tools. **SICs:** 5072 (Hardware); 5082 (Construction & Mining Machinery); 5084 (Industrial Machinery & Equipment); 5039 (Construction Materials Nec); 5169 (Chemicals & Allied Products Nec). **Emp:** 3. **Officers:** Alex Pye, Contact.

■ **13624** ■ **CBS Fasteners Inc.**
1345 N Brasher St.
Anaheim, CA 92807
Phone: (714)779-6368 **Fax:** (714)779-0934
Products: Fasteners. **SIC:** 5072 (Hardware). **Est:** 1978. **Sales:** $2,000,000 (2000). **Emp:** 24. **Officers:** G.W. Bozarth, President; John F. Cunningham, Treasurer.

■ **13625** ■ **Centennial Bolt Inc.**
555 Joliet St.
Denver, CO 80239-2006
Phone: (303)371-1370 **Fax:** (303)371-0805
E-mail: centbolt@aol.com
Products: Nuts; Bolts, screws, and anchors. **SIC:** 5072 (Hardware). **Est:** 1979. **Sales:** $4,000,000 (2000). **Emp:** 28. **Officers:** Mark Cordova, President.

■ **13626** ■ **Central Distribution Services, LLC**
5400 33rd St. SE
Grand Rapids, MI 49512
Phone: (616)940-3540
Free: (800)748-0054 **Fax:** (616)940-3564
URL: http://www.centdist.com
Products: Hardware, including power hand tools; Lawn and garden supplies; Electrical equipment and supplies; Plumbing equipment; Paint and painting supplies; Automotive equipment. **SICs:** 5072 (Hardware); 5083 (Farm & Garden Machinery); 5063 (Electrical Apparatus & Equipment); 5074 (Plumbing & Hydronic Heating Supplies); 5198 (Paints, Varnishes & Supplies). **Est:** 1998. **Sales:** $115,000,000 (2000). **Emp:** 275. **Former Name:** L.G. #Cook Distributors Inc. **Former Name:** Cook Distribution Services, LLC.

■ **13627** ■ **Century Fasteners Corp.**
50-20 Ireland St.
Elmhurst, NY 11373
Phone: (718)446-5000 **Fax:** (718)426-8119
Products: Connectors for electronic equipment. **SIC:** 5065 (Electronic Parts & Equipment Nec). **Sales:** $30,000,000 (2000). **Emp:** 135. **Officers:** Evan Stieglitz, President; George Stieglitz, CFO.

■ **13628** ■ **Century Fasteners, Inc.**
11333 Greenstone Ave.
Santa Fe Springs, CA 90670-4618
Phones: (213)583-6721 (213)583-9436
Fax: (213)232-5332
Products: Fasteners. **SIC:** 5072 (Hardware). **Est:** 1957. **Sales:** $5,000,000 (2000). **Emp:** 49. **Officers:** Harold C. Benson.

■ **13629** ■ **Century Saw and Tool Co. Inc.**
19347 Mount Elliot St.
Detroit, MI 48234
Phone: (313)893-2280 **Fax:** (313)893-3379
E-mail: centurysaw@yahoo.com
Products: Tools, including saws and hammers. **SIC:** 5072 (Hardware). **Est:** 1921. **Sales:** $3,200,000 (2000). **Emp:** 8. **Officers:** D.E. McGinnis, President & Treasurer.

■ **13630** ■ **Chamberlain Group Inc.**
845 Larch Ave.
Elmhurst, IL 60126
Phone: (630)279-3600 **Fax:** (630)530-6091
Products: Automatic garage door openers; Polishers, sanders, and grinders. **SICs:** 5063 (Electrical Apparatus & Equipment); 5072 (Hardware).

■ **13631** ■ **Chandler Products Co.**
1491 Chardon Rd.
Cleveland, OH 44117
Phone: (216)481-4400 **Fax:** (216)481-4427
Products: Bolts. **SIC:** 5072 (Hardware). **Est:** 1930. **Sales:** $10,000,000 (2000). **Emp:** 150.

■ **13632** ■ **Channellock Inc.**
1306 S Main St.
PO Box 519
Meadville, PA 16335
Phone: (814)724-8700 **Fax:** 800-962-2583
Products: Hand tools; Pliers; Screwdrivers. **SIC:** 5072 (Hardware).

■ **13633** ■ **Chubbuck Sales Inc.**
3536 S Whitingham Dr.
West Covina, CA 91792-2947
Phone: (909)869-0069
Products: Hardware. **SIC:** 5072 (Hardware). **Est:** 1980. **Sales:** $400,000 (2000). **Emp:** 2. **Officers:** Clyde Taylor, President; Diane Taylor, Secretary.

■ **13634** ■ **Clark Supply Co.**
PO Box 24
Falconer, NY 14733
Phone: (716)665-4120 **Fax:** (716)665-3638
URL: http://www.clark-supply.com
Products: Tools; Electrical equipment and supplies; Plumbing fixtures, equipment, and supplies; Heating fixtures, equipment, and supplies. **SICs:** 5063 (Electrical Apparatus & Equipment); 5074 (Plumbing & Hydronic Heating Supplies); 5072 (Hardware). **Est:** 1856. **Sales:** $3,500,000 (2000). **Emp:** 20. **Officers:** John L. Martin, President; John Martin Jr., VP & General Merchandising Mgr.

■ **13635** ■ **Claymore Sieck Co.**
311 E Chase St.
Baltimore, MD 21202
Phone: (410)685-4660
Free: (800)624-7134 **Fax:** (410)685-1547
Products: Durable and nondurable goods. **SICs:** 5099 (Durable Goods Nec); 5199 (Nondurable Goods Nec). **Sales:** $21,000,000 (2000). **Emp:** 40. **Officers:** Jeff Gilliams, CEO.

■ **13636** ■ **Cleco Industrial Fasteners, Inc.**
16701 Lathrop
Harvey, IL 60426-6029
Phone: (708)339-3600 **Fax:** (708)339-8648
Products: Bolts, nuts, rivets, screws, and washers. **SIC:** 5072 (Hardware). **Emp:** 37. **Officers:** Don Rosenberger, Quality Control & Purchasing Mgr.; George Laxton, Warehouse Mgr.; Martha Holloway, Data Processing Mgr.

■ **13637** ■ **Click Bond Inc.**
2151 Lockheed Way
Carson City, NV 89706
Phone: (702)885-8000 **Fax:** (702)883-0191
Products: Aeronautical equipment and supplies. **SIC:** 5072 (Hardware). **Sales:** $5,000,000 (2000). **Emp:** 65.

■ **13638** ■ **Cold Headers Inc.**
5514 N Elston Ave.
Chicago, IL 60630
Phone: (773)775-7900 **Fax:** (773)775-0779
Products: Screws; Nuts; Bolts. **SIC:** 5072 (Hardware). **Est:** 1963. **Sales:** $6,000,000 (2000). **Emp:** 65. **Officers:** Bruce Duncan, President; Rick Duncan, Vice President.

■ **13639** ■ **Coleman Industrial Supply Inc.**
1331 Industrial Way
PO Box 1516
Longview, WA 98632-1017
Phone: (206)425-3620 **Fax:** (206)425-9265
Products: Hardware fasteners; Bolts, nuts, rivets, screws, and washers. **SICs:** 5072 (Hardware); 5085 (Industrial Supplies). **Emp:** 29. **Officers:** C. R. Schneider.

■ **13640** ■ **Colonial Hardware Corp.**
163 Varick St.
New York, NY 10013
Phone: (212)741-8989 **Fax:** (212)741-8193
Products: Tools. **SIC:** 5072 (Hardware). **Est:** 1931. **Emp:** 50.

■ **13641** ■ **Columbus Hardware Supplies Inc.**
944 W 5th Ave.
Columbus, OH 43212
Phone: (614)294-8665 **Fax:** (614)294-8777
Products: Hammers; Power hand tools; Ladders. **SICs:** 5072 (Hardware); 5084 (Industrial Machinery &

Equipment). **Est:** 1884. **Sales:** $5,000,000 (2000). **Emp:** 24. **Officers:** Donald Bowers, President.

■ **13642** ■ **Components West**
6658 Hwy. 89
Ogden, UT 84405
Phone: (801)479-1997
Products: Fasteners and springs. **SIC:** 5072 (Hardware).

■ **13643** ■ **Contico International Inc.**
1101 Warson Rd.
St. Louis, MO 63132
Phone: (314)997-5900 **Fax:** (314)997-1270
Products: Hand and automotive tool boxes; Storage bins; Plastic shelving; Flower pots; Gun cases. **SICs:** 5099 (Durable Goods Nec); 5072 (Hardware). **Est:** 1967. **Emp:** 2,000. **Alternate Name:** Jack Berman.

■ **13644** ■ **Continental Midland**
PO Box 248
Millersport, OH 43046-9748
Phone: (740)467-2677 **Fax:** (740)467-3135
Products: Screws and bolts. **SIC:** 5072 (Hardware). **Sales:** $2,000,000 (2000). **Emp:** 49. **Officers:** R. Thornburg.

■ **13645** ■ **Contractors Heating and Supply Co.**
70 Santa Fe Dr.
Denver, CO 80223
Phone: (303)893-1120 **Fax:** (303)893-0732
Products: Power tools, drills, and hand sanders. **SICs:** 5075 (Warm Air Heating & Air-Conditioning); 5084 (Industrial Machinery & Equipment). **Est:** 1945. **Sales:** $12,000,000 (2000). **Emp:** 48. **Officers:** D.G. Brady, President.

■ **13646** ■ **Copeland Lumber Yard Inc.**
901 NE Glisan St.
Portland, OR 97232
Phone: (503)232-7181
Products: Lumber and wood products; Hardware. **SICs:** 5072 (Hardware); 5031 (Lumber, Plywood & Millwork). **Est:** 1913. **Sales:** $197,000,000 (2000). **Emp:** 999. **Officers:** H. J. Whitsell, Chairman of the Board; W. A. Whitsell, President; R. W. LaDeRoute, Vice President.

■ **13647** ■ **Copeland Lumber Yard Inc.**
901 NE Glisan St.
Portland, OR 97232
Phone: (503)232-7181 **Fax:** (503)233-9759
Products: Lumber and building materials; General-line of hardware. **SIC:** 5072 (Hardware). **Sales:** $175,000,000 (2000). **Emp:** 1,000. **Officers:** Helen J. Whitsell, CEO & Chairman of the Board; Michael Anderson, VP of Finance.

■ **13648** ■ **Cotter and Co.**
8600 W Bryn Mawr Ave.
Chicago, IL 60631-3579
Phone: (773)975-2700 **Fax:** (773)975-1712
Products: Hardware. **SIC:** 5072 (Hardware). **Sales:** $2,130,000,000 (2000). **Emp:** 4,200. **Officers:** Dan A. Cotter, CEO & President; Kerry Kirby, VP of Finance; Jerome Thompson, VP of Marketing; Steve Kirkwood, Dir. of Information Systems.

■ **13649** ■ **Crucible Service Center**
PO Box 445
Butler, WI 53007
Phone: (414)781-6710 **Fax:** (414)781-6743
Products: Steel tools. **SIC:** 5051 (Metals Service Centers & Offices). **Sales:** $15,000,000 (2000). **Emp:** 25. **Officers:** David A. Adamson, General Mgr.

■ **13650** ■ **Cummins Utility Supply**
513 N Nelson
Amarillo, TX 79107-7904
Phone: (806)373-1808
Free: (800)800-3096 **Fax:** (806)373-2313
Products: Wiring supplies; Hand tools. **SICs:** 5072 (Hardware); 5063 (Electrical Apparatus & Equipment). **Est:** 1952. **Emp:** 18. **Officers:** Rod Phillips.

■ **13651** ■ **C.A. Cunningham Co.**
545 Medford St.
PO Box 45
Charlestown, MA 02129
Phone: (617)242-5345
Free: (800)841-8102 **Fax:** (617)242-7651
Products: Builder's hardware. **SIC:** 5072 (Hardware). **Est:** 1880. **Emp:** 13. **Officers:** Jon Cunningham, e-mail: jonc@cacco.com; Robert Raposo, e-mail: robertr@cacco.com; Ralph Lawson.

■ **13652** ■ **Cutlery**
12503 A Wayzata Blvd.
Ridgedale Center
Minnetonka, MN 55343
Phone: (612)545-1484
Products: Knives, scissors, dart supplies, and sharpening tools. **SIC:** 5072 (Hardware). **Emp:** 40. **Officers:** Don Nelson.

■ **13653** ■ **Cutting Tools Inc.**
8601 73rd Ave. N
Brooklyn Park, MN 55428-1571
Phone: (612)535-7757
Free: (800)247-6669 **Fax:** (612)535-2345
E-mail: ctisales@cuttingtoolsincann.com
Products: Cutting tools; Abrasives; Measuring equipment. **SICs:** 5072 (Hardware); 5085 (Industrial Supplies). **Est:** 1980. **Emp:** 19. **Officers:** Ken Johnson, President; Dennis Struss, Vice President.

■ **13654** ■ **D and T Services Inc.**
123 N Columbus Ave.
Louisville, MS 39339
Phone: (601)773-5024
Products: Hardware supplies, including gloves and drill bits. **SICs:** 5072 (Hardware); 5136 (Men's/Boys' Clothing). **Est:** 1968. **Sales:** $2,000,000 (2000). **Emp:** 16. **Officers:** Jerry L. Donald, President; William Donald, Controller.

■ **13655** ■ **Danaher Tool Group**
1609 Old Missouri Rd.
Springdale, AR 72764-2699
Phone: (501)751-8500 **Fax:** (501)751-6914
Products: Tools. **SIC:** 5072 (Hardware). **Est:** 1970. **Sales:** $35,000,000 (2000). **Emp:** 650. **Officers:** B. Fred Turrentine.

■ **13656** ■ **Darling Bolt Co.**
PO Box 2035
Warren, MI 48090
Phone: (313)757-4100 **Fax:** (313)757-1555
Products: Cap screws, washers, nuts, and bolts. **SIC:** 5072 (Hardware). **Est:** 1957. **Sales:** $12,000,000 (2000). **Emp:** 50. **Officers:** D.S. Holl, President; B. Phillips, Controller; T.P. Heacock, Dir. of Marketing.

■ **13657** ■ **Decatur Hopkins**
800 John Quincy Adams
Taunton, MA 02780-1094
Phone: (508)824-8650 **Fax:** (508)824-1775
URL: http://www.dechop.com
Products: Tools and hardware, including screwdrivers, hammers, and nails. **SIC:** 5072 (Hardware). **Est:** 1905. **Sales:** $50,000,000 (2000). **Emp:** 200. **Officers:** William F. Hopkins Jr., President.

■ **13658** ■ **Delaware County Supply Co.**
1000 Randall Ave.
Boothwyn, PA 19061-3538
Phone: (610)485-1812 **Fax:** (610)485-1829
Products: Hardware; Exotic hardwood lumber. **SICs:** 5085 (Industrial Supplies); 5031 (Lumber, Plywood & Millwork); 5072 (Hardware). **Est:** 1924. **Emp:** 35. **Officers:** Alvin Tingle, Manager.

■ **13659** ■ **Delta Fastener Corp.**
7122 Old Katy Rd.
Houston, TX 77024-2112
Phone: (713)868-2351 **Fax:** (713)868-6219
E-mail: delta@texascompx.com
Products: Fasteners. **SIC:** 5072 (Hardware). **Est:** 1972. **Sales:** $3,000,000 (1999). **Emp:** 21. **Officers:** Steve Palmer, President.

■ **13660** ■ **Delta Industrial Systems Co.**
1275 Sawgrass Corporate Pkwy.
Sunrise, FL 33323-2812
Phone: (305)822-9977
Products: Aluminum window and door hardware. **SIC:** 5072 (Hardware). **Est:** 1978. **Sales:** $8,000,000 (2000). **Emp:** 18. **Officers:** Peter Coslett, President; Geoffrey S. DePass, Vice President; Lloyd R. Hepburn, Vice President.

■ **13661** ■ **Delta Wholesale Hardware Co.**
PO Box 729
Clarksdale, MS 38614
Phone: (601)627-4141 **Fax:** (601)627-2147
Products: Hardware. **SIC:** 5072 (Hardware). **Est:** 1905. **Sales:** $3,500,000 (2000). **Emp:** 35. **Officers:** Stovall Carter, President; Kenneth Hawes, Treasurer & Secty.; Tom Barron, Manager.

■ **13662** ■ **Denver Hardware Co.**
3200 Walnut St.
Denver, CO 80205
Phone: (303)292-3550
Products: Hardware. **SIC:** 5072 (Hardware). **Est:** 1945. **Sales:** $8,000,000 (2000). **Emp:** 25. **Officers:** Burton F. Kaatz, CEO; Martin Kaatz, Treasurer & Secty.

■ **13663** ■ **Denver Hardware Co.**
3200 Walnut St.
Denver, CO 80205
Phone: (303)292-3550
Products: Hardware. **SIC:** 5072 (Hardware). **Sales:** $8,000,000 (2000). **Emp:** 25.

■ **13664** ■ **Design House Inc.**
PO Box 1001
Germantown, WI 53022
Phone: (414)255-1970
Free: (800)558-1919 **Fax:** (414)255-9416
E-mail: dhi@execpc.com
Products: Locks; Lights; Bathroom accessories and fittings; Fasteners, including bolts, nuts, rivets, screws, and washers; Fans; Faucets; Doors; Cabinets; Wood products; Shutters;. Vanities. **SICs:** 5039 (Construction Materials Nec); 5031 (Lumber, Plywood & Millwork). **Est:** 1872. **Sales:** $70,000,000 (1999). **Emp:** 200. **Officers:** Kevin Keenan, President; Todd Witte, Sr. VP.

■ **13665** ■ **Dewco Milwaukee Sales**
6235 Industrial Ct.
Greendale, WI 53129
Phone: (414)421-2650
Free: (800)873-9703 **Fax:** (414)421-9396
Products: Abrasive products; Power hand tools; Hand tools. **SICs:** 5085 (Industrial Supplies); 5072 (Hardware). **Emp:** 49.

■ **13666** ■ **Disston Co.**
7345-G W Friendly Ave.
Greensboro, NC 27410-6252
Phone: (919)852-9220 **Fax:** (919)299-0616
Products: Saw blades; Tool and utensil cases; Saws. **SIC:** 5072 (Hardware).

■ **13667** ■ **Diversified Fastening**
501 Richings St.
CharLes City, IA 50616-1838
Phone: (515)228-1162
Free: (800)833-6417 **Fax:** (515)228-6124
Products: Bolts, nuts, rivets, screws, and washers. **SIC:** 5072 (Hardware). **Est:** 1978. **Emp:** 120. **Officers:** Dan Crawford.

■ **13668** ■ **DJ Associates, Inc.**
8411 S Zero St.
Ft. Smith, AR 72903-7097
Phone: (501)452-3987 **Fax:** (501)452-7752
E-mail: dja@pia.com
URL: http://www.pia.com/djassoc
Products: Forged and plastic hardware; Nylon webbing. **SICs:** 5072 (Hardware); 5131 (Piece Goods & Notions). **Est:** 1976. **Officers:** Michael P. Beck, Vice President.

■ 13669 ■ Drago Supply Co. Inc.
740 Houston Ave.
Port Arthur, TX 77640
Phone: (409)983-4911
Products: Hardware; Industrial supplies. SICs: 5072 (Hardware); 5085 (Industrial Supplies). Est: 1931. Sales: $63,000,000 (2000). Emp: 200. Officers: Joseph P. Drago, President & Chairman of the Board; Sam Drago, Exec. VP; Phil Drago Jr., Exec. VP; J.C. delaMoriniere, Vice President.

■ 13670 ■ Drapery Hardware of Florida
2147 NW 29th St.
Ft. Lauderdale, FL 33311
Phone: (954)735-1046
Free: (800)771-4402   Fax: (954)735-6912
URL: http://www.draperyhardware.com
Products: Drapery hardware. SIC: 5072 (Hardware). Est: 1972. Emp: 8. Officers: Sy Posner, President; Sandi Posner, Treasurer; Ron Posner, Vice President.

■ 13671 ■ Duo-Fast Corp. North Central Sales Div.
200 Laura Dr.
Addison, IL 60101
Phone: (708)543-7970
Products: Tools, including staplers and nailers. SIC: 5072 (Hardware). Est: 1950. Sales: $19,000,000 (2000). Emp: 60. Officers: T.B. Bienapfl, Manager.

■ 13672 ■ Duo-Fast Northeast
22 Tolland St.
East Hartford, CT 06108
Phone: (860)289-6861   Fax: (860)291-8784
Products: Staples and nails, adhesives and abrasives. SIC: 5072 (Hardware). Est: 1949. Sales: $8,000,000 (2000). Emp: 40. Officers: Richard Steier, CEO.

■ 13673 ■ Earnest Machine Products Co.
12502 Plaza Dr.
Parma, OH 44130
Phone: (216)362-1100   Fax: (216)362-9970
Products: Nuts and bolts. SIC: 5072 (Hardware). Est: 1948. Sales: $25,000,000 (2000). Emp: 130. Officers: John P. Zehnder, CEO; Philip Gentili, Controller; Joe Lonsway, Sales Mgr.; Tim Weber, Dir. of Information Systems.

■ 13674 ■ John A. Eberly Inc.
PO Box 8047
Syracuse, NY 13217
Phone: (315)449-3034   Fax: (315)476-3426
Products: Cutlery, tweezers and mill supplies. SICs: 5072 (Hardware); 5122 (Drugs, Proprietaries & Sundries); 5085 (Industrial Supplies). Sales: $1,000,000 (2000). Emp: 4. Officers: John Lee, CEO; Herb Jerry, Controller.

■ 13675 ■ Eckart and Finard Inc.
80 Weston St.
Hartford, CT 06120
Phone: (203)246-7411
Free: (800)243-9981   Fax: (203)247-1649
E-mail: fasteners@eckart-finard.com
URL: http://www.eckart-finard.com
Products: Fasteners; Electronic equipment; Adhesives; Abrasives; Cutting tools. SIC: 5072 (Hardware). Est: 1960. Sales: $6,000,000 (2000). Emp: 35. Officers: Marvin Rosenblatt, CEO; Kenneth Rosenblatt, VP of Marketing & Sales; Peter Butcher, VP of Operations.

■ 13676 ■ Econo Trading Company
500 S Independence Ave.
Rockford, IL 61102
Phone: (815)968-5735   Fax: (815)968-3504
Products: Hardware, including hinges, locks, pulls, catches, and knobs. SIC: 5072 (Hardware). Est: 1969. Sales: $500,000 (1999). Emp: 5. Officers: Penny B. VanScoy, General Mgr.

■ 13677 ■ E.K. Fasteners Inc.
15020 Marquardt Ave.
Santa Fe Springs, CA 90670-5704
Phone: (562)404-2121
Products: Fasteners. SIC: 5072 (Hardware). Est: 1967. Sales: $18,000,000 (2000). Emp: 34. Officers: Y. Kitagami, President; T. Kitagami, CFO; T. Iwasaki, Dir. of Marketing.

■ 13678 ■ El Paso Saw and Belting Supply Co.
1701 Texas St.
El Paso, TX 79901
Phone: (915)532-3677   Fax: (915)544-5674
Products: Sandpaper tools. SICs: 5072 (Hardware); 5085 (Industrial Supplies). Est: 1925. Sales: $7,000,000 (2000). Emp: 25. Officers: Patrick Gorman, President; Raul Florres, Finance Officer.

■ 13679 ■ Electronic Fasteners Inc.
PO Box 9182
Waltham, MA 02454
Phone: (617)890-7780
Products: Hardware, including bolts, nuts, rivets, screws, and washers. SIC: 5072 (Hardware). Est: 1960. Sales: $8,200,000 (2000). Emp: 45. Officers: Steven Damalas, President; Maryann Treska, Accounting Manager; Michael DeCenzo, Merchandising Mgr.

■ 13680 ■ Ellsworth Supply Company Inc.
340 E Main St.
Stratford, CT 06497-0328
Phone: (203)375-3317
Free: (800)499-9784   Fax: (203)380-2963
Products: Cutting tools, including saws; Sandblasting equipment and media. SICs: 5072 (Hardware); 5084 (Industrial Machinery & Equipment). Est: 1934. Sales: $800,000 (2000). Emp: 3. Officers: Marjorie Barrett, Owner.

■ 13681 ■ Emery Waterhouse Co.
PO Box 659
Portland, ME 04104
Phone: (207)775-2371   Fax: (207)775-1821
Products: Hardware; Housewares; Paint; Machinery. SICs: 5072 (Hardware); 5023 (Homefurnishings); 5084 (Industrial Machinery & Equipment); 5198 (Paints, Varnishes & Supplies). Est: 1842. Sales: $90,000,000 (2000). Emp: 300. Officers: Charles Hildrein Jr., President; Kirby Kramer, VP of Finance; Steven Frawley, Sr. VP of Marketing & Sales; Don Hills, VP of Information Systems; Ernie Lebel, VP of Human Resources.

■ 13682 ■ Empire Level Manufacturing Corp.
929 Empire Dr.
Mukwonago, WI 53149
Phone: (262)368-2000
Free: (800)558-0722   Fax: (262)368-2127
E-mail: empire@empirelevel.com
URL: http://www.empirelevel.com
Products: Hand tools, including levels, squares, and measuring tape; Underground warning tape. SIC: 5072 (Hardware). Est: 1919. Emp: 300. Officers: John Dwyer, Sales/Marketing Contact, e-mail: dwyerj@empirelevel.com.

■ 13683 ■ Empire Machinery and Supply Co.
3550 Virginia Beach Blvd.
Norfolk, VA 23501
Phone: (804)855-1011   Fax: (804)855-4496
Products: Building supplies, including screws and tools. SICs: 5085 (Industrial Supplies); 5072 (Hardware). Est: 1914. Sales: $18,000,000 (2000). Emp: 100. Officers: Wiley Kidd, CEO; Linwood Diggs, CFO; H.C. Turner Jr., Exec. VP of Marketing; Kevin Sweeney, Dir. of Systems.

■ 13684 ■ Empire Staple Co.
1710 Platte St.
Denver, CO 80202
Phone: (303)433-6803   Fax: (303)433-4015
Products: Building tools. SIC: 5072 (Hardware). Est: 1952. Emp: 50. Officers: William J. Spicer, Manager; Curt Robinson, Sales/Marketing Contact; Chris Merkel, Customer Service Contact; Mark Kozin, Human Resources Contact.

■ 13685 ■ Enderes Tool Co. Inc.
PO Box 240189
Apple Valley, MN 55124
Phone: (612)891-1200   Fax: (612)891-1202
Products: Screwdrivers; Chisels; Hardware. SIC: 5072 (Hardware). Sales: $7,000,000 (2000). Emp: 50. Officers: M. Bothum, President; T. Dahl, CFO; M. Palkovich.

■ 13686 ■ Harry J. Epstein Co.
301 W 8th
Kansas City, MO 64105-1567
Phone: (816)421-4752
Free: (800)821-5503   Fax: (816)421-4647
Products: American-made hand tools. SIC: 5072 (Hardware). Est: 1933. Sales: $2,000,000 (2000). Emp: 9. Officers: Kenneth C. Sackin, President; Steve Sackin, VP of Marketing & Sales.

■ 13687 ■ Equality Screw Co. Inc.
PO Box 1645
El Cajon, CA 92022
Phone: (619)562-6100
Free: (800)854-2886   Fax: (619)440-3979
E-mail: sales@eqscrew.com
URL: http://www.eqscrew.com
Products: Screws for cabinet and woodworking industries. SIC: 5072 (Hardware). Est: 1970. Sales: $4,000,000 (2000). Emp: 15. Officers: Steven E. Gumbiner, President; Linda Tuininga, Controller.

■ 13688 ■ Erb Hardware Co. Ltd.
PO Box 616
Lewiston, ID 83501
Phone: (208)746-0441   Fax: (208)746-5506
Products: Home remodeling equipment, including nails and lumber. SICs: 5072 (Hardware); 5039 (Construction Materials Nec); 5051 (Metals Service Centers & Offices). Est: 1897. Sales: $3,000,000 (2000). Emp: 30. Officers: R. Bennett, President; J. Bennett, Vice President; Orville C. Willard, VP of Marketing; Karla Dahlberg, Dir. of Data Processing.

■ 13689 ■ Evans Findings Company, Inc.
33 Eastern Ave.
East Providence, RI 02914
Phone: (401)434-5600   Fax: (401)434-6908
Products: Metal stampings. SIC: 5072 (Hardware). Est: 1928. Sales: $5,000,000 (2000). Emp: 55. Doing Business As: Evans Co.

■ 13690 ■ Fabsco Corp.
1745 W 124th St.
Calumet Park, IL 60827
Phone: (708)371-7500   Fax: (708)371-7524
E-mail: info@fabscocorp.com
URL: http://www.fabscocorp.com
Products: Anchor bolts and threaded rod. SIC: 5072 (Hardware). Est: 1960. Sales: $2,500,000 (2000). Emp: 23. Officers: J. C. O'Neill; Kevin O'Neill, Sales/Marketing Contact; Michael O'Neill, Managing Dir.

■ 13691 ■ Fairbanks Co.
PO Box 1871
Rome, GA 30161
Phone: (706)234-6701
Free: (800)831-0022   Fax: (706)234-6910
E-mail: fksco@aol.com
URL: http://www.fairbankscocoasters.com
Products: Casters; Wheels; Handtrucks. SIC: 5072 (Hardware). Est: 1887. Emp: 100. Officers: E. A. Brumbelow, VP of Production; Arlene Touchstone, Sales Mgr.; Andrew Rawlins, Purchasing Mgr.; Tony Grimes, Dir. of Engineering.

■ 13692 ■ Fairmont Tamper
PO Box 415
Fairmont, MN 56031-0415
Phone: (507)235-3361
Products: Power handtools. SIC: 5072 (Hardware). Sales: $110,000,000 (1994). Emp: 900. Officers: G. Robert Newman, President; Darrell M. Christensen, VP & Controller.

■ 13693 ■ Fairview True Value Hardware
68 Violet Ave.
Poughkeepsie, NY 12601-1521
Phone: (914)485-4700   Fax: (914)452-7156
Products: Hardware tools; Paint. SICs: 5072 (Hardware); 5198 (Paints, Varnishes & Supplies). Emp: 49. Officers: John Art Ackert; Harry Scherr IV, President.

■ 13694 ■ Fasnap Corp.
PO Box 1613
Elkhart, IN 46515
Phone: (219)264-1185
Free: (800)624-2058   Fax: (219)264-0802
E-mail: sales@fasnap.com
URL: http://www.fasnap.com
Products: Snap fasteners; Grommets; Washers; Upholstery button coverings; Bench mounted and automatic setting machines. SICs: 5072 (Hardware); 5085 (Industrial Supplies). Est: 1981. Sales: $5,500,000 (2000). Emp: 20. Officers: Paul E. Reed, Secretary; Sally Reed, Vice President; Steven Reed, President; Craig Miller, Sales Representative.

■ 13695 ■ Fastec Industrial
23348 County Rd. 6
Elkhart, IN 46514
Phone: (219)262-2505
Free: (800)837-2505   Fax: (219)266-0123
Products: Hardware, including screws, nuts, and bolts; Door locks. SIC: 5072 (Hardware). Est: 1979. Sales: $20,000,000 (2000). Emp: 100. Officers: J. Braddock, President; C. White, Exec. VP; M. Marshall, Vice President; Dennis Strahan, Sales/Marketing Contact.

■ 13696 ■ Fastenal Co.
2001 Theurer Blvd.
Winona, MN 55987-1500
Phone: (507)454-5374   Fax: (507)453-8049
Products: Bolts, screws, and nuts. SIC: 5072 (Hardware). Est: 1967. Sales: $398,000,000 (2000). Emp: 3,073. Officers: Robert A. Kierlin, CEO, President & Chairman of the Board; Daniel L. Florness, CFO & Treasurer; Robert Strauss, Sales Mgr.; Patrick J. Rice, Controller; Reyne Wisecupp, Dir of Human Resources.

■ 13697 ■ Fastener Controls Inc. (FASCON)
15915 Piuma Ave.
Cerritos, CA 90703-1526
Phone: (562)860-1097   Fax: (562)860-0987
Products: Bolts; Screws. SIC: 5046 (Commercial Equipment Nec). Est: 1966. Sales: $1,000,000 (1999). Emp: 6. Officers: Lynn W. Farmer, President.

■ 13698 ■ Fastener Supply Co.
1340 Amble Dr.
Charlotte, NC 28206
Phone: (704)596-7634
Free: (800)888-9519   Fax: (704)596-8160
Products: Bolts, nuts, rivets, screws, and washers. SICs: 5072 (Hardware); 5085 (Industrial Supplies). Emp: 60.

■ 13699 ■ Fasteners Inc.
PO Box 80604
Seattle, WA 98108
Phone: (206)763-2275
Free: (800)562-8392   Fax: (206)763-1941
Products: Fasteners, nuts, bolts, screws and washers. SIC: 5072 (Hardware). Sales: $9,000,000 (2000). Emp: 40. Officers: Scott Petterson, President; Robert Cosmo, Controller.

■ 13700 ■ Fasteners & Metal Products Corp.
30 Thayer Rd.
Waltham, MA 02454
Phone: (617)489-0414   Fax: (617)489-1171
Products: Hardware fasteners; Bolts, nuts, rivets, screws, and washers. SIC: 5072 (Hardware). Est: 1954. Sales: $5,000,000 (2000). Emp: 20. Officers: T. J. Hatzis.

■ 13701 ■ Fastner House
4601 Honeywell Dr.
Ft. Wayne, IN 46825-6270
Phone: (219)484-0702
Products: Nuts and bolts. SIC: 5072 (Hardware). Sales: $2,000,000 (1994). Emp: 10. Officers: Dick Miller, General Mgr.

■ 13702 ■ Faucet-Queens Inc.
401 Chaddick Dr.
Wheeling, IL 60090
Phone: (847)541-7777   Fax: (847)541-7708
Products: Tools; Hardware supplies, including screws, nuts, and fasteners; Plumbing accessories. SICs: 5072 (Hardware); 5074 (Plumbing & Hydronic

Heating Supplies). Est: 1945. Sales: $12,000,000 (2000). Emp: 53. Officers: John W. Lehman, President; Sonja Johnston, Dir. of Systems.

■ 13703 ■ Faucet-Queens Inc.
650 Forest Edge Dr.
Vernon Hills, IL 60061
Phone: (847)821-0777   Fax: (847)821-0277
Products: Hardware; Plumbing equipment. SICs: 5072 (Hardware); 5074 (Plumbing & Hydronic Heating Supplies). Sales: $15,000,000 (2000). Emp: 53. Officers: John W. Lehman, President; Bruce A. Rinnert, VP & Controller.

■ 13704 ■ Federal Screw Products Inc.
3917 N Kedzie Ave.
Chicago, IL 60618
Phone: (773)478-5744   Fax: (773)478-4147
Products: Screws; Nuts; Bolts; Fans. SIC: 5072 (Hardware). Est: 1931. Sales: $2,500,000 (2000). Emp: 25. Officers: A. Knott, President; C. Marc, Vice President.

■ 13705 ■ Fehr Bros. Industries Inc.
895 Kings Hwy.
Saugerties, NY 12477
Phone: (845)246-9525
Free: (800)431-3095   Fax: (845)246-3330
E-mail: fehr@fehr.com
URL: http://www.fehr.com
Products: Hardware and rigging hardware; Chain; Cable. SICs: 5085 (Industrial Supplies); 5072 (Hardware). Est: 1949. Sales: $13,600,000 (2000). Emp: 54. Officers: Richard Dooley, President, e-mail: info@fehr.com.

■ 13706 ■ First Choice Tool Co.
1210 Progress St.
PO Box 670
Sturgis, MI 49091
Phone: (616)651-7964
Free: (800)782-4659   Fax: (616)651-4412
E-mail: firstchoice@voyager.net
URL: http://www.firstchoicetool.com
Products: Hand tools, including sheet metal bending/forming tools; Snips, including aviation, tinner and utility; Wrenches. SIC: 5072 (Hardware). Officers: Stephen Deter, President; Aimee Audette, Customer Service Mgr.; Robert Besser, Sales/Marketing Contact.

■ 13707 ■ Fitchburg Hardware Company Inc.
692 N Main St.
Leominster, MA 01453
Phone: (978)534-4956
Products: Hardware, including nuts and bolts. SIC: 5072 (Hardware). Est: 1858. Sales: $4,500,000 (2000). Emp: 15. Officers: Marie B. Martino, President.

■ 13708 ■ Five Star Trading Company
PO Box 11451
Bainbridge Island, WA 98110-5451
Phone: (206)842-6542   Fax: (206)842-0536
Products: Hand tools; Farm equipment; Scrap paper. SICs: 5072 (Hardware); 5093 (Scrap & Waste Materials); 5083 (Farm & Garden Machinery). Officers: Stephen T. Smith, President.

■ 13709 ■ The Fletcher-Terry Company
225 Riverview Ave.
Waltham, MA 02454
Phone: (781)647-5560   Fax: (781)891-8375
Products: Tools, including glass cutters, point drivers, framing machines, and glaziers' tools. SICs: 5072 (Hardware); 5085 (Industrial Supplies). Officers: Joaquim Pires; Clinton McKim.

■ 13710 ■ Florida Bolt and Nut Co.
3875 Fiscal Ct.
Riviera Beach, FL 33404
Phone: (561)842-2658   Fax: (561)540-2658
E-mail: flabolt@worldnet.att.net
Products: Nuts; Bolts. SIC: 5072 (Hardware). Est: 1953. Sales: $2,000,000 (2000). Emp: 12. Officers: Cheryl A. Warner, President.

■ 13711 ■ Florida Bolt and Nut Co.
3875 Fiscal Ct.
Riviera Beach, FL 33404
Phone: (561)842-2658   Fax: (561)540-2658
Products: Hardware. SIC: 5072 (Hardware). Sales: $2,000,000 (2000). Emp: 12.

■ 13712 ■ Florida Hardware Co.
436 Cassat Ave.
Jacksonville, FL 32254
Phone: (904)783-1650   Fax: (904)783-4556
E-mail: fhcjax@bellsouth.net
Products: Hardware. SIC: 5072 (Hardware). Est: 1886. Sales: $20,000,000 (2000). Emp: 80.

■ 13713 ■ Foley-Belsaw Co.
6301 Equitable Rd.
Kansas City, MO 64120
Phone: (816)483-6400
Free: (800)821-3452   Fax: (816)483-5010
E-mail: foley@foley-belsaw.com
URL: http://www.foley-belsaw.com
Products: Sharpening equipment. SIC: 5072 (Hardware). Est: 1926. Officers: Joe Brennan, Sales Mgr.

■ 13714 ■ Foltz Manufacturing and Supply Co.
65 E Washington St.
Hagerstown, MD 21740
Phone: (301)739-1076   Fax: (301)891-1250
Products: Hand tools, including sand paper, hammers, and saws. SICs: 5072 (Hardware); 5051 (Metals Service Centers & Offices). Est: 1877. Sales: $4,000,000 (2000). Emp: 25. Officers: R.A. Foltz, President; Henry C. Foltz III, Treasurer.

■ 13715 ■ Frederick Trading Co.
7901 Trading Ln.
Frederick, MD 21705
Phone: (301)662-2161
Free: (800)995-8190   Fax: (301)662-7243
Products: Hardware and plumbing equipment. SICs: 5072 (Hardware); 5074 (Plumbing & Hydronic Heating Supplies). Sales: $103,000,000 (2000). Emp: 360. Officers: Bill Fondren, President.

■ 13716 ■ Fried Brothers Inc.
467 N 7th St.
Philadelphia, PA 19123
Phone: (215)627-3205
Free: (800)523-2924   Fax: (215)627-2676
E-mail: FBIsecurity@FBIsecurity.com
URL: http://www.FBIsecurity.com
Products: Door hardware; Safes; Access control; Locks; Keys; Door closers; Panic devices; Key machines and cabinets; Locksmith supplies. SIC: 5072 (Hardware). Est: 1922. Sales: $5,000,000 (1999). Emp: 25. Officers: Alex Ebrahimzadeh, President; A. Ebrahimzadeh, President.

■ 13717 ■ Frontier Fasteners Inc.
12710 Market
Houston, TX 77015
Phone: (713)451-4242   Fax: (713)451-6565
Products: Fasteners; Nuts and bolts; Screws. SIC: 5072 (Hardware). Est: 1981. Sales: $2,500,000 (2000). Emp: 15. Officers: Jerry Williams, President; Arnold Shaw, Vice President; Robyn Varnado, Secretary.

■ 13718 ■ Fulton Corp.
303 8th Ave.
Fulton, IL 61252
Phone: (815)589-3211
Free: (800)252-0002   Fax: (815)589-4433
E-mail: service@fultoncorp.com
URL: http://www.fultoncorp.com
Products: Hardware products; Mail boxes. SICs: 5072 (Hardware); 5099 (Durable Goods Nec). Est: 1969. Emp: 60. Officers: Dee Willoughby, President; Thomas C. Taylor, VP of Sales; Linda Fall.

■ 13719 ■ Funk Machine and Supply
1805 Yolande Ave.
Lincoln, NE 68521
Phone: (402)475-5477
Products: Nuts and bolts. SIC: 5072 (Hardware).

■ 13720 ■ **Garden Exchange Limited**
300 Keawe St.
Hilo, HI 96720
Phone: (808)961-2875 **Fax:** (808)961-9234
E-mail: gardenx@interpac.net
Products: Hardware; Garden equipment and supplies, including fertilizer and lawnmowers. **SICs:** 5072 (Hardware); 5083 (Farm & Garden Machinery); 5191 (Farm Supplies). **Est:** 1964. **Emp:** 17. **Officers:** Sachiko Ikeda, President; Jeffrey Enriques-Ikeda, Vice President; Lee Enriques, Sec. & Treas.; Russell Enriques, Treasurer.

■ 13721 ■ **General Fasteners Company Inc.**
11820 Globe St.
Livonia, MI 48150-1180
Phone: (313)591-9500 **Fax:** (313)591-6387
Products: Hardware, including fasteners, nuts, and bolts. **SIC:** 5072 (Hardware). **Est:** 1952. **Sales:** $56,000,000 (2000). **Emp:** 200. **Officers:** David H. Grossman, President; Alfred L. Winebarger, CFO; Robert Ramsey, Dir. of Sales.

■ 13722 ■ **General Tool and Supply Co.**
2705 NW Nicolai St.
Portland, OR 97210-1818
Phone: (503)226-3411
Free: (800)783-3411 **Fax:** (503)778-5518
URL: http://www.generaltool.com
Products: Tools, including saws, electrical tools, and hammers. **SICs:** 5085 (Industrial Supplies); 5072 (Hardware). **Est:** 1925. **Sales:** $46,000,000 (2000). **Emp:** 140. **Officers:** William Derville, President.

■ 13723 ■ **GLF/SAE**
125 Blaze Industrial Pky.
Berea, OH 44017-8004
Phone: (440)239-2015 **Fax:** (440)239-2000
Products: Bolts, nuts, rivets, screws, and washers; Hardware fasteners. **SIC:** 5072 (Hardware). **Emp:** 20. **Officers:** Alex Sluzniak. **Former Name:** Great Lakes Fastener, Inc.

■ 13724 ■ **Global Fastener Inc.**
10634 Control Place Dr.
Dallas, TX 75238-1310
Phone: (214)340-6068
Free: (800)553-7998 **Fax:** (214)340-3618
E-mail: globalf@flash.net
URL: http://www.globalfasteners.com
Products: Fasteners; Electronic hardware. **SICs:** 5072 (Hardware); 5065 (Electronic Parts & Equipment Nec); 5085 (Industrial Supplies). **Est:** 1983. **Emp:** 12. **Officers:** James Powdrill, President.

■ 13725 ■ **Globemaster Inc.**
9714 Old Katy Rd.
Houston, TX 77055
Phone: (713)464-8256
Products: Tool and tackle boxes. **SICs:** 5072 (Hardware); 5091 (Sporting & Recreational Goods). **Est:** 1967. **Sales:** $4,000,000 (2000). **Emp:** 65. **Officers:** John P. Lundeen, Vice President; Mike Ford, Controller; Patty Mosher, Sales Mgr.

■ 13726 ■ **GM International Inc.**
PO Box 1346
Elkhart, IN 46515
Phone: (219)295-1080 **Fax:** (219)295-1033
Products: Hardware; Fasteners. **SIC:** 5072 (Hardware). **Est:** 1968. **Sales:** $20,000,000 (2000). **Emp:** 75. **Officers:** Stan Hingle, President; Jeff Stetten, Treasurer.

■ 13727 ■ **Goff Custom Spring Inc.**
410 Township Rd. 219
Bellefontaine, OH 43311
Products: Springs. **SIC:** 5072 (Hardware).

■ 13728 ■ **Dave Grattan & Sons Inc.**
16147 Montoya St.
PO Box 2264
Irwindale, CA 91706-1147
Phone: (626)969-1703
Free: (800)468-9513 **Fax:** (626)334-7218
Products: Hardware fasteners. **SICs:** 5072 (Hardware); 5085 (Industrial Supplies). **Sales:** $8,000,000 (2000). **Emp:** 99.

■ 13729 ■ **Gulf Bolt & Supply**
403 E Brazos
PO Box 2112
Victoria, TX 77901
Phone: (512)575-6441
Free: (800)753-7884 **Fax:** (512)575-3584
Products: Bolts, nuts, rivets, screws, and washers. **SIC:** 5072 (Hardware). **Emp:** 19. **Officers:** Diane Shroller; Edward Kalinowski Sr.

■ 13730 ■ **H. and E. Brothers Inc.**
14021 Amargosa Rd.
Victorville, CA 92392
Phone: (760)241-7540
Products: Home improvement supplies and equipment. **SIC:** 5072 (Hardware). **Est:** 1952. **Sales:** $40,000,000 (2000). **Emp:** 350. **Officers:** E. M. Stein, President; Phillip Stein, CEO; Dee Dee Nielson, Dir. of Marketing.

■ 13731 ■ **Hafele America Co.**
PO Box 4000
Archdale, NC 27263
Phone: (910)889-2322
Free: (800)334-1873 **Fax:** (919)431-3831
Products: Furniture fittings. **SIC:** 5072 (Hardware). **Sales:** $2,000,000 (2000). **Emp:** 99. **Officers:** Wolfgang Hafele.

■ 13732 ■ **Hager Companies**
139 Victor St.
St. Louis, MO 63104
Phone: (314)772-4400 **Fax:** (314)772-0744
E-mail: http://www.hagerhinge.com
Products: Hardware, including hinges, door trim and accessories, weather-and threshold-stripping, and building materials. **SIC:** 5072 (Hardware). **Officers:** Steven N. Curran, Sales/Marketing Contact, e-mail: scurran@hagerhinge.com; Steve Welch, Customer Service Contact, e-mail: swelch@hagerhinge.com.

■ 13733 ■ **Handy Hardware Wholesale Inc.**
PO Box 12847
Houston, TX 77217
Phone: (713)644-1495 **Fax:** (713)644-3167
Products: Hardware. **SIC:** 5072 (Hardware). **Est:** 1961. **Sales:** $158,000,000 (1999). **Emp:** 290. **Officers:** James D. Tipton, President; Tina Kirbie, VP of Finance; Daniel H. King, VP of Merchandising; Duwayne Maurer, VP Mgt. Information Systems; David Washburn, VP of Warehouse & Delivery Operations.

■ 13734 ■ **Harco**
557 S Douglas St.
El Segundo, CA 90245-4891
Phone: (310)643-9400 **Fax:** (310)643-8007
Products: Nuts. **SIC:** 5072 (Hardware). **Sales:** $11,000,000 (2000). **Emp:** 49.

■ 13735 ■ **Hardlines Marketing Inc.**
PO Box 23080
Milwaukee, WI 53223
Phone: (414)351-4700
Free: (800)288-0304 **Fax:** (414)351-9110
Products: Paper and allied products; Tools; Paints and allied products; Metal window and door screens and metal weather strip; Automotive parts and supplies, New. **SICs:** 5072 (Hardware); 5113 (Industrial & Personal Service Paper); 5083 (Farm & Garden Machinery); 5198 (Paints, Varnishes & Supplies); 5013 (Motor Vehicle Supplies & New Parts). **Est:** 1977. **Sales:** $27,000,000 (2000). **Emp:** 100. **Officers:** S. Gendelman.

■ 13736 ■ **Hardware Distribution Warehouses Inc.**
6900 Woolworth Rd.
Shreveport, LA 71129
Phone: (318)686-8527
Free: (800)256-8527 **Fax:** (318)686-8550
URL: http://www.hdwinc.com
Products: Hardware. **SICs:** 5072 (Hardware); 5074 (Plumbing & Hydronic Heating Supplies); 5063 (Electrical Apparatus & Equipment). **Est:** 1970. **Sales:** $50,000,000 (1999). **Emp:** 200. **Officers:** Kenneth R. Beauvais, CEO & President; Wade Wilkerson, CFO; James Coghlan, VP of Sales; Bill Millerd, VP of Marketing & Merchandising; Mary Ann Burton, General

Mgr.; Stanton Horne, Director MIS. **Former Name:** South States, Inc.

■ 13737 ■ **Hardware Distributors Inc.**
2580 Getty St.
Muskegon, MI 49444
Phone: (616)733-2641
Free: (800)686-9950 **Fax:** (616)733-2643
Products: Lawn and garden supplies; Hand and power tools; Electrical supplies; Plumbing supplies; Paint. **SICs:** 5072 (Hardware); 5083 (Farm & Garden Machinery); 5063 (Electrical Apparatus & Equipment); 5198 (Paints, Varnishes & Supplies); 5074 (Plumbing & Hydronic Heating Supplies). **Est:** 1952. **Sales:** $6,500,000 (2000). **Emp:** 35. **Officers:** Arthur W. Brown, CEO; Steve Hegedus, CFO; Dan Workman, Dir. of Marketing; Barb Workman, Dir of Human Resources.

■ 13738 ■ **Hardware Imagination**
4300 NW 37th Ave.
Miami, FL 33142
Phone: (305)635-3300
Free: (800)821-3248 **Fax:** (305)635-1300
Products: Cabinetry materials, including plywood, laminate, hardware, adhesives. **SIC:** 5072 (Hardware). **Est:** 1984. **Sales:** $20,000,000 (1999). **Emp:** 80. **Officers:** Jim Roye, President; John Davis, Sec. & Treas.; Louis Perez, Human Resources.

■ 13739 ■ **Hardware Specialties Co.**
3419 11th Ave. SW
Seattle, WA 98134
Phone: (206)624-5785 **Fax:** (206)682-0186
Products: Marine electrical hardware. **SICs:** 5072 (Hardware); 5063 (Electrical Apparatus & Equipment). **Est:** 1946. **Sales:** $5,000,000 (2000). **Emp:** 19. **Officers:** Conrad Unger, CEO.

■ 13740 ■ **Hardware Specialty Company Inc.**
48-75 36th St.
Long Island City, NY 11101
Phone: (718)361-9393 **Fax:** (718)706-0238
Products: Hardware. **SIC:** 5072 (Hardware). **Est:** 1932. **Sales:** $40,000,000 (2000). **Emp:** 169. **Officers:** Edward Kaufman, President; Al Rozbruch, CFO; Peter Foyto, Dir. of Marketing.

■ 13741 ■ **Hardware Supply Company Inc.**
940 Chestnut
PO BOX 240
Terre Haute, IN 47808-0240
Phone: (812)232-9474
Free: (800)827-2707 **Fax:** (812)232-9473
Products: Hardware. **SICs:** 5072 (Hardware); 5085 (Industrial Supplies). **Est:** 1932. **Sales:** $2,000,000 (2000). **Emp:** 10. **Officers:** Mel Krueger; Troy Mann, Sales/Marketing Contact.

■ 13742 ■ **Hollis Harrell Co.**
PO Box 89
Hazlehurst, MS 39083
Phone: (601)894-4856
Products: Building materials, including nails, bolts, and wood. **SICs:** 5072 (Hardware); 5031 (Lumber, Plywood & Millwork); 5051 (Metals Service Centers & Offices). **Est:** 1938. **Sales:** $3,000,000 (2000). **Emp:** 13. **Officers:** William C. Harrell, President; Hollis Harrell, Vice President.

■ 13743 ■ **Harrington Tools Inc.**
4316 Alger St.
Los Angeles, CA 90039
Phone: (323)245-2142
Free: (800)331-6291 **Fax:** (818)500-8378
Products: Hand tools. **SIC:** 5072 (Hardware). **Est:** 1938. **Sales:** $7,000,000 (2000). **Emp:** 100. **Officers:** Michelle Harrington, President; Rick Hall, Vice President.

■ 13744 ■ **Hasson-Bryan Hardware Co.**
114 W Main
Morristown, TN 37814
Phone: (423)586-2283 **Fax:** (423)581-5506
Products: Hardware, including rulers, tapes, nails, and hammers; Pipes and fittings. **SICs:** 5072 (Hardware); 5085 (Industrial Supplies). **Est:** 1923. **Sales:** $5,000,000 (2000). **Emp:** 38. **Officers:** B.E. Davis, President & Treasurer.

■ 13745 ■ Hawaii Hardware Company Ltd.
550 Kilauea Ave.
Hilo, HI 96720
Phone: (808)935-3795 **Fax:** (808)935-5518
Products: Tools; Building supplies; Paints. **SICs:** 5072 (Hardware); 5039 (Construction Materials Nec); 5085 (Industrial Supplies); 5198 (Paints, Varnishes & Supplies).

■ 13746 ■ Hawley Industrial Supplies Inc.
1020 Fairfield Ave.
Bridgeport, CT 06605
Phone: (203)366-4541 **Fax:** (203)336-1918
Products: Hardware, including pipes, fitting, lathes, and drills. **SICs:** 5072 (Hardware); 5084 (Industrial Machinery & Equipment). **Est:** 1876. **Sales:** $10,000,000 (2000). **Emp:** 100. **Officers:** Joseph H. Stagg III, CEO & President.

■ 13747 ■ Heads & Threads Co.
2727 Shermer Rd.
Northbrook, IL 60062-7708
Products: Fasteners. **SIC:** 5072 (Hardware). **Emp:** 49.

■ 13748 ■ Heads and Threads Div.
2727 Shermer Rd.
Northbrook, IL 60062
Phone: (847)564-1100 **Fax:** (847)480-1787
Products: Steel fasteners. **SIC:** 5072 (Hardware). **Sales:** $54,000,000 (2000). **Emp:** 165. **Officers:** Lee Bookman, President; Myrna Neuman, Controller.

■ 13749 ■ Heads and Threads International, LLC
PO Box 39
Sayreville, NJ 08872-9998
Phone: (732)727-5800
Free: (800)929-1950 **Fax:** (732)727-5888
URL: http://www.headsandthreads.com
Products: Nuts and bolts. **SIC:** 5072 (Hardware). **Est:** 1953. **Sales:** $160,000,000 (2000). **Emp:** 320. **Officers:** Steve Schonholtz, President; Glenn Mayer, VP of Sales; Leah Mazur, Regional Mgr.; Peter Blake Jr., Dir. of Mktg. & Sales. **Former Name:** Gardenbolt International Corp.

■ 13750 ■ Heart of America Bolt
5185 Merriam Dr.
Shawnee Mission, KS 66203-2122
Phone: (913)384-0242 **Fax:** (913)384-0292
Products: Fasteners, including nuts, bolts, and washers. **SIC:** 5072 (Hardware). **Est:** 1978. **Emp:** 22. **Officers:** Edward R. Oshman; Robert D. Oshman, e-mail: roshman@aol.com.

■ 13751 ■ Herald Wholesalers Inc.
20830 Coolidge
Oak Park, MI 48237
Phone: (248)398-4560
Free: (800)323-5042 **Fax:** (248)398-2733
Products: Hardware; Builders' hardware; Plumbing fixtures, equipment, and supplies; Household appliances; Small electrical appliances; Cabinets; Windows; Door frames; Lighting equipment; Propeller fans and accessories, axial fans, and power roof ventilators; Mirrors; House furnishings. **SICs:** 5072 (Hardware); 5074 (Plumbing & Hydronic Heating Supplies); 5064 (Electrical Appliances—Television & Radio); 5031 (Lumber, Plywood & Millwork); 5023 (Homefurnishings). **Est:** 1956. **Emp:** 60. **Officers:** Gerald Katz, Pres./Owner.

■ 13752 ■ Heritage Industries
4605 Spring Rd.
Cleveland, OH 44131-1021
Phone: (216)398-8776 **Fax:** (216)661-5777
Products: Hand tools; Abrasive products. **SICs:** 5072 (Hardware); 5169 (Chemicals & Allied Products Nec). **Est:** 1985. **Emp:** 30.

■ 13753 ■ Hillman Fastener
10590 Hamilton Ave.
Cincinnati, OH 45248
Phone: (513)851-4900 **Fax:** (513)851-4997
Products: Nuts, bolts, and screws; Concrete fasteners. **SIC:** 5072 (Hardware). **Sales:** $46,000,000 (2000). **Emp:** 200. **Officers:** Max Hillman Jr., President; J. Gallagher, VP of Finance; Rick Hillman, VP of Marketing; Ken Foskey, Dir. of Data Processing.

■ 13754 ■ Hitachi Power Tools USA Ltd.
3950 Steve Reynolds
Norcross, GA 30093
Phone: (770)925-1774
Free: (800)829-4752 **Fax:** (770)279-4293
E-mail: hku-usa@hitachi-powertools.com
URL: http://www.hitachi.com
Products: Electric and pneumatic power tools and parts. **SIC:** 5072 (Hardware). **Est:** 1984. **Sales:** $120,000,000 (2000). **Emp:** 170. **Officers:** Masayoshi Ishizuka, President; Shoji Matsushima, Vice President; Steve Karagan.

■ 13755 ■ Holo-Krome Co.
PO Box 330635
West Hartford, CT 06110
Phone: (860)523-5235 **Fax:** 800-243-3149
Products: Fasteners. **SICs:** 5072 (Hardware); 5085 (Industrial Supplies). **Est:** 1929. **Emp:** 99.

■ 13756 ■ Homier Distributing Inc.
84 Commercial Rd.
Huntington, IN 46750-8800
Phone: (219)356-9477
Free: (800)348-5004 **Fax:** (219)356-4358
Products: Tools; Electric and electronic equipment. **SICs:** 5063 (Electrical Apparatus & Equipment); 5072 (Hardware). **Est:** 1958. **Emp:** 120. **Officers:** Charles Homier.

■ 13757 ■ Horizon Distribution Inc.
226 S 1st St.
Yakima, WA 98901
Phone: (509)453-3181
Free: (800)572-3806 **Fax:** (509)457-5769
Products: Hardware and industrial supplies. **SICs:** 5072 (Hardware); 5085 (Industrial Supplies). **Sales:** $24,000,000 (2000). **Emp:** 75. **Officers:** Ken Marble, President; Dan Marples, Finance Officer.

■ 13758 ■ House-Hasson Hardware Inc.
3125 Waterplant Rd.
Knoxville, TN 37914
Phone: (931)525-0471
Products: Hardware. **SIC:** 5072 (Hardware). **Sales:** $42,000,000 (1993). **Emp:** 178. **Officers:** Don Hasson, President; Robert Harless, VP & Secty.

■ 13759 ■ HPM Building Supply
380 Kanoelehua Ave.
Hilo, HI 96720
Phone: (808)935-0875 **Fax:** (808)961-4019
Products: Building supplies, including nails, hammers, and tools. **SIC:** 5072 (Hardware). **Est:** 1921. **Sales:** $47,000,000 (2000). **Emp:** 205. **Officers:** Robert M. Fujimoto, CEO & President; Michael K. Fujimoto, Exec. VP; Vern F. Berry, VP of Marketing & Sales; Linda Nako, Dir. of Information Systems; Thuy N. Fujimoto, Dir of Human Resources.

■ 13760 ■ Huffaker's Inc.
PO Box 790290
San Antonio, TX 78279
Phone: (210)344-8373 **Fax:** (210)344-0943
Products: Hardware. **SIC:** 5072 (Hardware). **Est:** 1914. **Sales:** $5,000,000 (2000). **Emp:** 29. **Officers:** George E. Nelson, President; James R. Cate, CEO; Kent Nelson, Vice President; Teresa Owens, Dir. of Data Processing.

■ 13761 ■ Ken R. Humke Co.
PO Box 5128
Portland, OR 97208
Phone: (503)222-9741
Products: Nuts and bolts. **SIC:** 5072 (Hardware).

■ 13762 ■ Ideal Division
3200 Parker Dr.
St. Augustine, FL 32095
Phone: (904)829-1000
Free: (800)221-0100 **Fax:** (904)825-1121
Products: Hose clamps. **SIC:** 5072 (Hardware). **Est:** 1913. **Emp:** 250. **Officers:** Ron Cervelli, General Mgr.; Ray Moylan, Marketing Mgr.; Valerie Salls, Human Resources Contact.

■ 13763 ■ IMA Tool Distributors
280 Midland Ave.
Saddle Brook, NJ 07663-6404
Phone: (201)791-8787
Products: Power driven hand tools; Hand tools, including machinery tools and saws; Metal cutting machine tools; Machine tool accessories. **SICs:** 5072 (Hardware); 5085 (Industrial Supplies); 5084 (Industrial Machinery & Equipment). **Officers:** Robert Sherman, President.

■ 13764 ■ Industrial Fasteners Corp.
7 Harbor Park Dr.
Port Washington, NY 11050
Phone: (516)484-4900 **Fax:** (516)484-5217
Products: Hardware; Hardware fasteners. **SIC:** 5072 (Hardware). **Est:** 1948. **Sales:** $20,000,000 (2000). **Emp:** 100. **Officers:** Bernard Feldman, President; Marty Chernick, Vice President; Glenn Rones, Co-President; Gary Rones, Co-President.

■ 13765 ■ Industrial Power Sales Inc.
8461 Garvey Dr.
Raleigh, NC 27616
Phone: (919)876-6115 **Fax:** (919)876-0729
E-mail: info@ipstools.com
URL: http://www.ipstools.com
Products: Power tools and parts. **SIC:** 5072 (Hardware). **Est:** 1979. **Sales:** $12,000,000 (2000). **Emp:** 45. **Officers:** Robert M. Lee Sr., CEO; Lloyd E. Nelson, CFO.

■ 13766 ■ International Screw & Bolt
7500 New Horizon Blvd.
Amityville, NY 11701
Phone: (631)225-6400
Free: (800)645-1234 **Fax:** (631)225-6499
Products: Bolts, nuts, rivets, screws, and washers; Anchors. **SIC:** 5072 (Hardware). **Est:** 1957. **Emp:** 49. **Officers:** Larry Englson.

■ 13767 ■ The IXL Group
Bernie, MO 63822
Phone: (573)293-5341 **Fax:** (573)293-5633
Products: Tool handles. **SIC:** 5072 (Hardware). **Officers:** David Ulm, Sales Mgr., e-mail: dulm@ameslandg.com.

■ 13768 ■ Jacon Fasteners and Electronics Inc.
9539 Vassar Ave.
Chatsworth, CA 91311
Phone: (818)700-2901 **Fax:** (818)709-7426
E-mail: sales@jacon.com
URL: http://www.jacon.com
Products: Fasteners. **SIC:** 5085 (Industrial Supplies). **Est:** 1956. **Sales:** $10,000,000 (1999). **Emp:** 37. **Officers:** Donald Wientjes, President; Sue Wientjes, Controller; William J. English, General Mgr.

■ 13769 ■ Jay-Cee Sales and Rivet Inc.
32861 Chelsey Dr.
Farmington, MI 48336
Phone: (248)478-2150
Free: (800)521-6777 **Fax:** (248)478-6416
E-mail: sales@rivetsinstock.com
URL: http://www.rivetsinstock.com
Products: Rivets. **SIC:** 5072 (Hardware). **Est:** 1948. **Sales:** $4,200,000 (2000). **Emp:** 13. **Officers:** Michael H. Clinton, President; Jerry Clinton, Controller; Cary Weitzman, Vice President.

■ 13770 ■ Leonard Jed Co.
1301 Covington St.
Baltimore, MD 21230
Phone: (410)685-1482 **Fax:** (410)685-2647
Products: Hardware, including fasteners, nuts and bolts, hammers, and screwdrivers; Scales. **SICs:** 5072 (Hardware); 5085 (Industrial Supplies). **Est:** 1870. **Sales:** $5,000,000 (2000). **Emp:** 30. **Officers:** Leonard Jed, President; Edward McLaughlin, Controller.

■ 13771 ■ Jennison Industrial Supply
PO Box 717
Bay City, MI 48707-0717
Phone: (517)895-5531 **Fax:** (517)895-5598
Products: Hoists; Jacks; Rope; Paint; Toolboxes; Gloves. **SICs:** 5072 (Hardware); 5198 (Paints, Varnishes & Supplies); 5084 (Industrial Machinery &

Equipment); 5085 (Industrial Supplies); 5136 (Men's/Boys' Clothing). **Est:** 1850. **Sales:** $4,000,000 (2000). **Emp:** 28. **Officers:** Steve Kopec, Store Mgr.

■ **13772** ■ **Jensen-Byrd Company Inc.**
PO Box 3708
Spokane, WA 99220
Phone: (509)624-1321 **Fax:** (509)838-2432
Products: Hardware tools. **SIC:** 5072 (Hardware). **Sales:** $74,000,000 (2000). **Emp:** 170. **Officers:** Mike Jensen, President; Doug Kauffman, VP of Finance.

■ **13773** ■ **Jensen Distribution Services**
PO Box 3708
Spokane, WA 99220
Phone: (509)624-1321 **Fax:** (509)838-2432
URL: http://www.jensenonline.com
Products: Paints and paint sundries; Hardware; Tools; Electrical supplies; Plumbing supplies; Lawn and garden equipment and supplies; Housewares. **SICs:** 5072 (Hardware); 5198 (Paints, Varnishes & Supplies); 5063 (Electrical Apparatus & Equipment); 5074 (Plumbing & Hydronic Heating Supplies); 5083 (Farm & Garden Machinery). **Est:** 1883. **Sales:** $70,000,000 (2000). **Emp:** 180. **Officers:** Mike Jensen, President; Doug Miller, Exec. VP; Ted Geocaris, Sales Mgr., e-mail: tedg@jensenonline.com. **Former Name:** Jensen-Byrd Company Inc.

■ **13774** ■ **Johnson Brothers**
223 Basalt
PO Box 1836
Idaho Falls, ID 83403-1836
Phone: (208)523-8600
Free: (800)276-2656 **Fax:** (208)522-3676
URL: http://www.jbros.com
Products: Door, cabinet hardware; Wood, metal doors; Flooring; Formica; Marvin windows, doors. **SIC:** 5072 (Hardware). **Est:** 1905. **Sales:** $6,000,000 (2000). **Emp:** 49. **Officers:** David L. Sargis. **Former Name:** Precision Door Hardware.

■ **13775** ■ **Jones Hardware Company Inc.**
115 E Independence St.
Shamokin, PA 17872
Phone: (570)648-4631 **Fax:** (570)648-3457
E-mail: jonesace@joneshardware.com
Products: Hardware and building material. **SIC:** 5072 (Hardware). **Est:** 1917. **Sales:** $4,200,000 (2000). **Emp:** 34. **Officers:** Robert F. Jones, President; Donald L. Blessing, Dir. of Marketing.

■ **13776** ■ **Joy Enterprises**
1104 53rd Court S
West Palm Beach, FL 33407-2350
Phone: (561)863-3205
Free: (800)500-3879 **Fax:** (561)863-3277
E-mail: mail@joyenterprises.com
URL: http://www.joyenterprises.com
Products: Sporting knives; Pocket knives; Swords; Martial arts equipment; Outdoor and sports equipment, including eyewear; Police and security equipment; Binoculars. **SICs:** 5048 (Ophthalmic Goods); 5091 (Sporting & Recreational Goods). **Est:** 1958. **Sales:** $4,000,000 (2000). **Emp:** 29. **Officers:** Alex Shelton, President, e-mail: alex@joyenterprises.com; Steven B. Shelton, Vice President, e-mail: bob@joyenterprises.com; Sandra Brunet, Sales/Marketing Contact, e-mail: sandra@joyenterprises.com; ct. **Former Name:** Joy Optical Co.

■ **13777** ■ **J.S. Screw Manufacturing Co.**
7040 Laurel Canyon
North Hollywood, CA 91615
Phone: (818)983-1715 **Fax:** (818)983-2864
Products: Screws; Bolts. **SIC:** 5072 (Hardware). **Sales:** $6,000,000 (2000). **Emp:** 99. **Officers:** Irwin Schwartzman.

■ **13778** ■ **JZ Allied International Holdings Inc.**
13207 Bradley Ave.
Sylmar, CA 91342
Phone: (818)364-2333
Products: Hardware; Power and hand tools. **SIC:** 5072 (Hardware).

■ **13779** ■ **Kagiya Trading Co. Ltd. of America**
PO Box 21052
Nashville, TN 37221
Phone: (615)298-1220 **Fax:** (615)298-1274
E-mail: kagiya-usa@msn.com
Products: Hardware; Surgical appliances and supplies; Pneumatic power driven hand tools; Hardwood lumber; Metric gauges; Construction equipment; Forklifts. **SICs:** 5072 (Hardware); 5031 (Lumber, Plywood & Millwork); 5047 (Medical & Hospital Equipment); 5084 (Industrial Machinery & Equipment). **Est:** 1981. **Emp:** 4. **Officers:** Richard T. Ebata, President.

■ **13780** ■ **Kansas City Bolt, Nut and Screw Co.**
1324 W 12th St.
Kansas City, MO 64101
Phone: (816)471-6979
Products: Fasteners. **SIC:** 5072 (Hardware). **Sales:** $24,000,000 (1992). **Emp:** 150. **Officers:** Brian Folk, President.

■ **13781** ■ **Kar Products**
461 N 3rd Ave.
Des Plaines, IL 60016
Phone: (847)296-6111 **Fax:** (847)299-6893
Products: Hardware fasteners; Bolts, nuts, rivets, screws, and washers. **SICs:** 5072 (Hardware); 5085 (Industrial Supplies). **Est:** 1950. **Sales:** $130,000,000 (2000). **Emp:** 1,000. **Officers:** Max Beshears, President; Leo Sofianos, VP & CFO; Scott Mccullough, VP of Marketing; Dave Kamath, VP of Information Systems; Tom D'Onofrio, Finance Officer.

■ **13782** ■ **Kass Industrial Supply Corp.**
443 E Tremont Ave.
Bronx, NY 10457
Phone: (718)299-6060
Products: Power tools. **SIC:** 5072 (Hardware). **Est:** 1953. **Sales:** $3,000,000 (2000). **Emp:** 40. **Officers:** Allen Kass, President; Ozong Etta, Controller.

■ **13783** ■ **Kemp Hardware and Supply Co.**
PO Box 529
Paramount, CA 90723
Phone: (562)634-2553
Products: Hardware supplies, including nuts, bolts, screws, and wire. **SICs:** 5072 (Hardware); 5051 (Metals Service Centers & Offices). **Est:** 1922. **Sales:** $2,500,000 (2000). **Emp:** 15. **Officers:** D.O. Kemp, President; J.S. Kemp, CFO.

■ **13784** ■ **Kentec Inc.**
3250 Centerville Hwy.
PO Box 390040
Snellville, GA 30039
Phone: (770)985-1907
Free: (800)241-0148 **Fax:** (770)985-6989
E-mail: kentec@mindspring.com
URL: http://www.kentec.com
Products: Hardware, including staples, staplers, nails, hammers, and nailers. **SIC:** 5072 (Hardware). **Est:** 1957. **Sales:** $28,000,000 (2000). **Emp:** 125. **Officers:** George W. Morgan, President.

■ **13785** ■ **Kett Tool Co.**
5055 Madison Rd.
Cincinnati, OH 45227-1494
Phone: (513)271-0333 **Fax:** (513)271-5318
Products: Saws and shears. **SICs:** 5085 (Industrial Supplies); 5072 (Hardware). **Est:** 1941. **Sales:** $6,000,000 (2000). **Emp:** 30. **Officers:** R. Hoffman, Chairman of the Board & Treasurer; W. Berlier, President; K. Conlon, Vice President.

■ **13786** ■ **A.L. Kilgo Co. Inc.**
180 Sand Island Rd.
Honolulu, HI 96819
Phone: (808)832-2200 **Fax:** (808)832-2201
Products: Hardware. **SIC:** 5072 (Hardware).

■ **13787** ■ **Klarman Sales Inc.**
8 Cloverwood Rd.
White Plains, NY 10605
Phone: (914)949-5130 **Fax:** (914)949-6313
Products: Hardware. **SIC:** 5072 (Hardware). **Officers:** Stan Klarman, Contact.

■ **13788** ■ **Knox Industrial Supplies Inc.**
1600 E McFadden Ave.
Santa Ana, CA 92705
Phone: (714)972-1010 **Fax:** (714)543-8758
Products: Tools. **SIC:** 5072 (Hardware). **Est:** 1932. **Sales:** $10,000,000 (2000). **Emp:** 65. **Officers:** David P. Knox, President; Gerda Reim, Controller; Dale A. Bower, VP of Marketing.

■ **13789** ■ **The Kruse Company**
4275 Thunderbird Ln.
Fairfield, OH 45014
Phone: (513)860-3600
Free: (800)729-3200 **Fax:** (513)860-3669
E-mail: service@thekrusecompany.com
URL: http://www.hardwarestoreonline.com
Products: Lawn and garden supplies; Paint; Screwdrivers; Hardware; Plumbing, electrical, and houseware tools. **SICs:** 5072 (Hardware); 5063 (Electrical Apparatus & Equipment); 5083 (Farm & Garden Machinery); 5198 (Paints, Varnishes & Supplies). **Est:** 1902. **Sales:** $52,000,000 (2000). **Emp:** 168. **Officers:** Terry O'Brien, President & CEO; Jack Pulskamp, VP of Finance, e-mail: jpulskamp@thekrusecompany.com; Norm Durfy, Vice President; Mark Houekamp, VP of Operations; Laura Dickhaut, Dir. of Marketing, e-mail: ldickhaut@thekrusecompany.com; Barb Frech, Customer Service Contact.

■ **13790** ■ **Lakeside Spring Products**
422 N Griffin St.
Grand Haven, MI 49417
Phone: (616)847-2706
Products: Springs; Coil. **SIC:** 5072 (Hardware).

■ **13791** ■ **Land, Air & Sea Tool Corp.**
5760 NW 72nd Ave.
Miami, FL 33166
Phone: (305)592-5501
Free: (800)792-8665 **Fax:** (305)592-9974
Products: Tools, including drill bit sharpeners. **SIC:** 5072 (Hardware). **Est:** 1994. **Officers:** Joanne Weaver, President. **Former Name:** Martek International Inc.

■ **13792** ■ **Langford Tool & Drill**
1125 Washington Ave. S
Minneapolis, MN 55405
Phone: (612)332-8571 **Fax:** (612)332-9137
Products: Construction fastening systems. **SICs:** 5085 (Industrial Supplies); 5082 (Construction & Mining Machinery). **Emp:** 49. **Officers:** David McCulloch; Tom Mertens.

■ **13793** ■ **Laredo Hardware Co.**
401 Market St.
Laredo, TX 78040
Phone: (956)722-0981 **Fax:** (956)722-0938
Products: Electrical equipment and supplies; Tools; Plumbing and heating valves and specialties. **SICs:** 5072 (Hardware); 5085 (Industrial Supplies); 5074 (Plumbing & Hydronic Heating Supplies); 5063 (Electrical Apparatus & Equipment). **Sales:** $6,000,000 (2000). **Emp:** 39. **Officers:** Armengol Guerra, Jr., President; Armengol Guerra, III, Vice President; Yolanda G. Guerra, Treasurer & Secty.

■ **13794** ■ **Leatherman Tool Group Inc.**
PO Box 20595
12106 NE Ainsworth Cl.
Portland, OR 97220
Phone: (503)253-7826
Free: (800)847-8665 **Fax:** (503)253-7830
E-mail: dsales@leatherman.com
URL: http://www.leatherman.com
Products: Tools. **SIC:** 5072 (Hardware). **Est:** 1983. **Emp:** 540. **Officers:** T.S. Leatherman, President; S. Leatherman, VP of US Sales; R. Bjorklund, VP of Marketing; N. Henry, VP of Finance; D. Stapp; J. Wilcox, Human Resources Contact.

■ 13795 ■ Lehigh-Armstrong Inc.
202 Boston Rd.
Billerica, MA 01862
Phone: (978)663-0010
Free: (800)225-1396 **Fax:** (978)663-5125
E-mail: sales@lehigh-armstrong.com
URL: http://www.Lehigh-Armstrong.com
Products: Fasteners, and Electronic equipment. **SIC:** 5072 (Hardware). **Est:** 1916. **Sales:** $4,000,000 (1999). **Emp:** 18. **Officers:** Mel Dalaklis, President; Anthony Eovine, Controller; Steve Dalakis, General Mgr.; Peter Krea, Customer Service Contact.

■ 13796 ■ Gary Kenneth Lilly Fasteners Inc.
PO Box 6005
Newark, DE 19714-6005
Phone: (302)366-7640
Products: Nuts and bolts. **SIC:** 5072 (Hardware). **Est:** 1961. **Sales:** $2,000,000 (2000). **Emp:** 30. **Officers:** Gary K. Lilly, President.

■ 13797 ■ H.G. Lipscomb and Co.
621 Murfreesboro Rd.
Nashville, TN 37210
Phone: (615)255-7401 **Fax:** (615)255-4729
Products: Hardware; Plumbing supplies; Paint. **SICs:** 5072 (Hardware); 5074 (Plumbing & Hydronic Heating Supplies); 5198 (Paints, Varnishes & Supplies). **Est:** 1893. **Sales:** $2,000,000 (2000). **Emp:** 25. **Officers:** H.Z. Lipscomb Jr., President.

■ 13798 ■ Little Rock Tool Service, Inc.
11600 Arch St.
PO Box 164720
Little Rock, AR 72206-4720
Phone: (501)888-2457
Free: (800)482-8922 **Fax:** (501)888-2445
E-mail: lrts@worlnet.att.net
Products: Cutting tools. **SIC:** 5072 (Hardware). **Est:** 1964. **Sales:** $12,000,000 (2000). **Emp:** 90. **Officers:** Jerry Victory; Mike Griffith, Marketing & Sales Mgr.; Jerry Victory, Customer Service Mgr.; Lisa Robnett, Human Resources.

■ 13799 ■ Locks Co.
2050 NE 151st St.
North Miami, FL 33162
Phone: (305)949-0700
Free: (800)288-0801 **Fax:** (305)949-3619
Products: Security and safety equipment. **SIC:** 5072 (Hardware). **Sales:** $6,000,000 (2000). **Emp:** 25.

■ 13800 ■ Lohr Structural Fasteners Inc.
PO Box 1387
2355 Wilson Rd.
Humble, TX 77396
Phone: (281)446-6766
Free: (800)782-4544 **Fax:** (281)446-7805
URL: http://www.lohrfasteners.com
Products: Structural fasteners. **SIC:** 5072 (Hardware). **Est:** 1979. **Emp:** 15. **Officers:** Ken Lohr, President; Jose Flores, Sales/Marketing Contact; Cassandra Humphries, Customer Service Contact; Christine Broders, Customer Service Contact. **Alternate Name:** LSF.

■ 13801 ■ Long Lewis Inc.
430 N 9th St.
Birmingham, AL 35203
Phone: (205)322-2561
Products: Hardware, including saws, drills, sanders, and hammers. **SIC:** 5072 (Hardware). **Est:** 1887. **Sales:** $85,000,000 (2000). **Emp:** 300. **Officers:** Vaughan Burrell, CEO; Mark H. Elliott, CFO; Ron Parker, Dir. of Marketing & Sales.

■ 13802 ■ Long Lewis Inc.
430 N 9th St.
Birmingham, AL 35203
Phone: (205)322-2561 **Fax:** (205)322-2561
Products: Automobile dealers; Hardware. **SIC:** 5072 (Hardware). **Sales:** $109,000,000 (2000). **Emp:** 234. **Officers:** Vaughan Burrell, CEO; Mark H. Elliott, CFO.

■ 13803 ■ Lord & Hodge, Inc.
362 Industrial Park Rd., Unit 4
PO Box 737
Middletown, CT 06457
Phone: (860)632-7006 **Fax:** (860)632-2192
Products: Grommets; Snap fasteners; Tooling; Vises. **SICs:** 5072 (Hardware); 5085 (Industrial Supplies). **Est:** 1945. **Emp:** 10. **Officers:** M. G. Smith, President; G. M. Lord, Vice President; Kevin Martin, Customer Service Contact.

■ 13804 ■ Lowell Corp.
PO Box 158
Worcester, MA 01613-0158
Phone: (508)835-2900
Free: (800)456-9355 **Fax:** (508)835-2944
E-mail: customerservice@lowellcorp.com
URL: http://www.lowellcorp.com
Products: Ratchet devices. **SIC:** 5072 (Hardware). **Est:** 1868. **Emp:** 35. **Officers:** Paul DiPierro, Marketing & Sales Mgr.; Donna Brote, Customer Service Mgr.

■ 13805 ■ Mahar Tool Supply Inc.
PO Box 1747
Saginaw, MI 48605
Phone: (517)799-5530 **Fax:** (517)799-0830
Products: Metal removal products; Coolants; Power tools; Abrasives. **SICs:** 5084 (Industrial Machinery & Equipment); 5072 (Hardware). **Est:** 1947. **Sales:** $60,000,000 (2000). **Emp:** 110. **Officers:** Barbara Mahar-Lincoln, CEO; Mike Kane, President; Frank Austin, Exec. VP; Deb Bierlein, Controller.

■ 13806 ■ Maintenance Warehouse/America Corp.
PO Box 85838
San Diego, CA 92186
Phone: (619)452-5555
Products: Hardware. **SIC:** 5072 (Hardware). **Sales:** $98,000,000 (2000). **Emp:** 380. **Officers:** J. Neeley, President; Ron Turk, CFO.

■ 13807 ■ Makita U.S.A. Inc.
14930 Northam St.
La Mirada, CA 90638
Phone: (714)522-8088 **Fax:** (714)522-8194
Products: Power handtools. **SIC:** 5072 (Hardware). **Sales:** $210,000,000 (2000). **Emp:** 650. **Officers:** Paul Fukatsu, President; Hiro Otsu, Controller.

■ 13808 ■ Malco Industries
162 Eastern Ave.
Lynn, MA 01902
Phone: (617)598-1990
Free: (800)696-4111 **Fax:** (781)598-9382
Products: Hardware, including hand tools and fasteners; Housewares, including containers and cookware. **SICs:** 5072 (Hardware); 5023 (Homefurnishings). **Est:** 1905. **Sales:** $2,000,000 (2000). **Emp:** 10. **Officers:** Alfred T. Goldstein, President. **Alternate Name:** Malden Mop and Brush Co.

■ 13809 ■ Malco Products Inc.
Hwy. 55 & County Rd., No. 136
Annandale, MN 55302
Phone: (320)274-8246
Free: (800)328-3530 **Fax:** (320)274-2269
Products: Hand tools; Sheet metal; Siding. **SICs:** 5085 (Industrial Supplies); 5051 (Metals Service Centers & Offices). **Sales:** $6,000,000 (2000). **Emp:** 150. **Officers:** Gerry Keymer.

■ 13810 ■ Mann Edge Tool Co. Collins Axe Div.
PO Box 351
Lewistown, PA 17044-0351
Phone: (717)248-9628 **Fax:** (717)248-4846
Products: Axes, picks, hammers, etc.; Handles. **SIC:** 5072 (Hardware).

■ 13811 ■ Manware Inc.
1511 South 700 West
Salt Lake City, UT 84104
Phone: (801)972-1212 **Fax:** (801)972-1537
E-mail: manaware@worldnet.att.com
Products: Industrial and construction products. **SIC:** 5072 (Hardware). **Est:** 1915. **Sales:** $10,000,000

(1999). **Emp:** 13. **Officers:** Clark Naylor, CEO; Pat Naylor; Steve Cutler.

■ 13812 ■ Marco Supply Company Inc.
812 Pocahantas Ave.
Roanoke, VA 24012
Phone: (703)344-6211
Products: Electrical construction tools and fasteners. **SICs:** 5063 (Electrical Apparatus & Equipment); 5072 (Hardware). **Sales:** $13,000,000 (1994). **Emp:** 55. **Officers:** David Jones, President.

■ 13813 ■ Marmon Group
15450 E Jefferson Ave.
Grosse Pointe, MI 48230
Phone: (313)331-5100
Products: Coil; Springs. **SIC:** 5072 (Hardware).

■ 13814 ■ Mass Hardware and Supply Inc.
170 High St.
Waltham, MA 02454
Phone: (781)893-6711 **Fax:** (781)893-7214
Products: Bolts, nuts, rivets, screws, and washers. **SIC:** 5072 (Hardware). **Est:** 1946. **Sales:** $12,000,000 (2000). **Emp:** 120. **Officers:** Ken Feeley, President; Timothy Casey, Vice President.

■ 13815 ■ A.G. Mauro Co.
310 Alpha Dr.
Pittsburgh, PA 15238
Phone: (412)782-6600 **Fax:** (412)963-6913
Products: Hardware, including bathroom hardware and supplies. **SIC:** 5072 (Hardware). **Sales:** $7,000,000 (2000). **Emp:** 75. **Officers:** Ray Mauro, President.

■ 13816 ■ Mayes Brothers Tool Manufacturing
713 Clairmont Rd.
Johnson City, TN 37605
Phone: (423)926-6171 **Fax:** (423)926-1723
Products: Squares and levels. **SIC:** 5072 (Hardware). **Est:** 1916. **Sales:** $9,400,000 (2000). **Emp:** 115. **Officers:** John H. Stevens.

■ 13817 ■ Mayhew Steel Products
PO Box 88
Shelburne Falls, MA 01370
Phone: (413)625-6351
Free: (800)872-0037 **Fax:** (413)625-6395
URL: http://www.mayhew.com
Products: Chisels, screwdrivers, pry bars, punches, extractors, and hand guards. **SIC:** 5072 (Hardware). **Est:** 1856. **Emp:** 65. **Officers:** John Lawless, President.

■ 13818 ■ McKim Group
225 Riverview Ave.
Waltham, MA 02454
Phone: (781)647-5560 **Fax:** (781)891-8375
Products: Tools; Hammers; Knives; Hardware. **SIC:** 5072 (Hardware).

■ 13819 ■ McLaughlin Industrial Distributors Inc.
7141 Paramount Blvd.
Pico Rivera, CA 90660
Phone: (213)723-2411 **Fax:** (562)948-4448
Products: Tools and tool boxes. **SIC:** 5072 (Hardware). **Est:** 1960. **Sales:** $9,000,000 (2000). **Emp:** 40. **Officers:** Harry Y. McLaughlin, CEO; Allen Markarian, Exec. VP & Treasurer.

■ 13820 ■ McLendon Hardware Inc.
710 S 2nd St.
Renton, WA 98055
Phone: (206)235-3555 **Fax:** (206)235-3569
Products: Hardware. **SIC:** 5072 (Hardware). **Est:** 1926. **Sales:** $37,000,000 (2000). **Emp:** 200. **Officers:** Gail R. McLendon-Baer, President; Debra Judd, Treasurer; Bruce Stevens, Dir. of Marketing & Sales.

■ 13821 ■ McMaster-Carr Supply Co. California
PO Box 54960
Los Angeles, CA 90054
Phone: (562)692-5911 **Fax:** (562)695-2323
Products: Hardware; Nails; Hammers; Saws; Rubber and plastic garden hose; Automatic fire sprinkler equipment. **SICs:** 5072 (Hardware); 5051 (Metals

Service Centers & Offices). **Est:** 1901. **Sales:** $13,000,000 (2000). **Emp:** 200. **Officers:** Robert Delaney, General Mgr.; Steve Finn, CFO; Robert Gabler, Dir. of Marketing; John McDonald, Dir of Human Resources.

■ 13822 ■ **Charles McMurray Co.**
2520 N Argyle
Fresno, CA 93727
Phone: (559)292-5751 **Fax:** (559)292-3749
URL: http://www.charlesmcmurray.com
Products: Hardware. **SIC:** 5072 (Hardware). **Est:** 1946. **Sales:** $31,000,000 (2000). **Emp:** 75. **Officers:** Louis McMurray, President; Terry Koressel, General Mgr.; Dave Coles, VP of Marketing.

■ 13823 ■ **MEBCO Contractors Supplies**
757 Front St.
Berea, OH 44017-1608
Phone: (440)234-5854
Free: (800)234-5854 **Fax:** (440)234-5678
Products: Caulking; Glazing tapes; Tools. **SICs:** 5169 (Chemicals & Allied Products Nec); 5072 (Hardware). **Est:** 1965. **Emp:** 4. **Officers:** Paul Kmec, President.

■ 13824 ■ **Medal, Inc.**
330 Vine Ave.
Sharon, PA 16146
Phone: (724)342-6839
Free: (800)942-8085 **Fax:** (724)342-2251
E-mail: medal@nauticom.net
Products: Hardware. **SIC:** 5072 (Hardware). **Est:** 1953. **Sales:** $6,000,000 (1999). **Emp:** 40. **Officers:** Richard R. Rose, VP & General Mgr.

■ 13825 ■ **Merit Fasteners Corp.**
2510 County Rd., Hwy. 427
Longwood, FL 32750
Phone: (407)331-4815
Free: (800)432-0642 **Fax:** (407)331-5015
Products: Nuts and bolts. **SIC:** 5072 (Hardware). **Sales:** $11,000,000 (2000). **Emp:** 48. **Officers:** Don Rogers, President; Linda Rogers Sprinkle, CFO.

■ 13826 ■ **Metropolis Metal Spinning and Stamping Inc.**
4551 Furman Ave.
Bronx, NY 10470
Phone: (718)325-5650 **Fax:** (718)655-6854
Products: Screw machine products, brass and aluminum sand castings, die casting, stampings, and electrical products. **SICs:** 5084 (Industrial Machinery & Equipment); 5051 (Metals Service Centers & Offices). **Sales:** $15,000,000 (1994). **Emp:** 120. **Officers:** Howard L. Puhn, President.

■ 13827 ■ **Mid-State Bolt and Nut Company Inc.**
PO Box 2039
Columbus, OH 43216
Phone: (614)253-8631 **Fax:** (614)253-1585
E-mail: mapone@cose.com
URL: http://www.msbolt.com
Products: Nuts, bolts, and screws. **SIC:** 5072 (Hardware). **Est:** 1946. **Sales:** $20,000,000 (2000). **Emp:** 100. **Officers:** B. Wilson, President; D. Breault, Controller; M. Peterson, Sales Mgr.; P. Entingh, Customer Service Contact, e-mail: custserv@iwaynet.net; D. Broehm, Exec. VP.

■ 13828 ■ **Midwest Bolt and Supply Inc.**
405 E 14th Ave.
North Kansas City, MO 64116
Phone: (816)842-7880
Products: Fasteners; Nuts; Bolts; Screws. **SIC:** 5072 (Hardware). **Est:** 1987. **Sales:** $9,000,000 (2000). **Emp:** 28. **Officers:** Paul Scharringhausen, President.

■ 13829 ■ **Miller Hardware Co.**
2 Necessity Ave.
Harrison, AR 72601
Phone: (501)741-3493 **Fax:** (501)741-2761
Products: Hardware. **SIC:** 5072 (Hardware). **Est:** 1931. **Sales:** $13,000,000 (2000). **Emp:** 88. **Officers:** T.M. Miller, President; Martha Kendrick, Treasurer & Secty.

■ 13830 ■ **Mining Construction Supply**
1780 E Benson Hwy.
Tucson, AZ 85714
Phone: (520)889-1100 **Fax:** (520)889-0801
Products: Tools, including power and hand; Compactors. **SIC:** 5072 (Hardware). **Emp:** 28.

■ 13831 ■ **Mitchell-Powers Hardware**
PO Box 2048
Bristol, TN 37621
Phone: (931)764-1153
Products: Hardware. **SIC:** 5072 (Hardware). **Sales:** $14,000,000 (1994). **Emp:** 80. **Officers:** James G. Allred, Vice President.

■ 13832 ■ **Mizutani USA**
31012 Huntwood Ave.
Hayward, CA 94544
Phones: (510)487-2100 (510)471-7018
Fax: (510)471-1727
Products: Bolts, nuts, rivets, screws, and washers; Hardware. **SIC:** 5072 (Hardware). **Sales:** $12,000,000 (2000). **Emp:** 55. **Officers:** John Mizutani, President.

■ 13833 ■ **MNP Fastener Distribution Group**
1500 W Bryn Mawr
Itasca, IL 60143
Phone: (217)621-1502
Products: Screws, bolts and nuts. **SIC:** 5072 (Hardware). **Sales:** $8,000,000 (1994). **Emp:** 25. **Officers:** Becky Valentin, Finance Officer.

■ 13834 ■ **Molls Inc.**
1509 S Telegraph
Bloomfield Hills, MI 48302
Phone: (248)334-4242 **Fax:** (248)334-8787
Products: Hardware; Drapery hardware. **SIC:** 5072 (Hardware). **Est:** 1941. **Emp:** 3. **Officers:** Suenther Paesel, President.

■ 13835 ■ **Monarch Brass and Copper Corp.**
PO Box S
New Rochelle, NY 10802
Phone: (914)235-3000
Products: Copper rods; Brass goods. **SICs:** 5051 (Metals Service Centers & Offices); 5074 (Plumbing & Hydronic Heating Supplies).

■ 13836 ■ **Monarch Machine and Tool Company Inc.**
PO Box 810
Pasco, WA 99301-0810
Phone: (509)547-7753 **Fax:** (509)547-6318
Products: Hardware and tools. **SIC:** 5072 (Hardware). **Est:** 1947. **Sales:** $1,500,000 (2000). **Emp:** 15. **Officers:** Doug J. Winters, President; Dottie Clark, Treasurer & Secty.

■ 13837 ■ **Monroe Hardware Co.**
101 N Sutherland Ave.
Monroe, NC 28110
Phone: (704)289-3121
Free: (800)222-1974 **Fax:** (704)289-2838
Products: Hardware. **SIC:** 5072 (Hardware). **Sales:** $99,000,000 (2000). **Emp:** 350. **Officers:** Greg Alfred, CEO; Bruce Allen, CFO.

■ 13838 ■ **M.K. Morse Co.**
PO Box 8677
Canton, OH 44711
Phone: (330)453-8187 **Fax:** (330)453-1111
Products: Saw blades, including hand, hack, and band saw blades; Hole saws; Cut off wheels; Mounted points; Abrasives. **SICs:** 5072 (Hardware); 5085 (Industrial Supplies).

■ 13839 ■ **Mott Equity Exchange**
509 Country Rd.
Mott, ND 58646
Phone: (701)824-3296
Products: Tires and inner tubes, new; Lumber and wood products; Hardware; Electrical equipment and supplies. **SICs:** 5072 (Hardware); 5031 (Lumber, Plywood & Millwork); 5065 (Electronic Parts & Equipment Nec); 5014 (Tires & Tubes). **Est:** 1911. **Sales:** $3,000,000 (2000). **Emp:** 15. **Officers:** Dale Ottmar, President; Ed Schultz, Manager.

■ 13840 ■ **MSC Industrial Supply Co.**
151 Sunnyside Blvd.
Plainview, NY 11803
Phone: (516)349-7100 **Fax:** (516)349-0265
Products: Tools; Industrial supplies; Janitorial supplies. **SICs:** 5072 (Hardware); 5085 (Industrial Supplies); 5087 (Service Establishment Equipment). **Est:** 1941. **Sales:** $63,000,000 (2000). **Emp:** 450. **Officers:** Mitchell Jacobson, President; Jean Haass, Dir. of Marketing; David Gillies, Dir. of Information Systems; Barbara Schwartz, Dir of Human Resources.

■ 13841 ■ **Mutual Services of Highland Park**
1393 Half Day Rd.
Highland Park, IL 60035
Phone: (847)432-0027
Products: Hardware, including screwdrivers, circular saws, and faucets; Paints; Hollow metal doors and frames; Paving brick and landscape walls. **SICs:** 5072 (Hardware); 5198 (Paints, Varnishes & Supplies); 5032 (Brick, Stone & Related Materials); 5074 (Plumbing & Hydronic Heating Supplies). **Est:** 1917. **Sales:** $9,000,000 (2000). **Emp:** 80. **Officers:** Dane E. Sheahen, CEO; Chris Sheahen, CFO.

■ 13842 ■ **Napa Auto Parts (Burlington, Vermont)**
703 Pine St.
Burlington, VT 05401-0506
Phone: (802)864-4568 **Fax:** (802)864-0365
Products: Hardware, auto parts and related accessories. **SICs:** 5072 (Hardware); 5013 (Motor Vehicle Supplies & New Parts). **Sales:** $2,000,000 (1994). **Emp:** 12. **Officers:** Kevin Heron, Manager.

■ 13843 ■ **Neill-LaVielle Supply Co.**
1711 S Floyd St.
Louisville, KY 40208
Phone: (502)637-5401
Free: (800)288-8789 **Fax:** (502)637-5450
Products: Tools, including screwdrivers, scales, and rulers; Hardware, including screws, nuts, and bolts. **SICs:** 5072 (Hardware); 5051 (Metals Service Centers & Offices); 5085 (Industrial Supplies). **Est:** 1881. **Sales:** $45,000,000 (2000). **Emp:** 150.

■ 13844 ■ **Nelson Roanoke Corp.**
7901 Trading Ln.
Frederick, MD 21701-3275
Products: Hardware. **SIC:** 5072 (Hardware). **Sales:** $17,000,000 (2000). **Emp:** 105.

■ 13845 ■ **Nelson-Roanoke Div.**
7901 Trading Ln.
Frederick, MD 21701-3275
Products: Hardware, home furnishings and industrial supplies. **SICs:** 5072 (Hardware); 5023 (Homefurnishings); 5085 (Industrial Supplies). **Sales:** $14,000,000 (1994). **Emp:** 54. **Officers:** Nicholas Felsh, President.

■ 13846 ■ **NFZ Products Inc.**
3343 Hollins Ferry Rd.
Baltimore, MD 21227
Phone: (410)242-0069
Free: (877)535-2142 **Fax:** (410)242-1328
URL: http://www.nfzproducts.com
Products: Knives, including pocket, and hunting products; Surgical knives; Scissors; Tweezers; Forceps; Leather jackets; Martial arts items. **SICs:** 5072 (Hardware); 5047 (Medical & Hospital Equipment); 5091 (Sporting & Recreational Goods). **Est:** 1986. **Sales:** $3,000,000 (2000). **Emp:** 6. **Officers:** Mohammad Aslam. **Former Name:** Knives & Things.

■ 13847 ■ **NJ Rivet Co.**
1785 Haddon Ave.
Camden, NJ 08103-3007
Phone: (609)963-2237 **Fax:** (609)963-2367
E-mail: sales@njrivet.com
URL: http://www.njrivet.com
Products: Semi-tubular and solid rivets. **SIC:** 5072 (Hardware). **Est:** 1934. **Sales:** $2,000,000 (2000). **Emp:** 24. **Officers:** Dennis L. Van Name, President, e-mail: dennisv@njrivet.com.

■ 13848 ■ Nor-Mar Sales Company Inc.
20835 Nordhoff St.
Chatsworth, CA 91311
Phone: (818)700-8804 **Fax:** (818)700-2979
URL: http://www.normarsales.com
Products: Builders hardware; Plumbing fixtures. **SICs:**
5072 (Hardware); 5074 (Plumbing & Hydronic Heating
Supplies). **Est:** 1973. **Emp:** 49. **Officers:** Norm
Kurnick.

■ 13849 ■ Normad Fastener Company Inc.
2442 Rosemead Blvd.
South el Monte, CA 91733
Phone: (626)443-0276
Products: Nuts; Bolts; Hydraulic hoses. **SICs:** 5085
(Industrial Supplies); 5072 (Hardware). **Est:** 1963.
Sales: $1,000,000 (2000). **Emp:** 10. **Officers:** Morris
F. Madsen, Owner; Chris Madsen, General Mgr.

■ 13850 ■ North Coast Distributing, Inc.
26565 Miles Rd.
Warrensville Heights, OH 44128
Phone: (216)292-6911 **Fax:** (216)292-7635
Products: Outdoor power equipment. **SIC:** 5072
(Hardware). **Est:** 1939. **Emp:** 65. **Officers:** John
Strang.

■ 13851 ■ North Texas Bolt, Nut & Screw, Inc.
1502 109th St.
Grand Prairie, TX 75050-1903
Phone: (972)647-0608
Free: (800)749-0608 **Fax:** (972)660-4936
E-mail: northtexasbolt@earthlink.net
URL: northtexasbolt.com
Products: Bolts, nuts, screws, and special parts. **SICs:**
5072 (Hardware); 5085 (Industrial Supplies). **Est:** 1972.
Sales: $5,000,000 (1999). **Emp:** 18. **Officers:** Anthony
A. Wright.

■ 13852 ■ Odell Hardware Company Inc.
PO Box 20688
Memphis, TN 38101-0140
Phone: (919)299-9121
Products: Hardware supplies. **SIC:** 5072 (Hardware).
Sales: $46,000,000 (2000). **Emp:** 200. **Officers:**
Mackie Stout, President.

■ 13853 ■ Omega Products Corporation
360-10 Knickerbocker Ave.
Bohemia, NY 11716
Phone: (516)563-7217
Free: (800)221-8665 **Fax:** (516)563-5041
Products: Hand tools; Keys and key accessories. **SIC:**
5072 (Hardware). **Emp:** 49. **Officers:** Ernest Sauer,
President; Mary Ann Rogers, Exec. VP.

■ 13854 ■ Matthew Opperman Co., Inc.
5713 SW 150th Ave.
Miami, FL 33193
Phone: (305)383-3929
Free: (800)719-2909 **Fax:** (305)388-9162
E-mail: moco@icanect.net
URL: http://www.matthewopperman.com
Products: Machinery; Abrasives; Power tools; Cutting
tools; Welding equipment; Safety equipment. **SIC:**
5072 (Hardware). **Est:** 1992. **Sales:** $1,000,000
(1999). **Emp:** 2.

■ 13855 ■ Orgill Inc.
2100 Latham St.
Memphis, TN 38109
Phone: (901)948-3381
Products: Hardware. **SIC:** 5072 (Hardware). **Est:**
1847. **Sales:** $436,000,000 (1999). **Emp:** 800.
Officers: William Fondren Jr., President. **Former
Name:** Orgill Brothers and Co.

■ 13856 ■ Osborn Machinery Company Inc.
424 N 4th St.
Clarksburg, WV 26301
Phone: (304)624-5636 **Fax:** (304)622-6266
Products: Electrical and plumbing supplies; Power
tools. **SICs:** 5072 (Hardware); 5074 (Plumbing &
Hydronic Heating Supplies); 5063 (Electrical Apparatus
& Equipment). **Est:** 1921. **Sales:** $3,000,000 (2000).
Emp: 17. **Officers:** James Rockwell, President; Harry
M. Kilmer, Treasurer & Secty.; Joe Nester, General
Mgr.

■ 13857 ■ OxTech Industries Inc.
PO Box 8
Oxford, NJ 07863-0008
Phone: (908)453-2151 **Fax:** (908)453-2991
Products: Screwdrivers; Plant hangers; Wall brackets.
SIC: 5072 (Hardware). **Est:** 1987. **Sales:** $1,300,000
(2000). **Emp:** 8. **Officers:** Roland E. Bakonyi,
President; Debra R. Stamm, General Mgr.

■ 13858 ■ Pacific Hardware & Specialties Inc.
7625 McKinley E
Tacoma, WA 98404-1764
Phone: (253)473-5670 **Fax:** (253)473-3288
Products: Hardware; Plumbing fittings and brass
goods. **SICs:** 5072 (Hardware); 5074 (Plumbing &
Hydronic Heating Supplies). **Sales:** $10,000,000
(2000). **Emp:** 42. **Officers:** Scott D. Langlow; Stephen
D. Langlow.

■ 13859 ■ Palmer Pipe and Supply Inc.
1909 Garden City Hwy.
Midland, TX 79702
Phone: (915)682-7337
Products: Hardware. **SIC:** 5072 (Hardware). **Est:**
1960. **Sales:** $3,000,000 (2000). **Emp:** 20. **Officers:**
Robert C. Palmer, President; Peggy Palmer, Vice
President; Buddy Cole, Dir. of Sales; John Couch, Dir.
of Operations.

**■ 13860 ■ Panama Machinery and Equipment
Co.**
PO Box 776
Everett, WA 98206
Phone: (206)682-3166
Products: Steel machine tools. **SIC:** 5084 (Industrial
Machinery & Equipment). **Sales:** $129,000,000 (2000).
Emp: 150. **Officers:** Manny B. Berman, Payroll Mgr.;
Sam Nelson, Controller.

■ 13861 ■ PanaVise Products International
PO Box 584
Skokie, IL 60076
Phone: (847)674-9888 **Fax:** (847)674-9808
Products: Hardware. **SIC:** 5072 (Hardware). **Officers:**
Gary Richter, President; Roy Vetzner, International
Sales Manager.

■ 13862 ■ The Parker Company
101 N 1st St.
Decatur, IN 46733
Phone: (219)724-3141
Free: (800)552-1795 **Fax:** (219)724-3142
Products: Hardware; Industrial supplies; Building
materials. **SIC:** 5072 (Hardware). **Est:** 1982. **Sales:**
$3,000,000 (2000). **Emp:** 38. **Officers:** Rick Parker;
Tom Rumschlag, Sales/Marketing Contact. **Former
Name:** Schafer Company Inc.

■ 13863 ■ Parker Metal Goods Corp.
PO Box 15052
Worcester, MA 01615-0052
Phone: (508)791-7131
Products: Shopping carts; Household hardware. **SIC:**
5072 (Hardware). **Sales:** $15,000,000 (2000). **Emp:**
200. **Officers:** Jordan Levy, CEO.

■ 13864 ■ Parts Associates Inc.
12420 Plaza Dr.
Cleveland, OH 44130
Phone: (216)433-7700
Free: (800)321-1128 **Fax:** (216)433-9051
URL: http://www.pai-net.com
Products: Fasteners; Chemicals; Aerosol paints.
SICs: 5072 (Hardware); 5169 (Chemicals & Allied
Products Nec); 5198 (Paints, Varnishes & Supplies).
Est: 1948. **Sales:** $35,000,000 (2000). **Emp:** 300.
Officers: D.B. Lamb, President & Treasurer; T.E.
Wright, VP of Sales.

**■ 13865 ■ Pensacola Mill Supply Company
Inc.**
3030 N E St.
Pensacola, FL 32501
Phone: (850)434-2701
Products: Tools, including screwdrivers, pliers, and
pulleys; Glue. **SIC:** 5072 (Hardware). **Est:** 1949. **Sales:**
$8,000,000 (2000). **Emp:** 52. **Officers:** Joel Roth,
President; James King, Vice President.

■ 13866 ■ Pentacon Inc.
10375 Richmond Ave., Ste. 700
Houston, TX 77042
Phone: (713)860-1000 **Fax:** (713)860-1001
E-mail: heather.holub@pentacon-inc.com
URL: http://www.pentacon-inc.com
Products: Fasteners, including screws, bolts, washers,
springs, and fittings. **SIC:** 5072 (Hardware). **Est:** 1998.
Sales: $186,473,000 (1999). **Emp:** 900. **Officers:**
Mark E. Baldwin, CEO & Chairman of the Board;
James C. Jackson, VP & Controller.

■ 13867 ■ K.M. Perezi & Associates
21007 NE 4th St.
Redmond, WA 98053
Phone: (425)868-9249 **Fax:** (425)868-9299
Products: Architectural and security hardware. **SIC:**
5072 (Hardware). **Est:** 1989. **Sales:** $2,000,000
(2000). **Emp:** 3. **Officers:** K. Perezi.

■ 13868 ■ John Perine Co.
820 S Adams
Seattle, WA 98108
Phone: (206)682-9755
Free: (800)347-0039 **Fax:** (206)682-9675
E-mail: jperineco@uswest.net
Products: Fasteners, including screws, nuts, and bolts.
SIC: 5072 (Hardware). **Est:** 1937. **Sales:** $7,000,000
(1999). **Emp:** 39. **Officers:** J.D. Perine, President &
Chairman of the Board; R.A. Sterlington, Exec. VP of
Finance; Douglas G. Carrossino, VP of Marketing.

■ 13869 ■ Piper Weatherford Co.
10755 Rockwall
Dallas, TX 75238-1219
Phone: (214)343-9000 **Fax:** (214)341-9995
Products: Hardware; Doors. **SICs:** 5072 (Hardware);
5031 (Lumber, Plywood & Millwork). **Emp:** 49.
Officers: Bob Boswell.

■ 13870 ■ Plano International
431 E South St.
Plano, IL 60545-1601
Phone: (630)552-3111 **Fax:** (630)552-9737
Products: Plastic tool, tote, and utility boxes. **SIC:**
5099 (Durable Goods Nec).

■ 13871 ■ Pleasants Hardware Co.
PO Box 5258
Winston-Salem, NC 27113-5258
Phone: (336)725-3067 **Fax:** (336)725-6921
URL: http://www.pleasants.com
Products: Architectural wood doors; Hollow metal
doors and frames; Finish hardware; Toilet partitions
and restroom accessories; Misc. specialty items. **SIC:**
5072 (Hardware). **Est:** 1913. **Sales:** $116,000,000
(2000). **Emp:** 410. **Officers:** W. Sam Smoak, President
& CFO; Charles R. Hummel Sr., CEO & Chairman of
the Board; Dan C. Holt, Vice President; Virginia F.
Cole, Contact.

■ 13872 ■ Poe Corp.
556 Perry Ave.
Greenville, SC 29611-4852
Phone: (864)271-9000 **Fax:** (864)271-9015
Products: Tools. **SIC:** 5072 (Hardware). **Sales:**
$25,000,000 (2000). **Emp:** 92. **Officers:** Crawford Poe;
Nelson C. Poe Jr.; Randolph S. Poe; Volney C. Allen.

■ 13873 ■ Porteous Fastener Co.
22795 S Utility
Carson, CA 90745
Phone: (310)549-9180
Free: (800)IAM-NUTS **Fax:** (310)513-6326
Products: Nuts, bolts, washers, and screws. **SIC:** 5072
(Hardware). **Est:** 1966. **Emp:** 400. **Officers:** J. B.
Porteous, Chairman of the Board; Barry Porteous,
President; Jay Hebert, VP of Sales, e-mail: jhebert@
porteousfastner.com; Pat Clearman, Human
Resources Contact.

■ 13874 ■ Porter Cable
3949 E Guasti Rd., Apt. A
Ontario, CA 91761-1549
Phone: (626)333-3566 **Fax:** (626)330-5900
Products: Portable power tools, including
screwdrivers. **SIC:** 5072 (Hardware). **Emp:** 725.

■ **13875** ■ **Primark Tool Group**
715 E Gray St., 3rd Fl.
Louisville, KY 40212-1615
Phone: (502)635-8100
Free: (800)242-7003 **Fax:** (502)635-8134
Products: Power tool accessories. **SICs:** 5072 (Hardware); 5085 (Industrial Supplies). **Officers:** Ralph Cox.

■ **13876** ■ **Primeco Inc. Southeast Div.**
PO Box 36217
Charlotte, NC 28236
Phone: (704)348-2600
Products: Trenchers; Air-compressors; Saws. **SICs:** 5072 (Hardware); 5084 (Industrial Machinery & Equipment). **Est:** 1932. **Sales:** $64,000,000 (2000). **Emp:** 350. **Officers:** Jerry Lane, Vice President; Wayne Coleman, VP of Sales; Ken Midyette, Dir. of Sales.

■ **13877** ■ **Prosperity Tool Corp.**
2006 National Guard Dr.
Plant City, FL 33567
Phone: (813)752-6602 **Fax:** (813)754-4655
Products: Tools. **SIC:** 5072 (Hardware).

■ **13878** ■ **Purchased Parts Group**
13599 Merriman Rd.
Livonia, MI 48150
Phone: (734)422-7900
Free: (800)482-4160 **Fax:** (734)422-1999
Products: Metal nuts and bolts. **SIC:** 5072 (Hardware). **Est:** 1977. **Sales:** $100,000,000 (2000). **Emp:** 350. **Officers:** Mike Turnbull, President.

■ **13879** ■ **QSN Manufacturing Inc.**
101 Frontier Wy.
Bensenville, IL 60106
Phone: (708)616-1500 **Fax:** (708)616-1666
Products: Fasteners. **SIC:** 5072 (Hardware). **Sales:** $70,000,000 (2000). **Emp:** 280.

■ **13880** ■ **Raleigh Hardware Co.**
PO Box 1183
Beckley, WV 25802
Phone: (304)253-7348 **Fax:** (304)253-3699
Products: Hardware, including screws, nails, and hammers. **SIC:** 5072 (Hardware). **Est:** 1909. **Sales:** $6,000,000 (2000). **Emp:** 45. **Officers:** Thomas H. Moss, President.

■ **13881** ■ **Ram Threading Inc.**
2640 Crockett
Beaumont, TX 77701
Phone: (409)833-2658 **Fax:** (409)832-4014
Products: Bolts, nuts, rivets, screws, and washers; Hardware fasteners. **SICs:** 5072 (Hardware); 5085 (Industrial Supplies). **Est:** 1983. **Emp:** 12. **Officers:** Antoine LeBlanc.

■ **13882** ■ **Ram Tool and Supply Co.**
PO Box 320979
Birmingham, AL 35232
Phone: (205)591-2527
Products: Hardware. **SIC:** 5072 (Hardware). **Sales:** $26,000,000 (1994). **Emp:** 80. **Officers:** Mariam Head, President; Joan Parker, Controller.

■ **13883** ■ **RB & W Corp.**
800 Mogadore Rd.
Kent, OH 44240-7535
Phone: (330)673-3446 **Fax:** (330)673-0154
Products: Nuts; Extrusion products. **SICs:** 5072 (Hardware); 5082 (Construction & Mining Machinery). **Sales:** $1,000,000 (2000). **Emp:** 189. **Officers:** Rick Johnston.

■ **13884** ■ **Red Devil Inc.**
2400 Vauxhall Rd.
Union, NJ 07083
Phone: (908)688-6900
Free: (800)247-3790 **Fax:** (908)688-8872
E-mail: staff@reddevil.com
URL: http://www.reddevil.com
Products: Hand tools; Caulking compounds and sealants. **SICs:** 5169 (Chemicals & Allied Products Nec); 5072 (Hardware). **Est:** 1872. **Sales:** $55,000,000 (2000). **Emp:** 225. **Officers:** John Primavera, VP of Marketing.

■ **13885** ■ **George D. Rhone Company Inc.**
109-27 West St.
Coleman, TX 76834
Phone: (915)625-4141
Products: Hardware, including nuts and bolts. **SIC:** 5072 (Hardware). **Est:** 1926. **Sales:** $3,000,000 (2000). **Emp:** 12. **Officers:** G.D. Rhone, President & Treasurer.

■ **13886** ■ **Riggs Supply Co.**
320 Cedar St.
Kennett, MO 63857
Phone: (573)888-4639 **Fax:** (573)888-0067
Products: Hardware; Building materials. **SICs:** 5072 (Hardware); 5039 (Construction Materials Nec). **Est:** 1859. **Emp:** 49. **Officers:** A. Riggs III, President & CEO; Michael E. Bell, Exec. VP & CFO; L. G. Riggs, Sr. VP; A. David Riggs, Treasurer & Secty.

■ **13887** ■ **Riggsbee Hardware & Industrial Supply**
1120 Sampson
Houston, TX 77003-3932
Phone: (713)224-6734
Free: (800)327-1192 **Fax:** (713)224-2916
Products: Hardware. **SICs:** 5072 (Hardware); 5085 (Industrial Supplies). **Est:** 1959. **Emp:** 49.

■ **13888** ■ **RJM Sales, Associates, Inc.**
1739 Chestnut St.
Glenview, IL 60025
Phone: (847)486-9133 **Fax:** (847)486-1309
E-mail: rjmsales@aol.com
Products: Doors; Hardware. **SICs:** 5072 (Hardware); 5031 (Lumber, Plywood & Millwork). **Est:** 1976. **Emp:** 5. **Officers:** Dick Morrison, Contact; Tom Morrison, Contact.

■ **13889** ■ **Robnet Inc.**
3701 Commerce Dr.
Baltimore, MD 21227
Phone: (410)247-7273 **Fax:** (410)536-4378
E-mail: robnetinc@aol.com
Products: Fasteners; Industrial supplies. **SICs:** 5072 (Hardware); 5085 (Industrial Supplies). **Est:** 1985. **Sales:** $2,000,000 (2000). **Emp:** 9. **Officers:** Elizabeth Rosen Edelstein, President; Robert Z. Edelstein, Vice President.

■ **13890** ■ **Rockford Bolt & Steel Co.**
126 Mill St.
Rockford, IL 61101-1491
Phone: (815)968-0514 **Fax:** (815)968-3111
E-mail: rockfordbolt@voyager.net
Products: Hardware fasteners. **SIC:** 5072 (Hardware). **Est:** 1863. **Sales:** $7,000,000 (2000). **Emp:** 98. **Officers:** Michael G. Rosman; John Moore; Joe Casica, Sales & Marketing Contact; Bob Petrina, Customer Service Contact; Lisa Borg, Human Resources Contact.

■ **13891** ■ **Rocknel Fastener Inc.**
5309 11th St.
PO Box 5087
Rockford, IL 61125-5087
Phone: (815)873-4000 **Fax:** (815)873-4011
URL: http://www.rocknel.com
Products: Hardware fasteners. **SIC:** 5072 (Hardware). **Est:** 1989. **Sales:** $26,000,000 (2000). **Emp:** 108. **Officers:** Eugene J. Werlich, President; N. Tanaka, Vice President; Jerry Derango, Sales Mgr.

■ **13892** ■ **Rods Indiana Inc.**
PO Box 369
Butler, IN 46721
Phone: (219)868-2172 **Fax:** (219)868-2173
Products: Hardware fasteners; Externally threaded fasteners (except aircraft). **SIC:** 5072 (Hardware). **Emp:** 12. **Officers:** Dan Dickerhoof.

■ **13893** ■ **Rooster Products International Inc./McGuire-Nicholas**
8154 Bracken Creek
San Antonio, TX 78266
Phone: (210)651-5288
Free: (800)255-9945 **Fax:** (210)651-5388
E-mail: dsershonskeeter@mindspring.com
Products: Tool pouches; Nail bags; Soft sided tuff wearline; Kneepads; Men's and boys' work clothing; Specialty bags and liners; Tool and utensil cases. **SICs:** 5072 (Hardware); 5136 (Men's/Boys' Clothing). **Sales:** $100,000,000 (2000). **Emp:** 1,500. **Officers:** Juan Pablo Cabrera, President. **Former Name:** Rooster Products International Inc.

■ **13894** ■ **Rose Caster Co.**
12402 Hubbell St.
Detroit, MI 48227
Phone: (313)272-8200 **Fax:** (313)272-1136
Products: Casters. **SIC:** 5072 (Hardware). **Est:** 1933. **Sales:** $4,000,000 (2000). **Emp:** 45. **Officers:** C.G. Sargent, President.

■ **13895** ■ **Ross-Frazer Supply Co.**
8th & Monterey
St. Joseph, MO 64503
Phone: (816)279-2731 **Fax:** (816)233-2653
Products: Power tools; Nuts and bolts; Gardening supplies. **SIC:** 5072 (Hardware). **Est:** 1868. **Sales:** $1,000,000 (2000). **Emp:** 12. **Officers:** Barry Bock, President; Dan Bock, Treasurer.

■ **13896** ■ **Royal Brass and Hose**
PO Box 51468
Knoxville, TN 37950-1468
Phone: (423)558-0224
Free: (800)669-9650 **Fax:** (423)558-8484
E-mail: sales@royalbrassandhose.com
URL: http://www.royalbrassandhose.com
Products: Brass fittings, fasteners, nuts, bolts; Hydrulic and industrial hoses; Adapters; Metric fittings. **SICs:** 5072 (Hardware); 5085 (Industrial Supplies). **Est:** 1947. **Sales:** $21,000,000 (2000). **Emp:** 150. **Officers:** Steve Edwards, Treasurer; P.A. Macdonald, VP of Finance; J. Ingram, President.

■ **13897** ■ **J.P. Ruklic Screw Company Inc.**
PO Box 1608
Homewood, IL 60430
Phone: (708)798-8282
Free: (800)323-7073 **Fax:** (708)798-8887
URL: http://www.nutsandbolts.net
Products: Fasteners, screws, and washers. **SIC:** 5072 (Hardware). **Est:** 1964. **Sales:** $5,000,000 (2000). **Emp:** 30. **Officers:** J.P. Ruklic, President & Treasurer, e-mail: JPRuklic@aol.com; Robert Feenwalt, Marketing & Sales Mgr.; Colleen Flaherty, Customer Service Mgr.

■ **13898** ■ **S and S Automotive Inc.**
740 N Larch Ave.
Elmhurst, IL 60126
Phone: (708)279-1600
Products: Fasteners. **SIC:** 5013 (Motor Vehicle Supplies & New Parts). **Est:** 1960. **Sales:** $40,000,000 (2000). **Emp:** 400. **Officers:** R. Kushner, President; James Withrow, Controller; E.W. Norris, Exec. VP of Marketing.

■ **13899** ■ **Saffron Supply Co.**
325 Commercial St.
Salem, OR 97301
Phone: (503)581-7501 **Fax:** (503)581-5056
Products: Hardware; Plumbing supplies; Electrical equipment. **SICs:** 5072 (Hardware); 5074 (Plumbing & Hydronic Heating Supplies); 5063 (Electrical Apparatus & Equipment). **Est:** 1910. **Sales:** $2,500,000 (2000). **Emp:** 20. **Officers:** Morris H. Saffron, President; Richard Gassner, VP of Finance.

■ **13900** ■ **Sales Systems Ltd.**
700 Florida Ave.
Portsmouth, VA 23707
Phone: (757)397-0763
Free: (800)368-3711 **Fax:** (757)393-3669
E-mail: sslss@aol.com
Products: Bolts, nuts, rivets, screws, and washers. **SIC:** 5072 (Hardware). **Est:** 1971. **Sales:** $24,000,000 (2000). **Emp:** 130. **Officers:** Bill Creecy, President; Martha Patterson, Controller.

■ **13901** ■ **Samson Hardware & Fairbanks**
100 N Turner St.
Fairbanks, AK 99701
Phone: (907)452-3110 **Fax:** (907)451-8036
Products: Hardware. **SIC:** 5072 (Hardware).

■ 13902 ■ Sanson and Rowland Inc.
PO Box 5768
Philadelphia, PA 19120
Phone: (215)329-9263 **Fax:** (215)456-9760
Products: Fasteners, nuts, bolts, and screws. **SIC:** 5072 (Hardware). **Est:** 1890. **Sales:** $3,000,000 (2000). **Emp:** 20. **Officers:** Richard L. Goodby, President; Richard W. Goodby, Chairman of the Board & Treasurer.

■ 13903 ■ Saria International Inc.
1200 Industrial Rd, Unit 2
San Carlos, CA 94070
Phone: (650)591-1440 **Fax:** (650)591-1976
E-mail: sariaintl@aol.com
URL: http://www.sariainternational.com
Products: Automotive chemicals and lubricants; Building materials; Hardware; Paints; Adhesives; Silicones; Bathroom accessories. **SICs:** 5013 (Motor Vehicle Supplies & New Parts); 5072 (Hardware); 5039 (Construction Materials Nec); 5031 (Lumber, Plywood & Millwork); 5198 (Paints, Varnishes & Supplies). **Est:** 1976. **Emp:** 9. **Officers:** Abby Azem, President.

■ 13904 ■ J.E. Sawyer and Company Inc.
PO Box 2177
Glens Falls, NY 12801
Phone: (518)793-4104
Free: (800)724-3983 **Fax:** (518)793-1993
E-mail: jesruss@superior.net
URL: http://www.jesawyer.com
Products: Steel products; Hardware; Plumbing fixtures, equipment, and supplies; Heating equipment; Tools, including power, air, and woodworking tools. **SICs:** 5072 (Hardware); 5085 (Industrial Supplies); 5074 (Plumbing & Hydronic Heating Supplies). **Est:** 1883. **Sales:** $12,000,000 (2000). **Emp:** 58. **Officers:** Russ Chatham, President & CEO, e-mail: jesruss@ superior.net; Dick Collins, Chairman of the Board; Fred Twiss, CFO.

■ 13905 ■ Sidney Scheinert & Son Inc.
PO Box 527
404 Midland Ave.
Saddle Brook, NJ 07663
Phone: (201)791-4600 **Fax:** (201)791-8551
E-mail: sssinc@msn.com
URL: http://www.scheinertscrews.com
Products: Screws, nuts, and bolts. **SIC:** 5072 (Hardware). **Est:** 1910. **Sales:** $10,000,000 (2000). **Emp:** 50. **Officers:** R. Scheinert.

■ 13906 ■ Schlafer Supply Company Inc.
PO Box 999
Appleton, WI 54912
Phone: (414)733-4433
Products: Fasteners, nuts, bolts, and screws. **SIC:** 5072 (Hardware). **Est:** 1876. **Sales:** $16,000,000 (2000). **Emp:** 50. **Officers:** Merle Mueller, CEO & President; Rick Boss, Treasurer.

■ 13907 ■ Scotty's Hardware Inc.
1931 Lake Tahoe Blvd.
PO Box 7737
South Lake Tahoe, CA 96150
Phone: (530)541-3601 **Fax:** (530)541-1937
Products: Hardware. **SIC:** 5072 (Hardware). **Emp:** 99. **Officers:** Mauro Capone.

■ 13908 ■ Selby Furniture Hardware Company Inc.
321 Rider Ave.
Bronx, NY 10451
Phone: (718)993-3700 **Fax:** 800-224-0058
E-mail: selbern@aol.com
URL: http://www.selbyexclusives.com
Products: Furniture parts; Hinges; Stays; Magnets. **SIC:** 5072 (Hardware). **Est:** 1949. **Sales:** $9,000,000 (2000). **Emp:** 40. **Officers:** Sanford L. Bruckner, CEO; Leonard Unger, CFO; Neil H. Bruckner, President; Frank Torres, Dir. of Marketing; Joseph Kovacs, Marketing & Sales Mgr.; Bill McHugh, Customer Service Mgr.

■ 13909 ■ Semcor Equipment & Manufacturing Corp.
18 Madison
Keyport, NJ 07735-1117
Phone: (732)264-6080
Free: (800)262-6080 **Fax:** (732)264-4621
Products: Tools. **SIC:** 5072 (Hardware). **Emp:** 99. **Officers:** Jack McMenamn.

■ 13910 ■ Senco of Florida Inc.
1602 N Goldenrod Rd.
Orlando, FL 32807-8345
Phone: (407)277-0412 **Fax:** (407)282-2207
Products: Fastening systems. **SICs:** 5072 (Hardware); 5099 (Durable Goods Nec). **Sales:** $24,400,000 (2000). **Emp:** 105. **Officers:** Robert J. Shluzas.

■ 13911 ■ Sentry/Liberty Hardware Distributors Inc.
2700 River Rd.
Des Plaines, IL 60018
Phone: (847)699-2323
Products: Tools; Paint; Building and heating supplies; Automotive supplies; Farm and pet supplies; Housewares. **SICs:** 5072 (Hardware); 5198 (Paints, Varnishes & Supplies); 5074 (Plumbing & Hydronic Heating Supplies); 5199 (Nondurable Goods Nec); 5023 (Homefurnishings).

■ 13912 ■ Service Plus Distributors Inc.
1900 Frost Rd. Ste. 101
Bristol, PA 19007
Phone: (215)785-4466 **Fax:** (215)785-5231
E-mail: sales@spdhardware.com
URL: http://www.spdhardware.com
Products: Hardware. **SIC:** 5072 (Hardware). **Est:** 1989. **Emp:** 30.

■ 13913 ■ Setko Fasteners Inc.
26 Main St.
Bartlett, IL 60103
Phone: (708)837-2831 **Fax:** (708)837-2896
Products: Lock nuts; Screws; Hex keys. **SIC:** 5072 (Hardware). **Est:** 1935. **Sales:** $6,000,000 (2000). **Emp:** 62. **Officers:** J. Brown, President; B. Blazier, VP of Finance; B. Vanni, Dir. of Marketing.

■ 13914 ■ Sewell Hardware Company Inc.
528 Clematis St.
West Palm Beach, FL 33401
Phone: (561)832-7171 **Fax:** (561)655-5248
Products: Hardware; Metal doors. **SICs:** 5072 (Hardware); 5085 (Industrial Supplies). **Est:** 1924. **Sales:** $10,000,000 (2000). **Emp:** 78. **Officers:** Chap Brown, Vice President; Bill Sewell, Vice President.

■ 13915 ■ Shank Spring Design Inc.
540 South St.
Piqua, OH 45356
Phone: (937)773-0116
Products: Springs. **SIC:** 5072 (Hardware).

■ 13916 ■ Shohet Frederick of New Hampshire Inc.
159 Frontage Rd.
Manchester, NH 03103-6013
Phone: (603)434-3050 **Fax:** (603)434-7937
Products: Hardware. **SIC:** 5072 (Hardware). **Officers:** Alvin Levy, President.

■ 13917 ■ Shook Builder Supply Co.
PO Box 1790
Hickory, NC 28603
Phone: (704)328-2051 **Fax:** (704)328-2425
Products: Hardware; Lumber. **SICs:** 5072 (Hardware); 5031 (Lumber, Plywood & Millwork).

■ 13918 ■ Shop Tools Inc.
892 Commercial
Palo Alto, CA 94303-4905
Phone: (650)494-8331 **Fax:** (650)494-8751
Products: Drills and saws. **SICs:** 5072 (Hardware); 5085 (Industrial Supplies). **Emp:** 49.

■ 13919 ■ Shur-Lok Corp.
PO Box 19584
Irvine, CA 92623
Phone: (949)474-6000
Products: Honeycomb sandwich fasteners and inserts,

bearing nuts and lockwashers. **SIC:** 5072 (Hardware). **Sales:** $22,000,000 (2000). **Emp:** 200. **Officers:** Peter Grefe, President; Mike Anglin, VP of Finance.

■ 13920 ■ SK Hand Tool Corp.
3535 W 47th St.
Chicago, IL 60632
Phone: (773)523-1300
Free: (800)822-5575 **Fax:** (773)523-2103
E-mail: marketing@skhandtool.com
URL: http://www.skhandtool.com
Products: Mechanics' hand tools. **SIC:** 5072 (Hardware). **Est:** 1921. **Emp:** 400. **Officers:** Bernard Roussel, President & CEO; Jim Chasm, VP of Marketing & Sales.

■ 13921 ■ Robert Skeels and Co.
19216 S Laurel Park Rd.
Compton, CA 90220
Phone: (310)639-7240 **Fax:** (310)639-7569
Products: Builders' hardware and locksmith supplies. **SIC:** 5072 (Hardware). **Sales:** $7,300,000 (2000). **Emp:** 40. **Officers:** Bob Lange, Finance General Manager.

■ 13922 ■ Smith Abrasives, Inc.
1700 Sleepy Valley Rd.
Hot Springs, AR 71901
Phone: (501)321-2244
Free: (800)221-4156 **Fax:** (501)321-9232
E-mail: http://www.getsharp.com
Products: Knife and tool sharpeners; Abrasive products. **SICs:** 5072 (Hardware); 5085 (Industrial Supplies). **Officers:** Richard Smith, President; Mike Skoug, Plant Mgr.; Marsha Batterton, Supervisor of Operations and Comm.; Gary Knupps, VP of Operations.

■ 13923 ■ Jay Smith Associates
840 Hinckley Rd., Ste. 221
Burlingame, CA 94010
Phone: (650)652-7800 **Fax:** (707)765-6327
Products: Building and security hardware. **SIC:** 5072 (Hardware). **Officers:** Jim Morgan, Contact.

■ 13924 ■ Smith Hardware Company Inc.
515 N George St.
Goldsboro, NC 27530
Phone: (919)735-6281 **Fax:** (919)738-5464
Products: Hardware; Farm machinery and equipment. **SICs:** 5072 (Hardware); 5083 (Farm & Garden Machinery). **Est:** 1899. **Sales:** $18,000,000 (2000). **Emp:** 105. **Officers:** Bill Prince, CEO; Edgar Best, Exec. VP.

■ 13925 ■ Snap-on Tools Corp.
PO Box 1410
Kenosha, WI 53141-1410
Phone: (414)656-5200
Products: Hand tools; Electrical tools; Industrial tools. **SICs:** 5084 (Industrial Machinery & Equipment); 5072 (Hardware); 5085 (Industrial Supplies). **Est:** 1920. **Sales:** $881,600,000 (2000). **Emp:** 9,000. **Officers:** Robert A. Cornog, CEO, President & Chairman of the Board; Michael F. Montemurro, Sr. VP & Finance Officer; Richard V. Caskey, VP of Marketing; Donald E. Lyons.

■ 13926 ■ Sona Enterprises
7828 Somerset Blvd., Ste. D
Paramount, CA 90723
Phone: (562)633-3002 **Fax:** (562)633-3583
Products: Scissors; Magnifying glasses; Knives. **SIC:** 5072 (Hardware).

■ 13927 ■ Sonin Inc.
301 Fields Ln., Ste. 201
Brewster, NY 10509
Phone: (845)277-4646
Free: (800)223-7511 **Fax:** (845)277-8154
E-mail: sonin@compuserve.com
URL: http://www.sonin.com
Products: Laser levels; Electrical measuring and testing equipment; Hand tools; Calculators; Moisture testing and sensing tools. **SICs:** 5065 (Electronic Parts & Equipment Nec); 5072 (Hardware). **Est:** 1987. **Officers:** Christopher Tufo, President; Narciso Rivera, Controller; Janet Tufo, Marketing & Sales Mgr.; Laura

Madison, Customer Service Mgr.; Howard Klein, VP of Sales.

■ 13928 ■ Southern Carbide Specialists Inc.
901 N Highland Ave.
PO Box 69
Quitman, GA 31643-0069
Phone: (912)263-8927
Free: (800)343-1573 Fax: (912)263-9268
Products: Hand operated saws; Saws; Medical equipment. SICs: 5072 (Hardware); 5047 (Medical & Hospital Equipment). Sales: $10,000,000 (2000). Emp: 49. Officers: Stanley Weiss.

■ 13929 ■ Southern Cross and O'Fallon
Building Products Co.
PO Box 907
O Fallon, MO 63366
Phone: (314)272-6226 Fax: (314)272-6220
Products: Hardware, including hammers and drills; Lumber. SICs: 5072 (Hardware); 5085 (Industrial Supplies); 5031 (Lumber, Plywood & Millwork). Sales: $20,000,000 (2000). Emp: 80. Officers: John A. Kelly, President.

■ 13930 ■ Southern Hardware Company Inc.
PO Box 2508
West Helena, AR 72390-0508
Phone: (501)572-6761 Fax: (501)572-2106
E-mail: tmiller@southernhardware.com
Products: Hardware; Plumbing; Electrical; Paint sundries. SIC: 5072 (Hardware). Est: 1952. Sales: $19,000,000 (2000). Emp: 60. Officers: Thomas G. Miller Jr., President.

■ 13931 ■ Spartan Tool Supply
1660 Alum Creek Dr.
Columbus, OH 43209-2709
Phone: (614)443-7607
Free: (800)848-1368 Fax: (614)445-4590
E-mail: sales@spartantoolco.com
URL: http://www.spartantoolco.com
Products: Power tools; Pneumatic tools; Hydraulic equipment; Cutting tools; Abrasives; Hand tools. SICs: 5072 (Hardware); 5085 (Industrial Supplies). Est: 1978. Emp: 49. Officers: Dick Bateman.

■ 13932 ■ Special-T-Metals Company Inc.
15850 W 108th St.
Shawnee Mission, KS 66219-1340
Phone: (913)492-9500
Products: Fasteners, including stainless steel, nuts, and bolts. SIC: 5072 (Hardware). Est: 1970. Sales: $15,000,000 (2000). Emp: 70. Officers: Richard Schwind, President; Jerry Cash, VP of Finance; Roger Taylor, Dir. of Marketing.

■ 13933 ■ Spencer Products Co.
1859 Summit Commerce Park
Twinsburg, OH 44087-2370
Phone: (216)475-8700
Products: Hardware. SIC: 5072 (Hardware). Sales: $15,000,000 (1994). Emp: 40. Officers: Robert Tuttle, CEO; Robbin Nichols, Controller.

■ 13934 ■ Spokane Hardware Supply Inc.
PO Box 2664
Spokane, WA 99220
Phone: (509)535-1663
Free: (800)888-1663 Fax: (509)535-2823
E-mail: shs@spokane-hardware.com
URL: http://www.spokane-hardware.com; www.thehardwarehut.com
Products: Hardware; Hand and power tools; Paint; Sundries. SICs: 5072 (Hardware); 5198 (Paints, Varnishes & Supplies). Est: 1945. Sales: $10,000,000 (2000). Emp: 38. Officers: Steve Northrop, President; Alan Grimsrud, Controller; Andy Foskett, Dir. of Marketing; Rick Reinbold, Vice President; Andy Foskett, Sales/Marketing Contact, e-mail: andy@spokane-hardware.com; Cindi Hayes, Customer Service Contact, e-mail: cindi@spokane-hardware.com; Alan Grimsrud, Human Resources Contact.

■ 13935 ■ Star Stainless Screw Co.
PO Box 288
Totowa, NJ 07511
Phone: (201)256-2300 Fax: (201)256-2423
Products: Hardware, including screws, nuts, and bolts. SIC: 5072 (Hardware). Est: 1949. Sales: $92,000,000 (2000). Emp: 280. Officers: Wayne Golden, President; Arnold Slavin, Controller.

■ 13936 ■ E. Stauber Wholesale Hardware
2105 Northwestern Ave.
Waukegan, IL 60087-4149
Phone: (847)623-7740 Fax: (847)623-7768
E-mail: eswhhowe@aol.com
Products: Hardware for doors. SIC: 5072 (Hardware). Est: 1958. Emp: 17. Officers: Constance Dannible, President; Richard Dannible, Vice President; David Gutantes, Vice President; JoAnn Boyda, Purchasing Agent.

■ 13937 ■ Stewart Fastener Corp.
101 Southside Dr.
Charlotte, NC 28217-1725
Phone: (704)527-4713
Free: (800)877-7770 Fax: (704)522-7522
E-mail: sales@stewartfastener.com
URL: http://www.stewartfastener.com
Products: Fasteners; Power and hand tools; Drill bits; Saw accessories; Anchoring systems. SICs: 5072 (Hardware); 5085 (Industrial Supplies). Est: 1961. Emp: 42. Officers: D. Ronald Stewart, President; Mike Bell, VP of Marketing & Sales. Doing Business As: Stewart Fastener and Tool.

■ 13938 ■ Stewart Supply Inc.
2369 Pecan Ct.
Haltom City, TX 76117
Phone: (817)834-7313 Fax: 888-829-3214
Products: Hardware. SIC: 5072 (Hardware). Sales: $5,000,000 (2000). Emp: 27.

■ 13939 ■ Stimpson Company Inc.
900 Sylvan Ave.
Bayport, NY 11705
Phone: (516)472-2000 Fax: (516)472-2425
E-mail: customer_service@stimpsonco.com
URL: http://www.stimpsonco.com
Products: Eyelets, grommets, washers, and hole plugs. SIC: 5072 (Hardware). Est: 1852. Sales: $40,000,000 (2000). Emp: 500. Officers: Ralph Rau, President; Edward J. DeWalters, Sales Mgr.; Ginger Farrell, Sales/Marketing Contact, e-mail: ginger_farrell@stimpsonco.com.

■ 13940 ■ A.L. Strasser Hardware Co.
910 Southwest Blvd.
Kansas City, KS 66103
Phone: (913)236-5858 Fax: (913)236-4737
Products: Hardware, including hammers and screwdrivers. SIC: 5072 (Hardware). Est: 1917. Sales: $7,000,000 (2000). Emp: 100. Officers: L.A. Strasser, President; Leroy Andrews, Treasurer; H.A. Strasser, Vice President; Jack Vogel, Dir. of Data Processing.

■ 13941 ■ Strong Tool Co.
1251 E 286th St.
Cleveland, OH 44132
Phone: (216)289-2450
Free: (800)362-0293 Fax: (216)289-4562
Products: Tools; Drills; Nonmetallic coated abrasive products and buffing wheels, polishing wheels, and laps; Bolts, nuts, rivets, screws, and washers; Saws. SICs: 5072 (Hardware); 5085 (Industrial Supplies). Sales: $33,000,000 (2000). Emp: 95. Officers: Bob Kraisner; Jon Griffee; John Siskovic.

■ 13942 ■ Sunline USA Group Inc.
Hwy. 29 N & Joe Brown Dr.
PO Box 13206
Greensboro, NC 27415
Phone: (919)375-1143 Fax: (919)375-1144
Products: Cabinet hardware. SIC: 5072 (Hardware).

■ 13943 ■ Sunny International Inc.
8900 NW 33rd St.
Miami, FL 33172
Phone: (305)591-3065
Free: (800)327-0032 Fax: (305)599-1301
E-mail: email@sunico.com
URL: http://www.sunico.com
Products: Power tools and parts; Hand tools. SICs: 5072 (Hardware); 5084 (Industrial Machinery & Equipment). Est: 1980. Sales: $8,000,000 (2000). Emp: 20. Officers: Ray Lee, General Mgr.; Jason Huang, President; Cecilian Sanchez, Manager; Jason Huang, Sales/Marketing Contact.

■ 13944 ■ Sunshine Industries Inc.
1111 E 200th St.
Cleveland, OH 44117
Phone: (216)383-9000 Fax: (216)383-8019
Products: Brooms; Hardware. SIC: 5072 (Hardware). Sales: $25,000,000 (1994). Emp: 112. Officers: Sheldon Leventhal, President; Joe Monroe, Controller.

■ 13945 ■ Supply Station Inc.
PO Box 13219
Sacramento, CA 95813-3219
Phone: (916)920-2919
Free: (800)783-7888 Fax: (916)920-2340
E-mail: info@supplystation.com
URL: http://www.supplystation.com
Products: Industrial equipment, including fasteners, automotive hoses, nuts, and bolts; Chemicals and abrasives; Paints; Lamps; Hand and power tools. SICs: 5072 (Hardware); 5084 (Industrial Machinery & Equipment); 5013 (Motor Vehicle Supplies & New Parts); 5085 (Industrial Supplies). Est: 1979. Sales: $2,000,000 (2000). Emp: 20. Officers: Bill Tolbert; Chuck Lenert.

■ 13946 ■ Surfa-Shield Corp.
2360 Thompson Bridge Rd., Apt P6
Gainesville, GA 30501-1624
Products: Home improvement equipment. SIC: 5072 (Hardware).

■ 13947 ■ Surpless, Dunn & Co.
2150 W Lawrence Ave.
Chicago, IL 60625-1496
Phone: (773)878-8300
Free: (800)621-5117 Fax: (773)878-8534
Products: Hardware; Industrial supplies. SICs: 5072 (Hardware); 5085 (Industrial Supplies). Est: 1889. Emp: 34. Officers: James B. Surpless.

■ 13948 ■ Techni-Tool, Inc.
1547 N Trooper Rd.
PO Box 1117
Worcester, PA 19490-1117
Phone: (610)941-2400
Free: (800)832-4866 Fax: (610)828-5623
E-mail: sales@techni-tool.com
URL: http://www.techni-tool.com
Products: Tools. SIC: 5072 (Hardware). Est: 1959. Emp: 236. Officers: Paul Weiss, Pres.; Stuart Weiss, V.P.; Haz Klein; Michael Ryan.

■ 13949 ■ Texas Mill Supply Inc.
200 Union Bower Ct., Ste. 214
Irving, TX 75061
Phone: (972)554-1111 Fax: (972)554-6043
Products: Tools. SIC: 5072 (Hardware). Emp: 14. Officers: Joe Casstevens.

■ 13950 ■ Texas Staple Company Inc.
2422 Bartlett St.
Houston, TX 77098
Phone: (713)524-8385
Products: Fasteners and related tools. SIC: 5072 (Hardware). Est: 1962. Sales: $2,000,000 (2000). Emp: 10. Officers: Wesley Oder, President; Linda B. Grant, Treasurer & Secty.; Stephen M. Bingham, Vice President.

■ 13951 ■ Thackeray Corp.
509 Madison Ave., Rm. 1714
New York, NY 10022-5501
Phone: (212)759-3695 Fax: (212)759-4481
Products: Hardware for builders. SIC: 5072 (Hardware). Sales: $19,100,000 (1994). Emp: 60.

Officers: Martin J. Rabinowitz, President & Chairman of the Board; Jules Ross, VP of Finance & Treasurer.

■ 13952 ■ Thomas Hardware, Parts and Fasteners Inc.
1001 Rockland St.
Reading, PA 19604-1596
Phone: (215)921-3558
Free: (800)634-4293 **Fax:** (215)921-9794
Products: Hardware supplies, including fasteners.
SIC: 5013 (Motor Vehicle Supplies & New Parts). **Est:** 1950. **Sales:** $12,000,000 (2000). **Emp:** 35. **Officers:** Brad Scribner, President; Darryl Steffey, Dir. of Systems.

■ 13953 ■ Thornton Industries, Inc.
5901 Courtesy Ln.
Shreveport, LA 71108
Phone: (318)636-7450 **Fax:** (318)636-9110
Products: Hand tools; Electric-powered hand tools; Brooms. **SICs:** 5072 (Hardware); 5074 (Plumbing & Hydronic Heating Supplies); 5084 (Industrial Machinery & Equipment). **Sales:** $6,000,000 (2000). **Emp:** 32. **Officers:** J. Blocker Thorton III; Ed Hughes.

■ 13954 ■ Threaded Fasteners Inc.
358 St. Louis St.
PO Box 2644
Mobile, AL 36652-2644
Phone: (205)432-0107 **Fax:** (205)432-0223
Products: Hardware, including nuts and bolts. **SICs:** 5072 (Hardware); 5085 (Industrial Supplies). **Emp:** 25. **Officers:** P. F. Martin.

■ 13955 ■ Thruway Fasteners Inc.
2910 Niagara Falls Blvd.
North Tonawanda, NY 14120
Phone: (716)694-1434
Products: Fasteners, nuts, bolts, and screws. **SIC:** 5072 (Hardware). **Est:** 1959. **Sales:** $35,000,000 (2000). **Emp:** 140. **Officers:** Paul G. Lemke, President; Diane Brennes, Controller.

■ 13956 ■ Time Saver Tool Corp.
PO Box 4299
Hammond, IN 46324
Phone: (219)845-2500 **Fax:** (219)845-2058
Products: Hand tools. **SIC:** 5072 (Hardware). **Est:** 1954. **Officers:** Tom Vlahos, President.

■ 13957 ■ Tool House Inc.
PO Box 80759
Lincoln, NE 68501
Phone: (402)476-6673
Products: Fasteners; Hand tools; Electric tools. **SIC:** 5072 (Hardware). **Est:** 1896. **Sales:** $5,000,000 (2000). **Emp:** 40. **Officers:** Paul Ahrendt, President.

■ 13958 ■ Tool Mart
750 Citracado Pkwy.
Escondido, CA 92025
Phone: (760)480-1444
Products: Mechanical tools; Woodworking tools. **SIC:** 5072 (Hardware). **Sales:** $10,000,000 (2000). **Emp:** 14. **Officers:** Allan Houch, Owner.

■ 13959 ■ Tool World
1160 Air Way Blvd.
El Paso, TX 79925
Phone: (915)779-5616
Free: (800)929-5022 **Fax:** (915)779-5624
Products: Power and hand tools, including carpentry, industrial, and gardening tools. **SIC:** 5084 (Industrial Machinery & Equipment). **Est:** 1980. **Sales:** $4,000,000 (2000). **Emp:** 12. **Officers:** Guenter Miller, President.

■ 13960 ■ Toolman Co.
721 Graywood Ave.
Elkhart, IN 46516-5418
Phone: (219)295-0296
Free: (800)942-0257 **Fax:** (219)295-5851
Products: Tools; Hand tools; Power tools and parts. **SICs:** 5072 (Hardware); 5084 (Industrial Machinery & Equipment). **Est:** 1964. **Sales:** $1,000,000 (2000). **Emp:** 15. **Officers:** Robert Steffen.

■ 13961 ■ TradeCom International Inc.
32750 Solon Road, Ste. 9
Solon, OH 44139
Phone: (440)248-9116 **Fax:** (440)248-9178
E-mail: tradecominternational@worldnet.att.net
URL: http://www.imex.com/wdiyc/members/tradecom.html
Products: Paint and varnish brushes; Rollers; Pads; Hardware. **SICs:** 5072 (Hardware); 5085 (Industrial Supplies); 5023 (Homefurnishings); 5169 (Chemicals & Allied Products Nec); 5074 (Plumbing & Hydronic Heating Supplies). **Est:** 1970. **Sales:** $3,000,000 (2000). **Emp:** 4. **Officers:** Edward S. Benhoff, President; Edward S. Benhoff, Sales/Marketing Contact.

■ 13962 ■ Trans-Atlantic Co.
440 Fairmount Ave.
Philadelphia, PA 19123
Phone: (215)629-0400
Free: (800)523-9956 **Fax:** (215)629-1282
E-mail: tacoj@aol.com
Products: Builders' and security hardware. **SIC:** 5072 (Hardware). **Est:** 1951. **Sales:** $8,000,000 (2000). **Emp:** 35. **Officers:** Norman Millman, CEO; B. Davis, Dir. of Marketing. **Also Known by This Acronym:** TACO.

■ 13963 ■ Travers Tool Co.
128-15 26th Ave.
Flushing, NY 11354
Phone: (718)886-7200
Free: (800)221-0270 **Fax:** (718)886-7895
Products: Tools. **SIC:** 5084 (Industrial Machinery & Equipment). **Sales:** $32,000,000 (2000). **Emp:** 150. **Officers:** Barry Zolot, President & Treasurer.

■ 13964 ■ Travers Tool Co., Inc.
128-15 26th Ave.
PO Box 541550
Flushing, NY 11354-0108
Phone: (718)886-7200
Free: (800)221-0270 **Fax:** (718)886-7895
E-mail: info@travers.com
URL: http://www.travers.com
Products: Cutting tools; Blades; Abrasives; Machine tools; Hand and power tools. **SIC:** 5072 (Hardware). **Est:** 1924. **Emp:** 150. **Officers:** David Trevas, Founder.

■ 13965 ■ Triangle Brass Manufacturing Co.
PO Box 23277
Los Angeles, CA 90023
Phone: (323)262-4191 **Fax:** 800-637-8746
E-mail: trimcobbw@aol.com
URL: http://www.trimcobbw.com
Products: Door hardware. **SIC:** 5072 (Hardware). **Sales:** $6,000,000 (2000). **Emp:** 140. **Officers:** Martin S. Simon; Ira J. Simon.

■ 13966 ■ Trophy Products Inc.
9714 Old Katy Rd.
Houston, TX 77055
Phone: (713)464-8256
Free: (800)275-2626 **Fax:** (713)464-4623
Products: Tool boxes; Tackle boxes. **SICs:** 5091 (Sporting & Recreational Goods); 5072 (Hardware). **Emp:** 99. **Officers:** R. L. Bernstein; H. D. Klebanoff; E. A. Perwien.

■ 13967 ■ True Value Regional Distributor
2150 Olympic St.
Springfield, OR 97477
Phone: (541)726-8243
Products: Hardware. **SIC:** 5072 (Hardware).

■ 13968 ■ TruServ Corp.
8600 W Bryn Mawr Ave.
Chicago, IL 60631-3505
Phone: (773)695-5000 **Fax:** (773)695-6558
URL: http://www.truevalue.com
Products: Hardware, gardening equipment, and home furnishings. **SICs:** 5072 (Hardware); 5083 (Farm & Garden Machinery); 5023 (Homefurnishings). **Est:** 1948. **Sales:** $4,500,000,000 (1999). **Emp:** 5,400. **Officers:** Donald Hoye, President & CEO; Len Kuhr, CFO; Brian Schnaber, COO.

■ 13969 ■ Twin City Hardware Company Inc.
1010 N Dale St.
St. Paul, MN 55117
Phone: (612)488-6701 **Fax:** (612)488-8510
Products: Hardware, including locks, cabinet hardware, knobs, poles, and hinges. **SIC:** 5072 (Hardware). **Est:** 1883. **Sales:** $7,000,000 (2000). **Emp:** 32. **Officers:** George H. Boomer Sr., President; Dave Shroyer, Controller.

■ 13970 ■ Ultra Hardware Products LLC
1777 Hylton Rd., Dept. AWDD 2000
Pennsauken, NJ 08110
Phone: (856)663-5050
Free: (800)426-6379 **Fax:** (856)663-1743
E-mail: info@ultrahardware.com
URL: http://www.ultrahardware.com
Products: Builders hardware; Commercial, storm door and window, and sliding door hardware; Padlocks; Cabinet hardware; Plumbing and accessories; Hand tools; Locksets; Faucets. **SICs:** 5072 (Hardware); 5074 (Plumbing & Hydronic Heating Supplies). **Est:** 1987. **Emp:** 120. **Officers:** Daniel Carpey, President; Ed Stein, VF; Rick Lipski, VP of Sales, e-mail: rlipski@ultrahardware.com; Jill Donaldson, Customer Service COntact, e-mail: jdonaldson@ultrahardware.com; Roger Mason, Dir. of Marketing.

■ 13971 ■ Union Butterfield Corp.
PO Box 50000
Asheville, NC 28813
Phone: 800-222-8665 **Fax:** 800-432-9482
E-mail: union.butterfield@worldnet.att.net
URL: http://www.unionbutterfield.com
Products: Cutting tools. **SIC:** 5072 (Hardware). **Est:** 1880. **Emp:** 161. **Officers:** Alan Fowler, VP of Sales.

■ 13972 ■ United Fastener and Supply Co.
12565 E Slauson Ave.
Whittier, CA 90606
Phone: (562)945-3302
Products: Nuts, bolts, and screws. **SIC:** 5072 (Hardware). **Est:** 1974. **Sales:** $2,000,000 (2000). **Emp:** 13. **Officers:** James W. Becker, President.

■ 13973 ■ United Hardware Distributing Co.
5005 Nathan Ln.
Plymouth, MN 55442
Phone: (612)559-1800 **Fax:** (612)557-2799
URL: http://www.unitedhardware.com
Products: Hardware, plumbing, paint and electrical, hand and power tools, farm & garden, farm supplies, housewares, sporting goods, automotive, toys, trim-a-tree, outdoor living. **SIC:** 5072 (Hardware). **Est:** 1945. **Sales:** $155,000,000 (1999). **Emp:** 370. **Officers:** David A. Heider, CEO & President; John Nitsche, VP & CFO; Alice Heroux, Customer Service Contact; Robert Branton, Sales/Marketing Contact; Wayne Castrovinci, Dir. of Information Systems; Renee Bourget, Human Resources Contact.

■ 13974 ■ United Manufacturers Supplies Inc.
80 Gordon Dr.
Syosset, NY 11791-4705
Phone: (516)496-4430
Free: (800)645-7260 **Fax:** (516)496-7968
E-mail: united@spacelab.net
Products: Hardware; Framing supplies; Moulding; Glass; Acrylic. **SICs:** 5072 (Hardware); 5031 (Lumber, Plywood & Millwork). **Sales:** $6,000,000 (2000). **Emp:** 99.

■ 13975 ■ U.S. Industrial Products Corp.
96-12 43rd Ave.
Corona, NY 11368
Phone: (718)335-3300
Free: (800)FOR-HDWE **Fax:** (718)565-1444
Products: Hardware. **SIC:** 5072 (Hardware). **Est:** 1945. **Sales:** $9,000,000 (2000). **Emp:** 49.

■ 13976 ■ U.S. Industrial Tool Supply
15101 Cleat
Plymouth, MI 48170-6015
Phones: (734)455-3388 800-521-7394
Free: (800)521-7394 **Fax:** (734)455-3256
URL: http://www.ustool.com
Products: Tools, including aircraft, sheet metal forming tools and air-operated hand tools. **SICs:** 5072 (Hardware); 5084 (Industrial Machinery & Equipment).

Est: 1955. **Sales:** $10,000,000 (2000). **Emp:** 45. **Officers:** William Marinovich.

■ **13977** ■ **Universal Fastener Co.**
5930 Old Mt. Holly Rd.
PO Box 668013
Charlotte, NC 28208
Phone: (704)392-5342
Free: (800)438-2922   **Fax:** (704)394-0904
Products: Snap fasteners (all types). **SIC:** 5072 (Hardware). **Est:** 1960. **Emp:** 49.

■ **13978** ■ **Vaughan and Bushnell Manufacturing**
PO Box 390
Hebron, IL 60034-0390
Phone: (815)648-2446   **Fax:** (815)648-4300
URL: http://www.vaughanmfg.com
Products: Hand tools. **SIC:** 5072 (Hardware). **Est:** 1869. **Sales:** $10,000,000 (2000). **Emp:** 499. **Officers:** H. A. Vaughan Jr.

■ **13979** ■ **Vaughan & Bushnell Manufacturing Co.**
225 Riverview Ave.
Waltham, MA 02454
Phone: (781)647-5560   **Fax:** (781)891-8375
Products: Hammers; Metal bars; Tools. **SIC:** 5072 (Hardware).

■ **13980** ■ **Vermont American Tool Co.**
800 Woodside Ave.
Fountain Inn, SC 29644-2029
Phone: (864)862-8000   **Fax:** (864)862-8041
Products: Tools. **SIC:** 5072 (Hardware). **Est:** 1985. **Sales:** $25,000,000 (2000). **Emp:** 275. **Officers:** George Hall III.

■ **13981** ■ **W C L Co.**
PO Box 3588
La Puente, CA 91744-0588
Phone: (626)968-5523   **Fax:** (626)369-9805
Products: Fasteners. **SIC:** 5072 (Hardware). **Est:** 1957. **Sales:** $4,000,000 (2000). **Emp:** 22. **Officers:** Lee Harper, President; J.C. Harper, Treasurer.

■ **13982** ■ **Wagner Hardware Co.**
PO Box 607
Mansfield, OH 44901
Phone: (419)522-7811   **Fax:** (419)526-6851
Products: Hardware, including nails and fasteners; Plumbing and electrical equipment and supplies; Lawn and garden supplies; Automotive products; Hand and power tools; Cleaning supplies. **SICs:** 5072 (Hardware); 5013 (Motor Vehicle Supplies & New Parts); 5169 (Chemicals & Allied Products Nec); 5199 (Nondurable Goods Nec). **Est:** 1895. **Sales:** $12,000,000 (2000). **Emp:** 52. **Officers:** Michael J. Brauchler, Corp. Secty.; James Arnold, Treasurer; Steve Jenkins, Asst. Treasurer; David J. Baumberger, Vice President; Dwayne Washer, Human Resources Contact; Dwayne Washer, President.

■ **13983** ■ **Wahler Brothers**
2549 N Halsted
Chicago, IL 60614
Phone: (773)248-1349
Products: Contractor supplies; Hardware; Janitor's supplies. **SICs:** 5072 (Hardware); 5087 (Service Establishment Equipment).

■ **13984** ■ **P.J. Wallbank Springs Inc.**
2121 Beard St.
Port Huron, MI 48060
Phone: (810)987-2992
Products: Springs and coil. **SIC:** 5072 (Hardware).

■ **13985** ■ **Watters and Martin Inc.**
3800 Village Ave.
Norfolk, VA 23502
Phone: (757)857-0651
Products: Hardware. **SIC:** 5072 (Hardware). **Sales:** $15,400,000 (1994). **Emp:** 88. **Officers:** James W. Griffiths, President; Bryan Jones, Treasurer & Secty.

■ **13986** ■ **Wayne Fasteners Inc.**
2611 Independence Dr.
Ft. Wayne, IN 46808-1391
Phone: (219)484-0393
Free: (800)994-0393   **Fax:** (219)483-8082
Products: Fasteners; MRO supplies. **SICs:** 5072 (Hardware); 5085 (Industrial Supplies). **Est:** 1976. **Emp:** 43. **Officers:** Thomas E. Mason; Charles T. Keller.

■ **13987** ■ **WBH Industries**
PO Box 98
Arlington, TX 76011
Phone: (817)649-5700
Products: Hardware, wood and metal door frames. **SICs:** 5072 (Hardware); 5031 (Lumber, Plywood & Millwork). **Sales:** $16,000,000 (1994). **Emp:** 50.

■ **13988** ■ **Webb Bolt and Nut Co.**
2830 Taft Ave.
Orlando, FL 32804
Phone: (407)841-1844   **Fax:** (407)423-1824
Products: Bolts, nuts, rivets, screws, and washers. **SIC:** 5072 (Hardware). **Emp:** 49. **Officers:** Stanley A. Webb.

■ **13989** ■ **Wedin International Inc., Ball Screw Manufacturing and Repair, Inc.**
1111 6th Ave.
Cadillac, MI 49601
Phone: (231)779-8650
Free: (800)759-3346   **Fax:** (231)779-8673
E-mail: wedin@michweb.net
URL: http://www.wedin.com
Products: Precision, semi-precision, and rolled thread ballscrews; Acme screws and brass nuts; Precision cut and ground gears and splines; Special lead bars and threads. **SICs:** 5072 (Hardware); 5085 (Industrial Supplies); 5051 (Metals Service Centers & Offices). **Est:** 1936. **Sales:** $10,000,000 (2000). **Emp:** 99. **Officers:** Jack N. Rabun Jr., Vice President.

■ **13990** ■ **Weingart & Sons**
1251 Randall Ave.
Bronx, NY 10474-6411
Phone: (718)589-1703   **Fax:** (718)617-1539
Products: Bolts, nuts, rivets, screws, and washers; Snap fasteners (all types); Power hand tools; Hardware. **SIC:** 5072 (Hardware). **Emp:** 15.

■ **13991** ■ **Carl Weissman and Sons Inc.**
PO Box 1609
Great Falls, MT 59403
Phone: (406)761-4848
Free: (800)334-5964   **Fax:** (406)791-6731
Products: Hardware, steel and auto parts and supplies. **SICs:** 5072 (Hardware); 5051 (Metals Service Centers & Offices); 5013 (Motor Vehicle Supplies & New Parts). **Sales:** $30,000,000 (2000). **Emp:** 175. **Officers:** J. Weissman, CEO & President; Arnold Schandelson, CFO.

■ **13992** ■ **Wells and Wade Hardware**
201 S Wenatchee Ave.
Wenatchee, WA 98801
Phone: (509)662-7173
Products: Hardware. **SIC:** 5072 (Hardware). **Sales:** $19,000,000 (1992). **Emp:** 70. **Officers:** Stan G. Jensen, President; Joe Donahou, Finance General Manager.

■ **13993** ■ **Wesche Co.**
10545 S Memorial
Tulsa, OK 74133
Phone: (918)583-7551   **Fax:** (918)583-1923
Products: Tools; Hardware. **SICs:** 5085 (Industrial Supplies); 5072 (Hardware). **Sales:** $4,000,000 (2000). **Emp:** 37. **Officers:** Robert A. Wesche.

■ **13994** ■ **West Union Corp.**
PO Box 3177
Memphis, TN 38173
Phone: (901)529-5700
Products: Hardware, including hammers and saws. **SIC:** 5072 (Hardware). **Est:** 1847. **Sales:** $420,000,000 (2000). **Emp:** 1,900. **Officers:** Micheal McDonnell, President; Bob Hawkins, Treasurer & Secty.; Charlie Epperson, VP of Human Resources.

■ **13995** ■ **Western Fastener Co.**
7373 Engineer Rd.
San Diego, CA 92111-1425
Phone: (619)292-5115   **Fax:** (619)292-0427
Products: Fasteners for electronic equipment. **SICs:** 5072 (Hardware); 5065 (Electronic Parts & Equipment Nec). **Est:** 1958. **Sales:** $5,000,000 (2000). **Emp:** 21. **Officers:** Scott Sutherland.

■ **13996** ■ **Western Tool Supply Inc.**
2315 25th St. SE
Salem, OR 97302
Phone: (503)588-8222
Products: Woodworking tools. **SIC:** 5082 (Construction & Mining Machinery). **Est:** 1981. **Sales:** $11,000,000 (2000). **Emp:** 50. **Officers:** Kevin Tiker, President.

■ **13997** ■ **Wilco Supply**
5960 Telegraph Ave.
Oakland, CA 94609-0047
Phone: (510)652-8522
Free: (800)745-5450   **Fax:** (510)653-5397
E-mail: wilco@wilcosupply.com
URL: http://www.wilcosupply.com
Products: Locks and hardware supplies. **SIC:** 5072 (Hardware). **Est:** 1953. **Sales:** $18,000,000 (2000). **Emp:** 52. **Officers:** H.D. Williams, President; Jonathan Clarner, CFO; Eric Heaton, Dir. of Marketing & Sales; Bob Williams, VP of Operations.

■ **13998** ■ **J.H. Williams Industrial Products, Inc.**
6969 Jamesson Rd.
PO Box 7577
Columbus, GA 31909
Phone: (706)563-9590   **Fax:** (706)561-0061
Products: Wrenches; Hand tools; Power tools and parts. **SIC:** 5072 (Hardware).

■ **13999** ■ **Wiurth Adams Nut and Bolt**
10100 85th Ave. N
Maple Grove, MN 55369
Phone: (763)424-3374
Products: Nuts and bolts. **SIC:** 5072 (Hardware). **Sales:** $30,000 (1999). **Emp:** 120. **Officers:** Winston Adams, CEO. **Former Name:** Adams Nut and Bolt Co.

■ **14000** ■ **Woodings-Verona Tool Works Inc.**
3801 Camden Ave.
Parkersburg, WV 26101
Free: (800)289-9889
E-mail: woodings@nb.net
URL: http://www.woodings-verona.com
Products: Tools. **SIC:** 5072 (Hardware). **Est:** 1873. **Emp:** 249. **Officers:** Gerald Potts, President.

■ **14001** ■ **Wynn's International Inc.**
PO Box 14143
Orange, CA 92863
Phone: (714)938-3700   **Fax:** (714)938-3739
Products: Industrial fluids, automotive chemicals, sealing products and locksmith supplies. **SIC:** 5072 (Hardware). **Sales:** $360,300,000 (1999). **Emp:** 2,121. **Officers:** James Carroll, Chairman of the Board; Seymour A. Schlosser, VP & CFO.

■ **14002** ■ **Yakima Hardware Co.**
226 S 1st St.
Yakima, WA 98901
Phone: (509)453-3181
Products: Hand tools; Lawn and garden supplies. **SICs:** 5072 (Hardware); 5083 (Farm & Garden Machinery). **Est:** 1889. **Sales:** $23,000,000 (2000). **Emp:** 75. **Officers:** Ken Marble, President; Dan Marple, Finance Officer; Ted Burton, Vice President.

■ **14003** ■ **Yarborough and Co.**
PO Box 308
High Point, NC 27261-0308
Phone: (919)861-2345   **Fax:** (919)861-4678
Products: Hardware. **SIC:** 5072 (Hardware). **Sales:** $25,000,000 (1993). **Emp:** 65. **Officers:** Gordon Yarborough, President; Dale Singley, Exec. VP of Finance.

■ **14004** ■ **Yeatman Architectural Hardware Inc.**
8030 Holly Ave.
Waldorf, MD 20601
Phone: (301)868-8850
Products: Doors and door frames; Commercial hardware, including doorknobs. **SICs:** 5072 (Hardware); 5031 (Lumber, Plywood & Millwork). **Est:** 1970. **Sales:** $1,500,000 (2000). **Emp:** 12. **Officers:**

Betty Loving, President; R.H. Yeatman Jr., Vice President.

■ **14005** ■ **Ziegler's Bolt & Nut House**
4848 Corporate St. SW
Canton, OH 44706-1907
Phone: (330)478-2542   **Fax:** (330)478-2031
Products: Bolts, nuts, rivets, screws, and washers; Hardware fasteners. **SICs:** 5072 (Hardware); 5085

(Industrial Supplies); 5051 (Metals Service Centers & Offices). **Sales:** $10,000,000 (2000). **Emp:** 90. **Officers:** Mike Young.

(22) Health and Beauty Aids

Entries in this section are arranged alphabetically by company name. When the company name is a personal name, the company name is alphabetized by the surname unless the first name or initial(s) are part of a trade name. See the User's Guide at the front of this directory for additional information.

■ **14006** ■ **78ic Beauty Supply & Salons**
Woodland Hills
7021 S Memorial, Ste. 147
Tulsa, OK 74133
Phone: (918)252-4486   **Fax:** (918)492-0278
E-mail: mdtar@aol.com
Products: Beauty supplies, including hair preparation.
SICs: 5122 (Drugs, Proprietaries & Sundries); 5087
(Service Establishment Equipment). **Est:** 1978. **Sales:**
$1,000,000 (2000). **Emp:** 49. **Officers:** Cheryl White,
Owner.

■ **14007** ■ **Aaraya Beauty Accents**
8827 W Ogden Ave., Ste. 122
Brookfield, IL 60513
Phone: (630)241-3366   **Fax:** (708)485-6571
Products: Wigs and hair pieces. **SIC:** 5199
(Nondurable Goods Nec).

■ **14008** ■ **Action Laboratories Inc.**
Via Martens
Anaheim, CA 92806
Phone: (714)630-5941
Free: (800)400-5696   **Fax:** (714)630-5941
URL: http://actionlab.com
Products: Skin and hair care products; Vitamins;
Toothpaste. **SIC:** 5122 (Drugs, Proprietaries &
Sundries). **Est:** 1963. **Sales:** $2,500,000 (2000). **Emp:**
8. **Officers:** James R. Bailey, President.

■ **14009** ■ **Aerial Company Inc.**
PO Box 197
Marinette, WI 54143
Phone: (715)735-9323   **Fax:** (715)735-9112
Products: Beauty products. **SIC:** 5087 (Service
Establishment Equipment). **Est:** 1912. **Sales:**
$32,000,000 (2000). **Emp:** 240. **Officers:** Ryan
Hmielewski, CEO & President; Mark Konrad,
Controller; Betsy Jaeger, VP of Sales; Al Demerath,
Manager; Roy Schwoerer, Manager.

■ **14010** ■ **Aerobic Life Industries Inc.**
2916 N 35th Ave., Ste. 8
Phoenix, AZ 85017-5264
Phone: (602)455-6380   **Fax:** (602)455-6397
Products: Health aids and foods; Skin and hair
creams; Water purification equipment. **SICs:** 5122
(Drugs, Proprietaries & Sundries); 5084 (Industrial
Machinery & Equipment). **Sales:** $19,000,000 (2000).
Emp: 28. **Officers:** Jason Pratt, President.

■ **14011** ■ **Agora Cosmetics Inc.**
580 Broadway, Ste. 1002
New York, NY 10012
Phone: (212)941-0890
Products: Cosmetics. **SIC:** 5122 (Drugs, Proprietaries
& Sundries).

■ **14012** ■ **Alberto-Culver International Inc.**
2525 Armitage Ave.
Melrose Park, IL 60160
Phone: (708)450-3000   **Fax:** (708)450-3354
Products: Toiletries and cosmetics. **SIC:** 5122 (Drugs,
Proprietaries & Sundries). **Sales:** $1,775,000,000
(2000). **Emp:** 11,000. **Officers:** John G. Horsman Jr.,
President; William Cernugel, Sr. VP & Finance Officer.

■ **14013** ■ **All City Barber & Beauty Supply**
408 S Main St.
Santa Ana, CA 92701
Phone: (714)835-8727
Free: (877)675-8727   **Fax:** (714)835-0286
Products: Beauty and barber shop accessories. **SICs:**
5122 (Drugs, Proprietaries & Sundries); 5087 (Service
Establishment Equipment). **Est:** 1957. **Emp:** 7.
Officers: Gary Nelson.

■ **14014** ■ **Allou Distributors Inc.**
50 Emjay Blvd.
Brentwood, NY 11717
Phone: (516)273-4000
Products: Beauty aids; Homefurnishings. **SICs:** 5122
(Drugs, Proprietaries & Sundries); 5023
(Homefurnishings). **Est:** 1962. **Sales:** $120,000,000
(2000). **Emp:** 150. **Officers:** Herman Jacobs,
President; David Shamilzadeh, CFO; Ramon Montes,
VP of Operations.

■ **14015** ■ **Allou Health and Beauty Care Inc.**
50 Emjay Blvd.
Brentwood, NY 11717
Phone: (516)273-4000   **Fax:** (516)273-5318
Products: Health and beauty aids, including
fragrances and non-perishable food products. **SICs:**
5122 (Drugs, Proprietaries & Sundries); 5149
(Groceries & Related Products Nec). **Sales:**
$301,800,000 (2000). **Emp:** 240. **Officers:** Victor
Jacobs, CEO & Chairman of the Board; David
Shamilzadeh, CFO.

■ **14016** ■ **Alma's Glow Products International**
1806 E Alondra Blvd.
Compton, CA 90221
Phone: (310)764-4247
Free: (800)552-4569   **Fax:** (310)764-2024
E-mail: almasglow@aol.com
URL: http://www.almasglow.com
Products: Hairgrowth preparations, including
shampoos; Miracle soaps and detergents. **SICs:** 5122
(Drugs, Proprietaries & Sundries); 5169 (Chemicals &
Allied Products Nec). **Est:** 1988. **Officers:** John W.
Jones; Alma Jones.

■ **14017** ■ **Almeda Beauty Shop**
10121 4th St. NW
Albuquerque, NM 87114-2211
Phone: (505)898-0686
Products: Service industry machinery; Barber and
beauty shop furniture and equipment; Beauty and
barber shop accessories. **SIC:** 5087 (Service
Establishment Equipment). **Officers:** Mary Salas,
Owner.

■ **14018** ■ **American Comb Corp.**
22 Kentucky Ave.
Paterson, NJ 07503
Phone: (973)523-6551
E-mail: americancomb@worldnet.att.net
URL: http://www.americancomb.com
Products: Personal goods. **SICs:** 5199 (Nondurable
Goods Nec); 5122 (Drugs, Proprietaries & Sundries).
Est: 1960. **Emp:** 10. **Officers:** Frank Bachrach,
President.

■ **14019** ■ **American Ex-Im Corp.**
805 Kearny
San Francisco, CA 94108
Phone: (415)362-2255   **Fax:** (415)362-4859
Products: Ginseng. **SIC:** 5122 (Drugs, Proprietaries &
Sundries).

■ **14020** ■ **Ammar Beauty Supply Co.**
223 W King St.
St. Augustine, FL 32084
Phone: (904)829-6544   **Fax:** (904)829-3032
Products: Beauty and barber shop accessories,
supplies, and equipment. **SICs:** 5087 (Service
Establishment Equipment); 5122 (Drugs, Proprietaries
& Sundries). **Est:** 1981. **Sales:** $700,000 (2000). **Emp:**
8. **Officers:** Jamal M. Ammar; Livia F. Ammar.

■ **14021** ■ **Amrion Inc.**
6565 Odell Pl.
Boulder, CO 80301-3306
Phone: (303)530-2525
Free: (800)492-3003   **Fax:** (303)530-2592
Products: Nutritional supplements including vitamins,
minerals, and herbs. **SIC:** 5122 (Drugs, Proprietaries &
Sundries). **Est:** 1987. **Sales:** $68,000,000 (2000).
Emp: 405. **Officers:** David Robinson, President.

■ **14022** ■ **Anderson Wholesale Co.**
PO Box 69
Muskogee, OK 74402
Phone: (918)682-5568   **Fax:** (918)682-7549
Products: Candy; Health and beauty aids;
Pharmaceuticals. **SICs:** 5122 (Drugs, Proprietaries &
Sundries); 5145 (Confectionery). **Est:** 1949. **Sales:**
$30,000,000 (2000). **Emp:** 200. **Officers:** John P.
Gilliam, President; Thomas Shelton, Dir. of Data
Processing; Mark Anderson, Vice President.

■ **14023** ■ **Applied Genetics Inc.**
205 Buffalo Ave.
Freeport, NY 11520
Phone: (516)868-9026
Products: Biological cosmetic raw materials. **SIC:**
5122 (Drugs, Proprietaries & Sundries). **Sales:**
$1,000,000 (2000). **Emp:** 13. **Officers:** Daniel B.
Yarosh, President.

■ **14024** ■ **Argos Enterprises**
101 Westfall Dr.
Syracuse, NY 13219
Phone: (315)468-0297   **Fax:** (315)468-2569
Products: Sun tanning lotions; Women's cosmetics;
Swimming pool accessories. **SICs:** 5122 (Drugs,
Proprietaries & Sundries); 5091 (Sporting &
Recreational Goods). **Officers:** Kenneth R.
Cosselmon, President.

■ **14025** ■ **Armstrong McCall**
PO Box 17068
Austin, TX 78760-7068
Phone: (512)444-1757   **Fax:** (512)444-4511
Products: Beauty supplies. **SIC:** 5122 (Drugs,
Proprietaries & Sundries). **Sales:** $17,000,000 (2000).
Emp: 100. **Officers:** John McCall, President; Vic Lacy,
Controller.

■ 14026 ■ **Arnold's Inc.**
PO Box 190260
Little Rock, AR 72219
Phone: (501)562-0675
Products: Beauty products; Hair and skin care items.
SIC: 5122 (Drugs, Proprietaries & Sundries). **Est:**
1884. **Sales:** $11,000,000 (2000). **Emp:** 100. **Officers:**
Harry Aburrow, President.

■ 14027 ■ **Auromere Inc.**
1291 Weber St.
Pomona, CA 91768
Phones: (909)629-0108   (909)629-8255
Free: (800)735-4691   **Fax:** (909)623-9877
Products: Body care products, including toothpaste;
Incense; Herbal tea; Food supplements. **SICs:** 5122
(Drugs, Proprietaries & Sundries); 5149 (Groceries &
Related Products Nec). **Est:** 1973. **Officers:** Danshina
Vanzetti, President; Michael Zucher, Vice President.

■ 14028 ■ **Austin House Inc.**
PO Box 665
Buffalo, NY 14226-0665
Phone: (716)825-2650
Free: (800)268-5157   **Fax:** (716)825-3200
Products: Travel accessories, including blow dryers,
miniature toothbrushes, and mouthwash. **SIC:** 5122
(Drugs, Proprietaries & Sundries). **Est:** 1974. **Sales:**
$85,000,000 (2000). **Emp:** 20. **Officers:** J. Taylor,
President; S. Taylor, Vice President.

■ 14029 ■ **Avon Products Inc.**
1345 Avenue of the Americas
New York, NY 10105-0302
Phone: (212)282-5000
Products: Cosmetics and perfume. **SIC:** 5092 (Toys &
Hobby Goods & Supplies). **Sales:** $5,212,700,000
(2000). **Emp:** 33,900. **Officers:** James E. Preston,
CEO & Chairman of the Board; Robert J. Corti, Sr. VP
& CFO.

■ 14030 ■ **Avon Products Inc. Newark**
  Regional Area
2100 Ogletown Rd.
Newark, DE 19712
Phone: (302)453-7700   **Fax:** (302)453-7788
Products: Health and beauty aids; Cosmetics;
Perfume. **SIC:** 5122 (Drugs, Proprietaries & Sundries).
Est: 1886. **Emp:** 550. **Officers:** Angelo Rossi,
Regional VP-NE Sales and Cust. Service; Keith Wargo,
Customer Service Director.

■ 14031 ■ **Awareness and Health Unlimited**
3509 N High St.
Columbus, OH 43214
Phone: (614)262-7087
Free: (800)533-7087   **Fax:** (614)262-0532
Products: Health care and beauty products, including
Chinese herbs and massage tools; Books and tapes.
SICs: 5122 (Drugs, Proprietaries & Sundries); 5192
(Books, Periodicals & Newspapers). **Est:** 1980.

■ 14032 ■ **B & A Distributing Inc.**
1800 Post Rd.
Warwick, RI 02886-1534
Phone: (401)739-9707
Products: Beauty and barber shop accessories. **SIC:**
5087 (Service Establishment Equipment). **Officers:**
Robert Rizzo, President.

■ 14033 ■ **B & G Beauty Supply Inc.**
1300 E Plumb Ln.
Reno, NV 89502-6915
Phone: (702)829-2704   **Fax:** (702)829-2706
Products: Service industry machinery; Barber and
beauty shop furniture and equipment. **SIC:** 5087
(Service Establishment Equipment). **Officers:** Joseph
Wright, President.

■ 14034 ■ **Baddour International**
4300 New Getwell Rd.
Memphis, TN 38118
Phone: (901)365-1191
Products: Plastic housewares; Sanitary paper
products; Household cleaning supplies; Health and
beauty aids, including toiletries. **SICs:** 5122 (Drugs,
Proprietaries & Sundries); 5023 (Homefurnishings);
5169 (Chemicals & Allied Products Nec). **Officers:**
Fred Akil, Manager.

■ 14035 ■ **Bean's Beauty Supply**
4405 Main St.
Philadelphia, PA 19127
Phone: (215)487-3333   **Fax:** (215)487-0202
Products: Beauty and barber shop accessories. **SIC:**
5087 (Service Establishment Equipment). **Officers:**
Michael Batt, Contact.

■ 14036 ■ **Beauty Aid Distributors**
PO Box 1405
Pocatello, ID 83204-1405
Phone: (208)232-5972
Products: Beauty salon and barber shop equipment
and supplies. **SIC:** 5087 (Service Establishment
Equipment). **Officers:** Harry Dudunake, Owner.

■ 14037 ■ **Beauty & Beauty Enterprises, Inc.**
30 Universal Pl.
Carlstadt, NJ 07072
Phone: (201)935-8887
Free: (800)474-6533   **Fax:** (201)939-5154
Products: Hairbrushes and combs; Artificial nails;
Cosmetics. **SIC:** 5122 (Drugs, Proprietaries &
Sundries). **Est:** 1986. **Sales:** $3,000,000 (2000). **Emp:**
5. **Officers:** Harry Hwang, President; Daniel Kim, Vice
President.

■ 14038 ■ **Belcam Inc.**
4 Montgomery St.
Rouses Point, NY 12979
Phone: (518)297-6641   **Fax:** (518)297-2943
Products: Toiletries. **SIC:** 5122 (Drugs, Proprietaries &
Sundries). **Est:** 1946. **Sales:** $35,000,000 (2000).
Emp: 250. **Officers:** M. Bellm, President; John Knot,
VP of Sales; L. Jerry Remilard, VP of Marketing &
Sales; Hugh Upton, Dir. of Information Systems; Fran
Wynnik, Dir of Human Resources.

■ 14039 ■ **Best Beauty Supply Co.**
516 Baltimore St.
Hanover, PA 17331
Phone: (717)637-4232
Free: (800)922-8075   **Fax:** (717)637-4232
Products: Beauty and barber shop accessories; Hair
preparations (including shampoos). **SICs:** 5122 (Drugs,
Proprietaries & Sundries); 5087 (Service Establishment
Equipment). **Est:** 1922. **Emp:** 3. **Officers:** Joel E.
Hastetter, Owner.

■ 14040 ■ **Billings Horn**
12881 166th St.
Cerritos, CA 90703-2103
Phone: (714)220-2313   **Fax:** (714)952-8931
Products: Health and beauty care, including shampoo
and medication. **SIC:** 5122 (Drugs, Proprietaries &
Sundries). **Emp:** 49.

■ 14041 ■ **Bindley Western**
9727 Tanner Rd.
Houston, TX 77041-7620
Phone: (713)460-8588   **Fax:** (713)460-2377
Products: Pharmaceutical preparations; Medicinal and
health supplies. **SIC:** 5122 (Drugs, Proprietaries &
Sundries). **Est:** 1968. **Emp:** 33. **Officers:** Dave
Bascom, Manager.

■ 14042 ■ **Bindley Western Drug Co.**
542 Covina Blvd.
San Dimas, CA 91773
Phone: (909)394-0067   **Fax:** (909)394-0796
Products: Pharmaceutical preparations; Medicinal and
health supplies. **SIC:** 5122 (Drugs, Proprietaries &
Sundries). **Emp:** 61. **Officers:** David Brinkley, Vice
President.

■ 14043 ■ **Bindley Western Drug Co.**
Carolina Division
Charlotte, NC 28203
Phone: (704)333-9393
Free: (800)800-4164   **Fax:** (704)588-7532
Products: Pharmaceutical preparations; Medicinal and
health supplies. **SIC:** 5122 (Drugs, Proprietaries &
Sundries). **Officers:** Ronald M. Glover, Vice President.

■ 14044 ■ **Bindley Western Drug Co. Dallas**
  Div.
4217 Mint Way
Dallas, TX 75237
Phone: (214)339-3744   **Fax:** (214)337-9407
Products: Pharmaceutical preparations; Medicinal and
health supplies. **SIC:** 5122 (Drugs, Proprietaries &
Sundries). **Emp:** 23. **Officers:** David N. Homeier, Vice
President.

■ 14045 ■ **Bindley Western Drug Co. Mid-**
  South Div.
8055 Troon Circle, Ste. F
Austell, GA 30168-7849
Phone: (404)739-5030   **Fax:** (404)739-8133
Products: Pharmaceutical preparations; Medicinal and
health supplies. **SIC:** 5122 (Drugs, Proprietaries &
Sundries). **Est:** 1968. **Emp:** 20. **Officers:** Keith Burks,
President; Sid Anderson, Vice President.

■ 14046 ■ **Bindley Western Drug Co.**
  Southeastern Div.
2600 Pitan Row
Orlando, FL 32809
Phone: (407)438-0500
Free: (800)800-4165   **Fax:** (407)438-2771
Products: Pharmaceutical preparations; Medicinal and
health supplies. **SIC:** 5122 (Drugs, Proprietaries &
Sundries). **Officers:** Gregory J. Olson, Vice President;
Nancy Vogt, Office Mgr.

■ 14047 ■ **Bindley Western Industries Inc.**
8909 Purdue Rd.
Indianapolis, IN 46268
Phone: (317)704-4000   **Fax:** (317)704-4629
Products: Pharmaceuticals. **SIC:** 5122 (Drugs,
Proprietaries & Sundries). **Est:** 1968. **Sales:**
$8,000,000,000 (1999). **Officers:** William E. Bindley,
CEO & Chairman of the Board; Michael D. McCormick,
Exec. VP; Thomas J. Salentine, Exec. VP & CFO; Keith
W. Burks, Exec. VP; Thomas J. Weakley, Dir of Human
Resources, e-mail: t.weakley@bindley.com.

■ 14048 ■ **Bindley Western Industries Inc.**
  Bindley Western Drug Div.
4212 W 71st St.
Indianapolis, IN 46268
Phone: (317)298-9900
Free: (800)377-8008   **Fax:** (317)297-5372
Products: Pharmaceutical preparations; Medicinal and
health supplies. **SIC:** 5122 (Drugs, Proprietaries &
Sundries). **Est:** 1968. **Emp:** 650. **Officers:** William E.
Bindley, CEO; Tom Salentine, Exec. VP & CFO.

■ 14049 ■ **Biopractic Group II Inc.**
PO Box 22164
Lehigh Valley, PA 18002-2164
Products: Skin care products and cosmetics. **SIC:**
5122 (Drugs, Proprietaries & Sundries). **Sales:**
$300,000 (2000). **Emp:** 2. **Officers:** Phillip Katzev,
President.

■ 14050 ■ **Blankinship Distributors Inc.**
1927 Vine St.
Kansas City, MO 64108
Phone: (816)842-6825
Products: Shampoos, relaxers, moisturizers, and oils.
SIC: 5122 (Drugs, Proprietaries & Sundries). **Sales:**
$21,000,000 (2000). **Emp:** 50. **Officers:** G. Lawrence
Blankinship, President.

■ 14051 ■ **Blistex Inc.**
1800 Swift Dr.
Oak Brook, IL 60523
Phone: (630)571-2870
Free: (800)837-1800   **Fax:** (630)571-3437
Products: Acne treatments and products for lactose
intolerance relief. **SIC:** 5122 (Drugs, Proprietaries &
Sundries). **Sales:** $28,500,000 (2000). **Emp:** 160.
Officers: David C. Arch, CEO; Patrick McKune, VP of
Finance.

■ 14052 ■ **Bottenfield's Inc.**
PO Box 769
Pittsburg, KS 66762
Phone: (316)231-3900   **Fax:** (316)231-3133
Products: Beauty supplies. **SIC:** 5122 (Drugs,
Proprietaries & Sundries). **Est:** 1922. **Sales:**

$6,000,000 (2000). **Emp:** 100. **Officers:** Jerry Bottenfield, President; Diane Slater, Controller.

■ 14053 ■ **Buy_Low Beauty Supply**
2738 N Pleasantburg Dr.
Greenville, SC 29609
Phone: (864)232-7996
Free: (800)428-9569 **Fax:** (864)233-6028
Products: Beauty supplies, including shampoos and conditioners. **SIC:** 5122 (Drugs, Proprietaries & Sundries). **Est:** 1976. **Sales:** $1,000,000 (2000). **Emp:** 10. **Officers:** Larry Rochester, Owner. **Former Name:** M.L. Wildey & Co.

■ 14054 ■ **Cache Beauty Supply Inc.**
2826 E Highland Dr.
PO Box 8070
Jonesboro, AR 72401
Phone: (870)972-5300
Free: (800)643-0333 **Fax:** (870)972-9050
E-mail: cache@cachebeauty.com
URL: http://www.cachebeauty.com
Products: Haircare and beauty products. **SICs:** 5122 (Drugs, Proprietaries & Sundries); 5087 (Service Establishment Equipment). **Est:** 1976. **Sales:** $1,000,000 (2000). **Emp:** 18. **Officers:** Joe Dickens, President; Bill Dickens, Treasurer & Secty.

■ 14055 ■ **Capps Beauty & Barber Inc.**
9034 E 31
Tulsa, OK 74145
Phones: (918)622-1652 (918)622-5161
Free: (800)364-6111 **Fax:** (918)622-5161
Products: Beauty supplies. **SIC:** 5122 (Drugs, Proprietaries & Sundries); 5087 (Service Establishment Equipment). **Est:** 1981. **Emp:** 14. **Officers:** Lou Capps, President; Les Capps, Vice President.

■ 14056 ■ **Cardinal Health-Behrens Inc.**
PO Box 2520
Waco, TX 76702-2520
Phone: (254)776-7583 **Free:** (800)567-5832
Products: Prescription drugs, including aspirin, laxatives, pain relievers, and over-the-counter drugs. **SIC:** 5122 (Drugs, Proprietaries & Sundries). **Est:** 1878. **Sales:** $3,000,000,000 (2000). **Emp:** 150. **Officers:** Robert D. Walter, CEO & Chairman of the Board; John C. Kane, President & COO; David Bearman, Exec. VP; Thomas S. Summer, VP & Treasurer.

■ 14057 ■ **Carewell Industries, Inc.**
PO Box 7016
Dover, DE 19903
Phone: (302)995-9277
Products: Toothbrushes. **SIC:** 5122 (Drugs, Proprietaries & Sundries). **Est:** 1989. **Sales:** $2,000,000 (2000). **Emp:** 6. **Officers:** Tony B. Gelbart, President; Ralph D'Angelo, Controller.

■ 14058 ■ **Carolina Salon Services**
684 Huey Rd.
Rock Hill, SC 29731-6528
Free: (800)277-1847
Products: Beauty and barber shop accessories. **SIC:** 5087 (Service Establishment Equipment).

■ 14059 ■ **Celestial Mercantile Corporation**
5 Eves Dr., Ste. 140
Marlton, NJ 08053
Phone: (856)985-8936 **Fax:** (856)985-9899
E-mail: celestial.mc@worldnet.att.net
Products: General merchandise, including cosmetics, sewing threads, chemical sundries, and pharmaceutical products; Automotive accessories. **SICs:** 5122 (Drugs, Proprietaries & Sundries); 5013 (Motor Vehicle Supplies & New Parts); 5131 (Piece Goods & Notions). **Est:** 1950. **Officers:** Lawrence Simon, President.

■ 14060 ■ **Cellulite Products Inc.**
6835 Valjean Ave.
Van Nuys, CA 91406
Phone: (818)989-5760
Products: Cosmetics. **SIC:** 5122 (Drugs, Proprietaries & Sundries).

■ 14061 ■ **Centre Beauty Supply**
4055 N Government Way Unit 4
Coeur D Alene, ID 83815-9230
Phone: (208)765-9197 **Fax:** (208)772-4853
Products: Service industry appliances; Beauty and barber shop accessories, including hair, skin, and nail care products. **SIC:** 5087 (Service Establishment Equipment). **Est:** 1985. **Emp:** 4. **Officers:** Marjorie Johnson, Owner.

■ 14062 ■ **Children's Art Corp.**
6342 Myrtle Dr.
Huntington Beach, CA 92647
Free: (800)373-7900 **Fax:** (714)847-6251
Products: Children's haircare and personal products. **SIC:** 5122 (Drugs, Proprietaries & Sundries). **Est:** 1994. **Sales:** $1,000,000 (2000). **Emp:** 4. **Officers:** Thomas Lloyd.

■ 14063 ■ **Cinema Secrets Inc.**
4400 Riverside Dr.
Burbank, CA 91505
Phone: (818)846-0579
Free: (800)808-0579 **Fax:** (818)846-0431
E-mail: info@cinemasecrets.com
URL: http://www.cinemasecrets.com
Products: Theatrical makeup and cosmetics. **SIC:** 5122 (Drugs, Proprietaries & Sundries). **Est:** 1984. **Emp:** 110. **Officers:** Daniel J. Stein, Owner; Michael R. Stein, Owner; Maurice D. Stein, Owner; Ron Vine, Contact; Sherry Kitchenmaster, Customer Service Mgr.; Bruce Gold, Human Resources Contact.

■ 14064 ■ **Clarins USA Inc.**
110 E 59th St.
New York, NY 10022-1304
Phone: (212)980-1800 **Fax:** (212)752-5710
Products: Cosmetics. **SIC:** 5122 (Drugs, Proprietaries & Sundries). **Sales:** $62,500,000 (2000). **Emp:** 350. **Officers:** Joseph M. Horowitz, President; Marc S. Rosenblum, VP of Finance.

■ 14065 ■ **Classic Beauty Supply and Service Center**
Glenmont Shopping Ctr.
12335 E Georgia Ave.
Wheaton, MD 20906
Phone: (301)946-2223
E-mail: david10177@aol.com
Products: Beauty and barber shop accessories; Appliances. **SICs:** 5087 (Service Establishment Equipment); 5064 (Electrical Appliances—Television & Radio). **Est:** 1986. **Emp:** 4. **Officers:** Brad Auslander, President; David Hurwitz, Sec. & Treas., e-mail: david10177@aol.com. **Former Name:** Classic Beauty Supplies.

■ 14066 ■ **Classic Fragrances Ltd.**
132 W 36th St.
New York, NY 10018
Phone: (212)929-2266 **Fax:** (212)929-1766
Products: Perfumes. **SIC:** 5122 (Drugs, Proprietaries & Sundries). **Est:** 1983. **Sales:** $3,000,000 (2000). **Emp:** 30. **Officers:** William Shnipper, President; Joseph Fernandez, Vice President.

■ 14067 ■ **Colette Malouf Inc.**
594 Broadway
New York, NY 10012
Phone: (212)941-9588 **Fax:** (212)431-9561
Products: Hair accessories; Jewelry. **SICs:** 5131 (Piece Goods & Notions); 5094 (Jewelry & Precious Stones). **Est:** 1987. **Sales:** $2,000,000 (2000). **Emp:** 12. **Officers:** Colette Malouf, President; Lisa Jay, President; Susan Keywork, Dir. of Marketing & Sales.

■ 14068 ■ **Color Me Beautiful Inc.**
14000 Thunderbolt Pl., Ste. E
Chantilly, VA 20151
Phone: (703)471-6400
Products: Cosmetics and skin care products. **SIC:** 5122 (Drugs, Proprietaries & Sundries). **Sales:** $31,000,000 (2000). **Emp:** 45. **Officers:** Steve DiAntonio, President; Leon Nelson, CFO.

■ 14069 ■ **Columbia Beauty Supply Co.**
PO Box 32786
Charlotte, NC 28232-2786
Phone: (704)845-2888
Free: (800)888-1825 **Fax:** (704)845-1405
Products: Hair and skin products. **SIC:** 5122 (Drugs, Proprietaries & Sundries). **Est:** 1920. **Officers:** Don Anderson, CEO & President; Waren Ramey, COO & VP. **Former Name:** State Beauty & Barbers Supply Co.

■ 14070 ■ **Compar Inc.**
70 E 55th St.
New York, NY 10022
Phone: (212)980-9620
Products: Fragrances. **SIC:** 5122 (Drugs, Proprietaries & Sundries). **Sales:** $51,000,000 (2000). **Emp:** 120. **Officers:** Fernando Aleu, President; Craig Morton, Dir. of Marketing.

■ 14071 ■ **Consolidated Midland Corp.**
20 Main St.
Brewster, NY 10509
Phone: (914)279-6108
Products: Vitamins. **SIC:** 5122 (Drugs, Proprietaries & Sundries).

■ 14072 ■ **Cornucopia Natural Foods Inc.**
4200 Shirley Dr.
Atlanta, GA 30336
Phone: (404)696-4667 **Fax:** (404)696-0786
Products: Cosmetics; Natural food. **SICs:** 5122 (Drugs, Proprietaries & Sundries); 5149 (Groceries & Related Products Nec).

■ 14073 ■ **Cosmetic Marketing Group**
PO Box 1138
Gresham, OR 97030-0244
Phone: (503)253-4327 **Fax:** (503)253-4966
Products: Beauty aids, including nail polish, make-up, conditioners, and lipstick. **SIC:** 5122 (Drugs, Proprietaries & Sundries). **Est:** 1974. **Sales:** $1,600,000 (2000). **Emp:** 45. **Officers:** M. Rodger Van Zanten. **Doing Business As:** The Curlery.

■ 14074 ■ **Cosmopolitan Trading Co.**
PO Box 7024
Minneapolis, MN 55407
Phone: (612)722-5512 **Fax:** (612)722-6164
Products: Cosmetics. **SIC:** 5122 (Drugs, Proprietaries & Sundries).

■ 14075 ■ **Coyote Vision USA**
PO Box 277
Pittsford, NY 14534
Phone: (716)385-7580
Free: (800)724-9401 **Fax:** (716)385-8524
E-mail: info@coyoteusa.com
URL: http://www.coyoteusa.com
Products: Sunglasses. **SIC:** 5048 (Ophthalmic Goods). **Sales:** $1,000,000 (2000). **Emp:** 30. **Officers:** Steven Carhart, President.

■ 14076 ■ **D & H Beauty Supply**
PO Box 14565
Grand Forks, ND 58206-1255
Phone: (701)746-5471 **Fax:** (701)746-5458
Products: Service industry machinery; Barber and beauty shop furniture and equipment; Beauty and barber shop accessories. **SIC:** 5087 (Service Establishment Equipment). **Officers:** Bruce Quammen, President.

■ 14077 ■ **Daiichi Fine Chemicals Inc.**
1 Overlook Point, Ste. 250
Lincolnshire, IL 60069
Phone: (847)634-7251 **Fax:** (847)634-7257
Products: Vitamins. **SIC:** 5122 (Drugs, Proprietaries & Sundries). **Sales:** $10,000,000 (2000). **Emp:** 15. **Officers:** Tim Jacobson, President; Sandy Mijares, Mgr. of Finance.

■ 14078 ■ **Dakota Drug Inc.**
PO Box 5009
Minot, ND 58702-5009
Phone: (701)852-2141
Products: Sundries; Candy; Smoking and chewing tobacco. **SICs:** 5122 (Drugs, Proprietaries & Sundries); 5194 (Tobacco & Tobacco Products); 5145 (Confectionery). **Est:** 1955. **Sales:** $80,000,000 (2000).

Emp: 63. **Officers:** Ted M. Scherr, CEO & President; Anna Marie Savelkoul; Jim Edwards, CFO; Jim Hatfield, Manager; Terry Narum, Dir of Human Resources.

■ 14079 ■ **Art Davidson & Associates**
PO Box 68
Waipahu, HI 96797-0068
Phone: (808)677-2422 **Fax:** (808)677-2411
Products: Toiletries and cosmetics. **SIC:** 5122 (Drugs, Proprietaries & Sundries). **Est:** 1978. **Emp:** 11. **Officers:** Arthur Davidson, President.

■ 14080 ■ **Al Davis Wholesale Co. Inc.**
767 Main St. W
Rochester, NY 14611
Phone: (716)328-6565
Products: Health and beauty items, including shampoos, conditioners, and cosmetics. **SIC:** 5122 (Drugs, Proprietaries & Sundries). **Est:** 1950. **Sales:** $6,000,000 (2000). **Emp:** 30. **Officers:** A. Davis, President.

■ 14081 ■ **Debra Inc.**
125 E 87th, Ste. 3C
New York, NY 10128
Phone: (212)534-6654 **Fax:** (212)534-6656
Products: Bulk finished cosmetics, including nail lacquers; Cosmetic raw materials; Cosmetic equipment and packaging components, including lipstick, mascara, and eyeliner containers; Compact cases and glass bottles; Glitter for the cosmetic, plastic, paint, and craft industries. **SICs:** 5122 (Drugs, Proprietaries & Sundries); 5199 (Nondurable Goods Nec). **Officers:** Ilisa Nash Daly, President.

■ 14082 ■ **Deodorant Stones of America**
9420 E Doubletree Ranch Rd., Ste. 101
Scottsdale, AZ 85258
Phone: (480)451-4981
Free: (800)279-9318 **Fax:** (480)451-5850
E-mail: dsa@primenet.com
Products: Deodorant crystals. **SIC:** 5122 (Drugs, Proprietaries & Sundries). **Est:** 1987. **Sales:** $1,000,000 (2000). **Emp:** 5. **Officers:** Larry Morris, Owner.

■ 14083 ■ **Dial Corp.**
15501 N Dial Blvd.
Scottsdale, AZ 85260-1619
Phone: (602)754-3425
Products: Soaps, detergents, and personal care products; Canned meats. **SIC:** 5149 (Groceries & Related Products Nec). **Sales:** $1,428,000,000 (2000). **Emp:** 2,533. **Officers:** Malcolm Jozoff, CEO, President & Chairman of the Board; Susan J. Riley, Sr. VP & CFO.

■ 14084 ■ **Diamond Products Co.**
PO Box 878
Seffner, FL 33584
Phone: (813)681-4611 **Fax:** (813)654-6707
Products: Over the counter pharmaceutical supplies, including peroxide, calamine lotion, and rubbing alcohol. **SIC:** 5122 (Drugs, Proprietaries & Sundries). **Emp:** 49.

■ 14085 ■ **The Dipper**
12216 Hodges
Houston, TX 77085
Phone: (713)721-4227
Free: (800)262-3049 **Fax:** (713)721-4577
Products: Scent related products. **SIC:** 5122 (Drugs, Proprietaries & Sundries).

■ 14086 ■ **F. Dohmen Co.**
PO Box 9
Germantown, WI 53022
Phone: (414)255-0022 **Fax:** (414)255-0041
Products: Drugs, proprietaries, and sundries. **SIC:** 5122 (Drugs, Proprietaries & Sundries). **Est:** 1858. **Sales:** $340,000,000 (2000). **Emp:** 275. **Officers:** John Dohmen, CEO; Terry Skeeba, Finance Officer.

■ 14087 ■ **Dolphin Acquisition Corp.**
600 Townsend
San Francisco, CA 94103
Phone: (415)487-3400 **Fax:** (415)487-3409
Products: Personal care products, including bath,

body lotion, and gel products. **SIC:** 5122 (Drugs, Proprietaries & Sundries). **Sales:** $2,000,000 (2000). **Emp:** 16. **Officers:** John C. Hansen, President.

■ 14088 ■ **E & B Beauty & Barber Supply**
1811 E Thayer Ave.
Bismarck, ND 58501-4780
Phones: (701)223-7408 (701)258-4707
Free: (888)258-4707
Products: Service industry machinery; Barber and beauty shop furniture and equipment. **SIC:** 5087 (Service Establishment Equipment). **Est:** 1978. **Sales:** $200,000 (2000). **Emp:** 3. **Officers:** Elsie Mazurek, Owner.

■ 14089 ■ **Eastern Atlantic Company Inc.**
111 Brook St.
Scarsdale, NY 10583
Phone: (914)472-6464 **Fax:** (914)472-1846
Products: Nutritional supplements. **SIC:** 5122 (Drugs, Proprietaries & Sundries). **Est:** 1952. **Sales:** $4,000,000 (2000). **Emp:** 6. **Officers:** Henry Weingartner, President; Ibrham Angel, Vice President.

■ 14090 ■ **Eastern Pharmaceuticals**
PO Box 299
Sunbury, NC 27979
Phone: (919)465-4405
Products: Cough syrup. **SIC:** 5122 (Drugs, Proprietaries & Sundries).

■ 14091 ■ **Edlis Inc.**
327 Blvd. of Allies
Pittsburgh, PA 15222
Phone: (412)261-2862
Free: (800)242-0536 **Fax:** (412)261-2865
Products: Hair and beauty and barber products. **SIC:** 5122 (Drugs, Proprietaries & Sundries). **Est:** 1888.

■ 14092 ■ **Edom Laboratories Inc.**
860 Grand Blvd.
Deer Park, NY 11729
Phone: (516)586-2266 **Fax:** (516)586-2385
Products: Vitamins, food supplements and cosmetics. **SIC:** 5122 (Drugs, Proprietaries & Sundries). **Sales:** $15,000,000 (2000). **Emp:** 20. **Officers:** A. Pollack, CEO.

■ 14093 ■ **Elite Supply Co.**
323 E 8th Ave.
Homestead, PA 15120
Phone: (412)461-9000
Free: (800)242-0535 **Fax:** (412)461-9069
E-mail: elitesupplyco@aol.com
Products: Beauty and barber shop accessories; Hair preparations; Cosmetics. **SICs:** 5122 (Drugs, Proprietaries & Sundries); 5087 (Service Establishment Equipment). **Est:** 1960. **Emp:** 6. **Officers:** Robert W. Gallowich, Owner.

■ 14094 ■ **Elk River Trading Co.**
5010 S 79 E Ave.
Tulsa, OK 74145
Phone: (918)622-7655 **Fax:** (918)622-7657
Products: Medicinal and health supplies. **SIC:** 5122 (Drugs, Proprietaries & Sundries). **Est:** 1989. **Officers:** Mark Parette, President.

■ 14095 ■ **En Garde Health Products Inc.**
7702-10 Balboa Blvd.
Van Nuys, CA 91406
Phone: (818)901-8505 **Fax:** (818)786-4699
Products: Oxygen products; Mind and memory products; Vitamins; Herbal extracts; Nutritional kits; Total body cleansers. **SIC:** 5122 (Drugs, Proprietaries & Sundries). **Sales:** $2,000,000 (2000). **Emp:** 10. **Officers:** A. Chaplan, Consultant.

■ 14096 ■ **Escada Beaute Ltd.**
1412 Broadway
New York, NY 10018
Phone: (212)852-5500
Products: Fragrances and cosmetics. **SIC:** 5122 (Drugs, Proprietaries & Sundries). **Sales:** $12,000,000 (2000). **Emp:** 30. **Officers:** Lawrence Appel, President; Lawrence Solomon, CFO; Martha Brady, VP of Sales.

■ 14097 ■ **Essence Beauty Supply**
4118 Central Ave. SE, Ste. D
Albuquerque, NM 87108-1177
Phone: (505)268-9704 **Fax:** (505)836-0355
Products: Beauty salon and barber shop equipment and supplies. **SIC:** 5087 (Service Establishment Equipment). **Est:** 1983. **Sales:** $72,000 (1999). **Emp:** 3. **Officers:** Lovie Hightower, Owner; Glen Chelf, Dir. of Marketing, e-mail: gchelf@lobo.net.

■ 14098 ■ **Eugene Trading Inc.**
3841 Broadway Pl.
Los Angeles, CA 90037
Phone: (213)231-1918 **Fax:** (213)231-2980
Products: Hair care items including hair brushes; Toys. **SICs:** 5122 (Drugs, Proprietaries & Sundries); 5092 (Toys & Hobby Goods & Supplies).

■ 14099 ■ **Gary Farn Ltd.**
249 Pepes Farm Rd.
Milford, CT 06460
Phone: (203)878-8900
Products: Perfume. **SIC:** 5122 (Drugs, Proprietaries & Sundries). **Sales:** $11,000,000 (2000). **Emp:** 15. **Officers:** Gary Farn, President.

■ 14100 ■ **Faulcon Industries**
133 Northeastern Blvd.
Nashua, NH 03062-1917
Phone: (603)882-1293
Products: Hair salon supplies. **SIC:** 5087 (Service Establishment Equipment). **Officers:** Joseph Kaitz, Owner.

■ 14101 ■ **Five Continent Enterprise Inc., PMB 4022**
5000 Birch St., Ste. 4000 W Tower
Newport Beach, CA 92660
Phone: (949)476-3649 **Fax:** (949)699-1629
E-mail: molecul1@ix.netcom.com
Products: Hydrolyzed collagen protein; Hydrdyzed chicken collagen type II. **SIC:** 5122 (Drugs, Proprietaries & Sundries). **Est:** 1983. **Sales:** $4,999,000 (2000). **Emp:** 10. **Officers:** Ahmad Alkayali, President.

■ 14102 ■ **Food For Health**
3655 W Washington St.
Phoenix, AZ 85009
Phone: (602)269-2371 **Fax:** (602)352-7553
Products: Health and natural foods; Nutritional supplements. **SIC:** 5122 (Drugs, Proprietaries & Sundries).

■ 14103 ■ **FoxMeyer Drug Co. Slidell Div.**
PO Box 2677
Slidell, LA 70459
Phone: (504)646-1006
Products: Health products. **SIC:** 5122 (Drugs, Proprietaries & Sundries). **Est:** 1984. **Sales:** $89,000,000 (2000). **Emp:** 80. **Officers:** John LeMaster, Manager; Bill Hamers, Sales Mgr.

■ 14104 ■ **Fragrance International Inc.**
398 E Rayen Ave.
Youngstown, OH 44505
Phone: (330)747-3341 **Fax:** (330)747-7200
Products: Cosmetics and perfumes. **SIC:** 5122 (Drugs, Proprietaries & Sundries). **Sales:** $18,000,000 (2000). **Emp:** 24. **Officers:** Brad Levy, President.

■ 14105 ■ **Freeda Vitamins Inc.**
36 E 41st St.
New York, NY 10017
Phone: (212)685-4980
Free: (800)777-3737 **Fax:** (212)685-7297
E-mail: freedavites@aol.com
URL: http://www.freedavitamins.com
Products: Vitamins. **SIC:** 5122 (Drugs, Proprietaries & Sundries). **Est:** 1928. **Emp:** 9. **Officers:** Philip W. Zimmerman, President; Sylvia Zimmerman, Vice President.

■ 14106 ■ **French Transit Ltd.**
398 Beach Rd.
Burlingame, CA 94010
Phone: (650)548-9600
Free: (800)829-7625 **Fax:** (650)548-9944
E-mail: info@thecrystal.com
URL: http://www.thecrystal.com
Products: Natural deodorants and cosmetics. **SIC:** 5122 (Drugs, Proprietaries & Sundries). **Sales:** $5,000,000 (2000). **Emp:** 7. **Officers:** Jerry Rosenblatt, President; Jerry Rosenblatt, CFO.

■ 14107 ■ **Eva Gabor International Ltd.**
5775 Deramus St.
Kansas City, MO 64120
Phone: (816)231-3700
E-mail: egil@evagabor.com
Products: Wigs. **SIC:** 5199 (Nondurable Goods Nec). **Est:** 1969. **Sales:** $17,300,000 (1999). **Emp:** 40. **Officers:** Michael Napolitano, President; Tony Sciara, COO.

■ 14108 ■ **Garner Wholesale Merchandisers Inc.**
305 Industrial Blvd.
Greenville, NC 27835
Phone: (919)758-1189
Products: Health and beauty aids. **SIC:** 5122 (Drugs, Proprietaries & Sundries).

■ 14109 ■ **Gemini Cosmetics**
1380 Greg St., Ste. 234
Sparks, NV 89431-6072
Phone: (702)359-3663
Free: (800)338-9091 **Fax:** (702)359-1649
E-mail: gemcos@hotmail.comm
URL: http://www.gemininails.com
Products: Cosmetic supplies, including makeup, manicure products, and manicure furniture. **SIC:** 5122 (Drugs, Proprietaries & Sundries). **Est:** 1983. **Sales:** $315,000 (2000). **Emp:** 2. **Officers:** Carol Coates, Owner.

■ 14110 ■ **General Merchandise Services Inc.**
PO Box 700
Bellefontaine, OH 43311
Phone: (513)592-7025 **Fax:** (513)599-5237
Products: Health and beauty care items, including makeup, shampoo, lotion, soap, and deodorant; Videos; Specialty food products. **SICs:** 5122 (Drugs, Proprietaries & Sundries); 5149 (Groceries & Related Products Nec). **Est:** 1973. **Sales:** $150,000,000 (2000). **Emp:** 340. **Officers:** James W. Donnelly, President; Mike Gardner, Controller; Jim Zedeker, Sales Mgr.; Andy Matt, Operations Mgr.; Jeff Schultz, Dir. of Marketing.

■ 14111 ■ **Geviderm Inc.**
3003 W Olive Ave.
Burbank, CA 91505
Phone: (818)841-3003
Products: Skin care products. **SIC:** 5122 (Drugs, Proprietaries & Sundries). **Sales:** $1,000,000 (1994). **Emp:** 2. **Officers:** Richard W. Clark, President.

■ 14112 ■ **Ginseng Co.**
PO Box 970
Simi Valley, CA 93062
Phone: (805)520-7500
Free: (800)423-5176 **Fax:** (805)520-7509
E-mail: Ginseng@GinsengCompany.com
URL: http://www.GinsengCompany.com
Products: Health food; Vitamins; Lotions; Ginseng products. **SICs:** 5122 (Drugs, Proprietaries & Sundries); 5149 (Groceries & Related Products Nec). **Est:** 1973. **Emp:** 14. **Officers:** Gary Raskin, President.

■ 14113 ■ **GMR Division MNH**
1199 Harlem Rd.
Buffalo, NY 14227-1700
Phone: (716)652-4547 **Fax:** (716)652-6909
Products: Health and beauty aids. **SIC:** 5122 (Drugs, Proprietaries & Sundries). **Emp:** 4. **Officers:** Albert Homer.

■ 14114 ■ **Golden Neo-Life Diamite International**
3500 Gateway Blvd.
Fremont, CA 94538
Phone: (510)651-0405 **Fax:** (510)657-7563
Products: Food supplements; Cleaning products. **SICs:** 5122 (Drugs, Proprietaries & Sundries); 5169 (Chemicals & Allied Products Nec). **Sales:** $92,000,000 (2000). **Emp:** 120. **Officers:** James Arnott, President; William P. Jarm, CFO.

■ 14115 ■ **V.F. Grace Inc.**
605 E 13th Ave.
Anchorage, AK 99501
Phone: (907)272-6431 **Fax:** (907)272-7000
Products: Health and beauty aids; Candy; Gardening supplies; Sporting goods, including camping, hiking, hunting, and fishing. **SICs:** 5122 (Drugs, Proprietaries & Sundries); 5091 (Sporting & Recreational Goods). **Est:** 1956. **Sales:** $35,000,000 (2000). **Emp:** 80. **Officers:** Charles R. Rush, President; Evelyn Rush, Vice President; Kent Harrington, General Mgr.; Tom Suellentrap, Dir. of Data Processing.

■ 14116 ■ **E.Z. Gregory Inc.**
PO Box 44268
Madison, WI 53744-4268
Phone: (608)271-2324
Free: (800)279-4499 **Fax:** (608)271-6525
Products: Health and beauty products; Toys; General merchandise. **SICs:** 5122 (Drugs, Proprietaries & Sundries); 5092 (Toys & Hobby Goods & Supplies). **Est:** 1930. **Sales:** $9,700,000 (1999). **Emp:** 70. **Officers:** Gary Hermanson, CEO & President; Kevin Van Kleek, Finance Officer; Kevin A. Jensen, VP of Sales.

■ 14117 ■ **Group One Capital Inc.**
1610 Des Peres Rd., Ste. 395
St. Louis, MO 63131
Phone: (314)821-5100 **Fax:** (314)821-6693
Products: Beauty products; Electrical supplies. **SICs:** 5087 (Service Establishment Equipment); 5063 (Electrical Apparatus & Equipment). **Sales:** $230,000,000 (2000). **Emp:** 2,000. **Officers:** Bruce A. Olson, President; Mark Crawford, VP of Finance.

■ 14118 ■ **GSK Products Inc.**
3422 W Wilshire, Ste. 13
Phoenix, AZ 85009
Phone: (602)278-6046
Products: Skin care products. **SIC:** 5122 (Drugs, Proprietaries & Sundries).

■ 14119 ■ **H & H Beauty & Barber Supply**
815 W South
Benton, AR 72015
Phone: (501)776-0237
Products: Hair preparations (including shampoos). **SIC:** 5122 (Drugs, Proprietaries & Sundries). **Est:** 1980. **Sales:** $80,000 (2000). **Emp:** 2. **Officers:** Cathy Hobbs; John Hobbs; Mike Cash.

■ 14120 ■ **Hair Depot Beauty Consultants**
315 16th St. SW
Minot, ND 58701-3518
Phone: (701)852-1008 **Free:** (800)472-2168
Products: Service industry machinery; Barber and beauty shop furniture and equipment. **SIC:** 5087 (Service Establishment Equipment). **Officers:** Karen Knatterud, Partner.

■ 14121 ■ **James F. Havice Inc.**
5 Industrial Park Rd.
Lewistown, PA 17044
Phone: (717)242-1427
Free: (800)327-0662 **Fax:** (717)242-2344
Products: Hair preparations (including shampoos); Cosmetics; School bags; Pet supplies; School supplies. **SICs:** 5122 (Drugs, Proprietaries & Sundries); 5099 (Durable Goods Nec); 5013 (Motor Vehicle Supplies & New Parts); 5092 (Toys & Hobby Goods & Supplies). **Est:** 1957. **Sales:** $25,000,000 (1999). **Emp:** 115. **Officers:** James F. Havice Jr., President; Dan Mowper, VP of Logistics; Chris Havice, VP & General Mgr.; John Hammel, VP of Logistics; Dan Momper, VP of Marketing; Bob Saxon, Special Projects/Buying.

■ 14122 ■ **Health Food Distributors**
1893 Northwood Dr.
Troy, MI 48084
Phone: (248)362-4545
Products: Medicinal and health supplies. **SIC:** 5122 (Drugs, Proprietaries & Sundries).

■ 14123 ■ **HealthComm International Inc.**
PO Box 1729
Gig Harbor, WA 98335
Phone: (253)858-6500
Products: Diet supplements, vitamins, and medical foods. **SICs:** 5149 (Groceries & Related Products Nec); 5122 (Drugs, Proprietaries & Sundries); 5141 (Groceries—General Line). **Sales:** $12,900,000 (2000). **Emp:** 40. **Officers:** Darrell Medcalf, President.

■ 14124 ■ **Helen of Troy Ltd.**
1 Helen of Troy Plz.
El Paso, TX 79912-1148
Phone: (915)779-6363
Products: Personal health and beauty electrical appliances, brushes, and hair notions. **SICs:** 5064 (Electrical Appliances—Television & Radio); 5122 (Drugs, Proprietaries & Sundries); 5131 (Piece Goods & Notions). **Sales:** $248,100,000 (2000). **Emp:** 318. **Officers:** Gerald J. Rubin, CEO & Chairman of the Board; Sam L. Henry, Sr. VP & CFO.

■ 14125 ■ **Helen of Troy Texas Corp.**
1 Helen of Troy Plz.
El Paso, TX 79912-1148
Phone: (915)779-6363 **Fax:** (915)774-4795
Products: Personal health and beauty electrical appliances, brushes, and hair notions. **SICs:** 5064 (Electrical Appliances—Television & Radio); 5122 (Drugs, Proprietaries & Sundries); 5131 (Piece Goods & Notions). **Sales:** $167,100,000 (2000). **Emp:** 285. **Officers:** Gerald J. Rubin, CEO & Chairman of the Board; Sam L. Henry, Sr. VP & CFO.

■ 14126 ■ **Hi-Fashion Cosmetics Inc.**
70 Herbert Ave.
Closter, NJ 07624
Phone: (201)767-5755 **Fax:** (201)767-3769
Products: Cosmetics. **SIC:** 5122 (Drugs, Proprietaries & Sundries).

■ 14127 ■ **HPF L.L.C.**
3275 Sunset Ln.
Hatboro, PA 19040
Phone: (215)442-0960
Free: (888)506-3267 **Fax:** (215)442-0966
E-mail: hpfllc@voicenet.com
URL: http://www.hpfonline.com
Products: Herbal supplements for cholesterol management, weight management, antioxidant, and cold and flu relief. **SIC:** 5122 (Drugs, Proprietaries & Sundries). **Sales:** $13,000,000 (2000). **Emp:** 4. **Officers:** Blaine Applegate, VP of Sales, e-mail: blainea@voicenet.com.

■ 14128 ■ **Idaho Barber & Beauty Supply Inc.**
PO Box 8044
Boise, ID 83707-2044
Phone: (208)376-0821 **Fax:** (208)376-5014
Products: Beauty, barber, and nail supplies and equipment. **SIC:** 5087 (Service Establishment Equipment). **Est:** 1929. **Officers:** Robert Copsey, President.

■ 14129 ■ **IDE-Interstate Inc.**
1500 New Horizon Blvd.
Amityville, NY 11701
Phone: (516)957-8300 **Fax:** (516)957-1678
Products: Pharmaceutical preparations; Cosmetics. **SIC:** 5122 (Drugs, Proprietaries & Sundries). **Est:** 1934. **Sales:** $86,000,000 (2000). **Emp:** 200. **Officers:** Ernest Sandler, President & Chairman of the Board; Peter Mc Cann, CFO; Ira M. Lawer, Dir. of Marketing; Donald Boyle, Dir. of Information Systems.

■ 14130 ■ **Imperial Distributors Inc.**
33 Sword St.
Auburn, MA 01501
Phone: (508)756-5156 **Fax:** (508)756-0395
Products: Health and beauty; General merchandise. **SIC:** 5122 (Drugs, Proprietaries & Sundries). **Est:** 1938. **Sales:** $120,000,000 (2000). **Emp:** 400.

Officers: Michael Sleeper, CEO & President; Herb Daitch, CFO; Allen Maciulewicz, Dir. of Marketing & Sales; Stephen Abramson, VP of Admin.

■ **14131** ■ **Interior Design Nutritionals**
75 W Center St.
Provo, UT 84601
Phone: (801)345-9000
Products: Nutritional beverages, foods, and supplements. **SICs:** 5149 (Groceries & Related Products Nec); 5122 (Drugs, Proprietaries & Sundries).

■ **14132** ■ **International Organic Products Inc.**
PO Box 2737
Laurel, MD 20709
Phone: (301)470-1160 **Fax:** (301)470-2632
Products: Fragrances and cosmetics. **SIC:** 5122 (Drugs, Proprietaries & Sundries). **Est:** 1983. **Sales:** $5,000,000 (2000). **Emp:** 12. **Officers:** Richard A. Boyd, President.

■ **14133** ■ **IQ Holdings Inc.**
16212 State Hwy. 249
Houston, TX 77086
Phone: (281)444-6454
Products: Hair spray and other personal care products; Insecticides; Automotive supplies. **SICs:** 5122 (Drugs, Proprietaries & Sundries); 5191 (Farm Supplies); 5013 (Motor Vehicle Supplies & New Parts). **Officers:** P. Yahanne Gupta, CEO.

■ **14134** ■ **Jaydon Inc.**
PO Box 4990
Rock Island, IL 61201
Phone: (309)787-4492 **Fax:** (309)787-4335
Products: Hair care products. **SIC:** 5122 (Drugs, Proprietaries & Sundries). **Est:** 1947. **Sales:** $60,000,000 (2000). **Emp:** 400. **Officers:** Jay M. Gellerman, President; James R. Tansey, VP of Finance & Admin.; Patrick Maupin, Sales/Marketing Contact; Judy Anderson, Customer Service Contact; James R. Tansey, Human Resources Contact.

■ **14135** ■ **Jay's Perfume Bar**
PO Box 524
Marlboro, NJ 07746
Products: Perfume. **SIC:** 5122 (Drugs, Proprietaries & Sundries). **Est:** 1985. **Emp:** 7. **Officers:** Jay Halpern; Marvin Winick.

■ **14136** ■ **J.D. Products**
PO Box 4067
Ann Arbor, MI 48106
Phone: (734)769-5640 **Fax:** (734)994-0436
Products: Perfume; Batteries; Convenience store items. **SIC:** 5122 (Drugs, Proprietaries & Sundries). **Est:** 1986. **Sales:** $1,000,000 (2000). **Emp:** 5. **Officers:** Jeff David, e-mail: jeff.david@juno.com. **Former Name:** Jacques DuBois Perfume Inc.

■ **14137** ■ **Jim's Beauty Supply**
302 Pearman Dairy Rd.
Anderson, SC 29625
Phone: (864)224-0577
Products: Beauty and barber shop accessories. **SIC:** 5087 (Service Establishment Equipment). **Officers:** Jim Freeman, Contact.

■ **14138** ■ **Steve Johnson & Associates**
66 E Escalon, No. 108
Fresno, CA 93710
Phone: (559)431-0320
Free: (800)445-1122 **Fax:** (559)431-0343
E-mail: sjassoc@lightspeed.net
Products: Hair preparations, including shampoos; Hair accessories. **SICs:** 5122 (Drugs, Proprietaries & Sundries); 5087 (Service Establishment Equipment). **Est:** 1979. **Sales:** $1,000,000 (2000). **Emp:** 9. **Officers:** Richard S. Johnson.

■ **14139** ■ **Jonel Inc.**
600 N Mcclurg Ct. #2505
Chicago, IL 60611
Phone: (312)454-1214 **Fax:** (312)266-1466
URL: http://www.jonelinc.com
Products: Manicure supplies. **SIC:** 5122 (Drugs, Proprietaries & Sundries). **Est:** 1970. **Emp:** 10.

■ **14140** ■ **Karemor Independent Distributor**
PO Box 271564
Nashville, TN 37227
Phone: (615)847-5273
Products: Vitamins. **SIC:** 5122 (Drugs, Proprietaries & Sundries).

■ **14141** ■ **Keen Jewelers**
419 9th St.
Huntington, WV 25701
Phone: (304)529-2514 **Fax:** (304)529-2514
Products: Hair preparations; Sunglasses; Toys and novelties; Jewelry. **SICs:** 5122 (Drugs, Proprietaries & Sundries); 5092 (Toys & Hobby Goods & Supplies); 5094 (Jewelry & Precious Stones); 5048 (Ophthalmic Goods). **Est:** 1958. **Officers:** Leonard Keen, President.

■ **14142** ■ **Kinray, Inc.**
152-35 10th Ave.
Whitestone, NY 11357
Phone: (718)767-1234 **Fax:** (718)767-4388
Products: Pharmaceuticals; Health and beauty aids; Medical equipment; Small electronics. **SICs:** 5122 (Drugs, Proprietaries & Sundries); 5047 (Medical & Hospital Equipment); 5063 (Electrical Apparatus & Equipment). **Est:** 1936. **Sales:** $735,000,000 (2000). **Officers:** Stewart Rahr, CEO & President; Bill Bodinger, CFO; Howard Hershberg, Human Resources Contact; Joseph Rahr, Founder.

■ **14143** ■ **Kiwi Brands**
447 Old Swede Rd.
Douglassville, PA 19518-1239
Phone: (610)385-3041 **Fax:** (610)385-3041
Products: Drugs; Sundries. **SIC:** 5122 (Drugs, Proprietaries & Sundries). **Est:** 1957. **Sales:** $140,000,000 (2000). **Emp:** 420. **Officers:** G. Michael Knowles, President; Thomas F. Rehr, VP of Finance; Bud P. Drago, VP of Marketing; Peter A. Panfile, Information Systems Mgr.; John W. McGough, VP of Human Resources.

■ **14144** ■ **Klabin Marketing**
2067 Broadway
New York, NY 10023
Phone: (212)877-3632
Free: (800)933-9440 **Fax:** (212)580-4329
E-mail: klabinmktg@aol.com
Products: Nutritional supplements. **SIC:** 5122 (Drugs, Proprietaries & Sundries). **Est:** 1988. **Officers:** George Klabin.

■ **14145** ■ **Knight Distributing Company Inc.**
2150 Boggs Rd., Ste. 370
Duluth, GA 30096
Phone: (770)623-2650
Products: Perfumes and cosmetics. **SIC:** 5122 (Drugs, Proprietaries & Sundries). **Sales:** $38,000,000 (1994). **Emp:** 50. **Officers:** Gary Rice, President.

■ **14146** ■ **KS Group International**
PO Box 19599
San Diego, CA 92159
Phone: (619)460-6355 **Fax:** (619)463-8431
Products: Cosmetics, toiletries, and hair products. **SIC:** 5122 (Drugs, Proprietaries & Sundries). **Officers:** S. Kan, Export Manager.

■ **14147** ■ **La Parfumerie Inc.**
750 Lexington Ave., 16th Fl.
New York, NY 10022
Phone: (212)754-6666
Free: (800)775-2541 **Fax:** (212)754-6817
Products: Perfumes and cosmetics. **SIC:** 5122 (Drugs, Proprietaries & Sundries). **Sales:** $18,000,000 (2000). **Emp:** 40. **Officers:** Francesco Borghese, CEO & President; Matthew Wenzler, Controller.

■ **14148** ■ **Lady Iris Cosmetic Company Inc.**
93-B S Railroad Ave.
Bergenfield, NJ 07621-1724
Phone: (201)384-3200
Free: (800)827-3220 **Fax:** (201)384-2390
E-mail: ladyirisco@juno.com
Products: Cosmetics. **SIC:** 5122 (Drugs, Proprietaries & Sundries). **Est:** 1927. **Sales:** $2,000,000 (1999). **Emp:** 10. **Officers:** S.C. Hosselet, President & Treasurer.

■ **14149** ■ **Lafayette Drug Company Inc.**
220 N University Ave.
Lafayette, LA 70502
Phone: (318)233-9041 **Fax:** (318)232-0738
Products: Health and beauty aids. **SIC:** 5122 (Drugs, Proprietaries & Sundries). **Est:** 1941. **Sales:** $9,400,000 (2000). **Emp:** 65. **Officers:** J.R. Chachere, President; M. Chachere, Dir. of Marketing.

■ **14150** ■ **J.F. Lazartigue Inc.**
764 Madison Ave.
New York, NY 10021
Phone: (212)249-9424
Free: (800)359-9345 **Fax:** (212)288-2625
URL: http://www.jflazartigue.com
Products: Hair care products. **SIC:** 5122 (Drugs, Proprietaries & Sundries). **Est:** 1988. **Sales:** $5,000,000 (2000). **Emp:** 25. **Officers:** Jean Francois Lazartigue, President.

■ **14151** ■ **Lee Brothers Corp.**
1555 S Jefferson Ave.
St. Louis, MO 63104
Phone: (314)773-6464 **Fax:** (314)773-6988
Products: Beauty supplies. **SIC:** 5122 (Drugs, Proprietaries & Sundries). **Est:** 1989. **Sales:** $2,000,000 (2000). **Emp:** 15. **Officers:** Chol Che Lee, President.

■ **14152** ■ **Liberty Natural Products**
8120 SE Stark St.
Portland, OR 97215
Phone: (503)256-1227
Free: (800)289-8427 **Fax:** (503)256-1182
E-mail: sales@libertynatural.com
URL: http://www.libertynatural.com
Products: Essential oils; Botanical ingredients. **SIC:** 5122 (Drugs, Proprietaries & Sundries). **Est:** 1982. **Officers:** Jim Dierking, e-mail: sales@libertynatural.com.

■ **14153** ■ **Linsey's Products Inc.**
2140 Martin Luther King Jr. Dr.
Atlanta, GA 30310
Phone: (404)696-3064 **Fax:** (404)696-3083
Products: Cosmetics for women of color. **SIC:** 5122 (Drugs, Proprietaries & Sundries). **Sales:** $300,000 (2000). **Emp:** 8. **Officers:** Ruby Linsey, President.

■ **14154** ■ **LRP Enterprises**
1275 Colusa Hwy., Ste. C
Yuba City, CA 95991
Phone: (530)743-4288 **Fax:** (530)742-5824
Products: Hair preparations; Hair goods. **SIC:** 5046 (Commercial Equipment Nec). **Est:** 1963. **Sales:** $425,000 (2000). **Emp:** 2. **Officers:** L.R. Perkins, Owner, e-mail: lrperkins@jps.net.

■ **14155** ■ **Lugo Hair Center Ltd.**
20 Snyder Ave.
Brooklyn, NY 11226
Phone: (718)284-0370
Products: Wigs. **SIC:** 5199 (Nondurable Goods Nec). **Sales:** $4,000,000 (2000). **Emp:** 10. **Officers:** Jose Lugo, President.

■ **14156** ■ **M and H Sales and Marketing Inc.**
155 White Plains Rd.
Tarrytown, NY 10591
Phone: (914)524-9100 **Fax:** (914)524-4140
E-mail: Rhudson@mhsales.com
URL: http://www.mhcom1/
Products: Beauty aids; Produce and frozen and dairy products; Grocery; Health food; Supplements; Natural specialties; Housewares. **SICs:** 5122 (Drugs, Proprietaries & Sundries); 5148 (Fresh Fruits & Vegetables); 5142 (Packaged Frozen Foods); 5149 (Groceries & Related Products Nec). **Est:** 1933. **Emp:** 500.

■ **14157** ■ **Macon Beauty Supply Co.**
PO Box 24690
Macon, GA 31212-4690
Phone: (912)474-2207
Free: (800)277-8104 **Fax:** (912)471-9483
Products: Beauty and barber shop accessories. **SIC:** 5087 (Service Establishment Equipment). **Officers:** Trey Norris, Contact.

■ **14158** ■ **Malone & Hyde**
4701 Central
Monroe, LA 71203
Phone: (318)323-8717 **Fax:** (318)323-6666
Products: Health and beauty aids; Ethnic products; Specialty foods. **SICs:** 5122 (Drugs, Proprietaries & Sundries); 5149 (Groceries & Related Products Nec).

■ **14159** ■ **Mercury Beauty Company Inc.**
9600 Lurline Ave.
Chatsworth, CA 91311
Phone: (818)998-1811 **Fax:** (818)341-5298
Products: Cosmetics; Hair preparations (including shampoos). **SIC:** 5122 (Drugs, Proprietaries & Sundries). **Est:** 1941. **Sales:** $25,000,000 (2000). **Emp:** 50. **Officers:** Paul Diamond, President; Lisa Lorenzian, VP of Finance & Admin.; John Lucy, Sr. VP of Sales.

■ **14160** ■ **Metagenics Inc.**
971 Calle Negocio
San Clemente, CA 92673
Phones: (714)366-0818   (714)366-2895
         (714)366-2895
Products: Vitamins. **SIC:** 5122 (Drugs, Proprietaries & Sundries).

■ **14161** ■ **Mid States Paper/Notion Co.**
810 Cherokee Ave.
Nashville, TN 37207
Phone: (615)226-1234 **Fax:** (615)226-1299
Products: Paper products; Cosmetics. **SICs:** 5122 (Drugs, Proprietaries & Sundries); 5113 (Industrial & Personal Service Paper). **Est:** 1953. **Sales:** $5,000,000 (2000). **Emp:** 30. **Officers:** Mike Crecelius, President; Eva Richardson, Controller.

■ **14162** ■ **Mikara Corp.**
3109 Louisiana Ave.
Minneapolis, MN 55427
Phone: (612)546-9500 **Fax:** (612)546-5212
Products: Beauty supplies, including rollers, shampoo, and make-up. **SIC:** 5122 (Drugs, Proprietaries & Sundries). **Est:** 1970. **Sales:** $20,000,000 (2000). **Emp:** 200. **Officers:** Michael P. Hicks, President. **Former Name:** National Beauty Inc.

■ **14163** ■ **Millbrook Distribution Services**
PO Box 790
Harrison, AR 72602-0790
Phone: (870)741-3425
Free: (800)643-8130 **Fax:** (870)365-3228
Products: Health and beauty aids, including toothpaste. **SIC:** 5122 (Drugs, Proprietaries & Sundries). **Est:** 1933. **Sales:** $250,000,000 (2000). **Emp:** 2,000. **Officers:** Bob Sigel, CEO & President; Doyle Patterson, VP of Marketing & Sales; Ken Savells, VP of Information Systems; Barry Beck, Dir of Human Resources.

■ **14164** ■ **Millbrook Distributors Inc.**
Rte. 56
Leicester, MA 01524
Phone: (508)892-8171 **Fax:** (508)892-4827
Products: Health and beauty aids; Specialty foods. **SICs:** 5122 (Drugs, Proprietaries & Sundries); 5149 (Groceries & Related Products Nec). **Sales:** $280,000,000 (2000). **Emp:** 500. **Officers:** Martin H. Sigel, Chairman of the Board; Robert A. Sigel, President.

■ **14165** ■ **MK Health Food Distributors**
7180 Lampson Ave.
Garden Grove, CA 92841-3914
Phone: (714)995-8858 **Fax:** (714)995-0381
Products: Vitamins. **SIC:** 5122 (Drugs, Proprietaries & Sundries). **Emp:** 49. **Officers:** George Kostka; Marianne Kostka.

■ **14166** ■ **Modern Overseas, Inc.**
311 California St.
San Francisco, CA 94111
Phone: (415)392-1531
Products: Nutritional supplements; Dental supplies. **SIC:** 5122 (Drugs, Proprietaries & Sundries). **Officers:** Mas Oishi, President.

■ **14167** ■ **Ruth More**
960 W Owens Ave.
Las Vegas, NV 89106-2516
Phone: (702)646-6463
Products: Beauty salon supplies. **SIC:** 5087 (Service Establishment Equipment). **Officers:** Ruth More, Owner.

■ **14168** ■ **Morgan and Sampson Pacific**
PO Box 3013
Los Alamitos, CA 90720
Phone: (714)220-4900
Products: Cough medicine. **SIC:** 5122 (Drugs, Proprietaries & Sundries). **Est:** 1930. **Sales:** $14,000,000 (2000). **Emp:** 100. **Officers:** Tom Paalman, President; Chip Carter, CFO.

■ **14169** ■ **Mustela USA**
N19 W6727 Commerce Ct.
Cedarburg, WI 53012
Phone: (414)377-6722
Free: (800)422-2987 **Fax:** (414)377-6867
E-mail: mustelausa@aol.com
Products: Infants' and children's skincare products. **SIC:** 5122 (Drugs, Proprietaries & Sundries). **Est:** 1987. **Sales:** $5,000,000 (2000). **Emp:** 12. **Officers:** Lynn Gagnon, President.

■ **14170** ■ **Natrol, Inc.**
21411 Prairie St.
Chatsworth, CA 91311
Phone: (818)739-6000
Free: (800)326-1520 **Fax:** (818)739-6001
URL: http://www.natrol.com
Products: Vitamins; Dietary supplements. **SIC:** 5122 (Drugs, Proprietaries & Sundries). **Est:** 1980. **Emp:** 300. **Officers:** Elliot Balbert.

■ **14171** ■ **Naturade Inc.**
14370 Myford Rd
Irvine, CA 92606
Phone: (949)573-4800
Free: (800)421-1830 **Fax:** (949)573-4824
URL: http://www.naturade.com
Products: Nutritional supplements. **SIC:** 5122 (Drugs, Proprietaries & Sundries). **Est:** 1926. **Sales:** $20,000,000 (1999). **Emp:** 50. **Officers:** Bill Stewart, CEO; Larry Batina, COO & CFO; John Hazlin, Sales/Marketing Contact, e-mail: JHazlin@ Naturade.com; Travis Turchi, Customer Service Contact, e-mail: TTurchi@Naturade.com.

■ **14172** ■ **Nature's Gate Herbal Cosmetics**
9200 Mason
Chatsworth, CA 91311
Phone: (818)882-2951 **Fax:** (818)341-3840
Products: All-natural cosmetics. **SIC:** 5122 (Drugs, Proprietaries & Sundries). **Est:** 1973. **Emp:** 250. **Officers:** Leo Weinstein, President; Shelley Rubenstein, Sales & Marketing Contact; Sarah Hinajosa, Customer Service Contact; Scott Cooper, Human Resources Contact.

■ **14173** ■ **Nature's Herbs**
600 E Quality Dr.
American Fork, UT 84003
Phone: (801)763-0700
Free: (800)437-2257 **Fax:** (801)763-0789
E-mail: village@naturesherbs.com
URL: http://www.naturesherbs.com
Products: Herbal products. **SIC:** 5122 (Drugs, Proprietaries & Sundries). **Est:** 1969. **Emp:** 100. **Officers:** Stephen Welling.

■ **14174** ■ **Network Marketing L.C.**
853 Broken Sound Pkwy. NW
Boca Raton, FL 33487-3694
Phone: (561)994-2090 **Fax:** (561)995-6583
Products: Weight control products, dietary supplements, and homeopathic remedies. **SIC:** 5122 (Drugs, Proprietaries & Sundries). **Sales:** $105,000,000 (2000). **Emp:** 290. **Officers:** Damon DeSantis, CEO; Stan Charlestein, CFO.

■ **14175** ■ **Neuman Distributors, Inc.**
250 Moonachie Rd.
Moonachie, NJ 07074
Phone: (201)941-2000 **Fax:** (201)931-0046
Products: Pharmaceuticals; Health and beauty aids.

SIC: 5122 (Drugs, Proprietaries & Sundries). **Sales:** $1,802,000,000 (2000). **Officers:** Samuel Toscano Jr., CEO & Chairman of the Board; Anthony Taccetta, Vice Chairman of the Board; Philip A. Piscopo, CFO; Barbara Toscano, Human Resources Contact.

■ **14176** ■ **New England Wholesale Drug Co.**
1150 W Chestnut St.
Brockton, MA 02301
Phone: (508)559-1550
Free: (800)800-4169 **Fax:** (508)559-1181
Products: Pharmaceutical preparations; Medicinal and health supplies. **SIC:** 5122 (Drugs, Proprietaries & Sundries). **Officers:** George E. Maloof, President.

■ **14177** ■ **New Man Barber & Beauty Supply**
12717 Lomas Blvd. NE
Albuquerque, NM 87112-6268
Phone: (505)293-8808
Products: Service industry machinery; Barber and beauty shop furniture and equipment; Beauty and barber shop accessories. **SIC:** 5087 (Service Establishment Equipment). **Officers:** Pete Maes, Partner.

■ **14178** ■ **New Mexico Beauty & Barber Supply**
1009 W 2nd St.
Roswell, NM 88201-3009
Phone: (505)622-4311
Products: Service establishment equipment; Beauty salon and barber shop equipment and supplies, including wigs and accessory items. **SIC:** 5087 (Service Establishment Equipment). **Officers:** William Wells, Owner.

■ **14179** ■ **Norstar Consumer Products Company Inc.**
206 Pegasus Ave.
Northvale, NJ 07647
Phone: (201)784-8155
Products: Health and beauty aids. **SIC:** 5122 (Drugs, Proprietaries & Sundries).

■ **14180** ■ **Nu-Dimension Beauty Supply Inc.**
10101 SW Arctic Dr.
Beaverton, OR 97005
Phone: (503)643-0129
Free: (800)999-6834 **Fax:** (503)526-9727
Products: Hair preparations (including shampoos); Cosmetics. **SIC:** 5122 (Drugs, Proprietaries & Sundries). **Est:** 1979. **Sales:** $2,900,000 (2000). **Emp:** 25. **Officers:** Bryan D. Heuvel, President; Linda Heuvel, Secretary.

■ **14181** ■ **Nu Skin International Inc.**
75 W Center St.
Provo, UT 84601
Phone: (801)345-1000 **Fax:** (801)345-2199
Products: Health care products, including shampoos, conditioners, lotions, vitamins, and nutrition drinks. **SIC:** 5122 (Drugs, Proprietaries & Sundries). **Est:** 1984. **Sales:** $1,230,000,000 (2000). **Emp:** 1,600. **Officers:** Blake Roney, CEO & President; Max Esplin, Controller; Raymond Beckham, Dir. of Corp. Communications; Brent Ririe, Dir. of Information Systems; Paul Swan, Dir of Human Resources.

■ **14182** ■ **Nutrition For Life International Inc.**
9101 Jameel Rd.
Houston, TX 77040
Phone: (713)460-1976 **Fax:** (713)460-4084
Products: Vitamins, minerals and skin care products. **SIC:** 5122 (Drugs, Proprietaries & Sundries). **Sales:** $69,700,000 (2000). **Emp:** 269. **Officers:** David P. Bertrand, President & Chairman of the Board; David O. Rodrigue, CFO.

■ **14183** ■ **Nutrition International Co.**
PO Box 50632
Irvine, CA 92619-0632
Phone: (714)854-4855 **Fax:** (714)854-6170
Products: Vitamins; Health foods. **SIC:** 5122 (Drugs, Proprietaries & Sundries). **Est:** 1964. **Sales:** $1,300,000 (2000). **Emp:** 50. **Officers:** L. Tung, President; C. Lin, VP of Finance.

■ 14184 ■ **Nutrition Medical Inc.**
5500 Wayzata Blvd., Ste. 800
Minneapolis, MN 55416-1249
Phone: (612)551-9595
Products: Generic and clinical nutrition products. **SIC:** 5122 (Drugs, Proprietaries & Sundries). **Sales:** $4,100,000 (2000). **Emp:** 22. **Officers:** William L. Rush, CEO, President & Chairman of the Board; Anwar H. Bhimani, CFO.

■ 14185 ■ **Optibal Co.**
5 Allison Dr.
Cherry Hill, NJ 08003-2309
Phone: (609)596-5757
Products: Vitamins. **SIC:** 5122 (Drugs, Proprietaries & Sundries). **Est:** 1979. **Sales:** $18,000,000 (2000). **Emp:** 50. **Officers:** David Fox, CEO.

■ 14186 ■ **Oral Logic Inc.**
7000 Hwy. 2 E
Minot, ND 58701
Phone: (701)852-5906 **Fax:** (701)852-1637
Products: Toothbrushes. **SIC:** 5122 (Drugs, Proprietaries & Sundries). **Sales:** $6,000,000 (2000). **Emp:** 60. **Officers:** Bruce Merrell, CEO; Richard Carlson, CFO; Kirk Klinkhammer, Dir. of Sales.

■ 14187 ■ **Parallel Traders Inc.**
8787 SW 132nd St.
Miami, FL 33176
Phone: (305)235-7058 **Fax:** (305)235-7058
Products: Perfumes. **SIC:** 5122 (Drugs, Proprietaries & Sundries).

■ 14188 ■ **Paramount Sales Co.**
548 Smithfield Ave.
Pawtucket, RI 02860
Phone: (401)728-4400 **Fax:** (401)722-4825
Products: Health and beauty aids; School supplies; Stationery; Toys, including stuffed animals and battery operated toys; Novelties. **SICs:** 5122 (Drugs, Proprietaries & Sundries); 5064 (Electrical Appliances—Television & Radio); 5112 (Stationery & Office Supplies); 5092 (Toys & Hobby Goods & Supplies). **Est:** 1936. **Sales:** $400,000 (2000). **Emp:** 3. **Officers:** Lestor Katz, President; Esther Katz, Vice President.

■ 14189 ■ **Parfums de Coeur Ltd.**
85 Old Kings Hwy. N
Darien, CT 06820
Phone: (203)655-8807
Products: Perfumes and fragrances. **SIC:** 5122 (Drugs, Proprietaries & Sundries). **Sales:** $110,000,000 (2000). **Emp:** 38. **Officers:** Mark Laracy, President; Ed Kaminski, VP of Finance & Admin.

■ 14190 ■ **Perfumania, Inc.**
11701 NW 101st Rd.
Miami, FL 33178
Phone: (305)889-1600 **Fax:** (305)888-0628
URL: http://www.perfumania.com
Products: Fragrances. **SIC:** 5122 (Drugs, Proprietaries & Sundries). **Sales:** $180,000,000 (1999). **Emp:** 1,600. **Officers:** Ilia Lekach, CEO; Donovan Cline, Chairman of the Board & Finance Officer; Claire Fair, Human Resources Contact; Jerome Falic, President.

■ 14191 ■ **Pola U.S.A. Inc.**
251 E Victoria St.
Carson, CA 90746
Phone: (310)527-9696
URL: http://www.pola.com
Products: Cosmetics. **SIC:** 5122 (Drugs, Proprietaries & Sundries). **Est:** 1975. **Sales:** $29,000,000 (2000). **Emp:** 38. **Officers:** Takashi Kuriki, President.

■ 14192 ■ **Pound International Corp.**
1221 Brickell, No. 1480
Miami, FL 33131
Phone: (305)530-8702
Free: (800)422-7883 **Fax:** (305)530-8912
E-mail: sales@stud100.com
Products: Health and beauty aids. **SIC:** 5122 (Drugs, Proprietaries & Sundries). **Est:** 1968. **Sales:** $1,000,000 (2000). **Emp:** 3. **Officers:** David Racklin, President; Dana C. Puerto, Vice President, e-mail: pintl@worldnet.att.net. **Alternate Name:** Stud Holdings Ltd.

■ 14193 ■ **Premier Inc. (Greenwich, Connecticut)**
Greenwich Office Park One
Greenwich, CT 06831
Phone: (203)622-5800
Products: Skin care and sun care products. **SIC:** 5122 (Drugs, Proprietaries & Sundries). **Sales:** $11,000,000 (1994). **Emp:** 15. **Officers:** Robert E. Albus, President.

■ 14194 ■ **Prime Natural Health Laboratories Inc.**
910 E Sandhill Ave.
Carson, CA 90746-5308
Phone: (310)515-5774 **Fax:** (310)515-1624
Products: Vitamins; Minerals. **SIC:** 5122 (Drugs, Proprietaries & Sundries). **Est:** 1971. **Sales:** $8,500,000 (2000). **Emp:** 125. **Officers:** Theodore Negrin, President.

■ 14195 ■ **Pro-Line Corp.**
2121 Panoramic Cir.
Dallas, TX 75212
Phone: (214)631-4247
Products: Hair care products. **SIC:** 5122 (Drugs, Proprietaries & Sundries). **Est:** 1970. **Sales:** $34,000,000 (2000). **Emp:** 275. **Officers:** C.J. Cottrell, CEO & Chairman of the Board; Robert Bobier, VP of Finance; Renee Brown, Dir. of Marketing.

■ 14196 ■ **Professional Education & Products Inc.**
20235 Bahama
Chatsworth, CA 91311
Phone: (818)718-6782
Free: (800)675-7682 **Fax:** (818)407-5636
Products: Hair preparations (including shampoos); Hair accessories; Cosmetics. **SICs:** 5122 (Drugs, Proprietaries & Sundries); 5087 (Service Establishment Equipment). **Est:** 1988. **Sales:** $1,500,000 (2000). **Emp:** 24. **Officers:** Harmon Greene, President; Louise Greene, Treasurer & Secty.; Lorelei Greene, Vice President. **Also Known by This Acronym:** Pro Ed.

■ 14197 ■ **Professional Salon Concepts Inc.**
48 Meadow Ave.
Joliet, IL 60436
Phone: (815)744-3384
Products: Shampoos; Conditioners. **SIC:** 5122 (Drugs, Proprietaries & Sundries). **Sales:** $40,000,000 (2000). **Emp:** 53. **Officers:** Steve Cowan, President.

■ 14198 ■ **Professional Salon Services**
16 Stafford Ct.
Cranston, RI 02920-4464
Phone: (401)463-5353
Free: (800)666-2580 **Fax:** (401)463-5807
Products: Service establishment equipment; Beauty salon and barber shop equipment and supplies; Hair care products. **SICs:** 5087 (Service Establishment Equipment); 5122 (Drugs, Proprietaries & Sundries). **Est:** 1980. **Sales:** $3,500,000 (2000). **Emp:** 30. **Officers:** Peter Garzone, President.

■ 14199 ■ **Progressive Distributors**
PO Box 295
Winthrop, ME 04364
Phone: (207)377-2251 **Fax:** (207)377-2251
Products: Health and beauty aids; Specialty foods; General merchandise. **SICs:** 5122 (Drugs, Proprietaries & Sundries); 5149 (Groceries & Related Products Nec); 5199 (Nondurable Goods Nec).

■ 14200 ■ **Prometex International Corp.**
PO Box 42404
Houston, TX 77042
Phone: (713)789-6562 **Fax:** (713)789-5536
Products: Vitamins, dietary supplements, and cosmetics. **SIC:** 5122 (Drugs, Proprietaries & Sundries). **Officers:** Jean Butterlin, Vice Pres. of Marketing.

■ 14201 ■ **Q Perfumes**
1965 Tubeway Ave.
City of Commerce, CA 90040
Phone: (213)728-3434 **Fax:** (213)728-4221
Products: Copies of designer fragrances. **SIC:** 5122 (Drugs, Proprietaries & Sundries).

■ 14202 ■ **Quality King Distributors Inc.**
2060 9th Ave.
Ronkonkoma, NY 11779
Phone: (631)737-5555
Free: (800)676-5554 **Fax:** (631)737-3309
URL: http://www.gkd.com
Products: Pharmaceuticals; Health and beauty care products; Fragrances; Non-perishable grocery items. **SICs:** 5122 (Drugs, Proprietaries & Sundries); 5149 (Groceries & Related Products Nec). **Est:** 1961. **Sales:** $1,708,000,000 (2000). **Emp:** 1,000. **Officers:** Glenn Nussdorf, President; Dennis Barkey, CFO.

■ 14203 ■ **Rack Service Company Inc.**
2601 Newcomb
Monroe, LA 71211
Phone: (318)322-1445 **Fax:** (318)322-1447
Products: Health aids; Toys; School supplies; Automotive supplies. **SICs:** 5122 (Drugs, Proprietaries & Sundries); 5199 (Nondurable Goods Nec); 5092 (Toys & Hobby Goods & Supplies). **Est:** 1944. **Sales:** $4,000,000 (2000). **Emp:** 42. **Officers:** Rickie Chambliss, President; Pat Dalton, VP of Finance; Steve Chambliss, VP of Operations; Jerry Hodge, Sales Mgr.; Mickey McCarty, VP & Merchandising Mgr.

■ 14204 ■ **Rainbow Distributing, Inc.**
2718 N Paulina
Chicago, IL 60614
Phone: (773)929-7629
Products: Medicinal and health supplies. **SIC:** 5122 (Drugs, Proprietaries & Sundries).

■ 14205 ■ **Rapid City Beauty & Barber Supply**
PO Box 7685
Rapid City, SD 57709-7685
Phone: (605)342-0435 **Fax:** (605)342-0713
Products: Service industry machinery; Barber and beauty shop furniture and equipment. **SIC:** 5087 (Service Establishment Equipment). **Officers:** Calvin Fuss, President.

■ 14206 ■ **Raylon Corp.**
345 Morgantown Rd.
PO Box 91
Reading, PA 19603
Phone: (610)376-4871
Free: (800)422-8166 **Fax:** (610)376-7677
E-mail: raylon91@aol.com
URL: http://www.raylon.com
Products: Beauty products and equipment. **SICs:** 5122 (Drugs, Proprietaries & Sundries); 5087 (Service Establishment Equipment). **Est:** 1953. **Emp:** 139. **Officers:** Howard Hafetz, President.

■ 14207 ■ **Raylon Corp.**
527 N White Horse Pike
Somerdale, NJ 08083
Phone: (609)435-6850 **Free:** (800)523-8213
Products: Beauty supplies. **SIC:** 5122 (Drugs, Proprietaries & Sundries).

■ 14208 ■ **Raylon Corp.**
2528 Monroeville Blvd.
Monroeville, PA 15146
Phone: (412)823-1047 **Fax:** (215)376-7677
Products: Shampoos; Permanents; Hair color; Nail color; Aroma therapy products, inclu ding aroma vera; Salon equipment. **SICs:** 5122 (Drugs, Proprietaries & Sundries); 5087 (Service Establishment Equipment).

■ 14209 ■ **Raylon Corp.**
3619 Walnut St.
Harrisburg, PA 17109
Phone: (717)652-7851
Free: (800)422-8166 **Fax:** (215)376-7677
Products: Beauty supplies. **SIC:** 5122 (Drugs, Proprietaries & Sundries).

■ 14210 ■ **RC International**
11222 I St.
Omaha, NE 68137-1296
Phone: (402)592-2102
Free: (800)433-3970 **Fax:** (402)593-0614
URL: http://www.rcinternational.com
Products: Toiletries and cosmetics; Hair accessories; HBC products; Private label products. **SIC:** 5122 (Drugs, Proprietaries & Sundries). **Est:** 1983. **Sales:** $10,000,000 (2000). **Emp:** 250. **Officers:** Bill

Cosentino, Vice President; Tanja Mardeson, e-mail: tmordeson@rcinternational.com; Al Gibbon, Customer Service Contact; Ron Rohlfs, Customer Service Contact; Gail Gust.

■ 14211 ■ Redy Inc.
1233 E Sahara Ave.
Las Vegas, NV 89104
Phone: (702)734-4801 **Fax:** (702)734-0774
Products: Service industry machinery; Barber and beauty shop equipment; Beauty and barber shop accessories; Clippers and tools. **SIC:** 5087 (Service Establishment Equipment). **Est:** 1977. **Emp:** 2.
Officers: Roy Mule, President.

■ 14212 ■ Reese Chemical Co.
10617 Frank Ave.
PO Box 1957
Cleveland, OH 44106
Phone: (216)231-6441
Free: (800)321-7178 **Fax:** (216)231-6444
E-mail: reese@atsapk.net
URL: http://www.reesechemical.com
Products: Pharmaceuticals. **SIC:** 5122 (Drugs, Proprietaries & Sundries). **Est:** 1907. **Sales:** $2,000,000 (2000). **Emp:** 25. **Officers:** George W. Reese III, President; Sandra Reese, Vice President.

■ 14213 ■ Reliv' International Inc.
PO Box 405
Chesterfield, MO 63006-0405
Phone: (636)537-9715 **Fax:** (636)537-9753
Products: Nutritional supplements, weight control products, granola bars, sport drink mixes, and skin care products. **SICs:** 5122 (Drugs, Proprietaries & Sundries); 5149 (Groceries & Related Products Nec).
Sales: $51,800,000 (2000). **Emp:** 228. **Officers:** Robert L. Montgomery, CEO, President & Chairman of the Board; David G. Kreher, CFO.

■ 14214 ■ Rexall Co.
6111 Broken Sound Pkwy. NW
Boca Raton, FL 33487-3625
Phone: (561)241-9400
Free: (800)255-7399 **Fax:** (561)995-6881
URL: http://www.rexallsundown.com
Products: Vitamins; Non-prescription remedies. **SIC:** 5122 (Drugs, Proprietaries & Sundries). **Est:** 1903.
Sales: $65,000,000 (2000). **Emp:** 500. **Officers:** Carl DeSantis, President; Geary Cotton, CFO; John Little, Dir. of Field Sales.

■ 14215 ■ Rexall Managed Care
851 Broken Sound Pkwy. NW
Boca Raton, FL 33487
Phone: (561)241-9400
Products: Vitamins and nutritional supplements; Over-the-counter medicines for HMO and healthcare facilities. **SIC:** 5122 (Drugs, Proprietaries & Sundries).

■ 14216 ■ Rexall Sundown Inc.
4031 Northeast 12th Terr.
Ft. Lauderdale, FL 33334
Phone: (561)241-9400
Products: Vitamins. **SIC:** 5122 (Drugs, Proprietaries & Sundries). **Sales:** $263,400,000 (2000). **Emp:** 820.
Officers: Christian Nast, CEO & President; Geary Cotton, VP, CFO & Treasurer.

■ 14217 ■ RIA International
123 Columbia Tpke. 104
Florham Park, NJ 07932
Phone: (973)301-2011
Free: (888)301-2011 **Fax:** (973)301-2012
E-mail: nj@ix.netcom.com
URL: http://www.riausa.com
Products: Pharmaceutical and nutritional products. **SIC:** 5122 (Drugs, Proprietaries & Sundries). **Est:** 1994. **Officers:** Kenia Catarra, Customer Service Contact.

■ 14218 ■ Richard Beauty Supply
4250 Normandy Court
Royal Oak, MI 48073
Phone: (248)549-3350 **Fax:** (248)549-7606
Products: Beauty supplies. **SIC:** 5122 (Drugs, Proprietaries & Sundries).

■ 14219 ■ Richards Products Inc.
PO Box 9000
Ft. Lauderdale, FL 33340
Phone: (954)978-0313
Products: Vitamins and health products. **SIC:** 5122 (Drugs, Proprietaries & Sundries). **Est:** 1966. **Sales:** $15,000,000 (2000). **Emp:** 20. **Officers:** Donald Montellese, Dir. of Sales.

■ 14220 ■ Rio Grande Trading Co.
1441 W 46th Ave., No. 8
Denver, CO 80211
Phone: (303)433-5700
Free: (800)373-5701 **Fax:** (303)433-6364
Products: Health foods; Body care items. **SICs:** 5122 (Drugs, Proprietaries & Sundries); 5149 (Groceries & Related Products Nec).

■ 14221 ■ Rite Way Barber & Beauty Supplies
5818 McClellan Blvd.
Anniston, AL 36206
Phone: (205)820-1124
E-mail: Ritewaybeauty@Prodigy.net
Products: Barber and beauty supplies. **SICs:** 5122 (Drugs, Proprietaries & Sundries); 5087 (Service Establishment Equipment). **Est:** 1973. **Sales:** $500,000 (2000). **Emp:** 7. **Officers:** Jerri Hensley, President.

■ 14222 ■ Rival/Pollenex
800 E 101 Terr., Ste. 100
Kansas City, MO 64131
Phone: (816)943-4100
Products: Health and beauty products. **SIC:** 5122 (Drugs, Proprietaries & Sundries). **Sales:** $75,000,000 (2000). **Emp:** 999. **Officers:** Richard Stern.

■ 14223 ■ Rocky Mountain Salon Consolidated
1413 Gold Ave.
Bozeman, MT 59715-2410
Phone: (406)586-2792
Free: (800)736-5340 **Fax:** (406)586-0943
Products: Service establishment equipment; Beauty salon and barber shop equipment and supplies. **SIC:** 5087 (Service Establishment Equipment). **Officers:** Scott Townley, Owner.

■ 14224 ■ Rothenberg and Schloss Inc.
6100 Broadmoor St.
Mission, KS 66202-3229
E-mail: rothsch@aol.com
Products: Personal care products, including hair care products; Pipes and lighters; Watches; Glasses. **SICs:** 5122 (Drugs, Proprietaries & Sundries); 5094 (Jewelry & Precious Stones). **Est:** 1874. **Sales:** $18,000,000 (2000). **Emp:** 55. **Officers:** Louis H. Ehrlich, Chairman of the Board; Ralph Harrell, Exec. VP.

■ 14225 ■ Royal Beauty & Barber
120 Baxter Ave. NW
PO Box 787
Knoxville, TN 37901
Phone: (865)637-0611
Products: Beauty and barber shop accessories. **SIC:** 5087 (Service Establishment Equipment). **Officers:** Al Jacobs, Contact.

■ 14226 ■ Royal Essence Ltd.
380 Mountain Rd., No. 1814
Union City, NJ 07087-7335
Phone: (201)864-0450 **Fax:** (201)864-0223
Products: Flavorings; Fragrances. **SICs:** 5122 (Drugs, Proprietaries & Sundries); 5149 (Groceries & Related Products Nec). **Est:** 1987. **Sales:** $1,000,000 (2000). **Emp:** 5. **Officers:** Howard E. Kennedy, President.

■ 14227 ■ Sally Beauty Company Inc.
PO Box 490
Denton, TX 76202
Phone: (940)898-7500 **Fax:** (940)898-7501
URL: http://www.sallybeauty.com
Products: Health and beauty aids; Salon equipment; Styling appliances; Professional products for hair, skin and nails. **SIC:** 5087 (Service Establishment Equipment). **Est:** 1969. **Sales:** $1,291,100,000 (2000).
Emp: 8,000. **Officers:** Michael H. Renzulli, CEO; Gary Robinson, CFO; Wayne Henderson, Salon Equipment Dir.; Richard Dowd, CIO; Gary Robinson.

■ 14228 ■ Salon Associates
956 W Webster
Chicago, IL 60616
Phone: (773)348-8460
Products: Beauty and barber shop accessories. **SIC:** 5087 (Service Establishment Equipment). **Officers:** Bob LaMonte, Contact.

■ 14229 ■ Sanofi Beaute Inc.
40 W 57th St.
New York, NY 10019-4001
Phone: (212)621-7300 **Fax:** (212)759-3738
Products: Cosmetics, including perfume. **SIC:** 5122 (Drugs, Proprietaries & Sundries). **Sales:** $240,000,000 (2000). **Emp:** 320. **Officers:** Lawrence Aiken, President; John Avagliano, VP of Finance; Linda Harper, VP of Sales.

■ 14230 ■ Schawbel Corp.
529 Main St.
Boston, MA 02129-1101
Phone: (617)241-7400 **Fax:** (617)492-4082
Products: Hair dryers and curlers. **SIC:** 5064 (Electrical Appliances—Television & Radio). **Sales:** $7,000,000 (2000). **Emp:** 10. **Officers:** William Schawbel, CEO; Thomas Paganetti, CFO.

■ 14231 ■ Scissors and Shears
849 Roger Williams Ave.
Rumford, RI 02916-2145
Phone: (401)434-4694 **Fax:** (401)435-3005
Products: Service industry machinery; Beauty and barber shop accessories; Metal cutting shears. **SIC:** 5087 (Service Establishment Equipment). **Officers:** James Olick, Owner.

■ 14232 ■ Paul Sebastian Inc.
PO Box 1544
Jackson, NJ 08527-0358
Products: Men's and women's cologne. **SIC:** 5122 (Drugs, Proprietaries & Sundries). **Emp:** 130.

■ 14233 ■ Sel-Leb Marketing, Inc.
495 River St.
Paterson, NJ 07524
Phone: (973)225-9880 **Fax:** (973)225-9840
Products: Fragrances; Cosmetics. **SIC:** 5122 (Drugs, Proprietaries & Sundries). **Est:** 1985. **Sales:** $18,000,000 (2000). **Emp:** 40. **Officers:** Jorge Lazaro, President; Paul Sharp, VP of Sales.

■ 14234 ■ Shaklee Corp.
444 Market St.
San Francisco, CA 94111
Phone: (415)954-3000 **Fax:** (415)986-0808
Products: Vitamins, cosmetics, and nutritious foods; Water treatment units. **SICs:** 5122 (Drugs, Proprietaries & Sundries); 5149 (Groceries & Related Products Nec); 5074 (Plumbing & Hydronic Heating Supplies). **Sales:** $1,690,000,000 (2000). **Emp:** 2,200.
Officers: Charles L. Orr, CEO & President; Angela Sabella, VP & CFO.

■ 14235 ■ R.G. Shakour Inc.
254 Turnpike Rd.
Westborough, MA 01581
Phone: (508)366-8282
Free: (800)262-9090 **Fax:** (508)898-3212
URL: http://www.rqshakour.com
Products: Professional beauty supplies and salon equipment. **SIC:** 5122 (Drugs, Proprietaries & Sundries). **Est:** 1928. **Sales:** $15,000,000 (1999).
Emp: 95. **Officers:** Jon Shakour, President; Renee G. Shakour, Vice President.

■ 14236 ■ Silver Sage
402 W 5050 N
Provo, UT 84604-5650
Phone: (801)571-6599
Products: Herbal diet supplements. **SIC:** 5122 (Drugs, Proprietaries & Sundries).

■ 14237 ■ Sime Health Ltd.
1200 6th Ave. S
Seattle, WA 98134
Phone: (206)622-9596
Products: Condoms; Latex gloves. **SIC:** 5122 (Drugs, Proprietaries & Sundries).

■ **14238** ■ **Simple Wisdom Inc.**
775 S Graham St.
Memphis, TN 38111
Phone: (901)458-4686
Products: Shampoo; Hair conditioner; Perfume; Hand and body lotion. **SIC:** 5122 (Drugs, Proprietaries & Sundries). **Est:** 1988. **Sales:** $100,000 (2000). **Emp:** 2. **Officers:** Mary Ann Davis, President; Larry Davis, Vice President.

■ **14239** ■ **C.D. Smith Drug Co.**
PO Box 789
St. Joseph, MO 64502
Phone: (816)232-5471   **Fax:** (816)279-1682
URL: http://www.cdsdrug
Products: Pharmaceuticals for personal care. **SIC:** 5122 (Drugs, Proprietaries & Sundries). **Est:** 1886. **Sales:** $220,000,000 (2000). **Emp:** 120. **Officers:** Robert Farley, President; Jeanne Matheisen, CFO; Richard M. Meehan, Dir. of Marketing.

■ **14240** ■ **S.O.E. Ltd.**
259 Radnor-Chester Rd., Ste. 210
Radnor, PA 19087
Phone: (610)971-6653
Products: Skincare products. **SIC:** 5122 (Drugs, Proprietaries & Sundries). **Sales:** $2,000,000 (2000). **Emp:** 3.

■ **14241** ■ **Solgar Vitamin and Herb Co.**
PO Box 330
Lynbrook, NY 11563
Phone: (516)599-2442
Products: Vitamins and herbs. **SIC:** 5122 (Drugs, Proprietaries & Sundries). **Est:** 1947. **Sales:** $100,000,000 (2000). **Emp:** 130. **Officers:** Allen Skolnick, President; Don Ruggiero, Controller.

■ **14242** ■ **Solis America Inc.**
1919 Stanley St.
Northbrook, IL 60062-5324
Phone: (847)310-6357
Products: Hair dryers, curling irons, and brushes; Espresso machines; Air cleaners. **SIC:** 5064 (Electrical Appliances—Television & Radio). **Sales:** $4,000,000 (1994). **Emp:** 9. **Officers:** Michael Gilbert, President.

■ **14243** ■ **Sondras Beauty Supply**
1407 Broad St.
Providence, RI 02905-2807
Phone: (401)781-1916
Products: Service industry machinery; Beauty and barber shop accessories. **SIC:** 5087 (Service Establishment Equipment). **Officers:** Sondra Murphy, Owner.

■ **14244** ■ **Specialty Catalog Corp.**
21 Bristol Dr.
South Easton, MA 02375
Phone: (508)238-0199   **Fax:** (508)238-3305
Products: Women's wigs and hairpieces. **SIC:** 5199 (Nondurable Goods Nec). **Sales:** $43,500,000 (2000). **Emp:** 349. **Officers:** Steven L. Bock, CEO & Chairman of the Board; J. William Heise, Sr. VP & CFO.

■ **14245** ■ **Stanley Home Products**
PO Box 729
Great Bend, KS 67530
Phone: (316)792-1711
Products: Home and personal care products. **SIC:** 5199 (Nondurable Goods Nec).

■ **14246** ■ **State Beauty Supply**
1721 Logan Ave.
Cheyenne, WY 82001-5005
Phone: (307)634-8984
Products: Service industry machinery; Beauty and barber shop accessories. **SIC:** 5087 (Service Establishment Equipment). **Officers:** Anthony Smith, Partner.

■ **14247** ■ **State Beauty Supply**
1522 Cerrillos Rd.
Santa Fe, NM 87505-3550
Phone: (505)988-4152
Products: Beauty salon and barber shop equipment and supplies. **SIC:** 5087 (Service Establishment Equipment). **Officers:** Diane Carter, Owner.

■ **14248** ■ **State Service Systems Inc.**
10405-B E 55th Pl.
Tulsa, OK 74146-6599
Phone: (918)627-8000   **Fax:** (918)627-8660
Products: Beauty supplies and equipment. **SIC:** 5087 (Service Establishment Equipment). **Sales:** $60,000,000 (2000). **Emp:** 60. **Officers:** Jamie Cheek, President; Jim Fielge, CFO.

■ **14249** ■ **Strickland Beauty & Barber Supply Inc.**
1245 N E St.
San Bernardino, CA 92405
Phone: (909)888-1359
Free: (800)491-2043   **Fax:** (949)888-1350
Products: Beauty and barber shop accessories. **SICs:** 5087 (Service Establishment Equipment); 5122 (Drugs, Proprietaries & Sundries). **Est:** 1978. **Sales:** $500,000 (2000). **Emp:** 8. **Officers:** John W. Strickland, President; Jewell E. Strickland, Secretary; John W. Strickland Jr., Vice President; Jewell L. Martin, Treasurer.

■ **14250** ■ **C.B. Sullivan Co. Inc.**
15 W Alice Ave.
Hooksett, NH 03106
Phone: (603)624-4752   **Fax:** (603)624-8621
Products: Professional beauty products and equipment. **SICs:** 5087 (Service Establishment Equipment); 5122 (Drugs, Proprietaries & Sundries). **Officers:** Charles Sullivan, President.

■ **14251** ■ **Sunhopper Inc.**
PO Box 2551
Elizabethtown, KY 42702-2551
Free: (800)537-4530
Products: Suntan oil. **SIC:** 5122 (Drugs, Proprietaries & Sundries). **Sales:** $200,000 (2000). **Emp:** 12. **Officers:** Doreen L. Fite, CEO & President.

■ **14252** ■ **Super-Nutrition Distributors Inc.**
1500 Hempstead Tpke., No. 100
East Meadow, NY 11554-1558
Phone: (516)897-2480
Free: (800)777-8844   **Fax:** (516)897-2580
URL: http://www.supernut.com
Products: Health food items, including vitamins, minerals, and supplements. **SICs:** 5122 (Drugs, Proprietaries & Sundries); 5149 (Groceries & Related Products Nec). **Est:** 1975. **Emp:** 140. **Officers:** Wes Burgar, President; Steven M. Falk, Vice President, e-mail: smfalk@msn.com; Bill Britton, Marketing & Sales Mgr.; Johanna Falber, Sales/Marketing Contact, e-mail: johannaf@supernut.com; Pam Pettit, Customer Service Contact, e-mail: pamp@supernit.com.

■ **14253** ■ **Swanson Health Products**
1318 39th St. NW
Fargo, ND 58102
Phone: (701)277-1662   **Fax:** 800-726-7691
Products: Vitamin supplements. **SIC:** 5122 (Drugs, Proprietaries & Sundries).

■ **14254** ■ **T & T Distributors**
4448 Technology Dr.
Fremont, CA 94538
Phone: (510)657-5220   **Fax:** (510)657-0432
E-mail: ttdist@aol.com
URL: http://www.wholesalecentral.com/tandt
Products: Lighters. **SIC:** 5122 (Drugs, Proprietaries & Sundries). **Est:** 1987. **Sales:** $300,000 (2000). **Emp:** 2.

■ **14255** ■ **Tamco Distributors Company Inc.**
365 Victoria Rd.
Youngstown, OH 44501
Phone: (330)792-2311   **Fax:** (330)797-7523
Products: Toiletries. **SIC:** 5122 (Drugs, Proprietaries & Sundries). **Sales:** $190,000,000 (2000). **Emp:** 275. **Officers:** David Schwartz, President; Sankar Krishnan, CFO.

■ **14256** ■ **Tec Laboratories Inc.**
PO Box 1958
Albany, OR 97321
Phone: (541)926-4577   **Fax:** (541)926-0218
Products: Outdoor protective lotions, cleansers, and insect repellent. **SIC:** 5122 (Drugs, Proprietaries & Sundries). **Est:** 1977. **Sales:** $3,000,000 (2000). **Emp:** 18. **Officers:** Steven Smith, President; Susan

Burchard, Controller; Larry Burris, Sales/Marketing Contact, e-mail: burris@teclabsinc.com.

■ **14257** ■ **Technical Marketing, Inc.**
1776 N Pine Island Rd., Ste. 306
Plantation, FL 33322
Phone: (954)370-0855   **Fax:** (954)474-3866
E-mail: tmusa@bellsouth.net
Products: Pharmaceuticals. **SIC:** 5122 (Drugs, Proprietaries & Sundries). **Est:** 1987. **Sales:** $1,000,000 (2000). **Emp:** 5. **Officers:** William Leibstone, President; Jean Claude Kappler. **Former Name:** William #Leibstone Associates, Inc.

■ **14258** ■ **Thompson's State Beauty Supply**
415 W 4th Ave.
Bloomington, IN 47404
Phone: (812)339-1959
Free: (800)882-1959   **Fax:** (812)339-1905
Products: Beauty and barber shop accessories. **SIC:** 5087 (Service Establishment Equipment). **Officers:** David Thompson, Contact. **Former Name:** Thompson Beauty Supply.

■ **14259** ■ **Threshold Enterprises Ltd.**
23 Janis Way
Scotts Valley, CA 95066
Phone: (408)438-6851
Free: (800)777-5677   **Fax:** (408)438-7410
Products: Health care products, including vitamins, herbal products, and natural body care. **SIC:** 5122 (Drugs, Proprietaries & Sundries). **Est:** 1983. **Emp:** 600.

■ **14260** ■ **Robyn Todd**
1495 Poleline Rd. E
Twin Falls, ID 83301-3588
Phone: (208)734-1488   **Fax:** (208)734-1581
Products: Service establishment equipment; Beauty salon and barber shop equipment and supplies. **SIC:** 5087 (Service Establishment Equipment). **Officers:** Jean Henderson, Owner.

■ **14261** ■ **Tree of Life Inc. Southeast**
1750 Tree Blvd.
PO Box 410
St. Augustine, FL 32085
Phone: (904)825-2240
Products: Medicinal and health supplies. **SIC:** 5122 (Drugs, Proprietaries & Sundries).

■ **14262** ■ **TRI-Alaska**
7215 Foxridge Circle, No. 2
Anchorage, AK 99518
Phone: (907)561-1956
Products: Beauty and barber shop accessories. **SIC:** 5087 (Service Establishment Equipment).

■ **14263** ■ **TRI-New England**
73 Reservoir Park Dr., No. 6
Rockland, MA 02370
Phone: (781)871-7886
Products: Beauty and barber shop accessories. **SIC:** 5087 (Service Establishment Equipment). **Officers:** Lisa Farkas, Contact.

■ **14264** ■ **Tri State Beauty Supply Inc.**
5200 Overland Rd.
Boise, ID 83705-2638
Phone: (208)345-1642   **Fax:** (208)345-1662
Products: Beauty salon and barber shop supplies. **SIC:** 5087 (Service Establishment Equipment). **Est:** 1970. **Emp:** 5. **Officers:** Richard Copsey, President.

■ **14265** ■ **TRI-Utah**
1155 N Industrial Park Dr.
Orem, UT 84057
Phone: (801)226-1308
Products: Beauty and barber shop accessories. **SIC:** 5087 (Service Establishment Equipment).

■ **14266** ■ **Tsuki's Hair Design**
1450 Ala Moana Blvd., Ste. 1241
Honolulu, HI 96814
Phone: (808)946-3902
Products: Beauty and barber shop accessories. **SIC:** 5087 (Service Establishment Equipment).

■ **14267** ■ **Tsumura International Inc.**
300 Lighting Way
Secaucus, NJ 07096-1578
Phone: (201)223-9000 **Fax:** (201)223-8278
Products: Fragrances; Children's toiletries. **SIC:** 5122
(Drugs, Proprietaries & Sundries). **Est:** 1987. **Sales:**
$180,000,000 (2000). **Emp:** 600. **Officers:** Howard
Hirsch, CEO & President; Norman Lavin, Exec. VP;
Katz Morita, Dir. of Marketing & Sales; Greg Sorrenson,
Dir. of Information Systems; Frank Quintilian, Human
Resources Mgr.

■ **14268** ■ **Ultimate Salon Services Inc.**
2621 Ridgepoint Dr., No. 120
Austin, TX 78754
Phone: (512)926-9193
Free: (800)999-7668 **Fax:** (512)926-1078
E-mail: Ultimate@Texas.net
Products: Hair care systems; Professional salon
products. **SIC:** 5122 (Drugs, Proprietaries & Sundries).
Est: 1990. **Emp:** 35. **Officers:** Laurie B. Spellman,
CEO; Gary Spellman, President; Ron Smith,
Sales/Marketing Contact; John Diaz, Customer Service
Contact; Christy Davis, Human Resources Contact.

■ **14269** ■ **United Beauty Equipment Co.**
91 N Lowell Rd.
Windham, NH 03087-1669
Phone: (603)434-8039
Products: Beauty salon equipment. **SIC:** 5087
(Service Establishment Equipment). **Est:** 1969. **Sales:**
$850,000 (2000). **Emp:** 2. **Officers:** James Slater,
Owner.

■ **14270** ■ **U.S. Export & Trading Company,
Inc.**
848 Harding St.
Escondido, CA 92027
Phone: (760)743-8211 **Fax:** (760)743-8140
Products: Vitamins. **SIC:** 5122 (Drugs, Proprietaries &
Sundries). **Est:** 1975. **Officers:** Lang Forehand,
President.

■ **14271** ■ **Vita Plus Industries Inc.**
953 E Sahara Ave.
Las Vegas, NV 89104
Phone: (702)733-8805
Free: (800)634-6747 **Fax:** (702)369-8597
Products: Dietary supplements; Skin moisturizers;
Vitamins and minerals. **SIC:** 5122 (Drugs, Proprietaries
& Sundries). **Est:** 1975. **Sales:** $1,000,000 (2000).
Emp: 20. **Officers:** Scott C. Goldsmith, CEO,
President & Chairman of the Board.

■ **14272** ■ **Vitality Distributiors Inc.**
940 NW 51st Pl.
Ft. Lauderdale, FL 33309-3103
Phone: (954)771-0445
Free: (800)226-VITA **Fax:** (954)771-4749
Products: Medicinal and health supplies. **SIC:** 5122
(Drugs, Proprietaries & Sundries). **Est:** 1967. **Emp:** 3.
Officers: Donald Scarborough, President; Lucille
Scarborough, Treasurer; Arthur J. Bishop, Vice
President.

■ **14273** ■ **The Vitamin Shoppe**
4700 Westside Ave.
North Bergen, NJ 07047
Phone: (201)866-7711
Free: (800)223-1216 **Fax:** (201)866-9513
Products: Vitamins. **SIC:** 5122 (Drugs, Proprietaries &
Sundries).

■ **14274** ■ **Vitamin Specialties Corp.**
8200 Ogontz Ave.
Wyncote, PA 19095
Phone: (215)885-3800
Free: (800)365-8482 **Fax:** (215)885-1310
Products: Vitamins and dietary supplements. **SIC:**
5122 (Drugs, Proprietaries & Sundries).

■ **14275** ■ **Walgreen Co.**
200 Wilmot Rd.
Deerfield, IL 60015
Phone: (847)940-2500
Products: Pharmaceuticals, health care products, and
cosmetics. **SIC:** 5122 (Drugs, Proprietaries &
Sundries). **Est:** 1901. **Sales:** $6,733,000,000 (2000).
Emp: 57,700. **Officers:** Charles R. Walgreen III, CEO
& Chairman of the Board; Charles D. Hunter, CFO;
Vernon A. Brunner, Sr. VP of Marketing; Gary A.
Pradarelli, Dir. of Information Systems; John A. Rubino.

■ **14276** ■ **Walsh Healthcare Solutions**
1702 Hampton Rd.
Texarkana, TX 75503
Phone: (903)255-2300 **Fax:** (903)735-4047
URL: http://www.walshdist.com
Products: Over-the-counter prescription drugs, aspirin,
pain relievers, and laxatives. **SIC:** 5122 (Drugs,
Proprietaries & Sundries). **Est:** 1920. **Sales:**
$600,000,000 (1999). **Emp:** 425. **Officers:** Ron
Nelson, President; Bob Boneroft, CFO; Hal Lower,
Treasurer; Greg Ashby, CIO; Randall Wilson, Dir. of
Purchasing. **Former Name:** Walsh Distribution Inc.

■ **14277** ■ **WeCare Distributors Inc.**
PO Box 669047
Charlotte, NC 28266
Phone: (704)393-1860
Products: Skin care products. **SIC:** 5122 (Drugs,
Proprietaries & Sundries).

■ **14278** ■ **Weider Health and Fitness Inc.**
21100 Erwin St.
Woodland Hills, CA 91367
Phone: (818)884-6800 **Fax:** (818)704-5734
Products: Fitness supplies, including exercise
equipment and clothing; Health care products, including
nutrients; Fitness magazines. **SICs:** 5122 (Drugs,
Proprietaries & Sundries); 5091 (Sporting &
Recreational Goods); 5192 (Books, Periodicals &
Newspapers). **Sales:** $210,000,000 (2000). **Emp:** 515.
Officers: Eric Weider, President & COO; Ron Novak,
CFO.

■ **14279** ■ **Wesco Merchandising**
7101 E Slauson Ave.
Los Angeles, CA 90040-3622
Phone: (213)269-0292
Products: Health and beauty aids; Automotive
supplies; Pet supplies. **SICs:** 5122 (Drugs,
Proprietaries & Sundries); 5013 (Motor Vehicle
Supplies & New Parts); 5199 (Nondurable Goods Nec).
Est: 1927. **Sales:** $40,000,000 (2000). **Emp:** 150.
Officers: Lou Bernardi, President; Pacita Diaz,
Controller; Bob Thompson, Exec. VP.

■ **14280** ■ **West Coast Beauty Supply**
5001 Industrial Way
Benicia, CA 94510
Phone: (707)748-4800 **Free:** (800)233-3141
Products: Beauty supplies. **SIC:** 5122 (Drugs,
Proprietaries & Sundries). **Est:** 1942. **Officers:** George
Clark, Founder; Marion Clark, Founder.

■ **14281** ■ **Wilcox Drug Company Inc.**
PO Box 391
Boone, NC 28607
Phone: (828)264-3615 **Fax:** (828)264-2831
Products: Roots, herbs, barks, and berries. **SIC:** 5148
(Fresh Fruits & Vegetables). **Sales:** $21,000,000
(2000). **Emp:** 45. **Officers:** Chuck Wanzer, General
Mgr.; Bill Pannell, CFO.

■ **14282** ■ **The Willing Group**
222 Saint Johns Ave.
Yonkers, NY 10704-2717
Phone: (914)964-5800 **Fax:** (914)964-5293
Products: Health and beauty aids; Cosmetics;
Pharmaceuticals; Food, including by-products. **SICs:**
5122 (Drugs, Proprietaries & Sundries); 5141
(Groceries—General Line). **Est:** 1965. **Sales:**
$10,000,000 (2000). **Emp:** 8. **Officers:** Louis J.
Goldstein, President.

■ **14283** ■ **Willis Distribution Beauty Supply**
4600 Homer Ohio Ln.
Groveport, OH 43125-9230
Phone: (614)836-0115 **Fax:** (614)836-0119
Products: Ethnic hair care products. **SIC:** 5122 (Drugs,
Proprietaries & Sundries).

■ **14284** ■ **X-S Beauty Supplies**
163 N Main St.
Port Chester, NY 10573-3303
Phone: (914)937-8787
Free: (800)366-8788 **Fax:** (914)937-6379
Products: Toiletries, including hair and skin care
products. **SIC:** 5122 (Drugs, Proprietaries & Sundries).
Est: 1980.

■ **14285** ■ **Yves Saint Laurent Parfums Corp.**
40 W 57th St.
New York, NY 10019
Phone: (212)621-7300 **Fax:** (212)621-7312
Products: Perfume. **SIC:** 5122 (Drugs, Proprietaries &
Sundries). **Est:** 1919. **Sales:** $200,000,000 (2000).
Emp: 185. **Officers:** Donald J. Loftus, CEO; Andrew
Chestnut, CFO.

(23) Heating and Cooling Equipment and Supplies

Entries in this section are arranged alphabetically by company name. When the company name is a personal name, the company name is alphabetized by the surname unless the first name or initial(s) are part of a trade name. See the User's Guide at the front of this directory for additional information.

■ **14286** ■ **A-1 Refrigeration Inc.**
1134 N 21st St.
Lincoln, NE 68503
Phone: (402)476-2323 **Fax:** (402)476-1160
Products: Commercial refrigeration, heating, and cooling equipment. **SICs:** 5078 (Refrigeration Equipment & Supplies); 5075 (Warm Air Heating & Air-Conditioning).

■ **14287** ■ **A & R Supply Co. Inc.**
296 S Pauline St.
Memphis, TN 38104
Phone: (901)527-0338 **Fax:** (901)527-5544
Products: Industrial air-conditioners, refrigeration, and heating equipment. **SICs:** 5075 (Warm Air Heating & Air-Conditioning); 5078 (Refrigeration Equipment & Supplies).

■ **14288** ■ **ABC Appliance Inc. White Automotive Association Div.**
3377 Fort St.
Lincoln Park, MI 48146-3634
Phone: (248)549-2300 **Fax:** (248)549-8161
Products: Air-conditioning equipment. **SIC:** 5075 (Warm Air Heating & Air-Conditioning). **Est:** 1943. **Sales:** $5,000,000 (2000). **Emp:** 40. **Officers:** Tony Defalco, Vice President; Ron Johnson, CFO.

■ **14289** ■ **ABCO Refrigeration Supply Corp.**
49-70 31st St.
Long Island City, NY 11101
Phone: (718)937-9000 **Fax:** (718)392-1296
Products: Air-conditioning and heating equipment and supplies. **SICs:** 5078 (Refrigeration Equipment & Supplies); 5075 (Warm Air Heating & Air-Conditioning). **Est:** 1949. **Sales:** $75,000,000 (2000). **Emp:** 150. **Officers:** J.A. Gottlieb, President; G. Moncher, Treasurer & Secty.

■ **14290** ■ **Able Distributors**
2501 N Central Ave.
Chicago, IL 60639
Phone: (773)889-5555
Products: Heating and cooling parts and products. **SIC:** 5075 (Warm Air Heating & Air-Conditioning).

■ **14291** ■ **ABR Wholesale, Inc.**
510 N Goodman St.
Rochester, NY 14609
Phone: (716)482-3601 **Fax:** (716)288-6955
Products: Heating and air-conditioning equipment and supplies. **SIC:** 5075 (Warm Air Heating & Air-Conditioning). **Est:** 1963. **Sales:** $12,000,000 (2000). **Emp:** 48. **Officers:** V.J. Monaco, CEO; Jody Monaco-McGarry, President.

■ **14292** ■ **AC & R Specialty Supply**
PO Box 1912
South Hackensack, NJ 07606
Phone: (201)652-7400 **Fax:** (201)343-2735
Products: Air-Conditioning and refrigeration supplies. **SICs:** 5075 (Warm Air Heating & Air-Conditioning); 5078 (Refrigeration Equipment & Supplies).

■ **14293** ■ **Acme Heat & Power**
21 Grand St.
Copiague, NY 11726
Phone: (516)842-7077 **Fax:** (516)842-1533
Products: Heating equipment. **SIC:** 5075 (Warm Air Heating & Air-Conditioning).

■ **14294** ■ **Acme Manufacturing Co.**
7500 State Rd.
Philadelphia, PA 19136
Phone: (215)338-2850 **Fax:** (215)335-1905
Products: Heating and cooling supplies. **SIC:** 5075 (Warm Air Heating & Air-Conditioning).

■ **14295** ■ **Acme Refrigeration**
5339 Choctaw Dr.
Baton Rouge, LA 70805
Phone: (504)355-2263
Free: (800)324-1852 **Fax:** (504)355-7666
Products: Air-conditioning and refrigeration equipment and supplies. **SICs:** 5078 (Refrigeration Equipment & Supplies); 5075 (Warm Air Heating & Air-Conditioning).

■ **14296** ■ **Acme Refrigeration of Baton Rouge Inc.**
11844 S Choctaw Dr.
Baton Rouge, LA 70815-2184
Phone: (225)273-1740 **Fax:** (225)273-1763
E-mail: acmecnt@eatel.net
URL: http://www.acmeref.com
Products: Equipment, parts, and supplies for heating, air conditioning, and refrigeration. **SIC:** 5075 (Warm Air Heating & Air-Conditioning). **Est:** 1945. **Emp:** 95. **Officers:** Adrian Kaiser, President.

■ **14297** ■ **ACR Group Inc.**
3200 Wilcrest Dr., Ste. 440
Houston, TX 77042-6019
Phone: (713)780-8532
Products: Heating and air-conditioning parts. **SIC:** 5075 (Warm Air Heating & Air-Conditioning). **Est:** 1980. **Sales:** $126,468,201 (2000). **Emp:** 350. **Officers:** Alex Trevino Jr., CEO & President; Anthony R. Maresca, Sr. VP & CFO.

■ **14298** ■ **ACR Supply Inc. (Houston, Texas)**
PO Box 630929
Houston, TX 77263
Phone: (713)787-6776 **Fax:** (713)787-6677
Products: Heating, ventilation, air conditioning, and refrigeration equipment. **SICs:** 5075 (Warm Air Heating & Air-Conditioning); 5078 (Refrigeration Equipment & Supplies). **Sales:** $30,000,000 (1994). **Emp:** 50. **Officers:** Alex Trevino Jr., President; Anthony Mareska, CFO.

■ **14299** ■ **Actrade International Corp.**
7 Penn Plz., Ste. 422
New York, NY 10001
Phone: (212)563-1036 **Fax:** (212)563-3271
Products: Air-ccnditioned; Bakery equipment. **SICs:** 5084 (Industrial Machinery & Equipment); 5075 (Warm Air Heating & Air-Conditioning). **Sales:** $43,000,000 (2000). **Emp:** 50. **Officers:** John Woerner, President.

■ **14300** ■ **AES of Norfolk Inc.**
3501 Progress Rd.
Norfolk, VA 23510
Phone: (757)857-6061
Free: (800)876-4237 **Fax:** (757)857-0695
Products: Cooling systems. **SIC:** 5075 (Warm Air Heating & Air-Conditioning). **Est:** 1947. **Sales:** $24,000,000 (2000). **Emp:** 40. **Officers:** Bruce Martin, Manager; Fran Dutcher.

■ **14301** ■ **AES of Oklahoma Inc.**
PO Box 270360
Oklahoma City, OK 73137
Phone: (405)947-8700
Products: Air conditioning and heating equipment. **SIC:** 5075 (Warm Air Heating & Air-Conditioning). **Sales:** $9,000,000 (2000). **Emp:** 30. **Officers:** Monte Hoover, General Mgr.

■ **14302** ■ **AES of Roanoke Inc.**
PO Box 4230
Roanoke, VA 24015
Phone: (540)343-8054
Free: (800)873-2377 **Fax:** (540)343-4250
Products: Heating and air-conditioning equipment. **SIC:** 5075 (Warm Air Heating & Air-Conditioning). **Est:** 1947. **Sales:** $14,000,000 (2000). **Emp:** 23. **Officers:** R.K. Taylor, President; Wayne Nicely, General Mgr.

■ **14303** ■ **Affiliated Holdings Inc.**
6009 Center St.
Omaha, NE 68106
Phone: (402)558-0988
Products: Electrical appliances; Heating and air-conditioning equipment. **SICs:** 5065 (Electronic Parts & Equipment Nec); 5075 (Warm Air Heating & Air-Conditioning).

■ **14304** ■ **Air O Quip Corp.**
PO Box 108308
Casselberry, FL 32718
Phone: (407)831-3600
Products: Air conditioning and heating equipment. **SICs:** 5075 (Warm Air Heating & Air-Conditioning); 5075 (Warm Air Heating & Air-Conditioning). **Est:** 1958. **Sales:** $23,000,000 (2000). **Emp:** 80. **Officers:** T.H. Burd, CEO.

■ **14305** ■ **Air Parts Inc.**
PO Box 170
Cumming, GA 30028
Phone: (404)781-6640
Products: Air-conditioning parts. **SIC:** 5075 (Warm Air Heating & Air-Conditioning).

■ **14306** ■ **Air Rite Filters Inc.**
1290 W 117th St.
Lakewood, OH 44107
Phone: (216)228-8200 **Fax:** (216)228-5651
Products: Air filters. **SIC:** 5075 (Warm Air Heating & Air-Conditioning). **Officers:** Dave Harris, President.

■ 14307 ■ **Air Systems Distributors Inc.**
5600 NW 84th Ave.
Miami, FL 33166
Phone: (305)592-3809 **Fax:** (305)592-3819
Products: Residential and commercial air conditioning equipment. **SIC:** 5075 (Warm Air Heating & Air-Conditioning).

■ 14308 ■ **Air Temperature Inc.**
802 Rozelle St.
Memphis, TN 38104
Phone: (901)278-7211 **Fax:** (901)278-4911
Products: Air conditioning equipment. **SIC:** 5075 (Warm Air Heating & Air-Conditioning). **Sales:** $18,000,000 (2000). **Emp:** 70. **Officers:** Larry Jones, Controller.

■ 14309 ■ **Airfan Engineered Products Inc.**
10259 Stanford Ave.
Garden Grove, CA 92840-4860
Phone: (213)723-3354
Products: Heating and air conditioning. **SIC:** 5075 (Warm Air Heating & Air-Conditioning). **Officers:** T. Haldeman, Chairman of the Board.

■ 14310 ■ **Ajax Supply Co.**
5714 Ayers
Corpus Christi, TX 78415
Phone: (512)855-6284
Products: Air conditioners; Heaters. **SIC:** 5074 (Plumbing & Hydronic Heating Supplies). **Est:** 1951. **Sales:** $10,000,000 (2000). **Emp:** 35. **Officers:** Bill Winston, CEO.

■ 14311 ■ **All City Refrigeration Co. Inc.**
32425 W 8 Mile Rd.
Livonia, MI 48152-1301
Phone: (248)478-8780 **Fax:** (248)476-8625
E-mail: ventura@ameritech.net
Products: Refrigeration equipment and supplies; Ice making machines. **SIC:** 5078 (Refrigeration Equipment & Supplies). **Est:** 1961. **Sales:** $3,000,000 (2000). **Emp:** 13. **Officers:** Helen Perpich, Owner.

■ 14312 ■ **All Seasons Engines Inc.**
126 S Main St.
Roswell, NM 88203
Phone: (505)625-0800 **Fax:** (505)622-5887
Products: Commercial refrigeration equipment, including reach-in and walk-in refrigerators. **SIC:** 5078 (Refrigeration Equipment & Supplies). **Officers:** William Rochelle, President.

■ 14313 ■ **AllerMed Corp.**
31 Steel Rd.
Wylie, TX 75098
Phone: (972)442-4898 **Fax:** (972)442-4897
Products: Dust collection and other air purification equipment for heating, ventilating, and air-conditioning systems; Filters. **SIC:** 5075 (Warm Air Heating & Air-Conditioning). **Est:** 1981. **Officers:** Boyd Hager, President; Betsy Blasdell, Dir. of Marketing.

■ 14314 ■ **Allied Fire Lite Fireplace**
310 Westhill Blvd.
Appleton, WI 54914
Phone: (920)733-4911 **Fax:** (920)733-8186
Products: Fireplace equipment; Patio equipment. **SICs:** 5074 (Plumbing & Hydronic Heating Supplies); 5021 (Furniture).

■ 14315 ■ **Allred's Inc.**
PO Box 57160
Salt Lake City, UT 84157-0160
Phone: (801)266-4413 **Fax:** (801)266-6741
Products: Heaters and air conditioners, including equipment and supplies; Electric equipment and supplies. **SICs:** 5075 (Warm Air Heating & Air-Conditioning); 5063 (Electrical Apparatus & Equipment). **Est:** 1949. **Sales:** $20,000,000 (2000). **Emp:** 80. **Officers:** Christine Allred, CEO; Bob Haag, Sales/Marketing Contact; Robert G. Allred, Customer Service Contact.

■ 14316 ■ **American Excelsior Co.**
200 S 49th Ave.
Phoenix, AZ 85043
Phone: (602)269-3860 **Fax:** (602)278-7914
Products: Evaporative cooler supplies; Foam and packaging supplies. **SICs:** 5078 (Refrigeration Equipment & Supplies); 5113 (Industrial & Personal Service Paper).

■ 14317 ■ **American Filtration Systems Inc.**
3668 Placentia Ct.
Chino, CA 91710
Phone: (909)613-1500 **Fax:** (909)613-1516
E-mail: amfilsys@mail.deltanet.com
Products: Air pollution control; Filtration products; Fans. **SICs:** 5075 (Warm Air Heating & Air-Conditioning); 5074 (Plumbing & Hydronic Heating Supplies). **Est:** 1989. **Sales:** $10,000,000 (1999). **Emp:** 9. **Officers:** Kenneth L. Wirtjes, President; Kim L. Feamster, Vice President.

■ 14318 ■ **American Hermetics, Inc.**
2935 E Ponce de Leon Ave.
Decatur, GA 30030
Phones: (404)373-8782 (404)378-0232
Products: Air conditioning compressors. **SIC:** 5075 (Warm Air Heating & Air-Conditioning). **Est:** 1974. **Sales:** $2,000,000 (2000). **Emp:** 15. **Officers:** Paul Sykes, President.

■ 14319 ■ **American Metals Supply Co. Inc.**
PO Box 1325
Springfield, IL 62705
Phone: (217)528-7553 **Fax:** (217)528-7920
Products: Heating and air-conditioning equipment, including pipes, fittings, and venting supplies. **SIC:** 5075 (Warm Air Heating & Air-Conditioning). **Est:** 1962. **Sales:** $8,000,000 (1999). **Emp:** 13. **Officers:** S. Hassebrock, President.

■ 14320 ■ **American Technotherm Corp.**
1 Barnes Ave.
Colchester, VT 05446
Phone: (802)655-4061 **Fax:** (802)655-7927
Products: Electrical equipment, including thermo storage heaters and controls. **SIC:** 5075 (Warm Air Heating & Air-Conditioning).

■ 14321 ■ **Amtrol International Inc.**
PO Box 1008
West Warwick, RI 02893-0908
Phone: (401)884-6300 **Fax:** (401)885-2567
Products: Refrigeration equipment and supplies. **SIC:** 5078 (Refrigeration Equipment & Supplies). **Officers:** Chester Kirk, Chairman of the Board.

■ 14322 ■ **Andrews Distributing Company Inc.**
PO Box 17557
Nashville, TN 37217-0557
Phone: (615)399-1776
Free: (800)264-4806 **Fax:** (615)360-8260
Products: Heaters; Air-conditioners, parts, and supplies. **SIC:** 5075 (Warm Air Heating & Air-Conditioning). **Est:** 1957. **Sales:** $47,000,000 (1999). **Emp:** 92. **Officers:** Peggy A. Andrews, CEO & President, e-mail: peggyandrews@isdn.net; Glenn D. Loper, VP of Sales, e-mail: glennloper@adcchat.com; Janet Booker-Davis, Controller, e-mail: janetbookerdavis@adcnash.com; John N. Andrews, Sr. Chairman of the Board, e-mail: johnandrews@adcnash.com.

■ 14323 ■ **Apex Supply Company Inc.**
2500 Button Gwinnett Dr.
Atlanta, GA 30340
Phone: (404)449-7000 **Fax:** (404)263-4834
URL: http://www.apexsupply.com
Products: Heating and air-conditioning supplies; Plumbing supplies; Industrial supplies. **SICs:** 5074 (Plumbing & Hydronic Heating Supplies); 5075 (Warm Air Heating & Air-Conditioning); 5039 (Construction Materials Nec). **Est:** 1955. **Sales:** $210,000,000 (1999). **Emp:** 565. **Officers:** Clyde Rodbell, Chairman; Sidney Rodbell, President.

■ 14324 ■ **Applied Power Corp.**
1210 Hornann Dr. SE
Lacey, WA 98503
Phone: (360)438-2110
Free: (800)777-7075 **Fax:** (360)438-2115
E-mail: info@appliedpower.com
URL: http://www.appliedpower.com
Products: Photovoltaic modules and components. **SIC:** 5074 (Plumbing & Hydronic Heating Supplies).
Est: 1981. **Sales:** $10,000,000 (2000). **Emp:** 50. **Officers:** Tim Ball, CEO; Tom Rawson, CFO; Tom Krueger, Dir. of Mktg. & Sales; Linda Smith, Human Resources Contact, e-mail: lsmith@appliedpower.com. **Former Name:** Solar Electric Specialties Co.

■ 14325 ■ **APR Supply Co.**
305 N 5th St.
Lebanon, PA 17046
Phone: (717)274-5999 **Fax:** (717)273-2150
URL: http://www.aprsupply.com
Products: Plumbing, heating, and cooling equipment. **SICs:** 5074 (Plumbing & Hydronic Heating Supplies); 5075 (Warm Air Heating & Air-Conditioning). **Est:** 1922. **Emp:** 90. **Officers:** M.R. Tice, CEO & Chairman of the Board, e-mail: rtice@aprsupply.com; Scott Weaver, COO, e-mail: sweaver@aprsupply.com; John Tice, Vice President, e-mail: jtice@aprsupply.com; Bruce R. Hoch, Sales/Marketing Contact, e-mail: bhoch@aprsupply.com.

■ 14326 ■ **Arctic Technical Services**
1318 Well St.
Fairbanks, AK 99701
Phone: (907)452-8368 **Fax:** (907)452-8007
E-mail: nrgtech@polarnet.com
URL: http://www.polarnet.com/~nrgtech
Products: Energy-efficient appliances and supplies. **SIC:** 5075 (Warm Air Heating & Air-Conditioning). **Est:** 1983. **Officers:** Philip G. Loudon, President; Marshall Nimner, Sales/Marketing Contact.

■ 14327 ■ **Associated Appliance Service**
2318 NW 12th St.
Oklahoma City, OK 73107-5606
Phone: (405)525-2003 **Fax:** (405)521-9679
Products: Refrigeration equipment and supplies. **SIC:** 5078 (Refrigeration Equipment & Supplies). **Officers:** Thomas Simer, Vice President.

■ 14328 ■ **Auer Steel & Heating Supply**
2935 W Silver Spring Dr.
Milwaukee, WI 53209
Phone: (414)463-1234 **Fax:** (414)463-0303
URL: http://www.auersteel.com
Products: Heating and air conditioning supplies. **SIC:** 5075 (Warm Air Heating & Air-Conditioning). **Est:** 1940. **Emp:** 125.

■ 14329 ■ **Authorized Refrigeration Parts Co.**
301 S Vandeventer Ave.
St. Louis, MO 63110
Phone: (314)371-2773 **Fax:** (314)371-5677
Products: Cooling equipment. **SICs:** 5078 (Refrigeration Equipment & Supplies); 5075 (Warm Air Heating & Air-Conditioning). **Est:** 1939. **Sales:** $4,000,000 (2000). **Emp:** 25. **Officers:** Gordon Bell, CEO & President; Greg Jones, CFO.

■ 14330 ■ **Automatic Equipment Sales of Virginia Inc.**
PO Box 27305
Richmond, VA 23261
Phone: (804)355-0651 **Fax:** (804)353-8940
Products: Heating and air-conditioning equipment. **SICs:** 5075 (Warm Air Heating & Air-Conditioning); 5074 (Plumbing & Hydronic Heating Supplies). **Est:** 1947. **Sales:** $325,000,000 (2000). **Emp:** 550. **Officers:** Ralph K. Taylor, President; Tom Holt, Controller; Bill Taylor, Sales Mgr.; John Cantrell, Dir. of Systems; Sue Wells, Controller.

■ 14331 ■ **Automatic Firing Inc.**
2100 Fillmore Ave.
Buffalo, NY 14214
Phone: (716)836-0300 **Fax:** (716)837-0561
Products: Heating equipment. **SICs:** 5075 (Warm Air Heating & Air-Conditioning); 5074 (Plumbing & Hydronic Heating Supplies). **Est:** 1947. **Sales:** $1,000,000 (2000). **Emp:** 10. **Officers:** Samuel Oliver, Partner; J. Pellegrino, VP of Finance; Fred J. Ruffino, VP of Marketing.

■ 14332 ■ Automatic Ice & Beverage Inc.
PO Box 110159
Birmingham, AL 35211-0159
Phone: (205)787-9640
Free: (800)476-4242 **Fax:** (205)787-9659
E-mail: autoicebev@aol.com
Products: Ice making machines; Beverage-dispensing equipment. **SIC:** 5078 (Refrigeration Equipment & Supplies). **Est:** 1966. **Sales:** $5,000,000 (2000). **Emp:** 21. **Officers:** Mark McMillan, President; Marjorie Elam, Treasurer & Secty.

■ 14333 ■ Baker Distributing Co.
7892 Baymeadows Way
Jacksonville, FL 32256
Phone: (904)733-9633 **Fax:** (904)730-9403
URL: http://www.bakerdist.com
Products: Commercial refrigeration equipment, parts, and supplies. **SICs:** 5078 (Refrigeration Equipment & Supplies); 5075 (Warm Air Heating & Air-Conditioning). **Est:** 1945. **Sales:** $180,000,000 (1999). **Emp:** 430. **Officers:** Carole Poindexter, President; Robert Pierce, VP of Sales; Wayne Oatman, VP of Operations; Randy Day, VP of Marketing.

■ 14334 ■ Baker Distributing Co.
2113 N Hamilton St.
PO Box 27527
Richmond, VA 23261
Phone: (804)353-7141
Free: (800)533-8444 **Fax:** (804)358-4822
Products: Heating, air-conditioning, and refrigeration equipment. **SICs:** 5075 (Warm Air Heating & Air-Conditioning); 5078 (Refrigeration Equipment & Supplies); 5074 (Plumbing & Hydronic Heating Supplies). **Officers:** Bill Warner.

■ 14335 ■ Baker-Hauser Co.
1601 W Detweiller Dr.
Peoria, IL 61615-1644
Phone: (309)692-5151 **Free:** (800)432-8212
Products: Refrigeration equipment. **SIC:** 5078 (Refrigeration Equipment & Supplies). **Est:** 1946. **Sales:** $6,000,000 (1999). **Emp:** 35. **Officers:** Stan Galat, General Mgr.

■ 14336 ■ Bales & Truitt Company Inc.
PO Box 818
Kernersville, NC 27285-0818
Phone: (910)996-3531
Free: (800)682-6951 **Fax:** (910)996-8438
Products: Refrigeration equipment and supplies; Air, water, oil and hydraulic filters; Lubricants; Air brake system and parts. **SICs:** 5078 (Refrigeration Equipment & Supplies); 5013 (Motor Vehicle Supplies & New Parts); 5085 (Industrial Supplies); 5172 (Petroleum Products Nec). **Est:** 1925. **Officers:** James H. Truitt Jr., Treasurer.

■ 14337 ■ Bar Beverage Control Inc.
4540 E Paris Ave. SE, A
Grand Rapids, MI 49512-5444
Phone: (616)698-8828
Products: Refrigeration equipment and supplies, including refrigerated beverage dispensers. **SIC:** 5078 (Refrigeration Equipment & Supplies). **Officers:** Donald Dunkelberg, President.

■ 14338 ■ Barnebey and Sutcliffe Corp.
835 N Cassady Ave.
Columbus, OH 43219
Phone: (614)258-9501 **Fax:** (614)258-3464
Products: Dust collection and other air purification equipment for heating, ventilating, and air-conditioning systems. **SIC:** 5075 (Warm Air Heating & Air-Conditioning). **Officers:** Amanda Fisher, Mktg. Coordinator.

■ 14339 ■ Barnett Supply Co. Inc.
PO Box 40891
Memphis, TN 38174-0891
Phone: (901)278-0440 **Fax:** (901)525-0729
Products: Refrigeration equipment and supplies, including ice making machines. **SIC:** 5078 (Refrigeration Equipment & Supplies). **Officers:** Clifford Barnett, President.

■ 14340 ■ BDT Engineering Company Inc. - Industrial Products Div.
4810 N 124th St.
Milwaukee, WI 53225-3601
Phone: (414)353-3112 **Fax:** (414)353-3304
Products: Heat exchange equipment. **SIC:** 5084 (Industrial Machinery & Equipment). **Est:** 1911. **Sales:** $10,000,000 (1999). **Emp:** 85. **Officers:** Ed Dusold, VP & General Mgr. **Former Name:** Senior Engineering Company Inc. Industrial Products.

■ 14341 ■ Bee Jay Refrigeration Inc.
4216 Springwood Ave.
Baltimore, MD 21206-1933
Phone: (410)483-3954 **Fax:** (410)483-6192
Products: Refrigeration equipment and supplies. **SIC:** 5078 (Refrigeration Equipment & Supplies). **Officers:** Joseph Berg, President.

■ 14342 ■ Behler-Young Co.
PO Box 946
Grand Rapids, MI 49509
Phones: (616)531-3400 (616)454-8080
Fax: (616)531-6740
Products: Heating and air-conditioning equipment. **SIC:** 5075 (Warm Air Heating & Air-Conditioning). **Sales:** $21,000,000 (1994). **Emp:** 170. **Officers:** Douglas R. Young, President; Joe Hrabovsky, CFO.

■ 14343 ■ G.W. Berkheimer Company Inc.
3460 Taft St.
Gary, IN 46408
Phone: (219)887-0141
Products: Heat and air conditioner equipment. **SIC:** 5075 (Warm Air Heating & Air-Conditioning). **Est:** 1933. **Sales:** $60,000,000 (2000). **Emp:** 200. **Officers:** George Primich, President; Dale Cobble, Treasurer.

■ 14344 ■ G.W. Berkheimer Company Inc. South Bend
612 Chapin St.
South Bend, IN 46601
Phone: (219)288-4741
Products: Heating, air conditioning, and ventilation products. **SIC:** 5075 (Warm Air Heating & Air-Conditioning). **Sales:** $8,000,000 (2000). **Emp:** 18. **Officers:** James P. Duchemin, General Mgr.

■ 14345 ■ Bev-Tech, Inc.
PO Box 130
York, ME 03909-0130
Phone: (207)363-2707
Free: (800)883-1554 **Fax:** (207)363-1885
Products: Ice cream and espresso machines; Frozen cocktail mix. **SICs:** 5078 (Refrigeration Equipment & Supplies); 5149 (Groceries & Related Products Nec); 5046 (Commercial Equipment Nec). **Officers:** Martin McNerney, President.

■ 14346 ■ Billings Distributing Corp.
260 Fulton St.
Fresno, CA 93721
Phone: (209)268-6314
Products: Air conditioners. **SIC:** 5075 (Warm Air Heating & Air-Conditioning). **Est:** 1951. **Sales:** $1,000,000 (2000). **Emp:** 5. **Officers:** Harry H. Billings, President; Loretta D. Billings, Exec. VP of Finance; David S. Billings, Dir. of Marketing.

■ 14347 ■ Biloff Manufacturing Co. Inc.
PO Box 726
Shafter, CA 93263
Phone: (661)746-3976
Free: (800)468-5677 **Fax:** (661)746-0426
Products: Ice merchandising cabinets. **SIC:** 5078 (Refrigeration Equipment & Supplies). **Officers:** Arlis Biloff, President.

■ 14348 ■ R.D. Bitzer Company Inc.
1330 Willow Ave.
Elkins Park, PA 19027
Phone: (215)224-2112 **Fax:** (215)635-0615
Products: Heating and air conditioning systems. **SIC:** 5075 (Warm Air Heating & Air-Conditioning). **Est:** 1929. **Sales:** $14,000,000 (2000). **Emp:** 5. **Officers:** W.Q. Bitzer, CEO; John H. Bitzer Jr., President.

■ 14349 ■ Blu-Ridge Sales Inc.
11613 Busy St.
Richmond, VA 23236-4059
Phone: (804)379-2774
Products: Refrigeration equipment and supplies. **SIC:** 5078 (Refrigeration Equipment & Supplies). **Officers:** Richard Bishop, President.

■ 14350 ■ BMI Equipment Dist.
5431 Old Alexandria Tpke.
Warrenton, VA 20187
Phone: (540)341-4330
Free: (800)446-0275 **Fax:** (540)341-4300
Products: Commercial refrigeration equipment. **SIC:** 5078 (Refrigeration Equipment & Supplies). **Est:** 1972. **Sales:** $1,000,000 (2000). **Emp:** 8. **Officers:** William Miller, President; Bill Miller Jr., Vice President; Christopher Miller, Sales Mgr.

■ 14351 ■ Boat Electric Co. Inc.
2520 Westlake Ave. N
Seattle, WA 98109-2234
Phone: (206)281-7570 **Fax:** (425)251-7511
Products: Refrigeration equipment and supplies for marine industry. **SIC:** 5078 (Refrigeration Equipment & Supplies). **Officers:** W. Bunn, President.

■ 14352 ■ Boise Refrigeration Service Co.
202 W 39th St.
Boise, ID 83714-6404
Phone: (208)344-0709
Free: (800)464-0709 **Fax:** (208)344-4457
E-mail: freon01.@aol.com
URL: http://www.boiserefrigeration.com
Products: Commercial refrigeration equipment and supplies; Commercial reach-in and walk-in refrigerators. **SIC:** 5078 (Refrigeration Equipment & Supplies). **Est:** 1983. **Sales:** $2,000,000 (2000). **Emp:** 22. **Officers:** Ronald Hiatt, President.

■ 14353 ■ Boston Stove Co.
155 John St.
Reading, MA 01867
Phone: (617)944-1045
Products: Pre-fabricated fireplaces. **SIC:** 5074 (Plumbing & Hydronic Heating Supplies). **Est:** 1856. **Sales:** $2,000,000 (2000). **Emp:** 5. **Officers:** Earl D. Kaufman, President; Don Kaufman, CFO.

■ 14354 ■ Bowman Refrigeration Inc.
1135 NW 46th St.
Seattle, WA 98107-4633
Phone: (206)706-3033 **Fax:** (206)706-3034
E-mail: scott@bowmanrefrigeration.com
Products: Industrial refrigeration equipment. **SIC:** 5078 (Refrigeration Equipment & Supplies). **Est:** 1987. **Sales:** $1,000,000 (2000). **Emp:** 7. **Officers:** David Bowman, President.

■ 14355 ■ BP Products Inc.
4780 Beidler Rd.
Willoughby, OH 44094
Phones: (440)975-4300 800-272-8546
Fax: (440)942-4416
URL: http://www.paulinproducts.com
Products: Propane heaters and lanterns. **SIC:** 5074 (Plumbing & Hydronic Heating Supplies). **Est:** 1982. **Officers:** James Paulin, Sales Mgr.

■ 14356 ■ Brackett Supply Inc.
PO Box 669046
Charlotte, NC 28208
Phone: (704)393-7827 **Fax:** (704)393-3311
Products: Heating and air-conditioning parts. **SIC:** 5075 (Warm Air Heating & Air-Conditioning). **Officers:** Dennis Brackett.

■ 14357 ■ Thomas Brannon
PO Box 1049
Flint, MI 48501-1049
Phone: (810)235-1322 **Fax:** (810)233-5724
Products: Refrigeration equipment and supplies. **SIC:** 5078 (Refrigeration Equipment & Supplies). **Officers:** Thomas Brannon, Owner.

■ **14358** ■ **Brauer Supply Co.**
4260 Forest Park
St. Louis, MO 63108
Phone: (314)534-7150 **Fax:** (314)534-1816
Products: Heating and air conditioning equipment and supplies. **SIC:** 5033 (Roofing, Siding & Insulation). **Est:** 1881. **Sales:** $14,000,000 (2000). **Emp:** 55. **Officers:** Jim Truesdell, President.

■ **14359** ■ **Brock-McVey Co.**
1100 Brock McVey Dr.
PO Box 55487
Lexington, KY 40555
Phone: (606)255-1412 **Fax:** (606)233-4387
Products: Plumbing, heating, air-conditioning, and electrical supplies. **SICs:** 5078 (Refrigeration Equipment & Supplies); 5075 (Warm Air Heating & Air-Conditioning). **Est:** 1935. **Sales:** $14,000,000 (2000). **Emp:** 200. **Officers:** John M. McDonald III, President; Steve Ales, Controller; John McDonald IV, Exec. VP & General Mgr., e-mail: johnivbrothersckmcvey.com; Lincoln Patrick, Dir. of Data Processing.

■ **14360** ■ **Browning Metal Products Co.**
7700 N Harker Dr., No. B
Peoria, IL 61615-1852
Phone: (309)682-1015
Products: Ventilation products. **SIC:** 5075 (Warm Air Heating & Air-Conditioning). **Sales:** $25,000,000 (2000). **Emp:** 20. **Officers:** Sam Ansley, President; Craig Nickelbein, Sales Mgr.

■ **14361** ■ **Bob Brown's Heating & Air Conditioning**
2616 N C St.
Ft. Smith, AR 72901-3444
Phone: (501)783-0217
Products: Air conditioning units; Furnaces. **SIC:** 5075 (Warm Air Heating & Air-Conditioning). **Emp:** 6. **Officers:** Robert Brown, President.

■ **14362** ■ **BSW Inc.**
4680 E 2nd St., Ste. A
Benicia, CA 94510
Phone: (707)745-8175 **Fax:** (707)745-9708
Products: Wood stoves, barbeques, and fireplaces. **SIC:** 5074 (Plumbing & Hydronic Heating Supplies).

■ **14363** ■ **Burke Engineering Company Inc.**
PO Box 3427
El Monte, CA 91733
Phone: (626)579-6763 **Fax:** (626)579-1156
Products: Heating and air conditioning parts and supplies. **SICs:** 5075 (Warm Air Heating & Air-Conditioning); 5078 (Refrigeration Equipment & Supplies). **Est:** 1949. **Sales:** $34,000,000 (2000). **Emp:** 140. **Officers:** Gary W. Burke, President; Kelly M. Burke, VP of Finance; Brian Wolf, VP of Marketing & Sales; Mike W. Burke, VP of Operations; Trevor Garner, Dir of Human Resources.

■ **14364** ■ **Butcher Air Conditioning Co.**
101 Boyce Rd.
Broussard, LA 70518
Phone: (318)837-2000 **Fax:** (318)837-2069
Products: Air-conditioning and heating equipment and supplies. **SIC:** 5075 (Warm Air Heating & Air-Conditioning). **Est:** 1949. **Sales:** $8,000,000 (2000). **Emp:** 25. **Officers:** T.P. Butcher, President; Tim Barrett, Controller; Jessie P. Touchet, Dir. of Marketing & Sales.

■ **14365** ■ **Butler & Sons Refrigeration**
PO Box 336
Childersburg, AL 35044-0336
Phone: (205)378-3480 **Fax:** (205)378-3480
Products: Commercial refrigeration equipment and supplies; Commercial reach-in and walk-in refrigerators. **SIC:** 5078 (Refrigeration Equipment & Supplies). **Officers:** Walter Butler, President.

■ **14366** ■ **Camco Services Inc.**
PO Box 24
Oak Hill, WV 25901-0024
Phone: (304)469-6445 **Free:** (800)343-2665
Products: Refrigeration and air conditioning equipment; Heating equipment. **SICs:** 5078 (Refrigeration Equipment & Supplies); 5075 (Warm Air Heating & Air-Conditioning). **Officers:** David Coleman, President.

■ **14367** ■ **Carrier Corp./Bldg Sys and Svc Di**
PO Box 23130
Oakland, CA 94623
Phone: (510)769-6000 **Fax:** (510)635-4406
Products: HVAC equipment, sells and services air conditioners. **SIC:** 5075 (Warm Air Heating & Air-Conditioning).

■ **14368** ■ **Carrier North Carolina**
4300 Golf Acres Dr.
Charlotte, NC 28208
Phone: (704)394-7311
Free: (800)927-6154 **Fax:** (704)392-0979
Products: Heating and air-conditioning equipment, parts, and supplies. **SIC:** 5075 (Warm Air Heating & Air-Conditioning). **Est:** 1949. **Sales:** $92,000,000 (2000). **Emp:** 180. **Officers:** Phil Smith, Regional General Mgr.; Dave Benfer, Carrier Sales Mgr.; Danny Adams, Bryant Sales Mgr.; Harry Bufkin, Totaline Sales Mgr.; Ernie Hunt, VP & Sales Mgr.; Harry Bafkin, VP & Sales Mgr.; John Clark, VP & Credit Mgr. **Former Name:** Thermo Industries Inc.

■ **14369** ■ **Carroll Air Systems Inc.**
3711 W Walnut St.
Tampa, FL 33607
Phone: (813)879-5790 **Fax:** (813)874-9553
E-mail: rwerking@carrollair.com
URL: http://www.carrollair.com
Products: Industrial air-conditioning equipment. **SIC:** 5075 (Warm Air Heating & Air-Conditioning). **Est:** 1972. **Sales:** $10,000,000 (2000). **Emp:** 26. **Officers:** James Carroll, President; Phil Carroll, Vice President.

■ **14370** ■ **Stanley Castor**
1017 Rte. 12
Westmoreland, NH 03467-9711
Phone: (603)399-7737 **Fax:** (603)399-7737
Products: Commercial refrigeration equipment and supplies, including refrigerated fixtures. **SIC:** 5078 (Refrigeration Equipment & Supplies). **Officers:** Stanley Castor, Owner.

■ **14371** ■ **Cavallero Heating and Air Conditioning Inc.**
5541 Hwy. 50 E
Carson City, NV 89706
Phone: (702)883-2066
Products: Heaters; Air-conditioners. **SIC:** 5075 (Warm Air Heating & Air-Conditioning). **Est:** 1976. **Sales:** $8,000,000 (2000). **Emp:** 75. **Officers:** Ken Cavallero, President.

■ **14372** ■ **Celsco Inc.**
5620 N Western Ave.
Oklahoma City, OK 73118-4008
Phone: (405)840-6006 **Fax:** (405)840-6016
Products: Refrigeration equipment and supplies. **SIC:** 5078 (Refrigeration Equipment & Supplies). **Officers:** Joe Blake, President.

■ **14373** ■ **Central Air Conditioning Distributor**
121 Sweeten Creek Rd.
Asheville, NC 28803
Products: Heating and cooling equipment and supplies. **SIC:** 5075 (Warm Air Heating & Air-Conditioning).

■ **14374** ■ **Central Air Conditioning Distributors Inc.**
100 Clanton Rd.
Charlotte, NC 28217
Phone: (704)523-0306 **Fax:** (704)523-0380
Products: Air conditioning units and supplies. **SICs:** 5064 (Electrical Appliances—Television & Radio); 5075 (Warm Air Heating & Air-Conditioning).

■ **14375** ■ **Central Engineering & Supply Co.**
2422 Butler St.
Box 35907
Dallas, TX 75235
Phone: (214)951-0270 **Fax:** (214)637-0749
Products: Air-conditioning and refrigeration equipment; Industrial tools, equipment, and supplies. **SICs:** 5075 (Warm Air Heating & Air-Conditioning); 5085 (Industrial Supplies); 5078 (Refrigeration Equipment & Supplies).

■ **14376** ■ **Central Equipment Distributing Co.**
1120 N Vermont Ave.
Oklahoma City, OK 73107-5008
Phone: (405)947-7867
Free: (800)522-6673 **Fax:** (405)947-7974
Products: Electrical appliances, including heating and air-conditioning equipment. **SIC:** 5064 (Electrical Appliances—Television & Radio). **Officers:** John Samara, President.

■ **14377** ■ **Central Plains Distributing Inc.**
13202 I St.
Omaha, NE 68137
Free: (800)779-8299 **Fax:** (402)334-1289
Products: Heating and air-conditioning equipment. **SIC:** 5075 (Warm Air Heating & Air-Conditioning).

■ **14378** ■ **Central VA Chimney**
Rte. 2, Box 253
Dillwyn, VA 23936
Phone: (804)983-2988
Products: Stainless steel chimney materials. **SIC:** 5074 (Plumbing & Hydronic Heating Supplies).

■ **14379** ■ **Century Air Conditioning and Maintenance Supply, Inc.**
1750 Enterprise Way
Marietta, GA 30067
Phone: (770)933-8833
Products: Air conditioning supplies. **SIC:** 5075 (Warm Air Heating & Air-Conditioning).

■ **14380** ■ **Century Air Conditioning Supply Inc.**
5381 Gulfton St.
Houston, TX 77081
Phone: (713)663-6661
Products: Air-conditioning equipment. **SIC:** 5075 (Warm Air Heating & Air-Conditioning).

■ **14381** ■ **Champion Distributors Inc.**
PO Box 691
Lecompte, LA 71346-0691
Phone: (318)776-5011
Products: Refrigeration equipment and supplies; Commercial refrigeration equipment. **SIC:** 5078 (Refrigeration Equipment & Supplies). **Officers:** Mac Bennett, President.

■ **14382** ■ **Chase Supply Co.**
12431 Vincennes Rd.
Blue Island, IL 60406-1640
Phone: (773)785-0500
Products: Heating and air-conditioning equipment. **SICs:** 5075 (Warm Air Heating & Air-Conditioning); 5074 (Plumbing & Hydronic Heating Supplies).

■ **14383** ■ **Chicago Furnace Supply Inc.**
4929 S Lincoln
Lisle, IL 60532
Phone: (708)971-0400 **Fax:** (708)971-0255
Products: Furnaces. **SICs:** 5074 (Plumbing & Hydronic Heating Supplies); 5075 (Warm Air Heating & Air-Conditioning). **Est:** 1901. **Sales:** $99,000,000 (2000). **Emp:** 25. **Officers:** Robert A. Lorenz, President; Richard R. Lorenz, Vice President.

■ **14384** ■ **Clarks Distributing Co.**
PO Box 33294
Charlotte, NC 28233
Phone: (704)375-4456 **Fax:** (704)375-0918
Products: Heating and air-conditioning equipment; Gas grills. **SICs:** 5075 (Warm Air Heating & Air-Conditioning); 5064 (Electrical Appliances—Television & Radio).

■ **14385** ■ **Climate Technologies**
43334 W 7 Mile Rd.
Northville, MI 48167-2280
Phone: (248)380-2020 **Fax:** (248)380-2025
E-mail: climatetechnologies@ameritech.net
Products: Commercial and industrial heating and air conditioning equipment. **SIC:** 5074 (Plumbing & Hydronic Heating Supplies). **Sales:** $5,000,000 (2000). **Emp:** 14. **Officers:** Walter Zimmerman, President.

■ 14386 ■ Climatic Control Company Inc.
5061 W State St.
Milwaukee, WI 53208
Phone: (414)259-9070
Free: (800)242-1656 **Fax:** (414)259-0613
E-mail: info@climaticcontrol.com
URL: http://www.climaticcontrol.com
Products: Heating and air conditioning controls, equipment and supplies. **SIC:** 5075 (Warm Air Heating & Air-Conditioning). **Est:** 1964. **Sales:** $12,000,000 (1999). **Emp:** 64. **Officers:** Larry L. Rector, President & CEO; Ron Mackiewicz, VP of Sales & Merchandising; Don Gall, Marketing Mgr.; Don St. Martin, VP of Operations.

■ 14387 ■ Climatic Corp.
PO Box 25189
Columbia, SC 29224-5189
Phone: (803)736-7770 **Fax:** (803)736-7841
Products: Air conditioning units; Heat units. **SICs:** 5064 (Electrical Appliances—Television & Radio); 5075 (Warm Air Heating & Air-Conditioning). **Est:** 1956. **Sales:** $95,000,000 (2000). **Emp:** 140. **Officers:** John H. Bailey, CEO & President; Richard F. Smith, Exec. VP; Roger Longnecker, Dir. of Marketing; William Hagen, Dir. of Systems; Cindee Baley.

■ 14388 ■ Coastal Supply Company Inc.
407 Harmon St.
Savannah, GA 31401
Phone: (912)233-9621
Products: Heating units; Air conditioning units; Heater parts; Air conditioning parts. **SIC:** 5075 (Warm Air Heating & Air-Conditioning). **Est:** 1961. **Sales:** $12,000,000 (2000). **Emp:** 55. **Officers:** Ralph O. Kessler, CEO; B. Stenger, CFO.

■ 14389 ■ Coastline Distributing
4120 NW 10th Ave.
Oakland Park, FL 33309-4601
Phone: (954)776-4811 **Fax:** (954)772-4818
Products: Air-conditioning equipment. **SICs:** 5075 (Warm Air Heating & Air-Conditioning); 5085 (Industrial Supplies). **Emp:** 15. **Officers:** Dan Pawlusiak, General Mgr.

■ 14390 ■ Coastline Distribution Inc.
601 Codisco Way
Sanford, FL 32771
Phone: (407)323-8500 **Fax:** (407)330-9488
Products: Heating and air-conditioning equipment and supplies. **SIC:** 5075 (Warm Air Heating & Air-Conditioning). **Est:** 1958. **Sales:** $71,000,000 (2000). **Emp:** 200. **Officers:** Mark Nelles, President; James Walker, VP & CFO.

■ 14391 ■ Cochrane Supply and Engineering, Inc.
30303 Stephenson Hwy.
Madison Heights, MI 48071-1633
Phone: (248)588-9260
Free: (800)482-4894 **Fax:** (248)588-9261
URL: http://www.cochranesupply.com
Products: HVAC accessories, including temperature controls and control systems. **SICs:** 5075 (Warm Air Heating & Air-Conditioning); 5078 (Refrigeration Equipment & Supplies). **Est:** 1967. **Sales:** $9,000,000 (2000). **Emp:** 30. **Officers:** Donald J. Cochrane, President; Scott Cochrane, Vice President; Don Cochrane Jr., Treasurer, e-mail: pziemba@cochranesupply.com; Jim Vanootighem, e-mail: jvanootighem@cochranesupply.com; Calvin Odom, e-mail: codom@cochranesupply.com.

■ 14392 ■ Colorado Commercial Refrigeration
12445 Mead Way
Littleton, CO 80125-9759
Phone: (303)791-7878 **Fax:** (303)791-7881
Products: Refrigeration equipment and supplies. **SIC:** 5078 (Refrigeration Equipment & Supplies). **Est:** 1982. **Emp:** 10. **Officers:** Nelson Rolph, President.

■ 14393 ■ Columbia Pipe and Supply
1120 W Pershing Rd.
Chicago, IL 60609
Phone: (312)927-6600 **Fax:** (312)927-8415
E-mail: columbiapipe.com
Products: Pipes; Valves and fittings; Heating and air conditioning units; Plumbing supplies; Milling supplies.

SICs: 5074 (Plumbing & Hydronic Heating Supplies); 5075 (Warm Air Heating & Air-Conditioning); 5085 (Industrial Supplies). **Est:** 1935. **Sales:** $50,000,000 (2000). **Emp:** 187. **Officers:** W.D. Arenberg, President; J.S. Harrison, Treasurer; T.P. Arenberg, Exec. VP of Marketing.

■ 14394 ■ Comfort Mart Dist. Inc.
520 Congress St.
Troy, NY 12180
Phone: (518)272-2022 **Fax:** (518)272-5498
Products: Heating, ventilation, and air conditioning parts and equipment. **SIC:** 5075 (Warm Air Heating & Air-Conditioning). **Est:** 1973. **Officers:** Judith Lapides, President; Irwin M. Lapides, Vice President.

■ 14395 ■ Comfort Supply Inc.
3500 S Hoover Rd.
Wichita, KS 67215
Phone: (316)945-8268
Products: Heating and cooling supplies. **SICs:** 5075 (Warm Air Heating & Air-Conditioning); 5074 (Plumbing & Hydronic Heating Supplies). **Est:** 1967. **Sales:** $5,000,000 (2000). **Emp:** 32. **Officers:** Herb Cundiff, President.

■ 14396 ■ Comfort Supply Inc.
PO Box 262806
Houston, TX 77207
Phone: (713)845-4705
Free: (800)856-7511 **Fax:** (713)466-4534
Products: Air-conditioners. **SIC:** 5075 (Warm Air Heating & Air-Conditioning). **Est:** 1981. **Sales:** $23,000,000 (2000). **Emp:** 100. **Officers:** Don Huslage, President.

■ 14397 ■ Comfortmaker Distribution
601 Codisco Way
Sanford, FL 32771
Phone: (407)323-8500
Products: Air conditioning supplies. **SIC:** 5075 (Warm Air Heating & Air-Conditioning). **Officers:** Mark Nelles, President.

■ 14398 ■ Commercial Equipment & Design, Inc.
904 E 16th St.
Wilmington, DE 19802
Phone: (302)656-7752
Free: (800)220-4048 **Fax:** (302)656-7798
URL: http://www.restaurantequip.baweb.com
Products: Refrigeration equipment and supplies for restaurants, taverns, pizza shops, markets, clubs, caterers, bakeries, delis, nursing homes, and church kitchens. **SIC:** 5078 (Refrigeration Equipment & Supplies). **Est:** 1992. **Emp:** 12. **Officers:** Eugene Blaine, Sales Mgr.

■ 14399 ■ Commercial Refrigeration Inc.
15870 Yoder Ave.
Caldwell, ID 83605-8342
Phone: (208)454-3031 **Fax:** (208)459-7695
Products: Refrigeration equipment and supplies. **SIC:** 5078 (Refrigeration Equipment & Supplies). **Officers:** Leonard Holst, President.

■ 14400 ■ Lyon Conklin and Company Inc.
2101 Race St.
Baltimore, MD 21230
Phone: (410)752-6800 **Fax:** (410)252-3201
Products: Heaters and air-conditioners. **SICs:** 5051 (Metals Service Centers & Offices); 5075 (Warm Air Heating & Air-Conditioning); 5074 (Plumbing & Hydronic Heating Supplies). **Est:** 1860. **Sales:** $90,000,000 (2000). **Emp:** 200. **Officers:** Jenny Allen, President; R.D. Bossle, Vice President.

■ 14401 ■ Continental Equipment Co.
2309 N Hullen St.
Metairie, LA 70001-1930
Phone: (504)835-5151
Free: (888)405-5151 **Fax:** (504)835-5199
URL: http://www.continentalequipment.net
Products: Refrigeration equipment and supplies; Refrigerated beverage dispensers; Food service equipment and supplies; Cooking equipment; Restaurant layout and design. **SIC:** 5078 (Refrigeration Equipment & Supplies). **Est:** 1975. **Sales:** $5,000,000

(2000). **Emp:** 21. **Officers:** Alan Shear, Owner, e-mail: ashear@continentalequipment.net.

■ 14402 ■ Control-Equip of Tennessee, Inc.
2044 E Magnolia Ave.
Knoxville, TN 37917-8026
Phone: (865)522-5656
Free: (800)567-4822 **Fax:** (865)523-8944
Products: Main control lines. **SIC:** 5078 (Refrigeration Equipment & Supplies). **Est:** 1987. **Sales:** $500,000 (2000). **Emp:** 3. **Officers:** Cleveland Moffett, President; Alexander Wade, Vice President. **Former Name:** Tennessee Control-Equip Inc.

■ 14403 ■ Convoy Servicing Co. Inc.
3323 Jane Ln.
Dallas, TX 75247
Phone: (214)638-3053 **Fax:** (214)638-4620
Products: Transport refrigeration units. **SIC:** 5078 (Refrigeration Equipment & Supplies). **Sales:** $10,000,000 (2000). **Emp:** 75. **Officers:** William Niseman, President.

■ 14404 ■ Cooling & Heating Inc.
70 Eglin Pkwy. NE
Ft. Walton Beach, FL 32548-4957
Phone: (850)244-6161 **Fax:** (850)664-0079
Products: Refrigeration and air conditioning equipment; Heating equipment; Electrical equipment and supplies; Metal sheets. **SICs:** 5075 (Warm Air Heating & Air-Conditioning); 5078 (Refrigeration Equipment & Supplies); 5063 (Electrical Apparatus & Equipment); 5051 (Metals Service Centers & Offices). **Est:** 1964. **Sales:** $1,000,000 (1999). **Emp:** 6. **Officers:** John Mark Gibson; Christianne Gibson; Lester A. Malone, Sales & Marketing Contact.

■ 14405 ■ Corken Steel Products Co.
PO Box 2650
Covington, KY 41012
Phone: (606)291-4664 **Fax:** (606)261-2665
Products: Heating and air-conditioning equipment and supplies. **SICs:** 5075 (Warm Air Heating & Air-Conditioning); 5033 (Roofing, Siding & Insulation). **Est:** 1955. **Sales:** $14,000,000 (2000). **Emp:** 75. **Officers:** D.I. Corken, President; D. Corken Jr., Treasurer; Richard C. Bucher Jr., Dir. of Marketing & Sales; Jeffrey S. Corken, Dir. of Data Processing.

■ 14406 ■ Cornforths
5625 N 7th St.
Phoenix, AZ 85014-2505
Phone: (602)277-6855 **Fax:** (602)277-7340
Products: Refrigeration equipment and supplies, including automotive refrigeration. **SIC:** 5078 (Refrigeration Equipment & Supplies). **Est:** 1948. **Emp:** 10. **Officers:** Wayne Cornofrth, President.

■ 14407 ■ Cosco Inc.
1369 Colburn St.
Honolulu, HI 96817
Phone: (808)845-2234
Free: (800)262-9399 **Fax:** (808)842-1736
Products: Refrigeration and air conditioning equipment and supplies. **SICs:** 5078 (Refrigeration Equipment & Supplies); 5075 (Warm Air Heating & Air-Conditioning). **Est:** 1961. **Sales:** $5,000,000 (2000). **Emp:** 20. **Officers:** Roberta Cosco, President. **Doing Business As:** Cosco Supply.

■ 14408 ■ Crystal Refrigeration Inc.
710 E 59th St.
Davenport, IA 52807-2627
Phone: (319)386-1000 **Fax:** (319)386-0088
Products: Refrigeration equipment and supplies; Food service equipment; Ice cream equipment. **SICs:** 5078 (Refrigeration Equipment & Supplies); 5046 (Commercial Equipment Nec). **Est:** 1986. **Sales:** $4,000,000 (2000). **Emp:** 17. **Officers:** Phillip Taylor, President.

■ 14409 ■ D & D Transport Refrigeration Services
PO Box 30737
Billings, MT 59107-0737
Phone: (406)656-6290
Free: (800)826-7161 **Fax:** (406)656-9943
Products: Refrigeration equipment and supplies; Refrigeration units for motor vehicles. **SIC:** 5078

(Refrigeration Equipment & Supplies). **Officers:** William Davies, President.

■ 14410 ■ Dakota Refrigeration Inc.
515 19th St. N
Fargo, ND 58102-4133
Phone: (701)235-9698 **Fax:** (701)235-5207
Products: Commercial refrigeration equipment and supplies. **SIC:** 5078 (Refrigeration Equipment & Supplies). **Officers:** James Kempel, President.

■ 14411 ■ Dales Mechanical Sales & Service
1701 E Main St.
Van Buren, AR 72956-4736
Phone: (501)474-6844
Products: Electric heating furnaces; Air-conditioning equipment; Plumbing fixtures, equipment, and supplies. **SICs:** 5075 (Warm Air Heating & Air-Conditioning); 5074 (Plumbing & Hydronic Heating Supplies). **Officers:** Lester Beckham, President.

■ 14412 ■ Dalton Supply Co. Inc.
PO Box 1246
Dalton, GA 30722-1246
Phone: (706)278-1264
Products: Plumbing, heating, and electrical supplies. **SICs:** 5074 (Plumbing & Hydronic Heating Supplies); 5075 (Warm Air Heating & Air-Conditioning); 5063 (Electrical Apparatus & Equipment). **Est:** 1940. **Sales:** $4,000,000 (1999). **Emp:** 15. **Officers:** Norman McCoy, President.

■ 14413 ■ Defreeze Corp.
20 Deerfoot Rd.
Southborough, MA 01772
Phone: (508)485-8512
Products: Commercial freezers; Fish processing equipment. **SICs:** 5064 (Electrical Appliances—Television & Radio); 5087 (Service Establishment Equipment). **Sales:** $500,000 (1992). **Emp:** 5. **Officers:** Alan Bezanson, President.

■ 14414 ■ M & T DeMar Inc.
4237 E University Dr.
Phoenix, AZ 85034-7315
Phone: (602)437-8002
Free: (800)279-8002 **Fax:** (602)437-8290
Products: Refrigeration equipment and supplies; Refrigerated beverage dispensers; Ice cream and yogurt machines; Ice makers. **SIC:** 5078 (Refrigeration Equipment & Supplies). **Officers:** Mark De Mar, President; Jeff Hawken, Dir. of Mktg. & Sales, e-mail: sales@americanbev.com.

■ 14415 ■ Dennis Refrigeration & Electric
23850 W 102nd Ter.
Shawnee Mission, KS 66227-4626
Phone: (913)764-6232 **Fax:** (913)764-2078
Products: Industrial refrigeration equipment; Construction and fabrication equipment. **SICs:** 5078 (Refrigeration Equipment & Supplies); 5039 (Construction Materials Nec). **Est:** 1973. **Emp:** 8. **Officers:** Dennis Harrington, Owner.

■ 14416 ■ Dennis Supply Co.
PO Box 3376
Sioux City, IA 51102
Phone: (712)255-7637
Products: Heating and refrigeration equipment. **SICs:** 5075 (Warm Air Heating & Air-Conditioning); 5078 (Refrigeration Equipment & Supplies). **Est:** 1936. **Sales:** $5,000,000 (2000). **Emp:** 40. **Officers:** Carter R. Dennis, CEO.

■ 14417 ■ DESA International Inc.
PO Box 90004
Bowling Green, KY 42102
Phone: (502)781-9600 **Fax:** (502)781-9400
Products: Warm air heating and cooling equipment; Chain saws; Dehumidifiers. **SICs:** 5075 (Warm Air Heating & Air-Conditioning); 5084 (Industrial Machinery & Equipment).

■ 14418 ■ Design Air
PO Box 39
Kimberly, WI 54136
Phone: (920)739-7005
Products: Heating and air-conditioning supplies. **SICs:**

5075 (Warm Air Heating & Air-Conditioning); 5074 (Plumbing & Hydronic Heating Supplies).

■ 14419 ■ Dey Distributing
1418 N Irwin Ave.
Green Bay, WI 54302-1614
Phone: (920)437-7022
Free: (800)397-4339 **Fax:** 800-728-3394
Products: Appliance parts; Furnaces and central air equipment; Gas grills. **SICs:** 5064 (Electrical Appliances—Television & Radio); 5075 (Warm Air Heating & Air-Conditioning). **Emp:** 6. **Officers:** John DeJardin.

■ 14420 ■ Dickson CC Co.
2100 Sigman Rd. NW
Conyers, GA 30012
Phone: (770)388-7373
Products: Air conditioning supply and parts. **SIC:** 5075 (Warm Air Heating & Air-Conditioning).

■ 14421 ■ Dickson CC Co.
1050 Industrial Park Dr.
Marietta, GA 30062
Phone: (770)425-0121
Products: Air conditioning supply and parts. **SIC:** 5075 (Warm Air Heating & Air-Conditioning).

■ 14422 ■ C.C. Dickson Co.
927 East Blvd.
Charlotte, NC 28203
Phone: (704)372-2604
Products: Heating and air-conditioning systems. **SICs:** 5075 (Warm Air Heating & Air-Conditioning); 5078 (Refrigeration Equipment & Supplies); 5074 (Plumbing & Hydronic Heating Supplies). **Sales:** $97,000,000 (2000). **Emp:** 416. **Officers:** C.C. Dickson Jr., President.

■ 14423 ■ Dugan Equipment & Supply Co.
PO Box 3040
Kansas City, KS 66103-0040
Phone: (913)236-4060
Free: (800)373-4061 **Fax:** (913)236-5231
Products: Refrigeration equipment, including commercial refrigerators. **SIC:** 5078 (Refrigeration Equipment & Supplies). **Est:** 1954. **Sales:** $3,000,000 (2000). **Emp:** 20. **Officers:** Robert Dugan, President.

■ 14424 ■ Duncan Supply Co. Inc.
910 N Illinois St.
Indianapolis, IN 46204
Phone: (317)634-1335
Free: (800)382-5528 **Fax:** (317)264-6689
URL: http://www.duncansupply.com
Products: Furnaces; Air-conditioners; Ice machines; Compressors. **SIC:** 5075 (Warm Air Heating & Air-Conditioning). **Est:** 1936. **Sales:** $22,000,000 (1999). **Emp:** 95. **Officers:** Rick Fine, President, e-mail: rickfine@duncansupply.com; Steven R. Pluckebaum, Controller, e-mail: stevenrpluckebaum@duncansupply.com; Tim Hunter, Vice President, e-mail: timhunter@duncansupply.com; Randy Roberson, Sales Mgr., e-mail: randyroberson@duncansupply.com.

■ 14425 ■ Earth Energy Technology and Supply Inc.
PO Box 219
Marietta, OK 73448
Phone: (405)276-9455 **Fax:** (405)276-9459
Products: Ground source heat pump supplies. **SIC:** 5075 (Warm Air Heating & Air-Conditioning). **Est:** 1988. **Sales:** $3,000,000 (2000). **Emp:** 12. **Officers:** Charles Young, President; Cathy Ershadi, Controller.

■ 14426 ■ Eastern Refrigeration Co.
275 Old Hartford Rd.
Colchester, CT 06415-0298
Phone: (860)859-0016
Products: Refrigeration equipment and supplies. **SIC:** 5078 (Refrigeration Equipment & Supplies). **Officers:** Pierre Belisle, President.

■ 14427 ■ Ecology Detergents Inc.
237 West Ave.
Stamford, CT 06902-5512
Phone: (203)324-0030 **Fax:** (203)356-9143
Products: Commercial refrigeration equipment,

including reach-in and walk-in refrigerators. **SIC:** 5078 (Refrigeration Equipment & Supplies). **Officers:** William Smith, President.

■ 14428 ■ ECS Marketing Services Inc.
PO Box 70189
Bellevue, WA 98007-0189
Phone: (425)883-3420 **Fax:** (425)883-9247
Products: Ventilation equipment. **SIC:** 5075 (Warm Air Heating & Air-Conditioning). **Est:** 1975. **Sales:** $6,000,000 (2000). **Emp:** 9. **Officers:** Donald Sundene, President.

■ 14429 ■ EDS Refrigeration Inc.
2920 Girard Blvd. NE
Albuquerque, NM 87107-1935
Phone: (505)884-0085 **Fax:** (505)884-0939
Products: Refrigeration equipment and supplies, including ice machines and resturant equipment. **SICs:** 5078 (Refrigeration Equipment & Supplies); 5046 (Commercial Equipment Nec). **Officers:** Edmond Paques, President.

■ 14430 ■ T.F. Ehrhart Co.
600 York St.
Quincy, IL 62306
Phone: (217)222-9103 **Fax:** (217)228-1788
Products: Air-conditioning and heating equipment. **SIC:** 5075 (Warm Air Heating & Air-Conditioning).

■ 14431 ■ Elixir Industries
17925 S Broadway
Gardena, CA 90248
Phone: (213)321-1191
Free: (800)421-1942 **Fax:** (310)323-1467
Products: Ventilating equipment and supplies. **SIC:** 5075 (Warm Air Heating & Air-Conditioning). **Est:** 1948. **Emp:** 500. **Officers:** Dave Whitt, President; Hoss Rassouli, Vice President; Steve Solomon, VP of Finance; Tom Martin, Corp. OEM. Sales & Mkt. Mgr.; Stanley Lipsey, Corp. Aftermarket Sales & Mkt. Mgr.

■ 14432 ■ Energy International Corp.
22226 Garrison St.
Dearborn, MI 48124-2208
Phone: (313)563-8000 **Fax:** (313)563-8001
E-mail: eicusa@ix.netcom.com
URL: http://www.energyintl.com
Products: Heating, air-conditioning, and ventilation equipment. **SICs:** 5063 (Electrical Apparatus & Equipment); 5074 (Plumbing & Hydronic Heating Supplies). **Est:** 1978. **Sales:** $12,000,000 (1999). **Emp:** 20. **Officers:** Ned M. Fawaz, President.

■ 14433 ■ Energy Plus
4811 Miller Trunk Hwy.
Duluth, MN 55811
Phone: (218)722-7818 **Fax:** (218)722-2146
Products: Chimneys, wood stoves, and fireplaces. **SIC:** 5074 (Plumbing & Hydronic Heating Supplies).

■ 14434 ■ EPPSCO Supply
6914 Industrial Ave.
El Paso, TX 79915-1108
Phone: (915)779-4800
Products: Air-conditioners; Heaters. **SICs:** 5075 (Warm Air Heating & Air-Conditioning); 5074 (Plumbing & Hydronic Heating Supplies). **Est:** 1906. **Sales:** $30,000,000 (2000). **Emp:** 90. **Officers:** M.P. Pelt, President; Robert Beckoff, CFO.

■ 14435 ■ Equipment Sales Corp.
703 Western Dr.
Mobile, AL 36607
Phone: (205)476-2220 **Fax:** (205)471-5602
Products: Air-conditioning equipment. **SIC:** 5075 (Warm Air Heating & Air-Conditioning). **Est:** 1951. **Sales:** $16,000,000 (2000). **Emp:** 45. **Officers:** Frank Raue Sr., President; Frank Raue Jr., Treasurer; H.L. Hughes Jr., Secretary.

■ 14436 ■ Evans Inc.
218 Pennsylvania Ave.
Virginia Beach, VA 23462-2514
Phone: (757)399-3044
Free: (800)446-8007 **Fax:** (757)393-4350
Products: Heating, ventilation, and air-conditioning parts; Appliance parts. **SICs:** 5075 (Warm Air Heating & Air-Conditioning); 5074 (Plumbing & Hydronic

Heating Supplies); 5063 (Electrical Apparatus & Equipment). **Est:** 1952. **Emp:** 51. **Officers:** Dan Evans, President; George E. Evans, VP of Sales.

■ 14437 ■ **Excelsior Manufacturing and Supply**
1465 E Industrial Dr.
Itasca, IL 60143
Phone: (708)773-5500 **Fax:** (708)773-5542
Products: Heating and air-conditioning equipment, including registers and shoe metal. **SICs:** 5074 (Plumbing & Hydronic Heating Supplies); 5074 (Plumbing & Hydronic Heating Supplies); 5075 (Warm Air Heating & Air-Conditioning). **Est:** 1886. **Sales:** $33,000,000 (2000). **Emp:** 200. **Officers:** John Brady, President & Treasurer.

■ 14438 ■ **Fabricated Systems of Atlanta**
4620 S Atlanta Rd. SE
Smyrna, GA 30080
Phone: (404)792-1696
Products: Air conditioning supply and parts. **SIC:** 5075 (Warm Air Heating & Air-Conditioning).

■ 14439 ■ **Fadson International Company**
PO Box 23036
Richfield, MN 55423
Phone: (612)861-7480 **Fax:** (612)888-7720
Products: Air-conditioning equipment; Electronic equipment; Food processing and packaging equipment; Medical equipment and supplies; Pollution control equipment. **SICs:** 5075 (Warm Air Heating & Air-Conditioning); 5047 (Medical & Hospital Equipment); 5065 (Electronic Parts & Equipment Nec); 5084 (Industrial Machinery & Equipment). **Officers:** Akin Fadamitan, Export Manager.

■ 14440 ■ **Fairfax Trailer Sales Inc.**
170 E Alton Ave.
East Alton, IL 62024
Phone: (618)254-7411 **Fax:** (618)251-4004
Products: Tubs; Showers; Furnaces; Siding; Air-conditioning units. **SICs:** 5039 (Construction Materials Nec); 5074 (Plumbing & Hydronic Heating Supplies); 5075 (Warm Air Heating & Air-Conditioning); 5033 (Roofing, Siding & Insulation). **Est:** 1958. **Sales:** $6,000,000 (2000). **Emp:** 25. **Officers:** Mike Howard, President; Cheryl Tilton, Controller; Tyler Mitchell, Dir. of Marketing & Sales; Cynthia Reames, Dir. of Data Processing.

■ 14441 ■ **Falgouts Refrigeration & Appliance Service**
PO Box 10206, Sta. 1
Houma, LA 70363-0206
Phone: (504)873-8460 **Fax:** (504)873-8498
Products: Commercial refrigeration equipment and supplies, including refrigerated fixtures. **SIC:** 5078 (Refrigeration Equipment & Supplies). **Est:** 1976. **Officers:** Peter Falgout, President.

■ 14442 ■ **Famous Enterprises Inc.**
PO Box 1889
Akron, OH 44309
Phone: (216)762-9621 **Fax:** (216)762-0510
Products: Room air conditioners and dehumidifiers; Plumbing fixtures, equipment, and supplies; Cabinets. **SICs:** 5085 (Industrial Supplies); 5074 (Plumbing & Hydronic Heating Supplies); 5065 (Electronic Parts & Equipment Nec). **Est:** 1933. **Sales:** $120,000,000 (2000). **Emp:** 650. **Officers:** Jay Blaushild, President; Mark Wiseman, Vice President; Marc Blaushield, Vice President; Dale Newman, Vice President.

■ 14443 ■ **Federal Corp.**
PO Box 26408
Oklahoma City, OK 73126
Phone: (405)239-7301
Free: (800)289-3331 **Fax:** (405)232-5438
E-mail: salesokc@federalcorp.com
URL: http://www.federalcorp.com
Products: Heating and air conditioning supplies. **SICs:** 5075 (Warm Air Heating & Air-Conditioning); 5074 (Plumbing & Hydronic Heating Supplies). **Est:** 1918. **Sales:** $8,000,000 (2000). **Emp:** 40. **Officers:** Alan Loeffler, President; Donald Ray, CFO; Virginia McFarland, Sales/Marketing Contact, e-mail: vmcfarland@federalcorp.com; Phil Ferguson, Customer Service Contact, e-mail: pferguson@

federalcorp.com; Margaret Watral, Human Resources Contact, e-mail: mwatral@federalcorp.com.

■ 14444 ■ **Ferguson Enterprises Inc.**
6525 E 42nd St.
Tulsa, OK 74145-4611
Phone: (918)628-1500 **Fax:** (918)628-1314
E-mail: fei.tulsa088@ferguson.com
URL: http://www.ferguson.com
Products: Plumbing supplies; Waterworks. **SICs:** 5075 (Warm Air Heating & Air-Conditioning); 5074 (Plumbing & Hydronic Heating Supplies). **Est:** 1953. **Emp:** 28. **Officers:** Anthony Dixon.

■ 14445 ■ **Ferguson Enterprises, Inc.**
PO Box 2778
Newport News, VA 23609-0778
Phone: (757)874-7795 **Fax:** (757)989-2501
URL: http://www.ferguson.com
Products: HVAC; Plumbing; Underground; Industrial PVF; Light fixtures; Sinks; Faucets; Tubs. **SIC:** 5074 (Plumbing & Hydronic Heating Supplies). **Est:** 1953. **Sales:** $3,000,000,000 (2000). **Emp:** 9,500. **Officers:** Charles A. Banks, CEO; Stewart P. Mitchell, VP & CFO; Claude Hornsby, Sr. VP of Branch Operations; Mike Grunkemeyer, Sr. VP of Business Development; John Garrett, Sr. VP of Logistics.

■ 14446 ■ **Ferguson Enterprises Inc.**
250 Long Rd.
King of Prussia, PA 19406-3099
Phone: (215)354-0575
Products: Heating and cooling equipment; Plumbing equipment. **SICs:** 5075 (Warm Air Heating & Air-Conditioning); 5074 (Plumbing & Hydronic Heating Supplies).

■ 14447 ■ **Fireplace Industries Inc.**
4386 S Federal Blvd.
Englewood, CO 80110-5311
Phone: (303)825-8600 **Fax:** (303)825-9145
Products: Gas fireplaces, gas logs, and glass fireplace doors. **SIC:** 5074 (Plumbing & Hydronic Heating Supplies). **Est:** 1973. **Sales:** $3,800,000 (2000). **Emp:** 21. **Officers:** C. Larry Grinage, President.

■ 14448 ■ **Fireside Distributors**
4013 Atlantic Ave.
PO Box 41226
Raleigh, NC 27629-1226
Phone: (919)872-4434 **Fax:** (919)327-0031
Products: Fireside equipment, including gas logs, piping, and chimney sweep supplies. **SICs:** 5074 (Plumbing & Hydronic Heating Supplies); 5099 (Durable Goods Nec). **Est:** 1965.

■ 14449 ■ **Fireside Distributors of Oregon, Inc.**
18389 SW Boones Ferry Rd.
Portland, OR 97224
Phone: (503)684-8535 **Fax:** (503)620-5699
Products: Fireplace products and supplies. **SIC:** 5074 (Plumbing & Hydronic Heating Supplies).

■ 14450 ■ **J.S. Fleming Associates Inc.**
28 Lord Rd.
Marlborough, MA 01752-4548
Phone: (508)460-0904 **Fax:** (508)460-0909
Products: Air-conditioning equipment; Air-conditioning room units, self-contained. **SICs:** 5064 (Electrical Appliances—Television & Radio); 5075 (Warm Air Heating & Air-Conditioning). **Officers:** Joseph Fleming, President.

■ 14451 ■ **Fountain Dispensers Co. Inc.**
35 Greenwich St.
Providence, RI 02907-2534
Phone: (401)461-8400 **Fax:** (401)461-8462
E-mail: fodico@aol.com
Products: Refrigeration equipment and supplies; Air cleaners; Ice machines. **SIC:** 5078 (Refrigeration Equipment & Supplies). **Est:** 1960. **Sales:** $900,000 (1999). **Emp:** 6. **Officers:** Francis W. Marceau, President.

■ 14452 ■ **Freeman Corp.**
11103 Ripley Ct.
Boise, ID 83704
Phone: (208)376-4341
Products: Refrigerator repair equipment. **SIC:** 5078

(Refrigeration Equipment & Supplies). **Officers:** Verlin Freeman, President.

■ 14453 ■ **French Refrigeration Co.**
RR 1, Box 241
Norway, ME 04268-9709
Phone: (207)743-6573
Products: Refrigeration equipment and supplies for offices, restaurants, and institutions. **SIC:** 5078 (Refrigeration Equipment & Supplies). **Officers:** Clarence French, Owner.

■ 14454 ■ **Furnace & Duct Supply Co.**
635 Elmwood Ave.
Providence, RI 02907
Phone: (401)941-3800 **Fax:** (401)941-3839
Products: Heating and cooling supplies. **SIC:** 5075 (Warm Air Heating & Air-Conditioning).

■ 14455 ■ **Gartner Refrigeration Inc.**
2331 W Superior St.
Duluth, MN 55806-1931
Phone: (218)722-4439
Free: (800)777-8515 **Fax:** (218)722-3422
Products: Refrigeration equipment and supplies. **SIC:** 5078 (Refrigeration Equipment & Supplies). **Officers:** Jack Gartner, President.

■ 14456 ■ **Carlton J. Gaskins**
357 W Main St.
Lake City, SC 29560-2315
Phone: (803)394-8830 **Fax:** (803)389-2778
Products: Refrigeration equipment and supplies. **SIC:** 5078 (Refrigeration Equipment & Supplies). **Officers:** Carlton Gaskins, Owner.

■ 14457 ■ **Geary Pacific Corp.**
1908 N Enterprise St.
Orange, CA 92865
Phone: (714)279-2950 **Fax:** (714)279-2940
Products: Heating, venting, and air conditioning equipment and supplies. **SIC:** 5075 (Warm Air Heating & Air-Conditioning). **Est:** 1961. **Emp:** 80. **Officers:** Pat Geary, President; Ken Abbott, VP & Controller.

■ 14458 ■ **Gemaire Distributors Inc.**
2151 W Hillsboro Blvd., Ste. 400
Deerfield Beach, FL 33442
Free: (800)226-2665 **Fax:** (954)426-0999
Products: Air conditioning equipment. **SIC:** 5075 (Warm Air Heating & Air-Conditioning).

■ 14459 ■ **General Heating and Cooling Co.**
820 Atlantic Ave.
North Kansas City, MO 64116
Phone: (816)471-1466 **Fax:** (816)842-4075
Products: Air conditioning and heating equipment. **SIC:** 5075 (Warm Air Heating & Air-Conditioning). **Sales:** $30,000,000 (1993). **Emp:** 150. **Officers:** Bob Heinzinger, President; Daniel Coon, Finance Officer.

■ 14460 ■ **General Motors Corporation - Harrison Div.**
200 Upper Mountain Rd.
Lockport, NY 14094-1896
Phone: (716)439-2011 **Fax:** (716)439-3237
Products: Heating, cooling, and ventilation systems. **SIC:** 5075 (Warm Air Heating & Air-Conditioning). **Sales:** $2,000,000,000 (2000). **Emp:** 13,000. **Officers:** Paul J. Tosch.

■ 14461 ■ **Gensco, Inc.**
1824 Ship Ave.
Anchorage, AK 99501
Phone: (907)274-6507 **Fax:** (907)274-9525
Products: Force air heating supplies. **SIC:** 5075 (Warm Air Heating & Air-Conditioning).

■ 14462 ■ **Gensco, Inc.**
2270 NE Argyle
Portland, OR 97213
Phone: (503)288-7473 **Fax:** (503)288-8523
Products: Air-conditioning and heating supplies. **SIC:** 5075 (Warm Air Heating & Air-Conditioning).

■ 14463 ■ Gensco, Inc.
3350 Pipebend Pl. NE
Salem, OR 97301
Phone: (503)585-1743 Fax: (503)585-3204
Products: Heating and air-conditioning supplies. SIC:
5075 (Warm Air Heating & Air-Conditioning).

■ 14464 ■ Gensco, Inc.
921 SE Armour Rd.
Bend, OR 97702
Phone: (541)388-1547 Fax: (541)388-2263
Products: Heating and air-conditioning supplies. SIC:
5075 (Warm Air Heating & Air-Conditioning). Officers:
Chris Sodeman.

■ 14465 ■ Gensco Inc.
4402 20th St. E
Tacoma, WA 98424
Phone: (253)922-3003
Products: Heating and air-conditioning equipment.
SIC: 5075 (Warm Air Heating & Air-Conditioning).

■ 14466 ■ Gensco, Inc.
1703 6th Ave. S
Seattle, WA 98134
Phone: (206)682-7591 Fax: (206)682-8359
Products: Heating and cooling equipment. SIC: 5075
(Warm Air Heating & Air-Conditioning).

■ 14467 ■ Gensco, Inc.
11155 120th NE
Kirkland, WA 98033
Phone: (425)822-9644 Fax: (425)822-3939
Products: Heating and air-conditioning equipment and
supplies, including sheet metal and furnaces. SICs:
5075 (Warm Air Heating & Air-Conditioning); 5074
(Plumbing & Hydronic Heating Supplies); 5051 (Metals
Service Centers & Offices).

■ 14468 ■ Gensco, Inc.
2501 River Rd.
Yakima, WA 98902
Phone: (509)248-6226 Fax: (509)453-8458
Products: Heating and cooling supplies. SIC: 5075
(Warm Air Heating & Air-Conditioning).

■ 14469 ■ Gensco, Inc.
1630 Division
Bellingham, WA 98226
Phone: (206)676-8874 Fax: (206)676-9927
Products: Heating and cooling supplies. SIC: 5075
(Warm Air Heating & Air-Conditioning). Officers: Ron
Dunsnee.

■ 14470 ■ Gills Automotive Inc.
275 Rimmon St.
Manchester, NH 03102-3714
Phone: (603)623-7193 Fax: (603)626-6388
Products: Refrigeration equipment and supplies,
including motor vehicle units. SIC: 5078 (Refrigeration
Equipment & Supplies). Officers: Gill Larivee,
President.

■ 14471 ■ Godby Products Inc.
7904 Rockville Rd.
Indianapolis, IN 46214
Phone: (317)271-8400 Fax: (317)271-8429
Products: Fireplaces. SIC: 5074 (Plumbing & Hydronic
Heating Supplies). Est: 1987. Sales: $3,000,000
(2000). Emp: 35. Officers: Dennis Godby, CEO;
Connie Lin, Controller; D. Bartle, Dir. of Marketing.

■ 14472 ■ Goodell's Refrigeration
801 E 4th St., Ste. 22
Gillette, WY 82716-4061
Phone: (307)686-7676
Products: Refrigeration equipment and supplies. SIC:
5078 (Refrigeration Equipment & Supplies). Officers:
Winfield Goodell, Owner.

■ 14473 ■ Goodwin Refrigeration Co. Inc.
2410 Reliance Ave.
Apex, NC 27502-7048
Phone: (919)387-5797 Fax: (919)387-7086
Products: Commercial reach-in and walk-in
refrigerators. SIC: 5078 (Refrigeration Equipment &
Supplies). Officers: Brentley Goodwin, President.

■ 14474 ■ Griffin Refrigeration Inc.
80 Eastway
Reading, MA 01867-1107
Phone: (781)942-1522 Fax: (781)944-1318
E-mail: grifbunker@cs.com
Products: Refrigeration. SICs: 5078 (Refrigeration
Equipment & Supplies); 5075 (Warm Air Heating & Air-
Conditioning). Est: 1963. Emp: 6. Officers: Richard
Griffin, President.

■ 14475 ■ Grover Brothers Equipment Inc.
1500 N Main St.
Hattiesburg, MS 39401-1911
Phone: (601)545-3505 Fax: (601)544-4801
Products: Restaurant equipment and supplies. SIC:
5078 (Refrigeration Equipment & Supplies). Officers:
Craig Grover, President.

■ 14476 ■ Habegger Corp.
4995 Winton Rd.
Cincinnati, OH 45232
Phone: (513)681-6313 Fax: (513)853-6642
Products: Heating and air conditioning equipment and
supplies. SIC: 5075 (Warm Air Heating & Air-
Conditioning). Est: 1952. Sales: $105,000,000 (2000).
Emp: 200. Officers: F. Habegger, President; S. Frey,
Controller; Bill Schmutte, Sales/Marketing Contact; Dan
Veit, Human Resources Contact.

■ 14477 ■ Hammond Sheet Metal Company
Inc.
119 Cass Ave.
St. Louis, MO 63102
Phone: (314)241-5922
Products: Heating and cooling equipment. SIC: 5075
(Warm Air Heating & Air-Conditioning). Est: 1903.
Sales: $45,000,000 (2000). Emp: 130. Officers: G.K.
Moser, President; Russ Hagen, Controller; Craig
Moser, Dir. of Marketing & Sales; Doris Stout, Dir. of
Data Processing; Fred Smith, Dir of Human Resources.

■ 14478 ■ Harken Inc.
PO Box 80150
Billings, MT 59108-0150
Phone: (406)252-1207 Fax: (406)248-4862
Products: Refrigeration equipment and supplies.
SICs: 5078 (Refrigeration Equipment & Supplies);
5083 (Farm & Garden Machinery). Officers: Kathleen
Keneally, President.

■ 14479 ■ Heat Inc.
9 Flagstone Dr.
Hudson, NH 03051
Phone: (603)889-0104
Free: (800)631-3141 Fax: (603)889-0736
SIC: 5075 (Warm Air Heating & Air-Conditioning). Est:
1958. Sales: $30,000,000 (1999). Emp: 26. Officers:
David Brassard, President.

■ 14480 ■ Heat-N-Glo Fireplaces
6665 W Hwy. 13
Savage, MN 55378
Phone: (612)985-6000
Free: (888)427-3973 Fax: (612)985-6001
E-mail: info@heatnglo.com
URL: http://www.heatnglo.com
Products: Gas and wood burning fireplaces and
stoves. SIC: 5074 (Plumbing & Hydronic Heating
Supplies). Est: 1975. Emp: 600.

■ 14481 ■ Heating-Cooling Distributors Inc.
757 E Murry St.
Indianapolis, IN 46227-1139
Phone: (317)791-4234 Fax: (317)248-8803
Products: Warm air heating and cooling equipment.
SIC: 5075 (Warm Air Heating & Air-Conditioning). Est:
1986. Sales: $3,500,000 (2000). Emp: 10. Officers:
Richard Hutchinson, President; Linda Wilborn, CFO.

■ 14482 ■ Heating and Cooling Supply Inc.
3980 Home Ave.
San Diego, CA 92105
Phone: (619)262-7543
Free: (800)883-4955 Fax: (619)262-5456
Products: Heating and cooling systems. SIC: 5075
(Warm Air Heating & Air-Conditioning).

■ 14483 ■ Heating Specialties of New
Hampshire
25 Pond St.
PO Box 621
Nashua, NH 03061
Phone: (603)882-2726
Free: (800)875-1515 Fax: (603)882-2728
E-mail: hsofnh@aol.com
Products: Heating, air conditioning and refrigeration
supplies. SIC: 5075 (Warm Air Heating & Air-
Conditioning). Est: 1963. Officers: Raymond Maynard,
President.

■ 14484 ■ HEPA Corp.
3071 E Coronado St.
Anaheim, CA 92806
Phone: (714)630-5700 Fax: (714)630-2894
Products: High-efficiency air filters for computer
rooms, cleanrooms, medical and computer disk drives.
SIC: 5075 (Warm Air Heating & Air-Conditioning).

■ 14485 ■ HIM Mechanical Systems Inc.
90 1st St.
Bridgewater, MA 02324-1054
Phone: (508)697-5000 Fax: (508)679-5812
Products: Commercial refrigeration equipment and
supplies. SIC: 5078 (Refrigeration Equipment &
Supplies). Officers: Mitchell Howard, President.

■ 14486 ■ Hinshaw Supply Company of
California
145 11th St.
San Francisco, CA 94103
Phone: (415)431-2376
Products: Refrigeration supplies. SIC: 5078
(Refrigeration Equipment & Supplies).

■ 14487 ■ Home Crafts, Inc.
760 Railroad Ave.
West Babylon, NY 11704
Phone: (516)669-0141 Fax: (516)669-0351
Products: Fireplaces and chimneys. SIC: 5074
(Plumbing & Hydronic Heating Supplies).

■ 14488 ■ Houston Trane
10555 Westpark Dr.
Houston, TX 77042
Phone: (281)530-4000 Fax: (713)266-6956
Products: Heating and air conditioning equipment and
supplies. SIC: 5075 (Warm Air Heating & Air-
Conditioning). Sales: $23,000,000 (1993). Emp: 100.
Officers: R.O. Hunton, CEO & President; Larry Bower,
Vice President.

■ 14489 ■ HRS Corp.
5009 Cleveland St.
Virginia Beach, VA 23462-2503
Phone: (757)490-2446 Fax: (757)490-2453
Products: Refrigeration equipment and supplies; Ice
making machines; Restaurant equipment and supplies.
SICs: 5078 (Refrigeration Equipment & Supplies);
5046 (Commercial Equipment Nec). Officers: Grover
Midgett, President.

■ 14490 ■ Hubbell Mechanical Supply Co.
PO Box 3813, GS
Springfield, MO 65808
Phone: (417)865-5531
Free: (800)492-4217 Fax: (417)865-0163
Products: Heating equipment; Plumbing supplies.
SICs: 5075 (Warm Air Heating & Air-Conditioning);
5074 (Plumbing & Hydronic Heating Supplies). Est:
1970. Sales: $4,000,000 (2000). Emp: 16. Officers:
Jack J. Hubbell, President.

■ 14491 ■ HVAC Sales and Supply Co.
3940 Senator St.
Memphis, TN 38118
Phone: (901)365-1137 Fax: (901)794-9655
Products: Heating equipment; Air-conditioning
equipment; Ventilating equipment and supplies. SICs:
5074 (Plumbing & Hydronic Heating Supplies); 5075
(Warm Air Heating & Air-Conditioning). Officers:
William Bomar, President.

■ 14492 ■ **Ice Systems & Supplies Inc.**
163 E Mount Gallant Rd.
Rock Hill, SC 29730-8977
Phone: (803)324-8791
Free: (800)662-1273   **Fax:** (803)324-5950
Products: Ice machines and related equipment. **SIC:** 5078 (Refrigeration Equipment & Supplies). **Est:** 1977. **Sales:** $7,500,000 (2000). **Emp:** 19. **Officers:** W. Rockwell, President.

■ 14493 ■ **ICEE Distributors Inc.**
1513 Swan Lake Rd.
Bossier City, LA 71111-5335
Phone: (318)746-4895   **Fax:** (318)746-1119
Products: Refrigeration equipment and supplies; Refrigerated beverage dispensers. **SIC:** 5078 (Refrigeration Equipment & Supplies). **Officers:** Joe Festervan, Chairman of the Board.

■ 14494 ■ **Illco Inc.**
PO Box 1330
Aurora, IL 60507
Phone: (708)892-7904   **Fax:** (708)892-0318
URL: http://www.illco.com
Products: Furnaces; Air-conditioning room units, self-contained; Electric water heaters; Valves and pipe fittings. **SICs:** 5074 (Plumbing & Hydronic Heating Supplies); 5078 (Refrigeration Equipment & Supplies). **Est:** 1929. **Sales:** $20,000,000 (2000). **Emp:** 65. **Officers:** John P. Glass III, CEO & President.

■ 14495 ■ **Indiana Supply Corp.**
3835 E 21st St.
Indianapolis, IN 46218
Phone: (317)359-5451
Free: (800)686-0195   **Fax:** (317)351-2134
Products: Heating and cooling supplies. **SIC:** 5075 (Warm Air Heating & Air-Conditioning). **Est:** 1955. **Emp:** 100. **Officers:** Stan Hurt, CEO; David Draga, President; Brian Redman, VP of Sales; Bill Thompson, VP of Operations; Bob Phillips, VP of Marketing.

■ 14496 ■ **J and B Supply Inc.**
PO Box 10450
Ft. Smith, AR 72917
Phone: (501)649-4915   **Fax:** (501)649-4911
Products: Plumbing, heating, and air-conditioning equipment and supplies. **SICs:** 5075 (Warm Air Heating & Air-Conditioning); 5074 (Plumbing & Hydronic Heating Supplies); 5063 (Electrical Apparatus & Equipment). **Est:** 1968. **Sales:** $30,000,000 (2000). **Emp:** 106. **Officers:** Steve Jones, President; Warren Thompson, Controller; Duane Bagwell, Dir. of Data Processing; Steve Pelpbury, Vice President.

■ 14497 ■ **Ken Jeter Store Equipment, Inc.**
5124 Cliff Gookin Blvd.
Tupelo, MS 38801-7001
Phone: (601)844-1192
Free: (800)336-1192   **Fax:** (601)844-1310
Products: Commercial foodservice equipment. **SIC:** 5078 (Refrigeration Equipment & Supplies). **Est:** 1971. **Emp:** 21. **Officers:** Kenneth Jeter, President; Pat Jeter, VP & Treasurer.

■ 14498 ■ **Johnson Controls, Inc.**
1600 Wilson Way SE
Smyrna, GA 30082
Phone: (770)436-2677
Products: Air conditioning supply and parts. **SIC:** 5075 (Warm Air Heating & Air-Conditioning).

■ 14499 ■ **Johnson Heater Corp.**
970 Executive Pkwy.
St. Louis, MO 63141-6302
Phone: (314)542-9494   **Fax:** (314)542-9445
Products: Heating equipment; Ventilating equipment and supplies. **SICs:** 5074 (Plumbing & Hydronic Heating Supplies); 5075 (Warm Air Heating & Air-Conditioning). **Est:** 1921. **Sales:** $5,000,000 (2000). **Emp:** 25. **Officers:** G.W. Lieberg, President.

■ 14500 ■ **Johnson Heating Supply**
232 NE 9th Ave.
Portland, OR 97232
Phone: (503)234-5071   **Fax:** (503)233-0451
Products: Heating equipment parts and supplies. **SICs:** 5075 (Warm Air Heating & Air-Conditioning); 5074 (Plumbing & Hydronic Heating Supplies).

■ 14501 ■ **Johnson Supply and Equipment Corp.**
10151 Stella Link
Houston, TX 77025
Phone: (713)661-6666   **Fax:** (713)661-3684
Products: Air conditioning and refrigeration equipment. **SICs:** 5075 (Warm Air Heating & Air-Conditioning); 5078 (Refrigeration Equipment & Supplies). **Sales:** $54,500,000 (2000). **Emp:** 240. **Officers:** Robert E. Uehlinger, President; Dennis Waitschies, VP of Operations.

■ 14502 ■ **George L. Johnston Company Inc.**
1200 Holden Ave.
Detroit, MI 48202
Products: Air-conditioning, heating and refrigeration equipment, parts and supplies. **SICs:** 5075 (Warm Air Heating & Air-Conditioning); 5078 (Refrigeration Equipment & Supplies). **Sales:** $499,000,000 (2000). **Emp:** 1,600. **Officers:** Dan Herrick, President.

■ 14503 ■ **Johnstone Supply**
3720 E Pikes Peak Ave.
Colorado Springs, CO 80909-6569
Phone: (719)550-0123
Free: (800)634-6344   **Fax:** (719)591-3725
E-mail: store30@JohnstoneSupply.com
URL: http://www.PlanetJohnStore.com
Products: Heating and air-conditioning parts; Electrical motors; Plumbing. **SICs:** 5075 (Warm Air Heating & Air-Conditioning); 5063 (Electrical Apparatus & Equipment); 5074 (Plumbing & Hydronic Heating Supplies). **Emp:** 13. **Officers:** J. Wieland, President.

■ 14504 ■ **Johnstone Supply**
3061 Kingston Ct.
Marietta, GA 30067
Phone: (404)768-7337
Products: Air conditioning supply and parts. **SIC:** 5075 (Warm Air Heating & Air-Conditioning).

■ 14505 ■ **Johnstone Supply**
6019 Goshen Springs Rd.
Norcross, GA 30071
Phone: (770)446-0400
Products: Air conditioning supply and parts. **SIC:** 5075 (Warm Air Heating & Air-Conditioning).

■ 14506 ■ **Jomar Distributors Inc.**
767 Waverly St.
Framingham, MA 01702-8512
Phone: (508)620-8885
Products: Heating equipment. **SIC:** 5074 (Plumbing & Hydronic Heating Supplies).

■ 14507 ■ **F.W. Kauphusman Inc.**
525 Steelhead Way
Boise, ID 83704-8374
Phone: (208)377-1600   **Fax:** (208)375-1254
Products: Air-conditioning equipment; Heating equipment. **SIC:** 5075 (Warm Air Heating & Air-Conditioning). **Officers:** Richard Kauphusman, President.

■ 14508 ■ **Kelmar Corp.**
201 Airport N
Ft. Wayne, IN 46825
Phone: (219)484-4141
Products: Blowers and fans; Heaters and burners; Air pollution control equipment and supplies; Air-conditioning equipment. **SIC:** 5075 (Warm Air Heating & Air-Conditioning). **Est:** 1983. **Sales:** $600,000 (2000). **Emp:** 2. **Officers:** Dan Kelly, Owner.

■ 14509 ■ **Kirsch Energy System**
146 Florence Ave.
Hawthorne, NJ 07506
Phone: (973)423-4488   **Fax:** (973)423-9491
URL: http://www.kirsch-energy.com
Products: Fuel oil; Heating and cooling equipment. **SIC:** 5075 (Warm Air Heating & Air-Conditioning). **Est:** 1936. **Sales:** $2,000,000 (1999). **Emp:** 9. **Officers:** Joseph J. Kirsch, CEO, e-mail: www.kirsch-energy.com; Guy Cebular, Customer Service Contact.

■ 14510 ■ **Kleeko Enterprises**
1907 S Cypress
Wichita, KS 67207
Phone: (316)682-9333   **Fax:** (316)685-4111
Products: Air purification equipment; Water treatment equipment. **SICs:** 5075 (Warm Air Heating & Air-Conditioning); 5074 (Plumbing & Hydronic Heating Supplies). **Officers:** Gerald D. Kruse, Vice President.

■ 14511 ■ **Kleenaire Corp.**
2117 Jefferson St.
Stevens Point, WI 54481
Phone: (715)344-2602
Products: Warm air heating and cooling equipment; Ventilating equipment and supplies. **SIC:** 5075 (Warm Air Heating & Air-Conditioning). **Est:** 1939. **Sales:** $3,000,000 (2000). **Emp:** 9. **Officers:** Walter J. Okray Jr., CEO & President; Thomas E. Okray, CFO.

■ 14512 ■ **Klinge Corp.**
PO Box 3608
York, PA 17402
Phone: (717)840-4500   **Fax:** (717)840-4501
Products: Container refrigeration units, mobile generator sets, railroad air conditioning and refrigeration equipment. **SICs:** 5075 (Warm Air Heating & Air-Conditioning); 5078 (Refrigeration Equipment & Supplies).

■ 14513 ■ **Kold Temp Refigeration Inc.**
PO Box 6387
Reno, NV 89503-6387
Phone: (702)323-0070
Products: Refrigeration equipment and supplies, including ice making machines. **SIC:** 5078 (Refrigeration Equipment & Supplies). **Officers:** Joseph Mangiapia, President.

■ 14514 ■ **J. M. Kopecky & Co.**
PO Box 24271
Omaha, NE 68124-0271
Phone: (402)331-9408   **Fax:** (402)331-9352
E-mail: jmkopecky@uswest.net
Products: Commercial refrigeration equipment and supplies, including reach-in and walk-in refrigerators. **SIC:** 5078 (Refrigeration Equipment & Supplies). **Officers:** John Kopecky, Chairman of the Board; John Kopecky, President. **Former Name:** Kopecky & Yates Inc.

■ 14515 ■ **Kru-Kel Co. Inc.**
PO Box 71501
North Charleston, SC 29405
Phone: (803)744-2558   **Fax:** (803)744-8729
Products: Refrigeration equipment and supplies; Heating equipment; Air conditioning equipment. **SIC:** 5078 (Refrigeration Equipment & Supplies). **Est:** 1971. **Sales:** $1,500,000 (2000). **Emp:** 7. **Officers:** Kurt Kruger, President.

■ 14516 ■ **Gustave A. Larson Co.**
W233 N2869 Roundy Cir. W
PO Box 910
Pewaukee, WI 53072
Phone: (262)542-0200   **Fax:** (262)542-1400
E-mail: info@galarson.com
URL: http://www.galarson.com
Products: Heating, refrigeration, and air-conditioning parts and supplies. **SICs:** 5078 (Refrigeration Equipment & Supplies); 5075 (Warm Air Heating & Air-Conditioning). **Est:** 1936. **Sales:** $100,000,000 (1999). **Emp:** 250. **Officers:** Andrew Larson, President; Gregg Turley, VP of Marketing & Sales; Frank Mirocha, VP of Operations; Scott Larson, VP of Finance; Sue Sinclair, VP of Inventory Management.

■ 14517 ■ **Lay International Consulting Services**
12826 Sanfield Dr.
St. Louis, MO 63146
Phone: (314)532-0517   **Fax:** (314)532-1989
Products: Warm air heating and air-conditioning equipment; Aluminum extruded products. **SIC:** 5075 (Warm Air Heating & Air-Conditioning). **Officers:** James Yeh, President.

■ 14518 ■ LDI MFG Co., Inc.
PO Box 400
Logansport, IN 46947-0400
Phone: (219)722-3124
Free: (800)366-2001 **Fax:** (219)722-7213
E-mail: ldihvac@mindspring.com
Products: Commercial heating, ventilating, and air-conditioning equipment and systems. **SIC:** 5075 (Warm Air Heating & Air-Conditioning). **Est:** 1946. **Sales:** $6,500,000 (1999). **Emp:** 65. **Officers:** R.G. Swennumson, CEO; C. Hall, CFO; Susan Erny, Sales/Marketing Contact; Carolyn Smith, Customer Service contact; Camille Hall, Human Resources.

■ 14519 ■ Lee's Refrigeration
2165 Wilder Ave.
Helena, MT 59601-1503
Phone: (406)442-2712
Products: Refrigeration equipment and supplies; Commercial refrigeration equipment, including reach-in and walk-in refrigerators. **SIC:** 5078 (Refrigeration Equipment & Supplies). **Officers:** Lee Mc Millan, President.

■ 14520 ■ Lees Refrigeration, Div. of Hussmann Corp.
1713 Democrat St.
Honolulu, HI 96819-3116
Phone: (808)847-3237 **Fax:** (808)842-1525
Products: Refrigeration equipment and supplies. **SIC:** 5078 (Refrigeration Equipment & Supplies). **Emp:** 15. **Officers:** larry Vowell, President. **Alternate Name:** Lees Refrigeration Sales & Service.

■ 14521 ■ Lehman's Commercial Service
1501 Michigan St.
Des Moines, IA 50314-3517
Phone: (515)243-1974 **Fax:** (515)243-1784
Products: Furnaces; Air-conditioning equipment; Unit coolers (refrigeration). **SICs:** 5075 (Warm Air Heating & Air-Conditioning); 5078 (Refrigeration Equipment & Supplies). **Officers:** Randy Lehman, President.

■ 14522 ■ Leming Supply Inc.
PO Box 4759
Lafayette, IN 47903-4759
Phone: (765)448-4553
Free: (800)428-7648 **Fax:** (765)447-7677
Products: Refrigeration equipment and supplies. **SIC:** 5078 (Refrigeration Equipment & Supplies). **Officers:** Manford Leming, President.

■ 14523 ■ Leonard Refrigeration & Heating Sales & Service
16119 Hubbell St.
Detroit, MI 48235-4026
Phone: (313)838-2240 **Fax:** (313)838-2240
Products: Refrigerator and heating systems repair. **SICs:** 5064 (Electrical Appliances—Television & Radio); 5075 (Warm Air Heating & Air-Conditioning). **Officers:** Norman Bibek, Partner.

■ 14524 ■ Leonard's Stone & Fireplace
12200 S I 35 W
Burleson, TX 76028
Phone: (817)293-2204 **Fax:** (817)293-9429
Products: Fireplaces. **SIC:** 5074 (Plumbing & Hydronic Heating Supplies).

■ 14525 ■ LKS International Inc.
4001 W Devon Ave.
Chicago, IL 60646
Phone: (773)283-6601 **Fax:** (773)283-6710
Products: Restaurant and commercial foodservice equipment and supplies. **SIC:** 5078 (Refrigeration Equipment & Supplies). **Sales:** $4,000,000 (2000). **Emp:** 6.

■ 14526 ■ Lloyd's Refrigeration Inc.
3550 W Tompkins Ave.
Las Vegas, NV 89103
Phone: (702)798-1010 **Fax:** (702)798-6531
Products: Refrigeration equipment and supplies. **SIC:** 5078 (Refrigeration Equipment & Supplies). **Officers:** Gary Lloyd, President.

■ 14527 ■ Lomanco Inc.
PO Box 519
Jacksonville, AR 72076
Phone: (501)982-6511 **Fax:** (501)982-1258
Products: Ventilation products, including turbines. **SIC:** 5075 (Warm Air Heating & Air-Conditioning). **Est:** 1946. **Sales:** $30,000,000 (2000). **Emp:** 300. **Officers:** Ted Belden, President; Jim Byro, CFO; Will Forde, Dir. of Marketing & Sales; Bill Bona, Dir. of Data Processing.

■ 14528 ■ Magic Refrigeration Co.
5423 S 99th East Ave.
Tulsa, OK 74146-5726
Phone: (918)664-2160
Free: (800)375-2160 **Fax:** 800-375-2160
Products: Refrigeration equipment and supplies; Ice making machines. **SIC:** 5078 (Refrigeration Equipment & Supplies). **Officers:** Ward Farmer, President.

■ 14529 ■ Magnum Equipment Inc.
5817 Plauche St.
New Orleans, LA 70123-4033
Phone: (504)733-5550
Free: (800)737-6322 **Fax:** (504)733-5545
Products: Commercial refrigeration equipment and supplies. **SIC:** 5078 (Refrigeration Equipment & Supplies). **Officers:** Thomas Maag, President.

■ 14530 ■ Maines Paper and Food Service Inc. Equipment and Supply Div.
PO Box 438
Conklin, NY 13748-0438
Phone: (607)772-0055 **Fax:** (607)729-2480
Products: Restaurant, refrigeration and air-conditioning equipment. **SICs:** 5046 (Commercial Equipment Nec); 5078 (Refrigeration Equipment & Supplies); 5075 (Warm Air Heating & Air-Conditioning). **Sales:** $17,000,000 (1994). **Emp:** 28. **Officers:** David Maines, President.

■ 14531 ■ Marco Sales Inc.
1100 Macklind Ave.
St. Louis, MO 63110
Phone: (314)768-4200
Products: Heating equipment; Air-conditioning equipment. **SIC:** 5075 (Warm Air Heating & Air-Conditioning). **Est:** 1957. **Sales:** $40,000,000 (2000). **Emp:** 75. **Officers:** A.B. Jokerst Jr., CEO & President.

■ 14532 ■ Market Equipment Company Inc.
1114 N Ruby St.
Spokane, WA 99202-1737
Phone: (509)325-4526 **Fax:** (509)326-9452
Products: Commercial refrigeration equipment and supplies. **SIC:** 5078 (Refrigeration Equipment & Supplies). **Officers:** Michael Schnell, President.

■ 14533 ■ Mason Supply Co.
PO Box 83585
Columbus, OH 43203
Phone: (614)253-8607
Free: (800)282-1846 **Fax:** (614)253-0061
E-mail: sales@masonsupply.com
URL: http://www.masonsupply.com
Products: Heating and cooling supplies; Refrigeration supplies; Commercial ice machines. **SICs:** 5078 (Refrigeration Equipment & Supplies); 5075 (Warm Air Heating & Air-Conditioning). **Est:** 1944. **Emp:** 80.

■ 14534 ■ McClintock and Bustad Inc.
25133 W Ave. Tibbitts
Valencia, CA 91355
Phone: (818)893-4609
Products: Heating and ventilation equipment and supplies. **SIC:** 5075 (Warm Air Heating & Air-Conditioning). **Est:** 1965. **Sales:** $2,000,000 (2000). **Emp:** 6. **Officers:** Joe Bustad, CEO.

■ 14535 ■ McCormick Refrigeration
1600 Front St.
Anniston, AL 36201
Phone: (205)831-2271 **Fax:** (205)831-5220
Products: Refrigeration equipment and supplies. **SIC:** 5078 (Refrigeration Equipment & Supplies). **Officers:** Robert McCormick, Owner.

■ 14536 ■ McCrudden Heating Supply
523 Williamson
Youngstown, OH 44502
Phone: (330)744-4108
Free: ((33))523-4108 **Fax:** (330)744-5665
E-mail: mccruddens@webtv.net
Products: Heating equipment and supplies. **SIC:** 5075 (Warm Air Heating & Air-Conditioning). **Est:** 1963. **Sales:** $7,850,000 (2000). **Emp:** 25. **Officers:** Charles McCrudden.

■ 14537 ■ A.Y. McDonald Supply Co.
PO Box 1364
Joplin, MO 64801
Phone: (417)623-7740 **Fax:** (417)623-6717
Products: Heating and air-conditioning equipment; Indoor fixtures, including bathtubs and toilets. **SICs:** 5075 (Warm Air Heating & Air-Conditioning); 5074 (Plumbing & Hydronic Heating Supplies).

■ 14538 ■ McKenney Supply Inc.
106 E Pleasure St.
Searcy, AR 72143-7710
Phone: (501)268-8422 **Fax:** (501)268-7337
Products: Industrial electric heating and air products. **SICs:** 5063 (Electrical Apparatus & Equipment); 5078 (Refrigeration Equipment & Supplies); 5075 (Warm Air Heating & Air-Conditioning). **Est:** 1969. **Emp:** 10. **Officers:** Frank McKenney, President; Anita McKenney, VP of Finance; M. Kent Jones, VP of Sales.

■ 14539 ■ Mechanical Refrigeration & AC
PO Box 3627
Little Rock, AR 72203-3627
Phone: (501)455-3590 **Fax:** (501)455-6584
Products: Refrigeration equipment and supplies. **SIC:** 5078 (Refrigeration Equipment & Supplies). **Est:** 1969. **Officers:** Jerry W. Davis, CEO.

■ 14540 ■ Mechanical Services of Orlando Inc.
9440 Sidney Hayes Rd.
Orlando, FL 32824
Phone: (407)857-3510
Products: Air-conditioning equipment; Heating equipment. **SIC:** 5075 (Warm Air Heating & Air-Conditioning).

■ 14541 ■ Metro Refrigeration Supply, Inc.
2050 Sigman Rd. NW
Conyers, GA 30012
Phone: (770)922-8606
Products: Refrigeration supply. **SIC:** 5078 (Refrigeration Equipment & Supplies).

■ 14542 ■ Metro Refrigeration Supply, Inc.
685 Thornton Way
Lithia Springs, GA 30122
Phone: (770)948-8400
Products: Refrigeration supplies and equipment. **SIC:** 5078 (Refrigeration Equipment & Supplies).

■ 14543 ■ Metro Refrigeration Supply, Inc.
3061 Kingston Ct.
Marietta, GA 30067
Phone: (770)953-0022
Products: Refrigeration supply. **SIC:** 5078 (Refrigeration Equipment & Supplies).

■ 14544 ■ Metropolitan AC & Refrigeration
PO Box 422
Everett, MA 02149-0003
Phone: (617)389-4300 **Fax:** (617)389-1110
Products: Air-conditioning equipment and supplies. **SIC:** 5075 (Warm Air Heating & Air-Conditioning). **Officers:** Philip Polcaro, President.

■ 14545 ■ R.E. Michel Company Inc.
1991 Mooreland Pkwy.
Annapolis, MD 21401
Phone: (410)267-7500 **Fax:** (410)280-2192
Products: Heating and air-conditioning equipment and supplies. **SIC:** 5075 (Warm Air Heating & Air-Conditioning).

■ 14546 ■ R.E. Michel Company Inc.
10820 Guilford Rd.
Annapolis Junction, MD 20701
Phone: (301)604-3747 **Fax:** (301)604-0896
Products: Heating and air-conditioning equipment and

supplies. **SIC:** 5075 (Warm Air Heating & Air-Conditioning).

■ **14547** ■ **R.E. Michel Company Inc.**
2509 Schuster Dr.
Cheverly, MD 20784
Phone: (301)322-4700 **Fax:** (301)773-7681
Products: Heating and air-conditioning equipment and supplies. **SIC:** 5075 (Warm Air Heating & Air-Conditioning).

■ **14548** ■ **R.E. Michel Company Inc.**
150-8 Airport Dr.
Westminster, MD 21157
Phone: (410)876-9144 **Fax:** (410)876-3441
Products: Heating and air-conditioning equipment and supplies. **SIC:** 5075 (Warm Air Heating & Air-Conditioning).

■ **14549** ■ **R.E. Michel Company Inc.**
1918 Tucker
Burlington, NC 27215
Phone: (919)228-1304 **Fax:** (919)229-4519
Products: Heating and air-conditioning equipment and supplies. **SIC:** 5075 (Warm Air Heating & Air-Conditioning).

■ **14550** ■ **R.E. Michel Company Inc.**
4141 Barringer Dr.
Charlotte, NC 28217
Phone: (704)523-5515 **Fax:** (704)523-5519
Products: Heating and air-conditioning equipment and supplies. **SIC:** 5075 (Warm Air Heating & Air-Conditioning).

■ **14551** ■ **R.E. Michel Company Inc.**
2200 Sullivan
Greensboro, NC 27405
Phone: (910)274-3844
Free: (800)876-6384 **Fax:** (910)272-8204
Products: Heating and air-conditioning equipment and supplies. **SIC:** 5075 (Warm Air Heating & Air-Conditioning).

■ **14552** ■ **R.E. Michel Company Inc.**
309 W 9th St.
Greenville, NC 27834
Phone: (919)758-0088 **Fax:** (919)758-2238
Products: Heating and air-conditioning equipment and supplies. **SIC:** 5075 (Warm Air Heating & Air-Conditioning).

■ **14553** ■ **R.E. Michel Company Inc.**
1310 Hodges St.
Raleigh, NC 27604
Phone: (919)821-5700
Free: (800)274-1310 **Fax:** (919)821-5799
Products: Heating and air-conditioning equipment and supplies. **SIC:** 5075 (Warm Air Heating & Air-Conditioning).

■ **14554** ■ **R.E. Michel Company Inc.**
4461 Sunset Ave.
Rocky Mount, NC 27804
Phone: (919)937-2089 **Fax:** (919)937-2916
Products: Heating and air-conditioning equipment and supplies. **SIC:** 5075 (Warm Air Heating & Air-Conditioning).

■ **14555** ■ **R.E. Michel Company Inc.**
410 Haled St.
Winston-Salem, NC 27127
Phone: (910)724-7000
Free: (800)876-6385 **Fax:** (910)761-8685
Products: Heating equipment and supplies; Refrigeration equipment and supplies. **SICs:** 5075 (Warm Air Heating & Air-Conditioning); 5078 (Refrigeration Equipment & Supplies).

■ **14556** ■ **R.E. Michel Company Inc.**
Bldg. 14E
Bound Brook, NJ 08805
Phone: (732)560-0560 **Fax:** (732)560-1686
Products: Air-conditioning equipment; Cast iron heating boilers, radiators, and convectors. **SIC:** 5075 (Warm Air Heating & Air-Conditioning).

■ **14557** ■ **R.E. Michel Company Inc.**
827 New York Ave.
Trenton, NJ 08638
Phone: (609)599-4535 **Fax:** (609)392-4646
Products: Refrigeration equipment and supplies; Heating equipment and supplies. **SICs:** 5075 (Warm Air Heating & Air-Conditioning); 5078 (Refrigeration Equipment & Supplies).

■ **14558** ■ **R.E. Michel Company Inc.**
749 N Delsea Dr.
Vineland, NJ 08360
Phone: (609)691-8448 **Fax:** (609)691-3427
Products: Refrigeration equipment and supplies; Heating supplies. **SICs:** 5075 (Warm Air Heating & Air-Conditioning); 5078 (Refrigeration Equipment & Supplies).

■ **14559** ■ **R.E. Michel Company Inc.**
116 Hawley Ave.
Syracuse, NY 13203
Phone: (315)474-6007 **Fax:** (315)474-2589
Products: Heating and air-conditioning equipment. **SIC:** 5075 (Warm Air Heating & Air-Conditioning).

■ **14560** ■ **R.E. Michel Company Inc.**
3412 S Ridge St. E
Ashtabula, OH 44004
Phone: (440)993-7881
Free: (800)727-4328 **Fax:** (440)992-0928
Products: Heating, air-conditioning, and refrigeration parts and equipment. **SICs:** 5075 (Warm Air Heating & Air-Conditioning); 5078 (Refrigeration Equipment & Supplies).

■ **14561** ■ **R.E. Michel Company Inc.**
4260 Lake Park Rd.
Youngstown, OH 44512
Phone: (330)782-6600
Free: (800)783-6600 **Fax:** (330)782-5771
Products: Heating, air-conditioning, and refrigeration parts. **SICs:** 5075 (Warm Air Heating & Air-Conditioning); 5078 (Refrigeration Equipment & Supplies).

■ **14562** ■ **R.E. Michel Company Inc.**
929 E Highland St.
Allentown, PA 18103
Phone: (215)434-6054 **Fax:** (215)434-9977
Products: Heating and cooling supplies. **SIC:** 5075 (Warm Air Heating & Air-Conditioning).

■ **14563** ■ **R.E. Michel Company Inc.**
1807 9th Ave.
Altoona, PA 16602
Phone: (814)942-6600 **Fax:** (814)942-7931
Products: Heating and cooling supplies. **SIC:** 5075 (Warm Air Heating & Air-Conditioning).

■ **14564** ■ **R.E. Michel Company Inc.**
5384 Enterprise Ave.
Bethel Park, PA 15102
Phone: (412)835-5500
Free: (800)351-3439 **Fax:** (412)835-8511
URL: http://www.remichel.com
Products: Heating and cooling supplies. **SIC:** 5075 (Warm Air Heating & Air-Conditioning).

■ **14565** ■ **R.E. Michel Company Inc.**
1028 Morton Ave.
Chester, PA 19013
Phone: (215)872-9420 **Fax:** (215)872-3355
Products: Heating and cooling supplies. **SIC:** 5075 (Warm Air Heating & Air-Conditioning).

■ **14566** ■ **R.E. Michel Company Inc.**
1302 Myrtle
Erie, PA 16501
Phone: (814)453-6664 **Fax:** (814)453-7105
Products: Heating and cooling supplies. **SIC:** 5075 (Warm Air Heating & Air-Conditioning).

■ **14567** ■ **R.E. Michel Company Inc.**
RD 6, Box 518
Woodward Rd.
Greensburg, PA 15601
Phone: (412)836-7646 **Fax:** (412)836-1339
Products: Heating and cooling supplies. **SIC:** 5075 (Warm Air Heating & Air-Conditioning).

■ **14568** ■ **R.E. Michel Company Inc.**
803 S 26th St.
Harrisburg, PA 17111
Phone: (717)564-7565 **Fax:** (717)564-9439
Products: Heating and cooling supplies. **SIC:** 5075 (Warm Air Heating & Air-Conditioning).

■ **14569** ■ **R.E. Michel Company Inc.**
511 W Roseville Rd.
Lancaster, PA 17604
Phone: (717)393-1790 **Fax:** (717)393-1891
Products: Heating and cooling supplies. **SIC:** 5075 (Warm Air Heating & Air-Conditioning).

■ **14570** ■ **R.E. Michel Company Inc.**
10 Leonburg Rd.
Mars, PA 16046
Phone: (412)776-0736 **Fax:** (412)776-6070
Products: Heating and cooling supplies. **SIC:** 5074 (Plumbing & Hydronic Heating Supplies). **Officers:** Bryan Champlin.

■ **14571** ■ **R.E. Michel Company Inc.**
177 Mercer St.
Meadville, PA 16335
Phone: (814)724-8046 **Fax:** (814)337-5183
Products: Heating and cooling supplies. **SIC:** 5075 (Warm Air Heating & Air-Conditioning).

■ **14572** ■ **R.E. Michel Company Inc.**
845 Williams Ln.
Reading, PA 19604
Phone: (215)929-3373 **Fax:** (215)929-8461
Products: Heating and cooling supplies. **SIC:** 5075 (Warm Air Heating & Air-Conditioning).

■ **14573** ■ **R.E. Michel Company. Inc.**
405 Gilligan St.
Scranton, PA 18508
Phone: (717)963-7881 **Fax:** (717)963-7883
Products: Heating and cooling supplies. **SIC:** 5075 (Warm Air Heating & Air-Conditioning).

■ **14574** ■ **R.E. Michel Company Inc.**
2420 Commercial Blvd.
State College, PA 16801
Phone: (814)234-1134
Products: Heating and cooling supplies. **SIC:** 5075 (Warm Air Heating & Air-Conditioning).

■ **14575** ■ **R.E. Michel Company Inc.**
140 W Berkeley St.
Uniontown, PA 15401
Phone: (412)438-4506 **Fax:** (412)438-6825
Products: Heating and cooling supplies. **SIC:** 5075 (Warm Air Heating & Air-Conditioning).

■ **14576** ■ **R.E. Michel Company Inc.**
2250 Manor Ave.
Upper Darby, PA 19082
Phone: (215)853-4570 **Fax:** (215)853-3929
Products: Heating and cooling supplies. **SIC:** 5075 (Warm Air Heating & Air-Conditioning).

■ **14577** ■ **R.E. Michel Company Inc.**
915 Eastern Rd.
Warrington, PA 18976
Phone: (215)343-2004 **Fax:** (215)343-1803
Products: Heating and cooling supplies. **SIC:** 5075 (Warm Air Heating & Air-Conditioning).

■ **14578** ■ **R.E. Michel Company Inc.**
322 W Towne Rd.
West Chester, PA 19380
Phone: (215)692-2966 **Fax:** (215)692-6812
Products: Heating and cooling supplies. **SIC:** 5075 (Warm Air Heating & Air-Conditioning). **Officers:** Steve Amway.

■ **14579** ■ **R.E. Michel Company Inc.**
1240 W Mark
York, PA 17404
Phone: (717)845-2681 **Fax:** (717)895-2083
Products: Heating and cooling supplies. **SIC:** 5075 (Warm Air Heating & Air-Conditioning).

■ 14580 ■ R.E. Michel Company Inc.
830 N Lincoln St.
Arlington, VA 22201
Phone: (703)524-8336
Products: Heating and cooling supplies. **SIC:** 5075 (Warm Air Heating & Air-Conditioning).

■ 14581 ■ R.E. Michel Company Inc.
604 Henry Ave.
Charlottesville, VA 22903
Phone: (804)977-4311 **Fax:** (804)293-3404
Products: Heating and air-conditioning equipment. **SIC:** 5075 (Warm Air Heating & Air-Conditioning).

■ 14582 ■ R.E. Michel Company Inc.
45 Sealtergood Dr.
Christiansburg, VA 24073
Phone: (540)381-0700 **Fax:** (540)382-1238
Products: Heating and air-conditioning equipment. **SIC:** 5075 (Warm Air Heating & Air-Conditioning).

■ 14583 ■ R.E. Michel Company Inc.
131 Industrial Dr.
Fredericksburg, VA 22408
Phone: (540)891-1534 **Fax:** (540)898-4580
Products: Heating and air-conditioning equipment. **SIC:** 5075 (Warm Air Heating & Air-Conditioning).

■ 14584 ■ R.E. Michel Company Inc.
26 Pleasant Hill Rd.
Harrisonburg, VA 22801
Phone: (540)433-7848 **Fax:** (540)433-3151
Products: Heating and air-conditioning equipment. **SIC:** 5075 (Warm Air Heating & Air-Conditioning).

■ 14585 ■ R.E. Michel Company Inc.
3116 Oddfellows Rd.
Lynchburg, VA 24501
Phone: (804)528-4441
Products: Heating and air-conditioning equipment. **SIC:** 5075 (Warm Air Heating & Air-Conditioning).

■ 14586 ■ R.E. Michel Company Inc.
9098 Owens Ct.
Manassas Park, VA 20111
Phone: (703)330-0771 **Fax:** (703)330-5704
Products: Heating and air-conditioning equipment. **SIC:** 5075 (Warm Air Heating & Air-Conditioning).

■ 14587 ■ R.E. Michel Company Inc.
2742 Gallows Rd.
Vienna, VA 22180
Phone: (703)698-6244 **Fax:** (703)698-6238
Products: Heating and air-conditioning equipment. **SIC:** 5075 (Warm Air Heating & Air-Conditioning). **Est:** 1935.

■ 14588 ■ R.E. Michel Company Inc.
2735 Ellsmore Ave.
Norfolk, VA 23513
Phone: (757)855-2011 **Fax:** (757)853-8387
Products: Heating and air-conditioning equipment. **SIC:** 5075 (Warm Air Heating & Air-Conditioning).

■ 14589 ■ R.E. Michel Company Inc.
401 5th St.
Petersburg, VA 23803
Phone: (804)862-3535 **Fax:** (804)861-2877
Products: Heating and air-conditioning equipment. **SIC:** 5075 (Warm Air Heating & Air-Conditioning).

■ 14590 ■ R.E. Michel Company Inc.
3900 Garwood
Portsmouth, VA 23701
Phone: (757)465-2516 **Fax:** (757)465-1184
Products: Heating and air-conditioning equipment. **SIC:** 5075 (Warm Air Heating & Air-Conditioning).

■ 14591 ■ R.E. Michel Company Inc.
1714 W Cary St.
Richmond, VA 23220
Phones: (804)358-9145 (804)231-4666
Products: Heating and air-conditioning supplies. **SIC:** 5075 (Warm Air Heating & Air-Conditioning).

■ 14592 ■ R.E. Michel Company Inc.
2419 Shenandoah Ave.
Roanoke, VA 24017
Phone: (540)344-1666 **Fax:** (540)345-1363
Products: Heating and air-conditioning supplies and equipment. **SIC:** 5075 (Warm Air Heating & Air-Conditioning).

■ 14593 ■ R.E. Michel Company Inc.
PO Box 56, US Rte. 13
Tasley, VA 23441
Phone: (757)787-8731 **Fax:** (757)787-8424
Products: Heating and air-conditioning equipment. **SIC:** 5075 (Warm Air Heating & Air-Conditioning).
Officers: Gary Bruch.

■ 14594 ■ R.E. Michel Company Inc.
2609 Dean Dr.
Virginia Beach, VA 23452
Phone: (757)463-7131 **Fax:** (757)340-3682
Products: Air-conditioning, heating, and refrigeration equipment. **SICs:** 5075 (Warm Air Heating & Air-Conditioning); 5078 (Refrigeration Equipment & Supplies).

■ 14595 ■ R.E. Michel Company Inc.
129 Kingsgate Pkwy.
Williamsburg, VA 23185
Phone: (757)229-0028
Products: Heating, refrigeration, and cooling equipment. **SICs:** 5075 (Warm Air Heating & Air-Conditioning); 5078 (Refrigeration Equipment & Supplies).

■ 14596 ■ R.E. Michel Company Inc.
130 Dye Dr.
Beckley, WV 25801
Phone: (304)255-2222 **Fax:** (304)253-9048
Products: Heating, cooling, and refrigeration equipment. **SICs:** 5075 (Warm Air Heating & Air-Conditioning); 5078 (Refrigeration Equipment & Supplies).

■ 14597 ■ R.E. Michel Company Inc.
1904 Bigley Ave.
Charleston, WV 25302
Phone: (304)345-3303 **Fax:** (304)343-6962
Products: Heating and cooling supplies. **SICs:** 5075 (Warm Air Heating & Air-Conditioning); 5074 (Plumbing & Hydronic Heating Supplies).

■ 14598 ■ R.E. Michel Company Inc.
716 30th St.
Huntington, WV 25702
Phone: (304)529-1054
Products: Heating and cooling supplies. **SICs:** 5075 (Warm Air Heating & Air-Conditioning); 5074 (Plumbing & Hydronic Heating Supplies).

■ 14599 ■ R.E. Michel Company Inc.
1089 Maple Dr.
Morgantown, WV 26505
Phone: (304)598-3729 **Fax:** (304)598-3881
Products: Heating and cooling supplies. **SICs:** 5075 (Warm Air Heating & Air-Conditioning); 5074 (Plumbing & Hydronic Heating Supplies).

■ 14600 ■ R.E. Michel Company Inc.
41 41st. St.
Wheeling, WV 26003
Phone: (304)232-4540 **Fax:** (304)232-6908
Products: Heating, air-conditioning, and refrigeration parts. **SICs:** 5075 (Warm Air Heating & Air-Conditioning); 5078 (Refrigeration Equipment & Supplies).

■ 14601 ■ R.E. Michel Company Inc.
1 R.E. Michel Dr.
Glen Burnie, MD 21060
Phone: (410)760-4000 **Fax:** (410)761-3703
Products: Heating, air conditioning and refrigeration equipment, parts and supplies. **SICs:** 5074 (Plumbing & Hydronic Heating Supplies); 5075 (Warm Air Heating & Air-Conditioning); 5078 (Refrigeration Equipment & Supplies). **Sales:** $130,000,000 (2000). **Emp:** 700. **Officers:** J.W.H. Michel, President; Ronald D. Miller, Exec. VP & CFO.

■ 14602 ■ Mid-Lakes Distributing Inc.
1029 W Adams St.
Chicago, IL 60607
Phone: (312)733-1033 **Fax:** (312)733-1721
E-mail: info@mid-lakes.com
Products: HVAC. **SIC:** 5075 (Warm Air Heating & Air-Conditioning). **Est:** 1959. **Sales:** $12,000,000 (1999). **Emp:** 32. **Officers:** John Harte, President; Tom Meyer, VP of Marketing & Sales; David Munro, Dir. of Systems.

■ 14603 ■ Mike's Refrigeration Inc.
209 Highway 52 E
Velva, ND 58790-7347
Products: Refrigeration equipment, including dairy equipment. **SIC:** 5078 (Refrigeration Equipment & Supplies). **Officers:** Michael Jungers, President.

■ 14604 ■ Miller Refrigeration Supply Co.
2915 N Jackson Hwy.
Sheffield, AL 35660-3434
Phone: (205)381-6000 **Fax:** (205)381-6001
Products: Refrigeration equipment and supplies; Heating and air conditioning. **SICs:** 5078 (Refrigeration Equipment & Supplies); 5075 (Warm Air Heating & Air-Conditioning). **Officers:** Donald Miller, President.

■ 14605 ■ Bud Miller Supply Inc.
PO Box 5738
Ft. Wayne, IN 46895-5738
Phone: (219)482-3778 **Fax:** (219)482-3759
Products: Refrigeration equipment and supplies. **SIC:** 5078 (Refrigeration Equipment & Supplies). **Officers:** Clifford Miller, CEO.

■ 14606 ■ Milwaukee Stove and Furnace Supply Company Inc.
5070 W State St.
Milwaukee, WI 53208
Phone: (414)258-0300
Products: Heating, ventilation, and air-conditioning systems. **SICs:** 5074 (Plumbing & Hydronic Heating Supplies); 5039 (Construction Materials Nec). **Est:** 1922. **Sales:** $20,000,000 (2000). **Emp:** 70. **Officers:** Tom Engler, President; Terry VerStraate, Controller.

■ 14607 ■ Mingledorffs Inc.
6675 Jones Mill Ct.
Norcross, GA 30092
Phone: (404)446-6311 **Fax:** (770)239-2200
URL: http://www.mingledorffs.com
Products: Air-conditioning equipment; Heating equipment. **SIC:** 5075 (Warm Air Heating & Air-Conditioning). **Est:** 1939. **Sales:** $136,000,000 (2000). **Emp:** 240. **Officers:** Robert M. Kesterton, Chairman of the Board; Bud Mingzedorff, CEO; Matthew Ranstead, Chairman of the Board & CFO.

■ 14608 ■ Mobile Fleet Service of Spokane
216 N Dyer Rd.
Spokane, WA 99212-0830
Phone: (509)535-3311 **Fax:** (509)535-3983
Products: Refrigeration units. **SIC:** 5078 (Refrigeration Equipment & Supplies). **Officers:** Gene Ressa, President.

■ 14609 ■ J.W. Moffett Co. Inc.
11329 Oldfield Dr.
Carmel, IN 46033-3777
Phone: (317)848-1171
Products: Drinking water coolers, water softening systems, and drinking water systems. **SICs:** 5078 (Refrigeration Equipment & Supplies); 5074 (Plumbing & Hydronic Heating Supplies). **Officers:** Eric Moffett, President.

■ 14610 ■ Moore Supply Co.
4332 W Ferdinand St.
Chicago, IL 60624-1017
Phone: (312)235-4400 **Fax:** (312)235-4351
Products: Air-conditioning and heating equipment and supplies. **SIC:** 5075 (Warm Air Heating & Air-Conditioning). **Est:** 1934. **Emp:** 19. **Officers:** Richard D. Moore, President; Robert S. Moore, Vice President.

■ 14611 ■ Mortemp Inc.
PO Box 24967
Seattle, WA 98124
Phone: (206)767-0140
Products: Temperature controls, including heating, ventilation, and air-conditioning. **SICs:** 5063 (Electrical Apparatus & Equipment); 5063 (Electrical Apparatus & Equipment). **Sales:** $9,000,000 (2000). **Emp:** 27. **Officers:** Jerry Peterson, President.

■ 14612 ■ **Mountain Sales & Service Inc.**
6759 E 50th Ave.
Commerce City, CO 80022-4618
Phone: (303)289-5558 **Fax:** (303)289-2830
Products: Refrigeration equipment, supplies, and service; Food service equipment. **SICs:** 5078 (Refrigeration Equipment & Supplies); 5046 (Commercial Equipment Nec). **Est:** 1981. **Emp:** 20. **Officers:** Richard Muckler, President.

■ 14613 ■ **MR Supply Inc.**
PO Box 3106
Huntington, WV 25702-0106
Phone: (304)529-4168
Free: (888)529-4168 **Fax:** (304)529-1620
E-mail: mrsply@aol.com
Products: Refrigeration and heating equipment and supplies; Air Filters. **SIC:** 5078 (Refrigeration Equipment & Supplies). **Est:** 1934. **Emp:** 12. **Officers:** Richard Brunton Sr., President, Dir. of Marketing & Sales; Richard Brunton II, Customer Service Contact.

■ 14614 ■ **Mulder Refrigeration**
1109 S Commerce Ave.
Sioux Falls, SD 57103
Phone: (605)338-1897 **Fax:** (605)338-1820
Products: Refrigeration equipment and supplies; Restaurant equipment. **SIC:** 5078 (Refrigeration Equipment & Supplies). **Officers:** Ardeen Mulder, Owner.

■ 14615 ■ **Mutual Manufacturing and Supply Co.**
3300 Spring Grove Ave.
Cincinnati, OH 45225
Phone: (513)541-2330
Products: Plumbing, heating, and industrial products; Hydronic and steam heating. **SICs:** 5074 (Plumbing & Hydronic Heating Supplies); 5085 (Industrial Supplies); 5074 (Plumbing & Hydronic Heating Supplies). **Est:** 1917. **Sales:** $130,000,000 (1999). **Emp:** 280. **Officers:** Tom Meueller, President; John Robinson, VP of Operations.

■ 14616 ■ **J.B. Myers Group Inc.**
1020 Duquesne Blvd.
Duquesne, PA 15110
Phone: (412)469-1010 **Fax:** (412)469-9633
E-mail: jbmeyers@sgi.net
Products: Heating and cooling equipment. **SIC:** 5075 (Warm Air Heating & Air-Conditioning). **Est:** 1946. **Emp:** 25. **Officers:** Jeffrey J. Wappler; Beverly Rannigan. **Former Name:** Myers Furnace Supply Co.

■ 14617 ■ **National Temperature Control Centers Inc.**
13324 Farmington Rd.
Livonia, MI 48150
Phone: (734)525-3000 **Fax:** (248)583-1665
Products: Refrigeration and air conditioning equipment; Heating equipment. **SICs:** 5075 (Warm Air Heating & Air-Conditioning); 5078 (Refrigeration Equipment & Supplies). **Est:** 1975. **Sales:** $44,000,000 (2000). **Emp:** 206. **Officers:** Tom Twells, President; Tom Totte, Controller; Mark Linton, VP of Marketing & Sales; E. Wietecha, Dir of Human Resources.

■ 14618 ■ **New Energy Distributing**
PO Box 87
Dyersville, IA 52040
Phone: (319)875-8891
Free: (800)852-1224 **Fax:** (319)875-2023
URL: http://www.newenergyinc.com
Products: Gas and wood products, including fireplaces, logs, and pipes; Venting. **SIC:** 5074 (Plumbing & Hydronic Heating Supplies). **Est:** 1979. **Emp:** 10. **Officers:** Rick Eudaley, President, e-mail: rick@newenergyinc.com; Barb Koopmann, Office Mgr., e-mail: barb@newenergyinc.com.

■ 14619 ■ **NGE Inc.**
2937 Tanager Ave.
Los Angeles, CA 90040
Phone: (213)685-8340 **Fax:** (213)726-1644
Products: Air-conditioning equipment; Fans. **SIC:** 5075 (Warm Air Heating & Air-Conditioning). **Est:** 1933. **Emp:** 48. **Officers:** Mark O'Donnell, President; Janet Hoffman, Operations Mgr.

■ 14620 ■ **George Nikiforov, Inc.**
200 Park Ave. S, Ste. 514
New York, NY 10003
Phone: (212)473-4555 **Fax:** (212)473-5925
E-mail: geonikinc@aol.com
URL: http://www.geonikinc.com
Products: Heating equipment, including burners and boilers; Air-conditioning equipment; Environmental water controls; Pumps and pumping equipment; Industrial blowers and fans; Valves, including solenoid and safety; Ignition transformers; Pressure gauges and thermometers; Pipe fittings. **SICs:** 5075 (Warm Air Heating & Air-Conditioning); 5084 (Industrial Machinery & Equipment); 5074 (Plumbing & Hydronic Heating Supplies). **Est:** 1983. **Sales:** $3,000,000 (2000). **Emp:** 7. **Officers:** George Nikiforov, President.

■ 14621 ■ **Noland Co.**
6607 Wilson Blvd.
Falls Church, VA 22044
Phone: (703)241-5000 **Fax:** (703)241-5288
Products: Heating and cooling supplies. **SIC:** 5075 (Warm Air Heating & Air-Conditioning).

■ 14622 ■ **Noland Co.**
10512 Balls Ford Rd.
Manassas, VA 20108
Phone: (703)369-5531 **Fax:** (703)369-9065
Products: Heating and cooling equipment; Plumbing equipment. **SICs:** 5075 (Warm Air Heating & Air-Conditioning); 5074 (Plumbing & Hydronic Heating Supplies).

■ 14623 ■ **Noland Co.**
6601 Lee Hwy.
Warrenton, VA 20186
Phone: (540)347-6660 **Fax:** (540)347-6483
Products: Heating, cooling, and plumbing equipment and supplies. **SIC:** 5075 (Warm Air Heating & Air-Conditioning).

■ 14624 ■ **Northeast Louisiana Heating & Air Distributing**
504 N 17th St.
Monroe, LA 71201-6440
Phone: (318)325-2040
Free: (800)348-5594 **Fax:** (318)387-5534
Products: Heating and air-conditioning. **SIC:** 5075 (Warm Air Heating & Air-Conditioning). **Officers:** Sam Ladart, President.

■ 14625 ■ **Northwest Diesel & Refrigeration Services**
601 Apollo Ave. NE
St. Cloud, MN 56304-0213
Phone: (320)252-6141
Free: (888)252-6141 **Fax:** (320)252-2114
Products: Refrigeration equipment and supplies, including truck units. **SIC:** 5078 (Refrigeration Equipment & Supplies). **Est:** 1970. **Sales:** $1,000,000 (2000). **Emp:** 5. **Officers:** Arden Gall, President.

■ 14626 ■ **O'Connor Company, Inc.**
PO Box 2253
Wichita, KS 67201
Phone: (316)263-3187 **Fax:** (316)267-0115
Products: Heating and air-conditioning supplies. **SIC:** 5075 (Warm Air Heating & Air-Conditioning).

■ 14627 ■ **O'Connor Company, Inc.**
1250 Saline
North Kansas City, MO 64116
Phone: (816)471-4011
Free: (800)800-3540 **Fax:** (816)471-7794
Products: Heating and air-conditioning equipment. **SICs:** 5075 (Warm Air Heating & Air-Conditioning); 5088 (Transportation Equipment & Supplies).

■ 14628 ■ **One Stop Distributing**
225 Gladstone
Idaho Falls, ID 83401
Phone: (208)523-9862 **Fax:** (208)523-9862
Products: Refrigeration equipment and supplies; Plumbing, electrical, and HVAC supplies. **SIC:** 5074 (Plumbing & Hydronic Heating Supplies). **Est:** 1999. **Sales:** $1,500,000 (2000). **Emp:** 5. **Officers:** Robert Bidstrup, President, e-mail: bob@idahonet.com. **Former Name:** Jewel Electric Inc.

■ 14629 ■ **Orbilt Compressors, Inc.**
140 Mendel Dr. SW
Atlanta, GA 30336
Phone: (404)699-1521
Products: Air conditioning supply and parts. **SIC:** 5075 (Warm Air Heating & Air-Conditioning).

■ 14630 ■ **Osgood SM Company Inc.**
6513 City W Pky.
Eden Prairie, MN 55344-3248
Phone: (612)937-2045 **Fax:** (612)937-9667
Products: Refrigeration parts. **SIC:** 5078 (Refrigeration Equipment & Supplies). **Officers:** Al Luehmann, Chairman of the Board.

■ 14631 ■ **Pameco Corp.**
1000 Center Pl.
Norcross, GA 30093-1725
Phone: (770)798-0700 **Free:** (800)933-3809
Products: Air conditioning and heating equipment. **SIC:** 5075 (Warm Air Heating & Air-Conditioning). **Sales:** $484,000,000 (2000). **Emp:** 1,587. **Officers:** Gerry Gurbacki, CEO & Chairman of the Board; Theodore R. Kallgren, VP & CFO.

■ 14632 ■ **Passage Supply Co.**
PO Box 9037
El Paso, TX 79982
Phone: (915)778-9377 **Fax:** (915)772-9602
Products: Heating and Cooling equipment and supplies. **SIC:** 5075 (Warm Air Heating & Air-Conditioning). **Sales:** $10,000,000 (2000). **Emp:** 23.

■ 14633 ■ **Patco Inc.**
6955 Central Hwy.
Pennsauken, NJ 08109
Phone: (609)665-5276
Products: Air conditioners. **SIC:** 5064 (Electrical Appliances—Television & Radio). **Sales:** $3,000,000 (2000). **Emp:** 11. **Officers:** Paul J. Thompson, President.

■ 14634 ■ **Pelreco Inc.**
323 Pine Point Rd.
Scarborough, ME 04074-8810
Phone: (207)282-3683 **Fax:** (207)284-2137
Products: Food service equipment; Refrigeration equipment and supplies, including commercial reach-in and walk-in refrigerators. **SIC:** 5078 (Refrigeration Equipment & Supplies). **Officers:** Henry Pelletier, President.

■ 14635 ■ **Phillips Ice Service Inc.**
438 State St.
Bowling Green, KY 42101-1241
Phone: (502)843-8901
Products: Ice making machines; Ice. **SICs:** 5078 (Refrigeration Equipment & Supplies); 5199 (Nondurable Goods Nec). **Officers:** Wayne Marion, President.

■ 14636 ■ **Picone Building Products**
180 Long Island Ave.
Holtsville, NY 11742
Phone: (516)289-5490 **Fax:** (516)289-5416
URL: http://www.fpli.com
Products: Fireplaces. **SIC:** 5074 (Plumbing & Hydronic Heating Supplies). **Est:** 1977. **Emp:** 10. **Officers:** Susan Picone, General Mgr.; Sal Picone, Marketing & Sales Mgr.

■ 14637 ■ **Pilottes Transport Refrigeration**
PO Box 195
Swansea, MA 02777-0195
Phone: (508)673-4779 **Fax:** (508)675-8510
Products: Truck refrigeration equipment; Refrigerated storage trailer. **SIC:** 5078 (Refrigeration Equipment & Supplies). **Est:** 1971. **Officers:** Richard Pilotte, President.

■ 14638 ■ **Plains Auto Refrigeration**
212 San Pedro SE
Albuquerque, NM 87108
Phone: (505)266-0055 **Fax:** (505)266-0033
Products: Refrigeration equipment and supplies, including motor vehicle units; Automotive electronic systems, including cruise control and audio systems. **SICs:** 5078 (Refrigeration Equipment & Supplies); 5013 (Motor Vehicle Supplies & New Parts); 5065

(Electronic Parts & Equipment Nec). **Est:** 1954. **Sales:** $1,000,000 (2000). **Emp:** 5. **Officers:** Wayne Cardwell, Owner.

■ **14639** ■ **Polar Refrigeration & Restaurant Equipment**
6446 Homer Dr.
Anchorage, AK 99518-1957
Phone: (907)349-3500 **Fax:** (907)344-7053
Products: Refrigeration equipment and supplies, including commercial refrigeration equipment; Restaurant equipment. **SIC:** 5078 (Refrigeration Equipment & Supplies).

■ **14640** ■ **Pomeco Corp.**
2119 Wheeler
Ft. Smith, AR 72901
Phone: (501)785-1439
Free: (800)736-1440 **Fax:** (501)782-4548
URL: http://www.pameco.com
Products: Commercial refrigeration, heating, and air-conditioning supplies. **SICs:** 5078 (Refrigeration Equipment & Supplies); 5074 (Plumbing & Hydronic Heating Supplies). **Officers:** Mark Miller, General Mgr. **Alternate Name:** Superior Supply Co.

■ **14641** ■ **Porta-Lung Inc.**
7854 Logan St.
Denver, CO 80229-5810
Phone: (303)288-7575 **Fax:** (303)288-7577
Products: Negative pressure ventilators. **SIC:** 5047 (Medical & Hospital Equipment). **Sales:** $200,000 (2000). **Emp:** 3. **Officers:** Walter W. Weingarten Jr., President.

■ **14642** ■ **Potter Distributing Inc.**
4037 Roger B. Chaffee
Grand Rapids, MI 49548
Phone: (616)531-6860 **Fax:** (616)531-9578
Products: Warm air heating and cooling equipment. **SIC:** 5075 (Warm Air Heating & Air-Conditioning). **Est:** 1960. **Sales:** $30,000,000 (2000). **Emp:** 50. **Officers:** Douglas Potter, President.

■ **14643** ■ **Pro Air Inc.**
28731 CR-6
Elkhart, IN 46514
Phone: (219)264-5494 **Fax:** (219)264-2194
Products: Recreational vehicle air conditioners; Automotive air-conditioning equipment; Air-conditioning equipment. **SIC:** 5075 (Warm Air Heating & Air-Conditioning). **Est:** 1978. **Sales:** $5,000,000 (2000). **Emp:** 47. **Officers:** Dennis Haeck; Dennis Mitchell.

■ **14644** ■ **Progressive Wholesale Supply Co.**
2445 Northline Industrial Dr.
Maryland Heights, MO 63043-3308
Phone: (314)567-5131
Products: Heaters and air-conditioners. **SIC:** 5075 (Warm Air Heating & Air-Conditioning). **Est:** 1976. **Sales:** $4,700,000 (2000). **Emp:** 9. **Officers:** Mike Decker, President.

■ **14645** ■ **Prybil Enterprises**
PO Box 6
North Liberty, IA 52317-0006
Phone: (319)626-2333 **Fax:** (319)626-2370
Products: Refrigeration and air conditioning equipment; Furnaces; Mobile vehicle refrigeration systems. **SICs:** 5078 (Refrigeration Equipment & Supplies); 5075 (Warm Air Heating & Air-Conditioning); 5074 (Plumbing & Hydronic Heating Supplies). **Officers:** Gerald Prybil, Owner.

■ **14646** ■ **R & B Service Co.**
8524 Vineyard Ridge Rd. NE
Albuquerque, NM 87122-2620
Phone: (505)822-0829
Products: Refrigeration equipment and supplies; Ice making machines. **SIC:** 5078 (Refrigeration Equipment & Supplies). **Officers:** Barry Deutsch, Partner.

■ **14647** ■ **R & E Supply Inc.**
PO Box 2010
Hot Springs National Park, AR 71914
Phone: (501)623-2541
Products: Refrigeration equipment and supplies. **SIC:** 5078 (Refrigeration Equipment & Supplies). **Officers:** Robert Miller, President.

■ **14648** ■ **Recife Importing & Exporting Inc.**
2260 State St.
Hamden, CT 06517
Phone: (203)624-3503 **Fax:** (203)562-9409
Products: Air-conditioning equipment; Athletic footwear. **SICs:** 5075 (Warm Air Heating & Air-Conditioning); 5139 (Footwear). **Officers:** John Busca Jr., General Mgr.

■ **14649** ■ **RECO**
24 NE 51st
Oklahoma City, OK 73105
Phone: (405)236-1511 **Fax:** (405)521-1862
Products: Refrigeration and air conditioning equipment; Heating equipment. **SICs:** 5078 (Refrigeration Equipment & Supplies); 5075 (Warm Air Heating & Air-Conditioning). **Est:** 1939. **Sales:** $10,000,000 (2000). **Emp:** 49. **Officers:** Max E. Harris, CEO; Jack Litteral, CFO; Harvey M. Harris, Dir. of Marketing.

■ **14650** ■ **Red River Electric & Refrigeration Supply**
810 Crossland Ave.
Clarksville, TN 37040-3765
Phone: (931)552-6580 **Fax:** (931)553-8472
Products: Refrigeration equipment and supplies. **SIC:** 5078 (Refrigeration Equipment & Supplies). **Officers:** Don Wilson, President.

■ **14651** ■ **Reeve's Refrigeration & Heating Supply**
PO Box 546
Minot, ND 58702-0546
Phone: (701)838-0702
Products: Refrigeration equipment and supplies. **SICs:** 5078 (Refrigeration Equipment & Supplies); 5074 (Plumbing & Hydronic Heating Supplies); 5075 (Warm Air Heating & Air-Conditioning). **Officers:** Reeves Elsie, President.

■ **14652** ■ **Refractory Products Co.**
770 Tollgate Rd.
Elgin, IL 60123
Phone: (708)697-2350 **Fax:** (708)697-2366
Products: Furnace insulation products. **SIC:** 5075 (Warm Air Heating & Air-Conditioning). **Est:** 1925. **Sales:** $7,000,000 (2000). **Emp:** 50. **Officers:** David S. Woodruff, President; Bruce T. Morton, CFO; William Buckley, Dir. of Marketing.

■ **14653** ■ **Refrigeration & Air-Conditioning Maintenance Co.**
PO Box 43477
Las Vegas, NV 89116-1477
Phone: (702)642-3224
Products: Refrigeration and air conditioning equipment. **SICs:** 5078 (Refrigeration Equipment & Supplies); 5075 (Warm Air Heating & Air-Conditioning). **Officers:** Doug Smith, President.

■ **14654** ■ **Refrigeration Contractors Inc.**
PO Box 661
Gresham, OR 97030-0163
Phone: (503)257-8668
Products: Refrigeration equipment and supplies. **SIC:** 5078 (Refrigeration Equipment & Supplies). **Officers:** Ralph Rogers, President.

■ **14655** ■ **Refrigeration Equipment Co.**
820 Atlantic Ave.
North Kansas City, MO 64116
Phone: (816)471-1466
Products: Refrigeration and air conditioning equipment. **SICs:** 5078 (Refrigeration Equipment & Supplies); 5075 (Warm Air Heating & Air-Conditioning). **Sales:** $20,000,000 (1992). **Emp:** 100. **Officers:** Bob Heinzinger, President; Daniel Coon, Controller.

■ **14656** ■ **Refrigeration Heating Inc.**
345 19th St. N
PO Box 989
Fargo, ND 58107-0989
Phone: (701)232-7070 **Fax:** (701)293-9043
Products: HVAC and refrigeration equipment and supplies. **SIC:** 5078 (Refrigeration Equipment & Supplies). **Est:** 1979. **Officers:** Chris Daly, President.

■ **14657** ■ **Refrigeration Sales Corp.**
3405 Perkins Ave.
Cleveland, OH 44114
Phone: (216)881-7800 **Fax:** (216)881-1526
Products: Heating and air-conditioning supplies. **SICs:** 5075 (Warm Air Heating & Air-Conditioning); 5078 (Refrigeration Equipment & Supplies). **Est:** 1946. **Sales:** $39,000,000 (2000). **Emp:** 113. **Officers:** W. Farr Jr., Chairman of the Board; William J. Wagner, Controller; James Darus, Commercial Mgr.; W. Farr III, VP of Sales & Marketing.

■ **14658** ■ **Refrigeration Sales Inc.**
PO Box 928
Jackson, MI 49204-0928
Phone: (517)784-8579 **Fax:** (517)784-7373
Products: Refrigeration equipment and supplies, including commercial refrigeration equipment. **SIC:** 5078 (Refrigeration Equipment & Supplies). **Officers:** Russell Lyke, President.

■ **14659** ■ **Refrigeration Suppliers Inc.**
412 Aberdeen Rd.
Hampton, VA 23661-1324
Phone: (757)622-7191 **Fax:** (757)623-7124
Products: Refrigeration equipment and supplies. **SIC:** 5078 (Refrigeration Equipment & Supplies). **Officers:** John Boyenton, Chairman of the Board.

■ **14660** ■ **Refrigeration Supply Co.**
907 Barry Pl. NW
Washington, DC 20001-2298
Phone: (202)462-2600 **Fax:** (202)462-9213
E-mail: rscdc@aol.com
URL: http://www.rscdc.com
Products: Commercial refrigeration equipment and supplies; Refrigerant recycling. **SIC:** 5078 (Refrigeration Equipment & Supplies). **Est:** 1934. **Emp:** 8. **Officers:** Nikki Mehta, President.

■ **14661** ■ **Refron Inc.**
38-18 33rd St.
Long Island City, NY 11101
Phone: (718)392-8002
Free: (800)4RE-FRON **Fax:** (718)392-8006
E-mail: custserv@refron.com
URL: http://www.refron.com
Products: Refrigerant gases and refrigerant reclamation services. **SICs:** 5078 (Refrigeration Equipment & Supplies); 5075 (Warm Air Heating & Air-Conditioning). **Est:** 1954. **Emp:** 50. **Officers:** Jay Kestenbaum, President; Star Baccari, Sales/Marketing Contact, e-mail: star@refron.com.

■ **14662** ■ **Restaurant Design & Development**
2885 Aurora Ave., Ste. 7
Boulder, CO 80303-2251
Phone: (303)449-9331 **Fax:** (303)449-9333
Products: Refrigeration equipment and supplies; Food service supplies. **SICs:** 5078 (Refrigeration Equipment & Supplies); 5046 (Commercial Equipment Nec). **Officers:** Ajit Acharya, President.

■ **14663** ■ **RI Refrigeration Supply Co.**
199 Branch Ave.
Providence, RI 02904-2739
Phone: (401)421-8422
Free: (800)221-7477 **Fax:** (401)331-7594
Products: Refrigeration equipment and supplies. **SIC:** 5078 (Refrigeration Equipment & Supplies). **Officers:** David Richardson, President.

■ **14664** ■ **Robertshaw Uni-Line North America**
PO Box 2000
Corona, CA 91718-2000
Phone: (909)734-2600 **Fax:** (909)737-8261
Products: HVAC equipment parts. **SIC:** 5075 (Warm Air Heating & Air-Conditioning). **Sales:** $40,900,000 (2000). **Emp:** 175. **Officers:** Gerry Wiley, VP & General Merchandising Mgr.

■ **14665** ■ **Robinson Fin Machines Inc.**
13670 Hwy. 68 S
Kenton, OH 43326-9302
Phone: (419)674-4152 **Fax:** (419)674-4154
E-mail: info@robfin.com
URL: http://www.robfin.com
Products: Cooling fins. **SIC:** 5075 (Warm Air Heating & Air-Conditioning). **Est:** 1983. **Sales:** $5,000,000

(2000). **Emp:** 45. **Officers:** Ruth A. Haushalter, President; David Haushalter, Sales/Marketing Contact, e-mail: robfin@kanton.com; Ruth Haushalter, Customer Service Contact; Sheryl Haushalter-Herron, Human Resources Contact.

■ **14666** ■ **Rood Utilities**
PO Box 216
Auburn, NY 13021
Phone: (315)252-7204
Free: (800)721-4004 **Fax:** (315)253-3073
Products: Heating equipment and supplies. **SIC:** 5075 (Warm Air Heating & Air-Conditioning).

■ **14667** ■ **W.A. Roosevelt Co.**
PO Box 1208
La Crosse, WI 54602-1208
Phone: (608)781-2000 **Fax:** (608)781-3355
Products: Heating and plumbing supplies; Electrical supplies; Refrigeration supplies. **SICs:** 5078 (Refrigeration Equipment & Supplies); 5075 (Warm Air Heating & Air-Conditioning); 5074 (Plumbing & Hydronic Heating Supplies); 5063 (Electrical Apparatus & Equipment). **Est:** 1868. **Sales:** $23,000,000 (2000). **Emp:** 76. **Officers:** Steve W. Reiman, President; Richard W. Spencer, CFO; Paul J. Hundt, Dir. of Marketing & Sales; Thomas M. Brindley, Exec. VP.

■ **14668** ■ **Roswell Winnelson Co.**
223 E 3rd St.
Roswell, NM 88201-6219
Phone: (505)623-8700
Free: (800)432-7840 **Fax:** (505)623-8700
Products: Refrigeration equipment and supplies. **SIC:** 5078 (Refrigeration Equipment & Supplies). **Officers:** Benjamin Fulkerson, President.

■ **14669** ■ **Royal Sovereign Corp.**
100 W Sheffield Ave.
Englewood, NJ 07631
Phone: (201)568-0830
Free: (800)397-1025 **Fax:** (201)568-1079
URL: http://www.royalsov.com
Products: Heating and cooling equipment; Laminating equipment and film. **SIC:** 5075 (Warm Air Heating & Air-Conditioning). **Est:** 1986. **Sales:** $15,000,000 (2000). **Emp:** 10. **Officers:** T.K. Lim, President; Jeffrey Paull, Sales/Marketing Contact. **Alternate Name:** Royal Centurian, Inc.

■ **14670** ■ **RTI Technologies, Inc.**
PO Box 3099
York, PA 17402-0099
Phone: (717)840-0678
Free: (800)468-2321 **Fax:** (717)755-8304
E-mail: rti@rtitech.com
URL: http://www.rtitech.com
Products: Refrigerant recycling equipment; Automotive service equipment. **SICs:** 5078 (Refrigeration Equipment & Supplies); 5013 (Motor Vehicle Supplies & New Parts). **Est:** 1990. **Emp:** 60. **Officers:** Steve Kijak, VP Field Sales, e-mail: s.kijak@attglobalnet; Allen Updegraff, VP Field Sales, e-mail: rti@attglobal.net; Jim Markle, VP of Marketing, e-mail: jem@rtitech.com; Jim Vinarski, President & CEO, e-mail: jav@rtitech.com; Ed Strausbaugh, Distribution Mgr., e-mail: ejs@rtitech.com.

■ **14671** ■ **Sabol and Rice Inc.**
PO Box 25957
Salt Lake City, UT 84125-0957
Phone: (801)973-2300 **Fax:** (801)972-5033
Products: Commercial heaters and air-conditioners. **SIC:** 5075 (Warm Air Heating & Air-Conditioning). **Est:** 1958. **Sales:** $11,000,000 (2000). **Emp:** 30. **Officers:** George Sabol Sr. Sr., President; Robert Rice, Secretary.

■ **14672** ■ **Salem Refrigeration Company Inc.**
600 Aureole St.
Winston-Salem, NC 27107-3250
Phone: (910)784-8815
Products: Commercial refrigeration equipment and supplies. **SIC:** 5078 (Refrigeration Equipment & Supplies). **Officers:** James Vernon, President.

■ **14673** ■ **Saunco Air Technologies**
PO Box 178
Hickman, CA 95323
Phone: (209)874-2357 **Fax:** (209)874-1174
Products: Air filtration systems. **SIC:** 5075 (Warm Air Heating & Air-Conditioning).

■ **14674** ■ **Sawnee Refrigeration & Welding Supply, Inc.**
PO Box 207
Cumming, GA 30028-0207
Phone: (770)889-2295
Products: Refrigeration supplies. **SIC:** 5078 (Refrigeration Equipment & Supplies).

■ **14675** ■ **Scatena York Company**
2000 Oakdale Ave.
San Francisco, CA 94124
Phone: (415)285-6600
Free: (800)752-6161 **Fax:** (415)695-1712
E-mail: mailbox@scatenayork.com
URL: http://www.criosbanc-scotenayork.com
Products: Refrigerated display cases. **SIC:** 5078 (Refrigeration Equipment & Supplies). **Est:** 1941. **Sales:** $4,500,000 (2000). **Emp:** 9. **Officers:** James A. Scatena Jr., President; John B. Cain, Treasurer; Don L. Dotson, VP of Sales.

■ **14676** ■ **Scott's Market Equipment Inc.**
RR 1, Box 275
Marsing, ID 83639-9525
Phone: (208)888-3886 **Fax:** (208)896-4263
Products: Refrigeration equipment and supplies, including refrigerated display equipment. **SIC:** 5078 (Refrigeration Equipment & Supplies). **Officers:** W. Scott, President.

■ **14677** ■ **Servidyne System**
PO Box 93846
Atlanta, GA 30377-0846
Products: Air conditioning supply and parts. **SIC:** 5075 (Warm Air Heating & Air-Conditioning).

■ **14678** ■ **Shelby-Skipwith Inc.**
PO Box 777
Memphis, TN 38101
Phone: (901)948-4481
Products: Heating and air-conditioning equipment. **SICs:** 5075 (Warm Air Heating & Air-Conditioning); 5074 (Plumbing & Hydronic Heating Supplies). **Est:** 1940. **Sales:** $12,000,000 (2000). **Emp:** 28. **Officers:** John Wallace, President; Evelyn Bennett, Treasurer & Secty.; Stoughton Outlan, Dir. of Marketing.

■ **14679** ■ **Shelton Winair Co.**
740 River Rd.
Shelton, CT 06484
Phone: (203)929-6319
Free: (800)972-2221 **Fax:** (203)929-6373
E-mail: sheltonwinair@email.msn.com
URL: http://www.sheltonwinair.com
Products: Heating, ventilating, and air-conditioning equipment and supplies; Adhesives; Rubber products. **SIC:** 5075 (Warm Air Heating & Air-Conditioning). **Est:** 1980. **Emp:** 15.

■ **14680** ■ **Shepler Refrigeration Inc.**
PO Box 12146
Portland, OR 97212-0146
Phone: (503)282-7255 **Fax:** (503)282-7567
Products: Refrigeration equipment and supplies. **SIC:** 5078 (Refrigeration Equipment & Supplies). **Est:** 1930. **Emp:** 30. **Officers:** Norman Keck, President.

■ **14681** ■ **Shoemaker of Indiana, Inc.**
711 S Main St.
South Bend, IN 46601-3009
Phone: (219)288-4661
Free: (800)582-5539 **Fax:** (219)288-4664
Products: Heating and air-conditioning equipment and supplies. **SICs:** 5078 (Refrigeration Equipment & Supplies); 5075 (Warm Air Heating & Air-Conditioning); 5074 (Plumbing & Hydronic Heating Supplies). **Officers:** Chuck Bybee, President.

■ **14682** ■ **Shollmier Distribution Inc.**
312 Time Saver
Harahan, LA 70123
Phone: (504)733-8662
Products: Heating and air conditioning equipment and supplies. **SIC:** 5075 (Warm Air Heating & Air-Conditioning).

■ **14683** ■ **Shore Distributors Inc.**
PO Box 2017
Salisbury, MD 21802-2017
Phone: (410)749-3121 **Fax:** (410)749-3121
Products: Heating, air-conditioning, and plumbing supplies. **SICs:** 5074 (Plumbing & Hydronic Heating Supplies); 5075 (Warm Air Heating & Air-Conditioning). **Est:** 1946. **Sales:** $15,000,000 (1999). **Emp:** 44. **Officers:** J.F. Morris, President; John A. Morris, Sales Mgr.; Gary Brown, Controller, e-mail: gbrown@shoredist.com.

■ **14684** ■ **Shurail Supply Inc.**
9124 Grand Ave. S
Bloomington, MN 55420
Phone: (952)884-8266
Free: (800)886-7487 **Fax:** (952)884-1211
Products: HVAC equipment and supplies; Contractor tools. **SIC:** 5075 (Warm Air Heating & Air-Conditioning). **Est:** 1965. **Sales:** $3,000,000 (2000). **Emp:** 15. **Officers:** Dorothy Martin; Debra Martin.

■ **14685** ■ **Sisco Products Inc.**
PO Box 549
Buford, GA 30518-0549
Phone: (404)945-2181 **Fax:** (404)932-5672
Products: Refrigeration equipment and supplies, including ice making machines. **SIC:** 5078 (Refrigeration Equipment & Supplies). **Officers:** David Koenig, President.

■ **14686** ■ **Skipper Heating, Air Conditioning & Fireplace Showroom**
3524 Green St.
Muskegon, MI 49444-3812
Phone: (231)739-4444 **Fax:** (231)733-7868
E-mail: skipperh@gte.net
Products: Heating and cooling systems; Gas and wood fireplaces; Gas grills and equipment. **SICs:** 5074 (Plumbing & Hydronic Heating Supplies); 5075 (Warm Air Heating & Air-Conditioning). **Est:** 1946. **Sales:** $1,726,000 (1999). **Emp:** 18. **Officers:** Thomas J. Skipper, President. **Former Name:** Skipper Heating and Air Conditioning.

■ **14687** ■ **S.M.S. Distributors**
451 Beech Ave.
PO Box 150
Woodbury Heights, NJ 08097
Phone: (609)853-5919
Free: (800)214-4910 **Fax:** (609)845-2042
E-mail: wbss@bellatlantic.net
URL: http://www.sms-chim-line.com
Products: Chimney liners and direct vent pipe. **SIC:** 5074 (Plumbing & Hydronic Heating Supplies). **Est:** 1986. **Sales:** $250,000 (2000). **Emp:** 3. **Officers:** Donald Steward Sr., President; Mark Murphy, Sales/Marketing Contact.

■ **14688** ■ **Thomas Somerville Co.**
105 Fairfax
Martinsburg, WV 25401
Phone: (304)263-4981
Products: Heating and cooling supplies. **SICs:** 5075 (Warm Air Heating & Air-Conditioning); 5074 (Plumbing & Hydronic Heating Supplies).

■ **14689** ■ **Soukup Brothers Mechanical Inc.**
3328 S Highland Dr.
Las Vegas, NV 89109-3427
Phone: (702)796-1600 **Fax:** (702)796-0809
Products: Refrigeration equipment and supplies; Ice making machines. **SIC:** 5078 (Refrigeration Equipment & Supplies). **Officers:** Dennis Soukup, President.

■ **14690** ■ **Southeast Wholesale Equipment Distributors Inc.**
4400 Zenith St.
Metairie, LA 70001-1208
Phone: (504)888-2700 **Fax:** (504)454-6950
Products: Refrigeration equipment and supplies; Ice

making machines. **SIC:** 5078 (Refrigeration Equipment & Supplies). **Officers:** Wayne Vidrine, President.

■ **14691** ■ **Southern California Air-Conditioning Distributors**
16900 E Chestnut St.
La Puente, CA 91748
Phone: (626)854-4500   **Fax:** (626)854-4690
Products: Air conditioning and heating equipment. **SIC:** 5075 (Warm Air Heating & Air-Conditioning). **Est:** 1915. **Sales:** $10,000,000 (2000). **Emp:** 160. **Officers:** John Staples, President; John Scarsi, Vice President; Dan Berliner, Sales Mgr.

■ **14692** ■ **Southern Refrigeration Corp.**
2026 Salem Ave.
Roanoke, VA 24027
Phone: (703)342-3493   **Fax:** (703)343-2163
Products: Parts for repairing air-conditioners. **SICs:** 5078 (Refrigeration Equipment & Supplies); 5075 (Warm Air Heating & Air-Conditioning). **Est:** 1947. **Sales:** $18,000,000 (2000). **Emp:** 61. **Officers:** John S. Lang Jr., President; Sidney Johnson, VP of Finance; Paul D. Kabler, General Mgr.

■ **14693** ■ **SPL Associates Inc.**
PO Box 759
Williston, VT 05495-0759
Phone: (802)864-9831
Products: Refrigeration equipment and supplies; Commercial refrigeration equipment, including reach-in and walk-in refrigerators. **SIC:** 5078 (Refrigeration Equipment & Supplies). **Officers:** Samuel Levin, President.

■ **14694** ■ **Squire Supply Corp.**
PO Box 8086
Columbus, OH 43201
Phone: (614)291-4676   **Fax:** (614)291-7972
Products: Heating and air-conditioning equipment. **SICs:** 5075 (Warm Air Heating & Air-Conditioning); 5074 (Plumbing & Hydronic Heating Supplies). **Est:** 1950. **Sales:** $2,000,000 (2000). **Emp:** 25. **Officers:** Jack Balogh, President; Tim Colter, CFO.

■ **14695** ■ **Bruce Stancil Refrigeration Services Inc.**
RR 4, Box 534
Wilson, NC 27893-9432
Phone: (919)237-7959
Products: Commercial refrigeration equipment and supplies. **SIC:** 5078 (Refrigeration Equipment & Supplies). **Officers:** Jackie Vaughn, President.

■ **14696** ■ **Standfix Air Distribution Products - ACME**
214 Commercial St.
Medina, NY 14103
Phone: (716)798-0300
Free: (800)229-0021   **Fax:** (716)798-0021
Products: Furnace pipes and fittings. **SIC:** 5075 (Warm Air Heating & Air-Conditioning). **Est:** 1904. **Emp:** 55. **Officers:** Chuck Kreppeneck, Branch Mgr. **Former Name:** Acme Manufacturing Co.

■ **14697** ■ **Stant Manufacturing Inc.**
1620 Columbia Ave.
Connersville, IN 47331
Phone: (765)825-3121   **Fax:** (765)825-0285
URL: http://www.stant.com
Products: Heating and air-conditioning supplies. **SICs:** 5013 (Motor Vehicle Supplies & New Parts); 5013 (Motor Vehicle Supplies & New Parts). **Est:** 1898. **Sales:** $100,000,000 (2000). **Emp:** 800. **Officers:** Lou Braga, Exec. VP & General Mgr.; Mike Lafuze, Finance Officer; Don Vogelsang, Controller; John Foote, VP of Human Resources; John Foote, VP of Human Resources.

■ **14698** ■ **Star Restaurant Equipment & Supplies**
PO Box 1716
Bismarck, ND 58502-1716
Phone: (701)255-7729
Products: Restaurant equipment and supplies. **SIC:** 5078 (Refrigeration Equipment & Supplies). **Est:** 1984. **Officers:** Cindy Steidler, Partner.

■ **14699** ■ **Star Steel Supply Co.**
24417 Groesbeck Hwy.
Warren, MI 48089-4723
Products: Ventilation fittings. **SIC:** 5075 (Warm Air Heating & Air-Conditioning). **Est:** 1919. **Sales:** $22,000,000 (2000). **Emp:** 100. **Officers:** Jeffrey R. Lee, CEO & President; Garlene Stephens, VP of Operations; Randy Mangeno, Dir. of Marketing.

■ **14700** ■ **Sturdvant Refrigeration/Air-Conditioning**
300 Hoohana St.
Kahului, HI 96732-2966
Phone: (808)871-6404   **Fax:** (808)871-6400
Products: Sheet metal; Air-conditioners for residential use. **SICs:** 5075 (Warm Air Heating & Air-Conditioning); 5051 (Metals Service Centers & Offices). **Est:** 1980. **Sales:** $2,500,000 (2000). **Emp:** 20. **Officers:** Steve Sturdevant, President.

■ **14701** ■ **Suburban Manufacturing Co.**
PO Box 399
Dayton, TN 37321
Phone: (423)775-2131   **Fax:** (423)775-2335
Products: Heating equipment; Recreational Vehicle accessories; Air-conditioning equipment; Recreational vehicle air conditioners. **SICs:** 5075 (Warm Air Heating & Air-Conditioning); 5013 (Motor Vehicle Supplies & New Parts). **Est:** 1946. **Emp:** 450.

■ **14702** ■ **Summit Wholesale**
38 Ganson Ave.
PO Box 921
Batavia, NY 14021
Phone: (716)343-7022   **Fax:** (716)343-5562
E-mail: summit@iinc.com
Products: Fireplace equipment. **SIC:** 5074 (Plumbing & Hydronic Heating Supplies). **Est:** 1987. **Sales:** $6,000,000 (2000). **Emp:** 15.

■ **14703** ■ **Superior Supply Co.**
14315 W 100 St.
Lenexa, KS 66215
Phone: (913)888-4467   **Fax:** (913)888-9017
Products: Heating, air-conditioning, and refrigeration supplies. **SICs:** 5075 (Warm Air Heating & Air-Conditioning); 5078 (Refrigeration Equipment & Supplies).

■ **14704** ■ **Superior Supply Co.**
2935 SW Van Buren
Topeka, KS 66611
Phone: (913)226-3571   **Fax:** (785)266-2429
Products: Heating, air-conditioning, and refrigeration supplies. **SICs:** 5075 (Warm Air Heating & Air-Conditioning); 5078 (Refrigeration Equipment & Supplies).

■ **14705** ■ **Superior Supply Co.**
1420 S 6th St.
St. Joseph, MO 64501
Phone: (816)233-9111   **Fax:** (816)233-2362
Products: Heating and air-conditioning equipment; Refrigeration equipment. **SICs:** 5075 (Warm Air Heating & Air-Conditioning); 5078 (Refrigeration Equipment & Supplies).

■ **14706** ■ **Superior Supply Co.**
1405 Illinois Ave.
Columbia, MO 65203
Phone: (573)449-0806   **Fax:** (573)875-2724
Products: Heating and air-conditioning equipment; Refrigeration equipment. **SICs:** 5075 (Warm Air Heating & Air-Conditioning); 5078 (Refrigeration Equipment & Supplies).

■ **14707** ■ **Superior Supply Co.**
RR 1, Box 105H
Linn Creek, MO 65052
Phone: (573)346-5914   **Fax:** (573)346-5915
Products: Heating, air-conditioning, and refrigeration equipment. **SICs:** 5075 (Warm Air Heating & Air-Conditioning); 5078 (Refrigeration Equipment & Supplies). **Former Name:** Pameco.

■ **14708** ■ **Superior Supply Co.**
1020 Illinois
Joplin, MO 64801
Phone: (417)781-1521   **Fax:** (417)781-4120
Products: Heating and air-conditioning equipment; Refrigeration equipment. **SICs:** 5075 (Warm Air Heating & Air-Conditioning); 5078 (Refrigeration Equipment & Supplies).

■ **14709** ■ **Superior Supply Company Inc.**
215 Laura
Wichita, KS 67211
Phone: (316)263-6212   **Fax:** (316)263-6251
Products: Heating and air-conditioning equipment and parts. **SIC:** 5075 (Warm Air Heating & Air-Conditioning). **Est:** 1954. **Sales:** $13,000,000 (2000). **Emp:** 50. **Officers:** Jack Simpson, President; Bill Bowles, CFO.

■ **14710** ■ **Tarrant Service Agency, Inc.**
2450 Valley Rd., Ste. 6
Reno, NV 89512-1609
Phone: (702)356-8141   **Fax:** (702)356-1459
Products: Commercial refrigeration equipment; Air conditioning machinery and parts. **SICs:** 5075 (Warm Air Heating & Air-Conditioning); 5078 (Refrigeration Equipment & Supplies). **Officers:** Rhio Moeller, Branch Manager.

■ **14711** ■ **Taylor Dakota Distributors**
517 Airport Rd.
Bismarck, ND 58504-6107
Phone: (701)223-2338   **Fax:** (701)223-0028
Products: Refrigeration equipment and supplies. **SIC:** 5078 (Refrigeration Equipment & Supplies). **Officers:** Tom Kambeitz, President.

■ **14712** ■ **Taylor Distributors of Indiana**
2605 Ardmore Ave.
Ft. Wayne, IN 46809-2956
Phone: (219)478-1551   **Free:** (800)874-3213
Products: Refrigeration equipment and supplies. **SIC:** 5078 (Refrigeration Equipment & Supplies). **Officers:** Grayston Witmer, President.

■ **14713** ■ **TD's Radio & TV**
316 W Main St.
Norman, OK 73069-1311
Phone: (405)321-5210   **Fax:** (405)321-5215
Products: Electrical appliances, including television sets and radios; Air conditioning appliances; Portable dehumidifiers. **SIC:** 5064 (Electrical Appliances—Television & Radio). **Officers:** Dean Waddell, Owner.

■ **14714** ■ **Teague Refrigeration Service**
PO Box 630
Deming, NM 88031-0630
Phone: (505)546-9691
Products: Refrigeration equipment and supplies; Ice making machines. **SIC:** 5078 (Refrigeration Equipment & Supplies). **Officers:** Leon Teague, Owner.

■ **14715** ■ **Tempaco Inc.**
PO Box 547667
Orlando, FL 32803
Phone: (407)898-3456   **Fax:** (407)898-7316
E-mail: info@tempaco.com
URL: http://www.tempaco.com
Products: Hvac Parts and controls. **SICs:** 5084 (Industrial Machinery & Equipment); 5075 (Warm Air Heating & Air-Conditioning). **Est:** 1946. **Sales:** $14,000,000 (2000). **Emp:** 32. **Officers:** Charles T. Clark, CEO & President; Maria Robinson, CFO; J. Mellon, VP ofCommunications; Marvin Ross, VP of Sales.

■ **14716** ■ **Tempco Supplies Inc.**
2034 S Southland Ave.
Gonzales, LA 70737-4158
Phone: (504)647-3330
Free: (800)880-3332   **Fax:** (504)647-4723
URL: http://www.Tempcosupplies.com
Products: Refrigeration equipment and supplies; Refrigerated display equipment Heating and air conditioning equipment and supplies; Ventilation equipment. **SIC:** 5078 (Refrigeration Equipment & Supplies). **Est:** 1988. **Sales:** $1,500,000 (2000). **Emp:** 5. **Officers:** Brian Lambert; Kenny Gautreau; Charles Gautreau, President.

■ 14717 ■ **Temperature Equipment Corp.**
17725 Volbrecht Rd.
Lansing, IL 60438
Phone: (708)418-0900   **Fax:** (708)418-5100
Products: Heating, air-conditioning, and refrigeration products, including replacement parts and supplies. **SICs:** 5075 (Warm Air Heating & Air-Conditioning); 5074 (Plumbing & Hydronic Heating Supplies); 5078 (Refrigeration Equipment & Supplies). **Est:** 1935. **Sales:** $90,000,000 (1999). **Emp:** 140. **Officers:** F.A. Mungo, President; R.F. Mungo, Exec. VP; Barry Masek, CFO.

■ 14718 ■ **Temperature Systems Inc.**
PO Box 9090
Madison, WI 53725-9090
Phone: (608)271-7500
Products: Heating and cooling systems. **SIC:** 5075 (Warm Air Heating & Air-Conditioning). **Est:** 1947. **Sales:** $18,000,000 (2000). **Emp:** 80. **Officers:** T. Riker, President; Bob Schmidt, Dir. of Systems.

■ 14719 ■ **Tesco Distributors Inc.**
300 Nye Ave.
Irvington, NJ 07111
Phone: (973)399-0333   **Fax:** (973)399-0599
Products: Air-conditioning and refrigeration equipment. **SICs:** 5075 (Warm Air Heating & Air-Conditioning); 5078 (Refrigeration Equipment & Supplies). **Sales:** $15,000,000 (2000). **Emp:** 65. **Officers:** Arnold Blun, President.

■ 14720 ■ **Tesdell Refrigeration Supply Inc.**
1800 Dixon St., No. H
Des Moines, IA 50316-2172
Phone: (515)288-3634
Free: (800)383-2369   **Fax:** (515)288-8704
Products: Warm air heating and cooling equipment. **SIC:** 5075 (Warm Air Heating & Air-Conditioning). **Officers:** Erik Tesdell, President.

■ 14721 ■ **Thermal Equipment Company Inc.**
RR 7, Box 1145
Thomasville, GA 31792-9541
Phone: (912)226-7110
Products: Refrigeration equipment and supplies; Ice making machines. **SIC:** 5078 (Refrigeration Equipment & Supplies). **Officers:** Larry Tuten, President.

■ 14722 ■ **Thermal Supply Inc.**
717 S Lander St.
Seattle, WA 98134
Phone: (206)624-4590
Products: Refrigeration equipment. **SIC:** 5078 (Refrigeration Equipment & Supplies). **Sales:** $31,000,000 (2000). **Emp:** 100. **Officers:** Bob Monroe, President.

■ 14723 ■ **Thermo King of Baltimore Inc.**
7135 Standard Dr.
Hanover, MD 21076-1320
Phone: (410)712-7200   **Fax:** (410)712-7204
Products: Commercial refrigeration equipment and supplies. **SIC:** 5078 (Refrigeration Equipment & Supplies). **Officers:** James Ward, President.

■ 14724 ■ **Thermo King of Chattanooga**
PO Box 71826
Chattanooga, TN 37407-0826
Phone: (423)622-2159   **Fax:** (423)622-9570
Products: Automobile air-conditioners. **SIC:** 5075 (Warm Air Heating & Air-Conditioning). **Officers:** Curtis Matthews, President.

■ 14725 ■ **Thermo King of Nashville Inc.**
PO Box 101011
Nashville, TN 37224-1011
Phone: (615)244-2996
Free: (800)999-8754   **Fax:** (615)244-3019
Products: Refrigeration equipment and supplies, including motor vehicle units. **SIC:** 5078 (Refrigeration Equipment & Supplies). **Officers:** Charles Miller, President.

■ 14726 ■ **Thermo King of Sioux Falls**
1709 N Cliff Ave.
Sioux Falls, SD 57103-0145
Phone: (605)334-5162   **Fax:** (605)334-1556
Products: Mobile vehicle refrigeration systems; Refrigeration and air conditioning equipment. **SIC:** 5078 (Refrigeration Equipment & Supplies). **Officers:** Ken Tschetter, Chairman of the Board.

■ 14727 ■ **Three States**
4001 Lakefront Ct.
Earth City, MO 63045-1413
Products: Heating and cooling vents. **SIC:** 5075 (Warm Air Heating & Air-Conditioning). **Est:** 1865. **Sales:** $5,500,000 (2000). **Emp:** 27. **Officers:** Bill Haines, President; A. Conary, Controller.

■ 14728 ■ **Three States Supply Co.**
PO Box 646
Memphis, TN 38101
Phone: (901)948-8651   **Fax:** (901)948-2454
Products: HVAC supplies, equipment, and parts; Sheet metal. **SICs:** 5075 (Warm Air Heating & Air-Conditioning); 5051 (Metals Service Centers & Offices). **Est:** 1945. **Sales:** $70,000,000 (2000). **Emp:** 235. **Officers:** Charles M. Brejot, President.

■ 14729 ■ **Total Supply**
1865 Beaver Ridge Cir.
Norcross, GA 30071
Phone: (770)417-1806
Products: Air conditioning supply and parts. **SIC:** 5075 (Warm Air Heating & Air-Conditioning).

■ 14730 ■ **Total Supply**
5158 Kennedy Rd.
Forest Park, GA 30297
Phone: (404)608-0062
Free: (800)209-1526   **Fax:** (404)609-0605
Products: Air conditioning supply, parts, and equipment. **SIC:** 5075 (Warm Air Heating & Air-Conditioning). **Est:** 1991. **Sales:** $30,000,000 (1999). **Emp:** 60.

■ 14731 ■ **Total Supply**
4620 S Atlanta Rd. SE
Smyrna, GA 30080
Phone: (404)792-1696
Products: Air conditioning supply and parts. **SIC:** 5075 (Warm Air Heating & Air-Conditioning).

■ 14732 ■ **Total Supply Inc.**
5158 Kennedy Rd., Ste. F
Forest Park, GA 30297
Phone: (404)608-0062
Products: Heating, ventilation, air conditioning, and refrigeration equipment. **SIC:** 5075 (Warm Air Heating & Air-Conditioning).

■ 14733 ■ **Traco Industrial Corp.**
461 W 126th
New York, NY 10027-2535
Phone: (212)865-7700   **Fax:** (212)222-6817
Products: Air conditioning, refrigeration, and heating equipment. **SICs:** 5075 (Warm Air Heating & Air-Conditioning); 5078 (Refrigeration Equipment & Supplies). **Emp:** 49.

■ 14734 ■ **Tradex Corporation**
PO Box 495188
Garland, TX 75049
Phone: (972)840-8805   **Fax:** (972)840-1265
Products: Heating equipment; Refrigeration equipment; Automotive parts and accessories; Vacuum cleaners; Lathes. **SICs:** 5075 (Warm Air Heating & Air-Conditioning); 5064 (Electrical Appliances—Television & Radio); 5013 (Motor Vehicle Supplies & New Parts); 5078 (Refrigeration Equipment & Supplies). **Officers:** Vincent Heinz, President; Tammy Heinz, Sales/Marketing Contact, e-mail: toheinz@aol.com. **Former Name:** Tradex International.

■ 14735 ■ **Trane Co**
3600 Pammel Creek
La Crosse, WI 54601
Phone: (608)787-2000   **Fax:** (608)787-2552
Products: A/C and refrigeration equipment. **SICs:** 5075 (Warm Air Heating & Air-Conditioning); 5078 (Refrigeration Equipment & Supplies). **Officers:** James Schultz, CEO.

■ 14736 ■ **Transport Refrigeration of Sioux Falls**
4622 N Cliff Ave.
Sioux Falls, SD 57104-0554
Phone: (605)332-3861   **Fax:** (605)332-4917
Products: Mobile vehicle refrigeration systems; Refrigeration and air conditioning equipment. **SICs:** 5078 (Refrigeration Equipment & Supplies); 5075 (Warm Air Heating & Air-Conditioning). **Officers:** Jim Keizer, President.

■ 14737 ■ **Tri-City Fuel and Heating Company Inc.**
PO Box 5708
West Columbia, SC 29171
Phone: (803)796-9172   **Fax:** (803)739-5636
Products: Heating units; Air-conditioners. **SICs:** 5075 (Warm Air Heating & Air-Conditioning); 5074 (Plumbing & Hydronic Heating Supplies). **Est:** 1920. **Sales:** $3,000,000 (2000). **Emp:** 30. **Officers:** Russell F. Schull, President.

■ 14738 ■ **Tri-State Distributors Inc.**
PO Box 247
Royston, GA 30662-0247
Phone: (706)245-6164   **Fax:** (706)245-8112
Products: Air-conditioning equipment; Heating equipment. **SICs:** 5074 (Plumbing & Hydronic Heating Supplies); 5075 (Warm Air Heating & Air-Conditioning). **Officers:** Steve Williams, Chairman of the Board.

■ 14739 ■ **Truck Thermo King Inc.**
PO Box 898
Harrisonburg, VA 22801-0898
Phone: (540)434-7004
Products: Mobile vehicle refrigeration systems. **SIC:** 5078 (Refrigeration Equipment & Supplies). **Officers:** Robert Plecker, President.

■ 14740 ■ **Turbex Heat Transfer Corp.**
PO Box 10208
Westminster, CA 92685-0208
Phone: (714)996-3270
Products: Condensers and evaporators. **SIC:** 5084 (Industrial Machinery & Equipment). **Sales:** $2,000,000 (2000). **Emp:** 14. **Officers:** Larry Carter, President; Kathy Shubin, Controller.

■ 14741 ■ **Twin City ICEE Inc.**
8136 Cypress St.
West Monroe, LA 71291-8290
Phone: (318)396-4266   **Fax:** (318)396-3431
Products: Refrigeration equipment and supplies. **SIC:** 5078 (Refrigeration Equipment & Supplies). **Officers:** Joseph Festervan, President.

■ 14742 ■ **Ultima**
345 E 103rd St.
New York, NY 10029
Phone: (212)534-8921
Products: Air-conditioning and refrigeration supplies. **SICs:** 5075 (Warm Air Heating & Air-Conditioning); 5078 (Refrigeration Equipment & Supplies).

■ 14743 ■ **Underwood HVAC, Inc.**
4450 Commerce SW
Atlanta, GA 30336
Phone: (404)691-1505
Products: Air conditioning supply and parts. **SIC:** 5075 (Warm Air Heating & Air-Conditioning).

■ 14744 ■ **United Automatic Heating Supplies**
2125 Superior Ave.
Cleveland, OH 44114
Phone: (216)621-5571
Free: (800)837-8247   **Fax:** (216)621-2789
Products: Heating and air-conditioning equipment. **SIC:** 5075 (Warm Air Heating & Air-Conditioning).

■ 14745 ■ **United Automatic Heating Supplies**
133 N Summit St.
Akron, OH 44304
Phone: (330)376-1011
Free: (800)686-9523   **Fax:** (330)376-4793
Products: Heating and air conditioning equipment. **SIC:** 5075 (Warm Air Heating & Air-Conditioning).

■ **14746** ■ **United Automatic Heating Supplies**
1087 N Meridian Rd.
Youngstown, OH 44509
Phone: (330)793-7672
Free: (800)837-5244 **Fax:** (330)793-4822
Products: Heating and air-conditioning equipment, parts, tools, and accessories. **SIC:** 5075 (Warm Air Heating & Air-Conditioning).

■ **14747** ■ **United Automatic Heating Supplies**
399 Phillips Ave.
Toledo, OH 43612
Phone: (419)478-4131
Free: (800)686-6471 **Fax:** (419)470-5505
Products: Train heating and air-conditioning equipment. **SIC:** 5075 (Warm Air Heating & Air-Conditioning).

■ **14748** ■ **United Refrigeration Inc.**
11401 Roosevelt Blvd.
Philadelphia, PA 19154
Phone: (215)698-9100
Free: (800)852-5132 **Fax:** (215)698-9493
E-mail: info@uri.com
URL: http://www.uri.com
Products: Refrigeration and condensing equipment; Heating, ventilating, and air conditioning equipment and parts; Controls; Motors; Electrical components; Pipes and fittings; Chemicals. **SICs:** 5078 (Refrigeration Equipment & Supplies); 5075 (Warm Air Heating & Air-Conditioning); 5169 (Chemicals & Allied Products Nec).
Est: 1945. **Sales:** $66,000,000 (2000). **Emp:** 270.
Officers: John H. Reilly, CEO & President; Carmen Carosella, Controller; Colin Dayton, VP of Sales.

■ **14749** ■ **Universal Management Consultants Inc.**
2017 Bainbridge Row Dr.
Louisville, KY 40207
Phone: (502)895-9903 **Fax:** (502)897-5872
URL: http://www.iglou.com/umc
Products: Filtering, heating, ventilating, and air-conditioning equipment; Oxygen and nitrogen generators; Medical equipment; General hardware; Air compressors, including paint spraying. **SICs:** 5075 (Warm Air Heating & Air-Conditioning); 5063 (Electrical Apparatus & Equipment); 5085 (Industrial Supplies); 5072 (Hardware). **Est:** 1978. **Emp:** 3. **Officers:** Edwin W. Moriarty, President, e-mail: edwin@iglou.com.

■ **14750** ■ **Utter Company Inc.**
955 W Pine St.
Lexington, KY 40508-2431
Phone: (606)252-8834 **Fax:** (606)252-8833
Products: Heating and air-conditioning supplies. **SICs:** 5075 (Warm Air Heating & Air-Conditioning); 5074 (Plumbing & Hydronic Heating Supplies). **Est:** 1959.
Sales: $3,000,000 (2000). **Emp:** 14. **Officers:** C.S. Utter, President; H.H. Slone, CFO.

■ **14751** ■ **Vair Corp.**
9305 Gerwig Ln. Q-R
Columbia, MD 21046
Phone: (410)995-6000
Free: (800)808-0800 **Fax:** (410)995-6580
Products: Refrigeration and air conditioning equipment; Heating equipment. **SICs:** 5078 (Refrigeration Equipment & Supplies); 5075 (Warm Air Heating & Air-Conditioning). **Est:** 1968. **Officers:** Philip Gardner, CEO; Mark Gardner, President.

■ **14752** ■ **W.R. Val Dere Co.**
712 S Hacienda Dr., No. 5
Tempe, AZ 85281-2949
Phone: (602)894-0980 **Fax:** (602)894-1310
Products: Refrigeration equipment and supplies, including refrigerated beverage dispensers; Water filters. **SIC:** 5078 (Refrigeration Equipment & Supplies).
Officers: William Dere, CEO.

■ **14753** ■ **Valley Controls & Supply Co.**
3192 Hall Ave.
Grand Junction, CO 81504-6036
Phone: (970)434-1374 **Fax:** (970)434-1068
Products: Heating equipment; Ventilating equipment and supplies; Refrigeration and air conditioning equipment; HVAC equipment and supplies. **SICs:** 5078 (Refrigeration Equipment & Supplies); 5075 (Warm Air Heating & Air-Conditioning); 5074 (Plumbing &

Hydronic Heating Supplies). **Est:** 1983. **Sales:** $3,250,000 (2000). **Emp:** 15. **Officers:** William Olsen, President.

■ **14754** ■ **Valley Controls and Supply Co.**
3192 Hall Ave.
Grand Junction, CO 81504-6036
Phone: (970)434-1374 **Fax:** (970)434-1068
Products: Heating and Cooling equipment and supplies. **SIC:** 5078 (Refrigeration Equipment & Supplies). **Sales:** $3,300,000 (2000). **Emp:** 15.

■ **14755** ■ **Village Products**
10 Lamy Dr.
Goffstown, NH 03045
Phone: (603)645-6060 **Fax:** (603)622-8689
Products: Fireplace equipment and supplies, including gas and wood stills. **SIC:** 5074 (Plumbing & Hydronic Heating Supplies).

■ **14756** ■ **The Bill Voorhees Company Inc.**
700 8th Ave. S
Nashville, TN 37203
Phone: (615)242-4481 **Fax:** (615)256-0729
Products: Central heat and air supplies. **SICs:** 5075 (Warm Air Heating & Air-Conditioning); 5072 (Hardware); 5064 (Electrical Appliances—Television & Radio). **Est:** 1959. **Sales:** $10,000,000 (1999). **Emp:** 18. **Officers:** William S. Voorhees, President; Joan Voorhees, Sec. & Treas.

■ **14757** ■ **Vorys Brothers Inc.**
834 W 3rd Ave.
Columbus, OH 43212
Phone: (614)294-4701 **Fax:** (614)294-0202
Products: Heating and air-conditioning equipment; Primary metals; Metals processing machinery. **SICs:** 5075 (Warm Air Heating & Air-Conditioning); 5084 (Industrial Machinery & Equipment). **Est:** 1925. **Sales:** $30,000,000 (2000). **Emp:** 49. **Officers:** Roger Wallace, CEO & President; Ted Morrison, Vice President.

■ **14758** ■ **Washita Refrigeration & Equipment Co.**
PO Box 577
Tishomingo, OK 73460-0577
Phone: (580)371-3112
Free: (800)235-9476 **Fax:** (580)371-3304
Products: Refrigeration equipment and supplies. **SIC:** 5078 (Refrigeration Equipment & Supplies). **Officers:** David Cribbs, President.

■ **14759** ■ **Weathertrol Supply Company Inc.**
2600 East University Dr.
Denton, TX 76209
Phone: (940)387-1778
Products: Refrigeration, air conditioning, and heating products. **SICs:** 5078 (Refrigeration Equipment & Supplies); 5075 (Warm Air Heating & Air-Conditioning).
Sales: $36,000,000 (2000). **Emp:** 130. **Officers:** Rocky Waite, President; Inez Baillio, VP of Finance.

■ **14760** ■ **Wesley Electric and Supply Inc.**
829 E Jefferson St.
Louisville, KY 40206
Phone: (502)585-3301 **Fax:** (502)499-6871
Products: Air-conditioning and heating equipment. **SIC:** 5075 (Warm Air Heating & Air-Conditioning).
Sales: $9,000,000 (2000). **Emp:** 40. **Officers:** Jack Slaughter, President; Brenda Slaughter, Controller.

■ **14761** ■ **Western Automation Inc.**
23011 Moulton Pkwy., H-2
Laguna Hills, CA 92653
Phone: (714)859-6988
Products: Air-conditioning equipment. **SIC:** 5063 (Electrical Apparatus & Equipment). **Est:** 1961. **Sales:** $20,000,000 (2000). **Emp:** 8. **Officers:** Michael D. Thompson, President.

■ **14762** ■ **Westside Development Inc.**
PO Box 2110
Covington, KY 41012
Phone: (606)431-4252 **Fax:** (606)431-1980
Products: Commercial refrigeration equipment and supplies. **SIC:** 5078 (Refrigeration Equipment & Supplies). **Officers:** Daniel Boone, President.

■ **14763** ■ **George F. Wheelock Company Inc.**
PO Box 10544
Birmingham, AL 35202-0544
Phone: (205)251-5268
Free: (800)247-7050 **Fax:** (205)324-3919
E-mail: gfwheelock@aol.com
URL: http://www.geofwheelock.com
Products: Heating and cooling equipment. **SIC:** 5075 (Warm Air Heating & Air-Conditioning). **Est:** 1888.
Emp: 12. **Officers:** George F. Wheelock III, President; Joey Henderson, VP & General Mgr.

■ **14764** ■ **White Inc.**
816 9th St. S
PO Box 3367
Great Falls, MT 59403-3367
Phone: (406)453-4307 **Fax:** (406)453-6112
Products: Commercial refrigeration equipment and supplies. **SIC:** 5078 (Refrigeration Equipment & Supplies). **Est:** 1938. **Emp:** 20. **Officers:** Rodger Widseth, President.

■ **14765** ■ **Wholesale Heating Supply Co.**
135 Orchard Lake Rd.
Pontiac, MI 48341
Phone: (313)338-6454 **Fax:** (313)338-6420
Products: Furnaces and heating devices. **SIC:** 5075 (Warm Air Heating & Air-Conditioning). **Sales:** $8,000,000 (2000). **Emp:** 35. **Officers:** Frank Waldorn, President; Sue Carter, Vice President.

■ **14766** ■ **Wichita Sheet Metal Supply Co.**
1601 S Sheridan St.
Wichita, KS 67213-1339
Phone: (316)942-9412
E-mail: griffitt@feist.com
URL: http://www.WSM_Industries.com
Products: Steel sheets; Heating supplies; Air-conditioners. **SICs:** 5075 (Warm Air Heating & Air-Conditioning); 5051 (Metals Service Centers & Offices); 5074 (Plumbing & Hydronic Heating Supplies). **Est:** 1951. **Sales:** $20,000,000 (1999). **Emp:** 99. **Officers:** Freda V. Moore, CEO & President; John Griffitt, Exec. VP.

■ **14767** ■ **Willar Corp.**
E 1212 Front
Spokane, WA 99202
Phone: (509)533-9911 **Fax:** (509)533-9884
Products: Refrigeration and air conditioning equipment; Heating equipment; Electronic systems and equipment; Plumbing fixtures, equipment, and supplies; Parts and attachments for small household appliances.
SICs: 5064 (Electrical Appliances—Television & Radio); 5074 (Plumbing & Hydronic Heating Supplies); 5075 (Warm Air Heating & Air-Conditioning); 5065 (Electronic Parts & Equipment Nec).

■ **14768** ■ **Willco Wholesale Distributors**
1601 W 8th St.
Muncie, IN 47302
Phone: (765)289-6606
Products: Heating equipment. **SIC:** 5075 (Warm Air Heating & Air-Conditioning).

■ **14769** ■ **Winterbottom Supply Co.**
PO Box 507
Waterloo, IA 50704-0507
Phone: (319)233-6123 **Fax:** (319)233-6126
Products: Commercial refrigeration equipment and supplies. **SIC:** 5078 (Refrigeration Equipment & Supplies). **Officers:** John Knight, President.

■ **14770** ■ **Yandle Witherspoon Supply**
PO Box 31548
Charlotte, NC 28231
Phone: (704)372-2780
Free: (800)476-2780 **Fax:** (704)334-4455
URL: http://www.yandlewitherspoon.com
Products: Heating and air-conditioning supplies. **SIC:** 5075 (Warm Air Heating & Air-Conditioning). **Est:** 1960.

■ **14771** ■ **Wittichen Supply Company Inc.**
1600 3rd Ave. S
Birmingham, AL 35233
Phone: (205)251-8500 **Fax:** (205)251-1050
Products: Heating and refrigeration equipment and supplies. **SICs:** 5075 (Warm Air Heating & Air-Conditioning); 5078 (Refrigeration Equipment &

Supplies). **Est:** 1946. **Sales:** $55,000,000 (2000). **Emp:** 150. **Officers:** David P. Henderson, CEO & President; Harry Hill, Controller; Charles R. Herring, General Mgr.

■ **14772** ■ **Wolpert Refrigeration Inc.**
4962 Dixie Hwy.
Saginaw, MI 48601-5452
Phone: (517)777-5270 **Fax:** (517)777-4851
Products: Refrigeration equipment and supplies. **SIC:** 5078 (Refrigeration Equipment & Supplies). **Officers:** Ralph Wolpert, President.

■ **14773** ■ **William Wurzbach Company Inc.**
1939 International Blvd.
Oakland, CA 94606
Phone: (510)261-0217 **Fax:** (510)534-9400
E-mail: info@wmwurzbach.com
URL: http://www.wmwurzbachco.com
Products: Equipment, parts, and supplies for commercial and industrial refrigeration and air conditioning. **SIC:** 5078 (Refrigeration Equipment & Supplies). **Est:** 1948. **Sales:** $18,000,000 (2000). **Emp:** 72. **Officers:** R. Wurzbach, President.

■ **14774** ■ **Yeomans Distributing Co.**
1503 W Altorfer Dr.
Peoria, IL 61615
Phone: (309)691-3282 **Fax:** (309)693-9306
Products: Heaters and air-conditioners. **SIC:** 5075 (Warm Air Heating & Air-Conditioning). **Est:** 1947. **Sales:** $17,000,000 (2000). **Emp:** 37. **Officers:** Murray M. Yeomans, President; A. Cioni, Treasurer.

■ **14775** ■ **York International Corp.**
160 Raritan Ctr. Pkwy., Ste. 6
Edison, NJ 08837
Phone: (732)469-5400 **Fax:** 800-995-5930
Products: Air-conditioning and heating equipment. **SIC:** 5075 (Warm Air Heating & Air-Conditioning).

■ **14776** ■ **York International Corp. Frick/Reco Div.**
5692 E Houston St.
San Antonio, TX 78220-1958
Phone: (210)661-9191 **Fax:** (210)662-6591
Products: Refrigeration and air conditioning equipment. **SIC:** 5078 (Refrigeration Equipment & Supplies). **Est:** 1960. **Officers:** Richard E. Clemens, General Mgr.; R. Glenn Fair, Marketing Mgr.; Sally Sandlin, Dir. of Operations.

■ **14777** ■ **Behler Young Co.**
3419 Lapeer Rd.
Flint, MI 48503
Phone: (810)743-1160 **Fax:** (810)743-2610
Products: Heating and air-conditioning equipment and supplies. **SIC:** 5075 (Warm Air Heating & Air-Conditioning).

■ **14778** ■ **Behler Young Co.**
929 Second St.
Kalamazoo, MI 49001
Phone: (616)343-5504 **Fax:** (616)343-4850
Products: Heating and air-conditioning equipment and supplies. **SIC:** 5075 (Warm Air Heating & Air-Conditioning).

■ **14779** ■ **Behler Young Co.**
1411 E High St.
Jackson, MI 49203-3315
Phone: (517)789-7191
Products: Heating and air-conditioning equipment and supplies. **SIC:** 5075 (Warm Air Heating & Air-Conditioning).

■ **14780** ■ **Behler Young Co.**
1244 E Carver St.
Traverse City, MI 49684
Phone: (616)946-7391 **Fax:** (616)946-1743
Products: Heating and air-conditioning equipment and supplies. **SIC:** 5075 (Warm Air Heating & Air-Conditioning).

■ **14781** ■ **Behler Young Co.**
3325 Enterprise
Saginaw, MI 48603
Phone: (517)799-4805
Free: (800)968-1693 **Fax:** (517)799-7455
Products: Heating and air-conditioning equipment and supplies. **SIC:** 5075 (Warm Air Heating & Air-Conditioning).

■ **14782** ■ **Behler Young Co.**
3100 W Main
Lansing, MI 48917
Phone: (517)371-1770
Free: (800)968-0328 **Fax:** (517)371-1521
Products: Heating and air-conditioning equipment and supplies. **SIC:** 5075 (Warm Air Heating & Air-Conditioning).

■ **14783** ■ **Behler Young Co.**
2440 S Industrial
Ann Arbor, MI 48104
Phone: (734)761-5511
Free: (800)968-4998 **Fax:** (734)761-7745
Products: Heating and air-conditioning equipment and

supplies. **SIC:** 5075 (Warm Air Heating & Air-Conditioning).

■ **14784** ■ **Behler Young Co.**
1075 Golf Dr.
Bloomfield, MI 48302
Phone: (248)335-6527 **Free:** (800)968-4998
URL: http://www.behler-young.com
Products: Heating and air-conditioning equipment and supplies. **SIC:** 5075 (Warm Air Heating & Air-Conditioning).

■ **14785** ■ **Behler Young Co.**
26444 Groesbeck Hwy.
Warren, MI 48089
Phone: (810)779-1730
Free: (800)968-4998 **Fax:** (810)775-8660
Products: Heating and air-conditioning equipment and supplies. **SIC:** 5075 (Warm Air Heating & Air-Conditioning).

■ **14786** ■ **Behler Young Co.**
12920 Inkster Rd.
Redford, MI 48239
Phone: (313)532-7990 **Fax:** (313)532-0681
Products: Heating and air-conditioning equipment and supplies. **SIC:** 5075 (Warm Air Heating & Air-Conditioning).

■ **14787** ■ **Young Supply Co.**
888 W Baltimore Ave.
Detroit, MI 48202
Phone: (313)875-3280 **Fax:** (313)875-3037
Products: Heating and air-conditioning supplies. **SIC:** 5078 (Refrigeration Equipment & Supplies). **Est:** 1948. **Sales:** $30,000,000 (2000). **Emp:** 110. **Officers:** Ronald Vallan, CEO & President; R. Stinson, Treasurer; Marlin Redmond, VP of Marketing.

■ **14788** ■ **Frank Young Supply North**
1913 Pickwick
Glenview, IL 60025
Phone: (847)657-7100 **Fax:** (847)657-7190
Products: Heating, air-conditioning, and ventilating equipment. **SIC:** 5075 (Warm Air Heating & Air-Conditioning).

■ **14789** ■ **Ziegler Repair**
925 Central
New Rockford, ND 58356
Phone: (701)947-2766
Products: Commercial refrigeration equipment and supplies. **SICs:** 5078 (Refrigeration Equipment & Supplies); 5075 (Warm Air Heating & Air-Conditioning). **Est:** 1970. **Sales:** $96,000 (2000). **Officers:** William Ziegler, Owner.

(24) Horticultural Supplies

Entries in this section are arranged alphabetically by company name. When the company name is a personal name, the company name is alphabetized by the surname unless the first name or initial(s) are part of a trade name. See the User's Guide at the front of this directory for additional information.

■ 14790 ■ **20th Century Nursery Landscape**
1348 Liberty Pike
Franklin, TN 37064
Phone: (615)790-2790 **Fax:** (615)790-2790
Products: Ground covers. **SIC:** 5193 (Flowers & Florists' Supplies).

■ 14791 ■ **A & A Plants**
5392 E NC 150 Hwy.
Browns Summit, NC 27214
Phone: (919)656-7881 **Fax:** (919)656-7833
Products: Plants, including shrubs and bushes. **SIC:** 5193 (Flowers & Florists' Supplies).

■ 14792 ■ **Aarons Creek Farms**
380 Greenhouse Dr.
Buffalo Junction, VA 24529
Phone: (804)374-2174
Free: (800)487-8502 **Fax:** (804)374-2055
URL: http://www.acfplugs.com
Products: Nursery plants; Bedding plants; Plugs; Perennials; Annuals; Vegetables. **SIC:** 5193 (Flowers & Florists' Supplies). **Est:** 1965. **Sales:** $3,000,000 (1999). **Emp:** 75.

■ 14793 ■ **Accawmacke Ornamentals**
PO Box 4
Tasley, VA 23441
Phone: (757)787-8128
Products: Flowers. **SIC:** 5193 (Flowers & Florists' Supplies).

■ 14794 ■ **Accent Nursery**
4448 Hwy. 92
Douglasville, GA 30135
Phone: (404)949-4144 **Fax:** (404)949-4144
Products: Outdoor plants. **SIC:** 5193 (Flowers & Florists' Supplies).

■ 14795 ■ **Air Conditioned Roses, Inc.**
PO Box 184
Pana, IL 62557
Phone: (217)562-2421
Free: (800)443-7673 **Fax:** (217)562-5880
Products: Fresh flowers. **SIC:** 5193 (Flowers & Florists' Supplies). **Est:** 1963. **Emp:** 8. **Officers:** Paul Dubre, Manager. **Former Name:** Illinois Roses Ltd.

■ 14796 ■ **Airport Greenhouse**
11330 Smith Rd.
Ft. Wayne, IN 46809
Phone: (219)747-3356 **Fax:** (219)747-9761
Products: Greenhouse plants; Mums and spring bedding plants. **SIC:** 5193 (Flowers & Florists' Supplies).

■ 14797 ■ **Ajo Way Garden & Nursery**
3220 E Ajo Way
Tucson, AZ 85713
Phone: (520)294-9611
Products: Bedding plants. **SIC:** 5193 (Flowers & Florists' Supplies).

■ 14798 ■ **Alan's Tropical Plants**
300 E Croton Way
Howey in the Hills, FL 34737-3215
Phone: (352)934-2920 **Fax:** (352)934-3105
Products: House plants. **SIC:** 5193 (Flowers & Florists' Supplies).

■ 14799 ■ **Alexander's Nursery**
6566 Kuamoo Rd. No. C
Kapaa, HI 96746
Phone: (808)822-5398
Products: Plants, flowers, and gardening and planting supplies. **SICs:** 5193 (Flowers & Florists' Supplies); 5191 (Farm Supplies).

■ 14800 ■ **Alma, Inc.**
270 Lancaster St.
Portland, ME 04101
Phone: (207)773-5667 **Fax:** (207)772-8338
Products: Flowers and florist supplies. **SIC:** 5193 (Flowers & Florists' Supplies).

■ 14801 ■ **Alpha Fern Co.**
PO Box 535
Pierson, FL 32180
Phone: (904)749-2786
Free: (800)313-8827 **Fax:** (904)749-3333
E-mail: alphafern@msn.com
Products: Floral greens. **SIC:** 5193 (Flowers & Florists' Supplies). **Est:** 1979. **Emp:** 25. **Officers:** Joe Strickland, Owner; John Wheeler, Owner.

■ 14802 ■ **Alvin Tree Farm, Inc.**
RR 7, Box 1
Alvin, TX 77511
Phone: (281)331-0190 **Fax:** (281)331-9651
E-mail: alvintreefarm@pdg.net
URL: http://www.freeweb.pdg.net/alvintreefarm1
Products: Trees; Ground covers; Ornamental shrubs. **SIC:** 5193 (Flowers & Florists' Supplies). **Est:** 1984.

■ 14803 ■ **American Nursery Products**
7010 S Yale, No. 101
Tulsa, OK 74136
Phone: (918)523-9665 **Fax:** (918)523-9771
Products: Trees, shrubs, and perennials. **SIC:** 5193 (Flowers & Florists' Supplies). **Est:** 1996. **Sales:** $24,000,000 (2000). **Emp:** 700. **Officers:** J. Wayne Fields, CEO & President; Charlotte Teehec, Treasurer.

■ 14804 ■ **Ameriglobe Irrigation Distributors**
19 Blandin Ave.
Framingham, MA 01702-7019
Phone: (508)820-4444
Products: Lawn and garden equipment and supplies. **SIC:** 5083 (Farm & Garden Machinery).

■ 14805 ■ **Andy's Discount Nursery & Landscape**
1807 Hwy. 85 N
Fayetteville, GA 30214
Phone: (404)461-6089 **Fax:** (404)461-7915
Products: Plants, shrubs, and trees. **SIC:** 5193 (Flowers & Florists' Supplies).

■ 14806 ■ **Angle Acres Greenhouse**
2855 Angle Rd.
Orchard Park, NY 14127
Phone: (716)674-8754 **Fax:** (716)674-4166
Products: Plants, including tropical and domestic varieties. **SIC:** 5193 (Flowers & Florists' Supplies).

■ 14807 ■ **Anthuriums of Hawaii**
530 Ainaola Dr.
Hilo, HI 96720
Phone: (808)959-8717
Free: (877)751-8717 **Fax:** (808)959-6868
Products: Flowers. **SIC:** 5193 (Flowers & Florists' Supplies). **Est:** 1974. **Emp:** 6. **Officers:** Ethel S. Yogi, Owner.

■ 14808 ■ **Apopka Trees & Shrubs**
1616 N Schopke Rd.
Apopka, FL 32712
Phone: (407)886-1060
Products: Trees and shrubs. **SIC:** 5193 (Flowers & Florists' Supplies).

■ 14809 ■ **H.T. Ardinger and Son Co.**
PO Box 569360
Dallas, TX 75356-9360
Phone: (214)631-9830 **Fax:** (214)634-1270
Products: Silk flowers and greenery; Silk Christmas trees and ornaments; Baskets. **SIC:** 5193 (Flowers & Florists' Supplies). **Est:** 1948. **Sales:** $70,000,000 (2000). **Emp:** 94. **Officers:** H.T. Ardinger, Owner.

■ 14810 ■ **Avalon Ornamentals**
16515 E Davenport Rd.
Winter Garden, FL 34787
Phone: (407)656-7687 **Fax:** (407)656-3535
Products: Ornamental plants. **SIC:** 5193 (Flowers & Florists' Supplies).

■ 14811 ■ **Avant Gardens Silk Plants**
6922 S Butte Ave.
Tempe, AZ 85283-4151
Phone: (602)940-1903
Products: Silk flowers, including cacti; Candles. **SICs:** 5193 (Flowers & Florists' Supplies); 5199 (Nondurable Goods Nec).

■ 14812 ■ **Babikow Greenhouses**
7838 Babikow Rd.
Baltimore, MD 21237
Phone: (410)391-4200
Products: Bedding plants. **SIC:** 5193 (Flowers & Florists' Supplies).

■ 14813 ■ **Bailey Nurseries Inc.**
1325 Bailey Rd.
St. Paul, MN 55119
Phone: (612)459-9744 **Fax:** (612)459-5100
Products: Nursery stock, including trees, shrubs, and plants. **SIC:** 5193 (Flowers & Florists' Supplies). **Est:** 1905. **Sales:** $28,000,000 (2000). **Emp:** 400. **Officers:** Gordon J. Bailey, President.

■ 14814 ■ **Baker's Nursery**
3408 Colwell Ave.
Tampa, FL 33614
Phone: (813)932-6527 **Fax:** (813)931-4815
Products: Plants. **SIC:** 5193 (Flowers & Florists'
Supplies).

■ 14815 ■ **Ball Horticultural Co.**
622 Town Rd.
PO Box 2698
West Chicago, IL 60185-2698
Phone: (630)231-3600 **Fax:** (630)231-3507
Products: Horticultural products. **SIC:** 5193 (Flowers &
Florists' Supplies). **Est:** 1905. **Sales:** $100,000,000
(2000). **Emp:** 465. **Officers:** Anna Caroline Ball, CEO
& President; Barrie L. Ricketts, CFO.

■ 14816 ■ **Ball Seed Co.**
622 Town Rd.
West Chicago, IL 60185
Phone: (630)231-3500
Products: Horticulture products. **SIC:** 5193 (Flowers &
Florists' Supplies).

■ 14817 ■ **Banner Place Nursery**
RR 3, Box 510
Sophia, NC 27350-9803
Phone: (919)861-1400
Products: Nursery equipment and supplies. **SIC:** 5193
(Flowers & Florists' Supplies).

■ 14818 ■ **Barrow's Greenhouses**
312 Main St.
Gorham, ME 04038
Phone: (207)839-3321
Products: Plants. **SIC:** 5193 (Flowers & Florists'
Supplies).

■ 14819 ■ **Barton's Greenhouse & Nursery**
Hwy. 26
Alabaster, AL 35007
Phone: (205)664-2964 **Fax:** (205)664-2965
Products: Annual plants. **SIC:** 5193 (Flowers &
Florists' Supplies).

■ 14820 ■ **Bartsch Greenhouses**
567 Wible Run Rd.
Pittsburgh, PA 15209
Phone: (412)486-3174 **Fax:** (412)487-9211
Products: Plants, including annuals and poinsettias.
SIC: 5193 (Flowers & Florists' Supplies).

■ 14821 ■ **Bath Beach Nurseries, Inc.**
8410 New Utrecht Ave.
Brooklyn, NY 11214
Phone: (718)256-8336
Products: Garden supplies. **SIC:** 5193 (Flowers &
Florists' Supplies).

■ 14822 ■ **Baton Rouge Landscape Co.**
12136 Oakwild Ave.
Baton Rouge, LA 70810-7109
Phone: (504)766-1203
Products: Landscaping products and supplies. **SIC:**
5193 (Flowers & Florists' Supplies).

■ 14823 ■ **Baucoms Nursery Farm**
10020 John Russell Rd.
Charlotte, NC 28213
Phone: (704)596-3220 **Fax:** (704)597-9401
Products: Indoor and outdoor plants. **SIC:** 5193
(Flowers & Florists' Supplies).

■ 14824 ■ **Bay Grove Nurseries, Inc.**
PO Box 377
Perryville, MD 21903-0377
Phone: (410)397-3337
Products: Shrubbery. **SIC:** 5193 (Flowers & Florists'
Supplies).

■ 14825 ■ **Bay State Florist Supply, Inc.**
36 Martone Pl.
Springfield, MA 01109
Phone: (413)736-7771
Products: Flowers and florist supplies. **SIC:** 5193
(Flowers & Florists' Supplies).

■ 14826 ■ **Beach Growers**
9176 W Atlantic Ave.
Delray Beach, FL 33446
Phone: (561)498-3030
Products: Foliage, including trees and plants. **SIC:**
5193 (Flowers & Florists' Supplies).

■ 14827 ■ **Beaty's Nursery**
1933 Mike Muncey Rd.
Mc Minnville, TN 37110
Phone: (931)934-2364 **Fax:** (931)934-2394
Products: Plants; Shade and ornamental trees. **SIC:**
5193 (Flowers & Florists' Supplies). **Est:** 1971.

■ 14828 ■ **Beautiful Plants by Charlie**
10421 State Rd. 579
Thonotosassa, FL 33592
Phone: (813)986-4473 **Fax:** (813)986-7678
Products: Hanging baskets and flowering plants. **SIC:**
5193 (Flowers & Florists' Supplies).

■ 14829 ■ **Dorothy Biddle Service**
348 Greeley Lake Rd.
Greeley, PA 18425-9799
Phone: (570)226-3239 **Fax:** (570)226-0349
E-mail: dbsfrog@ptd.net
URL: http://www.dorothybiddle.com
Products: Floral supplies. **SIC:** 5193 (Flowers &
Florists' Supplies). **Est:** 1936. **Sales:** $750,000 (2000).
Emp: 5. **Officers:** Lynne J. Dodson, Owner.

■ 14830 ■ **Brooks Nursery Inc.**
PO Box 263
Boling, TX 77420
Phone: (409)657-2465
Products: Color bedding plants. **SIC:** 5193 (Flowers &
Florists' Supplies). **Est:** 1987. **Sales:** $1,800,000
(2000). **Emp:** 35. **Officers:** Pete Brooks, President.

■ 14831 ■ **Buckeye Sales Inc.**
1009 Race St.
Cincinnati, OH 45202
Phone: (513)621-2391 **Free:** (800)825-9559
Products: Silk flowers and foliages, baskets, ribbon,
dried flowers, xmas decorations, floral and gift supplies.
SICs: 5193 (Flowers & Florists' Supplies); 5049
(Professional Equipment Nec). **Est:** 1975. **Emp:** 15.
Officers: Tom Cappel, President; Steve Cappel, Vice
President.

■ 14832 ■ **Bush Landscaping & Nursery**
2848 Lore Rd.
Anchorage, AK 99507
Phone: (907)344-2775 **Fax:** (907)349-4507
Products: Trees and shrubs; Wood chips and mulch;
Perennials. **SIC:** 5193 (Flowers & Florists' Supplies).

■ 14833 ■ **Capitol Wholesale Florists Inc.**
11740 Maumelle Blvd.
North Little Rock, AR 72113
Phone: (501)758-0006
Products: Flowers. **SIC:** 5193 (Flowers & Florists'
Supplies). **Est:** 1966. **Sales:** $2,000,000 (2000). **Emp:**
17. **Officers:** Wayne Burke, President; Gloria Gough,
Treasurer & Secty.

■ 14834 ■ **R.J. Carbone Co.**
1 Goddard Dr.
Cranston, RI 02920
Phone: (401)463-3333 **Fax:** (401)463-5787
Products: Plants and flowers. **SIC:** 5193 (Flowers &
Florists' Supplies).

■ 14835 ■ **Carbone Floral Distributors**
540 Albany St.
Boston, MA 02118
Phone: (617)728-7979
Products: Flowers. **SIC:** 5193 (Flowers & Florists'
Supplies).

■ 14836 ■ **CCC Associates Co.**
PO Box 3508
Montgomery, AL 36109
Phone: (334)272-2140
Free: (800)627-1387 **Fax:** (334)277-6023
Products: Potted plants; Flowers and florists supplies.
SIC: 5193 (Flowers & Florists' Supplies). **Est:** 1950.
Sales: $53,000,000 (2000). **Emp:** 640. **Officers:**
James L. Thompson Sr., CEO; James Thompson Jr.,

President; Betsy Spivey, Sales Mgr.; Don Bush, Dir. of
Systems; Regina Martin, Personnel Mgr.

■ 14837 ■ **Cedars Wholesale Floral Imports**
6151 B St.
Anchorage, AK 99518
Phone: (907)563-5566 **Fax:** (907)561-5566
Products: Flowers. **SIC:** 5193 (Flowers & Florists'
Supplies).

■ 14838 ■ **Celebrity, Inc.**
4520 Old Troup Rd.
Tyler, TX 75707
Phone: (903)561-3981 **Fax:** (903)581-2887
URL: http://www.celebrity-inc.com
Products: Artificial flowers; Foliage; Flower
arrangements; Christmas decorations, including trees
and wreaths; Textile products. **SICs:** 5193 (Flowers &
Florists' Supplies); 5131 (Piece Goods & Notions);
5199 (Nondurable Goods Nec). **Sales:** $125,200,000
(2000). **Officers:** Robert H. Patterson Jr., CEO; Lynn
Skillen, CFO; Mary Cowan, Human Resources
Contact.

■ 14839 ■ **Celebrity Inc. (Tyler, Texas)**
PO Box 6666
Tyler, TX 75707
Phone: (903)561-3981
Products: Artificial flowers. **SIC:** 5193 (Flowers &
Florists' Supplies). **Sales:** $125,100,000 (2000). **Emp:**
727. **Officers:** Robert H. Patterson Jr., CEO, President
& Chairman of the Board.

■ 14840 ■ **CFX, Inc.**
1800 NW 89th Pl.
Miami, FL 33172
Phone: (305)592-4478
Free: (800)883-3000 **Fax:** (305)513-6413
E-mail: cfxsales@gate.net
URL: http://www.cfxflowers.com
Products: Fresh cut flowers. **SIC:** 5193 (Flowers &
Florists' Supplies). **Est:** 1974. **Sales:** $34,000,000
(2000). **Emp:** 61.

■ 14841 ■ **Roman J. Claprood Co.**
242 N Grant Ave.
Columbus, OH 43215
Phone: (614)221-5515
Products: Flowers. **SIC:** 5193 (Flowers & Florists'
Supplies). **Est:** 1939. **Sales:** $4,000,000 (2000). **Emp:**
35. **Officers:** Floyd R. Claprood, President.

■ 14842 ■ **Cleveland Plant and Flower Co.**
2419 E 9th St.
Cleveland, OH 44115
Phone: (216)241-3290 **Fax:** (216)241-5390
Products: Flowers, including roses and carnations.
SIC: 5193 (Flowers & Florists' Supplies). **Est:** 1974.
Sales: $6,000,000 (2000). **Emp:** 60. **Officers:** Jim
Priest, CEO.

■ 14843 ■ **Color Spot Nurseries Inc.**
3478 Buskirk Ave.
Pleasant Hill, CA 94523
Phone: (925)934-4443 **Free:** (800)554-4065
Products: Florest. **SIC:** 5193 (Flowers & Florists'
Supplies). **Sales:** $206,000,000 (2000). **Emp:** 2,500.
Officers: Raju Boligala, President & COO; Joseph P.
O'Neill, CFO.

■ 14844 ■ **Conard-Pyle Co.**
372 Rose Hill Rd.
West Grove, PA 19390
Phone: (610)869-2426
Free: (800)458-6559 **Fax:** (610)869-0651
URL: http://www.starroses.com
Products: Wholesale container nursery. **SIC:** 5193
(Flowers & Florists' Supplies). **Est:** 1897. **Sales:**
$19,000,000 (2000). **Emp:** 300. **Officers:** Steven B.
Hutton, President; David Watkins, Treasurer; Richard
H. Hoback, Dir. of Marketing & Sales.

■ 14845 ■ **Concord Nurseries Inc.**
10175 Mile Black Rd.
North Collins, NY 14111
Phone: (716)337-2485
Free: (800)223-2211 **Fax:** 800-448-1267
E-mail: concordnurseriesinc@mci.com
Products: Plants and flowers. **SIC:** 5193 (Flowers &

Florists' Supplies). **Est:** 1894. **Sales:** $4,000,000 (2000). **Emp:** 60. **Officers:** David Taylor, President; Tom Suffoletto, Sales Mgr.

■ 14846 ■ Creative Distributors
96 Union Pk.
Boston, MA 02118
Phone: (617)426-5525
Products: Florist supplies. **SIC:** 5193 (Flowers & Florists' Supplies).

■ 14847 ■ Creighton & Son
123 Washington Ave.
Portland, ME 04101
Phone: (207)774-3812
Free: (800)CRA-YTON **Fax:** (207)774-6919
Products: Flowers and florists supplies. **SIC:** 5193 (Flowers & Florists' Supplies).

■ 14848 ■ Cuthbert Greenhouse Inc.
4900 Hendron Rd.
Groveport, OH 43125
Phone: (614)836-3866
Free: (800)321-1939 **Fax:** (614)836-3767
Products: Potted crops; Bedding annuals; Plugs. **SIC:** 5193 (Flowers & Florists' Supplies). **Est:** 1950. **Sales:** $6,000,000 (2000). **Emp:** 70. **Officers:** Wayne H. Cuthbert, President; Ronald F. Cuthbert, Vice President; Robert L. Cuthbert, Sec. & Treas.; Ronald C. Storm, Sales/Marketing Contact, e-mail: rcstorm@ cuthbertgreenhouse.com;David L. Cuthbert, Customer Service Contact.

■ 14849 ■ Cuthbert Greenhouse Inc.
4900 Hendron Rd.
Groveport, OH 43125
Phone: (614)836-3866
Free: (800)321-1939 **Fax:** (614)836-3767
Products: Horticultural supplies. **SIC:** 5193 (Flowers & Florists' Supplies). **Sales:** $6,000,000 (2000). **Emp:** 70.

■ 14850 ■ Cuthbert Greenhouse Inc.
4900 Hendron Rd.
Groveport, OH 43125
Phone: (614)836-3866
Free: (800)321-1939 **Fax:** (614)836-3767
Products: Horticultural supplies. **SIC:** 5193 (Flowers & Florists' Supplies). **Sales:** $6,000,000 (2000). **Emp:** 70.

■ 14851 ■ CWF Inc.
3015 Beechtree Dr.
Sanford, NC 27330
Phone: (919)775-3631
Products: Floral supplies. **SIC:** 5193 (Flowers & Florists' Supplies). **Sales:** $4,000,000 (2000). **Emp:** 24. **Officers:** Joanne Kirkman, Dir. of Admin.

■ 14852 ■ D'Anna B'Nana
15-1293 Auina Rd.
Pahoa, HI 96778
Phone: (808)965-6262 **Fax:** (808)965-6262
Products: Palm trees. **SIC:** 5193 (Flowers & Florists' Supplies).

■ 14853 ■ Davids and Royston Bulb Company Inc.
550 W 135th St.
Gardena, CA 90248
Phone: (310)532-2313 **Fax:** (310)532-8846
Products: Flower bulbs. **SIC:** 5193 (Flowers & Florists' Supplies). **Est:** 1938. **Sales:** $7,000,000 (2000). **Emp:** 20. **Officers:** Daniel Davids, President.

■ 14854 ■ Decorative Designs
301 W 92 St.
Bloomington, MN 55420-3632
Phone: (612)881-3389 **Fax:** (612)881-5161
Products: Plants, including silk plants; Planters. **SIC:** 5193 (Flowers & Florists' Supplies). **Est:** 1965. **Sales:** $1,000,000 (2000). **Emp:** 20. **Officers:** Renate M. Stone, CEO.

■ 14855 ■ Denver Wholesale Florists
PO Box 173354
Denver, CO 80217-3354
Phone: (303)399-0970
Products: Flowers. **SIC:** 5193 (Flowers & Florists' Supplies). **Est:** 1909. **Sales:** $32,000,000 (2000).

Emp: 750. **Officers:** John Shelton, CEO; Larry Hagen, CFO.

■ 14856 ■ Design Craft
225 W John Rowan Blvd.
Bardstown, KY 40004-2602
Phone: (502)348-4275 **Fax:** (502)348-2748
Products: Needlework; Silk flowers; Vases. **SICs:** 5193 (Flowers & Florists' Supplies); 5199 (Nondurable Goods Nec). **Sales:** $1,000,000 (2000). **Emp:** 49. **Officers:** Bernetta Evans.

■ 14857 ■ DIMON Inc.
PO Box 681
Danville, VA 24543
Phone: (804)792-7511 **Fax:** (804)791-0377
Products: Tobacco stemming and redrying. **SIC:** 5193 (Flowers & Florists' Supplies). **Sales:** $1,815,200,000 (1999). **Emp:** 3,200. **Officers:** Brian J. Harker, CEO & President; James A. Cooley, VP & CFO.

■ 14858 ■ Bill Doran Co.
619 W Jefferson St.
Rockford, IL 61105
Phone: (815)965-8791
Products: Floral supplies, including fresh flowers, silk flowers, greenery, and baskets. **SIC:** 5193 (Flowers & Florists' Supplies). **Sales:** $44,000,000 (2000). **Emp:** 200. **Officers:** Patricia D. La Fever, President.

■ 14859 ■ Evelyn's Floral
343 W Benson Blvd. No. 7
Anchorage, AK 99503
Phone: (907)561-7322
Free: (800)669-4820 **Fax:** (907)563-5292
Products: Fresh flowers; Gifts and novelties. **SIC:** 5193 (Flowers & Florists' Supplies).

■ 14860 ■ Evergreen Nurseries
PO Box 2788
Honolulu, HI 96803-2788
Phone: (808)259-9945 **Fax:** (808)259-7464
Products: Foliage. **SIC:** 5193 (Flowers & Florists' Supplies).

■ 14861 ■ First American Artificial Flowers Inc.
Bradley Pkwy.
Blauvelt, NY 10913
Phone: (914)353-0700
Free: (800)431-1990 **Fax:** (914)353-0341
Products: Artificial flowers. **SIC:** 5193 (Flowers & Florists' Supplies). **Est:** 1910. **Sales:** $3,000,000 (2000). **Emp:** 20. **Officers:** Samuel Berger, President; Sam Cohem, Secretary.

■ 14862 ■ First Coast Designs Inc.
7800 Bayberry Rd.
Jacksonville, FL 32256-6815
Phone: (904)730-9496 **Fax:** (904)737-9178
Products: Silk flowers, dry flowers, and pottery. **SIC:** 5193 (Flowers & Florists' Supplies). **Emp:** 49.

■ 14863 ■ Flora-Dec Saes, Inc.
373 N Nimitz Hwy.
Honolulu, HI 96817-5027
Phone: (808)537-6194 **Fax:** (808)528-1854
Products: Floral supplies. **SIC:** 5193 (Flowers & Florists' Supplies). **Est:** 1966.

■ 14864 ■ Floral Acres Inc.
PO Box 540939
Lake Worth, FL 33454-0939
Products: Tropical foliage. **SIC:** 5193 (Flowers & Florists' Supplies). **Est:** 1955. **Sales:** $6,000,000 (2000). **Emp:** 115. **Officers:** A. Rosacker Jr., President; Leif Johansen, Dir. of Marketing & Sales.

■ 14865 ■ Floralife Inc.
120 Tower Dr.
Burr Ridge, IL 60521
Phone: (630)325-8587 **Fax:** (630)325-4924
Products: Horticultural supplies. **SIC:** 5199 (Nondurable Goods Nec).

■ 14866 ■ Paul Florence Turfgrass
13600 Watkins Rd.
Marysville, OH 43040
Phone: (937)642-7487
Products: Turfgrass, mulches, and sod. **SIC:** 5193 (Flowers & Florists' Supplies).

■ 14867 ■ Florexotica Hawaii
826A Queen St.
Honolulu, HI 96813
Phone: (808)842-5166 **Fax:** (808)842-5165
E-mail: lei@florexotica.com
URL: http://www.florexotica.com
Products: Silk flowers and plants; Christmas decorations. **SICs:** 5193 (Flowers & Florists' Supplies); 5199 (Nondurable Goods Nec). **Est:** 1980. **Sales:** $1,000,000 (1999). **Emp:** 3. **Officers:** Patrick Stender, President; Lei-Ann Durant, VP; Marinda Kennedy, Sales/Marketing Contact, e-mail: mkatsflorexotica.com.

■ 14868 ■ Florimex Worldwide Inc.
512 Bridge St.
Danville, VA 24541
Phone: (804)792-7511 **Free:** (800)222-2939
Products: Fresh-cut flowers. **SIC:** 5193 (Flowers & Florists' Supplies). **Sales:** $443,000,000 (2000). **Emp:** 1,450. **Officers:** Dwight L. Ferguson, President & COO; Ritchie L. Bond, Sr. VP & CFO.

■ 14869 ■ Flower Warehouse
1308 Loagan
Costa Mesa, CA 92626
Phone: (714)545-0310
Products: Flowers. **SIC:** 5193 (Flowers & Florists' Supplies).

■ 14870 ■ Forrest-Keeling Nursery
Hwy. 79 S
Elsberry, MO 63343
Phone: (573)898-5571 **Fax:** (573)898-5803
Products: Trees and bushes. **SIC:** 5193 (Flowers & Florists' Supplies). **Est:** 1945. **Sales:** $2,000,000 (2000). **Emp:** 80. **Officers:** H.A. Steavenson, CEO & President; Hugh K. Steavenson, CFO.

■ 14871 ■ Frinks Greenhouses Inc.
418 W 13th St.
Cedar Falls, IA 50613
Phone: (319)266-3517
Products: Potted plants, bedding plants, and geraniums. **SIC:** 5193 (Flowers & Florists' Supplies). **Est:** 1951. **Sales:** $2,000,000 (2000). **Emp:** 12. **Officers:** Maurice F. Frink, President & Treasurer.

■ 14872 ■ Gardener's Supply Co.
128 Intervale Rd.
Burlington, VT 05401
Phone: (802)660-3500 **Fax:** (802)660-3501
Products: Flowers. **SIC:** 5193 (Flowers & Florists' Supplies). **Est:** 1983. **Sales:** $22,000,000 (2000). **Emp:** 140. **Officers:** William Raap, President; Cindy Davis, CFO.

■ 14873 ■ Goble's Flower Farm
RR2 BOX 200
Kula, HI 96790
Phone: (808)878-6079 **Fax:** (808)878-6079
Products: Flowers. **SIC:** 5193 (Flowers & Florists' Supplies).

■ 14874 ■ Good Earth Farm, Inc.
55 Pleasant Hill Rd.
Freeport, ME 04032
Phone: (207)865-9544 **Fax:** (207)865-1600
Products: Dried flowers. **SIC:** 5193 (Flowers & Florists' Supplies).

■ 14875 ■ Good Floral Distributors
Grove St. Extension
Houlton, ME 04730
Phone: (207)532-2040
Free: (800)660-2040 **Fax:** (207)532-1270
Products: Florists' supplies, including cut flowers. **SIC:** 5193 (Flowers & Florists' Supplies). **Est:** 1984. **Emp:** 5.

■ 14876 ■ **Green Connection Inc.**
804 E 15th Ave.
Anchorage, AK 99501
Phone: (907)276-7836 **Fax:** (907)276-7258
Products: Plants. **SIC:** 5193 (Flowers & Florists' Supplies).

■ 14877 ■ **Green Mountain Florist Supply**
State Hwy. 2
Montpelier, VT 05602
Phone: (802)223-7600 **Fax:** (802)229-0948
Products: Flowers; Flower supplies. **SIC:** 5193 (Flowers & Florists' Supplies).

■ 14878 ■ **The Greenhouse**
PO Box 4627
Kailua Kona, HI 96745-4627
Phone: (808)329-1979
Products: Gardening supplies; Plants. **SICs:** 5193 (Flowers & Florists' Supplies); 5083 (Farm & Garden Machinery).

■ 14879 ■ **Greenleaf Wholesale Florist**
3712 Edith Blvd. NE
PO Box 6364
Albuquerque, NM 87107-2218
Phone: (505)344-2331
Free: (800)578-5323 **Fax:** (505)345-8572
E-mail: abqgwf@aol.com
Products: Flowers and florists' supplies, including ribbon, wire, dried flowers, and pots. **SIC:** 5193 (Flowers & Florists' Supplies). **Est:** 1974. **Emp:** 17.
Officers: Ray Kitayama; Tim Matsumo, President, e-mail: tmatsuno@greenleaf.com.

■ 14880 ■ **Greenleaf Wholesale Florists**
PO Box 537
Brighton, CO 80601
Phone: (303)659-8000 **Fax:** (303)659-4022
Products: Fresh and silk flowers. **SIC:** 5193 (Flowers & Florists' Supplies). **Est:** 1959. **Sales:** $37,000,000 (2000). **Emp:** 340. **Officers:** Dwight Matsuno, President; Dennis Kitayama, CFO; John Horiuchi, Dir. of Sales; Connie Wasmundt, Dir. of Data Processing; Sonja Kimberling, Office Mgr.

■ 14881 ■ **Halifax Floral Co., Inc.**
395 Promenade St.
Providence, RI 02908
Phone: (401)751-4333 **Fax:** (401)751-5319
Products: Plants, cut flowers, and florist supplies. **SIC:** 5193 (Flowers & Florists' Supplies).

■ 14882 ■ **Hashimoto Nursery**
PO Box 525
Pahoa, HI 96778
Phone: (808)965-9522
Products: Cut flowers. **SIC:** 5193 (Flowers & Florists' Supplies).

■ 14883 ■ **Hawaii Protea Corp.**
Haleakala Hwy.
Kula, HI 96790
Phone: (808)878-2525 **Fax:** (808)878-2704
Products: Tropical flowers. **SIC:** 5193 (Flowers & Florists' Supplies).

■ 14884 ■ **Hawaiian Greenhouse, Inc.**
PO Box 1
Pahoa, HI 96778
Phone: (808)965-8351 **Fax:** (808)965-9401
Products: Flowers. **SIC:** 5193 (Flowers & Florists' Supplies).

■ 14885 ■ **Alexander Hay Greenhouses, Inc.**
75 Oakwood Ave.
North Haledon, NJ 07508
Phone: (973)427-1193 **Fax:** (973)427-6856
Products: Flowers and plants. **SIC:** 5193 (Flowers & Florists' Supplies).

■ 14886 ■ **Hill Floral Products**
2117 Peacock Rd.
Richmond, IN 47374
Phone: (765)973-6600 **Fax:** (765)962-2920
Products: Flowers and florists supplies. **SIC:** 5193 (Flowers & Florists' Supplies).

■ 14887 ■ **Hilo Farmer's Exchange**
318 Kinoole St.
Hilo, HI 96720
Phone: (808)935-6697 **Fax:** (808)961-6520
Products: Lawn and garden supplies. **SICs:** 5193 (Flowers & Florists' Supplies); 5191 (Farm Supplies).

■ 14888 ■ **A.H. Hoffman Inc.**
PO Box 266
Lancaster, NY 14086
Phone: (716)684-8111 **Fax:** (716)684-3722
Products: Plant food; Potting soils, peat moss, and specialty soil products. **SIC:** 5193 (Flowers & Florists' Supplies). **Est:** 1899. **Sales:** $6,000,000 (2000). **Emp:** 50. **Officers:** Guenter H. Burkhardt, President.

■ 14889 ■ **Ho'Owaiwia Farms**
RR 1, Box 199A
Papaikou, HI 96781
Phone: (808)964-5222 **Fax:** (808)964-5078
Products: Landscape materials. **SIC:** 5193 (Flowers & Florists' Supplies).

■ 14890 ■ **Roy Houff Co.**
6200 S Oak Pk. Ave.
Chicago, IL 60638
Phone: (312)586-8118 **Fax:** (312)586-8789
Products: Cut flowers. **SIC:** 5193 (Flowers & Florists' Supplies). **Sales:** $38,000,000 (2000). **Emp:** 225. **Officers:** Roy Houff, Chairman of the Board; Henry Kite, CFO.

■ 14891 ■ **I.E.F. Corp.**
PO Box 1088
Spanaway, WA 98387
Phone: (253)535-5289
Free: (800)275-1665 **Fax:** (253)846-1552
Products: Horticultural supplies. **SIC:** 5193 (Flowers & Florists' Supplies). **Sales:** $4,000,000 (2000). **Emp:** 15.

■ 14892 ■ **Inouye Lei Flowers, Inc.**
3222 Ala Laulani St.
Honolulu, HI 96818
Phone: (808)839-0064
Products: Flowers. **SIC:** 5193 (Flowers & Florists' Supplies).

■ 14893 ■ **Interior Plant Designs, Ltd.**
5333 A St.
Anchorage, AK 99518
Phone: (907)563-2535 **Fax:** (907)563-3418
Products: Interior plants. **SIC:** 5193 (Flowers & Florists' Supplies).

■ 14894 ■ **Interior Tropicals, Inc.**
275 Market St.,Ste. 531
Minneapolis, MN 55405-1626
Products: Plants. **SIC:** 5193 (Flowers & Florists' Supplies).

■ 14895 ■ **International Decoratives Company Inc.**
PO Box 777
Valley Center, CA 92082
Phone: (760)749-2682
Free: (800)582-0128 **Fax:** (760)749-3677
E-mail: koala@inetworld.net
Products: Preserved foliage; Pastel Eucalyptus. **SIC:** 5193 (Flowers & Florists' Supplies). **Est:** 1969. **Sales:** $1,400,000 (2000). **Emp:** 45. **Officers:** R.E. Russell, President; Kathy Russell, Treasurer & Secty.

■ 14896 ■ **Jiffy Foam, Inc.**
PO Box 3609
Newport, RI 02840
Phone: (401)846-7870 **Fax:** (401)847-9966
Products: Floral and modelling foam. **SIC:** 5193 (Flowers & Florists' Supplies).

■ 14897 ■ **Jirdon Agri Chemicals Inc.**
PO Box 516
Morrill, NE 69358
Phone: (308)247-2126
Free: (800)445-5454 **Fax:** (308)247-2128
E-mail: jirdonag@prairieweb.com
Products: Lawn and garden chemicals. **SICs:** 5193 (Flowers & Florists' Supplies); 5169 (Chemicals & Allied Products Nec). **Est:** 1972. **Sales:** $11,500,000 (2000). **Emp:** 50. **Officers:** William L. Siegel,

President; Jennifer M. McGinley, Controller; Esther Seigel, Secretary.

■ 14898 ■ **JML Sales Corp.**
15326 E Valley Blvd.
La Puente, CA 91744
Phone: (626)369-3778 **Fax:** (626)336-8458
Products: Artificial flowers; Trees; Vases; Baskets; Green foliage. **SIC:** 5193 (Flowers & Florists' Supplies). **Sales:** $7,000,000 (2000). **Emp:** 10. **Officers:** Manuel See.

■ 14899 ■ **Johnston Florist Inc.**
14179 Lincoln
North Huntingdon, PA 15642
Phone: (412)751-2821 **Fax:** (412)751-2961
Products: Flowers and flower arrangements. **SIC:** 5193 (Flowers & Florists' Supplies). **Est:** 1898. **Sales:** $5,000,000 (2000). **Emp:** 150. **Officers:** Earle S. Guffey, Chairman of the Board.

■ 14900 ■ **K and D Exports Imports Corp.**
225 5th Ave.
New York, NY 10010
Phone: (212)683-8670 **Fax:** (212)683-8670
Products: Silk flowers. **SIC:** 5193 (Flowers & Florists' Supplies). **Est:** 1974. **Sales:** $4,500,000 (2000). **Emp:** 35. **Officers:** Diane Eamtrakul, CEO; John R. Good, CFO; Michael Hylland, President.

■ 14901 ■ **Kamuela Roses, Inc.**
1124 Kohou St.
Honolulu, HI 96817
Phone: (808)847-6748
Products: Flowers. **SIC:** 5193 (Flowers & Florists' Supplies).

■ 14902 ■ **Karthauser and Sons Inc.**
W147 N Fond du Lac Ave.
Germantown, WI 53022
Phone: (414)255-7815 **Fax:** (414)255-6920
Products: Plants and flowers. **SIC:** 5193 (Flowers & Florists' Supplies). **Sales:** $6,000,000 (2000). **Emp:** 20. **Officers:** Brad Gerald, President.

■ 14903 ■ **K.D. Farms, Inc.**
Kawela
Kaunakakai, HI 96748
Phone: (808)567-6024
Products: Flowers and florists' supplies. **SIC:** 5193 (Flowers & Florists' Supplies).

■ 14904 ■ **Kervar Inc.**
119-121 W 28th St.
New York, NY 10001
Phone: (212)564-2525
Free: (888)453-7827 **Fax:** (212)594-0030
E-mail: kervar@injersey.com
URL: http://www.kervar.com
Products: Floral products. **SIC:** 5193 (Flowers & Florists' Supplies). **Est:** 1980. **Emp:** 8. **Officers:** Dennis Bernstein, CEO.

■ 14905 ■ **Kim Originals Inc.**
PO Box 825
Sedalia, MO 65302-0825
Phone: (660)826-2500
Free: (800)467-5467 **Fax:** (660)827-0711
Products: Silk flowers. **SIC:** 5193 (Flowers & Florists' Supplies). **Est:** 1960. **Sales:** $6,500,000 (2000). **Emp:** 40. **Officers:** Loretta E. Cline, CEO & President; Craig Cline, CFO; Tom Williams, Vice President.

■ 14906 ■ **Knutson Farms Inc.**
16406 78th St. E
Sumner, WA 98390-2900
Phone: (253)863-5107
Products: Flowers, including daffodils and tulips. **SIC:** 5193 (Flowers & Florists' Supplies). **Est:** 1956. **Sales:** $3,000,000 (2000). **Emp:** 100. **Officers:** R. Knutson, President.

■ 14907 ■ **Koba Nurseries & Landscaping**
41-709 Mokulama St.
Waimanalo, HI 96795
Phone: (808)259-5954 **Fax:** (808)259-9712
Products: Plants, trees, sod, grass, and shrubs. **SIC:** 5193 (Flowers & Florists' Supplies).

■ **14908** ■ **Kobayashi Farm & Nursery**
PO Box 525
Captain Cook, HI 96704
Phone: (808)328-9861   **Fax:** (808)328-8023
Products: Fresh flowers. **SIC:** 5193 (Flowers & Florists' Supplies).

■ **14909** ■ **Kula Farm**
751E Pulehuiki Rd.
Kula, HI 96790
Phone: (808)878-1046
Free: (800)525-5852   **Fax:** (808)878-2746
Products: Fresh flowers. **SIC:** 5193 (Flowers & Florists' Supplies).

■ **14910** ■ **W. Lee Flowers and Company Inc.**
PO Box 1629
Lake City, SC 29560
Phone: (803)389-2731   **Fax:** (803)389-4199
Products: Florist supplies, including flowers, seeds, and pots. **SIC:** 5193 (Flowers & Florists' Supplies). **Est:** 1929. **Sales:** $68,000,000 (2000). **Emp:** 170. **Officers:** W. Henry Johnson, President; Bill Garner, Controller; L.H. Jordon, VP of Sales; Carl Jordon, Dir. of Systems.

■ **14911** ■ **Lee Wholesale Floral Inc.**
620 15th St.
Lubbock, TX 79401
Phone: (806)765-8309   **Fax:** (806)762-3138
Products: Flowers and florists supplies. **SIC:** 5193 (Flowers & Florists' Supplies). **Est:** 1954. **Sales:** $3,500,000 (2000). **Emp:** 27. **Officers:** Sue Lee, President; Perry Lee, General Mgr.

■ **14912** ■ **Lloyd's Carnation**
357 IHE Pl.
Kula, HI 96790
Phone: (808)878-6235
Products: Orchids. **SIC:** 5193 (Flowers & Florists' Supplies).

■ **14913** ■ **Lorelei's Exotic Leis & Flower**
PO Box 173
Makawao, HI 96768
Phone: (808)572-0181
Products: Leis and flowers. **SIC:** 5193 (Flowers & Florists' Supplies).

■ **14914** ■ **Mahealani Farms Inc.**
PO Box 247
Hana, HI 96713
Phone: (808)248-7533
Free: (800)456-4262   **Fax:** (808)248-7253
E-mail: hanatrop@mau.net
URL: http://www.hanatropicals.com
Products: Flowers, including orchids and bromeliads; Plants, including palms. **SIC:** 5193 (Flowers & Florists' Supplies). **Est:** 1980. **Sales:** $250,000 (2000). **Emp:** 4. **Officers:** Anthony J. Pu, Owner; Susan J. Pu, CFO. **Doing Business As:** Hana Tropicals.

■ **14915** ■ **Mahoney's Garden Center**
242 Cambridge St.
Winchester, MA 01890
Phone: (781)729-5900   **Fax:** (781)729-5900
Products: Garden center. **SIC:** 5193 (Flowers & Florists' Supplies). **Sales:** $25,000,000 (2000). **Emp:** 300. **Officers:** Paul Mahoney, Owner.

■ **14916** ■ **Marshall Pottery Inc.**
4901 Elysian Fields Rd.
PO Box 1839
Marshall, TX 75671
Phone: (903)938-9201
Free: (800)POT-USA1   **Fax:** (903)938-8222
E-mail: askus@marshallpottery.net
URL: http://www.marshallpottery.com
Products: Flower pots; Handturned stoneware pottery. **SICs:** 5193 (Flowers & Florists' Supplies); 5199 (Nondurable Goods Nec). **Est:** 1895. **Sales:** $10,500,000 (2000).

■ **14917** ■ **Maui Blooms**
300 Ohukoi Rd., Ste. C 304
Kihei, HI 96753
Phone: (808)874-0875
Free: (800)451-0618   **Fax:** (808)875-4104
Products: Fresh and dried flowers. **SIC:** 5193 (Flowers & Florists' Supplies).

■ **14918** ■ **Maui Tropicals & Foliage**
1111 E Kuiaha Rd.
Haiku, HI 96708
Phone: (808)572-9600
Products: Flowers and foliages. **SIC:** 5193 (Flowers & Florists' Supplies).

■ **14919** ■ **J.M. McConkey and Company Inc.**
PO Box 1690
Sumner, WA 98390
Phone: (253)863-8111   **Fax:** (253)863-5833
URL: http://www.mcconkeyco.com
Products: Horticultural products. **SIC:** 5083 (Farm & Garden Machinery). **Est:** 1964. **Sales:** $20,000,000 (2000). **Emp:** 100. **Officers:** Edward McConkey, President; Dennis Dody, Controller; D. Knievel, VP of Marketing.

■ **14920** ■ **McKay Nursery Company Inc.**
PO Box 185
Waterloo, WI 53594
Phone: (920)478-2121   **Fax:** (920)478-3615
Products: Plants. **SIC:** 5193 (Flowers & Florists' Supplies). **Est:** 1897. **Sales:** $8,000,000 (1999). **Emp:** 120. **Officers:** Jerry Draeger, President; Tim Jonas, Treasurer & Secty.

■ **14921** ■ **Metrolina Greenhouses Inc.**
16400 Huntersville Concord Rd.
Huntersville, NC 28078
Phone: (704)875-1371
Free: (800)222-2905   **Fax:** (704)875-6741
Products: Plants, including bedding plants; Hanging baskets; Flowers, including potted annuals, poinsettas and mums. **SIC:** 5193 (Flowers & Florists' Supplies). **Est:** 1973. **Sales:** $35,000,000 (2000). **Emp:** 250. **Officers:** Tom Van Wingerden, President; Art Van Wingerden, Vice President, e-mail: art@metrolinagreenhouses.com; Vickie Van Wingerden, Treasurer.

■ **14922** ■ **Mid American Growers**
Rte. 89
Granville, IL 61326
Phone: (815)339-6831
Free: (800)892-6888   **Fax:** (815)339-2747
E-mail: dthiu@midamg.com
Products: Flowers and plants. **SIC:** 5193 (Flowers & Florists' Supplies). **Est:** 1970. **Sales:** $20,000,000 (1999). **Emp:** 250. **Officers:** N. Vanwingerden, President.

■ **14923** ■ **Mt. Eden Floral Co.**
531 E Evelyn Ave.
Mountain View, CA 94041
Phone: (650)903-5020   **Fax:** (650)903-3251
E-mail: sales@mteden.com
Products: Flowers and florists supplies. **SIC:** 5193 (Flowers & Florists' Supplies). **Est:** 1915. **Sales:** $27,000,000 (2000). **Emp:** 250. **Officers:** Robert Shibata, President; Karen Chuang, CFO; Henry Kakinami, Dir. of Marketing & Sales. **Former Name:** Mount Eden Nursery Co.

■ **14924** ■ **Charles H. Mueller Co.**
7091 N River Rd.
New Hope, PA 18938
Phone: (215)862-2033
Products: Flower bulbs; Tulips; Daffodils. **SIC:** 5193 (Flowers & Florists' Supplies).

■ **14925** ■ **Multi-Grow Investments Inc.**
9831 Oakwood Cir.
VilLa Park, CA 92861-1221
Phone: (909)627-7676   **Fax:** (909)627-6556
Products: Groundcovers. **SIC:** 5193 (Flowers & Florists' Supplies). **Est:** 1972. **Sales:** $2,000,000 (2000). **Emp:** 50. **Officers:** Howard M. Lee, President.

■ **14926** ■ **Musser Forests Inc.**
PO Box 340
Indiana, PA 15701
Phone: (412)465-5686   **Fax:** (412)465-9893
Products: Nursery stock, including plants, seeds, and crafts. **SIC:** 5193 (Flowers & Florists' Supplies). **Est:** 1928. **Sales:** $6,000,000 (2000). **Emp:** 290. **Officers:** Fred Musser Jr., President; Norman Miller, CFO; Nancy Musser, VP of Marketing.

■ **14927** ■ **NAPCO & LBK Marketing Corp.**
7800 Bayberry Rd.
Jacksonville, FL 32256-6815
Phone: (904)737-8500   **Fax:** (904)737-9178
Products: Flowers and florists supplies. **SIC:** 5193 (Flowers & Florists' Supplies). **Emp:** 99.

■ **14928** ■ **Nordlie Inc.**
262 E Montcalm St.
Detroit, MI 48201
Phone: (313)963-2400   **Fax:** (313)963-0951
Products: Floral goods. **SIC:** 5193 (Flowers & Florists' Supplies). **Est:** 1928. **Sales:** $52,000,000 (2000). **Emp:** 100. **Officers:** Kevin Smith, CEO; Thomas Addison, CFO.

■ **14929** ■ **Nortex Wholesale Nursery Inc.**
1300 W Brown
Wylie, TX 75098
Phone: (972)442-5451
Free: (800)880-5451   **Fax:** (972)442-5919
Products: Plants, including bedding plants; Herbs; Foliage. **SIC:** 5193 (Flowers & Florists' Supplies). **Est:** 1951. **Sales:** $2,800,000 (1999). **Emp:** 65. **Officers:** Jon Pinkus, President.

■ **14930** ■ **Of Distinction, Inc. - The Silk Plant Co.**
2110 W 98 St.
Bloomington, MN 55431-2506
Phone: (612)888-5654
Products: Plants. **SIC:** 5193 (Flowers & Florists' Supplies).

■ **14931** ■ **Orchid Plantation, Inc.**
14-4970 Kaimu-Kapoho Rd.
Pahoa, HI 96778
Phone: (808)965-6295   **Fax:** (808)965-6295
E-mail: opi@turquoise.net
Products: Orchids, including potted orchids. **SIC:** 5193 (Flowers & Florists' Supplies). **Est:** 1989. **Sales:** $300,000 (1999). **Emp:** 10. **Officers:** Elton Mow, MG.

■ **14932** ■ **Oregon Floral Distributors**
1130 Anderson Ln.
Springfield, OR 97477
Phone: (541)746-8497
Free: (800)888-6113   **Fax:** (541)746-1109
E-mail: oregonfloral@home.com
URL: http://www.oregonfloral.com
Products: Flowers and floral products. **SIC:** 5193 (Flowers & Florists' Supplies). **Est:** 1989. **Emp:** 15.

■ **14933** ■ **Orkin Lawn Care**
2170 Piedmont Rd. NE
Atlanta, GA 30324
Phone: (404)888-2777
Products: Lawn care chemicals. **SICs:** 5193 (Flowers & Florists' Supplies); 5169 (Chemicals & Allied Products Nec).

■ **14934** ■ **Outer Bay Trading Co.**
186 Porters Point Rd.
PO Box 125
Colchester, VT 05446
Phone: (802)864-7628   **Fax:** (802)864-7628
Products: Florist supplies, including roses and bouquets. **SIC:** 5193 (Flowers & Florists' Supplies). **Est:** 1986.

■ **14935** ■ **Pacific Floral Exchange, Inc.**
16-685 Milo St.
PO Box 1989
Keaau, HI 96749
Phone: (808)966-7427
Free: (800)752-7779   **Fax:** (808)966-7684
E-mail: pacflor@aloha.net
Products: Tropical flowers, including anthiriums, orchids, protea, heliconia, ginger, blooming plants, and tropical foliage. **SIC:** 5193 (Flowers & Florists' Supplies). **Est:** 1989. **Sales:** $3,000,000 (2000). **Emp:** 40. **Officers:** Grayson Inouye, President; Henry Terada, Vice President; Michael Inouye, Sales/Marketing Contact; Michael Inouye, Sales & Marketing Contact.

■ 14936 ■ Pallian & Co.
PO Box 1704
Wells, ME 04090
Phone: (207)646-1600
Products: Baskets, reeds, topiaries, and dried flower arrangements. **SIC:** 5193 (Flowers & Florists' Supplies).

■ 14937 ■ Paradise Flower Farms Inc.
352 Ihe Pl. No.B
Kula, HI 96790
Phone: (808)878-2591 **Fax:** (808)878-1864
Products: Spring flowers, including roses and chrysanthemums. **SIC:** 5193 (Flowers & Florists' Supplies).

■ 14938 ■ Pasqua Florist & Greenhouse
659 Metacom Ave.
Warren, RI 02885
Phone: (401)245-7511
Products: Potted plants. **SIC:** 5193 (Flowers & Florists' Supplies).

■ 14939 ■ Pearl's Garden Center
PO Box 213
Captain Cook, HI 96704
Phone: (808)323-3009
Products: Garden supplies. **SICs:** 5193 (Flowers & Florists' Supplies); 5191 (Farm Supplies).

■ 14940 ■ Pennock Co.
3027 Stokley St.
Philadelphia, PA 19129
Phone: (215)844-6600
Products: Flowers and floral supplies. **SIC:** 5193 (Flowers & Florists' Supplies). **Sales:** $76,000,000 (2000). **Emp:** 400. **Officers:** Wayne Collins, President; Robert Billings, Treasurer.

■ 14941 ■ Perennial Gardens
PO Box 770106
Eagle River, AK 99577
Phone: (907)688-2821 **Fax:** (907)688-6292
Products: Garden supplies, including bedding plants, indoor and outdoor fertilizers, lime, soils, and moss. **SICs:** 5193 (Flowers & Florists' Supplies); 5191 (Farm Supplies).

■ 14942 ■ Pikes Peak Greenhouses, Inc.
PO Box 7070
Colorado Springs, CO 80933
Phone: (719)475-2770
Products: Cut flowers; Bedding plants. **SIC:** 5193 (Flowers & Florists' Supplies). **Est:** 1904. **Emp:** 24. **Officers:** Timothy Haley, President. **Former Name:** Pikes Peak Wholesale Florist Inc.

■ 14943 ■ Quintal Farms
PO Box 462
Kurtistown, HI 96760
Phone: (808)966-7370 **Fax:** (808)966-7370
Products: Nursery supplies, including cut flowers and plants. **SIC:** 5193 (Flowers & Florists' Supplies).

■ 14944 ■ G. Reising and Co.
70 La Prenda
Millbrae, CA 94030-2119
Phone: (650)259-0700
Free: (800)442-4720 **Fax:** (650)259-0777
Products: Floral products. **SIC:** 5193 (Flowers & Florists' Supplies). **Est:** 1933. **Sales:** $3,000,000 (2000). **Emp:** 25. **Officers:** Richard F. Reising, President; Matthew J. Reising, CFO; Max G. Reising, Dir. of Marketing.

■ 14945 ■ Roak's Seven-Acre Greenhouses
963 Washington Ave.
Portland, ME 04103
Phone: (207)772-5523
Products: Potted plants. **SIC:** 5193 (Flowers & Florists' Supplies).

■ 14946 ■ Sally's Flower Shop
333 Main St.
Winooski, VT 05404
Phone: (802)655-3894
Products: Flowers. **SIC:** 5193 (Flowers & Florists' Supplies).

■ 14947 ■ Jerry Schluckbier Inc.
2760 Industrial Row
Troy, MI 48098
Phone: (248)280-0844 **Fax:** (248)280-1256
E-mail: jsifaith@aol.com
Products: Horticultural supplies. **SIC:** 5193 (Flowers & Florists' Supplies). **Officers:** Gerald Schluckbier, President.

■ 14948 ■ Sequoia Floral International
3245 Santa Rosa Ave.
Santa Rosa, CA 95407
Phone: (707)525-0780 **Fax:** (707)525-0719
E-mail: sequoiafloralintl@prodigy.net
Products: Cut flowers, bouquets, dried manufacturing and floral supplies. **SIC:** 5193 (Flowers & Florists' Supplies). **Est:** 1976. **Sales:** $6,000,000 (2000). **Emp:** 50. **Officers:** Bill Horn; Pam Soares, Marketing & Sales Mgr.; Mike Bertoli, Human Resources; Jim Fitzpatrick. **Former Name:** Sequoia Wholesale Florist Inc.

■ 14949 ■ Sharion's Silk Flower Outlet
905 Lovers Lane Rd. SE
Calhoun, GA 30701-4633
Phone: (706)625-5519
Free: (800)465-8468 **Fax:** (706)625-8468
E-mail: sste9697@aol.com
URL: http://www.sharion'ssilkflower.com
Products: Floral and supplies; Home decor items. **SIC:** 5193 (Flowers & Florists' Supplies). **Est:** 1980. **Sales:** $900,000 (2000). **Emp:** 5. **Officers:** Sharion Stewart, Owner. **Former Name:** Stewart Crafts Inc.

■ 14950 ■ Silk and Morgan Inc.
33866 Woodward Ave.
Birmingham, MI 48009-0914
Phone: (248)644-4411
Free: (888)820-6599 **Fax:** (248)642-5230
E-mail: blossoms@blossomsbirmingham.com
URL: http://www.blossomsbirmingham.com
Products: Flowers; Gifts; Party decor; Home decor. **SIC:** 5193 (Flowers & Florists' Supplies). **Est:** 1975. **Sales:** $2,500,000 (2000). **Emp:** 25. **Officers:** Norman H. Silk, President, e-mail: norm@blossomsbirmingham.com; Dale R. Morgan, Vice President, e-mail: dale@blosssomsbirmingham.com. **Doing Business As:** Blossoms.

■ 14951 ■ Skinner Nursery Inc.
7415 SW 22nd Ct.
Topeka, KS 66614-6070
Phone: (785)478-0123
Products: Nursery stock; Fertilizer. **SICs:** 5193 (Flowers & Florists' Supplies); 5191 (Farm Supplies). **Est:** 1892. **Sales:** $200,000 (2000). **Emp:** 2. **Officers:** Robert E. Skinner, President.

■ 14952 ■ South Cedar Greenhouses
23111 Cedar Ave. S
Farmington, MN 55024-8017
Phone: (612)469-3202
Products: Plants. **SIC:** 5193 (Flowers & Florists' Supplies).

■ 14953 ■ Southern Floral Co.
1313 W 20th
Houston, TX 77008-1639
Phone: (713)880-1300 **Fax:** (713)867-0211
Products: Flowers and floral supplies. **SIC:** 5193 (Flowers & Florists' Supplies). **Est:** 1927. **Emp:** 150. **Officers:** R.H. Weatherford.

■ 14954 ■ Southern Importers Inc.
PO Box 8579
Greensboro, NC 27419
Phone: (336)292-4521
Free: (800)334-9658 **Fax:** (336)852-6397
E-mail: sales@southernimporters.com
URL: http://www.southernimporters.com
Products: Horticultural products, including Canadian sphagnum, peat moss, bark (pine, hardwood, cedar, cypress); Soils, premium products including professional potting and planting mix, seed starter (both of these in attractive, stand up packaging); Black deco mulch, red monterey mulch, mulch and feed; Lawn boster. **SIC:** 5193 (Flowers & Florists' Supplies). **Est:** 1959. **Sales:** $20,000,000 (2000). **Emp:** 20. **Officers:** J. D. Camia, Chief Operating Officer; Roger Welgold, Natl. Sales Mgr.

■ 14955 ■ Spokane Flower Growers
PO Box 53
Spokane, WA 99210
Phone: (509)624-0121 **Fax:** (509)747-8509
Products: Floral supplies. **SIC:** 5193 (Flowers & Florists' Supplies). **Est:** 1925. **Sales:** $4,000,000 (2000). **Emp:** 30. **Officers:** Alan E. Lesher, General Mgr.

■ 14956 ■ Stein Garden and Gifts
5400 S 27th St.
Milwaukee, WI 53221
Phone: (414)761-5404 **Fax:** (414)761-5420
Products: Garden supplies, florist supplies and fresh cut flowers. **SIC:** 5193 (Flowers & Florists' Supplies). **Sales:** $50,000,000 (2000). **Emp:** 1,000. **Officers:** Jack Stein, Owner.

■ 14957 ■ Gerald Stevens Inc.
301 E LasOlas Blvd.
Ft. Lauderdale, FL 33301
Phone: (954)713-5000
Free: (800)333-8483 **Fax:** (561)563-9958
Products: Flowers and gifts. **SIC:** 5193 (Flowers & Florists' Supplies). **Sales:** $110,600,000 (1999). **Emp:** 3,775. **Officers:** Gerald R. Geddis, CEO & President; Albert Detz, CFO.

■ 14958 ■ Super American Import
5400 NW 161 St.
Miami, FL 33014
Phone: (305)625-0772 **Fax:** (305)625-7604
Products: Silk flowers; Gift items. **SICs:** 5193 (Flowers & Florists' Supplies); 5199 (Nondurable Goods Nec).

■ 14959 ■ Synnestvedt Co.
24550 W Hwy. 120
Round Lake, IL 60073
Phone: (847)546-4834 **Fax:** (847)546-9065
E-mail: synnco@aol.com
URL: http://www.synnestvedt.com
Products: Trees; Shrubs; Liners and containers; Perennials. **SIC:** 5193 (Flowers & Florists' Supplies). **Est:** 1943. **Sales:** $2,000,000 (2000). **Emp:** 70. **Officers:** Matthew Synnestvedt, President.

■ 14960 ■ Tennessee Florist Supply Inc.
PO Box 3022
Knoxville, TN 37927
Phone: (423)524-7451 **Fax:** (423)637-8155
Products: Flowers. **SIC:** 5193 (Flowers & Florists' Supplies). **Est:** 1953. **Sales:** $9,000,000 (2000). **Emp:** 70. **Officers:** Dennis Pierce, President; J. Talent, Treasurer & Secty.; M. Talent, Dir. of Marketing.

■ 14961 ■ Teters Floral Products Inc.
PO Box 210
Bolivar, MO 65613
Phone: (417)326-7654 **Fax:** (417)326-8061
Products: Flowers. **SIC:** 5193 (Flowers & Florists' Supplies). **Est:** 1957. **Sales:** $77,000,000 (2000). **Emp:** 700. **Officers:** H.W. Godfrey, President; Duane Williams, Exec. VP of Finance; Steve Harrill, Exec. VP of Sales; Kenneth Hatfield, Exec. VP of Operations; Ron Erven, Dir of Human Resources.

■ 14962 ■ Tonkadale Greenhouses
3739 Tonkawood Rd.
Minnetonka, MN 55345-1445
Phone: (612)938-1445
Products: Plants. **SIC:** 5193 (Flowers & Florists' Supplies).

■ 14963 ■ Tropical Gardens of Maui
Iao Valley Rd.
Wailuku, HI 96793
Phone: (808)244-3085 **Fax:** (808)242-6152
Products: Orchids. **SIC:** 5193 (Flowers & Florists' Supplies).

■ 14964 ■ U.A.F. L.P.
6610 Anderson Rd.
Tampa, FL 33634
Phone: (813)885-6936 **Fax:** (813)882-9918
Products: Fresh flowers. **SIC:** 5193 (Flowers & Florists' Supplies). **Sales:** $13,000,000 (2000). **Emp:** 120. **Officers:** Bill McClure, President.

■ **14965** ■ **Ulery Greenhouse Co.**
PO Box 1108
Springfield, OH 45501
Phone: (937)325-5543
Free: (800)722-5143 **Fax:** (937)325-1824
E-mail: ulery@cfanet.com
Products: Plants and flowers. **SIC:** 5193 (Flowers & Florists' Supplies). **Est:** 1908. **Sales:** $5,000,000 (1999). **Emp:** 62. **Officers:** P.D. Ulery, President; W.E. Ulery, Finance Officer; Jeff S. Ulery, VP of Marketing & Sales, e-mail: jeff@ulerygreenhouse.com; Michele Donovan, Customer Service Contact, e-mail: michele@ulerygreenhouse.com.

■ **14966** ■ **United Floral Supply Inc.**
PO Box 2518
North Canton, OH 44720
Phone: (330)966-9160
Products: Fresh flowers. **SIC:** 5193 (Flowers & Florists' Supplies). **Sales:** $6,000,000 (2000). **Emp:** 22. **Officers:** Patty Streb, President.

■ **14967** ■ **U.S.A. Floral Products**
1025 Thomas Jefferson NW
Ste. 300 E
Washington, DC 20007
Phone: (202)333-0800 **Fax:** (202)333-0803
E-mail: growth@usafp.com
URL: http://www.usafp.com
Products: Flowers and floral products. **SIC:** 5193 (Flowers & Florists' Supplies). **Est:** 1997. **Officers:** Michael W. Broomfield, CEO; G. Andrew Cooke, CFO; Dwight Ferguson, COO & President.

■ **14968** ■ **Van Ness Water Gardens Inc.**
2460 N Euclid Ave.
Upland, CA 91784-1199
Phone: (909)982-2425
Free: (800)205-2425 **Fax:** (909)949-7217
E-mail: vnwg@vnwg.com
Products: Water garden plants and related supplies. **SIC:** 5193 (Flowers & Florists' Supplies). **Est:** 1922. **Sales:** $400,000 (2000). **Emp:** 15. **Officers:** William Uber, President; Caroline Uber, Controller.

■ **14969** ■ **Van Wingerden International Inc.**
556 Jeffress Rd.
Fletcher, NC 28732
Phone: (704)891-4116 **Fax:** (704)891-8581
Products: Potted plants; Fresh flowers. **SIC:** 5193 (Flowers & Florists' Supplies). **Est:** 1970. **Sales:** $20,000,000 (2000). **Emp:** 250. **Officers:** Bert Lemkes, President; T. Burnette, Dir. of Marketing.

■ **14970** ■ **Van Zyverden, Inc.**
PO Box 550
Meridian, MS 39302-0550
Phone: (601)679-8274 **Fax:** (601)679-8039
URL: http://www.vanzyverdenusa.com
Products: Flower bulbs. **SIC:** 5191 (Farm Supplies). **Est:** 1952. **Sales:** $32,000,000 (2000). **Emp:** 250. **Officers:** Jacqueline Van Zyverden Hogan, Co-Owner & Chairman of the Board; Robert A. Van Zyverden, CEO & Chairman of the Board; Patsy McMillian, Controller; Nick Burkardt, President. **Former Name:** Van Zyverden Brothers, Inc.

■ **14971** ■ **Vermont Flower Exchange**
47 Woodstock Ave.
Rutland, VT 05701
Phone: (802)775-1836
Products: Fresh flowers; Floral supplies; Balloons. **SIC:** 5193 (Flowers & Florists' Supplies). **Est:** 1976. **Emp:** 10. **Officers:** Ronald Ayres, President; Gary Ayres, SCT; Judy Wood, General Mgr.

■ **14972** ■ **Volcano Flowers & Greenery**
PO Box 966
Volcano, HI 96785
Phone: (808)967-7450
Products: Flowers. **SIC:** 5193 (Flowers & Florists' Supplies).

■ **14973** ■ **Watanabe Floral, Inc.**
1607 Hart St.
Honolulu, HI 96817
Phone: (808)848-1026 **Fax:** (808)848-1033
Products: Flowers and dried flower arrangements. **SIC:** 5193 (Flowers & Florists' Supplies).

■ **14974** ■ **Watanabe Floral, Inc.**
Lalamilo Farm Area, Lot 2
Kamuela, HI 96743
Phone: (808)885-7588 **Fax:** (808)885-6900
Products: Roses. **SIC:** 5193 (Flowers & Florists' Supplies).

■ **14975** ■ **Wetsel Inc.**
PO Box 791
Harrisonburg, VA 22801
Phone: (540)434-6753 **Fax:** (540)434-4894
Products: Lawn and garden distributors. **SIC:** 5193 (Flowers & Florists' Supplies). **Sales:** $60,000,000 (1999). **Emp:** 180. **Officers:** Floyd Grigsby, President & General Mgr.

■ **14976** ■ **Wight Nurseries Inc.**
PO Box 390
Cairo, GA 31728
Phone: (912)377-3033 **Fax:** (912)377-9394
Products: Outdoor plants, including bushes. **SIC:** 5193

(Flowers & Florists' Supplies). **Est:** 1887. **Sales:** $19,000,000 (2000). **Emp:** 520. **Officers:** Richard VanLandingham, President; Bob Jones, VP of Finance; Charles Culbreth, VP of Marketing; Bob Szczepanski, Dir. of Systems; Jerry Lee, VP of Human Resources.

■ **14977** ■ **Wilderness Nursery**
Box 6078-A
Palmer, AK 99645
Phone: (907)745-6205 **Fax:** (907)745-6206
Products: Outdoor plants, including annuals, perennials, trees, and shrubs. **SIC:** 5193 (Flowers & Florists' Supplies).

■ **14978** ■ **Dave Wilson Nursery**
19701 Lake Rd.
Hickman, CA 95323
Phone: (209)874-1821 **Fax:** (209)874-1920
Products: Bare root trees. **SIC:** 5193 (Flowers & Florists' Supplies). **Est:** 1938. **Sales:** $4,000,000 (2000). **Emp:** 100. **Officers:** Robert Woolley, President; Chuck Quiring, Controller; Truman Hise, Vice President.

■ **14979** ■ **A. Yamashiro, Inc.**
746 Bannister St.
Honolulu, HI 96819
Phone: (808)841-8726 **Fax:** (808)845-8843
Products: Fresh flowers. **SIC:** 5193 (Flowers & Florists' Supplies). **Est:** 1970. **Sales:** $800,000 (2000). **Emp:** 6.

■ **14980** ■ **Yoder Brothers Inc.**
115 3rd St. SE
Barberton, OH 44203
Phone: (330)745-2143 **Fax:** (330)745-3098
Products: Potted plants. **SIC:** 5193 (Flowers & Florists' Supplies). **Est:** 1920. **Emp:** 1,500. **Officers:** Thomas D. Doak, President; Thomas W. Wancheck, VP of Finance.

■ **14981** ■ **Zeigler's Market**
315 N Ridgewood, US 1
Edgewater, FL 32132
Phone: (904)427-6136
Free: (800)831-2365 **Fax:** (904)427-6136
Products: Produce; Plants, including flowers and trees. **SIC:** 5193 (Flowers & Florists' Supplies).

■ **14982** ■ **Zieger and Sons Inc.**
6215 Ardleigh St.
Philadelphia, PA 19138
Phone: (215)438-7060
Products: Florist supplies. **SIC:** 5193 (Flowers & Florists' Supplies). **Est:** 1910. **Sales:** $15,000,000 (1999). **Emp:** 160. **Officers:** P.C. Zieger, President.

(25) Household Appliances

Entries in this section are arranged alphabetically by company name. When the company name is a personal name, the company name is alphabetized by the surname unless the first name or initial(s) are part of a trade name. See the User's Guide at the front of this directory for additional information.

■ 14983 ■ **1st Source Parts Center**
3442 Stanford NE
Albuquerque, NM 87107
Phone: (505)884-0166
Free: (800)388-3442 **Fax:** (505)884-9107
E-mail: adale@bigfoot.com
URL: http://www.1stsourceparts.com
Products: Parts for major household appliances, including washing machines and refrigerators. **SICs:** 5063 (Electrical Apparatus & Equipment); 5065 (Electronic Parts & Equipment Nec). **Est:** 1963. **Emp:** 116. **Officers:** Mark F. Williams.

■ 14984 ■ **A-1 Janitorial Supply & Equipment**
1419 Eastway Dr.
Charlotte, NC 28205-2205
Phone: (704)537-9921 **Fax:** (704)567-9833
Products: Electrical appliances, including televisions and radios; Vacuum cleaners. **SIC:** 5064 (Electrical Appliances—Television & Radio). **Officers:** Hwaja Mc Intyre, President.

■ 14985 ■ **A-1 Telecom Inc.**
PO Box 336
Niles, MI 49120-0336
Phone: (616)683-3870 **Fax:** (616)683-0937
Products: Electrical appliances; CB and amateur radios; Antennas and accessories. **SIC:** 5064 (Electrical Appliances—Television & Radio). **Officers:** Sam Ammori, President.

■ 14986 ■ **A-Air Conditioning Contractor**
27332 Van Dyke Ave.
Warren, MI 48093-2850
Phone: (313)372-5500 **Fax:** (810)758-6677
Products: Electrical appliances, including television sets and radios; Household appliance parts. **SIC:** 5064 (Electrical Appliances—Television & Radio). **Officers:** Robert Williams, Owner.

■ 14987 ■ **AA Water Service**
300 N White Sands Blvd., No. C
Alamogordo, NM 88310-7062
Phone: (505)434-2977
Products: Water service supplies, including water softeners, reverse osmosis machines, coolers, water bottles, and dispenser bottled water. **SICs:** 5078 (Refrigeration Equipment & Supplies); 5074 (Plumbing & Hydronic Heating Supplies).

■ 14988 ■ **AAA Distributors Inc.**
PO Box 415
Braddock Heights, MD 21714-0415
Phone: (301)428-0330
Free: (800)426-9967 **Fax:** (301)698-0146
Products: Office equipment and supplies. **SIC:** 5064 (Electrical Appliances—Television & Radio). **Sales:** $2,000,000 (2000). **Emp:** 5.

■ 14989 ■ **AAT Communications Systems Corp.**
1854 Hylan Blvd.
Staten Island, NY 10305
Phone: (718)351-4782
Free: (800)622-6224 **Fax:** (718)351-2525
Products: Sound and entertainment equipment and

supplies. **SIC:** 5064 (Electrical Appliances—Television & Radio). **Sales:** $8,000,000 (2000). **Emp:** 55.

■ 14990 ■ **Absolute Appliance Distributors Inc.**
4295 Cromwell Rd., Ste. 403
Chattanooga, TN 37421
Phone: (615)490-0015
Products: Home appliances. **SIC:** 5064 (Electrical Appliances—Television & Radio).

■ 14991 ■ **Accardos Appliance Parts & Services**
8640 Oak St.
New Orleans, LA 70118-1222
Phone: (504)866-1951
Products: Small electrical appliances; Household appliances; Major appliance parts; Television sets; Radios. **SIC:** 5064 (Electrical Appliances—Television & Radio). **Officers:** Peter Accardo, Owner.

■ 14992 ■ **Ace Appliances Inc.**
2450 N Sherwood Forest Blvd.
Baton Rouge, LA 70815
Phone: (504)275-6220
Products: Kitchen appliances, including refrigerators; Washers and dryers. **SIC:** 5064 (Electrical Appliances—Television & Radio). **Est:** 1954. **Sales:** $5,500,000 (2000). **Emp:** 32. **Officers:** James Kennison, President.

■ 14993 ■ **ADI Jacksonville**
2757 Earnest St.
Jacksonville, FL 32205
Phone: (904)384-0620 **Fax:** (904)384-8871
Products: Appliances. **SIC:** 5064 (Electrical Appliances—Television & Radio).

■ 14994 ■ **Advance Refrigeration Co.**
1177 Industrial Dr.
Bensenville, IL 60106
Phone: (708)766-2000 **Fax:** (708)766-2147
Products: Household appliances and parts. **SIC:** 5064 (Electrical Appliances—Television & Radio). **Est:** 1960. **Sales:** $10,000,000 (2000). **Emp:** 50. **Officers:** Donald P. Leach, President; Chuck Cardwell, Controller; Ralgh G. Hinkle, VP of Marketing & Sales.

■ 14995 ■ **AIMS Multimedia**
9710 De Soto Ave.
Chatsworth, CA 91311-4409
Phone: (818)773-4300
Free: (800)367-2467 **Fax:** (818)341-6700
Products: Sound and entertainment equipment and supplies. **SIC:** 5064 (Electrical Appliances—Television & Radio).

■ 14996 ■ **Alaska Housewares Inc.**
501 West 58th Ave.
Anchorage, AK 99518-1431
Phone: (907)561-2240 **Fax:** (907)561-2088
Products: Electrical appliances, including television and radio; Houseware products; Automotive paint. **SICs:** 5064 (Electrical Appliances—Television & Radio); 5023 (Homefurnishings); 5198 (Paints, Varnishes & Supplies). **Officers:** Richard Emery, President.

■ 14997 ■ **Albert Trading Co.**
PO Box 433
West Bend, WI 53095
Phone: (414)334-9295 **Fax:** (414)335-3037
Products: Small electrical household appliances; Mirrors; Electric coffeemakers. **SICs:** 5064 (Electrical Appliances—Television & Radio); 5023 (Homefurnishings). **Officers:** Gerald Albert, President.

■ 14998 ■ **Algert Company, Inc.**
2121 E Del Amo Blvd.
Compton, CA 90220
Phone: (213)632-7777 **Fax:** (213)483-6856
Products: Air-conditioners; Kitchen cabinets; Electrical appliances, including kitchen ranges, refrigerators, and washers. **SICs:** 5064 (Electrical Appliances—Television & Radio); 5075 (Warm Air Heating & Air-Conditioning); 5031 (Lumber, Plywood & Millwork). **Officers:** Geert Jensen, President.

■ 14999 ■ **All Brand Appliance Parts Inc.**
170 N Blackhorse Pike
Mt. Ephraim, NJ 08059
Phone: (609)933-2300 **Fax:** (609)933-3762
Products: Commercial and residential appliance parts. **SIC:** 5064 (Electrical Appliances—Television & Radio). **Officers:** Richard Presant.

■ 15000 ■ **All Brand Appliance Parts of Pennsylvania**
949 E Main St.
Norristown, PA 19401
Phone: (215)277-5175 **Fax:** (215)275-8876
Products: Appliance parts. **SIC:** 5064 (Electrical Appliances—Television & Radio). **Officers:** Salvatore Falconi.

■ 15001 ■ **Allen Appliance Distributors**
6505 St. Vincent Ave.
Shreveport, LA 71136-6480
Phone: (318)868-6541
Free: (800)551-8737 **Fax:** (318)865-6102
Products: Appliances. **SIC:** 5064 (Electrical Appliances—Television & Radio). **Sales:** $4,000,000 (2000). **Emp:** 12. **Officers:** David Taylor, General Mgr.

■ 15002 ■ **Allied Telecommunications Inc.**
PO Box 2106
Richmond, IN 47375-2106
Phone: (765)935-1538 **Fax:** (765)966-6485
Products: Sound and entertainment equipment and supplies. **SIC:** 5064 (Electrical Appliances—Television & Radio). **Sales:** $10,000,000 (2000). **Emp:** 44.

■ 15003 ■ **Allstate/GES Appliance Inc.**
2001 N 23rd Ave.
Phoenix, AZ 85009-2918
Phone: (602)252-6507 **Fax:** (602)258-4736
Products: Household appliances. **SIC:** 5064 (Electrical Appliances—Television & Radio). **Est:** 1970. **Sales:** $15,000,000 (2000). **Emp:** 45. **Officers:** E. R. Goodwin, President.

■ **15004** ■ **Allyn International Corp.**
1075 Santa Fe Dr.
Denver, CO 80204-3900
Phone: (303)825-5200 **Fax:** (303)825-5078
Products: Household sewing machines. **SIC:** 5064 (Electrical Appliances—Television & Radio). **Officers:** Albert Rose, President.

■ **15005** ■ **Altron International**
314 W Walton Blvd.
Pontiac, MI 48340-1041
Phone: (248)334-2519
Free: (800)922-9078 **Fax:** (248)334-3558
Products: Sound and entertainment equipment and supplies. **SIC:** 5064 (Electrical Appliances—Television & Radio). **Sales:** $5,000,000 (2000). **Emp:** 20.

■ **15006** ■ **Ambex Inc.**
1917 Drew St.
Clearwater, FL 33765
Phone: (727)442-2727
E-mail: info@ambexroasters.com
URL: http://www.ambexroasters.com
Products: Coffee roasters; Coffee. **SICs:** 5046 (Commercial Equipment Nec); 5149 (Groceries & Related Products Nec). **Est:** 1995. **Emp:** 4.

■ **15007** ■ **Amco-McLean Corp.**
766 McLean Ave.
Yonkers, NY 10704
Phone: (914)237-4000 **Fax:** (914)237-4341
Products: Television, video, car and portable audio equipment, fax machines, phones and microwave ovens. **SIC:** 5064 (Electrical Appliances—Television & Radio). **Sales:** $7,000,000 (2000). **Emp:** 12. **Officers:** Joe Bonda, President.

■ **15008** ■ **American Appliance Parts Co. Inc.**
1180 Sherman Ave.
Hamden, CT 06514-1322
Phone: (203)248-4444 **Fax:** (203)281-6301
Products: Major appliance parts. **SICs:** 5065 (Electronic Parts & Equipment Nec); 5063 (Electrical Apparatus & Equipment). **Est:** 1945. **Emp:** 2. **Officers:** John Malatesta, President.

■ **15009** ■ **American International Exports**
8834 Monard Dr.
Silver Spring, MD 20910-1815
Phone: (301)585-7448 **Fax:** (301)585-1804
Products: Electrical appliances. **SIC:** 5064 (Electrical Appliances—Television & Radio). **Officers:** Robert Dhyani, President.

■ **15010** ■ **American Sewing Machine Distributors**
165 Middle Tpke. W
Manchester, CT 06040-4024
Phone: (860)649-0545 **Fax:** (860)649-0545
Products: Sewing machines. **SIC:** 5064 (Electrical Appliances—Television & Radio). **Officers:** Aaron Cheerman, President.

■ **15011** ■ **Anaheim Manufacturing Co.**
PO Box 4146
Anaheim, CA 92803
Phone: (714)524-7770 **Fax:** (714)996-7073
Products: Domestic garbage disposers. **SIC:** 5064 (Electrical Appliances—Television & Radio). **Sales:** $22,900,000 (2000). **Emp:** 130. **Officers:** Thomas Dugan, President; Ron Williams, VP of Finance.

■ **15012** ■ **Anaheim Marketing International**
4332 E La Palma Ave.
Anaheim, CA 92807
Phone: (714)993-1707 **Fax:** (714)993-1930
E-mail: info@go-ami.com
URL: http://www.go-ami.com
Products: Household appliances; Commercial and industrial garbage and trash compactors. **SICs:** 5064 (Electrical Appliances—Television & Radio); 5046 (Commercial Equipment Nec). **Est:** 1985. **Sales:** $7,000,000 (1999). **Emp:** 15. **Officers:** Edward E. Chavez, President; Lisa Ortega, Vice President, e-mail: anaheimktg@aol.com.

■ **15013** ■ **Apco Inc.**
1834 Bagwell St.
Flint, MI 48503-4406
Phone: (810)732-8933 **Fax:** (810)732-8980
Products: Home appliance parts. **SIC:** 5065 (Electronic Parts & Equipment Nec). **Emp:** 49.

■ **15014** ■ **Apco Inc.**
3305 S Pennsylvania
Lansing, MI 48910-4732
Phone: (517)882-5785
Free: (800)519-2726 **Fax:** (517)882-2640
E-mail: apco@voyager.net
URL: http://www.apcoinc.com
Products: Household appliance parts; Commercial heating and cooling equipment; Apartment maintenance supplies. **SICs:** 5065 (Electronic Parts & Equipment Nec); 5075 (Warm Air Heating & Air-Conditioning); 5087 (Service Establishment Equipment). **Est:** 1947. **Emp:** 49. **Officers:** D. A. Nussdorfer.

■ **15015** ■ **API Appliance Parts Inc.**
1645 Old County Rd.
San Carlos, CA 94070-1347
Phone: (650)591-4467
Free: (800)950-7278 **Fax:** (650)591-3508
URL: http://partsforappliances.com
Products: Appliance parts; Heating and air-conditioning equipment and supplies. **SICs:** 5065 (Electronic Parts & Equipment Nec); 5075 (Warm Air Heating & Air-Conditioning); 5064 (Electrical Appliances—Television & Radio). **Est:** 1964. **Emp:** 140. **Officers:** Len Berberich; Mark Berberich, Sales/Marketing Contact.

■ **15016** ■ **Appliance Dealer Supply Co.**
6237 E 22nd St.
Tucson, AZ 85711-5230
Phone: (602)252-7506
Free: (800)821-8195 **Fax:** (602)258-3091
Products: Household appliance parts. **SICs:** 5065 (Electronic Parts & Equipment Nec); 5063 (Electrical Apparatus & Equipment). **Officers:** Paul Zeller, President.

■ **15017** ■ **Appliance Distributors Unlimited**
729 Erie Ave.
Takoma Park, MD 20912
Phone: (301)608-2600 **Fax:** (301)608-9499
Products: Household appliances; Small electrical appliances. **SIC:** 5064 (Electrical Appliances—Television & Radio). **Officers:** Tom Oliff, President.

■ **15018** ■ **Appliance Parts Center Inc.**
222 E 8th St.
National City, CA 91950
Phone: (619)474-6781
Free: (800)777-7909 **Fax:** (619)474-0463
URL: http://www.appliancepartscenter.com
Products: Major appliance parts; Heating and cooling equipment parts. **SICs:** 5065 (Electronic Parts & Equipment Nec); 5075 (Warm Air Heating & Air-Conditioning). **Est:** 1962. **Sales:** $6,750,000 (2000). **Emp:** 50. **Officers:** John Meints, e-mail: jomeints@worldnet.att.net.

■ **15019** ■ **Appliance Parts Co.**
2742 W Medowell Rd.
Phoenix, AZ 85009
Phone: (602)269-6385 **Fax:** (602)269-2088
Products: Major appliance parts. **SIC:** 5063 (Electrical Apparatus & Equipment).

■ **15020** ■ **Appliance Parts Co.**
2001 S Western Ave.
Las Vegas, NV 89102
Phone: (702)382-6532 **Fax:** (702)382-3487
Products: Parts for ranges, refrigerators, and large appliances. **SIC:** 5064 (Electrical Appliances—Television & Radio). **Officers:** Dick Wilkie.

■ **15021** ■ **Appliance Parts Co. Inc.**
94-472 Ukee St.
Waipahu, HI 96797
Phone: (808)676-2664 **Fax:** (808)676-3552
Products: Parts for appliances, including refrigerators, washing machines, and mixers. **SICs:** 5064 (Electrical Appliances—Television & Radio); 5065 (Electronic Parts & Equipment Nec). **Officers:** Dave Dumas.

■ **15022** ■ **Appliance Parts Distributors Inc.**
1175 William St.
Buffalo, NY 14240
Phone: (716)856-5005 **Fax:** (716)856-4779
Products: Appliance parts. **SICs:** 5064 (Electrical Appliances—Television & Radio); 5065 (Electronic Parts & Equipment Nec). **Officers:** Leonard Jarmusz.

■ **15023** ■ **Appliance Parts Distributors Inc.**
400 Bristol Pke.
PO Box 40
Croydon, PA 19021
Phone: (215)785-6282 **Fax:** (215)785-5138
Products: Appliance parts. **SICs:** 5064 (Electrical Appliances—Television & Radio); 5065 (Electronic Parts & Equipment Nec). **Officers:** Stephan R. Bieber.

■ **15024** ■ **Appliance Parts Inc.**
14105 13th Ave. N
Plymouth, MN 55441-4369
Phone: (612)333-0931 **Fax:** (612)333-2847
Products: Appliance parts. **SIC:** 5064 (Electrical Appliances—Television & Radio). **Officers:** William T. Fredrick.

■ **15025** ■ **Appliance Parts Inc.**
228 14th St., Ste 101
Tuscaloosa, AL 35401-7408
Phone: (205)345-2828 **Fax:** (205)345-2892
Products: Washing machines; Household clothes dryers; Major appliance parts. **SIC:** 5064 (Electrical Appliances—Television & Radio). **Officers:** James Walker, President.

■ **15026** ■ **Appliance Parts Inc.**
PO Box 6001
Alexandria, LA 71307-6001
Phone: (318)448-3454 **Fax:** (318)443-3859
Products: Household appliance parts; Air conditioner and refrigerator parts and supplies; Air conditioning and heating systems; Duct grills. **SICs:** 5064 (Electrical Appliances—Television & Radio); 5075 (Warm Air Heating & Air-Conditioning). **Officers:** Fred Lambert, President.

■ **15027** ■ **Appliance Parts of Lake Charles**
1700 Common St.
Lake Charles, LA 70601-6136
Phone: (318)439-1797
Products: Major appliance parts. **SIC:** 5065 (Electronic Parts & Equipment Nec). **Officers:** Bruce Coleman, President.

■ **15028** ■ **Appliance Parts & Supply Co.**
805 Church St.
Mobile, AL 36602-1112
Phone: (205)432-6634
Products: Refrigerator and electrical appliance parts. **SIC:** 5064 (Electrical Appliances—Television & Radio). **Officers:** Fred Hybart, President.

■ **15029** ■ **Appliance Parts Warehouse Inc.**
2311 E 23rd St.
PO Box 71925
Chattanooga, TN 37407
Phone: (423)698-1731 **Fax:** (423)698-1731
Products: Major appliance parts, including furnace, air-conditioner, washer, and dryer parts. **SICs:** 5063 (Electrical Apparatus & Equipment); 5064 (Electrical Appliances—Television & Radio). **Officers:** John Rewcastle.

■ **15030** ■ **Appliance Recycling Centers of America Inc.**
7400 Excelsior Blvd.
Minneapolis, MN 55426
Phone: (612)930-9000 **Fax:** (612)930-1800
URL: http://www.appliancesmart.com
Products: Recycled appliances, sold thru our retail stores. **SICs:** 5093 (Scrap & Waste Materials); 5064 (Electrical Appliances—Television & Radio). **Est:** 1976. **Sales:** $11,900,000 (1999). **Emp:** 158. **Officers:** Edward R. Cameron, CEO & President; Dennis McGrath, Customer Service Contact; Lyndy Janzig, Human Resources Contact.

■ 15031 ■ **Arizona Appliance Parts**
6237 E 22nd St.
Tucson, AZ 85711
Phone: (520)748-2222   **Fax:** (520)790-6666
Products: Appliance parts. **SIC:** 5064 (Electrical Appliances—Television & Radio). **Officers:** Dennis Anderson, Partner.

■ 15032 ■ **Arizona Coin & Commercial Laundry Equipment**
1831 W Buckeye Rd.
Phoenix, AZ 85007-3522
Phone: (602)258-9274
Products: Major electrical appliances, including washers and dryers. **SICs:** 5087 (Service Establishment Equipment); 5064 (Electrical Appliances—Television & Radio). **Officers:** Leroy Aman, Partner.

■ 15033 ■ **Arizona Wholesale Supply Co.**
PO Box 2979
Phoenix, AZ 85062
Phone: (602)258-7901   **Fax:** (602)258-8335
E-mail: builder@awsco.net
URL: http://www.builderappliances.com/arizona
Products: Appliances; Fireplaces; Grills; Bathtubs. **SIC:** 5064 (Electrical Appliances—Television & Radio). **Est:** 1944. **Sales:** $100,000,000 (1999). **Emp:** 250. **Officers:** T.W. Thomas, President & Chairman of the Board; Ned Dryer, Controller; Bill Parks, Vice President; Sue Zawarus, Dir. of Data Processing; Bill Abbott; J.T. Taylor.

■ 15034 ■ **Armstrong International Inc. Three Rivers Div.**
816 Maple St.
Three Rivers, MI 49093
Phone: (616)273-1415   **Fax:** (616)279-7602
Products: Industrial humidifiers. **SIC:** 5075 (Warm Air Heating & Air-Conditioning). **Sales:** $45,000,000 (2000). **Emp:** 300. **Officers:** Gus Armstrong, President; David Dykstra, Controller.

■ 15035 ■ **Arrow-Cold Control Appliance Parts Co.**
PO Box 171275
Kansas City, KS 66117-0275
Phone: (913)371-4677
Free: (800)255-0289   **Fax:** (913)371-3256
Products: Major appliances and HVAC parts and equipment. **SICs:** 5064 (Electrical Appliances—Television & Radio); 5075 (Warm Air Heating & Air-Conditioning). **Est:** 1951. **Emp:** 10. **Officers:** Betty Budd, President.

■ 15036 ■ **Arrowhead Supply Inc.**
18 N 19th Ave. W
Duluth, MN 55806-2127
Phone: (218)722-6699   **Fax:** (218)722-0518
Products: Kitchen and bath appliances. **SIC:** 5064 (Electrical Appliances—Television & Radio). **Officers:** Edward Aamodt, President.

■ 15037 ■ **Associated Sales**
4201 W Camelback Rd.
Phoenix, AZ 85019-2860
Phone: (602)242-7561   **Fax:** (602)973-4904
Products: Kitchen appliances. **SIC:** 5064 (Electrical Appliances—Television & Radio). **Officers:** William Adams, President.

■ 15038 ■ **Astro-Pure Water Purifiers**
3025 SW 2nd Ave.
Ft. Lauderdale, FL 33315-3309
Phone: (954)832-0630   **Fax:** (954)832-0729
Products: Water purification and water treatment equipment and supplies. **SIC:** 5074 (Plumbing & Hydronic Heating Supplies). **Est:** 1971. **Sales:** $500,000 (2000). **Emp:** 16. **Officers:** R.L. Stefl, President; Mary C. Stefl, Vice President.

■ 15039 ■ **Atlantic Communications Inc.**
PO Box 596
Bangor, ME 04402-0596
Phone: (207)947-2575
Free: (800)300-2575   **Fax:** (207)947-2859
Products: Sound and entertainment equipment and supplies. **SIC:** 5064 (Electrical Appliances—Television & Radio). **Sales:** $1,300,000 (2000). **Emp:** 9.

■ 15040 ■ **Auto Chlor System Inc.**
746 Poplar Ave.
Memphis, TN 38105
Phone: (901)579-2300   **Fax:** (901)684-0600
Products: Commercial appliances. **SIC:** 5064 (Electrical Appliances—Television & Radio). **Sales:** $19,000,000 (1994). **Emp:** 80. **Officers:** George Griesbeck, President; Bill F. Dutton, CFO.

■ 15041 ■ **AVAC Corp.**
666 University Ave. W
St. Paul, MN 55104-4801
Phone: (651)222-0763
Free: (800)328-9430   **Fax:** (651)224-2674
E-mail: bojacker@AVAcorp.com
URL: http://www.AVAcorp.com
Products: Vacuum cleaners and accessories. **SIC:** 5064 (Electrical Appliances—Television & Radio). **Est:** 1952. **Sales:** $3,000,000 (2000). **Emp:** 12. **Officers:** Russell Battisto, President, e-mail: Russ@AVAcorp.com.

■ 15042 ■ **Avon Appliance & Electric Co. Inc.**
PO Box 407
Avon, CT 06001-0407
Phone: (860)678-1927   **Fax:** (860)678-1779
Products: Electrical appliances, including washers, dryers, dishwashers, refrigerators, microwaves, and trash disposals. **SIC:** 5064 (Electrical Appliances—Television & Radio). **Officers:** Stephen Brighenti, President.

■ 15043 ■ **Ayre Acoustics Inc.**
2300 Central Ave Ste. B
Boulder, CO 80301
Phone: (303)442-7300   **Fax:** (303)442-7301
Products: Designs and high-end audio equipment. **SIC:** 5064 (Electrical Appliances—Television & Radio). **Officers:** Charles Hansen, President.

■ 15044 ■ **B & B Appliance Parts of Mobile**
PO Box 6707
Mobile, AL 36660-0707
Phone: (205)478-8485   **Fax:** (205)478-9509
Products: Electrical appliances, including television sets and radios; Household appliance parts. **SIC:** 5064 (Electrical Appliances—Television & Radio). **Officers:** Lonnie Brown, President.

■ 15045 ■ **Barnsley-Weis Associates Inc.**
10130 SW North Dakota St.
Tigard, OR 97223-4236
Phone: (503)624-8758   **Fax:** (503)624-2547
Products: Electrical appliances. **SIC:** 5064 (Electrical Appliances—Television & Radio). **Officers:** Rudy Barnsley, President.

■ 15046 ■ **Beam of Denver Inc.**
750 E 71st Ave. B
Denver, CO 80229-6800
Phone: (303)286-7123
Products: Vacuum cleaning systems. **SIC:** 5064 (Electrical Appliances—Television & Radio). **Officers:** Don Mohr, President.

■ 15047 ■ **Belco Athletic Laundry Equipment Co.**
PO Box 241655
Charlotte, NC 28224-1655
Phone: (704)525-2078
Products: Laundry equipment, including washers and dryers. **SIC:** 5087 (Service Establishment Equipment). **Sales:** $3,000,000 (2000). **Emp:** 12. **Officers:** William Beall, President.

■ 15048 ■ **Bell Parts Supply Inc.**
2609 45th St.
Highland, IN 46322
Phone: (219)924-1200   **Fax:** (219)924-1266
Products: Electrical appliances and parts. **SIC:** 5064 (Electrical Appliances—Television & Radio). **Officers:** Jule Bell, President.

■ 15049 ■ **Bennies Warehouse Distribution Center**
R.D. 1, Rural Box 1997
Berwick, PA 18603
Phone: (570)759-2201   **Fax:** (570)759-2206
Products: Electronic consumer products. **SIC:** 5064

(Electrical Appliances—Television & Radio). **Sales:** $4,000,000 (2000). **Emp:** 8. **Officers:** Bennie Naunczek, Owner; Judy Naunczek, Vice President.

■ 15050 ■ **Bermil Industries Corp.**
461 Doughty Blvd.
Inwood, NY 11096
Phone: (516)371-4400   **Fax:** (516)371-4204
Products: Commercial laundry equipment. **SIC:** 5087 (Service Establishment Equipment). **Sales:** $11,000,000 (2000). **Emp:** 70. **Officers:** Archie Abrams, CFO.

■ 15051 ■ **Bernina of America Inc.**
3500 Thayer Ct.
Aurora, IL 60504-6182
Phone: (630)978-2500
Products: Sewing machines. **SIC:** 5064 (Electrical Appliances—Television & Radio). **Sales:** $27,000,000 (2000). **Emp:** 50. **Officers:** Martin Favre, President; Michael Perich, VP & CFO.

■ 15052 ■ **Birnberg & Sons Inc.**
516 N Prior Ave.
St. Paul, MN 55104
Phone: (612)645-4521   **Fax:** (612)645-5958
Products: Small electrical appliances; Small electric household appliances, except fans; Television sets; Radio receivers. **SIC:** 5064 (Electrical Appliances—Television & Radio). **Est:** 1888. **Emp:** 12. **Officers:** Herman Birnberg, President.

■ 15053 ■ **Black and Decker Corp. Products Service Div.**
626 Hanover Pike
Hampstead, MD 21074
Phone: (410)239-5000   **Fax:** (410)239-5227
Products: Appliances; Electronic equipment. **SICs:** 5072 (Hardware); 5063 (Electrical Apparatus & Equipment). **Est:** 1910. **Sales:** $172,700,000 (2000). **Emp:** 1,000. **Officers:** Bud Schreiber, Director; Heber Anderson, Dir. of Operations; Brad Drummond, Information Systems Mgr.; Kent Aderholt, Dir of Human Resources.

■ 15054 ■ **Blodgett Supply Co. Inc.**
PO Box 759
Williston, VT 05495-0759
Phone: (802)864-9831   **Fax:** (802)864-3645
Products: Small electrical appliances; Household appliances; Television sets; Radios. **SIC:** 5064 (Electrical Appliances—Television & Radio). **Officers:** Samuel Levin, President.

■ 15055 ■ **Bose Corp.**
3550 E 40th St.
Yuma, AZ 85365
Phone: (520)726-1820   **Fax:** (520)344-1364
Products: Speakers. **SIC:** 5064 (Electrical Appliances—Television & Radio).

■ 15056 ■ **Boyd Distributing Co. Inc.**
1400 W 3rd Ave.
Denver, CO 80223
Phone: (303)534-7706   **Fax:** (303)623-1838
Products: Signs; Major appliances; Kitchen products; Golf carts; Turf equipment; Cleaning and janitorial supplies. **SICs:** 5064 (Electrical Appliances—Television & Radio); 5091 (Sporting & Recreational Goods); 5087 (Service Establishment Equipment); 5169 (Chemicals & Allied Products Nec). **Est:** 1945. **Sales:** $13,000,000 (2000). **Emp:** 58. **Officers:** Dan Boyd, CEO; Jack Ryan, Dir. of Marketing.

■ 15057 ■ **Brey Appliance Parts Inc.**
1345 Geronimo
El Paso, TX 79925
Phone: (915)778-2739   **Fax:** (915)778-3074
Products: Household appliances. **SIC:** 5064 (Electrical Appliances—Television & Radio). **Officers:** Sam Shallenberger.

■ 15058 ■ **Briel America Inc.**
256 S Livingston Ave.
Livingston, NJ 07039
Phone: (973)716-0999   **Fax:** (973)716-9888
Products: Espresso machines. **SIC:** 5046 (Commercial Equipment Nec). **Sales:** $900,000 (1993). **Emp:** 5. **Officers:** Walter Nachtigall, President.

■ 15059 ■ The Brightman Co.
10411 Baur Blvd.
St. Louis, MO 63132
Phone: (314)993-2233 **Fax:** (314)993-0532
Products: Major appliances, including stoves, televisions, and stereos; Floor coverings, including vinyl and tile; Microwaves; Vacuum cleaners; Whirlpool tubs. **SICs:** 5064 (Electrical Appliances—Television & Radio); 5023 (Homefurnishings); 5074 (Plumbing & Hydronic Heating Supplies). **Est:** 1951. **Sales:** $10,000,000 (2000). **Emp:** 39. **Officers:** J.R. Brightman, Chairman of the Board; H.P. Brightman, President; Dale DeLarber, Exec. VP.

■ 15060 ■ Broich Enterprises Inc.
6440 City West Pky.
Eden Prairie, MN 55344
Phone: (952)941-2270 **Fax:** (952)941-3066
Products: Major appliances. **SIC:** 5064 (Electrical Appliances—Television & Radio). **Officers:** Walter Broich, President.

■ 15061 ■ Brown Appliance Parts Co. Inc.
857 N Central Ave.
PO Box 27010
Knoxville, TN 37927
Phone: (423)525-9363 **Fax:** (423)525-7360
Products: Appliance parts. **SIC:** 5064 (Electrical Appliances—Television & Radio). **Officers:** Mack Brown.

■ 15062 ■ Brown-Rogers-Dixson Co.
675 N Main St.
Winston-Salem, NC 27102-2111
Phone: (910)722-1112 **Fax:** (910)721-0685
Products: Appliances; Hardware. **SICs:** 5072 (Hardware); 5064 (Electrical Appliances—Television & Radio). **Est:** 1880. **Sales:** $9,000,000 (2000). **Emp:** 30. **Officers:** Carl Dixson, CEO & President; Ronald Dixson, Exec. VP.

■ 15063 ■ Buckeye Vacuum Cleaner Supply Co. Inc.
2870 Plant Atkinson Rd.
Smyrna, GA 30080-7240
Phone: (404)351-7300 **Fax:** (404)351-7307
Products: Vacuum cleaner parts. **SIC:** 5064 (Electrical Appliances—Television & Radio). **Officers:** Kenard Strauss, President.

■ 15064 ■ Builder Contract Sales Inc.
PO Box 14829
SurfsiDe Beach, SC 29587-4829
Phone: (803)651-3303 **Fax:** (803)651-4034
Products: Major appliances; Floor coverings. **SICs:** 5064 (Electrical Appliances—Television & Radio); 5023 (Homefurnishings). **Officers:** Tim Helms, President.

■ 15065 ■ Builderway Inc.
PO Box 429
Simpsonville, SC 29681-0429
Phone: (803)297-6266
Products: Electrical appliances, including ranges, washers, freezers, and refrigerators; Lumber. **SICs:** 5031 (Lumber, Plywood & Millwork); 5064 (Electrical Appliances—Television & Radio). **Sales:** $98,000,000 (2000). **Emp:** 350. **Officers:** Newell LaVoy, President; Truman Hornsby, Vice President.

■ 15066 ■ Burgess Lighting and Distributing
10358 Lee Hwy.
Fairfax, VA 22030
Phone: (703)385-6660
Products: Lighting fixtures, including lamps. **SIC:** 5023 (Homefurnishings).

■ 15067 ■ C & C Distributors
12463 Little Fawn Rd.
Gulfport, MS 39503-7691
Phone: (228)868-1220
Products: Vacuum cleaners. **SIC:** 5087 (Service Establishment Equipment).

■ 15068 ■ C/D/R/ Inc.
300 Delware Ave., Ste. 1704
Wilmington, DE 19801
Phone: (302)427-5865
Products: Ceiling fans, light kits, and related accessories. **SIC:** 5023 (Homefurnishings).

■ 15069 ■ C and L Supply Inc.
PO Box 578
Vinita, OK 74301
Phone: (918)256-6411 **Fax:** (918)256-3836
Products: Appliances, including stoves and refrigerators; Plumbing supplies; Electrical supplies. **SICs:** 5074 (Plumbing & Hydronic Heating Supplies); 5075 (Warm Air Heating & Air-Conditioning); 5063 (Electrical Apparatus & Equipment); 5064 (Electrical Appliances—Television & Radio). **Est:** 1955. **Sales:** $18,000,000 (2000). **Emp:** 73. **Officers:** Fred B. Kidd, President; Kathy L. Kidd, Treasurer & Secty.; Jesse Hale, VP of Marketing.

■ 15070 ■ Cain and Bultman Inc.
PO Box 2815
Jacksonville, FL 32204
Phone: (904)356-4812
Free: (800)356-2687 **Fax:** (904)798-1099
Products: Televisions and floor coverings. **SICs:** 5064 (Electrical Appliances—Television & Radio); 5023 (Homefurnishings). **Sales:** $44,000,000 (2000). **Emp:** 80. **Officers:** M.A. Sandifer, President; Art Cahoon, CFO.

■ 15071 ■ Caloric Corp.
PO Box 6255
Florence, SC 29502
Phone: (803)667-1191
Free: (800)843-0304 **Fax:** (803)679-1311
Products: Ranges. **SIC:** 5064 (Electrical Appliances—Television & Radio). **Officers:** Thomas L'Esperance, President.

■ 15072 ■ Camsco Wholesalers Inc.
291 Hwy. 51 C-1
Ridgeland, MS 39157-3934
Phone: (601)856-5550 **Fax:** (601)856-5552
Products: Electrical appliances, including television sets, radios, refrigerators, and freezers. **SIC:** 5064 (Electrical Appliances—Television & Radio). **Officers:** Gilbert Sollek, President.

■ 15073 ■ Cange & Associates International
3725 Orchid Gln
Escondido, CA 92025-7916
Phone: (619)276-7301 **Fax:** (619)276-7301
Products: Household appliances. **SIC:** 5064 (Electrical Appliances—Television & Radio). **Officers:** Robert P. Cange, President.

■ 15074 ■ Capitol Sales Company Inc.
3110 Neil Armstrong Blvd.
St. Paul, MN 55121-2234
Phone: (612)688-6830
Free: (800)447-5196 **Fax:** (612)688-0107
Products: Sound and entertainment equipment and supplies. **SIC:** 5064 (Electrical Appliances—Television & Radio).

■ 15075 ■ Caribiner International
525 N Washington Ave.
Minneapolis, MN 55401
Phone: (612)333-1271
Free: (800)292-4125 **Fax:** (612)333-0225
Products: Audio visual equipment and supplies, rental and staging. Presentation technology for communications needs to organizations. **SIC:** 5064 (Electrical Appliances—Television & Radio). **Sales:** $220,000,000 (2000). **Emp:** 400. **Officers:** Dan Knotts, Sr. VP.

■ 15076 ■ Carolina C and E Inc.
651 Pilot View St.
Winston-Salem, NC 27101-2717
Phone: (336)788-9191
Free: (800)441-9191 **Fax:** (336)650-1124
Products: Sound and entertainment equipment and supplies. **SIC:** 5064 (Electrical Appliances—Television & Radio). **Sales:** $6,000,000 (2000). **Emp:** 50.

■ 15077 ■ Carswell Distributing Co.
PO Box 4193
Winston-Salem, NC 27115-4193
Phone: (910)767-7700 **Fax:** (910)767-8802
Products: Household appliances; Consumer electronics; Lawn and garden equipment. **SICs:** 5064 (Electrical Appliances—Television & Radio); 5083 (Farm & Garden Machinery); 5063 (Electrical

Apparatus & Equipment). **Est:** 1948. **Emp:** 60. **Officers:** William Parsley, President.

■ 15078 ■ Jeff Cash
5512 Old Wake Forest Rd.
Raleigh, NC 27609-5014
Phone: (919)790-1331 **Fax:** (919)790-1390
Products: Electrical appliances and parts. **SIC:** 5064 (Electrical Appliances—Television & Radio). **Officers:** Jeff Cash, Owner.

■ 15079 ■ Cashwell Appliance Parts Inc.
3485 Clinton Rd.
Fayetteville, NC 28302
Phone: (919)323-1111 **Fax:** (919)323-5067
Products: Major appliance parts; Heating and air conditioning systems parts. **SICs:** 5064 (Electrical Appliances—Television & Radio); 5075 (Warm Air Heating & Air-Conditioning). **Officers:** Jimmy Cashwell.

■ 15080 ■ Castle Distributors Inc.
137 Pleasant Hill Rd.
Scarborough, ME 04074-9309
Phone: (207)883-8901 **Fax:** (207)883-0158
Products: Kitchen and bath cabinetry; Major appliances; Solid surface counter tops. **SICs:** 5064 (Electrical Appliances—Television & Radio); 5031 (Lumber, Plywood & Millwork). **Est:** 1973. **Sales:** $2,000,000 (2000). **Emp:** 9. **Officers:** William Levandowski Jr., President.

■ 15081 ■ Central Distributing Co.
PO Box 1229
San Antonio, TX 78293
Phone: (210)225-1541 **Fax:** (210)225-2228
Products: Kitchen appliances. **SIC:** 5064 (Electrical Appliances—Television & Radio). **Est:** 1953. **Sales:** $6,500,000 (2000). **Emp:** 18. **Officers:** Seth Newberger, President; Jim Bowman, CFO.

■ 15082 ■ Central Supply Division of Central Consolidated Inc.
PO Box 631009
Houston, TX 77263-1009
Phone: (713)688-6660 **Fax:** (713)688-0646
Products: Appliance parts. **SIC:** 5063 (Electrical Apparatus & Equipment). **Officers:** Buzz Buvinghausen.

■ 15083 ■ Charter Distributing Inc.
509 South St.
Easton, MD 21601-3845
Phone: (410)822-2323 **Fax:** (410)820-7123
Products: Cooking appliances. **SIC:** 5064 (Electrical Appliances—Television & Radio). **Officers:** Christophe Spurry, President.

■ 15084 ■ Choquette and Company Inc.
PO Box 88
Seekonk, MA 02771
Phone: (508)761-4300
Products: Electrical appliances; Electronic equipment. **SICs:** 5064 (Electrical Appliances—Television & Radio); 5065 (Electronic Parts & Equipment Nec). **Est:** 1924. **Sales:** $30,000,000 (2000). **Emp:** 50. **Officers:** Robert G. Choquette, President; David Lefrancois, Controller; Paul Collins, Dir. of Marketing.

■ 15085 ■ R.J. Clarkson Co. Inc.
4436 Augusta Rd.
Lexington, SC 29073-7945
Phone: (803)356-4710 **Fax:** (803)356-0796
Products: Electrical appliances. **SIC:** 5064 (Electrical Appliances—Television & Radio). **Officers:** Robert Clarkson, Chairman of the Board.

■ 15086 ■ Cloud Brothers Inc.
1617 N Bendix Dr.
South Bend, IN 46628-2836
Phone: (219)289-0395 **Fax:** (219)289-0397
URL: http://www.Cloudbrothers.com
Products: Kitchen and bath appliances and supplies. **SIC:** 5064 (Electrical Appliances—Television & Radio). **Emp:** 11. **Officers:** Bruce Auger, President.

■ 15087 ■ **Coast Appliance Parts Co.**
2606 Lee Ave.
South el Monte, CA 91733
Phone: (626)579-1500 **Fax:** (626)579-2559
E-mail: perry@coastparts.com
URL: http://www.coastparts.com
Products: Appliance parts; Electric motors. **SICs:** 5065 (Electronic Parts & Equipment Nec); 5063 (Electrical Apparatus & Equipment). **Est:** 1958. **Emp:** 75. **Officers:** Perry Erickson, CEO.

■ 15088 ■ **Coastline Parts Co.**
818 Snow Hill Rd.
Salisbury, MD 21801
Phone: (410)742-8634 **Fax:** (410)742-2187
Products: Appliance parts. **SICs:** 5063 (Electrical Apparatus & Equipment); 5064 (Electrical Appliances—Television & Radio). **Officers:** James M. Elliott.

■ 15089 ■ **Collins Appliance Parts Inc.**
1533 Metropolitan St.
Pittsburgh, PA 15233
Phones: (412)321-3700 (412)323-1234
Free: (800)366-9969 **Fax:** (412)323-1232
Products: Parts and attachments for small household appliances. **SIC:** 5065 (Electronic Parts & Equipment Nec). **Est:** 1932. **Sales:** $2,500,000 (2000). **Emp:** 21. **Officers:** Jay Collins.

■ 15090 ■ **Colorado Prime Foods**
500 Bl County Blvd., Ste. 400
Farmingdale, NY 11735-3996
Phone: (516)694-1111 **Free:** (800)933-9652
Products: Refrigerators and grills. **SIC:** 5064 (Electrical Appliances—Television & Radio). **Sales:** $350,000,000 (2000). **Emp:** 2,000. **Officers:** Bill Dordelman, CEO; Tom Taylor, VP of Finance.

■ 15091 ■ **Commercial Dishwashers**
5001 NE 82nd Ave.
Portland, OR 97220-4928
Phone: (503)284-3449
Products: Electrical appliances, including televisions, radios, and dishwashers. **SIC:** 5064 (Electrical Appliances—Television & Radio). **Officers:** Gary Miller, Partner.

■ 15092 ■ **Commercial Washer Dryer Sales Co.**
PO Box 2858
Gaithersburg, MD 20886-2858
Phone: (301)258-9030 **Fax:** (301)670-9289
Products: Major electrical appliances, including electric and gas clothes dryers. **SIC:** 5064 (Electrical Appliances—Television & Radio). **Officers:** Albert Fries, President.

■ 15093 ■ **Conair Corp.oration**
7475 N Glen Harbor Blvd.
Glendale, AZ 85307
Phone: (623)872-8750 **Fax:** (623)872-7022
Products: Personal care products, telephones and kitchen appliances (distribution depot). **SIC:** 5064 (Electrical Appliances—Television & Radio).

■ 15094 ■ **Connecticut Appliance & Fireplace Distributors, LLC**
50 Graham Pl.
Southington, CT 06489-1511
Phone: (860)621-9313 **Fax:** (860)621-2151
E-mail: sales@cafd.com
URL: http://www.cafd.com
Products: Kitchen appliances; Fireplaces; Chimneys; Gas grills; Patio heaters; Sinks; Faucets. **SICs:** 5064 (Electrical Appliances—Television & Radio); 5074 (Plumbing & Hydronic Heating Supplies); 5087 (Service Establishment Equipment). **Officers:** Douglas W. DuPont, Managing Member.

■ 15095 ■ **Contract Kitchen Distributors**
12002 Old Baltimore Pike
Beltsville, MD 20705-1412
Phone: (301)595-4477 **Fax:** (301)937-6934
Products: Electrical appliances, including television sets, radios, and other household appliances. **SIC:** 5064 (Electrical Appliances—Television & Radio). **Officers:** Ken Adams, President.

■ 15096 ■ **Cook Brothers Inc.**
240 N Ashland
Chicago, IL 60607
Phone: (773)384-4663 **Fax:** (773)376-2665
Products: Appliances; Jewelry. **SICs:** 5064 (Electrical Appliances—Television & Radio); 5094 (Jewelry & Precious Stones).

■ 15097 ■ **Cramer Co. Inc.**
811 E Waterman St.
Wichita, KS 67202-4729
Phone: (316)263-6145 **Fax:** (316)263-0800
Products: Household appliances; Prefabricated fireplaces; Wood kitchen cabinets and cabinetwork, stock line. **SICs:** 5064 (Electrical Appliances—Television & Radio); 5031 (Lumber, Plywood & Millwork); 5074 (Plumbing & Hydronic Heating Supplies). **Officers:** Doug Cramer, President.

■ 15098 ■ **Creative Technologies Corp.**
170 53rd St.
Brooklyn, NY 11232
Phone: (718)492-8400 **Fax:** (718)492-3878
Products: Small kitchen appliances including electric motor-driven pasta machines and food grillers. **SIC:** 5064 (Electrical Appliances—Television & Radio). **Sales:** $5,000,000 (2000). **Emp:** 33. **Officers:** David Guttmann, CEO & Chairman of the Board; Sarah Newman, Controller.

■ 15099 ■ **Crescent Electric Supply (Appleton, Wisconsin)**
PO Box 1157
Appleton, WI 54912
Phone: (920)734-4517
Products: Electrical appliances. **SIC:** 5063 (Electrical Apparatus & Equipment). **Sales:** $20,000,000 (2000). **Emp:** 39. **Officers:** Ron Buxman, Manager.

■ 15100 ■ **Cruse Communication Co.**
4903 Dawn Ave.
East Lansing, MI 48823-5689
Phone: (517)332-3579 **Fax:** (517)332-7757
Products: Sound and entertainment equipment and supplies. **SIC:** 5064 (Electrical Appliances—Television & Radio).

■ 15101 ■ **Curtis Co.**
731 E Brooks Rd.
Memphis, TN 38116
Phone: (901)332-1414 **Fax:** (901)398-6187
Products: Major appliance parts. **SICs:** 5063 (Electrical Apparatus & Equipment); 5065 (Electronic Parts & Equipment Nec). **Officers:** Waymon Turner.

■ 15102 ■ **Custom Radio Corp.**
4012 Merchant Rd.
Ft. Wayne, IN 46818-1246
Phone: (219)489-2062 **Fax:** (219)489-2647
Products: Electrical appliances. **SIC:** 5064 (Electrical Appliances—Television & Radio). **Officers:** Ronald Miller, President.

■ 15103 ■ **D and H Distributing Co.**
2525 N 7th St.
Harrisburg, PA 17110
Phone: (717)236-8001
Free: (800)877-1200 **Fax:** (717)255-7838
Products: Televisions, radios, kitchen cabinets, appliances, computers and peripheral parts. **SICs:** 5064 (Electrical Appliances—Television & Radio); 5099 (Durable Goods Nec); 5065 (Electronic Parts & Equipment Nec); 5045 (Computers, Peripherals & Software). **Sales:** $429,000,000 (2000). **Emp:** 400. **Officers:** Izzy Schwab, CEO & Chairman of the Board; Robert J. Miller, CFO.

■ 15104 ■ **D & L Appliance Parts Company, Inc.**
2100 Freedom Dr.
Charlotte, NC 28208-5154
Phone: (704)374-0400
Free: (800)432-5068 **Fax:** (704)377-1138
Products: Parts and supplies for major appliances; Heating and air-conditioning systems. **SICs:** 5064 (Electrical Appliances—Television & Radio); 5075 (Warm Air Heating & Air-Conditioning); 5065 (Electronic Parts & Equipment Nec). **Est:** 1955. **Emp:** 85. **Officers:** R.B. Brackett.

■ 15105 ■ **Davitt and Hanser Music Co.**
4940 Delhi Ave.
Cincinnati, OH 45238
Phone: (513)451-5000 **Fax:** (513)347-2298
Products: Sound and entertainment equipment and supplies. **SIC:** 5064 (Electrical Appliances—Television & Radio). **Sales:** $20,000,000 (2000). **Emp:** 45.

■ 15106 ■ **Dayton Appliance Parts Co.**
122 Sears St.
Dayton, OH 45402
Phone: (937)224-3531 **Fax:** (937)224-3437
Products: Appliance parts. **SIC:** 5064 (Electrical Appliances—Television & Radio). **Officers:** James Houtz.

■ 15107 ■ **Deering Banjo Co.**
7936-D Lester Ave.
Lemon Grove, CA 91945
Phone: (619)464-8252
Free: (800)845-7791 **Fax:** (619)464-0833
Products: Sound and entertainment equipment and supplies. **SIC:** 5064 (Electrical Appliances—Television & Radio). **Sales:** $800,000 (2000). **Emp:** 15.

■ 15108 ■ **D'ELIA Associates of Connecticut Inc.**
4 Laser Ln.
Wallingford, CT 06492-1928
Phone: (203)234-0667
Free: (800)356-3803 **Fax:** (203)234-1826
Products: Electrical appliances, including refrigerators and freezers. **SIC:** 5064 (Electrical Appliances—Television & Radio). **Est:** 1965. **Officers:** Charles D. Callahan, President.

■ 15109 ■ **DeLonghi America Inc.**
Park 80 W, Plaza One
Saddle Brook, NJ 07663
Phone: (201)909-4000 **Fax:** (201)909-8550
URL: http://www.delonghiusa.com
Products: Kitchen; Home comfort; Floor care products. **SIC:** 5064 (Electrical Appliances—Television & Radio). **Est:** 1982. **Emp:** 50. **Officers:** James McCusker, President.

■ 15110 ■ **Derby Industries Inc.**
4451 Robards Ln.
Louisville, KY 40218-4513
Phone: (502)966-4206 **Fax:** (502)466-4431
Products: Electrical appliances. **SIC:** 5064 (Electrical Appliances—Television & Radio). **Officers:** Raymond Loyd, President.

■ 15111 ■ **Distribution Holdings Inc.**
4 Triad Ctr., Ste. 800
Salt Lake City, UT 84180
Phone: (801)575-6500 **Fax:** (801)575-6507
Products: Electrical appliances. **SIC:** 5064 (Electrical Appliances—Television & Radio). **Sales:** $240,000,000 (2000). **Emp:** 500. **Officers:** S. Whitfield Lee, CEO.

■ 15112 ■ **Diversified Distributors**
PO Box 41248
Charleston, SC 29423-1248
Phone: (803)760-0299
Products: Small electrical appliances; Household appliances; Television sets; Radios. **SIC:** 5064 (Electrical Appliances—Television & Radio).

■ 15113 ■ **Herman Dodge & Son Inc.**
547 Library St.
San Fernando, CA 91340-2523
Phone: (818)362-6771 **Fax:** (818)367-6282
Products: Coffee urns; Small electric household appliances, except fans; Kitchenware. **SICs:** 5199 (Nondurable Goods Nec); 5023 (Homefurnishings). **Est:** 1951. **Emp:** 49.

■ 15114 ■ **Douglas/Quikut**
PO Box 29
Walnut Ridge, AR 72476-0029
Phone: (870)886-6774 **Fax:** (870)886-9162
Products: Vacuum cleaners; Knives. **SICs:** 5064 (Electrical Appliances—Television & Radio); 5072 (Hardware). **Emp:** 220. **Officers:** Nathan Howard, General Mgr.; David Fortune, Operating Officer; Dave Kohlmeyer, Controller.

■ 15115 ■ Drillot Corporation
PO Box 97
Suwanee, GA 30024-0097
Phone: (404)932-7282 **Fax:** (404)932-7292
Products: Household appliances. **SIC:** 5064 (Electrical Appliances—Television & Radio). **Officers:** John Drillot, President.

■ 15116 ■ Drug Guild Distributors Inc.
350 Meadowland Pkwy.
Secaucus, NJ 07094
Phone: (201)348-3700
Products: Appliances, including microwaves, toasters, and hair dryers; Pharmaceuticals; Sundries. **SICs:** 5064 (Electrical Appliances—Television & Radio); 5122 (Drugs, Proprietaries & Sundries). **Est:** 1946. **Sales:** $522,300,000 (2000). **Emp:** 325. **Officers:** Roman Englander, CEO & President; Jay J. Reba, VP of Finance; Alan Glenn, Sr. VP.

■ 15117 ■ DSI Distributing, Inc.
9190 Corporation Dr.
Indianapolis, IN 46256
Phone: (317)845-4400
Free: (800)888-8876 **Fax:** (317)849-5732
URL: http://www.cssnps.com
Products: Satellite systems; Audio and video equipment. **SIC:** 5064 (Electrical Appliances—Television & Radio). **Est:** 1980. **Sales:** $230,000,000 (2000). **Emp:** 300. **Officers:** Dave Robison, e-mail: daverobison@dsinps.com. **Former Name:** DSI Systems Inc.

■ 15118 ■ Eastern Electric
PO Box 211088
West Palm Beach, FL 33421-1088
Phone: (561)640-3233 **Fax:** (561)640-0322
Products: Kitchen supplies, including irons, blenders, and mixers. **SIC:** 5064 (Electrical Appliances—Television & Radio). **Sales:** $12,000,000 (2000). **Emp:** 50. **Officers:** Ken Springer, President.

■ 15119 ■ El Rancho Laundry Equipment
PO Box 1941
Taos, NM 87571-1941
Phone: (505)758-8729
Products: Laundry equipment. **SIC:** 5064 (Electrical Appliances—Television & Radio). **Officers:** Abe Montoya, Owner.

■ 15120 ■ Electrical Appliance Service Co.
1450 Howard St.
San Francisco, CA 94103-2523
Phone: (415)777-0314
Free: (800)795-5848 **Fax:** (415)543-2170
Products: Home electric appliance parts. **SICs:** 5063 (Electrical Apparatus & Equipment); 5065 (Electronic Parts & Equipment Nec). **Officers:** Gary Tribulato.

■ 15121 ■ Electronic Supply
222 7th Ave.
Huntington, WV 25701-1926
Phone: (304)523-6443
Free: (800)523-7293 **Fax:** (304)523-6445
E-mail: esupply1@ezwv.com
Products: Air-conditioning equipment, including self-contained room units; Electronic parts. **SIC:** 5064 (Electrical Appliances—Television & Radio). **Est:** 1947. **Sales:** $1,000,000 (1999). **Emp:** 7. **Officers:** Houston Hodge, President; Gordon Farmer, Vice President.

■ 15122 ■ European Crafts/USA
3637 Cahuenga Blvd.
Hollywood, CA 90068
Phone: (213)851-4070
Free: (800)851-0750 **Fax:** (213)851-0148
Products: Sound and entertainment equipment and supplies. **SIC:** 5064 (Electrical Appliances—Television & Radio).

■ 15123 ■ Evansville Appliance Parts
900 E Diamond Ave.
Evansville, IN 47711
Phone: (812)423-8867 **Fax:** (812)423-6833
Products: Major appliance parts. **SIC:** 5064 (Electrical Appliances—Television & Radio). **Officers:** J.D. Joergens.

■ 15124 ■ Export of International Appliances
8820 Monard Dr.
Silver Spring, MD 20910-1815
Phone: (301)589-4610 **Fax:** (301)585-7937
Products: Electrical appliances. **SIC:** 5064 (Electrical Appliances—Television & Radio). **Officers:** Naresh Jain, President.

■ 15125 ■ Familian Corp.
2750 S Towne Ave.
Pomona, CA 91766-6205
Phone: (818)374-4200
Free: (888)747-3888 **Fax:** (818)786-5703
Products: Washers and dryers. **SIC:** 5064 (Electrical Appliances—Television & Radio). **Est:** 1926. **Sales:** $325,300,000 (2000). **Emp:** 1,400. **Officers:** Jeffrey Yunickel, CEO & Chairman of the Board; Leonard Gross, Exec. VP & CFO; Jeff Van Wagenen, VP of Marketing; Steve Dunn, Dir. of Information Systems; Karen Gorham, Personnel Mgr.

■ 15126 ■ Fantec Inc.
PO Box 45669
Baton Rouge, LA 70895-5669
Phone: (504)275-5900 **Fax:** (504)275-1000
Products: Ceiling fan parts. **SIC:** 5064 (Electrical Appliances—Television & Radio). **Officers:** John Marshall, President.

■ 15127 ■ John W. Fiedler
N5612 N Wall St.
Spokane, WA 99205-6436
Phone: (509)487-7466 **Fax:** (509)487-7966
Products: Vacuum cleaners. **SIC:** 5064 (Electrical Appliances—Television & Radio). **Officers:** John Fiedler, Owner.

■ 15128 ■ Filco Inc.
1433 Fulton Ave.
Sacramento, CA 95822
Phone: (916)739-6021
Products: Appliances; Electronic equipment. **SICs:** 5065 (Electronic Parts & Equipment Nec); 5064 (Electrical Appliances—Television & Radio). **Sales:** $7,000,000 (2000). **Emp:** 100. **Officers:** David Saca, President.

■ 15129 ■ Flower Films and Video
10341 San Pablo Ave.
El Cerrito, CA 94530
Phone: (510)525-0942 **Fax:** (510)525-1204
Products: Sound and entertainment equipment and supplies. **SIC:** 5064 (Electrical Appliances—Television & Radio).

■ 15130 ■ Folkcraft Instruments
High and Wheeler Sts.
Winsted, CT 06098
Phone: (860)379-9857 **Fax:** (860)379-7685
Products: Sound and entertainment equipment and suppliess. **SIC:** 5064 (Electrical Appliances—Television & Radio).

■ 15131 ■ Fox Appliance Parts of Atlanta Inc.
PO Box 16217
Atlanta, GA 30321-0217
Phone: (404)363-3313
Free: (800)342-5369 **Fax:** (404)362-2989
Products: Parts and attachments for small household appliances; Unitary air conditioners. **SIC:** 5064 (Electrical Appliances—Television & Radio). **Officers:** Patrick Fox, Treasurer.

■ 15132 ■ Fox Appliance Parts of Augusta Inc.
PO Box 14369
Augusta, GA 30919
Phone: (706)737-3400 **Fax:** (706)737-2487
URL: http://www.foxparts.com
Products: Major appliance parts. **SIC:** 5064 (Electrical Appliances—Television & Radio). **Officers:** Richard S. Fox.

■ 15133 ■ Fox Appliance Parts of Columbus Inc.
2508 Cusseta Rd.
PO Box 3158
Columbus, GA 31903
Phone: (706)687-2267 **Fax:** (706)687-7198
Products: Major appliance parts. **SIC:** 5064 (Electrical Appliances—Television & Radio). **Officers:** J.R. Fox.

■ 15134 ■ Fox Appliance Parts of Macon Inc.
6357 Hawkinsville Rd.
PO Box 13486
Macon, GA 31208-3486
Phone: (912)788-1793
Free: (800)342-7130 **Fax:** (912)781-0608
E-mail: foxmacon@aol.com
URL: http://www.foxparts.com
Products: Major appliance parts; Heating and air conditioning equipment, parts, and supplies. **SICs:** 5064 (Electrical Appliances—Television & Radio); 5075 (Warm Air Heating & Air-Conditioning). **Est:** 1948. **Officers:** Billy Fox; Denny Fox, Sales/Marketing Contact; Marc Fox, Human Resources Contact.

■ 15135 ■ Freed Appliance Distributing
2969 Red Hawk Dr.
Grand Prairie, TX 75052-7622
Phone: (817)478-5421
Free: (800)772-7423 **Fax:** (817)478-5425
Products: Kitchen appliances. **SIC:** 5064 (Electrical Appliances—Television & Radio).

■ 15136 ■ Fretz Corp.
2001 Woodhaven Rd.
Philadelphia, PA 19116
Phone: (215)671-8300
Free: (800)222-8300 **Fax:** (215)671-8340
URL: http://www.fretz.com
Products: Appliances. **SIC:** 5064 (Electrical Appliances—Television & Radio). **Est:** 1932. **Sales:** $22,000,000 (1999). **Emp:** 27. **Officers:** Thomas J. Dolan, President.

■ 15137 ■ G & E Parts Center, Inc.
1212 Bluff Rd.
PO Box 1074
Columbia, SC 29202
Phone: (803)771-4346
Free: (800)226-6600 **Fax:** (803)256-6593
Products: Major appliance parts. **SICs:** 5064 (Electrical Appliances—Television & Radio); 5065 (Electronic Parts & Equipment Nec). **Est:** 1955. **Officers:** Keith Bishop.

■ 15138 ■ G & N Appliance Parts
1525 S 4th Ave.
Tucson, AZ 85713
Phone: (520)624-2102
Products: Washer and dryer parts. **SIC:** 5065 (Electronic Parts & Equipment Nec).

■ 15139 ■ G & N Appliance Parts
2742 W Mcdowell Rd
Phoenix, AZ 85009-1417
Phone: (602)269-6385
Free: (800)293-2726 **Fax:** (602)269-2088
Products: Household appliance parts. **SICs:** 5065 (Electronic Parts & Equipment Nec); 5063 (Electrical Apparatus & Equipment). **Officers:** Richard Wilkie, Owner.

■ 15140 ■ G & N Distributors Inc.
6229 Vance Rd. 1
Chattanooga, TN 37421-2979
Phone: (423)892-2842 **Fax:** (423)894-5950
Products: Electrical appliances, including televisions, radios, and washing machines. **SIC:** 5064 (Electrical Appliances—Television & Radio). **Officers:** William Gaddis, President.

■ 15141 ■ Gaggenau USA Corp.
5551 McFadden Ave.
Huntington Beach, CA 92649-1317
Products: Kitchen appliances. **SIC:** 5064 (Electrical Appliances—Television & Radio). **Sales:** $16,000,000 (2000). **Emp:** 14. **Officers:** Ron Rhinerson, President.

■ 15142 ■ **Gas Equipment Distributors**
535 W Thompson Ln., No. B
Nashville, TN 37211
Phone: (615)242-1377
Products: Barbeque equipment and supplies. **SIC:** 5064 (Electrical Appliances—Television & Radio).

■ 15143 ■ **Gateway Appliance Distributing Co.**
19204 68th S
Kent, WA 98032
Phone: (253)872-7838
Free: (800)231-7838 **Fax:** (253)872-2149
URL: http://www.gatedist.com
Products: Kitchen appliances, including ranges, dishwashers, range hoods, and barbecues; Plumbing supplies and equipment, including sinks and faucets. **SICs:** 5064 (Electrical Appliances—Television & Radio); 5074 (Plumbing & Hydronic Heating Supplies). **Est:** 1991. **Emp:** 20. **Officers:** Neal Gillan, Vice President; Paul Casey, Sales Mgr.

■ 15144 ■ **Gemini Ex-Im**
11310 Riverview Dr.
Houston, TX 77077
Phone: (281)497-0045
Products: Appliances. **SIC:** 5064 (Electrical Appliances—Television & Radio).

■ 15145 ■ **Gene Schick Co.**
3544 Arden Rd.
Hayward, CA 94545-3921
Phone: (650)589-7850 **Fax:** (650)589-8421
Products: Appliances. **SIC:** 5064 (Electrical Appliances—Television & Radio). **Sales:** $7,000,000 (1993). **Emp:** 15. **Officers:** Gene Schick, President.

■ 15146 ■ **Genes Appliance Parts Inc.**
788 Gorham St.
Lowell, MA 01852-4636
Phone: (978)453-2896 **Fax:** (978)453-7277
Products: Parts and attachments for small household appliances. **SIC:** 5064 (Electrical Appliances—Television & Radio). **Officers:** Gerard Beaudry, President.

■ 15147 ■ **Genesis Technologies Inc.**
PO Box 3789
Eagle, CO 81631
Phone: (970)328-9515 **Fax:** (970)328-9522
Products: Loudspeaker sound systems. **SIC:** 5064 (Electrical Appliances—Television & Radio).

■ 15148 ■ **Glindmeyer Distributors Co.**
PO Box 19003
New Orleans, LA 70119
Phone: (504)486-6646
Free: (800)466-1754 **Fax:** (504)488-7221
Products: Appliances and electronics. **SICs:** 5064 (Electrical Appliances—Television & Radio); 5065 (Electronic Parts & Equipment Nec). **Est:** 1969. **Sales:** $7,000,000 (2000). **Emp:** 16. **Officers:** Vincent Salamone, President.

■ 15149 ■ **Global Access Entertainment Inc.**
212 NW 4th Ave.
Hallandale, FL 33009-4015
Phone: (954)458-7505 **Fax:** (954)458-8554
Products: Sound and entertainment equipment and supplies. **SIC:** 5064 (Electrical Appliances—Television & Radio). **Sales:** $5,000,000 (2000). **Emp:** 25.

■ 15150 ■ **Goldberg Company Inc.**
PO Box 4590
Glen Allen, VA 23058-4590
Phone: (804)228-5700 **Fax:** (804)228-5701
Products: Mobile electronics. **SIC:** 5064 (Electrical Appliances—Television & Radio). **Sales:** $1,000,000 (2000). **Emp:** 11. **Officers:** Leroy B. Goldberg, Chairman of the Board; R. Danny Bache, Treasurer & Secty.

■ 15151 ■ **GPX Inc.**
108 Madison St.
St. Louis, MO 63102
Phone: (314)621-3314 **Fax:** (314)621-0869
Products: Electrical and electronic equipment and supplies. **SIC:** 5064 (Electrical Appliances—Television & Radio). **Sales:** $200,000,000 (2000). **Emp:** 500.

■ 15152 ■ **Great American Floor Care Center**
2318 Adams Ave.
Huntington, WV 25704-1320
Phone: (304)429-3565 **Fax:** (304)429-1364
Products: Electrical appliances; Vacuum cleaners. **SIC:** 5064 (Electrical Appliances—Television & Radio). **Est:** 1961. **Sales:** $1,000,000 (2000). **Emp:** 6. **Officers:** Jeff Maddox, President.

■ 15153 ■ **Greer Appliance Parts Inc.**
1018 S Rockford
PO Box 4563
Tulsa, OK 74159-0563
Phone: (918)587-3346
Free: (800)299-3012 **Fax:** (918)582-8810
Products: Parts and attachments for small household appliances. **SICs:** 5064 (Electrical Appliances—Television & Radio); 5065 (Electronic Parts & Equipment Nec). **Est:** 1933. **Emp:** 40. **Officers:** Glen Greer, President.

■ 15154 ■ **Gulf Central Corp.**
7819 Professional Pl.
Tampa, FL 33637
Phone: (813)985-3185
Free: (800)282-3892 **Fax:** (813)988-2385
E-mail: glfcntrl@ix.netcom.com
URL: http://www.glfcntrl.com
Products: Household appliances; Gas grills. **SIC:** 5064 (Electrical Appliances—Television & Radio). **Est:** 1963. **Sales:** $6,000,000 (1999). **Emp:** 18. **Officers:** S.C. Plumley, President; Vivian Plumley, Vice President; Barry Jones, VP of Sales.

■ 15155 ■ **Guy T. Gunter Jr. & Associates**
174 14th St. NW
Atlanta, GA 30318-7802
Phone: (404)874-7529 **Fax:** (404)876-3830
Products: Electrical appliances, including television sets, radios, and kitchen equipment; Gas appliances. **SIC:** 5064 (Electrical Appliances—Television & Radio). **Est:** 1952. **Officers:** Guy Gunter, President.

■ 15156 ■ **Hadco Inc.**
PO Box 97
Suwanee, GA 30024
Phone: (404)932-7282
Free: (800)222-6649 **Fax:** (404)932-7292
Products: Cooking appliances. **SIC:** 5064 (Electrical Appliances—Television & Radio). **Officers:** John Orillot.

■ 15157 ■ **Hall Electric Supply Co., Inc. (HESCO)**
PO Box 124
Arlington, MA 02476-0984
Phone: (781)438-3800
Free: (800)444-3726 **Fax:** (781)438-3833
Products: Major appliances, parts, and accessories. **SICs:** 5064 (Electrical Appliances—Television & Radio); 5065 (Electronic Parts & Equipment Nec). **Est:** 1941. **Officers:** K.E. Hall, General Mgr.

■ 15158 ■ **Hamburg Brothers**
40 24th St.
Pittsburgh, PA 15222
Phone: (412)227-6200
Products: Consumer electroincs, including TV's, VCR's, DVD players, stereo equipment. **SIC:** 5064 (Electrical Appliances—Television & Radio). **Est:** 1920. **Officers:** Dennis Holzer, President; Richard Weaver, CEO & CFO.

■ 15159 ■ **Hamilton Appliance Parts Inc.**
1832 McCalla Ave.
Knoxville, TN 37915-1419
Phone: (423)525-0418
Products: Appliance parts. **SIC:** 5064 (Electrical Appliances—Television & Radio). **Officers:** Samuel Hamilton, President.

■ 15160 ■ **Hanessian Mercantile Co.**
PO Box 2079
Nogales, AZ 85628-2079
Phone: (520)287-3211 **Fax:** (520)287-6015
Products: Major household appliances. **SIC:** 5064 (Electrical Appliances—Television & Radio). **Officers:** Nubar Hanessian, President.

■ 15161 ■ **Harman Appliance Sales**
334 N 115th St.
Omaha, NE 68154-2523
Phone: (402)334-1883 **Fax:** (402)334-7949
Products: Major kitchen appliances; Jacuzzi covers. **SICs:** 5064 (Electrical Appliances—Television & Radio); 5091 (Sporting & Recreational Goods). **Officers:** Sheila Harman, President.

■ 15162 ■ **Harmony International Corporation**
3337 Kraft Ave. SE
Grand Rapids, MI 49512
Phone: (616)949-6342 **Fax:** (616)949-1102
E-mail: harmonyhlw@aol.com
Products: Household appliances, including electric ranges, dishwashers, refrigerators, and freezers; Air-conditioning room units; Ice makers; Vacuum cleaners. **SICs:** 5064 (Electrical Appliances—Television & Radio); 5075 (Warm Air Heating & Air-Conditioning); 5078 (Refrigeration Equipment & Supplies); 5074 (Plumbing & Hydronic Heating Supplies). **Est:** 1977. **Sales:** $4,000,000 (2000). **Emp:** 6. **Officers:** Harlan Wilson, President.

■ 15163 ■ **Harris Appliance Parts Company Inc.**
110 Hwy. 29 N Bypass
PO Box 1867
Anderson, SC 29622
Phone: (864)225-7433 **Fax:** (864)224-7443
Products: Major appliance parts. **SIC:** 5064 (Electrical Appliances—Television & Radio). **Est:** 1947. **Emp:** 8. **Officers:** Diane Brock.

■ 15164 ■ **Hart-Greer Ltd.**
3313 1st Ave. N
Birmingham, AL 35222-1203
Phone: (205)320-0095
Products: Appliances, including washers and dryers. **SIC:** 5064 (Electrical Appliances—Television & Radio). **Est:** 1972. **Sales:** $12,000,000 (2000). **Emp:** 25. **Officers:** Jack Scott, President; Walter Barnett, CFO.

■ 15165 ■ **Henderson and Baird Hardware Company Inc.**
1100 Sycamore St.
Greenwood, MS 38930
Phone: (601)453-3221
Products: Hardware, including plumbing and electrical supplies; Housewares, including fans and vacuum cleaners. **SICs:** 5072 (Hardware); 5064 (Electrical Appliances—Television & Radio). **Sales:** $18,000,000 (2000). **Emp:** 90. **Officers:** Harry H. Carter, President; Jamie S. Bledsoe, CFO; David Reaves, Sales Mgr.; Melissa Hazelwood, Dir of Personnel.

■ 15166 ■ **Heral Enterprises Inc.**
PO Box 193666
Little Rock, AR 72219-3666
Phone: (501)568-2090
Free: (800)482-1104 **Fax:** (501)568-0731
Products: Electrical appliances, including television sets, radios, and vacuum cleaners. **SIC:** 5064 (Electrical Appliances—Television & Radio). **Est:** 1974. **Officers:** Gary Heral, President.

■ 15167 ■ **Hermitage Electric Supply Corp.**
PO Box 24990
Nashville, TN 37202-4990
Phone: (615)843-3300
Free: (800)998-0939 **Fax:** (615)242-4443
URL: http://www.hermitagelighting.com
Products: Antiques; Decorative accessories; Lighting; Household appliances; Kitchen and bath products. **SICs:** 5064 (Electrical Appliances—Television & Radio); 5063 (Electrical Apparatus & Equipment); 5021 (Furniture). **Est:** 1942. **Emp:** 65. **Officers:** Jack Fleischer, President, e-mail: jfleischer@hermitagelighting.com

■ 15168 ■ **High Country Kitchens**
7001 W Colfax Ave.
Lakewood, CO 80215-4108
Phone: (303)233-6782 **Fax:** (303)837-1831
Products: Electrical appliances; Countertops. **SICs:** 5064 (Electrical Appliances—Television & Radio); 5039 (Construction Materials Nec). **Officers:** Robert Munson, President.

■ 15169 ■ **Hitachi Home Electronics (America) Inc. Visual Technologies Div.**
3890 Steve Reynolds Blvd.
Norcross, GA 30093
Phone: (770)279-5600
Free: (800)448-2244 **Fax:** (770)279-5696
Products: Blank. **SIC:** 5064 (Electrical Appliances—Television & Radio). **Officers:** T. Itoh, CEO.

■ 15170 ■ **Home & Farm Center Inc.**
RR, Box 4490
Rutland, VT 05701
Phone: (802)773-3877
Products: Major appliances. **SIC:** 5064 (Electrical Appliances—Television & Radio). **Officers:** Richard Hoenes, President.

■ 15171 ■ **The Hoover Co.**
101 E Maple St.
North Canton, OH 44720
Phone: (330)499-9200
Free: (800)891-5696 **Fax:** (330)497-5816
URL: http://www.hoover.com
Products: Vacuums. **SIC:** 5064 (Electrical Appliances—Television & Radio). **Est:** 1908. **Officers:** Keith G. Minton, President; Jerry F. Lauer, VP of Sales; G. Baker, Sales/Marketing Contact, e-mail: gbaker@hoover.com.

■ 15172 ■ **Hosey and Port Sales Corp.**
PO Box 275
Medfield, MA 02052-0275
Phone: (508)359-4115 **Fax:** (508)359-5217
Products: Cooking appliances. **SIC:** 5064 (Electrical Appliances—Television & Radio). **Officers:** John Hosey, President.

■ 15173 ■ **Hutchs TV and Appliance**
50 E Main St.
Lehi, UT 84043-2142
Phone: (801)768-3461 **Fax:** (801)768-9434
Products: Electrical appliances, including television sets, radios, camcorders, satellite sytems, and vacuums. **SIC:** 5064 (Electrical Appliances—Television & Radio). **Est:** 1948. **Officers:** H. Hutchings, President.

■ 15174 ■ **Ideal Appliance Parts Inc.**
PO Box 7007
Metairie, LA 70010-7007
Phone: (504)888-4232 **Fax:** (504)888-4258
Products: Electrical appliances, including television sets, radios, and other household appliances. **SIC:** 5064 (Electrical Appliances—Television & Radio). **Officers:** Norman Joseph, President.

■ 15175 ■ **Independent Distribution Services Inc.**
3000 Waterview Ave.
Baltimore, MD 21230
Phone: (410)539-3000 **Fax:** (410)576-8472
Products: Major appliances; Outdoor power equipment; Wine. **SICs:** 5064 (Electrical Appliances—Television & Radio); 5182 (Wines & Distilled Beverages). **Est:** 1896. **Sales:** $75,000,000 (2000). **Emp:** 150. **Officers:** John Mulkey, President, e-mail: jmulkey@zamoiski.com; Paul Zeller, Treasurer; Don Waksmuncki, Treasurer.

■ 15176 ■ **Indiana Soft Water Service Inc.**
6901 E 38th St.
Indianapolis, IN 46226
Phone: (317)925-6484
Products: Water softeners and related equipmment. **SIC:** 5074 (Plumbing & Hydronic Heating Supplies). **Sales:** $5,000,000 (2000). **Emp:** 80. **Officers:** Tom Stewart, General Mgr.

■ 15177 ■ **International Piecework Controls Co.**
PO Box 1909
Edison, NJ 08818-1909
Phone: (732)225-8844
Products: Sewing machines, home refrigerators, and other consumer appliances. **SIC:** 5064 (Electrical Appliances—Television & Radio).

■ 15178 ■ **Jack Spratt Woodwind Shop**
11 Park Ave.
Old Greenwich, CT 06870-0277
Phone: (203)637-1176
Free: (800)626-9277 **Fax:** (203)637-7555
Products: Sound and entertainment equipment and supplies. **SIC:** 5064 (Electrical Appliances—Television & Radio). **Sales:** $100,000 (2000). **Emp:** 2.

■ 15179 ■ **Jacoby Appliance Parts**
269 Main St.
Hackensack, NJ 07601
Phone: (201)489-6444 **Fax:** (201)489-4648
Products: Major appliance parts, including washer, dryer, stove, and refrigerator parts. **SICs:** 5064 (Electrical Appliances—Television & Radio); 5065 (Electronic Parts & Equipment Nec). **Officers:** Jules R. Jacoby.

■ 15180 ■ **Jarrell Distributors Inc.**
2651 Fondren Dr.
Dallas, TX 75206
Phone: (214)363-7211 **Fax:** (214)363-3100
Products: Household appliances. **SIC:** 5064 (Electrical Appliances—Television & Radio). **Est:** 1947. **Sales:** $12,000,000 (2000). **Emp:** 30. **Officers:** K.L. Lipshie, President; Larry Eubanks, VP of Operations.

■ 15181 ■ **JCA Technology Group, A TVC Company**
130 Industrial Dr.
Chambersburg, PA 17201-0444
Phone: (717)263-8258
Free: (800)233-7600 **Fax:** (717)263-1547
Products: Sound and entertainment equipment and supplies. **SIC:** 5064 (Electrical Appliances—Television & Radio).

■ 15182 ■ **Jetmore Distributing**
3343 Merrick Rd.
Wantagh, NY 11793
Phone: (516)826-1166
Free: (800)481-1166 **Fax:** (516)826-1152
Products: Barbeque grills; Spray paint; Grill pans. **SICs:** 5064 (Electrical Appliances—Television & Radio); 5198 (Paints, Varnishes & Supplies). **Est:** 1971.

■ 15183 ■ **Kaman Music Corp. Los Angeles**
1215 W Walnut St.
Compton, CA 90224-5686
Phone: (310)537-1712
Free: (800)262-7826 **Fax:** (310)632-7463
Products: Sound and entertainment equipment and suppliess. **SIC:** 5064 (Electrical Appliances—Television & Radio). **Sales:** $30,000,000 (2000). **Emp:** 50.

■ 15184 ■ **Kaufman Supply**
PO Box 44984
Atlanta, GA 30336
Phone: (404)699-8750
Products: Electrical appliances, washers and driers, hardware and plumbing supplies for mobile homes and apartments. **SICs:** 5064 (Electrical Appliances—Television & Radio); 5074 (Plumbing & Hydronic Heating Supplies); 5072 (Hardware). **Sales:** $102,000,000 (2000). **Emp:** 300. **Officers:** Richard L. Kaufman, CEO; Gert Docterman, VP of Operations.

■ 15185 ■ **Kellco & Associates**
635 N 7th St.
Tooele, UT 84074
Phone: (435)882-5125 **Fax:** (435)882-1920
Products: Office equipment; Plastic shapes; Hand tools; Household radios; Electrical small appliances. **SICs:** 5064 (Electrical Appliances—Television & Radio); 5044 (Office Equipment); 5162 (Plastics Materials & Basic Shapes); 5072 (Hardware). **Officers:** Linda Kell, General Mgr.

■ 15186 ■ **Kennewick Industry and Electric Supply**
113 E Columbia Dr.
Kennewick, WA 99336-3799
Phone: (509)582-5156
Free: (800)544-5156 **Fax:** (509)582-5156
Products: Electrical and electronic equipment and supplies. **SIC:** 5064 (Electrical Appliances—Television & Radio). **Sales:** $9,200,000 (2000). **Emp:** 49.

■ 15187 ■ **Key Boston Inc.**
126 Grove St.
Franklin, MA 02038
Phone: (508)528-4500 **Fax:** (508)528-3476
Products: Electric appliances. **SIC:** 5064 (Electrical Appliances—Television & Radio). **Sales:** $22,000,000 (2000). **Emp:** 40. **Officers:** Richard Karp, President.

■ 15188 ■ **King Kitchens Inc.**
6075 E Shelby Dr., Ste. 1
Memphis, TN 38141
Phone: (901)362-9651
Products: Kitchen cabinets; Household appliances. **SIC:** 5064 (Electrical Appliances—Television & Radio). **Est:** 1962. **Sales:** $6,000,000 (2000). **Emp:** 30. **Officers:** Howard Willingham, CEO & President.

■ 15189 ■ **Kitchen Distributors Maryland**
2221 Greenspring Dr.
Timonium, MD 21093-3115
Phone: (410)252-6200 **Fax:** (410)252-6866
Products: Kitchen materials, including cabinets, appliances, and counter tops. **SICs:** 5031 (Lumber, Plywood & Millwork); 5064 (Electrical Appliances—Television & Radio). **Emp:** 75.

■ 15190 ■ **Klaus Companies**
8400 N Allen Rd.
Peoria, IL 61615
Phone: (309)691-4840 **Fax:** (309)693-1724
Products: Household appliances; Small electrical appliances. **SIC:** 5064 (Electrical Appliances—Television & Radio). **Est:** 1912. **Sales:** $30,000,000 (2000). **Emp:** 100. **Officers:** Robert Klaus, President; Ronald Henderson, Controller.

■ 15191 ■ **KLH Research and Development Corp.**
PO Box 1085
Sun Valley, CA 91353
Phone: (818)767-2843 **Fax:** (818)767-8246
Products: Hi-fi speaker systems. **SIC:** 5064 (Electrical Appliances—Television & Radio). **Sales:** $11,000,000 (2000). **Emp:** 50. **Officers:** Sylvia Chall, VP of Finance.

■ 15192 ■ **Knogo North America Inc.**
350 Wireless Blvd.
Hauppauge, NY 11788
Phone: (516)232-2100
Free: (800)645-4224 **Fax:** (516)232-2124
Products: Anti-shoplifting devices: cameras and video monitors. **SICs:** 5064 (Electrical Appliances—Television & Radio); 5045 (Computers, Peripherals & Software). **Sales:** $28,000,000 (2000). **Emp:** 220.

■ 15193 ■ **KSC Industries Inc.**
8653 Ave.nida Costa Norte
San Diego, CA 92154
Phone: (619)671-0110
Products: Speakers. **SIC:** 5064 (Electrical Appliances—Television & Radio). **Sales:** $16,000,000 (2000). **Emp:** 185. **Officers:** Jeff King, President.

■ 15194 ■ **Kultur, White Star, Duke International Films Ltd. Inc.**
195 Hwy 36
West Long Branch, NJ 07764
Phone: (732)229-2343 **Fax:** (732)229-0066
Products: Sound and entertainment equipment and supplies. **SIC:** 5064 (Electrical Appliances—Television & Radio).

■ 15195 ■ **L & D Appliance Corp.**
11969 Telegraph Rd.
Santa Fe Springs, CA 90670
Phone: (562)946-1105 **Fax:** (562)941-9483
E-mail: lndappl@worldnet.att.net
URL: http://www.lndappl.com
Products: Air conditioners; Electric household appliances, including washers, dryers, and refrigerators. **SICs:** 5064 (Electrical Appliances—Television & Radio); 5075 (Warm Air Heating & Air-Conditioning). **Est:** 1956. **Sales:** $10,000,000 (2000). **Emp:** 30. **Officers:** Henry Hsu, Treasurer, e-mail: henryh@lndappl.com.

■ **15196** ■ **L and W Enterprises Inc.**
PO Box 190
Kearney, NE 68848-0190
Phone: (308)237-2185
Products: Appliances. **SIC:** 5064 (Electrical Appliances—Television & Radio). **Est:** 1953. **Sales:** $8,000,000 (2000). **Emp:** 85. **Officers:** L. Loescher, President; Marc Loescher, CFO.

■ **15197** ■ **Lafayette Electronics Supply Inc.**
PO Box 4549
Lafayette, IN 47903
Phone: (765)447-9660
Free: (800)842-1527 **Fax:** (765)447-6967
Products: Electronic parts and equipment for sound systems, LAN networks and industrial controls. **SICs:** 5064 (Electrical Appliances—Television & Radio); 5064 (Electrical Appliances—Television & Radio); 5063 (Electrical Apparatus & Equipment). **Sales:** $1,000,000 (2000). **Emp:** 10. **Officers:** Ron D. Hurst, President; Anita Hines-Hurst, VP of Finance.

■ **15198** ■ **Lapure Water Coolers**
4219 Central Ave.
St. Petersburg, FL 33713
Phone: (727)327-8764 **Fax:** (727)327-2148
Products: Water filtration equipment, including filtration water coolers, filter units, water softeners and reverse osmosis equipment. **SICs:** 5078 (Refrigeration Equipment & Supplies); 5074 (Plumbing & Hydronic Heating Supplies). **Est:** 1990. **Sales:** $600,000 (2000). **Emp:** 9. **Officers:** David Alexander, President; Rand Mosteller, Vice President.

■ **15199** ■ **Lasonic Electronics Corp.**
1827 W Valley Blvd.
Alhambra, CA 91803
Phone: (626)281-3957 **Fax:** (626)576-7314
Products: Radios and cassettes. **SIC:** 5064 (Electrical Appliances—Television & Radio). **Sales:** $18,000,000 (2000). **Emp:** 30. **Officers:** Hong-Xi Chen, President; Wilfred Lau, CFO.

■ **15200** ■ **S.K. Lavery Appliance Co.**
1003 Farmington Ave.
West Hartford, CT 06107-2103
Phone: (860)523-5271 **Fax:** (860)232-8950
Products: Household appliances. **SIC:** 5064 (Electrical Appliances—Television & Radio). **Officers:** Samuel Lavery, President.

■ **15201** ■ **Lazy-Man, Inc.**
616 Hardwick St.
PO Box 327
Belvidere, NJ 07823
Phone: (908)475-5315
Free: (800)475-1950 **Fax:** (908)475-3165
Products: Camping and outdoor cooking equipment. **SICs:** 5074 (Plumbing & Hydronic Heating Supplies); 5099 (Durable Goods Nec). **Est:** 1936. **Officers:** G.D. McGlaughlin Jr., President. **Former Name:** Chicago Combustion Corporation.

■ **15202** ■ **Ledgerwood-Herwig Associates Ltd.**
119 S Easton Rd.
Glenside, PA 19038-4525
Products: Small electrical appliances; Household appliances; Television sets; Radios. **SIC:** 5064 (Electrical Appliances—Television & Radio). **Officers:** Patrick Ledgerwood, President.

■ **15203** ■ **I. Lehrhoff and Company Inc.**
50 Camptown Rd.
Maplewood, NJ 07040
Phone: (973)374-5300 **Fax:** (973)374-5524
Products: Appliances, including toasters, microwaves, and blenders. **SIC:** 5064 (Electrical Appliances—Television & Radio). **Est:** 1918. **Sales:** $52,000,000 (2000). **Emp:** 68. **Officers:** Arthur Lehrhoff, CEO; Julius Lehrhoff, Treasurer; Daniel Lehrhoff, President.

■ **15204** ■ **Lello Appliances Corp.**
355 Murray Hills Pkwy.
East Rutherford, NJ 07073
Phone: (201)939-2555
Products: Electric kitchen appliances. **SIC:** 5064 (Electrical Appliances—Television & Radio). **Sales:** $2,000,000 (1993). **Emp:** 5. **Officers:** G. Buzzy, President; R. Spata, Controller.

■ **15205** ■ **Liberty Distributors Inc.**
PO Box 48168
Wichita, KS 67201-8168
Phone: (316)264-7393
Products: Appliances, including stoves. **SIC:** 5064 (Electrical Appliances—Television & Radio). **Est:** 1969. **Sales:** $2,500,000 (2000). **Emp:** 8. **Officers:** Louis Taylor, President; Karen Warne, Controller.

■ **15206** ■ **Madison Appliance Parts Inc.**
1226 Williamson St.
Madison, WI 53703
Phone: (608)257-2589 **Fax:** (608)257-6967
Products: Appliance parts. **SIC:** 5063 (Electrical Apparatus & Equipment). **Officers:** William E. Brandt.

■ **15207** ■ **Madison Electric Co.**
31855 Van Dyke Ave.
Warren, MI 48093-1047
Phone: (810)825-0200 **Fax:** (810)825-0225
Products: General line of electric and electronic appliances and equipment. **SIC:** 5064 (Electrical Appliances—Television & Radio). **Sales:** $90,000,000 (2000). **Emp:** 220. **Officers:** Joseph Schneider, President; Ben Rosenthal, Treasurer & Secty.

■ **15208** ■ **Magnamusic Distributors Inc.**
74 Amenia Union Rd.
Sharon, CT 06069
Phone: (860)364-5431 **Fax:** (860)364-5168
Products: Sound and entertainment equipment and supplies. **SIC:** 5064 (Electrical Appliances—Television & Radio).

■ **15209** ■ **Manufacturing Distributors**
2444 Lycoming Creek Rd.
Williamsport, PA 17701
Phone: (570)494-4770
Products: Vacuum cleaners. **SIC:** 5064 (Electrical Appliances—Television & Radio).

■ **15210** ■ **Marcone Appliance Parts**
17300 Marquardt Ave.
Cerritos, CA 90703
Phone: (626)289-3735
Free: (800)242-4666 **Fax:** (626)576-7491
Products: Controls for major appliances; Major appliance parts. **SIC:** 5064 (Electrical Appliances—Television & Radio). **Est:** 1947. **Emp:** 20. **Officers:** Annette Sharpe.

■ **15211** ■ **Marcone Appliance Parts Center**
4410 Alamo Dr.
Tampa, FL 33605
Phone: (813)247-4410
Free: (800)282-6636 **Fax:** (813)247-3832
Products: Appliance parts. **SIC:** 5063 (Electrical Apparatus & Equipment). **Emp:** 150. **Officers:** Mitch Markow; Jim Souers.

■ **15212** ■ **Marcone Appliance Parts Center**
641 Monterey Pass Rd.
Monterey Park, CA 91754
Phone: (213)283-7741 **Fax:** (626)576-7491
Products: Appliance parts. **SIC:** 5064 (Electrical Appliances—Television & Radio). **Officers:** Annette Sharpe.

■ **15213** ■ **Marcone Appliance Parts Center Inc.**
2300 Clark Ave.
St. Louis, MO 63103
Phone: (314)231-7141 **Fax:** (314)231-5481
Products: Major appliance parts; Parts and attachments for small household appliances. **SICs:** 5065 (Electronic Parts & Equipment Nec); 5064 (Electrical Appliances—Television & Radio). **Est:** 1932. **Sales:** $13,000,000 (2000). **Emp:** 350. **Officers:** Mitchell Markow, President; Malcom Klearman, VP of Finance; Jeff Diamond, Sales Mgr.

■ **15214** ■ **Marta Cooperative of America**
15150 N Hayden Rd., Ste. 106
Scottsdale, AZ 85260
Phone: (602)443-0211
Free: (800)229-4101 **Fax:** 800-229-7751
Products: Electrical appliances. **SIC:** 5064 (Electrical Appliances—Television & Radio). **Sales:** $2,000,000 (1994). **Emp:** 20. **Officers:** Joseph P. Verdi, Director; Wendy Pitts, Controller.

■ **15215** ■ **Martin Industries Inc.**
301 E Tennessee St.
PO Box 128
Florence, AL 35631
Phone: (256)767-0330 **Fax:** (256)740-5192
E-mail: sales@martinindustries.com
URL: http://www.martinindustries.com
Products: Gas fireplaces; Gas logs; Gas grills; Utility trailers. **SIC:** 5064 (Electrical Appliances—Television & Radio). **Est:** 1905.

■ **15216** ■ **Masda Corp.**
22 Troy Rd.
Whippany, NJ 07981
Phone: (973)386-1100 **Fax:** (973)884-8963
Products: Outdoor gas barbecues, wood burning stoves and other energy products. **SIC:** 5074 (Plumbing & Hydronic Heating Supplies). **Sales:** $13,000,000 (1994). **Emp:** 30. **Officers:** Walter Blanke, Treasurer.

■ **15217** ■ **Masda Corp. New England**
11 Rodgers Rd.
Ward Hill, MA 01835
Phone: (978)373-3649
Free: (800)446-2732 **Fax:** (978)373-4651
Products: Gas grills; Gas and wood heating equipment; Gas logs and fireplaces. **SICs:** 5074 (Plumbing & Hydronic Heating Supplies); 5064 (Electrical Appliances—Television & Radio). **Est:** 1984. **Emp:** 5. **Officers:** Jon Freitas, Division Mgr.; Mel Brown, Sales Mgr.

■ **15218** ■ **May & Company Inc.**
PO Box 1111
Jackson, MS 39215-1111
Phone: (601)354-5781
Free: (800)398-0749 **Fax:** (601)355-4804
Products: Electrical appliances repair parts; Portable power tools; Gas grill parts. **SIC:** 5064 (Electrical Appliances—Television & Radio). **Est:** 1948. **Sales:** $250,000 (2000). **Emp:** 7. **Officers:** Andrew May, President.

■ **15219** ■ **W.L. May Company Inc.**
1120 Southeast Madison St.
PO Box 14368
Portland, OR 97214
Phone: (503)231-9398 **Fax:** (503)239-3995
Products: Appliance parts. **SICs:** 5065 (Electronic Parts & Equipment Nec); 5064 (Electrical Appliances—Television & Radio). **Officers:** Edward Cohen Jr.

■ **15220** ■ **Maycor Appliance Parts and Service Co.**
240 Edwards St. SE
Cleveland, TN 37311
Phone: (423)472-3333 **Fax:** (423)478-0476
Products: Appliance parts. **SIC:** 5065 (Electronic Parts & Equipment Nec). **Sales:** $49,000,000 (2000). **Emp:** 525. **Officers:** Nelson Wooldridge, President.

■ **15221** ■ **Maytag Corp.**
403 W 4th St. N
Newton, IA 50208
Phone: (515)792-8000 **Fax:** (515)791-8578
Products: Washing machines; Dryers; Refrigerators. **SIC:** 5064 (Electrical Appliances—Television & Radio). **Sales:** $870,000,000 (2000). **Emp:** 3,500. **Officers:** Richard Haines, President.

■ **15222** ■ **McCombs Supply Co.**
815 S 26th St.
Harrisburg, PA 17111
Phone: (717)558-7571
Free: (800)692-7473 **Fax:** (717)558-9097
Products: Major appliance parts. **SIC:** 5064 (Electrical Appliances—Television & Radio). **Officers:** Ken McCombs Jr.; Ken McCombs, III.

■ 15223 ■ **McCombs Supply Company Inc.**
346 N Marshall St.
Lancaster, PA 17604
Phone: (717)299-3866
Free: (800)732-0499 **Fax:** (717)393-5243
E-mail: mccombs@redrose.net
Products: Major appliance parts. **SIC:** 5064 (Electrical Appliances—Television & Radio). **Est:** 1960. **Officers:** Ken McCombs Jr.; Ken McCombs III.

■ 15224 ■ **McDaniels Sales Co.**
16839 S US 27
Lansing, MI 48906
Phone: (517)482-0748 **Fax:** (517)482-8929
Products: Kitchen cabinets to be built in; Household appliances. **SICs:** 5064 (Electrical Appliances—Television & Radio); 5031 (Lumber, Plywood & Millwork). **Est:** 1958. **Sales:** $5,000,000 (2000). **Emp:** 30. **Officers:** David Jessup, President.

■ 15225 ■ **McPhails Inc.**
PO Box 1789
Rohnert Park, CA 94927-1789
Phone: (707)769-9800 **Fax:** (707)769-7972
Products: Electrical appliances and propane gas. **SICs:** 5064 (Electrical Appliances—Television & Radio); 5172 (Petroleum Products Nec). **Sales:** $10,000,000 (2000). **Emp:** 25. **Officers:** Bruce MacPhail, President; Dennis Parsons, CFO.

■ 15226 ■ **Ellis Meares & Son Inc.**
PO Box 187
Fair Bluff, NC 28439-0187
Phone: (910)649-7521 **Fax:** (910)649-6220
Products: Household appliances; Electronic systems and equipment. **SIC:** 5064 (Electrical Appliances—Television & Radio). **Est:** 1901. **Emp:** 30. **Officers:** Carl Meares, President.

■ 15227 ■ **Metro Builders Supply Inc.**
5313 S Mingo
Tulsa, OK 74145-8102
Phone: (918)622-7692 **Fax:** (918)622-6940
Products: Household appliances. **SIC:** 5064 (Electrical Appliances—Television & Radio). **Officers:** Nick Stavros, President.

■ 15228 ■ **Michael Supply Company Inc.**
301 East St. S
Talladega, AL 35160-2452
Phone: (205)362-6144 **Fax:** (205)362-6145
Products: Plumbing hardware; Appliances. **SICs:** 5064 (Electrical Appliances—Television & Radio); 5074 (Plumbing & Hydronic Heating Supplies). **Officers:** John Robbs, President.

■ 15229 ■ **Mid-South Appliance Parts Inc.**
PO Box 193458
Little Rock, AR 72219-3458
Phone: (501)376-8351 **Fax:** (501)376-4233
Products: Electrical appliances, including televisions and radios; Household applianc e parts. **SICs:** 5064 (Electrical Appliances—Television & Radio); 5065 (Electronic Parts & Equipment Nec). **Officers:** Leonard Kremers, President.

■ 15230 ■ **Middle Tennessee Utility District**
P.O Box 670
Smithville, TN 37166
Phone: (615)597-4300 **Fax:** (615)597-6331
E-mail: mtng@mtng.com
URL: http://www.mtng.com
Products: Stoves, heaters, dryers and other gas appliances. **SICs:** 5074 (Plumbing & Hydronic Heating Supplies); 5064 (Electrical Appliances—Television & Radio). **Est:** 1955. **Sales:** $30,000,000 (2000). **Emp:** 140. **Officers:** Leslie B. Enoch II, CEO.

■ 15231 ■ **Midwest Electric Inc.**
PO Box 1198
Sioux City, IA 51102-1198
Phone: (712)252-4574
Free: (800)232-6262 **Fax:** (712)252-0140
Products: Electric household appliances. **SIC:** 5064 (Electrical Appliances—Television & Radio). **Officers:** Vernon Stolen, President.

■ 15232 ■ **Midwest Sales and Service Inc.**
917 S Chapin St.
South Bend, IN 46601
Phone: (219)287-3365 **Fax:** (219)287-3429
Products: Consumer appliances. **SIC:** 5064 (Electrical Appliances—Television & Radio). **Sales:** $9,000,000 (2000). **Emp:** 17. **Officers:** Trell Wechter, CEO; Trell Wechter, President & CFO.

■ 15233 ■ **Milwaukee Appliance Parts Company Inc.**
3455 N 124th St.
Brookfield, WI 53005
Phone: (414)781-0111
Free: (800)657-0711 **Fax:** (414)781-7124
Products: Major appliance parts. **SIC:** 5065 (Electronic Parts & Equipment Nec). **Est:** 1950. **Emp:** 10. **Officers:** Bert Badtke.

■ 15234 ■ **Miracle Exclusives, Inc.**
PO Box 8
Port Washington, NY 11050
Phone: (516)621-3333
Free: (800)645-6360 **Fax:** (516)621-1997
Products: Juice machines; Grain mills; Stainless steel Cookware; Pressure cookers; Dehydrator; Soybean milk machines; Yogurt makers; Wheatgrass juicers; Sprouters; Scales. **SIC:** 5064 (Electrical Appliances—Television & Radio). **Est:** 1963. **Sales:** $3,000,000 (2000). **Emp:** 10. **Officers:** Ernest E. Brunswick, President, e-mail: miracleexc@juno.com.

■ 15235 ■ **MITO Corp.**
54905 County Rd. 17
Elkhart, IN 46516
Phone: (219)295-2441
Free: (800)433-6486 **Fax:** (219)522-5480
Products: Sound and entertainment equipment and supplies. **SIC:** 5064 (Electrical Appliances—Television & Radio). **Sales:** $12,000,000 (2000). **Emp:** 42.

■ 15236 ■ **MMRF Inc.**
PO Box 7049
Charlotte, NC 28241-7049
Phone: (704)588-5558 **Fax:** (704)588-7021
Products: Small electrical appliances; Household appliances; Television sets; Radios. **SIC:** 5064 (Electrical Appliances—Television & Radio). **Officers:** Rees Russell, Vice President.

■ 15237 ■ **Modern Mass Media Inc.**
PO Box 950
Chatham, NJ 07928
Phone: (973)635-6000 **Fax:** (973)635-3404
Products: Installation and rental of business and professional audio visual and video products. **SIC:** 5064 (Electrical Appliances—Television & Radio). **Sales:** $12,000,000 (2000). **Emp:** 50. **Officers:** Chip Del Coro, President; Carl Del Coro, Exec. VP of Finance.

■ 15238 ■ **Modern Supply Company Inc.**
PO Box 22997
Knoxville, TN 37933-0997
Phone: (423)966-4567 **Fax:** (423)675-5711
Products: Electrical appliances, including televisions, radios, heating and air conditioning equipment; Cabinets; Lighting; Plumbing. **SICs:** 5064 (Electrical Appliances—Television & Radio); 5063 (Electrical Apparatus & Equipment); 5074 (Plumbing & Hydronic Heating Supplies); 5031 (Lumber, Plywood & Millwork). **Officers:** Mitchell Robinson, President.

■ 15239 ■ **Molay Supply Inc.**
801 1st Ave. N
Birmingham, AL 35203
Phone: (205)322-4321
Products: Kitchen appliances. **SIC:** 5064 (Electrical Appliances—Television & Radio). **Sales:** $1,000,000 (1993). **Emp:** 4. **Officers:** Paul Molay, Secretary.

■ 15240 ■ **MOORE Co.**
333 SE 2nd Ave.
Portland, OR 97214
Phone: (503)234-5000
Free: (800)828-2300 **Fax:** (503)238-1603
Products: Consumer electronics. **SIC:** 5064 (Electrical Appliances—Television & Radio). **Sales:** $13,000,000 (2000). **Emp:** 18. **Officers:** Gary A. Taylor, President; K.C. Rawls, VP & CFO.

■ 15241 ■ **Moore Discount Inc.**
101 & 107 S White St.
Athens, TN 37303
Phone: (423)745-6070 **Fax:** (423)745-9162
Products: Furniture; Major household appliances. **SICs:** 5064 (Electrical Appliances—Television & Radio); 5021 (Furniture). **Officers:** Carrie Moore, President.

■ 15242 ■ **Moulinex Appliances Inc.**
7 Reuten Dr.
Closter, NJ 07624
Phone: (201)784-0073
Products: Household appliances. **SIC:** 5064 (Electrical Appliances—Television & Radio). **Sales:** $20,000,000 (1992). **Emp:** 70. **Officers:** Thierry Schwarz, CEO & President; Christopher Plancon, CFO.

■ 15243 ■ **Murray Lighting Inc.**
PO Box 1544
Denton, TX 76201
Phone: (817)387-9571
Products: Appliances; Lighting fixtures. **SICs:** 5063 (Electrical Apparatus & Equipment); 5064 (Electrical Appliances—Television & Radio). **Est:** 1955. **Sales:** $6,000,000 (2000). **Emp:** 20. **Officers:** Patricia Murray, CEO; R. Murray, Treasurer & Secty.

■ 15244 ■ **Music Industries Inc.**
99 Tulip Ave., Ste. 101
Floral Park, NY 11001
Phone: (516)352-4110
Free: (800)431-6699 **Fax:** (516)352-0754
Products: Sound and entertainment equipment and supplies. **SIC:** 5064 (Electrical Appliances—Television & Radio). **Sales:** $13,000,000 (2000). **Emp:** 16.

■ 15245 ■ **National Electric Supply Co.**
702 Carmony Rd. NE
Albuquerque, NM 87107-4134
Phone: (505)345-3577 **Fax:** (505)344-5801
Products: Electrical appliance parts. **SIC:** 5065 (Electronic Parts & Equipment Nec). **Officers:** Brit Lawrence, President.

■ 15246 ■ **Nelco Sewing Machine Sales Corp.**
164 W 25th St.
New York, NY 10001
Phone: (212)924-7604 **Fax:** (212)633-6380
Products: Sewing machines. **SIC:** 5064 (Electrical Appliances—Television & Radio). **Est:** 1940. **Sales:** $9,000,000 (2000). **Emp:** 45. **Officers:** L. Jolson, President; Barbara Jolson, Vice President.

■ 15247 ■ **New Resource Inc.**
106 Longwinter Dr.
Norwell, MA 02061
Phone: (617)871-2020
Free: (800)872-4434 **Fax:** (617)871-9905
Products: Sound and entertainment equipment and supplies. **SIC:** 5064 (Electrical Appliances—Television & Radio). **Sales:** $7,000,000 (2000). **Emp:** 7.

■ 15248 ■ **NewSound L.L.C.**
PO Box 669
Waterbury, VT 05676
Phone: (802)244-7858 **Fax:** (802)244-1808
Products: Sound and entertainment equipment and supplies. **SIC:** 5064 (Electrical Appliances—Television & Radio).

■ 15249 ■ **Newton Appliance Sales & Service**
PO Box 292
Newton, GA 31770-0292
Phone: (912)734-5554
Products: Electrical appliances. **SIC:** 5064 (Electrical Appliances—Television & Radio). **Officers:** Herman Coker, President.

■ 15250 ■ **Newtown Appliance Sales & Services**
98-723 Kuahao Pl. B.
Pearl City, HI 96782-3103
Phone: (808)488-1614 **Fax:** (808)487-7666
Products: Electrical appliances, including televisions and radios; Large appliances, including washers,

dryers, refrigerators, and ranges. **SIC:** 5064 (Electrical Appliances—Television & Radio). **Officers:** Wilfred Nishimoto, President.

■ **15251** ■ **NMC Corp.**
477 Madison Ave., Ste. 701
New York, NY 10022
Phone: (212)207-4560
Products: Durable goods. **SIC:** 5099 (Durable Goods Nec). **Sales:** $1,400,000 (2000). **Emp:** 28. **Officers:** Marvin Greenfield, President & Treasurer.

■ **15252** ■ **Nor-Mon Distributing Inc.**
1134 SE Stark
Portland, OR 97214
Phone: (503)234-6215   **Fax:** (503)234-2891
Products: Hardware tools; Major appliance parts. **SICs:** 5064 (Electrical Appliances—Television & Radio); 5065 (Electronic Parts & Equipment Nec). **Est:** 1981. **Emp:** 9. **Officers:** Norman Chusid, President; Jose Rodriguez, General Mgr.; Monte Chusid, Vice President; D. Singer, Human Resources Contact.

■ **15253** ■ **North Star Sales Co.**
5401 Fairbanks St., Ste. 3
Anchorage, AK 99518-1261
Phone: (907)561-1164   **Fax:** (907)561-3145
Products: Sound and entertainment equipment and supplies. **SIC:** 5064 (Electrical Appliances—Television & Radio).

■ **15254** ■ **Northeast Group Inc.**
4 Arlington Rd.
Needham, MA 02494
Phone: (781)449-4223   **Fax:** (781)449-7785
Products: Sound and entertainment equipment and supplies. **SIC:** 5064 (Electrical Appliances—Television & Radio). **Sales:** $30,000,000 (2000). **Emp:** 12.

■ **15255** ■ **Northwest Wholesale Distributors**
11427 SE Foster Rd.
Portland, OR 97266-4041
Phone: (503)232-7114
Free: (800)234-8227   **Fax:** (503)232-1115
Products: Electrical appliances, including vacuum cleaners. **SIC:** 5064 (Electrical Appliances—Television & Radio). **Officers:** John Stark, Chairman of the Board.

■ **15256** ■ **Oakton Distributors Inc.**
PO Box 1425
Elk Grove Village, IL 60007
Phone: (847)228-5858
Free: (800)262-5866   **Fax:** (847)228-5803
URL: http://www.oakton.com
Products: Household appliances. **SIC:** 5064 (Electrical Appliances—Television & Radio). **Est:** 1955. **Sales:** $43,300,000 (2000). **Emp:** 40. **Officers:** Marvin Friedman, CEO & President, e-mail: marv@oakton.com.

■ **15257** ■ **Roy J. O'Donnell Co. Inc.**
2256 S Delaware St.
Denver, CO 80223-4138
Phone: (303)778-7575   **Fax:** (303)744-7587
Products: Electrical entertainment equipment, including television sets; Small housewares. **SIC:** 5064 (Electrical Appliances—Television & Radio). **Officers:** Daniel O Donnell, President.

■ **15258** ■ **OK Distributing Company Inc.**
208 NW 132nd St.
Oklahoma City, OK 73114-2306
Phone: (405)751-8833
Free: (800)375-8833   **Fax:** (405)751-9234
Products: Gas and electrical appliances. **SIC:** 5064 (Electrical Appliances—Television & Radio). **Est:** 1977. **Emp:** 7. **Officers:** J. Poarch, Chairman of the Board.

■ **15259** ■ **Olsen Audio Group Inc.**
7845 E Evans Rd.
Scottsdale, AZ 85260
Phone: (480)998-7140   **Fax:** (480)998-7192
Products: Microphone windscreens and components; professional audio equipment. **SIC:** 5064 (Electrical Appliances—Television & Radio). **Officers:** Lynn Clark, CFO.

■ **15260** ■ **Oregon Equipment Co. Inc.**
110 E 2nd St.
The Dalles, OR 97058-1704
Phone: (541)296-2915   **Fax:** (541)296-8073
Products: Electrical appliances, including dishwashers. **SIC:** 5064 (Electrical Appliances—Television & Radio). **Officers:** Hewitt Hillis, President.

■ **15261** ■ **Owens Electric Supply Inc.**
PO Box 3427
Wilmington, NC 28406
Phone: (910)791-6058   **Fax:** (910)395-1376
Products: Sound and entertainment equipment and supplies. **SIC:** 5064 (Electrical Appliances—Television & Radio). **Sales:** $5,000,000 (2000). **Emp:** 12.

■ **15262** ■ **Pacific Intertrade Corporation**
4165 Thousand Oaks Blvd., Ste. 301
Westlake Village, CA 91362
Phone: (805)495-5239   **Fax:** (805)495-9392
Products: Lawn and garden machinery; Electrical appliances. **SICs:** 5064 (Electrical Appliances—Television & Radio); 5083 (Farm & Garden Machinery). **Officers:** Robert G. Lees, President.

■ **15263** ■ **Palmieri Associates**
369 Passaic Ave., Ste. 116
Fairfield, NJ 07004
Phone: (973)882-1266   **Fax:** (973)882-1221
Products: Electrical and electronic equipment and supplies. **SIC:** 5064 (Electrical Appliances—Television & Radio).

■ **15264** ■ **Panasonic Broadcast and Television Systems Co.**
1 Panasonic Way
Secaucus, NJ 07094
Phone: (201)348-7621
Products: Broadcast and professional audio and video equipment. **SIC:** 5064 (Electrical Appliances—Television & Radio). **Officers:** Warren Allgyer, President.

■ **15265** ■ **Park Supply Co. Inc.**
1702 Hwy. 11 N
Picayune, MS 39466-2032
Phone: (601)798-1141   **Fax:** (601)798-7135
E-mail: parkms@ametro.net
Products: Plumbing supplies; Appliances; Electrical products. **SICs:** 5064 (Electrical Appliances—Television & Radio); 5074 (Plumbing & Hydronic Heating Supplies); 5063 (Electrical Apparatus & Equipment). **Est:** 1964. **Emp:** 13. **Officers:** George Drummond, Chairman of the Board.

■ **15266** ■ **Partners 4 Design Inc.**
275 Market St., Ste. 109
Minneapolis, MN 55405-1622
Phone: (612)476-4444   **Fax:** (612)447-4444
Products: Kitchen cabinets to be built in; Household appliances. **SICs:** 5064 (Electrical Appliances—Television & Radio); 5031 (Lumber, Plywood & Millwork). **Officers:** John Idstrom, President.

■ **15267** ■ **Pearsol Appliance Company**
3127 Main St.
Dallas, TX 75226-1584
Phone: (214)939-0930
Free: (800)527-7385   **Fax:** (214)939-0936
E-mail: pearsol@juno.com
URL: http://www.pearsol.com
Products: Household appliance parts and supplies; Small household appliances. **SIC:** 5064 (Electrical Appliances—Television & Radio). **Est:** 1943. **Sales:** $900,000 (2000). **Emp:** 10. **Officers:** Tom Harrington.

■ **15268** ■ **Pearsol's Parts Center**
2319 Gilbert Ave.
Cincinnati, OH 45206
Phone: (513)221-1195   **Fax:** (513)221-0401
Products: Home appliance parts. **SIC:** 5064 (Electrical Appliances—Television & Radio). **Officers:** Ronald Ellis.

■ **15269** ■ **Pelican Plumbing Supply Inc.**
139 Plantation Rd.
Harahan, LA 70123
Phone: (504)733-6300   **Fax:** (504)733-1181
Products: Kitchenware; Electric garbage disposals;

Electric water heaters; Bathroom accessories and fittings. **SICs:** 5064 (Electrical Appliances—Television & Radio); 5074 (Plumbing & Hydronic Heating Supplies); 5075 (Warm Air Heating & Air-Conditioning). **Est:** 1954. **Sales:** $5,000,000 (2000). **Emp:** 38.

■ **15270** ■ **Pells Radio Center**
415 N Mitchell
Cadillac, MI 49601-1838
Phone: (616)775-3141
Free: (800)459-3434   **Fax:** (616)775-8333
Products: Kitchen appliances; Televisons; Stereos; Furnaces. **SICs:** 5064 (Electrical Appliances—Television & Radio); 5075 (Warm Air Heating & Air-Conditioning). **Emp:** 18. **Officers:** John Putvin.

■ **15271** ■ **Pennsylvania Sewing Machine Co.**
215 Vandale Dr.
Houston, PA 15342-1250
Phone: (724)746-8800
Free: (800)245-0708   **Fax:** (724)746-8807
E-mail: pennsewl@pulsenet.com
Products: Industrial sewing machinery. **SIC:** 5064 (Electrical Appliances—Television & Radio). **Est:** 1981. **Sales:** $5,100,000 (2000). **Emp:** 15. **Officers:** Robert Matusic, President.

■ **15272** ■ **PHD, Inc.**
29309 Clayton Ave.
Wickliffe, OH 44092
Phone: (440)944-3500   **Fax:** (440)944-8380
URL: http://www.phdusa.com
Products: Small electric items; Housewares. **SIC:** 5064 (Electrical Appliances—Television & Radio). **Est:** 1977. **Sales:** $120,000,000 (2000). **Emp:** 150. **Officers:** Richard F. Henry, CEO & Chairman of the Board, e-mail: henryr@phdusa.com. **Former Name:** Professional Housewares Distributors Inc.

■ **15273** ■ **Pioneer Electronics (USA) Inc.**
PO Box 1720
Long Beach, CA 90801
Phone: (310)835-6177   **Fax:** (310)816-0402
Products: Audio and video equipment; Electrical machinery; Electronic components. **SICs:** 5064 (Electrical Appliances—Television & Radio); 5065 (Electronic Parts & Equipment Nec). **Sales:** $432,000,000 (2000). **Emp:** 900.

■ **15274** ■ **Plainsco Inc.**
15 N Kline St.
Aberdeen, SD 57401
Phone: (605)225-7100
Products: Electric appliances, plumbing and heating equipment. **SICs:** 5063 (Electrical Apparatus & Equipment); 5074 (Plumbing & Hydronic Heating Supplies). **Sales:** $39,000,000 (1993). **Emp:** 130. **Officers:** Dennis Logan, CEO; Lloys Hodgin, CFO.

■ **15275** ■ **Morton Pollack Enterprises Inc.**
6500 Flotilla St.
Los Angeles, CA 90040
Phone: (213)721-8832   **Fax:** (213)726-8904
Products: Clothes washers and dryers; Coin-operated laundry equipment and supplies. **SICs:** 5064 (Electrical Appliances—Television & Radio); 5085 (Industrial Supplies). **Est:** 1962. **Sales:** $25,000,000 (2000). **Emp:** 45. **Officers:** Morton Pollack, CEO; Eric Steinberg, President; Brad Pollack, Exec. VP.

■ **15276** ■ **Postema Sales Co. Inc.**
3396 Chicago Dr. SW
Grandville, MI 49418-1086
Phone: (616)532-6181   **Fax:** (616)532-0613
Products: Small electrical appliances; Household appliances. **SIC:** 5064 (Electrical Appliances—Television & Radio). **Officers:** Frederick Postema, President.

■ **15277** ■ **Potter Distributing Inc.**
4037 Roger B. Chaffee
Grand Rapids, MI 49548
Phone: (616)531-6860   **Fax:** (616)531-9578
Products: Large household appliances. **SIC:** 5064 (Electrical Appliances—Television & Radio). **Sales:** $25,000,000 (2000). **Emp:** 45. **Officers:** Doug Potter, President; Martin Denbraber, Controller.

■ 15278 ■ **Power Equipment Company**
2373 S Kinnickinnic Ave.
Milwaukee, WI 53207
Phone: (414)744-3210
Free: (800)242-3939 **Fax:** (414)744-6751
Products: Appliance repair parts and motors. **SIC:** 5063 (Electrical Apparatus & Equipment). **Est:** 1931. **Officers:** Dan Wiken. **Alternate Name:** 100,000 Parts.

■ 15279 ■ **John Preston Fuels**
PO Box 369
Ossipee, NH 03864-0369
Phone: (603)539-2807
Products: Stoves, grills, and fireplace screens; Cast iron goods; Oil lamps and kerosene wicks. **SICs:** 5074 (Plumbing & Hydronic Heating Supplies); 5199 (Nondurable Goods Nec).

■ 15280 ■ **Pro-Mark Corp.**
10707 Craighead Dr.
Houston, TX 77025
Phone: (713)666-2525
Free: (800)822-1492 **Fax:** (713)669-8000
Products: Sound and entertainment equipment and supplies. **SIC:** 5064 (Electrical Appliances—Television & Radio).

■ 15281 ■ **Prudential Builders Center**
PO Box 3088
Spokane, WA 99220
Phone: (509)535-2401
Free: (800)767-5567 **Fax:** (509)534-9145
Products: Kitchen appliances and cabinets, custom TV's, vacuums and electronic parts. **SICs:** 5064 (Electrical Appliances—Television & Radio); 5065 (Electronic Parts & Equipment Nec). **Sales:** $5,000,000 (2000). **Emp:** 9. **Officers:** Steve Brandon, President.

■ 15282 ■ **Prudential Distributors Inc.**
PO Box 3088
Spokane, WA 99220
Phone: (509)535-2401
Products: Household appliances. **SIC:** 5064 (Electrical Appliances—Television & Radio). **Est:** 1945. **Sales:** $1,000,000 (2000). **Emp:** 25. **Officers:** Stephen Brandon, President.

■ 15283 ■ **Pure Water Centers**
1155 Chest Dr., No. 109
Foster City, CA 94404
Free: (800)989-2837 **Fax:** (818)734-1440
Products: Mechanical drinking water coolers. **SIC:** 5078 (Refrigeration Equipment & Supplies).

■ 15284 ■ **Pure Water Centers, Inc.**
2419 N Black Canyon Hwy., Ste. 10
Phoenix, AZ 85009
Phone: (602)254-6323
Free: (800)989-2837 **Fax:** (602)253-1880
E-mail: purewatercenter@worldnet.alt.net
Products: Water filtration systems, water coolers, water conditioning systems sales, services, parts. **SIC:** 5078 (Refrigeration Equipment & Supplies). **Emp:** 14. **Former Name:** Acqua Group of Arizona.

■ 15285 ■ **Quality Sew and Vac**
224 W 3rd St.
Grand Island, NE 68801-5916
Phone: (308)382-7310
Free: (800)431-0032 **Fax:** (308)382-7329
Products: Household items. **SIC:** 5064 (Electrical Appliances—Television & Radio). **Sales:** $1,000,000 (2000). **Emp:** 8.

■ 15286 ■ **Quick-Rotan Inc.**
120 S La Salle St., #1450
Chicago, IL 60603-3403
Products: Sewing machines and parts. **SIC:** 5063 (Electrical Apparatus & Equipment). **Sales:** $3,000,000 (2000). **Emp:** 15. **Officers:** Paul Manos, President.

■ 15287 ■ **R & R Mill Company**
PO Box 187
Smithfield, UT 84335-0187
Phone: (435)563-3333 **Fax:** (435)563-4093
Products: Corn and grain mills; Food Dehydrators; Juicers. **SICs:** 5064 (Electrical Appliances—Television & Radio); 5046 (Commercial Equipment Nec); 5083 (Farm & Garden Machinery). **Officers:** Ralph Roylance, President.

■ 15288 ■ **Refrigeration and Electric Supply Co.**
1222 Spring St.
Little Rock, AR 72202
Phone: (501)374-6373
Products: Refrigerator parts; Electrical supplies, including wire and cable. **SICs:** 5078 (Refrigeration Equipment & Supplies); 5063 (Electrical Apparatus & Equipment). **Est:** 1949. **Sales:** $15,000,000 (2000). **Emp:** 50. **Officers:** Carl H. Miller Jr., President; Elaine King, Treasurer & Secty.; Robert Miller, Vice President.

■ 15289 ■ **Robert Reiser and Co.**
725 Dedham St.
Canton, MA 02021
Phone: (617)821-1290
Products: Food processing equipment, including blenders, mixers, and dicers; Packaging equipment. **SICs:** 5084 (Industrial Machinery & Equipment); 5064 (Electrical Appliances—Television & Radio).

■ 15290 ■ **Rep Associates Inc.**
5209 Point Fosdick Dr. NW, Ste. 206
Gig Harbor, WA 98335-1728
Phone: (253)851-8098 **Fax:** (253)858-8596
Products: Sound and entertainment equipment and supplies. **SIC:** 5064 (Electrical Appliances—Television & Radio). **Sales:** $4,000,000 (2000). **Emp:** 5.

■ 15291 ■ **Riccar America Co.**
1800 E Walnut Ave.
Fullerton, CA 92831
Phone: (714)669-1760
Products: Vacuum cleaners and sewing machines. **SIC:** 5064 (Electrical Appliances—Television & Radio). **Sales:** $11,000,000 (2000). **Emp:** 30. **Officers:** Craig Neal, President.

■ 15292 ■ **Richlund Enterprises**
608 3rd St.
Kentwood, LA 70444
Phone: (504)229-3252
Free: (800)736-4127 **Fax:** (504)299-4956
E-mail: richlund@tightspot.net
URL: http://www.appliancebuzz.com
Products: Washers, hardware; Household clothes dryers; Dishwashing machines; Commercial and industrial garbage and trash compactors; Ice-making machines and liquid chillers. **SICs:** 5064 (Electrical Appliances—Television & Radio); 5084 (Industrial Machinery & Equipment); 5072 (Hardware); 5078 (Refrigeration Equipment & Supplies). **Sales:** $2,000,000 (2000). **Emp:** 6. **Officers:** Beryl Billiot, President, e-mail: bbilliot@appliancebuzz.com. **Former Name:** Richlund Sales Inc.

■ 15293 ■ **Roldan Products Corp.**
13545 Barrett Pkwy. Dr.
Ste. 302
Ballwin, MO 63021
Phone: (314)822-7222 **Fax:** (314)822-7223
E-mail: Roldanprod@aol.com
URL: http://www.Roldan-export.com
Products: Commercial cooking equipment, including gas stoves; Portable lamps; Lighting louvers and diffusers; Women's jewelry; Household electrical cooking stoves. **SICs:** 5064 (Electrical Appliances—Television & Radio); 5074 (Plumbing & Hydronic Heating Supplies); 5063 (Electrical Apparatus & Equipment); 5094 (Jewelry & Precious Stones). **Est:** 1926. **Emp:** 4. **Officers:** Joe Roldan, Chairman.

■ 15294 ■ **Roth Distributing Co.**
11300 W 47th St.
Minnetonka, MN 55343-8849
Phone: (952)933-4428 **Fax:** (952)935-8795
URL: http://www.rothdistributing.com
Products: Kitchen appliances; Solid surface products. **SICs:** 5064 (Electrical Appliances—Television & Radio); 5023 (Homefurnishings); 5039 (Construction Materials Nec). **Est:** 1960. **Officers:** James Merrick, President.

■ 15295 ■ **Roth Distributing Co.**
15845 E 32nd Ave., Ste. 2A
Aurora, CO 80011
Phone: (303)373-9090 **Fax:** (303)373-2006
URL: http://www.rothdistributing.com
Products: Electrical appliances. **SICs:** 5064 (Electrical Appliances—Television & Radio); 5023 (Homefurnishings). **Est:** 1960. **Sales:** $61,000,000 (1999). **Emp:** 65. **Officers:** James Merrick, President; John Thielen, Vice President; David Kreider, Sec. & Treas.

■ 15296 ■ **Rowenta Inc.**
196 Boston Ave.
Medford, MA 02155
Phone: (781)396-0600 **Fax:** (617)497-4082
Products: Electrical appliances. **SIC:** 5064 (Electrical Appliances—Television & Radio). **Est:** 1988. **Officers:** Paul Pofcher, Director.

■ 15297 ■ **R.T. Rude Corp.**
129 W 53rd Ave.
Anchorage, AK 99518-1602
Phone: (907)563-9994 **Fax:** (907)563-9996
Products: Electronic parts and equipment, including home appliances; Home cleaning products; Marine equipment. **SICs:** 5065 (Electronic Parts & Equipment Nec); 5064 (Electrical Appliances—Television & Radio); 5088 (Transportation Equipment & Supplies); 5169 (Chemicals & Allied Products Nec). **Officers:** Robert Rude, President.

■ 15298 ■ **Russ Doughten Films Inc.**
5907 Meredith Dr.
Des Moines, IA 50322
Phone: (515)278-4737
Free: (800)247-3456 **Fax:** (515)278-4738
Products: Sound and entertainment equipment and supplies. **SIC:** 5064 (Electrical Appliances—Television & Radio).

■ 15299 ■ **S & S Appliance Service Co.**
601 Graymont Ave. N
Birmingham, AL 35203-2523
Phone: (205)324-1673 **Fax:** (205)320-2491
Products: Major appliances, including refrigerators, stoves, washing machines, and dryers. **SIC:** 5064 (Electrical Appliances—Television & Radio). **Officers:** Duel Speegle, President.

■ 15300 ■ **S/S Electronics Inc.**
1412 44th St. NW
Fargo, ND 58108-3067
Phone: (701)281-3855 **Fax:** (701)281-2960
Products: Electrical appliances. **SIC:** 5064 (Electrical Appliances—Television & Radio). **Est:** 1970. **Emp:** 22. **Officers:** T. Mark Sample, President.

■ 15301 ■ **Sadco Inc.**
PO Box 250547
Montgomery, AL 36125-0547
Phone: (205)288-5100 **Fax:** (205)288-5103
E-mail: sadco1953@mindspring.com
Products: Furniture; Electronics; Appliances. **SICs:** 5064 (Electrical Appliances—Television & Radio); 5021 (Furniture). **Officers:** Herbert Levy, Chairman of the Board.

■ 15302 ■ **St. Paul Appliance Center Inc.**
7618 Lyndale Ave. S
Minneapolis, MN 55423-4028
Phone: (612)861-5960 **Fax:** (612)861-5250
Products: Small electrical appliances; Sewing machines; Television sets; Radio receivers; Parts and attachments for small household appliances. **SIC:** 5064 (Electrical Appliances—Television & Radio). **Officers:** Patrick O Brien, President.

■ 15303 ■ **Sarco Inc.**
2416 2nd Ave.
Seattle, WA 98121-1425
Phone: (206)441-5977 **Fax:** (206)441-4162
Products: Restaurant and commercial foodservice equipment and supplies. **SIC:** 5064 (Electrical Appliances—Television & Radio). **Sales:** $300,000 (2000). **Emp:** 4.

■ 15304 ■ Scholl Oil and Transport Co.
PO Box 148
Holyoke, CO 80734-0148
Phone: (970)854-3300
Free: (800)876-0281 **Fax:** (970)854-3304
Products: Sound and entertainment equipment and supplies. **SIC:** 5064 (Electrical Appliances—Television & Radio).

■ 15305 ■ Schutte and Koerting Div.
2233 State Rd.
Bensalem, PA 19020
Phone: (215)639-0900 **Fax:** (215)639-1597
Products: Packaged vacuum systems. **SIC:** 5087 (Service Establishment Equipment). **Sales:** $127,100,000 (2000). **Emp:** 100. **Officers:** T.R. Kling, General Mgr.; H.V. Schramm, Comptroller.

■ 15306 ■ Schwarz Service Co.
603 Main St.
Ruma, IL 62278
Phone: (618)282-2028 **Fax:** (618)539-3743
Products: Stove parts. **SIC:** 5064 (Electrical Appliances—Television & Radio). **Est:** 1982. **Sales:** $1,000,000 (2000). **Emp:** 2. **Officers:** Helena Schwarz, President & Treasurer.

■ 15307 ■ Servall Co.
2501 S Cedar St.
Lansing, MI 48910-3137
Phone: (517)487-9550
Free: (800)899-0559 **Fax:** (517)487-2902
Products: Major appliance parts. **SIC:** 5065 (Electronic Parts & Equipment Nec). **Est:** 1976. **Sales:** $850,000 (1999). **Emp:** 2. **Officers:** Jim Nelson, Manager; Brian Davis.

■ 15308 ■ Servall Co.
6761 10 Mile Rd.
Center Line, MI 48015
Phones: (810)754-1818 (313)872-3658
Fax: (810)754-2260
Products: Appliance parts. **SIC:** 5064 (Electrical Appliances—Television & Radio). **Sales:** $21,000,000 (2000). **Emp:** 150. **Officers:** Kenneth Adler; Ken Adler, President & Treasurer; Anthony Nosis, Dir. of Sales.

■ 15309 ■ Servall Co.
1834 E 55th St.
Cleveland, OH 44103
Phone: (216)431-4400
Free: (800)362-2406 **Fax:** (216)431-7415
Products: Appliance parts, including parts for heating and cooling units. **SICs:** 5064 (Electrical Appliances—Television & Radio); 5075 (Warm Air Heating & Air-Conditioning). **Officers:** Kim Adler.

■ 15310 ■ Sewing Center Supply Co.
9631 NE Colfax St.
Portland, OR 97220-1232
Phone: (503)252-1452 **Fax:** (503)252-7280
Products: Electrical appliances, including televisions, radios, and sewing machines. **SIC:** 5064 (Electrical Appliances—Television & Radio). **Officers:** Richard Hunt, President.

■ 15311 ■ Sharp Wholesale Corp.
73-09 88th St.
Glendale, NY 11385
Phone: (718)459-0756 **Fax:** (718)459-0758
Products: Sewing machines. **SIC:** 5064 (Electrical Appliances—Television & Radio).

■ 15312 ■ Siano Appliance Distributors Inc.
5372 Pleasantview Rd.
Memphis, TN 38128
Phone: (901)382-5833
Products: Home appliances. **SIC:** 5064 (Electrical Appliances—Television & Radio). **Sales:** $6,000,000 (2000). **Emp:** 10. **Officers:** Ralph Siano, President.

■ 15313 ■ Singer Sewing Co.
PO Box 1909
Edison, NJ 08818-1909
Phone: (732)225-8844 **Fax:** (732)248-8432
Products: Sewing machines. **SIC:** 5064 (Electrical Appliances—Television & Radio).

■ 15314 ■ SJA Industries Inc.
1357 Kuehner Dr.
Simi Valley, CA 93063
Phone: (805)527-8899 **Fax:** (805)527-8088
Products: Car stereo speakers and loudspeakers. **SIC:** 5064 (Electrical Appliances—Television & Radio). **Officers:** George Wu, President.

■ 15315 ■ Small Appliance Repair Inc.
1500 Albany Ave.
Hartford, CT 06112-2113
Phone: (860)246-7424
Products: Household electrical appliances and parts, including vacuum cleaners. **SIC:** 5064 (Electrical Appliances—Television & Radio). **Officers:** Wallace Gitberg, President.

■ 15316 ■ Smeed Communication Services
PO Box 2099
Eugene, OR 97402
Phone: (541)686-1654 **Fax:** (541)334-1199
Products: Communications and telephone equipment, sound and voice mail. **SIC:** 5064 (Electrical Appliances—Television & Radio). **Officers:** Glen Smeed, President.

■ 15317 ■ W.H. Smith Kitchen Specialties
129 Winfield Rd.
St. Albans, WV 25177-1500
Phone: (304)727-2952 **Fax:** (304)727-2953
Products: Household appliances; Bathroom accessories and fittings; Kitchenware. **SICs:** 5064 (Electrical Appliances—Television & Radio); 5023 (Homefurnishings). **Officers:** W. Smith, Owner.

■ 15318 ■ Solinger and Associates
1 E Delaware Pl., Ste. 208
Chicago, IL 60611-1452
Phone: (312)951-1011
Products: Household stoves; Cooking utensils. **SICs:** 5064 (Electrical Appliances—Television & Radio); 5074 (Plumbing & Hydronic Heating Supplies); 5023 (Homefurnishings). **Sales:** $2,000,000 (1994). **Emp:** 5. **Officers:** Jeffrey W. Solinger, President.

■ 15319 ■ Sound Around Inc.
1600 63rd St.
Brooklyn, NY 11204
Phone: (718)236-8000 **Fax:** (718)236-2400
Products: Sound and entertainment equipment and supplies. **SIC:** 5064 (Electrical Appliances—Television & Radio). **Sales:** $37,000,000 (2000). **Emp:** 150.

■ 15320 ■ Southern States Industrial Sales
PO Box 885
Paris, TN 38242-0885
Phone: (901)642-0885
Products: Electrical appliances, including televisions and other household appliances. **SIC:** 5064 (Electrical Appliances—Television & Radio). **Officers:** Jerry Delk, President.

■ 15321 ■ Standard Appliance Parts Corporation
4814 Ayers St.
PO Box 7199
Corpus Christi, TX 78415
Phone: (512)853-9823 **Fax:** (512)853-4582
Products: Appliance parts and supplies. **SICs:** 5064 (Electrical Appliances—Television & Radio); 5065 (Electronic Parts & Equipment Nec). **Est:** 1950. **Emp:** 20. **Officers:** Glenn D. Peek; Suanne Peek Smith.

■ 15322 ■ Sun Electrical Appliance Sales & Service
4554 E Princess Anne Rd.
Norfolk, VA 23502-1614
Phone: (757)855-3052
Free: (800)347-4197 **Fax:** (757)857-6544
Products: Household appliances. **SIC:** 5064 (Electrical Appliances—Television & Radio). **Officers:** H. Vaughan, President.

■ 15323 ■ Sunkyong America Inc.
110 E 55th, 17th Fl.
New York, NY 10022
Phone: (212)906-8100
Products: Major appliances and supplies. **SICs:** 5064 (Electrical Appliances—Television & Radio); 5045 (Computers, Peripherals & Software); 5085 (Industrial Supplies). **Officers:** Youngman Kim, President.

■ 15324 ■ Sunseri's Inc.
2258 St. Claude Ave.
PO Box 3127, Bywater Station
New Orleans, LA 70117
Phone: (504)944-6762 **Fax:** (504)888-3790
Products: Appliance parts. **SICs:** 5063 (Electrical Apparatus & Equipment); 5064 (Electrical Appliances—Television & Radio). **Officers:** Joe Sunseri.

■ 15325 ■ Sunseri's Inc.
4500 I-10 Service Rd. S
Metairie, LA 70001
Phone: (504)888-3773 **Fax:** (504)888-3790
Products: Major appliance parts. **SICs:** 5063 (Electrical Apparatus & Equipment); 5065 (Electronic Parts & Equipment Nec).

■ 15326 ■ Superior Appliance Service Co.
1050 Scribner Ave. NW
Grand Rapids, MI 49504-4212
Phone: (616)459-3271 **Fax:** (616)459-3272
Products: Small electrical appliances. **SIC:** 5064 (Electrical Appliances—Television & Radio). **Officers:** Jerry Wells, Owner.

■ 15327 ■ T & E Timers Inc.
53 E 10 Mile Rd.
Madison Heights, MI 48071-4202
Phone: (248)543-1156 **Free:** (800)521-0258
Products: Appliance parts. **SIC:** 5065 (Electronic Parts & Equipment Nec). **Officers:** Thomas Perkowski, President.

■ 15328 ■ Tacony Corp.
1760 Gilsinn Ln.
Fenton, MO 63026
Phone: (314)349-3000 **Fax:** (314)349-2333
URL: http://www.tacony.com
Products: Sewing machines; Vacuum cleaners; Ceiling fans; Commercial janitorial equipment. **SICs:** 5064 (Electrical Appliances—Television & Radio); 5065 (Electronic Parts & Equipment Nec). **Est:** 1946. **Sales:** $120,000,000 (2000). **Emp:** 270. **Officers:** Kenneth J. Tacony, President, e-mail: k.tacony@tacony.com; H. William Hinderer III, CFO; John Maloney, VP of Marketing & Sales, e-mail: j.maloney@tacony.com.

■ 15329 ■ Tadiran Electronic Industries Inc.
10 E 53rd St.
New York, NY 10022-6102
Phone: (212)751-3600 **Fax:** (212)751-8181
Products: Electronic products, including refrigerators and stoves; Military electronic equipment. **SICs:** 5065 (Electronic Parts & Equipment Nec); 5064 (Electrical Appliances—Television & Radio). **Sales:** $1,116,800,000 (2000). **Emp:** 8,260. **Officers:** Israel Zamir, CEO & President; Edward A. Hoffman, VP of Finance.

■ 15330 ■ Tampa Appliance Parts Corp.
9840 Currie Davis Dr.
Tampa, FL 33619
Phone: (813)623-3131
Free: (800)282-0661 **Fax:** (813)620-1143
Products: Appliance parts. **SICs:** 5063 (Electrical Apparatus & Equipment); 5064 (Electrical Appliances—Television & Radio). **Officers:** Margaret Bush.

■ 15331 ■ Target Appliances
6316 Reisterstown Rd.
Baltimore, MD 21215-2309
Phone: (410)358-4433 **Fax:** (410)358-4980
Products: Major electrical appliances. **SIC:** 5064 (Electrical Appliances—Television & Radio). **Officers:** Ted Gamerman, President.

■ 15332 ■ Target Distributing Co.
11730 Parklawn Dr.
Rockville, MD 20852
Phone: (301)770-9400 **Fax:** (301)881-5463
Products: Telecommunication products. **SIC:** 5064 (Electrical Appliances—Television & Radio). **Sales:** $25,000,000 (2000). **Emp:** 38. **Officers:** Dick Warsaw, President; Robert Warsaw, Vice President.

■ **15333** ■ **Target Premiums Inc.**
1075 Old Norcross Rd., Ste. E
Lawrenceville, GA 30045-3302
Phone: (404)972-5121 **Fax:** (404)978-0132
Products: Electrical appliances; Electronics. **SIC:** 5064
(Electrical Appliances—Television & Radio). **Officers:**
Bruce Kessler, President.

■ **15334** ■ **TDI Air Conditioning Appliances**
2600 E 5th St.
Tyler, TX 75701
Phone: (903)597-8381 **Fax:** (903)593-9638
Products: Central heating and air-conditioning units;
Appliances, including ovens, refrigerators, microwaves,
disposals, freezers, washers, and dryers. **SICs:** 5064
(Electrical Appliances—Television & Radio); 5075
(Warm Air Heating & Air-Conditioning). **Emp:** 60.

■ **15335** ■ **TEAC America Inc. Data Storage
Products Div.**
PO Box 750
Montebello, CA 90640
Phone: (323)726-0303 **Fax:** (323)727-7656
Products: Electronic sound equipment, airborne video
recorders. **SIC:** 5064 (Electrical Appliances—
Television & Radio). **Sales:** $57,000,000 (2000). **Emp:**
200. **Officers:** Les Luzar, General Mgr.; Scott Elrich,
Mgr. of Finance.

■ **15336** ■ **Texas Sales Co.**
PO Box 1826
El Paso, TX 79949
Phone: (915)772-1177
Products: Electrical appliances, televisions, jewelry
and watches. **SICs:** 5064 (Electrical Appliances—
Television & Radio); 5094 (Jewelry & Precious Stones).
Sales: $24,000,000 (1992). **Emp:** 100. **Officers:** Jack
Schlusselburg, President.

■ **15337** ■ **Thermo King Atlanta Inc.**
PO Box 1305
Forest Park, GA 30298-1305
Phone: (404)361-4019 **Fax:** (404)363-8951
Products: Major appliances and parts, including
refrigerators and freezers. **SIC:** 5064 (Electrical
Appliances—Television & Radio). **Officers:** Bobby
Williamson, President.

■ **15338** ■ **TIC Industries Co.**
15224 E Stafford St.
City of Industry, CA 91744-4418
Phone: (626)968-0211
Free: (800)779-6664 **Fax:** (626)968-1363
Products: Sound and entertainment equipment and
supplies. **SIC:** 5064 (Electrical Appliances—Television
& Radio). **Sales:** $10,000,000 (2000). **Emp:** 49.

■ **15339** ■ **Toner Cable Equipment Inc.**
969 Horsham Rd.
Horsham, PA 19044
Phone: (215)675-2053
Free: (800)523-5947 **Fax:** (215)675-7543
Products: Sound and entertainment equipment and
supplies. **SIC:** 5064 (Electrical Appliances—Television
& Radio).

■ **15340** ■ **TR Systems**
2652 US Hwy. 41 W
Marquette, MI 49855-2257
Phone: (906)228-5757 **Fax:** (906)228-6362
Products: Vacuum cleaners. **SIC:** 5064 (Electrical
Appliances—Television & Radio). **Officers:** Tom Ross,
President.

■ **15341** ■ **Trek Corp.**
801 W Madison St.
Waterloo, WI 53594
Phone: (920)478-4700 **Fax:** (920)478-4200
Products: Appliances. **SIC:** 5064 (Electrical
Appliances—Television & Radio). **Est:** 1960. **Sales:**
$511,000,000 (2000). **Emp:** 1,850. **Officers:** Richard
A. Burke, CEO & President; Joseph Siefkes, VP of
Finance; John Knapp, Dir. of Systems.

■ **15342** ■ **Trevarrow Inc.**
1295 N Opdyke Rd.
Auburn Hills, MI 48326-2648
Phone: (248)377-2300
Free: (800)482-1948 **Fax:** (248)377-2392
E-mail: Trevarrow@Trevarrowinc.com
URL: http://www.trevarrowinc.com
Products: Appliances. **SIC:** 5064 (Electrical
Appliances—Television & Radio). **Est:** 1928. **Sales:**
$30,000,000 (2000). **Emp:** 60. **Officers:** Bruce H.
Trevarrow, President; Virginia E. Trevarrow, Vice
President; Laurence E. Trevarrow III, Treasurer; Amy
Trevarrow-Palma, Corp. Secty.; Dean Striler,
Sales/Marketing Contact.

■ **15343** ■ **Tribles of Maryland Inc.**
901 Southern Ave.
Oxon Hill, MD 20745-4359
Phone: (301)894-6161
Free: (800)874-2537 **Fax:** (301)505-2547
E-mail: tribles@tribles.com
Products: Household appliance parts. **SICs:** 5064
(Electrical Appliances—Television & Radio); 5065
(Electronic Parts & Equipment Nec). **Est:** 1945.
Officers: John Trible, President; Preston Trible, Vice
President.

■ **15344** ■ **Turner Appliance**
1638 Tulip Dr.
Indianapolis, IN 46227-5034
Phone: (317)788-9180
Products: Electrical appliances, including televisions,
radios, and washing machines. **SIC:** 5064 (Electrical
Appliances—Television & Radio). **Officers:** Kevin
Noone, Owner.

■ **15345** ■ **Turner Sherwood Corp.**
PO Box 161038
Memphis, TN 38186-1038
Phone: (901)332-1414
Free: (800)332-1945 **Fax:** (901)398-6187
Products: Electrical appliances. **SIC:** 5064 (Electrical
Appliances—Television & Radio). **Officers:** Jerry
Brasher, President.

■ **15346** ■ **Twin City Supply Company**
233 Harris Ave.
Providence, RI 02903
Phone: (401)331-5930
Free: (800)556-7544 **Fax:** (401)421-2133
Products: Refrigeration and appliance parts. **SICs:**
5064 (Electrical Appliances—Television & Radio); 5078
(Refrigeration Equipment & Supplies). **Est:** 1955. **Emp:**
16. **Officers:** Henry Dziadosz; Stephen Dziadosz.

■ **15347** ■ **Uni Distribution Co.**
10 Universal City Plz., No. 400
Universal City, CA 91608
Phone: (818)777-1000 **Fax:** (818)777-6420
Products: Sound and entertainment equipment and
supplies. **SIC:** 5064 (Electrical Appliances—Television
& Radio). **Sales:** $1,000,000,000 (2000). **Emp:** 1,100.

■ **15348** ■ **United Sewing Machine Distributing**
916 SW D Ave.
Lawton, OK 73501-4531
Phone: (580)353-8800
Products: Sewing machines. **SIC:** 5064 (Electrical
Appliances—Television & Radio). **Officers:** Henry
Herzig, President.

■ **15349** ■ **Universal Service and Supply**
3605 W Twain Ave.
Las Vegas, NV 89103-1901
Phone: (702)876-0333 **Fax:** (702)876-5994
Products: Electrical appliances. **SIC:** 5064 (Electrical
Appliances—Television & Radio). **Officers:** Patrick
Miller, President.

■ **15350** ■ **Universal Sewing Supply Inc.**
1011 E Park Indus. Dr.
St. Louis, MO 63130
Phone: (314)862-0800
Free: (800)325-3340 **Fax:** (314)725-8808
E-mail: unisew@universalsewing.com
URL: http://www.universalsewing.com
Products: Sewing machine parts. **SIC:** 5064 (Electrical
Appliances—Television & Radio). **Est:** 1956. **Sales:**
$25,000,000 (2000). **Emp:** 100. **Officers:** Phil

Samuels, President; Steven R. Sinn, VP of Sales;
Clifford Samuels, Vice President.

■ **15351** ■ **V & V Appliance Parts Inc.**
27 W Myrtle Ave.
Youngstown, OH 44507
Phone: (330)743-5144 **Fax:** (330)743-3221
Products: Appliance parts. **SICs:** 5064 (Electrical
Appliances—Television & Radio); 5065 (Electronic
Parts & Equipment Nec). **Officers:** Victor Lazar.

■ **15352** ■ **Vacuum Center Central Michigan**
G4099 S Saginaw St.
Burton, MI 48529-1645
Phone: (810)742-8954 **Fax:** (810)742-3720
Products: Vacuum cleaners and parts. **SIC:** 5064
(Electrical Appliances—Television & Radio). **Officers:**
Lawrence Ruhstorfer, President.

■ **15353** ■ **Valdez**
7420 Sunset Blvd.
Los Angeles, CA 90046
Phone: (213)874-9998
Products: Sound and entertainment equipment and
supplies. **SIC:** 5064 (Electrical Appliances—Television
& Radio). **Sales:** $200,000 (2000). **Emp:** 2.

■ **15354** ■ **Valley Appliance Parts Co.**
719 Hamburg Tpke.
Pompton Lakes, NJ 07442-1433
Phone: (973)835-2157 **Fax:** (973)835-5545
Products: Major appliance parts, including washer,
dryer, refrigerator, dishwasher, and range parts. **SICs:**
5064 (Electrical Appliances—Television & Radio); 5065
(Electronic Parts & Equipment Nec). **Emp:** 30.
Officers: Richard Henches.

■ **15355** ■ **Valley Sales Company Inc.**
PO Box 53
West Springfield, MA 01090-0053
Phone: (413)732-7754 **Fax:** (413)736-1229
Products: Sound and entertainment equipment and
supplies. **SIC:** 5064 (Electrical Appliances—Television
& Radio). **Sales:** $1,800,000 (2000). **Emp:** 8.

■ **15356** ■ **Vanderheyden Distributing Inc.**
PO Box 3685
South Bend, IN 46619-0685
Phone: (219)232-8291 **Fax:** (219)239-4684
Products: Electrical appliances. **SIC:** 5064 (Electrical
Appliances—Television & Radio). **Officers:** August
Vanderheyden, Chairman of the Board.

■ **15357** ■ **Video Aided Instruction Inc.**
182 Village Rd.
Roslyn Heights, NY 11577
Phone: (516)621-0012
Free: (800)966-8378 **Fax:** (516)484-8785
Products: Sound and entertainment equipment and
supplies. **SIC:** 5064 (Electrical Appliances—Television
& Radio).

■ **15358** ■ **Vihon Associates**
3620 Dekalb T Pkwy., Ste. 2013
Atlanta, GA 30340
Phone: (404)457-2970 **Fax:** (404)457-2972
Products: Electrical appliances. **SIC:** 5064 (Electrical
Appliances—Television & Radio). **Officers:** Greg
Vihon, Partner.

■ **15359** ■ **Viking Distributing Company Inc.**
685 Market St.
Medford, OR 97504-6125
Phone: (541)773-4928
Products: Appliances, including sewing machines.
SIC: 5064 (Electrical Appliances—Television & Radio).
Officers: E. Smith, President.

■ **15360** ■ **VillaWare Manufacturing Co.**
1420 E 36th St.
Cleveland, OH 44114
Phone: (216)391-6650
Products: Kitchenware, such as pasta makers and
meat grinders. **SIC:** 5023 (Homefurnishings).

■ **15361** ■ **Vita-Mix Corp.**
8615 Usher Rd.
Cleveland, OH 44138
Phone: (440)235-4840 **Fax:** (440)235-3726
Products: Electrical appliances, including blenders

and fans. **SIC:** 5064 (Electrical Appliances—Television & Radio). **Sales:** $30,000,000 (1994). **Emp:** 100. **Officers:** Fred Weiss, Treasurer.

■ **15362** ■ **Wagner Appliance Parts Inc.**
1840 E Race St.
Allentown, PA 18103-9584
Phone: (215)264-0681 **Fax:** 800-992-4637
Products: Appliance parts. **SIC:** 5064 (Electrical Appliances—Television & Radio). **Officers:** Jeffrey Wagner.

■ **15363** ■ **Walker Vacuum Supply**
1400 S Van Buren St.
Enid, OK 73703-7853
Phone: (580)234-1712
Products: Small electrical appliances; Household vacuum cleaners; Televisions; Radios. **SIC:** 5064 (Electrical Appliances—Television & Radio). **Officers:** William Walker, Owner.

■ **15364** ■ **Warren Distributing Corp.**
PO Box 26628
Raleigh, NC 27611
Phone: (919)828-9100 **Fax:** (919)828-8896
Products: Appliances. **SIC:** 5064 (Electrical Appliances—Television & Radio). **Est:** 1945. **Sales:** $18,600,000 (2000). **Emp:** 29. **Officers:** Robert S. Warren Jr., President; James Finch, Controller; R. Warren III, VP of Marketing.

■ **15365** ■ **Washer and Refrigeration Supply Company Inc.**
716 2nd Ave., North
Birmingham, AL 35201
Phone: (205)322-8693
Free: (800)322-4WRS **Fax:** (205)324-4596
Products: Washer and refrigerator supplies. **SICs:** 5063 (Electrical Apparatus & Equipment); 5065 (Electronic Parts & Equipment Nec); 5078 (Refrigeration Equipment & Supplies). **Officers:** Dave Smith.

■ **15366** ■ **Washington Electric Membership Cooperative**
PO Box 598
Sandersville, GA 31082
Phone: (912)552-2577
Products: Appliances. **SIC:** 5064 (Electrical Appliances—Television & Radio). **Est:** 1937. **Sales:** $86,000,000 (2000). **Emp:** 100. **Officers:** T.L. Bray, Director; Leon Powell, Treasurer & Secty.; Larry E. Renfroe, Dir. of Data Processing.

■ **15367** ■ **Water-Vac Distributors-Rainbow**
649 Mckinney Rd.
Mt. Airy, NC
Phone: (336)789-7979
Products: Vacuum cleaning systems. **SIC:** 5064 (Electrical Appliances—Television & Radio).

■ **15368** ■ **WCI International Co.**
3 Parkway Ctr.
Pittsburgh, PA 15220
Phone: (412)928-0252
Products: Consumer appliances. **SIC:** 5064 (Electrical Appliances—Television & Radio). **Sales:** $32,000,000 (2000). **Emp:** 131. **Officers:** J. Rushworth, President; Joe Standeven, Exec. VP of Finance.

■ **15369** ■ **Welbilt Corp.**
2227 Welbilt Blvd.
New Port Richey, FL 34655-5130
Phone: (727)375-7010
Products: Household appliances; Heating systems; Food service equipment. **SICs:** 5064 (Electrical Appliances—Television & Radio); 5046 (Commercial

Equipment Nec); 5074 (Plumbing & Hydronic Heating Supplies). **Est:** 1907. **Sales:** $450,000,000 (2000). **Emp:** 3,000. **Officers:** Andre Roake, CEO; Patrick Clark, VP of Finance.

■ **15370** ■ **Western Cascade Equipment Co.**
13456 SE 27th Pl.
Bellevue, WA 98005-4211
Phone: (425)562-9400 **Fax:** (425)562-6594
Products: Washers and dryers; Drycleaning equipment. **SICs:** 5087 (Service Establishment Equipment); 5064 (Electrical Appliances—Television & Radio). **Est:** 1987. **Sales:** $5,000,000 (2000). **Emp:** 20. **Officers:** Andy Jacoby, VP of Marketing & Sales.

■ **15371** ■ **White Sewing Machine Co.**
PO Box 458012
Cleveland, OH 44145-8012
Phone: (216)252-3300 **Fax:** (216)252-3311
Products: Household sewing machines. **SIC:** 5064 (Electrical Appliances—Television & Radio). **Sales:** $46,200,000 (2000). **Emp:** 100. **Officers:** Bengt Gerborg, President; Dave Mechenbier, Controller.

■ **15372** ■ **Wholesale Builder Supply Inc.**
51740 Grand River Ave.
Wixom, MI 48393-2303
Phone: (248)347-6290
Free: (800)722-4405 **Fax:** (248)347-6284
Products: Electrical appliances, including televisions, radios, and dishwashers. **SIC:** 5064 (Electrical Appliances—Television & Radio). **Officers:** Richard Mc Kimmy, President.

■ **15373** ■ **Williams Distributing Co.**
658 Richmond NW
Grand Rapids, MI 49504-2036
Phone: (616)456-1613 **Fax:** (616)456-8091
Products: Kitchen cabinets; Appliances; Heating and cooling equipment; Outdoor power equipment; Windows and doors; Fireplaces. **SICs:** 5031 (Lumber, Plywood & Millwork); 5064 (Electrical Appliances—Television & Radio). **Est:** 1968. **Sales:** $50,000,000 (2000). **Emp:** 120. **Officers:** James C. Williams; Charlie Readle, Sales/Marketing Contact; Mike Kosten, Customer Service Contact; Mary Lynn Dornbos, Human Resources Contact.

■ **15374** ■ **Charlie Wilson's Appliance Co.**
202 E Market St.
Louisville, KY 40202-1218
Phone: (502)583-0604 **Fax:** (502)583-0608
E-mail: cwappl@iglow.com
Products: Small electrical appliances; Household appliances; Television sets; Radios. **SICs:** 5064 (Electrical Appliances—Television & Radio); 5063 (Electrical Apparatus & Equipment). **Est:** 1950. **Officers:** Charles Wilson, President.

■ **15375** ■ **Wishing Well Video Distributing Co.**
PO Box 1008
Silver Lake, WI 53170
Phone: (414)889-8501
Free: (800)888-9355 **Fax:** (414)889-8591
Products: Sound and entertainment equipment and supplies. **SIC:** 5064 (Electrical Appliances—Television & Radio). **Sales:** $1,000,000 (2000). **Emp:** 24.

■ **15376** ■ **W.L. Roberts Inc.**
3791 Air Park
Memphis, TN 38118
Phone: (901)362-2080
Products: Consumer appliances and electronics. **SIC:** 5064 (Electrical Appliances—Television & Radio). **Sales:** $10,000,000 (2000). **Emp:** 17. **Officers:** Don Holmes, President; Betty Holmes, Vice President.

■ **15377** ■ **Wonderful World of Imports**
1820 6th Ave. SE, Ste. U
Decatur, AL 35601-6044
Phone: (256)353-9610 **Fax:** (256)350-1652
E-mail: ttandto@aol.com
Products: Electrical appliances, including television sets, radios, and household appliances. **SIC:** 5064 (Electrical Appliances—Television & Radio). **Est:** 1973. **Emp:** 5. **Officers:** E Vassar, President.

■ **15378** ■ **Woodson and Bozeman Inc.**
PO Box 18450
Memphis, TN 38181-0450
Phone: (901)362-1500
Free: (800)876-4243 **Fax:** (901)362-1509
Products: Home appliances. **SIC:** 5064 (Electrical Appliances—Television & Radio). **Sales:** $24,000,000 (2000). **Emp:** 45. **Officers:** Ed Bozeman, President; John Conant, CFO.

■ **15379** ■ **Woolworth Corp.**
233 Broadway
New York, NY 10279-0003
Phone: (212)553-2000 **Fax:** (212)553-2094
Products: Appliances, including stoves and refrigerators; Pots and pans; Clothes; Housewares. **SICs:** 5064 (Electrical Appliances—Television & Radio); 5023 (Homefurnishings); 5136 (Men's/Boys' Clothing); 5137 (Women's/Children's Clothing).

■ **15380** ■ **World Wide Pictures Inc.**
1201 Hennepin Ave.
Minneapolis, MN 55403
Phone: (612)338-3335
Free: (800)745-4318 **Fax:** (612)338-3029
Products: Sound and entertainment equipment and supplies. **SIC:** 5064 (Electrical Appliances—Television & Radio).

■ **15381** ■ **Wright and Wilhelmy Co.**
11005 E St.
Omaha, NE 68137
Phone: (402)593-0600 **Fax:** (402)593-0610
URL: http://www.wrightandw.com
Products: Small electrical appliances; Sporting goods. **SICs:** 5064 (Electrical Appliances—Television & Radio); 5091 (Sporting & Recreational Goods). **Est:** 1871. **Sales:** $19,000,000 (2000). **Emp:** 95. **Officers:** G. Harting, President & Treasurer; Harold Ronnfeldt, Sr. VP of Sales; Ron Herzinger, Data Processing Mgr.; Dave Stoecklien, Sr. VP of Marketing and Merchandising.

■ **15382** ■ **Xcell International Corp.**
646 Blackhawk Dr.
Westmont, IL 60559
Phone: (630)323-0107 **Fax:** (630)323-0217
Products: Spices and seasonings. **SICs:** 5064 (Electrical Appliances—Television & Radio); 5023 (Homefurnishings); 5149 (Groceries & Related Products Nec). **Sales:** $28,000,000 (2000). **Emp:** 50.

■ **15383** ■ **Zamoiski Company Inc.**
3000 Waterview Ave.
Baltimore, MD 21230-3510
Phone: (410)539-3000
Free: (800)950-5900 **Fax:** (410)576-7787
E-mail: jmulkey@zamoiski.com
URL: http://www.zamoiski.com
Products: Electrical appliances; Lawn and garden equipment, including lawn mowers, riding mowers, and snow throwers. **SIC:** 5064 (Electrical Appliances—Television & Radio). **Est:** 1896. **Officers:** John Mulkey, President.

(26) Household Items

Entries in this section are arranged alphabetically by company name. When the company name is a personal name, the company name is alphabetized by the surname unless the first name or initial(s) are part of a trade name. See the User's Guide at the front of this directory for additional information.

■ 15384 ■ **A & S Suppliers**
1970 W 84 St.
Hialeah, FL 33014
Phone: (305)557-1688 **Fax:** (305)557-1067
Products: Bed linens; Table linens; Hotel towels; Baby comforters and blankets; Drapes; Aprons. **SICs:** 5023 (Homefurnishings); 5137 (Women's/Children's Clothing). **Officers:** Armando Rodriguez, President.

■ 15385 ■ **AAA Glass Corp.**
2800 E 12th
Los Angeles, CA 90023-3622
Phone: (213)263-2177 **Fax:** (213)265-4844
Products: Glassware. **SIC:** 5023 (Homefurnishings).
Emp: 108. **Officers:** Leo Barth.

■ 15386 ■ **Abrahams Oriental Rugs**
5120 Wood Way
Houston, TX 77056
Phone: (713)622-4444 **Fax:** (713)622-8928
Products: Oriental rugs. **SIC:** 5023 (Homefurnishings).
Sales: $4,000,000 (1999). **Emp:** 10. **Officers:** Samuel Abraham, CEO.

■ 15387 ■ **Accent Lamp and Shade Co. Inc.**
PO Box 95128
Newton, MA 02495
Phone: (617)527-3900 **Fax:** (617)332-3608
E-mail: accenthkd@aol.com
Products: Lamps and shades. **SICs:** 5023 (Homefurnishings); 5063 (Electrical Apparatus & Equipment). **Est:** 1971. **Sales:** $6,000,000 (2000).
Emp: 40. **Officers:** Haig K. Deranian.

■ 15388 ■ **Adleta Corp.**
1645 Diplomat Dr.
Carrollton, TX 75006
Phone: (972)620-5600
Free: (800)423-5382 **Fax:** (972)620-4768
Products: Floor coverings. **SIC:** 5023 (Homefurnishings). **Sales:** $40,000,000 (2000). **Emp:** 102. **Officers:** Jack Adleta, President; Roger Stieben, Controller.

■ 15389 ■ **ADO Corp.**
851 Simuel Rd.
Spartanburg, SC 29301-8830
Phone: (864)574-2731 **Fax:** (864)574-5835
Products: Draperies and drapery material. **SICs:** 5023 (Homefurnishings); 5131 (Piece Goods & Notions).
Emp: 130. **Officers:** Richard H. Shelton III.

■ 15390 ■ **AFGD**
3350 Ball St.
Birmingham, AL 35234
Phone: (205)841-6785
Free: (800)753-2341 **Fax:** (205)841-4308
E-mail: http://www.afg.com/afgd/
Products: Glass products, including flat glass and insulated windows. **SIC:** 5039 (Construction Materials Nec). **Officers:** Todd French.

■ 15391 ■ **Air Flow Shutters Shade**
1825 NE 144th St.
North Miami, FL 33181-1419
Phone: (305)949-7416
Products: Draperies, shutters, and mini-blinds. **SICs:** 5023 (Homefurnishings); 5031 (Lumber, Plywood & Millwork). **Sales:** $1,000,000 (2000). **Emp:** 22.
Officers: David Monuse.

■ 15392 ■ **Airtex Consumer Products**
150 Industrial Park Rd.
Cokato, MN 55321
Phone: (320)286-2696 **Fax:** (320)286-2428
Products: Pillow forms; Cotton batting. **SIC:** 5199 (Nondurable Goods Nec). **Sales:** $2,500,000 (2000).
Emp: 50. **Officers:** Greg Winsperger.

■ 15393 ■ **Alicia Comforts**
5 Cook
Brooklyn, NY 11206
Phone: (718)384-2100 **Fax:** (718)384-7634
Products: Linens; Pillows; Sheets and pillowcases; Bedspreads and bedsets; Comforters; Fabric, including white goose down, poly and lambswool fill. **SIC:** 5023 (Homefurnishings). **Est:** 1979. **Sales:** $1,000,000 (2000). **Emp:** 24. **Officers:** Jay B. Rosenfeld, President; Helen Rosenfeld, Sec. & Treas.

■ 15394 ■ **Allegheny Inc.**
3600 William Flynn Hwy.
Allison Park, PA 15101
Phone: (412)486-5500
Free: (800)933-9336 **Fax:** (412)486-8950
Products: Floorcovering equipment and supplies. **SIC:** 5023 (Homefurnishings). **Sales:** $2,000,000 (2000).
Emp: 12.

■ 15395 ■ **Allure Home Creation Company Inc.**
85 Fulton St.
Boonton, NJ 07005
Phone: (973)402-8888 **Fax:** (973)334-2383
Products: Home furnishings, including curtains and drapes. **SIC:** 5023 (Homefurnishings). **Sales:** $25,000,000 (1994). **Emp:** 50. **Officers:** Stanley Ho, President; Dan Harris, Vice President.

■ 15396 ■ **American Commercial Inc.**
20633 S Fordyce Ave.
Long Beach, CA 90810
Phone: (310)886-3700 **Fax:** (310)763-0625
Products: Dishes and crystal. **SIC:** 5023 (Homefurnishings). **Sales:** $50,000,000 (2000). **Emp:** 200. **Officers:** Alfred J. Blake, President; Norman Higo, VP of Finance.

■ 15397 ■ **American Cut Crystal**
1150 Broadway
Hewlett, NY 11557-2338
Phone: (516)569-1300 **Fax:** (516)569-5656
E-mail: a.c.c.@worldnet.att.net
Products: Crystal products, including vases and glassware. **SIC:** 5023 (Homefurnishings). **Est:** 1938.
Emp: 40. **Officers:** Marvin Wolf, President; Eleanor Wolf, Vice President.

■ 15398 ■ **American Hotel Register Co.**
2775 Shermer Rd.
Northbrook, IL 60062
Phone: (847)564-4000
Free: (800)323-5686 **Fax:** (847)564-4109
Products: Linens; Hardware. **SICs:** 5023 (Homefurnishings); 5072 (Hardware). **Est:** 1896.
Sales: $50,000,000 (2000). **Emp:** 250. **Officers:** James F. Leahy.

■ 15399 ■ **American Pacific Enterprises Inc.**
70 W 40th St.
New York, NY 10018
Phone: (212)944-6799
Products: Quilts. **SIC:** 5023 (Homefurnishings).

■ 15400 ■ **American Textile Co.**
PO Box 4006
Pittsburgh, PA 15201-0006
Phone: (412)681-9404
Free: (800)289-2826 **Fax:** (412)681-3582
Products: Textiles; Bedspreads and bedsets; Table linens. **SIC:** 5023 (Homefurnishings). **Sales:** $10,000,000 (2000). **Emp:** 160. **Officers:** Reid W. Ruttenberg, CEO & Chairman of the Board; Jack Ouellette, President; C. Lance Ruttenberg, Vice President.

■ 15401 ■ **AMS Imports Inc.**
23 Ash Ln.
Amherst, MA 01002
Phone: (413)253-2644
Free: (800)648-1816 **Fax:** (413)256-0434
E-mail: ams@amsimports.com
URL: http://www.amsimports.com
Products: Rugs. **SIC:** 5023 (Homefurnishings). **Est:** 1980. **Sales:** $1,000,000 (2000). **Emp:** 3. **Officers:** Anne Schewe, President; Jared Quinn, Dir. of Mktg. & Sales.

■ 15402 ■ **Amway Distributors**
858 Todd Preis Dr.
Nashville, TN 37221
Phone: (615)646-4060
Products: Housewares and cleaning products. **SIC:** 5023 (Homefurnishings).

■ 15403 ■ **Andrea by Sadek**
19 E 26th St.
New York, NY 10010
Phone: (212)679-8121
Products: Decorative accessories. **SIC:** 5023 (Homefurnishings).

■ 15404 ■ **Arabel Inc.**
16301 NW 49th Ave.
Miami, FL 33014
Phone: (305)623-8302
Free: (800)759-5959 **Fax:** (305)624-0714
E-mail: arabel@arabel.com
URL: http://www.arabel.com
Products: Vertical and wood blinds. **SIC:** 5023 (Homefurnishings). **Est:** 1986. **Sales:** $10,000,000 (2000). **Emp:** 22. **Officers:** Howard Rothman, President.

■ 15405 ■ C.F. Archer Associates
RD 2, 2976 Persse Rd.
Lafayette, NY 13084
Phone: (315)677-3263 **Fax:** (315)677-3263
Products: Glassware. **SIC:** 5023 (Homefurnishings).

■ 15406 ■ Architectural Surfaces, Inc.
560 N Nimitz Hwy., No. 29-217E
Honolulu, HI 96817-5330
Phone: (808)523-7866
Free: (800)523-7886 **Fax:** (808)523-8199
E-mail: asi@pixi.com
URL: http://www.asi-hawaii.com
Products: Wallpaper; Wallcoverings; Floorcoverings; Moldings; Metal finishes; Acoustic panels; Specialty paint finishes. **SICs:** 5023 (Homefurnishings); 5031 (Lumber, Plywood & Millwork); 5198 (Paints, Varnishes & Supplies). **Est:** 1984. **Emp:** 5. **Officers:** Paul Rasmussen, President; Jill Lumeng, Vice President.

■ 15407 ■ Artmark Chicago Ltd.
4136 United Pky.
Schiller Park, IL 60176-1708
Phone: (312)266-1111 **Fax:** (312)266-1985
Products: Houseware; Giftware. **SICs:** 5023 (Homefurnishings); 5199 (Nondurable Goods Nec). **Est:** 1945. **Sales:** $20,000,000 (2000). **Emp:** 80. **Officers:** Richard Lozins, President; Robert Lozins, Exec. VP; Robert Baer, Vice President.

■ 15408 ■ Ashbrook & Associates
1271 N Blue Gum St.
Anaheim, CA 92806-2414
Phone: (714)765-5900
Free: (888)867-3618 **Fax:** (714)765-5904
E-mail: Timash@earthlink.net
Products: Window coverings. **SIC:** 5023 (Homefurnishings). **Est:** 1967. **Emp:** 10. **Officers:** Rick Ashbrook.

■ 15409 ■ Asmara Inc.
Fargo Bldg.
Boston, MA 02210
Phone: (617)261-0222 **Fax:** (617)261-0228
Products: Rugs. **SIC:** 5023 (Homefurnishings). **Sales:** $2,000,000 (2000). **Emp:** 13. **Officers:** Abid Ilahi, President; Angela Hague, Marketing Mgr.

■ 15410 ■ Atlas Textile Company Inc.
PO Box 911008
Commerce, CA 90091-1008
Phone: (213)888-8700 **Fax:** (213)888-8795
Products: Towels, sheets, and home textiles. **SIC:** 5131 (Piece Goods & Notions). **Sales:** $60,000,000 (2000). **Emp:** 120. **Officers:** Benjamin Kaye, President; Harry Simon, Treasurer & Secty.

■ 15411 ■ B and F System Inc.
3920 S Walton Walker
Dallas, TX 75236-0036
Phone: (214)333-2111 **Fax:** (214)333-2137
E-mail: bnfservice@bnfusa.com
URL: http://www.bnfusa.com
Products: Household products, including cookware, tools, cutlery, sport knives, and gift items. **SICs:** 5023 (Homefurnishings); 5199 (Nondurable Goods Nec). **Est:** 1950. **Emp:** 95.

■ 15412 ■ Back to Basics Products Inc.
11660 S State St.
Draper, UT 84020-9455
Phone: (801)571-7349
Free: (800)688-1989 **Fax:** (801)571-6061
E-mail: service@backtobasicsproducts.com
URL: http://www.backtobasicsproducts.com
Products: Home canning equipment; Ice shavers and accessories. **SIC:** 5023 (Homefurnishings). **Est:** 1971. **Sales:** $8,000,000 (2000). **Emp:** 12. **Officers:** Bill Beesley, VP of Sales; Tom Daniels, President.

■ 15413 ■ H.W. Baker Linen Co.
PO Box 544
Mahwah, NJ 07430
Phone: (201)825-2000 **Fax:** (201)825-0649
Products: Linens for hotels, hospitals, and nursing homes. **SIC:** 5023 (Homefurnishings). **Sales:** $51,000,000 (1994). **Emp:** 200. **Officers:** D.E. Hymans, President & Treasurer; J.L. Hymans, Exec. VP of Finance.

■ 15414 ■ Bakertowne Company, Inc.
136 Cherry Valley Ave.
West Hempstead, NY 11552
Phone: (516)489-6002
Free: (800)989-8696 **Fax:** (516)489-6087
Products: Kitchenware; Furniture hardware; Industrial fittings. **SICs:** 5023 (Homefurnishings); 5072 (Hardware); 5085 (Industrial Supplies). **Est:** 1975. **Sales:** $5,000,000 (2000). **Emp:** 7. **Officers:** Tim Sennett, Vice President; Carl Barone, Vice President; Lou Kahn, Vice President; Paul Goldman, President.

■ 15415 ■ Bath/Kitchen & Tile Supply Co.
103 Greenbank Rd.
Wilmington, DE 19808
Phone: (302)992-9200
Products: Bath accessories; Kitchen accessories; Tile products. **SICs:** 5023 (Homefurnishings); 5032 (Brick, Stone & Related Materials). **Emp:** 50.

■ 15416 ■ Bay Colony Mills Inc.
PO Box 2396
Providence, RI 02906-0396
Phone: (401)831-3505 **Fax:** (401)731-4816
Products: Bedding products; Finished products. **SIC:** 5023 (Homefurnishings). **Officers:** Joseph Mc Osker, President.

■ 15417 ■ BDD Inc.
4318 E University Dr.
Phoenix, AZ 85034-7318
Phone: (602)437-0549 **Fax:** (520)327-0123
Products: Window coverings. **SIC:** 5023 (Homefurnishings). **Sales:** $2,200,000 (2000). **Emp:** 49. **Officers:** James W. Miller.

■ 15418 ■ Benthin Systems, Inc.
79 N Industrial Pk.
510 North Ave.
Sewickley, PA 15143
Phone: (412)749-5200
Free: (800)366-0089 **Fax:** (412)749-5206
Products: Window coverings. **SIC:** 5023 (Homefurnishings). **Est:** 1980. **Sales:** $14,000,000 (2000). **Emp:** 110. **Officers:** Doreen Carraway; Donald Dugan; William Dugan; Michael Dugan. **Former Name:** Swnteca.

■ 15419 ■ Bergquists Imports Inc.
1412 S Hwy. 33
Cloquet, MN 55720-2627
Phone: (218)879-3343
Free: (800)328-0853 **Fax:** (218)879-0010
E-mail: bbergqu106@aol.com
URL: http://www.bergquistimports.com
Products: Scandinavian gift products; Crystals; Candleholders; Christmas ornaments. **SICs:** 5023 (Homefurnishings); 5099 (Durable Goods Nec). **Est:** 1948. **Emp:** 15. **Officers:** Barry Bergquist; Joan Lampi, Customer Service Mgr.

■ 15420 ■ Best Brands Home Products, Inc.
325 5th Ave., Ste. 518
New York, NY 10016
Phone: (212)684-7456
Free: (800)684-1236 **Fax:** (212)684-7630
E-mail: att@bestbrands.com
URL: http://www.bestbrands.com
Products: Table linens; Bedding, bath, and beach tablecloth and placement products; Kitchen textile. **SICs:** 5023 (Homefurnishings); 5131 (Piece Goods & Notions). **Est:** 1958. **Sales:** $2,000,000 (2000). **Emp:** 25. **Officers:** Jack Albert, President; Ronnie Gindi, Exec. VP; Cari Bennett, Production Mgr.; David Meyer, Dir. of Operations.

■ 15421 ■ Bicor Processing Corp.
362 Dewitt Ave.
Brooklyn, NY 11207
Phone: (718)649-9595 **Fax:** (718)927-1269
E-mail: bicor@iname.com
Products: Pillows. **SIC:** 5023 (Homefurnishings). **Est:** 1970. **Officers:** Allan Berg, President; Eileen Berg, Customer Service Mgr.; Harry Small, Sales & Marketing Contact.

■ 15422 ■ Blyth Industries Inc.
100 Field Point Rd.
Greenwich, CT 06830-6442
Phone: (203)661-1926
Products: Candle accessories including holders, lamps, and rings. **SIC:** 5199 (Nondurable Goods Nec). **Sales:** $331,300,000 (2000). **Emp:** 2,100. **Officers:** Robert B. Goergen, CEO, President & Chairman of the Board; Howard E. Rose, VP & CFO.

■ 15423 ■ Bomaine Corp.
2716 Ocean Park Blvd., Ste. 1065
Santa Monica, CA 90405
Phone: (310)450-2303
Products: Home furnishings. **SIC:** 5023 (Homefurnishings). **Sales:** $67,000,000 (2000). **Emp:** 500. **Officers:** G.M. Bronstein, President; Kenji Onishi, Controller.

■ 15424 ■ Bon Motif Co.
4045 Horton St.
Emeryville, CA 94608
Phone: (510)655-2000 **Fax:** (510)655-1600
E-mail: Bonmotif@compuserve.com
Products: Rugs. **SIC:** 5023 (Homefurnishings). **Sales:** $7,000,000 (2000). **Emp:** 20. **Officers:** David Himy, President.

■ 15425 ■ Boone-Davis Inc.
1346 N Knollwood Cir.
Anaheim, CA 92801
Phone: (714)229-9900
Free: (800)275-2343 **Fax:** (714)229-8900
Products: Picture frames; Clocks; Business card holder, recipe file boxes, CD cabinet holder. **SICs:** 5023 (Homefurnishings); 5094 (Jewelry & Precious Stones). **Officers:** Patrice Boone, President.

■ 15426 ■ Boston Warehouse Trading Corp.
59 Davis Ave.
Norwood, MA 02062
Phone: (617)769-8550
Products: Kitchen giftware. **SIC:** 5023 (Homefurnishings). **Sales:** $11,000,000 (2000). **Emp:** 45. **Officers:** Peter Jenkins, President.

■ 15427 ■ Boutross Imports Inc.
209 25th St.
Brooklyn, NY 11232
Phone: (718)965-0070
Free: (800)227-7781 **Fax:** (718)965-9837
E-mail: boutrossco@aol.com
URL: http://www.boutross.com
Products: Linens, including baby and table linens; Handkerchiefs. **SICs:** 5023 (Homefurnishings); 5131 (Piece Goods & Notions). **Est:** 1894. **Sales:** $2,000,000 (2000). **Emp:** 12. **Officers:** Michael E. Boutross.

■ 15428 ■ Bowen Supply Inc.
PO Box 947015
Ft. Worth, TX 76147-9015
Phone: (912)924-9076
Products: Venetian blinds; Mobile homes. **SICs:** 5023 (Homefurnishings); 5012 (Automobiles & Other Motor Vehicles). **Est:** 1964. **Emp:** 65. **Officers:** Harold P. Bowen, CEO & Chairman of the Board; Mary Gillis, Treasurer & Secty.; Stuart Howell, VP of Marketing.

■ 15429 ■ Brewster Wallcovering Co.
67 Pacella Park Dr.
Randolph, MA 02368
Phone: (781)963-4800
Free: (800)366-1700 **Fax:** (781)963-8805
E-mail: info@brewsterwallcovering.com
URL: http://www.brewsterwallcovering.com
Products: Wallpaper and borders; Textiles and accessories; Alternative wall systems; Fabrics; Valances. **SICs:** 5198 (Paints, Varnishes & Supplies); 5023 (Homefurnishings); 5031 (Lumber, Plywood & Millwork); 5131 (Piece Goods & Notions). **Est:** 1954. **Emp:** 500. **Officers:** Kenneth Grandberg, President; Peter Ciaccia, CFO.

■ 15430 ■ Brunschwig and Fils Inc.
75 Virginia Rd.
North White Plains, NY 10603
Phone: (914)684-5800
Products: Wallcoverings and wallpaper; Furniture;

Trim; Mirrors; Carpeting; Tables; Lamps. **SICs:** 5131 (Piece Goods & Notions); 5021 (Furniture); 5023 (Homefurnishings); 5198 (Paints, Varnishes & Supplies). **Sales:** $33,000,000 (2000). **Emp:** 300. **Officers:** T. Peardon Jr., President; R.A. Williamson, VP & CFO.

■ **15431** ■ **Buck Knives Inc.**
1900 Weld Blvd.
El Cajon, CA 92022
Phone: (619)449-1100
Free: (800)735-2825 **Fax:** (760)729-2825
Products: Knives. **SIC:** 5072 (Hardware). **Sales:** $30,000,000 (2000). **Emp:** 499. **Officers:** Charles T. Buck. **Alternate Name:** Buck Work-Man.

■ **15432** ■ **Burlington Futon Co. Inc.**
388 Pine St.
Burlington, VT 05401-4779
Phone: (802)658-6685 **Fax:** (802)862-7169
Products: Beds and bedding. **SIC:** 5023 (Homefurnishings). **Officers:** Mark Binkhorst, President.

■ **15433** ■ **C-Mor Co.**
7 Jewell St.
Garfield, NJ 07026
Phone: (201)478-3900
Free: (800)631-3830 **Fax:** (201)478-0249
E-mail: morshade@aol.com
Products: Window shades and blinds. **SICs:** 5199 (Nondurable Goods Nec); 5023 (Homefurnishings). **Est:** 1946. **Sales:** $11,000,000 (2000). **Emp:** 100. **Officers:** Robert A. Gershuny, President.

■ **15434** ■ **Nancy Calhoun Inc.**
PO Box 130
Corona, CA 92878-0130
Phone: (714)529-4700
Products: Dinnerware, including serving pieces, glassware, and flatware. **SIC:** 5023 (Homefurnishings). **Sales:** $6,500,000 (2000). **Emp:** 40. **Officers:** Nancy Calhoun, President.

■ **15435** ■ **Carpet Mart & Wallpaper Outlet**
1271 Manheim Pke.
Lancaster, PA 17601
Phone: (717)299-2381
Products: Carpets; Blinds; Tilee. **SICs:** 5198 (Paints, Varnishes & Supplies); 5023 (Homefurnishings).

■ **15436** ■ **Carvel Hall Inc.**
PO Box 271
Crisfield, MD 21817
Phone: (410)968-0500 **Fax:** (410)968-1260
Products: Kitchen cutlery. **SIC:** 5023 (Homefurnishings). **Est:** 1895. **Sales:** $2,000,000 (2000). **Emp:** 38. **Officers:** James Robellsed, General Mgr.; Mike Lewis, CFO; Ann Butler, Dir of Human Resources.

■ **15437** ■ **Casa Linda Draperies**
4111 Elva St.
Dallas, TX 75227-3813
Phone: (214)388-4721 **Fax:** (214)381-6090
Products: Draperies and mini-blinds. **SIC:** 5023 (Homefurnishings). **Sales:** $1,000,000 (2000). **Emp:** 49. **Officers:** A. C. Riskind.

■ **15438** ■ **Casella Lighting Co.**
111 Rhode Island St.
San Francisco, CA 94103
Phone: (415)626-9600 **Fax:** (415)626-4539
Products: Electrical and electronic equipment and supplies. **SIC:** 5023 (Homefurnishings). **Sales:** $4,900,000 (2000). **Emp:** 29.

■ **15439** ■ **Castec Window Shading Inc.**
7531 Coldwater Canyon Ave.
North Hollywood, CA 91605-2007
Phone: (818)503-8300
Free: (800)828-2500 **Fax:** 800-932-3323
Products: Window blinds and shades. **SIC:** 5023 (Homefurnishings). **Emp:** 99. **Officers:** G. J. Castellaw.

■ **15440** ■ **Century-Federman Wallcoverings Inc.**
18 Holly Hill Cir.
Marshfield, MA 02050-1728
Phone: (781)337-9300 **Fax:** (781)335-5353
Products: Wallcovering materials, including wallpaper and fabric wallcovering. **SIC:** 5198 (Paints, Varnishes & Supplies). **Est:** 1979. **Sales:** $2,000,000 (2000). **Emp:** 10. **Officers:** Paul V. Hankey, President.

■ **15441** ■ **Chantal Cookware Corp.**
2030 W Sam Houston
Houston, TX 77043
Phone: (713)467-9949
Products: Cookware. **SICs:** 5023 (Homefurnishings); 5087 (Service Establishment Equipment).

■ **15442** ■ **Chernov Brothers Inc.**
219 Larchwood Dr.
Warwick, RI 02886-8551
Phone: (401)751-4910
Products: Curtains, drapes, sheets, towels, and blankets. **SIC:** 5023 (Homefurnishings). **Officers:** Edward Chernov, President.

■ **15443** ■ **Childers & Associates**
6800 W 115th St., Ste. 110
Overland Park, KS 66211
Phone: (913)345-8844
Free: (800)341-6692 **Fax:** (913)345-8496
E-mail: mchilders@blitz-it.net
Products: Glassware; Home Decor; Lighting; General giftware. **SIC:** 5023 (Homefurnishings). **Est:** 1980. **Emp:** 8. **Officers:** Julie Childers; Mo Childers.

■ **15444** ■ **Cinti Floor Co.**
5162 Broerman Ave.
Cincinnati, OH 45217
Phone: (513)641-4500 **Fax:** (513)482-4204
Products: Floorcovering equipment and supplies. **SIC:** 5023 (Homefurnishings). **Sales:** $1,000,000 (2000). **Emp:** 49.

■ **15445** ■ **CK Associates**
PO Box 23127
Lexington, KY 40523
Phone: (859)266-2171
Free: (800)318-6910 **Fax:** (859)266-3921
Products: Glassware. **SIC:** 5023 (Homefurnishings).

■ **15446** ■ **Clauss Cutlery Co.**
225 Riverview Ave.
Waltham, MA 02454
Phone: (781)647-5560 **Fax:** (781)891-8375
Products: Cutlery. **SIC:** 5072 (Hardware).

■ **15447** ■ **Closet Centers America**
6700 Distribution Dr.
Beltsville, MD 20705-1401
Phone: (301)595-4100 **Fax:** (301)595-4104
Products: Closet organizers. **SIC:** 5023 (Homefurnishings). **Emp:** 32. **Officers:** Michael Kaperst.

■ **15448** ■ **Closet City Ltd.**
619 Bethlehem Pke.
PO Box 779
Montgomeryville, PA 18936-0779
Phone: (215)855-4400
Free: (800)342-0070 **Fax:** (215)362-0901
E-mail: closetcity@erols.com
URL: http://www.closetcity.com
Products: Closet organizers; Home offices; Wall beds; Garage storage systems. **SIC:** 5023 (Homefurnishings). **Emp:** 49.

■ **15449** ■ **Coast Cutlery Co.**
PO Box 5821
Portland, OR 97228
Phone: (503)234-4545
Free: (800)426-5858 **Fax:** (503)234-4422
URL: http://www.coastcutlery.com
Products: Sports cutlery; Multi-tools. **SIC:** 5072 (Hardware). **Est:** 1919. **Emp:** 49. **Officers:** David C. Brands, Owner; Mike Hill, Sales Mgr., e-mail: mikehill@prnw.net; Nancy Morgan, Customer Service Mgr.; Bob Wells, Operations Mgr.; Barry Leach.

■ **15450** ■ **Coleman Interior Service Co.**
3233 Rhode Island Ave.
Mt. Rainier, MD 20712
Phone: (301)699-0730 **Fax:** (301)699-0733
Products: Draperies; Valances; Bedspreads; Headboards; Window Treatments. **SIC:** 5023 (Homefurnishings). **Est:** 1955. **Sales:** $150,000 (2000). **Emp:** 5. **Officers:** C.D. Steinberg.

■ **15451** ■ **Columbus Wallcovering Co.**
2301 Shermer Rd.
Northbrook, IL 60062
Phone: (708)882-7474 **Fax:** (708)882-7578
Products: Wallpaper and wallcoverings. **SIC:** 5198 (Paints, Varnishes & Supplies). **Sales:** $6,000,000 (1994). **Emp:** 12. **Officers:** Tim Schorn, General Mgr.; Donald S. Smith, Mgr. of Finance.

■ **15452** ■ **Consolidated Tile and Carpet Co.**
15100 Ravinia Ave.
Orland Park, IL 60462-3745
Phone: (708)403-5000 **Fax:** (708)403-5030
Products: Floorcovering equipment and supplies. **SIC:** 5023 (Homefurnishings). **Sales:** $10,000,000 (2000). **Emp:** 100.

■ **15453** ■ **Contract Decor Inc.**
1243 N Gene Autrey Trail
Palm Springs, CA 92262
Phone: (760)320-5566
Free: (800)631-7013 **Fax:** (760)320-3673
E-mail: mail@contract_decor.com
Products: Curtains; Bedspreads and bedsets; Window blinds and shades; Cubicle curtains; Draperies. **SICs:** 5023 (Homefurnishings); 5198 (Paints, Varnishes & Supplies). **Est:** 1976. **Sales:** $6,500,000 (1999). **Emp:** 15. **Officers:** Marc Stewart, President.

■ **15454** ■ **Cook's Mart Ltd.**
3000 E 3rd. Ave.
Denver, CO 80206
Phone: (303)388-5933
Products: Pots and pans; Cookbooks; Household appliances. **SICs:** 5046 (Commercial Equipment Nec); 5023 (Homefurnishings); 5064 (Electrical Appliances—Television & Radio); 5192 (Books, Periodicals & Newspapers).

■ **15455** ■ **Laura Copenhaver Industries Inc.**
PO Box 149 Dept. D
Marion, VA 24354
Phone: (540)783-4663
Products: Bed canopies and quilts. **SIC:** 5023 (Homefurnishings). **Est:** 1916. **Sales:** $1,000,000 (2000). **Emp:** 20. **Officers:** Tom Copenhaver, President.

■ **15456** ■ **Cork Supply International Inc.**
537 Stone Rd.
Benicia, CA 94510
Phone: (707)746-0353 **Fax:** (707)746-7471
Products: Winecorks. **SIC:** 5199 (Nondurable Goods Nec). **Sales:** $10,000,000 (2000). **Emp:** 20. **Officers:** Jochen Michalski, President; Justin Davis, Sales Mgr.

■ **15457** ■ **Corning Inc.**
Houghton Park
Corning, NY 14831
Phone: (607)974-9000 **Fax:** (607)974-7095
Products: Glass products, including fine crystal. **SIC:** 5023 (Homefurnishings). **Emp:** 49.

■ **15458** ■ **Couzon USA**
298 Federal St.
PO Box 905
Greenfield, MA 01302-0905
Phone: (413)774-3481
Free: (800)544-1781 **Fax:** (413)773-5399
URL: http://www.couzon.com
Products: Stainless steel flatware. **SIC:** 5023 (Homefurnishings). **Est:** 1934. **Sales:** $30,000,000 (2000). **Officers:** N. Leanne Travis, Dir. of Operations; Alain Poujol, Vice President.

■ 15459 ■ **Coyle Inc.**
250 W Beltline Hwy.
Madison, WI 53713
Phone: (608)257-0291
Free: (800)842-6953 **Fax:** (608)258-7248
URL: http://www.coylecarpet.com
Products: Blinds; Flooring, including ceramic, tile, hardwood, laminate and carpeting. **SICs:** 5032 (Brick, Stone & Related Materials); 5023 (Homefurnishings); 5198 (Paints, Varnishes & Supplies). **Est:** 1943. **Sales:** $7,000,000 (2000). **Emp:** 40. **Officers:** P.E. Coyle, President.

■ 15460 ■ **Coyne Mattress Co. Ltd.**
94-134 Leowwena St.
Waipahu, HI 96797
Phone: (808)671-4071 **Fax:** (808)676-5822
Products: Bedding. **SIC:** 5023 (Homefurnishings). **Est:** 1898. **Sales:** $6,200,000 (2000). **Emp:** 53. **Officers:** Donald E. Lee, President; Herbert Lee, VP of Finance.

■ 15461 ■ **Coyne's Inc.**
7400 Boone Ave., N
Brooklyn Park, MN 55428
Phone: (612)425-8666
Free: (800)336-8666 **Fax:** (612)425-1653
Products: Glassware. **SIC:** 5023 (Homefurnishings).

■ 15462 ■ **Craftmade International Inc.**
PO Box 1037
Coppell, TX 75019-1037
Phone: (972)393-3800
Free: (800)527-2578 **Fax:** (972)304-3754
URL: http://www.craftmade.com
Products: Ceiling fans and lamps. **SICs:** 5023 (Homefurnishings); 5063 (Electrical Apparatus & Equipment). **Est:** 1985. **Sales:** $40,900 (1999). **Emp:** 100. **Officers:** James R. Ridings, CEO, President & Chairman of the Board; Kathy Oher, CFO; Clifford Crimmings, VP of Marketing.

■ 15463 ■ **Creative Specialties Inc.**
20969 Ventura Blvd., Ste. 21
Woodland Hills, CA 91364-2364
Phone: (818)367-2131 **Fax:** (818)367-2558
Products: Household metal, brass and porcelain bath accessories, wood towel racks, toilet seats, and lock sets. **SIC:** 5099 (Durable Goods Nec). **Sales:** $9,000,000 (2000). **Emp:** 60. **Officers:** C. Sweetman, President; Janet Peterson, Controller.

■ 15464 ■ **Crystal Clear Industries Inc.**
2 Bergen Tpk.
Ridgefield Park, NJ 07660
Phone: (201)440-4200
Products: Lead crystal and glass giftware, serveware, tabletop accessories, holloware, and lighting. **SICs:** 5023 (Homefurnishings); 5063 (Electrical Apparatus & Equipment). **Sales:** $97,400,000 (2000). **Emp:** 325. **Officers:** Abraham Lefkowitz, President; Morty Roth, CFO.

■ 15465 ■ **Custom Drapery and Blinds Inc.**
1312 Live Oak St.
Houston, TX 77003
Phone: (713)225-9211 **Fax:** (713)225-0805
Products: Custom blinds, drapes, and carpets. **SIC:** 5023 (Homefurnishings). **Est:** 1960. **Sales:** $14,000,000 (2000). **Emp:** 110. **Officers:** A.R. Klein, President; Mark Garrison, Controller.

■ 15466 ■ **Dandee Creations Ltd.**
94 Thames
Brooklyn, NY 11237-1620
Phone: (718)366-5911 **Fax:** (718)628-4902
Products: Lamps and shades. **SICs:** 5023 (Homefurnishings); 5063 (Electrical Apparatus & Equipment). **Emp:** 20. **Officers:** Mel Palchik.

■ 15467 ■ **Davic Drapery Co.**
410 S Maple Ave.
Falls Church, VA 22046-4222
Phone: (703)532-6600 **Fax:** (703)532-6601
Products: Draperies. **SIC:** 5023 (Homefurnishings). **Sales:** $820,000 (2000). **Emp:** 34. **Officers:** Sayeda Kazmi.

■ 15468 ■ **Decorative Aides Co. Inc.**
317 St. Paul Ave.
Jersey City, NJ 07306
Phone: (201)656-8813
Free: (800)875-4852 **Fax:** (201)656-0511
Products: Windows; Furniture trimmings; Knitting mills; Macrame for vertical blinds; Decorative trimming, cords, tassels, and tiebacks. **SIC:** 5023 (Homefurnishings). **Est:** 1977. **Emp:** 50. **Officers:** Terry L. Bressler, President.

■ 15469 ■ **Derr Flooring Co.**
525 Davisville Rd.
Willow Grove, PA 19090
Phone: (215)657-6300 **Fax:** (215)657-9830
Products: Flooring. **SIC:** 5023 (Homefurnishings). **Sales:** $22,000,000 (1993). **Emp:** 65. **Officers:** C.H. Derr Sr., CEO & President; W.M. Meehan, CFO.

■ 15470 ■ **W.N. Desherbinin Products Inc.**
PO Box 63
Hawleyville, CT 06440-0063
Phone: (203)791-0494
Free: (800)458-0010 **Fax:** (203)797-1385
E-mail: lampparts@wndesherbinin.com
URL: http://www.wndesherbinin.com
Products: Lamps and lighting fixtures. **SIC:** 5063 (Electrical Apparatus & Equipment). **Est:** 1940. **Sales:** $4,000,000 (2000). **Emp:** 30. **Officers:** Lawrence Greenhaus, President; Cindy Sfaelos, Vice President; Connie Kaufman, Vice President.

■ 15471 ■ **Design Center of the Americas**
1855 Griffin Rd.
Dania Beach, FL 33004
Phone: (954)920-7997
Free: (800)57D-COTA **Fax:** (954)920-8066
E-mail: dcota@dcota.com
URL: http://www.dcota.com
Products: House furnishings. **SIC:** 5023 (Homefurnishings). **Est:** 1985. **Sales:** $6,000,000 (2000). **Emp:** 26. **Officers:** Marvin I. Danto, CEO & Chairman of the Board; James H. Danto, President; Joan A. Kerns, Exec. VP & General Mgr.

■ 15472 ■ **Design/Craft Fabric Corp.**
7227 Oak Park Ave.
Niles, IL 60714
Phone: (847)647-2022
Free: (800)755-1010 **Fax:** (847)647-1015
Products: Decorative and fire retardant fabrics; Window blinds and Velcro products. **SIC:** 5023 (Homefurnishings). **Sales:** $6,000,000 (2000). **Emp:** 30. **Officers:** Mark Weiner, CEO.

■ 15473 ■ **Designer's Den Inc.**
1869 W Harvard Ave.
Atlanta, GA 30337
Phone: (404)767-8763
Free: (800)426-2644 **Fax:** (404)767-4168
E-mail: designden1@aol.com
Products: House furnishings; Professional supplies. **SIC:** 5023 (Homefurnishings). **Est:** 1969. **Sales:** $900,000 (1999). **Emp:** 12. **Officers:** Winston Jones, President.

■ 15474 ■ **Dilmaghani and Company Inc.**
540 Central Ave.
Scarsdale, NY 10583
Phone: (914)472-1700 **Fax:** (914)472-5154
URL: http://www.flyingcarpet.com
Products: Oriental, area, and custom-made rugs. **SIC:** 5023 (Homefurnishings). **Est:** 1923. **Emp:** 15. **Officers:** Dennis A. Dilmagham, President.

■ 15475 ■ **Dimock, Gould and Co.**
190 22nd St.
Moline, IL 61265
Phone: (309)797-0650 **Fax:** (309)764-9922
Products: Kitchen cabinets and marble vanity top manufacturer. **SIC:** 5023 (Homefurnishings). **Sales:** $6,000,000 (2000). **Emp:** 15. **Officers:** Gordon R. Ainsworth, President; Daryl Nelson, Treasurer & Secty.

■ 15476 ■ **Dixie Store Fixtures and Sales Company Inc.**
2425 1st Ave. N
Birmingham, AL 35203
Phone: (205)322-2442 **Fax:** (205)322-2445
Products: Light fixtures; Ceiling fans. **SICs:** 5046 (Commercial Equipment Nec); 5063 (Electrical Apparatus & Equipment). **Est:** 1921. **Sales:** $8,000,000 (2000). **Emp:** 40. **Officers:** Francis G. Cypress, CEO; M.C Kramer, Vice President; J.L Harris, Secretary.

■ 15477 ■ **D.J.H. Inc.**
PO Box 1975
Hallandale, FL 33008-1975
Phone: (305)620-1990 **Fax:** (305)620-1775
E-mail: djhmiami@aol.com
URL: http://www.djhinc.com
Products: Household products. **SICs:** 5023 (Homefurnishings); 5064 (Electrical Appliances—Television & Radio). **Est:** 1993. **Sales:** $3,500,000 (2000). **Emp:** 8. **Officers:** Marvin Tuchklaper, President.

■ 15478 ■ **Edward Don and Co.**
2500 S Harlem Ave.
North Riverside, IL 60546
Phone: (708)442-9400 **Fax:** (708)442-0436
Products: Silverware; Napkins; Ashtrays; Candles; Pots and pans; Linen. **SICs:** 5023 (Homefurnishings); 5199 (Nondurable Goods Nec); 5113 (Industrial & Personal Service Paper). **Est:** 1922. **Sales:** $250,000,000 (2000). **Emp:** 1,100. **Officers:** Robert E. Don, CEO & Chairman of the Board; James P. Jones, CFO; Paul Burgoyne, VP of Marketing.

■ 15479 ■ **Down Lite International**
106 Northeast Dr.
Loveland, OH 45140
Phone: (513)677-3696 **Fax:** (513)677-3812
Products: Down feather products, including bedding, pillows, and clothing. **SIC:** 5023 (Homefurnishings). **Est:** 1977. **Sales:** $35,000,000 (2000). **Emp:** 150. **Officers:** Larry Werthaiser, e-mail: lwerthaiser@ downlite.com.

■ 15480 ■ **Drapery Stitch of Delphos**
PO Box 307
50 Summers Ln.
Delphos, OH 45833
Phone: (419)692-3921 **Fax:** (419)692-4050
Products: Draperies. **SIC:** 5023 (Homefurnishings). **Sales:** $1,000,000 (2000). **Emp:** 49. **Officers:** Donald J. Beckmann.

■ 15481 ■ **Drulane/ Palmer Smith**
PO Box 570
Farmington, WV 26571-0570
Phone: (304)825-6697
Free: (800)825-2697 **Fax:** (304)825-1103
E-mail: drulane@mindspring.com
Products: Table, kitchen, art, and novelty glassware; Kitchenware; Bathroom accessories and fittings; Bedspreads and bedsets. **SICs:** 5023 (Homefurnishings); 5199 (Nondurable Goods Nec). **Est:** 1988. **Sales:** $2,000,000 (2000). **Emp:** 49. **Former Name:** Drulane Co.

■ 15482 ■ **Duchess Royale Inc.**
4350 S Winchester Ave.
Chicago, IL 60609-3193
Phone: (773)651-5555 **Fax:** (773)651-8081
Products: Sponges. **SIC:** 5199 (Nondurable Goods Nec). **Sales:** $1,000,000 (2000). **Emp:** 29. **Officers:** Walter F. Bogusz.

■ 15483 ■ **Andrew Dutton Co.**
284 Bodwell St.
Avon, MA 02322-1119
Phone: (508)586-4100
Free: (800)800-2511 **Fax:** (508)559-1397
URL: http://www.Andrewdutton.com
Products: Homefurnishings, including upholstery, shades, and blinds. **SIC:** 5023 (Homefurnishings). **Est:** 1880. **Sales:** $6,000,000 (2000). **Emp:** 54. **Officers:** W. Colby, President; David MacCord, Treasurer.

■ **15484** ■ **East Hampton Industries Inc.**
PO Box 5066
Ft. Lauderdale, FL 33310
Phone: (516)371-5553
Free: (800)645-1188 **Fax:** 800-323-2248
Products: Asphalt paving mix. **SIC:** 5023 (Homefurnishings). **Sales:** $500,000 (2000). **Emp:** 2. **Officers:** Arnie Beiss, President; Ian Beiss, VP of Finance.

■ **15485** ■ **Ebbtide & Associates**
60 Red Bluff Rd.
Okatie, SC 29910-3916
Phone: (803)524-7721 **Fax:** (803)522-9474
Products: Lamps and shades. **SICs:** 5023 (Homefurnishings); 5063 (Electrical Apparatus & Equipment). **Emp:** 6. **Officers:** Mary Hyland; William Hyland.

■ **15486** ■ **Eide Industries Inc.**
16215 Piuma Ave.
Cerritos, CA 90703-1528
Phone: (310)402-8335
Free: (800)422-6827 **Fax:** (310)924-2233
Products: Canvas awnings and bags. **SIC:** 5199 (Nondurable Goods Nec). **Est:** 1938. **Sales:** $4,000,000 (2000). **Emp:** 55. **Officers:** D.J. Araiza, President; Joe Belli, Dir. of Marketing & Sales.

■ **15487** ■ **A.L. Ellis Inc.**
278 Court
PO Box 6127
Plymouth, MA 02362-6127
Phone: (508)746-1941 **Fax:** (508)746-5669
Products: Curtains; Draperies; Bedspreads and bedsets. **SIC:** 5023 (Homefurnishings). **Est:** 1920. **Sales:** $5,000,000 (2000). **Emp:** 70. **Officers:** A.L. Ellis III, President & Treasurer.

■ **15488** ■ **Empress Linen Import Co.**
16400 Ventura Blvd., Ste. 331
Encino, CA 91436-2123
Phone: (818)784-9511
Products: Linens; Towels and washcloths. **SIC:** 5023 (Homefurnishings). **Emp:** 1.

■ **15489** ■ **Emser International**
8431 Santa Monica Blvd.
Los Angeles, CA 90069-4209
Phone: (213)650-2000 **Fax:** (213)654-3190
Products: Rugs; Ceramic tile; Apparel fabrics. **SICs:** 5023 (Homefurnishings); 5032 (Brick, Stone & Related Materials); 5131 (Piece Goods & Notions). **Emp:** 75.

■ **15490** ■ **Equity Industries Corp.**
5721 Bayside Rd.
Virginia Beach, VA 23455
Phone: (757)460-2483 **Fax:** (757)464-1144
Products: Clocks. **SIC:** 5094 (Jewelry & Precious Stones). **Est:** 1979. **Sales:** $10,000,000 (1999). **Emp:** 25. **Officers:** Lee Rivers, President; Keith Kibiloski, Dir. of Marketing & Sales.

■ **15491** ■ **Euro Classic Distributors Inc.**
9474 NW 13th St., Bay 76
Miami, FL 33172-2810
Phone: (305)591-3283 **Fax:** (305)591-8275
Products: Bathroom accessories and fittings. **SIC:** 5023 (Homefurnishings). **Est:** 1983. **Sales:** $25,000 (2000). **Emp:** 1. **Officers:** Rosario Dominguez, President.

■ **15492** ■ **Excalibur Cutlery & Gifts**
PO Box 1818
Eugene, OR 97440
Phone: (541)484-4779 **Fax:** (541)343-2851
Products: Cutlery and related supplies. **SIC:** 5072 (Hardware). **Est:** 1978. **Sales:** $5,000,000 (1999). **Emp:** 65. **Officers:** Charles Warren, President.

■ **15493** ■ **FABTEX Inc.**
111 Woodbine Ln.
Danville, PA 17821
Phone: (570)275-7500
Free: (800)778-2791 **Fax:** (570)275-4026
Products: Draperies; Bedspreads and bedsets; Window blinds and shades. **SIC:** 5023 (Homefurnishings). **Est:** 1986. **Sales:** $20,000,000 (2000). **Emp:** 300. **Officers:** Robert W. Snyder,

President; R. Craig Davis, Exec. VP; William P. Friese, Vice President.

■ **15494** ■ **Fallani and Cohn**
415 Rte. 303
Tappan, NY 10983
Phone: (914)683-7631
Products: Table linens. **SIC:** 5023 (Homefurnishings).

■ **15495** ■ **Federal Wholesale Company Inc.**
734 Myron St.
Hubbard, OH 44425
Phone: (330)534-1171 **Fax:** (330)534-3826
Products: Household supplies; Plastics. **SICs:** 5023 (Homefurnishings); 5162 (Plastics Materials & Basic Shapes). **Sales:** $85,000,000 (2000). **Emp:** 400.

■ **15496** ■ **Filter Fresh of Northern Virginia Inc.**
PO Box 3284
Merrifield, VA 22116
Phone: (703)207-9033
Products: Coffee urns. **SIC:** 5046 (Commercial Equipment Nec).

■ **15497** ■ **Finn Distributing Co. Inc.**
PO Box 940
Wichita, KS 67201-0940
Phone: (316)265-1624
Free: (800)876-3466 **Fax:** (316)265-1626
Products: Household furniture; Wood kitchen cabinets; Household appliances. **SICs:** 5021 (Furniture); 5064 (Electrical Appliances—Television & Radio). **Sales:** $1,200,000 (2000). **Emp:** 3. **Officers:** John Finn, President; Bob Finn, General Mgr.

■ **15498** ■ **First National Trading Company Inc.**
855 Avenue of the Americas
New York, NY 10016
Phone: (212)695-0610
Products: Quilts and household linens. **SIC:** 5023 (Homefurnishings). **Sales:** $38,000,000 (1992). **Emp:** 200. **Officers:** Paul Shen, President; George Santos, Controller.

■ **15499** ■ **Flexi-Wall Systems**
PO Box 89
Liberty, SC 29657
Phone: (864)843-3104
Free: (800)843-5394 **Fax:** (864)843-9318
E-mail: flexiwall@prodigg.net
URL: http://www.flexiwall.com
Products: Wallcovering products. **SIC:** 5198 (Paints, Varnishes & Supplies). **Est:** 1969. **Sales:** $2,000,000 (2000). **Emp:** 6. **Officers:** Jim Gilbert, Director; Crystal Dyar, Sales/Marketing Contact.

■ **15500** ■ **Flo-Pac Pacific Div.**
11690 Pacific Ave.
Fontana, CA 92335-6960
Phone: (909)681-3747 **Fax:** (909)681-4997
E-mail: pacific@flo-pac.com
URL: http://www.flo-pac.com
Products: Push brooms; Rotary brushes; Mops; Cleaning tools. **SICs:** 5199 (Nondurable Goods Nec); 5085 (Industrial Supplies). **Est:** 1931. **Sales:** $9,000,000 (2000). **Emp:** 65. **Officers:** Theodore Alm, General Mgr.; Kerry O'Brien, VP of Sales. **Former Name:** Pacific Coast Brush Company Inc.

■ **15501** ■ **Florida Clock & Supplies Inc.**
9706 SE Hwy. 441
Belleview, FL 34420
Phone: (352)245-6524
Free: (800)780-6524 **Fax:** (352)245-6013
Products: Clocks. **SIC:** 5094 (Jewelry & Precious Stones). **Est:** 1986. **Sales:** $500,000 (2000). **Emp:** 6. **Officers:** Steve Ambler, President.

■ **15502** ■ **Foge Jensen Imports**
PO Box 727
Napa, CA 94559-0727
Phone: (707)226-9123
Free: (800)788-0409 **Fax:** (707)224-6670
Products: Furniture and articles not otherwise classified, housewares and glass. **SIC:** 5023 (Homefurnishings).

■ **15503** ■ **Forbo America Inc.**
1105 N Market St., Ste. 1300
Wilmington, DE 19801
Phone: (302)427-2139
Products: Wallpaper and supplies. **SIC:** 5198 (Paints, Varnishes & Supplies). **Sales:** $26,600,000 (1993). **Emp:** 54. **Officers:** Doug Grimes, CEO; Gene Chace, CFO.

■ **15504** ■ **Forbo Wallcoverings Inc.**
3 Killdeer Ct.
PO Box 457
Bridgeport, NJ 08014
Phone: (609)467-3800 **Fax:** (609)467-4880
Products: Wallpaper. **SICs:** 5198 (Paints, Varnishes & Supplies); 5023 (Homefurnishings). **Est:** 1972. **Sales:** $8,000,000 (2000). **Emp:** 3. **Officers:** Gene Chace, President; Steve Levine, VP of Sales & Marketing.

■ **15505** ■ **Forschner Group Inc.**
1 Research Dr.
Shelton, CT 06484-6226
Phone: (203)929-5391 **Fax:** (203)929-3786
Products: Knives; Watches; Potpourri; Sunglasses. **SICs:** 5199 (Nondurable Goods Nec); 5094 (Jewelry & Precious Stones); 5023 (Homefurnishings). **Est:** 1855. **Sales:** $126,600,000 (2000). **Emp:** 198. **Officers:** James W. Kennedy, CEO & Chairman of the Board; Tod Cunningham, Exec. VP & CFO.

■ **15506** ■ **Framers On Peachtree**
2351 Peachtree Rd. NE
Atlanta, GA 30305-4147
Phone: (404)237-2888
Products: Mirror and picture frames. **SIC:** 5023 (Homefurnishings). **Emp:** 15. **Officers:** Terry Jones.

■ **15507** ■ **Freund, Freund and Company Inc.**
102 Franklin St.
New York, NY 10013-2982
Phone: (212)226-3753 **Fax:** (212)431-6869
Products: Pillow protectors; Mattress pads; Ticking; Textile converters. **SIC:** 5023 (Homefurnishings). **Est:** 1845. **Sales:** $1,300,000 (2000). **Emp:** 5. **Officers:** David J. Freund, President.

■ **15508** ■ **Frieling USA Inc.**
1812-A Center Park Dr.
Charlotte, NC 28217
Phone: (704)357-1080
Products: Plasticware utensils and dishes; Table tops. **SIC:** 5023 (Homefurnishings). **Sales:** $900,000 (2000). **Emp:** 3. **Officers:** Monica Schnacke, President.

■ **15509** ■ **Function Junction Inc.**
306 Delaware St.
Kansas City, MO 64105-1216
Phone: (816)471-6000 **Fax:** (816)471-3220
Products: Homefurnishings; Kitchenware. **SIC:** 5023 (Homefurnishings). **Est:** 1997. **Sales:** $2,000,000 (2000). **Emp:** 25. **Officers:** Steve Eberman, President.

■ **15510** ■ **B.R. Funsten and Co.**
825 Van Ness Ave., Ste. 201
San Francisco, CA 94109-7837
Phone: (415)674-0530 **Fax:** (415)674-3452
Products: Homefurnishings. **SIC:** 5023 (Homefurnishings). **Est:** 1957. **Sales:** $77,000,000 (2000). **Emp:** 140. **Officers:** Jim Funsten, President; Don Jackson, CFO.

■ **15511** ■ **Garci Plastics Industries**
1730 W 38th Pl.
Hialeah, FL 33012-7099
Phone: (305)558-8930
Free: (800)327-0066 **Fax:** (305)362-3708
Products: Plastic housewares, including ceiling panels and vertical blinds. **SICs:** 5162 (Plastics Materials & Basic Shapes); 5023 (Homefurnishings). **Sales:** $7,000,000 (2000). **Emp:** 49. **Officers:** Hugo E. Rams, Vice President; Eduardo Rams, President.

■ **15512** ■ **Fred P. Gattas Company Inc.**
5000 Summer Ave.
Memphis, TN 38122
Phone: (901)767-2930
Products: Furniture; Crystal; Diamonds. **SICs:** 5043 (Photographic Equipment & Supplies); 5023 (Homefurnishings); 5094 (Jewelry & Precious Stones).

Est: 1957. **Sales:** $28,000,000 (2000). **Emp:** 110. **Officers:** Fred Gattas Jr., President; Andrew D. Gattas, Treasurer & Secty.

■ 15513 ■ **Genesis Manufacturing, Inc.**
PO Box 252
Albertville, AL 35950
Phone: (205)878-1003
Free: (800)788-3536 **Fax:** (205)891-0513
Products: Lamp shades. **SIC:** 5023 (Homefurnishings). **Est:** 1995. **Sales:** $3,000,000 (2000). **Emp:** 39. **Officers:** George Stewart; Angie Higgins, Customer Service Mgr.; Joey Davidson, Human Resources. **Former Name:** Alabama Lamp, Inc.

■ 15514 ■ **Gibson Overseas Inc.**
2410 Yates Ave.
Los Angeles, CA 90040-1918
Phone: (323)832-8900 **Fax:** (323)832-0900
E-mail: gibsonla@aol.com
URL: http://www.gibsonusa.com
Products: Fine china; Mugs; Stainless cutlery; Household glassware; Dinnerware. **SIC:** 5023 (Homefurnishings). **Est:** 1979. **Emp:** 200. **Officers:** Soloman Gabbay.

■ 15515 ■ **Grabarczyk Associates**
578 San Remo Cir.
Inverness, FL 34450
Phone: (352)344-1449 **Fax:** (352)344-8132
Products: Glassware. **SIC:** 5023 (Homefurnishings).

■ 15516 ■ **Gregg Manufacturing Co.**
143 Tuttle Ave.
Fredericktown, OH 43019-1029
Phone: (740)694-4926
Products: Lamps; Lighting fixtures. **SICs:** 5023 (Homefurnishings); 5063 (Electrical Apparatus & Equipment). **Sales:** $1,000,000 (2000). **Emp:** 49. **Officers:** R. S. Gregg.

■ 15517 ■ **Haleyville Drapery Manufacturing**
PO Box 695
Haleyville, AL 35565-9201
Phone: (205)486-9257 **Fax:** (205)486-4788
Products: Drapery. **SIC:** 5023 (Homefurnishings). **Sales:** $30,000,000 (2000). **Emp:** 499. **Officers:** Robin Johnson.

■ 15518 ■ **Hanco M. Handelsman Co.**
1323 S Michigan Ave.
Chicago, IL 60605
Phone: (312)427-0784
Free: (800)621-4454 **Fax:** (312)427-8787
Products: Canvas bags; Drawstring sacks; Aprons. **SIC:** 5023 (Homefurnishings). **Est:** 1918. **Officers:** Stuart Berger, President.

■ 15519 ■ **James G. Hardy and Company Inc.**
352 7th Ave., Ste. 1223
New York, NY 10001
Phone: (212)689-6680 **Fax:** (212)686-1827
Products: Linens; Towels; Robes; Slippers. **SICs:** 5023 (Homefurnishings); 5139 (Footwear); 5136 (Men's/Boys' Clothing); 5137 (Women's/Children's Clothing). **Est:** 1924. **Sales:** $10,000,000 (1999). **Emp:** 30. **Officers:** Marc Gudowitz, Vice President, e-mail: mghardy@earthlink.net.

■ 15520 ■ **Harold Import Company Inc.**
140 LeHigh Ave.
Lakewood, NJ 08701
Phone: (732)367-2800
Products: Kitchen tools and utensils. **SIC:** 5023 (Homefurnishings).

■ 15521 ■ **Hawaiian Housewares, Ltd.**
99-1305 Koaha Pl.
Aiea, HI 96701
Phone: (808)453-8000 **Fax:** (808)456-5043
Products: Housewares; Pet supplies; Health and beauty care. **SICs:** 5023 (Homefurnishings); 5013 (Motor Vehicle Supplies & New Parts); 5072 (Hardware); 5122 (Drugs, Proprietaries & Sundries).

■ 15522 ■ **Haywin Textile Products Inc.**
PO Box 229013
Brooklyn, NY 11222-9013
Phone: (718)384-0317 **Fax:** (718)387-7179
Products: Sheets and towels. **SIC:** 5023 (Homefurnishings). **Sales:** $20,000,000 (2000). **Emp:** 30. **Officers:** Alfred Haft, President.

■ 15523 ■ **Heines Custom Draperies**
27223 Hwy. Blvd.
Katy, TX 77450-1040
Phone: (281)391-3103 **Fax:** (281)391-6878
Products: Draperies. **SIC:** 5023 (Homefurnishings). **Sales:** $1,500,000 (2000). **Emp:** 49. **Officers:** Victor Grisbee.

■ 15524 ■ **The Helman Group Ltd.**
1701 Pacific Ave., No. 280
Oxnard, CA 93033
Phone: (805)487-7772
Free: (800)217-1958 **Fax:** (805)487-9975
URL: http://www.thehelmangroup.com
Products: Housewares. **SICs:** 5023 (Homefurnishings); 5074 (Plumbing & Hydronic Heating Supplies). **Est:** 1969. **Sales:** $20,000,000 (1999). **Emp:** 30. **Officers:** Barry Helman, CEO; Andrew Helman, President; Gregg Bond, President. **Former Name:** LA Fads Inc.

■ 15525 ■ **J.L. Henderson and Co.**
2533 Peralta St.
Oakland, CA 94607-1795
Phone: (510)839-1900 **Fax:** (510)839-1944
Products: Food; Housewares, including dishes and towels; Boating equipment and supplies, including engines. **SICs:** 5141 (Groceries—General Line); 5023 (Homefurnishings). **Est:** 1941. **Sales:** $37,800,000 (2000). **Emp:** 72. **Officers:** M. John Henderson, President & Chairman of the Board; Don Wycoff, CFO; Tim Henderson, Sales Mgr.

■ 15526 ■ **Hercules Sales, Inc.**
1465 Durham Hwy.
PO Box 1057
Roxboro, NC 27573
Phone: (919)597-2275 **Fax:** (919)597-5200
Products: Kitchen and bath products. **SIC:** 5023 (Homefurnishings).

■ 15527 ■ **Heritage Lace Inc.**
PO Box 328
Pella, IA 50219
Phone: (515)628-4949 **Fax:** (515)628-1689
Products: Ready-made lace curtains, lace table cloths, place mats, runners, doilies, and curtain lace fabric. **SICs:** 5023 (Homefurnishings); 5131 (Piece Goods & Notions). **Sales:** $52,000,000 (2000). **Emp:** 140. **Officers:** Mark De Cook, President.

■ 15528 ■ **Hi-Jac Corporation**
PO Box 132
Ft. Payne, AL 35967-0132
Phone: (205)845-0461
Products: Coasters. **SIC:** 5023 (Homefurnishings). **Officers:** Evelyn Davis, President.

■ 15529 ■ **Hoboken Wood Flooring Corp.**
70 Demarest Dr.
Wayne, NJ 07470-6702
Phone: (973)694-2888 **Fax:** (973)694-6885
Products: Wood and vinyl floor coverings. **SICs:** 5031 (Lumber, Plywood & Millwork); 5023 (Homefurnishings). **Sales:** $77,000,000 (1994). **Emp:** 190. **Officers:** John Sakosits, Chairman of the Board; Thomas Dougherty, VP & CFO.

■ 15530 ■ **Home Fasions Distributor**
655 Post Rd.
Wells, ME 04090
Phone: (207)646-3437
Products: Towels and linens. **SIC:** 5023 (Homefurnishings).

■ 15531 ■ **Home Interiors and Gifts Inc.**
4550 Spring Valley Rd.
Dallas, TX 75244-3705
Phone: (972)386-1000 **Fax:** (972)386-1065
Products: Decorative home accessories. **SIC:** 5023 (Homefurnishings). **Emp:** 1,000.

■ 15532 ■ **HomeBase Inc.**
3345 Michelson Dr.
Irvine, CA 92612-0650
Phone: (949)442-5000
URL: http://www.homebase.com
Products: Home improvement products; Food and general products. **SICs:** 5039 (Construction Materials Nec); 5031 (Lumber, Plywood & Millwork); 5141 (Groceries—General Line); 5149 (Groceries & Related Products Nec). **Sales:** $1,500,000 (1999). **Emp:** 10,000. **Officers:** Herbert J. Zarkin, CEO & President.

■ 15533 ■ **Horizon West Draperies**
4613 Palm Dr.
La Canada, CA 91011-2012
Phone: (213)589-6242 **Fax:** (213)589-6247
Products: Commercial and residential draperies. **SIC:** 5023 (Homefurnishings). **Emp:** 99. **Officers:** Neal Elisco.

■ 15534 ■ **Horn EB Replacement Service**
429 Washington St.
Boston, MA 02108-5278
Phone: (617)542-7752
Free: (800)835-0297 **Fax:** (617)542-2932
E-mail: ebhorn@compvserve.com
Products: Jewelry and watches; Figurines; Pens; Sunglasses; Clocks; China; Silver. **SICs:** 5094 (Jewelry & Precious Stones); 5048 (Ophthalmic Goods); 5023 (Homefurnishings); 5199 (Nondurable Goods Nec). **Officers:** Richard Finn, President.

■ 15535 ■ **Houseware Warehouse Inc.**
PO Box 1330
Edgewater, FL 32132-1330
Phone: (904)423-7848 **Fax:** (904)423-2599
Products: Housewares. **SIC:** 5023 (Homefurnishings). **Est:** 1987. **Sales:** $2,500,000 (2000). **Emp:** 8. **Officers:** Chuck Theroux, President; Michelle Theroux, Vice President.

■ 15536 ■ **Hunter and Company of North Carolina**
PO Box 2363
High Point, NC 27261
Phone: (336)883-4161
Free: (800)523-8387 **Fax:** (336)889-3270
URL: http://www.hunterwallpaper.com
Products: Wallcoverings and blinds. **SICs:** 5198 (Paints, Varnishes & Supplies); 5023 (Homefurnishings). **Est:** 1949. **Sales:** $9,000,000 (1999). **Emp:** 37. **Officers:** W.H. McInnis, Chairman of the Board; James L. McInnis, Treasurer & Secty.; Aaron (Rocky) Rice, President.

■ 15537 ■ **Ichikoh Manufacturing Inc.**
6601 Midland
Shelbyville, KY 40065
Phone: (502)633-4936 **Fax:** (502)633-6251
Products: Mirrors. **SIC:** 5023 (Homefurnishings). **Emp:** 300.

■ 15538 ■ **In Products Inc.**
4601 W 47th St.
Chicago, IL 60632-4801
Phone: (773)585-9779 **Fax:** (773)585-9812
Products: Lamps. **SICs:** 5023 (Homefurnishings); 5063 (Electrical Apparatus & Equipment). **Est:** 1970. **Emp:** 49. **Officers:** Joe Ramski.

■ 15539 ■ **Incentive Associates Inc.**
6803 W 64th St., Ste. 114
Shawnee Mission, KS 66202
Phone: (913)722-2848 **Fax:** (913)722-6854
E-mail: associate@ix.netcom.com
Products: Clocks and watches; Wenger swiss army knives; Clothing with logos; Prepaid phone cards; Cameras; Tools; Blankets; Golf equipment; Plastic cups; Umbrellas; Towels; Crystal. **SICs:** 5064 (Electrical Appliances—Television & Radio); 5136 (Men's/Boys' Clothing); 5137 (Women's/Children's Clothing); 5199 (Nondurable Goods Nec); 5091 (Sporting & Recreational Goods). **Est:** 1983. **Emp:** 4. **Officers:** John Buckley, President.

■ 15540 ■ **Indiana Wholesalers Inc.**
PO Box 5245
Evansville, IN 47716
Phone: (812)476-1373
Products: Interior home improvement supplies. **SICs:** 5023 (Homefurnishings); 5031 (Lumber, Plywood & Millwork). **Est:** 1942. **Sales:** $5,000,000 (2000). **Emp:** 20. **Officers:** Charlie Reising, President.

■ 15541 ■ **International Tile and Supply Corp.**
1288 S La Brea Ave.
Los Angeles, CA 90019
Phone: (213)931-1761 **Fax:** (213)935-8667
Products: Wall tile; Ceramic floor tile. **SIC:** 5032 (Brick, Stone & Related Materials).

■ 15542 ■ **Ivystone Group**
528 Trestle Pl.
Downingtown, PA 19335
Phone: (610)873-1040
Free: (800)327-9036 **Fax:** (610)873-1138
Products: Glassware. **SIC:** 5023 (Homefurnishings).

■ 15543 ■ **Jacobs Trading Co.**
901 N 3rd St.
Minneapolis, MN 55401
Phone: (612)349-2300 **Fax:** (612)349-2390
E-mail: operator@jacobstrading.com
URL: http://www.customerreturns.com
Products: General merchandise; Customer returns; Excess; Closeout. **SICs:** 5199 (Nondurable Goods Nec); 5199 (Nondurable Goods Nec). **Est:** 1967. **Sales:** $100,000,000 (2000). **Emp:** 30. **Officers:** Andy Estoclet, CEO; Steve Mocol, CFO.

■ 15544 ■ **Jaunty Co., Inc.**
1850 Beverly Blvd.
Los Angeles, CA 90057
Phone: (213)413-3333
Free: (800)323-3342 **Fax:** (213)413-0828
E-mail: info@eddia.com
URL: http://www.eddia.com
Products: Rugs; Porcelain. **SIC:** 5023 (Homefurnishings). **Est:** 1979. **Sales:** $10,000,000 (2000). **Emp:** 18. **Officers:** Eddie Mirarooni, President; Kami Navid, Marketing Mgr.

■ 15545 ■ **Jenkins Metal Corp. Hunting Classics Limited Div.**
PO Box 2089
Gastonia, NC 28053
Phone: (704)867-6394 **Fax:** (704)867-0491
Products: Knives. **SIC:** 5091 (Sporting & Recreational Goods). **Sales:** $7,000,000 (2000). **Emp:** 100. **Officers:** Robert B. Jenkin Jr., President; Sonny Willis, Controller.

■ 15546 ■ **K & T Lamp & Shade Company Inc.**
2860 State Rte. 121 N
Mayfield, KY 42066
Phone: (502)247-5762 **Fax:** (502)247-9688
Products: Lamps; Lampshades. **SICs:** 5023 (Homefurnishings); 5063 (Electrical Apparatus & Equipment). **Est:** 1969. **Sales:** $3,000,000 (2000). **Emp:** 14. **Officers:** Dan Burgess; James Burgess.

■ 15547 ■ **K-Tel International (USA) Inc.**
2605 Fernbrook Ln. N
Minneapolis, MN 55447
Phone: (612)509-9416 **Fax:** (612)559-6803
Products: Consumer products including, massagers and food product machinery. **SICs:** 5064 (Electrical Appliances—Television & Radio); 5099 (Durable Goods Nec); 5084 (Industrial Machinery & Equipment). **Sales:** $9,000,000 (2000). **Emp:** 65. **Officers:** David Weiner, President.

■ 15548 ■ **Key-Duncan Wallcoverings**
1729 Research Dr.
Louisville, KY 40299
Phone: (502)491-5080 **Fax:** (502)491-5085
Products: Wall coverings and supplies. **SIC:** 5198 (Paints, Varnishes & Supplies).

■ 15549 ■ **King Koil Sleep Product**
PO Box 830067
San Antonio, TX 78283-0067
Phone: (972)225-4300 **Fax:** (972)225-4330
Products: Bedding. **SIC:** 5023 (Homefurnishings). **Sales:** $3,000,000 (2000). **Emp:** 33. **Officers:** Carl McCalvin.

■ 15550 ■ **Kitchen Specialties Inc.**
7921A W Broad St., Ste. 133
Richmond, VA 23294
Phone: (804)965-0860
Products: Kitchen supplies. **SIC:** 5023 (Homefurnishings).

■ 15551 ■ **Kitchens Inc. of Paducah**
905 Harrison St.
Paducah, KY 42001-1827
Phone: (502)442-9496 **Fax:** (502)442-9497
Products: Kitchenware; Bathroom accessories and fittings. **SICs:** 5023 (Homefurnishings); 5074 (Plumbing & Hydronic Heating Supplies); 5072 (Hardware). **Officers:** F. Jones, President.

■ 15552 ■ **Kittrich Corp.**
14555 Alondra Blvd.
La Mirada, CA 90638-5602
Phone: (213)582-0665 **Fax:** (213)581-3742
Products: Vertical blinds. **SIC:** 5023 (Homefurnishings). **Emp:** 49.

■ 15553 ■ **Kmart Corp.**
3100 W Big Beaver Rd.
Troy, MI 48084
Phone: (248)643-1000
Products: General merchandise, including household items, clothing, sporting goods, and gifts and novelties. **SICs:** 5023 (Homefurnishings); 5136 (Men's/Boys' Clothing); 5137 (Women's/Children's Clothing); 5091 (Sporting & Recreational Goods); 5199 (Nondurable Goods Nec).

■ 15554 ■ **Koch-Bailey Associates**
302 W 5400 S, Ste. 109
Salt Lake City, UT 84107-8232
Phone: (801)261-5802
Free: (800)658-5963 **Fax:** (801)261-8722
Products: Giftware. **SIC:** 5023 (Homefurnishings). **Est:** 1978. **Emp:** 25. **Officers:** Glen R. Smith, Agency President; William E. Budge, VP of Sales. **Former Name:** Koch-Bailey & Associates.

■ 15555 ■ **Koch-Bailey and Associates**
9226 N 5th Ave.
Phoenix, AZ 85021
Phone: (602)870-9429
Free: (800)658-5963 **Fax:** (602)371-8387
Products: Household items. **SIC:** 5023 (Homefurnishings).

■ 15556 ■ **Koval Marketing Inc.**
11208 47th Ave. W
Mukilteo, WA 98275
Phone: (425)347-4249 **Fax:** (425)347-2368
Products: Home and outdoor products; Pet supplies and food; Office products. **SICs:** 5023 (Homefurnishings); 5099 (Durable Goods Nec); 5199 (Nondurable Goods Nec); 5112 (Stationery & Office Supplies). **Sales:** $100,000,000 (2000). **Emp:** 35. **Officers:** Roy Koval, Owner; Chuck Williamson, President.

■ 15557 ■ **Kraft Hardware Inc.**
306 E 61st St.
New York, NY 10021
Phone: (212)838-2214 **Fax:** (212)644-9254
Products: Decorative bathroom accessories. **SIC:** 5023 (Homefurnishings). **Sales:** $7,500,000 (2000). **Emp:** 49. **Officers:** Stan Saperstein.

■ 15558 ■ **Kwik-Affix Products**
5942 Richard St.
Jacksonville, FL 32216
Phone: (904)448-1180
Free: (800)685-5945 **Fax:** (904)448-1182
Products: Materials for window coverings. **SIC:** 5023 (Homefurnishings). **Est:** 1982. **Emp:** 8. **Officers:** Herbert Gleinser, President.

■ 15559 ■ **Langlois Stores Inc.**
3000 Henry St.
Muskegon, MI 49441-4016
Phone: (616)733-2528
Free: (800)606-7600 **Fax:** (616)733-0545
Products: Electrical appliances, including televisions and radios; Furniture; Hot tubs. **SICs:** 5064 (Electrical Appliances—Television & Radio); 5091 (Sporting & Recreational Goods); 5021 (Furniture). **Officers:** Robert Langlois, President.

■ 15560 ■ **Homer Laughlin China Co.**
Harrison St.
Newell, WV 26050-1299
Phone: (304)387-1300
Free: (800)452-4462 **Fax:** (304)389-0593
Products: China. **SIC:** 5023 (Homefurnishings). **Est:** 1871. **Emp:** 800.

■ 15561 ■ **Lawrin Lighting, Inc.**
PO Box 2128
Columbus, MS 39704-2128
Phone: (601)289-1711
Free: (800)824-5376 **Fax:** (601)289-6685
Products: Lamps and shades. **SICs:** 5023 (Homefurnishings); 5063 (Electrical Apparatus & Equipment). **Est:** 1946. **Emp:** 49. **Officers:** Scott Berry, CEO; Phil Williams, President.

■ 15562 ■ **Le Creuset of America Inc.**
PO Box 575
Yemassee, SC 29945
Phone: (803)943-4308
Products: Cast iron cookware. **SIC:** 5046 (Commercial Equipment Nec). **Est:** 1977. **Sales:** $12,000,000 (2000). **Emp:** 50. **Officers:** Finn Schjorring, CEO; Faye Gooding, VP of Finance & Admin.; John McKeever, VP of Sales.

■ 15563 ■ **Lee Jay Bed and Bath**
1 Federal St. #Hanify
Boston, MA 02110
Products: Bed sheets; Comforters; Towels. **SIC:** 5023 (Homefurnishings).

■ 15564 ■ **Geo Zolton Lefton Co.**
3622 S Morgan St.
Chicago, IL 60609
Phone: (773)254-4344
Free: (800)938-1800 **Fax:** (773)254-4545
URL: www.gzlefton.com
Products: China. **SIC:** 5023 (Homefurnishings). **Est:** 1941. **Sales:** $20,000,000 (2000). **Emp:** 60. **Officers:** George Z. Lefton, CEO; Steven Lefton Sharp, CEO; Chris Sebastian, Treasurer; Mark Holmen, VP of Sales, e-mail: mholmen@leftonco.com; Theresa Fredericks, Customer Service Contact, e-mail: tfredericks@leftonco.com; Chris Sebastian, Human Resources Contact, e-mail: csebast@leftonco.com.

■ 15565 ■ **Geo H. Lehleitner and Company Inc.**
202 Crofton Rd.
Kenner, LA 70062
Phone: (504)466-6678
Products: Home furnishings. **SIC:** 5023 (Homefurnishings).

■ 15566 ■ **Leifheit Sales Inc.**
1140 Broadway, No. 502
New York, NY 10001
Phone: (212)679-5260
Products: Plastic goods, including can openers. **SIC:** 5023 (Homefurnishings).

■ 15567 ■ **Harris Levy, Inc.**
278 Grand St.
New York, NY 10002-4488
Phone: (212)226-3102
Free: (800)221-7750 **Fax:** (212)334-9360
Products: Kitchen towels; Down comforters. **SIC:** 5023 (Homefurnishings). **Est:** 1894. **Emp:** 49. **Officers:** Robert L. Levy.

■ 15568 ■ **Lifetime Hoan Corp.**
1 Merrick Ave.
Westbury, NY 11590
Phone: (516)683-6000 **Fax:** (516)683-6116
Products: Household products including cutlery,

kitchenware and cutting boards. **SICs:** 5072 (Hardware); 5023 (Homefurnishings). **Sales:** $100,000,000 (2000). **Emp:** 527. **Officers:** Milton L. Cohen, President & Chairman of the Board; Jeffrey Siegel, President.

■ 15569 ■ **Lipper International Inc.**
230 5th Ave.
New York, NY 10001
Phone: (212)686-6076 **Fax:** (212)889-8657
Products: Woodenware and porcelain. **SIC:** 5023 (Homefurnishings). **Est:** 1947. **Emp:** 38. **Officers:** Amy Lipper, President; Joseph Leighton, Vice President; Laura Lipper Richardson, Vice President.

■ 15570 ■ **Little Rock Drapery Co.**
7501 Kanis Rd.
PO Box 55003
Little Rock, AR 72215
Phone: (501)227-5900
Free: (800)482-9956 **Fax:** (501)954-9540
Products: Custom-made rollershades; Laminated shades; Draperies; Drapery hardware. **SICs:** 5023 (Homefurnishings); 5072 (Hardware). **Est:** 1967. **Emp:** 2. **Officers:** Walter H. Ahring III, Warehouse Mgr.

■ 15571 ■ **Loomcraft Textiles Inc.**
645 N Lakeview Pkwy.
Vernon Hills, IL 60061
Phone: (847)680-0000
Free: (800)621-5588 **Fax:** (847)680-0092
E-mail: loom645@aol.com
Products: Draperies; Furniture and automotive fabrics. **SICs:** 5131 (Piece Goods & Notions); 5023 (Homefurnishings). **Est:** 1950. **Sales:** $41,300,000 (1999). **Emp:** 60. **Officers:** Ron Frankel, President; Andrew Goldwasser, Sales/Marketing Contact.

■ 15572 ■ **J.M. Lynne Company Inc.**
PO Box 1010
Smithtown, NY 11787
Phone: (516)582-4300 **Fax:** (516)582-4112
Products: Wallpaper. **SIC:** 5198 (Paints, Varnishes & Supplies). **Sales:** $21,000,000 (1994). **Emp:** 100. **Officers:** Jonathan Landsberg, President.

■ 15573 ■ **William P. Mahne Company Inc.**
1920 S Vandeventer
St. Louis, MO 63103
Fax: (314)771-2094
Products: Silverware and plated ware; Flatware; China. **SIC:** 5023 (Homefurnishings). **Est:** 1946. **Sales:** $2,000,000 (2000). **Emp:** 10. **Officers:** William R. Mahne, CEO; Jan Bettison, Treasurer.

■ 15574 ■ **Malik International Enterprises Ltd.**
Merchandise-Mart
PO Box 3194
Chicago, IL 60654
Phone: (773)334-6785 **Fax:** (773)334-6785
Products: Seafood; Housewares. **SICs:** 5023 (Homefurnishings); 5146 (Fish & Seafoods). **Officers:** Raymond H. Malik, President & CEO.

■ 15575 ■ **Maran-Wurzell Glass and Mirror Co.**
2300 E Slauson Ave.
Huntington Park, CA 90255
Phone: (213)233-4256 **Fax:** (213)581-7212
Products: Glass and mirrors. **SICs:** 5023 (Homefurnishings); 5039 (Construction Materials Nec). **Est:** 1939. **Sales:** $11,000,000 (2000). **Emp:** 60. **Officers:** J. Weiser, President; Charlotte Harlow, Controller.

■ 15576 ■ **Marburn Stores Inc.**
225 Walker St.
CliffsiDe Park, NJ 07010
Phone: (201)943-0222
Products: Domestic curtains and linens. **SIC:** 5023 (Homefurnishings). **Est:** 1956. **Sales:** $19,000,000 (1999). **Emp:** 200. **Officers:** B.C. Hinden, President.

■ 15577 ■ **Marcus Brothers**
1755 McDonald Ave.
Brooklyn, NY 11230-6906
Phones: (718)645-4565 (718)998-0218
Free: (800)862-7287 **Fax:** (718)376-0385
E-mail: marcusbros@juno.com
URL: http://www.members.aol.com/charlie15/marcus1.htm
Products: Infant crib blankets, comforters, crib sheets, and gift sets. **SICs:** 5023 (Homefurnishings); 5137 (Women's/Children's Clothing). **Est:** 1921. **Sales:** $2,000,000 (1999). **Emp:** 50. **Officers:** S. Marcus.

■ 15578 ■ **Markuse Corp.**
10 Wheeling Ave.
Woburn, MA 01801
Phone: (617)932-9444 **Fax:** (617)933-1930
Products: Hand tools, jewelry, metal goods, furniture and articles not otherwise classified, housewares and glass. **SIC:** 5023 (Homefurnishings).

■ 15579 ■ **Martexport Inc.**
654 Madison Ave., Ste. 1409
New York, NY 10021
Phone: (212)935-0300 **Fax:** (212)689-3886
Products: Home furnishings; Gifts and novelties. **SICs:** 5023 (Homefurnishings); 5199 (Nondurable Goods Nec). **Sales:** $20,000,000 (1994). **Emp:** 10. **Officers:** Martin Kalkstein, President; Jack Martin, Vice President.

■ 15580 ■ **Masterpiece Crystal**
PO Drawer A
Jane Lew, WV 26378
Phone: (304)884-7841
Free: (800)624-3114 **Fax:** (304)884-7842
Products: Pressed and blown glassware. **SIC:** 5023 (Homefurnishings). **Sales:** $2,000,000 (2000). **Emp:** 35. **Officers:** Bill Hogan. **Former Name:** Mason Glassware Co.

■ 15581 ■ **McArthur Towels, Inc.**
700 Moore St.
Box 448
Baraboo, WI 53913
Phone: (608)356-8922
Free: (800)356-9168 **Fax:** (608)356-7587
E-mail: sales@mcarthur-towels.com
URL: http://www.mcarthur-towels.com
Products: Athletic, licensed, and custom towels; Gift items. **SICs:** 5023 (Homefurnishings); 5091 (Sporting & Recreational Goods). **Est:** 1885. **Sales:** $25,000,000 (1999). **Emp:** 65. **Officers:** Gregg H. McArthur, President; Thomas Ryter, Sales/Marketing Contact, e-mail: tryter@mcarthur-towels.com.

■ 15582 ■ **McArthur Towels Inc.**
700 Moore St.
Baraboo, WI 53913
Phone: (608)356-8922
Free: (800)356-9168 **Fax:** (608)356-7587
Products: Household items. **SIC:** 5023 (Homefurnishings). **Sales:** $16,000,000 (2000). **Emp:** 40.

■ 15583 ■ **McCarthy Drapery Company Inc.**
909 Glencastle Way
Raleigh, NC 27606-3475
Phone: (919)834-1928
Products: Draperies. **SIC:** 5023 (Homefurnishings). **Sales:** $10,000,000 (2000). **Emp:** 99.

■ 15584 ■ **H.J. McCarty & Son**
PO Box 1359
Newburyport, MA 01950-8357
Phone: (978)462-8111
Products: Draperies; Drapery hardware; Drapery material; Shades, blinds and curtain and drapery rods, poles, and other hardware. **SICs:** 5023 (Homefurnishings); 5072 (Hardware). **Est:** 1866. **Sales:** $5,000,000 (2000). **Officers:** H.J. McCarty, Owner.

■ 15585 ■ **Messina and Zucker Inc.**
295 5th Ave.
New York, NY 10016
Phone: (212)889-3750 **Fax:** (212)779-1060
E-mail: sales@zucker.net
URL: http://www.messinaandzucker.com
Products: Blankets, bedspreads, comforters, and sheets; Tablecloths; Towels; Pillows; Rugs; Kitchen textiles. **SIC:** 5023 (Homefurnishings). **Est:** 1967. **Officers:** C.S. Zucker, President, e-mail: clyde@zucker.net.

■ 15586 ■ **Metro Marketing Inc.**
2851 E Las Hermanas St.
East Rancho Dominguez, CA 90221
Phone: (310)898-1888 **Fax:** (310)898-1937
Products: Household supplies. **SIC:** 5023 (Homefurnishings). **Est:** 1976. **Emp:** 49. **Officers:** Salim Rajan; Warren Kashuk. **Doing Business As:** Metro/Thebe, Inc.

■ 15587 ■ **Meyda Tiffany**
One Meyda Fine Pl.
55 Oriskany Blvd.
Yorkville, NY 13495
Phone: (315)768-3711
Free: (800)222-4009 **Fax:** (315)768-1428
E-mail: salesteam@meyda.com
URL: http://www.meyda.com
Products: Tiffany lamps and decorative lighting. **SICs:** 5023 (Homefurnishings); 5063 (Electrical Apparatus & Equipment). **Est:** 1974. **Emp:** 75. **Officers:** Robert Cohen, President.

■ 15588 ■ **Mid-America Export Inc.**
9650 E Colfax Ave.
Aurora, CO 80010-5010
Phone: (303)364-3800 **Fax:** (303)366-1110
Products: Kitchen equipment. **SIC:** 5023 (Homefurnishings). **Officers:** Ki Cho, President.

■ 15589 ■ **Misco Shawnee Inc.**
2200 Forte Ct.
Maryland Heights, MO 63043
Phone: (314)739-3337 **Fax:** (314)739-8163
Products: Flooring. **SIC:** 5023 (Homefurnishings). **Sales:** $38,000,000 (2000). **Emp:** 100. **Officers:** Courtney A. Gould, Chairman of the Board; James Gould, President & CFO.

■ 15590 ■ **Mottahedeh and Co.**
225 5th Ave.
New York, NY 10010
Phone: (212)685-3050
Free: (800)242-3050 **Fax:** (212)889-9483
URL: http://www.mottahedeh.com
Products: China; Silverware; Brassware; Porcelain ware. **SIC:** 5023 (Homefurnishings). **Est:** 1924. **Officers:** Wendy Kvalheim, President; Pauline Kelbly, Sr. VP of Sales.

■ 15591 ■ **Mr. Hardwoods**
210 Commerce Way
Jupiter, FL 33458
Phone: (561)746-9663
Free: (800)226-9664 **Fax:** (561)743-0447
Products: Floorcovering equipment and supplies. **SIC:** 5023 (Homefurnishings).

■ 15592 ■ **Neuwirth Co.**
225 5th Ave.
New York, NY 10010.
Phone: (212)685-6420
Free: (800)638-9478 **Fax:** (212)685-6684
E-mail: neuwirthco@worldnet.att.net
Products: Glassware. **SIC:** 5023 (Homefurnishings). **Est:** 1930. **Sales:** $5,000,000 (2000). **Emp:** 8. **Officers:** Robert A. Neuwirth, President; David A. Neuwirth, Dir. of Marketing & Sales.

■ 15593 ■ **New Options on Waste Inc.**
877 S Pearl St.
Albany, NY 12202
Phone: (518)433-0033
Products: Household products; Debris recycling. **SIC:** 5093 (Scrap & Waste Materials). **Sales:** $20,000,000 (1994). **Emp:** 55. **Officers:** Richard Deitz, President.

■ **15594** ■ **Newell P.R. Ltd.**
PO Box 3379
Carolina, PR 00984-3379
Phone: (787)769-8885 **Fax:** (787)768-6610
Products: Glassware; Hardware; Writing instrurments;
Office supplies; Picture frames. **SICs:** 5023
(Homefurnishings); 5112 (Stationery & Office
Supplies); 5072 (Hardware). **Est:** 1968. **Sales:**
$13,000,000 (2000). **Emp:** 26. **Officers:** Hiram
Va'zquas, General Mgr.

■ **15595** ■ **Nolarec Industries, Inc.**
Pinehurst Rd.
PO Box 1065
Aberdeen, NC 28315
Phone: (919)944-7187
Products: Lamps. **SICs:** 5023 (Homefurnishings);
5063 (Electrical Apparatus & Equipment). **Sales:**
$2,000,000 (2000). **Emp:** 49. **Officers:** Charles
Stevens.

■ **15596** ■ **Noonoo Rug Company Inc.**
100 Park Plaza Dr.
Secaucus, NJ 07094
Phone: (201)330-0101 **Fax:** (201)330-8805
E-mail: noonoorug@aol.com
URL: http://www.noonoo.com
Products: Hand knotted carpet collections from India,
Pakistan, and Nepal. **SIC:** 5023 (Homefurnishings).
Est: 1930. **Emp:** 11. **Officers:** Eugene D. Newman,
President, e-mail: edncpwc@aol.com.

■ **15597** ■ **Nordic Products Inc.**
2215 Merrill Creek Pky.
Everett, WA 98203
Phone: (425)261-1000 **Fax:** (425)261-1001
Products: Kitchen gadgets. **SIC:** 5023
(Homefurnishings). **Est:** 1974. **Emp:** 50.

■ **15598** ■ **Noritake Company Inc.**
75 Seaview Dr.
Secaucus, NJ 07094-1806
Phone: (201)319-0600
Free: (800)562-1991 **Fax:** (201)319-1954
Products: Tableware and china. **SIC:** 5023
(Homefurnishings). **Sales:** $51,000,000 (1993). **Emp:**
200. **Officers:** K. Tomita, President; T. Seno,
Controller.

■ **15599** ■ **Noury and Sons Ltd.**
5 Sampson St.
Saddle Brook, NJ 07663-5911
Phone: (201)867-6900 **Fax:** (201)368-0739
E-mail: ifo@nourijon.com
URL: http://www.nourison.com
Products: Oriental rugs. **SIC:** 5023 (Homefurnishings).
Est: 1980. **Sales:** $45,000,000 (2000). **Emp:** 100.
Officers: Paul Peykar, President.

■ **15600** ■ **Novelty Cord and Tassel Company
Inc.**
107-20 Ave. D
Brooklyn, NY 11236-1911
Phone: (718)272-8800 **Fax:** (718)272-0446
Products: Trimmings, drapery tie backs, and roller
shade accessories. **SIC:** 5023 (Homefurnishings). **Est:**
1906. **Emp:** 50. **Officers:** Charles J. Imershein,
President; William L. Imershein, CEO; Arthur
Ackerman, Sales/Marketing Contact.

■ **15601** ■ **Ohio Kitchen and Bath**
19000 Miles Ave.
Cleveland, OH 44128
Phone: (216)587-1222 **Fax:** (216)587-1531
Products: Plumbing supplies; Counter tops; Cabinets;
Appliances. **SICs:** 5023 (Homefurnishings); 5064
(Electrical Appliances—Television & Radio); 5074
(Plumbing & Hydronic Heating Supplies). **Est:** 1929.
Sales: $9,000,000 (2000). **Emp:** 40. **Officers:** Dale
Kramer, President.

■ **15602** ■ **Orrefors Inc.**
140 Bradford Dr.
Berlin, NJ 08009
Phone: (609)768-5400 **Fax:** (609)768-9726
Products: Swedish crystal, including glasses, giftware,
and bowls. **SICs:** 5023 (Homefurnishings); 5199
(Nondurable Goods Nec). **Sales:** $19,000,000 (2000).
Emp: 75. **Officers:** Richard Kaplan, President; William

Dougherty, VP of Finance; Robin Spink, Marketing
Mgr.; Rodrick Bennett, Dir. of Information Systems.

■ **15603** ■ **Ostrow Textile L.L.C.**
PO Box 10550
Rock Hill, SC 29731
Phone: (803)324-4284 **Fax:** (803)324-7942
Products: Household decor and linens, including bed
sheets, curtains, and bath towels. **SIC:** 5023
(Homefurnishings). **Est:** 1912. **Sales:** $46,000,000
(2000). **Emp:** 520. **Officers:** Joel J. Ostrow, President;
Broni Holcombe, Controller; Larry Simon, Dir. of
Marketing; Ralph Brashe, Dir. of Systems.

■ **15604** ■ **Otagiri Mercantile Company Inc.**
475 Ecceles Ave.
South San Francisco, CA 94080
Phone: (650)871-4080
Products: Homefurnishings and household glassware.
SIC: 5023 (Homefurnishings). **Sales:** $51,000,000
(1994). **Emp:** 200. **Officers:** T. Hirokawa, President; M.
Oto, VP of Finance.

■ **15605** ■ **Over and Back Inc.**
200 13th Ave.
Ronkonkoma, NY 11779
Phone: (516)981-1110
Products: Tableware. **SIC:** 5023 (Homefurnishings).

■ **15606** ■ **Charles D. Owen Manufacturing
Company Inc.**
PO Box 457
875 Warren Wilson Rd.
Swannanoa, NC 28778
Phone: (704)298-6802
Free: (800)447-0112 **Fax:** (704)299-0901
URL: http://www.blanketsandthrows.com
Products: Blankets. **SIC:** 5023 (Homefurnishings).
Est: 1974. **Emp:** 600. **Officers:** Brian Harper,
Telemarketing Sales Manager, e-mail: BKHarp@
aol.com.

■ **15607** ■ **Pacific Drapery Co.**
3801 30th
San Diego, CA 92104-3609
Phone: (619)295-6031
Products: Draperies and upholstery. **SIC:** 5023
(Homefurnishings). **Sales:** $3,000,000 (2000). **Emp:**
49.

■ **15608** ■ **Pacific Home Furnishings**
98-735 Kuahoa Pl.
Pearl City, HI 96782
Phone: (808)487-3881 **Fax:** (808)486-2201
Products: Floor and wallcoverings. **SICs:** 5023
(Homefurnishings); 5198 (Paints, Varnishes &
Supplies). **Est:** 1952. **Emp:** 29. **Officers:** Gary
Grimoto, VP & Treasurer; Tommy Lee, President &
Secty.

■ **15609** ■ **Pampered Chef**
350 S Route 53
Addison, IL 60101
Phone: (708)261-8900
Products: Kitchen tools and utensils. **SIC:** 5023
(Homefurnishings).

■ **15610** ■ **Pande Cameron/Fritz and La Rue**
200 Lexington Ave.
New York, NY 10016
Phone: (212)686-8330
Products: Oriental rugs. **SIC:** 5023 (Homefurnishings).

■ **15611** ■ **Paradise Manufacturing Company
Inc.**
2840 E 26th St.
Los Angeles, CA 90023
Phone: (213)269-2106 **Fax:** (213)355-1230
Products: Patio cushions and umbrellas. **SIC:** 5023
(Homefurnishings). **Est:** 1934. **Sales:** $40,000,000
(2000). **Emp:** 150. **Officers:** Robert Sachs, CEO.

■ **15612** ■ **Paragon Interiors Inc.**
1614 Eisenhower Dr. N
Goshen, IN 46526-5381
Phone: (219)533-8641 **Fax:** (219)534-2510
Products: Draperies; Bedspreads and bedsets;
Window shades and accessories. **SIC:** 5023

(Homefurnishings). **Sales:** $2,000,000 (2000). **Emp:**
75. **Officers:** Nyal J. Weaver.

■ **15613** ■ **Parkway Drapery Co.**
27209 W Warren
Dearborn Heights, MI 48127-1804
Phone: (313)565-7300
Free: (800)482-0225 **Fax:** (313)565-7888
Products: Window blinds and shades; Draperies. **SIC:**
5023 (Homefurnishings). **Sales:** $4,000,000 (2000).
Emp: 49. **Officers:** Tony Zaguroli. **Doing Business
As:** Designer Vertical Blinds.

■ **15614** ■ **Patented Products Inc.**
513 Market St.
Danville, OH 43014-0601
Phone: (740)599-6842
Free: (800)990-4622 **Fax:** (740)599-6848
Products: Bedwarmers. **SIC:** 5023 (Homefurnishings).
Est: 1939. **Sales:** $1,000,000 (2000). **Emp:** 25.
Officers: Larry W. Grindle, President; Dan Grindle, VP
of Operations.

■ **15615** ■ **PD60 Distributors Inc.**
5065 Avalon Ridge Pky.
Norcross, GA 30071-4738
Phone: (770)446-0042 **Fax:** (770)446-0467
E-mail: pdsixty@mindspring.com
Products: Sewing machines; Sewing machine parts.
SIC: 5064 (Electrical Appliances—Television & Radio).
Est: 1988. **Sales:** $3,900,000 (2000). **Emp:** 20.
Officers: Paul Yee, President.

■ **15616** ■ **Penthouse Industries Inc.**
84 N 9th St.
Brooklyn, NY 11211
Phone: (718)384-5800
Free: (800)228-5803 **Fax:** (718)486-8535
Products: Curtains; Draperies; Bedspreads and
bedsets; House furnishings. **SIC:** 5023
(Homefurnishings). **Sales:** $6,000,000 (2000). **Emp:**
102. **Officers:** Irving Wilensky, Chairman of the Board;
Steven Wilensky, President.

■ **15617** ■ **Perfection Products Inc.**
22672 Lambert St., Ste. 620
Lake Forest, CA 92630
Phone: (949)770-3489
Free: (800)229-3489 **Fax:** (949)770-4090
Products: Household items. **SIC:** 5023
(Homefurnishings). **Sales:** $2,000,000 (2000). **Emp:**
15.

■ **15618** ■ **Robert H. Peterson Co.**
14724 E Proctor Ave.
City of Industry, CA 91746
Phone: (626)369-5085 **Fax:** (626)369-5979
Products: Gas fire logs; Barbecues. **SICs:** 5023
(Homefurnishings); 5099 (Durable Goods Nec). **Est:**
1949. **Emp:** 100. **Officers:** William S. White; Jerry
Scott, Sales/Marketing Contact.

■ **15619** ■ **Phelans**
728 3rd Ave. SE
Cedar Rapids, IA 52401-1612
Phone: (319)363-9634 **Fax:** (319)362-2163
Products: Wallcoverings, wallpaper; Paints and allied
products; Draperies; Window blinds and shades;
Furniture and fixtures; Carpets; Lamps; Asphalt and
vinyl asbestos floor tile. **SICs:** 5023 (Homefurnishings);
5198 (Paints, Varnishes & Supplies); 5021 (Furniture);
5063 (Electrical Apparatus & Equipment); 5032 (Brick,
Stone & Related Materials). **Sales:** $4,000,000 (2000).
Emp: 33. **Officers:** Paul Phelan.

■ **15620** ■ **Piedmont Distribution Centers**
PO Box 7123
Charlotte, NC 28241
Phone: (704)588-2867
Products: Housewares; Food. **SICs:** 5023
(Homefurnishings); 5141 (Groceries—General Line).

■ **15621** ■ **Portmeirion USA**
91 Great Hill Rd.
Naugatuck, CT 06770
Phone: (203)723-1471
Products: Home furnishings; Dinnerware. **SIC:** 5023
(Homefurnishings). **Sales:** $9,000,000 (1993). **Emp:**
35. **Officers:** R.B. Stone, President.

■ 15622 ■ Pottery Manufacturing and Distributing Inc.
18881 S Hoover St.
Gardena, CA 90248-4284
Phone: (310)323-7754
Free: (800)991-9914 **Fax:** (310)323-6613
Products: Gifts and novelties. **SIC:** 5023 (Homefurnishings).

■ 15623 ■ L. Powell Co.
PO Box 1408
Culver City, CA 90232-1408
Phone: (310)204-2224 **Fax:** (310)841-0842
Products: Homefurnishing. **SIC:** 5023 (Homefurnishings). **Sales:** $110,000,000 (2000). **Emp:** 120. **Officers:** Richard Powell, President; Larry Hirota, VP & CFO.

■ 15624 ■ The Premium Connection
6165 S Pecos
Las Vegas, NV 89120
Phone: (702)434-6900
Free: (800)683-0933 **Fax:** (702)434-9715
URL: http://www.premconnect.com
Products: Radios; Clocks; Desk accessories; Housewares. **SIC:** 5023 (Homefurnishings). **Est:** 1985. **Sales:** $10,000,000 (2000). **Emp:** 26. **Officers:** Ron Worth, President, e-mail: ron.worth@premconnect.com; Hyla Worth, Vice President.

■ 15625 ■ Princess House Inc.
470 Miles Standish Blvd.
Taunton, MA 02780
Phone: (508)823-0713 **Fax:** (508)823-5182
Products: Lead crystal products. **SIC:** 5023 (Homefurnishings). **Est:** 1963. **Sales:** $66,800,000 (2000). **Emp:** 630. **Officers:** James Northrop, CEO & President; Mark Doherty, VP of Finance; Elizabeth Bowes, VP of Marketing.

■ 15626 ■ Quality Sew & Vac
224 W 3rd St.
Grand Island, NE 68801-5916
Phone: (308)382-7310
Free: (800)431-0032 **Fax:** (308)382-7329
Products: Industrial and commercial vacuum cleaners; Industrial sewing machines; Ceiling fans. **SIC:** 5064 (Electrical Appliances—Television & Radio). **Est:** 1969. **Sales:** $1,000,000 (2000). **Emp:** 8. **Officers:** Ronald Von Behren, Owner.

■ 15627 ■ Queens Decorative Wallcoverings Inc.
83-59 Smedley St.
Jamaica, NY 11435
Phone: (718)523-4323 **Fax:** (718)526-7971
Products: Wallpaper. **SIC:** 5198 (Paints, Varnishes & Supplies). **Est:** 1978. **Emp:** 3. **Officers:** Joseph Singer, President.

■ 15628 ■ Rada Manufacturing Co.
PO Box 838
Waverly, IA 50677
Phone: (319)352-5454 **Fax:** (319)352-0770
E-mail: Customerservice@radamfg.com
URL: http://www.radacutlery.com
Products: Cutlery. **SIC:** 5072 (Hardware). **Est:** 1948. **Officers:** Gary Nelson, President, e-mail: gnelson@radamfg.com; Dan Kielman, Sales Mgr.; Linda Hankes, Customer Service, e-mail: lhankes@radamfg.com.

■ 15629 ■ Ramallah Inc.
880 Hanna Dr.
American Canyon, CA 94589
Phone: (707)649-0900 **Fax:** (707)649-0932
Products: Linens. **SIC:** 5023 (Homefurnishings). **Emp:** 210.

■ 15630 ■ RB Rubber Products Inc.
904 NE 10th Ave.
McMinnville, OR 97128
Phone: (503)472-4691
Free: (800)525-5530 **Fax:** (503)434-4455
Products: Rubber flooring from recycled rubber. **SIC:** 5023 (Homefurnishings). **Officers:** Ronald Bogh, CEO, President & Chairman of the Board; Paul Gilson, Exec. VP & CFO.

■ 15631 ■ Reliable Fabrics Inc.
PO Box 6176
Chelsea, MA 02150
Phone: (617)387-5321
Free: (800)682-4567 **Fax:** (617)387-9352
URL: http://www.Reliablefabrics.com
Products: Draperies; Drapery hardware; Window blinds and shades; Shades, blinds and curtain and drapery rods, poles, and other hardware. **SICs:** 5023 (Homefurnishings); 5072 (Hardware). **Est:** 1933. **Sales:** $1,000,000 (2000). **Emp:** 15. **Officers:** Charles M. Schultz, President; Dr. Kalman Kobrin, Vice President.

■ 15632 ■ Rembrandt Lamps
3757 S Ashland
Chicago, IL 60609
Phone: (773)247-7500 **Fax:** 800-234-3757
Products: Lamps, furniture, and accessories. **SICs:** 5023 (Homefurnishings); 5063 (Electrical Apparatus & Equipment); 5021 (Furniture). **Est:** 1906. **Sales:** $10,000,000 (2000). **Emp:** 45. **Officers:** Ronald Harris.

■ 15633 ■ Rev-A-Shelf, Inc.
2409 Plantside Dr.
Louisville, KY 40299
Phone: (502)499-5835 **Fax:** (502)491-2215
Products: Kitchen cabinet accessories, including spice racks. **SICs:** 5023 (Homefurnishings); 5031 (Lumber, Plywood & Millwork). **Emp:** 499.

■ 15634 ■ Revere Mills Inc.
7313 N Harlem Ave.
Niles, IL 60714
Phone: (847)647-7070
Free: (800)367-8258 **Fax:** (847)647-6979
E-mail: reveremill@aol.com
Products: Domestic houseware items, including shower curtains, sheets, and bath mats. **SICs:** 5023 (Homefurnishings); 5131 (Piece Goods & Notions). **Est:** 1916. **Sales:** $20,000,000 (2000). **Emp:** 40. **Officers:** Justin Gideon, CEO; Mitesh Shah, Controller; Dan Harris, Dir. of Marketing; John Vandenberge, President; Sue Rivera, Dir. of Operations.

■ 15635 ■ Richard-Ginori 1735, Inc.
41 Madison Ave., 6th Fl.
New York, NY 10010
Phone: (212)213-6884 **Fax:** (212)696-0784
E-mail: ginori1735@aol.com
Products: Porcelain dinnerware. **SIC:** 5023 (Homefurnishings). **Est:** 1960. **Sales:** $2,500,000 (2000). **Emp:** 3. **Officers:** Carol Whitehouse, General Mgr. **Former Name:** Pozzi-Ginori Corporation of America.

■ 15636 ■ Riedel Crystal of America Inc.
24 Aero Rd.
Bohemia, NY 11716
Phone: (516)567-7575
Products: Crystal products, including glasses and gift items. **SICs:** 5023 (Homefurnishings); 5199 (Nondurable Goods Nec).

■ 15637 ■ Rodwell Sales
3640 Concord Rd.
York, PA 17402-8629
Phone: (717)848-2732
Free: (800)443-2205 **Fax:** (717)845-5799
Products: Hearth brooms. **SIC:** 5199 (Nondurable Goods Nec).

■ 15638 ■ Roga International Div. Export-Import Marketing
413 E 1st St.
PO Box 6026
Rome, GA 30162
Phone: (706)295-5181 **Fax:** (706)295-3648
Products: Braided, hooked, and other carpet and rugs; Noncurrent-carrying wiring devices. **SICs:** 5023 (Homefurnishings); 5063 (Electrical Apparatus & Equipment). **Officers:** Rodney C. Hardeman Jr., President.

■ 15639 ■ Romac Export Management Corp.
2242 S Hobart Blvd.
Los Angeles, CA 90018-2149
Phone: (213)734-2922 **Fax:** (213)732-4087
E-mail: romacxport@aol.com
Products: Homefurnishings; Flooring, including carpet, wood, vinyl, and tile; Clothing; Gift items; Sporting goods; Building materials; Personal care products; Stationary; Greeting cards; Furniture; Children's products; Artworks. **SICs:** 5023 (Homefurnishings); 5091 (Sporting & Recreational Goods); 5136 (Men's/Boys' Clothing); 5099 (Durable Goods Nec); 5039 (Construction Materials Nec). **Est:** 1978. **Sales:** $4,000,000 (2000). **Emp:** 4. **Officers:** Roberta Best, CEO; Masaharu Ich'uyo, President; Bennet Best, Vice President.

■ 15640 ■ Maya Romanoff Corp.
1730 W Greenleaf Ave.
Chicago, IL 60626-2412
Phone: (773)465-6909 **Fax:** (773)465-7089
Products: Shears; Wallcoverings, including wallpaper with stone finishes, wood veneers, and metallics; Sheets. **SICs:** 5023 (Homefurnishings); 5198 (Paints, Varnishes & Supplies). **Est:** 1969. **Emp:** 30. **Officers:** Maya Romanoff, President.

■ 15641 ■ Rosanna Inc.
1239 S King St.
Seattle, WA 98144-2024
Phone: (206)325-8883 **Fax:** (206)325-8096
Products: Dishware; Flatware; Tabletop accessories. **SIC:** 5023 (Homefurnishings). **Est:** 1982. **Sales:** $2,870,617 (2000). **Emp:** 10. **Officers:** Rosanna Bowles, President, e-mail: rosanna@nwlmk.com; Sharon Beals, National Sales Coordinator; Heather Rathbun, Customer Service Mgr.; Mimmo Rosati, Vice President. **Former Name:** Rosanna Imports Inc.

■ 15642 ■ Royal Doulton USA Inc.
700 Cottontail Ln.
Somerset, NJ 08873
Phone: (732)356-7880
Products: China and porcelain. **SIC:** 5023 (Homefurnishings). **Est:** 1945. **Sales:** $8,400,000 (2000). **Emp:** 176. **Officers:** Ronald Jones, CEO.

■ 15643 ■ Royal Prestige of Missouri Inc.
3470 Hampton Ave. No. 206
St. Louis, MO 63139
Phone: (314)481-9888
Products: Housewares; Kitchen supplies. **SIC:** 5023 (Homefurnishings). **Sales:** $7,000,000 (2000). **Emp:** 30. **Officers:** J. Willenbrock, President.

■ 15644 ■ The Rug Barn Inc.
PO Box 1187
Abbeville, SC 29620
Phone: (864)446-2123
Products: Decorative home furnishings. **SIC:** 5023 (Homefurnishings). **Sales:** $176,700,000 (2000). **Emp:** 2,050. **Officers:** Ernie Ruddock, President; Tom Pless, Controller. **Former Name:** Decorative Home Accents Inc.

■ 15645 ■ Charles Sadek Import Company Inc.
125 Beachwood Ave.
New Rochelle, NY 10802
Phone: (914)633-8090 **Fax:** (914)633-8552
Products: China dishes; Brass; Silver. **SIC:** 5023 (Homefurnishings). **Sales:** $19,000,000 (2000). **Emp:** 76. **Officers:** Sanford J. Sadek, President.

■ 15646 ■ Saladmaster Inc.
912 113th St.
Arlington, TX 76011
Phone: (817)633-3555 **Fax:** (817)633-5544
Products: Kitchenware. **SIC:** 5023 (Homefurnishings). **Est:** 1947. **Sales:** $7,000,000 (2000). **Emp:** 100. **Officers:** Peter B. Menke, President; Jeffrey D. Nelson, CFO; J. William Francisco, Dir. of Marketing.

■ 15647 ■ Salco Inc.
1420 Major St.
Salt Lake City, UT 84115-5306
Phone: (801)487-7841
Free: (800)453-9135 **Fax:** (801)487-7845
Products: Household items. **SIC:** 5023

(Homefurnishings). **Sales:** $6,000,000 (2000). **Emp:** 56.

■ 15648 ■ **Salton/Maxium Housewares Inc.**
550 Business Center Dr.
Mt. Prospect, IL 60056
Phone: (847)803-4600 **Fax:** (847)803-1186
Products: Designs and markets kitchen and home appliances. **SIC:** 5023 (Homefurnishings). **Sales:** $306,000,000 (2000). **Emp:** 219. **Officers:** Leonard Dreimann, CEO; David C. Sabin, Chairman of the Board.

■ 15649 ■ **Arthur Sanderson and Sons North America Ltd.**
285 Grand Ave.
Englewood, NJ 07631
Phone: (201)894-8400 **Fax:** (201)894-8815
Products: Wallpaper and fabric. **SIC:** 5131 (Piece Goods & Notions). **Sales:** $25,000,000 (2000). **Emp:** 25. **Officers:** Bill Wagner, President.

■ 15650 ■ **Seabrook Wallcoverings Inc.**
1325 Farmville Rd.
Memphis, TN 38122
Phone: (901)320-3500
Products: Wallcoverings. **SIC:** 5198 (Paints, Varnishes & Supplies). **Sales:** $127,000,000 (2000). **Emp:** 490. **Officers:** James Seabrook Jr., President; Larry Cooksey, VP of Finance.

■ 15651 ■ **Shaheen Carpet Mills**
PO Box 167
Resaca, GA 30735-0167
Phone: (706)629-9544 **Fax:** (706)625-5341
Products: Floorcovering equipment and supplies. **SIC:** 5023 (Homefurnishings). **Sales:** $10,000,000 (2000). **Emp:** 49.

■ 15652 ■ **Shapco Inc.**
640 Wheeling Rd.
Wheeling, IL 60090-5707
Phone: (847)229-1435
Free: (800)878-8894 **Fax:** (847)229-1843
Products: Shades, blinds, and curtain and drapery rods, poles, and other hardware; Drapery hardware. **SICs:** 5023 (Homefurnishings); 5072 (Hardware). **Est:** 1986.

■ 15653 ■ **Signature Housewares Inc.**
671 Via Alondra, Ste. 801
Camarillo, CA 93012
Phone: (805)484-6666 **Fax:** (805)987-6637
Products: Housewares, including dishes, rugs, and curtains. **SIC:** 5023 (Homefurnishings). **Est:** 1985. **Sales:** $10,000,000 (2000). **Emp:** 10. **Officers:** Keith Morrison, President; Yoshi Aoyama, VP of Finance.

■ 15654 ■ **Fitz and Floyd Silvestri Corporation Inc.**
501 Corporate Drive
Lewisville, TX 75057
Phone: (972)918-0098 **Fax:** (972)454-1208
Products: China and giftware. **SICs:** 5023 (Homefurnishings); 5199 (Nondurable Goods Nec). **Est:** 1958. **Sales:** $62,500,000 (2000). **Emp:** 250. **Officers:** Arthur Bylin, CEO; John Walker, VP of Finance; Pat Harkin, VP of Sales; John King, VP of Operations; Bobby Aldredge, Dir of Human Resources.

■ 15655 ■ **S.P. Skinner Company Inc.**
91 Great Hill Rd.
Naugatuck, CT 06770
Phone: (203)723-1471
Products: Dishes, glassware, and figurines. **SIC:** 5023 (Homefurnishings). **Est:** 1930. **Sales:** $9,000,000 (2000). **Emp:** 35. **Officers:** David T. Hardy, Exec. VP.

■ 15656 ■ **Skyline Distributing Co.**
PO Box 2053
Great Falls, MT 59403-2053
Phone: (406)453-0061 **Fax:** (406)453-0061
Products: Crafts; Floral supplies; Gifts; Home decor; Silk floral; Trees, Holiday items. **SICs:** 5023 (Homefurnishings); 5193 (Flowers & Florists' Supplies). **Est:** 1965. **Emp:** 7. **Officers:** Irene G. Russell, Owner.

■ 15657 ■ **Laurence Smith Distributors**
3044 E Commerce Rd.
Midland, MI 48642
Phone: (517)835-7313
Products: Windows. **SIC:** 5023 (Homefurnishings).

■ 15658 ■ **L.E. Smith Glass Co.**
PO Box 963
Mt. Pleasant, PA 15666
Phone: (412)547-3544 **Fax:** (412)547-2077
Products: Decorative glass. **SIC:** 5023 (Homefurnishings). **Sales:** $10,000,000 (2000). **Emp:** 200. **Officers:** R. D. Ritcher.

■ 15659 ■ **Soil Shield International**
40780 Fremont Blvd.
Fremont, CA 94538
Phone: (510)490-6600 **Fax:** (510)490-4130
Products: Fabric protection and cleaning products for upholstery and carpets. **SIC:** 5169 (Chemicals & Allied Products Nec). **Sales:** $12,500,000 (1993). **Emp:** 50. **Officers:** Michael Connolly, President; Pamela Meggers, Vice President.

■ 15660 ■ **Solar Graphic Inc.**
3337 22nd Ave. S
St. Petersburg, FL 33712
Phone: (813)327-4288
Free: (800)869-8468 **Fax:** (813)321-6004
E-mail: solargx@aol.com
URL: http://www.solargraphics.com
Products: Tinted windows; Storefront advertising. **SICs:** 5023 (Homefurnishings); 5031 (Lumber, Plywood & Millwork). **Est:** 1981. **Sales:** $700,000 (2000). **Emp:** 16. **Officers:** Richard Purdum, President.

■ 15661 ■ **Sorrell Interiors**
2341 Recreation Dr.
West Bloomfield, MI 48324
Phone: (810)683-6030
Products: Window, wall, and floor coverings. **SICs:** 5023 (Homefurnishings); 5198 (Paints, Varnishes & Supplies). **Est:** 1958. **Sales:** $150,000 (2000). **Emp:** 1. **Officers:** Herb Benson, Owner.

■ 15662 ■ **Southern Distributors Inc.**
818 Perry St.
Richmond, VA 23224-2230
Phone: (804)231-1128 **Fax:** (804)230-4533
Products: Toys; Housewares; School supplies; Batteries; Makeup; Hosiery; Film; Baby items; Seasonal items; Watches; Candy; Pet supplies; Sewing notions. **SICs:** 5023 (Homefurnishings); 5092 (Toys & Hobby Goods & Supplies); 5063 (Electrical Apparatus & Equipment); 5122 (Drugs, Proprietaries & Sundries); 5112 (Stationery & Office Supplies). **Est:** 1948. **Emp:** 22. **Officers:** Harry Cohen, President; Frank Cohen, Vice President.

■ 15663 ■ **Southern Interiors Inc.**
2541 Farrisview Blvd.
Memphis, TN 38118-1502
Phone: (901)363-7357 **Fax:** (901)363-7359
Products: Draperies. **SIC:** 5023 (Homefurnishings). **Sales:** $1,000,000 (2000). **Emp:** 49. **Officers:** Joe D. Wicker.

■ 15664 ■ **The Spiral Collection, Inc.**
1500 S Western Ave.
Chicago, IL 60608
Phone: (312)738-0622
Free: (800)227-2154 **Fax:** (312)738-9756
E-mail: spiral@ais.net
URL: http://www.easypedestal.com
Products: Paper and steel decorative accessories. **SIC:** 5199 (Nondurable Goods Nec). **Est:** 1994. **Sales:** $2,000,000 (2000). **Emp:** 30. **Officers:** Melissa Garfinkle; Charlotte Garfinkle, Sales/Marketing Contact. **Alternate Name:** Spiral. **Alternate Name:** Flute.

■ 15665 ■ **Stage Inc.**
PO Box 9657
Knoxville, TN 37940
Phone: (615)577-5551 **Fax:** (615)573-7984
Products: Stage curtains. **SIC:** 5099 (Durable Goods Nec). **Sales:** $15,000,000 (1994). **Emp:** 2. **Officers:** J. Donald Mitchell, President.

■ 15666 ■ **Standard Textile Company Inc.**
3130 Frederick Ave.
Baltimore, MD 21229-3804
Phone: (410)233-4400 **Fax:** (410)233-6317
E-mail: standardtextile@erols.com
Products: Home linens, including sheets, blankets, pillows, and towels. **SICs:** 5023 (Homefurnishings); 5131 (Piece Goods & Notions). **Emp:** 45. **Officers:** Edward Grinspan; David Mandl.

■ 15667 ■ **Stanley Roberts Inc.**
65 Industrial Rd.
Lodi, NJ 07644
Phone: (973)778-5900
Products: Flatware and cutlery. **SICs:** 5094 (Jewelry & Precious Stones); 5023 (Homefurnishings). **Sales:** $25,000,000 (1992). **Emp:** 100. **Officers:** Edward Pomeranz, Owner.

■ 15668 ■ **Stark Carpet Corp.**
979 3rd Ave.
New York, NY 10022
Phone: (212)752-9000 **Fax:** (212)758-4342
Products: Carpets, area and oriental rugs. **SIC:** 5023 (Homefurnishings). **Sales:** $117,000,000 (2000). **Emp:** 300. **Officers:** John S. Stark, CEO; Hy Needleman, CFO.

■ 15669 ■ **Stover Broom**
PO Box 1704
Lewiston, ME 04241
Phone: (207)784-1591 **Fax:** (207)784-3915
Products: Brooms and brushes. **SIC:** 5023 (Homefurnishings). **Officers:** John Campbell, President.

■ 15670 ■ **Stuart's Federal Fireplace, Inc.**
PO Box 252172
West Bloomfield, MI 48325-2172
Phone: (248)557-3344 **Fax:** (248)443-4694
Products: Fireplaces; Grills; Hot tubs and spas. **SICs:** 5023 (Homefurnishings); 5074 (Plumbing & Hydronic Heating Supplies). **Est:** 1946. **Sales:** $800,000 (2000). **Emp:** 10. **Officers:** Peter Stuart, President.

■ 15671 ■ **Sultan and Sons Inc.**
650 SW 9th Ter.
Pompano Beach, FL 33069
Phone: (954)782-6600
Free: (800)299-6601 **Fax:** (954)786-8650
Products: Custom draperies and bedspreads. **SIC:** 5023 (Homefurnishings). **Est:** 1924. **Sales:** $13,500,000 (2000). **Emp:** 202. **Officers:** Ezra Sulton, President; Tom Turner, Vice President; Murray Maratchi, Exec. VP.

■ 15672 ■ **Super Glass Corp.**
1020 E 48th St.
Brooklyn, NY 11203
Phone: (718)469-9300 **Fax:** (718)469-5480
E-mail: superglasscorp@aol.com
Products: Glass vases. **SIC:** 5023 (Homefurnishings). **Est:** 1938. **Sales:** $7,000,000 (2000). **Emp:** 100. **Officers:** B. Friedman, President; E. Kay, CFO; Howard Friedman, Dir. of Marketing.

■ 15673 ■ **Superior Linen Company Inc.**
PO Box 250
Hackensack, NJ 07601
Phone: (201)343-3300
Products: Draperies; Linens; Tablecloths; Washtowels; Napkins. **SICs:** 5023 (Homefurnishings); 5113 (Industrial & Personal Service Paper). **Est:** 1967. **Sales:** $4,000,000 (2000). **Emp:** 25. **Officers:** Paul J. Lieberman, Owner; Stuart Richman, CEO; Herb Fink, Vice President.

■ 15674 ■ **Surface Technology Corp.**
15909 1/2 49th St. S
Gulfport, FL 33707
Phone: (813)323-0212 **Fax:** (813)321-5609
Products: Counter tops. **SICs:** 5023 (Homefurnishings); 5031 (Lumber, Plywood & Millwork). **Est:** 1988. **Emp:** 50. **Officers:** Philip Lacey; Howard Berger; John McCarthy.

■ 15675 ■ **Swiff-Train Co.**
2500 Agnes St.
Corpus Christi, TX 78405
Phone: (512)883-1707 **Fax:** (512)883-9653
Products: Floorcovering equipment and supplies. **SIC:** 5023 (Homefurnishings).

■ 15676 ■ **Swiss Army Brands Inc.**
1 Research Dr.
Shelton, CT 06484
Phone: (203)929-6391 **Fax:** (203)925-1092
Products: Pocket knives; Sunglasses; Watches. **SICs:** 5094 (Jewelry & Precious Stones); 5072 (Hardware). **Est:** 1855. **Sales:** $130,000,000 (2000). **Emp:** 223. **Officers:** J. Merrick Taggart, President; Thomas Lupinski, Sr. VP & CFO; Ted Richardson, VP of Marketing; Joan Bowman, VP of Human Resources.

■ 15677 ■ **Syracuse China Corp.**
PO Box 4820
Syracuse, NY 13221
Phone: (315)455-5671 **Fax:** (315)455-4575
Products: China. **SIC:** 5023 (Homefurnishings). **Sales:** $30,000,000 (2000). **Emp:** 1,000. **Officers:** Chester D. Amond, President; Charles S. Goodman.

■ 15678 ■ **Szco Supplier Inc.**
PO Box 6353
Baltimore, MD 21230-0353
Phone: (410)547-6999
Free: (800)547-6998 **Fax:** (410)547-7391
E-mail: Szco@ixinetcom.com
Products: Scissors and knives. **SIC:** 5072 (Hardware). **Est:** 1984. **Emp:** 16. **Officers:** Jamil Chaurdry, President.

■ 15679 ■ **T and A Supply Co.**
1105 Westlake Ave. N
Seattle, WA 98109
Phone: (206)282-3770
Free: (800)562-2857 **Fax:** (206)284-0591
Products: Floorcovering equipment and supplies. **SIC:** 5023 (Homefurnishings). **Sales:** $60,000,000 (2000). **Emp:** 140.

■ 15680 ■ **T-Fal Corp.**
25 Riverside Dr.
Pine Brook, NJ 07058
Phone: (973)575-1060 **Fax:** (973)575-0207
Products: Non-stick cookware; Small electric appliances. **SICs:** 5023 (Homefurnishings); 5063 (Electrical Apparatus & Equipment). **Est:** 1976. **Sales:** $200,000,000 (2000). **Emp:** 310. **Officers:** Greg Infeld, President; Jacques Nadeau, VP of Finance; Don Moulder, VP of Sales; Jean Paul Ciquier, VP of Marketing; Jan Bramball, VP of Human Resources.

■ 15681 ■ **Takahashi Trading Corp.**
200 Rhode Island St.
San Francisco, CA 94103
Phone: (415)431-8300
Free: (800)222-9415 **Fax:** (415)621-1741
Products: Plates and ceramics. **SIC:** 5023 (Homefurnishings). **Est:** 1948. **Sales:** $14,000,000 (1999). **Emp:** 30. **Officers:** Henry Takahashi, President; Masako M. Suzuki, CFO; Rob Ramos, Dir. of Marketing & Sales.

■ 15682 ■ **Tasso Wallcovering**
1020 NW 6th St., Ste. H
Deerfield Beach, FL 33442-7711
Phone: (954)429-3883 **Fax:** (954)429-8208
E-mail: tassousa@aol.com
URL: http://www.tassousa.com
Products: Wallcoverings, and wallpaper. **SICs:** 5023 (Homefurnishings); 5198 (Paints, Varnishes & Supplies). **Est:** 1890. **Emp:** 6. **Officers:** Dich Roos.

■ 15683 ■ **THC Systems Inc.**
395 N Service Rd No. 300
Melville, NY 11747
Phone: (516)753-3700 **Fax:** (516)753-3728
Products: Chinaware. **SIC:** 5023 (Homefurnishings). **Est:** 1925. **Sales:** $18,000,000 (2000). **Emp:** 100. **Officers:** Allan Conseur, President; Morty Cohen, CFO; Barry Goldberg, Dir. of Marketing.

■ 15684 ■ **Tianjin-Philadelphia Rug Co.**
231 W Mount Pleasant
Philadelphia, PA 19119
Phone: (215)247-3535
Products: Oriental rugs. **SIC:** 5023 (Homefurnishings). **Sales:** $1,000,000 (2000). **Emp:** 6. **Officers:** Richard Maloumian, President.

■ 15685 ■ **Towle Manufacturing Co.**
144 Addison St.
East Boston, MA 02128-9115
Phone: (617)568-1300 **Fax:** (617)568-9185
Products: Sterling silver and stainless steel flatware and accessories. **SIC:** 5023 (Homefurnishings). **Sales:** $56,000,000 (2000). **Emp:** 180. **Officers:** Leonard Florence, Chairman of the Board; E. Merle Randolph, CFO.

■ 15686 ■ **Toyo Trading Co.**
13000 S Spring St.
Los Angeles, CA 90061
Phone: (310)660-0300
Free: (800)669-8696 **Fax:** (310)715-2459
Products: Decorative Accessories. **SIC:** 5023 (Homefurnishings). **Sales:** $7,000,000 (2000). **Emp:** 18. **Officers:** Randy Nakayama, President.

■ 15687 ■ **Trans World Investments, Ltd.**
1126 Pine Croft Dr.
West Columbia, SC 29170
Phone: (803)794-5152
Products: Household furnishings, including carpets and rugs; Farm machinery and equipment. **SICs:** 5023 (Homefurnishings); 5083 (Farm & Garden Machinery). **Officers:** Jackson L. Cobb, President.

■ 15688 ■ **Trend Pacific Inc.**
2580 Corporate Pl., Ste. F109
Monterey Park, CA 91754-7633
Phone: (323)266-8925 **Fax:** (323)266-8944
E-mail: trendpac@aol.com
Products: Ceramic mugs. **SIC:** 5023 (Homefurnishings). **Est:** 1963. **Emp:** 5. **Officers:** Frank Ige.

■ 15689 ■ **Twin Panda Inc./Katha Diddel Home Collection**
225 5th Ave., Ste. 804
New York, NY 10010
Phone: (212)725-6045 **Fax:** 800-438-8946
E-mail: customerservice@kathodiddel.com
URL: http://www.kathodiddel.com
Products: Needlepoint goods, including pillows, rugs, and linens; Hook rugs. **SIC:** 5023 (Homefurnishings). **Est:** 1980. **Sales:** $2,000,000 (1999). **Emp:** 9. **Officers:** Katha Diddel, President, e-mail: kathadiddel@aol.com.

■ 15690 ■ **TWT Moulding Company Inc.**
PO Box 1425
Brownwood, TX 76804
Phone: (915)643-2521 **Fax:** (915)646-0311
Products: Molding-picture framing. **SIC:** 5099 (Durable Goods Nec). **Est:** 1957. **Sales:** $4,000,000 (2000). **Emp:** 16. **Officers:** Richard Wall, Chairman of the Board; Clois Broome, Controller; Darlene Kennedy, Dir. of Sales.

■ 15691 ■ **Ulster Linen Company, Inc.**
148 Madison Ave.
New York, NY 10016-6780
Phone: (212)684-5534 **Fax:** (212)689-0937
E-mail: Ulster@ulsterlinen.com
URL: http://www.ulsterlinen.com
Products: Household linens and linen piece goods. **SIC:** 5023 (Homefurnishings). **Est:** 1933. **Emp:** 8.

■ 15692 ■ **UMBRA U.S.A. Inc.**
1705 Broadway
Buffalo, NY 14212
Free: (800)387-5122 **Fax:** (716)299-6168
URL: http://www.umbra.com
Products: Household supplies; Cabinet hardware; Drapery; Furniture. **SICs:** 5023 (Homefurnishings); 5072 (Hardware). **Est:** 1984. **Emp:** 200.

■ 15693 ■ **Urken Supply Company Inc.**
27 Witherspoon
Princeton, NJ 08540-3201
Phone: (609)924-3076 **Fax:** (609)924-6769
Products: Furniture hardware; Plumbing fixtures, equipment, and supplies; Window blinds and shades. **SIC:** 5023 (Homefurnishings). **Emp:** 49. **Officers:** Irv Urken.

■ 15694 ■ **USA Plastics Inc.**
306A Mcknight Pk. Dr.
Pittsburgh, PA 15237
Phone: (412)367-0594 **Fax:** (412)367-2016
E-mail: usapla@usaor.net
Products: Food storage containers. **SIC:** 5023 (Homefurnishings). **Est:** 1988. **Sales:** $4,000,000 (2000). **Officers:** Max Lees, President.

■ 15695 ■ **Variety Distributors Inc.**
702 Spring St.
Harlan, IA 51537
Phone: (712)755-2184 **Fax:** (712)755-5041
Products: Draperies; Giftware; Furniture. **SICs:** 5023 (Homefurnishings); 5199 (Nondurable Goods Nec); 5021 (Furniture). **Est:** 1945. **Sales:** $16,000,000 (2000). **Emp:** 65. **Officers:** Richard Mudler, President; Clarence W. Smith, General Mgr.; Jeff Evers, Sales Mgr.

■ 15696 ■ **Villeroy and Boch Tableware Ltd.**
5 Vaughn Dr., Ste. 303
Princeton, NJ 08540
Phone: (609)734-7800 **Fax:** (609)734-7840
Products: China. **SIC:** 5023 (Homefurnishings). **Sales:** $40,000,000 (2000). **Emp:** 80. **Officers:** Benard Reuter, President; Tom Price, CFO.

■ 15697 ■ **VMC/USA**
7618 Slate Ridge Blvd.
Reynoldsburg, OH 43068
Phone: (614)759-9800 **Fax:** (614)759-9802
Products: Servingware. **SIC:** 5023 (Homefurnishings). **Est:** 1988. **Sales:** $200,000,000 (2000). **Emp:** 3. **Officers:** Claude Feltrin, Director; Didier Paresys, Finance Officer; Philippe Rapacz, Dir. of Sales.

■ 15698 ■ **VVP America Inc.**
965 Ridgelake Blvd.
Memphis, TN 38120
Phone: (901)767-7111 **Fax:** (901)683-9351
Products: Glass; Mirrors. **SIC:** 5039 (Construction Materials Nec). **Est:** 1992. **Sales:** $650,000,000 (2000). **Emp:** 2,500. **Officers:** Mark Burke, CEO & President; John Wagner, VP of Finance; Jim Charles, Dir. of Marketing; John Jameson, Dir. of Data Processing; William Minderman, VP of Admin.

■ 15699 ■ **Waechtersbach U.S.A.**
4201 NE 34th St.
Kansas City, MO 64117
Phone: (816)455-3800
Products: Ceramic dinnerware, including mugs, plates, and bowls. **SIC:** 5023 (Homefurnishings). **Sales:** $5,000,000 (2000). **Emp:** 20. **Officers:** Susan Jones, President.

■ 15700 ■ **Wal-Mart Stores Inc.**
702 SW 8th St.
Bentonville, AR 72716
Phones: (501)273-4000 (501)273-4314
Products: Household appliances, including coffee makers; Homefurnishings, including kitchen supplies; Toys. **SICs:** 5023 (Homefurnishings); 5064 (Electrical Appliances—Television & Radio); 5092 (Toys & Hobby Goods & Supplies). **Sales:** $8,066,000,000 (2000).

■ 15701 ■ **Wang's International, Inc.**
PO Box 18447
Memphis, TN 38181-0447
Phone: (901)362-2111
Free: (800)829-2647 **Fax:** 800-733-9290
URL: http://www.wangs.com
Products: Home decor products; Giftware. **SICs:** 5023 (Homefurnishings); 5199 (Nondurable Goods Nec). **Est:** 1976. **Emp:** 800.

■ 15702 ■ **Washington Forge Inc.**
28 Harrison Ave.
Englishtown, NJ 07726
Phone: (732)446-7777
Products: Cutlery. **SIC:** 5072 (Hardware). **Sales:** $4,000,000 (1994). **Emp:** 18. **Officers:** Marco McGuiness, Vice President; Raymond Rohr, CFO.

■ 15703 ■ **Watermark Association of Artisans Inc.**
Hwy. 158 E
Camden, NC 27921
Phone: (252)338-0853
Free: (800)982-8337 **Fax:** (252)338-1444
E-mail: watermark@interpath.com
URL: http://www.watermarkusa.com
Products: Tabletop accessories. **SIC:** 5023 (Homefurnishings). **Est:** 1978. **Sales:** $1,000,000 (2000). **Emp:** 14. **Officers:** Kimberly Sawyer, Director.

■ 15704 ■ **Wedgwood U.S.A. Inc.**
PO Box 1454
Wall, NJ 07719
Phone: (908)938-5800
Products: Crystal and china. **SIC:** 5023 (Homefurnishings). **Est:** 1940. **Sales:** $60,000,000 (2000). **Emp:** 140. **Officers:** Chris McGillary, President; Tony Cappiello, CFO; Don Hendrickson, VP of Admin.

■ 15705 ■ **Wesco Fabrics Inc.**
4001 Forest St.
Denver, CO 80216
Phone: (303)388-4101 **Fax:** (303)388-3908
Products: Draperies; Bed spreads; Vertical blinds. **SIC:** 5023 (Homefurnishings). **Est:** 1946. **Sales:** $14,000,000 (2000). **Emp:** 200. **Officers:** Richard Gentry, President; Jim Webb, Controller.

■ 15706 ■ **Westfield Decorator Fashions**
PO Box 419
Westfield, IN 46074
Phone: (317)896-2521
Products: Custom window coverings. **SIC:** 5023 (Homefurnishings). **Officers:** Miller F. Myers, CEO; Burton F. Myers, CFO.

■ 15707 ■ **H. Lynn White Inc.**
8208 Nieman Rd.
Lenexa, KS 66214
Phone: (913)492-4100
Free: (800)999-4483 **Fax:** (913)492-0416
Products: Custom window coverings, wall coverings, and floor coverings. **SICs:** 5023 (Homefurnishings); 5198 (Paints, Varnishes & Supplies). **Est:** 1950. **Sales:**

$3,500,000 (2000). **Emp:** 25. **Officers:** William H. Hare Jr., Chairman of the Board; Gary G. Kusck, President.

■ 15708 ■ **W.A. Wilson and Sons Inc.**
6 Industrial Park
Wheeling, WV 26003
Phone: (304)232-2200 **Fax:** (304)232-6413
Products: Glass and paint. **SICs:** 5039 (Construction Materials Nec); 5198 (Paints, Varnishes & Supplies). **Sales:** $13,200,000 (1994). **Emp:** 65. **Officers:** Robert H. Hartong, President; Barry Larson, Controller.

■ 15709 ■ **Windows of the World**
1855 Griffin Rd., Ste. A123
Dania, FL 33004
Phones: (954)921-8336 (305)945-5074
Fax: (954)921-8557
Products: Decorative window treatments; Fabrics; Wallcoverings. **SIC:** 5023 (Homefurnishings). **Emp:** 15. **Officers:** Sonia Najman, Sales & Marketing Contact, e-mail: sonia@sindowsoftheworld.com.

■ 15710 ■ **The Wine Enthusiast Companies**
PO Box 39
Pleasantville, NY 10570
Phone: 800-356-8466 **Fax:** (914)345-3129
Products: Wine cellars; Racks. **SIC:** 5023 (Homefurnishings). **Sales:** $10,000,000 (2000). **Emp:** 49. **Officers:** Adam Strum.

■ 15711 ■ **Wipeco Corp.**
855 N Cicero Ave.
Chicago, IL 60651
Phone: (773)261-0225 **Fax:** (773)261-0225
Products: Wipers; Towels; Rags. **SIC:** 5023 (Homefurnishings). **Sales:** $5,000,000 (2000). **Emp:** 85. **Officers:** Courtney Shanken, CEO; Jeff Shanken, Dir. of Marketing & Sales.

■ 15712 ■ **WMF of America**
85 Price Pkwy.
Farmingdale, NY 11735
Phone: (631)293-3990
Free: (800)999-6347 **Fax:** (631)293-3561
E-mail: info@wmf-usa.wmf.com
Products: Flatware; Giftware; Cookware; Storage systems; Spice mills. **SIC:** 5023 (Homefurnishings). **Est:** 1953. **Sales:** $33,000,000 (2000). **Emp:** 40. **Officers:** Ray Teilborg, President; Joseph Milack, Controller; Emma Popolow, VP of Marketing & Sales; Peter Braley, VP of Marketing & Sales; Sherrie Eggerud, Eastern Regional Sales Mgr. **Former Name:** WMF Hutsehenrouther USA.

■ 15713 ■ **WMF Hutschenreuther USA**
85 Price Pkwy.
Farmingdale, NY 11735
Phone: (516)293-3990 **Fax:** (516)293-3561
Products: Homefurnishings. **SIC:** 5023 (Homefurnishings). **Est:** 1953. **Sales:** $33,000,000 (2000). **Emp:** 40. **Officers:** Mark J. Roland, President; Marlene V. Freed, VP of Operations.

■ 15714 ■ **Wonderly Company Inc.**
25 Cornell St.
PO Box 1458
Kingston, NY 12401
Phone: (914)331-0148 **Fax:** (914)331-6218
E-mail: wonderly@mhv.net
URL: http://www.wonderlys.com
Products: Custom draperies and bedspreads. **SIC:** 5023 (Homefurnishings). **Est:** 1919. **Sales:** $3,000,000 (2000). **Emp:** 99. **Officers:** C.E. Wonderly Jr.

■ 15715 ■ **Worldwide Manufacturing Inc.**
12910 SW 89th Ct.
Miami, FL 33176-5803
Phone: (305)235-5585
Free: (800)327-8053 **Fax:** (305)235-8851
Products: Bathroom accessories and fittings. **SICs:** 5023 (Homefurnishings); 5074 (Plumbing & Hydronic Heating Supplies). **Est:** 1968. **Sales:** $2,000,000 (2000). **Emp:** 49. **Officers:** Sondra Seiderman.

■ 15716 ■ **Zak Designs Inc.**
S 1604 Garfield Rd.
Spokane, WA 99224
Phone: (509)244-0555 **Fax:** (509)244-0704
Products: Dinnerware. **SICs:** 5023 (Homefurnishings); 5094 (Jewelry & Precious Stones). **Sales:** $66,000,000 (2000). **Emp:** 180. **Officers:** Irving L. Zakheim, CEO & President; Michelle Miller, Controller.

■ 15717 ■ **Zeroll Co.**
PO Box 999
Ft. Pierce, FL 34954
Phone: (561)461-3811
Free: (800)872-5000 **Fax:** (561)461-1061
E-mail: info@zeroll.com
URL: http://www.zeroll.com
Products: Ice cream scoops; Ice cream spades; Dishers; Kitchen utensils. **SIC:** 5023 (Homefurnishings). **Est:** 1935. **Sales:** $7,500,000 (2000). **Emp:** 40. **Officers:** Thomas M. Funka Sr., President; Lenny Van Valkenburg, General Mgr.; Dayna Bennett, Human Resources Contact.

(27) Industrial Machinery

Entries in this section are arranged alphabetically by company name. When the company name is a personal name, the company name is alphabetized by the surname unless the first name or initial(s) are part of a trade name. See the User's Guide at the front of this directory for additional information.

■ **15718** ■ **1st Call McCall Heating and Clng**
1650 NE Lombard St.
Portland, OR 97211
Phone: (503)231-3311 **Fax:** (503)286-5194
Products: Sheet metal work; Installs heating and air conditioning equipment; Oil equipment. **SICs:** 5084 (Industrial Machinery & Equipment); 5172 (Petroleum Products Nec). **Officers:** Kevin Kelly, Owner.

■ **15719** ■ **A-1 Air Compressor Corp.**
679 W Winthrop Ave.
Addison, IL 60101
Phone: (630)543-2606 **Fax:** (630)543-2614
Products: Assemble and repair air compressors, vacuum systems, compressed air dryers and filters. **SIC:** 5084 (Industrial Machinery & Equipment).

■ **15720** ■ **A and A Mechanical Inc.**
1101 Ulrich Ave.
Louisville, KY 40219
Phone: (502)968-0164
Products: HVAC equipment. **SICs:** 5074 (Plumbing & Hydronic Heating Supplies); 5075 (Warm Air Heating & Air-Conditioning). **Sales:** $18,000,000 (1992). **Emp:** 80. **Officers:** William T. Allen, President.

■ **15721** ■ **AA Electric S.E. Inc.**
2011 S Combee Rd.
Lakeland, FL 33801
Phone: (863)665-6941
Free: (800)237-8274 **Fax:** (863)665-1435
E-mail: aabfl@concentric.net
URL: http://www.a-aelectric.com
Products: Industrial controls. **SIC:** 5085 (Industrial Supplies). **Est:** 1961. **Sales:** $14,200,000 (1999). **Emp:** 37. **Officers:** Edward J. Kirk, President; Rhoda Kirk, Treasurer & Secty.

■ **15722** ■ **Aaron Equipment Co.**
735 E Green St.
Bensenville, IL 60106
Phone: (630)350-2200 **Fax:** (630)350-9047
E-mail: sales@aaronequipment.com
URL: http://www.aaronequipment.com
Products: Plastics-working machinery; Chemical manufacturing machinery. **SIC:** 5084 (Industrial Machinery & Equipment). **Est:** 1939. **Sales:** $10,000,000 (2000). **Emp:** 90. **Officers:** Jerrold V. Cohen, President.

■ **15723** ■ **ABB Power Generation**
5309 Commonwealth Center Pkwy, Ste. 400
Midlothian, VA 23112
Phone: (804)763-2000 **Fax:** (804)763-2187
Products: Steam and gas engine turbines. **SIC:** 5084 (Industrial Machinery & Equipment). **Est:** 1971. **Sales:** $200,000,000 (2000). **Emp:** 240. **Officers:** Hans Levander, President; Paul Packard, Finance Officer; Jim Grant, VP of Marketing & Sales; Paul Attanasio, Dir. of Data Processing; John E. Cotton Jr., Dir of Human Resources.

■ **15724** ■ **Robert Abel and Company Inc.**
195 Merrimac St.
Woburn, MA 01888
Phone: (781)935-7860 **Fax:** (781)935-7457
Products: Industrial trucks and forklifts. **SIC:** 5084 (Industrial Machinery & Equipment). **Est:** 1922. **Sales:** $25,000,000 (2000). **Emp:** 85. **Officers:** Michael Romano, President; Maurice Maher, CFO; J.L. Croce, President.

■ **15725** ■ **Aberdeen Dynamics**
17717 E Admiral Pl.
PO Box 582510
Tulsa, OK 74158
Phones: (918)437-8000 (918)437-9000
Fax: (918)437-8420
Products: Hydraulic components. **SIC:** 5084 (Industrial Machinery & Equipment).

■ **15726** ■ **Abrasive Specialists Inc.**
7521 Commerce Ln.
Minneapolis, MN 55432
Phone: (612)571-4111
Free: (800)843-1614 **Fax:** (612)571-5026
E-mail: abrspec@aol.com
Products: Cutting tools; Machine tool accessories, including machine lube. **SICs:** 5084 (Industrial Machinery & Equipment); 5085 (Industrial Supplies). **Est:** 1976. **Sales:** $10,000,000 (2000). **Emp:** 25. **Officers:** Dennis Olsen, President; Jaime Olsen, General Mgr.

■ **15727** ■ **Abrasive-Tool Corp.**
1555 Emerson St.
Rochester, NY 14606
Phone: (716)254-4500 **Fax:** (716)254-2247
Products: Abrasive, cutting and precision tools, machine tool accessories and, industrial coolant. **SICs:** 5084 (Industrial Machinery & Equipment); 5085 (Industrial Supplies). **Sales:** $20,000,000 (2000). **Emp:** 42. **Officers:** Michael T. Hanna, President & CFO.

■ **15728** ■ **AC Sales Company Ltd.**
1080 E 29th St.
Hialeah, FL 33013
Phone: (305)696-7880 **Fax:** (305)693-7835
Products: Woodworking machinery. **SIC:** 5084 (Industrial Machinery & Equipment). **Est:** 1956. **Sales:** $1,000,000 (2000). **Emp:** 16. **Officers:** Silvia Tosco, Manager.

■ **15729** ■ **Accessorie Air Compressor Systems Inc.**
1858 N Case St.
Orange, CA 92865-4241
Phone: (714)634-2292 **Fax:** (714)974-3008
Products: Compressors. **SIC:** 5084 (Industrial Machinery & Equipment). **Sales:** $3,000,000 (2000). **Emp:** 18.

■ **15730** ■ **Accurate Air Engineering Inc.**
PO Box 5526
Compton, CA 90224
Phone: (310)537-1350 **Fax:** (310)537-1374
Products: Compressors. **SIC:** 5084 (Industrial

Machinery & Equipment). **Sales:** $15,000,000 (2000). **Emp:** 60.

■ **15731** ■ **ACI Controls**
5604 Business Ave.
Cicero, NY 13039
Phone: (315)452-1171 **Fax:** (315)452-4608
Products: Industrial equipment. **SIC:** 5084 (Industrial Machinery & Equipment).

■ **15732** ■ **ACM Equipment Rental and Sales Co.**
4010 South 22nd St.
Phoenix, AZ 85040-1437
Phone: (602)232-0600
Free: (877)700-7368 **Fax:** (602)232-0620
URL: http://www.acmeq.com
Products: Cranes; Lifts; Boom trucks; Sweepers; Loader parts; Fork lifts. **SIC:** 5084 (Industrial Machinery & Equipment). **Est:** 1990. **Sales:** $55,000,000 (1999). **Emp:** 180. **Officers:** Ken Sharp, VP & General Merchandising Mgr.; Ron Bear, VP of Sales; Steve McClain, Vice President; Albert Perez, Sales & Marketing Contact, e-mail: aperez@acmeq.com; Paul Phillimore, Customer Service Contact, e-mail: pphillimore@acmeq.com.

■ **15733** ■ **Acme-Dixie Inc.**
PO Box 218
Westlake, LA 70669
Phone: (318)882-6467 **Fax:** (318)882-6011
Products: Industrial equipment, including man-lifts, welding equipment, and sand blasters. **SIC:** 5084 (Industrial Machinery & Equipment). **Est:** 1936. **Sales:** $31,000,000 (2000). **Emp:** 150. **Officers:** John T. Banken, President; Glen Bergeron, CFO; Charlie Willis, VP of Marketing; Tammy Lemaire, VP of Operations.

■ **15734** ■ **Acrowood Corp.**
PO Box 1028
Everett, WA 98206
Phone: (425)258-3555 **Fax:** (425)252-7622
E-mail: acrowood@whidbey.net
URL: http://www.acrowood.com
Products: Woodyard, chip processing, and saw mill machinery. **SIC:** 5084 (Industrial Machinery & Equipment). **Est:** 1892. **Emp:** 100. **Officers:** Farhang Javid, CEO; Philip Hutmacher, Treasurer & Secty.; Shannon R. Javid, President.

■ **15735** ■ **ADCO Equipment Inc.**
3455 San Gabriel River Pkwy.
Pico Rivera, CA 90660
Phone: (213)623-8514
Products: Pumps; Generators; Forklifts. **SIC:** 5084 (Industrial Machinery & Equipment). **Est:** 1955. **Sales:** $18,000,000 (2000). **Emp:** 90. **Officers:** Lonnie E. Duncan, President & Chairman of the Board; Don Taylor, Treasurer & Secty.; Chris Rhoades, Dir. of Marketing.

■ **15736** ■ **Advanced Equipment Company Inc.**
PO Box 3370
Capitol Heights, MD 20791
Phone: (301)336-0200
Products: Industrial equipment. **SIC:** 5084 (Industrial

Machinery & Equipment). **Est:** 1966. **Sales:** $1,000,000 (2000). **Emp:** 17. **Officers:** Jerry Yochelson, President; Janet Dusseau, Dir. of Sales.

■ **15737** ■ **Advanced Industrial Products, Inc.**
2125 Whitney Ave.
Gretna, LA 70056
Phone: (504)367-1257
Free: (800)259-1516   **Fax:** (504)366-0841
E-mail: aipi@iamerica.net
Products: Industrial equipment, including hoses and pumps. **SIC:** 5084 (Industrial Machinery & Equipment). **Est:** 1979. **Officers:** Jack Lopipero, President.

■ **15738** ■ **Advanced Test Equipmnt Rentals**
PO Box 910036
San Diego, CA 92191
Phone: (858)558-6500   **Fax:** (858)558-6570
Products: Rents, sells, calibrates and repairs electronic test equipment; Environmental, optical and communications equipment. **SIC:** 5084 (Industrial Machinery & Equipment). **Officers:** James Berg, President.

■ **15739** ■ **Adwood Corp.**
PO Box 1195
High Point, NC 27261
Phone: (336)884-1846
Free: (800)397-1860   **Fax:** (336)841-6493
E-mail: mail@adwood.com
URL: http://www.adwood.com
Products: Woodworking machinery and supplies. **SIC:** 5084 (Industrial Machinery & Equipment). **Est:** 1981. **Sales:** $5,000,000 (2000). **Emp:** 18. **Officers:** Rudolf Stockinger, COO; Steven McHugh, General Mgr.

■ **15740** ■ **AEROGO, Inc.**
1170 Andover Pk. W
Seattle, WA 98188-3909
Phone: (206)575-3344
Free: (800)426-4757   **Fax:** (206)575-3505
E-mail: info@aerogo.com
URL: http://www.aerogo.com
Products: General industrial machinery. **SIC:** 5084 (Industrial Machinery & Equipment). **Est:** 1967. **Emp:** 75. **Officers:** Jack Byrne, President.

■ **15741** ■ **AGA Welding**
905 Belden Ave., SE
Canton, OH 44711
Phone: (330)453-8414   **Fax:** (330)453-8005
Products: Gas cutting and welding equipment (torches, cutting machines); Butane gas. **SICs:** 5084 (Industrial Machinery & Equipment); 5172 (Petroleum Products Nec). **Est:** 1955. **Sales:** $6,000,000 (2000). **Emp:** 22. **Officers:** Robert Diamond, President.

■ **15742** ■ **Air-Dreco**
1833 Johanna
Houston, TX 77055
Phone: (281)602-5500
Products: Hydraulic and pneumatic power products. **SIC:** 5085 (Industrial Supplies). **Officers:** Tom Brown, President; George Siller, VP of Finance.

■ **15743** ■ **Air & Hydraulic Engineering**
585 Old Norcross Rd., Ste. F
Lawrenceville, GA 30045-8702
Phone: (404)458-3115   **Fax:** (404)459-4029
Products: Hydraulic equipment and supplies. **SIC:** 5084 (Industrial Machinery & Equipment).

■ **15744** ■ **Air & Hydraulic Equipment, Inc.**
PO Box 3247
Chattanooga, TN 37404-0247
Phone: (423)756-2000
Free: (800)277-4466   **Fax:** (423)756-2084
E-mail: aneinc@aol.com
Products: Hydraulics; Pneumatics. **SIC:** 5084 (Industrial Machinery & Equipment). **Est:** 1971. **Sales:** $10,000,000 (2000). **Emp:** 55. **Officers:** Dick Lafollette, CEO; Cliff Keur, Marketing & Sales Mgr.; Scott Ehmig, Marketing & Sales Mgr.; Craig Deimling, Customer Service Contact; Frances Flowers, Human Resources.

■ **15745** ■ **Air Power Inc.**
PO Box 5406
High Point, NC 27262
Phone: (910)886-5081   **Fax:** (910)889-2745
Products: Pneumatic equipment. **SIC:** 5084 (Industrial Machinery & Equipment). **Est:** 1967. **Sales:** $20,200,000 (2000). **Emp:** 66. **Officers:** W.A. Ball, President; Alice F. Ball, Treasurer & Secty.; T.E. Rankin, General Mgr.; C.L. Ridge, Manager.

■ **15746** ■ **Airgas**
500 Codell Dr.
Lexington, KY 40509
Phone: (606)252-0343   **Fax:** (606)266-5816
Products: Welding equipment (stud welding, induction, electron beam, friction, plasma, etc.). **SICs:** 5084 (Industrial Machinery & Equipment); 5087 (Service Establishment Equipment). **Est:** 1982. **Emp:** 30. **Officers:** Butch Smith, Regional VP; Central Welding Supplies FR.

■ **15747** ■ **Airgas West**
9950 4th St.
Rancho Cucamonga, CA 91730
Phone: (909)987-6295   **Fax:** (909)987-9607
Products: Welding supplies; Gases, safety supplies, industrial coatings, tools. **SICs:** 5084 (Industrial Machinery & Equipment); 5169 (Chemicals & Allied Products Nec); 5085 (Industrial Supplies). **Est:** 1946. **Emp:** 600. **Officers:** Matt Whitton, District Manager. **Former Name:** Airco A and R Equipment Co.

■ **15748** ■ **AirSep Corporation**
290 Creekside Dr.
Buffalo, NY 14228-2070
Phone: (716)691-0202
Free: (800)320-0303   **Fax:** (716)691-0707
Products: Medical equipment; Special industrial machinery. **SICs:** 5084 (Industrial Machinery & Equipment); 5047 (Medical & Hospital Equipment). **Est:** 1987. **Officers:** Ravinder Bansal, CEO & Chairman of the Board; Joseph Priest, President & COO; Edward Vrana, Sr. VP.

■ **15749** ■ **Akron Overseas Inc.**
PO Box 5418
Akron, OH 44334
Phone: (330)864-6411   **Fax:** (330)864-9300
Products: Tires; Hydraulic pumps; Roof coatings. **SICs:** 5084 (Industrial Machinery & Equipment); 5014 (Tires & Tubes); 5033 (Roofing, Siding & Insulation). **Officers:** Willem Adams, Export Manager.

■ **15750** ■ **Alaska Industrial Hardware, Inc.**
2192 Viking Dr.
Anchorage, AK 99501
Phone: (907)276-7201   **Fax:** (907)258-3054
Products: Tools, including compressors and generators. **SICs:** 5084 (Industrial Machinery & Equipment); 5072 (Hardware).

■ **15751** ■ **Alban Tractor Company Inc.**
PO Box 9595
Baltimore, MD 21237
Phone: (410)686-7777
Free: (800)492-6994   **Fax:** (410)686-3729
E-mail: info@albancat.com
URL: http://www.albancat.com
Products: Tractors; Heavy equipment; Commercial diesel engines. **SICs:** 5084 (Industrial Machinery & Equipment); 5083 (Farm & Garden Machinery). **Est:** 1927. **Emp:** 480. **Officers:** James C. Alban IV, President; Frank Izzo, VP of Finance; James Stewart, VP of Sales; Robert Marano, VP of Service; Mike Burke, Customer Service Contact, e-mail: mburke@albancat.com. **Former Name:** Alban Engine Power Systems. **Former Name:** Alban Machinery and Hydraulic Services.

■ **15752** ■ **Alden Corp.**
251 Munson Rd.
Wolcott, CT 06716
Phone: (203)879-4889
Free: (800)832-5336   **Fax:** (203)879-6097
E-mail: alden@aldn.com
URL: http://www.aldn.com
Products: Drill-out broken bolt extractors. **SIC:** 5084 (Industrial Machinery & Equipment). **Est:** 1990. **Sales:** $4,000,000 (2000). **Emp:** 25. **Officers:** Don Desaulniers; Peter Bergamo, Sales /Marketing Contact; Kathy Lang, Customer Service Contact, e-mail: katlan@aldn.com; Dale Dosaulniers, Human Resources Contact.

■ **15753** ■ **Alfa Laval Celleco Inc.**
1000 Laval Blvd.
Lawrenceville, GA 30043
Phone: (770)963-2100   **Fax:** (770)339-6132
Products: Papermaking machinery. **SIC:** 5084 (Industrial Machinery & Equipment). **Sales:** $48,000,000 (2000). **Emp:** 55. **Officers:** John Sams, President; Bob Ross, CFO.

■ **15754** ■ **All American Truck Brokers**
PO Box 12365
Wilmington, DE 19850
Phone: (302)654-6101
Products: Dump trucks. **SIC:** 5084 (Industrial Machinery & Equipment).

■ **15755** ■ **G.B. Allan and Co.**
PO Box 816146
Dallas, TX 75381-6146
Phone: (972)620-7655
Free: (800)422-8727   **Fax:** (972)241-7126
E-mail: gballan@flash.net
Products: Industrial steam and process control equipment, including underground storage tanks, humidifiers, valves, and water heaters. **SIC:** 5084 (Industrial Machinery & Equipment). **Est:** 1940. **Sales:** $7,000,000 (2000). **Emp:** 14. **Officers:** Richard Hitz, President.

■ **15756** ■ **Allegheny High Lift Inc.**
R.D. 6, Box 510
Greensburg, PA 15601
Phone: (412)836-1535
Products: Forklifts; Aerial lifts. **SIC:** 5084 (Industrial Machinery & Equipment). **Est:** 1981. **Sales:** $12,000,000 (2000). **Emp:** 70. **Officers:** William Scott, President; Kim Scott, Controller; Bill Scott Jr., Dir. of Marketing.

■ **15757** ■ **Allied Industrial Equipment Corp.**
9388 Dielman Industrial Dr.
St. Louis, MO 63132
Phone: (314)569-2100
Free: (800)467-8900   **Fax:** (314)569-2595
E-mail: gschaffer@alliedindustrial.com
URL: http://www.alliedindustrial.com
Products: Industrial equipment, including forklifts. **SIC:** 5084 (Industrial Machinery & Equipment). **Est:** 1979. **Sales:** $24,000,000 (1999). **Emp:** 74. **Officers:** Steve Mattis, President; Charles Howes, Controller; Joel Donze, Operations Mgr.

■ **15758** ■ **Allied Trading Companies**
PO Box 3603
Chattanooga, TN 37415
Phone: (423)877-2000   **Fax:** (423)877-1111
Products: Raw materials; Textile equipment. **SICs:** 5131 (Piece Goods & Notions); 5084 (Industrial Machinery & Equipment). **Est:** 1979.

■ **15759** ■ **Allied Transmission, Inc.**
215 K Central Ave.
Farmingdale, NY 11735
Phone: (718)335-1800
Products: Industrial products. **SIC:** 5084 (Industrial Machinery & Equipment).

■ **15760** ■ **Allstates Textile Machinery Inc.**
PO Box 266
Anderson, SC 29622
Phone: (864)226-6195   **Fax:** (864)226-0968
E-mail: sales@allstatestextile.com
URL: http://www.allstatestextile.com
Products: Used textile machinery. **SIC:** 5084 (Industrial Machinery & Equipment). **Est:** 1967. **Emp:** 3. **Officers:** Richard J. Willis IV, President.

■ **15761** ■ **Alphatronics Engineering Corp.**
154 Talamine Ct
Colorado Springs, CO 80907
Phone: (719)520-5880   **Fax:** (719)520-5882
Products: Semiconductor test equipment. **SIC:** 5084 (Industrial Machinery & Equipment). **Officers:** John Sanders, President.

■ **15762** ■ **AM-DYN-IC Fluid Power**
3755 Linden Ave. SE
Grand Rapids, MI 49548
Phone: (616)241-4695 **Fax:** (616)241-4394
Products: Hydraulic equipment. **SIC:** 5084 (Industrial Machinery & Equipment).

■ **15763** ■ **Amchem Inc.**
155 N New Boston St.
Woburn, MA 01801
Phone: (781)938-0700 **Fax:** (781)935-8395
Products: Industrial machine tools. **SIC:** 5084 (Industrial Machinery & Equipment). **Est:** 1976. **Sales:** $5,000,000 (2000). **Emp:** 9. **Officers:** Philip Haigh, President; Cheryl Johnson, Office Mgr.

■ **15764** ■ **American Barmag Corp.**
PO Box 7046
Charlotte, NC 28241
Phone: (704)588-0072 **Fax:** (704)588-2047
Products: Man-made fibers machinery. **SIC:** 5084 (Industrial Machinery & Equipment). **Est:** 1965. **Sales:** $100,000,000 (2000). **Emp:** 120. **Officers:** Kay Schnaidt, Exec. VP.

■ **15765** ■ **American Chemical Works Co.**
PO Box 6031
Providence, RI 02940
Phone: (401)421-0828 **Fax:** (401)421-5909
Products: Jewelry chemicals. **SIC:** 5084 (Industrial Machinery & Equipment). **Sales:** $8,000,000 (2000). **Emp:** 20. **Officers:** Bruce Holland, President.

■ **15766** ■ **American Export Trading Company**
10919 Van Owen
North Hollywood, CA 91605
Phone: (818)985-5114 **Fax:** (818)985-5771
Products: Industrial machinery and equipment; Industrial supplies. **SICs:** 5084 (Industrial Machinery & Equipment); 5085 (Industrial Supplies). **Officers:** Stanley W. Epstein, President.

■ **15767** ■ **American Industrial Tool Co.**
4710 Mission Rd.
Mission, KS 66205
Phone: (913)432-4332 **Fax:** (913)432-0943
Products: Cylinders; Valves; Hoists; Pneumatic tools; Compressors. **SICs:** 5084 (Industrial Machinery & Equipment); 5072 (Hardware); 5085 (Industrial Supplies). **Emp:** 49. **Officers:** Tom Wilson.

■ **15768** ■ **American Laubscher Corp.**
80 Finn Ct.
Farmingdale, NY 11735
Phone: (516)694-5900 **Fax:** (516)293-0935
Products: Industrial supplies. **SIC:** 5084 (Industrial Machinery & Equipment). **Sales:** $19,000,000 (2000). **Emp:** 55.

■ **15769** ■ **American Printing Equipment Inc.**
PO Box 678
Addison, IL 60101
Phone: (630)832-5858 **Fax:** (630)832-5884
Products: Printing presses. **SIC:** 5084 (Industrial Machinery & Equipment). **Est:** 1970. **Sales:** $2,000,000 (2000). **Emp:** 4. **Officers:** Raymond L. Pawlak, President.

■ **15770** ■ **American Rotary Tools Company Inc.**
30 Beechwood Ave.
PO Box 809
Port Washington, NY 11050-0232
Phones: (516)883-2887 (516)883-2888
Free: (800)645-3824 **Fax:** (516)767-2397
E-mail: ArtcoTools@aol.com
Products: Metal deburring and polishing supplies; Mold and die maker's equipment. **SICs:** 5084 (Industrial Machinery & Equipment); 5085 (Industrial Supplies). **Est:** 1929. **Sales:** $2,000,000 (2000). **Emp:** 15. **Officers:** Wolfgang Klich, President; Santina Borthwick, Vice President.

■ **15771** ■ **Amida Industries Inc.**
PO Box 3147
Rock Hill, SC 29732
Phone: (803)324-3011
Free: (800)433-3026 **Fax:** (803)366-1101
E-mail: amidasales@juno.com
URL: http://www.amida.com
Products: Light towers; Material handlers, sprayers, generators, and dumpers. **SICs:** 5063 (Electrical Apparatus & Equipment); 5084 (Industrial Machinery & Equipment). **Est:** 1971. **Emp:** 200. **Officers:** Irvin Plowden Sr.; Ed McLelland, Admin. Sales Mgr.

■ **15772** ■ **Anatel Corp.**
2200 Central Ave.
Boulder, CO 80301
Phone: (303)442-5533
Free: (800)373-0531 **Fax:** (303)447-8365
Products: Process control instruments and equipment. **SIC:** 5084 (Industrial Machinery & Equipment). **Sales:** $12,000,000 (2000). **Emp:** 94. **Officers:** Jack Yamamori, President; Steve Wolfe, VP of Finance.

■ **15773** ■ **Anderson and Vreeland Inc.**
PO Box 1246
Caldwell, NJ 07007
Phone: (973)227-2270 **Fax:** (973)882-6621
Products: Printing equipment. **SIC:** 5043 (Photographic Equipment & Supplies). **Est:** 1961. **Sales:** $70,000,000 (2000). **Emp:** 150. **Officers:** W.K. Anderson, President; Ray Booker, Controller.

■ **15774** ■ **Applied Energy Company Inc.**
11431 Chairman Dr.
Dallas, TX 75243
Phone: (214)349-1171 **Fax:** (214)349-2037
Products: Fluid power hydraulics for industrial and commercial use. **SIC:** 5084 (Industrial Machinery & Equipment). **Est:** 1967. **Sales:** $11,000,000 (2000). **Emp:** 45. **Officers:** James E. Steedly Jr., President; Noel Gamadia, CFO; Fred Santa Maria, Vice President.

■ **15775** ■ **Applied Industrial Technologies**
8475 N 87th St.
PO Box 23488
Milwaukee, WI 53224
Phone: (414)355-5500 **Fax:** (414)355-1775
Products: Industrial products, including conveyors and power transmissions; Fluid power. **SIC:** 5084 (Industrial Machinery & Equipment).

■ **15776** ■ **Arbor Handling Services Inc.**
PO Box 91
Willow Grove, PA 19090
Phone: (215)657-2700
Products: Industrial machinery and equipment. **SIC:** 5084 (Industrial Machinery & Equipment). **Sales:** $18,000,000 (1994). **Emp:** 65. **Officers:** Mike Timken, Controller.

■ **15777** ■ **Arizona Welding Equipment Co.**
4030 W Lincoln St.
Phoenix, AZ 85009-5398
Phone: (602)269-2151 **Fax:** (602)278-8607
Products: Industrial machinery. **SIC:** 5084 (Industrial Machinery & Equipment). **Est:** 1941. **Sales:** $15,800,000 (2000). **Emp:** 96. **Officers:** William A. Meyer, President; Betty Pierson, Treasurer & Secty.

■ **15778** ■ **Armstrong Bros. Tool Co.**
5200 W Armstrong Ave.
Chicago, IL 60646
Phone: (773)763-3333 **Fax:** (773)763-2922
Products: Mechanics' hand service tools; Tools. **SIC:** 5084 (Industrial Machinery & Equipment).

■ **15779** ■ **Aro Corp.**
1725 US Hwy. 1 N
Southern Pines, NC 28387
Phone: (919)692-8700 **Fax:** (919)692-7822
Products: Pneumatic tools and engine start-up systems. **SIC:** 5084 (Industrial Machinery & Equipment). **Sales:** $6,000,000 (2000). **Emp:** 499. **Officers:** Harry G. Leidich.

■ **15780** ■ **Aronson-Campbell Industrial Supply Inc.**
1700 136th PL, NE
Bellevue, WA 98005-2328
Products: Industrial equipment, including power tools and hand tools; Solvents. **SICs:** 5084 (Industrial Machinery & Equipment); 5169 (Chemicals & Allied Products Nec). **Est:** 1890. **Sales:** $14,000,000 (2000). **Emp:** 23. **Officers:** John Buckberger, President; Bruce Buckberger, Vice President.

■ **15781** ■ **Assembly Automation Industries**
1858 Business Center Dr.
Duarte, CA 91010
Phone: (626)303-2777 **Fax:** (626)303-8874
Products: Pneumatic screw driving equipment. **SIC:** 5084 (Industrial Machinery & Equipment). **Officers:** Francis Frost, President.

■ **15782** ■ **Associated Bearings**
115 N Jackson
Topeka, KS 66603
Phone: (785)232-5508 **Fax:** (785)235-3826
Products: Industrial equipment, including power transmissions, bearings, belts, and pulleys. **SICs:** 5084 (Industrial Machinery & Equipment); 5085 (Industrial Supplies).

■ **15783** ■ **Associated Bearings**
2029 Wyandotte
Kansas City, MO 64108
Phone: (816)421-0407 **Fax:** (816)283-3287
Products: Industrial equipment, including power transmissions, bearings, belts, and pulleys. **SICs:** 5084 (Industrial Machinery & Equipment); 5085 (Industrial Supplies).

■ **15784** ■ **Associated Material Handling Industries Inc.**
1230 Brookville Way
Indianapolis, IN 46239-1048
Phone: (317)576-0300 **Fax:** (317)577-0383
Products: Forklifts. **SIC:** 5084 (Industrial Machinery & Equipment). **Sales:** $6,000,000 (2000). **Emp:** 23.

■ **15785** ■ **Astral Precision Equipment Co.**
800 Busse Rd.
Elk Grove Village, IL 60007
Phone: (847)439-1650
Products: Tooling; Tool and die machinery and parts. **SIC:** 5084 (Industrial Machinery & Equipment). **Est:** 1957. **Sales:** $3,000,000 (2000). **Emp:** 14. **Officers:** Xavier F. Kaufmann, President.

■ **15786** ■ **Atec Inc.**
12600 Executive Dr.
Stafford, TX 77477-3064
Phone: (281)276-2700 **Fax:** (281)240-2682
Products: Scientific and measurement devices. **SIC:** 5084 (Industrial Machinery & Equipment). **Sales:** $12,500,000 (2000). **Emp:** 100.

■ **15787** ■ **Athens Material Handling Inc.**
PO Box 6685
Athens, GA 30604
Phone: (706)543-7410
Products: Forklifts; Material handling supplies. **SIC:** 5084 (Industrial Machinery & Equipment). **Sales:** $4,000,000 (2000). **Emp:** 14. **Officers:** Dennis Graves, President.

■ **15788** ■ **Atlantic Fluid Power**
111 Bridge Rd.
Hauppauge, NY 11788
Phone: (516)234-3131 **Fax:** (516)234-3283
Products: Hydraulic and pneumatic equipment. **SIC:** 5084 (Industrial Machinery & Equipment).

■ **15789** ■ **Atlantic Trading Company Ltd.**
225 W 34th St., Ste. 2015
New York, NY 10122
Phone: (212)268-4487
Free: (888)482-2725 **Fax:** (212)268-4487
Products: Petroleum, fuels, and related equipment. **SIC:** 5084 (Industrial Machinery & Equipment). **Sales:** $5,000,000 (2000). **Emp:** 4.

■ 15790 ■ Atlas Lift Truck Rentals
5050 River Rd.
Schiller Park, IL 60176
Phone: (847)678-3450 **Fax:** (847)678-1750
E-mail: wholesale@atlaslift.com
URL: http://www.atlaslift.com
Products: Material handling equipment, including lift trucks; Construction equipment. **SICs:** 5084 (Industrial Machinery & Equipment); 5082 (Construction & Mining Machinery). **Est:** 1951. **Sales:** $90,000,000 (2000). **Emp:** 250. **Officers:** Harold Birndorf, President; Howard Bernstein, Chairman of the Board, e-mail: bernstein@atlaslift.com.

■ 15791 ■ Atlas Machine and Supply Inc.
7000 Global Dr.
Louisville, KY 40258-1976
Phone: (502)584-7262 **Fax:** (502)589-0310
Products: Industrial machinery and supplies. **SIC:** 5084 (Industrial Machinery & Equipment). **Est:** 1907. **Sales:** $13,000,000 (2000). **Emp:** 120. **Officers:** Robert N. Gimmel, President; Mike Coatney, Controller; Richard Gimmel Jr., Dir. of Marketing & Sales.

■ 15792 ■ ATS Machinery and Equipment Co.
515 S Maxwell Rd.
Peoria, IL 61607
Phone: (309)697-5530 **Fax:** (309)695-5541
Products: Used machine tools. **SIC:** 5084 (Industrial Machinery & Equipment). **Est:** 1947. **Sales:** $3,000,000 (2000). **Emp:** 14. **Officers:** John McEllin, President; Randy Blaudan, Dir. of Sales.

■ 15793 ■ Automatic Pump and Equipment Company Inc.
PO Box 26012
Beaumont, TX 77720-6012
Phone: (409)866-2314 **Fax:** (409)866-6501
Products: Pumps. **SIC:** 5084 (Industrial Machinery & Equipment). **Est:** 1946. **Sales:** $7,000,000 (2000). **Emp:** 23. **Officers:** Ronald Moye, President; T.H. Kent, Vice President; Larry Walker, VP & General Merchandising Mgr.

■ 15794 ■ B & J Industrial Supply Co.
PO Box 80526
Seattle, WA 98108
Phone: (206)762-4430
Free: (800)767-4430 **Fax:** (206)762-5329
URL: http://www.industsupply.com
Products: Industrial tools. **SICs:** 5084 (Industrial Machinery & Equipment); 5085 (Industrial Supplies). **Est:** 1936. **Emp:** 90. **Officers:** Martin Burkland, President.

■ 15795 ■ Babush Conveyor Corp.
10605 W Glenbrook Ct.
Milwaukee, WI 53224
Phone: (414)362-7100 **Fax:** (414)354-0441
E-mail: babushsales@babush.com
URL: http://www.babush.com
Products: Conveyors for packages, cartons, and pallets. **SIC:** 5084 (Industrial Machinery & Equipment). **Est:** 1924. **Sales:** $6,000,000 (1999). **Emp:** 30. **Officers:** Chris Shult, President. **Former Name:** Babush Corp.

■ 15796 ■ Babush Corp.
PO Box 660
Menomonee Falls, WI 53052
Phone: (414)255-5300 **Fax:** (414)255-1808
Products: Industrial machinery. **SIC:** 5084 (Industrial Machinery & Equipment). **Sales:** $5,000,000 (2000). **Emp:** 11.

■ 15797 ■ The Bag Connection Inc.
459 SW 9th St.
Dundee, OR 97115
Phone: (503)538-8180 **Fax:** (503)538-0418
Products: Systems for recycling; maintenance program for industrial sling bulk bags. **SIC:** 5084 (Industrial Machinery & Equipment).

■ 15798 ■ Bailey Company Inc.
PO Box 80565
Nashville, TN 37208
Phone: (615)242-0351
Products: Heavy equipment. **SICs:** 5084 (Industrial Machinery & Equipment); 5082 (Construction & Mining Machinery). **Est:** 1954. **Sales:** $49,800,000 (2000). **Emp:** 302. **Officers:** Gordon Morrow, President; Bert Bailey, CFO.

■ 15799 ■ BAL RV Products Group
365 W Victoria St.
Compton, CA 90220
Phone: (310)639-4000
Free: (800)347-2232 **Fax:** (310)639-7411
E-mail: buyajack@aol.com
URL: http://www.norcoindustries.com
Products: Stabilizing jacks; Accessories for travel trailers, fifth wheel trailers, and motor homes. **SICs:** 5084 (Industrial Machinery & Equipment); 5013 (Motor Vehicle Supplies & New Parts). **Est:** 1964. **Emp:** 100. **Officers:** Andy Tallman, Chairman of the Board; Jeff Few, President; Bernie Garceau, VP of Sales, e-mail: bgarceau@aol.com.

■ 15800 ■ A.O. Barnes Co.
PO Box 2539
Anderson, IN 46018
Phone: (765)643-5364 **Fax:** (765)643-5915
Products: Abrasives; Perishable tooling. **SICs:** 5084 (Industrial Machinery & Equipment); 5085 (Industrial Supplies). **Est:** 1935. **Sales:** $1,500,000 (2000). **Emp:** 9. **Officers:** James Hauke, President.

■ 15801 ■ Barone Inc.
5879 W 58th Ave.
Arvada, CO 80002
Phone: (303)424-4497 **Fax:** (303)424-4476
Products: Fabricates and builds equipment and machinery. **SIC:** 5084 (Industrial Machinery & Equipment). **Officers:** Frank Barone, President.

■ 15802 ■ Barton Group Inc.
1505 Corporate Ave.
Memphis, TN 38132
Phone: (901)345-5294
Products: Industrial machinery. **SIC:** 5084 (Industrial Machinery & Equipment). **Sales:** $6,000,000 (1993). **Emp:** 20. **Officers:** Richard Barton, President.

■ 15803 ■ Rudolf Bass Inc.
45 Halladay St.
Jersey City, NJ 07304
Phone: (201)433-3800
Free: (800)526-3003 **Fax:** (201)433-6853
E-mail: rbassmachy@aol.com
Products: New and used woodworking machines. **SIC:** 5084 (Industrial Machinery & Equipment). **Est:** 1918. **Sales:** $4,000,000 (2000). **Emp:** 12. **Officers:** Edwin L. Bass, President; Richard H. Bass, CFO.

■ 15804 ■ Bass Woodworking Machinery
1080 E 29th St.
Hialeah, FL 33013-3518
Phone: (305)691-2277
Free: (800)432-5440 **Fax:** (305)836-5483
Products: Industrial machinery. **SIC:** 5084 (Industrial Machinery & Equipment). **Sales:** $1,000,000 (2000). **Emp:** 8.

■ 15805 ■ Bass Woodworking Machinery, Inc.
PO Box 173932
Hialeah, FL 33017-3932
Phone: (305)691-2277
Free: (800)432-5440 **Fax:** (305)836-5483
E-mail: basswwmachinery@aol.com
Products: Woodworking machinery, and accessories. **SICs:** 5084 (Industrial Machinery & Equipment); 5072 (Hardware). **Est:** 1918. **Sales:** $1,000,000 (1999). **Emp:** 8. **Officers:** Richard Bass, President; Silvia Secades, Vice President; Lazaro Castro, Sales/Marketing Contact.

■ 15806 ■ Louis P. Batson Co.
PO Box 3978
Greenville, SC 29608
Phone: (864)242-5262 **Fax:** (864)271-4535
E-mail: batson@lpbatson.com
URL: http://www.lpbatson.com
Products: Textile machinery and supplies; Industrial machinery; Paper and plastic machinery and supplies. **SICs:** 5084 (Industrial Machinery & Equipment); 5085 (Industrial Supplies). **Est:** 1948. **Emp:** 50. **Officers:** Louis P. Batson Jr., CEO; Elliott Batson, President; Glenn Batson, Vice President; Dreugh Batson, Group Mgr.; Stan Bell, Group Mgr.

■ 15807 ■ Battey Machinery Co.
PO Box 33
Rome, GA 30162-0033
Phone: (706)291-4141
Products: Industrial machinery. **SIC:** 5084 (Industrial Machinery & Equipment). **Est:** 1901. **Sales:** $18,000,000 (2000). **Emp:** 100. **Officers:** Jack F. Cumming, CEO; V.B. Yeargan Jr., Treasurer & Secty.; Joel K. Dyer, Dir. of Systems.

■ 15808 ■ Baum Iron Co.
1221 Harney St.
Omaha, NE 68102
Phone: (402)345-4122 **Fax:** (402)345-0663
Products: Hydraulic equipment. **SIC:** 5084 (Industrial Machinery & Equipment).

■ 15809 ■ Baumer Electric Ltd.
122 Spring St., No. C-6
Southington, CT 06489
Phone: (860)621-2121
Free: (800)937-9336 **Fax:** (860)628-6280
E-mail: sales.us@baumerelectric.com
URL: http://www.baumerelectric.com
Products: Sensors. **SICs:** 5084 (Industrial Machinery & Equipment); 5063 (Electrical Apparatus & Equipment). **Est:** 1988. **Sales:** $7,000,000 (1999). **Emp:** 20. **Officers:** Ed Leese, Distribution Mgr.; Stephen Petronio, Engineering Mgr.; Linda Collin, Customer Service Contact.

■ 15810 ■ Bayou Import-Export Corp.
2110 31st Ct.
Kenner, LA 70065
Phone: (504)461-8797 **Fax:** (504)467-7901
E-mail: conscreen@aol.com
Products: Screen printing machinery, supplies, and equipment; Industrial machinery and supplies. **SIC:** 5084 (Industrial Machinery & Equipment). **Sales:** $750,000 (1999). **Officers:** Victor Garcia, President; Anne Donato, Vice President.

■ 15811 ■ Bearing Distributors Inc.
25 S 6th St.
PO Box 537
Princeton, IL 61356
Phone: (815)875-3386 **Fax:** (815)879-0500
E-mail: princeton@bdi-usa.com
Products: Ball bearings; Power transmissions. **SICs:** 5084 (Industrial Machinery & Equipment); 5085 (Industrial Supplies). **Est:** 1935. **Emp:** 6. **Officers:** Brad Oeder; Mike Green.

■ 15812 ■ Bearings & Drives Inc.
3012 Freeman St.
PO Box 5267
Chattanooga, TN 37406
Phone: (423)624-8333 **Fax:** (423)624-8335
Products: Industrial power transmissions; Hydraulic power equipment. **SIC:** 5084 (Industrial Machinery & Equipment).

■ 15813 ■ Beckwith Kuffel Industries Inc.
5930 1st Ave. S
Seattle, WA 98108-3248
Phone: (206)767-6700
Free: (800)767-6700 **Fax:** (206)767-6230
URL: http://www.b-k.com
Products: Industrial compressors and pumps. **SIC:** 5084 (Industrial Machinery & Equipment). **Est:** 1979. **Sales:** $12,000,000 (2000). **Emp:** 40. **Officers:** G. Beckwith; L. Kuffel; Mike Pierson, Sales & Marketing Contact.

■ 15814 ■ B.E.E. Industrial Supply Inc.
25634 Nickel Pl.
Hayward, CA 94545-3222
Phone: (510)293-3180 **Fax:** (510)293-3190
Products: Abrasive products; Brushes; Dies; Drills; Metal cutting machine tools; Hardware fasteners; Hand tools; Polishers, sanders, and grinders. **SICs:** 5085 (Industrial Supplies); 5072 (Hardware); 5084 (Industrial Machinery & Equipment). **Est:** 1975. **Sales:** $3,000,000 (2000). **Emp:** 11.

■ 15815 ■ **Behr Machinery and Equipment Corp.**
PO Box 1318
Rockford, IL 61105
Phone: (815)987-2640 **Fax:** (815)987-2650
Products: Machinery; Machine tools. **SIC:** 5084 (Industrial Machinery & Equipment). **Est:** 1985. **Sales:** $1,200,000 (2000). **Emp:** 4. **Officers:** R.L. Schou, Chairman of the Board; James R. Schou, President.

■ 15816 ■ **C. Behrens Machinery Co.**
Danvers Indust. Park
Danvers, MA 01923
Phone: (978)774-4200
Products: Machinery, including turret punch presses. **SIC:** 5084 (Industrial Machinery & Equipment). **Sales:** $6,000,000 (2000). **Emp:** 20. **Officers:** Richard Jacob, President.

■ 15817 ■ **Bencruz Enterprises Corporation**
7820 SW 93rd Ave.
Miami, FL 33173
Phone: (305)595-2668 **Fax:** (305)598-7618
Products: Industrial machinery and equipment. **SIC:** 5084 (Industrial Machinery & Equipment). **Officers:** Ben R. Cruz, Intl. Consultant.

■ 15818 ■ **Berendsen Fluid Power, Inc.**
3528 Roger Chaffe Memorial Dr.
Wyoming, MI 49548
Phone: (616)452-4560 **Fax:** (616)452-5768
Products: Hydraulics equipment and supplies. **SICs:** 5084 (Industrial Machinery & Equipment); 5085 (Industrial Supplies). **Former Name:** Lucas Fluid Power Inc.

■ 15819 ■ **Louis Berkman Co.**
PO Box 820
Steubenville, OH 43952
Phone: (740)283-3722 **Fax:** (740)283-3621
Products: Industrial machinery and hardware. **SICs:** 5084 (Industrial Machinery & Equipment); 5072 (Hardware). **Sales:** $100,000,000 (2000). **Emp:** 800. **Officers:** Louis Berkman, President; John Koren, Controller.

■ 15820 ■ **The Berns Co.**
1250 W 17th St.
Long Beach, CA 90813
Phone: (562)437-0471
Free: (800)421-3773 **Fax:** (562)436-1074
E-mail: bernsco@aol.com
URL: http://www.thebernsco.com
Products: Forklifts and replacement parts. **SIC:** 5084 (Industrial Machinery & Equipment). **Est:** 1956. **Sales:** $5,000,000 (2000). **Emp:** 35. **Officers:** Dan Berns, President & Chairman of the Board; Steve Berns, Dir. of Marketing. **Alternate Name:** Forklift Parts Mfg. Co. Inc.

■ 15821 ■ **Best Label Company Inc./IMS Div.**
2943 Whipple Rd.
Union City, CA 94587
Phone: (510)489-5400 **Fax:** (510)489-2914
Products: Auto marking equipment, custom pressure sensitive labels and labeling machines. **SICs:** 5084 (Industrial Machinery & Equipment); 5112 (Stationery & Office Supplies). **Officers:** Ernest Wong, CEO.

■ 15822 ■ **BET Plant Services USA Inc.**
4067 Industrial Park Dr., #3A
Norcross, GA 30071-1638
Products: Industrial machinery and equipment. **SIC:** 5084 (Industrial Machinery & Equipment). **Sales:** $4,750,000,000 (2000). **Emp:** 12,500. **Officers:** Ralph A. Trallo, President.

■ 15823 ■ **Beta Supply Co.**
PO Box 5217
Houston, TX 77262
Phone: (713)921-3600 **Fax:** (713)921-3313
E-mail: info@betaintl.com
URL: http://www.betaintl.com
Products: Valves and fittings for the petrochemical, oil and gas, and pipeline industries. **SIC:** 5085 (Industrial Supplies). **Est:** 1976. **Sales:** $23,500,000 (2000). **Emp:** 308. **Officers:** Robert Goldsmith, President; Rafael Ramos, General Mgr., e-mail: rramos@betaintl.com.

■ 15824 ■ **Bimex Incorporated**
3617 Shallford Rd.
Atlanta, GA 30340
Phone: (404)451-2525 **Fax:** (404)457-1827
Products: Machinery accessories, including router bits; Chemical belt cleaner; Industrial machinery. **SICs:** 5084 (Industrial Machinery & Equipment); 5169 (Chemicals & Allied Products Nec). **Officers:** D.C. Benson, Universal Marketing Manager.

■ 15825 ■ **Binks Manufacturing Co.**
9201 W Belmont Ave.
Franklin Park, IL 60131-2887
Phone: (847)671-3000 **Fax:** (847)671-6489
Products: Spray guns; Pumps; Compressors. **SIC:** 5084 (Industrial Machinery & Equipment). **Est:** 1890. **Sales:** $222,200,000 (2000). **Emp:** 1,623. **Officers:** Burke B. Roche, CEO & President; Doran J. Unschuld, VP & Secty.; Stephen Kennedy, Dir. of Marketing; Lloyd McRoy, Dir. of Information Systems; James Lindquist, Dir of Human Resources.

■ 15826 ■ **Bishop Ladder Co. Inc.**
1400 Park St.
Hartford, CT 06106
Phone: (860)951-3246
Products: Ladders and scaffolds. **SIC:** 5084 (Industrial Machinery & Equipment). **Est:** 1873. **Sales:** $2,000,000 (2000). **Emp:** 6. **Officers:** Robert Rider, President.

■ 15827 ■ **Black Equipment Co. Inc.**
PO Box 5286
Evansville, IN 47716
Phone: (812)477-6481 **Fax:** (812)474-4346
Products: Industrial machinery, including forklift trucks, conveyors, advance industrial sweepers and scrubbers, loaders, industrial vehicles, and floor care equipment. **SIC:** 5084 (Industrial Machinery & Equipment). **Est:** 1956. **Sales:** $13,000,000 (2000). **Emp:** 80. **Officers:** Kenneth F. Bonnell, President; Milton J. Black, Chairman of the Board; James Black, Vice President.

■ 15828 ■ **Bohl Equipment Co.**
534 Laskey Rd.
Toledo, OH 43612
Phone: (419)476-7525 **Fax:** (419)476-0558
Products: Forklifts; Overhead cranes; Industrial equipment parts. **SIC:** 5084 (Industrial Machinery & Equipment). **Est:** 1953. **Sales:** $16,000,000 (2000). **Emp:** 75. **Officers:** R.A. Bohl, President; S.C. Bohl, VP of Finance; Robert D. Bohl, VP of Sales.

■ 15829 ■ **Bolliger Corp.**
P.O. Box 2949
Spartanburg, SC 29304
Phone: (864)582-1900
Products: Textile machinery. **SIC:** 5084 (Industrial Machinery & Equipment).

■ 15830 ■ **Bollinger Healthcare**
222 W Airport Fwy.
Irving, TX 75062-6322
Free: (800)858-4568 **Fax:** (214)721-9188
Products: Industrial equipment, including supports and weights. **SIC:** 5084 (Industrial Machinery & Equipment). **Emp:** 82.

■ 15831 ■ **Bore Technology Inc.**
5977 Hutchinson Rd.
Batavia, OH 45103
Phone: (513)625-8374
Products: Nickel plating equipment. **SIC:** 5084 (Industrial Machinery & Equipment). **Est:** 1988. **Sales:** $900,000 (2000). **Emp:** 5. **Officers:** Bill Moeller, President.

■ 15832 ■ **Bornell Supply Company Inc.**
8550 North 25A
PO Box 1138
Piqua, OH 45356
Phone: (937)773-5323 **Fax:** (937)773-8015
Products: Mechanical power transmission equipment. **SIC:** 5084 (Industrial Machinery & Equipment). **Est:** 1949. **Sales:** $6,000,000 (2000). **Emp:** 20. **Officers:** Clinton G. Wander Jr., President.

■ 15833 ■ **Robert Bosch Corp. Packaging Machinery Div.**
PO Box 579
Bridgman, MI 49106-0579
Phone: (616)466-4149 **Fax:** (616)466-4149
Products: Packaging machinery. **SIC:** 5084 (Industrial Machinery & Equipment). **Sales:** $59,000,000 (2000). **Emp:** 69. **Officers:** Peter F. Loveland, Exec. VP.

■ 15834 ■ **Robert Bosch Power Tools**
9401 James Ave. S
Bloomington, MN 55431-2500
Phone: (612)881-6979 **Fax:** (612)881-7046
Products: Power tools and parts. **SIC:** 5084 (Industrial Machinery & Equipment). **Emp:** 3. **Officers:** Mark Napadano.

■ 15835 ■ **Boshco Inc.**
42 Manning Rd.
Billerica, MA 01821
Phone: (978)667-1911
Free: (800)442-4430 **Fax:** (978)671-0011
E-mail: contact@boshco.com
URL: http://www.boshco.com
Products: Woodworking equipment. **SIC:** 5084 (Industrial Machinery & Equipment). **Est:** 1942. **Sales:** $5,000,000 (2000). **Emp:** 15. **Officers:** Peter B. Boshco, President; Randall R. Boshco, Vice President.

■ 15836 ■ **Boshco Inc.**
42 Manning Rd.
Billerica, MA 01821
Phone: (978)667-1911
Free: (800)442-4430 **Fax:** (978)671-0011
Products: Industrial machinery. **SIC:** 5084 (Industrial Machinery & Equipment). **Sales:** $5,000,000 (2000). **Emp:** 15.

■ 15837 ■ **Bostwick-Braun Lorain Div.**
5000 Grove Ave.
Lorain, OH 44055-3612
Phone: (440)277-8288 **Fax:** (440)277-0858
E-mail: bblor@centuryinter.net
URL: http://www.bostwick-braun.com
Products: Industrial tools; Construction supplies. **SICs:** 5084 (Industrial Machinery & Equipment); 5082 (Construction & Mining Machinery). **Emp:** 25. **Former Name:** Kohlmyer Supply Co.

■ 15838 ■ **BPC Supply Co.**
2753 Midland Dr.
Ogden, UT 84401
Phone: (801)399-5564
Products: Conveyors, Hydraulic power transmission. **SIC:** 5084 (Industrial Machinery & Equipment).

■ 15839 ■ **Bracken Company Inc.**
109 Lindberg Ave.
Methuen, MA 01844
Phone: (978)685-2200
Free: (800)878-2725 **Fax:** (978)686-3685
Products: Industrial machinery. **SIC:** 5084 (Industrial Machinery & Equipment). **Est:** 1950. **Sales:** $12,000,000 (2000). **Emp:** 30. **Officers:** Paul C. Bracken Jr., President; Dave Schuettner, Treasurer.

■ 15840 ■ **Brance-Krachy Company Inc.**
PO Box 1724
Houston, TX 77011
Phone: (713)225-6661
Free: (800)454-9451 **Fax:** (713)225-5044
E-mail: sales@brancekrachy.com
Products: Industrial equipment and supplies. **SICs:** 5063 (Electrical Apparatus & Equipment); 5065 (Electronic Parts & Equipment Nec). **Est:** 1926. **Sales:** $17,000,000 (2000). **Emp:** 60. **Officers:** Vickie Goree, President.

■ 15841 ■ **Branom Instrument Company Inc.**
PO Box 80307
Seattle, WA 98108
Phone: (206)762-6050
Free: (800)767-6051 **Fax:** (206)767-5669
Products: Pneumatic and electronic control panels for process control; Electrical meters. **SIC:** 5084 (Industrial Machinery & Equipment). **Sales:** $10,000,000 (2000). **Emp:** 75. **Officers:** William Branom, CEO.

■ 15842 ■ Braymar Precision Inc.
1889 W Commonwealth Ave., Ste. P
Fullerton, CA 92833-3028
Phone: (714)870-1411
Free: (888)BRA-YMAR **Fax:** (714)870-4267
Products: Fasteners; Inserts; Fittings and standoffs.
SICs: 5084 (Industrial Machinery & Equipment); 5085
(Industrial Supplies). **Est:** 1979. **Sales:** $2,500,000
(2000). **Emp:** 12. **Officers:** Mark F. Reihl, President;
Brad W. Reihl, VP of Operations; Jay K. Reihl, VP of
Marketing & Sales.

■ 15843 ■ Brehob Corp.
1334 S Meridian St.
Indianapolis, IN 46225
Phone: (317)231-8080
Free: (800)632-4451 **Fax:** (317)231-8082
E-mail: brehob@brehob.com
URL: http://www.brehob.com
Products: Electrical cranes; Hoists; Air compressors;
Electric motors. **SICs:** 5063 (Electrical Apparatus &
Equipment); 5075 (Warm Air Heating & Air-
Conditioning); 5084 (Industrial Machinery &
Equipment). **Est:** 1953. **Sales:** $30,000,000 (2000).
Emp: 175. **Officers:** James P. Smither, Chairman of
the Board.

■ 15844 ■ Brennan-Hamilton Co.
PO Box 2626
South San Francisco, CA 94083
Phone: (650)589-2700 **Fax:** (650)589-9209
Products: Industrial cutting tools. **SICs:** 5084
(Industrial Machinery & Equipment); 5085 (Industrial
Supplies). **Est:** 1955. **Sales:** $4,000,000 (2000). **Emp:**
7. **Officers:** Elaine Bergin, President; Tom Bergin,
Treasurer & Secty.

■ 15845 ■ Briggs-Weaver Inc.
306 Airline Dr. Ste. 100A
Coppell, TX 75019
Phone: (972)304-7200
Free: (877)292-2737 **Fax:** (972)304-7300
E-mail: sales@briggsweaver.com
URL: http://www.briggsweaver.com
Products: Maintenance, repair and operations
supplies (MRO); Industrial supplies. **SICs:** 5084
(Industrial Machinery & Equipment); 5085 (Industrial
Supplies); 5049 (Professional Equipment Nec). **Est:**
1896. **Emp:** 110. **Officers:** Terry Taylor, President, e-
mail: ttaylor@briggsweaver.com; Joe Dugger, Exec.
VP, e-mail: jdugger@briggsweaver.com; Rick Floeck,
VP of Finance, e-mail: rfloeck@briggsweaver.com;
Patrick McDonald, VP of Marketing & Sales, e-mail:
pmcdonald@briggsweaver.com; Hank Rist, VP of
Operations, e-mail: hrist@briggsweaver.com.

■ 15846 ■ Brodie Inc.
10 Ballard Rd.
Lawrence, MA 01843
Phone: (508)682-6300 **Fax:** (508)686-0608
Products: Forklifts. **SIC:** 5084 (Industrial Machinery &
Equipment). **Est:** 1948. **Sales:** $35,000,000 (2000).
Emp: 112. **Officers:** Walter J. Schumman, President;
Barbara Cogan, Controller.

■ 15847 ■ Brookline Machine Co.
87 Belmont St., No. 1
North Andover, MA 01845-2304
Phone: (978)689-0750
Products: Hydraulics equipment and supplies,
including drive lines. **SIC:** 5084 (Industrial Machinery &
Equipment).

■ 15848 ■ D.P. Brown of Pennsylvania Corp.
710 Street Rd.
Bensalem, PA 19020
Phone: (215)245-6800 **Fax:** (215)245-0509
Products: Power machinery, pulleys, and retractors;
Power transmissions; Conveying equipment. **SICs:**
5063 (Electrical Apparatus & Equipment); 5084
(Industrial Machinery & Equipment). **Est:** 1894. **Sales:**
$4,000,000 (2000). **Emp:** 14. **Officers:** E.B. Thomas
Jr., CEO & President.

■ 15849 ■ Browne Dreyfus International Ltd.
305 Madison Ave., Ste. 420
New York, NY 10165
Phone: (212)867-7700 **Fax:** (212)867-7820
E-mail: info@bdi-ltd.com
URL: http://www. bdi-ltd.com
Products: Specialty automotive tools; Welding
equipment; Garage equipment. **SIC:** 5084 (Industrial
Machinery & Equipment). **Est:** 1989. **Emp:** 12.
Officers: Jan Philip Browne, Managing Dir.; Ed Smith,
Customer Service Contact, e-mail: esmith@bdi-
ltd.com.

■ 15850 ■ Bruening Bearings Inc.
3600 Euclid Ave.
Cleveland, OH 44115
Phone: (216)881-8900 **Fax:** (216)391-9110
Products: Industrial machines and supplies. **SICs:**
5084 (Industrial Machinery & Equipment); 5085
(Industrial Supplies). **Sales:** $52,000,000 (1994). **Emp:**
256. **Officers:** John C. Dannemiller, CEO & Chairman
of the Board; John R. Whitten, VP & Treasurer.

■ 15851 ■ Brungart Equipment Company Inc.
3930 Pinson Valley Pkwy.
Birmingham, AL 35217-1856
Phone: (205)520-2000 **Fax:** (205)520-2031
Products: Industrial equipment. **SIC:** 5084 (Industrial
Machinery & Equipment). **Sales:** $48,200,000 (2000).
Emp: 220. **Officers:** Ken Brown, President; Don
Wallace, CFO.

■ 15852 ■ Bryan Equipment Sales Inc.
457 Wards Corner Rd.
Loveland, OH 45140
Phone: (513)248-2000 **Fax:** (513)248-0398
E-mail: info@bryanequipment.com
Products: Power tools. **SICs:** 5084 (Industrial
Machinery & Equipment); 5083 (Farm & Garden
Machinery). **Est:** 1948. **Sales:** $55,000,000 (1999).
Emp: 60. **Officers:** Frederick Bryan III, Owner and
Chairman; J. Thomas Jones, President; Tom Mattei,
VP & Treasurer; Casey McGrath, Sales & Marketing
Contact; Julie Phelps, Customer Service Contact; Lisa
Taylor, Human Resources Contact.

■ 15853 ■ P.R. Bryant Corp.
2229 Massachusetts Ave.
Indianapolis, IN 46218-4341
Phone: (317)262-0695
Products: Used machinery. **SIC:** 5084 (Industrial
Machinery & Equipment). **Est:** 1964. **Sales:**
$1,000,000 (2000). **Emp:** 5. **Officers:** Paul R. Bryant,
Owner; Mary Bryant, Treasurer & Secty.; Steve Lee,
Vice President.

■ 15854 ■ Buckeye Industrial Supply Company
3989 Groves Rd.
PO Box 328967
Columbus, OH 43232
Phone: (614)864-8400
Free: (800)686-8400 **Fax:** (614)864-1818
E-mail: bisbuckeye@aol.com
URL: http://www.bisbuckeye.com
Products: Metal cutting machine tools; Regrinds.
SICs: 5084 (Industrial Machinery & Equipment); 5085
(Industrial Supplies). **Est:** 1947. **Emp:** 26. **Officers:**
Jack Meizlish, President; Brent Meizlish, VP of
Operations; Rick Meizlish, VP of Sales; Jean Funk,
Admin. Asst.

■ 15855 ■ Bullington Lift Trucks
2790 Broadway
PO Box 763
Macon, GA 31298
Phone: (912)788-0520
Free: (800)950-5438 **Fax:** (912)784-1525
E-mail: bullift@mindspring.com
Products: Forklifts; Dock equipment; Material handling
equipment; Commercial lawn care equipment; Farm
equipment; Parts for forklifts and tractors. **SICs:** 5084
(Industrial Machinery & Equipment); 5083 (Farm &
Garden Machinery); 5082 (Construction & Mining
Machinery); 5013 (Motor Vehicle Supplies & New
Parts). **Est:** 1969. **Sales:** $4,000,000 (2000). **Emp:** 24.
Officers: F.L. Bullington, Chairman of the Board;
Danny Bullington, President; Eddy Billington, Vice
President; Toby Billington, Vice President.

■ 15856 ■ B.H. Bunn Co.
2730 Drane Field Rd.
Lakeland, FL 33811-1395
Phone: (813)647-1555
Free: (800)222-2866 **Fax:** (813)686-2866
E-mail: bunnytyco@aol.com
Products: Package tying machines. **SIC:** 5085
(Industrial Supplies). **Est:** 1907. **Sales:** $3,000,000
(2000). **Emp:** 15. **Officers:** Richard B. Bunn, CEO;
Richard B. Bunn, Chairman of the Board.

■ 15857 ■ Burch Body Works Inc.
22 N Monroe St.
Rockford, MI 49341
Phone: (616)866-4421 **Fax:** (616)866-4454
Products: Hoist systems. **SIC:** 5084 (Industrial
Machinery & Equipment). **Est:** 1866. **Sales:**
$1,000,000 (2000). **Emp:** 11. **Officers:** David Klinger,
President.

■ 15858 ■ Burgmaster
12975 Clarence Center Rd.
Akron, NY 14001-1321
Products: Drill press machines; Spare parts. **SIC:**
5084 (Industrial Machinery & Equipment). **Sales:**
$1,000,000 (2000). **Emp:** 4. **Officers:** G. Welter, Vice
President.

■ 15859 ■ Burnett Engraving Co. Inc.
1351 N Hudley
Anaheim, CA 92806
Phone: (714)632-0870 **Fax:** (714)632-8734
Products: Engraving and stamping supplies;
Embossing seals. **SIC:** 5049 (Professional Equipment
Nec). **Est:** 1963. **Sales:** $1,000,000 (2000). **Emp:** 18.
Officers: James D. Pinckney, CEO; Janel Everidge,
Sales/Marketing Contact; Michael Pinckney,
Sales/Marketing Contact; Janel Everidge, Customer
Service Contact.

■ 15860 ■ Troy Burns Co.
6723 Asher Ave.
PO Box 4050
Little Rock, AR 72204
Phone: (501)562-1111
Free: (800)643-8807 **Fax:** (501)565-4316
E-mail: tburns@aristotle.net
Products: Materials handling equipment. **SICs:** 5084
(Industrial Machinery & Equipment); 5082
(Construction & Mining Machinery). **Est:** 1946. **Sales:**
$1,600,000 (1999). **Emp:** 5. **Officers:** Troy Burns Jr.,
President.

■ 15861 ■ C. Design International Inc.
1967 Quincy Ct.
Glendale Heights, IL 60139
Phone: (708)582-2600 **Fax:** (708)582-2605
Products: Printing, packaging, and labeling equipment
and supplies. **SIC:** 5084 (Industrial Machinery &
Equipment). **Est:** 1991. **Sales:** $8,000,000 (2000).
Emp: 20. **Officers:** Ringo Suek, President.

■ 15862 ■ C & J Tool & Gage Co.
4830 S Division Ave.
Grand Rapids, MI 49548
Phone: (616)534-6071 **Fax:** (616)534-2055
Products: Precision measuring tools; Cutting tools;
Carbide, HSS. **SICs:** 5084 (Industrial Machinery &
Equipment); 5072 (Hardware). **Est:** 1981. **Sales:**
$3,000,000 (2000). **Emp:** 14. **Officers:** Robert Lock,
President.

■ 15863 ■ Calcom Inc.
3433 Edward
Santa Clara, CA 95051
Phone: (408)727-5353 **Fax:** (408)727-5265
Products: Printing trades machinery, equipment, and
supplies. **SICs:** 5084 (Industrial Machinery &
Equipment); 5199 (Nondurable Goods Nec). **Emp:** 2.

■ 15864 ■ Calkins Fluid Power, Inc.
E 5417 Broadway
Spokane, WA 99212
Phone: (509)536-7642
Free: (800)541-0713 **Fax:** (509)534-7310
E-mail: cfpspokane@calkinsmfg.com
URL: http://www.calkinsmfg.com
Products: Hydraulic equipment and supplies. **SIC:**

5084 (Industrial Machinery & Equipment). **Former Name:** Calkins Distributing.

■ **15865** ■ **Call Associates Inc.**
4230 Kiernan Ave., No. 210
Modesto, CA 95356-9323
Phone: (650)875-1911 **Free:** (800)266-7537
Products: Industrial controls and heaters. **SIC:** 5084 (Industrial Machinery & Equipment). **Est:** 1960. **Sales:** $1,000,000 (2000). **Officers:** Gene Wilkens; Joyce P. Call, VP of Finance.

■ **15866** ■ **Callis-Thompson, Inc.**
Rte. 13 S
Harrington, DE 19952
Phone: (302)398-3068 **Fax:** (302)398-4622
Products: Liquid handling equipment. **SIC:** 5084 (Industrial Machinery & Equipment).

■ **15867** ■ **Caltrol Inc.**
PO Box 5020
Glendora, CA 91740
Phone: (818)963-1010 **Fax:** (818)963-9629
Products: Control and relief valves; Regulators; Electric activators; Control systems. **SICs:** 5084 (Industrial Machinery & Equipment); 5063 (Electrical Apparatus & Equipment). **Est:** 1985. **Sales:** $50,000,000 (2000). **Emp:** 170. **Officers:** Ben Rector, President; George Haslam, Controller; Jim McGrath, Sales Dir.; Bonnie Flores, Personnel Mgr.

■ **15868** ■ **Cam Industries, Inc.**
215 Philadelphia St.
PO Box 227
Hanover, PA 17331
Phone: (717)637-5988 **Fax:** (717)637-9329
E-mail: cam@camindustries.com
URL: http://www.camindustries.com
Products: Industrial machinery. **SIC:** 5084 (Industrial Machinery & Equipment). **Est:** 1965. **Sales:** $3,000,000 (1999). **Emp:** 40. **Officers:** C.A. McGough III, President; Charles A. McGough, Sales/Marketing Contact; Patricia Staub, Customer Service Contact; Bill Marquis.

■ **15869** ■ **Campbell Group**
100 Production Dr.
Harrison, OH 45030
Phone: (513)367-3152 **Fax:** (513)367-3176
Products: Pneumatic and hydraulic hand tools; Compressors; Paint spray equipment; Winches. **SIC:** 5084 (Industrial Machinery & Equipment).

■ **15870** ■ **M.E. Canfield Co.**
8314 E Slavson Ave.
Pico Rivera, CA 90660
Phone: (213)264-5050 **Fax:** (562)949-5984
URL: http://www.powerlift.com
Products: Conveyors; Racks. **SICs:** 5084 (Industrial Machinery & Equipment); 5046 (Commercial Equipment Nec). **Est:** 1909. **Sales:** $4,000,000 (2000). **Emp:** 10. **Officers:** Brad Christman, Sales Mgr.

■ **15871** ■ **Cannon Engineering and Equipment Co. LLC**
2011 Heide
Troy, MI 48084
Phone: (248)362-0560 **Fax:** (248)362-2296
E-mail: ceecotroy@aol.com
Products: Aerial buckets; Hydraulic cranes. **SIC:** 5084 (Industrial Machinery & Equipment). **Est:** 1964. **Sales:** $4,000,000 (1999). **Emp:** 19. **Officers:** Richard J. Ryan, President; Vickie L. Greig, Human Resources Contact.

■ **15872** ■ **Carbro Corp.**
15724 Condon Ave.
PO Box 278
Lawndale, CA 90260
Phone: (310)643-8400 **Fax:** (310)643-9703
E-mail: cabrocorp@aol.com
Products: Carbide cutting tools. **SIC:** 5084 (Industrial Machinery & Equipment). **Est:** 1969. **Sales:** $4,000,000 (2000). **Emp:** 55. **Officers:** Ed Plano; Frank Barela, Sales & Marketing Contact.

■ **15873** ■ **Cardinal Carryor Inc.**
1055 Grade Ln.
Louisville, KY 40213
Phone: (502)363-6641 **Fax:** (502)363-6644
E-mail: lift@cardinalcarryor.com
URL: http://www.cardinalcarryor.com
Products: Material handling equipment. **SIC:** 5084 (Industrial Machinery & Equipment). **Est:** 1947. **Sales:** $20,000,000 (2000). **Emp:** 88. **Officers:** Ben L. Brumleve, President & General Mgr.; Brad Baker, VP, Treasurer, and Operations Manager; Pat Plamp, VP, Equipment Sales; Mark Archer, VP, Aftermarket Services; Linda Pike, Corp. Secty.

■ **15874** ■ **Cardinal Carryor Inc.**
1055 Grade Ln.
Louisville, KY 40213
Phone: (502)363-6641 **Fax:** (502)363-6644
Products: Industrial machinery. **SIC:** 5084 (Industrial Machinery & Equipment).

■ **15875** ■ **Cardinal State Fasteners**
1130 Kingwood Ave.
Norfolk, VA 23502-5603
Phone: (757)855-2041 **Fax:** (757)857-8339
Products: Machine tools for home workshops, laboratories, garages; Service industry machinery and parts. **SICs:** 5084 (Industrial Machinery & Equipment); 5085 (Industrial Supplies). **Emp:** 49. **Officers:** Robert Stephenson.

■ **15876** ■ **Carloss Well Supply Co.**
4000 Runway Rd.
Memphis, TN 38118
Phone: (901)360-8047
Free: (800)238-7313 **Fax:** (901)360-8113
E-mail: www.carloss.com
Products: Pumps; Engines for generators. **SIC:** 5084 (Industrial Machinery & Equipment). **Est:** 1881. **Sales:** $7,000,000 (2000). **Emp:** 30. **Officers:** Robert McConnell, President; Bill Anderson, VP of Operations.

■ **15877** ■ **Carlson Dimond and Wright**
2338 Morrissey Ave.
Warren, MI 48091
Phone: (734)758-6611 **Fax:** (734)758-6038
Products: Industrial drive systems and components. **SIC:** 5084 (Industrial Machinery & Equipment).

■ **15878** ■ **Carolina Handling Inc.**
PO Box 7548
Charlotte, NC 28241
Phone: (704)357-6273
Free: (800)688-8802 **Fax:** (704)329-3858
URL: http://www.caralina-handling.com
Products: Fork lifts; Warehouse equipment. **SIC:** 5084 (Industrial Machinery & Equipment). **Est:** 1966. **Sales:** $60,000,000 (2000). **Emp:** 300. **Officers:** T.B. Hilton, President; D. Heicnemer, VP of Sales; J. Swittenburg, VP of Product Development.

■ **15879** ■ **Carotek Inc.**
PO Box 1395
Matthews, NC 28106
Phone: (704)847-4406 **Fax:** (704)847-4485
E-mail: carotek@carotek.com
URL: http://www.carotek.com
Products: Pumps, blowers, and digital equipment. **SIC:** 5039 (Construction Materials Nec). **Est:** 1964. **Sales:** $60,000,000 (2000). **Emp:** 140. **Officers:** J. Addison Bell, CEO & CFO.

■ **15880** ■ **Catey Controls**
535 Moore Ln.
Billings, MT 59101
Phone: (406)259-3703 **Fax:** (406)259-7248
Products: Hydraulic equipment. **SIC:** 5084 (Industrial Machinery & Equipment).

■ **15881** ■ **Catey Controls**
3102 W Broadway
PO Box 7496
Missoula, MT 59807
Phone: (406)728-7860 **Fax:** (406)549-3720
Products: Hydraulic controls; Pneumatic controls; **SIC:** 5084 (Industrial Machinery & Equipment).

■ **15882** ■ **CBW Automation Inc.**
3939 Automation Way
Ft. Collins, CO 80525
Phone: (970)229-9500 **Fax:** (970)229-9600
Products: Special trade machinery. **SIC:** 5084 (Industrial Machinery & Equipment). **Officers:** David Carson, President.

■ **15883** ■ **CESSCO Rental and Sales Inc.**
703 E Scott St.
Wichita Falls, TX 76307
Phone: (940)766-0238
Products: Industrial equipment; Construction equipment. **SICs:** 5084 (Industrial Machinery & Equipment); 5082 (Construction & Mining Machinery). **Est:** 1964. **Sales:** $1,800,000 (2000). **Emp:** 20. **Officers:** Elizabeth V. Hansard, CEO.

■ **15884** ■ **Chaneaco Supply Co.**
32 Park Ave.
Washington, PA 15301
Phone: (724)222-0960 **Fax:** (724)222-5545
E-mail: chaneaco@chaneaco.com
URL: http://www.chaneaco.com
Products: Pipe, valves, and fittings; Oilfield supplies; Industrial supplies. **SICs:** 5084 (Industrial Machinery & Equipment); 5085 (Industrial Supplies). **Est:** 1974. **Sales:** $800,000 (2000). **Emp:** 4. **Officers:** Charles N. Eason, President.

■ **15885** ■ **Chew International Bascom Div.**
495 River St.
Paterson, NJ 07524
Phone: (973)345-1802 **Fax:** (973)631-8566
Products: Container loads. **SIC:** 5084 (Industrial Machinery & Equipment). **Officers:** Ralph Chew, President.

■ **15886** ■ **Chicago Machine Tool Co.**
2150 Touhy Ave.
Elk Grove Village, IL 60007
Phone: (708)364-4700 **Fax:** (708)364-0852
Products: Industrial machines. **SIC:** 5084 (Industrial Machinery & Equipment). **Est:** 1945. **Sales:** $11,000,000 (2000). **Emp:** 25. **Officers:** Francis J. Myers Jr., CEO; John J. Myers, President.

■ **15887** ■ **Choquettes' Used Trucks & Equipment**
1230 Glendale Ave.
Sparks, NV 89431
Phone: (775)358-1500 **Fax:** (775)359-5671
E-mail: choquettes@netscape.net
Products: Used Trucks; New and used snow removal equipment. **SIC:** 5084 (Industrial Machinery & Equipment). **Est:** 1983. **Sales:** $2,000,000 (2000). **Emp:** 11. **Officers:** Gene Choquette, Owner.

■ **15888** ■ **Cimarron Corporation Inc.**
PO Box 5519
Greenville, SC 29606
Phone: (864)288-5475 **Fax:** (864)297-5081
Products: Weaving looms. **SIC:** 5084 (Industrial Machinery & Equipment). **Sales:** $400,000 (2000). **Emp:** 2. **Officers:** W.H. Jewell, President; John Van Hee, VP of Finance.

■ **15889** ■ **Clarklift Corporation of Indiana**
6902 E 32nd St.
Indianapolis, IN 46226
Phone: (317)545-6631
Products: Forklifts. **SIC:** 5084 (Industrial Machinery & Equipment). **Est:** 1935. **Sales:** $11,000,000 (2000). **Emp:** 65. **Officers:** Michael C. Branic, President; James R. Thieman, Controller; V.D. Agnelneri, VP of Sales.

■ **15890** ■ **Clarklift of Dalton Inc.**
PO Box 1045
Dalton, GA 30722-1045
Phone: (706)278-1104 **Fax:** (706)278-0460
Products: Heavy machinery and parts, including lift trucks. **SIC:** 5084 (Industrial Machinery & Equipment). **Est:** 1967. **Sales:** $25,000,000 (2000). **Emp:** 100. **Officers:** Patrick Sain, President; Bill Gleaton, Controller; Michael Sain, Dir. of Marketing.

■ 15891 ■ Clarklift of Detroit Inc.
PO Box 487
Troy, MI 48099
Phone: (248)528-2100
Free: (800)462-7862 **Fax:** (248)740-2613
URL: http://www.clarkliftdetroit.com
Products: Fork lift trucks. **SIC:** 5084 (Industrial Machinery & Equipment).

■ 15892 ■ Clarklift of Minnesota Inc.
501 W 78th St.
Bloomington, MN 55420
Phone: (952)887-5400 **Fax:** (952)881-3030
URL: http://www.clarkliftofmn.com
Products: Material handling equipment; Forklift trucks. **SIC:** 5084 (Industrial Machinery & Equipment). **Est:** 1949. **Sales:** $28,000,000 (2000). **Emp:** 140. **Officers:** Clayton Schubert, President.

■ 15893 ■ Clausing Industrial Inc.
1819 N Pitcher St.
Kalamazoo, MI 49007
Phone: (616)345-7155
Products: Industrial tools, including band saws, grinders, mills, and press brakes. **SIC:** 5084 (Industrial Machinery & Equipment).

■ 15894 ■ CMA International
7515 Topton St., Ste. 100
New Carrollton, MD 20784
Phone: (301)577-9340 **Fax:** (301)577-7019
E-mail: jaschaff@wam.umd.edu
Products: Transportation equipment; Metal forgings and stampings; Electrical measuring and testing equipment; Medical eyemasks; Pump gaskets; Epoxy sealants; Concrete waterproofing. **SICs:** 5084 (Industrial Machinery & Equipment); 5088 (Transportation Equipment & Supplies); 5051 (Metals Service Centers & Offices); 5085 (Industrial Supplies); 5063 (Electrical Apparatus & Equipment). **Est:** 1986. **Emp:** 2. **Officers:** John A. Schaffer, Director.

■ 15895 ■ Coffin Turbo Pump Inc.
PO Box 9833
Englewood, NJ 07631
Phone: (201)568-4700 **Fax:** (201)568-4716
E-mail: info@coffinturbopump.com
URL: http://www.coffinturbopump.com
Products: Pumps and pumping equipment. **SIC:** 5084 (Industrial Machinery & Equipment). **Est:** 1925. **Sales:** $15,000,000 (2000). **Emp:** 50.

■ 15896 ■ Cognex Corp.
2060 Challenger Dr.
Alameda, CA 94501-1037
Phone: (510)749-4000 **Fax:** (510)865-9927
Products: Website inspection machines for various industries. **SIC:** 5084 (Industrial Machinery & Equipment). **Officers:** Richard Rombach, Chairman of the Board.

■ 15897 ■ Coker International Trading Inc.
PO Box 443
Sandy Springs, SC 29677
Phone: (864)287-5000 **Fax:** (864)287-5300
Products: Textile machinery. **SIC:** 5084 (Industrial Machinery & Equipment). **Officers:** Jackson R. Coker, President.

■ 15898 ■ Colorado Clarklift Inc.
4105 Globeville Rd.
Denver, CO 80216
Phone: (303)292-5438
Products: Forklifts. **SIC:** 5082 (Construction & Mining Machinery). **Sales:** $57,000,000 (1992). **Emp:** 80. **Officers:** John Faulkner, President.

■ 15899 ■ Columbine International
5441 Merchant Cir.
Placerville, CA 95667
Phone: (530)622-2791
Free: (800)635-6693 **Fax:** (530)622-2704
E-mail: columbine@directcon.net
URL: http://www.columbineint.com
Products: Thermoplastic welding equipment. **SIC:** 5084 (Industrial Machinery & Equipment). **Est:** 1982. **Sales:** $5,000,000 (2000). **Emp:** 25. **Officers:** Greg A. Yaple.

■ 15900 ■ Comer Inc.
PO Box 410305
Charlotte, NC 28241
Phone: (704)588-8400 **Fax:** (704)588-2222
E-mail: tbounds@comerusa.com
URL: http://www.powertransmission.com
Products: Agricultural and industrial machinery gear drives. **SIC:** 5084 (Industrial Machinery & Equipment). **Est:** 1986. **Sales:** $50,000,000 (2000). **Emp:** 25. **Officers:** Roger Mortara, Sales Mgr.; Nancy Smith, Customer Service Contact; Tawnee Bounds, Human Resources Contact.

■ 15901 ■ Comet Industries Inc.
4800 Deramus
Kansas City, MO 64120
Phone: (816)245-9400 **Fax:** (816)245-9460
Products: General industrial machinery; Railroad equipment and supplies. **SICs:** 5084 (Industrial Machinery & Equipment); 5085 (Industrial Supplies); 5088 (Transportation Equipment & Supplies). **Est:** 1963. **Sales:** $6,000,000 (2000). **Emp:** 400. **Officers:** Edwin Johnson, President; Larry Pagel, Vice President.

■ 15902 ■ Commercial Body Corp.
PO Box 1119
San Antonio, TX 78294
Phone: (210)224-1931
Free: (800)292-1931
Fax: (210)224-6885
Products: Cherrypickers and other utility equipment. **SIC:** 5084 (Industrial Machinery & Equipment). **Sales:** $25,000,000 (2000). **Emp:** 120. **Officers:** Gary L. Grist, CEO; Roger Buchhorn, Controller.

■ 15903 ■ Common Equipment Co.
PO Box 988
Peoria, IL 61603
Phone: (309)672-9300 **Fax:** (309)672-9321
Products: Forklift trucks. **SIC:** 5084 (Industrial Machinery & Equipment). **Est:** 1953. **Sales:** $12,000,000 (2000). **Emp:** 54. **Officers:** S.J. Statler, President; J. Bannon, Vice President; J.M. Zieglowsky, Exec. VP.

■ 15904 ■ Component Technology
1225 Illinois St.
Des Moines, IA 50314
Phone: (515)244-7411
Free: (800)333-7411 **Fax:** (515)244-4264
URL: http://www.certifiedpower.com
Products: Hydraulics. **SIC:** 5084 (Industrial Machinery & Equipment).

■ 15905 ■ Component Technology
3303 Washington Blvd.
St. Louis, MO 63103
Phone: (314)535-7411 **Fax:** (314)535-3103
Products: Pumps. **SIC:** 5084 (Industrial Machinery & Equipment).

■ 15906 ■ Component Technology
200 Indiana Ave.
Toledo, OH 43624
Phone: (419)243-7411 **Fax:** (419)255-3742
Products: Hydraulic parts and equipment. **SIC:** 5084 (Industrial Machinery & Equipment).

■ 15907 ■ Components & Equipment International
849 W Main St.
PO Box 903
Kent, OH 44240
Phone: (330)673-8886 **Fax:** (330)673-3785
Products: Pneumatic and hydraulic hand tools. **SIC:** 5084 (Industrial Machinery & Equipment).

■ 15908 ■ Connell Motor Truck Company Inc.
PO Box 8467
Stockton, CA 95208
Phone: (209)948-3434 **Fax:** (209)464-9731
Products: Forklifts and parts. **SICs:** 5012 (Automobiles & Other Motor Vehicles); 5013 (Motor Vehicle Supplies & New Parts). **Est:** 1947. **Sales:** $4,300,000 (2000). **Emp:** 42. **Officers:** Sheldon Heckman, President; Mary Cox, Comptroller; Robert Carr, Sales Mgr.

■ 15909 ■ Connie's Enterprise
PO Box 11238
Jacksonville, FL 32239
Phone: (904)353-0604 **Fax:** (904)355-1525
Products: Petroleum, fuels, and related equipment. **SIC:** 5084 (Industrial Machinery & Equipment). **Sales:** $7,000,000 (2000). **Emp:** 35.

■ 15910 ■ Consolidated Tool Manufacturers Inc.
10927 Franklin Ave.
Franklin Park, IL 60131
Phone: (708)451-9050 **Fax:** (847)678-0946
Products: Cutting tools. **SIC:** 5084 (Industrial Machinery & Equipment). **Est:** 1962. **Sales:** $700,000 (2000). **Emp:** 8. **Officers:** Stan Dawinski, President.

■ 15911 ■ Continental Screen Printing Supply
2110 31st Ct.
Kenner, LA 70065-4537
Phone: (504)461-8797 **Fax:** (504)467-7901
E-mail: conscreen@aol.com
URL: http://www.members.aol.com/conscreen/bienvenidu
Products: Screen printing machinery, equipment, and supplies. **SIC:** 5084 (Industrial Machinery & Equipment). **Est:** 1991. **Sales:** $750,000 (1999). **Officers:** Victor Garcia, President; Anne Donato, Vice President.

■ 15912 ■ Control Sales Inc.
PO Box 469
Beech Grove, IN 46107
Phone: (317)786-2272 **Fax:** (317)786-0022
E-mail: sales@control-sales.com
URL: http://www.control-sales.com
Products: Industrial motor controls. **SICs:** 5063 (Electrical Apparatus & Equipment); 5084 (Industrial Machinery & Equipment). **Est:** 1975. **Sales:** $4,600,000 (2000). **Emp:** 8. **Officers:** Earl McKenny, President.

■ 15913 ■ Controltech
PO Box 1524
San Carlos, CA 94070
Phone: (650)593-2111 **Fax:** (650)593-9629
Products: Designs and custom control panels; Control systems and regulators. **SIC:** 5084 (Industrial Machinery & Equipment). **Officers:** Art von Wronski, President.

■ 15914 ■ Conveyor & Drive Equipment
PO Box 191100
St. Louis, MO 63119
Phone: (314)961-1200 **Fax:** (314)961-6052
Products: Conveyors and conveying equipment. **SIC:** 5084 (Industrial Machinery & Equipment).

■ 15915 ■ Coordinated Equipment Co.
1707 E Anaheim St.
Wilmington, CA 90744
Phone: (310)834-8535 **Fax:** (310)834-2991
Products: Testing of bulky material handling devices, cable, chain, wire rope; Retails used heavy equipment. **SIC:** 5084 (Industrial Machinery & Equipment). **Sales:** $900,000 (2000). **Emp:** 15. **Officers:** Carol J. Countryman, VP & CFO.

■ 15916 ■ CPS Distributors Inc.
4275 Forest St.
Denver, CO 80216
Phone: (303)394-6040 **Fax:** (303)394-2667
Products: Industrial and farm machinery. **SIC:** 5084 (Industrial Machinery & Equipment). **Est:** 1900. **Sales:** $17,000,000 (2000). **Emp:** 63. **Officers:** Jack Bentley, President; Alan C. Bergold, CFO; D. Champlin, VP of Marketing.

■ 15917 ■ Crader Distributing Co.
Rte. 3, Box 3135
Marble Hill, MO 63764
Phone: (573)238-2676
Products: Chain saws; Lawn and garden equipment. **SICs:** 5084 (Industrial Machinery & Equipment); 5083 (Farm & Garden Machinery). **Est:** 1943. **Sales:** $27,000,000 (1999). **Emp:** 40.

■ **15918** ■ **Crane Engineering Sales Inc.**
PO Box 38
Kimberly, WI 54136
Phone: (920)733-4425
Products: Industrial machinery and equipment. **SIC:** 5084 (Industrial Machinery & Equipment). **Sales:** $23,000,000 (1994). **Emp:** 64. **Officers:** Mark Schwei, President; Peggy Campbell, Controller.

■ **15919** ■ **Creative Engineering and Manufacturing Corp.**
3510 Mattingly Rd.
Buckner, KY 40010-8801
Phone: (502)241-7144
Free: (800)626-5388 **Fax:** (502)241-7170
Products: Textile industries machinery. **SIC:** 5084 (Industrial Machinery & Equipment). **Est:** 1976. **Sales:** $650,000 (2000). **Emp:** 15. **Officers:** M. E. Tueskoes, President; Irmi Tueskoes, Vice President.

■ **15920** ■ **Crellin Handling Equipment Inc.**
12 Commercial Way
East Providence, RI 02914
Phone: (401)438-6400 **Fax:** (401)431-1380
Products: Forklifts; Batteries; Scrubbers/sweepers; Racks/shelving storage equipment; Dock equipment. **SIC:** 5084 (Industrial Machinery & Equipment). **Est:** 1956. **Sales:** $13,000,000 (2000). **Emp:** 95. **Officers:** Richard Crellin, President; Douglas Crellin, Vice President, e-mail: dcrellin@crellin.com; Rick Farrell, Sales Mgr.; Larry Reynolds, Sales/Marketing Contact; Michele Etzold, Human Resources Contact.

■ **15921** ■ **CSL and Associates Inc.**
10 Commerce St., Ste. B
Destin, FL 32541-2359
Phone: (850)650-6602
Free: (800)622-6069 **Fax:** (850)650-6606
E-mail: service@smokersoutpost.com
URL: http://www.smokersoutpost.com
Products: Waste receptacles. **SIC:** 5199 (Nondurable Goods Nec). **Est:** 1991. **Sales:** $2,800,000 (2000). **Emp:** 7. **Officers:** Carol Luedecke, President.

■ **15922** ■ **Cummins Diesel Sales Inc.**
2690 Cleveland Ave. N
St. Paul, MN 55113
Phone: (612)636-1000
Free: (800)642-0085 **Fax:** (612)638-2442
Products: Industrial machinery. **SIC:** 5084 (Industrial Machinery & Equipment). **Sales:** $27,000,000 (2000). **Emp:** 200.

■ **15923** ■ **Cummins Great Plains Diesel Inc.**
5515 Center St.
Omaha, NE 68106
Phone: (402)551-7678 **Fax:** (402)551-1952
Products: Industrial diesel engines. **SIC:** 5084 (Industrial Machinery & Equipment). **Sales:** $216,000,000 (2000). **Emp:** 250. **Officers:** William Hanley, Chairman of the Board; Don Baldwin, CFO.

■ **15924** ■ **Cummins Mid-South Inc.**
1784 E Brooks Rd.
Memphis, TN 38116
Phone: (901)345-1784 **Fax:** (901)345-7424
Products: Stock parts, including injectors and cylinder heads. **SIC:** 5084 (Industrial Machinery & Equipment). **Sales:** $63,000,000 (2000). **Emp:** 200. **Officers:** Thomas Lemmons, General Mgr.; Jeff Reeves, Finance Officer.

■ **15925** ■ **Custom Manufacturing Co.**
5501 S Lamar
Dallas, TX 75215
Phone: (214)428-5173
Products: Metal stamping equipment and supplies. **SIC:** 5084 (Industrial Machinery & Equipment).

■ **15926** ■ **Cutters Exchange Inc.**
PO Box 7001
Murfreesboro, TN 37133
Phone: (615)895-8070
Products: Industrial machinery. **SIC:** 5084 (Industrial Machinery & Equipment). **Sales:** $12,000,000 (1990). **Emp:** 70. **Officers:** Michael T. Ferris, Vice President; Brock Qualls, VP of Finance.

■ **15927** ■ **D & F Distributors**
2317 Cruzen St.
Nashville, TN 37211
Phone: (615)259-9090 **Fax:** (615)259-9095
Products: Pumps. **SIC:** 5084 (Industrial Machinery & Equipment). **Est:** 1983. **Emp:** 31.

■ **15928** ■ **Daewoo Equipment Corp.**
4350 Emery Industrial Pkwy.
Warrensville Heights, OH 44128
Phone: (216)595-1212
Products: Lift trucks. **SIC:** 5084 (Industrial Machinery & Equipment).

■ **15929** ■ **Danville Gasoline & Oil Co. Inc.**
Leverenz Automotive & Truck Parts
201 W Main St.
Danville, IL 61832-5709
Phone: (217)442-8500
Free: (800)252-6879 **Fax:** (217)442-0052
E-mail: wtliv@soltec.net
Products: Lubricants; Auto parts. **SIC:** 5082 (Construction & Mining Machinery). **Est:** 1916. **Sales:** $3,900,000 (2000). **Emp:** 15. **Officers:** W.T. Leverenz IV, President.

■ **15930** ■ **Dapra Corp.**
66 Granby St.
Bloomfield, CT 06002
Phone: (860)242-8539
Free: (800)243-3344 **Fax:** (860)242-3017
E-mail: dapracorp@aol.com
URL: http://www.dapra.com
Products: Indexable carbide milling cutters; Rotary index tables; Vises; Dot peen marking systems; Power scrapers. **SIC:** 5084 (Industrial Machinery & Equipment). **Est:** 1956. **Sales:** $15,000,000 (2000). **Emp:** 40. **Officers:** Tom Watson, President & CEO; Marie-Louise Pratt, Chairman of the Board.

■ **15931** ■ **J. Dashew Inc.**
2709 Frederick Ave.
Baltimore, MD 21223
Phone: (410)233-1660
Free: (800)638-3170 **Fax:** (410)945-7245
Products: Industrial machines and equipement. **SIC:** 5084 (Industrial Machinery & Equipment). **Sales:** $12,000,000 (1992). **Emp:** 40.

■ **15932** ■ **Theo. H. Davies and Company Ltd.**
560 N Nimitz Hwy., Ste. 207
Honolulu, HI 96817-5315
Phone: (808)531-5971
Products: Mining machinery. **SIC:** 5082 (Construction & Mining Machinery). **Sales:** $300,000,000 (1990). **Emp:** 3,000. **Officers:** David A. Heenan, CEO & President; Martin Jaskot, Exec. VP & CFO.

■ **15933** ■ **John Day Co.**
PO Box 3541
Omaha, NE 68110
Phone: (402)455-8000 **Fax:** (402)457-3812
Products: Industrial material handling, safety and agricultural equipment. **SICs:** 5084 (Industrial Machinery & Equipment); 5083 (Farm & Garden Machinery). **Sales:** $30,000,000 (2000). **Emp:** 125. **Officers:** Jere Fonda; Judy Bunkers, Sales/Marketing Contact, e-mail: judyb@johnday.com; Bill Brandis, Customer Service Contact.

■ **15934** ■ **Bob Dean Supply Inc.**
2624 Hanson St.
Ft. Myers, FL 33901-7488
Phone: (941)332-1131 **Fax:** (941)332-7746
Products: Pumps; Power tools; Paints. **SICs:** 5085 (Industrial Supplies); 5084 (Industrial Machinery & Equipment); 5198 (Paints, Varnishes & Supplies). **Est:** 1947. **Sales:** $8,000,000 (2000). **Emp:** 70. **Officers:** Robert S. Dean Jr., President; William Tubb, Controller.

■ **15935** ■ **Dearborn Fabricating and Engineering Corp.**
19440 Glendale Ave.
Detroit, MI 48223
Phone: (313)273-2800 **Fax:** (313)273-5252
Products: Conveyor systems. **SIC:** 5084 (Industrial Machinery & Equipment). **Est:** 1947. **Sales:** $70,000,000 (2000). **Emp:** 140. **Officers:** J. Paisley, President; William Kiley, Controller; President.

■ **15936** ■ **Decatur Custom Tool Inc.**
410 N Jasper St.
Decatur, IL 62521
Phone: (217)423-3639
URL: http://www.dctools.com
Products: Industrial cutting tools. **SIC:** 5084 (Industrial Machinery & Equipment). **Est:** 1966. **Sales:** $14,000,000 (2000). **Emp:** 43. **Officers:** J.E. Gahwiler, President, e-mail: jegahwiler@dctools.com; Mike Moran, Sales Mgr.

■ **15937** ■ **Deco Tool Supply Co.**
415 W 76th St.
Davenport, IA 52808
Phone: (319)386-5970 **Fax:** (319)386-1321
Products: Metal working tools. **SIC:** 5084 (Industrial Machinery & Equipment). **Sales:** $31,400,000 (2000). **Emp:** 100. **Officers:** Dennis Quinn, President.

■ **15938** ■ **Decorative Engineering and Supply Inc.**
17000 S Western Ave.
PO Box 559
Gardena, CA 90248-0559
Phone: (310)532-4013
Free: (800)473-2124 **Fax:** (310)329-2215
E-mail: deceng@earthlink.com
Products: Industrial spray equipment. **SICs:** 5084 (Industrial Machinery & Equipment); 5198 (Paints, Varnishes & Supplies). **Est:** 1950. **Sales:** $1,000,000 (2000). **Emp:** 6. **Officers:** Frank Miller, President, Dir. of Marketing & Sales.

■ **15939** ■ **Delta Materials Handling Inc.**
4676 Clarke Rd.
Memphis, TN 38141
Phone: (901)795-7230
Products: Forklift trucks. **SIC:** 5084 (Industrial Machinery & Equipment). **Est:** 1960. **Sales:** $15,000,000 (2000). **Emp:** 90. **Officers:** Joseph Costa, President & CFO.

■ **15940** ■ **Denver Air Machinery Co.**
1421 Blake St.
Denver, CO 80202-1334
Phone: (303)893-0507 **Fax:** (303)893-0509
Products: Machinery parts. **SIC:** 5084 (Industrial Machinery & Equipment). **Est:** 1946. **Sales:** $1,000,000 (2000). **Emp:** 12. **Officers:** E. James White, President.

■ **15941** ■ **Dependable Foundry Equipment Co.**
PO Box 1687
Tualatin, OR 97062
Phone: (503)692-5552 **Fax:** (503)692-4477
Products: Foundry equipment. **SIC:** 5084 (Industrial Machinery & Equipment). **Sales:** $11,000,000 (2000). **Emp:** 75. **Officers:** Russ Tromey, President.

■ **15942** ■ **Derda Inc.**
1195 W Bertrand Rd.
Niles, MI 49120-8772
Phone: (616)683-6666
Products: Wood working equipment. **SIC:** 5084 (Industrial Machinery & Equipment). **Est:** 1946. **Sales:** $3,000,000 (2000). **Emp:** 10. **Officers:** John Derda, President; Rebecca McKee, Treasurer.

■ **15943** ■ **Desoutter Inc.**
1800 Overview Dr.
Rock Hill, SC 29730
Free: (888)298-2905 **Fax:** 800-232-6611
Products: Pneumatic tooling. **SIC:** 5084 (Industrial Machinery & Equipment). **Est:** 1968. **Sales:** $8,000,000 (2000). **Emp:** 25. **Officers:** Thomas R. Boik, Vice President; Chris Vizachero, Production Mgr.

■ **15944** ■ **Detroit Air Compressor and Pump Co.**
3205 Bermuda
Ferndale, MI 48220
Phone: (248)544-2982 **Fax:** (248)544-2027
Products: Air and gas compressors and vacuum pumps; Blowers and fans; Compressed air and gas dryers. **SIC:** 5084 (Industrial Machinery & Equipment). **Est:** 1927. **Sales:** $3,000,000 (2000). **Emp:** 18. **Officers:** Gretchen Bornor Cole, President.

■ 15945 ■ **Deuer Manufacturing Co.**
225 Riverview Ave.
Waltham, MA 02454
Phone: (781)647-5560 **Fax:** (781)891-8375
Products: Winches. **SIC:** 5084 (Industrial Machinery &
Equipment).

■ 15946 ■ **Dev-Air Corp.**
380 N Morehall Rd.
Malvern, PA 19355
Phone: (215)647-3677 **Fax:** (215)640-0853
Products: Hydraulic and pneumatic equipment parts.
SIC: 5084 (Industrial Machinery & Equipment). **Est:**
1968. **Sales:** $3,000,000 (2000). **Emp:** 14. **Officers:**
Richard T. Devaney, President.

■ 15947 ■ **DeVlieg-Bullard Services Group**
10100 Forest Hills Rd.
Rockford, IL 61114
Phone: (815)544-8120 **Fax:** (815)544-8191
Products: Heavy machinery parts. **SIC:** 5084
(Industrial Machinery & Equipment). **Est:** 1990. **Sales:**
$34,000,000 (2000). **Emp:** 275. **Officers:** Richard
Sappenfield, President; Richard Tetrick, VP of Finance;
Anthony Graceffa, Dir. of Marketing.

■ 15948 ■ **D.I. Engineering Corp. of America**
1658 Cole Blvd., Bldg. 6, Ste. 290
Golden, CO 80401
Phone: (303)231-0045 **Fax:** (303)231-0050
Products: Can making machinery. **SIC:** 5084
(Industrial Machinery & Equipment). **Officers:** Hiroshi
Yamazaki, Exec. Vice President.

■ 15949 ■ **Diamond Industrial Tools Inc.**
6712 Crawford Avenue
Lincolnwood, IL 60712
Phone: (847)676-9700
Free: (800)441-7771 **Fax:** (847)676-0043
E-mail: toditinc@aol.com
URL: http://www.diamondindustrialtools.com
Products: Abrasive grinding wheels, diamond and
CBN wheels, saws, and precision grinding machines.
SICs: 5084 (Industrial Machinery & Equipment); 5085
(Industrial Supplies). **Est:** 1968. **Sales:** $5,000,000
(1999). **Emp:** 21. **Officers:** Harry G. Sachsel,
President.

■ 15950 ■ **Die-A-Matic Corp.**
650 N State St.
York, PA 17403
Phone: (717)846-9300
Free: (888)343-2628 **Fax:** 800-643-5224
URL: http://www.dieamatic.com
Products: Hydraulic and pneumatic equipment. **SIC:**
5085 (Industrial Supplies). **Est:** 1956. **Sales:**
$22,000,000 (2000). **Emp:** 130. **Officers:** R.A. Gross,
CEO; Greg Plitt, Controller; Jon Newman, COO.

■ 15951 ■ **Dillon Supply Co.**
PO Box 1111
Raleigh, NC 27602
Phone: (919)832-7771 **Fax:** (919)828-3110
Products: Industrial machinery, supplies, and metals.
SICs: 5084 (Industrial Machinery & Equipment); 5085
(Industrial Supplies); 5051 (Metals Service Centers &
Offices). **Sales:** $120,000,000 (1992). **Emp:** 400.
Officers: Robert L. McCann, President.

■ 15952 ■ **Dixie Mill Inc.**
901 Tchoupitoulas St.
New Orleans, LA 70130
Phone: (504)525-6101 **Fax:** (504)525-3089
Products: Machine and cutting tools. **SIC:** 5084
(Industrial Machinery & Equipment). **Est:** 1918. **Sales:**
$5,000,000 (2000). **Emp:** 47. **Officers:** Richard M.
Cahn, President; Warren Scull, Controller.

■ 15953 ■ **William Dixon Co.**
750 Washington Ave.
Carlstadt, NJ 07072
Phone: (201)939-6700 **Fax:** (201)939-5067
Products: Small precision tools. **SIC:** 5072
(Hardware). **Sales:** $27,000,000 (2000). **Emp:** 200.
Officers: J. Canzoneri, President & CFO.

■ 15954 ■ **DJ's Alaska Rentals, Inc.**
405 Boniface Pkwy.
Anchorage, AK 99504
Phone: (907)333-6561 **Fax:** (907)333-6564
Products: Paint sprayers; Mowers; Loaders. **SICs:**
5198 (Paints, Varnishes & Supplies); 5083 (Farm &
Garden Machinery); 5084 (Industrial Machinery &
Equipment).

■ 15955 ■ **DNB Engineering Inc.**
3535 W Commonwealth Ave.
Fullerton, CA 92833
Phone: (714)870-7781 **Fax:** (714)870-5081
Products: EMI, RFI, lightning, EMC, EMP, tempest
engineering and test laboratory; Product safety and
ISO 90000 certifications. **SIC:** 5084 (Industrial
Machinery & Equipment). **Officers:** Alwyn Broaddus,
President.

■ 15956 ■ **Do All Foreign Sales Corp.**
254 N Laurel Ave.
Des Plaines, IL 60016
Phone: (847)803-7350 **Fax:** (847)824-0936
Products: Machine cutting tools; Industrial supplies;
Electrical apparatus, including measuring instruments.
SICs: 5084 (Industrial Machinery & Equipment); 5085
(Industrial Supplies); 5063 (Electrical Apparatus &
Equipment). **Officers:** Bruno Gruaz, VP of International
Operations.

■ 15957 ■ **Dodge Chicago/IBT**
4643 W 138th St.
Crestwood, IL 60445
Phone: (708)396-1402 **Fax:** (708)396-0735
Products: Industrial equipment and supplies. **SICs:**
5084 (Industrial Machinery & Equipment); 5085
(Industrial Supplies).

■ 15958 ■ **Dorsey Millwork Inc.**
36 Railroad Ave.
Albany, NY 12205
Phone: (518)489-2542
Products: Millwork. **SIC:** 5031 (Lumber, Plywood &
Millwork). **Sales:** $14,000,000 (1994). **Emp:** 50.
Officers: Ed Dorsey Sr., President; Ed Dorsey Jr.,
Controller.

■ 15959 ■ **Downard Hydraulics Inc.**
PO Box 1212
Princeton, WV 24740
Phone: (304)487-1492
Products: Hydraulic equipment. **SIC:** 5084 (Industrial
Machinery & Equipment). **Est:** 1975. **Sales:**
$4,800,000 (2000). **Emp:** 100. **Officers:** D.E.
Downard, President; Pam Parker, Controller; Don
Downard Jr., VP of Operations.

■ 15960 ■ **Dozier Equipment Co.**
770 South 70th St.
Milwaukee, WI 53214
Phone: (414)443-0581
Free: (800)251-1234 **Fax:** 800-336-6608
URL: http://www.chdist.com
Products: Equipment, including safety glasses and
cranes. **SIC:** 5084 (Industrial Machinery & Equipment).
Est: 1953. **Sales:** $15,000,000 (2000). **Emp:** 500.
Officers: Dave Stark, President; Karen Wagner, Dir of
Human Resources.

■ 15961 ■ **Drago Supply Company Inc.**
740 Houston Ave.
Port Arthur, TX 77640
Phone: (409)983-4911 **Fax:** (409)982-8248
Products: Industrial and mill equipment. **SICs:** 5084
(Industrial Machinery & Equipment); 5085 (Industrial
Supplies). **Sales:** $164,000,000 (2000). **Emp:** 200.
Officers: Joseph P. Drago, President.

■ 15962 ■ **Dresser Industries Inc.**
PO Box 718
Dallas, TX 75221
Phone: (214)740-6000
Free: (800)990-0376 **Fax:** (214)740-6584
Products: Upstream and downstream pumps; Mining
machinery; Construction equipment. **SIC:** 5084
(Industrial Machinery & Equipment). **Sales:**
$2,848,800,000 (2000). **Emp:** 31,300. **Officers:**
William E. Bradford, CEO & Chairman of the Board;
Gary V. Morris, Exec. VP & CFO.

■ 15963 ■ **Drilex Corporation**
10628 N Camino Rosas Nuevas
Tucson, AZ 85737-7081
Phone: (520)886-0956 **Fax:** (520)886-1178
Products: Industrial machinery; Mining machinery.
SICs: 5084 (Industrial Machinery & Equipment); 5082
(Construction & Mining Machinery). **Est:** 1980.
Officers: Holland W. Phillips, President.

■ 15964 ■ **Drillers Supply Inc.**
6000 Brittmoore Rd.
Houston, TX 77041
Phone: (713)466-7711
Products: Drilling supplies, including drill bits. **SIC:**
5084 (Industrial Machinery & Equipment). **Sales:**
$7,000,000 (2000). **Emp:** 20. **Officers:** Faber
McMullen, President.

■ 15965 ■ **DS America Inc.**
5110 Tollview Dr.
Rolling Meadows, IL 60008
Phone: (847)870-7400 **Fax:** (847)870-0149
Products: Pre-press equipment; Electrical equipment.
SICs: 5084 (Industrial Machinery & Equipment); 5063
(Electrical Apparatus & Equipment). **Est:** 1967. **Sales:**
$76,300,000 (2000). **Emp:** 165. **Officers:** Kennard S.
Cloud, President; Hiro Matsuo, VP of Finance; Dan
Regan, VP of Operations; Sallie Knanishu, Personnel
Mgr.

■ 15966 ■ **DTC Tool Corp.**
850 Mahler Rd.
Burlingame, CA 94010
Phone: (650)697-1414
Free: (800)486-8300 **Fax:** (650)697-4848
Products: Metal cutting tools; Small cutting tools for
machine tools and metalworking machinery. **SICs:**
5084 (Industrial Machinery & Equipment); 5085
(Industrial Supplies).

■ 15967 ■ **Durable Packaging Corp.**
3139 W Chicago Ave.
Chicago, IL 60622
Phone: (773)638-4140 **Fax:** (773)638-2493
Products: Packaging machines. **SIC:** 5084 (Industrial
Machinery & Equipment). **Officers:** Lawrence Ulrich,
President.

■ 15968 ■ **Durkopp Adler America Inc.**
3025 Northwoods Pkwy.
Norcross, GA 30071
Phone: (404)446-8162
Free: (800)235-1075 **Fax:** (770)448-1545
URL: http://www.durkoppadler.com
Products: Industrial sewing machines. **SICs:** 5064
(Electrical Appliances—Television & Radio); 5084
(Industrial Machinery & Equipment). **Sales:**
$46,000,000 (2000). **Emp:** 95. **Officers:** John Couch,
President; Jurgen Gonetz, Controller.

■ 15969 ■ **DXP Enterprises Inc.**
7272 Pinemont
Houston, TX 77040
Phone: (713)996-4700
Products: Industrial machinery and equipment. **SIC:**
5084 (Industrial Machinery & Equipment). **Sales:**
$203,400,000 (2000). **Emp:** 706. **Officers:** David R.
Little, CEO & Chairman of the Board; Gary A. Allcorn,
Sr. VP & CFO.

■ 15970 ■ **Dynafluid Products, Inc.**
1638 Production Rd.
Jeffersonville, IN 47130
Phone: (812)288-8285 **Fax:** (812)283-1584
Products: Hydraulic and pneumatic components. **SIC:**
5084 (Industrial Machinery & Equipment).

■ 15971 ■ **Dynamic Technology**
2416-A Over Dr.
Lexington, KY 40510
Phone: (606)281-0045 **Fax:** (606)255-9701
Products: Hydraulic and pneumatic equipment and
supplies. **SIC:** 5084 (Industrial Machinery &
Equipment).

■ **15972** ■ **Dynamic Technology**
11584 Commonwealth Dr.
Louisville, KY 40299-2340
Phone: (502)968-3603 **Fax:** (502)968-1504
Products: Hydraulic and pneumatic equipment and supplies. **SIC:** 5084 (Industrial Machinery & Equipment).

■ **15973** ■ **Eagle International, Inc.**
520 Ralph St.
Sarasota, FL 34242
Phone: (941)349-6124 **Fax:** (941)349-6893
Products: Paper ruling printing machinery; Used paper converting pulpmill machinery; Stationery paper mill machinery; Printing bindery equipment; Typesetting machinery. **SIC:** 5084 (Industrial Machinery & Equipment). **Officers:** H. Carter Castilow, President.

■ **15974** ■ **Eastern Lift Truck Co.**
PO Box 307
Maple Shade, NJ 08052-0307
Phone: (856)779-8880
Free: (888)779-8880 **Fax:** (856)482-8804
E-mail: sales@easternlifttrucks.com
URL: http://www.easternlifttrucks.com
Products: Fork lift trucks. **SIC:** 5084 (Industrial Machinery & Equipment). **Est:** 1971. **Sales:** $30,000,000 (2000). **Emp:** 165. **Officers:** Edward Gallagher, Controller, e-mail: sales@easternlifttruck.com; J. Michael Pruitt, President, e-mail: sales@easternlifttruck.com; J. Daniel Pruitt, Vice President; J. Daniel Pruitt, Vice President.

■ **15975** ■ **ebm Industries, Inc.**
100 Hyde Rd.
Farmington, CT 06034
Phone: (860)674-1515 **Fax:** (860)674-8536
E-mail: sales@ebm.com
URL: http://www.ebm.com
Products: Fans and blowers. **SIC:** 5084 (Industrial Machinery & Equipment). **Est:** 1981. **Emp:** 402. **Officers:** Bob Sobolewski, President; Jeffrey Oswald, VP of Finance. **Former Name:** ebm Papst Inc.

■ **15976** ■ **Ecorse Sales and Machinery Inc.**
75 Southfield
Ecorse, MI 48229
Phone: (313)383-2100
Products: Rebuilt screw machines. **SIC:** 5084 (Industrial Machinery & Equipment). **Est:** 1950. **Sales:** $5,000,000 (2000). **Emp:** 25. **Officers:** Steve Johnson, CEO.

■ **15977** ■ **Edgerton Forge Inc.**
257 E Morrison
Edgerton, OH 43517
Phone: (419)298-2333 **Fax:** (419)298-3487
Products: Iron and steel forgings; Tools for automotive use. **SICs:** 5013 (Motor Vehicle Supplies & New Parts); 5085 (Industrial Supplies); 5072 (Hardware). **Sales:** $7,000,000 (2000). **Emp:** 80.

■ **15978** ■ **Edlo Sales and Engineering Inc.**
407 Yorktown Road
Logansport, IN 46947
Phone: (219)753-0502
Free: (800)552-3102 **Fax:** (219)722-5331
E-mail: edlosales@cqc.com
Products: Assembly Tools; Air and electric cutting tools. **SIC:** 5084 (Industrial Machinery & Equipment). **Est:** 1963. **Sales:** $7,000,000 (2000). **Emp:** 17. **Officers:** Timothy Offutt, President; Karla C. Padfield, CEO.

■ **15979** ■ **Electric Motor Engineering Inc.**
25501 Arctic Ocean Dr.
Lake Forest, CA 92630
Phone: (714)583-9802 **Fax:** (714)583-9785
Products: Motors; Fans. **SICs:** 5063 (Electrical Apparatus & Equipment); 5084 (Industrial Machinery & Equipment). **Est:** 1952. **Sales:** $3,000,000 (2000). **Emp:** 12. **Officers:** Richard C. Hubbell, President.

■ **15980** ■ **Electro-Matic Products Inc.**
23409 Industrial Park Ct.
Farmington Hills, MI 48335
Phone: (248)478-1182 **Fax:** (248)478-1472
Products: Industrial electrical apparatus, programmable interfaces and electrical assembling.

SIC: 5084 (Industrial Machinery & Equipment). **Sales:** $47,000,000 (2000). **Emp:** 150.

■ **15981** ■ **Electronic Product Tool**
10-6 Technology Dr.
Setauket, NY 11733
Phone: (516)751-3333
Free: (800)221-4378 **Fax:** (516)751-3792
E-mail: sales@epttool.com
URL: http://www.epttool.com
Products: Electronic tools, including soldering and desoldering equipment. **SIC:** 5065 (Electronic Parts & Equipment Nec). **Est:** 1990. **Sales:** $1,700,000 (1999). **Emp:** 6. **Officers:** Edward Zito, Owner.

■ **15982** ■ **T.J. Elias Sales & Service, Inc.**
2716 E 31st St.
Minneapolis, MN 55406
Phone: (612)721-1825
Free: (800)527-3413 **Fax:** (612)721-1774
Products: Commercial and industrial sewing machines. **SIC:** 5084 (Industrial Machinery & Equipment). **Officers:** Steve Elias, Contact.

■ **15983** ■ **Emco Inc.**
2318 Arty Ave
PO Box 34549
Charlotte, NC 28208
Phone: (704)372-8281
Free: (800)741-8281 **Fax:** (704)372-6732
Products: Industrial power transmission equipment. **SIC:** 5084 (Industrial Machinery & Equipment). **Est:** 1954. **Emp:** 53. **Officers:** Gary Peabody, Controller; Teresa M. Anderson, Sales/Marketing Contact; Pam Swinne, Human Resources Contact.

■ **15984** ■ **Emery Air Charter Inc.**
PO Box 6067
Rockford, IL 61125
Phone: (815)968-8287 **Fax:** (815)968-2889
Products: Fuel base operator. **SIC:** 5172 (Petroleum Products Nec). **Sales:** $8,000,000 (1994). **Emp:** 40. **Officers:** John C. Emery, President.

■ **15985** ■ **Enco Manufacturing Co.**
400 Nevada Pacific Hwy.
Fernley, NV 89408
Free: (800)873-3626 **Fax:** 800-965-5857
Products: General industrial machinery; Industrial supplies. **SICs:** 5084 (Industrial Machinery & Equipment); 5085 (Industrial Supplies). **Est:** 1940. **Sales:** $60,000,000 (2000). **Emp:** 300. **Officers:** Charles Vsiskin, President.

■ **15986** ■ **Enfield Overseas Trade Co.**
17 W Forest Dr.
Enfield, CT 06082
Phone: (860)749-8659 **Fax:** (860)749-8659
Products: New and used plastic processing machinery; Used machine tools; New and used lift trucks and forklifts. **SIC:** 5084 (Industrial Machinery & Equipment). **Est:** 1970. **Officers:** William G. Camp, President; Monika Ibanez, Vice President; Vic Pileika, Vice President.

■ **15987** ■ **Engine Center Inc.**
2351 Hilton
Ferndale, MI 48220
Phone: (248)399-0002 **Fax:** (248)399-3142
Products: Industrial engines. **SIC:** 5084 (Industrial Machinery & Equipment). **Est:** 1935. **Sales:** $5,000,000 (2000). **Emp:** 16. **Officers:** Robert E. Tell, President.

■ **15988** ■ **Engine Distributors Inc.**
332 S 17th St.
Camden, NJ 08105
Phone: (609)365-8631
Products: Industrial machine engines. **SIC:** 5084 (Industrial Machinery & Equipment). **Est:** 1970. **Sales:** $14,000,000 (2000). **Emp:** 30. **Officers:** Glen Cummins Jr., President; Steve Mattson, Controller; Anthony De Marco, VP of Marketing.

■ **15989** ■ **Engine and Equipment Co. Inc.**
20321 Susana Rd.
Rancho Dominguez, CA 90220-5723
Phone: (310)604-9488
Products: Power equipment; Engines; Generators;

Hydraulic systems. **SICs:** 5084 (Industrial Machinery & Equipment); 5063 (Electrical Apparatus & Equipment). **Est:** 1952. **Sales:** $8,500,000 (2000). **Emp:** 63. **Officers:** James H. Crawford, President; Des O'Dwyer, Sales Mgr.

■ **15990** ■ **Engineered Drives**
Rte. 1, Dancehall Rd.
Milton, PA 17847
Phone: (717)742-8751 **Fax:** (717)742-2624
Products: Industrial products. **SIC:** 5084 (Industrial Machinery & Equipment).

■ **15991** ■ **Engineered Sales Inc.**
18 Progress Pkwy.
Maryland Heights, MO 63043
Phone: (314)878-4500 **Fax:** (314)878-7022
Products: Hydraulic and pneumatic equipment and supplies. **SICs:** 5084 (Industrial Machinery & Equipment); 5085 (Industrial Supplies). **Est:** 1964. **Sales:** $23,000,000 (2000). **Emp:** 51. **Officers:** Bud Hoffner, e-mail: budhoffner@engineeredsales.com.

■ **15992** ■ **Engineering Equipment Co.**
1020 W 31st St., Ste. 125
Downers Grove, IL 60515
Phone: (630)963-7800 **Fax:** (630)963-7123
E-mail: engreqmt@aol.com
URL: http://www.engineeringequipment.com
Products: Metalworking machinery; Fabricated structural metal products; Construction and mining machinery; Hardware; Firefighting trucks and equipment; Street sweepers; Utility service vehicles. **SICs:** 5084 (Industrial Machinery & Equipment); 5051 (Metals Service Centers & Offices); 5045 (Computers, Peripherals & Software); 5082 (Construction & Mining Machinery); 5072 (Hardware). **Officers:** F.J. Cullen, Vice President.

■ **15993** ■ **Garrett Enumclaw Co.**
803 Roosevelt Ave.
Enumclaw, WA 98022
Phone: (206)825-2511
Products: Machinery. **SIC:** 5082 (Construction & Mining Machinery). **Est:** 1939. **Sales:** $12,000,000 (2000). **Emp:** 86. **Officers:** Dwight A. Garrett, CEO; Ron Olson, Controller.

■ **15994** ■ **Envirosystems Equipment Company Inc.**
4100 E Michigan St.
Tucson, AZ 85714
Phone: (520)584-9001 **Fax:** (520)584-9211
Products: industrial machinery for dust collection and paint stripping. **SIC:** 5084 (Industrial Machinery & Equipment). **Sales:** $3,000,000 (2000). **Emp:** 30. **Officers:** Mathew Pobloske, President.

■ **15995** ■ **Equality Trading**
17051 Malta Circle
Huntington Beach, CA 92649
Phone: (714)377-0125 **Fax:** (714)377-0125
Products: Metal forming machine tools; Welding and soldering equipment; Hardware, including fasteners, buckles, and snaps; Home furnishings; Fabricated wire products. **SICs:** 5084 (Industrial Machinery & Equipment); 5051 (Metals Service Centers & Offices); 5023 (Homefurnishings); 5072 (Hardware). **Officers:** Ron Winger, President.

■ **15996** ■ **Equipment Inc.**
PO Box 1987
Jackson, MS 39215-1987
Phone: (601)948-3272 **Fax:** (601)948-3282
Products: Industrial equipment. **SIC:** 5084 (Industrial Machinery & Equipment). **Est:** 1951. **Sales:** $10,000,000 (2000). **Emp:** 64. **Officers:** Joe Schmelzer, President & Treasurer; Richard Donnell, CFO; Eddie Batte, VP of Marketing & Sales; Jennifer Parker, Human Resources Mgr.

■ **15997** ■ **Equipment and Technology, Inc.**
PO Box 8766
Jacksonville, FL 32239
Phone: (904)744-3400 **Fax:** (904)745-5319
E-mail: lprt@mediaone.net
Products: Shrimp farming and processing equipment. **SIC:** 5084 (Industrial Machinery & Equipment). **Sales:**

$3,000,000 (2000). **Emp:** 1. **Officers:** Lee Lippert, President. **Former Name:** Lippert International.

■ **15998** ■ **Erie Industrial Supply Co.**
931 Greengarden Rd.
Erie, PA 16501-1525
Phone: (814)452-3231
Free: (800)999-0575 **Fax:** (814)456-7176
E-mail: eis931@erie.net
URL: http://www.eisc.com
Products: Industrial supplies, including high speed cutting tools, sanding belts, and machinery. **SIC:** 5084 (Industrial Machinery & Equipment). **Est:** 1943. **Sales:** $14,000,000 (2000). **Emp:** 30. **Officers:** Dan C. Zambrzycki, President; Albert J. Gusky, Controller; Lynn M. Miller, Dir. of Data Processing; Dena Zambrzycki, Office Mgr.; Dena Zambrzycki, Office Mgr.

■ **15999** ■ **Evans Hydro**
18128 South Santa Fe Ave.
Rancho Dominguez, CA 90220
Phone: (310)608-5801 **Fax:** (310)608-0963
E-mail: evanspump@earthlink.net
Products: Pumps; Pump parts and service; Motors. **SIC:** 5084 (Industrial Machinery & Equipment). **Est:** 1929. **Sales:** $5,000,000 (1999). **Emp:** 26. **Officers:** James Byrom, President; Kim Dixon, Controller; Chris Madden, Sales/Marketing Contact; Kathy King, Customer Service Contact, e-mail: kathyk@hydroaire.com. **Alternate Name:** Evans Pump Equipment Inc.

■ **16000** ■ **Evansville Auto Parts Inc.**
9000 N Kentucky Ave.
Evansville, IN 47725-1396
Phone: (812)425-8264 **Fax:** (812)428-5705
Products: Machinery parts, including components for compressors and generators. **SICs:** 5084 (Industrial Machinery & Equipment); 5085 (Industrial Supplies); 5063 (Electrical Apparatus & Equipment). **Est:** 1912. **Sales:** $2,000,000 (2000). **Emp:** 15. **Officers:** W.D. Walton, President; Dennis Seib, CFO; David Dazey, Operations Mgr.

■ **16001** ■ **Ex-Cell-O North American Sales and Service Inc.**
6015 Center Dr.
Sterling Heights, MI 48312-2667
Phone: (810)939-1330
Products: Rebuilt boring and transfer machines; Parts for woodworking and boring machines. **SIC:** 5084 (Industrial Machinery & Equipment).

■ **16002** ■ **Eyelet Enterprises Inc.**
69 Tenean St.
Boston, MA 02122-3401
Phone: (617)282-4700 **Fax:** (617)282-4560
Products: Eyelets; Eyelet machinery. **SIC:** 5084 (Industrial Machinery & Equipment). **Est:** 1960. **Sales:** $1,000,000 (2000). **Emp:** 14. **Officers:** William Zimbone, President.

■ **16003** ■ **Fabricating and Production Machinery Inc.**
PO Box 240
Sturbridge, MA 01566
Phone: (508)347-3500
Free: (800)222-8187 **Fax:** (508)347-7799
E-mail: machines@fpminc.com
URL: http://www.fpminc.com
Products: Machine tools. **SIC:** 5084 (Industrial Machinery & Equipment). **Est:** 1985. **Sales:** $5,000,000 (2000). **Emp:** 11. **Officers:** Joseph S. Lowkes, President.

■ **16004** ■ **Falk Corp.**
4970 Joule St.
Reno, NV 89502-4119
Phone: (702)856-6155 **Fax:** (702)856-2114
Products: Paratransmission products. **SIC:** 5084 (Industrial Machinery & Equipment). **Est:** 1972. **Sales:** $7,000,000 (2000). **Emp:** 5. **Officers:** Robert Behl, General Mgr.

■ **16005** ■ **Fallsway Equipment Company Inc.**
PO Box 4537
Akron, OH 44310-0537
Phone: (216)633-6000
Free: (800)458-7941 **Fax:** (216)633-6080
Products: Lift trucks. **SIC:** 5013 (Motor Vehicle Supplies & New Parts). **Est:** 1959. **Sales:** $17,500,000 (2000). **Emp:** 140. **Officers:** Harry F. Fairhurst, President; J. Scott Rainey, VP of Finance; Ronald Ober, VP of Marketing.

■ **16006** ■ **Famous Manufacturing Co.**
PO Box 1889
Akron, OH 44309
Phone: (330)762-9621
Products: HVAC equipment. **SIC:** 5075 (Warm Air Heating & Air-Conditioning). **Sales:** $140,000,000 (1992). **Emp:** 600. **Officers:** Dave Ross, President.

■ **16007** ■ **FGH Systems Inc.**
2 Richwood Pl.
Denville, NJ 07834
Phone: (973)625-8114
Products: Molding machines. **SIC:** 5084 (Industrial Machinery & Equipment). **Est:** 1977. **Sales:** $6,000,000 (2000). **Emp:** 20. **Officers:** Frank G. Hohmann, CEO.

■ **16008** ■ **Field Tool Supply Co.**
2358 N Seeley Ave.
Chicago, IL 60647
Phones: (312)541-6500 800-621-8824
Fax: 800-221-3519
URL: http://www.Fiecotool.com
Products: Tools, including cutting and hand; Abrasives; Measuring instruments; Cutting fluids; Shop supplies. **SIC:** 5084 (Industrial Machinery & Equipment). **Est:** 1983. **Sales:** $7,000,000 (1999). **Emp:** 20. **Officers:** Mark Friefeld, President.

■ **16009** ■ **Flexbar Machine Corp.**
250 Gibbs Rd.
Central Islip, NY 11722-2612
Phone: (516)582-8440
Free: (800)879-7575 **Fax:** (516)582-8487
URL: http://www.flexbar.com
Products: Machine tools and accessories; Measuring instruments. **SIC:** 5084 (Industrial Machinery & Equipment). **Est:** 1965. **Sales:** $5,500,000 (2000). **Emp:** 24. **Officers:** J.S. Adler, President; M. Cruz, VP of Finance; L. Valenti, Dir. of Marketing; J. Weiner, Dir. of Data Processing.

■ **16010** ■ **Flexo-Printing Equipment Corp.**
1298 Helmo Ave. N
Oakdale, MN 55128
Phone: (612)731-9499 **Fax:** (612)731-0525
Products: specialty equipment and products. **SIC:** 5084 (Industrial Machinery & Equipment). **Sales:** $1,000,000 (2000). **Emp:** 3.

■ **16011** ■ **Florig Equipment**
35 Industrial Pkwy.
Woburn, MA 01801
Phone: (781)935-6462 **Fax:** (781)933-6932
Products: Mobile hydraulic equipment. **SIC:** 5084 (Industrial Machinery & Equipment).

■ **16012** ■ **Florig Equipment**
775 Marconi Ave.
Ronkonkoma, NY 11779
Phone: (516)467-2200 **Fax:** (516)467-4548
Products: Mobile hydraulics. **SIC:** 5084 (Industrial Machinery & Equipment).

■ **16013** ■ **Florig Equipment**
906 Ridge Pike
Conshohocken, PA 19428
Phone: (215)825-0900 **Fax:** (215)825-0909
Products: Hydraulic pumps. **SIC:** 5084 (Industrial Machinery & Equipment).

■ **16014** ■ **Florig Equipment**
113 Lyle Ln.
Nashville, TN 37210
Phone: (615)242-2554 **Fax:** (615)244-8963
Products: Pumps and hydraulic equipment and parts. **SIC:** 5084 (Industrial Machinery & Equipment).

■ **16015** ■ **Florig Equipment of Buffalo, Inc.**
188 Creekside Dr.
Amherst, NY 14228
Phone: (716)691-9000 **Fax:** (716)691-5720
Products: Hydraulic equipment. **SIC:** 5084 (Industrial Machinery & Equipment).

■ **16016** ■ **Florig Equipment of Portland, Inc.**
27 Washington Ave.
Scarborough, ME 04074
Phone: (207)883-9751 **Fax:** (207)883-8959
Products: Mobile hydraulic equipment. **SIC:** 5084 (Industrial Machinery & Equipment). **Est:** 1987. **Sales:** $2,000,000 (2000). **Emp:** 4. **Officers:** Edward Florig, President; John Woodman, Vice President.

■ **16017** ■ **Flowmatic Systems**
11611 SW 147th Ct.
PO Box 1139
Dunnellon, FL 34432
Phone: (352)465-2000 **Fax:** (352)465-2010
E-mail: info@flowmatic.com
URL: http://www.flowmatic.com
Products: Reverse osmosis components; Filter housings. **SIC:** 5084 (Industrial Machinery & Equipment). **Officers:** Doug Brane, President; Scott Brane, Vice President.

■ **16018** ■ **Fluid-Dynamic Midwest Inc.**
229 Wrightwood Ave.
Elmhurst, IL 60126
Phone: (630)530-5500 **Fax:** (630)530-5513
Products: Hydraulic fluid power systems. **SIC:** 5084 (Industrial Machinery & Equipment).

■ **16019** ■ **Fluid Power Equipment**
PO Box 1287
Mills, WY 82644
Phone: (307)472-6000 **Fax:** (307)472-1801
Products: Hydraulic equipment. **SIC:** 5084 (Industrial Machinery & Equipment).

■ **16020** ■ **Fluid Power Inc.**
10451 Mill Run Circle, Ste. 40-D
Owings Mills, MD 21117
Phone: (410)646-1545 **Fax:** (410)646-1656
Products: Hydraulic equipment; Lubrication equipment. **SIC:** 5084 (Industrial Machinery & Equipment).

■ **16021** ■ **Fluid Power Inc.**
534 Township Line Rd.
Blue Bell, PA 19422
Phone: (215)643-0350 **Fax:** (215)643-4017
Products: Hydraulic equipment, including valves and pumps. **SIC:** 5084 (Industrial Machinery & Equipment).

■ **16022** ■ **Fluid Power Inc.**
135 Burgs Ln.
York, PA 17406
Phone: (717)252-1535 **Fax:** (717)252-1539
Products: Hydraulic and pneumatic equipment; Lubrication equipment. **SIC:** 5084 (Industrial Machinery & Equipment).

■ **16023** ■ **Fluid-Tech, Inc.**
1226 Trapper Cir. NW
Roanoke, VA 24012-1138
Phone: (910)765-3955
Free: (800)868-4903 **Fax:** (919)768-2926
Products: Pneumatic and hydraulic equipment and supplies. **SICs:** 5084 (Industrial Machinery & Equipment); 5085 (Industrial Supplies).

■ **16024** ■ **FMH Material Handling Solutions, Inc.**
1054 Hawkins Blvd.
El Paso, TX 79915
Phone: (915)778-8368
Free: (800)592-1035 **Fax:** (915)778-3579
E-mail: johnfaulkner@fmhsolutions.com
URL: http://www.fmhsolutions.com
Products: Forklifts and parts; Material handling products; Rack and shelving. **SIC:** 5084 (Industrial Machinery & Equipment). **Est:** 1978. **Emp:** 79.

■ **16025** ■ **FMH Material Handling Solutions, Inc.**
4105 Globeville Rd.
Denver, CO 80216
Phone: (303)292-5438
Free: (800)451-6739 **Fax:** (303)297-3426
URL: http://www.clarkliftusa.com
Products: Forklifts and parts. **SIC:** 5084 (Industrial Machinery & Equipment). **Est:** 1961. **Sales:** $14,000,000 (2000). **Emp:** 60. **Officers:** John Faulkner, President; Bruce Murray, Vice President.

■ **16026** ■ **Foley Holding Co.**
3506 W Harry St.
Wichita, KS 67213
Phone: (316)943-4237 **Fax:** (316)943-0827
Products: Materials handling equipment. **SICs:** 5082 (Construction & Mining Machinery); 5084 (Industrial Machinery & Equipment). **Sales:** $39,000,000 (1993). **Emp:** 55. **Officers:** Bill Sanders, President.

■ **16027** ■ **FORCE America Inc.**
501 E Cliff Rd., Ste. 100
Burnsville, MN 55337
Phone: (612)707-1300 **Fax:** (612)707-1330
URL: http://www.forceamerica.com
Products: Hydraulic products and equipment. **SIC:** 5084 (Industrial Machinery & Equipment). **Officers:** Ken Slipka, CEO & Chairman of the Board; Steve Loeffler, President & COO.

■ **16028** ■ **Force America Inc.**
420 NW Business Park Ln.
Kansas City, MO 64150
Phone: (816)587-6363
Free: (800)383-4724 **Fax:** (816)587-6464
URL: http://www.forceamerica.com
Products: Hydraulic components. **SIC:** 5084 (Industrial Machinery & Equipment). **Former Name:** Mid-America Power Drives.

■ **16029** ■ **Force Machinery Company Inc.**
PO Box 3729
Union, NJ 07083
Phone: (908)688-8270 **Fax:** (908)964-3935
URL: http://www.forcemachinery.com
Products: Woodworking machinery and specialty power tools. **SIC:** 5084 (Industrial Machinery & Equipment). **Est:** 1952. **Sales:** $4,200,000 (2000). **Emp:** 25. **Officers:** George Force, President; James Force, Exec. VP; Matt Walton, Customer Service Contact; Anne T. Barnett, Human Resources Contact.

■ **16030** ■ **Forest City Tool Co.**
620 23rd St. NW
Hickory, NC 28601
Phone: (704)322-4266 **Free:** (800)543-7940
Products: Wood working equipment, including drills, lathes, and router bits. **SIC:** 5084 (Industrial Machinery & Equipment). **Est:** 1890. **Sales:** $16,000,000 (2000). **Emp:** 235. **Officers:** Delores Hare, Sales Mgr.

■ **16031** ■ **Fort Dodge Machine Supply Company Inc.**
PO Box 974
Ft. Dodge, IA 50501
Phone: (515)576-2161 **Fax:** (515)576-1618
Products: Agricultural and industrial machine parts. **SICs:** 5084 (Industrial Machinery & Equipment); 5083 (Farm & Garden Machinery). **Est:** 1920. **Sales:** $5,000,000 (2000). **Emp:** 23. **Officers:** James A. Fletcher, President; David Fletcher, Vice President.

■ **16032** ■ **Forte Industrial Equipment Systems Inc.**
6037 Commerce Ct.
Mason, OH 45040
Phone: (513)398-2800 **Fax:** (513)563-5568
Products: Conveyor equipment. **SIC:** 5084 (Industrial Machinery & Equipment). **Est:** 1980. **Sales:** $5,000,000 (2000). **Emp:** 20. **Officers:** E. Forte, President; Dave Kling, Controller.

■ **16033** ■ **Forte Industries**
6037 Commerce Ct
Mason, OH 45040
Phone: (513)398-2800 **Fax:** (513)398-2837
Products: Materials handling equipment and systems

integration; engineering services. **SIC:** 5084 (Industrial Machinery & Equipment).

■ **16034** ■ **Fortron/Source Corp.**
47443 Fremont Blvd.
Fremont, CA 94538
Phone: (510)440-0188 **Fax:** (510)440-0928
URL: http://www.fsusa.com
Products: Power tools and parts. **SIC:** 5084 (Industrial Machinery & Equipment). **Est:** 1983. **Sales:** $15,000,000 (2000). **Emp:** 20. **Officers:** Jackson Wang, President; Jack Wang, Mgr. of Finance; Monica Mao, Dir. of Marketing.

■ **16035** ■ **Fosburg & McLaughlin Inc.**
615 Addison St.
PO Drawer 2069
Berkeley, CA 94702
Phone: (510)845-8283
Products: Mobile hydraulic equipment. **SIC:** 5084 (Industrial Machinery & Equipment).

■ **16036** ■ **John Henry Foster Company of St. Louis Inc.**
PO Box 5820
St. Louis, MO 63134
Phone: (314)427-0600 **Fax:** (314)427-3502
Products: Pneumatic and hydraulic equipment. **SIC:** 5084 (Industrial Machinery & Equipment). **Sales:** $15,000,000 (1992). **Emp:** 49. **Officers:** Robert Gau, President.

■ **16037** ■ **Michael Fox Auctioneers Inc.**
3835 Naylors Ln.
Baltimore, MD 21208
Phone: (410)653-4000 **Fax:** (410)653-4069
Products: General industrial machinery. **SIC:** 5084 (Industrial Machinery & Equipment). **Est:** 1946. **Sales:** $58,000,000 (2000). **Emp:** 20. **Officers:** David S. Fox, President; Linda Smith, Controller.

■ **16038** ■ **Michael Fox International Inc.**
3835 Naylors Ln.
Baltimore, MD 21208
Phone: (410)653-4000
Free: (800)722-3334 **Fax:** (410)653-4069
URL: http://www.michaelfox.com
Products: Industrial machinery. **SIC:** 5084 (Industrial Machinery & Equipment). **Est:** 1946. **Sales:** $75,000,000 (1999). **Emp:** 35. **Officers:** David S. Fox, President, e-mail: dfox@michaelfox.com. **Former Name:** Michael Fox Auctioneers Inc.

■ **16039** ■ **Frank & Thomas, Inc.**
111 Smith Hines Rd.
Thomas Centre, Ste. G
Greenville, SC 29607
Phone: (864)288-5050
Free: (800)832-7746 **Fax:** (864)234-7544
E-mail: info@frank1-thomas.com
URL: http://www.frank1-thomas.com
Products: Textile machinery and parts. **SIC:** 5084 (Industrial Machinery & Equipment). **Est:** 1946. **Emp:** 7. **Officers:** A. W. Thomas III, President.

■ **16040** ■ **Fraza Equipment Inc.**
15725 E 12 Mile Rd.
Roseville, MI 48066
Phone: (810)778-6111 **Fax:** (810)778-9795
E-mail: fraza@wnol.net
URL: http://www.fraza.com
Products: Material handling equipment, including hi-lows, forklifts, aerial equipment and lift trucks. **SIC:** 5084 (Industrial Machinery & Equipment). **Est:** 1938. **Sales:** $17,000,000 (2000). **Emp:** 90. **Officers:** Terry Fraza, President; Gary Nienaltowski, Chairman of the Board & CFO; Gary Lowe, Sales Mgr.

■ **16041** ■ **R.K. Fromm, Inc.**
3561 Copley Cir.
PO Box 4224
Copley, OH 44321-0224
Phone: (330)666-6737 **Fax:** (330)666-0673
Products: Electrical controls. **SIC:** 5084 (Industrial Machinery & Equipment). **Est:** 1976. **Sales:** $2,000,000 (2000). **Emp:** 7. **Officers:** Robert K. Fromm, President; Charles V. Koester, Vice President.

■ **16042** ■ **Frost Engineering Service Co.**
PO Box 26770
Santa Ana, CA 92799-6770
Phone: (714)549-9222 **Fax:** (510)568-2166
Products: Jet pumps, gauges, valves, lubricators, and oil systems. **SIC:** 5084 (Industrial Machinery & Equipment). **Est:** 1954. **Sales:** $3,000,000 (2000). **Emp:** 10. **Officers:** E. Vernon Frost, Chairman of the Board; Steve Williams, President.

■ **16043** ■ **Fuchs Machinery Inc.**
5401 F St.
Omaha, NE 68117-2827
Phone: (402)734-1991 **Fax:** (402)734-3619
Products: Industrial machinery. **SIC:** 5084 (Industrial Machinery & Equipment). **Est:** 1923. **Sales:** $24,000,000 (2000). **Emp:** 75. **Officers:** J.M. Fuchs, CEO & Chairman of the Board; Tom Peterson, Controller; T. Berger, COO & President; Bill Kiefer, Sales/Marketing Contact.

■ **16044** ■ **G-Riffco**
1011 Currie Ave. N
Minneapolis, MN 55403
Phone: (612)338-7355
Products: Industrial equipment. **SIC:** 5084 (Industrial Machinery & Equipment).

■ **16045** ■ **Gaffey Inc.**
9655 Alawhe Dr.
Claremore, OK 74017-4366
Phone: (918)836-6827
Products: Overhead cranes, parts, and hoists. **SIC:** 5084 (Industrial Machinery & Equipment). **Est:** 1972. **Sales:** $7,000,000 (2000). **Emp:** 90. **Officers:** A. Gaffey, President.

■ **16046** ■ **Gahr Machine Co.**
19199 St. Clair Ave.
Cleveland, OH 44117-1090
Phone: (216)531-0053 **Fax:** (216)531-0595
URL: http://www.gahrmachine.com
Products: Used machines, mills, turrets, and lathes. **SIC:** 5084 (Industrial Machinery & Equipment). **Est:** 1947. **Sales:** $5,000,000 (1999). **Emp:** 30. **Officers:** William P. Rhea, President, e-mail: bill@ghrmachine.com; Gregg Rickettson, Dir. of Marketing.

■ **16047** ■ **Gardner and Meredith Inc.**
PO Box 4837
Chattanooga, TN 37405
Phone: (615)756-4722
Products: Solder; Computer peripherals; Cutting tools; Rivet and fastener machines. **SICs:** 5085 (Industrial Supplies); 5045 (Computers, Peripherals & Software); 5084 (Industrial Machinery & Equipment). **Sales:** $2,000,000 (1994). **Emp:** 10. **Officers:** David Gardner, President.

■ **16048** ■ **Gavlick Machinery Corporation**
100 Franklin St.
PO Box 370
Bristol, CT 06011-0370
Phone: (860)589-2900 **Fax:** (860)589-0863
E-mail: gavlick@att.net
URL: http://www.gavlick.com
Products: Used industrial machinery. **SIC:** 5084 (Industrial Machinery & Equipment). **Officers:** Richard Gavlick, President.

■ **16049** ■ **GE Machine Tool Services**
PO Box 32036
Louisville, KY 40232
Phone: (502)969-3126 **Fax:** (502)969-6321
Products: Steel working machinery. **SIC:** 5084 (Industrial Machinery & Equipment). **Est:** 1960. **Sales:** $12,000,000 (2000). **Emp:** 40. **Officers:** Brian Runkle, President; Art Sims, Controller. **Former Name:** Advance Machinery Company Inc.

■ **16050** ■ **Gehr Industries**
7400 E Slauson Ave.
Los Angeles, CA 90040-3308
Phone: (213)728-5558 **Fax:** (213)887-8051
Products: Pumps and pumping equipment. **SIC:** 5084 (Industrial Machinery & Equipment).

■ 16051 ■ **Gelber Industries**
1001 Cambridge Dr.
Elk Grove Village, IL 60007-2453
Phone: (708)437-4500 **Fax:** (708)437-2002
Products: Industrial machinery and supplies. **SICs:** 5084 (Industrial Machinery & Equipment); 5085 (Industrial Supplies). **Sales:** $15,000,000 (1994). **Emp:** 80. **Officers:** Lou Mattaliano, President.

■ 16052 ■ **General Air Service and Supply Company Inc.**
1105 Zuni St.
Denver, CO 80204
Phone: (303)892-7003 **Fax:** (303)595-9036
URL: http://www.generalair.com
Products: Welding products and gases. **SICs:** 5084 (Industrial Machinery & Equipment); 5169 (Chemicals & Allied Products Nec); 5172 (Petroleum Products Nec). **Est:** 1970. **Sales:** $22,000 (2000). **Emp:** 105. **Officers:** Gary Armstrong, President, e-mail: garmstrong@generalair.com.

■ 16053 ■ **General Automation Manufacturing Inc.**
35444 Mound Rd.
Sterling Heights, MI 48310
Phone: (810)268-0300 **Fax:** (810)268-1741
Products: Industrial presses. **SIC:** 5084 (Industrial Machinery & Equipment). **Est:** 1961. **Sales:** $400,000 (2000). **Emp:** 4. **Officers:** Joseph E. Suminski.

■ 16054 ■ **General Electric Co. Marine and Industrial Engines Div.**
1 Neumann Way, No. S158
Cincinnati, OH 45215
Phone: (513)552-5370 **Fax:** (513)552-5001
Products: Gas turbines. **SIC:** 5084 (Industrial Machinery & Equipment). **Est:** 1950. **Sales:** $650,000,000 (2000). **Emp:** 110. **Officers:** Richard R. Ruegg, General Mgr.; Jeff Rodgers, Mgr. of Finance; Richard Cull, Marketing Mgr.; E. Eugene Custer, Human Resources Mgr.

■ 16055 ■ **General Handling Systems Inc.**
701 E Plano Pkwy.
Plano, TX 75074-6758
Phone: (972)424-9339
Free: (888)424-9339 **Fax:** (972)424-6817
Products: Overhead bridge cranes; Hoists; Monorail systems. **SICs:** 5084 (Industrial Machinery & Equipment); 5088 (Transportation Equipment & Supplies). **Est:** 1968. **Sales:** $2,500,000 (2000). **Emp:** 5. **Officers:** Daniel M. Dantzler, President; Duane Dantzler, Accountant, e-mail: d.l.dantzler@inetmail.att.net.

■ 16056 ■ **General Industrial Tool and Supply Inc.**
12540 Sherman Way
North Hollywood, CA 91605
Phone: (818)983-0520 **Fax:** (818)503-6200
E-mail: genindust@aol.com
Products: Power hand tools; Machine tools for home workshops, laboratories, garages. **SICs:** 5084 (Industrial Machinery & Equipment); 5083 (Farm & Garden Machinery). **Est:** 1955. **Sales:** $8,000,000 (2000). **Emp:** 42. **Officers:** Mary Sawin.

■ 16057 ■ **General Supply and Paper Co.**
1 George Ave.
Wilkes Barre, PA 18705-2511
Phone: (717)823-1194 **Fax:** (717)822-6065
Products: Paper and paper products. **SIC:** 5084 (Industrial Machinery & Equipment). **Sales:** $4,000,000 (2000). **Emp:** 15.

■ 16058 ■ **Al George Inc.**
PO Box 3604
Lafayette, LA 70502
Phone: (337)233-0626 **Fax:** (337)233-0828
URL: http://www.agiindustries.com
Products: Pumps and pump parts. **SIC:** 5084 (Industrial Machinery & Equipment). **Est:** 1968. **Sales:** $3,000,000 (2000). **Emp:** 35. **Officers:** David B. George, CEO; John M. George, CFO.

■ 16059 ■ **Geraghty Industrial Equipment Inc.**
4414 11th St.
Rockford, IL 61109
Phone: (815)397-4450 **Fax:** (815)397-4456
Products: Fork lifts. **SIC:** 5084 (Industrial Machinery & Equipment). **Est:** 1956. **Sales:** $12,000,000 (2000). **Emp:** 48. **Officers:** Gerald Risch, CEO; Dale Nash, VP of Finance; H.J. Santel, VP of Marketing & Sales.

■ 16060 ■ **Gerhardt's International, Inc.**
PO Box 36334
Houston, TX 77236
Phone: (713)789-8860 **Fax:** (713)789-4732
Products: Generator sets, units, and parts; Steam engines and turbines parts; Diesel engines; Industrial engine and turbine accessories; Electrical equipment, including internal combustable engines. **SICs:** 5084 (Industrial Machinery & Equipment); 5063 (Electrical Apparatus & Equipment); 5085 (Industrial Supplies). **Officers:** Fred Johnston, VP and General Manager.

■ 16061 ■ **Paul H. Gesswein and Co.**
255 Hancock Ave.
Bridgeport, CT 06605
Phone: (203)366-5400 **Fax:** (203)366-3953
Products: Jewelry supplies, including die cutters and polishing stones. **SIC:** 5049 (Professional Equipment Nec). **Est:** 1914. **Sales:** $20,000,000 (2000). **Emp:** 80. **Officers:** Dwight Gesswein, President.

■ 16062 ■ **Getz Bros. & Company Inc.**
150 Post St., Ste. 500
San Francisco, CA 94108-4707
Phone: (415)772-5500 **Fax:** (415)772-5659
E-mail: info@getz.com
URL: http://www.getz.com
Products: Medical equipment; Building materials; Chemicals; Plastics; Health and beauty supplies; Industrial products. **SICs:** 5039 (Construction Materials Nec); 5021 (Furniture); 5169 (Chemicals & Allied Products Nec). **Est:** 1871. **Sales:** $500,000,000 (1999). **Emp:** 2,100. **Officers:** Adel Michael, VP & CFO; Ray Simkins, Pres., Medical Operations; Jeffrey Li, Pres., Commercial Operations.

■ 16063 ■ **Gierston Tool Company Inc.**
382 Upper Oakwood Ave.
PO Box 2247
Elmira, NY 14903
Phone: (607)733-7191 **Fax:** (607)733-1295
E-mail: gierston@gierston.com
URL: http://www.gierston.com
Products: Industrial tools, including cutting, abrasive, machine, and hand tools. **SICs:** 5084 (Industrial Machinery & Equipment); 5085 (Industrial Supplies). **Est:** 1939. **Sales:** $8,900,000 (2000). **Emp:** 25. **Officers:** T. Carlson, President; R. Maxa, Sr. VP; L. Diggs, Sr. VP.

■ 16064 ■ **Gilbert and Richards Inc.**
70 State St.
North Haven, CT 06473
Phone: (203)239-4646 **Fax:** (203)234-8371
E-mail: office@gilbertandrichards.com
URL: http://www.gilbertandrichards.com
Products: Milling and boring machines; Lathes; Drills; Saws. **SIC:** 5084 (Industrial Machinery & Equipment). **Est:** 1946. **Sales:** $8,000,000 (2000). **Emp:** 16. **Officers:** Dale A. Monegan, President.

■ 16065 ■ **Giles and Ransome Inc.**
2975 Galloway Rd.
Bensalem, PA 19020
Phone: (215)639-4300 **Fax:** (215)245-2831
Products: Heavy equipment, including earth moving equipment and forklifts; Engines. **SICs:** 5084 (Industrial Machinery & Equipment); 5082 (Construction & Mining Machinery); 5013 (Motor Vehicle Supplies & New Parts). **Est:** 1916. **Sales:** $200,000,000 (2000). **Emp:** 585. **Officers:** Wayne L. Bromley Jr., President; Dennis Runyen, Exec. VP; Jeff Speer, VP of Sales; Dale Hulse, Information Systems Mgr.; Richard Smith, Dir of Human Resources.

■ 16066 ■ **GL&V/Celleco Inc.**
1000 Laval Blvd.
Lawrenceville, GA 30043
Phone: (404)963-2100
Products: Pulp and paper industry parts; Cleaners; Screens. **SICs:** 5084 (Industrial Machinery & Equipment); 5085 (Industrial Supplies). **Sales:** $20,000,000 (2000). **Emp:** 65. **Officers:** Greg Bruyea, President. **Former Name:** Celleco Hedemora Inc.

■ 16067 ■ **Global House**
PO Box 993
Sanford, NC 27331
Phone: (919)776-2391
Products: Industrial pumps and pumping equipment; Construction machinery. **SICs:** 5084 (Industrial Machinery & Equipment); 5082 (Construction & Mining Machinery). **Officers:** John Kelley, President.

■ 16068 ■ **Global Products Company**
3221 Rosemead Place
Rosemead, CA 91770
Phone: (626)288-5353
Products: Water pollution control equipment; Industrial pumps; Office equipment; Water purification equipment. **SICs:** 5084 (Industrial Machinery & Equipment); 5074 (Plumbing & Hydronic Heating Supplies); 5044 (Office Equipment). **Officers:** Gilbert Ng, Managing Director.

■ 16069 ■ **Globe Machinery and Supply Co.**
4060 Dixon St.
Des Moines, IA 50313
Phone: (515)262-0088
Free: (800)362-2804 **Fax:** (515)262-8261
Products: Industrial machinery and supplies. **SIC:** 5084 (Industrial Machinery & Equipment). **Sales:** $26,000,000 (1999). **Emp:** 100. **Officers:** Harold Thoreson, CEO & President; Scott A. Manhart, CFO.

■ 16070 ■ **Godwin Company, Inc.**
1175 W 16th St.
Indianapolis, IN 46202
Phone: (317)637-3325 **Fax:** (317)263-9625
Products: Forklift trucks. **SIC:** 5084 (Industrial Machinery & Equipment).

■ 16071 ■ **Gonzalez International Inc.**
28 Allegheny Ave., Ste. 1212
Baltimore, MD 21204
Phone: (301)321-1577 **Fax:** (301)321-1090
Products: Industrial machinery and equipment. **SIC:** 5084 (Industrial Machinery & Equipment). **Officers:** Julio Gonzalez, President.

■ 16072 ■ **Gosiger Inc.**
108 McDonough St.
Dayton, OH 45402
Phone: (937)228-5174
Free: (800)888-4188 **Fax:** (937)228-5189
URL: http://www.gosiger.com
Products: Machine tools, including saws and grinders; Automation and engineered systems; Robotics. **SIC:** 5084 (Industrial Machinery & Equipment). **Est:** 1922. **Sales:** $140,000,000 (2000). **Emp:** 190. **Officers:** Jane G. Haley, President; Jerry L. Gecowets, Exec. VP.

■ 16073 ■ **Grainger, Inc.**
35 Corporate Cir.
Albany, NY 12203
Phone: (518)869-1414
Products: Industrial equipment and supplies, including motors and gliders. **SIC:** 5084 (Industrial Machinery & Equipment).

■ 16074 ■ **Gray Machinery Co.**
77 E Palantine Rd.
Prospect Heights, IL 60070
Phone: (847)537-7700 **Fax:** (847)537-9307
E-mail: sales@graymachinery.com
URL: http://www.graymachinery.com
Products: Fabrication and production machinery; Used metalworking machine tools; Toolroom equipment. **SIC:** 5084 (Industrial Machinery & Equipment). **Est:** 1966. **Sales:** $10,000,000 (2000). **Emp:** 20. **Officers:** Glenn R. Gray, President; Melvin A. Teichman, Vice President. **Former Name:** Gray Industrial Investments Inc.

■ **16075** ■ **Grays Harbor Equipment Inc.**
401 S F St.
Aberdeen, WA 98520
Phone: (206)532-8643 **Fax:** (206)532-8646
Products: Industrial equipment. **SIC:** 5084 (Industrial Machinery & Equipment). **Est:** 1920. **Sales:** $900,000 (2000). **Emp:** 7. **Officers:** William L. Perry, President; Ada G. Isaacson, Treasurer & Secty.

■ **16076** ■ **Greaves Company Inc.**
PO Box 99267
Seattle, WA 98199
Phone: (206)284-0660 **Fax:** (206)244-2673
Products: Industrial fluid process controls. **SIC:** 5084 (Industrial Machinery & Equipment). **Est:** 1932. **Sales:** $4,000,000 (2000). **Emp:** 10. **Officers:** Frank A. Robinson, President.

■ **16077** ■ **GreenTek Inc.**
1600 NW Washington Blvd.
Grants Pass, OR 97526
Phone: (541)471-7111 **Fax:** (541)471-7116
Products: Research and development; Airborne particulate monitors. **SIC:** 5084 (Industrial Machinery & Equipment).

■ **16078** ■ **J.M. Grimstad, Inc.**
6203 Chancellor Dr.
Cedar Falls, IA 50613
Phone: (319)277-8550 **Fax:** (319)277-1691
Products: Hydraulic fluid power systems; Pneumatic fluid power systems. **SIC:** 5084 (Industrial Machinery & Equipment).

■ **16079** ■ **J.M. Grimstad Inc.**
1001 S 84th St.
PO Box 14517
Milwaukee, WI 53214
Phone: (414)258-5200 **Fax:** (414)258-3414
E-mail: info@grimstad.com
URL: http://www.grimstad.com
Products: Hydraulic, filtration, and pneumatic equipment; Electrical power units. **SICs:** 5084 (Industrial Machinery & Equipment); 5063 (Electrical Apparatus & Equipment). **Est:** 1934. **Emp:** 60. **Officers:** Jodie Gruber, Sales/Marketing Contact; Mona Trawicki, Customer Service Contact.

■ **16080** ■ **Grinders Clearing House Inc.**
13301 E 8 Mile Rd.
Warren, MI 48089
Phone: (810)771-1500 **Fax:** (810)771-5958
Products: Used equipment. **SIC:** 5084 (Industrial Machinery & Equipment). **Sales:** $10,000,000 (2000). **Emp:** 50. **Officers:** Chuck Thornton, President.

■ **16081** ■ **A. Gusmer Co.**
PO Box 846
Cranford, NJ 07016
Phones: (908)272-9400 (908)272-8735
(908)272-8735
Products: Industrial machinery and supplies; Farm product raw materials. **SICs:** 5084 (Industrial Machinery & Equipment); 5159 (Farm-Product Raw Materials Nec). **Officers:** Louis C. Uribe, Dir. of Sales.

■ **16082** ■ **J. Lee Hackett Co.**
23550 Haggerty Rd.
Farmington, MI 48335-2636
Phone: (313)478-0200
Products: Machinery parts. **SIC:** 5084 (Industrial Machinery & Equipment). **Est:** 1923. **Sales:** $125,000,000 (2000). **Emp:** 38. **Officers:** J. Lee Juett, President; Richard L. Kelm, CFO; John L. McCartney, Sr. VP.

■ **16083** ■ **Haggard and Stocking Associates Inc.**
5318 Victory Dr.
Indianapolis, IN 46203
Phone: (317)788-4661
Free: (800)622-4824 **Fax:** (317)788-1645
Products: Cutting wheels, abrasive wheels, carbides, drills, reamers and material handling equipment. **SIC:** 5084 (Industrial Machinery & Equipment). **Sales:** $37,000,000 (1999). **Emp:** 47. **Officers:** Bill Holden, President.

■ **16084** ■ **Hallidie Machinery Company Inc.**
PO Box 3536
Seattle, WA 98124
Phone: (206)583-0600 **Fax:** (206)624-7528
Products: Machine tools. **SIC:** 5084 (Industrial Machinery & Equipment). **Est:** 1900. **Sales:** $20,000,000 (2000). **Emp:** 40. **Officers:** Lawrence E. Myhre, President; William Cavender, Treasurer; Jim D. Ellis, Vice President; Beverly Gorman, Dir of Human Resources.

■ **16085** ■ **Handi-Ramp Inc.**
1414 Armour Blvd.
Mundelein, IL 60060
Phone: (847)816-7525
Free: (800)876-RAMP **Fax:** (847)816-7689
Products: Wheelchair and loading ramps; Dock boards. **SIC:** 5084 (Industrial Machinery & Equipment). **Est:** 1958.

■ **16086** ■ **Handling Systems Inc.**
2659 E Magnolia St.
Phoenix, AZ 85034-6923
Phone: (602)275-2228
Free: (800)229-9977 **Fax:** (602)275-2424
E-mail: handsys@handlingsystems.com
URL: http://www.handlingsystems.com
Products: Forklifts; Conveyors; Mezzanines; Racking and shelving. **SIC:** 5084 (Industrial Machinery & Equipment). **Est:** 1981. **Sales:** $20,000,000 (2000). **Emp:** 75. **Officers:** Charles Martiny, President, e-mail: chuck@handlingsystems.com.

■ **16087** ■ **Hansco Technologies, Inc.**
17 Philips Pkwy.
Montvale, NJ 07645
Phone: (201)391-0700 **Fax:** (201)391-4261
E-mail: sales@hanscotech.com
URL: http://www.hanscotech.com
Products: Machine tools. **SIC:** 5084 (Industrial Machinery & Equipment). **Est:** 1992. **Sales:** $10,000,000 (2000). **Emp:** 30. **Officers:** Hans U. Berlinger, President, e-mail: hberlinger@hanscotech.com; Michael J. Campbell, CFO; Monika Frost, Manager, e-mail: mfrost@hanscotech.com; Theo Halliday, Dir of Human Resources, e-mail: thalliday@hansotech.com.

■ **16088** ■ **Harbor Tool Supply Inc.**
20 SW Park Ave.
Westwood, MA 02090
Phone: (781)329-4432
Products: Power and hand tools, including cutting tools and abrasives. **SICs:** 5084 (Industrial Machinery & Equipment); 5072 (Hardware).

■ **16089** ■ **Harris Industrial Gases Inc.**
8475 Auburn Blvd.
Citrus Heights, CA 95610
Phone: (916)725-2168 **Fax:** (916)725-2117
E-mail: harris@harrisindustrialgases.com
URL: http://www.harrisindustrialgases.com
Products: Welding equipment; Industrial gases. **SIC:** 5084 (Industrial Machinery & Equipment). **Est:** 1936. **Sales:** $3,599,612 (2000). **Emp:** 24. **Officers:** Kathleen Harris, President; Rhonda Pratt, Controller. **Former Name:** Harris Welding Supply.

■ **16090** ■ **Harris Pump and Supply Co.**
603 Parkway View Dr., No. 6
Pittsburgh, PA 15205-1412
Phone: (412)787-7867 **Fax:** (412)787-7696
Products: Industrial tools, including power drives; Machinery supplies. **SICs:** 5085 (Industrial Supplies); 5084 (Industrial Machinery & Equipment). **Est:** 1896. **Sales:** $8,000,000 (2000). **Emp:** 34. **Officers:** Timothy Williams, President; David Whitlinger, Controller; Ray Johnson, Vice President.

■ **16091** ■ **Haskel International, Inc.**
100 E Graham Pl.
Burbank, CA 91502
Phone: (818)843-4000 **Fax:** (818)841-4291
E-mail: sales@haskel.com
URL: http://www.haskel.com
Products: Hydraulic and pneumatic pumps. **SICs:** 5084 (Industrial Machinery & Equipment); 5085 (Industrial Supplies). **Est:** 1946. **Sales:** $54,000,000

(2000). **Emp:** 260. **Officers:** R. Needham, President; P. Duffy, VP of Marketing.

■ **16092** ■ **M.L. Hauser Company**
PO Box 6174
Clearwater, FL 33758-6174
Phone: (813)855-5465 **Fax:** (813)855-7707
Products: Electrical equipment; Lumber and millwork; Furniture; Fresh fruits and vegetables; Industrial machinery. **SICs:** 5084 (Industrial Machinery & Equipment); 5063 (Electrical Apparatus & Equipment); 5031 (Lumber, Plywood & Millwork); 5021 (Furniture); 5148 (Fresh Fruits & Vegetables). **Officers:** Michael L. Hauser, General Mgr.

■ **16093** ■ **Hawaiian Fluid Power**
803 Ahua St.
Honolulu, HI 96819
Phone: (808)833-4516 **Fax:** (808)839-6471
Products: Hydraulics. **SIC:** 5084 (Industrial Machinery & Equipment).

■ **16094** ■ **Hawera Inc.**
PO Box 402
South Elgin, IL 60177-0402
Phone: (630)653-3044
Free: (800)869-7460 **Fax:** (630)653-7760
Products: Tools, including drill bits and levels. **SICs:** 5084 (Industrial Machinery & Equipment); 5072 (Hardware). **Est:** 1978. **Emp:** 10. **Officers:** Don Fraser, Vice President.

■ **16095** ■ **Hawkins Chemical Inc.**
3100 E Hennepin Ave.
Minneapolis, MN 55413-2923
Phone: (612)331-6910
Free: (800)328-5460 **Fax:** (612)331-5304
Products: Industrial machinery and equipment. **SIC:** 5084 (Industrial Machinery & Equipment). **Est:** 1938. **Sales:** $87,700,000 (2000). **Emp:** 151. **Officers:** Dean L. Hahn, CEO & Chairman of the Board; Howard M. Hawkins, VP & Treasurer.

■ **16096** ■ **Heavy Machines Inc.**
3926 E Raines Rd.
Memphis, TN 38118-6936
Phone: (901)260-2200
Free: (800)238-5591 **Fax:** (901)260-2276
E-mail: general@heavymachinesinc.com
URL: http://www.heavymachinesinc.com
Products: Industrial machines, including cranes, stackers, porters, loaders, handlers, and trucks. **SIC:** 5084 (Industrial Machinery & Equipment). **Est:** 1971. **Sales:** $45,000,000 (2000). **Emp:** 180. **Officers:** Richard O. Wilson Jr., CEO; William F. Bailey, Sr. VP. **Alternate Name:** Melanie J. #Hall.

■ **16097** ■ **E.P. Heller Co.**
21 Samson Ave.
Madison, NJ 07940-2261
Phone: (973)377-2878 **Fax:** (973)514-1022
Products: Carbide cutting tools. **SICs:** 5084 (Industrial Machinery & Equipment); 5072 (Hardware). **Est:** 1960. **Sales:** $3,000,000 (2000). **Emp:** 36. **Officers:** Eugene P. Heller.

■ **16098** ■ **Herc-U-Lift Inc.**
5655 Hwy. 12 W
PO Box 187
Maple Plain, MN 55359-0187
Phone: (612)479-2501
Free: (800)362-3500 **Fax:** (612)479-2296
Products: Material handling equipment, including forklifts. **SIC:** 5084 (Industrial Machinery & Equipment). **Est:** 1968. **Sales:** $31,000,000 (1999). **Emp:** 115. **Officers:** Les Nielsen, President; Brad Ellingson, Treasurer; Jack Piche, Dir. of Marketing.

■ **16099** ■ **Hermes Machine Tool Company Inc.**
5 Gardner Rd.
Fairfield, NJ 07004
Phone: (973)227-9150
Free: (800)639-6224 **Fax:** (973)227-9364
E-mail: hermes@newmach.com
URL: http://www.newmach.com
Products: Heavy large equipment including lathes, milling equipment, and drills. **SIC:** 5084 (Industrial Machinery & Equipment). **Est:** 1958. **Sales:**

$10,000,000 (2000). **Emp:** 20. **Officers:** G. Bard, President; T. Bard, Vice President; N. Bard, Vice President.

■ 16100 ■ **Highway Equipment and Supply Co.**
1016 W Church St.
Orlando, FL 32854
Phone: (407)843-6310   **Fax:** (407)849-0740
Products: Industrial engines. **SIC:** 5085 (Industrial Supplies). **Est:** 1942. **Sales:** $7,000,000 (2000). **Emp:** 25. **Officers:** E.A. Snyder, Chairman of the Board; Jeffrey Passmore, President.

■ 16101 ■ **Fred Hill and Son Co.**
2101 Hornig Rd.
Philadelphia, PA 19116
Phone: (215)698-2200
Free: (800)523-0112   **Fax:** (215)698-4539
Products: Materials handling equipment. **SIC:** 5084 (Industrial Machinery & Equipment). **Sales:** $20,000,000 (2000). **Emp:** 65. **Officers:** Kenneth Shaw Jr., President; Martin O'Halloran, Controller.

■ 16102 ■ **Hirschmann Corp.**
123 Powerhouse Rd.
Roslyn Heights, NY 11577
Phone: (516)484-0500
Products: Industrial machinery and equipment. **SIC:** 5084 (Industrial Machinery & Equipment). **Sales:** $22,000,000 (1994). **Emp:** 45. **Officers:** E.J. Dunki, President; Thomas Haughey, Treasurer.

■ 16103 ■ **Hixon Manufacturing and Supply**
1001 Smithfield Dr.
Ft. Collins, CO 80524
Phone: (970)482-0111   **Fax:** (970)482-0428
Products: Measuring and controlling devices for surveying. **SIC:** 5084 (Industrial Machinery & Equipment). **Officers:** Tim Hixon, President.

■ 16104 ■ **Hobart Arc Welding Systems**
11933 Woodruff Ave.
Downey, CA 90241-5601
Phone: (714)521-7514
Products: Welding machinery. **SIC:** 5084 (Industrial Machinery & Equipment). **Est:** 1962. **Sales:** $1,000,000 (2000). **Emp:** 9. **Officers:** Glen Irving, Manager.

■ 16105 ■ **Hobart Corp.**
701 S Ridge Ave.
Troy, OH 45373-0815
Phone: (513)332-3000
Free: (800)960-1190   **Fax:** (937)332-2633
URL: http://www.hobartcorp.com
Products: Machines for baking, cooking, refrigeration, dishwashing, waste handling, preparation, weighing, wrapping, and labeling. **SIC:** 5084 (Industrial Machinery & Equipment). **Est:** 1897. **Emp:** 1,200.

■ 16106 ■ **Hockman Lewis Ltd.**
200 Executive Dr.
West Orange, NJ 07052
Phone: (973)325-3838   **Fax:** (973)325-7974
E-mail: sales@hl-ltd.com
Products: Service station equipment; Automotive service equipment. **SICs:** 5084 (Industrial Machinery & Equipment); 5049 (Professional Equipment Nec). **Est:** 1933. **Emp:** 35. **Officers:** Garrett E. Pearce, President; J. Gregory Hockman, Vice President, e-mail: jgh@hl-ltd.com.

■ 16107 ■ **Hoffman Brothers**
5290 N Pearl St.
Rosemont, IL 60018
Phone: (847)671-1550
Free: (800)323-9120   **Fax:** (847)671-1320
Products: Industrial sewing machines; Die cutting machines; Embroidery machines. **SIC:** 5084 (Industrial Machinery & Equipment). **Officers:** Scott Hoffman.

■ 16108 ■ **Hoist Liftruck Manufacturing**
6499 W 65th St.
Bedford Park, IL 60638
Phone: (708)458-2200   **Fax:** (708)458-1176
Products: Truck hoists and cranes. **SIC:** 5084 (Industrial Machinery & Equipment).

■ 16109 ■ **Holloway Brothers Tools Inc.**
PO Box 3055
Wilmington, DE 19804-0055
Phone: (302)322-5441   **Fax:** (302)328-7024
URL: http://www.hollowaytools.com
Products: Industrial machinery and supplies. **SICs:** 5084 (Industrial Machinery & Equipment); 5085 (Industrial Supplies). **Est:** 1946. **Sales:** $8,000,000 (2000). **Emp:** 40. **Officers:** Eric Holloway, President; Steven R. Graham, CFO; Joe Tanner, Vice President.

■ 16110 ■ **Holloway Brothers Tools Inc.**
PO Box 3055
Wilmington, DE 19804-0055
Phone: (302)322-5441   **Fax:** (302)328-7024
Products: Industrial machinery. **SIC:** 5084 (Industrial Machinery & Equipment). **Sales:** $8,000,000 (2000). **Emp:** 40.

■ 16111 ■ **Holox Ltd.**
1885 Broadway
Macon, GA 31201-2903
Phone: (912)746-6211   **Free:** (800)652-6087
Products: Welding equipment. **SIC:** 5084 (Industrial Machinery & Equipment). **Sales:** $29,000,000 (1993). **Emp:** 200. **Officers:** Rod Woods, General Mgr.

■ 16112 ■ **Hope Group**
PO Box 840
Northborough, MA 01532-0840
Phone: (508)393-7660   **Fax:** (508)393-8203
Products: Air compressors, fittings, industrial rubber hoses, pneumatic, hydraulic equipment and electronic control systems. **SICs:** 5084 (Industrial Machinery & Equipment); 5085 (Industrial Supplies). **Sales:** $178,000,000 (2000). **Emp:** 100. **Officers:** Carey Rhoten, President & Treasurer.

■ 16113 ■ **Horner Electric Inc.**
1521 E Washington St.
Indianapolis, IN 46201
Phone: (317)639-4261   **Fax:** (317)639-6875
Products: Pumps; Hoists; Motors; Variable frequency drives. **SICs:** 5063 (Electrical Apparatus & Equipment); 5084 (Industrial Machinery & Equipment). **Est:** 1949. **Sales:** $9,000,000 (2000). **Emp:** 75. **Officers:** Mary E. Horner, President; David Margolius, CFO; Philip Horner, Vice President.

■ 16114 ■ **E.C. Horrigan & Associates**
4509 Taylor Ln.
Warrensville Heights, OH 44128
Phone: (216)831-8090   **Fax:** (216)831-0411
Products: Motion control products; Power transmission products. **SIC:** 5084 (Industrial Machinery & Equipment).

■ 16115 ■ **Hosokawa Micron International Inc.**
780 3rd Ave. Ste. 3201
New York, NY 10017
Phone: (212)826-3830   **Fax:** (212)826-6612
Products: Power handling equipment and industrial mixers. **SICs:** 5084 (Industrial Machinery & Equipment); 5085 (Industrial Supplies). **Emp:** 2,000. **Officers:** Isa Sato, President.

■ 16116 ■ **Hougen Manufacturing Inc.**
PO Box 2005
Flint, MI 48501
Phone: (810)732-5840   **Fax:** (810)732-3553
Products: Magnetic drills. **SIC:** 5084 (Industrial Machinery & Equipment). **Est:** 1959. **Sales:** $12,000,000 (2000). **Emp:** 125. **Officers:** Randall B. Hougen, President; M. Maclean, CFO; Patrick J. Carmody, Dir. of Marketing & Sales; Richard C. Grega, Dir. of Data Processing.

■ 16117 ■ **Howden Fan Co.**
1 Westinghouse Plz.
HyDe Park, MA 02136
Phone: (617)361-3700
Products: Industrial fans. **SIC:** 5084 (Industrial Machinery & Equipment). **Est:** 1970.

■ 16118 ■ **Hub Tool and Supply Inc.**
PO Box 11647
Wichita, KS 67202
Phone: (316)265-9608
Products: Industrial cutting tools and drill bits. **SIC:** 5084 (Industrial Machinery & Equipment).

■ 16119 ■ **Hubbard Industrial Supply Co.**
901 W 2nd St.
Flint, MI 48502
Phone: (810)234-8681
Free: (800)875-4811   **Fax:** (810)234-6142
E-mail: www.info@HubbardSupply.com
URL: http://www.HubbardSupply.com
Products: Industrial machinery and supplies. **SICs:** 5084 (Industrial Machinery & Equipment); 5085 (Industrial Supplies). **Est:** 1865. **Emp:** 80. **Officers:** Robert Fuller.

■ 16120 ■ **Hull Lift Truck Inc.**
28747 U.S 33 W
Elkhart, IN 46516
Phone: (219)293-8651   **Fax:** (219)674-9769
Products: Materials handling equipment. **SIC:** 5084 (Industrial Machinery & Equipment). **Est:** 1964. **Sales:** $28,000,000 (2000). **Emp:** 140. **Officers:** Robert L. Hull, President; Carey R. Bert, Controller.

■ 16121 ■ **Hutchins Manufacturing Co.**
49 N Lotus Ave.
Pasadena, CA 91107
Phones: (818)792-8211   (818)792-8281
Fax: (818)792-8574
E-mail: mail@hutchinsmfg.com
URL: http://www.hutchinsmfg.com
Products: Pneumatic sanders and accessories. **SIC:** 5084 (Industrial Machinery & Equipment). **Sales:** $6,000,000 (2000). **Emp:** 60. **Officers:** Daniel H. Kay Jr., Sales & Marketing Contact; Shirley O'Neill, Human Resources Contact.

■ 16122 ■ **Hydra-Power, Inc.**
14630 28th Ave. N
Minneapolis, MN 55447
Phone: (612)559-2930   **Fax:** (612)559-6519
Products: Hydraulic components. **SIC:** 5084 (Industrial Machinery & Equipment).

■ 16123 ■ **Hydra-Power Systems Inc.**
12135 Esther Lama Dr., Ste. G
El Paso, TX 79938-7728
Phone: (915)860-9919
Products: Hydraulic and pneuatic tools. **SIC:** 5084 (Industrial Machinery & Equipment). **Sales:** $9,000,000 (1994). **Emp:** 30. **Officers:** Tom Brown, President; Jeff Moore, VP of Finance.

■ 16124 ■ **Hydradyene Hydraulics Inc.**
2537 I-85 S
Charlotte, NC 28208
Phone: (704)392-6185
Free: (800)432-6194   **Fax:** (704)393-8949
Products: Hydraulic and pumping equipment components. **SIC:** 5084 (Industrial Machinery & Equipment). **Sales:** $1,000,000 (2000). **Emp:** 6. **Officers:** Charles Rubright, General Mgr.

■ 16125 ■ **Hydradyne Hydraulics**
2537 I-85 S
Charlotte, NC 28208
Phone: (704)392-6185
Free: (800)432-6194   **Fax:** (704)393-8949
Products: Commercial hydraulic equipment, including pumps, motors, and valves. **SIC:** 5084 (Industrial Machinery & Equipment). **Est:** 1964. **Sales:** $2,000,000 (2000). **Emp:** 11. **Officers:** Charles Rubright, General Mgr.

■ 16126 ■ **Hydraquip Corp.**
1119 111th St.
Arlington, TX 76011
Phone: (972)660-7230   **Fax:** (972)660-1076
Products: Hydraulics and fluid power equipment. **SIC:** 5084 (Industrial Machinery & Equipment).

■ 16127 ■ Hydraquip Corp.
PO Box 925009
Houston, TX 77292-5009
Phone: (713)680-1951 **Fax:** (713)680-9799
Products: Hydraulic and pneumatic valves, filters, and brakes; Power units. **SIC:** 5084 (Industrial Machinery & Equipment). **Est:** 1951. **Emp:** 65.

■ 16128 ■ Hydraquip Corp.
618-A W Rhapsody
San Antonio, TX 78216
Phone: (210)341-8896 **Fax:** (210)341-0801
Products: Hydraulic equipment, including belts, straps, and brakes. **SICs:** 5084 (Industrial Machinery & Equipment); 5085 (Industrial Supplies).

■ 16129 ■ Hydraulic and Air Controls
PO Box 28208
Columbus, OH 43228
Phone: (614)276-8141
Products: Hydraulic and pneumatic products. **SIC:** 5082 (Construction & Mining Machinery). **Sales:** $32,000,000 (2000). **Emp:** 45. **Officers:** John Taylor, President; Cindy Lewis, Controller.

■ 16130 ■ Hydraulic Controls Inc.
4700 San Pablo Ave.
Emeryville, CA 94608
Phone: (510)658-8300
Free: (800)847-6900 **Fax:** (510)658-3133
E-mail: hciemeryville@2xtreme.net
URL: http://www.hydraulic-controls.com
Products: Hydraulic and pneumatic cylinders, pumps, and motors. **SIC:** 5084 (Industrial Machinery & Equipment). **Est:** 1965. **Sales:** $55,000,000 (2000). **Emp:** 212. **Officers:** Richard A. Cotter, CEO & President.

■ 16131 ■ Hydro-Abrasive Machining Inc.
8831 Miner St.
Los Angeles, CA 90002
Phone: (323)587-1342 **Fax:** (323)587-1814
E-mail: hydromachine@earthlink.net
URL: http://www.hydromachine.com
Products: Waterjet cutting of metals and composites; Composite panels fabrication. **SIC:** 5049 (Professional Equipment Nec). **Est:** 1949. **Sales:** $2,800,000 (1999). **Emp:** 30. **Officers:** Richard Woolman, President; Michael L. Woolman, Sales Mgr.

■ 16132 ■ Hydro Dyne Inc.
PO Box 443
Massillon, OH 44648
Phone: (330)832-5076 **Fax:** (330)832-8163
Products: Heat transfer equipment. **SIC:** 5084 (Industrial Machinery & Equipment). **Est:** 1967. **Sales:** $2,500,000 (2000). **Emp:** 50. **Officers:** Rose Ann Dare, President.

■ 16133 ■ Hydro-Power Inc.
PO Box 2181
Terre Haute, IN 47802-0181
Phone: (812)232-0156 **Fax:** (812)232-8068
E-mail: hydrpwr@aol.com
URL: http://www.hydropower.com
Products: Industrial water pumps; Cranes; Compressors. **SIC:** 5084 (Industrial Machinery & Equipment). **Est:** 1969. **Sales:** $15,000,000 (2000). **Emp:** 60. **Officers:** J.R. White, President; Joe J. Goda, CFO; John Petry, Sales Mgr.

■ 16134 ■ Hyster MidEast
3480 Spring Grove Ave.
Cincinnati, OH 45223
Phone: (513)541-0401 **Fax:** (513)853-8458
URL: http://www.hystermideast.com
Products: Waste reduction equipment; Material handling equipment; Systems design and engineering. **SICs:** 5084 (Industrial Machinery & Equipment); 5085 (Industrial Supplies). **Est:** 1934. **Emp:** 300. **Officers:** R.W. Risheill, General Mgr.; Rick Schimpf, Controller; Jennifer Kingma, Sales/Marketing Contact, e-mail: jkingma@bode-finn.com. **Former Name:** Bode-Finn Co.

■ 16135 ■ Hyster New England, Inc.
358 Second Ave.
Waltham, MA 02451
Phone: (781)890-7950
Free: (800)234-5438 **Fax:** (781)890-4259
URL: http://www.hysterneweng.com
Products: Forklift trucks and service; Allied products. **SIC:** 5084 (Industrial Machinery & Equipment). **Est:** 1997. **Sales:** $60,000,000 (2000). **Emp:** 280. **Officers:** Charles F. Haywood, President. **Former Name:** Lewis-Boyle Inc.

■ 16136 ■ IBT Inc.
PO Box 2982
Shawnee Mission, KS 66201
Phone: (913)677-3151
Free: (800)332-2114 **Fax:** (913)677-3752
E-mail: ibtinfo@ibtinc.com
URL: http://www.ibtinc.com
Products: Warehouse equipment; Power transmission products; Conveying equipment products; Industrial rubber products; Industrial drives and controls; Industrial automation products. **SICs:** 5085 (Industrial Supplies); 5084 (Industrial Machinery & Equipment). **Est:** 1949. **Sales:** $120,000,000 (2000). **Emp:** 449. **Officers:** Stephen R. Cloud, CEO & President; Wayne L. Shields, Treasurer; Ron Aupperle, VP of Marketing & Sales; Larry Brand, VP of Operations; Janet Clayton, Dir of Human Resources.

■ 16137 ■ IBT Inc.
4323 Woodson
Woodson Terrace, MO 63134
Phone: (314)428-4284 **Fax:** (314)428-1048
URL: http://www.ibtinc.com
Products: Industrial power transmissions; Belts; Bearings; Pulleys. **SICs:** 5084 (Industrial Machinery & Equipment); 5085 (Industrial Supplies).

■ 16138 ■ ICC Instrument Company Inc.
1483 E Warner Ave.
Santa Ana, CA 92705
Phone: (714)540-4966 **Fax:** (714)540-5327
Products: Sells, repairs and provides traceable calibration of process and test equipment; ISO 9002 registered. **SIC:** 5084 (Industrial Machinery & Equipment).

■ 16139 ■ Ideal Machinery and Supply Co.
109 E Main St.
Plainville, CT 06062
Phone: (860)747-1651
Free: (800)559-1651 **Fax:** (860)793-9139
E-mail: idealms@idealms.com
URL: http://www.idealms.com
Products: Cutting tools; Cutting fluids; Drills; Sanding belts; Grinders. **SICs:** 5084 (Industrial Machinery & Equipment); 5085 (Industrial Supplies). **Est:** 1918. **Sales:** $7,000,000 (2000). **Emp:** 16. **Officers:** Art Hoerle, President; Theo Hoerle, Vice President, e-mail: Theo@idealms.com.

■ 16140 ■ IKR Corporation
17 S Briar Hollow Ln., Ste. 202
Houston, TX 77027
Phone: (713)627-3520 **Fax:** (713)627-9508
Products: Industrial machinery. **SIC:** 5084 (Industrial Machinery & Equipment). **Est:** 1979. **Officers:** Richard A. Koehler, President.

■ 16141 ■ Ilapak Inc.
105 Pheasant Run
Newtown, PA 18940
Phone: (215)579-2900
Products: Liquid filler machinery, equipment, and supplies. **SICs:** 5084 (Industrial Machinery & Equipment); 5085 (Industrial Supplies).

■ 16142 ■ Illinois Auto Electric Co.
656 County Line Rd.
Elmhurst, IL 60126
Phone: (630)833-4300 **Fax:** (630)832-6104
E-mail: info@iaeco.net
URL: http://www.illinoisautoelectric.com
Products: Transport refrigeration; Air cooled engines; Diesel rebuilding for locomotives. **SICs:** 5084 (Industrial Machinery & Equipment); 5078 (Refrigeration Equipment & Supplies); 5088

(Transportation Equipment & Supplies). **Est:** 1915. **Sales:** $40,000,000 (2000). **Emp:** 250.

■ 16143 ■ Illinois Carbide Tool Co.
1322 Belvidere Rd.
Waukegan, IL 60085
Phone: (847)244-1110 **Fax:** (847)249-0693
Products: Small cutting tools for machine tools and metalworking machinery. **SIC:** 5084 (Industrial Machinery & Equipment). **Est:** 1954. **Sales:** $3,500,000 (1999). **Emp:** 25. **Officers:** A.G. Mini, CEO; John Mini, President; Michael Mini, VP of Marketing.

■ 16144 ■ IM/EX Port Inc.
4417 Provens Dr.
Akron, OH 44319
Phone: (330)896-3056 **Fax:** (330)896-3056
Products: Industrial machinery and equipment. **SIC:** 5084 (Industrial Machinery & Equipment). **Officers:** Susan Bailey, President.

■ 16145 ■ IMT Corp.
330 Greco Ave., Ste. 103
Coral Gables, FL 33146-1800
Phone: (305)441-7680
Free: (800)735-0070 **Fax:** (305)441-7682
Products: Active in US and Can, Experts in Polyurethane Equipment Low P., High P. Mold concepts clamping designs, rotary tables, conveyors, machines. **SIC:** 5084 (Industrial Machinery & Equipment).

■ 16146 ■ IMT Inc.
2313 North Shore Rd.
Bellingham, WA 98226
Phone: 800-248-1752 **Fax:** (206)738-9217
Products: Industrial plastics machinery. **SIC:** 5084 (Industrial Machinery & Equipment). **Officers:** David Netka, President.

■ 16147 ■ Indeck Power Equipment Co.
1111 Willis Ave.
Wheeling, IL 60090
Phone: (708)541-8300 **Fax:** (708)541-9984
Products: General industrial machinery. **SIC:** 5084 (Industrial Machinery & Equipment). **Est:** 1958. **Sales:** $20,000,000 (2000). **Emp:** 60. **Officers:** G.R. Forsythe, Chairman of the Board; L. Lagowski, VP of Finance; John G. Williamson, VP of Marketing & Sales.

■ 16148 ■ Indianapolis Belting & Supply
8900 E 30th St.
Indianapolis, IN 46219
Phone: (317)898-2411
Free: (800)382-5523 **Fax:** (317)899-6475
Products: Industrial equipment and supplies including belts, bearings, and power transmissions; Coated abrasives; Band-saw blades; Fluid power. **SICs:** 5084 (Industrial Machinery & Equipment); 5085 (Industrial Supplies). **Est:** 1954.

■ 16149 ■ Industrial Belting & Transmission, Inc.
4061 McCollum Ct.
PO Box 32215
Louisville, KY 40232
Phone: (502)456-6100
Free: (800)264-BELT **Fax:** (502)452-9744
E-mail: indbelt@indbelt.com
URL: http://www.indbelt.com
Products: Bulk material handling components; Conveyor belts; Electical motion control components; Power transmission components. **SIC:** 5084 (Industrial Machinery & Equipment). **Est:** 1977. **Sales:** $18,500,000 (2000). **Emp:** 50. **Officers:** Mark Deich, Vice President, e-mail: madeich@aol.com. **Former Name:** Industrial Belt & Transmissions.

■ 16150 ■ Industrial Development & Procurement
4000 Town Center, Ste. 480
Southfield, MI 48075
Phone: (248)358-5383
Products: Office and accounting machines; Metal forgings and stampings; Industrial machinery; Electrical industrial apparatus; Motor vehicles. **SICs:** 5084 (Industrial Machinery & Equipment); 5044 (Office Equipment); 5051 (Metals Service Centers & Offices);

5012 (Automobiles & Other Motor Vehicles); 5063 (Electrical Apparatus & Equipment). **Officers:** Brooks G. Rawlins, Dir. of Intl. Trade.

■ **16151** ■ **Industrial Municipal Equipment Inc.**
PO Box 369
West Islip, NY 11795-0369
Phone: (516)567-9000
Products: Industrial equipment and supplies. **SIC:** 5084 (Industrial Machinery & Equipment).

■ **16152** ■ **Industrial Pipe & Steel**
9936 Rush
South el Monte, CA 91733-2637
Phone: (626)443-9467
Free: (800)423-4981   **Fax:** (626)579-4602
E-mail: info@ipstool.com
URL: http://www.ipstool.com
Products: General industrial machinery. **SICs:** 5084 (Industrial Machinery & Equipment); 5085 (Industrial Supplies). **Est:** 1962. **Sales:** $11,000,000 (2000). **Emp:** 55. **Officers:** Joe Schorr; Bob Entrikin, Sales/Marketing Contact; Kevin Armour, Customer Service Contact; Kevin Chapman, Human Resources Contact.

■ **16153** ■ **Industrial Source**
PO Box 2330
Eugene, OR 97402
Phone: (541)344-1438   **Fax:** (541)344-0611
Products: Welding equipment. **SIC:** 5084 (Industrial Machinery & Equipment). **Est:** 1945. **Sales:** $5,000,000 (1999). **Emp:** 35. **Officers:** Robert G. Laing, President; Brent P. Laing, Vice President. **Alternate Name:** Eugene Welders Supply Co.

■ **16154** ■ **Industrial Supply Co.**
1635 South 300 West
Salt Lake City, UT 84130
Phone: (801)484-8644   **Fax:** (801)487-0469
URL: http://www.Indsupply.com
Products: Industrial tools and supplies. **SICs:** 5084 (Industrial Machinery & Equipment); 5085 (Industrial Supplies). **Est:** 1914. **Sales:** $430,000,000 (1999). **Emp:** 130. **Officers:** Chris Bateman, VP of Marketing & Sales; Jon Richards, VP & CFO; Phillip Thompson; Randy Evans, Sales/Marketing Contact, e-mail: revan@Indsupply.com.

■ **16155** ■ **Industrial Supply Solutions, Inc.**
PO Box 1866
Charleston, WV 25327
Phone: (304)346-5341   **Fax:** (304)346-5347
E-mail: info@indssi.com
URL: http://www.indssi.com
Products: Industrial supplies. **SIC:** 5085 (Industrial Supplies). **Est:** 1946. **Sales:** $30,000,000 (1999). **Emp:** 100. **Officers:** Frank Carmazzi, President; Angela Hutchinson, CFO; Perry Bennhardt, Vice President; Mike Lear, Vice President; Joe Canmazzi, Vice President. **Former Name:** Persingers Inc.

■ **16156** ■ **Industrial Tool Products Inc.**
919 N Central Ave.
Wood Dale, IL 60191
Phone: (630)766-4040   **Fax:** (630)766-4166
Products: Pneumatic tools, including screwdrivers, hoists, and hammers. **SICs:** 5084 (Industrial Machinery & Equipment); 5085 (Industrial Supplies). **Est:** 1945. **Sales:** $14,000,000 (2000). **Emp:** 40. **Officers:** Herbert Newham, President; Robert McNelis, Vice President.

■ **16157** ■ **Inland Empire Equipment Inc.**
1762 S Sycamore Ave.
Rialto, CA 92376
Phone: (909)877-0657   **Fax:** (909)877-5351
Products: Material moving equipment, including forklifts. **SIC:** 5084 (Industrial Machinery & Equipment). **Est:** 1970. **Sales:** $22,000,000 (2000). **Emp:** 200. **Officers:** Dianne Loomis, President; Rich Engle, Corporate General Manager; Dick Patrick, Sales/Marketing Contact; Elmer Karhu, Customer Service Contact; Diane Miller, Human Resources Contact.

■ **16158** ■ **Inland Industries Inc.**
PO Box 15999
Shawnee Mission, KS 66285-5999
Phone: (913)492-9050
Products: Newspaper presses. **SIC:** 5084 (Industrial Machinery & Equipment). **Est:** 1910. **Sales:** $62,000,000 (2000). **Emp:** 200. **Officers:** Clark Murray, President.

■ **16159** ■ **Inland Newspaper Machinery Corp.**
PO Box 15999
Shawnee Mission, KS 66285-5999
Phone: (913)492-9050
Free: (800)255-6746   **Fax:** (913)492-6217
E-mail: inmc1@inlandnews.com
URL: http://www.inlandnews.com
Products: Newspaper presses. **SIC:** 5084 (Industrial Machinery & Equipment). **Est:** 1910. **Sales:** $6,000,000 (2000). **Emp:** 50. **Officers:** Beau Campbell, President; J. Burton, VP of Finance.

■ **16160** ■ **Inotek Technologies Corp.**
11212 Indian Trl.
Dallas, TX 75229
Phone: (972)243-7000   **Fax:** (972)243-2924
Products: Instrument repairing and calibrating service. **SIC:** 5084 (Industrial Machinery & Equipment). **Sales:** $25,500,000 (2000). **Emp:** 76. **Officers:** David L. White, CEO; Susan I. Williamson, CFO.

■ **16161** ■ **Integrated Process Equipment Corp.**
911 Bern Ct. Ste. 110
San Jose, CA 95112
Phone: (408)436-2170
Products: Semiconductor wafer processing equipment. **SIC:** 5084 (Industrial Machinery & Equipment). **Sales:** $189,000,000 (2000). **Emp:** 1,100. **Officers:** R.D. McDaniel, CEO & President; John S. Hodgson, VP, CFO & Treasurer.

■ **16162** ■ **Integrated Systems Inc.**
1904 SE Ochoco St.
Portland, OR 97222
Phone: (503)654-7886   **Fax:** (503)654-7868
Products: Conveyors and conveying equipment. **SIC:** 5084 (Industrial Machinery & Equipment). **Officers:** Steve Heston, President.

■ **16163** ■ **Intermarket Imports Inc.**
PO Box 39
Guilderland Center, NY 12085-0039
Phone: (518)869-3223   **Fax:** (518)869-5988
Products: Tools; Hydraulic lifts; Jacks. **SICs:** 5084 (Industrial Machinery & Equipment); 5085 (Industrial Supplies). **Est:** 1972. **Sales:** $6,000,000 (2000). **Emp:** 30. **Officers:** Joseph A. Milot, President; Cindy Slagh, Vice President.

■ **16164** ■ **International Machine Tool Ltd.**
2461 N Clybourn Ave.
Chicago, IL 60614
Phone: (773)871-5282
Products: Gear cutting machines. **SIC:** 5084 (Industrial Machinery & Equipment). **Est:** 1973. **Sales:** $1,000,000 (2000). **Emp:** 3. **Officers:** Bert Schwesig, President; Werner Schwesig, Secretary.

■ **16165** ■ **International Marketing Specialists Inc.**
4108 McAlice Ct.
Plano, TX 75093
Phone: (972)758-7226
Free: (800)814-2516   **Fax:** (972)758-7226
E-mail: wmathews@concentric.net
URL: http://www.used autoclaves.com
Products: Industrial equipment; Auto claves. **SIC:** 5084 (Industrial Machinery & Equipment). **Est:** 1983.

■ **16166** ■ **International Medcom**
7497 Kennedy Rd.
Sebastopol, CA 95472
Phone: (707)823-0336   **Fax:** (707)823-7207
Products: Radiation monitoring equipment; Detection instruments. **SIC:** 5084 (Industrial Machinery & Equipment). **Officers:** Rachel Sythe, CFO.

■ **16167** ■ **Interstate Detroit Diesel Inc.**
2501 E 80th St.
Minneapolis, MN 55425
Phone: (612)854-5511
Products: Engines; Generators. **SIC:** 5084 (Industrial Machinery & Equipment). **Sales:** $100,000,000 (2000). **Emp:** 560. **Officers:** Jeff Caswell, CEO; Harry Lindstrom, VP of Finance; Kerry J. Kline, VP of Marketing; F. Hamblin, Dir. of Data Processing.

■ **16168** ■ **Interstate Welding Sales Corp.**
1801 Marinette Ave.
Marinette, WI 54143
Phone: (715)732-7950
Free: (800)261-7950   **Fax:** (715)732-7940
URL: http://www.iweld.com
Products: Safety supplies; Gases; Tools; Abrasives; Rental and repair; Welding equipment; Fire safety equipment; Fasteners. **SICs:** 5084 (Industrial Machinery & Equipment); 5085 (Industrial Supplies). **Est:** 1969. **Sales:** $50,000,000 (1999). **Emp:** 215. **Officers:** David Higley, President; William Higley, Exec. VP of Business Development.

■ **16169** ■ **Intramar Inc.**
10497 Town & Country Way, Ste. 225
Houston, TX 77024
Phone: (713)984-2791   **Fax:** (713)984-2379
E-mail: intramar@worldnet.att.net
Products: Industrial machinery and spare parts; Construction equipment; Hotel furniture. **SICs:** 5084 (Industrial Machinery & Equipment); 5021 (Furniture); 5082 (Construction & Mining Machinery). **Est:** 1987. **Sales:** $4,000,000 (2000). **Emp:** 6. **Officers:** W.S. Renshaw, President.

■ **16170** ■ **Investrade Import & Export**
1040 Woodrow
Wichita, KS 67203
Phone: (316)265-9630   **Fax:** (316)265-9630
Products: Metal cutting tools and sawing machinery; Steel; Computers; Precision measuring equipment; Nuts and screws. **SICs:** 5084 (Industrial Machinery & Equipment); 5072 (Hardware); 5051 (Metals Service Centers & Offices); 5045 (Computers, Peripherals & Software). **Officers:** Marco Seabra, Director of Business Operations.

■ **16171** ■ **Ion Tech Inc.**
2330 E Prospect Rd.
Ft. Collins, CO 80525
Phone: (970)221-1807   **Fax:** (970)493-1439
Products: Thin film etching and deposition equipment and services. **SIC:** 5084 (Industrial Machinery & Equipment).

■ **16172** ■ **Ion Technologies Corp.**
4815 Para Dr.
Cincinnati, OH 45237-5009
Phone: (513)641-3100   **Fax:** (513)641-3560
E-mail: info@ion-tech.com
URL: http://www.ion-tech.com
Products: Electrostatic power coating equipment; Liquid spray guns. **SIC:** 5084 (Industrial Machinery & Equipment). **Est:** 1987. **Sales:** $6,000,000 (2000). **Emp:** 25. **Officers:** John O. Graves, President; Peter Parker, VP of Engineering; Paul Gollnitz, Controller; Donald S. Tyler, VP of Sales.

■ **16173** ■ **Iowa Machinery and Supply Company Inc.**
1711 2nd Ave.
Des Moines, IA 50314
Phone: (515)288-0123   **Fax:** (515)288-3733
URL: http://www.iowamach.com
Products: Industrial equipment and supplies, including forklifts and air compressors. **SICs:** 5084 (Industrial Machinery & Equipment); 5085 (Industrial Supplies). **Est:** 1903. **Sales:** $25,000,000 (1999). **Emp:** 96. **Officers:** Robert Hollwager, Chairman of the Board; Darrell Randall, President.

■ **16174** ■ **IPS of California**
70 Glenn Way
San Carlos, CA 94070
Phone: (650)592-1742   **Fax:** (650)592-3544
Products: Digital video image processing systems. **SIC:** 5084 (Industrial Machinery & Equipment). **Officers:** Shirley Boice, Treasurer.

■ 16175 ■ Ison Equipment Inc.
Hwy. 8 E
Monico, WI 54501
Phone: (715)487-5583   Fax: (715)487-5968
Products: Industrial tractors. SIC: 5084 (Industrial Machinery & Equipment). Sales: $30,000,000 (2000). Emp: 75. Officers: A. Ison Jr., President; John Ison, Dir. of Marketing.

■ 16176 ■ Isspro Inc.
PO Box 11177
Portland, OR 97211
Phone: (503)288-4488
Free: (800)888-8065   Fax: (503)249-2999
Products: Designs, engineers, and markets vehicle instrumentation systems for the heavy-duty vehicular market-agricultural, industrial, construction, large truck plants and OEMs. SIC: 5084 (Industrial Machinery & Equipment). Sales: $23,500,000 (2000). Emp: 175. Officers: A Kevin Roli, President; Dennis Cromwell, CFO.

■ 16177 ■ ITS/Intertrade Scientific, Inc.
176 Bolton Rd.
Vernon, CT 06066
Phone: (860)871-0401   Fax: (860)871-9233
Products: Industrial machinery, including electrical testing equipment. SICs: 5084 (Industrial Machinery & Equipment); 5063 (Electrical Apparatus & Equipment). Officers: Joseph J. Mahar, Operations Manager.

■ 16178 ■ IVI Corp.
265 Oak St.
Pembroke, MA 02359
Phone: (781)826-3195   Fax: (781)826-1195
Products: Industrial vacuum equipment for coating. SIC: 5084 (Industrial Machinery & Equipment). Sales: $1,000,000 (2000). Emp: 20. Officers: George Mackertich, President.

■ 16179 ■ Izumi International, Inc.
1 Pelham Davis Circle
Greenville, SC 29615
Phone: (864)288-8001   Fax: (864)288-7272
Products: Industrial machinery, including textile machinery and parts. SIC: 5084 (Industrial Machinery & Equipment). Officers: Ichiro Izumi, President.

■ 16180 ■ J and L Strong Tool Co.
1251 E 286th St.
Cleveland, OH 44132
Phone: (216)289-2450   Fax: (216)289-4562
Products: Cutting tools; Abrasives. SICs: 5084 (Industrial Machinery & Equipment); 5085 (Industrial Supplies). Sales: $80,000,000 (1999). Emp: 111. Officers: Jeff Crowl, Controller.

■ 16181 ■ Jackson Welding Supply
1421 W Carson St.
Pittsburgh, PA 15219
Phone: (412)391-4500   Fax: (412)281-2299
Products: Welding machinery and equipment. SIC: 5084 (Industrial Machinery & Equipment). Est: 1944. Sales: $4,000,000 (2000). Emp: 25. Officers: J. Mazziotti Jr., President.

■ 16182 ■ Henry R. Jahn and Son Inc.
26 Broadway 20th Fl.
New York, NY 10004
Phone: (212)509-7920   Fax: (212)344-4728
E-mail: ferrex@ferrex.com
URL: http://www.ferrex.com
Products: Construction and road building machinery; Steel mill and cement plant demolition equipment; Electric welding apparatus. SICs: 5084 (Industrial Machinery & Equipment); 5082 (Construction & Mining Machinery). Est: 1914. Sales: $11,000,000 (2000). Emp: 35. Officers: William Ferretti, President; Tim Byrnes, Controller; James Robinson, VP of Marketing & Sales.

■ 16183 ■ Jarvis Supply Co.
PO Box 645
Winfield, KS 67156
Phone: (316)221-3113
Products: Auto parts; Industrial machinery. SICs: 5013 (Motor Vehicle Supplies & New Parts); 5084 (Industrial Machinery & Equipment); 5085 (Industrial Supplies); 5198 (Paints, Varnishes & Supplies); 5082 (Construction & Mining Machinery). Est: 1930. Sales: $12,000,000 (2000). Emp: 82. Officers: Chris Jarvis, President; Jeff Long, CFO.

■ 16184 ■ JC Industrial Motor Service Inc.
30121 Groesbeck Hwy.
Roseville, MI 48066
Phone: (810)779-4663   Fax: (313)779-3550
Products: Motors. SIC: 5084 (Industrial Machinery & Equipment). Est: 1946. Sales: $12,000,000 (2000). Emp: 35. Officers: Jerome G. Cohen, President; Hiram Cohen, Vice President; Ken Hayes, Dir. of Marketing.

■ 16185 ■ Jealco International, Inc.
435 Jones Dr.
Roswell, GA 30075
Phone: (404)998-2124   Fax: (404)998-0726
Products: Industrial equipment, including fans, blowers, and material handling supplies; Power transmission equipment; Hardware, including casters and wheels. SICs: 5084 (Industrial Machinery & Equipment); 5072 (Hardware); 5085 (Industrial Supplies). Officers: Jose E. Almeida, President.

■ 16186 ■ Jefferds Corp.
Rte. 35 W
PO Box 757
St. Albans, WV 25177
Phone: (304)755-8111   Fax: (304)755-7544
E-mail: name@Jefferds.com
URL: http://www.jefferds.com
Products: Forklifts; Trucks; Cranes; Dock equipment. SIC: 5084 (Industrial Machinery & Equipment). Est: 1947. Sales: $58,000,000 (2000). Emp: 320. Officers: K. Richard Sinclair, CEO & President; J.C. Jefferds III, CFO; Dennis Dunlap, Sales/Marketing Contact; John V. DeRito, Customer Service Contact; Ann Schoolcraft, Human Resources Contact.

■ 16187 ■ Jensen Tools Inc.
7815 S 46th St.
Phoenix, AZ 85044
Phone: (602)968-6231
Free: (800)426-1194   Fax: (602)438-1690
Products: Tools and testing equipment for the electronics industry. SIC: 5084 (Industrial Machinery & Equipment). Sales: $46,000,000 (2000). Emp: 150. Officers: Gary Treiber, Exec. VP; Norm Slone, VP & Controller.

■ 16188 ■ JLK Direct Distribution Inc.
PO Box 231
Latrobe, PA 15650-0231
Phone: (724)539-5000
Products: Metalworking consumables and related products, including cutting tools, carbide, abrasives, drills, machine tool accessories, hand tools, and other industrial supplies. SICs: 5084 (Industrial Machinery & Equipment); 5085 (Industrial Supplies). Sales: $316,200,000 (2000). Emp: 833. Officers: Michael W. Ruprich, President; Michael J. Mussog, VP & CFO.

■ 16189 ■ J.M. Equipment Co.
819 S 9th St.
Modesto, CA 95351
Phone: (209)522-3271   Fax: (209)522-5980
Products: Forklifts. SIC: 5084 (Industrial Machinery & Equipment). Est: 1936. Sales: $86,000,000 (2000). Emp: 45. Officers: Ed Henriques, President; Ramond Azevedo, CEO; Vincent Victorine, CFO; Rosemary Midor, Office Mgr.

■ 16190 ■ Johnston Industrial Supply Co.
1435 N Nias
Springfield, MO 65802-2236
Phone: (417)869-1887   Fax: (417)869-9913
Products: Industrial tools, including grinding wheels, screw drivers, braces, and saws; Cutting, power, and hand tools; Abrasives; Material handling equipment. SICs: 5084 (Industrial Machinery & Equipment); 5085 (Industrial Supplies); 5082 (Construction & Mining Machinery); 5072 (Hardware). Est: 1968. Sales: $27,000,000 (2000). Emp: 80. Officers: G.W. Johnston Jr., President; Walt Johnston, Vice President; Patricia S. Johnston, Dir. of Sales; Susie Johnston, Treasurer.

■ 16191 ■ Joint Production Technology Inc.
15381 Hallmark Ct.
Macomb, MI 48042
Phone: (810)786-0080   Fax: (810)786-0088
URL: http://www.jptonline.com
Products: Special industrial machinery; Tools. SICs: 5084 (Industrial Machinery & Equipment); 5085 (Industrial Supplies). Est: 1971. Sales: $4,300,000 (2000). Emp: 34. Officers: Robert B. Peuterbaugh, President.

■ 16192 ■ Grady W. Jones Company of Memphis Inc.
3965 Old Getwell Rd.
Memphis, TN 38118
Phone: (901)365-8830   Fax: (901)368-5102
Products: Forklifts and conveyor systems. SIC: 5084 (Industrial Machinery & Equipment). Est: 1944. Sales: $16,000,000 (1994). Emp: 95. Officers: Grady W. Jones Jr., President; Ron Fisher, Treasurer & Secty.

■ 16193 ■ Grady W. Jones of Little Rock Inc.
PO Box 97
North Little Rock, AR 72115
Phone: (501)945-2394   Fax: (501)945-0695
Products: Forklift trucks. SIC: 5084 (Industrial Machinery & Equipment). Est: 1956. Sales: $7,000,000 (2000). Emp: 55. Officers: James S. Jones, President; Charles R. Fisher, CFO; Roy Bradley, Sales Mgr.

■ 16194 ■ Joseph Industries Inc.
10039 Aurora Hudson Rd.
Streetsboro, OH 44241
Phone: (330)528-0091
Products: Materials handling equipment. SIC: 5084 (Industrial Machinery & Equipment).

■ 16195 ■ JWS Technologies Inc.
490 Stelton Rd.
Piscataway, NJ 08854
Phone: (908)752-4500   Fax: (908)752-6989
Products: Welding machinery and equipment. SIC: 5084 (Industrial Machinery & Equipment). Sales: $28,000,000 (2000). Emp: 65. Officers: J.P. Lyons, President; Dave Johnson, Controller; Kirk Johnson, Marketing Mgr.

■ 16196 ■ Kalamazoo International, Inc.
70 Van Buren
PO Box 271
South Haven, MI 49090
Phone: (616)637-2178   Fax: (616)637-2272
Products: Metal cargo protection devices; Foundry temperature sensing equipment; Paintmaking equipment; Label dispensing machinery; Metal security seals. SICs: 5084 (Industrial Machinery & Equipment); 5051 (Metals Service Centers & Offices). Officers: John C. Jensen, Mgr. Dir.

■ 16197 ■ Kaman Corp.
PO Box 1
Bloomfield, CT 06002
Phone: (203)243-8311
Products: Bearing, power transmission, fluid power, linear motion, materials handling, and electric drive items. SIC: 5085 (Industrial Supplies). Sales: $1,044,800,000 (2000). Emp: 4,318. Officers: Charles H. Kaman, CEO & Chairman of the Board; Robert M. Garneau, Exec. VP & CFO.

■ 16198 ■ Kaman Industrial Technology
1600 Commerce Ave.
Boise, ID 83705-5307
Phone: (208)343-1841   Fax: (208)345-7706
Products: Hydraulic power transmissions; Electrical equipment; Gearing equipment. SICs: 5084 (Industrial Machinery & Equipment); 5063 (Electrical Apparatus & Equipment).

■ 16199 ■ C.C. and F.F. Keesler Inc.
PO Box 299
Prospect Park, PA 19076
Phone: (215)534-0700   Fax: (215)534-9923
Products: Heavy equipment; Cranes; Trailers. SIC: 5084 (Industrial Machinery & Equipment). Est: 1926. Sales: $5,000,000 (2000). Emp: 14. Officers: Fredrick F. Keesler, President; Rick Keesler, Treasurer; Steve Keesler, Sales Mgr.

■ 16200 ■ Keizer Associates
55 Mississippi St.
San Francisco, CA 94107
Phone: (415)621-0881 **Fax:** (415)621-0881
Products: Pumps and pumping equipment. **SIC:** 5084 (Industrial Machinery & Equipment).

■ 16201 ■ Kelleigh Corporation
Export Dept.
10 E Athens Ave., Ste. 202
Ardmore, PA 19003
Phone: (610)642-9850 **Fax:** (610)642-9195
Products: Photopolymer platemaking equipment. **SIC:** 5084 (Industrial Machinery & Equipment). **Officers:** S.L. Barrow-Amor.

■ 16202 ■ Kelly Tractor Co.
8255 NW 58th St.
Miami, FL 33166
Phone: (305)592-5360 **Fax:** (305)477-2024
Products: Industrial tractors; Agricultural tractors. **SICs:** 5084 (Industrial Machinery & Equipment); 5083 (Farm & Garden Machinery). **Est:** 1933. **Sales:** $150,000,000 (2000). **Emp:** 500. **Officers:** L. Patrick Kelly, President & Chairman of the Board; Nicholas D. Kelly, Vice President; Barbara Dossey, Dir. of Marketing; Patricia Sandmeyer, Personnel Mgr.

■ 16203 ■ Kennametal Inc. Metalworking Systems Div.
PO Box 231
Latrobe, PA 15650
Phone: (724)539-5000 **Fax:** (724)539-4142
Products: Consumable metalworking tools. **SIC:** 5084 (Industrial Machinery & Equipment). **Sales:** $522,000,000 (2000). **Emp:** 750. **Officers:** Philip Weihl, General Mgr.; Ron Szymanski, Controller.

■ 16204 ■ Keo Cutters Inc.
PO Box 717
Warren, MI 48089-1509
Phone: (810)771-2050 **Fax:** (810)771-2062
Products: Small cutting tools for machine tools and metalworking machinery; Metal cutting machine tools. **SIC:** 5084 (Industrial Machinery & Equipment). **Est:** 1941. **Sales:** $6,000,000 (2000). **Emp:** 63. **Officers:** Ken Milner.

■ 16205 ■ Kerr Pump and Supply Inc.
PO Box 37160
Oak Park, MI 48237
Phone: (248)543-3880 **Fax:** (248)543-3236
E-mail: sales@kerrpump.com
URL: http://www.kerrpump.com
Products: Pumps, air compressors, blowers and vacuum pumps; Mixers; Tanks; Custom package systems; Hydronic specialties. **SIC:** 5084 (Industrial Machinery & Equipment). **Est:** 1905. **Sales:** $15,000,000 (2000). **Emp:** 50. **Officers:** John A. Sloan, President; John Watson, Finance Officer; F. Gerald Putt, Exec. VP of Marketing.

■ 16206 ■ Key Oil Co.
PO Box 123
Houston, TX 77001
Phone: (713)222-2041
Products: Rebuilt machinery. **SIC:** 5084 (Industrial Machinery & Equipment). **Est:** 1952. **Sales:** $6,000,000 (2000). **Emp:** 13. **Officers:** Peter S. Wareing, President; Walt L. Adkins, Treasurer & Secty.; Paul Fontenot, Dir. of Marketing & Sales.

■ 16207 ■ Keystone STIHL, Inc.
RR 4 Box 1572
Mifflintown, PA 17059-9556
Products: Chain saws; Lawn and garden equipment. **SICs:** 5084 (Industrial Machinery & Equipment); 5083 (Farm & Garden Machinery).

■ 16208 ■ Klingelhofer Corp.
PO Box 1098
Mountainside, NJ 07092
Phone: (908)232-7200 **Fax:** (908)232-1841
Products: Cold sawing machinery, including saw blades, band sawing machines, deburring machines. **SIC:** 5084 (Industrial Machinery & Equipment). **Est:** 1936. **Sales:** $5,000,000 (2000). **Emp:** 15. **Officers:** A.L. Klingelhofer, President; Fred Schaefer, Vice President.

■ 16209 ■ Henry Knese, Inc.
22-44 119th St.
College Point, NY 11356
Phone: (718)353-9300 **Fax:** (718)886-2972
Products: Pumps and pumping equipment; Electrical motors and generators. **SICs:** 5084 (Industrial Machinery & Equipment); 5063 (Electrical Apparatus & Equipment). **Officers:** Gregory S. Knese, Treasurer.

■ 16210 ■ Knitting Machine and Supply Company Inc.
1257 Westfield Ave.
Clark, NJ 07066
Phone: (732)382-9898 **Fax:** (732)382-9479
Products: Knitting machinery. **SIC:** 5084 (Industrial Machinery & Equipment). **Est:** 1940. **Sales:** $4,000,000 (2000). **Emp:** 15. **Officers:** Allen D. Van Anda, President, Chairman of the Board & Treasurer.

■ 16211 ■ Knudson Manufacturing Inc.
10401 W 120th Ave.
Broomfield, CO 80021
Phone: (303)469-2101 **Fax:** (303)469-7994
Products: Roll forming equipment. **SIC:** 5084 (Industrial Machinery & Equipment).

■ 16212 ■ Koike America Inc.
635 W Main St.
Arcade, NY 14009
Phone: (716)492-2400
Free: (800)252-5232 **Fax:** (716)457-3517
E-mail: info@koike.com
URL: http://www.koike.com
Products: Thermal, plasma, and laser cutting machines; Welding positioners; Turning rolls and manipulators. **SIC:** 5084 (Industrial Machinery & Equipment). **Est:** 1946. **Sales:** $40,000,000 (2000). **Emp:** 185. **Officers:** John Capozzi, President; Dennis Johnson, Sales Mgr.

■ 16213 ■ Kolda Corp.
16770 Hedgecroft, Ste. 708
Houston, TX 77060
Phone: (281)448-8995
Products: Industrial equipment. **SIC:** 5085 (Industrial Supplies).

■ 16214 ■ Komatsu America Industries Corp.
199 E Thorndale Ave.
Wood Dale, IL 60191
Phone: (708)860-3000
Products: Press brakes and press machines. **SIC:** 5084 (Industrial Machinery & Equipment). **Est:** 1985. **Sales:** $7,000,000 (2000). **Emp:** 24. **Officers:** James Gratz, Vice President; Henry Kato, President; James Landowski, Sales Mgr.

■ 16215 ■ Komerex Industries, Inc.
4401 Edison St.
Houston, TX 77009
Phone: (713)691-6399 **Fax:** (713)691-6399
Products: Industrial equipment, including gas compressor replacement parts and internal combustion engine parts; Shrimp and seafood; Purchase owner finance real estate mortgage notes ($60,000-600,000); Annuities; Lottery winnings; Cash streams; Accounts receivables (factoring). **SICs:** 5084 (Industrial Machinery & Equipment); 5146 (Fish & Seafoods). **Est:** 1985. **Officers:** James Stibbs, Mgr. Dir.

■ 16216 ■ Komori America Corp.
5520 Meadowbrook Industrial Ct.
Rolling Meadows, IL 60008
Phone: (708)806-9000
Products: Printing presses, other than lithographic; Printing presses, lithographic. **SIC:** 5084 (Industrial Machinery & Equipment). **Sales:** $31,000,000 (2000). **Emp:** 100. **Officers:** Hiro Inagaki, President.

■ 16217 ■ Komp Equipment Company Inc.
PO Box 1489
Hattiesburg, MS 39403-1489
Phone: (601)582-8215 **Fax:** (601)582-0100
Products: Industrial equipment. **SIC:** 5084 (Industrial Machinery & Equipment). **Est:** 1889. **Sales:** $5,000,000 (2000). **Emp:** 20. **Officers:** George P. Komp, CEO.

■ 16218 ■ Kornylak Corp.
400 Heaton St.
Hamilton, OH 45011
Phone: (513)863-1277
Free: (800)837-5676 **Fax:** (513)863-7644
E-mail: kornylak@kornylak.com
URL: http://www.kornylak.com
Products: Conveyors; Insulation; Vehicles; Wheels. **SIC:** 5084 (Industrial Machinery & Equipment). **Est:** 1946. **Sales:** $7,000,000 (2000). **Emp:** 54. **Officers:** T. Kornylak, President; Anne G. McAdams, Sales/Marketing Contact.

■ 16219 ■ Koyo Corporation of USA
47771 Halyard St.
Plymouth, MI 48170
Phone: (734)454-4107
Products: Centerless grinders. **SIC:** 5084 (Industrial Machinery & Equipment).

■ 16220 ■ A. Krieg Consulting and Trading Inc.
119 Maple Vale Dr.
Woodbridge, CT 06525
Phone: (203)393-3672 **Fax:** (203)393-1293
Products: Power handtools; Machine tools, including drills; Welding equipment; Construction machinery; Medical equipment, including whirlpool baths. **SICs:** 5084 (Industrial Machinery & Equipment); 5072 (Hardware); 5047 (Medical & Hospital Equipment); 5082 (Construction & Mining Machinery). **Officers:** Adrian Krieg, President.

■ 16221 ■ Kruger Trailer Inc.
RR 1 Box 67
Georgetown, DE 19947
Phone: (302)856-2577 **Fax:** (302)856-2578
Products: Flatbed trailers. **SIC:** 5084 (Industrial Machinery & Equipment).

■ 16222 ■ KSB Inc.
4415 Sarellen Rd.
Richmond, VA 23231
Phone: (804)222-1818 **Fax:** (804)226-6961
Products: Industrial machinery and equipement. **SIC:** 5084 (Industrial Machinery & Equipment). **Est:** 1969. **Sales:** $120,200,000 (2000). **Emp:** 383. **Officers:** Peter Raab, President; Kevin Sciuk, CFO; Ron Webb, Dir. of Marketing & Sales.

■ 16223 ■ J.W. Kuehn Company Inc.
1504 Cliff Rd. E
Burnsville, MN 55337-1415
Phone: (612)890-4881 **Fax:** (612)890-1484
Products: Material handling equipment, including conveyers, tanks, column lifts, and bins. **SIC:** 5084 (Industrial Machinery & Equipment). **Est:** 1962. **Sales:** $1,000,000 (2000). **Emp:** 4. **Officers:** JoAnn E. LeClair, President.

■ 16224 ■ Kustom Tool Works Inc.
28310 Crocker Ave.
Valencia, CA 91355
Phone: (805)295-8610 **Fax:** (805)257-3522
Products: Machining tools. **SIC:** 5084 (Industrial Machinery & Equipment). **Est:** 1989. **Sales:** $5,000,000 (2000). **Emp:** 7. **Officers:** Earl T. Bayless, Owner; Murriel Brady, Dir. of Sales.

■ 16225 ■ L.A. Liquid Handling Systems
15411 S Broadway St.
Gardena, CA 90248
Phone: (213)321-8992 **Fax:** (213)532-8794
Products: Pumps. **SIC:** 5084 (Industrial Machinery & Equipment). **Est:** 1965. **Sales:** $7,000,000 (2000). **Emp:** 26. **Officers:** Richard Stingley, President.

■ 16226 ■ Lake Welding Supply Co.
363 Ottawa St.
Muskegon, MI 49442
Phone: (231)722-3773
Free: (800)873-5253 **Fax:** (231)725-9113
URL: http://www.Lakewelding.com
Products: Grinding wheels; Safety equipment; Welding equipment; Gases. **SICs:** 5084 (Industrial Machinery & Equipment); 5172 (Petroleum Products Nec). **Est:** 1953. **Sales:** $7,000,000 (2000). **Emp:** 34. **Officers:** J. Freriks, President; G. Teerman, Treasurer.

■ **16227** ■ **Lamination Services Inc.**
4040 Willow Lake Blvd.
Memphis, TN 38175
Phone: (901)794-3032
Free: (800)737-3032 **Fax:** (901)795-4074
E-mail: time@lamserv.com
URL: http://www.lamserv.com
Products: Lamination supplies and equipment; Photo ID equipment and supplies; Photo ID and imaging systems. **SICs:** 5043 (Photographic Equipment & Supplies); 5049 (Professional Equipment Nec); 5084 (Industrial Machinery & Equipment). **Est:** 1975. **Sales:** $5,000,000 (2000). **Emp:** 60. **Officers:** Mason Ezzell, President; Glenn Brown, Sales/Marketing Contact, e-mail: jgb@lamserv.com; Darryl Hollingsworth, Customer Service Contact; Mary K. Berry, Human Resources Contact.

■ **16228** ■ **C.R. Laurence Company Inc.**
2503 E Vernon Ave.
Los Angeles, CA 90058
Phone: (213)588-1281 **Fax:** (213)581-6522
Products: Industrial abrasive products; Power hand tools for the glass industry; Chemical sealants. **SICs:** 5084 (Industrial Machinery & Equipment); 5169 (Chemicals & Allied Products Nec). **Est:** 1921. **Sales:** $68,000,000 (2000). **Emp:** 400. **Officers:** Bernard P. Harris, Chairman of the Board; D. Friese, President; Ed Ankin, CFO; Paul M. Daniels, Dir. of Marketing; Dave Scott, Dir. of Data Processing.

■ **16229** ■ **LCI Corp.**
PO Box 16348
Charlotte, NC 28297-8804
Phone: (704)394-8341
Products: Cartridge heaters; Extrusion control equipment. **SIC:** 5084 (Industrial Machinery & Equipment). **Est:** 1963. **Sales:** $28,000,000 (2000). **Emp:** 110. **Officers:** Robert P. Barbee, President; H.S. Trimakas, Controller.

■ **16230** ■ **L.C.I. Process Division**
PO Box 16348
Charlotte, NC 28297-8804
Phone: (704)394-8341 **Fax:** (704)392-8507
Products: Chemical processing machinery. **SIC:** 5084 (Industrial Machinery & Equipment).

■ **16231** ■ **Leamco-Ruthco**
PO Box 60050
Midland, TX 79711
Phone: (915)561-5837 **Fax:** (915)563-2375
URL: http://www.weathford.com
Products: Pumping equipment, including plastic bearings. **SIC:** 5084 (Industrial Machinery & Equipment). **Est:** 1962. **Sales:** $21,000,000 (2000). **Emp:** 248. **Officers:** Paul Ellis, General Mgr.; Craig Scott, CFO; Sam Burnes, Marketing & Sales Mgr.

■ **16232** ■ **Lee Engineering Supply Company, Inc.**
150 Plauche St.
New Orleans, LA 70123
Phone: (504)733-3333 **Fax:** (504)734-8114
Products: Pumps and pumping equipment. **SIC:** 5084 (Industrial Machinery & Equipment).

■ **16233** ■ **Lift Truck Sales and Service Inc.**
2720 Nicholson Rd.
Kansas City, MO 64120
Phone: (816)241-6360
Products: Forklifts. **SIC:** 5084 (Industrial Machinery & Equipment). **Est:** 1980. **Sales:** $100,000 (2000). **Emp:** 65. **Officers:** Jerry Stevens, President; Conrad Maslowski, Vice President.

■ **16234** ■ **Liftech Handling Inc.**
6847 Elliott Dr.
East Syracuse, NY 13057
Phone: (315)463-7333
Products: Forklifts and parts. **SIC:** 5084 (Industrial Machinery & Equipment). **Sales:** $22,000,000 (2000). **Emp:** 150. **Officers:** Joe Verzino, President; Ed Pietruniak, CFO.

■ **16235** ■ **Frank Lill and Son Inc.**
656 Basket Rd.
Webster, NY 14580
Phone: (716)265-0490 **Fax:** (716)265-1842
Products: Power boilers. **SIC:** 5074 (Plumbing & Hydronic Heating Supplies). **Sales:** $28,000,000 (2000). **Emp:** 200. **Officers:** Charles G. Lill, President; Ed Johnson, Controller.

■ **16236** ■ **The Lincoln Electric Co**
9804 Norwalk Blvd.
Santa Fe Springs, CA 90670
Phone: (562)906-7700 **Fax:** (562)906-7711
Products: Electric welders, welding electrodes and electric motors. **SIC:** 5084 (Industrial Machinery & Equipment).

■ **16237** ■ **Lindsey Completion Systems**
PO Box 2512
Odessa, TX 79760
Phone: (915)337-5541
Products: Oil well production tools. **SIC:** 5084 (Industrial Machinery & Equipment). **Sales:** $2,000,000 (2000). **Emp:** 2. **Officers:** Charlie Holtz, General Mgr.

■ **16238** ■ **Litchfield Packaging Machinery Corp.**
PO Box 419
Morris, CT 06763
Phone: (860)567-2011 **Fax:** (860)567-2012
E-mail: litchpac@wtco.net
Products: Packaging and bottling machinery. **SIC:** 5084 (Industrial Machinery & Equipment). **Est:** 1970. **Sales:** $3,000,000 (2000). **Emp:** 5. **Officers:** Ric Edwards, Vice President.

■ **16239** ■ **Livingston & Haven, Inc.**
11616 Wilmar Blvd.
Charlotte, NC 28273
Phone: (704)525-7910 **Fax:** (704)525-5093
Products: Hydraulic fluid power systems; Pneumatic fluid power systems; Electric and electronic equipment. **SICs:** 5084 (Industrial Machinery & Equipment); 5063 (Electrical Apparatus & Equipment).

■ **16240** ■ **Livingston & Haven, Inc.**
7523 Irmo Dr.
Columbia, SC 29212
Free: (800)825-4969 **Fax:** (803)781-9118
Products: Hydraulics and pneumatics. **SIC:** 5084 (Industrial Machinery & Equipment).

■ **16241** ■ **Livingston & Haven, Inc.**
316 Nancy Lynn Ln., Ste. 12B
Knoxville, TN 37919
Phone: (423)584-1124 **Fax:** (423)584-1125
URL: http://www.lhtech.com
Products: Fluid power products. **SIC:** 5084 (Industrial Machinery & Equipment). **Est:** 1947. **Emp:** 180. **Officers:** Clifton Vann IV, President, e-mail: scb@lhtech.com; Susan Berger, Sales & Marketing Contact, e-mail: gar@lhtech.com; Garry Reid, Customer Service Contact, e-mail: grm@lhtech.com; Gloria Mack, Human Resources Contact; Tim Gillig, Div. Mgr., e-mail: gar@lhtech.com.

■ **16242** ■ **Lombardini USA Inc.**
2150 Boggs Rd.
Duluth, GA 30026
Phone: (404)623-3554 **Fax:** (404)623-8833
Products: Engines for heavy equipment and generators. **SIC:** 5084 (Industrial Machinery & Equipment). **Est:** 1978. **Sales:** $9,000,000 (2000). **Emp:** 12. **Officers:** James R. McPherson Jr., CFO.

■ **16243** ■ **London Litho Aluminum Company Inc.**
7100 N Lawndale Ave.
Lincolnwood, IL 60712
Phone: (847)679-4600
Free: (800)695-2104 **Fax:** (847)679-6453
Products: Printing equipment and supplies. **SIC:** 5084 (Industrial Machinery & Equipment). **Sales:** $169,000,000 (2000). **Emp:** 250. **Officers:** Eric London, President; William Ramsey, Controller.

■ **16244** ■ **Long Island Transmission Corp.**
495 Smith St.
Farmingdale, NY 11735
Phone: (516)454-9000 **Fax:** (516)454-9155
Products: Industrial power transmission equipment. **SIC:** 5063 (Electrical Apparatus & Equipment). **Est:** 1955. **Sales:** $11,000,000 (2000). **Emp:** 45. **Officers:** Victor Cangro Jr., CEO; Lawrence A. Cangro, CFO.

■ **16245** ■ **LOR Inc.**
PO Box 647
Atlanta, GA 30301
Phone: (404)888-2750
Products: Hydraulic and pumping equipment components. **SIC:** 5084 (Industrial Machinery & Equipment). **Sales:** $5,000,000 (2000). **Emp:** 7. **Officers:** Joe Young, General Mgr.

■ **16246** ■ **Lotus Group**
2411 Hamilton Mill Rd.
Charlotte, NC 28270
Phone: (704)366-5505 **Fax:** (704)366-0262
Products: Chemical preparations; Textile machinery; Fabric millinery; Electronic components; Office machines. **SICs:** 5084 (Industrial Machinery & Equipment); 5044 (Office Equipment); 5169 (Chemicals & Allied Products Nec). **Officers:** Abe Warshenbrot, President.

■ **16247** ■ **Louisiana Chemical Equipment Co.**
PO Box 65064
Baton Rouge, LA 70896-5064
Phone: (504)923-3602
Products: Chemical processing equipment. **SIC:** 5169 (Chemicals & Allied Products Nec). **Sales:** $15,000,000 (2000). **Emp:** 35. **Officers:** Alvin Rotenberg, Exec. VP.

■ **16248** ■ **Louisiana Welding Supply Company Inc.**
1931 Plank Rd.
Baton Rouge, LA 70802
Phone: (504)343-9212 **Fax:** (504)343-9211
Products: Welding equipment. **SIC:** 5084 (Industrial Machinery & Equipment). **Est:** 1945. **Sales:** $7,000,000 (2000). **Emp:** 40. **Officers:** Charles White, President; Paul Haygood, Controller.

■ **16249** ■ **LPKF Laser and Electronics**
28220 SW Boberg Rd.
Wilsonville, OR 97070
Phone: (503)454-4200 **Fax:** (503)682-7151
Products: systems for the fabrication of prototype printed circuit boards. **SIC:** 5084 (Industrial Machinery & Equipment). **Officers:** Bill Boggs, President; Stephan Schmidt, General Mgr.

■ **16250** ■ **LU International**
500 N Highland Ave.
Los Angeles, CA 90036-2020
Phone: (213)994-0878
Products: Industrial machinery; Sporting and recreational goods; Nursery products; Farm and garden machinery; Electrical appliances. **SICs:** 5084 (Industrial Machinery & Equipment); 5091 (Sporting & Recreational Goods); 5193 (Flowers & Florists' Supplies); 5083 (Farm & Garden Machinery); 5064 (Electrical Appliances—Television & Radio). **Officers:** Randy J. Lu, Owner.

■ **16251** ■ **Lynch Machinery Co.**
PO Box 1217
Havertown, PA 19083
Phone: (215)789-1210
Products: Machine tools for the plate metal industry. **SIC:** 5084 (Industrial Machinery & Equipment). **Sales:** $7,000,000 (2000). **Emp:** 25. **Officers:** Robert Rachor, President.

■ **16252** ■ **M and M Supply Co.**
PO Box 548
Duncan, OK 73534-0548
Phone: (580)252-7879 **Fax:** (580)252-7708
Products: Petroleum, fuels, and related equipment. **SIC:** 5084 (Industrial Machinery & Equipment). **Sales:** $15,000,000 (2000). **Emp:** 60.

■ 16253 ■ Machine Drive
8919 Rossash Rd.
Cincinnati, OH 45236
Phone: (513)793-7077
Products: Variable machine drives. **SIC:** 5084
(Industrial Machinery & Equipment).

■ 16254 ■ Machine Tool and Supply Corp.
PO Box 1927
Jackson, TN 38302
Phone: (901)424-3400
Products: Industrial maintenance and cutting tools.
SIC: 5084 (Industrial Machinery & Equipment).

■ 16255 ■ Machine and Welding Supply Co.
PO Box 1708
Dunn, NC 28335
Phone: (910)892-4016 **Fax:** (910)892-3575
URL: http://www.mwsc.com
Products: Industrial, medical and specialty gases,
welding and heavy metal equipment and supplies.
SICs: 5169 (Chemicals & Allied Products Nec); 5172
(Petroleum Products Nec); 5084 (Industrial Machinery
& Equipment); 5085 (Industrial Supplies). **Est:** 1954.
Sales: $40,000,000 (2000). **Emp:** 200. **Officers:**
Emmett C. Aldredge Jr., President; Emmett C.
Aldredge Jr., President.

■ 16256 ■ Machinery Sales Co.
4400 S Soto St.
Los Angeles, CA 90058
Phone: (213)588-8111 **Fax:** (213)587-2125
Products: Lathes; Milling machines. **SIC:** 5084
(Industrial Machinery & Equipment). **Est:** 1938. **Sales:**
$35,000,000 (2000). **Emp:** 55. **Officers:** Richard C.
Rivett, Chairman of the Board; John Ramsey,
Controller; Gary Smith, VP of Marketing & Sales.

■ 16257 ■ Machinery Systems Inc.
614 E State Pkwy.
Schaumburg, IL 60173
Phone: (847)882-8085 **Fax:** (847)882-2894
E-mail: msi@machsys.com
URL: http://www.machinery-system.com
Products: Industrial machinery and equipment;
Machine tools. **SIC:** 5084 (Industrial Machinery &
Equipment). **Est:** 1977. **Sales:** $31,000,000 (2000).
Emp: 55. **Officers:** Joseph J. Romanowski, CEO &
President; Ron Mager, VP of Operations.

■ 16258 ■ MacQueen Equipment Inc.
595 Aldine St.
St. Paul, MN 55104
Phone: (612)645-5726
Free: (800)832-6417 **Fax:** (612)645-6668
E-mail: mqequip@aol.com
Products: Recycling equipment, including street
sweepers and plows. **SIC:** 5084 (Industrial Machinery &
Equipment). **Est:** 1961. **Sales:** $11,000,000 (2000).
Emp: 35. **Officers:** William Garber, President.

■ 16259 ■ N.J. Malin and Associates Inc.
PO Box 797
Addison, TX 75001-0797
Phone: (972)458-2680 **Fax:** (903)458-2680
Products: Forklifts. **SIC:** 5084 (Industrial Machinery &
Equipment). **Est:** 1971. **Sales:** $24,000,000 (2000).
Emp: 100. **Officers:** William Hyde, President; Wally
Maya, CFO.

■ 16260 ■ Mannesmann Corp.
450 Park Ave., 24th Fl.
New York, NY 10022
Phone: (212)826-0040
Free: (800)356-9235 **Fax:** (212)826-0074
Products: Hydraulic pumps, automobile parts,
industrial machinery. **SIC:** 5013 (Motor Vehicle
Supplies & New Parts). **Sales:** $3,300,000,000 (2000).
Emp: 1,000. **Officers:** Peter P. Wittgenstein,
President; Manfred Becker, Exec. VP of Finance.

■ 16261 ■ Manufacturers Supplies Co.
4220 Rider Trail N
Earth City, MO 63045
Phone: (314)770-0880 **Fax:** (314)770-0990
Products: Industrial die cutting equipment and related
products. **SIC:** 5084 (Industrial Machinery &
Equipment). **Est:** 1907. **Sales:** $9,000,000 (2000).

Emp: 45. **Officers:** Robert F. Goellner, President; Bob
Goellner Jr., Vice President.

■ 16262 ■ Mapal Aaro, Inc.
4032 Dove Rd.
Port Huron, MI 48060-1025
Phone: (810)364-8020 **Fax:** (810)364-4750
E-mail: mapalaaro@aol.com
Products: Carbide and diamond cutting tools. **SIC:**
5084 (Industrial Machinery & Equipment). **Est:** 1975.
Sales: $5,000,000 (2000). **Emp:** 55. **Officers:** Gary G.
Peacock.

■ 16263 ■ J Mar and Sons Inc.
119 Butterfield Rd.
North Aurora, IL 60542-1313
Phone: (630)851-0814 **Fax:** (630)896-7154
Products: Garage service equipment. **SIC:** 5013
(Motor Vehicle Supplies & New Parts). **Sales:**
$3,000,000 (2000). **Emp:** 30. **Officers:** Joe Peters,
President.

■ 16264 ■ Mark-Costello Co.
1145 Dominguez St., Ste. J
Carson, CA 90746
Phone: (310)637-1851 **Fax:** (310)762-2330
Products: Waste compactors. **SIC:** 5046 (Commercial
Equipment Nec). **Sales:** $3,000,000 (2000). **Emp:** 14.
Officers: Hugh Gilliland, Vice President.

■ 16265 ■ MarketForce, Ltd.
PO Box 3343
Palos Verdes Peninsula, CA 90274
Phone: (310)541-8679 **Fax:** (310)541-4559
E-mail: marforce@aol.com
Products: Industrial machinery and equipment. **SIC:**
5084 (Industrial Machinery & Equipment). **Est:** 1958.
Emp: 4. **Officers:** J.A. Lembeck, General Mgr.; E.L.
Baumgartner.

■ 16266 ■ W.P. and R.S. Mars Co.
215 E 78th St.
Bloomington, MN 55420
Phone: (612)884-9388 **Fax:** (612)884-1329
E-mail: marsblm@cpinternet.com
Products: Industrial tools and supplies. **SICs:** 5085
(Industrial Supplies); 5084 (Industrial Machinery &
Equipment). **Est:** 1923. **Sales:** $20,000,000 (1999).
Emp: 84. **Officers:** Robert S. Mars III, President.

■ 16267 ■ Frank Martin Sons Inc.
PO Box 10
Ft. Kent Mills, ME 04744
Phone: (207)834-3171 **Fax:** (207)834-3115
Products: Machinery parts. **SIC:** 5084 (Industrial
Machinery & Equipment). **Sales:** $4,000,000 (2000).
Emp: 16. **Officers:** Reno Ouellette, President; Steven
Ouellette, Accountant; David Ouellette, Dir. of
Marketing.

■ 16268 ■ Marvitec Export Corporation
1475 NW 97th Ave.
Miami, FL 33172
Phones: (305)593-1475 (305)593-1476
Fax: (305)591-9200
E-mail: sales@marvitec.com
URL: http://www.marvitec.com
Products: Welding equipment and spare parts;
Hydraulic jacks; Construction equipment spare parts;
Hydraulic motors and pumps. **SICs:** 5084 (Industrial
Machinery & Equipment); 5039 (Construction Materials
Nec). **Est:** 1976. **Sales:** $1,500,000 (2000). **Emp:** 4.
Officers: Jose L. Rueda, President, e-mail: joserueda-
sr@marvitec.com.

■ 16269 ■ Mascon Inc.
5 Commonwealth Ave.
Woburn, MA 01801
Phone: (781)938-5800 **Fax:** (781)933-8161
E-mail: export@mascon.com
URL: http://www.mascon.com
Products: HASL machines; Wastewater treatment
chemicals and equipment; Flux, oil, solder, tin, and
process chemicals for manufacturing of printed circuit
boards. **SICs:** 5084 (Industrial Machinery &
Equipment); 5169 (Chemicals & Allied Products Nec).
Est: 1981. **Officers:** James Huang, President & CEO;
James Chen, Chairman of the Board.

■ 16270 ■ Mascon Inc.
5 Commonwealth Ave.
Woburn, MA 01801
Phone: (781)938-5800 **Fax:** (781)933-8161
Products: Industrial machinery. **SIC:** 5084 (Industrial
Machinery & Equipment).

■ 16271 ■ F.C. Mason Co.
PO Box 318
St. Johns, MI 48879
Phone: (517)224-3291 **Fax:** (517)224-2001
Products: Hydraulic equipment; Power transmission
equipment; Agricultural replacement parts. **SIC:** 5084
(Industrial Machinery & Equipment). **Est:** 1898. **Sales:**
$4,000,000 (2000). **Emp:** 24. **Officers:** E.A. Idzkowski,
President; E.K. Moore, VP & Corporate Secretary; Ken
Sexton, Controller/Sales Mgr.

■ 16272 ■ Material Handling Services Inc.
315 E Fullerton Ave.
Carol Stream, IL 60188
Phone: (630)665-7200 **Fax:** (630)665-4669
Products: Forklift trucks; Racking; Warehouse
equipment. **SIC:** 5084 (Industrial Machinery &
Equipment). **Est:** 1981. **Sales:** $55,000,000 (2000).
Emp: 234. **Officers:** G. Risch, President; Dale Nash,
Controller; Brian Butler, VP of Sales.

■ 16273 ■ Materials Handling Equipment Corp.
7433 U.S Hwy. 30 E
Ft. Wayne, IN 46803
Phone: (219)749-0475 **Fax:** (219)749-0879
Products: Industrial handling equipment, including lift
trucks, overhead cranes, conveyors, rack equipment,
and dock equipment. **SIC:** 5084 (Industrial Machinery &
Equipment). **Est:** 1949. **Sales:** $18,000,000 (2000).
Emp: 95. **Officers:** Tom R. Fisher, President.

■ 16274 ■ Matthews International Corp., Marking Systems Div.
6515 Penn Ave.
Pittsburgh, PA 15206
Phone: (412)665-2500 **Fax:** (412)665-2550
E-mail: info@matthewsinternational.com
URL: http://www.matthewsmarketing.com
Products: Printing equipment; Contract and inkjet
printing; Indenting industrial marking systems. **SICs:**
5084 (Industrial Machinery & Equipment); 5085
(Industrial Supplies). **Est:** 1850. **Sales:** $44,000,000
(2000). **Emp:** 300. **Officers:** Robert J. Schwartz,
President; Michelle Spaulding, Sales/Marketing
Contact, e-mail: spaulding@
matthewsinternational.com; Karen Sciulli, Customer
Service Contact, e-mail: sciulli@
matthewsinternational.com.

■ 16275 ■ Mausner Equipment Company Inc.
651 Pierce Pl.
East Meadow, NY 11554
Phone: (516)481-1600
Products: Tools; Gauges; Instruments. **SICs:** 5084
(Industrial Machinery & Equipment); 5051 (Metals
Service Centers & Offices). **Est:** 1937. **Sales:**
$20,000,000 (2000). **Emp:** 108. **Officers:** Seymour
Mausner, President; Dorothy Mausner, Treasurer.

■ 16276 ■ Mazzei Injector Corp.
500 Rooster Dr.
Bakersfield, CA 93307
Phone: (805)363-6500 **Fax:** (805)363-7500
URL: http://www.mazzei-injector.com
Products: Special industrial machinery; Water
treatment systems. **SICs:** 5084 (Industrial Machinery &
Equipment); 5074 (Plumbing & Hydronic Heating
Supplies). **Est:** 1976. **Officers:** Angelo Mazzei; Bob
Tebbe.

■ 16277 ■ MBM Corp. (Charleston, South Carolina)
PO Box 40249
Charleston, SC 29423-0249
Phone: (843)552-2700
Free: (800)223-2508 **Fax:** (843)760-3813
E-mail: sales@mbmcorp.com
Products: Paper handling equipment. **SIC:** 5084
(Industrial Machinery & Equipment). **Est:** 1936. **Sales:**
$25,000,000 (2000). **Emp:** 48. **Officers:** W. Golde,
President; Ned Ginsburg, Controller.

■ 16278 ■ **James McGraw Inc.**
PO Box 85620
Richmond, VA 23285
Phone: (804)233-3071
Free: (800)288-6060 **Fax:** (804)230-2833
Products: Industrial machinery and supplies. **SICs:** 5084 (Industrial Machinery & Equipment); 5085 (Industrial Supplies). **Sales:** $126,000,000 (2000). **Emp:** 160. **Officers:** Chuck Yahn, CEO; Robin Goodman, Controller.

■ 16279 ■ **McKee-Pitts Industrials Inc.**
506 N 2nd St.
Ft. Smith, AR 72901
Phone: (501)782-0373
Products: Pneumatic tools. **SIC:** 5084 (Industrial Machinery & Equipment). **Sales:** $11,000,000 (1994). **Emp:** 35.

■ 16280 ■ **P.C. McKenzie Co.**
PO Box 112638
Pittsburgh, PA 15241
Phone: (412)257-8866
Products: Industrial boilers. **SIC:** 5074 (Plumbing & Hydronic Heating Supplies).

■ 16281 ■ **Frank G.W. McKittrick Company Inc.**
PO Box 929
North Chelmsford, MA 01863
Phone: (978)458-6391 **Fax:** (978)251-3270
Products: New & used industrial machinery. **SIC:** 5084 (Industrial Machinery & Equipment). **Est:** 1922. **Sales:** $2,000,000 (2000). **Emp:** 5. **Officers:** Philip R. McKittrick, President & CFO; Anthony J. Menegoni, CFO.

■ 16282 ■ **McMillan Conroy Machinery**
PO Box 3069
Milford, CT 06460
Phone: (203)882-5301 **Fax:** (203)882-5306
E-mail: sales@mcmillanconroy.com
URL: http://www.mcmillanconroy.com
Products: Used industrial wiredrawing machines; Used industrial tube machinery; Used rolling mill machinery. **SIC:** 5084 (Industrial Machinery & Equipment). **Officers:** John Conroy, Vice President, e-mail: john@mcmillanconroy.com.

■ 16283 ■ **Mechanical Drives Inc.**
1510 E 26th St.
Chattanooga, TN 37401
Phone: (423)622-1153 **Fax:** (423)698-1625
Products: Industrial equipment, including motors, bearings, and belts. **SICs:** 5084 (Industrial Machinery & Equipment); 5063 (Electrical Apparatus & Equipment); 5085 (Industrial Supplies).

■ 16284 ■ **Mechanical Equipment Company Inc.**
PO Box 689
Matthews, NC 28106
Phone: (704)847-2100 **Fax:** (704)847-2349
Products: Pumps; Heat exchangers; Water and wastewater equipment; Rotary joints. **SICs:** 5084 (Industrial Machinery & Equipment); 5074 (Plumbing & Hydronic Heating Supplies). **Est:** 1940. **Sales:** $10,000,000 (1999). **Emp:** 33. **Officers:** Walter H. Lee, President.

■ 16285 ■ **Mechanical Finishing Co.**
PO Box 1872
Meriden, CT 06450-1872
Phone: (203)235-4412 **Fax:** (203)235-4515
Products: Finishing media and compounds. **SIC:** 5084 (Industrial Machinery & Equipment). **Sales:** $1,000,000 (2000). **Emp:** 5. **Officers:** T.C. Andrew, President; Michelle Govoni, Office Mgr.

■ 16286 ■ **MEE Material Handling Equipment**
11721 W Carmen Ave.
Milwaukee, WI 53225
Phone: (414)353-3300
Products: Forklifts. **SIC:** 5084 (Industrial Machinery & Equipment). **Sales:** $14,000,000 (2000). **Emp:** 66. **Officers:** James F. Heyrman, President.

■ 16287 ■ **Melco Embroidery Systems**
1575 W 124th Ave.
Westminster, CO 80234
Phone: (303)457-1234
Products: computerized embroidery systems. **SIC:** 5084 (Industrial Machinery & Equipment). **Sales:** $36,000,000 (2000). **Emp:** 200. **Officers:** Art Brunner, President.

■ 16288 ■ **Melin Tool Company Inc.**
3370 W 140th St.
Cleveland, OH 44111
Phone: (216)251-7471
Free: (800)521-1078 **Fax:** 800-521-1558
Products: Cobalt and carbide cutting tools. **SIC:** 5084 (Industrial Machinery & Equipment). **Sales:** $3,300,000 (2000). **Emp:** 48. **Officers:** Michael J. Wochna, President.

■ 16289 ■ **Metaresearch Inc.**
9220 SW Barbur Blvd., Ste. 119
Portland, OR 97219
Phone: (503)248-4131 **Fax:** (503)230-2627
Products: Sells industrial instruments, process control and related products. **SIC:** 5084 (Industrial Machinery & Equipment). **Officers:** Lee Buhler, President.

■ 16290 ■ **Methods and Equipment Associates**
24860 Hathaway Dr.
Farmington Hills, MI 48335
Phone: (248)442-2773 **Fax:** (248)442-2727
E-mail: mande@rust.net
Products: Machine tools. **SIC:** 5084 (Industrial Machinery & Equipment). **Est:** 1962. **Sales:** $17,000,000 (2000). **Emp:** 25. **Officers:** T.A. Kleinhardt, President.

■ 16291 ■ **MGA Research Corp.**
PO Box 71
1290 Main Rd.
Akron, 07400, 14001
Phone: (716)542-5515
Products: Automotive testing equipment. **SIC:** 5085 (Industrial Supplies).

■ 16292 ■ **M.H. Equipment Corp.**
309 NE Rock Island Ave.
PO Box 528
Peoria, IL 61651-0528
Phone: (309)686-4030
Free: (800)322-0810 **Fax:** (309)686-4017
E-mail: mhequip@aol.com
URL: http://www.mhequipment.com
Products: Lift trucks. **SICs:** 5084 (Industrial Machinery & Equipment); 5012 (Automobiles & Other Motor Vehicles). **Est:** 1952. **Sales:** $20,000,000 (2000). **Emp:** 130. **Officers:** John S. Wieland, President; R.R. Creamean, VP & Treasurer.

■ 16293 ■ **Micro Metrology Inc.**
9553 Vassar Ave.
Chatsworth, CA 91311
Phone: (818)993-4971 **Fax:** (818)701-5516
Products: Repair, sales and calibration of precision measuring equipment. **SIC:** 5084 (Industrial Machinery & Equipment). **Officers:** Allen Ganner, Owner.

■ 16294 ■ **Mid-America Industrial Equipment Co.**
1601 N Corrington
Kansas City, MO 64120
Phone: (816)483-5000 **Fax:** (816)483-5721
E-mail: maiekci@swbell.net
Products: Industrial tractors. **SIC:** 5084 (Industrial Machinery & Equipment). **Est:** 1979.

■ 16295 ■ **Mid-America Power Drives**
1601 Airport Rd.
Waukesha, WI 53188
Phone: (414)896-3500 **Fax:** (414)896-3510
Products: Hydraulics systems equipment and supplies. **SICs:** 5084 (Industrial Machinery & Equipment); 5085 (Industrial Supplies).

■ 16296 ■ **Mid-Atlantic STIHL, Inc.**
5017 Neal Rd.
PO Box 2507
Durham, NC 27705
Phone: (919)383-7411
Products: Chain saws; Lawn and garden equipment. **SICs:** 5084 (Industrial Machinery & Equipment); 5083 (Farm & Garden Machinery).

■ 16297 ■ **Midvale Industries Inc.**
6310 Knox Industrial Dr.
St. Louis, MO 63139-3092
Phone: (314)647-5604
Products: Industrial equipment and supplies. **SICs:** 5084 (Industrial Machinery & Equipment); 5085 (Industrial Supplies).

■ 16298 ■ **Midwest Machinery**
12500 S Dupont Ave.
Burnsville, MN 55337
Phone: (612)890-8880
Free: (800)950-3298 **Fax:** (612)890-7046
Products: Industrial machinery. **SIC:** 5084 (Industrial Machinery & Equipment). **Sales:** $30,000,000 (2000). **Emp:** 80.

■ 16299 ■ **Midwest Refrigeration Supply Inc.**
4717 F St.
Omaha, NE 68117
Phone: (402)733-4900 **Fax:** (402)731-0823
Products: Compressors. **SIC:** 5084 (Industrial Machinery & Equipment). **Sales:** $400,000 (2000). **Emp:** 2.

■ 16300 ■ **Mill-Log Equipment Company Inc.**
PO Box 8099
Coburg, OR 97408
Phone: (503)485-2203
Products: Heavy duty equipment, including converters and marine goods. **SIC:** 5084 (Industrial Machinery & Equipment). **Est:** 1946. **Sales:** $3,500,000 (2000). **Emp:** 14. **Officers:** Dennis Hoff, President; Donna Lovewell, Treasurer & Secty.

■ 16301 ■ **Miller Industrial Tools Inc.**
20315-19 Nordhoff St.
Chatsworth, CA 91311
Phone: (818)983-1805
Free: (800)423-2383 **Fax:** (818)785-4768
Products: Industrial tools. **SIC:** 5084 (Industrial Machinery & Equipment). **Est:** 1945. **Sales:** $4,000,000 (2000). **Emp:** 32.

■ 16302 ■ **Miller Machinery Corp.**
PO Box 668
Killingworth, CT 06419
Phone: (860)663-3511 **Fax:** (860)663-2871
E-mail: miller.machinery@snet.net
URL: http://www.miller-machinery.com
Products: Metalworking extruding and grinding machinery; Rolling mill machinery. **SIC:** 5084 (Industrial Machinery & Equipment). **Est:** 1964. **Sales:** $23,000,000 (1999). **Emp:** 22. **Officers:** Martin Miller, President; E. Laskorin, Sales/Marketing Contact; J. Listano, Customer Service Contact; Mark Miller, Human Resources Contact.

■ 16303 ■ **Miller Welding Supply Company Inc.**
1635 W Spenser St.
Appleton, WI 54912
Phone: (920)734-9821 **Fax:** (920)735-4063
Products: Welding equipment. **SIC:** 5084 (Industrial Machinery & Equipment). **Est:** 1953. **Sales:** $8,000,000 (2000). **Emp:** 51. **Officers:** K.L. Booher, President.

■ 16304 ■ **Glen Mills Inc.**
395 Allwood Rd.
Clifton, NJ 07012-1704
Phone: (973)777-0777 **Fax:** (973)777-0070
Products: Scientific and measurement devices. **SIC:** 5084 (Industrial Machinery & Equipment). **Sales:** $2,000,000 (2000). **Emp:** 15.

■ 16305 ■ **Mills Wilson George Inc.**
1847 Vanderhorn Dr.
Memphis, TN 38134
Phone: (901)373-5100 **Fax:** (901)373-5155
Products: Industrial equipment. **SIC:** 5084 (Industrial Machinery & Equipment). **Est:** 1960. **Sales:** $7,000,000 (2000). **Emp:** 12. **Officers:** Jim Bruther, President.

■ 16306 ■ **Minnesota Supply Co.**
6470 Flying Cloud Dr.
Eden Prairie, MN 55344
Phone: (612)941-9390 **Fax:** (612)941-9390
Products: Industrial equipment; Construction supplies. **SICs:** 5084 (Industrial Machinery & Equipment); 5082 (Construction & Mining Machinery). **Est:** 1919. **Sales:** $25,000,000 (2000). **Emp:** 108. **Officers:** Peter Carlson, Chairman of the Board; Peter Carlson, CFO.

■ 16307 ■ **Mississippi Valley STIHL, Inc.**
3023 W Farmington Rd.
Peoria, IL 61604
Phone: (309)676-1304 **Fax:** (309)676-2047
Products: Chain saws; Lawn and garden equipment. **SICs:** 5084 (Industrial Machinery & Equipment); 5083 (Farm & Garden Machinery). **Est:** 1978. **Sales:** $10,000,000 (2000). **Emp:** 26. **Officers:** Mike Joynt, President; Walter Greenberg, Vice President; Sheila Elsey, Sales Consultant, e-mail: sheilae@mvstihl.com.

■ 16308 ■ **Missouri Export Trading Company**
1845 E Blaine
Springfield, MO 65803
Phone: (417)865-9283 **Fax:** (417)862-1971
Products: New diesel engines and generator sets; Used heavy duty diesel engines and component cores for remanufacturers. **SIC:** 5084 (Industrial Machinery & Equipment). **Officers:** Joe Jenkins, President.

■ 16309 ■ **Mitchell-Hughes Co.**
PO Box 747
Wofford Heights, CA 93285
Phone: (760)376-4430 **Fax:** (760)376-4435
Products: Vacuum pick-up tools for scientific and electronic applications; Hand tools and specialty electronic production aids. **SIC:** 5084 (Industrial Machinery & Equipment). **Sales:** $1,000,000 (1999). **Emp:** 3. **Officers:** David D. Davis, President.

■ 16310 ■ **Mitee-Bite Products Inc.**
PO Box 430
Center Ossipee, NH 03814
Phone: (603)539-4538
Free: (800)543-3580 **Fax:** (603)539-2183
E-mail: mitee.bite@rscs.net
URL: http://www.miteebite.com
Products: Clamping devices for the machine tool industry. **SIC:** 5084 (Industrial Machinery & Equipment). **Est:** 1985. **Emp:** 14. **Officers:** Maurice E. Bishop.

■ 16311 ■ **Mitek Industries Inc.**
PO Box 7359
St. Louis, MO 63177
Phone: (314)434-1200 **Fax:** (314)434-5343
Products: Press machinery; Connection plates; Footwear. **SIC:** 5084 (Industrial Machinery & Equipment). **Est:** 1969. **Sales:** $250,000,000 (2000). **Emp:** 1,100. **Officers:** E.M. Toombs, CEO & Chairman of the Board; R.D. Burnhardt, Sr. VP & Finance Officer; D.P. Sordo, Sr. VP; Bill Watson, Dir of Human Resources.

■ 16312 ■ **Mitsui & Co. (USA), Inc. Seattle Branch**
1001 4th Ave., Ste. 3950
Seattle, WA 98154
Phone: (206)223-5604 **Fax:** (206)223-5618
URL: http://www.Mitsui.com
Products: Industrial machinery; Lumber; Vans; Seafoods; General merchandise. **SICs:** 5084 (Industrial Machinery & Equipment); 5051 (Metals Service Centers & Offices); 5031 (Lumber, Plywood & Millwork); 5111 (Printing & Writing Paper). **Officers:** S. Kumajima, Sr. VP.

■ 16313 ■ **Mizen International, Inc.**
1603 Greenmount St.
Rockford, IL 61107
Phone: (815)968-9700 **Fax:** (815)968-9710
Products: Packaging machinery; Paper pulp mill machinery; Blow molding machinery; Board games. **SICs:** 5084 (Industrial Machinery & Equipment); 5092 (Toys & Hobby Goods & Supplies). **Officers:** Neil Mizen, President.

■ 16314 ■ **MJL Corp.**
1 Brozzini Court No. 1A
Greenville, SC 29615
Phone: (864)234-5992 **Fax:** (864)234-5785
Products: Textile cutting machines; Die cutting machines. **SIC:** 5084 (Industrial Machinery & Equipment). **Sales:** $11,000,000 (2000). **Emp:** 15. **Officers:** Joe Bucknery, CEO.

■ 16315 ■ **Mobile Power and Hydraulics**
1721 S 7th St.
St. Louis, MO 63104
Phone: (314)231-9522
Products: Hydraulic equipment. **SIC:** 5084 (Industrial Machinery & Equipment). **Sales:** $1,000,000 (2000). **Emp:** 6. **Officers:** John Pullan, General Mgr.

■ 16316 ■ **Modec Inc.**
4725 Oakland St.
Denver, CO 80266
Phone: (303)373-2696 **Fax:** (303)373-2699
Products: Decontamination units. **SIC:** 5084 (Industrial Machinery & Equipment).

■ 16317 ■ **Modern Group Ltd.**
PO Box 710
Bristol, PA 19007
Phone: (215)943-9100 **Fax:** (215)943-8901
E-mail: modern@moderngroup.com
URL: http://www.moderngroup.com
Products: Forklift trucks. **SIC:** 5084 (Industrial Machinery & Equipment). **Est:** 1946. **Sales:** $150,000,000 (1999). **Emp:** 570. **Officers:** David E. Griffith, CEO & President; George Wilkinson, Exec. VP & CFO; Don Sherow, Dir. of Materials, e-mail: sheowD@moderngroup.com; Nancy Lee, CFO; Tom Callahan, Human Resources Contact, e-mail: callahot@moderngroup.com.

■ 16318 ■ **Mohawk Machinery Inc.**
10601 Glendale Rd.
Cincinnati, OH 45215
Phone: (513)771-1952 **Fax:** (513)771-5120
E-mail: sales@mohawkmachinery.com
URL: http://www.mohawkmachinery.com
Products: Metal working machinery. **SIC:** 5084 (Industrial Machinery & Equipment). **Est:** 1956. **Sales:** $5,000,000 (2000). **Emp:** 30. **Officers:** Bill Molloy, President; Joe Harpenau, Dir. of Marketing.

■ 16319 ■ **Monarch Industries Incorporated U.S.A.**
9201 Pennsylva Ave. S, Ste. 12
Bloomington, MN 55431
Phone: (612)884-0226 **Free:** (800)665-0247
Products: Pumps; Hydraulic cylinders; Utility mixers. **SIC:** 5084 (Industrial Machinery & Equipment). **Est:** 1973. **Sales:** $72,000,000 (2000). **Emp:** 600. **Officers:** Gene Dunn, CEO; Dan O'Rourke, CFO.

■ 16320 ■ **Joe Money Machinery Co.**
4400 Lewisburg Rd.
Birmingham, AL 35207
Phone: (205)841-7000
Products: Industrial machinery. **SIC:** 5082 (Construction & Mining Machinery). **Est:** 1937. **Sales:** $16,000,000 (2000). **Emp:** 80. **Officers:** Charles S. Money, President; Geane Armstrong, Finance Officer; Joe D. McCaleb, Dir. of Marketing & Sales.

■ 16321 ■ **Morgan Graphic Supply**
224 Townsend St.
San Francisco, CA 94107
Phone: (415)777-2850 **Fax:** (415)777-2763
Products: Supplies and equipment for printing industry; Desktop publishing. **SIC:** 5084 (Industrial Machinery & Equipment).

■ 16322 ■ **Morpol Industrial Corporation Ltd.**
7071 Orchard Lake Rd., Ste. 320
West Bloomfield, MI 48322
Phone: (248)855-9320 **Fax:** (248)855-9370
Products: Industrial machinery and equipment; Petroleum products. **SICs:** 5084 (Industrial Machinery & Equipment); 5172 (Petroleum Products Nec). **Officers:** Frank D. Paulus, Vice President.

■ 16323 ■ **The Robert E. Morris Co.**
17 Talcot Notch Rd.
Farmington, CT 06032
Phone: (203)678-0200
Products: Machinery; Tools. **SICs:** 5084 (Industrial Machinery & Equipment); 5072 (Hardware). **Est:** 1941. **Sales:** $86,000,000 (2000). **Emp:** 150. **Officers:** Michael Wicken, President; John Bowen, VP of Finance; Lee B. Morris, Chairman of the Board.

■ 16324 ■ **S.G. Morris Co.**
699 Miner Rd.
Cleveland, OH 44143
Phone: (440)473-1640 **Fax:** (440)473-6205
E-mail: sgmmail@sgmorris.com
URL: http://www.sgmorris.com
Products: Hydraulic and pneumatic pumps. **SIC:** 5084 (Industrial Machinery & Equipment). **Est:** 1932.

■ 16325 ■ **S.G. Morris Co.**
27439 Holiday Ln.
Perrysburg, OH 43551
Phone: (419)874-8716 **Fax:** (419)874-9150
Products: Hydraulic and pneumatic pumps. **SIC:** 5084 (Industrial Machinery & Equipment).

■ 16326 ■ **S.G. Morris Co.**
699 Miner Rd.
Highland Heights, OH 44143
Phone: (440)473-1640 **Fax:** (440)473-6205
Products: Industrial machinery and supplies including hydraulics and pneumatics. **SICs:** 5084 (Industrial Machinery & Equipment); 5085 (Industrial Supplies). **Sales:** $23,000,000 (2000). **Emp:** 58. **Officers:** Robert Cermak, CFO.

■ 16327 ■ **Morrison Industrial Equipment Co.**
1825 Monroe Ave. NW
Grand Rapids, MI 49505
Phone: (616)361-2673 **Fax:** (616)361-0885
Products: Industrial equipment, including lift trucks and power tools. **SIC:** 5084 (Industrial Machinery & Equipment). **Est:** 1953. **Sales:** $15,000,000 (2000). **Emp:** 250. **Officers:** Albert Morrison, President.

■ 16328 ■ **Morrow Equipment Company L.L.C.**
PO Box 3306
Salem, OR 97302-0306
Phone: (503)585-5721 **Fax:** (503)363-1172
Products: Industrial cranes. **SIC:** 5084 (Industrial Machinery & Equipment). **Est:** 1968. **Sales:** $55,000,000 (2000). **Emp:** 175. **Officers:** Christian Chalupny, President; Tom Manz, Controller.

■ 16329 ■ **MPBS Industries**
2820 E Washington Blvd.
Los Angeles, CA 90023
Phone: (323)268-8514
Free: (800)421-6265 **Fax:** (323)268-6305
E-mail: info@mpbs.com
URL: http://www.mpbs.com
Products: Cutlery, including butcher's cutlery; Packing, packaging, and bottling machinery; Food products machinery. **SIC:** 5084 (Industrial Machinery & Equipment). **Est:** 1966. **Sales:** $6,000,000 (2000). **Emp:** 30. **Officers:** M. Dernburg, President; Renee Dernburg, Sec. & Treas.; Renee Dernburg, Sec. & Treas.

■ 16330 ■ **Murata of America Inc.**
PO Box 667609
Charlotte, NC 28266
Phone: (704)394-8331
Products: Textile industries machinery. **SIC:** 5084 (Industrial Machinery & Equipment). **Sales:** $70,000,000 (2000). **Emp:** 70. **Officers:** Takao Watanabe, President; W.A. Gaddis, Finance Officer.

■ **16331** ■ **Murphy Elevator Company Inc.**
128 E Main St.
Louisville, KY 40202
Phone: (502)587-1225
Products: Elevators. **SIC:** 5084 (Industrial Machinery
& Equipment). **Est:** 1932. **Sales:** $6,000,000 (2000).
Emp: 40. **Officers:** D. Gregory Carlisle, President.

■ **16332** ■ **Muscle Shoals Mack Sales Inc.**
PO Box 535
Tuscumbia, AL 35674
Phone: (256)383-9546   **Fax:** (256)383-2741
Products: Mack trucks. **SIC:** 5084 (Industrial
Machinery & Equipment). **Sales:** $50,000,000 (2000).
Emp: 60. **Officers:** Morris Britton, President.

■ **16333** ■ **Mustang Industrial Equipment Co.**
PO Box 15713
Houston, TX 77020
Phone: (713)675-1552   **Fax:** (713)670-3431
Products: Forklifts. **SIC:** 5084 (Industrial Machinery &
Equipment). **Est:** 1970. **Sales:** $30,000,000 (2000).
Emp: 120. **Officers:** Louis Tucker, President; Mark
Slator, VP & General Merchandising Mgr.

■ **16334** ■ **Mutual Sales Corp.**
2447 W Belmont Ave.
Chicago, IL 60618
Phone: (773)935-9440   **Fax:** (773)935-3043
Products: Industrial power tools; Fasteners. **SICs:**
5084 (Industrial Machinery & Equipment); 5085
(Industrial Supplies). **Emp:** 30. **Officers:** R. R.
Baumann.

■ **16335** ■ **J.E. Myles Inc.**
310 Executive Dr.
Troy, MI 48083-4587
Phone: (248)583-1020
Free: (800)968-5364   **Fax:** (248)583-6998
E-mail: sales@jem-cp-r.com
URL: http://www.jemyles.com
Products: Hydraulic, pneumatic, handling, and
assembly equipment. **SIC:** 5084 (Industrial Machinery
& Equipment). **Est:** 1959. **Sales:** $5,000,000 (2000).
Emp: 35. **Officers:** J. Ed Myles, President; Scott
Myles, VP of Operations, e-mail: smyles@rust.net;
Colin Myles, Dir. of Sales & Marketing.

■ **16336** ■ **Nalpak Video Sales, Inc.**
1937-C Friendship Dr.
El Cajon, CA 92020
Phone: (619)258-1200   **Fax:** (619)258-0925
E-mail: Bob@nalpak.com
URL: http://www.nalpak.com
Products: Cases; Charts; Carts; Soft side bags;
Material handling equipment. **SIC:** 5099 (Durable
Goods Nec). **Est:** 1980. **Emp:** 7. **Officers:** Robert S.
Kaplan, President; David Northup, Sales/Marketing
Contact, e-mail: david@nalpak.com; Pam Stringfellow,
Customer Service Contact, e-mail: Pam@nalpak.com;
Debbie Singer, Human Resources Contact, e-mail:
Debbie@nalpak.com.

■ **16337** ■ **Nance Corp.**
PO Box 29828
Richmond, VA 23242-9828
Phone: (804)784-5266   **Fax:** (804)784-4561
Products: Materials handling equipment; Conveyors
and conveying equipment. **SIC:** 5084 (Industrial
Machinery & Equipment). **Est:** 1960. **Sales:**
$5,500,000 (2000). **Emp:** 12. **Officers:** R.E. Nance,
President.

■ **16338** ■ **Nasco Inc.**
2100 Old Hwy. 8
St. Paul, MN 55112-1802
Phone: (612)780-2000   **Fax:** (612)638-1826
Products: Welding and industrial safety supplies. **SIC:**
5084 (Industrial Machinery & Equipment). **Sales:**
$72,000,000 (2000). **Emp:** 230. **Officers:** Craig Loos,
President; Mike Muenver, Controller.

■ **16339** ■ **Nation Wide Die Steel and
Machinery Co.**
PO Box 639
De Soto, MO 63020
Phone: (314)586-7979   **Fax:** (314)586-5997
Products: Die cutters. **SIC:** 5084 (Industrial Machinery
& Equipment). **Sales:** $900,000 (2000). **Emp:** 10.

Officers: Frank Gray, President; Michael Gray,
Controller; Robert Catlett, Dir. of Information Systems.

■ **16340** ■ **National Equipment Corp.**
322 Bruckner Blvd.
Bronx, NY 10454
Phone: (212)585-0200   **Fax:** (212)993-2650
Products: Machinery for food processing and tea
bagging. **SIC:** 5084 (Industrial Machinery &
Equipment). **Est:** 1912. **Sales:** $7,000,000 (2000).
Emp: 108. **Officers:** R.A. Greenberg, Vice President;
C.H. Greenberg, CFO.

■ **16341** ■ **National Industrial Hardware Inc.**
462 N 4th St.
Philadelphia, PA 19123
Phone: (215)627-1091
Free: (800)334-9582   **Fax:** (215)627-7329
Products: Power hand tools; Drills; Saws; Metal
cutting machine tools; Chisels; Fabricated industrial
parts. **SICs:** 5084 (Industrial Machinery & Equipment);
5072 (Hardware). **Est:** 1939. **Sales:** $4,000,000
(2000). **Emp:** 32. **Officers:** Robert Kirschenstein,
President & CFO; Jerry Ruttenberg, VP of Marketing &
Sales; Mimi Harris, General Mgr.

■ **16342** ■ **National Oil Well Inc.**
555 N Center St.
Casper, WY 82601-1946
Products: Oil field supplies, including drillers and
finders. **SIC:** 5084 (Industrial Machinery & Equipment).
Sales: $6,000,000 (2000). **Emp:** 18. **Officers:** Bob
Smith, CEO.

■ **16343** ■ **National Sales Engineering**
35545 Schoolcraft Rd.
Livonia, MI 48150
Phone: (734)591-3030   **Fax:** (734)591-7640
Products: Machine tools, including lathes and mills.
SIC: 5084 (Industrial Machinery & Equipment). **Est:**
1918. **Sales:** $9,000,000 (2000). **Emp:** 20. **Officers:**
F.D. Schultz, President; R.J. Weidenbach, VP of
Finance; Robert G. Braund, VP of Marketing.

■ **16344** ■ **Nationwide Ladder and Equipment
Company Inc.**
180 Rockingham Rd.
Windham, NH 03087
Phone: (603)434-6911
Free: (800)228-2519   **Fax:** (603)434-0807
Products: Construction materials and machinery. **SIC:**
5084 (Industrial Machinery & Equipment). **Sales:**
$5,000,000 (2000). **Emp:** 30.

■ **16345** ■ **NC Machinery Co.**
PO Box 3562
Seattle, WA 98124-3562
Phone: (425)251-9800
Free: (800)562-4735   **Fax:** (425)251-5886
Products: Industrial machinery and equipment. **SIC:**
5084 (Industrial Machinery & Equipment). **Sales:**
$340,000,000 (2000). **Emp:** 1,100. **Officers:** John
Harnish, CEO & President; Dave Wendta, VP, CFO &
Treasurer.

■ **16346** ■ **Neita Product Management**
PO Box 1479
White River Junction, VT 05001
Phone: (802)765-4011   **Fax:** (802)765-4229
Products: Industrial machinery and equipment;
Industrial instruments; Wood construction panels;
Chemicals and lubricants; Plastic materials and
shapes. **SICs:** 5084 (Industrial Machinery &
Equipment); 5169 (Chemicals & Allied Products Nec);
5162 (Plastics Materials & Basic Shapes); 5031
(Lumber, Plywood & Millwork). **Officers:** Thomas
Essex, VP of Sales.

■ **16347** ■ **Nelson-Jameson Inc.**
PO Box 647
Marshfield, WI 54449-0647
Phone: (715)387-1151
Free: (800)826-8302   **Fax:** (715)387-8746
E-mail: sales@nelsonjameson.com
URL: http://www.nelsonjameson.com
Products: Sanitation; Maintenance; Laboratory
products for food and dairy processing plants. **SICs:**
5085 (Industrial Supplies); 5084 (Industrial Machinery &
Equipment); 5199 (Nondurable Goods Nec). **Est:** 1947.

Sales: $48,000,000 (2000). **Emp:** 85. **Officers:** J.E.
Nelson, Chairman of the Board; Jerry Lippert, VP &
General Mgr.; Murray Smith, Dir. of Mktg. & Sales; Ray
Mullins, Customer Service Mgr.; Ron Hendrickson, Dir
of Human Resources.

■ **16348** ■ **Nestor Sales Co.**
PO Box 1650
Pinellas Park, FL 33780
Phone: (813)535-6411
Products: Industrial air tools and hydraulic equipment.
SIC: 5084 (Industrial Machinery & Equipment). **Sales:**
$35,000,000 (1994). **Emp:** 165. **Officers:** Robert
Nestor, President; Michael Huling, Vice President.

■ **16349** ■ **Norman Equipment Company Inc.**
9850 S Industrial Dr.
Bridgeview, IL 60455
Phone: (708)430-4000   **Fax:** (708)430-3027
URL: http://www.normanequipment.com
Products: Fluid power and filtration components and
systems; Process and electrical controls. **SIC:** 5084
(Industrial Machinery & Equipment). **Est:** 1946. **Emp:**
150. **Officers:** Phillip Netznik, CEO; Frank Milos,
President.

■ **16350** ■ **North Country Equipment Inc.**
3603 Hwy. 2 W
Grand Rapids, MN 55744
Phone: (218)326-9427
Products: Industrial equipment; Construction
equipment; Forestry equipment. **SICs:** 5084 (Industrial
Machinery & Equipment); 5082 (Construction & Mining
Machinery). **Est:** 1969. **Sales:** $13,000,000 (2000).
Emp: 42. **Officers:** Richard Le Beau, Owner; Art
Olson, Controller.

■ **16351** ■ **Northern Machine Tool Co.**
761 Alberta Ave.
Muskegon, MI 49441-3002
Phone: (616)755-1603   **Fax:** (616)759-7917
Products: Tool and die machinery. **SIC:** 5084
(Industrial Machinery & Equipment). **Sales:** $1,000,000
(2000). **Emp:** 35. **Officers:** Steve Olsen.

■ **16352** ■ **Northern Truck Equip. Corp.**
47213 Schweigers Cir.
Sioux Falls, SD 57101-1104
Phone: (605)543-5206   **Fax:** (605)543-5219
Products: Motorized Vehicless. **SIC:** 5084 (Industrial
Machinery & Equipment). **Sales:** $4,000,000 (2000).
Emp: 26.

■ **16353** ■ **Northland Industrial Truck Company
Inc.**
6 Jonspin Rd.
Wilmington, MA 01887
Phone: (978)658-5900   **Fax:** (978)658-8837
Products: Motorized vehicles. **SIC:** 5084 (Industrial
Machinery & Equipment). **Sales:** $30,000,000 (2000).
Emp: 100.

■ **16354** ■ **Northwestern Equipment Supply**
635 Gilman St.
Berkeley, CA 94710-1330
Phone: (510)527-4080   **Fax:** (510)527-4164
Products: Welding equipment, including cetelyn and
oxygen tanks. **SIC:** 5085 (Industrial Supplies). **Emp:**
20. **Officers:** Dennis Vandermark.

■ **16355** ■ **Nott-Atwater Co**
PO Box 13365
Spokane, WA 99213
Phone: (509)922-4522   **Fax:** (509)922-9820
Products: Gaskets; Conveyor belts; Sheet rubber.
SICs: 5084 (Industrial Machinery & Equipment); 5162
(Plastics Materials & Basic Shapes). **Officers:** Jim
Hemingway, President.

■ **16356** ■ **Numatics Inc./Microsmith Div**
7741 E Gray Rd Ste 5
Scottsdale, AZ 85260
Phone: (480)443-4773   **Fax:** (480)443-4753
Products: Industrial controls for fluid power circuit
board assembly. **SIC:** 5084 (Industrial Machinery &
Equipment). **Officers:** Jeff Welker, President.

■ 16357 ■ **Jack Ogle & Co.**
1131 Poplar Pl.,S
Seattle, WA 98144
Phone: (206)324-3425 **Fax:** (206)323-2294
Products: Hydraulic and pneumatic equipment. **SIC:** 5084 (Industrial Machinery & Equipment). **Est:** 1949. **Sales:** $5,000,000 (2000). **Emp:** 30. **Officers:** C. Aguirre, CEO & President; J. Wilkinson, VP of Marketing & Sales; P. Bowra, VP of Finance.

■ 16358 ■ **Ohio Belt & Transmission**
300 N Westwood
PO Box 404
Toledo, OH 43697
Phone: (419)535-5665 **Fax:** (419)535-6868
URL: http://www.ohiobelting.com
Products: Motion-control products. **SIC:** 5084 (Industrial Machinery & Equipment). **Est:** 1913.

■ 16359 ■ **Ohio Overseas Corp.**
520 Madison Ave.
Toledo, OH 43604
Phone: (419)241-4334 **Fax:** (419)241-5033
E-mail: ohiooverseas@aol.com
Products: Refinery supplies, and spare parts. **SICs:** 5084 (Industrial Machinery & Equipment); 5085 (Industrial Supplies). **Est:** 1978. **Sales:** $2,000,000 (2000). **Emp:** 6. **Officers:** Michael Sugheir, Vice President; Lori Lipscomb, Sales/Marketing Contact.

■ 16360 ■ **OKI Systems Ltd.**
4665 Interstate Dr.
Cincinnati, OH 45246
Phone: (513)874-2600 **Fax:** (513)874-8755
Products: Forklift trucks; Material handling equipment. **SIC:** 5084 (Industrial Machinery & Equipment). **Est:** 1970. **Emp:** 376. **Officers:** David Reder, President; Gary Knapp, CFO. **Former Name:** OKI Systems Inc.

■ 16361 ■ **Omni-X Inc.**
2751 W Mansfield Ave.
Englewood, CO 80110
Phone: (303)789-3575 **Fax:** (303)789-4755
Products: Tube bending products. **SIC:** 5084 (Industrial Machinery & Equipment). **Officers:** Alexandr Slouka, President.

■ 16362 ■ **Orbit Fluid Power Co.**
301 W 25th St.
PO Box 886
Stuttgart, AR 72160
Phone: (870)673-2584 **Fax:** (870)673-1980
Products: Hydraulic power units. **SIC:** 5084 (Industrial Machinery & Equipment).

■ 16363 ■ **Orbital Trading Co.**
PO Box 2342
Culver City, CA 90230
Phone: (213)301-4705 **Fax:** (213)973-6069
Products: Industrial machinery, including drilling robots; Computer work stations. **SICs:** 5084 (Industrial Machinery & Equipment); 5044 (Office Equipment). **Officers:** William L. Thomas, VP of Marketing.

■ 16364 ■ **Orenco Systems Inc.**
814 Airway Ave.
Sutherlin, OR 97479
Phone: (541)459-4449 **Fax:** (541)459-2884
Products: Fluid power pumps and motors for wastewater pumping and treatment systems. **SIC:** 5084 (Industrial Machinery & Equipment). **Officers:** Tim Willhoft, Treasurer.

■ 16365 ■ **Osgood Machinery Inc.**
800 Commerce Pkwy. W
Lancaster, NY 14086-1738
Phone: (716)684-7700
Free: (800)666-7701 **Fax:** (716)684-0459
E-mail: info@osgoodmachinery.com
URL: http://www.osgoodmachinery.com
Products: Machine tools for metal working, lathes, milling machines, and grinders. **SIC:** 5084 (Industrial Machinery & Equipment). **Est:** 1902. **Emp:** 40. **Officers:** Robert A. Mikulek Sr., President; Anthony R. Mikulec, Principal.

■ 16366 ■ **Owsley and Sons Inc.**
Gold Hill Rd. & I-77
Ft. Mill, SC 29715
Phone: (803)548-3636 **Fax:** (803)548-3141
Products: Cranes; Generators. **SICs:** 5084 (Industrial Machinery & Equipment); 5063 (Electrical Apparatus & Equipment). **Est:** 1936. **Sales:** $26,000,000 (2000). **Emp:** 115. **Officers:** T.R. Owsley, President; Sam O. Smith, Treasurer; J.D. Wall, VP of Marketing.

■ 16367 ■ **Pabco Fluid Power Co.**
361 W Morley Dr.
Saginaw, MI 48601
Phone: (517)753-6100 **Fax:** (517)753-0421
Products: Pumps. **SIC:** 5084 (Industrial Machinery & Equipment).

■ 16368 ■ **Pabco Fluid Power Co.**
7830 N Central Dr.
Westerville, OH 43081-9671
Phone: (614)548-6444 **Fax:** (614)548-5258
Products: Hydraulic and pneumatics equipment. **SIC:** 5084 (Industrial Machinery & Equipment).

■ 16369 ■ **Pabco Fluid Power Co.**
PO Box 691007
Cincinnati, OH 45269
Phone: (513)941-6200
Free: (800)727-2226 **Fax:** (513)941-6452
Products: Hydraulic equipment, power units and conveyors. **SIC:** 5084 (Industrial Machinery & Equipment). **Sales:** $33,000,000 (2000). **Emp:** 100. **Officers:** Jim Coffaro, President.

■ 16370 ■ **Pacific Airgas Inc.**
3591 N Columbia Blvd.
Portland, OR 97217-7463
Phone: (503)283-2294
Products: Industrial machinery. **SIC:** 5084 (Industrial Machinery & Equipment). **Sales:** $20,000,000 (2000). **Emp:** 150. **Officers:** Patricia Paddock, President; Duane Pfaff, Controller.

■ 16371 ■ **Pacific Detroit Diesel Allison Co.**
5061 N Lagoon Ave.
Portland, OR 97217
Phone: (503)283-0505 **Fax:** (503)240-4692
Products: Diesel engines, generators and transmissions; Engine, generators and transmission repairs. **SIC:** 5084 (Industrial Machinery & Equipment). **Sales:** $350,000,000 (2000). **Emp:** 350. **Officers:** J.R. Tyrrell, President; Kevin Burnette, Controller.

■ 16372 ■ **Pacific Fibers, Inc.**
33 E Ashland Ave.
Phoenix, AZ 85004
Phone: (602)254-9452 **Fax:** (602)258-4681
Products: Textile machinery; Industrial cotton gins; Raw cotton. **SICs:** 5084 (Industrial Machinery & Equipment); 5159 (Farm-Product Raw Materials Nec). **Officers:** Guenter Wassmann, President.

■ 16373 ■ **Pacific Fluid Systems Corp.**
1925 NW Quimby Ave.
Portland, OR 97209
Phone: (503)222-3295 **Fax:** (503)228-6036
Products: Hydraulics equipment and supplies. **SIC:** 5084 (Industrial Machinery & Equipment).

■ 16374 ■ **Pacific Fluids Systems Inc.**
PO Box 835
West Sacramento, CA 95691
Phone: (916)372-0660 **Fax:** (916)372-0492
Products: Fluid power components and systems; Hydraulic power units. **SIC:** 5084 (Industrial Machinery & Equipment). **Officers:** Michael Jacobs, CEO.

■ 16375 ■ **Pacific Machinery Inc.**
3651 Lala Rd.
Lihue, HI 96766
Phone: (808)245-4057 **Fax:** (808)245-8506
Products: Heavy equipment and parts. **SIC:** 5084 (Industrial Machinery & Equipment).

■ 16376 ■ **Pacific STIHL, Inc.**
11096 Midway
Chico, CA 95926
Phone: (530)343-1657
Products: Chain saws; Lawn and garden equipment.

SICs: 5084 (Industrial Machinery & Equipment); 5083 (Farm & Garden Machinery).

■ 16377 ■ **Pacific Utility Equipment Co.**
PO Box 23009
Portland, OR 97281
Phone: (503)620-0611 **Fax:** (503)684-7579
URL: http://www.pacutil.com
Products: Utility and municipal equipment. **SICs:** 5084 (Industrial Machinery & Equipment); 5082 (Construction & Mining Machinery). **Est:** 1967. **Sales:** $64,000,000 (2000). **Emp:** 239. **Officers:** Roy Goecks, President; Debbie Pack, VP of Finance; Steve Lapsley; Glen Pursley, Information Systems Mgr.; Steve Hawks, Human Resources Mgr.; Joe Nowak, General Sales Manager.

■ 16378 ■ **Pacon Machines Corp.**
PO Box 1236
Madison, CT 06443-1236
Phone: (203)245-1940 **Fax:** (203)245-1794
Products: Imported machinery. **SIC:** 5084 (Industrial Machinery & Equipment). **Est:** 1954. **Sales:** $2,000,000 (2000). **Emp:** 5. **Officers:** Wolfram Aurin, President; Kay Aurin, Vice President.

■ 16379 ■ **Pantropic Power Products Inc.**
8205 NW 58th St.
Miami, FL 33166
Phone: (305)592-4944 **Fax:** (305)477-1943
Products: Industrial engines, generators, and marine engines. **SIC:** 5084 (Industrial Machinery & Equipment). **Est:** 1986. **Sales:** $51,200,000 (2000). **Emp:** 160. **Officers:** Luis Botas, President; Fernando Cabrera, CFO; Richard Cassano, Sales/Marketing Contact, e-mail: rcassano@pantropic.com; George Lauder, Customer Service Ccntact, e-mail: glauder@pantropic.com.

■ 16380 ■ **Parrish-Keith-Simmons Inc.**
PO Box 25307
Nashville, TN 37202
Phone: (615)244-4554
Products: Hand and industrial tools. **SICs:** 5084 (Industrial Machinery & Equipment); 5072 (Hardware).

■ 16381 ■ **Parry Corp.**
925 S Main St.
Akron, OH 44311
Phone: (330)376-2242
Products: Welding supplies. **SIC:** 5084 (Industrial Machinery & Equipment).

■ 16382 ■ **Parsons Air Gas Inc. (Riverside, California)**
PO Box 5489
Riverside, CA 92517
Phone: (909)686-3481
Products: Welding supplies. **SIC:** 5084 (Industrial Machinery & Equipment). **Sales:** $17,000,000 (1994). **Emp:** 75. **Officers:** Glenn Skirvin, Controller.

■ 16383 ■ **Pathon Co.**
PO Box 443
Medina, OH 44258
Phone: (330)721-8000 **Fax:** (330)723-1569
Products: Metal finishing equipment and supplies. **SICs:** 5084 (Industrial Machinery & Equipment); 5085 (Industrial Supplies). **Est:** 1977. **Sales:** $800,000 (2000). **Emp:** 6. **Officers:** Kevin Ditto, President; Randy Vivost, Sales Mgr.

■ 16384 ■ **Patten Corp.**
10851 Bloomfield
PO Box 1129
Los Alamitos, CA 90720-1129
Phones: (562)598-6688 (714)821-6640
Fax: (562)594-0318
E-mail: info@pattencorp.com
URL: http://www.pattencorp.com
Products: Industrial equipment, including flow meters, thermometers, level controls, gas monitors, air flow measurement equipment, tank gauges, and rupture disks. **SIC:** 5084 (Industrial Machinery & Equipment). **Est:** 1960. **Emp:** 12. **Officers:** James Patten, President; Dave Davis, Purchasing.

■ 16385 ■ **PBI Market Equipment Inc.**
2667 Gundry Ave.
Signal Hill, CA 90806
Phone: (562)595-4785 **Fax:** (562)426-2262
Products: Supermarket equipment. **SIC:** 5046
(Commercial Equipment Nec). **Sales:** $20,000,000
(1994). **Emp:** 85. **Officers:** T.L. Everson, President; K.
Everson, CFO.

■ 16386 ■ **Pearce Industries Inc.**
PO Box 35068
Houston, TX 77235-5068
Phone: (713)723-1050 **Fax:** (713)551-0454
Products: Generators, engine parts, front-end loaders,
and compressors. **SICs:** 5084 (Industrial Machinery &
Equipment); 5082 (Construction & Mining Machinery).
Est: 1958. **Sales:** $180,000,000 (2000). **Emp:** 700.
Officers: Louis M. Pearce III, CEO; Robert J. Jesse,
VP of Finance & Admin.; G.M. Green, Dir. of Sales;
John MacNawara, Data Processing Mgr.; John Gutta,
Dir. of Industrial Relations.

■ 16387 ■ **Pearl Equipment Co.**
4717 Centennial Blvd.
Nashville, TN 37209
Phone: (615)383-8703 **Fax:** (615)297-3463
E-mail: pearl@edge.com
URL: http://www.pearlequip.com
Products: Fabrication machinery; Punch presses;
Brakes and shears. **SIC:** 5084 (Industrial Machinery &
Equipment). **Sales:** $8,000,000 (2000). **Emp:** 25.
Officers: Milton E. Wilson, CEO; Richard H. Levy,
President; Kenneth R. Heindrichs, Sales/Marketing
Contact, e-mail: ken26@edge.net.

■ 16388 ■ **Pearse Pearson Co.**
1370 Main St.
Millis, MA 02054
Phone: (508)376-2947 **Fax:** (508)376-4888
Products: Hydraulics and pneumatics equipment. **SIC:**
5084 (Industrial Machinery & Equipment).

■ 16389 ■ **Pederson-Sells Equipment**
30 N 25th St.
Ft. Dodge, IA 50501
Phone: (515)573-8129
Free: (800)248-8129 **Fax:** (515)955-2019
Products: Hydraulic components. **SIC:** 5084 (Industrial
Machinery & Equipment). **Est:** 1953. **Emp:** 40.

■ 16390 ■ **Perfect Fit Industries, Inc.**
201 Cuthbertson St.
PO Box 709
Monroe, NC 28110
Phone: (704)753-4161 **Fax:** (704)753-8927
Products: Industrial equipment, including internal
combustion engines; Electronic equipment. **SICs:** 5084
(Industrial Machinery & Equipment); 5065 (Electronic
Parts & Equipment Nec). **Officers:** John P. Cali,
International Marketing Manager.

■ 16391 ■ **Perfection Type Inc.**
1050 33rd Ave. SE, No. 1000
Minneapolis, MN 55414-2707
Phone: (612)917-8444 **Fax:** (612)917-8440
E-mail: perfection@bigplanet.com
Products: Printing equipment, including printing
presses. **SIC:** 5084 (Industrial Machinery &
Equipment). **Est:** 1925. **Sales:** $2,500,000 (2000).
Emp: 16. **Officers:** M. Libby, President; Bruce
Mattson, Sales Mgr.

■ 16392 ■ **Perry Videx, LLC**
25 Mt. Laurel Rd.
Hainesport, NJ 08036
Phone: (609)267-1600 **Fax:** (609)267-4499
URL: http://www.perryvidex.com
Products: Industrial equipment and machinery,
including used plastics machinery, used packaging
machinery, and used chemical machinery; Used mining
machinery. **SICs:** 5084 (Industrial Machinery &
Equipment); 5082 (Construction & Mining Machinery).
Emp: 75. **Officers:** Gregg P. Epstein, President;
Leonard Jacobs, Vice President; Ken Miller, Vice
President. **Former Name:** Perry Machinery Corp.

■ 16393 ■ **Peterson Machine Tool Co.**
PO Box 278
Shawnee Mission, KS 66201
Phone: (913)432-7500
Free: (800)255-6308 **Fax:** (913)432-8970
E-mail: petersonmachine@att.net
URL: http://www.petersonmachine.com
Products: Automotive engine rebuilding equipment.
SIC: 5084 (Industrial Machinery & Equipment). **Est:**
1962. **Sales:** $16,000,000 (1999). **Emp:** 80. **Officers:**
Fred Dellett Jr., President; Gary Baker, CFO; Lyle
Haley, Marketing & Sales Mgr.

■ 16394 ■ **Petro-Chem Equipment Co.**
PO Box 358
Baton Rouge, LA 70821
Phone: (504)292-8400
Products: Industrial equipment; Meters; Valves;
Pumps. **SIC:** 5084 (Industrial Machinery & Equipment).
Sales: $2,000,000 (2000). **Emp:** 13. **Officers:** Ad
Laplace, President.

■ 16395 ■ **Pfaff Pegasus of USA Inc.**
7270 McGinnis Ferry Rd.
Suwanee, GA 30024-1245
Phone: (404)623-1909 **Fax:** (404)623-3575
Products: Industrial sewing machines. **SIC:** 5084
(Industrial Machinery & Equipment). **Sales:**
$35,000,000 (2000). **Emp:** 67. **Officers:** Hans
Neuberger, CEO & President; John W. Yoder, VP of
Finance; Takoao Sakurai, VP of Marketing.

■ 16396 ■ **Picanol of America Inc.**
PO Box 5519
Greenville, SC 29606
Phone: (803)288-5475 **Fax:** (803)297-5081
Products: Textile industries machinery. **SIC:** 5084
(Industrial Machinery & Equipment). **Est:** 1970. **Sales:**
$7,000,000 (2000). **Emp:** 25. **Officers:** James C.
Thomas, President; John C. Van Hee, VP of Finance.

■ 16397 ■ **PID, Inc.**
PO Box 230
Augusta, ME 04332-0230
Phone: (207)623-8101
Free: (800)243-8743 **Fax:** (207)621-4122
E-mail: info@pidinc.com
Products: Industrial instrumentation. **SIC:** 5084
(Industrial Machinery & Equipment). **Est:** 1984. **Emp:**
27.

■ 16398 ■ **Piedmont Clarklift Inc.**
PO Box 16328
Greenville, SC 29606
Phone: (864)297-1330 **Fax:** (864)288-5874
E-mail: 7623-0@clarkmhc.com
Products: Forklifts; Batteries and chargers; Racks and
shelving. **SIC:** 5084 (Industrial Machinery &
Equipment). **Est:** 1976. **Sales:** $12,000,000 (2000).
Emp: 62. **Officers:** Jerry Prince, President; C. Bostic,
Treasurer & Secty.; Steve R. Johnson, VP of
Marketing; Rick Butler, Dir. of Information Systems.

■ 16399 ■ **Pilgrim Instrument & Controls**
38 Union St.
East Walpole, MA 02032
Phone: (508)668-3500
Free: (800)536-7990 **Fax:** (508)668-4181
Products: Industrial instrumentation. **SIC:** 5084
(Industrial Machinery & Equipment).

■ 16400 ■ **Pioneer Equipment Inc.**
3738 E Miami St.
Phoenix, AZ 85040
Phone: (602)437-4312 **Fax:** (602)437-0174
Products: Compressors. **SIC:** 5084 (Industrial
Machinery & Equipment). **Sales:** $5,000,000 (2000).
Emp: 23.

■ 16401 ■ **Pioneer Machinery Inc.**
PO Box 250
Lexington, SC 29071
Phone: (803)356-0123 **Free:** (800)922-5406
Products: Logging equipment; Industrial trucks. **SICs:**
5082 (Construction & Mining Machinery); 5084
(Industrial Machinery & Equipment). **Sales:**
$250,000,000 (2000). **Emp:** 350. **Officers:** Garner
Scott, CEO & Chairman of the Board; Jim Wise,
President.

■ 16402 ■ **PLM Transportation Equipment
Corp.**
1 Market Plz., Ste. 800, Steuart Twr.
San Francisco, CA 94105-1301
Phone: (415)974-1399
Free: (800)227-0830 **Fax:** (415)882-0860
Products: Transportation equipment. **SIC:** 5088
(Transportation Equipment & Supplies). **Sales:**
$1,100,000 (2000). **Emp:** 10. **Officers:** Douglas P.
Goodrich, President; Michael Allgood, VP & CFO.

■ 16403 ■ **PMC Machinery, Inc.**
14600 Keel St.
Plymouth, MI 48170-6004
Phone: (734)459-3270 **Fax:** (734)459-4382
E-mail: pmcmachinery@worldnet.att.net
URL: http://www.pmcmachinery.com
Products: Machine tools. **SIC:** 5084 (Industrial
Machinery & Equipment). **Est:** 1983. **Sales:**
$82,000,000 (1999). **Emp:** 70. **Officers:** Robert Bloch,
President; Barbara Bloch, Secretary; John Hirzel, CFO;
Norman Paszko, Sales Mgr.; Al Bolon, VP of Sales.

■ 16404 ■ **PMH Associates**
9945 Wild Grape Dr.
San Diego, CA 92131
Phone: (619)695-3878 **Fax:** (619)693-4288
Products: Industrial equipment, including vacuum
furnaces, ovens, and pumps; Laboratory equipment,
including vacuum pumps; Electronic equipment,
including semiconductors and flat panel display. **SICs:**
5084 (Industrial Machinery & Equipment); 5049
(Professional Equipment Nec); 5065 (Electronic Parts &
Equipment Nec). **Officers:** Peter M. Hauser, President.

■ 16405 ■ **PNB Trading, Inc.**
100 Stuyvesant Rd.
Pittsford, NY 14534
Phone: (716)383-8149 **Fax:** (716)383-1370
Products: Industrial machinery and equipment;
Industrial supplies. **SICs:** 5084 (Industrial Machinery &
Equipment); 5085 (Industrial Supplies). **Officers:** Peter
N. Borys, President & CEO.

■ 16406 ■ **Pneumatrek, Inc.**
3066 South 300 West
PO Box 15601
Salt Lake City, UT 84115
Phone: (801)486-2178 **Fax:** (801)466-0737
Products: Hydraulics; Pneumatics. **SIC:** 5084
(Industrial Machinery & Equipment).

■ 16407 ■ **PNR International Ltd.**
1435 Joyce Ave.
Palatine, IL 60067-5725
Phone: (847)934-1705 **Fax:** (847)934-8118
E-mail: pnr12atsprodigy.net
Products: Torque calibration equipment. **SIC:** 5084
(Industrial Machinery & Equipment). **Est:** 1986. **Sales:**
$500,000 (1999). **Emp:** 3. **Officers:** Peter Salter,
President; Ruth Salter, Secretary.

■ 16408 ■ **Pocahontas Welding Supply Co.**
1319 Norfolk Ave., Ste.
Roanoke, VA 24013
Phone: (540)344-0934 **Fax:** (540)344-2967
Products: Industrial gases; Welding equipment,
including blowtorches and goggles. **SICs:** 5084
(Industrial Machinery & Equipment); 5169 (Chemicals
& Allied Products Nec). **Est:** 1949. **Sales:** $5,500,000
(2000). **Emp:** 30. **Officers:** W.H. Wood, Manager; Don
Parsons, Controller.

■ 16409 ■ **Poclain Hydraulics Inc.**
PO Box 801
Sturtevant, WI 53177
Phone: (262)554-6566 **Fax:** (262)554-4860
E-mail: info-america@poclain-hydraulics.com
URL: http://www.poclain-hydraulics.com
Products: Hydraulic motors, pumps, valves, and
electronics. **SIC:** 5084 (Industrial Machinery &
Equipment). **Emp:** 100. **Officers:** Laurent Bataille,
CEO; Tom Shinners, Controller.

■ 16410 ■ **Joseph E. Podgor Co. Inc.**
7055 Central Hwy.
Pennsauken, NJ 08109-4699
Phone: (609)663-7878
Free: (800)257-8226 **Fax:** (609)663-9467
Products: Screen printing supplies and equipment.
SICs: 5084 (Industrial Machinery & Equipment); 5199 (Nondurable Goods Nec). **Est:** 1931. **Emp:** 40.

■ 16411 ■ **Potomac Industrial Trucks Inc.**
800 Ritchie Rd.
Capitol Heights, MD 20743
Phone: (301)336-1700
Products: Forklifts and equipment handling machinery.
SIC: 5012 (Automobiles & Other Motor Vehicles).
Sales: $22,000,000 (2000). **Emp:** 150. **Officers:** Theodore Wolff Jr., President; Paul Willbanks, VP of Finance.

■ 16412 ■ **Powell Tool Supply Inc.**
PO Box 1854
South Bend, IN 46634-6709
Phone: (219)289-4811 **Fax:** (219)289-3504
E-mail: ptsinc@sbt-infinet
Products: Industrial equipment. **SIC:** 5084 (Industrial Machinery & Equipment). **Est:** 1948. **Sales:** $10,000,000 (2000). **Emp:** 25. **Officers:** Alfred Eaton, President.

■ 16413 ■ **Power Drives and Bearings Div.**
801 S 20th St.
Omaha, NE 68108
Phone: (402)344-7323
Products: Fluid power components and bearings. **SIC:** 5085 (Industrial Supplies).

■ 16414 ■ **Power Lift Corp.**
8314 E Slauson Ave.
Pico Rivera, CA 90660
Phone: (562)949-1000 **Fax:** (562)949-5984
E-mail: marketing@powerlift.com
URL: http://www.powerlift.com
Products: Industrial equipment, including lift trucks, utility vehicles, sweepers, scrubbers, and spare parts.
SICs: 5084 (Industrial Machinery & Equipment); 5085 (Industrial Supplies). **Est:** 1993. **Sales:** $42,000,000 (2000). **Emp:** 220. **Officers:** Richard Cowan, President; Gary Ortiz, VP & General Mgr.; Jon Sims, Sales Mgr.; Stephen Rapier, Dir. of Marketing; Paul Difuccia, VP of Sales & Marketing.

■ 16415 ■ **Power Machinery Center**
3450 E Camino Ave.
Oxnard, CA 93030
Phone: (805)485-0577 **Fax:** (805)983-2773
Products: Forklifts and rackings. **SIC:** 5084 (Industrial Machinery & Equipment). **Est:** 1950. **Sales:** $9,500,000 (2000). **Emp:** 60. **Officers:** Richard Power, President; John Danzi, Controller; John Power, Vice President.

■ 16416 ■ **Power Pumps Inc.**
2820 Seaboard Ln.
Long Beach, CA 90805
Phone: (562)531-3333
URL: http://www.powerpumps.com
Products: Industrial pumps. **SIC:** 5084 (Industrial Machinery & Equipment). **Est:** 1954. **Sales:** $11,000,000 (2000). **Emp:** 34. **Officers:** F.V. Keenan, President, e-mail: fkeenan@powerpumps.com.

■ 16417 ■ **Power & Pumps, Inc.**
400 Pittman St.
PO Box 2153
Orlando, FL 32801
Phone: (305)843-7400 **Fax:** (407)423-9786
Products: Pumps and pump parts. **SIC:** 5084 (Industrial Machinery & Equipment).

■ 16418 ■ **Power Tool & Machinery**
2506 S Orchard St.
Boise, ID 83705-3799
Phone: (208)336-1551 **Fax:** (208)343-9567
Products: Power tools and machines. **SIC:** 5084 (Industrial Machinery & Equipment). **Est:** 1942. **Emp:** 9. **Officers:** Bob Ohlson; Russ Brown.

■ 16419 ■ **Prairie Tool Co.**
110 Prairie Tool Dr.
Prairie du Chien, WI 53821-2027
Phone: (608)326-6111 **Fax:** (608)326-6444
Products: Grinding, polishing, buffing, honing, and lapping tools. **SIC:** 5084 (Industrial Machinery & Equipment). **Est:** 1920. **Sales:** $1,000,000 (2000).
Emp: 49. **Officers:** W.L. Herreid.

■ 16420 ■ **Praxair Distribution, Inc.**
4030 W Lincoln St.
Phoenix, AZ 85009-5398
Phone: (602)269-2151
Free: (800)246-9353 **Fax:** (602)278-8607
Products: Welding supplies, including gases, rods, machinery, and face shields. **SIC:** 5084 (Industrial Machinery & Equipment). **Est:** 1941. **Sales:** $15,800,000 (2000). **Emp:** 96. **Officers:** Steve Bogard, General Mgr.; Tim Walters, Sales Mgr.; Al Hummels, Retail Manager. **Former Name:** Arizona Welding Equipment Co.

■ 16421 ■ **Praxair Distribution/W. Div.**
767 Industrial Rd.
San Carlos, CA 94070
Phone: (650)592-7304 **Fax:** (650)592-2909
Products: Industrial, medical and specialty gases; Welding supplies and equipment. **SICs:** 5084 (Industrial Machinery & Equipment); 5169 (Chemicals & Allied Products Nec).

■ 16422 ■ **Precision Industries**
909 Broadway
West Burlington, IA 52655
Phone: (319)753-6233 **Fax:** (319)753-6235
Products: Bearings, hydraulics, pneumatics, and lubricants. **SICs:** 5084 (Industrial Machinery & Equipment); 5085 (Industrial Supplies).

■ 16423 ■ **Precision Tool and Supply**
7510 Lawndale
Houston, TX 77012
Phone: (713)923-9381
Free: (800)537-9790 **Fax:** (713)923-9859
Products: Small cutting tools for machine tools and metalworking machinery. **SICs:** 5084 (Industrial Machinery & Equipment); 5072 (Hardware). **Est:** 1951.
Emp: 37. **Officers:** D. E. Lanier.

■ 16424 ■ **Pressotechnik Ltd.**
4250 Weaver Pkwy.
Warrenville, IL 60555-3924
Phone: (630)543-4400
Products: Air-over hydraulic presses. **SIC:** 5084 (Industrial Machinery & Equipment).

■ 16425 ■ **Prime Label Div.**
3626 Stern Ave.
St. Charles, IL 60174
Phone: (630)443-3626
Products: Industrial machinery and equipment. **SIC:** 5084 (Industrial Machinery & Equipment). **Sales:** $6,100,000 (1993). **Emp:** 45. **Officers:** Joseph Rooney, General Mgr.

■ 16426 ■ **Printers Supply of Indiana Inc.**
PO Box 886
Indianapolis, IN 46206
Phone: (317)263-5298
Free: (800)627-4479 **Fax:** (317)263-5294
E-mail: psi@indy.net
Products: Graphic arts supplies and equipment. **SIC:** 5084 (Industrial Machinery & Equipment). **Est:** 1959.
Sales: $7,000,000 (2000). **Emp:** 40. **Officers:** R. Duane Henry, President; Robert Kratoska, Sales/Marketing Contact.

■ 16427 ■ **Printers Xchange Inc.**
2839 Galahad Dr.
Atlanta, GA 30345
Phone: (404)321-3762
Products: Printing trades machinery, equipment, and supplies. **SIC:** 5084 (Industrial Machinery & Equipment).

■ 16428 ■ **Probe Technology Corp.**
2424 Walsh Ave.
Santa Clara, CA 95051
Phone: (408)980-1740 **Fax:** (408)492-0450
Products: Probe cards and probing equipment. **SIC:** 5084 (Industrial Machinery & Equipment). **Officers:** R Mende, President; Bill Downey, CFO.

■ 16429 ■ **Process Equipment Inc.**
26569 Corporate Ave.
Hayward, CA 94545
Phone: (510)782-5122 **Fax:** (510)284-3500
Products: Food processing and standard stainless steel equipment; Specialty pharmaceutical instruments.
SIC: 5084 (Industrial Machinery & Equipment). **Sales:** $1,500,000 (2000). **Emp:** 8.

■ 16430 ■ **Procon Products**
910 Ridgely Rd.
Murfreesboro, TN 37129
Phone: (615)890-5710 **Fax:** (615)896-7729
E-mail: mail@proconpump.com
URL: http://www.proconpump.com
Products: Pumps. **SIC:** 5084 (Industrial Machinery & Equipment). **Est:** 1950. **Emp:** 100.

■ 16431 ■ **Stanley M. Proctor Co.**
2016 Midway Ave.
Twinsburg, OH 44087
Phone: (216)425-7814 **Fax:** (216)425-3222
Products: Hydraulic and pneumatic equipment. **SIC:** 5084 (Industrial Machinery & Equipment). **Est:** 1955.
Sales: $11,000,000 (2000). **Emp:** 30. **Officers:** John D. Proctor, CEO & President.

■ 16432 ■ **Production Machinery Inc.**
9000 Yellow Brick Rd.
Baltimore, MD 21237
Phone: (410)574-2110 **Fax:** (410)574-4790
E-mail: info@promaco.com
URL: http://www.promaco.com
Products: Roll bending machines; Cold saws; Material handling equipment; Portable magnetic drills. **SIC:** 5084 (Industrial Machinery & Equipment). **Est:** 1957.
Sales: $1,200,000 (1999). **Emp:** 6. **Officers:** R. Schmidt, CEO; M. Doyle, CFO; D. Gettier, General Mgr.

■ 16433 ■ **Pumps, Parts and Service Inc.**
PO Box 7788
Charlotte, NC 28241
Phone: (704)588-1338
Products: Industrial pump systems. **SIC:** 5084 (Industrial Machinery & Equipment). **Sales:** $14,000,000 (2000). **Emp:** 45. **Officers:** Ray Miller, President.

■ 16434 ■ **Purity Cylinder Gases Inc.**
PO Box 9390
Grand Rapids, MI 49509-0390
Phone: (616)532-2375 **Fax:** (616)532-1022
Products: Gas products; Welding equipment. **SICs:** 5084 (Industrial Machinery & Equipment); 5169 (Chemicals & Allied Products Nec). **Est:** 1938. **Sales:** $17,000,000 (2000). **Emp:** 100. **Officers:** Gary Nyhuis, President; Chuck Miesch, Accountant.

■ 16435 ■ **Quimby Corp.**
1603 NW 14th Ave.
Portland, OR 97209
Phone: (503)221-1100 **Fax:** (503)241-9549
Products: Industrial supplies. **SIC:** 5084 (Industrial Machinery & Equipment). **Sales:** $9,500,000 (2000).
Emp: 45.

■ 16436 ■ **Raco Industrial Corp.**
2100 S Wolf Rd.
Des Plaines, IL 60018
Phone: (847)298-8600
Free: (888)411-4879 **Fax:** (847)635-8976
E-mail: sales@raco.com
URL: http://www.raco.com
Products: Metal-working machinery, including grinders, mills, presses and shears. **SIC:** 5084 (Industrial Machinery & Equipment). **Est:** 1953. **Sales:** $7,000,000 (1999). **Emp:** 24. **Officers:** R.C. Atherton, Chairman of the Board; John C. Boecher, President.

■ **16437** ■ **Rand & Jones Enterprises Co., Inc.**
137 Wickham Dr.
Williamsville, NY 14221
Phone: (716)632-2180
Free: (800)688-2368 **Fax:** (716)632-7831
Products: Bathroom products; Kitchen cabinets; Plumbing materials; Countertops. **SICs:** 5084 (Industrial Machinery & Equipment); 5031 (Lumber, Plywood & Millwork); 5074 (Plumbing & Hydronic Heating Supplies). **Officers:** Joan C. Yang, President.

■ **16438** ■ **Rank America Inc.**
5 Concourse Pkwy Ste. 2400
Atlanta, GA 30328
Phone: (404)392-9029 **Fax:** (404)392-0585
Products: Industrial machinery. **SIC:** 5084 (Industrial Machinery & Equipment). **Sales:** $500,000,000 (1991). **Emp:** 6,000. **Officers:** John Watson, Exec. VP of Finance.

■ **16439** ■ **Rapid Air Corp.**
4601 Kishwaukee St.
Rockford, IL 61109
Phone: (815)397-2578 **Fax:** (815)398-3887
Products: Press room equipment. **SIC:** 5084 (Industrial Machinery & Equipment). **Sales:** $1,000,000 (2000). **Emp:** 62. **Officers:** R.D. Nordlof, President; James M. Beers, Dir. of Marketing.

■ **16440** ■ **Raymond Sales Corp.**
PO Box 130
Greene, NY 13778-0130
Phone: (607)656-2311
Products: Materials handling equipment and systems. **SIC:** 5084 (Industrial Machinery & Equipment).

■ **16441** ■ **RDO Equipment Co.**
12500 S Dupont Ave.
Burnsville, MN 55337
Phone: (952)890-8880
Free: (800)950-3298 **Fax:** (952)890-7046
URL: http://www.rdoequipment.com
Products: Industrial tractors. **SIC:** 5084 (Industrial Machinery & Equipment). **Est:** 1990. **Sales:** $30,000,000 (1999). **Emp:** 80. **Officers:** Ron Saar, VP & General Merchandising Mgr.; Judy Norman, Accountant. **Former Name:** Midwest Machinery.

■ **16442** ■ **Read-Ferry Company Ltd.**
22 Wilkins Ave.
Haddonfield, NJ 08033
Phone: (609)795-5510
Products: Industrial pollution control equipment, including dust collectors. **SIC:** 5084 (Industrial Machinery & Equipment). **Est:** 1965. **Sales:** $11,000,000 (2000). **Emp:** 4. **Officers:** H. William Blakeslee, Owner.

■ **16443** ■ **Reading Crane and Engineering Co.**
11 Vanguard Dr.
Reading, PA 19606-3765
Phone: (610)582-7203 **Fax:** (610)582-7208
URL: http://www.readingcrane.com
Products: Overhead cranes. **SIC:** 5084 (Industrial Machinery & Equipment). **Sales:** $12,000,000 (2000). **Emp:** 75. **Officers:** Jim Friedman, President; Audrey Stroman, Controller; Randy R. Gross, President.

■ **16444** ■ **Albert Rebel and Associates Inc.**
PO Box 712548
Los Angeles, CA 90071-7548
Phone: (909)594-9515
Products: Machinery. **SIC:** 5084 (Industrial Machinery & Equipment).

■ **16445** ■ **Reif Carbide Tool Company, Inc.**
11055 E 9 Mile Rd.
PO Box 862
Warren, MI 48090
Phone: (810)754-1890 **Fax:** (810)754-0378
E-mail: rctc@mindspring.com
Products: Carbide cutting tools. **SIC:** 5084 (Industrial Machinery & Equipment). **Est:** 1946. **Sales:** $2,000,000 (2000). **Emp:** 25. **Officers:** Fred John Reif; Jim Dennis.

■ **16446** ■ **John Reiner & Company, Inc.**
601 Commercial Ave.
Carlstadt, NJ 07072
Phone: (201)460-9444 **Fax:** (201)460-0363
Products: Industrial engines; Gasoline; Fuel. **SICs:** 5084 (Industrial Machinery & Equipment); 5172 (Petroleum Products Nec). **Est:** 1927. **Sales:** $2,000,000 (2000). **Emp:** 8. **Officers:** Gary James Briskie, e-mail: garry.briskie@tenhoevebros.com.

■ **16447** ■ **REM Sales Inc.**
34 Bradley Park Rd.
East Granby, CT 06026
Phone: (203)653-0071 **Fax:** (203)653-0393
E-mail: rem.sales@snet.net
Products: Tuning and machinery centers; Tuning and milling machines. **SIC:** 5084 (Industrial Machinery & Equipment). **Est:** 1957. **Sales:** $22,000,000 (2000). **Emp:** 36. **Officers:** Lee B. Morris, President; Bob Whelan, CFO; James MacGregor, VP of Engineering; Betty Kopiel; Linda Merchant, Sales & Marketing Contact; Dave Bailey, Customer Service Contact.

■ **16448** ■ **Repete Corp.**
PO Box 900
Sussex, WI 53089
Phone: (414)246-4541 **Fax:** (414)246-7166
URL: http://www.repete.com
Products: Control systems. **SIC:** 5084 (Industrial Machinery & Equipment). **Est:** 1965. **Sales:** $5,000,000 (2000). **Emp:** 40. **Officers:** Norm Peterson, e-mail: n-peterson@execpc; Dick Jorgensen; Mike Nelson, Sales & Marketing Contact; Jay Davis, Sales & Marketing Contact; Bernd Hess, Customer Service Contact; Gladys Beitsch, Human Resources Contact.

■ **16449** ■ **Rex Supply Co.**
PO Box 266
Houston, TX 77001
Phone: (713)222-2251
Free: (800)369-0669 **Fax:** (713)225-5737
E-mail: rexmkt@neosoft.com
URL: http://www.rex-supply.com
Products: Industrial tools; Machine tools; Shop supplies. **SIC:** 5084 (Industrial Machinery & Equipment). **Est:** 1946. **Sales:** $30,000,000 (2000). **Emp:** 125. **Officers:** Joe Madden, President; Brenda Whipple, Controller.

■ **16450** ■ **RHM Fluid Power Inc.**
375 Manufacturers Dr.
Westland, MI 48186
Phone: (734)326-5400 **Fax:** (734)326-0339
E-mail: rhmfp3@wwnet.com
URL: http://www.rhmfluidpower.com
Products: Hydraulic, lubrication, pneumatic, and coolant components and systems; Air compressors. **SIC:** 5084 (Industrial Machinery & Equipment). **Est:** 1958. **Sales:** $28,000,000 (2000). **Emp:** 75. **Officers:** Emil F. Muccino Jr., VP & Secty.; William W. Tulloch, President; Jeffrey M. Verona, Vice President; Joe Brandis, Sales/Marketing Contact; Neal LeBlanc, Customer Service Contact; Margaret Aghababian, Human Resources Contact.

■ **16451** ■ **Richards Machine and Cutting Tools Inc.**
PO Box 471
Gretna, LA 70054
Phone: (504)368-1004
Free: (800)223-2689 **Fax:** (504)368-1007
E-mail: richmach@bellsouth.net
URL: http://www.richardsmachine.com
Products: Machine tools; Metal cutting tools; Perishable cutting tools. **SIC:** 5084 (Industrial Machinery & Equipment). **Est:** 1966. **Emp:** 10. **Officers:** N.B. Delph, President; Red Freeze, Sales/Marketing Contact.

■ **16452** ■ **L.L. Richards Machinery Company Inc.**
PO Box 516
Butler, WI 53007-0516
Phone: (414)771-3120 **Fax:** (414)771-7367
Products: Plant machinery. **SIC:** 5084 (Industrial Machinery & Equipment). **Est:** 1937. **Sales:** $10,000,000 (2000). **Emp:** 15. **Officers:** J.R. Richards, President; Greg Hoesly, CFO.

■ **16453** ■ **Riekes Equipment Co.**
6703 L St.
Omaha, NE 68131
Phone: (402)593-1181
Products: Industrial trucks; Material handling equipment. **SIC:** 5084 (Industrial Machinery & Equipment). **Sales:** $14,000,000 (2000). **Emp:** 45. **Officers:** Duncan J. Murphy, President; Allen Eggert, Controller.

■ **16454** ■ **Ringhaver Equipment Co.**
PO Box 30169
Tampa, FL 33630
Phone: (813)671-3700 **Fax:** (813)671-3118
URL: http://www.ringhaver.com
Products: Heavy earthmoving, small construction equipment; Cranes; Power Systems. **SIC:** 5084 (Industrial Machinery & Equipment). **Est:** 1986. **Emp:** 700. **Officers:** Lance Ringhaver, President; Tim Geddes, Exec. VP; Mike O'Keefe, Treasurer; Brian Rose, Controller; Ernie Stein, Human Resources Mgr.

■ **16455** ■ **Roberts Motor Co.**
550 NE Columbia Blvd.
Portland, OR 97211
Phone: (503)240-6282
Products: Heavy trucks. **SIC:** 5084 (Industrial Machinery & Equipment). **Sales:** $58,000,000 (2000). **Emp:** 73. **Officers:** Vittz J. Ramsdell, President; Patrick Howard, Treasurer & Secty.

■ **16456** ■ **Rockford Industrial Welding Supply Inc.**
4646 Linden Rd.
Rockford, IL 61109-3300
Phone: (815)226-1900
Products: Welding supplies. **SIC:** 5084 (Industrial Machinery & Equipment). **Sales:** $65,000,000 (2000). **Emp:** 75. **Officers:** Gary R. Bertrand, President; Dave Wiles, Controller.

■ **16457** ■ **Rocky Mountain Conveyor and Equipment**
6666 E 47th Avenue Dr.
Denver, CO 80216-3409
Phone: (303)333-5778
Free: (800)223-3740 **Fax:** (303)333-6986
E-mail: sales@rmce.com
Products: Conveyors; Sensors; Control techniques drives. **SIC:** 5084 (Industrial Machinery & Equipment).

■ **16458** ■ **Rogers Machinery Company Inc.**
PO Box 230429
Portland, OR 97281
Phone: (503)639-0808 **Fax:** (503)639-0111
Products: Compressed air, vacuum and pump systems. **SIC:** 5084 (Industrial Machinery & Equipment). **Sales:** $40,000,000 (2000). **Emp:** 190. **Officers:** W Novak, President; Ann Davidson, Treasurer.

■ **16459** ■ **Roll-Rite Corp.**
26265 Research Rd.
Hayward, CA 94545
Phone: 800-345-9305 **Fax:** 800-436-1444
E-mail: rollrite@roll-rite.com
URL: http://www.roll-rite.com
Products: Material handling equipment; Casters and wheels. **SICs:** 5084 (Industrial Machinery & Equipment); 5085 (Industrial Supplies). **Est:** 1935. **Sales:** $21,000 (1999). **Emp:** 12. **Officers:** Mario Sequeira, President.

■ **16460** ■ **Ross-Willoughby Co.**
PO Box 182054
Columbus, OH 43218-2054
Phone: (614)486-4311
Free: (800)282-8979 **Fax:** (614)486-7331
Products: Industrial tools. **SIC:** 5084 (Industrial Machinery & Equipment). **Sales:** $25,000,000 (1999). **Emp:** 99. **Officers:** L. P. Schultz, President; M. A. Kirk, VP of Supply; A. D. West, Treasurer.

■ **16461** ■ **Royal Supply Inc.**
PO Box 629
Elyria, OH 44036-0629
Phone: (440)322-5411
Free: (800)222-5411 **Fax:** (440)322-9090
E-mail: mailbox@royalsupply.com
URL: http://www.royalsupply.com
Products: Industrial equipment. **SIC:** 5085 (Industrial Supplies). **Est:** 1957. **Sales:** $5,000,000 (2000). **Emp:** 22. **Officers:** Ted Altfeld, President; Bob Vollick, COO & VP.

■ **16462** ■ **RSL Trading Company, Inc.**
2494 Bayshore Blvd., Ste. 250
Dunedin, FL 34698
Phone: (813)736-6770 **Fax:** (813)736-6773
Products: Machine tools, including bending and metalworking. **SIC:** 5084 (Industrial Machinery & Equipment). **Officers:** Robert S. Liu, President.

■ **16463** ■ **Rudel Machinery Company Inc.**
25 South St.
Hopkinton, MA 01748
Phone: (508)497-0942 **Fax:** (508)435-0502
Products: Industrial machinery. **SIC:** 5084 (Industrial Machinery & Equipment). **Sales:** $22,000,000 (2000). **Emp:** 22. **Officers:** John K. Wendt, Chairman of the Board; James Ensinger, Treasurer.

■ **16464** ■ **Ruth Corp.**
PO Box 220
Holland, OH 43528
Phone: (419)865-6555 **Fax:** (419)865-8169
Products: New and used pipe machinery. **SIC:** 5084 (Industrial Machinery & Equipment). **Est:** 1957. **Sales:** $3,500,000 (2000). **Emp:** 10. **Officers:** Jack H. Ruth, President; Gari A. Ruth, Vice President; Jennifer Harris, Office Mgr.; David F. Ruth, Vice President.

■ **16465** ■ **Rutland Tool and Supply Company Inc.**
2225 Workman Mill Rd.
PO Box 997
Whittier, CA 90601
Phone: (562)566-5010 **Free:** (800)289-4787
E-mail: rutlandtool@earthlink.net
URL: rutlandtool.com
Products: Hand tools, industrial tools, milling machines, and drills. **SICs:** 5084 (Industrial Machinery & Equipment); 5072 (Hardware).

■ **16466** ■ **S. and S. Machinery Co.**
140 53rd St.
Brooklyn, NY 11232
Phone: (718)492-7400 **Fax:** (718)439-3930
Products: Boring mills; Blades. **SIC:** 5084 (Industrial Machinery & Equipment). **Est:** 1939. **Sales:** $20,000,000 (2000). **Emp:** 100. **Officers:** Jed Srybnik, President; Ben Movasegni, CFO.

■ **16467** ■ **S.A.C.M. Textile Inc.**
Hwy. 29
Lyman, SC 29365
Phone: (864)877-1886 **Fax:** (864)877-4171
Products: Textile machinery. **SIC:** 5084 (Industrial Machinery & Equipment). **Est:** 1972. **Sales:** $4,000,000 (2000). **Emp:** 7. **Officers:** J. Schittley, President.

■ **16468** ■ **Salem Sales Associates**
2407 Central Ave.
PO Box 9323
Charlotte, NC 28205
Phone: (704)375-3328 **Fax:** (704)375-3458
Products: Industrial equipment. **SIC:** 5084 (Industrial Machinery & Equipment).

■ **16469** ■ **Sales International**
17922 Star of India Ln.
Carson, CA 90746
Phone: (310)538-5725 **Fax:** (310)538-4057
Products: Die-casting equipment. **SIC:** 5084 (Industrial Machinery & Equipment). **Est:** 1966. **Sales:** $10,000,000 (2000). **Emp:** 10. **Officers:** M. Hayakawa, Partner.

■ **16470** ■ **Sanford Process Corp.**
65 North Ave.
Natick, MA 01760
Phone: (508)653-7860 **Fax:** (508)653-7832
URL: http://www.sandfordprocess.thomasregister.com
Products: Equipment for hard anodizing process and systems. **SIC:** 5084 (Industrial Machinery & Equipment). **Est:** 1962. **Sales:** $1,000,000 (2000). **Emp:** 6. **Officers:** Leonid Lerner, General Mgr.; William Corcoran, President.

■ **16471** ■ **Saurer Textile Systems Charlotte**
4200 Performance Rd.
Charlotte, NC 28214
Phone: (704)394-8111 **Fax:** (704)393-1502
E-mail: info@stsc.saurer.com
Products: Textile machinery, including twisting and winding machines. **SIC:** 5084 (Industrial Machinery & Equipment). **Est:** 1969. **Sales:** $20,000 (2000). **Emp:** 37. **Officers:** Helmut Leksa, CEO & President; George Rickles, VP of Finance & CFO. **Former Name:** American Volkmann Corp.

■ **16472** ■ **Schoonmaker Service Parts Co.**
PO Box 621
Petaluma, CA 94953-0621
Phone: (707)763-8100 **Fax:** (707)763-8240
Products: Large diesel machine engines. **SIC:** 5084 (Industrial Machinery & Equipment). **Est:** 1898. **Sales:** $900,000 (2000). **Emp:** 6. **Officers:** W. Troy Padgett, President; Nancy L. Padgett, CFO.

■ **16473** ■ **Scotsco Inc.**
13101 SE 84th Ave.
Clackamas, OR 97015-9733
Phone: (503)777-4726 **Fax:** (503)653-7938
Products: Outdoor power equipment. **SIC:** 5084 (Industrial Machinery & Equipment). **Est:** 1971. **Sales:** $15,000,000 (2000). **Emp:** 40. **Officers:** Wendall O. Walker, President; James De Forest, Controller; Steve Byerly, Vice President.

■ **16474** ■ **Scott Machinery Co.**
4055 South 500 West
Salt Lake City, UT 84123
Phone: (801)262-7441
Free: (800)734-7441 **Fax:** (801)261-1857
URL: http://www.scottmcahineeryco.com
Products: Industrial machinery, including tractors. **SICs:** 5082 (Construction & Mining Machinery); 5084 (Industrial Machinery & Equipment). **Est:** 1968. **Sales:** $45,000,000 (2000). **Emp:** 90. **Officers:** David M. Scott, President; R.N. Patrick, Controller; David T. Foulger, VP of Sales; Bill Kleman, VP Product Support.

■ **16475** ■ **Screen Industry Art Inc.**
214 Industrial Dr.
Soddy-Daisy, TN 37379
Phone: (423)332-6190 **Fax:** (423)332-6293
Products: Screen printing; Textile printers. **SIC:** 5084 (Industrial Machinery & Equipment). **Officers:** Glen Roberson, President.

■ **16476** ■ **Sea-Pac Inc.**
PO Box 2707
Gardena, CA 90247
Phone: (310)324-3835
Products: Tuna canning machines. **SIC:** 5084 (Industrial Machinery & Equipment). **Est:** 1962. **Sales:** $5,000,000 (2000). **Emp:** 40. **Officers:** W.A. Larson, President; T. Luthi, Treasurer & Secty.; Frank A. Islas, VP of Marketing.

■ **16477** ■ **Seaboard Industrial Supply**
151 N 3rd St.
Philadelphia, PA 19106-1914
Phone: (215)627-5652 **Fax:** (215)627-3425
Products: Pneumatic tools and air handling equipment. **SICs:** 5084 (Industrial Machinery & Equipment); 5072 (Hardware). **Emp:** 99. **Officers:** Anthony Vail.

■ **16478** ■ **Sebastian Equipment Company Inc.**
1801 Joplin St.
Joplin, MO 64802
Phone: (417)623-3300
Products: Industrial equipment, including carbines and grinders. **SIC:** 5085 (Industrial Supplies). **Est:** 1940.

Sales: $7,600,000 (2000). **Emp:** 36. **Officers:** Greg Scheurich, President; R. Scheurich, Treasurer.

■ **16479** ■ **Sees & Faber-Berlin Inc.**
1611 Grove Ave.
Jenkintown, PA 19046-2303
Phone: (215)887-4899 **Fax:** (215)887-3314
Products: Fabricated industrial parts; Industrial and commercial service machines; Fasteners, standards and special; Trimming spades for refractory trade. **SICs:** 5084 (Industrial Machinery & Equipment); 5085 (Industrial Supplies). **Est:** 1888. **Emp:** 49. **Officers:** Ralph Berlin.

■ **16480** ■ **Seghers Better Technology**
3114 Emery Cir.
Austell, GA 30168
Phone: (770)739-4205 **Fax:** (770)739-0117
E-mail: seghers-usa@bettertechnology.com
URL: http://www.bettertechnology.com
Products: Industrial paint-stripping and plastic-stripping machinery. **SIC:** 5074 (Plumbing & Hydronic Heating Supplies). **Est:** 1986. **Sales:** $3,000,000 (2000). **Emp:** 8. **Officers:** L. Ceyssens, President. **Former Name:** Seghers Dinamec Inc.

■ **16481** ■ **Seika Machinery, Inc.**
3528 Torrance Blvd., Ste. 100
Torrance, CA 90503
Phone: (310)540-7310 **Fax:** (310)540-7930
URL: http://www.seikausa.com
Products: Electronics; Carts, racks, and accessories. **SIC:** 5046 (Commercial Equipment Nec). **Sales:** $8,000,000 (2000). **Emp:** 10. **Officers:** T. Shumizu, President; Hiro Suganura, Exec. VP, e-mail: hiro@seika.com.

■ **16482** ■ **Sellers Process Equipment Co.**
394 E Church Rd., Ste. A
King of Prussia, PA 19406-2694
Phone: (610)279-2448
Free: (888)270-6509 **Fax:** (610)279-3940
URL: http://www.sellersprocess.com
Products: Pumps, including food, pharmaceutical, and dairy. **SIC:** 5084 (Industrial Machinery & Equipment). **Est:** 1970. **Sales:** $4,000,000 (2000). **Emp:** 10. **Officers:** Ken Boschen, President; William Sellers, Secretary/Chairman.

■ **16483** ■ **Sepco-Industries Inc.**
PO Box 1697
Houston, TX 77251
Phone: (713)937-0330
Products: Pumps. **SIC:** 5084 (Industrial Machinery & Equipment). **Est:** 1908. **Sales:** $90,000,000 (2000). **Emp:** 450. **Officers:** David R. Little, President; Gary allcorn, Sr. VP & Finance Officer.

■ **16484** ■ **Sewing Machines Distributors**
1292 Foster Rd.
Las Cruces, NM 88001
Phone: (505)522-8717
Products: Sewing machines. **SIC:** 5084 (Industrial Machinery & Equipment).

■ **16485** ■ **Shearer Industrial Supply Co.**
PO Box 1272
York, PA 17405
Phone: (717)767-7575
Free: (800)682-9718 **Fax:** (717)767-7570
Products: Cutting tools; Abrasives. **SICs:** 5084 (Industrial Machinery & Equipment); 5085 (Industrial Supplies). **Est:** 1923. **Sales:** $60,000,000 (2000). **Emp:** 185. **Officers:** Andrew Shearer, President; Larry Julius, Treasurer & Secty.; Bill Schenck, VP of Marketing & Sales; Darlene Kroh, Dir. of Information Systems.

■ **16486** ■ **Sheats Supply Services, Inc.**
6121 E 30th St.
Indianapolis, IN 46219-1002
Phone: (317)542-1070
Free: (800)860-8665 **Fax:** (317)545-6000
E-mail: info@sheats.com
URL: http://www.sheats.com
Products: Industrial cutting tools. **SICs:** 5084 (Industrial Machinery & Equipment); 5085 (Industrial Supplies). **Est:** 1967. **Sales:** $5,000,000 (1999). **Emp:** 25. **Officers:** Nancy L. Sheats, Chairman of the Board

& Finance Officer; Jeffrey D. Sheats, President; Buddy D. Sheats, CFO, e-mail: Bud@Sheats.com; Don Richey, Customer Service Mgr., e-mail: Don@Sheats.com; Jeff Sheats, Human Resources Contact, e-mail: jeff@Sheats.com.

■ 16487 ■ Shibamoto America, Inc.
2395 Pleasantdale Rd., No. 1
Doraville, GA 30340
Phone: (404)446-9232 Fax: (404)446-9234
Products: Industrial strapping machines; Chain link fencing; Steel products; Tension control bolts; Fish. SICs: 5084 (Industrial Machinery & Equipment); 5051 (Metals Service Centers & Offices); 5039 (Construction Materials Nec); 5146 (Fish & Seafoods). Officers: Ken Noguchi, Vice President.

■ 16488 ■ Sid Tool Company Inc.
151 Sunnyside Blvd.
Plainview, NY 11803
Phone: (516)349-7100 Fax: (516)349-0265
Products: Tools and machinery items, including screws and screwdrivers. SICs: 5085 (Industrial Supplies); 5084 (Industrial Machinery & Equipment). Est: 1941. Sales: $430,000,000 (2000). Emp: 2,000. Officers: Mitchell Jacobson, CEO & President; Shelley Boxer, VP & CFO; David Gillies, VP of Information Systems; Barbara Schwartz, VP of Human Resources.

■ 16489 ■ Sierra Concepts Corp.
9912 S Pioneer Blvd.
Santa Fe Springs, CA 90670
Phone: (562)949-8311
Products: Machine tools. SIC: 5084 (Industrial Machinery & Equipment). Sales: $225,000,000 (2000). Emp: 450. Officers: W.J. Ellison, CEO & President; Klaus Rindt, Controller.

■ 16490 ■ Siggins Co.
512 E 12th Ave.
North Kansas City, MO 64116
Phone: (816)421-7670
Free: (800)353-3218 Fax: (816)421-2162
E-mail: sigginsinfo@siggins.net
URL: http://www.siggins.net
Products: Shelving; Bulk material handling conveyors and conveying systems. SICs: 5046 (Commercial Equipment Nec); 5084 (Industrial Machinery & Equipment). Est: 1946. Emp: 28. Officers: Sandra Higman; Don adams, Customer Service Contact, e-mail: dadams@siggins.net.

■ 16491 ■ Silent Hoist and Crane Co.
841-877 63rd St.
Brooklyn, NY 11220
Phone: (718)238-2525 Fax: (718)680-7651
Products: Forklift trucks. SIC: 5084 (Industrial Machinery & Equipment). Est: 1918. Sales: $5,000,000 (2000). Emp: 50. Officers: E.M. Wunsch, Vice President; Peter E. Wunsch, Treasurer; John Ahlbrand, Vice President.

■ 16492 ■ Silver State Welding Supply Inc.
3560 Losee Rd.
North Las Vegas, NV 89030
Phone: (702)734-2182
Products: Welding machines; Helmets; Earplugs. SICs: 5084 (Industrial Machinery & Equipment); 5085 (Industrial Supplies). Sales: $6,000,000 (2000). Emp: 22. Officers: Bob Conklin, General Mgr.; Jerry Fisher, General Mgr.

■ 16493 ■ Simpson Industries Inc.
47603 Halyard Dr.
Plymouth, MI 48170-2429
Phone: (248)540-6200 Fax: (248)540-7484
Products: Machine components. SIC: 5084 (Industrial Machinery & Equipment). Sales: $193,000,000 (2000). Emp: 1,400. Officers: Robert W. Navarre, CEO & Chairman of the Board; Roy E. Parrott, COO & President.

■ 16494 ■ Singer Products Export Company Inc.
PO Box 484
Hartsdale, NY 10530-0484
Phone: (914)722-0400 Fax: (914)722-0404
Products: Battery manufacturing equipment; Motor vehicle parts and accessories. SICs: 5084 (Industrial Machinery & Equipment); 5013 (Motor Vehicle Supplies & New Parts). Officers: Richard J. Singer, President.

■ 16495 ■ Sisco Equipment Rental and Sales Inc.
3506 W Harry St.
Wichita, KS 67213
Phone: (316)943-4237 Fax: (316)943-0827
Products: Heavy equipment, including forklifts, cranes, and street sweepers. SICs: 5082 (Construction & Mining Machinery); 5084 (Industrial Machinery & Equipment). Sales: $9,000,000 (2000). Emp: 55. Officers: Bill Sanders, President; Alan Sands, Controller; Bill Murphy, VP & General Merchandising Mgr.

■ 16496 ■ Robert M. Slife and Associates
2754 Woodhill Rd.
Cleveland, OH 44104
Phone: (216)791-3500 Fax: (216)791-3505
Products: Industrial equipment. SIC: 5084 (Industrial Machinery & Equipment). Est: 1951. Sales: $7,000,000 (2000). Emp: 38. Officers: Robert Slife, President.

■ 16497 ■ Harold E. Smith Co.
3630 Concord Rd.
York, PA 17402-8629
Phone: (717)397-2874
Free: (800)437-6484 Fax: (717)397-6886
Products: Cutting tools, including saws, lathes, and drills; Fasteners, including nuts and bolts. SICs: 5085 (Industrial Supplies); 5084 (Industrial Machinery & Equipment). Est: 1940. Sales: $7,000,000 (2000). Emp: 36.

■ 16498 ■ Smith-Koch Inc.
886 Tryens Rd.
Aston, PA 19014
Phone: (610)459-1212 Fax: (610)459-3992
E-mail: tjksk@aol.com
URL: http://www.smith-koch.com
Products: Pumps, including fluid systems. SIC: 5084 (Industrial Machinery & Equipment). Est: 1920. Sales: $8,500,000 (2000). Emp: 27. Officers: Toby Koch, President.

■ 16499 ■ SMW Systems Inc.
9828 S Arlee Ave.
Santa Fe Springs, CA 90670
Phone: (562)949-7991
Free: (800)423-4651 Fax: (562)864-1391
Products: Machine tool accessories. SIC: 5084 (Industrial Machinery & Equipment). Sales: $12,000,000 (1999). Emp: 60. Officers: L. Atkins, President; Steve Brown, Controller.

■ 16500 ■ Smyth-Despard Company Inc.
800 Broad St.
PO Box 4789
Utica, NY 13504-4789
Phone: (315)732-2154 Fax: (315)732-6598
Products: General industrial machinery; Pumps; Hydraulic and pneumatic cylinders. SICs: 5084 (Industrial Machinery & Equipment); 5085 (Industrial Supplies); 5074 (Plumbing & Hydronic Heating Supplies). Emp: 23. Officers: Thomas Jenny.

■ 16501 ■ Solares Florida Corp.
7625 NW 54th St.
Miami, FL 33166
Phone: (305)592-0593 Fax: (305)592-0400
E-mail: rmsolares@solaresflorida.com
URL: http://www.solaresflorida.com
Products: Petroleum equipment specializing in bulk plants, loading terminals, flow/level/pressure/temperature instruments and controls. SICs: 5084 (Industrial Machinery & Equipment); 5085 (Industrial Supplies); 5063 (Electrical Apparatus & Equipment); 5047 (Medical & Hospital Equipment); 5074 (Plumbing & Hydronic Heating Supplies). Est: 1975. Sales: $15,000,000 (1999). Emp: 30. Officers: Alberto E. Solares, President; Ignacio Solares, Vice President; Rosa M. Solares, Sec. & Treas., e-mail: rmsolares@solaresflorida.com; Orlando Muniz, Customer Service Contact; Tracy Hernandez, Human Resources Contact.

■ 16502 ■ A.R. Soltis & Co., Inc.
34443 Industrial Dr.
Livonia, MI 48150
Phone: (734)522-1957 Fax: (734)522-1988
Products: Grinding wheels; Sanding discs; Sand paper; Abrasives; Carbide; Coolants. SICs: 5084 (Industrial Machinery & Equipment); 5085 (Industrial Supplies).

■ 16503 ■ Sommer and Maca Industries Inc.
5501 W Ogden Ave.
Cicero, IL 60804-3507
Phone: (773)242-2871
Free: (800)323-9200 Fax: (708)863-5462
E-mail: somacausa@aol.com
URL: http://www.somaca.com
Products: Glass machinery; Glass supplies for glass installers. SICs: 5084 (Industrial Machinery & Equipment); 5039 (Construction Materials Nec). Est: 1920. Sales: $40,000,000 (2000). Emp: 225. Officers: A.L. Maca, CEO; Richard Carroll, President; J.P. Johnson, Exec. VP.

■ 16504 ■ Sonics and Materials Inc.
53 Church Hill Rd.
Newtown, CT 06470
Phone: (203)270-4600
Free: (800)745-1105 Fax: (203)270-4610
E-mail: info@sonicsandmaterials.com
URL: http://www.sonicsandmaterials.com
Products: Ultrasonic plastic welding equipment. SIC: 5084 (Industrial Machinery & Equipment). Est: 1969. Sales: $9,500,000 (2000). Emp: 90. Officers: Robert S. Soloff, President.

■ 16505 ■ Soule Steam Feed Works
PO Box 5757
Meridian, MS 39302
Phone: (601)693-1982
Free: (800)647-6288 Fax: (601)483-8923
E-mail: soule@cybertron.com
URL: http://www.soule-miner.com
Products: Industrial equipment; Steam feed equipment; Power transmissions; MRO supplies; Machining services; Iron castings; Band and circular saw blades. SICs: 5084 (Industrial Machinery & Equipment); 5085 (Industrial Supplies). Est: 1893. Sales: $3,000,000 (2000). Emp: 32. Officers: Robert G. Soule, e-mail: bob@soule-miner.com; Rick Morris, Sales & Marketing Contact; Jack Ward, Customer Service Contact.

■ 16506 ■ Soule Steam Feed Works
PO Box 5757
Meridian, MS 39302
Phone: (601)693-1982
Free: (800)647-6288 Fax: (601)483-8923
Products: Industrial machinery. SIC: 5084 (Industrial Machinery & Equipment). Sales: $3,000,000 (2000). Emp: 32.

■ 16507 ■ South-Tex Treaters Inc.
PO Box 60480
Midland, TX 79711
Phone: (915)563-2766 Fax: (915)563-1729
Products: Gas separating equipment; Gas generating equipment; Gas detection systems. SIC: 5084 (Industrial Machinery & Equipment). Est: 1986. Sales: $10,000,000 (1999). Emp: 40. Officers: David C. Morrow, President.

■ 16508 ■ Southern Belting & Transmission
218 Ottley Dr. NE
Atlanta, GA 30324
Phone: (404)875-1655
Free: (800)241-1094 Fax: (404)876-2916
E-mail: info@southernbelting.com
URL: http://www.southernbelting.com
Products: Motion control equipment. SIC: 5084 (Industrial Machinery & Equipment).

■ 16509 ■ Southern Ice Equipment Distributor
4217 W Northside Dr., No. B
Jackson, MS 39213
Phone: (601)923-3332
Products: Ice making equipment machines. SIC: 5084 (Industrial Machinery & Equipment).

■ 16510 ■ **Southern Machinery Company Inc.**
PO Box 110768
Nashville, TN 37222-0768
Phone: (615)832-3365
Products: Conveying equipment. SIC: 5084 (Industrial Machinery & Equipment). **Est:** 1958. **Sales:** $7,000,000 (2000). **Emp:** 25. **Officers:** Glen Eaden, President.

■ 16511 ■ **Southern Minnesota Machinery Sales Inc.**
210 South St.
Dodge Center, MN 55927
Phone: (507)374-6346
Free: (800)770-5638 **Fax:** (507)374-6824
E-mail: smms@clear.lakes.com
URL: http://www.sominn.com
Products: Industrial machinery. SIC: 5084 (Industrial Machinery & Equipment). **Est:** 1972. **Sales:** $4,000,000 (2000). **Emp:** 10. **Officers:** George McNeilus, President; Shari McNeilus, CFO.

■ 16512 ■ **Southern Pump and Filter Inc.**
2883 Directors Cove
Memphis, TN 38131-0398
Phone: (901)332-4890 **Fax:** (901)346-4350
Products: specialty equipment and products. SIC: 5084 (Industrial Machinery & Equipment). **Sales:** $1,500,000 (2000). **Emp:** 4.

■ 16513 ■ **Southern Pump and Tank Co.**
PO Box 31516
Charlotte, NC 28231
Phone: (704)596-4373
Free: (800)477-2826 **Fax:** (704)599-7700
E-mail: sales@southernpump.com
URL: http://www.southernpump.com
Products: Liquid handling equipment, pumps, and tanks for gas stations, convenience stores, and manufacturing industry. SIC: 5084 (Industrial Machinery & Equipment). **Est:** 1935. **Sales:** $60,000,000 (1999). **Emp:** 223. **Officers:** Charley Tew, COO; Mark Allison, CFO.

■ 16514 ■ **Southwest DoAll Industrial Supply**
514 Riverdale Dr.
Glendale, CA 91204
Phone: (818)243-3153
Products: Industrial tools. SIC: 5072 (Hardware). **Sales:** $25,000,000 (1992). **Emp:** 130. **Officers:** David Crawford, President; Jim Blakley, Controller.

■ 16515 ■ **Southwest Hallowell Inc.**
637 S Rockford Dr.
Tempe, AZ 85281
Phone: (602)966-3988 **Fax:** (602)966-5947
Products: Material handling equipment. SIC: 5084 (Industrial Machinery & Equipment). **Est:** 1981. **Sales:** $1,700,000 (2000). **Emp:** 7. **Officers:** Scott Garrison, President.

■ 16516 ■ **Spar Tek Industries Inc.**
PO Box 17375
Portland, OR 97217
Phone: (503)283-4749 **Fax:** (503)289-1621
Products: Plywood equipment. SIC: 5084 (Industrial Machinery & Equipment).

■ 16517 ■ **Spectronics Inc.**
11230 NW Reeves St.
Portland, OR 97229
Phone: (503)643-8030 **Fax:** (503)526-0157
Products: High accuracy optical non-contact measurement products for physical distance. SIC: 5084 (Industrial Machinery & Equipment). **Sales:** $400,000 (2000). **Emp:** 5. **Officers:** Wallace E. Masters, President; Shirley Masters, Treasurer.

■ 16518 ■ **Standard Machine and Equipment Co.**
PO Box 1187
Uniontown, PA 15401
Phone: (412)438-0536 **Fax:** (412)438-1322
Products: Industrial demolition equipment. SIC: 5084 (Industrial Machinery & Equipment). **Sales:** $7,000,000 (2000). **Emp:** 150. **Officers:** Frank Carlow, CEO.

■ 16519 ■ **Star Cutter Co.**
PO Box 376
Farmington, MI 48332-0376
Phone: (248)474-8200 **Fax:** (248)474-9518
URL: http://www.starcutter.com
Products: Sharpening machines; Film coatings; Carbide pre-forms; Reamers; Drills. SICs: 5084 (Industrial Machinery & Equipment); 5162 (Plastics Materials & Basic Shapes). **Est:** 1927. **Emp:** 800. **Officers:** Brad Lawton, President; Boyd E. Moilanen, VP of Finance; M. Woodhouse, VP of Marketing & Sales; Bill Maples, Marketing Mgr.; Diana Johnson, Manager; Tim Zoia, Human Resources Mgr.

■ 16520 ■ **Star Middle East USA Inc.**
4801 Woodway Dr., Ste. 300 E
Houston, TX 77056
Phone: (713)871-1121 **Fax:** (713)871-0327
Products: Water well drilling equipment; Oil field equipment. SICs: 5084 (Industrial Machinery & Equipment); 5082 (Construction & Mining Machinery). **Est:** 1982. **Emp:** 4. **Officers:** J. Qasem, Contact; F. Qasem, Sales/Marketing Contact.

■ 16521 ■ **Steel Industries Inc.**
12600 Beech Daly Rd.
Redford, MI 48239
Phone: (313)535-8505
Free: (877)783-3599 **Fax:** (313)534-2165
E-mail: info@steelindustriesinc.com
URL: http://www.steelindustriesinc.com
Products: Open die forging, seamless steel rolled rings, and bar products. SIC: 5051 (Metals Service Centers & Offices). **Est:** 1913. **Sales:** $14,000,000 (2000). **Emp:** 105. **Officers:** Keith Woodland, President; John Samson, Marketing Coordinator, e-mail: jsamson@steelindustriesinc.com; Charles Finneran, International Sales Manager, e-mail: cfinneran@steelindustriesinc.com; Renay Wheeler, Dir of Human Resources, e-mail: rwheeler@steelindustriesinc.com.

■ 16522 ■ **Steelhead Inc.**
PO Box 21370
San Antonio, TX 78221-0370
Phone: (210)628-1066 **Fax:** (210)628-1818
Products: Packing, packaging, and bottling machinery; Air pollution control equipment and supplies. SIC: 5084 (Industrial Machinery & Equipment).

■ 16523 ■ **Stewart & Stevenson**
5717 I-10 E
San Antonio, TX 78219
Phone: (210)662-1000 **Fax:** (210)662-9832
Products: Industrial equipment, including forklifts and irrigation equipment; Diesel engines. SIC: 5084 (Industrial Machinery & Equipment).

■ 16524 ■ **Stewart and Stevenson Services Inc. Texas**
PO Box 1637
Houston, TX 77251
Phone: (713)868-7700
Products: Machinery. SICs: 5084 (Industrial Machinery & Equipment); 5078 (Refrigeration Equipment & Supplies). **Officers:** Bob H. O'Neal, President; Robert L. Hargrave, VP of Finance.

■ 16525 ■ **STIHL Northwest**
PO Box 999
Chehalis, WA 98532
Phone: (360)748-8694 **Fax:** (360)748-1469
Products: Chain saws; Lawn and garden power tools. SICs: 5084 (Industrial Machinery & Equipment); 5083 (Farm & Garden Machinery).

■ 16526 ■ **STIHL Southeast, Inc.**
2250 Principal Row
Orlando, FL 32837
Phone: (407)240-7900
Products: Chain saws; Lawn and garden equipment. SICs: 5084 (Industrial Machinery & Equipment); 5083 (Farm & Garden Machinery).

■ 16527 ■ **STIHL Southwest Inc.**
Hwy. 270 N
PO Box 518
Malvern, AR 72104
Phone: (501)332-2788
Products: Chain saws; Lawn and garden equipment. SICs: 5084 (Industrial Machinery & Equipment); 5083 (Farm & Garden Machinery).

■ 16528 ■ **Stiles Machinery Inc.**
3965 44th St.
Grand Rapids, MI 49512
Phone: (616)698-7500
Products: Panel processing and woodworking machinery. SIC: 5084 (Industrial Machinery & Equipment). **Sales:** $22,000,000 (1992). **Emp:** 70. **Officers:** Peter Kleinschmidt, President.

■ 16529 ■ **Stokes Equipment Co.**
1001 Horsham Rd.
Horsham, PA 19044
Phone: (215)672-6100
Free: (800)220-1099 **Fax:** (215)443-9348
URL: http://www.stokesequipment.com
Products: Industrial equipment, including conveyors. SIC: 5084 (Industrial Machinery & Equipment). **Est:** 1942. **Sales:** $9,000,000 (2000). **Emp:** 30. **Officers:** Thomas Swaintak, President; Peter Rice, Sales Mgr.

■ 16530 ■ **Strategic Distribution Inc.**
475 Steamboat Rd.
Greenwich, CT 06830
Phone: (203)629-8750 **Fax:** (203)629-8554
Products: Industrial products. SIC: 5099 (Durable Goods Nec). **Sales:** $80,000,000 (1994). **Emp:** 400. **Officers:** Andrew M. Bursky, President.

■ 16531 ■ **Studer Industrial Tool**
PO Box 11343
Pittsburgh, PA 15238
Phone: (412)828-2470 **Fax:** (412)826-1180
Products: Electrical industrial tools, including saws, drills, and grinders. SIC: 5084 (Industrial Machinery & Equipment). **Est:** 1978. **Sales:** $4,200,000 (2000). **Emp:** 20. **Officers:** M.A. Studer, President; A.O. Pivirotto, Dir. of Marketing.

■ 16532 ■ **Stultz Fluid Power**
190 Rand Rd.
Portland, ME 04102
Phone: (207)828-4727 **Fax:** (207)828-4728
Products: Hydraulic and pneumatic equipment. SIC: 5084 (Industrial Machinery & Equipment).

■ 16533 ■ **Weldon F. Stump & Company Inc.**
1313 Campbell St.
PO Box 3155
Toledo, OH 43607-0155
Phone: (419)243-6221
Free: (800)537-3498 **Fax:** (419)243-7277
E-mail: stumpco@aol.com
URL: http://www.stumpco.com
Products: Used metal working equipment. SIC: 5084 (Industrial Machinery & Equipment). **Est:** 1964. **Sales:** $8,000,000 (2000). **Emp:** 30. **Officers:** Weldon F. Stump, President; Raymond G. Darr, Controller; Robert S. Stump, Vice President.

■ 16534 ■ **Suhner Manufacturing, Inc.**
Hwy. 411 S
PO Box 1234
Rome, GA 30162-1234
Phone: (706)235-8046 **Fax:** (706)235-8045
E-mail: suhner@bellsouth.net
URL: http://www.suhner.com
Products: Flexible shafting; Abrasive power tools. SICs: 5084 (Industrial Machinery & Equipment); 5072 (Hardware). **Est:** 1976. **Sales:** $10,000,000 (2000). **Emp:** 170. **Officers:** Paul Luthi, President; Karl Waechtler, Vice President; Donny Terry, Customer Service Contact. **Former Name:** Suhner Industrial Products Corporation.

■ 16535 ■ Summers Induserve Supply
400 Buffalo St.
PO Box 210
Johnson City, TN 37605-0210
Phone: (423)461-4700
Free: (800)634-6313 **Fax:** (423)926-5120
E-mail: summers@mounet.com
URL: http://www.sum_ind.com
Products: Industrial and automotive tools; precision tools; cutting tools; abrasives; safety supplies; jan./san.. **SICs:** 5084 (Industrial Machinery & Equipment); 5072 (Hardware); 5013 (Motor Vehicle Supplies & New Parts). **Emp:** 60. **Officers:** R. Glenn Shaw, CEO.
Former Name: Summers Hardware & Supply Co.

■ 16536 ■ Summit Handling Systems Inc.
11 Defco Park Rd.
North Haven, CT 06473
Phone: (203)239-5351 **Fax:** (203)234-8090
E-mail: sumhand@aol.com
Products: Material handling equipment, including forklifts. **SIC:** 5084 (Industrial Machinery & Equipment). **Est:** 1953. **Sales:** $10,000,000 (2000). **Emp:** 65. **Officers:** L.T. McKevitt, President; Richard George, Human Resources Contact.

■ 16537 ■ Sun Distributors L.P.
1 Logan Sq.
Philadelphia, PA 19103
Phone: (215)665-3650 **Fax:** (215)282-1309
Products: Glass; Maintenance supplies; Hydraulic and electric power equipment. **SICs:** 5084 (Industrial Machinery & Equipment); 5039 (Construction Materials Nec). **Est:** 1976. **Sales:** $655,700,000 (2000). **Emp:** 4,350. **Officers:** Donald T. Marshall, CEO & Chairman of the Board; Louis J. Cissone, Sr. VP & CFO.

■ 16538 ■ Sundstrand Fluid Handling Corp.
14845 W 64th Ave.
Arvada, CO 80007
Phone: (303)425-0800 **Fax:** (303)425-0896
Products: Compressors and high-speed, magnet drive and centrifugal pumps and blowers. **SIC:** 5084 (Industrial Machinery & Equipment). **Sales:** $252,000,000 (2000). **Emp:** 1,500. **Officers:** Pat Thomas, President; Brenda Stone, Finance Officer.

■ 16539 ■ SunSource Technology Services
5390 E Ponce de Leon Ave., Ste. E
Stone Mountain, GA 30083
Phone: (770)491-6900
Free: (800)288-4831 **Fax:** (770)441-9827
URL: http://www.sun-source.com
Products: Hydraulic equipment; Pneumatic equipment; Electronic motion control systems. **SICs:** 5084 (Industrial Machinery & Equipment); 5063 (Electrical Apparatus & Equipment). **Est:** 1959. **Sales:** $650,000,000 (2000). **Emp:** 1,000. **Officers:** Ken Evans, President; Barry Pullin, Sales/Marketing Contact; Kevin Gorham, Human Resources Contact.
Former Name: Activation Inc.

■ 16540 ■ Supa Machinery Sales Inc.
2727 3 Mile Rd.
PO Box 361
Franksville, WI 53126
Phone: (262)835-3400 **Fax:** (262)835-3419
E-mail: sales@supamachinery.com
URL: http://www.supamachinery.com
Products: Industrial metalworking machinery and equipment. **SIC:** 5084 (Industrial Machinery & Equipment). **Est:** 1973. **Emp:** 20. **Officers:** Gerald Kolb, CEO; Gerald Kolb, CEO.

■ 16541 ■ Swiss Precision Instruments
PO Box 3135
Garden Grove, CA 92842-3135
Phone: (213)721-1818
Free: (800)492-7788 **Fax:** 800-637-8349
Products: Precision measuring tools; Precision mechanical springs. **SIC:** 5084 (Industrial Machinery & Equipment). **Est:** 1962. **Sales:** $20,000,000 (2000). **Emp:** 99. **Officers:** Kurt Oetiker.

■ 16542 ■ Sydnor Hydrodynamics Inc.
2111 Magnolia St.
Richmond, VA 23261
Phone: (804)643-2725
Products: Water pumps; Drill wells; Plumbing supplies.

SICs: 5084 (Industrial Machinery & Equipment); 5074 (Plumbing & Hydronic Heating Supplies). **Est:** 1889. **Sales:** $30,000,000 (2000). **Emp:** 95. **Officers:** G.S. Sydnor Jr., President; Steve Marusco, Controller; Grayson Harding, Dir. of Sales.

■ 16543 ■ Sygnet
PO Box 47953
Minneapolis, MN 55447
Phone: (612)473-0732 **Free:** (888)223-8770
URL: http://www.hind-sight.com
Products: Industrial equipment, including temperature recording devices; Motor vehicle accessories; Polyurethene coatings; Trailer hitching alignment systems. **SICs:** 5085 (Industrial Supplies); 5084 (Industrial Machinery & Equipment); 5169 (Chemicals & Allied Products Nec); 5013 (Motor Vehicle Supplies & New Parts). **Est:** 1988. **Officers:** Gene Deterling, President.

■ 16544 ■ Symtech Inc.
PO Box 2627
Spartanburg, SC 29304
Phone: (864)578-7101 **Fax:** (864)578-7107
Products: Textile machinery. **SIC:** 5084 (Industrial Machinery & Equipment). **Est:** 1985. **Emp:** 65. **Officers:** Hans J. Balmer, CEO; Lucia Balmer, CFO; Rodger Hartwig, Sales Mgr.

■ 16545 ■ Talladega Machinery and Supply Company Inc.
301 N Johnson Ave.
Talladega, AL 35160
Phone: (256)362-4124
Free: (800)289-8672 **Fax:** (256)761-2565
Products: Industrial supplies, machinery parts, and manufacturing. **SIC:** 5084 (Industrial Machinery & Equipment). **Sales:** $45,000,000 (1999). **Emp:** 269. **Officers:** Gary M. Heacock, President; Stan Hartdegen, Accounting Manager.

■ 16546 ■ Tampa Armature Works Inc.
PO Box 3381
Tampa, FL 33601
Phone: (813)621-5661 **Fax:** (813)622-7040
Products: Industrial equipment, including motors, generators, and compressors; Fertilizers, feed, and chemical farm products. **SICs:** 5063 (Electrical Apparatus & Equipment); 5169 (Chemicals & Allied Products Nec). **Est:** 1921. **Sales:** $45,000,000 (2000). **Emp:** 375. **Officers:** J.A. Turner III, President; Charles B. Shupe, Treasurer; Carey Webb, Sales Mgr.; Joseph Hodges, Information Systems Mgr.

■ 16547 ■ Tamrock USA
1 Driltech Dr.
Alachua, FL 32615
Phone: (904)462-4610 **Fax:** (904)462-3247
Products: Drills. **SIC:** 5084 (Industrial Machinery & Equipment). **Emp:** 49. **Officers:** Seppo Kivimaki.

■ 16548 ■ Tate & Lyle Enterprises, Inc.
2801 Ponce De Leon Blvd., Ste. 1055
Coral Gables, FL 33134
Phone: (305)448-2845
Products: Industrial machinery, equipment, and supplies; Farm machinery and equipment. **SICs:** 5084 (Industrial Machinery & Equipment); 5083 (Farm & Garden Machinery); 5085 (Industrial Supplies). **Officers:** C. Joe Coote, President.

■ 16549 ■ Tavdi Company, Inc.
300 County Rd.
PO Box 298
Barrington, RI 02806
Phone: (401)245-2932 **Fax:** (401)245-0737
Products: Plastics materials and basic shapes; Chemicals and allied products; Industrial machinery and equipment. **SICs:** 5084 (Industrial Machinery & Equipment); 5162 (Plastics Materials & Basic Shapes); 5169 (Chemicals & Allied Products Nec). **Officers:** Ismail Saltuk, President.

■ 16550 ■ Taylor-Dunn Manufacturing Co.
2114 W Ball Rd.
Anaheim, CA 92804
Phone: (714)956-4040
Free: (800)688-8680 **Fax:** (714)956-3130
E-mail: wctd@aol.com
URL: http://www.taylor-dunn.com
Products: Electric industrial and commercial vehicles including burden carriers, tow tractors, and personnel carriers. **SICs:** 5084 (Industrial Machinery & Equipment); 5012 (Automobiles & Other Motor Vehicles). **Est:** 1949. **Officers:** Tim Everett.

■ 16551 ■ Robert Taylor & Sons, Inc.
381 W Ironwood Dr.
South Salt Lake, UT 84115
Phone: (801)486-1335 **Fax:** (801)486-0206
Products: Industrial equipment. **SIC:** 5084 (Industrial Machinery & Equipment). **Est:** 1932. **Sales:** $5,000,000 (2000). **Emp:** 28. **Officers:** Bob Taylor.

■ 16552 ■ TCI Machinery Inc.
1720 Industrial Pke.
PO Box 939
Gastonia, NC 28053
Phone: (704)867-8331 **Fax:** (704)861-1016
E-mail: tci@tcimachinery.com
URL: http://www.tcimachinery.com
Products: Textile machinery and parts; Battery powered industrial vehicle equipment and parts. **SIC:** 5084 (Industrial Machinery & Equipment). **Est:** 1988. **Emp:** 24. **Officers:** Hannes Charen, CEO.

■ 16553 ■ TEC Industrial
PO Box 4770
Davenport, IA 52808
Phone: (319)323-3233 **Fax:** (319)323-5161
Products: Motors; Motor repairs; Hoists and hoist parts. **SIC:** 5084 (Industrial Machinery & Equipment). **Est:** 1939. **Sales:** $15,000,000 (2000). **Emp:** 150. **Officers:** Rich Harris, Vice President. **Former Name:** Industrial Engineering Equipment Co.

■ 16554 ■ TechniStar Corp.
1198 Boston Ave.
Longmont, CO 80501
Phone: (303)651-0188 **Fax:** (303)651-5600
Products: Robotic-based, flexible automation systems for food packaging and industrial use. **SIC:** 5084 (Industrial Machinery & Equipment). **Sales:** $12,000,000 (2000). **Emp:** 80. **Officers:** Glenn Maddalon, CEO & President.

■ 16555 ■ Tekmatex Inc.
PO Box 667429
Charlotte, NC 28266
Phone: (704)394-5131 **Fax:** (704)393-5008
Products: Woodworking machinery; Textile machinery. **SIC:** 5084 (Industrial Machinery & Equipment). **Est:** 1962. **Sales:** $95,000,000 (2000). **Emp:** 51. **Officers:** Yoichi Ishi, President; Robert H. Meadows.

■ 16556 ■ Televan Sales Inc.
5451 Sylvia Ave.
Dearborn Heights, MI 48125
Phone: (313)292-7150
Free: (800)886-7151 **Fax:** (313)292-7153
Products: Hydraulic components, including pumps, valves, cylinders, hose assemblies and power units. **SIC:** 5084 (Industrial Machinery & Equipment). **Est:** 1949. **Sales:** $1,500,000 (2000). **Emp:** 10. **Officers:** Daniel Dismondy.

■ 16557 ■ Ternes Register System
4851 White Bear Pkwy.
St. Paul, MN 55110-3325
Phone: (612)633-2361 **Fax:** (612)633-2373
Products: Printing equipment, including benders and punches. **SIC:** 5084 (Industrial Machinery & Equipment). **Sales:** $6,000,000 (2000). **Emp:** 80. **Officers:** James N. Ternes, President; Eric C. Ternes, Vice President; David S. Martin, Dir. of Marketing; Diane Prescott, Personnel Mgr.

■ 16558 ■ TES (USA) Corp.
1 World Trade Ctr., Ste. 1147
New York, NY 10048
Phone: (212)775-0555 **Fax:** (212)524-0970
Products: Pumps and pumping equipment. **SIC:** 5084
(Industrial Machinery & Equipment).

■ 16559 ■ Tetra Laval Convenience Food Inc.
PO Box 358
Avon, MA 02322
Phone: (508)588-2600 **Fax:** (508)588-1791
Products: Restaurant and commercial foodservice
equipment and supplies. **SIC:** 5084 (Industrial
Machinery & Equipment). **Sales:** $200,000,000 (2000).
Emp: 150.

■ 16560 ■ Textiles South Inc.
10100 NW 116th Way
Miami, FL 33178
Phone: (305)887-9191 **Fax:** (305)887-3339
Products: Textile industries machinery. **SIC:** 5084
(Industrial Machinery & Equipment). **Sales:** $3,000,000
(2000). **Emp:** 8. **Officers:** Jay Grossman, President.

■ 16561 ■ Think and Tinker Ltd.
PO Box 408
Monument, CO 80132
Phone: (719)488-9640 **Fax:** (719)481-0464
Products: Printed circuit board prototyping equipment
and supplies—etchers, dry film, laminators and plating
equipment; Carbide cutting tools. **SIC:** 5084 (Industrial
Machinery & Equipment). **Officers:** Ron Reed,
President.

**■ 16562 ■ Thompson and Johnson Equipment
Company Inc.**
6926 Fly Rd.
East Syracuse, NY 13057
Phone: (315)437-2881 **Fax:** (315)437-5034
E-mail: tjequip@aol.com
URL: http://www.thompsonjohnson.com
Products: Forklifts; Skid steerloaders; Industrial
batteries and chargers; Industrial floor sweepers and
scrubbers. **SIC:** 5084 (Industrial Machinery &
Equipment). **Est:** 1954. **Sales:** $21,000,000 (2000).
Emp: 108. **Officers:** David Schneckenburger,
President.

■ 16563 ■ Thomson National Press Co.
115 Dean Ave.
Franklin, MA 02038
Phone: (508)528-2000 **Fax:** (508)528-6869
Products: Die cutting equipment; Foil stamping
equipment. **SIC:** 5084 (Industrial Machinery &
Equipment). **Est:** 1923. **Sales:** $5,000,000 (2000).
Emp: 25. **Officers:** A.F. St. Andre, President; Richard
Cutter; Janet Giorgio.

■ 16564 ■ Tilia, Inc.
568 Howard St., 2nd Fl.
San Francisco, CA 94105
Phone: (415)243-9890
Free: (800)777-5452 **Fax:** (415)777-2634
Products: Vacuum packaging machines. **SIC:** 5064
(Electrical Appliances—Television & Radio). **Est:** 1985.
Sales: $18,000,000 (2000). **Emp:** 30. **Officers:** Linda
S. Graebner, President; Delores Silva, CFO; Chris
Johnson, Dir. of Marketing.

■ 16565 ■ Tool Service Corp.
PO Box 26248
Milwaukee, WI 53226
Phone: (414)476-7600
Products: Abrasive, carbide, and cutting tools. **SIC:**
5084 (Industrial Machinery & Equipment). **Est:** 1945.
Sales: $18,000,000 (2000). **Emp:** 50. **Officers:** Ross
R. Conklin, President.

■ 16566 ■ Toolkraft Distributing
352 Longhill St.
Springfield, MA 01108
Phone: (413)737-7331 **Fax:** (413)736-7701
Products: Stationary woodworking power tools. **SIC:**
5084 (Industrial Machinery & Equipment). **Sales:**
$1,000,000 (2000). **Emp:** 4. **Officers:** Clement J.
Deliso Sr., Owner.

■ 16567 ■ Toombs Truck and Equipment Co.
1800 Walcutt Rd.
Columbus, OH 43228-9612
Phone: (614)876-1181 **Fax:** (614)876-1135
Products: Equipment for trucks and diggers. **SIC:**
5084 (Industrial Machinery & Equipment). **Est:** 1932.
Sales: $10,000,000 (2000). **Emp:** 33. **Officers:**
Richard Thut, Vice President.

■ 16568 ■ Tornos Technologies U.S. Corp.
PO Box 325
Brookfield, CT 06804-0325
Phone: (203)775-4319 **Fax:** (203)775-4281
Products: Swiss screw machines. **SIC:** 5084
(Industrial Machinery & Equipment). **Est:** 1959. **Sales:**
$16,000,000 (2000). **Emp:** 32. **Officers:** Thomas F.
Dierks, President & Treasurer.

■ 16569 ■ Toshiba Tungaloy America Inc.
1375 E Irving Park Rd.
Itasca, IL 60143
Phone: (630)285-9500
Free: (800)542-3222 **Fax:** (630)285-9523
Products: Metal cutting machine tools. **SIC:** 5084
(Industrial Machinery & Equipment). **Sales:**
$15,000,000 (2000). **Emp:** 60. **Officers:** Shuji
Washida, President; Tom Krakowiak, Controller.

■ 16570 ■ Tower Equipment Company Inc.
385 Front St. N, Ste. 201
Issaquah, WA 98027-2929
Phone: (425)889-8886 **Fax:** (425)867-3924
Products: Pumps and valves; Engineering supplies.
SICs: 5084 (Industrial Machinery & Equipment); 5049
(Professional Equipment Nec). **Est:** 1950. **Sales:**
$1,000,000 (2000). **Emp:** 4. **Officers:** Raymond H.
Svenson, President & Chairman of the Board.

■ 16571 ■ Towlift Inc.
1395 Valley Belt Rd.
Cleveland, OH 44131
Phone: (216)749-6800 **Fax:** (216)749-0873
URL: http://www.towlift.com
Products: Forklift equipment. **SIC:** 5084 (Industrial
Machinery & Equipment). **Est:** 1965. **Sales:**
$25,000,000 (1999). **Emp:** 240. **Officers:** David H.
Cannon, President; David Bongorno, VP of Finance;
Joe Buchtinec, VP of Sales.

■ 16572 ■ T.R. Trading Co.
PO Box 310279
New Braunfels, TX 78131
Phone: (512)629-9203 **Fax:** (512)620-0470
Products: General industrial machinery; Electronic
components; Incinerators; Filters; Industrial sewing
machines; Marine supplies (dunnage). **SIC:** 5084
(Industrial Machinery & Equipment). **Est:** 1986. **Emp:**
4. **Officers:** William T. Hovestadt, President.

■ 16573 ■ Trade America
1862 Akron-Peninsula Rd.
Akron, OH 44313
Phone: (330)923-5300
Products: Industrial trucks; Tires; Medical rubber
goods; Rubber machinery; Farm machinery. **SICs:**
5084 (Industrial Machinery & Equipment); 5047
(Medical & Hospital Equipment); 5014 (Tires & Tubes);
5083 (Farm & Garden Machinery). **Officers:** Michael J.
Janovic, President.

■ 16574 ■ Transco Industries Inc.
PO Box 20429
Portland, OR 97294
Phone: (503)256-1955 **Fax:** (503)256-0723
Products: Mining machinery and equipment;
Conveying systems and vehicle washing equipment.
SIC: 5084 (Industrial Machinery & Equipment).

■ 16575 ■ TransLogic Corp.
10825 E 47th Ave.
Denver, CO 80239
Phone: (303)371-7770
Free: (800)525-1841 **Fax:** (303)373-7932
Products: conveyor transport systems; Pneumatic
tube systems. **SIC:** 5084 (Industrial Machinery &
Equipment). **Sales:** $60,000,000 (2000). **Emp:** 270.
Officers: Charlie Kegley, CEO & President; Bob
Rasmussen, CFO.

**■ 16576 ■ Transmission Equipment
International Inc.**
134 S Turnpike Rd.
Wallingford, CT 06492
Phone: (203)269-8751 **Fax:** (203)284-8349
Products: Industrial machines and parts. **SIC:** 5084
(Industrial Machinery & Equipment). **Est:** 1948. **Sales:**
$2,000,000 (2000). **Emp:** 8. **Officers:** James
Gambardella, President. **Former Name:** Transmission
Equipment Co.

■ 16577 ■ Transupport Inc.
53 Turbine Way
Merrimack, NH 03054-4161
Phone: (603)424-3111 **Fax:** (603)424-1888
URL: http://www.transupport.com
Products: Gas turbine engines; Fuel boost pumps;
Governors and controls. **SIC:** 5084 (Industrial
Machinery & Equipment). **Est:** 1972. **Sales:**
$10,000,000 (2000). **Emp:** 5. **Officers:** Harold Foote,
President; Ken Foote, VP of Marketing.

■ 16578 ■ Tri Lift
180 Main St.
New Haven, CT 06512
Phone: (203)467-1686
Products: Forklifts. **SIC:** 5084 (Industrial Machinery &
Equipment). **Sales:** $11,000,000 (2000). **Emp:** 72.
Officers: S. Murgo, President; Nicholas J. Carolla, Dir.
of Marketing.

■ 16579 ■ Tri-Line Corp.
250 Summit Point Dr.
Henrietta, NY 14467-9607
Phone: (716)377-3370 **Fax:** (716)377-7314
Products: Hydraulic and pneumatic equipment. **SIC:**
5084 (Industrial Machinery & Equipment).

■ 16580 ■ Tri-Star Industrial Supply Inc.
10435 Baur Blvd.
St. Louis, MO 63132
Phone: (314)997-0600 **Fax:** (314)997-1929
Products: Industrial tools. **SIC:** 5084 (Industrial
Machinery & Equipment). **Sales:** $20,000,000 (1994).
Emp: 67. **Officers:** George L. Sachs, President.

■ 16581 ■ Triangle Industrial Sales, Inc.
3000 Town Ctr., No. 501
Southfield, MI 48075-1173
Phone: (248)352-6688 **Fax:** (248)352-6758
Products: Automotive production equipment. **SIC:**
5084 (Industrial Machinery & Equipment).

■ 16582 ■ Trinet Industries Inc.
19811 Colima Rd., No. 410
Walnut, CA 91789
Phone: (714)594-4676 **Fax:** (714)594-1409
Products: Packaging machinery; Steel mill equipment.
SIC: 5084 (Industrial Machinery & Equipment).
Officers: Howard Pak, CEO.

■ 16583 ■ Triumph Twist Drill Co.
1 Precision Plz.
Crystal Lake, IL 60014
Phone: (815)459-6250 **Fax:** (815)369-4763
Products: Drilling bits. **SIC:** 5084 (Industrial Machinery
& Equipment). **Est:** 1961. **Sales:** $30,000,000 (2000).
Emp: 499. **Officers:** Mark Harwell.

**■ 16584 ■ Tru-Form Tool and Manufacturing
Industries Inc.**
14511 Anson Ave.
Santa Fe Springs, CA 90670
Phone: (562)802-2041
Free: (800)262-6266 **Fax:** (562)924-8896
URL: http://www.tru-form.com
Products: Custom clips, brackets, wire forms, metal
stampings, springs, and assemblies. **SIC:** 5085
(Industrial Supplies). **Sales:** $10,000,000 (1999). **Emp:**
90. **Officers:** Vern Hildebrandt; Vern Hildebrandt Jr.;
Kathy Teixeira, Estimator.

■ 16585 ■ Tynan Equipment Co.
5926 Stockberger Pl.
Indianapolis, IN 46241
Phone: (317)247-8474 **Fax:** (317)247-6843
Products: Industrial trucks; Fork lifts. **SIC:** 5084
(Industrial Machinery & Equipment). **Est:** 1960. **Sales:**

$6,000,000 (2000). **Emp:** 50. **Officers:** Michael J. Tynan, President; Linda Carver, Controller.

■ 16586 ■ **Udelson Equipment Co.**
1400 Brookpark Rd.
Cleveland, OH 44109
Phone: (216)398-7300
Products: Used heavy equipment. **SIC:** 5084 (Industrial Machinery & Equipment). **Est:** 1920. **Sales:** $32,000,000 (2000). **Emp:** 100. **Officers:** Alan Udelson, CEO; Allen Myers, CFO.

■ 16587 ■ **Union Carbide Corp., IPX Services**
Bldg. 82, Rm. 426
PO Box 8004
South Charleston, WV 25303
Phone: (304)747-7000
Products: Industrial equipment and spare parts; Valve and pipe fittings; Electronic equipment and supplies; Industrial petrochemicals. **SICs:** 5084 (Industrial Machinery & Equipment); 5085 (Industrial Supplies); 5172 (Petroleum Products Nec); 5063 (Electrical Apparatus & Equipment). **Officers:** Kurt A. Heringhausen, Manager.

■ 16588 ■ **United Conveyor Corp.**
2100 Norman Drive W
Waukegan, IL 60085
Phone: (847)473-5900 **Fax:** (847)473-5959
E-mail: info@unitedconveyor.com
URL: http://www.unitedconveyor.com
Products: Conveyors; Abrasive material handling systems. **SIC:** 5084 (Industrial Machinery & Equipment). **Est:** 1920. **Sales:** $50,000,000 (2000). **Emp:** 350. **Officers:** D.N. Basler, President; David Hoyem, Treasurer; D.E. Charhut, VP of Product Sales & Technology; Fred Schroeder, Controller.

■ 16589 ■ **United Engines Inc.**
PO Box 75079
Oklahoma City, OK 73147
Phone: (405)947-3321 **Fax:** (405)947-3406
Products: Remanufacture and modify heavy equipment transmissions and diesel engines. **SIC:** 5084 (Industrial Machinery & Equipment). **Sales:** $121,000,000 (2000). **Emp:** 140. **Officers:** Jay Morton, President.

■ 16590 ■ **U.S. Amada Ltd.**
7025 Firestone Blvd.
Buena Park, CA 90621
Phone: (714)670-2121
Products: Sheet metalworking machinery. **SIC:** 5084 (Industrial Machinery & Equipment).

■ 16591 ■ **U.S. Equipment Co.**
20580 Hoover Rd.
Detroit, MI 48205
Phone: (313)526-8300 **Fax:** (313)526-5303
Products: Used metalworking production machinery. **SIC:** 5084 (Industrial Machinery & Equipment). **Est:** 1947. **Sales:** $12,000,000 (2000). **Emp:** 40. **Officers:** George A. Simon II; President.

■ 16592 ■ **U.S. Extrusion Tool and Die**
1110 Trumbull Ave.
Girard, OH 44420
Phone: (330)759-2944 **Fax:** (330)759-8166
Products: Aluminum extrusion dies. **SIC:** 5084 (Industrial Machinery & Equipment). **Est:** 1957. **Sales:** $2,000,000 (2000). **Emp:** 40. **Officers:** A. Papiernik, President.

■ 16593 ■ **U.S. International**
801 N Curtis Ave.
Alhambra, CA 91801
Phone: (626)281-1804 **Fax:** (626)281-0633
Products: Diesel engine parts. **SIC:** 5084 (Industrial Machinery & Equipment). **Est:** 1976. **Officers:** Dennis Harrington.

■ 16594 ■ **U.S. Machinery, Inc.**
1775 S West St.
PO Box 13356
Wichita, KS 67213
Phone: (316)942-2120 **Fax:** (316)942-2206
E-mail: info@usmweb.com
URL: http://www.usmweb.com
Products: Skidster and rubber track loaders. **SIC:** 5084 (Industrial Machinery & Equipment).

■ 16595 ■ **Universal Process Equipment Inc.**
1180 Rte. 130 S
Robbinsville, NJ 08691
Phone: (609)443-4545 **Fax:** (609)259-0644
E-mail: upe@upe.com
URL: http://www.upe.com
Products: Used processing equipment. **SIC:** 5084 (Industrial Machinery & Equipment). **Sales:** $20,000,000 (2000). **Emp:** 75. **Officers:** Ronald H. Gale, President; Jan Gale, VP & CFO; Violet Persichilli; Jeffrey Shapiro, COO.

■ 16596 ■ **Vacuum Pump Systems Inc.**
PO Box 1826
Gainesville, GA 30503-1826
Phone: (404)532-0260 **Fax:** (404)536-1005
Products: Vacuum pumps and motors. **SIC:** 5084 (Industrial Machinery & Equipment). **Officers:** Bobby Tow, President.

■ 16597 ■ **Valley Industrial Trucks Inc.**
1152 Meadowbrook St.
Youngstown, OH 44512
Phone: (330)788-4081 **Fax:** (330)788-5432
Products: Fork lifts; Dock levelers; Material handling equipment. **SIC:** 5084 (Industrial Machinery & Equipment). **Est:** 1956. **Sales:** $7,000,000 (2000). **Emp:** 45. **Officers:** Ron Doll, President; D. D'Alesio, VP of Marketing.

■ 16598 ■ **Valley National Gases, Inc.**
1151 Findley St.
Cincinnati, OH 45214
Phone: (513)241-5840 **Fax:** (513)241-0191
Products: Industrial gas welding equipment. **SIC:** 5084 (Industrial Machinery & Equipment). **Emp:** 40. **Officers:** Laurence Bandi, President. **Former Name:** Weldco Inc.

■ 16599 ■ **Valley Welding Supply Co.**
67 43rd St.
Wheeling, WV 26003
Phone: (304)232-1541
E-mail: valgas@vngas.com
Products: Welding products; Industrial gases; Propane; Fire safety equipment; Specialty gases. **SICs:** 5169 (Chemicals & Allied Products Nec); 5084 (Industrial Machinery & Equipment). **Est:** 1962. **Sales:** $100,000,000 (2000). **Emp:** 500. **Officers:** Gary E. West, Chairman of the Board; Lawrence E. Bandi, President & CEO; John Bushwack, Exec. VP & COO; Robert D. Scherich, CFO; K. Crawford, Data Processing Mgr.; Gerald A. McGlumphy, Comptroller.

■ 16600 ■ **Oliver H. Van Horn Company Inc.**
4100 Euphrosine St.
New Orleans, LA 70150
Phone: (504)821-4100
Free: (800)800-7070 **Fax:** (504)822-2449
URL: http://www.ohvanhorn.com
Products: Machine tools; Industrial supplies. **SICs:** 5085 (Industrial Supplies); 5084 (Industrial Machinery & Equipment). **Est:** 1903. **Sales:** $20,000,000 (2000). **Emp:** 75. **Officers:** L.E. Eagan, CEO, e-mail: le@ohvanhorn.com; C.J. Van Horn, President, e-mail: cvh@ohvanhorn.com.

■ 16601 ■ **Veeco Process Metrology**
2650 E Elvira Rd.
Tucson, AZ 85706
Phone: (520)741-1297
Free: (800)366-9956 **Fax:** (520)294-1799
Products: Metrology instruments; Precision optical and magnetic media test measurement equipment; Laser triangulation measurement systems. **SIC:** 5084 (Industrial Machinery & Equipment). **Sales:** $40,000,000 (2000). **Emp:** 125. **Officers:** Edward Braun, President.

■ 16602 ■ **Virginia Carolina Tools Inc.**
PO Box 3488
West Columbia, SC 29169
Phone: (803)791-8691 **Fax:** (803)791-0686
Products: Cutting tools. **SICs:** 5084 (Industrial Machinery & Equipment); 5072 (Hardware). **Emp:** 49.

■ 16603 ■ **Virginia Materials**
3306 Peterson St.
Norfolk, VA 23509
Phone: (757)855-0155
Free: (800)743-0094 **Fax:** (757)857-5631
E-mail: sales@sandblaster.com
URL: http://www.sandblaster.com
Products: Sand blasters; Abrasives. **SICs:** 5084 (Industrial Machinery & Equipment); 5085 (Industrial Supplies). **Est:** 1957. **Sales:** $6,000,000 (1999). **Emp:** 18. **Officers:** John Burns, General Mgr.; Ben Burns, Customer Service Contact. **Alternate Name:** Virginia Materials and Supplies, Inc.

■ 16604 ■ **Jerry K. Vlcek Corp.**
3760 Black Forest Ln.
Yorba Linda, CA 92886
Phone: (714)970-1285 **Fax:** (714)970-9080
Products: Hoses, including rubber; Air compressors; Air-conditioning tools; Garage service equipment; Motor vehicle tools. **SICs:** 5084 (Industrial Machinery & Equipment); 5085 (Industrial Supplies); 5075 (Warm Air Heating & Air-Conditioning); 5087 (Service Establishment Equipment). **Officers:** Jerry K. Vlcek, President.

■ 16605 ■ **Voell Machinery Company Inc.**
PO Box 2103
Waukesha, WI 53187
Phone: (262)786-6640 **Fax:** (262)786-1576
E-mail: vmach@execpc.com
URL: http://www.voellmachinery.com
Products: Industrial machine tools. **SIC:** 5084 (Industrial Machinery & Equipment). **Est:** 1932. **Sales:** $7,000,000 (2000). **Emp:** 13. **Officers:** Robert Voell, President; Tom Voell, Vice President, e-mail: TomV@Voellmachinery.com.

■ 16606 ■ **Vogel Tool & Die Corp.**
1825 N 32nd
Stone Park, IL 60165-1003
Phone: (708)345-0160 **Fax:** (708)345-0535
E-mail: info@vogeltool.com
URL: http://www.vogeltool.com
Products: Tools for fabricating picket fence; Notching pipe and tube; Cut off, piercing and slotting for tube. **SICs:** 5085 (Industrial Supplies); 5084 (Industrial Machinery & Equipment). **Est:** 1938. **Sales:** $3,000,000 (2000). **Emp:** 42. **Officers:** H. Loren Vogel.

■ 16607 ■ **Volland Electric Equipment Corp.**
75 Innsbruck Dr.
Buffalo, NY 14227
Phone: (716)656-9900
Free: (800)782-6877 **Fax:** (716)656-8899
E-mail: info@volland.com
URL: http://www.volland.com
Products: Industrial machine motors; Cranes and hoists; Reactors; Generators and reducers; Transformers. **SIC:** 5084 (Industrial Machinery & Equipment). **Est:** 1943. **Sales:** $15,000,000 (2000). **Emp:** 85. **Officers:** Ronald Graham, e-mail: rgraham@volland.com.

■ 16608 ■ **Voorhies Supply Company Inc.**
401 W St. Peter St.
New Iberia, LA 70560
Phone: (318)364-2431 **Fax:** (318)365-0548
Products: Industrial tools; Welding equipment; Lawn mowers; Metal; Pipes. **SICs:** 5084 (Industrial Machinery & Equipment); 5051 (Metals Service Centers & Offices); 5085 (Industrial Supplies); 5083 (Farm & Garden Machinery). **Est:** 1949. **Sales:** $10,000,000 (2000). **Emp:** 70. **Officers:** Paul E. Voorhies II, President; Preston J. Guillotte, Treasurer; Ken McGrew, Vice President.

■ 16609 ■ Voss Equipment Inc.
15241 Commercial Ave.
Harvey, IL 60426
Phone: (708)596-7000 **Fax:** (708)596-6791
E-mail: yalevoss@aol.com
Products: Fork-lifting trucks. **SIC:** 5084 (Industrial Machinery & Equipment). **Sales:** $20,000,000 (2000). **Emp:** 85. **Officers:** Peter W. Voss Jr., President; Thomas J Mateja, Controller; George Sefer, Dir. of Marketing & Sales; Peter W. Voss III, Operations Mgr.

■ 16610 ■ WAFAB International
208 Lindbergh Ave.
Livermore, CA 94550
Phone: (925)455-5252 **Fax:** (925)455-5351
Products: Equipment for the wafer fabrication industry; Wet processing equipment. **SIC:** 5084 (Industrial Machinery & Equipment).

■ 16611 ■ Wagner Hydraulic Equipment Co.
10528 Venice Blvd.
Culver City, CA 90232-3308
Phone: (562)272-2091 **Fax:** (562)842-3905
E-mail: wagnerhydr@aol.com
Products: Hydraulic pumps, valves, blowers, wheels, and strainers. **SIC:** 5084 (Industrial Machinery & Equipment). **Est:** 1952. **Sales:** $1,500,000 (2000). **Emp:** 5. **Officers:** William R. Wagner, President; Jeanine A. Herman, CFO; Roger Wagner.

■ 16612 ■ Wallace Coast Machinery Co.
5225 7th St. E
Tacoma, WA 98424
Phone: (253)922-7433
Products: Custom machinery. **SIC:** 5084 (Industrial Machinery & Equipment). **Sales:** $4,000,000 (1994). **Emp:** 5. **Officers:** Darrell W. Jesse Sr., CEO & CFO.

■ 16613 ■ Waltman's Inc.
PO Box 3648
Modesto, CA 95352
Phone: (209)522-1001
Products: Engines and machines. **SICs:** 5013 (Motor Vehicle Supplies & New Parts); 5084 (Industrial Machinery & Equipment). **Est:** 1958. **Sales:** $700,000 (2000). **Emp:** 10. **Officers:** D.G. Wallace, President; Lisa Adams, CFO.

■ 16614 ■ Ward Technologies Inc.
5010 S Ash Ave
Tempe, AZ 85282
Phone: (480)831-5500 **Fax:** (480)839-5422
Products: Constant temperature baths; Semiconductor process equipment; Tanks. **SIC:** 5084 (Industrial Machinery & Equipment). **Sales:** $2,000,000 (1999). **Emp:** 5. **Officers:** Howard L. Ward, President.

■ 16615 ■ Warehouse Equipment Inc.
2500 York Rd.
Elk Grove Village, IL 60007
Phone: (847)595-9400 **Fax:** (847)595-2126
E-mail: rtrenu@weinet.com
URL: http://www.weinet.com
Products: Material handling equipment. **SIC:** 5084 (Industrial Machinery & Equipment). **Est:** 1970. **Sales:** $100,000,000 (2000). **Emp:** 150. **Officers:** M. Scheck, President; Kevin O'Leary, Controller; Robert A. Trenn, VP of Marketing.

■ 16616 ■ WEB Machinery Co.
PO Box 248
Jamestown, NY 14701
Phone: (716)488-1935
Products: New and used metal and wood working equipment. **SIC:** 5084 (Industrial Machinery & Equipment). **Est:** 1925. **Sales:** $6,000,000 (2000). **Emp:** 15. **Officers:** Myron J. Koplik, President.

■ 16617 ■ Weber Industries Inc.
84M New Hampshire Ave.
St. Louis, MO 63123
Phone: (314)631-9200 **Fax:** (314)631-3738
Products: Pumps. **SIC:** 5084 (Industrial Machinery & Equipment).

■ 16618 ■ Max Weiss Company Inc.
8625 W Bradley Rd.
Milwaukee, WI 53224-2893
Phone: (414)355-8220
Free: (888)649-3477 **Fax:** (414)355-4698
URL: http://www.maxweiss.com
Products: Structural steel forming and rolling; Fabricator. **SICs:** 5084 (Industrial Machinery & Equipment); 5085 (Industrial Supplies). **Est:** 1946. **Sales:** $3,500,000 (2000). **Emp:** 25. **Officers:** Raymond Weiss.

■ 16619 ■ Welders Equipment Company Inc.
PO Box 2609
Victoria, TX 77902
Phone: (512)578-0307
Products: Welding equipment. **SIC:** 5084 (Industrial Machinery & Equipment). **Est:** 1929. **Sales:** $40,000,000 (2000). **Emp:** 130. **Officers:** David P. Engel, President; Robert Lobe, Exec. VP of Finance.

■ 16620 ■ Weldon Tool Co.
6030 Carey Dr.
Cleveland, OH 44125
Phone: (216)642-5454 **Fax:** (216)229-4910
Products: Cutting tools. **SICs:** 5084 (Industrial Machinery & Equipment); 5072 (Hardware). **Est:** 1918. **Emp:** 300. **Officers:** George Briggs.

■ 16621 ■ Wenger Manufacturing Inc.
PO Box 130
Sabetha, KS 66534
Phone: (785)284-2133
Free: (800)347-3594 **Fax:** (785)284-3771
E-mail: marketing@wenger.com
URL: http://www.wenger.com
Products: Extrusion cooking systems for foods and feeds. **SIC:** 5084 (Industrial Machinery & Equipment). **Est:** 1935. **Sales:** $40,000,000 (2000). **Emp:** 250. **Officers:** L.G. Wenger, President; G.L. Howard, CFO.

■ 16622 ■ Werres Corp.
807 E South St.
Frederick, MD 21701
Phone: (301)620-4000 **Fax:** (301)770-6043
Products: Material handling equipment, including forklifts, conveyors, and stackers. **SIC:** 5084 (Industrial Machinery & Equipment). **Sales:** $40,000,000 (2000). **Emp:** 100. **Officers:** Dan Senecal, President.

■ 16623 ■ West Coast Machine Tools
PO Box 88179
Seattle, WA 98138
Phone: (253)872-7540 **Fax:** (253)872-7544
Products: Metal working machine tools. **SIC:** 5084 (Industrial Machinery & Equipment). **Sales:** $3,000,000 (2000). **Emp:** 10. **Officers:** S. Krom, President.

■ 16624 ■ Westco./DoAll Industrial Distribution
166 Riverside Industrial Pkwy.
Portland, ME 04103-1431
Phone: (207)774-5812 **Fax:** (207)878-7607
Products: Industrial tools. Bandsaw machines and blades. **SIC:** 5084 (Industrial Machinery & Equipment). **Emp:** 7. **Former Name:** Gage Co. Westco Industrial Distribution.

■ 16625 ■ Western Branch Diesel Inc.
PO Box 7788
Portsmouth, VA 23707-0788
Phone: (757)673-7000 **Fax:** (757)673-7190
Products: Generators and diesel engines. **SIC:** 5084 (Industrial Machinery & Equipment). **Est:** 1946. **Sales:** $48,000,000 (1999). **Emp:** 281. **Officers:** Herbert A. Haneman Jr., President; R.K. Butler, CFO; C. Gould, Dir. of Marketing & Sales; Neil Blair, Dir. of Data Processing; George Schmidt, Dir. of Data Processing.

■ 16626 ■ Western Fluid Power
4242 S Eagleson Rd., Unit 108
Boise, ID 83705
Phone: (208)362-2032 **Fax:** (208)362-2096
Products: Hydraulic and pneumatic equipment and supplies. **SIC:** 5084 (Industrial Machinery & Equipment).

■ 16627 ■ Western Fluid Power
3410 W 11th St.
Eugene, OR 97402
Phone: (541)484-9666 **Fax:** (541)345-4161
Products: Fluid power products. **SIC:** 5084 (Industrial Machinery & Equipment).

■ 16628 ■ Western Fluid Power
4309 NW St. Helens Rd.
Portland, OR 97210
Phone: (503)228-6666
Free: (800)783-5843 **Fax:** (503)228-7318
Products: Cylinders; Power units; Filters, motors, pumps, and valves. **SICs:** 5084 (Industrial Machinery & Equipment); 5085 (Industrial Supplies). **Est:** 1970. **Emp:** 50.

■ 16629 ■ Westmark Industries Inc.
6701 McEwan Rd.
Lake Oswego, OR 97035
Phone: (503)620-0945 **Fax:** (503)639-6749
Products: Pressure sensitive labels; label printing machinery. **SIC:** 5084 (Industrial Machinery & Equipment). **Officers:** Michael Offer, President.

■ 16630 ■ Whitten Pumps Inc.
502 County Line Rd.
Delano, CA 93215
Phone: (805)725-0250 **Fax:** (805)725-6553
Products: Pumps. **SIC:** 5084 (Industrial Machinery & Equipment). **Est:** 1914. **Sales:** $7,100,000 (2000). **Emp:** 80. **Officers:** R.E. Whitten, President; D.E. Dyar, Secretary.

■ 16631 ■ Wickman Corp.
10325 Capital Ave.
Oak Park, MI 48237
Phone: (248)548-3822 **Fax:** (248)548-3832
Products: Diamond grinding wheels. **SIC:** 5084 (Industrial Machinery & Equipment). **Est:** 1948. **Sales:** $10,000,000 (2000). **Emp:** 75. **Officers:** Ben F. Stormes II, President; Jeffrey C. Kelchner, VP of Finance; John Guenther, VP of Marketing.

■ 16632 ■ Wigglesworth Machine Co.
PO Box 166
East Boston, MA 02128
Phone: (617)567-7210 **Fax:** (617)561-0265
Products: Heavy machinery, including drills and grinders. **SIC:** 5084 (Industrial Machinery & Equipment). **Est:** 1928. **Sales:** $2,000,000 (2000). **Emp:** 10. **Officers:** Albert G. Wigglesworth Jr., President; Brian D. Besse, Controller.

■ 16633 ■ A.R. Wilfley and Sons Inc.
PO Box 2330
Denver, CO 80201
Phone: (303)779-1777 **Fax:** (303)779-1277
Products: Centrifugal pumps and pumping equipment. **SIC:** 5084 (Industrial Machinery & Equipment). **Sales:** $27,000,000 (2000). **Emp:** 175. **Officers:** Michael Wilfley, President.

■ 16634 ■ Willamette Electric Products Co.
810 N Graham St.
Portland, OR 97227
Phone: (503)288-7361
Free: (800)949-7361 **Fax:** (503)288-7684
Products: Reand sells automobile and electrical parts—clutches and water pumps. **SIC:** 5084 (Industrial Machinery & Equipment). **Sales:** $5,000,000 (2000). **Emp:** 98. **Officers:** Elliott Quinn, Owner.

■ 16635 ■ W.W. Williams Co.
835 W Goodale Blvd.
Columbus, OH 43212
Phone: (614)228-5000 **Fax:** (614)228-4490
Products: Industrial machinery. **SIC:** 5084 (Industrial Machinery & Equipment). **Est:** 1912. **Sales:** $100,000,000 (1999). **Emp:** 1,100. **Officers:** Robert G. Peyton, President; William S. Williams, CEO & Chairman of the Board.

■ 16636 ■ Williams Equipment Co.
14808 W 117th St.
PO Box 3237
Olathe, KS 66063
Phone: (913)764-9326 **Fax:** (913)764-8372
Products: Hydraulic and pneumatic equipment,

including pumps, gauges, and controllers. **SIC:** 5084 (Industrial Machinery & Equipment).

■ **16637** ■ **Wilson Co.**
PO Box 9100
Addison, TX 75001
Phone: (972)931-8666   **Fax:** (972)248-7472
E-mail: info@wilson-company.com
URL: http://www.wilson-company.com
Products: Air and hydraulic equipment. **SIC:** 5084 (Industrial Machinery & Equipment). **Est:** 1965. **Sales:** $25,000,000 (2000). **Emp:** 90. **Officers:** Richard A. Bills, President; Cheryl Marshall, Vice President; Jerry Herrin, VP of Marketing.

■ **16638** ■ **Wilton Corp.**
300 S Hicks Rd.
Palatine, IL 60067
Phone: (847)934-6000   **Fax:** (847)934-6730
Products: Industrial equipment and machinery, including vises and clamps, drilling, sawing, and grinding equipment, abrasives, and power brushes. **SICs:** 5084 (Industrial Machinery & Equipment); 5072 (Hardware).

■ **16639** ■ **Winchester Equipment Co.**
620 Penn Ave.
Winchester, VA 22601
Phone: (540)667-2244
Products: Forklifts. **SIC:** 5084 (Industrial Machinery & Equipment). **Est:** 1957. **Sales:** $4,900,000 (2000). **Emp:** 27. **Officers:** Douglas C. Rinkler, CEO & CFO; Harold F. Ford, Dir. of Marketing.

■ **16640** ■ **Windmoeller and Hoelscher Corp.**
23 New England Way
Lincoln, RI 02865
Phone: (401)333-2770
Free: (800)854-8702   **Fax:** (401)333-6491
E-mail: info@whcorp.com
Products: Printing presses; Extruders; Converting machinery; Bag-production machinery. **SIC:** 5084 (Industrial Machinery & Equipment). **Est:** 1977. **Sales:** $75,000,000 (2000). **Emp:** 50. **Officers:** James K. Feeney, President & Treasurer; Henry F. Taylor, VP of Finance; Hans A. Deamer, Sr. VP of Sales.

■ **16641** ■ **Windsor Industries Inc. (Englewood, Colorado)**
1351 W Stanford Ave.
Englewood, CO 80110
Phone: (303)762-1800   **Fax:** (303)762-0817
Products: Floor cleaning machines and equipment. **SIC:** 5084 (Industrial Machinery & Equipment). **Sales:** $55,000,000 (2000). **Emp:** 300. **Officers:** Carl Hatton, President.

■ **16642** ■ **Wisconsin Bearing**
206 Hood St.
La Crosse, WI 54601
Phone: (608)785-1200
Products: Belts, pulleys, shifts, motors, and chains. **SIC:** 5084 (Industrial Machinery & Equipment).

■ **16643** ■ **Wisconsin Lift Truck Corp.**
3125 Intertech Drive
Brookfield, WI 53045
Phone: (262)781-8010
Free: (800)236-2379   **Fax:** (262)781-2531
E-mail: wltmktg@wisconsinlift.com
URL: http://www.wisconsinlift.com
Products: Industrial machinery, including forklift trucks, aerial equipment, skid steer loaders, rough terrain lift trucks, side loaders, and hand pallet trucks; Industrial cleaning equipment; Mini excavators. **SIC:** 5084 (Industrial Machinery & Equipment). **Est:** 1962. **Sales:** $100,000,000 (1999). **Emp:** 570. **Officers:** Otto J. Wolter, CEO & President, e-mail: owolter@wisconsinlift.com; Steven Kletzien, VP & CFO, e-mail: kletzien@wisconsinlift.com; Dave Oldenburg, Marketing Mgr., e-mail: doldenbu@wisconsinlift.com; Sharon Cerny, Dir of Human Resources, e-mail: scerny@wisconsinlift.com; Shawn Presser, Manager; Jeff Keough, Marketing & Sales Mgr.; Bill Bywater, Customer Service Contact; John Wolter, Sales Mgr., e-mail: jwolter@wisconsinlift.com.

■ **16644** ■ **Wisner Manufacturing Inc.**
1165 Globe Ave.
Mountainside, NJ 07092
Phone: (908)233-4200   **Fax:** (908)233-7331
Products: Large machinery, including milk machines. **SIC:** 5084 (Industrial Machinery & Equipment). **Est:** 1908. **Sales:** $7,000,000 (2000). **Emp:** 21. **Officers:** Tom Malatesta, CEO.

■ **16645** ■ **WMT Machine Tool Company Inc.**
600 Hollister Rd.
Teterboro, NJ 07608
Phone: (201)288-2400
Products: Machinery, including hand and power tools. **SIC:** 5084 (Industrial Machinery & Equipment). **Est:** 1936. **Sales:** $6,000,000 (2000). **Emp:** 20. **Officers:** Neal McKean, President.

■ **16646** ■ **Wolff Corp.**
11204 W Greenfield
Milwaukee, WI 53214
Phone: (414)257-2555   **Fax:** (414)771-8211
E-mail: wolff@execpc.com
Products: Rotary gear pumps; Hydraulic valves and pumps; Computer parts. **SICs:** 5084 (Industrial Machinery & Equipment); 5045 (Computers, Peripherals & Software). **Officers:** Harry Olson, General Mgr.

■ **16647** ■ **Womack Machine**
2010 Shea Rd.
Dallas, TX 75235
Phone: (214)357-3871   **Fax:** (214)350-9322
Products: Hydraulic and pneumatic equipment. **SIC:** 5084 (Industrial Machinery & Equipment).

■ **16648** ■ **Womack Machine**
2300 Wirt Rd.
Houston, TX 77055
Phone: (713)956-6400   **Fax:** (713)956-2539
Products: Hydraulic and pneumatic equipment. **SIC:** 5084 (Industrial Machinery & Equipment).

■ **16649** ■ **Womack Machine Supply**
PO Box 35027
Dallas, TX 75235
Phone: (214)357-3871
Products: Hydraulic and pnuematic machinery. **SIC:** 5084 (Industrial Machinery & Equipment). **Officers:** Robert C. Womack, President; Kenneth Cason, Treasurer.

■ **16650** ■ **World Wide Laser Service Corp.**
1340 W San Pedro St.
PO Box 1940
Gilbert, AZ 85299-1940
Phone: (602)892-8566
Free: (800)815-8566   **Fax:** (602)497-9661
URL: http://www.wlsc.com
Products: Industrial laser marking systems, parts, and repairs. **SIC:** 5084 (Industrial Machinery & Equipment). **Est:** 1986. **Sales:** $5,000,000 (2000). **Emp:** 40. **Officers:** James Souza, President; Alesha Sovza, Sales Contact; Susan Kienzle, Customer Service Contact.

■ **16651** ■ **Wrenn Brungart**
PO Box 410050
Charlotte, NC 28241
Phone: (704)587-1003   **Fax:** (704)588-4266
Products: Material handling equipment and supplies. **SIC:** 5084 (Industrial Machinery & Equipment). **Est:** 1943. **Sales:** $230,000,000 (1999). **Emp:** 1,050. **Officers:** Stan Sewell, President; Courts Holland, VP of Finance; Dan Reed, Data Processing Mgr.; James Holmes, Dir of Personnel.

■ **16652** ■ **A.L. Xander Co. Inc.**
PO Box 98
Corry, PA 16407-0098
Phone: (814)665-8268   **Fax:** (814)664-7343
Products: Hydraulic and pneumatic components and seals. **SIC:** 5084 (Industrial Machinery & Equipment). **Est:** 1952. **Sales:** $9,000,000 (2000). **Emp:** 30. **Officers:** A.L. Xander, President; Debra Poe, Accountant; John Xander, Sales Mgr.; Tom Xander, Admin. Mgr.

■ **16653** ■ **XWW Alloys, Inc.**
6200 N Telegraph Rd.
Dearborn Heights, MI 48127
Phone: (313)274-0500   **Fax:** (313)274-5549
Products: Welding equipment. **SIC:** 5084 (Industrial Machinery & Equipment). **Est:** 1959. **Sales:** $1,000,000 (2000). **Emp:** 14. **Officers:** John J. Everton, CEO; Robert Kujawski, President.

■ **16654** ■ **Yale/Chase Materials Handling, Inc.**
2615 Pellissier Place
PO Box 1231
La Puente, CA 91749
Phone: (562)699-0501   **Fax:** (562)692-6678
Products: Forklifts; Used equipment parts. **SICs:** 5084 (Industrial Machinery & Equipment); 5085 (Industrial Supplies). **Est:** 1993. **Sales:** $30,000,000 (2000). **Emp:** 110. **Officers:** Roger Ketelsleger, CEO; R.D. Paradis, CFO.

■ **16655** ■ **Yancey Machine Tool Co.**
4110 SW Macadam Ave.
Portland, OR 97201
Phone: (503)228-7259   **Fax:** (503)228-8180
Products: Machine tools. **SIC:** 5084 (Industrial Machinery & Equipment). **Est:** 1959. **Sales:** $2,000,000 (2000). **Emp:** 12. **Officers:** R.M. Yancey, President; Grace E. Yancey, Secretary.

■ **16656** ■ **Yang Machine Tool Co.**
4920 E La Palma Ave.
Anaheim, CA 92807
Phone: (714)693-0705
Products: Machining equipment. **SIC:** 5084 (Industrial Machinery & Equipment).

■ **16657** ■ **A.B. Young Cos.**
PO Box 90287
Indianapolis, IN 46290-0287
Phone: (317)844-7001
Free: (800)886-7001   **Fax:** (317)848-2606
E-mail: info@abyoung.com
URL: http://www.abyoung.com
Products: Industrial power and process equipment. **SIC:** 5085 (Industrial Supplies). **Est:** 1952. **Sales:** $13,000,000 (2000). **Emp:** 30. **Officers:** Bruce H. Young, President.

■ **16658** ■ **Zagar Inc.**
24000 Lakeland Blvd.
Cleveland, OH 44132
Phone: (216)731-0500   **Fax:** (216)731-8591
E-mail: sales@zagarinc.com
URL: http://www.zagar.com
Products: Mining machinery, including drills. **SIC:** 5085 (Industrial Supplies). **Est:** 1937. **Sales:** $7,000,000 (2000). **Emp:** 80. **Officers:** John F. Zagar; Randal E. Roberts, Marketing & Sales Mgr.; William Hanigan, Human Resources.

■ **16659** ■ **Zed Group Inc.**
IMC Box 6475
Chelsea, MA 02150
Phone: (617)889-2220   **Fax:** (617)889-0170
E-mail: zedgroup@worldnet.att.net
Products: Soldering irons and machinery; Industrial assembly machinery; Vision magnifiers; High precision hand tools; Magnifiers; Printed circuit board repair kits. **SICs:** 5084 (Industrial Machinery & Equipment); 5085 (Industrial Supplies). **Est:** 1970. **Emp:** 87. **Officers:** Robert Zisa, President; Clifford Watts, Sales/Marketing Contact; Elmer Shirks, Customer Service Contact; Henry Anderson, Human Resources Contact.

■ **16660** ■ **Zima Corp.**
PO Box 6010
Spartanburg, SC 29304
Phone: (864)576-5810   **Fax:** (864)591-1985
Products: Finishing machinery. **SIC:** 5084 (Industrial Machinery & Equipment). **Est:** 1969. **Sales:** $2,000,000 (2000). **Emp:** 27. **Officers:** K. Zimmerli, President; Rudy Mikelonis, Controller; Harry DeLoach, Dir. of Marketing & Sales.

■ 16661 ■ Zimmer Machinery Corp.
PO Box 5561
Spartanburg, SC 29304
Phone: (864)463-4352
Free: (800)458-3194 **Fax:** (864)463-4670
E-mail: info@zimmer-usa.com
URL: http://www.zimmer-usa.com
Products: Textile machinery. **SIC:** 5084 (Industrial Machinery & Equipment). **Est:** 1969. **Emp:** 38. **Officers:** Roland J.P. Zimmer, President, e-mail: roland@zimmer-usa.com. **Former Name:** Zimmer Machinery America Inc.

■ 16662 ■ Zoeller Co.
3649 Cane Run Rd.
PO Box 16347
Louisville, KY 40211-1961
Phone: (502)778-2731
Free: (800)928-PUMP **Fax:** (502)774-3624
E-mail: info@zoeller.com
URL: http://www.zoeller.com
Products: Pumps. **SIC:** 5084 (Industrial Machinery & Equipment). **Est:** 1939. **Sales:** $60,000,000 (2000). **Emp:** 240. **Officers:** Donald R. Fleming, CEO & Chairman of the Board; Bobby Ragland, President; John Zoeller, Exec. VP; Michael A. Babrowski, VP of Marketing, e-mail: mikeb@zoeller.com; Jeanine Burke, Customer Service Mgr., e-mail: jeanine@zoeller.com; Joe Shoemaker, Human Resources Mgr., e-mail: joes@zoeller.com.

■ 16663 ■ Zonne Industrial Tool Co.
11945 Rivera Rd.
Santa Fe Springs, CA 90670
Phone: (562)945-2951
Free: (888)729-9931 **Fax:** (562)945-2951
Products: Machine components and air components. **SIC:** 5084 (Industrial Machinery & Equipment). **Est:** 1925. **Sales:** $2,000,000 (2000). **Emp:** 9. **Officers:** Jay H. Ritenour, President; Thomas Bayes, VP of Operations.

(28) Industrial Supplies

Entries in this section are arranged alphabetically by company name. When the company name is a personal name, the company name is alphabetized by the surname unless the first name or initial(s) are part of a trade name. See the User's Guide at the front of this directory for additional information.

■ 16664 ■ **A-C Supply Inc.**
8220 W Sleske
Milwaukee, WI 53223
Phone: (414)357-7350 **Fax:** (414)357-8164
Products: Bearings and power transmission equipment. **SICs:** 5085 (Industrial Supplies); 5084 (Industrial Machinery & Equipment); 5063 (Electrical Apparatus & Equipment). **Est:** 1969. **Sales:** $40,000,000 (2000). **Emp:** 160. **Officers:** Tom Schuster, President; Pat Lange, Controller; Gary Holtzen, Dir. of Data Processing.

■ 16665 ■ **A. Louis Supply Co.**
5610 Main Ave.
Ashtabula, OH 44004-7200
Phone: (440)997-5161 **Fax:** (440)992-5165
E-mail: alsco@alltel.net
Products: Industrial supplies and electrical hardware. **SICs:** 5085 (Industrial Supplies); 5063 (Electrical Apparatus & Equipment). **Est:** 1905. **Sales:** $5,000,000 (2000). **Emp:** 30. **Officers:** G.R. Coblitz, President.

■ 16666 ■ **A & W Bearings & Supply**
PO Box 561069
Dallas, TX 75247
Phone: (214)630-7681 **Fax:** (214)630-4049
Products: Bearings; Belts; Chains; Sprockets. **SIC:** 5085 (Industrial Supplies).

■ 16667 ■ **ABCO Welding and Industrial Supply**
PO Box 296
Waterford, CT 06385
Phone: (860)442-0363 **Fax:** (860)447-3347
Products: Welding supplies; Industrial supplies. **SIC:** 5085 (Industrial Supplies). **Est:** 1922. **Sales:** $8,000,000 (2000). **Emp:** 44. **Officers:** William R. McCourt, President; Barry Colvin, CFO; Frank Hanney, Sales Mgr.; Kent Lacey, Dir. of Systems.

■ 16668 ■ **Abrasive Products Inc.**
PO Box 250
Fortville, IN 46040
Phone: (317)485-7701 **Fax:** (317)485-6771
Products: Abrasive products; Nonmetallic sized grains, powders, and flour abrasives. **SIC:** 5085 (Industrial Supplies). **Sales:** $8,000,000 (2000). **Emp:** 52. **Officers:** Clark Hyland, President; Mike Ray, Treasurer.

■ 16669 ■ **Acme-Danneman Company Inc.**
480 Canal St.
New York, NY 10013-1803
Phone: (212)966-4204 **Fax:** (212)925-8042
Products: Industrial hardware, including pumps and hoses. **SICs:** 5084 (Industrial Machinery & Equipment); 5085 (Industrial Supplies). **Est:** 1920. **Sales:** $1,000,000 (2000). **Emp:** 6. **Officers:** John W. Powers, President; J. Normand La Rochelle, Treasurer; Alfred Sternfels, Sales Mgr.

■ 16670 ■ **Acorn Paper Products Co**
PO Box 23965
Los Angeles, CA 90023
Phone: (323)268-0507 **Fax:** (323)262-8517
Products: Corrugated boxes; Die cutting. **SICs:** 5085 (Industrial Supplies); 5113 (Industrial & Personal Service Paper). **Officers:** Richard Seff, CEO.

■ 16671 ■ **Acro Electronics Corp.**
1101 W Chicago Ave.
East Chicago, IN 46312
Phone: (219)397-8681
Free: (800)288-2276 **Fax:** (219)397-2068
E-mail: acro@netnitco.net
URL: http://www.acroelectronics.com
Products: Industrial equipment and supplies. **SICs:** 5084 (Industrial Machinery & Equipment); 5085 (Industrial Supplies). **Est:** 1954. **Emp:** 14. **Officers:** Art Garcia, CEO; David Bergin.

■ 16672 ■ **Aero Tec Laboratories Inc.**
Spear Rd. Industrial Park
Ramsey, NJ 07446
Phone: (201)825-1400 **Fax:** (201)825-1962
Products: Fuel cells. **SIC:** 5085 (Industrial Supplies). **Est:** 1970. **Sales:** $4,000,000 (2000). **Emp:** 50. **Officers:** P.J. Regna, President; David Dack, VP of Sales.

■ 16673 ■ **Aggregate Equipment and Supply**
1601 N Main St.
Rockford, IL 61110
Phone: (309)694-6644
Free: (800)322-1590 **Fax:** (309)694-3308
URL: http://www.aggregate-equipment.com
Products: Construction Equipment. **SICs:** 5085 (Industrial Supplies); 5084 (Industrial Machinery & Equipment); 5072 (Hardware). **Emp:** 16. **Officers:** Kevin O'Hara.

■ 16674 ■ **Aggregate Equipment and Supply**
301 N Madison St.
Rockford, IL 61110
Phone: (815)968-2418
Free: (800)747-9322 **Fax:** (815)968-1521
Products: Industrial supplies. **SIC:** 5085 (Industrial Supplies).

■ 16675 ■ **AGL Welding Supply Company Inc.**
PO Box 1707
Clifton, NJ 07015
Phone: (201)478-5000
Products: Welding supplies; Industrial equipment and supplies. **SICs:** 5084 (Industrial Machinery & Equipment); 5169 (Chemicals & Allied Products Nec). **Est:** 1927. **Sales:** $13,000,000 (2000). **Emp:** 99. **Officers:** Patrick M. Fenelon, President; David M. Malin, VP of Finance; Kevin J. Brancato, VP of Marketing.

■ 16676 ■ **Aimtek Inc. Welding Supply Div.**
201 Washington St.
Auburn, MA 01501
Phone: (508)832-5035
Free: (800)772-0104 **Fax:** (508)832-5043
E-mail: sales@aimtek.com
URL: http://www.aimtek.com
Products: Industrial supplies and equipment, including welding machines. **SICs:** 5085 (Industrial Supplies); 5084 (Industrial Machinery & Equipment). **Est:** 1973. **Sales:** $7,000,000 (2000). **Emp:** 25. **Officers:** Amar Kapur, President; Jay Kapur, General Mgr.; Rita Kapur, Customer Service Contact.

■ 16677 ■ **Air-Oil Products Corp.**
2400 E Burnside St.
Portland, OR 97214
Phone: (503)234-0866
Free: (800)242-2672 **Fax:** (503)232-2615
URL: http://www.air-oil.com
Products: Seals and pneumatics. **SIC:** 5085 (Industrial Supplies). **Est:** 1963. **Sales:** $9,000,000 (2000). **Emp:** 35. **Officers:** Mitchell A. Massey, President, e-mail: mitchm@air-oil.com.

■ 16678 ■ **Airco Gas and Gear**
5430 W Morris St.
Indianapolis, IN 46241
Phone: (317)243-6601
Products: Industrial gases. **SICs:** 5169 (Chemicals & Allied Products Nec); 5085 (Industrial Supplies). **Est:** 1929. **Sales:** $31,000,000 (2000). **Emp:** 100. **Officers:** Jerry Gordon, General Mgr.

■ 16679 ■ **Airgas Inc.**
PO Box 6675
Radnor, PA 19087-5240
Phone: (610)687-5253 **Fax:** (610)687-1052
Products: Industrial specialty medical gas; Welding gas and supplies. **SICs:** 5169 (Chemicals & Allied Products Nec); 5085 (Industrial Supplies). **Est:** 1986. **Sales:** $1,158,800,000 (2000). **Emp:** 6,400. **Officers:** Peter McCausland, CEO & Chairman of the Board; Thomas C. Deas Jr., VP & CFO; Rudi Endres, VP of Marketing; Ronald Beebe, VP of Admin.

■ 16680 ■ **Airgas Intermountain**
1118 NE Frontage Rd.
Ft. Collins, CO 80524-9218
Phone: (970)490-7700 **Fax:** (970)490-7750
URL: http://www.airgas.com
Products: Welding supplies; Safety equipment and supplies; Industrial, medical, and specialty gas. **SICs:** 5084 (Industrial Machinery & Equipment); 5122 (Drugs, Proprietaries & Sundries). **Est:** 1953. **Sales:** $70,000,000 (1999). **Emp:** 325. **Officers:** Jim Johnston, President, e-mail: jimjohnston@airgas.com.
Former Name: Air Gas Inc.

■ 16681 ■ **Airgas-North Central**
10 W 4th St.
Waterloo, IA 50701
Phone: (319)233-3540 **Fax:** (319)233-6871
URL: http://www.airgas.com
Products: Welding supplies; Cylinder and bulk gases; Safety products. **SICs:** 5084 (Industrial Machinery &

Equipment); 5085 (Industrial Supplies). **Est:** 1982. **Sales:** $60,000,000 (1999). **Emp:** 398. **Officers:** Jeff Allen, President; Mike Allison, VP of Finance & Admin.; Tim Helms, Dir. of Information Systems; Bonnie Bowers, Dir of Human Resources; Bonnie Bowers, Dir of Human Resources. **Former Name:** Great Lakes Airgas Inc.

■ 16682 ■ **Airline Hydraulics Corp.**
I-95 Business Ctr.
Bensalem, PA 19020
Phone: (215)638-4700
Free: (800)999-7378 **Fax:** (215)638-1707
E-mail: airline@airlinehyd.com
URL: http://www.airlinehyd.com
Products: Hydraulics; Pneumatics; Automation; Electric controls. **SICs:** 5085 (Industrial Supplies); 5065 (Electronic Parts & Equipment Nec). **Est:** 1950. **Sales:** $40,000,000 (2000). **Emp:** 160. **Officers:** Joseph Loughran, President; Russell Pickus, Controller; James Moorehead, VP of Marketing & Sales.

■ 16683 ■ **All Line Inc.**
31 W 310 91st St.
Naperville, IL 60564
Phone: (630)820-1800 **Fax:** (630)820-1830
Products: Rope and cord; Wire rope. **SIC:** 5085 (Industrial Supplies). **Est:** 1978. **Sales:** $6,000,000 (2000). **Emp:** 48. **Officers:** R.A. Moore, President; J.A. Eriksen, Exec. VP of Finance; John Haugan, Sales/Marketing Contact.

■ 16684 ■ **Allen Refractories Co.**
131 Shackelford Rd.
Pataskala, OH 43062
Phone: (740)927-8000 **Fax:** (740)927-9404
Products: Refractory products. **SIC:** 5085 (Industrial Supplies). **Est:** 1970. **Sales:** $9,000,000 (2000). **Emp:** 35. **Officers:** James A. Shackelford, President & Treasurer; Margaret O. Shackelford, General Counsel/Exec. VP.

■ 16685 ■ **Allied Bearing Supply**
416 S Utica
PO Box 3263
Tulsa, OK 74104
Phone: (918)583-0164
Free: (800)331-2692 **Fax:** (918)584-2107
E-mail: tulsa@alliedbearings.com
URL: http://www.alliedbearings.com
Products: Bearings and power transmission equipment. **SICs:** 5085 (Industrial Supplies); 5063 (Electrical Apparatus & Equipment). **Est:** 1934.

■ 16686 ■ **Allied Box Co.**
1931 Stout Field West Dr.
Indianapolis, IN 46241-4020
Phone: (317)352-0083
Products: Paper and paper products. **SIC:** 5113 (Industrial & Personal Service Paper). **Sales:** $2,000,000 (2000). **Emp:** 8.

■ 16687 ■ **Allied Purchasing**
1334 18th St. SW
Mason City, IA 50401
Phone: (515)423-1824
Products: Industrial supplies. **SIC:** 5085 (Industrial Supplies).

■ 16688 ■ **Allied Tools Inc.**
PO Box 34367
Louisville, KY 40232
Phone: (502)966-4114 **Fax:** (502)968-2942
Products: Abrasives, cutting tools and electronic gauging equipment. **SICs:** 5085 (Industrial Supplies); 5084 (Industrial Machinery & Equipment); 5063 (Electrical Apparatus & Equipment). **Sales:** $2,000,000 (2000). **Emp:** 7. **Officers:** Gary Hebner, President.

■ 16689 ■ **AlliedSignal Hardware Product Group**
120 S Webber Dr.
Chandler, AZ 85226
Phone: (602)365-2611 **Fax:** (602)365-4067
Products: Ball bearings for the aircraft, machine tool and instrumentation industries. **SIC:** 5085 (Industrial Supplies). **Sales:** $10,000,000 (2000). **Emp:** 30. **Officers:** Jack O'Donnell, President.

■ 16690 ■ **Aloha Tap & Die Inc.**
1240 Mookaula
Honolulu, HI 96817-4621
Phone: (808)845-7252 **Fax:** (808)842-7555
Products: Taps, dies, drill bits, and fasteners. **SICs:** 5072 (Hardware); 5085 (Industrial Supplies); 5084 (Industrial Machinery & Equipment). **Emp:** 49.

■ 16691 ■ **Alta Sales Inc.**
110 S 1200 W
Lindon, UT 84042
Phone: (801)785-1114 **Fax:** (801)785-4333
Products: Valves; Purification equipment. **SICs:** 5085 (Industrial Supplies); 5084 (Industrial Machinery & Equipment). **Est:** 1952. **Sales:** $1,500,000 (2000). **Emp:** 10. **Officers:** Jerrie Wilson, President. **Doing Business As:** Alta-Robbin.

■ 16692 ■ **AM-DYN-IC Fluid Power**
25340 Terra Industrial Dr.
Chesterfield, MI 48051
Phone: (810)949-6860 **Fax:** (810)949-0370
Products: Hydraulic components. **SIC:** 5085 (Industrial Supplies).

■ 16693 ■ **Ambraco Inc.**
Hwy. 61-151 S
Dubuque, IA 52001
Phone: (319)583-3035
Free: (800)225-8946 **Fax:** (319)583-3531
E-mail: ambracol@mwci.net
URL: http://www.ambraco.com
Products: Twine; Packaging materials. **SIC:** 5085 (Industrial Supplies). **Est:** 1983. **Sales:** $25,000,000 (2000). **Emp:** 7. **Officers:** Stephen J. Dodds, CEO.

■ 16694 ■ **American Industrial Supply**
519 Potrero Ave.
San Francisco, CA 94110
Phone: (415)826-1144 **Fax:** (415)552-3300
Products: Industrial supplies. **SIC:** 5087 (Service Establishment Equipment). **Est:** 1968. **Sales:** $20,000,000 (2000). **Emp:** 6. **Officers:** George Herbst, President.

■ 16695 ■ **American Laubscher Corp.**
80 Finn Ct.
Farmingdale, NY 11735
Phone: (516)694-5900 **Fax:** (516)293-0935
Products: Screw machine parts; Micromolded plastics; Ceramics; Gears. **SICs:** 5084 (Industrial Machinery & Equipment); 5162 (Plastics Materials & Basic Shapes); 5085 (Industrial Supplies). **Est:** 1950. **Sales:** $19,000,000 (2000). **Emp:** 55. **Officers:** H.R. Lehmann, President; L.W. Miller, Vice President.

■ 16696 ■ **Ameru Trading Co.**
1043 Sterling Rd., Ste. 201
Herndon, VA 20170
Phone: (703)709-1900 **Fax:** (703)709-2524
Products: Ball bearings and tapered rolles bearings. **SIC:** 5085 (Industrial Supplies). **Est:** 1990. **Officers:** Robert A. Mix, President.

■ 16697 ■ **Ames Industries Inc.**
2537 Curtiss St.
Downers Grove, IL 60515
Phone: (630)964-2440 **Fax:** (630)964-0497
Products: Recoat rubber rollers for folding machines, printers and photo copiers; Typewriter platens. **SIC:** 5085 (Industrial Supplies). **Sales:** $97,000,000 (2000). **Emp:** 750.

■ 16698 ■ **Anchor Sales Associates Inc.**
614 Heron Dr., Unit 9
Bridgeport, NJ 08014
Phone: (856)467-1133 **Fax:** (856)467-5466
Products: Industrial pumps; Electric variable speed drills; Motors, including gear motors. **SIC:** 5084 (Industrial Machinery & Equipment). **Est:** 1981. **Sales:** $2,000,000 (2000). **Emp:** 8. **Officers:** Robert Taraska, President.

■ 16699 ■ **Anle Paper Company Inc.**
100 Progress Rd.
Lombard, IL 60148
Phone: (630)629-9700 **Fax:** (630)639-9770
Products: Disposable paper products. **SIC:** 5113 (Industrial & Personal Service Paper). **Sales:**

$40,000,000 (2000). **Emp:** 132. **Officers:** David Niedelman, Payroll Mgr.; Harry Mandell, Controller.

■ 16700 ■ **Apache Hose and Belting Inc.**
4805 Bowling St. SW
PO Box 1719
Cedar Rapids, IA 52406-1719
Phone: (319)365-0471
Free: (800)553-5455 **Fax:** (319)365-2522
E-mail: info@apachehb.com
URL: http://www.apachehb.com
Products: Hose and accessories; Conveyor belts and accessories; Cut rubber parts; Preassembled/coupled hose assemblies; Custom fabricated belting products. **SIC:** 5085 (Industrial Supplies). **Est:** 1963. **Sales:** $51,000,000 (2000). **Emp:** 275.

■ 16701 ■ **Applied Industrial Tech**
205 Industrial Park Blvd.
PO Box 1628
Tullahoma, TN 37388
Phone: (931)455-6990 **Fax:** (931)455-9039
Products: Motors; Industrial products. **SICs:** 5084 (Industrial Machinery & Equipment); 5085 (Industrial Supplies). **Est:** 1991. **Emp:** 4.

■ 16702 ■ **Applied Industrial Tech, Inc.**
1240 Polk Ave.
Nashville, TN 37210
Phone: (615)244-6462
Products: Hydraulic equipment and supplies; Bearings and motors. **SIC:** 5085 (Industrial Supplies).

■ 16703 ■ **Applied Industrial Technologies**
PO Box 5426
Willowick, OH 44095-0426
Phone: (216)426-4000 **Free:** (800)322-3460
URL: http://www.appliedindustrial.com
Products: Bearings for industrial machinery; Industrial rubber products; Inner motion components; Power transmission products; Fluid power components. **SIC:** 5085 (Industrial Supplies). **Est:** 1923. **Sales:** $1,160,000,000 (2000). **Emp:** 5,000. **Officers:** John C. Dannemiller.

■ 16704 ■ **Applied Industrial Technologies**
1948 Plaza Dr.
Benton Harbor, MI 49022-2210
Phone: (616)927-4425
Free: (800)552-2548 **Fax:** (616)927-1173
Products: Industrial parts and supplies, including belts, bearings, and power transmissions. **SICs:** 5085 (Industrial Supplies); 5084 (Industrial Machinery & Equipment); 5063 (Electrical Apparatus & Equipment).

■ 16705 ■ **Applied Industrial Technologies, Inc.**
8021 New Jersey Ave.
Hammond, IN 46323
Phone: (219)844-5090 **Fax:** (219)844-1899
Products: Industrial parts including belts, pulleys, and reducers. **SICs:** 5084 (Industrial Machinery & Equipment); 5085 (Industrial Supplies). **Former Name:** Dodge Chicago Industrial Bearings.

■ 16706 ■ **Applied Industrial Technologies, Inc.**
2130 Industrial St.
Wisconsin Rapids, WI 54495
Phone: (715)421-1730
Free: (800)637-2324 **Fax:** (715)423-0959
URL: http://www.appliedindustrial.com
Products: Industrial power transmissions. **SICs:** 5085 (Industrial Supplies); 5085 (Industrial Supplies).

■ 16707 ■ **Aramsco, Inc.**
1655 Imperial Way
Thorofare, NJ 08086
Phone: (609)848-5330
Free: (800)767-6933 **Fax:** (609)848-0802
URL: http://www.aramsco.com
Products: Industrial supplies; Clothing; Hazmat supplies. **SICs:** 5085 (Industrial Supplies); 5136 (Men's/Boys' Clothing); 5047 (Medical & Hospital Equipment). **Est:** 1966. **Sales:** $47,000,000 (2000). **Emp:** 125. **Officers:** William Kennworthy, President; David Naylor, Sales/Marketing Contact; Denice Ashby, Customer Service Contact. **Former Name:** Herbert #Abrams Co. Inc.

■ **16708** ■ **Arctic Industrial Supply**
6510 Arctic Spur Rd.
Anchorage, AK 99518
Phone: (907)561-1520
Products: Clinder gas. **SIC:** 5169 (Chemicals & Allied Products Nec).

■ **16709** ■ **Arizona Sealing Devices Inc.**
150 E Alamo Dr.
Chandler, AZ 85225
Phone: (602)892-7325
Products: O-rings; Seals; Gaskets. **SIC:** 5085 (Industrial Supplies). **Sales:** $400,000 (2000). **Emp:** 2. **Officers:** Liisa Hamelin, President.

■ **16710** ■ **Armitage Industrial Supply, Inc.**
4930 W Belmont Ave.
Chicago, IL 60641-4331
Phone: (773)202-8300 **Fax:** (773)202-8569
Products: Industrial supplies; Tools; Needles, pins, and fasteners; General industrial machinery; Paints and allied products; Hand tools; Power tools and parts; Mill supplies; Gears; Electrical equipment and supplies; Plumbing fixtures, equipment, and supplies; Lubricating oils and greases; Batteries; Furnaces; Air-conditioning equipment; Hard surface floor coverings; Cabinets; Specialty cleaning and sanitation products; Major appliance parts. **SICs:** 5085 (Industrial Supplies); 5072 (Hardware); 5074 (Plumbing & Hydronic Heating Supplies); 5063 (Electrical Apparatus & Equipment); 5198 (Paints, Varnishes & Supplies). **Est:** 1974. **Sales:** $1,000,000 (2000). **Emp:** 8. **Officers:** Richard Steele, President.

■ **16711** ■ **E.G. Artz Inc.**
PO Box 97
Brookfield, WI 53008
Phone: (262)781-5700
Free: (800)242-2088 **Fax:** (262)781-6336
Products: Shelving; Work benches; Ladders. **SIC:** 5085 (Industrial Supplies). **Est:** 1930. **Sales:** $6,000,000 (2000). **Emp:** 21. **Officers:** Richard T. Artz, Sec. & Treas.; Susan C. Artz, Chairman; Paul D. Ziemer Jr., President.

■ **16712** ■ **Associated Industrial Supply Co.**
PO Box 208
Columbia, SC 29202-0208
Phone: (803)765-0990
Products: Industrial supplies for factories, including pipe and fittings. **SIC:** 5085 (Industrial Supplies). **Est:** 1902. **Sales:** $50,000,000 (2000). **Emp:** 200. **Officers:** Robert McBeth, CEO; Phillip Holson, CFO; Jack Lee, VP of Sales.

■ **16713** ■ **Associated Material Handling Industries Inc.**
550 Kenoe Blvd.
Carol Stream, IL 60188-1838
Phone: (630)588-8800
Free: (800)755-7201 **Fax:** (630)588-8815
URL: http://www.associated-allied.net
Products: Industrial equipment. **SIC:** 5084 (Industrial Machinery & Equipment). **Est:** 1960. **Emp:** 227. **Officers:** Gordon Demaine, President; Andrew Konopka, VP of Finance; Dave LeMaster, VP of Marketing & Sales; Charlie Maguire, VP of Technical Support; Greg Stashuk, VP of Aftermarket.

■ **16714** ■ **Associated Packaging Inc.**
215 Connell St.
Goodlettsville, TN 37072
Phone: (615)859-3737 **Fax:** (615)851-1451
Products: Paper and paper products. **SIC:** 5113 (Industrial & Personal Service Paper). **Sales:** $29,000,000 (2000). **Emp:** 25.

■ **16715** ■ **Atlanta Broom Company Inc.**
4750 Bakers Ferry Rd. SW
Atlanta, GA 30336-2246
Phone: (404)696-4600
Free: (800)696-6919 **Fax:** (404)691-3183
Products: Industrial and personal service paper and plastic products. **SIC:** 5113 (Industrial & Personal Service Paper). **Sales:** $20,000,000 (2000). **Emp:** 65. **Officers:** Herman Fishman, President; Steve Mote, General Manager, Finance.

■ **16716** ■ **Atlantic Corp.**
8400 Triad Dr.
Greensboro, NC 27409
Phone: (919)668-0081
Products: Paper and paper products. **SIC:** 5113 (Industrial & Personal Service Paper). **Sales:** $150,000,000 (2000). **Emp:** 350.

■ **16717** ■ **Aztech Controls Corp.**
324 S Bracken Ln.
Chandler, AZ 85224-4700
Phone: (480)782-6000
Free: (800)238-4590 **Fax:** (480)782-6040
E-mail: dramacier@aztechcontrols.com
Products: Gauges; Tubing; Filters, pumps, and fittings; Valves; Tanks; Actuators; High tech instrumentation components. **SICs:** 5085 (Industrial Supplies); 5084 (Industrial Machinery & Equipment); 5088 (Transportation Equipment & Supplies). **Est:** 1986. **Emp:** 70. **Officers:** Pat Frazier, CEO & President.

■ **16718** ■ **Babbitt Steam Specialty Co.**
PO Box 51208
New Bedford, MA 02745
Phone: (508)995-9533
Free: (800)727-4323 **Fax:** (508)995-2701
E-mail: tbssco@aol.com
URL: http://www.babbitsteam.com
Products: Industrial supplies, including sprockets, rims, guides, valve openers, and pipe fitting valves. **SIC:** 5085 (Industrial Supplies). **Est:** 1907. **Sales:** $10,000,000 (2000). **Emp:** 42. **Officers:** Edwin V. Babbitt III, President; John I. Babbitt Jr., CFO; Robert Tracey, Dir. of Marketing & Sales; Anne Polk, Dir. of Data Processing.

■ **16719** ■ **Baltimore Hydraulics Inc.**
708 E 25th St.
Baltimore, MD 21218-5436
Phone: (410)467-8088
Free: (800)947-8088 **Fax:** (410)467-0074
E-mail: tiohydro@msn.com
URL: http://www.baltimorhydraulics.com
Products: Hydraulics repairs and supplies. **SICs:** 5085 (Industrial Supplies); 5083 (Farm & Garden Machinery); 5084 (Industrial Machinery & Equipment). **Est:** 1962. **Emp:** 49. **Officers:** Gordon Kauffman.

■ **16720** ■ **Barker Pipe Fittings Inc.**
271 Lancaster Ave.
Frazer, PA 19355
Phone: (215)644-7400 **Fax:** (215)647-4011
Products: Industrial pipe, valves, and fittings. **SIC:** 5074 (Plumbing & Hydronic Heating Supplies). **Est:** 1923. **Sales:** $11,000,000 (2000). **Emp:** 50. **Officers:** Carol Barker, President; Robert Barker, CFO.

■ **16721** ■ **E. J Bartells Co.**
PO Box 5477
Kennewick, WA 99336
Phone: (509)582-4985 **Fax:** (509)582-5889
Products: Sells refractory and industrial insulation products; insulation materials and supplies. **SICs:** 5085 (Industrial Supplies); 5075 (Warm Air Heating & Air-Conditioning).

■ **16722** ■ **Bartlett Bearing Co. Inc.**
4320 H St.
Philadelphia, PA 19124
Phone: (215)743-8963
Free: (800)523-3382 **Fax:** (215)744-1980
E-mail: Bartlett97@aol.com
Products: Bearings. **SIC:** 5085 (Industrial Supplies). **Est:** 1952. **Sales:** $7,400,000 (2000). **Emp:** 27. **Officers:** G.L. Musser, President; S.L. Limeburner, CFO; Victor McDevitt, Sales Mgr.

■ **16723** ■ **Barton Truck Center Inc.**
PO Box 30154
Memphis, TN 38130
Phone: (901)345-5294
Products: Heavy equipment parts. **SIC:** 5085 (Industrial Supplies).

■ **16724** ■ **E.A. Baumbach Manufacturing Co.**
650 W Grand Ave.
Elmhurst, IL 60126
Phone: (630)941-0505
Products: Springs. **SIC:** 5085 (Industrial Supplies).

Est: 1911. **Sales:** $900,000 (2000). **Emp:** 3. **Officers:** Earl A. Baumbach Jr., President; Mark Baumbach, Dir. of Sales.

■ **16725** ■ **A.J. Baxter and Co. Inc.**
10171 W Jefferson Ave.
River Rouge, MI 48218
Phone: (313)843-1153
Products: Industrial supplies. **SIC:** 5085 (Industrial Supplies). **Est:** 1943. **Sales:** $5,000,000 (2000). **Emp:** 22. **Officers:** Charles Jackson, President.

■ **16726** ■ **Bay Rubber Co.**
404 Pendleton Way
Oakland, CA 94621
Phone: (510)635-9151
Free: (800)229-7822 **Fax:** (510)430-9815
Products: Rubber. **SIC:** 5085 (Industrial Supplies). **Sales:** $2,500,000 (2000). **Emp:** 10.

■ **16727** ■ **Bearing Belt Chain Co.**
3501 Aldebaran St.
Las Vegas, NV 89102
Phone: (702)876-4225 **Fax:** (702)364-0842
E-mail: ray@bearing.com
URL: http://www.bearing.com
Products: Bearing belt chains; Conveyors; Power transmission products. **SIC:** 5085 (Industrial Supplies). **Est:** 1959. **Sales:** $7,000,000 (1999). **Emp:** 25. **Officers:** S. Philpott, President; Dale Augustin, General Mgr. **Alternate Name:** BBC Industrial Supply Co.

■ **16728** ■ **Bearing Belt and Chain Inc.**
729 E Buckeye Rd.
Phoenix, AZ 85034
Phone: (602)252-6541
Products: Bearings; Sprockets; Conveyor belts. **SIC:** 5085 (Industrial Supplies). **Est:** 1957. **Sales:** $10,000,000 (2000). **Emp:** 35. **Officers:** Richard J. Linkowski, President.

■ **16729** ■ **Bearing Distributors**
8000 Hub Pkwy.
Cleveland, OH 44125
Phone: (216)642-9100 **Fax:** (216)642-9573
URL: http://www.bdi-usa.com
Products: Bearings; Chains; Paint; Pillow blocks; Retaining rings; Seals; Shafting; T-track; Power transmission; Fluid power equipment. **SICs:** 5085 (Industrial Supplies); 5198 (Paints, Varnishes & Supplies). **Est:** 1935. **Sales:** $250,000,000 (2000). **Emp:** 499. **Officers:** David Hooser, President, e-mail: dhooser@bdi-usa.com; John A. Neuman, CFO, e-mail: jneuman@bdi-usa.com; Carl G. James, VP & Secty., e-mail: cjames@bdi-usa.com; Chris Shaffer, Dir. of Information Systems, e-mail: cshaffer@bdi-usa.com.

■ **16730** ■ **Bearing Distributors**
PO Box 3490
East Chicago, IN 46312
Phone: (219)398-3300 **Fax:** (219)398-3277
Products: Bearings; Power transmission equipment and supplies; Motors. **SICs:** 5085 (Industrial Supplies); 5013 (Motor Vehicle Supplies & New Parts).

■ **16731** ■ **Bearing Distributors Inc.**
1036 Atando Ave.
PO Box 33716
Charlotte, NC 28233
Phone: (704)375-0061 **Fax:** (704)342-1973
Products: Motors; Pulleys; Belts; Bearings. **SICs:** 5085 (Industrial Supplies); 5063 (Electrical Apparatus & Equipment).

■ **16732** ■ **Bearing Engineers Inc.**
27 Argonaut
Aliso Viejo, CA 92656
Phone: (949)586-7442
Free: (800)372-7402 **Fax:** (949)586-7786
E-mail: socalsales@bearingengineers.com
URL: http://www.bearingengineers.com
Products: Linear motion bearings; Motion control products; Electro-mechanical systems. **SIC:** 5085 (Industrial Supplies). **Est:** 1956. **Sales:** $16,000,000 (2000). **Emp:** 35. **Officers:** Robert R. Bloom, CEO; James Yamada, Controller; Joe Uhrig, President.

■ **16733** ■ **Bearing Enterprises Inc.**
203 Brighton Ave.
Boston, MA 02134
Phone: (617)782-1400
Products: Ball bearings; Aerosol sprays; Lubricants and greases; V-belts. **SICs:** 5085 (Industrial Supplies); 5172 (Petroleum Products Nec). **Est:** 1961. **Sales:** $8,000,000 (2000). **Emp:** 38. **Officers:** Edward X. Greene, President.

■ **16734** ■ **Bearings and Drives Inc.**
9508 E Rush St.
South el Monte, CA 91733
Phone: (626)575-1307 **Fax:** (626)443-3438
Products: Bearings for machinery. **SIC:** 5085 (Industrial Supplies). **Est:** 1946. **Sales:** $6,000,000 (2000). **Emp:** 30. **Officers:** Gaye Duncan, President; E. W. Murphy Jr., Vice President.

■ **16735** ■ **Bearings and Drives, Inc.**
PO Box 1842
Athens, GA 30603-1842
Phone: (706)546-8640 **Fax:** (706)546-8682
Products: Industrial bearings and drive trains. **SICs:** 5084 (Industrial Machinery & Equipment); 5085 (Industrial Supplies).

■ **16736** ■ **Bearings and Drives, Inc.**
363 1st St. SW
PO Box 83
Cleveland, TN 37312
Phone: (423)472-3291 **Fax:** (423)472-3383
Products: Industrial supplies. **SIC:** 5085 (Industrial Supplies).

■ **16737** ■ **Bearings and Drives, Inc.**
2540 NW 74th Pl.
Gainesville, FL 32653
Phone: (352)375-0568 **Fax:** (352)377-5432
E-mail: brgsdrvs@msa.com
Products: Industrial supplies; Electric motors. **SICs:** 5085 (Industrial Supplies); 5063 (Electrical Apparatus & Equipment).

■ **16738** ■ **Bearings & Drives Unlimited, Inc.**
Bethlehem Pike & Cherry Ln.
Souderton, PA 18964
Phone: (215)723-0938
Products: Bearings, drives, and belts. **SIC:** 5085 (Industrial Supplies).

■ **16739** ■ **Bearings Inc.**
PO Box 6925
Cleveland, OH 44101-9986
Phone: (216)881-8900 **Fax:** (216)881-8988
Products: Ball bearings, unmounted; Electric motors; Conveyors and conveying equipment; Controlling instruments and accessories; Sprockets. **SICs:** 5085 (Industrial Supplies); 5065 (Electronic Parts & Equipment Nec); 5084 (Industrial Machinery & Equipment); 5063 (Electrical Apparatus & Equipment). **Est:** 1923. **Sales:** $814,000,000 (2000). **Emp:** 4,225. **Officers:** John C. Dannemiller, President & COO; John C. Robinson, Vice President.

■ **16740** ■ **Bearings Incorporated of Kentucky**
PO Box 17286
Louisville, KY 40217
Phone: (502)637-1445 **Fax:** (502)635-1427
Products: Bearings; Sprockets; Chains. **SICs:** 5085 (Industrial Supplies); 5084 (Industrial Machinery & Equipment). **Est:** 1944. **Sales:** $5,500,000 (2000). **Emp:** 15. **Officers:** Bill McCarty, General Mgr.; Robert Pfeiffer, Treasurer.

■ **16741** ■ **Bearings & Industrial Supply Co., Inc.**
431 Irmen Dr.
Addison, IL 60101
Phone: (630)628-1966
Free: (800)826-9870 **Fax:** (630)628-0116
E-mail: bearings4u@aol.com
URL: http://www.bearingsnow.com
Products: Bearings; Power transmission units; Industrial products; Pump parts; Electrical parts. **SICs:** 5085 (Industrial Supplies); 5084 (Industrial Machinery & Equipment); 5013 (Motor Vehicle Supplies & New Parts). **Est:** 1983. **Sales:** $4,000,000 (1999). **Emp:** 14. **Officers:** Narendra Khandwala, President; Bela

Khandwala, Sec. & Treas.; Bipin Shah, Customer Service Contact, e-mail: bearings4u@aol.com.

■ **16742** ■ **Bearings Service & Supply**
1327 N Market
Box 7497
Shreveport, LA 71137-7497
Phone: (318)424-1447
Free: (800)458-9318 **Fax:** (318)424-9737
URL: http://www.bearserco.com
Products: Bearings. **SIC:** 5085 (Industrial Supplies). **Est:** 1972. **Emp:** 78.

■ **16743** ■ **Bearings Service & Supply, Inc.**
2129 Peters Rd.
Harvey, LA 70058-1736
Phone: (504)366-4111 **Fax:** (504)366-4136
Products: Industrial supplies, including bearings, belts, and reducers. **SIC:** 5085 (Industrial Supplies).

■ **16744** ■ **Beck Packaging Corp.**
PO Box 20250
Lehigh Valley, PA 18002-0250
Phone: (610)264-0551
Free: (800)722-2325 **Fax:** (610)264-7465
Products: Paper, plastics, and packaging machinery. **SICs:** 5113 (Industrial & Personal Service Paper); 5162 (Plastics Materials & Basic Shapes); 5084 (Industrial Machinery & Equipment). **Sales:** $10,000,000 (2000). **Emp:** 30. **Officers:** Irwin Beck, President.

■ **16745** ■ **Beckley Equipment Co.**
2850 University Dr.
Saginaw, MI 48603
Phone: (517)793-5922
Free: (800)933-3220 **Fax:** (517)793-0524
Products: Industrial supplies. **SIC:** 5085 (Industrial Supplies).

■ **16746** ■ **Beemer Precision Inc.**
230 New York Dr.
Ft. Washington, PA 19034
Phone: (215)646-8440
Products: Bearings; O-rings; K-couplings. **SIC:** 5085 (Industrial Supplies). **Est:** 1930. **Sales:** $7,500,000 (2000). **Emp:** 55. **Officers:** A.J. Diesinger Jr., Chairman of the Board; Hal Myer, President.

■ **16747** ■ **Belting Industry Company Inc.**
20 Boright Ave.
Kenilworth, NJ 07033
Phone: (908)272-8591 **Fax:** (908)272-3825
Products: Industrial belts, including conveyor belts and belting. **SIC:** 5085 (Industrial Supplies). **Est:** 1958. **Sales:** $8,000,000 (2000). **Emp:** 100. **Officers:** W.S. Cooper, President; Paul West, CFO; Rita J. Kae, Dir. of Marketing & Sales.

■ **16748** ■ **Beltservice Corp.**
4143 N Rider Trail
Earth City, MO 63045-1102
Phone: (314)344-8500
Free: (800)727-2358 **Fax:** (314)344-8511
E-mail: beltservice@worldnet.att.net
URL: http://www.beltservice.com
Products: Conveyor belting, including food, package handling, heavy duty, coal feeder, filtration, magnetic separator, light duty, and corrugated sidewall belting. **SIC:** 5085 (Industrial Supplies). **Est:** 1969. **Emp:** 300. **Officers:** R.E. Engelsmann, President; W.R. Engelsmann, Chairman of the Board; M. Gray, Finance Officer; Ned Pauley, Marketing & Sales Mgr.; Thomas Acker, COO. **Alternate Name:** Beltwall Division of Beltservice Corp.

■ **16749** ■ **L.A. Benson Company Inc.**
PO Box 2137
Baltimore, MD 21203
Phone: (410)342-9225
Products: Industrial supplies. **SIC:** 5085 (Industrial Supplies). **Est:** 1911. **Sales:** $6,000,000 (2000). **Emp:** 30. **Officers:** Lew Benson III, President.

■ **16750** ■ **Berg Bag Co.**
410 3rd Ave. N
Minneapolis, MN 55401
Phone: (612)332-8845
Products: Storage equipment and containers. **SIC:**

5113 (Industrial & Personal Service Paper). **Sales:** $5,000,000 (2000). **Emp:** 10.

■ **16751** ■ **Berry Bearing Co.**
1605 Alton Rd.
Birmingham, AL 35210-3770
Products: Ball bearings; Industrial equipment. **SICs:** 5084 (Industrial Machinery & Equipment); 5085 (Industrial Supplies). **Sales:** $180,000,000 (2000). **Emp:** 1,200. **Officers:** Gardner Larned, President; James McQuetty, VP of Finance; Bob Tonderau, Dir. of Marketing; James Hopper, Dir. of Systems.

■ **16752** ■ **Bertsch Co.**
1655 Steele Ave. SW
Grand Rapids, MI 49507
Phone: (616)452-3251 **Fax:** (616)452-8114
Products: Industrial supplies, including pipes, valves, and fittings. **SICs:** 5085 (Industrial Supplies); 5084 (Industrial Machinery & Equipment). **Est:** 1875. **Sales:** $72,000,000 (2000). **Emp:** 400. **Officers:** John R. Bertsch, President; Gary Blynt, Treasurer; C. Chenevert, Dir. of Marketing; Ric Gajewski, Dir. of Information Systems; Jim Decker, Dir. of Operations.

■ **16753** ■ **Black and Co.**
1717 E Garfield Ave.
Decatur, IL 62525
Phone: (217)428-4424
Free: (800)829-2434 **Fax:** (217)428-1439
Products: Industrial supplies, including tools, safety supplies, and solvents. **SIC:** 5085 (Industrial Supplies). **Est:** 1920. **Sales:** $62,000,000 (2000). **Emp:** 197. **Officers:** Jeffrey Black, President; Donna Thorpe, Secretary; Kevin Krause, Dir. of Marketing.

■ **16754** ■ **Bolk Industrial Supply Corp.**
PO Box 279
Vincennes, IN 47591
Phone: (812)882-4090 **Fax:** (812)882-4294
Products: Bearings, pipes, chains, and hoses. **SIC:** 5085 (Industrial Supplies). **Est:** 1916. **Sales:** $1,000,000 (2000). **Emp:** 9. **Officers:** Patricia L. Bolk, President.

■ **16755** ■ **Bonita Pioneer Packaging Prods**
7333 SW Bonita Rd.
Portland, OR 97224
Phone: (503)684-6542 **Fax:** (503)639-5965
Products: Boxes and shopping bags, gift wrap and retail bags for retail industries. **SIC:** 5113 (Industrial & Personal Service Paper).

■ **16756** ■ **Bonneville Industrial**
45 South 1500 West
Orem, UT 84058
Phone: (801)225-7770 **Fax:** (801)224-1456
URL: http://www.biscotools.com
Products: Industrial supplies. **SIC:** 5085 (Industrial Supplies). **Est:** 1977. **Sales:** $5,000,000 (2000). **Emp:** 18. **Officers:** Greg Lupus, President.

■ **16757** ■ **Boring and Smith Industries Div.**
2500 Royal Pl.
Tucker, GA 30084
Phone: (404)934-6341
Products: General industrial supplies. **SIC:** 5085 (Industrial Supplies). **Sales:** $13,000,000 (1994). **Emp:** 50. **Officers:** Douglas C. Smith, General Mgr.; Peter Covert, Controller.

■ **16758** ■ **Bossert Industrial Supply Inc.**
5959 W Howard St.
Niles, IL 60714
Phone: (708)647-0515 **Fax:** (708)647-7476
Products: Industrial supplies, including cutting tools, abrasives, and fixtures. **SIC:** 5085 (Industrial Supplies). **Est:** 1917. **Emp:** 486. **Officers:** Robert Brudzinski, President; Tom Brury, Finance Officer; Nancy Tirrell, Manager; John Radke, Dir. of Systems; Donald Grau, Dir of Human Resources.

■ **16759** ■ **Bowman Distribution**
PO Box 6908
Cleveland, OH 44101-9990
Phone: (216)416-7200 **Fax:** (216)416-7403
URL: http://www.barnesgroupinc.com
Products: Fasteners; Welding parts; Automatic parts. **SICs:** 5085 (Industrial Supplies); 5013 (Motor Vehicle

Supplies & New Parts); 5072 (Hardware). **Est:** 1933. **Sales:** $213,400,000 (2000). **Emp:** 10,200. **Officers:** Don Crist, Exec. VP of Mgt. Information Systems; James Bonvissuto, Controller; John Wierda, Dir. of Sales, e-mail: jwierda@bowman-bgi.com; Jeff Taylor, Customer Service Contact, e-mail: jtaylor@bowman-bgi.com; Ken Sloan, Human Resources Contact, e-mail: ksloan@bowman-bgi.com.

■ **16760** ■ **Boyer Steel Inc.**
19640 Charleston Ave.
Detroit, MI 48203
Phone: (313)368-8760 **Fax:** (313)368-8769
Products: Steel tubing. **SIC:** 5085 (Industrial Supplies). **Est:** 1936. **Sales:** $3,000,000 (2000). **Emp:** 10. **Officers:** Marylin Paielli, President; R.A. Paielli, Treasurer.

■ **16761** ■ **Boyle Machine and Supply Co.**
PO Box 352
Peabody, MA 01960-6852
Phone: (978)531-1920 **Fax:** (978)532-2263
Products: Tools, including saws, blades, wrenches and hammers. **SIC:** 5085 (Industrial Supplies). **Est:** 1932. **Sales:** $1,000,000 (2000). **Emp:** 13. **Officers:** Gloria Hennessey, President.

■ **16762** ■ **N.H. Bragg and Sons**
92 Perry Rd.
Bangor, ME 04402-0927
Phone: (207)947-8611 **Fax:** (207)947-6752
E-mail: nhbragg@nhbragg.com
URL: http://www.nhbragg.com
Products: Equipment and parts for welding, automotive, and industrial use. **SICs:** 5085 (Industrial Supplies); 5013 (Motor Vehicle Supplies & New Parts). **Est:** 1854. **Sales:** $20,000,000 (1999). **Emp:** 150. **Officers:** John W. Bragg, President; Sam Cronkite, Comptroller; Eric Clyve, Sales Mgr.

■ **16763** ■ **Brake Systems Inc.**
2221 NE Hoyt St.
Portland, OR 97232
Phone: (503)236-2116 **Fax:** (503)239-5005
Products: New brake products; rebrake components. **SIC:** 5085 (Industrial Supplies). **Sales:** $10,000,000 (1999). **Emp:** 32. **Officers:** Harry Dozier, President; Katie Dozier, Treasurer.

■ **16764** ■ **Brammall Supply Co.**
PO Box 396
Benton Harbor, MI 49023
Phone: (616)926-2111
Products: Industrial supplies, including abrasives, nuts, and power tools. **SIC:** 5085 (Industrial Supplies). **Est:** 1879. **Sales:** $5,000,000 (2000). **Emp:** 16. **Officers:** K. Ankli, President; T. Lauren, Controller.

■ **16765** ■ **Branom Instrument Co. Inc.**
8435 N Interstate Pl.
Portland, OR 97217
Phone: (503)283-2555 **Fax:** (503)283-2652
Products: Industrial instruments. **SIC:** 5084 (Industrial Machinery & Equipment).

■ **16766** ■ **Britain's Steel and Supplies**
1335 S Pacific Ave.
Yuma, AZ 85365
Phone: (520)782-4731
Products: Industrial fasteners; Pumps; Tools. **SIC:** 5085 (Industrial Supplies).

■ **16767** ■ **Bro Tex Company Inc., Wiping Cloth Div.**
800 Hampden Ave.
St. Paul, MN 55114
Phone: (612)645-5721
Free: (800)328-2282 **Fax:** (612)646-1876
Products: Paper and paper products. **SIC:** 5113 (Industrial & Personal Service Paper).

■ **16768** ■ **Bruckner Supply Co. Inc.**
36 Harbor Park Dr.
Port Washington, NY 11050-4602
Phone: (516)484-6070 **Fax:** (516)484-1255
Products: Industrial supplies. **SIC:** 5085 (Industrial Supplies). **Sales:** $15,000,000 (2000). **Emp:** 50. **Officers:** Eli Rosenbaum, CEO & President.

■ **16769** ■ **Brushtech Inc.**
PO Box 1130
Plattsburgh, NY 12901
Phone: (518)563-8420 **Fax:** (518)563-0581
Products: Steel products; Brushes. **SICs:** 5085 (Industrial Supplies); 5072 (Hardware).

■ **16770** ■ **Buck-Hilkert Inc.**
1001 E Broadway
Logansport, IN 46947-0510
Phone: (219)753-2555 **Fax:** (219)722-1827
Products: Industrial hardware. **SIC:** 5085 (Industrial Supplies). **Officers:** Larry Long, President.

■ **16771** ■ **Buckeye Rubber and Packing Co.**
23940 Mercantile Rd.
Beachwood, OH 44122
Phone: (216)464-8900 **Fax:** (216)831-0254
Products: O-rings. **SIC:** 5085 (Industrial Supplies). **Est:** 1937. **Sales:** $11,000,000 (2000). **Emp:** 65. **Officers:** E.E. Klemm, President.

■ **16772** ■ **Buford Brothers Inc.**
909 Division St.
Nashville, TN 37203
Phone: (615)256-4681 **Fax:** (615)256-8413
Products: Industrial supplies. **SICs:** 5085 (Industrial Supplies); 5084 (Industrial Machinery & Equipment). **Est:** 1837. **Sales:** $16,000,000 (2000). **Emp:** 42. **Officers:** Bill Young, President.

■ **16773** ■ **Bussert Industrial Supply Inc.**
8211 Bavaria Dr. E
Macedonia, OH 44056-2259
Phone: (216)441-3000
Products: Gears, tools, wheels, motors and other industrial supplies and equipment. **SICs:** 5085 (Industrial Supplies); 5084 (Industrial Machinery & Equipment). **Sales:** $12,000,000 (1994). **Emp:** 30. **Officers:** Jerry Vanderhide, Manager.

■ **16774** ■ **C-Tech Systems Div.**
6450 Carlson Dr.
Eden Prairie, MN 55346
Phone: (612)974-1700 **Fax:** (612)906-7624
Products: Industrial fasteners. **SIC:** 5072 (Hardware). **Sales:** $11,000,000 (2000). **Emp:** 80. **Officers:** D. Brandt, Sr. VP of Operations.

■ **16775** ■ **California Industrial Rubber Company Inc.**
2732 S Cherry Ave.
Fresno, CA 93706
Phone: (209)485-1487
Products: Industrial supplies. **SIC:** 5085 (Industrial Supplies). **Sales:** $16,000,000 (1993). **Emp:** 93. **Officers:** Larry Cane Sr., President; Carol Anne Cane, Controller.

■ **16776** ■ **Calolympic Glove and Safety Company Inc.**
PO Box 2323
Riverside, CA 92516-2323
Phone: (909)369-0165
Free: (800)421-6630 **Fax:** (909)369-0950
Products: Security and safety equipment. **SIC:** 5085 (Industrial Supplies). **Sales:** $10,200,000 (2000). **Emp:** 30.

■ **16777** ■ **Campbell Supply Co.**
710 S Oak St.
Iowa Falls, IA 50126
Phone: (515)648-4621
Free: (800)782-5134 **Fax:** (515)648-4624
E-mail: campbell@iafalls.com
Products: Industrial supplies, including hand tools and fasteners. **SICs:** 5085 (Industrial Supplies); 5072 (Hardware). **Est:** 1963. **Sales:** $6,000,000 (2000). **Emp:** 48. **Officers:** C. John Campbell, President; Robert N. Campbell, Vice President; Keith Theis, Sales Mgr.

■ **16778** ■ **Cannon Equipment West**
12822 Monarch St.
Garden Grove, CA 92841
Phone: (714)373-5800 **Fax:** (714)898-3584
Products: Material handling equipment, fold-up carts, wire displays and fixtures. **SIC:** 5085 (Industrial Supplies). **Sales:** $10,000,000 (2000). **Emp:** 120.

■ **16779** ■ **Capitol Corp.**
233 E Rankin St.
Jackson, MS 39202
Phone: (601)969-9266
Products: Welding supplies; Environmental supplies. **SIC:** 5085 (Industrial Supplies). **Est:** 1950. **Sales:** $8,200,000 (2000). **Emp:** 59. **Officers:** Von Dunaway, Chairman of the Board; Dean Dunaway, President; Jim Garner, VP of Sales.

■ **16780** ■ **Carbide Tooling & Design**
1232 51st Ave.
Oakland, CA 94601-5602
Phone: (510)532-7669
Free: (800)231-9071 **Fax:** (510)532-6104
Products: Carbide tools. **SICs:** 5085 (Industrial Supplies); 5084 (Industrial Machinery & Equipment). **Sales:** $650,000 (2000). **Emp:** 9. **Officers:** L.C. Montanelli. **Former Name:** Oakland Carbide Engineering.

■ **16781** ■ **Carolina Fluid Components**
9309 Stockport Pl.
Charlotte, NC 28273
Phone: (704)588-6101 **Fax:** (704)588-6115
E-mail: info@cfcsite.com
URL: http://www.cfcsite.com
Products: Fluid power components. **SIC:** 5085 (Industrial Supplies). **Est:** 1978. **Emp:** 90. **Officers:** Jack Marks, CEO; Marty Jenkins, President; Ed Jarnac, Sales/Marketing Contact, e-mail: ejarnac@cfcsite.com; George Beckett, Customer Service Contact.

■ **16782** ■ **Carolina Hardware & Supply, Inc.**
218 W 2nd Loop Rd.
PO Box 13559
Florence, SC 29504-1559
Phone: (803)662-0702 **Fax:** (803)662-2411
Products: Industrial supplies. **SIC:** 5085 (Industrial Supplies). **Est:** 1983. **Emp:** 45. **Officers:** John Frank III, Vice President.

■ **16783** ■ **Carpenter Brothers Inc.**
4555 W Schroeder Dr.
Milwaukee, WI 53223-1400
Phone: (414)354-6555 **Fax:** (414)354-6610
Products: Foundry supplies, including sands and abrasives. **SIC:** 5085 (Industrial Supplies). **Est:** 1917. **Sales:** $9,000,000 (2000). **Emp:** 30. **Officers:** John E. Carpenter, President; John Ryan, Controller.

■ **16784** ■ **A.A. Casey Co.**
5124 Nebraska Ave.
Tampa, FL 33603-2364
Phone: (813)234-8831
Free: (800)329-8831 **Fax:** (813)238-9527
Products: Hand tools, including electrical, pneumatic and hydraulic; Tools, including hand saws, saw blades, and hoists; Pumps; Genrators; Fasteners; Threading equipment; Pipe bending equipment. **SICs:** 5085 (Industrial Supplies); 5084 (Industrial Machinery & Equipment); 5072 (Hardware). **Est:** 1959. **Emp:** 49.

■ **16785** ■ **Cedar Rapids Welding Supply Inc.**
PO Box 453
Cedar Rapids, IA 52406
Phone: (319)365-1466 **Fax:** (319)365-1469
Products: Gases; Wire; Welding supplies. **SICs:** 5169 (Chemicals & Allied Products Nec); 5084 (Industrial Machinery & Equipment). **Est:** 1941. **Sales:** $3,000,000 (2000). **Emp:** 17. **Officers:** Bryan Ellis, President.

■ **16786** ■ **Cee Kay Supply Co.**
5835 Manchester Ave.
St. Louis, MO 63110
Phone: (314)644-3500 **Fax:** (314)644-4336
URL: http://www.ceekay.com
Products: Welding supplies; Cylinder and welding gases. **SICs:** 5084 (Industrial Machinery & Equipment); 5169 (Chemicals & Allied Products Nec). **Est:** 1951. **Sales:** $20,000,000 (2000). **Emp:** 100. **Officers:** Thomas Dunn, President; Ned Lane, Exec. VP; Maryann Boughnou, Controller; Larry Greiner, VP of Operations.

■ **16787** ■ **Central Jersey Supply Co.**
PO Box 549
Perth Amboy, NJ 08862-0549
Phone: (732)826-7400 **Fax:** (732)826-7928
E-mail: centersup@aol.com
Products: Industrial supplies, including pipes, valves, and fittings. **SICs:** 5085 (Industrial Supplies); 5074 (Plumbing & Hydronic Heating Supplies). **Est:** 1946. **Sales:** $8,100,000 (2000). **Emp:** 30. **Officers:** S. Horwitz, President; D. Horwitz, VP of Finance; A. Horwitz, VP of Marketing.

■ **16788** ■ **Central States Airgas Inc.**
200 S 23rd St.
Fairfield, IA 52556-4203
Phone: (515)472-3141 **Fax:** (515)472-3041
Products: Welding supplies; Janitorial supplies. **SICs:** 5169 (Chemicals & Allied Products Nec); 5084 (Industrial Machinery & Equipment). **Est:** 1961. **Sales:** $13,000,000 (2000). **Emp:** 80. **Officers:** Dick Johnson, President; Gary Puls, Controller; Jeff Allen, Sales Mgr.

■ **16789** ■ **Centro, Inc.**
3315 Overton Crossing
PO Box 27161
Memphis, TN 38167-0161
Phone: (901)357-1261
Free: (800)238-6672 **Fax:** (901)357-1379
URL: http://www.centromemphis.com
Products: Valves; Thermometers; Gauges; Meters; Filters. **SICs:** 5085 (Industrial Supplies); 5084 (Industrial Machinery & Equipment). **Est:** 1970. **Sales:** $14,000,000 (1999). **Emp:** 44. **Officers:** Hollis A. Henson, President, e-mail: hollisa@centromemphis.com; Jack Herida, Sales/Marketing Contact, e-mail: jherida@centromemphis.com.

■ **16790** ■ **Chamberlin Rubber Company Inc.**
PO Box 22700
Rochester, NY 14692
Phone: (716)427-7780 **Fax:** (716)427-2429
E-mail: sales@crubber.com
URL: http://www.crubber.com
Products: Industrial hydraulic hose, fittings, and gaskets. **SIC:** 5085 (Industrial Supplies). **Est:** 1865. **Sales:** $8,000,000 (2000). **Emp:** 39. **Officers:** William E. Lanigan, President; Stephen Hayes, Treasurer; Jerome Stomper, VP of Marketing & Sales.

■ **16791** ■ **Carter Chambers Supply Inc.**
PO Box 15705
Baton Rouge, LA 70895
Phone: (504)926-2123 **Fax:** (504)926-1289
Products: Valves; Instrumentation. **SIC:** 5085 (Industrial Supplies). **Est:** 1959. **Sales:** $35,000,000 (2000). **Emp:** 125. **Officers:** Louis Bonnecaze Jr. Jr., President; Greg Stelly, Controller; Greg Stelly, Controller.

■ **16792** ■ **Charken Co. Inc.**
PO Box 13052
Pittsburgh, PA 15243
Phone: (412)745-7979 **Fax:** (412)745-8060
Products: Industrial supplies; Hardware fasteners; Bolts, nuts, rivets, screws, and washers. **SICs:** 5085 (Industrial Supplies); 5072 (Hardware). **Est:** 1955. **Sales:** $12,000,000 (2000). **Emp:** 70. **Officers:** C. Charles Watterson, President.

■ **16793** ■ **Chase Industries Inc.**
5400 Renaissance Tower 1201 Elm St.
Dallas, TX 75270
Products: Industrial engineers materials. **SIC:** 5085 (Industrial Supplies). **Sales:** $433,000,000 (2000). **Emp:** 700. **Officers:** Martin V. Alonzo, CEO; Michael T. Segraves, VP & CFO.

■ **16794** ■ **Cheler Corp.**
PO Box 1750
Seattle, WA 98111-1750
Phone: (206)624-9699 **Fax:** (206)762-8014
Products: Industrial supplies. **SIC:** 5085 (Industrial Supplies). **Est:** 1916. **Sales:** $30,000,000 (2000). **Emp:** 1,500. **Officers:** Chad E. Ernst, President; Beatrice J. Winn, Controller; Carl F. Teichman, VP of Marketing; Charles R. Rogers, VP of Admin.; Jason R. Stevens, General Mgr.

■ **16795** ■ **Chemung Supply Corp.**
PO Box 527
Elmira, NY 14902
Phone: (607)733-5506 **Fax:** (607)732-5379
Products: Corrugated metal; Plastic pipe; Highway supplies. **SICs:** 5051 (Metals Service Centers & Offices); 5162 (Plastics Materials & Basic Shapes). **Est:** 1932. **Sales:** $16,000,000 (1999). **Emp:** 45. **Officers:** Jerry Stemerman, President.

■ **16796** ■ **China House Trading Co.**
2040 Westlake Ave. N
Seattle, WA 98109
Phone: (206)283-1301 **Fax:** (206)283-1443
Products: Industrial equipment and supplies. **SIC:** 5085 (Industrial Supplies). **Est:** 1985. **Sales:** $600,000 (2000). **Emp:** 3. **Officers:** John Still, President.

■ **16797** ■ **Churubusco Distribution Service Center**
PO Box 245
Churubusco, IN 46723
Phone: (219)693-2111 **Fax:** (219)693-6351
Products: Machine parts, including gaskets; Automobile parts. **SICs:** 5013 (Motor Vehicle Supplies & New Parts); 5085 (Industrial Supplies). **Sales:** $45,000,000 (2000). **Emp:** 200. **Officers:** John Zale, Manager; Deborah Carlson, Controller.

■ **16798** ■ **CIMID Corp.**
50 S Center St.
Orange, NJ 07050
Phone: (973)672-5000 **Fax:** (973)672-0059
Products: Polishing, finishing, and grinding products. **SIC:** 5084 (Industrial Machinery & Equipment). **Sales:** $4,000,000 (2000). **Emp:** 7. **Officers:** Frederick E. Eiden, President.

■ **16799** ■ **Cincinnati Gasket Packing Manufacturing Inc.**
40 Illinois Ave.
Cincinnati, OH 45215
Phone: (513)761-3458 **Fax:** (513)761-2994
Products: Gaskets for industrial machinery. **SIC:** 5085 (Industrial Supplies). **Est:** 1907. **Sales:** $6,000,000 (2000). **Emp:** 55. **Officers:** L.J. Uhlenbrock, President & Treasurer.

■ **16800** ■ **Clean Seal**
PO Box 2919
South Bend, IN 46680-2919
Phone: (219)299-1888
Free: (800)366-3682 **Fax:** (219)299-8044
E-mail: cleanseal@cleanseal.com
URL: http://www.cleanseal.com
Products: Extruded and lathe cut mechanical rubber goods. **SIC:** 5085 (Industrial Supplies). **Est:** 1978. **Emp:** 70. **Officers:** Bill Dawson, Vice President; Bill Dorton, Distribution Mgr.

■ **16801** ■ **Clemmons Corp.**
PO Box 4697
Wilmington, NC 28406
Phone: (910)763-3131
Free: (800)768-3131 **Fax:** (910)763-3939
Products: Cylinders; Pumps; Motors; Hoses; Fittings. **SIC:** 5085 (Industrial Supplies). **Est:** 1985. **Sales:** $3,000,000 (2000). **Emp:** 10. **Officers:** Paul Clemmons, President; Weston Clemmons, Vice President, e-mail: Weston9378@aol.com.

■ **16802** ■ **Clisby Agency Inc.**
4300 H St.
Philadelphia, PA 19124
Phone: (215)535-3900
Free: (800)783-3277 **Fax:** (215)535-3901
Products: Power transmission products; Chains, bearings, and gears. **SICs:** 5085 (Industrial Supplies); 5063 (Electrical Apparatus & Equipment). **Est:** 1953. **Officers:** Robert Clisby; Richard Clisby, Sales/Marketing Contact.

■ **16803** ■ **Colonial Hardware Corp.**
163 Varick St.
New York, NY 10013
Phone: (212)741-8989
Free: (800)345-8665 **Fax:** (212)741-8193
Products: Industrial supplies and other hardware. **SICs:** 5085 (Industrial Supplies); 5072 (Hardware).

Sales: $13,000,000 (2000). **Emp:** 40. **Officers:** Michael O'Connell, President; Sheldon Aaron, Controller.

■ **16804** ■ **Commonwealth Tool Specialty Inc.**
PO Box 20039
Roanoke, VA 24018-0502
Phone: (540)989-4368 **Fax:** (540)772-0443
Products: Cutting tools. **SIC:** 5085 (Industrial Supplies). **Est:** 1981. **Sales:** $8,000,000 (2000). **Emp:** 25. **Officers:** E. Staley Jr., President; J. Griffith, VP of Finance; J. Addington, Dir. of Marketing.

■ **16805** ■ **Con-Tech International, Inc.**
PO Box 53313
New Orleans, LA 70153
Phone: (504)523-4785 **Fax:** (504)522-7322
Products: Industrial drum parts and supplies; Plastic bags and resins; Groceries; Metal processing chemicals; Packaging machinery and equipment. **SICs:** 5085 (Industrial Supplies); 5162 (Plastics Materials & Basic Shapes); 5149 (Groceries & Related Products Nec); 5169 (Chemicals & Allied Products Nec); 5084 (Industrial Machinery & Equipment). **Officers:** R. Evans, CEO.

■ **16806** ■ **Connect Air International Inc.**
4240 B St NW
Auburn, WA 98001
Phone: (253)813-5599 **Fax:** (253)813-5699
Products: Custom molded cable assemblies; Bulk wire and cable for computer peripheral manufacturers and electronic system installers. **SIC:** 5085 (Industrial Supplies).

■ **16807** ■ **Continental International**
6723 S Hanna
Ft. Wayne, IN 46816
Phone: (219)447-7000
Free: (800)348-1888 **Fax:** (219)447-9966
E-mail: conintl@aol.com
URL: http://www.contintl.com
Products: Industrial supplies, including seals and abrasives. **SIC:** 5085 (Industrial Supplies). **Est:** 1970. **Sales:** $18,000,000 (2000). **Emp:** 56. **Officers:** Ronald Clem, President, e-mail: ronaldclem@aol.com; Lona Butts, VP of Operations; Debbie Felton, VP of Marketing & Sales, e-mail: abrasivegl@aol.com.

■ **16808** ■ **Contractors Parts Supply, Inc.**
55 Lyerly Bldg. 313
Houston, TX 77022
Phone: (713)695-7162 **Fax:** (713)695-7810
Products: Hydraulic crane parts; Cables; Sling bearings. **SICs:** 5085 (Industrial Supplies); 5084 (Industrial Machinery & Equipment).

■ **16809** ■ **Control Specialties Inc.**
PO Box 266724
Houston, TX 77207
Phone: (713)644-5353 **Fax:** (713)845-1515
Products: Control valves and transmitters. **SIC:** 5085 (Industrial Supplies). **Est:** 1966. **Sales:** $20,000,000 (2000). **Emp:** 70. **Officers:** Randy R. Pennington Jr., President; Dee Whisenhunt, CFO; Gene Johnson, VP of Sales.

■ **16810** ■ **Cook Iron Store Co.**
PO Box 1237
Rochester, NY 14603
Phone: (716)454-5840
Free: (800)724-1540 **Fax:** (716)325-4465
E-mail: cookiron@mindspring.com
Products: Industrial supplies. **SIC:** 5085 (Industrial Supplies). **Est:** 1907. **Sales:** $7,000,000 (2000). **Emp:** 34. **Officers:** Edward W. Page, President; Stephen M. Wichtowski, VP & Sales Mgr.; Terry K. Page, Secretary.

■ **16811** ■ **Corrosion Fluid Products Corp.**
24450 Indoplex Ct.
Farmington Hills, MI 48335
Phone: (248)478-0100 **Fax:** (248)478-8970
Products: Corrosion resistant pipe, valves, pumps, and hose. **SIC:** 5085 (Industrial Supplies). **Est:** 1968. **Sales:** $28,000,000 (2000). **Emp:** 80. **Officers:** J. Andronaco.

■ 16812 ■ Coulter Welding Inc.
2816 S Broadway
Minot, ND 58701-7114
Phone: (701)852-4044
Products: Welding equipment and supplies. SIC: 5084 (Industrial Machinery & Equipment).

■ 16813 ■ Coyle Mechanical Supply
PO Box 578
Granite City, IL 62040
Phone: (618)797-1760   Fax: (618)797-1764
Products: Industrial pipes, valves, and fittings. SIC: 5085 (Industrial Supplies). Est: 1968. Sales: $12,000,000 (2000). Emp: 30. Officers: Jerry T. Coyle, President.

■ 16814 ■ Cruzen Equipment Company Inc.
160 W Mallory Ave.
Memphis, TN 38109
Phone: (901)774-3130
Products: Pumps; Greasing equipment; Industrial supplies, including glass products, valves, and meters. SICs: 5084 (Industrial Machinery & Equipment); 5085 (Industrial Supplies). Sales: $17,000,000 (2000). Emp: 55. Officers: Phillip Cruzen, President.

■ 16815 ■ CTI Abrasives and Tools
2650 S Grand Ave.
Santa Ana, CA 92705
Phone: (714)662-0909   Fax: (714)662-3121
Products: Precision and cutting tools; Abrasives. SIC: 5085 (Industrial Supplies).

■ 16816 ■ J.A. Cunningham Equipment Inc.
2025 Trenton Ave.
Philadelphia, PA 19125
Phone: (215)426-6650   Fax: (215)426-8927
Products: Welding equipment. SIC: 5085 (Industrial Supplies). Est: 1946. Sales: $14,000,000 (2000). Emp: 50. Officers: Paul D. Cunningham, CEO & CFO.

■ 16817 ■ Curtis Fluid Controls, Inc.
2170 S Lipan
Denver, CO 80223
Phone: (303)922-4564
Free: (800)395-2861   Fax: (303)922-4597
Products: Mobile and industrial hydraulic systems and components. SICs: 5085 (Industrial Supplies); 5084 (Industrial Machinery & Equipment). Est: 1974. Sales: $2,500,000 (2000). Emp: 10. Officers: C. Lang, President; S. Lang, VP, Secty. & Treasurer; Bo Harris.

■ 16818 ■ Dabney-Hoover Supply Company Inc.
61 W Georgia Ave.
Memphis, TN 38103
Phone: (901)523-8061
Products: Industrial and mill supplies. SIC: 5085 (Industrial Supplies). Est: 1946. Sales: $4,500,000 (2000). Emp: 20. Officers: Charles W. Hoover III, President; Roger S. Terry, Treasurer & Secty.

■ 16819 ■ Dacotah Paper Co.
3940 15th NW
Fargo, ND 58108
Phone: (701)281-1730   Fax: (701)281-9799
Products: Industrial and personal service paper. SIC: 5113 (Industrial & Personal Service Paper). Sales: $40,000,000 (2000). Emp: 105. Officers: M.D. Mohr, President; M.D. Mohr, CFO.

■ 16820 ■ Davies Supply Co.
6601 W Grand Ave.
Chicago, IL 60707-2298
Phone: (773)637-7800   Fax: (773)637-7033
Products: Industrial supplies. SIC: 5085 (Industrial Supplies). Est: 1877. Sales: $5,000,000 (2000). Emp: 33. Officers: William B. Davies, CEO; John S. Birkos, President; George A. Fuka, Dir. of Marketing & Sales; W.C. Porter, Dir. of Data Processing.

■ 16821 ■ Davis Supply Co. Inc.
PO Box 437
Brewton, AL 36427-0437
Phone: (205)867-6864
Free: (800)239-3115   Fax: (205)867-6867
Products: Fasteners; Mill supplies; Chains; Gloves. SICs: 5085 (Industrial Supplies); 5136 (Men's/Boys' Clothing); 5137 (Women's/Children's Clothing); 5072 (Hardware). Est: 1976. Emp: 4.

■ 16822 ■ De Lille Oxygen Co.
772 Marion Rd.
Columbus, OH 43207
Phone: (614)444-1177   Fax: (614)444-0733
E-mail: info@delille.com
URL: http://www.delille.com
Products: Industrial and specialty gases; Welding supplies. SICs: 5169 (Chemicals & Allied Products Nec); 5085 (Industrial Supplies). Est: 1925. Sales: $11,000,000 (2000). Emp: 60. Officers: Jim O'Conner, President; Tom Smith, Controller.

■ 16823 ■ Dees Corp.
110 Industrial Dr., No. 105
Pottstown, PA 19464-3460
Phone: (610)574-2900
Products: Hydraulic equipment components. SIC: 5085 (Industrial Supplies).

■ 16824 ■ Dees Fluid Power
7611 White Pine Rd.
Richmond, VA 23234
Phone: (804)275-9222   Fax: (804)275-8808
Products: Hydraulic parts. SICs: 5085 (Industrial Supplies); 5084 (Industrial Machinery & Equipment).

■ 16825 ■ Delaware Valley Hydraulics
325 Quigley Blvd.
New Castle, DE 19720
Phone: (302)322-1555
Products: Hydraulics equipment and supplies. SIC: 5085 (Industrial Supplies).

■ 16826 ■ Denali Industrial Supply Inc.
3933 Spenard Rd.
Anchorage, AK 99517
Phone: (907)248-0090
Products: Fasteners; Tools; Safety supplies. SIC: 5085 (Industrial Supplies).

■ 16827 ■ Derkin and Wise Inc.
PO Box 1015
Toledo, OH 43697
Phone: (419)248-4411   Fax: (419)248-4419
Products: Industrial materials. SIC: 5085 (Industrial Supplies). Est: 1959. Sales: $4,000,000 (2000). Emp: 15. Officers: Mark S. Derkin, President; J.A. Derkin, VP of Finance.

■ 16828 ■ Desselle-Maggard Corp.
PO Box 86630
Baton Rouge, LA 70879
Phone: (504)753-3290   Fax: (504)751-5545
Products: Industrial valves and instrumentation. SIC: 5084 (Industrial Machinery & Equipment). Est: 1984.

■ 16829 ■ Detroit Ball Bearing Company Executive Offices
1400 Howard St.
Detroit, MI 48216
Phone: (313)963-6011   Fax: (313)963-5427
Products: Bearings, power transmissions and industrial supplies. SIC: 5085 (Industrial Supplies). Sales: $355,000,000 (1999). Emp: 1,000. Officers: James T. Moore, President; Steven P. Mellos, Sr. VP & Treasurer.

■ 16830 ■ Detroit Gas Products Co.
1200 Farrow Ave.
Ferndale, MI 48220
Phone: (248)543-4012   Fax: (248)543-9819
Products: Welding supplies, including gases, hard hats, welding rods, and wires. SICs: 5085 (Industrial Supplies); 5169 (Chemicals & Allied Products Nec). Est: 1948. Sales: $6,000,000 (2000). Emp: 20. Officers: Thomas Arndt, President & Treasurer.

■ 16831 ■ Dewald Fluid Power Company Inc.
1023 W 8th St.
Mishawaka, IN 46544
Phone: (219)255-4776
Products: Air and hydraulic equipment components. SIC: 5085 (Industrial Supplies). Est: 1960. Sales: $5,000,000 (2000). Emp: 20. Officers: Nick DeCicco, President; Kirk Demeulenaere, General Mgr.; Phil Haslett, Sales Mgr.

■ 16832 ■ Dills Supply Co./Division of Dayton Supply and Tool
242 Leo St.
Dayton, OH 45404
Phone: (937)228-3201
Free: ((93)247-5416   Fax: (937)228-8284
Products: Industrial and contractor supplies. SIC: 5085 (Industrial Supplies). Est: 1945. Sales: $5,500,000 (2000). Emp: 27.

■ 16833 ■ Divesco Inc.
5000 Hwy. 80 E
Jackson, MS 39208
Phone: (601)932-1934   Fax: (601)932-5698
Products: Valves and pumps. SIC: 5084 (Industrial Machinery & Equipment). Est: 1979. Sales: $1,000,000 (2000). Emp: 5. Officers: Thomas F. Westbrook Jr., President; S. Kay Fisher, Vice President; Tom Westbrook, Sales/Marketing Contact, e-mail: tom@divesco.com.

■ 16834 ■ Dixie Industrial Supply Co.
2100 The Oaks Pkwy.
Belmont, NC 28012
Phone: (704)820-1000   Fax: (704)820-1104
Products: Grinding wheels; Conveyer belts; Pipes; Fittings; Hoses; MROP, including cutting tools and hand tools. SIC: 5085 (Industrial Supplies). Est: 1963. Emp: 300. Officers: Charles Lingenfelter, President; Bill McGough, Controller; Laura Wright, Dir of Personnel.

■ 16835 ■ Dixie Industrial Supply Div.
PO Box 1127
Belmont, NC 28012-1127
Phone: (704)482-5641
Products: Industrial supplies including boxes. SIC: 5085 (Industrial Supplies). Sales: $54,000,000 (2000). Emp: 250. Officers: Peter Covert, Controller.

■ 16836 ■ DoAll Co.
254 N Laurel Ave.
Des Plaines, IL 60016
Phone: (847)824-1122
Free: (800)923-6255   Fax: (847)699-7524
Products: Industrial supplies, industrial machinery and equipment. SICs: 5085 (Industrial Supplies); 5084 (Industrial Machinery & Equipment). Sales: $232,000,000 (1999). Emp: 120. Officers: David Crawford, Sr. VP; Stephen Stoppenbrink, Vice President; M.L. Wilkie, President.

■ 16837 ■ Douglas and Sons, Inc.
231 W Cedar St.
Kalamazoo, MI 49007
Phone: (616)344-2860   Fax: (616)344-4048
Products: Power washing supplies, including roller covers. SIC: 5085 (Industrial Supplies).

■ 16838 ■ Doussan Inc.
PO Box 52407
New Orleans, LA 70152
Phone: (504)948-7561   Fax: (504)942-4324
Products: Industrial power tools and supplies; Gases. SICs: 5085 (Industrial Supplies); 5169 (Chemicals & Allied Products Nec). Est: 1945. Sales: $24,000,000 (2000). Emp: 110. Officers: Jeff Ellis, President; John Olsen, Controller.

■ 16839 ■ S.E. Drey and Co. Inc.
9135 Harrison Park Ct.
PO Box 26499
Indianapolis, IN 46226
Phone: (317)543-5640
Free: (800)222-8053   Fax: (317)543-5641
E-mail: sedrey@concentric.net
URL: http://www.sedrey.com
Products: Industrial materials; Casters and wheels; Material handling equipment. SICs: 5085 (Industrial Supplies); 5084 (Industrial Machinery & Equipment). Est: 1959. Sales: $950,000 (2000). Emp: 6. Officers: Don Curtis, President.

■ 16840 ■ Duncan Co.
425 NE Hoover
Minneapolis, MN 55413-2926
Phone: (612)331-1776
Free: (800)677-1776   Fax: (612)331-4735
Products: Machine tool accessories; Parts for metal

forming machine tools. **SICs:** 5085 (Industrial Supplies); 5084 (Industrial Machinery & Equipment). **Est:** 1928. **Sales:** $10,000,000 (2000). **Emp:** 35. **Officers:** Eric Duncan.

■ **16841** ■ **Duncan-Edward Co.**
PO Box 14038
Ft. Lauderdale, FL 33302
Phone: (954)467-1461
Products: Industrial tools. **SIC:** 5085 (Industrial Supplies). **Est:** 1945. **Sales:** $4,000,000 (2000). **Emp:** 20. **Officers:** Scott Debrauwere, President; Bob Slaughter, Treasurer; L. Lankford, Dir. of Marketing.

■ **16842** ■ **Duncan Equipment Co.**
PO Box 40
Duncan, OK 73533
Phone: (405)255-1216 **Fax:** (405)255-0409
Products: Industrial supplies. **SICs:** 5085 (Industrial Supplies); 5084 (Industrial Machinery & Equipment). **Est:** 1949. **Sales:** $24,000,000 (2000). **Emp:** 93. **Officers:** John O. Moore, President; John Smith, Treasurer.

■ **16843** ■ **Dynamic Technology**
2608 Nordic Rd.
Dayton, OH 45414
Phone: (937)274-3007 **Fax:** (937)274-2502
Products: Hydraulic and pneumatic products. **SICs:** 5085 (Industrial Supplies); 5084 (Industrial Machinery & Equipment).

■ **16844** ■ **Dynamic Technology**
2323 Crowne Point Dr.
Cincinnati, OH 45241-5405
Phone: (513)793-4992 **Fax:** (513)793-4990
Products: Hydraulic parts. **SIC:** 5085 (Industrial Supplies).

■ **16845** ■ **Economy Paper Company Inc.**
1175 E Main St.
Rochester, NY 14601
Phone: (716)482-5340 **Fax:** (716)482-2089
Products: Paper and paper products. **SIC:** 5113 (Industrial & Personal Service Paper). **Sales:** $10,000,000 (2000). **Emp:** 43.

■ **16846** ■ **A. Ehrke & Co.**
31100 Bainbridge Rd.
Solon, OH 44139
Phone: (440)248-9400 **Fax:** (440)248-9170
Products: Valves. **SIC:** 5085 (Industrial Supplies).

■ **16847** ■ **EIS Com-Kyl**
41444 Christy St.
Fremont, CA 94538
Phone: (510)979-0070
Free: (800)722-1123 **Fax:** (510)438-6180
Products: Manufacturing supplies. **SIC:** 5085 (Industrial Supplies). **Former Name:** Com-Kyl.

■ **16848** ■ **Empire Airgas**
1200 Sullivan St.
Elmira, NY 14901
Phone: 800-666-6523 **Fax:** 800-333-6523
Products: Industrial gases including propane and helium; Welding supplies; Industrial tools. **SICs:** 5169 (Chemicals & Allied Products Nec); 5084 (Industrial Machinery & Equipment); 5085 (Industrial Supplies). **Est:** 1991. **Sales:** $25,000,000 (2000). **Emp:** 135. **Officers:** Chuck Graves, President; Richard R. Schillo, General Mgr.

■ **16849** ■ **Empire Refactory Sales Inc.**
219 Murray St.
Ft. Wayne, IN 46803
Phone: (219)456-5656 **Fax:** (219)744-3564
Products: Refractory materials. **SIC:** 5085 (Industrial Supplies). **Est:** 1936. **Sales:** $10,000,000 (1999). **Emp:** 40. **Officers:** Larry E. Snell, President; Bill Sale, VP & Treasurer; Leanna Rondot, Customer Service Contact, e-mail: lrondo@mixi.net.

■ **16850** ■ **Emuge Corp.**
104 Otis St.
Northborough, MA 01532
Phone: (508)393-1300 **Fax:** (508)393-1310
E-mail: emuge@emuge.cOm
URL: http://www.emuge.com
Products: Machine taps and dies; End mills; Thread mills; Precision work holding and clamping; Tapping fluid; Gear hobs. **SIC:** 5085 (Industrial Supplies). **Est:** 1983. **Sales:** $6,000,000 (2000). **Emp:** 20. **Officers:** Peter Matysiak, President; Alan D Shepherd, Sales/Marketing Contact.

■ **16851** ■ **Engine Service and Supply Co.**
1902 N Grant
Odessa, TX 79761
Phone: (915)337-2386 **Fax:** (915)337-0181
Products: Industrial tools, parts, and supplies. **SICs:** 5085 (Industrial Supplies); 5084 (Industrial Machinery & Equipment). **Est:** 1945. **Sales:** $7,000,000 (2000). **Emp:** 35. **Officers:** Vance Cobb.

■ **16852** ■ **Exotic Rubber and Plastics Corp.**
PO Box 395
Farmington, MI 48332
Phone: (810)477-2122 **Fax:** (810)477-0427
Products: Hydraulics equipment and supplies, including rubber and plastic sheets, hoses, tubes, and pipes. **SICs:** 5199 (Nondurable Goods Nec); 5085 (Industrial Supplies). **Est:** 1962. **Sales:** $18,000,000 (2000). **Emp:** 130. **Officers:** A.B. Marino, President; Thomas Marino, Exec. VP of Finance & Operations; J.E. Brevik, Exec. VP.

■ **16853** ■ **Expanko Cork Co.**
PO Box 384
West Chester, PA 19380
Phone: (610)436-8300
Free: (800)345-6202 **Fax:** (610)344-0288
E-mail: sales@expanko.com
URL: http://www.expanko.com
Products: Cork. **SIC:** 5085 (Industrial Supplies). **Est:** 1945. **Emp:** 8. **Officers:** D.E. McKee, President; Ann M. Young, Controller; Robert Mckee, Sales/Marketing Contact, e-mail: rmckee@expanko.com; G. Phipps, Customer Service Contact.

■ **16854** ■ **Exploration Supplies of Houma Inc.**
9077 Park Ave.
Houma, LA 70360
Phone: (504)851-1000
Free: (800)737-3977 **Fax:** (504)876-3312
E-mail: ramorris@mobiletel.com
Products: Industrial supplies. **SIC:** 5085 (Industrial Supplies). **Est:** 1960. **Sales:** $4,000,000 (2000). **Emp:** 30. **Officers:** John D. Morris, President; Robert A. Morris, Vice President.

■ **16855** ■ **Fairmont Supply Co. (Washington, Pennsylvania)**
PO Box 501
Washington, PA 15301
Phone: (724)223-2200
Free: (800)245-9900 **Fax:** (724)223-2335
Products: Industrial material and management supplies. **SIC:** 5085 (Industrial Supplies). **Sales:** $291,000,000 (2000). **Emp:** 640. **Officers:** Charles Whirlow, President; Ronald Rapp, Controller.

■ **16856** ■ **Fairmont Supply Co. Western Operations**
565 South 300 W
Price, UT 84501
Phone: (435)636-3100
Free: (800)332-6934 **Fax:** (435)636-3105
URL: http://www.fairmontsupply.com
Products: Mining, safety and industrial products. **SICs:** 5082 (Construction & Mining Machinery); 5084 (Industrial Machinery & Equipment). **Est:** 1921. **Sales:** $225,000,000 (2000). **Emp:** 600. **Officers:** Van Compagni, General Mgr.

■ **16857** ■ **Fauver Co.**
1500 E Avis Dr.
Madison Heights, MI 48071
Phone: (734)585-5252 **Fax:** (734)585-1183
Products: Hydraulic and pneumatic equipment and supplies, including pumps and air cylinders; Electrical switches; Oil and air filters. **SICs:** 5085 (Industrial

Supplies); 5063 (Electrical Apparatus & Equipment). **Est:** 1923. **Sales:** $90,000,000 (2000). **Emp:** 300. **Officers:** Frank Brayton, President; Charles Dale, CFO; Therese Mosier, Dir. of Information Systems.

■ **16858** ■ **Faxon Engineering Company Inc.**
467 New Park Ave.
West Hartford, CT 06110
Phone: (860)236-4266
Products: Hydraulic hoses. **SIC:** 5085 (Industrial Supplies). **Est:** 1947. **Sales:** $4,000,000 (2000). **Emp:** 25. **Officers:** J.N. Clark, President & Treasurer; Kevin Rourke, VP of Marketing.

■ **16859** ■ **J. Fegely Inc.**
1810 West High St.
PO Box 619
Pottstown, PA 19464
Phone: (610)323-9120
Free: (800)523-5400 **Fax:** (610)326-0446
E-mail: jfegely@ptd.net
URL: http://www.jfegely.com
Products: Industrial tools; Janitorial supplies; Cutting tools and accessories. **SICs:** 5085 (Industrial Supplies); 5087 (Service Establishment Equipment). **Est:** 1851. **Sales:** $50,000,000 (2000). **Emp:** 115. **Officers:** Tom A. McCaslin IV, CEO; Joseph R. Homa, President & COO.

■ **16860** ■ **Filtemp Sales, Inc.**
PO Box 15860
Phoenix, AZ 85060
Phone: (602)243-4245 **Fax:** (602)243-4263
E-mail: filtemp@azlink.com
URL: http://www.filtemp.com
Products: Filters; Pumps; Tanks; Fans; Heat exchangers. **SICs:** 5074 (Plumbing & Hydronic Heating Supplies); 5085 (Industrial Supplies). **Est:** 1972. **Sales:** $6,000,000 (2000). **Emp:** 14. **Officers:** George Metro, Vice President, e-mail: gmetro@azlink.com; John Gaspers, President, e-mail: jgaspers@azlink.com.

■ **16861** ■ **Findley Welding Supply Inc.**
1326 E 12th St.
Erie, PA 16503
Phone: (814)456-5311
Products: Welding supplies, including torches, tanks, safety equipment, and masks. **SIC:** 5085 (Industrial Supplies). **Est:** 1936. **Sales:** $15,000,000 (2000). **Emp:** 70. **Officers:** G. Seeds, President.

■ **16862** ■ **Fine Organics Corp.**
PO Box 2277
Clifton, NJ 07015
Phone: (973)472-6800
Free: (800)526-7481 **Fax:** (973)472-6810
Products: Industrial organic chemicals and specialty cleaners and polishes. **SIC:** 5085 (Industrial Supplies). **Sales:** $4,000,000 (2000). **Emp:** 20. **Officers:** W.J. Reidy, CEO; Charles Gentile, Controller.

■ **16863** ■ **First International Trading Company**
2231 South Pacific Ave.
San Pedro, CA 90731
Phone: (310)514-8427 **Fax:** (310)514-2552
Products: Industrial supplies, including engine filters; Industrial oils and greases; Brake fluid; Chemical adhesives; Electronic components. **SICs:** 5085 (Industrial Supplies); 5172 (Petroleum Products Nec); 5065 (Electronic Parts & Equipment Nec); 5169 (Chemicals & Allied Products Nec). **Officers:** Richard Peterson, Vice President.

■ **16864** ■ **First Line Marketing, Inc.**
636 South Alaska
Seattle, WA 98108
Phone: (206)622-3335 **Fax:** (206)622-4821
Products: Industrial supplies; Industrial machinery and equipment. **SICs:** 5085 (Industrial Supplies); 5084 (Industrial Machinery & Equipment). **Officers:** Kurtis A. Nicholson, Account Manager.

■ **16865** ■ **Fitch Industrial Welding Supply Inc.**
PO Box 2067
Lawton, OK 73501
Phone: (580)353-4950
Free: (800)256-4950 **Fax:** (580)355-8663
E-mail: fitch@sirinet.net
URL: http://www.fitchindustrial.com
Products: Welding supplies and gases. **SICs:** 5085 (Industrial Supplies); 5169 (Chemicals & Allied Products Nec). **Est:** 1950. **Sales:** $10,000,000 (2000). **Emp:** 37. **Officers:** Frederick L. Fitch, President; Hazel Lee Fitch, Vice President.

■ **16866** ■ **T.J. Fleming Co.**
647 Southwest Blvd.
Kansas City, KS 66103
Phone: (913)236-9000
Products: Hoses. **SIC:** 5085 (Industrial Supplies). **Est:** 1946. **Sales:** $3,000,000 (2000). **Emp:** 5. **Officers:** Joseph R. Fleming, President; Robert Evilsizer, Treasurer & Secty.

■ **16867** ■ **Flickinger Co.**
3200 Bayshore Rd., Unit 3
Benicia, CA 94510
Phone: (707)747-9095 **Free:** (800)747-9997
Products: Industrial valves. **SIC:** 5085 (Industrial Supplies). **Sales:** $37,000,000 (1992). **Emp:** 170. **Officers:** Mark Stannard, Manager.

■ **16868** ■ **Flo-Products Co.**
2305 Millpark Rd.
Maryland Heights, MO 63043
Phone: (314)428-4000 **Fax:** (314)428-4097
E-mail: customerservice@flo-products.com
URL: http://www.flo-products.com
Products: Hydraulic and pneumatic components. **SIC:** 5085 (Industrial Supplies). **Est:** 1959. **Sales:** $12,000,000 (2000). **Emp:** 34. **Officers:** Dick Widmyer, President; Greg Stone, VP of Finance.

■ **16869** ■ **Florida Bearings Inc.**
3164 N Miami Ave.
Miami, FL 33127
Phone: (305)573-8424 **Fax:** (305)573-7366
Products: Industrial parts, including bearings, seals, and pulleys. **SIC:** 5085 (Industrial Supplies). **Est:** 1943. **Sales:** $5,000,000 (2000). **Emp:** 27. **Officers:** Al Marchetti, President; Aurora Suarez, Controller; Bruce Marchetti, Dir. of Marketing.

■ **16870** ■ **Fluid-Air Components L.L.C.**
PO Box 55848
Portland, OR 97238
Phone: (503)254-9292 **Fax:** (503)252-4163
Products: Fluid power systems and air components; Hydraulic and pneumatic components and systems. **SIC:** 5085 (Industrial Supplies). **Officers:** Eric Nelson, CFO.

■ **16871** ■ **Forge Industries Inc.**
4450 Market St.
Youngstown, OH 44512
Phone: (330)782-8301
Products: Industrial supplies. **SIC:** 5085 (Industrial Supplies).

■ **16872** ■ **Forged Vessel Connections Inc.**
PO Box 38421
Houston, TX 77238-8421
Phone: (713)688-9705
Free: (800)231-2701 **Fax:** (713)688-1846
E-mail: fvc@forgedvesselconn.com
URL: http://www.forgedvesselconn.com
Products: Flanges for pressure vessels. **SICs:** 5085 (Industrial Supplies); 5085 (Industrial Supplies). **Est:** 1976. **Sales:** $25,000,000 (2000). **Emp:** 95. **Officers:** James C. Fiadler; Dennis Mican, Sales/Marketing Contact, e-mail: dmican@forgedvesselconn.com; Bula Brandon, Customer Service Contact, e-mail: bbrandon@forgedvesselconn.com; Reuana Carroll, Human Resources Contact, e-mail: rcarroll@forgedvesselconn.com.

■ **16873** ■ **Forman Inc.**
2036 Lord Baltimore Dr.
Baltimore, MD 21244
Phone: (410)298-7500
Free: (800)446-2853 **Fax:** (410)298-2089
Products: Disposable products, cups, toilet paper and janitorial supplies. **SIC:** 5113 (Industrial & Personal Service Paper). **Sales:** $48,000,000 (2000). **Emp:** 70. **Officers:** J.J. Mucha, CEO; F.A. Mucha, Treasurer.

■ **16874** ■ **W.J. Foss Co.**
380 Union St., No. LL24
West Springfield, MA 01089-4123
Phone: (413)737-0206 **Fax:** (413)737-0390
Products: Industrial supplies. **SICs:** 5085 (Industrial Supplies); 5063 (Electrical Apparatus & Equipment). **Est:** 1912. **Sales:** $1,000,000 (2000). **Emp:** 11. **Officers:** Richard Grimaldi, President.

■ **16875** ■ **L.B. Foster Co.**
415 Holiday Dr.
Pittsburgh, PA 15220
Phone: (412)928-3400
Free: (800)255-4500 **Fax:** (412)928-7891
Products: Pipe and pipe coatings for utilities. **SIC:** 5039 (Construction Materials Nec). **Sales:** $220,300,000 (2000). **Emp:** 526. **Officers:** Lee B. Foster II, CEO & President; Roger F. Nejes, Sr. VP & CFO.

■ **16876** ■ **Foundry Service Supply Inc.**
7 Greenwood Pl.
Baltimore, MD 21208
Phone: (410)486-6238 **Fax:** (410)486-7071
Products: Foundry supplies, including files and sand. **SIC:** 5085 (Industrial Supplies). **Est:** 1950. **Sales:** $5,000,000 (2000). **Emp:** 14. **Officers:** Henry M. Witmyer, President & Treasurer.

■ **16877** ■ **Fournier Rubber and Supply Co.**
1341 Norton Ave.
Columbus, OH 43212
Phone: (614)294-6453 **Fax:** (614)294-0644
Products: Sheet rubber; Gaskets; Hose assemblies; Fittings; Spray equipment; Couplings. **SIC:** 5085 (Industrial Supplies). **Est:** 1933. **Sales:** $6,000,000 (2000). **Emp:** 22. **Officers:** Dennis K. Davison, President; Kevin Hissrich, VP of Finance.

■ **16878** ■ **Frederickseal, Inc.**
461 Straw Rd.
Manchester, NH 03102
Phone: (603)668-0900
Free: (800)258-3017 **Fax:** (603)623-4444
E-mail: info@frederickseal.com
URL: http://www.frederickseal.com
Products: Sealing materials & devices: including mechanical seals, packing, gasketing, o-rings, hydraulic and pneumatic seals; Boiler supplies. **SIC:** 5085 (Industrial Supplies). **Est:** 1969. **Sales:** $1,500,000 (1999). **Emp:** 16. **Officers:** Anthony J. Frederick Jr., President, e-mail: tony@frederickseal.com; Brent Smith, Inside Sales; Sandra Cox, Human Resources Contact.

■ **16879** ■ **Freeman Manufacturing and Supply**
1101 Moore Rd.
Avon, OH 44011
Phone: (440)934-1902 **Fax:** (440)934-7200
Products: Patterns for wax, pattern letters and epoxies; Repairing and reproducing. **SIC:** 5085 (Industrial Supplies).

■ **16880** ■ **Friedman Bag Company Inc.**
PO Box 866004
Los Angeles, CA 90086
Phone: (213)628-2341
Products: agricultural bags. **SICs:** 5113 (Industrial & Personal Service Paper); 5199 (Nondurable Goods Nec). **Sales:** $203,000,000 (2000). **Emp:** 300. **Officers:** Alvin Lanfeld, President.

■ **16881** ■ **Fugitt Rubber & Supply Company, Inc.**
1900 Thomas Rd.
Memphis, TN 38134-6315
Phone: (901)525-7897
Free: (800)423-1724 **Fax:** (901)377-5257
Products: Rubber and plastic hose and belting; Seals,

gaskets, and packing. **SIC:** 5085 (Industrial Supplies). **Officers:** Harold Gaither, President.

■ **16882** ■ **Fulton, Mehring & Hauser Company, Inc.**
PO Box 2466
York, PA 17405-2466
Phone: (717)843-9054 **Fax:** (717)845-1347
E-mail: fmh@cyberia.com
URL: http://www.industry.net/fulton.mehring
Products: Industrial supplies. **SIC:** 5085 (Industrial Supplies). **Est:** 1901. **Sales:** $6,500,000 (2000). **Emp:** 29. **Officers:** M.S. Paules, President; Don Taylor, CFO; Rick Herr, Information Systems Mgr.

■ **16883** ■ **Fulton Supply Co.**
342 Nelson St. SW
PO Box 4028
Atlanta, GA 30313
Phone: (404)688-3400
Free: (800)241-7090 **Fax:** (404)681-1845
Products: Nonmetallic coated abrasive products and buffing wheels, polishing wheels, and laps; Metal cutting machine tools; Power hand tools; Gauges; Valves; Precision measuring tools; Material handling equipment; Machine tool accessories; Machine tools, metal cutting types; Pumps; Compressors; Parts and attachments for pumps; Safety products; Railroad equipment and supplies. **SICs:** 5085 (Industrial Supplies); 5084 (Industrial Machinery & Equipment); 5072 (Hardware); 5088 (Transportation Equipment & Supplies). **Est:** 1914. **Sales:** $22,000,000 (2000). **Emp:** 99.

■ **16884** ■ **Furniture Makers Supply Co.**
PO Box 728
Lexington, NC 27292
Phone: (336)956-2722
Free: (800)845-2127 **Fax:** (336)956-2918
Products: Abrasive products; Textile tape; Adhesives and sealants. **SICs:** 5085 (Industrial Supplies); 5169 (Chemicals & Allied Products Nec). **Est:** 1952. **Sales:** $10,000,000 (2000). **Emp:** 45. **Officers:** Dan E. Smith, President; Robert Ketchie, Chairman of the Board; Charles Parks Jr., Sec. & Treas.

■ **16885** ■ **Gage Co.**
PO Box 658
Library, PA 15129-0658
Phone: (412)255-6904 **Fax:** (412)255-6905
Products: Industrial supplies, including pipes, valves, and copper tubing. **SICs:** 5074 (Plumbing & Hydronic Heating Supplies); 5085 (Industrial Supplies). **Est:** 1892. **Sales:** $176,000,000 (2000). **Emp:** 600. **Officers:** Robert A. Chute, CEO; Gary Van Luven, Vice Chairman of the Board & CFO; Lloyd Morgan, President.

■ **16886** ■ **Gage Co. Central Div.**
5420 W 84th St.
Indianapolis, IN 46268
Phone: (317)872-8876
Free: (800)886-4243 **Fax:** (317)876-2573
E-mail: gageco@internetmci.com
URL: http://www.thegage.com
Products: Industrial supplies, including pipes, valves, fittings, and rubber products; Cutting tools. **SIC:** 5085 (Industrial Supplies). **Est:** 1892. **Sales:** $7,000,000 (2000). **Emp:** 26. **Officers:** Tom Russell, Manager.

■ **16887** ■ **Gardena Industrial Supply and Hardware Co.**
17010 S Vermont
Gardena, CA 90247
Phone: (310)527-9500
Products: Industrial supplies including drills, braces, adhesives, and blades. **SIC:** 5085 (Industrial Supplies).

■ **16888** ■ **Gary's Machinery Inc.**
1442 E Lincoln Ave.
Orange, CA 92865-1934
Phone: (714)283-1900 **Fax:** (714)279-4765
Products: Machine parts. **SIC:** 5085 (Industrial Supplies). **Est:** 1959. **Sales:** $3,000,000 (2000). **Emp:** 3. **Officers:** Gary L. Rawley, President.

■ **16889** ■ **Gas Technics of Ohio**
14788 York Rd.
North Royalton, OH 44133
Phone: (440)237-8770
Products: Medical and industrial gases. **SIC:** 5169 (Chemicals & Allied Products Nec).

■ **16890** ■ **Gates InterAmerica**
3609 N 29th Ave.
Hollywood, FL 33020
Phone: (954)926-7510   **Fax:** (954)926-8024
Products: Hydraulic belts and hoses, including automotive. **SICs:** 5085 (Industrial Supplies); 5013 (Motor Vehicle Supplies & New Parts). **Est:** 1911. **Sales:** $38,000,000 (2000). **Emp:** 13,500. **Officers:** J. Riess, President; E.V. Heath, Mgr. Dir.

■ **16891** ■ **Gear Motions Inc.**
1750 Milton Ave.
Syracuse, NY 13209
Phone: (315)488-0100   **Fax:** (315)488-0196
Products: Gears and shafts for large machinery. **SIC:** 5085 (Industrial Supplies). **Est:** 1970. **Sales:** $8,000,000 (2000). **Emp:** 97. **Officers:** S.R. Haines II, President; Nelson A. Puccia, VP of Finance; Stephen H. Haines, Dir. of Marketing.

■ **16892** ■ **Geib Industries Inc.**
3220 Wolf Rd.
Franklin Park, IL 60131
Phone: (847)455-4550   **Fax:** (847)455-4559
Products: Air compressors, hydraulic hoses and fittings. **SIC:** 5085 (Industrial Supplies). **Est:** 1960. **Sales:** $12,000,000 (2000). **Emp:** 35. **Officers:** Robert Geib, President.

■ **16893** ■ **General Tool & Supply Co.**
5614 7th Ave. S
PO Box 80904
Seattle, WA 98108
Phone: (206)762-1500
Free: (800)321-3305   **Fax:** (206)767-7026
E-mail: custseerv@generaltool.com
URL: http://www.generaltool.com
Products: Tools; Industrial supplies; Electronic systems and equipment. **SICs:** 5085 (Industrial Supplies); 5065 (Electronic Parts & Equipment Nec); 5084 (Industrial Machinery & Equipment). **Est:** 1927. **Sales:** $48,000,000 (2000). **Emp:** 150. **Officers:** William Derville, President; George Stonecliffe, Vice President; Jim Miller, Vice President; Ken Smith, Vice President.

■ **16894** ■ **Patsy Georgino and Sons Inc.**
PO Box 300
Penfield, PA 15849
Phone: (814)637-5301
Products: Industrial supplies, including drill bits, oils, grease, and cutting tools. **SIC:** 5085 (Industrial Supplies). **Sales:** $6,000,000 (2000). **Emp:** 20. **Officers:** Donald Georgino, President & Treasurer; Patsy F. Georgino, Vice President.

■ **16895** ■ **The John M. Glass Co., Inc.**
7504 Crews Dr.
PO Box 26189
Lawrence, IN 46226
Phone: (317)547-0727
Free: (800)628-1960   **Fax:** (317)547-0722
Products: Foundry supplies; Safety equipment; Pneumatic tools; Hoists; Crucibles; Abrasives; Chisels; Hot melt adhesives and epoxies; industrial vibrators; Electric tools and hoists; Chaplest; Chills; Ferrules; Wire shapes; Screw machine parts. **SICs:** 5085 (Industrial Supplies); 5084 (Industrial Machinery & Equipment). **Est:** 1919. **Sales:** $3,000,000 (2000). **Emp:** 6. **Officers:** F. Wolfla, President; R.A. Wolfla, Vice President.

■ **16896** ■ **Global Expediting and Marketing Co.**
PO Box 611
Avondale Estates, GA 30002
Phone: (404)296-2839   **Fax:** (404)296-9596
Products: Spare parts. **SIC:** 5085 (Industrial Supplies). **Est:** 1974. **Sales:** $1,000,000 (2000). **Emp:** 4. **Officers:** Owen Beckner, President; David Beckner, Vice President.

■ **16897** ■ **Globe Machinery and Supply Co.**
4060 Dixon St.
Des Moines, IA 50313
Phone: (515)262-0088
Free: (800)362-2804   **Fax:** (515)262-8261
Products: Industrial tools and supplies. **SIC:** 5085 (Industrial Supplies). **Est:** 1893. **Sales:** $27,000,000 (2000). **Emp:** 95. **Officers:** Harold Thoreson, CEO & President.

■ **16898** ■ **Goddard Industries Inc.**
PO Box 165
Worcester, MA 01613-0765
Phone: (508)852-2435   **Fax:** (508)852-2443
E-mail: valve@goddardvalve.com
Products: Cryogenic valves for storage and transfer of liquified gases. **SICs:** 5074 (Plumbing & Hydronic Heating Supplies); 5085 (Industrial Supplies). **Est:** 1959. **Sales:** $10,100,000 (2000). **Emp:** 50. **Officers:** Saul I. Reck, Chairman of the Board & Treasurer; S.J. Vinciguerra, President; Donald R. Nelson, Vice President; Leon A. Shriber, VP of Sales.

■ **16899** ■ **Goodall Rubber Co.**
790 Birney Hwy.
Aston, PA 19014-1443
Free: (800)562-8002
Products: Industrial supplies. **SIC:** 5085 (Industrial Supplies). **Sales:** $164,000,000 (2000). **Emp:** 502. **Officers:** Joseph Mika, CEO; Donald A. Stout, VP of Finance.

■ **16900** ■ **Gooding Rubber Co. (La Grange, Illinois)**
411 E Plainfield Rd.
La Grange, IL 60525
Phone: (708)354-2270   **Fax:** (708)354-2348
Products: Industrial hoses and belts. **SIC:** 5085 (Industrial Supplies). **Sales:** $25,000,000 (2000). **Emp:** 80. **Officers:** John Mork, President; Kim Heis, Dir. of Operations.

■ **16901** ■ **Goodyear Tire Rubber Co.**
3151 S Vaughn Way, Ste. 410
Aurora, CO 80014
Phone: (303)695-2413   **Fax:** (303)695-2424
Products: Industrial rubber products, including conveyor belts and hoses. **SICs:** 5085 (Industrial Supplies); 5014 (Tires & Tubes). **Sales:** $2,000,000 (2000). **Emp:** 5.

■ **16902** ■ **Goss Supply Co.**
620 Marietta St.
PO BOX 2580
Zanesville, OH 43702-2580
Phone: (740)454-2571
Free: (800)222-4677   **Fax:** (740)454-7344
Products: Industrial supplies. **SIC:** 5085 (Industrial Supplies). **Est:** 1950. **Emp:** 50. **Officers:** Clarence Goss, President; Terry Goss, Vice President; Roger Whitt, Sales Mgr.; Andy Goss, Marketing.

■ **16903** ■ **Graphic Sciences Inc.**
7515 NE Ambassador Pl
Portland, OR 97220
Phone: (503)460-0203   **Fax:** (503)460-0225
Products: Printing ink. **SIC:** 5085 (Industrial Supplies). **Sales:** $23,000,000 (1999). **Emp:** 119. **Officers:** William K. Wishart, President; Cindy Cummings, Controller.

■ **16904** ■ **Grayco Products**
1025 Old Country Rd.
Westbury, NY 11590
Phone: (516)997-9200   **Fax:** (516)997-9617
Products: Industrial supplies; Safety equipment; Foodservice equipment. **SICs:** 5085 (Industrial Supplies); 5046 (Commercial Equipment Nec). **Est:** 1969. **Sales:** $1,000,000 (2000). **Emp:** 20. **Officers:** Herbert Ginsberg, President; Robert Ginsberg, Vice President; Nancy Berger, Treasurer.

■ **16905** ■ **Great Falls Paper Co.**
600 2nd St. S
Great Falls, MT 59405
Phone: (406)453-7671
Free: (800)992-7671   **Fax:** (406)453-7673
Products: Paper and paper products. **SIC:** 5113

(Industrial & Personal Service Paper). **Sales:** $1,000,000 (2000). **Emp:** 8.

■ **16906** ■ **Great Western Airgas Inc.**
2584 U.S Hwy. 6 and 50
Grand Junction, CO 81505
Phone: (303)243-1944
Products: Oxygen; Nitrogen. **SICs:** 5084 (Industrial Machinery & Equipment); 5169 (Chemicals & Allied Products Nec). **Est:** 1991. **Sales:** $3,300,000 (2000). **Emp:** 14. **Officers:** Dennis Schafer, General Mgr.

■ **16907** ■ **Carl Green and Co.**
3351 O'Brian Rd. SW
Grand Rapids, MI 49504
Phone: (616)453-1046
Products: Nonmetallic coated abrasive products and buffing wheels, polishing wheels, and laps; Abrasive products. **SICs:** 5085 (Industrial Supplies); 5084 (Industrial Machinery & Equipment). **Est:** 1967. **Emp:** 3. **Officers:** Carl E. Green, President.

■ **16908** ■ **Greensboro Pipe Company Inc.**
3102 Randleman Rd.
Greensboro, NC 27406
Phone: (919)275-9156
Products: Industrial pipes, valves, and fittings, including drainage, pressure, culverts, PVC, CPVC, stainless steel, and plastic. **SICs:** 5085 (Industrial Supplies); 5074 (Plumbing & Hydronic Heating Supplies). **Est:** 1970. **Sales:** $5,000,000 (2000). **Emp:** 18. **Officers:** Garvie Chambers, President.

■ **16909** ■ **Greno Industries Inc.**
P.O Box 542
Schenectady, NY 12301
Phone: (518)393-4195   **Fax:** (518)393-4182
Products: Industrial supplies. **SIC:** 5085 (Industrial Supplies). **Sales:** $11,000,000 (1994). **Emp:** 80. **Officers:** Vince Greno, President.

■ **16910** ■ **R.D. Grier and Sons Co.**
317 Railroad Ave.
Salisbury, MD 21802
Phone: (410)749-4131
Products: Industrial supplies, including oils, greases, pipes, and pipe fittings. **SIC:** 5085 (Industrial Supplies). **Est:** 1888. **Sales:** $7,600,000 (2000). **Emp:** 40. **Officers:** T. Grier, President.

■ **16911** ■ **Grinnell Supply Sales Co**
1600 E Orangethorpe Ave.
Fullerton, CA 92831
Phone: (714)773-1166   **Fax:** (714)879-2319
Products: Piping valves, fittings and pipe hangers. **SIC:** 5085 (Industrial Supplies).

■ **16912** ■ **Groth Corp.**
PO Box 15293
Houston, TX 77220-5293
Phone: (713)675-6151   **Fax:** (713)675-3714
URL: http://www.grothcorp.com
Products: Pressure vacuum relief valves; Gas blanketing regulators; Rupture discs. **SIC:** 5085 (Industrial Supplies). **Est:** 1960. **Sales:** $30,000,000 (2000). **Emp:** 140. **Officers:** Ed Groth Jr., Consultant; Dorna Rohrman, Personnel Mgr.; Ken Shaw, President.

■ **16913** ■ **GRS Industrial Supply Co.**
405 Grandville Ave. NW
Grand Rapids, MI 49503
Phone: (616)458-3601
Free: (800)442-8781   **Fax:** (616)458-3172
URL: http://www.JLindustrial.com
Products: Industrial tools, including nuts and bolts, hand tools, and power tools. **SIC:** 5085 (Industrial Supplies). **Est:** 1938. **Sales:** $16,000,000 (2000). **Emp:** 42. **Officers:** Michael Obrecht; Todd Lloyd.

■ **16914** ■ **GT Sales and Manufacturing Inc.**
PO Box 9408
Wichita, KS 67277
Phone: (316)943-2171   **Fax:** (316)943-4800
Products: Industrial supplies. **SIC:** 5085 (Industrial Supplies). **Est:** 1946. **Sales:** $17,000,000 (2000). **Emp:** 61. **Officers:** N.M. Onofrio Jr., President; M Freeman, General Mgr.

■ **16915** ■ **Gusmer Enterprises Inc.**
27 North Ave. E
Cranford, NJ 07016
Phone: (908)272-9400 **Fax:** (908)272-8735
Products: Industrial equipment and supplies. **SICs:** 5084 (Industrial Machinery & Equipment); 5085 (Industrial Supplies). **Sales:** $40,000,000 (2000). **Emp:** 170. **Officers:** William E. Gusner, CEO; Murray D. Hauser, CFO & Treasurer.

■ **16916** ■ **Guyan Machinery Company Inc.**
PO Box 150
Chapmanville, WV 25508-0150
Phone: (304)855-4501
Products: Screens, including dryer and vibrating screens. **SIC:** 5082 (Construction & Mining Machinery). **Est:** 1913. **Sales:** $24,000,000 (2000). **Emp:** 150. **Officers:** Cecil Cline, President; R.L. Porter, VP of Finance.

■ **16917** ■ **GWS Supply, Inc.**
2375 W Nordale Dr.
Appleton, WI 54914
Phone: (920)739-6066 **Fax:** (920)739-6319
Products: Industrial supplies. **SIC:** 5085 (Industrial Supplies).

■ **16918** ■ **Haasco Inc.**
27 U.S Hwy. 41 S
Henderson, KY 42420
Phone: (270)826-8808
Free: (800)737-8808 **Fax:** (270)826-8812
E-mail: haasco@henderson.net
Products: Hydraulic and pneumatic equipment and supplies. **SICs:** 5085 (Industrial Supplies); 5084 (Industrial Machinery & Equipment).

■ **16919** ■ **Hagerty Brothers Co.**
PO Box 1500
Peoria, IL 61655
Phone: (309)699-7251 **Fax:** (309)698-3149
Products: Industrial steel products. **SICs:** 5051 (Metals Service Centers & Offices); 5085 (Industrial Supplies). **Sales:** $107,900,000 (2000). **Emp:** 145. **Officers:** Randy Fellerhoff, President; Stan Butler, Controller.

■ **16920** ■ **Haggard and Stocking Associates Inc.**
5318 Victory Dr.
Indianapolis, IN 46203
Phone: (317)788-4661 **Fax:** (317)788-1645
Products: Industrial and MRO equipment and supplies. **SICs:** 5085 (Industrial Supplies); 5084 (Industrial Machinery & Equipment). **Est:** 1973. **Sales:** $25,000,000 (2000). **Emp:** 62. **Officers:** Herbert C. Haggard; J.B. Bachman, Sales Mgr.; Karen Barryhill, Customer Service; Paul Mills, Human Resources.

■ **16921** ■ **Haldeman-Homme Inc.**
430 Industrial Blvd.
Minneapolis, MN 55413
Phone: (612)331-4880
Free: (800)795-0696 **Fax:** (612)378-2236
URL: http://www.haldemanhomme.com
Products: Laboratory casework space-saver systems, hardwood flooring, industrial storage and materials handling equipment and institutional casework. **SICs:** 5046 (Commercial Equipment Nec); 5085 (Industrial Supplies). **Est:** 1924. **Sales:** $17,000,000 (2000). **Emp:** 80. **Officers:** Mike Propp, President; K.C. Gunther, Treasurer.

■ **16922** ■ **Hardesty Welding Supply Div.**
PO Box 6136
Evansville, IN 47719-0136
Phone: (812)425-5288 **Fax:** (812)425-2737
Products: Welding supplies; Gases and helium. **SICs:** 5085 (Industrial Supplies); 5169 (Chemicals & Allied Products Nec). **Est:** 1969. **Sales:** $10,100,000 (2000). **Emp:** 20. **Officers:** Del Stogsdill, Operations Mgr.

■ **16923** ■ **Hardware and Supply Company of Chester Inc.**
PO Box 678
Chester, PA 19016-0678
Phone: (610)876-6116
Free: (800)347-9393 **Fax:** (610)872-7544
Products: Industrial hardware; Supply maintenance.

SIC: 5085 (Industrial Supplies). **Est:** 1942. **Sales:** $3,700,000 (2000). **Emp:** 24. **Officers:** Patricia V. Steinberg, President.

■ **16924** ■ **Harley Industries Inc.**
PO Box 470203
Tulsa, OK 74147-0203
Phone: (918)492-9706
Products: Engines, pumps, gauges, and valves. **SIC:** 5085 (Industrial Supplies). **Est:** 1936. **Sales:** $13,000,000 (2000). **Emp:** 54. **Officers:** Gene Maxon, President; K. Nellis, VP & CFO; Dennis Noise, Dir. of Marketing.

■ **16925** ■ **Harris Supply Company Inc.**
36 Central Pl.
Wellsville, NY 14895
Phone: (716)593-5811
Free: (800)626-1660 **Fax:** (716)593-5184
Products: Plumbing supplies; HVAC supplies; Electrical supplies. **SICs:** 5074 (Plumbing & Hydronic Heating Supplies); 5065 (Electronic Parts & Equipment Nec); 5085 (Industrial Supplies). **Est:** 1923. **Sales:** $10,000,000 (2000). **Emp:** 55. **Officers:** Daniel C. Harris Jr., Chairman of the Board; Kevin O. Harris, President; Robert Ross, Controller; Rhonda Gates, Exec. Asst.

■ **16926** ■ **Hatfield and Company Inc.**
206 S Town East Blvd.
Mesquite, TX 75149
Phone: (972)288-7625 **Fax:** (972)289-9063
E-mail: djennings@hatfieldandcompany.com
URL: http://www.hatfield.org
Products: Gauges, valves, and filters, loading arms. **SICs:** 5084 (Industrial Machinery & Equipment); 5085 (Industrial Supplies). **Est:** 1958. **Sales:** $35,000,000 (2000). **Emp:** 76. **Officers:** George R. Hatfield, CEO, e-mail: grhatfield@hatfieldandcompany.com; George Boles, VP & CFO, e-mail: gboles@ hatfieldandcompany.com; Stephen B. Rogers, President & COO, e-mail: srogers@ hatfieldandcompany.com; Harvey Sparhawk, Chief of Information Operations, e-mail: hsparhawk@ hatfieldandcompany.com; Mabel Peery, Dir of Human Resources.

■ **16927** ■ **C.W. Hayden Company Inc.**
306 Rodman Rd.
Auburn, ME 04211-1030
Phone: (207)783-2054
Free: (800)333-2054 **Fax:** (207)783-2724
Products: Marine and industrial supplies. **SICs:** 5085 (Industrial Supplies); 5169 (Chemicals & Allied Products Nec); 5088 (Transportation Equipment & Supplies). **Est:** 1948. **Emp:** 24. **Officers:** Chris Hayden, Vice President; Thomas W. Hayden, Treasurer; John A. Hayden, President.

■ **16928** ■ **Heatbath Corp.**
PO Box 2978
Springfield, MA 01102
Phone: (413)543-3381 **Fax:** (413)543-2378
Products: Industrial processing equipment. **SIC:** 5084 (Industrial Machinery & Equipment). **Sales:** $19,000,000 (2000). **Emp:** 100. **Officers:** E.A. Walen, President; Peter Chrzanowski, Controller.

■ **16929** ■ **Helicoflex Co.**
PO Box 9889
Columbia, SC 29290
Phone: (803)783-1880
Products: Metallic o-rings. **SIC:** 5085 (Industrial Supplies). **Sales:** $14,000,000 (2000). **Emp:** 46. **Officers:** Randy Colvin, General Mgr.

■ **16930** ■ **Hitachi Maxco Ltd.**
1630 Albritton Dr.
Kennesaw, GA 30144
Phone: (404)424-9350 **Fax:** (404)424-9145
Products: Roller chains; Chemicals, including solder paste; Waste water chains; Industrial tow trucks; Sugar mill chains. **SICs:** 5085 (Industrial Supplies); 5169 (Chemicals & Allied Products Nec). **Officers:** Robert Lozano, Import-Export Mgr.

■ **16931** ■ **Hoke Controls**
1 Madison St., No. B
East Rutherford, NJ 07073-1605
Phone: (973)812-0682 **Fax:** (973)812-0183
Products: Instrument valves and fittings. **SIC:** 5085 (Industrial Supplies). **Est:** 1964. **Sales:** $1,000,000 (2000). **Emp:** 10. **Officers:** Jeff Arnold, General Mgr.

■ **16932** ■ **Hopper Specialty West, Inc.**
2824 Vassar NE
Albuquerque, NM 87107
Phone: (505)884-1939
Free: (800)748-2922 **Fax:** (505)888-1472
Products: Hydraulic and industrial hosing. **SIC:** 5085 (Industrial Supplies).

■ **16933** ■ **H.S. Industrial Equipment**
55 Mushroom Blvd.
Rochester, NY 14623
Phone: (716)424-4800
Free: (800)836-8758 **Fax:** (716)424-4803
Products: Industrial equipment and materials; Electrostatic refinishing. **SICs:** 5085 (Industrial Supplies); 5084 (Industrial Machinery & Equipment). **Est:** 1960. **Emp:** 13.

■ **16934** ■ **Hub/Industrial Mill Supply Co.**
8813 Grow Dr.
Pensacola, FL 32514
Phone: (850)484-8202 **Fax:** (850)484-7559
Products: Industrial mill supplies; Pipe valves and fittings. **SICs:** 5085 (Industrial Supplies); 5074 (Plumbing & Hydronic Heating Supplies). **Est:** 1966. **Sales:** $4,000,000 (2000). **Emp:** 11. **Officers:** Barry Camp, President; Jim Golden, CFO.

■ **16935** ■ **T.F. Hudgins Inc.**
PO Box 920901
Houston, TX 77292
Phone: (713)682-3651 **Fax:** (713)682-1109
Products: Lead roofing and plumbing materials. **SICs:** 5085 (Industrial Supplies); 5084 (Industrial Machinery & Equipment). **Est:** 1947. **Sales:** $45,000,000 (1999). **Emp:** 80. **Officers:** Kirk Coffman, President.

■ **16936** ■ **Huntsville/Redstone Paper Co.**
PO Box 3368
Huntsville, AL 35810
Phone: (205)851-2100
Free: (800)444-7452 **Fax:** (205)851-2115
Products: Paper and paper products. **SIC:** 5113 (Industrial & Personal Service Paper). **Sales:** $6,500,000 (2000). **Emp:** 25.

■ **16937** ■ **IDG**
3950 Virginia Ave.
Cincinnati, OH 45227
Phone: (513)271-0618
Free: (800)589-7220 **Fax:** (513)271-6031
URL: http://www.IDGINC.com
Products: Industrial supplies. **SIC:** 5085 (Industrial Supplies). **Est:** 1912. **Sales:** $50,000,000 (2000). **Emp:** 101. **Officers:** Jeff Hayes, President; Greg Chicoine, VP of Operations; Jeff Poplis, Dir. of Marketing. **Former Name:** Scallan Supply Co.

■ **16938** ■ **IEI Investments Inc.**
1630 N Meridian St.
Indianapolis, IN 46202-1496
Phone: (317)926-3351
Products: Flexible gas pipe. **SIC:** 5051 (Metals Service Centers & Offices). **Sales:** $2,000,000 (1994). **Emp:** 4. **Officers:** Carl L. Chapman, President; Steven M. Schein, VP & Treasurer.

■ **16939** ■ **IGC Energy Inc.**
1630 N Meridian St.
Indianapolis, IN 46202-1496
Phone: (317)926-3351
Products: Flexible gas pipe. **SIC:** 5051 (Metals Service Centers & Offices). **Sales:** $2,000,000 (1993). **Emp:** 4. **Officers:** Paul T. Baker, President; Niel C. Ellerbrook, VP of Finance.

■ **16940** ■ **Impex International**
PO Box 214067
Auburn Hills, MI 48321
Phone: (248)852-4032 **Fax:** (248)852-4032
Products: Bearings, pillow blocks, and flanges;

Chains, clutches, couplings, and sprockets; Lubrication equipment parts; Hydraulic pumps and motors; Pneumatic valves. **SICs:** 5085 (Industrial Supplies); 5084 (Industrial Machinery & Equipment). **Officers:** Sujit Jain, President.

■ 16941 ■ **Independent Foundry Supply Co.**
6463 E Canning St.
Los Angeles, CA 90040
Phone: (323)725-1051 **Fax:** (323)725-0973
E-mail: ifsco@aol.com
URL: http://www.foundry-supplies.com
Products: Foundry supplies. **SIC:** 5085 (Industrial Supplies). **Est:** 1935. **Sales:** $2,000,000 (2000). **Emp:** 9. **Officers:** H.J. Ritchie, President.

■ 16942 ■ **Indiana Oxygen Co.**
PO Box 78588
Indianapolis, IN 46278-0588
Phone: (317)290-0003 **Fax:** (317)328-5009
Products: Welding gases. **SICs:** 5169 (Chemicals & Allied Products Nec); 5084 (Industrial Machinery & Equipment). **Est:** 1915. **Sales:** $29,000,000 (2000). **Emp:** 70. **Officers:** Walter L. Brant, President; David Kaplan, CFO; Jim Fuller, VP of Sales.

■ 16943 ■ **Indiana Supply Corp.**
3835 E 21st St.
Indianapolis, IN 46218
Phone: (317)359-5451 **Fax:** (317)351-3252
Products: Industrial supplies, construction and metal materials. **SICs:** 5085 (Industrial Supplies); 5039 (Construction Materials Nec); 5051 (Metals Service Centers & Offices). **Sales:** $30,000,000 (2000). **Emp:** 90. **Officers:** Dave Draga, President; Tracy Jaisle, Controller.

■ 16944 ■ **Indianapolis Welding Supply Inc.**
315 W McCarty St.
Indianapolis, IN 46225
Phone: (317)632-2446
Products: Welding supplies, including oxygen, propane, and helium. **SICs:** 5084 (Industrial Machinery & Equipment); 5169 (Chemicals & Allied Products Nec).

■ 16945 ■ **Indresco, Inc.**
PO Box 650
Pine Brook, NJ 07058-0650
Phone: (914)969-6681 **Fax:** (914)969-6989
Products: Pneumatic and hydraulic hand tools. **SICs:** 5085 (Industrial Supplies); 5072 (Hardware). **Emp:** 49.

■ 16946 ■ **Industrial Distribution Group, Inc.**
2500 Royal Pl.
Tucker, GA 30084-3035
Phone: (770)243-9000 **Fax:** (770)243-9040
URL: http://www.idg-corp.com
Products: Industrial supplies. **SIC:** 5085 (Industrial Supplies). **Est:** 1997. **Sales:** $285,000,000 (2000). **Emp:** 950. **Officers:** Martin S. Pinson, CEO; Douglass C. Smith, COO.

■ 16947 ■ **Industrial Gas and Supply Co.**
518 Alabama St.
Bristol, TN 37620
Phone: (615)968-1536
Products: Welding supplies. **SIC:** 5084 (Industrial Machinery & Equipment). **Est:** 1958. **Sales:** $13,000,000 (2000). **Emp:** 125. **Officers:** David H. Luther, President; Al Hutchinson, VP of Finance; Richard Watson, Exec. VP of Operations; Roger Painter, VP of Admin.; Patricia Bailey, Secretary.

■ 16948 ■ **Industrial Safety Supply Co.**
176 Newington Rd.
West Hartford, CT 06107
Phone: (860)233-9881
Products: Industrial supplies including plastic rods, films, tubes, material handling and firefighting equipment. **SICs:** 5085 (Industrial Supplies); 5084 (Industrial Machinery & Equipment); 5087 (Service Establishment Equipment). **Sales:** $18,000,000 (2000). **Emp:** 100. **Officers:** Henry F. Bonk, CEO; William F. Bonk, President.

■ 16949 ■ **Industrial Steel and Wire Co.**
1901 N Narragansett
Chicago, IL 60639
Phone: (312)804-0404 **Fax:** (312)804-0408
E-mail: info@industeel.com
Products: Steel wire and strips for springs; Stampers. **SICs:** 5051 (Metals Service Centers & Offices); 5085 (Industrial Supplies). **Est:** 1936. **Sales:** $30,000,000 (2000). **Emp:** 100. **Officers:** Ralph D. Furlong, President; Wayne Bennett, Controller; M. Zemcik, Exec. VP of Marketing & Sales.

■ 16950 ■ **Industrial Supplies Co.**
1225 Cottman Ave.
Philadelphia, PA 19111
Phone: (215)742-6200 **Fax:** (215)745-6210
Products: Industrial supplies. **SIC:** 5085 (Industrial Supplies).

■ 16951 ■ **Industrial Supply Co.**
322-328 N 9th St.
PO Box 179
Terre Haute, IN 47808-0179
Phone: (812)234-1569
Free: (800)234-4726 **Fax:** (812)234-0436
E-mail: sales@ind-supply.com
URL: http://www.ind-supply.com
Products: Plumbing; Hydronics; Mill supplies; MRO supplies. **SICs:** 5085 (Industrial Supplies); 5074 (Plumbing & Hydronic Heating Supplies); 5075 (Warm Air Heating & Air-Conditioning). **Est:** 1915. **Sales:** $15,000,000 (2000). **Emp:** 50. **Officers:** Harley R. Ireland III, President; Donald M. Ireland, Vice President, e-mail: dmi@ind-supply.com; Jack Simpson, Sales Mgr., e-mail: jls@ind-supply.com; M. Ruth Ridener, Human Resources Contact, e-mail: rw@ind-supply.com.

■ 16952 ■ **Industrial Supply Co.**
12905 Hwy. 55
Plymouth, MN 55441
Phone: (612)559-0033
Free: (800)627-9434 **Fax:** (612)559-3148
E-mail: www.industrialsupplyco.com
URL: http://www.idustrialsupplyco.com
Products: Industrial supplies, including bearings and power transmission products. **SIC:** 5085 (Industrial Supplies). **Est:** 1939. **Sales:** $16,000,000 (2000). **Emp:** 48. **Officers:** Mark Koch, Owner & Pres.; Mike Benusa, Sales Coordinator.

■ 16953 ■ **Industrial Supply Co.**
1408 Northland Dr., Ste. 103
Mendota Heights, MN 55120
Phone: (651)405-1526 **Fax:** (651)405-3892
Products: Industrial bearings, belts, and motors. **SICs:** 5084 (Industrial Machinery & Equipment); 5085 (Industrial Supplies); 5063 (Electrical Apparatus & Equipment).

■ 16954 ■ **Industrial Supply Co.**
1100 W Russell Ave.
Sioux Falls, SD 57104
Phone: (605)336-3471 **Fax:** (605)336-3492
Products: Industrial supplies. **SIC:** 5085 (Industrial Supplies).

■ 16955 ■ **Industrial Supply Co.**
3109 E Voorhees St.
Danville, IL 61834
Phone: (217)446-5029
Free: (877)336-4726 **Fax:** (217)446-5360
URL: www.ind-supply.com
Products: Plumbing, hydronics, MRO, and mill supplies. **SICs:** 5085 (Industrial Supplies); 5074 (Plumbing & Hydronic Heating Supplies); 5075 (Warm Air Heating & Air-Conditioning). **Est:** 1915. **Officers:** Harley R. Ireland III, President; Donald M. Ireland, Vice President.

■ 16956 ■ **Industrial Supply Company Inc.**
(Salt Lake City, Utah)
PO Box 30600
Salt Lake City, UT 84130
Phone: (801)484-8644 **Fax:** (801)487-0469
Products: Industrial supplies. **SIC:** 5085 (Industrial Supplies). **Sales:** $40,000,000 (1994). **Emp:** 125. **Officers:** Philip Thompson III, CEO; Denny Frandsen, VP & CFO.

■ 16957 ■ **Industrial Supply Corp.**
326 Ohio
Waynesboro, VA 22980-4516
Phone: (540)946-4500
Free: (800)572-2064 **Fax:** (540)946-4525
Products: Industrial supplies. **SIC:** 5085 (Industrial Supplies). **Emp:** 24. **Officers:** C. D. Lambert.

■ 16958 ■ **Industrial Supply Corp.**
PO Box 6356
Richmond, VA 23230
Phone: (804)355-8041 **Fax:** (804)358-0726
Products: Drills; Sprockets; Brooms; Saws. **SIC:** 5085 (Industrial Supplies). **Est:** 1934. **Sales:** $11,000,000 (2000). **Emp:** 65. **Officers:** Julius W. Crowell Jr., Chairman of the Board; John Lloyd, President; Doug Sims, Sales Mgr.; Barbara Robertson, Dir. of Data Processing; Lee Atkinson, Controller.

■ 16959 ■ **Industrial Tools and Abrasives Inc.**
PO Box 71809
Chattanooga, TN 37407
Phone: (423)266-1265 **Fax:** (423)267-8860
Products: Abrasives; Cutting tools; Saw blades. **SICs:** 5085 (Industrial Supplies); 5072 (Hardware). **Est:** 1876. **Sales:** $6,000,000 (2000). **Emp:** 40. **Officers:** R.L. McCann, President; Bobby Brantley, Exec. VP; Tim Pfenning, Vice President.

■ 16960 ■ **Intech Corp.**
250 Herbert Ave.
Closter, NJ 07624
Phone: (201)767-8066 **Fax:** (201)767-7797
E-mail: intechpower@carroll.com
URL: http://www.intechpower.com
Products: Gears; Rollers. **SIC:** 5085 (Industrial Supplies). **Est:** 1983. **Sales:** $2,000,000 (1999). **Emp:** 8. **Officers:** Georg Bartosch, President; Ruth Emblin, Marketing Mgr. **Alternate Name:** Intech Power-Core.

■ 16961 ■ **Interlectric Corp.**
1401 Lexington Ave.
Warren, PA 16365
Phone: (814)723-6061
Products: Industrial, commercial and residential lighting and tanning bulbs. **SIC:** 5063 (Electrical Apparatus & Equipment). **Sales:** $3,500,000 (2000). **Emp:** 80. **Officers:** Steven Rothenberg, CEO & President.

■ 16962 ■ **Interstate Co.**
2601 E 80th St.
Minneapolis, MN 55425-1378
Phone: (612)854-2044
Products: Industrial equipment and supplies. **SICs:** 5084 (Industrial Machinery & Equipment); 5085 (Industrial Supplies). **Sales:** $120,000,000 (2000). **Emp:** 560. **Officers:** Jeff Caswell, CEO; Harry Lindstrom, CFO.

■ 16963 ■ **Interstate Welding Sales Corp.**
1801 Marinette Ave.
Marinette, WI 54143
Phone: (715)732-7950 **Fax:** (715)732-7940
Products: Fasteners; Fire equipment service and supplies; Safety equipment; Tools and abrasives; Industrial gases. **SIC:** 5085 (Industrial Supplies). **Sales:** $50,000,000 (1999). **Emp:** 200. **Officers:** Dave Higley, President.

■ 16964 ■ **Stuart C. Irby Co.**
PO Box 1819
Jackson, MS 39215-1819
Phone: (601)969-1811
Free: (800)844-1811 **Fax:** (601)960-7380
E-mail: prevost@irby.com
URL: http://www.irby.com
Products: Residential utilities; Industrial supplies. **SICs:** 5063 (Electrical Apparatus & Equipment); 5085 (Industrial Supplies). **Est:** 1926. **Sales:** $252,000,000 (2000). **Emp:** 576. **Officers:** Stuart M. Irby, President; Mike Anthony, Vice President; Liles Williams, Vice President; Charles R. Campbell III, Vice President; Alvon H. Doty, Vice President; Charles L. Irby, Vice President.

■ 16965 ■ **Island Spring & Drive Shaft Co.**
7309 Grand Ave.
Pittsburgh, PA 15225
Phone: (412)264-6714
Free: (800)837-4713 **Fax:** (412)264-6722
E-mail: dank@pointspring.com
URL: http://www.pointspring.com
Products: Hydraulic parts; Specialty springs; Drive shafts. **SIC:** 5085 (Industrial Supplies). **Est:** 1926. **Emp:** 25. **Officers:** Dan Kubisiak.

■ 16966 ■ **JacksonLea**
75 Progress Ln.
Waterbury, CT 06705
Phone: (203)753-5116 **Fax:** (203)754-3770
Products: Compounds; Buffing wheels. **SICs:** 5085 (Industrial Supplies); 5085 (Industrial Supplies); 5169 (Chemicals & Allied Products Nec). **Est:** 1923. **Sales:** $6,000,000 (2000). **Emp:** 40. **Officers:** Robert C. Nelson, General Mgr.

■ 16967 ■ **Jacksonville Mechanical Supply Inc.**
618 Richlands Hwy.
Jacksonville, NC 28540
Phone: (252)455-8328
Products: Mechanical supplies. **SIC:** 5039 (Construction Materials Nec).

■ 16968 ■ **E. James and Company Inc.**
1725 W Division St.
Chicago, IL 60622
Phone: (773)227-1881
Free: (800)927-2358 **Fax:** (773)227-3124
E-mail: ejcotpp@hotmail.com
URL: http://www.ejames.com
Products: V-belts, hose assemblies and clamps; Sheet rubber; Mats, and matting supplies. **SIC:** 5085 (Industrial Supplies). **Est:** 1953. **Sales:** $4,000,000 (2000). **Emp:** 20. **Officers:** Michael Romano, President; Paul Delort, Customer Service Contact.

■ 16969 ■ **Jarett Industries Inc.**
134 Brentwood
South Orange, NJ 07079-1141
Phone: (201)539-4410 **Fax:** (201)539-1132
Products: Hydraulic hose and fittings. **SIC:** 5084 (Industrial Machinery & Equipment). **Est:** 1931. **Sales:** $3,000,000 (2000). **Emp:** 18. **Officers:** S.H. Weisman, President.

■ 16970 ■ **Jasper Engineering and Equipment Co.**
3800 5th Ave. W
Hibbing, MN 55746-2816
Phone: (218)262-3421 **Fax:** (218)262-4936
URL: http://www.jaspereng.com
Products: Pumps; Scrubbers; Lubricants; Process control equipment. **SICs:** 5084 (Industrial Machinery & Equipment); 5172 (Petroleum Products Nec); 5085 (Industrial Supplies). **Est:** 1958. **Sales:** $9,000,000 (2000). **Emp:** 29. **Officers:** Tom D. Jamar, President; Kevin Gargano, VP of Finance; Tim W. Rasch, VP of Marketing; Peg Arthurs, Data Processing Mgr.

■ 16971 ■ **Jolley Industrial Supply Company Inc.**
105-109 Agate Way
Sharon, PA 16146
Phone: (412)981-5400 **Fax:** (412)981-7740
Products: Mill supplies. **SIC:** 5085 (Industrial Supplies). **Est:** 1950. **Sales:** $4,000,000 (2000). **Emp:** 25. **Officers:** Richard C. Jolley, President; Ann Jolley, Treasurer & Secty.; Bill Donato, Vice President.

■ 16972 ■ **Jonesboro Winnelson Co.**
804 Dee Str.
PO Box 637
Jonesboro, AR 72403-0637
Phone: (501)932-4543
Free: (800)242-3316 **Fax:** (501)932-9086
Products: Plumbing and industrial supplies. **SICs:** 5085 (Industrial Supplies); 5074 (Plumbing & Hydronic Heating Supplies). **Est:** 1964. **Emp:** 4. **Officers:** Bobby Warren, President.

■ 16973 ■ **Juno Industries Inc.**
4355 Drane Field Rd.
Lakeland, FL 33811
Phone: (813)646-1493 **Fax:** (813)646-1295
Products: Industrial supplies, pipe valves, instrumentation and plastic fabrication. **SICs:** 5169 (Chemicals & Allied Products Nec); 5085 (Industrial Supplies); 5084 (Industrial Machinery & Equipment). **Sales:** $20,000,000 (1994). **Emp:** 106. **Officers:** W.B. Moore, President; Tom Hodge, Controller.

■ 16974 ■ **Justis Supply Company Inc.**
821 E Main
Farmington, NM 87401
Phone: (505)325-0291 **Fax:** (505)327-5647
Products: Industrial supplies. **SIC:** 5085 (Industrial Supplies). **Sales:** $2,500,000 (2000). **Emp:** 35. **Officers:** Dan E. Brack, CEO & President.

■ 16975 ■ **Kalamazoo Mill Supply Co.**
1820 Lake St.
Kalamazoo, MI 49001
Phone: (616)349-9641
Free: (800)878-6455 **Fax:** (616)349-9888
Products: Industrial supplies. **SIC:** 5085 (Industrial Supplies). **Est:** 1941. **Sales:** $9,500,000 (2000). **Emp:** 44. **Officers:** A.V. Kimball Jr., President; W. Fulkerson, Treasurer; A. Kimball III, Dir. of Marketing.

■ 16976 ■ **Kaman Industrial**
240 E Verdugo Ave.
Burbank, CA 91502
Phone: (818)845-8571 **Fax:** (818)845-4252
Products: Bearings and power transmission products. **SIC:** 5085 (Industrial Supplies). **Est:** 1958. **Sales:** $3,200,000 (2000). **Emp:** 20. **Officers:** John Henry, Branch Mgr.

■ 16977 ■ **Kaman Industrial Technologies**
2601 S 24th St.
Phoenix, AZ 85034
Phone: (602)273-1641 **Fax:** (602)273-7926
Products: 80,000 bearing, power transmission, fluid power, linear motion, materials handling and electronic drive items; Hoses. **SICs:** 5085 (Industrial Supplies); 5063 (Electrical Apparatus & Equipment).

■ 16978 ■ **Kansas City Rubber and Belting Co.**
1815 Prospect Ave.
Kansas City, MO 64127
Phone: (816)483-8580 **Fax:** (816)483-8583
Products: Rubber. **SIC:** 5085 (Industrial Supplies). **Sales:** $2,000,000 (2000). **Emp:** 15.

■ 16979 ■ **Kansas Oxygen Inc.**
PO Box 3007
Hutchinson, KS 67504-3007
Phone: (316)665-5551 **Fax:** (316)665-0471
Products: Welding and industrial gases. **SIC:** 5084 (Industrial Machinery & Equipment). **Est:** 1946. **Sales:** $14,000,000 (2000). **Emp:** 110. **Officers:** Richard Hollowell, President; Steve Howell, CFO; Tom Mohr, Dir. of Marketing; Lisa Krause, Dir of Human Resources.

■ 16980 ■ **Kar Products, Inc.**
1085 Telegraph
Reno, NV 89502
Phone: (702)786-0811 **Fax:** (702)786-1690
Products: Industrial hardware. **SICs:** 5085 (Industrial Supplies); 5084 (Industrial Machinery & Equipment).

■ 16981 ■ **Keen Compressed Gas Co.**
PO Box 15146
Wilmington, DE 19850-5146
Phone: (302)594-4545 **Fax:** (302)594-4569
Products: Welding gases. **SIC:** 5169 (Chemicals & Allied Products Nec). **Est:** 1919. **Sales:** $10,000,000 (2000). **Emp:** 100. **Officers:** J. Merrill Keen, President; D. Haas, CFO; Willard Keen, Sales Mgr.

■ 16982 ■ **Kelly Pipe Co.**
11700 Bloomfield Ave.
Santa Fe Springs, CA 90670
Phone: (562)868-0456
Free: (800)305-3559 **Fax:** (562)863-4695
E-mail: sales@kellypipe.com
URL: http://www.kellypipe.com
Products: Steel pipes. **SIC:** 5051 (Metals Service Centers & Offices). **Est:** 1898. **Emp:** 140. **Officers:** Earle Cohen, CEO; George T. LaBollita, Exec. VP; John Wolfson, VP & General Mgr. of Branches.

■ 16983 ■ **Kelly Supply Company of Iowa**
PO Box 1328
Grand Island, NE 68802
Phone: (308)382-5670
Products: Industrial maintenance and operating supplies. **SICs:** 5074 (Plumbing & Hydronic Heating Supplies); 5063 (Electrical Apparatus & Equipment); 5084 (Industrial Machinery & Equipment); 5085 (Industrial Supplies). **Est:** 1889. **Sales:** $5,000,000 (2000). **Emp:** 25. **Officers:** Jeff Kelly, President; Arlon Krueger, Controller.

■ 16984 ■ **Kendall Industrial Supplies Inc.**
702 N 20th St.
Battle Creek, MI 49015
Phone: (616)965-2211 **Fax:** (616)965-3164
Products: Industrial presses; Lathes; Industrial supplies. **SIC:** 5085 (Industrial Supplies). **Est:** 1900. **Sales:** $12,000,000 (2000). **Emp:** 63. **Officers:** Axel Johnson, President; James Treadwell, Vice President; William Kein, Sales Mgr.; Sandy Roepke, Dir. of Data Processing; Kathy Devine, Dir of Human Resources.

■ 16985 ■ **Kennametal**
550 Virginia Dr.
Ft. Washington, PA 19034
Phone: (215)654-5330
Free: (800)446-7738 **Fax:** 800-447-6698
Products: Carbide and industrial supplies. **SICs:** 5085 (Industrial Supplies); 5169 (Chemicals & Allied Products Nec).

■ 16986 ■ **Kennedy Manufacturing Co.**
520 E Sycamore
Van Wert, OH 45891-1377
Phone: (419)238-2442
Free: (800)413-8665 **Fax:** (419)238-5644
E-mail: kmcinfo@kennedymfg.com
URL: http://www.kennedymfg.com
Products: Industrial quality tool chests, roller cabinets, and work stations. **SIC:** 5085 (Industrial Supplies). **Est:** 1911. **Sales:** $28,000,000 (1999). **Emp:** 300. **Officers:** D. Thompson, President; B. Susaeta, National Sales Mgr.; K. Wise, VE; M. Hurless, VP of Operations.

■ 16987 ■ **R. G. Kenrick Company Inc.**
G-3530 Flushing Rd.
Flint, MI 48504
Phone: (810)733-7440 **Fax:** (810)733-7534
Products: Hydraulics; Pneumatics. **SIC:** 5085 (Industrial Supplies). **Sales:** $2,500,000 (2000). **Emp:** 12.

■ 16988 ■ **Kentucky Bearings Service**
1111 Majaun Rd.
Lexington, KY 40511
Phone: (606)231-8288 **Fax:** (606)231-8956
Products: Industrial supplies. **SIC:** 5085 (Industrial Supplies).

■ 16989 ■ **Kentucky Mine Supply Co.**
PO Box 779
Harlan, KY 40831
Phone: (606)573-3850
Products: Mining supplies; Plumbing supplies, including pipes, valves, and fittings; Tools; Welding equipment and supplies; Safety supplies; Hoses and rubber goods; Fasteners; Hoists and jacks; Steel products; Pumps; Electrical supplies; Wire and cable; Paint; Lubricants. **SICs:** 5084 (Industrial Machinery & Equipment); 5074 (Plumbing & Hydronic Heating Supplies); 5085 (Industrial Supplies); 5051 (Metals Service Centers & Offices); 5198 (Paints, Varnishes & Supplies). **Est:** 1917. **Sales:** $5,000,000 (2000). **Emp:** 15. **Officers:** James M. Bushnell, President; Ann Heck, Treasurer; Terry Kirk, Vice President.

■ 16990 ■ Kentucky Welding Supply
PO Box 638
Prestonsburg, KY 41653
Phone: (606)874-8001
Products: Oxygen and acetylene welding supplies.
SICs: 5084 (Industrial Machinery & Equipment); 5085
(Industrial Supplies). **Est:** 1983. **Sales:** $2,000,000
(2000). **Emp:** 15. **Officers:** Paul Day, Manager.

■ 16991 ■ Kibar Bearings
165 Jordan Rd.
Troy, NY 12180-8386
Phone: (518)283-8002 **Fax:** (518)274-1167
Products: Ball bearings. **SIC:** 5085 (Industrial
Supplies). **Sales:** $4,000,000 (2000). **Emp:** 55.
Officers: A J Sperrazza.

■ 16992 ■ Knight Corp.
PO Box 332
Ardmore, PA 19003
Phone: (215)853-2161
Free: (800)FIL-TER4 **Fax:** (215)853-1080
E-mail: pgknight@knightcorp.com
Products: Filters. **SIC:** 5085 (Industrial Supplies). **Est:**
1973. **Sales:** $6,000,000 (2000).

■ 16993 ■ Lamons Beaumont Bolt & Gasket
PO Box 1710
Beaumont, TX 77704
Phone: (409)838-6304 **Fax:** (409)838-6336
E-mail: bbgbmt@pnx.com
URL: http://www.lamonsgasket.com
Products: Industrial fasteners. **SICs:** 5085 (Industrial
Supplies); 5072 (Hardware). **Est:** 1970. **Sales:**
$10,000,000 (2000). **Emp:** 54. **Officers:** Michael J.
Vaughn. **Former Name:** Beaumont Bolt & Gasket.

■ 16994 ■ Laube Technology Inc.
P.O Box 6079
Camarillo, CA 93011
Phone: (805)388-1050
Free: (888)355-2823 **Fax:** (805)388-3433
E-mail: info@laube.com
URL: http://www.laube.com
Products: Industrial fasteners; Electronic components;
Custom keyboard and control panel assemblies. **SICs:**
5065 (Electronic Parts & Equipment Nec); 5072
(Hardware); 5085 (Industrial Supplies). **Est:** 1948.
Sales: $20,000,000 (2000). **Emp:** 29. **Officers:** Claude
Ising, President; Lydia Banes, CFO.

■ 16995 ■ Lawson Products Inc.
1666 E Touhy Ave.
Des Plaines, IL 60018
Phone: (847)827-9666
Free: (800)448-8985 **Fax:** (847)827-1525
URL: http://www.lawsonproducts.com
Products: Industrial supplies. **SIC:** 5085 (Industrial
Supplies). **Est:** 1952. **Sales:** $191,000,000 (1999).
Emp: 1,000. **Officers:** Sidney L. Port, Chairman of the
Exec. Committee; Robert Washlow, CEO & Chairman
of the Board; Jeffrey B. Belford; Roger Cannon, Office
of the President; Julie Kampert, Sales/Marketing
Contact, e-mail: jkampert@lawsonproducts.com.

■ 16996 ■ Lempco Industries Inc.
5490 Dunham Rd.
Cleveland, OH 44137
Phone: (216)475-2400 **Fax:** 800-221-6310
Products: Industrial parts for machinery. **SIC:** 5085
(Industrial Supplies). **Est:** 1918. **Sales:** $22,000,000
(2000). **Emp:** 200. **Officers:** J.J. Strnad, President &
Chairman of the Board; R.H. Myles, Exec. VP of
Finance.

■ 16997 ■ Leon's Molds
1404 Memorial Dr.
Waycross, GA 31501-1947
Phone: (912)285-1813
Products: Industrial molds. **SIC:** 5085 (Industrial
Supplies). **Officers:** Leon Griffin, Owner.

■ 16998 ■ Lewis Supply Company Inc.
PO Box 220
Memphis, TN 38101
Phone: (901)525-6871
Products: Industrial supplies for safety, maintenance,
and production. **SIC:** 5085 (Industrial Supplies). **Est:**
1918. **Sales:** $21,500,000 (2000). **Emp:** 100. **Officers:**

Michael S. Burnham Jr., President; Earl F. Blair,
Controller; Steve Humbert, Dir. of Data Processing.

■ 16999 ■ Liconix Industries Inc.
3611 164th St.
Flushing, NY 11358-2003
Phone: (718)961-6008 **Fax:** (718)278-7087
Products: Casters. **SICs:** 5045 (Computers,
Peripherals & Software); 5065 (Electronic Parts &
Equipment Nec). **Est:** 1975. **Sales:** $1,000,000 (2000).
Emp: 6. **Officers:** Patrick Chen, President; Joyce
Chen, CFO; Jenny Ung, Secretary.

■ 17000 ■ Lindquist Industrial Supply Co.
13 Hamden Park Dr.
Hamden, CT 06517
Phone: (203)497-1510 **Fax:** (203)497-1511
Products: Industrial supplies. **SIC:** 5085 (Industrial
Supplies). **Sales:** $15,000,000 (2000). **Emp:** 40.
Officers: J. Drummond, President; Maurice Harmon,
Controller.

■ 17001 ■ Linear Industries Ltd
1850 Enterprise Way
Monrovia, CA 91016
Phone: (626)303-1130 **Fax:** (626)303-2035
Products: Linear motion components, bearings,
shafts, ball screw and spline, position tables and
controls. **SICs:** 5085 (Industrial Supplies); 5088
(Transportation Equipment & Supplies).

**■ 17002 ■ Lipe-Rollway Corp. International
Div.**
7600 Morgan Rd.
Liverpool, NY 13090
Phone: (315)457-6211
Products: Roller bearings. **SIC:** 5085 (Industrial
Supplies). **Sales:** $11,200,000 (2000). **Emp:** 21.
Officers: Carl Lossner, President.

■ 17003 ■ Logan and Whaley Company Inc.
PO Box 1089
Marshall, TX 75671
Phone: (903)938-4377 **Fax:** (903)938-6631
URL: http://www.LoganWhaley.com
Products: Industrial supplies and safety supplies. **SIC:**
5085 (Industrial Supplies). **Est:** 1884. **Sales:**
$10,000,000 (2000). **Emp:** 30. **Officers:** Tom Whaley
Jr., President; Tom Whaley Sr., CFO.

■ 17004 ■ Losey and Company Inc.
3700 Hartley Ave.
Easton, PA 18045-3757
Phone: (215)253-3511
Products: Industrial supplies, including nuts, bolts,
wrenches, and flashlights. **SIC:** 5085 (Industrial
Supplies). **Est:** 1865. **Sales:** $3,600,000 (2000). **Emp:**
23. **Officers:** A. Richard Kreitz, President; Gene
Lowell, Vice President; Shirley Frable, Controller; Toni
Venanzi, Dir. of Systems.

■ 17005 ■ Louisiana Mill Supply
109 N City Service Hwy.
Sulphur, LA 70663
Phone: (318)625-2900 **Fax:** (318)625-4551
Products: Industrial tools and supplies. **SIC:** 5085
(Industrial Supplies). **Emp:** 16. **Officers:** Jeff Byrley,
Branch Manager.

■ 17006 ■ Louisiana Mill Supply
10093 Rayco Sandres Rd.
Gonzales, LA 70737
Phone: (504)644-4100
Free: (800)852-8305 **Fax:** (504)644-5400
Products: Industrial and mill supplies. **SIC:** 5085
(Industrial Supplies). **Emp:** 14. **Officers:** Tommy
Campbell, Branch Manager.

■ 17007 ■ Bert Lowe Supply Co.
5402 E Diana
Tampa, FL 33610-1926
Phone: (813)621-7784
Free: (800)922-1431 **Fax:** (813)623-6999
E-mail: blstpa1@gte.net
Products: Industrial supplies and equipment. **SICs:**
5085 (Industrial Supplies); 5084 (Industrial Machinery &
Equipment). **Est:** 1952. **Sales:** $4,000,000 (2000).
Emp: 20.

■ 17008 ■ Lumberton Industries Inc.
PO Box 443
Medina, OH 44258
Phone: (330)723-1700
Free: (800)677-2153 **Fax:** (330)723-1569
Products: Nonmetallic abrasive products(including
diamond abrasives). **SIC:** 5085 (Industrial Supplies).
Est: 1990. **Sales:** $950,000 (2000). **Emp:** 6. **Officers:**
Randal F. Virost, President; Kevin Ditto, Controller.

■ 17009 ■ M & M Sales & Equipment
2639 Kermit Hwy.
Odessa, TX 79763-2542
Phone: (915)332-1481
Free: (800)592-4516 **Fax:** (915)332-7433
Products: Machine shop supplies. **SIC:** 5085
(Industrial Supplies). **Emp:** 49. **Officers:** Joe Abbott.

■ 17010 ■ Mackay Industrial Sales Inc.
2131 Kalamazoo SE
Grand Rapids, MI 49507
Phone: (616)241-1671 **Fax:** (616)241-2753
Products: Gears; Machine chain; Miscellaneous
machinery products, including flexible metal hose and
tubing, metal bellows, etc.; Motors. **SICs:** 5085
(Industrial Supplies); 5063 (Electrical Apparatus &
Equipment). **Est:** 1946. **Sales:** $5,000,000 (2000).
Emp: 25. **Officers:** D.J. Tyizynski, CEO; C.S. Cadman
III, Treasurer.

■ 17011 ■ Magnum Corp.
32400 Telegraph Rd., No. 102
Bingham Farms, MI 48025
Phone: (810)433-1170 **Fax:** (313)334-1735
Products: Machine parts and gears. **SIC:** 5085
(Industrial Supplies). **Sales:** $19,000,000 (2000). **Emp:**
150. **Officers:** Martin Abel, President; Lisa Proctor,
Finance Officer.

■ 17012 ■ Mahoning Valley Supply Co.
PO Box 5498
Poland, OH 44514-0498
Phone: (330)758-6601
Products: Welding supplies; Industrial supplies; Safety
supplies. **SICs:** 5085 (Industrial Supplies); 5084
(Industrial Machinery & Equipment). **Est:** 1937. **Sales:**
$9,000,000 (2000). **Emp:** 40. **Officers:** David Williams,
President; Marcia Bortner, Treasurer; M. Gollings, Dir.
of Marketing; W. D. Truran, Dir. of Data Processing.

■ 17013 ■ The Manderscheid Co.
624 W Adams St.
Chicago, IL 60661
Phone: (312)782-8662 **Fax:** (312)782-6245
Products: Industrial supplies, including abrasives,
adhesives, and sealants; Industrial buffing and
polishing equipment; Office supplies, including tape.
SICs: 5085 (Industrial Supplies); 5084 (Industrial
Machinery & Equipment); 5112 (Stationery & Office
Supplies). **Officers:** G. Richad Matteucci, Vice
President.

■ 17014 ■ Manson Tool and Supply Co.
732 Commerce St.
PO Box 204
Thornwood, NY 10594-0204
Phone: (914)769-7056
Free: (800)431-1040 **Fax:** 800-941-1950
E-mail: info@mansontool.com
URL: http://www.mansontool.com
Products: Small cutting tools for machine tools and
metalworking machinery; Measuring and controlling
devices; Polishers, sanders and grinders. **SIC:** 5085
(Industrial Supplies). **Est:** 1950. **Emp:** 8. **Officers:**
Ronald Haines, President. **Alternate Name:** Main Tool
Supply. **Alternate Name:** Van Emmerik Tool and
Supply.

■ 17015 ■ Manufactured Rubber Products Inc.
4501 Tacony St.
Philadelphia, PA 19124
Phone: (215)533-3600
Products: Gasket fabricators. **SIC:** 5085 (Industrial
Supplies). **Est:** 1942. **Sales:** $6,000,000 (2000). **Emp:**
28. **Officers:** Edmond Furia, President.

■ **17016** ■ **R.J. Marshall Co.**
26776 W 12 Mile Rd.
Southfield, MI 48034
Phone: (248)353-4100
Free: (800)338-7900 **Fax:** (248)948-6460
Products: Process minerals and chemicals. **SIC:** 5085 (Industrial Supplies). **Sales:** $30,000,000 (2000). **Emp:** 90.

■ **17017** ■ **Martensen Enterprises Inc.**
1721 W Culver St.
Phoenix, AZ 85007
Phone: (602)271-9048 **Fax:** (602)253-5289
Products: Construction materials and machinery. **SIC:** 5085 (Industrial Supplies). **Sales:** $3,000,000 (2000). **Emp:** 15.

■ **17018** ■ **The Massey Company Inc.**
PO Box 26
Mt. Holly, NC 28120
Phone: (704)827-9661 **Fax:** (704)827-8979
Products: Pipe valves and fittings; Actuation and instrumentation. **SIC:** 5085 (Industrial Supplies). **Est:** 1923. **Sales:** $11,000,000 (2000). **Emp:** 35. **Officers:** Henry H. Massey Jr., Chairman of the Board; Thad R Chesson, CEO & Secretary; Michael Reavis, VP of Marketing; Thomas Nelson, Vice President; Thomas Keigher, Vice President; David S. Massey, President & Treasurer.

■ **17019** ■ **Material Sales Company Inc.**
25885 W 8 Mile Rd.
Redford, MI 48240-1047
Phone: (313)534-1320 **Fax:** (313)534-8854
Products: Small cutting tools for machine tools and metalworking machinery. **SIC:** 5084 (Industrial Machinery & Equipment). **Emp:** 12.

■ **17020** ■ **McComb Wholesale Paper Co.**
PO Box 463
McComb, MS 39649
Phone: (601)684-5521
Products: Paper and paper products. **SIC:** 5113 (Industrial & Personal Service Paper). **Sales:** $600,000 (2000). **Emp:** 7.

■ **17021** ■ **McGill Hose and Coupling Inc.**
PO Box 408
East Longmeadow, MA 01028
Phone: (413)525-3977
Products: Hose and fittings. **SIC:** 5085 (Industrial Supplies). **Est:** 1962. **Sales:** $3,000,000 (2000). **Emp:** 15. **Officers:** Harry McGill, President; Bill Watkins, Marketing Mgr.

■ **17022** ■ **McGraw Group Inc.**
576 Griffith Rd.
Charlotte, NC 28217
Phone: (704)525-9423 **Fax:** (704)522-0249
Products: Hydraulic and electrical equipment; Industrial supplies and machine tools. **SICs:** 5084 (Industrial Machinery & Equipment); 5085 (Industrial Supplies); 5013 (Motor Vehicle Supplies & New Parts). **Former Name:** Industrial Transmissions Inc.

■ **17023** ■ **James McGraw Inc.**
PO Box 85620
Richmond, VA 23285
Phone: (804)233-3071 **Fax:** (804)231-9120
Products: Industrial machinery and supplies. **SICs:** 5085 (Industrial Supplies); 5063 (Electrical Apparatus & Equipment); 5072 (Hardware); 5084 (Industrial Machinery & Equipment). **Est:** 1866. **Sales:** $37,000,000 (1993). **Emp:** 160. **Officers:** Ken Fisketson.

■ **17024** ■ **McGuire Bearing**
5516 1st Ave. S
Seattle, WA 98108
Phone: (206)767-3283
Free: (800)562-7206 **Fax:** (206)763-2181
Products: Bearings; Power transmission components. **SICs:** 5085 (Industrial Supplies); 5063 (Electrical Apparatus & Equipment).

■ **17025** ■ **McGuire Bearing**
4230 E Mission Ave.
Spokane, WA 99202-4407
Phone: (509)535-1511
Free: (800)541-4114 **Fax:** (509)535-6685
Products: Bearings; Belts; Roller chains and related power transmission supplies. **SIC:** 5085 (Industrial Supplies).

■ **17026** ■ **McGuire-Nicholas Co., Inc.**
PMB 170
1175 Baker St., Ste. D13
Costa Mesa, CA 92626-4139
Phone: (213)722-6961 **Fax:** (213)722-5816
Products: Tool pouches and holders; Nail bags; Work aprons; Knee pads; Support belts. **SIC:** 5085 (Industrial Supplies).

■ **17027** ■ **McJunkin Corp.**
PO Box 513
Charleston, WV 25322
Phone: (304)348-5211 **Fax:** (304)348-4922
Products: Industrial supplies, including pipes, valves, and fittings. **SIC:** 5085 (Industrial Supplies). **Est:** 1921. **Sales:** $270,000,000 (2000). **Emp:** 1,250. **Officers:** H.B. Wehrle III, CEO & President; Michael H. Wehrle, Sr. VP & CFO; S.D. Wehrle, Sr. VP of Sales; H.R. Hill, VP of Information Systems; William Board, Dir of Personnel.

■ **17028** ■ **McLean International Marketing Inc.**
PO Box 535
Mequon, WI 53092
Phone: (414)242-0958 **Fax:** (414)242-6644
Products: Security and safety equipment. **SIC:** 5085 (Industrial Supplies). **Sales:** $1,000,000 (2000). **Emp:** 3.

■ **17029** ■ **MDC Industries Inc.**
Collins St. & Willard St.
PO Box 12730
Philadelphia, PA 19134-0730
Phone: (215)426-5925
Free: (800)682-1311 **Fax:** (215)426-8277
URL: http://www.mdcindust.com
Products: Industrial abrasives. **SIC:** 5085 (Industrial Supplies). **Est:** 1959. **Sales:** $3,000,000 (2000). **Emp:** 10. **Officers:** A. Schwab, President; Charles Schwab, VP of Marketing & Sales, e-mail: cschwab@mdcindust.com; Bernice Ferretti, Office Mgr.; Florence Haines, Customer Service Contact; Joseph Carroll, Vice President.

■ **17030** ■ **Meriden Cooper Corp.**
112 Golden Street Pk.
Meriden, CT 06450
Phone: (203)237-8448 **Fax:** (203)238-1314
Products: Industrial thermometers and pressure gauges. **SIC:** 5085 (Industrial Supplies). **Emp:** 12.
Officers: Joseph Cooper, CEO.

■ **17031** ■ **Metric & Multistandard Components Corp.**
120 Old Saw Mill River Rd.
Hawthorne, NY 10532
Phone: (914)769-5020
Free: (800)431-2792 **Fax:** (914)769-5049
Products: Metric industrial supplies. **SIC:** 5085 (Industrial Supplies). **Est:** 1963. **Sales:** $18,000,000 (1999). **Emp:** 110. **Officers:** Joseph A. Voves, President, e-mail: joe4metric@aol.com; Ivo Peske, General Mgr.

■ **17032** ■ **O.E. Meyer Co.**
PO Box 479
Sandusky, OH 44871-0479
Phone: (419)625-3054 **Fax:** (419)625-3999
Products: Gases; Welding supplies. **SICs:** 5085 (Industrial Supplies); 5169 (Chemicals & Allied Products Nec). **Sales:** $12,900,000 (2000). **Emp:** 78.
Officers: Rodney S. Belden, CEO.

■ **17033** ■ **Michigan Airgas**
311 Columbus Ave.
Bay City, MI 48706
Phone: (517)894-4101 **Fax:** (517)894-1181
Products: Welding supplies; Industial gases, including oxygen. **SICs:** 5169 (Chemicals & Allied Products Nec); 5085 (Industrial Supplies). **Est:** 1936. **Sales:**

$31,000,000 (2000). **Emp:** 150. **Officers:** Steven Clark, President; Ron Beebe, VP of Finance; Jeff Polerecky, Sales Mgr.

■ **17034** ■ **Mid-America Airgas Inc.**
PO Box 1117
Bowling Green, KY 42102-1117
Phone: (502)842-9486
Free: (888)520-9353 **Fax:** (502)843-0413
Products: Industrial gases and welding supplies. **SICs:** 5169 (Chemicals & Allied Products Nec); 5084 (Industrial Machinery & Equipment). **Sales:** $71,000,000 (2000). **Emp:** 140. **Officers:** Bob Hillyard, President; Dale Gentry, Controller.

■ **17035** ■ **Mid-America Power Drives**
30 N 25th St.
Ft. Dodge, IA 50501-4336
Phone: (515)955-7711 **Fax:** (515)955-2367
Products: Hydraulic parts. **SIC:** 5085 (Industrial Supplies).

■ **17036** ■ **Mid-South Oxygen Company Inc.**
1385 Corporate Ave.
Memphis, TN 38116
Phone: (901)396-5050 **Fax:** (901)396-5020
Products: Gases. **SICs:** 5169 (Chemicals & Allied Products Nec); 5085 (Industrial Supplies). **Sales:** $21,000,000 (2000). **Emp:** 120. **Officers:** George Valentine, President; L. Franks, Treasurer.

■ **17037** ■ **Mid-Valley Supply Co.**
1912 S 1st St.
Ironton, OH 45638
Phone: (614)532-3500
Free: (800)848-0999 **Fax:** (614)532-0233
Products: Industrial supplies. **SIC:** 5085 (Industrial Supplies). **Est:** 1946. **Sales:** $25,000,000 (2000).
Emp: 75. **Officers:** Lee H. Dunbar, President.

■ **17038** ■ **Mill Supplies Corp.**
PO Box 12120
Lansing, MI 48901-2120
Phone: (517)372-6610
Free: (800)648-6455 **Fax:** (517)372-4471
Products: Industrial supplies, including fittings and power tools. **SICs:** 5085 (Industrial Supplies); 5084 (Industrial Machinery & Equipment). **Est:** 1924. **Sales:** $5,000,000 (1999). **Emp:** 14. **Officers:** Gerald P. Kelley, President; Fran Kelley, Secretary; Joseph Newman, Vice President; Jeff Mason, Treasurer.

■ **17039** ■ **Mill Supplies Inc.**
5105 Industrial Rd.
PO Box 11286
Ft. Wayne, IN 46825-5266
Phone: (219)484-8566
Free: (800)589-5353 **Fax:** (219)483-0006
Products: Industrial, construction, and safety supplies. **SIC:** 5085 (Industrial Supplies). **Est:** 1959. **Sales:** $16,000,000 (2000). **Emp:** 65. **Officers:** Janet Beckstein, CEO.

■ **17040** ■ **Miller Bearings Inc.**
1635 N Magnolia Ave.
Ocala, FL 34475
Phone: (352)732-4141 **Fax:** (352)368-1799
Products: Industrial equipment and parts, including power transmissions and bearings. **SICs:** 5084 (Industrial Machinery & Equipment); 5085 (Industrial Supplies).

■ **17041** ■ **Miller Bearings Inc.**
17 S Westmoreland Dr.
Orlando, FL 32805
Phone: (407)425-9078 **Fax:** (407)648-4474
Products: Ball bearings, power transmission and electromechanical products. **SICs:** 5085 (Industrial Supplies); 5063 (Electrical Apparatus & Equipment). **Sales:** $39,000,000 (2000). **Emp:** 120. **Officers:** Bill Kiley, CEO; Craig O. Faber, VP of Finance.

■ 17042 ■ Milligan-Spika Co.
463 Roland Way
PO Box 14006
Oakland, CA 94621
Phone: (510)562-6667
Free: (800)773-9909 **Fax:** (510)430-0807
E-mail: sales@milliganspika.com
URL: http://www.milliganspika.com
Products: Process piping, sensors, and controls; Gas, liquid, steam, metering and control. **SICs:** 5085 (Industrial Supplies); 5084 (Industrial Machinery & Equipment). **Est:** 1957. **Sales:** $1,200,000 (1999). **Emp:** 9. **Officers:** Shel Milligan Jr.; Stan Orlik.

■ 17043 ■ Mine Supply Co.
PO Box 1330
Carlsbad, NM 88220
Phone: (505)887-2888 **Fax:** (505)887-1162
E-mail: minesup@caverns.com
Products: Industrial maintenance parts. **SIC:** 5085 (Industrial Supplies). **Est:** 1946. **Sales:** $23,000,000 (2000). **Emp:** 65. **Officers:** Jack L. Skinner, CEO & President; J.C. Skinner, VP & CFO; Randy Bailey, Dir. of Marketing.

■ 17044 ■ Minnesota Mining & Manufacturing Co. Do-It-Yourself Div.
3M Center, Bldg. 223-4S-02
St. Paul, MN 55144-1000
Phone: (612)733-2931 **Fax:** (612)737-2501
Products: Abrasive products; Natural base glues and adhesives; Industrial safety devices, including first-aid kits and face and eye masks; Paint and varnish removers; Automotive maintenance equipment. **SICs:** 5085 (Industrial Supplies); 5013 (Motor Vehicle Supplies & New Parts); 5198 (Paints, Varnishes & Supplies).

■ 17045 ■ MLT International Inc.
PO Box 338
Line Lexington, PA 18932-0338
Phone: (215)699-5313
Products: Industrial products; Materials handling products; Medical equipment and supplies. **SICs:** 5085 (Industrial Supplies); 5084 (Industrial Machinery & Equipment); 5047 (Medical & Hospital Equipment). **Sales:** $13,000,000 (1994). **Emp:** 12. **Officers:** D.J. Burns, President.

■ 17046 ■ Modern Material Handling Co.
PO Box 5658
Greenville, SC 29606-5658
Phone: (864)242-9990
Free: (800)255-9390 **Fax:** (864)271-2892
Products: Hand tracks; Insulated freezer clothing. **SICs:** 5085 (Industrial Supplies); 5136 (Men's/Boys' Clothing). **Officers:** Ben Reed, President.

■ 17047 ■ Monahan Paper Co.
175 2nd St.
Oakland, CA 94607
Phone: (510)835-4670 **Fax:** (510)273-4585
Products: Paper and paper products. **SIC:** 5113 (Industrial & Personal Service Paper). **Sales:** $7,000,000 (2000). **Emp:** 30.

■ 17048 ■ Moonachie Co.
1 Graphic Place
PO Box 393
Moonachie, NJ 07074
Phone: (201)641-2211 **Fax:** (201)641-2189
Products: Machine and auto valves. **SICs:** 5085 (Industrial Supplies); 5013 (Motor Vehicle Supplies & New Parts).

■ 17049 ■ Mooney General Paper Co.
1451 Chestnut Ave.
Hillside, NJ 07205
Phone: (973)926-3800 **Fax:** (973)926-0425
Products: Paper, plastic products and packaging supplies for the food industry. **SICs:** 5113 (Industrial & Personal Service Paper); 5162 (Plastics Materials & Basic Shapes). **Sales:** $54,000,000 (2000). **Emp:** 78. **Officers:** Gary Riemer, President; Gary Reimer, CFO.

■ 17050 ■ Moore Brothers Div.
1725 69th St.
Sacramento, CA 95819
Phone: (916)454-9353
Products: Welding supplies; Nitrogen; Nitrous Oxide; Oxygen. **SICs:** 5169 (Chemicals & Allied Products Nec); 5085 (Industrial Supplies).

■ 17051 ■ Moore Drums Inc.
2819 Industrial Ave.
Charleston, SC 29405
Phone: (803)744-7448 **Fax:** (803)744-2740
Products: Petroleum, fuels, and related equipment. **SIC:** 5085 (Industrial Supplies). **Sales:** $8,000,000 (2000). **Emp:** 100.

■ 17052 ■ Morrison Industries Inc.
PO Box P
Grand Rapids, MI 49501
Phone: (616)361-2673
Products: Material handling equipment. **SIC:** 5084 (Industrial Machinery & Equipment). **Sales:** $50,000,000 (1993). **Emp:** 300. **Officers:** Jack Morrison, CEO.

■ 17053 ■ Morse Distribution Inc.
PO Box 490
Bellingham, WA 98227
Phone: (360)734-2400 **Fax:** (360)676-2897
Products: Steel service center. **SICs:** 5085 (Industrial Supplies); 5051 (Metals Service Centers & Offices). **Sales:** $15,000,000 (2000). **Emp:** 60. **Officers:** Robert I. Morse, President; Richard D. Olsen, VP & CFO.

■ 17054 ■ Mosier Fluid Power of Ohio Inc.
2495 Technical Dr.
Miamisburg, OH 45342
Phone: (937)847-9846
Products: Hydraulic and pneumatic valve gauges. **SIC:** 5085 (Industrial Supplies). **Est:** 1949. **Sales:** $6,000,000 (2000). **Emp:** 15. **Officers:** Steve C. Stamas, President; T.J. Steuve, VP & Treasurer.

■ 17055 ■ Motion Industries
7701 N 67th St.
Milwaukee, WI 53223
Phone: (414)365-8780 **Fax:** (414)365-8787
URL: http://www.motionindustries.com
Products: Bearings and power transmission parts; hydraulic and industrial hoses; fluid power; electrical drives. **SIC:** 5085 (Industrial Supplies). **Former Name:** Wisconsin Bearing.

■ 17056 ■ Motion Industries, Atlantic Tracy Div.
190 Rand Rd.
Portland, ME 04102-1408
Phone: (207)854-9721
Free: (800)224-5774 **Fax:** (207)854-3490
Products: Power transmission equipment and supplies; Electric motors; Bearings; Rubber and plastic belts and belting, flat; Sprockets; Power transmission chain. **SICs:** 5085 (Industrial Supplies); 5084 (Industrial Machinery & Equipment); 5063 (Electrical Apparatus & Equipment).

■ 17057 ■ Motion Industries Inc.
1605 Alton Rd.
PO Box 1477
Birmingham, 26300, 35210
Phone: (205)956-1122
Free: (800)526-9328 **Fax:** (205)951-1175
URL: http://www.motion-industries.com
Products: Industrial supplies. **SIC:** 5085 (Industrial Supplies). **Est:** 1946. **Sales:** $2,000,000,000 (2000). **Emp:** 6,000. **Officers:** Willam Stevens, CEO; G. Harold Dunaway, CFO.

■ 17058 ■ Mt. Ellis Paper Company Inc.
Gateway International Park
New Windsor, NY 12553
Phone: (914)567-1100 **Fax:** (914)567-1146
Products: Paper and paper products. **SIC:** 5113 (Industrial & Personal Service Paper). **Sales:** $27,000,000 (2000). **Emp:** 59.

■ 17059 ■ MS Rubber Co.
715 E McDowell Rd.
Jackson, MS 39204-5908
Phone: (601)948-2575
Free: (800)748-9083 **Fax:** (601)360-1703
E-mail: mrubber@aol.com
Products: Gaskets; Protective clothing; Rubber hose; Mechanical rubber goods; Plastics, hydraulic hose, conveyor belting. **SICs:** 5199 (Nondurable Goods Nec); 5162 (Plastics Materials & Basic Shapes). **Est:** 1963. **Sales:** $5,100,000 (2000). **Emp:** 31. **Officers:** Ella Ruth Hebert, Chairman of the Board; Greg Hebert, CEO; Pearl Storment, Vice President; Pearl Storment, Sales/Marketing Contact; Bob Neugent, Customer Service Contact; Susan Foster, Human Resources Contact. **Alternate Name:** Miss Rubber & Specialty.

■ 17060 ■ MSC Industrial Direct Inc.
75 Mckess Rd.
Melville, NY 11747
Phone: (516)812-2000
Free: (800)645-7270 **Fax:** (516)812-1703
URL: http://www.mscdirect.com
Products: Industrial products, including cutting tools, abrasives, and welding and electrical supplies; Safety equipment. **SIC:** 5084 (Industrial Machinery & Equipment). **Est:** 1941. **Sales:** $750,000,000 (2000). **Emp:** 2,700. **Officers:** Mitchell Jacobson, CEO & President; Shelley Boxer, VP & CFO. **Former Name:** MSC Industrial Supply Company Inc.

■ 17061 ■ Multifacet Industrial Supply Company Inc.
PO Box 207
Burlington, NJ 08016
Phone: (609)386-6900
Products: Industrial supplies. **SIC:** 5085 (Industrial Supplies). **Sales:** $3,000,000 (2000). **Emp:** 12. **Officers:** W.T. Whitehurst, President.

■ 17062 ■ Munnell & Sherrill Inc.
PO Box 13249
Portland, OR 97213
Phone: (503)281-0021 **Fax:** (503)287-4950
Products: Mill supplies. **SIC:** 5085 (Industrial Supplies). **Est:** 1915. **Sales:** $18,000,000 (2000). **Emp:** 62. **Officers:** Salvatore Mangone, President; Gary L. Butts, Vice President; Michael D. Burrell, Secretary; Thomas E. Price, Jr., Treasurer.

■ 17063 ■ Murdock Electric and Supply Co.
PO Box 2775
Wichita, KS 67201
Phone: (316)262-0401 **Fax:** (316)262-4987
Products: Power transmissions, belts, bearings, and pulleys. **SICs:** 5084 (Industrial Machinery & Equipment); 5013 (Motor Vehicle Supplies & New Parts).

■ 17064 ■ Murdock Industrial Inc.
310 Water St.
Akron, OH 44308
Phone: (330)535-7105 **Fax:** (330)535-1125
E-mail: mfmurdock@earthlink.net
Products: Industrial supplies, including rubber, safety equipment, conveyorbelt and hydraulic hose; Aeroqup; Thermoid; Garlock and SIA Adhesives. **SIC:** 5085 (Industrial Supplies). **Est:** 1904. **Sales:** $5,000,000 (2000). **Emp:** 20. **Officers:** Tony Price, President; Philip Jones, Vice President. **Former Name:** M.F. #Murdock Co.

■ 17065 ■ J.E. Myles Inc.
310 Executive Dr.
Troy, MI 48084
Phone: (313)583-1020 **Fax:** (313)583-6998
Products: Fluid power products; Hydraulic power supplies, hose assemblies, and test machines. **SIC:** 5085 (Industrial Supplies). **Sales:** $5,000,000 (2000). **Emp:** 37. **Officers:** J. Ed Myles, President; Scott Myles, VP of Operations.

■ 17066 ■ National Compressed Gases Inc.
24 McDermott Rd.
North Haven, CT 06473
Phone: (203)624-5144
Products: Compressed air and gases; Medical gases. **SIC:** 5169 (Chemicals & Allied Products Nec). **Est:**

1980. **Sales:** $3,000,000 (2000). **Emp:** 28. **Officers:** Joseph Bango, Vice President.

■ **17067** ■ **National Welders Supply Company Inc.**
PO Box 31007
Charlotte, NC 28231
Phone: (704)333-5475
Free: (800)866-4422 **Fax:** (704)342-0260
URL: http://www.nwsco.com
Products: Welding supplies; Industrial gases. **SICs:** 5085 (Industrial Supplies); 5084 (Industrial Machinery & Equipment); 5169 (Chemicals & Allied Products Nec). **Est:** 1941. **Sales:** $100,000,000 (2000). **Emp:** 750. **Officers:** Richard Lake, CEO & President; A.W. Demart, Sr. VP of Finance; Tom Sheridan, Human Resources Contact, e-mail: tom_sheridan@nwsco.com.

■ **17068** ■ **National Welding Supply of Algona**
PO Box 496
Algona, IA 50511
Phone: (515)295-7261 **Fax:** (515)295-7263
Products: Welding supplies. **SICs:** 5169 (Chemicals & Allied Products Nec); 5084 (Industrial Machinery & Equipment); 5085 (Industrial Supplies). **Est:** 1940. **Sales:** $1,000,000 (2000). **Emp:** 9. **Officers:** Duane Larson, Manager.

■ **17069** ■ **Neff Engineering Co.**
PO Box 8604
Ft. Wayne, IN 46898
Phone: (219)489-6007 **Fax:** (219)489-6204
Products: Hydraulics. **SIC:** 5085 (Industrial Supplies). **Sales:** $5,000,000 (2000). **Emp:** 20. **Officers:** John W. Neff, President; Harry M. Neff, General Mgr.

■ **17070** ■ **Neill-LaVielle Supply Co.**
1711 S Floyd St.
Louisville, KY 40208
Phone: (502)637-5401
Products: Steel flame cutting. **SIC:** 5085 (Industrial Supplies). **Sales:** $51,000,000 (2000). **Emp:** 165. **Officers:** Richard Pfeiffer, President.

■ **17071** ■ **Nekoosa Corp.**
PO Box 129
Nekoosa, WI 54457
Phone: (715)886-3800
Products: Industrial supplies. **SIC:** 5085 (Industrial Supplies). **Est:** 1918. **Sales:** $10,000,000 (2000). **Emp:** 58. **Officers:** T.L. Olson, President; Larry Grosskopf, Controller.

■ **17072** ■ **Nelson-Dunn Inc.**
940 S Vail Ave.
Montebello, CA 90640-5420
Phone: (323)724-3705
Free: (800)635-3866 **Fax:** (323)722-8136
URL: http://www.nelsondunn.com
Products: Hydraulic hoses and gaskets. **SIC:** 5085 (Industrial Supplies). **Est:** 1959. **Sales:** $5,500,000 (2000). **Emp:** 24. **Officers:** Kevin B. Dunn, President.

■ **17073** ■ **New York Twist Drill Inc.**
5368 E Rockton Rd.
South Beloit, IL 61080
Free: (800)645-3830 **Fax:** 800-543-0972
E-mail: customerservice@newyorktwistdrill.com
URL: http://www.newyorktwistdrill.com
Products: Drilling bits; Small cutting tools for machine tools and metalworking machinery. **SICs:** 5084 (Industrial Machinery & Equipment); 5072 (Hardware). **Sales:** $30,000,000 (2000). **Emp:** 100. **Officers:** E. P. Campbell; Mike Dabson, E-com Manager, e-mail: mdabson@newyorktwistdrill.com.

■ **17074** ■ **Newmans Inc.**
1300 Gazin St.
Houston, TX 77020
Phone: (713)675-8631
Products: General industrial supplies. **SIC:** 5085 (Industrial Supplies). **Sales:** $43,000,000 (1994). **Emp:** 200. **Officers:** Ray Baker, President; Frank Carter, CFO.

■ **17075** ■ **Norfolk Bearing & Supply Co.**
3512 Princess Anne Rd.
PO Box 12825
Norfolk, VA 23502
Phone: (757)853-3691 **Fax:** (757)855-5861
Products: Bearings; Transmission parts; Sprockets. **SICs:** 5084 (Industrial Machinery & Equipment); 5085 (Industrial Supplies).

■ **17076** ■ **Garland C. Norris Co.**
PO Box 28
Apex, NC 27502
Phone: (919)387-1059 **Fax:** (919)387-1325
Products: Industrial and personal service paper. **SIC:** 5113 (Industrial & Personal Service Paper). **Sales:** $23,000,000 (2000). **Emp:** 43. **Officers:** J.A. King, President; J.A. King II, CFO.

■ **17077** ■ **Walter Norris Co.**
5530 Milton Pkwy.
Rosemont, IL 60018
Phone: (847)671-7410
Free: (800)345-0316 **Fax:** (847)671-4538
Products: Pumps; Valves; Cylinders; Motors. **SICs:** 5084 (Industrial Machinery & Equipment); 5085 (Industrial Supplies). **Est:** 1940. **Sales:** $26,000,000 (2000). **Emp:** 100. **Officers:** Frank Brayton, President; Don Adamitis, VP of Finance.

■ **17078** ■ **Northeast Airgas Inc.**
PO Box 1647
Salem, NH 03079-1142
Phone: (603)890-4600 **Free:** (800)821-9852
Products: Gases, including industrial, lab, and medical; Welding and safety equipment. **SICs:** 5169 (Chemicals & Allied Products Nec); 5084 (Industrial Machinery & Equipment); 5085 (Industrial Supplies). **Est:** 1988. **Sales:** $25,000,000 (2000). **Emp:** 50. **Officers:** John Musselman, President; Mark Lagasse, CFO.

■ **17079** ■ **Northeast Industrial Components Co.**
PO Box 868
Bristol, RI 02809
Phone: (401)253-2555
Products: Industrial products. **SIC:** 5162 (Plastics Materials & Basic Shapes). **Sales:** $300,000 (2000). **Emp:** 1. **Officers:** John Mac Intyre, President.

■ **17080** ■ **Northeast Steel and Machine Products**
PO Box 9007
Forestville, CT 06010-9007
Phone: (860)589-2700 **Fax:** (860)584-8561
E-mail: nes@ntplx.net
Products: Wire, not insulated. **SIC:** 5085 (Industrial Supplies). **Est:** 1968. **Sales:** $7,500,000 (2000). **Emp:** 24. **Officers:** A. Weaver, President; Jeanne S. Weaver, Vice President.

■ **17081** ■ **Northern Indiana Supply Company Inc.**
PO Box 447
Kokomo, IN 46903
Phone: (765)459-4151 **Fax:** (765)459-5749
E-mail: nisco@holli.com
Products: Industrial supplies, including pipe valves and fittings, lockers, and shelves. **SIC:** 5085 (Industrial Supplies). **Est:** 1933. **Sales:** $12,400,000 (2000). **Emp:** 43. **Officers:** James Gardenhire, President; James Gardenhire, President.

■ **17082** ■ **Northern Industrial Supply Inc.**
2800 E Holland Ave.
Saginaw, MI 48601
Phone: (517)753-2414
Products: Industrial supplies, including main line power transmissions. **SIC:** 5085 (Industrial Supplies). **Est:** 1934. **Sales:** $7,000,000 (2000). **Emp:** 28. **Officers:** Andy Anderson, President; Jeffrey Pickelman, Controller; Eric Anderson, VP of Marketing.

■ **17083** ■ **Novelty Machine and Supply Company Inc.**
901 5th St.
Sioux City, IA 51102
Phone: (712)255-0114
Products: Industrial supplies, including pump lines and

automatic transmissions. **SICs:** 5085 (Industrial Supplies); 5084 (Industrial Machinery & Equipment). **Est:** 1880. **Sales:** $8,000,000 (2000). **Emp:** 23. **Officers:** John A. Olson, President.

■ **17084** ■ **Nudo Products Inc.**
2508 S Grand E
Springfield, IL 62703
Phone: (217)528-5636
Free: (800)826-4132 **Fax:** (217)528-8722
Products: Multiweb laminations and foil. **SIC:** 5085 (Industrial Supplies). **Est:** 1956. **Sales:** $30,000,000 (2000). **Emp:** 50.

■ **17085** ■ **O-Rings Inc.**
PO Box 65675
Los Angeles, CA 90065
Phone: (323)343-9500
Free: (800)421-6669 **Fax:** (323)343-9505
E-mail: orings@usa.net
URL: http://www.orings.com
Products: O-rings and gaskets. **SIC:** 5085 (Industrial Supplies). **Est:** 1958. **Officers:** S.K. Lee, President; Richard Kelly, Sales/Marketing Contact; Cliff Stevens, Customer Service Contact; Cliff Stevens, Customer Service Contact.

■ **17086** ■ **Ohio Brake & Clutch**
1460 Wolf Creek Trl.
PO Box 325
Sharon Center, OH 44274
Phone: (216)781-0805 **Fax:** (330)239-4995
Products: Industrial components. **SICs:** 5084 (Industrial Machinery & Equipment); 5085 (Industrial Supplies).

■ **17087** ■ **Ohio Pipe Valves and Fittings Inc.**
3900 Trent Ave.
Cleveland, OH 44109
Phone: (216)631-6000 **Fax:** (216)631-4874
Products: Pipes; Valves; Fittings; Thermometers; Gages; Steam traps; Valve actuation and modification. **SICs:** 5085 (Industrial Supplies); 5074 (Plumbing & Hydronic Heating Supplies). **Est:** 1911. **Sales:** $6,000,000 (2000). **Emp:** 20. **Officers:** E.G. Resch, President.

■ **17088** ■ **Oklahoma Rig and Supply Company Inc.**
PO Box 249
Muskogee, OK 74402
Phone: (918)687-5441 **Fax:** (918)682-5936
Products: Oilfield and industrial supplies. **SICs:** 5072 (Hardware); 5084 (Industrial Machinery & Equipment); 5085 (Industrial Supplies). **Sales:** $40,000,000 (1993). **Emp:** 100. **Officers:** Robert B. Thompson, President.

■ **17089** ■ **Omega Optical, Inc.**
3 Grove St.
Brattleboro, VT 05301
Phone: (802)254-2690 **Fax:** (802)254-3937
E-mail: info@omegafilters.com
URL: http://www.omegafilters.com
Products: Optical filters. **SIC:** 5085 (Industrial Supplies). **Est:** 1969. **Sales:** $8,000,000 (1999). **Emp:** 130. **Officers:** Dr. Robert L. Johnson, President & Technical Dir.; Cheryl Aaron, Marketing Coord.

■ **17090** ■ **Omni Services Inc.**
25 Union St.
Worcester, MA 01608
Phone: (508)799-2746 **Fax:** (508)799-2844
Products: Hydraulic equipment and parts, including couplings and fittings. **SIC:** 5085 (Industrial Supplies). **Sales:** $10,000,000 (1999). **Emp:** 72. **Officers:** Robert Mitchell, CFO; Chuck Connors, President.

■ **17091** ■ **Oren Van Aman Company Inc.**
PO Box 5266
Ft. Wayne, IN 46895
Phone: (219)625-3844 **Fax:** (219)625-4447
Products: Industrial sales. **SIC:** 5085 (Industrial Supplies). **Sales:** $90,000,000 (2000). **Emp:** 20.

■ **17092** ■ **OSG Tap and Die Inc.**
676 E Fullerton Ave.
Glendale Heights, IL 60139
Phone: (708)790-1400
Products: Drills; Taps; Dies; End mills. **SICs:** 5084

(Industrial Machinery & Equipment); 5085 (Industrial Supplies). **Est:** 1968. **Sales:** $65,000,000 (2000). **Emp:** 370. **Officers:** George Osawa, President.

■ **17093** ■ **Owensboro Supply Company Inc.**
PO Box 2029
Owensboro, KY 42302
Phone: (502)683-8318 **Fax:** (502)926-6268
Products: Industrial supplies; Oil. **SICs:** 5085 (Industrial Supplies); 5172 (Petroleum Products Nec). **Est:** 1966. **Sales:** $2,100,000 (2000). **Emp:** 7. **Officers:** H.M. Morgan, President.

■ **17094** ■ **Pacific Abrasive Supply Co.**
7100 Village Dr.
Buena Park, CA 90621
Phone: (714)994-2040
Free: (800)755-2042 **Fax:** (714)994-4723
E-mail: pasco@gateway.net
Products: Coated abrasive products, including belts; Discs; Sheets and rolls. **SIC:** 5085 (Industrial Supplies). **Est:** 1920. **Sales:** $20,000,000 (2000). **Emp:** 81. **Officers:** David M. Yeager, President.

■ **17095** ■ **Pacific Fibre and Rope Company Inc.**
PO Box 187
Wilmington, CA 90748
Phones: (310)834-4567 800-825-7673
Fax: (310)835-6781
E-mail: pacific@worldnet.att.net
Products: Rope; Rope ladders; Fiber; Cargo and gangway nets. **SIC:** 5085 (Industrial Supplies). **Est:** 1928. **Sales:** $2,000,000 (2000). **Emp:** 14. **Officers:** A. Goldman, President & CEO.

■ **17096** ■ **Pacific Handy Cutter Inc.**
PO Box 10869
Costa Mesa, CA 92627
Phone: (714)662-1033
Free: (800)229-2233 **Fax:** (714)662-7595
E-mail: info@pacifichandycutter.com
Products: Cutting tools; Sundries; Blades and scrapers. **SICs:** 5085 (Industrial Supplies); 5072 (Hardware). **Est:** 1950. **Sales:** $12,000,000 (2000). **Emp:** 55. **Officers:** Gerry Schmidt; Katitza Schmidt; Robert B. Wenk.

■ **17097** ■ **Pacific Industrial Supply Company Inc.**
PO Box 24045
Seattle, WA 98124
Phone: (206)682-2100
Free: (800)622-3434 **Fax:** (206)623-2173
E-mail: sales@pacificindustrial.com
URL: http://www.pacific_industrial.com
Products: Hydraulic equipment; Steel; Cable, wire, and rope; Marine supplies; Hand tools; Industrial supplies. **SICs:** 5085 (Industrial Supplies); 5051 (Metals Service Centers & Offices). **Est:** 1985. **Sales:** $15,000,000 (2000). **Emp:** 48. **Officers:** Howard K. Brown, President; C. Leon Frazier, Vice President; Woody Haizlip, Sales/Marketing Contact.

■ **17098** ■ **Packers Engineering and Equipment Company Inc.**
6720 N 16th St.
Omaha, NE 68112
Phone: (402)451-1252 **Fax:** (402)451-1555
Products: Packing house supplies and parts. **SICs:** 5085 (Industrial Supplies); 5046 (Commercial Equipment Nec). **Est:** 1949. **Sales:** $60,000,000 (2000). **Emp:** 165. **Officers:** Jerry Byrnes, President; John T. Byrnes, Vice President.

■ **17099** ■ **Parker Hannifin Corp. Fluidpower Sales Div.**
PO Box 3500
Troy, MI 48007-3500
Phone: (248)589-2400 **Fax:** (248)589-4769
Products: Pneumatic and hydraulic components. **SIC:** 5085 (Industrial Supplies). **Est:** 1971. **Sales:** $10,000,000 (2000). **Emp:** 35. **Officers:** Richard Marbrey, General Mgr.; Ian Panton, Controller.

■ **17100** ■ **Patron Transmission**
75 Allen Blvd.
Farmingdale, NY 11735
Phone: (516)293-8084 **Fax:** (516)293-1925
Products: Sprockets, belts, conveyors, bearings and pumps. **SICs:** 5085 (Industrial Supplies); 5084 (Industrial Machinery & Equipment).

■ **17101** ■ **Patterson Sales Associates**
PO Box 13156
Savannah, GA 31416-0156
Phone: (912)598-0086 **Fax:** (912)598-0174
Products: Paper and paper products. **SIC:** 5113 (Industrial & Personal Service Paper). **Sales:** $1,000,000 (2000). **Emp:** 2.

■ **17102** ■ **R.E. Peacock Co./Southwestern Cordage Co.**
3942 S Memorial Dr.
Tulsa, OK 74145
Phone: (918)627-0206
Free: (800)331-4079 **Fax:** (918)627-1459
Products: Rope; Military supplies. **SIC:** 5085 (Industrial Supplies). **Est:** 1957. **Emp:** 10.

■ **17103** ■ **Henry A. Petter Supply Co.**
PO Box 2350
Paducah, KY 42001
Phone: (270)443-2441
Free: (800)626-3940 **Fax:** (270)575-6900
URL: http://www.petterusa.com
Products: Industrial supplies; Janitorial supplies; Paper; Office supplies; Electrical supplies; Pipes; Valves; Fittings; Safety supplies. **SICs:** 5085 (Industrial Supplies); 5087 (Service Establishment Equipment); 5112 (Stationery & Office Supplies). **Est:** 1890. **Sales:** $20,000,000 (1999). **Emp:** 200. **Officers:** Robert Petter, CEO, e-mail: petter@petterusa.com; Robert Petter Jr, Exec. VP; John Sircy, Chairman of the Board & Finance Officer.

■ **17104** ■ **Pikotek**
PO Box 260438
Lakewood, CO 80226
Phone: (303)988-1242 **Fax:** (303)988-1922
Products: critical service gaskets, mechanical seals and insulation sets. **SIC:** 5085 (Industrial Supplies). **Officers:** Thomas Wallace, President.

■ **17105** ■ **Pioneer Industrial Corp.**
400 Russell Blvd.
St. Louis, MO 63104
Phone: (314)771-0700
Free: (800)505-PUMP **Fax:** (314)771-2904
URL: http://www.pioneerindustrial.com
Products: Industrial supplies; Valves; Pumps. **SIC:** 5085 (Industrial Supplies). **Sales:** $6,700,000 (2000). **Emp:** 60. **Officers:** William Pfitzinger, President, e-mail: bpfitzinger@pioneerindustrial.com; Terry Hickey, Vice President, e-mail: thickey@pioneerindustrial.com. **Former Name:** Zoltek Companies Inc. Equipment and Services Div.

■ **17106** ■ **Pipe Valve and Fitting Co.**
PO Box 5806
Denver, CO 80217
Phone: (303)289-5811
Free: (800)525-0157 **Fax:** (303)287-7005
E-mail: pvfco@msn.com
Products: Pipes, valves, and steel fittings. **SICs:** 5085 (Industrial Supplies); 5051 (Metals Service Centers & Offices). **Est:** 1962. **Sales:** $4,500,000 (2000). **Emp:** 18. **Officers:** Gary D. Sommerfeld, President; Gary D. Sommerfeld, President.

■ **17107** ■ **Piping Supply Company Inc.**
3008 N Hickory St.
Chattanooga, TN 37406
Phone: (615)698-8996
Products: Industrial pipe fittings and valves. **SIC:** 5085 (Industrial Supplies). **Est:** 1966. **Sales:** $14,000,000 (2000). **Emp:** 20. **Officers:** Chris Warren, President; Peggy Hale, CFO.

■ **17108** ■ **Plant Service Co.**
6th & Bingham
Pittsburgh, PA 15203
Phone: (412)381-4664
Free: (800)426-9599 **Fax:** (412)381-7260
Products: Industrial supplies; Hand tools; Abrasives; Cutting tools. **SICs:** 5085 (Industrial Supplies); 5072 (Hardware). **Emp:** 49. **Officers:** Lee Frazier; Jim Russell.

■ **17109** ■ **PMC Specialties Group**
3302 Ingleside Rd.
Cleveland, OH 44122
Phone: (216)921-3848
Products: Inks. **SICs:** 5085 (Industrial Supplies); 5169 (Chemicals & Allied Products Nec).

■ **17110** ■ **Praxair Gas Tech**
12000 Roosevelt Rd.
Hillside, IL 60162
Phone: (708)449-9300
Products: Gases; Safety supplies; Welding supplies. **SICs:** 5085 (Industrial Supplies); 5084 (Industrial Machinery & Equipment); 5047 (Medical & Hospital Equipment); 5169 (Chemicals & Allied Products Nec). **Officers:** Ronald Castle, General Mgr. **Former Name:** Linde Gases of the Midwest Inc.

■ **17111** ■ **Precision Bearing**
1144 27th Ave. SW
Cedar Rapids, IA 52404
Phone: (319)365-5276 **Fax:** (319)365-9132
Products: Bearings, hydraulics, pneumatics and pumps. **SICs:** 5084 (Industrial Machinery & Equipment); 5085 (Industrial Supplies).

■ **17112** ■ **Precision Bearing Co.**
1919 Cornhusker Hwy.
Lincoln, NE 68521-1878
Phone: (402)474-7700
Free: (800)742-7011 **Fax:** (402)474-0141
Products: Industrial supplies. **SIC:** 5085 (Industrial Supplies).

■ **17113** ■ **Precision Bearing Co.**
2503 S 13th St.
Norfolk, NE 68701
Phone: (402)371-6777 **Fax:** (402)371-4476
Products: Bearings; Motors; Belts; Industrial lubricants. **SICs:** 5085 (Industrial Supplies); 5063 (Electrical Apparatus & Equipment); 5172 (Petroleum Products Nec).

■ **17114** ■ **Precision Industrial Distributors Inc.**
5151 Oceanus Dr.
Huntington Beach, CA 92649
Phone: (714)379-1380
Products: Industrial machine tools. **SIC:** 5085 (Industrial Supplies). **Sales:** $1,300,000 (2000). **Emp:** 5. **Officers:** John Szot, President.

■ **17115** ■ **Precision Speed Instruments Inc.**
PO Box 27400
Phoenix, AZ 85061
Phone: (602)973-1055
Free: (800)873-1055 **Fax:** (602)242-8577
Products: Transmission protection devices; instruments, gauges and ancillary products. **SIC:** 5085 (Industrial Supplies). **Sales:** $1,000,000 (2000). **Emp:** 4. **Officers:** Ann Bogert, President.

■ **17116** ■ **Price Engineering Company, Inc.**
N8 W22577 Johnson Dr.
Waukesha, WI 53186
Phone: (262)547-2700 **Fax:** (262)547-0416
E-mail: sales@priceeng.com
URL: http://www.priceeng.com
Products: Hydraulic, electrical, and pneumatic parts; Robotic and automation equipment. **SIC:** 5085 (Industrial Supplies). **Est:** 1953. **Sales:** $30,000,000 (1999). **Emp:** 100. **Officers:** Tom Price Sr., President; Tom Price Jr., Vice President; Tom Bauman, VP of Marketing; Scott Conrad, Customer Service Contact, e-mail: sconrad@priceeng.com; Chris Johnson, Human Resources Contact, e-mail: cjohnson@priceeng.com.

■ **17117** ■ **Process Supplies & Accessories, Inc.**
6700 Baum Drive, Ste. 18
Knoxville, TN 37919
Phone: (423)588-0392 **Fax:** (423)584-4760
Products: Instruments. **SICs:** 5049 (Professional Equipment Nec); 5084 (Industrial Machinery & Equipment).

■ **17118** ■ **Processors Equipment & Hardware**
1605 Mono Dr.
Modesto, CA 95355
Phone: (209)524-1404 **Fax:** (209)524-0112
Products: Industrial supplies. **SIC:** 5085 (Industrial Supplies). **Emp:** 5.

■ **17119** ■ **Production Tool Supply**
PO Box 987
Warren, MI 48089
Phone: (810)755-7770
Free: (800)366-3600 **Fax:** 800-545-8655
URL: http://www.ptsxpress.com
Products: Industrial tools, including surface grinders and micrometers. **SICs:** 5085 (Industrial Supplies); 5084 (Industrial Machinery & Equipment). **Est:** 1951. **Sales:** $220,000,000 (1999). **Emp:** 500. **Officers:** Mark Kahn, President; Michael Brenner, Controller; David Francis, Distribution Mgr.; Richard Coleman, Dir. of Systems; Pamela Mack, Dir of Human Resources.

■ **17120** ■ **Production Tool Supply of Jackson**
PO Box 963
Jackson, MI 49204-0963
Phone: (517)787-5300
Free: (800)992-0092 **Fax:** (517)787-3767
URL: http://www.pts-tools.com
Products: Industrial supplies. **SIC:** 5085 (Industrial Supplies). **Est:** 1966. **Sales:** $8,000,000 (2000). **Emp:** 23. **Officers:** Dennis Ruede, General Mgr.; Michael Brenner, CFO.

■ **17121** ■ **Pump Engineering Co.**
9807 Jordan Cir.
Santa Fe Springs, CA 90670
Phone: (562)946-6864 **Fax:** (562)944-4768
E-mail: sales@pumpeco.com
Products: Industrial products, including pumps and pump parts. **SIC:** 5085 (Industrial Supplies). **Est:** 1946. **Sales:** $7,500,000 (2000). **Emp:** 28. **Officers:** J.L. Hamilton, President.

■ **17122** ■ **Pump Systems Inc.**
15000 Bolsa Chica Rd.
Huntington Beach, CA 92649
Phone: (714)898-0313
Products: Industrial supplies. **SIC:** 5084 (Industrial Machinery & Equipment). **Est:** 1952. **Sales:** $20,000,000 (2000). **Emp:** 25. **Officers:** L. Statler, President; J. Statler, CFO.

■ **17123** ■ **Purvis Bearings**
3000 Airport Fwy.
Ft. Worth, TX 76111
Phone: (817)831-4581 **Fax:** (817)831-3465
Products: Industrial equipment, including bearings, belts, and reducers. **SIC:** 5085 (Industrial Supplies).

■ **17124** ■ **Quaker City Paper Co.**
300 N Sherman St.
York, PA 17405
Phone: (717)843-9061
Free: (800)533-2553 **Fax:** (717)843-7850
Products: Paper and paper products. **SIC:** 5113 (Industrial & Personal Service Paper). **Sales:** $12,000,000 (2000). **Emp:** 67.

■ **17125** ■ **Quality Mill Supply Company Inc.**
PO Box 508
Columbus, IN 47201
Phone: (812)379-9585 **Fax:** (812)379-2810
Products: Drills; Children's clothing accessories; Abrasive products. **SICs:** 5085 (Industrial Supplies); 5084 (Industrial Machinery & Equipment); 5137 (Women's/Children's Clothing). **Est:** 1944. **Sales:** $18,000,000 (2000). **Emp:** 65. **Officers:** Alan G. Gilbert, President; C.J. Zauss, Treasurer; Mike Baker, Sales Mgr.

■ **17126** ■ **Quimby Corp.**
1603 NW 14th Ave.
Portland, OR 97209
Phone: (503)221-1100
Free: (800)743-1109 **Fax:** (503)241-9549
E-mail: Sales@Quimbycorp.com
URL: http://www.Quimbycorp.com
Products: Welding and industrial supplies, safety equipment, compressed gases. **SICs:** 5084 (Industrial Machinery & Equipment); 5085 (Industrial Supplies); 5169 (Chemicals & Allied Products Nec). **Est:** 1956. **Sales:** $11,000,000 (1999). **Emp:** 45. **Officers:** Wayne M. Quimby, President; Joe Smith, Sales Mgr.; Tom Minkler, Operations Mgr.

■ **17127** ■ **R and W Supply Inc.**
PO Box 270
Littlefield, TX 79339
Phone: (806)385-4447
Free: (800)477-1191 **Fax:** (806)385-4449
E-mail: rwsupply@worldnet.att.net
URL: http://www.rwsupply.com
Products: Heaters; Grills; Gas equipment, including hoses, nozzles, pumps, filters, tanks, valves, and fittings. **SIC:** 5085 (Industrial Supplies). **Est:** 1946. **Sales:** $10,000,000 (2000). **Emp:** 23. **Officers:** Shawn Pickrell, President; Linda Pickrell, Treasurer & Secty.

■ **17128** ■ **Ramclif Supply Co.**
1212 East Mason Avenue
York, PA 17403
Phone: (717)854-5534
Free: (800)723-7055 **Fax:** (717)848-1380
URL: http://www.ramclif.com
Products: Industrial supplies, including shop, safety, plumbing, heating, and air conditioning equipment; Abrasives; Precision, cutting, and hand tools. **SICs:** 5085 (Industrial Supplies); 5074 (Plumbing & Hydronic Heating Supplies); 5075 (Warm Air Heating & Air-Conditioning). **Est:** 1954. **Sales:** $10,000,000 (1999). **Emp:** 35. **Officers:** Jeffrey W. Peters, President, e-mail: jeffpeters@ramclif.com; Paul W. Green, JR., VP & Secty., e-mail: paulgreen@ramclif.com; Stephen M. Green, VP & Treasurer, e-mail: stevegreen@ramclif.com; Gary Wineholt, Sales/Marketing Contact, e-mail: garywineholt@ramclif.com; Dawn Weaver, Human Resources Contact, e-mail: dawnweaver@ramclif.com.

■ **17129** ■ **Randall-Graw Company Inc.**
PO Box 3119
La Crosse, WI 54602
Phone: (608)784-6228
Products: Welding supplies. **SIC:** 5084 (Industrial Machinery & Equipment). **Est:** 1946. **Sales:** $15,000,000 (2000). **Emp:** 60. **Officers:** R.B. Graw, President; L. Fossen, VP of Finance; O. Midtlien, Dir. of Marketing.

■ **17130** ■ **F. Raniville Company Inc.**
PO Box 888283
Grand Rapids, MI 49588-8283
Phone: (616)957-3200 **Fax:** (616)957-8927
Products: Conveyor belting. **SIC:** 5085 (Industrial Supplies). **Est:** 1874. **Sales:** $2,000,000 (2000). **Emp:** 9. **Officers:** Robert H. Beaman, President.

■ **17131** ■ **Rapid Controls Inc.**
PO Box 8390
Rapid City, SD 57709-8390
Phone: (605)348-7688 **Fax:** (605)341-5496
E-mail: info@rapidcontrols.com
URL: http://www.rapidcontrols.com
Products: Industrial controls. **SIC:** 5085 (Industrial Supplies). **Est:** 1987. **Sales:** $700,000 (2000). **Emp:** 6. **Officers:** David Deeny, Owner.

■ **17132** ■ **Raufeisen Enterprises**
513 31st St.
Rock Island, IL 61201
Phone: (309)794-1111
Free: (800)778-5739 **Fax:** (309)794-1811
E-mail: info@heenan.com
URL: http://www.heenen.com
Products: Hydraulics and pneumatics. **SIC:** 5085 (Industrial Supplies). **Est:** 1931. **Sales:** $15,000,000 (1999). **Emp:** 38. **Officers:** Todd B. Raufeisen, President.

■ **17133** ■ **Reed Manufacturing Co.**
1425 W 8th St.
Erie, PA 16502
Phone: (814)452-3691
Free: (800)666-3691 **Fax:** (814)455-1697
E-mail: reedmfg@ncinter.net
URL: http://www.reedmfgco.com
Products: Pipe tools; Vises; Hand tools. **SIC:** 5085 (Industrial Supplies). **Est:** 1896. **Emp:** 100. **Officers:** Ralph T. Wright, President; Scott K. Wright, VP of Marketing & Sales.

■ **17134** ■ **Refco IDG.**
730 Main St.
PO Box 8
Boylston, MA 01505-0008
Phone: (508)869-2106
Free: (800)225-7400 **Fax:** (508)869-6516
Products: Cutting tools; Abrasives; Safety supplies. **SICs:** 5085 (Industrial Supplies); 5084 (Industrial Machinery & Equipment). **Est:** 1959. **Sales:** $35,000,000 (2000). **Emp:** 92. **Officers:** Mark W. Fuller, Vice President.

■ **17135** ■ **Reichman, Crosby, Hays Inc.**
3150 Carrier
Memphis, TN 38116
Phone: (901)345-2200
Products: Industrial mill supplies, including grinding wheels, drill bits, and hand and power tools. **SICs:** 5085 (Industrial Supplies); 5072 (Hardware). **Est:** 1895. **Sales:** $13,000,000 (2000). **Emp:** 44. **Officers:** Gene Langley, CEO.

■ **17136** ■ **Reid Tool Supply Co.**
2265 Black Creek Rd.
Muskegon, MI 49444
Phone: (616)777-3951
Free: (800)253-0421 **Fax:** (616)773-4485
Products: Industrial supplies and equipment. **SICs:** 5085 (Industrial Supplies); 5084 (Industrial Machinery & Equipment). **Est:** 1948. **Sales:** $27,000,000 (2000). **Emp:** 82. **Officers:** Paul Reid, CEO; Rick Goodwin, CFO.

■ **17137** ■ **RG Group Inc.**
PO Box 2824
York, PA 17405
Phone: (717)846-9300
Free: (877)870-2692 **Fax:** (717)845-7786
E-mail: customer.service@rg-group.com
URL: http://www.rg-group.com
Products: Hydraulic, pneumatic, and connector components. **SIC:** 5085 (Industrial Supplies). **Est:** 1956. **Sales:** $22,000,000 (2000). **Emp:** 130. **Officers:** Jon Newman, President & COO, e-mail: jon.newman@rg-group.com; Greg Plitt, CFO, e-mail: greg.plitt@rg-group.com.

■ **17138** ■ **Rice Welding Supply Co.**
10141 Market St.
Houston, TX 77029
Phone: (713)674-2012
Products: Clinder gas. **SIC:** 5169 (Chemicals & Allied Products Nec).

■ **17139** ■ **RKR Corp.**
4600 Grape St.
Denver, CO 80216
Phone: (303)321-7610
Products: Pipes, valves, and pipe fittings industry. **SIC:** 5051 (Metals Service Centers & Offices).

■ **17140** ■ **Robco International Corporation/Advanced Technology International**
PO Box 707
Oak Park, IL 60303
Phone: (708)524-1880 **Fax:** (708)524-2015
E-mail: info@-intl.com
URL: http://www.ati-intl.com
Products: Electrical regulators; Industrial supplies, including pumps, vacuums, chemical soldering fluxes, and welding supplies; Hardware clamps. **SICs:** 5085 (Industrial Supplies); 5084 (Industrial Machinery & Equipment); 5063 (Electrical Apparatus & Equipment); 5072 (Hardware). **Est:** 1974. **Emp:** 7. **Officers:** Robert F. Begani, President.

■ **17141** ■ **Roberts and Brune Co.**
939 Broadway
PO Box 5100
Redwood City, CA 94063
Phone: (650)366-3833
Free: (800)792-7473 **Fax:** (650)366-1134
URL: http://www.robertsbrune.com
Products: Pipes, valves, and fittings; Tools for water, sewer, and storm drainage. **SICs:** 5085 (Industrial Supplies); 5084 (Industrial Machinery & Equipment). **Sales:** $5,000,000 (2000). **Emp:** 12. **Officers:** Reed Mack, President, e-mail: rmack@riconet.net.

■ **17142** ■ **Rockford Industrial Welding Supply Inc.**
4646 Linden Rd.
Rockford, IL 61109-3300
Phone: (815)226-1900
Products: Welding supplies and gases. **SICs:** 5085 (Industrial Supplies); 5169 (Chemicals & Allied Products Nec). **Est:** 1955. **Sales:** $11,000,000 (2000). **Emp:** 55. **Officers:** Gary R. Bertrand, President; Dave Wiles, Controller; Terry Bennett, Sales Mgr.

■ **17143** ■ **A.J. Rod Co. Inc.**
5011 Navigation Blvd.
Houston, TX 77011
Phone: (713)921-6111
Free: (800)392-3714 **Fax:** (713)926-4704
E-mail: ajrodco@aol.com
URL: http://www.members.aol.com/ajrodco/index.htm
Products: Cutting tools. **SIC:** 5085 (Industrial Supplies). **Est:** 1948. **Sales:** $7,000,000 (2000). **Emp:** 25. **Officers:** Johnny Rutherford, President.

■ **17144** ■ **R.A. Rodriguez Inc.**
20 Seaview Blvd.
Port Washington, NY 11050-4618
Phone: (516)625-8080 **Fax:** (516)621-2424
URL: http://www.rodriguez-usa.com
Products: Precision ball and roller bearings for aerospace, industrial, and automotive applications. **SIC:** 5085 (Industrial Supplies). **Est:** 1929. **Emp:** 80. **Officers:** R.A. Rodriguez, President; Peter Rodriguez, Vice President; Robert Rodriguez, Vice President; Bill Randazzo, Customer Service Contact, e-mail: billr@rodriguez-usa.com.

■ **17145** ■ **B.W. Rogers Co.**
PO Box 1030
Akron, OH 44309
Phone: (330)315-3100 **Fax:** (330)762-5505
URL: http://www.bwrogers.com
Products: Pneumatic and hydraulic parts. **SIC:** 5085 (Industrial Supplies). **Est:** 1928. **Sales:** $25,000,000 (2000). **Emp:** 95. **Officers:** R. Rogers, President; F. Hague, VP of Finance; Andrew C. Dalzell, Dir. of Marketing.

■ **17146** ■ **Root Brothers Manufacturing and Supply Co.**
10317 S Michigan St.
Chicago, IL 60628
Phone: (773)264-5000 **Fax:** (773)264-6365
Products: Mill supplies. **SIC:** 5085 (Industrial Supplies).

■ **17147** ■ **Rowland Co.**
4900 N 20th St.
PO Box 12278
Philadelphia, PA 19144
Phone: (215)455-4900 **Fax:** (215)455-8888
E-mail: rowland2@ix.netcom.com
URL: http://www.rowland2.com
Products: Industrial brake linings; Industrial brakes and clutches. **SIC:** 5085 (Industrial Supplies).

■ **17148** ■ **Rubber and Accessories Inc.**
PO Box 777
Eaton Park, FL 33840
Phone: (863)665-6115
Free: (800)282-1734 **Fax:** (863)665-4540
E-mail: 212ra@gte.net
URL: http://www.rubberandaccessories.com
Products: Industrial hoses and conveyor belts. **SIC:** 5085 (Industrial Supplies). **Est:** 1972. **Sales:** $13,000,000 (2000). **Emp:** 50. **Officers:** Harry K. Robb Jr., President.

■ **17149** ■ **Rubin Brothers Company Inc.**
PO Box 5750
Harrisburg, PA 17110
Phone: (717)234-7071
Products: Wiping rags. **SIC:** 5093 (Scrap & Waste Materials). **Est:** 1945. **Sales:** $8,000,000 (2000). **Emp:** 40. **Officers:** Robert L. Rubin, CEO & President; Stewart Rubin, Treasurer; Steven Rubin, Secretary.

■ **17150** ■ **RVS Controls Co.**
380 Lapp Rd.
Malvern, PA 19355
Phone: (610)889-9910
Products: Industrial controls and instruments. **SIC:** 5084 (Industrial Machinery & Equipment). **Sales:** $1,000,000 (1999). **Emp:** 12. **Officers:** Richard Smith, President.

■ **17151** ■ **J. R. Sack Company Inc.**
1632 Leonard NW
Grand Rapids, MI 49504
Phone: (616)453-5757 **Fax:** (616)453-6144
Products: Blast cleaning equipment, replacement parts, abrasives, fluxes, belts, and buckets. **SICs:** 5085 (Industrial Supplies); 5084 (Industrial Machinery & Equipment). **Emp:** 8. **Officers:** Joseph R. Sack, President.

■ **17152** ■ **Saddle Brook Controls**
280 Midland Ave.
Saddle Brook, NJ 07663
Phone: (201)791-0233 **Fax:** (201)791-0393
Products: Industrial control products. **SICs:** 5065 (Electronic Parts & Equipment Nec); 5085 (Industrial Supplies). **Est:** 1933. **Sales:** $4,000,000 (2000). **Emp:** 16. **Officers:** Gary Laurita, President; Felix Akintunde, Controller.

■ **17153** ■ **SAF-T-GARD International, Inc.**
205 Huehl Rd.
Northbrook, IL 60062
Phone: (847)291-1600
Free: (800)548-4273 **Fax:** (847)291-1610
E-mail: safety@saftgard.com
URL: http://www.saftgard.com
Products: Industrial safety products; Personal protective equipment. **SICs:** 5136 (Men's/Boys' Clothing); 5137 (Women's/Children's Clothing); 5099 (Durable Goods Nec). **Est:** 1936. **Emp:** 50. **Officers:** Richard A. Rivkin, President, e-mail: rrivkin@saftgard.com; Robert A. Drell, CFO, e-mail: rdrell.saftgard@flashcom.net; David Hunter, VP, Industrial Sales, e-mail: sales@safetgard.com. **Alternate Name:** Voltgard.

■ **17154** ■ **Safety West**
15200 Don Julian Rd.
La Puente, CA 91745
Phone: (626)968-9444
Free: (800)237-3105 **Fax:** (626)330-0443
E-mail: info@safetywestinc.com
URL: http://www.safetywest.com
Products: Industrial safety products, including gloves and protective clothing. **SIC:** 5085 (Industrial Supplies). **Est:** 1984. **Sales:** $12,000,000 (2000). **Emp:** 27.

■ **17155** ■ **Sager Spuck Statewide Supply Company Inc.**
PO Box 918
Albany, NY 12201-0918
Phone: (518)436-4711 **Fax:** (518)436-3532
Products: Mill supplies, including pipes, valves, air pumps, and compressors. **SIC:** 5085 (Industrial Supplies). **Est:** 1923. **Sales:** $10,000,000 (2000). **Emp:** 44. **Officers:** Thomas S. Frederick, President; Larry Decker, CFO; David W. Bender, VP of Marketing & Sales.

■ **17156** ■ **St. Louis Coke and Foundry**
2817 Hereford St.
St. Louis, MO 63139
Phone: (314)772-7500
Products: Foundry supplies. **SICs:** 5051 (Metals Service Centers & Offices); 5085 (Industrial Supplies). **Est:** 1874. **Sales:** $9,000,000 (2000). **Emp:** 13. **Officers:** Robert E. Woods Jr., President; Karen R. Woods, Dir of Human Resources.

■ **17157** ■ **St. Louis Paper and Box Co.**
PO Box 8260
St. Louis, MO 63156
Phone: (314)531-7900
Free: (800)779-7901 **Fax:** (314)531-0968
Products: Packaging supplies and packaging equipment and machinery. **SICs:** 5113 (Industrial & Personal Service Paper); 5084 (Industrial Machinery & Equipment). **Sales:** $11,000,000 (1999). **Emp:** 32. **Officers:** William Livingston Jr., CEO.

■ **17158** ■ **John Sakash Company Inc.**
433 Romans Rd.
Elmhurst, IL 60126
Phone: (630)833-3940 **Fax:** (630)833-9830
Products: Wire; Ropes; Chains. **SIC:** 5085 (Industrial Supplies). **Est:** 1958. **Sales:** $7,500,000 (2000). **Emp:** 45. **Officers:** John W. Sakash, President; Paul Slavik, Treasurer & Secty.; Pat Norket, Sales Mgr.

■ **17159** ■ **Sarco Inc.**
PO Box 893
Voorhees, NJ 08043
Phone: (609)795-0699
Products: Valves. **SIC:** 5085 (Industrial Supplies).

■ **17160** ■ **Saxonburg Ceramics Inc.**
PO Box 688
Saxonburg, PA 16056
Phone: (412)352-1561
Free: (800)245-1270 **Fax:** (412)352-3580
Products: Industrial ceramics. **SIC:** 5085 (Industrial Supplies). **Est:** 1924. **Sales:** $10,000,000 (2000). **Emp:** 160. **Officers:** Furman South IV, President; Conan S. McManus, Dir. of Sales & Marketing.

■ **17161** ■ **Scott Industrial Systems Inc.**
PO Box 1387
Dayton, OH 45401
Phone: (937)233-8146 **Fax:** (937)233-1020
Products: Industrial machinery and equipment. **SIC:** 5084 (Industrial Machinery & Equipment). **Est:** 1953. **Sales:** $20,000,000 (2000). **Emp:** 74. **Officers:** M. Bryan, President; H. Phillips, Controller.

■ **17162** ■ **Seaman Mill Supplies Co.**
1317 Chester St.
Reading, PA 19601
Phone: (215)376-5711
Products: Industrial supplies. **SIC:** 5085 (Industrial Supplies). **Est:** 1950. **Sales:** $5,000,000 (2000). **Emp:** 13. **Officers:** Andrew B. Shearer, President; Larry Julius, Treasurer; Jeffery Darr, VP of Marketing & Sales.

■ **17163** ■ **Seelye Plastics Inc.**
9700 Newton Ave.
Bloomington, MN 55431
Phone: (612)881-2658 **Fax:** (612)881-3503
Products: Industrial plastic products, machining and fabrication. **SIC:** 5072 (Hardware). **Emp:** 125. **Officers:** Joe Petrich, President.

■ **17164** ■ **Sekisui TA Industries Inc.**
7089 Belgrave Ave.
Garden Grove, CA 92841
Phone: (714)898-0344 **Fax:** (714)772-6799
Products: Carton sealing equipment; Broad line of pressure sensitive tapes. **SIC:** 5085 (Industrial Supplies). **Sales:** $40,000,000 (2000). **Emp:** 175. **Officers:** Marty Tanaka, President; Tim Koontz, VP of Finance.

■ **17165** ■ **Semmelmeyer-Corby Co.**
5432 Highland Park Dr.
St. Louis, MO 63110
Phone: (314)371-4777 **Fax:** (314)371-4777
E-mail: semcor@worldinter.net
Products: Industrial machinery and supplies, including conveyor belts, hoses, lined pipes, and valves. **SICs:** 5085 (Industrial Supplies); 5084 (Industrial Machinery & Equipment). **Est:** 1907. **Sales:** $10,000,000 (2000). **Emp:** 45. **Officers:** R. Freedman, President & Treasurer.

■ 17166 ■ Senior Flexonics Inc. Dearborn Industrial Products Div.
PO Box 307
Westmont, IL 60559
Phone: (815)886-1140 **Fax:** (815)886-4550
Products: Metal hose, including fabricated hose; Rubber products, including belts. **SIC:** 5085 (Industrial Supplies). **Sales:** $15,000,000 (2000). **Emp:** 50. **Officers:** David M. Dambek, VP & General Merchandising Mgr.; Carol Wissmiller, Controller; Graig Fuhs, Marketing & Sales Mgr.

■ 17167 ■ Sepco Bearing and P.T. Group
6618 E Hwy. 332
Freeport, TX 77541
Phone: (409)233-4491 **Fax:** (409)233-8605
Products: Ball bearings; Chains; Seals; Power transmission products. **SICs:** 5085 (Industrial Supplies); 5063 (Electrical Apparatus & Equipment).

■ 17168 ■ Serson Supply Inc.
3701 W 49th St.
Chicago, IL 60632
Phone: (773)847-6210
Free: (800)228-2863 **Fax:** (773)847-0238
E-mail: sales@serson.com
URL: http://www.serson.com
Products: Industrial supplies, including abrasives, cutting tools, fasteners, MRO. **SICs:** 5085 (Industrial Supplies); 5072 (Hardware). **Est:** 1907. **Sales:** $5,000,000 (2000). **Emp:** 30. **Officers:** W.E. Barnes, President; R.J. Serson Jr., Vice President; J.J. Barnes, Secretary.

■ 17169 ■ Servsteel Inc.
214 Westbridge Dr.
Morgan, PA 15064
Phone: (412)221-8600
Products: Refractory ceramics. **SICs:** 5051 (Metals Service Centers & Offices); 5085 (Industrial Supplies).

■ 17170 ■ Sharp Products International, Inc.
PO Box 4339
Wallingford, CT 06492-4050
Phone: (203)284-2627 **Fax:** (203)284-8550
Products: Screen printing supplies and equipment. **SICs:** 5198 (Paints, Varnishes & Supplies); 5085 (Industrial Supplies). **Officers:** Ghaus Ghori, President.

■ 17171 ■ Shima American Corp.
945 Larch Ave.
Elmhurst, IL 60126
Phone: (630)833-9400 **Fax:** (630)530-1670
Products: Seal bearings; Cutting tools; Indexible inserts. **SIC:** 5085 (Industrial Supplies). **Est:** 1963. **Sales:** $23,000,000 (2000). **Emp:** 27. **Officers:** Koshi Shima, Vice President; Hajime Itoh, CFO; M. Katayama, Dir. of Sales.

■ 17172 ■ Shingle & Gibb Co.
Moorestown West Corp.
845 Lancer Dr.
Moorestown, NJ 08057
Phone: (609)234-8500 **Fax:** (609)273-7640
Products: Drives and motion control equipment. **SIC:** 5084 (Industrial Machinery & Equipment).

■ 17173 ■ Shook and Fletcher Insulation Co.
PO Box 380501
Birmingham, AL 35238
Phone: (205)991-7606 **Fax:** (205)991-7745
URL: http://www.sfiwlo@aol.com
Products: Commercial and industrial insulation. **SIC:** 5033 (Roofing, Siding & Insulation). **Est:** 1949. **Sales:** $25,000,000 (2000). **Emp:** 130. **Officers:** Wayne W. Killion, President; David Jackson, Exec. VP of Finance.

■ 17174 ■ Shuster Corp.
4 Wright St.
New Bedford, MA 02740
Phone: (508)999-3261
Free: (800)343-8409 **Fax:** (508)990-2157
E-mail: sales@shustercorp.com
URL: http://www.shustercorp.com
Products: Industrial Supplies; Marine supplies; Power transmission products; Filtration systems. **SIC:** 5085 (Industrial Supplies). **Est:** 1916. **Sales:** $6,000,000 (2000). **Emp:** 42. **Officers:** Steven Shuster, CEO & President.

■ 17175 ■ Silliter/Klebes Industrial Supplies Inc.
13 Hamden Park Dr.
Hamden, CT 06517
Phone: (203)497-1500 **Fax:** (203)497-1501
Products: Industrial supplies, including carbines, chemicals, cutting tools, and braces. **SICs:** 5085 (Industrial Supplies); 5063 (Electrical Apparatus & Equipment). **Est:** 1933. **Sales:** $140,000,000 (2000). **Emp:** 50. **Officers:** Jay Drummond, President; Moe Harmon, Controller.

■ 17176 ■ Slip-Not Belting Corp.
PO Box 89
Kingsport, TN 37662
Phone: (423)246-8141 **Fax:** (423)246-7728
Products: Leather and synthetic belting. **SIC:** 5085 (Industrial Supplies). **Est:** 1917. **Sales:** $4,000,000 (2000). **Emp:** 61. **Officers:** David B. Shivell, President; Edwin B. Neale, Treasurer.

■ 17177 ■ Smith-Thompson Co.
9433 E 51st St., Ste. F
Tulsa, OK 74145
Phone: (918)665-6044 **Fax:** (918)665-6047
Products: Ball, butterfly, and globe valves; Metering and measurement equipment. **SICs:** 5074 (Plumbing & Hydronic Heating Supplies); 5085 (Industrial Supplies).

■ 17178 ■ Smith-Thompson Inc.
PO Box 2249
Amarillo, TX 79105
Phone: (806)372-6751
Free: (800)323-4008 **Fax:** (806)372-6444
Products: Ball valves. **SIC:** 5085 (Industrial Supplies).

■ 17179 ■ Snow Filtration Co.
6386 Gano Rd.
West Chester, OH 45069-4809
Phone: (513)777-6200
Products: Nonwoven and woven industrial filter media. **SIC:** 5199 (Nondurable Goods Nec). **Sales:** $22,000,000 (1994). **Emp:** 120. **Officers:** Stephen G. Vollmer, President.

■ 17180 ■ Sooner Airgas Inc.
2701 W Reno
Oklahoma City, OK 73108
Phone: (405)235-8621 **Fax:** (405)239-2840
Products: Welding supplies. **SICs:** 5084 (Industrial Machinery & Equipment); 5169 (Chemicals & Allied Products Nec).

■ 17181 ■ South Bend Supply Company Inc.
PO Box 1996
South Bend, IN 46634
Phone: (219)232-1421
Products: Industrial supplies, including sheet metal, conditioning systems, and plumbing supplies. **SICs:** 5085 (Industrial Supplies); 5074 (Plumbing & Hydronic Heating Supplies). **Est:** 1906. **Sales:** $22,000,000 (2000). **Emp:** 93. **Officers:** Jeff Stuber, Branch President.

■ 17182 ■ Southern Belting & Transmissions
6021 Coca Cola Blvd.
Columbus, GA 31907
Phones: (706)561-6946 (706)875-1651
Fax: (706)561-2510
Products: Industrial and engineering parts and supplies, including belts, transmissions, and bearings. **SIC:** 5085 (Industrial Supplies).

■ 17183 ■ Southern California Airgas Inc.
4007 Paramount Blvd., No. 100
Lakewood, CA 90712-4138
Phone: (310)329-7517 **Fax:** (310)523-9373
Products: Welding supplies; Industrial gases. **SICs:** 5084 (Industrial Machinery & Equipment); 5085 (Industrial Supplies). **Est:** 1993. **Sales:** $50,000,000 (2000). **Emp:** 340. **Officers:** Mark Straka, President; T.W. Cherry, VP of Finance.

■ 17184 ■ Southern Filters Inc.
284 Snow Dr.
Birmingham, AL 35209
Phone: (205)942-5817
Products: Industrial and automotive air conditioner filters. **SICs:** 5085 (Industrial Supplies); 5075 (Warm Air Heating & Air-Conditioning).

■ 17185 ■ Southern Fluid Power
2900 Dodds Ave.
Chattanooga, TN 37407
Phone: (423)698-5888 **Fax:** (423)698-5913
Products: Industrial parts. **SIC:** 5085 (Industrial Supplies).

■ 17186 ■ Southern Hardware and Supply Company Ltd.
PO Box 1792
Monroe, LA 71210
Phone: (318)387-5000
URL: http://www.cust2.america.net/jemarx/
Products: Industrial supplies and machinery, including electric and manual hand tools and valves. **SICs:** 5085 (Industrial Supplies); 5084 (Industrial Machinery & Equipment); 5072 (Hardware). **Est:** 1890. **Sales:** $1,000,000 (2000). **Emp:** 25. **Officers:** J.E. Marx III, President.

■ 17187 ■ Southern Rubber Company Inc.
PO Box 7039
Greensboro, NC 27417-0039
Phone: (919)299-2456 **Fax:** (919)294-4970
Products: Industrial rubber and gaskets. **SIC:** 5085 (Industrial Supplies). **Est:** 1925. **Sales:** $8,000,000 (2000). **Emp:** 46. **Officers:** H. Edward Bowman, President; David Delman, Vice President.

■ 17188 ■ Southwest Wire Rope Inc.
1902 Federal Rd.
Houston, TX 77015
Phone: (713)453-8518
Products: Wire rope. **SIC:** 5051 (Metals Service Centers & Offices). **Est:** 1969. **Sales:** $15,000,000 (2000). **Emp:** 50. **Officers:** Charles R. Maher, President; James Black, VP of Finance; Harry Urech, VP of Sales; John D. Lamerton, Director.

■ 17189 ■ Southwire Co.
3555 W Washington St.
Phoenix, AZ 85009
Phone: (602)233-1777 **Fax:** (602)233-9456
Products: Copper and aluminum cable wire. **SIC:** 5085 (Industrial Supplies).

■ 17190 ■ Specialty Products Inc.
PO Box 565
Fairfield, AL 35064-0565
Phone: (205)785-1116 **Fax:** (205)785-4322
Products: Industrial, hydraulic hose, and conveyor belting. **SIC:** 5085 (Industrial Supplies). **Est:** 1963. **Sales:** $2,000,000 (2000). **Emp:** 20. **Officers:** Mark Anderson, President; Mitch Mitchell, Dir. of Sales.

■ 17191 ■ Spencer Industries
1930 Rudkin Rd.
Yakima, WA 98903
Phone: (509)248-0580
Free: (800)572-8351 **Fax:** (509)575-0250
URL: http://www.spencer-ind.com
Products: Chain gears. **SIC:** 5085 (Industrial Supplies). **Est:** 1946. **Emp:** 7.

■ 17192 ■ Spencer Industries Inc.
8410 Dallas Ave.
Seattle, WA 98108
Phone: (206)763-0210 **Fax:** (206)767-2514
URL: http://www.spencer-ind.com
Products: Hydraulics. **SIC:** 5085 (Industrial Supplies). **Est:** 1945. **Sales:** $42,000,000 (2000). **Emp:** 120. **Officers:** Charles Harris, President; John Hoyt, VP of Finance; John Mahoney, Dir. of Marketing.

■ 17193 ■ Sprunger Corp.
PO Box 1621
2300 California Rd.
Elkhart, IN 46515-1621
Phone: (219)262-2476
Free: (800)582-0319 **Fax:** (219)264-0578
E-mail: elkcases@aol.com
Products: Replacement parts for stationary power tools. **SIC:** 5084 (Industrial Machinery & Equipment). **Est:** 1947. **Sales:** $1,000,000 (2000). **Emp:** 19. **Officers:** D.D. Fahlbeck.

■ 17194 ■ **Standard Supply and Hardware Company Inc.**
PO Box 60620
New Orleans, LA 70160
Phone: (504)586-8400
Free: (800)866-6652 **Fax:** (504)586-3105
URL: http://www.stdsupply.com
Products: Industrial supplies; Safety supplies. **SICs:** 5084 (Industrial Machinery & Equipment); 5085 (Industrial Supplies); 5039 (Construction Materials Nec). **Est:** 1909. **Sales:** $40,000,000 (2000). **Emp:** 160. **Officers:** Evans Hadden, President; Manuel Merlos, COO; P. Rigney, Dir. of Marketing; P. Barrios, Dir. of Data Processing; Pat Parenton, Sales Mgr., e-mail: pparenton@stdsupply.com.

■ 17195 ■ **J.J. Stangel Co.**
PO Box 280
Manitowoc, WI 54221-0280
Phone: (414)684-3313 **Fax:** (414)684-1252
Products: Industrial supplies, including abrasives, adhesives, hand tools, and electrical tools. **SICs:** 5085 (Industrial Supplies); 5169 (Chemicals & Allied Products Nec). **Est:** 1917. **Sales:** $12,500,000 (2000). **Emp:** 42. **Officers:** John J. Zimmer, President; Joe Zimmer, VP of Finance.

■ 17196 ■ **Stark Co.**
432 W Allegheny Arms
Philadelphia, PA 19133
Phone: (215)425-2222 **Fax:** (215)425-3560
Products: Paper and paper products. **SIC:** 5113 (Industrial & Personal Service Paper). **Sales:** $4,000,000 (2000). **Emp:** 21.

■ 17197 ■ **State Seal Co.**
4135 E Wood St.
Phoenix, AZ 85040
Phone: (602)437-1532 **Fax:** (602)437-4332
Products: Seals, packing, hose, fittings, valves and machined plastics; Fabricates gaskets. **SICs:** 5085 (Industrial Supplies); 5162 (Plastics Materials & Basic Shapes).

■ 17198 ■ **Steam Supply Co.**
PO Box 24703
Seattle, WA 98124
Phone: (206)622-4690
Products: Steam valves and gauges. **SIC:** 5085 (Industrial Supplies). **Sales:** $39,000,000 (1993). **Emp:** 181. **Officers:** Ed Ries, President.

■ 17199 ■ **Jewell Strickland Auto**
PO Box 2026
Wilmington, NC 28402-2026
Phone: (910)762-8533 **Fax:** (919)763-4811
Products: Industrial bearings and automobile parts. **SICs:** 5085 (Industrial Supplies); 5013 (Motor Vehicle Supplies & New Parts). **Emp:** 49.

■ 17200 ■ **Stutz Co.**
4450 W Carroll Ave.
Chicago, IL 60624
Phone: (773)287-1068 **Fax:** (773)287-4303
Products: Metal finishing equipment and supplies; Abrasive finishing compositions. **SICs:** 5084 (Industrial Machinery & Equipment); 5085 (Industrial Supplies). **Est:** 1921. **Sales:** $8,000,000 (1999). **Emp:** 30. **Officers:** George L. Stutz, President; Patti Ruff, Office Mgr.; Gerry Stutz, Vice President.

■ 17201 ■ **Sumter Machinery Company Inc.**
PO Box 700
Sumter, SC 29151-0700
Phone: (803)773-1441
Free: (800)922-0405 **Fax:** (803)773-4960
Products: Industrial supplies and construction castings. **SICs:** 5085 (Industrial Supplies); 5082 (Construction & Mining Machinery). **Est:** 1904. **Sales:** $4,500,000 (2000). **Emp:** 50.

■ 17202 ■ **Sunbelt Supply Co.**
8363 Market St. Rd.
Houston, TX 77029
Phone: (713)672-2222
Free: (800)825-8365 **Fax:** (713)672-2725
Products: Valves; Metal fittings, flanges, and unions for piping systems. **SIC:** 5085 (Industrial Supplies). **Emp:** 49. **Officers:** Brent Scheps.

■ 17203 ■ **Sunset Industrial Parts**
16121 S Piuma Ave.
Cerritos, CA 90701
Phone: (562)809-8300 **Fax:** (562)403-3828
Products: Bearings; Industrial supplies. **SIC:** 5085 (Industrial Supplies). **Emp:** 25.

■ 17204 ■ **SunSource**
5750 W Erie St.
Chandler, AZ 85226
Phone: (602)254-8414 **Fax:** (602)258-7268
Products: Hydraulic and pneumatic service and sales. Engineering design. **SIC:** 5085 (Industrial Supplies). **Est:** 1949. **Sales:** $9,000,000 (2000). **Emp:** 40. **Officers:** Ken Elans, President; Chuck Freeman, CFO. **Former Name:** Air-Draulics Co.

■ 17205 ■ **SuperGrind Co.**
PO Box 538
Mentor, OH 44061
Phone: (440)257-6277 **Fax:** (440)257-6405
URL: http://www.supergrind.com
Products: Industrial diamond tools, including grinding wheels, cutting tools, polishing supplies, and abrasives. **SICs:** 5085 (Industrial Supplies); 5072 (Hardware). **Est:** 1989. **Officers:** C.M. Kretz, Sales Mgr.

■ 17206 ■ **Superior Group Inc.**
PO Box 6760
Radnor, PA 19087-8760
Phone: (610)964-2000
Products: Carbon, stainless steel, aluminum, and nickel alloy pipe, tubing, and fittings. **SIC:** 5051 (Metals Service Centers & Offices).

■ 17207 ■ **Sutton-Garten Co.**
901 N Senate Ave.
Indianapolis, IN 46202
Phone: (317)264-3236 **Fax:** (317)264-3233
Products: Welding supplies, including torches and gases. **SICs:** 5085 (Industrial Supplies); 5169 (Chemicals & Allied Products Nec). **Est:** 1918. **Sales:** $4,000,000 (2000). **Emp:** 16. **Officers:** Pat Garten, President.

■ 17208 ■ **Svetlana Electron Devices, Inc.**
8200 S Memorial Pky.
Huntsville, AL 35802
Phone: (205)882-1344 **Fax:** (205)880-8077
URL: http://www.svetlana.com
Products: Vacuum tubes. **SIC:** 5085 (Industrial Supplies). **Officers:** George Badger, President.

■ 17209 ■ **Swing Machinery and Equipment Company Inc.**
106 W Rhapsody
San Antonio, TX 78216-3104
Phone: (210)342-9588 **Fax:** (210)340-5634
URL: http://www.swingmachinery.com
Products: Industrial supplies; Industrial and commercial service machines; Metalworking machinery; Abrasives; Air and electric tools; Safety equipment. **SICs:** 5085 (Industrial Supplies); 5084 (Industrial Machinery & Equipment); 5051 (Metals Service Centers & Offices). **Est:** 1947. **Emp:** 49.

■ 17210 ■ **System Brunner USA Inc.**
275 Edgemont Ter.
Teaneck, NJ 07666
Phone: (201)907-0868 **Fax:** (201)907-0821
Products: Control strips; Test forms; Color control software: Measuring devices. **SIC:** 5084 (Industrial Machinery & Equipment). **Est:** 1983. **Officers:** Nina Bachrach, Dir. of Business Development; Raphael Bachrach, Technical Dir.

■ 17211 ■ **T and A Industrial Distributors**
12550 Robin Ln.
Brookfield, WI 53005-1398
Phone: (414)384-6000
Products: Cutting tools and abrasives. **SIC:** 5085 (Industrial Supplies). **Sales:** $14,000,000 (2000). **Emp:** 65. **Officers:** James E. Ketter, President.

■ 17212 ■ **Tapco USA, Inc.**
5605 Pike Rd.
Loves Park, IL 61111
Phone: (815)877-4039
Free: (800)827-7787 **Fax:** (815)877-6143
URL: http://www.tapcousa.com
Products: Taps; Thread grinding; Resharpening. **SICs:** 5085 (Industrial Supplies); 5084 (Industrial Machinery & Equipment). **Est:** 1975. **Sales:** $800,000 (2000). **Emp:** 7. **Officers:** John A. Cotton, President; Greg Schmidt, Sales/Marketing Contact; Susan Hickey, Human Resources Contact. **Alternate Name:** Cutting Tools & Abrasives.

■ 17213 ■ **Taylor-Parker Co.**
1130 Kingwood Ave.
Norfolk, VA 23502
Phone: (804)855-2041
Products: Machine tools and industrial supplies, including wrenches, lathes, sanders, and hammers. **SIC:** 5085 (Industrial Supplies). **Est:** 1865. **Sales:** $4,000,000 (2000). **Emp:** 19. **Officers:** R.L. McCann, President; Bob Brantly, Exec. VP & Controller.

■ 17214 ■ **Taylor Simkins Inc.**
1235 Tower Trails
El Paso, TX 79907
Phone: (915)544-4252 **Fax:** (915)544-3411
Products: Gases; Welding supplies. **SICs:** 5169 (Chemicals & Allied Products Nec); 5084 (Industrial Machinery & Equipment).

■ 17215 ■ **Tek-Matic, Inc.**
7324 Forest Hills Rd.
Loves Park, IL 61111
Phone: (815)282-1775 **Fax:** (815)282-1862
Products: Power transmission products, including chains, belts, and sprockets. **SICs:** 5085 (Industrial Supplies); 5084 (Industrial Machinery & Equipment).

■ 17216 ■ **Tennessee Mat Company Inc.**
PO Box 100186
Nashville, TN 37224
Phone: (615)254-8381
Free: (800)264-3030 **Fax:** (615)255-4428
Products: Carpet top matting, rubber products, rubber and vinyl entrance, safety, anti-fatigue industrial matting and dock bumpers. **SIC:** 5085 (Industrial Supplies). **Sales:** $35,000,000 (2000). **Emp:** 170. **Officers:** Elliot Greenberg, President.

■ 17217 ■ **Tepco Corp.**
Box 1160
Rapid City, SD 57709
Phone: (605)343-7200 **Fax:** (605)343-7240
E-mail: tepco@rapidnet.com
URL: http://www.rapidnet.com/tepco
Products: Industrial parts; Electronic equipment, including FM radio translators and transmittors and radio frequency amplifiers and equipment. **SICs:** 5085 (Industrial Supplies); 5065 (Electronic Parts & Equipment Nec). **Est:** 1957. **Emp:** 4. **Officers:** Don K. Lefevre; Karin Simpson, Sales/Marketing Contact.

■ 17218 ■ **George B. Tewes Company Inc.**
323 S Date Ave.
Alhambra, CA 91803
Phone: (818)281-6300 **Fax:** (818)281-2706
Products: Industrial felt. **SIC:** 5085 (Industrial Supplies). **Est:** 1934. **Sales:** $1,000,000 (2000). **Emp:** 4. **Officers:** John W. Gough, President; Raymond J. Tewes, VP of Marketing & Sales.

■ 17219 ■ **Texas Mill Inc.**
601 Foreman Rd.
Orange, TX 77630-9082
Phone: (409)886-5686 **Fax:** (409)886-0897
Products: Industrial supplies, including wrenches and power tools. **SICs:** 5085 (Industrial Supplies); 5072 (Hardware). **Emp:** 49. **Officers:** Monty Legro.

■ 17220 ■ **Texas Mill Inc.**
905 W Cotton
Longview, TX 75604
Phone: (903)758-7005 **Fax:** (903)758-3095
Products: Industrial and mill supplies, including gloves and tools. **SIC:** 5085 (Industrial Supplies). **Emp:** 14. **Officers:** Monty Legro, Owner; Frank Schindler, Vice President.

■ 17221 ■ Texas Mill Inc.
PO Box 167
Fairfield, TX 75840-0167
Phone: (512)446-7366
Products: Industrial supplies. **SIC:** 5085 (Industrial Supplies).

■ 17222 ■ Texas Mill Inc.
4801 Leopard St.
Corpus Christi, TX 78408
Phone: (512)887-0000
Free: (800)223-9955 **Fax:** (512)884-2168
Products: Industrial and mill supplies, including rubber boots, rainsuits, tools, paints, sockets, and hoists. **SICs:** 5085 (Industrial Supplies); 5084 (Industrial Machinery & Equipment). **Emp:** 13. **Officers:** Monte Legro, President and Owner; Frank Schindler, Vice President.

■ 17223 ■ Texas Mill Supply and Manufacturing Company Inc.
2413 Avenue K
Galena Park, TX 77547
Phone: (713)675-2421 **Fax:** (713)675-0068
Products: Industrial tools; Safety products; Janitorial products. **SICs:** 5085 (Industrial Supplies); 5087 (Service Establishment Equipment); 5084 (Industrial Machinery & Equipment). **Est:** 1965. **Sales:** $150,000,000 (1999). **Emp:** 550. **Officers:** Monta K. Legro, President; Leonard Truett, CFO; Bill Herrington, Vice President; Rick Brown, VP of Operations; Boyd Noble, National Accounts Mgr.

■ 17224 ■ Texas Rubber Supply Inc.
2436 Irving Blvd.
Dallas, TX 75207
Phone: (214)631-3143
Free: (800)366-2904 **Fax:** (214)631-3651
Products: Rubber. **SIC:** 5085 (Industrial Supplies). **Sales:** $7,500,000 (2000). **Emp:** 60.

■ 17225 ■ W.E. Thew Supply Company Inc.
PO Box 2426
Green Bay, WI 54306
Phone: (920)436-4520 **Fax:** (920)436-4531
Products: Industrial supplies. **SIC:** 5085 (Industrial Supplies). **Est:** 1920. **Sales:** $14,000,000 (1994). **Emp:** 50.

■ 17226 ■ Thompson and Cooke Inc.
4200 Kenilworth Ave.
Bladensburg, MD 20710
Phone: (301)864-6380 **Fax:** (301)864-8749
Products: Industrial supplies, including abrasives and cutting tools. **SICs:** 5084 (Industrial Machinery & Equipment); 5085 (Industrial Supplies). **Est:** 1937. **Sales:** $2,500,000 (2000). **Emp:** 12. **Officers:** A.J. Thompson, President; L.B. Gaigon, VP & General Merchandising Mgr.

■ 17227 ■ Geo. S. Thomson Company Inc.
PO Box 17
El Paso, TX 79999
Phone: (915)544-8000 **Fax:** (915)544-3429
E-mail: gst@flash.net
Products: Industrial supplies, including compressors, valves, paint, and painting tools. **SICs:** 5085 (Industrial Supplies); 5084 (Industrial Machinery & Equipment); 5198 (Paints, Varnishes & Supplies). **Est:** 1902. **Sales:** $7,000,000 (1999). **Emp:** 30. **Officers:** Michael B. Huey, President; Richard Pinney, Division Mgr.; Jim Rivera, Operations Mgr.

■ 17228 ■ Thorpe Insulation Co.
215 S 14th St.
Phoenix, AZ 85034
Phone: (602)258-6861 **Fax:** (602)495-9766
Products: Fabricates fiberglass duct systems for commercial industries; Insulation contractor; Commercial and industrial insulation products for plumbing, heating and mechanical applications. **SIC:** 5085 (Industrial Supplies).

■ 17229 ■ Thrall Distribution Inc.
PO Box 15190
Loves Park, IL 61111
Phone: (815)282-3100
Products: Industrial supplies and equipment. **SICs:** 5085 (Industrial Supplies); 5084 (Industrial Machinery &

Equipment). **Sales:** $164,000,000 (2000). **Emp:** 500. **Officers:** Steven Cosgrove, President; Mitzi Stride, Controller.

■ 17230 ■ T.L.K. Industries Inc.
902 Ogden Ave.
Superior, WI 54880
Phone: (715)392-6253 **Fax:** (715)392-6256
Products: Non-ferrous metals; Oil absorbents. **SICs:** 5093 (Scrap & Waste Materials); 5085 (Industrial Supplies). **Est:** 1982. **Sales:** $1,300,000 (2000). **Emp:** 10. **Officers:** Andy Karon, Owner.

■ 17231 ■ Torque-A-Matic
12822 E Indiana
Spokane, WA 99216
Phone: (509)928-0535 **Fax:** (509)928-0539
Products: Industrial engines; Power transmissions; Belts, bearings, and pulleys. **SICs:** 5084 (Industrial Machinery & Equipment); 5085 (Industrial Supplies); 5063 (Electrical Apparatus & Equipment).

■ 17232 ■ Trade Development Corporation of Chicago
2049 Century Park E, Ste. 480
Los Angeles, 41400, 90067
Phone: (310)556-8091 **Fax:** (310)556-3088
E-mail: china-trade@worldnet.att.net
URL: http://www.chinatradedevelopmentcom
Products: Liquid pumps; Gas boosters; Cylinder testing equipment. **SICs:** 5085 (Industrial Supplies); 5084 (Industrial Machinery & Equipment). **Est:** 1979. **Sales:** $1,000,000 (1999). **Emp:** 10. **Officers:** Michael R.A. Wade, President. **Doing Business As:** China Trade Development Corp.

■ 17233 ■ Transmission Products, Inc.
3024 Bells Rd.
PO Box 24657
Richmond, VA 23234
Phone: (804)233-8351 **Fax:** (804)233-5723
Products: Industrial transmission parts. **SIC:** 5063 (Electrical Apparatus & Equipment).

■ 17234 ■ Transmission Products, Inc.
1519 11th St. NE
PO Box 5326
Roanoke, VA 24012
Phone: (540)344-2093
Free: (800)827-7849 **Fax:** (540)342-6819
Products: Industrial transmission parts. **SICs:** 5085 (Industrial Supplies); 5063 (Electrical Apparatus & Equipment).

■ 17235 ■ Tri-Power MPT
1447 S Main St.
Akron, OH 44301
Phone: (330)773-3307
Free: (800)362-7551 **Fax:** (330)773-3300
E-mail: info@tri-power.com
URL: http://www.tri-power.com
Products: Power transmission equipment, motion control products, and machine safety products. **SICs:** 5085 (Industrial Supplies); 5063 (Electrical Apparatus & Equipment). **Est:** 1954. **Sales:** $10,000,000 (2000). **Emp:** 18. **Officers:** Richard R. Wiley, President; Ronald J. Wiley, Vice President; Roger A. Wiley, Vice President.

■ 17236 ■ Troy Belting Supply Co.
70 Cohoes Rd.
Watervliet, NY 12189
Phone: (518)272-4920 **Fax:** (518)272-0531
Products: Industrial rubber products, electric motors and power transmission/material handling equipment. **SICs:** 5085 (Industrial Supplies); 5063 (Electrical Apparatus & Equipment); 5084 (Industrial Machinery & Equipment). **Sales:** $15,000,000 (2000). **Emp:** 76. **Officers:** G.L. Smith, President.

■ 17237 ■ Tryon Trading, Inc.
PO Box 40
Tryon, NC 28782
Phone: (704)859-6999 **Fax:** (704)859-6060
E-mail: tryonusa@teleplex.net
URL: http://www.tryontrading.com
Products: Industrial valves and controllers; Measuring equipment, including pressure and temperature; Board level electronic components; Industrial meters. **SICs:**

5085 (Industrial Supplies); 5084 (Industrial Machinery & Equipment); 5049 (Professional Equipment Nec); 5065 (Electronic Parts & Equipment Nec). **Est:** 1987. **Officers:** Bud Mackay, President.

■ 17238 ■ Tubular Products of Texas Inc.
4515 Brittmoore Rd.
Houston, TX 77041
Phone: (713)937-3900 **Fax:** (713)937-7947
Products: Pipes, pup joints, crossovers, and blast joints. **SIC:** 5085 (Industrial Supplies). **Est:** 1976. **Sales:** $10,000,000 (2000). **Emp:** 7. **Officers:** James F. Bass, CEO.

■ 17239 ■ Ultra Hydraulics Inc.
1110 Claycraft Rd., Ste. A
Columbus, OH 43230-6630
Phone: (614)759-9000 **Fax:** (614)759-9046
Products: Gear pumps; Motors. **SICs:** 5084 (Industrial Machinery & Equipment); 5085 (Industrial Supplies). **Est:** 1977. **Sales:** $6,000,000 (2000). **Emp:** 22. **Officers:** G. Scott, VP & General Merchandising Mgr.; James E. Campbell, CFO & Treasurer.

■ 17240 ■ Unibri International
PO Box 7671
Algonquin, IL 60102
Phone: (847)458-7262 **Fax:** (847)458-7284
E-mail: unibri@aol.com
URL: http://www.unibri.com
Products: Industrial supplies, including plastic safety shields, cleaners, and headwear; Industrial equipment, including water presses, compressors and sandblasting nozzles; Foundry supplies. **SICs:** 5085 (Industrial Supplies); 5084 (Industrial Machinery & Equipment). **Est:** 1991. **Emp:** 2. **Officers:** Chris Hindley, President.

■ 17241 ■ Union Paper Company Inc.
10 Admiral St.
Providence, RI 02908
Phone: (401)274-7000 **Fax:** (401)331-1910
Products: Paper and paper products. **SIC:** 5113 (Industrial & Personal Service Paper). **Sales:** $7,000,000 (2000). **Emp:** 165.

■ 17242 ■ United Paper Company Inc.
4101 Sarellen Rd.
Richmond, VA 23231
Products: Paper food service products. **SIC:** 5113 (Industrial & Personal Service Paper). **Sales:** $34,000,000 (2000). **Emp:** 50. **Officers:** Paul Burns, President.

■ 17243 ■ U.S. Rigging Supply Corp.
4001 W Carriage Dr.
Santa Ana, CA 92704
Phone: (714)545-7444
Free: (800)624-1116 **Fax:** (714)545-3311
E-mail: sales@usrigging.com
URL: http://www.usrigging.com
Products: Wire-rope, swage fittings, copper and stainless splicing sleeves, shackles, snap hooks, thimbles, turnbuckles, rigging hardware, wire rope cutters and swagers, cable assemblies, tree support systems, rope, and cordage. **SIC:** 5072 (Hardware). **Est:** 1974. **Sales:** $3,000,000 (2000). **Emp:** 20. **Officers:** Gaylord C. Whipple, President.

■ 17244 ■ United World Supply Co.
103 N Ben Jordan
Victoria, TX 77901-8628
Phone: (512)575-0464
Free: (800)688-8121 **Fax:** (512)575-0424
Products: Tools; Industrial supplies; Farm machinery and equipment. **SICs:** 5085 (Industrial Supplies); 5084 (Industrial Machinery & Equipment); 5083 (Farm & Garden Machinery). **Emp:** 9.

■ 17245 ■ Universal Sales Engineering Inc.
5060 E 62nd St.
Indianapolis, IN 46220
Phone: (317)255-3181 **Fax:** (317)253-0658
Products: Heavy machinery parts. **SIC:** 5084 (Industrial Machinery & Equipment). **Est:** 1967. **Sales:** $2,700,000 (2000). **Emp:** 8. **Officers:** Ken Pendleton, President.

■ 17246 ■ Frank J. Upchurch Co.
PO Box 669107
Charlotte, NC 28266
Phone: (704)394-4186 **Fax:** (704)399-4285
Products: Textile machinery parts. **SIC:** 5084
(Industrial Machinery & Equipment). **Est:** 1957. **Sales:**
$5,000,000 (2000). **Emp:** 10. **Officers:** Frank J.
Upchurch Sr., President; Patricia O'Neill, CFO; Gettis
Upchurch, Dir. of Marketing & Sales.

■ 17247 ■ Valiac Inc.
208 College Crossing
Rolling Meadows, IL 60008-2155
Phone: (847)776-1010 **Fax:** (847)776-1023
Products: Three piece ball valves. **SIC:** 5085
(Industrial Supplies). **Est:** 1988. **Sales:** $200,000
(2000). **Emp:** 1. **Officers:** Claude I. Benusiglio, CEO &
President.

■ 17248 ■ Vallen Safety Supply Co.
PO Box 3587
Houston, TX 77253
Phone: (713)462-8700
Free: (800)482-5536 **Fax:** 800-303-8256
Products: Industrial safety supplies. **SIC:** 5047
(Medical & Hospital Equipment). **Sales:** $1,000,000
(2000). **Emp:** 6. **Officers:** Butch Hutton, Exec. VP;
Wayne Hankamer, Sr. VP.

■ 17249 ■ Valley Welders Supply Inc.
320 N 11th St.
Billings, MT 59101
Phone: (406)256-3330 **Fax:** (406)256-3343
Products: Welding and industrial supplies. **SIC:** 5085
(Industrial Supplies). **Est:** 1949. **Sales:** $13,000,000
(2000). **Emp:** 95. **Officers:** Ron Adkins, President.

■ 17250 ■ Valley Welding Supply Inc.
PO Box 12609
Salem, OR 97309
Phone: (503)581-6400
Products: Welding supplies. **SIC:** 5084 (Industrial
Machinery & Equipment). **Est:** 1936. **Sales:**
$5,000,000 (2000). **Emp:** 35. **Officers:** Mark Lottis,
President; John Lottis, Treasurer & Secty.; Dick
Wilkinson, Sales Mgr.

■ 17251 ■ Van Sant Equipment Corp.
185 Oberlin Ave., N
Lakewood, NJ 08701-4525
Phone: (732)363-5158
Free: (800)872-5797 **Fax:** (732)363-6367
Products: Industrial supplies; Building equipment;
Polystyrene plastic; Chemical products; Dow
styrofoam; Hoses; Generators and pumps. **SICs:** 5085
(Industrial Supplies); 5084 (Industrial Machinery &
Equipment); 5063 (Electrical Apparatus & Equipment);
5169 (Chemicals & Allied Products Nec). **Emp:** 17.
Officers: Gordon L. Strout Jr.

■ 17252 ■ Victor Machinery Exchange Inc.
251 Centre St.
New York, NY 10013-3214
Phone: (212)226-3494
Free: (800)723-5359 **Fax:** (212)941-8465
E-mail: sales@victornet.com
URL: http://www.victornet.com
Products: Precision measuring tools; Cutting tools and
accessories for machine tools and metalworking. **SICs:**
5085 (Industrial Supplies); 5084 (Industrial Machinery &
Equipment). **Est:** 1918. **Emp:** 49.

■ 17253 ■ Victory White Metal Co.
6100 Roland Ave.
Cleveland, OH 44127
Phone: (216)271-1400
Free: (800)635-5050 **Fax:** (216)271-6430
E-mail: sales@vwmc.com
Products: Soldering supplies. **SIC:** 5085 (Industrial
Supplies). **Est:** 1920. **Sales:** $40,000,000 (2000).
Emp: 100. **Officers:** Joseph B. Sturman, President;
Alex J. Stanwick, Treasurer.

■ 17254 ■ Viking Distributing Company Inc.
1225 6th St.
San Francisco, CA 94107
Phone: (415)824-3750 **Fax:** (415)882-4261
Products: Construction and industrial supplies,
including power tools. **SICs:** 5085 (Industrial Supplies);

5039 (Construction Materials Nec); 5084 (Industrial
Machinery & Equipment). **Emp:** 113. **Officers:** Al
Malatesta.

■ 17255 ■ Viking Formed Products
23925 Reedy Dr.
Elkhart, IN 46514
Phone: (219)262-9250
Free: (800)262-9250 **Fax:** (219)262-3019
URL: http://www.vikingformedproducts.com
Products: Fiberglass molds; Thermoform plastic parts.
SICs: 5085 (Industrial Supplies); 5162 (Plastics
Materials & Basic Shapes); 5084 (Industrial Machinery
& Equipment). **Est:** 1989. **Sales:** $25,000,000 (2000).
Emp: 300. **Officers:** Kevin Gibson, President; Andy
Murray, VP of Operations.

■ 17256 ■ Virginia Welding Supply Company Inc.
PO Box 1268
Charleston, WV 25325
Phone: (304)346-0875 **Fax:** (304)345-0401
Products: Welding supplies. **SIC:** 5085 (Industrial
Supplies). **Est:** 1948. **Sales:** $25,000,000 (2000).
Emp: 170. **Officers:** William V. Accuosti, President;
Don Parsons, Controller; David Bauer, VP of Sales.

■ 17257 ■ Vogel Tool and Die Corp.
1825 N 32nd
Stone Park, IL 60165-1003
Phone: (708)345-0160 **Fax:** (708)345-0535
Products: Industrial machinery. **SIC:** 5085 (Industrial
Supplies). **Sales:** $3,000,000 (2000). **Emp:** 42.

■ 17258 ■ Voto Manufacturing Sales Company Inc.
500 N 3rd St.
Steubenville, OH 43952
Phone: (740)282-3621 **Fax:** (740)282-5441
Products: Wire rope, hoses, fittings, and blades. **SIC:**
5085 (Industrial Supplies). **Est:** 1938. **Sales:**
$12,000,000 (2000). **Emp:** 60. **Officers:** James V.
Wolbert, President; Gary Folden, CFO; Barry Stewart,
Exec. VP; William Warner, Vice President.

■ 17259 ■ Wagner-Smith Co.
PO Box 672
Dayton, OH 45401
Phone: (937)298-7481
Products: Industrial pumps and equipment. **SIC:** 5084
(Industrial Machinery & Equipment). **Sales:**
$50,000,000 (1994). **Emp:** 200. **Officers:** P.H.
Wagner, President.

■ 17260 ■ Henry Walke Co.
1415 E Bessemer Ave.
Greensboro, NC 27405-7111
Phone: (919)275-9511 **Fax:** (919)273-8447
Products: Measuring tools and cutting tools; Industrial
supplies. **SICs:** 5085 (Industrial Supplies); 5084
(Industrial Machinery & Equipment). **Emp:** 49.

■ 17261 ■ James Walker Co.
7109 Industrial Rd.
Baltimore, MD 21208
Phone: (410)486-3950 **Fax:** (410)486-5176
Products: Lifting devices; Industrial hardware,
including shackles. **SICs:** 5085 (Industrial Supplies);
5084 (Industrial Machinery & Equipment). **Est:** 1911.
Sales: $1,000,000 (2000). **Emp:** 20. **Officers:** H.
James Watson Jr., President; Steven Sneeringer,
Chairman of the Board & Finance Officer; James F.
Connor, Dir. of Marketing & Sales.

■ 17262 ■ P.G. Walker and Son Inc.
PO Box 762
Springfield, MO 65801-0762
Phone: (417)862-1745
Products: Industrial gases. **SIC:** 5085 (Industrial
Supplies). **Est:** 1937. **Sales:** $16,000,000 (2000).
Emp: 100. **Officers:** John A. Wyrsch, President; Terry
Jones, Controller; Earl Dyck, Dir. of Marketing.

■ 17263 ■ Washington Belt & Drive
PO Box 58
Wenatchee, WA 98807-0058
Phone: (509)547-1661 **Fax:** (509)547-1685
Products: Industrial belting and packing hose; Speed
changers, drives, and gears. **SICs:** 5084 (Industrial

Machinery & Equipment); 5063 (Electrical Apparatus &
Equipment); 5085 (Industrial Supplies).

■ 17264 ■ Washington Belt & Drive
425 N Way
Box 387
Colville, WA 99114
Phone: (509)452-5669
Products: Industrial supplies, including gear belts and
motors. **SICs:** 5085 (Industrial Supplies); 5063
(Electrical Apparatus & Equipment).

■ 17265 ■ Washington Belt & Drive
4201 Airport Way S
Seattle, WA 98108
Phone: (206)623-5650 **Fax:** (206)622-7888
Products: Belts and drives. **SIC:** 5085 (Industrial
Supplies).

■ 17266 ■ Washington Belt & Drive
PO Box 58
Wenatchee, WA 98801
Phone: (509)663-8591 **Fax:** (509)453-6577
Products: Industrial supplies, including gear belts and
motors. **SICs:** 5084 (Industrial Machinery &
Equipment); 5063 (Electrical Apparatus & Equipment);
5085 (Industrial Supplies).

■ 17267 ■ Water Works and Industrial Supply Co., Inc.
PO Box 585
Huntington, WV 25710
Phone: (304)525-7888
Free: (800)642-3402 **Fax:** (304)522-6267
Products: Industrial supplies, including pipes, waste
and wastewater industry supplies. **SIC:** 5085 (Industrial
Supplies). **Est:** 1950. **Sales:** $6,000,000 (2000). **Emp:**
21. **Officers:** Sandra Deppner Wright, President.

■ 17268 ■ Welco Gases Corp.
425 Avenue P
Newark, NJ 07105
Phone: (973)589-7895 **Free:** (888)935-2642
Products: Compressed industrial, medical and
specialty gases and welding supplies. **SIC:** 5169
(Chemicals & Allied Products Nec). **Sales:**
$21,000,000 (2000). **Emp:** 75. **Officers:** Robert F.
Aliessandro, President; Paul D'Aloia, VP of Finance.

■ 17269 ■ Welders Supply Inc.
430 S Industrial Blvd.
Dallas, TX 75207
Phone: (214)748-4721
Products: Welding supplies. **SIC:** 5085 (Industrial
Supplies). **Est:** 1940. **Sales:** $7,000,000 (2000). **Emp:**
35. **Officers:** Carl R. Squibb, CEO & President.

■ 17270 ■ Welding Industrial Supply Inc.
2200 N Western Ave.
Chicago, IL 60647
Phone: (773)384-7622 **Fax:** (773)384-7273
Products: Welding supplies, including welders, gas
propane, rods, machines, and regulators. **SIC:** 5085
(Industrial Supplies). **Est:** 1950. **Sales:** $15,000,000
(2000). **Emp:** 50. **Officers:** Craig Devries, President;
Roger Yackey, Vice President.

■ 17271 ■ Weldstar Co.
PO Box 1150
Aurora, IL 60504
Phone: (708)859-3100
Products: Welding rods, gases, hats, shields. **SIC:**
5085 (Industrial Supplies). **Est:** 1936. **Sales:**
$13,000,000 (2000). **Emp:** 40. **Officers:** John V.
Winkle, President; Joseph Winkle, Treasurer & Secty.;
James Berry, Sales Mgr.

■ 17272 ■ Welsco Inc.
PO Box 1058
North Little Rock, AR 72115-1058
Phone: (501)771-1204 **Fax:** (501)771-4062
E-mail: mail@welsco.com
URL: http://www.welsco.com
Products: Welding supplies; Industrial gases. **SICs:**
5084 (Industrial Machinery & Equipment); 5085
(Industrial Supplies); 5169 (Chemicals & Allied
Products Nec). **Est:** 1941. **Sales:** $21,000,000 (2000).
Emp: 100. **Officers:** Angela Harrison, CEO &
Chairman of the Board; Robert Bosnears, President;

David Cagle, COO; Gerald Perrier, Regional Sales Mgr.; Raymond Digby, Regional Sales Mgr.

■ **17273** ■ **West Coast Ship Chandlers Inc.**
2665 Magnolia St.
Oakland, CA 94607
Phone: (510)444-7200 **Fax:** (510)444-7216
E-mail: sales@westcoastship.com
URL: http://www.westcoastship.com
Products: Marine and industrial supplies. **SICs:** 5085 (Industrial Supplies); 5088 (Transportation Equipment & Supplies). **Est:** 1953. **Sales:** $6,000,000 (2000). **Emp:** 22. **Officers:** Charlie Michelson, Owner, e-mail: charlie.michelson@westcoastship.com.

■ **17274** ■ **West Coast Wire Rope and Rigging Inc.**
PO Box 5999
Portland, OR 97228
Phone: (503)228-9353
Products: Wire rope. **SIC:** 5051 (Metals Service Centers & Offices). **Sales:** $74,000,000 (2000). **Emp:** 100. **Officers:** Karen Newton, President; Dale Hanson, Controller.

■ **17275** ■ **West Penn Laco Inc.**
331 Ohio
Pittsburgh, PA 15209-2798
Phone: (412)821-3608 **Fax:** (412)821-8187
Products: Welding supplies; Industrial gases; Automotive paints. **SICs:** 5085 (Industrial Supplies); 5169 (Chemicals & Allied Products Nec); 5198 (Paints, Varnishes & Supplies). **Est:** 1928. **Sales:** $8,500,000 (2000). **Emp:** 40. **Officers:** William E. Richards, CEO; Neil MacKay, General Mgr.; Howard MacKay, Sales Mgr.

■ **17276** ■ **Western Rubber and Supply Inc.**
PO Box 56117
Hayward, CA 94545
Phone: (510)441-6500 **Fax:** (510)441-9790
Products: Custom molded and extruded rubber parts—vibration and motor mounts, grommets, O-rings, vacuum cups and bumpers; Custom fabricates die-cut parts—mouse and counter pads. **SIC:** 5085 (Industrial Supplies). **Officers:** Don Ulery, Chairman of the Board.

■ **17277** ■ **Westmoreland Industrial Supply Co.**
RD 12
Greensburg, PA 15601
Phone: (412)242-3814
Products: Industrial supplies and tools, including grinding wheels, cutting tools, abrasives, nuts, and bolts. **SICs:** 5085 (Industrial Supplies); 5084 (Industrial Machinery & Equipment). **Est:** 1929. **Sales:** $2,000,000 (2000). **Emp:** 8. **Officers:** Paul Shrum, CEO.

■ **17278** ■ **White River Paper Company Inc.**
PO Box 455
White River Junction, VT 05001-0455
Phone: (802)295-3188
Free: (800)639-7226 **Fax:** (802)295-5494
Products: Paper and paper products. **SIC:** 5113 (Industrial & Personal Service Paper). **Sales:** $12,000,000. **Emp:** 45.

■ **17279** ■ **White Water Manufacturing**
1700 Nebraska Ave.
Grants Pass, OR 97527
Phone: (541)476-1344 **Fax:** (541)476-7533
Products: Inflatable rafts and catarafts, kayaks and dry bags. **SICs:** 5085 (Industrial Supplies); 5091 (Sporting & Recreational Goods); 5099 (Durable Goods Nec).

■ **17280** ■ **Ralph C. Williams Inc.**
429 Waynesburg Rd. SE
Canton, OH 44707
Phone: (330)452-6548
Free: (800)362-6522 **Fax:** (330)452-8445
Products: Hoses and fittings; Lubricants; Tools. **SICs:**

5085 (Industrial Supplies); 5172 (Petroleum Products Nec); 5072 (Hardware). **Est:** 1954. **Sales:** $3,000,000 (1999). **Emp:** 30. **Officers:** George A. German, President.

■ **17281** ■ **Williamson & Co.**
9 Shelter Dr.
Greer, SC 29650
Phone: (864)848-1011 **Fax:** (864)848-4310
E-mail: lestcoll@aol.com
Products: Roll packaging. **SIC:** 5085 (Industrial Supplies). **Est:** 1973. **Emp:** 52. **Officers:** Dan F. Williamson; Lester T. Collins, Sales & Marketing Contact; Larry Williamson, Human Resources Contact.

■ **17282** ■ **Wilton Corp.**
PO Box 88839
Chicago, IL 60680
Phone: (847)934-6000 **Fax:** (847)934-6730
Products: Tools, machinery and brushes. **SIC:** 5085 (Industrial Supplies). **Sales:** $80,000,000 (2000). **Emp:** 500. **Officers:** Rosemarie Egan, VP of Finance.

■ **17283** ■ **Wisconsin Bearing**
695 Sullivan Dr.
Fond du Lac, WI 54935
Phone: (920)923-7500
Products: Bearings. **SIC:** 5085 (Industrial Supplies).

■ **17284** ■ **Wisconsin Bearing**
2125 S Stroughton
Madison, WI 53716
Phone: (608)221-3328
Products: Bearings and pearl blocks. **SICs:** 5085 (Industrial Supplies); 5084 (Industrial Machinery & Equipment).

■ **17285** ■ **Wisconsin Bearing**
3669 Enterprise Dr.
Sheboygan, WI 53083-2663
Phone: (920)467-2621 **Fax:** (920)467-6131
Products: Bearings. **SIC:** 5085 (Industrial Supplies).

■ **17286** ■ **Walter A. Wood Supply Co.**
4509 Rossville Blvd.
Chattanooga, TN 37407
Phone: (423)867-1033 **Fax:** (423)867-7944
Products: Industrial supplies. **SICs:** 5085 (Industrial Supplies); 5072 (Hardware). **Est:** 1913. **Sales:** $19,300,000 (2000). **Emp:** 80. **Officers:** J. Leon Henry, President.

■ **17287** ■ **Woodlawn Hardware**
4290 Katonah Ave.
Bronx, NY 10470-2095
Phone: (718)324-2178 **Fax:** (718)324-6547
Products: Industrial supplies; Electrical equipment and supplies; Insulated wire; Hardwood flooring; Ceramic wall and floor tile; Power tools and parts; Hardware. **SICs:** 5085 (Industrial Supplies); 5063 (Electrical Apparatus & Equipment); 5023 (Homefurnishings); 5072 (Hardware); 5051 (Metals Service Centers & Offices). **Est:** 1957. **Emp:** 49. **Officers:** Frank Milito, Owner, e-mail: fmilito@aol.com.

■ **17288** ■ **F.B. Wright Co.**
PO Box 770
Dearborn, MI 48121
Phone: (313)843-8250 **Fax:** (313)843-8450
Products: Gaskets and hoses. **SIC:** 5085 (Industrial Supplies). **Est:** 1938. **Sales:** $30,000,000 (2000). **Emp:** 135. **Officers:** William J. Reno, CEO & Chairman of the Board; J. Doerr, VP of Finance; John Dallacqua, VP of Marketing; Richard Steffes, Dir. of Data Processing.

■ **17289** ■ **Wyo-Ben Inc.**
PO Box 1979
Billings, MT 59103
Phone: (406)652-6351
Free: (800)548-7055 **Fax:** (406)656-0748
E-mail: email@wyoben.com
Products: Drilling supplies. **SIC:** 5032 (Brick, Stone & Related Materials). **Est:** 1950. **Sales:** $30,000,000 (1999). **Emp:** 105. **Officers:** David Brown, President; D.A. Buckingham, Treasurer; R. Stichman, Dir. of Marketing.

■ **17290** ■ **Xpedx**
613 Main St.
Wilmington, MA 01887
Phone: (978)988-7447 **Fax:** (978)988-8525
Products: Personal and service paper and sanitation chemical preparations. **SICs:** 5113 (Industrial & Personal Service Paper); 5169 (Chemicals & Allied Products Nec). **Sales:** $208,000,000 (2000). **Emp:** 300.

■ **17291** ■ **Herman W. Yecies Inc.**
PO Box 688
Passaic, NJ 07055
Phone: (973)777-7200 **Fax:** (973)777-0954
Products: Industrial supplies; Safety equipment; Hand tools. **SICs:** 5084 (Industrial Machinery & Equipment); 5085 (Industrial Supplies). **Est:** 1902. **Sales:** $2,000,000 (2000). **Emp:** 9. **Officers:** Roberta Yecies, President.

■ **17292** ■ **A.B. Young Cos.**
PO Box 90287
Indianapolis, IN 46290-0287
Phone: (317)844-7001
Free: (800)886-7001 **Fax:** (317)848-2606
Products: Industrial machinery. **SIC:** 5085 (Industrial Supplies). **Sales:** $13,000,000 (2000). **Emp:** 30.

■ **17293** ■ **Young and Vann Supply Co.**
PO Box 757
Birmingham, AL 35201
Phone: (205)252-5161 **Fax:** (205)326-4465
Products: Industrial supplies. **SIC:** 5085 (Industrial Supplies). **Est:** 1906. **Sales:** $18,000,000 (2000). **Emp:** 65. **Officers:** Gary Mercer, President; Jim Johnson, VP of Sales; Marleen Pinkerton, Controller; John Kinabrew, Sales Mgr.

■ **17294** ■ **Zatkoff Seals and Packings Co.**
23230 Industrial Park Dr.
Farmington, MI 48335-2850
Phone: (248)478-2400
Free: (800)967-3257 **Fax:** (248)478-3392
E-mail: info@zatkoff.com
URL: http://www.zatkoff.com
Products: Seals and packings, including o-rings, gaskets, and adhesives. **SIC:** 5085 (Industrial Supplies). **Est:** 1959. **Sales:** $50,000,000 (2000). **Emp:** 150. **Officers:** Roger Zatkoff, CFO; Gary Zatkoff, President.

■ **17295** ■ **Zenith Supply Company Inc.**
50 32nd St.
Pittsburgh, PA 15201
Phone: (412)391-9570 **Fax:** (412)391-5160
Products: Pressure seals; Carbon steel and forged steel valves. **SIC:** 5074 (Plumbing & Hydronic Heating Supplies). **Est:** 1951. **Sales:** $12,000,000 (2000). **Emp:** 80. **Officers:** Sheldon Marstine, President.

■ **17296** ■ **Ziff Co.**
180 Shrewsbury St.
West Boylston, MA 01583
Free: (888)997-4515
Products: Paper, plastic and floor cleaning products. **SICs:** 5113 (Industrial & Personal Service Paper); 5169 (Chemicals & Allied Products Nec). **Sales:** $62,000,000 (2000). **Emp:** 90.

(29) Jewelry

Entries in this section are arranged alphabetically by company name. When the company name is a personal name, the company name is alphabetized by the surname unless the first name or initial(s) are part of a trade name. See the User's Guide at the front of this directory for additional information.

■ 17297 ■ **14 Carats Ltd.**
314 S Beverly Dr.
Beverly Hills, CA 90212
Phone: (310)551-1212 **Fax:** (310)551-0519
Products: Jewelry. **SIC:** 5094 (Jewelry & Precious Stones). **Est:** 1962. **Sales:** $13,000,000 (2000). **Emp:** 40. **Officers:** Cheryl Alpert, President, e-mail: cheryl@xivkarats.com. **Former Name:** Lory's West Inc.

■ 17298 ■ **A La Carte Jewelry**
1006 Pine St.
Yankton, SD 57078-3056
Phone: (605)665-4179
Products: Jewelry. **SIC:** 5094 (Jewelry & Precious Stones). **Officers:** Rod Wipf, Owner.

■ 17299 ■ **A-Mark Precious Metals Inc.**
100 Wilshire Blvd., 3rd Fl.
Santa Monica, CA 90401
Phone: (310)319-0200 **Fax:** (310)319-0279
E-mail: main@amark.com
URL: http://www.amark.com
Products: Precious metals, including gold, silver, platinum, and palladium in coins, bar, and grain form, used for investment, manufacturing, and industrial products. **SIC:** 5094 (Jewelry & Precious Stones). **Est:** 1965. **Sales:** $1,000,000,000 (1999). **Emp:** 30. **Officers:** Deborah Spinosa, COO & Exec. VP; Yolanda Estrada, Marketing Representative, e-mail: yestrada@amark.com; Taleen Khatchadourian, Marketing Representative, e-mail: taleen@amark.com; Cathy Fu, Sales/Marketing Contact; Carey Wehrli, Human Resources Contact, e-mail: cwehrli@amark.com.

■ 17300 ■ **A & Z Pearls Inc.**
550 S Hill, Ste. 660
Los Angeles, CA 90013-2401
Phone: (213)627-3030 **Fax:** (213)627-1038
Products: Jewelry; Pearls. **SIC:** 5094 (Jewelry & Precious Stones). **Emp:** 9.

■ 17301 ■ **Abco International**
PO Box 574125
Orlando, FL 32857-4125
Phone: (407)896-6000 **Fax:** (407)896-5458
E-mail: abco11@juno.com
URL: http://www.wholesalecentral.com/abco
Products: Jewelry. **SIC:** 5094 (Jewelry & Precious Stones). **Est:** 1980. **Sales:** $5,300,000 (1999). **Emp:** 16. **Officers:** Burt Weinberg.

■ 17302 ■ **Accessory Wholesale**
550 Wholesalers Pkwy. C
Harahan, LA 70123-3308
Phone: (504)736-0357 **Fax:** (504)734-8638
Products: Costume jewelry. **SIC:** 5094 (Jewelry & Precious Stones). **Officers:** Mike Gietl, Owner.

■ 17303 ■ **Adirondack Silver**
PO Box 13536
Albany, NY 12212
Phone: (518)456-8110
Free: (800)SILVER-2 **Fax:** (518)456-8132
Products: Sterling silver jewelry. **SIC:** 5094 (Jewelry & Precious Stones).

■ 17304 ■ **Alaska Trophy Manufacturing**
845 E Loop Dr.
Anchorage, AK 99501-3739
Phone: (907)272-2172
Products: Jewelry; Precious stones (gems); Trophies. **SIC:** 5094 (Jewelry & Precious Stones). **Officers:** Joseph Bradshaw, President.

■ 17305 ■ **Allan Distributors**
801 Water St., No. 105
Framingham, MA 01701-3200
Phone: (508)877-8655
Products: Jewelry. **SIC:** 5094 (Jewelry & Precious Stones).

■ 17306 ■ **Almanzan**
PO Box 10113
Oakland, CA 94610-0113
Phone: (510)532-8700 **Free:** (800)345-4441
Products: Jewelry. **SIC:** 5094 (Jewelry & Precious Stones). **Emp:** 49.

■ 17307 ■ **Amadom Corp.**
801 E Aztec Ave.
Gallup, NM 87301-5509
Phone: (505)722-5452 **Fax:** (505)722-0979
Products: Jewelry and precious stones. **SIC:** 5094 (Jewelry & Precious Stones). **Officers:** Frank Budick, President.

■ 17308 ■ **American Jewelry Sales**
PO Box 19309
Johnston, RI 02919
Phones: (401)942-8080 (401)447-4212
Fax: (401)273-4970
Products: Costume jewelry. **SIC:** 5094 (Jewelry & Precious Stones).

■ 17309 ■ **Amerind Inc.**
580 5th Ave.
New York, NY 10036
Phone: (212)382-0210 **Fax:** (212)382-1165
Products: Diamonds and precious stones. **SIC:** 5094 (Jewelry & Precious Stones). **Est:** 1960. **Sales:** $4,000,000 (2000). **Emp:** 10. **Officers:** Solomon Gad, President.

■ 17310 ■ **Anka Co. Inc.**
12 Greco Ln., Ste. 18
Warwick, RI 02886-1242
Phone: (401)467-6868
Free: (800)556-7768 **Fax:** (401)467-2159
Products: Jewelry; Precious stones (gems). **SIC:** 5094 (Jewelry & Precious Stones). **Officers:** Anthony Masi, Vice President.

■ 17311 ■ **Antwerp Diamond Distributing Inc.**
587 5th Ave.
New York, NY 10017
Phone: (212)319-3300 **Fax:** (212)207-8168
Products: Diamonds for jewelry purposes. **SIC:** 5094 (Jewelry & Precious Stones). **Est:** 1950. **Sales:** $21,000,000 (2000). **Emp:** 32.

■ 17312 ■ **Apex Technologies**
392 5th Ave.
New York, NY 10018
Phone: (212)268-3535
Products: Fashion jewelry and home accessories. **SIC:** 5094 (Jewelry & Precious Stones). **Sales:** $4,800,000 (2000). **Emp:** 35.

■ 17313 ■ **Arlington Coin Co.**
140 Gansett Ave.
Cranston, RI 02910-2549
Phone: (401)942-3188
Products: Coins for the jewelry industry. **SIC:** 5094 (Jewelry & Precious Stones). **Officers:** David Ledversis, Owner.

■ 17314 ■ **Art Cathedral Metal Inc.**
PO Box 6146
Providence, RI 02940-6146
Phone: (401)273-7200
Free: (800)472-6435 **Fax:** (401)273-6262
Products: Jewelry. **SIC:** 5094 (Jewelry & Precious Stones). **Sales:** $10,000,000 (2000). **Emp:** 200.

■ 17315 ■ **Art's Theatrical Supply**
3306 83rd
Lubbock, TX 79423
Phone: (806)792-2136
Free: (800)338-1500 **Fax:** (806)792-0131
Products: Rhinestones, sequins, and beads. **SIC:** 5094 (Jewelry & Precious Stones).

■ 17316 ■ **E.H. Ashley & Company Inc.**
PO Box 15067
Riverside, RI 02915-0067
Phone: (401)431-0950
Free: (800)735-7424 **Fax:** 800-735-7423
Products: Jewelry; Precious stones (gems). **SIC:** 5094 (Jewelry & Precious Stones). **Officers:** Otto Hoffer, Chairman of the Board.

■ 17317 ■ **ASO Enterprises**
171 Elmgrove Ave.
Providence, RI 02906-4222
Phone: (401)331-7051 **Fax:** (401)273-8850
Products: Jewelry and precious stones. **SIC:** 5094 (Jewelry & Precious Stones). **Officers:** Odile Von Heyden, Owner.

■ 17318 ■ **Atlas Diamond Co.**
760 Market St., Ste. 765
San Francisco, CA 94102-2302
Phone: (415)433-5123 **Free:** (800)752-8527
Products: Diamonds for jewelry purposes. **SIC:** 5094 (Jewelry & Precious Stones). **Emp:** 5.

■ 17319 ■ **Aurafin Corp.**
14001 NW 4th St.
Sunrise, FL 33325
Phone: (954)846-8099
Products: Gold jewelry. **SIC:** 5094 (Jewelry & Precious Stones).

■ **17320** ■ **Aurea Italia Inc.**
16 Florence St.
Providence, RI 02904-3527
Phone: (401)232-3303
Products: Jewelry; Precious stones (gems). **SIC:** 5094 (Jewelry & Precious Stones). **Officers:** Larry Buteau, President.

■ **17321** ■ **Aurora Arts & Krafts**
1426 E 26th Ave.
Anchorage, AK 99508-3935
Phone: (907)279-0330
Products: Jade products; Gold products. **SIC:** 5094 (Jewelry & Precious Stones). **Officers:** O. Martin, Partner.

■ **17322** ■ **Ayre & Ayre Silversmiths**
PO Box 1049
Moriarty, NM 87035-1049
Phone: (505)832-4344
Products: Brass goods; Silver goods; Jewelry. **SIC:** 5094 (Jewelry & Precious Stones). **Officers:** Robert Ayre, Partner.

■ **17323** ■ **B & V Inc.**
5701 Central NE
Albuquerque, NM 87108
Phone: (505)265-8911   **Fax:** (505)842-9631
Products: American indian art; Jewelry; Kachinas; Pottery. **SIC:** 5094 (Jewelry & Precious Stones). **Est:** 1974. **Officers:** Victoria Madden, President.

■ **17324** ■ **Baba International Inc.**
7177 Pembrooke Rd.
Pembroke Pines, FL 33023
Phone: (954)989-1100   **Fax:** (954)989-2354
E-mail: babainc@aol.com
URL: http://www.wholesalecentral.com/baba
Products: Custom jewelry; Gift items. **SICs:** 5094 (Jewelry & Precious Stones); 5199 (Nondurable Goods Nec).

■ **17325** ■ **Baker's Fine Jewelry and Gifts**
760 W 22nd St.
Norfolk, VA 23517
Phone: (757)625-2529   **Fax:** (757)622-0983
Products: Gifts; Jewelry. **SICs:** 5094 (Jewelry & Precious Stones); 5199 (Nondurable Goods Nec). **Est:** 1919. **Sales:** $750,000,000 (2000). **Emp:** 17.

■ **17326** ■ **L.G. Balfour Co.**
7211 Circle South Rd.
Austin, TX 78745-6603
Phone: (512)222-3600
Free: (800)622-2727   **Fax:** (512)226-5294
Products: Fraternal, college, and school jewelry and emblems. **SIC:** 5094 (Jewelry & Precious Stones). **Est:** 1913. **Sales:** $105,000,000 (2000). **Emp:** 1,000. **Officers:** L. James Santerre, Vice Chm.

■ **17327** ■ **Ballanda Corp.**
10020 Pioneer Blvd., Ste. 105
Santa Fe Springs, CA 90670
Phone: (562)801-6192
Free: (800)827-2328   **Fax:** (562)801-6197
E-mail: accounting@ballanda.com
Products: Watches and clocks; Electronics. **SICs:** 5094 (Jewelry & Precious Stones); 5064 (Electrical Appliances—Television & Radio). **Est:** 1976. **Sales:** $5,000,000 (2000). **Emp:** 17. **Officers:** Caleb Law, President.

■ **17328** ■ **Bartky Mineralogical Enterprises Inc.**
375 Walnut St.
Livingston, NJ 07039-5011
Phone: (973)992-9451
Free: (800)523-7625   **Fax:** (973)992-9553
Products: Semi-precious minerals and finished products, including pen sets, book ends, and jewelry. **SIC:** 5094 (Jewelry & Precious Stones). **Est:** 1987. **Sales:** $3,000,000 (2000). **Emp:** 6. **Officers:** Cynthia Bartky, President; Murray Bartky, CFO.

■ **17329** ■ **Baume and Mercier**
663 5th Ave.
New York, NY 10022
Phone: (212)593-0444
Products: Watches. **SIC:** 5094 (Jewelry & Precious

Stones). **Sales:** $25,000,000 (1993). **Emp:** 100. **Officers:** Steven P. Kaiser, President.

■ **17330** ■ **Bazar Inc. Sales Co.**
793 Waterman Ave.
East Providence, RI 02914-1713
Phone: (401)434-2595   **Fax:** (401)434-0814
Products: Jewelry; Precious stones (gems). **SIC:** 5094 (Jewelry & Precious Stones). **Officers:** Banice Bazar, President.

■ **17331** ■ **The Bell Group**
7500 Bluewater Rd. NW
Albuquerque, NM 87121-1962
Phone: (505)839-3000
Free: (800)545-6566   **Fax:** (505)839-3001
E-mail: andrea.hill@riogrande.com
URL: http://www.riogrande.com
Products: Jewelry supplies, tools, and findings. **SIC:** 5072 (Hardware). **Est:** 1944. **Emp:** 400. **Officers:** Hugh Bell, Director; Eddie Bell, Director; Allan Bell, Director; Andrea Hill, Director. **Doing Business As:** Rio Grande, Neutec, Sonic Mill, West Coast.

■ **17332** ■ **Bellini Jewelry Co.**
1478 Atwood Ave.
Johnston, RI 02919
Phone: (401)521-2233   **Fax:** (401)521-1177
E-mail: babol@aol.com
URL: http://www.buyri.com
Products: Jewelry; Precious metals; Precious gems. **SIC:** 5094 (Jewelry & Precious Stones). **Est:** 1973. **Sales:** $290,000 (2000). **Emp:** 5. **Officers:** Angelo Lauro, Owner.

■ **17333** ■ **Belmar Inc.**
554 Killingly St.
Johnston, RI 02919-5227
Phone: (401)454-4430   **Fax:** (401)454-4432
Products: Collectors' miniatures. **SIC:** 5094 (Jewelry & Precious Stones). **Officers:** Robert Pesare, President.

■ **17334** ■ **Bennett Brothers Inc.**
30 E Adams St.
Chicago, IL 60603
Phone: (312)263-4800
URL: http://www.BennettBrothers.com
Products: Durable goods; Jewelry; Home furnishings. **SICs:** 5099 (Durable Goods Nec); 5094 (Jewelry & Precious Stones); 5023 (Homefurnishings). **Emp:** 100. **Officers:** G.K. Bennett, President; G. Kirk Bennett Jr., Vice President.

■ **17335** ■ **Samuel Benoit**
879 Waterman Ave.
East Providence, RI 02914-1313
Phone: (401)431-1520   **Fax:** (401)431-0670
Products: Costume jewelry. **SIC:** 5094 (Jewelry & Precious Stones). **Est:** 1990. **Sales:** $500,000 (2000). **Emp:** 4. **Officers:** Samuel Benoit, Owner.

■ **17336** ■ **Benold's Jewelers**
2900 W Anderson Ln., Ste. F
Austin, TX 78757
Phone: (512)452-6491   **Fax:** (512)454-8541
Products: Jewelry and gifts. **SIC:** 5094 (Jewelry & Precious Stones). **Emp:** 30. **Officers:** Harold Laves. **Former Name:** Laves Jewelry Co.

■ **17337** ■ **Benras Watch Co.**
1550 W Carroll
Chicago, IL 60607
Phone: (312)243-3300
Free: (800)621-4445   **Fax:** (312)243-6500
Products: Watches; Diamonds. **SIC:** 5094 (Jewelry & Precious Stones). **Emp:** 499.

■ **17338** ■ **Bijoux Terner L.P.**
7200 NW 7th St.
Miami, FL 33126
Phone: (305)266-9000
Products: Costume jewelry, including earrings, necklaces, and bracelets. **SIC:** 5094 (Jewelry & Precious Stones). **Sales:** $88,000,000 (2000). **Emp:** 350. **Officers:** Salomon Terner, President; Leo Schuck, VP of Finance; Rosa Terner, VP of Marketing.

■ **17339** ■ **Sid Birzon Inc.**
686 Main St.
Buffalo, NY 14202
Phone: (716)856-8255
Free: (800)783-8250   **Fax:** (716)856-8262
E-mail: sidbirinc@aol.com
Products: Closeout name brand watches. **SIC:** 5094 (Jewelry & Precious Stones). **Est:** 1951. **Sales:** $2,100,000 (2000). **Emp:** 10. **Officers:** Sidney Birzon, President; Gerald Bizon, Vice President.

■ **17340** ■ **Black Hills Gold Colema**
PO Box 6400
Rapid City, SD 57701-4670
Phone: (605)394-3700   **Fax:** (605)394-3750
Products: Jewelry. **SIC:** 5094 (Jewelry & Precious Stones). **Sales:** $20,000,000 (1999). **Emp:** 300. **Officers:** Dwight Sobczak SR.; Dwight Sobczak JR., Sales/Marketing Contact; Dan Sobczak; Gogie Enstad, Customer Service Contact; Jim Anderson, Human Resource Contact.

■ **17341** ■ **Blake Brothers**
13 Columbia Dr. Unit 3
Amherst, NH 03031-2319
Phone: (603)377-8058
Free: (800)8-BLAKE-8   **Fax:** (603)377-0631
Products: Sterling silver jewelry. **SIC:** 5094 (Jewelry & Precious Stones).

■ **17342** ■ **Joseph Blank Inc.**
15 W 47th St.
New York, NY 10036
Phone: (212)575-9050   **Fax:** (212)302-8521
E-mail: blank@polygon.net
URL: http://www.josephblank.com
Products: Loose stones for jewelry. **SIC:** 5094 (Jewelry & Precious Stones). **Est:** 1919. **Sales:** $10,000,000 (2000). **Emp:** 10. **Officers:** M. Blank, President; Marjorie Ann Blank, VP of Marketing & Sales; Douglas Blank, Sec. & Treas.

■ **17343** ■ **Blue Canyon Jewelry**
10918 Cochiti Rd. SE
Albuquerque, NM 87123-3350
Phone: (505)298-3096
Products: Jewelry; Precious stones (gems). **SIC:** 5094 (Jewelry & Precious Stones). **Officers:** James Smith, Owner.

■ **17344** ■ **Blue Pearl**
PO Box 5127
Gainesville, FL 32602
Products: Jewelry; Paper goods and printed matter; Cosmetics; Cleaning preparations. **SICs:** 5199 (Nondurable Goods Nec); 5111 (Printing & Writing Paper).

■ **17345** ■ **Blue Ribbon Awards**
1935 S Lennox Ave.
Casper, WY 82601-4944
Phone: (307)266-6401
Products: Trophies; Awards. **SIC:** 5094 (Jewelry & Precious Stones). **Officers:** Barbara Millay, President.

■ **17346** ■ **Bock Jewelry Co. Inc.**
6019 Berkshire Lane
Dallas, TX 75225-5706
Phone: (214)692-9000   **Fax:** (214)692-1117
Products: Jewelry. **SIC:** 5094 (Jewelry & Precious Stones).

■ **17347** ■ **Borel Jules & Co.**
1110 Grand
Kansas City, MO 64106-2306
Phone: (816)421-6110
Free: (800)776-6862   **Fax:** (816)421-2596
Products: Jewelers and watchmakers tools and supplies; Precision tools. **SIC:** 5094 (Jewelry & Precious Stones). **Est:** 1921. **Sales:** $6,000,000 (2000). **Emp:** 50. **Officers:** Mark Borel, President.

■ **17348** ■ **Bortman Trading Co.**
PO Box 134
Center Sandwich, NH 03227-0134
Phone: (603)284-7068
Products: Jewelry; Precious stones (gems). **SIC:** 5094 (Jewelry & Precious Stones). **Officers:** David Bortman, Owner.

■ **17349** ■ **Bruce Breton & Co. Inc.**
427 Amherst St.
Nashua, NH 03063-1258
Phone: (603)882-2050
Products: Jewelry; Precious stones (gems); Precious metal. **SIC:** 5094 (Jewelry & Precious Stones).
Officers: Bruce Breton, President.

■ **17350** ■ **Broadway Style Showroom No. 1**
2850D Stirling Rd.
Hollywood, FL 33020
Phone: (954)922-6336 **Fax:** (954)922-4839
Products: Fashion and costume jewelry. **SIC:** 5094 (Jewelry & Precious Stones).

■ **17351** ■ **Harold Brown Jewelry Inc.**
316 W Bender Blvd.
Hobbs, NM 88240-2269
Phone: (505)392-6046 **Fax:** (505)392-6046
Products: Jewelry; Precious stones (gems). **SIC:** 5094 (Jewelry & Precious Stones). **Officers:** Harold Brown, President.

■ **17352** ■ **Donald Bruce and Co.**
3600 N Talman Ave.
Chicago, IL 60618
Phone: (312)477-8100 **Fax:** (312)477-6293
Products: Costume jewelry. **SIC:** 5094 (Jewelry & Precious Stones). **Sales:** $51,000,000 (2000). **Emp:** 205. **Officers:** Lewis Solomon, Owner; David Toppin, CFO; Donald Mahoney, Dir of Human Resources.

■ **17353** ■ **Brunos Turquoise Trading Post**
PO Box 60307
Boulder City, NV 89006-0307
Products: Jewelry; Precious stones (gems). **SIC:** 5094 (Jewelry & Precious Stones). **Officers:** Bruno Liquori, Owner.

■ **17354** ■ **Bulova Corp.**
1 Bulova Ave.
Woodside, NY 11377-7874
Phone: (718)204-3300 **Fax:** (718)204-3546
Products: Watches and clocks. **SIC:** 5094 (Jewelry & Precious Stones). **Est:** 1911. **Sales:** $109,200,000 (2000). **Emp:** 430. **Officers:** Herbert C. Hofmann, CEO & President; John T. O'Reilly, Controller; Phillip Shaw, Dir. of Marketing; Larry DiOrio, Dir. of Information Systems; Eleanor Smith, Dir of Personnel.

■ **17355** ■ **Buy-Lines Co.**
5444 Melrose Ave.
Los Angeles, CA 90038
Phone: (323)463-4855
Products: Glass beads. **SICs:** 5094 (Jewelry & Precious Stones); 5099 (Durable Goods Nec).

■ **17356** ■ **California Time Inc.**
1250 S Broadway
Los Angeles, CA 90015
Phone: (213)749-9949 **Fax:** (213)749-2846
Products: Watches. **SIC:** 5094 (Jewelry & Precious Stones).

■ **17357** ■ **Capri Jewelry Inc.**
392 5th Ave.
New York, NY 10018
Phone: (212)947-5280 **Fax:** (212)643-8064
Products: Watches, rings, chains, and earrings. **SIC:** 5094 (Jewelry & Precious Stones). **Sales:** $41,000,000 (2000). **Emp:** 70. **Officers:** Saul Smith, President.

■ **17358** ■ **Carat Diamond Corp.**
1156 Avenue of the Americas
New York, NY 10036-2702
Phone: (212)869-8666
Free: (800)223-0530 **Fax:** (212)840-6738
Products: Jewelry. **SIC:** 5094 (Jewelry & Precious Stones). **Emp:** 6.

■ **17359** ■ **Jim Carr Inc.**
100 Bridge St.
Pelham, NH 03076
Phone: (603)635-3143
Products: Jewelry and precious stones; Coins; Medals and trophies. **SIC:** 5094 (Jewelry & Precious Stones). **Officers:** Jim Carr, President.

■ **17360** ■ **Cartier Inc.**
653 5th Ave.
New York, NY 10022
Phone: (212)753-0111
Products: Jewelry including watches, rings, and necklaces. **SIC:** 5094 (Jewelry & Precious Stones). **Est:** 1847. **Sales:** $120,000,000 (2000). **Emp:** 300. **Officers:** Simon Critchel, President; Gary Saage Jr., VP of Finance; Herve Martin, Vice President; Eric Tanner, Dir. of Information Systems; Lyle Kishbaugh.

■ **17361** ■ **Cas Ker Co.**
2121 Spring Grove Ave.
Cincinnati, OH 45214-1721
Phone: (513)241-7073
Free: (800)587-0408 **Fax:** (513)241-5848
Products: Jewelry; Watches and parts. **SIC:** 5094 (Jewelry & Precious Stones). **Sales:** $5,250,000 (2000). **Emp:** 30.

■ **17362** ■ **Casio, Inc.**
570 Mt. Pleasant Ave.
Dover, NJ 07801
Phone: (973)361-5400 **Free:** (800)962-2746
Products: Watches; Batteries; Computers. **SICs:** 5044 (Office Equipment); 5045 (Computers, Peripherals & Software); 5094 (Jewelry & Precious Stones). **Est:** 1970. **Sales:** $630,000,000 (2000). **Emp:** 250. **Officers:** John J. McDonald, CEO & President; Joseph D'Agostino, CFO; Dennis Reer, Dir. of Marketing; James Griffen, Dir. of Systems; Doug Poff, Dir of Personnel.

■ **17363** ■ **Cates Associates**
Route 32
East Vassalboro, ME 04935
Phone: (207)923-3101
Products: Jewelry; Precious stones (gems). **SIC:** 5094 (Jewelry & Precious Stones). **Officers:** Coralene Cates, Owner.

■ **17364** ■ **Cathedral Art Metal Inc.**
PO Box 6146
Providence, RI 02940-6146
Phone: (401)273-7200
Free: (800)472-6435 **Fax:** (401)273-6262
E-mail: camco@cathedralart.com
Products: Jewelry, including precious stones (gems), sterling silver, religious, and gift. **SICs:** 5094 (Jewelry & Precious Stones); 5199 (Nondurable Goods Nec). **Est:** 1920. **Sales:** $10,000,000 (2000). **Emp:** 200. **Officers:** Leo Tracey, President; Barbara Omlsted, Sales/Marketing Contact; Diane Andrade, Customer Service Contact; Dave Stebner, Human Resources Contact.

■ **17365** ■ **Cellino Inc.**
31 W 47th St., No. 103
New York, NY 10036-2808
Phone: (212)382-0959
Products: Jewelry. **SIC:** 5094 (Jewelry & Precious Stones). **Emp:** 6.

■ **17366** ■ **Chatham Created Gems Inc.**
111 Maiden Ln., 5th Fl.
San Francisco, CA 94108
Phone: (415)397-8450
Free: (800)222-2002 **Fax:** (415)397-8466
E-mail: tcemerald@aol.com
URL: http://www.chatham.com
Products: Created gems. **SIC:** 5094 (Jewelry & Precious Stones). **Est:** 1938. **Sales:** $9,500,000 (1999). **Emp:** 120. **Officers:** Thomas Chatham, President, e-mail: tcemerald@aol.com; John Chatham, Partner.

■ **17367** ■ **Chiefs Discount Jewelers Inc.**
1724 Post Rd.
Warwick, RI 02888-5941
Phone: (401)737-4331
Products: Jewelry and precious stones. **SIC:** 5094 (Jewelry & Precious Stones). **Officers:** David Manzi, President.

■ **17368** ■ **Chipita Accessories**
110 E 7th St.
Walsenburg, CO 81089
Phone: (719)738-3991 **Fax:** (719)738-2130
Products: Hand-beaded jewelry including necklaces

and bracelets. **SIC:** 5094 (Jewelry & Precious Stones). **Est:** 1983. **Sales:** $1,700,000 (2000). **Emp:** 54. **Officers:** Joan Eagle, President; Ben Eagle, CFO & Treasurer; William Reiners, Dir. of Information Systems.

■ **17369** ■ **Citizen Watch Company of America Inc.**
1200 Wall St. W
Lyndhurst, NJ 07071
Phone: (201)438-8150
Free: (800)767-9112 **Fax:** (201)438-4161
Products: Watches. **SIC:** 5094 (Jewelry & Precious Stones). **Est:** 1975. **Sales:** $100,000,000 (2000). **Emp:** 300. **Officers:** Laurence Grunstein, President; Mike Calev, Controller; Keith Boughton, VP of Sales; Noreen Schaffer, Personnel Mgr.

■ **17370** ■ **Citra Trading Corp.**
590 5th Ave.
New York, NY 10036
Phone: (212)354-1000
Products: Pearls, gold, and diamonds. **SIC:** 5094 (Jewelry & Precious Stones). **Est:** 1960. **Sales:** $44,000,000 (2000). **Emp:** 50. **Officers:** H. Chitrik, President.

■ **17371** ■ **CJC Holdings Inc.**
PO Box 149056
Austin, TX 78714-9056
Phone: (512)444-0571 **Fax:** (512)444-7618
Products: Jewelry, including class rings, pendants, and wedding rings. **SIC:** 5094 (Jewelry & Precious Stones). **Sales:** $120,000,000 (2000). **Emp:** 1,100. **Officers:** John T. Waugh, President; Charlyn A. Cook, VP of Marketing; Jeffrey H. Brennan, CFO. **Doing Business As:** Artcarved Class Rings. **Doing Business As:** R. Johns Ltd. **Doing Business As:** Artcarved Bridal. **Doing Business As:** Orange Blossom. **Doing Business As:** Artcarved College Rings.

■ **17372** ■ **Clamor Impex Inc.**
214 NE 1st St.
Miami, FL 33132
Phone: (305)379-1701 **Fax:** (305)379-1702
E-mail: clamorimpx@aol.com
URL: http://www.wholesalecentral.com/clamor/
Products: Watches. **SIC:** 5094 (Jewelry & Precious Stones). **Est:** 1991. **Sales:** $3,000,000 (1999). **Emp:** 7. **Officers:** Sam Todwala; Kerfegar Mehta.

■ **17373** ■ **Clark Sales Co.**
PO Box 900398
Sandy, UT 84093
Phone: (801)942-7021 **Fax:** (801)942-2918
Products: Sterling silver jewelry. **SIC:** 5094 (Jewelry & Precious Stones). **Est:** 1982. **Emp:** 3. **Officers:** Charles Clark, Owner.

■ **17374** ■ **Colossal Jewelry and Accessories Inc.**
217 Hergesell Ave.
Maywood, NJ 07607
Phone: (201)556-0202
Free: (800)252-4206 **Fax:** (201)556-0205
E-mail: colossal@webspan.net
URL: http://www.colossaljewelry.com
Products: Costume jewelry; Hair accessories; Nail polish; Cosmetics. **SICs:** 5094 (Jewelry & Precious Stones); 5131 (Piece Goods & Notions); 5122 (Drugs, Proprietaries & Sundries).

■ **17375** ■ **Colossal Jewelry and Accessories Inc.**
406 N Midland Ave.
Saddle Brook, NJ 07663
Phone: (201)794-6533
Free: (800)252-4206 **Fax:** (201)794-6537
Products: Jewelry. **SIC:** 5094 (Jewelry & Precious Stones).

■ **17376** ■ **Connoisseurs Products Corp.**
17 Presidential Way
Woburn, MA 01801-1040
Phone: (781)932-3949
Free: (800)851-5333 **Fax:** (781)932-4755
E-mail: connoisseure@mindspring.com
Products: Jewelry, including silver and metal cleaners.

SIC: 5094 (Jewelry & Precious Stones). **Est:** 1972. **Emp:** 45. **Officers:** D. Dorfman; John Boyd, VP of Marketing; John Archambault, Human Resources Contact.

■ **17377** ■ **Connor & Son**
PO Box 6016
Incline Village, NV 89450-6016
Phone: (702)831-2741
Products: Jewelry; Precious stones (gems). **SIC:** 5094 (Jewelry & Precious Stones). **Officers:** Robert Connor, Owner.

■ **17378** ■ **David Cooke Co.**
57 E Carpenter St.
Valley Stream, NY 11580-4403
Phone: (516)785-0565
Free: (800)645-6644   **Fax:** (516)785-0565
Products: Fine jewelry. **SIC:** 5094 (Jewelry & Precious Stones).

■ **17379** ■ **Elaine Coyne Galleries**
Peachtree Business Center
3039 Amwiler Rd., Ste. 120
Atlanta, GA 30360
Phone: (404)448-8101
Free: (800)741-2523   **Fax:** (404)448-8096
Products: Women's clothing accessories; Jewelry. **SICs:** 5094 (Jewelry & Precious Stones); 5137 (Women's/Children's Clothing). **Est:** 1974. **Emp:** 6. **Officers:** Elaine Coyne, President; Richard Turner, Vice-President.

■ **17380** ■ **Craftown Inc.**
109 A McArthur Ct.
Nicholasville, KY 40356-9109
Phone: (859)885-4720
Free: (800)962-8656   **Fax:** (859)887-2321
Products: Costume equestrian jewelry. **SIC:** 5094 (Jewelry & Precious Stones). **Est:** 1975. **Officers:** Bobby Holman, President. **Doing Business As:** The Finishing Touch of KY.

■ **17381** ■ **Creative Imports Inc.**
205 Hallene Rd. 210B
Warwick, RI 02886-2450
Phone: (401)738-8240   **Fax:** (401)738-8328
Products: Costume jewelry. **SIC:** 5094 (Jewelry & Precious Stones). **Est:** 1986. **Officers:** Louis Demascole, President.

■ **17382** ■ **Cres Jewelry Factory Inc.**
PO Box 800
West New York, NJ 07093-0800
Products: Jewelry, made of platinum metals and karat gold; Diamonds for jewelry purposes. **SIC:** 5094 (Jewelry & Precious Stones). **Emp:** 49.

■ **17383** ■ **Judy Crosby's Americana Arts I**
PO Box 7365
Albuquerque, NM 87194-7365
Phone: (505)266-2324   **Fax:** (505)266-2522
Products: Jewelry and precious stones, including Native American jewelry. **SIC:** 5094 (Jewelry & Precious Stones). **Officers:** Judy Crosby, President.

■ **17384** ■ **Crumrine Manufacturing Jewelers**
145 Catron Dr.
Reno, NV 89512-1001
Phone: (702)786-3712   **Fax:** (702)786-8466
Products: Costume jewelry and costume novelties. **SIC:** 5094 (Jewelry & Precious Stones). **Est:** 1948. **Sales:** $5,000,000 (2000). **Emp:** 80. **Officers:** Marjorie M. Crumrine, Chairman of the Board; David Crumrine, President; Judy Pepper.

■ **17385** ■ **Crystaline North America Inc.**
1170-B Pontiac Ave.
Cranston, RI 02920-7926
Phone: (401)461-2104   **Fax:** (401)461-2105
E-mail: cnacorp@aol.com
Products: Silver and costume jewelry. **SIC:** 5094 (Jewelry & Precious Stones). **Officers:** George Holl, President; Maureen Kelley, Sales/Marketing Contact; Tammy Donley, Customer Service Contact.

■ **17386** ■ **Cuba Buckles**
PO Box 1327
Cuba, NM 87013-1327
Phone: (505)289-3918   **Free:** (800)451-2098
Products: Jewelry and precious stones. **SIC:** 5094 (Jewelry & Precious Stones). **Est:** 1979. **Emp:** 2. **Officers:** Stewart Otto, Owner.

■ **17387** ■ **Dallas Gold and Silver Exchange Inc.**
2817 Forest Ln.
Dallas, TX 75234
Phone: (972)484-3662   **Fax:** (972)241-0646
URL: http://www.dgse.com
Products: Jewelry. **SIC:** 5094 (Jewelry & Precious Stones). **Est:** 1965. **Sales:** $16,000,000 (2000). **Emp:** 23. **Officers:** L.S. Smith, CEO & Chairman of the Board; John Benson, CFO.

■ **17388** ■ **Davenport Organisation**
1 Merrill Industrial Dr., Ste. 18
Hampton, NH 03842-1981
Phone: (603)926-9266   **Fax:** (603)926-4499
Products: Jewelry; Precious stones (gems); Precious metal; Diamonds for jewelry purposes. **SIC:** 5094 (Jewelry & Precious Stones). **Officers:** Dallas Davenport, Owner.

■ **17389** ■ **Dave's Jewelry & Giftware**
PO Box 740
Pelham, NH 03076
Phone: (603)635-2881   **Fax:** (603)635-2881
Products: Jewelry and precious stones; Giftware. **SICs:** 5094 (Jewelry & Precious Stones); 5199 (Nondurable Goods Nec). **Officers:** David Provencal, Owner.

■ **17390** ■ **A.J. Denison Co. Inc.**
1 East St.
Riverside, RI 02915-4414
Phone: (401)433-3232   **Fax:** (401)437-1888
Products: Custom and specialized jewelry. **SIC:** 5094 (Jewelry & Precious Stones). **Est:** 1923. **Emp:** 8. **Officers:** Lawerence Merlino, President.

■ **17391** ■ **Denver Merchandise Mart**
451 E 58th Ave.
Denver, CO 80216
Phone: (303)292-6278
Free: (800)289-6278   **Fax:** (303)298-1503
Products: Jewelry; Furniture; Gifts; Apparel. **SICs:** 5094 (Jewelry & Precious Stones); 5021 (Furniture); 5099 (Durable Goods Nec); 5136 (Men's/Boys' Clothing). **Est:** 1965. **Sales:** $19,000,000 (2000). **Emp:** 75. **Officers:** Darrell Hare, General Mgr.

■ **17392** ■ **Desert Indian Traders**
1009 W Highway 66
Gallup, NM 87301-6830
Phone: (505)722-5554   **Fax:** (505)722-5615
Products: Jewelry and precious stones. **SIC:** 5094 (Jewelry & Precious Stones). **Officers:** Mohammad Rasheed, Owner.

■ **17393** ■ **Desert Star Jewelry Manufacturing**
10901 Acoma SE
Albuquerque, NM 87123
Phone: (505)296-6238   **Fax:** (505)296-0120
Products: Jewelry. **SIC:** 5094 (Jewelry & Precious Stones).

■ **17394** ■ **Design Accessories Inc.**
3636 Aerial Way Dr.
Roanoke, VA 24018
Phone: (540)344-8958   **Fax:** (540)342-6073
URL: http://www.designmktg.com
Products: Jewelry. **SIC:** 5094 (Jewelry & Precious Stones). **Emp:** 8. **Officers:** Cynthia Dillon-Lawrence, e-mail: c.dillon@designmktg.com.

■ **17395** ■ **J. and S.S. DeYoung Inc.**
38 Newbury St.
Boston, MA 02116-3210
Phone: (617)266-0100   **Fax:** (617)424-1616
Products: Jewelry, including earrings, bracelets, necklaces, and rings. **SIC:** 5094 (Jewelry & Precious Stones). **Est:** 1835. **Sales:** $30,000,000 (2000). **Emp:** 25. **Officers:** Joseph Samuel, CEO.

■ **17396** ■ **Direct Diamonds Distributors**
333 Washington St.
Boston, MA 02108
Phone: (617)523-0444
Products: Diamonds. **SIC:** 5094 (Jewelry & Precious Stones).

■ **17397** ■ **Divinci Ltd.**
4220 Pinecrest Cir. W
Las Vegas, NV 89121-4924
Phone: (702)458-1349   **Fax:** (702)456-8072
Products: Jewelry; Precious stones (gems). **SIC:** 5094 (Jewelry & Precious Stones). **Est:** 1973. **Officers:** Shava Spector, President.

■ **17398** ■ **Don-Lin Jewelry Co. Inc.**
39 Haskins St.
Providence, RI 02903
Phone: (401)274-0165   **Fax:** (401)272-6866
Products: Jewelry and precious stones. **SIC:** 5094 (Jewelry & Precious Stones). **Officers:** Donald St. Angelo, President.

■ **17399** ■ **Downey Designs International Inc.**
2265 Executive Dr.
Indianapolis, IN 46241
Phone: (317)248-9888
Products: Jewelry. **SIC:** 5094 (Jewelry & Precious Stones). **Sales:** $55,000,000 (1992). **Emp:** 240. **Officers:** David G. Downey, CEO & Chairman of the Board; Nancy Mills, VP & CFO.

■ **17400** ■ **Max Duraffourg Gem Company Inc.**
PO Box 568
Bedford, NY 10506-0568
Phone: (914)234-9784
Products: Synthetic stones, including emeralds and rubies. **SIC:** 5094 (Jewelry & Precious Stones). **Est:** 1963. **Sales:** $500,000 (2000). **Emp:** 3. **Officers:** Pierre Zweigart, President.

■ **17401** ■ **Dynamic Concepts Inc.**
98 Sheffield Rd.
Cranston, RI 02920-6040
Phone: (401)942-0381   **Fax:** (401)942-2534
Products: Jewelry. **SIC:** 5094 (Jewelry & Precious Stones). **Officers:** Gerald Shaulson, President.

■ **17402** ■ **E Big Inc.**
PO Box 385
Meridian, ID 83642-0385
Phone: (208)888-3606
Products: Jewelry; Precious stones (gems). **SIC:** 5094 (Jewelry & Precious Stones). **Officers:** Ellie Herndon, President.

■ **17403** ■ **Eagle Trophy**
32 Shannon Rd.
Salem, NH 03079-1843
Phone: (603)893-6536
Products: Jewelry and precious stones; Coins; Medals and trophies. **SIC:** 5094 (Jewelry & Precious Stones). **Officers:** Kenneth De Santis, Owner.

■ **17404** ■ **East Continental Gems Inc.**
580 5th Ave.
New York, NY 10036
Phone: (212)575-0944   **Fax:** (212)944-6254
URL: http://www.eastcontinentalgems.com
Products: Precious stones, including diamonds, emeralds, sapphires, and rubies; Jewelry. **SIC:** 5094 (Jewelry & Precious Stones). **Est:** 1972. **Sales:** $5,000,000 (2000). **Emp:** 3. **Officers:** Eli Mirzoeff, President, e-mail: mirzoef@ibm.net; Adam Mirzoeff, Vice President.

■ **17405** ■ **Eastrade Inc.**
609 5th Ave.
New York, NY 10017
Phone: (212)752-8448
Products: Precious stones, including emeralds, rubies, and sapphires. **SIC:** 5094 (Jewelry & Precious Stones). **Est:** 1946. **Sales:** $500,000 (2000). **Emp:** 2. **Officers:** Michael Dymant, President.

■ 17406 ■ **Jerry Elkins Inc.**
1010 W Highway 66
Gallup, NM 87301-6845
Phone: (505)722-3878 **Fax:** (505)722-2003
Products: Jewelry; Precious stones (gems). **SIC:** 5094
(Jewelry & Precious Stones). **Officers:** Jerry Elkins,
President.

■ 17407 ■ **Ellis Tanner Trading Co.**
1980 Hwy. 602
Gallup, NM 87305-0636
Phone: (505)722-7776 **Fax:** (505)722-4144
Products: Jewelry. **SIC:** 5094 (Jewelry & Precious
Stones).

■ 17408 ■ **Elvee/Rosenberg Inc.**
11 W 37th St.
New York, NY 10018-6235
Phone: (212)575-0767
Free: (877)575-0767 **Fax:** (212)575-0931
E-mail: sales@elveerosenberg.com
URL: http://www.elveerosenberg.com
Products: Costume jewelry parts, including beads,
pearls, crystals, and stones; Bead stringing supplies.
SIC: 5094 (Jewelry & Precious Stones). **Est:** 1914.
Sales: $4,000,000 (2000). **Emp:** 19. **Officers:** Chester
Hochbaum, President; Melanie Holzberg, Sales Mgr.

■ 17409 ■ **Evvan Importers Inc.**
589 5th Ave.
New York, NY 10017
Phone: (212)319-3100
Free: (800)43E-VVAN **Fax:** (212)319-3460
E-mail: evvan@aol.com
Products: Natural precious and semi-precious stones;
Precious stones (gems). **SIC:** 5094 (Jewelry &
Precious Stones). **Est:** 1968. **Emp:** 15. **Officers:** Elliot
Eshaghian; Jackie Cohen, Sales/Marketing Contact.

■ 17410 ■ **Excelsior International Corp.**
PO Box 1268
Providence, RI 02901-1268
Phone: (401)737-7388 **Fax:** (401)737-7330
Products: Watches with imported movements or
modules. **SIC:** 5094 (Jewelry & Precious Stones).
Officers: Lambert Chang, President.

■ 17411 ■ **Export USA**
2530 Lakefield Way
Sugar Land, TX 77479
Phone: (281)980-5370
Products: Jewelry; Water and air filters; Metal
anchors. **SICs:** 5094 (Jewelry & Precious Stones);
5085 (Industrial Supplies); 5051 (Metals Service
Centers & Offices). **Officers:** Lacey Jean Mizell, Export
Manager.

■ 17412 ■ **Fantasy Diamond Corp.**
1550 W Carroll Ave.
Chicago, IL 60607
Phone: (312)421-4444
Free: (800)621-4445 **Fax:** (312)243-6500
Products: Jewelry, including diamond rings, earrings
and pendants. **SIC:** 5094 (Jewelry & Precious Stones).
Est: 1878. **Sales:** $11,000,000 (2000). **Emp:** 65.
Officers: Louis Price, President.

■ 17413 ■ **Feibelman & Krack**
PO Box 8045
Cranston, RI 02920-0045
Phone: (401)943-6370 **Fax:** (401)942-1160
Products: Fashion jewelry. **SIC:** 5094 (Jewelry &
Precious Stones). **Est:** 1967. **Emp:** 4. **Officers:** H.
Feibelman, Owner.

■ 17414 ■ **Field and Associates Inc.**
269 SE 5th Ave.
Delray Beach, FL 33483
Phone: (561)278-0545 **Fax:** (561)278-8463
Products: Golf tournament and business awards,
including watches, rings, plaques, ceramics, artwork,
and luggage. **SICs:** 5094 (Jewelry & Precious Stones);
5099 (Durable Goods Nec); 5199 (Nondurable Goods
Nec). **Est:** 1981. **Sales:** $3,500,000 (2000). **Emp:** 12.
Officers: Chuck Field, President; Susan Field, Exec.
VP.

■ 17415 ■ **Fire Mountain Gems**
28195 Redwood Hwy.
Cave Junction, OR 97523-9304
Phone: (541)592-2222
Free: (800)423-2319 **Fax:** (541)592-3103
E-mail: firemtn@cdsnet.net
URL: http://www.firemtn.com
Products: Jewelers' findings and materials; Jewelers'
materials and lapidary work; Jewelry. **SIC:** 5094
(Jewelry & Precious Stones). **Est:** 1974. **Sales:**
$15,000,000 (2000). **Emp:** 115. **Officers:** Stuart
Freedman, President, e-mail: stuart@cdsnet.net; Chris
Freedman, Secretary; Connie Gammel, Customer
Service Contact; Scott Kasiah, Human Resources
Contact.

■ 17416 ■ **Fragments Inc.**
107 Green St.
New York, NY 10012
Phone: (212)226-8878 **Fax:** (212)226-6187
Products: Costume and fine jewelry. **SIC:** 5094
(Jewelry & Precious Stones). **Est:** 1984. **Sales:**
$3,000,000 (1999). **Emp:** 6. **Officers:** Janet Goldman,
President; Jimmy Moore, Vice President.

■ 17417 ■ **Fremont Coin Co. Inc.**
317 Fremont St.
Las Vegas, NV 89101-5607
Phone: (702)382-1469
Products: Gold, silver, and coins. **SIC:** 5094 (Jewelry
& Precious Stones). **Officers:** Phil Carlino, Chairman of
the Board.

■ 17418 ■ **Friedman and Co.**
PO Box 8025
Savannah, GA 31412
Phone: (912)233-9333
Free: (800)545-9033 **Fax:** (912)238-4873
Products: Jewelry. **SIC:** 5094 (Jewelry &
Precious Stones). **Est:** 1925. **Sales:** $137,600,000 (2000). **Emp:**
1,500. **Officers:** Bradleu J. Stinn, President & CEO;
Robert S. Morris, Exec. VP; John G. Call, COO.

■ 17419 ■ **Frontier**
35 York St., 11th Fl.
Brooklyn, NY 11201
Phone: (718)855-3030
Free: (800)338-2338 **Fax:** (718)855-3303
Products: Watches. **SIC:** 5094 (Jewelry & Precious
Stones). **Est:** 1982. **Sales:** $3,600,000 (2000). **Emp:**
11. **Officers:** Stephen Cheung.

■ 17420 ■ **G & S Jewelry Manufacturing**
10016 Cochiti Rd. SE
Albuquerque, NM 87123
Phone: (505)293-7398
Free: (800)922-0834 **Fax:** (505)293-3446
Products: Jewelry, including sterling silver and
costume. **SIC:** 5094 (Jewelry & Precious Stones).

■ 17421 ■ **Gamzon Brothers Inc.**
21 W 46th St.
New York, NY 10036
Phone: (212)719-2550 **Fax:** (212)764-0533
Products: Jewelers' tools and supplies. **SIC:** 5094
(Jewelry & Precious Stones). **Est:** 1947. **Sales:**
$5,000,000 (2000). **Emp:** 27. **Officers:** R. Gamzon,
President; Jack Feldheim, Vice President; Stephen
Winer, Secretary.

■ 17422 ■ **Donald & Rema Gee**
1349 Commanche Dr.
Las Vegas, NV 89109-3112
Phone: (702)735-9637
Products: Jewelry; Precious stones (gems); Precious
metal; Diamonds for jewelry purposes. **SIC:** 5094
(Jewelry & Precious Stones). **Officers:** Donald Gee,
Partner.

■ 17423 ■ **Gem East Corp.**
2124 2nd Ave.
Seattle, WA 98121
Phone: (206)441-1700 **Fax:** (206)448-1801
Products: Jewelry, including diamonds and 14 karat
gold. **SIC:** 5094 (Jewelry & Precious Stones). **Sales:**
$6,000,000 (2000). **Emp:** 99. **Officers:** Pat Druxman;
Hal Staehle.

■ 17424 ■ **Gem Enterprises, Inc.**
12 E Broadway
Derry, NH 03038-2410
Phone: (603)432-1920
Products: Jewelry; Precious stones (gems). **SIC:** 5094
(Jewelry & Precious Stones). **Officers:** Greg
Germanton, President.

■ 17425 ■ **Gem-La Jewelry Inc.**
964 Mineral Spring Ave.
North Providence, RI 02904-4933
Phone: (401)724-3150 **Fax:** (401)725-3150
Products: Jewelry, including costume jewelry; Box
goods; Rings; Closeouts. **SIC:** 5094 (Jewelry &
Precious Stones). **Est:** 1975. **Emp:** 2. **Officers:** Shirley
Gemma.

■ 17426 ■ **Gem Platinum Manufacturing Co.**
48 W 48th St.
New York, NY 10036
Phone: (212)819-0850
Products: Platinum and gems. **SIC:** 5094 (Jewelry &
Precious Stones). **Est:** 1923. **Sales:** $12,000,000
(2000). **Emp:** 15. **Officers:** Howard Schliff, President;
Larry Liman, Vice President.

■ 17427 ■ **Gemcarve**
1116 17th St. W
Billings, MT 59102-4130
Phone: (406)259-9622
Products: Jewelry; Precious stones (gems). **SIC:** 5094
(Jewelry & Precious Stones). **Officers:** Earl Moos,
Owner.

■ 17428 ■ **GemTek Enterprises Inc.**
983 Cranston St.
Cranston, RI 02920
Phone: (401)946-6760 **Fax:** (401)946-8436
URL: http://www.gemtekenterprises.com
Products: Costume jewelry; Sterling silver and gold
jewelry, including bracelets and rings. **SIC:** 5094
(Jewelry & Precious Stones). **Est:** 1990. **Sales:**
$1,500,000 (2000). **Emp:** 6. **Officers:** Robert Krupa,
President.

■ 17429 ■ **Genal Strap Inc.**
31-00 47th Ave.
Long Island City, NY 11101
Phone: (718)706-8700 **Fax:** (718)706-8978
Products: Watch bands and batteries. **SICs:** 5094
(Jewelry & Precious Stones); 5063 (Electrical
Apparatus & Equipment). **Sales:** $18,000,000 (2000).
Emp: 60. **Officers:** Aaron Greenwald, President.

■ 17430 ■ **Gerson Company Inc.**
6100 Broadmoor St.
Shawnee Mission, KS 66202
Phone: (913)262-7400
Free: (800)999-7401 **Fax:** (913)262-3568
URL: http://www.gersoncompany.com
Products: Costume jewelry; Watches; Seasonal; Trim
a tree; Home decor. **SIC:** 5094 (Jewelry & Precious
Stones). **Est:** 1938. **Sales:** $76,000,000 (2000). **Emp:**
300. **Officers:** Peter Gerson, Chairman of the Board;
John C. Hjalmarson, CEO; James S. Gerson,
President, e-mail: jimgerson@gersoncompany.com.

■ 17431 ■ **Michael Giordano International**
7 W 36th St.
New York, NY 10018
Phone: (212)239-1800 **Fax:** (212)629-0953
Products: Costume jewelry. **SIC:** 5094 (Jewelry &
Precious Stones). **Est:** 1989. **Sales:** $3,000,000
(2000). **Emp:** 30. **Officers:** Michael Giordino,
President.

■ 17432 ■ **Global Importing Inc.**
20 Polk St.
Johnston, RI 02919-2321
Phone: (401)232-2700 **Fax:** (401)232-1250
Products: Jewelry; Precious stones (gems). **SIC:** 5094
(Jewelry & Precious Stones). **Officers:** Debra Scorpio,
President.

■ 17433 ■ Barry Glucksman & Associates
31 Algonquin Dr.
Warwick, RI 02888-5301
Phone: (401)463-9933 **Fax:** (401)274-3465
E-mail: amerapt@juno.com
Products: Jewelry; Gifts; Inspirational plaques; Picture frames; Key chains. **SICs:** 5094 (Jewelry & Precious Stones); 5199 (Nondurable Goods Nec). **Est:** 1983. **Sales:** $3,000,000 (2000). **Emp:** 5. **Officers:** Barry Glucksman, President.

■ 17434 ■ Gold Father's Jewelry, Inc.
3830 E Flamingo Rd., Ste. C-1, No. 173
Las Vegas, NV 89121
Phone: 800-642-2545 **Fax:** (702)891-8837
Products: Jewelry, including gold layered jewelry, charms, cubic zirconium items, and chain by the inch. **SIC:** 5094 (Jewelry & Precious Stones). **Est:** 1983. **Officers:** Patty McClirk, Owner. **Former Name:** Gold Father's.

■ 17435 ■ Gold Findings Company Inc.
55 W 47th
New York, NY 10036-2834
Phone: (212)354-7816 **Fax:** (718)891-8651
Products: Gold jewelry. **SIC:** 5094 (Jewelry & Precious Stones). **Emp:** 4.

■ 17436 ■ Gold & Silver Exchange
6101 Menaul Blvd. NE
Albuquerque, NM 87110-3319
Phone: (505)884-9230 **Fax:** (505)884-9230
Products: Jewelry and precious stones and metals, including gold bullion and platinum. **SIC:** 5094 (Jewelry & Precious Stones). **Officers:** David Castle, Owner.

■ 17437 ■ H.R. Goldman Co.
3350 N Durango Dr., Apt. 1101
Las Vegas, NV 89129-7271
E-mail: hrgoldmanco@worldnet.att.net
URL: http://www.home.att.net/~hrgoldmanco
Products: Earrings and hair accessories. **SICs:** 5094 (Jewelry & Precious Stones); 5199 (Nondurable Goods Nec).

■ 17438 ■ Gordon Brothers Corp.
40 Broad St., Ste. 11
Boston, MA 02109
Phone: (617)422-6218
Free: (800)366-3006 **Fax:** (617)422-6222
E-mail: jewelry@gordonbrothers.com
URL: http://www.gbjewelry.com
Products: Fine jewelry. **SIC:** 5094 (Jewelry & Precious Stones). **Est:** 1903. **Officers:** Greg Mazure, Vice President; Richard Lawler, President & CEO; Robert Radest, Vice President.

■ 17439 ■ Alan Gordon & Co.
6517 N May
Oklahoma City, OK 73116-4811
Phone: (405)848-1688 **Fax:** (405)848-2084
Products: Diamonds; Rings. **SIC:** 5094 (Jewelry & Precious Stones). **Est:** 1878. **Sales:** $500,000 (2000). **Emp:** 5. **Officers:** Alan N. Gordon, President; Arthur Alan Gordon, Vice President.

■ 17440 ■ Mike Graham Co.
5505 Osuna Rd. NE, Ste. F
Albuquerque, NM 87109-2542
Phone: (505)884-4653 **Fax:** (505)881-7666
Products: Jewelry and precious stones. **SIC:** 5094 (Jewelry & Precious Stones). **Officers:** Mike Graham, President.

■ 17441 ■ The Green Company, Inc.
15550 W 109th St.
Lenexa, KS 66219-1308
Phone: (913)888-8880 **Fax:** (913)888-8937
E-mail: green@thegreencompany.com
URL: http://www.thegreencompany.com
Products: Jewelry. **SIC:** 5094 (Jewelry & Precious Stones). **Est:** 1885. **Sales:** $3,250,000 (2000). **Emp:** 35. **Officers:** William P. Schutte, President; Jack M. Hinkle, Vice President; J.P. Hildebrand, Vice President; Marcia Lawrence, Sales/Marketing Contact; Gwen Schroeder, Customer Service Contact.

■ 17442 ■ Hahn Watch & Jewelry Co.
102-30 66th Rd., Apt. 11H
Forest Hills, NY 11375-2090
Products: Watches and parts; Jewelry, including diamonds. **SIC:** 5094 (Jewelry & Precious Stones). **Emp:** 2. **Officers:** Fred Hahn.

■ 17443 ■ Hallock Coin Jewelry
2060 W Lincoln Ave.
Anaheim, CA 92801-5301
Phone: (714)956-2360 **Fax:** (714)635-8247
Products: Jewelry, including pendants and chains. **SIC:** 5094 (Jewelry & Precious Stones). **Emp:** 25. **Officers:** George Hallock.

■ 17444 ■ Hardy Turquoise Co.
PO Box 1598
Apache Junction, AZ 85217-1598
Phone: (520)463-2371
Products: Raw turquoise. **SIC:** 5094 (Jewelry & Precious Stones). **Est:** 1976. **Sales:** $700,000 (2000). **Emp:** 3. **Officers:** Leonard Hardy, President.

■ 17445 ■ Harold Jewelry Inc.
96 Bowery 5th Fl.
New York, NY 10013-4727
Phone: (212)695-4905 **Fax:** (212)629-6817
Products: Necklaces, charms, chains, rings, and bracelets. **SIC:** 5094 (Jewelry & Precious Stones). **Est:** 1981. **Sales:** $15,000,000 (2000). **Emp:** 50. **Officers:** Harold Ha, President.

■ 17446 ■ Heartline
905 Early St.
Santa Fe, NM 87501-4237
Phone: (505)983-6777 **Fax:** (505)983-0810
Products: Jewelry; Precious stones (gems); Precious metal. **SIC:** 5094 (Jewelry & Precious Stones). **Officers:** Douglas Magnus, Owner.

■ 17447 ■ G.A. Heaton Co.
6595 Highway 49N
Mariposa, CA 95338
Phone: (209)377-8227
Products: Costume jewelry. **SIC:** 5094 (Jewelry & Precious Stones).

■ 17448 ■ Heuer Time and Electronics Corp.
960 S Springfield Ave.
Springfield, NJ 07081
Phone: (973)467-1890 **Fax:** (973)467-8938
Products: Watches. **SIC:** 5094 (Jewelry & Precious Stones). **Est:** 1976. **Sales:** $5,000,000 (2000). **Emp:** 100. **Officers:** Fred Reffsin, President; Walter Crawford, VP of Finance; Carol Shainswit, Dir. of Marketing.

■ 17449 ■ Honolulu Wholesale Jewelry Exchange
1525 Kalakaua Ave.
Honolulu, HI 96826
Phone: (808)942-7474
Free: (800)843-8533 **Fax:** (808)942-5454
E-mail: royal@rhhj.com
URL: http://www.rhhj.com
Products: Hawaiian jewelry and diamonds. **SIC:** 5094 (Jewelry & Precious Stones). **Est:** 1972. **Emp:** 118. **Officers:** Maggie Breeder, CEO.

■ 17450 ■ Horn EB Replacement Service
429 Washington St.
Boston, MA 02108-5278
Phone: (617)542-7752
Free: (800)835-0297 **Fax:** (617)542-2932
Products: Household items. **SIC:** 5094 (Jewelry & Precious Stones).

■ 17451 ■ William Hubb
PO Box 7072
Incline Village, NV 89452-7072
Phone: (702)832-0102
Products: Jewelry and precious stones. **SIC:** 5094 (Jewelry & Precious Stones). **Officers:** William Hubb, Owner.

■ 17452 ■ Idaho Coin Galleries
302 Main Ave. N
Twin Falls, ID 83301-5956
Phone: (208)733-8593
Products: Jewelry and precious stones; Precious metals. **SIC:** 5094 (Jewelry & Precious Stones). **Officers:** Howard Kinsfather, President.

■ 17453 ■ Import Ltd.
5249 N 35th St.
Milwaukee, WI 53209
Phone: (414)461-1240 **Fax:** (414)461-8590
Products: Jewelry. **SIC:** 5094 (Jewelry & Precious Stones). **Est:** 1934. **Emp:** 65. **Officers:** Stacy Terris, CEO.

■ 17454 ■ Import Wholesale Co.
11351 Harry Hines Blvd.
Dallas, TX 75229
Phone: (972)247-3772
Products: Jewelry; Ottomans; Handbags. **SICs:** 5094 (Jewelry & Precious Stones); 5137 (Women's/Children's Clothing); 5023 (Homefurnishings).

■ 17455 ■ Indian Den Traders
1208 E Hwy. 66
Gallup, NM 87301-6513
Phone: (505)722-4141 **Fax:** (505)722-4137
Products: Indian arts and crafts. **SIC:** 5094 (Jewelry & Precious Stones). **Officers:** Edward Gomez, Owner.

■ 17456 ■ Indian Mission Jewelry
PO Box 230
Prewitt, NM 87045-0230
Phone: (505)876-2721
Products: Jewelry; Natural precious and semi-precious stones; Silver ore. **SIC:** 5094 (Jewelry & Precious Stones). **Officers:** Charles Popperwell, Owner.

■ 17457 ■ Indian Trade Center Inc.
3306 E Hwy. 66
Gallup, NM 87301
Phone: (505)722-6666 **Fax:** (505)722-7794
Products: Pottery and Native American jewelry. **SIC:** 5094 (Jewelry & Precious Stones). **Est:** 1974. **Sales:** $6,000,000 (2000). **Emp:** 29. **Officers:** Mohammad Aysheh, President.

■ 17458 ■ Insonic Technology, Inc.
1240 S Hill St.
Los Angeles, CA 90015
Phone: (213)746-2109 **Fax:** (213)746-7737
E-mail: insonic@ix.netcom.com
Products: Watches; Electronic organizers. **SICs:** 5094 (Jewelry & Precious Stones); 5112 (Stationery & Office Supplies). **Sales:** $53,000,000 (2000). **Emp:** 68. **Officers:** Ron Bagheri, Marketing & Sales Mgr.; Fredy Miranda, Customer Service Contact; Rodrigo Echavarria, Human Resources. **Former Name:** Enterprices.

■ 17459 ■ International Bullion and Metal Brokers Inc.
49 W 24th St.
New York, NY 10010
Phone: (212)929-8800
Free: (800)622-8889 **Fax:** (212)929-0928
Products: Finished jewelry and manufacturing. **SIC:** 5094 (Jewelry & Precious Stones). **Est:** 1980. **Emp:** 120. **Officers:** Steve Kovacs, President.

■ 17460 ■ International Cultured Pearl & Jewelry Co.
71 W 47th
New York, NY 10036-2878
Phones: (212)869-5141 (212)869-5142 (212)869-5143
Free: (800)223-2484 **Fax:** (212)869-5140
Products: Pearl jewelry, including cultured pearl necklaces, earrings, and bracelets; Natural black diamonds. **SIC:** 5094 (Jewelry & Precious Stones). **Est:** 1951. **Sales:** $2,000,000 (2000). **Emp:** 49. **Officers:** Robert Schwager; Ronny Schwager.

■ 17461 ■ International Importers Inc.
2761 N 29th Ave.
Hollywood, FL 33020
Phone: (954)920-6344 **Fax:** (954)921-7747
Products: Custom jewelry, including necklaces, rings, and broaches. **SIC:** 5094 (Jewelry & Precious Stones).

■ 17462 ■ Interstate Wholesale Inc.
5500 W 14th St.
Sioux Falls, SD 57106-0206
Phone: (605)336-0999
Products: Costume jewelry. **SIC:** 5094 (Jewelry & Precious Stones). **Officers:** Aleene Wobbema, President.

■ 17463 ■ IPX
103 Indian Trail Rd.
Oak Brook, IL 60521
Phone: (630)323-1223 **Fax:** (630)323-1223
Products: Antique watches. **SIC:** 5094 (Jewelry & Precious Stones). **Officers:** Peter Foyo, Export Coordinator.

■ 17464 ■ Judith Jack LLC
392 5th Ave.
New York, NY 10018
Phone: (212)695-4004
Free: (800)431-0017 **Fax:** (212)695-4094
Products: Jewelry. **SIC:** 5094 (Jewelry & Precious Stones). **Est:** 1978. **Emp:** 65. **Officers:** M. Horowitz.

■ 17465 ■ Jamco
4309 Hilton NE
Albuquerque, NM 87110
Phone: (505)256-1092 **Fax:** (505)881-0255
Products: Watch bands; Indian jewelry. **SIC:** 5094 (Jewelry & Precious Stones). **Officers:** Joann Mc Natt, Owner.

■ 17466 ■ Jay's Indian Arts Inc.
2227 E 7th Ave.
Flagstaff, AZ 86004
Phone: (520)526-2439 **Fax:** (520)526-6368
Products: Gift items including silver and Indian jewelry and art. **SICs:** 5199 (Nondurable Goods Nec); 5094 (Jewelry & Precious Stones).

■ 17467 ■ JDS Industries Inc.
2704 W 3rd St.
Sioux Falls, SD 57104-6210
Phone: (605)339-4010
Products: Coins, medals, and trophies. **SIC:** 5094 (Jewelry & Precious Stones). **Officers:** Darwin Sletten, President.

■ 17468 ■ J. Jenkins Sons Company Inc.
1801 Whitehead Rd.
Baltimore, MD 21207
Phone: (410)265-5200 **Fax:** (410)298-4809
Products: Jewelry, including rings, class rings, and service award jewelry; Plaques. **SIC:** 5094 (Jewelry & Precious Stones). **Est:** 1902. **Sales:** $6,000,000 (2000). **Emp:** 80. **Officers:** Gabe Sparagana.

■ 17469 ■ The Jewelers of Las Vegas
2400 Western Ave.
Las Vegas, NV 89102-4810
Phone: (702)382-7413 **Fax:** (702)382-3307
Products: Jewelry and precious stones. **SIC:** 5094 (Jewelry & Precious Stones). **Officers:** Mordichai Yerushalmi, President.

■ 17470 ■ Jewelmasters Inc.
3123 Commerce Pky.
Miramar, FL 33025-3944
Phone: (561)655-7260 **Fax:** (561)659-4976
Products: Fine jewelry. **SIC:** 5094 (Jewelry & Precious Stones). **Est:** 1912. **Sales:** $46,062,000 (2000). **Emp:** 99. **Officers:** Josef J. Barr, CEO & Chairman of the Board.

■ 17471 ■ Jewelry By Dyan & Eduardo
2762 W Union Ave.
Las Cruces, NM 88005-4313
Phone: (505)523-8031
Products: Jewelry and precious stones. **SIC:** 5094 (Jewelry & Precious Stones). **Officers:** Dyan Tintor, Partner.

■ 17472 ■ Jewelry Exchange Inc.
549 E Sahara Ave.
Las Vegas, NV 89104-2730
Phone: (702)369-0669
Products: Jewelry and precious stones. **SIC:** 5094 (Jewelry & Precious Stones). **Officers:** Lester Finver, President.

■ 17473 ■ Jewelry Trend Inc.
White Horse Sq.
Box 56
Helen, GA 30545
Phone: (706)878-3080
Free: (800)432-2439 **Fax:** (706)878-3078
Products: Jewelry. **SIC:** 5094 (Jewelry & Precious Stones).

■ 17474 ■ JGL Inc.
1901 Beverly Blvd.
Los Angeles, CA 90057-9906
Phone: (213)413-0220
Free: (800)421-8745 **Fax:** (213)413-0265
Products: Jewelry. **SIC:** 5094 (Jewelry & Precious Stones). **Est:** 1971. **Emp:** 19. **Officers:** Anil Mehta.

■ 17475 ■ JJ Gold International Inc.
20227 NE 15th Ct.
North Miami Beach, FL 33179
Phone: (305)654-8833 **Fax:** (305)654-8868
Products: Costume jewelry. **SIC:** 5094 (Jewelry & Precious Stones).

■ 17476 ■ Martin and Osa Johnson Safari Museum
111 N Grant Ave.
Chanute, KS 66720
Phone: (316)431-2730 **Fax:** (316)431-3848
E-mail: osajohns@safarimuseum.com
Products: Jewelry. **SIC:** 5094 (Jewelry & Precious Stones). **Est:** 1961. **Emp:** 4. **Officers:** Conrad G. Froehlich, Director; Barbara E. Henshall, Curator; Oella L. Baughn, Museum Store Mgr. **Former Name:** Safari Museum Press.

■ 17477 ■ J.R.N. Inc.
1342 Featherbed Ln.
Venice, FL 34292
Phone: (941)485-7517
Free: (800)842-0431 **Fax:** (941)485-4957
E-mail: WorleysWonder@Hotmail.com
URL: http://www.WorleysWonder.net
Products: Jewelry; Glass cleaner; Metal cleaner. **SICs:** 5094 (Jewelry & Precious Stones); 5094 (Jewelry & Precious Stones). **Est:** 1988. **Sales:** $150,000,000 (2000). **Emp:** 2. **Officers:** J.R. Normile, President, e-mail: JRN@Gate.net.

■ 17478 ■ Judee K Creations Inc.
7623 Fulton
North Hollywood, CA 91605
Phone: (818)765-4653
Free: (800)334-4363 **Fax:** (818)765-4895
Products: Costume jewelry. **SIC:** 5094 (Jewelry & Precious Stones). **Est:** 1972.

■ 17479 ■ K & J Jewelry Manufacturing
1521 24th Ave. S, No. A2
Grand Forks, ND 58201-6736
Phone: (701)746-6678
Products: Jewelry; Precious stones (gems); Precious metal. **SIC:** 5094 (Jewelry & Precious Stones). **Officers:** Hilary Klinicke, President.

■ 17480 ■ K & M Associates
PO Box 9567
Providence, RI 02940-9567
Phone: (401)461-4300 **Fax:** (401)785-9230
Products: Jewelry; Precious stones (gems). **SIC:** 5094 (Jewelry & Precious Stones). **Officers:** Joseph Bingle, Contact.

■ 17481 ■ Kabana Inc.
616 Indian School Rd.
Albuquerque, NM 87102
Phone: (505)843-9330 **Fax:** (505)843-9624
Products: Jewelry. **SIC:** 5094 (Jewelry & Precious Stones). **Sales:** $6,000,000 (2000). **Emp:** 499. **Officers:** Stavros Eleftheriou.

■ 17482 ■ William J. Kappel Wholesale Co.
535 Liberty Ave.
Pittsburgh, PA 15222
Phone: (412)471-6400
Products: Jewelry. **SIC:** 5094 (Jewelry & Precious Stones). **Sales:** $25,000,000 (1992). **Emp:** 100. **Officers:** William D. Kappel, President.

■ 17483 ■ Kardas/Jelinek Gemstones
52 Fisher Rd.
Great Falls, MT 59405-8114
Phone: (406)454-1138
Products: Jewelry; Precious stones (gems); Precious metal. **SIC:** 5094 (Jewelry & Precious Stones). **Officers:** Kathryn Jelinek, Owner.

■ 17484 ■ Karmily Gem Corp.
580 5th Ave.
New York, NY 10036-4793
Phone: (212)354-1828
Free: (800)933-GEMS **Fax:** (212)840-6178
Products: Jewelry; including diamonds, rubies, sapphires, and emeralds. **SIC:** 5094 (Jewelry & Precious Stones). **Est:** 1975. **Emp:** 49.

■ 17485 ■ Richard W. Kaye Inc.
760 Market
San Francisco, CA 94102-2401
Phone: (415)781-0524 **Fax:** (415)781-0526
Products: Jewelry. **SIC:** 5094 (Jewelry & Precious Stones). **Emp:** 4.

■ 17486 ■ Kaye Pearl Co.
4131 58th St.
Woodside, NY 11377
Phone: (718)446-7720 **Fax:** (718)899-7229
E-mail: fshncraft@aol.com
Products: Jewelry. **SIC:** 5094 (Jewelry & Precious Stones). **Est:** 1952. **Sales:** $2,000,000 (2000). **Emp:** 30. **Officers:** Robert Bassoff, President; Jack Partubio, VP of Sales.

■ 17487 ■ Kenilworth Creations Inc.
PO Box 9541
Providence, RI 02940-9541
Phone: (401)739-1458 **Fax:** (401)732-4356
Products: Jewelry; Precious stones (gems). **SIC:** 5094 (Jewelry & Precious Stones). **Officers:** Sheila Ekeblad, President.

■ 17488 ■ Rob E. Kennedy
1334 S Las Vegas
Las Vegas, NV 89104-1103
Phone: (702)386-2998
Products: Jewelry; Precious stones (gems). **SIC:** 5094 (Jewelry & Precious Stones). **Officers:** Rob Kennedy, Owner.

■ 17489 ■ Key Imports
1621 Braman Ave.
Ft. Myers, FL 33901
Phone: (941)337-0889 **Fax:** (941)337-0889
Products: Jewelry. **SIC:** 5094 (Jewelry & Precious Stones).

■ 17490 ■ Khalsa Trading Co. Inc.
PO Box 36930
Albuquerque, NM 87176-6930
Phone: (505)255-8278 **Fax:** (505)255-3877
Products: Sterling silver jewelry; Native American jewelry. **SIC:** 5094 (Jewelry & Precious Stones). **Est:** 1981. **Emp:** 12. **Officers:** Gurubachan Khalsa, President. **Alternate Name:** Karin #Feeney.

■ 17491 ■ Kim International Mfg., L.P.
14840 Landmark Blvd., No. 310
Dallas, TX 75240
Phone: (972)385-7555
Free: (800)275-5555 **Fax:** (972)385-0080
Products: Fine jewelry. **SIC:** 5094 (Jewelry & Precious Stones). **Est:** 1976. **Emp:** 70. **Officers:** Bong K. Kim. **Former Name:** Kim Imports Inc.

■ 17492 ■ Kitsinian Jewelers
6743 Odessa Ave.
Van Nuys, CA 91406
Phone: (818)988-9961 **Fax:** (818)988-9592
Products: Fine jewelry. **SIC:** 5094 (Jewelry & Precious Stones). **Emp:** 49. **Officers:** S. A. Kitsinian.

■ 17493 ■ Jane Koplewitz
PO Box 4392
Burlington, VT 05406
Phone: (802)862-6336
Products: Jewelry; Precious stones (gems). **SIC:** 5094 (Jewelry & Precious Stones). **Officers:** Jane Koplewitz, Owner.

■ 17494 ■ K's Merchandise Mart Inc.
3103 N Charles St.
Decatur, IL 62526
Phone: (217)875-1440   **Fax:** (217)875-5202
Products: Jewelry; Sporting and athletic goods; Baby goods; Household supplies. **SICs:** 5094 (Jewelry & Precious Stones); 5091 (Sporting & Recreational Goods); 5199 (Nondurable Goods Nec). **Est:** 1959. **Sales:** $288,000,000 (2000). **Emp:** 1,800. **Officers:** David K. Eldridge, President; Richard B. Powers, VP & CFO; Don Ouellette, VP of Marketing; Ken Greenwell, Dir. of Systems; Jan Baughman, Office Mgr.

■ 17495 ■ S.J. Kurman & Co.
175 5th Ave.
New York, NY 10010
Phone: (212)677-7664   **Fax:** (212)460-8359
Products: Earrings, bracelets, and necklaces. **SIC:** 5094 (Jewelry & Precious Stones).

■ 17496 ■ L.A. Silver
640 S Hill St., Booth H24
Los Angeles, CA 90014
Phone: (213)624-8669   **Fax:** (213)624-5221
Products: Silver jewelry. **SIC:** 5094 (Jewelry & Precious Stones).

■ 17497 ■ Lapis Lazuli Jewelry Distributors
860 Worcester Rd.
Framingham, MA 01702-5260
Phone: (508)875-2836
Products: Jewelry. **SIC:** 5094 (Jewelry & Precious Stones).

■ 17498 ■ S. LaRose, Inc.
3223 Yanceyville St.
PO Box 21208
Greensboro, NC 27420
Phone: (336)621-1936
Free: (800)537-4513   **Fax:** (336)621-0706
E-mail: info@SLaRose.com
URL: http://www.SlaRose.com
Products: Watches; Clocks; Parts; Movements; Tools. **SIC:** 5094 (Jewelry & Precious Stones). **Est:** 1936. **Emp:** 45. **Officers:** James S. Laing, President, e-mail: JimLaing@SLaRose.com; Rick Dunnuck, Vice President, e-mail: Rdunnuck@SLaRose.com; Jane L. Laing, CEO.

■ 17499 ■ Lasting Impressions Inc.
Box 22065, Dept. LH
Orlando, FL 32830
Phone: (407)263-6883
Products: Costume jewelry and related gift items. **SIC:** 5094 (Jewelry & Precious Stones). **Est:** 1980.

■ 17500 ■ Lata Export and Import
1114 S Main St.
Los Angeles, CA 90015
Phone: (213)749-4378   **Fax:** (213)749-1439
Products: Jewelry, including costume, ethnic, and semi-precious; Flags; Caps; Findings. **SICs:** 5094 (Jewelry & Precious Stones); 5099 (Durable Goods Nec).

■ 17501 ■ Lavdas Jewelry Ltd.
3671 E 12 Mile Rd.
Warren, MI 48092
Phone: (810)751-8275   **Fax:** (810)751-4129
Products: Fine jewelry. **SIC:** 5094 (Jewelry & Precious Stones). **Est:** 1979. **Sales:** $11,000,000 (2000). **Emp:** 20. **Officers:** Nick Lavdas, Owner.

■ 17502 ■ Victor H. Levy Inc.
1355 S Flower St.
Los Angeles, CA 90015
Phone: (213)749-8247   **Fax:** (213)744-0626
Products: Costume jewelry. **SIC:** 5094 (Jewelry & Precious Stones). **Est:** 1951. **Sales:** $3,000,000 (2000). **Emp:** 30. **Officers:** May Fine, CEO; Gary M. Fine, President.

■ 17503 ■ Loews Corp.
667 Madison Ave.
New York, NY 10021-8087
Phone: (212)545-2000   **Fax:** (212)545-2525
Products: Watches. **SIC:** 5094 (Jewelry & Precious Stones). **Sales:** $69,577,100,000 (2000). **Emp:** 35,900. **Officers:** Laurence A. Tisch, CEO & Chairman of the Board; Peter W. Keegan, Sr. VP & CFO.

■ 17504 ■ Longhill Partners Inc.
PO Box 237
Woodstock, VT 05091-0237
Phone: (802)457-4000   **Fax:** (802)457-4004
Products: Jewelry and precious stones; Spirituality and Jewish enlightenment books. **SICs:** 5094 (Jewelry & Precious Stones); 5192 (Books, Periodicals & Newspapers). **Officers:** Stuart Matlins, President.

■ 17505 ■ Lory's West Inc.
314 S Beverly Dr.
Beverly Hills, CA 90212
Phone: (310)551-1212   **Fax:** (310)551-0519
Products: Diamond, silver, and gold jewelry; Picture frames; Costume jewelry. **SIC:** 5094 (Jewelry & Precious Stones). **Est:** 1962. **Sales:** $13,000,000 (2000). **Emp:** 40. **Officers:** Bruce Faber, President.

■ 17506 ■ Lyles-DeGrazier Co.
PO Box 58263
Dallas, TX 75258
Phone: (214)747-3558
Products: Jewelry. **SIC:** 5094 (Jewelry & Precious Stones). **Est:** 1949. **Sales:** $5,000,000 (2000). **Emp:** 10. **Officers:** Scott Polk, President.

■ 17507 ■ Magic Novelty Company Inc.
308 Dyckman St.
New York, NY 10034
Phone: (212)304-2777   **Fax:** (212)567-2809
E-mail: sales@magicnovelty.com
URL: http://www.magicnovelty.com
Products: Jewelers' findings. **SIC:** 5094 (Jewelry & Precious Stones). **Est:** 1940. **Sales:** $10,000,000 (1999). **Emp:** 100. **Officers:** Alex Neuburger; Stephen Neuburger; Steven Lastella, Sales & Customer Service Contact.

■ 17508 ■ Maine Entrepreneurs Group
19 Cottage St.
Portland, ME 04103-4413
Phone: (207)772-8967   **Fax:** (207)772-8720
Products: Sugar; American lumber; Jewelry; Precious stones. **SICs:** 5094 (Jewelry & Precious Stones); 5141 (Groceries—General Line); 5031 (Lumber, Plywood & Millwork). **Officers:** P. Vachon, President.

■ 17509 ■ Skip Maisel Inc.
510 Central Ave. SW
Albuquerque, NM 87102-3114
Phone: (505)242-6526   **Fax:** (505)242-8450
Products: Jewelry; Natural precious and semi-precious stones; Silver ore. **SIC:** 5094 (Jewelry & Precious Stones). **Officers:** Albert Maisel, President.

■ 17510 ■ Majesti Watch Company Inc.
70 W 36th St.
New York, NY 10018
Phone: (212)239-0444   **Fax:** (212)629-4371
E-mail: jpiontnica@aol.com
Products: Watches. **SIC:** 5094 (Jewelry & Precious Stones). **Est:** 1954. **Sales:** $6,000,000 (2000). **Emp:** 49. **Officers:** Joseph Piontnica, President; Jack Piontnica, Dir. of Sales; Aliza Piontnica, Dir. of Data Processing.

■ 17511 ■ Marcel Watch Corp.
200 Meadowlands Pkwy.
Secaucus, NJ 07094-2302
Phone: (201)330-5600
Free: (800)422-6053   **Fax:** (973)645-9247
Products: Clocks; Watches and parts. **SIC:** 5094 (Jewelry & Precious Stones). **Est:** 1959. **Sales:** $10,000,000 (2000). **Emp:** 25. **Officers:** Dan Bob, Warehouse Mgr.

■ 17512 ■ Gina Marie Sales
43 Oak Grove Blvd.
North Providence, RI 02911-2608
Phone: (401)232-0863
Products: Costume jewelry. **SIC:** 5094 (Jewelry & Precious Stones).

■ 17513 ■ Marketing Group Inc. (Harvey, Illinois)
10 S Wacker Dr. Ste. 3500
Chicago, IL 60606-7407
Phone: (708)331-0200
Products: Watches and clocks; Hats and bags; Calculators. **SICs:** 5094 (Jewelry & Precious Stones); 5099 (Durable Goods Nec). **Sales:** $21,500,000 (1994). **Emp:** 45. **Officers:** Michael D. Gurley, President; John A. Pionke, Controller.

■ 17514 ■ Maryland Import/Export, Inc.
4248 Cherry Valley Dr.
Olney, MD 20832
Phone: (301)774-2960   **Fax:** (301)774-8230
Products: Jewelry; Dairy products. **SICs:** 5094 (Jewelry & Precious Stones); 5143 (Dairy Products Except Dried or Canned). **Officers:** Bruce Ensor, President.

■ 17515 ■ Mask-Off Corp.
582 Manville Rd.
Woonsocket, RI 02895-5550
Phone: (401)232-0100   **Fax:** (401)232-0103
Products: Jewelry; Precious stones (gems). **SIC:** 5094 (Jewelry & Precious Stones). **Officers:** Anthony Fandetti, President.

■ 17516 ■ Frank Mastoloni and Sons Inc.
608 5th Ave.
New York, NY 10020
Phone: (212)757-7278   **Fax:** (212)582-0884
Products: Cultured pearls. **SIC:** 5094 (Jewelry & Precious Stones). **Sales:** $25,000,000 (2000). **Emp:** 35. **Officers:** Francis J. Mastoloni Sr., President; Raymond L. Mastoloni Sr., Treasurer & Secty.; Edward J. Mastoloni, Vice President.

■ 17517 ■ Mathews Enterprises
2345 Filbert St., Ste. 204
San Francisco, CA 94123
Phone: (415)563-1595   **Fax:** (415)563-0526
Products: Jewelry. **SIC:** 5094 (Jewelry & Precious Stones). **Est:** 1976. **Sales:** $500,000 (2000). **Officers:** Philip D. Mathews, Owner.

■ 17518 ■ Mayers Jewelry Company Inc.
2004 Grant St.
Hollywood, FL 33020-3546
Phone: (954)921-1422   **Fax:** (954)921-1441
Products: Jewelry. **SIC:** 5094 (Jewelry & Precious Stones). **Sales:** $10,000,000 (2000). **Emp:** 80. **Officers:** Sam Ziefer.

■ 17519 ■ McCrone Associates
PO Box 8439
Warwick, RI 02888-0597
Phone: (401)738-3115
Products: Jewelry; Precious stones (gems). **SIC:** 5094 (Jewelry & Precious Stones). **Officers:** Leo McCrone, President.

■ 17520 ■ Merchants Overseas Inc.
41 Bassett St.
Providence, RI 02903-4633
Phone: (401)331-5603
Free: (800)333-4144   **Fax:** (401)331-5430
E-mail: mopvd@ids.net
Products: Jewelry. **SIC:** 5094 (Jewelry & Precious Stones). **Est:** 1949. **Officers:** Stanley J. Wachtenheim, President.

■ 17521 ■ Merchants Overseas Inc.
41 Bassett St.
Providence, RI 02903-4633
Phone: (401)331-5603
Free: (800)333-4144   **Fax:** (401)331-5430
Products: Jewelry. **SIC:** 5094 (Jewelry & Precious Stones).

■ 17522 ■ **Merrimack Jewelers Inc.**
356 Daniel Webster Hwy.
Merrimack, NH 03054-4131
Phone: (603)424-3434
Products: Jewelry; Precious stones (gems). **SIC:** 5094
(Jewelry & Precious Stones). **Officers:** George Slaybe,
President.

■ 17523 ■ **Henry Meyer Diamond Company**
Inc.
400 Madison Ave.
New York, NY 10017
Phone: (212)644-1114 **Fax:** (212)755-0371
Products: Diamonds. **SIC:** 5094 (Jewelry & Precious
Stones). **Est:** 1914. **Sales:** $3,000,000 (2000). **Emp:** 5.
Officers: Charles A. Meyer, President.

■ 17524 ■ **MGD Enterprises**
PO Box 412
Midwest, WY 82643-0412
Phone: (307)437-9216
Products: Jewelry; Precious stones (gems). **SIC:** 5094
(Jewelry & Precious Stones). **Officers:** David Rector,
Owner.

■ 17525 ■ **Missoula Gold & Silver Exchange**
2020 Brooks St.
Missoula, MT 59801-6646
Phone: (406)728-5786 **Fax:** (406)543-5450
Products: Jewelry; Precious stones (gems); Precious
metal. **SIC:** 5094 (Jewelry & Precious Stones).
Officers: Kent Hakes, President.

■ 17526 ■ **J.P. Morton Company Inc.**
PO Box 741188
Los Angeles, CA 90004
Phone: (213)487-1440 **Fax:** (213)380-5350
E-mail: jpmortonco@earthlink.net
Products: Precious and semi-precious stones and
diamonds. **SIC:** 5094 (Jewelry & Precious Stones).
Est: 1954. **Sales:** $3,100,000 (2000). **Emp:** 9.
Officers: J.P. Morton, CEO; Christopher P. Morton,
Vice President.

■ 17527 ■ **H.E. Murdock Inc.**
88 Main St.
Waterville, ME 04901-6602
Phone: (207)873-7036 **Fax:** (207)872-0915
Products: Jewelry; Precious stones (gems); Precious
metal. **SIC:** 5094 (Jewelry & Precious Stones).
Officers: Jeffery Corey, President.

■ 17528 ■ **C.S. Nacol Jewelry**
3703 Twin City Hwy.
Port Arthur, TX 77642
Phone: (409)962-8522
Products: Jewelry. **SIC:** 5094 (Jewelry & Precious
Stones). **Est:** 1896. **Sales:** $11,000,000 (2000). **Emp:**
100. **Officers:** Charles S. Nacol, President; Susie
Sonnier, Controller; Habeeb Nacol, VP of Marketing.

■ 17529 ■ **Nakai Trading Co.**
8605 Central Ave. NW
Albuquerque, NM 87121-2102
Phone: (505)836-1053 **Fax:** (505)836-1056
E-mail: nakai8605@gateway.net
Products: Handmade Indian jewelry. **SIC:** 5094
(Jewelry & Precious Stones). **Est:** 1974. **Sales:**
$1,000,000 (2000). **Emp:** 15. **Officers:** Gilo Lopez,
Partner; Grace Brawnek, President.

■ 17530 ■ **Narragansett Trading Co. Ltd.**
PO Box 7322
Warwick, RI 02886-8545
Phone: (401)884-2985 **Fax:** (401)885-7703
Products: Natural precious and semi-precious stones.
SIC: 5094 (Jewelry & Precious Stones). **Est:** 1984.
Sales: $1,000,000 (2000). **Emp:** 6. **Officers:** Richard
H. Volk, President.

■ 17531 ■ **Navajo Manufacturing Co.**
5801 Logan St., AW8
Denver, CO 80216
Phone: (303)292-3090
Free: (800)525-5097 **Fax:** (303)298-8059
E-mail: catalog@navajomfg.com
Products: Native American jewelry, t-shirts, and
handcrafts. **SIC:** 5094 (Jewelry & Precious Stones).
Est: 1978. **Emp:** 70. **Officers:** Larry Rupp, President;

Gordon Levy, CEO; Phil Britton, Sales/Marketing
Contact; Bob Hodge, Sales/Marketing Contact.

■ 17532 ■ **Stephen L. Nevitt**
210 Bonnyvale Rd.
Brattleboro, VT 05301-8521
Phone: (802)257-4442
Products: Jewelry and precious stones. **SIC:** 5094
(Jewelry & Precious Stones). **Officers:** Stephen Nevitt,
Owner.

■ 17533 ■ **Nice Time & Electronics Inc.**
1140 Broadway, Ste. 808
New York, NY 10001
Phone: (212)481-0251 **Fax:** (212)481-0259
Products: Watches. **SIC:** 5094 (Jewelry & Precious
Stones).

■ 17534 ■ **North American Investment**
Services
PO Box 35733
Albuquerque, NM 87176-5733
Phone: (505)888-0561 **Fax:** (505)260-3105
Products: Precious metals. **SIC:** 5094 (Jewelry &
Precious Stones). **Officers:** Ron Brown, Owner.

■ 17535 ■ **North American Treasures Inc.**
PO Box 4338
Helena, MT 59604-4338
Phone: (406)227-8256
Products: Jewelry; Precious stones (gems). **SIC:** 5094
(Jewelry & Precious Stones). **Officers:** Larry Lafrance,
President.

■ 17536 ■ **North American Watch Corp.**
125 Chubb Ave.
Lyndhurst, NJ 07071
Phone: (201)460-4800 **Fax:** (201)460-8384
Products: Watches. **SIC:** 5094 (Jewelry & Precious
Stones). **Est:** 1961. **Sales:** $100,000,000 (2000). **Emp:**
543. **Officers:** E. Grinberg, President; B. Diamond,
CFO.

■ 17537 ■ **Odyssey Jewelry Inc.**
1920 Westminster St.
Providence, RI 02909-2802
Phone: (401)421-2230
Free: (800)535-9179 **Fax:** (401)831-0835
E-mail: odysseyjewelry@juno.com
URL: http://www.wholesalecentral.com/odyssey
Products: Costume jewelry. **SIC:** 5094 (Jewelry &
Precious Stones). **Est:** 1974. **Officers:** Robert Di Iorio,
President; Peter Di Iorio, Sales/Marketing Contact.

■ 17538 ■ **Olympia Gold Inc.**
11540 Wiles Rd., Ste. 2
Coral Springs, FL 33076
Phone: (954)345-6991
Free: (800)395-7774 **Fax:** (954)344-4360
E-mail: permagold@aol.com
URL: http://www.olympiagold.com
Products: Jewelry. **SIC:** 5094 (Jewelry & Precious
Stones). **Est:** 1989. **Sales:** $2,000,000 (2000). **Emp:**
10. **Officers:** Skip Wilson, CEO.

■ 17539 ■ **Orient Express**
814 Branch Ave.
Providence, RI 02904-1707
Phone: (401)751-7056 **Fax:** (401)272-2887
Products: Costume jewelry. Hair accessories. **SICs:**
5094 (Jewelry & Precious Stones); 5131 (Piece Goods
& Notions). **Est:** 1983. **Emp:** 37. **Officers:** Bernard
Maceroni, Managing Dir.

■ 17540 ■ **Original Designs Inc.**
44 40 11th
Long Island City, NY 11101-5105
Phone: (718)706-8989
Free: (800)458-4300 **Fax:** (718)392-0774
Products: Jewelry, made of platinum metals and karat
gold. **SIC:** 5094 (Jewelry & Precious Stones). **Est:**
1936. **Sales:** $35,000,000 (2000). **Emp:** 260. **Officers:**
Victor Weinman.

■ 17541 ■ **OroAmerica Inc.**
443 N Varney St.
Burbank, CA 91502
Phones: (818)848-5555 800-423-5284
Free: (800)423-2246 **Fax:** (818)841-4342
Products: Jewelry, made of platinum metals and karat
gold. **SIC:** 5094 (Jewelry & Precious Stones). **Sales:**
$180,000,000 (2000). **Emp:** 300.

■ 17542 ■ **Parkville Imports Inc.**
1019 N Stadium Dr.
Tempe, AZ 85281
Phone: (602)921-8485
Free: (800)627-3051 **Fax:** (602)921-9213
Products: Accessories; Jewelry; Novelties. **SICs:** 5094
(Jewelry & Precious Stones); 5092 (Toys & Hobby
Goods & Supplies). **Officers:** Barry Greenberg,
President.

■ 17543 ■ **Ronald Hayes Pearson Inc.**
RR 1, Box 158
Deer Isle, ME 04627-9709
Phone: (207)348-2535 **Fax:** (207)348-2535
E-mail: cahecker@media2.hypernet.com
Products: Jewelry. **SIC:** 5094 (Jewelry & Precious
Stones). **Est:** 1948. **Emp:** 3. **Officers:** Carolyn A.
Hecker, President.

■ 17544 ■ **S.A. Peck & Co.**
55 E Washington Blvd.
Chicago, IL 60602-2103
Phone: (312)977-0300
Free: (800)922-0090 **Fax:** (312)977-0324
E-mail: sapeck@interaccess.com
URL: http://www.sapeck.com
Products: Jewelry. **SIC:** 5094 (Jewelry & Precious
Stones). **Est:** 1922. **Sales:** $10,000,000 (2000). **Emp:**
30. **Officers:** Joseph Murphy, President; Michael
Holtzman, Vice President.

■ 17545 ■ **Ed Pereira Inc.**
1725 Pontiac Ave.
Cranston, RI 02920-4477
Phone: (401)397-4200 **Fax:** (401)397-5804
Products: Jewelry; Precious stones (gems). **SIC:** 5094
(Jewelry & Precious Stones). **Officers:** Joan Pereira,
President.

■ 17546 ■ **Perm Inc.**
7575 SW 134th St.
Miami, FL 33156-6843
Phone: (305)591-2366 **Fax:** (305)591-9358
Products: Jewelry. **SIC:** 5094 (Jewelry & Precious
Stones). **Emp:** 49.

■ 17547 ■ **Persin and Robbin Jewelers**
24 S Dunton St.
Arlington Heights, IL 60005
Phone: (847)253-7900 **Fax:** (847)253-2953
Products: Gold jewelry including bracelets, rings,
necklaces, and chains. **SIC:** 5094 (Jewelry & Precious
Stones). **Est:** 1958. **Sales:** $5,000,000 (2000). **Emp:**
35. **Officers:** Janet Robbin, President & Treasurer.

■ 17548 ■ **Samuel Platzer Company Inc.**
31 W 47th St.
New York, NY 10036
Phone: (212)719-2000
Products: Jewelry. **SIC:** 5094 (Jewelry & Precious
Stones). **Est:** 1923. **Sales:** $3,000,000 (2000). **Emp:** 4.
Officers: David J. Platzer, President; Frances Platzer,
Finance Officer; Nancy Platzer, Dir. of Marketing.

■ 17549 ■ **Polishers & Jewelers Supply Inc.**
PO Box 3448
Providence, RI 02909-0448
Phone: (401)454-2888
Products: Jewelry; Precious stones (gems). **SIC:** 5094
(Jewelry & Precious Stones). **Officers:** Ralph Liscio,
President.

■ 17550 ■ **J.O. Pollack L.L.C.**
1700 W Irving Park Rd.
Chicago, IL 60613-2559
Phone: (773)477-2100
Free: (800)621-1904 **Fax:** (773)477-2521
E-mail: jopollack4@aol.com
URL: http://www.jopollack.com
Products: Fraternity and sorority jewelry; Nursing

jewelry. SIC: 5094 (Jewelry & Precious Stones). Est: 1900. Sales: $5,000,000 (1999). Emp: 45. Officers: Kenneth V. Hachikian, President, e-mail: kvhach@ preferredgreek.com.

■ 17551 ■ Polson's Rock Shop
2461 S Holmes Ave.
Idaho Falls, ID 83404-6971
Phone: (208)529-8184
Products: Jewelry; Precious stones (gems). SIC: 5094 (Jewelry & Precious Stones). Officers: Ivan Polson, Owner.

■ 17552 ■ Pow Wow Indian Jewelry
1821 W Hwy. 66 Ave.
Gallup, NM 87301-6805
Phone: (505)863-4426   Fax: (505)722-6433
Products: Jewelry; Precious stones (gems). SIC: 5094 (Jewelry & Precious Stones). Officers: Jim Rashid, Owner.

■ 17553 ■ Norman W. Pullen Inc.
PO Box 10600
Portland, ME 04104-0600
Phone: (207)772-2211
Products: Jewelry; Precious stones (gems); Precious metal. SIC: 5094 (Jewelry & Precious Stones). Officers: Norman Pullen, President.

■ 17554 ■ Pyramid Studios
10 State St.
Ellsworth, ME 04605
Phone: (207)667-3321
Products: Jewelry; Precious stones (gems). SIC: 5094 (Jewelry & Precious Stones). Officers: David Herrington, Owner.

■ 17555 ■ Quintel/Consort Watch Co.
44 Century Dr.
Wheeling, IL 60090
Phone: (847)541-3333
Products: Watches. SIC: 5094 (Jewelry & Precious Stones).

■ 17556 ■ Rare Coins
44 W 1st St.
Reno, NV 89501-1402
Phone: (702)322-4166
Products: Jewelry; Precious stones (gems); Precious metals bullions. SIC: 5094 (Jewelry & Precious Stones). Officers: Tony Mitchell, Owner.

■ 17557 ■ Raymond Jewelers
695 Haddon Ave.
Collingswood, NJ 08108-3722
Phone: (609)854-5186
Products: Jewelry. SIC: 5094 (Jewelry & Precious Stones). Emp: 3. Officers: Debra Wolf.

■ 17558 ■ Schweichert Reed Inc.
PO Box 245
Midlothian, VA 23113-0245
Phone: (804)794-5402   Fax: (804)794-0946
Products: Class rings. SIC: 5094 (Jewelry & Precious Stones). Officers: K Schweickert, President.

■ 17559 ■ Regency Collection Inc.
200 Northridge Dr.
Acworth, GA 30101
Phone: (770)529-4270
Free: (800)786-5756   Fax: (770)529-4268
E-mail: dbodie@mindspring.com
Products: Jewelry. SIC: 5094 (Jewelry & Precious Stones). Est: 1997. Sales: $500,000 (2000). Emp: 3. Officers: Deborah Bodie, President.

■ 17560 ■ Regency Collection Inc.
2880 Holcomb Bridge Rd., Ste. 544
Alpharetta, GA 30022
Phone: (770)650-8420
Free: (800)786-5756   Fax: (770)650-8419
Products: Jewelry. SIC: 5094 (Jewelry & Precious Stones). Sales: $500,000 (2000). Emp: 3.

■ 17561 ■ Irving Remar
22 Anson Rd.
Portland, ME 04102-2202
Phone: (207)772-8007
Products: Jewelry; Precious stones (gems). SIC: 5094

(Jewelry & Precious Stones). Officers: Irving Remar, Owner.

■ 17562 ■ Republic Jewelry & Coin Co.
212 Center St.
Auburn, ME 04210-6150
Phone: (207)782-9492   Fax: (207)782-7351
Products: Jewelry; Precious stones and metals; Diamonds. SIC: 5094 (Jewelry & Precious Stones). Officers: Daniel Cunliffe, President.

■ 17563 ■ Rhode Island Wholesale Jewelry
PO Box 19758
Johnston, RI 02919
Phone: (401)943-5980
Free: (800)422-1055   Fax: (401)943-0930
E-mail: riwholesale@aol.com
URL: http://www.wholesalejewelry4u.com
Products: Costume jewelry. SIC: 5094 (Jewelry & Precious Stones).

■ 17564 ■ William Richey Design Ltd.
20 Main St.
Camden, ME 04843-1704
Phone: (207)236-4731   Fax: (207)236-7141
Products: Jewelry and semi-precious stones. SIC: 5094 (Jewelry & Precious Stones). Officers: William Richey, President.

■ 17565 ■ Ridco Inc.
2707 Mt. Rushmore Rd.
PO Box 5600
Rapid City, SD 57701-5600
Phone: (605)343-2226   Fax: (605)343-8653
Products: Jewelry. SIC: 5094 (Jewelry & Precious Stones). Emp: 125. Officers: Jesse B. Riddle.

■ 17566 ■ RMP Enterprises Inc.
La Fonda Hotel
100 E San Francisco St.
Santa Fe, NM 87501
Phone: (505)983-5552   Fax: (505)984-1203
Products: Jewelry; Precious stones (gems). SIC: 5094 (Jewelry & Precious Stones). Officers: Robert Pettus, President.

■ 17567 ■ M.L. Roberts Inc.
8 Industrial Ln.
Johnston, RI 02919
Phone: (401)421-0600   Fax: (401)273-4970
Products: Jewelry and precious stones; Jewelers' findings. SIC: 5094 (Jewelry & Precious Stones). Officers: Michael Molk, President.

■ 17568 ■ Rocket Jewelry Box Inc.
125 E 144th St.
Bronx, NY 10451-5435
Phone: (212)292-5370   Fax: (212)402-2021
Products: Jewelry boxes. SIC: 5199 (Nondurable Goods Nec). Sales: $4,000,000 (2000). Emp: 99. Officers: Michael Kaplan.

■ 17569 ■ Roeden Inc.
PO Box 50050
Henderson, NV 89016-0050
Phone: (702)798-2800   Fax: (702)798-5137
Products: Jewelry, including wholesale custom jewelry. SIC: 5094 (Jewelry & Precious Stones). Officers: Dennis Cravero, President.

■ 17570 ■ Rolyn Inc.
189 Macklin St.
Cranston, RI 02920
Phone: (401)944-0844
Free: (800)8-CHANTE   Fax: (401)944-5040
E-mail: rolyninc@aol.com
URL: http://www.chante.com
Products: Sterling silver jewelry. SIC: 5094 (Jewelry & Precious Stones). Est: 1962. Sales: $5,000,000 (2000). Emp: 40. Officers: Douglas M. Ricci, CEO; Anthony A. Rendine, Vice President; Sheldon Jacob, Dir. of Marketing.

■ 17571 ■ Roma Chain Manufacturing
21 SE 1st Ave., Ste. 300
Miami, FL 33131
Phone: (305)374-1169
Free: (800)633-7662   Fax: (305)374-3979
E-mail: romchain@bellsouth.net
Products: Gold-filled and gold-layered jewelry. SIC: 5094 (Jewelry & Precious Stones). Est: 1985.

■ 17572 ■ Romanoff International Supply Corp.
9 Deforest St.
Amityville, NY 11701
Phone: (631)842-2400
Free: (800)221-7448   Fax: (631)842-0028
E-mail: romanoffl@aol.com
URL: http://www.romanoff.com
Products: Jewelry tools and equipment. SIC: 5094 (Jewelry & Precious Stones). Est: 1949. Sales: $10,000,000 (2000). Emp: 50. Officers: Bob Romanoff, President; Evan Douglas, CFO.

■ 17573 ■ Ronald Hayes Pearson Inc.
RR 1, Box 158
Deer Isle, ME 04627-9709
Phone: (207)348-2535   Fax: (207)348-2535
Products: Jewelry. SIC: 5094 (Jewelry & Precious Stones).

■ 17574 ■ H.M. Rose Goldsmith
801 Scalp Ave.
Johnstown, PA 15904-3314
Phone: (814)266-9430
Free: (800)338-4292   Fax: (814)269-2194
E-mail: info@hm-rose.com
URL: http://www.hmrosejewelers.com
Products: Loose colored gems, custom jewelry, and diamonds. SIC: 5094 (Jewelry & Precious Stones). Est: 1987. Emp: 49. Officers: H.M. Rose; Margie Rose.

■ 17575 ■ Royal Chain Inc.
2 W 46th Ave.
New York, NY 10036
Phone: (212)382-3340
Free: (800)622-0960   Fax: (212)730-7616
Products: Jewelry, including 14 and 10 karat gold chains, bracelets, earrings, bangles, platinum chains. SIC: 5094 (Jewelry & Precious Stones). Est: 1978. Sales: $50,000,000 (1999). Emp: 35. Officers: Paul Maroof, President; Fred Sherman, Vice President; Shaun Yafeh, Vice President.

■ 17576 ■ Royal Stones Corp.
1212 Avenue of the Americas, Ste. 2301
New York, NY 10036-1601
Phone: (212)944-2211
Free: (800)223-4166   Fax: (212)764-7025
E-mail: stoneroyal@aol.com
URL: http://www.royalstones.com
Products: Diamonds for jewelry purposes; Natural precious and semi-precious stones. SIC: 5094 (Jewelry & Precious Stones). Emp: 49. Officers: Michael Aharonoff, President.

■ 17577 ■ RTC Manufacturing
1011 S Bowen Rd.
Arlington, TX 76013-2292
Phone: (817)461-8101   Fax: (817)548-9482
Products: 14 karat gold jewelry. SIC: 5094 (Jewelry & Precious Stones). Sales: $2,000,000 (2000). Emp: 25. Officers: Don Fields.

■ 17578 ■ Ru-Mart Metal Specialties
767 Hartford Ave.
Johnston, RI 02919
Phone: (401)421-3055   Fax: (401)272-2618
Products: Metal stampings for jewelry, gifts, and crafts. SIC: 5094 (Jewelry & Precious Stones). Est: 1969. Sales: $750,000 (2000). Emp: 12. Officers: Anthony Bertoldi, President; Joseph Bertoldi, Vice President; Elaine Cyr, Dir. of Marketing.

■ 17579 ■ Ru-Mart Metal Specialties
767 Hartford Ave.
Johnston, RI 02919
Phone: (401)421-3055   Fax: (401)272-2618
Products: Jewelry. SIC: 5094 (Jewelry & Precious Stones). Sales: $800,000 (2000). Emp: 12.

■ 17580 ■ **Rubins Stone House**
36 NE 1st St., Ste. 335
Miami, FL 33132-2403
Phone: (305)374-5816 **Fax:** (305)375-0550
Products: Gemstones. **SIC:** 5094 (Jewelry & Precious Stones). **Emp:** 11.

■ 17581 ■ **Susan Ryan Jewelry**
3715 Espejo St. NE
Albuquerque, NM 87111-3430
Phone: (505)294-5275 **Fax:** (505)323-1316
E-mail: srjewelry@compuserve.com
URL: http://www.allsterling.com
Products: Costume jewelry. **SIC:** 5094 (Jewelry & Precious Stones). **Est:** 1988. **Officers:** Susan Ryan, Owner; Charles Ryan, Owner.

■ 17582 ■ **S & T Jewelers**
631 S Hill St., No. A
Los Angeles, CA 90014-1712
Phone: (213)623-1121
Free: (800)338-2128 **Fax:** (213)623-1128
Products: Jewelry. **SIC:** 5094 (Jewelry & Precious Stones). **Est:** 1982. **Emp:** 49. **Officers:** Shavel Einelhury; Tony Moreh.

■ 17583 ■ **Saettele Jewelers Inc.**
8182 Maryland Ave. 205
St. Louis, MO 63105
Phone: (314)725-8182
Products: Diamonds and gold jewelry. **SIC:** 5094 (Jewelry & Precious Stones). **Sales:** $300,000 (2000). **Emp:** 3. **Officers:** Gustave Saettele, President.

■ 17584 ■ **Sago Imports Inc.**
1140 Broadway, Ste. 707
New York, NY 10001
Phone: (212)685-2580 **Fax:** (212)689-9445
Products: Costume jewelry; Clothing. **SICs:** 5094 (Jewelry & Precious Stones); 5137 (Women's/Children's Clothing).

■ 17585 ■ **Salvors Inc.**
200 Greene St.
Key West, FL 33040
Phone: (305)325-7106
Products: Coins. **SICs:** 5094 (Jewelry & Precious Stones); 5094 (Jewelry & Precious Stones).

■ 17586 ■ **Samuels Jewelers**
320 W Kimberly Rd.
Davenport, IA 52806-5995
Phone: (319)391-4362 **Fax:** (319)391-0208
Products: Jewelry. **SIC:** 5094 (Jewelry & Precious Stones). **Emp:** 99.

■ 17587 ■ **Sanchez Fine Jewelers**
PO Box 848
Jackson, WY 83001-0848
Phone: (307)733-9439 **Fax:** (307)733-7340
Products: Jewelry; Precious stones (gems). **SIC:** 5094 (Jewelry & Precious Stones). **Officers:** Anthony Sanchez, Owner.

■ 17588 ■ **Sandaga**
1231 Broadway
New York, NY 10001
Phone: (212)532-6820 **Fax:** (212)213-6409
Products: Costume jewelry. **SIC:** 5094 (Jewelry & Precious Stones).

■ 17589 ■ **Sassounian Inc.**
404 W 7th, Ste. 614
Los Angeles, CA 90014-1613
Phones: (213)627-1206 (213)627-1206
Free: (800)544-4419 **Fax:** (213)623-6981
Products: Jewelers' materials and lapidary work. **SIC:** 5094 (Jewelry & Precious Stones). **Emp:** 49. **Officers:** Paul Sassounian, Warehouse Mgr.

■ 17590 ■ **Sausalito Craftworks**
PO Box 1792
Sausalito, CA 94966
Phone: (415)332-3392
Free: (800)332-3393 **Fax:** (415)332-2607
Products: Brass, copper, and sterling silver bracelets and earrings. **SIC:** 5094 (Jewelry & Precious Stones). **Est:** 1974.

■ 17591 ■ **Leo Schachter and Company Inc.**
579 5th Ave.
New York, NY 10017
Phone: (212)688-2000
Products: Diamonds. **SIC:** 5094 (Jewelry & Precious Stones). **Sales:** $11,000,000 (2000). **Emp:** 20. **Officers:** Leo Schachter, President.

■ 17592 ■ **E. Schreiber Inc.**
580 5th Ave.
New York, NY 10036
Phone: (212)382-0280
Products: Diamonds. **SIC:** 5094 (Jewelry & Precious Stones). **Est:** 1972. **Sales:** $20,000,000 (2000). **Emp:** 20. **Officers:** Emanuel Schreiber, President.

■ 17593 ■ **Sea Level Products International**
2815 Junipero Ave., Ste. 110
Signal Hill, CA 90806-2111
Phone: (562)985-0076
Free: (800)777-0062 **Fax:** (562)988-2920
Products: Jewelry. **SIC:** 5094 (Jewelry & Precious Stones). **Emp:** 5. **Officers:** Salvador Enciso.

■ 17594 ■ **Security Silver and Gold Exchange**
PO Box 1774
Boise, ID 83701-1774
Phone: (208)343-5050 **Free:** (800)635-5350
Products: Precious metals bullions. **SIC:** 5094 (Jewelry & Precious Stones). **Officers:** Henry Pahlas, President.

■ 17595 ■ **Seiko Corporation of America**
1111 MacArthur Blvd.
Mahwah, NJ 07430
Phone: (201)529-5730
Products: Watches and clocks. **SIC:** 5094 (Jewelry & Precious Stones). **Est:** 1970. **Sales:** $500,000,000 (2000). **Emp:** 700. **Officers:** T. Mitome, President; Ron Leyno, Sr. VP & Finance Officer; Jonathon Nettelfield, VP of Admin. & Development; John Mattaliano, VP of Information Systems; Carolyn Procopio, Dir of Human Resources.

■ 17596 ■ **Seiko Time West**
840 Apollo St., Ste. 100
El Segundo, CA 90245
Phone: (310)640-3308 **Fax:** (310)640-1017
Products: Watches and clocks. **SIC:** 5094 (Jewelry & Precious Stones). **Est:** 1971. **Sales:** $3,000,000 (2000). **Emp:** 12. **Officers:** William Saunders, Exec. VP.

■ 17597 ■ **Seville Watch Corp.**
587 5th Ave.
New York, NY 10018
Phone: (212)355-3450 **Fax:** (212)355-3720
Products: Watches. **SIC:** 5094 (Jewelry & Precious Stones). **Est:** 1980. **Sales:** $29,000,000 (2000). **Emp:** 50. **Officers:** Benny Shabtai, Owner.

■ 17598 ■ **Shil La Art Gems, Inc.**
50 W 47th, Rm. 204
New York, NY 10036-8682
Phone: (212)719-1298 **Fax:** (212)944-0128
Products: Gem stones. **SIC:** 5094 (Jewelry & Precious Stones). **Emp:** 49.

■ 17599 ■ **Shiprock Trading Post**
PO Box 906
Shiprock, NM 87420-0906
Phone: (505)368-4585 **Fax:** (505)368-5583
Products: Navajo weavings, sculptures, and jewelry. **SIC:** 5094 (Jewelry & Precious Stones). **Officers:** Jed Foutz, Owner.

■ 17600 ■ **Shirts Unlimited**
1181 Rock Blvd.
Sparks, NV 89431-0933
Phone: (702)359-8755
Products: Trophies. **SIC:** 5094 (Jewelry & Precious Stones). **Officers:** Bill Reels, Owner.

■ 17601 ■ **Shube Manufacturing Inc.**
600 Moon SE
Albuquerque, NM 87123
Phone: (505)275-7677
Free: (800)545-5082 **Fax:** (505)275-8182
E-mail: shubesmfg@aol.com
URL: http://www.shubes.com
Products: Silver jewelry; Fine pewter figurines. **SIC:** 5094 (Jewelry & Precious Stones). **Est:** 1975. **Sales:** $10,000,000 (2000). **Emp:** 200. **Officers:** Tom Kirkland, Sales Mgr.

■ 17602 ■ **Silver City**
607 S Hill St., No. 946
Los Angeles, CA 90014
Phone: (213)689-1488 **Fax:** (213)489-7922
Products: Sterling silver jewelry and watches. **SIC:** 5094 (Jewelry & Precious Stones). **Est:** 1985.

■ 17603 ■ **Silver Dust Trading Inc.**
120 W Highway 66
Gallup, NM 87301-6226
Phone: (505)722-4848 **Fax:** (505)722-4848
Products: Jewelry and precious stones, including turquoise. **SIC:** 5094 (Jewelry & Precious Stones). **Officers:** Cynthia Ferrari, President.

■ 17604 ■ **A Silver Lining Inc.**
PO Box 477
Boothbay Harbor, ME 04538-0477
Phone: (207)633-4103
Products: Jewelry; Precious stones (gems). **SIC:** 5094 (Jewelry & Precious Stones). **Officers:** Anthony Heyl, President.

■ 17605 ■ **Silver Ray**
6908 Central Ave. SE
Albuquerque, NM 87108-1855
Phone: (505)265-0444
Products: Silver and gold filled jewelry. **SIC:** 5094 (Jewelry & Precious Stones). **Officers:** Ray Quintana, Owner.

■ 17606 ■ **Silver Sun Wholesale Inc.**
2011 Central Ave. NW
Albuquerque, NM 87104-1403
Phone: (505)246-9692 **Fax:** (505)246-9719
Products: Sterling silver jewelry. **SIC:** 5094 (Jewelry & Precious Stones). **Officers:** Deanna Olson, President.

■ 17607 ■ **SilverSource**
2118 Wilshire Blvd., No. 1155
Santa Monica, CA 90403
Phone: (310)828-8922
Free: (888)925-RING **Fax:** (310)712-8873
URL: http://www.silversource.com
Products: Sterling silver jewelry with real gemstones. **SIC:** 5094 (Jewelry & Precious Stones). **Est:** 1994. **Emp:** 2. **Officers:** Charles Henry Frieder, Owner, e-mail: Charlie@silversource.com.

■ 17608 ■ **SKL Company Inc.**
511 Victor St.
Saddle Brook, NJ 07663-6118
Phone: (201)845-5566 **Fax:** (201)843-5723
Products: Jewelry; Clothing. **SICs:** 5094 (Jewelry & Precious Stones); 5137 (Women's/Children's Clothing). **Est:** 1953. **Sales:** $2,000,000 (2000). **Emp:** 8. **Officers:** Howard Levine, President; James Levine, Manager.

■ 17609 ■ **SMH (US) Inc.**
35 E 21st St.
New York, NY 10010
Phone: (212)271-1400 **Fax:** (212)505-6159
Products: Watches and clocks; Watch and clock repair. **SIC:** 5094 (Jewelry & Precious Stones). **Sales:** $200,000,000 (2000). **Emp:** 400. **Officers:** Roland Streule, CEO & President; Joe Mella, CFO.

■ 17610 ■ **Snow & Stars Corp.**
18 Delaine St.
Providence, RI 02909-2429
Phone: (401)421-4134
Products: Jewelry; Precious stones (gems); Jewelers' findings. **SIC:** 5094 (Jewelry & Precious Stones). **Officers:** Shuzo Sugano, President.

■ 17611 ■ Somersault Ltd.
PO Box 1771
New York, NY 10016
Phone: (212)213-4774
Products: Watches; Jewelry. **SIC:** 5094 (Jewelry & Precious Stones). **Sales:** $2,000,000 (2000). **Emp:** 15. **Officers:** Ken Fuld, President; Elaine Fuld, Sales Mgr.

■ 17612 ■ South Pacific Wholesale
PO Box 249
East Montpelier, VT 05651
Phone: (802)223-1354
Free: (800)336-2162 **Fax:** (802)223-4044
E-mail: sopacvt@aol.com
URL: http://www.beading.com
Products: Jewelry; Precious gems. **SIC:** 5094 (Jewelry & Precious Stones). **Est:** 1977. **Officers:** Willis Backus, Owner.

■ 17613 ■ Southern Watch Inc.
1239 Broadway, Ste. 1406
New York, NY 10001
Phone: (212)689-3995 **Fax:** (212)689-6246
Products: Watches. **SIC:** 5094 (Jewelry & Precious Stones).

■ 17614 ■ Southwestern Gold Inc.
PO Box 9083
Albuquerque, NM 87119-9083
Phone: (505)881-3636 **Fax:** (505)883-8957
Products: Jewelry and precious stones; Coins; Medals; Trophies. **SIC:** 5094 (Jewelry & Precious Stones). **Officers:** Phil Karler, Secretary.

■ 17615 ■ Southwestern Jewelry & Gifts
1117 S White Sands Blvd.
Alamogordo, NM 88310-7251
Phone: (505)437-9828
Products: Jewelry; Precious stones (gems). **SIC:** 5094 (Jewelry & Precious Stones). **Officers:** Tom Davis, President.

■ 17616 ■ W.M. Spaman Jewellers
112 W South
Kalamazoo, MI 49007-4711
Phone: (616)345-2073
Products: Jewelry. **SIC:** 5094 (Jewelry & Precious Stones). **Est:** 1950. **Emp:** 49. **Officers:** Richard Emig, President.

■ 17617 ■ Samuel Spil Co.
Box 220074
Charlotte, NC 28222
Phone: (704)364-3051
Free: (800)858-1362 **Fax:** (704)364-9458
Products: Gold jewelry. **SIC:** 5094 (Jewelry & Precious Stones).

■ 17618 ■ Stange Co.
2324 Weldon Pkwy.
St. Louis, MO 63146
Phone: (314)432-2000
Free: (800)432-3307 **Fax:** (314)432-3308
Products: Jewelry. **SIC:** 5094 (Jewelry & Precious Stones). **Est:** 1919. **Sales:** $2,000,000 (2000). **Emp:** 25. **Officers:** David P. Bouchein; James L. Wilhite.

■ 17619 ■ Stanley-Lawrence Co.
2535 S Fairfax Ave.
Culver City, CA 90232
Phone: (562)933-7136 **Fax:** (562)933-3245
Products: Fine jewelry and gifts. **SIC:** 5094 (Jewelry & Precious Stones). **Est:** 1922. **Sales:** $1,000,000 (2000). **Emp:** 10. **Officers:** Lawrence Hartman, President; Steve Hartman, Exec. VP of Finance.

■ 17620 ■ Star Jewelry Enterprises Inc.
1914 Westminster St.
Providence, RI 02909-2802
Phone: (401)751-8335
Products: Jewelry; Precious stones (gems). **SIC:** 5094 (Jewelry & Precious Stones). **Officers:** Kevin Montella, President.

■ 17621 ■ Henri Stern Watch Agency Inc.
1 Rockefeller Plz.
New York, NY 10020
Phone: (212)581-0870
Products: Watches. **SIC:** 5094 (Jewelry & Precious Stones). **Est:** 1859. **Sales:** $5,000,000 (2000). **Emp:** 20. **Officers:** Werner Sonn, CEO; Hank Edelman, President.

■ 17622 ■ David G. Steven Inc.
663 5th Ave.
New York, NY 10022
Phone: (212)593-0444
Products: Men's and women's watches. **SIC:** 5094 (Jewelry & Precious Stones). **Sales:** $25,000,000 (1994). **Emp:** 100. **Officers:** Steven P. Kaiser, President; Robert Dembner, CFO.

■ 17623 ■ H.S. Strygler Company Inc.
595 Madison Ave.
New York, NY 10022
Phone: (212)758-4100 **Fax:** (212)758-4128
Products: Jewelry, including stones, semi-precious stones, and diamonds. **SIC:** 5094 (Jewelry & Precious Stones). **Est:** 1937. **Sales:** $7,000,000 (2000). **Emp:** 13. **Officers:** H.S. Strygler, President; Rosa Strygler, Treasurer.

■ 17624 ■ The Sultan Co.
3049 Ualena St., No. 14
Honolulu, HI 96819-1942
Phone: (808)923-4971 **Fax:** (808)923-4970
Products: Jewelry. **SIC:** 5094 (Jewelry & Precious Stones). **Sales:** $28,000,000 (2000). **Emp:** 300. **Officers:** Edward D. Sultan Jr., Chairman of the Board; Harold E. Johnson, President.

■ 17625 ■ Sun Fashion Designs Inc.
PO Box 10745
Prescott, AZ 86304
Phone: (520)778-9585
Free: (800)398-7802 **Fax:** (520)778-9587
E-mail: sfd@primenet.com
Products: Gold-plated and silver-bonded jewelry; Sterling silver jewelry; Costume jewelry. **SIC:** 5094 (Jewelry & Precious Stones). **Est:** 1976. **Sales:** $4,500,000 (2000). **Emp:** 25. **Officers:** Joe Witck, President & Owner.

■ 17626 ■ Sun Sales
California Mart, Ste. A-988
110 E 9th St.
Los Angeles, CA 90079
Phone: (213)489-9739 **Fax:** (213)489-1882
Products: Fashion accessories, including hair pieces and costume jewelry; Sterling silver jewelry; Jewelry design. **SICs:** 5094 (Jewelry & Precious Stones); 5199 (Nondurable Goods Nec).

■ 17627 ■ Sunwest Silver Co.
324 Lomas Blvd. NW
Albuquerque, NM 87102
Phone: (505)243-3781 **Fax:** (505)843-6183
Products: Jewelry. **SIC:** 5094 (Jewelry & Precious Stones). **Sales:** $2,000,000 (2000). **Emp:** 49. **Officers:** Ernest Montoya.

■ 17628 ■ Swedes Sales
RR 1 Box 16
Raynesford, MT 59469
Phone: (406)735-4430
Products: Jewelry. **SIC:** 5094 (Jewelry & Precious Stones). **Officers:** Lawrence Malmberg, Owner.

■ 17629 ■ S.A. Swift Ltd.
PO Box 111
Waterville, ME 04903-0111
Phone: (207)872-2078 **Fax:** (207)872-6736
Products: Sterling silver jewelry. **SIC:** 5094 (Jewelry & Precious Stones). **Officers:** Stephen Swift, President.

■ 17630 ■ Tacoa Inc.
385 5th Ave., Ste. 700
New York, NY 10016-2203
Phone: (212)889-5497
Free: (800)833-8144 **Fax:** (212)545-1559
Products: Jewelry. **SIC:** 5094 (Jewelry & Precious Stones). **Emp:** 75.

■ 17631 ■ Ellis Tanner Trading Co.
1980 Hwy. 602
Gallup, NM 87305-0636
Phone: (505)722-7776 **Fax:** (505)722-4144
E-mail: etanner@cia-g.com
URL: http://www.cia-g.com/etanner
Products: Jewelry; Precious stones (gems). **SIC:** 5094 (Jewelry & Precious Stones). **Officers:** Ellis Tanner, President.

■ 17632 ■ Taramax U.S.A., Inc.
600 Warren Ave.
Spring Lake Heights, NJ 07762
Phone: (732)282-0300 **Fax:** (732)282-0404
Products: Watches. **SIC:** 5094 (Jewelry & Precious Stones). **Est:** 1993. **Emp:** 20. **Officers:** Thomas Venables, President.

■ 17633 ■ Taxor Inc.
1201 W Foothill Blvd.
Azusa, CA 91702
Phone: (626)969-2688
Free: (800)282-8332 **Fax:** (626)969-2688
E-mail: watches@taxor.com
URL: http://www.taxor.com
Products: Watches. **SIC:** 5094 (Jewelry & Precious Stones).

■ 17634 ■ Teneff Jewelry Inc.
W 510 Riverside Ave., Ste. 303
Spokane, WA 99201
Phone: (509)747-1038
Products: 14-karat gold jewelry. **SIC:** 5094 (Jewelry & Precious Stones). **Est:** 1945. **Sales:** $1,000,000 (2000). **Emp:** 22. **Officers:** Steven Teneff, President.

■ 17635 ■ Terryberry Co.
2033 Oak Industrial Dr. NE
Grand Rapids, MI 49505-6011
Phone: (616)458-1391
Free: (800)253-0882 **Fax:** (616)458-5292
Products: Jewelry. **SIC:** 5094 (Jewelry & Precious Stones). **Sales:** $15,000,000 (2000). **Emp:** 120. **Officers:** George Byam.

■ 17636 ■ Thunderbird Silver Co.
4250 E Main St., Ste. 105E
Farmington, NM 87402-8635
Phone: (505)327-1696 **Fax:** (505)327-1696
Products: Jeweler supplies, including sheet metal, wires, beading supplies, sterling silver, nickel silver, and brass. **SIC:** 5094 (Jewelry & Precious Stones). **Officers:** Randy Garrett, Owner.

■ 17637 ■ Timco Jewelers Corp.
59 Center St.
Rutland, VT 05701
Phone: (802)773-3377
Products: Jewelry; Precious stones (gems). **SIC:** 5094 (Jewelry & Precious Stones). **Officers:** Tim Schneller, President.

■ 17638 ■ Time Service Inc.
245 23rd St.
Toledo, OH 43624
Phone: (419)241-4181
Free: (800)537-0260 **Fax:** (419)241-4594
Products: Jewelry stores. **SIC:** 5094 (Jewelry & Precious Stones). **Sales:** $18,000,000 (2000). **Emp:** 400. **Officers:** Lawrence S. Goldberg, President; Arthur Geiger, Treasurer.

■ 17639 ■ Tin-Nee-Ann Trading Co.
923 Cerrillos Rd.
Santa Fe, NM 87504-0566
Phone: (505)988-1630
Free: (800)255-5491 **Fax:** (505)988-2938
E-mail: tinneeann2@aol.com
Products: Jewelry; Indian arts; Trophy mounts. **SIC:** 5094 (Jewelry & Precious Stones). **Est:** 1974. **Officers:** Dee Christen, Owner.

■ 17640 ■ Todisco Jewelry Inc.
30-00 47th Ave.
Long Island City, NY 11101
Phone: (212)997-1963 **Fax:** (718)784-7366
Products: Jewelry, including rings, earrings, and pendants. **SIC:** 5094 (Jewelry & Precious Stones). **Emp:** 75. **Officers:** Frank Todisco.

■ 17641 ■ Tool Craft Inc.
767 Hartford Ave.
Johnston, RI 02919
Phone: (401)521-9630 Fax: (401)521-6502
Products: Jewelry findings and stampings. SIC: 5094 (Jewelry & Precious Stones). Est: 1969. Sales: $1,300,000 (2000). Emp: 20. Officers: Anthony Bertoldi, President; Joseph Bertoldi, Vice President; Elaine Cye, Dir. of Marketing.

■ 17642 ■ Touch Adjust Clip Co. Inc.
1687 Roosevelt Ave.
Bohemia, NY 11716-1428
Phone: (516)589-3077
Free: (888)571-8222 Fax: (516)589-7489
E-mail: touchajust@aol.com
URL: http://www.mjsa.polygon.net/~10530
Products: Jeweler's findings and materials. SIC: 5094 (Jewelry & Precious Stones). Est: 1965. Sales: $2,500,000 (2000). Emp: 28. Officers: Richard Haug; Frank Grande, Sales/Marketing Contact; Susan Angstasia, Customer Service Contact.

■ 17643 ■ Troica Enterprise Inc.
241 5th Ave., Ste. 402
New York, NY 10016
Phone: (212)686-7777 Fax: (212)686-6732
Products: Watches and clocks. SIC: 5094 (Jewelry & Precious Stones).

■ 17644 ■ Tryon Mercantile Inc.
790 Madison Ave.
New York, NY 10021
Phone: (212)570-4180 Fax: (212)772-1286
Products: Diamond/jewelry consultants and jewelry auction analysts offering expertise on retail sales development and forecasting. Industries served: diamonds, jewelry, and auctions worldwide. SIC: 5094 (Jewelry & Precious Stones). Emp: 1.

■ 17645 ■ Turquoise World
2933 San Mateo Blvd. NE
Albuquerque, NM 87110-3156
Phone: (505)881-6219
Products: Jewelry; Precious stones (gems). SIC: 5094 (Jewelry & Precious Stones). Officers: Monte Carrico, Owner.

■ 17646 ■ Universal Jewelers & Trading Co.
6900 Central Ave. SE
Albuquerque, NM 87108-1855
Phone: (505)255-2225 Fax: (505)262-0081
Products: Sterling silver; Indian and southwestern jewelry. SIC: 5094 (Jewelry & Precious Stones). Est: 1975. Officers: Norman Assed, Owner. Former Name: Universal Jewelers Inc.

■ 17647 ■ Vitriesse Glass Studio
4 Andover Rd.
PO Box 23
Weston, VT 05161
Phone: (802)824-6634 Fax: (802)824-6644
Products: Glass beaded jewelry. SIC: 5094 (Jewelry & Precious Stones). Est: 1982. Emp: 12. Officers: Lucy Bergamini, Owner.

■ 17648 ■ Waldeck Jewelers
9817 Acoma Rd. SE
Albuquerque, NM 87123-3301
Phone: (505)299-2227
Free: (800)688-9999 Fax: (505)296-0333
Products: Jewelry. SIC: 5094 (Jewelry & Precious Stones). Est: 1972. Sales: $2,000,000 (2000). Emp: 49. Officers: Steve Waldeck, President; Steve Wilkins, Vice President.

■ 17649 ■ Waliga Imports and Sales Inc.
1467 Atwood Ave.
Johnston, RI 02919-7704
Phone: (401)272-6777 Fax: (401)274-0920
Products: Jewelry, including precious stones, custom jewelry, and costume jewelry. SIC: 5094 (Jewelry & Precious Stones). Est: 1974. Emp: 21. Officers: William Waliga, President.

■ 17650 ■ George Walton's Gold Diamond Co.
4300 Old Seward Hwy.
Anchorage, AK 99503-6034
Phone: (907)562-2571 Fax: (907)562-7778
Products: Jewelry; Precious stones (gems); Precious metal. SIC: 5094 (Jewelry & Precious Stones). Officers: George Walton, President.

■ 17651 ■ Watches
401 S Los Angeles St. 3
Los Angeles, CA 90013
Phone: (213)680-7733 Fax: (213)680-9193
Products: Watches. SIC: 5094 (Jewelry & Precious Stones).

■ 17652 ■ Webster Watch Company Associates LLC
44 E 32nd St.
New York, NY 10016
Phone: (212)889-3560
Free: (800)289-8963 Fax: (212)213-2649
E-mail: wwc1@aol.com
Products: Watches. SIC: 5094 (Jewelry & Precious Stones). Est: 1956. Sales: $10,000,000 (1999). Emp: 25. Officers: J. Robbins, President, e-mail: julesr@websterwatch.com; David Robbins, CFO, e-mail: davidr@websterwatch.com; Linda Robbins, VP of Sales, e-mail: lindar@websterwatch.com.

■ 17653 ■ Wedlo Inc.
1816 3rd Ave. N
Birmingham, AL 35203-3102
Phone: (205)322-4444 Fax: (205)252-6827
Products: Jewelry. SIC: 5094 (Jewelry & Precious Stones). Est: 1956. Sales: $40,000,000 (2000). Emp: 360. Officers: Robert A. Keller, CEO & President; Rich Wiggins, CFO; Jan Adams, Dir. of Advertising; Harold Sharker, Exec. VP; Alissa Varnon, Human Resources Mgr.

■ 17654 ■ Wel-Met Corp.
930 Wellington Ave.
Cranston, RI 02910-3721
Phone: (401)467-3222
Products: Jewelry. SIC: 5094 (Jewelry & Precious Stones). Officers: William Garey, President.

■ 17655 ■ Wheatland Rock Shop
1808 9th St.
Wheatland, WY 82201-2143
Phone: (307)322-2192 Free: (888)518-6111
URL: http://www.silverbybentley.com
Products: Jewelry; Precious stones and gems; New arrowheads, gold and silver. SIC: 5094 (Jewelry & Precious Stones). Est: 1979. Emp: 1. Officers: Roger Bentley, Owner, e-mail: adele@silverbybentley.com.

■ 17656 ■ Wildflower Jewelry
3359 Osceola St.
Denver, CO 80212
Phone: (303)433-5346
Free: (800)959-2286 Fax: (303)433-7511
E-mail: flrjewl@eazy.net
URL: http://www.flowered-jewel.com
Products: Floral jewelry. SIC: 5094 (Jewelry & Precious Stones). Est: 1983. Emp: 6. Officers: Heide Hetter. Alternate Name: Wildflower Collection.

■ 17657 ■ Wilkerson Jewelers
222 S Main
Stuttgart, AR 72160-4355
Phone: (870)673-4441 Fax: (870)673-7947
Products: Gold. SIC: 5094 (Jewelry & Precious Stones). Emp: 49. Officers: Bob Wilkerson.

■ 17658 ■ Winkler Group, Ltd.
321 Veazie St.
Providence, RI 02904-2120
Phone: (401)272-2885 Fax: (401)272-2887
Products: Jewelry; Precious stones (gems). SIC: 5094 (Jewelry & Precious Stones). Est: 1960. Emp: 37. Officers: Traci Maceroni, CEO; Heidi Loomis, CFO; Doreen Troy; Bernie Maceroni, Sales/Mktg.

■ 17659 ■ Harry Winston Inc.
718 5th Ave.
New York, NY 10019
Phone: (212)245-2000
Products: Diamonds. SIC: 5094 (Jewelry & Precious Stones). Est: 1932. Sales: $38,000,000 (2000). Emp: 150. Officers: Ronald Winston, President; Robert Benvenuto, CFO; Joan Gendelman, Dir of Personnel.

■ 17660 ■ Wittnauer International
145 Huguenot St.
New Rochelle, NY 10802
Phone: (914)654-7200
Free: (800)431-1863 Fax: (914)654-7263
Products: Watches. SIC: 5094 (Jewelry & Precious Stones). Est: 1880. Emp: 200. Officers: Robert Coleman, CEO; Charles D. Watkins, President & COO; Stephen D'Angelo, CFO; Lawrence Crider, VP of Marketing and Promotions. Former Name: Longines-Wittnauer Watch Co.

■ 17661 ■ Charles Wolf and Sons Inc.
1212 Avenue of the Americas
New York, NY 10036
Phone: (212)719-4410
Products: Diamonds. SIC: 5094 (Jewelry & Precious Stones). Est: 1921. Sales: $22,000,000 (2000). Emp: 30. Officers: Jack Wolf, President; Leon Wolf, Vice President.

■ 17662 ■ World Wide Imports of Orlando Inc.
1511 S Lake Pleasant Rd.
Apopka, FL 32703
Phone: (407)886-0090 Fax: (407)886-4902
Products: Jewelry. SIC: 5094 (Jewelry & Precious Stones).

■ 17663 ■ Wuite Traders International
PO Box 70608
Sunnyvale, CA 94086
Phone: (408)766-2717 Fax: (408)733-2717
Products: Jewelry, silverware, and china; Surgical and medical plate ware; Men's and boys' clothing. SICs: 5094 (Jewelry & Precious Stones); 5136 (Men's/Boys' Clothing); 5047 (Medical & Hospital Equipment). Officers: Harold Kuykendall, Export Mgr.

■ 17664 ■ Yeh Dah Ltd.
98-1805 Piki St.
Aiea, HI 96701-1625
Phone: (808)487-7085 Fax: (808)487-7085
Products: Watch bands. SIC: 5094 (Jewelry & Precious Stones). Officers: Donald Yap, President.

■ 17665 ■ Yong's Watch & Clock Repair
2700 State St. 13
Las Vegas, NV 89109-1604
Phone: (702)892-9776
Products: Jewelry; Precious stones (gems). SIC: 5094 (Jewelry & Precious Stones). Officers: Yong Yi, Owner.

■ 17666 ■ York Novelty Import Inc.
10 W 37th St.
New York, NY 10018
Phone: (212)594-7040
Free: (800)223-6676 Fax: (212)594-8226
Products: Jewelers' findings and materials; Costume jewelry. SIC: 5094 (Jewelry & Precious Stones). Emp: 15. Officers: M. Bookstein.

■ 17667 ■ Zack Trading
2724 S Park Rd.
Hallandale, FL 33009-3833
Phone: (954)983-9100
Free: (800)777-7767 Fax: (954)894-0600
E-mail: zack@zacktrading.com
URL: http://www.zacktrading.com
Products: Jewelry, including costume, Christian, sterling, and trendy jewelry. SIC: 5094 (Jewelry & Precious Stones). Est: 1986. Officers: Heidi Zack; Gary Zack.

(30) Livestock and Farm Products

Entries in this section are arranged alphabetically by company name. When the company name is a personal name, the company name is alphabetized by the surname unless the first name or initial(s) are part of a trade name. See the User's Guide at the front of this directory for additional information.

■ **17668** ■ **3K Livestock**
35375 Hwy. 228
Brownsville, OR 97327
Phone: (541)466-5161 **Fax:** (541)466-5535
Products: Lambs. **SIC:** 5154 (Livestock).

■ **17669** ■ **4 Seasons Livestock**
PO Box 509
Choteau, MT 59422-0509
Phone: (406)466-2169 **Fax:** (406)466-2169
Products: Livestock. **SIC:** 5154 (Livestock). **Officers:** Douglas Crary, Owner.

■ **17670** ■ **A & K Feed and Grain Company Inc.**
PO Box 158
Lime Springs, IA 52155
Phone: (319)566-2291
Products: Grain and feed. **SICs:** 5153 (Grain & Field Beans); 5191 (Farm Supplies). **Est:** 1946. **Sales:** $9,000,000 (2000). **Emp:** 15. **Officers:** Dale Schwade, President.

■ **17671** ■ **ABJ Enterprises Inc.**
PO Box 428
Dunn, NC 28335
Phone: (910)892-1357 **Fax:** (910)892-0547
Products: Cotton. **SIC:** 5159 (Farm-Product Raw Materials Nec). **Sales:** $7,000,000 (2000). **Emp:** 12. **Officers:** Alsey B. Johnson, CEO; John A. Johnson, President & CFO.

■ **17672** ■ **Ada Farmers Exchange Co.**
332 W Lincoln Ave.
Ada, OH 45810
Phone: (419)634-3030
Products: Animal feed and grain; Chemicals and fertilizer. **SICs:** 5153 (Grain & Field Beans); 5191 (Farm Supplies). **Sales:** $10,000,000 (2000). **Emp:** 93. **Officers:** George Secor, General Mgr.

■ **17673** ■ **Adair Feed and Grain Co.**
PO Box 417
Adair, IA 50002
Phone: (515)742-3855 **Fax:** (515)742-5083
Products: Livestock equipment; Grains, including seed and corn. **SIC:** 5191 (Farm Supplies). **Est:** 1960. **Sales:** $9,000,000 (2000). **Emp:** 10. **Officers:** Randy Crawford, President & Treasurer.

■ **17674** ■ **Adams-Dougherty Livestock Brokerage**
803 E Rice St.
Sioux Falls, SD 57103-0157
Phone: (605)336-3830
Products: Livestock; Cattle; Hogs. **SIC:** 5154 (Livestock). **Officers:** Clare Vollan, President.

■ **17675** ■ **Adams Group Inc.**
1020 East St.
Woodland, CA 95776
Phone: (530)662-7351
Products: Grain. **SIC:** 5153 (Grain & Field Beans).

■ **17676** ■ **Addison County Commodity Sales**
PO Box 214
Middlebury, VT 05753
Phone: (802)388-2639
Products: Cattle. **SIC:** 5154 (Livestock).

■ **17677** ■ **ADM-Growmark Inc.**
PO Box 1470
Decatur, IL 62525
Phone: (217)424-5900 **Fax:** (217)424-5990
Products: Grain. **SIC:** 5153 (Grain & Field Beans). **Sales:** $790,000,000 (2000). **Emp:** 650. **Officers:** Bernal Kraft, President; Doug J. Schmalz, Controller; Marvin Rau, VP of Marketing; Richard E. Burket.

■ **17678** ■ **AG Cooperative Service Inc.**
2420 Clinton Rd.
Sedalia, MO 65301
Phone: (660)826-5327
Products: Grain; Chemicals; Petroleum. **SICs:** 5191 (Farm Supplies); 5169 (Chemicals & Allied Products Nec); 5172 (Petroleum Products Nec). **Est:** 1957. **Sales:** $8,200,000 (2000). **Emp:** 22. **Officers:** Bill Pittman, President; Carroll Gregg, General Mgr.

■ **17679** ■ **Ag Partners Co. Cannon Falls Div.**
PO Box 308
Cannon Falls, MN 55009
Phone: (507)263-4651
Products: Farming supplies, including grain. **SICs:** 5153 (Grain & Field Beans); 5191 (Farm Supplies). **Est:** 1946. **Sales:** $17,000,000 (2000). **Emp:** 10. **Officers:** Greg Schwambeck, General Mgr.; Joe Morgan, Manager.

■ **17680** ■ **Agiand Co-op**
PO Box 125
Oakland, NE 68045
Phone: (402)685-5613
Products: Grain elevator. **SIC:** 5153 (Grain & Field Beans). **Est:** 1915. **Officers:** Dale Johnson, President; Dennis Behrens, Manager.

■ **17681** ■ **Agland Coop**
PO Box 466
Hooper, NE 68031
Phone: (402)654-3323 **Fax:** (402)654-3866
Products: Farm supplies, including grain, wheat, corn, milo, feed for hogs and cattle, and petroleum. **SICs:** 5153 (Grain & Field Beans); 5191 (Farm Supplies); 5172 (Petroleum Products Nec). **Est:** 1915. **Sales:** $12,000,000 (2000). **Emp:** 25. **Officers:** Dale J. Johnson, General Mgr. **Former Name:** Elkhorn Valley Co.

■ **17682** ■ **AGP Grain Co.**
Rte. 1, Box 56
Glenvil, NE 68941
Phone: (402)726-2266 **Fax:** (402)726-2269
Products: Grain. **SIC:** 5153 (Grain & Field Beans). **Est:** 1960. **Sales:** $5,000,000 (2000). **Emp:** 2. **Officers:** Jim Lindsay, CEO. **Alternate Name:** Anan Grain Co.

■ **17683** ■ **Agrex Inc.**
9300 W 110th St. No. 500
Overland Park, KS 66210
Phone: (913)345-5400
Products: Corn, soybeans, and sorghum. **SIC:** 5153 (Grain & Field Beans). **Sales:** $40,000,000 (2000). **Emp:** 47. **Officers:** Junko Kishida, President; Joe Milkowski, Controller; Joe Guenley, VP of Marketing.

■ **17684** ■ **Agri Grain Marketing**
PO Box 8129
Des Moines, IA 50301
Phone: (515)224-2600
Free: (800)247-4134 **Fax:** (515)224-2651
Products: Grain. **SIC:** 5153 (Grain & Field Beans). **Est:** 1986. **Sales:** $1,000,000,000 (2000). **Emp:** 125. **Officers:** Peter Reed, General Mgr.; Julie Andrews, Accounting Manager; Mark Metzger, Dir. of Sales.

■ **17685** ■ **AGRI Sales**
254 Main St.
Sunfield, MI 48890
Phone: (517)566-8031 **Fax:** (517)566-8995
Products: Grain elevators; Grain. **SIC:** 5153 (Grain & Field Beans). **Est:** 1965. **Sales:** $6,000,000 (2000). **Emp:** 10. **Officers:** Ross Thomas, Manager. **Former Name:** Mueller Bean Co.

■ **17686** ■ **Agri Sales Inc.**
385 Morley Dr.
Saginaw, MI 48605
Phone: (517)753-5432 **Fax:** (517)753-5218
Products: Beans and grains. **SIC:** 5153 (Grain & Field Beans). **Est:** 1937. **Sales:** $18,000,000 (2000). **Emp:** 100. **Officers:** Eugene Mueller, President; James L. Dale, Controller; Neil French, General Mgr.

■ **17687** ■ **AgriPro Seeds Inc.**
6700 Antioch Rd.
PO Box 2962
Shawnee Mission, KS 66204
Phone: (913)384-4940 **Fax:** (913)384-0208
Products: Agricultural products including, wheat, corn, soybeans, sunflowers, and alfalfa. **SICs:** 5191 (Farm Supplies); 5191 (Farm Supplies). **Est:** 1973. **Sales:** $55,000,000 (2000). **Emp:** 280. **Officers:** Milton Allen, President; Craig Jensen, Controller; Darwin Allred, Dir. of Materials.

■ **17688** ■ **Agway Inc.**
PO Box 4933
Syracuse, NY 13221
Phone: (315)449-6436 **Fax:** (315)449-6253
Products: Feed, fertilizer, pet food and farm production supplies. **SICs:** 5159 (Farm-Product Raw Materials Nec); 5172 (Petroleum Products Nec). **Sales:** $1,562,900,000 (2000). **Emp:** 7,000. **Officers:** Peter O'Neill, VP of Finance.

■ **17689** ■ **Alabama Farmers Cooperative Inc.**
PO Box 2227
Decatur, AL 35609-2227
Phone: (256)353-6843 **Fax:** (256)350-1770
Products: Grain. **SIC:** 5153 (Grain & Field Beans). **Sales:** $250,000,000 (2000). **Emp:** 600. **Officers:**

Thomas Paulk, CEO & President; Joe Lovvorn, Treasurer.

■ 17690 ■ **Allen Brothers Feed Inc.**
300 3rd St.
Kentwood, LA 70444
Phone: (504)229-5521
Products: Animal feed. **SIC:** 5191 (Farm Supplies). **Est:** 1952. **Sales:** $4,000,000 (2000). **Emp:** 9. **Officers:** Bruce Meyer, President; Maggie Meyer, Treasurer & Secty.

■ 17691 ■ **Alliance Grain Co.**
PO Box 546
Gibson City, IL 60936
Phone: (217)784-4284
Products: Corn and beans. **SIC:** 5153 (Grain & Field Beans). **Sales:** $60,000,000 (2000). **Emp:** 35. **Officers:** Robert Landow, President; Steve Kelly, General Mgr.

■ 17692 ■ **Allied International Marketing Corp.**
380 Maple Ave., Ste. 202
Vienna, VA 22180
Phone: (703)255-6400 **Fax:** (703)255-0921
E-mail: aimcorp@erols.com
Products: Grain; Fertilizers; Agricultural medical equipment; Flour. **SICs:** 5191 (Farm Supplies); 5153 (Grain & Field Beans); 5099 (Durable Goods Nec); 5141 (Groceries—General Line). **Est:** 1984. **Sales:** $1,000,000 (2000). **Officers:** Gebreyes Begna, President.

■ 17693 ■ **Allied Order Buyers, Inc.**
1908 Hwy. 20
Lawton, IA 51030
Phones: (712)944-5175 (712)252-3614
Fax: (712)255-8046
Products: Livestock. **SIC:** 5154 (Livestock).

■ 17694 ■ **Allied Order Buyers, Inc.**
333 Livestock Exchange Bldg.
Sioux City, IA 51101
Phone: (712)252-3614 **Fax:** (712)255-8046
Products: Livestock. **SIC:** 5154 (Livestock).

■ 17695 ■ **Amber NFO Reload Corp.**
RR 3
Anamosa, IA 52205
Phone: (319)462-2968
Products: Livestock. **SIC:** 5154 (Livestock).

■ 17696 ■ **American Legend Cooperative**
PO Box 58308
Seattle, WA 98188
Phone: (425)251-3100
Products: Furs. **SIC:** 5159 (Farm-Product Raw Materials Nec). **Sales:** $4,000,000 (1994). **Emp:** 35. **Officers:** Claudia Campbell, President; Kathy Domagala, Controller.

■ 17697 ■ **Amherst Cooperative Elevator Inc.**
PO Box 115
Amherst, CO 80721
Phone: (303)854-3141 **Fax:** (303)854-3764
Products: Grains, including corn, wheat, oats, and soy beans. **SICs:** 5153 (Grain & Field Beans); 5172 (Petroleum Products Nec). **Est:** 1941. **Sales:** $20,000,000 (2000). **Emp:** 19. **Officers:** C.W. Krogmeier, President; Gary Peintner, CFO.

■ 17698 ■ **Amsko Fur Corp.**
247 W 30th St.
New York, NY 10001
Phone: (212)736-9035 **Fax:** (212)629-6229
Products: Furs, skins, and hides. **SIC:** 5159 (Farm-Product Raw Materials Nec). **Officers:** Jack Skoknick, President.

■ 17699 ■ **Andale Farmers Cooperative Company Inc.**
PO Box 18
Andale, KS 67001
Phone: (316)444-2141
Products: Grain and farming supplies. **SICs:** 5153 (Grain & Field Beans); 5191 (Farm Supplies). **Sales:** $30,000,000 (1993). **Emp:** 45. **Officers:** Bill York, Finance General Manager.

■ 17700 ■ **Andelain Farm**
14740 Mud College Rd.
Thurmont, MD 21788
Phone: (301)271-4191 **Fax:** (301)271-3718
Products: School and show horses. **SIC:** 5154 (Livestock).

■ 17701 ■ **Andres and Wilton Farmers Grain and Supply Co.**
28451 S Rte. 45
Peotone, IL 60468
Phone: (708)258-3268
Products: Grain. **SICs:** 5153 (Grain & Field Beans); 5191 (Farm Supplies). **Est:** 1913. **Sales:** $5,000,000 (2000). **Emp:** 7. **Officers:** G. Koehler, President; Allan Mundt, Treasurer; Robert Kline, Manager.

■ 17702 ■ **Anthony Farmers Cooperative and Elevator Co.**
PO Box 111
Anthony, KS 67003
Phone: (316)842-5181
Products: Grain; Chemicals; Fertilizer; Petroleum. **SICs:** 5153 (Grain & Field Beans); 5169 (Chemicals & Allied Products Nec); 5172 (Petroleum Products Nec); 5191 (Farm Supplies). **Est:** 1916. **Sales:** $10,600,000 (2000). **Emp:** 28. **Officers:** John Walker, President; Larry Wood, CFO.

■ 17703 ■ **Arcadia Livestock, Inc.**
PO Box 27
Arcadia, WI 54612
Phone: (608)323-7795
Products: Livestock; Meat. **SICs:** 5154 (Livestock); 5147 (Meats & Meat Products).

■ 17704 ■ **Ardrosson Farms**
Darby-Paoli Rd.
PO Box 567
Villanova, PA 19085
Phone: (215)688-2651
Products: Cattle; Milk. **SICs:** 5154 (Livestock); 5143 (Dairy Products Except Dried or Canned).

■ 17705 ■ **Arizona Grain Inc.**
PO Box 11188
Casa Grande, AZ 85230
Phone: (602)836-8228
Products: Wheat, corn, oats, and seed. **SICs:** 5153 (Grain & Field Beans); 5191 (Farm Supplies). **Sales:** $18,000,000 (2000). **Emp:** 21. **Officers:** John Skelley, CEO; Dwayne Mann, CFO.

■ 17706 ■ **Ashland Farmers Elevator Co.**
PO Box 199
Ashland, IL 62612
Phone: (217)476-3318 **Fax:** (217)476-3936
Products: Grain; Feed; Seed. **SICs:** 5153 (Grain & Field Beans); 5191 (Farm Supplies). **Est:** 1907. **Sales:** $8,000,000 (2000). **Emp:** 8. **Officers:** Donald Mohoney, President; Patricia Edwards, General Mgr.

■ 17707 ■ **Ashmore Grain Co. Inc.**
PO Box 100
Ashmore, IL 61912
Phone: (217)349-8221
Products: Beans and corn. **SIC:** 5153 (Grain & Field Beans). **Sales:** $20,000,000 (2000). **Emp:** 20. **Officers:** Earl Clapp, Partner; Charles Barbee, Partner; Larry Clapp, Dir. of Marketing & Sales.

■ 17708 ■ **Assumption Cooperative Grain Co.**
104 W North St.
Assumption, IL 62510
Phone: (217)226-3213
Free: (800)252-6542 **Fax:** (217)226-3244
E-mail: acoopmainel.ccipost.net
URL: http://www.acoop.com
Products: Grain; Petroleum. **SICs:** 5153 (Grain & Field Beans); 5172 (Petroleum Products Nec). **Est:** 1934. **Sales:** $45,000,000 (2000). **Emp:** 28. **Officers:** Robert Adcock, President; Thomas Bressner, General Mgr.; Terry Lush, Sales/Marketing Contact; Tom Bressner, Customer Service Contact; Mike Snyder, Human Resources Contact.

■ 17709 ■ **Atchison County Farmers Union Cooperative Association**
PO Drawer B
Atchison, KS 66002
Phone: (913)367-0318
Products: Grain. **SIC:** 5153 (Grain & Field Beans). **Est:** 1917. **Sales:** $27,000,000 (2000). **Emp:** 45. **Officers:** Milton Hines, President; Mark Shields, Controller; William Nienstedt, General Mgr.

■ 17710 ■ **Atherton Grain Co.**
PO Box 366
Walnut, IL 61376
Phone: (815)379-2177
Products: Grain. **SIC:** 5153 (Grain & Field Beans). **Est:** 1928. **Sales:** $8,000,000 (2000). **Emp:** 15. **Officers:** Roy A. Atherton, President & CFO.

■ 17711 ■ **Auction Livestock, Inc.**
Old Highway 10 E
Perham, MN 56573
Phone: (218)346-3415 **Fax:** (218)346-9004
Products: Livestock; Meat. **SICs:** 5154 (Livestock); 5147 (Meats & Meat Products).

■ 17712 ■ **Augusta Farmers Cooperative Co.**
410 W Green St.
Augusta, IL 62311
Phone: (217)392-2184
Products: Grain elevator. **SIC:** 5153 (Grain & Field Beans). **Est:** 1920. **Sales:** $5,000,000 (2000). **Emp:** 7. **Officers:** William Finney, President; Edward Widener, General Mgr.

■ 17713 ■ **Austinville Elevator**
77 Sunset St.
Austinville, IA 50608
Phone: (515)847-2832
Products: Grain, including corn, wheat, and rice. **SICs:** 5153 (Grain & Field Beans); 5191 (Farm Supplies); 5072 (Hardware). **Est:** 1953. **Sales:** $12,000,000 (2000). **Emp:** 15. **Officers:** John Commons, General Mgr.

■ 17714 ■ **B & B Buyers Inc.**
RR 1, Box 26
Chinook, MT 59523-9703
Phone: (406)357-3800
Products: Livestock; Cattle. **SIC:** 5154 (Livestock). **Officers:** Mark Billmayer, President.

■ 17715 ■ **B & B Cattle Co.**
PO Box 1850
Palestine, TX 75802
Phone: (903)729-6277
Free: (800)328-3433 **Fax:** (903)729-1192
Products: Cattle. **SIC:** 5154 (Livestock).

■ 17716 ■ **B & J Cattle Co.**
18th & Minnesota Ave.
Billings, MT 59103
Phone: (406)252-6072 **Fax:** (406)245-8002
Products: Cattle; Sheep. **SIC:** 5154 (Livestock).

■ 17717 ■ **Bailey's Slaughter House**
PO Box 696
Hardwick, VT 05843
Phone: (802)472-5578
Products: Cattle and beef; Pigs; Sheep. **SICs:** 5154 (Livestock); 5147 (Meats & Meat Products).

■ 17718 ■ **Baker Agri Sales Inc.**
3415 W Main St.
Sedalia, MO 65301
Phone: (816)826-5955
Products: Agricultural products. **SICs:** 5191 (Farm Supplies); 5122 (Drugs, Proprietaries & Sundries). **Est:** 1964. **Sales:** $2,000,000 (2000). **Emp:** 8. **Officers:** D.A. Baker, President.

■ 17719 ■ **Bales Continental Commission Co.**
PO Box 1337
Huron, SD 57350
Phone: (605)352-8682 **Fax:** (605)352-9374
Products: Livestock; Auctioning livestock. **SIC:** 5154 (Livestock). **Officers:** Jerry Bales, President.

■ **17720** ■ **Balthauser & Moyer**
Exchange Bldg.
West Fargo, ND 58078-1100
Phone: (701)282-4245
Products: Livestock. **SIC:** 5154 (Livestock). **Officers:**
Herbert Paulson, Owner.

■ **17721** ■ **Bar Lazy K Bar Ranch Inc.**
PO Box 337
Presho, SD 57568-0337
Phone: (605)669-2767
Products: Livestock; Cattle. **SIC:** 5154 (Livestock).
Officers: Delmer Volmer, President.

■ **17722** ■ **J.T. Barham and Co.**
22711 Main St.
Capron, VA 23829
Phone: (804)658-4239 **Fax:** (804)658-4608
Products: Fertilizer; Feed; Seed; Grain elevator. **SICs:**
5159 (Farm-Product Raw Materials Nec); 5191 (Farm
Supplies). **Est:** 1888. **Sales:** $3,000,000 (2000). **Emp:**
22. **Officers:** Ira H. Barham, Owner.

■ **17723** ■ **Barretts Equine Sales Ltd.**
PO Box 2010
Pomona, CA 91769
Phone: (909)629-3099 **Fax:** (909)629-2155
Products: Horses. **SIC:** 5159 (Farm-Product Raw
Materials Nec). **Est:** 1989. **Sales:** $1,000,000 (2000).
Emp: 5. **Officers:** Gerald McMahon, President & CFO.

■ **17724** ■ **Barta International Sales Corp.**
2400 Vallejo St.
San Francisco, CA 94123
Phone: (415)346-6090
Products: Hides and skins. **SIC:** 5159 (Farm-Product
Raw Materials Nec). **Officers:** Ivan Andreas Barta,
Vice President.

■ **17725** ■ **Bartlett and Co. (Headquarters)**
4800 Main St.
Kansas City, MO 64112
Phone: (816)753-6300
Free: (800)888-6300 **Fax:** (816)753-0062
Products: Grain merchants and storage; Flour mills;
Cattle feed lots. **SIC:** 5153 (Grain & Field Beans). **Est:**
1933. **Sales:** $795,000,000 (1999). **Emp:** 525.
Officers: Paul D. Bartlett, CEO & Chairman of the
Board; Arnold Wheeler, Sec. & Treas.; James B.
Hebenstreit, President.

■ **17726** ■ **Beattie Farmers Union Cooperative**
Association
PO Box 79
Beattie, KS 66406
Phone: (785)353-2237 **Fax:** (785)353-2236
Products: Grain. **SIC:** 5153 (Grain & Field Beans).
Est: 1950. **Sales:** $13,000,000 (2000). **Emp:** 22.
Officers: Charles Gerstner, CEO; Larry Preuss,
General Mgr.

■ **17727** ■ **Belle Fourche Livestock Exchange**
PO Box 126
Belle Fourche, SD 57717-0126
Phone: (605)892-2655 **Fax:** (605)892-3142
Products: Livestock. **SIC:** 5154 (Livestock). **Officers:**
Dean Strong, President.

■ **17728** ■ **Bement Grain Company Inc.**
400 E Bodman St.
Bement, IL 61813
Phone: (217)678-2261
Products: Grain elevator. **SIC:** 5153 (Grain & Field
Beans). **Est:** 1903. **Sales:** $11,000,000 (2000). **Emp:**
17. **Officers:** Roger Hendrix, CEO; Dean Creviston,
Treasurer & Secty.; Richard Thomas, Manager.

■ **17729** ■ **Benson-Quinn Co.**
1075 Grain Exchange
Minneapolis, MN 55415
Phone: (612)340-5900
Products: Grain; Meat. **SICs:** 5153 (Grain & Field
Beans); 5147 (Meats & Meat Products). **Est:** 1920.
Sales: $92,000,000 (2000). **Emp:** 175. **Officers:**
Lawrence Neumann, President; Carl Myers, Vice
President.

■ **17730** ■ **George Benz and Sons Inc.**
5th & Minnesota St.
St. Paul, MN 55101
Phone: (612)224-1351
Products: Raw milk. **SIC:** 5143 (Dairy Products Except
Dried or Canned). **Est:** 1902. **Sales:** $28,000,000
(2000). **Emp:** 140. **Officers:** George Benz, President.

■ **17731** ■ **Bessman Price Auctioneers**
PO Box 353
Madison, SD 57042-0353
Phone: (605)256-9156 **Fax:** (605)256-9516
Products: Livestock; Auctioning livestock. **SIC:** 5154
(Livestock). **Officers:** Wayne Bessman, Partner.

■ **17732** ■ **Bethany Grain Company Inc.**
PO Box 350
Bethany, IL 61914-0350
Phone: (217)665-3392
Products: Grain elevator. **SIC:** 5153 (Grain & Field
Beans). **Est:** 1907. **Sales:** $7,000,000 (2000). **Emp:** 5.
Officers: Harry L. Bennett, President; Kevin Walker,
General Mgr.

■ **17733** ■ **A.M. Bickley Inc.**
PO Box 91
Marshallville, GA 31057
Phone: (912)967-2291
Products: Farm commodities. **SICs:** 5159 (Farm-
Product Raw Materials Nec); 5153 (Grain & Field
Beans). **Est:** 1957. **Sales:** $13,000,000 (2000). **Emp:**
25. **Officers:** A.M. Bickley Jr., President; John S.
Bickley, Treasurer & Secty.

■ **17734** ■ **Billingsley Ranch Outfitters**
Equipment
PO Box 768
Glasgow, MT 59230-0768
Phone: (406)367-5577 **Fax:** (406)367-5578
Products: Livestock. **SIC:** 5154 (Livestock). **Officers:**
Dorothy Billingsley, President.

■ **17735** ■ **Blackfoot Livestock Commission**
Company Inc.
PO Box 830
Blackfoot, ID 83221
Phone: (208)785-0500
Products: Livestock, including cows and horses. **SIC:**
5154 (Livestock). **Est:** 1926. **Sales:** $3,000,000 (2000).
Emp: 6. **Officers:** J. Clarke Bayne, President.

■ **17736** ■ **Blackwell Cooperative Elevator**
Association
410 N Main St.
Blackwell, OK 74631
Phone: (580)363-1461
Products: Wheat. **SIC:** 5153 (Grain & Field Beans).
Est: 1922. **Sales:** $2,000,000 (2000). **Emp:** 17.
Officers: Charles Boesch, President; Ray Kirk,
General Mgr.

■ **17737** ■ **Blanchard Valley Farmers**
Cooperative
PO Box 607
McComb, OH 45858
Phone: (419)293-2311 **Fax:** (419)293-3040
Products: Farm supplies, including grain, feed, seed,
and fertilizer. **SICs:** 5153 (Grain & Field Beans); 5191
(Farm Supplies). **Est:** 1913. **Sales:** $20,000,000
(2000). **Emp:** 52. **Officers:** Jerry Silveus, President.

■ **17738** ■ **Bliss Cooperative Grain Co.**
PO Box 549
Marland, OK 74644
Phone: (580)268-3316
Products: Grain. **SIC:** 5153 (Grain & Field Beans).
Est: 1920. **Sales:** $3,000,000 (2000). **Emp:** 5.
Officers: Wilbur Ingmire, President; Richard Cockrell,
CFO; Gregory Miller, Dir. of Marketing.

■ **17739** ■ **Jack S. Bloxham**
348 Bootlegger Tr.
Black Eagle, MT 59414-0328
Phone: (406)761-4492 **Free:** (800)761-4492
Products: Livestock. **SIC:** 5154 (Livestock). **Officers:**
Jack Bloxham, Owner.

■ **17740** ■ **Bluff Springs Farmers Elevator Co.**
PO Box 50
Bluff Springs, IL 62622
Phone: (217)323-2815 **Fax:** (217)323-1134
Products: Grain, corn, seed, and beans. **SICs:** 5153
(Grain & Field Beans); 5191 (Farm Supplies). **Est:**
1908. **Sales:** $13,000,000 (2000). **Emp:** 30. **Officers:**
Ronald Kuhlman, President; Marlin McCormick,
General Mgr.

■ **17741** ■ **Bobb Brothers Inc.**
PO Box 306
Leesburg, OH 45135
Phone: (513)780-2241
Products: Grain, including corn and wheat. **SIC:** 5153
(Grain & Field Beans). **Est:** 1950. **Sales:** $12,000,000
(2000). **Emp:** 12. **Officers:** Paul Bobb, President.

■ **17742** ■ **Robert L. Boedeker**
PO Box 482
Lander, WY 82520-0482
Phone: (307)332-3703
Products: Livestock. **SIC:** 5154 (Livestock). **Officers:**
Robert Boedeker, Owner.

■ **17743** ■ **D.E. Bondurant Grain Company Inc.**
PO Box 280
Ness City, KS 67560
Phone: (913)798-3322 **Fax:** (913)798-3330
Products: Grains, including corn, wheat, and soybean.
SICs: 5153 (Grain & Field Beans); 5191 (Farm
Supplies). **Est:** 1888. **Sales:** $29,500,000 (2000).
Emp: 23. **Officers:** Robert F. Gantz, President.

■ **17744** ■ **Bottineau Farmers Elevator Inc.**
PO Box 7
Bottineau, ND 58318
Phone: (701)228-2294
Products: Grain. **SIC:** 5153 (Grain & Field Beans).
Est: 1939. **Sales:** $28,000,000 (2000). **Emp:** 18.
Officers: Doug Bremner, President; Orville Wilhelm,
Treasurer; Del Haberman, General Mgr.

■ **17745** ■ **Bradfordton Cooperative**
Association Inc.
4440 West Jefferson St.
Springfield, IL 62707
Phone: (217)546-1206
Products: Grain elevator; Corn and beans; Seed.
SICs: 5153 (Grain & Field Beans); 5191 (Farm
Supplies). **Est:** 1919. **Sales:** $4,000,000 (1999). **Emp:**
6. **Officers:** William Frey, President; Jacob Hermes,
Treasurer & Secty.; Mike Huber, General Mgr.

■ **17746** ■ **Bricelyn Elevator Association**
PO Box 368
Bricelyn, MN 56014
Phone: (507)653-4448 **Fax:** (507)653-4500
Products: Grain elevators; Grain; Feed; Fertilizer and
fertilizer materials. **SICs:** 5153 (Grain & Field Beans);
5191 (Farm Supplies). **Est:** 1919. **Sales:** $42,800,000
(2000). **Emp:** 9. **Officers:** A. Legred, President; H.
Assmus, Treasurer & Secty.

■ **17747** ■ **Britton Livestock Sales Inc.**
S Hwy. 27
Britton, SD 57430
Phone: (605)448-5911 **Fax:** (605)448-2668
Products: Livestock; Auctioning livestock. **SIC:** 5154
(Livestock). **Emp:** 25. **Officers:** Keith Jensen,
President. **Former Name:** Britton Livestock Auction,
Inc.

■ **17748** ■ **Brooks Farmers Cooperative**
Association
PO Box 8
Brooks, MN 56715
Phone: (218)698-4275
Products: Grain elevator. **SICs:** 5153 (Grain & Field
Beans); 5191 (Farm Supplies). **Est:** 1940. **Sales:**
$7,000,000 (2000). **Emp:** 7. **Officers:** John LaCrosse,
President; Rodney Myhre, General Mgr.

■ **17749** ■ **Broussard Rice Mill Inc.**
PO Drawer 160
Mermentau, LA 70556-0160
Phone: (318)824-2409 **Fax:** (318)824-8537
Products: Milled rice and byproducts. **SIC:** 5153

(Grain & Field Beans). **Sales:** $25,000,000 (2000). **Emp:** 49. **Officers:** J. B. Broussard.

■ 17750 ■ **BTR Farmers Co-op**
PO Box 244
Leeds, ND 58346
Phone: (701)466-2231
Products: Wheat. **SIC:** 5153 (Grain & Field Beans).

■ 17751 ■ **Buchanan Farmers Elevator Co.**
PO Box 100
Buchanan, ND 58420
Phone: (701)252-6622 **Fax:** (701)252-6655
Products: Grain elevator. **SIC:** 5153 (Grain & Field Beans). **Est:** 1939. **Sales:** $6,100,000 (2000). **Emp:** 4. **Officers:** Travis Traut, General Mgr.; Gary Neys, Treasurer & Secty.

■ 17752 ■ **Buckeye Cooperative Elevator Co.**
PO Box 2037
Buckeye, IA 50043
Phone: (515)855-4141 **Fax:** (515)855-4278
E-mail: buckeye@cnsinternet.com
Products: Corn; Grain; Fertilizer; Feed. **SICs:** 5153 (Grain & Field Beans); 5191 (Farm Supplies); 5172 (Petroleum Products Nec). **Est:** 1945. **Sales:** $20,000,000 (2000). **Emp:** 23. **Officers:** Larry Zoske, President; Bruce Stofferan, General Mgr.

■ 17753 ■ **Buckingham Cooperative Co.**
1236 Dwan St.
Buckingham, IA 50612
Phone: (319)478-2331
Products: Grain elevator. **SIC:** 5153 (Grain & Field Beans). **Est:** 1966. **Sales:** $15,000,000 (2000). **Emp:** 6. **Officers:** H. Foss, President.

■ 17754 ■ **Bunge Corp.**
11720 Borman Dr.
St. Louis, MO 63146
Phone: (314)872-3030 **Fax:** (314)872-0110
URL: http://www.bungecorp.com
Products: Dry corn milling; Corn flaking grits; Corn meal, corn flour, bulgar wheat; Corn oil; Hominy feed; Corn soy blend; Soybean processing, including soybean meal and soybean oil; Edible oils and bakery products, including cooking and frying oils, shortenings, margarine; Bakery mixes, bakery concentrates; Frozen bakery products; Toppings and filling; Syrups. **SIC:** 5153 (Grain & Field Beans). **Est:** 1923. **Sales:** $2,570,000,000 (2000). **Emp:** 3,000. **Officers:** John E. Klein, President; Michael Scharf, CFO; Fred Sands; Dexter Frye; Richard McWard.

■ 17755 ■ **Burgess Brothers Grain Inc.**
U.S Hwy. 51 S
Clinton, KY 42031
Phone: (502)653-4346
Products: Grain including wheat, corn, and beans. **SIC:** 5153 (Grain & Field Beans). **Est:** 1974. **Sales:** $6,000,000 (2000). **Emp:** 5. **Officers:** Orville Burgess Jr., President.

■ 17756 ■ **Burnett Dairy Cooperative**
11631 State Rd. 70
Grantsburg, WI 54840-0188
Phone: (715)689-2468 **Fax:** (715)689-2135
Products: Farm supplies. **SIC:** 5191 (Farm Supplies). **Est:** 1967. **Sales:** $37,000,000 (2000). **Emp:** 125. **Officers:** James Melin, President; Tim Swenson, Bookkeeper.

■ 17757 ■ **Bushland Grain Cooperative**
PO Box 129
Bushland, TX 79012
Phone: (806)358-2411 **Fax:** (806)358-2413
Products: Grain. **SIC:** 5153 (Grain & Field Beans). **Est:** 1939. **Sales:** $2,500,000 (2000). **Emp:** 4. **Officers:** Sidney Sharp, President.

■ 17758 ■ **Calcot Ltd.**
PO Box 259
Bakersfield, CA 93302
Phone: (661)327-5961 **Fax:** (661)861-9870
URL: http://www.calcot.com
Products: Raw cotton. **SIC:** 5159 (Farm-Product Raw Materials Nec). **Est:** 1927. **Sales:** $418,000,000 (1999). **Emp:** 185. **Officers:** Tom W. Smith, President; Robert W. Norris, Sr. VP & Finance Officer; Steve

Newman, VP of Data Processing; Mary Joe Pasek, Personnel Mgr.

■ 17759 ■ **Caldwell Supply Company Inc.**
PO Box T
Hazleton, PA 18201
Phone: (717)455-7511 **Fax:** (717)455-0385
Products: Farm supplies. **SICs:** 5191 (Farm Supplies); 5072 (Hardware); 5083 (Farm & Garden Machinery). **Sales:** $92,000,000 (1992). **Emp:** 230. **Officers:** Ralph Caldwell III, President; Jim Karafonda, Controller.

■ 17760 ■ **Calumet Industries Inc.**
Rte. 2, Box 30
Calumet, OK 73014
Phone: (405)262-2263
Products: Surplus grain; Veterinarian supplies. **SICs:** 5191 (Farm Supplies); 5153 (Grain & Field Beans). **Est:** 1977. **Sales:** $14,000,000 (2000). **Emp:** 40. **Officers:** Connie Todd, President.

■ 17761 ■ **Art Camenzind Dairy Cattle**
10406 State St.
Omaha, NE 68122
Phones: (402)571-0522 (402)571-0737
Fax: (402)571-7360
Products: Dairy cattle. **SIC:** 5154 (Livestock).

■ 17762 ■ **Robert G. Candee**
Rte. 4, Box 2010
Richey, MT 59259
Phone: (406)773-5674
Products: Livestock; Cattle. **SIC:** 5154 (Livestock). **Officers:** Robert Candee, Owner.

■ 17763 ■ **Capital Ford New Holland Inc.**
PO Box 16568
Little Rock, AR 72231-6568
Phone: (501)834-9999
Products: Tractor parts. **SICs:** 5082 (Construction & Mining Machinery); 5083 (Farm & Garden Machinery). **Sales:** $10,500,000 (2000). **Emp:** 25. **Officers:** Doug Meyer, President & CFO.

■ 17764 ■ **Carolina Cotton Growers Association Inc.**
209 Oberlin Rd.
Raleigh, NC 27605
Phone: (919)833-2048
Products: Raw cotton. **SIC:** 5159 (Farm-Product Raw Materials Nec). **Est:** 1922. **Sales:** $5,000,000 (2000). **Emp:** 15. **Officers:** J. Cox, President & Treasurer.

■ 17765 ■ **Carrollton Farmers Elevator Co.**
PO Box 264
Carrollton, IL 62016
Phone: (217)942-6922
Products: Grain. **SIC:** 5153 (Grain & Field Beans). **Est:** 1919. **Sales:** $9,800,000 (2000). **Emp:** 8. **Officers:** Chris Howard, General Mgr.

■ 17766 ■ **Carwell Elevator Company Inc.**
PO Box 187
Cherry Valley, AR 72324
Phone: (501)588-3381
Products: Grain. **SIC:** 5153 (Grain & Field Beans). **Est:** 1955. **Sales:** $24,000,000 (2000). **Emp:** 50. **Officers:** J.L. Carwell Jr., President; W.B. Carwell, General Mgr.

■ 17767 ■ **Castlewood Farmers Elevator**
PO Box 200
Castlewood, SD 57223
Phone: (605)793-2181
Products: Grain; Seeds. **SICs:** 5153 (Grain & Field Beans); 5191 (Farm Supplies). **Est:** 1912. **Sales:** $7,000,000 (2000). **Emp:** 6. **Officers:** Garret TeKrony, President; Robert Bruinsma, General Mgr.

■ 17768 ■ **Cenex Harvest States Cooperatives**
PO Box 64594
St. Paul, MN 55164
Phone: (651)451-5151 **Fax:** (651)451-5568
Products: Grain. **SIC:** 5153 (Grain & Field Beans). **Sales:** $5,607,400,000 (2000). **Emp:** 2,404. **Officers:** John D. Johnson, CEO & President; Tom F. Baker, VP of Finance.

■ 17769 ■ **Centennial Commodities Inc.**
4000 N Bayou Hills Ln.
Parker, CO 80134
Phone: (303)840-0644 **Fax:** (303)840-0650
E-mail: drybeans@aol.com
Products: Dry beans; Popcorn. **SIC:** 5153 (Grain & Field Beans). **Est:** 1985. **Sales:** $3,000,000 (2000). **Emp:** 2. **Officers:** Dick Simpson, President.

■ 17770 ■ **Central Commodities Ltd.**
1140 W Locust St.
Belvidere, IL 61008
Phone: (815)544-3455 **Fax:** (815)544-3457
Products: Corn. **SIC:** 5153 (Grain & Field Beans). **Est:** 1957. **Sales:** $18,300,000 (2000). **Emp:** 11. **Officers:** Robert R. Mickey, President; Gary Hulstedt, General Mgr.

■ 17771 ■ **Central Connecticut Cooperative Farmers Association**
PO Box 8500
Manchester, CT 06040
Phone: (203)649-4523
Products: Grain. **SICs:** 5153 (Grain & Field Beans); 5191 (Farm Supplies); 5144 (Poultry & Poultry Products). **Est:** 1938. **Sales:** $55,000,000 (2000). **Emp:** 65. **Officers:** Bob Jacquire, Chairman of the Board; Emmanuel Hirth, CFO.

■ 17772 ■ **Central Livestock Association**
PO Box 419
South St. Paul, MN 55075
Phone: (651)451-1844 **Fax:** (651)451-1774
Products: Livestock. **SIC:** 5154 (Livestock). **Sales:** $40,000,000 (2000). **Emp:** 125. **Officers:** D. G. Kampmier, President; Mark Esch, Controller.

■ 17773 ■ **CGB Enterprises Inc.**
PO Box 249
Mandeville, LA 70470
Phone: (504)867-3500 **Fax:** (504)867-3506
Products: Grain. **SIC:** 5153 (Grain & Field Beans). **Sales:** $140,000,000 (2000). **Emp:** 825. **Officers:** Richard Wilcox, CEO & President; Gary Wunsch, Exec. VP & CFO.

■ 17774 ■ **Chamberlain Livestock Auction**
PO Box 244
Chamberlain, SD 57325-0244
Phone: (605)734-6037
Products: Livestock; Auctioning livestock. **SIC:** 5154 (Livestock). **Officers:** Robert Jorgenson, Owner.

■ 17775 ■ **Chapin Farmers Elevator Co.**
PO Box 349
Chapin, IL 62628
Phone: (217)472-5771
Products: Farm products; Grain. **SICs:** 5153 (Grain & Field Beans); 5159 (Farm-Product Raw Materials Nec). **Est:** 1908. **Sales:** $9,700,000 (2000). **Emp:** 7. **Officers:** Alvin Saunderson Jr., President; Kenneth Crews, General Mgr.; Douglas K. Renoud, Manager.

■ 17776 ■ **A.W. Cherry & Son**
PO Box 3260
Bowling Green, KY 42102
Phone: (502)782-1902 **Fax:** (502)782-0456
Products: Cattle. **SIC:** 5154 (Livestock).

■ 17777 ■ **Chickasha Cotton Oil Co.**
PO Box 2710
Chandler, AZ 85244
Phone: (602)963-5300 **Fax:** (602)821-5888
Products: Cottonseed oil mill; cotton ginning; crop financing. **SIC:** 5159 (Farm-Product Raw Materials Nec). **Sales:** $212,000,000 (2000). **Emp:** 450. **Officers:** Ryoichi Kondo, President & Chairman of the Board.

■ 17778 ■ **Chokio Equity Exchange Inc.**
PO Box 126
Chokio, MN 56221
Phone: (612)324-2477
Products: Grain. **SIC:** 5153 (Grain & Field Beans). **Sales:** $3,000,000 (1993). **Emp:** 8. **Officers:** Steve Negen, General Mgr.

■ 17779 ■ Cisco Cooperative Grain Inc.
PO Box 69
Cisco, IL 61830
Phone: (217)669-2141 **Fax:** (217)669-2331
Products: Grain. **SIC:** 5153 (Grain & Field Beans).
Est: 1900. **Sales:** $15,000,000 (2000). **Emp:** 11.
Officers: Dale Huisinga, President; Michelle Burns,
Office Mgr.

■ 17780 ■ CJ Cattle Co. Inc.
PO Box 3177
Butte, MT 59702-3177
Phone: (406)494-2670 **Fax:** (406)494-2672
Products: Livestock. **SIC:** 5154 (Livestock). **Officers:**
Craig Britton, President.

■ 17781 ■ Clayton H. Clark
RFD 3 Box 1900
Skowhegan, ME 04976
Phone: (207)474-5825
Products: Livestock. **SIC:** 5154 (Livestock).

■ 17782 ■ Clifton Grain Inc.
PO Box 293
Chebanse, IL 60922-0293
Phone: (815)694-2397
Products: Beans and corn. **SIC:** 5153 (Grain & Field
Beans). **Est:** 1983. **Sales:** $4,000,000 (2000). **Emp:** 6.
Officers: James Goldtrap, President; Jeff Lambert,
Treasurer & Secty.

■ 17783 ■ Clinton Landmark Inc.
PO Box 512
Wilmington, OH 45177
Phone: (513)382-1633
Products: Agricultural products. **SICs:** 5191 (Farm
Supplies); 5153 (Grain & Field Beans). **Est:** 1933.
Sales: $12,000,000 (2000). **Emp:** 40. **Officers:** Marvin
L. Chamberlin, President & Chairman of the Board;
James Hafler, CEO.

■ 17784 ■ Clovis Livestock Auction
PO Box 187
Clovis, NM 88102-0187
Phone: (505)762-4422 **Fax:** (505)762-4421
Products: Livestock; Auctioning livestock. **SIC:** 5154
(Livestock). **Officers:** Dick Moore, Partner.

■ 17785 ■ Co-op Country Farmers Elevator
PO Box 604
Renville, MN 56284
Phone: (612)329-8377
URL: http://www.coopcountry.com
Products: Grain; Fertilizer; Feed. **SICs:** 5153 (Grain &
Field Beans); 5191 (Farm Supplies). **Sales:**
$32,000,000 (2000). **Emp:** 40. **Officers:** Craig Hebrink,
President; Lynne Payne, Controller. **Former Name:**
Cooperative Country Farmer's Elevator.

■ 17786 ■ Colusa Elevator Company Inc.
PO Box 26
Colusa, IL 62329
Phone: (217)755-4221
Products: Grain. **SIC:** 5153 (Grain & Field Beans).
Sales: $23,000,000 (2000). **Emp:** 30. **Officers:** Donald
P. Griffiths Sr., CEO & President; Jean McEnte, CFO.

■ 17787 ■ Colwell Cooperative
PO Box 605
Charles City, IA 50616
Phone: (515)228-3123 **Fax:** (515)228-3141
Products: Feed and agricultural grain. **SICs:** 5153
(Grain & Field Beans); 5191 (Farm Supplies). **Est:**
1937. **Sales:** $11,565,000 (1999). **Emp:** 16. **Officers:**
John Fox, President; Richard Schrader, Treasurer &
Secty.; Gayle Melcher, General Mgr.

■ 17788 ■ Commodity Specialists Co.
301 4th Ave., 780 Grain Exchange Bldg.
Minneapolis, MN 55415
Phone: (612)330-9889 **Fax:** (612)330-9890
Products: Merchants of agricultural commodities. **SIC:**
5159 (Farm-Product Raw Materials Nec). **Sales:**
$70,000,000 (2000). **Emp:** 130. **Officers:** Philip J.
Lindau, CEO & President; O. William Mikkelson, CFO.

■ 17789 ■ ConAgra Grain Co.
11 Conagra Dr.
Omaha, NE 68102-5011
Products: Grains, corn, and rice. **SIC:** 5153 (Grain &
Field Beans). **Sales:** $670,000,000 (2000). **Emp:**
1,260. **Officers:** Thomas Racciatti, President; Pauline
Woulfe, Controller; Roberta Mellen, Dir of Human
Resources.

■ 17790 ■ Connell Grain Growers Inc.
PO Box 220
Connell, WA 99326
Phone: (509)234-2641
Products: Grain. **SIC:** 5153 (Grain & Field Beans).
Est: 1930. **Sales:** $18,000,000 (2000). **Emp:** 11.
Officers: Kent Hansen, General Mgr.

■ 17791 ■ Consolidated Cooperative Inc.
PO Box 48
Gowrie, IA 50543
Phone: (515)352-3851
Products: Grain and farm supplies, and industrial oil.
SICs: 5153 (Grain & Field Beans); 5191 (Farm
Supplies); 5172 (Petroleum Products Nec). **Sales:**
$44,000,000 (1992). **Emp:** 42. **Officers:** Alan Kohtz,
General Mgr.

■ 17792 ■ Continental Grain Co.
277 Park Ave.
New York, NY 10172
Phone: (212)207-5100 **Fax:** (212)207-5043
Products: Wheat, corn, and soybeans; Meat products,
including pork, beef, and poultry. **SICs:** 5153 (Grain &
Field Beans); 5147 (Meats & Meat Products). **Est:**
1813. **Sales:** $15,000,000,000 (2000). **Emp:** 14,500.
Officers: Paul J. Freibourg, CEO & Chairman of the
Board; James J. Bigham, CFO; Keith Johnson, VP of
Information Systems; Dwight Coffin, VP & Secty.

■ 17793 ■ Cooksville Grain Co.
PO Box 200
Cooksville, IL 61730
Phone: (309)725-3214 **Fax:** (309)725-3216
Products: Corn and beans. **SIC:** 5153 (Grain & Field
Beans). **Est:** 1906. **Sales:** $10,000,000 (2000). **Emp:**
4. **Officers:** Frank Sylvester, General Mgr.

■ 17794 ■ Cooperative Elevator Co.
4878 Mill St.
Elkton, MI 48731
Phone: (517)375-2281 **Fax:** (517)375-2282
Products: Grain; Corn; Wheat; Oats; Canned dry
beans. **SIC:** 5153 (Grain & Field Beans). **Est:** 1989.
Sales: $59,000,000 (2000). **Emp:** 110. **Officers:** John
P. Kohr, CEO.

■ 17795 ■ Cooperative Elevator, Sebewaing
969 E Pine St.
Sebewaing, MI 48759
Phone: (517)883-3030
Products: Grain. **SICs:** 5153 (Grain & Field Beans);
5191 (Farm Supplies); 5172 (Petroleum Products Nec).
Officers: Melvin Kuhl, General Mgr.

■ 17796 ■ Cooperative Grain and Supply
PO Box 8
Bazine, KS 67516
Phone: (785)398-2271
Free: (877)294-4427 **Fax:** (785)398-2273
E-mail: grainbin@ruralnet.com
Products: Grain; Chemical; Fertilizers; Feed; Fuels.
SICs: 5153 (Grain & Field Beans); 5191 (Farm
Supplies); 5159 (Farm-Product Raw Materials Nec);
5172 (Petroleum Products Nec). **Est:** 1927. **Sales:**
$9,000,000 (1999). **Emp:** 12. **Officers:** Allen Janke,
Chairman of the Board; Linda Cox, General Mgr.

■ 17797 ■ Cooperative Grain and Supply
PO Box 7
Roseland, NE 68973
Phone: (402)756-6201
Products: Grain, field beans, feeds and fertilizers.
SICs: 5153 (Grain & Field Beans); 5191 (Farm
Supplies). **Sales:** $21,000,000 (1992). **Emp:** 27.
Officers: Glen Wiens, President; David Bruggeman,
Finance General Manager.

■ 17798 ■ Cooperative Sampo Corp.
Box 220
Menahga, MN 56464
Phone: (218)564-4534 **Fax:** (218)564-4534
Products: Grain elevator. **SIC:** 5153 (Grain & Field
Beans). **Est:** 1903. **Sales:** $7,000,000 (2000). **Emp:**
62. **Officers:** Jon Lenzen, CEO.

■ 17799 ■ Coshocton Grain Co.
PO Box 606
Coshocton, OH 43812
Phone: (614)622-0941 **Fax:** (614)622-1911
Products: Grain. **SIC:** 5153 (Grain & Field Beans).
Est: 1948. **Sales:** $10,300,000 (2000). **Emp:** 12.
Officers: Brent Porteus, President.

■ 17800 ■ Cottonwood Sales Yard
PO Box 178
Cottonwood, ID 83522-0178
Phone: (208)962-3284
Products: Livestock. **SIC:** 5154 (Livestock). **Officers:**
Urban Arnzen, Owner.

■ 17801 ■ Coulter Elevator
PO Box 177
Coulter, IA 50431
Phone: (515)866-6921 **Fax:** (515)866-6811
Products: Grain and farm supplies. **SICs:** 5153 (Grain
& Field Beans); 5191 (Farm Supplies). **Sales:**
$2,000,000 (1994). **Emp:** 9. **Officers:** Vic Steding,
Manager.

■ 17802 ■ Country Star Coop
PO Box 428
New Washington, OH 44854
Phone: (419)492-2548
Products: Grain elevators. **SICs:** 5153 (Grain & Field
Beans); 5191 (Farm Supplies). **Est:** 1930. **Sales:**
$42,000,000 (2000). **Emp:** 50. **Officers:** Howard Von
Stein, President; Ron Dentinger, General Mgr.

■ 17803 ■ Craighead Farmers Cooperative
Rte. 2, Box 348
Bono, AR 72416
Phone: (870)932-3623
Products: Farm supplies. **SIC:** 5191 (Farm Supplies).
Sales: $24,000,000 (1994). **Emp:** 100. **Officers:** Mike
Eaton, Finance General Manager.

■ 17804 ■ Crowley Grain Drier Inc.
PO Box 677
Crowley, LA 70526
Phone: (318)783-3284
Products: Seed rice. **SIC:** 5153 (Grain & Field Beans).
Est: 1945. **Sales:** $6,000,000 (2000). **Emp:** 26.
Officers: Lawrence Trahan, CEO; Dave Trahan, VP of
Finance.

■ 17805 ■ Culver-Fancy Prairie Cooperative
Co.
PO Box 222
Athens, IL 62613
Phone: (217)636-7171 **Fax:** (217)636-8060
Products: Corn; Soybeans. **SIC:** 5153 (Grain & Field
Beans). **Est:** 1965. **Sales:** $14,000,000 (2000). **Emp:**
8. **Officers:** Dean Baugher, President; Matthew W.
Winterbauer, Treasurer & Secty.; Gary Chandler,
General Mgr.

■ 17806 ■ Cyclone Grain Co.
4079 E County Rd. 400 S
Frankfort, IN 46041-8630
Phone: (765)654-4466 **Fax:** (765)654-4468
Products: Grain elevator. **SIC:** 5153 (Grain & Field
Beans). **Est:** 1968. **Sales:** $5,000,000 (2000). **Emp:** 5.
Officers: Robert L. Heilman, Partner.

■ 17807 ■ Cylinder Cooperative Elevator
PO Box 67
Cylinder, IA 50528
Phone: (712)424-3335
Products: Grain. **SIC:** 5153 (Grain & Field Beans).
Sales: $6,000,000 (2000). **Emp:** 10. **Officers:** Richard
Berkland, President; Harry Borman, General Mgr.

■ 17808 ■ Dalhart Consumers Fuel and Grain Association Inc.

PO Box 671
Dalhart, TX 79022
Phone: (806)249-5695 **Fax:** (806)249-5897
Products: Gasoline; Grain. **SICs:** 5153 (Grain & Field Beans); 5171 (Petroleum Bulk Stations & Terminals); 5191 (Farm Supplies). **Est:** 1933. **Sales:** $16,000,000 (2000). **Emp:** 25. **Officers:** David Noble, President; Ed Green, General Mgr.

■ 17809 ■ Damascus Peanut Co.

State Hwy. 200 W
Damascus, GA 31741
Phone: (912)725-3353 **Fax:** (912)725-3338
Products: Raw peanuts. **SIC:** 5159 (Farm-Product Raw Materials Nec). **Est:** 1949. **Sales:** $17,000,000 (2000). **Emp:** 100. **Officers:** Joe Bryan, President.

■ 17810 ■ Danforth-Gilman Grain Co.

PO Box 166
Danforth, IL 60930
Phone: (815)269-2390
Products: Corn and soybeans. **SIC:** 5153 (Grain & Field Beans). **Est:** 1908. **Sales:** $11,000,000 (2000). **Emp:** 7. **Officers:** Eugene Tammen, President.

■ 17811 ■ Daniel Piroutek

HCR 1 Box6-A
Milesville, SD 57553
Phone: (605)544-3316 **Fax:** (605)544-3316
Products: Livestock and farm products. **SIC:** 5154 (Livestock).

■ 17812 ■ Davenport Union Warehouse Co.

10th & Jefferson
Davenport, WA 99122
Phone: (509)725-7081 **Fax:** (509)725-6755
Products: Grain, including wheat and barley. **SIC:** 5153 (Grain & Field Beans). **Est:** 1909. **Sales:** $10,000,000 (2000). **Emp:** 6. **Officers:** Dale Williams, President; Ed Stoner, Manager.

■ 17813 ■ Davis Grain Corp.

5512 Bainbridge Blvd.
Chesapeake, VA 23324
Phone: (804)543-2041
Products: Corn; Soybeans. **SIC:** 5153 (Grain & Field Beans). **Est:** 1953. **Sales:** $46,000,000 (2000). **Emp:** 70. **Officers:** Russell Davis, Chairman of the Board.

■ 17814 ■ DeBruce Grain Inc.

2702 Rock Creek Pkwy., Ste. 4
Kansas City, MO 64117-2519
Phone: (816)421-8182
Products: Grain. **SIC:** 5153 (Grain & Field Beans). **Sales:** $60,000,000 (2000). **Emp:** 70. **Officers:** Larry Kittoe, President; Jerry Byrnes, Controller.

■ 17815 ■ DeKalb-Pfizer Genetics, Crawfordsville Div.

PO Box 683
Crawfordsville, IN 47933-0683
Phone: (765)362-2104
Products: Farm supplies. **SIC:** 5191 (Farm Supplies). **Officers:** B Thada, Manager.

■ 17816 ■ Delphos Co-Op Association Inc.

413 W 1st St.
Delphos, KS 67436
Phone: (785)523-4213
Products: Grain. **SIC:** 5153 (Grain & Field Beans). **Sales:** $12,000,000 (1994). **Emp:** 14. **Officers:** Kent Baldock, President.

■ 17817 ■ Delta International

PO Box 188
Fairfield, CT 06430
Phone: (203)255-1969 **Fax:** (203)254-2906
E-mail: Berkseek@connix.com
URL: http://www.delta-trade-intl.com
Products: Agricultural products; Tires and tire retreading equipment. **SICs:** 5148 (Fresh Fruits & Vegetables); 5014 (Tires & Tubes); 5159 (Farm-Product Raw Materials Nec). **Est:** 1978. **Sales:** $2,000,000 (1999). **Emp:** 2. **Officers:** Gerald L. Berk, President, e-mail: berkseek@connix.com. **Former Name:** The First Delta Corporation.

■ 17818 ■ Demeter Inc.

PO Box 465
Fowler, IN 47944
Phone: (317)884-0600 **Fax:** (317)884-0933
Products: Corn; Wheat; Beans. **SIC:** 5153 (Grain & Field Beans). **Est:** 1944. **Sales:** $200,000,000 (2000). **Emp:** 150. **Officers:** Donald Brouillette, President; Larry Callahan, Controller; Al Dewit, Dir. of Marketing; Steve Puetz, Dir. of Data Processing; James Deckara, Dir of Human Resources.

■ 17819 ■ Donovan Farmers Cooperative Elevator Inc.

PO Box 159
Donovan, IL 60931
Phone: (815)486-7325
Products: Corn; Soybeans; Fertilizer. **SICs:** 5153 (Grain & Field Beans); 5191 (Farm Supplies). **Est:** 1905. **Sales:** $13,700,000 (2000). **Emp:** 18. **Officers:** Johnnie G. Hoyer, President; Doug Anderson, Manager.

■ 17820 ■ Dorchester Farmers Cooperative

N Depot St.
Dorchester, NE 68343
Phone: (402)946-2211
Products: Farm supplies. **SICs:** 5153 (Grain & Field Beans); 5191 (Farm Supplies). **Sales:** $31,000,000 (1994). **Emp:** 45. **Officers:** Jim Herrem, President.

■ 17821 ■ Louis Dreyfus Corp. Allenberg Cotton Company Div.

PO Box 3254
Cordova, TN 38018-3254
Phone: (901)383-5000 **Fax:** (901)383-5010
Products: Raw cotton; Textiles. **SIC:** 5159 (Farm-Product Raw Materials Nec). **Est:** 1870. **Sales:** $96,000,000 (2000). **Emp:** 180. **Officers:** John Goss, CEO & President; William Zarfoss, CFO; T.C. Brookes, Dir. of Data Processing; Patsy Schoonover, Human Resources Mgr.

■ 17822 ■ Louis Dreyfus Corp.

PO Box 810
Wilton, CT 06897-0810
Phone: (203)761-2000 **Fax:** (203)761-8321
Products: Grain; Beans; Coffee; Sugar; Petroleum. **SICs:** 5153 (Grain & Field Beans); 5159 (Farm-Product Raw Materials Nec); 5172 (Petroleum Products Nec). **Est:** 1860. **Sales:** $1,710,000,000 (2000). **Emp:** 2,000. **Officers:** John Goss, President; Jerry Dubrowski, VP & Treasurer; John Lombardi, Dir. of Information Systems; Veronica Pitaro, Dir of Human Resources.

■ 17823 ■ Driscoll Grain Cooperative Inc.

PO Box 208
Driscoll, TX 78351
Phone: (512)387-6242 **Fax:** (512)387-6242
Products: Grain, including corn. **SIC:** 5153 (Grain & Field Beans). **Est:** 1950. **Sales:** $4,000,000 (2000). **Emp:** 12. **Officers:** Dan Felder, President; Ronald K. Goldman, General Mgr.

■ 17824 ■ Dunavant Enterprises Inc.

3797 New Getwell Rd.
Memphis, TN 38118
Phone: (901)369-1500 **Fax:** (901)369-1608
E-mail: info@dunavant.com
URL: http://www.dunavant.com
Products: Raw cotton. **SIC:** 5159 (Farm-Product Raw Materials Nec). **Est:** 1970. **Sales:** $1,200,000,000 (2000). **Emp:** 700. **Officers:** W.B. Dunavant Jr., CEO & Chairman of the Board; William B. Dunavant III, President; Louis Baioni, Exec. VP & CFO; Cheryl Cooley, Dir of Human Resources.

■ 17825 ■ Earlville Farmers Cooperative

602 Railroad St.
Earlville, IL 60518
Phone: (815)246-8461 **Fax:** (815)246-7163
Products: Grain, including corn and wheat. **SIC:** 5153 (Grain & Field Beans). **Est:** 1905. **Sales:** $14,000,000 (2000). **Emp:** 12. **Officers:** David Grey, President; Robert Leonard, Controller.

■ 17826 ■ Edmonson Wheat Growers Inc.

PO Box 32
Edmonson, TX 79032
Phone: (806)864-3327 **Fax:** (806)864-3325
Products: Grain. **SICs:** 5153 (Grain & Field Beans); 5191 (Farm Supplies). **Est:** 1934. **Sales:** $10,300,000 (2000). **Emp:** 12. **Officers:** Jack Witten, President; Royce Duckett, General Mgr.

■ 17827 ■ Effingham Equity

PO Box 488
Effingham, IL 62401
Phone: (217)342-4101 **Fax:** (217)347-7601
Products: Feed. **SICs:** 5153 (Grain & Field Beans); 5172 (Petroleum Products Nec). **Sales:** $80,000,000 (2000). **Emp:** 225. **Officers:** Harry Fehrenbacher, President; Dale Semple, CFO.

■ 17828 ■ El Toro Land and Cattle Co.

PO Box G
Heber, CA 92249
Phone: (619)352-6312
Products: Livestock. **SIC:** 5154 (Livestock). **Est:** 1965. **Sales:** $12,000,000 (2000). **Emp:** 65. **Officers:** Robert Odell, President.

■ 17829 ■ Elburn Cooperative Co.

PO Box U
Elburn, IL 60119
Phone: (630)365-6444
Products: Grain and farm supplies. **SICs:** 5153 (Grain & Field Beans); 5191 (Farm Supplies). **Sales:** $19,000,000 (2000). **Emp:** 21. **Officers:** Eldon Gould, President; Richard Viddle, Treasurer.

■ 17830 ■ Eldridge Cooperative Co.

111 W Davenport St.
Eldridge, IA 52748
Phone: (319)285-9615 **Fax:** (319)285-7495
Products: Grain and farm supplies. **SICs:** 5153 (Grain & Field Beans); 5191 (Farm Supplies). **Sales:** $45,000,000 (2000). **Emp:** 90. **Officers:** Ron Ralfs, President; Sara Meyer, Controller.

■ 17831 ■ Ellsworth-William Cooperative Co.

PO Box C
Ellsworth, IA 50075-0190
Phone: (515)836-4411 **Fax:** (515)836-2114
Products: Grain, including corn and soybeans; Feed. **SICs:** 5153 (Grain & Field Beans); 5191 (Farm Supplies). **Est:** 1935. **Sales:** $21,000,000 (2000). **Emp:** 25. **Officers:** Randy Olson, President; Mark Lunde, Treasurer; Kurt Ross, General Mgr.

■ 17832 ■ Elwood Line Grain and Fertilizer Co.

PO Box 127
Momence, IL 60954
Phone: (815)472-4842 **Fax:** (815)472-2775
Products: Grains; Fertilizer. **SICs:** 5153 (Grain & Field Beans); 5191 (Farm Supplies). **Est:** 1969. **Sales:** $7,000,000 (2000). **Emp:** 10. **Officers:** Elwood Line, President.

■ 17833 ■ EMP Co-op Inc.

1519 Everson Rd.
Woodburn, IN 46797
Phone: (219)632-4284
Products: Grain and farm supplies. **SICs:** 5153 (Grain & Field Beans); 5191 (Farm Supplies). **Sales:** $13,000,000 (2000). **Emp:** 22. **Officers:** Jerry Schaefer, President; Greg Baumert, Controller.

■ 17834 ■ Equity Cooperative Elevator Co.

Main St.
Sheyenne, ND 58374
Phone: (701)996-2231
Products: Grain and feed. **SIC:** 5153 (Grain & Field Beans). **Est:** 1906. **Sales:** $4,700,000 (2000). **Emp:** 6. **Officers:** Tom Smith, CEO; Lauren Jordre, Treasurer & Secty.

■ 17835 ■ Equity Elevator and Trading Co.

PO Box 69
Wood Lake, MN 56297
Phone: (507)485-3153
Free: (800)248-5427 **Fax:** (507)485-3180
Products: Grain, farm supplies, agronomy and feed. **SICs:** 5153 (Grain & Field Beans); 5191 (Farm

Supplies). **Sales:** $30,000,000 (2000). **Emp:** 15. **Officers:** Roger Hanson, General Mgr.

■ **17836** ■ **Equity Grain and General Merchant Exchange**
PO Box 46
Mullinville, KS 67109
Phone: (316)548-2222
Products: Grains, including wheat, corn, milo, and soybean. **SIC:** 5153 (Grain & Field Beans). **Est:** 1913. **Sales:** $4,000,000 (2000). **Emp:** 5. **Officers:** Ron Freeman, CEO.

■ **17837** ■ **Erickson's Sheep Co.**
PO Box 1781
Billings, MT 59102
Phone: (406)259-1010
Products: Livestock; Sheep. **SIC:** 5154 (Livestock). **Officers:** George Erickson, Owner.

■ **17838** ■ **Evangeline Farmers Cooperative**
521 Lithcote Rd.
Ville Platte, LA 70586
Phone: (318)363-1046
Products: Farm supplies and fuel oil. **SICs:** 5191 (Farm Supplies); 5172 (Petroleum Products Nec). **Est:** 1966. **Sales:** $6,500,000 (2000). **Emp:** 20. **Officers:** Bill Brunet, President.

■ **17839** ■ **Farm Service Elevator Co.**
PO Box 933
Willmar, MN 56201
Phone: (612)235-1080 **Fax:** (612)235-7731
Products: Grain. **SIC:** 5153 (Grain & Field Beans). **Est:** 1953. **Sales:** $25,000,000 (2000). **Emp:** 50. **Officers:** Virgil Stangeland, Vice President; Ronald Hanson, Treasurer & Secty.; Ivan Willroth, Dir. of Marketing; Gary Ascheman, Dir. of Data Processing; Jim Sieben, Dir of Human Resources.

■ **17840** ■ **Farmers Co-op Elevator and Mercantile Association**
PO Box 909
Dighton, KS 67839
Phone: (316)397-5343
Products: Grain, corn, wheat, and milo. **SICs:** 5191 (Farm Supplies); 5191 (Farm Supplies). **Est:** 1915. **Sales:** $23,000,000 (2000). **Emp:** 20. **Officers:** Rad Roehl, President; Floyd G. Barber, CFO.

■ **17841** ■ **Farmers Cooperative Association**
Kansas St. & Railroad
Brewster, KS 67732
Phone: (785)694-2281
Products: Grains, including milo, sunflowers, corn, and wheat. **SIC:** 5153 (Grain & Field Beans). **Est:** 1915. **Sales:** $6,000,000 (2000). **Emp:** 14. **Officers:** Lyman Goetsch, President.

■ **17842** ■ **Farmers Cooperative Association**
Main St.
Lindsay, NE 68644
Phone: (402)428-2305 **Fax:** (402)428-2108
Products: Grain and feed. **SICs:** 5153 (Grain & Field Beans); 5191 (Farm Supplies); 5031 (Lumber, Plywood & Millwork). **Sales:** $12,000,000 (2000). **Emp:** 10. **Officers:** Gary Jarecki, General Mgr.

■ **17843** ■ **Farmers Cooperative Association**
PO Box 608
Clinton, OK 73601
Phone: (580)323-1467
Products: Wheat; Fertilizer. **SICs:** 5153 (Grain & Field Beans); 5191 (Farm Supplies). **Est:** 1920. **Sales:** $1,000,000 (2000). **Emp:** 9. **Officers:** Bill Friesen, President.

■ **17844** ■ **Farmers Cooperative Association**
PO Box 127
Brule, NE 69127
Phone: (308)287-2304 **Fax:** (308)287-2238
Products: Feed and seed. **SICs:** 5153 (Grain & Field Beans); 5191 (Farm Supplies). **Est:** 1914. **Sales:** $9,000,000 (2000). **Emp:** 15. **Officers:** Tom Struckman, President; Timothy Jimenez, General Mgr.; Darwin Hawk, Manager.

■ **17845** ■ **Farmers Cooperative Association**
PO Box 100
Milroy, MN 56263
Phone: (507)336-2555
Products: Dog, cat, and other pet food; Corn; Oats; Wheat; Unshelled beans. **SICs:** 5153 (Grain & Field Beans); 5191 (Farm Supplies); 5149 (Groceries & Related Products Nec). **Est:** 1905. **Sales:** $5,000,000 (2000). **Emp:** 10. **Officers:** Mike Swalboski, President; Tom Grimes, General Mgr.

■ **17846** ■ **Farmers Cooperative Association**
105 Jackson St.
Jackson, MN 56143
Phone: (507)847-4160
Products: Fertilizers, grain and other farm products. **SICs:** 5191 (Farm Supplies); 5153 (Grain & Field Beans). **Sales:** $30,000,000 (1994). **Emp:** 40. **Officers:** Tom Underwood, Chairman of the Board; Wayne Gordon, Finance General Manager.

■ **17847** ■ **Farmers Cooperative Association (York, Nebraska)**
Rte. 2 Box 3
York, NE 68467
Phone: (402)362-6691
Products: Grain and farm supplies. **SICs:** 5153 (Grain & Field Beans); 5191 (Farm Supplies). **Sales:** $30,000,000 (1994). **Emp:** 30. **Officers:** Mike McLain, President; Bud Mooney, Controller.

■ **17848** ■ **Farmers Cooperative (Carmen, Oklahoma)**
PO Box 100
Carmen, OK 73726
Phone: (580)987-2234
Products: Grain. **SIC:** 5153 (Grain & Field Beans). **Sales:** $12,000,000 (1994). **Emp:** 24. **Officers:** Stacy Herbst, Finance Office Manager.

■ **17849** ■ **Farmers Cooperative Co.**
1303 9th Ave.
Manson, IA 50563
Phone: (712)469-3388 **Fax:** (712)469-2221
Products: Beans and corn; Fertilizers. **SICs:** 5153 (Grain & Field Beans); 5191 (Farm Supplies); 5172 (Petroleum Products Nec). **Est:** 1911. **Sales:** $18,000,000 (2000). **Emp:** 15. **Officers:** Kevin Hartkemeyer, President.

■ **17850** ■ **Farmers Cooperative Co.**
PO Box 248
Wolcott, IN 47995
Phone: (219)279-2115
Products: Grains, corn, soybean and wheat. **SIC:** 5153 (Grain & Field Beans). **Est:** 1944. **Sales:** $7,900,000 (2000). **Emp:** 4. **Officers:** Dennis Brooks, President; Joe Ruemler, Manager.

■ **17851** ■ **Farmers Cooperative Co.**
PO Box 160
Pocahontas, IA 50574
Phone: (712)335-3575 **Fax:** (712)335-3583
Products: Corn and beans. **SICs:** 5153 (Grain & Field Beans); 5191 (Farm Supplies). **Est:** 1918. **Sales:** $19,700,000 (2000). **Emp:** 24. **Officers:** Marv Allen, President; Ronald Tasler, General Mgr.

■ **17852** ■ **Farmers Cooperative Co.**
304 Ellsworth St.
Dows, IA 50071
Phone: (515)852-4136 **Fax:** (515)852-4139
Products: Grain, including corn and beans. **SICs:** 5153 (Grain & Field Beans); 5191 (Farm Supplies). **Est:** 1917. **Sales:** $30,000,000 (2000). **Emp:** 25. **Officers:** Orlin Schwab, President; John Trewin, Controller.

■ **17853** ■ **Farmers Cooperative Co.**
PO Box 179
Greenfield, IA 50849
Phone: (515)743-2161
Products: Grain, farm supplies, fencing and feeding machinery. **SICs:** 5153 (Grain & Field Beans); 5191 (Farm Supplies); 5039 (Construction Materials Nec); 5083 (Farm & Garden Machinery). **Sales:** $16,500,000 (1994). **Emp:** 29. **Officers:** Robert W. Lilly, President; Gale Johnston, Finance General Manager.

■ **17854** ■ **Farmers Cooperative Co. (Dike, Iowa)**
S Main St.
Dike, IA 50624
Phone: (319)989-2416
Products: Grain. **SICs:** 5153 (Grain & Field Beans); 5143 (Dairy Products Except Dried or Canned); 5191 (Farm Supplies). **Officers:** James Raymond, General Mgr.; James Raymond, CFO.

■ **17855** ■ **Farmers Cooperative Co. (Hinton, Iowa)**
PO Box 1046
Hinton, IA 51024
Phone: (712)947-4212
Products: Grain and farm supplies. **SICs:** 5153 (Grain & Field Beans); 5191 (Farm Supplies). **Sales:** $30,000,000 (1993). **Emp:** 28. **Officers:** James Carlson, General Mgr.; Roger Pfleeger, Finance Officer.

■ **17856** ■ **Farmers Cooperative Co. (Milligan, Nebraska)**
PO Box 97
Milligan, NE 68406
Phone: (402)629-4275
Products: Grain and printing paper. **SICs:** 5153 (Grain & Field Beans); 5111 (Printing & Writing Paper). **Sales:** $17,000,000 (1994). **Emp:** 17. **Officers:** Galen Kuska, President.

■ **17857** ■ **Farmers Cooperative Co. (Readlyn, Iowa)**
PO Box 339
Readlyn, IA 50668-0339
Phone: (319)279-3396
Products: Grain and farm supplies. **SICs:** 5153 (Grain & Field Beans); 5191 (Farm Supplies). **Sales:** $23,000,000 (2000). **Emp:** 25. **Officers:** Curt Brandt, President; Bruce Buxton, Mgr. of Finance.

■ **17858** ■ **Farmers Cooperative Co. (Woolstock, Iowa)**
PO Box 157
Woolstock, IA 50599
Phone: (515)839-5532
Products: Grain and farm supplies. **SICs:** 5153 (Grain & Field Beans); 5191 (Farm Supplies). **Sales:** $11,000,000 (2000). **Emp:** 12. **Officers:** John Peterson, General Mgr.

■ **17859** ■ **Farmers Cooperative Compress**
PO Box 2877
Lubbock, TX 79408
Phone: (806)763-9431 **Fax:** (806)763-3281
Products: Cotton warehouse; Cotton merchant. **SIC:** 5159 (Farm-Product Raw Materials Nec). **Sales:** $132,000,000 (2000). **Emp:** 160. **Officers:** Ron Hartke, President & General Mgr.; Linda May, Treasurer.

■ **17860** ■ **Farmers Cooperative of El Campo**
PO Box 826
El Campo, TX 77437
Phone: (409)543-6284 **Fax:** (409)543-9004
Products: Agricultural products, including milo, cotton, and corn. **SICs:** 5159 (Farm-Product Raw Materials Nec); 5153 (Grain & Field Beans); 5191 (Farm Supplies). **Est:** 1982. **Sales:** $38,000,000 (2000). **Emp:** 48. **Officers:** Jimmy Roppolo, General Mgr.; April Graves, Controller.

■ **17861** ■ **Farmers Cooperative Elevator**
PO Box 38
Oslo, MN 56744
Phone: (218)695-2301
Products: Grain; Feed. **SICs:** 5153 (Grain & Field Beans); 5191 (Farm Supplies). **Sales:** $5,000,000 (2000). **Emp:** 4. **Officers:** H. Zola, President; Clark Klava, Manager.

■ **17862** ■ **Farmers Cooperative Elevator**
PO Box 67
Sharon, ND 58277
Phone: (701)524-1770
Products: Grain and petroleum products. **SICs:** 5153 (Grain & Field Beans); 5172 (Petroleum Products Nec). **Sales:** $4,000,000 (1993). **Emp:** 3. **Officers:** Tom Amundson, Finance General Manager.

■ 17863 ■ **Farmers Cooperative Elevator Association**
PO Box 130
Crowell, TX 79227
Phone: (940)684-1234
Products: Grain and feed. **SICs:** 5153 (Grain & Field Beans); 5191 (Farm Supplies). **Est:** 1934. **Sales:** $3,000,000 (2000). **Emp:** 4. **Officers:** F.W. Riethmayer, CEO; Bill Hord, General Mgr.

■ 17864 ■ **Farmers Cooperative Elevator Co.**
PO Box 247
Cavalier, ND 58220
Phone: (701)265-8439
Products: Corn and beans. **SIC:** 5153 (Grain & Field Beans). **Est:** 1929. **Sales:** $4,700,000 (2000). **Emp:** 4. **Officers:** Ron Steinke, President; Cecil Watson, Treasurer & Secty.; Orlo Mostad, Sales Mgr.

■ 17865 ■ **Farmers Cooperative Elevator Co.**
PO Box 150
Blairsburg, IA 50034
Phone: (515)325-6252
Products: Grains, including corn, wheat, and soybean; Propane. **SICs:** 5153 (Grain & Field Beans); 5169 (Chemicals & Allied Products Nec). **Est:** 1937. **Sales:** $8,000,000 (2000). **Emp:** 10. **Officers:** Larry Carstens, President; Richard K. Williams, Manager.

■ 17866 ■ **Farmers Cooperative Elevator Co.**
PO Box 1009
Dawson, MN 56232-1009
Phone: (320)769-2408
Products: Grain; Feed. **SICs:** 5153 (Grain & Field Beans); 5191 (Farm Supplies). **Est:** 1927. **Sales:** $12,000,000 (2000). **Emp:** 8. **Officers:** Maynard Kemen, Chairman of the Board; Tom Collins, General Mgr.

■ 17867 ■ **Farmers Cooperative Elevator Co.**
3rd St. & Railroad Tracks
Echo, MN 56237
Phone: (507)925-4126
Products: Grain. **SICs:** 5153 (Grain & Field Beans); 5153 (Grain & Field Beans); 5191 (Farm Supplies). **Est:** 1907. **Sales:** $26,000,000 (2000). **Emp:** 21. **Officers:** John Brandts, Manager.

■ 17868 ■ **Farmers Cooperative Elevator Co.**
PO Box 316
Garden Plain, KS 67050
Phone: (316)535-2221 **Fax:** (316)535-2518
Products: Grain and farm supplies. **SICs:** 5153 (Grain & Field Beans); 5191 (Farm Supplies). **Sales:** $10,800,000 (1993). **Emp:** 26. **Officers:** L. Zoglman, President; Terry Kohler, Finance General Manager.

■ 17869 ■ **Farmers Cooperative Elevator Co. (Everly, Iowa)**
701 N Main St.
Everly, IA 51338
Phone: (712)834-2238
Products: Grain and field beans. **SIC:** 5153 (Grain & Field Beans). **Sales:** $49,000,000 (1994). **Emp:** 62. **Officers:** Thomas Goeken, President; Ralph Braufey, Controller.

■ 17870 ■ **Farmers Cooperative Elevator (Martelle, Iowa)**
124 Morley Rd.
Martelle, IA 52305
Phone: (319)482-3101
Products: Grain and farm supplies. **SICs:** 5153 (Grain & Field Beans); 5191 (Farm Supplies); 5171 (Petroleum Bulk Stations & Terminals). **Officers:** A Holcomb, President.

■ 17871 ■ **Farmers Cooperative Elevator and Supply**
116 E 6th
Newkirk, OK 74647
Phone: (580)362-3376
Products: Grain elevator; Wheat and corn; Chemicals; Fertilizers. **SICs:** 5153 (Grain & Field Beans); 5169 (Chemicals & Allied Products Nec); 5191 (Farm Supplies). **Est:** 1927. **Sales:** $9,000,000 (2000). **Emp:** 22.

■ 17872 ■ **Farmers Cooperative Grain Co.**
PO Box 12
Dalton City, IL 61925-0012
Phone: (217)874-2392
Products: Grain. **SIC:** 5153 (Grain & Field Beans). **Est:** 1906. **Sales:** $4,000,000 (2000). **Emp:** 7. **Officers:** Dean Freeland, President; Jerome Rode, General Mgr.

■ 17873 ■ **Farmers Cooperative Grain and Seed**
E 8th & Dewey Sts.
Thief River Falls, MN 56701
Phone: (218)681-6281
Products: Grain and farm supplies. **SICs:** 5153 (Grain & Field Beans); 5191 (Farm Supplies). **Sales:** $12,000,000 (1993). **Emp:** 15. **Officers:** Gary Anderson, Finance General Manager.

■ 17874 ■ **Farmers Cooperative Grain and Supply**
PO Box 47
Burdett, KS 67523
Phone: (316)525-6226
Products: Grain, wheat, milo, and corn. **SIC:** 5153 (Grain & Field Beans). **Est:** 1910. **Sales:** $4,000,000 (2000). **Emp:** 9. **Officers:** Leon Steffen, President; Jim Ray, Manager.

■ 17875 ■ **Farmers Cooperative Mill Elevator**
106 S Broadway Ave.
Carnegie, OK 73015
Phone: (580)654-1016
Products: Grain and petroleum products. **SICs:** 5153 (Grain & Field Beans); 5172 (Petroleum Products Nec). **Sales:** $27,000,000 (1994). **Emp:** 32. **Officers:** Faye Holand, Bookkeeper.

■ 17876 ■ **Farmers Cooperative (Odebolt, Iowa)**
205 E 1st St.
Odebolt, IA 51458
Phone: (712)668-2211
Products: Grain and farm supplies. **SICs:** 5153 (Grain & Field Beans); 5191 (Farm Supplies). **Sales:** $33,000,000 (1992). **Emp:** 30. **Officers:** R. Richey, Mgr. of Finance.

■ 17877 ■ **Farmers Cooperative of Pilger**
PO Box 326
Pilger, NE 68768-0326
Phone: (402)396-3414
Products: Grain and farm supplies. **SICs:** 5153 (Grain & Field Beans); 5191 (Farm Supplies). **Sales:** $17,000,000 (1993). **Emp:** 20. **Officers:** Ken Wolverton, President.

■ 17878 ■ **Farmers Cooperative Society (Sioux Center, Iowa)**
317 3rd St. NW
Sioux Center, IA 51250
Phone: (712)722-2671
Products: Farm supplies and grain. **SICs:** 5191 (Farm Supplies); 5153 (Grain & Field Beans). **Sales:** $44,000,000 (1994). **Emp:** 78. **Officers:** Kenneth Ehrp, Mgr. of Finance.

■ 17879 ■ **Farmer's Elevator Co-op**
PO Box 67
Swanton, NE 68445
Phone: (402)448-2040 **Fax:** (402)448-2395
Products: Grain elevators. **SIC:** 5153 (Grain & Field Beans). **Sales:** $16,000,000 (2000). **Emp:** 21. **Officers:** Robert Blankers, CEO.

■ 17880 ■ **Farmers Elevator Co.**
434 1st St.
Chappell, NE 69129
Phone: (308)874-2245
Free: (800)633-5803 **Fax:** (308)874-2405
Products: Grain elevator. **SIC:** 5153 (Grain & Field Beans). **Est:** 1914. **Sales:** $25,000,000 (2000). **Emp:** 34. **Officers:** Mike Pollnow, General Mgr.; Nancy Rooney, Controller.

■ 17881 ■ **Farmers Elevator Co.**
PO Box 37
Rock Valley, IA 51247
Phone: (712)476-5321
Products: Grain. **SIC:** 5153 (Grain & Field Beans). **Est:** 1899. **Sales:** $15,000,000 (2000). **Emp:** 30. **Officers:** John C. Groeneweg, President; G. Zomermaand, General Mgr.

■ 17882 ■ **Farmers Elevator Co.**
201 E Campbell
Ransom, IL 60470
Phone: (815)586-4221 **Fax:** (815)586-4248
Products: Grains, corn, and beans. **SICs:** 5153 (Grain & Field Beans); 5191 (Farm Supplies). **Est:** 1904. **Sales:** $15,000,000 (2000). **Emp:** 10. **Officers:** Michael Welbourne, General Mgr.

■ 17883 ■ **Farmers Elevator Co.**
Railroad Ave.
Circle, MT 59215
Phone: (406)485-3313
Products: Grain. **SIC:** 5153 (Grain & Field Beans). **Est:** 1931. **Sales:** $3,000,000 (2000). **Emp:** 20. **Officers:** Harvey Eiever, President.

■ 17884 ■ **Farmers Elevator Company of Manteno**
PO Box 667
Manteno, IL 60950
Phone: (815)468-3461 **Fax:** (815)468-6849
Products: Corn and beans. **SIC:** 5153 (Grain & Field Beans). **Est:** 1913. **Sales:** $10,000,000 (2000). **Emp:** 5. **Officers:** Thomas Taden, General Mgr.

■ 17885 ■ **Farmers Elevator Co. Richey Div.**
PO Box 37
Richey, MT 59259
Phone: (406)773-5758
Products: Grain elevator; Wheat and barley. **SIC:** 5153 (Grain & Field Beans). **Sales:** $300,000 (2000). **Emp:** 2. **Officers:** Rob Schriver, President.

■ 17886 ■ **Farmers Elevator and Exchange Inc.**
PO Box 65
Wapello, IA 52653
Phone: (319)523-5351 **Fax:** (319)523-5514
Products: Grain. **SIC:** 5153 (Grain & Field Beans). **Est:** 1917. **Sales:** $9,000,000 (2000). **Emp:** 23. **Officers:** Raymond Fisher, General Mgr.

■ 17887 ■ **Farmers Elevator of Fergus Falls**
406 E Junius St.
Fergus Falls, MN 56537
Phone: (218)736-2894
Products: Grain; Feed. **SICs:** 5153 (Grain & Field Beans); 5191 (Farm Supplies). **Est:** 1912. **Sales:** $12,000,000 (2000). **Emp:** 6. **Officers:** Tom Jennen, President.

■ 17888 ■ **Farmers Elevator Inc.**
Box 280
Temple, OK 73568
Phone: (580)342-6495
Products: Grain. **SIC:** 5153 (Grain & Field Beans). **Est:** 1916. **Sales:** $2,500,000 (2000). **Emp:** 6. **Officers:** Robert Spurlock, President; Becky Tomah, Bookkeeper.

■ 17889 ■ **Farmers Elevator and Supply Co.**
E Market St.
Morrison, IL 61270
Phone: (815)772-4029
Free: (888)877-7301 **Fax:** (815)772-2588
Products: Grain; Farm supplies. **SICs:** 5153 (Grain & Field Beans); 5191 (Farm Supplies). **Est:** 1919. **Sales:** $12,000,000 (2000). **Emp:** 15. **Officers:** Doug Vandermyde, President.

■ 17890 ■ **Farmer's Fur House**
R.R.1
PO Box 28
Cayuga, ND 58013-9718
Phone: (701)427-5526
Products: Farm-product raw materials, including hides and furs. **SIC:** 5159 (Farm-Product Raw Materials Nec). **Officers:** Daro Crandall, Owner.

■ **17891** ■ **Farmers Gin Company Inc.**
PO Box 295
Clinton, KY 42031
Phone: (502)653-2731 **Fax:** (502)653-2403
Products: Grain and farm supplies. **SICs:** 5153 (Grain & Field Beans); 5191 (Farm Supplies). **Sales:** $7,000,000 (2000). **Emp:** 20. **Officers:** Kenny Ward, President.

■ **17892** ■ **Farmers Grain Company of Chestnut**
100 W Olive St.
Chestnut, IL 62518
Phone: (217)796-3513 **Fax:** (217)796-3364
Products: Grains. **SIC:** 5153 (Grain & Field Beans). **Est:** 1917. **Sales:** $12,000,000 (2000). **Emp:** 10. **Officers:** Allan Opperman, President; Don Adams, Manager.

■ **17893** ■ **Farmers Grain Company of Dorans**
PO Box 715
Mattoon, IL 61938
Phone: (217)234-4955
Products: Grain; Feed. **SICs:** 5153 (Grain & Field Beans); 5191 (Farm Supplies). **Est:** 1906. **Sales:** $6,000,000 (2000). **Emp:** 7. **Officers:** Douglas Blume, President; Mark Knaus, Manager.

■ **17894** ■ **Farmers Grain Company Inc.**
PO Box 477
Pond Creek, OK 73766
Phone: (580)532-4273
Products: Grain. **SIC:** 5153 (Grain & Field Beans). **Est:** 1917. **Sales:** $7,000,000 (2000). **Emp:** 12. **Officers:** Kent Prickett, General Mgr.

■ **17895** ■ **Farmers Grain Company of Julesburg**
PO Box 296
Julesburg, CO 80737
Phone: (970)474-2537
Products: Wheat; Corn. **SIC:** 5153 (Grain & Field Beans). **Est:** 1942. **Sales:** $6,000,000 (1999). **Emp:** 6. **Officers:** James G. Kontny, President.

■ **17896** ■ **Farmers Grain Cooperative**
PO Box 9550
Ogden, UT 84409
Phone: (801)621-7803
Products: Corn; Wheat; Barley. **SIC:** 5153 (Grain & Field Beans). **Est:** 1938. **Sales:** $64,000,000 (2000). **Emp:** 100. **Officers:** Lewis S. Spears, Exec. VP; Alan F. Barron, Treasurer; Grif MaAuliffe, Merchandising Mgr.; Scott Campbell, Dir. of Data Processing.

■ **17897** ■ **Farmers Grain Dealers Inc.**
PO Box 4887
Des Moines, IA 50306
Phone: (515)223-7400
Products: Corn; Dry beans; Grain elevators. **SIC:** 5153 (Grain & Field Beans). **Sales:** $25,000,000 (2000). **Emp:** 12. **Officers:** Hal Richard, President.

■ **17898** ■ **Farmers Grain and Seed**
PO Box 1568
Nyssa, OR 97913
Phone: (541)372-2201 **Fax:** (541)372-3948
Products: Grain. **SIC:** 5153 (Grain & Field Beans). **Est:** 1945. **Sales:** $1,000,000 (2000). **Emp:** 2. **Officers:** Nancy DeBoer, Owner; Mike Couch, Dir. of Marketing & Sales; Carolyn Shoemaker, Dir. of Admin.

■ **17899** ■ **Farmers Grain and Supply Company Inc.**
409 Main
Follett, TX 79034
Phone: (806)653-3561
Products: Wheat and milo. **SICs:** 5153 (Grain & Field Beans); 5191 (Farm Supplies). **Sales:** $3,000,000 (2000). **Emp:** 12. **Officers:** K. Jett, President; Bill Cornett, Treasurer & Secty.

■ **17900** ■ **Farmers Grain Terminal**
PO Box 1232
Tallulah, LA 71282
Phone: (318)574-0564 **Fax:** (318)574-0569
Products: Grain. **SIC:** 5153 (Grain & Field Beans). **Sales:** $20,000,000 (2000). **Emp:** 5. **Officers:** Alex Curtis, President.

■ **17901** ■ **Farmers Livestock Marketing Association**
84 Rte. 127
PO Box 435
Greenville, IL 62246
Phone: (618)664-1432
Free: (800)743-9110 **Fax:** (618)664-2868
E-mail: farmer@papadoes.com
URL: http://www.famerslivestock.com
Products: Livestock, including cattle, sheep, and hogs. **SIC:** 5154 (Livestock). **Est:** 1925. **Sales:** $75,000,000 (1999). **Emp:** 22. **Officers:** Bill McKinney, General Mgr.

■ **17902** ■ **Farmers Shipping and Supply**
PO Box 128
Edmore, ND 58330
Phone: (701)644-2271 **Fax:** (701)644-2396
Products: Grain. **SIC:** 5153 (Grain & Field Beans). **Est:** 1914. **Sales:** $9,000,000 (2000). **Emp:** 5. **Officers:** Ken Spanier, General Mgr.

■ **17903** ■ **Farmers Soybean Corp.**
PO Box 749
Blytheville, AR 72316-0749
Phone: (501)763-8191
Products: Grain, including soybeans and wheat. **SICs:** 5153 (Grain & Field Beans); 5191 (Farm Supplies). **Est:** 1951. **Sales:** $20,000,000 (2000). **Emp:** 17. **Officers:** Paul C. Hughes, CEO & President.

■ **17904** ■ **Farmers Union Co-op**
600 W Broad St.
PO Box 8
Blue Springs, NE 68318-0008
Phone: (402)645-3356 **Fax:** (402)645-8114
Products: Grain elevator. **SIC:** 5153 (Grain & Field Beans). **Est:** 1919. **Sales:** $4,000,000 (2000). **Emp:** 7. **Officers:** Nick Savener, President; Dennis Morgan, General Mgr.

■ **17905** ■ **Farmers Union Cooperative Association**
Rte. 1
Nora, NE 68961
Phone: (402)225-4177
Products: Grain elevator. **SIC:** 5153 (Grain & Field Beans). **Est:** 1911. **Sales:** $7,000,000 (2000). **Emp:** 20. **Officers:** Jim Lynch, President; Doug Muehlich, General Mgr.

■ **17906** ■ **Farmers Union Cooperative Association (Mead, Nebraska)**
PO Box 154
Mead, NE 68041
Phone: (402)624-3255
Products: Grain and farm supplies. **SIC:** 5153 (Grain & Field Beans). **Officers:** Mark Gustafson, President.

■ **17907** ■ **Farmers Union Cooperative Co.**
PO Box 135
Friend, NE 68359-0135
Phone: (402)947-4291
Products: Grain elevator. **SIC:** 5153 (Grain & Field Beans). **Est:** 1919. **Sales:** $8,000,000 (2000). **Emp:** 10. **Officers:** Dave Bruntz, President; Doris Schlegelmilch, Bookkeeper; Dennis Heng, General Mgr.

■ **17908** ■ **Farmers Union Cooperative Elevator Co.**
PO Box 36
Wray, CO 80758
Phone: (970)332-4703
Products: Grain, including wheat. **SIC:** 5153 (Grain & Field Beans). **Est:** 1917. **Sales:** $1,100,000 (2000). **Emp:** 11. **Officers:** Chris Wisdom, President; Brent Ostman, General Mgr.

■ **17909** ■ **Farmers Union Elevator Co.**
PO Box 390
Lindsborg, KS 67456
Phone: (785)227-3361 **Fax:** (785)227-4457
Products: Grain elevators. **SIC:** 5153 (Grain & Field Beans). **Sales:** $10,000,000 (2000). **Emp:** 20. **Officers:** Steve Biehler, General Mgr.

■ **17910** ■ **Farmers Union Grain Cooperative**
PO Box 8
Edgeley, ND 58433
Phone: (701)493-2481
Products: Grains, including corn, soybeans, and wheat. **SICs:** 5153 (Grain & Field Beans); 5191 (Farm Supplies). **Est:** 1939. **Sales:** $12,000,000 (2000). **Emp:** 9. **Officers:** Mike Brandenburg, President.

■ **17911** ■ **Farmers Union Oil Co. (Ellendale, North Dakota)**
PO Box 219
Ellendale, ND 58436
Phone: (701)349-3280
Products: Farm supplies. **SIC:** 5191 (Farm Supplies). **Sales:** $4,900,000 (2000). **Emp:** 30. **Officers:** Kevin Brokaw, President; Jeff Schaefer, CFO.

■ **17912** ■ **Farmland Grain Div.**
10100 N Executive Hills Dr.
Kansas City, MO 64153
Phone: (816)459-3300 **Fax:** (816)459-3395
Products: Grain. **SIC:** 5153 (Grain & Field Beans). **Sales:** $1,060,000,000 (2000). **Emp:** 400. **Officers:** John Bernardi, Exec. VP, Chairman of the Board & CEO; Charlie Deis, Controller.

■ **17913** ■ **Farmland Industries Inc. Union Equity Exchange Div.**
PO Box 3408
Enid, OK 73702
Phone: (580)233-5100
Products: Wheat; Grain; Soybeans; Milo. **SIC:** 5153 (Grain & Field Beans). **Est:** 1926. **Sales:** $900,000,000 (2000). **Emp:** 338. **Officers:** William R. Allen Jr., CEO & President; Edwin Wallace, CFO; Fred Howard, Sr. VP of Marketing.

■ **17914** ■ **Farmland Service Cooperative**
PO Box 80
Gothenburg, NE 69138
Phone: (308)537-7141
Products: Grain and farm supplies. **SICs:** 5153 (Grain & Field Beans); 5191 (Farm Supplies). **Sales:** $46,000,000 (1994). **Emp:** 100. **Officers:** James Rubenthaler, President; Stan Mitchell, Controller.

■ **17915** ■ **W.D. Felder & Co.**
PO Box 815
Lubbock, TX 79408
Phone: (806)763-6630 **Fax:** (806)762-5031
Products: Raw cotton. **SIC:** 5159 (Farm-Product Raw Materials Nec). **Est:** 1904. **Officers:** Tom Smith.

■ **17916** ■ **Ferguson Cattle Co. Inc.**
PO Box 3286
Bozeman, MT 59772-3286
Phone: (406)586-1648
Products: Livestock; Cattle. **SIC:** 5154 (Livestock). **Officers:** Jeff Ferguson, President.

■ **17917** ■ **Fessenden Cooperative Association**
PO Box 126
Fessenden, ND 58438
Phone: (701)547-3291
Products: Grain, grain products and farm-related supplies. **SICs:** 5153 (Grain & Field Beans); 5191 (Farm Supplies). **Sales:** $36,300,000 (1992). **Emp:** 25. **Officers:** Lyle Wipf, General Mgr.

■ **17918** ■ **Finger Lakes Livestock Exchange Inc.**
Rte. 5 & Rte. 20
Canandaigua, NY 14424
Phone: (716)394-1515
Products: Livestock. **SIC:** 5154 (Livestock). **Est:** 1964. **Sales:** $15,000,000 (2000). **Emp:** 28. **Officers:** R. Parker, Owner; Barbara Parker, Treasurer & Secty.

■ **17919** ■ **Fisher Farmers Grain and Coal Co.**
1 Main St.
Dewey, IL 61840
Phone: (217)897-1111 **Fax:** (217)897-1979
Products: Grain and farm supplies. **SICs:** 5153 (Grain & Field Beans); 5191 (Farm Supplies). **Sales:** $45,000,000 (1992). **Emp:** 30. **Officers:** Louis Schwing Jr., President; John Cummings, Finance General Manager.

■ 17920 ■ Four Circle Cooperative
PO Box 99
Bird City, KS 67731
Phone: (785)734-2331 **Fax:** (785)734-2481
Products: Grain elevator. **SIC:** 5153 (Grain & Field Beans). **Est:** 1914. **Sales:** $15,000,000 (2000). **Emp:** 17. **Officers:** Ned Smith, President.

■ 17921 ■ Four Seasons F.S. Inc.
N 6055 State Rd. 40
Elk Mound, WI 54739
Phone: (715)835-3194
Products: Grain, fertilizer, seed, feed, chemical, livestock equipment and grain bins. **SIC:** 5153 (Grain & Field Beans). **Sales:** $59,000,000 (2000). **Emp:** 65. **Officers:** James Sharpee, President; Dave Christensen, CFO.

■ 17922 ■ Fowler Elevator Inc.
PO Box L
Newtown, MO 64667
Phone: (660)794-5435
Products: Grain. **SIC:** 5153 (Grain & Field Beans). **Est:** 1946. **Sales:** $10,000,000 (2000). **Emp:** 20. **Officers:** John J. Fowler, President.

■ 17923 ■ Fowler Equity Exchange Inc.
Hwy. 54 & Main St.
Fowler, KS 67844
Phone: (316)646-5262 **Fax:** (316)646-5372
Products: Farming products, including grain, feed, seed, fertilizer, petroleum products, seed cleaning and farm supply products. **SIC:** 5153 (Grain & Field Beans). **Est:** 1914. **Sales:** $8,800,000 (2000). **Emp:** 12. **Officers:** Brent Marshall, President & General Mgr.

■ 17924 ■ C.B. Fox Co.
220 Camp St.
New Orleans, LA 70130
Phone: (504)588-9211
Products: Grain. **SIC:** 5153 (Grain & Field Beans). **Est:** 1894. **Sales:** $2,000,000 (2000). **Emp:** 4. **Officers:** Joel M. Pratt, President & Treasurer.

■ 17925 ■ Foxley Grain
814 N 5th St.
PO Box 512
Clear Lake, IA 50428
Phone: (515)357-6131 **Fax:** (515)357-7168
Products: Soybeans, black soybeans, Azuki, and corn. **SIC:** 5153 (Grain & Field Beans). **Officers:** Kim F. Pleggenkuhle, Manager.

■ 17926 ■ Fredonia Cooperative Association
PO Box 538
Fredonia, KS 66736
Phone: (316)378-2191
Products: Grain elevator. **SIC:** 5153 (Grain & Field Beans). **Est:** 1948. **Sales:** $7,000,000 (2000). **Emp:** 9. **Officers:** Everett Metzger, General Mgr.

■ 17927 ■ Frenchman Valley Farmer's Cooperative
143 Broadway Ave.
Imperial, NE 69033
Phone: (308)882-4381
Free: (800)538-2667 **Fax:** (308)882-3242
Products: Grain elevator. **SIC:** 5191 (Farm Supplies). **Est:** 1965. **Sales:** $52,000,000 (2000). **Emp:** 130. **Officers:** Rand Levy, President; Tim Greene, CFO; Duane Brammer, General Mgr.

■ 17928 ■ Frick Hog Buying & Trucking
PO Box 661
Yankton, SD 57078-0661
Phone: (605)665-6839
Products: Livestock; Hogs. **SIC:** 5154 (Livestock). **Officers:** John Frick, President.

■ 17929 ■ Frick's Services Inc.
PO Box 40
Wawaka, IN 46794
Phone: (219)761-3311
Products: Farm supplies and grain. **SICs:** 5191 (Farm Supplies); 5153 (Grain & Field Beans). **Sales:** $75,000,000 (1992). **Emp:** 100. **Officers:** Merrill B. Frick, CFO.

■ 17930 ■ Frontier Cooperative Co.
PO Box 379
David City, NE 68632
Phone: (402)367-3019
Products: Grain and farm supplies. **SICs:** 5153 (Grain & Field Beans); 5191 (Farm Supplies). **Sales:** $52,000,000 (1994). **Emp:** 50. **Officers:** G. Stara, General Mgr.

■ 17931 ■ Funks Grove Grain Co.
PO Box 246
McLean, IL 61754
Phone: (309)874-2771
Products: Grain. **SIC:** 5153 (Grain & Field Beans). **Sales:** $4,200,000 (2000). **Emp:** 5. **Officers:** Rick Jannusch, President; Katie Rousey, Treasurer.

■ 17932 ■ Gallagher's Inc.
1450 Sheldon Rd.
St. Albans, VT 05478
Phone: (802)524-5336
Products: Cattle. **SIC:** 5154 (Livestock). **Former Name:** S.R. & T.M. Gallagher.

■ 17933 ■ Garrard County Stockyard
PO Box 654
Lancaster, KY 40444
Phone: (606)792-2118
Products: Livestock, including cows, bulls, steers, and heifers. **SIC:** 5154 (Livestock). **Est:** 1939. **Sales:** $30,000,000 (2000). **Emp:** 50. **Officers:** E. Freeman, President; R.C. Freeman, Chairman of the Board & Finance Officer.

■ 17934 ■ Garwood Implement and Supply Co.
PO Box 428
Garwood, TX 77442
Phone: (409)758-3221 **Fax:** (409)758-3844
Products: Dried rice. **SIC:** 5153 (Grain & Field Beans). **Est:** 1936. **Sales:** $10,000,000 (2000). **Emp:** 25. **Officers:** William N. Lehrer, President.

■ 17935 ■ Gass Horse Supply
476 Main St.
Orono, ME 04473-0476
Phone: (207)866-2075 **Free:** (800)439-2075
Products: Horse supplies and equipment. **SICs:** 5159 (Farm-Product Raw Materials Nec); 5083 (Farm & Garden Machinery). **Est:** 1909. **Emp:** 1. **Officers:** John Gass, Owner. **Former Name:** Gass Sales Stables.

■ 17936 ■ Gateway Co-Op
PO Box 125
Galva, IL 61434
Phone: (309)932-2081 **Fax:** (309)932-3136
E-mail: gateway@inw.net
Products: Grain; Farm supplies. **SICs:** 5153 (Grain & Field Beans); 5191 (Farm Supplies). **Est:** 1899. **Sales:** $42,400,000 (2000). **Emp:** 94. **Officers:** L. Wayne Krieg, General Mgr.; Kathy Huffman, Office Mgr.; Scott Sallee, Dir. of Marketing & Sales.

■ 17937 ■ General Genetics Inc.
13811 Cypress Ave.
Sand Lake, MI 49343-9639
Phone: (616)636-8876 **Fax:** (616)636-4914
Products: Animal health products; Bull semen. **SIC:** 5159 (Farm-Product Raw Materials Nec). **Officers:** Richard Van Hoven, President.

■ 17938 ■ Genesee Union Warehouse Company Inc.
PO Box 67
Genesee, ID 83832
Phone: (208)285-1141 **Fax:** (208)285-1716
E-mail: guw@turbonet.com
Products: Barley; Wheat; Peas; Lentils; Chickpeas. **SICs:** 5153 (Grain & Field Beans); 5191 (Farm Supplies). **Est:** 1916. **Sales:** $13,400,000 (2000). **Emp:** 14. **Officers:** Bill Wood, General Mgr.; Mike Martinez, Manager; Sam White, Grain Dept. Mgr.

■ 17939 ■ Genetic Leaders International
193 Woodburn Pl.
Advance, NC 27006-9456
Phone: (910)998-3958 **Fax:** (910)998-3958
Products: Livestock. **SIC:** 5154 (Livestock). **Officers:** P. Simmons, Owner.

■ 17940 ■ Doug Gilmou Inc.
RRNo. 1, Box 15A
Barnet, VT 05821
Phone: (802)633-2575 **Fax:** (802)633-4380
Products: Cattle; Auctioning livestock. **SIC:** 5154 (Livestock). **Officers:** Doug Gilmou, President.

■ 17941 ■ Ging and Co.
PO Box 248
Farina, IL 62838
Phone: (618)245-3333
Products: Seed; Grain. **SICs:** 5153 (Grain & Field Beans); 5191 (Farm Supplies). **Est:** 1898. **Sales:** $9,000,000 (2000). **Emp:** 11. **Officers:** Stanley Soldner, General Mgr.

■ 17942 ■ Glen's Peanuts and Grains Inc.
1668 N M 88
Portales, NM 88130-9670
Phone: (505)276-8201 **Fax:** (505)276-8394
E-mail: gpeanuts@yucca.net
Products: Dealers in raw, roasted, farm products; roasted/salted processed or shelled peanuts; processed, unshelled peanuts. **SIC:** 5159 (Farm-Product Raw Materials Nec). **Est:** 1977. **Sales:** $2,100,000 (1999). **Emp:** 18. **Officers:** Glen McAfee, President; Eldon McAfee, Vice President.

■ 17943 ■ Gligorea Livestock
PO Box 6628
Sheridan, WY 82801-7102
Phone: (307)674-7600
Products: Livestock. **SIC:** 5154 (Livestock). **Officers:** Gene Gligorea, Partner.

■ 17944 ■ Otto Goedecke Inc.
PO Box 387
Hallettsville, TX 77964
Phone: (512)798-3261 **Fax:** (512)798-3262
Products: Cotton. **SIC:** 5159 (Farm-Product Raw Materials Nec). **Est:** 1932. **Sales:** $2,500,000 (2000). **Emp:** 6. **Officers:** Otto E. Goedecke, President.

■ 17945 ■ H. E. Goldberg & Co., Inc.
9050 M. L. King Way S
Seattle, WA 98118
Phone: (206)722-8200
Free: (800)722-8201 **Fax:** (206)722-0435
E-mail: hegcofur@aol.com
URL: http://www.hegoldbergfur.com
Products: Furskins. **SIC:** 5159 (Farm-Product Raw Materials Nec). **Officers:** J. Irwin Goldberg, President.

■ 17946 ■ Golden Belt Cooperative Association Inc.
PO Box 138
Ellis, KS 67637
Phone: (785)726-3115
Products: Grain elevator. **SIC:** 5153 (Grain & Field Beans). **Est:** 1903. **Sales:** $5,000,000 (2000). **Emp:** 12. **Officers:** Peter D. Johnson, President; Gary Kohl, Treasurer & Secty.

■ 17947 ■ Good Seed and Grain Company Inc.
PO Box 157
Hamburg, IA 51640
Phone: (712)382-1238 **Fax:** (712)382-2001
Products: Grain, including white and yellow corn and soybeans. **SIC:** 5153 (Grain & Field Beans). **Est:** 1917. **Sales:** $10,000,000 (2000). **Emp:** 15. **Officers:** Richard Dittberner, General Mgr.

■ 17948 ■ Goodhue Elevator Association Cooperative
PO Box 218
Goodhue, MN 55027
Phone: (612)923-4496
Products: Grain elevator. **SIC:** 5153 (Grain & Field Beans). **Est:** 1905. **Sales:** $4,000,000 (2000). **Emp:** 20. **Officers:** Bill Ahlbrecht, General Mgr.

■ 17949 ■ Gooding Livestock Community Co.
Lee'Mark W
822 Ambassador Dr.
Henderson, NV 89015-9629
Products: Livestock. **SIC:** 5154 (Livestock). **Officers:** Tony Barth, Owner.

■ 17950 ■ **Goodland Cooperative Equity Exchange Inc.**
PO Box 998
Goodland, KS 67735
Phone: (913)899-3681
Products: Grain elevator. **SIC:** 5153 (Grain & Field Beans). **Est:** 1915. **Sales:** $40,000,000 (2000). **Emp:** 45. **Officers:** Steve Evert, President; Randy Schoenphaler, Controller.

■ 17951 ■ **Graham Grain Co.**
200 Voorhees St.
Terre Haute, IN 47802
Phone: (812)232-1044
Products: Grain. **SIC:** 5153 (Grain & Field Beans). **Sales:** $17,000,000 (2000). **Emp:** 11. **Officers:** John Cook, General Mgr.

■ 17952 ■ **Grain Growers Cooperative (Cimarron, Kansas)**
PO Box 508
Cimarron, KS 67835
Phone: (316)335-5101
Products: Grain, farm supplies. **SICs:** 5153 (Grain & Field Beans); 5191 (Farm Supplies). **Officers:** Larry Scott, CEO.

■ 17953 ■ **Grain Land Co-op**
Hwy. 22
Minnesota Lake, MN 56068
Phone: (507)462-3315 **Fax:** (507)462-3316
Products: Grain; Products of petroleum refining; Agricultural chemicals. **SICs:** 5153 (Grain & Field Beans); 5172 (Petroleum Products Nec); 5191 (Farm Supplies). **Sales:** $1,900,000 (2000). **Emp:** 2. **Officers:** Mike Christensen, President.

■ 17954 ■ **Grain Land Cooperative**
PO Box 65
Blue Earth, MN 56013
Phone: (507)526-3211 **Fax:** (507)526-4614
Products: Grain. **SICs:** 5153 (Grain & Field Beans); 5191 (Farm Supplies). **Est:** 1914. **Emp:** 220. **Officers:** Don Gales, General Mgr.; Bill Erickson, CFO.

■ 17955 ■ **Grainland Cooperative**
RR 1, Box 860
Eureka, IL 61530
Phone: (309)467-2355
Products: Grain. **SIC:** 5153 (Grain & Field Beans). **Est:** 1904. **Sales:** $9,000,000 (2000). **Emp:** 7. **Officers:** Ed Wyss, President; Jeff Brooks, General Mgr. **Former Name:** Farmers Grain Cooperative of Eureka.

■ 17956 ■ **Grainland Cooperative**
RR 1, Box 860
Eureka, IL 61530
Phone: (309)744-2218 **Fax:** (309)744-2416
E-mail: glsecor@elpaso.net
Products: Grain elevator; Corn and beans; Farming supplies. **SICs:** 5153 (Grain & Field Beans); 5191 (Farm Supplies). **Est:** 1903. **Sales:** $35,000,000 (2000). **Emp:** 11. **Officers:** Ed Wyss, President. **Former Name:** Secor Elevator Copmany Inc.

■ 17957 ■ **Grand Prairie Cooperative**
PO Box 10
Sadorus, IL 61872
Phone: (217)598-2312
Products: Grain. **SIC:** 5153 (Grain & Field Beans). **Sales:** $50,000,000 (1992). **Emp:** 50. **Officers:** Dennis Montavon, Finance General Manager.

■ 17958 ■ **Grandview Hatchery & Locker Plant**
716 10th Ave.
Belle Fourche, SD 57717-1509
Phone: (605)892-3866
Products: Farm-product raw materials; Farm animals; Chicks. **SIC:** 5159 (Farm-Product Raw Materials Nec). **Officers:** Fred Carlson, Partner.

■ 17959 ■ **Gray Storage and Dryer Company Inc.**
Hwy. 129 N
Ocilla, GA 31774
Phone: (912)468-9451
Products: Peanuts. **SIC:** 5159 (Farm-Product Raw Materials Nec). **Est:** 1954. **Sales:** $32,000,000 (2000).

Emp: 60. **Officers:** Jack Gray, President; Gloria Hudson, Treasurer & Secty.

■ 17960 ■ **Great Bend Cooperative Association**
PO Box 68
Great Bend, KS 67530
Phone: (316)793-3533 **Fax:** (316)792-1999
Products: Grain elevator. **SICs:** 5153 (Grain & Field Beans); 5191 (Farm Supplies). **Est:** 1959. **Sales:** $16,500,000 (2000). **Emp:** 47. **Officers:** Danny Leroy, President; Frank Riedl, Controller.

■ 17961 ■ **Great Plains Co-op**
PO Box 137
Benedict, NE 68316
Phone: (402)732-6622
Products: Grain and farm supplies. **SICs:** 5153 (Grain & Field Beans); 5191 (Farm Supplies). **Sales:** $26,000,000 (1993). **Emp:** 40. **Officers:** Jim Biermann, Manager; Bonnie Tindall, Controller.

■ 17962 ■ **Greeley Elevator Co.**
700 6th St.
Greeley, CO 80631
Phone: (970)352-2575
Products: Feed; Beans. **SICs:** 5153 (Grain & Field Beans); 5191 (Farm Supplies). **Est:** 1920. **Sales:** $2,000,000 (2000). **Emp:** 5. **Officers:** Matt Geib, Manager.

■ 17963 ■ **Green Seed Co.**
1080 Highway 29 N
Athens, GA 30601-1124
Phone: (706)548-7333
Products: Farm supplies. **SIC:** 5191 (Farm Supplies). **Sales:** $34,000,000 (1994). **Emp:** 200. **Officers:** Alan Rosoff, President.

■ 17964 ■ **Gregory Livestock**
1109 Felton Ave.
Gregory, SD 57533-1145
Phone: (605)835-9408
Products: Livestock. **SIC:** 5154 (Livestock). **Officers:** Gary Stinton, Owner.

■ 17965 ■ **GROWMARK Inc.**
1701 Towanda Ave.
Bloomington, IL 61701
Phone: (309)557-6000 **Fax:** (309)829-8532
Products: Farm supplies, petroleum and grain. **SICs:** 5191 (Farm Supplies); 5171 (Petroleum Bulk Stations & Terminals); 5153 (Grain & Field Beans). **Sales:** $330,000,000 (2000). **Emp:** 845. **Officers:** Norm Jones, CEO; Vern McGinnis, VP & CFO.

■ 17966 ■ **Gruen Export Co.**
6310 N Port Washington Rd.
PO Box 17287
Milwaukee, WI 53217
Phone: (414)964-4880 **Fax:** (414)964-0278
Products: Hides; Leather tanning and finishing. **SICs:** 5159 (Farm-Product Raw Materials Nec); 5199 (Nondurable Goods Nec). **Officers:** Steven O. Gruen, President.

■ 17967 ■ **G.A. Hackler Livestock**
3880 W Franklin Rd.
Meridian, ID 83642-5442
Phone: (208)888-1732
Products: Livestock; Cattle. **SIC:** 5154 (Livestock). **Officers:** G. Hackler, Partner.

■ 17968 ■ **Hahn and Phillips Grease Company Inc.**
PO Box 130
Marshall, MO 65340
Phone: (660)886-9688 **Fax:** (660)886-7173
Products: Inedible animal greases, tallows, and proteins. **SICs:** 5191 (Farm Supplies); 5149 (Groceries & Related Products Nec); 5199 (Nondurable Goods Nec). **Est:** 1957. **Sales:** $35,000,000 (2000). **Emp:** 42. **Officers:** Larry R. Phillips, President; Terry Clark, Vice President; W.E. Phillips, CEO.

■ 17969 ■ **Hahnaman-Albrecht Inc.**
1318 E State St.
Rockford, IL 61104-2228
Phone: (815)288-7330
Products: Fertilizer; Grain, corn, wheat, and soybeans. **SIC:** 5153 (Grain & Field Beans). **Est:** 1984. **Sales:** $55,000,000 (2000). **Emp:** 65. **Officers:** Dean Hamilton, CEO; Jeffrey D. Hamilton, CFO.

■ 17970 ■ **Raymond Haider**
407 12th St. NW
Mandan, ND 58554-1932
Phone: (701)663-7236
Products: Livestock; Cattle. **SIC:** 5154 (Livestock). **Officers:** Raymond Haider, Owner.

■ 17971 ■ **Hallock Cooperative Elevator Co.**
310 S Atlantic St.
Hallock, MN 56728
Phone: (218)843-2624
Products: Grain. **SIC:** 5153 (Grain & Field Beans). **Est:** 1967. **Sales:** $15,000,000 (2000). **Emp:** 3. **Officers:** Kim Turner, General Mgr.

■ 17972 ■ **Halstad Elevator Co.**
PO Box 87
Halstad, MN 56548
Phone: (218)456-2135
Products: Grain; Fertilizer; Chemicals. **SICs:** 5153 (Grain & Field Beans); 5191 (Farm Supplies). **Est:** 1898. **Sales:** $14,000,000 (2000). **Emp:** 10. **Officers:** Robin H. Stene, General Mgr.; Michelle Wescott, Bookkeeper.

■ 17973 ■ **Hamilton Elevator Company Inc.**
PO Box 177
Campus, IL 60920
Phone: (815)567-3311 **Fax:** (815)567-3430
Products: Grain and field beans. **SIC:** 5153 (Grain & Field Beans). **Sales:** $5,000,000 (2000). **Emp:** 6. **Officers:** Rodney W. Carlson, President & CFO; Maureen Carlson, Secretary.

■ 17974 ■ **Harco Distributing Co.**
PO Box 913
Stuttgart, AR 72160
Phone: (870)673-4071 **Fax:** (870)673-6521
Products: Agricultural equipment, including seed and grain testing equipment; Seeds. **SICs:** 5153 (Grain & Field Beans); 5191 (Farm Supplies); 5083 (Farm & Garden Machinery). **Officers:** Doug Hartz, President.

■ 17975 ■ **Hardy Cooperative Elevator Co.**
PO Box 8
Hardy, IA 50545
Phone: (515)824-3221
Products: Corn; Beans; Fertilizers; Chemicals. **SICs:** 5153 (Grain & Field Beans); 5191 (Farm Supplies); 5169 (Chemicals & Allied Products Nec). **Est:** 1915. **Sales:** $26,000,000 (2000). **Emp:** 20. **Officers:** M. Worland, CEO; Larry Meyers, Information Systems Mgr.

■ 17976 ■ **Harmony Co-op**
212 S Division St.
Colby, WI 54421
Phone: (715)223-2306
Products: Farm supplies, petroleum products and hardware. **SICs:** 5191 (Farm Supplies); 5172 (Petroleum Products Nec); 5072 (Hardware). **Sales:** $9,900,000 (1994). **Emp:** 27. **Officers:** Ronald Schmidt, President; Arleen Christophersen, Bookkeeper.

■ 17977 ■ **B.H. Harrison Livestock Co.**
903 Butler Ferry Rd.
Bainbridge, GA 31717
Phone: (912)246-5344
Products: Livestock, including hogs. **SIC:** 5154 (Livestock).

■ 17978 ■ **Hartman Hide and Fur Company Inc.**
PO Box 518
Detroit Lakes, MN 56502
Phone: (218)847-5681 **Fax:** (218)847-8570
Products: Raw furs; Hides. **SIC:** 5159 (Farm-Product Raw Materials Nec). **Sales:** $5,000,000 (2000). **Emp:** 9. **Officers:** Ed Hartman; S.M. Hartman, Partner.

■ **17979** ■ **Hartsburg Grain Co.**
PO Box 80
Hartsburg, IL 62643
Phone: (217)642-5211
Products: Grain; Corn; Lumber. **SICs:** 5153 (Grain & Field Beans); 5031 (Lumber, Plywood & Millwork). **Est:** 1903. **Sales:** $6,000,000 (2000). **Emp:** 4. **Officers:** Jeff Duckworth, CEO.

■ **17980** ■ **Jacob Hartz Seed Company Inc.**
901 N Park Ave.
Stuttgart, AR 72160
Phone: (501)673-8565 **Fax:** (501)673-1476
Products: Soybeans, wheat, and rice. **SIC:** 5153 (Grain & Field Beans). **Est:** 1925. **Sales:** $26,500,000 (2000). **Emp:** 80. **Officers:** Danny Kennedy, President; Larry Spooner, Dir. of Marketing; Allen Stone, Dir. of Information Systems; Betty Burton, Dir of Personnel.

■ **17981** ■ **Harvest States Cooperatives Line Elevator Div.**
PO Box 432
Montevideo, MN 56265
Phone: (320)269-6531
Products: Grain. **SIC:** 5153 (Grain & Field Beans). **Est:** 1906. **Sales:** $40,000,000 (2000). **Emp:** 27. **Officers:** Jeff Spence, General Mgr.

■ **17982** ■ **Harvest States Soybean Processing**
PO Box 3247
Mankato, MN 56001
Phone: (507)625-7911
Free: (800)642-5365 **Fax:** (507)345-2254
Products: Soybean Meal, refined soybean oil, and soy flour. **SIC:** 5153 (Grain & Field Beans). **Sales:** $450,000,000 (2000). **Emp:** 195. **Officers:** James D. Tibbets.

■ **17983** ■ **Donald Hauck**
PO Box 1914
Minot, ND 58702-1914
Phone: (701)839-7595
Products: Livestock. **SIC:** 5154 (Livestock). **Officers:** Donald Hauck, Owner.

■ **17984** ■ **Haverhill Cooperative**
PO Box 50
Haverhill, IA 50120
Phone: (515)475-3221 **Fax:** (515)496-5225
Products: Grain. **SIC:** 5191 (Farm Supplies). **Est:** 1929. **Sales:** $12,000,000 (2000). **Emp:** 8. **Officers:** Mark Klamfoth, Manager.

■ **17985** ■ **Hay Land and Livestock Inc.**
PO Box 52
Pinedale, WY 82941-0052
Phone: (307)367-4522
Products: Livestock. **SIC:** 5154 (Livestock). **Officers:** Joseph Hay, President.

■ **17986** ■ **Heartland Co-op (Trumbull, Nebraska)**
PO Box 73
Trumbull, NE 68980
Phone: (402)743-2381
Products: Grain and farm supplies. **SICs:** 5153 (Grain & Field Beans); 5191 (Farm Supplies). **Sales:** $54,000,000 (1994). **Emp:** 63. **Officers:** Dennis Salmen, General Mgr.; Dennis Asmus, Accountant.

■ **17987** ■ **Hector Farmers Elevator**
141 Ash Ave. E
Hector, MN 55342
Phone: (320)848-2273
Products: Grain; Farm supplies. **SICs:** 5153 (Grain & Field Beans); 5191 (Farm Supplies). **Est:** 1912. **Sales:** $3,000,000 (2000). **Emp:** 12. **Officers:** John Washburn, Manager.

■ **17988** ■ **Heinold Hog Market Inc.**
PO Box 375
Kouts, IN 46347
Phone: (219)766-2211 **Fax:** (219)766-3224
Products: Hogs. **SIC:** 5154 (Livestock). **Est:** 1987. **Sales:** $160,000,000 (2000). **Emp:** 225. **Officers:** Terry Miller, President; Larry Sievers, Chairman of the Board & CFO.

■ **17989** ■ **Chester Heitmann**
504 E Railroad St.
Cut Bank, MT 59427-3018
Phone: (406)873-2051
Products: Merchants of raw farm products; Feathers; Hides; Pelts. **SIC:** 5159 (Farm-Product Raw Materials Nec). **Officers:** Chester Heitmann, Owner.

■ **17990** ■ **Hennepin Cooperative Seed Exchange Inc.**
8175 Lewis Rd.
Golden Valley, MN 55427
Phone: (612)545-7702
Products: Feed and seed. **SIC:** 5191 (Farm Supplies). **Sales:** $8,000,000 (1994). **Emp:** 35. **Officers:** Paul Oie, Finance General Manager.

■ **17991** ■ **Heraa Inc.**
PO Box 591
Veguita, NM 87062-0591
Phone: (505)864-6935 **Fax:** (505)864-4144
Products: Livestock; Cattle. **SIC:** 5154 (Livestock). **Officers:** Iman Ghoreishi, President.

■ **17992** ■ **Hereford Grain Corp.**
PO Box 910
Hereford, TX 79045-0910
Phone: (806)364-3755 **Fax:** (806)364-0708
Products: Wheat, milo, and corn. **SICs:** 5153 (Grain & Field Beans); 5191 (Farm Supplies). **Est:** 1953. **Sales:** $17,000,000 (2000). **Emp:** 33. **Officers:** Frank Brorman, President; Joe Artho, Treasurer.

■ **17993** ■ **Herkimer Cooperative Business Association**
317 Brenecke
Bremen, KS 66412
Phone: (785)744-3226
Products: Grain elevator. **SIC:** 5191 (Farm Supplies). **Est:** 1916. **Sales:** $6,500,000 (2000). **Emp:** 17. **Officers:** James Leseberg, President.

■ **17994** ■ **Herreid Livestock Market**
PO Box 67
Herreid, SD 57632-0067
Phone: (605)437-2265 **Fax:** (605)437-2634
Products: Livestock. **SIC:** 5154 (Livestock). **Officers:** Herman Schumacher, Partner.

■ **17995** ■ **Hettinger Cooperative Equity Exchange**
Railroad Right of Way
Hettinger, ND 58639
Phone: (701)567-2408
Free: (800)249-2408 **Fax:** (701)567-2003
Products: Grain. **SIC:** 5153 (Grain & Field Beans). **Est:** 1914. **Sales:** $5,000,000 (1999). **Emp:** 5. **Officers:** Terry Henderson, CEO; Eugene Burrer, Treasurer & Secty.

■ **17996** ■ **Hiawatha Grain Co.**
4111 Central Ave. NE, No. 212
Columbia Heights, MN 55421
Phone: (612)789-5270 **Fax:** (612)789-5290
Products: Grains; Screenings; Malt sprouts. **SIC:** 5153 (Grain & Field Beans). **Est:** 1920. **Sales:** $1,000,000 (2000). **Emp:** 2. **Officers:** John P. Fudali Jr., President.

■ **17997** ■ **High Plains Cooperative**
PO Box 520
Kimball, NE 69145
Phone: (308)235-4655 **Fax:** (308)235-2107
E-mail: hpc@megavision.com
URL: http://www.hpcoop.com
Products: Grain. **SIC:** 5153 (Grain & Field Beans). **Est:** 1930. **Sales:** $22,000,000 (2000). **Emp:** 51. **Officers:** S. Hillius, General Mgr.

■ **17998** ■ **Highmore Auction**
PO Box 504
Highmore, SD 57345-0245
Phone: (605)852-2211
Products: Livestock. **SIC:** 5154 (Livestock). **Officers:** Nathan Shaull, Owner.

■ **17999** ■ **C.F. Hill Grain Co. Inc.**
116 Aisne St.
Bartlett, TX 76511
Phone: (254)527-3311
Products: Grain; Fertilizer and fertilizer materials. **SICs:** 5153 (Grain & Field Beans); 5191 (Farm Supplies). **Est:** 1974. **Sales:** $4,400,000 (2000). **Emp:** 4. **Officers:** James C. Hill, President; Ernest Fisher, Treasurer & Secty.; Tommy Hill, Vice President.

■ **18000** ■ **Hillsdale Cooperative Elevator**
PO Box 265
Hillsdale, IL 61257
Phone: (309)658-2218
Products: Grain. **SIC:** 5153 (Grain & Field Beans). **Est:** 1921. **Sales:** $2,000,000 (2000). **Emp:** 6. **Officers:** Rod Stinson, President; Victor Johnson, President.

■ **18001** ■ **Hoegemeyer Hybrids Inc.**
1755 Hoegemeyer Rd.
Hooper, NE 68031
Phone: (402)654-3399
Free: (800)245-4631 **Fax:** (402)654-3342
E-mail: hoeghyb@corn1.com
URL: http://www.corn1.com
Products: Seed. **SIC:** 5153 (Grain & Field Beans). **Est:** 1937. **Sales:** $10,000,000 (2000). **Emp:** 35. **Officers:** Tom Hoegemeyer, President; Steven Ziegler, CFO; Sue Stenberg, Dir. of Marketing.

■ **18002** ■ **Holmquist Grain and Lumber Co.**
200 N Logan Ave.
PO Box 127
Oakland, NE 68045
Phone: (402)685-5641 **Fax:** (402)685-5131
Products: Grain; Lumber and wood products; Feed. **SICs:** 5153 (Grain & Field Beans); 5031 (Lumber, Plywood & Millwork); 5191 (Farm Supplies). **Est:** 1883. **Sales:** $16,300,000 (2000). **Emp:** 40. **Officers:** Robert L. Peters, President; Larry J. Larson, Treasurer & Secty.

■ **18003** ■ **Holyrood Cooperative Grain and Supply Co.**
200 E Santa Fe St.
Holyrood, KS 67450
Phone: (913)252-3233
Products: Grain. **SIC:** 5153 (Grain & Field Beans). **Est:** 1906. **Sales:** $12,000,000 (2000). **Emp:** 15. **Officers:** Roger Corn, Manager.

■ **18004** ■ **Hoople Farmers Grain Co.**
PO Box 140
Hoople, ND 58243
Phone: (701)894-6116
Products: Fertilizer and fertilizer materials; Grain; Petroleum and its products. **SICs:** 5153 (Grain & Field Beans); 5172 (Petroleum Products Nec). **Est:** 1906. **Sales:** $4,200,000 (2000). **Emp:** 8. **Officers:** Steve O'Berg, President.

■ **18005** ■ **Horpestad Ranch Inc.**
PO Box 93
Lavina, MT 59046-0093
Phone: (406)636-4831
Products: Livestock. **SIC:** 5154 (Livestock). **Officers:** Fred Horpestad, President.

■ **18006** ■ **Hub Grain Company Inc.**
HCR 1, Box 62
Friona, TX 79035
Phone: (806)265-3215
Products: Grain. **SIC:** 5153 (Grain & Field Beans).

■ **18007** ■ **Humphreys Coop Tipton Location**
500 S Broadway
Tipton, OK 73570
Phone: (580)667-5251 **Fax:** (580)667-4328
Products: Raw cotton; Seed; Grain elevator. **SICs:** 5153 (Grain & Field Beans); 5191 (Farm Supplies); 5159 (Farm-Product Raw Materials Nec). **Est:** 1929. **Sales:** $6,000,000 (2000). **Emp:** 50. **Officers:** Scott Lovett, Location Mgr. **Former Name:** Tipton Farmers Cooperative.

■ 18008 ■ Vernon Hunsdon
RFD 2, Box 801
Chester, VT 05143-9801
Phone: (802)875-3624
Products: Livestock. **SIC:** 5154 (Livestock). **Officers:** Vernon Hunsdon, Owner.

■ 18009 ■ Hutchinson Coop Elevator
PO Box 158
Hutchinson, MN 55350
Phone: (612)587-4647
E-mail: hutchele@hutchtel.net
Products: Grain; Farming supplies. **SICs:** 5153 (Grain & Field Beans); 5191 (Farm Supplies). **Est:** 1998. **Sales:** $6,100,000 (2000). **Emp:** 9. **Officers:** Larry Peterson, Manager. **Alternate Name:** Farmers Elevator Co.

■ 18010 ■ Idaho Livestock Auction Co.
PO Box 2187
Idaho Falls, ID 83403-2187
Phone: (208)522-7211
Products: Livestock; Auctioning livestock. **SIC:** 5154 (Livestock). **Officers:** Leon Skelton, Owner.

■ 18011 ■ International Service Group
3000 Langford Rd., Ste. 700
Norcross, GA 30071
Phone: (404)447-8777 **Fax:** (404)246-9885
Products: Bulk unprocessed and shelled peanuts. **SIC:** 5159 (Farm-Product Raw Materials Nec). **Officers:** Bob Kopec, President.

■ 18012 ■ Interstate Commodities Inc.
PO Box 607
Troy, NY 12180
Phone: (518)272-7212
Products: Grain. **SIC:** 5153 (Grain & Field Beans). **Est:** 1947. **Sales:** $58,000,000 (2000). **Emp:** 10. **Officers:** Victor A. Oberting Jr., President; Gary Oberting, Finance Officer.

■ 18013 ■ Iowa Soybean Association
4554 114th St.
Urbandale, IA 50322-5410
Phone: (515)223-1423 **Fax:** (515)223-4331
Products: Soybeans. **SIC:** 5153 (Grain & Field Beans). **Officers:** Kirk Leeds, Field Programs Director.

■ 18014 ■ Italgrani Elevator Co.
7900 Van Buren Ave.
St. Louis, MO 63111
Phone: (314)638-1447 **Fax:** (314)752-7621
Products: Flour. **SIC:** 5153 (Grain & Field Beans). **Est:** 1979. **Sales:** $100,000,000 (1999). **Emp:** 35. **Officers:** James Meyer, Exec. VP of Finance; Patrick Beem, Dir. of Marketing; Debbie Muenchau, Dir. of Information Systems; Beverly Moore, Dir of Human Resources.

■ 18015 ■ Iuka Cooperative Inc.
PO Box 175
Iuka, KS 67066
Phone: (316)546-2231
Products: Grain and farm supplies. **SICs:** 5153 (Grain & Field Beans); 5191 (Farm Supplies). **Sales:** $29,000,000 (1994). **Emp:** 50. **Officers:** David Brehm, President; Terry Coulter, Controller.

■ 18016 ■ J & L Livestock
200 N Phillips Ave.
Sioux Falls, SD 57104
Phone: (605)338-6232
Products: Livestock; Cattle. **SIC:** 5154 (Livestock). **Officers:** Wally Jansma, Partner.

■ 18017 ■ J & R Mercantile Ltd.
PO Box 5052
Gallup, NM 87305-5049
Phone: (505)722-6015
Products: Livestock; Grain and seeds. **SICs:** 5154 (Livestock); 5191 (Farm Supplies). **Officers:** Ron Blackwell, Partner.

■ 18018 ■ Jacobson Cattle Co.
PO Box 874
Baker, MT 59313-0874
Phone: (406)778-3110
Products: Livestock; Cattle. **SIC:** 5154 (Livestock). **Officers:** Gerald Jacobson, Owner.

■ 18019 ■ JaGee Corp.
PO Box 9600
Ft. Worth, TX 76147
Phone: (817)335-5881 **Fax:** (817)335-1905
Products: Grains. **SIC:** 5153 (Grain & Field Beans). **Sales:** $95,000,000 (1991). **Emp:** 255. **Officers:** Richard F. Garvey, President; Deborah Quillin, Treasurer.

■ 18020 ■ Jamestown Livestock Sales
RR 3
Jamestown, ND 58401-9803
Phone: (701)252-2111
Free: (800)718-2111 **Fax:** (701)752-4160
E-mail: nenow@daktel.com
URL: http://www.JamestownLivestock.uswestdex.com
Products: Livestock. **SIC:** 5154 (Livestock). **Emp:** 30. **Officers:** Roger Nenow, Owner; Lois Nenow, Owner.

■ 18021 ■ Jarvis-Paris-Murphy Company Inc.
PO Box 1848
Waco, TX 76703
Phone: (254)756-7261
Products: Grain, corn, and wheat. **SIC:** 5153 (Grain & Field Beans). **Est:** 1955. **Sales:** $6,500,000 (2000). **Emp:** 12. **Officers:** Gary R. Murphy, President; John Woelfel, Manager.

■ 18022 ■ Jasper County Farm Bureau Cooperative
PO Box 238
Rensselaer, IN 47978
Phone: (219)866-7131 **Fax:** (219)866-7490
Products: Grains and farm supplies. **SICs:** 5153 (Grain & Field Beans); 5191 (Farm Supplies). **Sales:** $60,000,000 (1992). **Emp:** 115. **Officers:** Donald L. Misch, General Mgr.; Kevin P. Benner, Treasurer & Secty.

■ 18023 ■ Jensen Lloyd and Willis
110 Dakota Ave. N
Huron, SD 57350-1630
Phone: (605)352-9309 **Fax:** (605)352-9309
Products: Veterinary instruments; Feed. **SIC:** 5047 (Medical & Hospital Equipment). **Officers:** Lloyd Jensen, Partner.

■ 18024 ■ Jimbo's Jumbos Inc.
PO Box 465
Edenton, NC 27932
Phone: (919)482-2193 **Fax:** (919)482-7857
Products: Peanuts. **SIC:** 5159 (Farm-Product Raw Materials Nec). **Est:** 1946. **Sales:** $190,000,000 (2000). **Emp:** 650. **Officers:** J. Tilmon Keel Jr., CEO & Chairman of the Board; Richard Lamnus, VP & CFO.

■ 18025 ■ Johnston Elevator Co.
307 N McEwan
Clare, MI 48617-1454
Phone: (517)386-7271 **Fax:** (517)386-4116
Products: Grain and feed. **SICs:** 5191 (Farm Supplies); 5153 (Grain & Field Beans). **Emp:** 15.

■ 18026 ■ Kalispell Livestock Auction
PO Box 914
Kalispell, MT 59903-0914
Phone: (406)752-1448 **Fax:** (406)752-4040
Products: Livestock. **SIC:** 5154 (Livestock). **Est:** 1965. **Officers:** Richard Carpenter, President.

■ 18027 ■ Kanorado Cooperative Association
Box 40
Kanorado, KS 67741
Phone: (785)399-2321
Products: Grain elevator. **SIC:** 5153 (Grain & Field Beans). **Est:** 1915. **Sales:** $5,000,000 (2000). **Emp:** 8. **Officers:** W. James Cody, President; Ken Ketter, Marketing Mgr.

■ 18028 ■ Kathryn Farmers Mutual Elevators Inc.
PO Box 196
Kathryn, ND 58049
Phone: (701)796-7861
Products: Fine grains. **SIC:** 5153 (Grain & Field Beans). **Est:** 1905. **Sales:** $2,800,000 (2000). **Emp:** 5. **Officers:** Ken Clauson, President; Ron Olthoff, General Mgr.

■ 18029 ■ Kaufman Grain Co.
PO Box 96
Cissna Park, IL 60924
Phone: (815)457-2185
Products: Grain elevator. **SIC:** 5153 (Grain & Field Beans). **Est:** 1946. **Sales:** $12,000,000 (2000). **Emp:** 15. **Officers:** Kevin Kaufman, General Mgr.

■ 18030 ■ Keller Grain and Feed Inc.
7977 Main St.
Greenville, OH 45331
Phone: (937)448-2116 **Fax:** (937)448-2102
Products: Feed, grains, and seeds. **SICs:** 5153 (Grain & Field Beans); 5191 (Farm Supplies). **Est:** 1933. **Sales:** $21,000,000 (2000). **Emp:** 38. **Officers:** David W. Keller, President; J.K. Keller, Treasurer & Secty.

■ 18031 ■ Dennis Kelly
226 W 5th St.
Winner, SD 57580-1715
Phone: (605)842-1824
Products: Livestock. **SIC:** 5154 (Livestock). **Officers:** Dennis Kelly, Owner.

■ 18032 ■ Kemp Grain Company Inc.
405 W Walnut St.
Lexington, IL 61753
Phone: (309)365-2241 **Fax:** (309)365-2261
Products: Hardware, including hammers; Grain elevator; Corn and grain. **SICs:** 5153 (Grain & Field Beans); 5072 (Hardware). **Est:** 1946. **Sales:** $9,000,000 (2000). **Emp:** 9. **Officers:** George P. Kemp, President.

■ 18033 ■ Dale B. Kendall
East Barnet Rd.
Barnet, VT 05821
Phone: (802)633-2626
Products: Livestock. **SIC:** 5154 (Livestock). **Officers:** Dale Kendall, Partner.

■ 18034 ■ King Grain Company Inc.
120 N 1st St.
Muleshoe, TX 79347
Phone: (806)272-4541
Products: Grain. **SIC:** 5153 (Grain & Field Beans). **Est:** 1950. **Sales:** $4,000,000 (2000). **Emp:** 7. **Officers:** Max King, President.

■ 18035 ■ Kist Livestock Auction Co.
PO Box 1313
Mandan, ND 58554-7313
Phone: (701)663-9573 **Fax:** (701)663-9860
Products: Livestock. **SIC:** 5154 (Livestock). **Officers:** Fred Kist, President.

■ 18036 ■ Klein Brothers Ltd.
PO Box 609
Stockton, CA 95201
Phone: (209)948-6802
Products: Dry beans. **SIC:** 5153 (Grain & Field Beans). **Sales:** $11,000,000 (2000). **Emp:** 21. **Officers:** Bud Klein, President.

■ 18037 ■ Norman Klinker
RR 1, Box 184
Fairfield, MT 59436-9713
Phone: (406)467-2945
Products: Livestock; Cattle. **SIC:** 5154 (Livestock). **Officers:** Norman Klinker, Owner.

■ 18038 ■ Knightstown Elevator Inc.
PO Box 65
Knightstown, IN 46148
Phone: (765)345-2181 **Fax:** (765)345-7683
Products: Grain elevator. **SIC:** 5153 (Grain & Field Beans). **Est:** 1973. **Sales:** $5,000,000 (2000). **Emp:** 8. **Officers:** Thomas R. Haase, President.

■ 18039 ■ Kokomo Grain Company Inc.
239 N Mill St.
Greentown, IN 46936
Phone: (765)457-7536
Products: Grain, including corn and wheat; Beans. **SIC:** 5153 (Grain & Field Beans). **Sales:** $3,000,000 (2000). **Emp:** 5. **Officers:** Raymond Ortman, Owner.

■ 18040 ■ Kragnes Farmers Elevator
9749 21st St., N
Moorhead, MN 56560-7247
Phone: (218)233-4247 **Fax:** (218)233-9292
Products: Grain; Fertilizer and related materials;
Seeds; Chemicals. **SICs:** 5153 (Grain & Field Beans);
5191 (Farm Supplies). **Est:** 1911. **Sales:** $15,000,000
(2000). **Emp:** 10. **Officers:** Terry Eiden, CEO.

■ 18041 ■ La Porte County Cooperative
PO Box 160
La Porte, IN 46350
Phone: (219)362-2156 **Fax:** (219)326-1058
Products: Petroleum products; Grain. **SICs:** 5153
(Grain & Field Beans); 5172 (Petroleum Products Nec).
Est: 1927. **Sales:** $59,000,000 (2000). **Emp:** 140.
Officers: George Vanbierdonck, President.

■ 18042 ■ Lake Preston Cooperative Association
106 2nd Ave. NW
Lake Preston, SD 57249
Phone: (605)847-4414 **Fax:** (605)847-4435
Products: Grain. **SIC:** 5191 (Farm Supplies). **Est:**
1938. **Sales:** $30,000,000 (2000). **Emp:** 25. **Officers:**
Arnold Wienk, President.

■ 18043 ■ Lamont Grain Growers Inc.
Main St.
Lamont, WA 99017
Phone: (509)257-2206 **Fax:** (509)257-2207
Products: Grain; Wheat; Barley. **SIC:** 5153 (Grain &
Field Beans). **Est:** 1934. **Sales:** $4,000,000 (2000).
Emp: 4. **Officers:** Brian Madison, General Mgr.

■ 18044 ■ Lapeer County Cooperative Inc.
155 S Saginaw St.
Lapeer, MI 48446
Phone: (313)664-2907
Products: Grain and farm supplies. **SICs:** 5153 (Grain
& Field Beans); 5191 (Farm Supplies). **Sales:**
$22,000,000 (1992). **Emp:** 75. **Officers:** Donald
Currey, General Mgr.; Paul Elsen, Controller.

■ 18045 ■ Latah County Grain Growers Inc.
PO Box 9086
Moscow, ID 83843
Phone: (208)882-7581
Products: Grain, including wheat, oats, and barley.
SIC: 5153 (Grain & Field Beans). **Est:** 1930. **Sales:**
$8,000,000 (2000). **Emp:** 14. **Officers:** Alan Lyon,
President; David I. Strong, General Mgr.

■ 18046 ■ Latham Seed Co.
131 180th St.
Alexander, IA 50420
Phone: (641)692-3258 **Fax:** (641)692-3250
URL: http://www.lathamseeds.com
Products: Soybean seeds and oats. **SIC:** 5153 (Grain
& Field Beans). **Est:** 1947. **Sales:** $8,000,000 (2000).
Emp: 24. **Officers:** Willard J. Latham, President;
Donald Latham, Vice President.

■ 18047 ■ Lawrence County Exchange
PO Box 487
Moulton, AL 35650
Phone: (256)974-9213
Products: Grain, feed, fertilizer and agricultural
chemicals. **SICs:** 5153 (Grain & Field Beans); 5191
(Farm Supplies). **Sales:** $21,000,000 (1994). **Emp:** 25.
Officers: Gene Pickens, President; Lloyd Rutherford,
Finance General Manager.

■ 18048 ■ Layne and Myers Grain Co.
PO Box 86
New Market, IN 47965
Phone: (765)866-0175
Products: Grain elevator. **SICs:** 5153 (Grain & Field
Beans); 5191 (Farm Supplies). **Est:** 1941. **Sales:**
$25,000,000 (2000). **Emp:** 15. **Officers:** David Myers,
President; Rebecca Nelson, Treasurer & Secty.; James
Myers, Dir. of Marketing & Sales.

■ 18049 ■ Le Roy Cooperative Association Inc.
PO Box 248
Le Roy, KS 66857
Phone: (316)964-2225 **Fax:** (316)964-2465
Products: Grains, feed, and chemicals. **SICs:** 5153

(Grain & Field Beans); 5191 (Farm Supplies); 5169
(Chemicals & Allied Products Nec). **Est:** 1960. **Sales:**
$14,000,000 (2000). **Emp:** 17. **Officers:** Karry Trostle,
President; Donald Meats.

■ 18050 ■ Lea County Livestock Marketing
PO Box 712
Lovington, NM 88260-0712
Phone: (505)396-5381
Products: Livestock; Auctioning livestock. **SIC:** 5154
(Livestock). **Officers:** Mack Hendershot, President.

■ 18051 ■ Lemmon Livestock Inc.
PO Box 477
Lemmon, SD 57638-0477
Phone: (605)374-3877 **Fax:** (605)374-3215
Products: Livestock. **SIC:** 5154 (Livestock). **Officers:**
Paul Huffman, Owner.

■ 18052 ■ G. Levor and Company Inc.
PO Box 866
Gloversville, NY 12078
Phone: (518)725-3185 **Fax:** (518)725-1379
Products: Goat skins; Deerskin and elkskin gloves.
SIC: 5199 (Nondurable Goods Nec). **Est:** 1967. **Sales:**
$1,700,000 (2000). **Emp:** 11. **Officers:** Andrew
Studenic, President; Leslie Smrtic, Controller; George
E. Bradt, Dir. of Operations.

■ 18053 ■ Lewis-Simpson Ranch
PO Box 5
Robert Lee, TX 76945
Phone: (915)453-2555 **Fax:** (915)453-2556
Products: Livestock. **SIC:** 5154 (Livestock). **Est:** 1976.
Sales: $4,000,000 (2000). **Emp:** 5. **Officers:** Bill
Simpson, General Mgr.; Barbara Davis, Controller.

■ 18054 ■ Lewis-Simpson Ranch
PO Box 5
Robert Lee, TX 76945
Phone: (915)453-2555 **Fax:** (915)453-2556
Products: Livestock and farm products. **SIC:** 5154
(Livestock). **Sales:** $4,000,000 (2000). **Emp:** 5.

■ 18055 ■ Lewiston Grain Growers
PO Box 467
Lewiston, ID 83501
Phone: (208)743-8551 **Fax:** (208)746-0721
Products: Grains. **SIC:** 5153 (Grain & Field Beans).
Sales: $40,000,000 (2000). **Emp:** 59. **Officers:** Carl
Younce, General Mgr.; Ken Blakeman, Manager.

■ 18056 ■ Lewiston Livestock Market Inc.
PO Box 711
Lewiston, ID 83501-0711
Phone: (208)743-5506 **Fax:** (208)746-4442
Products: Livestock. **SIC:** 5154 (Livestock). **Officers:**
Douglas Bickford, President.

■ 18057 ■ Lewistown Livestock Auction
PO Box 1190
Lewistown, MT 59457-1190
Phone: (406)538-3471
Products: Livestock; Auctioning livestock. **SIC:** 5154
(Livestock). **Officers:** Richard Swanz, Owner.

■ 18058 ■ Lexington Trotters and Breeders Association
PO Box 420
Lexington, KY 40585
Phone: (606)255-0752 **Fax:** (606)231-0217
Products: Race horses. **SIC:** 5159 (Farm-Product
Raw Materials Nec). **Est:** 1875. **Sales:** $10,000,000
(2000). **Emp:** 50. **Officers:** John A. Cashman Jr. Jr.,
President; Mike J. Lang, Treasurer.

■ 18059 ■ R.Q. Line & Co.
803 E Rice St.
3rd Fl., Livestock Exchange Bldg.
Sioux Falls, SD 57103
Phone: (605)336-3170
Products: Livestock. **SIC:** 5154 (Livestock). **Officers:**
Frank L. Schneider, President; Gloria E. Schneider,
Vice President.

■ 18060 ■ John Linn
RR 2 Box 276
Richmond, VT 05477-0276
Phone: (802)434-4882
Products: Merchants of raw farm products; Feathers;

Hides; Pelts. **SIC:** 5159 (Farm-Product Raw Materials
Nec). **Officers:** John Linn, Owner.

■ 18061 ■ Linton Livestock Market Inc.
PO Box 365
Napoleon, ND 58561-0365
Phone: (701)254-4581
Products: Livestock. **SIC:** 5154 (Livestock). **Officers:**
Kelly Fischer, President.

■ 18062 ■ Lloyds Buying Service
701 14th Ave. N
Greybull, WY 82426-1514
Phone: (307)765-4666
Products: Livestock. **SIC:** 5154 (Livestock). **Officers:**
Lloyd Groseclose, Owner.

■ 18063 ■ Logsdon Service Inc.
PO Box 308
Wayland, MO 63472
Phone: (660)754-6417
Products: Chemicals, seeds, and grain. **SICs:** 5153
(Grain & Field Beans); 5169 (Chemicals & Allied
Products Nec); 5191 (Farm Supplies). **Est:** 1945.
Sales: $10,000,000 (2000). **Emp:** 20. **Officers:** Steve
Logsdon, CEO; John Logsdon, Vice President.

■ 18064 ■ Long & Hansen Commission Co.
803 E Rice
Sioux Falls, SD 57101
Phone: (605)336-3640
Products: Livestock; Cattle. **SIC:** 5154 (Livestock).
Officers: Roger Stanley, President.

■ 18065 ■ Lowe's Pellets and Grain Co.
R.R. 4, Box 46
Greensburg, IN 47240
Phone: (812)663-7863
Products: Grain. **SIC:** 5153 (Grain & Field Beans).
Sales: $15,000,000 (2000). **Emp:** 35. **Officers:** Don
Lowe, President.

■ 18066 ■ Ludlow Cooperative Elevator Company Inc.
PO Box 155
Ludlow, IL 60949
Phone: (217)396-4111
Products: Grain elevator. **SIC:** 5153 (Grain & Field
Beans). **Est:** 1904. **Sales:** $50,000,000 (2000). **Emp:**
25. **Officers:** David Hastings, General Mgr.; John
Cowell, Controller.

■ 18067 ■ Lyford Gin Association
PO Box 70
Lyford, TX 78569
Phone: (210)347-3541
Products: Grain; Cotton. **SICs:** 5083 (Farm & Garden
Machinery); 5083 (Farm & Garden Machinery); 5172
(Petroleum Products Nec). **Est:** 1938. **Sales:**
$19,000,000 (2000). **Emp:** 20. **Officers:** Russell
Klostermann, President; Steve Marshall, CFO.

■ 18068 ■ M & R Trading Inc.
514 W Maloney
Gallup, NM 87301-0687
Phone: (505)722-9020
Products: Livestock; Feed; Cans; Gasoline. **SICs:**
5154 (Livestock); 5191 (Farm Supplies); 5172
(Petroleum Products Nec). **Officers:** Frank Mraz,
President.

■ 18069 ■ Macon Ridge Farmers Association
PO Box 428
Sicily Island, LA 71368
Phone: (318)389-5349
Products: Farm supplies and petroleum products.
SICs: 5191 (Farm Supplies); 5172 (Petroleum
Products Nec). **Sales:** $6,000,000 (2000). **Emp:** 16.
Officers: W.D. Hackney, President.

■ 18070 ■ Madison Farmers Elevator Co.
PO Box F
Madison, SD 57042
Phone: (605)256-4584 **Fax:** (605)256-2529
Products: Grain, including corn, wheat, and beans;
Fertilizers; Chemicals; Herbicides; Insecticides. **SICs:**
5153 (Grain & Field Beans); 5191 (Farm Supplies);
5169 (Chemicals & Allied Products Nec). **Est:** 1908.

Sales: $12,000,000 (2000). **Emp:** 18. **Officers:** Arley Raastid, General Mgr.

■ **18071** ■ **Madison Landmark Inc.**
254 W High St.
London, OH 43140
Phone: (740)852-2062
Products: Grain and farm supplies. **SICs:** 5153 (Grain & Field Beans); 5191 (Farm Supplies). **Sales:** $16,500,000 (1994). **Emp:** 50. **Officers:** Eugene Fisher, President.

■ **18072** ■ **Magness Huron Livestock Exchange**
560 7th St., NE
Huron, SD 57350
Phone: (605)352-8759   **Fax:** (605)352-8772
Products: Livestock; Auctioning livestock. **SIC:** 5154 (Livestock). **Officers:** Gordon Magness, President.

■ **18073** ■ **Mahaska Farm Service Co.**
PO Box 1040
Oskaloosa, IA 52577-1040
Phone: (515)672-2589   **Fax:** (515)673-9735
Products: Grain and field beans, fertilizer, livestock feed and supplies. **SICs:** 5153 (Grain & Field Beans); 5191 (Farm Supplies). **Sales:** $16,300,000 (2000). **Emp:** 51. **Officers:** Bob Farber, General Mgr.; Lin Yoder, Controller.

■ **18074** ■ **Mapleton Grain Co.**
111 N Front St.
Mapleton, IA 51034
Phone: (712)882-2733
Products: Grain; Corn; Oats. **SIC:** 5153 (Grain & Field Beans). **Est:** 1959. **Sales:** $3,000,000 (2000). **Emp:** 9. **Officers:** Gene Elmquist, President.

■ **18075** ■ **Martinsburg Farmers Elevator Co.**
PO Box 130
Martinsburg, MO 65264-0130
Phone: (573)492-6218
Products: Grain. **SIC:** 5153 (Grain & Field Beans). **Est:** 1920. **Sales:** $8,200,000 (2000). **Emp:** 10. **Officers:** Ronald Blaue, President; Mike Gibson, Bookkeeper; Robert Morrison, General Mgr.

■ **18076** ■ **Maynard Cooperative Co.**
PO Box 215
Maynard, IA 50655
Phone: (319)637-2285
Products: Grain and livestock. **SICs:** 5153 (Grain & Field Beans); 5154 (Livestock). **Sales:** $27,000,000 (2000). **Emp:** 31. **Officers:** Darren Cittig, President; Steve Callender, Controller.

■ **18077** ■ **McBee Grain and Trucking Inc.**
PO Box 74
Bluffton, OH 45817
Phone: (419)358-5931
E-mail: mcbeegrain@aol.com
Products: Grain; Feed. **SICs:** 5153 (Grain & Field Beans); 5191 (Farm Supplies). **Est:** 1971. **Sales:** $3,000,000 (2000). **Emp:** 9. **Officers:** Lyle R. McKanna, CEO; Jeff McKanna, Vice President.

■ **18078** ■ **C.E. McChesney Co.**
PO Box 236
Gladstone, IL 61437
Phone: (309)627-2374   **Fax:** (309)627-2539
Products: Grain; Recycled goods. **SICs:** 5153 (Grain & Field Beans); 5093 (Scrap & Waste Materials). **Est:** 1960. **Sales:** $3,000,000 (2000). **Emp:** 12. **Officers:** Charles McChesney, Owner.

■ **18079** ■ **McClesky Mills Inc.**
292 Rhodes St.
Smithville, GA 31787
Phone: (912)846-2003   **Fax:** (912)846-4805
Products: Shelled peanuts. **SIC:** 5159 (Farm-Product Raw Materials Nec). **Sales:** $95,000,000 (2000). **Emp:** 100. **Officers:** Jerry M. Chandler, President; William H. Marshall Jr., CFO.

■ **18080** ■ **M.W. McCoy Cattle Co.**
PO Box 1781
Billings, MT 59103-1781
Phone: (406)248-7331   **Fax:** (406)248-7331
Products: Livestock. **SIC:** 5154 (Livestock). **Officers:** Mike McCoy, Owner.

■ **18081** ■ **McCraken Livestock Inc.**
RR 2, Box 244
St. Albans, VT 05478-9802
Phone: (802)524-2991
Products: Livestock. **SIC:** 5154 (Livestock). **Officers:** John McCraken, President.

■ **18082** ■ **McDonald Livestock Co.**
851 Arena Rd.
West Fargo, ND 58078
Phone: (701)282-3206
Products: Livestock; Auctioning livestock. **SIC:** 5154 (Livestock). **Officers:** Richard Samson, President.

■ **18083** ■ **McGeary Grain Inc.**
PO Box 299
Lancaster, PA 17608
Phone: (717)394-6843
Free: (800)624-3279   **Fax:** (717)394-6931
E-mail: sales@mcgearygrain.com
URL: http://www.mcgearygrain.com
Products: Grain; Feed ingredients; Certified organics, including feed and flour. **SIC:** 5153 (Grain & Field Beans). **Est:** 1983. **Sales:** $20,000,000 (2000). **Emp:** 17. **Officers:** D.R. Poorbaugh, President.

■ **18084** ■ **McLaughlin Livestock Auction**
PO Box 559
Mc Laughlin, SD 57642-0559
Phones: (605)823-4821   (605)823-4497
Fax: (605)823-4230
Products: Livestock. **SIC:** 5154 (Livestock). **Officers:** Dallas D. Schott, President.

■ **18085** ■ **Medford Co-operative Inc.**
PO Box 407
Medford, WI 54451-0407
Phone: (715)748-2056
Free: (800)348-6909   **Fax:** (715)748-2166
E-mail: info@medfordcoop.com
URL: http://www.medfordcoop.com
Products: Feed; Fertilizer; Grain bins; Metal fencing supplies; Petroleum bulk station; Bulk petroleum; Propane; Auto acessories; Auto Repairs; Hardware; Clothing; Groceries; Heating, electrical, and plumbing sales and installations. **SICs:** 5191 (Farm Supplies); 5039 (Construction Materials Nec); 5171 (Petroleum Bulk Stations & Terminals). **Est:** 1911. **Sales:** $18,000,000 (2000). **Emp:** 125. **Officers:** Ralph Zuleger, President; Andrew Stotka, Controller; Donald Purvis, Vice President; JoAnn Smith, Secretary; Graham Courtney Jr., Treasurer & General Mgr.

■ **18086** ■ **Mendota Farm Cooperative Supply Inc.**
PO Box 407
Mendota, IL 61342
Phone: (815)539-6772   **Fax:** (815)539-6772
Products: Lumber; Grain. **SIC:** 5153 (Grain & Field Beans). **Est:** 1908. **Sales:** $3,000,000 (2000). **Emp:** 14. **Officers:** Jon Dinges, General Mgr.

■ **18087** ■ **Merchant's Grain Inc.**
PO Box 398
Selma, NC 27576
Phone: (919)965-2303
Products: Farm supplies. **SIC:** 5191 (Farm Supplies). **Officers:** John Barmmeier, President.

■ **18088** ■ **Michigan Agricultural Commodities**
PO Box 96
Blissfield, MI 49228
Phone: (517)486-2171
Products: Agricultural supplies; Livestock. **SICs:** 5153 (Grain & Field Beans); 5154 (Livestock). **Est:** 1918. **Sales:** $18,000,000 (2000). **Emp:** 11. **Officers:** Ken Lake, General Mgr.

■ **18089** ■ **Michigan Livestock Exchange**
6400 Bentley Rd.
Williamston, MI 48895-9641
Phone: (517)337-2856   **Fax:** (517)336-1510
Products: Livestock. **SIC:** 5154 (Livestock). **Est:** 1922. **Sales:** $500,000,000 (2000). **Emp:** 200. **Officers:** Thomas H. Reed, CEO & President; Gregory Beck, VP of Finance; Michael Bigelow, VP of Marketing; Jon Hansen, VP of Admin.; Virgie A. Jellinek, Dir of Human Resources.

■ **18090** ■ **Michigan Peat Div.**
PO Box 3006
Houston, TX 77253
Phone: (713)522-0711
Products: t. **SIC:** 5193 (Flowers & Florists' Supplies). **Sales:** $125,000,000 (2000). **Emp:** 80. **Officers:** Mark E. Kuebler, President; J. David Newman, Vice President.

■ **18091** ■ **Mid Columbia Producers Inc.**
PO Box 344
Moro, OR 97039
Phone: (503)565-3737   **Fax:** (503)565-3653
Products: Grains, including wheat. **SIC:** 5153 (Grain & Field Beans). **Est:** 1930. **Sales:** $21,000,000 (2000). **Emp:** 25. **Officers:** David Pinkerton, President; Bill Conn, Controller; Charles Carlson, General Mgr.

■ **18092** ■ **Mid-Iowa Cooperative (Beaman, Iowa)**
PO Box 80
Beaman, IA 50609
Phone: (515)366-2740
Products: Grain, field beans, feed, fertilizers and other farm supplies. **SICs:** 5153 (Grain & Field Beans); 5191 (Farm Supplies). **Sales:** $63,000,000 (2000). **Emp:** 70. **Officers:** Mark Lynch, President.

■ **18093** ■ **Mid-Wood Inc.**
12818 E Gypsy Lane Rd.
Bowling Green, OH 43402
Phone: (419)352-5231
Products: Grain elevators. **SIC:** 5153 (Grain & Field Beans). **Est:** 1967. **Sales:** $38,000,000 (2000). **Emp:** 70. **Officers:** Tom Dorman, General Mgr.; Joe Boroff, Controller.

■ **18094** ■ **Midland Bean Co.**
PO Box 484
Dove Creek, CO 81324
Phone: (303)677-2215
Products: Dried pinto beans. **SIC:** 5153 (Grain & Field Beans). **Est:** 1952. **Sales:** $12,000,000 (2000). **Emp:** 14. **Officers:** Rodney Tanner, President.

■ **18095** ■ **Midland Cooperative Inc. Wilcox Div.**
PO Box 188
Wilcox, NE 68982
Phone: (308)478-5231
Products: Corn and grain; Fertilizers. **SICs:** 5153 (Grain & Field Beans); 5191 (Farm Supplies). **Est:** 1956. **Sales:** $7,000,000 (2000). **Emp:** 12. **Officers:** Keith Lukasiewicz, General Mgr.

■ **18096** ■ **Midland Marketing Cooperative, Inc.**
PO Box 639
Hays, KS 67601-0639
Phone: (785)628-3221
Products: Grains including wheat, oats, soybean, milo, corn, and sunflower; Dry and liquid fertilizer; Anhydrous ammonia; Diesel fuel; Gasoline; Propane; Tires; Agricultural chemicals; Feed; Seed; Lubricants. **SICs:** 5153 (Grain & Field Beans); 5191 (Farm Supplies). **Est:** 1915. **Sales:** $32,000,000 (2000). **Emp:** 41. **Officers:** Vance Westhusin, CEO.

■ **18097** ■ **Midwest Cooperatives**
PO Box 787
Pierre, SD 57501
Phone: (605)224-5935
Products: Grain and farm supplies. **SICs:** 5153 (Grain & Field Beans); 5191 (Farm Supplies). **Sales:** $45,000,000 (1994). **Emp:** 20.

■ 18098 ■ Milan Farmers Elevator
PO Box 32
Milan, MN 56262
Phone: (320)734-4435 **Fax:** (320)734-4437
Products: Feed, including wheat, oats, and corn.
SICs: 5153 (Grain & Field Beans); 5191 (Farm
Supplies). **Est:** 1945. **Sales:** $5,000,000 (2000). **Emp:**
6. **Officers:** Mark Streed, President; Lois Lovehaug,
CFO.

■ 18099 ■ C.C. Miller Corp.
PO Box 396
Morrisville, VT 05661-0396
Phone: (802)888-3670
Products: Livestock. **SIC:** 5154 (Livestock). **Officers:**
Clarence Miller, President.

■ 18100 ■ Miller Livestock Sales Co.
PO Box 237
Bassett, NE 68714-0237
Phone: (402)853-2461
Products: Livestock. **SIC:** 5154 (Livestock). **Officers:**
Jay Anderberg, Owner.

■ 18101 ■ A.E. Miller Stockyards
N Main
Delphos, OH 45833
Phone: (419)695-1851
Products: Livestock. **SIC:** 5154 (Livestock).

■ 18102 ■ Minier Cooperative Grain Co.
PO Box 650
Minier, IL 61759
Phone: (309)392-2424 **Fax:** (309)392-3343
Products: Grain elevator. **SIC:** 5153 (Grain & Field
Beans). **Est:** 1907. **Sales:** $20,000,000 (2000). **Emp:**
7. **Officers:** Keith D. Swigart, General Mgr., e-mail:
keith@trianglenet.net; Duane Haning, President.

■ 18103 ■ Minn-Kota AG Products Inc.
PO Box 175
Breckenridge, MN 56520
Phone: (218)643-8464
Free: (800)253-6527 **Fax:** (218)643-4252
Products: Grain. **SIC:** 5191 (Farm Supplies). **Est:**
1985. **Sales:** $32,000,000 (2000). **Emp:** 30. **Officers:**
George M. Schuler III, President; Marilyn Anderson,
Controller.

■ 18104 ■ Minneola Cooperative Inc.
PO Box 376
Minneola, KS 67865
Phone: (316)885-4235
Products: Grain elevators; Farm supplies. **SICs:** 5153
(Grain & Field Beans); 5191 (Farm Supplies). **Est:**
1912. **Sales:** $6,000,000 (2000). **Emp:** 15. **Officers:**
Tom Sterezker, President.

**■ 18105 ■ Minster Farmers Cooperative
Exchange Inc.**
PO Box 100
Minster, OH 45865
Phone: (419)628-2367
Free: (888)628-2505 **Fax:** (419)628-2978
Products: Grain; Feed; Agronomy. **SICs:** 5153 (Grain
& Field Beans); 5143 (Dairy Products Except Dried or
Canned). **Est:** 1920. **Sales:** $30,000,000 (2000). **Emp:**
35. **Officers:** Jeff Schaefer, President; Henry Albers,
Treasurer & Secty.

■ 18106 ■ Missouri Swine Export Federation
6235 Cunningham Dr., Rte. 11
Columbia, MO 65202
Phone: (573)445-8375 **Fax:** (573)446-2398
Products: Livestock, including swine. **SIC:** 5154
(Livestock). **Officers:** Don Nikodim, Executive Director.

■ 18107 ■ Moews Seed Company Inc.
Hwy. 89 S
Granville, IL 61326
Phone: (815)339-2201
Products: Corn. **SIC:** 5191 (Farm Supplies). **Est:**
1920. **Sales:** $21,000,000 (2000). **Emp:** 100. **Officers:**
Thomas Navin, President; Dave Trapkus, Comptroller;
Kermit Land, Dir. of Marketing & Sales.

■ 18108 ■ Moffatt Hay Co.
2216 Smedley Rd.
Carlsbad, NM 88220
Phone: (505)236-6392 **Fax:** (505)236-6313
Products: Raw farm materials, including hay and feed.
SIC: 5159 (Farm-Product Raw Materials Nec).
Officers: C.M. Moffatt, Owner.

■ 18109 ■ Monica Elevator Co.
19213 N Main St.
Princeville, IL 61559
Phone: (309)385-4938
Products: Grain elevators. **SIC:** 5153 (Grain & Field
Beans). **Sales:** $5,000,000 (2000). **Emp:** 8. **Officers:**
Norm Stahl, President.

■ 18110 ■ Monroeville Co-op Grain
82 Townsend Ave.
Norwalk, OH 44857
Phone: (419)465-2583 **Fax:** (419)663-3531
Products: Grain; Feed. **SICs:** 5153 (Grain & Field
Beans); 5191 (Farm Supplies). **Sales:** $23,000,000
(2000). **Emp:** 44. **Officers:** Bob Sunderman, General
Mgr.

■ 18111 ■ Montana International Lvstk
4385 Wylie Dr.
Helena, MT 59601-9567
Phone: (406)227-5208 **Fax:** (406)227-8194
Products: Livestock, including cattle, sheep, and
horses; Dairy products. **SICs:** 5154 (Livestock); 5143
(Dairy Products Except Dried or Canned). **Est:** 1975.
Sales: $500,000 (2000). **Emp:** 5. **Officers:** Gibson
Goodman, Partner. **Doing Business As:** Running W
Cattle Co.

■ 18112 ■ Montezuma Cooperative Exchange
PO Box 98
Montezuma, KS 67867
Phone: (316)846-2231
Products: Grain. **SICs:** 5153 (Grain & Field Beans);
5191 (Farm Supplies). **Officers:** Dale Allen, CEO.

■ 18113 ■ Monticello Grain Company Inc.
420 W Marion St.
Monticello, IL 61856
Phone: (217)762-2163 **Fax:** (217)762-9732
Products: Grain, including corn and beans. **SIC:** 5153
(Grain & Field Beans). **Est:** 1903. **Sales:** $20,000,000
(2000). **Emp:** 12.

■ 18114 ■ Mooney Cattle Co. Inc.
4801 Umatilla Ave.
Boise, ID 83709-6142
Phone: (208)362-5091 **Fax:** (208)362-0163
Products: Livestock; Cattle. **SIC:** 5154 (Livestock).
Officers: Richard Mooney, President.

■ 18115 ■ Morazan
104 Open Buckle Rd
Vaughn, MT 59487-9514
Products: Sheep; Goats; Rabbit. **SIC:** 5154
(Livestock). **Est:** 1993. **Former Name:** Broken Arrow.

■ 18116 ■ Morgan Grain and Feed Co.
PO Box 248
Morgan, MN 56266
Phone: (507)249-3157
Free: (800)449-3157 **Fax:** (507)249-3507
Products: Prepared animal feed and dry fertilizer. **SIC:**
5191 (Farm Supplies). **Sales:** $14,100,000 (2000).
Emp: 15. **Officers:** Richard A. Potter, President.

■ 18117 ■ Morrisonville Farmers Cooperative
PO Box 17
Morrisonville, IL 62546
Phone: (217)526-3123
Products: Grain elevator. **SIC:** 5153 (Grain & Field
Beans). **Est:** 1919. **Sales:** $18,000,000 (2000). **Emp:**
10. **Officers:** Glenn Fesser, President.

■ 18118 ■ Morrow County Grain Growers Inc.
Hwy. 207
Lexington, OR 97839
Phone: (541)989-8221 **Fax:** (541)989-8229
URL: http://www.mcgg.net
Products: Grain; Seed; Case IH equipment. **SICs:**
5191 (Farm Supplies); 5153 (Grain & Field Beans).
Est: 1930. **Sales:** $40,000,000 (2000). **Emp:** 60.

Officers: Steve Hill, President; Chris Meyer, General
Mgr.

■ 18119 ■ Moultrie Grain Association
Rte. 1, Box 147
Arthur, IL 61911
Phone: (217)543-2157 **Fax:** (217)543-2158
Products: Grain. **SIC:** 5153 (Grain & Field Beans).
Sales: $12,000,000 (2000). **Emp:** 12. **Officers:** John
Stinson, President.

■ 18120 ■ Mount Pulaski Farmers Grain
PO Box 77
Mt. Pulaski, IL 62548
Phone: (217)792-5711
Products: Grain elevator. **SIC:** 5153 (Grain & Field
Beans). **Est:** 1905. **Sales:** $7,500,000 (2000). **Emp:** 7.
Officers: Russ Adams, General Mgr.; Melody Reed,
Dir. of Information Systems.

■ 18121 ■ Mt. Union Cooperative Elevator
PO Box 57
Mt. Union, IA 52644
Phone: (319)865-1450 **Fax:** (319)865-1452
Products: Fertilizers; Grains, including corn and
beans; Petroleum, oil, and gasoline. **SICs:** 5153 (Grain
& Field Beans); 5191 (Farm Supplies); 5172
(Petroleum Products Nec). **Est:** 1946. **Sales:**
$16,000,000 (2000). **Emp:** 18. **Officers:** Kirby Moon,
President; Tim Edwards, General Mgr.

**■ 18122 ■ Moweaqua Farmers Cooperative
Grain Co.**
PO Box 146
Moweaqua, IL 62550
Phone: (217)768-4416
Products: Grain elevator. **SIC:** 5153 (Grain & Field
Beans). **Sales:** $12,000,000 (2000). **Emp:** 7. **Officers:**
James Hedges, CEO.

■ 18123 ■ Munsell Livestock
PO Box 1408
MiLes City, MT 59301-1408
Phone: (406)232-1644
Products: Livestock. **SIC:** 5154 (Livestock). **Officers:**
Wesley Munsell, President.

■ 18124 ■ Napoleon Livestock Auction
PO Box 3
Napoleon, ND 58561-0003
Phone: (701)754-2216 **Fax:** (701)754-2953
Products: Livestock. **SIC:** 5154 (Livestock). **Officers:**
George Bitz, President.

■ 18125 ■ Nathan Segal and Company Inc.
2100 W Loop 610 S
Houston, TX 77027
Phone: (713)621-2000
Products: Grain and feed ingredients. **SIC:** 5153
(Grain & Field Beans). **Sales:** $29,000,000 (1993).
Emp: 15. **Officers:** Jack Goldfield, President; Zane
Segal, Treasurer & Secty.

■ 18126 ■ NC Plus Hybrids Coop.
3820 N 56th
Lincoln, NE 68504
Phone: (402)467-2517
Free: (800)279-7999 **Fax:** (402)467-4217
E-mail: lincoln@nc-plus.com
URL: http://www.nc-plus.com
Products: Seed; Corn; Alfalfa; Sorghum; Soybean.
SICs: 5191 (Farm Supplies); 5153 (Grain & Field
Beans). **Est:** 1958. **Sales:** $39,000,000 (2000). **Emp:**
115. **Officers:** Larry Schuett, President, e-mail:
lschuett@nc-plus.com.

■ 18127 ■ Nehawka Farmers Cooperative
PO Box 159
Nehawka, NE 68413
Phone: (402)227-2715 **Fax:** (402)227-2062
Products: Feed; Grain; Fertilizer; Hardware; Tires;
Petroleum. **SICs:** 5153 (Grain & Field Beans); 5014
(Tires & Tubes); 5072 (Hardware); 5172 (Petroleum
Products Nec). **Est:** 1902. **Sales:** $11,000,000 (2000).
Emp: 21. **Officers:** Keith Stone, President; Arlo Cole,
Treasurer; Stan Stark, General Mgr.

■ **18128** ■ **Todd Nelson**
2301 Highway 95
Council, ID 83612-5233
Phone: (208)253-6052
Products: Livestock. **SIC:** 5154 (Livestock). **Officers:** Todd Nelson, Partner.

■ **18129** ■ **Neowa F.S. Inc.**
PO Box 127
Maynard, IA 50655
Phone: (319)637-2281
Products: Feed, fertilizer, livestock equipment and petroleum. **SICs:** 5191 (Farm Supplies); 5083 (Farm & Garden Machinery); 5172 (Petroleum Products Nec). **Sales:** $56,000,000 (1994). **Emp:** 40. **Officers:** John P. Flynn, General Mgr.; Darryl Dolf, Finance Officer.

■ **18130** ■ **NEW Cooperative Inc.**
PO Box 818
Ft. Dodge, IA 50501
Phone: (515)955-2040 **Fax:** (515)955-5565
Products: Grain. **SIC:** 5153 (Grain & Field Beans). **Est:** 1973. **Sales:** $240,000,000 (2000). **Emp:** 145. **Officers:** Brent Banty, General Mgr.; Danny Jannsen, Sales Mgr.

■ **18131** ■ **Newark Farmers Grain Co.**
203 N Johnson St.
Newark, IL 60541
Phone: (815)695-5141 **Fax:** (815)695-5651
Products: Grain; Fertilizer and fertilizer materials; Field, garden, and flower seeds. **SICs:** 5153 (Grain & Field Beans); 5191 (Farm Supplies). **Est:** 1930. **Sales:** $14,000,000 (2000). **Emp:** 8. **Officers:** Jerome Whalen, General Mgr.

■ **18132** ■ **Nokomis Equity Elevator Co.**
301 E State St.
Nokomis, IL 62075
Phone: (217)563-8612
Products: Grain elevator. **SIC:** 5153 (Grain & Field Beans). **Est:** 1929. **Sales:** $12,000,000 (2000). **Emp:** 12. **Officers:** Larry Ernst, General Mgr.

■ **18133** ■ **Nomura and Company Inc.**
40 Broderick Rd.
Burlingame, CA 94010
Phone: (415)692-5457 **Fax:** (415)692-8297
Products: Milled rice and byproducts. **SIC:** 5153 (Grain & Field Beans). **Est:** 1948. **Sales:** $25,000,000 (2000). **Emp:** 10. **Officers:** George Okamoto, President.

■ **18134** ■ **W.H. Nored Cotton Co.**
PO Box 1009
Greenwood, MS 38935-1009
Phone: (601)453-3772 **Fax:** (601)455-3838
Products: Cotton. **SIC:** 5159 (Farm-Product Raw Materials Nec). **Est:** 1951. **Sales:** $12,500,000 (1994). **Emp:** 3. **Officers:** Bobby Nored, President.

■ **18135** ■ **North American Fur Producers New York Inc.**
1275 Valley Brook Ave.
Lyndhurst, NJ 07071-3519
Phone: (201)933-3366
Products: Raw fur pelts. **SIC:** 5137 (Women's/Children's Clothing). **Est:** 1970. **Sales:** $49,000,000 (2000). **Emp:** 150. **Officers:** Michael Mengar, CEO & President; Doug Fizel, Sr. VP.

■ **18136** ■ **North Central Commodities, Inc.**
PO Box 13055
Grand Forks, ND 58208-3055
Phone: (701)746-7436 **Fax:** (701)746-9243
Products: Sunflower seeds; Dry beans and peas. **SICs:** 5153 (Grain & Field Beans); 5159 (Farm-Product Raw Materials Nec). **Officers:** Paul Montgomery, Manager.

■ **18137** ■ **North Central Cooperative Elevator**
PO Box 313
Clarion, IA 50525
Phone: (515)532-2881 **Fax:** (515)532-2273
Products: Grain elevators. **SIC:** 5153 (Grain & Field Beans). **Sales:** $45,000,000 (2000). **Emp:** 50. **Officers:** Al Struthers, General Mgr.

■ **18138** ■ **North Central Farm Service Inc.**
PO Box 337
Hampton, IA 50441-0337
Phone: (515)456-2571
Products: Grain. **SIC:** 5153 (Grain & Field Beans). **Sales:** $10,000,000 (1994). **Emp:** 50. **Officers:** Jack Hendrickson, General Mgr.

■ **18139** ■ **North East Kingdom Sales, Inc.**
PO Box 550
Barton, VT 05822-0296
Phone: (802)525-4774 **Fax:** (802)525-3997
Products: Livestock; Farm machinery and equipment. **SICs:** 5154 (Livestock); 5191 (Farm Supplies). **Officers:** James T. Young, President; Raymond LeBlanc, Vice President.

■ **18140** ■ **Northeast Cooperative**
445 S Main St.
West Point, NE 68788
Phone: (402)372-5303
Products: Grain and animal feed additives. **SICs:** 5153 (Grain & Field Beans); 5191 (Farm Supplies). **Sales:** $25,000,000 (1994). **Emp:** 42. **Officers:** Jim Meier, Controller.

■ **18141** ■ **Northeast Hide & Fur Corp.**
RR 1, Box 890
Waterboro, ME 04087-9606
Phone: (207)247-4444 **Fax:** (207)247-4522
Products: Hides; Pelts. **SIC:** 5159 (Farm-Product Raw Materials Nec). **Officers:** Antonio Andreotola, President.

■ **18142** ■ **Northeast Texas Farmers Cooperative Inc.**
PO Box 489
Sulphur Springs, TX 75482
Phone: (903)885-3143
Products: Farm supplies. **SIC:** 5191 (Farm Supplies). **Sales:** $25,000,000 (1994). **Emp:** 121. **Officers:** Richard Thomas, General Mgr.; Lanny R. Dodd, Controller.

■ **18143** ■ **Northwest Grain**
PO Box 128
St. Hilaire, MN 56754
Phone: (218)964-5252
URL: http://www.northwestgrain.com
Products: Grain; Argonomy; Confectionary sunflowers. **SICs:** 5153 (Grain & Field Beans); 5191 (Farm Supplies). **Est:** 1952. **Sales:** $73,000,000 (2000). **Emp:** 75. **Officers:** Tim Miller, General Mgr.; Rob LaCoursiere, Controller; Ben Bjerken, Dir. of Marketing; David Giles, General Mgr. **Former Name:** St. Hilaire Cooperative Elevators.

■ **18144** ■ **Northwest Grain Growers, Inc.**
PO Box 310
Walla Walla, WA 99362
Phone: (509)525-6510 **Fax:** (509)529-6050
URL: http://www.nwgrgr.com
Products: Wheat; Barley. **SIC:** 5153 (Grain & Field Beans). **Est:** 1929. **Sales:** $94,600,000 (2000). **Emp:** 36. **Officers:** Edward Chvatal, President. **Former Name:** Walla Walla Grain Growers, Inc.

■ **18145** ■ **Northwest Iowa Cooperative**
PO Box 218
Ashton, IA 51232
Phone: (712)724-6171
Products: Grain. **SICs:** 5153 (Grain & Field Beans); 5191 (Farm Supplies). **Est:** 1981. **Sales:** $17,000,000 (2000). **Emp:** 21. **Officers:** Kermit DeBoom, President; Robert Harten, General Mgr.

■ **18146** ■ **Northwood Cooperative Elevator**
PO Box 227
Northwood, IA 50459
Phone: (515)324-2753 **Fax:** (515)324-2765
Products: Grain and farm supplies. **SICs:** 5153 (Grain & Field Beans); 5191 (Farm Supplies). **Sales:** $18,000,000 (2000). **Emp:** 20. **Officers:** Larry L. Wright, President.

■ **18147** ■ **Northwood Equity Elevators**
PO Box 380
Northwood, ND 58267
Phone: (701)587-5291
Products: Grain elevator. **SIC:** 5153 (Grain & Field Beans). **Est:** 1915. **Sales:** $9,000,000 (2000). **Emp:** 8. **Officers:** Scott Ostlie, General Mgr.

■ **18148** ■ **Ocheyedan Cooperative Elevator Association**
Box 69
Ocheyedan, IA 51354
Phone: (712)758-3621
Free: (800)779-2107 **Fax:** (712)758-3625
Products: Grain, seeds and other farm supplies. **SICs:** 5153 (Grain & Field Beans); 5191 (Farm Supplies). **Est:** 1906. **Sales:** $35,000,000 (2000). **Emp:** 35. **Officers:** Doug Radunz, President; Dennis Mass, Finance General Manager.

■ **18149** ■ **Odessa Trading Company Inc.**
PO Box 277
Odessa, WA 99159
Phone: (509)982-2661
Products: Grain; Tractor supplies. **SICs:** 5153 (Grain & Field Beans); 5083 (Farm & Garden Machinery). **Est:** 1928. **Sales:** $13,000,000 (2000). **Emp:** 26. **Officers:** Jerry Wacker, CEO; Mark Cronrath, Marketing Mgr.

■ **18150** ■ **Odessa Union Warehouse Co-op**
PO Box 247
Odessa, WA 99159-0247
Phone: (509)982-2691 **Fax:** (509)982-2970
URL: http://www.odessaunion.com
Products: Grain elevator. **SIC:** 5153 (Grain & Field Beans). **Est:** 1903. **Sales:** $22,000,000 (2000). **Emp:** 28. **Officers:** Bill Bell, President; Marvin Greenwald, General Mgr.; Mike Conklin, Manager; Keith Bailey, Marketing Mgr., e-mail: keith@odessaunion.com.

■ **18151** ■ **Ohsman and Sons Co.**
400 8th St. SE
PO Box 1196
Cedar Rapids, IA 52406
Phone: (319)365-7546 **Fax:** (319)365-7550
E-mail: mail@ohsman.com
Products: Wool; Furs; Hides; Leather. **SIC:** 5159 (Farm-Product Raw Materials Nec). **Est:** 1891. **Sales:** $50,000,000 (2000). **Emp:** 15. **Officers:** Michael Ohsman, President; Gary Osborne, Manager.

■ **18152** ■ **Oils of Aloha**
66935 Kaukonahua Rd.
PO Box 685
Waialua, HI 96791
Phone: (808)637-5620
Free: (800)367-6010 **Fax:** (808)637-6194
E-mail: info@oilsofaloha.com
URL: http://www.oils-of-aloha.com
Products: Edible and cosmetic nut oils. **SIC:** 5159 (Farm-Product Raw Materials Nec). **Est:** 1988. **Sales:** $1,000,000 (2000). **Emp:** 10. **Officers:** Dana G. Gray.

■ **18153** ■ **O.K. Grain Co.**
Box 156
Litchfield, IL 62056
Phone: (217)324-6151
Products: Grains, including corn, beans, and wheat. **SIC:** 5153 (Grain & Field Beans). **Est:** 1960. **Sales:** $15,000,000 (2000). **Emp:** 14. **Officers:** L.L. Herndon Jr., President & CFO.

■ **18154** ■ **Old Dominion Grain Corp.**
P. O. Box 18
West Point, VA 23181
Phone: (804)843-2922
Free: (800)552-6991 **Fax:** (804)843-4670
Products: Grain. **SIC:** 5153 (Grain & Field Beans). **Sales:** $19,000,000 (2000). **Emp:** 15. **Officers:** P.L. Harrell, President.

■ **18155** ■ **Olton Grain Cooperative Inc.**
PO Drawer M
Olton, TX 79064
Phone: (806)285-2638
Products: Grain elevator and farm supplies. **SICs:** 5153 (Grain & Field Beans); 5191 (Farm Supplies). **Sales:** $12,000,000 (1992). **Emp:** 15. **Officers:** E.W. Richards, Finance General Manager.

■ 18156 ■ **Orleans Commissions Sales**
PO Box 55
Orleans, VT 05860
Phone: (802)754-8533
Products: Livestock. **SIC:** 5154 (Livestock).

■ 18157 ■ **Ottawa Cooperative Association Inc.**
302 N Main St.
Ottawa, KS 66067
Phone: (785)242-5170
Products: Grain elevator. **SIC:** 5153 (Grain & Field Beans). **Est:** 1952. **Sales:** $13,800,000 (2000). **Emp:** 23. **Officers:** Gene Maxwell, President; Adrian DeRousseau, General Mgr.

■ 18158 ■ **Pacific Southwest Seed and Grain Inc.**
PO Box 5540
Yuma, AZ 85366
Phone: (520)782-2571 **Fax:** (520)782-4656
Products: Wheat; Seed. **SICs:** 5191 (Farm Supplies); 5153 (Grain & Field Beans). **Est:** 1988. **Sales:** $9,000,000 (2000). **Emp:** 24. **Officers:** Steven Leffler, President.

■ 18159 ■ **Paoli Farmers Cooperative Elevator Co.**
PO Box 5649
Paoli, CO 80746
Phone: (970)774-7234 **Fax:** (970)774-6320
Products: Grain, wheat, and corn. **SIC:** 5153 (Grain & Field Beans). **Est:** 1919. **Sales:** $5,000,000 (2000). **Emp:** 7. **Officers:** Steve Bahnsen, General Mgr.

■ 18160 ■ **Parshall Farmers Union Co-op Inc.**
PO Box 128
Parshall, ND 58770
Phone: (701)862-3113 **Fax:** (701)862-4103
Products: Grain elevator. **SIC:** 5153 (Grain & Field Beans). **Est:** 1915. **Sales:** $8,700,000 (2000). **Emp:** 12. **Officers:** Dick Hauge, President & Chairman of the Board; Harold Rasmusson, General Mgr.

■ 18161 ■ **Pendleton Grain Growers Inc.**
1000 Dorion SW
Pendleton, OR 97801
Phone: (541)276-7611
Free: (800)422-7611 **Fax:** (541)278-5055
URL: http://www.pggcounty.com
Products: Grain; Farm supplies; Animal feed; Petroleum and propane; Lawn and garden; Pumps and irrigation. **SICs:** 5153 (Grain & Field Beans); 5191 (Farm Supplies); 5072 (Hardware); 5172 (Petroleum Products Nec). **Est:** 1930. **Sales:** $105,000,000 (2000). **Emp:** 300. **Officers:** Albert Gosiak, President.

■ 18162 ■ **Perdue Farms Grain Div.**
PO Box 1537
Salisbury, MD 21802
Phone: (410)543-3650 **Fax:** (410)860-4226
Products: Grain. **SIC:** 5153 (Grain & Field Beans). **Sales:** $163,000,000 (2000). **Emp:** 832. **Officers:** Richard Willey, VP & General Merchandising Mgr.

■ 18163 ■ **Lynn Perry**
PO Box 867
Shelby, MT 59474-0867
Phone: (406)434-2040
Products: Livestock. **SIC:** 5154 (Livestock). **Officers:** Lynn Perry, Owner.

■ 18164 ■ **Perryton Equity Exchange**
PO Drawer 889
Perryton, TX 79070
Phone: (806)435-4016 **Fax:** (806)435-7194
Products: Grain. **SICs:** 5153 (Grain & Field Beans); 5191 (Farm Supplies); 5172 (Petroleum Products Nec). **Est:** 1919. **Sales:** $47,000,000 (2000). **Emp:** 120. **Officers:** Edgar Womble, General Mgr.; Steve Ewing, Controller.

■ 18165 ■ **Pickrell Cooperative Elevator Association**
Main St.
Pickrell, NE 68422
Phone: (402)673-3280
Products: Grain; Feed; Fertilizers. **SICs:** 5153 (Grain & Field Beans); 5191 (Farm Supplies). **Est:** 1905.

Sales: $7,500,000 (2000). **Emp:** 13. **Officers:** Leonard Buhr, President.

■ 18166 ■ **Pine City Cooperative Association**
600 6th St.
Pine City, MN 55063
Phone: (612)629-2581
Products: Farm supplies, petroleum products and lumber. **SICs:** 5191 (Farm Supplies); 5172 (Petroleum Products Nec); 5031 (Lumber, Plywood & Millwork). **Sales:** $10,000,000 (1993). **Emp:** 50. **Officers:** Craig Mold, President.

■ 18167 ■ **Pine Island Farmers Elevator Co.**
PO Box 1037
Pine Island, MN 55963
Phone: (507)356-8313 **Fax:** (507)356-8881
Products: Grain elevator. **SIC:** 5153 (Grain & Field Beans). **Sales:** $15,000,000 (2000). **Emp:** 30. **Officers:** Tim Clemmens, General Mgr.

■ 18168 ■ **Piqua Farmers Cooperative Association**
PO Box 67
Piqua, KS 66761
Phone: (316)468-2535
Products: Grain elevator. **SIC:** 5153 (Grain & Field Beans). **Est:** 1956. **Sales:** $3,000,000 (2000). **Emp:** 11. **Officers:** John Hasstedt, President; Marvin Lynch, Manager.

■ 18169 ■ **Daniel Piroutek**
HCR 1 Box6-A
Milesville, SD 57553
Phone: (605)544-3316 **Fax:** (605)544-3316
E-mail: piroutek@wcenet.com
URL: http://www.sdauctions.com
Products: Livestock; Cattle. **SIC:** 5154 (Livestock). **Est:** 1976. **Emp:** 3. **Officers:** Daniel Piroutek, Owner.

■ 18170 ■ **Plains Cotton Cooperative Association**
3301 E 50th St.
Lubbock, TX 79408
Phone: (806)763-8011 **Fax:** (806)762-7400
URL: http://www.pcca.com
Products: Cotton. **SIC:** 5159 (Farm-Product Raw Materials Nec). **Est:** 1953. **Sales:** $1,000,000,000 (1999). **Emp:** 1,300. **Officers:** Van May, President; Bill Morton, CFO; David Stanford, VP of Marketing; Joe Tubb, VP of Information Systems.

■ 18171 ■ **Plains Equity Exchange**
PO Box 157
Plains, KS 67869
Phone: (316)563-7269
Products: Grain elevator. **SICs:** 5153 (Grain & Field Beans); 5171 (Petroleum Bulk Stations & Terminals); 5191 (Farm Supplies). **Est:** 1913. **Sales:** $14,000,000 (2000). **Emp:** 22. **Officers:** Vonn Richardson, Chairman of the Board; Elwin Tyson, General Mgr.

■ 18172 ■ **Henry G. Pohlman Farms**
Henry St.
Malinta, OH 43535
Phone: (419)256-7282
Products: Cattle. **SIC:** 5154 (Livestock). **Est:** 1890. **Sales:** $2,000,000 (2000). **Emp:** 7. **Officers:** Henry F. Pohlman, Partner.

■ 18173 ■ **Pomeroy Grain Growers Inc.**
PO Box 220
Pomeroy, WA 99347
Phone: (509)843-1694 **Fax:** (509)847-1695
Products: Grain elevator. **SIC:** 5153 (Grain & Field Beans). **Est:** 1930. **Sales:** $18,000,000 (2000). **Emp:** 16. **Officers:** Charles Woody, CFO.

■ 18174 ■ **Pond International Inc.**
1559 Hidden Valley Rd.
Sandy, UT 84092-5724
Phone: (801)571-4365
Free: (800)644-6475 **Fax:** (801)571-1814
E-mail: pond@aol.com
Products: Agricultural products; Clothing. **SICs:** 5159 (Farm-Product Raw Materials Nec); 5136 (Men's/Boys' Clothing). **Est:** 1982. **Emp:** 30. **Officers:** Eugene Yamada, President.

■ 18175 ■ **Pontiac Livestock Sales**
Rte. 116 E
Pontiac, IL 61764
Phone: (815)844-6951
Products: Livestock, including pigs, sheep, cows, and horses. **SIC:** 5154 (Livestock). **Est:** 1952. **Sales:** $3,000,000 (2000). **Emp:** 15. **Officers:** Frank R. Trainor, Partner.

■ 18176 ■ **Prairie Livestock L.L.C.**
Barton Ferry Rd.
West Point, MS 39773
Phone: (601)494-5651 **Fax:** (601)494-2672
Products: Cattle. **SIC:** 5154 (Livestock). **Est:** 1964. **Sales:** $100,000,000 (2000). **Emp:** 25. **Officers:** James D. Bryan, President; Carolyn Skelton, Controller; Sharon Duke, Dir. of Data Processing; Phil McClellan, Human Resources Mgr.

■ 18177 ■ **Prewitt Cattle Co.**
815 3rd St. Ne
Sidney, MT 59270-4717
Phone: (406)482-5251 **Fax:** (406)482-6644
Products: Livestock. **SIC:** 5154 (Livestock). **Officers:** Chantz Prewitt, President.

■ 18178 ■ **Prins Grain Co.**
R.R. 1
Holland, MN 56139
Phone: (507)347-3131
Products: Grains and feed. **SICs:** 5153 (Grain & Field Beans); 5191 (Farm Supplies). **Est:** 1972. **Sales:** $6,000,000 (2000). **Emp:** 12. **Officers:** Mike Lingen, General Mgr.

■ 18179 ■ **Prinz Grain and Feed Inc.**
PO Box 265
West Point, NE 68788
Phone: (402)372-2495 **Fax:** (402)372-3228
Products: Grain and feed. **SICs:** 5153 (Grain & Field Beans); 5191 (Farm Supplies). **Sales:** $11,200,000 (1994). **Emp:** 19. **Officers:** Leonard W. Prinz, President.

■ 18180 ■ **Producers Cooperative Association of Girard**
PO Box 323
Girard, KS 66743
Phone: (316)724-8241 **Fax:** (316)724-8243
Products: Grain elevator. **SIC:** 5153 (Grain & Field Beans). **Est:** 1948. **Sales:** $16,000,000 (2000). **Emp:** 50. **Officers:** Bill Huston, CEO.

■ 18181 ■ **Producers Livestock Marketing Association**
PO Box 540477
North Salt Lake, UT 84054
Phone: (801)292-2424
Products: Pigs, cattle, and horses. **SIC:** 5154 (Livestock). **Est:** 1935. **Sales:** $140,000,000 (2000). **Emp:** 200. **Officers:** Mike Urrutia, President; John Butler, Controller.

■ 18182 ■ **Protection Co-op Supply**
PO Box 338
Protection, KS 67127
Phone: (316)622-4619
Products: Grain elevator. **SIC:** 5153 (Grain & Field Beans). **Est:** 1926. **Sales:** $10,000,000 (2000). **Emp:** 17. **Officers:** Kendall D. Poland, General Mgr.

■ 18183 ■ **Public Auction Yards**
PO Box 1781
Billings, MT 59103-1781
Phone: (406)245-6447 **Fax:** (406)259-6888
Products: Livestock. **SIC:** 5154 (Livestock). **Officers:** Pat Goggins, Owner.

■ 18184 ■ **Pyramid Agri-Products International**
Rte. 3, Box 33-A
Larned, KS 67550
Phone: (316)285-7211 **Fax:** (316)285-6566
Products: Beef livestock; Poultry; Packaged frozen meats; Grain, including alfalfa. **SICs:** 5153 (Grain & Field Beans); 5154 (Livestock); 5144 (Poultry & Poultry Products); 5142 (Packaged Frozen Foods). **Officers:** John Woods, Owner.

■ 18185 ■ Quad County Cooperative
PO Box 4
Exeter, NE 68351
Phone: (402)266-5951 **Fax:** (402)266-2101
Products: Grain, corn, wheat, and milo. **SICs:** 5153 (Grain & Field Beans); 5191 (Farm Supplies); 5172 (Petroleum Products Nec). **Est:** 1916. **Sales:** $12,000,000 (2000). **Emp:** 25. **Officers:** Gerry Geiger, President; Edwin Wilkensen, Manager; Don Mullen, General Mgr.; Timothy Lehman, Dir. of Merchandising.

■ 18186 ■ Quaker City Hide Co.
25 Washington Ln., Ste. 6A
Wyncote, PA 19095-1400
Phone: (215)886-2400 **Fax:** (215)886-9487
E-mail: qchide@erols.com
Products: Raw hides and skins; Pet supplies. **SICs:** 5159 (Farm-Product Raw Materials Nec); 5149 (Groceries & Related Products Nec); 5199 (Nondurable Goods Nec). **Est:** 1876. **Emp:** 5. **Officers:** Jeff Sternfeld, President.

■ 18187 ■ Quaker City Hide Co.
25 Washington Ln., Ste. 6A
Wyncote, PA 19095-1400
Phone: (215)886-2400 **Fax:** (215)886-9487
Products: Livestock and farm products. **SIC:** 5159 (Farm-Product Raw Materials Nec).

■ 18188 ■ Radium Cooperative Co.
Rte. 2
Radium, KS 67550
Phone: (316)982-4364
Products: Grain elevator. **SIC:** 5153 (Grain & Field Beans). **Est:** 1904. **Sales:** $5,000,000 (2000). **Emp:** 22. **Officers:** W.S. Symns, President; Steven Hays, Manager; Beryl Conkle, Manager.

■ 18189 ■ Randall Farmers Cooperative Union
PO Box 95
Randall, KS 66963
Phone: (785)739-2312 **Fax:** (785)739-2313
Products: Grain elevator. **SIC:** 5153 (Grain & Field Beans). **Est:** 1926. **Sales:** $9,000,000 (2000). **Emp:** 9. **Officers:** Steve Dunstan, President; Charles Houghton, General Mgr.

■ 18190 ■ H.G. Randall Inc.
PO Box 221
Tomah, WI 54660
Phone: (608)372-4539
Products: Dairy cattle. **SIC:** 5154 (Livestock). **Sales:** $6,000,000 (2000). **Emp:** 7. **Officers:** Howard Randall, President.

■ 18191 ■ Rangen Inc.
PO Box 706
Buhl, ID 83316-0706
Phone: (208)543-6421 **Fax:** (208)543-6090
Products: Fish; Cattle; Beans. **SICs:** 5146 (Fish & Seafoods); 5154 (Livestock); 5153 (Grain & Field Beans). **Est:** 1925. **Sales:** $27,000,000 (2000). **Emp:** 180. **Officers:** Chris Rangen, President; J. Wayne Courtney, Controller.

■ 18192 ■ Redfield Livestock Auction Inc.
PO Box 356
Redfield, SD 57469
Phone: (605)472-2360
Products: Livestock; Auctioning livestock. **SIC:** 5154 (Livestock). **Officers:** Gilbert Lutter, President.

■ 18193 ■ Redwood Valley Co-op Elevator
PO Box 393
Redwood Falls, MN 56283
Phone: (507)637-2914
Products: Grain; Feed. **SICs:** 5153 (Grain & Field Beans); 5191 (Farm Supplies). **Est:** 1976. **Sales:** $13,000,000 (2000). **Emp:** 8. **Officers:** Michael Kohout, General Mgr.

■ 18194 ■ Reese Farmers Inc.
9715 Saginaw
Reese, MI 48757
Phone: (517)868-4146 **Fax:** (517)868-9831
Products: Grain; Dry feed. **SICs:** 5153 (Grain & Field Beans); 5191 (Farm Supplies). **Est:** 1974. **Sales:** $20,000,000 (2000). **Emp:** 18. **Officers:** Robert Elbers, President; John Findlay, Secretary.

■ 18195 ■ Revere Elevator Company Inc.
Main St. & Railrd Track
Revere, MN 56166
Phone: (507)752-7341
Products: Grain. **SIC:** 5153 (Grain & Field Beans). **Est:** 1991. **Sales:** $3,500,000 (2000). **Emp:** 2. **Officers:** Raymond Haack, CEO; Brian Berg, CFO.

■ 18196 ■ Rhode Island Tack Shop Inc.
PO Box 803
North Scituate, RI 02857
Phone: (401)934-0097
Free: (800)429-0097 **Fax:** (401)934-2330
Products: Horses. **SIC:** 5159 (Farm-Product Raw Materials Nec). **Est:** 1992. **Sales:** $450,000 (2000). **Emp:** 3. **Officers:** Carleton Swedberg, President.
Former Name: Pine Grove Stable Inc.

■ 18197 ■ Rickett Grain Co.
PO Box 32
Forest City, IL 61532
Phone: (309)597-2331
Products: Grain. **SIC:** 5153 (Grain & Field Beans). **Est:** 1947. **Sales:** $9,000,000 (2000). **Emp:** 6. **Officers:** E. Rickett, President; Lynn Coers, Manager.

■ 18198 ■ Rio Farmers Union Cooperative
PO Box 246
Rio, WI 53960
Phone: (920)992-3114
Products: Grain and feed; Fertilizer. **SICs:** 5153 (Grain & Field Beans); 5191 (Farm Supplies). **Est:** 1932. **Sales:** $13,000,000 (2000). **Emp:** 39. **Officers:** Ralph Berger, President; R.W. Vogts, Treasurer & Secty.; Myron Bandt, General Mgr.

■ 18199 ■ Rivard's Quality Seeds Inc.
PO Box 303
Argyle, MN 56713
Phone: (218)437-6638 **Fax:** (218)437-6392
Products: Clean grain, wheat, and barley. **SIC:** 5153 (Grain & Field Beans). **Est:** 1968. **Sales:** $3,000,000 (2000). **Emp:** 10. **Officers:** L. Rivard, President; K. Schuster, CFO.

■ 18200 ■ River Spring Cooperative
PO Box 87
Old Fort, OH 44861
Phone: (419)992-4223
Products: Grain elevators. **SIC:** 5153 (Grain & Field Beans). **Est:** 1913. **Sales:** $2,000,000 (2000). **Emp:** 3. **Officers:** Mike Myers, General Mgr.

■ 18201 ■ Robbins Livestock Auction
PO Box 17004
Missoula, MT 59808-7004
Phone: (406)728-3052
Products: Livestock. **SIC:** 5154 (Livestock). **Officers:** Dave Robbins, Partner.

■ 18202 ■ Roberts Brothers Inc.
PO Box 109
Shawboro, NC 27973
Phone: (919)232-2798 **Fax:** (252)232-2571
Products: Grain. **SIC:** 5153 (Grain & Field Beans). **Est:** 1959. **Sales:** $1,700,000 (2000). **Emp:** 6. **Officers:** Wade E. Morgan, President; Jo Ann R. Morgan, Treasurer & Secty.

■ 18203 ■ Rolla Cooperative Equity Exchange
PO Box 196
Rolla, KS 67954
Phone: (316)593-4335
Products: Grain; Chemicals; Fertilizer. **SICs:** 5153 (Grain & Field Beans); 5169 (Chemicals & Allied Products Nec); 5191 (Farm Supplies). **Est:** 1918. **Sales:** $8,000,000 (2000). **Emp:** 20. **Officers:** Ted King, General Mgr.

■ 18204 ■ Rolla Cooperative Grain Co.
116 Front St. S Box 177
Rolla, ND 58367
Phone: (701)477-5612 **Fax:** (701)477-3054
Products: Barley; Wheat, including durum wheat. **SIC:** 5153 (Grain & Field Beans). **Est:** 1921. **Sales:** $4,000,000 (2000). **Emp:** 5. **Officers:** Robert Dunlop, President; Steve Lange, Treasurer; L Guderjahn, Dir. of Marketing.

■ 18205 ■ Rosamond Cooperative
PO Box 37
Rosamond, IL 62083
Phone: (217)562-2363
Products: Grain elevator. **SIC:** 5153 (Grain & Field Beans). **Est:** 1919. **Sales:** $10,500,000 (2000). **Emp:** 9. **Officers:** James Wilcox, President; R. Bishop, Vice President.

■ 18206 ■ Rosholt Farmers Cooperative Elevator Co.
PO Box 16
Rosholt, SD 57260
Phone: (605)537-4236 **Fax:** (605)537-4336
Products: Grain and farm supplies. **SICs:** 5153 (Grain & Field Beans); 5191 (Farm Supplies). **Sales:** $20,000,000 (1994). **Emp:** 9. **Officers:** Richard Sando, President.

■ 18207 ■ Roswell Livestock Auction Co.
PO Box 2041
Roswell, NM 88202-2041
Phone: (505)622-5580 **Fax:** (505)625-5680
Products: Livestock. **SIC:** 5154 (Livestock). **Officers:** Larry Wooton, President.

■ 18208 ■ Roswell Wool LLC
212 E 4th St.
Roswell, NM 88201
Phone: (505)622-3360 **Fax:** (505)622-3161
E-mail: rwool@zianet.com
URL: http://www.rt66.com/~markw/
Products: Dealers in raw farm products; Raw wool; Commission merchants. **SIC:** 5159 (Farm-Product Raw Materials Nec). **Est:** 1992. **Sales:** $5,000,000 (2000). **Emp:** 5. **Officers:** Mike Corn, Owner & Manager.
Former Name: Wool Growers Central Storage Co.

■ 18209 ■ Route 16 Grain Cooperative
301 E State St.
Nokomis, IL 62075
Phone: (217)563-8612
Products: Farm supplies, chemicals and grain. **SICs:** 5191 (Farm Supplies); 5153 (Grain & Field Beans). **Sales:** $12,000,000 (1994). **Emp:** 20.

■ 18210 ■ John Rueb Associates Inc.
250 Beechwood Dr.
Boise, ID 83709-0944
Phone: (208)345-8265
Products: Dealers in raw farm products; Feathers; Hides; Pelts. **SIC:** 5159 (Farm-Product Raw Materials Nec). **Officers:** John Rueb, President.

■ 18211 ■ Rugby Farmers Union Elevator Co.
105 E Dewey St.
Rugby, ND 58368-0286
Phone: (701)776-5214 **Fax:** (701)776-6437
Products: Grain. **SICs:** 5153 (Grain & Field Beans); 5191 (Farm Supplies). **Est:** 1940. **Sales:** $7,000,000 (2000). **Emp:** 15. **Officers:** Steve Fritle, President; Duane Johnston, General Mgr.

■ 18212 ■ Rumbold and Kuhn Inc.
PO Box 26
Princeville, IL 61559
Phone: (309)385-4846 **Fax:** (309)695-2020
Products: Grain elevator. **SIC:** 5153 (Grain & Field Beans). **Est:** 1953. **Sales:** $35,000,000 (2000). **Emp:** 4. **Officers:** E. Rumbold, President; Ezra Rumbold, Treasurer & Secty.; Bruce Graham, Dir. of Marketing.

■ 18213 ■ Rural Serv Inc.
PO Box 870
Fremont, OH 43420
Phone: (419)332-6468
Products: Grain and farm supplies. **SICs:** 5153 (Grain & Field Beans); 5191 (Farm Supplies). **Sales:** $21,600,000 (1992). **Emp:** 65. **Officers:** Tom Antesberger, President.

■ 18214 ■ Herbert A. Russell
RR 8C54, Box 240
Nye, MT 59061
Phone: (406)328-6296
Products: Livestock; Cattle. **SIC:** 5154 (Livestock). **Officers:** Herbert Russell, Owner.

■ **18215** ■ **Ruth Farmers Elevator Inc.**
4600 Ruth Rd.
Ruth, MI 48470
Phone: (517)864-3391 **Fax:** (517)864-3434
Products: Grain. **SIC:** 5153 (Grain & Field Beans).
Est: 1936. **Sales:** $21,000,000 (2000). **Emp:** 38.
Officers: Paul Holdwick, Chairman of the Board; Earl
Booms, Treasurer; Gerald Geiger, General Mgr.

■ **18216** ■ **S-T Leather Co.**
2135 S James Rd., Bay F
Columbus, OH 43232
Phone: (614)235-1900 **Fax:** (614)235-1945
Products: Skins; Hardware. **SIC:** 5199 (Nondurable
Goods Nec). **Est:** 1948. **Officers:** Andrea Marcum,
Manager.

■ **18217** ■ **St. Albans Commission Sales**
RR 2, Box 244
St. Albans, VT 05478
Phone: (802)524-2991 **Fax:** (802)524-5581
Products: Livestock. **SIC:** 5154 (Livestock).

■ **18218** ■ **St. Angsar Mills Inc.**
PO Box 370
St. Ansgar, IA 50472-0370
Phone: (515)736-4520
E-mail: stamills@smig.net
Products: Grain and feed. **SIC:** 5153 (Grain & Field
Beans). **Est:** 1930. **Sales:** $12,000,000 (2000). **Emp:**
13. **Officers:** Edward J. Kleinwort, President; J.R.
Kleinwort, COO.

■ **18219** ■ **St. John Grain Growers Inc.**
PO Box 6
St. John, WA 99171
Phone: (509)648-3316
Products: Wheat and barley. **SIC:** 5153 (Grain & Field
Beans). **Est:** 1929. **Sales:** $3,000,000 (2000). **Emp:** 8.
Officers: Mack Mills, President; Tom Jeffries,
Manager.

■ **18220** ■ **Salado Cattle Co.**
PO Box 38
Salado, TX 76571
Phone: (254)947-5132 **Fax:** (254)947-8175
Products: Cattle. **SIC:** 5154 (Livestock). **Sales:**
$3,000,000 (2000). **Emp:** 4. **Officers:** C.B. Hodge,
President; Glen Hodge, Vice President; Claude Hodge,
Marketing & Sales Mgr.

■ **18221** ■ **Sanborn Farmers Elevator**
PO Box 67
Sanborn, MN 56083
Phone: (507)648-3851 **Fax:** (507)648-3826
Products: Grain; Feed; Seed; Bulk petroleum. **SICs:**
5153 (Grain & Field Beans); 5191 (Farm Supplies).
Est: 1914. **Sales:** $17,000,000 (2000). **Emp:** 13.
Officers: Bernell Hillesheim, President; Ken Kostner,
Vice President.

■ **18222** ■ **Satanta Cooperative Grain**
PO Box 99
Satanta, KS 67870
Phone: (316)649-2230
Products: Grain; Fertilizer; Oil. **SICs:** 5153 (Grain &
Field Beans); 5172 (Petroleum Products Nec); 5191
(Farm Supplies). **Est:** 1929. **Sales:** $11,000,000
(2000). **Emp:** 17. **Officers:** Don Clough, General Mgr.

■ **18223** ■ **S.C. Farm Bureau Marketing
Association**
724 Knox Abbott Dr.
Cayce, SC 29033
Phone: (803)796-6700
Products: Grain. **SIC:** 5153 (Grain & Field Beans).
Sales: $11,300,000 (2000). **Emp:** 12. **Officers:** David
Winkles, President; Bob Fallaw, CFO.

■ **18224** ■ **Jacob Schmalenberge**
PO Box 39
Hebron, ND 58638-0039
Phone: (701)878-4948
Products: Livestock. **SIC:** 5154 (Livestock). **Officers:**
Jacob Schmalenberge, Owner.

■ **18225** ■ **J.M. Schultz Seed Co.**
PO Box 211
Dieterich, IL 62424
Phone: (217)925-5212
Products: Corn, soybeans, and grain. **SIC:** 5153
(Grain & Field Beans). **Est:** 1903. **Sales:** $8,000,000
(2000). **Emp:** 25. **Officers:** Jim Knapp, Vice President;
Gary Parker, Controller; Tom Lizer, Sales Mgr.

■ **18226** ■ **Scott and Muscatine's Service Co.**
PO Box 609
Walcott, IA 52773
Phone: (319)284-6293
Products: Farm products. **SIC:** 5191 (Farm Supplies).
Sales: $16,000,000 (2000). **Emp:** 50. **Officers:** Merle
Anderson, General Mgr.; Merel Anderson, General
Mgr.

■ **18227** ■ **The Scoular Co.**
2027 Dodge St.
Omaha, NE 68102
Phone: (402)342-3500
Free: (800)488-3500 **Fax:** (402)342-5568
URL: http://www.scoular.com
Products: Grain; Corn; Oats; Wheat; Beans; Feed
ingredients; Food ingredients; Grain and grain by-
product merchandising; Grain storage. **SICs:** 5153
(Grain & Field Beans); 5191 (Farm Supplies). **Est:**
1892. **Sales:** $2,000,000,000 (1999). **Emp:** 400.
Officers: Duane A. Fischer, President; Timothy Regan,
CFO; John Heck, Exec. VP; Randal L. Linville, CEO.

■ **18228** ■ **Seed Resource Inc.**
1401 W 6th St.
Tulia, TX 79088
Phone: (806)995-3882 **Free:** (800)724-4306
Products: Sorghum, sudan grass, ryes, and millets.
SIC: 5191 (Farm Supplies). **Sales:** $5,800,000 (2000).
Emp: 35.

■ **18229** ■ **Senrenella Enterprises Inc.**
7911 Amherst Ave.
St. Louis, MO 63130
Phone: (314)863-9249 **Fax:** (314)863-4666
E-mail: senrenella@earthlink.net
Products: Rice and food products. **SIC:** 5153 (Grain &
Field Beans). **Est:** 1978. **Officers:** Allen L. McKellar,
President.

■ **18230** ■ **Sexauer Company Inc.**
PO Box 58
Brookings, SD 57006-0058
Phone: (605)692-6171
Products: Feed and fertilizer. **SIC:** 5191 (Farm
Supplies). **Sales:** $35,000,000 (1994). **Emp:** 100.
Officers: Richard Niemeyer, CFO.

■ **18231** ■ **Seymour Livestock Trucking**
2809 S Montana St.
Butte, MT 59701-3122
Phone: (406)723-5255
Products: Livestock; Cattle. **SIC:** 5154 (Livestock).
Officers: Martin Seymour, Owner.

■ **18232** ■ **Shipman Elevator Co.**
PO Box 349
Shipman, IL 62685
Phone: (618)836-5568 **Fax:** (618)836-5567
Products: Grain; Fertilizer. **SICs:** 5153 (Grain & Field
Beans); 5191 (Farm Supplies). **Est:** 1919. **Sales:**
$23,000,000 (2000). **Emp:** 22. **Officers:** Brad Huette,
President.

■ **18233** ■ **Shoshone Sales Yard Inc.**
PO Box 276
Shoshone, ID 83352-0276
Phone: (208)886-2281 **Fax:** (208)886-2282
Products: Livestock. **SIC:** 5154 (Livestock). **Est:** 1960.
Sales: $14,808,532 (2000). **Emp:** 35. **Officers:** Pete
Peterson, President.

■ **18234** ■ **Simplot AgriSource**
PO Box 70013
418 S 9th St., Ste. 308
Boise, ID 83707-2700
Phone: (208)672-2700
Products: Grains. **SIC:** 5153 (Grain & Field Beans).
Est: 1987. **Emp:** 70. **Officers:** Skip Kellogg, General
Mgr. **Doing Business As:** J.R. Simplot Co.

■ **18235** ■ **Slay Industries Inc.**
1441 Hampton Ave.
St. Louis, MO 63139
Phone: (314)647-7529 **Fax:** (314)647-8084
Products: Grain; Oats; Crude oil; Chemical
preparations; Fertilizer and fertilizer materials. **SICs:**
5191 (Farm Supplies); 5169 (Chemicals & Allied
Products Nec); 5172 (Petroleum Products Nec). **Emp:**
600.

■ **18236** ■ **Jess Smith and Sons Inc.**
2905 F St.
Bakersfield, CA 93301
Phone: (805)325-7231 **Fax:** (805)325-9745
Products: Raw cotton. **SIC:** 5159 (Farm-Product Raw
Materials Nec). **Sales:** $5,700,000 (2000). **Emp:** 15.
Officers: Ernest Schroeder, CEO; Albert Pacini,
Controller.

■ **18237** ■ **Smith Southside Feed and Grain
Inc.**
PO Box 446
Bowling Green, KY 42101
Phone: (502)529-5651
Products: Livestock feed and farm feeders, and grain.
SIC: 5191 (Farm Supplies). **Est:** 1970. **Sales:**
$1,500,000 (2000). **Emp:** 6. **Officers:** L. Eugene
Smith, President.

■ **18238** ■ **Snipes Webb Trailer & Livestock
Co.**
5100 Broadway Blvd. SE
Albuquerque, NM 87105-7416
Phone: (505)877-2471 **Fax:** (505)873-8190
Products: Livestock, including horse trailers. **SIC:**
5154 (Livestock). **Officers:** W Snipes, Owner.

■ **18239** ■ **South Central Cooperative**
310 Logan St.
Holdrege, NE 68949
Phone: (308)995-8626
Products: Grain, feed, seed, fertilizer and agricultural
chemicals. **SICs:** 5153 (Grain & Field Beans); 5191
(Farm Supplies). **Sales:** $60,000,000 (1992). **Emp:** 60.
Officers: Mike Meier, Comptroller; Ron Jergens, CEO.

■ **18240** ■ **South Dakota Livestock Sale**
PO Box 164
Watertown, SD 57201-0164
Phone: (605)886-4804
Products: Livestock; Cattle. **SIC:** 5154 (Livestock).
Officers: Raymond O Farrell, Vice President.

■ **18241** ■ **South Dakota Wheat Growers
Association**
PO Box 1460
Aberdeen, SD 57401
Phone: (605)225-5500 **Fax:** (605)228-0859
Products: Grain; Fuel; Fertilizer. **SICs:** 5153 (Grain &
Field Beans); 5191 (Farm Supplies); 5171 (Petroleum
Bulk Stations & Terminals). **Est:** 1923. **Sales:**
$254,000,000 (2000). **Emp:** 250. **Officers:** Verland
Losinger, General Mgr.; Nick Kukla, Controller; Keith
Hainy, Dir. of Marketing; ShirLee Sudemeyer, Data
Processing Mgr.; Orville Wiest, Dir of Human
Resources.

■ **18242** ■ **South Omaha Supply**
3310 H St.
Omaha, NE 68107
Phone: (402)731-3100
Products: Feed and farm supplies. **SIC:** 5191 (Farm
Supplies). **Sales:** $15,000,000 (1994). **Emp:** 31.
Officers: Joe Hahn, General Mgr.

■ **18243** ■ **Southeast Cooperative Service Co.**
Hwy. 25 S
Advance, MO 63730
Phone: (573)722-3522
Products: Grain; Feed; Fertilizer; Chemicals; Seed;
Petroleum. **SICs:** 5191 (Farm Supplies); 5153 (Grain &
Field Beans). **Est:** 1946. **Sales:** $12,000,000 (1999).
Emp: 39. **Officers:** C.D. Stewart, President; Mike
Galloway, General Mgr.

■ **18244** ■ **Southern States Madisonville Cooperative**
1001 Pride Ave.
Madisonville, KY 42431
Phone: (502)821-3325 **Fax:** (502)825-9448
Products: Farm supplies including feed and fertilizer.
SIC: 5191 (Farm Supplies). **Sales:** $6,000,000 (2000).
Emp: 17. **Officers:** David Brumfield, General Mgr.

■ **18245** ■ **Southwest Cooperative Wholesale**
1821 E Jackson St.
Phoenix, AZ 85034
Phone: (602)254-5644 **Fax:** (602)254-5644
Products: Farm, plumbing, electrical and hardware
supplies. **SICs:** 5191 (Farm Supplies); 5074 (Plumbing
& Hydronic Heating Supplies); 5063 (Electrical
Apparatus & Equipment); 5072 (Hardware). **Sales:**
$7,500,000 (1994). **Emp:** 45. **Officers:** Emil Rovey,
President.

■ **18246** ■ **Southwest Hide Co.**
250 Beechwood Dr., Ste. 180
Boise, ID 83709-0944
Phone: (208)378-8000 **Fax:** (208)377-9069
Products: Leather; Hides and skins, including cattle
and pig. **SICs:** 5159 (Farm-Product Raw Materials
Nec); 5199 (Nondurable Goods Nec). **Est:** 1956.
Officers: Clark C. Fidler, Director.

■ **18247** ■ **Southwestern Irrigated Cotton Growers Association**
PO Box 1709
El Paso, TX 79949
Phone: (915)581-5441 **Fax:** (915)581-4138
Products: Raw cotton, cottonseed. **SIC:** 5159 (Farm-
Product Raw Materials Nec). **Sales:** $60,000,000
(1999). **Emp:** 50. **Officers:** David L. Hand, President.

■ **18248** ■ **Speartex Grain Co.**
PO Box 248
Spearman, TX 79081
Phone: (806)659-3711 **Fax:** (806)659-2872
Products: Agricultural goods; Cattle. **SICs:** 5154
(Livestock); 5191 (Farm Supplies). **Sales:** $9,000,000
(2000). **Emp:** 30. **Officers:** C.M. Archer, General Mgr.

■ **18249** ■ **Spokane Seed Co.**
PO Box 11007
Spokane, WA 99211-1007
Phone: (509)535-3671 **Fax:** (509)535-0874
E-mail: spokseed@spokaneseed.com
Products: Dried peas, lentils, and garbanzo beans.
SIC: 5153 (Grain & Field Beans). **Est:** 1908. **Sales:**
$26,000,000 (2000). **Emp:** 50. **Officers:** Peter
Johnstone, CEO & President; Jeff White, Treasurer.

■ **18250** ■ **Stanford Grain Co.**
Main St.
Stanford, IL 61774
Phone: (309)379-2141 **Fax:** (309)379-2321
Products: Corn; Beans. **SIC:** 5153 (Grain & Field
Beans). **Est:** 1895. **Sales:** $7,000,000 (2000). **Emp:** 4.
Officers: Jim Lynch, President; J. Capraun, General
Mgr.

■ **18251** ■ **Staple Cotton Cooperative Association**
PO Box 547
Greenwood, MS 38935
Phone: (601)453-6231 **Fax:** (601)453-6233
Products: Raw cotton. **SIC:** 5159 (Farm-Product Raw
Materials Nec). **Est:** 1921. **Sales:** $705,000,000
(2000). **Emp:** 153. **Officers:** Woods E. Eastland,
President & Chairman of the Board; Mack L. Alford, VP
& Treasurer; Meredith Allen, VP of Marketing; L.A.
Gnemi, VP of Systems; R.E. Dilatush, Jr., VP of Human
Resources.

■ **18252** ■ **Steele-Siman & Co.**
803 E Rice St.
Sioux Falls, SD 57103-0157
Phone: (605)336-0593
Products: Livestock. **SIC:** 5154 (Livestock). **Officers:**
Don Stencil, Partner.

■ **18253** ■ **S.S. Steiner Inc.**
655 Madison Ave.
New York, NY 10021
Phone: (212)838-8900 **Fax:** (212)593-4238
E-mail: info@hopsteiner.com
Products: Hops; Hops extracts and oils. **SICs:** 5159
(Farm-Product Raw Materials Nec); 5099 (Durable
Goods Nec). **Est:** 1845. **Emp:** 99.

■ **18254** ■ **E.J. Steinke Ranches Inc.**
5561 West 129 North
Idaho Falls, ID 83402-5254
Phone: (208)522-5159
Products: Livestock. **SIC:** 5154 (Livestock). **Officers:**
Allen Steinke, President.

■ **18255** ■ **Jesse C. Stewart Co.**
360 Broadmoor Ave.
Pittsburgh, PA 15228
Phone: (412)343-0600
Products: Grains. **SICs:** 5153 (Grain & Field Beans);
5191 (Farm Supplies). **Est:** 1896. **Sales:** $14,000,000
(2000). **Emp:** 10. **Officers:** Robert Danik, President &
Chairman of the Board; William Ryan Jr., Vice
President.

■ **18256** ■ **Stockmen's Livestock Exchange**
PO Box 1209
Dickinson, ND 58602-1209
Phone: (701)225-8156
Free: (800)472-2667 **Fax:** (701)225-9832
Products: Livestock. **SIC:** 5154 (Livestock). **Emp:** 54.
Officers: Larry Schnell, President.

■ **18257** ■ **Stockmen's Livestock Market**
PO Box 280
Yankton, SD 57078-0280
Phone: (605)665-9641
Products: Livestock; Auctioning livestock. **SIC:** 5154
(Livestock). **Officers:** Gail Sohler, President.

■ **18258** ■ **Stones Inc.**
PO Box 974
Bainbridge, GA 31717
Phone: (912)246-2929 **Fax:** (912)246-9083
Products: Farm feed and seed. **SIC:** 5191 (Farm
Supplies). **Sales:** $20,200,000 (2000). **Emp:** 120.
Officers: Joe M. Higdon, President; Laura S. Bridges,
Treasurer.

■ **18259** ■ **Stonington Cooperative Grain Co.**
PO Box 350
Stonington, IL 62567
Phone: (217)325-3211
Products: Grain elevator. **SIC:** 5153 (Grain & Field
Beans). **Est:** 1935. **Sales:** $24,000,000 (2000). **Emp:**
12. **Officers:** John Callan, President; Tom Johnson,
CFO.

■ **18260** ■ **Stotler Grain Co.**
1010 W Clark St.
Champaign, IL 61821-3326
Phone: (217)356-9011
Products: Grain. **SIC:** 5153 (Grain & Field Beans).
Est: 1935. **Sales:** $1,000,000 (2000). **Emp:** 1.
Officers: Howard Stotler, Partner.

■ **18261** ■ **Stratford Farmers Cooperative**
PO Box 14
Stratford, WI 54484
Phone: (715)687-4136
Products: Farm and gardening supplies and
equipment. **SICs:** 5191 (Farm Supplies); 5083 (Farm &
Garden Machinery). **Sales:** $10,500,000 (1994). **Emp:**
45. **Officers:** F. Brenner, Finance General Manager.

■ **18262** ■ **Stratford Grain and Supply Cooperative**
719 Commercial St.
Stratford, IA 50249
Phone: (515)838-2410
Products: Grain; Feed; Chemicals. **SICs:** 5153 (Grain
& Field Beans); 5191 (Farm Supplies); 5169
(Chemicals & Allied Products Nec). **Est:** 1909. **Sales:**
$7,000,000 (2000). **Emp:** 14. **Officers:** Arnold Carlson,
CEO; Steve Phillips, Manager.

■ **18263** ■ **Sturgis Livestock Exchange**
PO Box 1059
Sturgis, SD 57785-1059
Phone: (605)347-2575 **Fax:** (605)347-4069
Products: Livestock. **SIC:** 5154 (Livestock). **Officers:**
Paul Schultes, Contact.

■ **18264** ■ **Stuttgart Industrial Service Inc.**
1056 Old England Hwy.
Stuttgart, AR 72160
Phone: (870)673-2801 **Fax:** (870)673-4139
Products: Grain and feed handling equipment. **SIC:**
5084 (Industrial Machinery & Equipment). **Sales:**
$2,000,000 (2000). **Emp:** 16. **Officers:** Lynn Staton,
President; Lucille Staton, Treasurer & Secty.

■ **18265** ■ **Sublette Cooperative, Inc.**
Rte. 1, Box 56B
Copeland, KS 67837
Phone: (316)668-5615 **Fax:** (316)675-2288
Products: Grain; Fertilizer; Agricultural chemicals;
Petroleum. **SICs:** 5153 (Grain & Field Beans); 5191
(Farm Supplies). **Est:** 1929. **Sales:** $19,000,000
(1999). **Emp:** 31. **Officers:** James Axtell, General Mgr.;
Gaylord Sanneman, Information Systems Mgr.

■ **18266** ■ **Sublette Farmers Elevator Co.**
PO Box 289
Sublette, IL 61367
Phone: (815)849-5222 **Fax:** (815)849-5288
Products: Grain; Lumber; Building materials. **SICs:**
5153 (Grain & Field Beans); 5031 (Lumber, Plywood &
Millwork); 5191 (Farm Supplies). **Est:** 1919. **Sales:**
$9,100,000 (2000). **Emp:** 9. **Officers:** Gerald Henkel,
President; Steven B. Klein, CFO.

■ **18267** ■ **Sullivan Inc.**
PO Box 703
Ulysses, KS 67880
Phone: (316)356-1219 **Fax:** (316)353-1127
Products: Grain; Feed; Seed. **SICs:** 5153 (Grain &
Field Beans); 5191 (Farm Supplies). **Est:** 1922. **Sales:**
$28,000,000 (2000). **Emp:** 23. **Officers:** Jerry L.
Sullivan, President; R. Lynn Teeter, CFO; Keric J.
Sullivan, Operations Mgr.

■ **18268** ■ **Sully Cooperative Exchange Inc.**
PO Box 250
Sully, IA 50251-0250
Phone: (515)594-4115
Products: Grain and feed. **SICs:** 5153 (Grain & Field
Beans); 5191 (Farm Supplies). **Est:** 1920. **Sales:**
$30,000,000 (2000). **Emp:** 60. **Officers:** Howard
VanderGrend, General Mgr.; Charles James,
Controller.

■ **18269** ■ **Suncook Tanning Corp.**
PO Box 3009
Peabody, MA 01960
Phone: (978)532-0707
Products: Cow hide. **SIC:** 5099 (Durable Goods Nec).
Est: 1965. **Sales:** $3,500,000 (2000). **Emp:** 3.
Officers: Michael M. Ossoff, President; Melvin R.
Ossoff, VP of Marketing.

■ **18270** ■ **Superior Cooperative Elevator Co.**
603 Railroad St.
Superior, IA 51363
Phone: (712)858-4491
Free: (800)242-3625 **Fax:** (712)858-4610
Products: Grain, farm supplies and petroleum. **SICs:**
5153 (Grain & Field Beans); 5191 (Farm Supplies);
5171 (Petroleum Bulk Stations & Terminals). **Sales:**
$45,000,000 (2000). **Emp:** 30. **Officers:** Garry Strube,
Manager.

■ **18271** ■ **Sutton Ranches**
PO Box 33
Onida, SD 57564-0033
Phone: (605)258-2540 **Fax:** (605)258-2840
Products: Farm-product raw materials; Farm animals,
including horses, cattle, and rodeo stock. **SICs:** 5159
(Farm-Product Raw Materials Nec); 5154 (Livestock).
Officers: James Sutton, Partner.

■ **18272** ■ **Syracuse Cooperative Exchange**
PO Box 946
Syracuse, KS 67878
Phone: (316)384-5751 **Fax:** (316)384-5752
E-mail: syrcoop@pld.com
Products: Grain. **SIC:** 5153 (Grain & Field Beans).
Est: 1945. **Sales:** $13,000,000 (2000). **Emp:** 17.
Officers: Richard Rile, General Mgr.

■ **18273** ■ **Tabor Grain Co.**
4666 Faries Pkwy.
Decatur, IL 62525
Phone: (217)424-5200 **Fax:** (217)424-5990
URL: http://www.admworld.com
Products: Grains. **SICs:** 5153 (Grain & Field Beans);
5191 (Farm Supplies). **Est:** 1966. **Sales:** $878,000,000
(2000). **Emp:** 175. **Officers:** Burnell D. Kraft,
President; Harold Murphy, Controller; Marvin Rau, VP
of Merchandising.

■ **18274** ■ **Taintor Cooperative Co.**
1380 Hwy. 63 S, Box 512
New Sharon, IA 50207
Phone: (515)637-4097
Free: (800)747-0663 **Fax:** (515)637-4292
Products: Grain and farm supplies. **SICs:** 5153 (Grain
& Field Beans); 5191 (Farm Supplies). **Sales:**
$10,500,000 (2000). **Emp:** 25. **Officers:** Dennis
Hunwardsen, General Mgr.

■ **18275** ■ **Tama-Benton Cooperative Co.**
PO Box 459
Dysart, IA 52224
Phone: (319)476-3666 **Fax:** (319)476-4329
Products: Grain elevator. **SICs:** 5153 (Grain & Field
Beans); 5191 (Farm Supplies); 5172 (Petroleum
Products Nec). **Est:** 1947. **Sales:** $19,000,000 (2000).
Emp: 25. **Officers:** Keith Bader, President; John
Schneider, Treasurer & Secty.; Jim Hegge, General
Mgr.

■ **18276** ■ **Jesse R. Taylor Co.**
405 S 10th St.
Opelika, AL 36801
Phone: (334)745-5774 **Fax:** (334)749-7120
Products: Farm-product raw materials. **SIC:** 5159
(Farm-Product Raw Materials Nec). **Sales:** $5,000,000
(2000). **Emp:** 4. **Officers:** Jesse R. Taylor, President.

■ **18277** ■ **Terral Seed, Inc.**
PO Box 826
Lake Providence, LA 71254
Phone: (318)559-2840 **Fax:** (318)559-2888
E-mail: terralsd@bayou.com
Products: Soybeans; Wheat; Rice; Corn. **SIC:** 5191
(Farm Supplies). **Est:** 1950. **Sales:** $24,000,000
(2000). **Emp:** 65. **Officers:** Thomas Terral, President;
Larry J. Mullen, Treasurer & Secty. **Former Name:**
Terral-Norris Seed Company Inc.

■ **18278** ■ **Texas-West Indies Co.**
PO Box 110
El Campo, TX 77437
Phone: (409)543-2741
Products: Grain. **SIC:** 5153 (Grain & Field Beans).
Sales: $10,200,000 (1993). **Emp:** 12. **Officers:** Jim
Leslie, Treasurer & Secty.

■ **18279** ■ **Thomas & Jones Sales
Management**
808 Arapaho St.
Cheyenne, WY 82009-4214
Phone: (307)632-5118
Products: Livestock. **SIC:** 5154 (Livestock). **Officers:**
Thomas Jones, Partner.

■ **18280** ■ **Thorpe Livestock Inc.**
PO Box 1827
Aberdeen, SD 57401-1827
Phone: (605)225-2062 **Fax:** (605)225-1637
Products: Livestock. **SIC:** 5154 (Livestock). **Officers:**
James Thorpe, President.

■ **18281** ■ **Ben Tilton & Sons, Inc.**
470 Bradford Rd.
RR 2, Box 470
East Corinth, ME 04427
Phone: (207)285-3467 **Fax:** (207)285-7212
Products: Livestock; General merchandise. **SICs:**

5154 (Livestock); 5199 (Nondurable Goods Nec); 5099
(Durable Goods Nec). **Officers:** Benjamin Tilton,
President.

■ **18282** ■ **Sumner H. Tilton**
66 Clinton St.
Concord, NH 03301-2355
Phone: (603)225-6161
Products: Livestock. **SIC:** 5154 (Livestock). **Officers:**
Sumner Tilton, Owner.

■ **18283** ■ **Timberline Feed Lot Inc.**
PO Box 1710
Worland, WY 82401-1710
Phone: (307)347-4388 **Fax:** (307)347-6248
Products: Livestock. **SIC:** 5154 (Livestock). **Officers:**
Phillip Huber, President.

■ **18284** ■ **E.H. Tindall Inc.**
357 Lawrence Station
Lawrenceville, NJ 08648
Phone: (609)587-5740
Products: Grain, including soybeans and corn. **SIC:**
5153 (Grain & Field Beans). **Est:** 1969. **Sales:**
$3,500,000 (2000). **Emp:** 6. **Officers:** Earl H. Tindall,
President & Treasurer.

■ **18285** ■ **Top of Iowa Coop**
PO Box 181
Joice, IA 50446
Phone: (515)588-3131
Products: Corn and beans. **SICs:** 5153 (Grain & Field
Beans); 5191 (Farm Supplies). **Est:** 1945. **Sales:**
$55,000,000 (2000). **Emp:** 45. **Officers:** Richard
Hanna, President.

■ **18286** ■ **Tourbillon Farm**
401 Snake Hill Rd.
North Scituate, RI 02857-9806
Phone: (401)934-2221
Free: (888)934-2221 **Fax:** (401)934-2988
E-mail: tourbillon@worldnet.att.net
URL: http://www.tourbillontrailers.com
Products: Horses; Horse trailers. **SICs:** 5159 (Farm-
Product Raw Materials Nec); 5083 (Farm & Garden
Machinery). **Emp:** 8. **Officers:** Julian Forge, Owner.

■ **18287** ■ **Tradigrain Inc.**
889 Ridge Lake Blvd.
Memphis, TN 38120
Phone: (901)684-1496
Products: Grain. **SIC:** 5153 (Grain & Field Beans).
Sales: $4,000,000 (2000). **Emp:** 9. **Officers:** William
Adams, President.

■ **18288** ■ **Trainor Grain and Supply Co.**
R.R. 2, Box 44, Wing Sta.
Forrest, IL 61741
Phone: (815)832-5512
Products: Grain and fertilizer. **SICs:** 5153 (Grain &
Field Beans); 5191 (Farm Supplies). **Sales:**
$21,000,000 (1993). **Emp:** 25. **Officers:** John A.
Trainor, President.

■ **18289** ■ **Joseph Trenk and Sons**
171 Thomas St.
Newark, NJ 07114
Phone: (201)589-5778
Products: Chickens. **SIC:** 5144 (Poultry & Poultry
Products). **Est:** 1924. **Sales:** $2,000,000 (2000). **Emp:**
6. **Officers:** David Trenk, CEO & President.

■ **18290** ■ **Tri Central Co-op**
PO Box 176
Ashkum, IL 60911
Phone: (815)698-2327
Products: Grain. **SICs:** 5153 (Grain & Field Beans);
5191 (Farm Supplies). **Est:** 1915. **Sales:** $12,500,000
(2000). **Emp:** 15. **Officers:** Melvin Marcotte, President;
Paul Foster Jr., General Mgr.

■ **18291** ■ **Tri-Line Farmers Cooperative**
PO Box 65
Clarkfield, MN 56223
Phone: (612)669-7501
Products: Grain. **SIC:** 5153 (Grain & Field Beans).
Est: 1984. **Sales:** $45,000,000 (2000). **Emp:** 28.
Officers: Tom Listul, President; Rodney Olson,
General Mgr.

■ **18292** ■ **Trinidad Bean and Elevator Co.**
PO Box 128
Greeley, CO 80632-0128
Phone: (970)352-0346 **Fax:** (303)571-5256
Products: Beans. **SIC:** 5153 (Grain & Field Beans).
Est: 1958. **Sales:** $50,000,000 (2000). **Emp:** 150.
Officers: Carl Hartman, President.

■ **18293** ■ **Trinidad-Benham Corp.**
PO Box 378007
Denver, CO 80237
Phone: (303)220-1400 **Fax:** (303)220-1490
Products: Beans and rice; Popcorn; Household
aluminum foil. **SICs:** 5153 (Grain & Field Beans); 5149
(Groceries & Related Products Nec); 5199 (Nondurable
Goods Nec). **Est:** 1917. **Sales:** $180,000,000 (1999).
Emp: 450. **Officers:** Carl C. Hartman, President; Larry
Cotham, VP of Marketing; Linda Walmsley, VP of
Human Resources; Jim Branson, VP of Sales; Gary
Peters, VP of Finance.

■ **18294** ■ **Triple S Ranch Supply**
2635 SE Hwy 54
El Dorado, KS 67042-9347
Phone: (316)321-7514 **Free:** (800)782-1017
Products: Livestock feed; Clothing; Tires;
Convenience store items. **SIC:** 5191 (Farm Supplies).
Est: 1984. **Officers:** Steve Stanfield, Partner.

■ **18295** ■ **Troy Elevator Inc.**
PO Box 190
Bloomfield, IA 52537
Phone: (515)675-3375 **Fax:** (515)675-3371
Products: Grain elevator. **SIC:** 5153 (Grain & Field
Beans). **Sales:** $16,000,000 (2000). **Emp:** 18.
Officers: Carolyn Ensminger, President & Treasurer.

■ **18296** ■ **Twomey Co.**
1 State St.
Smithshire, IL 61478
Phone: (309)325-7100
Products: Grain, corn, and beans. **SIC:** 5191 (Farm
Supplies). **Est:** 1945. **Sales:** $28,000,000 (2000).
Emp: 70. **Officers:** J. Craig Twomey, President; John
Twomey, VP & Treasurer.

■ **18297** ■ **Ulysses Cooperative Supply Co.**
PO Box 947
Ulysses, KS 67880
Phone: (316)356-1241
Products: Grain. **SIC:** 5153 (Grain & Field Beans).
Est: 1930. **Sales:** $35,000,000 (2000). **Emp:** 45.
Officers: Maurice Stein, General Mgr.

■ **18298** ■ **Randy J. Unger Cattle Marketing**
PO Box 103
Watertown, SD 57201-0103
Phone: (605)882-1129 **Fax:** (605)882-1129
Products: Livestock; Cattle. **SIC:** 5154 (Livestock).
Officers: Randy Unger, Owner.

■ **18299** ■ **Union Elevator and Warehouse Co.**
PO Box 370
Lind, WA 99341
Phone: (509)677-3441 **Fax:** (509)677-3623
Products: Grain. **SIC:** 5153 (Grain & Field Beans).
Est: 1908. **Sales:** $15,000,000 (2000). **Emp:** 13.
Officers: Ralph A. Gering, President & Chairman of the
Board; Randy Roth, Manager.

■ **18300** ■ **Union Seed Company Inc.**
PO Box 339
Nampa, ID 83653-0339
Phone: (208)466-3568 **Fax:** (208)466-3684
Products: Alfalfas, clovers, and grasses. **SIC:** 5191
(Farm Supplies). **Est:** 1909. **Sales:** $12,000,000
(2000). **Emp:** 22. **Officers:** Jerry L. Jones, President.

■ **18301** ■ **United Co-op**
PO Box 37
Bigelow, MN 56117
Phone: (507)683-2731 **Fax:** (507)683-2518
Products: Farming products. **SICs:** 5153 (Grain &
Field Beans); 5191 (Farm Supplies). **Est:** 1980. **Sales:**
$20,000,000 (2000). **Emp:** 24. **Officers:** Marv
Masching, CEO.

■ 18302 ■ **United Farmers Elevator Co.**
PO Box 47
Murdock, MN 56271
Phone: (320)875-2811 **Fax:** (320)875-2813
Products: Grains including corn, beans, wheat, and oats. **SIC:** 5153 (Grain & Field Beans). **Est:** 1982. **Sales:** $5,000,000 (2000). **Emp:** 26. **Officers:** Robert Schoen, President; Jerry Baker, General Mgr.

■ 18303 ■ **United Farmers Mercantile Cooperative**
203 W Oak St.
Red Oak, IA 51566
Phone: (712)623-2575 **Fax:** (712)623-9154
Products: Grain elevator and feed. **SIC:** 5153 (Grain & Field Beans). **Sales:** $35,000,000 (2000). **Emp:** 50. **Officers:** Fred Hossle, President; Jim Rice, Finance General Manager.

■ 18304 ■ **United Producers, Inc.**
5909 Cleveland Ave.
Columbus, OH 43231
Phone: (614)890-6666
Free: (800)456-3276 **Fax:** (614)890-4776
E-mail: info@pla-corp.com
URL: http://www.uproducers.com
Products: Livestock marketing and related services, and agricultural financing. **SIC:** 5154 (Livestock). **Est:** 1934. **Sales:** $500,000,000 (2000). **Emp:** 110. **Officers:** W. Dennis Bolling, President & CEO; Joe Werstak, CFO; Jeff Hording, Vice President; Jeff Hording, Vice President. **Former Name:** Producers Livestock Association.

■ 18305 ■ **U.S. World Trade Corp.**
111 SW 5th Ave., Ste. 1900
Portland, OR 97204
Phone: (503)275-4100 **Fax:** (503)275-5078
Products: Grains; Fresh fruits; Grass seeds; Finfish; Millwork. **SICs:** 5153 (Grain & Field Beans); 5148 (Fresh Fruits & Vegetables); 5031 (Lumber, Plywood & Millwork); 5191 (Farm Supplies); 5146 (Fish & Seafoods). **Officers:** Lothar E. Paesler, General Mgr.

■ 18306 ■ **Unity Grain and Supply Co.**
PO Box 229
Hammond, IL 61929
Phone: (217)578-3013
Products: Grains, including corn and beans. **SIC:** 5153 (Grain & Field Beans). **Est:** 1918. **Sales:** $14,000,000 (2000). **Emp:** 12. **Officers:** Sam Dick, President.

■ 18307 ■ **Universal Semen Sales Inc.**
2626 2nd Ave. S
Great Falls, MT 59405-3004
Phone: (406)453-0374
Free: (800)227-8774 **Fax:** (406)453-0510
E-mail: unisemen@mtn-webtech.com
Products: Bovine semen. **SIC:** 5159 (Farm-Product Raw Materials Nec). **Est:** 1975. **Officers:** Jack Ganje, President.

■ 18308 ■ **Ursa Farmers Cooperative**
202 W Maple St.
Ursa, IL 62376
Phone: (217)964-2111 **Fax:** (217)964-2260
Products: Grain; Feed. **SICs:** 5153 (Grain & Field Beans); 5191 (Farm Supplies). **Est:** 1920. **Sales:** $82,000,000 (2000). **Emp:** 42. **Officers:** Gerald Jenkins, General Mgr.; Ken Buckert, Controller.

■ 18309 ■ **Utah Wool Marketing Association**
855 South 500 West
Salt Lake City, UT 84101
Phone: (801)328-1507 **Fax:** (801)531-6838
Products: Raw wool. **SIC:** 5159 (Farm-Product Raw Materials Nec). **Est:** 1926. **Sales:** $2,000,000 (2000). **Emp:** 10. **Officers:** J.R. Broadbent, President; Will Hart Griggs, Manager.

■ 18310 ■ **Utica Cooperative Grain Company Inc.**
PO Box 216
Utica, NE 68456
Phone: (402)534-2411
Products: Grain; Feed. **SICs:** 5153 (Grain & Field Beans); 5191 (Farm Supplies). **Est:** 1912. **Sales:** $9,500,000 (2000). **Emp:** 12. **Officers:** Martin Linhorst, President; Leon Blanchet, General Mgr.

■ 18311 ■ **V and M Cotton Co.**
PO Box 167
Inverness, MS 38753
Phone: (601)265-5801
Products: Raw cotton. **SIC:** 5159 (Farm-Product Raw Materials Nec). **Est:** 1982. **Sales:** $2,000,000 (2000). **Emp:** 2. **Officers:** Charles M. Harris, CEO.

■ 18312 ■ **Valders Cooperative**
PO Box 10
Valders, WI 54245
Phone: (414)775-4131
Products: Grain. **SIC:** 5191 (Farm Supplies). **Est:** 1946. **Sales:** $19,000,000 (2000). **Emp:** 91. **Officers:** Bill Hoeltke, General Mgr.

■ 18313 ■ **Valley Forge Leather Co.**
314 Old Lancaster Rd.
Merion Station, PA 19066
Phone: (610)668-2121 **Fax:** (610)668-9545
Products: Calfskins, kipskins, deer skins, wet blue hides, and cattle hides. **SIC:** 5159 (Farm-Product Raw Materials Nec). **Officers:** Robert Spiewak, Sales Manager.

■ 18314 ■ **Valley Seed Co.**
PO Box 11188
Casa Grande, AZ 85230-1188
Phone: (520)836-8713 **Fax:** (520)421-0832
Products: Grains and seed. **SIC:** 5153 (Grain & Field Beans).

■ 18315 ■ **Van Horn Hybrids Inc.**
PO Box 380
Cerro Gordo, IL 61818
Phone: (217)677-2131
Products: Corn; Beans. **SIC:** 5153 (Grain & Field Beans). **Est:** 1934. **Sales:** $9,000,000 (2000). **Emp:** 18. **Officers:** Roger Oliver, President & CFO.

■ 18316 ■ **Vermillion Elevator Co.**
PO Box 49
Vermillion, MN 55085
Phone: (612)437-4439
Products: Grain; Chemicals. **SICs:** 5191 (Farm Supplies); 5169 (Chemicals & Allied Products Nec). **Est:** 1942. **Sales:** $7,000,000 (2000). **Emp:** 8. **Officers:** Gregory Ries, President.

■ 18317 ■ **V.H. Associates Inc.**
PO Box 380
Cerro Gordo, IL 61818
Phone: (217)677-2131
Products: Grain, field beans, seed, feed and fertilizers. **SICs:** 5153 (Grain & Field Beans); 5191 (Farm Supplies). **Sales:** $20,000,000 (2000). **Emp:** 22. **Officers:** Roger Oliver, President & CFO; Bill Hinton, VP & Secty.

■ 18318 ■ **Vintage Sales Stables Inc.**
3451 Lincoln Hwy. E
Paradise, PA 17562-9621
Phone: (717)768-8204 **Fax:** (717)442-8031
Products: Operation of livestock auction markets. **SIC:** 5154 (Livestock). **Est:** 1850. **Sales:** $59,000,000 (2000). **Emp:** 50. **Officers:** Robert Frame, President; Denise Frame, Vice President.

■ 18319 ■ **Vista Trading Corp.**
16800 Greenspoint Park Dr., Ste. 225 N
Houston, TX 77060
Phone: (281)876-8110
Products: Bulk grain. **SIC:** 5153 (Grain & Field Beans).

■ 18320 ■ **W-L Research Inc.**
8701 W US Hwy. 14
Evansville, WI 53536-8752
Phone: (608)882-4100
Products: Alfalfa varieties. **SIC:** 5191 (Farm Supplies). **Sales:** $12,700,000 (2000). **Emp:** 25.

■ 18321 ■ **Wabash Elevator Co.**
PO Box 338
Uniontown, KY 42461
Phone: (502)822-4241
Products: Grain. **SIC:** 5191 (Farm Supplies). **Est:** 1900. **Sales:** $17,000,000 (2000). **Emp:** 16. **Officers:** Raymond Turner, Owner.

■ 18322 ■ **Wagner Livestock Auction**
PO Box 548
Wagner, SD 57380-0548
Phone: (605)384-5551
Products: Livestock. **SIC:** 5154 (Livestock). **Officers:** Dale Wagner, Owner.

■ 18323 ■ **Wagner Mills Inc.**
PO Box 545
Schuyler, NE 68661
Phone: (402)352-2471
Products: Grain. **SIC:** 5153 (Grain & Field Beans). **Est:** 1939. **Sales:** $9,000,000 (2000). **Emp:** 18. **Officers:** Leroy Trofholz, President; Bernie Friedrichsen, Controller.

■ 18324 ■ **Walker River Pute Tribal Council**
PO Box 220
Schurz, NV 89427-0220
Phone: (702)773-2306 **Fax:** (702)773-2585
Products: Livestock; Auctioning livestock. **SIC:** 5154 (Livestock). **Officers:** Anita Collins, Chairman of the Board.

■ 18325 ■ **Ward and Van Scoy Inc.**
PO Box 359
Owego, NY 13827
Phone: (607)687-2712
Products: Grain, feed, and soybean oil. **SICs:** 5191 (Farm Supplies); 5191 (Farm Supplies). **Est:** 1948. **Sales:** $4,000,000 (2000). **Emp:** 15. **Officers:** Richard Van Scoy, CEO & President; C. Michael Ward, Vice President.

■ 18326 ■ **Watertown Livestock Auction, Inc.**
PO Box 256
Watertown, SD 57201-0476
Phone: (605)886-5052 **Fax:** (605)886-0248
Products: Livestock. **SIC:** 5154 (Livestock). **Officers:** Roger Koedam, President; Sid Koedam, Vice President; Gerrit Wiekamp, Treasurer & Secty.

■ 18327 ■ **Watonwan Farm Services Co.**
PO Box 68
Truman, MN 56088
Phone: (507)776-2831
Free: (800)657-3282 **Fax:** (507)776-2871
E-mail: wfsinfo@wfsag.com
URL: http://www.wfsag.com
Products: Grain. **SIC:** 5153 (Grain & Field Beans). **Est:** 1937. **Sales:** $150,000,000 (2000). **Emp:** 325. **Officers:** Ed Bosanko, President & General Mgr.; William Day, Chairman of the Board & Finance Officer.

■ 18328 ■ **Watonwan Farm Services Co. Ormsby Div.**
PO Box 458
Ormsby, MN 56162
Phone: (507)736-2961
Products: Grain elevator; Fertilizers. **SICs:** 5153 (Grain & Field Beans); 5191 (Farm Supplies). **Est:** 1979. **Sales:** $1,000,000 (2000). **Emp:** 2. **Officers:** John Miest, General Mgr.

■ 18329 ■ **Fred Webb Inc.**
PO Box 6084
Greenville, NC 27835
Phone: (919)758-2141 **Fax:** (919)830-3276
Products: Grain. **SIC:** 5153 (Grain & Field Beans). **Est:** 1948. **Sales:** $68,000,000 (2000). **Emp:** 8. **Officers:** James Fred Webb, President; Jim A. King, Secretary; Jeffery Edwards, Vice President.

■ 18330 ■ **Keith E. Wegnar Livestock Inc.**
PO Box 543
Casselton, ND 58012-0543
Phone: (701)282-8582
Products: Livestock; Cattle. **SIC:** 5154 (Livestock). **Officers:** Keith Wegnar, President.

■ 18331 ■ **Weil Brothers Cotton Inc.**
4444 Park Blvd.
Montgomery, AL 36116
Phone: (205)244-1800 **Fax:** (205)271-4238
Products: Raw cotton. **SIC:** 5159 (Farm-Product Raw Materials Nec). **Est:** 1878. **Sales:** $100,000,000 (2000). **Emp:** 100. **Officers:** Robert S. Weil Sr., CEO & Chairman of the Board; James E. McGhee, Treasurer.

■ 18332 ■ Weiser Livestock Commission
PO Box 648
Weiser, ID 83672-0648
Phone: (208)549-0564
Products: Livestock. **SIC:** 5154 (Livestock). **Officers:** Donald Withers, Treasurer.

■ 18333 ■ Wendell Farmers Elevator Co.
PO Box 228
Wendell, MN 56590
Phone: (218)458-2127
Products: Grain. **SIC:** 5153 (Grain & Field Beans). **Est:** 1969. **Sales:** $4,500,000 (2000). **Emp:** 3. **Officers:** Charles Foss, President; Randy Olson, Manager.

■ 18334 ■ Wensman Seed Co.
PO Box 190
Wadena, MN 56482
Phone: (218)631-2954
Free: (800)456-4894 **Fax:** (218)631-4195
E-mail: wensman@wcta.net
URL: http://www.wensmanseed.com
Products: Seed corn; Soybeans; Alfalfa; Sunflower seeds. **SIC:** 5159 (Farm-Product Raw Materials Nec). **Former Name:** Peterson-Biddick Co.

■ 18335 ■ West Bend Elevator Co.
PO Box 49
West Bend, IA 50597-0049
Phone: (515)887-7211 **Fax:** (515)887-7291
E-mail: info@westbendelev.com
URL: http://www.westbendelev.com
Products: Grain. **SIC:** 5153 (Grain & Field Beans). **Est:** 1908. **Sales:** $80,000,000 (2000). **Emp:** 115. **Officers:** Joe Anniss, General Mgr.; Chad Meyer, Dir. of Marketing; Bill Hocraffer, Dir. of Marketing.

■ 18336 ■ West Central Cooperative
406 1st St.
Ralston, IA 51459
Phone: (712)667-3200
URL: http://www.west-central.com
Products: Corn and beans. **SICs:** 5153 (Grain & Field Beans); 5191 (Farm Supplies). **Est:** 1933. **Sales:** $200,000,000 (1999). **Emp:** 225. **Officers:** Don Pottroff, President; Jeffrey Stroburg, CEO.

■ 18337 ■ West Lyon Cooperative Inc.
PO Box 310
Inwood, IA 51240
Phone: (712)753-4528 **Fax:** (712)753-2226
Products: Grain and farm supplies. **SICs:** 5153 (Grain & Field Beans); 5191 (Farm Supplies). **Sales:** $36,000,000 (2000). **Emp:** 40. **Officers:** Carl Stuvick, CEO & President; W.R. Hinhouse, Controller.

■ 18338 ■ West Nesbitt Inc.
59 Court St.
Binghamton, NY 13901
Phone: (607)432-6500
Products: Diary; Feed; Cattle, horses, and pigs. **SICs:** 5153 (Grain & Field Beans); 5154 (Livestock); 5191 (Farm Supplies). **Est:** 1925. **Sales:** $5,000,000 (2000). **Emp:** 35. **Officers:** B. Richard Tonoli, CEO.

■ 18339 ■ Reginald West
RR 1, Box 1495
Franklin, VT 05457
Phone: (802)285-6600
Products: Cattle. **SIC:** 5154 (Livestock).

■ 18340 ■ Western Iowa Cooperative
150 Main St.
Hornick, IA 51026
Phone: (712)874-3211 **Fax:** (712)847-3230
Products: Grain. **SIC:** 5153 (Grain & Field Beans). **Est:** 1919. **Sales:** $52,000,000 (2000). **Emp:** 50. **Officers:** Steve Longval, President; Robert Kendall, Treasurer.

■ 18341 ■ Western Livestock Inc.
PO Box 850
Dickinson, ND 58602-0850
Phone: (701)225-8145 **Fax:** (701)225-8145
Products: Livestock. **SIC:** 5154 (Livestock). **Officers:** Patrick Brien, President.

■ 18342 ■ Wheaton Dumont Cooperative Elevator Inc.
1115 Broadway Ave.
Wheaton, MN 56296
Phone: (612)563-8152
Products: Grain. **SIC:** 5153 (Grain & Field Beans). **Est:** 1905. **Sales:** $30,000,000 (2000). **Emp:** 17. **Officers:** Orval Kohls, General Mgr.; David Holthusen, Controller.

■ 18343 ■ Wheeler Brothers
420 Santa Fe
Alva, OK 73717
Phone: (580)327-0141 **Fax:** (580)327-1802
Products: Grain, including wheat; Fertilizer. **SICs:** 5153 (Grain & Field Beans); 5191 (Farm Supplies). **Sales:** $5,500,000 (2000). **Emp:** 7. **Officers:** Dean Goll, President.

■ 18344 ■ Wheeler Brothers Grain Company Inc.
PO Box 29
Watonga, OK 73772
Phone: (580)623-7223 **Fax:** (580)623-2686
Products: Grain. **SIC:** 5153 (Grain & Field Beans). **Sales:** $60,000,000 (2000). **Emp:** 70. **Officers:** Steve Smola, President; Rick Cowen, Treasurer & Secty.

■ 18345 ■ Whitaker Farmers Cooperative Grain Co.
7690 E 9000 N Rd.
Grant Park, IL 60940
Phone: (815)465-6681 **Fax:** (815)465-6861
E-mail: whitcoop@keynet.net
Products: Grain, including wheat, oats, and beans. **SICs:** 5153 (Grain & Field Beans); 5191 (Farm Supplies). **Est:** 1945. **Sales:** $3,000,000 (2000). **Emp:** 5. **Officers:** Russell Koehn, President; Gerry Bertrand, Manager.

■ 18346 ■ Whitman County Growers Inc.
PO Box 151
Colfax, WA 99111
Phone: (509)397-4381
Products: Grain. **SIC:** 5153 (Grain & Field Beans). **Est:** 1972. **Sales:** $20,000,000 (2000). **Emp:** 20. **Officers:** J. Richard Clonninger, President; Robert J. Holmes, CFO.

■ 18347 ■ Whittemore Cooperative Elevator
502 Railroad
Whittemore, IA 50598
Phone: (515)884-2271
Products: Grain. **SIC:** 5191 (Farm Supplies). **Est:** 1947. **Sales:** $9,000,000 (2000). **Emp:** 25. **Officers:** Roy Beenken, General Mgr.

■ 18348 ■ Wilbur-Ellis Co.
1200 Westlake Ave. N, Ste. 1000
Seattle, WA 98109
Phone: (206)284-1300 **Fax:** (206)281-8604
Products: Legumes; Animal feed. **SICs:** 5191 (Farm Supplies); 5153 (Grain & Field Beans). **Officers:** Ronald Patton, Manager.

■ 18349 ■ Will-Du Page Service Co.
100 Manhattan Rd.
Joliet, IL 60433
Phone: (815)740-2840
Products: Farm supplies. **SIC:** 5191 (Farm Supplies). **Sales:** $16,000,000 (2000). **Emp:** 45. **Officers:** Ronald Hack, President; Paul Zabel, Controller.

■ 18350 ■ Lyle L. Williams
22601 154th Ave.
Box Elder, SD 57719-0184
Phone: (605)923-3133
Products: Livestock, including cattle and sheep. **SIC:** 5154 (Livestock). **Est:** 1969. **Sales:** $12,000,000 (2000). **Officers:** Lyle Williams, Owner; Myron Williams, Partner.

■ 18351 ■ Williamsville Farmers Cooperative Grain Co.
PO Box 169
Williamsville, IL 62693
Phone: (217)566-3321
Products: Grain; Feed. **SICs:** 5153 (Grain & Field Beans); 5191 (Farm Supplies). **Est:** 1921. **Sales:**

$7,500,000 (2000). **Emp:** 7. **Officers:** Norman E. Constant, President; Floyd Olesen, Vice President.

■ 18352 ■ Willow Hill Grain Inc.
PO Box 213
Willow Hill, IL 62480
Phone: (618)455-3201
Products: Grain. **SIC:** 5153 (Grain & Field Beans). **Est:** 1966. **Sales:** $5,000,000 (2000). **Emp:** 8. **Officers:** D.L. Huisinga, Owner.

■ 18353 ■ Wilmont Farmers Elevator Co.
PO Box 219
Wilmont, MN 56185
Phone: (507)926-5141
Free: (800)367-5141 **Fax:** (507)926-5142
Products: Grain; Feed chemicals; Fertilizer; Farm-related products, including bins, wagons, and sprayers. **SICs:** 5153 (Grain & Field Beans); 5191 (Farm Supplies). **Est:** 1914. **Sales:** $15,000,000 (2000). **Emp:** 12. **Officers:** Bob Newman, President; Tom Ramerth, Dir. of Marketing.

■ 18354 ■ Wilson Seeds Inc.
PO Box 391
Harlan, IA 51537
Phone: (712)755-3841
Products: Corn. **SIC:** 5191 (Farm Supplies). **Est:** 1926. **Sales:** $8,000,000 (2000). **Emp:** 50. **Officers:** John Crabtree, President; Bill Jenkinson, Controller; William Dinslage, Dir. of Marketing & Sales.

■ 18355 ■ Windom Sales Company Inc.
PO Box 53
Windom, MN 56101
Phone: (507)831-2694
Products: Livestock. **SIC:** 5154 (Livestock). **Est:** 1940. **Sales:** $1,000,000 (2000). **Emp:** 1. **Officers:** H.N. Trotter, President.

■ 18356 ■ Wishek Livestock Market Inc.
PO Box 401
Wishek, ND 58495-0401
Phone: (701)452-2306 **Fax:** (701)452-2508
Products: Livestock. **SIC:** 5154 (Livestock). **Officers:** Curtis Rohweder, President.

■ 18357 ■ Wolcott and Lincoln Inc.
4800 Main St.
Kansas City, MO 64112
Phone: (816)753-6750 **Fax:** (816)531-6876
Products: Grain. **SIC:** 5153 (Grain & Field Beans). **Sales:** $43,000,000 (2000). **Emp:** 80. **Officers:** Daniel Gibson, General Mgr.; Rich Williams, Controller.

■ 18358 ■ Wolverton Farmers Elevator
PO Box 69
Wolverton, MN 56594
Phone: (218)995-2565
Products: Grain elevator. **SICs:** 5153 (Grain & Field Beans); 5191 (Farm Supplies). **Est:** 1929. **Sales:** $12,000,000 (2000). **Emp:** 7. **Officers:** Curt Bjertness, General Mgr.; Mark Sundstrom, President.

■ 18359 ■ Worland Livestock Auction Inc.
PO Box 33
Worland, WY 82401-0033
Phone: (307)347-9201 **Fax:** (307)347-2842
Products: Livestock. **SIC:** 5154 (Livestock). **Officers:** Terry Warneke, Owner; Rick Warneke, Owner.

■ 18360 ■ L.C. Wormell
305 Bridgeton Rd.
Westbrook, ME 04092
Phones: (207)829-5161 (207)773-7498
Products: Livestock; Dairy products. **SICs:** 5154 (Livestock); 5143 (Dairy Products Except Dried or Canned). **Alternate Name:** L.C. #Wormell Livestock.

■ 18361 ■ Wright Lorenz Grain Company Inc.
PO Box 2420
Salina, KS 67402-2420
Phone: (913)827-3687 **Fax:** (913)827-9361
Products: Grain, corn, wheat, milo, and soybeans. **SICs:** 5153 (Grain & Field Beans); 5191 (Farm Supplies). **Est:** 1946. **Sales:** $80,000,000 (2000). **Emp:** 40. **Officers:** Don R. Timmel, President; Larry Geibler, Controller.

■ 18362 ■ Ronald J. Wright
48 Community Dr.
Newport, VT 05855
Phone: (802)334-6115 **Fax:** (802)334-1591
E-mail: wrient@together.net
URL: http://www.sover.net/.
Products: Livestock; Sporting goods; Clothing; Antiques; Furniture. **SICs:** 5154 (Livestock); 5136 (Men's/Boys' Clothing); 5137 (Women's/Children's Clothing); 5091 (Sporting & Recreational Goods). **Est:** 1990. **Sales:** $1,500,000 (2000). **Emp:** 10. **Officers:** Ronald Wright, Owner.

■ 18363 ■ Yale Farmers Cooperative
PO Box 128-127
Yale, SD 57386
Phone: (605)599-2911
Free: (800)599-2911 **Fax:** (605)599-2808
E-mail: yalecoop@basec.net
Products: Grain, feed, fertilizer; Petroleum; Chemical; Service station. **SIC:** 5153 (Grain & Field Beans). **Est:** 1913. **Sales:** $23,000,000 (2000). **Emp:** 18. **Officers:** Gary Doering, General Mgr.; Connie Doering, Mgr. of Finance; Brad Wedel, President; Raymond Hofer, Vice President; Darby Fast, Secretary; John Fox, Director.

■ 18364 ■ Ypsilanti Equity Elevator Company Inc.
PO Box 287
Ypsilanti, ND 58497
Phone: (701)489-3379
Products: Grain, field beans, feed, seed, fertilizers and agricultural chemicals. **SICs:** 5153 (Grain & Field Beans); 5191 (Farm Supplies). **Sales:** $11,000,000 (1993). **Emp:** 6. **Officers:** Dick Christensen, Fiance General Manager.

■ 18365 ■ Zenchiku Land and Cattle Co.
4600 Carrigan Ln.
Dillon, MT 59725
Phone: (406)683-5474
Products: Livestock. **SIC:** 5154 (Livestock). **Officers:** John Morse, President.

(31) Luggage and Leather Goods

Entries in this section are arranged alphabetically by company name. When the company name is a personal name, the company name is alphabetized by the surname unless the first name or initial(s) are part of a trade name. See the User's Guide at the front of this directory for additional information.

■ **18366** ■ **Accesories That Matter**
320 5th Ave., #609
New York, NY 10001
Phone: (212)947-3012
Products: Handbags and other small leather goods. **SICs:** 5199 (Nondurable Goods Nec); 5137 (Women's/Children's Clothing). **Sales:** $3,000,000 (2000). **Emp:** 4. **Officers:** A. Roy, CEO.

■ **18367** ■ **Airway Industries Inc.**
Airway Park
Ellwood City, PA 16117
Phone: (724)752-0012 **Fax:** (724)752-3444
Products: Luggage. **SIC:** 5099 (Durable Goods Nec). **Sales:** $91,000,000 (1994). **Emp:** 180. **Officers:** Thomas Falloon, President; Joe Sergi, VP of Finance.

■ **18368** ■ **AmeriBag Inc.**
55 Greenkill Ave.
Kingston, NY 12401
Phone: (914)339-1292 **Fax:** (914)339-1294
E-mail: salesinfo@ameribag.com
URL: http://www.ameribag.com
Products: Leather and chiefly leather goods. **SIC:** 5099 (Durable Goods Nec). **Est:** 1987. **Sales:** $4,000,000 (1999). **Emp:** 52. **Officers:** Irwin Gaffin, CEO & President; Margery Gaffin, Vice President; Carey Goldberg, Dir. of Sales, e-mail: ccgold@aol.com.

■ **18369** ■ **American Accessories International Inc.**
901 E Summit Hill Dr., No. 302
Knoxville, TN 37915-1200
Phone: (423)525-9100 **Fax:** (423)525-0889
Products: Cosmetic bags; Tote bags. **SICs:** 5199 (Nondurable Goods Nec); 5099 (Durable Goods Nec). **Est:** 1983. **Sales:** $20,000,000 (2000). **Emp:** 25. **Officers:** Eric L. Zeanah, President; Mary Stewart, Accountant.

■ **18370** ■ **Amex Hides Ltd.**
3220 88th St.
Flushing, NY 11369
Phone: (212)777-5557 **Fax:** (212)995-8010
Products: Hides. **SIC:** 5159 (Farm-Product Raw Materials Nec). **Est:** 1908. **Sales:** $1,000,000 (2000). **Emp:** 2. **Officers:** Patricia Tolvar, President; Sally Peres, Controller.

■ **18371** ■ **Art Craft Wallets Inc.**
380 Lafayette St.
New York, NY 10003
Phone: (212)674-3332 **Fax:** (212)674-3677
Products: Leather goods, including wallets. **SIC:** 5199 (Nondurable Goods Nec). **Est:** 1950. **Emp:** 50. **Officers:** Edward Kandler, Sales & Marketing Contact; Joe Kandler, Customer Service Contact.

■ **18372** ■ **Atchison Leather Products**
201 Main
Atchison, KS 66002-2838
Phone: (913)367-6431
Free: (800)255-6023 **Fax:** (913)367-7353
Products: Leather products, including tool aprons, pouches and holders. **SIC:** 5199 (Nondurable Goods Nec). **Est:** 1908. **Sales:** $5,000,000 (2000). **Emp:** 100.

Officers: Sue Schuler, Account Mgr., e-mail: sue@atchisonproducts.com.

■ **18373** ■ **Atwood Leather Cutting**
PO Box 3882
Hickory, NC 28603-3882
Phone: (704)322-7020 **Fax:** (704)322-7021
Products: Leather. **SIC:** 5199 (Nondurable Goods Nec). **Emp:** 19. **Officers:** Al Woodward.

■ **18374** ■ **Bag Bazaar Ltd.**
1 E 33rd St.
New York, NY 10016
Phone: (212)689-3508 **Fax:** (212)696-2098
Products: Handbags. **SIC:** 5137 (Women's/Children's Clothing). **Sales:** $50,000,000 (2000). **Emp:** 90. **Officers:** David Sutton, CEO; Robert Frankel, Controller; Ronnie Hersh, Dir. of Marketing; Joe Zipper, Dir. of Data Processing; Giti Reiss, Dir of Human Resources.

■ **18375** ■ **Beggs and Cobb Corp.**
139 Lynnfield St.
Peabody, MA 01960
Phone: (978)532-3080 **Fax:** (978)531-1183
Products: Split leather. **SIC:** 5199 (Nondurable Goods Nec). **Sales:** $1,000,000 (2000). **Emp:** 5. **Officers:** Robert E. Remis, President; Michael Gordon, Controller.

■ **18376** ■ **Berman Leather Company Inc.**
229 A St.
Boston, MA 02210-1309
Phone: (617)426-0870 **Fax:** (617)357-8564
E-mail: berman@ma.ultranet
URL: http://www.bermanleather.com
Products: Finished leather products and leather crafting materials. **SICs:** 5199 (Nondurable Goods Nec); 5099 (Durable Goods Nec). **Est:** 1905. **Sales:** $3,000,000 (1999). **Emp:** 10. **Officers:** Robert S. Berman, President.

■ **18377** ■ **Border Leather Corp.**
261 Broadway
Chula Vista, CA 91910-2319
Phone: (619)691-1657
Free: (800)732-6936 **Fax:** (619)691-0159
E-mail: borderleather@4dcomm.com
Products: Leather goods and raw leather material. **SIC:** 5199 (Nondurable Goods Nec). **Est:** 1983. **Emp:** 8. **Officers:** Gloria Gold; Deborah Biezonsky, General Mgr.; Daneil Biezonsky.

■ **18378** ■ **Bugatti Inc.**
100 Condor St.
East Boston, MA 02128
Phone: (617)567-7600
Free: (800)284-2887 **Fax:** (617)567-5541
E-mail: customerservice@bugatti.com
URL: http://www.bugatti.com
Products: Leather goods. **SIC:** 5199 (Nondurable Goods Nec). **Est:** 1972. **Emp:** 49. **Officers:** Terry L. Scheller.

■ **18379** ■ **California Wallet Co. Inc.**
3728 Rockwell Ave.
El Monte, CA 91731
Phone: (626)443-6888 **Fax:** (626)443-8597
Products: Nylon products, including wallets, fannypacks, and tote bags. **SIC:** 5099 (Durable Goods Nec).

■ **18380** ■ **Carina International Inc.**
4657 N Pulaski St.
Chicago, IL 60630
Phone: (773)509-0016 **Fax:** 800-441-6779
Products: Luggage; Portfolios, briefcases, and handbags. **SIC:** 5099 (Durable Goods Nec).

■ **18381** ■ **Caye's Luggage**
PO Box 891
Portland, OR 97207-0891
Phone: (503)227-4322 **Fax:** (503)227-4324
Products: Luggage and luggage accessories. **SIC:** 5099 (Durable Goods Nec). **Est:** 1923. **Emp:** 6. **Officers:** M. Kornberg.

■ **18382** ■ **Chicago Case International**
PO Box 584
Skokie, IL 60076
Phone: (847)674-9888 **Fax:** (847)674-9808
Products: Carrying cases; Computer cases; Demonstration products. **SIC:** 5099 (Durable Goods Nec).

■ **18383** ■ **Clipper Products**
675 Cincinnati-Batavia Pike
Cincinnati, OH 45245
Phone: (513)528-7011
Free: (800)543-0324 **Fax:** (513)528-7676
E-mail: sales@clipperproducts.com
URL: http://www.clipperproducts.com
Products: Occupational luggage cases, sample cases, binocular and camera cases; Carts. **SIC:** 5099 (Durable Goods Nec). **Est:** 1969. **Emp:** 15. **Officers:** David J. Durham, President & CEO; Rose Moppin, Controller.

■ **18384** ■ **Columbia Impex Corp.**
16112-A NW 13th Ave.
Miami, FL 33169-5748
Phone: (305)625-0511 **Fax:** (305)621-1193
E-mail: ColumbiImplex@altavista.com
Products: Reptile and exotic leathers. **SIC:** 5199 (Nondurable Goods Nec). **Est:** 1971. **Sales:** $2,500,000 (2000). **Emp:** 4. **Officers:** Ruben Villanueva, Manager. **Alternate Name:** King Cobra.

■ **18385** ■ **Cromwell Leather Group**
147 Palmer Ave.
Mamaroneck, NY 10543
Phone: (914)381-0100 **Fax:** (914)381-0046
E-mail: sales@cromwellgroup.com
Products: Leather. **SIC:** 5199 (Nondurable Goods Nec). **Emp:** 40. **Officers:** Thomas J. Fleisch, President & Treasurer. **Former Name:** Excel Tanning Corp.

■ 18386 ■ Custom Leathercraft Manufacturing
811 W 58th St.
Los Angeles, CA 90037
Phone: (213)752-2221
Free: (800)325-0455 **Fax:** (213)752-9429
Products: Leather belts; Leather goods. **SIC:** 5199
(Nondurable Goods Nec).

■ 18387 ■ Diamond Leather Inc.
11401 Gateway W
El Paso, TX 79936-6419
Phones: (915)598-1874 (915)598-2225
Free: (800)426-6105 **Fax:** (915)594-2786
Products: Leather. **SIC:** 5199 (Nondurable Goods
Nec). **Sales:** $1,800,000 (2000). **Emp:** 49. **Officers:**
Mauricio Lewkowicz.

■ 18388 ■ Dimensional Graphics Corp. Risto Division
325 N Jackson Ave.
PO Box 1893
Mason City, IA 50401
Phone: (515)423-8931
Free: (800)392-0890 **Fax:** (515)423-0912
URL: http://www.dimensionalgrafix.com
Products: Sewn leather and vinyl products. **SIC:** 5199
(Nondurable Goods Nec). **Est:** 1953. **Sales:**
$2,000,000 (1999). **Emp:** 60. **Officers:** Paul M. Gold,
President, e-mail: paul@dimensionalgrafix.com; Barry
Groh, Vice President, e-mail: barry@
dimensionalgrafix.com; John Sandvig, Sales Contact;
Carolyn Gold, Marketing Contact, e-mail: carolyn@
dimesionalgrafix.com; Jim Trimble, Customer Service
Contact, e-mail: jim@dimensionalgrafix.com. **Also
Known by This Acronym:** MEID.

■ 18389 ■ Dover Handbag Corp.
20 W 33rd St.
New York, NY 10001
Phone: (212)563-7055
Products: Backpacks, diaper bags, and purses. **SICs:**
5137 (Women's/Children's Clothing); 5159 (Farm-
Product Raw Materials Nec). **Est:** 1949. **Sales:**
$2,000,000 (2000). **Emp:** 8. **Officers:** Trevor Brentall,
President.

■ 18390 ■ Eagle Creek
3055 Enterprise Ct.
Vista, CA 92083-8347
Phone: (760)471-7600 **Fax:** (760)471-2536
Products: Travel gear. **SIC:** 5099 (Durable Goods
Nec). **Emp:** 99.

■ 18391 ■ Ebinger Brothers Leather Co.
44 Mitchell Rd.
Ipswich, MA 01938
Phone: (978)356-5701
Free: (800)343-8120 **Fax:** (978)356-9832
URL: http://www.ebingerleather.com
Products: Leather products, including key rings,
luggage tags, and clothing accessories. **SIC:** 5199
(Nondurable Goods Nec). **Est:** 1947. **Sales:**
$4,000,000 (2000). **Emp:** 26. **Officers:** K.A. Ebinger,
President; Peter Olson, Sales Mgr.; Christopher
Ebinger, General Mgr.

■ 18392 ■ Elco Manufacturing Company Inc.
39 W 19th St.
New York, NY 10011-4225
Phone: (212)255-4300 **Fax:** (212)255-4331
Products: Personal leather goods; Stationery
specialties. **SIC:** 5199 (Nondurable Goods Nec). **Est:**
1904. **Sales:** $1,000,000 (2000). **Emp:** 15. **Officers:** S.
Weintraub, President.

■ 18393 ■ Excel Tanning Corp.
715 Mamaroneck Ave.
Mamaroneck, NY 10543
Phone: (914)381-0100 **Fax:** (914)381-0046
Products: Luggage and leather goods. **SIC:** 5199
(Nondurable Goods Nec). **Sales:** $1,000,000 (2000).
Emp: 40.

■ 18394 ■ Patrick Farrell Imports Inc.
675 Anita St., Ste. C6
Chula Vista, CA 91911-4660
Phone: (619)482-1513
Free: (800)350-2252 **Fax:** (619)482-7210
Products: Leather goods. **SIC:** 5199 (Nondurable
Goods Nec). **Est:** 1976.

■ 18395 ■ GMS Corp.
1680 Carolina Dr.
Elk Grove Village, IL 60007-2926
Phone: (847)985-9419
Products: Leather and chiefly leather goods;
Briefcases; Attache cases. **SICs:** 5199 (Nondurable
Goods Nec); 5099 (Durable Goods Nec). **Est:** 1982.
Emp: 10. **Officers:** S.N. Goyal, Vice President.

■ 18396 ■ H & J Leather Finishing
312 N Perry
Johnstown, NY 12095-1211
Phone: (518)762-7775 **Fax:** (518)762-2576
Products: Finished leathers. **SIC:** 5199 (Nondurable
Goods Nec). **Emp:** 49. **Officers:** Herman Dimaio.

■ 18397 ■ Hillmer's Luggage & Leather
115 SE 6th Ave.
Topeka, KS 66603-3564
Phone: (785)233-2314 **Fax:** (785)233-2315
Products: Luggage; Leather and chiefly leather goods.
SICs: 5099 (Durable Goods Nec); 5199 (Nondurable
Goods Nec). **Est:** 1922. **Emp:** 10. **Officers:** Walt
Hillmer, President.

■ 18398 ■ Hunter Co., Inc.
3300 W 71st Ave.
Westminster, CO 80030-5303
Phone: (303)427-4626
Free: (800)676-4868 **Fax:** (303)428-3980
Products: Holsters, slings, and gun cases; Knife
cases; Leather and nylon shooting accessories. **SICs:**
5199 (Nondurable Goods Nec); 5099 (Durable Goods
Nec). **Est:** 1952. **Sales:** $5,000,000 (2000). **Emp:** 68.
Officers: James Holtzclaw Jr., CEO & President.

■ 18399 ■ I.J.K. Sales Corp.
935 Cliffside Ave.
North Woodmere, NY 11581
Phone: (516)791-9129 **Fax:** (516)791-9108
Products: Luggage. **SIC:** 5099 (Durable Goods Nec).
Est: 1963. **Sales:** $10,000,000 (2000). **Emp:** 6.
Officers: Irv Kay, President.

■ 18400 ■ Import Leather Inc.
PO Box 1070
Exeter, NH 03833
Phone: (603)778-8484 **Fax:** (603)778-0374
Products: Imported leather. **SIC:** 5199 (Nondurable
Goods Nec). **Sales:** $8,000,000 (2000). **Emp:** 35.
Officers: Jonathon S. Shafmaster, President; Dan
Wilson, CFO.

■ 18401 ■ Infocase Inc.
2437 Williams Ave.
Cincinnati, OH 45212
Phone: (513)396-6744
Free: (800)248-4844 **Fax:** (513)924-1907
E-mail: info@infocase.com
URL: http://www.infocase.com
Products: Customized computer cases for laptop
computers and peripherals. **SIC:** 5199 (Nondurable
Goods Nec). **Est:** 1992. **Sales:** $3,000,000 (2000).
Emp: 5. **Officers:** William E. Howard, President.
Former Name: Quickcom.

■ 18402 ■ Jolie Handbags/Uptown Ltd.
10 W 33rd St.
New York, NY 10001
Phone: (212)736-6677 **Fax:** (212)564-5053
Products: Women's handbags and purses. **SIC:** 5137
(Women's/Children's Clothing). **Est:** 1971. **Sales:**
$3,000,000 (2000). **Emp:** 200. **Officers:** Gary Stein.

■ 18403 ■ L & S Trading Co.
2311 Bobolink Cove
Memphis, TN 38134
Phone: (901)377-7655
Products: Leather goods. **SIC:** 5199 (Nondurable
Goods Nec). **Officers:** Mike Stetson, President.

■ 18404 ■ Las Cruces Leather Co.
745 E Lohman Ave.
Las Cruces, NM 88001-3372
Phone: (505)523-0388 **Fax:** (505)524-8071
Products: Fine leather goods and supplies. **SIC:** 5199
(Nondurable Goods Nec). **Officers:** Teresa Amezquita,
Owner.

■ 18405 ■ Leather Connection
165 Classon Ave.
Brooklyn, NY 11205
Phone: (718)783-1120
Free: (800)832-1132 **Fax:** (718)783-1147
Products: Leather goods. **SIC:** 5099 (Durable Goods
Nec). **Est:** 1986. **Sales:** $2,000,000 (2000). **Emp:** 4.

■ 18406 ■ Leather Loft Stores
PO Box 1070
Exeter, NH 03833
Phone: (603)778-8484
Products: Leather handbags, jackets, and luggage.
SICs: 5199 (Nondurable Goods Nec); 5099 (Durable
Goods Nec).

■ 18407 ■ Liberty Leather Products Company Inc.
165 Classon Ave.
Brooklyn, NY 11205
Phone: (718)783-1100
Free: (800)832-1132 **Fax:** (718)783-1147
Products: Attache cases; Briefcases; Leather goods.
SIC: 5099 (Durable Goods Nec). **Est:** 1986. **Sales:**
$2,000,000 (2000). **Emp:** 5.

■ 18408 ■ Lifestyle International Inc.
110 S Enterprise Ave.
Secaucus, NJ 07094
Phone: (201)863-2426 **Fax:** (201)963-9140
Products: Luggage. **SIC:** 5099 (Durable Goods Nec).
Est: 1982. **Sales:** $25,000,000 (2000). **Emp:** 25.
Officers: D.H. Palk, President; C.Y. Kim, CFO; Larry
Shick, Exec. VP.

■ 18409 ■ Luggage America Inc.
1840 S Wilmington Ave.
Compton, CA 90220-5118
Phone: (310)223-2990
Free: (800)225-2990 **Fax:** (310)223-2999
E-mail: info@luggageamerica.com
URL: http://www.luggageamerica.com
Products: Luggage. **SIC:** 5099 (Durable Goods Nec).
Est: 1980. **Sales:** $25,000,000 (2000). **Emp:** 24.
Officers: Chris Yu, President. **Doing Business As:**
Olympia International.

■ 18410 ■ M-Bin International Imports
3136 Norbrook Dr.
Memphis, TN 38116
Phone: (901)398-6802
Free: (800)223-5031 **Fax:** (901)344-8602
E-mail: mbinintl@aol.com
URL: http://www.mbinintl.com
Products: Leather coats and jackets; Knives; Caps.
SICs: 5199 (Nondurable Goods Nec); 5091 (Sporting &
Recreational Goods). **Sales:** $4,000,000 (1999). **Emp:**
7. **Officers:** Abdul Shaikh, President.

■ 18411 ■ Marlo Bags
111 Marquardt Dr.
Wheeling, IL 60090-6427
Phone: (847)215-1400
Free: (800)437-8773 **Fax:** (847)808-4155
E-mail: info@marlobags.com
URL: http://www.marlobags.com
Products: Handbags; Ladies Golf accessories. **SIC:**
5137 (Women's/Children's Clothing). **Est:** 1933. **Sales:**
$10,000,000 (2000). **Emp:** 17. **Officers:** Martin Faber,
President; Michael Faber, Vice President.

■ 18412 ■ Maryland Leather Inc.
1012 Russell St.
Baltimore, MD 21230
Phone: (410)547-6999
Free: (800)547-6998 **Fax:** (410)547-7391
Products: Leather products, including wallets and
purses. **SIC:** 5199 (Nondurable Goods Nec).

■ **18413** ■ **Monarch Luggage Company Inc.**
5 Delavan St.
Brooklyn, NY 11231
Phone: (718)858-6900 **Fax:** (718)934-9110
Products: Canvas luggage. **SIC:** 5099 (Durable Goods
Nec). **Est:** 1946. **Sales:** $25,000,000 (2000). **Emp:**
400.

■ **18414** ■ **Oklahoma Leather Products Inc.**
500 26th St., NW
Miami, OK 74354
Phone: (918)542-6651 **Fax:** (918)542-6653
Products: Leather and chiefly leather goods. **SIC:**
5199 (Nondurable Goods Nec). **Est:** 1974. **Emp:** 130.

■ **18415** ■ **Orsen-Porter-Rockwell International**
888 Brannan St., No. 2105
San Francisco, CA 94103
Phone: (415)558-8994 **Fax:** (415)558-8995
Products: Women's handbags and purses; Leather
coats and jackets; Leather goods. **SICs:** 5199
(Nondurable Goods Nec); 5136 (Men's/Boys' Clothing);
5137 (Women's/Children's Clothing). **Emp:** 49.

■ **18416** ■ **Ossoff Leather**
40 Endicott
Peabody, MA 01960-3122
Phone: (978)532-0707 **Fax:** (978)532-5289
Products: Leather goods. **SIC:** 5199 (Nondurable
Goods Nec). **Sales:** $2,000,000 (2000). **Emp:** 49.
Officers: Michael Ossoff; Hyman Ossoff.

■ **18417** ■ **Pacific Hide & Leather Company,
Inc.**
14000 S Broadway
Los Angeles, CA 90061
Phone: (562)321-6730 **Fax:** (310)329-3474
Products: Leather and leather goods. **SIC:** 5199
(Nondurable Goods Nec).

■ **18418** ■ **Pantera International Corp.**
320 5th Ave. N
New York, NY 10001
Phone: (212)279-1170 **Fax:** (212)967-3954
Products: Women's handbags. **SIC:** 5137
(Women's/Children's Clothing). **Est:** 1986. **Sales:**
$2,000,000 (2000). **Emp:** 8. **Officers:** Arnold Simon,
President.

■ **18419** ■ **Philadelphia Hide Brokerage**
1000 S Lenola Rd.
Maple Shade, NJ 08052-1604
Phone: (609)439-0707
Products: Leather and rawhide. **SIC:** 5199
(Nondurable Goods Nec). **Sales:** $3,000,000 (2000).
Emp: 10. **Officers:** Michael Halpert, CEO & CFO.

■ **18420** ■ **Phillippe of California Inc.**
10 W 33rd St.
New York, NY 10001
Phone: (212)564-9191 **Fax:** (212)947-8473
Products: Handbags. **SIC:** 5137 (Women's/Children's
Clothing). **Est:** 1956. **Sales:** $5,000,000 (2000). **Emp:**
10. **Officers:** Bob Zeinoun, CEO.

■ **18421** ■ **Preston Leather Products**
44 Mitchell Rd.
PO Box 594
Ipswich, MA 01938-0594
Phone: (978)356-5701
Free: (800)343-8120 **Fax:** (978)356-9832
E-mail: janet@prestonleather.com
URL: http://www.prestonleather.com
Products: Leather skins and hide; Leather belts, bags,
and accesories; Canvas products. **SICs:** 5199
(Nondurable Goods Nec); 5099 (Durable Goods Nec).
Est: 1970. **Officers:** Christopher Ebinger, e-mail:
chris@ebingerleather.com.

■ **18422** ■ **Regal Bag Corp.**
PO Box 8
Newburgh, NY 12551-0008
Phone: (914)562-4922 **Fax:** (914)565-0927
Products: Handbags. **SIC:** 5137 (Women's/Children's
Clothing). **Est:** 1946. **Sales:** $20,000,000 (2000). **Emp:**
110. **Officers:** William Kaplan, President; Scott
Leibowitz, Controller; John Boronyak, Dir. of Marketing;
Paul Cooper, Dir. of Data Processing.

■ **18423** ■ **Regal Shearing**
39 W 960 Midan Dr.
Elburn, IL 60119
Phone: (630)232-6063
Free: (800)472-5593 **Fax:** (630)232-8702
Products: Sheepskin seat covers, including covers for
bikes, cars, and boats; Leatherr. **SICs:** 5099 (Durable
Goods Nec); 5199 (Nondurable Goods Nec). **Est:**
1984. **Sales:** $100,000 (2000). **Emp:** 1. **Officers:** Kern
L. Fischer, General Mgr.

■ **18424** ■ **Rico Industries Inc.**
1712 S Michigan Ave.
Chicago, IL 60616
Phone: (312)427-0313 **Fax:** (312)427-1887
Products: Leather wallets. **SIC:** 5199 (Nondurable
Goods Nec). **Est:** 1944. **Sales:** $5,000,000 (2000).
Emp: 75. **Officers:** Cary Schack, President; Bernard
Schack, CFO.

■ **18425** ■ **Robert Manufacturing Company Inc.**
1055 E 35th St.
Hialeah, FL 33013
Phone: (305)691-5311 **Fax:** (305)696-3949
Products: Bags, including gym bags, duffel bags, and
backpacks. **SICs:** 5199 (Nondurable Goods Nec); 5099
(Durable Goods Nec). **Est:** 1970. **Sales:** $2,500,000
(2000). **Emp:** 94. **Officers:** Peter Levine, President;
Harry Zimmerman, Treasurer & Secty.

■ **18426** ■ **Shafmaster Company Inc.**
PO Box 1070
Exeter, NH 03833
Phone: (603)778-8484 **Fax:** (603)778-0374
Products: Leather. **SIC:** 5199 (Nondurable Goods
Nec). **Sales:** $20,000,000 (2000). **Emp:** 100. **Officers:**
Jonathan S. Shafmaster, President; Daniel Wilson,
CFO.

■ **18427** ■ **Silver Blue Associated Ltd.**
320 5th Ave.
New York, NY 10001
Phone: (212)563-5858 **Fax:** (212)563-5935
Products: Women's handbags and purses; Luggage;
Leather goods. **SICs:** 5199 (Nondurable Goods Nec);
5099 (Durable Goods Nec). **Sales:** $2,000,000 (2000).
Emp: 4. **Officers:** Sarita Silver, President.

■ **18428** ■ **Silver Blue Associated Ltd.**
320 5th Ave.
New York, NY 10001
Phone: (212)563-5858 **Fax:** (212)563-5935
Products: Luggage and leather goods. **SIC:** 5199
(Nondurable Goods Nec). **Sales:** $2,000,000 (2000).
Emp: 4.

■ **18429** ■ **Sirco International Corp.**
13337 South St.
Cerritos, CA 90703-7300
Products: Handbags. **SICs:** 5199 (Nondurable Goods
Nec); 5137 (Women's/Children's Clothing). **Est:** 1964.
Sales: $33,300,000 (2000). **Emp:** 163. **Officers:**
Yutaka Yamaguchi, President; Robert Majernik, CFO;
Candy Braun, Dir of Personnel.

■ **18430** ■ **Skyway Luggage Co.**
30 Wall St.
Seattle, WA 98121
Phone: (206)441-5300 **Fax:** (206)441-5306
E-mail: info@skywayluggage.com
Products: Luggage. **SIC:** 5099 (Durable Goods Nec).
Est: 1909. **Sales:** $10,000,000 (1999). **Emp:** 100.
Officers: H.L. Kotkins Jr., President; William Willhoit,
Exec. VP & CFO.

■ **18431** ■ **South Bay Leather Corp.**
3065 Beyer Blvd., Ste. B-101
San Diego, CA 92154
Phone: (619)428-7535
Free: (800)845-5991 **Fax:** (619)428-0926
Products: Luggage and leather goods. **SIC:** 5199
(Nondurable Goods Nec). **Est:** 1988. **Sales:**
$1,000,000 (2000). **Emp:** 9.

■ **18432** ■ **Spradling International Inc.**
200 Cahaba Valley Pkwy. N
PO Box 1668
Pelham, AL 35124
Phone: (205)985-4206
Free: (800)333-0955 **Fax:** (205)985-9176
E-mail: sales@spradlingvinyl.com
URL: http://www.spradlingvinyl.com
Products: Leather; Vinyl. **SIC:** 5199 (Nondurable
Goods Nec). **Est:** 1964. **Emp:** 48. **Officers:** Mark
Goldstone, President; Kathy Streich, Treasurer; Chuck
Streich, VP of Sales.

■ **18433** ■ **Sterco New York Inc.**
1380 N Jerusalem Rd.
North Merrick, NY 11566-1011
Phone: (516)845-4525 **Fax:** (516)845-4034
Products: Saddlery; Leather jackets; Ball bearings.
SICs: 5199 (Nondurable Goods Nec); 5085 (Industrial
Supplies).

■ **18434** ■ **Michael Stevens Ltd.**
712 5th Ave., Fl. 12
New York, NY 10019-4108
Phone: (212)947-5595 **Fax:** (212)967-8439
Products: Small leather and vinyl handbags. **SIC:**
5137 (Women's/Children's Clothing). **Sales:**
$83,000,000 (2000). **Emp:** 200. **Officers:** Barbara
Khouri, President.

■ **18435** ■ **TENBA Quality Cases, Ltd.**
50 Washington St.
Brooklyn, NY 11201
Phone: (718)222-9870 **Fax:** (718)222-9871
E-mail: tenba@tenba.com
URL: http://www.tenba.com
Products: Occupational luggage cases, sample cases,
binocular and camera cases; Computer accessories.
SICs: 5099 (Durable Goods Nec); 5046 (Commercial
Equipment Nec). **Emp:** 49. **Officers:** Robert Weinreb.

■ **18436** ■ **TENBA Quality Cases Ltd.**
503 Broadway
New York, NY 10012-4401
Phone: (212)966-1013 **Fax:** (212)334-0841
Products: Luggage and leather goods. **SIC:** 5099
(Durable Goods Nec).

■ **18437** ■ **Texas Leather Trim Inc.**
2422 Blue Smoke Ct. S
Ft. Worth, TX 76105-1009
Phone: (817)535-5883
Free: (800)880-0248 **Fax:** (817)535-8643
E-mail: tltleather@waymark.net
Products: Leather and leather products; Footwear
components; Golf and corporate gifts. **SIC:** 5199
(Nondurable Goods Nec). **Est:** 1968. **Sales:**
$4,200,000 (2000). **Emp:** 40. **Officers:** John C.
Cooper; Gregory S. Cooper.

■ **18438** ■ **Viva Handbags Inc.**
1803 S Hope St.
Los Angeles, CA 90015
Phone: (213)748-3932 **Fax:** (213)748-1146
E-mail: vivabags@aol.com
Products: Women's handbags and purses; Apparel
belts; Leather goods. **SICs:** 5137 (Women's/Children's
Clothing); 5199 (Nondurable Goods Nec). **Est:** 1981.
Emp: 25. **Officers:** Irma Castillo.

■ **18439** ■ **Louis Vuitton North America Inc.**
130 E 59th St., 10th Fl.
New York, NY 10022
Phone: (212)572-9700
Products: Handbags and luggage. **SICs:** 5137
(Women's/Children's Clothing); 5099 (Durable Goods
Nec). **Sales:** $75,000,000 (2000). **Emp:** 300. **Officers:**
David Daniel, President; Tom Nelson, Controller.

■ **18440** ■ **Walach Leather Splitting**
22 Pierpont St.
Peabody, MA 01960-5663
Phones: (978)531-2040 (978)LEA-THER
Products: Leather pieces; Leather working machinery.
SIC: 5199 (Nondurable Goods Nec). **Est:** 1964. **Emp:**
49. **Officers:** Dennis Walach.

■ **18441** ■ **Warden Leathers Inc.**
PO Box 842
Gloversville, NY 12078
Phone: (518)725-6447   **Fax:** (518)756-3710
Products: Finished leather. **SIC:** 5199 (Nondurable Goods Nec). **Est:** 1968. **Sales:** $4,000,000 (2000). **Emp:** 12. **Officers:** Warren Dennie, President.

■ **18442** ■ **Warehouse Outlet Stores Inc.**
95 Montgomery St.
Paterson, NJ 07501-1117
Phone: (973)278-9702
Free: (800)942-6322   **Fax:** (973)278-9673
Products: Women's handbags and purses. **SIC:** 5137 (Women's/Children's Clothing). **Est:** 1987. **Emp:** 15. **Officers:** Bruce Hardesty, President; Jose A. Giro, Vice President. **Doing Business As:** Who's Bags.

■ **18443** ■ **Harry Weiss Inc.**
870 5th Ave., No. 8F
New York, NY 10021-4953
Phone: (212)631-0684   **Fax:** (212)951-7405
Products: Women's handbags. **SIC:** 5137 (Women's/Children's Clothing). **Est:** 1972. **Sales:** $4,200,000 (2000). **Emp:** 13. **Officers:** Harry Weiss, President; Linda Aultman, Controller; Jean Shargel, Vice President.

■ **18444** ■ **West Ridge Designs**
1236 NW Flanders
Portland, OR 97209
Phone: (503)248-0053   **Fax:** (503)274-7685
Products: Backpacks. **SIC:** 5199 (Nondurable Goods Nec). **Sales:** $1,000,000 (2000). **Emp:** 30. **Officers:** Dann Morris.

■ **18445** ■ **Westport Corp.**
331 Changebridge Rd.
PO Box 2002
Pine Brook, NJ 07058
Phone: (973)575-0110
Free: (800)524-0629   **Fax:** (973)575-8197
URL: http://www.mundi.westport.com
Products: Leather goods. **SIC:** 5199 (Nondurable Goods Nec). **Est:** 1969. **Sales:** $71,000,000 (2000). **Emp:** 100. **Officers:** Richard Florin, CEO; John Florin, Sales/Marketing Contact, e-mail: johnf@ mundiwestport.com; Maria Caballero, Customer Service Contact, e-mail: mariac@mundiwestport.com.

■ **18446** ■ **World Network Trading Corp.**
7311 NW 12th St., Ste. 19
Miami, FL 33101
Phone: (305)762-4653   **Fax:** (305)762-6419
Products: Leather goods, including briefcases, backpacks, purses, and portfolios. **SIC:** 5199 (Nondurable Goods Nec). **Emp:** 12.

■ **18447** ■ **Worldwide Dreams LLC**
350 Fifth Ave., Ste. 2101
New York, NY 10118
Phone: (212)273-9200
Free: (800)221-8828   **Fax:** (212)273-9599
Products: Small leather goods. **SIC:** 5199 (Nondurable Goods Nec). **Est:** 1998. **Sales:** $98,000,000 (2000). **Emp:** 150. **Officers:** Roger Gimbel, Chairman of the Board; Allan Feldman, CEO; John Margaritis, President; Donn Liles, President, IT Div.; Geoffrey Gimbel, CFO. **Former Name:** Roger Gimbel Accessories Inc.

(32) Marine

Entries in this section are arranged alphabetically by company name. When the company name is a personal name, the company name is alphabetized by the surname unless the first name or initial(s) are part of a trade name. See the User's Guide at the front of this directory for additional information.

■ 18448 ■ **A.E.R. Supply, Inc.**
2301 Nasa Rd., No. 1
PO Box 349
Seabrook, TX 77586
Phone: (281)474-3276
Free: (800)767-7606 **Fax:** (281)474-2714
Products: Marine supplies (dunnage). **SIC:** 5088 (Transportation Equipment & Supplies).

■ 18449 ■ **American Industrial Exports Ltd.**
39 Spring St.
Ramsey, NJ 07446
Phone: (201)785-1280 **Fax:** (201)785-1283
E-mail: aminexusa@aol.com
Products: Marine accessories, flow meters, pressure gauges, and thermometers; Flashlights; Safety equipment; Laundry equipment; Window washing equipment and supplies. **SICs:** 5088 (Transportation Equipment & Supplies); 5047 (Medical & Hospital Equipment); 5063 (Electrical Apparatus & Equipment); 5136 (Men's/Boys' Clothing). **Officers:** Leonard A. Becker, Owner.

■ 18450 ■ **Argo International Corp.**
140 Franklin St.
New York, NY 10013
Phone: (212)431-1700 **Fax:** (212)431-2206
URL: http://www.argointl.com
Products: Electrical and mechanical equipment and components; Marine supplies and equipment; Industrial equipment, including machine parts and compressors. **SICs:** 5088 (Transportation Equipment & Supplies); 5084 (Industrial Machinery & Equipment). **Est:** 1952. **Sales:** $90,000,000 (2000). **Emp:** 250. **Officers:** John Calicchio, CEO & Chairman of the Board; Douglas J. Alpuche, CFO; John Santacroce, COO; Dominic Linsalata, Dir. of Data Processing.

■ 18451 ■ **Barbour Marine Supply**
410 Hedrick St.
PO Box 248
Beaufort, NC 28516
Phone: (252)728-2136
Free: (800)682-2643 **Fax:** (252)728-1217
E-mail: barbours@mail.clis.com
Products: Marine supplies and industrial supplies. **SICs:** 5088 (Transportation Equipment & Supplies); 5085 (Industrial Supplies). **Est:** 1919. **Emp:** 12. **Officers:** Nelson B. Gillikin, General Mgr.; Bryan Gillikin, President; Jack Booth, Vice President.

■ 18452 ■ **Barclay Marine Distributors Corp.**
2323 W Fulton St.
Chicago, IL 60612
Phone: (312)829-0500 **Fax:** (312)829-6533
Products: Marine supplies (dunnage). **SIC:** 5088 (Transportation Equipment & Supplies). **Officers:** Ken Masters, Sales Mgr.; Doug Morichika, Purchasing Agent.

■ 18453 ■ **Barclay Marine Distributors Corp.**
24600 Maplehurst Dr.
Clinton Township, MI 48036
Phone: (810)469-9910 **Fax:** (810)469-9918
Products: Marine supplies (dunnage). **SIC:** 5088

(Transportation Equipment & Supplies). **Officers:** Pat Johnson, General Mgr.

■ 18454 ■ **Barclay Marine Distributors Corp.**
1755 Buerkle Rd.
White Bear Lake, MN 55110
Phone: (612)770-8515 **Fax:** (612)770-1575
Products: Marine supplies (dunnage). **SIC:** 5088 (Transportation Equipment & Supplies). **Officers:** Bill Hatch, General Mgr.

■ 18455 ■ **Barclay Marine Distributors Corp.**
55 Design Dr.
Kansas City, MO 64116
Products: Marine supplies (dunnage). **SIC:** 5088 (Transportation Equipment & Supplies).

■ 18456 ■ **Beacon Supply Co.**
821 Industry Rd.
Kenner, LA 70062-6868
Phone: (504)467-9200
Products: Marine supplies (dunnage). **SIC:** 5088 (Transportation Equipment & Supplies). **Officers:** Erol Hymel, General Mgr.; Bob Garrett, Purchasing Agent.

■ 18457 ■ **C.C. Beckman Co.**
11 Commercial St.
New Bedford, MA 02740
Phone: (508)994-9674 **Fax:** (508)990-2785
Products: Marine products, including boat pumps, lights, anchors, and hardware. **SIC:** 5013 (Motor Vehicle Supplies & New Parts). **Est:** 1924. **Sales:** $4,000,000 (2000). **Emp:** 27. **Officers:** C.E. Beckman, President & Treasurer.

■ 18458 ■ **Bell Industries**
500 Hardman Ave.
PO Box 538
South St. Paul, MN 55075
Phone: (612)450-9020 **Fax:** (612)450-0844
Products: Marine supplies (dunnage). **SIC:** 5088 (Transportation Equipment & Supplies). **Officers:** Dan Huettl, General Mgr.; Rich Foss, Purchasing Agent.

■ 18459 ■ **Bell Industries**
Fulton Dr.
Germantown, WI 53022
Phone: (414)781-1860
Products: Marine supplies (dunnage). **SIC:** 5088 (Transportation Equipment & Supplies). **Officers:** Rod Sunbled, General Mgr.; Dan Yesko, Purchasing Agent.

■ 18460 ■ **Benrock Inc.**
4841 Lewis Rd.
Stone Mountain, GA 30083
Products: Marine supplies (dunnage). **SIC:** 5088 (Transportation Equipment & Supplies).

■ 18461 ■ **Benrock of Oklahoma**
15233 E Skelly Dr.
Tulsa, OK 74116
Phone: (918)437-2371
Products: Marine supplies (dunnage). **SIC:** 5088 (Transportation Equipment & Supplies). **Officers:** Rick Willis, General Mgr.

■ 18462 ■ **John A. Biewer**
2555 Busha Hwy.
Marysville, MI 48040
Phone: (810)364-9744
Free: (800)352-3523 **Fax:** (810)364-7540
Products: Marine equipment and supplies; Fishing and hunting equipment and supplies. **SIC:** 5088 (Transportation Equipment & Supplies). **Est:** 1916. **Emp:** 26. **Officers:** Scott Biewer, President; James Biewer, Sec. & Treas., e-mail: jbiewer@ameritech.net.

■ 18463 ■ **Big Island Marine**
73-4840 Kanalani St.
Kailua Kona, HI 96740
Phone: (808)329-3719 **Fax:** (808)326-4791
Products: Marine equipment and supplies. **SIC:** 5088 (Transportation Equipment & Supplies). **Est:** 1978. **Sales:** $900,000 (2000). **Emp:** 8. **Officers:** John F. Villesvik, Owner.

■ 18464 ■ **Blue Water Ship Store**
2030 FM 2094
PO Box 989
Kemah, TX 77565
Phone: (281)334-7583 **Fax:** (281)334-3147
Products: Marine supplies (dunnage). **SIC:** 5088 (Transportation Equipment & Supplies). **Officers:** Paul Brown, Owner and Purchasing Agent.

■ 18465 ■ **Boat America Corp.**
880 S Pickett St.
Alexandria, VA 22304
Phone: (703)370-4202 **Fax:** (703)461-2852
Products: Marine supplies (dunnage). **SIC:** 5088 (Transportation Equipment & Supplies). **Officers:** Jim Georgiadis, General Mgr.; Lisa George, Purchasing Agent; Jeff Young, Production Mgr.; Connie Springer, Production Mgr.

■ 18466 ■ **The Boat Locker**
1543 Post Rd. E
Westport, CT 06880
Phone: (203)259-7808 **Fax:** (203)254-3311
Products: Boats. **SIC:** 5091 (Sporting & Recreational Goods). **Est:** 1984. **Sales:** $2,000,000 (2000). **Emp:** 4. **Officers:** Scott Hardy.

■ 18467 ■ **Boater's World**
6711 Ritz Way
Beltsville, MD 20705
Phone: (301)953-9611
Products: Marine supplies (dunnage). **SIC:** 5088 (Transportation Equipment & Supplies). **Officers:** Bob Carey, General Mgr.

■ 18468 ■ **Bob's Machine Shop**
1501 33rd St. SE
Ruskin, FL 33570
Phone: (813)645-3966 **Fax:** (813)645-7267
Products: Outboard motors. **SIC:** 5091 (Sporting & Recreational Goods).

■ 18469 ■ R.G. Brewer, Inc.
161 E Boston Post Rd.
Mamaroneck, NY 10543
Phone: (914)698-3232 **Fax:** (914)698-3408
Products: Marine supplies (dunnage). **SIC:** 5088
(Transportation Equipment & Supplies). **Officers:** John
Johnson, General Mgr.

■ 18470 ■ Brewers Chandlery East
19 Novelty Ln.
Essex, CT 06426
Phone: (860)767-8267 **Fax:** (860)388-0260
Products: Marine equipment and supplies. **SIC:** 5088
(Transportation Equipment & Supplies). **Officers:** Mark
Hanrahan, Purchasing Agent.

■ 18471 ■ Brown Marine Service Inc.
PO Box 1415
Pensacola, FL 32596
Phone: (850)453-3471
Free: (800)234-3471 **Fax:** (850)457-1662
E-mail: bdc@brownmarine.com
URL: http://www.brownmarine.com
Products: Truck, car, and boat parts; Diesel engines
and parts; Commercial marine vessels; Heavy
equipment export. **SICs:** 5088 (Transportation
Equipment & Supplies); 5013 (Motor Vehicle Supplies
& New Parts). **Est:** 1958. **Sales:** $6,500,000 (1999).
Emp: 75. **Officers:** Warren T. Brown, President;
Shirley F. Bryan, Treasurer; Estill Lundsford, Sales.

■ 18472 ■ Brown Ship Chandlery Inc.
36 Union Wharf
Portland, ME 04101-4607
Phone: (207)772-3796 **Fax:** (207)772-8471
Products: Transportation equipment. **SICs:** 5088
(Transportation Equipment & Supplies); 5085
(Industrial Supplies). **Officers:** Charles Poole,
President.

■ 18473 ■ Byfield Marine Supply LLC
175 Olive Rd.
Pensacola, FL 32514
Phone: (850)477-8011
Free: (800)237-3741 **Fax:** (850)478-3011
E-mail: byfieldmarine@aol.com
Products: Marine supplies. **SIC:** 5088 (Transportation
Equipment & Supplies). **Est:** 1987. **Emp:** 25. **Officers:**
Fred Byfield, President. **Former Name:** Byfield Marine
Supply Co.

■ 18474 ■ Cape Water Sports
337 Main St.
Rte. 28
Harwich Port, MA 02646
Phone: (508)432-7079 **Fax:** (508)432-8407
Products: Boats. **SIC:** 5091 (Sporting & Recreational
Goods).

■ 18475 ■ Carolina Rim and Wheel Co.
PO Box 30126
Charlotte, NC 28230
Phone: (704)334-7276
Free: (800)532-6219 **Fax:** (704)334-7270
URL: http://www.carolinarim.com
Products: Boat trailer tires and rims; Truck rim and
wheel; Oil and air filters; Brakes, including air and
hydraulic; Brake drums; Suspension parts; Trailer
parts. **SICs:** 5014 (Tires & Tubes); 5013 (Motor Vehicle
Supplies & New Parts). **Est:** 1928. **Sales:** $10,000,000
(2000). **Emp:** 70. **Officers:** John McClemments,
President & Treasurer; Thomas M. Stewart, VP &
Secty., e-mail: tstewart@carolinarim.com.

■ 18476 ■ Cascade Yachts, Inc.
7030 NE 42nd
Portland, OR 97218
Phone: (503)287-5794 **Fax:** (503)287-5794
Products: Yachts; Yachting equipment and supplies,
including engine systems, furling systems, and
accessories. **SIC:** 5091 (Sporting & Recreational
Goods). **Est:** 1989. **Sales:** $1,000,000 (2000). **Emp:** 8.
Officers: L.J. Geerling, President.

■ 18477 ■ Certified Parts Corp.
PO Box 8468
Janesville, WI 53547-8468
Phone: (608)752-9441 **Fax:** (608)752-3528
E-mail: cpc@certifiedpartscorp.com
URL: http://www.certifiedpartscorp.com
Products: Parts for PWC; Go karts; Mini bikes;
Snowmobiles; ATV's. **SICs:** 5088 (Transportation
Equipment & Supplies); 5091 (Sporting & Recreational
Goods); 5013 (Motor Vehicle Supplies & New Parts).
Est: 1982. **Emp:** 12. **Officers:** James Grafft, President.

■ 18478 ■ Chapman Marine Supply
2201 SE Indian St., A-5
Stuart, FL 34997
Phone: (561)283-9110
Free: (800)245-3622 **Fax:** (561)283-9116
E-mail: sales@chapmanmarine.com
URL: http://www.chapmanmarine.com
Products: Marine supplies; Paints; Tapes; Sandpaper;
Sealants; Outriggers; Rod holders; Filters; Cordage;
Electrical products; Plumbing products; Pumps; Hoses.
SICs: 5088 (Transportation Equipment & Supplies);
5198 (Paints, Varnishes & Supplies); 5085 (Industrial
Supplies); 5063 (Electrical Apparatus & Equipment).
Est: 1985. **Emp:** 12. **Officers:** Robert V. Chapman Jr.,
President; Artie Jo Chapman, Vice President, Human
Resources Contact.

■ 18479 ■ Churchill Brothers
1130 W Marine View Dr.
Everett, WA 98201-1500
Phone: (425)259-3500 **Fax:** 800-222-6127
Products: Marine canvas and interiors. **SIC:** 5091
(Sporting & Recreational Goods). **Officers:** Oscar
Hoglund, Owner.

■ 18480 ■ Coast Distribution
1400 N Fiesta Blvd.
Gilbert, AZ 85234
Phone: (602)497-0083
Products: Marine supplies (dunnage). **SIC:** 5088
(Transportation Equipment & Supplies).

■ 18481 ■ Coast Distribution
PO Box 1449
Morgan Hill, CA 95038-1449
Products: Marine supplies (dunnage). **SIC:** 5088
(Transportation Equipment & Supplies). **Officers:** Dave
Berger, Contact.

■ 18482 ■ Coast Distribution
175 Greenfield Rd.
Lancaster, PA 17601
Products: Marine supplies (dunnage). **SIC:** 5088
(Transportation Equipment & Supplies).

■ 18483 ■ Coast Marine
7133 Burns
Ft. Worth, TX 76118
Phone: (972)247-9080
Products: Marine supplies (dunnage). **SIC:** 5088
(Transportation Equipment & Supplies). **Officers:** Alan
Aldi, Warehouse Manager.

■ 18484 ■ Coast Marine Distribution
230A Kelsey Ln.
Tampa, FL 33619
Phone: (813)622-7427 **Fax:** (813)621-6346
Products: Marine supplies (dunnage). **SIC:** 5088
(Transportation Equipment & Supplies). **Officers:** Ron
Grimaldi, Sales Mgr.

■ 18485 ■ Coastal Distributors, Inc.
PO Box 358
South Boston, MA 02127-0913
Phone: (781)749-7130 **Fax:** (781)740-4796
Products: Marine supplies (dunnage). **SIC:** 5088
(Transportation Equipment & Supplies). **Officers:**
Robert Rugerri, General Mgr.

■ 18486 ■ Colie Sailmakers
1649 Bay Ave.
Point Pleasant, NJ 08742
Phone: (732)892-4344 **Fax:** (732)899-8965
Products: Boats. **SIC:** 5091 (Sporting & Recreational
Goods).

■ 18487 ■ Composite Engineering Inc.
277 Baker Ave.
Concord, MA 01742
Phone: (978)371-3132 **Fax:** (978)369-3162
Products: Boats. **SIC:** 5091 (Sporting & Recreational
Goods).

■ 18488 ■ CYN
1661 N Elston Ave.
Chicago, IL 60622
Phone: (773)227-7627 **Fax:** (773)227-8655
Products: Marine supplies (dunnage). **SIC:** 5088
(Transportation Equipment & Supplies). **Officers:** Tony
Macaitis, General Mgr.

■ 18489 ■ Defender Industries
42 Great Neck Rd.
Waterford, CT 06385
Phone: (860)701-3400
Free: (800)628-8225 **Fax:** (860)654-1616
Products: Marine supplies. **SIC:** 5088 (Transportation
Equipment & Supplies). **Est:** 1938. **Emp:** 80. **Officers:**
Sheldon Lance, General Mgr.; Andrew Lance, Vice
President; Steven Lance, Vice President.

■ 18490 ■ Defender Marine Supply NY
321 Main St.
New Rochelle, NY 10801
Phone: (914)632-2318 **Fax:** (914)632-8540
Products: Marine supplies (dunnage). **SIC:** 5088
(Transportation Equipment & Supplies). **Emp:** 25.
Officers: Andrew Lance, President; Steven Lance.

■ 18491 ■ Dinghy Shop International
334 S Bayview Ave.
PO Box 431
Amityville, NY 11701
Phone: (516)264-0005 **Fax:** (516)598-8540
E-mail: dinghyshop@pipeline.com
URL: http://www.dinghyshop.com
Products: Small sailboats and kayaks. **SIC:** 5091
(Sporting & Recreational Goods). **Est:** 1993. **Officers:**
James Koehler; Susan Koehler. **Alternate Name:**
International Dinghy Shop.

■ 18492 ■ Diversified Marine Products
1914 Mateo St.
Los Angeles, CA 90021
Phone: (213)624-5595 **Fax:** (213)689-0986
Products: Marine accessories. **SIC:** 5088
(Transportation Equipment & Supplies). **Est:** 1947.
Sales: $1,500,000 (2000). **Emp:** 50. **Officers:** Daniel
Solomon, CEO; Doug Knecht, CFO; Jeff Magaziner,
Vice President.

■ 18493 ■ Doc Freeman's
1401 NW Leary Way
Seattle, WA 98107
Phone: (206)633-1500
Free: (800)423-8641 **Fax:** (206)789-5800
E-mail: docfreemans@seanet.com
URL: http://www.docfreemans.com
Products: Marine equipment. **SIC:** 5088
(Transportation Equipment & Supplies). **Est:** 1947.
Sales: $8,000,000 (2000). **Emp:** 59. **Officers:** Lee
Knudson, Owner and CEO; Amos Cordova Jr., Vice
President; Lowry Chamberlain, Customer Service
Contact; Richard Whistler, Human Resources Contact.

■ 18494 ■ Donovan Marine
115 W South St.
Albemarle, NC 28001
Phone: (704)983-5050
Free: (800)222-0174 **Fax:** (704)982-1481
Products: Marine accessories. **SIC:** 5088
(Transportation Equipment & Supplies). **Est:** 1913.
Sales: $30,000,000 (2000). **Emp:** 65. **Officers:** Alex
Furr, General Mgr.; Ken Furr, Purchasing Agent.

■ 18495 ■ Donovan Marine
4757 S Loop E
Houston, TX 77033
Phone: (713)734-4171 **Fax:** (713)734-1674
Products: Marine supplies (dunnage). **SIC:** 5088
(Transportation Equipment & Supplies).

■ 18496 ■ **Donovan Marine Inc.**
400 N Carrollton Ave.
PO Box 19100
New Orleans, LA 70179
Phone: (504)488-5731 **Fax:** (504)486-3258
Products: Marine supplies (dunnage). **SIC:** 5088
(Transportation Equipment & Supplies). **Officers:**
Benton Smallpage, President.

■ 18497 ■ **Easton Wholesale Co.**
PO Box 839
Easton, MD 21601
Phone: (410)822-0600 **Fax:** (410)822-1286
Products: Marine supplies (dunnage). **SIC:** 5088
(Transportation Equipment & Supplies). **Officers:** Tom
Cover, General Mgr.; Phil Greenhawk, Purchasing
Agent.

■ 18498 ■ **C.G. Edwards & Co.**
272 Dorchester Ave.
Boston, MA 02127
Phone: (617)268-4111 **Fax:** (617)268-8845
Products: Marine supplies (dunnage). **SIC:** 5088
(Transportation Equipment & Supplies). **Officers:** Mark
Edwards, Purchasing Agent.

■ 18499 ■ **Englund Marine Supply**
Foot of 15th St.
Astoria, OR 97103
Phone: (503)325-4341
Free: (800)228-7051 **Fax:** (503)325-6421
Products: Marine supplies (dunnage). **SIC:** 5088
(Transportation Equipment & Supplies). **Est:** 1944.
Emp: 35. **Officers:** John Englund, General Mgr., e-
mail: englund@pacifier.com; Ron Fox, Purchasing
Agent.

■ 18500 ■ **Fall City Boat Works**
3015 Upper River Rd.
Louisville, KY 40207
Phone: (502)897-6521
Products: Marine supplies (dunnage). **SIC:** 5088
(Transportation Equipment & Supplies). **Officers:** Herb
Miller Jr., General Manager and Purchasing Agent.

■ 18501 ■ **Fawcett Boat Supplies Inc.**
110 Compromise St.
Annapolis, MD 21401
Phone: (410)267-8681
Free: (800)456-9151 **Fax:** (410)267-7547
E-mail: fawcboat@bellatlantic.net
URL: http://www.fawcettboat.com
Products: Boat and marine supplies. **SIC:** 5091
(Sporting & Recreational Goods). **Est:** 1948. **Emp:** 35.
Officers: Gregory Kaufman, President; Richard
Terhorst, Vice President.

■ 18502 ■ **Fiber Glass West**
4604 Alawai Rd., No. 8
Waimea, HI 96796
Phone: (808)338-1162
Products: Fiberglass for boats. **SIC:** 5085 (Industrial
Supplies).

■ 18503 ■ **Fisheries Supply Co. Industrial Div.**
1900 N Northlake Way
Seattle, WA 98103
Phone: (206)632-4462
Free: (800)426-6930 **Fax:** (206)634-4600
E-mail: mail@fisheriessupply.com
URL: http://www.fisheriessupply.com
Products: Marine hardware; Parts for Ford
automobiles. **SICs:** 5088 (Transportation Equipment &
Supplies); 5013 (Motor Vehicle Supplies & New Parts).
Est: 1928. **Sales:** $18,000,000 (2000). **Emp:** 80.
Officers: Carl Sutter, President; Tim Carey,
Sales/Marketing Contact, e-mail: tcarey@
fisheriessupply.com; Jeff Leach, Customer Service
Contact, e-mail: jleach@fisheriessupply.com.

■ 18504 ■ **Fisherman's Marine Supply**
901 N Columbia Blvd.
Portland, OR 97217
Phone: (503)283-0044
Products: Marine supplies (dunnage). **SIC:** 5088
(Transportation Equipment & Supplies).

■ 18505 ■ **Freeport Marine Supply**
47 W Merrick Rd.
Freeport, NY 11520
Phone: (516)379-2610
Free: (800)645-2565 **Fax:** (516)379-2909
E-mail: sales@freeportmarine.com
Products: Marine supplies; Engine parts; Marine
electronics. **SIC:** 5088 (Transportation Equipment &
Supplies). **Est:** 1939. **Officers:** Irwin Ross, General
Mgr.

■ 18506 ■ **Getaway Sailing**
2701 Boston St.
Baltimore, MD 21224
Phone: (410)342-3110 **Fax:** (410)732-6131
Products: Boats. **SIC:** 5091 (Sporting & Recreational
Goods).

■ 18507 ■ **Glenn-Mar Marine Supply, Inc.**
6870 142nd Ave. N
Largo, FL 33771
Phone: (813)536-1955 **Fax:** (813)539-1248
Products: Marine supplies. **SIC:** 5088 (Transportation
Equipment & Supplies). **Est:** 1971. **Emp:** 40. **Officers:**
Glenn Rabbass, President; Robert Nealy, Sales Mgr.

■ 18508 ■ **Gold Coast Marine Distribution**
640 SW Flagler Dr.
Ft. Lauderdale, FL 33335
Phone: (954)463-8281 **Fax:** (954)462-8412
Products: Marine supplies (dunnage). **SIC:** 5088
(Transportation Equipment & Supplies). **Officers:** Don
Mains, General Mgr.; Ray Derry, Purchasing Agent.

■ 18509 ■ **Great Lakes Power Products**
5727 Old Boonville Hwy.
Evansville, IN 47715
Phone: (812)422-4893 **Fax:** (812)422-4911
Products: Marine transmissions and equipment,
including convertors, control cables, and pump drives;
Industrial transmissions and equipment, including
conveyors, control cables, pump drives, and drive lines.
SICs: 5088 (Transportation Equipment & Supplies);
5084 (Industrial Machinery & Equipment).

■ 18510 ■ **Great Lakes Power Products**
7455 Tyler Blvd.
Mentor, OH 44060-8389
Phone: (440)951-5111 **Fax:** (440)953-1052
Products: Marine engines, motors, air compressors,
pumps, and parts. **SIC:** 5088 (Transportation
Equipment & Supplies).

■ 18511 ■ **Greenwich Trading Co.**
22 South St.
Norwalk, CT 06854
Phone: (203)853-0041 **Fax:** (203)853-8055
Products: Alternative fragrances; Marine supplies;
Paint. **SICs:** 5088 (Transportation Equipment &
Supplies); 5198 (Paints, Varnishes & Supplies); 5122
(Drugs, Proprietaries & Sundries). **Officers:** Daniel J.
Lyons, President.

■ 18512 ■ **Gulf Coast Marine Supply Inc.**
501 Stimrad Rd.
Mobile, AL 36610
Phone: (205)452-8066
Products: Marine pipes, valves, and fittings. **SIC:** 5088
(Transportation Equipment & Supplies). **Est:** 1935.
Sales: $9,000,000 (2000). **Emp:** 100. **Officers:** Marvin
Mostellar Jr., President; Lil Bowab, Finance Officer.

■ 18513 ■ **Gulf King Marine**
322 Huff St.
Aransas Pass, TX 78336-5619
Phone: (512)758-3223
Products: Marine supplies (dunnage). **SIC:** 5088
(Transportation Equipment & Supplies). **Officers:**
Buddy Herndon, Owner; Buster Mott, Purchasing
Agent.

■ 18514 ■ **Gunderland Marine Supply, Inc.**
1221 Cantwell Ln.
PO Box 9758
Corpus Christi, TX 78407
Phone: (512)882-4231 **Fax:** (512)888-5622
Products: Marine and industrial supplies. **SIC:** 5088
(Transportation Equipment & Supplies). **Est:** 1919.

Sales: $3,500,000 (2000). **Emp:** 25. **Officers:** Ken
Gunderland, Owner; Josie Alman, Purchasing Agent.

■ 18515 ■ **H and L Marine Woodworking Inc.**
2965 Harcourt St.
East Rancho Dominguez, CA 90221
Phone: (310)638-8746
Products: Marine supplies (dunnage). **SIC:** 5088
(Transportation Equipment & Supplies).

■ 18516 ■ **Hamilton Marine**
PO Box 227
Searsport, ME 04974
Phone: (207)548-6302 **Fax:** 800-969-6352
Products: Marine and boating supplies, including sails,
nautical gear, and clothing; Commercial fishing
supplies. **SIC:** 5088 (Transportation Equipment &
Supplies).

■ 18517 ■ **Hannays**
1708 Central Ave. NE
Minneapolis, MN 55413
Phone: (612)781-7411 **Fax:** (612)781-4325
Products: Marine products. **SIC:** 5088 (Transportation
Equipment & Supplies).

■ 18518 ■ **Hardin Marine Inc.**
1280 S Anaheim Blvd.
Anaheim, CA 92805-6201
Phone: (714)956-9100
Products: Boats, marine engines, and parts. **SIC:**
5088 (Transportation Equipment & Supplies). **Est:**
1968. **Sales:** $6,000,000 (2000). **Emp:** 35. **Officers:**
Barry Lieberman, CEO & President; Debbie
Kapanoske, Controller; Marv Marter, Dir. of Marketing.

■ 18519 ■ **Hardware & Marine Co. of Alabama**
1875 N Conception St. Rd.
Mobile, AL 36610
Phone: (334)452-3423 **Fax:** (334)452-3425
Products: Marine supplies (dunnage). **SIC:** 5088
(Transportation Equipment & Supplies). **Officers:**
Laura Leon, General Mgr.

■ 18520 ■ **Hern Marine**
7341 Dixie Hwy.
Fairfield, OH 45014
Phone: (513)874-2628
Products: Marine supplies (dunnage). **SIC:** 5088
(Transportation Equipment & Supplies).

■ 18521 ■ **Hopkins-Carter Company Inc.**
3701 NW 21st St.
Miami, FL 33142
Phone: (305)635-7377
Products: Marine supplies. **SIC:** 5088 (Transportation
Equipment & Supplies).

■ 18522 ■ **HSS Group**
PO Box 310
San Pedro, CA 90732
Phone: (310)547-1181 **Fax:** (310)832-3744
URL: http://www.harborship.com
Products: Marine industry supplies; Wine and distilled
beverages. **SICs:** 5088 (Transportation Equipment &
Supplies); 5182 (Wines & Distilled Beverages). **Est:**
1932. **Sales:** $5,000,000 (1999). **Emp:** 10. **Officers:**
Jeff Crouthamel, President.

■ 18523 ■ **Imtra Corp.**
30 Samuel Barnet Blvd.
New Bedford, MA 02745
Phone: (508)995-7000 **Fax:** (508)998-5359
Products: Marine products, including clothing, chains,
ropes, anchor recovery, outboard motors, and more.
SIC: 5091 (Sporting & Recreational Goods). **Sales:**
$9,000,000 (2000). **Emp:** 30. **Officers:** Bill Farnham,
President; Ned Rogerson, CFO.

■ 18524 ■ **Indmar Products Industrial Div.**
5400 Old Millington Rd.
Millington, TN 38053
Phone: (901)353-9930 **Fax:** (901)358-4292
Products: Inboard marine engines and equipment.
SIC: 5088 (Transportation Equipment & Supplies).

■ **18525** ■ **Industrial Liaison Inc.**
17835 Sky Park Cir. C
Irvine, CA 92614
Phone: (949)261-7079 **Fax:** (949)261-8606
Products: Saddlery and rodeo equipment; Marine supplies. **SICs:** 5088 (Transportation Equipment & Supplies); 5091 (Sporting & Recreational Goods). **Est:** 1973. **Sales:** $1,500,000 (2000). **Emp:** 10. **Officers:** John Pearce, President; Tomko Y. Pearce, Controller; Andre Mendoza, Sales Mgr.

■ **18526** ■ **K.L. Jack & Co.**
145 Warren Ave.
Portland, ME 04103-1103
Phone: (207)878-3600 **Fax:** (207)878-3304
Products: Marine crafts and supplies; Industrial fasteners; Cutting supplies. **SIC:** 5088 (Transportation Equipment & Supplies). **Officers:** Kenneth Jack, President.

■ **18527** ■ **Jacobi Hardware Co., Inc.**
721 Surry St.
PO Drawer 3728
Wilmington, NC 28406
Phone: (919)763-1644
Products: Marine supplies (dunnage). **SIC:** 5088 (Transportation Equipment & Supplies). **Officers:** John Cain, General Mgr.; Walter Craven, Purchasing Agent.

■ **18528** ■ **Jamestown Distributors Inc.**
PO Box 348
Jamestown, RI 02835-0348
Phone: (401)423-2520
Free: (800)423-0030 **Fax:** 800-423-0542
Products: Transportation equipment and supplies; Marine crafts and supplies. **SIC:** 5088 (Transportation Equipment & Supplies). **Officers:** William Murdock, President.

■ **18529** ■ **Johnson Supply Co.**
50 S East St.
PO Box 449
Pensacola, FL 32501
Phone: (850)434-7103
Products: Marine supplies (dunnage). **SIC:** 5088 (Transportation Equipment & Supplies). **Officers:** Jim Johnson, General Manager and Purchasing Agent.

■ **18530** ■ **JPA Electronics Supply Inc.**
Park 80 W, Plaza 1
Saddle Brook, NJ 07663
Phone: (201)845-0980 **Fax:** (201)845-5139
Products: Electronic components, modules, and boards for industrial, military, and space applications. **SIC:** 5065 (Electronic Parts & Equipment Nec). **Est:** 1984. **Sales:** $11,000,000 (2000). **Emp:** 13. **Officers:** Hidekazu Okubo, General Mgr.

■ **18531** ■ **Keller Marine Service Inc.**
PO Box 0190
Port Trevorton, PA 17864
Phone: (717)374-8169 **Fax:** (717)374-5356
Products: RV and Marine accessories. **SIC:** 5088 (Transportation Equipment & Supplies). **Officers:** G. Michael Keller, President; Lori Morrow, Dir. of Sales; Robert Keister, General Mgr.; Jonas Lantz, Marketing & Sales Mgr.

■ **18532** ■ **Kellogg Marine Supply Inc.**
129 Mill Rock Rd.
PO Box 809
Old Saybrook, CT 06475-0809
Phone: (860)388-4277
Free: (800)243-9303 **Fax:** (860)388-0260
E-mail: mail@kelloggmarine.com
URL: http://www.kelloggmarine.com
Products: Marine supplies (dunnage). **SIC:** 5088 (Transportation Equipment & Supplies). **Est:** 1962. **Sales:** $40,000,000 (2000). **Emp:** 140. **Officers:** Jerry Pressman, President; Bob Staehle, General Mgr., e-mail: bstaehle@kelloggmarine.com. **Former Name:** Kellogg Marine, Inc.

■ **18533** ■ **Ken Dor Corp.**
5721 W Ryan St.
Franklin, WI 53132
Phone: (414)421-8484 **Fax:** (414)421-7236
Products: Marine supplies. **SIC:** 5088 (Transportation Equipment & Supplies).

■ **18534** ■ **T.A. King & Son Inc.**
PO Box 190
Jonesport, ME 04649-0190
Phone: (207)497-2274 **Fax:** (207)497-2123
Products: Marine crafts and supplies; Marine supplies. **SIC:** 5088 (Transportation Equipment & Supplies). **Officers:** Thomas King, President.

■ **18535** ■ **Kirkland Marine Co.**
3506 Stone Way N
Seattle, WA 98103
Phone: (206)633-1155
Products: Boating equipment and supplies. **SIC:** 5088 (Transportation Equipment & Supplies).

■ **18536** ■ **Knutson Distributors**
15 Mill Dam Rd.
Huntington, NY 11743
Phone: (516)673-4144
Products: Marine supplies (dunnage). **SIC:** 5088 (Transportation Equipment & Supplies). **Officers:** John Calabreeze, Purchasing Agent.

■ **18537** ■ **Kona Marine Supply**
74-425 Kealakehe Pkwy., No. 8
Kailua Kona, HI 96740
Phone: (808)329-1012 **Fax:** (808)326-4179
Products: Boat accessories, including trailers and trailer parts, paints, safety equipment, cleaning supplies, filter systems, and oil. **SICs:** 5091 (Sporting & Recreational Goods); 5198 (Paints, Varnishes & Supplies); 5172 (Petroleum Products Nec); 5169 (Chemicals & Allied Products Nec); 5084 (Industrial Machinery & Equipment).

■ **18538** ■ **Kremer Marine**
1408 Cowan Rd.
Gulfport, MS 39507
Phone: (228)896-1629
Products: Marine supplies. **SIC:** 5088 (Transportation Equipment & Supplies). **Est:** 1922. **Sales:** $1,000,000 (2000). **Emp:** 18. **Officers:** Charles Kremer, General Mgr.; Henry Kremer, Vice President.

■ **18539** ■ **L.A. Marine Hardware**
345 N Beacon St.
San Pedro, CA 90731
Phone: (310)831-9261
Products: Marine supplies (dunnage). **SIC:** 5088 (Transportation Equipment & Supplies). **Officers:** Anthony Iocanno, Purchasing Agent.

■ **18540** ■ **Lambs Yacht Center**
3376 Lakeshore Blvd.
PO Box 7038
Jacksonville, FL 32210
Phone: (904)384-5577
Products: Marine supplies (dunnage). **SIC:** 5088 (Transportation Equipment & Supplies). **Officers:** Frank Surface, General Mgr.; Jeff Todd, Purchasing Agent.

■ **18541** ■ **Land-N-Sea Distribution East**
2968A Ravenswood Rd.
Ft. Lauderdale, FL 33335
Phone: (954)792-5436 **Fax:** (954)581-4867
Products: Marine supplies (dunnage). **SIC:** 5088 (Transportation Equipment & Supplies). **Officers:** Pierre Giraud, General Mgr.; Mike Sulser, Purchasing Agent.

■ **18542** ■ **Land-N-Sea Distribution West**
5900 Youngquist Rd.
Ft. Myers, FL 33908
Phone: (941)433-5686 **Fax:** (941)433-3550
Products: Marine supplies (dunnage). **SIC:** 5088 (Transportation Equipment & Supplies). **Officers:** Scott Lewis, General Mgr.; Mike Sulser, Purchasing Agent.

■ **18543** ■ **Land-N-Sea—Norfolk**
1340 Azalea Garden Rd.
Norfolk, VA 23502
Phone: (757)853-7658
Products: Marine supplies (dunnage). **SIC:** 5088 (Transportation Equipment & Supplies). **Officers:** Bob Nagel, General Mgr.; Jim Holloway, Purchasing Agent.

■ **18544** ■ **Leader Creek Marina**
536 E 48th Ave.
Anchorage, AK 99503-7315
Phone: (907)561-8141 **Fax:** (907)562-5974
Products: Transportation equipment and supplies; Marine crafts and supplies. **SIC:** 5088 (Transportation Equipment & Supplies). **Officers:** Rod Egemo, Owner.

■ **18545** ■ **Leo J. Distributors**
1000 Minnesota Ave.
Duluth, MN 55802
Phone: (218)722-1757
Products: Marine supplies (dunnage). **SIC:** 5088 (Transportation Equipment & Supplies). **Officers:** Joel Johnson, General Manager and Purchasing Agent.

■ **18546** ■ **Lewis Marine Supply**
220 SW 32 St.
PO Box 21107
Ft. Lauderdale, FL 33335
Phone: (954)523-4371 **Fax:** (954)764-0185
E-mail: lms@lewismarine.com
URL: http://www.lewismarine.com
Products: Marine supplies. **SIC:** 5088 (Transportation Equipment & Supplies). **Est:** 1956. **Emp:** 100. **Officers:** John Stephens, Vice President; Ginger Keimel, Director.

■ **18547** ■ **LFS Inc.**
851 Coho Way
Bellingham, WA 98225
Phone: (360)734-3336
Free: (800)426-8860 **Fax:** (360)734-4058
E-mail: bham@lfsinc.com
URL: http://www.lfsinc.com
Products: Marine supplies (dunnage). **SIC:** 5088 (Transportation Equipment & Supplies). **Est:** 1967. **Officers:** Bill Stevens, Purchasing Agent; Philip Kolody.

■ **18548** ■ **Little River Marine Co.**
PO Box 986
Gainesville, FL 32602
Phone: (352)378-5025
Free: (800)247-4591 **Fax:** (352)378-5044
Products: Boats and rowing shells. **SIC:** 5091 (Sporting & Recreational Goods). **Est:** 1977. **Sales:** $500,000 (2000). **Emp:** 7. **Officers:** William Larson, President; Steve Larson, Vice President.

■ **18549** ■ **Llewellyn Supply**
507 N Figueroa St.
Wilmington, CA 90744
Phone: (310)834-2508
Free: (800)423-9800 **Fax:** (310)518-1480
E-mail: info@llsupplyco.com
Products: Marine hardware; Paints; Cordage. **SICs:** 5088 (Transportation Equipment & Supplies); 5198 (Paints, Varnishes & Supplies). **Est:** 1936. **Sales:** $5,000,000 (1999). **Emp:** 17. **Officers:** Chris Bowen Sr., Vice President, e-mail: chrissr@llsupplyco.com.

■ **18550** ■ **Lorenz & Jones Marine Distributors, Inc.**
1920 SE Delaware Ave.
Ankeny, IA 50021
Phone: (515)964-4205
Products: Marine supplies (dunnage). **SIC:** 5088 (Transportation Equipment & Supplies). **Officers:** Thomas Lorenz Sr., President.

■ **18551** ■ **Lowrance Electronics Inc.**
12000 E Skelly Dr.
Tulsa, OK 74128
Phone: (918)437-6881 **Fax:** (918)438-6149
URL: http://www.lowrance.com
Products: Fish locaters and global positioning systems. **SIC:** 5065 (Electronic Parts & Equipment Nec). **Est:** 1957. **Sales:** $89,753,000 (1999). **Emp:** 850. **Officers:** Darrell Lowrance.

■ **18552** ■ **J.J.W. Luden & Co., Inc.**
Concord at Charlotte St.
Charleston, SC 29403
Phone: (803)723-7829
Products: Marine supplies (dunnage). **SIC:** 5088 (Transportation Equipment & Supplies). **Officers:** Frank Drayton, General Manager and Purchasing Agent.

■ **18553** ■ **M & E Marine Supply, Inc.**
PO Box 601, Rte. 130
Collingswood, NJ 08108
Phone: (609)858-1010
Products: Marine supplies (dunnage). **SIC:** 5088
(Transportation Equipment & Supplies).

■ **18554** ■ **Mackinaw Sales Inc.**
2955 Crestwood Cir.
East Lansing, MI 48823
Phone: (517)351-7210 **Fax:** (517)351-7210
Products: Outdoor goods and supplies; Marine
equipment and supplies. **SIC:** 5091 (Sporting &
Recreational Goods).

■ **18555** ■ **Magee Marine Supply**
9946 Fancher Rd.
Brewerton, NY 13029-9762
Phone: (315)676-2411
Products: Marine supplies (dunnage). **SIC:** 5088
(Transportation Equipment & Supplies).

■ **18556** ■ **Manset Marine Supply Co.**
PO Box 709
Rockland, ME 04841
Phone: (207)596-6464
Free: (800)322-6500 **Fax:** (207)596-5615
Products: Marine equipment, including boats. **SIC:**
5088 (Transportation Equipment & Supplies).

■ **18557** ■ **Marathon Boat Yard**
2059 Overseas Hwy.
Marathon, FL 33050
Phone: (305)743-6641
Products: Marine supplies (dunnage). **SIC:** 5088
(Transportation Equipment & Supplies). **Officers:**
Diane Van Buren, General Mgr.

■ **18558** ■ **Marco Marine Seattle, IMFS Div.**
2300 W Commodore Way
Seattle, WA 98199
Phone: (206)285-3200 **Fax:** (206)282-8520
E-mail: ror@marcoseattle.com
Products: Marine equipment and supplies;
Commercial fishing products. **SICs:** 5088
(Transportation Equipment & Supplies); 5091 (Sporting
& Recreational Goods). **Est:** 1953. **Emp:** 300.

■ **18559** ■ **Marine Equipment & Supply**
1401 Metropolitan Ave.
PO Box 598
Thorofare, NJ 08086
Phone: (856)853-8320
Free: (800)257-7908 **Fax:** (856)853-1858
Products: Marine supplies (dunnage); Shrink wrap;
Remanufactured engines. **SICs:** 5088 (Transportation
Equipment & Supplies); 5091 (Sporting & Recreational
Goods). **Est:** 1910. **Emp:** 80. **Officers:** Donald
Kirkland Jr., President; Jim Del Cioppo, VP of
Marketing & Sales. **Also Known by This Acronym:**
MESCO.

■ **18560** ■ **Marine & Industrial Supply**
8330 Harry Hines Blvd.
Dallas, TX 75235
Phone: (214)631-2300 **Fax:** (214)631-5124
Products: Marine supplies (dunnage). **SIC:** 5088
(Transportation Equipment & Supplies).

■ **18561** ■ **Marine Rescue Products Inc.**
PO Box 3484
Newport, RI 02840-0991
Phone: (401)847-9144 **Fax:** (401)848-9577
Products: Lifeguard equipment; First aid equipment.
SIC: 5088 (Transportation Equipment & Supplies).
Officers: Rian Wilkinson, President.

■ **18562** ■ **Marinovich Trawl Co.**
PO Box 1416
Biloxi, MS 39533-1416
Phone: (228)436-6429
Products: Marine supplies (dunnage). **SIC:** 5088
(Transportation Equipment & Supplies). **Officers:**
Steve Marinovich, General Mgr.

■ **18563** ■ **Maschmedt and Associates**
12304 32nd Ave. NE
Seattle, WA 98125
Phone: (206)364-6304
Products: Boating equipment and supplies. **SIC:** 5088
(Transportation Equipment & Supplies). **Sales:**
$11,000,000 (1993). **Emp:** 40. **Officers:** Bob
Maschmedt, President.

■ **18564** ■ **McCaughey Brothers**
500 Bay Flat Rd.
Bodega Bay, CA 94923
Phone: (707)875-3935
Products: Marine supplies (dunnage). **SIC:** 5088
(Transportation Equipment & Supplies). **Officers:** Ned
McCaughey, General Manager and Purchasing Agent.

■ **18565** ■ **McGill Distributors**
1903 Longstreet St. N
Kingstree, SC 29556
Phone: (803)354-7404 **Fax:** (803)354-3263
Products: Marine supplies (dunnage). **SIC:** 5088
(Transportation Equipment & Supplies).

■ **18566** ■ **Melvin Village Marina Inc.**
PO Box 165
Melvin Village, NH 03850-0165
Phone: (603)544-3583
Products: Boats, motors, and trailers. **SIC:** 5088
(Transportation Equipment & Supplies). **Officers:**
Thomas Young, President.

■ **18567** ■ **Merritt Marine Supply**
2621 NE 4th St.
Pompano Beach, FL 33064
Phone: (954)946-5350
Products: Marine supplies (dunnage). **SIC:** 5088
(Transportation Equipment & Supplies). **Officers:** Jim
Hogan, General Manager and Purchasing Agent.

■ **18568** ■ **Mid-South Engine Systems Inc.**
2063 Bonn St.
Harvey, LA 70058
Phone: (504)347-2470
Products: Marine engines. **SIC:** 5088 (Transportation
Equipment & Supplies).

■ **18569** ■ **Midnight Sun Boat Company, Inc.**
201 N Bragaw St.
Anchorage, AK 99508
Phone: (907)279-3925 **Fax:** (907)279-6325
Products: Marine supplies(dunnage). **SIC:** 5088
(Transportation Equipment & Supplies). **Est:** 1958.
Sales: $1,000,000 (2000). **Emp:** 4.

■ **18570** ■ **Midwest Marine Supply Co.**
24300 E Jefferson Ave.
St. Clair Shores, MI 48080
Phone: (810)778-8950
Free: (800)860-1540 **Fax:** (810)778-6108
Products: Marine equipment, including engines, parts,
paint, epoxy, air conditioning, pumps, and steering
systems. **SIC:** 5088 (Transportation Equipment &
Supplies). **Est:** 1968. **Emp:** 10. **Officers:** Mike
Kennedy, Vice President; Bob Kennedy, President.

■ **18571** ■ **Moes Marine Service**
2022 W Wind Rd.
Oshkosh, WI 54901
Phone: (920)231-2799 **Fax:** (920)231-0442
Products: Marine parts and accessories. **SIC:** 5088
(Transportation Equipment & Supplies).

■ **18572** ■ **J.A. Moody Co.**
Phoenixville Pike
Malvern, PA 19355
Phone: (215)647-3810 **Fax:** (215)647-3833
Products: Marine valves and power fluid equipment.
SIC: 5085 (Industrial Supplies). **Sales:** $10,000,000
(2000). **Emp:** 12. **Officers:** Frank E. Buzan, President.

■ **18573** ■ **Morgan Recreational Supply**
7263 Victor Pittsford Rd., Box F
Victor, NY 14564
Phone: (716)924-7188 **Fax:** (716)924-4410
Products: Marine supplies (dunnage). **SIC:** 5088
(Transportation Equipment & Supplies). **Officers:** Scott
Scudder, General Mgr.; Tim Prokop, Purchasing Agent.

■ **18574** ■ **Nabo Industries**
31 Cornelia St.
New York, NY 10014
Phone: (212)645-6942 **Fax:** (212)645-6853
Products: Kayaks, boat paddles, canoes, and water
sports equipment. **SIC:** 5091 (Sporting & Recreational
Goods). **Est:** 1991. **Officers:** Nicholas Daddazio,
President.

■ **18575** ■ **Nautical & Industrial Supply Inc.**
2536 SE Clayton St.
Stuart, FL 34997
Phone: (561)283-4010
Free: (800)343-7592 **Fax:** (561)283-4327
Products: Marine, auto, aircraft paint, and refinishing
supplies; Specialty industrial supplies. **SICs:** 5088
(Transportation Equipment & Supplies); 5085
(Industrial Supplies). **Est:** 1969. **Officers:** Ben Posdal.

■ **18576** ■ **Ocean Products Research, Inc.**
Rte. 645
Diggs, VA 23045
Phone: (804)725-3406
Free: (800)627-6008 **Fax:** (804)725-4906
E-mail: opradmin@inna.net
URL: http://www.opr-rope.com
Products: Industrial fishing products, including rope
and net; Paint. **SICs:** 5085 (Industrial Supplies); 5198
(Paints, Varnishes & Supplies); 5088 (Transportation
Equipment & Supplies). **Est:** 1964. **Sales:** $3,200,000
(2000). **Emp:** 20. **Officers:** James M. Hutson, Vice
President, e-mail: tuygieii@inna.net.

■ **18577** ■ **Ocean State Yacht Brokerage and
Marine Services**
801 Oaklawn Ave.
Cranston, RI 02920-2819
Phone: (401)946-2628
Products: Transportation equipment and supplies;
Marine crafts and supplies. **SIC:** 5088 (Transportation
Equipment & Supplies). **Officers:** Ronald Cataldi,
President.

■ **18578** ■ **Oceana Ltd.**
1811 VA St.
PO Box 6691
Annapolis, MD 21401
Phone: (410)269-6022 **Fax:** (410)268-6528
Products: Marine supplies (dunnage); Aircraft parts
and auxiliary equipment. **SIC:** 5088 (Transportation
Equipment & Supplies). **Est:** 1980. **Officers:** Ross
Glover.

■ **18579** ■ **Overtons Sports Center, Inc.**
111 Red Banks Rd.
Greenville, NC 27835
Phone: (919)355-7600
Products: Marine supplies (dunnage). **SIC:** 5088
(Transportation Equipment & Supplies). **Officers:**
Warren Rogers, Purchasing Agent.

■ **18580** ■ **Pacific O.E.M. Supply**
3500 W Garry Ave.
Santa Ana, CA 92704
Phone: (714)688-5795 **Fax:** (714)668-5799
Products: Marine supplies (dunnage). **SIC:** 5088
(Transportation Equipment & Supplies). **Officers:**
George Uyemura, Owner.

■ **18581** ■ **Padre Island Supply**
9830 S Padre Island Dr.
Corpus Christi, TX 78418
Phone: (512)937-1473
Products: Marine supplies (dunnage). **SIC:** 5088
(Transportation Equipment & Supplies). **Officers:** Bill
Fortran, Owner; Susan Parsons, Purchasing Agent.

■ **18582** ■ **Paxton Company Inc.**
PO Box 12103
Norfolk, VA 23541
Phone: (757)853-6781
Free: (800)234-7290 **Fax:** (757)853-7709
Products: Industrial marine equipment. **SIC:** 5088
(Transportation Equipment & Supplies). **Sales:**
$53,000,000 (2000). **Emp:** 70. **Officers:** Guy Beale Jr.,
President; Margaret Beale, Treasurer & Secty.

■ **18583** ■ **Performance Catamarans Inc.**
1800 E Borchard Ave.
Santa Ana, CA 92705-4694
Phone: (714)835-6416 **Fax:** (714)541-6643
Products: Boats. **SIC:** 5091 (Sporting & Recreational
Goods). **Est:** 1988. **Sales:** $3,000,000 (2000). **Emp:**
49.

■ **18584** ■ **Port Supply**
500 Westridge Dr.
Watsonville, CA 95076
Phone: (831)728-4417
Free: (800)621-6885 **Fax:** 800-825-7678
E-mail: custserv@portsupply.com
URL: http://www.portsupply.com
Products: Marine supplies. **SIC:** 5088 (Transportation
Equipment & Supplies). **Est:** 1978. **Sales:**
$100,000,000 (2000). **Emp:** 100. **Officers:** Scott Miller,
General Mgr.

■ **18585** ■ **Porta-Bote International**
1074 Independence Ave.
Mountain View, CA 94043
Phone: (650)961-5334
Free: (800)227-8882 **Fax:** (650)961-3800
E-mail: dist@porta-bote.com
URL: http://www.porta-bote.com
Products: Boats. **SIC:** 5091 (Sporting & Recreational
Goods). **Est:** 1973. **Officers:** Sandy Kaye, President;
Paul Mintz, Vice President.

■ **18586** ■ **Post Marine**
65 River St.
New Rochelle, NY 10801
Phone: (914)235-9800 **Fax:** (914)235-9008
URL: http://www.postmarine.com
Products: Marine supplies (dunnage). **SIC:** 5088
(Transportation Equipment & Supplies). **Est:** 1918.
Sales: $5,000,000 (2000). **Emp:** 21. **Officers:** Mike
Gravinese, President.

■ **18587** ■ **Post Yacht Supplies**
PO Box 571
Manasquan, NJ 08736-0571
Phone: (732)892-2214 **Fax:** (732)899-7903
Products: Marine supplies (dunnage). **SIC:** 5088
(Transportation Equipment & Supplies). **Officers:** Tom
Adams, General Manager and Purchasing Agent.

■ **18588** ■ **Proper Tighe Marine**
PO Box 537
Danville, CA 94526-0537
Products: Marine supplies (dunnage). **SIC:** 5088
(Transportation Equipment & Supplies). **Officers:** Kirby
Eaton, General Mgr.; Rocky Santaferraro, Purchasing
Agent.

■ **18589** ■ **Radar Marine Electronics**
16 Squalicum Mall
Bellingham, WA 98225
Phone: (206)733-2012 **Fax:** (206)733-2383
Products: Marine electronics. **SIC:** 5065 (Electronic
Parts & Equipment Nec). **Emp:** 8. **Officers:** William E.
Pulse.

■ **18590** ■ **Radio Holland U.S.A.**
8943 Gulf Fwy.
Houston, TX 77017
Phone: (713)943-3325
Products: Marine electronics. **SICs:** 5063 (Electrical
Apparatus & Equipment); 5065 (Electronic Parts &
Equipment Nec). **Officers:** Jacob Plenter, CEO.

■ **18591** ■ **Reilly-Benton Company Inc.**
1645 Tchoupitoulas St.
New Orleans, LA 70152
Phone: (504)586-1711
Products: Boat insulation. **SIC:** 5088 (Transportation
Equipment & Supplies). **Est:** 1941. **Sales:** $11,000,000
(2000). **Emp:** 50. **Officers:** Warren K. Watters,
President; Balad Tebo, Vice President.

■ **18592** ■ **Rockland Boat, Inc.**
20 Park Dr.
Rockland, ME 04841
Phone: (207)594-8181 **Fax:** (207)594-8161
Products: Marine supplies. **SIC:** 5088 (Transportation
Equipment & Supplies).

■ **18593** ■ **Rockland Marine Corp.**
79 Mechanic St.
Rockland, ME 04841
Phone: (207)594-7860 **Fax:** (207)594-8032
E-mail: rockmar@medcoast.com
Products: Marine supplies(dunnage). **SIC:** 5088
(Transportation Equipment & Supplies). **Est:** 1991.
Sales: $2,000,000 (2000). **Emp:** 30.

■ **18594** ■ **Rolls Battery Engineering Inc.**
PO Box 671
Salem, MA 01970
Phone: (508)745-3333 **Fax:** (508)741-8956
Products: Marine batteries. **SIC:** 5063 (Electrical
Apparatus & Equipment). **Est:** 1956. **Sales:**
$7,000,000 (2000). **Emp:** 5. **Officers:** John J. Surrette,
President.

■ **18595** ■ **Roloff Manufacturing Corp.**
PO Box 7002
Kaukauna, WI 54130-7002
Phone: (920)766-3501 **Fax:** (920)766-3896
E-mail: rmfgcorp@execpd.com
URL: http://www.roloffanchors.com
Products: Marine anchors and accessories; Dock
fittings; Gray iron castings. **SICs:** 5088 (Transportation
Equipment & Supplies); 5091 (Sporting & Recreational
Goods). **Est:** 1944. **Emp:** 50. **Officers:** R.J. Roloff,
President & Treasurer; Harold W. Roloff, Chairman of
the Board; D.H. Roloff, Vice President; Danielle J.
Heraly, Human Resources Contact.

■ **18596** ■ **Rotometals Inc.**
980 Harrison St.
San Francisco, CA 94107
Phone: (415)392-3285
Free: (800)779-1102 **Fax:** (415)896-1636
Products: Ship equipment, including anodes. **SIC:**
5051 (Metals Service Centers & Offices). **Est:** 1939.
Sales: $2,000,000 (2000). **Emp:** 4. **Officers:** Gary
Hora, President.

■ **18597** ■ **Sailing Inc.**
5401 N Marginal Rd.
Cleveland, OH 44114
Free: (800)450-7245 **Fax:** (216)361-0996
Products: Boats. **SIC:** 5091 (Sporting & Recreational
Goods).

■ **18598** ■ **The Sailor's Supply**
231 E Beach Dr.
Panama City, FL 32401
Phone: (850)769-5007
Products: Marine supplies (dunnage). **SIC:** 5088
(Transportation Equipment & Supplies).

■ **18599** ■ **Salks Hardware & Marine Inc.**
2524 W Shore Rd.
Warwick, RI 02886-3848
Phone: (401)739-1027
Products: Marine supplies. **SIC:** 5088 (Transportation
Equipment & Supplies). **Officers:** Harold Salk,
President.

■ **18600** ■ **Paul R. Salomon Co.**
5000 Grand River St.
Detroit, MI 48208
Phone: (313)894-2323 **Fax:** (313)894-5816
E-mail: sales@paulnslaeomonmsn.com
URL: http://www.paulnsalomsn.com
Products: Marine supplies; Electric supplies; Dry cell
batteries; Light bulbs; Fishing tackle; Netting. **SICs:**
5088 (Transportation Equipment & Supplies); 5063
(Electrical Apparatus & Equipment); 5091 (Sporting &
Recreational Goods). **Est:** 1936. **Sales:** $1,650,000
(2000). **Emp:** 6. **Officers:** Marvin Salomon, Gen. Mgr.
and Purchasing Agent.

■ **18601** ■ **San Diego Marine Exchange**
2636 Shelter Island Dr.
San Diego, CA 92106
Phone: (619)223-7159
Free: (800)336-SDMX **Fax:** (619)223-7586
E-mail: www.sandiegomarine.com
Products: Marine supplies. **SIC:** 5088 (Transportation
Equipment & Supplies). **Est:** 1957. **Sales:** $8,000,000
(1999). **Emp:** 30. **Officers:** Dale Donnelly, Owner;
Jerry Pollard, General Mgr.

■ **18602** ■ **Sea Coast Distributors, Inc.**
105 Wartburg Ave.
Copiague, NY 11726
Phone: (516)842-2338
Free: (800)645-5857 **Fax:** (516)842-2021
Products: Marine equipment and supplies. **SIC:** 5088
(Transportation Equipment & Supplies). **Est:** 1978.
Sales: $4,000,000 (2000). **Emp:** 25. **Officers:** Ron
Destefanis, President; Walter Werner.

■ **18603** ■ **Sea Containers America Inc.**
1155 Ave. of the Amer.
New York, NY 10036
Phone: (212)302-5055
Products: Marine sports advertising materials. **SIC:**
5088 (Transportation Equipment & Supplies). **Est:**
1965. **Sales:** $8,000,000 (2000). **Emp:** 16. **Officers:** R.
Lynch, President; L. Mazure, Controller.

■ **18604** ■ **Seaboard Manufacturing Co.**
2010 Atlantic Hwy.
Warren, ME 04864
Phone: (207)273-2718
Products: Lobster traps and trap building supplies.
SIC: 5088 (Transportation Equipment & Supplies). **Est:**
1958. **Sales:** $990,000 (2000). **Emp:** 6. **Officers:** Jeff
Kenniston, Owner.

■ **18605** ■ **Seaboard Marine**
2947 W 5th St.
Oxnard, CA 93030
Products: Marine equipment and supplies. **SIC:** 5088
(Transportation Equipment & Supplies). **Est:** 1982.

■ **18606** ■ **Sealand Power Industries, Inc.**
568 E Elizabeth Ave.
PO Box 1400
Linden, NJ 07036-0004
Phone: (908)486-7600
Free: (800)225-0004 **Fax:** (908)486-1056
Products: Marine, industrial, and military parts and
equipment. **SIC:** 5088 (Transportation Equipment &
Supplies).

■ **18607** ■ **Seaside Supply Stores**
803 S Palos Verdes
San Pedro, CA 90731-3719
Phone: (310)831-0251 **Fax:** (310)514-2951
E-mail: seaside@pacbell.net
Products: Marine hardware; Marine and industrial
supply. **SIC:** 5088 (Transportation Equipment &
Supplies). **Est:** 1941. **Sales:** $2,600,000 (1999). **Emp:**
10. **Officers:** John Meyers; Mario Meyers.

■ **18608** ■ **Seattle Marine Industrial Division**
2121 W Commodore
Seattle, WA 98199-0098
Phone: (206)285-5010 **Fax:** (206)285-7925
Products: Marine supplies including hardware, tools,
and commercial fishing gear. **SICs:** 5091 (Sporting &
Recreational Goods); 5072 (Hardware).

■ **18609** ■ **Seattle Ship Supply**
PO Box 70438
Seattle, WA 98107-0438
Phone: (206)283-7000
Products: Marine supplies (dunnage). **SIC:** 5088
(Transportation Equipment & Supplies). **Officers:** Ted
Bautom, General Mgr.; Rick Reinholsten, Purchasing
Agent.

■ **18610** ■ **Shores Marine**
24910 Jefferson
St. Clair Shores, MI 48080
Phone: (810)778-3200
Products: Marine supplies (dunnage). **SIC:** 5088
(Transportation Equipment & Supplies). **Officers:** Mike
Tusa Sr., General Mgr.; Mike Tusa Jr., Purchasing
Agent.

■ **18611** ■ **Skipper Shop**
PO Box 519
Puerto Real, PR 00740
Phone: (787)863-5530 **Fax:** (787)860-2360
Products: Boats. **SIC:** 5091 (Sporting & Recreational
Goods).

■ 18612 ■ Larry Smith Electronics
1619 Broadway
Riviera Beach, FL 33404-5627
Phone: (561)844-3592 **Fax:** (561)844-1608
E-mail: isei@gate.net
URL: http://www.marine-electronics.com
Products: Marine electronics. **SICs:** 5088 (Transportation Equipment & Supplies); 5088 (Transportation Equipment & Supplies). **Est:** 1956. **Emp:** 46. **Officers:** Larry Smith; Tom Lambert.

■ 18613 ■ Spartan Lobster Traps Inc.
4 Walts Way
Narragansett, RI 02882-3438
Phone: (401)789-5350
Products: Transportation equipment and supplies; Marine crafts and supplies. **SIC:** 5088 (Transportation Equipment & Supplies). **Officers:** Bruce Kopf, President.

■ 18614 ■ Standard Marine Supply Co.
Stock Island/Div.
1st & Maloney Ave.
Key West, FL 33040
Phone: (305)294-2515
Products: Marine supplies (dunnage). **SIC:** 5088 (Transportation Equipment & Supplies). **Officers:** Elton Brewer, General Mgr.

■ 18615 ■ Standard Marine Supply Co.
2nd & Alachua St.
PO Box 477
Fernandina Beach, FL 32034
Phone: (904)261-3671
Products: Marine supplies (dunnage). **SIC:** 5088 (Transportation Equipment & Supplies). **Officers:** David Hardee, General Manager and Purchasing Agent.

■ 18616 ■ Standard Marine Supply Corp.
120 N 20th St.
PO Box 5001
Tampa, FL 33675
Phone: (813)248-2905 **Fax:** (813)247-4386
Products: Marine hardware. **SIC:** 5088 (Transportation Equipment & Supplies). **Officers:** James Hardee Jr., General Manager and Purchasing Agent.

■ 18617 ■ Clarence Sterling & Son
1014 W Main St.
Crisfield, MD 21817
Phone: (410)968-1222
Products: Marine supplies (dunnage). **SIC:** 5088 (Transportation Equipment & Supplies). **Officers:** John Somers, General Manager and Purchasing Agent.

■ 18618 ■ Stover Greenlight Auto & Marine
Rte. 1, Junction 52 & N
Stover, MO 65078
Phone: (573)377-4621
Products: Marine supplies (dunnage). **SIC:** 5088 (Transportation Equipment & Supplies). **Officers:** Bob Blonstein, President; Diane Blonstein, Vice President.

■ 18619 ■ Norman Sutliff & Son
PO Box 1157
Kodiak, AK 99615
Phone: (907)486-5797
Products: Marine supplies (dunnage). **SIC:** 5088 (Transportation Equipment & Supplies).

■ 18620 ■ Svendsen's Boat Works
1851 Clement Ave.
Alameda, CA 94501
Phone: (510)522-2886 **Fax:** (510)522-0870
Products: Marine supplies and equipment; Full-service boat repair yard; Metal and rail maker shop on site. **SIC:** 5088 (Transportation Equipment & Supplies). **Officers:** Svend Svendsen, President.

■ 18621 ■ Svendsen's Marine Distribution
1851 Clement Ave.
Alameda, CA 94501
Phone: (510)522-7860
Free: (800)824-2391 **Fax:** (510)522-0870
URL: http://www.svendsens.com
Products: Marine supplies; Marine hardware. **SIC:** 5088 (Transportation Equipment & Supplies). **Officers:**

Sven Svendsen, General Mgr.; Don McLeish, Purchasing Agent.

■ 18622 ■ Tacoma Fiberglass
2406 Port of Tacoma Rd.
Tacoma, WA 98422
Phone: (253)272-1258
Products: Marine supplies (dunnage). **SIC:** 5088 (Transportation Equipment & Supplies). **Officers:** Bob Reed, General Manager and Purchasing Agent.

■ 18623 ■ Nelson A. Taylor Company Inc.
66 Kingsboro Ave.
Gloversville, NY 12078
Phone: (518)725-0681 **Fax:** (518)725-4335
URL: http://www.taylormadegroup.com
Products: Flags, boat covers, and windshields. **SICs:** 5091 (Sporting & Recreational Goods); 5013 (Motor Vehicle Supplies & New Parts); 5199 (Nondurable Goods Nec). **Est:** 1897. **Sales:** $137,000,000 (2000). **Emp:** 1,200. **Officers:** James W. Taylor, Chairman of the Board; Dennis Flint, President.

■ 18624 ■ Thego Corporation/Acme Marine Hoist, inc.
690 Montauk Hwy.
Bayport, NY 11705
Phone: (516)472-3030 **Fax:** (516)472-3103
Products: Marine supplies; Boat hoists. **SIC:** 5088 (Transportation Equipment & Supplies). **Est:** 1957. **Sales:** $2,000,000 (2000). **Emp:** 8. **Officers:** Hugo Klingele, President; Carole Catera, Secretary.

■ 18625 ■ Tiger Enterprises
Columbia Falls Rd.
Addison, ME 04606
Phone: (207)483-6000 **Fax:** (207)483-4729
Products: Boat equipment and supplies. **SICs:** 5091 (Sporting & Recreational Goods); 5088 (Transportation Equipment & Supplies).

■ 18626 ■ Ullman Sails
957 N Lime Ave.
Sarasota, FL 34237
Phone: (941)951-0189 **Fax:** (941)955-4758
Products: Sailboats. **SIC:** 5091 (Sporting & Recreational Goods).

■ 18627 ■ United Marine Inc.
490 Northwind S River Dr.
Miami, FL 33128
Phone: (305)545-8445
Free: (800)432-5966 **Fax:** (305)325-1241
Products: Boat accessories. **SIC:** 5088 (Transportation Equipment & Supplies). **Emp:** 120. **Officers:** Gary E. Scarborough.

■ 18628 ■ Universal Marine
1 Venetian Dr.
Portage Des Sioux, MO 63373
Phone: (314)899-0940
Free: (800)325-6123 **Fax:** (314)899-1101
Products: Marine supplies (dunnage). **SIC:** 5088 (Transportation Equipment & Supplies). **Est:** 1972. **Sales:** $500,000 (2000). **Emp:** 4. **Officers:** Warren Spielman, General Manager and Purchasing Agent; Jered Lee Bontradee.

■ 18629 ■ Vida Paint & Supply Co.
PO Box 2706
Morgan City, LA 70380
Phone: (504)385-2884 **Fax:** (504)385-0705
E-mail: vidamc@vidapaint.com
URL: http://www.vidapaint.com
Products: Marine supplies (dunnage). **SIC:** 5088 (Transportation Equipment & Supplies). **Est:** 1973. **Sales:** $5,000,000 (2000). **Emp:** 30. **Officers:** Jules Arceneaux, General Mgr.; Lee Shilling, Purchasing Agent; David L. Kirkpatrick, President.

■ 18630 ■ Vida Paint & Supply Co.
100 Bond St.
Houma, LA 70360
Phone: (504)868-1005 **Fax:** (504)873-9092
E-mail: vidahma@vidapaint.com
URL: http://www.vidapaint.com
Products: Marine supplies (dunnage). **SIC:** 5088 (Transportation Equipment & Supplies). **Officers:** Lester "Bif" Bourgeois, General Mgr.; Jimmy Hardin.

■ 18631 ■ Vita-Plate Battery, Inc.
PO Box 727
Port Clinton, OH 43452
Products: Marine supplies (dunnage). **SIC:** 5088 (Transportation Equipment & Supplies). **Officers:** Bob Ravis, General Mgr.; Dennis Howerth, Purchasing Agent.

■ 18632 ■ Warren Marine Supply Inc.
15 Read Ave.
Warren, RI 02885-2213
Phone: (401)245-5333
Products: Transportation equipment and supplies; Marine crafts and supplies. **SIC:** 5088 (Transportation Equipment & Supplies). **Officers:** Robert Frost, President.

■ 18633 ■ Washington Chain and Supply
PO Box 3645
Seattle, WA 98124
Phone: (206)623-8500
Free: (800)851-3429 **Fax:** (206)621-9834
E-mail: info@wachain.com
URL: http://www.wachain.com
Products: Marine supplies, including anchors, chains, wire rope, shackles, and blocks. **SICs:** 5088 (Transportation Equipment & Supplies); 5099 (Durable Goods Nec). **Est:** 1976. **Sales:** $9,000,000 (2000). **Emp:** 30. **Officers:** D. Castle, President; Bert Cehovet, Vice President; Darrell Castle, Sales/Marketing Contact, e-mail: darrell@wachain.com; Craig Clarey, Customer Service Contact, e-mail: craig@wachain.com.

■ 18634 ■ Washington Chain and Supply Inc.
PO Box 3645
Seattle, WA 98124
Phone: (206)623-8500 **Fax:** (206)621-9834
Products: Wholesales chains, shackles and bindings for marine, construction and transportation industries; Release hooks for mooring and towing. **SICs:** 5085 (Industrial Supplies); 5072 (Hardware). **Officers:** Darrell Castle, President.

■ 18635 ■ Washington Marina Co.
1300 Maine Ave. SW
Washington, DC 20024
Phone: (202)554-0222
Products: Marine supplies (dunnage). **SIC:** 5088 (Transportation Equipment & Supplies). **Officers:** Bob Stickell, General Mgr.; Allen Simmons, Purchasing Agent.

■ 18636 ■ Wesmac Enterprises
PO Box 606
Union, ME 04862-0606
Phone: (207)785-2636 **Fax:** (207)785-2635
Products: Transportation equipment and supplies; Marine crafts and supplies; Non-recreational boats; Fiberglass. **SICs:** 5088 (Transportation Equipment & Supplies); 5033 (Roofing, Siding & Insulation). **Officers:** Malcolm Pettegrow, Partner.

■ 18637 ■ West Marine Corp.
120 Allied Dr.
Dedham, MA 02026
Phone: (617)329-2430
Products: Boat accessories. **SIC:** 5088 (Transportation Equipment & Supplies). **Est:** 1850. **Sales:** $3,000,000 (2000). **Emp:** 12. **Officers:** Randy Repass, President.

■ 18638 ■ Wholesale Marine Supply Co. of Alaska, Inc.
PO Box 102900
Anchorage, AK 99510-2900
Phone: (907)279-7754 **Fax:** (907)279-6325
Products: Marine supplies (dunnage). **SIC:** 5088 (Transportation Equipment & Supplies). **Est:** 1958. **Emp:** 6. **Officers:** Stanley Pickles, President.

■ 18639 ■ Wilcox Marine Supply Inc.
PO Box 99
Mystic, CT 06355
Phone: (860)536-4206 **Fax:** (860)536-8326
Products: Boating supplies, including life jackets, waxes, and cleaners. **SIC:** 5088 (Transportation Equipment & Supplies).

■ 18640 ■ Wildwasser Sport U.S.A. Inc.
PO Box 4617
Boulder, CO 80306
Phone: (303)444-2336 **Fax:** (303)444-2375
E-mail: www.wildnet.com
Products: Kayaks. **SIC:** 5091 (Sporting & Recreational Goods). **Est:** 1984. **Sales:** $2,000,000 (2000). **Emp:** 15. **Officers:** Landis Arnold, President.

■ 18641 ■ Williams and Wells Corp.
100 State St.
Moonachie, NJ 07074
Phone: (201)440-1800
Products: Ship chandlers. **SIC:** 5088 (Transportation Equipment & Supplies). **Sales:** $26,000,000 (1993). **Emp:** 50. **Officers:** Stuart Margolins, President; Rene Mounier, Controller.

■ 18642 ■ Wind Line Sails
1524 Glencoe Ave.
Highland Park, IL 60035
Phone: (847)433-0551 **Fax:** (630)932-0622
Products: Boats. **SIC:** 5091 (Sporting & Recreational Goods).

■ 18643 ■ Wolf Warehouse Distributors
312 E Market St.
New Albany, IN 47150
Phone: (812)944-2264
Products: Marine supplies (dunnage). **SIC:** 5088 (Transportation Equipment & Supplies).

■ 18644 ■ World Trade Network, Ltd.
16920 28th Ave. N
Minneapolis, MN 55447
Phone: (763)473-3825 **Fax:** (763)473-3521
E-mail: ben@wtnltd.com
URL: http://www.wtnltd.com
Products: Marine electronics; Marine safety equipment; Industrial equipment and spare parts. **SICs:** 5088 (Transportation Equipment & Supplies); 5085 (Industrial Supplies); 5065 (Electronic Parts & Equipment Nec). **Est:** 1984. **Sales:** $2,000,000 (2000). **Emp:** 4. **Officers:** Ben Kyriagis, e-mail: ben@wtnlto.com.

■ 18645 ■ ZF Group NAO
7310 Turfway Rd. No. 450
Florence, KY 41042
Phone: (606)282-4300 **Fax:** (606)282-4311
SIC: 5013 (Motor Vehicle Supplies & New Parts). **Est:** 1979. **Emp:** 1,467. **Officers:** Jim Orchard, CEO.
Former Name: ZF Industries Inc.

■ 18646 ■ Zidell Marine Corp.
3121 SW Moody Ave.
Portland, OR 97201
Phone: (503)228-8691
Free: (800)547-9259 **Fax:** (503)228-6750
Products: Barges. **SIC:** 5088 (Transportation Equipment & Supplies). **Est:** 1952. **Sales:** $59,000,000 (2000). **Emp:** 100. **Officers:** Jay Zidell, President; Kathy Thompson, Treasurer. **Alternate Name:** Zidell Inc.

■ 18647 ■ Zimco Marine
400 Washington St.
PO Drawer AE
Port Isabel, TX 78578
Phone: (956)943-2762 **Fax:** (956)943-1405
E-mail: gwlzimco@aol.com
Products: Marine supplies (dunnage). **SIC:** 5088 (Transportation Equipment & Supplies). **Est:** 1986. **Emp:** 80. **Officers:** Walt Zimmerman, Owner; Inocente Zurita, Operations Mgr.

■ 18648 ■ Jerry Zimmerman
253 Molasses Ln.
Mt. Pleasant, SC 29464
Phone: (803)881-1223 **Fax:** (803)881-1223
Products: Boats. **SIC:** 5091 (Sporting & Recreational Goods).

■ 18649 ■ Zodiac of North America
PO Box 400
Stevensville, MD 21666
Phone: (410)643-4141 **Fax:** (410)643-4491
E-mail: info@zodiac.com
URL: http://www.zodiac.com
Products: Inflatable boats and life rafts. **SICs:** 5091 (Sporting & Recreational Goods); 5088 (Transportation Equipment & Supplies). **Est:** 1965. **Officers:** J.J. Marie, President.

(33) Medical, Dental, and Optical Equipment

Entries in this section are arranged alphabetically by company name. When the company name is a personal name, the company name is alphabetized by the surname unless the first name or initial(s) are part of a trade name. See the User's Guide at the front of this directory for additional information.

■ 18650 ■ **21st Century Holdings Inc.**
2170 W State Rd. 434, Ste. 200
Longwood, FL 32779
Phone: (407)880-7200
Products: Electro-therapy devices. **SIC:** 5047 (Medical & Hospital Equipment). **Sales:** $1,300,000 (1990). **Emp:** 12. **Officers:** John Frankum, President; Thomas V. Behan, CFO.

■ 18651 ■ **A & A Reconditioned Medical**
8601 Kenilworth Dr.
Springfield, VA 22151
Phone: (703)978-4510
Products: Used medical equipment. **SIC:** 5047 (Medical & Hospital Equipment). **Officers:** Bill Peabody, Owner.

■ 18652 ■ **A-Dec International Inc.**
PO Box 111
Newberg, OR 97132-0111
Phone: (503)538-9471 **Fax:** (503)537-2742
Products: Dental equipment and supplies. **SIC:** 5047 (Medical & Hospital Equipment). **Officers:** George Austin, President.

■ 18653 ■ **A & W Medical & Oxygen Supply**
100 Sampson St.
Clinton, NC 28328-4037
Phone: (910)592-3882 **Fax:** (910)592-2120
Products: Medical equipment; Hospital equipment. **SIC:** 5047 (Medical & Hospital Equipment). **Officers:** Charles Adams, President.

■ 18654 ■ **A-Welders & Medical Supply**
PO Box 3457
Knoxville, TN 37927-3457
Phone: (865)522-8350 **Fax:** (865)522-8414
Products: Medical and hospital equipment and supplies; Industrial welding supplies; Medical and industrial gases. **SICs:** 5047 (Medical & Hospital Equipment); 5085 (Industrial Supplies). **Officers:** Glenn Madgett, President.

■ 18655 ■ **Abbey Pharmaceutical Services Inc.**
1771 W Diehl Rd.
Naperville, IL 60563
Phone: (630)305-8000 **Fax:** (630)305-8190
Products: Catheters and feeding tubes. **SIC:** 5047 (Medical & Hospital Equipment). **Est:** 1987. **Sales:** $75,000,000 (2000). **Emp:** 175. **Officers:** Tim Burfield, President.

■ 18656 ■ **Accutron Inc.**
2020 W Melinda Ln.
Phoenix, AZ 85027
Phone: (602)780-2020 **Fax:** (602)780-0444
Products: Medical and hospital equipment; Dental equipment and supplies. **SIC:** 5047 (Medical & Hospital Equipment). **Officers:** Raymond Blasdell, Treasurer.

■ 18657 ■ **Adco Inc.**
1320 Leighton Ave., Ste. B
Anniston, AL 36201-4614
Phone: (205)236-2593
Products: Medical and hospital equipment and supplies, including hearing aids. **SIC:** 5047 (Medical &

Hospital Equipment). **Officers:** Don Whitlow, Vice President.

■ 18658 ■ **ADCO Surgical Supply Inc.**
PO Box 1328
Bangor, ME 04402-1328
Phone: (207)942-5273
Free: (800)727-5273 **Fax:** (207)941-9392
URL: http://www.medicalmailorder.com
Products: Surgical equipment and supplies. **SIC:** 5047 (Medical & Hospital Equipment). **Est:** 1963. **Sales:** $6,000,000 (2000). **Emp:** 32. **Officers:** William J. Clifford Jr., VP & General Mgr.; Karen Wright, Controller; Diane Simpson, Sales Mgr.; Kurt Kitchen, Dir. of Data Processing.

■ 18659 ■ **Adtek Co.**
PO Box 264
Sellersburg, IN 47172-0264
Phone: (812)246-5418 **Fax:** (812)246-6107
Products: X-Ray equipment and consumables. **SIC:** 5047 (Medical & Hospital Equipment). **Est:** 1984. **Sales:** $20,000,000 (2000). **Emp:** 23. **Officers:** A. Snyder, President.

■ 18660 ■ **Advanced Imaging Technologies Inc.**
212 S Hydraulic St., Ste. 200
Wichita, KS 67211
Phone: (316)267-7844 **Fax:** (316)267-1345
Products: X-Ray equipment and supplies. **SIC:** 5047 (Medical & Hospital Equipment). **Est:** 1985. **Sales:** $6,000,000 (2000). **Emp:** 29. **Officers:** Michael G. Puls, President.

■ 18661 ■ **Advanced Medical Systems Inc.**
935 Horsham Rd., Ste. M
Horsham, PA 19044
Phone: (215)443-5424
Free: (800)473-5414 **Fax:** (215)672-6740
Products: I.V. lines. **SIC:** 5047 (Medical & Hospital Equipment). **Est:** 1980. **Sales:** $7,000,000 (2000). **Emp:** 30. **Officers:** John Sasso, President; Veronica Haug, Vice President; David Lloyd, VP of Sales.

■ 18662 ■ **Advanced Scientific Inc.**
PO Box 101
Chalmette, LA 70044-0101
Phone: (504)277-7562 **Fax:** (504)277-7566
Products: Medical equipment; Hospital equipment. **SIC:** 5047 (Medical & Hospital Equipment). **Officers:** Ronald Zibilich, President.

■ 18663 ■ **Aero Products Corp.**
700 Aero Ln.
Sanford, FL 32771-6656
Phone: (407)330-5911 **Fax:** (407)331-3528
Products: Emergency medical equipment, including back boards and bandages. **SIC:** 5047 (Medical & Hospital Equipment). **Est:** 1979. **Sales:** $35,000,000 (2000). **Emp:** 120. **Officers:** Scott L. Barnes, President.

■ 18664 ■ **Affiliated Medical Research**
180 Robert Curry Dr.
Martinsville, IN 46151-8076
Phone: (765)342-0578 **Fax:** (765)342-0719
Products: Medical and surgical equipment and supplies. **SIC:** 5047 (Medical & Hospital Equipment). **Est:** 1976. **Sales:** $10,000,000 (2000). **Emp:** 10. **Officers:** Daniel Hallman, President.

■ 18665 ■ **Airgas Safety**
PO Box 1010
W185 N11300 Whitney Dr.
Germantown, WI 53022-8210
Phone: (414)255-7300
Free: (800)558-8900 **Fax:** (414)255-7307
URL: http://www.airgas.com
Products: First aid and industrial equipment. **SICs:** 5047 (Medical & Hospital Equipment); 5084 (Industrial Machinery & Equipment). **Est:** 1944. **Emp:** 300. **Officers:** Jim Meyer, Exec. VP.

■ 18666 ■ **Akin Industries, Inc.**
147 Commerce Dr.
Monticello, AR 71655
Phone: (501)367-6263
Free: (800)395-2981 **Fax:** (501)367-5230
Products: Nursing home furniture, including tables, chairs, sofas and beds; Hospitality furniture. **SIC:** 5047 (Medical & Hospital Equipment). **Est:** 1985. **Sales:** $23,000,000 (2000). **Emp:** 180. **Officers:** Mike Akin, President; Richard Akin, Chairman of the Board.

■ 18667 ■ **AKMS, Inc.**
PO Box 50329
Columbia, SC 29250
Phone: (803)695-5001 **Fax:** (803)695-1997
E-mail: staff@braceguard.com
URL: http://www.braceguard.com
Products: Orthodontic brace shields. **SIC:** 5047 (Medical & Hospital Equipment). **Est:** 1983. **Officers:** Dr. A. Keith Amstutz, President. **Former Name:** A-K Medical Software Inc.

■ 18668 ■ **Aladdin Synergetics Inc.**
555 Marriot Dr., No. 400
Nashville, TN 37214
Phone: (615)748-3830
Free: (800)888-8018 **Fax:** (615)748-3678
E-mail: foodserv@aladdin-inc.com
URL: http://www.aladdin-inc.com
Products: Meal delivery systems. **SIC:** 5047 (Medical & Hospital Equipment). **Est:** 1968. **Officers:** Fred Meyer, General Mgr.; Marty Rothschild, VP of Marketing; Gary Yarbrough, New Business Development; Steve Avery, VP of Sales; Rich Nicorvo, VP of Finance.

■ 18669 ■ **ALARIS Medical Systems Inc.**
10221 Wateridge Cir.
San Diego, CA 92121
Phone: (619)458-7000 **Fax:** (619)458-7760
Products: Intravenous infusion and patient monitoring products. **SIC:** 5047 (Medical & Hospital Equipment). **Sales:** $140,700,000 (2000). **Emp:** 1,400. **Officers:** William J. Mercer, CEO & President.

■ 18670 ■ Aleutian Pribilof Island Association
201 E 3rd Ave.
Anchorage, AK 99501-2503
Phone: (907)276-2700 **Fax:** (907)276-4894
Products: Medical equipment; Janitors' supplies; Medicinal products. **SICs:** 5047 (Medical & Hospital Equipment); 5087 (Service Establishment Equipment).

■ 18671 ■ Alfreds Processor Sales & Service
122 W Union St.
Kenner, LA 70062-4822
Phone: (504)464-5914 **Fax:** (504)467-7423
Products: Medical equipment; Hospital equipment; X-ray apparatus. **SIC:** 5047 (Medical & Hospital Equipment). **Officers:** Alfred Williams, Owner.

■ 18672 ■ Allegiance Healthcare Corporation Hospital Supply/Scientific Products
1450 Waukegan Rd.
Mc Gaw Park, IL 60085
Phone: (847)689-8410
URL: http://www.allegiance.net
Products: Medical, surgical, and laboratory equipment and supplies. **SIC:** 5047 (Medical & Hospital Equipment). **Sales:** $4,500,000,000 (2000). **Emp:** 20,000. **Officers:** Lester B. Knight, CEO & Chairman of the Board.

■ 18673 ■ ALM Surgical Equipment Inc.
1820 N Lemon St.
Anaheim, CA 92801-1009
Phone: (714)578-1234 **Fax:** (714)540-7363
Products: Surgical supplies, including tables, lights, gas columns, headlamps, and video systems. **SIC:** 5047 (Medical & Hospital Equipment). **Sales:** $7,000,000 (2000). **Emp:** 80. **Officers:** George Crispin, President.

■ 18674 ■ American Ambulance
1401 E Washington St.
Phoenix, AZ 85034
Phone: (602)255-0131 **Fax:** (602)254-5362
Products: Ambulance equipment and supplies. **SIC:** 5047 (Medical & Hospital Equipment). **Est:** 1982. **Sales:** $1,000,000 (2000). **Emp:** 100. **Officers:** Howard Robinson, President.

■ 18675 ■ American Health Systems Inc.
PO Box 26688
Greenville, SC 29616-1688
Phone: (843)234-0496 **Fax:** (843)234-0499
Products: Medical and hospital equipment. **SIC:** 5047 (Medical & Hospital Equipment). **Sales:** $3,000,000 (1994). **Emp:** 50. **Officers:** Donald Bolt, President; Tammy Yeargin, Controller.

■ 18676 ■ American Homepatient, Inc.
42014 Veterans Ave.
Hammond, LA 70403
Phone: (504)542-4343
Free: (800)375-4343 **Fax:** (504)543-0254
Products: Respiratory equipment. **SIC:** 5047 (Medical & Hospital Equipment). **Officers:** William Hunt, General Mgr. **Former Name:** Lifecare Medical Inc.

■ 18677 ■ American Medical Export Inc.
316 Van Buren Ave.
Teaneck, NJ 07666
Phone: (201)836-1429
Products: Medical X-ray equipment; Electrocardiographs and electroencephalographs; Medical diagnostic apparatus. **SIC:** 5047 (Medical & Hospital Equipment). **Officers:** Marilyn C. Goodlow, Vice President.

■ 18678 ■ American Respiratory Inc.
3220 E 21st St.
Tulsa, OK 74114-1814
Phone: (918)664-9173 **Fax:** (918)747-4920
Products: Medical and hospital equipment and supplies. **SIC:** 5047 (Medical & Hospital Equipment). **Officers:** Dave Daniel, President.

■ 18679 ■ American Scientific Technology, L.L.C.
2541 Welland Ave. SE, Ste. A
Atlanta, GA 30316-4135
Phone: (404)243-6166 **Fax:** (404)243-6196
Products: Medical and hospital equipment and

supplies. **SIC:** 5047 (Medical & Hospital Equipment). **Officers:** Dean Heard, President. **Former Name:** New World Technology Inc.

■ 18680 ■ Amigo Mobility International Inc.
6693 Dixie Hwy.
Bridgeport, MI 48722
Phone: (517)777-0910
Free: (800)821-2710 **Fax:** (517)777-8184
E-mail: webmaster@myamigo.com
URL: http://www.myamigo.com
Products: Power operated vehicles. **SIC:** 5047 (Medical & Hospital Equipment). **Est:** 1968. **Sales:** $10,000,000 (1999). **Emp:** 94. **Officers:** Allan Thieme, President; Sara Kristal, Sales & Marketing Contact; Deb Kapa, Customer Service Contact; Andrea Lupo, Human Resources Contact.

■ 18681 ■ Anabolic Laboratories Inc.
17802 Gillette Ave.
Irvine, CA 92614
Phone: (949)863-0340
Products: Professional healthcare provider supplies. **SIC:** 5047 (Medical & Hospital Equipment). **Sales:** $44,000,000 (2000). **Emp:** 250. **Officers:** Steven Brown, President; Mark Nishi, Controller.

■ 18682 ■ Anderson Home Health Supply
4063 Henderson Blvd.
Tampa, FL 33629
Phone: (813)289-3811
Products: Home health care products. **SIC:** 5047 (Medical & Hospital Equipment). **Est:** 1981. **Sales:** $500,000 (2000). **Emp:** 3. **Officers:** Marianne S. Schweitzer, CEO; Richard J. Schweitzer, President; Christine Stapleton, President; Jon Pratt, Vice President.

■ 18683 ■ Anderson Medical Inc.
4024 Beresford Rd.
Charlotte, NC 28211-3808
Phone: (704)442-1990 **Fax:** (704)365-1779
Products: Medical equipment; Hospital equipment; Orthopedic appliances and parts. **SIC:** 5047 (Medical & Hospital Equipment). **Est:** 1986. **Officers:** Fred Anderson, President.

■ 18684 ■ Anderson's Wheelchair Therapeutic Supply
1117 2nd St. SW
Rochester, MN 55902-1936
Phone: (507)288-0113 **Fax:** (507)288-0410
Products: Medical equipment; Hospital equipment; Wheel chairs. **SIC:** 5047 (Medical & Hospital Equipment). **Officers:** Gretchen Anderson, President.

■ 18685 ■ Anesthesia Equipment Supply
24301 Roberts Dr.
Black Diamond, WA 98010-9205
Phone: (253)631-8008 **Fax:** (206)886-1350
Products: Medical and hospital equipment and supplies. **SIC:** 5047 (Medical & Hospital Equipment). **Officers:** Mario Sorci, President.

■ 18686 ■ Angeles Medical Supply Inc.
PO Box 2366
Port Angeles, WA 98362-0305
Phone: (425)452-4724 **Fax:** (206)457-3263
Products: Medical equipment; Hospital equipment; Hospital furniture; Oxygen tents. **SIC:** 5047 (Medical & Hospital Equipment). **Officers:** Gary Gano, President.

■ 18687 ■ Apex Medical Corp.
800 S Van Eps Ave.
PO Box 1235
Sioux Falls, SD 57101-1235
Phone: (605)332-6689
Free: (800)328-2935 **Fax:** (605)332-6818
E-mail: apexmed@apexmedical.com
URL: http://www.apexmedical.com
Products: Home health care products. **SIC:** 5047 (Medical & Hospital Equipment). **Est:** 1976. **Sales:** $10,000,000 (1999). **Emp:** 90. **Officers:** Rich Miller, Controller; Duane Wagner, VP of Operations; Brian Wicklow, VP of Marketing & Sales, e-mail: bwicklow@apexmedical.com.

■ 18688 ■ Archbold Health Services Inc.
400 Old Albany Rd.
Thomasville, GA 31792
Phone: (912)227-6800
Products: Medical equipment. **SIC:** 5047 (Medical & Hospital Equipment). **Sales:** $35,000,000 (2000). **Emp:** 128. **Officers:** Ken E. Beverly, President; Clay Campbell, Exec. VP of Finance.

■ 18689 ■ Area Access Inc.
8117 Ransell Rd.
Falls Church, VA 22042-1015
Phone: (703)573-2111
Free: (800)333-2732 **Fax:** (703)207-0446
URL: http://www.areaaccess.com
Products: Wheelchair lifts; Scooters; Elevators and handicapped vehicle modifications. **SIC:** 5047 (Medical & Hospital Equipment). **Est:** 1983. **Sales:** $3,000,000 (2000). **Emp:** 20. **Officers:** Scott Hobson, President; Cliff Wenn, Sales/Marketing Contact; Phil Reed, Customer Service Contact.

■ 18690 ■ Arizona Therapy Source
338 N 16th St.
Phoenix, AZ 85006-3706
Phone: (602)252-5891
Free: (800)996-3006 **Fax:** (602)252-7789
URL: http://www.aztherapysource.com
Products: Physical therapy equipment and supplies. **SIC:** 5047 (Medical & Hospital Equipment). **Est:** 1959. **Sales:** $350,000 (2000). **Emp:** 3. **Officers:** Alan Stotts, President. **Former Name:** Medical Electronics Sales & Service.

■ 18691 ■ Armstrong Medical Industries Inc.
PO Box 700
Lincolnshire, IL 60069
Phone: (847)913-0101 **Fax:** (847)913-0138
Products: Medical equipment. **SIC:** 5047 (Medical & Hospital Equipment). **Est:** 1957. **Emp:** 94. **Officers:** Warren G. Armstrong, President; Rose West, CFO; George Mede, VP of Marketing & Sales.

■ 18692 ■ Aseptico, Inc.
PO Box 1548
Woodinville, WA 98072-1548
Phone: (425)487-3157
Free: (800)426-5913 **Fax:** (360)668-8722
E-mail: info@aseptico.com
URL: http://www.aseptico.com
Products: Lab motors; Implant units; Endodontic units; Portable equipment. **SIC:** 5047 (Medical & Hospital Equipment). **Est:** 1975. **Sales:** $4,000,000 (2000). **Emp:** 50. **Officers:** Glenn Kazen, President; Doug Kazen, CFO; Ken Goff, Dir. of Marketing & Sales. **Former Name:** North Pacific Dental, Inc.

■ 18693 ■ Associated Healthcare Systems Inc.
85 Woodridge Dr.
West Amherst, NY 14228
Phone: (716)564-4500
Products: Medical equipment. **SIC:** 5047 (Medical & Hospital Equipment). **Sales:** $26,000,000 (2000). **Emp:** 90. **Officers:** Donald White, CEO & President; Scott Kovel, Finance Officer.

■ 18694 ■ Associated Medical Supply Inc.
15210 N 75th St.
Scottsdale, AZ 85260
Phone: (480)998-1684
Free: (800)637-2513 **Fax:** (480)991-3395
Products: Medical and hospital equipment; Veterinarian's supplies. **SIC:** 5047 (Medical & Hospital Equipment). **Officers:** Michael Shumsky, President.

■ 18695 ■ Associated X-Ray Corp.
PO Box 120559
East Haven, CT 06512-0559
Phone: (203)466-2446 **Fax:** (203)466-2448
Products: Medical equipment; Hospital equipment; Hospital furniture; X-ray apparatus. **SIC:** 5047 (Medical & Hospital Equipment). **Officers:** Gary Johnson, President.

■ 18696 ■ Atecs Corp.
156 Mokauea St.
Honolulu, HI 96819-3105
Phone: (808)845-2991 **Fax:** (808)842-0921
Products: Medical and industrial equipments and

supplies. SICs: 5047 (Medical & Hospital Equipment); 5084 (Industrial Machinery & Equipment); 5085 (Industrial Supplies). Est: 1967. Sales: $2,000,000 (2000). Emp: 6. Officers: Ronald Sciulli, President; Thomas Sciulli, Vice President; Aida Sciulli, CEO/Owner.

■ 18697 ■ Athmann Industrial Medical Supply
PO Box 26445
Indianapolis, IN 46226-0445
Phone: (317)898-3344
Free: (800)456-2467   Fax: (317)898-5222
Products: Medical equipment; Hospital equipment. SIC: 5047 (Medical & Hospital Equipment). Officers: Susan Athmann, President.

■ 18698 ■ Attention Medical Co.
1419 Dunn Dr.
Carrollton, TX 75006
Phone: (972)245-0908   Fax: (972)446-4325
Products: Medical supplies and equipment. SIC: 5047 (Medical & Hospital Equipment). Est: 1983. Sales: $21,100,000 (2000). Emp: 90. Officers: David Stanley, CEO & President; Thomas P. Drake, CFO; Rosewell G. Capron, VP of Marketing & Sales; Lori Ewing, Data Processing Mgr.; Julie Garrison, Human Resources Mgr.

■ 18699 ■ Avionix Medical Devices
PO Box 9669
Midland, TX 79708
Phone: (915)686-0188
Free: (800)627-8914   Fax: (915)685-1161
Products: Medical equipment. SIC: 5047 (Medical & Hospital Equipment). Est: 1989. Officers: A.V. Prakash, President.

■ 18700 ■ B & B Medical Service Inc.
2236 NW 10th St., Bldg. 103
Oklahoma City, OK 73107-5658
Phone: (405)235-9548
Free: (800)372-9548   Fax: (405)272-0889
Products: Medical and hospital equipment, including therapy equipment. SIC: 5047 (Medical & Hospital Equipment). Officers: W. Long, President.

■ 18701 ■ B C Sales Co., Inc.
2395 SW 1st Ave.
Fruitland, ID 83619-3745
Phone: (208)452-4707
Free: (800)452-4707   Fax: (208)452-5860
Products: Safety shoes; Gloves; Safety supplies. SIC: 5047 (Medical & Hospital Equipment). Est: 1983. Sales: $3,500,000 (1999). Emp: 23. Officers: Greg Bieker, President; Sue Rose, Human Resources Contact.

■ 18702 ■ B & J Enterprises Inc.
1001 Highway 25 N
Heber Springs, AR 72543-2010
Phone: (501)362-3727   Fax: (501)362-7997
Products: Medical equipment; Hospital equipment. SIC: 5047 (Medical & Hospital Equipment). Officers: Barry Niemi, President.

■ 18703 ■ Baxter Healthcare Corp.
Converters/Custom Sterile Div.
1500 Waukegan Rd.
Mc Gaw Park, IL 60085
Phone: (847)473-1500   Fax: (847)785-2458
Products: Custom sterile products; Surgery equipment; Draperies; Gloves. SIC: 5047 (Medical & Hospital Equipment). Sales: $170,000,000 (2000). Emp: 700. Officers: Joe Damico, President.

■ 18704 ■ Beck-Lee Inc.
PO Box 528
Stratford, CT 06615-0528
Phone: (203)332-7678
Free: (800)235-2852   Fax: (203)384-1932
E-mail: info@becklee.com
URL: http://www.becklee.com
Products: Medical supplies, including exam gloves and cardiology supplies. SIC: 5047 (Medical & Hospital Equipment). Officers: Thomas Carpenter, Chairman of the Board; William Lichtenberger, Vice President.

■ 18705 ■ Bedsole Medical Companies Inc.
3280 Dauphin St., Ste. 115-C
Mobile, AL 36606-4050
Phone: (205)476-3635   Fax: (205)471-5979
Products: Medical equipment; Hospital equipment. SIC: 5047 (Medical & Hospital Equipment). Officers: M. Bedsole, President.

■ 18706 ■ Best Labs
PO Box 20468
St. Petersburg, FL 33742
Phone: (813)525-0255   Fax: (813)527-8518
Products: Hearing aids; Batteries. SICs: 5063 (Electrical Apparatus & Equipment); 5047 (Medical & Hospital Equipment). Est: 1976. Sales: $4,000,000 (2000). Emp: 44. Officers: Harvey L. Romanek, President; Barbara Perkinson, Comptroller.

■ 18707 ■ Big Sky Fire Equipment
207 W Janeaux
Lewistown, MT 59457-3036
Phone: (406)538-9303
Products: Medical equipment; Hospital equipment; Hospital furniture; Oxygen tents. SIC: 5047 (Medical & Hospital Equipment). Officers: Joe Moline, Partner.

■ 18708 ■ Binson's Hospital Supplies Inc.
26834 Lawrence Ave.
Center Line, MI 48015
Phone: (810)755-2300
Products: Hospital supplies, including respirators, bedding, gauze, and bandages. SIC: 5047 (Medical & Hospital Equipment). Est: 1953. Sales: $48,000,000 (2000). Emp: 165. Officers: Jim Binson, President; Yvonne Lapworth, CFO.

■ 18709 ■ Bio-Medical Imaging Inc.
PO Box 5364
Winston-Salem, NC 27113-5364
Phone: (336)768-9506   Fax: (336)768-0309
Products: Medical and hospital equipment, including X-ray apparatus. SIC: 5047 (Medical & Hospital Equipment). Est: 1980. Emp: 6. Officers: Margaret Ferrell, Treasurer; Graham Ferrell, President.

■ 18710 ■ Bio Medical Life Systems Inc.
PO Box 1360
Vista, CA 92085-1360
Phone: (619)727-5600   Fax: (619)727-4220
Products: Medical equipment, including electrical stimulation devices. SIC: 5047 (Medical & Hospital Equipment). Est: 1982. Sales: $3,000,000 (2000). Emp: 25. Officers: Richard Saxon, CEO.

■ 18711 ■ Bio-Medical Resources Inc.
2150 W 6th Ave.
Broomfield, CO 80020
Phone: (303)469-1746   Fax: (303)469-1748
Products: Medical equipment, including thermometers. SIC: 5047 (Medical & Hospital Equipment). Est: 1977. Sales: $3,000,000 (2000). Emp: 13. Officers: Denny Dickenson, President.

■ 18712 ■ Biocoustics Instruments Inc.
6925 Oakland Mills Rd., Ste. H
Columbia, MD 21045-4714
Phone: (410)995-6131
Free: (800)366-4616   Fax: (410)381-5674
Products: Medical equipment. SIC: 5047 (Medical & Hospital Equipment). Est: 1981. Emp: 12. Officers: Alfred King, President.

■ 18713 ■ Biomedical Research & Development Laboratories, Inc.
8561 Atlas Dr.
Gaithersburg, MD 20877-4135
Phone: (301)948-6506   Fax: (301)869-5570
Products: Medical equipment; Hospital equipment; Laboratory and scientific equipment. SIC: 5047 (Medical & Hospital Equipment). Officers: Bruce Kroener, President.

■ 18714 ■ Biopool International Inc.
6025 Nicolle St.
Ventura, CA 93003
Phone: (805)654-0643   Fax: (805)654-0681
Products: Biological test kits. SIC: 5047 (Medical & Hospital Equipment). Sales: $15,000,000 (2000). Emp:

117. Officers: Michael D. Bick, CEO & Chairman of the Board; Robert K. Foote, CFO.

■ 18715 ■ Biosound Esaote Inc.
8000 Castleway Dr.
Indianapolis, IN 46250-1943
Phone: (317)849-1793
Free: (800)428-4374   Fax: (317)841-8616
E-mail: info@biomail.com
URL: http://www.Biosound.com
Products: Medical diagnostic ultrasound equipment. SIC: 5047 (Medical & Hospital Equipment). Sales: $34,000,000 (2000). Emp: 100. Officers: Fabrizio Landi, President; Tom Feick, Exec. VP & CFO.

■ 18716 ■ Biotronik Inc.
6024 Jean Rd.
Lake Oswego, OR 97035-5369
Phone: (503)635-3594
Free: (800)547-0394   Fax: (503)635-9936
E-mail: cha@biotronikusa.com
Products: Medical devices, pacemakers, leads, and accessory products. SIC: 5047 (Medical & Hospital Equipment). Est: 1963. Emp: 2,200. Officers: Professor Schaldach, President.

■ 18717 ■ F.R. Blankenstein Co. Inc.
PO Box 986
Natchez, MS 39121-0986
Phone: (601)445-5618   Fax: (601)445-0413
Products: Medical and hospital equipment; Welding equipment; Safety supplies; Swimming pool supplies. SICs: 5047 (Medical & Hospital Equipment); 5084 (Industrial Machinery & Equipment); 5091 (Sporting & Recreational Goods). Officers: F. Blankenstein, President.

■ 18718 ■ Bodyline Comfort Systems
3730 Kori Rd.
Jacksonville, FL 32257
Phone: (904)262-4068
Free: (800)874-7715   Fax: (904)262-2225
E-mail: info@bodyline.com
URL: http://www.bodyline.com
Products: Support braces; Pillows. SIC: 5047 (Medical & Hospital Equipment). Est: 1968.

■ 18719 ■ Branches Medical Inc.
3652 NW 16th St.
Lauderhill, FL 33311
Phone: (305)321-6339
Products: Medical equipment. SIC: 5047 (Medical & Hospital Equipment). Est: 1989. Sales: $2,000,000 (2000). Emp: 10. Officers: Hamish Reed, CEO; Cynthia Reed, President & CFO.

■ 18720 ■ Browns Medical Imaging
14315 C Cir.
Omaha, NE 68144-3349
Phone: (402)330-2168
Free: (800)701-9729   Fax: (402)330-1120
Products: X-ray Equipment and supplies. SIC: 5047 (Medical & Hospital Equipment). Officers: Daniel Brown, President; Jim Ciurej, Sales/Marketing Contact.

■ 18721 ■ Buhl Animal Clinic
201 11th Ave. S
Buhl, ID 83316-1301
Phone: (208)543-4326
Products: Medical and hospital equipment; Veterinarians' equipment and supplies. SIC: 5047 (Medical & Hospital Equipment). Officers: E Hammerquist, Partner.

■ 18722 ■ Burke Inc.
1800 Merriam Ln.
Kansas City, KS 66106
Phone: (913)722-5658   Fax: (913)722-2614
Products: Medical equipment. SIC: 5047 (Medical & Hospital Equipment). Est: 1958. Sales: $20,000,000 (2000). Emp: 65. Officers: Du Wayne Kramer, President; Ron Kruse, Vice President.

■ 18723 ■ Burkhart Dental Supply
PO Box 11265
Tacoma, WA 98411-0265
Phone: (253)474-7761   Fax: (253)472-4773
Products: Dental equipment and supplies. SIC: 5047

(Medical & Hospital Equipment). **Officers:** Perry Burkhart, Chairman of the Board.

■ **18724** ■ **Campagna Inc.**
173 State St.
Bristol, RI 02809-2205
Phone: (401)253-8808
Products: Medical equipment; Hospital equipment; Optometric equipment and supplies; Surgical equipment. **SIC:** 5047 (Medical & Hospital Equipment). **Officers:** Vincent Campagna, President.

■ **18725** ■ **Cantel Medical Corp.**
1135 Broad St., Ste. 203
Clifton, NJ 07013
Phone: (973)470-8700   **Fax:** (973)471-0054
URL: http://www.cantelmedical.com
Products: Infection prevention and control products; Diagnostic equipment; Medical and surgical equipment; Precision instruments; Industrial equipment. **SICs:** 5047 (Medical & Hospital Equipment); 5043 (Photographic Equipment & Supplies); 5049 (Professional Equipment Nec); 5084 (Industrial Machinery & Equipment). **Est:** 1963. **Sales:** $50,102,000 (1999). **Emp:** 170. **Officers:** James P. Reilly, CEO & President; Craig A. Sheldon, VP & Controller; Charles M. Diker, Chairman of the Board; Alan J. Hirschfield, Vice Chairman of the Board; Darwin C. Dornbush, Secretary; Joanna Zisa Albrecht, Asst. Secty.; Darwin C. Dornbush, Secretary; Joanna Zisa-Albrecht, Asst. Secretary. **Former Name:** Cantel Industries Inc.

■ **18726** ■ **Care Medical Equipment Inc.**
1877 NE 7th Ave.
Portland, OR 97212-3905
Phone: (503)288-8174
Free: (800)952-9566   **Fax:** (503)288-8817
Products: Medical and hospital equipment, including home care and rehabilitation products. **SIC:** 5047 (Medical & Hospital Equipment). **Officers:** Donald Adler, President.

■ **18727** ■ **Carlisle Medical Inc.**
PO Box 9814
Mobile, AL 36691-0814
Phone: (205)344-7988
Free: (800)553-1783   **Fax:** (205)343-5587
Products: Medical equipment. **SIC:** 5047 (Medical & Hospital Equipment). **Officers:** Donnie Carlisle, President.

■ **18728** ■ **Carolina First Aid Inc.**
PO Box 147
Pfafftown, NC 27040-0147
Phone: (910)922-3916   **Fax:** (910)922-3532
Products: Medical equipment; Hospital equipment. **SIC:** 5047 (Medical & Hospital Equipment). **Officers:** Will Partin, President.

■ **18729** ■ **Carpenter-Dent-Sublett No. 1**
PO Box 1747
Bowling Green, KY 42102-1747
Phone: (502)781-5310
Free: (800)452-3065   **Fax:** (502)843-9071
Products: Home medical equipment. **SIC:** 5047 (Medical & Hospital Equipment). **Officers:** David Hancock, President.

■ **18730** ■ **Catheter Research Inc.**
6131 W 80th St.
Indianapolis, IN 46278
Phone: (317)872-0074   **Fax:** (317)872-0169
Products: Catheters. **SIC:** 5047 (Medical & Hospital Equipment). **Est:** 1984. **Sales:** $900,000 (2000). **Emp:** 7. **Officers:** John Steen, CEO & President.

■ **18731** ■ **L.D. Caulk Co.**
PO Box 359
Milford, DE 19963
Phone: (302)422-4511   **Fax:** (302)422-0258
Products: Dental products. **SIC:** 5047 (Medical & Hospital Equipment). **Sales:** $90,000,000 (2000). **Emp:** 500. **Officers:** T.L. Whiting, Vice President; Charles E. Jackson, Controller; Thomas C. Burns, Dir. of Sales; Paul Rials, Dir. of Data Processing.

■ **18732** ■ **Central Nebraska Home Care**
PO Box 1146
Kearney, NE 68848-1146
Phone: (308)234-6094   **Fax:** (308)234-6442
Products: Medical equipment; Hospital equipment. **SIC:** 5047 (Medical & Hospital Equipment). **Officers:** Steve Duennerman, Director.

■ **18733** ■ **Central Virginia Medical Inc.**
5406 B. Distributor Dr.
Richmond, VA 23225-6106
Phone: (804)233-5508   **Fax:** (804)230-0761
Products: Medical equipment; Hospital equipment. **SIC:** 5047 (Medical & Hospital Equipment). **Officers:** Donald Smith, President.

■ **18734** ■ **Charmant Incorporated USA**
400 American Rd.
Morris Plains, NJ 07950-2400
Phone: (201)538-1511   **Fax:** (201)538-0762
Products: Optical equipment and supplies. **SIC:** 5048 (Ophthalmic Goods). **Est:** 1984. **Sales:** $40,000,000 (2000). **Emp:** 175. **Officers:** Masao Otani, President; Cheryl Weber, CFO.

■ **18735** ■ **Charron Medical Equipment Inc.**
1 E Hollis St.
Nashua, NH 03060-2942
Phone: (603)889-7220
Products: Medical equipment; Hospital equipment. **SIC:** 5047 (Medical & Hospital Equipment). **Officers:** Paul Charron, President.

■ **18736** ■ **Checkpoint International**
PO Box 280883
East Hartford, CT 06128-0883
Phone: (860)724-1811   **Fax:** (860)289-1310
Products: Scientific instruments; Air pollution control equipment; Computers, peripherals, and software; Farm equipment; Medical and hospital equipment. **SICs:** 5047 (Medical & Hospital Equipment); 5075 (Warm Air Heating & Air-Conditioning); 5045 (Computers, Peripherals & Software); 5083 (Farm & Garden Machinery). **Officers:** Emmanuel E. Ochieke, President.

■ **18737** ■ **Chelsea Clock Co. Inc.**
284 Everett Ave.
Chelsea, MA 02150
Phone: (617)884-0250
Free: (800)435-2001   **Fax:** (617)884-3608
Products: Clocks; Thermometers. **SIC:** 5047 (Medical & Hospital Equipment). **Est:** 1897. **Sales:** $2,000,000 (2000). **Emp:** 99. **Officers:** Richard F. Leavitt.

■ **18738** ■ **Chem-Tronics Inc.**
PO Box 627
Leavenworth, KS 66048-1097
Phone: (913)651-3930
Free: (800)332-3930   **Fax:** (913)682-5109
Products: Medical equipment; Hospital equipment; Veterinary instruments. **SIC:** 5047 (Medical & Hospital Equipment). **Officers:** Seth Fox, President.

■ **18739** ■ **Cherney & Associates, Inc.**
28910 Indian Valley Rd.
Rancho Palos Verdes, CA 90275-4805
Phone: (310)541-6620   **Fax:** (310)541-9540
Products: Surgical equipment; Medical equipment and supplies. **SIC:** 5047 (Medical & Hospital Equipment). **Officers:** Alison Cherney, CEO.

■ **18740** ■ **Chesapeake Medical Systems**
7 Cedar St.
Cambridge, MD 21613
Phone: (410)228-0221
Free: (800)333-5643   **Fax:** (410)228-4561
Products: Medical equipment; Hospital equipment; X-ray apparatus; Hospital furniture. **SIC:** 5047 (Medical & Hospital Equipment). **Officers:** Mike Halsey, President.

■ **18741** ■ **Chicopee Medical Supplies**
920 Front St.
Chicopee, MA 01020-1724
Phone: (413)594-8383
Free: (800)622-8191   **Fax:** (413)594-8552
Products: Medical equipment; Hospital equipment. **SIC:** 5047 (Medical & Hospital Equipment). **Officers:**

Eugene Kirejczyk, President; Mike Rauomski, Sales & Marketing Contact.

■ **18742** ■ **Cho-Pat Inc.**
PO Box 293
Hainesport, NJ 08036
Phone: (609)261-1336
Free: (800)221-1601   **Fax:** (609)261-7593
E-mail: sales@cho-pat.com
URL: http://www.cho-pat.com
Products: Sports medical devices, including knee and arm braces. **SIC:** 5047 (Medical & Hospital Equipment). **Est:** 1979. **Emp:** 24. **Officers:** George Gauvry, President; Carol Budd, Customer Service Contact.

■ **18743** ■ **Choice Medical Inc.**
6311 Clearspring Rd.
Baltimore, MD 21212-2602
Phone: (410)377-3753
Products: Medical equipment; Hospital equipment. **SIC:** 5047 (Medical & Hospital Equipment). **Officers:** Sean Coyle, President.

■ **18744** ■ **Clarksville Pharmacy Inc.**
602 McKennon St.
Clarksville, AR 72830-3524
Phone: (501)754-8402   **Fax:** (501)754-6616
Products: Medical equipment; Hospital equipment. **SIC:** 5047 (Medical & Hospital Equipment). **Officers:** Dixie White, President.

■ **18745** ■ **CMP Industries Inc.**
PO Box 350
Albany, NY 12201
Phones: (518)434-3147   800-833-2343
Free: (800)888-5868   **Fax:** (518)434-1288
Products: Dental laboratory equipment. **SIC:** 5047 (Medical & Hospital Equipment). **Est:** 1889. **Sales:** $9,000,000 (2000). **Emp:** 62. **Officers:** William Regan, CEO & President; Edward J. Civiok Jr., Treasurer; Richard C. Adamson, Dir. of Marketing; Robert J. Briggs, Dir. of Admin.

■ **18746** ■ **Colonial Medical Supplies**
915 S Orange Ave.
Orlando, FL 32806
Phone: (407)849-6455
Free: (800)747-0246   **Fax:** (407)849-6458
E-mail: info@Colonialmed.com
URL: http://www.Colonialmed.com
Products: Wheelchairs; Hospital beds; Bedside commodes. **SIC:** 5047 (Medical & Hospital Equipment). **Est:** 1981. **Sales:** $10,000,000 (2000). **Emp:** 35. **Officers:** Betty Bruinsma, CEO.

■ **18747** ■ **Columbia Diagnostics Inc.**
1127 International Pky., No. 201
Fredericksburg, VA 22406-1142
Phone: (703)569-7511
Products: Medical equipment; Hospital equipment. **SIC:** 5047 (Medical & Hospital Equipment). **Officers:** Robert Meinershagen, President.

■ **18748** ■ **Commercial/Medical Electronics**
PO Box 690206
Tulsa, OK 74169-0206
Phone: (918)749-6151
Free: (800)324-4844   **Fax:** (918)749-3023
Products: Medical equipment; Hospital equipment; Electromedical equipment. **SIC:** 5047 (Medical & Hospital Equipment). **Est:** 1976. **Sales:** $100,000 (2000). **Emp:** 11. **Officers:** Hugh Holly, Owner.

■ **18749** ■ **Complete Medical Products Inc.**
2052 N Decatur Rd.
Decatur, GA 30033
Phone: (404)728-0010
Free: (800)525-4119   **Fax:** (404)728-0010
Products: Rehabilitative supplies. **SIC:** 5047 (Medical & Hospital Equipment). **Est:** 1986. **Sales:** $1,000,000 (2000). **Emp:** 5. **Officers:** James K. McNeely, President; Kathy Conliff, Controller.

■ **18750** ■ **Cone Instruments Inc.**
5201 Naiman Pkwy.
Solon, OH 44139
Phone: (216)248-1035
Free: (800)321-6964 **Fax:** (216)248-9477
E-mail: cone.instru@worldnet.att.net
Products: Medical supplies, including ultrasound equipment. **SIC:** 5047 (Medical & Hospital Equipment). **Est:** 1976. **Sales:** $9,300,000 (2000). **Emp:** 30. **Officers:** Jay Cone, President; Patti Ramsay, Secretary; Greg Stanislawski, Dir. of Marketing & Sales.

■ **18751** ■ **Conger Dental Supply Co.**
1917 SW Gage Blvd.
Topeka, KS 66604-3390
Phone: (785)271-8073
Free: (800)255-3983 **Fax:** (785)271-8078
SIC: 5047 (Medical & Hospital Equipment). **Officers:** Lloyd Bauman, Owner.

■ **18752** ■ **Connecticut Physicians & Surgeons**
PO Box 429
Norwalk, CT 06852-0429
Phone: (203)838-2354
Products: Medical equipment; Hospital equipment; Surgical equipment. **SIC:** 5047 (Medical & Hospital Equipment). **Officers:** Gerard McShane, President.

■ **18753** ■ **Consumer Care Products Inc.**
1446 Pilgrim Rd.
Plymouth, WI 53073
Phone: (920)893-4614 **Fax:** (920)893-6195
E-mail: ccpi@consumercareinc.com
URL: http://www.consumercareinc.com; www.polylock.com
Products: Durable medical equipment, rehab, and special ed supplies and equipment; High performance mushroom tape; Fastener systems; Floor traction materials; Custom fabrications/sewing. **SIC:** 5047 (Medical & Hospital Equipment). **Est:** 1978. **Sales:** $1,000,000 (2000). **Emp:** 12. **Officers:** Dr. Terrand B. Grall.

■ **18754** ■ **Cooley Medical Equipment Inc.**
490 S Lake Dr.
Prestonsburg, KY 41653-1359
Phone: (606)886-9267 **Fax:** (606)886-8657
Products: Medical and hospital equipment and supplies. **SIC:** 5047 (Medical & Hospital Equipment). **Officers:** Gary Bailey, President.

■ **18755** ■ **Cora Medical Products Inc.**
3615 Goodlett St.
Memphis, TN 38118-6213
Phone: (901)794-7174 **Fax:** (901)362-8603
Products: Medical equipment; Hospital equipment. **SIC:** 5047 (Medical & Hospital Equipment). **Officers:** Mike Cohen, President.

■ **18756** ■ **Corinthian Healthcare Systems**
8227 Northwest Blvd.
Indianapolis, IN 46278-1378
Phone: (317)875-9026 **Fax:** (317)876-0557
Products: Medical and hospital equipment and supplies. **SIC:** 5047 (Medical & Hospital Equipment). **Officers:** Lyman Eaton, Chairman of the Board.

■ **18757** ■ **CPS Marketing Corporation**
2000 Main St., Ste. 500
Ft. Myers, FL 33901
Phone: (941)466-8343 **Fax:** (941)332-7092
Products: Citrus fruits; Furniture; Computers; Aircraft engines; Medical equipment. **SICs:** 5047 (Medical & Hospital Equipment); 5148 (Fresh Fruits & Vegetables); 5021 (Furniture); 5045 (Computers, Peripherals & Software); 5088 (Transportation Equipment & Supplies). **Officers:** Christian P. Swartz, President.

■ **18758** ■ **Crescent City Pharmaceutical**
200 Loyola Ave.
New Orleans, LA 70112-2002
Phone: (504)524-2254
Free: (800)256-2007 **Fax:** (504)528-9310
Products: Medical and hospital equipment. **SIC:** 5047 (Medical & Hospital Equipment). **Est:** 1951. **Emp:** 15. **Officers:** Frank Smith, President.

■ **18759** ■ **W. C. Cressy & Sons Inc.**
Old Alewive Rd.
Kennebunk, ME 04043
Phone: (207)985-6111
Products: Wheelchair lifts; Ramps; Buses. **SIC:** 5047 (Medical & Hospital Equipment).

■ **18760** ■ **Crystal Home Health Care Inc.**
15819 Schoolcraft St.
Detroit, MI 48227-1749
Phone: (313)493-4900
Free: (800)493-4902 **Fax:** (313)493-4904
E-mail: bob@e-homehealth.com
URL: http://www.e-homehealth.com
Products: Medical and hospital equipment and supplies. **SIC:** 5047 (Medical & Hospital Equipment). **Est:** 1985. **Sales:** $1,500,000 (2000). **Emp:** 20. **Officers:** Robert McPherson, President.

■ **18761** ■ **CUI Corp.**
1160 Mark Ave.
Carpinteria, CA 93013
Phone: (805)684-7617 **Fax:** (805)684-6475
Products: Medical products; Silicone products including breast implants. **SIC:** 5047 (Medical & Hospital Equipment). **Est:** 1975. **Sales:** $7,000,000 (2000). **Emp:** 90. **Officers:** Gerry Campbell, President; Jack Barlow, Sales Mgr.; Terry Young, Dir of Human Resources.

■ **18762** ■ **Culver Products Co. Inc.**
PO Box 230
Culver, IN 46511-0230
Phone: (219)842-3465 **Fax:** (219)842-3933
Products: Dental equipment and supplies. **SIC:** 5047 (Medical & Hospital Equipment). **Officers:** Thomas Pugh, President.

■ **18763** ■ **Dalco International, Inc.**
8433 Glazebrook Ave.
Richmond, VA 23228
Phone: (804)266-7702 **Fax:** (804)266-7740
E-mail: mail@dalcointernational.com
URL: http://www.dalcointernational.com
Products: Orthopedic splints and braces. **SIC:** 5047 (Medical & Hospital Equipment). **Est:** 1982. **Officers:** Leif Daleng, President.

■ **18764** ■ **James W. Daly Inc.**
PO Box 6041
Peabody, MA 01961
Phone: (978)532-6900
Products: Medical and hospital supplies, including stethoscopes and wheelchairs. **SIC:** 5047 (Medical & Hospital Equipment). **Est:** 1929. **Sales:** $720,000,000 (2000). **Emp:** 300. **Officers:** Thomas Slagle, President; David Canniff, Controller; John Kilgour, Dir. of Sales.

■ **18765** ■ **Datex-Ohmeda, Inc.**
3 Highwood Dr.
Tewksbury, MA 01876
Phone: (978)640-0460
Free: (800)345-2700 **Fax:** (978)640-0469
URL: http://www.datex-ohmeda.com
Products: Anesthesia delivery systems; Patient monitors; Supplies and accessories; Information systems; Support services.s. **SIC:** 5047 (Medical & Hospital Equipment). **Est:** 1900. **Emp:** 3,500. **Officers:** Richard Atkin, President. **Former Name:** Datex Medical Instrumentation Inc.

■ **18766** ■ **Alan G. Day Corp.**
PO Box 5245
Lutherville Timonium, MD 21094-5245
Phone: (410)561-9995 **Fax:** (410)560-1372
Products: Physical therapy equipment and supplies; Exercise equipment. **SICs:** 5047 (Medical & Hospital Equipment); 5091 (Sporting & Recreational Goods). **Officers:** Jennifer Day, President.

■ **18767** ■ **DE International Inc.**
1377 Barclay Cir., Ste. F
Marietta, GA 30060-2907
Phone: (404)422-8836 **Free:** (800)233-5409
Products: Chiropractic equipment. **SIC:** 5047 (Medical & Hospital Equipment). **Officers:** Sidney Williams, President.

■ **18768** ■ **De-Tec Inc.**
1744 W Genesee St.
Syracuse, NY 13204
Phone: (315)487-0909
Products: Anaesthesia machines. **SIC:** 5047 (Medical & Hospital Equipment).

■ **18769** ■ **Delta-Southland International**
PO Box 3606
Kingsport, TN 37664-0606
Phone: (423)378-5997 **Fax:** (423)378-3635
Products: Medical and hospital equipment and supplies. **SIC:** 5047 (Medical & Hospital Equipment). **Officers:** Wallace Boyd, President.

■ **18770** ■ **Dental Enterprises Inc.**
795 S Jason St.
Denver, CO 80223-3911
Phone: (303)777-6717 **Fax:** (303)777-6726
Products: Dental equipment and supplies. **SIC:** 5047 (Medical & Hospital Equipment). **Est:** 1977. **Sales:** $1,500,000 (2000). **Emp:** 9. **Officers:** James Riedel, President; Steven Pacheco, Vice President.

■ **18771** ■ **Dentec Corp.**
25560 W Lake Shore Dr.
Barrington, IL 60010-1461
Phone: (847)241-5966
Free: (800)942-7192 **Fax:** (847)241-0323
Products: Dental equipment and supplies. **SIC:** 5047 (Medical & Hospital Equipment). **Officers:** A. Wayne Lackey, President.

■ **18772** ■ **Derma-Therm Inc.**
155 Edgewater Rd.
Inman, SC 29349-6911
Phone: 800-788-1106
Products: Chiropractic equipment. **SIC:** 5047 (Medical & Hospital Equipment). **Officers:** Walter Pierce, President.

■ **18773** ■ **DeRoyal**
200 Debusk Ln.
Powell, TN 37849
Phone: (615)938-7828
Products: Medical restraints; Orthopedic, cardiovascular, and related medical products. **SIC:** 5047 (Medical & Hospital Equipment). **Emp:** 2,500. **Former Name:** DeRoyal Industries Inc.

■ **18774** ■ **Diagnostic Equipment Service Corp.**
PO Box 303
Norfolk, MA 02056-0303
Phone: (508)520-0040 **Fax:** (508)520-7055
URL: http://www.descomed.com
Products: Medical and hospital equipment. **SICs:** 5047 (Medical & Hospital Equipment); 5085 (Industrial Supplies). **Est:** 1970. **Sales:** $4,000,000 (2000). **Emp:** 27. **Officers:** Robert Cecca, President.

■ **18775** ■ **Dialysis Clinic Inc.**
1600 Hayes St., Ste. 300
Nashville, TN 37203-3020
Phone: (615)327-3061 **Fax:** (615)259-2513
Products: Medical equipment; Hospital equipment. **SIC:** 5047 (Medical & Hospital Equipment). **Officers:** Mark Penick, Controller.

■ **18776** ■ **Dixon Medical Inc.**
3445 Sexton Woods Dr.
Atlanta, GA 30341-2622
Phone: (404)457-0602 **Fax:** (404)454-7548
Products: Medical equipment. **SIC:** 5047 (Medical & Hospital Equipment). **Officers:** William Dixon, President.

■ **18777** ■ **Dockters X-Ray Inc.**
7515 18th Ave. NW
Seattle, WA 98117-5430
Phone: (206)784-7768 **Fax:** (206)784-1007
E-mail: dxi@aa.net
Products: Medical and hospital X-ray equipment. **SIC:** 5047 (Medical & Hospital Equipment). **Est:** 1985. **Sales:** $1,000,000 (2000). **Emp:** 4. **Officers:** Don Dockter, President.

■ **18778** ■ **J.P. Donico & Associates**
1754 West 24th St.
Erie, PA 16502
Phone: (814)454-6000 **Fax:** (814)456-7470
Products: Medical and hospital equipment; Drugs, proprietaries, and sundries; Groceries; Electric water heaters; Air pollution control equipment. **SICs:** 5122 (Drugs, Proprietaries & Sundries); 5047 (Medical & Hospital Equipment); 5149 (Groceries & Related Products Nec); 5064 (Electrical Appliances—Television & Radio); 5075 (Warm Air Heating & Air-Conditioning). **Officers:** John Paul Donico, President.

■ **18779** ■ **Down River Home Health Supply**
3138 Biddle St.
Riverview, MI 48192-5916
Phone: (734)285-3800 **Fax:** (734)285-1190
Products: Medical equipment; Hospital equipment; Hospital furniture; Surgical equipment. **SIC:** 5047 (Medical & Hospital Equipment). **Officers:** Leon Sturtz, President.

■ **18780** ■ **Dura Med Inc.**
285 Southland Dr.
Lexington, KY 40503-1934
Phone: (606)278-2858 **Free:** (800)272-2858
Products: Medical and hospital equipment; Technical aids for the handicapped. **SIC:** 5047 (Medical & Hospital Equipment). **Officers:** Gary Goodwin, President.

■ **18781** ■ **Durr-Fillauer Medical Inc.**
PO Box 244009
Montgomery, AL 36124-4009
Phone: (205)241-8800 **Fax:** (205)241-8845
Products: Medical equipment and supplies, including pharmaceuticals and instruments. **SICs:** 5047 (Medical & Hospital Equipment); 5122 (Drugs, Proprietaries & Sundries). **Est:** 1896. **Sales:** $950,500,000 (2000). **Emp:** 1,362. **Officers:** W.A. Williamson Jr., CEO & Chairman of the Board; Richard L. Klein, Sr. VP & CFO; Charles E. Adair, President & COO; Ben McDavid, Dir of Human Resources.

■ **18782** ■ **Eastern Maine Healthcare**
489 State St.
Bangor, ME 04401
Phone: (207)945-7000
Products: Medical and hospital equipment. **SIC:** 5047 (Medical & Hospital Equipment). **Officers:** Robert Brandow, President.

■ **18783** ■ **Econ Equipment & Supplies Inc.**
35350 Union Lake Rd.
Harrison Township, MI 48045-3146
Phone: (810)791-4040
Free: (800)875-4040 **Fax:** (810)791-3939
Products: Medical equipment; Hospital equipment; Dental equipment and supplies. **SIC:** 5047 (Medical & Hospital Equipment). **Officers:** Roger Leduc, CEO.

■ **18784** ■ **EEV, Inc.**
4 Westchester Plaza
Elmsford, NY 10523
Phone: (914)592-6050 **Fax:** (914)682-8922
E-mail: info@eevine.com
URL: http://www.eev.com
Products: CCD's and ccd cameras; Linac magnetrons for medical applications; Marine radar components; Power tubes for UHFTV transmitters and chemical and gas sensors. **SICs:** 5047 (Medical & Hospital Equipment); 5065 (Electronic Parts & Equipment Nec). **Est:** 1977. **Emp:** 37. **Officers:** Rudy Winter, COO & Exec. VP; Mike Kirk, VP Commercial Div.; Howard Paul, VP Industrial, Scientific & Gov Div.

■ **18785** ■ **ELA Medical Inc.**
2950 Xenium Ln. N, Ste. 120
Plymouth, MN 55441-2623
Phone: (612)935-2033 **Fax:** (612)935-1080
Products: Medical and hospital equipment, including pace makers. **SIC:** 5047 (Medical & Hospital Equipment). **Officers:** James Stasik, Vice President.

■ **18786** ■ **Elan Pharmaceuticals**
2 Thurber Blvd.
Smithfield, RI 02917
Phone: (401)868-6400 **Fax:** (401)233-6480
Products: Medical equipment; Rubber druggist and

medical sundries such as water bottles, pacifiers, gloves, etc. **SIC:** 5047 (Medical & Hospital Equipment). **Est:** 1986. **Sales:** $30,800,000 (2000). **Emp:** 210. **Officers:** James T. O'Brien, COO.

■ **18787** ■ **Electro-Med Co. Inc.**
PO Box 18366
Louisville, KY 40261-0366
Phone: (502)459-6603 **Fax:** (502)454-6604
Products: Durable medical equipment. **SIC:** 5047 (Medical & Hospital Equipment). **Officers:** James Tittle, President.

■ **18788** ■ **Elevators Etc.**
6802 Ringgold Rd.
Chattanooga, TN 37412
Phone: (423)267-5438
Free: (800)451-8336 **Fax:** (423)265-7477
E-mail: liftu@aol.com
URL: http://www.elevatorsetc.com
Products: Equipment for the handicapped, including elevators, stairlifts, wheelchair lifts, and dumbwaiters. **SIC:** 5047 (Medical & Hospital Equipment). **Est:** 1988. **Emp:** 20. **Officers:** Gordon Hulgan III, President. **Alternate Name:** EMR Accessibilty.

■ **18789** ■ **Elite Denture Center**
2625 St. Johns Ave.
Billings, MT 59102-4656
Phone: (406)652-6999
Products: Dental equipment and supplies; Dental laboratory equipment and supplies. **SIC:** 5047 (Medical & Hospital Equipment). **Officers:** Wayne Kernall, Partner.

■ **18790** ■ **EMP International Corp.**
PO Box 1226
Abingdon, VA 24210
Phone: (540)628-5970 **Fax:** (540)628-5562
E-mail: empco@preferred.com
Products: Oxygen analyzers for combustion control and boiler control applications. **SICs:** 5047 (Medical & Hospital Equipment); 5084 (Industrial Machinery & Equipment). **Est:** 1975. **Emp:** 15. **Officers:** N.J. Patel, CEO.

■ **18791** ■ **Endolite North America Ltd.**
105 Westpark Rd.
Centerville, OH 45459
Phone: (937)291-3636
Products: Artificial limbs and prosthetic components. **SIC:** 5047 (Medical & Hospital Equipment). **Sales:** $4,000,000 (2000). **Emp:** 12. **Officers:** Lanny Wiggins, General Mgr.; Kevin Hickey, Controller.

■ **18792** ■ **Enos Home Oxygen Therapy Inc.**
PO Box 8756
New Bedford, MA 02742-8756
Phone: (508)992-2146
Free: (800)473-4669 **Fax:** (508)999-2724
Products: Medical and hospital equipment; Furniture; Oxygen therapy equipment. **SIC:** 5047 (Medical & Hospital Equipment). **Est:** 1950. **Sales:** $1,200,000 (2000). **Emp:** 23. **Officers:** R. Enos, President.

■ **18793** ■ **Etac USA Inc.**
2325 Park Lawn Dr., Ste. J
Waukesha, WI 53186-2938
Phone: (414)796-4600
E-mail: etac1usa@exepc.com
Products: Wheelchairs; Four-wheel walkers; Daily living and bath aids. **SIC:** 5047 (Medical & Hospital Equipment). **Sales:** $1,000,000 (2000). **Emp:** 30. **Officers:** Brian Rourke, Regional Sales Mgr.

■ **18794** ■ **Extech Ltd.**
PO Box 659
Wilsonville, OR 97070
Phone: (503)682-7278 **Fax:** (503)682-3252
Products: Environmental process control monitoring and analysis equipment. **SICs:** 5047 (Medical & Hospital Equipment); 5144 (Poultry & Poultry Products). **Est:** 1970. **Officers:** L.C. Fromm, Exec. Vice Pres.; G. Fromm, Sales & Marketing Contact.

■ **18795** ■ **Falls Welding & Fabricating, FWF Medical Products Div.**
608 Grant St.
Akron, OH 44311
Phone: (330)253-3437
Free: (800)231-6444 **Fax:** (330)253-2278
E-mail: sales@fwfmedicalproducts.com
URL: http://www.fwfmedicalproducts.com
Products: Medical carts and racks for oxygen delivery and storage. **SIC:** 5047 (Medical & Hospital Equipment). **Est:** 1965. **Sales:** $300,000 (1999). **Emp:** 4. **Officers:** Ross R. Holden, President. **Former Name:** Falls Welding & Fabrication, Medical Products Div.

■ **18796** ■ **Fertility Technologies Inc.**
313 Speen St.
Natick, MA 01760
Phone: (508)653-3900
Products: Diagnostic and therapeutic products. **SIC:** 5047 (Medical & Hospital Equipment). **Sales:** $1,000,000 (1993). **Emp:** 15. **Officers:** J. Tyler Dean, President.

■ **18797** ■ **Fillauer Inc.**
PO Box 5189
2710 Amnicola Hwy.
Chattanooga, TN 37406-0189
Phone: (423)624-0946
Free: (800)251-6398 **Fax:** (423)624-1402
URL: http://www.fillauer.com
Products: Prosthetic and orthotic devices. **SIC:** 5047 (Medical & Hospital Equipment). **Est:** 1914. **Sales:** $12,900,000 (1999). **Emp:** 95. **Officers:** Kenneth D. Driver, President & COO; Ed Connelly, VP & CFO; Fran Varner, Sales/Marketing Contact; Tom Johnson, Human Resources Contact.

■ **18798** ■ **First Aid Plus Inc.**
4626 Illinois Ave.
Louisville, KY 40213-1923
Phone: (502)499-9797 **Fax:** (502)456-0580
Products: Medical and hospital equipment and supplies. **SIC:** 5047 (Medical & Hospital Equipment). **Officers:** Chris Meiners, President.

■ **18799** ■ **Flex-Foot Inc.**
27418 Laguna Hills Dr., No. A
Aliso Viejo, CA 92656
Phone: (714)362-3883
Products: Prosthetic devices. **SIC:** 5047 (Medical & Hospital Equipment). **Sales:** $2,000,000 (2000). **Emp:** 20. **Officers:** John Fosberg, President.

■ **18800** ■ **Forcean Inc.**
10338 Ilona Ave.
Los Angeles, CA 90064
Phone: (213)551-1293 **Fax:** (213)551-1307
Products: Electronic communications equipment; Medical and hospital equipment and supplies, including surgical instruments; Computers and peripheral equipment. **SICs:** 5047 (Medical & Hospital Equipment); 5065 (Electronic Parts & Equipment Nec); 5045 (Computers, Peripherals & Software). **Officers:** Paul Cheuk, President.

■ **18801** ■ **Fuji Medical Systems USA Inc.**
419 West Ave.
Stamford, CT 06902-6300
Phone: (203)353-0300 **Fax:** (203)353-0926
Products: Medical X-ray film. **SIC:** 5047 (Medical & Hospital Equipment). **Est:** 1965. **Sales:** $51,000,000 (2000). **Emp:** 200. **Officers:** Dennis Nagami, CEO & Chairman of the Board; John J. Weber, CFO; John A. Taggart, VP of Sales; Peter Guyton, Dir. of Information Systems.

■ **18802** ■ **Fukuda Denshi USA, Inc.**
17725 NE 65th St., Bldg. C
Redmond, WA 98052
Phone: (425)881-7737
Free: (800)365-6668 **Fax:** (425)869-2018
URL: http://www.fukuda.com
Products: EKG, monitoring, and ultrasound machines. **SIC:** 5047 (Medical & Hospital Equipment). **Sales:** $12,000,000 (2000). **Emp:** 33. **Officers:** Robert Steurer, Exec. VP. **Former Name:** Fukuda Denshi America Corp.

■ 18803 ■ Gainor Medical U.S.A. Inc.
PO Box 353
McDonough, GA 30253-0353
Phone: (404)474-0474 Fax: (404)474-0424
Products: Medical disposables. SIC: 5047 (Medical & Hospital Equipment). Est: 1986. Sales: $90,000,000 (2000). Emp: 49. Officers: Mark Gainor, CEO & President; J. Michael Highland, CFO; Ado A. Strentse, VP of Marketing & Sales; Robin Rupe, Dir. of Data Processing; John Harris, Dir of Human Resources.

■ 18804 ■ Gaspro
2305 Kam Hwy.
Honolulu, HI 96819
Phone: (808)842-2222 Fax: (808)842-2131
Products: Medical equipment; Industrial regulators and gauges; Safety equipment; Welding supplies. SICs: 5047 (Medical & Hospital Equipment); 5084 (Industrial Machinery & Equipment). Est: 1910. Sales: $35,000,000 (2000). Emp: 135. Officers: Jim Webb, President; Michael Kenny, Vice President.

■ 18805 ■ General Biomedical Service Inc.
1900 25th St.
Kenner, LA 70062
Phone: (504)468-8597
Free: (800)558-9449 Fax: (504)469-3723
E-mail: info@generalbiomedical.com
URL: http://www.generalbiomedical.com
Products: Respiratory and anesthesia equipment and supplies. SIC: 5047 (Medical & Hospital Equipment). Est: 1982. Officers: Barbara Chauvin, President; Ron Messina, Sales/Marketing Contact, e-mail: us_sales@generalbiomedical.com.

■ 18806 ■ General Imaging Corp.
7151 Savannah Dr.
Newburgh, IN 47630-2184
Phone: (812)853-9294 Fax: (812)853-9268
Products: Medical equipment; Hospital equipment. SIC: 5047 (Medical & Hospital Equipment). Officers: Bob Lewis, President.

■ 18807 ■ General Medical Corp.
PO Box 27452
Richmond, VA 23261
Phone: (804)264-7500 Fax: (804)264-6779
Products: Medical supplies, tools, and equipment. SIC: 5047 (Medical & Hospital Equipment). Est: 1950. Sales: $750,000,000 (2000). Emp: 1,860. Officers: Steven B. Nielsen, CEO & President; Don Garber, Sr. VP & Finance Officer; Bruce Glickstein, Sr. VP of Marketing & Sales; Nancy Witschey, VP of Data Processing; Alan Jensen.

■ 18808 ■ Genesis Medical Equipment
3909 Beecher Rd.
Flint, MI 48532-3602
Phone: (810)733-6322
Products: Medical equipment; Hospital equipment; Hospital furniture. SIC: 5047 (Medical & Hospital Equipment). Officers: Richard Haener, Partner.

■ 18809 ■ Gensia Sicor Inc.
19 Hughes
Irvine, CA 92618
Phone: (949)455-4700 Fax: (949)457-2852
Products: Surgical instruments. SIC: 5047 (Medical & Hospital Equipment). Sales: $168,100,000 (2000). Emp: 1,200. Officers: Carlo Salvi, CEO; John W. Sayward, VP, CFO & Treasurer.

■ 18810 ■ Georgia Steel and Chemical Co.
10810 Guilford Rd., Ste. 104
Annapolis Junction, MD 20701-1118
Phone: (301)317-5502 Fax: (301)470-6313
Products: Chemical cleaning agents for respirators. SIC: 5169 (Chemicals & Allied Products Nec). Sales: $1,000,000 (2000). Emp: 15. Officers: Thomas G. O'Neill, President.

■ 18811 ■ Geriatric Medical & Surgical
395 3rd St.
Everett, MA 02149
Phone: (617)387-5936
Free: (800)523-0528 Fax: (617)389-1527
Products: Medical and surgical supplies; Disposable products; Pharmaceuticals. SICs: 5047 (Medical & Hospital Equipment); 5122 (Drugs, Proprietaries & Sundries). Est: 1953. Officers: Arthur Siegal, President.

■ 18812 ■ Godbee Medical Distributors
PO Box 7
Jemison, AL 35085-0007
Phone: (205)755-1771 Fax: (205)755-1772
Products: Medical equipment; Hospital equipment; Hospital furniture; Surgical appliances and supplies. SIC: 5047 (Medical & Hospital Equipment). Officers: Sidney Godbee, President.

■ 18813 ■ Godbee Medical Distributors
324 Montevallo Rd.
Alabaster, AL 35007
Phone: (205)664-4455
Products: Hospital equipment and supplies. SIC: 5047 (Medical & Hospital Equipment).

■ 18814 ■ Mike Graeffs Eastside Drugs
8506 E Mill Plain Blvd.
Vancouver, WA 98664-2011
Phone: (206)694-3353 Fax: (206)694-4460
Products: Medical equipment; Hospital equipment; Gifts and novelties; Candy; Pharmaceutical preparations. SICs: 5047 (Medical & Hospital Equipment); 5145 (Confectionery); 5122 (Drugs, Proprietaries & Sundries); 5199 (Nondurable Goods Nec). Officers: Michael Graeff, President.

■ 18815 ■ Great Lakes Orthopedics Inc.
13601 Pioneer Trl
Eden Prairie, MN 55347-2613
Phone: (612)920-1520 Fax: (612)920-2208
Products: Medical and hospital equipment and supplies. SIC: 5047 (Medical & Hospital Equipment). Officers: Gary Bongard, President.

■ 18816 ■ Greenville Health Corp.
701 Grove Rd.
Greenville, SC 29605
Phone: (864)455-6220 Fax: (864)455-5714
Products: Home care equipment; Pain therapy equipment. SIC: 5122 (Drugs, Proprietaries & Sundries). Est: 1986. Sales: $4,000,000 (2000). Emp: 75. Officers: Frank Pinckney, President; Robert W. Champion, Finance Officer.

■ 18817 ■ Grogan's Healthcare Supply Inc.
1016 S Broadway
Lexington, KY 40504
Phone: (606)254-6661 Fax: (606)254-6666
Products: Medical equipment and supplies. SIC: 5047 (Medical & Hospital Equipment). Sales: $16,000,000 (2000). Emp: 88. Officers: Alan Grogan, CEO; Doug Ragland, CFO.

■ 18818 ■ GTS Scientific Inc.
PO Box 7555
Gaithersburg, MD 20898-7555
Phone: (301)929-1444 Fax: (301)948-6972
Products: Medical equipment; Hospital equipment; Laboratory and scientific equipment. SIC: 5047 (Medical & Hospital Equipment). Officers: Anthony Guerra, President.

■ 18819 ■ Gulf South Medical Supply Inc.
426 Christine Dr.
Ridgeland, MS 39157
Phone: (601)856-5900 Fax: (601)856-8695
Products: Medical and hospital equipment and supplies. SIC: 5047 (Medical & Hospital Equipment). Est: 1982. Officers: Thomas Hixon, President.

■ 18820 ■ Haffner X-Ray Company Inc.
PO Box 344
Noblesville, IN 46060-0344
Phone: (317)773-5171
Free: (800)382-2722 Fax: (317)773-5172
Products: X-ray equipment; Automatic film processors, including accessories and supplies. SICs: 5047 (Medical & Hospital Equipment); 5043 (Photographic Equipment & Supplies). Est: 1967. Emp: 9. Officers: Richard Haffner, President.

■ 18821 ■ Hal-Hen Company Inc.
14-33 31st Ave.
Long Island City, NY 11106
Phone: (718)392-6020
Free: (800)242-5436 Fax: (718)482-1884
Products: Hearing aids and accessories. SIC: 5047 (Medical & Hospital Equipment). Est: 1946. Emp: 50. Officers: Joseph A. Vespe, Dir. of Operations.

■ 18822 ■ Hamilton Medical Inc.
PO Box 30008
Reno, NV 89520-3008
Phone: (702)858-3200 Fax: (702)856-5621
E-mail: thompson@hammedl.com
URL: http://www.hammedl.com
Products: Ventilators and supplies. SIC: 5047 (Medical & Hospital Equipment). Est: 1984. Officers: Max Walchli, President.

■ 18823 ■ Handicapped Driving Aids of Michigan Inc.
3990 2nd St.
Wayne, MI 48184
Phone: (734)595-4400 Fax: (734)595-4520
Products: Medical equipment and supplies; Hospital equipment; Vehicular equipment, including wheelchair lifts. SIC: 5047 (Medical & Hospital Equipment). Officers: Leon Sturtz, CEO.

■ 18824 ■ Happy Harry's Healthcare Inc.
311 Ruthar Dr.
Newark, DE 19711
Phone: (302)454-3390
Products: Durable medical equipment. SIC: 5047 (Medical & Hospital Equipment).

■ 18825 ■ Harmony Enterprises America
7 Backus Ave., Ste. 1515
Danbury, CT 06810-7427
Phone: (203)748-3411 Fax: (203)798-1182
Products: Specialty medical devices and supplies; Latex condoms; Industrial chemicals. SICs: 5047 (Medical & Hospital Equipment); 5122 (Drugs, Proprietaries & Sundries); 5169 (Chemicals & Allied Products Nec). Officers: Yin-Min Lin, President.

■ 18826 ■ Harris Discount Supply
7506 Melrose Ln., A
Oklahoma City, OK 73127-5163
Phone: (405)341-6963
Products: Medical equipment; Hearing aids; Dental equipment and supplies. SIC: 5047 (Medical & Hospital Equipment). Officers: Michael Harris, Owner.

■ 18827 ■ Harris Enterprises Inc.
12111 W Markham St., No. 14-174
Little Rock, AR 72211-2734
Phone: (501)225-6350 Fax: (501)225-9141
Products: Medical equipment; Hospital equipment; Industrial safety devices, including first-aid kits and face and eye masks. SIC: 5047 (Medical & Hospital Equipment). Officers: Everett Harris, President.

■ 18828 ■ Hartzler's Inc. Exporters
PO Box 661625
Arcadia, CA 91066
Phone: (626)796-6606 Fax: (626)445-5223
Products: Orthopedic braces and medical supplies; Sports medicine products; Canes, crutches, and walkers; Dried fruit and fruit concentrates. SICs: 5047 (Medical & Hospital Equipment); 5149 (Groceries & Related Products Nec). Officers: Mitzie Hartzler, President.

■ 18829 ■ Harvard Apparatus, Inc.
84 October Hill Rd.
Holliston, MA 01746
Free: (800)272-2775 Fax: (508)429-5732
E-mail: bioscience@harvardapparatus.com
URL: http://www.harvardapparatus.com
Products: Life science research products. SIC: 5047 (Medical & Hospital Equipment). Est: 1904. Officers: Chane Graziano, CEO; David Green, President; Mara Potter, Marketing & Sales Mgr.

■ 18830 ■ **Hazra Associates, Inc.**
2996 Burnbrick Rd.
PO Box 397
Bath, OH 44210
Phone: (330)659-4055 **Fax:** (330)659-3326
E-mail: 75674-1540@compuserve.com
Products: Surgical and medical instruments and appliances; X-ray and electromedical apparatus. **SIC:** 5047 (Medical & Hospital Equipment). **Est:** 1981. **Emp:** 3. **Officers:** Bilas Hazra, President.

■ 18831 ■ **HCI Corp./International Marketing Services**
10 E Washington St.
PO Box 936
Lexington, VA 24450-0936
Phone: (540)463-1095 **Fax:** (540)464-1174
Products: Medical equipment; Household and industrial chemicals; Plastics; Poultry products. **SICs:** 5047 (Medical & Hospital Equipment); 5162 (Plastics Materials & Basic Shapes); 5169 (Chemicals & Allied Products Nec); 5144 (Poultry & Poultry Products). **Est:** 1986. **Officers:** Hugh M. Henderson, President.

■ 18832 ■ **Healthcare Services International**
6679 Rutledge Dr.
Fairfax Station, VA 22039
Phone: (703)425-1546 **Fax:** (703)478-0147
Products: Dental equipment and supplies; X-ray apparatus; Ophthalmic goods; Surgical and medical instruments. **SICs:** 5047 (Medical & Hospital Equipment); 5048 (Ophthalmic Goods). **Officers:** S.N. Singh, President.

■ 18833 ■ **Hearing Aid Centers of America**
PO Box 3055
Kalamazoo, MI 49003-3055
Phone: (616)324-0301
Free: (800)253-3252 **Fax:** (616)324-2387
E-mail: home@hacofamerica.com
URL: http://www.hacofamerica.com
Products: Hearing aids; Assistive listening devices; Signaling systems. **SIC:** 5047 (Medical & Hospital Equipment). **Est:** 1946. **Sales:** $2,000,000 (1999). **Emp:** 15. **Officers:** Ronald Slager, CEO.

■ 18834 ■ **Henry Schein Inc. Dental Div.**
135 Duryea Rd.
Melville, NY 11747
Phone: (516)843-5500 **Fax:** (516)843-5665
Products: Health services equipment. **SIC:** 5047 (Medical & Hospital Equipment). **Sales:** $669,000,000 (2000). **Emp:** 2,000. **Officers:** Stanley M. Bergman, CEO, President & Chairman of the Board; Steven Paladino, Sr. VP & CFO.

■ 18835 ■ **Gary A. Hill**
3516 Neal Dr.
Knoxville, TN 37918-5229
Phone: (423)922-8314 **Fax:** (423)922-0453
Products: Medical equipment; Hospital equipment. **SIC:** 5047 (Medical & Hospital Equipment). **Officers:** Gary Hill, Owner.

■ 18836 ■ **Holladay Surgical Supply Co.**
2551 Landmark Dr.
Winston-Salem, NC 27103-6717
Phone: (910)760-2111
Free: (800)227-7602 **Fax:** (910)768-7731
Products: Medical, hospital, and surgical equipment, including furniture. **SIC:** 5047 (Medical & Hospital Equipment). **Est:** 1943. **Sales:** $3,200,000 (2000). **Emp:** 12. **Officers:** Noland Brown, President.

■ 18837 ■ **Home-Bound Medical Care Inc.**
2165 Sticer Cove, Ste. 1
Memphis, TN 38134
Phone: (901)386-5082 **Fax:** (901)382-0681
Products: Medical equipment. **SIC:** 5047 (Medical & Hospital Equipment). **Sales:** $20,000,000 (2000). **Emp:** 550. **Officers:** Kyle Altman, CEO; Randall Greer, CFO.

■ 18838 ■ **Home Diagnostics Inc.**
2300 NW 55th Ct.
Ft. Lauderdale, FL 33309
Phone: (954)677-9201
Free: (800)342-7226 **Fax:** (954)677-9203
Products: Glucose testing systems. **SIC:** 5047 (Medical & Hospital Equipment). **Sales:** $9,000,000

(1993). **Emp:** 90. **Officers:** George H. Holley, CEO & President.

■ 18839 ■ **Home Edco Home Care**
100 Dowd
Bangor, ME 04402-1156
Phone: (207)942-6505 **Fax:** (207)990-2127
Products: Medical and hospital equipment, including home care equipment. **SIC:** 5047 (Medical & Hospital Equipment). **Officers:** Arthur Blank, President.

■ 18840 ■ **Home Medical Supply Inc.**
265 West 1230 North
Provo, UT 84604-2546
Phone: (801)374-8101 **Fax:** (801)374-8126
Products: Medical equipment; Hospital equipment. **SIC:** 5047 (Medical & Hospital Equipment). **Est:** 1986. **Sales:** $1,000,000 (2000). **Emp:** 8. **Officers:** Larry Barney, President.

■ 18841 ■ **HomeReach Inc.**
404 E Wilson Bridge Rd., No. G-H
Worthington, OH 43085
Phone: (614)786-7060
Free: (800)229-7060 **Fax:** (614)786-7070
Products: Medical supplies, including intravenous equipment. **SIC:** 5047 (Medical & Hospital Equipment). **Est:** 1987. **Sales:** $5,000,000 (2000). **Emp:** 18. **Officers:** Mike Lazar, President; Jill Costanzo, Marketing Mgr.

■ 18842 ■ **Horizon Medical Inc.**
324 State St.
St. Paul, MN 55107-1608
Phone: (612)298-0843 **Fax:** (612)298-0018
Products: Surgical instruments, including suture needles, and eye, ear, nose, and throat instruments. **SIC:** 5047 (Medical & Hospital Equipment). **Officers:** Timothy Scanlan, President.

■ 18843 ■ **Howmedica Mountain States, Inc.**
1182 W 2450 S, No. A
Salt Lake City, UT 84119-8510
Phone: (801)484-8244 **Fax:** (801)484-8493
Products: Medical equipment; Orthopedic appliances (braces), including parts. **SIC:** 5047 (Medical & Hospital Equipment). **Officers:** Mike Carr, President.

■ 18844 ■ **HSO Corp.**
9595 153rd Ave. NE
Redmond, WA 98052
Phone: (425)822-1966 **Fax:** (425)869-9022
Products: Medical and hospital equipment; Hospital furniture; Oxygen therapy equipment. **SICs:** 5047 (Medical & Hospital Equipment); 5021 (Furniture). **Officers:** Martin Mc Curry, President.

■ 18845 ■ **Hudson Home Health Care Inc.**
72 Pane Rd.
Newington, CT 06111-5521
Phone: (860)667-4871
Free: (800)321-4442 **Fax:** (860)666-2714
E-mail: info@hudsonhhc.com
URL: http://www.hudsonhhc.com
Products: Medical equipment. **SIC:** 5047 (Medical & Hospital Equipment). **Est:** 1980. **Emp:** 55. **Officers:** Shirley Curley, President.

■ 18846 ■ **Huntleigh Technology Inc.**
40 Christopher Way
Eatontown, NJ 07724-3327
Phone: (732)446-2500
Free: (800)223-1218 **Fax:** (732)446-1938
Products: Intermittent pneumatic compression systems and medical ultrasonics. **SIC:** 5047 (Medical & Hospital Equipment). **Est:** 1977. **Sales:** $30,000,000 (2000). **Emp:** 100. **Officers:** Robert Riedel, President; William Guidetti, Vice President; Kelly Lama, Marketing Mgr.; Len Nass, Operations Officer.

■ 18847 ■ **Hutchinson Health Care Services**
803 E 30th Ave.
Hutchinson, KS 67502-4341
Phone: (316)665-0528
Free: (800)247-0292 **Fax:** (316)665-0586
E-mail: healthequip@mindspring.com
URL: http://www.health-equip.com
Products: Medical and hospital equipment and supplies. **SIC:** 5047 (Medical & Hospital Equipment).

Est: 1983. **Sales:** $2,000,000 (2000). **Emp:** 25. **Officers:** Jack Wortman, President.

■ 18848 ■ **Hyperbaric Oxygen Therapy Systems Inc.**
3224 Hoover Ave.
National City, CA 91950-7224
Phone: (619)336-2022 **Fax:** (619)336-2017
Products: Hyperbaric chambers. **SIC:** 5047 (Medical & Hospital Equipment). **Sales:** $1,200,000 (2000). **Emp:** 110. **Officers:** W.T. Gurnee, CEO & CFO; R.G. Williscroft, Dir. of Data Processing.

■ 18849 ■ **Imaging Concepts Inc.**
8237 Hermitage Rd.
Richmond, VA 23228-3031
Phone: (804)261-1921
Free: (800)228-0060 **Fax:** (804)262-3096
Products: Diagnostic ultrasound equipment. **SIC:** 5047 (Medical & Hospital Equipment). **Officers:** William Williams, President; Ann C. Williams, Corp. Safety.

■ 18850 ■ **Implant Dynamic**
37724 Hills Tech Dr.
Farmington Hills, MI 48331-3416
Phone: (248)489-4290 **Fax:** (248)489-4292
Products: Medical equipment; Hospital equipment; Orthopedic instruments, such as bone drills, bone plate; Orthopedic appliances (braces), including parts. **SIC:** 5047 (Medical & Hospital Equipment). **Officers:** Jerry Kee, President.

■ 18851 ■ **G.A. Ingram Co.**
12600 Newburgh Rd.
Livonia, MI 48150-1002
Phone: (313)591-1515 **Fax:** (313)591-2163
Products: Medical equipment and supplies. **SIC:** 5047 (Medical & Hospital Equipment). **Est:** 1973. **Sales:** $11,000,000 (2000). **Emp:** 10. **Officers:** Eugene McGorisk, Chairman of the Board; Dan Lear, Marketing & Sales Mgr.; Michelle Salveta, Customer Service Contact; Terry Pomroy, Dir of Human Resources.

■ 18852 ■ **Inmed Corp.**
2450 Meadowbrook Pkwy.
Duluth, GA 30096-4635
Phone: (404)623-0816 **Fax:** (404)623-1829
Products: Medical equipment; Medicinal products. **SICs:** 5047 (Medical & Hospital Equipment); 5122 (Drugs, Proprietaries & Sundries). **Est:** 1975. **Sales:** $25,000,000 (2000). **Emp:** 60. **Officers:** Wolfgang Lenz, President; Martha Holmes, Controller; David Emm, Dir. of Marketing & Sales; Norman Kelly, Dir. of Data Processing.

■ 18853 ■ **Integrated Medical Systems**
2717 19th Pl. S
Birmingham, AL 35209-1919
Phone: (205)879-3840 **Fax:** (205)879-3842
Products: Medical equipment; Hospital equipment. **SIC:** 5047 (Medical & Hospital Equipment). **Officers:** Farrell Robinson, President.

■ 18854 ■ **Interactive Medical Technologies Ltd.**
7348 Bellaire Ave.
North Hollywood, CA 91605-4301
Phone: (310)312-9652
Products: Medical equipment. **SIC:** 5047 (Medical & Hospital Equipment).

■ 18855 ■ **Intercontinental Trade Development**
PO Box 10838
Rockville, MD 20849-0838
Phone: (301)921-8200
Products: Medical equipment; Hospital equipment. **SIC:** 5047 (Medical & Hospital Equipment). **Officers:** Mark Zuares, President.

■ 18856 ■ **International Diagnostic Systems Corp.**
PO Box 799
St. Joseph, MI 49085-0799
Phone: (616)428-8400 **Fax:** (616)428-0093
E-mail: contactus@ids-kits.com
Products: Diagnostic test kits. **SIC:** 5122 (Drugs, Proprietaries & Sundries). **Est:** 1985. **Sales:** $1,000,000 (1999). **Emp:** 12. **Officers:** Deborah K.

Morris, President. **Also Known by This Acronym:** IDS.

■ **18857** ■ **International Domestic Development Corp.**
4511 Bragg Blvd.
Fayetteville, NC 28303
Phone: (919)864-5515
Products: X-ray apparatus. **SIC:** 5047 (Medical & Hospital Equipment). **Est:** 1977. **Sales:** $1,000,000 (2000). **Emp:** 15. **Officers:** Rex Harris, President.

■ **18858** ■ **International Healthcare Products**
4222 S Pulaski Rd.
Chicago, IL 60632
Phone: (773)247-7422
Free: (800)423-7886 **Fax:** (773)890-4669
E-mail: marketing@faricoinfo.com
URL: http://www.fabricoinfo.com/bathomatic
Products: Hydraulic bath lifts. **SIC:** 5047 (Medical & Hospital Equipment). **Est:** 1980. **Emp:** 80. **Officers:** Ashley Ross.

■ **18859** ■ **International Surgical Systems**
PO Box 16538
Phoenix, AZ 85011-6538
Phone: (602)277-2000 **Fax:** (602)277-9130
Products: Medical equipment; Hospital equipment. **SIC:** 5047 (Medical & Hospital Equipment). **Officers:** Steven Hansen, President.

■ **18860** ■ **International Trade Group**
5726 Monticello Ave.
Dallas, TX 75206
Phone: (214)827-0246 **Fax:** (214)823-2223
Products: Medical equipment and supplies; Electrical industrial controls; Computers; Motor vehicle parts. **SICs:** 5047 (Medical & Hospital Equipment); 5063 (Electrical Apparatus & Equipment); 5045 (Computers, Peripherals & Software); 5013 (Motor Vehicle Supplies & New Parts). **Officers:** George Smith, President.

■ **18861** ■ **Interroyal Hospital Supply Corp.**
168 Canal St., Ste. 600
New York, NY 10013
Phone: (212)334-0990 **Fax:** (212)431-7128
Products: Metal bedside cabinets; Medical instruments and apparatus; Metal commercial and library shelving; Wood partitions and storage systems; Hospital furniture and beds. **SICs:** 5047 (Medical & Hospital Equipment); 5046 (Commercial Equipment Nec). **Officers:** Hydook Mantashian, Dir. Intl. Div.

■ **18862** ■ **Interwest Home Medical Inc.**
235 E6100 S
Salt Lake City, UT 84107
Phone: (801)261-5100 **Fax:** (801)266-5319
Products: Home medical equipment. **SIC:** 5047 (Medical & Hospital Equipment). **Sales:** $24,800,000 (2000). **Emp:** 250. **Officers:** James E. Robinson, CEO, President & Chairman of the Board; Que H. Christensen, Sr. VP of Corp. Development.

■ **18863** ■ **Interwest Medical Equipment Distributors Inc.**
235 E 6100 S
Salt Lake City, UT 84107-7349
Phone: (801)261-5100
Free: (800)468-1000 **Fax:** (801)266-5319
Products: Medical equipment for home respiratory care. **SIC:** 5047 (Medical & Hospital Equipment). **Sales:** $28,600,000 (2000). **Emp:** 325. **Officers:** James E. Robinson, CEO & President; Bret A. Hardy, VP & Controller.

■ **18864** ■ **ISC/BioExpress**
420 N Kays Dr.
Kaysville, UT 84037
Phone: (801)547-5047
Free: (800)999-2901 **Fax:** (801)547-5051
E-mail: isc@bioexpress.com
URL: http://www.bioexpress.com
Products: Laboratory supplies, equipment, and chemicals for molecular biology, tissue culture, and immunology. **SIC:** 5047 (Medical & Hospital Equipment). **Est:** 1985. **Sales:** $25,000,000 (2000). **Emp:** 55. **Officers:** Cynthia Lundberg, President.

■ **18865** ■ **J & J Supply, Inc.**
120 E Main St.
Shawnee, OK 74801-6906
Phone: (405)878-0729 **Fax:** (405)878-0162
Products: Medical equipment; Hospital equipment. **SIC:** 5047 (Medical & Hospital Equipment). **Officers:** Herman Jones, President.

■ **18866** ■ **J & L Medical Supply Corp.**
PO Box 24067
Tempe, AZ 85285-4067
Phone: (602)967-9203 **Fax:** (602)345-2425
Products: Medical and hospital equipment, including orthopedic equipment. **SIC:** 5047 (Medical & Hospital Equipment). **Officers:** Ross Frazier, President.

■ **18867** ■ **Jaco Co.**
4848 Ronson Ct.
San Diego, CA 92111
Phone: (619)278-7743 **Fax:** (619)299-5472
Products: Surgical appliances and supplies; Laboratory professional equipment; Medical and hospital equipment. **SIC:** 5047 (Medical & Hospital Equipment). **Officers:** Jaime Munoz, President.

■ **18868** ■ **Janos Technology Inc.**
HCR 33, Rte. 35, Box 25
Townshend, VT 05353
Phone: (802)365-7714 **Fax:** (802)365-4596
E-mail: optics@janostech.com
URL: http://www.janostech.com
Products: IR optics; Optical assemblies. **SIC:** 5048 (Ophthalmic Goods). **Est:** 1970. **Sales:** $8,000,000 (2000). **Emp:** 80. **Officers:** Bruce C. Gardner, President; David I. Kaneshiro, VP of Tech. Sales & Engineering; Irwin A. Lampron, Mgr. of Finance.

■ **18869** ■ **Justlin Medical Inc.**
21717 NE 161st St.
Woodinville, WA 98072-7460
Phone: (425)861-4770
Free: (800)343-7786 **Fax:** (425)861-4772
Products: Medical and surgical equipment and supplies. **SIC:** 5047 (Medical & Hospital Equipment). **Est:** 1982. **Sales:** $2,000,000 (2000). **Emp:** 8. **Officers:** Tom Thomason, President.

■ **18870** ■ **Kako International Inc.**
0110 SW Curry St.
Portland, OR 97201-4375
Phone: (503)222-4801 **Fax:** (503)222-4813
Products: Medical equipment. **SIC:** 5047 (Medical & Hospital Equipment). **Est:** 1986. **Sales:** $600,000 (2000). **Emp:** 4. **Officers:** Kate Lagrand, President.

■ **18871** ■ **Kalamazoo Dental Supply**
710 Gibson St.
Kalamazoo, MI 49007
Phone: (616)345-0260
Free: (800)858-7805 **Fax:** (616)345-3977
Products: Medical equipment; Hospital equipment; Dental equipment and supplies. **SIC:** 5047 (Medical & Hospital Equipment). **Officers:** Gary Gray, Owner.

■ **18872** ■ **Kane X-Ray Company Inc.**
2134 Espey Ct., Ste. 12
Crofton, MD 21114-2437
Phone: (301)261-3645
Free: (800)238-8074 **Fax:** (410)721-6995
Products: Medical and hospital equipment and furniture; X-ray machines; Tubes. **SIC:** 5047 (Medical & Hospital Equipment). **Officers:** Daniel Kane, President.

■ **18873** ■ **Kentec Medical Inc.**
17871 Fitch
Irvine, CA 92614
Phone: (949)863-0810 **Fax:** (949)724-8923
Products: Medical equipment, including blood filters and neonatal and intensive care monitors. **SIC:** 5047 (Medical & Hospital Equipment). **Est:** 1970. **Sales:** $13,000,000 (2000). **Emp:** 32. **Officers:** Steve Becsi, President, e-mail: sbecsi@kentecmedical.com.

■ **18874** ■ **Kentucky Dental Supply Co. Inc.**
PO Box 12130
Lexington, KY 40580-2130
Phone: (606)299-6291 **Fax:** (606)299-0248
Products: Dental equipment and supplies. **SIC:** 5047

(Medical & Hospital Equipment). **Officers:** Carle Mahan, Treasurer.

■ **18875** ■ **Kentucky Home Care Services, Inc.**
790 N Dixie Ave., Ste. 500
Elizabethtown, KY 42701-2503
Phone: (502)737-2900
Free: (800)248-8921 **Fax:** (502)769-4699
Products: Home oxygen and medical equipment. **SIC:** 5047 (Medical & Hospital Equipment). **Officers:** David Fields, President & CEO.

■ **18876** ■ **Keomed Inc.**
11515 K Tel Dr.
Minnetonka, MN 55343-8845
Phone: (612)944-7306 **Fax:** (612)944-0881
Products: Medical and hospital equipment, including anesthetic and critical care equipment. **SIC:** 5047 (Medical & Hospital Equipment). **Officers:** Desmond Keogh, President.

■ **18877** ■ **Knit-Rite Inc.**
PO Box 410208
Kansas City, MO 64141-0208
Phone: (816)221-5200
Free: (800)462-4707 **Fax:** (816)221-2896
Products: Prosthetics and supplies, including socks. **SIC:** 5047 (Medical & Hospital Equipment). **Est:** 1923. **Sales:** $10,000,000 (2000). **Emp:** 55. **Officers:** W.B. Smith, President; Ron Hercules, Vice President; Robert L. Hickam, Dir. of Marketing; David Gordon, Dir. of Systems.

■ **18878** ■ **A. Kuhlman and Co.**
3939 Woodward Ave.
Detroit, MI 48201
Phone: (313)831-4050 **Fax:** (313)831-1393
Products: Surgical equipment, including scalpels, picks, and scissors. **SIC:** 5047 (Medical & Hospital Equipment). **Est:** 1867. **Sales:** $10,000,000 (2000). **Emp:** 16. **Officers:** Henry M. Kuhlman, President.

■ **18879** ■ **La Pointique International**
PO Box 6504
Bellevue, WA 98008-0504
Phone: (206)575-8843 **Fax:** (206)575-8843
Products: Knee and elbow support equipment. **SIC:** 5047 (Medical & Hospital Equipment). **Officers:** Theresa Wong, Vice President.

■ **18880** ■ **Lab Safety Supply Inc.**
401 S Wright Rd.
PO Box 1368
Janesville, WI 53547-1368
Phone: (608)754-2345
Free: (800)356-0783 **Fax:** 800-543-9910
E-mail: custsvc@labsafety.com
URL: http://www.labsafety.com
Products: Personal safety equipment; Industrial supplies; Material handling equipment; Spill cleanup products; Facilities maintenance; Janitorial equipment; Signs, tapes, and labels. **SICs:** 5122 (Drugs, Proprietaries & Sundries); 5087 (Service Establishment Equipment); 5047 (Medical & Hospital Equipment); 5085 (Industrial Supplies). **Est:** 1974. **Emp:** 650. **Officers:** Larry J. Loizzo, President, e-mail: prez@labsafety.com.

■ **18881** ■ **Labomed, Inc.**
2921 S Lacienega Blvd.
Culver City, CA 90232
Phone: (310)202-0814
Free: (800)548-6907 **Fax:** (310)202-7286
URL: http://www.laborned.com
Products: Medical equipment. **SIC:** 5047 (Medical & Hospital Equipment). **Est:** 1978. **Sales:** $1,000,000 (2000). **Emp:** 10. **Officers:** Jack Baker, Manager; Jack Gilbert. **Former Name:** Best American Co.

■ **18882** ■ **Laboratory Supply Company**
PO Box 9289
Louisville, KY 40209
Phone: (502)363-1891 **Fax:** (502)364-1609
E-mail: labsco@labsco.com
URL: http://www.labsco.com
Products: Medical and laboratory equipment and supplies, including chemistry analyzer machines, exam tables, and consumables. **SIC:** 5047 (Medical & Hospital Equipment). **Est:** 1972. **Sales:** $56,000,000

(1999). **Emp:** 182. **Officers:** Charles E. Davis Sr., President & Treasurer; Charles E. Davis Jr., Secretary. **Alternate Name:** LABSCO.

■ 18883 ■ **LDC Corporation of America**
7 E Glenolden Ave.
Glenolden, PA 19036
Phone: (610)586-0986
Free: (800)782-6324 **Fax:** (610)586-0847
Products: Wheel chairs; Medical equipment; Products for physically challenged. **SIC:** 5047 (Medical & Hospital Equipment). **Emp:** 2. **Officers:** Jacques Dallery, President.

■ 18884 ■ **Lease Surgical Inc.**
101 S Cleveland Ave.
Sioux Falls, SD 57103-2034
Phone: (605)338-1033
Products: Medical equipment; Hospital equipment. **SIC:** 5047 (Medical & Hospital Equipment). **Officers:** William Lease, President.

■ 18885 ■ **Ralph Leasure & Associates Inc.**
10555 Guilford Rd.
Suite #113
Jessup, MD 20794-9110
Phone: (301)317-0070
Free: (800)486-KNEE **Fax:** (301)317-0776
E-mail: r/a@erols.com
URL: http://www.surgicalbusiness.com
Products: Medical equipment; Hospital equipment; Orthopedic instruments; Blood collecting and processing equipment. **SIC:** 5047 (Medical & Hospital Equipment). **Est:** 1980. **Officers:** Ralph Leasure, President, e-mail: rll@home.com; Karla Payball, Customer Service Contact, e-mail: kadqueb@aol.com.

■ 18886 ■ **Leeward Inc.**
1121 Hempshire St., No. 135
Richardson, TX 75080
Phone: (972)690-9778 **Fax:** (972)690-1351
Products: Medical instruments and equipment. **SIC:** 5047 (Medical & Hospital Equipment). **Sales:** $1,500,000 (2000). **Emp:** 4. **Officers:** Tom Sampson, President.

■ 18887 ■ **Leisegang Medical Inc.**
6401 Congress Ave.
Boca Raton, FL 33487
Phone: (561)994-0202
Free: (800)448-4450 **Fax:** (561)998-0846
E-mail: www.leisegang.com
Products: Medical equipment. **SIC:** 5047 (Medical & Hospital Equipment). **Est:** 1986. **Sales:** $5,000,000 (2000). **Emp:** 35. **Officers:** W. Speyer, President; John Miller, Sales & Marketing Contact; Julie Durnbaugh, Customer Service Contact; Jane Klaffer, Human Resources Contact.

■ 18888 ■ **Leisure-Lift, Inc.**
1800 Merriam Ln.
Kansas City, KS 66106
Phone: (913)722-5658
Free: (800)255-0285 **Fax:** (913)722-2614
E-mail: leisurlift@aol.com
URL: http://www.pacesaver.com
Products: Wheelchairs; Scooters; Liftchairs. **SIC:** 5047 (Medical & Hospital Equipment). **Est:** 1958. **Sales:** $20,000,000 (2000). **Emp:** 65. **Officers:** Du Wayne Kramer, President; Ron Kruse, Vice President; Ron Weldan, Sales/Marketing Contact, e-mail: scooter.ron@worldnet.com; Mike Wade, Customer Service Contact; Ron Kruse, Human Resources Contact. **Alternate Name:** Burke Inc.

■ 18889 ■ **LeJoy Uniforms Inc.**
608 23rd St. S
Birmingham, AL 35233-2325
Phone: (205)252-8654 **Fax:** (205)252-0501
Products: Medical equipment; Hospital equipment. **SIC:** 5047 (Medical & Hospital Equipment). **Officers:** Leonard Nichols, President.

■ 18890 ■ **LeMare Medical Inc.**
PO Box 526743
Miami, FL 33172
Phone: (305)591-1152 **Fax:** (305)358-9608
Products: Medical equipment. **SIC:** 5047 (Medical &

Hospital Equipment). **Est:** 1925. **Sales:** $7,000,000 (2000). **Emp:** 7. **Officers:** Julio E. Estay, President.

■ 18891 ■ **Lintex Corp.**
2609 Territorial Rd.
St. Paul, MN 55114-1074
Phone: (612)646-6600 **Fax:** (612)646-3210
Products: Hospital beds; Linens. **SICs:** 5047 (Medical & Hospital Equipment); 5021 (Furniture). **Est:** 1954. **Sales:** $18,000,000 (2000). **Emp:** 70. **Officers:** John Sleizer, President; Tom Folz, Controller; Tim Phippen, Vice President; Geoff Mayo, VP of Operations.

■ 18892 ■ **Lors Medical Corp.**
PO Box 1718
Roanoke Rapids, NC 27870-7718
Phone: (919)537-0031
Products: Oxygen; Home medical equipment. **SIC:** 5047 (Medical & Hospital Equipment). **Est:** 1979. **Sales:** $8,500,000 (2000). **Emp:** 82. **Officers:** Donald Lynch, President; Dorothy A. Boehm, Controller.

■ 18893 ■ **Luxury Liners**
14545 Valley View Ave., Ste. R
Santa Fe Springs, CA 90670
Phone: (562)921-1813
Free: (800)247-4203 **Fax:** (562)921-1404
E-mail: atoll@earthlink.net
Products: Wheel chairs, seating systems, and wheel chair accessories; Prosthetics. **SIC:** 5047 (Medical & Hospital Equipment). **Est:** 1981. **Officers:** Richard Pasillas, President; Rudy Oceguera, Vice President.

■ 18894 ■ **Lynn Medical Instrument Co.**
PO Box 7027
Bloomfield Hills, MI 48302-7027
Phone: (248)338-4571 **Fax:** (248)338-6242
Products: Medical equipment; Hospital equipment; Hospital furniture; Patient monitoring equipment. **SIC:** 5047 (Medical & Hospital Equipment). **Officers:** Louis Fagnani, President.

■ 18895 ■ **Lyntech Corp.**
10177 S 77th East Ave.
Tulsa, OK 74133-6802
Phone: (918)299-1321
Products: Medical equipment; Hospital equipment. **SIC:** 5047 (Medical & Hospital Equipment). **Officers:** Robert Lynch, President.

■ 18896 ■ **Mabis Healthcare Inc.**
28690 N Ballard Dr.
Lake Forest, IL 60045
Phone: (847)680-6811
Free: (800)728-6811 **Fax:** (847)680-9646
URL: http://www.mabis.net
Products: Blood pressure monitors; Stethoscopes; Thermometers; Rubber goods. **SIC:** 5047 (Medical & Hospital Equipment). **Est:** 1992. **Sales:** $20,000,000 (2000). **Emp:** 35. **Officers:** Mike Mazza, President.

■ 18897 ■ **Magnivision**
1500 S 66th Ave.
Hollywood, FL 33023
Phone: (954)986-9000 **Fax:** (954)986-9004
Products: Optical goods including lenses, frames, and optical accessories. **SIC:** 5048 (Ophthalmic Goods). **Emp:** 350. **Former Name:** Al Nyman and Son.

■ 18898 ■ **Main Line International Inc.**
151 Ben Burton Cr.
Bogart, GA 30622
Phone: (706)227-1800
Free: (800)397-9020 **Fax:** (706)227-3633
E-mail: info@mlimedical.com
URL: http://www.mlinedical.com
Products: Diagnostic ultrasound equipment. **SIC:** 5047 (Medical & Hospital Equipment). **Est:** 2000. **Officers:** John Shirreffs, Director.

■ 18899 ■ **Major Medical Supply Co. Inc.**
687 Laconia Rd.
Belmont, NH 03220-3921
Phone: (603)267-7406 **Fax:** (603)267-8231
Products: Medical and hospital equipment and furniture; Surgical equipment and supplies. **SIC:** 5047 (Medical & Hospital Equipment). **Officers:** William Sussenberger, President.

■ 18900 ■ **Manchester Medical Supply Inc.**
PO Box 300
Manchester, CT 06045-0831
Phone: (860)649-9015
Products: Medical and hospital equipment and supplies. **SIC:** 5047 (Medical & Hospital Equipment). **Officers:** Roger Talbot, President.

■ 18901 ■ **Master Works International**
100 Dogwood Dr.
Marietta, GA 30068-3301
Phone: (404)565-5220 **Fax:** (404)565-5331
Products: Dental laboratory equipment and supplies. **SIC:** 5047 (Medical & Hospital Equipment). **Officers:** Tokuo Masuda, President.

■ 18902 ■ **Mastermans**
PO Box 411
Auburn, MA 01501-0411
Phone: (508)755-7861 **Fax:** (508)755-1543
Products: Medical equipment; Hospital equipment; Industrial safety devices, including first-aid kits and face and eye masks. **SIC:** 5047 (Medical & Hospital Equipment). **Officers:** Benson Masterman, Partner.

■ 18903 ■ **MBI Inc.**
1353 Arville St.
Las Vegas, NV 89102-1608
Phone: (702)259-1999
E-mail: mbimedical@msn.com
Products: Medical and hospital equipment, including X-ray machines, film, processors, stress testing treadmills, and autoclaves. **SIC:** 5047 (Medical & Hospital Equipment). **Est:** 1983. **Sales:** $2,070,000 (2000). **Emp:** 13. **Officers:** Scott Graham, President; Darla Graham, Sec. & Treas. **Doing Business As:** MBI X-Ray & Medical Supply.

■ 18904 ■ **McAbee Medical Inc.**
1401 6th Ave. SE
Decatur, AL 35601-4200
Phone: (205)351-7747 **Fax:** (205)351-7740
Products: Medical equipment; Hospital equipment. **SIC:** 5047 (Medical & Hospital Equipment). **Officers:** John McAbee, President.

■ 18905 ■ **McKesson General Medical Corp.**
PO Box 27452
Richmond, VA 23228
Phone: (804)264-7500
Products: Medical equipment and supplies. **SIC:** 5047 (Medical & Hospital Equipment). **Sales:** $1,200,000,000 (2000). **Emp:** 3,000. **Officers:** Paul C. Julian, President.

■ 18906 ■ **McQueary Brothers Drug Co.**
PO Box 5955
Springfield, MO 65801
Phone: (417)869-2577
Free: (800)747-2577 **Fax:** (417)831-5207
Products: Pharmaceuticals. **SIC:** 5122 (Drugs, Proprietaries & Sundries). **Sales:** $100,000,000 (2000). **Emp:** 80. **Officers:** William T. McQueary, Chairman of the Board; Fred McQueary, CFO.

■ 18907 ■ **Med Dent Service Corp.**
25 Falmouth Rd.
Falmouth, ME 04105-1841
Phone: (207)781-2293 **Fax:** (207)781-5089
Products: Medical equipment; Hospital equipment. **SIC:** 5047 (Medical & Hospital Equipment). **Officers:** Herbert Olsen, President.

■ 18908 ■ **Med-Lab Supply Company Inc.**
923 NW 27th Ave.
Miami, FL 33125
Phone: (305)642-5144
Products: X-ray equipment. **SIC:** 5047 (Medical & Hospital Equipment). **Est:** 1965. **Sales:** $9,000,000 (2000). **Emp:** 56. **Officers:** Gonzalo Diaz, CEO; Augie Maquiera, Controller; A. Diaz, Vice President.

■ 18909 ■ **Med-Tech Inc.**
32035 Edward Ave.
Madison Heights, MI 48071-1419
Phone: (248)589-3109 **Fax:** (248)588-3747
Products: Medical equipment; Hospital equipment. **SIC:** 5047 (Medical & Hospital Equipment). **Officers:** Pingree Ianitelli, President.

■ **18910** ■ **Meddev Corp.**
2468 Embarcadero Way
Palo Alto, CA 94303-3313
Phone: (650)494-1153
Free: (800)543-2789 **Fax:** (650)494-1464
E-mail: info@meddev-corp.com
URL: http://www.meddev-corp.com
Products: Medical equipment; Surgical and medical
instruments and apparatus. **SIC:** 5047 (Medical &
Hospital Equipment). **Est:** 1971. **Sales:** $2,000,000
(2000). **Emp:** 15. **Officers:** Richard G. Grey,
Treasurer; Richard P. Jobe, Chairman of the Board &
President.

■ **18911** ■ **Medi-Globe Corp.**
6202 S Maple Ave.
Tempe, AZ 85283-2861
Phone: (602)897-2772 **Fax:** (602)897-2878
E-mail: info@mediglobe.com
URL: http://www.mediglobe.com
Products: Instruments for flexible endoscopy. **SIC:**
5047 (Medical & Hospital Equipment). **Est:** 1988.
Sales: $9,000,000 (2000). **Emp:** 35. **Officers:** Stefan
Wohnhas, CEO & President; Brian Karler, Exec. VP.

■ **18912** ■ **Medi Inc. - School Health Div.**
75 York Ave.
PO Box 302
Randolph, MA 02368
Phone: (781)961-1232
Free: (800)225-8634 **Fax:** (781)961-5750
Products: Medical equipment; Medicinal and health
supplies; Athletic training and nursing supplies. **SIC:**
5047 (Medical & Hospital Equipment). **Est:** 1984.
Sales: $9,000,000 (2000). **Emp:** 35. **Officers:** William
J. Mc Gilivray, Owner.

■ **18913** ■ **Medical Devices Inc.**
12211 Old Shelbyville Ra., Ste. C
Louisville, KY 40243
Phone: (502)244-5200 **Fax:** (502)244-4452
Products: Medical equipment; Hospital equipment.
SIC: 5047 (Medical & Hospital Equipment). **Officers:**
Dale Allison, President.

■ **18914** ■ **Medical Equipment Repair Services Inc.**
6092 Clark Center Ave.
Sarasota, FL 34238
Phone: (941)921-2584 **Fax:** (941)924-6158
Products: Respiratory systems equipment. **SIC:** 5047
(Medical & Hospital Equipment). **Sales:** $5,000,000
(2000). **Emp:** 17. **Officers:** Jeff Klemz, Dir. of
Operations; Karen Beasly, Accounting Manager.

■ **18915** ■ **Medical Equipment Resale, Inc.**
45031 Grand River
PO Box 7006
Novi, MI 48376-7006
Phone: (248)380-7951
Free: (800)962-4419 **Fax:** (248)380-7954
E-mail: meri@wwnet.net
URL: http://www.medequipresale.com
Products: Medical and hospital equipment and
supplies. **SIC:** 5047 (Medical & Hospital Equipment).
Est: 1980. **Emp:** 6. **Officers:** Ira Rubin, President.
Doing Business As: Medical Equipment Resale, Inc.

■ **18916** ■ **Medical Imaging Inc.**
PO Box 4023
Camp Verde, AZ 86322-4023
Phone: (602)943-4759 **Fax:** (602)581-8429
Products: X-ray film and supplies; Dark room film
processors. **SICs:** 5047 (Medical & Hospital
Equipment); 5043 (Photographic Equipment &
Supplies).

■ **18917** ■ **Medical Imaging Services Inc.**
800 Central Ave.
Jefferson, LA 70121-1305
Phone: (504)733-9729 **Fax:** (504)733-9715
Products: Medical equipment; Hospital equipment; X-
ray apparatus. **SIC:** 5047 (Medical & Hospital
Equipment). **Officers:** Terry Ancar, President.

■ **18918** ■ **Medical International Inc.**
PO Box 166
Spring Lake, NJ 07762
Phone: (732)974-1550 **Fax:** (732)974-1554
Products: Surgical instruments and appliances;
Laboratory and scientific instruments; Medical
instruments and supplies. **SIC:** 5047 (Medical &
Hospital Equipment). **Est:** 1987. **Officers:** Carol Myers,
President.

■ **18919** ■ **Medical Marketing Inc.**
1771 South 900 West, No. 50
Salt Lake City, UT 84104-1700
Phone: (801)977-0168 **Fax:** (801)972-3448
Products: Medical equipment; Hospital equipment.
SIC: 5047 (Medical & Hospital Equipment). **Officers:**
Robert Frost, President.

■ **18920** ■ **Medical Mart Inc.**
465-G S Herlong Ave.
Rock Hill, SC 29732
Phone: (803)366-5544
Products: Medical equipment; Hospital equipment.
SIC: 5047 (Medical & Hospital Equipment). **Officers:**
Robert Loftin, President.

■ **18921** ■ **Medical Procedures Inc.**
2223 Eastern Ave.
Baltimore, MD 21231-3112
Phone: (410)522-3451
Products: Medical equipment; Hospital equipment.
SIC: 5047 (Medical & Hospital Equipment). **Officers:**
Jack McGlasson, President.

■ **18922** ■ **Medical Scientific Service**
11004 Los Arboles Ave. NE
Albuquerque, NM 87112-1721
Phone: (505)298-6639 **Fax:** (505)292-0148
E-mail: mssabqnm@aol.com
Products: Medical equipment; Hospital equipment;
Hospital furniture. **SIC:** 5047 (Medical & Hospital
Equipment). **Est:** 1972. **Sales:** $100,000 (2000). **Emp:**
4. **Officers:** Michael G. Erick, President, e-mail:
mgerick@aol.com.

■ **18923** ■ **Medical Specialists Company Inc.**
7770 Iliff Ave., Ste. D
Denver, CO 80231-5326
Phone: (303)750-2002
Free: (800)873-3414 **Fax:** (303)750-2043
E-mail: medspecial@aol.com
URL: http://www.medicalspecialistsnet
Products: Physical therapy and chiropractic
equipment; Personal health and wellness products and
supplies; Ergonomic products; Corporate health
products. **SIC:** 5047 (Medical & Hospital Equipment).
Est: 1955. **Emp:** 20. **Officers:** Mark Graves, Vice
President.

■ **18924** ■ **Medical Supplies Inc.**
146 Kennedy Memorial Dr.
Waterville, ME 04901-5133
Phone: (207)873-6151 **Fax:** (207)873-3199
Products: Medical equipment; Hospital equipment;
Hospital furniture. **SIC:** 5047 (Medical & Hospital
Equipment). **Officers:** Richard Upham, President.

■ **18925** ■ **MediQuip International**
1865 Summit Ave., Ste. 600
Plano, TX 75074
Phone: (972)423-1600 **Fax:** (972)423-6423
Products: Medical equipment. **SIC:** 5047 (Medical &
Hospital Equipment). **Sales:** $30,000,000 (2000). **Emp:**
90. **Officers:** Ralph Armstrong, CEO & President.

■ **18926** ■ **Memphis Serum Company Inc.**
PO Box 16203
Memphis, TN 38186-0203
Phone: (901)332-4694
Free: (800)582-6227 **Fax:** (901)396-2823
Products: Medical equipment; Hospital equipment;
Veterinary instruments. **SIC:** 5047 (Medical & Hospital
Equipment). **Officers:** John Adams, President.

■ **18927** ■ **Menlo Tool Company Inc.**
PO Box 5127
Warren, MI 48090-5127
Phone: (810)756-6010 **Fax:** (810)756-1821
Products: Medical and hospital equipment, including

carbide tools and dental drill bits. **SIC:** 5047 (Medical &
Hospital Equipment). **Officers:** Frank Kastelic,
President.

■ **18928** ■ **Mercy National Purchasing Inc.**
55 Shuman Blvd.
Naperville, IL 60563-8469
Phone: (708)355-5500 **Fax:** (630)355-7080
Products: Hospital equipment and supplies, including
light bulbs and x-ray machines. **SIC:** 5047 (Medical &
Hospital Equipment). **Est:** 1967. **Sales:** $4,000,000
(2000). **Emp:** 17. **Officers:** Warren Rhodes, President,
e-mail: mgray@memi.org.

■ **18929** ■ **Mercy Resource Management, Inc.**
55 Shuman Blvd.
Naperville, IL 60563-8469
Phone: (630)355-5500 **Fax:** (630)355-7080
URL: http://www.mrmi.org
Products: Medical and hospital equipment;
Pharmaceuticals. **SIC:** 5047 (Medical & Hospital
Equipment). **Est:** 1967. **Sales:** $1,000,000,000 (2000).
Emp: 13. **Officers:** Michael Gray, CEO & President.
Former Name: Mercy National Purchasing Inc.

■ **18930** ■ **Meridian Synapse Corporation**
12020 Synapse Valley, No. 100
Reston, VA 20191
Phone: (703)318-0464 **Fax:** (703)318-7234
Products: Medical and hospital equipment and
supplies. **SIC:** 5047 (Medical & Hospital Equipment).
Officers: Michael Cole, President.

■ **18931** ■ **Merriam-Graves Corp.**
1361 Union St.
West Springfield, MA 01089
Phone: (413)781-6550 **Fax:** (413)739-4071
Products: Medical equipment; Hospital equipment.
SIC: 5047 (Medical & Hospital Equipment). **Officers:**
Henry Wakeman, President.

■ **18932** ■ **Merriam-Graves Corp.**
806 River Rd.
Charlestown, NH 03603
Phone: (603)542-8768
Free: (800)333-8095 **Fax:** (603)542-6153
URL: http://www.merriamgraves.com
Products: Medical equipment; Chemicals. **SICs:** 5047
(Medical & Hospital Equipment); 5169 (Chemicals &
Allied Products Nec). **Est:** 1966. **Emp:** 250. **Officers:**
Donald Wakeman, President; Henry K. Wakeman IV,
COO, e-mail: wakeman@merriam-graves.com; Gregg
Tewksbury, CFO; John Brennan, VP of Marketing.
Former Name: Kitcher Corp.

■ **18933** ■ **Metropolitan Medical Inc.**
360-4 McGhee Rd.
Winchester, VA 22603
Phones: 800-336-0318 (540)662-8000
Free: (800)336-0318 **Fax:** 800-590-0081
E-mail: sales@metropolitanmedicalcom
URL: http://www.metropolitanmedical.com
Products: Medical equipment, including respiratory
and critical care; Anesthesia; Biomedical engineering;
Medical gas systems. **SIC:** 5047 (Medical & Hospital
Equipment). **Est:** 1971. **Emp:** 28. **Officers:** Donald G.
Morley, President, e-mail: donm@
metropolitanmedical.com.

■ **18934** ■ **Metropolitan X-Ray Sales Inc.**
24558 Michigan Ave.
Dearborn, MI 48124-1711
Phone: (313)278-7373 **Fax:** (313)278-0434
Products: Medical equipment; Hospital equipment; X-
ray apparatus. **SIC:** 5047 (Medical & Hospital
Equipment). **Officers:** John Kill, President.

■ **18935** ■ **Meyers Medical Inc.**
1112 Baywater Dr.
West Columbia, SC 29170-3119
Phone: (803)791-7436
Products: Medical equipment; Hospital equipment;
Orthopedic appliances (braces), including parts. **SIC:**
5047 (Medical & Hospital Equipment). **Officers:**
William Meyers, President.

■ 18936 ■   Micro Ear Technology Inc.
PO Box 59124
Minneapolis, MN 55459-0124
Phone: (612)934-3001
Free: (800)635-3455   **Fax:** (612)934-2037
Products: Hearing aids. **SIC:** 5047 (Medical & Hospital
Equipment). **Officers:** Larry Hagen, President.

■ 18937 ■   Mid-Michigan Regional Health Systems
4005 Orchard Dr.
Midland, MI 48640-6102
Phone: (517)839-3398   **Fax:** (517)839-3307
Products: Medical equipment; Hospital equipment.
SIC: 5047 (Medical & Hospital Equipment). **Officers:**
Terence Moore, President.

■ 18938 ■   Midland Hospital Supply Inc.
PO Box 2685
Fargo, ND 58108
Phone: (701)235-4451   **Fax:** (701)235-7920
Products: Medical and surgical equipment and
supplies. **SIC:** 5047 (Medical & Hospital Equipment).
Est: 1947. **Sales:** $15,000,000 (2000). **Emp:** 33.
Officers: Richard W. Larson, President; Faye Y.
DuBord, CFO; Robert Sutton, Exec. VP.

■ 18939 ■   Midwest Vision Distributors Inc.
Hwy. 23 E, Box 1167
St. Cloud, MN 56301
Phone: (612)252-6006   **Fax:** (612)259-7220
Products: Ophthalmic goods. **SIC:** 5048 (Ophthalmic
Goods). **Sales:** $11,000,000 (1993). **Emp:** 230.
Officers: Myrel A. Neumann, President; Patrick Miller,
VP of Finance.

■ 18940 ■   MIRA Inc.
87 Rumford Ave.
Waltham, MA 02454
Phone: (617)894-2200   **Fax:** (617)647-1855
Products: Surgical instruments, including suture
needles, and eye, ear, nose, and throat instruments.
SIC: 5047 (Medical & Hospital Equipment). **Est:** 1968.
Sales: $1,000,000 (2000). **Emp:** 10. **Officers:** Dan
O'Brien, President; Ray Lynds, CFO; William Manning,
Dir. of Marketing.

■ 18941 ■   Mississippi Serum Distributors
165 Wilmington St.
PO Box 8776
Jackson, MS 39284-8776
Phone: (601)372-8434   **Fax:** (601)371-3045
Products: Medical equipment; Hospital equipment;
Veterinary instruments. **SIC:** 5047 (Medical & Hospital
Equipment). **Officers:** Stephen Pittman, President.

■ 18942 ■   Missoula Hearing
601 S Orange St.
Missoula, MT 59801-2611
Phone: (406)549-1951   **Fax:** (406)542-5682
Products: Medical and hospital equipment and
supplies. **SIC:** 5047 (Medical & Hospital Equipment).
Est: 1970. **Emp:** 3. **Officers:** Dudley Anderson,
President.

■ 18943 ■   Mitchell Home Medical
4811 Carpenter Rd.
Ypsilanti, MI 48197
Phone: (734)572-0203
Free: (800)420-0202   **Fax:** (734)572-0281
Products: Oxygen and respiratory equipment, DME,
supplies. **SIC:** 5047 (Medical & Hospital Equipment).
Est: 1967. **Sales:** $2,000,000 (1999). **Emp:** 20.
Officers: Mitch Michaluk, Owner. **Former Name:** Ann
Arbor Therapy Oxygen Inc.

■ 18944 ■   Mitchell Orthopedic Supply Inc.
PO Box 634
Brentwood, TN 37024-0634
Phone: (615)377-6900   **Fax:** (615)377-6319
Products: Medical equipment; Hospital equipment;
Orthopedic appliances (braces), including parts. **SIC:**
5047 (Medical & Hospital Equipment). **Officers:**
Lawrence Mitchell, President.

■ 18945 ■   MKM Inc.
543 Newfield Ave.
Stamford, CT 06905-3302
Phone: (203)324-3055   **Fax:** (203)359-1903
Products: Medical equipment; Hospital equipment.
SIC: 5047 (Medical & Hospital Equipment). **Officers:**
Tyrone Mak, President.

■ 18946 ■   MMI Inc.
PO Box 305
Southfield, MI 48037
Phone: (248)358-1940
Free: (800)344-1644   **Fax:** (248)358-2219
Products: Radiology products; O.R. prep products,
including disposable gowns and caps. **SIC:** 5047
(Medical & Hospital Equipment). **Est:** 1960. **Emp:** 19.
Officers: H.R. Mattler; Steve Mattler.

■ 18947 ■   Morgan Scientific, Inc.
151 Essex St.
Haverhill, MA 01832-5564
Phone: (978)521-4440   **Fax:** (978)521-4445
E-mail: support@morgansci.com
URL: http://www.morgansci.com
Products: Medical equipment; Hospital equipment;
Compost monitoring. **SIC:** 5047 (Medical & Hospital
Equipment). **Est:** 1980. **Officers:** Patrick Morgan,
President. **Former Name:** P.K. Morgan Instruments
Inc.

■ 18948 ■   William Morris Associates
PO Box 709
Asheville, NC 28802-0709
Phone: (704)255-7721
Free: (800)243-3112   **Fax:** (704)254-9185
Products: Medical and hospital equipment and
supplies. **SIC:** 5047 (Medical & Hospital Equipment).
Officers: William Morris, President.

■ 18949 ■   Mountain Aire Medical Equipment
3975 Interpark Dr.
Colorado Springs, CO 80907-5067
Phone: (719)592-0333
Free: (800)659-9110   **Fax:** (719)592-0335
Products: Medical equipment; Hospital equipment;
Oxygen tents. **SIC:** 5047 (Medical & Hospital
Equipment). **Officers:** Debra Byington, President.

■ 18950 ■   Mountain Imaging Inc.
1109 S Plaza Way 274
Flagstaff, AZ 86001-6317
Phone: (520)774-0027   **Fax:** (520)774-0603
Products: Medical and hospital equipment, including
X-ray film and supplies. **SIC:** 5047 (Medical & Hospital
Equipment). **Officers:** Randy Brogdon, President.

■ 18951 ■   Mountain States Medical Inc.
5220 Pinemont Dr.
Salt Lake City, UT 84123-4607
Phone: (801)261-2255   **Fax:** (801)261-2242
Products: Medical, hospital, and surgical equipment.
SIC: 5047 (Medical & Hospital Equipment). **Officers:**
Robert Wrigley, President.

■ 18952 ■   Mourad & Associated International Trade
PO Box 633
Rosemead, CA 91770
Phone: (626)572-9134   **Fax:** (626)571-0191
Products: Medical equipment, including surgical
instruments and apparatus, electromedical equipment,
and electrocardiographs. **SIC:** 5047 (Medical &
Hospital Equipment). **Officers:** Jaime Mourad,
President.

■ 18953 ■   MRS Industries Inc.
PO Box 773
Rocky Hill, CT 06067-0773
Phone: (860)828-9624
Free: (800)452-1344   **Fax:** (860)828-7772
E-mail: mrsind@aol.com
URL: http://www.mrsindustries.com
Products: Industrial safety and cleanroom supplies.
SICs: 5047 (Medical & Hospital Equipment); 5084
(Industrial Machinery & Equipment). **Officers:** Michael
Shelto, President.

■ 18954 ■   Nada Concepts Inc.
771 NE Harding St.
Minneapolis, MN 55413
Phone: (612)623-4436
Free: (800)722-2587   **Fax:** (612)331-1613
Products: Orthopedic back supports. **SIC:** 5047
(Medical & Hospital Equipment). **Est:** 1985. **Emp:** 4.
Officers: Victor Toso, President.

■ 18955 ■   Nasco West
PO Box 3837
Modesto, CA 95352-3837
Phone: (209)545-1600
Free: (800)558-9595   **Fax:** (209)545-1669
Products: Art and school supplies; Medical training
equipment. **SICs:** 5047 (Medical & Hospital
Equipment); 5112 (Stationery & Office Supplies).
Sales: $10,000,000 (2000). **Emp:** 80. **Officers:** Tom
Swafford, Exec. VP.

■ 18956 ■   Nassifs Professional Pharmacy
PO Box 778
North Adams, MA 01247-0778
Phone: (413)663-3845   **Fax:** (413)664-9730
Products: Medical equipment; Hospital equipment;
Surgical equipment; Pharmaceutical preparations.
SICs: 5047 (Medical & Hospital Equipment); 5122
(Drugs, Proprietaries & Sundries). **Officers:** Allen
Nassif, President.

■ 18957 ■   National Medical Excess
733 Brush Ave.
Bronx, NY 10465-1839
Phone: (914)665-2777
Free: (800)872-5407   **Fax:** (914)665-2101
Products: Medical equipment. **SIC:** 5047 (Medical &
Hospital Equipment). **Est:** 1989. **Sales:** $4,000,000
(2000). **Emp:** 5. **Officers:** John Wittenberg, President.

■ 18958 ■   NCS Healthcare
3200 E Reno Ave.
Del City, OK 73115-6603
Phone: (405)670-2939
Free: (800)421-4123   **Fax:** (405)670-2726
Products: Medical equipment; Hospital equipment;
Hospital furniture. **SIC:** 5047 (Medical & Hospital
Equipment). **Est:** 1982. **Sales:** $4,000,000 (2000).
Emp: 30. **Officers:** Gail Benjamin, Director.

■ 18959 ■   Nebraska Medical Mart II
720 E 23rd St.
Fremont, NE 68025
Phone: (402)727-4270   **Fax:** (402)727-7682
Products: Medical equipment; Hospital equipment;
Home oxygen. **SIC:** 5047 (Medical & Hospital
Equipment). **Officers:** Mike Keithley, President; Joe
Woolridge, General Mgr.

■ 18960 ■   New Mexico Orthopedic Supplies
4821 Central Ave. NE
Albuquerque, NM 87108-1226
Phone: (505)255-8673   **Fax:** (505)265-8965
Products: Orthopedic equipment and supplies. **SIC:**
5047 (Medical & Hospital Equipment). **Officers:**
Seymour Lefton, President.

■ 18961 ■   Nihon Kohden America Inc.
2601 Campus Dr.
Irvine, CA 92612
Phone: (714)250-3959   **Fax:** (714)250-3210
Products: Medical equipment. **SIC:** 5047 (Medical &
Hospital Equipment). **Est:** 1979. **Sales:** $37,500,000
(2000). **Emp:** 100. **Officers:** Hitoshi Adachi, President;
Michael Osawa, Accountant; R. Hecker, Dir. of
Marketing; Mike Ohsawa, Controller; Maureen Soll, Dir
of Human Resources.

■ 18962 ■   Nowak Dental Supplies Inc.
PO Box 1489
Chalmette, LA 70044-1489
Phone: (504)944-0395   **Fax:** (504)949-2149
Products: Medical equipment; Hospital equipment;
Dental equipment and supplies; Dental laboratory
equipment and supplies. **SIC:** 5047 (Medical & Hospital
Equipment). **Officers:** Bernard Nowak, President.

■ 18963 ■ **Nuclear Associates**
100 Voice Rd.
Carle Place, NY 11514
Phone: (516)741-6360
Free: (888)466-8257 **Fax:** (516)741-2166
E-mail: sales@nucl.com
URL: http://www.nucl.com
Products: Hospital equipment, including imaging instruments and accessories for: diagnostic radiology, radiation therapy and protection, ultrasound, mammography, nuclear medecine, health physics, MRI and industrial radiography. **SIC:** 5047 (Medical & Hospital Equipment). **Est:** 1966. **Sales:** $14,000,000 (2000). **Emp:** 42. **Officers:** Martin J. Ratner, General Mgr.; Gary Poynter, Controller.

■ 18964 ■ **Nyle International Corp.**
PO Box 1107
Bangor, ME 04401
Phone: (207)942-4851
Products: Surgical and medical equipment. **SIC:** 5047 (Medical & Hospital Equipment). **Officers:** Samuel Nyer, CEO & Treasurer.

■ 18965 ■ **O2 Emergency Medical Care Service Corp.**
5950 Pine Tree Dr.
West Bloomfield, MI 48322-1412
Phone: (734)661-0581 **Fax:** (734)477-0771
Products: Medical equipment and supplies. **SIC:** 5047 (Medical & Hospital Equipment). **Sales:** $8,000,000 (1994). **Emp:** 35. **Officers:** Donald Stern, President.

■ 18966 ■ **Office Pavilion/MBI Systems Inc.**
1201 Mercer St.
Seattle, WA 98109-5512
Phone: (206)343-5800
Free: (800)798-2309 **Fax:** (206)343-0231
Products: Office furniture. **SICs:** 5047 (Medical & Hospital Equipment); 5021 (Furniture). **Est:** 1980. **Emp:** 49. **Officers:** Henry R. Snider.

■ 18967 ■ **Omnimedical Inc.**
3700 E Columbia St., No. 100
Tucson, AZ 85714-3412
Products: Medical and hospital equipment, including surgical equipment and supplies; Hospital furniture. **SICs:** 5047 (Medical & Hospital Equipment); 5021 (Furniture). **Officers:** William Graue, President.

■ 18968 ■ **On-Gard Systems Inc.**
2323 Delgany St.
Denver, CO 80202
Phone: (303)825-5210 **Fax:** (303)293-2095
Products: Medical equipment, including waste disposal systems. **SIC:** 5047 (Medical & Hospital Equipment). **Est:** 1989. **Sales:** $2,000,000 (2000). **Emp:** 38. **Officers:** Mark E. Weiss, President; Thomas J. Bauer, VP of Marketing & Sales.

■ 18969 ■ **Ortho-Care Southeast Inc.**
632-D Matthews Mint Hill Rd.
Matthews, NC 28105-2797
Phone: (704)845-2690
Free: (800)845-2690 **Fax:** (704)847-1513
Products: Orthopedic appliances (braces), including parts. **SIC:** 5047 (Medical & Hospital Equipment). **Officers:** Mike Springs, President.

■ 18970 ■ **Otake Instrument Inc.**
1314 S King St., Ste. 615
Honolulu, HI 96814-1941
Phone: (808)592-8933 **Fax:** (808)592-8929
Products: Medical equipment; Laboratory and scientific equipment. **SIC:** 5047 (Medical & Hospital Equipment). **Est:** 1981. **Sales:** $500,000 (2000). **Emp:** 2. **Officers:** Jean Otake, President.

■ 18971 ■ **Otto Dental Supply Company Inc.**
1010 Front St.
Conway, AR 72032-4306
Phone: (501)327-9511
Products: Dental equipment and supplies; Dental professional equipment and supplies. **SIC:** 5047 (Medical & Hospital Equipment). **Est:** 1970. **Officers:** W. Otto, President.

■ 18972 ■ **Owens and Minor Inc.**
PO Box 27626
Glen Allen, VA 23060-7626
Phone: (804)747-9794 **Fax:** (804)270-7281
URL: http://www.owens-minor.com
Products: Medical and surgical supplies. **SICs:** 5047 (Medical & Hospital Equipment); 5122 (Drugs, Proprietaries & Sundries). **Est:** 1882. **Sales:** $3,186,373,000 (1999). **Emp:** 2,761. **Officers:** G. Gilmer Minor III, Chairman of the Board; Craig R. Smith, President & CFO.

■ 18973 ■ **Oxygen Co. Inc.**
2205 Perl Rd.
Richmond, VA 23230-2007
Phone: (804)673-6500 **Fax:** (804)673-6508
Products: Medical equipment; Hospital equipment. **SIC:** 5047 (Medical & Hospital Equipment). **Officers:** Wayne Sale, President.

■ 18974 ■ **Pacific Criticare Inc.**
91-340 Komohana St.
Kapolei, HI 96707-1737
Phone: (808)671-5090 **Fax:** (808)671-2492
Products: Medical and hospital equipment and supplies. **SIC:** 5047 (Medical & Hospital Equipment). **Officers:** Robert Shipp, President.

■ 18975 ■ **T.H. Page Inc.**
6600 France Ave. S, Ste. 162
Minneapolis, MN 55435-1802
Phone: (612)920-7221
Free: (800)682-3940 **Fax:** (612)920-4422
Products: Medical and hospital equipment and supplies, including orthopedic equipment. **SIC:** 5047 (Medical & Hospital Equipment). **Officers:** Thomas Page, President.

■ 18976 ■ **Panoramic Corp.**
4321 Goshen Rd.
Ft. Wayne, IN 46818
Phone: (219)489-2291 **Fax:** (219)489-5683
Products: Medical equipment; X-ray apparatus; Dental equipment and supplies; Hospital furniture. **SIC:** 5047 (Medical & Hospital Equipment). **Officers:** Eric Stetzel, President.

■ 18977 ■ **Para-Pharm Inc.**
1213 Main St.
Willimantic, CT 06226-1907
Phone: (860)423-1661 **Fax:** (860)423-4334
SIC: 5047 (Medical & Hospital Equipment). **Officers:** James Wojnar, President.

■ 18978 ■ **Paradise Optical Co.**
848 S Beretania No. 100-A
Honolulu, HI 96813
Phone: (808)523-5021
Products: Optical equipment and supplies. **SIC:** 5048 (Ophthalmic Goods).

■ 18979 ■ **Peakwon International Inc.**
107 St. Francis St., No. 2411
Mobile, AL 36602
Phone: (205)433-4769 **Fax:** (205)438-4164
Products: Medical equipment; Computer and peripheral equipment; Military ordnance. **SICs:** 5047 (Medical & Hospital Equipment); 5045 (Computers, Peripherals & Software); 5099 (Durable Goods Nec). **Officers:** M. Rene Henry, Export Manager.

■ 18980 ■ **Performance Medical Group, Inc.**
803 Cajundome Blvd.
Lafayette, LA 70506-2307
Phone: (318)237-1924 **Fax:** (318)232-9143
E-mail: 103006,1326@compuserve.com
URL: http://www.performancemed.com
Products: Medical equipment; Hospital equipment; Hospital furniture; X-ray apparatus. **SIC:** 5047 (Medical & Hospital Equipment). **Est:** 1969. **Emp:** 45. **Officers:** Michael Mouton, President.

■ 18981 ■ **Peripheral Visions Inc.**
27635 Covington Way SE
Kent, WA 98042-9120
Phone: (253)630-4045 **Fax:** (253)630-8211
URL: http://www.peripheralvisions.com
Products: Clinical chemistry analyzer parts and supplies. **SIC:** 5047 (Medical & Hospital Equipment). **Officers:** Diana Laverdure, President.

■ 18982 ■ **Permark, Inc.**
450 Raritan Center Pkwy.
Edison, NJ 08837
Phone: (732)225-3700
Free: (800)282-5228 **Fax:** (732)225-3767
E-mail: permark@aol.com
URL: http://www.permark.com
Products: Micropigmentation systems. **SIC:** 5047 (Medical & Hospital Equipment). **Est:** 1990. **Sales:** $1,300,000 (1999). **Emp:** 7. **Officers:** Joseph M. Cooperstein, CEO & President. **Former Name:** Micropigmentation Devices Inc.

■ 18983 ■ **Roy L. Perry Supply Company Inc.**
501 S 5th St.
Phoenix, AZ 85004-2548
Phone: (602)254-4450 **Fax:** (602)258-4669
Products: Medical equipment; Hospital equipment. **SIC:** 5047 (Medical & Hospital Equipment). **Est:** 1921. **Sales:** $600,000 (2000). **Emp:** 5. **Officers:** Don Oens, Controller.

■ 18984 ■ **Pharm-Med Inc.**
39023 Harper Ave.
Clinton Township, MI 48036-3226
Phone: (810)468-1207 **Fax:** 800-848-0149
Products: Medical equipment; Hospital equipment. **SIC:** 5047 (Medical & Hospital Equipment). **Officers:** Thomas Jantz, President.

■ 18985 ■ **Pharmacies In Medisav Homecare**
8820 Rogers Ave.
Ft. Smith, AR 72903-5245
Phone: (501)452-2210
Free: (800)633-4728 **Fax:** (501)452-6632
E-mail: ft4u70a@prodigy.com
Products: Medical equipment; Hospital equipment. **SIC:** 5047 (Medical & Hospital Equipment). **Est:** 1985. **Officers:** Joe Larkin, President.

■ 18986 ■ **Phoenix Group HI-TEC Corp.**
600 Stewart St., Ste. 1728
Seattle, WA 98101-1217
Phone: (206)727-2286
Free: (888)808-9208 **Fax:** (206)727-2277
E-mail: jamesc@phoenixhitec.com
URL: http://www.phoenixhitec.com
Products: Medical and industrial equipment and supplies. **SIC:** 5047 (Medical & Hospital Equipment). **Est:** 1990. **Sales:** $10,000,000 (2000). **Emp:** 30. **Officers:** Wayne Tsien, President.

■ 18987 ■ **PhotoVision Inc.**
3251 Progress Dr., Ste. B
Orlando, FL 32826
Phone: (407)382-2772 **Fax:** (407)382-2701
Products: Medical lasers. **SIC:** 5047 (Medical & Hospital Equipment).

■ 18988 ■ **Physician Sales and Service Inc.**
4245 Southpoint Blvd., Ste. 300
Jacksonville, FL 32216-6187
Phone: (904)281-0011
Products: Disposable medical equipment, including bandages, syringes, and blood analysis supplies. **SIC:** 5047 (Medical & Hospital Equipment). **Est:** 1983. **Sales:** $483,300,000 (2000). **Emp:** 2,072. **Officers:** Patrick C. Kelly, CEO, President & Chairman of the Board; David A. Smith, Exec. VP & CFO; L. Darlene Kelly, Chief Info. Officer.

■ 18989 ■ **Physicians Supply Co.**
2650 S 1030 W
Salt Lake City, UT 84119-2469
Products: Hospital beds; Toilets; Toilet paper; Diapers. **SICs:** 5047 (Medical & Hospital Equipment); 5046 (Commercial Equipment Nec). **Est:** 1923. **Sales:** $8,000,000 (2000). **Emp:** 35. **Officers:** R.G. Dorius, President; Lloyd Francom, Dir. of Marketing.

■ **18990** ■ **Polar Electro Inc.**
370 Crossways Park Dr.
Woodbury, NY 11797-2050
Phone: (516)364-0400
Free: (800)290-6330 **Fax:** (516)364-5454
URL: http://www.polarusa.com
Products: Heart-rate monitors. **SIC:** 5047 (Medical &
Hospital Equipment). **Est:** 1989. **Emp:** 80. **Officers:**
Philippe Duleyrie, President; Thomas F. McCoy, Exec.
VP; Jukka Jumisko, Controller; Christine Ombres,
Human Resources Contact.

■ **18991** ■ **Precision Instruments Inc.**
801 S Rancho Dr., Ste. 3B
Las Vegas, NV 89106-3860
Phone: (702)382-8899 **Fax:** (702)382-4116
Products: Medical equipment; Hospital equipment;
Orthopedic appliances (braces), including parts. **SIC:**
5047 (Medical & Hospital Equipment). **Officers:** Ron
Emes, President.

■ **18992** ■ **Precision Technology Inc.**
(Norwood, New Jersey)
50 Maple St.
Norwood, NJ 07648
Phone: (201)767-1600 **Fax:** (201)767-6739
Products: Orthopedic equipment. **SIC:** 5047 (Medical
& Hospital Equipment). **Sales:** $4,000,000 (2000).
Emp: 40. **Officers:** Ira Housman, President.

■ **18993** ■ **Premier Medical Supplies Inc.**
4566 Emery Indstl Pkwy
Cleveland, OH 44128-5702
Phone: (216)831-2777 **Fax:** (216)831-7168
Products: Home care goods, including beds,
wheelchairs, and bandages; Home oxygen; Disposable
medical products. **SIC:** 5047 (Medical & Hospital
Equipment). **Sales:** $5,000,000 (2000). **Emp:** 20.
Officers: Claude A. McCann, President.

■ **18994** ■ **Prescotts Inc.**
PO Box 609
Monument, CO 80132-0609
Phone: (719)481-3353
Free: (800)438-3937 **Fax:** (719)488-2268
E-mail: prescott@surgicalmicroscopes.com
URL: http://www.surgicalmicroscopes.com
Products: Surgical microscopes and accessories.
SICs: 5047 (Medical & Hospital Equipment); 5048
(Ophthalmic Goods). **Est:** 1985. **Sales:** $6,000,000
(1999). **Emp:** 18. **Officers:** Warren Knop, President;
Joe Redner, Sales/Marketing Contact.

■ **18995** ■ **J.A. Preston Corp.**
PO Box 89
Jackson, MI 49204-0089
Phone: (517)787-1600
Free: (800)631-7277 **Fax:** (517)789-3299
Products: Therapeutic appliances and supplies. **SIC:**
5047 (Medical & Hospital Equipment).

■ **18996** ■ **Prime Care Medical Supplies Inc.**
30-68 Whitestone Expwy
Flushing, NY 11354
Phone: (718)353-3311
Products: Medical equipment and supplies. **SIC:** 5047
(Medical & Hospital Equipment).

■ **18997** ■ **Pro-Chem Ltd. Inc.**
409 S Schultz Rd.
Long Grove, IA 52756
Phone: (319)355-6666
Free: (800)373-6666 **Fax:** (319)358-6266
Products: Medical equipment; Hospital equipment; X-
ray apparatus. **SIC:** 5047 (Medical & Hospital
Equipment). **Officers:** Paul Marietta, President.

■ **18998** ■ **Pro-Med Supplies Inc.**
PO Box 201331
Bloomington, MN 55420-6331
Phone: (612)884-1518 **Fax:** (612)884-9547
Products: Medical equipment; Hospital equipment;
Surgical and medical instruments and apparatus. **SIC:**
5047 (Medical & Hospital Equipment). **Officers:** Henry
Deyle, President.

■ **18999** ■ **Promatek Medical Systems Inc.**
1851 Black Rd.
Joliet, IL 60435
Phone: (815)725-6766
Free: (800)327-3422 **Fax:** (815)744-3908
Products: Medical equipment. **SIC:** 5047 (Medical &
Hospital Equipment). **Sales:** $2,500,000 (2000). **Emp:**
5. **Officers:** William Devries, Vice President.

■ **19000** ■ **PTC International**
401 E Pratt St., Ste. 2235
Baltimore, MD 21202-3003
Phone: (301)546-3966 **Fax:** (301)546-3805
Products: Steel wire and related products; Fertilizers,
including mixing; Pharmaceutical preparations;
Prepared animal feeds; Surgical and medical
instruments. **SICs:** 5047 (Medical & Hospital
Equipment); 5051 (Metals Service Centers & Offices);
5191 (Farm Supplies); 5122 (Drugs, Proprietaries &
Sundries). **Officers:** Tai Young Lee, President.

■ **19001** ■ **Quality Control Consultants**
3087 Bellbrook Center Dr.
Memphis, TN 38116-3506
Phone: (901)396-2916
Products: Medical and hospital equipment;
Processors. **SIC:** 5047 (Medical & Hospital
Equipment). **Officers:** John Frankenberger, President.

■ **19002** ■ **Quality Monitor Systems**
1950 Victor Pl.
Colorado Springs, CO 80915-1501
Phone: (719)596-2187
Free: (800)743-5747 **Fax:** (719)596-0322
URL: http://www.quakmonsys.com
Products: Medical equipment; Hospital equipment.
SIC: 5047 (Medical & Hospital Equipment). **Est:** 1986.
Sales: $1,015,968 (2000). **Emp:** 10. **Officers:** Dennis
Heath, Chairman of the Board, e-mail: dennis@
qualmonsys.com; Stanley Helm, President, e-mail:
stan@qualmonsys.com; James Clark, Vice President,
e-mail: jim@qualmonsys.com.

■ **19003** ■ **Quantum Labs Inc.**
9851 13th Ave. N
Minneapolis, MN 55441-5003
Phone: (612)545-1984
Free: (800)328-8213 **Fax:** (612)545-7613
Products: Medical equipment; Hospital equipment;
Dental equipment and supplies. **SIC:** 5047 (Medical &
Hospital Equipment). **Officers:** Michael Stefanson,
President.

■ **19004** ■ **Queen City Home Health Care Inc.**
10780 Reading Rd.
Cincinnati, OH 45241-2531
Phone: (513)681-8811
Products: Medical equipment. **SIC:** 5047 (Medical &
Hospital Equipment).

■ **19005** ■ **R5 Trading International Inc.**
PO Box 3355
Princeton, NJ 08543
Phone: (609)951-9512 **Fax:** (609)951-9513
Products: Medical equipment, including X-ray
equipment and ultrasonics; Medical and surgical
supplies; Telecommunications equipment;
Homefurnishings. **SICs:** 5047 (Medical & Hospital
Equipment); 5023 (Homefurnishings); 5065 (Electronic
Parts & Equipment Nec). **Officers:** R. Stephen Winget,
President.

■ **19006** ■ **R & B Orthopedics Inc.**
7000 Hampton Center, Ste. G
Morgantown, WV 26505-1705
Phone: (304)598-0416
Products: Medical equipment; Hospital equipment;
Orthopedic appliances (braces), including parts. **SIC:**
5047 (Medical & Hospital Equipment). **Officers:**
Thomas Harris, President.

■ **19007** ■ **R-K Market**
PO Box 940
Belfield, ND 58622-0940
Phone: (701)575-4354
Products: Medical equipment; Hospital equipment.
SIC: 5047 (Medical & Hospital Equipment). **Officers:**
Nita Northrop, Partner.

■ **19008** ■ **Radiology Resources Inc.**
20 Aegean Dr., Ste. 8
Methuen, MA 01844-1580
Phone: (781)935-4470
Products: Medical and hospital equipment, including
furniture, X-ray machines, and tubes. **SIC:** 5047
(Medical & Hospital Equipment). **Officers:** Charles
Moreland, President.

■ **19009** ■ **Radiology Services Inc.**
PO Box 72
Georgetown, MA 01833-0072
Phone: (978)352-2050
Free: (800)352-9729 **Fax:** (978)352-7283
Products: X-ray supplies and accessories. **SIC:** 5047
(Medical & Hospital Equipment). **Officers:** Roy
Hayward, President.

■ **19010** ■ **RadServ Inc.**
21540 Plummer St.
Chatsworth, CA 91311-4103
Products: Radiology and radiation oncology
equipment. **SIC:** 5047 (Medical & Hospital Equipment).

■ **19011** ■ **Rainhart Co.**
PO Box 4533
Austin, TX 78765
Phone: (512)452-8848
Free: (800)628-0021 **Fax:** (512)452-9883
Products: Laboratory testing equipment for federal
agencies, private contractors and laboratories. **SIC:**
5084 (Industrial Machinery & Equipment). **Sales:**
$2,000,000 (2000). **Emp:** 15. **Officers:** Robert Durr,
President; Homer L. Johnson, CFO.

■ **19012** ■ **Ransdell Surgical Inc.**
PO Box 34518
Louisville, KY 40232-4518
Phone: (502)584-6311
Products: Surgical instruments, including suture
needles and eye, ear, nose, and throat instruments.
SIC: 5047 (Medical & Hospital Equipment). **Est:** 1958.
Sales: $59,000,000 (2000). **Emp:** 100. **Officers:**
Micheal Ransdell, President; Rick Schmidt, CFO;
Joseph Speiden, Dir. of Marketing; Brian Harper, Dir. of
Data Processing.

■ **19013** ■ **Red Ball Medical Supply Inc.**
PO Box 7316
Shreveport, LA 71137-7316
Phone: (318)424-8393
Products: Medical and hospital equipment. **SIC:** 5047
(Medical & Hospital Equipment). **Est:** 1978. **Sales:**
$2,500,000 (2000). **Emp:** 25. **Officers:** Judy Kennedy.

■ **19014** ■ **Redline Healthcare Corp.**
8121 10th Ave. N
Golden Valley, MN 55427
Phone: (612)545-5757 **Fax:** (612)545-8207
Products: Home hospital equipment. **SIC:** 5047
(Medical & Hospital Equipment). **Est:** 1961. **Sales:**
$220,000,000 (2000). **Emp:** 750. **Officers:** Rob Carr,
President; Rob Carr, CFO; Timothy Pawlik, VP of
Marketing & Sales; James Reinstatler, Dir. of
Information Systems; Diana L. Kincade, Dir of Human
Resources.

■ **19015** ■ **Regional Home Care Inc.**
125 Tolman Ave.
Leominster, MA 01453-1912
Phone: (978)840-0113
Free: (800)229-6267 **Fax:** (978)840-0115
Products: Medical equipment; Hospital equipment.
SIC: 5047 (Medical & Hospital Equipment). **Officers:**
Cabot Carabott, President.

■ **19016** ■ **Rehab Medical Equipment Inc.**
PO Box 1869
Collegedale, TN 37315-1869
Phone: (423)899-8172
Products: Medical and hospital equipment and
supplies, including orthopedic equipment and supplies.
SIC: 5047 (Medical & Hospital Equipment). **Officers:**
Allen Hughes, President.

■ 19017 ■ **Remedpar Inc.**
101 Old Stone Bridge Rd.
Goodlettsville, TN 37072-3201
Phone: (615)859-1303 **Fax:** (615)859-4165
Products: Medical equipment; Hospital equipment; X-ray apparatus; Hospital furniture. **SIC:** 5047 (Medical & Hospital Equipment). **Officers:** Edward Sloan, President.

■ 19018 ■ **Renishaw Inc.**
623 Cooper Ct.
Schaumburg, IL 60173
Phone: (847)843-3666 **Fax:** (847)843-1744
E-mail: renmktsvcs@aol.com
URL: http://www.renishaw.com
Products: Medical probes. **SIC:** 5047 (Medical & Hospital Equipment). **Est:** 1981. **Sales:** $60,000,000 (2000). **Emp:** 76. **Officers:** Leo Somerville, President; Kenneth J. Scharmann, Controller; Barry Rogers, Sales/Marketing Contact.

■ 19019 ■ **Respiratory Homecare Inc.**
40 E Broad St.
Cookeville, TN 38501-3210
Phone: (931)528-5894 **Fax:** (931)528-6023
Products: Medical and hospital equipment and supplies. **SIC:** 5047 (Medical & Hospital Equipment). **Officers:** Lindsey Scurlock, President.

■ 19020 ■ **RF Management Corp.**
95 Madison Dr.
Morristown, NJ 07960
Phone: (973)292-2833
Products: Medical equipment. **SIC:** 5047 (Medical & Hospital Equipment).

■ 19021 ■ **RGH Enterprises Inc.**
2300 Edison Blvd.
Twinsburg, OH 44087
Phone: (330)963-6996
Free: (800)321-0591 **Fax:** (330)963-6839
Products: Medical and surgical supplies; Hospital equipment; Wheelchairs and crutches. **SIC:** 5047 (Medical & Hospital Equipment). **Est:** 1990. **Sales:** $25,000,000 (2000). **Emp:** 102. **Officers:** Ron G. Harrington, President.

■ 19022 ■ **Rieger Medical Supply Co.**
3111 E Central Ave.
Wichita, KS 67214-4816
Phone: (316)684-0589 **Fax:** (316)684-6408
Products: Medical equipment; Hospital equipment. **SIC:** 5047 (Medical & Hospital Equipment). **Officers:** Ernest Rieger, President.

■ 19023 ■ **RLP Inc.**
PO Box 37889
Phoenix, AZ 85069-7889
Phone: (602)943-0625
Free: (800)535-5998 **Fax:** (602)395-1325
Products: Ophthalmic frames; Ophthalmic goods. **SIC:** 5048 (Ophthalmic Goods). **Officers:** Ralph Powers, President.

■ 19024 ■ **Roane-Barker Inc.**
PO Box 2880
Greenville, SC 29602-2880
Phone: (864)234-0598
Free: (800)868-4272 **Fax:** (864)234-0598
Products: Diagnostic apparatus; Medical equipment; Hospital equipment. **SIC:** 5047 (Medical & Hospital Equipment). **Officers:** Ralph Falls, President.

■ 19025 ■ **Roberts Oxygen Company Inc.**
PO Box 5507
Rockville, MD 20855
Phone: (301)948-8100 **Fax:** (301)294-1950
Products: Medical and hospital equipment; Oxygen therapy equipment. **SIC:** 5047 (Medical & Hospital Equipment). **Officers:** William Roberts, Chairman of the Board.

■ 19026 ■ **Rushmore Health Care Products**
821 Mount Rushmore Rd.
Rapid City, SD 57701-3602
Phone: (605)341-1725 **Fax:** (605)341-0167
Products: Medical and hospital equipment, including X-ray and life services. **SIC:** 5047 (Medical & Hospital Equipment). **Officers:** W. Vanneman, President.

■ 19027 ■ **Rx Rocker Corp.**
3541 Old Conejo Rd., Ste. 101
Newbury Park, CA 91320
Phone: (805)499-0696
Free: (800)762-5371 **Fax:** (805)499-8644
Products: Wheel chairs. **SIC:** 5047 (Medical & Hospital Equipment). **Est:** 1989. **Sales:** $1,000,000 (2000). **Emp:** 10. **Officers:** Willard D. Eyer, President.

■ 19028 ■ **St. Jude Medical Inc.**
1 Lillehei Plz.
St. Paul, MN 55117
Phone: (612)483-2000 **Fax:** (612)490-4333
Products: Heart valves; Cardiac rhythm management systems; Catheters. **SIC:** 5047 (Medical & Hospital Equipment). **Officers:** Ronald Matricaria, CEO & Chairman of the Board.

■ 19029 ■ **St. Louis Ostomy Distributors Inc.**
PO Box 6520
Holliston, MA 01746-6520
Phone: (508)535-3535
Free: (800)365-3232 **Fax:** (508)535-7301
Products: Ostomy products; Incontinence, urological, and wound care products; Orthopedic appliances (braces), including parts. **SIC:** 5047 (Medical & Hospital Equipment). **Est:** 1983. **Emp:** 20. **Officers:** Michael J. Quinn, President.

■ 19030 ■ **Sales and Marketing Services Inc.**
PO Box 815
Columbia, MD 21044
Phone: (410)799-7040 **Fax:** (410)799-1070
Products: Medical and surgical instruments and supplies. **SIC:** 5047 (Medical & Hospital Equipment). **Sales:** $10,000,000 (1994). **Emp:** 36. **Officers:** W. Richard Smith, President.

■ 19031 ■ **Sammons Preston**
4 Sammons Ct.
Bolingbrook, IL 60440
Phone: (630)226-1300
Free: (800)323-5547 **Fax:** (630)226-1388
Products: Medical equipment. **SIC:** 5047 (Medical & Hospital Equipment). **Sales:** $43,800,000 (2000). **Emp:** 150. **Officers:** Edward Donnelly, President; Joe Dietrich, Finance Officer.

■ 19032 ■ **San Jose Surgical Supply Inc.**
902 S Bascom Ave.
San Jose, CA 95128
Phone: (408)293-9033
Products: Medical equipment. **SIC:** 5047 (Medical & Hospital Equipment). **Sales:** $10,000,000 (2000). **Emp:** 35. **Officers:** Dennis Collins, President.

■ 19033 ■ **Sandler Medical Services**
1244 6th Ave.
Des Moines, IA 50314-2715
Phone: (515)244-4236
Products: Medical equipment; Hospital equipment and furniture. **SIC:** 5047 (Medical & Hospital Equipment). **Officers:** Ray Sprague, President.

■ 19034 ■ **Schuco Inc.**
1720 Sublette Ave.
St. Louis, MO 63110-1927
Phone: (314)726-2000
Products: Respiratory equipment. **SIC:** 5047 (Medical & Hospital Equipment).

■ 19035 ■ **Sema Inc.**
360 Industrial Ln.
Birmingham, AL 35211
Phone: (205)945-8612 **Fax:** (205)945-4933
SIC: 5047 (Medical & Hospital Equipment). **Est:** 1982. **Officers:** Jerry Akers, President.

■ 19036 ■ **Service Drug of Brainerd Inc.**
218 W Washington St.
Brainerd, MN 56401-2922
Phone: (218)829-3664
Products: Medical equipment; Hospital equipment. **SIC:** 5047 (Medical & Hospital Equipment). **Officers:** Steven Wiewel, President.

■ 19037 ■ **Service Engineering Co.**
8621 Barefoot Industrial Rd.
Raleigh, NC 27613
Phone: (919)783-6116
Free: (800)334-5528 **Fax:** (919)782-8234
E-mail: rspi@mindspring.com
URL: http://www.serviceeng.com
Products: Medical equipment; Commercial cooking equipment; Ice-making machines and liquid chillers. **SICs:** 5047 (Medical & Hospital Equipment); 5046 (Commercial Equipment Nec). **Est:** 1973. **Sales:** $1,000,000 (2000). **Emp:** 9. **Officers:** Nelson Hinton, President. **Former Name:** Med Con Ltd.

■ 19038 ■ **sjs X-Ray Corp.**
PO Box 148
Mt. Pleasant, SC 29465-0148
Phone: (843)884-8943
Free: (800)999-2364 **Fax:** (843)884-8510
E-mail: sjsbdog@juno.com
Products: Medical equipment; Hospital equipment; Physicians' supplies; Hospital furniture. **SIC:** 5047 (Medical & Hospital Equipment). **Est:** 1985. **Sales:** $1,200,000 (2000). **Emp:** 7. **Officers:** Stephen Sutcliffe, President, e-mail: grumley3@juno.com. **Former Name:** X-Ray SJS Corp.

■ 19039 ■ **Sklar Instrument Company Inc.**
889 S Matlack St.
West Chester, PA 19382
Phone: (610)430-3200 **Fax:** (610)429-0500
E-mail: surgi@sklarcorp.com
URL: http://www.sklarcorp.com
Products: Medical equipment; Surgical instruments, including suture needles, and eye, ear, nose, and throat instruments. **SIC:** 5047 (Medical & Hospital Equipment). **Est:** 1892. **Sales:** $18,000,000 (1999). **Emp:** 70. **Officers:** Don Taylor, President.

■ 19040 ■ **Skyland Hospital Supply Inc.**
PO Box 51970
Knoxville, TN 37950-1970
Phone: (423)546-2524 **Fax:** (423)546-9357
Products: Medical and hospital equipment and supplies. **SIC:** 5047 (Medical & Hospital Equipment). **Officers:** Edward Albers, Chairman of the Board.

■ 19041 ■ **Skytron**
PO Box 888615
Grand Rapids, MI 49588-8615
Phone: (616)957-1950
Free: (800)759-8766 **Fax:** (616)957-5053
E-mail: skytron@aol.com
URL: http://www.medicom.com/skytron
Products: Medical and hospital equipment and supplies. **SIC:** 5047 (Medical & Hospital Equipment). **Est:** 1972. **Officers:** David Mehney, President; Dennis Doar, Exec. VP; Dave Sterkenburg, Customer Service Contact. **Former Name:** The KMW Group Inc.

■ 19042 ■ **Smith-Holden Inc.**
99 Corliss St.
Providence, RI 02904
Phone: (401)331-0742
Products: Dental products. **SIC:** 5047 (Medical & Hospital Equipment). **Est:** 1850. **Sales:** $15,500,000 (2000). **Emp:** 100. **Officers:** Cyril Buckley Jr., President; Carter Buckley, Treasurer; Richard S. Stenmann, Dir. of Marketing.

■ 19043 ■ **SNA Inc.**
436 Atwells Ave.
Providence, RI 02909-1031
Phone: (401)274-1110
Products: Medical equipment; Hospital equipment. **SIC:** 5047 (Medical & Hospital Equipment). **Officers:** Nancy Kim, President.

■ 19044 ■ **Sontek Industries Inc.**
20 Pond Park Rd.
Hingham, MA 02043-4327
Phone: (781)749-3055 **Fax:** (781)740-1151
Products: Disposable items used in the health care industry for respiratory therapy and critical care. **SIC:** 5047 (Medical & Hospital Equipment). **Est:** 1982. **Officers:** Garry Prime, President; Mark Newbert, Marketing Mgr.

■ **19045** ■ **South Jersey X-Ray Supply Co.**
8015 Rte. 130 S
Delran, NJ 08075
Phone: (609)461-4261 **Fax:** (609)461-9307
Products: X-ray supplies. **SIC:** 5047 (Medical & Hospital Equipment). **Est:** 1968. **Sales:** $35,000,000 (2000). **Emp:** 70. **Officers:** Ray J. Eveland, President; Paul Eisenstein, Controller; John Fitzpatrick, VP of Marketing.

■ **19046** ■ **Southern Prosthetic Supply**
PO Box 406
Alpharetta, GA 30009-0406
Phone: (770)442-9870
Free: (800)867-7776 **Fax:** (770)442-0379
URL: http://www.spsco.com
Products: Orthotic appliances; Artificial limbs (prosthetic). **SIC:** 5047 (Medical & Hospital Equipment). **Officers:** Ron May, President & COO. **Former Name:** J.E. Hanger Incorporated of Georgia.

■ **19047** ■ **Spar Medical Inc.**
1606 Green Springs Hwy. S
Birmingham, AL 35205-4547
Phone: (205)252-2992 **Fax:** (205)252-0469
Products: Medical equipment; Hospital equipment. **SIC:** 5047 (Medical & Hospital Equipment). **Officers:** James Sparacio, President.

■ **19048** ■ **Special Care Medical Inc.**
PO Box 21564
Columbia, SC 29221-1564
Phone: (803)926-0161 **Fax:** (803)926-0345
Products: Medical equipment; Hospital equipment. **SIC:** 5047 (Medical & Hospital Equipment). **Officers:** David McLendon, President.

■ **19049** ■ **Specialties of Surgery Inc.**
PO Box 560
Jenks, OK 74037-0560
Phone: (918)299-4970 **Fax:** (918)299-6875
Products: Medical equipment; Hospital equipment. **SIC:** 5047 (Medical & Hospital Equipment). **Officers:** Terry Newell, President.

■ **19050** ■ **Specialty Surgical Instrumentation Inc.**
200 River Hills Dr.
Nashville, TN 37210
Phone: (615)883-9090
Products: Surgical equipment. **SIC:** 5047 (Medical & Hospital Equipment).

■ **19051** ■ **Spinal Analysis Machine**
660 Middlegate Rd.
Henderson, NV 89015-2608
Phone: (702)565-2633 **Fax:** (702)565-7985
Products: Medical equipment and supplies; Diagnostic equipment. **SIC:** 5047 (Medical & Hospital Equipment). **Officers:** Robyn Lange, President.

■ **19052** ■ **Standard Medical Imaging Inc.**
9002 Red Branch Rd.
Columbia, MD 21045
Phone: (410)997-1500
Free: (800)952-9729 **Fax:** (410)992-9729
URL: http://www.standardmed.com
Products: X-ray equipment and supplies, including film and film processors, diagnostic opaques, and chemicals. **SIC:** 5047 (Medical & Hospital Equipment). **Est:** 1954. **Sales:** $59,000,000 (2000). **Emp:** 205. **Officers:** Roger C. Norden, President; James F. Krieger, Sr. VP; Robert C. Tahaney, Sales/Marketing Contact, e-mail: rtahaney@standardmed.com; Charlene Schroeder, Customer Service Contact, e-mail: cschroeder@standardmed.com; Cheryl Pagel, Human Resources Contact, e-mail: cpagel@standardmed.com.

■ **19053** ■ **Stat Surgical Center Inc.**
291 Main St.
Falmouth, MA 02540-2751
Phone: (508)548-1342 **Fax:** (508)540-9475
Products: Medical equipment; Hospital equipment. **SIC:** 5047 (Medical & Hospital Equipment). **Officers:** Paul Dussault, President.

■ **19054** ■ **Stemmans Inc.**
PO Box 156
Carencro, LA 70520-0156
Phone: (318)234-2382
Products: Medical equipment; Hospital equipment; Veterinary instruments. **SIC:** 5047 (Medical & Hospital Equipment). **Officers:** Donald Stemmans, President.

■ **19055** ■ **Stepic Corp.**
37-31 30th St.
Long Island City, NY 11101
Phone: (718)784-2220 **Fax:** (718)784-0828
Products: Critical care products, primarily anesthesia related. **SIC:** 5047 (Medical & Hospital Equipment). **Sales:** $18,000,000 (2000). **Emp:** 53. **Officers:** Steven Picheny, President.

■ **19056** ■ **Steri-Systems Corp.**
PO Box 909
Auburn, GA 30011-0909
Phone: (404)963-1429 **Fax:** (404)995-7067
Products: Medical equipment; Hospital equipment. **SIC:** 5047 (Medical & Hospital Equipment). **Officers:** John Durden, President.

■ **19057** ■ **Stolls Medical Rentals Inc.**
2500 E Main St.
Waterbury, CT 06705-2803
Phone: (203)757-9818
Free: (800)750-0316 **Fax:** (203)753-4791
Products: Medical equipment; Hospital equipment. **SIC:** 5047 (Medical & Hospital Equipment). **Officers:** Robert McCormack, President.

■ **19058** ■ **Stuart Medical Inc.**
Donohue & Luxor Rd., 1 Stuart Pl
Greensburg, PA 15601
Phone: (412)837-5700 **Fax:** (412)834-6009
Products: Hospital equipment and supplies. **SIC:** 5047 (Medical & Hospital Equipment). **Sales:** $350,000,000 (2000). **Emp:** 1,200. **Officers:** Richard P. Byington, CEO & President; H. Richard Howie, CFO; Tom Sherry, Exec. VP; Joe Kriss, VP of Information Systems; Martin Clancy, Human Resources Mgr.

■ **19059** ■ **Sullivan Dental Products Inc.**
10920 W Lincoln Ave.
West Allis, WI 53227
Phone: (414)321-8881 **Fax:** (414)321-5163
Products: Dental equipment and products, including gauze and cotton balls. **SIC:** 5047 (Medical & Hospital Equipment). **Est:** 1980. **Sales:** $241,600,000 (2000). **Emp:** 1,015. **Officers:** Robert E. Doering, CEO & President; Timothy J. Sullivan, VP & CFO; Kevin J. Ackeret, VP of Sales.

■ **19060** ■ **Summertree Medisales**
1380 Tulilp St., Ste. O
Longmont, CO 80501
Phone: (303)651-5226 **Fax:** (303)678-4837
Products: Medical and hospital equipment and supplies. **SIC:** 5047 (Medical & Hospital Equipment). **Officers:** Linda Thompson, Manager; Jacquie Shank, Customer Service Contact. **Former Name:** Summertree Corp.

■ **19061** ■ **Summit Instruments Corp.**
76 Woolens Rd.
Elkton, MD 21921-1816
Phone: (410)398-7250
Products: Medical equipment; Hospital equipment; Hospital furniture; Surgical instruments, including suture needles, and eye, ear, nose, and throat instruments. **SIC:** 5047 (Medical & Hospital Equipment). **Officers:** Peter Groop, President.

■ **19062** ■ **Summit Trading Co.**
4623 Old York Rd.
Philadelphia, PA 19140
Products: Medical and hospital equipment. **SIC:** 5047 (Medical & Hospital Equipment). **Officers:** Lynn Beamon, President.

■ **19063** ■ **Sun Medical Equipment and Supply Co.**
1072 W 14th Mile Rd.
Clawson, MI 48017
Phone: (248)280-2020
Products: Hospital equipment and supplies for the

home. **SIC:** 5047 (Medical & Hospital Equipment). **Sales:** $8,000,000 (2000). **Emp:** 30. **Officers:** Greg Jameson, Director.

■ **19064** ■ **Surgical Instrument Associates**
4220 Park Glen Rd.
Minneapolis, MN 55416-4758
Phone: (612)922-4444 **Fax:** (612)922-5309
Products: Operating room accessories. **SIC:** 5047 (Medical & Hospital Equipment). **Est:** 1977. **Officers:** Brian Arcari, President.

■ **19065** ■ **Surgitec**
4325 Laurel, Ste. 103
Anchorage, AK 99508-5338
Phone: (907)562-7733 **Fax:** (907)562-7686
Products: Medical equipment; Surgical equipment. **SIC:** 5047 (Medical & Hospital Equipment). **Est:** 1980. **Sales:** $2,000,000 (2000). **Emp:** 4. **Officers:** Gregg Crawford, Owner.

■ **19066** ■ **Syncor International Corp.**
20001 Prairie St.
Chatsworth, CA 91311
Phone: (818)886-7400
Products: Nuclear medicine equipment. **SIC:** 5047 (Medical & Hospital Equipment). **Est:** 1985. **Sales:** $332,500,000 (2000). **Emp:** 2,161. **Officers:** Gene R. McGrevin, CEO & President; Michael E. Mikity, VP & CFO.

■ **19067** ■ **Syrvet, Inc.**
16200 Walnut St.
Waukee, IA 50263
Phone: (515)987-5554
Free: (800)727-5203 **Fax:** (515)987-5553
E-mail: supervet@syrvet.com
URL: http://www.syrvet.com
Products: Veterinary instruments and animal health supplies. **SIC:** 5047 (Medical & Hospital Equipment). **Est:** 1987. **Emp:** 13. **Officers:** Daniel Klein, President.

■ **19068** ■ **Systems Medical Co. Inc.**
PO Box 61
Owosso, MI 48867-0061
Phone: (517)725-9314 **Fax:** (517)723-5534
Products: Medical and hospital equipment and supplies. **SIC:** 5047 (Medical & Hospital Equipment). **Officers:** Steven Grudzien, President.

■ **19069** ■ **Talon Associates International, Inc.**
1275 First Ave., Ste. 104
New York, NY 10021
Phone: (212)535-9580 **Fax:** (212)988-5920
Products: Medical equipment and instruments; Signs and advertising displays. **SICs:** 5047 (Medical & Hospital Equipment); 5099 (Durable Goods Nec). **Officers:** David M. Talon, Mgr. Dir.

■ **19070** ■ **Tamarack Ltd.**
PO Box 70
Lanark, WV 25860
Phone: (304)255-6500
Products: Medical equipment; Hospital equipment. **SIC:** 5047 (Medical & Hospital Equipment). **Officers:** Al Subbaraya, President.

■ **19071** ■ **Tecan US Inc.**
PO Box 13953
Durham, NC 27709-3953
Phone: (919)361-5200 **Fax:** (919)361-5201
Products: Medical equipment; Hospital equipment. **SIC:** 5047 (Medical & Hospital Equipment). **Officers:** Jean Rufener, President.

■ **19072** ■ **Technical Products Inc.**
2416 Park Central Blvd.
Decatur, GA 30035
Phone: (404)981-8434 **Fax:** (404)981-8438
Products: Medical equipment; Hospital equipment; Hospital furniture; Surgical instruments, including suture needles, and eye, ear, nose, and throat instruments. **SIC:** 5047 (Medical & Hospital Equipment). **Officers:** Norbert Thompson, President.

■ 19073 ■ Tens of Charlotte Inc.
10201 Thomas Payne Cir
Charlotte, NC 28277
Phone: (704)846-2098
Products: Medical equipment. SIC: 5047 (Medical & Hospital Equipment). Officers: Marieta S. Smith, President.

■ 19074 ■ Theraquip Inc.
PO Box 16327
Greensboro, NC 27416-0327
Phone: (910)665-1395   Fax: (910)665-3563
Products: Medical equipment; Hospital equipment. SIC: 5047 (Medical & Hospital Equipment). Officers: Charles Bullock, President.

■ 19075 ■ Thermafil/Tulsa Dental Products
5001 E 68th St., Ste. 500
Tulsa, OK 74136-3324
Phone: (918)493-6598
Free: (800)662-1202   Fax: (918)493-6599
Products: Dental equipment and supplies. SIC: 5047 (Medical & Hospital Equipment). Officers: Bruce Thompson, Chief Operating Officer.

■ 19076 ■ Thigpen Pharmacy Inc.
PO Box 760
Pikeville, NC 27863-0760
Phone: (919)242-5565
Products: Medical equipment; Hospital equipment; Hospital furniture. SIC: 5047 (Medical & Hospital Equipment). Officers: Walter Thigpen, President.

■ 19077 ■ Thompson Dental Company Inc.
PO Box 49
Columbia, SC 29202
Phone: (803)799-4920
Products: Dental professional equipment and supplies. SIC: 5047 (Medical & Hospital Equipment). Est: 1899. Sales: $31,000,000 (2000). Emp: 232. Officers: Perrin DesPortes, President.

■ 19078 ■ Thrifty Medical Supply Inc.
6815 NW 10th St., No. 4
Oklahoma City, OK 73127-4249
Phone: (405)787-3985
Free: (800)375-3099   Fax: (405)495-2749
Products: Medical equipment; Hospital equipment; Dental equipment and supplies. SIC: 5047 (Medical & Hospital Equipment). Officers: Willis Smith, President.

■ 19079 ■ Timm Medical Systems
6585 City W Pkwy.
Eden Prairie, MN 55344
Phone: (952)947-9410   Fax: (952)947-9411
URL: http://www.timmmedical.com
Products: Medical devices for the diagnosis and treatment of erectile dysfunction (ED) and urinary incontinence. SIC: 5047 (Medical & Hospital Equipment). Est: 1998. Sales: $18,000,000 (2000). Emp: 115. Officers: Julian Osbon, COO; Price Dunaway, Sr. VP of Operations; Jakc Pahl, President; Jerald Mattys, CEO; Joseph Hafermann, CFO; Mark McKoskey, VP of Operations & Business Development. Former Name: Osbon Medical Systems Ltd.

■ 19080 ■ Toray Marketing and Sales (America) Inc.
140 Cypress Station Dr., Ste. 210
Houston, TX 77090
Phone: (281)587-2299
Free: (800)662-1777   Fax: (281)587-9933
Products: Medical equipment, including dialyzers. SIC: 5047 (Medical & Hospital Equipment). Est: 1987. Sales: $1,000,000 (2000). Emp: 7. Officers: Masanori Kamiura, President; David Marsh, Dir. of Marketing & Sales; Dennis Metcalf, Dir. of Information Systems; Dennis Metcalf, Dir. of Information Systems.

■ 19081 ■ Toshiba America Medical Systems Inc.
2441 Michelle Dr.
Tustin, CA 92780
Phone: (714)730-5000
Products: X-ray, ultrasound, CT, and MRI equipment. SIC: 5047 (Medical & Hospital Equipment). Sales: $400,000,000 (2000). Emp: 400. Officers: Takashi Hayashi, President; Arnold Raymon, VP of Finance; Frank Parker, VP of Marketing; Bob McKay, Dir. of Corp. Communications; Margaret O'Dowd, Dir of Human Resources.

■ 19082 ■ Trademark Dental Ceramics Inc.
1684 Barnett Shoals Rd.
Athens, GA 30605-3007
Phone: (706)549-9960
Products: Dental equipment and supplies. SIC: 5047 (Medical & Hospital Equipment). Officers: Richard Askew, President.

■ 19083 ■ Tradex International Corp.
PO Box 8415
Newport Beach, CA 92660
Phone: (949)458-9808   Fax: (949)458-9808
Products: Medical instruments and equipment. SICs: 5047 (Medical & Hospital Equipment); 5191 (Farm Supplies). Officers: Robert Slater, President.

■ 19084 ■ Treasure Valley X-Ray Inc.
PO Box 7772
Boise, ID 83707-1772
Phone: (208)323-1968
Products: Medical equipment; Hospital equipment; Hospital furniture; X-ray apparatus. SIC: 5047 (Medical & Hospital Equipment). Officers: Richard Fedrizzi, President.

■ 19085 ■ Tri-State Hospital Supply Corp.
8200 Utah
Merrillville, IN 46410
Phone: (219)942-6723
Free: (800)326-0207   Fax: (219)942-6782
Products: Hospital equipment, including trays and stirrup kits. SIC: 5047 (Medical & Hospital Equipment).

■ 19086 ■ Tri-State Medical Supply Inc.
846 Pelham Pkwy.
Pelham, NY 10803-2710
Phone: (516)420-1700
Products: Medical equipment. SIC: 5047 (Medical & Hospital Equipment). Sales: $9,000,000 (1994). Emp: 35. Officers: Todd A. Sternbach, President.

■ 19087 ■ Tri-State Surgical Corp.
4353 N Mozart
Chicago, IL 60618
Phone: (773)267-8800   Fax: (773)267-2046
Products: Surgical equipment. SIC: 5047 (Medical & Hospital Equipment).

■ 19088 ■ Troxler World Trade Corp.
3008 Cornwallis Rd.
PO Box 12057
Research Triangle Park, NC 27709
Phone: (919)549-8661   Fax: (919)549-0761
E-mail: troxint@mindspring.com
Products: Laboratory and scientific instruments, including moisture and density nuclear devices. SICs: 5047 (Medical & Hospital Equipment); 5049 (Professional Equipment Nec); 5065 (Electronic Parts & Equipment Nec). Est: 1950. Officers: Suzanne Babcock, VP of Admin.

■ 19089 ■ Tru-Care Health Systems Inc.
5004 N Portland Ave.
Oklahoma City, OK 73112-6122
Phone: (405)949-9969
Products: Medical equipment; Hospital equipment; Therapeutic appliances and supplies. SIC: 5047 (Medical & Hospital Equipment). Officers: Bob Mc Gerry, President.

■ 19090 ■ Ulster Scientific Inc.
PO Box 819
New Paltz, NY 12561
Phone: (914)255-2200
Free: (800)431-8233   Fax: (914)255-3299
Products: Laboratory equipment; Homecare supplies; Laboratory safety products. SIC: 5047 (Medical & Hospital Equipment). Est: 1977. Sales: $12,000,000 (2000). Emp: 50. Officers: Peter F. Lordi Jr., CEO.

■ 19091 ■ United Biomedical Inc.
PO Box 377
Andover, KS 67002-0377
Phone: (316)733-5350   Fax: (316)733-1028
Products: Used medical and hospital equipment. SIC: 5047 (Medical & Hospital Equipment). Est: 1987.

Sales: $350,000 (2000). Emp: 5. Officers: Jeffrey Heck, President, e-mail: jheck46219@aol.com; Linda Heck, Sec. & Treas.

■ 19092 ■ United Pharmaceutical & Medical Supply Co.
1338 W Fremont St.
Stockton, CA 95203-2626
Phone: (510)568-5555   Fax: (510)568-6011
Products: Medical equipment; Pharmaceutical preparations. SIC: 5047 (Medical & Hospital Equipment). Officers: George P. Gee, Contact.

■ 19093 ■ United Service Dental Chair
5669 147th St. N
Hugo, MN 55038-9302
Phone: (612)429-8660   Fax: (612)429-1096
Products: Dental and medical chairs. SIC: 5047 (Medical & Hospital Equipment). Officers: Michael Haider, President.

■ 19094 ■ U.S.-China Industrial Exchange Inc.
7201 Wisconsin Ave., Ste. 703
Bethesda, MD 20814
Phone: (301)215-7777   Fax: (301)215-7719
Products: Medical equipment; Construction, mining, and other industrial machinery; Scientific research instrumentation. SICs: 5047 (Medical & Hospital Equipment); 5082 (Construction & Mining Machinery); 5049 (Professional Equipment Nec). Sales: $23,800,000 (2000). Emp: 237. Officers: Roberta Lipson, CEO & President; Lawrence Pemble, Exec. VP of Finance.

■ 19095 ■ United States Medical Corp.
7205 E Kemper Rd.
Cincinnati, OH 45249-1030
Phone: (513)489-5595
Products: Surgical equipment. SIC: 5047 (Medical & Hospital Equipment). Sales: $12,000,000 (2000). Emp: 50. Officers: Paul Rogers, President.

■ 19096 ■ U.S. Medical Supply Co.
3731 Northcrest Rd., Ste. 10
Atlanta, GA 30340-3416
Phone: (404)457-2677   Fax: (404)452-1149
Products: Medical equipment. SIC: 5047 (Medical & Hospital Equipment). Officers: Michael Childs, President.

■ 19097 ■ Up-Rad Inc.
PO Box 289
Leonardtown, MD 20650-0289
Phone: (301)739-4556
Products: Medical equipment; Hospital equipment; Dental equipment and supplies. SIC: 5047 (Medical & Hospital Equipment). Officers: Karen Updegrave, President.

■ 19098 ■ Valley Forge Scientific Corp.
136 Greentree Rd.
Oaks, PA 19456
Phones: (215)666-7500   (610)666-7500
Fax: (610)666-7565
Products: Surgical equipment; Medical equipment; Dental equipment and supplies; Optometric equipment and supplies. SICs: 5047 (Medical & Hospital Equipment); 5048 (Ophthalmic Goods). Sales: $600,000 (2000). Emp: 9. Officers: Jerry L. Malis, CEO, President & Chairman of the Board; Thomas J. Gilloway, Exec. VP & CFO.

■ 19099 ■ ValuNet Div.
2060 Craigshire Rd.
St. Louis, MO 63146
Phone: (314)542-1956
Products: Medical equipment. SIC: 5047 (Medical & Hospital Equipment).

■ 19100 ■ Venice Convalescent Aids Medical Supply
620 Cypress Ave.
Venice, FL 34292
Phone: (941)485-3366   Fax: (941)484-9872
Products: Convalescent equipment for the home. SIC: 5047 (Medical & Hospital Equipment). Est: 1979. Sales: $500,000 (2000). Emp: 5. Officers: Carolyn Archer, President.

■ 19101 ■ VHA Supply Co.
220 E Los Colinas
Irving, TX 75039
Phone: (972)830-0000
Products: Hospital equipment. **SIC:** 5047 (Medical & Hospital Equipment). **Est:** 1985. **Sales:** $40,000,000 (2000). **Emp:** 120. **Officers:** Dwight Winstead, President & COO; Don Burg, VP of Finance.

■ 19102 ■ Viking Traders, Inc.
5 Cold Hill Rd. S, Ste. 18
Mendham, NJ 07945
Phone: (973)543-3211
Products: Medical and surgical equipment and supplies; Sporting and athletic goods. **SICs:** 5047 (Medical & Hospital Equipment); 5091 (Sporting & Recreational Goods). **Officers:** Steve Swanbeck, President.

■ 19103 ■ Vivax Medical Corp.
139 Center St.
PO Box 1400
Bristol, CT 06010
Phone: (860)589-8200   **Fax:** (860)589-5944
E-mail: sales@vivaxmedicalcorp.com
URL: http://www.vivaxmedicalcorp.com
Products: Hospital beds. **SIC:** 5047 (Medical & Hospital Equipment). **Est:** 1984. **Officers:** Thomas Ellen, President.

■ 19104 ■ VNA of Rhode Island Inc.
157 Waterman St.
Providence, RI 02906-3126
Phone: (401)444-9770
Products: Medical equipment; Hospital equipment. **SIC:** 5047 (Medical & Hospital Equipment). **Officers:** Jane Mac Kenzie, President.

■ 19105 ■ Watkins Pharmaceutical & Surgical Supply
1391 E Sherman Blvd.
Muskegon, MI 49444
Phone: (616)739-7158   **Fax:** (616)739-8024
Products: Medical and hospital equipment, including furniture and supplies and home health equipment and supplies. **SIC:** 5047 (Medical & Hospital Equipment). **Officers:** Sidney Miller, Owner.

■ 19106 ■ Welding Equipment & Supply/All State Medical Gases
255 Field Point Rd.
Greenwich, CT 06830
Phone: (203)869-4388   **Fax:** (203)869-3652
URL: http://www.wesasm.com
Products: Medical and hospital equipment and supplies; Welding equipment; Industrial gases; Propane. **SICs:** 5047 (Medical & Hospital Equipment); 5084 (Industrial Machinery & Equipment). **Est:** 1953. **Sales:** $11,000,000 (2000). **Emp:** 65. **Officers:** John Barry III, President, e-mail: jbarry@wesasm.com; John Ell, Human Resources Contact; John Morrell; Jim Spencer; Ed Dougherty, Sales/Marketing Contact; John Kinosh, Customer Service Contact. **Former Name:** Greenwich Propane Inc. **Former Name:** New England Propane Inc.

■ 19107 ■ Kenyon Wells & Associates
PO Box 429
Lexington, SC 29071-0429
Phone: (803)359-6020   **Fax:** (803)359-9270
Products: Medical equipment; Hospital equipment. **SIC:** 5047 (Medical & Hospital Equipment). **Officers:** Kenyon Wells, President.

■ 19108 ■ Westmed Specialties Inc.
1420 20th St., NW, Ste. B
Auburn, WA 98001-3413
Phone: (206)431-8480   **Fax:** (206)431-8616
Products: Medical equipment; Hospital equipment. **SIC:** 5047 (Medical & Hospital Equipment). **Est:** 1989. **Emp:** 10. **Officers:** Garry Skelton, President.

■ 19109 ■ WINMED Products Co.
PO Box 61556
Ft. Myers, FL 33906-1556
Phone: (941)791-4000
Free: (800)544-5155   **Fax:** (941)791-6000
E-mail: winmed@usacomputers.net
URL: http://www.winmedproducts.com
Products: Medical equipment. **SIC:** 5047 (Medical & Hospital Equipment). **Est:** 1991. **Emp:** 8. **Officers:** Bruce C. Russell; Chris King, Sales/Marketing Contact. **Former Name:** Winnie Walker Co.

■ 19110 ■ Wolverine X-Ray Sales and Service
21277 Bridge St.
Southfield, MI 48034
Phone: (810)352-8600
Free: (800)534-9886   **Fax:** (810)352-0555
Products: X-ray apparatus; Lead and shielding devices. **SIC:** 5047 (Medical & Hospital Equipment). **Est:** 1943. **Emp:** 17. **Officers:** Walter E. Carrigan.

■ 19111 ■ Worldwide Medical
1084 Flynt Dr., Bldg. A
Jackson, MS 39208
Phone: (601)932-1525   **Fax:** (601)936-2468
Products: Electromedical and x-ray apparatus; Medical laboratory analysis instruments; Laboratory sterilizers; Medical diagnostic equipment; Surgical instruments and supplies. **SIC:** 5047 (Medical & Hospital Equipment). **Officers:** Mike Yarbro, President.

■ 19112 ■ X-Ray Products Corp.
PO Box 896
Atascadero, CA 93423-0896
Phone: (562)949-8394   **Fax:** (562)948-5904
Products: X-ray machines and supplies. **SIC:** 5084 (Industrial Machinery & Equipment). **Est:** 1939. **Sales:** $10,000,000 (2000). **Emp:** 55. **Officers:** Richard C. Stark, President; Gertrude Hart, Controller.

■ 19113 ■ Yellow River Systems
401 Broadway, Ste. 703
New York, NY 10013
Phone: (212)714-2789   **Fax:** (212)714-0288
E-mail: yrsinc@yahoo.com
Products: Computers, peripherals and software; Medical and hospital equipment; Scientific research and educational instruments and equipment; Manufacturing and construction machinery; Electronic components. **SICs:** 5047 (Medical & Hospital Equipment); 5091 (Sporting & Recreational Goods); 5082 (Construction & Mining Machinery); 5045 (Computers, Peripherals & Software); 5023 (Homefurnishings). **Sales:** $1,500,000 (1999). **Emp:** 5. **Officers:** Thomas Chen, President.

■ 19114 ■ Zee Medical Service Co.
PO Box 849
Wolfeboro Falls, NH 03896-0849
Phone: (603)569-6284
Free: (800)640-1615   **Fax:** (603)569-5191
Products: Medical and safety equipment. **SIC:** 5047 (Medical & Hospital Equipment). **Officers:** William Climo, Owner.

■ 19115 ■ Jackson Zimmer & Associates
PO Box 279
Oakley, UT 84055-0279
Phone: (801)486-3516   **Fax:** (801)486-3522
Products: Medical and hospital equipment; Orthopedic equipment and supplies. **SIC:** 5047 (Medical & Hospital Equipment). **Officers:** Jesse Jackson, President.

(34) Medical, Dental, and Optical Supplies

Entries in this section are arranged alphabetically by company name. When the company name is a personal name, the company name is alphabetized by the surname unless the first name or initial(s) are part of a trade name. See the User's Guide at the front of this directory for additional information.

■ 19116 ■ **3-D Optical Lab Inc.**
1370 S Bertolsen Rd.
PO Box 2842
Eugene, OR 97402
Phone: (541)683-3898 **Fax:** (541)342-8533
Products: Ophthalmic goods. **SIC:** 5048 (Ophthalmic Goods).

■ 19117 ■ **A Plus Medical, Inc.**
948 Walton Way
Augusta, GA 30901-2893
Phone: (404)321-9478
Free: (800)241-4636 **Fax:** (706)722-0279
Products: Powered wheelchair systems and parts. **SIC:** 5047 (Medical & Hospital Equipment). **Est:** 1973. **Emp:** 20. **Officers:** Richard Grigg, Contact.

■ 19118 ■ **Abana Pharmaceuticals Inc.**
PO Box 46903
St. Louis, MO 63146-6903
Phone: (314)390-2133
Products: Pharmaceuticals. **SIC:** 5122 (Drugs, Proprietaries & Sundries). **Sales:** $23,000,000 (2000). **Emp:** 30. **Officers:** Dale Eads, President.

■ 19119 ■ **Abbey Home Healthcare**
131 Cheshire Ln., No. 500
Minnetonka, MN 55305-1058
Phone: (612)827-8251
Products: Powered wheelchair systems and parts. **SIC:** 5047 (Medical & Hospital Equipment). **Officers:** Lee Delie, Contact.

■ 19120 ■ **Abbey Medical Inc.**
PO Box 9100
Fountain Valley, CA 92728-9100
Phone: (714)957-2000
Products: Home health care products. **SICs:** 5047 (Medical & Hospital Equipment); 5122 (Drugs, Proprietaries & Sundries). **Est:** 1924. **Sales:** $227,300,000 (2000). **Emp:** 3,200. **Officers:** Timothy M. Aitken, CEO & President; Richard J. Rapp, CFO & Treasurer; Sarah L. Eames, VP of Marketing; Thomas J. Wiedel, VP, CFO & Chief Acct. Officer; James F. Philipp.

■ 19121 ■ **Academy Optical Inc.**
PO Box 809
Presque Isle, ME 04769-0809
Phone: (207)764-4900 **Fax:** (207)764-5497
Products: Ophthalmic goods; Ophthalmic frames. **SIC:** 5048 (Ophthalmic Goods).

■ 19122 ■ **Accu Rx Optical**
100 Federal Way
Johnston, RI 02919
Phone: (401)454-2920 **Fax:** 800-234-2371
Products: Ophthalmic goods. **SIC:** 5048 (Ophthalmic Goods).

■ 19123 ■ **AcryMed Inc.**
12232 SW Garden Pl.
Portland, OR 97223
Phone: (503)624-9830 **Fax:** (503)639-0846
URL: http://www.acrymed.com
Products: Wound dressing products. **SIC:** 5122

(Drugs, Proprietaries & Sundries). **Est:** 1993. **Emp:** 12. **Officers:** Bruce L. Gibbins, Chairman, CTO; Jack McMaken, CEO & President, e-mail: jmcmaken@acrymed.com.

■ 19124 ■ **Action Laboratories Inc.**
Via Martens
Anaheim, CA 92806
Phone: (714)630-5941 **Fax:** (714)630-5941
Products: Health and beauty aids. **SIC:** 5122 (Drugs, Proprietaries & Sundries). **Sales:** $2,500,000 (2000). **Emp:** 8.

■ 19125 ■ **ADI Medical**
5745 W Howard
Niles, IL 60714
Phone: (847)647-7699 **Fax:** (847)647-7629
E-mail: adimedical@msn.com
URL: http://www.adimedical.com
Products: Medical supplies. **SIC:** 5047 (Medical & Hospital Equipment). **Est:** 1988. **Officers:** Joe Zhu, CEO; Ling Liu, President.

■ 19126 ■ **Adtek Co.**
PO Box 264
Sellersburg, IN 47172-0264
Phone: (812)246-5418 **Fax:** (812)246-6107
Products: Medical, dental, and optical equipment. **SIC:** 5047 (Medical & Hospital Equipment). **Sales:** $20,000,000 (2000). **Emp:** 23.

■ 19127 ■ **AJC International Inc.**
5188 Roswell Rd.
Atlanta, GA 30342
Phone: (404)252-6750
Free: (800)252-3663 **Fax:** (404)252-9340
Products: Food, including frozen poultry, pork, beef, seafood, fruit and vegetables. **SIC:** 5141 (Groceries—General Line). **Sales:** $400,000,000 (2000). **Emp:** 150. **Officers:** Gerald L. Allison, CEO.

■ 19128 ■ **Akin Medical Equipment International**
PO Box 412632
Kansas City, MO 64141
Phone: (816)753-3219 **Fax:** (816)531-2271
Products: Chemicals; Water purification equipment; Air purification equipment; Medical supplies and equipment; Dental supplies; Over-the-counter pharmaceuticals and nutritional food supplements; Sugar; Cocoa; Coffee. **SICs:** 5047 (Medical & Hospital Equipment); 5169 (Chemicals & Allied Products Nec); 5074 (Plumbing & Hydronic Heating Supplies); 5075 (Warm Air Heating & Air-Conditioning); 5122 (Drugs, Proprietaries & Sundries). **Est:** 1974. **Emp:** 4. **Officers:** Hon. John Akin, President; Rev. Grace Akin, Vice President.

■ 19129 ■ **AKMS Inc.**
PO Box 50329
Columbia, SC 29250
Phone: (803)695-5001 **Fax:** (803)695-1997
Products: Medical, dental, and optical equipment. **SIC:** 5047 (Medical & Hospital Equipment).

■ 19130 ■ **Akorn Inc.**
2500 Mill Brook Dr.
Buffalo Grove, IL 60089
Phone: 800-93-AKORN **Fax:** (847)236-3823
Products: Ophthalmic pharmaceuticals. **SIC:** 5122 (Drugs, Proprietaries & Sundries). **Est:** 1971. **Sales:** $450,000 (2000). **Emp:** 350. **Officers:** John N. Kapoor, Chairman of the Board; Floyd Benjamin, President; Scott Zion, Sr. VP & General Mgr.

■ 19131 ■ **Alanco Eyewear**
8117 NE 13th Ave.
Vancouver, WA 98665
Phone: (360)574-0065
Free: (800)551-6500 **Fax:** (360)573-7805
E-mail: aloeye@aol.com
Products: Ophthalmic frames. **SIC:** 5048 (Ophthalmic Goods). **Est:** 1981. **Sales:** $1,000,000 (2000). **Emp:** 8. **Officers:** Alan Weintraub, President, e-mail: alo@pacifier.com. **Former Name:** Alanco Optical Inc.

■ 19132 ■ **Albers Inc.**
PO Box 51030
Knoxville, TN 37950-1030
Phone: (423)524-5492 **Fax:** (423)637-2308
Products: Pharmacy supplies. **SIC:** 5122 (Drugs, Proprietaries & Sundries). **Est:** 1864. **Sales:** $170,000,000 (2000). **Emp:** 170. **Officers:** John M. Walz, CEO & President.

■ 19133 ■ **Alcide Corp.**
8561 154th Ave. NE
Redmond, WA 98052
Phone: (425)882-2555 **Fax:** (425)861-0173
Products: Develops and markets unique biocidal products, including anti-infective products, disinfecting products and an antimicrobial for controlling food borne pathogens on poultry. **SIC:** 5122 (Drugs, Proprietaries & Sundries). **Sales:** $11,200,000 (1999). **Emp:** 15. **Officers:** Joseph Sasenick, CEO & President; John P. Richards, Exec. VP & CFO.

■ 19134 ■ **Allegiance Corp.**
1430 Waukegan Rd.
Mc Gaw Park, IL 60085
Phone: (847)578-4240 **Fax:** (847)578-4438
Products: Medical supplies; Laboratory supplies. **SIC:** 5047 (Medical & Hospital Equipment). **Sales:** $4,350,800,000 (2000). **Emp:** 19,800. **Officers:** Lester B. Knight, CEO & Chairman of the Board; Peter B. McKee, Sr. VP & CFO.

■ 19135 ■ **Allegiance Healthcare Corporation Hospital Supply/Scientific Products**
1450 Waukegan Rd.
Waukegan, IL 60085
Phone: (847)689-8410
Products: Medical, dental, and optical equipment. **SIC:** 5047 (Medical & Hospital Equipment). **Sales:** $4,500,000,000 (2000). **Emp:** 20,000.

■ **19136** ■ **Allentown Optical Corp.**
525 Business Park Ln.
PO Box 25003
Allentown, PA 18103
Phone: (215)433-5269
Free: (800)322-9021 **Fax:** (215)435-7865
Products: Ophthalmic goods. **SIC:** 5048 (Ophthalmic Goods).

■ **19137** ■ **Allied Medical, Inc.**
690 S Mendenhall Rd.
Memphis, TN 38117
Phone: (901)683-3543
Free: (800)422-2126 **Fax:** (901)683-0109
Products: Powered wheelchair systems and parts; Respiratory services; Home medical equipment. **SIC:** 5047 (Medical & Hospital Equipment). **Est:** 1973. **Emp:** 24. **Officers:** Rebecca Dyer, President.

■ **19138** ■ **Allied Safety Inc.**
5959 W Howard St.
Niles, IL 60714
Phone: (847)647-4000
Products: Safety equipment, including earplugs and goggles. **SIC:** 5047 (Medical & Hospital Equipment). **Est:** 1964. **Sales:** $60,000,000 (2000). **Emp:** 240. **Officers:** Fred E. Loepp, President; Ron Wiedeman, VP of Sales; Joe Becker, Dir of Human Resources.

■ **19139** ■ **Allred Optical Laboratory**
845 Church St. N
Concord, NC 28025-4300
Phone: (704)788-3937 **Fax:** (704)782-1512
Products: Ophthalmic goods. **SIC:** 5048 (Ophthalmic Goods). **Officers:** Ralph Allred, President.

■ **19140** ■ **American Health Supplies**
7610 225th St., SE
Woodinville, WA 98072
Phone: (425)486-4875 **Fax:** (425)485-2573
Products: Optical pharmaceuticals. **SICs:** 5048 (Ophthalmic Goods); 5122 (Drugs, Proprietaries & Sundries). **Officers:** Steven Hines, President.

■ **19141** ■ **American Medical Industries**
330 1/2 E 3rd St.
Dell Rapids, SD 57022
Phone: (605)428-5501 **Fax:** (605)428-5502
E-mail: ezhealth@sd.cybernex.net
URL: http://www.ezhealthcare.com
Products: Pill crushers and splitters, medication organizers, and pill timers; Home healthcare publications; Medical products for humans and animals. **SIC:** 5122 (Drugs, Proprietaries & Sundries). **Est:** 1986. **Officers:** Jim Fiocchi, President; Dan Anderson, Vice President.

■ **19142** ■ **American Medical Services**
825 W Huron
Pontiac, MI 48341
Phone: (248)338-6118
Products: Medical equipment and supplies. **SIC:** 5047 (Medical & Hospital Equipment). **Sales:** $3,000,000 (2000). **Emp:** 16. **Officers:** Larry L. Gaskins, General Mgr.; Barbara Etapa, Finance Officer.

■ **19143** ■ **American Medserve Corp.**
184 Shuman Blvd., Ste. 200
Naperville, IL 60563
Phone: (708)717-2904
Products: Pharmaceuticals. **SIC:** 5122 (Drugs, Proprietaries & Sundries). **Officers:** Timothy L. Burfield, CEO & President.

■ **19144** ■ **American Plasma Services L.P**
1925 Century Park E #1970
Los Angeles, CA 90067-2701
Products: Plasma. **SIC:** 5047 (Medical & Hospital Equipment).

■ **19145** ■ **Americo International Trading, Ltd.**
13607 Belinda Court
Houston, TX 77069
Phone: (281)580-2343 **Fax:** (281)580-0609
Products: Medical supplies; Industrial machinery and equipment; Industrial supplies; New and refurbished medical equipment. **SICs:** 5047 (Medical & Hospital Equipment); 5084 (Industrial Machinery & Equipment);

5085 (Industrial Supplies). **Officers:** Bryan K. Oldham, Vice President.

■ **19146** ■ **AmeriNet/SupportHealth**
2204 Lakeshore Dr., Ste. 140
Birmingham, AL 35209
Phone: (205)802-1682
Free: (800)426-7971 **Fax:** (205)802-1687
URL: http://www.amerinet-gpo.com
Products: Medical and surgical supplies; Pharmaceuticals; Laboratory products. **SICs:** 5047 (Medical & Hospital Equipment); 5122 (Drugs, Proprietaries & Sundries). **Est:** 1989. **Sales:** $200,000,000 (2000). **Emp:** 5. **Officers:** Ronald Pollini R. Ph., Sr. Program Mgr., Pharmacy Svcs.; Barbara Odom, Sr. Program Mgr., Medical/Surgical Svcs.; Bill O'Donovan, Program Mgr. Laboratory Svcs.; Amanda Adams CPht, Program Coordinator Pharmacy Svcs.; Pamela Walden, Program Coordinator, Medical/Surgical. **Former Name:** SupportHealth Inc.

■ **19147** ■ **AmeriSource Corp.**
PO Box 959
Valley Forge, PA 19482-0959
Phone: (610)296-4480 **Fax:** (610)647-0141
Products: Pharmaceuticals. **SIC:** 5122 (Drugs, Proprietaries & Sundries). **Sales:** $78,000,000,000 (2000). **Emp:** 3,000. **Officers:** R. David Yost, CEO; Kurt J. Hilzinger, Sr. VP & CFO.

■ **19148** ■ **AmeriSource Corp. Orlando Div.**
2100 Directors Row
Orlando, FL 32809-6234
Phone: (407)856-6239 **Fax:** (407)245-6907
Products: Pharmaceuticals. **SIC:** 5122 (Drugs, Proprietaries & Sundries). **Est:** 1896. **Sales:** $61,000,000 (2000). **Emp:** 80. **Officers:** Jeff Greer, General Mgr.; George Balch, Manager; Kyle Mead, Dir. of Marketing & Sales; Ben Malari, Information Systems Mgr.

■ **19149** ■ **AmeriSource Corp. (Paducah, Kentucky)**
PO Box 330
Paducah, KY 42001-0330
Phone: (502)444-7300 **Fax:** (502)444-7047
Products: Pharmaceutical supplies. **SIC:** 5122 (Drugs, Proprietaries & Sundries). **Sales:** $453,000,000 (2000). **Emp:** 325. **Officers:** Denise Gillerland, VP & General Merchandising Mgr.

■ **19150** ■ **AmeriSource Health Corp.**
PO Box 959
Valley Forge, PA 19482-0959
Phone: (610)296-4480 **Fax:** (610)647-0141
Products: Generic pharmaceuticals; Health and beauty aids. **SIC:** 5122 (Drugs, Proprietaries & Sundries). **Est:** 1988. **Sales:** $5,551,700,000 (2000). **Emp:** 3,000. **Officers:** R. David Yost, CEO & President; Kurt J. Hilzinger, VP, CFO & Treasurer.

■ **19151** ■ **AmeriSource-Lynchburg Div.**
PO Box 10069
Lynchburg, VA 24506-0069
Phone: (804)239-6971 **Fax:** (804)582-4755
Products: Drugs. **SIC:** 5122 (Drugs, Proprietaries & Sundries). **Est:** 1897. **Sales:** $130,000,000 (2000). **Emp:** 200. **Officers:** Dave Farley, General Mgr.; David R. Wright, Vice President; Charlie W. Black, VP of Marketing. **Former Name:** Alco Health Services Corp.

■ **19152** ■ **Anda Generics Inc.**
4001 SW 47th Ave., Bldg. 201
Ft. Lauderdale, FL 33314
Phone: (954)584-0300 **Free:** (800)331-2632
Products: Pharmaceuticals. **SIC:** 5122 (Drugs, Proprietaries & Sundries). **Sales:** $15,700,000 (1994). **Emp:** 75. **Officers:** Alan Cohen, President.

■ **19153** ■ **Andover Corp.**
4 Commercial Dr.
Salem, NH 03079
Phone: (603)686-0660 **Fax:** (603)893-6508
E-mail: sales@andcorp.com
URL: http://www.andcorp.com
Products: Optical interference filters. **SIC:** 5048 (Ophthalmic Goods). **Est:** 1979. **Emp:** 45. **Officers:** Richard J. Bennett, President; William E. Grenier, VP of Marketing & Sales, e-mail: weg@andcorp.com; John

Cotton, Vice President; Debra Maddox, Customer Service Contact, e-mail: deb@andcorp.com.

■ **19154** ■ **Anodyne Inc.**
10912 Greenbrier Rd.
Minnetonka, MN 55305-3474
Phone: (612)831-6130 **Fax:** (612)831-6130
Products: Electromedical supplies. **SIC:** 5047 (Medical & Hospital Equipment).

■ **19155** ■ **Apotheca Inc.**
1622 N 16th St.
Phoenix, AZ 85006
Phone: (602)252-5244 **Fax:** (602)258-4082
Products: Pharmaceuticals, including vitamins. **SIC:** 5122 (Drugs, Proprietaries & Sundries). **Est:** 1973. **Sales:** $4,000,000 (2000). **Emp:** 13. **Officers:** Mitchell Herseth, President; Bonnie Herseth, VP & Treasurer.

■ **19156** ■ **Apothecary Products Inc.**
11750 12th Ave. S
Burnsville, MN 55337
Phones: (612)890-1940 800-328-2742
Free: (800)328-1584 **Fax:** (612)890-0418
E-mail: pillminder@aol.com
Products: Medical alert supplies; Pill containers; Dosage aids; Pharmacy equipment and supplies. **SIC:** 5047 (Medical & Hospital Equipment). **Est:** 1974. **Sales:** $30,000,000 (2000). **Emp:** 210. **Officers:** T. Noble, CEO; Ellen Davis, Sr. VP; John Creel, President; Hal Edwards, Sales/Marketing Contact; Kay Johnson, Customer Service Contact; Don Shaffer, Human Resources Contact.

■ **19157** ■ **Apria Healthcare**
2041 Ave. C, Ste. 400
Bethlehem, PA 18017
Phone: (610)266-6333
Free: (800)842-2525 **Fax:** (610)266-6187
Products: Home medical equipment. Home respiratory equipment (oxygen, nebulizers, cpap, ventilators). Infusion services. **SICs:** 5047 (Medical & Hospital Equipment); 5049 (Professional Equipment Nec). **Est:** 1994. **Officers:** Carol Policelli, Branch Mgr. **Former Name:** Abbey.

■ **19158** ■ **Arco Pharmaceuticals Inc.**
90 Orville Dr.
Bohemia, NY 11716
Phone: (516)567-9500 **Fax:** (516)244-1787
Products: Pharmaceuticals; Vitamins; Cosmetics. **SIC:** 5122 (Drugs, Proprietaries & Sundries). **Est:** 1960. **Sales:** $43,000,000 (2000). **Emp:** 500. **Officers:** Scott Rudolph, CEO, President & Chairman of the Board; Harvey Kamil, Exec. VP & CFO; B. Drucker, VP of Sales.

■ **19159** ■ **Area Access Inc.**
8117 Ransell Rd.
Falls Church, VA 22042-1015
Phone: (703)573-2111
Free: (800)333-2732 **Fax:** (703)207-0446
Products: Medical, dental, and optical equipment. **SIC:** 5047 (Medical & Hospital Equipment). **Sales:** $3,000,000 (2000). **Emp:** 20.

■ **19160** ■ **Arkansas Optical Co.**
PO Box 9004
North Little Rock, AR 72119-9004
Phone: (501)372-1923
Products: Ophthalmic goods; Optometric equipment and supplies. **SIC:** 5048 (Ophthalmic Goods). **Officers:** Mary Thompson, President.

■ **19161** ■ **Ray Arndt Optical Supplies**
820 NW 18th Ave.
Portland, OR 97209-2317
Phone: (503)223-6106 **Fax:** (503)223-1471
Products: Ophthalmic goods. **SIC:** 5048 (Ophthalmic Goods). **Officers:** John Parr, President.

■ **19162** ■ **Ashmore Optical Co. Inc.**
PO Box 2961
Charleston, WV 25330-2961
Phone: (304)344-2366
Free: (800)564-8308 **Fax:** (304)344-2369
Products: Ophthalmic goods; Optometric equipment and supplies. **SIC:** 5048 (Ophthalmic Goods). **Officers:** Paul Burdette, President.

■ 19163 ■ **Asia Pacific Trading Co.**
35 W 31st St.
New York, NY 10001
Phone: (212)736-5220
Free: (800)437-0031 **Fax:** (212)967-9320
Products: Sunglasses and accessories. **SIC:** 5048
(Ophthalmic Goods).

■ 19164 ■ **Associated Medical**
2901 S Hampton Rd.
Philadelphia, PA 19154
Phone: (215)677-0589
Products: Medical supplies. **SIC:** 5047 (Medical &
Hospital Equipment). **Emp:** 60. **Officers:** Phyllis
Forman, President.

■ 19165 ■ **Associated Services for the Blind**
919 Walnut St.
Philadelphia, PA 19107
Phone: (215)627-0600
Free: (800)876-5456 **Fax:** (215)922-0692
Products: Aids and services for the blind, including
canes, talking watches, recorders, adaptive equipment,
and games. **SIC:** 5047 (Medical & Hospital Equipment).
Est: 1980. **Sales:** $100,000 (2000). **Emp:** 2. **Officers:**
Dolores Ferrar-Godzieba.

■ 19166 ■ **Asuka Corp.**
7800 River Rd.
North Bergen, NJ 07047
Phone: (201)861-5450 **Fax:** (201)861-1523
Products: Self-aligning optical fiber splicers; UV curing
optical fiber related products; Pure liquid gelatin, for
electrical and medical purposes; UV curing adhesives
for optical and electrical purposes. **SICs:** 5049
(Professional Equipment Nec); 5169 (Chemicals &
Allied Products Nec). **Officers:** R. Kanda, President.

■ 19167 ■ **Atecs Corp.**
156 Mokauea St.
Honolulu, HI 96819-3105
Phone: (808)845-2991 **Fax:** (808)842-0921
Products: Medical, dental, and optical equipment. **SIC:**
5047 (Medical & Hospital Equipment). **Sales:**
$2,000,000 (2000). **Emp:** 6.

■ 19168 ■ **Atlantis Eyewear, Inc.**
177 Elmdale Rd.
North Scituate, RI 02857-1308
Phone: (401)353-4930 **Fax:** (401)353-3440
Products: Eyeglass frames. **SIC:** 5048 (Ophthalmic
Goods).

■ 19169 ■ **Auto Suture Company U.S.A.**
150 Glover Ave.
Norwalk, CT 06856
Phone: (203)845-1000
Free: (800)321-0263 **Fax:** 800-544-8772
URL: http://www.ossurg.com
Products: Sutures; Staples; Surgical instruments;
Minimally invasive, cardiovascular and diagnostic
breast technologies. **SIC:** 5047 (Medical & Hospital
Equipment). **Est:** 1967. **Emp:** 2,350.

■ 19170 ■ **Avatex Corp.**
5910 N Central Expy.
Dallas, TX 75206
Phone: (214)365-7450 **Fax:** (214)365-7499
Products: Pharmaceuticals; Developer of electronic
ordering and inventory control systems; Franchiser of
general variety and craft stores and holding company.
SIC: 5122 (Drugs, Proprietaries & Sundries). **Sales:**
$117,200,000 (2000). **Emp:** 13. **Officers:** Abbey J.
Butler, CEO & Chairman of the Board; Grady E.
Schleier, VP, CFO & Treasurer.

■ 19171 ■ **Avon-Glendale Home Medical
Equipment and Supplies Inc.**
PO Box 17776
Los Angeles, CA 90017
Phone: (213)487-1180
Products: Hospital equipment and supplies, including
beds, bandages, gauze, stockings, and support socks.
SIC: 5047 (Medical & Hospital Equipment). **Est:** 1971.
Sales: $4,000,000 (2000). **Emp:** 18. **Officers:** Alan
Dubin, President.

■ 19172 ■ **Avon Products Inc. Northeast
Regional Area**
2100 Ogletown Rd.
Newark, DE 19712
Phone: (302)453-7700 **Fax:** (302)453-7788
Products: Cosmetics. **SIC:** 5122 (Drugs, Proprietaries
& Sundries). **Sales:** $458,000,000 (2000). **Emp:** 600.
Officers: Angelo Rossi, VP of Sales.

■ 19173 ■ **B & G Optics**
1320 Unity St.
Philadelphia, PA 19124
Phone: (215)289-2480 **Fax:** (215)289-4046
Products: Ophthalmic goods. **SIC:** 5048 (Ophthalmic
Goods).

■ 19174 ■ **Barnes Wholesale Drug Company
Inc.**
PO Box 17010
Inglewood, CA 90308
Phone: (310)641-1885 **Fax:** (310)649-3206
URL: http://www.barneswholesale.com
Products: Pharmaceuticals. **SIC:** 5122 (Drugs,
Proprietaries & Sundries). **Est:** 1948. **Sales:**
$250,000,000 (1999). **Emp:** 110. **Officers:** Robert
Schwartz, President, e-mail: bschwartz@
barneswholesale.com.

■ 19175 ■ **Barry Optical Co., Inc.**
281 Clinton St.
PO Box 456
Hempstead, NY 11550
Phones: (516)481-9656 (516)481-9555
Free: (800)522-7795 **Fax:** (516)481-7270
Products: Ophthalmic goods. **SIC:** 5048 (Ophthalmic
Goods).

■ 19176 ■ **Bauer Optical Co.**
23-25 Spring St.
PO Box 350
Ossining, NY 10562-0350
Phone: (914)944-9016 **Fax:** (914)944-9004
E-mail: baueropt@aol.com
Products: Ophthalmic goods. **SIC:** 5048 (Ophthalmic
Goods). **Est:** 1940. **Emp:** 4. **Officers:** Ed Klotz, Owner.

■ 19177 ■ **Baxter International Inc. (Deerfield,
Illinois)**
1 Baxter Pkwy.
Deerfield, IL 60015
Phone: (847)948-2000
Products: Health care products, including aspirin,
laxatives, and diet pills; Diapers. **SIC:** 5122 (Drugs,
Proprietaries & Sundries). **Est:** 1931. **Sales:**
$6,138,000,000 (2000). **Emp:** 37,000. **Officers:**
Vernon R. Loucks Jr., CEO & Chairman of the Board;
Harry M. Jansen Kraemer Jr., Sr. VP & CFO.

■ 19178 ■ **Baylor Biomedical Services**
2625 Elm St.
Dallas, TX 75226
Phone: (214)820-2176
Products: Powered wheelchair systems and parts.
SIC: 5047 (Medical & Hospital Equipment). **Officers:**
Chad Johnson, Contact.

■ 19179 ■ **Beauty and Beauty Enterprises Inc.**
30 Universal Pl.
Carlstadt, NJ 07072
Phone: (201)935-8887
Free: (800)474-6533 **Fax:** (201)939-5154
Products: Health and beauty aids. **SIC:** 5122 (Drugs,
Proprietaries & Sundries). **Sales:** $3,000,000 (2000).
Emp: 5.

■ 19180 ■ **Beck-Lee Inc.**
PO Box 425
Stratford, CT 06615-0425
Phone: (203)332-7678
Free: (800)235-2852 **Fax:** (203)384-1932
Products: Medical, dental, and optical equipment. **SIC:**
5047 (Medical & Hospital Equipment).

■ 19181 ■ **Beehive Botanicals Inc.**
Rte. 8, Box 8257
Hayward, WI 54843
Phone: (715)634-4274
Free: (800)283-4274 **Fax:** (715)634-3523
E-mail: beehive@win.bright.net
URL: http://www.beehive-botanicals.com
Products: Bee related products; Botanicals; Raw
material; Consumer goods. **SIC:** 5122 (Drugs,
Proprietaries & Sundries). **Est:** 1972. **Emp:** 49.

■ 19182 ■ **Benedict Optical**
341 Bennett Ln.
Lewisville, TX 75067
Phone: (972)221-4141
Free: (800)423-2361 **Fax:** 800-275-4666
Products: Ophthalmic goods. **SIC:** 5048 (Ophthalmic
Goods).

■ 19183 ■ **Bergen Brunswig Corp.**
1765 Fremont Dr.
Salt Lake City, UT 84104
Phone: (801)972-4131 **Fax:** (801)975-0948
Products: Pharmaceutical items. **SIC:** 5122 (Drugs,
Proprietaries & Sundries).

■ 19184 ■ **Bergen Brunswig Corp.**
4000 Metropolitan Dr.
Orange, CA 92868-3510
Phone: (714)385-4000
Free: (800)840-5131 **Fax:** (714)385-1442
Products: Pharmaceuticals, proprietary medicines,
cosmetics, toiletries and electronic products. **SICs:**
5122 (Drugs, Proprietaries & Sundries); 5065
(Electronic Parts & Equipment Nec). **Sales:**
$21,246,000,000 (1999). **Emp:** 13,000. **Officers:**
Donald R. Roden, CEO & President; Neil F. Dimick,
Exec. VP & CFO.

■ 19185 ■ **Bernell Corp.**
PO Box 4637
South Bend, IN 46601
Phone: (219)234-3200
Free: (800)227-2252 **Fax:** (219)233-8422
Products: Ophthalmic goods; Optometric equipment
and supplies. **SIC:** 5048 (Ophthalmic Goods). **Officers:**
Jeffrey Beardsley, CEO.

■ 19186 ■ **B.G. Industries Inc.**
8550 Balboa Blvd., Ste. 214
Northridge, CA 91325
Phone: (818)894-0744
Products: Medical supplies. **SIC:** 5047 (Medical &
Hospital Equipment).

■ 19187 ■ **Bindley Western Industries Inc.**
8909 Purdue Rd.
Indianapolis, IN 46268-3135
Phone: (317)704-4000
Free: (800)800-4162 **Fax:** (317)704-4601
Products: Pharmaceuticals, healthcare products and
beauty aids. **SIC:** 5122 (Drugs, Proprietaries &
Sundries). **Sales:** $7,449,000,000 (1999). **Emp:** 1,254.
Officers: William E. Bindley, CEO & Chairman of the
Board; Thomas J. Salentine, Exec. VP & CFO.

■ 19188 ■ **Bindley Western Industries Inc.
Kendall Div.**
PO Box 1060
Shelby, NC 28150
Phone: (704)482-2481
Products: Pharmaceuticals and sundries. **SIC:** 5122
(Drugs, Proprietaries & Sundries). **Sales:**
$109,000,000 (2000). **Emp:** 104. **Officers:** C. Rush
Hamrick III, General Mgr.

■ 19189 ■ **Bingham Enterprises Inc.**
13540 Lake City Way
Seattle, WA 98125
Phone: (206)367-3128
Free: (800)574-1172 **Fax:** (206)367-1465
URL: http://www.binghams.com/med-co
Products: Packaging materials; Laboratory and
hospital supplies. **SIC:** 5047 (Medical & Hospital
Equipment). **Est:** 1973. **Emp:** 6. **Officers:** R. Larry
Bingham, President, e-mail: rlb@eskimo.com. **Doing
Business As:** Med-Co. **Doing Business As:** B.E.I.
Packaging.

■ 19190 ■ Bio-Dental Technologies Corp.
11291 Sunrise Park Dr.
Rancho Cordova, CA 95742
Phone: (916)638-8147 **Fax:** (916)638-0116
Products: Dental products. **SIC:** 5047 (Medical & Hospital Equipment). **Sales:** $33,100,000 (2000). **Emp:** 124. **Officers:** Curtis M. Rocca III, CEO & President; Terry E. Bane, CFO.

■ 19191 ■ Bio Instruments Inc.
271 Silver Lake Rd.
St. Paul, MN 55112
Phone: (612)631-3380 **Fax:** (612)631-9595
Products: Cardiovascular supplies for open heart surgery. **SIC:** 5047 (Medical & Hospital Equipment). **Officers:** Richard Rog, President.

■ 19192 ■ Bioject Medical Technologies Inc.
7620 SW Bridgeport Rd.
Portland, OR 97224
Phone: (503)639-7221 **Fax:** (503)624-9002
Products: Develops and needle-free medical injection devices. **SIC:** 5047 (Medical & Hospital Equipment). **Sales:** $2,600,000 (2000). **Emp:** 30. **Officers:** James C. O'Shea, CEO, President & Chairman of the Board; Michael A. Temple, VP, CFO & Treasurer.

■ 19193 ■ Blankinship Distributors Inc.
1927 Vine St.
Kansas City, MO 64108
Phone: (816)842-6825 **Fax:** (816)421-2823
Products: Hair care and confectionery products. **SICs:** 5122 (Drugs, Proprietaries & Sundries); 5145 (Confectionery). **Sales:** $4,000,000 (2000). **Emp:** 6. **Officers:** G. Lawrence Blankinship, President.

■ 19194 ■ Blue Grass Optical Co.
140 S Forbes Rd.
Lexington, KY 40511
Phone: (606)255-0743 **Fax:** (606)233-9883
Products: Ophthalmic goods. **SIC:** 5048 (Ophthalmic Goods). **Officers:** Jon Durkin, President.

■ 19195 ■ BNA Optical Supply Inc.
2819 Columbine Pl.
Nashville, TN 37204-3103
Phone: (615)383-7036
Free: (800)528-9127 **Fax:** (615)269-7197
Products: Ophthalmic goods; Optometric equipment and supplies. **SIC:** 5048 (Ophthalmic Goods). **Officers:** Steve Mullins, President.

■ 19196 ■ James A. Bock Pharmaceutical, Inc.
PO Box 785
Wilmington, OH 45177
Phone: (937)382-4545 **Fax:** (937)382-5611
Products: Orthopedic products; Chemical fuel oil additive; Chemical boiler water treatments; Pharmaceuticals; vitamins and nutritional supplements. **SICs:** 5122 (Drugs, Proprietaries & Sundries); 5047 (Medical & Hospital Equipment); 5169 (Chemicals & Allied Products Nec). **Officers:** James A. Bock, President.

■ 19197 ■ Bradley Pharmaceuticals Inc.
383 Rte. 46 W
Fairfield, NJ 07004-2402
Phone: (973)882-1505 **Fax:** (973)575-5366
URL: http://www.bradpharm.com
Products: Pharmaceuticals. **SIC:** 5122 (Drugs, Proprietaries & Sundries). **Est:** 1985. **Sales:** $18,800,000 (1999). **Emp:** 110. **Officers:** Daniel Glassman, CEO & Chairman of the Board.

■ 19198 ■ Brentwood Medical Products Inc.
3300 Fujita St.
Torrance, CA 90505
Phone: (310)530-5955
Free: (800)624-8950 **Fax:** (310)530-1421
Products: Medical supplies. **SIC:** 5047 (Medical & Hospital Equipment). **Sales:** $5,000,000 (2000). **Emp:** 22. **Officers:** Delbert A. Freeman, President; Sandra Dancy, Accounting Manager.

■ 19199 ■ Briggs Corp.
PO Box 1698
Des Moines, IA 50306
Phone: (515)327-6400
Free: (800)247-2343 **Fax:** 800-222-1996
Products: Medical supplies. **SIC:** 5047 (Medical & Hospital Equipment). **Est:** 1948. **Sales:** $20,000,000 (2000). **Emp:** 275. **Officers:** Phil Bolge, COO; Ken Flaskerud, CFO; B. Klitsch, VP of Customer Services.

■ 19200 ■ Brinkmann Instruments Inc.
1 Cantiague Rd.
Westbury, NY 11590-0207
Phone: (516)334-7500
Free: (800)645-3050 **Fax:** (516)334-7506
Products: Scientific and measurement devices. **SIC:** 5047 (Medical & Hospital Equipment).

■ 19201 ■ Brittain Merchandising
PO Box 449
Lawton, OK 73502
Phone: (580)355-4430
Products: Drugs, proprietaries and stationery. **SICs:** 5122 (Drugs, Proprietaries & Sundries); 5112 (Stationery & Office Supplies). **Sales:** $46,000,000 (1999). **Emp:** 50. **Officers:** L.D. Brittain, President; Shirley Crumpton, Treasurer.

■ 19202 ■ Brothers' Optical Lab, Inc.
2125 S Manchester Ave.
Anaheim, CA 92802
Phone: (714)634-9303
Free: (800)531-3112 **Fax:** (714)634-3317
Products: Ophthalmic goods. **SIC:** 5048 (Ophthalmic Goods).

■ 19203 ■ James Brudnick Company Inc.
219 Medford St.
Malden, MA 02148
Phone: (781)321-6800
Products: Pharmaceuticals; Tobacco; Candy products. **SICs:** 5122 (Drugs, Proprietaries & Sundries); 5194 (Tobacco & Tobacco Products); 5145 (Confectionery). **Sales:** $77,000,000 (2000). **Emp:** 100. **Officers:** Richard Brudnick, President.

■ 19204 ■ BTE Import-Export
11765 West Ave., No. 253
San Antonio, TX 78216
Phone: (210)663-0979 **Fax:** (210)377-0505
E-mail: wmsbte584@cs.com
URL: http://www.blowoutcenter.com/1715
Products: Druggists' sundries, including skin and wound care; Medical equipment and supplies; Cosmetics; Exotic wild game meat snacks; Internet auction website. **SICs:** 5122 (Drugs, Proprietaries & Sundries); 5141 (Groceries—General Line); 5094 (Jewelry & Precious Stones); 5047 (Medical & Hospital Equipment). **Est:** 1984. **Sales:** $45,250 (2000). **Emp:** 1. **Officers:** Cecil Williams, CEO.

■ 19205 ■ Burrows Co.
230 West Palatine Rd.
Wheeling, IL 60090
Phone: (847)537-7300 **Fax:** (847)537-7786
Products: Medical and surgical supplies and equipment; Food-warming equipment; Textiles. **SICs:** 5047 (Medical & Hospital Equipment); 5046 (Commercial Equipment Nec); 5131 (Piece Goods & Notions). **Sales:** $100,000,000 (2000). **Emp:** 450. **Officers:** George J. Burrows, President & CFO; Scott Schroeder, CFO.

■ 19206 ■ W.A. Butler Co.
5600 Blazer Pkwy.
Dublin, OH 43017
Phone: (614)761-9095 **Fax:** (614)761-1045
URL: http://www.wabutler.com
Products: Medical supplies, including veterinary drugs. **SICs:** 5122 (Drugs, Proprietaries & Sundries); 5047 (Medical & Hospital Equipment). **Est:** 1953. **Sales:** $500,000,000 (1999). **Emp:** 700. **Officers:** Howard Deputy, President & CEO; Leo McNeil, Vice Chairman of the Board & CFO; Kevin Vasquez, Exec. VP & COO; David Stone, VP of Marketing & Sales; Fred Bravo, VP of Operations.

■ 19207 ■ Buttrey Food & Drug
999 W Utah Ave.
Payson, UT 84651
Phone: (801)465-4831 **Fax:** (801)565-3672
Products: Food; Pharmaceuticals. **SICs:** 5122 (Drugs, Proprietaries & Sundries); 5141 (Groceries—General Line). **Officers:** Kent Thompson.

■ 19208 ■ Caldwell and Bloor Company Inc.
80 W 3rd St.
Mansfield, OH 44902
Phone: (419)522-3011 **Fax:** (419)524-7542
Products: Medical equipment and supplies. **SIC:** 5047 (Medical & Hospital Equipment). **Sales:** $500,000 (2000). **Emp:** 15. **Officers:** Thomas H. Bloor, President; James McKown, Treasurer.

■ 19209 ■ Caltag Lab
1849 Bayshore Hwy.
Burlingame, CA 94010
Phone: (650)652-0468 **Fax:** (650)652-9030
Products: Immunological research products. **SIC:** 5122 (Drugs, Proprietaries & Sundries).

■ 19210 ■ Canyon State Opthalmaic Lab, Inc.
2123 S Priest Rd., Ste. 203
Tempe, AZ 85282
Phone: (602)967-5834 **Free:** (800)624-7186
SIC: 5048 (Ophthalmic Goods).

■ 19211 ■ Capstone Pharmacy Services
7170 Standard Dr.
Hanover, MD 21076-1321
Phone: (410)646-7373
Free: (800)766-2761 **Fax:** (410)525-3691
Products: Pharmaceuticals. **SIC:** 5122 (Drugs, Proprietaries & Sundries). **Est:** 1995. **Sales:** $200,000,000 (2000). **Emp:** 1,500. **Officers:** Dirk Allison, President; Jim Shelton, Vice President.

■ 19212 ■ Cardinal Health Inc.
5555 Glendon Ct.
Dublin, OH 43016
Phone: (614)717-5000 **Fax:** (614)761-8919
Products: Pharmaceuticals; Medical supplies. **SICs:** 5122 (Drugs, Proprietaries & Sundries); 5047 (Medical & Hospital Equipment). **Est:** 1971. **Sales:** $8,862,000,000 (2000). **Emp:** 4,800. **Officers:** John C. Kane, President & COO; David Bearman, Exec. VP & CFO; John C. Kane, President & COO; William H. Bottlinger, Dir. of Information Systems; Carole W. Tomko, Dir of Human Resources.

■ 19213 ■ Cardinal Optics, Inc.
Rt. 133 Clarendon Rd.
West Rutland, VT 05777
Phone: (802)438-5426
Products: Chemical dyes; Optic lens materials. **SIC:** 5048 (Ophthalmic Goods).

■ 19214 ■ Caremed
5702 Hwy. 49
Hattiesburg, MS 39401
Phone: (601)584-4300
Products: Powered wheelchair systems and parts. **SIC:** 5047 (Medical & Hospital Equipment). **Officers:** Mike Barlow, Contact.

■ 19215 ■ Caribe Optical Lab/Lens
Urb Lariviera
Ave. Dediego 929
Rio Piedras, PR 00926
Phone: (787)781-4945 **Fax:** (787)793-0766
Products: Ophthalmic goods. **SIC:** 5048 (Ophthalmic Goods).

■ 19216 ■ Carl Beatty and Associates
7659 Lake Shore Dr.
Owings, MD 20736
Phone: (301)855-0154
Free: (888)736-9848 **Fax:** (301)855-2769
Products: Veterinary products. **SIC:** 5047 (Medical & Hospital Equipment).

■ 19217 ■ **Carlton Optical Distributors**
9419 E San Salvador Dr., Ste. 102
Scottsdale, AZ 85258-5510
Phone: (480)860-1801
Free: (800)457-6115 **Fax:** (480)860-2502
Products: Ophthalmic goods; Eye glasses; Ophthalmic frames. **SIC:** 5048 (Ophthalmic Goods). **Est:** 1975. **Sales:** $1,500,000 (2000). **Emp:** 5. **Officers:** Steven J. Henke, President.

■ 19218 ■ **Carnrick Laboratories Inc.**
65 Horsehill Rd.
Cedar Knolls, NJ 07927
Phone: (973)267-2670 **Fax:** (973)267-2289
Products: Pharmaceuticals. **SIC:** 5122 (Drugs, Proprietaries & Sundries). **Est:** 1899. **Sales:** $84,000,000 (2000). **Emp:** 140. **Officers:** Edmond Bergeron, President; Donna Vanden Bosch, Treasurer; Brenda Phillips, Secretary.

■ 19219 ■ **Carolina Vet Supply**
PO Box 2812
Shelby, NC 28150
Phone: (704)482-7158 **Free:** (800)209-8101
Products: Veterinary products. **SIC:** 5047 (Medical & Hospital Equipment). **Sales:** $300,000 (2000). **Emp:** 1.

■ 19220 ■ **Cascade Optical Inc.**
6740 Cascade Rd. SE
Grand Rapids, MI 49546-6850
Phone: (616)942-9886
Products: Ophthalmic goods; Ophthalmic frames. **SIC:** 5048 (Ophthalmic Goods). **Officers:** Robert Conens, President.

■ 19221 ■ **C.D.C. Optical Lab Inc.**
20724 Cattle Dr.
Redding, CA 96003
Phone: (530)223-0152
Free: (800)273-2735 **Fax:** (530)223-0152
Products: Ophthalmic goods. **SIC:** 5048 (Ophthalmic Goods).

■ 19222 ■ **Celestial Mercantile Corporation**
5 Eves Dr., Ste. 140
Marlton, NJ 08053
Phone: (609)985-8936 **Fax:** (609)985-9899
Products: Health and beauty aids. **SIC:** 5122 (Drugs, Proprietaries & Sundries).

■ 19223 ■ **Cenna International Corp.**
7 Post Office Rd., 7F
Waldorf, MD 20602-2744
Phones: (301)932-8666 (301)932-4153
(301)932-4049
Free: (800)847-6984 **Fax:** (301)843-6149
E-mail: md0351@share.com
Products: Medical products; Computer hardware; Scientific, laboratory, test, and measurement equipment; Electrical supplies. **SICs:** 5047 (Medical & Hospital Equipment); 5045 (Computers, Peripherals & Software); 5063 (Electrical Apparatus & Equipment). **Est:** 1988. **Sales:** $3,000,000 (2000). **Emp:** 7. **Officers:** Shaheer Yousaf, President; Adeel A. Shah, Vice President; Mohammad Bilal, VP Government and Commercial Sales.

■ 19224 ■ **Central Medical Inc.**
3836 Minnehaha Ave.
Minneapolis, MN 55406-3230
Phone: (612)724-0474
Free: (800)666-5431 **Fax:** (612)724-7849
E-mail: centralmed@Pop.mns.uswest.net
Products: Medical surgery products, including open heart, vascular, anasthesia, critical care, dialysis products, cardiac care lab, interventional radiology, and biopsy products. **Est:** 1970. **Officers:** Sam Currow, President; Sam Curro, President.

■ 19225 ■ **Central Optical of Youngstown Inc.**
PO Box 6210
Youngstown, OH 44501
Phone: (330)783-9660
Free: (800)322-6678 **Fax:** (330)783-9721
Products: Ophthalmic goods. **SIC:** 5048 (Ophthalmic Goods).

■ 19226 ■ **Centrex Inc.**
38 West 32nd St.
New York, NY 10001
Phone: (212)695-3320 **Fax:** (212)967-1436
E-mail: centrexinc@msn.com
Products: Ophthalmic lenses. **SIC:** 5048 (Ophthalmic Goods). **Est:** 1938. **Officers:** T.A. Brill, President.

■ 19227 ■ **Chadwick Optical Inc.**
PO Box 485
White River Junction, VT 05001-0485
Phone: (802)295-5933 **Fax:** (802)295-5933
Products: Ophthalmic goods; Ophthalmic frames. **SIC:** 5048 (Ophthalmic Goods). **Officers:** Bruno Saccarelli, President.

■ 19228 ■ **Chemins Company Inc.**
PO Box 2498
Colorado Springs, CO 80901
Phone: (719)579-9650
Free: (800)777-7161 **Fax:** (719)579-9651
Products: Ddietary supplements and nutrients; Minerals, vitamins, amino acids, herbs, protein, creams, lotions and beverages. **SIC:** 5122 (Drugs, Proprietaries & Sundries). **Sales:** $70,000,000 (1999). **Emp:** 211. **Officers:** James Cameron, CEO & President; Dorothy Coulter, CFO.

■ 19229 ■ **Children's Art Corp.**
6342 Myrtle Dr.
Huntington Beach, CA 92647
Free: (800)373-7900 **Fax:** (714)847-6251
Products: Health and beauty aids. **SIC:** 5122 (Drugs, Proprietaries & Sundries). **Sales:** $1,000,000 (2000). **Emp:** 4.

■ 19230 ■ **City Optical Company Inc./Division of The Tavel Optical Group**
2839 Lafayette Rd.
Indianapolis, IN 46222-2147
Phone: (317)924-1300 **Fax:** (317)924-3741
E-mail: lstavel@taveloptical.com
URL: http://www.taveloptical.com
Products: Glasses and contacts; complete vision care. **SIC:** 5048 (Ophthalmic Goods). **Est:** 1940. **Emp:** 250. **Officers:** Larry S. Tavel MD, CEO.

■ 19231 ■ **Claflin Co.**
1070 Willett Ave.
East Providence, RI 02915
Phone: (401)437-1870 **Fax:** (401)433-5281
E-mail: claflinco@worldnet.att.net
Products: Medical and surgical supplies. **SIC:** 5047 (Medical & Hospital Equipment).

■ 19232 ■ **Arthur V. Clancy, Jr.**
625 S Gay St.
Knoxville, TN 37902-1608
Phone: (423)523-4161 **Fax:** (423)522-9367
Products: Ophthalmic goods. **SIC:** 5048 (Ophthalmic Goods). **Officers:** Arthur Clancy, Owner.

■ 19233 ■ **Classic Optical Inc.**
21177 Hilltop St.
Southfield, MI 48034
Phone: (248)358-5895 **Fax:** (313)869-5545
Products: Eyeglasses and frames. **SIC:** 5048 (Ophthalmic Goods). **Est:** 1968. **Sales:** $15,000,000 (2000). **Emp:** 95. **Officers:** Steven Feldman, President; Jon Vintzel, Controller; Philip Gach, Exec. VP.

■ 19234 ■ **Clear Optics Inc.**
430 Alta Vista St., No. 1
Santa Fe, NM 87505-4104
Phone: (505)983-5075 **Free:** (800)221-0213
Products: Ophthalmic lenses. **SIC:** 5048 (Ophthalmic Goods). **Est:** 1975. **Officers:** Tate Hall, President.

■ 19235 ■ **Clinical Homecare Corp. Haemotronic Ltd.**
45 Kulick Rd.
Fairfield, NJ 07004
Phone: (201)575-0614
Products: I.V. solutions. **SIC:** 5047 (Medical & Hospital Equipment).

■ 19236 ■ **Clintec Nutrition Co.**
3 Pkwy. N, No. 500
Deerfield, IL 60015
Phone: (847)317-2800 **Fax:** (708)317-3186
Products: Nutrition products for I.V. use. **SIC:** 5122 (Drugs, Proprietaries & Sundries). **Est:** 1986. **Sales:** $400,000,000 (2000). **Emp:** 2,000. **Officers:** Phillip Laughlin, President; Rock Foster, VP of Finance; Gerald Carino, VP of Sales.

■ 19237 ■ **Coates Optical Lab Inc.**
PO Box 20200
Montgomery, AL 36125
Phone: (205)288-2021
Products: Ophthalmic goods; Eye glasses. **SIC:** 5048 (Ophthalmic Goods). **Officers:** Pete Coates, President.

■ 19238 ■ **Cobb Optical Lab Inc.**
78 NW 37th St.
Miami, FL 33127
Phone: (305)576-1700 **Fax:** (305)576-7088
Products: Ophthalmic goods. **SIC:** 5048 (Ophthalmic Goods).

■ 19239 ■ **Colonial Hospital Supply Co. Inc.**
555 Oakwood Rd.
Lake Zurich, IL 60047
Phone: (847)438-2900 **Fax:** (847)438-9645
Products: Hospital supplies. **SIC:** 5047 (Medical & Hospital Equipment). **Est:** 1952. **Sales:** $87,000,000 (2000). **Emp:** 300. **Officers:** Ben Welch, President; Richard Ruminski, Controller; Al Anderson, Exec. VP.

■ 19240 ■ **Colorado Serum Co.**
PO Box 16428
Denver, CO 80216
Phone: (303)295-7527 **Fax:** (303)295-1923
Products: Biotech and biological products; Veterinary instruments. **SIC:** 5122 (Drugs, Proprietaries & Sundries). **Emp:** 100. **Officers:** J Huff, President; Majon Huff, Treasurer.

■ 19241 ■ **ComoTec**
5130 Commercial Dr., Ste. E
Melbourne, FL 32940-7175
Phone: (407)638-4244 **Fax:** (407)638-4249
Products: Ophthalmic goods; Optometric equipment and supplies. **SIC:** 5048 (Ophthalmic Goods). **Sales:** $1,700,000 (2000). **Emp:** 4. **Officers:** Patrick Lange, Contact; Barry Swanson, Contact.

■ 19242 ■ **Complete Medical Products Inc.**
2052 N Decatur Rd.
Decatur, GA 30033
Phone: (404)728-0010
Products: Medical supplies. **SIC:** 5047 (Medical & Hospital Equipment). **Emp:** 5. **Officers:** James K. McNeely, President; Kathy Conliff, Controller.

■ 19243 ■ **Complete Medical Supplies Inc.**
10 Ford Products Rd.
Valley Cottage, NY 10989
Phone: (914)353-0434
Free: (800)242-2674 **Fax:** (914)353-1379
E-mail: completemedical@worldnet.att.net
URL: http://www.completemedical.com
Products: Rehabilitation and home health care supplies. **SIC:** 5047 (Medical & Hospital Equipment). **Est:** 1988. **Emp:** 38. **Officers:** Seth Klein, Vice President; Barbara Harris, President; Manny Levy, Nat'l Sales Mgr.; Angelo Soto, Customer Service Contact.

■ 19244 ■ **Connecticut Optical**
PO Box 572
Waterbury, CT 06720
Phones: (203)573-9107 (203)753-5109
Free: (800)992-3608 **Fax:** 800-525-4059
Products: Ophthalmic goods. **SIC:** 5048 (Ophthalmic Goods).

■ 19245 ■ **The Consulting Scientists**
44 Murray Hill Sq.
Murray Hill, NJ 07974
Phone: (908)508-0690 **Fax:** (908)508-0691
Products: Pharmaceutical RandD, Organo-Fluoro Compunds, Expert Witness. Providing consulting services or temporary, part time or bench chemistry in specialty of organic synthesis. **SIC:** 5122 (Drugs, Proprietaries & Sundries).

■ 19246 ■ **Consumer Care Products Inc.**
PO Box 684
Sheboygan, WI 53082-0684
Phone: (920)459-8353 **Fax:** (920)459-9070
Products: Medical, dental, and optical equipment. **SIC:**
5047 (Medical & Hospital Equipment).

■ 19247 ■ **Contact Optical Center Inc.**
12301 N Grant, Unit G
Denver, CO 80241
Phone: (303)457-1118
Free: (800)875-1313 **Fax:** (303)457-0091
E-mail: coc@unidial.com
Products: Soft contact lenses. **SIC:** 5048 (Ophthalmic
Goods). **Officers:** Craig Thornton, Treasurer.

■ 19248 ■ **Continental Safety Equipment Inc.**
899 Apollo Rd.
Eagan, MN 55121
Phone: (651)454-7233
Free: (800)844-7003 **Fax:** (651)454-3217
E-mail: safetysales@aol.com
Products: Safety products, including goggles, gloves,
and respirators. **SIC:** 5047 (Medical & Hospital
Equipment). **Est:** 1945. **Sales:** $8,000,000 (1999).
Emp: 30. **Officers:** A.B. Westerberg, President;
George R. Blank, Sales Mgr.

■ 19249 ■ **Continental Sales Co.**
4890 Ironton, Unit G1
Denver, CO 80239
Phone: (303)373-2390
Products: Ophthalmic goods. **SIC:** 5048 (Ophthalmic
Goods).

■ 19250 ■ **Continental Sales Co. of America**
PO Box 1002
Santa Cruz, CA 95061
Phone: (408)426-7423
Free: (800)662-3903 **Fax:** 800-288-2721
Products: Ophthalmic goods. **SIC:** 5048 (Ophthalmic
Goods).

■ 19251 ■ **Continental Trading Co. Inc.**
4807 Colley Ave.
Norfolk, VA 23508-2036
Phone: (757)440-0617
Products: Ophthalmic goods. **SIC:** 5048 (Ophthalmic
Goods). **Est:** 1952. **Officers:** Allen Morrison, President.

■ 19252 ■ **Copeland Optical Inc.**
738 S Perry Ln., Ste. 17
Tempe, AZ 85281
Phone: (602)267-0682 **Fax:** (602)968-0092
Products: Ophthalmic goods. **SIC:** 5048 (Ophthalmic
Goods). **Doing Business As:** Laser Optics.

■ 19253 ■ **Cornell Surgical Co.**
30 New Bridge Rd.
Bergenfield, NJ 07621-4304
Phone: (201)384-9000
Free: (800)COR-NELL **Fax:** (201)384-9111
E-mail: info@cornellsurgical.com
URL: http://www.cornellsurgical.com
Products: Medical, surgical, hospital equipment
supplies. **SIC:** 5047 (Medical & Hospital Equipment).
Est: 1945. **Sales:** $5,000,000 (2000). **Emp:** 19.
Officers: Howard Shiffman, President.

■ 19254 ■ **County Optical Inc.**
PO Box 909
Caribou, ME 04736-0909
Phone: (207)493-3329 **Fax:** (207)493-3320
Products: Ophthalmic goods. **SIC:** 5048 (Ophthalmic
Goods). **Officers:** William Belanger, President.

■ 19255 ■ **Cramer Products, Inc.**
PO Box 1001
Gardner, KS 66030
Phone: (913)856-7511 **Fax:** (913)884-5626
E-mail: info@cramersportsmed.com
URL: http://www.cramersportsmed.com
Products: Sports medicine equipment and supplies.
SIC: 5122 (Drugs, Proprietaries & Sundries). **Est:**
1918. **Sales:** $15,000,000 (2000). **Emp:** 75. **Officers:**
Thomas K. Rogge, President & CEO; Dennis Katzer,
Controller; Jack Patterson, VP of Sales; Sharon
Kramer, Dir of Human Resources.

■ 19256 ■ **Creative Health Products**
5148 Saddle Ridge Rd.
Plymouth, MI 48170
Phone: (734)996-5900
Free: (800)742-4478 **Fax:** (734)996-4650
E-mail: sales@chponline.com
URL: http://www.chponline.com
Products: Fitness testing and measuring equipment;
Medicinal and health supplies; Health and medical
books. **SIC:** 5047 (Medical & Hospital Equipment). **Est:**
1976. **Sales:** $2,700,000 (2000). **Emp:** 11. **Officers:**
Marlene Donoghue, President; Wallace Donoghue,
Treasurer & Secty.

■ 19257 ■ **Creative Rehab**
1817 State St.
Racine, WI 53404
Phone: (414)635-0211
Products: Powered wheelchair systems and parts.
SIC: 5047 (Medical & Hospital Equipment). **Officers:**
Jim Cook, Contact.

■ 19258 ■ **Crown Optical Co. Inc.**
15 Commerce St.
Greenville, RI 02828
Phone: (401)949-3400
Free: (800)955-2769 **Fax:** (401)949-3904
Products: Lenses. **SIC:** 5048 (Ophthalmic Goods).

■ 19259 ■ **Crown Optical Ltd.**
2111 Van Deman St.
Baltimore, MD 21224
Phone: (410)685-7373
Free: (800)638-9382 **Fax:** (301)685-0173
Products: Ophthalmic goods. **SIC:** 5048 (Ophthalmic
Goods).

■ 19260 ■ **Crutcher Dental Inc.**
849 S 3rd St.
Louisville, KY 40203
Phone: (502)584-5104
Free: (800)385-4234 **Fax:** (502)584-4756
Products: Dental supplies; Sponges. **SIC:** 5047
(Medical & Hospital Equipment). **Est:** 1897. **Sales:**
$4,000,000 (2000). **Emp:** 22. **Officers:** Dorothy F.
Lauch, President; Rosemary Roberts, CFO; Sally
Drake, Dir. of Marketing & Sales; Tammy Wisehart, Dir.
of Data Processing.

■ 19261 ■ **Crystal Home Health Care Inc.**
15819 Schoolcraft St.
Detroit, MI 48227-1749
Phone: (313)493-4900
Free: (800)493-4902 **Fax:** (313)493-4904
Products: Medical, dental, and optical equipment. **SIC:**
5047 (Medical & Hospital Equipment). **Sales:**
$1,500,000 (2000). **Emp:** 20.

■ 19262 ■ **Cumberland Optical Company Inc.**
806 Olympic St.
Nashville, TN 37203
Phone: (615)254-5868
Products: Eyeglasses. **SIC:** 5048 (Ophthalmic
Goods). **Est:** 1959. **Sales:** $6,500,000 (2000). **Emp:**
65. **Officers:** Kenneth W. Wyatt, President.

■ 19263 ■ **Cunningham Sales Corp.**
180 Cedar Hill St.
Marlborough, MA 01752-3017
Phone: (508)481-2940
Products: Ophthalmic goods. **SIC:** 5048 (Ophthalmic
Goods). **Officers:** Robert Cunningham, President.

■ 19264 ■ **Custom Healthcare Systems**
919 W 21st St.
Norfolk, VA 23517-1515
Phone: (757)622-8334
Free: (800)933-4440 **Fax:** (757)622-8436
Products: Surgical and medical instruments and
apparatus. **SIC:** 5047 (Medical & Hospital Equipment).
Officers: Larry Heath, President.

■ 19265 ■ **Custom Labs**
2641 2nd St.
Macon, GA 31206
Phone: (912)742-2615
Products: Ophthalmic goods. **SIC:** 5048 (Ophthalmic
Goods).

■ 19266 ■ **Custom Labs**
6398 Hwy. 85
PO Box 488
Riverdale, GA 30274
Phone: (404)997-3344
Free: (800)241-5322 **Fax:** (404)994-0038
Products: Ophthalmic goods. **SIC:** 5048 (Ophthalmic
Goods).

■ 19267 ■ **Custom Vision Optical**
2341 Charles St.
PO Box 28019
Dallas, TX 75228
Phone: (214)321-4347
Free: (800)443-2518 **Fax:** (972)988-7241
Products: Ophthalmic goods. **SIC:** 5048 (Ophthalmic
Goods).

■ 19268 ■ **CVK Corp.**
3725 Ingersoll Ave.
Des Moines, IA 50312-3410
Phone: (515)279-2020 **Fax:** (515)255-8002
E-mail: cvkcorp@sprintmail.com
Products: Ophthalmic goods. **SIC:** 5048 (Ophthalmic
Goods). **Est:** 1953. **Sales:** $6,000,000 (2000). **Emp:**
85. **Officers:** Vincent Copple, President.

■ 19269 ■ **D & K Healthcare Resources, Inc.**
8000 Maryland Ave., Ste. 920
St. Louis, MO 63105
Phone: (314)727-3485
Free: (888)727-3485 **Fax:** (314)727-5759
URL: http://www.dkwd.com
Products: Prescription and over-the-counter
pharmaceuticals. **SIC:** 5122 (Drugs, Proprietaries &
Sundries). **Sales:** $815,000,000 (2000). **Emp:** 324.
Officers: J. Hord Armstrong III, CEO & Chairman of
the Board; Martin D. Wilson, President & COO.
Alternate Name: D and K Wholesale Drugs Inc.
Former Name: D and K Wholesale Drug Inc.

■ 19270 ■ **D & K Wholesale Drug, Inc.**
2040 Creative Dr., No. 300
Lexington, KY 40505-4283
Phone: (606)254-5534 **Fax:** (606)233-9587
Products: Pharmaceutical products. **SIC:** 5122 (Drugs,
Proprietaries & Sundries). **Est:** 1941. **Sales:**
$100,000,000 (2000). **Emp:** 50. **Officers:** W. VanMeter
Alford, President; Martin D. Wilson, President; Hord
Armstrong, CEO.

■ 19271 ■ **Dako Corp.**
6392 Via Real
Carpinteria, CA 93013
Phone: (805)566-6655 **Fax:** (805)566-6688
Products: R and D, marketing and selling of research;
Diagnostic devices on antibodies antiserum. **SIC:** 5047
(Medical & Hospital Equipment). **Officers:** Viggo
Harboe, President.

■ 19272 ■ **Datex-Ohmeda Inc.**
2 Highwood Dr.
Tewksbury, MA 01876
Phone: (978)640-0460 **Fax:** (978)640-0469
Products: Equipment and systems for anesthesia and
critical care providers. **SIC:** 5047 (Medical & Hospital
Equipment). **Sales:** $153,000,000 (2000). **Emp:** 450.
Officers: Richard W. J. Aiken, CEO & President.

■ 19273 ■ **DBL Labs**
30840 Joseph St.
PO Box 280
St. Joseph, MN 56374
Phone: (320)363-7211
Free: (800)888-0222 **Fax:** 800-888-9624
Products: Ophthalmic goods. **SIC:** 5048 (Ophthalmic
Goods).

■ 19274 ■ **Decot Hy-Wyd Sport Glasses, Inc.**
PO Box 15830
Phoenix, AZ 85060-5830
Phone: (602)955-7625
Free: (800)528-1901 **Fax:** (602)955-7151
E-mail: decot@sportglasses.com
URL: http://www.sportglasses.com
SIC: 5048 (Ophthalmic Goods). **Est:** 1949. **Sales:**
$1,600,000 (2000). **Emp:** 10. **Officers:** Robert Decot,
Chairman of the Board; Susan Decot, President.

■ 19275 ■ **Delta Enterprises Inc.**
PO Box 647
Fairbury, NE 68352-0647
Phone: (402)729-3366 **Fax:** (402)729-3569
Products: Ophthalmic goods. **SIC:** 5048 (Ophthalmic Goods). **Officers:** J. Thayer, President.

■ 19276 ■ **Delta Hi-Tech Inc.**
3762 S 150 E
Salt Lake City, UT 84115
Phone: (801)263-0975
Free: (800)378-0909 **Fax:** (801)263-9487
E-mail: deltahitech@rmi.net
Products: Insulin syringes, 28,29 and 30 guage (short needle). **SIC:** 5047 (Medical & Hospital Equipment). **Est:** 1989. **Sales:** $1,500,000 (2000). **Emp:** 5. **Officers:** Glade James, President; Jan Frank, Dir. of Sales.

■ 19277 ■ **Derma Sciences Inc.**
214 Carnegie Ctr., Ste. 100
Princeton, NJ 08540
Phone: (609)514-4744
Free: (800)825-4325 **Fax:** (609)514-0502
URL: http://www.dermasciences.com
Products: Derma grain spray; Ointment; Wet dressings. **SICs:** 5122 (Drugs, Proprietaries & Sundries); 5047 (Medical & Hospital Equipment). **Est:** 1984. **Sales:** $4,000,000 (2000). **Emp:** 16. **Officers:** Edward J. Quilty, CEO & Chairman of the Board; Stephen T. Wills, VP & CFO.

■ 19278 ■ **Deschutes Optical**
20332 Empire Rd., Ste. F-5
PO Box 7229
Bend, OR 97708
Phone: (503)288-8244 **Fax:** 800-388-2649
Products: Ophthalmic goods. **SIC:** 5048 (Ophthalmic Goods).

■ 19279 ■ **De'Vons Optics Inc.**
10823 Bell Ct.
Rancho Cucamonga, CA 91730
Phone: (909)466-4700
Free: (888)333-8667 **Fax:** (909)466-4703
Products: Reading glasses, sunglasses, and goggles. **SIC:** 5048 (Ophthalmic Goods). **Est:** 1983. **Sales:** $2,000,000 (2000). **Emp:** 5. **Officers:** James Lai, Sales/Marketing Contact.

■ 19280 ■ **Diamond Optical Corp.**
101 French Ave., Ste. A
Braintree, MA 02184-6503
Phone: (781)848-5999
Free: (800)232-8117 **Fax:** (781)843-4839
Products: Ophthalmic goods. **SIC:** 5048 (Ophthalmic Goods). **Officers:** Wayne Roache, President.

■ 19281 ■ **Discount Drugs Wisconsin Inc.**
4945 Wyconda Rd.
Rockville, MD 20852
Phone: (301)230-8930 **Fax:** (301)230-2772
URL: http://www.rodmans.com
Products: Discount drug and gourmet food. **SIC:** 5149 (Groceries & Related Products Nec). **Est:** 1958. **Sales:** $24,000,000 (2000). **Emp:** 160. **Officers:** Leonard Rodman, CEO; Arvind G. Chitale, Finance Officer.

■ 19282 ■ **Dispensers Optical Service Corp.**
PO Box 35000
Louisville, KY 40232
Phones: (502)491-3440 (502)491-8547
Free: (800)626-4545
Products: Ophthalmic goods. **SIC:** 5048 (Ophthalmic Goods).

■ 19283 ■ **Dittmar Inc.**
101 E Laurel Ave.
Cheltenham, PA 19012
Phone: (215)379-5533 **Fax:** (215)663-0163
Products: Surgical equipment, including trays, tubes, and scissors. **SIC:** 5047 (Medical & Hospital Equipment). **Est:** 1932. **Sales:** $5,000,000 (2000). **Emp:** 50. **Officers:** J. Nowak, President; David C. Santaspirt, Dir. of Marketing.

■ 19284 ■ **Diversified Ophthalmics Inc.**
PO Box 2530
Spokane, WA 99220-2530
Phone: (509)324-6364
Free: (800)542-2020 **Fax:** (509)324-2357
Products: Ophthalmic goods, including contact lenses. **SIC:** 5048 (Ophthalmic Goods). **Officers:** W. Herston, Division Mgr.

■ 19285 ■ **Diversified Ophthalmics, Inc.**
250 McCullough St.
Cincinnati, OH 45226-2145
Phone: (513)321-7988
Free: (800)622-2281 **Fax:** (513)321-6355
Products: Ophthalmic products. **SIC:** 5048 (Ophthalmic Goods). **Est:** 1977.

■ 19286 ■ **Dockters X-Ray Inc.**
7515 18th Ave. NW
Seattle, WA 98117-5430
Phone: (206)784-7768 **Fax:** (206)784-1007
Products: Medical, dental, and optical equipment. **SIC:** 5047 (Medical & Hospital Equipment). **Sales:** $1,000,000 (2000). **Emp:** 4.

■ 19287 ■ **The F. Dohmen Co./Anoka**
1101 Lund Blvd.
Anoka, MN 55303
Phones: (612)656-2300 (612)656-2311
Products: Pharmaceuticals. **SIC:** 5122 (Drugs, Proprietaries & Sundries). **Est:** 1918. **Sales:** $220,000,000 (2000). **Emp:** 80. **Officers:** Jeffery Rehovsky, Divisional Vice President; Allan V. Lueck, Dir. of Finance; Douglas Rewerts, Director of Sales, Anoka Division. **Former Name:** Northwestern Drug Co.

■ 19288 ■ **Donley Medical Supply Co.**
PO Box 83108
Lincoln, NE 68501
Phone: (402)474-3222
Free: (800)742-7571 **Fax:** (402)474-3256
Products: Medical supplies, including bandages, syringes, beds, wheelchairs, and walkers. **SIC:** 5047 (Medical & Hospital Equipment). **Est:** 1920. **Sales:** $4,000,000 (2000). **Emp:** 28. **Officers:** Michael G. Dodge, General Mgr.

■ 19289 ■ **DRG International Inc.**
1167 U.S Hwy. 22
Mountainside, NJ 07092
Phone: (908)233-2075 **Fax:** (908)233-0758
E-mail: corp@drgintl.com
URL: http://www.drgintl.com
Products: Medical supplies; Diagnostic tests for immunology, Diabetes, gynecology, tumor markers, infectious diseases, toxicology, drug detection; Medical digital graphic image processing systems for angiography, X-ray, ultrasound, and endoscopy. **SIC:** 5047 (Medical & Hospital Equipment). **Est:** 1970. **Sales:** $12,000,000 (2000). **Emp:** 65. **Officers:** Cyril E. Geacintov, President; E. Geacintov, Vice President.

■ 19290 ■ **Drogueria Betances**
PO Box 368
Caguas, PR 00726
Phone: (787)746-0951
Free: (800)981-8151 **Fax:** (787)744-4838
E-mail: joannacr@coquinet.com
Products: Pharmaceuticals. **SIC:** 5122 (Drugs, Proprietaries & Sundries). **Est:** 1962. **Sales:** $96,000,000 (2000). **Emp:** 100. **Officers:** Luis Cartagena, President; Alejandro Cartagena, Vice President; Joanna Cartagena, Dir. of Sales.

■ 19291 ■ **Drogueria J.M. Blanco**
PO Box 364129
San Juan, PR 00936-4929
Phone: (787)793-6262 **Fax:** (787)273-2748
Products: Medicine; Personal care products. **SICs:** 5122 (Drugs, Proprietaries & Sundries); 5047 (Medical & Hospital Equipment).

■ 19292 ■ **Drug Center, Inc.**
GPO Box 3687
San Juan, PR 00936
Phone: (787)724-5115
Products: Pharmaceuticals. **SIC:** 5122 (Drugs, Proprietaries & Sundries).

■ 19293 ■ **Duffens Optical**
900 Lynn St.
PO Box 631
Hannibal, MO 63401
Phones: (573)221-9200 800-221-3266
Free: (800)392-3429 **Fax:** (573)221-3640
Products: Ophthalmic goods. **SIC:** 5048 (Ophthalmic Goods).

■ 19294 ■ **Duffens Optical**
PO Box 897
Denver, CO 80201
Phone: (303)623-5301
Free: (800)999-5367 **Fax:** (303)623-1830
Products: Ophthalmic goods. **SIC:** 5048 (Ophthalmic Goods).

■ 19295 ■ **Dunlaw Optical Laboratories**
PO Box 3110
Lawton, OK 73502-3110
Phone: (580)355-8410
Free: (800)678-4525 **Fax:** 800-365-3409
E-mail: dunlan@sirinet.net
Products: Ophthalmic goods; Safety glasses. **SIC:** 5048 (Ophthalmic Goods). **Est:** 1984. **Sales:** $2,000,000 (2000). **Emp:** 13. **Officers:** Dennis Foster, President.

■ 19296 ■ **Durr Medical Corp.**
PO Box 165
Columbia, SC 29202
Phone: (803)791-5900
Products: Medical supplies. **SIC:** 5047 (Medical & Hospital Equipment). **Est:** 1896. **Sales:** $241,400,000 (2000). **Officers:** Cullen F. Smith, President & COO; Phillip G. Young, VP & Controller; R. Michael Davenport, VP of Marketing.

■ 19297 ■ **Dyna Corp.**
6300 Yarrow Dr.
Carlsbad, CA 92009
Phone: (760)438-2511
Free: (800)854-2706 **Fax:** 800-662-3962
Products: Emergency medical supplies and equipment. **SIC:** 5047 (Medical & Hospital Equipment). **Est:** 1967. **Sales:** $18,000,000 (2000). **Emp:** 120. **Officers:** Robert DeBussey, President; Charles Climenson, CFO; Jan Amato, Dir. of Sales; Ralph Davis, Dir. of Admin.; Gary Leupold, Vice President.

■ 19298 ■ **Dynamic Medical Equipment Ltd.**
51 Rushmore St.
Westbury, NY 11590
Phones: (516)333-1472 (718)470-1880
Products: Powered wheelchair systems and parts. **SIC:** 5047 (Medical & Hospital Equipment). **Officers:** Allen Channin, Contact.

■ 19299 ■ **E-Y Laboratories Inc.**
107 N Amphlett Blvd.
San Mateo, CA 94401
Phone: (650)342-3296 **Fax:** (650)342-2648
Products: R and D for specialty biochemical reagents for research and in-vitro diagnostic rapid test kits. **SIC:** 5122 (Drugs, Proprietaries & Sundries).

■ 19300 ■ **Eagle Optical**
205 E Boone Ave.
Spokane, WA 99202-1707
Phone: (509)624-4565 **Fax:** (509)747-5492
Products: Ophthalmic goods, including frames. **SIC:** 5048 (Ophthalmic Goods).

■ 19301 ■ **Eastern Ophthalmic Supply & Repair**
PO Box 9666
Knoxville, TN 37940-0666
Phone: (865)579-3010
URL: http://www.kiddeast@aol.com
Products: Ophthalmic goods. **SIC:** 5048 (Ophthalmic Goods). **Officers:** Jerry Gibson, President.

■ 19302 ■ **Eclyptic Inc.**
136 W Orion St., Ste. 3
Tempe, AZ 85283-5602
Phone: (602)438-0799 **Fax:** (602)838-4934
E-mail: info@veatchinstruments.com
URL: http://www.veatchinstructments.com
Products: Ophthalmic goods; Digital imaging. **SICs:**

5048 (Ophthalmic Goods); 5065 (Electronic Parts & Equipment Nec). **Est:** 1910. **Sales:** $45,000,000 (2000). **Emp:** 14. **Officers:** Tom Veatch, President; Kyna Veasett, Sales/Marketing Contact, e-mail: kyna@veatchinstruments.com.

■ **19303** ■   **Edcat Enterprises**
733 N Beach St.
Daytona Beach, FL 32114
Phone: (904)253-2385
Free: (800)274-3566   **Fax:** (904)258-1582
Products: Massage Therapy products; Nutritional and medical posters. **SICs:** 5199 (Nondurable Goods Nec); 5122 (Drugs, Proprietaries & Sundries).

■ **19304** ■   **Empire Equities Inc.**
14735 SW Peachtree Dr.
Tigard, OR 97224-1486
Products: Pharmaceutical preparations; Surgical and orthopedic equipment. **SICs:** 5047 (Medical & Hospital Equipment); 5122 (Drugs, Proprietaries & Sundries). **Officers:** John Lang, President.

■ **19305** ■   **Enos Home Oxygen Therapy Inc.**
PO Box 8756
New Bedford, MA 02742-8756
Phone: (508)992-2146
Free: (800)473-4669   **Fax:** (508)999-2724
Products: Medical, dental, and optical equipment. **SIC:** 5047 (Medical & Hospital Equipment). **Sales:** $1,200,000 (2000). **Emp:** 23.

■ **19306** ■   **Eon Labs Manufacturing, Inc.**
227-15 N Conduit Ave.
Laurelton, NY 11413
Phone: (718)276-8600
Free: (800)526-0225   **Fax:** (718)276-1735
Products: Generic pharmaceuticals, including antibiotics, analgesics, sulfones, and psychotherapeutic drugs. **SIC:** 5122 (Drugs, Proprietaries & Sundries). **Est:** 1993. **Sales:** $10,000,000 (2000). **Emp:** 200. **Officers:** Dr. Bernard Hampl, President; Frank J. Della Fera, VP of Sales & Marketing; William Holt, CFO.

■ **19307** ■   **ERW International, Inc.**
PO Box 690
Barrington, IL 60011
Phone: (847)381-7972   **Fax:** (847)381-5892
Products: Medical equipment; Security mirrors; Label printing machines. **SICs:** 5047 (Medical & Hospital Equipment); 5084 (Industrial Machinery & Equipment). **Est:** 1978. **Officers:** Kathy Umlauf, President.

■ **19308** ■   **Etac USA Inc.**
2325 Park Lawn Dr.
Waukesha, WI 53186-2938
Phone: (414)796-4600   **Fax:** (414)882-0668
Products: Rehab products, wheel chairs, walkers, ADL's and bath products. **SIC:** 5047 (Medical & Hospital Equipment). **Sales:** $2,000,000 (2000). **Emp:** 10. **Officers:** Carola Oberg, President; Cynthia Lutz, CFO.

■ **19309** ■   **Evans Optical**
PO Box 2030
Havre, MT 59501-2030
Phone: (406)265-1276   **Free:** (800)865-1276
Products: Opthalmic goods, including frames. **SIC:** 5048 (Ophthalmic Goods). **Est:** 1982. **Sales:** $200,000 (2000). **Officers:** Bill Evans, Partner.

■ **19310** ■   **Everest and Jennings International Ltd.**
3601 Rider Tr. S
Earth City, MO 63045
Phone: (314)512-7000
Products: Home care beds. **SIC:** 5047 (Medical & Hospital Equipment). **Sales:** $19,000,000 (2000). **Emp:** 180.

■ **19311** ■   **Execu-Flow Systems, Inc.**
1 Ethel Rd., No. 106
Edison, NJ 08817
Phone: (732)287-9191   **Fax:** (732)287-2329
Products: Medical sulfur. **SIC:** 5169 (Chemicals & Allied Products Nec). **Est:** 1981. **Sales:** $7,000,000 (2000). **Emp:** 75. **Officers:** Michael J. Custode,

President; Kenneth R. Erb, Treasurer & Secty.; Larry G. Drappi, Exec. VP of Marketing & Sales.

■ **19312** ■   **Experimental Applied Sciences**
555 Corp.orate Cir
Golden, CO 80401
Phone: (303)384-0080   **Fax:** (303)384-0173
Products: Body-building monthly magazine publishing. **SIC:** 5122 (Drugs, Proprietaries & Sundries). **Officers:** Mike Fitzman, Director.

■ **19313** ■   **Express International Corp.**
PO Box 47
Flushing, NY 11352
Phone: (718)358-0200
Products: Hospital supplies; Skin and hair care products; Medical and surgical disposables. **SICs:** 5122 (Drugs, Proprietaries & Sundries); 5047 (Medical & Hospital Equipment). **Officers:** Marlene Mossayebi, President.

■ **19314** ■   **Express Optical Lab**
16-18 Bridge St.
Brownsville, PA 15417-2310
Phone: (412)785-2160
Free: (800)342-2881   **Fax:** (412)785-4365
Products: Ophthalmic goods. **SIC:** 5048 (Ophthalmic Goods).

■ **19315** ■   **Extend-A-Life Inc.**
1010 S Arroyo Pkwy.
Pasadena, CA 91105
Phone: (626)441-1223   **Fax:** (626)447-1293
Products: Security and safety equipment. **SIC:** 5047 (Medical & Hospital Equipment). **Sales:** $300,000 (2000). **Emp:** 4.

■ **19316** ■   **Eye Care Inc.**
5858 Line Ave.
Shreveport, LA 71106
Phones: (318)869-4443   (318)865-0017
Free: (800)533-9638   **Fax:** (318)868-4738
Products: Ophthalmic goods. **SIC:** 5048 (Ophthalmic Goods). **Est:** 1984. **Sales:** $1,100,000 (2000). **Emp:** 11. **Officers:** Robert Landry, President; Terry DeMarche; M.D. Pickering; Glen Coullard.

■ **19317** ■   **Eye Kraft Optical Inc.**
PO Box 400
St. Cloud, MN 56302
Phone: (320)251-0141
Free: (888)455-2022   **Fax:** (320)251-0148
E-mail: eyekraft@cloudnet.com
URL: http://www.eyekraft.com
Products: Ophthalmic goods. **SIC:** 5048 (Ophthalmic Goods). **Est:** 1954. **Emp:** 75. **Officers:** James Negard.

■ **19318** ■   **Eyeglass Shoppe**
508 Atkinson Dr.
Honolulu, HI 96814
Phone: (808)949-1595   **Fax:** (808)949-7781
Products: Eyeglasses; Contact lenses. **SIC:** 5048 (Ophthalmic Goods).

■ **19319** ■   **F and M Distributors Inc.**
25800 Sherwood Ave.
Warren, MI 48091
Phone: (734)758-1400   **Fax:** (810)758-0380
Products: Drug store supplies. **SIC:** 5122 (Drugs, Proprietaries & Sundries). **Est:** 1955. **Sales:** $43,000,000 (2000). **Emp:** 4,300. **Officers:** Frank Newman, President; Laura Kendall, CFO; Patty Klein, VP of Marketing.

■ **19320** ■   **Fairwind Sunglasses Trading Company Inc.**
8301 Biscayne Blvd.
Miami, FL 33138
Phone: (305)758-0057
Free: (800)327-2266   **Fax:** (305)758-0719
E-mail: sales@fairwindco.com
URL: http://www.fairwindco.com
Products: Sunglasses; Reading glasses. **SIC:** 5048 (Ophthalmic Goods). **Est:** 1978. **Emp:** 15. **Officers:** Auden Lin.

■ **19321** ■   **Falls Welding and Fabrication, Medical Products Div.**
608 Grant St.
Akron, OH 44311
Phone: (330)253-3437
Free: (800)231-6444   **Fax:** (330)253-2278
Products: Medical, dental, and optical equipment. **SIC:** 5047 (Medical & Hospital Equipment). **Sales:** $500,000 (2000). **Emp:** 5.

■ **19322** ■   **Far-Vet Supply Co.**
635 Prior Ave. N
St. Paul, MN 55104
Phone: (612)646-8788
Free: (800)328-9483   **Fax:** (612)646-4507
E-mail: farvet@farvet.com
Products: Pharmaceutical supplies and drugs. **SIC:** 5122 (Drugs, Proprietaries & Sundries). **Est:** 1936. **Sales:** $12,000,000 (2000). **Emp:** 34. **Officers:** Tom Gitis, President; Laura Skaalrud, Controller.

■ **19323** ■   **FEA Industries, Inc.**
1 N Morton Ave.
Morton, PA 19070
Phone: (215)876-2002
Free: (800)327-2002   **Fax:** (215)876-6140
Products: Ophthalmic goods. **SIC:** 5048 (Ophthalmic Goods).

■ **19324** ■   **Fisher Healthcare**
9999 Veterans Memorial Dr.
Houston, TX 77038-2499
Free: (800)640-0640   **Fax:** 800-290-0290
Products: Scientific and measurement devices. **SIC:** 5047 (Medical & Hospital Equipment). **Sales:** $500,000,000 (2000). **Emp:** 350.

■ **19325** ■   **Fisher Scientific Co.**
2000 Park Lane Dr.
Pittsburgh, PA 15275
Phone: (412)490-8300   **Fax:** (412)562-5344
Products: Laboratory equipment and supplies. **SICs:** 5047 (Medical & Hospital Equipment); 5049 (Professional Equipment Nec). **Sales:** $1,299,000,000 (2000). **Emp:** 4,000.

■ **19326** ■   **Forest Medical Products Inc.**
PO Box 989
Hillsboro, OR 97123
Phone: (503)640-3012   **Fax:** (503)640-4008
Products: Dental equipment and supplies. **SIC:** 5047 (Medical & Hospital Equipment). **Officers:** Franklin Mascarenhas, Treasurer.

■ **19327** ■   **Fortune Personnel Consultants of Springfield Inc.**
180 Denslow Rd., Unit 4
East Longmeadow, MA 01028
Phone: (413)525-3800   **Fax:** (413)525-2971
Products: Specialists in nationwide search and recruitment for the medical device and pharmaceutical industries. We are a nationally recognized and respected firm specializing in engineering, product development, regulatory affairs, clinical affairs, and quality manufacturing personnel. **SIC:** 5122 (Drugs, Proprietaries & Sundries). **Emp:** 5.

■ **19328** ■   **FoxMeyer Drug Co.**
PO Box 814204
Dallas, TX 75381
Phone: (972)446-9090   **Fax:** (972)446-4467
Products: Drugs. **SIC:** 5122 (Drugs, Proprietaries & Sundries). **Est:** 1977. **Sales:** $2,800,000,000 (2000). **Emp:** 2,500. **Officers:** Robert King, CEO & President; Dennis Letham, CFO; Mike Webster, Sr. VP of Sales; Sandy Stevens.

■ **19329** ■   **FoxMeyer Drug Co. Carol Stream Div.**
520 E North Ave.
Carol Stream, IL 60188-2125
Phone: (630)462-6501
Products: Pharmaceuticals. **SIC:** 5122 (Drugs, Proprietaries & Sundries). **Est:** 1987. **Sales:** $520,000,000 (2000). **Emp:** 200. **Officers:** Tom Anderson, President.

■ **19330** ■ **Franklin Medical Products**
1320 Airport Rd.
Montrose, CO 81401
Phone: (970)249-0677 **Fax:** (970)249-0643
Products: Contract manufacturing and disposable medical product packaging. **SIC:** 5047 (Medical & Hospital Equipment). **Officers:** George Glumac, President.

■ **19331** ■ **Franz Optical Company Inc.**
2041 E Burnside St.
Gresham, OR 97030
Phone: (503)667-2303 **Fax:** (503)666-2083
E-mail: mdybludoc@aol.com
Products: Ophthalmic goods. **SIC:** 5048 (Ophthalmic Goods). **Est:** 1997. **Emp:** 4. **Officers:** Tera S. Palmblad, President. **Former Name:** Portland Optical Company Inc.

■ **19332** ■ **Future Med, Inc.**
654 E Capitol St. NE
Washington, DC 20002
Phone: (202)546-8036 **Fax:** (202)546-8057
Products: Medical instruments and supplies. **SIC:** 5047 (Medical & Hospital Equipment). **Officers:** L. Holtsman, President.

■ **19333** ■ **Future Optics Inc.**
PO Box 1408
Jackson, TN 38302-1408
Phones: (901)424-5751 800-238-3816
Free: (800)372-8211 **Fax:** (901)422-6595
Products: Optical products and supplies. **SIC:** 5048 (Ophthalmic Goods). **Est:** 1977. **Emp:** 28. **Officers:** Frank Flew, President; Bill Landers, Vice President; Rick Barnett, Treasurer.

■ **19334** ■ **Jack Gell and Co.**
5700 Federal Ave.
Detroit, MI 48209
Phone: (313)554-2000
Products: Hospital and hotel linens, including sheets, pillowcases, blankets, and towels; Hospital uniforms; Furniture, including tables and chairs. **SIC:** 5047 (Medical & Hospital Equipment). **Est:** 1946. **Sales:** $9,000,000 (2000). **Emp:** 25. **Officers:** L. Gell-Prouhet, President; T. Seeber, Dir. of Marketing & Sales.

■ **19335** ■ **Gemini Cosmetics**
1380 Greg St., Ste. 234
Sparks, NV 89431-6072
Phone: (702)359-3663
Free: (800)338-9091 **Fax:** (702)359-9130
Products: Health and beauty aids. **SIC:** 5122 (Drugs, Proprietaries & Sundries). **Sales:** $300,000 (2000). **Emp:** 2.

■ **19336** ■ **General Drug Co.**
PO Box 1110
Mishawaka, IN 46546-1110
Products: Pharmaceutical drugs. **SIC:** 5122 (Drugs, Proprietaries & Sundries). **Sales:** $144,000,000 (2000). **Emp:** 78. **Officers:** Tom Morris, General Mgr.; Chuck Nell, Sales Mgr.

■ **19337** ■ **General Injectables and Vaccines Inc.**
PO Box 9
Bastian, VA 24314
Phone: (540)688-4121
Products: Medical supplies. **SIC:** 5047 (Medical & Hospital Equipment).

■ **19338** ■ **Generic Distributors L.P.**
1611 Olive St.
Monroe, LA 71201
Phone: (318)388-8850
Products: Pharmaceuticals. **SIC:** 5122 (Drugs, Proprietaries & Sundries). **Sales:** $6,000,000 (2000). **Emp:** 23. **Officers:** Don Couzillon, President.

■ **19339** ■ **Girzen, Res.**
9508 Locust Hill Dr.
Great Falls, VA 22066
Phone: (703)757-9123
Products: Provides regulatory services to medical device companies. Industries served: medical. **SIC:** 5047 (Medical & Hospital Equipment). **Emp:** 1.

■ **19340** ■ **Global Optics Inc.**
1255 Ontario Rd.
Green Bay, WI 54311
Phone: (920)432-1502 **Fax:** (920)432-5483
Products: Ophthalmic lenses. **SIC:** 5048 (Ophthalmic Goods). **Sales:** $4,000,000 (1999). **Emp:** 19. **Officers:** Amos Williams, President & Treasurer.

■ **19341** ■ **Golden State Medical Supply Inc.**
27644 Newhall Ranch Rd., Unit 40
Valencia, CA 91355-4017
Phone: (661)295-8101
E-mail: gsms@earthlink.net
Products: Pharmaceuticals (unit of use); Medical and surgical supplies. **SICs:** 5122 (Drugs, Proprietaries & Sundries); 5047 (Medical & Hospital Equipment). **Est:** 1986. **Sales:** $3,000,000 (2000). **Emp:** 6. **Officers:** Jim Stroud, CEO & President; Wanda Stroud, VP of Operations.

■ **19342** ■ **R.W. Greeff Company Inc.**
777 W Putnam Ave.
Greenwich, CT 06830
Phone: (203)532-2900
Products: Pharmaceutical chemicals. **SIC:** 5122 (Drugs, Proprietaries & Sundries). **Est:** 1918. **Sales:** $11,000,000 (2000). **Emp:** 26. **Officers:** E.G. Knoblock Jr., CEO; Jack Sarekgest, CFO; Rolf W. Spaeth, President.

■ **19343** ■ **Grogan's, Inc.**
1016 S Broadway
Lexington, KY 40504
Phone: (606)254-6661 **Fax:** (606)254-6666
E-mail: grogans@gte.net
URL: http://www.grogans.com
Products: Wheelchairs, including powered, manual, and sport. **SIC:** 5047 (Medical & Hospital Equipment). **Est:** 1960. **Emp:** 90. **Officers:** Dan Pickett, Contact.

■ **19344** ■ **Gulf States Optical Labs Inc.**
PO Box 60023
New Orleans, LA 70160-0023
Phone: (504)834-1646
Free: (800)662-7889 **Fax:** (504)834-2580
Products: Ophthalmic goods. **SIC:** 5048 (Ophthalmic Goods). **Officers:** Pierre Bezou, Owner & Pres.

■ **19345** ■ **H Enterprises International Inc.**
120 S 6th St., Ste. 2300
Minneapolis, MN 55402
Phone: (612)340-8849
Products: Disposable medical supplies. **SIC:** 5047 (Medical & Hospital Equipment). **Sales:** $38,000,000 (2000). **Emp:** 130. **Officers:** John Byrne, President; Mike Gorman, CFO.

■ **19346** ■ **Howard Hall Div.**
777 W Putnam Ave.
Greenwich, CT 06830
Phone: (203)532-2900 **Fax:** (203)532-2980
E-mail: info@rwgreeff.com
URL: http://www.rwgreeff.com
Products: Chemical preparations; Fine chemicals and intermediates for the pharmaceutical, electronics, beverage, rubber, plastics, and other industries. **SIC:** 5169 (Chemicals & Allied Products Nec). **Est:** 1968. **Sales:** $12,000,000 (2000). **Emp:** 10. **Officers:** Jeffrey O. Brown, Sales Mgr., e-mail: jbrown@rwgreeff.com. **Former Name:** Howard Hall International.

■ **19347** ■ **Hamilton Medical Inc.**
PO Box 30008
Reno, NV 89520-3008
Phone: (702)858-3200 **Fax:** (702)856-5621
Products: Medical, dental, and optical equipment. **SIC:** 5047 (Medical & Hospital Equipment).

■ **19348** ■ **Hampton Vision Center**
10 Depot Sq.
Hampton, NH 03842
Phone: (603)926-2722
Products: Eyeglass frames and lenses. **SIC:** 5048 (Ophthalmic Goods).

■ **19349** ■ **Handy Care**
15900 Crenshaw Blvd., No. 1377
Gardena, CA 90249
Phone: (562)634-3937 **Fax:** (562)634-0612
Products: Medicinal and health supplies; Industrial supplies. **SICs:** 5047 (Medical & Hospital Equipment); 5085 (Industrial Supplies). **Est:** 1989. **Sales:** $2,000,000 (2000). **Emp:** 10.

■ **19350** ■ **Hartwell Medical Corp.**
6352 Corte Del Abeto, Ste. J
Carlsbad, CA 92009-1408
Phone: (760)438-5500
Free: (800)633-5900 **Fax:** (760)438-2783
Products: Emergency medical supplies. **SIC:** 5047 (Medical & Hospital Equipment). **Est:** 1989. **Sales:** $1,500,000 (2000). **Emp:** 7. **Officers:** Gary R. Williams, President.

■ **19351** ■ **Hawaiian Sunglass Co.**
1200 College Walk No. 112
Honolulu, HI 96817
Phone: (808)945-3134 **Fax:** (808)944-8292
E-mail: mrsell@lava.net
Products: Sunglasses. **SIC:** 5048 (Ophthalmic Goods). **Est:** 1969. **Emp:** 4.

■ **19352** ■ **Hayes Medical Inc.**
1115 Windfield Way
El Dorado Hills, CA 95762
Phone: (916)355-7100
Free: (800)240-0500 **Fax:** (916)355-7190
Products: Orthopedic devices. **SIC:** 5047 (Medical & Hospital Equipment). **Sales:** $8,000,000 (1999). **Emp:** 40. **Officers:** Dan E. Hayes Jr., CEO; Charles Eyler, CFO.

■ **19353** ■ **Health Care Services, Inc.**
342 4th Ave.
Huntington, WV 25701
Phone: (304)525-9184 **Fax:** (304)525-9152
Products: Hospital products; Home hospital equipment and supplies. **SIC:** 5047 (Medical & Hospital Equipment). **Est:** 1974. **Officers:** Fred Silverstein, President.

■ **19354** ■ **Health Services Corporation of America**
PO Box 1689
Cape Girardeau, MO 63702-1689
Phone: (573)334-7711 **Fax:** (573)335-4453
Products: Pharmaceuticals. **SIC:** 5122 (Drugs, Proprietaries & Sundries). **Est:** 1969. **Sales:** $97,000,000 (2000). **Emp:** 126. **Officers:** Tom Jamieson, President; Tim Goodman, VP of Finance.

■ **19355** ■ **HealthStyles, Inc.**
201 Santa Monica Blvd., Ste. 400
Santa Monica, CA 90401
Phone: (310)451-9476 **Fax:** (310)393-1147
E-mail: info@health-e-styles.com
URL: http://www.health-e-styles.com
Products: Alternative healthcare products. **SIC:** 5122 (Drugs, Proprietaries & Sundries). **Est:** 1999. **Sales:** $10,000,000 (2000). **Emp:** 7. **Officers:** Larry Namer, CEO; Nataly Scherbalova, Exec. VP. **Former Name:** Comspan Inc.

■ **19356** ■ **Heard Optical Co.**
PO Box 1448
Long Beach, CA 90801-1448
Phone: (562)595-4461
Free: (800)366-8116 **Fax:** (562)492-6385
Products: Ophthalmic goods. **SIC:** 5048 (Ophthalmic Goods).

■ **19357** ■ **HemaCare Corp.**
4954 Van Nuys Blvd.
Sherman Oaks, CA 91403
Phone: (818)986-3883
Free: (888)481-1538 **Fax:** (818)986-1417
E-mail: mailroom@hemacare.com
URL: http://www.hemacare.com
Products: Blood component products and blood plasmas, including plateletpheresis concentrate. **SIC:** 5122 (Drugs, Proprietaries & Sundries). **Est:** 1978. **Sales:** $19,000,000 (1999). **Emp:** 150. **Officers:** William Nicely, CEO; David Fractor, CFO, e-mail: dfractor@hemacare.com; Alan Darlington, Chairman of

the Board, e-mail: adarlington@hemacare.com; JoAnn Stover, Corp. Secty., e-mail: jstover@hemacare.com.

■ 19358 ■ HI-Tech Optical Inc.
3157 Christy Way
Saginaw, MI 48603-2226
Phone: (517)799-9390
Free: (800)848-2266 **Fax:** (517)799-3711
E-mail: Hitechop@concentric.com
Products: Ophthalmic goods; Ophthalmic frames. **SIC:** 5048 (Ophthalmic Goods). **Officers:** Neil Coon, Secretary.

■ 19359 ■ John W.W. Holden, Inc.
628 Union Ave.
Providence, RI 02909
Phone: (401)944-1515 **Fax:** (401)943-5050
Products: Optical accessories. **SIC:** 5048 (Ophthalmic Goods). **Est:** 1923. **Emp:** 9. **Officers:** R. Marshall, President; L. Marshall, Vice President.

■ 19360 ■ Holladay Surgical Supply Co.
2551 Landmark Dr.
Winston-Salem, NC 27103-6717
Phone: (910)760-2111
Free: (800)227-7602 **Fax:** (910)768-7731
Products: Medical, dental, and optical equipment. **SIC:** 5047 (Medical & Hospital Equipment). **Sales:** $3,200,000 (2000). **Emp:** 12.

■ 19361 ■ Honolulu Optical
1450 Ala Moana Blvd., Ste. 2250
Honolulu, HI 96814-4665
Phone: (808)536-3959 **Fax:** (808)524-4936
Products: Optical equipment and supplies, including prescription and non-prescription glasses, contacts, and sunglasses. **SIC:** 5048 (Ophthalmic Goods).

■ 19362 ■ House of Plastic Inc.
329 W 14 Mile Rd.
Clawson, MI 48017-1926
Phone: (248)549-3400
Products: Ophthalmic goods; Contact lenses. **SIC:** 5048 (Ophthalmic Goods). **Officers:** Victor Frohriep, President.

■ 19363 ■ Huntleigh Technology Inc.
227 Rte. 33 E
Manalapan, NJ 07726
Phone: (732)446-2500
Free: (800)223-1218 **Fax:** (732)446-1938
Products: Medical, dental, and optical equipment. **SIC:** 5047 (Medical & Hospital Equipment). **Sales:** $30,000,000 (2000). **Emp:** 100.

■ 19364 ■ I See Optical Co.
44 W Church St.
Blackwood, NJ 08012
Phone: (609)227-9300
Free: (800)257-7724 **Fax:** 800-348-4733
Products: Ophthalmic goods. **SIC:** 5048 (Ophthalmic Goods).

■ 19365 ■ Ideal Optics Inc.
4000 Cumberland Parkway Blvd., Ste. 500
Atlanta, GA 30339
Phone: (404)432-0048
Free: (800)554-7353 **Fax:** (404)434-8291
Products: Contact lenses. **SIC:** 5048 (Ophthalmic Goods). **Officers:** Dennis McClung, President.

■ 19366 ■ I.F. Optical Co. Inc.
2812 W Touhy Ave.
Chicago, IL 60645
Phones: (773)761-8969 (773)761-3323
Free: (800)972-5847 **Fax:** (773)761-3601
E-mail: chaoopt@aol.com
Products: Ophthalmic goods. **SIC:** 5048 (Ophthalmic Goods). **Est:** 1972.

■ 19367 ■ Illmo Rx Service Inc.
PO Box 14520
St. Louis, MO 63178
Phones: (314)434-6858 800-325-4636
Free: (800)392-1710 **Fax:** (314)434-6428
Products: Ophthalmic goods. **SIC:** 5048 (Ophthalmic Goods).

■ 19368 ■ Independent Drug Co.
235 Northeast Ave.
Tallmadge, OH 44278-1492
Phone: (330)633-9411 **Fax:** (330)633-9642
Products: Pharmaceutical preparations. **SIC:** 5122 (Drugs, Proprietaries & Sundries). **Est:** 1932. **Emp:** 43.
Officers: James S. Eden Jr.

■ 19369 ■ Index 53 Optical
St. Stephen
PO Box 1111
St. Cloud, MN 56302
Phone: (320)252-9380
Free: (800)328-7035 **Fax:** (320)654-9502
Products: Ophthalmic goods. **SIC:** 5048 (Ophthalmic Goods).

■ 19370 ■ Industrial Vision Corp.
1976 Arsenal St.
St. Louis, MO 63118
Phone: (314)892-9995
Products: Safety glasses. **SIC:** 5048 (Ophthalmic Goods). **Sales:** $2,000,000 (2000). **Emp:** 15. **Officers:** John Stewart, President.

■ 19371 ■ Infolab Inc.
PO Box 1309
Clarksdale, MS 38614
Phone: (601)627-2283 **Fax:** (601)627-1913
Products: Medical supplies, including bandages and needles. **SICs:** 5122 (Drugs, Proprietaries & Sundries); 5047 (Medical & Hospital Equipment). **Est:** 1968.
Sales: $46,000,000 (2000). **Emp:** 75. **Officers:** I.D. Spradling, President.

■ 19372 ■ Information Sales and Marketing Company Inc.
PO Box 2772
Covington, LA 70434
Phone: (504)892-6700
Free: (800)843-7215 **Fax:** (504)892-5089
E-mail: ism@i-55.com
Products: Laboratory supplies, including blood collection tubes, gloves, beakers, and flasks; Reusable shipping containers for computers and specialized equipment. **SIC:** 5047 (Medical & Hospital Equipment).
Sales: $1,000,000 (2000). **Emp:** 5. **Officers:** Donna Hunstock, President.

■ 19373 ■ Integrated Medical Inc.
8100 S Akron St., Ste. 320
Englewood, CO 80112-3508
Phone: (303)792-0069
Free: (800)333-7617 **Fax:** (303)792-0702
Products: Physical therapy supplies. **SIC:** 5047 (Medical & Hospital Equipment). **Est:** 1976. **Sales:** $5,000,000 (2000). **Emp:** 30. **Officers:** Dennis Mc Gimsey, President.

■ 19374 ■ Integrated Orbital Implants Inc.
12526 High Bluff Dr., No. 300
San Diego, CA 92130
Phone: (619)792-3565
Products: Optical implanting supplies. **SIC:** 5048 (Ophthalmic Goods). **Est:** 1989. **Sales:** $1,000,000 (2000). **Emp:** 5. **Officers:** Arthur Perry, President.

■ 19375 ■ H. Interdonati, Inc.
PO Box 262
Cold Spring Harbor, NY 11724
Phone: (516)367-6613
Products: Chemical food additives and pharmaceuticals. **SICs:** 5169 (Chemicals & Allied Products Nec); 5122 (Drugs, Proprietaries & Sundries).
Officers: Joseph Hoffman, Sales Mgr.

■ 19376 ■ International Eyewear Inc.
PO Box 32308
Baltimore, MD 21282-2308
Phone: (410)486-8300
Free: (800)638-1888 **Fax:** (410)486-7908
Products: Ophthalmic goods; Ophthalmic frames. **SIC:** 5048 (Ophthalmic Goods). **Officers:** Lester Goldberg, President.

■ 19377 ■ International Optical Supply Co.
5027 South 300 West
Salt Lake City, UT 84107-4707
Phone: (801)269-1119
Free: (800)443-6889 **Fax:** (801)269-1127
E-mail: partywicks@uswest.net
Products: Ophthalmic goods. **SIC:** 5048 (Ophthalmic Goods). **Est:** 1986. **Officers:** Jerry McWillis, President.

■ 19378 ■ International Trade & Telex Corp.
2621 E 20th
PO Box 91291
Long Beach, CA 90809
Phone: (213)435-3492 **Fax:** (562)426-2005
E-mail: reittc@gte.net
Products: Medical supplies; Environmental/hazardous wastes supplies; Poultry. **SICs:** 5047 (Medical & Hospital Equipment); 5144 (Poultry & Poultry Products); 5013 (Motor Vehicle Supplies & New Parts). **Emp:** 3. **Officers:** M.L. Haynes, President.

■ 19379 ■ Intraoptics Inc.
1611 Owen Dr., Ste. C
Fayetteville, NC 28304-3400
Phone: (910)323-9797
Products: Ophthalmic goods; Optometric equipment and supplies. **SIC:** 5048 (Ophthalmic Goods). **Officers:** William Philbrick, President.

■ 19380 ■ ISC/BioExpress
420 N Kays Dr.
Kaysville, UT 84037
Phone: (801)547-5047
Free: (800)999-2901 **Fax:** (801)547-5051
Products: Medical, dental, and optical equipment. **SIC:** 5047 (Medical & Hospital Equipment). **Sales:** $25,000,000 (2000). **Emp:** 55.

■ 19381 ■ ITG Laboratories Inc.
702 Marshall St., Ste. 280
Redwood City, CA 94063
Phone: (650)361-1891
Products: Wound dressing supplies. **SIC:** 5122 (Drugs, Proprietaries & Sundries).

■ 19382 ■ I.V. Therapy Associates
4055 Faber Pl. Dr., No. 105
Charleston, SC 29405
Phone: (803)747-0847
Products: Pharmaceutical preparations, including antibiotics. **SIC:** 5122 (Drugs, Proprietaries & Sundries). **Est:** 1988. **Sales:** $19,000,000 (2000). **Emp:** 25. **Officers:** Mark Hohenwarter, President.

■ 19383 ■ J.A. Optronics
7337 Old Alexandria Ferry Rd.
Clinton, MD 20735-1832
Phone: (301)868-5316
Free: (800)888-0090 **Fax:** (301)868-9402
Products: Ophthalmic goods; Optomeric equipment and supplies. **SIC:** 5048 (Ophthalmic Goods). **Est:** 1970. **Sales:** $1,000,000 (2000). **Emp:** 8. **Officers:** James Arthur, Owner.

■ 19384 ■ Jeffers Vet Supply
PO Box 100
Dothan, AL 36302
Phone: (334)793-6257
Free: (800)533-3377 **Fax:** (334)793-5179
Products: Veterinary products. **SIC:** 5047 (Medical & Hospital Equipment).

■ 19385 ■ Jerry's At Misquamicut Inc.
PO Box 371
Westerly, RI 02891-0371
Phone: (401)596-3155
Free: (800)872-3827 **Fax:** (401)596-3979
Products: Optometric equipment and supplies. **SIC:** 5048 (Ophthalmic Goods). **Officers:** Gerald Swerdlick, President.

■ 19386 ■ JM Smith Corp.
PO Box 1779
Spartanburg, SC 29304
Phone: (864)582-1216 **Fax:** (864)591-0333
Products: Prescription drugs. **SIC:** 5122 (Drugs, Proprietaries & Sundries). **Sales:** $200,000,000 (2000). **Emp:** 350. **Officers:** Bill Cobb, President; Jimmy Wilson, Treasurer & Controller.

■ 19387 ■ **Joy Enterprises**
1104 53rd Court S
West Palm Beach, FL 33407-2350
Phone: (561)863-3205
Free: (800)500-3879 **Fax:** (561)863-3277
Products: Hardware. **SIC:** 5048 (Ophthalmic Goods).
Sales: $4,000,000 (2000). **Emp:** 29.

■ 19388 ■ **Joy Optical Co.**
1104 53rd Court S
West Palm Beach, FL 33407-2350
Phone: (561)863-3205
Free: (800)500-3879 **Fax:** (561)863-3277
E-mail: mail@joyenterprises.com
URL: http://www.joyoptical.com
Products: Eyewear; Sporting knives. **SICs:** 5048 (Ophthalmic Goods); 5091 (Sporting & Recreational Goods). **Est:** 1958. **Sales:** $4,000,000 (2000). **Emp:** 29. **Officers:** Alex Shelton, President; Steven B. Shelton, Vice President; Sandra Brunet, Sales/Marketing Contact. **Alternate Name:** Joy Enterprises.

■ 19389 ■ **K and K Pet Talk**
2901 Bartlett
Tucson, AZ 85741
Phone: (520)887-4926 **Fax:** (520)888-2293
Products: Veterinary products. **SIC:** 5047 (Medical & Hospital Equipment).

■ 19390 ■ **K and K Vet Supply**
3190 A American St.
Springdale, AR 72765-1756
Phone: (501)751-1516 **Fax:** (501)751-1744
Products: Veterinary products. **SIC:** 5047 (Medical & Hospital Equipment).

■ 19391 ■ **K & S Distributors**
5817 Tibby Rd.
Bensalem, PA 19020
Phone: (215)750-1381
Products: Pharmaceuticals. **SIC:** 5047 (Medical & Hospital Equipment).

■ 19392 ■ **Kamaaina Vision Center Inc.**
508 Atkinson Dr.
Honolulu, HI 96814-4728
Phone: (808)949-1595 **Fax:** (808)949-7781
Products: Ophthalmic goods. **SIC:** 5048 (Ophthalmic Goods). **Officers:** Anthony Miller, President.

■ 19393 ■ **Kasperek Optical Inc.**
3620 Biddle St.
Riverview, MI 48192-6559
Phone: (734)283-0844
Free: (800)288-2700 **Fax:** (734)283-0703
Products: Ophthalmic goods; Ophthalmic frames. **SIC:** 5048 (Ophthalmic Goods). **Officers:** Michael Kasperek, President.

■ 19394 ■ **Kendell Co**
740 Vintage Ave.
Ontario, CA 91764
Phone: (909)987-0042 **Fax:** (909)987-6884
Products: Surgical dressings. **SIC:** 5047 (Medical & Hospital Equipment).

■ 19395 ■ **Kentucky Buying Cooperative Int.**
140 Venture Ct., Suite 1
Lexington, KY 40509
Phone: (606)253-9688
Free: (800)928-7777 **Fax:** (606)253-9669
Products: Veterinary products. **SIC:** 5047 (Medical & Hospital Equipment). **Sales:** $4,000,000 (1999). **Emp:** 23.

■ 19396 ■ **Kinray Inc.**
152-35 10th Ave
Whitestone, NY 11357
Phone: (718)767-1234
Products: Drugs, health and beauty products; Medical equipment; Small electronics. **SIC:** 5122 (Drugs, Proprietaries & Sundries). **Sales:** $900,000,000 (2000). **Emp:** 275. **Officers:** Stewart Rahr, CEO; Bill Bodinger, CFO.

■ 19397 ■ **Klabin Marketing**
2067 Broadway
New York, NY 10023
Phone: (212)877-3632
Free: (800)933-9440 **Fax:** (212)580-4329
Products: Health and beauty aids. **SIC:** 5122 (Drugs, Proprietaries & Sundries).

■ 19398 ■ **Gerard Kluyskens Company Inc.**
295 5th Ave.
New York, NY 10016
Phone: (212)685-5710 **Fax:** (212)685-5719
E-mail: mail@gkci.com
Products: Optical supplies, including eyeglasses and parts. **SIC:** 5048 (Ophthalmic Goods). **Est:** 1912. **Sales:** $6,000,000 (2000). **Emp:** 21. **Officers:** John Piciocchi, President.

■ 19399 ■ **Koley's Medical Supply Company Inc.**
505 Crown Point Ave.
Omaha, NE 68110
Phone: (402)455-4444
Products: Hospital supplies, including bedpans, gowns, and bedsheets. **SIC:** 5047 (Medical & Hospital Equipment).

■ 19400 ■ **Krall Optometric Professional LLC**
1415 N Sanborn Blvd.
Mitchell, SD 57301-1015
Phone: (605)996-2020 **Fax:** (605)996-7769
Products: Ophthalmic goods; Optometric equipment and supplies. **SIC:** 5048 (Ophthalmic Goods). **Est:** 1900. **Emp:** 9. **Officers:** Jeff Krall, Managing Partner. **Former Name:** Karl Optometric Clinic.

■ 19401 ■ **Kramer Laboratories Inc.**
8778 SW 8th St.
Miami, FL 33174
Phone: (305)223-1287
Products: Pharmaceutical products. **SIC:** 5122 (Drugs, Proprietaries & Sundries). **Sales:** $5,000,000 (2000). **Emp:** 5. **Officers:** Gloria Rodriguez, Vice President.

■ 19402 ■ **Krelitz Industries Inc.**
800 N 3rd St.
Minneapolis, MN 55401-1104
Phone: (612)339-7401
Products: Pharmaceutical and over-the-counter drugs. **SIC:** 5122 (Drugs, Proprietaries & Sundries). **Est:** 1926. **Sales:** $254,500,000 (2000). **Emp:** 190. **Officers:** Barry M. Krelitz, CEO & President; Dennis J. Allingham, Sr. VP & CFO; Richard M. Meehan, VP of Marketing & Sales.

■ 19403 ■ **Laboratory & Biomedical Supplies Inc.**
12625 High Bluff Dr., Ste. 311
San Diego, CA 92130-2054
Phone: (619)259-2626 **Fax:** (619)259-1342
E-mail: labsusa@aol.com
Products: Diagnostic kits, biochemicals, and laboratory products. **SIC:** 5047 (Medical & Hospital Equipment). **Est:** 1987. **Sales:** $2,500,000 (2000). **Emp:** 5. **Officers:** Silvia I. Dreyfuss, General Mgr. **Also Known by This Acronym:** LABS.

■ 19404 ■ **Langley Optical Company Inc.**
8140 Marshall Dr.
Lenexa, KS 66214
Phone: (913)492-5379
Free: (800)888-5379 **Fax:** (913)492-8508
Products: Ophthalmic goods. **SIC:** 5048 (Ophthalmic Goods).

■ 19405 ■ **Lawrence Eyewear**
115 Edwin Rd., Ste. 2
South Windsor, CT 06074-2413
Phone: (860)289-4465 **Fax:** (860)528-8416
Products: Ophthalmic goods; Ophthalmic frames. **SIC:** 5048 (Ophthalmic Goods). **Officers:** Lawrence Ruffino, President.

■ 19406 ■ **J.F. Lazartigue Inc.**
764 Madison Ave.
New York, NY 10021
Phone: (212)249-9424
Free: (800)359-9345 **Fax:** (212)288-2625
Products: Hair care treatment products. **SIC:** 5122

(Drugs, Proprietaries & Sundries). **Sales:** $3,600,000 (2000). **Emp:** 26. **Officers:** Bertrand Thiery, General Mgr.; Alexia Van de Maele, Accounting Manager.

■ 19407 ■ **Charles Leich Div.**
PO Box 869
Evansville, IN 47708
Phone: (812)428-6700 **Fax:** (812)428-7625
Products: Pharmacueticals. **SICs:** 5122 (Drugs, Proprietaries & Sundries); 5047 (Medical & Hospital Equipment). **Est:** 1854. **Sales:** $50,000,000 (2000). **Emp:** 50. **Officers:** R.M. Leich Jr., President; Jack Laroy, Comptroller; C. Funke, Dir. of Marketing; J.A. Alstadt, Dir. of Data Processing; C.O. Smith, VP of Operations.

■ 19408 ■ **Leisure-Lift Inc.**
1800 Merriam Ln.
Kansas City, KS 66106
Phone: (913)722-5658
Free: (800)255-0285 **Fax:** (913)722-2614
Products: Medical, dental, and optical equipment. **SIC:** 5047 (Medical & Hospital Equipment). **Sales:** $20,000,000 (2000). **Emp:** 65.

■ 19409 ■ **Lenco, Inc.**
175 Quality Ln.
Rutland, VT 05701-4995
Phone: (802)865-0604 **Fax:** (802)865-0667
Products: Optical products. **SIC:** 5048 (Ophthalmic Goods).

■ 19410 ■ **Lenco Inc.**
42 Evergreen Ave.
PO Box 979
Rutland, VT 05702-0979
Phone: (802)775-2505
Products: Ophthalmic goods; Ophthalmic frames. **SIC:** 5048 (Ophthalmic Goods). **Officers:** Harold Leonard, President.

■ 19411 ■ **Lens Co.**
1350 S King St., Ste. 314
Honolulu, HI 96814-2008
Phone: (808)599-5454 **Fax:** (808)521-1241
Products: Contact lenses. **SIC:** 5048 (Ophthalmic Goods).

■ 19412 ■ **Lens Express Inc.**
350 SW 12th Ave.
Deerfield Beach, FL 33442
Phone: (954)421-5800
Free: (800)568-3937 **Fax:** 800-732-5367
URL: http://www.lensexpress.com
Products: Eyecare and contact lens solutions. **SIC:** 5048 (Ophthalmic Goods). **Est:** 1986. **Sales:** $50,000,000 (2000). **Emp:** 250. **Officers:** Brian O'Neill, Exec. VP; Mendo Akdag, President; Harvey Berkowitz, VP of Operations.

■ 19413 ■ **Lensland**
416 Waverly Ave.
Mamaroneck, NY 10543
Phones: (914)381-4540 (914)381-0523
(914)381-4455 **Fax:** (914)381-4509
Products: Ophthalmic goods. **SIC:** 5048 (Ophthalmic Goods).

■ 19414 ■ **Liberty Natural Products**
8120 SE Stark St.
Portland, OR 97215
Phone: (503)256-1227
Free: (800)289-8427 **Fax:** (503)256-1182
Products: Health and beauty aids. **SIC:** 5122 (Drugs, Proprietaries & Sundries).

■ 19415 ■ **Life-Tech Inc.**
PO Box 36221
Houston, TX 77236
Phone: (713)495-9411 **Fax:** (713)495-7960
Products: Medical, dental, and optical equipment. **SIC:** 5047 (Medical & Hospital Equipment). **Sales:** $11,000,000 (2000). **Emp:** 120.

■ **19416** ■ **Eli Lilly and Co. Pharmaceutical Div.**
Lilly Corporate Ctr.
Indianapolis, IN 46285
Phone: (317)267-2157
Products: Pharmaceuticals. **SIC:** 5122 (Drugs, Proprietaries & Sundries). **Est:** 1940. **Sales:** $400,000,000 (2000). **Emp:** 1,935.

■ **19417** ■ **Lotus Light Inc.**
PO Box 1008
Silver Lake, WI 53170
Phone: (414)889-8501
Products: Natural medicines. **SIC:** 5122 (Drugs, Proprietaries & Sundries). **Est:** 1977. **Sales:** $38,000,000 (2000). **Emp:** 50. **Officers:** Santosh Krisky, President.

■ **19418** ■ **Luffeys Medical & Surgical Supplies**
PO Box 4745
2000 B Tower Dr.
Monroe, LA 71211-4745
Phone: (318)388-4036 **Fax:** (318)322-8123
Products: Medical supplies for hospitals, physicians, nursing homes, and home health care. **SIC:** 5047 (Medical & Hospital Equipment). **Est:** 1965. **Emp:** 25. **Officers:** George Luffey, President; Eddie Kincaid, Vice President; John Luffey, Sec. & Treas.; Richard Osbon, Purchasing Agent.

■ **19419** ■ **Luxury Liners**
14545 Valley View Ave., Ste. R
Santa Fe Springs, CA 90670
Phone: (562)921-1813
Free: (800)247-4203 **Fax:** (562)921-1404
Products: Medical, dental, and optical equipment. **SIC:** 5047 (Medical & Hospital Equipment).

■ **19420** ■ **Luzerne Optical Labs, Ltd.**
180 N Wilkes Barre Blvd.
PO Box 998
Wilkes Barre, PA 18703-0998
Phone: (570)822-3183
Free: (800)432-8096 **Fax:** (570)823-4299
E-mail: vision@luzerneoptical.com
URL: http://www.luzerneoptical.com
Products: Ophthalmic goods, including spectacle lenses, frames, custom made gas perm contacts, low vision spectacles, magnifiers, soft contact lenses and solutions, sunglasses, eyeglass cases, telescopes, binoculars, riflescopes, eye patches, anti-reflective coatings, and safety glasses. **SIC:** 5048 (Ophthalmic Goods). **Est:** 1973. **Sales:** $20,000,000 (2000). **Emp:** 160. **Officers:** Jack Dougherty, President; Lorraine Dougherty, Vice President; Neil Dougherty, Marketing & Sales Mgr.; John G. Dougherty, Vice President.

■ **19421** ■ **Maats Enterprises**
PO Box 4129
Philadelphia, PA 19144
Phone: (215)457-4134 **Fax:** (215)457-1176
Products: Medical, dental, and hospital supplies; Motor vehicle parts and supplies; Sporting and recreational goods; Poultry and poultry products; Computer and peripheral equipment. **SICs:** 5047 (Medical & Hospital Equipment); 5013 (Motor Vehicle Supplies & New Parts); 5045 (Computers, Peripherals & Software); 5091 (Sporting & Recreational Goods); 5144 (Poultry & Poultry Products). **Officers:** Matthew A. Afolabi, President.

■ **19422** ■ **Marine Optical Inc.**
5 Hampden Dr.
South Easton, MA 02375
Phone: (508)238-8700
Products: Eyeglass frames. **SIC:** 5048 (Ophthalmic Goods). **Est:** 1925. **Sales:** $2,300,000 (2000). **Emp:** 100. **Officers:** Michael Ferrara, President.

■ **19423** ■ **Marmac Distributors Inc.**
4 Craftsman Rd.
East Windsor, CT 06088
Phone: (203)623-9926
Products: Pharmaceuticals. **SIC:** 5122 (Drugs, Proprietaries & Sundries). **Est:** 1969. **Sales:** $240,000,000 (2000). **Emp:** 105. **Officers:** John G. Dewees, VP & General Merchandising Mgr.; Alex Stachtiarks, Controller; Chip Caney, Dir. of Marketing.

■ **19424** ■ **Masbeirn Corp.**
5353 W Colfax Ave.
Denver, CO 80214-1811
Phone: (303)232-6244 **Fax:** (303)235-0472
Products: Ophthalmic goods. **SIC:** 5048 (Ophthalmic Goods). **Officers:** William Masler, President.

■ **19425** ■ **Mason Distributors**
5105 NW 159th St.
Hialeah, FL 33014-6336
Phone: (305)624-5557
Products: Pharmaceuticals. **SIC:** 5122 (Drugs, Proprietaries & Sundries).

■ **19426** ■ **Maxcare International Inc.**
1626 Delaware Ave.
Des Moines, IA 50317
Phone: (515)265-6565 **Fax:** (515)265-9900
Products: Medical disposables; Cleaning mitts; Cosmetics; Health foods; Burn ointment. **SICs:** 5122 (Drugs, Proprietaries & Sundries); 5047 (Medical & Hospital Equipment). **Officers:** Paul Singh, President.

■ **19427** ■ **Mays Chemical Co.**
5611 E 71st St.
Indianapolis, IN 46220
Phone: (317)842-8722 **Fax:** (317)576-9630
E-mail: wgmays@mayschem.com
URL: http://www.mayschem.com
Products: Food, pharmaceutical, industrial, and automotive chemicals. **SIC:** 5169 (Chemicals & Allied Products Nec). **Est:** 1980. **Sales:** $150,000,000 (2000). **Emp:** 170. **Officers:** William G. Mays, President; Bill West, Controller; John T. Thompson, VP of Marketing & Sales; Bill Creuziger, Dir. of Systems; T. Mays, Dir of Human Resources.

■ **19428** ■ **MBI Inc.**
1353 Arville St.
Las Vegas, NV 89102-1608
Phone: (702)259-1999
Products: Medical, dental, and optical equipment. **SIC:** 5047 (Medical & Hospital Equipment). **Sales:** $2,100,000 (2000). **Emp:** 13.

■ **19429** ■ **M.C. International**
455 Market St., Ste. 210
San Francisco, CA 94105
Phone: (415)836-6760 **Fax:** (415)836-6774
E-mail: mcmail@mcexportsf.com
URL: http://www.mcexportsf.com
SICs: 5047 (Medical & Hospital Equipment); 5169 (Chemicals & Allied Products Nec); 5122 (Drugs, Proprietaries & Sundries). **Est:** 1958. **Sales:** $40,000,000 (2000). **Emp:** 80.

■ **19430** ■ **F.H. McGary Optical Co.**
PO Box 675
Bangor, ME 04402-0675
Phone: (207)945-6429 **Fax:** (207)945-4348
Products: Ophthalmic goods; Optometric equipment and supplies. **SIC:** 5048 (Ophthalmic Goods). **Officers:** Robert McGary, President.

■ **19431** ■ **McGee Eye Fashions Inc.**
510 Commerce Park Dr.
Marietta, GA 30060-2719
Phone: (404)422-0010 **Fax:** (404)422-0012
Products: Ophthalmic frames. **SIC:** 5048 (Ophthalmic Goods). **Officers:** Wayne McGee, President.

■ **19432** ■ **McKesson Drug**
PO Box 27088
Salt Lake City, UT 84127-0088
Phone: (801)977-9500 **Fax:** (801)973-0332
Products: Pharmaceuticals. **SIC:** 5122 (Drugs, Proprietaries & Sundries).

■ **19433** ■ **McKesson Drug Co.**
1 Post St.
San Francisco, CA 94104
Phone: (415)983-8300 **Fax:** (415)983-7160
Products: Drugs. **SIC:** 5122 (Drugs, Proprietaries & Sundries). **Est:** 1833. **Sales:** $7,898,000,000 (2000). **Emp:** 4,408. **Officers:** Tom Simone, President; Chuck Falkenroth, VP & Controller; Fred Toney, Sr. VP of Marketing & Sales; Hank Wilde, Exec. VP of Operations; Susan Weir, Sr. VP of Human Resources.

■ **19434** ■ **McKesson Drug Co.**
1 Post St.
San Francisco, CA 94104
Phone: (415)983-8300 **Fax:** (415)983-8955
Products: Bottled water, pharmaceuticals and beauty aids. **SIC:** 5122 (Drugs, Proprietaries & Sundries). **Sales:** $10,750,000,000 (2000). **Emp:** 6,000.

■ **19435** ■ **McKesson HBOC Inc.**
1 Post St.
San Francisco, CA 94104
Phone: (415)983-8300 **Fax:** (415)983-7160
Products: Pharmaceuticals; Health and beauty care products. **SIC:** 5122 (Drugs, Proprietaries & Sundries). **Sales:** $20,857,300,000 (2000). **Emp:** 13,700. **Officers:** Mark A. Pulido, CEO & President; Richard H. Hawkins, VP & CFO.

■ **19436** ■ **McKesson Health Systems**
1 Post St.
San Francisco, CA 94104
Phone: (415)983-8300
Products: Pharmaceuticals. **SIC:** 5122 (Drugs, Proprietaries & Sundries).

■ **19437** ■ **McKesson Pharmaceutical Inc.**
PO Box 1831
Phoenix, AZ 85001
Phone: (602)272-7916 **Fax:** (602)278-6687
Products: Pharmaceutical preparations. **SIC:** 5122 (Drugs, Proprietaries & Sundries).

■ **19438** ■ **McLeod Optical Company Inc.**
PO Box 6045
Providence, RI 02940-6045
Phone: (401)467-3000
Products: Ophthalmic goods. **SIC:** 5048 (Ophthalmic Goods). **Officers:** Edwin McLeod, President.

■ **19439** ■ **Med-X International, Inc.**
PO Box 101
Tenafly, NJ 07670
Phone: (201)387-8556 **Fax:** (201)387-8499
E-mail: topmed@aol.com
Products: Medical products, including disposables. **SIC:** 5047 (Medical & Hospital Equipment). **Est:** 1982. **Sales:** $2,000,000 (2000). **Emp:** 3. **Officers:** Gary Malajian, President.

■ **19440** ■ **Medeiros Optical Service**
1118 Fort St. Mall
Honolulu, HI 96813-2707
Phone: (808)536-8243 **Fax:** (808)531-0755
Products: Ophthalmic goods. **SIC:** 5048 (Ophthalmic Goods). **Officers:** Lorraine Brown, Owner.

■ **19441** ■ **Medi Inc.**
75 york Ave.
Randolph, MA 02368
Phone: (617)961-1232
Free: (800)225-8634 **Fax:** (617)961-5750
Products: Medical, dental, and optical equipment. **SIC:** 5047 (Medical & Hospital Equipment). **Sales:** $8,500,000 (2000). **Emp:** 25.

■ **19442** ■ **Medical Advisory Systems Inc.**
8050 Southern Maryland Blvd.
Owings, MD 20736
Phone: (410)257-9504 **Fax:** (410)257-2704
Products: Medical supplies. **SIC:** 5122 (Drugs, Proprietaries & Sundries). **Sales:** $1,800,000 (1994). **Emp:** 20. **Officers:** Thomas M. Hall, CEO; Ronald W. Pickett, President & Treasurer.

■ **19443** ■ **Medical Dynamics Inc.**
99 Inverness Dr.E
Englewood, CO 80112
Phone: (303)790-2990
Free: (800)525-1294 **Fax:** (303)799-1378
Products: Miniature scopes and video systems for medical and dental diagnosis and surgical procedures. **SIC:** 5047 (Medical & Hospital Equipment). **Sales:** $7,900,000 (2000). **Emp:** 20. **Officers:** Van Horsley, CEO & President; Pat Horsley-Adair, Treasurer.

■ **19444** ■ **Medical Electronics Sales and Service**
338 N 16th St.
Phoenix, AZ 85006-3706
Phone: (602)252-5891
Free: (800)996-3006 **Fax:** (602)252-7789
Products: Medical, dental, and optical equipment. **SIC:** 5047 (Medical & Hospital Equipment). **Sales:** $400,000 (2000). **Emp:** 3.

■ **19445** ■ **Medical Equipment Resale Inc.**
45031 Grand River
Novi, MI 48376-7006
Phone: (248)380-7951
Free: (800)962-4419 **Fax:** (248)380-7954
Products: Medical, dental, and optical equipment. **SIC:** 5047 (Medical & Hospital Equipment).

■ **19446** ■ **Medical Specialists Company Inc.**
7770 Iliff Ave., Ste. D
Denver, CO 80231-5326
Phone: (303)750-2002
Free: (800)873-3414 **Fax:** (303)750-2043
Products: Medical, dental, and optical equipment. **SIC:** 5047 (Medical & Hospital Equipment).

■ **19447** ■ **Medical Specialties Company Inc.**
58 Norfolk Ave.
South Easton, MA 02375-0600
Phone: (508)238-8590
Products: Medical supplies and equipment. **SIC:** 5047 (Medical & Hospital Equipment). **Sales:** $58,000,000 (2000). **Emp:** 175. **Officers:** Jim Damicone, President; John Sills, CFO.

■ **19448** ■ **MELIBRAD**
PO Box 19689
Las Vegas, NV 89132-0689
Phone: (702)895-9033
Free: (800)634-6786 **Fax:** (702)895-9231
Products: Ophthalmic goods. **SIC:** 5048 (Ophthalmic Goods). **Est:** 1965. **Officers:** Larry J. Elton, President. **Former Name:** DRP Corp.

■ **19449** ■ **Merck-Medco Managed Care Inc.**
100 Summit Ave.
Montvale, NJ 07645
Phone: (201)358-5400 **Fax:** (201)476-2660
Products: Pharmacueticals. **SIC:** 5122 (Drugs, Proprietaries & Sundries). **Est:** 1983. **Emp:** 6,000. **Officers:** Pear Losberg, President; JoAnn Reed, Sr. VP & Finance Officer; Roger C. Holstein, Exec. VP of Marketing & Sales; Thomas P. Apker, Sr. VP of Information Systems.

■ **19450** ■ **Mercy National Purchasing Inc.**
55 Shuman Blvd.
Naperville, IL 60563-8469
Phone: (708)355-5500 **Fax:** (630)355-7080
Products: Medical, dental, and optical equipment. **SIC:** 5047 (Medical & Hospital Equipment). **Sales:** $4,000,000 (2000). **Emp:** 17.

■ **19451** ■ **Mesa Optical**
1225 N 23rd St., Ste. 103
Grand Junction, CO 81501
Phone: (970)241-9166
Free: (800)237-4219 **Fax:** (970)242-7316
Products: Ophthalmic goods. **SIC:** 5048 (Ophthalmic Goods).

■ **19452** ■ **MGM Optical Laboratory**
621 Ave. De Diego
Puerto Nuevo, PR 00920
Phone: (787)781-6299 **Fax:** (787)781-6499
SIC: 5048 (Ophthalmic Goods). **Est:** 1989. **Sales:** $2,600,000 (2000). **Emp:** 29. **Officers:** Manuel Mirando M.D., President; Gabriel Garcia, VP & Gen. Mgr.

■ **19453** ■ **Miami-Luken Inc.**
265 S Pioneer Blvd.
Springboro, OH 45066
Phone: (513)743-7775 **Fax:** (513)743-7786
Products: Pharmaceuticals; Home health care; Candy. **SIC:** 5122 (Drugs, Proprietaries & Sundries). **Est:** 1962. **Sales:** $80,000,000 (2000). **Emp:** 85. **Officers:** William M. Powers, President; James Lyons, CFO.

■ **19454** ■ **Micro Bio-Medics Inc.**
846 Pelham Pkwy.
Pelham Manor, NY 10803
Phone: (914)738-8400 **Fax:** (914)738-9538
Products: Medical supplies. **SIC:** 5047 (Medical & Hospital Equipment). **Sales:** $43,400,000 (2000). **Officers:** Bruce J. Haber, President.

■ **19455** ■ **Midark Optical**
23908 I-30, Ste. A
Alexander, AR 72002
Phones: (501)847-0271 (501)847-3526
Free: (800)643-5756 **Fax:** (501)847-2421
Products: Ophthalmic goods. **SIC:** 5048 (Ophthalmic Goods).

■ **19456** ■ **Middlefield Optical Company, Inc.**
14561 Old State Rd.
PO Box 1079
Middlefield, OH 44062
Phone: (440)632-0107
Free: (800)331-5407 **Fax:** 800-368-5329
E-mail: middlefld@aol.com
Products: Ophthalmic goods. **SIC:** 5048 (Ophthalmic Goods). **Est:** 1974. **Sales:** $2,000,000 (2000). **Emp:** 19. **Officers:** Jeff Schleger, President; Dale Schleger, Vice President; Pam Taylor, Sec. & Treas.

■ **19457** ■ **Midland Medical Supply Co.**
4850 Old Cheney Rd.
Lincoln, NE 68516
Phone: (402)423-8877
Free: (800)762-2895 **Fax:** (402)423-2931
Products: Medical supplies and equipment. **SIC:** 5047 (Medical & Hospital Equipment). **Sales:** $18,000,000 (2000). **Emp:** 55. **Officers:** Al Borchhardt, President.

■ **19458** ■ **Midwest Labs**
1450 N Dayton
Chicago, IL 60622
Phone: (773)261-3131
Free: (800)247-2525 **Fax:** (773)261-9407
Products: Ophthalmic goods. **SIC:** 5048 (Ophthalmic Goods). **Est:** 1973. **Sales:** $6,000,000 (2000). **Emp:** 55. **Officers:** Jack Winjum; Lois Winjum.

■ **19459** ■ **Midwest Labs, Inc.**
117 Salem St.
PO Box 519
Indianola, IA 50125
Phone: (515)961-6593
Free: (800)247-2525 **Fax:** (515)961-0515
E-mail: midwest1@dwx.com
Products: Ophthalmic goods. **SIC:** 5048 (Ophthalmic Goods). **Est:** 1973. **Sales:** $6,000,000 (2000). **Emp:** 50. **Officers:** Jack Winjum, President; Lois Winjum, Vice President.

■ **19460** ■ **Midwest Lens**
14304 W 100 St.
Lenexa, KS 66215
Phone: (913)894-1030 **Free:** (800)444-4158
Products: Ophthalmic goods. **SIC:** 5048 (Ophthalmic Goods).

■ **19461** ■ **Midwest Medical Supply Company Inc.**
13400 Lakefront Dr.
Bridgeton, MO 63044
Phone: (314)291-2900
Free: (800)736-2115 **Fax:** (314)298-7957
E-mail: midwest@cyberjunction.net
URL: http://www.midwestmedical.com
Products: Medical supplies for servicing acute care, alternate care, long term, and home care. **SIC:** 5047 (Medical & Hospital Equipment). **Est:** 1970. **Sales:** $55,000,000 (2000). **Emp:** 180. **Officers:** Merrill Klearman, President; John Hoffman, CFO; Regina Frey, Dir of Human Resources; Tom Harris, Exec. VP.

■ **19462** ■ **Midwest Optical Laboratories, Inc.**
PO Box 842
Dayton, OH 45401
Phone: (937)878-6667
Free: (800)762-9504 **Fax:** (937)878-6137
Products: Ophthalmic goods. **SIC:** 5048 (Ophthalmic Goods).

■ **19463** ■ **J.S. Milam Optical Co. Inc.**
PO Box 700
Nashville, TN 37202-0700
Phone: (615)242-3372 **Fax:** 800-342-8384
Products: Ophthalmic lenses. **SIC:** 5048 (Ophthalmic Goods). **Officers:** John Milam, President.

■ **19464** ■ **Miller's Adaptive Technologies**
2023 Romig Rd.
Akron, OH 44320
Phones: (330)753-9799 (330)753-9600
Free: (800)837-4544 **Fax:** (330)572-2603
E-mail: mjm@millers.com
Products: Modular hardware and components adaptable for wheelchair seating systems. **SIC:** 5047 (Medical & Hospital Equipment). **Est:** 1949. **Officers:** David A. McInturff, Sales/Marketing Contact, e-mail: dam@millers.com; Matthew J. McCourry, Customer Service Contact, e-mail: mjm@millers.com. **Former Name:** Millers Rents & Sells.

■ **19465** ■ **Millers Rents & Sells**
5410 Warner Rd.
Cleveland, OH 44125
Phone: (216)642-1447
Products: Powered wheelchair systems and parts. **SIC:** 5047 (Medical & Hospital Equipment). **Officers:** Rob Miller, Contact.

■ **19466** ■ **Moore Industries Inc.**
PO Box 311
Bradley, IL 60915
Phone: (815)932-5500
Products: Medical technologies, including needleless injectors for diabetics. **SIC:** 5047 (Medical & Hospital Equipment).

■ **19467** ■ **Moore Medical Corp.**
PO Box 1500
New Britain, CT 06050
Phone: (860)826-3600 **Fax:** (860)223-2382
URL: http://www.mooremedical.com
Products: Medical and pharmaceutical supplies. **SICs:** 5122 (Drugs, Proprietaries & Sundries); 5047 (Medical & Hospital Equipment). **Est:** 1969. **Sales:** $286,300,000 (2000). **Emp:** 356. **Officers:** David V. Harper, Exec. VP & CFO; Richard A. Bucchi, Exec. VP of Marketing & Sales; Kenneth Kollmeyer, Exec. VP of Operations.

■ **19468** ■ **More Mobility**
333 W Blaine St.
McAdoo, PA 18237
Phone: (717)929-1456
Free: (800)368-9333 **Fax:** (717)929-1478
E-mail: dave46@ptd.net
Products: Powered wheelchair systems and parts. **SIC:** 5047 (Medical & Hospital Equipment). **Est:** 1984. **Sales:** $300,000 (2000). **Emp:** 5. **Officers:** Al Mertz, CEO; Dave Bowen.

■ **19469** ■ **Motloid Co.**
300 N Elizabeth St., 2N
Chicago, IL 60607
Phone: (312)226-2454
Free: (800)662-5021 **Fax:** (312)226-2480
E-mail: sales@yates-motloid.com
URL: http://www.yates-motloid.com
Products: Dental supplies and equipment.t. **SIC:** 5063 (Electrical Apparatus & Equipment). **Emp:** 20. **Officers:** Ronald I. Schwarcz, President; Mona G. Zemsky, Marketing Mgr., e-mail: mona@yates-motloid.com; Maria Ramirez, Customer Service Contact, e-mail: mramirez@yates-motloid.com; Alison James, Human Resources Contact, e-mail: alison@yates-motloid.com.

■ **19470** ■ **Multi Vision Optical**
202 Professional Bldg.
PO Box 229
Wheeling, WV 26003
Phone: (304)232-9820
Products: Ophthalmic goods. **SIC:** 5048 (Ophthalmic Goods).

■ 19471 ■ Multifocal Rx Lens Lab
216 Valley Hill Rd.
Riverdale, GA 30274
Phone: (404)478-2121
Free: (800)241-9030 **Fax:** 800-448-0078
Products: Ophthalmic goods. **SIC:** 5048 (Ophthalmic Goods).

■ 19472 ■ Mustela USA
N19 W6727 Commerce Ct.
Cedarburg, WI 53012
Phone: (414)377-6722
Free: (800)422-2987 **Fax:** (414)377-6867
Products: Health and beauty aids. **SIC:** 5122 (Drugs, Proprietaries & Sundries). **Sales:** $5,000,000 (2000). **Emp:** 12.

■ 19473 ■ N.A. Marketing Inc.
RR 5, Box 5
Augusta, ME 04330
Phone: (207)623-2393
Free: (800)280-6489 **Fax:** (207)621-2784
E-mail: namarket@mint.net
URL: http://www.magnummagnets.com
Products: Magnetic therapy products. **SIC:** 5049 (Professional Equipment Nec). **Est:** 1979. **Officers:** Arnold Haskell, President. **Former Name:** Haskell Associates Inc.

■ 19474 ■ N.A. Marketing Inc.
RR 5, Box 5
Augusta, ME 04330
Phone: (207)623-2393
Free: (800)280-6489 **Fax:** (207)621-2784
Products: Medical, dental, and optical supplies. **SIC:** 5048 (Ophthalmic Goods).

■ 19475 ■ Natcom International
1944 Scudder Dr.
Akron, OH 44320
Phone: (330)867-6774
Free: (800)984-9071 **Fax:** (330)864-7475
E-mail: natcomi@ibm.net
Products: Medical supplies; Laboratory equipment; Wood products; Outdoor camping equipment. **SICs:** 5047 (Medical & Hospital Equipment); 5031 (Lumber, Plywood & Millwork); 5091 (Sporting & Recreational Goods). **Est:** 1978. **Sales:** $2,000,000 (2000). **Emp:** 10. **Officers:** Walter Nagel, President; T. Bussell, Vice President.

■ 19476 ■ National Keystone Mizzy Tridynamics
616 Hollywood Ave.
Cherry Hill, NJ 08002
Phone: (609)663-4700 **Fax:** (609)663-0381
Products: Dental products. **SIC:** 5047 (Medical & Hospital Equipment). **Officers:** Gloria Berger, Exec. VP.

■ 19477 ■ National Medical Excess
144 E Kingsbridge Rd.
Mt. Vernon, NY 10550
Phone: (914)665-2777
Free: (800)872-5407 **Fax:** (914)665-2101
Products: Medical, dental, and optical equipment. **SIC:** 5047 (Medical & Hospital Equipment). **Sales:** $4,000,000 (2000). **Emp:** 5.

■ 19478 ■ National Optical Co. Inc.
PO Box 4746
Monroe, LA 71211-4746
Phone: (318)387-2121 **Fax:** (318)322-9688
Products: Ophthalmic goods. **SIC:** 5048 (Ophthalmic Goods). **Officers:** Ronald Phillips, President.

■ 19479 ■ National Specialty Services Inc.
556 Metroplex Dr.
Nashville, TN 37211
Phone: (615)833-7530
Free: (800)879-5569 **Fax:** 800-289-9285
Products: Pharmaceuticals, therapeutic plasma, and medical supplies. **SIC:** 5122 (Drugs, Proprietaries & Sundries). **Sales:** $90,000,000 (2000). **Emp:** 130. **Officers:** Harry Travis, VP & General Merchandising Mgr.; Michael Szabo, Controller.

■ 19480 ■ NCS Healthcare
3200 E Reno Ave.
Del City, OK 73115-6603
Phone: (405)670-2939
Free: (800)421-4123 **Fax:** (405)670-2726
Products: Medical, dental, and optical equipment. **SIC:** 5047 (Medical & Hospital Equipment). **Sales:** $4,000,000 (2000). **Emp:** 30.

■ 19481 ■ Nelson Hawaiian, Ltd.
2080 S King No. 203
Honolulu, HI 96826
Phone: (808)941-3844 **Fax:** (808)945-9234
E-mail: nelhawaii@aol.com
Products: Sunglasses. **SIC:** 5048 (Ophthalmic Goods).

■ 19482 ■ Neostyle Eyewear Corp.
2605 State St.
San Diego, CA 92103
Phone: (619)299-0755
Products: Eyeglass frames. **SIC:** 5048 (Ophthalmic Goods). **Sales:** $14,000,000 (2000). **Emp:** 55. **Officers:** Helmut Igel, President.

■ 19483 ■ Neptune Polarized Sunglasses
PO Box 837
Kailua Kona, HI 96745
Phone: (808)329-6338
Free: (800)800-8180 **Fax:** (808)326-2508
Products: Polarized sunglasses. **SIC:** 5048 (Ophthalmic Goods). **Est:** 1986.

■ 19484 ■ Nethercott's Optical
1641 Cara Loop
Anchorage, AK 99515
Phone: (907)345-6112
Products: Optical glass cutters. **SIC:** 5048 (Ophthalmic Goods).

■ 19485 ■ Neuman Distributors Inc.
175 Railroad Ave.
Ridgefield, NJ 07657-2312
Phone: (201)941-2000
Products: Pharmaceuticals and medical supplies. **SICs:** 5122 (Drugs, Proprietaries & Sundries); 5047 (Medical & Hospital Equipment). **Sales:** $1,200,000,000 (2000). **Emp:** 750. **Officers:** Samuel Toscano Jr., CEO & Chairman of the Board; Phil Piscopo, CFO.

■ 19486 ■ Neuman Health Services Inc.
175 Railroad Ave.
Ridgefield, NJ 07657-2312
Phone: (201)941-2000
Products: Pharmaceuticals and medical supplies. **SICs:** 5122 (Drugs, Proprietaries & Sundries); 5047 (Medical & Hospital Equipment).

■ 19487 ■ NeuroCom International Inc.
9570 SE Lawnfield Rd.
Clackamas, OR 97015
Phone: (503)653-2144 **Fax:** (503)653-1991
Products: Electromedical and electrotherapeutic apparatus for balance and equilibrium disorders. **SIC:** 5047 (Medical & Hospital Equipment). **Officers:** Lewis Nashner, President.

■ 19488 ■ Neville Optical Inc.
PO Box 2250
Westover, WV 26502-2250
Phone: (304)291-1087
Free: (800)338-0148 **Fax:** (304)291-1071
Products: Ophthalmic goods. **SIC:** 5048 (Ophthalmic Goods). **Est:** 1987. **Sales:** $900,000 (2000). **Emp:** 12. **Officers:** George Neville, President.

■ 19489 ■ New City Optical Company Inc.
1107-1109 Wilso Dr.
Desoto Business Park
Baltimore, MD 21223
Phone: (301)646-3500
Free: (800)638-3536 **Fax:** (410)247-1630
Products: Ophthalmic goods. **SIC:** 5048 (Ophthalmic Goods).

■ 19490 ■ New City Optical Company Inc.
5819 Ward Ct.
Virginia Beach, VA 23455
Phone: (757)460-0939 **Fax:** (757)460-3563
Products: Ophthalmic goods. **SIC:** 5048 (Ophthalmic Goods).

■ 19491 ■ New England Serum Co.
U.S Rte. 1
Topsfield, MA 01983
Phone: (978)887-2368
Free: (800)637-3786 **Fax:** (978)887-9149
Products: Veterinary products. **SIC:** 5047 (Medical & Hospital Equipment).

■ 19492 ■ New Hampshire Optical Co.
40 Terrill Park Dr.
PO Box 1375
Concord, NH 03301
Phone: (603)225-7121
Free: (800)852-3717 **Fax:** (603)225-4834
E-mail: nhortattotalnetnh.net
Products: Ophthalmic goods; Eye glasses; Ophthalmic lenses. **SIC:** 5048 (Ophthalmic Goods). **Est:** 1984. **Emp:** 50. **Officers:** Jack Bresslin, President.

■ 19493 ■ The Newton Group, Inc.
PO Box 900
Newton, IA 50208
Products: Ophthalmic goods; Optometric equipment and supplies. **SIC:** 5048 (Ophthalmic Goods).

■ 19494 ■ The Newton Group, Inc. - Newton Lab
623 N 19th Ave. E
Newton, IA 50208-1839
Free: (800)234-7739
Products: Ophthalmic goods. **SIC:** 5048 (Ophthalmic Goods).

■ 19495 ■ Niagara Medical
707 Lowell Ave.
Erie, PA 16505
Free: (800)447-5438
Products: Powered wheelchair systems and parts. **SIC:** 5047 (Medical & Hospital Equipment). **Officers:** Harry Lochbaum, Contact.

■ 19496 ■ Nightingale Medical Equipment Services Inc.
6161 Stewart Rd.
Cincinnati, OH 45227
Phone: (513)271-5115
Products: Powered wheelchair systems and parts. **SIC:** 5047 (Medical & Hospital Equipment). **Officers:** Joe McFarland, Contact.

■ 19497 ■ North American Vision Services
59 Hanse Ave.
Freeport, NY 11520
Phone: (516)546-7507
Free: (800)678-4277 **Fax:** (516)623-1355
Products: Optical machinery; Refracting equipment; Optical solutions, bulbs, frames, and lenses. **SIC:** 5048 (Ophthalmic Goods). **Est:** 1979. **Emp:** 29. **Officers:** Jim Metz.

■ 19498 ■ North Atlantic Services Inc.
39 Angus Ln.
Greenwich, CT 06831-4402
Phone: (203)661-9249
Free: (800)223-5127 **Fax:** 800-626-6933
Products: Ophthalmic goods. **SIC:** 5048 (Ophthalmic Goods). **Est:** 1982. **Officers:** Anthony Sax, President.

■ 19499 ■ North Carolina Mutual Wholesale Drug Co.
PO Box 411
Durham, NC 27702
Phone: (919)596-2151 **Fax:** (919)596-1453
Products: Drugs. **SIC:** 5122 (Drugs, Proprietaries & Sundries). **Est:** 1952. **Sales:** $240,000,000 (2000). **Emp:** 150. **Officers:** Donald Peterson, CEO; Mike Broome, Controller; William V. O'Quinn, Dir. of Marketing.

■ 19500 ■ North Central Optical Co.
3682 29th St.
Grand Rapids, MI 49512
Phone: (616)949-8988 **Fax:** 800-336-3794
Products: Ophthalmic goods, including frames. **SIC:** 5048 (Ophthalmic Goods). **Officers:** Patrick Crowe, President.

■ 19501 ■ Novo Nordisk North America Inc.
405 Lexington Ave., Ste. 6200
New York, NY 10017
Phone: (212)867-0123
Products: Insulin and diabetes care products. **SIC:** 5122 (Drugs, Proprietaries & Sundries).

■ 19502 ■ Novo Nordisk Pharmaceuticals Inc.
100 Overlook Ctr., No. 200
Princeton, NJ 08540
Phone: (609)987-5800 **Fax:** (609)921-8082
Products: Insulin and insulin injecting pens. **SIC:** 5122 (Drugs, Proprietaries & Sundries). **Est:** 1989. **Sales:** $125,000,000 (2000). **Emp:** 360. **Officers:** Kenneth Capuano, President; Phil Fornecker, VP of Finance; Norman Ferzoco, VP of Sales; Joseph Perignat, Dir. of Information Systems; Sarajane Mackenzie, VP of Human Resources.

■ 19503 ■ Nu Skin Enterprises Inc.
75 W Center St.
Provo, UT 84601
Phone: (801)345-6100 **Fax:** (801)345-3099
Products: Skin care products and nutritional supplements. **SIC:** 5122 (Drugs, Proprietaries & Sundries). **Sales:** $894,200,000 (1999). **Emp:** 3,000. **Officers:** Steven J. Lund, CEO & President; Corey B. Lindley, CFO.

■ 19504 ■ Obrig Hawaii Contact Lens Lab
1481 S King
Honolulu, HI 96814
Phone: (808)949-2020 **Fax:** (808)946-6961
Products: Contact lenses. **SIC:** 5048 (Ophthalmic Goods).

■ 19505 ■ Ohio Valley-Clarksburg Inc.
PO Box 6295
Wheeling, WV 26003
Phone: (304)242-9526 **Fax:** (304)243-1197
Products: Pharmaceuticals. **SIC:** 5122 (Drugs, Proprietaries & Sundries). **Est:** 1914. **Sales:** $310,000,000 (2000). **Emp:** 200. **Officers:** Jim Worley, Vice President; Alvey Squires, Dir. of Sales.

■ 19506 ■ Oliver Peoples Inc.
8600 Sunset Blvd.
Los Angeles, CA 90069-0290
Phone: (310)657-5475 **Fax:** (310)657-2372
Products: Optical frames, clips, and cases. **SIC:** 5048 (Ophthalmic Goods). **Est:** 1987. **Sales:** $8,000,000 (2000). **Emp:** 25. **Officers:** Thomas M. Werner, President; Dore Chodorow, CFO; Larry Leight, Dir. of Marketing & Sales; Lind Veitch, Dir. of Information Systems.

■ 19507 ■ Omega Optical Co.
13515 N Stemmons Fwy.
Dallas, TX 75234
Phone: (972)241-4141
Free: (800)366-6342 **Fax:** 800-877-0329
Products: Ophthalmic goods. **SIC:** 5048 (Ophthalmic Goods).

■ 19508 ■ Ophthalmic Instrument Co. Inc.
178 Page St.
Stoughton, MA 02072
Phone: (781)341-5010
Free: (800)272-2070 **Fax:** (781)341-5020
Products: Ophthalmic goods. **SIC:** 5048 (Ophthalmic Goods). **Officers:** Werner Mueller, President.

■ 19509 ■ Optech Inc.
41 Keenan St.
PO Box 228
West Bridgewater, MA 02379
Phone: (508)583-3010
Free: (800)242-0297 **Fax:** (508)583-4458
SIC: 5048 (Ophthalmic Goods).

■ 19510 ■ Optek Inc.
PO Box 42276
Mesa, AZ 85274-2276
Phone: (602)233-0888
Free: (800)528-1186 **Fax:** (602)233-3323
Products: Ophthalmic goods; Contact lenses. **SIC:** 5048 (Ophthalmic Goods). **Officers:** Gary Ulmer, President.

■ 19511 ■ Optical Associates
PO Box 189
Albany, OR 97321-0058
Phone: (541)926-6077 **Fax:** (541)926-0605
Products: Ophthalmic goods. **SIC:** 5048 (Ophthalmic Goods). **Officers:** Rodney Bourdage, Partner.

■ 19512 ■ Optical Center Laboratory Inc.
930 E Lewiston Ave.
Ferndale, MI 48220-1451
Phone: (248)548-6210 **Fax:** (248)548-6214
E-mail: ocl@concentric.com
Products: Ophthalmic goods. **SIC:** 5048 (Ophthalmic Goods). **Est:** 1950. **Emp:** 30. **Officers:** Gary Laskowsky, Contact.

■ 19513 ■ Optical Laboratory of New Bedford
PO Box H-3101
New Bedford, MA 02741
Phone: (508)997-9779 **Fax:** (508)993-0211
Products: Ophthalmic goods. **SIC:** 5048 (Ophthalmic Goods).

■ 19514 ■ Optical Measurements Inc.
1900 E 14 Mile Rd.
Madison Heights, MI 48071-1545
Phone: (248)588-8084 **Fax:** (248)588-8009
Products: Ophthalmic goods; Optometric equipment and supplies. **SIC:** 5048 (Ophthalmic Goods). **Officers:** Thomas Anger, President.

■ 19515 ■ Optical One, Inc.
PO Box 489
Youngstown, OH 44502
Phone: (330)743-8518
Free: (800)223-3200 **Fax:** (330)743-0966
Products: Ophthalmic goods. **SIC:** 5048 (Ophthalmic Goods).

■ 19516 ■ Optical Plastics
PO Box 4115
Clackamas, OR 97015
Phone: (503)655-4787
Free: (800)547-3156 **Fax:** (503)655-3153
Products: Ophthalmic goods. **SIC:** 5048 (Ophthalmic Goods).

■ 19517 ■ Optical Suppliers Inc.
99-1253 Halawa Valley St.
Aiea, HI 96701
Phone: (808)486-2933 **Fax:** (808)486-6458
Products: Prescription eyeglasses. **SIC:** 5048 (Ophthalmic Goods).

■ 19518 ■ Optical Supply
1526 Plainsfield NE
Grand Rapids, MI 49505
Phone: (616)361-6000
Free: (800)632-9207 **Fax:** (616)361-8369
Products: Ophthalmic goods. **SIC:** 5048 (Ophthalmic Goods).

■ 19519 ■ Optique Paris Miki
2134 Kalakaua Ave.
Honolulu, HI 96815
Phone: (808)922-4310 **Fax:** (808)923-2736
Products: Sunglasses and frames. **SIC:** 5048 (Ophthalmic Goods). **Est:** 1976.

■ 19520 ■ Ortho-Tex Inc.
10408A Gulfdale
San Antonio, TX 78216
Phone: (210)490-3340
Free: (800)323-6816 **Fax:** (210)490-3322
Products: Orthopedic and rehabilitation equipment and supplies. **SIC:** 5047 (Medical & Hospital Equipment). **Sales:** $7,500,000 (2000). **Emp:** 12. **Officers:** J. Randolph Harig, President; Cheryl Harig, Treasurer.

■ 19521 ■ Owens and Minor Inc. Augusta Div.
777 Lewiston Rd.
Grovetown, GA 30813
Phone: (706)738-2571 **Fax:** (706)860-3313
Products: Medical supplies. **SIC:** 5047 (Medical & Hospital Equipment). **Sales:** $27,000,000 (2000). **Emp:** 33. **Officers:** Brad Parsons, Manager.

■ 19522 ■ PanVera Corp.
545 Science Dr.
Madison, WI 53711
Phone: (608)233-9450
Free: (800)791-1400 **Fax:** (608)233-3007
Products: Biomedical products; Medical research instruments. **SICs:** 5122 (Drugs, Proprietaries & Sundries); 5047 (Medical & Hospital Equipment). **Sales:** $6,200,000 (2000). **Emp:** 39. **Officers:** Ralph Kauten, President; Tom Burke, Exec. VP of Finance.

■ 19523 ■ Paradise Optical Co.
Pearlridge Center
Aiea, HI 96701
Phone: (808)488-6869
Products: Eyeglasses and contact lenses. **SIC:** 5048 (Ophthalmic Goods).

■ 19524 ■ Paramount Sales Co.
548 Smithfield Ave.
Pawtucket, RI 02860
Phone: (401)728-4400
Products: Health and beauty aids. **SIC:** 5122 (Drugs, Proprietaries & Sundries). **Sales:** $400,000 (2000). **Emp:** 3.

■ 19525 ■ ParMed Pharmaceuticals Inc.
4220 Hyde Pk. Blvd.
Niagara Falls, NY 14305
Phone: (716)284-5666 **Fax:** (716)284-8031
Products: Over-the-counter and prescription pharmaceuticals. **SIC:** 5122 (Drugs, Proprietaries & Sundries). **Est:** 1968. **Sales:** $35,000,000 (2000). **Emp:** 100. **Officers:** D. Palmo, VP & General Merchandising Mgr.; R. Vaccaro, Finance Officer; J. Hillman, VP of Marketing & Sales; P. Santuro; L. Wert, Human Resources Contact.

■ 19526 ■ Parnell Pharmaceuticals Inc.
PO Box 5130
Larkspur, CA 94977-5130
Phone: (415)256-1800
Free: (800)457-4276 **Fax:** (415)256-8099
E-mail: mail@parnellpharm.com
URL: http://www.parnellpharm.com
Products: Pharmaceuticals. **SIC:** 5122 (Drugs, Proprietaries & Sundries). **Est:** 1981. **Sales:** $3,000,000 (1999). **Emp:** 8. **Officers:** Francis Parnell, CEO & President; John Parnell, Vice President.

■ 19527 ■ Pascal Company Inc.
PO Box 1478
Bellevue, WA 98009
Phone: (425)827-4694 **Fax:** (425)827-6893
Products: Dental products, including sterilizing solutions, packing cord, prophy paste; Specialized instruments. **SIC:** 5047 (Medical & Hospital Equipment). **Officers:** Benjamin Paschall, CEO.

■ 19528 ■ Pasch Optical Lab
4589 W Morrison Rd.
Denver, CO 80219
Phone: (303)922-7537
Free: (800)888-0036 **Fax:** (303)922-4911
Products: Ophthalmic goods. **SIC:** 5048 (Ophthalmic Goods).

■ 19529 ■ Patterson Dental Co.
1031 Mendota Heights Rd.
St. Paul, MN 55120
Phone: (612)686-1600
Products: Dental equipment and supplies. **SIC:** 5047 (Medical & Hospital Equipment). **Sales:** $878,800,000 (1999). **Emp:** 3,300. **Officers:** Peter L. Frechette, CEO & President; Ronald E. Ezerski, Exec. VP & Treasurer.

■ 19530 ■ Peninsula Laboratories Inc.
601 Taylor Way
San Carlos, CA 94070
Phone: (650)592-5392 **Fax:** (650)595-4071
Products: Biologically active peptides, includes

synthesis of peptides under CGMP for clinical applications; specializes in synthesizing modified amino acids and small molecules for peptidomemetics. **SIC:** 5047 (Medical & Hospital Equipment). **Officers:** Hiroshi Morihara, CEO.

■ 19531 ■ **Perferx Optical Co. Inc.**
PO Box 285
Dalton, MA 01226
Phone: (413)684-2550 **Free:** (800)343-1428
SIC: 5048 (Ophthalmic Goods). **Officers:** John Enright, President.

■ 19532 ■ **Perfumania Inc.**
11701 NW 101 Street Rd.
Miami, FL 33178
Phone: (305)889-1600
Free: (800)927-1777 **Fax:** (305)592-5774
Products: Perfumes. **SIC:** 5122 (Drugs, Proprietaries & Sundries). **Sales:** $175,300,000 (2000). **Emp:** 1,834. **Officers:** Ilia Lekach, CEO & Chairman of the Board; Donovan Chin, CFO.

■ 19533 ■ **Perfusion Services of Baxter Healthcare Corp.**
16818 Via Del Campo Ct.
San Diego, CA 92127
Phone: (619)485-5599
Free: (800)348-4565 **Fax:** (619)485-5107
Products: Disposable hospital supplies. **SIC:** 5047 (Medical & Hospital Equipment). **Sales:** $140,000,000 (2000). **Emp:** 1,000. **Officers:** King Nelson, CEO & President; John Dahldorf, CFO.

■ 19534 ■ **Perigon Medical Dist. Corp.**
70 Sea Ln.
Farmingdale, NY 11735
Phone: (631)777-8899 **Fax:** (631)777-8383
URL: http://www.perigonmed.com
Products: Medical supplies. **SIC:** 5047 (Medical & Hospital Equipment). **Sales:** $15,000,000 (1994). **Emp:** 23. **Officers:** M. Chase, President; David Chase, Vice President. **Former Name:** Life Care Medical Products.

■ 19535 ■ **Peterson's Rental**
2809 Vaughn Rd., Northwest Bypass
Great Falls, MT 59404
Phone: (406)771-7368 **Fax:** (406)771-7368
Products: Antiseptic products. **SIC:** 5122 (Drugs, Proprietaries & Sundries).

■ 19536 ■ **Pfizer Inc. Distribution Center**
230 Brighton Rd.
Clifton, NJ 07012
Phone: (973)470-7700 **Fax:** (973)470-7823
Products: Prescription drugs and consumer health products. **SIC:** 5122 (Drugs, Proprietaries & Sundries). **Est:** 1958. **Sales:** $43,000,000 (2000). **Emp:** 100. **Officers:** James P. McKenna, Manager; Thomas Clinton, Operations Mgr.; Ronald Ontywein, Dir. of Data Processing; David Fitzgerald, Dir of Personnel.

■ 19537 ■ **Pharmacy Corporation of America**
1871 Lefthand Cir.
Longmont, CO 80501
Phone: (303)626-7788 **Fax:** (303)623-1167
Products: Pharmaceuticals. **SIC:** 5122 (Drugs, Proprietaries & Sundries). **Est:** 1972. **Sales:** $110,000,000 (2000). **Emp:** 1,000. **Officers:** David Redmond, Sr. VP & CFO; David L. Redmond, Sr. VP & CFO; Ron G. Roma, Sr. VP of Sales.

■ 19538 ■ **PharMerica Inc./PMSI**
175 Kelsey Ln.
Tampa, FL 33619
Phone: (813)626-7788 **Free:** (800)237-7676
Products: Pharmaceuticals for nursing homes, correctional, facilities, HMOs, and workers compensation; DME, nursing services, transportation, and custom rehabilitation; Orthotics and prosthetics; Hearing aids; TENS units. **SIC:** 5122 (Drugs, Proprietaries & Sundries). **Sales:** $451,700,000 (2000). **Emp:** 7,496. **Officers:** C. Arnold Renschler, CEO & President; James D. Shelton, Exec. VP & CFO. **Former Name:** PharMerica Inc.

■ 19539 ■ **Philips Medical Systems North America Co.**
PO Box 860
Shelton, CT 06484
Phone: (203)926-7674 **Fax:** (203)926-6099
Products: Medical diagnostic imaging and therapy equipment. **SIC:** 5047 (Medical & Hospital Equipment). **Sales:** $373,300,000 (2000). **Emp:** 1,600. **Officers:** William Curran, VP of Finance.

■ 19540 ■ **Physicians Optical Supply Inc.**
Box 31193
Omaha, NE 68101-1275
Phone: (402)558-5200 **Fax:** (402)558-2278
Products: Ophthalmic goods; Eye glasses. **SIC:** 5048 (Ophthalmic Goods). **Officers:** Robert Gregg, President.

■ 19541 ■ **Piedmont Optical Co.**
Rte. 70 E off Airport Rd.
PO Box 1470
Raleigh, NC 27602
Phone: (919)787-0151
Free: (800)662-7526 **Fax:** 800-768-7433
Products: Ophthalmic goods. **SIC:** 5048 (Ophthalmic Goods).

■ 19542 ■ **Pittman International**
1400 N Jefferson St.
Anaheim, CA 92807
Phone: (714)572-9195 **Fax:** (714)528-8062
Products: Veterinary products. **SIC:** 5047 (Medical & Hospital Equipment).

■ 19543 ■ **Plastoptics Inc.**
2328 W Sinto Ave.
Spokane, WA 99201-2948
Phone: (509)535-1529
Free: (800)333-1529 **Fax:** (509)535-1526
Products: Lenses and optical goods. **SIC:** 5048 (Ophthalmic Goods). **Est:** 1979. **Officers:** Eugene Headley, President.

■ 19544 ■ **Plunkett Optical Inc.**
PO Box 21
Ft. Smith, AR 72902-0021
Phone: (501)783-2001 **Free:** (800)272-4730
Products: Orthopedic appliances (braces), including parts. **SIC:** 5048 (Ophthalmic Goods). **Officers:** Bill Plunkett, President.

■ 19545 ■ **PML Inc.**
PO Box 570
Wilsonville, OR 97070
Phone: (503)570-2500 **Fax:** (503)570-2501
Products: Diagnostic microbiological culture media. **SIC:** 5047 (Medical & Hospital Equipment). **Sales:** $13,600,000 (2000). **Emp:** 166. **Officers:** Kenneth L. Minton, CEO & President; James N. Weider, CFO.

■ 19546 ■ **PML Microbiologicals Inc.**
PO Box 570
Wilsonville, OR 97070
Phone: (503)570-2500 **Fax:** (503)570-2501
Products: Diagnostic microbiological culture media. **SIC:** 5047 (Medical & Hospital Equipment). **Sales:** $14,000,000 (2000). **Emp:** 175.

■ 19547 ■ **Polar Electro Inc.**
370 Crossways Park Dr.
Woodbury, NY 11797
Phone: (516)364-0400
Free: (800)290-6330 **Fax:** (516)364-5454
Products: Wireless heart rate monitors; Repair of wireless heart rate monitors. **SIC:** 5047 (Medical & Hospital Equipment). **Sales:** $30,000,000 (2000). **Emp:** 65. **Officers:** Burt Birnbaum, President; Jukka Jumisko, Controller.

■ 19548 ■ **Polo-Ray Sunglass, Inc.**
7596 Harwin Dr.
Houston, TX 77036-1817
Phone: (713)975-8252
Free: (800)777-7656 **Fax:** (713)975-8257
E-mail: info@poloray.com
URL: http://www.poloray.com
Products: Sunglasses and reading glasses. **SIC:** 5048 (Ophthalmic Goods). **Est:** 1986. **Emp:** 10. **Officers:** Minly Sung.

■ 19549 ■ **Precision Optical Co.**
PO Box 280423
East Hartford, CT 06128-0423
Phone: (860)289-6023 **Fax:** (860)289-0164
Products: Ophthalmic goods. **SIC:** 5048 (Ophthalmic Goods). **Officers:** Richard Welch, President.

■ 19550 ■ **Precision Optical Laboratory**
PO Box 68
Gallaway, TN 38036-0068
Phone: (901)867-2991 **Fax:** 800-451-8047
Products: Ophthalmic lenses. **SIC:** 5048 (Ophthalmic Goods). **Officers:** Billy Stallings, Chairman of the Board.

■ 19551 ■ **Priority Healthcare Corp.**
250 Technology Park, No. 124
Lake Mary, FL 32746-6232
Phone: (407)869-7001
Products: Pharmaceuticals and medical supplies. **SIC:** 5122 (Drugs, Proprietaries & Sundries). **Sales:** $158,200,000 (2000). **Emp:** 130. **Officers:** Robert L. Myers, CEO & President; Donald J. Perfetto, VP, CFO & Treasurer.

■ 19552 ■ **Private Eyes Sunglasses Shop**
390 5th Ave.
New York, NY 10018-8104
Phone: (212)760-2455 **Free:** (800)628-8205
Products: Sunglasses; Eyewear cases and chains. **SIC:** 5048 (Ophthalmic Goods). **Former Name:** Private Eyes. **Alternate Name:** Tomichi Studio.

■ 19553 ■ **PRN Pharmaceutical Services Inc.**
8351 W Rockville Rd.
Indianapolis, IN 46234
Phone: (317)273-1552
Products: Pharmaceuticals. **SIC:** 5122 (Drugs, Proprietaries & Sundries). **Sales:** $104,000,000 (2000). **Emp:** 150. **Officers:** Caroline Copen, CEO.

■ 19554 ■ **Professional Dental Technologies Inc.**
633 Lawrence St.
Batesville, AR 72501
Phone: (870)698-2300
Free: (800)228-5595 **Fax:** (870)698-5554
Products: Dental hygiene products. **SIC:** 5047 (Medical & Hospital Equipment). **Sales:** $23,800,000 (2000). **Emp:** 332. **Officers:** William T. Evans, CEO; Robert E. Christian, Sr. VP & Treasurer.

■ 19555 ■ **Professional Medical Services Inc.**
175 Kelsey Ln.
Tampa, FL 33619
Phone: (813)626-7788 **Free:** (800)237-7676
Products: DME; Nursing service; Transportation; Custom rehabilitation; Orthotics and prosthetics; Hearing aids and TENs units for workers' comp patients. **SIC:** 5122 (Drugs, Proprietaries & Sundries). **Sales:** $52,000,000 (2000). **Emp:** 400. **Officers:** C. Arnold Renschler, President; Jim Shelton, CFO.

■ 19556 ■ **Professional Ophthalmic Labs Inc.**
3772 Peters Creek Rd. Ext.
Roanoke, VA 24005
Phones: (540)345-7303 800-476-4050
Free: (800)476-0167 **Fax:** (540)345-0167
E-mail: polinc@ixnetcom.com
URL: http://www.polinc.net
Products: Ophthalmic goods, including safety and prescription glasses, frames, and cases. **SIC:** 5048 (Ophthalmic Goods). **Sales:** $2,000,000 (2000). **Emp:** 32. **Officers:** Diane C. Strickler.

■ 19557 ■ **Professional Optical**
255 Haywood St.
Asheville, NC 28801
Phone: (704)252-2172
Free: (800)476-8770 **Fax:** (704)252-2657
Products: Ophthalmic goods. **SIC:** 5048 (Ophthalmic Goods).

■ **19558** ■ **Professional Optical Supply**
PO Box 1930
Dallas, TX 75204
Phone: (214)826-5610
Free: (800)492-4176 **Fax:** (214)821-3006
Products: Ophthalmic goods. **SIC:** 5048 (Ophthalmic Goods).

■ **19559** ■ **Protocol Systems Inc.**
8500 SW Creekside Pl
Beaverton, OR 97008-7107
Phone: (503)526-8500 **Fax:** (503)526-4200
Products: Designs, and markets vital signs monitoring instrumentation and systems. **SIC:** 5047 (Medical & Hospital Equipment). **Sales:** $66,300,000 (1999). **Emp:** 353. **Officers:** Robert F. Adrion, CEO & President; Craig M. Swanson, VP & CFO.

■ **19560** ■ **Proxycare Inc.**
4700 SW 51st St., Ste. 215
Ft. Lauderdale, FL 33314-5500
Phone: (954)791-5400 **Free:** (800)977-7699
Products: Pharmaceuticals. **SIC:** 5122 (Drugs, Proprietaries & Sundries). **Sales:** $7,600,000 (2000). **Emp:** 12. **Officers:** Luis Cruz, CEO; Bennett Marks, CFO.

■ **19561** ■ **Pulmonary Data Service**
PO Box 400
Louisville, CO 80027
Phone: (303)666-8100 **Fax:** (303)666-9886
Products: Medical diagnostic pulmonary equipment including spirometers, filters and dosimeters. **SIC:** 5047 (Medical & Hospital Equipment).

■ **19562** ■ **Qualis Inc.**
4600 Park Ave.
Des Moines, IA 50321
Phone: (515)243-3000
Free: (800)334-4514 **Fax:** (515)282-1417
Products: Marketing private label, contract and custom and house brand pharmaceutical products. **SIC:** 5122 (Drugs, Proprietaries & Sundries). **Sales:** $15,000,000 (2000). **Emp:** 180. **Officers:** Roxi Downing, CEO & Chairman of the Board; Paul Strayer, CFO.

■ **19563** ■ **Quality Care Pharmaceuticals Inc.**
3000 W Warner Ave.
Santa Ana, CA 92704
Phone: (714)754-5800
Products: Pharmaceuticals. **SIC:** 5122 (Drugs, Proprietaries & Sundries).

■ **19564** ■ **Quigley Corp.**
Landmark Bldg.
10 S Clinton St.
Doylestown, PA 18901
Phone: (215)345-0919 **Fax:** (215)345-5920
Products: Medicinal and health supplies; Food. **SICs:** 5122 (Drugs, Proprietaries & Sundries); 5141 (Groceries—General Line). **Est:** 1989.

■ **19565** ■ **Rack Service Company Inc.**
2601 Newcomb
Monroe, LA 71211
Phone: (318)322-1445 **Fax:** (318)322-1447
Products: Health and beauty aids. **SIC:** 5122 (Drugs, Proprietaries & Sundries). **Sales:** $4,000,000 (2000). **Emp:** 42.

■ **19566** ■ **Rally Products, Inc.**
109 Hillside Ave.
Londonderry, NH 03053
Phone: (603)434-2123 **Fax:** (603)434-9568
Products: Safety eyewear. **SIC:** 5048 (Ophthalmic Goods).

■ **19567** ■ **Rand-Scot Inc.**
401 Linden Center Dr.
Ft. Collins, CO 80524
Phone: (970)484-7967
Products: Manually operated patient lifts; Disabled patient movers. **SIC:** 5047 (Medical & Hospital Equipment). **Officers:** Joel Lerich, President.

■ **19568** ■ **Ransdell Surgical Inc.**
PO Box 4517
Louisville, KY 40204-0517
Phone: (502)584-6311
Products: Medical, dental, and optical equipment. **SIC:** 5047 (Medical & Hospital Equipment). **Sales:** $59,000,000 (2000). **Emp:** 100.

■ **19569** ■ **Read Optical Inc.**
414 Yellowstone Ave.
Pocatello, ID 83201-4532
Phone: (208)234-4160
Products: Ophthalmic goods. **SIC:** 5048 (Ophthalmic Goods). **Officers:** Reed Howell, President.

■ **19570** ■ **Redline Healthcare Corp.**
8121 10th Ave. N
Golden Valley, MN 55427
Phone: (612)545-5757 **Fax:** (612)545-8207
Products: Medical, dental, and optical equipment. **SIC:** 5047 (Medical & Hospital Equipment). **Sales:** $220,000,000 (2000). **Emp:** 750.

■ **19571** ■ **Fred Reed Optical Co. Inc.**
PO Box 94150
Albuquerque, NM 87199-4150
Phone: (505)265-3531
Products: Ophthalmic goods. **SIC:** 5048 (Ophthalmic Goods).

■ **19572** ■ **Reese Chemical Co.**
10617 Frank Ave.
Cleveland, OH 44106
Phone: (216)231-6441 **Fax:** (216)231-6444
Products: Health and beauty aids. **SIC:** 5122 (Drugs, Proprietaries & Sundries). **Sales:** $3,000,000 (2000). **Emp:** 40.

■ **19573** ■ **Reese Pharmaceutical Co.**
PO Box 1957
Cleveland, OH 44106
Phone: (216)231-6441
Free: (800)321-7178 **Fax:** (216)231-6444
E-mail: reese@apk.net
URL: http://www.reesechemical.com
Products: Pharmaceuticals. **SIC:** 5122 (Drugs, Proprietaries & Sundries). **Est:** 1907. **Sales:** $2,000,000 (2000). **Emp:** 25. **Officers:** George W. Reese III, President; Sandra Reese, Vice President.

■ **19574** ■ **Rehab Equipment Co.**
PO Box 17374
Winston-Salem, NC 27116-7374
Phone: (919)765-6630
Products: Powered wheelchair systems and parts. **SIC:** 5047 (Medical & Hospital Equipment). **Officers:** Rick Espinoza, Contact.

■ **19575** ■ **Rehab Specialties**
308 E 6th St.
Erie, PA 16507
Phone: (814)454-2863
Products: Powered wheelchair systems and parts. **SIC:** 5047 (Medical & Hospital Equipment).

■ **19576** ■ **The Rehab Tech Center**
Rehab Institute of Pittsburgh
6301 Northumberland St.
Pittsburgh, PA 15217
Phone: (412)521-9000
Products: Powered wheelchair systems and parts. **SIC:** 5047 (Medical & Hospital Equipment). **Officers:** Kim Henry, Contact.

■ **19577** ■ **Rehab Technology of Colorado**
5855 Stapleton Dr. N, Ste. A150
Denver, CO 80216
Phone: (303)322-6544
Products: Powered wheelchair systems and parts. **SIC:** 5047 (Medical & Hospital Equipment). **Officers:** Allen Harrison, Contact.

■ **19578** ■ **Respironics Colorado Inc.**
1401 W 122nd Ave.
Westminster, CO 80234
Phone: (303)457-9234
Free: (800)659-9235 **Fax:** (303)255-9000
Products: Medical respiratory equipment. **SIC:** 5047 (Medical & Hospital Equipment). **Sales:** $20,000,000 (2000). **Emp:** 150. **Officers:** Dennis Meteny, CEO & President.

■ **19579** ■ **Rexall Co.**
6111 Broken Sound Pkwy. NW
Boca Raton, FL 33487-3625
Phone: (561)241-9400
Free: (800)255-7399 **Fax:** (561)995-6881
Products: Health and beauty aids. **SIC:** 5122 (Drugs, Proprietaries & Sundries). **Sales:** $65,000,000 (2000). **Emp:** 500.

■ **19580** ■ **RGH Enterprises Inc.**
2300 Edison Blvd.
Twinsburg, OH 44087
Phone: (330)963-6996
Free: (800)321-0591 **Fax:** (330)963-6839
Products: Medical, dental, and optical equipment. **SIC:** 5047 (Medical & Hospital Equipment). **Sales:** $25,000,000 (2000). **Emp:** 102.

■ **19581** ■ **Richmond Optical Co.**
PO Box 4377
Hayward, CA 94540
Phone: (510)783-1420
Free: (800)972-0918 **Fax:** (510)783-3059
Products: Ophthalmic goods. **SIC:** 5048 (Ophthalmic Goods).

■ **19582** ■ **RLI Corp.**
9025 N Lindbergh Dr.
Peoria, IL 61615
Phone: (309)692-1000
Free: (800)331-4929 **Fax:** (309)692-1068
Products: Ophthalmic goods, including contact lenses. **SIC:** 5048 (Ophthalmic Goods). **Est:** 1965. **Sales:** $284,500,000 (2000). **Emp:** 392. **Officers:** Gerald D. Stephens, President; Joseph E. Dondanville, VP & CFO; George C. Schmid, VP of Marketing; Gregory J. Tiemeier, VP of Information Systems; Michael E. Quine, VP of Human Resources.

■ **19583** ■ **Robertson Optical Labs, Inc.**
1812 Washington St.
Columbia, SC 29202
Phone: (803)553-3365 **Fax:** (803)254-1978
Products: Ophthalmic goods. **SIC:** 5048 (Ophthalmic Goods).

■ **19584** ■ **Rochester Drug Cooperative Inc.**
PO Box 1670
Rochester, NY 14603
Phone: (716)271-7220 **Fax:** (716)271-3551
Products: Over-the-counter and prescription drugs, including aspirin, laxatives, and pain relievers. **SIC:** 5122 (Drugs, Proprietaries & Sundries). **Est:** 1905. **Sales:** $60,000,000 (2000). **Emp:** 55. **Officers:** Laurence F. Doud III, President; L. Carlascio, Treasurer; Alward M. Emmans, General Mgr.; David Rosen, Dir. of Data Processing; Dorothy Graham, Dir of Human Resources.

■ **19585** ■ **Rocky Mountain Instrument Co**
106 Laser Dr., Ste. 1
Lafayette, CO 80026
Phone: (303)651-2211 **Fax:** (303)664-5001
Products: Ooptical instruments and lenses. **SIC:** 5048 (Ophthalmic Goods). **Officers:** Yubong Hahn, President.

■ **19586** ■ **Rorer West Inc.**
655 Spice Island Dr.
Sparks, NV 89431
Phone: (702)353-4100 **Fax:** (702)353-4109
Products: Pharmeceuticals. **SIC:** 5122 (Drugs, Proprietaries & Sundries). **Est:** 1903. **Sales:** $170,000,000 (2000). **Emp:** 12. **Officers:** Roy W. Kemp, General Mgr.

■ **19587** ■ **Rosemont Pharmaceutical Corp.**
301 S Cherokee St.
Denver, CO 80223
Phone: (303)733-7207
Free: (800)445-8091 **Fax:** (303)733-9793
Products: Generic pharmaceutical products. **SIC:** 5122 (Drugs, Proprietaries & Sundries). **Sales:** $16,200,000 (2000). **Emp:** 95. **Officers:** Donald Waters, President.

■ 19588 ■ Rota Systems Inc.
PO Box 361
Derby, KS 67037-0361
Phone: (316)788-4531
Free: (800)835-1136 **Fax:** (316)788-1982
Products: Ophthalmic goods. **SIC:** 5048 (Ophthalmic Goods). **Officers:** Hollis Baker, Chairman of the Board.

■ 19589 ■ Rozin Optical Export Corp.
33-01 38th Ave.
Long Island City, NY 11101
Phone: (718)786-1201 **Fax:** (718)786-1406
Products: Frames; Optical supplies. **SIC:** 5048 (Ophthalmic Goods). **Est:** 1920. **Sales:** $13,000,000 (2000). **Emp:** 52. **Officers:** A. Rozin, President; Rudolph Kochman, Dir. of Marketing; Irina Kanevsky, Dir. of Systems.

■ 19590 ■ Rx Medical Services Corp.
888 E Las Olas Blvd., Ste. 210
Ft. Lauderdale, FL 33301
Phone: (954)462-1711 **Fax:** (954)462-5411
Products: Healthcare services, the operation and management of hospital and clinics and the wholesale distribution of pharmaceutical products. **SIC:** 5122 (Drugs, Proprietaries & Sundries). **Sales:** $20,000,000 (2000). **Emp:** 341. **Officers:** Mihael L. Goldberg, CEO & Chairman of the Board; Cotton S. Mather, CFO.

■ 19591 ■ Safety Optical
2110 Congress Pkwy.
PO Box 828
Athens, TN 37303
Phone: (423)745-9420
Free: (800)572-7311 **Fax:** 800-525-1439
Products: Ophthalmic goods. **SIC:** 5048 (Ophthalmic Goods).

■ 19592 ■ Salem Optical Co. Inc.
915 Brookstown Ave.
Winston-Salem, NC 27101
Phone: (919)725-4286
Free: (800)642-0493 **Fax:** (919)761-8615
Products: Ophthalmic goods. **SIC:** 5048 (Ophthalmic Goods).

■ 19593 ■ Salt Lake Optical Inc.
315 E 3rd St. S
PO Box 297
Salt Lake City, UT 84111
Phone: (801)328-4791
Products: Ophthalmic goods. **SIC:** 5048 (Ophthalmic Goods).

■ 19594 ■ Schein Pharmaceutical Inc.
100 Campus Dr.
Florham Park, NJ 07932
Phone: (973)593-5500 **Fax:** (973)593-5590
Products: Generic medication. **SIC:** 5122 (Drugs, Proprietaries & Sundries). **Est:** 1965. **Sales:** $476,000,000 (2000). **Emp:** 1,900. **Officers:** Martin Sperber, CEO & Chairman of the Board; Dariush Ashrafi, Exec. VP & CFO; Bob Shanks, Dir. of Marketing; Paul Kleutghen, VP of Operations; Paul Kirkwood, VP of Human Resources.

■ 19595 ■ Scherer Laboratories Inc.
2301 Ohio Dr., Ste. 234
Plano, TX 75093
Phone: (972)612-6225
Products: Pharmaceuticals. **SIC:** 5122 (Drugs, Proprietaries & Sundries). **Sales:** $1,000,000 (2000). **Emp:** 1. **Officers:** John Girardi, VP & General Mgr.

■ 19596 ■ Schmidt Laboratories
PO Box 1264
St. Cloud, MN 56302
Phone: (320)255-9787
Free: (800)962-5037 **Fax:** 800-553-8540
Products: Ophthalmic goods. **SIC:** 5048 (Ophthalmic Goods).

■ 19597 ■ Schneider Optics Inc.
285 Oser Ave.
Hauppauge, NY 11788
Phone: (631)761-5000 **Fax:** (631)761-5090
E-mail: info@schneideroptics.com
URL: http://www.schneideroptics.com
Products: Optical lenses and optical glass filters. **SIC:** 5048 (Ophthalmic Goods). **Sales:** $6,000,000 (2000). **Emp:** 15. **Officers:** Ron Leven, Sr. VP; Dwight Lindsey, Sr. VP. **Former Name:** Schneider Corp.

■ 19598 ■ Schroeder Optical Company Inc.
PO Box 12100
Roanoke, VA 24022-2100
Phone: (540)345-6736
Free: (800)628-4146 **Fax:** 800-344-4329
Products: Ophthalmic goods; Optometric equipment and supplies. **SIC:** 5048 (Ophthalmic Goods). **Officers:** Robert Schroeder, President.

■ 19599 ■ Scotland Yard
1001 Columbia St.
Newport, KY 41071
Phone: (606)581-0140
Free: (800)957-3540 **Fax:** (606)491-2931
Products: Veterinary products. **SIC:** 5047 (Medical & Hospital Equipment). **Sales:** $100,000 (2000). **Emp:** 1.

■ 19600 ■ Scott Drug Co.
PO Box 34649
Charlotte, NC 28234
Phone: (704)375-9841
Products: Over-the-counter pharmaceuticals. **SIC:** 5122 (Drugs, Proprietaries & Sundries). **Est:** 1891. **Sales:** $25,000,000 (2000). **Emp:** 75. **Officers:** Donald H. Ahern, CEO & Finance Officer.

■ 19601 ■ Sealey Optical Co.
3611 Maryland Ct.
C-3370
Richmond, VA 23233
Phone: (804)747-8700
Free: (800)229-5367 **Fax:** (804)270-1374
Products: Ophthalmic goods. **SIC:** 5048 (Ophthalmic Goods).

■ 19602 ■ Segura Products Co.
406 Fulton St.
Middlesex, NJ 08846-1527
Phone: (732)968-2295 **Fax:** (732)424-1988
Products: Pharmaceuticals; Perfumes; Skin and hair care products. **SIC:** 5122 (Drugs, Proprietaries & Sundries). **Est:** 1979. **Sales:** $25,000,000 (2000). **Emp:** 3. **Officers:** C.E. Marshall; Ed Marshall, Customer Service Contact. **Alternate Name:** Selene Export Company.

■ 19603 ■ Anthony Seow Company Inc.
PO Box 1284
Orem, UT 84057
Phone: (801)225-6612 **Fax:** (801)224-3607
E-mail: aseow1@aol.com
Products: Pharmaceuticals; Health and nutritional products; Cosmetics and skin care products; Encapsulating machine; Herbs and herb extracts. **SIC:** 5122 (Drugs, Proprietaries & Sundries). **Est:** 1983. **Officers:** Anthony Seow, Manager.

■ 19604 ■ Sermel Inc.
PO Box 359
Indianola, IA 50125-0359
Phone: (515)961-4222
E-mail: sermel@aol.com
URL: http://www.members.aol.com/sermel/index.html
Products: Ophthalmic goods. **SIC:** 5048 (Ophthalmic Goods). **Est:** 1970. **Officers:** Red Kuhn, President.

■ 19605 ■ Shared Service Systems Inc.
1725 S 20th St.
Omaha, NE 68108
Phone: (402)536-5300
Products: Medical supplies. **SIC:** 5047 (Medical & Hospital Equipment). **Sales:** $36,000,000 (2000). **Emp:** 140. **Officers:** Alvin Chamberlain, President.

■ 19606 ■ Shaws-Healthtick
1542 NE Weidler St.
Portland, OR 97232-1411
Phone: (503)288-4226
Products: Foam for prosthetic breasts; Swimming suits, bras, and maternity hosiery; Orthopedic garments and back braces. **SICs:** 5047 (Medical & Hospital Equipment); 5137 (Women's/Children's Clothing). **Emp:** 11.

■ 19607 ■ Sheridan Optical Co.
108 Clinton Ave.
PO Box 8
Pitman, NJ 08071
Phone: (609)582-0963 **Fax:** (609)582-1970
Products: Ophthalmic goods. **SIC:** 5048 (Ophthalmic Goods).

■ 19608 ■ Sierra Optical
4757 Morena Blvd.
San Diego, CA 92117-3462
Phone: (619)490-3490
Free: (800)544-2015 **Fax:** 800-748-5801
Products: Ophthalmic goods. **SIC:** 5048 (Ophthalmic Goods).

■ 19609 ■ Sietec Inc.
320 Westway, Ste. 530
Arlington, TX 76018-1099
Phone: (817)468-3377 **Fax:** (817)472-2907
Products: Parts and accessories for medical imaging equipment. **SIC:** 5047 (Medical & Hospital Equipment). **Sales:** $2,000,000 (2000). **Emp:** 4. **Officers:** Michael G. Puls, President; Thomas Hoefert, CFO.

■ 19610 ■ Sigma America
6024 Mission St.
Daly City, CA 94014
Phone: (650)992-1820
Free: (800)433-5443 **Fax:** (650)992-1866
Products: Sunglasses; Binoculars. **SIC:** 5048 (Ophthalmic Goods).

■ 19611 ■ Sigma-Tau Pharmaceuticals Inc.
800 S Frederick Ave.
Gaithersburg, MD 20877
Phone: (301)948-1041
Free: (800)447-0169 **Fax:** (301)948-1862
URL: http://www.sigmatau.com
Products: Pharmaceuticals for carnitine deficiency. **SIC:** 5122 (Drugs, Proprietaries & Sundries). **Sales:** $56,000,000 (1999). **Emp:** 101. **Officers:** C. Kenneth Mehring, Exec. VP & General Mgr.; Don Zelm, VP of Finance.

■ 19612 ■ Silhouette Optical Ltd.
266 Union St.
Northvale, NJ 07647
Phone: (201)768-8600
Products: Eyeglass frames. **SIC:** 5048 (Ophthalmic Goods).

■ 19613 ■ Silton USA Corp.
64-68 185th St.
Fresh Meadows, NY 11365
Phone: (718)445-8832 **Fax:** (718)359-3634
E-mail: silton@accesshub.net
Products: Sunglasses and reading glasses; Optical frames. **SIC:** 5048 (Ophthalmic Goods). **Est:** 1987.

■ 19614 ■ Singer Optical Co. Inc.
PO Box 3557
Evansville, IN 47734-3557
Phone: (812)423-1179 **Fax:** (812)423-1179
Products: Ophthalmic goods. **SIC:** 5048 (Ophthalmic Goods). **Officers:** Roger Singer, President.

■ 19615 ■ Siouxland Ophthalmics Lab Inc.
415 E 9th St.
Sheldon, IA 51201
Phone: (712)324-4352
Free: (800)831-8583 **Fax:** 800-628-3584
Products: Ophthalmic goods. **SIC:** 5048 (Ophthalmic Goods).

■ 19616 ■ Smith Drug Co.
PO Box 1779
Spartanburg, SC 29304
Phone: (864)582-1216 **Fax:** (864)591-0333
URL: http://www.smithdrugco.com
Products: Pharmaceuticals. **SIC:** 5122 (Drugs, Proprietaries & Sundries). **Est:** 1944. **Sales:** $400,000,000 (1999). **Emp:** 179. **Officers:** Ken Couch, President; Jimmy Wilson, CFO; Ron Bailey, VP of Marketing; Bobby Hawkins, VP of Operations; Rick Simerly, VP of Business Development.

■ 19617 ■ Socoloff Health Supply Inc.
6665 Corners Industrial, Ste. C
Norcross, GA 30092-3661
Phone: (404)448-8541 **Fax:** (404)448-7433
Products: Ophthalmic equipment, including supplies and surgical goods. **SIC:** 5048 (Ophthalmic Goods).
Officers: Morris Socoloff, President.

■ 19618 ■ Soderburg Optical Services
230 Eva St.
St. Paul, MN 55164
Phone: (612)291-1400 **Free:** (800)755-5655
E-mail: cogiles@ix.netcom.com
URL: http://www.soseyes.com
Products: Ophthalmic goods including contact lenses and refracting equipment. **SIC:** 5048 (Ophthalmic Goods). **Est:** 1945. **Sales:** $36,000,000 (2000). **Emp:** 360. **Officers:** Aloys Willenbring, CEO & President.

■ 19619 ■ Sola International Inc.
2420 Sand Hill Rd. Ste. 200
Menlo Park, CA 94025
Phone: (650)324-6868 **Fax:** (650)324-6850
Products: Ophthalmic eyeglass lenses. **SIC:** 5048 (Ophthalmic Goods). **Sales:** $529,800,000 (1999). **Emp:** 7,450. **Officers:** John E. Heine, CEO & President; Steven M. Neil, Exec. VP & CFO.

■ 19620 ■ Somerset Pharmaceuticals Inc.
5215 W Laurel St.
Tampa, FL 33607-1728
Phone: (813)288-0040
Products: Eldepryl drugs. **SIC:** 5122 (Drugs, Proprietaries & Sundries). **Sales:** $160,000,000 (2000). **Emp:** 42. **Officers:** Eric Ragghianti, Controller.

■ 19621 ■ Sound Optical
PO Box 1798
Tacoma, WA 98401
Phone: (253)474-0610
Free: (800)562-8135 **Fax:** (253)474-1436
Products: Ophthalmic goods. **SIC:** 5048 (Ophthalmic Goods). **Est:** 1954. **Emp:** 70.

■ 19622 ■ South Border Imports, Inc.
6925 216th St. SW, Ste. D
Lynnwood, WA 98036-7358
Phone: (425)776-1151
Free: (800)216-3362 **Fax:** (425)776-0275
Products: Sunglasses; Reading glasses; Energy snacks. **SIC:** 5048 (Ophthalmic Goods). **Est:** 1985. **Emp:** 12. **Officers:** Joseph McLaughlin, President. **Doing Business As:** Emerald Sunglass Co.

■ 19623 ■ Southeastern Optical Corp.
PO Box 12700
Roanoke, VA 24027
Phone: (540)989-8644
Free: (800)456-0088 **Fax:** 800-937-2638
Products: Ophthalmic goods. **SIC:** 5048 (Ophthalmic Goods). **Officers:** George Shields, President.

■ 19624 ■ Southern Micro Instruments
1700 Enterprise Way, Ste. 112
Marietta, GA 30067
Phone: (770)956-0343
Free: (800)241-3312 **Fax:** (770)953-4490
E-mail: sales@southernmicro.com
URL: http://www.southernmicro.com
Products: Optical instruments; Microscopes; Imaging Systems. **SIC:** 5048 (Ophthalmic Goods). **Est:** 1979. **Emp:** 37. **Officers:** Horst Van Schellenbeck, President.

■ 19625 ■ Southern Optical Co.
103 J & L Dr.
PO Box 8006
Goldsboro, NC 27530-8006
Phone: (919)735-2084
Free: (800)672-4780 **Fax:** (919)734-8552
Products: Ophthalmic goods. **SIC:** 5048 (Ophthalmic Goods).

■ 19626 ■ Southern Optical Co.
PO Box 2227
Greenville, SC 29602
Phone: (864)232-6762
Free: (800)999-4805 **Fax:** (864)233-7563
Products: Ophthalmic goods. **SIC:** 5048 (Ophthalmic Goods).

■ 19627 ■ Southern Optical, Inc.
PO Box 21328
Greensboro, NC 27420
Phones: (919)272-8146 (919)275-0498
Free: (800)909-4806
Products: Ophthalmic goods. **SIC:** 5048 (Ophthalmic Goods).

■ 19628 ■ Southern Prosthetic Supply Co.
PO Box 406
Alpharetta, GA 30009
Phone: (770)442-9870
Free: (800)767-7776 **Fax:** (770)442-0379
Products: Medical supplies, including prosthetics and orthotics. **SIC:** 5047 (Medical & Hospital Equipment). **Est:** 1950. **Sales:** $45,000,000 (2000). **Emp:** 75. **Officers:** Ivan Sabel, Chairman of the Board; Connie Withers, VP of Sales; A.G. Tidwell, COO.

■ 19629 ■ Southern Wholesale Co.
PO Box 5151
Rome, GA 30162-5151
Phone: (706)235-8155 **Fax:** (706)235-8158
Products: Drug, toy, hobby and variety items. **SICs:** 5199 (Nondurable Goods Nec); 5122 (Drugs, Proprietaries & Sundries); 5092 (Toys & Hobby Goods & Supplies). **Sales:** $81,000,000 (1993). **Emp:** 300. **Officers:** John Howard Jr., President; James Brown, Controller.

■ 19630 ■ SpaceLabs Medical Inc.
PO Box 97013
Redmond, WA 98073
Phone: (425)882-3700 **Fax:** (425)885-4877
Products: Patient monitoring and clinical information systems. **SIC:** 5047 (Medical & Hospital Equipment). **Sales:** $274,200,000 (2000). **Emp:** 1,500. **Officers:** Carl Lombardi, Chairman of the Board; James Richmar, CFO.

■ 19631 ■ Spectranetics Corp.
96 Talamine Ct.
Colorado Springs, CO 80907
Phone: (719)633-8333
Free: (800)633-2248 **Fax:** (719)633-2248
Products: Laser systems and catheters used for heart angioplasty surgery. **SIC:** 5047 (Medical & Hospital Equipment). **Sales:** $27,800,000 (1999). **Emp:** 192. **Officers:** Joseph A. Largey, CEO & President; Paul samek, VP of Finance.

■ 19632 ■ Spectrum Labs Inc.
PO Box 1685
Mesa, AZ 85211
Phone: (480)464-8971 **Fax:** (480)898-0611
Products: Testing laboratory and services; veterinary dermapathological supplies. **SIC:** 5047 (Medical & Hospital Equipment). **Officers:** Mervyn Levin, President.

■ 19633 ■ SPRI Medical Products Corp.
Ballert International Div.
642 Anthony Trl
Northbrook, IL 60062-2540
Phone: (847)272-7211
Free: (800)345-3456 **Fax:** (847)272-0420
Products: Orthopedic appliances (braces), including parts; Medical equipment. **SIC:** 5047 (Medical & Hospital Equipment). **Est:** 1980. **Emp:** 10. **Officers:** M. Kesselman, President.

■ 19634 ■ SST Corp.
PO Box 1649
Clifton, NJ 07012
Phone: (973)473-4300 **Fax:** (973)473-4326
Products: Bulk pharmaceuticals, vitamins, fine chemicals and chemical intermediates. **SICs:** 5122 (Drugs, Proprietaries & Sundries); 5169 (Chemicals & Allied Products Nec). **Sales:** $75,000,000 (2000). **Emp:** 36. **Officers:** George H. Turner II, President; Mark Goldberg, Controller.

■ 19635 ■ Standard Drug Co.
1 CVS Dr., No. E
Woonsocket, RI 02895-0988
Phone: (401)765-1500
Products: Over-the-counter and prescription drugs. **SIC:** 5122 (Drugs, Proprietaries & Sundries). **Est:** 1919. **Officers:** Charles Conaway, President.

■ 19636 ■ Stanis Trading Corp.
PO Box 562
Shoreham, NY 11786
Phone: (516)744-1208 **Fax:** (516)744-4970
Products: Medical and surgical dressings; Communications equipment. **SICs:** 5047 (Medical & Hospital Equipment); 5065 (Electronic Parts & Equipment Nec). **Officers:** Y.A. Shikari, President.

■ 19637 ■ State Optical Company, Inc.
1144 Fort St. Mall
Honolulu, HI 96813
Phone: (808)531-2761
Products: Eye glasses; Contact lenses. **SIC:** 5048 (Ophthalmic Goods).

■ 19638 ■ Steinberg Brothers Inc.
PO Box 205
Amsterdam, NY 12010-0205
Phone: (212)246-0808 **Fax:** (518)843-0437
Products: Latex gloves. **SIC:** 5122 (Drugs, Proprietaries & Sundries). **Sales:** $6,000,000 (2000). **Emp:** 499.

■ 19639 ■ Stone Medical Supply Corp.
PO Box 1701
Mt. Vernon, NY 10551-1701
Phone: (516)783-6262 **Fax:** (516)783-6826
Products: Medical supplies. **SIC:** 5047 (Medical & Hospital Equipment). **Est:** 1964. **Sales:** $8,000,000 (2000). **Emp:** 40. **Officers:** Andrew D. Stone, President & Chairman of the Board; Jan D. Bengelsdorf, Treasurer; Norman Shore, Dir. of Sales.

■ 19640 ■ Stuart's Hospital Supply Co.
1 Stuart Plz.
Greensburg, PA 15601
Phone: (412)271-3200
Products: Medical and surgical supplies, including bandages and scalpels; Hospital beds; First aid kits. **SIC:** 5047 (Medical & Hospital Equipment).

■ 19641 ■ Style Eyes Inc.
833 W 16th St.
Newport Beach, CA 92663
Phone: (949)548-5355 **Fax:** (949)548-5655
E-mail: info@styleeyes.com
URL: http://www.styleeyes.com
Products: Sunglasses. **SIC:** 5048 (Ophthalmic Goods). **Est:** 1977. **Sales:** $10,000,000 (2000). **Emp:** 25. **Officers:** P. Kahn, President. **Former Name:** Style Eyes of California.

■ 19642 ■ Suburban Ostomy Supply Company Inc.
75 October Hill Rd.
Holliston, MA 01746
Phone: (508)429-1000
Products: Medical supplies to the home health care industry. **SIC:** 5047 (Medical & Hospital Equipment). **Sales:** $94,400,000 (2000). **Emp:** 251. **Officers:** Donald H. Benovitz, President; Stephen N. Aschettino, VP, CFO & Treasurer.

■ 19643 ■ Sun Design Ltd.
PO Box 35
Watertown, CT 06795-0035
Phone: (860)274-9830
Free: (800)322-6748 **Fax:** (860)274-7694
E-mail: tabery@gate.net
URL: http://www.sundesigne.simplenet.com
Products: Reading glasses; Sunglasses. **SIC:** 5048 (Ophthalmic Goods). **Est:** 1982. **Sales:** $1,000,000 (2000). **Emp:** 12. **Officers:** John Hutchinson, President.

■ 19644 ■ Superior Pharmaceutical Co.
1385 Kemper Meadow
Cincinnati, OH 45240
Phone: (513)851-3600
Free: (800)826-5035 **Fax:** (513)742-6472
E-mail: superpharm@aol.com
URL: http://www.superpharm.com
Products: Pharmaceuticals; Generic goods. **SIC:** 5122 (Drugs, Proprietaries & Sundries). **Est:** 1986. **Sales:** $32,000,000 (2000). **Emp:** 65. **Officers:** Dennis B. Smith, CEO & President; William Van Metre, Dir. of Wholesale Relations; Greg Stofko, Dir. of Government Bids and Contracts.

■ 19645 ■ Swift Instruments, Inc.
952 Dorchester Ave.
Boston, MA 02125
Phone: (617)436-2960
Free: (800)446-1116 **Fax:** (617)436-3232
E-mail: swiftl@tiac.net
URL: http://www.swift-optics.com
Products: Weather and optical instruments, including microscopes, prism binoculars, spotting scopes, astronomical telescopes, riflescopes, and specialty magnifiers. **SIC:** 5048 (Ophthalmic Goods). **Est:** 1926. **Sales:** $14,000,000 (2000). **Emp:** 50. **Officers:** Humphrey Swift, President; Harold Mercer, VP & Treasurer; Bruce K. Mercer, VP & Sales Mgr.; Jane Y. Gilliland, Customer Service Contact.

■ 19646 ■ Symd Inc.
99-1253 Halawa Valley St.
Aiea, HI 96701-3281
Phone: (808)486-2933 **Fax:** (808)486-6458
Products: Ophthalmic goods. **SIC:** 5048 (Ophthalmic Goods). **Officers:** Yorio Shigemura, Chairman of the Board.

■ 19647 ■ Tactilitics Inc.
4760 Walnut St. Ste. 105
Boulder, CO 80301
Phone: (303)442-7746
Products: Radio frequency monitor systems for fall prevention in healthcare facilities. **SIC:** 5047 (Medical & Hospital Equipment). **Officers:** George Beggs, President.

■ 19648 ■ Target Industries Inc.
1 Pleasant St.
Cohasset, MA 02025
Phone: (781)383-6440
Free: (800)225-1812 **Fax:** (781)383-2589
E-mail: marketing@abboptical.com
URL: http://www.abboptical.com
Products: Optical products. **SIC:** 5048 (Ophthalmic Goods). **Est:** 1972. **Sales:** $50,000,000 (2000). **Emp:** 60.

■ 19649 ■ Taylor Optical Supplies Inc.
28 W Adams Ave., Ste. 1005
Detroit, MI 48226-1617
Phone: (313)962-6595 **Fax:** (313)962-5904
Products: Ophthalmic goods; Optometric equipment and supplies. **SIC:** 5048 (Ophthalmic Goods). **Officers:** Ralph Marco, President.

■ 19650 ■ Technical Marketing Inc.
1776 N Pine Island Rd., Ste. 306
Plantation, FL 33322
Phone: (954)370-0855 **Fax:** (954)474-3866
Products: Health and beauty aids. **SIC:** 5122 (Drugs, Proprietaries & Sundries). **Sales:** $1,000,000 (2000). **Emp:** 5.

■ 19651 ■ Tennessee Wholesale Drug Co.
200 Cumberland Bend
Nashville, TN 37228
Phone: (615)244-8110 **Fax:** (615)254-1565
Products: Drugs, including over-the-counter medications. **SIC:** 5122 (Drugs, Proprietaries & Sundries). **Sales:** $60,000,000 (2000). **Emp:** 400. **Officers:** James E. Richards, President; George Rodford, Controller; Mike Hohlfeld, VP of Sales.

■ 19652 ■ Tetra Sales U.S.A.
201 Tabor Rd.
Morris Plains, NJ 07950
Phone: (973)540-2000 **Fax:** (973)540-4453
Products: Pharmaceuticals; Consumer health products; Gum and candies. **SICs:** 5122 (Drugs, Proprietaries & Sundries); 5145 (Confectionery). **Sales:** $40,000,000 (2000). **Emp:** 35. **Officers:** Alan Mintz, President.

■ 19653 ■ Teva Pharmaceutical USA
650 Cathill Rd.
Sellersville, PA 18960
Phone: (215)256-8400 **Fax:** (215)256-7855
Products: Generic prescription pharmaceuticals. **SIC:** 5122 (Drugs, Proprietaries & Sundries). **Sales:** $240,000,000 (2000). **Emp:** 1,200. **Officers:** William A. Fletcher, CEO; Peter Terreri, Sr. VP & CFO; Paul Simon, Dir. of Marketing; Ann Overton, Dir. of Data Processing; Marge Cauley, Dir of Human Resources.

■ 19654 ■ Thau-Nolde Inc.
1884 Lackland Hill Pkwy., Ste. 9
St. Louis, MO 63146-3569
Phone: (314)531-6660
Products: Dental supplies, including toothbrushes and dental floss. **SIC:** 5047 (Medical & Hospital Equipment). **Est:** 1909. **Sales:** $4,000,000 (2000). **Emp:** 35. **Officers:** P.T. Rudloff, President; Michael Thau, Treasurer & Secty.; Jack G. Sanders, Vice President.

■ 19655 ■ F.D. Titus and Sons Inc.
20420 Business Pkwy.
Walnut, CA 91789-2938
Phone: (626)330-4571
Products: Medical supplies; Medical office furniture. **SIC:** 5047 (Medical & Hospital Equipment).

■ 19656 ■ TMC Orthopedic Supplies Inc.
4747 Bellaire Blvd.
Bellaire, TX 77401
Phone: (713)669-1800
Products: Orthopedic equipment. **SIC:** 5047 (Medical & Hospital Equipment). **Sales:** $5,400,000 (2000). **Emp:** 38. **Officers:** Joe Sansone, President.

■ 19657 ■ TNT Optical Supply, Inc.
8035 McDermitt Dr., Apt. 86
Davison, MI 48423-2970
Phone: (810)793-6261
Free: (800)521-3937 **Fax:** (810)793-2952
Products: Optical supplies. **SIC:** 5048 (Ophthalmic Goods). **Est:** 1982. **Emp:** 10. **Officers:** Thomas Hanson, President.

■ 19658 ■ Toshiba America Medical Systems Inc.
PO Box 2068
Tustin, CA 92780
Phone: (714)730-5000 **Fax:** (714)730-4022
Products: Medical equipment; scanners, MRI machines and X-ray machines. **SIC:** 5047 (Medical & Hospital Equipment). **Sales:** $85,000,000 (2000). **Emp:** 250. **Officers:** Masamichi Katsurada, President; Kenji Saito, VP of Finance.

■ 19659 ■ Total Orthopedic Div.
18978 Bonanza Way
Gaithersburg, MD 20879-1513
Phone: (301)840-9027 **Fax:** (301)840-9411
Products: Medical and orthopedic supplies. **SIC:** 5047 (Medical & Hospital Equipment). **Est:** 1976. **Sales:** $1,000,000 (2000). **Emp:** 7. **Officers:** Michael J. Hanik, CEO; George Beck, CFO; Leeja Nichols, Dir. of Marketing & Sales; Bruce Small, Dir. of Information Systems.

■ 19660 ■ Tri-Lite Optical
256 Burgen Blvd.
West Paterson, NJ 07424
Phones: (201)337-1717 (973)256-1155
Products: Ophthalmic goods. **SIC:** 5048 (Ophthalmic Goods).

■ 19661 ■ Tri-State Optical Co. Inc.
PO Box 30005
Shreveport, LA 71130-0005
Phone: (318)425-7432
Free: (800)621-1139 **Fax:** (318)425-8797
Products: Ophthalmic goods and frames. **SIC:** 5048 (Ophthalmic Goods). **Est:** 1952. **Officers:** Betty McCraw, President.

■ 19662 ■ Triconic Labs Inc.
7 Canal St.
Center Moriches, NY 11934
Phone: (516)878-2333
Free: (800)281-5367 **Fax:** (516)878-2721
Products: Ophthalmic goods. **SIC:** 5048 (Ophthalmic Goods).

■ 19663 ■ Trident Medical International
7687 Winton Dr.
Indianapolis, IN 46268
Phone: (317)870-4461
Free: (800)870-4467 **Fax:** (317)876-3643
Products: piratory therapy and anasthesia products. **SICs:** 5047 (Medical & Hospital Equipment); 5065 (Electronic Parts & Equipment Nec); 5023 (Homefurnishings); 5045 (Computers, Peripherals & Software). **Sales:** $100,000,000 (2000). **Emp:** 50. **Officers:** Robert Richmond, CEO; David Weiseman, Controller.

■ 19664 ■ Trioptics, Inc.
PO Box 2138
Milwaukee, WI 53201
Phone: (414)481-9822
Free: (800)288-3890 **Fax:** (414)481-8772
Products: Ophthalmic goods. **SIC:** 5048 (Ophthalmic Goods).

■ 19665 ■ Troy Biologicals Inc.
1238 Rankin St.
Troy, MI 48083-6004
Phone: (248)585-9720
Free: (800)521-0445 **Fax:** (248)585-2490
E-mail: info@troybio.com
URL: http://www.troybio.com
Products: Medical supplies. **SIC:** 5047 (Medical & Hospital Equipment). **Est:** 1976. **Sales:** $8,000,000 (2000). **Emp:** 25. **Officers:** Robert Ricketts, President; Tom Ricketts, e-mail: tom@troybio.com; Janine Deighan, Dir. of Merchandising, e-mail: janiae@troybio.com.

■ 19666 ■ Tuscaloosa Optical Dispensary
PO Box 1790
Tuscaloosa, AL 35403-1790
Phone: (205)752-2564
Products: Ophthalmic goods. **SIC:** 5048 (Ophthalmic Goods). **Officers:** Wayne Anders, Secretary.

■ 19667 ■ Twin City Optical Inc.
PO Box 267
Minneapolis, MN 55440
Phone: (612)546-6126 **Fax:** (612)546-8989
Products: Ophthalmic goods. **SIC:** 5048 (Ophthalmic Goods).

■ 19668 ■ UDL Laboratories, Inc.
PO Box 2629
Loves Park, IL 61132-2629
Phone: (815)282-1201
Products: Pharmaceuticals. **SIC:** 5122 (Drugs, Proprietaries & Sundries). **Emp:** 150. **Officers:** John W. Ford, Sr. VP of Sales & Marketing; Sherri MacDonald, Sr. VP of Operations.

■ 19669 ■ Ultra Lens
6611 NW 15th Way
Ft. Lauderdale, FL 33309
Phone: (954)975-8600
Free: (800)327-3718 **Fax:** (954)975-3352
Products: Ophthalmic goods. **SIC:** 5048 (Ophthalmic Goods).

■ 19670 ■ Uni-Patch
PO Box 271
Wabasha, MN 55981
Phone: (612)565-2601
Free: (800)328-9454 **Fax:** (612)565-3971
URL: http://www.uni-patch.com
Products: Electromedical supplies. **SIC:** 5047 (Medical & Hospital Equipment). **Est:** 1978. **Sales:** $12,000,000 (2000). **Emp:** 200.

■ 19671 ■ Unichem Industries Inc.
1 Bayberry Close
Piscataway, NJ 08854
Phone: (732)463-8442 **Fax:** (732)463-9343
E-mail: unichem@juno.com
Products: Pharmaceuticals; Chemicals; Metal scraps; Plastic materials; Stainless steel sheets and coils; Plastic scraps. **SICs:** 5122 (Drugs, Proprietaries & Sundries); 5169 (Chemicals & Allied Products Nec); 5051 (Metals Service Centers & Offices); 5162 (Plastics Materials & Basic Shapes). **Est:** 1982. **Emp:** 5. **Officers:** Kishore Sanghvi, President.

■ 19672 ■ **Union Standard Equipment Co.**
801 E 141st St.
Bronx, NY 10454
Phone: (718)585-0200 **Fax:** (718)993-2650
URL: http://www.unionmachinery.com
Products: Food & pharmaceutical packaging and processing machinery. **SICs:** 5084 (Industrial Machinery & Equipment); 5122 (Drugs, Proprietaries & Sundries). **Est:** 1912. **Sales:** $10,000,000 (1999). **Emp:** 100. **Officers:** Richard Greenberg, Vice President.

■ 19673 ■ **Uniquity**
PO Box 10
Galt, CA 95632-0010
Phone: (209)745-2111
Free: (800)521-7771 **Fax:** (209)745-4430
E-mail: uniquity@lodinet.com
Products: Mental health products; Anger management tools; Vibrator attachments. **SIC:** 5047 (Medical & Hospital Equipment). **Est:** 1971. **Emp:** 3. **Officers:** Reuven E. Epstein, Owner.

■ 19674 ■ **United Exporters**
1095 Market St., Ste. 701
San Francisco, CA 94103
Phone: (415)255-9393 **Fax:** (415)255-9392
Products: Medical equipment and supplies; Electronic components; Industrial products. **SICs:** 5047 (Medical & Hospital Equipment); 5065 (Electronic Parts & Equipment Nec). **Est:** 1947. **Sales:** $3,000,000 (2000). **Emp:** 4. **Officers:** M. De Hes-Berkowitz, President.

■ 19675 ■ **United Medical Supply Company Inc.**
5117 NE Pkwy.
Ft. Worth, TX 76106
Phone: (817)626-8261 **Fax:** (817)626-8425
Products: Medical and hospital supplies, including scalpels and gauze. **SIC:** 5047 (Medical & Hospital Equipment).

■ 19676 ■ **United Optical Co.**
PO Box 6400
Salt Lake City, UT 84106
Phone: (801)486-1001
Products: Ophthalmic goods; Optometric equipment and supplies. **SIC:** 5048 (Ophthalmic Goods). **Officers:** Michael Simmons, President.

■ 19677 ■ **United Optical Corp.**
PO Box 1147
Shawnee, OK 74802-1147
Phone: (405)275-1228
Free: (800)553-5150 **Fax:** 800-553-5166
Products: Ophthalmic frames; Ophthalmic goods. **SIC:** 5048 (Ophthalmic Goods). **Officers:** W. James, CEO.

■ 19678 ■ **United Research Laboratories Inc.**
1100 Orthodox St.
Philadelphia, PA 19124
Phone: (215)288-6500
Free: (800)523-3684 **Fax:** (215)807-1090
URL: http://www.urlmutual.com
Products: Generic pharmaceuticals. **SIC:** 5122 (Drugs, Proprietaries & Sundries). **Est:** 1946. **Sales:** $150,000,000 (2000). **Emp:** 350. **Officers:** Richard H. Roberts Ph.D., President; Gregory Hayer, VP of Sales; Michael Gurchiek, Sr. VP of Sales & Marketing.

■ 19679 ■ **U.S. Clinical Products**
2552 Summit Ave., No. 406
Plano, TX 75074
Phone: (214)424-6268 **Fax:** (214)644-0081
Products: Disposable masks, gloves, shoe covers, and waste bags. **SIC:** 5047 (Medical & Hospital Equipment). **Est:** 1981. **Sales:** $7,000,000 (2000). **Emp:** 27. **Officers:** Kenneth Moore, General Mgr.

■ 19680 ■ **United States Medical Corp.**
7205 E Kemper Rd.
Cincinnati, OH 45249-1030
Phone: (513)489-5595
Products: Medical, dental, and optical equipment. **SIC:** 5047 (Medical & Hospital Equipment). **Sales:** $12,000,000 (2000). **Emp:** 50.

■ 19681 ■ **United States Pharmaceutical Corp.**
96 North 5th West, Ste. 200
Bountiful, UT 84010
Phone: (801)295-1000 **Fax:** (801)295-9134
Products: Vitamins and nutrients; Medical and surgical instruments and supplies; Cosmetics and toiletries; Dental equipment and supplies; Pharmaceuticals. **SICs:** 5122 (Drugs, Proprietaries & Sundries); 5047 (Medical & Hospital Equipment). **Officers:** Ronald G. George, President.

■ 19682 ■ **U.S. Safety Corp.**
8101 Lenexa Dr.
Lenexa, KS 66214
Phone: (913)599-5555
Free: (800)821-5218 **Fax:** 800-252-5002
Products: Ophthalmic goods. **SIC:** 5048 (Ophthalmic Goods).

■ 19683 ■ **Universal Case Company Inc./Designer Optical**
474 S Perkins
Memphis, TN 38117-3803
Phone: (901)767-8640 **Fax:** (901)683-3172
Products: Ophthalmic goods; Ophthalmic frames. **SIC:** 5048 (Ophthalmic Goods). **Officers:** Arthur King, President.

■ 19684 ■ **Universal Marine Medical Supply Co.**
PO Box 199035
Brooklyn, NY 11219
Phone: (718)438-4804
Free: (800)828-9581 **Fax:** (718)972-2355
Products: Maritime pharmaceuticals. **SIC:** 5047 (Medical & Hospital Equipment). **Est:** 1977. **Sales:** $10,000,000 (2000). **Emp:** 18. **Officers:** Dr. Julius Nasso.

■ 19685 ■ **Universal Products Enterprises**
1243 Bay Area, No. 1805
Houston, TX 77058
Phone: (281)480-2129
Products: Pharmaceutical products. **SIC:** 5122 (Drugs, Proprietaries & Sundries). **Est:** 1988. **Emp:** 25. **Officers:** Anthony Smith, President.

■ 19686 ■ **Universal/Univis Inc.**
110 Frank Mossveig Dr.
Attleboro, MA 02703
Phone: (508)226-9630
Free: (800)899-5432 **Fax:** (508)226-9690
Products: Ophthalmic goods, including frames. **SIC:** 5048 (Ophthalmic Goods). **Est:** 1988. **Officers:** Charles Hoff, Chairman of the Board.

■ 19687 ■ **The Validation Group Inc.**
1100 E Hector St., Ste. 415
Conshohocken, PA 19428
Free: (800)691-1171 **Fax:** (610)940-9861
Products: Provides full compliance and validation services to the medical device, pharmaceutical, and biotech industries. The company has completed more than 150 projects in the United States, Canada, Europe, and South Africa. **SIC:** 5122 (Drugs, Proprietaries & Sundries). **Emp:** 60.

■ 19688 ■ **Vallen Safety Supply Co.**
12850 E Florence Ave.
Santa Fe Springs, CA 90670
Phone: (562)946-0076
Free: (800)482-5536 **Fax:** (562)941-5644
Products: Industrial safety equipment, including gloves, suits, eyewear, earwear, boots, monitors, and first-aid equipment and supplies. **SIC:** 5047 (Medical & Hospital Equipment). **Est:** 1943. **Sales:** $2,000,000 (2000). **Emp:** 22. **Officers:** Jim Thompson, President; Scott Olson, CFO; Jeffrey S. Dellerson, General Mgr.

■ 19689 ■ **Vermillion Wholesale Drug Company Inc.**
PO Box 1239
Opelousas, LA 70571-1239
Phone: (318)942-4976
Products: Non-prescription drugs, personal care items, toiletries and small kitchen items including pots and pans. **SIC:** 5122 (Drugs, Proprietaries & Sundries). **Sales:** $1,000,000 (2000). **Emp:** 13. **Officers:** Carl Schwartzenburg, President.

■ 19690 ■ **Vision Plastics USA, Inc.**
3500 La Touche No. 110
Anchorage, AK 99508
Phone: (907)562-2845 **Fax:** (907)562-2956
Products: Eyeglasses and lenses. **SIC:** 5048 (Ophthalmic Goods). **Former Name:** Vision Plastic Wholesale.

■ 19691 ■ **Vista Laboratories Inc.**
3711 E Atlanta Ave.
Phoenix, AZ 85040-2960
Phone: (602)257-8555
Free: (800)352-5465 **Fax:** 800-368-5782
Products: Ophthalmic goods. **SIC:** 5048 (Ophthalmic Goods).

■ 19692 ■ **VZ Ltd.**
945 W Wilshire
Oklahoma City, OK 73116
Phone: (405)843-8886 **Fax:** (405)841-6866
E-mail: vzsrehab@aol.com
URL: http://www.vzrehab.com
Products: Wheelchair and seating systems and accessories; Durable medical equipment, including hospital beds, bathroom safety equipment, oxygen equipment, and access products. **SIC:** 5047 (Medical & Hospital Equipment). **Est:** 1969. **Sales:** $2,000,000 (2000). **Emp:** 12. **Officers:** Stephanie Veazey, Contact. **Doing Business As:** Best Rents. **Doing Business As:** Bill Veazey's Rehab & Home Care Equipment.

■ 19693 ■ **Wallace Opticians Inc.**
3040 Vine St.
Lansing, MI 48912-4623
Phone: (517)332-8628
Products: Ophthalmic goods. **SIC:** 5048 (Ophthalmic Goods). **Officers:** Jack Wallace, President.

■ 19694 ■ **Walman Optical Co.**
801 12th Ave. N
Minneapolis, MN 55411
Phone: (612)520-6000
Free: (800)873-9256 **Fax:** (612)520-6069
Products: Ophthalmic goods. **SIC:** 5048 (Ophthalmic Goods).

■ 19695 ■ **Wendel Walters Optical Inc.**
1624 Linwood Blvd.
Oklahoma City, OK 73106-5026
Phone: (405)235-5301
Products: Ophthalmic goods. **SIC:** 5048 (Ophthalmic Goods). **Officers:** Wendel Walters, President.

■ 19696 ■ **Wasserott's Medical Services Inc.**
PO Box 195
Luzerne, PA 18709-0195
Phone: (717)287-2176
Products: Medical supplies. **SIC:** 5047 (Medical & Hospital Equipment).

■ 19697 ■ **West Penn Optical**
2576 W 8th St.
Colony Plaza
Erie, PA 16505
Phone: (814)833-1194
Products: Ophthalmic goods. **SIC:** 5048 (Ophthalmic Goods).

■ 19698 ■ **Westbrook Pharmaceutical and Surgical Supply Co.**
1910 Cochran Rd.
Pittsburgh, PA 15220
Phone: (412)561-6532
Products: Pharmaceutical supplies; Surgical supplies; Medical equipment, including beds. **SICs:** 5122 (Drugs, Proprietaries & Sundries); 5047 (Medical & Hospital Equipment). **Est:** 1980. **Sales:** $1,200,000 (2000). **Emp:** 14. **Officers:** Raymond Westbrook, President; Peggy Westbrook, CFO; Parris Westbrook, VP of Marketing.

■ 19699 ■ **Western Carolina Optical Inc.**
PO Box 1596
Asheville, NC 28802-1596
Phone: (828)258-1706
Free: (800)771-6131 **Fax:** (828)258-0206
Products: Opthalmic goods; Opthalmic frames. **SIC:**

5048 (Ophthalmic Goods). **Est:** 1985. **Officers:** Gerry Shaw, President.

■ **19700** ■   **Western Stockmen's Inc.**
223 Rodeo Ave.
Caldwell, ID 83605
Phone: (208)459-0777
Free: (800)624-9425   **Fax:** (208)455-4859
Products: Dry pet food and animal feeds; Veterinary pharmaceuticals and instruments. **SICs:** 5047 (Medical & Hospital Equipment); 5122 (Drugs, Proprietaries & Sundries). **Sales:** $40,000,000 (2000). **Emp:** 70. **Officers:** Ray Kaufman, President.

■ **19701** ■   **Wheelchair Pit-Stop**
28 E Decatur Ave.
Pleasantville, NJ 08232
Phone: (609)645-1610
Products: Powered wheelchair systems and parts. **SIC:** 5047 (Medical & Hospital Equipment). **Officers:** Bill Mooney, Contact.

■ **19702** ■   **Whitby Pharmaceuticals Inc.**
PO Box 85054
Richmond, VA 23261-5054
Phone: (804)254-4400   **Fax:** (804)995-5083
Products: Pharmaceuticals. **SIC:** 5122 (Drugs, Proprietaries & Sundries).

■ **19703** ■   **White Cross Corporation, Inc.**
350 Theo Frend Ave.
Rye, NY 10580
Phone: (914)921-0600   **Fax:** (914)921-0971
Products: Pharmaceutical preparations; Flavoring extracts; Medicinal chemicals, including antibiotics; Inorganic paint pigments; Industrial inorganic chemicals. **SICs:** 5122 (Drugs, Proprietaries & Sundries); 5169 (Chemicals & Allied Products Nec); 5149 (Groceries & Related Products Nec). **Est:** 1914. **Officers:** Joseph T. Raho, Vice President.

■ **19704** ■   **White and White Pharmacy Inc.**
PO Box 801
Grand Rapids, MI 49518-0801
Phone: (616)956-6100   **Fax:** (616)956-7603
Products: Pharmaceuticals. **SIC:** 5194 (Tobacco & Tobacco Products). **Est:** 1883. **Sales:** $25,100,000 (2000). **Emp:** 160. **Officers:** Thomas Ouellette, President; James Irwin, CFO; Mollie Linstrom, Marketing Mgr.

■ **19705** ■   **Williams Optical Laboratory Inc.**
PO Box 1246
Nashville, TN 37202
Phone: (615)256-6631
Free: (800)257-1750   **Fax:** (615)259-2303
Products: Ophthalmic goods. **SIC:** 5048 (Ophthalmic Goods).

■ **19706** ■   **Williams Physicians and Surgeons Supplies**
PO Box 27
Shreveport, LA 71161
Phone: (318)424-8186   **Fax:** (318)424-4863
Products: Medical supplies, including bandages. **SIC:**

5047 (Medical & Hospital Equipment). **Est:** 1946. **Sales:** $7,200,000 (2000). **Emp:** 35. **Officers:** J.H. Cotton, President; T. Cotton, Treasurer.

■ **19707** ■   **Wilmington Hospital Supply**
PO Box 3516
Wilmington, NC 28406
Phone: (919)763-5157   **Fax:** (919)762-6022
Products: Hospital supplies, including syringes, tubes, and IVs. **SIC:** 5047 (Medical & Hospital Equipment). **Est:** 1959. **Sales:** $5,000,000 (2000). **Emp:** 30. **Officers:** Gerald Shelton, CEO; Jane Lane, Controller.

■ **19708** ■   **Wilson Optical Company Inc.**
8990 Summerford Ln.
El Paso, TX 79907
Phone: (915)859-3415
Free: (800)592-2205   **Fax:** (915)858-0220
Products: Opthalmic goods. **SIC:** 5048 (Ophthalmic Goods). **Est:** 1976.

■ **19709** ■   **Winchester Optical**
758 Pre Emption Rd.
Geneva, NY 14456
Phone: (315)789-3911
Free: (800)462-7300   **Fax:** (315)789-2468
Products: Ophthalmic goods. **SIC:** 5048 (Ophthalmic Goods).

■ **19710** ■   **Winchester Optical**
1219 W Southern Ave.
PO Box 3248
Williamsport, PA 17701-0248
Phone: (717)323-7141
Free: (800)332-8599   **Fax:** (717)323-3133
Products: Ophthalmic goods. **SIC:** 5048 (Ophthalmic Goods).

■ **19711** ■   **Winchester Optical Company Inc.**
1935 Lake St.
Elmira, NY 14902
Phone: (607)734-4251
Free: (800)847-9357   **Fax:** (607)732-0901
Products: Ophthalmic goods. **SIC:** 5048 (Ophthalmic Goods).

■ **19712** ■   **Winchester Surgical Supply Co.**
PO Box 35488
Charlotte, NC 28235-5488
Phone: (704)372-2240
Products: Surgical supplies, including syringes and needles. **SIC:** 5047 (Medical & Hospital Equipment). **Est:** 1919. **Sales:** $15,000,000 (2000). **Emp:** 77. **Officers:** H.W. Stewart II, CEO & President; D.E. Hoffman, VP of Finance; Yates C. Farris, Dir. of Marketing & Sales; Banks M. Huntley, Dir. of Data Processing; Virginia Williams, Dir of Human Resources.

■ **19713** ■   **WOS Inc.**
PO Box 10387
Green Bay, WI 54307-0387
Phone: (920)336-0690
Free: (800)242-8088   **Fax:** (920)336-5576
Products: Ophthalmic goods. **SIC:** 5048 (Ophthalmic Goods). **Est:** 1949.

■ **19714** ■   **Xetal Inc.**
3590 Oceanside Rd.
Oceanside, NY 11572
Phone: (516)594-0005
Products: Medical products, including isolation gowns, face masks, gauze, latex gloves, needles, and syringes; Health and beauty aids; Chemicals for infection control. **SIC:** 5047 (Medical & Hospital Equipment). **Sales:** $14,600,000 (2000). **Emp:** 13. **Officers:** Jan Stahl, CEO; Peter Steil, President & CFO.

■ **19715** ■   **Yates & Bird**
300 N Elizabeth St., 2N
Chicago, IL 60607
Phone: (312)226-2412
Free: (800)662-5021   **Fax:** (312)226-2480
E-mail: sales@yates-motloid.com
URL: http://www.yates-motloid.com
Products: Dental lab supplies and equipment. **SIC:** 5063 (Electrical Apparatus & Equipment). **Emp:** 20. **Officers:** Ronald I. Schwarcz, President; Mona G. Zemsky, Marketing Mgr., e-mail: mona@yates-motloid.com; Maria Ramirez, Customer Service Contact, e-mail: mramirez@yates-motloid.com; Alison James, Human Resources Contact, e-mail: alison@yates-motloid.com.

■ **19716** ■   **York Hannover Health Care Inc.**
75 South Church Street
Pittsfield, MA 01201
Phone: (413)448-2111
Products: Provides prescription and non prescription medications and pharmacy related services to nursing homes and similar facilities. **SIC:** 5122 (Drugs, Proprietaries & Sundries). **Sales:** $200,000 (2000). **Emp:** 10. **Officers:** Thomas M. Clarke, CEO & President; David M. Fancher, CFO.

■ **19717** ■   **W.F. Young Inc.**
111 Lyman St.
Springfield, MA 01103
Phone: (413)737-0201
Free: (800)628-9653   **Fax:** (413)739-7942
E-mail: info@absorbine.com
URL: http://www.absorbine.com
Products: Over-the-counter pharmaceuticals including foot, muscle and veterinary products. **SIC:** 5122 (Drugs, Proprietaries & Sundries). **Est:** 1892. **Emp:** 26. **Officers:** Tyler F. Young, CEO & President; Adam Raczkowski, COO.

■ **19718** ■   **Zee Service Inc.**
22 Corporate Park
Irvine, CA 92606-3112
Phone: (714)252-9500   **Fax:** (714)855-2158
Products: First aid supplies. **SIC:** 5047 (Medical & Hospital Equipment). **Est:** 1953. **Sales:** $60,000,000 (2000). **Emp:** 300. **Officers:** D. Taylor, President; Robert Bancroft, VP of Finance; Ken Bray, VP of Sales; Barry Cole, Dir. of Data Processing; Ron Hondragon, Dir of Human Resources.

(35) Metals

Entries in this section are arranged alphabetically by company name. When the company name is a personal name, the company name is alphabetized by the surname unless the first name or initial(s) are part of a trade name. See the User's Guide at the front of this directory for additional information.

■ 19719 ■ **A-1 Metal Services Corp.**
1275 Railroad St., Ste. A
Corona, CA 91718
Phone: (714)774-2800
Products: Unfabricated steel. **SIC:** 5051 (Metals Service Centers & Offices). **Est:** 1974. **Sales:** $3,000,000 (2000). **Emp:** 13. **Officers:** E.R. Daly, President; Rollie Bennett, General Mgr.

■ 19720 ■ **A-Mark Financial Corp.**
100 Wilshire Blvd., 3rd Fl.
Santa Monica, CA 90401
Phone: (310)319-0200
Products: Precious metals. **SIC:** 5094 (Jewelry & Precious Stones). **Sales:** $7,000,000 (1992). **Emp:** 30. **Officers:** Steven C. Markoff, President.

■ 19721 ■ **AA & A Enterprises Inc.**
23-25 Lake Shore Dr. E
PO Box 284
Dunkirk, NY 14048
Phone: (716)366-0002 **Free:** (800)342-0751
Products: Aluminum; Trailer side kits and components;; Telescoping tent poles and accessories; Boat cover support poles; Marine hardware. **SICs:** 5051 (Metals Service Centers & Offices); 5013 (Motor Vehicle Supplies & New Parts); 5072 (Hardware). **Est:** 1977. **Emp:** 3. **Officers:** Sam Avny, VP of Sales; Pauline Avny, President & Treasurer.

■ 19722 ■ **Aaron Scrap Metals, Div. of Commercial Metals Co.**
PO Box 607069
Orlando, FL 32860-7069
Phone: (407)293-6584
Products: Metal products, machinery, equipment, and supplies; Copper; Aluminum; Secondary metals recycling. **SICs:** 5051 (Metals Service Centers & Offices); 5084 (Industrial Machinery & Equipment). **Est:** 1968. **Sales:** $15,000,000 (2000). **Emp:** 25. **Officers:** Greg Ledet, General Mgr.

■ 19723 ■ **ABC Metals Inc.**
PO Box 7012
Logansport, IN 46947-7012
Phone: (219)753-0471
Free: (800)238-8470 **Fax:** (219)753-6110
URL: http://www.abcmetals.com
Products: Copper alloys. **SIC:** 5051 (Metals Service Centers & Offices). **Est:** 1973. **Sales:** $26,000,000 (1999). **Emp:** 64. **Officers:** Jack Bell, President; James Bauer, VP of Finance; Kerry Swedun, VP of Sales; Barbara Williams, Dir. of Data Processing.

■ 19724 ■ **ABM International Corp.**
275 Kisco Ave.
Mt. Kisco, NY 10549
Phone: (914)241-2828
Products: Stainless steel tubing and pipes. **SIC:** 5051 (Metals Service Centers & Offices). **Est:** 1954. **Sales:** $10,000,000 (2000). **Emp:** 20. **Officers:** Jack J. Schnapp, President; John Mutone, Controller.

■ 19725 ■ **Actron Steel**
2866 Cass Rd.
Traverse City, MI 49684
Phone: (616)947-3981
Products: Steel. **SIC:** 5051 (Metals Service Centers & Offices).

■ 19726 ■ **ACuPowder International, LLC**
901 Lehigh Ave.
Union, NJ 07083
Phone: (908)851-4500 **Fax:** (908)851-4597
E-mail: acupowder@acupowder.com
URL: http://www.acupowder.com
Products: Metal powders. **SIC:** 5051 (Metals Service Centers & Offices). **Est:** 1995. **Sales:** $40,000,000 (1999). **Emp:** 80. **Officers:** Edul Daver, President; Michael Kudryk, CFO. **Former Name:** Alcan Aluminum Corp, Alcan Powder and Pigments.

■ 19727 ■ **Ada Iron and Metal Co.**
PO Box 306
Ada, OK 74820
Phone: (580)332-1165
Products: Iron; Metal. **SIC:** 5051 (Metals Service Centers & Offices). **Est:** 1914. **Sales:** $1,000,000 (2000). **Emp:** 16. **Officers:** Laura Benham, President.

■ 19728 ■ **Admiral Metals**
1821 Oregon Pke.
Lancaster, PA 17601
Phone: (717)519-1565
Products: Aluminum, brass, and steel. **SIC:** 5051 (Metals Service Centers & Offices).

■ 19729 ■ **Admiral Metals Inc.**
11 Forbes Rd.
Woburn, MA 01801
Phone: (781)933-8300 **Fax:** (781)937-4469
Products: Metals service center: brass, copper, aluminum and stainless steel cutting. **SIC:** 5051 (Metals Service Centers & Offices).

■ 19730 ■ **Admiral Steel**
4152 W 123rd St.
Alsip, IL 60803-1869
Phone: (708)388-9600
Free: (800)323-7055 **Fax:** (708)388-9317
E-mail: info@admiralsteel.com
URL: http://www.admiralsteel.com
Products: Steel. **SIC:** 5051 (Metals Service Centers & Offices). **Est:** 1949. **Sales:** $10,000,000 (2000). **Emp:** 45. **Officers:** Mark J. Tolliver, CEO.

■ 19731 ■ **Advance Steel Co.**
9635 French Rd.
Detroit, MI 48213
Phone: (313)571-6700 **Fax:** (313)571-6707
Products: Steel service center: galvanized, hot and cold rolled steel; slitting. **SIC:** 5051 (Metals Service Centers & Offices). **Officers:** Robert Stewart, Owner.

■ 19732 ■ **Aerodyne Ulbrich Alloys**
125 S Satellite Rd.
South Windsor, CT 06074
Phone: (860)289-6011
Products: High temperature metals for the aerospace industry, power generation, medical, oil patch, and marine industries. **SIC:** 5051 (Metals Service Centers & Offices). **Sales:** $12,000,000 (1994). **Emp:** 25. **Officers:** Edward Williams, President.

■ 19733 ■ **Aerospace Tube & Pipe**
9165 Olema Ave.
Hesperia, CA 92345
Phone: (760)956-8000
Products: Stainless steel and high temperature tube, pipe, and fittings; Aluminum, titanium, alloy steel, carbon, nickel and nickel alloy tube and pipe — 1/16" O.D. - 24" O.D. seamless and welded AMS-MILT-ASME-ASTM specifications. **SICs:** 5051 (Metals Service Centers & Offices); 5085 (Industrial Supplies); 5014 (Tires & Tubes). **Est:** 1975. **Sales:** $63,000,000 (1999). **Emp:** 63. **Officers:** Betty Knight, CEO; Wayne Moore, General Mgr. **Former Name:** West Coast Tube and Pipe.

■ 19734 ■ **AFCO Metals Inc.**
PO Box 95010
Little Rock, AR 72295-5010
Phone: (501)490-2255 **Fax:** (501)490-5201
Products: Metals service center. **SIC:** 5051 (Metals Service Centers & Offices). **Est:** 1962. **Sales:** $220,000,000 (2000). **Emp:** 300. **Officers:** Steve Makarewicz, President; Mike Rowland, VP & General Mgr.; Mike Nichols, Information Systems Mgr.; Tamara Capps, Human Resources Mgr.

■ 19735 ■ **Affiliated Metals**
450 Billy Mitchell Rd.
Salt Lake City, UT 84122-0990
Phone: (801)363-1711 **Free:** (800)748-4711
URL: http://www.affiliatedmetals.com
Products: Building materials including stainless bars, plates, angles, tubing and pipe, sheet aluminum bars, sheets, plates, angles, and extrusions. **SIC:** 5051 (Metals Service Centers & Offices). **Est:** 1962. **Sales:** $22,000,000 (2000). **Emp:** 57. **Officers:** Jess R. Peterson, Manager, e-mail: jpeterson@rsac.com.

■ 19736 ■ **Affiliated Metals Co.**
PO Box 1306
Granite City, IL 62040
Free: (888)597-6059
Products: Metals service center: cutting, slitting and processing. **SIC:** 5051 (Metals Service Centers & Offices). **Emp:** 140. **Officers:** Greg Poth, CFO.

■ 19737 ■ **Air Engineering Co. Inc.**
2308 Pahounui Dr.
Honolulu, HI 96819
Phone: (808)848-1040
Products: Sheet metal for air-conditioning units. **SICs:** 5051 (Metals Service Centers & Offices); 5075 (Warm Air Heating & Air-Conditioning). **Est:** 1960. **Sales:** $9,000,000 (2000). **Emp:** 75. **Officers:** William Hulick, President.

■ 19738 ■ **Airport Metals**
6099 Triangle Dr.
Los Angeles, CA 90040
Phone: (323)722-2500 **Fax:** (323)722-2626
Products: Metals and fabricates sheet metal. **SIC:**

5051 (Metals Service Centers & Offices). **Officers:** Larry Blivas, President.

■ **19739** ■ **Aladdin Steel Inc.**
Rte. 16 E
Gillespie, IL 62033
Phone: (217)839-2121
Free: (800)637-4455 **Fax:** (217)839-3823
Products: Steel. **SIC:** 5051 (Metals Service Centers & Offices). **Est:** 1976. **Sales:** $20,000,000 (2000). **Emp:** 105. **Officers:** E. Eschbacher, President; D. Kernich, Dir. of Marketing.

■ **19740** ■ **Alamo Iron Works**
PO Box 231
San Antonio, TX 78291-0231
Phone: (210)223-6161
Free: (800)292-7817 **Fax:** (210)704-8351
E-mail: aiw@aiwnet.com
URL: http://www.aiwnet.com
Products: Round bar iron. **SICs:** 5051 (Metals Service Centers & Offices); 5085 (Industrial Supplies). **Est:** 1878. **Sales:** $80,000,000 (2000). **Emp:** 460. **Officers:** Tony Koch, President; Mark Sobotik, VP of Finance; Rudy Fuselier, Exec. VP; Mickey Holzhaus, VP of Steel Divisions; Bill Bell, VP of Sales; Richard Ochoa, VP of Product Sales.

■ **19741** ■ **Alaskan Copper & Brass Co.**
3223 6th S
PO Box 3546
Seattle, WA 98134
Phone: (206)623-5800
Free: (800)552-7661 **Fax:** (206)382-7335
E-mail: acbsea@alascop.com
URL: http://www.alascop.com
Products: Corrosion resistant metal products of copper, brass, bronze, aluminum, stainless steel, and copper-nickel in sheet, plate, pipe, tube, rod, and bar form. **SIC:** 5051 (Metals Service Centers & Offices). **Est:** 1913. **Sales:** $50,000,000 (2000). **Emp:** 200. **Officers:** William M. Rosen; Kermit Rosen Jr.; Donald Rosen; Alan Rosen; Alex Rosen, Sales/Marketing Contact, e-mail: amr@alascop.com.

■ **19742** ■ **Alcan Aluminum Corp. Metal Goods Service Center Div.**
8800 Page Blvd.
St. Louis, MO 63114
Phone: (314)427-1234 **Fax:** (314)427-7806
Products: Metals, including aluminum, copper, steel, and brass. **SIC:** 5051 (Metals Service Centers & Offices). **Sales:** $110,000,000 (2000). **Emp:** 150. **Officers:** John Horstmeyer, President; John Schoonover, Controller; Mark Gosselin, Sales Mgr.

■ **19743** ■ **Alco Iron and Metal Co.**
1091 Doolittle Dr.
San Leandro, CA 94577
Phone: (510)562-1107
Products: Iron and metals. **SIC:** 5051 (Metals Service Centers & Offices). **Sales:** $3,000,000 (2000). **Emp:** 50. **Officers:** Ken Kantor, President.

■ **19744** ■ **All American Recycling Div.**
PO Box 1556
Ocala, FL 34478
Phone: (904)622-0101
Products: Steel, aluminum, copper, and brass. **SIC:** 5051 (Metals Service Centers & Offices). **Sales:** $15,000,000 (2000). **Emp:** 25. **Officers:** Jack Lovett, General Mgr.

■ **19745** ■ **All Foils Inc.**
4597 Van Epps Rd.
Brooklyn Heights, OH 44131
Phone: (216)661-0211
Free: (800)521-0054 **Fax:** (216)398-4161
Products: Aluminum, copper, stainless steel, and other metals in foil and light sheet. **SIC:** 5051 (Metals Service Centers & Offices). **Sales:** $15,000,000 (2000). **Emp:** 70. **Officers:** Eric J. Henkel, President; Karen Mittman, Controller.

■ **19746** ■ **Allegheny Rodney Strip Svc Ctr**
PO Box 366
Skokie, IL 60076
Phone: (847)676-5900 **Fax:** (847)676-5909
Products: Metals service centers: stainless steel strip. **SIC:** 5051 (Metals Service Centers & Offices).

■ **19747** ■ **Sam Allen and Son Inc.**
PO Box 430002
Pontiac, MI 48343
Phone: (248)335-8141 **Fax:** (248)335-8714
Products: Metals. **SIC:** 5051 (Metals Service Centers & Offices). **Est:** 1905. **Sales:** $6,000,000 (2000). **Emp:** 85. **Officers:** Barry D. Briskin, President; John Annal, Controller; Oliver M. Provenzano, Dir. of Marketing & Sales; Kiron Kothari, Controller.

■ **19748** ■ **Allen Steel Co.**
1340 South 200 West
Salt Lake City, UT 84115
Phone: (801)484-8591 **Fax:** (801)484-6541
Products: Steel bars, plates, and beams. **SIC:** 5051 (Metals Service Centers & Offices). **Est:** 1947. **Sales:** $4,000,000 (2000). **Emp:** 40. **Officers:** Robert Allen Jr., President; Ken Eaton, VP of Sales.

■ **19749** ■ **Alliance Metals Inc.**
905 Fern Hill Rd.
West Chester, PA 19380
Phone: (215)436-8600 **Fax:** (215)436-6335
Products: Aluminum. **SIC:** 5051 (Metals Service Centers & Offices). **Est:** 1970. **Sales:** $50,000,000 (2000). **Emp:** 100. **Officers:** Bradley B. Evans, President & CFO.

■ **19750** ■ **Alliance Steel Corp.**
275 Old Higgins Rd.
Des Plaines, IL 60018
Phone: (708)297-7000 **Fax:** (708)297-0318
E-mail: isteel2@aol.com
Products: Steel; Rust and stain removers. **SICs:** 5051 (Metals Service Centers & Offices); 5169 (Chemicals & Allied Products Nec). **Est:** 1974. **Sales:** $3,000,000 (2000). **Emp:** 14. **Officers:** Andrew Gross, President; Tim Scully, Contact; Tom McKneil, Sales Contact; Diane Bishop, Customer Service Contact.

■ **19751** ■ **Allied-Crawford Steel**
7135 Bryhawke Cir.
North Charleston, SC 29418
Phone: (803)552-6300 **Fax:** (803)552-3354
Products: Steel bars, shoots, plates, WF beams, pipes, and tubing. **SIC:** 5051 (Metals Service Centers & Offices). **Est:** 1984. **Sales:** $10,000,000 (2000). **Emp:** 49. **Officers:** Russ Williams, General Mgr.; Carl O. Rowe, Controller.

■ **19752** ■ **Allied Metals Inc.**
2220 Canada Dry St.
Houston, TX 77023
Phone: (713)923-9491 **Fax:** (713)923-5224
Products: Stainless and aluminum products. **SIC:** 5051 (Metals Service Centers & Offices). **Est:** 1950. **Sales:** $29,000,000 (2000). **Emp:** 40. **Officers:** Matt Keith, General Mgr., e-mail: mattkeith@hughessupply.com.

■ **19753** ■ **Alloy Tool Steel Inc.**
13525 E Freeway Dr.
Santa Fe Springs, CA 90670
Phone: (310)921-8605
Free: (800)288-9800 **Fax:** (310)802-1728
Products: Tool, alloy, and stainless steel. **SIC:** 5051 (Metals Service Centers & Offices). **Est:** 1974. **Sales:** $12,000,000 (2000). **Emp:** 20. **Officers:** David Chen, General Mgr.

■ **19754** ■ **Almetals Co.**
51035 Grand River Ave.
Wixom, MI 48393
Phone: (248)348-7722 **Fax:** (248)348-7627
Products: Metals. **SIC:** 5051 (Metals Service Centers & Offices). **Sales:** $22,000,000 (1994). **Emp:** 30. **Officers:** James Chain, President.

■ **19755** ■ **Alpha Steel Corp.**
141-141st St.
Hammond, IN 46327
Phone: (219)933-1000 **Fax:** (219)933-1114
Products: Steel. **SIC:** 5051 (Metals Service Centers & Offices). **Sales:** $20,000,000 (1993). **Emp:** 45. **Officers:** Robert Kotrba, General Mgr.; Doug Hutchison, Treasurer.

■ **19756** ■ **Alps Wire Rope Corp.**
1947 Quincy Ct.
Glendale Heights, IL 60139
Phone: (708)893-3888
Free: (800)424-9984 **Fax:** (708)893-8164
Products: Wire rope. **SIC:** 5051 (Metals Service Centers & Offices). **Est:** 1967. **Sales:** $6,000,000 (2000). **Emp:** 25. **Officers:** J.E. Benner, CEO & President.

■ **19757** ■ **Alps Wire Rope Corp.**
1947 Quincy Ct.
Glendale Heights, IL 60139
Phone: (708)893-3888
Products: Metals. **SIC:** 5051 (Metals Service Centers & Offices). **Sales:** $6,000,000 (2000). **Emp:** 20.

■ **19758** ■ **Alro Metals Service Center**
PO Box 3031
Boca Raton, FL 33431-0931
Phone: (407)997-6766
Products: Metals for machining and building materials. **SIC:** 5051 (Metals Service Centers & Offices). **Est:** 1968. **Sales:** $30,000,000 (2000). **Emp:** 125. **Officers:** B. Glick, President.

■ **19759** ■ **Alro Steel Corp.**
PO Box 927
Jackson, MI 49204
Phone: (517)787-5500 **Fax:** (517)787-6398
Products: Steel. **SIC:** 5051 (Metals Service Centers & Offices). **Est:** 1948. **Sales:** $780,000,000 (2000). **Emp:** 1,050. **Officers:** Mark Alyea, President; Leo Hollenbeck, Treasurer & Secty.; Dick Hoogerwerf, Dir. of Sales; Joe Richards, Dir. of Data Processing; Ron Henman, Dir of Human Resources.

■ **19760** ■ **Alro Steel Corp.**
1800 W Willow St.
Lansing, MI 48915
Phone: (517)371-9600
Products: Steel. **SIC:** 5051 (Metals Service Centers & Offices).

■ **19761** ■ **Alro Steel Corp.**
2301 S Walnut St.
Muncie, IN 47302
Phone: (765)282-5335
Products: Steel. **SIC:** 5051 (Metals Service Centers & Offices).

■ **19762** ■ **Alta Industries Ltd.**
PO Box 510
Salt Lake City, UT 84110
Phone: (801)972-8160
Products: Steel products. **SIC:** 5051 (Metals Service Centers & Offices). **Sales:** $23,000,000 (1993). **Emp:** 100. **Officers:** W. Pat King, CEO & President; Robert Elkington, CFO.

■ **19763** ■ **Alumax Building Products**
28921 E Hwy. 74
Sun City, CA 92586
Phone: (714)928-1000 **Fax:** (714)928-1008
Products: Aluminum; Fabricated steel plate (stacks and weldments). **SIC:** 5051 (Metals Service Centers & Offices).

■ **19764** ■ **Aluminum Distributors Inc.**
2107 Gardner Rd.
Broadview, IL 60153
Phone: (708)681-1900
Products: Metals. **SIC:** 5051 (Metals Service Centers & Offices). **Sales:** $20,000,000 (2000). **Emp:** 25.

■ 19765 ■ Aluminum and Stainless Inc.
PO Box 3484
Lafayette, LA 70502
Phone: (337)837-4381
Free: (800)252-9074 **Fax:** (337)837-5439
Products: Metals, including stainless steel, aluminum, brass, and copper. **SIC:** 5051 (Metals Service Centers & Offices). **Est:** 1969. **Sales:** $21,000,000 (2000). **Emp:** 26. **Officers:** O.P. Montagnet, CEO & President; Joseph Wolf, CFO; Al LeBlanc, Dir. of Marketing & Sales.

■ 19766 ■ Amalco Metals Inc.
33955 7th St.
Union City, CA 94587-3521
Phone: (510)487-1300 **Fax:** (510)489-6091
Products: Aluminum. **SIC:** 5051 (Metals Service Centers & Offices). **Est:** 1972. **Sales:** $18,000,000 (2000). **Emp:** 70. **Officers:** Patrick McCarthy, President; Stacey Wardell, VP of Marketing.

■ 19767 ■ Ambassador Steel Company Inc.
1469 E Atwater St.
Detroit, MI 48207
Phone: (313)259-6600 **Fax:** (313)259-0671
Products: Cold and hot-rolled steel. **SIC:** 5051 (Metals Service Centers & Offices). **Est:** 1951. **Sales:** $20,000,000 (2000). **Emp:** 50. **Officers:** Hymen Freedland, President; Jerry Carnaghi, Controller.

■ 19768 ■ American Alloy Steel Inc.
PO Box 40469
Houston, TX 77240
Phone: (713)462-8081 **Fax:** (713)462-8342
Products: Steel service center: cutting. **SIC:** 5051 (Metals Service Centers & Offices). **Officers:** Arthur Moore, President; Russell Brown, CFO.

■ 19769 ■ American Industries Inc.
PO Box 10086
Portland, OR 97210
Phone: (503)226-1511 **Fax:** (503)225-0211
Products: Steel. **SIC:** 5051 (Metals Service Centers & Offices). **Est:** 1944. **Sales:** $85,000,000 (2000). **Emp:** 300. **Officers:** Neil Thornton, President; Robert Duffy, VP of Finance; Greg Melcher, Sales Mgr.; Larry Potter, Data Processing Mgr.; Sherri Lynch, Human Resources Mgr.

■ 19770 ■ American Metals Corp.
1499 Parkway Blvd.
West Sacramento, CA 95691
Phone: (916)371-7700
Products: Metals. **SIC:** 5051 (Metals Service Centers & Offices).

■ 19771 ■ American Steel Builders International, Corp. & Copper Valley Concrete
7011 N Camino Martin
Tucson, AZ 85741
Phone: (520)744-6950 **Fax:** (520)744-6973
SIC: 5051 (Metals Service Centers & Offices). **Est:** 1981. **Sales:** $7,000,000 (1999). **Emp:** 70. **Officers:** Mike Finkelstein, President; Brian Kelly, V.

■ 19772 ■ American Steel L.L.C.
PO Box 10086
Portland, OR 97210
Phone: (503)226-1511
Products: Steel. **SIC:** 5051 (Metals Service Centers & Offices). **Officers:** Neil R. Thornton, CEO & President.

■ 19773 ■ American Tank and Fabricating Co
12314 Elmwood Ave.
Cleveland, OH 44111
Phone: (216)252-1500 **Fax:** (216)252-4871
Products: Steel service center: heavy steel plate fabricating. **SIC:** 5051 (Metals Service Centers & Offices).

■ 19774 ■ AMI Metals Inc.
1738 Gen. George Patton Dr.
Brentwood, TN 37027
Phone: (615)377-0400 **Fax:** (615)377-0103
Products: Metals. **SIC:** 5051 (Metals Service Centers & Offices). **Officers:** Robin L. Koop, President.

■ 19775 ■ AMS International Corp.
10718 Carmel Commons Blvd., Ste. 230
Charlotte, NC 28226
Phone: (704)543-8404
Products: Steel. **SIC:** 5051 (Metals Service Centers & Offices).

■ 19776 ■ Amsco Steel Company Inc.
3430 McCart St.
Ft. Worth, TX 76110
Phone: (817)926-3355
Free: (800)772-2743 **Fax:** (817)923-2860
URL: http://www.amscosteel.com
Products: Steel products, including bars, angles, sheets, coils, strips and plates. **SIC:** 5051 (Metals Service Centers & Offices). **Est:** 1952. **Sales:** $30,000,000 (1999). **Emp:** 60. **Officers:** Steve Sikes, CEO.

■ 19777 ■ Amsco Steel Products Co.
PO Box 97545
Wichita Falls, TX 76307-7545
Phone: (940)723-2715 **Fax:** (940)723-2519
Products: Steel plates and bars. **SIC:** 5051 (Metals Service Centers & Offices). **Est:** 1952. **Sales:** $4,000,000 (2000). **Emp:** 20. **Officers:** Ralph Surles, President.

■ 19778 ■ Amstek Metal
PO Box 3848
Joliet, IL 60434-3848
Phone: (815)725-2520 **Fax:** (815)725-1710
Products: Metals; Wire; Springs. **SIC:** 5051 (Metals Service Centers & Offices). **Est:** 1898. **Sales:** $21,000,000 (2000). **Emp:** 42. **Officers:** J.B. Stevens Jr., CEO; Leo Rossi, Controller; R.W. Piwonka, Vice President.

■ 19779 ■ Amtex Steel Inc.
700 Central Ave.
University Park, IL 60466-3138
Phone: (773)927-1080 **Fax:** (773)927-8162
Products: Steel. **SIC:** 5051 (Metals Service Centers & Offices). **Est:** 1978. **Sales:** $15,000,000 (2000). **Emp:** 45. **Officers:** Royce Spencer, President; Michael J. Flynn, CFO & Treasurer; Michael Spencer, Marketing & Sales Mgr.; Marry Sharp, Dir. of Data Processing; Sharon Pennington, Customer Service Contact.

■ 19780 ■ Anaheim Extrusion Co. Inc.
PO Box 6380
Anaheim, CA 92816
Phone: (714)630-3111
Free: (800)660-3318 **Fax:** (714)630-1823
E-mail: anexco@pacbell.net
Products: Aluminum; Extruded aluminum rod, bar, and other extruded shapes. **SIC:** 5051 (Metals Service Centers & Offices). **Est:** 1974. **Sales:** $25,000,000 (2000). **Emp:** 71. **Officers:** D. Baione, CEO; L. Gaddis, General Mgr.; P. Silverstein, Sales/Marketing Contact.

■ 19781 ■ The Anderson Group
6489 Ridings Rd.
Syracuse, NY 13206
Phone: (315)437-7556 **Fax:** (315)463-1533
E-mail: anderson@aiusa.com
Products: Portable wireless credit card verification system; Electronic equipment and supplies; Shelf labels; Signs; Steel shapes. **SICs:** 5051 (Metals Service Centers & Offices); 5084 (Industrial Machinery & Equipment); 5065 (Electronic Parts & Equipment Nec). **Est:** 1967. **Sales:** $10,000,000 (1999). **Emp:** 9. **Officers:** Philip D. Anderson, President. **Alternate Name:** Electronic Signage Systems Inc.

■ 19782 ■ Ansam Metals Corp.
PO Box 3408
1026 E Patapsco Ave.
Baltimore, MD 21225
Phone: (410)355-8220 **Fax:** (410)355-0513
Products: Nonferrous metals. **SIC:** 5051 (Metals Service Centers & Offices). **Officers:** Samuel S. Kahan, President; Jack Zager Sr., Vice President.

■ 19783 ■ Arrow Thompson Metals Inc.
6880 Troost Ave.
North Hollywood, CA 91605
Phone: (818)765-0522
Products: Stainless steel. **SIC:** 5051 (Metals Service

Centers & Offices). **Sales:** $13,000,000 (1993). **Emp:** 35. **Officers:** Hank Williams, General Mgr.; Nitz Fraser, Controller.

■ 19784 ■ Art Iron Inc.
PO Box 964
Toledo, OH 43697
Phone: (419)241-1261
Free: (800)472-1113 **Fax:** (419)242-9768
Products: Steel, aluminum, stainless steel, and tool steel. **SIC:** 5051 (Metals Service Centers & Offices). **Est:** 1905. **Emp:** 400. **Officers:** Donald Schlatter, President; Mel Retcher, CFO; Tom Kabat, Dir. of Marketing; Ernie Samas, Dir of Human Resources.

■ 19785 ■ Asheville Steel & Salvage Co.
314 Riverside Dr.
Asheville, NC 28801
Phone: (828)252-1061
Products: Steel. **SIC:** 5051 (Metals Service Centers & Offices).

■ 19786 ■ Asoma Corp.
105 Corporate Park Dr.
White Plains, NY 10604
Phone: (914)251-5400 **Fax:** (914)251-1073
Products: Metals; Minerals. **SICs:** 5051 (Metals Service Centers & Offices); 5052 (Coal, Other Minerals & Ores). **Est:** 1923. **Sales:** $180,000,000 (2000). **Emp:** 47. **Officers:** Glenn W. Peel, President; Sal Purpura, Exec. VP & CFO; Ernest Hirscheimer, Exec. VP; Jose Estacio, Dir. of Data Processing; Nancy Kovar, VP of Admin.

■ 19787 ■ Associated Steel Corp.
18200 Miles Rd.
Cleveland, OH 44128-0335
Phone: (216)475-8000
Products: Metals. **SIC:** 5051 (Metals Service Centers & Offices). **Sales:** $17,000,000 (1994). **Emp:** 50. **Officers:** Theodore H. Cohen Jr., President & Chairman of the Board; Marvin Gutterman, Treasurer.

■ 19788 ■ AST USA Inc.
222 Bloomingdale Rd., No. 401
White Plains, NY 10605-1511
Phone: (914)428-6010 **Fax:** (914)428-7930
Products: Stainless steel; Electrical steel; Wires. **SIC:** 5051 (Metals Service Centers & Offices). **Est:** 1976. **Sales:** $100,000,000 (1999). **Emp:** 20. **Officers:** Mario Pecciarini, Exec. VP; Stefano Coluzzi, Controller; Fabio Balboni, Vice President.

■ 19789 ■ Atlas Inc.
8550 Aetna Rd.
Cleveland, OH 44105
Phone: (216)441-3800
Products: Recycled scrap metal products. **SIC:** 5093 (Scrap & Waste Materials). **Sales:** $95,000,000 (2000). **Emp:** 215. **Officers:** Anthony J. Giordano Jr., President; Peter Toth, VP of Finance.

■ 19790 ■ Atlas Metal and Iron Corp.
318 Walnut St.
Denver, CO 80204
Phone: (303)825-7166
Products: Ferrous and non-ferrous metal scrap. **SIC:** 5093 (Scrap & Waste Materials). **Sales:** $37,000,000 (1992). **Emp:** 100. **Officers:** Donald Rosen, President.

■ 19791 ■ Atlas Steel Products Co.
7990 Bavaria Rd.
Twinsburg, OH 44087-2252
Phone: (216)425-1600 **Fax:** (216)963-0020
E-mail: info@atlassteel.com
URL: http://www.atlassteel.com
Products: Flat rolled carbon; Stainless steel, including aluminized, galvanized, galvanneal, galvalume, cold rolled, coils, sheets, blanks and tubing. **SIC:** 5051 (Metals Service Centers & Offices). **Est:** 1957. **Sales:** $43,800,000 (2000). **Emp:** 60. **Officers:** Lawrence J. Burr, CEO & President; Patrick Hanrahan, VP of Finance; Edward Basta, VP, Technology and Market Dev.; Joanne Meredith, VP of Human Resources.

■ **19792** ■ **Austin, D L Steel Supply Corp.**
PO Box 166
Collinsville, IL 62234
Phone: (618)345-7200 **Fax:** (618)345-7203
Products: Metal service center; Sheet, plate, ornamental, structural steel and metal fabricating; Stainless steel heat and corrosion resistant super alloys, roof mats, mining products, anchors, inserts and wire mesh; Perforated, expanded and bar grating; Threaded rod and all metal products. **SIC:** 5051 (Metals Service Centers & Offices). **Sales:** $6,000,000 (1999). **Emp:** 6. **Officers:** David L. Austin Sr., President; K. C. Austin, Treasurer.

■ **19793** ■ **Austin Metal and Iron Company Inc.**
PO Box 2115
Austin, TX 78768
Phone: (512)472-6452
Products: Steel piping and fixtures. **SIC:** 5051 (Metals Service Centers & Offices). **Est:** 1913. **Sales:** $2,500,000 (2000). **Emp:** 15. **Officers:** Robert Shapiro, CEO; Milton Simons, Treasurer.

■ **19794** ■ **Auto-Blankers**
1301 Alabama Ave.
Flint, MI 48505
Phone: (810)767-4300
Products: Steel. **SIC:** 5051 (Metals Service Centers & Offices).

■ **19795** ■ **Avesta Sheffield—North American Division, Inc.**
425 N Martingale Rd., No. 2000
Schaumburg, IL 60173-2218
Phone: (847)517-4050
Free: (800)833-8703 **Fax:** 800-545-8617
URL: http://www.avestasheffield.com
Products: Stainless steel. **SIC:** 5051 (Metals Service Centers & Offices). **Est:** 1992. **Sales:** $153,000,000 (2000). **Emp:** 206. **Officers:** Michael Rinker, President; Greg Hamilton, CFO.

■ **19796** ■ **Azco Steel Co.**
100 Midland Ave.
Saddle Brook, NJ 07663-6152
Phone: (201)791-0600
Products: High strength steel. **SIC:** 5051 (Metals Service Centers & Offices). **Est:** 1945. **Sales:** $10,000,000 (2000). **Emp:** 30. **Officers:** Ben Rosenzweig, President.

■ **19797** ■ **B and B Surplus Inc.**
7020 Rosedale Hwy.
Bakersfield, CA 93308
Phone: (805)589-0381 **Fax:** (805)589-5508
Products: Pipe; Steel. **SIC:** 5051 (Metals Service Centers & Offices). **Est:** 1963. **Sales:** $12,000,000 (2000). **Emp:** 40. **Officers:** Ron B. Boylan, President; Donice Boylan, CFO.

■ **19798** ■ **Baird Steel Inc.**
2926 W Main St.
Whistler, AL 36612
Phone: (205)457-9513
Products: Steel. **SIC:** 5051 (Metals Service Centers & Offices). **Est:** 1941. **Sales:** $10,000,000 (2000). **Emp:** 23. **Officers:** John Caldwell, President.

■ **19799** ■ **Balco Metals Inc. Recycling World**
9780 S Meridian Blvd., Ste. 180
Englewood, CO 80112-5926
Products: Metals. **SIC:** 5051 (Metals Service Centers & Offices).

■ **19800** ■ **Baldwin Steel Co.**
500 Rte 440
Jersey City, NJ 07305
Phone: (201)333-7000 **Fax:** (201)333-6077
E-mail: d.masini@baldwinsteel.com
URL: http://www.baldwinsteel.com
Products: Galvanized products. **SIC:** 5051 (Metals Service Centers & Offices). **Sales:** $180,000,000 (2000). **Emp:** 200. **Officers:** Robert Welter, President; Vincent Casantino, Treasurer.

■ **19801** ■ **Baltimore Scrap Corp.**
1600 Carbon Ave.
Baltimore, MD 21226
Phone: (410)355-4455
Products: Scrap metal. **SIC:** 5093 (Scrap & Waste Materials).

■ **19802** ■ **Bangor Steel**
123 Dowd Rd.
Bangor, ME 04401
Phone: (207)947-2773
Products: Steel. **SIC:** 5051 (Metals Service Centers & Offices).

■ **19803** ■ **Banner Service Corp.**
494 E Lies Rd.
Carol Stream, IL 60188
Phone: (630)653-7500
Free: (800)323-9732 **Fax:** (630)653-7555
E-mail: info@bargrind.com
URL: http://www.bargrind.com
Products: Centerless grinding; Bars, including carbon, stainless, aluminum, brass, and chrome-plated stainless steel. **SIC:** 5051 (Metals Service Centers & Offices). **Est:** 1961. **Sales:** $25,000,000 (2000). **Emp:** 62. **Officers:** Kirk Sneeden, CEO; L. Ferro, Controller; Bob McGourty, General Mgr.

■ **19804** ■ **Baron Drawn Steel Corp.**
PO Box 3275
Toledo, OH 43607
Phone: (419)531-5525
Free: (800)537-8850 **Fax:** (419)537-0754
Products: Steel service center: cutting, shearing, pickling, cold extrusion wires, carbon and alloy cold drawn steel bars and shapes. **SIC:** 5051 (Metals Service Centers & Offices). **Sales:** $25,000,000 (2000). **Emp:** 200. **Officers:** Peter Gasiorski, President.

■ **19805** ■ **Basin Pipe & Metal**
6960 Hwy. 70 N
Alamogordo, NM 88310
Phone: (505)437-6272
Products: Metals; Pipes. **SIC:** 5051 (Metals Service Centers & Offices).

■ **19806** ■ **Baszile Metals Service Inc.**
2554 E 25th St.
Los Angeles, CA 90058
Phone: (213)583-6922 **Fax:** (323)588-9542
E-mail: bbaszile@aol.com
URL: http://www.baszile.com
Products: Aluminum sheet, plate, rod, and bar. **SIC:** 5051 (Metals Service Centers & Offices). **Est:** 1974. **Sales:** $17,000,000 (2000). **Emp:** 23. **Officers:** Barry Baszile, President; Janet Baszile, Vice President; Dwight Stangle, Sales Mgr.

■ **19807** ■ **Bellesteel Industries Inc.**
PO Box 490
East Boston, MA 02128
Phone: (617)569-9100
Products: Steel. **SIC:** 5051 (Metals Service Centers & Offices). **Est:** 1950. **Sales:** $45,000,000 (2000). **Emp:** 50. **Officers:** Daniel Greiff, President; Elliot Sadow, Controller.

■ **19808** ■ **Belmont Steel Corp.**
2424 Oakton St.
Evanston, IL 60202-2796
Phone: (847)866-2100
Products: Hot and cold-rolled steel. **SIC:** 5051 (Metals Service Centers & Offices). **Est:** 1947. **Sales:** $85,000,000 (2000). **Emp:** 175. **Officers:** Joseph B. Pringle, President; LouAnn Mackowiak, VP of Finance & Admin.; John Hughes, VP of Marketing & Sales; Ed Linhart, Controller; Bill Beckert, Dir of Human Resources.

■ **19809** ■ **Benco Steel Inc.**
PO Box 2053
Hickory, NC 28603
Phone: (828)328-1714
Products: Steel. **SIC:** 5051 (Metals Service Centers & Offices). **Sales:** $18,000,000 (1994). **Emp:** 25. **Officers:** Joel White, Owner; Janice Elliot, Vice President.

■ **19810** ■ **Benedict-Miller Inc.**
PO Box 912
Lyndhurst, NJ 07071
Phone: (201)438-3000
Free: (800)526-6372 **Fax:** (201)438-4962
E-mail: info@benedict-miller.com
URL: http://www.benedict-miller.com
Products: Steel, including heat treated steel and commercial hardening. **SIC:** 5051 (Metals Service Centers & Offices). **Est:** 1940. **Sales:** $15,000,000 (2000). **Emp:** 100. **Officers:** J.P. Benedict, President & CEO; Walt Las, Sales Mgr.; Walt Las, Sales Mgr.

■ **19811** ■ **Benjamin Metals Co.**
PO Box 59906
Los Angeles, CA 90059
Phone: (213)321-1700 **Fax:** (213)770-0102
Products: Aluminum sheets and scrap. **SICs:** 5051 (Metals Service Centers & Offices); 5093 (Scrap & Waste Materials). **Est:** 1946. **Sales:** $30,000,000 (2000). **Emp:** 79. **Officers:** M. Benjamin, President; E. Purvis, Exec. VP.

■ **19812** ■ **Benjamin Steel Company Inc.**
777 Benjamin Dr.
Springfield, OH 45502-8846
Phone: (513)322-8000 **Fax:** (513)327-0451
Products: Steel. **SIC:** 5051 (Metals Service Centers & Offices). **Est:** 1969. **Sales:** $30,000,000 (2000). **Emp:** 200. **Officers:** Vincent J. Demana, President; Pat Guariello, Dir. of Systems.

■ **19813** ■ **Berg Steel Corp.**
4306 Normandy Ct.
Royal Oak, MI 48073
Phone: (248)549-6066 **Fax:** (248)549-0103
Products: Steel. **SIC:** 5051 (Metals Service Centers & Offices). **Est:** 1971. **Sales:** $20,000,000 (2000). **Emp:** 17. **Officers:** N.F. Berg, President.

■ **19814** ■ **Berkshire Valley**
PO Box 150
Adams, MA 01220
Phone: (413)743-4240
Free: (800)984-0591 **Fax:** (413)743-4240
E-mail: bvinc@bcn.net
URL: http://www.berkshirevalleyinc.com
Products: Metal and polyurethane for model trains. **SIC:** 5051 (Metals Service Centers & Offices). **Est:** 1989. **Emp:** 3.

■ **19815** ■ **Berlin Enterprises Inc.**
3200 Sheffield Ave.
Hammond, IN 46320
Phone: (219)933-0233 **Fax:** (219)933-0890
Products: Steel. **SIC:** 5051 (Metals Service Centers & Offices). **Sales:** $93,000,000 (2000). **Emp:** 80. **Officers:** Melvin Berlin, CEO.

■ **19816** ■ **Berlin Metals Inc.**
3200 Sheffield Ave.
Hammond, IN 46327
Phone: (219)933-0111
Free: (800)754-8867 **Fax:** (219)933-0692
URL: http://www.berlinmetals.com
Products: Coil slitting; Light gauge metals. **SIC:** 5051 (Metals Service Centers & Offices). **Est:** 1959. **Emp:** 85. **Officers:** Melvin Berlin, Chairman of the Board; Roy Berlin, President.

■ **19817** ■ **Berwick Steel Co**
PO Box 27278
Columbus, OH 43227
Phone: (614)866-1338 **Fax:** (614)866-6457
Products: Steel service center. **SIC:** 5051 (Metals Service Centers & Offices). **Officers:** Oak Okamura, President.

■ **19818** ■ **Berwick Steel Co.**
100 Steelway Pl.
Piqua, OH 45356
Phone: (937)778-8884
Products: Steel. **SIC:** 5051 (Metals Service Centers & Offices).

■ **19819** ■ **Besco Steel Supply, Inc.**
1801 Linder Industrial Dr.
Nashville, TN 37209
Phone: (615)251-8087
Products: Steel. **SIC:** 5051 (Metals Service Centers & Offices).

■ **19820** ■ **Bethlehem Steel Export Corp.**
701 E 3rd St.
Bethlehem, PA 18016
Phone: (215)694-2424
Products: Steel. **SIC:** 5051 (Metals Service Centers & Offices). **Sales:** $18,000,000 (1993). **Emp:** 25.
Officers: David Post, President.

■ **19821** ■ **BFI Recyclery**
964 Hazel St.
Akron, OH 44305
Phone: (330)434-9183
Products: Metals, plastics, and paper recycling. **SIC:** 5093 (Scrap & Waste Materials). **Sales:** $3,000,000 (1990). **Emp:** 8. **Officers:** Richard B. Jones, Manager.

■ **19822** ■ **BHP Trading Inc.**
111 W Ocean Blvd.
Long Beach, CA 90802
Phone: (562)491-1441
Products: Steel. **SIC:** 5051 (Metals Service Centers & Offices). **Est:** 1926. **Sales:** $9,000,000 (2000). **Emp:** 45. **Officers:** P. Spitzer, President; J. Demanett, VP of Finance & Admin.; L. Tries, VP Marketing & Development.

■ **19823** ■ **BICO Akron Inc.**
3100 Gilchrist Rd.
Mogadore, OH 44260
Phone: (330)794-1716 **Fax:** (330)733-7189
Products: Steel. **SIC:** 5051 (Metals Service Centers & Offices). **Est:** 1896. **Sales:** $8,000,000 (2000). **Emp:** 75. **Officers:** Michael A. Ensminger, CEO.

■ **19824** ■ **Bissett Steel Co**
9005 Bank St.
Cleveland, OH 44125
Phone: (216)447-4000 **Fax:** (216)447-1288
Products: Metal service center: cold drawn and hot rolled bars, stainless steel bars; turned, ground and polished shafting. **SIC:** 5051 (Metals Service Centers & Offices).

■ **19825** ■ **Bloch Steel Industries**
PO Box 24063
Seattle, WA 98124
Phone: (206)763-0200
Products: Steel. **SIC:** 5051 (Metals Service Centers & Offices). **Est:** 1920. **Sales:** $10,000,000 (2000). **Emp:** 50. **Officers:** Leo D. Bloch, CEO; Tom Thompson, Controller.

■ **19826** ■ **Block Steel Corp.**
6101 W Oakton
Skokie, IL 60077
Phone: (847)966-3000 **Fax:** (847)996-5906
E-mail: info@blocksteel.com
URL: http://www.blocksteel.com
Products: Aluminized and galvanized sheet steel. **SIC:** 5051 (Metals Service Centers & Offices). **Est:** 1948.
Sales: $50,000,000 (1999). **Emp:** 130. **Officers:** Larry Wolfson, President; Steve Wysocki, CFO; J. Block, VP of Sales; Don Morgan, VP of Marketing; Joe Block, Dir of Human Resources.

■ **19827** ■ **Blue Mountain Steel**
10097 US Highway 50 E
Carson City, NV 89701
Phone: (775)246-7770
Products: Steel. **SIC:** 5051 (Metals Service Centers & Offices).

■ **19828** ■ **BMG Metals Inc.**
PO Box 7536
Richmond, VA 23231
Phone: (804)226-1024
Products: Steel. **SIC:** 5051 (Metals Service Centers & Offices).

■ **19829** ■ **Bobco Metal Co.**
2000 S Alameda St.
Los Angeles, CA 90058
Phone: (213)748-5171
Free: (800)262-2605 **Fax:** (213)748-7869
Products: Steel Service Center; Ferrous and nonferrous metals. **SIC:** 5051 (Metals Service Centers & Offices). **Emp:** 40. **Officers:** Hamid Shooshani, President; Fred Shooshani, General Mgr.

■ **19830** ■ **Boman and Kemp Steel and Supply Inc.**
PO Box 9725
Ogden, UT 84409
Phone: (801)731-0615 **Fax:** (801)731-5785
Products: Sheet and structural steel. **SIC:** 5051 (Metals Service Centers & Offices). **Est:** 1968. **Sales:** $75,000,000 (2000). **Emp:** 120. **Officers:** Jeff R. Kemp, President; Mel Kemp, CEO.

■ **19831** ■ **Borg Compressed Steel Corp.**
1032 N Lewis Ave.
Tulsa, OK 74110
Phone: (918)587-2437 **Fax:** (918)587-2520
Products: Aluminum; Steel. **SIC:** 5051 (Metals Service Centers & Offices). **Est:** 1946. **Sales:** $41,000,000 (2000). **Emp:** 70. **Officers:** Harry Schwartz, President; Paul A. Schwartz, Treasurer.

■ **19832** ■ **Harry Brainum Junior Inc.**
360 McGuinness Blvd.
Brooklyn, NY 11222
Phone: (718)389-4080
Free: (800)540-7272 **Fax:** (718)383-1646
Products: Steel sheets and coils. **SIC:** 5051 (Metals Service Centers & Offices). **Est:** 1918. **Sales:** $10,000,000 (2000). **Emp:** 25. **Officers:** G. Brainum, President.

■ **19833** ■ **Bralco Metals Div.**
15090 Northam St.
La Mirada, CA 90638-5757
Phone: (714)736-4800
Free: (800)628-1864 **Fax:** (714)736-4840
E-mail: sales@bralco.com
Products: Metals, including aluminum, brass, copper, sheet and rod, and carbon steel. **SIC:** 5051 (Metals Service Centers & Offices). **Est:** 1944. **Sales:** $77,000,000 (2000). **Emp:** 125. **Officers:** Michael Hubbart, General Mgr.

■ **19834** ■ **Breen International**
5458 Steubenville Pike, No. 1st Fl.
McKees Rocks, PA 15136-1412
Phone: (724)695-8990 **Fax:** (724)695-3230
E-mail: breenint@aol.com
URL: http://www.breenint.com
Products: Tin plates; Stainless steel products; Galvanized-prepainted steel. **SIC:** 5051 (Metals Service Centers & Offices). **Est:** 1984. **Sales:** $7,500,000 (2000). **Emp:** 7. **Officers:** James P. Breen, President; Leslie Breen, VP of Sales; Kurt Tuszynski, Customer Service Contact; Judy Roth, Human Resources Contact. **Former Name:** Montour Metals Inc.

■ **19835** ■ **Bridgeport Steel Co.**
1034 Bridgeport Ave.
Milford, CT 06460
Phone: (203)874-2591
Free: (800)972-7272 **Fax:** (203)874-0509
E-mail: sales@bridgeportsteel.com
URL: http://www.bridgeportsteel.com
Products: Alloy Bar; Steel. **SIC:** 5051 (Metals Service Centers & Offices). **Est:** 1947. **Sales:** $11,000,000 (2000). **Emp:** 15. **Officers:** James Hudson, President & Treasurer.

■ **19836** ■ **Brina Steel Products Inc.**
2230 E 17th St.
Erie, PA 16504
Phone: (814)898-2842
Products: Steel products. **SIC:** 5051 (Metals Service Centers & Offices).

■ **19837** ■ **Bronze and Plastic Specialties Inc.**
2025 Inverness Ave.
Baltimore, MD 21230
Phone: (410)644-0440 **Fax:** (410)646-5161
Products: Bronze; Plastic; Fabrics. **SICs:** 5085 (Industrial Supplies); 5162 (Plastics Materials & Basic Shapes). **Sales:** $6,000,000 (2000). **Emp:** 40.
Officers: Richard G. Scherr, President.

■ **19838** ■ **Brown-Campbell Co**
1383 S Woodward Ave., Ste. 200
Bloomfield Hills, MI 48302
Phone: (248)338-4980 **Fax:** (248)338-4072
Products: Steel service center. **SIC:** 5051 (Metals Service Centers & Offices). **Est:** 1953. **Officers:** Murdoch Campbell, President.

■ **19839** ■ **Brown Metals Co.**
4225 Airport Dr.
Ontario, CA 91761
Phone: (909)390-3199 **Fax:** (909)390-3182
Products: Thin gauge stainless steel. **SIC:** 5051 (Metals Service Centers & Offices). **Officers:** Lance Brown, President.

■ **19840** ■ **Brown Steel Div.**
PO Box 16505
Columbus, OH 43216
Phone: (614)443-4881 **Fax:** (614)443-6371
Products: Unfabricated steel. **SIC:** 5051 (Metals Service Centers & Offices). **Est:** 1892. **Sales:** $15,000,000 (2000). **Emp:** 65. **Officers:** H. James Detty, CEO.

■ **19841** ■ **Buffalo Structural Steel**
20 John James Audobon Pkwy.
West Amherst, NY 14228
Phone: (716)639-7714 **Fax:** (716)639-7718
Products: Sheet steel; Coils. **SIC:** 5051 (Metals Service Centers & Offices). **Est:** 1977. **Sales:** $20,000,000 (2000). **Emp:** 60. **Officers:** J.C. Wright, President; Erv Gretzinger, Treasurer & Secty.; Deborah Riccione, Dir. of Marketing.

■ **19842** ■ **Bundy Enterprises Inc.**
2522 State Rd.
Bensalem, PA 19020
Phone: (215)245-1099
Products: Steel. **SIC:** 5051 (Metals Service Centers & Offices).

■ **19843** ■ **Burger Iron Co.**
1324 Firestone Pkwy.
Akron, OH 44301
Phone: (330)253-5121 **Fax:** (330)255-4539
Products: Steel products. **SIC:** 5051 (Metals Service Centers & Offices). **Est:** 1896. **Sales:** $34,000,000 (2000). **Emp:** 265. **Officers:** T.M. Fiocca, CEO & President; Frank Gazzillo, VP & Gen. Mgr.

■ **19844** ■ **Burgon Tool Steel Company Inc.**
20 Durham St.
Portsmouth, NH 03801
Phone: (603)430-9200 **Fax:** (603)430-4004
Products: Steel service center: tool steel cutting, slitting, shearing and fabricating. **SIC:** 5051 (Metals Service Centers & Offices).

■ **19845** ■ **Busby Metals Inc.**
55 Davids Dr.
Hauppauge, NY 11788
Phone: (631)434-3400
Free: (800)552-8729 **Fax:** (631)434-3409
E-mail: info@busbymetals.com
URL: http://www.busbymetals.com
Products: Copper, brass, and bronze products. **SIC:** 5051 (Metals Service Centers & Offices). **Est:** 1947.
Sales: $7,000,000 (2000). **Emp:** 12. **Officers:** Carl Orr, President; John Harkin, Vice President.

■ **19846** ■ **Cain Steel and Supply Co.**
PO Box 1369
Tuscaloosa, AL 35403
Phone: (205)349-2751
Products: Unfabricated steel. **SIC:** 5051 (Metals Service Centers & Offices). **Est:** 1932. **Sales:** $5,000,000 (2000). **Emp:** 35. **Officers:** Billy Minges, President.

■ 19847 ■ California Steel Services Inc.
1212 S Mountain View
San Bernardino, CA 92408
Phone: (909)796-2222
Free: (800)323-7227 **Fax:** (909)796-8888
E-mail: calsteel@msn.com
URL: http://www.calsteel.com
Products: General steel. **SIC:** 5051 (Metals Service Centers & Offices). **Est:** 1983. **Sales:** $1,600,000 (2000). **Emp:** 54. **Officers:** Parviz Razavian, President.

■ 19848 ■ Camalloy Inc.
PO Box 248
Washington, PA 15301
Phone: (724)228-1880
Free: (800)245-4940 **Fax:** (724)222-0336
URL: http://www.camalloy.com
Products: Stainless steel; Stainless plate; Bar; Industrial tapes; Adhesives and abrasives. **SICs:** 5051 (Metals Service Centers & Offices); 5169 (Chemicals & Allied Products Nec); 5085 (Industrial Supplies). **Est:** 1969. **Sales:** $14,000,000 (1999). **Emp:** 24. **Officers:** William Campbell, President; Frank Bennett, Vice President; Connie Howard, Treasurer.

■ 19849 ■ Cambridge Street Metal Company Inc.
500 Lincoln St.
Allston, MA 02134
Phone: (617)254-7580
Free: (800)254-7580 **Fax:** (617)254-3552
Products: Metals. **SIC:** 5051 (Metals Service Centers & Offices). **Est:** 1932. **Sales:** $8,000,000 (2000). **Emp:** 12. **Officers:** Harry Indursky, CEO & President; Robert Dumont, Treasurer; Randy Raymond, Vice President.

■ 19850 ■ Camden Iron and Metal Co.
1500 S 6th St.
Camden, NJ 08104
Phone: (609)365-7500
Products: Metals, including copper, aluminum, iron, and brass. **SIC:** 5051 (Metals Service Centers & Offices).

■ 19851 ■ Cape & Island Steel Co.
200 Airport Way
Hyannis, MA 02601
Phone: (508)775-2022
Products: Steel. **SIC:** 5051 (Metals Service Centers & Offices).

■ 19852 ■ Capitol Metals Company Inc.
4131 E Washington St.
Phoenix, AZ 85034
Phone: (602)275-4131 **Fax:** (602)273-0316
Products: Metals service center. **SIC:** 5051 (Metals Service Centers & Offices).

■ 19853 ■ Capitol Steel Inc.
PO Box 66636
Baton Rouge, LA 70896
Phone: (504)356-4631 **Fax:** (504)355-8562
Products: Steel. **SIC:** 5051 (Metals Service Centers & Offices). **Sales:** $20,000,000 (2000). **Emp:** 77. **Officers:** Tim Distefano, General Mgr.; Jim Richardson, Controller.

■ 19854 ■ Carbon and Alloy Metals Inc.
PO Box 1756
Houston, TX 77251
Phone: (713)690-5518 **Free:** (800)392-7720
E-mail: steelsales@carbonandalloy.com
URL: http://www.carbonandalloy.com
Products: Carbon and steel bars and plates. **SIC:** 5051 (Metals Service Centers & Offices). **Est:** 1985. **Sales:** $16,000,000 (2000). **Emp:** 38. **Officers:** Everett Hruska, President; David McIlheran, CFO.

■ 19855 ■ Cardel Sales Inc.
211 Parkwest Dr.
Pittsburgh, PA 15275-1003
Phone: (412)322-5400
Free: (800)232-3900 **Fax:** (412)322-7678
Products: Copper and copper-base alloy wire. **SIC:** 5051 (Metals Service Centers & Offices). **Emp:** 30. **Officers:** Gary Bahm.

■ 19856 ■ Cargill Steel & Wire
600 Cowan St.
Nashville, TN 37207
Phone: (615)782-8500
Products: Steel. **SIC:** 5051 (Metals Service Centers & Offices).

■ 19857 ■ Carlyle Inc.
PO Box 58999
Tukwila, WA 98138
Phone: (425)251-0700 **Fax:** (425)251-8826
Products: Wires, cables and connectors; fiber and cable assembly plant. **SIC:** 5051 (Metals Service Centers & Offices).

■ 19858 ■ Carolina Steel Corp.
1115 Old Lenoir Rd.
Hickory, NC
Phone: (828)322-9420
Products: Steel. **SIC:** 5051 (Metals Service Centers & Offices).

■ 19859 ■ Carolina Steel Corp.
PO Box 20888
Greensboro, NC 27420
Phone: (336)275-9711 **Fax:** (336)691-5772
Products: Metals service center: cutting, slitting, shearing and steel fabricating. **SIC:** 5051 (Metals Service Centers & Offices). **Sales:** $84,000,000 (2000). **Emp:** 450. **Officers:** W Reeves, President.

■ 19860 ■ Carpenter Technology/Steel Div
PO Box 58880
Los Angeles, CA 90058
Phone: (323)587-9131 **Fax:** (323)587-8145
Products: Specialty metals, stainless steel, nickel base alloys. **SIC:** 5051 (Metals Service Centers & Offices).

■ 19861 ■ Carson Masonry and Steel Supply
4783 US Highway 50 E
Carson City, NV 89701
Phone: (775)882-3832
Products: Masonry supplies. **SIC:** 5051 (Metals Service Centers & Offices).

■ 19862 ■ A.M. Castle and Co.
3400 N Wolf Rd.
Franklin Park, IL 60131
Phone: (847)455-7111
Free: (800)BUY-CSTL **Fax:** (847)455-9346
URL: http://www.amcastle.com
Products: Steel, including bars, coils, sheets, and plates. **SIC:** 5051 (Metals Service Centers & Offices). **Est:** 1890. **Sales:** $750,000,000 (1999). **Emp:** 1,500. **Officers:** G. Thomas McKane, CEO & President; Edward F. Culliton, VP & CFO; Steven V. Hooks, VP of Merchandising; Henry Winters, VP of Operations; Thomas D. Prendergast, VP of Human Resources.

■ 19863 ■ A.M. Castle and Co. Hy-Alloy Steels Div.
4527 Columbia Ave.
Hammond, IN 46327
Phone: (773)582-3200
Products: Steel and carbon-alloy steel. **SIC:** 5051 (Metals Service Centers & Offices). **Est:** 1945. **Sales:** $60,000,000 (2000). **Emp:** 75. **Officers:** Gise Van Baren, President; William Burlein, Dir. of Sales.

■ 19864 ■ Castle Metals Inc.
298 Crescentville Rd.
Cincinnati, OH 45246
Phone: (513)772-7000
Products: Specialty metals. **SICs:** 5051 (Metals Service Centers & Offices); 5052 (Coal, Other Minerals & Ores).

■ 19865 ■ Cavexsa USA Inc.
3701 Commercial Ave., Ste. 12
Northbrook, IL 60062-1830
Phone: (708)730-0030
Products: Steel bars. **SIC:** 5051 (Metals Service Centers & Offices). **Est:** 1976. **Sales:** $3,000,000 (2000). **Emp:** 3. **Officers:** M. Fernandez, Exec. VP.

■ 19866 ■ CCC Steel Inc.
2576 E Victoria St.
Rancho Dominguez, CA 90220
Phone: (310)637-0111 **Fax:** (310)637-7998
E-mail: sales@ccc-steel.com
URL: http://www.cccsteel.com
Products: Steel. **SIC:** 5051 (Metals Service Centers & Offices). **Est:** 1968. **Sales:** $62,000,000 (1999). **Emp:** 62. **Officers:** Bernd D. Hildebrandt, President; Gary Fajack, CFO.

■ 19867 ■ Central Steel Supply Company Inc.
99 Foley St.
Somerville, MA 02145
Phone: (617)625-3232
Free: (800)345-3232 **Fax:** (617)666-3027
URL: http://www.centralsteelsupply.com
Products: Steel products. **SIC:** 5051 (Metals Service Centers & Offices). **Est:** 1949. **Sales:** $10,000,000 (2000). **Emp:** 35. **Officers:** Walter Lipsett, Chairman of the Board; John de Vries, President, e-mail: johnnyd@gis.net.

■ 19868 ■ Central Steel and Wire Co
PO Box 5100
Chicago, IL 60680
Phone: (773)471-3800 **Fax:** 800-232-9279
Products: Metals service center: cutting, slitting, burning and shearing. **SIC:** 5051 (Metals Service Centers & Offices). **Est:** 1909.

■ 19869 ■ Centrotrade Minerals and Metals Inc.
521 5th Ave., 30th Fl.
New York, NY 10175-0003
Phone: (212)808-4900 **Fax:** (212)808-5546
Products: Copper concentrates. **SIC:** 5051 (Metals Service Centers & Offices). **Est:** 1988. **Sales:** $6,000,000 (1999). **Emp:** 10. **Officers:** William Ridgway, President, e-mail: bridgway@ctmm.com.

■ 19870 ■ Century Steel Corp.
300 E Joe Orr Rd.
Chicago Heights, IL 60411
Phone: (708)758-0900 **Fax:** (708)758-4902
Products: Steel, including hot-rolled, galvanized, and cold-rolled. **SIC:** 5051 (Metals Service Centers & Offices). **Est:** 1938. **Sales:** $85,000,000 (2000). **Emp:** 190. **Officers:** James T. Reid, President; Bernie Babel, Treasurer; Irwin Muchman, VP of Marketing; Gene Kijanowski, Data Processing Mgr.; Justine Wheeler, Personnel Mgr.

■ 19871 ■ Chapin and Bangs Co. Inc.
PO Box 1117
Bridgeport, CT 06601
Phone: (203)333-4183
Products: Steel. **SIC:** 5051 (Metals Service Centers & Offices). **Est:** 1888. **Sales:** $19,000,000 (1999). **Emp:** 105. **Officers:** Richard M. Hoyt, President; Brian H. Williams, Exec. VP; William H. Doelling, VP of Marketing; Donals M. Walker, VP of Sales.

■ 19872 ■ Chapman-Dyer Steel Manufacturing
PO Box 27365
Tucson, AZ 85726
Phone: (520)623-6318 **Fax:** (520)623-1227
Products: Steel. **SIC:** 5051 (Metals Service Centers & Offices). **Est:** 1946. **Sales:** $3,500,000 (2000). **Emp:** 13. **Officers:** M.B. Chapman, President & Chairman of the Board; Elmer L. Jones, Treasurer; Stephen A. Chapman, Vice President.

■ 19873 ■ Charles Bluestone Co.
PO Box 326
Elizabeth, PA 15037
Phone: (412)384-7400 **Fax:** (412)384-7406
Products: Nonferrous metals. **SIC:** 5093 (Scrap & Waste Materials). **Sales:** $35,000,000 (1992). **Emp:** 35. **Officers:** Paul Haveson, President; Deborah Clark, Controller.

■ 19874 ■ Chatham Steel Corp.
PO Box 2567
Savannah, GA 31498
Phone: (912)233-4182
Products: Steel; Pipe. **SIC:** 5051 (Metals Service Centers & Offices). **Est:** 1915. **Sales:** $150,000,000 (2000). **Emp:** 305. **Officers:** Arnold Tenenbaum, CEO

& President; G.K. Matthews, CFO; Bert M. Tenenbaum, VP of Marketing; J. Byrd, Dir. of Information Systems; Ronald Kronowitz.

■ 19875 ■ **Chemung Supply Corp.**
PO Box 527
Elmira, NY 14902
Phone: (607)733-5506 **Fax:** (607)732-5379
Products: Industrial supplies. **SIC:** 5051 (Metals Service Centers & Offices). **Sales:** $16,000,000 (2000). **Emp:** 60.

■ 19876 ■ **Chicago Tube and Iron Co.**
2531 W 48th St.
Chicago, IL 60632
Phone: (312)523-1441 **Fax:** (312)523-1375
Products: Iron; Metal tubing. **SIC:** 5051 (Metals Service Centers & Offices). **Est:** 1914. **Sales:** $140,000,000 (2000). **Emp:** 400. **Officers:** Robert B. Haigh, CEO & Chairman of the Board; John F. McGlone, VP & CFO; Thomas M. Moran, Dir. of Systems; Daniel L. Shoaf, Dir of Human Resources.

■ 19877 ■ **Choice Metals**
36 Cote Ave.
Goffstown, NH 03045
Phone: (603)626-5500
Free: (800)621-6267 **Fax:** (603)626-5502
Products: Metal products. **SIC:** 5051 (Metals Service Centers & Offices).

■ 19878 ■ **Christy Metals Company Inc.**
PO Box 8206
Northfield, IL 60093
Phone: (708)729-5744 **Fax:** (708)729-5759
Products: Metals. **SIC:** 5051 (Metals Service Centers & Offices). **Est:** 1963. **Sales:** $15,000,000 (2000). **Emp:** 30. **Officers:** Creighton Helms, Owner; Christy Helms, President; Sandy Berens, General Mgr.; Steve Mitterer, Dir. of Data Processing; Judy Muncer, Dir of Human Resources; Sherrie Schram, Distribution Mgr.

■ 19879 ■ **Cincinnati Steel Products**
4540 Steel Pl.
Cincinnati, OH 45209
Phone: (513)871-4444 **Fax:** (513)321-9608
E-mail: cinsteel@aol.com
Products: Steel. **SIC:** 5051 (Metals Service Centers & Offices). **Est:** 1933. **Sales:** $12,000,000 (2000). **Emp:** 52. **Officers:** J.S. Todd, CEO; T.H. Rutter, Treasurer; R.W. Lutts, President; K.S. Miller; Tom Brown, Sales Mgr.

■ 19880 ■ **Coil Center Corp.**
1415 Durant Dr.
Howell, MI 48843
Phone: (517)548-0100 **Fax:** (517)548-9289
Products: Steel service center. **SIC:** 5013 (Motor Vehicle Supplies & New Parts). **Sales:** $1,000,000 (1993). **Emp:** 40. **Officers:** Ken Ohashi, Exec. VP; James Bartkovich, Controller.

■ 19881 ■ **Coil Plus Pennsylvania Inc.**
5135 Milnor St. & Bleigh St.
Philadelphia, PA 19136
Phone: (215)331-5200
Products: Processed steel. **SIC:** 5051 (Metals Service Centers & Offices). **Est:** 1969. **Sales:** $40,000,000 (2000). **Emp:** 60. **Officers:** David Kinka, President; Hugh Graney, Dir of Human Resources; James J. Lehr, Dir. of Marketing & Sales; Betty Chaput, Dir. of Data Processing.

■ 19882 ■ **Columbia Iron and Metal Co.**
6600 Grant Ave.
Cleveland, OH 44105
Phone: (216)883-4972
Products: Raw metal and steel. **SIC:** 5051 (Metals Service Centers & Offices). **Est:** 1937. **Sales:** $11,700,000 (2000). **Emp:** 32. **Officers:** David P. Miller, Chairman of the Board; James D. Larr, VP of Finance & Treasurer; Gerald Mink, Dir. of Marketing & Sales.

■ 19883 ■ **Columbia National Group Inc.**
6600 Grant Ave.
Cleveland, OH 44105
Phone: (216)883-4972 **Fax:** (216)341-3483
Products: Scrap metals. **SIC:** 5093 (Scrap & Waste Materials). **Sales:** $180,000,000 (2000). **Emp:** 500. **Officers:** David Miller, President; Steve Ruscher, VP & CFO.

■ 19884 ■ **Columbia Ventures Corp.**
1220 Main St. Ste. 200
Vancouver, WA 98660
Phone: (360)693-1336 **Fax:** (360)693-1735
Products: Aluminum extrusions; aluminum fabrication and recycling. **SICs:** 5051 (Metals Service Centers & Offices); 5093 (Scrap & Waste Materials). **Sales:** $160,000,000 (2000). **Emp:** 1,000. **Officers:** Kenneth Peterson, CEO & President; Richard A. Roman, Sr. VP & CFO.

■ 19885 ■ **Columbus Metals Supply Inc.**
302 7th Ave. S
Columbus, MS 39701
Phone: (601)329-3889
Free: (800)742-6552 **Fax:** (601)327-5380
Products: Metals. **SIC:** 5051 (Metals Service Centers & Offices). **Est:** 1990. **Sales:** $3,000,000 (2000). **Emp:** 7. **Officers:** J.D. Rankin, President.

■ 19886 ■ **Combined Metals of Chicago L.P.**
2401 W Grant St.
Bellwood, IL 60104
Phone: (708)547-8800 **Fax:** (708)547-1037
Products: Stainless steel. **SIC:** 5051 (Metals Service Centers & Offices). **Sales:** $100,000,000 (2000). **Emp:** 100. **Officers:** Herbert F. Sass, General Mgr.; Glen Rolbiecki, Controller.

■ 19887 ■ **Commercial Alloys Corp.**
1831 Highland Rd.
Twinsburg, OH 44087-2222
Phone: (330)405-5440
Free: (800)221-3239 **Fax:** (330)405-5431
E-mail: cac@stratos.net
URL: http://www.aluminumscrap.com
Products: Nonferrous metals, including aluminum and zinc. **SIC:** 5051 (Metals Service Centers & Offices). **Est:** 1983. **Sales:** $150,000,000 (2000). **Emp:** 80. **Officers:** Jerry Brown, President, e-mail: kingjb@stratos.net.

■ 19888 ■ **Commercial Metals Co.**
7800 Stemmons Frwy.
Dallas, TX 75247-4227
Phone: (214)689-4300 **Fax:** (214)689-5586
E-mail: admin@commercialmetals.com
URL: http://www.commercialmetals.com
Products: Primary metal products. **SIC:** 5051 (Metals Service Centers & Offices). **Est:** 1915. **Sales:** $2,251,442 (1999). **Emp:** 8,000. **Officers:** Stanley A. Rabin, Chairman, CEO, and President; William B. Larson, VP and CFO.

■ 19889 ■ **Commodity Steel and Processing Inc.**
PO Box 3758
Center Line, MI 48015-0758
Phone: (810)758-1040 **Fax:** (313)758-2589
Products: Steel. **SIC:** 5051 (Metals Service Centers & Offices). **Est:** 1967. **Sales:** $12,000,000 (2000). **Emp:** 60. **Officers:** L.H. Golden, President; Sid Blackman, CFO; G. Hamilton, Dir. of Marketing.

■ 19890 ■ **Commonwealth Metal Corp.**
560 Sylvan Avenue
PO Box 1426
Englewood Cliffs, NJ 07632-0426
Phone: (201)569-2000
Free: (800)772-2119 **Fax:** (201)569-8628
E-mail: cwl!postmaster@commwel.attmail.com
URL: http://www.comercialmetals.com
Products: Nonferrous metal products. **SIC:** 5051 (Metals Service Centers & Offices). **Est:** 1965. **Sales:** $150,000,000 (2000). **Emp:** 55. **Officers:** Charles J. Shrem, CEO & President; Steven I. Halpern, Controller; Charles J. Schaffer, VP of Sales.

■ 19891 ■ **Complex Steel Wire Corp.**
36254 Annapolis
Wayne, MI 48184-2044
Phone: (734)326-1600
Free: (800)521-0666 **Fax:** (734)326-7421
Products: Wire mesh rack decking. **SIC:** 5051 (Metals

Service Centers & Offices). **Est:** 1970. **Emp:** 49. **Officers:** V. Fedell.

■ 19892 ■ **Confederate Steel Corp.**
PO Box 266386
Houston, TX 77207
Phone: (713)643-8526 **Fax:** (713)643-2032
Products: Reinforced steel for the construction industry. **SIC:** 5051 (Metals Service Centers & Offices). **Sales:** $3,000,000 (2000). **Emp:** 30. **Officers:** C.H. Underwood, CEO & President.

■ 19893 ■ **Consumers Steel Products Co.**
8510 Bessemer Ave.
Cleveland, OH 44127
Phone: (216)883-7171 **Fax:** (216)883-3417
Products: Hot, flat, rolled, and constructional steel. **SIC:** 5051 (Metals Service Centers & Offices). **Est:** 1943. **Sales:** $15,000,000 (2000). **Emp:** 25. **Officers:** Arnold Applebaum, Partner.

■ 19894 ■ **Contractors Steel Co.**
36555 Amrhein Rd.
Livonia, MI 48150
Phone: (313)464-4000 **Fax:** (313)464-2026
Products: Steel. **SIC:** 5051 (Metals Service Centers & Offices). **Est:** 1960. **Sales:** $60,000,000 (2000). **Emp:** 170. **Officers:** Donald R. Simon, President.

■ 19895 ■ **Copper and Brass Sales**
414 MacDade Blvd.
Collingdale, PA 19023
Phone: (215)586-1800 **Fax:** (610)586-0232
Products: Metal. **SIC:** 5051 (Metals Service Centers & Offices). **Est:** 1948. **Sales:** $15,000,000 (2000). **Emp:** 105. **Officers:** Frank Kavani, General Mgr.

■ 19896 ■ **Copper and Brass Sales Inc.**
17401 10 Mile Rd.
Eastpointe, MI 48021
Phone: (313)775-7710
Free: (800)926-2600 **Fax:** (313)775-5078
Products: Aluminum and aluminum-base alloy wire; Aluminum bars; Alloys, including yellow and leaded yellow brass; Brass, bronze, and copper foundries; Steel products; Nickel and nickel-base alloy mill shapes; Magnesium; Stainless steel. **SIC:** 5051 (Metals Service Centers & Offices). **Est:** 1931. **Emp:** 1,100. **Officers:** W.K. Howenstein, Chairman of the Board; M.J. Fitzsimons, President; D.K. Fitzsimons, Exec. VP.

■ 19897 ■ **Copper and Brass Sales Inc.**
17401 E 10 Mile Rd.
Eastpointe, MI 48021
Phone: (810)775-7710
Free: (800)926-2600 **Fax:** (810)775-5078
Products: Metals service center. **SIC:** 5051 (Metals Service Centers & Offices). **Est:** 1931. **Sales:** $1,502,000,000 (1999). **Emp:** 1,250. **Officers:** William Sabol, President.

■ 19898 ■ **Copper and Brass Sales Inc.**
2131 Garfield Ave.
Los Angeles, CA 90040
Phone: (323)726-7610 **Fax:** (323)726-2916
Products: Metals; Copper, brass, tubing, sheets, rods and bar. **SIC:** 5051 (Metals Service Centers & Offices).

■ 19899 ■ **Corey Steel Co.**
PO Box 5137
Chicago, IL 60680
Phone: (708)863-8000
Products: Steel products, including bars and sheets; Brass bars; Aluminum cans. **SIC:** 5051 (Metals Service Centers & Offices). **Est:** 1924. **Sales:** $50,000,000 (2000). **Emp:** 200. **Officers:** P.J. Darling II, CEO & President; R.M. Perez, Controller; J.W. Kenefick, Marketing Mgr.; Richard Bosworth, Dir. of Systems.

■ 19900 ■ **Corporacion del Cobre U.S.A. Inc.**
177 Broad St.
Stamford, CT 06901-2048
Phone: (203)425-4321 **Fax:** (203)425-4322
URL: http://www.codelco.com
Products: Copper. **SIC:** 5051 (Metals Service Centers & Offices). **Est:** 1974. **Sales:** $2,000,000 (2000). **Emp:** 3. **Officers:** Michael Galetzki, Dir. of Sales.

■ 19901 ■ Coulter Steel and Forge Co.
PO Box 8008
Emeryville, CA 94662
Phone: (510)420-3500 **Fax:** (510)420-3555
Products: Forge for titanium, aluminum and steel bars, rings, discs and shaped parts. **SIC:** 5051 (Metals Service Centers & Offices). **Sales:** $13,500,000 (2000). **Emp:** 73. **Officers:** Thomas Coulter, President; Robert Barney, Treasurer.

■ 19902 ■ Coutinho Caro and Company Inc.
300 First Stamford Pl.
Stamford, CT 06902
Phone: (203)356-4840
Products: Steel. **SIC:** 5051 (Metals Service Centers & Offices). **Est:** 1954. **Sales:** $11,000,000 (2000). **Emp:** 15. **Officers:** B.H. Huelbert, CEO; John Forbes, VP of Finance & Admin.

■ 19903 ■ Cragin Metals L.L.C.
2900 N Kearsarge Ave.
Chicago, IL 60641
Phone: (773)283-2201 **Fax:** (773)283-5699
Products: Steel service center: shearing and cutting. **SIC:** 5051 (Metals Service Centers & Offices). **Sales:** $5,000,000 (1999). **Emp:** 27. **Officers:** Thomas H. Weber, President.

■ 19904 ■ Crest Steel Corp.
1250 E 223rd St., Ste. 108
Carson, CA 90745-4214
Phone: (310)830-2651
Free: (800)421-1111 **Fax:** (310)835-2279
Products: Steel service center. **SIC:** 5051 (Metals Service Centers & Offices). **Sales:** $96,700,000 (2000). **Emp:** 130. **Officers:** Randy Putnam, President; Dave Zertuche, CFO.

■ 19905 ■ The Crispin Co.
2929 Allen Pkwy., Ste. 2222
Houston, TX 77019
Phone: (713)224-8000 **Fax:** (713)224-1120
E-mail: steelcrisp@aol.com
Products: Steel, including semi-finished, wire, rod, strand cable, rope, tubing, and pipe. **SIC:** 5051 (Metals Service Centers & Offices). **Officers:** Andre A. Crispin, Chairman of the Board; Jacque Bouchez, President.

■ 19906 ■ Crown Steel Sales Inc.
3355 W 31st St.
Chicago, IL 60623
Phone: (312)376-1700 **Fax:** (312)376-8650
Products: Hot-rolled steel. **SIC:** 5051 (Metals Service Centers & Offices). **Est:** 1939. **Sales:** $11,500,000 (2000). **Emp:** 65. **Officers:** R.L. Reineman, President; V.M. Leach, VP of Finance; R. Townsend, Dir. of Marketing & Sales.

■ 19907 ■ Crucible Service Center
568 Brick Church Park Dr.
Nashville, TN 37207-3200
Phone: (615)361-6699
Products: Steel. **SIC:** 5051 (Metals Service Centers & Offices).

■ 19908 ■ Crucible Service Centers
5639 W Genesee St.
Camillus, NY 13031-0991
Phone: (315)487-0800 **Fax:** (315)487-4028
Products: Steel products, including cutting and extracting tools. **SICs:** 5051 (Metals Service Centers & Offices); 5084 (Industrial Machinery & Equipment). **Est:** 1989. **Sales:** $282,300,000 (2000). **Emp:** 380. **Officers:** Harry O'Brien, President; T.S. Furtch, CFO; G.J. Kropf, VP of Sales; S. Walsh, Human Resources Mgr.

■ 19909 ■ Crystal Lite Manufacturing Co
18500 SW 108th Ave.
Tualatin, OR 97062
Phone: (503)692-3024 **Fax:** (503)692-9042
Products: Precision sheet metal work. **SIC:** 5051 (Metals Service Centers & Offices).

■ 19910 ■ Curtze Steel Inc.
1103 Bacon St.
Erie, PA 16511
Phone: (814)456-2008 **Fax:** (814)456-2000
Products: Hot rolled steel products. **SIC:** 5051 (Metals Service Centers & Offices). **Est:** 1956. **Emp:** 9.

■ 19911 ■ Cutter Precision Metals Inc.
PO Box 88488
Seattle, WA 98138
Phone: (206)575-4120
Free: (800)426-4724 **Fax:** (206)854-7401
URL: http://www.cuttermetals.com
Products: Cut non-ferrous metals. **SIC:** 5051 (Metals Service Centers & Offices). **Est:** 1976. **Sales:** $16,000,000 (2000). **Emp:** 26. **Officers:** Kirklan Voll, President; Pete Ratanafopa, Controller.

■ 19912 ■ Cutter Precision Metals Inc.
700 Comstock St.
Santa Clara, CA 95054
Phone: (408)727-0333 **Fax:** (408)988-2304
Products: Double disc, blanchard and centerless grinding; Aluminum, stainless steel and copper base alloy products. **SIC:** 5051 (Metals Service Centers & Offices).

■ 19913 ■ D and B Steel Co.
5221 W 164th St.
Cleveland, OH 44142
Phone: (216)267-5500
Products: Flat-rolled, stripped steel. **SIC:** 5051 (Metals Service Centers & Offices). **Est:** 1953. **Sales:** $8,000,000 (2000). **Emp:** 28. **Officers:** Michael Schmidt, President & Treasurer.

■ 19914 ■ Dailey Metal Group Inc.
1113 N Sherman Ave., No. 3
Madison, WI 53701
Phone: (608)244-5542
Products: Metal. **SIC:** 5051 (Metals Service Centers & Offices).

■ 19915 ■ Dakota Steel and Supply Co.
PO Box 2920
Rapid City, SD 57709-2920
Phone: (605)394-7200 **Fax:** (605)394-7224
Products: Steel bars and sheets, including structural and reinforcing. **SIC:** 5051 (Metals Service Centers & Offices). **Est:** 1953. **Sales:** $12,000,000 (2000). **Emp:** 70. **Officers:** Robert A. Heibult, President.

■ 19916 ■ Darco Enterprises Inc.
1600 S Laflin St.
Chicago, IL 60608
Phone: (312)243-3000
URL: http://www.darcoent.com
Products: Steel, metal lithography. **SIC:** 5051 (Metals Service Centers & Offices). **Est:** 1944. **Emp:** 50. **Officers:** H.A. Friedman, President; Reuben Friedman, CFO.

■ 19917 ■ Dave Steel Co. Inc.
PO Box 2630
Asheville, NC 28802
Phone: (828)252-2771 **Fax:** (828)252-0041
E-mail: dsco@davesteel.com
URL: http://www.davesteel.com
Products: Steel products, including hot-rolled steel. **SIC:** 5051 (Metals Service Centers & Offices). **Est:** 1929. **Sales:** $14,000,000 (2000). **Emp:** 85. **Officers:** A.J. Dave, President; William Lewin, VP of Finance; Jeffrey Dave, Exec. VP; Tim Heffner, VP of Marketing & Sales.

■ 19918 ■ Davis Salvage Co.
3337 E Washington St.
Phoenix, AZ 85034
Phone: (602)267-7208 **Fax:** (602)267-8920
Products: Steel; Aluminum; Copper; Brass. **SIC:** 5051 (Metals Service Centers & Offices). **Est:** 1953. **Sales:** $4,000,000 (2000). **Emp:** 22. **Officers:** Toddy Tamaroff, President; June Tamaroff, Vice President.

■ 19919 ■ DC Metals Inc.
380 S Danebo St.
Eugene, OR 97402
Phone: (503)344-3741
Products: Scrap metal. **SIC:** 5093 (Scrap & Waste Materials).

■ 19920 ■ Decker Steel & Supply Co.
1625 Ash St.
Erie, PA 16503
Phone: (814)454-2446
Free: (800)443-5344 **Fax:** (814)453-7867
E-mail: deckersteel@msn.com
URL: http://www.deckersteel.com
Products: HVAC products, stainless and carbon pipe, valves and fittings. **SIC:** 5051 (Metals Service Centers & Offices). **Est:** 1929. **Emp:** 6.

■ 19921 ■ Decker Steel and Supply Inc.
4500 Train Ave.
Cleveland, OH 44102
Phone: (216)281-7900 **Fax:** (216)281-1441
Products: Steel; Fittings. **SICs:** 5051 (Metals Service Centers & Offices); 5085 (Industrial Supplies). **Est:** 1929. **Sales:** $5,700,000 (2000). **Emp:** 28. **Officers:** John W. Decker, President; Glenn W. Carrathers, Treasurer; Kenneth S. Ross, Vice President.

■ 19922 ■ Del Paso Pipe and Steel Inc.
1113 Del Paso Blvd.
Sacramento, CA 95815
Phone: (916)925-1792 **Fax:** (916)925-2361
Products: Steel. **SIC:** 5051 (Metals Service Centers & Offices). **Est:** 1939. **Sales:** $10,000,000 (2000). **Emp:** 16. **Officers:** Harlan Karnofsky, President; Donna Karnofsky, Finance Officer.

■ 19923 ■ Delta Engineering and Manufacturing Co.
19500 SW Teton Ave.
Tualatin, OR 97062
Phone: (503)692-4435 **Fax:** (503)692-5030
Products: Contract manufacturing of precision sheet metal, primarily for the medical, electronic and telecommunications industries. **SIC:** 5051 (Metals Service Centers & Offices). **Officers:** Gary Wooden, President.

■ 19924 ■ Delta Steel Inc.
111 Beasley Rd.
Jackson, MS 39206
Phone: (601)956-4141
Products: Steel products. **SIC:** 5051 (Metals Service Centers & Offices).

■ 19925 ■ Denbo Iron and Metal Company Inc.
PO Box 1553
Decatur, AL 35602-1553
Phone: (256)353-6351 **Fax:** (256)351-9246
Products: Scrap iron and metal recycler. **SIC:** 5093 (Scrap & Waste Materials). **Sales:** $30,000,000 (1994). **Emp:** 80. **Officers:** Morley Denbo, CEO & President; Betty Cowart, Controller.

■ 19926 ■ Denman and Davis
1 Broad St.
Clifton, NJ 07011
Phone: (201)684-3900
Products: Steel bars and coils. **SIC:** 5051 (Metals Service Centers & Offices). **Sales:** $24,000,000 (2000). **Emp:** 100. **Officers:** David Deinzer, President.

■ 19927 ■ Dennen Steel Corp.
PO Box 3200
Grand Rapids, MI 49501
Phone: (616)784-2000 **Fax:** (616)784-0070
Products: Steel coils and sheets. **SIC:** 5051 (Metals Service Centers & Offices). **Est:** 1980. **Sales:** $50,000,000 (2000). **Emp:** 100. **Officers:** Andrew Dennen, CEO; Michael Mehlman, Sr. VP; Peter Dennen, Vice President.

■ 19928 ■ Dexter Sales Inc.
860A Waterman Ave.
East Providence, RI 02914
Phone: (401)431-2170 **Fax:** (401)438-9360
URL: http://www.dextersalesinc.com
Products: Aluminum, brass, copper, and steel mill

products. **SIC:** 5051 (Metals Service Centers & Offices). **Est:** 1990. **Emp:** 5. **Officers:** Alan Samdperil, President, e-mail: asamperil@aol.com.

■ 19929 ■ T.W. Dick Company Inc.
1-25 Summer St.
Gardiner, ME 04345
Phone: (207)582-5350 **Fax:** (207)582-5353
Products: Steel. **SIC:** 5051 (Metals Service Centers & Offices). **Est:** 1890. **Sales:** $1,000,000 (2000). **Emp:** 11. **Officers:** Paul Raeaume, President; Cynthia Petingill, Finance Officer.

■ 19930 ■ Dick's Superior Metal Sales
4298 Acker Rd.
Madison, WI 53701
Phone: (608)244-9332
Products: Metal. **SIC:** 5051 (Metals Service Centers & Offices).

■ 19931 ■ Diehl Steel Co
PO Box 17010
Cincinnati, OH 45217
Phone: (513)242-8900 **Fax:** (513)242-8988
Products: Steel service center: cutting and blanchard grinding. **SIC:** 5051 (Metals Service Centers & Offices).

■ 19932 ■ Dimco Steel, Inc.
3901 S Lamar St.
Dallas, TX 75215
Phone: (214)428-8336
Free: (877)428-8336 **Fax:** (214)428-1929
E-mail: dimco@flash.net
URL: http://www.dimcosteel.com
Products: New structural steel. **SIC:** 5051 (Metals Service Centers & Offices). **Est:** 1946. **Sales:** $6,000,000 (2000). **Emp:** 20. **Officers:** E.L. Duggan, President. **Former Name:** Duggan Industries Inc.

■ 19933 ■ Diversified Metals Inc.
49 Main St.
Monson, MA 01057
Phone: (413)267-5101
Free: (800)628-3035 **Fax:** (413)267-3151
E-mail: sales@diversifiedmetals.com
URL: http://www.diversifiedmetals.com
Products: Metals. **SIC:** 5051 (Metals Service Centers & Offices). **Sales:** $15,000,000 (2000). **Emp:** 25. **Officers:** K. Hamel, President; Donna Kuhn, Controller.

■ 19934 ■ Dixie Pipe Sales Inc.
PO Box 300650
Houston, TX 77230
Phone: (713)796-2021
Free: (800)733-3494 **Fax:** (713)799-8628
E-mail: sales@dixiepipe.com
Products: Carbon and steel pipes. **SIC:** 5051 (Metals Service Centers & Offices). **Est:** 1951. **Sales:** $40,000,000 (1999). **Emp:** 60. **Officers:** J. Durham, President; Charles McGuire, Sales & Marketing Contact.

■ 19935 ■ Doral Steel Inc.
1500 Coining Dr.
Toledo, OH 43612
Phone: (419)476-0011 **Fax:** (419)476-3008
Products: Steel. **SIC:** 5051 (Metals Service Centers & Offices). **Sales:** $50,000,000 (1994). **Emp:** 50. **Officers:** Cam Smith, President; Richard Jones, Controller.

■ 19936 ■ Du-Wald Steel Corp.
1100 Umatilla St.
Denver, CO 80204
Phone: (303)571-5530
Products: Ferrous and non-ferrous metal scrap. **SIC:** 5093 (Scrap & Waste Materials). **Sales:** $26,000,000 (1992). **Emp:** 70. **Officers:** Gary Yourtz, President.

■ 19937 ■ Dublin Metal Corp.
6001 Tain Dr., No. 200
Dublin, OH 43017
Phone: (614)761-9502
Products: Metals. **SIC:** 5051 (Metals Service Centers & Offices).

■ 19938 ■ DuBose Steel Incorporated of North Carolina
PO Box 1098
Roseboro, NC 28382
Phone: (919)525-4161 **Fax:** (919)525-5066
Products: Steel. **SIC:** 5051 (Metals Service Centers & Offices). **Est:** 1954. **Sales:** $23,000,000 (2000). **Emp:** 63. **Officers:** Donald K. Kempf, CEO & President.

■ 19939 ■ Duferco Trading Corp.
100 Metro Park S
Laurence Harbor, NJ 08878-2001
Products: Steel. **SIC:** 5051 (Metals Service Centers & Offices). **Sales:** $3,000,000,000 (2000). **Emp:** 150. **Officers:** Bruno Balfo, President; Bob Nordeen, CFO.

■ 19940 ■ Duhig and Co.
14275 Wicks Blvd.
San Leandro, CA 94577
Phone: (510)352-6460 **Fax:** (510)352-1042
Products: Plumbing materials and fixtures. **SIC:** 5051 (Metals Service Centers & Offices). **Sales:** $16,000,000 (2000). **Emp:** 48.

■ 19941 ■ Dura Metals Inc.
620 28th Ave.
Bellwood, IL 60104-1901
Phone: (708)547-7701 **Fax:** (708)547-7718
Products: Stainless steel. **SIC:** 5051 (Metals Service Centers & Offices). **Est:** 1978. **Sales:** $1,000,000 (2000). **Emp:** 6. **Officers:** Patricia White, CEO; LouAnne Johannesson, Sales Mgr.; Chris Johannesson, Dir. of Sales.

■ 19942 ■ Durrett-Sheppard Steel Co.
6800 E Baltimore St.
Baltimore, MD 21224
Phone: (410)633-6800 **Fax:** (410)633-4325
Products: Hot-rolled steel. **SIC:** 5051 (Metals Service Centers & Offices). **Est:** 1963. **Sales:** $38,000,000 (2000). **Emp:** 150. **Officers:** G.M. Durrett, President & Treasurer; Henry Hyson, Controller; Richard Raynor, Sales Mgr.; James Maskeroni, Dir. of Data Processing; Leslie Rohde, Dir of Human Resources.

■ 19943 ■ E and E Steel Company Inc.
2187 S Garfield Ave.
City of Commerce, CA 90040
Phone: (213)723-0947
Products: Steel sheets. **SIC:** 5051 (Metals Service Centers & Offices). **Est:** 1966. **Sales:** $9,000,000 (2000). **Emp:** 13. **Officers:** R. Alperson, President; Merill Bodily, Treasurer.

■ 19944 ■ E & L Steel Co. Inc.
176 American Way
Madison, MS 39110
Phone: (601)853-4277
Products: Steel. **SIC:** 5051 (Metals Service Centers & Offices).

■ 19945 ■ E. M J Co
5311 Clinton Dr.
Houston, TX 77020
Phone: (713)672-1621 **Fax:** (713)672-0528
Products: Steel service center. **SIC:** 5051 (Metals Service Centers & Offices).

■ 19946 ■ Eastern Wire Products
498 Kinsley Ave.
Providence, RI 02909
Phone: (401)861-1350
Free: (800)486-3181 **Fax:** (401)274-3988
E-mail: ewpewp@aol.com
Products: Wire products; Displays. **SIC:** 5051 (Metals Service Centers & Offices). **Est:** 1954. **Sales:** $6,000,000 (2000). **Emp:** 100. **Officers:** Frederick Granoff, Marketing & Sales Mgr.; Burt Weiser, Sales/Marketing Contact; Rachel Conti, Customer Service Contact.

■ 19947 ■ Easton Steel Service Inc.
PO Box 599
Easton, MD 21601
Phone: (410)822-1393
Free: (800)394-2442 **Fax:** (410)822-2019
Products: Steel service center: cutting service. Concrete reinforcing steel fabrication. **SIC:** 5051 (Metals Service Centers & Offices). **Sales:**

$5,500,000,000 (1999). **Emp:** 30. **Officers:** Chris Marvel, President.

■ 19948 ■ Eaton Steel Corp.
10221 Capital Ave.
Oak Park, MI 48237
Phone: (248)398-3434
Products: Steel. **SIC:** 5051 (Metals Service Centers & Offices). **Est:** 1963. **Sales:** $9,500,000 (2000). **Emp:** 45. **Officers:** A.E. Goodman, President & Treasurer; Aaron Goodman, VP of Marketing.

■ 19949 ■ Edgcomb Corp.
555 State Rd.
Bensalem, PA 19020
Phone: (215)245-3300 **Fax:** (215)245-3257
Products: Steel. **SIC:** 5051 (Metals Service Centers & Offices). **Est:** 1923. **Sales:** $800,000,000 (2000). **Emp:** 1,250. **Officers:** Francois Jubien, President; Robert Tamburrino, CFO; Ed Haggerty, Vice President; Les Wilson, VP of Information Systems; David Metro, VP of Human Resources.

■ 19950 ■ Edgcomb Metals Co. New England Div.
385 W Hollis St.
Nashua, NH 03061
Phone: (603)883-7731
Products: Metal, including steel and copper. **SIC:** 5051 (Metals Service Centers & Offices). **Est:** 1952. **Sales:** $50,000,000 (2000). **Emp:** 120. **Officers:** Joseph Canastra, General Mgr.; Gary Tapp, Controller; Michael Jordan, Dir. of Sales.

■ 19951 ■ Egger Steel Co.
PO Box E
Sioux Falls, SD 57101
Phone: (605)336-2490
Products: Steel. **SIC:** 5051 (Metals Service Centers & Offices). **Sales:** $20,000,000 (2000). **Emp:** 150. **Officers:** Steve E. Egger, President; Cliff Carlson, Controller.

■ 19952 ■ Ellwood Quality Steels Co.
700 Moravia St.
New Castle, PA 16101
Phone: (724)658-6502
Products: Steel. **SIC:** 5051 (Metals Service Centers & Offices).

■ 19953 ■ Enco Materials Inc.
PO Box 1275
Nashville, TN 37202
Phone: (615)256-3192
Products: Steel; Concrete. **SICs:** 5051 (Metals Service Centers & Offices); 5032 (Brick, Stone & Related Materials). **Est:** 1964. **Sales:** $51,000,000 (2000). **Emp:** 150. **Officers:** Peter Dawkins, President; Phillip Hood, Controller; Randy Pleiman, Purchasing Manager.

■ 19954 ■ Energy and Process Corp.
PO Box 125
Tucker, GA 30085
Phone: (770)934-3101
Free: (800)241-9460 **Fax:** (770)938-8903
E-mail: epsales@energyandprocess.com
URL: http://www.energyandprocess.com
Products: Metals; industrial supplies; piping. **SICs:** 5051 (Metals Service Centers & Offices); 5085 (Industrial Supplies). **Est:** 1966. **Sales:** $80,000,000 (2000). **Emp:** 300. **Officers:** Mark T. Capallo, President. **Former Name:** Hub Inc.

■ 19955 ■ Jack Engle and Co.
PO Box 01705
Los Angeles, CA 90001
Phone: (213)589-8111
Products: Aluminum, copper, and brass high-temperature alloys and steel. **SIC:** 5093 (Scrap & Waste Materials).

■ 19956 ■ Erie Concrete Steel
1301 Cranberry St.
Erie, PA 16501
Phone: (814)453-4969
Products: Steel products. **SIC:** 5051 (Metals Service Centers & Offices).

■ 19957 ■ Erie Concrete and Steel Supply Co.
PO Box 10336
Erie, PA 16514
Phone: (814)453-4969 **Fax:** (814)455-7917
Products: Steel. **SIC:** 5051 (Metals Service Centers & Offices). **Est:** 1913. **Sales:** $9,000,000 (2000). **Emp:** 26. **Officers:** Scott McCain, President; Jim Barnett, Sales Mgr.

■ 19958 ■ Erie Steel Products Inc.
2420 W 15th St.
Erie, PA 16505
Phone: (814)459-2715
Products: Steel products. **SIC:** 5051 (Metals Service Centers & Offices).

■ 19959 ■ Everett Anchor and Chain
PO Box 776
Everett, WA 98206
Phone: (206)682-3166 **Fax:** (206)682-2977
Products: Steel items, including plates and beams. **SICs:** 5051 (Metals Service Centers & Offices); 5039 (Construction Materials Nec). **Sales:** $6,000,000 (2000). **Emp:** 49. **Officers:** Leonard Berman, General Mgr.; Manney Berman, CEO.

■ 19960 ■ Extrusions Inc.
2401 Main St.
Ft. Scott, KS 66701
Phone: (316)223-1111 **Fax:** (316)223-1139
Products: Aluminum. **SIC:** 5051 (Metals Service Centers & Offices). **Est:** 1986. **Sales:** $12,000,000 (1999). **Emp:** 140.

■ 19961 ■ F and S Alloys and Minerals Corp.
605 3rd Ave.
New York, NY 10158
Phone: (212)490-1356 **Fax:** (212)557-8457
Products: Metals, including aluminum, tin, zinc, alloys, and silicons. **SICs:** 5051 (Metals Service Centers & Offices); 5052 (Coal, Other Minerals & Ores). **Est:** 1976. **Sales:** $31,000,000 (2000). **Emp:** 50. **Officers:** Roger Engel, President; Alan Hurwitz, CFO; Manfred Roescher, Dir. of Marketing & Sales; Marta Tyshynsky, Dir. of Information Systems; Larry Lundrew, Dir of Human Resources.

■ 19962 ■ Fabwel Inc.
1838 Middlebury St.
Elkhart, IN 46516
Phone: (219)522-8473 **Fax:** (219)522-5451
Products: Fabricated steel plate (stacks and weldments); Aluminum. **SIC:** 5051 (Metals Service Centers & Offices). **Est:** 1972. **Sales:** $80,000,000 (2000). **Emp:** 400. **Officers:** Edward Welter, CEO & President; John Gardner, CFO; R. M. Stout Jr., Exec. VP; Lewis Rawls, Exec. VP.

■ 19963 ■ Factory Steel and Metal Supply Co., LLC
14020 Oakland
Detroit, MI 48203
Phone: (313)883-6300 **Fax:** (313)883-4883
E-mail: factory42@juno.com
Products: Metals, including steel, aluminum, stainless, chrome molly, brass, and copper. **SIC:** 5051 (Metals Service Centers & Offices). **Est:** 1946. **Sales:** $4,000,000 (2000). **Emp:** 20. **Officers:** David Snow, Controller; Joe Bricker; Herman Halon, Sales/Marketing Contact; Misha Johnson, Human Resources Contact.

■ 19964 ■ Ed Fagan Inc.
769 Susquehanna Ave.
Franklin Lakes, NJ 07417
Phone: (201)891-4003
Products: Metals. **SIC:** 5051 (Metals Service Centers & Offices). **Sales:** $18,000,000 (1993). **Emp:** 25. **Officers:** Ed Fagan, President.

■ 19965 ■ Farwest Steel Corp.
PO Box 889
Eugene, OR 97440
Phone: (541)686-2000
Free: (800)452-5091 **Fax:** (541)683-9250
Products: Steel service center. **SIC:** 5051 (Metals Service Centers & Offices). **Sales:** $170,000,000 (2000). **Emp:** 280. **Officers:** Richard E. Jones, CEO & President; Dave Forester, VP of Finance.

■ 19966 ■ Fay Industries
PO Box 360947
Strongsville, OH 44136
Phone: (440)572-5030 **Fax:** (440)572-5614
Products: Steel service center: sawcutting service. **SIC:** 5051 (Metals Service Centers & Offices).

■ 19967 ■ Fedco Steel Corp.
785 Harrison Ave.
Harrison, NJ 07029
Phone: (201)481-1424
Products: Unfabricated steel. **SIC:** 5051 (Metals Service Centers & Offices).

■ 19968 ■ Fedor Steel Co.
2833 N Telegraph Rd.
Monroe, MI 48162
Phone: (734)242-2940
Products: Steel. **SIC:** 5051 (Metals Service Centers & Offices).

■ 19969 ■ Feralloy Corp.
8755 W Higgins Rd.
Chicago, IL 60631
Phone: (312)380-1500 **Fax:** (312)380-1535
E-mail: info@feralloy.com
URL: http://www.feralloy.com
Products: Steel coils, rolled and coated sheets. **SIC:** 5051 (Metals Service Centers & Offices). **Est:** 1955. **Sales:** $500,000,000 (1999). **Emp:** 500. **Officers:** Frank M. Walker, President; Michael F. Bogacki, VP of Finance; Paul J. Cusumano, Mgr. Natl. Accounts; William Butler, Dir. of Data Processing; Walter Burzynski, Controller; James A. Magnetta, General Mgr. Purchasing.

■ 19970 ■ Feralloy Corp. Birmingham Div.
1435 Red Hat Rd.
Decatur, AL 35601-7588
Phone: (205)252-5605 **Fax:** (205)251-8339
Products: Steel. **SIC:** 5051 (Metals Service Centers & Offices). **Est:** 1957. **Sales:** $47,000,000 (2000). **Emp:** 58. **Officers:** J.B. Atkinson, General Mgr.; Ken Thompson, Controller.

■ 19971 ■ Feralloy Corp. Midwest Div.
12550 Stony Island Ave.
Chicago, IL 60633
Phone: (773)646-4900 **Fax:** (773)646-3489
Products: Cold rolled steel sheet and strip. **SIC:** 5051 (Metals Service Centers & Offices). **Sales:** $54,000,000 (2000). **Emp:** 60. **Officers:** N.J. Murphy, President; Chuck De'Allisso, General Mgr.

■ 19972 ■ Feralloy Corp./Western Div
936 Performance Dr.
Stockton, CA 95206
Phone: (209)234-0548 **Fax:** (209)234-0549
Products: Carbon steel. **SIC:** 5051 (Metals Service Centers & Offices).

■ 19973 ■ Feralloy Processing Co
6600 George Nelson Dr.
Portage, IN 46368
Phone: (219)787-8773 **Fax:** (219)787-8426
Products: Steel service center: steel slitting and temper mill roll. **SIC:** 5051 (Metals Service Centers & Offices). **Officers:** Chuck D'Alessio, President.

■ 19974 ■ Aaron Ferer and Sons Co.
909 Abbott Dr.
Omaha, NE 68102
Phone: (402)342-2436 **Fax:** (402)342-6391
Products: Ferrous and non-ferrous metal scrap. **SIC:** 5051 (Metals Service Centers & Offices). **Sales:** $50,000,000 (2000). **Emp:** 60. **Officers:** Harvey D. Ferer, CEO; Matthew D. Ferer, Treasurer.

■ 19975 ■ Ferguson Metals, Inc.
3475 Symmes Rd.
Hamilton, OH 45015
Phone: (513)860-6500
Free: (800)347-2376 **Fax:** (513)874-6857
E-mail: salesquote@fergusonmetals.com
URL: http://www.fergusonmetals.com
Products: Stainless steel and high temperature alloys. **SIC:** 5051 (Metals Service Centers & Offices). **Est:** 1982. **Sales:** $15,000,000 (2000). **Emp:** 75. **Officers:** H. Wayne Furguson, CEO; Angela S. Halsey, Dir. of Marketing, e-mail: angela.halsey@aerospacealloys.com; Charles O'Donnell, VP of Sales.
Former Name: Aerospace Alloys Inc.

■ 19976 ■ Ferguson Steel Co.
2935 Howard St.
Port Huron, MI 48060
Phone: (810)985-5178
Products: Steel. **SIC:** 5051 (Metals Service Centers & Offices).

■ 19977 ■ Ferranti Steel and Aluminum Inc.
722 Frelinghuysen Ave.
Newark, NJ 07114
Phone: (973)824-8496
Free: (800)336-1018 **Fax:** (973)824-5224
E-mail: ferrantisteel@earthlink.net
Products: Steel bars; Stainless steel; Aluminim bars; Hi-temp bars; Vacmelted bars. **SIC:** 5051 (Metals Service Centers & Offices). **Est:** 1947. **Sales:** $9,000,000 (2000). **Emp:** 50. **Officers:** Armand J. Ferranti, CEO; Raymond Ferranti, VP & CFO.

■ 19978 ■ Ferro Union Inc.
1000 W Francisco St.
Torrance, CA 90502
Phone: (310)538-9900 **Fax:** (310)323-4267
Products: Steel pipes and angles. **SIC:** 5051 (Metals Service Centers & Offices). **Est:** 1927. **Sales:** $300,000,000 (2000). **Emp:** 400. **Officers:** Steven W. Scheinkman, President; Rich Schlatter, Controller; John Reynolds, VP of Purchasing; Lesley Robert, VP of Sales; Mary Brown, VP & Controller; Jodie VanRyckegan, VP of Information Systems.

■ 19979 ■ Fisher Brothers Steel Corp.
PO Box 592
Englewood, NJ 07631
Phone: (201)567-2400 **Fax:** (201)567-9530
Products: Square and rectangular tubing; Structural pipe; Hot Rolled steel; Fence pipe; Galvanized tubing; Guard rail; Expanded metal; Grating; Roof deck. **SIC:** 5051 (Metals Service Centers & Offices). **Est:** 1910. **Sales:** $30,000,000 (1999). **Emp:** 125. **Officers:** J.L. Fisher, President.

■ 19980 ■ Florida Extruders International Inc.
2540 Jewett Ln.
Sanford, FL 32771-1600
Phone: (407)323-3300 **Fax:** (407)322-3337
URL: http://www.pmark.com/fei
Products: Aluminum extrusions; Windows; Sliding glass and screen doors. **SIC:** 5051 (Metals Service Centers & Offices). **Est:** 1989. **Sales:** $50,000,000 (1999). **Emp:** 500. **Officers:** J.G. Lehman, President.

■ 19981 ■ Ford Steel Co
PO Box 54
Maryland Heights, MO 63043
Phone: (314)567-4680 **Fax:** (314)567-5762
Products: Steel service center: impact and abrasion resistant wear steels. **SIC:** 5051 (Metals Service Centers & Offices). **Officers:** James Theodorow, Treasurer.

■ 19982 ■ Four Corners Welding & Gas
606 E Hwy. 66
Gallup, NM 87301
Phone: (505)722-3845
Products: Welding; Gas. **SICs:** 5051 (Metals Service Centers & Offices); 5172 (Petroleum Products Nec).

■ 19983 ■ Francosteel Corp.
345 Hudson St.
New York, NY 10014
Phone: (212)633-1010 **Fax:** (212)633-1774
Products: Steel. **SIC:** 5051 (Metals Service Centers & Offices). **Est:** 1939. **Sales:** $500,000,000 (2000). **Emp:** 218. **Officers:** Michael Longchampt, President; Jean-Paul Fouillade, CFO; Gilbert Romano, Sr. VP of Marketing; Pierre Combal, Dir. of Information Systems; Joy Freeman, Dir of Personnel.

■ 19984 ■ Franklin Town Metals and Cores
145 McVail St.
Baltimore, MD 21229
Phone: (410)362-7470
Products: Scrap metal. **SIC:** 5093 (Scrap & Waste Materials).

■ 19985 ■ Fraser Steel Co.
PO Box 160
Albertville, MN 55301-0160
Phone: (612)535-5616
Products: Steel tubing. **SIC:** 5051 (Metals Service Centers & Offices). **Est:** 1969. **Sales:** $5,000,000 (2000). **Emp:** 25. **Officers:** Donald Fraser, President.

■ 19986 ■ Frederick Steel Co.
200 W North Bend Rd.
Cincinnati, OH 45216
Phone: (513)821-6400
Products: Steel products, including reinforcing bars and cold drawn bar stock. **SIC:** 5051 (Metals Service Centers & Offices). **Est:** 1933. **Sales:** $30,000,000 (2000). **Emp:** 45. **Officers:** Herbert Byer, President; Mark Kurtz, VP of Finance; Dave Barker, Manager; Gareth Turner, Dir of Personnel.

■ 19987 ■ Freeport Steel Co.
PO Box 11453
Pittsburgh, PA 15238
Phone: (412)820-7040   **Fax:** (412)820-7045
E-mail: freeport79@aol.com
Products: Steel, including galvanized sheet and coil. **SIC:** 5051 (Metals Service Centers & Offices). **Est:** 1979. **Sales:** $10,000,000 (1999). **Emp:** 15. **Officers:** Walter Reineman, CEO & President; Erich E. Schaefer, Vice President.

■ 19988 ■ Frejoth International Corp.
2050 N Durfee Ave.
South El Monte, CA 91733
Phone: (626)443-8652   **Fax:** (626)442-2108
Products: Metal, including sheet metal; Woodworking products. **SICs:** 5084 (Industrial Machinery & Equipment); 5051 (Metals Service Centers & Offices). **Est:** 1980. **Sales:** $900,000 (1994). **Emp:** 3. **Officers:** J. Chen, CEO.

■ 19989 ■ Friedman Industries Inc.
PO Box 21147
Houston, TX 77226
Phone: (713)672-9433
Free: (800)572-8671   **Fax:** 800-486-7896
Products: Fabricated steel pipe. **SIC:** 5051 (Metals Service Centers & Offices). **Est:** 1965. **Sales:** $124,700,000 (2000). **Emp:** 135. **Officers:** William Crow, President; Benny Harper, Sr. VP & Finance Officer.

■ 19990 ■ Friedman Steel Company Inc.
PO Box 430
Greenville, MS 38701
Phone: (601)378-2722
Products: Steel, including angle and flat sheets. **SIC:** 5051 (Metals Service Centers & Offices). **Sales:** $10,000,000 (2000). **Emp:** 100. **Officers:** Barry Friedman, President.

■ 19991 ■ Fullerton Metals Co.
3000 Shermer Rd.
Northbrook, IL 60065-3002
Phone: (708)291-2400   **Fax:** (708)291-2475
Products: Metals, including brass, copper, and aluminum. **SIC:** 5051 (Metals Service Centers & Offices). **Est:** 1943. **Sales:** $90,000,000 (2000). **Emp:** 140. **Officers:** Kenneth J. Riskind, CEO & President; Joseph Marzullo, Sr. VP & Finance Officer; Dennis Grottola, VP of Sales; Rob Fiorito, Information Systems Mgr.

■ 19992 ■ R.J. Gallagher Co.
7901 El Rio
Houston, TX 77054
Phone: (713)748-4501
Products: Metals. **SIC:** 5051 (Metals Service Centers & Offices). **Sales:** $83,000,000 (1993). **Emp:** 225. **Officers:** R.J. Gallagher Jr., President; Don Callegari, Controller.

■ 19993 ■ Gallagher Steel Co.
19515 Mack Ave.
Grosse Pointe, MI 48236
Phone: (313)884-0835
Products: Steel. **SIC:** 5051 (Metals Service Centers & Offices).

■ 19994 ■ Gallup Welding Co.
903 W Wilson Ave.
Gallup, NM 87301
Phone: (505)863-4882
Products: Welding. **SIC:** 5051 (Metals Service Centers & Offices).

■ 19995 ■ GCF Inc.
105 Dorothy St.
Buffalo, NY 14206
Phone: (716)823-9900
Products: Scrap metal. **SIC:** 5093 (Scrap & Waste Materials).

■ 19996 ■ General Steel Corp.
3344 E 80th St.
Cleveland, OH 44127
Phone: (216)883-4200
Products: Metal products. **SIC:** 5051 (Metals Service Centers & Offices). **Sales:** $37,000,000 (1994). **Emp:** 50. **Officers:** James LaMantia, President.

■ 19997 ■ General Steel Fabricators
927 Schifferdecker
Joplin, MO 64801
Phone: (417)623-2224   **Fax:** (417)623-2204
Products: Steel products and machinery; Tanks; Conveyors; Bucket elevators; Dryers; Petro-chemical piping. **SICs:** 5051 (Metals Service Centers & Offices); 5084 (Industrial Machinery & Equipment); 5085 (Industrial Supplies). **Sales:** $6,500,000 (2000). **Emp:** 50. **Officers:** Paul Howey, General Mgr.

■ 19998 ■ General Steel Warehouse Inc.
PO Box 2037
Lubbock, TX 79408
Phone: (806)763-7327   **Fax:** (806)592-8859
Products: Steel. **SIC:** 5051 (Metals Service Centers & Offices). **Sales:** $4,000,000 (2000). **Emp:** 16. **Officers:** Robert Rogers, President; Willie Mae Rogers, Treasurer.

■ 19999 ■ Gensco, Inc.
2913 Marvin Rd. NE
Olympia, WA 98516
Phone: (206)491-8393   **Fax:** (206)491-9328
Products: Sheet metal; Heating equipment supplies. **SICs:** 5051 (Metals Service Centers & Offices); 5075 (Warm Air Heating & Air-Conditioning).

■ 20000 ■ Genzink Steel
40 E 64th St.
Holland, MI 49423
Phone: (616)392-1437   **Fax:** (616)392-2423
Products: Steel service center: structural steel fabricating and welding. **SIC:** 5051 (Metals Service Centers & Offices). **Officers:** Ken Genzink, Chairman of the Board.

■ 20001 ■ Genzink Steel
40 E 64th St.
Holland, MI 49423
Phone: (616)392-1437   **Fax:** (616)392-2423
Products: Steel service center: structural steel fabricating and welding. **SIC:** 5051 (Metals Service Centers & Offices). **Officers:** Ken Genzink, Chairman of the Board.

■ 20002 ■ Georgetown Unimetal Sales
1901 Roxborough Rd., No. 220
Charlotte, NC 28211
Phone: (704)365-2205
Products: Wire rod steel. **SIC:** 5051 (Metals Service Centers & Offices). **Sales:** $256,000,000 (2000). **Emp:** 8. **Officers:** Richard Holzworth, President.

■ 20003 ■ J. Gerber and Company Inc.
11 Penn Plz.
New York, NY 10001-2057
Phone: (212)631-1200   **Fax:** (212)631-1316
Products: Steel; Wire. **SIC:** 5051 (Metals Service Centers & Offices). **Est:** 1937. **Sales:** $250,000,000 (2000). **Emp:** 70. **Officers:** Geoffrey Clain, CEO & President; Martin B. Edgnel, VP of Finance; Reggie Chua, Data Processing Mgr.

■ 20004 ■ Gerrard Steel of Illinois
25th Ave. & Main St.
Melrose Park, IL 60160
Phone: (708)681-9190   **Fax:** (708)681-9198
Products: Steel. **SIC:** 5051 (Metals Service Centers & Offices). **Sales:** $8,000,000 (1993). **Emp:** 20. **Officers:** Morris Peterson, President.

■ 20005 ■ Gibbs Wire and Steel Co.
PO Box 520
Southington, CT 06489
Phone: (203)621-0121
Products: Steel strips; Wire. **SIC:** 5051 (Metals Service Centers & Offices). **Est:** 1956. **Sales:** $50,000,000 (2000). **Emp:** 130. **Officers:** C. Wayne Gibbs, President; William Torres, VP & Treasurer; John Cleaver, VP of Sales.

■ 20006 ■ Gibraltar Steel Corp.
PO Box 2028
Buffalo, NY 14219-0228
Phone: (716)826-6500   **Fax:** (716)856-0084
Products: Cold rolled strip and strapping steel. **SIC:** 5051 (Metals Service Centers & Offices). **Sales:** $449,700,000 (2000). **Emp:** 1,450. **Officers:** Brian J. Lipke, CEO, President & Chairman of the Board; Walter T. Erazmus, CFO & Treasurer.

■ 20007 ■ Gibraltar Steel Products
635 S Park Ave.
Buffalo, NY 14210
Phone: (716)826-6500   **Fax:** (716)826-4254
Products: Steel service center: burnouts, bars, angles and fabricating. **SIC:** 5051 (Metals Service Centers & Offices). **Sales:** $621,900,000 (1999). **Emp:** 3,100. **Officers:** Brian Lipke, CEO; Walter Erazmus, CFO.

■ 20008 ■ Global Steel Trading Inc.
1199 E 5000N Rd
Bourbonnais, IL 60914
Phone: (815)936-4500   **Fax:** (815)936-4501
Products: Metals service center: flame cutting. **SIC:** 5051 (Metals Service Centers & Offices).

■ 20009 ■ Globe Iron Construction Company Inc.
PO Box 2354
Norfolk, VA 23501
Phone: (804)625-2542
Free: (800)476-4562   **Fax:** (804)628-0111
E-mail: gicco@pilot.infi.net
URL: http://www.pilot.infi.net/~gicco
Products: Structural steel, including angle beams, plates, and bars; Fabrication; Distribution. **SICs:** 5051 (Metals Service Centers & Offices); 5039 (Construction Materials Nec). **Est:** 1923. **Sales:** $29,000,000 (2000). **Emp:** 160. **Officers:** Arthur Peregoff, CEO & Chairman of the Board; Lee Peregoff, Pres., Treas. & Controller; Morgan L. Steele, VP & General Mgr.; Shirey Luck, Office Mgr.; Kevin R. Sullivan, Director.

■ 20010 ■ M. Glosser and Sons Inc.
72 Messenger St.
Johnstown, PA 15902
Phone: (814)533-2800
Products: Metal and industrial supplies. **SICs:** 5051 (Metals Service Centers & Offices); 5085 (Industrial Supplies). **Sales:** $52,000,000 (1994). **Emp:** 70. **Officers:** Ray Lackner, Finance Officer.

■ 20011 ■ GMA Industries Inc.
PO Box 74037
Romulus, MI 48174-0037
Phone: (734)595-7300
Free: (800)869-9946   **Fax:** (734)595-1310
URL: http://www.gma.ind.com
Products: Steel abrasives. Aluminum oxide, cut wire, glass bead. **SIC:** 5051 (Metals Service Centers & Offices). **Est:** 1982. **Sales:** $3,500,000 (2000). **Emp:** 20. **Officers:** Carl F. Stevens, President; Colleen Stevens, Treasurer; David Printz, Sales/Marketing Contact; Heather Martin, Customer Service Contact. **Former Name:** General Metal and Abrasives Co.

■ 20012 ■ Goldin Industries Inc.
PO Box 2909
Gulfport, MS 39505-2909
Phone: (601)896-6216
Products: Steel products; Metal roofing and roof

drainage equipment. **SICs:** 5093 (Scrap & Waste Materials); 5051 (Metals Service Centers & Offices). **Sales:** $20,000,000 (2000). **Emp:** 140. **Officers:** Jack Goldin, President.

■ 20013 ■ **D.F. Goldsmith Chemical and Metal Corp.**
909 Pitner Ave.
Evanston, IL 60202
Phone: (847)869-7800   **Fax:** (847)869-2531
E-mail: goldchem@aol.com
URL: http://www.dfgoldsmith.com
Products: Mercury; Gold; Chloride compounds; Silver and silver salts. **SIC:** 5051 (Metals Service Centers & Offices). **Est:** 1960. **Sales:** $5,000,000 (2000). **Emp:** 8. **Officers:** D.F. Goldsmith, President.

■ 20014 ■ **Goode's Welding Inc.**
926 E Mcgaffey St.
Roswell, NM 88201
Phone: (505)622-3490
Products: Welding. **SIC:** 5051 (Metals Service Centers & Offices).

■ 20015 ■ **Grand Haven Steel Products**
1605 Marion Ave.
Grand Haven, MI 49417
Phone: (616)847-7793
Products: Steel. **SIC:** 5051 (Metals Service Centers & Offices).

■ 20016 ■ **Graves Oil & Butane Co.**
105 Dale St. SE
Albuquerque, NM 87101
Phone: (505)877-3753
Products: Oil and butane. **SIC:** 5172 (Petroleum Products Nec).

■ 20017 ■ **Grayline Housewares**
455 Kehoe Blvd.
Carol Stream, IL 60188
Phone: (708)682-3330
Free: (800)222-7388   **Fax:** (708)682-3363
Products: PCV coated steel. **SIC:** 5051 (Metals Service Centers & Offices).

■ 20018 ■ **Great Central Steel Co.**
9801 S 76th Ave.
Bridgeview, IL 60455
Phone: (708)599-8090
Products: Steel. **SIC:** 5051 (Metals Service Centers & Offices). **Est:** 1945. **Sales:** $11,000,000 (2000). **Emp:** 15. **Officers:** Eugene Wagner, President; Mary Ann Bakes, Office Mgr.

■ 20019 ■ **Great Lakes Forge, Inc.**
2465 N Aero Pk. Ct.
Traverse City, MI 49686
Phone: (231)947-4931
Free: (800)748-0271   **Fax:** (231)947-5836
E-mail: sales@glforge.com
URL: http://www.glforge.com
Products: Steel. **SIC:** 5051 (Metals Service Centers & Offices). **Emp:** 13. **Former Name:** Grand Traverse Forging and Steel.

■ 20020 ■ **Great Plains Stainless Inc.**
1004 N 129 E Ave.
Tulsa, OK 74116
Phone: (918)437-5400
Free: (800)345-5757   **Fax:** (918)437-5440
E-mail: grplains@gpss.com
URL: http://www.gpss.com
Products: Stainless steel, pipe, fittings, and flanges. **SIC:** 5051 (Metals Service Centers & Offices). **Est:** 1983. **Sales:** $10,000,000 (2000). **Emp:** 22. **Officers:** Joseph Gibbons, President; James Gibbons, VP & General Mgr.; Tom Gibbons, Sales Mgr.; Michael Gibbons; Jim Henry, Marketing Mgr., e-mail: jhenry@ gpss.com; Reggie Tinker, e-mail: rtinker@gpss.com.

■ 20021 ■ **Great Western Steel Co.**
2310 W 58th St.
Chicago, IL 60636
Phone: (312)434-5800   **Fax:** (312)434-3033
Products: Flat rolled steel. **SIC:** 5051 (Metals Service Centers & Offices). **Est:** 1918. **Sales:** $23,000,000 (2000). **Emp:** 43. **Officers:** J.W. Malec, President; D.W. Flynn, CFO; W.D. Kliesner, Dir. of Marketing;

N.D. Wonsetler, Dir. of Information Systems; J.C. Ward, Dir of Human Resources.

■ 20022 ■ **Green Bay Supply Company Inc.**
2331 Topaz Dr.
Hatfield, PA 19440
Phone: (215)822-1844   **Fax:** (215)997-1922
Products: Stainless steel bars. **SIC:** 5051 (Metals Service Centers & Offices). **Est:** 1976. **Sales:** $48,000,000 (2000). **Emp:** 50. **Officers:** Richard C. Hazen, President.

■ 20023 ■ **Grossman Iron and Steel Co.**
5 N Market St.
St. Louis, MO 63102
Phone: (314)231-9423
Products: Iron and steel recycling. **SIC:** 5093 (Scrap & Waste Materials). **Sales:** $20,000,000 (1994). **Emp:** 100. **Officers:** David Grossman, President; Skip Grossman, Vice President.

■ 20024 ■ **H and D Steel Service Inc.**
9960 York Alpha Dr.
North Royalton, OH 44133
Phone: (440)237-3390   **Fax:** (440)237-4540
Products: Metals service center: slitting, shearing and cutting. **SIC:** 5051 (Metals Service Centers & Offices). **Officers:** Raymond Schreiber, President.

■ 20025 ■ **Habot Steel Company Inc.**
1180 Fahs St.
York, PA 17404
Phone: (717)848-6080   **Fax:** (717)848-6217
Products: Plate steel. **SIC:** 5051 (Metals Service Centers & Offices). **Est:** 1962. **Sales:** $1,500,000 (2000). **Emp:** 9. **Officers:** David Bottomley, President; Harry R. Bottomley, Vice President.

■ 20026 ■ **Hadro Aluminum & Metal Corp.**
4001 G St.
Philadelphia, PA 19124
Phone: (215)427-0100
Free: (800)638-2521   **Fax:** (215)427-1963
Products: Aluminum, brass, and copper sheets, bars, and ram rods; Magnesium rods and plates. **SIC:** 5051 (Metals Service Centers & Offices). **Est:** 1968. **Sales:** $5,000,000 (2000). **Emp:** 24. **Officers:** Hy Gorman, President.

■ 20027 ■ **Hansen Machine Co.**
13040 Greenly St.
Holland, MI 49424
Phone: (616)399-8880
Products: Metal stampings, plastic office chairs and auto accessories. **SIC:** 5013 (Motor Vehicle Supplies & New Parts). **Sales:** $16,000,000 (2000). **Emp:** 150. **Officers:** Ann Foy, President.

■ 20028 ■ **Harris Welco**
1051 York Rd.
PO Box 69
Kings Mountain, NC 28086
Phone: (704)739-6421   **Fax:** (704)739-2801
URL: http://www.jwharris.com
Products: Welding metals and accessories. **SICs:** 5051 (Metals Service Centers & Offices); 5084 (Industrial Machinery & Equipment). **Est:** 1944. **Sales:** $70,000,000 (1999). **Emp:** 215. **Officers:** William H. Roland Jr., President; William H. Roland Jr., Sales/Marketing Contact, e-mail: broland@ jwharris.com; David McGuirt, Customer Service Contact, e-mail: dmcguirt@jwharris.com; Rachael Whitaker, Human Resources Contact, e-mail: rwhitaker@jwharis.com. **Alternate Name:** Thermacote Welco Co.

■ 20029 ■ **Harvey Titanium Ltd.**
1330 Colorado Ave.
Santa Monica, CA 90404-3478
Phone: (310)829-0021
Products: Titanium and specialty metals. **SIC:** 5051 (Metals Service Centers & Offices). **Sales:** $70,000,000 (2000). **Emp:** 60. **Officers:** Barry Harvey, CEO & President.

■ 20030 ■ **Hascall Steel Company Inc.**
4165 Spartan Industrial Dr. SW
Grandville, MI 49418
Phone: (616)531-8600   **Fax:** (616)531-7555
Products: Steel service center: slitting, shearing and slearing. **SIC:** 5051 (Metals Service Centers & Offices). **Sales:** $36,000,000 (1999). **Emp:** 110. **Officers:** Dag Hascall, President; Chris VanWiagerden, Controller.

■ 20031 ■ **R.W. Hebard and Associates Inc.**
825 3rd Ave.
New York, NY 10022
Phone: (212)421-4590   **Fax:** (212)355-2159
Products: Steel. **SIC:** 5051 (Metals Service Centers & Offices). **Est:** 1945. **Sales:** $7,000,000 (2000). **Emp:** 75. **Officers:** Fred Lamesch, CEO & President; Joseph McNamara, CFO; Hans Mueller, Marketing & Sales Mgr.

■ 20032 ■ **Heidtman Steel Products Inc.**
PO Box 1793
Toledo, OH 43603
Phone: (419)691-4646   **Free:** (800)521-9531
Products: Steel service center: coil cutting, shearing, sawing, slitting and pickling. **SIC:** 5051 (Metals Service Centers & Offices). **Sales:** $229,000,000 (2000). **Emp:** 900. **Officers:** John Bates, CEO & President; Thomas Kaspitzke, Treasurer.

■ 20033 ■ **Henderson Steel Corp.**
PO Box 3760
Meridian, MS 39303
Phone: (601)484-3000
Products: Structural metal. **SIC:** 5051 (Metals Service Centers & Offices). **Sales:** $17,000,000 (1994). **Emp:** 30. **Officers:** Roger C. Henderson, President.

■ 20034 ■ **Hercules Industries**
1310 W Evans Ave.
Denver, CO 80223
Phone: (303)937-1000   **Fax:** (303)937-0903
URL: http://www.herculesindustries.com
Products: Sheet metal products; HVAC products. **SICs:** 5074 (Plumbing & Hydronic Heating Supplies); 5075 (Warm Air Heating & Air-Conditioning). **Est:** 1962. **Sales:** $25,000,000 (2000). **Emp:** 120. **Officers:** W.M. Newland, President.

■ 20035 ■ **Hi-Way Products Inc.**
500 Ash St.
Ida Grove, IA 51445
Phone: (712)364-3763   **Fax:** (712)364-3764
E-mail: hwyprod@pionet.net
Products: Steel and aluminum products, including handrails and guardrails. **SICs:** 5051 (Metals Service Centers & Offices); 5039 (Construction Materials Nec). **Est:** 1969. **Sales:** $5,000,000 (2000). **Emp:** 8. **Officers:** Richard Bogue, President; Mark Bogue, Vice President.

■ 20036 ■ **Hickman, Williams and Co.**
17370 Laurel Park Dr. N, Ste. 330
Livonia, MI 48152
Phone: (734)462-1890
Products: Materials used in the iron and steel industries. **SIC:** 5052 (Coal, Other Minerals & Ores). **Sales:** $286,000,000 (2000). **Emp:** 175. **Officers:** R.L. Damschroder, CEO & President; Arthur L. Haack, CFO.

■ 20037 ■ **Hickman, Williams and Co., Black Products Div.**
13513 S Calumet Ave.
Chicago, IL 60827-1834
Phone: (773)468-9700
Products: Carbon raisers and release agents; Alloys for the steel industry. **SIC:** 5051 (Metals Service Centers & Offices). **Sales:** $6,000,000 (2000). **Emp:** 10. **Officers:** Joe Costabile, General Mgr.

■ 20038 ■ **Highway Metal Services Inc.**
4735 W 150th St.
Cleveland, OH 44135
Phone: (216)676-1500   **Fax:** (216)676-1501
Products: Metals service center: cutting and shearing. **SIC:** 5051 (Metals Service Centers & Offices).

■ 20039 ■ **Hill Steel & Builders Supplies**
6110 Birch Rd.
Flint, MI 48507
Phone: (810)232-6194
Products: Steel; Building supplies. **SIC:** 5051 (Metals Service Centers & Offices).

■ 20040 ■ **Hinely Aluminum Inc.**
3645 Southside Industrial Pkwy., Ste. 101
Atlanta, GA 30354
Phone: (404)361-1944 **Fax:** (404)361-1109
Products: Aluminum. **SIC:** 5051 (Metals Service Centers & Offices). **Sales:** $14,000,000 (1993). **Emp:** 20. **Officers:** Robert Hinely, President.

■ 20041 ■ **Hinkle Metals and Supply Company Inc.**
PO Box 11441
Birmingham, AL 35202
Phone: (205)326-3300 **Fax:** (205)322-3724
Products: Steel service center. **SIC:** 5051 (Metals Service Centers & Offices).

■ 20042 ■ **J. Henry Holland Corp.**
PO Box 5100
Virginia Beach, VA 23455
Phone: (757)460-3300 **Fax:** (757)363-1910
Products: Wire rope. **SIC:** 5051 (Metals Service Centers & Offices). **Sales:** $14,000,000 (2000). **Emp:** 45. **Officers:** William Cutrell, President; Kelly Ellis, Comptroller; Larry D. Lusk, VP of Sales.

■ 20043 ■ **Holston Steel Services**
300 Piedmont Ave.
Bristol, VA 24201
Phone: (540)466-6000
Products: Steel. **SIC:** 5051 (Metals Service Centers & Offices).

■ 20044 ■ **Hoogovens Aluminium Corp.**
PO Box 2127
Secaucus, NJ 07096
Phone: (201)866-7776
Free: (800)631-3717 **Fax:** (201)866-6146
Products: Aluminum service center: cutting, slitting and shearing service. **SIC:** 5051 (Metals Service Centers & Offices). **Sales:** $120,000,000 (2000). **Emp:** 62. **Officers:** R. Johnson, President; J. Abrams, CFO.

■ 20045 ■ **H.H. Howard Corp.**
4837 S Kedzie Ave.
Chicago, IL 60632
Phone: (773)254-0400 **Fax:** (773)254-0496
Products: Steel. **SIC:** 5051 (Metals Service Centers & Offices). **Est:** 1941. **Sales:** $4,000,000 (2000). **Emp:** 50. **Officers:** Hugh C. Howard, Chairman of the Board; Richard A. Myers, President; Gregg S. Vagstad, Vice President.

■ 20046 ■ **Hugo Neu-Proler Co.**
901 New Dock St.
Terminal Island, CA 90731
Phone: (213)775-6626
Products: Scrap metal processing. **SIC:** 5093 (Scrap & Waste Materials).

■ 20047 ■ **Huntco Steel Inc.**
PO Box 10507
Springfield, MO 65808
Phone: (417)881-6697 **Fax:** (417)881-7285
Products: Steel service center: cutting, slitting and shearing. **SIC:** 5051 (Metals Service Centers & Offices).

■ 20048 ■ **Huntington Steel and Supply Company Inc.**
PO Box 1178
Huntington, WV 25714
Phone: (304)522-8218
Free: (800)888-9780 **Fax:** (304)525-4282
E-mail: sales@huntingtonsteel.com
URL: http://www.huntingtonsteel.com
Products: Steel, including plate, sheet, angle, channel, structural, and fabricated. **SIC:** 5051 (Metals Service Centers & Offices). **Est:** 1904. **Sales:** $12,000,000 (2000). **Emp:** 85. **Officers:** Michael J. Emerson, President; Marc Rutherford, Controller; Gary G. Moore, Service Center Mgr.

■ 20049 ■ **Huron Steel Company Inc.**
PO Box 34367
Detroit, MI 48234
Phone: (313)366-6400 **Fax:** (313)366-1394
Products: Steel bars and laterals. **SIC:** 5051 (Metals Service Centers & Offices). **Est:** 1939. **Sales:** $9,000,000 (2000). **Emp:** 25. **Officers:** Don K. Maurer, VP & General Merchandising Mgr.; Herman Rucker, Controller.

■ 20050 ■ **Huron Valley Steel Corp.**
41000 Huron River Dr.
Belleville, MI 48111
Phone: (734)697-3400 **Fax:** (734)697-4445
Products: Recycle scrap metals. **SIC:** 5093 (Scrap & Waste Materials). **Sales:** $134,000,000 (2000). **Emp:** 300. **Officers:** Leynold Fritz, President; Mark Gaffney, Controller.

■ 20051 ■ **Hurwitz Brothers Iron and Metal Company Inc.**
PO Box 5
Buffalo, NY 14220
Phone: (716)823-2863
Products: Metal; Iron. **SIC:** 5051 (Metals Service Centers & Offices). **Est:** 1894. **Sales:** $6,000,000 (2000). **Emp:** 20. **Officers:** Donald S. Hurwitz Jr., President; Michael Knowles, Treasurer.

■ 20052 ■ **Hynes Industries Inc.**
PO Box 2459
Youngstown, OH 44509
Phone: (216)799-3221 **Fax:** (216)799-9098
Products: Steel; Coiled and wire steel. **SIC:** 5051 (Metals Service Centers & Offices). **Est:** 1925. **Sales:** $29,000,000 (2000). **Emp:** 180. **Officers:** W.J. Bresnahan, President; E.C. Clarke, VP of Finance; J.E. Kearns, Dir of Personnel.

■ 20053 ■ **Ilva USA Inc.**
10 Bank St.
White Plains, NY 10606
Phone: (914)428-6010
Products: Metals. **SIC:** 5051 (Metals Service Centers & Offices). **Est:** 1976. **Sales:** $70,000,000 (2000). **Emp:** 20. **Officers:** Enrico Chevallard, President; Vans Letterman, Treasurer.

■ 20054 ■ **Independent Steel Co.**
PO Box 472
Valley City, OH 44280-0472
Phone: (216)225-7741 **Fax:** (216)273-6265
Products: Steel. **SIC:** 5051 (Metals Service Centers & Offices). **Est:** 1958. **Sales:** $36,000,000 (2000). **Emp:** 50. **Officers:** A.L. Schwertner, CEO; D. Nix, Vice President; D. Demian, Marketing & Sales Mgr.

■ 20055 ■ **Industrial Material Corp.**
7701 Harborside Dr.
Galveston, TX 77554
Phone: (409)744-4538 **Fax:** (409)744-1844
Products: Steel service center: steel processing, fabricating and painting. **SIC:** 5051 (Metals Service Centers & Offices).

■ 20056 ■ **Industrial Metal Processing Inc.**
PO Box 578
Lyman, SC 29365-0578
Phone: (864)233-2747
Products: Scrap metal, steel, copper, aluminum, brass and stainless steel. **SIC:** 5093 (Scrap & Waste Materials). **Sales:** $23,000,000 (1994). **Emp:** 80. **Officers:** James Knight, President; Mike Munafo, CFO.

■ 20057 ■ **Industrial Metals of the South Inc.**
PO Box 10507
New Orleans, LA 70112
Phone: (504)586-9191 **Fax:** (504)528-1041
Products: Aluminum and stainless metals. **SIC:** 5051 (Metals Service Centers & Offices). **Est:** 1965. **Sales:** $16,000,000 (2000). **Emp:** 21. **Officers:** John J. Gelpi Jr., President; Marilyn Hetter, Treasurer.

■ 20058 ■ **Industrial Steel and Machine Sales**
2712 Lackland Dr.
Waterloo, IA 50702
Phone: (319)296-1816 **Fax:** (319)296-3630
Products: Steel; Steel machines and metal working equipment. **SICs:** 5051 (Metals Service Centers & Offices); 5084 (Industrial Machinery & Equipment). **Est:** 1973. **Sales:** $1,500,000 (2000). **Emp:** 9. **Officers:** J.H. Earnest, President; Bob Bartz, Vice President; Kathy Earnest, Sec. & Treas.

■ 20059 ■ **Industrial Steel Service Center**
1700 W Cortland Ct.
Addison, IL 60101
Phone: (630)543-0660 **Fax:** (630)620-1146
Products: Steel. **SIC:** 5051 (Metals Service Centers & Offices). **Est:** 1969. **Sales:** $10,000,000 (2000). **Emp:** 50. **Officers:** P.L. Mehalic, President; M. Mehalic, VP of Marketing.

■ 20060 ■ **Industrial Steel Warehouse Inc.**
PO Box 3207
Longview, TX 75606
Phone: (903)759-4454 **Fax:** (903)759-4187
Products: Structural steel. **SICs:** 5051 (Metals Service Centers & Offices); 5039 (Construction Materials Nec). **Est:** 1936. **Sales:** $12,000,000 (2000). **Emp:** 30. **Officers:** Irving Falk, President; Morris Milstein, Exec. VP; Theral Hargis, Vice President.

■ 20061 ■ **Industrial Tube & Steel**
29 Ormsbee Ave.
Westerville, OH 43081
Phone: (614)899-0657
Products: Steel. **SIC:** 5051 (Metals Service Centers & Offices).

■ 20062 ■ **Industrial Tube and Steel Corp.**
1303 Home Ave.
Akron, OH 44310
Phone: (330)633-8125 **Fax:** (330)633-9756
Products: Steel service center: steel cutting and slitting steel tubing and cast iron bars. **SIC:** 5051 (Metals Service Centers & Offices). **Officers:** Richard Siess, President.

■ 20063 ■ **Infra Metals**
5208 24th Ave.
Tampa, FL 33619
Phone: (813)626-6005
Free: (800)693-1361 **Fax:** (813)626-8032
E-mail: fl@infra-metals.com
Products: Steel. **SIC:** 5051 (Metals Service Centers & Offices). **Est:** 1995. **Emp:** 35. **Officers:** Peter McGivney, General Mgr.; John Walmsley, Branch Mgr.

■ 20064 ■ **Infra Metals**
PO Box 1247
Hallandale, FL 33008-1247
Phone: (954)454-9505
Free: (800)432-1146 **Fax:** (954)454-9515
E-mail: fl@infra-metals.com
URL: http://www.infra-metals.com
Products: Nonferrous metals. **SIC:** 5051 (Metals Service Centers & Offices). **Est:** 1992. **Sales:** $20,000,000 (2000). **Emp:** 30. **Officers:** Peter McGivney, General Mgr.

■ 20065 ■ **Inland Steel Industries Inc.**
30 W Monroe St.
Chicago, IL 60603
Phone: (312)346-0300 **Fax:** (312)899-3589
Products: Steel. **SIC:** 5051 (Metals Service Centers & Offices). **Est:** 1986. **Sales:** $4,584,100,000 (2000). **Emp:** 14,695. **Officers:** Robert J. Darnall, CEO, President & Chairman of the Board; Jay M. Gratz, VP & CFO; H. William Howard, VP of Information Systems; Judd R. Cool, VP of Human Resources.

■ 20066 ■ **Integrity Steel Co**
6300 Sterling Dr N
Sterling Heights, MI 48312
Phone: (810)826-3700 **Fax:** (810)268-6980
Products: Metals service center: cutting, plate burning and grinding and plate sewing. **SIC:** 5051 (Metals Service Centers & Offices). **Emp:** 25. **Officers:** Bayrd Bergers, President.

■ 20067 ■ **Interstate Steel Co.**
401 E Touhy Ave.
Des Plaines, IL 60017
Phone: (847)827-5151
Free: (800)323-9800 **Fax:** (847)827-7216
URL: http://www.InterstateSteelCo.com
Products: Steel. **SIC:** 5051 (Metals Service Centers &

Offices). **Est:** 1945. **Sales:** $135,000,000 (2000). **Emp:** 110. **Officers:** Robert D. Gifford, President.

■ **20068** ■ **Interstate Steel Supply Co**
1800 Byberry Rd.
Philadelphia, PA 19116
Phone: (215)673-0300 **Fax:** (215)969-0334
Products: Steel service center; Steel processing. **SIC:** 5051 (Metals Service Centers & Offices).

■ **20069** ■ **Interstate Steel Supply Co.**
1800 E Byberry Rd.
Philadelphia, PA 19116
Phone: (215)673-0300 **Fax:** (215)969-0334
URL: http://www.metalsusa.com
Products: Carbon and alloy structural steell. **SIC:** 5051 (Metals Service Centers & Offices). **Est:** 1949. **Sales:** $100,000,000 (2000). **Emp:** 250. **Officers:** A.W. Bradburd, Chairman of the Board; J. Magasko, Vice President; J. Urban, VP of Marketing & Sales; D. Everett, Comptroller.

■ **20070** ■ **Iron Mike's Welding & Fab**
1535 N Dort Hwy.
Flint, MI 48506
Phone: (810)234-2996
Products: Steel and sheet metal. **SIC:** 5051 (Metals Service Centers & Offices).

■ **20071** ■ **J & F Steel Corporation**
2424 Oakton St.
Evanston, IL 60202-2796
Phone: (847)866-2100 **Fax:** (847)866-2101
Products: Steel. **SIC:** 5051 (Metals Service Centers & Offices). **Est:** 1947. **Sales:** $85,000,000 (2000). **Emp:** 175. **Officers:** Jack Schoettert, President; Tammy Graham, Vice President; Tom Smid, Branch Mgr. **Former Name:** Belmont Steel Corp.

■ **20072** ■ **J and J Steel and Supply Co.**
PO Box 1886
Odessa, TX 79760
Phone: (915)332-4351 **Fax:** (915)332-9731
Products: Oil field storage tanks. **SIC:** 5051 (Metals Service Centers & Offices). **Sales:** $4,000,000 (2000). **Emp:** 24.

■ **20073** ■ **Jacklin Steel Supply Co.**
2410 Aero Park Dr.
Traverse City, MI 49686
Phone: (616)946-8434
Products: Steel. **SIC:** 5051 (Metals Service Centers & Offices). **Est:** 1947. **Sales:** $10,000,000 (2000). **Emp:** 55. **Officers:** George Barker, President.

■ **20074** ■ **Jackson Iron and Metal Co.**
PO Box 1327
Jackson, MI 49204-1166
Phone: (517)787-1731 **Fax:** (517)787-8815
Products: Iron and metal recyclers. **SIC:** 5093 (Scrap & Waste Materials). **Sales:** $50,000,000 (1994). **Emp:** 130. **Officers:** Bill Kanter, VP & Controller.

■ **20075** ■ **Jeffrey's Steel Company Inc.**
PO Box 2763
Mobile, AL 36652
Phone: (334)456-4531
Free: (800)277-6778 **Fax:** (334)432-5618
E-mail: sales@jeffsteel.com
URL: http://www.metalsusa.com
Products: Structural steel. **SIC:** 5051 (Metals Service Centers & Offices). **Est:** 1968. **Sales:** $130,000,000 (2000). **Emp:** 340. **Officers:** Toby Jeffreys, CEO & President; Leon Jeffreys, Chairman of the Board.

■ **20076** ■ **Jim's Supply Company Inc.**
PO Box 668
Bakersfield, CA 93302
Phone: (661)324-6514 **Fax:** (661)324-6566
Products: Sells steel, used pipe and vineyard stakes; Vineyard stakes, posts and crossarms. **SIC:** 5051 (Metals Service Centers & Offices). **Officers:** Doreen Boylan, President.

■ **20077** ■ **Jonner Steel Industries**
6349 Strong
Detroit, MI 48211
Phone: (313)262-5700 **Fax:** (313)262-5769
Products: Metal service center: steel sheets and

blanks; processing, decoiling and shearing. **SIC:** 5051 (Metals Service Centers & Offices). **Officers:** Gerald Gunner, President; Thomas Bonk, CFO.

■ **20078** ■ **E. Jordan Brookes Company Inc.**
PO Box 910908
Los Angeles, CA 90091-0908
Phone: (323)722-8100 **Fax:** (323)888-2275
Products: Metals, including copper, brass, and bronze; Industrial plastics. **SICs:** 5051 (Metals Service Centers & Offices); 5162 (Plastics Materials & Basic Shapes). **Est:** 1936. **Emp:** 75. **Officers:** Robert J. Brookes, CEO; Ed Sarell, CFO; Roger Craddock, Sales Mgr.; Robert J. Brookes Jr., President.

■ **20079** ■ **Earle M. Jorgensen Co.**
3050 E Birch St.
Brea, CA 92821
Phone: (714)579-8823
Free: (800)336-5365 **Fax:** (714)577-3765
URL: http://www.emjmetals.com
Products: Aluminum and steel bar, sheet, plate, structurals, tubing, and pipe. **SIC:** 5051 (Metals Service Centers & Offices). **Est:** 1924. **Sales:** $1,000,000,000 (2000). **Emp:** 1,900. **Officers:** Maurice S. Nelson Jr., CEO & President; William Johnson, VP of Finance.

■ **20080** ■ **Jorgensen Steel Co.**
1900 Mitchell Blvd.
Schaumburg, IL 60193
Phone: (708)307-6100 **Fax:** (708)307-6114
Products: Cold finished steel bars and bar shapes; Steel pipe and tubes. **SIC:** 5051 (Metals Service Centers & Offices). **Est:** 1948. **Sales:** $16,000,000 (2000). **Emp:** 381. **Officers:** Al Moir, General Mgr.; D. Robison, Mgr. of Finance; Gregg Stevenson, VP Marketing & Development; Jerry Riano, Mgr. of Insustrial Relations.

■ **20081** ■ **K and F Industries Inc.**
(Indianapolis, Indiana)
PO Box 1206
Indianapolis, IN 46206
Phone: (317)783-2385 **Fax:** (317)782-9686
Products: Nonferrous metal scraps. **SIC:** 5093 (Scrap & Waste Materials). **Sales:** $40,000,000 (2000). **Emp:** 90. **Officers:** Martin J. Kroot, President; Gregory Kroot, CFO.

■ **20082** ■ **K and M Metals Inc.**
845 Alexander Ave.
Tacoma, WA 98421
Phone: (253)863-6800
Products: Metals. **SIC:** 5051 (Metals Service Centers & Offices).

■ **20083** ■ **Kalamazoo Mill Supply Co.**
PO Box 2421
Kalamazoo, MI 49003
Phone: (616)349-9641
Free: (800)878-6455 **Fax:** (616)349-9888
Products: Steel service center: flame cutting. **SICs:** 5051 (Metals Service Centers & Offices); 5085 (Industrial Supplies). **Sales:** $13,000,000 (2000). **Emp:** 49.

■ **20084** ■ **Kalamazoo Steel Processing Inc.**
PO Box 169
Kalamazoo, MI 49004
Phone: (616)344-9778 **Fax:** (616)344-2251
Products: Steel service center: leveling, shearing and slitting. **SIC:** 5051 (Metals Service Centers & Offices). **Officers:** Darren Draves, President.

■ **20085** ■ **Kanawha Steel and Equipment Inc.**
PO Box 3203
Charleston, WV 25332
Phone: (304)343-8801
Products: Steel products. **SIC:** 5082 (Construction & Mining Machinery). **Est:** 1935. **Sales:** $17,000,000 (2000). **Emp:** 90. **Officers:** Tom Horn Jr., President; Ray Hart, Vice President.

■ **20086** ■ **Kane Steel Co.**
PO Box 829
Millville, NJ 08332
Phone: (609)825-2200
Products: Steel. **SIC:** 5051 (Metals Service Centers & Offices). **Est:** 1955. **Sales:** $59,000,000 (2000). **Emp:**

80. **Officers:** Clifford Kane, President; J. Cohen, CFO; Ken Weinstein, Dir. of Marketing & Sales.

■ **20087** ■ **Kasle Steel Corp.**
PO Box 33536
Detroit, MI 48232
Phone: (313)943-2500
Free: (800)225-2753 **Fax:** (313)943-2551
E-mail: kasneilson@compuserve.com
Products: Steel. **SIC:** 5051 (Metals Service Centers & Offices). **Est:** 1935. **Sales:** $170,000,000 (2000). **Emp:** 500. **Officers:** Roger Kasle, President; David Yates, CFO; Reg Campbell, VP of Marketing.

■ **20088** ■ **Kataman Metals Inc.**
770 Bonhomme St., Ste. 550
St. Louis, MO 63105
Phone: (314)863-6699
Products: Primary and scrap metal. **SIC:** 5051 (Metals Service Centers & Offices). **Sales:** $228,000,000 (2000). **Emp:** 15. **Officers:** Warren J. Gelman, President; Russell Kasper, CFO.

■ **20089** ■ **M. Katch and Company Inc.**
503 Branner St.
Topeka, KS 66607
Phone: (785)234-2691
Products: Steel. **SIC:** 5051 (Metals Service Centers & Offices). **Est:** 1930. **Sales:** $9,000,000 (2000). **Emp:** 24. **Officers:** William S. Burns, President; Hershel Tkatch, President.

■ **20090** ■ **Kaw River Shredding Inc.**
PO Box 3010
Kansas City, KS 66103-0010
Phone: (913)621-2711
Products: Processed steel. **SIC:** 5051 (Metals Service Centers & Offices). **Est:** 1994. **Sales:** $28,000,000 (2000). **Emp:** 38. **Officers:** Richard Galamba, President; Raynard Brown, Vice President.

■ **20091** ■ **Kearney's Metals Inc.**
PO Box 2926
Fresno, CA 93745
Phone: (559)233-2591
Products: Aluminum and stainless steel. **SIC:** 5051 (Metals Service Centers & Offices). **Est:** 1965. **Sales:** $20,000,000 (2000). **Emp:** 100. **Officers:** Michael Kearney, Manager.

■ **20092** ■ **Keelor Steel Inc.**
5101 N Boone Ave.
Minneapolis, MN 55428
Phone: (612)535-1431 **Fax:** (612)535-9840
Products: Steel. **SIC:** 5051 (Metals Service Centers & Offices). **Est:** 1949. **Sales:** $50,000,000 (2000). **Emp:** 200. **Officers:** Tim LaPerre, President; Richard Faue, Dir. of Marketing & Sales.

■ **20093** ■ **Keibler-Thompson Corp.**
130 Entrance Way
New Kensington, PA 15068
Phone: (724)335-9161 **Fax:** (724)335-6189
Products: Steel mill refractory and demolition machinery and repairing. **SIC:** 5051 (Metals Service Centers & Offices). **Officers:** Mern Kemble, CEO; B Long, Treasurer.

■ **20094** ■ **Kemeny Overseas Products Corporation**
233 S Wacker
Chicago, IL 60606
Phone: (312)663-5161 **Fax:** (312)879-0379
Products: Cold-rolled and galvanized steel; Steel tinplate. **SIC:** 5051 (Metals Service Centers & Offices). **Officers:** A. Gabor, President.

■ **20095** ■ **Ken-Mac Metals Inc.**
17901 Englewood Dr.
Cleveland, OH 44130
Phone: (440)234-7500 **Fax:** (440)234-4459
E-mail: lparsonskentuckymacohcom
Products: Aluminum and stainless sheet metal. **SIC:** 5051 (Metals Service Centers & Offices). **Est:** 1962. **Sales:** $200,000,000 (1999). **Emp:** 200. **Officers:** L.E. Parsons, President; Sue Trusso, Human Resources Contact.

■ 20096 ■ **Kenilworth Steel Co**
106 E Market St Ste. 807
Warren, OH 44481
Phone: (330)373-1885 **Fax:** (330)399-2144
Products: Steel plate service center. **SIC:** 5051
(Metals Service Centers & Offices).

■ 20097 ■ **Kenwal Steel Corp.**
8223 W Warren Ave.
Dearborn, MI 48126
Phone: (313)739-1000 **Fax:** (313)933-5339
Products: Steel. **SIC:** 5051 (Metals Service Centers &
Offices). **Est:** 1946. **Sales:** $120,000,000 (2000). **Emp:**
150. **Officers:** Kenneth Eisenberg, CEO & Chairman of
the Board; Mary Ann Hoenscheid, Controller; David
Bazzy, COO & President; Diane Chmura, Personnel
Mgr. **Former Name:** Kenwal Products Corp.

■ 20098 ■ **Keystone Iron and Metal Company
Inc.**
4903 E Carson St.
Pittsburgh, PA 15207
Phone: (412)462-1520 **Fax:** (412)462-8047
Products: Iron; Primary metal products. **SIC:** 5051
(Metals Service Centers & Offices). **Est:** 1954. **Sales:**
$7,000,000 (2000). **Emp:** 20. **Officers:** W. Thompson,
President; Mary H. Thompson, Controller; M.L.
Thompson, Controller; Dennis M. Thompson, Dir. of
Marketing & Sales.

■ 20099 ■ **Keystone Steel Sales Inc.**
400 Barretto St.
Bronx, NY 10474
Phone: (718)542-8400 **Fax:** (212)378-5934
Products: Steel coils. **SIC:** 5051 (Metals Service
Centers & Offices). **Est:** 1965. **Sales:** $5,000,000
(2000). **Emp:** 12. **Officers:** J. Greenberg, President;
Larry Greenberg, Vice President.

■ 20100 ■ **Keystone Tube Co.**
13527 S Halsted St.
Chicago, IL 60629
Phone: (708)568-0800 **Fax:** (708)841-3724
Products: Carbon and alloy tubular products. **SIC:**
5051 (Metals Service Centers & Offices). **Sales:**
$21,000,000 (1994). **Emp:** 100. **Officers:** Marc
Biolchin, CEO & President; Steven Fisher, CFO.

■ 20101 ■ **KG Specialty Steel Inc.**
2001 Elizabeth St.
North Brunswick, NJ 08902
Phone: (732)297-9500 **Fax:** (732)422-1370
Products: Stainless steel products, including angles,
rounds, flats, seamless pipe, welded pipe, weld fittings,
and flanges. **SIC:** 5051 (Metals Service Centers &
Offices). **Est:** 1969. **Sales:** $80,000,000 (2000). **Emp:**
72. **Officers:** Ken Elkin, President.

■ 20102 ■ **Kgs Steel, Inc.**
4717 Centennial Blvd.
Nashville, TN 37209
Phone: (615)460-4620
Products: Steel. **SIC:** 5051 (Metals Service Centers &
Offices).

■ 20103 ■ **Kivort Steel Inc.**
380 Hudson
Waterford, NY 12188
Phone: (518)590-7233
Free: (800)462-2616 **Fax:** (518)235-2042
Products: Steel service center: processing, cutting,
slitting and shearing. **SIC:** 5051 (Metals Service
Centers & Offices). **Emp:** 22. **Officers:** Stanley Kivort,
President.

■ 20104 ■ **Klein Steel Service Inc.**
811 West Ave.
Rochester, NY 14611
Phone: (716)328-4000 **Fax:** (716)328-0470
Products: Steel service center. **SIC:** 5051 (Metals
Service Centers & Offices). **Officers:** Arnold Klein,
President.

■ 20105 ■ **Klockner Namasco Corp.**
5775 Glenridge Dr. NE, No. C
Atlanta, GA 30328-5380
Products: Metals. **SIC:** 5051 (Metals Service Centers
& Offices). **Est:** 1970. **Sales:** $480,000,000 (2000).

Emp: 650. **Officers:** F.W. Mueller, CEO & President;
George Budenbender, Sr. VP & Controller.

■ 20106 ■ **Kojemi Corp.**
PO Box 795
Syosset, NY 11791-0795
Phone: (516)921-5250 **Fax:** (516)921-5063
Products: Copper. **SIC:** 5051 (Metals Service Centers
& Offices). **Sales:** $800,000 (2000). **Emp:** 3. **Officers:**
Joe Spiciarich, President.

■ 20107 ■ **Koons Steel Inc.**
PO Box 476
Parker Ford, PA 19457
Phone: (610)495-9100
Free: (800)654-3441 **Fax:** (610)495-9101
Products: Metals service center: structural steel. **SIC:**
5051 (Metals Service Centers & Offices). **Sales:**
$54,000,000 (1999). **Emp:** 45. **Officers:** Frank Koons
III, President; Walter Meisinger, Controller.

■ 20108 ■ **J. Kozel and Son Inc.**
1150 Scottsville Rd.
Rochester, NY 14624
Phone: (716)436-9807
Products: Steel. **SIC:** 5051 (Metals Service Centers &
Offices). **Sales:** $4,000,000 (2000). **Emp:** 20. **Officers:**
Burt Kozel, President.

■ 20109 ■ **Kreher Steel Co.**
812 Lexington Dr. Ste. 100
Plano, TX 75075-2357
Phone: (972)578-9116
Products: Steel. **SIC:** 5051 (Metals Service Centers &
Offices).

■ 20110 ■ **Kreher Steel Company Inc.**
1550 N 25th Ave.
Melrose Park, IL 60160
Phone: (708)279-0058 **Fax:** (708)345-8293
URL: http://www.kreher.com
Products: Unfabricated steel, including carbon, alloy,
stainless and tool steel. **SIC:** 5051 (Metals Service
Centers & Offices). **Est:** 1979. **Sales:** $130,000,000
(1999). **Emp:** 100. **Officers:** Thomas Kreher,
President.

■ 20111 ■ **James H. Kurtz Steel**
18881 Sherwood
Detroit, MI 48234
Phone: (313)892-1212 **Fax:** (313)892-5834
Products: Steel products; Cold finished steel bars and
bar shapes. **SIC:** 5051 (Metals Service Centers &
Offices). **Sales:** $20,000,000 (2000). **Emp:** 100.
Officers: Bruce Kennedy, President; Ralph McKelvey,
CFO.

■ 20112 ■ **L and M Shape Burning Inc.**
PO Box 5289
Compton, CA 90224
Phone: (310)639-4222 **Fax:** (310)631-2577
Products: Steel plates. **SIC:** 5051 (Metals Service
Centers & Offices). **Sales:** $1,500,000 (2000). **Emp:**
12. **Officers:** G. Chuchua, President.

■ 20113 ■ **La Barge Pipe and Steel**
901 N 10th St.
St. Louis, MO 63101
Phone: (314)231-3400
Free: (800)LAB-ARGE **Fax:** (314)982-9395
URL: http://www.labargepipe.com
Products: Steel pipe. **SIC:** 5051 (Metals Service
Centers & Offices). **Est:** 1953. **Sales:** $60,000,000
(2000). **Emp:** 175. **Officers:** P.L. LaBarge III, CEO;
Stephen J. Kozak, Sales/Marketing Contact.

■ 20114 ■ **Lafayette Steel Co.**
3600 N Military St.
Detroit, MI 48210
Phone: (313)894-4552 **Fax:** (313)894-7930
Products: Steel. **SIC:** 5051 (Metals Service Centers &
Offices). **Est:** 1946. **Sales:** $116,000,000 (2000). **Emp:**
235. **Officers:** Bruce Bisballe, President; William T.
Corbett, VP of Finance; Walter Kuckelman, VP of
Sales; Dan Zemon, Exec. VP; John Quoziente,
Personnel Mgr.

■ 20115 ■ **Lake Steel Inc.**
PO Box 31748
Amarillo, TX 79120-1748
Phone: (806)383-7141 **Fax:** (806)383-0130
Products: Steel. **SIC:** 5051 (Metals Service Centers &
Offices). **Est:** 1949. **Sales:** $32,000,000 (1999). **Emp:**
79. **Officers:** Lane Seliger, President; Dewayne Ekrut,
Treasurer; David St. Clair, Dir of Personnel.

■ 20116 ■ **Lapham-Hickey Steel Corp.**
PO Box 57
St. Louis, MO 63166
Phone: (314)535-8200
Products: Beams and steel sheets. **SIC:** 5051 (Metals
Service Centers & Offices). **Sales:** $25,000,000 (2000).
Emp: 50. **Officers:** James Nickolson, General Mgr.;
Linda Pitman, CFO; Dan Kuenzle, Dir. of Marketing.

■ 20117 ■ **Lapham-Hickey Steel Corp.**
5500 W 73rd St.
Chicago, IL 60638
Phone: (708)496-6111
Free: (800)323-8443 **Fax:** (708)496-8504
E-mail: L-Hsales@Lapham-Hickey.com
URL: http://www.Lapham-Hickey.com
Products: Steel; Carbon; Bar products; Plate products;
Tubular products. **SIC:** 5051 (Metals Service Centers &
Offices). **Est:** 1926. **Sales:** $36,000,000 (1999). **Emp:**
300. **Officers:** W.M. Hickey Jr., President; Robert
Piland, VP of Finance; Richard O'Connell, VP &
General Merchandising Mgr.; Robert Carlisle, Dir. of
Data Processing.

■ 20118 ■ **Lapham-Hickey Steel Corp.**
2585 W 20th Ave.
Oshkosh, WI 54901
Phone: (920)233-8502
Products: Steel. **SIC:** 5051 (Metals Service Centers &
Offices).

■ 20119 ■ **Lapham-Hickey Steel Corp. Clifford
Metal Div.**
200 Corliss St.
Providence, RI 02904
Phone: (401)861-4100 **Fax:** (401)331-8127
Products: Steel. **SIC:** 5051 (Metals Service Centers &
Offices). **Est:** 1938. **Sales:** $9,000,000 (2000). **Emp:**
32. **Officers:** Michael D. Lawlor, President; Lisa
Harrington, CFO; Michael Lawlor, Dir. of Marketing;
Joseph Salum, Dir. of Data Processing; Linda Dwyer,
Office Mgr.

■ 20120 ■ **Leeco Steel Products Inc.**
8255 S Lemont Rd., No. 100
Darien, IL 60561
Phone: (773)762-4800
Free: (800)621-4366 **Fax:** (773)762-8466
Products: Specialty steel plates. **SIC:** 5051 (Metals
Service Centers & Offices). **Sales:** $42,000,000 (2000).
Emp: 50. **Officers:** Les O'Donnell, President; Jim
Miloch, CFO.

■ 20121 ■ **Leico Industries Inc.**
250 W 57th St.
New York, NY 10107
Phone: (212)765-5290 **Fax:** (212)582-5085
Products: High purity metals; Calibration equipment;
Triple-point-of-water cells. **SICs:** 5051 (Metals Service
Centers & Offices); 5085 (Industrial Supplies). **Est:**
1966. **Emp:** 17. **Officers:** Leon L. Eisenmann,
President.

■ 20122 ■ **Lenox Junk Co.**
1170 Massachusetts Ave.
Dorchester, MA 02125
Phone: (617)288-2841
Products: Scrap metal. **SIC:** 5093 (Scrap & Waste
Materials).

■ 20123 ■ **Charles Leonard Inc.**
13130 S Normandie Ave.
Gardena, CA 90249-2128
Phone: (310)715-7464 **Fax:** (310)715-7474
Products: Metal for binders; Vinyl film. **SIC:** 5051
(Metals Service Centers & Offices). **Est:** 1960. **Sales:**
$5,000,000 (2000). **Emp:** 10. **Officers:** Kenneth D.
Sherman, President; Sherry Sherman, VP of
Operations; Sherry Sherman, VP of Operations.

■ 20124 ■ Levand Steel and Supply Corp.
PO Box 24846
Los Angeles, CA 90024
Phone: (310)823-4453 **Fax:** (310)823-3583
Products: Sheet metal; Scrap metal; Ballast and counterweight metals. **SICs:** 5051 (Metals Service Centers & Offices); 5093 (Scrap & Waste Materials). **Est:** 1972. **Officers:** Joseph Cordner, President.

■ 20125 ■ L Levine & Co.
1899 River Rd.
Cincinnati, OH 45204
Phone: (513)471-5900
Products: Steel pipes. **SIC:** 5051 (Metals Service Centers & Offices).

■ 20126 ■ Levinson Steel Co.
110 Riossler Rd., Ste. 300C
Pittsburgh, PA 15220-1014
Phone: (412)572-3400
Products: Steel. **SIC:** 5051 (Metals Service Centers & Offices). **Sales:** $120,000,000 (2000). **Emp:** 170. **Officers:** William Bennett, CEO & President; Ken Thomas, VP & Controller.

■ 20127 ■ Lexington Steel Corp.
5443 W 70th Pl.
Bedford Park, IL 60638
Phone: (708)594-9200 **Fax:** (708)594-5233
Products: Steel. **SIC:** 5051 (Metals Service Centers & Offices). **Sales:** $60,000,000 (2000). **Emp:** 70. **Officers:** Robert Douglass, CEO; Robert Blumenschein, VP of Sales.

■ 20128 ■ Liebovich Brothers Inc.
2116 Preston St.
Rockford, IL 61102
Phone: (815)987-3200
Products: . **SIC:** 5051 (Metals Service Centers & Offices). **Est:** 1939. **Sales:** $130,000,000 (2000). **Emp:** 300. **Officers:** Gregory Liebovich, President; W.J. Rineberg, CFO.

■ 20129 ■ Lincoln Machine
4317 Progressive Ave.
Lincoln, NE 68504
Phone: (402)434-9140
Products: Metals. **SIC:** 5051 (Metals Service Centers & Offices).

■ 20130 ■ Lindquist Steels Inc.
PO Box 9718
Stratford, CT 06497
Phone: (203)377-2828
Products: Hot and cold-rolled steel. **SIC:** 5051 (Metals Service Centers & Offices). **Est:** 1944. **Sales:** $6,000,000 (2000). **Emp:** 45. **Officers:** Richard M. Hoyt, CEO; Gene Sullivan, Treasurer & Secty.; Robert B. Gibby, Vice President.

■ 20131 ■ Line Power Manufacturing Co.
329 Williams St.
Bristol, VA
Phone: (540)466-8200
Products: Foundries of brass, bronze, and aluminum. **SIC:** 5051 (Metals Service Centers & Offices).

■ 20132 ■ Liston Brick Company of Corona Inc.
PO Box 1869
Corona, CA 91718
Phone: (909)277-4221 **Fax:** (909)277-8382
Products: Aluminum ingots. **SIC:** 5051 (Metals Service Centers & Offices). **Est:** 1974. **Sales:** $30,000,000 (2000). **Emp:** 70. **Officers:** Walter Hall, CEO; Howard Hall, Sr. VP; Cynthia Gates, Controller.

■ 20133 ■ Lockhart Co.
PO Box 1165
Pittsburgh, PA 15230
Phone: (412)771-2600 **Fax:** (412)771-2737
Products: Used, scrap, and recycled materials. **SIC:** 5051 (Metals Service Centers & Offices). **Sales:** $40,000,000 (2000). **Emp:** 95.

■ 20134 ■ Lorbec Metals USA Ltd.
3415 Western Rd.
Flint, MI 48506
Phone: (810)736-0961
Products: Metal. **SIC:** 5051 (Metals Service Centers & Offices).

■ 20135 ■ Arthur Louis Steel Co.
PO Box 518
Ashtabula, OH 44005-0518
Phone: (440)997-5545 **Fax:** (440)992-9726
E-mail: alsteel@knownet.net
Products: Steel. **SIC:** 5051 (Metals Service Centers & Offices). **Est:** 1950. **Sales:** $6,000,000 (2000). **Emp:** 35. **Officers:** J.H. Kanicki, CEO & President.

■ 20136 ■ Lovejoy Industries, Inc.
1761 Elmore St.
Cincinnati, OH 45223
Phone: (513)541-1400
Free: (800)301-2277 **Fax:** (513)541-1485
E-mail: lovejoy04@fuse.net
Products: Steel. **SIC:** 5051 (Metals Service Centers & Offices). **Est:** 1989. **Sales:** $30,000,000 (1999). **Emp:** 130. **Officers:** Mike Randall, General Mgr.

■ 20137 ■ Lovejoy Industries Inc.
10160 Philipp Pkwy.
Streetsboro, OH 44241
Phone: (330)656-0001
Free: (800)326-6455 **Fax:** (330)656-4040
Products: Metals. **SIC:** 5051 (Metals Service Centers & Offices). **Sales:** $29,000,000 (2000). **Emp:** 70. **Officers:** Robert B. Lovejoy, President; Patrick Campbell, CFO.

■ 20138 ■ Loveman Steel Corp.
PO Box 46430
Bedford Heights, OH 44146-0430
Phone: (440)232-6200
Free: (800)568-3626 **Fax:** (440)232-0914
E-mail: lovemanstl@aol.com
URL: http://www.lovemansteel.com
Products: Steel. **SIC:** 5051 (Metals Service Centers & Offices). **Est:** 1928. **Sales:** $13,000,000 (2000). **Emp:** 88. **Officers:** Ralph Loveman, President; Jim Loveman, CFO.

■ 20139 ■ Lusk Metals and Plastics
PO Box 24013
Oakland, CA 94623
Phone: (510)785-6400 **Fax:** (510)786-9680
Products: Metal and plastic materials. **SICs:** 5051 (Metals Service Centers & Offices); 5162 (Plastics Materials & Basic Shapes). **Sales:** $63,000,000 (2000). **Emp:** 54. **Officers:** Eric Schnieder, President; Gary Peterson, Controller.

■ 20140 ■ Maas-Hansen Steel Corp.
PO Box 58364
Vernon, CA 90058
Phone: (213)583-6321
Free: (800)847-8335 **Fax:** (213)586-9535
Products: Steel sheet metal. **SIC:** 5051 (Metals Service Centers & Offices). **Est:** 1929. **Sales:** $100,000,000 (2000). **Emp:** 95. **Officers:** Leon Banks, President; Carlin Warner, Controller.

■ 20141 ■ Macsteel Service Centers USA - Edgcomb Metals Div.
555 State Rd.
Bensalem, PA 19020
Phone: (215)245-3300 **Fax:** (215)245-3257
URL: http://www.macsteelusa.com
Products: Carbon, stainless, aluminum flat rolled, general line and plate products; Tubing and piping; Prepainted metals and other specialties. **SIC:** 5051 (Metals Service Centers & Offices). **Est:** 1995. **Emp:** 1,800. **Officers:** Michael Hoffman, President & CEO. **Former Name:** Edgcomb Metals Co.

■ 20142 ■ Macuch Steel Products Inc.
PO Box 3285
Augusta, GA 30914
Phone: (706)823-2420 **Fax:** (706)823-2439
Products: Steel service center; steel fabricating. **SIC:** 5051 (Metals Service Centers & Offices). **Sales:** $15,000,000 (1999). **Emp:** 88. **Officers:** Edwin R. Macuch, President; Nancy A. Sheahan, Controller.

■ 20143 ■ Magnum Diversified Industries Inc.
279 Jenckes Hill Rd.
Smithfield, RI 02917-1905
Phone: (401)942-5021
Products: Metal, including copper, silver, and nickel. **SIC:** 5051 (Metals Service Centers & Offices).

■ 20144 ■ Magnum Steel and Trading Inc.
5 E Main St.
Hudson, OH 44236
Phone: (330)655-9365 **Fax:** (330)656-9368
Products: Scrap metal and raw materials. **SIC:** 5093 (Scrap & Waste Materials). **Sales:** $20,000,000 (2000). **Emp:** 6. **Officers:** Paolo A. Giorgi, President.

■ 20145 ■ Maiale Metal Products
1496 Hawthorne Rd.
Grosse Pointe, MI 48236
Phone: (313)885-5540
Products: Steel. **SIC:** 5051 (Metals Service Centers & Offices).

■ 20146 ■ Majestic Steel Service Inc.
5300 Majestic Pkwy.
Bedford Heights, OH 44146
Phone: (216)786-2666
Free: (800)321-5590 **Fax:** (216)786-0576
Products: Steel, including flat-rolled, galavanized, aluminized, bonderized, galvalume, cold-rolled. **SIC:** 5051 (Metals Service Centers & Offices). **Est:** 1979. **Sales:** $190,000,000 (2000). **Emp:** 100. **Officers:** Dennis Leebow, CEO & Chairman of the Board; Peter Doyle, Exec. VP; Kevin Ginley.

■ 20147 ■ Manhattan Brass and Copper Company Inc.
PO Box 780145
Maspeth, NY 11378
Phone: (718)381-5300
Free: (800)221-7575 **Fax:** (718)821-5229
Products: Brass, copper, and aluminum products. **SIC:** 5051 (Metals Service Centers & Offices). **Est:** 1938. **Sales:** $20,000,000 (2000). **Emp:** 40. **Officers:** Mark Bernstein, President; Jim Graham, CFO; Trevor Griffiths, Customer Service Contact; Robert Schwartz, Customer Service Contact.

■ 20148 ■ Mannesmann Pipe and Steel Corp.
1990 Post Oak Blvd., No. 1800
Houston, TX 77056
Phone: (713)960-1900 **Fax:** (713)960-1063
Products: Metal pipes; Steel. **SIC:** 5051 (Metals Service Centers & Offices). **Est:** 1952. **Sales:** $500,000,000 (2000). **Emp:** 80. **Officers:** Rudolf Georg, President; Tim A. Taylor, VP of Finance.

■ 20149 ■ Manufacturers Steel Supply Company Inc.
400 Edwin St.
St. Louis, MO 63103-2492
Phone: (314)371-5600 **Fax:** (314)371-5604
Products: Flat rolled steel. **SIC:** 5051 (Metals Service Centers & Offices). **Est:** 1953. **Sales:** $5,000,000 (2000). **Emp:** 20. **Officers:** Earon Barnes Jr., President & Treasurer; Richard L. Schumacher, Controller; James L. Schaper, Sales Mgr.; Judi G. Smith, Dir. of Data Processing.

■ 20150 ■ Manutec Inc.
2475 W Hampton Ave.
Milwaukee, WI 53209
Phone: (414)449-3332 **Fax:** (414)449-5035
Products: Metal fabricating: steel, aluminum, stainless; cylinders, booms, trailers, buckets, backhoes, conveyors, industrial furnaces, machinery bases, mining and construction equipment components, tanks, pumps. **SIC:** 5051 (Metals Service Centers & Offices). **Sales:** $6,500,000 (1999). **Emp:** 60. **Officers:** Irv Palmer, President.

■ 20151 ■ Mapes and Sprowl Steel Ltd.
1100 E Devon Ave.
Elk Grove Village, IL 60007
Phone: (708)364-0055 **Fax:** (708)364-0137
Products: Metal slitting and shearing. **SIC:** 5051 (Metals Service Centers & Offices). **Sales:** $20,000,000 (1994). **Emp:** 25. **Officers:** Gary Hamity, President; Charles V. Keating Sr., Controller.

■ 20152 ■ **Markle Steel Co.**
PO Box 2346
Houston, TX 77252-2346
Phone: (713)225-1141
Products: Hot-rolled steel. **SIC:** 5051 (Metals Service Centers & Offices). **Est:** 1903. **Sales:** $30,000,000 (1999). **Emp:** 126. **Officers:** J. Brooks Williams, President.

■ 20153 ■ **Markovits and Fox**
PO Box 611420
San Jose, CA 95161-1420
Phone: (408)453-7888   **Fax:** (408)453-7211
Products: Metals; Recycled metals. **SICs:** 5051 (Metals Service Centers & Offices); 5093 (Scrap & Waste Materials). **Est:** 1886. **Sales:** $65,000,000 (2000). **Emp:** 110. **Officers:** Marvin B. Fox, CEO; David L. Mighdoll, CFO.

■ 20154 ■ **Marlen Trading Company Inc.**
4101 Curtis Ave.
Baltimore, MD 21226
Phone: (410)355-3300
Products: Steel. **SIC:** 5051 (Metals Service Centers & Offices). **Est:** 1966. **Sales:** $8,000,000 (2000). **Emp:** 20. **Officers:** Leonard L. Levin, President; Debbie Lopez, Controller.

■ 20155 ■ **Marmon/Keystone Corp.**
PO Box 992
Butler, PA 16001
Phone: (724)283-3000   **Fax:** (724)283-0558
URL: http://www.marmonkeystone.com
Products: Pipe and tubing. **SIC:** 5051 (Metals Service Centers & Offices). **Est:** 1907. **Sales:** $60,000,000 (2000). **Emp:** 1,400. **Officers:** Norman E. Gottschalk Jr., President, e-mail: ngottschalk@mail.marmonkeystone.com; Andrew Seka, Exec. VP & Controller; Mike Conley, Vice President/Commercial; Jay Powell, Dir. of Information Systems.

■ 20156 ■ **Mascotech Forming Technologies**
690 W Maple
Troy, MI 48084
Phone: (248)362-1844   **Fax:** (248)362-8501
Products: Iron and steel forgings. **SIC:** 5051 (Metals Service Centers & Offices). **Est:** 1955. **Sales:** $21,000,000 (2000). **Emp:** 150. **Officers:** R.K. Trentham, President; M. Koziol, CFO; C.C. Minton, Dir. of Marketing.

■ 20157 ■ **Matex Products, Inc.**
14812 Detroit Ave.
Cleveland, OH 44107
Phone: (216)228-9911
Free: (800)67M-ATEX   **Fax:** (216)521-3709
Products: Planetary gear reducers. **SIC:** 5051 (Metals Service Centers & Offices). **Est:** 1980. **Sales:** $1,000,000 (1999). **Emp:** 5. **Officers:** H.A. Van Hala, President, e-mail: vanhala@matexgears.com; R.C. Van Hala, Treasurer; H.A. Van Hala, Sales/Marketing Contact. **Former Name:** Van Hala Industrial Co.

■ 20158 ■ **Maurice Pincoffs Company Inc.**
PO Box 920919
Houston, TX 77292
Phone: (713)681-5461   **Fax:** (713)681-8521
Products: Stainless steel, farm supplies and exercise equipment. **SICs:** 5051 (Metals Service Centers & Offices); 5191 (Farm Supplies); 5091 (Sporting & Recreational Goods). **Sales:** $80,000,000 (2000). **Emp:** 100. **Officers:** John I. Griffin, President; Taft Symonds, Chairman of the Board & CFO.

■ 20159 ■ **Maxco Inc.**
PO Box 80737
Lansing, MI 48908
Phone: (517)321-3130
Products: Steel mesh; Paint products; Steel rods. **SICs:** 5051 (Metals Service Centers & Offices); 5198 (Paints, Varnishes & Supplies). **Est:** 1946. **Sales:** $74,000,000 (2000). **Emp:** 620. **Officers:** Max A. Coon, Comptroller; Vincent Shunsky, VP of Finance & Treasurer; Eric L. Cross, Director.

■ 20160 ■ **May Steel Corp.**
100 Continental Dr.
Columbus, WI 53925
Phone: (920)623-2540
Products: Steel. **SIC:** 5051 (Metals Service Centers & Offices).

■ 20161 ■ **McCarthy Steel Inc.**
PO Box 1887
Bakersfield, CA 93303
Phone: (805)324-6715   **Fax:** (805)324-6710
Products: Steel and steel products, including steel tanks and structural steel. **SICs:** 5051 (Metals Service Centers & Offices); 5039 (Construction Materials Nec). **Est:** 1909. **Sales:** $6,500,000 (2000). **Emp:** 100. **Officers:** Robert E. McCarthy, President; Michael McCarthy Sr., VP of Finance; Richard F. Giles, Sales Mgr.

■ 20162 ■ **McNichols Co.**
PO Box 30300
Tampa, FL 33630-3300
Phone: (813)289-4100
Free: (800)237-3820   **Fax:** (813)289-3820
E-mail: sales@mcnichols.com
URL: http://www.mcnichols.com
Products: Grating, including safety, bar, and fiberglass; Metals; Wire cloth. **SIC:** 5051 (Metals Service Centers & Offices). **Est:** 1952. **Sales:** $70,000,000 (2000). **Emp:** 211. **Officers:** E.H. McNichols, President; Herb Goetschivs, CFO; W.J. Tuxhorn, Dir. of Marketing; L.D. Moulds, Dir of Human Resources.

■ 20163 ■ **Meier Metal Servicenters Inc.**
1471 E 9 Mile Rd.
Hazel Park, MI 48030
Phone: (810)645-5090   **Fax:** (810)645-6042
Products: Aluminum metal. **SIC:** 5051 (Metals Service Centers & Offices). **Est:** 1945. **Sales:** $48,000,000 (2000). **Emp:** 125. **Officers:** W.J. Targett, President; J.D. Bohrer, Controller.

■ 20164 ■ **Melton Steel Corp.**
7204 Navigation Blvd.
Houston, TX 77011
Phone: (713)928-5451   **Fax:** (713)928-2840
Products: Structural steel. **SICs:** 5051 (Metals Service Centers & Offices); 5039 (Construction Materials Nec). **Est:** 1948. **Sales:** $14,000,000 (2000). **Emp:** 20. **Officers:** Walter Melton, CEO; Linda Thompson, Controller.

■ 20165 ■ **Meridian National Corp.**
805 Chicago St.
Toledo, OH 43611
Phone: (419)729-3918
Products: Flat-rolled steel. **SIC:** 5051 (Metals Service Centers & Offices). **Sales:** $56,600,000 (2000). **Emp:** 152. **Officers:** William D. Feniger, CEO & President; James L. Rosino, VP, CFO & Treasurer.

■ 20166 ■ **Merit USA**
620 Clark Ave.
Pittsburg, CA 94565
Phone: (925)432-6900
Free: (800)445-6374   **Fax:** (925)427-6427
Products: Steel. **SIC:** 5051 (Metals Service Centers & Offices). **Sales:** $26,000,000 (2000). **Emp:** 60. **Officers:** Pete Ryner, CEO & President; Carol Brombough, Controller.

■ 20167 ■ **Merritt Machine Inc.**
2124 Snowhill Dr.
Mt. Airy, NC 27030
Phone: (336)789-1600
Products: Steel. **SIC:** 5051 (Metals Service Centers & Offices).

■ 20168 ■ **Mervis Industries Inc.**
PO Box 827
Danville, IL 61834
Phone: (217)442-5300
Free: (800)637-3016   **Fax:** (217)477-9245
URL: http://www.merris.com
Products: Scrap iron, metal and construction materials. **SICs:** 5093 (Scrap & Waste Materials); 5039 (Construction Materials Nec). **Est:** 1930. **Sales:** $60,000,000 (2000). **Emp:** 300. **Officers:** Louis L. Mervis, President; Michael A. Smith, CFO.

■ 20169 ■ **Metal Management Inc.**
500 N Dearborn St., Ste. 405
Chicago, IL 60610
Phone: (312)645-0700
Products: Scrap metal and recycled metal products. **SIC:** 5093 (Scrap & Waste Materials). **Sales:** $65,200,000 (2000). **Emp:** 376. **Officers:** Gerald M. Jacobs, CEO; Robert C. Larry, VP & CFO.

■ 20170 ■ **Metal Service and Supply Inc.**
916 Harrison St.
Indianapolis, IN 46202
Phone: (317)634-8720   **Fax:** (317)634-9549
Products: Steel products; Rolled and drawn nonferrous metals; Galvanized or other coated sheets; Aluminum. **SIC:** 5051 (Metals Service Centers & Offices). **Est:** 1974. **Sales:** $30,000,000 (2000). **Emp:** 60. **Officers:** Richard E. Skidmore, Chairman of the Board; Dennis McBride, Controller.

■ 20171 ■ **The Metal Store**
14506 Industrial Ave. S
Maple Heights, OH 44137
Phone: (216)663-0458   **Fax:** (216)663-0709
E-mail: sales@themetalstore.com
URL: http://www.themetalstore.com
Products: Metals, including steel(stainless and aluminum). **SIC:** 5051 (Metals Service Centers & Offices). **Est:** 1989. **Sales:** $1,000,000 (2000). **Emp:** 4. **Officers:** G. Harold Goodwin, President. **Former Name:** Metal Store of Cleveland Inc.

■ 20172 ■ **MetalCenter Inc.**
PO Box 60482
Los Angeles, CA 90060
Phone: (213)582-2272
Free: (800)448-0001   **Fax:** (310)944-1346
Products: Aluminum and stainless steel. **SIC:** 5051 (Metals Service Centers & Offices). **Sales:** $60,000,000 (2000). **Emp:** 114. **Officers:** Joe D. Crider, President; Dave Hannah, CFO; Robert Thommen, VP & Gen. Mgr.

■ 20173 ■ **Metallurg International Resources**
6 E 43rd St., Fl. 12
New York, NY 10017-4609
Phone: (212)835-0200
Free: (800)762-2424   **Fax:** (212)687-9623
Products: Metals, including ores. **SIC:** 5051 (Metals Service Centers & Offices). **Est:** 1991. **Emp:** 3. **Officers:** Eric Jackson, President; David Henderson, Commercial Director.

■ 20174 ■ **Metalmart Inc.**
12225 Coast Dr.
Whittier, CA 90601
Phone: (562)692-9081   **Fax:** (562)699-6868
Products: Metals; Metal service center. **SIC:** 5051 (Metals Service Centers & Offices).

■ 20175 ■ **Metals Engineering Co.**
PO Box 237
Monroe, CT 06468
Phone: (203)268-7325   **Fax:** (203)452-9737
Products: Casting materials, including alloyed metals. **SIC:** 5051 (Metals Service Centers & Offices). **Est:** 1960. **Sales:** $300,000 (2000). **Emp:** 4. **Officers:** Frank M. Christiano, President.

■ 20176 ■ **Metals USA Inc.**
3 Riverway, Ste. 600
Houston, TX 77056
Phone: (713)965-0990
Products: Metals. **SIC:** 5051 (Metals Service Centers & Offices). **Sales:** $507,000,000 (2000). **Emp:** 2,700. **Officers:** Arthur L. French, CEO, President & Chairman of the Board; Michael Kirksey, Sr. VP & CFO.

■ 20177 ■ **Metalwest**
1774 W 2800 S
Ogden, UT 84401
Phone: (801)399-5700
Products: Steel. **SIC:** 5051 (Metals Service Centers & Offices).

■ 20178 ■ **Metron Steel Corp.**
12900 S Metron Dr.
Chicago, IL 60633
Phone: (773)646-4000
Products: Hot rolled steel. **SIC:** 5051 (Metals Service Centers & Offices). **Est:** 1950. **Sales:** $100,000,000 (2000). **Emp:** 165. **Officers:** Richard E. O'Tolle, VP & General Merchandising Mgr.; Edward Nembrgut, Sr. VP & Finance Officer; John Swanson, Sales Mgr.; George Jaamrok, Dir. of Information Systems; Jim Barnhouse, Dir. of Admin.

■ 20179 ■ **Miami Valley Steel Service Inc.**
201 Fox Dr.
Piqua, OH 45356
Phone: (937)773-7127
Products: Steel. **SIC:** 5051 (Metals Service Centers & Offices).

■ 20180 ■ **Mickey's Mobile Metal Mending**
100 7th St.
Alamogordo, NM 88310
Phone: (505)437-6437
Products: Metal. **SIC:** 5051 (Metals Service Centers & Offices).

■ 20181 ■ **Mid-City Iron and Metal Corp.**
2104 E 15th St.
Los Angeles, CA 90021
Phone: (213)747-4281 **Fax:** (213)749-5772
URL: http://www.adamssteel.com
Products: Steel. **SIC:** 5093 (Scrap & Waste Materials). **Est:** 1948. **Sales:** $13,000,000 (2000). **Emp:** 14. **Officers:** George Adams, President; Tammi Shank, General Mgr.

■ 20182 ■ **Mid-East Materials Co.**
25611 Colleen
Oak Park, MI 48237
Phone: (248)968-0043 **Fax:** (248)968-2042
Products: Stainless steel, aluminum, brass, and copper sheets, plates, bars, and tubes. **SIC:** 5051 (Metals Service Centers & Offices). **Est:** 1974. **Sales:** $250,000 (2000). **Emp:** 4. **Officers:** Morris Carmen, Owner; Benno Levi, Treasurer; Sybil Carmen, President.

■ 20183 ■ **Mid-State Industries LLC**
PO Box 68
Arcola, IL 61910
Phone: (217)268-3900 **Fax:** (217)268-3906
Products: Steel service center: metal cutting and slitting. **SIC:** 5051 (Metals Service Centers & Offices).

■ 20184 ■ **Mid-West Materials Inc.**
3687 Shepard Rd.
PO Box 345
Perry, OH 44081
Phone: (440)259-5200
Free: (800)321-4143 **Fax:** (440)259-5204
E-mail: sales@mid-westmaterials.com
URL: http://www.mid-westmaterials.com
Products: Hot rolled steel and strip, hrpo, hi tensile, high carbon, galvanized alumnized, galvannealed. **SIC:** 5051 (Metals Service Centers & Offices). **Est:** 1952. **Sales:** $46,000,000 (1999). **Emp:** 100. **Officers:** Noreen Goldstein, President; Michael Alley, Treasurer; Scott Koppelman, COO; Brian Robbins, CEO; Sales/Marketing Contact, e-mail: sales@mid-westmaterials.com; Customer Service Contact, e-mail: sales@mid-westmaterials.com; Human Resources Contact.

■ 20185 ■ **Mid-West Steel Supply Co.**
1328 N 2nd St.
Minneapolis, MN 55411
Phone: (612)333-6868 **Fax:** (612)333-6872
Products: Steel and aluminum bars and sheets; Brass and stainless steel tubings. **SIC:** 5051 (Metals Service Centers & Offices). **Sales:** $2,000,000 (2000). **Emp:** 4. **Officers:** Jerry Rako, President.

■ 20186 ■ **Midland Aluminum Corp.**
4635 W 160th St.
Cleveland, OH 44135
Phone: (216)267-8044
Free: (800)321-1820 **Fax:** (216)267-7983
E-mail: sales@midlandalum.com
URL: http://www.midlandalum.com
Products: Aluminum; Stainless steel; Brass; Copper. **SIC:** 5051 (Metals Service Centers & Offices). **Est:** 1967. **Sales:** $20,000,000 (1999). **Emp:** 42. **Officers:** Chuck Pariano, President; Anne Roberts, Office Mgr.; Patrick Records, Vice President.

■ 20187 ■ **Midland Steel**
1615 Dublin Rd.
Midland, MI 48642
Phone: (517)631-6466
Products: Steel. **SIC:** 5051 (Metals Service Centers & Offices).

■ 20188 ■ **Midland Steel Warehouse Co.**
1120 Leggett Ave.
Bronx, NY 10474
Phone: (718)328-4600 **Fax:** (212)328-4929
Products: Steel sheets and coils. **SIC:** 5051 (Metals Service Centers & Offices). **Est:** 1970. **Sales:** $55,000,000 (2000). **Emp:** 75. **Officers:** R. Allen, President; Steven Spellman, Controller; J. Benes, Sales Mgr.

■ 20189 ■ **Midwest Coil Processing**
720 E 111th St.
Chicago, IL 60628
Phone: (312)468-2121
Products: Sheet steel. **SIC:** 5051 (Metals Service Centers & Offices). **Sales:** $200,000,000 (2000). **Emp:** 272. **Officers:** Tim LaPerre, President; Paul Staker, Controller.

■ 20190 ■ **Midwest Metallics L.P.**
135 S LaSalle St., Ste. 3600
Chicago, IL 60603-4110
Phone: (708)594-7171
Products: Scrap metal. **SIC:** 5093 (Scrap & Waste Materials).

■ 20191 ■ **Midwest Metals Inc.**
PO Box 4050
Davenport, IA 52808
Phone: (319)324-5243 **Fax:** (319)326-5372
Products: Steel. **SIC:** 5051 (Metals Service Centers & Offices). **Est:** 1990. **Sales:** $11,000,000 (2000). **Emp:** 30. **Officers:** Eugene W. Pierce III, Owner.

■ 20192 ■ **Mill Steel Co.**
PO Box 8827
Grand Rapids, MI 49518
Phone: (616)949-6700 **Fax:** (616)977-9300
Products: Steel service center: flat roll steel, cutting and slitting. **SIC:** 5051 (Metals Service Centers & Offices). **Officers:** William Buck, President.

■ 20193 ■ **Millard Metal Service Center**
PO Box 9054
Braintree, MA 02184-9054
Phone: (617)848-1400 **Fax:** (617)848-0337
Products: Metal. **SIC:** 5051 (Metals Service Centers & Offices). **Est:** 1941. **Sales:** $20,000,000 (2000). **Emp:** 100. **Officers:** D.A. Millard Jr., CEO; John Mason, Treasurer; Edward Torri, VP of Sales; David K. Millard, VP of Information Systems.

■ 20194 ■ **Miller Metal Service Corp.**
2400 Bond St.
University Park, IL 60466
Phone: (708)534-7200 **Fax:** (708)534-7211
Products: Steel service center: cutting, shearing, slitting, milling and resquared blanks. **SIC:** 5051 (Metals Service Centers & Offices). **Officers:** Wayne Miller, CEO.

■ 20195 ■ **Millitrade International Inc.**
6245 S Central Ave.
Phoenix, AZ 85040
Phone: (602)276-2400 **Fax:** (602)276-1096
Products: Steel products; Scrap metals; Rice. **SICs:** 5051 (Metals Service Centers & Offices); 5093 (Scrap & Waste Materials); 5149 (Groceries & Related Products Nec). **Est:** 1983. **Officers:** Peter Popat, Vice President.

■ 20196 ■ **Mills Alloy Steel Co.**
10160 Phillips Pkwy.
Streetsboro, OH 44241
Phone: (330)656-0001
Free: (800)326-6455 **Fax:** (330)656-4040
Products: Raw steel, including bars and plates. **SIC:** 5051 (Metals Service Centers & Offices). **Est:** 1988. **Sales:** $25,000,000 (2000). **Emp:** 65. **Officers:** Robert B. Lovejoy, President; Mary D. Turk, Controller.

■ 20197 ■ **Mine and Mill Supply Co.**
2500 S Combee Rd.
Lakeland, FL 33801
Phone: (863)665-5601
Free: (800)282-8489 **Fax:** (863)667-1907
E-mail: minemill@aol.com
URL: http://www.minemill.com
Products: Steel; Abrasives; Paint; Pipe; Valves; Tools. **SICs:** 5082 (Construction & Mining Machinery); 5085 (Industrial Supplies); 5072 (Hardware); 5198 (Paints, Varnishes & Supplies); 5169 (Chemicals & Allied Products Nec). **Est:** 1908. **Sales:** $12,000,000 (2000). **Emp:** 67. **Officers:** Leon Handley, President; Charles E. Fitzgerald, Finance Officer.

■ 20198 ■ **Misaba Steel Products Inc.**
3213 S Saginaw Rd.
Midland, MI 48640
Phone: (517)496-2720
Products: Steel products. **SIC:** 5051 (Metals Service Centers & Offices).

■ 20199 ■ **Mitsui and Company (U.S.A.) Inc.**
200 Park Ave.
New York, NY 10166
Phone: (212)878-4000 **Fax:** (212)878-4800
Products: Metal, steel, machinery, inorganic chemicals, petrochemicals, fertilizers and foods. **SICs:** 5051 (Metals Service Centers & Offices); 5084 (Industrial Machinery & Equipment); 5169 (Chemicals & Allied Products Nec); 5149 (Groceries & Related Products Nec). **Sales:** $13,143,000,000 (2000). **Emp:** 11,250. **Officers:** Masayoshi Furuhata, CEO & President; Kazuya Imai, Treasurer.

■ 20200 ■ **Momentum Metals Inc.**
PO Box 814045
Dallas, TX 75381
Phone: (972)241-1242
Products: Metal products. **SIC:** 5051 (Metals Service Centers & Offices). **Sales:** $1,000,000 (2000). **Emp:** 2. **Officers:** Dave Brock, President.

■ 20201 ■ **Monarch Steel Co.**
2464 Clybourn Ave.
Chicago, IL 60614
Phone: (773)929-2050
Free: (800)554-5655 **Fax:** (773)929-2737
Products: Cold and hot rolled steel; Galvanized steel. **SIC:** 5051 (Metals Service Centers & Offices). **Est:** 1957. **Sales:** $8,000,000 (2000). **Emp:** 16. **Officers:** P. Wynbrandt, President.

■ 20202 ■ **Monarch Steel Company Inc.**
4389 Martin Ave.
Cleveland, OH 44127
Phone: (216)883-8001 **Fax:** (216)883-8036
Products: Metal service center: slitting, shearing and leveling. **SIC:** 5051 (Metals Service Centers & Offices).

■ 20203 ■ **Monico Alloys Inc.**
2301 E 15th St.
Los Angeles, CA 90021
Phone: (213)629-4767 **Fax:** (213)627-2880
Products: Alloys. **SIC:** 5051 (Metals Service Centers & Offices). **Est:** 1979. **Sales:** $20,000,000 (2000). **Emp:** 50. **Officers:** Saul H. Zenk, President.

■ 20204 ■ **Morin Steel**
4 Stone Rd.
Alfred, ME 04002
Phone: (207)324-2112
Products: Steel. **SIC:** 5051 (Metals Service Centers & Offices).

■ 20205 ■ Morse Industries Inc.
PO Box 1779
Kent, WA 98035
Phone: (253)852-1399 **Fax:** (253)520-9942
Products: Metals; Metal service center. **SIC:** 5051
(Metals Service Centers & Offices). **Sales:**
$48,000,000 (1999). **Emp:** 40. **Officers:** Terry Morse,
President.

■ 20206 ■ Morweco Steel Co.
2911 N 20th St.
Philadelphia, PA 19132-1536
Products: Steel products. **SIC:** 5051 (Metals Service
Centers & Offices).

■ 20207 ■ Moses Lake Steel Supply Inc.
PO Box 1122
Moses Lake, WA 98837
Phone: (509)765-1741
Free: (800)765-1791 **Fax:** (509)766-2496
Products: Steel and fasteners. **SICs:** 5051 (Metals
Service Centers & Offices); 5072 (Hardware). **Sales:**
$1,300,000 (1999). **Emp:** 24. **Officers:** R Wayne
Rimple, President.

■ 20208 ■ Mound Steel Corp.
25 Mound Park Dr.
Springboro, OH 45066
Phone: (513)748-2937 **Fax:** (513)748-9763
E-mail: moundsteel@your-net.com
Products: Steel. **SIC:** 5051 (Metals Service Centers &
Offices). **Est:** 1964. **Sales:** $12,000,000 (2000). **Emp:**
65. **Officers:** Thomas C. Miller, President; Kenneth R.
Weartz, Chairman of the Board & CFO; Russ Ballard,
Sales Mgr.

■ 20209 ■ MP-Tech Inc.
1724-B Armitage Ct.
Addison, IL 60101
Phone: (708)916-9510 **Fax:** (708)916-9521
Products: Zinc and aluminum. **SIC:** 5093 (Scrap &
Waste Materials).

■ 20210 ■ MPL Industries, Inc.
12900 Preston Rd., LB 18
Dallas, TX 75230
Phone: (972)233-0757
Free: (800)231-4600 **Fax:** (972)788-2516
Products: Steel pipe and tubes; Metals, including
semi-fabricated steel and aluminum; Mill depot stock.
SIC: 5051 (Metals Service Centers & Offices). **Est:**
1977. **Sales:** $6,000,000 (1999). **Emp:** 10. **Officers:**
M.P. Long, President; M.A. Mitchell, CFO; Carlos
Breeden, Sales/Marketing Contact, e-mail: sometco@
aol.com.

■ 20211 ■ Mulach Steel Corp.
100 Leetsdale Industrial Dr.
Leetsdale, PA 15056
Phone: (412)257-1111
Products: Steel. **SIC:** 5051 (Metals Service Centers &
Offices). **Sales:** $11,000,000 (1992). **Emp:** 25.
Officers: Steven C. Thomas, CEO; R. Horsmon, CFO.

■ 20212 ■ Namasco
PO Drawer 450469
Houston, TX 77245
Phone: (713)433-7211
Free: (800)736-4555 **Fax:** (713)434-0041
Products: Structural steel, plates, and bar products.
SICs: 5051 (Metals Service Centers & Offices); 5039
(Construction Materials Nec). **Est:** 1955. **Sales:**
$30,000,000 (2000). **Emp:** 40. **Officers:** Ben Pritchard,
Branch Mgr.; Kirk Johnson, Controller.

■ 20213 ■ Namasco Corp.
5775 Glenridge Dr.
Bldg. C, Ste. 110
Atlanta, GA 30328
Phone: (404)267-8800 **Fax:** (404)267-8844
Products: Steel. **SIC:** 5051 (Metals Service Centers &
Offices). **Est:** 1970. **Sales:** $940,000,000 (2000). **Emp:**
1,100. **Officers:** Barney O'Brien, CEO & President; K.
Johnson, VP of Finance; Martin Flanigan, VP of
Marketing; Lloyd Burkhart; Joe Costa, Human
Resources Contact, e-mail: jcosta@namasco.com; D.
Falcone, Marketing Analyst, e-mail: dfalcone@
compuserve.com. **Former Name:** Klockner Namasco
Corp.

■ 20214 ■ Namasco Div.
PO Box 446
Middletown, OH 45042
Phone: (513)422-4586 **Fax:** (513)422-6333
Products: Slit steel. **SIC:** 5051 (Metals Service
Centers & Offices). **Est:** 1965. **Sales:** $27,000,000
(2000). **Emp:** 100. **Officers:** Rick Johnson, Manager;
Mike Cushard, Controller.

■ 20215 ■ Napa Pipe Corp.
1025 Kaiser Rd.
Napa, CA 94558
Phone: (707)257-5000 **Free:** (800)556-5300
Products: Large diameter roll pipes. **SIC:** 5051 (Metals
Service Centers & Offices). **Est:** 1987. **Sales:**
$90,000,000 (2000). **Emp:** 250. **Officers:** Thomas B.
Boklund, CEO; L. Ray Adams, VP of Finance; Robert
R. Mausshardt, VP of Marketing; K. Martin Green, Dir.
of Systems; Michael A. Brundy, Dir of Human
Resources.

■ 20216 ■ Napco Steel Inc.
1800 Arthur Dr.
West Chicago, IL 60185
Phone: (630)293-1900
Free: (800)292-8010 **Fax:** (630)293-0881
E-mail: napranger@aol.com
Products: Steel. **SIC:** 5051 (Metals Service Centers &
Offices). **Est:** 1976. **Sales:** $18,000,000 (2000). **Emp:**
45. **Officers:** M.J. Napoli Jr., President; Teri Napoli-
Estes, Dir. of Systems; J.M. Jourdan, Controller; J.R.
Napoli, Vice President.

■ 20217 ■ Nashville Steel Corp.
7211 Centennial Blvd.
Nashville, TN 37209
Phone: (615)350-7933
Products: Steel. **SIC:** 5051 (Metals Service Centers &
Offices). **Est:** 1960. **Sales:** $29,000,000 (2000). **Emp:**
40. **Officers:** O.B. Johnson Jr., President.

■ 20218 ■ National Compressed Steel Corp.
PO Box 5246
Kansas City, KS 66119
Phone: (913)321-3358 **Fax:** (913)321-3245
Products: Aluminum, brass, and bronze ingots; Lead
and zinc alloys. **SIC:** 5051 (Metals Service Centers &
Offices). **Est:** 1954. **Sales:** $6,500,000 (2000). **Emp:**
45. **Officers:** Al G. Galamba Jr., President; Irwin
Sackinerwin, Treasurer & Secty.; Mark Eibs, General
Mgr.

■ 20219 ■ National Material L.P.
1965 Pratt Blvd.
Elk Grove Village, IL 60007
Phone: (847)806-7200 **Fax:** (847)806-7220
Products: Steel and ferrous scrap metal. **SICs:** 5051
(Metals Service Centers & Offices); 5093 (Scrap &
Waste Materials). **Sales:** $891,000,000 (2000). **Emp:**
1,200. **Officers:** Michael Tang, CEO; Jack Sorenson,
Controller.

■ 20220 ■ National Metal Processing Inc.
6440 Mack Ave.
Detroit, MI 48207
Phone: (313)571-4100
Products: Metals. **SIC:** 5051 (Metals Service Centers
& Offices).

■ 20221 ■ National Titanium Corp.
2187 S Garfield Ave.
Los Angeles, CA 90040
Phone: (213)728-7370
Products: Titanium. **SIC:** 5051 (Metals Service
Centers & Offices). **Est:** 1972. **Sales:** $3,300,000
(2000). **Emp:** 21. **Officers:** William H. Blake, President.

■ 20222 ■ National Tube Supply Co
925 Central Ave.
University Park, IL 60466
Phone: (708)534-2700 **Fax:** (708)534-0200
Products: Steel service center: hot finished carbon
and alloy seamless, cold drawn on seamless and cut to
length. **SIC:** 5051 (Metals Service Centers & Offices).

■ 20223 ■ New Process Steel Corp.
5800 Westview Dr.
Houston, TX 77055
Phone: (713)686-9631
Free: (800)392-4989 **Fax:** (713)686-5358
Products: Galvanized steel. **SIC:** 5051 (Metals Service
Centers & Offices). **Est:** 1950. **Sales:** $350,000,000
(2000). **Emp:** 350. **Officers:** Richard E. Fant,
President; Phil Kelly, CFO.

■ 20224 ■ New York Wire Co.
152 N Main St.
Mt. Wolf, PA 17347
Phone: (717)266-5626 **Fax:** (717)260-5871
E-mail: info@ny-wire.com
URL: http://www.ny-wire.com
Products: Screening; Aluminum and aluminum-base
alloy wire. **SIC:** 5051 (Metals Service Centers &
Offices). **Est:** 1888. **Emp:** 500. **Former Name:** Root
Corp.

■ 20225 ■ Newark Wire Cloth Co.
351 Verona Ave.
Newark, NJ 07104
Phone: (973)483-7700
Free: (800)221-0392 **Fax:** (973)483-6315
E-mail: sales@newarkwire.com
URL: http://www.newarkwire.com
Products: Wire cloth and fabricated wire cloth parts.
SIC: 5051 (Metals Service Centers & Offices). **Est:**
1911. **Sales:** $3,500,000 (1999). **Emp:** 35. **Officers:**
R.W. Campbell, President. **Former Name:** Newark
Wire Cloth Inc.

■ 20226 ■ Nissho Iwai American Corp.
1211 Avenue of the Americas
New York, NY 10036-8880
Phone: (212)704-6500 **Fax:** (212)704-6543
Products: Ferrous and non-ferrous metals, machinery,
marine, aircraft, electronics, realty, construction,
energy, chemicals, food and textiles. **SICs:** 5051
(Metals Service Centers & Offices); 5031 (Lumber,
Plywood & Millwork); 5141 (Groceries—General Line).
Sales: $1,910,000,000 (2000). **Emp:** 425. **Officers:**
Akira Yokouchi, CEO, President & Chairman of the
Board; Masanobu Kondo, Exec. VP of Finance.

■ 20227 ■ Nitek Metal Service Inc.
212 Apache Dr.
Jackson, MS 39212
Phone: (601)373-4010 **Fax:** (601)373-0809
Products: Metals service center: slitting. **SIC:** 5051
(Metals Service Centers & Offices). **Officers:** George
Bolm, General Mgr.; Paula usry, Controller.

■ 20228 ■ Noffsinger Manufacturing Co
PO Box 488
Greeley, CO 80632
Phone: (970)352-0463
Free: (800)525-8922 **Fax:** (970)352-3017
Products: Steel rod draper, belted chain and
galvanized wire sizing belts. **SIC:** 5051 (Metals Service
Centers & Offices). **Officers:** Bob Noffsonger,
President; Ed Walters, Controller.

■ 20229 ■ Noftz Sheet Metal
2737 Penn Ave.
Pittsburgh, PA 15222
Phone: (412)471-1983 **Fax:** (412)471-0512
Products: Sheet metal; Registers; Grills. **SIC:** 5051
(Metals Service Centers & Offices).

■ 20230 ■ Non-Ferrous Processing Corp.
551 Stewart Ave.
Brooklyn, NY 11222
Phone: (718)384-5400
Products: Scrap metals. **SIC:** 5093 (Scrap & Waste
Materials).

■ 20231 ■ Norfolk Iron and Metal Co.
PO Box 1129
Norfolk, NE 68702-1129
Phone: (402)371-1810
Free: (800)228-8100 **Fax:** (402)371-8635
URL: http://www.norfolkiron.com
Products: Carbon steel products. **SIC:** 5051 (Metals
Service Centers & Offices). **Est:** 1908. **Sales:**
$125,000,000 (2000). **Emp:** 325. **Officers:** Richard
Robinson, CEO & President; Steve Ball, CFO; Brad

Zust, VP of Sales; Jay Fleecs, Human Resources Contact; Ron Herian, Human Resources Mgr.

■ **20232** ■ **North American Wire Products**
30000 Solon Rd.
Solon, OH 44139
Phone: (440)248-7600
Free: (800)701-WIRE **Fax:** (440)248-5491
URL: http://www.nawire.com
Products: Steel. **SIC:** 5051 (Metals Service Centers & Offices). **Est:** 1983. **Sales:** $20,000,000 (2000). **Emp:** 80. **Officers:** Bradley Martin, President; Patrick DeMarco, VP of Finance; Jackie Shields, Sales/Marketing Contact, e-mail: jshields@nawire.com; Regina Swinerton, Human Resources Contact, e-mail: rswinerton@nawire.com. **Former Name:** Martin Enterprises Inc.

■ **20233** ■ **North Shore Supply Company Inc.**
PO Box 9940
Houston, TX 77213
Phone: (713)453-3533
Free: (877)453-3533 **Fax:** (713)450-6227
E-mail: sales@nssco.com
URL: http://www.nssco.com
Products: Pipe, steel, fittings, coil processing, material handling equipment, palletrack and shelving. **SIC:** 5051 (Metals Service Centers & Offices). **Est:** 1955. **Sales:** $30,000,000 (2000). **Emp:** 152. **Officers:** William K. Nemzin, Chairman of the Board.

■ **20234** ■ **North Star Recycling Co.**
7650 Edinborough Way
Edina, MN 55435
Phone: (952)367-3500
Free: (800)328-1944 **Fax:** (952)367-3591
URL: http://www.cargillsteel.com
Products: Steel. **SICs:** 5093 (Scrap & Waste Materials); 5051 (Metals Service Centers & Offices). **Sales:** $50,000,000 (2000). **Emp:** 90. **Officers:** Jim Thompson, President; Terry Forrest Jr., CFO.

■ **20235** ■ **North State Metals Inc.**
468 Oakgrove Cloverhill Ch. Rd.
Lawndale, NC 28090
Phone: (704)538-1452
Products: Steel. **SIC:** 5051 (Metals Service Centers & Offices).

■ **20236** ■ **North States Steel Corp.**
811 Eagle Dr.
Bensenville, IL 60106
Phone: (708)595-5500 **Fax:** (708)595-5513
Products: Steel sheets. **SIC:** 5051 (Metals Service Centers & Offices). **Est:** 1971. **Sales:** $5,000,000 (2000). **Emp:** 17. **Officers:** Robert A. Walsh, President; Robert W. Walsh, Vice President.

■ **20237** ■ **Northern Industries Inc.**
4677 W Cal Sag Rd.
Crestwood, IL 60445
Phone: (708)371-1300 **Fax:** (708)371-3308
Products: Steel. **SIC:** 5051 (Metals Service Centers & Offices). **Sales:** $35,000,000 (2000). **Emp:** 65. **Officers:** Frank L. Gentile, CEO & Chairman of the Board.

■ **20238** ■ **Northern Steel Corp.**
364 E Ave.
Oswego, NY 13126
Phone: (315)343-1374 **Fax:** (315)343-2934
Products: Hot and cold rolled steel. **SIC:** 5051 (Metals Service Centers & Offices). **Est:** 1940. **Sales:** $15,000,000 (2000). **Emp:** 21. **Officers:** William Caruso, Vice President; George Caruso, Treasurer & Secty.; G. Caruso, Controller.

■ **20239** ■ **Northstar Steel and Aluminum Inc.**
PO Box 4886
Manchester, NH 03108
Phone: (603)668-3600
Free: (800)258-3515 **Fax:** (603)629-9943
E-mail: cs@nstarsteel.com
Products: Steel and aluminum. **SIC:** 5051 (Metals Service Centers & Offices). **Est:** 1970. **Sales:** $25,000,000 (2000). **Emp:** 65. **Officers:** James McVane, President.

■ **20240** ■ **Norton Metal Products Inc.**
1350 Lawson Rd.
Ft. Worth, TX 76131-2723
Phone: (817)232-0404 **Fax:** (817)577-1634
URL: http://www.nortonmetals.com
Products: Metals. **SIC:** 5051 (Metals Service Centers & Offices). **Est:** 1952. **Sales:** $20,000,000 (2000). **Emp:** 20. **Officers:** Larry Dunlap, President; Tim Colglazier, CFO; Larry Yates, Vice President.

■ **20241** ■ **Nova Steel Processing Inc.**
315 Park Ave.
Tipp City, OH 45371
Phone: (937)667-6255 **Fax:** (937)667-6783
Products: Steel service center: steel processing. **SIC:** 5051 (Metals Service Centers & Offices).

■ **20242** ■ **O'Brien Steel Service**
PO Box 5699
Peoria, IL 61601
Phone: (309)671-5800
Free: (800)322-4450 **Fax:** (309)671-5213
Products: Steel structurals, plates, sheets, and bars. **SIC:** 5051 (Metals Service Centers & Offices). **Est:** 1975. **Sales:** $50,000,000 (2000). **Emp:** 100. **Officers:** J.P. O'Brien, President; G. Brown, Controller; Michael O'Brien, Vice President.

■ **20243** ■ **Ohio Alloy Steels Inc.**
PO Box 1286
Youngstown, OH 44501
Phone: (216)743-5137 **Fax:** (216)743-4425
Products: Steels, including carbon, alloy, and tool. **SIC:** 5051 (Metals Service Centers & Offices). **Est:** 1971. **Sales:** $30,000,000 (2000). **Emp:** 70. **Officers:** John D. Morris, President; William F. Baker, VP of Finance.

■ **20244** ■ **Oilfield Pipe and Supply Inc.**
1730 S 11th St.
St. Louis, MO 63104-3475
Phone: (314)231-0404
Products: Steel pipes. **SIC:** 5051 (Metals Service Centers & Offices). **Est:** 1976. **Sales:** $5,000,000 (2000). **Emp:** 10. **Officers:** Curt Bolliger, President.

■ **20245** ■ **Okaya U.S.A. Inc.**
400 Kelby St., 16th Fl.
Ft. Lee, NJ 07024
Phone: (201)224-6000 **Fax:** (201)224-8144
Products: Steel. **SIC:** 5051 (Metals Service Centers & Offices). **Sales:** $26,000,000 (1993). **Emp:** 35. **Officers:** Minoru Itoh, President; Shinichi Watanabe, Treasurer.

■ **20246** ■ **Olympic Steel Inc.**
5096 Richmond Rd.
Bedford, OH 44146
Phone: (216)292-3800
Free: (800)321-6290 **Fax:** (216)292-0308
E-mail: bgould@olysteel.com
URL: http://www.olysteel.com
Products: Hot-rolled sheet, plate steel, tube, coil, stainless sheet, plate, and coated metal products. **SIC:** 5051 (Metals Service Centers & Offices). **Est:** 1954. **Sales:** $560,100,000 (2000). **Emp:** 952. **Officers:** Michael D. Siegal, CEO, President & Chairman of the Board; R. Louis Schneeberger, CFO; David Wolfort, COO.

■ **20247** ■ **Olympic Steel Inc. Chicago Div.**
1901 Mitchell Blvd.
Schaumburg, IL 60193
Phone: (708)437-8980
Products: Flat-rolled carbon and stainless steel. **SIC:** 5051 (Metals Service Centers & Offices). **Est:** 1954. **Sales:** $39,000,000 (2000). **Emp:** 55. **Officers:** Richard A. Galante Jr. Jr., General Mgr.; Ray Salata, Controller.

■ **20248** ■ **Olympic Steel Inc. Eastern Steel and Metal Div.**
1 Eastern Steel Rd.
Milford, CT 06460
Phone: (203)878-9381
Products: Steel, including coated, slit, sheeted, and hot- and cold-rolled steel. **SIC:** 5051 (Metals Service Centers & Offices). **Est:** 1932. **Sales:** $210,000,000 (2000). **Emp:** 380. **Officers:** Michael Siegal, President;

Louis Schneeberger, VP of Finance; Ronald Stalle, Dir. of Information Systems.

■ **20249** ■ **Olympic Steel Inc. Juster Steel Div.**
625 Xenium Ln. N
Minneapolis, MN 55441
Phone: (612)544-7100 **Fax:** (612)544-0975
Products: Flat-rolled steel products. **SIC:** 5051 (Metals Service Centers & Offices). **Est:** 1954. **Sales:** $65,000,000 (2000). **Emp:** 105. **Officers:** Jerald E. James, General Mgr.; K. Sams, CFO; Howard Harris, Dir. of Marketing.

■ **20250** ■ **O'Neal Metals Co.**
PO Box 71900
Chattanooga, TN 37407
Phone: (423)867-4820
Free: (800)572-7302 **Fax:** (423)867-4147
Products: Metals service center. **SIC:** 5051 (Metals Service Centers & Offices). **Sales:** $30,000,000 (1999). **Emp:** 35. **Officers:** Bill Sylvester, General Manager, Finance.

■ **20251** ■ **O'Neal Steel Inc.**
PO Box 2623
Birmingham, AL 35202
Phone: (205)599-8000 **Fax:** (205)599-8041
Products: Metal. **SIC:** 5051 (Metals Service Centers & Offices). **Sales:** $1,773,000,000 (2000). **Emp:** 2,395. **Officers:** Max DeJonge, CEO & President; Don Freriks, Exec. VP & CFO.

■ **20252** ■ **O'Neal Steel Inc. Evansville**
1323 Burch Dr.
Evansville, IN 47711
Phone: (812)867-8700
Free: (800)547-3014 **Fax:** (812)867-8777
URL: http://www.onealsteel.com
Products: Metal. **SIC:** 5051 (Metals Service Centers & Offices). **Sales:** $15,000,000 (2000). **Emp:** 55. **Officers:** Jeff Robertson, General Mgr.

■ **20253** ■ **O'Neal Steel Inc. (Waterloo, Iowa)**
PO Box 1798
Waterloo, IA 50704
Phone: (319)235-6521
Products: Metal. **SIC:** 5051 (Metals Service Centers & Offices). **Sales:** $17,000,000 (1994). **Emp:** 90. **Officers:** Max DeJonge, President; Glenn Davis, Exec. VP of Finance.

■ **20254** ■ **Orion Group (USA), Ltd.**
4826 Rio Vista Ave.
San Jose, CA 95129
Phone: (408)554-1685 **Fax:** (408)554-1761
Products: Metal. **SIC:** 5051 (Metals Service Centers & Offices). **Officers:** William Johnson, VP of Operations.

■ **20255** ■ **Orleans Materials and Equipment Company Inc.**
PO Box 26307
New Orleans, LA 70186
Phone: (504)288-6361 **Fax:** (504)282-6633
Products: Steel. **SIC:** 5051 (Metals Service Centers & Offices). **Est:** 1931. **Sales:** $22,000,000 (2000). **Emp:** 100. **Officers:** J.J. Housey, Chairman of the Board.

■ **20256** ■ **Ottawa River Steel Co.**
805 Chicago St.
Toledo, OH 43611
Phone: (419)729-1655
Products: Metals. **SIC:** 5051 (Metals Service Centers & Offices).

■ **20257** ■ **Otter Recycling**
570 Otter St.
Bristol, PA 19007
Phone: (215)788-9327
Products: Aluminum; Brass; Copper. **SICs:** 5093 (Scrap & Waste Materials); 5051 (Metals Service Centers & Offices).

■ **20258** ■ **Outokumpu Metals (USA) Inc.**
129 Fairfield Way
Bloomingdale, IL 60108
Phone: (708)307-1300 **Fax:** (708)980-8891
Products: Copper radiator strips. **SIC:** 5051 (Metals Service Centers & Offices). **Est:** 1932. **Sales:**

$7,000,000 (2000). **Emp:** 10. **Officers:** Erkki Karstunen, President.

■ **20259** ■ **Pacesetter Steel Service Inc.**
PO Box 100007
Kennesaw, GA 30144
Phone: (770)919-8000 **Fax:** (770)919-7225
Products: Metals service center: steel slitting, leveling, embossing and industrial prepainting. **SIC:** 5051 (Metals Service Centers & Offices). **Officers:** Steven Leebow, President.

■ **20260** ■ **Pacific Hide and Fur Depot Inc.**
PO Box 1549
Great Falls, MT 59403-1549
Phone: (406)761-8801 **Fax:** (406)453-4269
Products: New steel and recycled items. **SICs:** 5051 (Metals Service Centers & Offices); 5093 (Scrap & Waste Materials). **Sales:** $110,000,000 (2000). **Emp:** 500. **Officers:** Noble E. Vosburg, President; Dave Richards, Controller.

■ **20261** ■ **Pacific Machinery and Tool Steel Co.**
3445 NW Luzon St.
Portland, OR 97210-1694
Phone: (503)226-7656 **Fax:** (503)226-7588
Products: Steel, carbon, alloys, cast iron tubings, and drill rods. **SIC:** 5051 (Metals Service Centers & Offices). **Est:** 1912. **Sales:** $32,000,000 (2000). **Emp:** 43. **Officers:** W.J. Ulrich, President.

■ **20262** ■ **Pacific Metal Co.**
3400 SW Bond Ave.
Portland, OR 97201
Phone: (503)227-0691
Products: Aluminum. **SIC:** 5051 (Metals Service Centers & Offices). **Est:** 1876. **Sales:** $58,000,000 (2000). **Emp:** 140. **Officers:** D.E. Peck, CEO.

■ **20263** ■ **Pacific Steel and Recycling**
Short & Gaylord St.
Butte, MT 59701
Phone: (406)782-0402
Products: Steel. **SIC:** 5051 (Metals Service Centers & Offices).

■ **20264** ■ **Pako Steel Inc.**
2424 State Rd.
Bensalem, PA 19020
Phone: (215)639-7256
Products: Steel. **SIC:** 5051 (Metals Service Centers & Offices).

■ **20265** ■ **Parker Steel Co.**
4239 Monroe St.
Toledo, OH 43606
Phone: (419)473-2481
Free: (800)333-4140 **Fax:** (419)471-2655
E-mail: sales@metricmetal.com
URL: http://www.metricmetal.com
Products: Metric size metals in various shapes, including steel, alloy and stainless steel, aluminum, brass, and copper. **SIC:** 5051 (Metals Service Centers & Offices). **Est:** 1955. **Sales:** $14,000,000 (2000). **Emp:** 20. **Officers:** L. Goldner, President; Paul Goldner, VP of Finance; Mark Goldner, VP of Purchasing. **Alternate Name:** Metric Metal.

■ **20266** ■ **Pasminco Inc.**
70 St. George Ave.
Stamford, CT 06905
Phone: (203)325-4232 **Fax:** (203)325-4816
Products: Zinc sheets, bars. **SIC:** 5051 (Metals Service Centers & Offices). **Est:** 1989. **Sales:** $31,000,000 (2000). **Emp:** 2. **Officers:** Win Degraff, President; Fred LaValle, Treasurer.

■ **20267** ■ **PDM Steel Service Centers Div.**
PO Box 310
Stockton, CA 95201-0310
Phone: (209)943-0513 **Fax:** (209)943-1606
Products: Carbon steel products. **SIC:** 5051 (Metals Service Centers & Offices). **Sales:** $170,000,000 (2000). **Emp:** 470. **Officers:** E. Halecky, President; W.J. Nixon, VP of Finance.

■ **20268** ■ **Pechiney Corp.**
475 Steamboat Rd.
Greenwich, CT 06830
Phone: (203)661-4600 **Fax:** (203)869-5161
Products: Aluminum; Aluminum cans. **SIC:** 5051 (Metals Service Centers & Offices). **Sales:** $2,780,000,000 (2000). **Emp:** 28,000. **Officers:** Michel Simonnard, CEO; Jean-Francois Faivre, CFO; Francois Dalla Bona, VP of Marketing & Sales; Romulo Salazar, Dir of Human Resources.

■ **20269** ■ **Pechiney World Trade (USA) Inc.**
475 Steamboat Rd.
Greenwich, CT 06830
Phone: (203)622-8300 **Fax:** (203)622-8669
Products: Metals. **SIC:** 5051 (Metals Service Centers & Offices). **Est:** 1921. **Sales:** $1,900,000 (1999). **Emp:** 130. **Officers:** Bruno Poux-Guillaume, CEO; Thomas Sliker, Exec. VP; Jean Pierre Lager, VP of Aluminum; Gary Tamboryn, VP of Copper; Tim Palmer, VP of Aluminum Semis and Ferro Alloys; Dennis Delaney, VP of Chemicals; Jeff Beck, Ores and Concentrates.

■ **20270** ■ **Penn Stainless Products Inc.**
PO Box 9001
Quakertown, PA 18951-9001
Phone: (215)536-3053
Free: (800)222-6144 **Fax:** (215)536-3255
E-mail: info@pennstainless.com
URL: http://www.pennstainless.com
Products: Stainless steel, including angles, bars, fittings, flanges, pipes, plates, sheets, and tubing. **SIC:** 5051 (Metals Service Centers & Offices). **Est:** 1979. **Sales:** $36,000,000 (2000). **Emp:** 88. **Officers:** James W. Seward, President, e-mail: jseward@pennstainless.com; Thomas M. Paulovitz, Vice President, e-mail: tpaulovitz@pennstainless.com; Leonard G. Grabosky, Controller & Credit Mgr., e-mail: lengrabosky@pennstainless.com; Philip J. O'Donnell, Outside Sales Mgr., e-mail: podonnell@pennstainless.com; Richard C. Finnerty, Inside Sales Mgr., e-mail: rfinnerty@pennstainless.com; Kirk D. Fell, Material Mgr., e-mail: kfell@pennstainless.com; Robert A. Jellen, Plant Mgr., e-mail: bjellen@pennstainless.com; James B. Schuler, Quality Assurance, e-mail: jschuler@pennstainless.com.

■ **20271** ■ **Pennsylvania Steel Co.**
1717 Woodhaven Dr.
Bensalem, PA 19020
Phone: (215)633-9600
Products: Steel. **SIC:** 5051 (Metals Service Centers & Offices).

■ **20272** ■ **Perlow Steel Corp.**
2900 S 25th Ave.
Broadview, IL 60153
Phone: (708)865-1200 **Fax:** (708)865-1217
Products: Carbon and alloy bars. **SIC:** 5051 (Metals Service Centers & Offices). **Est:** 1955. **Sales:** $18,000,000 (2000). **Emp:** 30. **Officers:** L. Perlow, CEO & President; S. Perlow, CFO.

■ **20273** ■ **Petersen Aluminum Corp.**
1005 Tonne Rd.
Elk Grove Village, IL 60007-4978
Phone: (847)228-7150 **Fax:** (847)956-7968
Products: Aluminum and steel. **SIC:** 5051 (Metals Service Centers & Offices). **Sales:** $47,000,000 (2000). **Emp:** 150. **Officers:** Mike Petersen, CEO & President.

■ **20274** ■ **Petroleum Pipe and Supply Inc.**
PO Box 545
Carnegie, PA 15106
Phone: (412)279-7710 **Fax:** (412)279-9029
Products: Pipes and pipe fittings. **SIC:** 5051 (Metals Service Centers & Offices). **Est:** 1945. **Sales:** $5,000,000 (2000). **Emp:** 20. **Officers:** Paul Maisch, President.

■ **20275** ■ **Phillip Metals Inc.**
PO Box 1182
Nashville, TN 37202
Phone: (615)271-3300
Free: (800)624-2216 **Fax:** (615)254-6416
Products: Scrap processers. **SIC:** 5093 (Scrap & Waste Materials). **Sales:** $43,000,000 (2000). **Emp:** 200. **Officers:** Phillip Fracassi, President.

■ **20276** ■ **Pickands Mather, Ltd.**
1422 Euclid Ave., Ste. 1630
Cleveland, OH 44115
Phone: (216)694-5300
Products: Ferro alloys, including pig iron and filter cores. **SIC:** 5051 (Metals Service Centers & Offices). **Est:** 1883. **Sales:** $150,000,000 (2000). **Emp:** 42. **Officers:** Sam R. Zickel, President; John E. Tumas, Controller; Edward D. Gesdorf, Vice President; Yvette Curlee, Controller. **Former Name:** Pickands Mathers Sales, Inc.

■ **20277** ■ **Pielet Brothers Scrap, Iron and Metal L.P.**
135 S L Salle St.
Chicago, IL 60603-4159
Phone: (708)594-7171
Products: Ferrous metal scrap and waste metals. **SIC:** 5093 (Scrap & Waste Materials). **Sales:** $41,000,000 (1992). **Emp:** 250. **Officers:** Jim Pielet, President; John Porter, Controller.

■ **20278** ■ **Pierce Aluminum Company Inc.**
PO Box 100
Canton, MA 02021
Phone: (617)828-9005
Products: Aluminum products, including pipes and foil. **SIC:** 5051 (Metals Service Centers & Offices). **Sales:** $28,300,000 (2000). **Emp:** 79. **Officers:** R.W. Pierce Jr., President.

■ **20279** ■ **Pimalco Inc.**
6833 W Willis Rd. Ste. 5050
Chandler, AZ 85226
Phone: (520)796-1098 **Fax:** (520)796-0369
Products: Aerospace aluminum alloys—forged ingots and rods, extruded shapes, extruded and drawn tubing. **SIC:** 5051 (Metals Service Centers & Offices). **Sales:** $126,000,000 (2000). **Emp:** 750. **Officers:** Niles Evans, President; Greg Nelson, VP of Finance.

■ **20280** ■ **Pioneer Aluminum Inc.**
PO Box 23947
Los Angeles, CA 90023
Phone: (213)268-7211
Products: Aluminum for aerospace industry. **SIC:** 5051 (Metals Service Centers & Offices). **Est:** 1956. **Sales:** $52,000,000 (2000). **Emp:** 135. **Officers:** John P. Cassel, President & Chairman of the Board; S. Harris, VP of Finance; Robert M. Lamdry, VP of Marketing & Sales; Ray Ball, VP Marketing & Development.

■ **20281** ■ **Pioneer Steel Corp.**
7447 Intervale St.
Detroit, MI 48238
Phone: (313)933-9400 **Fax:** (313)933-1621
Products: Steel service center: flame cutting and processing. **SIC:** 5051 (Metals Service Centers & Offices). **Officers:** Donald Sazama, President.

■ **20282** ■ **Pioneer Steel and Tube Distributors**
1660 Lincoln St., Ste. 2300
Denver, CO 80264-2301
Phone: (303)289-3201
Free: (800)525-1266 **Fax:** (303)289-6381
E-mail: Pioneerpipe.com
Products: Steel pipes. **SIC:** 5051 (Metals Service Centers & Offices). **Est:** 1974. **Sales:** $60,000,000 (1999). **Emp:** 35. **Officers:** Mike Harris, Sr. VP & COO.

■ **20283** ■ **Pipe Distributors Inc.**
PO Box 23237
Houston, TX 77228
Phone: (713)635-4200 **Fax:** (713)635-8465
E-mail: housales@pipedistributorsinccom
Products: Steel pipe. **SIC:** 5051 (Metals Service Centers & Offices). **Est:** 1960. **Emp:** 59. **Officers:** Stanley T. Rawley, President; T. Paul Burchfield, Sr. VP; Chuck Zagst, Sr. VP.

■ **20284** ■ **Pitt-Des Moines Inc.**
3400 Grand Ave.
Pittsburgh, PA 15225
Phone: (412)331-3000 **Fax:** (412)331-7403
Products: Steel fabrications, including water tanks and bridges. **SIC:** 5051 (Metals Service Centers & Offices). **Est:** 1916. **Sales:** $474,500,000 (2000). **Emp:** 2,006.

Officers: William W, McKee, CEO & President; R.A. Byers, VP of Finance & Treasurer.

■ 20285 ■ Plant and Flanged Equipment
4000 85th Ave. N
Minneapolis, MN 55443
Phone: (612)424-8400 **Fax:** (612)424-1141
Products: Plumbing Materials and fixtures. **SIC:** 5051 (Metals Service Centers & Offices). **Sales:** $3,000,000 (2000). **Emp:** 10.

■ 20286 ■ PMX Industries Inc.
5300 Willow Creek Dr.
Cedar Rapids, IA 52404-4303
Phone: (319)368-7700 **Fax:** (319)368-7701
Products: Brass and copper. **SIC:** 5051 (Metals Service Centers & Offices). **Est:** 1989. **Sales:** $150,000,000 (2000). **Emp:** 600. **Officers:** Mi Ahn, President.

■ 20287 ■ Pohang Steel America Corp.
2530 Arnold, No. 170
Martinez, CA 94553
Phone: (510)228-9720
Products: Steel. **SIC:** 5051 (Metals Service Centers & Offices).

■ 20288 ■ Joseph G. Pollard Company Inc.
200 Atlantic Ave.
New Hyde Park, NY 11040
Phone: (516)746-0842
Free: (800)437-1146 **Fax:** (516)746-0852
E-mail: Info@pollardwater.com
URL: http://www.pollardwater.com
Products: Pipeline equipment; Leak detection; Line tracing equipment; Safety, lab supplies, wastewater tools, waterworks tool and supplies. **SIC:** 5051 (Metals Service Centers & Offices). **Est:** 1837. **Sales:** $8,000,000 (2000). **Emp:** 29. **Officers:** Brian Dougan, President; W. Lawrence Smith, VP of Finance; Mike Baker, Customer Service Mgr.

■ 20289 ■ Port Everglades Steel Corp.
PO Box 5768
Ft. Lauderdale, FL 33310
Phone: (954)942-9400 **Fax:** (954)942-6123
Products: Steel coils and bars. **SIC:** 5051 (Metals Service Centers & Offices). **Est:** 1953. **Sales:** $50,000,000 (2000). **Emp:** 15. **Officers:** Ira Vernon, President; Del Benzenhafer, VP of Finance; Mark Grygo, Accounting Supervisor.

■ 20290 ■ Potomac Steel and Supply Inc.
7801 Loisdale Rd.
Springfield, VA 22150
Phone: (703)550-7300
Products: Steel products. **SIC:** 5051 (Metals Service Centers & Offices). **Est:** 1946. **Sales:** $13,000,000 (2000). **Emp:** 22. **Officers:** James E. Pohlmann, President; John A. Pohlmann, Treasurer & Secty.

■ 20291 ■ Precision Aluminum and Sawing Service Inc.
PO Box 2278
Huntington Park, CA 90255
Phone: (213)583-0021 **Fax:** (213)587-1482
Products: Aluminum sheets. **SIC:** 5051 (Metals Service Centers & Offices). **Est:** 1969. **Sales:** $2,700,000 (2000). **Emp:** 22. **Officers:** James R. Fults, President; Randy Martin, General Mgr.

■ 20292 ■ Precision Metals Inc.
5265 N 124th St.
Milwaukee, WI 53225
Phone: (414)781-3240 **Fax:** (414)781-3643
Products: Custom hollow metals. **SIC:** 5051 (Metals Service Centers & Offices). **Est:** 1956. **Sales:** $5,500,000 (2000). **Emp:** 40. **Officers:** Theodore M. Koenigs, President & Treasurer.

■ 20293 ■ Precision Steel Warehouse Inc.
3500 N Wolf Rd.
Franklin Park, IL 60131
Phone: (847)455-7000 **Fax:** (847)455-1341
E-mail: Precisionsteel@psteel.com
URL: http://www.Precisionsteel.com
Products: Custom cut steel. **SIC:** 5051 (Metals Service Centers & Offices). **Est:** 1940. **Sales:** $60,000,000 (1999). **Emp:** 200. **Officers:** Terry A. Piper, CEO &

President; Raymond Lucchetti, VP of Finance; Dennis Spitz, Sales Mgr.

■ 20294 ■ Primary Industries (USA) Inc.
EAB Plz.
Uniondale, NY 11556
Phone: (516)794-1122 **Fax:** (516)794-8989
Products: Steel products. **SIC:** 5051 (Metals Service Centers & Offices). **Est:** 1915. **Sales:** $8,000,000 (2000). **Emp:** 12. **Officers:** Richard Siniscalchi, President; Murray Relis, Treasurer.

■ 20295 ■ Primary Steel Inc.
PO Box 1716
Middletown, CT 06457
Phone: (860)343-5111 **Fax:** (860)343-5101
Products: Metal service center. **SIC:** 5051 (Metals Service Centers & Offices). **Sales:** $250,000,000 (1999). **Emp:** 315. **Officers:** Charles Pompea, CEO; Harcourt Davis, CFO.

■ 20296 ■ Pro-Chem Corp.
9536 Ann St.
Santa Fe Springs, CA 90670
Phone: (562)946-9210 **Fax:** (562)944-9210
Products: Metal finishing processes and equipment. **SIC:** 5051 (Metals Service Centers & Offices). **Est:** 1972. **Sales:** $1,000,000 (2000). **Emp:** 5. **Officers:** Pat Patterson, President; Sylvia R. Tommer, Treasurer & Secty.

■ 20297 ■ ProCoil Corp.
5260 S Haggerty Rd.
Canton, MI 48188
Phone: (734)397-3700 **Fax:** (734)397-0029
Products: Steel service center: slitting, shearing and blanking. **SIC:** 5051 (Metals Service Centers & Offices).

■ 20298 ■ Production Carbide and Steel
PO Box 987
Warren, MI 48090
Phone: (313)755-2240 **Fax:** (313)756-3434
Products: High-speed tool steel. **SIC:** 5051 (Metals Service Centers & Offices). **Est:** 1952. **Sales:** $8,000,000 (2000). **Emp:** 14. **Officers:** D.D. Kahn, Chairman of the Board; Michael Brenner, Controller; Denny Taylor, General Mgr.; William Reno, Dir. of Data Processing; Pamela Mack, Dir of Human Resources.

■ 20299 ■ Production Supply Co.
4342 Michoud Blvd.
New Orleans, LA 70129
Phone: (504)254-0505
Products: Marine aluminum. **SIC:** 5051 (Metals Service Centers & Offices). **Est:** 1966. **Sales:** $12,000,000 (2000). **Emp:** 38. **Officers:** Newton Reynolds, President; Carolyn Lemone, Office Mgr.; Guy Bumpis, Sales Mgr.

■ 20300 ■ Production Supply Co.
4342 Michoud Blvd.
New Orleans, LA 70129
Phone: (504)254-0505 **Fax:** (504)254-9043
Products: Metals. **SIC:** 5051 (Metals Service Centers & Offices). **Sales:** $36,000,000 (2000). **Emp:** 33. **Officers:** Newton Reynolds, President; Stacey Robertson, Office Manager, Finance.

■ 20301 ■ Prosteel Service Centers Inc.
PO Box 5067
Delanco, NJ 08075
Phone: (609)461-8300
Products: Hot and cold-rolled galvanized steel. **SIC:** 5051 (Metals Service Centers & Offices). **Sales:** $20,000,000 (2000). **Emp:** 46. **Officers:** William Phillips, Vice President; William Carolan, Controller; Catherine McDade, Dir. of Admin.

■ 20302 ■ Puget Sound Pipe and Supply Inc.
7816 S 202nd St.
Kent, WA 98032
Phone: (253)796-9350 **Fax:** (253)796-9355
Products: Metal service center—pipes, valves and fittings. **SIC:** 5051 (Metals Service Centers & Offices). **Officers:** Gary Stratiner, President.

■ 20303 ■ Pusan Pipe America Inc.
9615 Norwalk Blvd., No. B
Santa Fe Springs, CA 90670-2931
Phone: (310)692-0600
Products: Steel pipes. **SIC:** 5051 (Metals Service Centers & Offices). **Est:** 1978. **Sales:** $35,000,000 (2000). **Emp:** 10. **Officers:** B.J. Lee, CEO; H. Kim, CFO.

■ 20304 ■ Queensboro Steel Corp.
PO Box 1769
Wilmington, NC 28402
Phone: (919)763-6237 **Fax:** (919)763-2320
Products: Cold finished steel bars and bar shapes. **SIC:** 5051 (Metals Service Centers & Offices). **Est:** 1952. **Sales:** $37,000,000 (2000). **Emp:** 225. **Officers:** S.L. Alper, Chairman of the Board; Mark Alper, President; Jeffrey Bruner, Dir. of Marketing; Michael Durham, Dir. of Systems.

■ 20305 ■ Quikservice Steel Co.
515 Madison St.
Muskogee, OK 74403
Phone: (918)687-5307
Products: Steel. **SIC:** 5051 (Metals Service Centers & Offices).

■ 20306 ■ R and S Steel Co.
4600 N Wabash, Ste. A
Denver, CO 80216
Phone: (303)321-9660
Products: Structural steel. **SIC:** 5051 (Metals Service Centers & Offices).

■ 20307 ■ Radnor Alloys Inc.
PO Box 269
Wayne, PA 19087
Phone: (215)687-3770
Products: Chrome and stainless steel, including pipes, fittings, and valves. **SIC:** 5051 (Metals Service Centers & Offices). **Sales:** $70,000,000 (2000). **Emp:** 95. **Officers:** John Dockray, President.

■ 20308 ■ Rafferty-Brown Steel Co.
PO Box 18927
Greensboro, NC 27419
Phone: (336)855-6300 **Fax:** (336)299-9882
Products: Steel service center. **SIC:** 5051 (Metals Service Centers & Offices). **Sales:** $65,000,000 (2000). **Emp:** 102. **Officers:** Robert Wood, President.

■ 20309 ■ Rebco West/Vistawall
9272 Hyssop Dr.
Rancho Cucamonga, CA 91730-6108
Phone: (909)481-6144
Products: Metals; metal service center. **SIC:** 5051 (Metals Service Centers & Offices).

■ 20310 ■ Red Bud Industries Inc.
200 B and E Industrial Dr.
Red Bud, IL 62278
Phone: (618)282-3801 **Fax:** (618)282-6718
Products: Metal processing, coil feeding, slitting and shearing machinery. **SIC:** 5051 (Metals Service Centers & Offices).

■ 20311 ■ Regal Steel Supply Inc.
PO Box 1050
Stockton, CA 95201
Phone: (209)943-3223 **Fax:** (209)943-3229
Products: Steel beams. **SICs:** 5051 (Metals Service Centers & Offices); 5039 (Construction Materials Nec). **Est:** 1990. **Sales:** $20,000,000 (2000). **Emp:** 24. **Officers:** Dennis Pfeiffer, Vice President.

■ 20312 ■ Reliance Sheet and Strip Co.
2301 W 10th St.
Antioch, CA 94509
Phone: (510)706-1061
Products: Steel. **SIC:** 5051 (Metals Service Centers & Offices). **Est:** 1949. **Sales:** $13,000,000 (2000). **Emp:** 18. **Officers:** Roger Abendroth, CEO; Peter Rooney, Treasurer & Secty.

■ 20313 ■ Reliance Steel and Aluminum Co.
PO Box 60482
Los Angeles, CA 90060
Phone: (213)582-2272 **Fax:** (213)582-2801
Products: Carbon steel products. **SIC:** 5051 (Metals

Service Centers & Offices). **Est:** 1939. **Sales:** $653,900,000 (2000). **Emp:** 1,400. **Officers:** Joe D. Crider, CEO & Chairman of the Board; Steven S. Weis, CFO; Greg Mollins, VP of Marketing; Yvette Schiotis, Dir of Human Resources.

■ **20314** ■ **Reliance Steel Co.**
2537 E 27th St.
Los Angeles, CA 90058
Phone: (323)583-6111 **Fax:** (323)581-1254
Products: Carbon steel sheet, plate, bars, structurals, pipe and tubing. **SIC:** 5051 (Metals Service Centers & Offices). **Est:** 1980.

■ **20315** ■ **Renco Corp.**
30 Rockefeller Plz.
New York, NY 10112
Phone: (212)541-6000 **Fax:** (212)541-6197
Products: Steel fabrication; Military vehicles; Office furniture. **SIC:** 5051 (Metals Service Centers & Offices). **Sales:** $1,170,000,000 (2000). **Emp:** 7,000. **Officers:** Ira Rennert, CEO & Chairman of the Board; Roger Fay, VP of Finance.

■ **20316** ■ **Reserve Iron and Metal L.P.**
4431 W 130th St.
Cleveland, OH 44135
Phone: (216)671-3000 **Fax:** (216)671-8887
Products: Iron; Metal. **SICs:** 5051 (Metals Service Centers & Offices); 5093 (Scrap & Waste Materials). **Sales:** $120,000,000 (2000). **Emp:** 150.

■ **20317** ■ **Reynolds Aluminum Supply**
3900 Pinson Valley Pkwy.
Birmingham, AL 35217
Phone: (205)853-7100
Products: Steel and aluminum. **SIC:** 5051 (Metals Service Centers & Offices).

■ **20318** ■ **Reynolds Aluminum Supply Co.**
6603 W Broad St.
Richmond, VA 23230
Phone: (804)281-2000 **Fax:** (804)281-3627
Products: Aluminum, stainless steel and nickel products including sheet, plate bars and pipe. **SIC:** 5051 (Metals Service Centers & Offices). **Sales:** $750,000,000 (2000). **Emp:** 875. **Officers:** Donald T. Cowles, President; Everett P. Chesley, VP of Admin.

■ **20319** ■ **Rhoda Brothers-Steel & Welding**
131 S Union St.
Lima, OH 45801
Phone: (419)228-7121
Products: Steel. **SIC:** 5051 (Metals Service Centers & Offices).

■ **20320** ■ **Richards and Conover Steel Co.**
6333 St. John Ave.
Kansas City, MO 64123
Phone: (816)483-9100 **Fax:** (816)483-6983
Products: Flat-rolled steel products. **SIC:** 5051 (Metals Service Centers & Offices). **Est:** 1857. **Sales:** $25,000,000 (2000). **Emp:** 120. **Officers:** S.L. Sawyer, President & CFO; William Smith, Exec. VP; James Dillon, Data Processing Mgr.

■ **20321** ■ **Richardson Trident Co**
405 N Plano Rd.
Richardson, TX 75081
Phone: (972)231-5176 **Fax:** (972)889-1885
Products: Metals service center. **SIC:** 5051 (Metals Service Centers & Offices). **Officers:** Tom Bentley, President.

■ **20322** ■ **Rickard Metals Inc.**
1707 S Grove Ave.
Ontario, CA 91761
Phone: (909)947-4922 **Fax:** (909)947-4909
Products: Alloys, including titanium, stainless steel, and aluminum. **SIC:** 5051 (Metals Service Centers & Offices). **Est:** 1985. **Sales:** $4,000,000 (2000). **Emp:** 7. **Officers:** Peggy Rickard, President & CFO.

■ **20323** ■ **Robert-James Sales Inc.**
PO Box 7999
Buffalo, NY 14225-7999
Phone: (716)874-6300
Products: Steel pipes, valves, and fittings. **SICs:** 5051 (Metals Service Centers & Offices); 5085 (Industrial

Supplies). **Est:** 1972. **Sales:** $37,000,000 (2000). **Emp:** 155. **Officers:** James Bokor, President; Robert Glidden Jr., Partner; Bill Barto, Exec. VP; Jon Duffit, Data Processing Mgr.

■ **20324** ■ **J.H. Roberts Industries Inc.**
3158 Des Plaines Ave.
Des Plaines, IL 60018
Phone: (708)699-0080 **Fax:** (708)699-0082
Products: Metals. **SIC:** 5051 (Metals Service Centers & Offices). **Sales:** $200,000,000 (2000). **Emp:** 700. **Officers:** John H. Roberts, Chairman of the Board; Lawrence A. Collins, Treasurer.

■ **20325** ■ **Robinson Steel Company Inc.**
4303 Kennedy Ave.
East Chicago, IN 46312
Phone: (219)398-4600
Products: Rolled and flattened steel. **SIC:** 5051 (Metals Service Centers & Offices). **Est:** 1986. **Sales:** $115,000,000 (2000). **Emp:** 100. **Officers:** Paul Labriola, President; Michael Gandio, VP of Finance.

■ **20326** ■ **Roll and Hold Warehousing and Distribution**
1745 165th St.
Hammond, IN 46320
Phone: (219)853-1125
Products: Rods; Metal plates; Cold finished steel bars and bar shapes. **SIC:** 5051 (Metals Service Centers & Offices).

■ **20327** ■ **Rolled Steel Co.**
2525 Arthur Ave.
Elk Grove Village, IL 60007
Phone: (847)981-8370 **Fax:** (847)981-8383
Products: Steel. **SIC:** 5051 (Metals Service Centers & Offices). **Est:** 1946. **Sales:** $6,000,000 (2000). **Emp:** 10. **Officers:** Jack Place, General Mgr.

■ **20328** ■ **Rolled Steel Products Corp.**
2187 S Garfield Ave.
Los Angeles, CA 90040
Phone: (213)723-8836
Free: (800)400-7833 **Fax:** (213)888-9866
Products: Metals. **SIC:** 5051 (Metals Service Centers & Offices). **Sales:** $28,100,000 (2000). **Emp:** 67. **Officers:** R. Alperson, President; Kyoo Lee, Controller.

■ **20329** ■ **Ron's Steel Sales**
846 South St.
Biddeford, ME 04005
Phone: (207)499-2736
Products: Steel products. **SIC:** 5051 (Metals Service Centers & Offices).

■ **20330** ■ **Rose Industries Inc. (Houston, Texas)**
PO Box 7887
Houston, TX 77270
Phone: (713)880-7000 **Fax:** (713)880-7733
Products: Scrap metal. **SIC:** 5093 (Scrap & Waste Materials). **Sales:** $22,000,000 (2000). **Emp:** 60. **Officers:** Jules H. Rose, President; Irving B. Rose, CEO.

■ **20331** ■ **Rose Metal Products Inc.**
PO Box 3238
Springfield, MO 65808
Phone: (417)865-1676 **Fax:** (417)865-7673
E-mail: rmp@dialus.com
Products: Sheet metal products. **SICs:** 5051 (Metals Service Centers & Offices); 5199 (Nondurable Goods Nec). **Est:** 1960. **Sales:** $5,000,000 (1999). **Emp:** 50. **Officers:** Ron Buchanan, President; Richard Splitter, Controller; Jim Skinner, Dir. of Marketing & Sales.

■ **20332** ■ **Royal Metals Company Inc.**
120 Mokauea
Honolulu, HI 96819
Phone: (808)845-3222 **Fax:** (808)841-1150
Products: Metal. **SIC:** 5051 (Metals Service Centers & Offices).

■ **20333** ■ **Roy's Welding & Wrought Iron**
28 Mcdonald Rd.
Alamogordo, NM 88310
Phone: (505)434-1696
Products: Wrought iron. **SIC:** 5051 (Metals Service Centers & Offices).

■ **20334** ■ **J. Rubin and Co.**
305 Peoples Ave.
Rockford, IL 61104
Phone: (815)964-9471
Products: Steel. **SIC:** 5051 (Metals Service Centers & Offices). **Sales:** $186,000,000 (2000). **Emp:** 250. **Officers:** Phillip E. Rubin, President; Mark Klein, CFO.

■ **20335** ■ **Rubin, Jack and Sons Inc.**
PO Box 3005
Compton, CA 90223
Phone: (310)635-5407 **Fax:** (310)632-1177
Products: Wire rope and slings and rigging supplies. **SIC:** 5051 (Metals Service Centers & Offices). **Officers:** Phil Mandel, CFO.

■ **20336** ■ **Rubin Steel Co.**
1430 Fruitville Pke.
Lancaster, PA 17601
Phone: (717)397-3613 **Fax:** (717)299-3922
Products: Steel products. **SIC:** 5051 (Metals Service Centers & Offices). **Est:** 1914. **Officers:** Stephen E. Rubin.

■ **20337** ■ **RuMar Manufacturing Corp.**
PO Box 193
Mayville, WI 53050
Phone: (920)387-2104 **Fax:** (920)387-2367
E-mail: rumar2@internetwis.com
URL: http://www.rumar.com
Products: Sheet metal. **SIC:** 5051 (Metals Service Centers & Offices). **Est:** 1972. **Sales:** $17,000,000 (2000). **Emp:** 150. **Officers:** Ross Galbreath, President; F. Laufenberg, VP of Finance; Nick Hechimovich, Dir. of Marketing; Dennis Gassner, Vice President.

■ **20338** ■ **J D Rush Company Inc.**
5900 E Lerdo Hwy.
Shafter, CA 93263
Phone: (661)392-1900 **Fax:** (661)399-2728
Products: Tubular goods; Metals and pipe. **SIC:** 5051 (Metals Service Centers & Offices). **Est:** 1933. **Officers:** Earl Lindley, CFO.

■ **20339** ■ **Russel Metals-Bahcall Group**
975 N Meade St.
PO Box 1054
Appleton, WI 54912-1054
Phone: (920)734-9271
Free: (800)875-7624 **Fax:** (920)730-5858
Products: Carbon steel service center; Steel pipe, tube, bars, and shapes. **SIC:** 5051 (Metals Service Centers & Offices). **Est:** 1900. **Sales:** $75,000,000 (2000). **Emp:** 250. **Officers:** Tom Plesha, VP & COO; Michael Silverman, Controller; Jim Wright, Sales Mgr.

■ **20340** ■ **Ryan Equipment Co., Inc.**
749 Creel Dr.
Wood Dale, IL 60191
Phone: (708)595-5711 **Fax:** (708)595-5794
Products: Metal products. **SIC:** 5051 (Metals Service Centers & Offices).

■ **20341** ■ **Ryerson Coil Processing Co.**
5101 Boone Ave., N
Minneapolis, MN 55428
Phone: (612)535-1431 **Fax:** (612)535-9840
Products: Metal service center specializing in carbon steel sheet and coil. **SIC:** 5051 (Metals Service Centers & Offices). **Sales:** $100,000,000 (2000). **Emp:** 350. **Officers:** Tim LaPerre, President; John Zimmerman, Controller.

■ **20342** ■ **Joseph T. Ryerson and Son Inc.**
PO Box 8000
Chicago, IL 60680
Phone: (773)762-2121 **Fax:** (773)861-2518
Products: Steel. **SIC:** 5051 (Metals Service Centers & Offices). **Est:** 1842. **Sales:** $1,666,000,000 (2000). **Emp:** 5,000. **Officers:** Carl G. Lusted, President; C. E.

Erickson, Controller; John Suppes, Dir. of Marketing; Richard Michell, Dir of Personnel.

■ 20343 ■ **Ryerson-Thypin - Div. of Ryerson Tull**
45 Saratoga Blvd.
Ayer, MA 01432-5216
Phone: (978)784-2800
Free: (800)842-1261   **Fax:** (978)784-2800
URL: http://www.ryersontull.com
Products: Steel. **SIC:** 5051 (Metals Service Centers & Offices). **Sales:** $50,000,000 (2000). **Officers:** Tim Farrell, General Mgr.; Tom Lapointe, Operations Mgr.; Terry Bartel, Sales Mgr. **Former Name:** Thypin Steel Company of New England Inc.

■ 20344 ■ **Ryerson Tull Inc.**
2621 West 15th Pl.
Chicago, IL 60608
Phone: (773)762-2121
Products: Metals. **SIC:** 5051 (Metals Service Centers & Offices). **Sales:** $2,789,400,000 (2000). **Emp:** 5,400. **Officers:** Neil S. Novich, CEO & President; Jay M. Gratz, VP & CFO.

■ 20345 ■ **Ryerson Tull Inc.**
PO Box 34275
Seattle, WA 98124
Phone: (206)242-3400   **Fax:** (206)242-1270
Products: Metals service center: aluminum, brass, stainless steel and carbon alloy. **SIC:** 5051 (Metals Service Centers & Offices).

■ 20346 ■ **S I Metals**
N5820 Johnson Rd.
Portage, WI 53901
Phone: (608)742-9039
Products: Metal. **SIC:** 5051 (Metals Service Centers & Offices).

■ 20347 ■ **S and I Steel Supply Div.**
PO Box 341
Memphis, TN 38101
Phone: (901)948-0395   **Fax:** (901)948-5870
URL: http://www.primarysteel.com
Products: Steel plate; Floor plate; Pipe. **SIC:** 5051 (Metals Service Centers & Offices). **Est:** 1964. **Emp:** 12. **Officers:** John White, President & General Mgr. **Former Name:** Primary Steel, Inc.

■ 20348 ■ **S and R Metals Inc.**
2070 Randolph St.
Huntington Park, CA 90255
Phone: (213)583-8904   **Fax:** (213)583-0906
Products: Hot-rolled steel. **SIC:** 5051 (Metals Service Centers & Offices). **Est:** 1955. **Sales:** $25,000,000 (2000). **Emp:** 55. **Officers:** Steve Miller, President.

■ 20349 ■ **Sabel Steel Service**
PO Drawer 4747
Montgomery, AL 36103
Phone: (205)265-6771
Products: Steel. **SICs:** 5051 (Metals Service Centers & Offices); 5093 (Scrap & Waste Materials). **Sales:** $40,000,000 (1994). **Emp:** 220. **Officers:** Keith Sabel, President; P.F. Brown, Controller.

■ 20350 ■ **Sampson Steel Corp.**
PO Box 2392
Beaumont, TX 77704
Phone: (409)838-1611
Free: (800)627-1999   **Fax:** (409)838-0448
Products: HR carbon steel bars; Structurals; Plates; Sheets; CF bars; Pipe; Structural tubing; Expanded metal; Bar grating. **SIC:** 5051 (Metals Service Centers & Offices). **Est:** 1916. **Sales:** $13,000,000 (2000). **Emp:** 65. **Officers:** Harold M. Eisen, President, e-mail: hme@sampsonsteeelcorp.com; Scott McClusky, Controller; Stephen A. Eisen, Vice President, e-mail: seisen@sampsonsteelcorp.com; Jay L. Eisen, Vice President, e-mail: jleisen@sampsonsteelcorp.com. **Former Name:** Eisen Industries Inc.

■ 20351 ■ **Samuel Specialty Metals Inc.**
4 Essex Ave.
Bernardsville, NJ 07924-2265
Phone: (201)884-2222   **Fax:** (201)992-4784
Products: Metal bars; Stainless steel. **SIC:** 5051 (Metals Service Centers & Offices). **Est:** 1983. **Sales:**

$220,000,000 (2000). **Emp:** 300. **Officers:** Wayne Bassett, President; Anna Christakos, Controller.

■ 20352 ■ **Samuels Recycling Co. Green Bay Div.**
PO Box 10917
Green Bay, WI 54307
Phone: (920)494-3451   **Fax:** (920)494-1548
Products: Scrap metal. **SIC:** 5093 (Scrap & Waste Materials). **Sales:** $12,000,000 (2000). **Emp:** 120. **Officers:** Gene Timmerman, General Mgr.

■ 20353 ■ **Savoye Packaging Corp.**
2050 S 10th St.
San Jose, CA 95112-4112
Phone: (408)745-0614   **Fax:** (408)745-0595
Products: Aluminum. **SIC:** 5051 (Metals Service Centers & Offices). **Est:** 1991. **Sales:** $33,000,000 (2000). **Emp:** 45. **Officers:** Victor Monia, President; Marcy Holzinger, Treasurer.

■ 20354 ■ **Sawing and Shearing Services Inc.**
13500 Western Ave.
Blue Island, IL 60406
Phone: (708)388-9955   **Fax:** (708)388-7199
Products: Steel service center: cutting and shearing. **SIC:** 5051 (Metals Service Centers & Offices).

■ 20355 ■ **ScanSteel Service Center Inc.**
PO Box 2667
Clarksville, IN 47131
Phone: (812)284-4141   **Fax:** (812)284-4395
Products: Hot-rolled carbon steel. **SIC:** 5051 (Metals Service Centers & Offices). **Est:** 1985. **Sales:** $11,000,000 (2000). **Emp:** 47. **Officers:** T.P. Scanlan Sr., President; T.P. Scanlan Jr., CFO.

■ 20356 ■ **Emil A. Schroth Inc.**
PO Box 496
Farmingdale, NJ 07727
Phone: (908)938-5015
Products: Non-ferrous metals. **SIC:** 5051 (Metals Service Centers & Offices). **Est:** 1931. **Sales:** $12,000,000 (2000). **Emp:** 25. **Officers:** Emil A. Schroth Jr., President; John Fodor, CFO; Steve Samaha, Dir. of Marketing & Sales.

■ 20357 ■ **Scion Steel Co.**
23800 Blackstone Rd.
Warren, MI 48089
Phone: (810)755-4000   **Fax:** (810)755-4064
Products: Structural steel. **SICs:** 5051 (Metals Service Centers & Offices); 5039 (Construction Materials Nec). **Est:** 1985. **Sales:** $13,000,000 (2000). **Emp:** 22. **Officers:** Carlos Hurches, President; Richard Costantini, VP & CFO.

■ 20358 ■ **Scott Stainless Steel**
6201 W Howard St.
Niles, IL 60714
Phone: (847)647-1000
Free: (888)278-2465   **Fax:** (847)647-1999
E-mail: sales@scottstainless.com
URL: http://www.scottstainless.com
Products: Raw stainless steel; Stainless steel sheet and coil. **SIC:** 5051 (Metals Service Centers & Offices). **Est:** 1953. **Sales:** $5,000,000 (2000). **Emp:** 7. **Officers:** L.R. Scott, President.

■ 20359 ■ **Sennett Steel Corp.**
1200 E 14 Mile Rd.
Madison Heights, MI 48071
Phone: (734)585-6040
Products: Steel. **SIC:** 5051 (Metals Service Centers & Offices). **Sales:** $140,000,000 (1993). **Emp:** 200. **Officers:** John H. Sennett, President & Treasurer.

■ 20360 ■ **Service Steel Aerospace Corp.**
PO Box 2333
Tacoma, WA 98401
Phone: (253)627-2910   **Fax:** (253)627-2911
Products: Steel service center, stainless and alloy bars and forgings. **SIC:** 5051 (Metals Service Centers & Offices).

■ 20361 ■ **SFI-Gray Steel Services Inc.**
3510 Maury St.
Houston, TX 77009
Phone: (713)225-0899   **Fax:** (713)222-8106
Products: Metals service center: steel flame cutting. **SIC:** 5051 (Metals Service Centers & Offices). **Officers:** Doug Gray, Owner.

■ 20362 ■ **SFK Steel Inc.**
3130 N Palafox St.
Pensacola, FL 32522
Phone: (850)434-0851   **Fax:** (850)438-9399
Products: Steel. **SIC:** 5051 (Metals Service Centers & Offices). **Est:** 1959. **Sales:** $5,000,000 (2000). **Emp:** 40. **Officers:** Marvin Kaiman, President; Jim Williams, CFO; Jay S. Kaiman, Dir. of Marketing; David Kaiman, Dir of Human Resources.

■ 20363 ■ **Sharon Piping and Equipment Inc.**
2188 Spicer Cove
Memphis, TN 38134
Phone: (901)385-7015
Products: Stainless steel fittings and pipes. **SIC:** 5051 (Metals Service Centers & Offices).

■ 20364 ■ **Showa Denko America Inc.**
489 5th Ave., Fl. 18
New York, NY 10017-6105
Phone: (212)210-8730
Products: Chemicals; Metals, including aluminum. **SICs:** 5051 (Metals Service Centers & Offices); 5169 (Chemicals & Allied Products Nec).

■ 20365 ■ **Sierra Alloys Company Inc.**
5467 Ayon Ave.
Irwindale, CA 91706
Phone: (626)969-6711
Free: (800)423-1897   **Fax:** (626)969-6719
E-mail: info@sierraalloys.com
Products: Metal; Titanium; Stainless and alloy steel; Inconel. **SIC:** 5051 (Metals Service Centers & Offices). **Est:** 1974. **Sales:** $25,000,000 (2000). **Emp:** 35. **Officers:** J.P. Augustyn, President.

■ 20366 ■ **Sierra Pacific Steel Inc.**
PO Box 6024
Hayward, CA 94540-6024
Phone: (510)785-4474
Products: Steel. **SIC:** 5051 (Metals Service Centers & Offices).

■ 20367 ■ **Simsmetal USA Corp. C and C Metals Div.**
11320 Dismantle Ct.
Rancho Cordova, CA 95742
Phone: (916)635-8750   **Fax:** (916)635-0995
Products: New and used steel and other metals. **SICs:** 5051 (Metals Service Centers & Offices); 5093 (Scrap & Waste Materials). **Officers:** Frank Cemo, General Mgr.

■ 20368 ■ **Singer Steel Co.**
1 Singer Dr.
Streetsboro, OH 44241-0279
Phone: (330)562-7200
Free: (877)746-4371   **Fax:** (330)362-7557
Products: Coiled and hot-rolled steel. **SIC:** 5051 (Metals Service Centers & Offices). **Est:** 1923. **Sales:** $42,000,000 (2000). **Emp:** 55. **Officers:** B. Alexander, CEO; E. Shaw, VP of Finance.

■ 20369 ■ **Singer Steel Inc.**
PO Box 3528
Enid, OK 73702
Phone: (580)233-0411   **Fax:** (580)233-2430
Products: Hot and cold-rolled steel. **SIC:** 5051 (Metals Service Centers & Offices). **Sales:** $25,000,000 (2000). **Emp:** 25. **Officers:** Richard A. Singer, President; David Martens, VP of Finance; Bill Howard, VP of Marketing.

■ 20370 ■ **Siskin Steel and Supply Company Inc.**
PO Box 1191
Chattanooga, TN 37401-1191
Phone: (423)756-3671   **Fax:** (423)756-3671
Products: Metals, including steel, copper, and aluminum. **SIC:** 5051 (Metals Service Centers & Offices). **Est:** 1900. **Sales:** $100,000,000 (2000). **Emp:** 400. **Officers:** Mervin Pregulman, CEO & President;

James R. Avriett, VP & CFO; Jerry D. Pearson, VP of Marketing & Sales; Kevin Sneary, Exec. VP; Dan Williams, Dir of Human Resources.

■ 20371 ■ Smith Pipe and Steel Co.
735 N 19th Ave.
Phoenix, AZ 85009
Phone: (602)257-9494
Free: (800)352-4596   Fax: (602)252-0291
Products: Steel. SIC: 5051 (Metals Service Centers & Offices). Est: 1938. Sales: $45,000,000 (2000). Emp: 122. Officers: Jack Waddell, VP & General Merchandising Mgr.; Eric Offenberger, Comptroller; Rick Resner, Dir. of Marketing.

■ 20372 ■ SOGEM-Afrimet Inc.
1212 6th Ave.
New York, NY 10036
Phone: (212)764-0880   Fax: (212)764-8851
Products: Metals, except precious; Chemical preparations. SICs: 5051 (Metals Service Centers & Offices); 5169 (Chemicals & Allied Products Nec). Est: 1926. Sales: $250,000,000 (2000). Emp: 50. Officers: Robert Podewif, President; Steve Springer, CFO; Maria Macchiarulo, Personnel Mgr.

■ 20373 ■ South Bay Foundry, Inc.
9444 Abraham Way
Santee, CA 92071-2853
Phone: (619)596-3825   Fax: (619)596-3715
Products: Cast iron and steel. SIC: 5051 (Metals Service Centers & Offices). Est: 1989. Sales: $10,000,000 (2000). Emp: 50. Officers: Bill Rogers, President.

■ 20374 ■ South Main Metal Building
4900 S Main St.
Roswell, NM 88201
Phone: (505)623-8842
Products: Metals. SIC: 5051 (Metals Service Centers & Offices).

■ 20375 ■ Southwark Metal Manufacturing Co.
1600 Washington Ave.
Philadelphia, PA 19146
Phone: (215)735-3401
Free: (800)523-1052   Fax: (215)735-0411
Products: Sheet metal. SIC: 5051 (Metals Service Centers & Offices).

■ 20376 ■ Southwest Stainless Inc.
8505 Monroe Ave.
Houston, TX 77061
Phone: (713)943-3790
Products: Stainless steel. SIC: 5051 (Metals Service Centers & Offices). Sales: $89,000,000 (1993). Emp: 120. Officers: Mike Stanwood, President.

■ 20377 ■ Southwest Steel
300 N 17th St.
Las Cruces, NM 88001
Phone: (505)526-5412
Products: Steel. SIC: 5051 (Metals Service Centers & Offices).

■ 20378 ■ Southwest Steel Supply Co.
3401 Morganford Rd.
St. Louis, MO 63116
Phone: (314)664-6100
Free: (888)777-7970   Fax: (314)772-3017
Products: Flat rolled steel. SIC: 5051 (Metals Service Centers & Offices). Est: 1949. Sales: $43,000,000 (2000). Emp: 99. Officers: Karl Shiotani, President; Ken Minagawa, Controller; Mark McCluskey, Sales Mgr.

■ 20379 ■ Southwestern Ohio Steel Inc.
PO Box 148
Hamilton, OH 45012-0148
Phone: (513)896-2700   Fax: (513)785-2323
Products: Cold and hot rolled steel. SIC: 5051 (Metals Service Centers & Offices). Est: 1945. Sales: $250,000,000 (2000). Emp: 500. Officers: Gary D. Johns, CEO & President; Michael Janson, Exec. VP of Finance; John Smurda, VP of Sales; Larry Wells, VP of Information Systems; Joseph Brefeld, Human Resources Contact.

■ 20380 ■ Southwestern Suppliers Inc.
6815 E 14th Ave.
PO Box 75069
Tampa, FL 33675-0069
Phone: (813)626-2193
Free: (800)282-2867   Fax: (813)628-0511
Products: Rebar; Wire products, including wire mesh; Nails; Automated fasteners; Polyfilm; Concrete accessories; Lumber accessories. SICs: 5082 (Construction & Mining Machinery); 5051 (Metals Service Centers & Offices). Est: 1960. Sales: $35,000,000 (2000). Emp: 70. Officers: Martin P. Koch, President, e-mail: mkoch@sowes.com; Frederick MacFawn, VP & Treasurer, e-mail: fmacfawn@sowes.com.

■ 20381 ■ Specialty Metals Industries
42299 Winchester Rd.
Temecula, CA 92590
Phone: (909)693-1300   Fax: (909)693-1301
Products: Metals distribution center; Metal fabrication, specializing in tubular steel. SIC: 5051 (Metals Service Centers & Offices).

■ 20382 ■ Specialty Metals and Minerals Inc.
2355 Tecumseh St.
Baton Rouge, LA 70802
Phone: (504)358-0400   Fax: (504)358-0868
E-mail: specialtymetals.mindspring.com
Products: Non-ferrous materials, lead, arsenic, antimony, tin, selenium, and red iron oxide. SIC: 5051 (Metals Service Centers & Offices). Est: 1981. Sales: $5,500,000 (2000). Emp: 36. Officers: Fred Giumond, President. Alternate Name: Specialty Metals.

■ 20383 ■ Specialty Metals Supply Inc.
750 Ridgewood Rd.
Ridgeland, MS 39157
Phone: (601)956-8555
Products: Metal products. SIC: 5051 (Metals Service Centers & Offices).

■ 20384 ■ Specialty Pipe and Tube Co.
PO Box 3116
Warren, OH 44485
Phone: (330)394-2512
Free: (800)366-7473   Fax: (330)394-6218
Products: Steel pipe and tubing. SIC: 5051 (Metals Service Centers & Offices). Sales: $12,000,000 (2000). Emp: 55. Officers: James Beatty, President.

■ 20385 ■ St Lawrence Steel Corp.
PO Box 2490
Streetsboro, OH 44241
Phone: (330)562-9000   Fax: (330)562-1100
Products: Steel plate fabricating. SIC: 5051 (Metals Service Centers & Offices).

■ 20386 ■ Standard Metals Inc.
440 Ledyard St.
Hartford, CT 06114
Phone: (860)296-5663
Free: (800)243-2224   Fax: (860)296-9877
E-mail: info@standardmetals.com
URL: http://www.standardmetals.com
Products: Copper based alloys; Water jet cutting machines. SIC: 5051 (Metals Service Centers & Offices). Est: 1980. Sales: $3,500,000 (2000). Emp: 10. Officers: Steve Buzash, President; Brian Weinstein, Vice President; Ed Kennelly, Vice President.

■ 20387 ■ Standard Steel and Wire Corp.
2450 W Hubbard St.
Chicago, IL 60612
Phone: (312)226-6100   Fax: (312)226-6141
Products: Flat-rolled steel. SIC: 5051 (Metals Service Centers & Offices). Est: 1920. Sales: $11,000,000 (2000). Emp: 26. Officers: Marguerite Hack, President; Christine Hack, CFO; Dennis Hack, Dir. of Marketing & Sales.

■ 20388 ■ Standard Tube Sales Corp.
PO Box 479
Marlborough, MA 01752
Phone: (508)481-7100   Fax: (508)481-5859
Products: Steel. SIC: 5051 (Metals Service Centers & Offices). Est: 1937. Sales: $14,000,000 (2000). Emp: 45. Officers: Francis Walsh, President; Jeffery Maloney, Controller.

■ 20389 ■ STATCO Engineering and Fabricators Inc.
7595 Reynolds Cir.
Huntington Beach, 24860, 92647
Phone: (714)375-6300
Free: (800)421-0362   Fax: (714)375-6314
E-mail: statcohb@statco-engineering.com
Products: Sanitary products; Stainless steel. SIC: 5051 (Metals Service Centers & Offices). Est: 1982. Sales: $59,000,000 (2000). Emp: 165. Officers: Jim Statham, President; Mark Etcheverry, Sales/Marketing Contact.

■ 20390 ■ State Line Supply Co.
1333 E Main St.
Bradford, PA 16701
Phone: (814)362-7433   Fax: (814)362-7437
Products: Structural steel. SICs: 5051 (Metals Service Centers & Offices); 5039 (Construction Materials Nec). Est: 1900. Sales: $3,000,000 (2000). Emp: 16. Officers: David Zuckerman, CEO & President; Robert P. Douglas, VP of Finance; Thomas Vinciquera, Sales Mgr.; Pat Vigliotta, Dir. of Data Processing.

■ 20391 ■ State Pipe and Supply Inc.
PO Box 3286
Santa Fe Springs, CA 90670
Phone: (562)695-5555   Fax: (562)692-1054
Products: Carbon steel pipes and fittings. SICs: 5051 (Metals Service Centers & Offices); 5074 (Plumbing & Hydronic Heating Supplies). Est: 1946. Officers: Honggie Kim, President.

■ 20392 ■ Steel City Corp.
PO Box 1227
Youngstown, OH 44501
Phone: (330)792-7663
Free: (800)321-0350   Fax: (330)792-7951
E-mail: steelcity@onecom.com; hardware@scity.com
URL: http://www.scity.com
Products: Steel products, including fence posts, mailboxes, tool organizers, and work bench legs. SICs: 5051 (Metals Service Centers & Offices); 5162 (Plastics Materials & Basic Shapes). Est: 1939. Sales: $28,000,000 (1999). Emp: 60. Officers: Kenneth Fibus, President; Stephen A. Speece, VP of Production; Jeff Bresler, Mgr. Dir., e-mail: jbresler@scity.com; JoAnn Reese, e-mail: jreesesciencety.com.

■ 20393 ■ Steel Co.
12500 Stoney Isle. Ave.
Chicago, IL 60633
Phone: (773)646-3600
Products: High carbon material; Sheet steel; Levelers. SIC: 5051 (Metals Service Centers & Offices). Est: 1971. Sales: $9,000,000 (2000). Emp: 69. Officers: K. Rajkumar, President; Avinash C. Gupta, Exec. VP of Finance.

■ 20394 ■ Steel Engineers Inc.
716 W Mesquite Rd.
Las Vegas, NV 89106
Phone: (702)386-0023   Fax: (702)386-6723
Products: Reinforcement steel; Aluminum sheets; Nuts and bolts. SIC: 5051 (Metals Service Centers & Offices). Est: 1968. Sales: $30,000,000 (2000). Emp: 200. Officers: Mike Zech, President.

■ 20395 ■ Steel Inc.
6245 Clermont St.
Commerce City, CO 80022
Phone: (303)287-0331
URL: http://www.etimberline.com
Products: Structural steel sheets. SICs: 5051 (Metals Service Centers & Offices); 5039 (Construction Materials Nec). Sales: $30,000,000 (2000). Emp: 90. Officers: Danial J. McCallin, President.

■ 20396 ■ Steel Industries Inc.
12600 Beech Daly Rd.
Detroit, MI 48239
Phone: (313)531-1140   Fax: (313)534-0988
Products: Steel. SIC: 5051 (Metals Service Centers & Offices). Est: 1913. Sales: $14,000,000 (2000). Emp: 105. Officers: Paul Sakmar, President.

■ **20397** ■ **Steel Manufacturing and Warehouse Co.**
PO Box 02-5668
Kansas City, MO 64102
Phone: (816)842-9143 **Fax:** (816)842-9148
Products: Steel sheets. **SIC:** 5051 (Metals Service Centers & Offices). **Est:** 1921. **Sales:** $40,000,000 (2000). **Emp:** 55. **Officers:** Charles Donnelly Jr., President; David Flint, CFO.

■ **20398** ■ **Steel and Pipe Supply Co.**
PO Box 1688
Manhattan, KS 66502
Phone: (785)537-2222 **Fax:** (785)587-5176
Products: Carbon steel; Piping. **SIC:** 5051 (Metals Service Centers & Offices). **Est:** 1951. **Sales:** $96,000,000 (2000). **Emp:** 175. **Officers:** Dennis A. Mullin, President; Philip Brokenicky, CFO; Mike Ross, Marketing Mgr.

■ **20399** ■ **Steel Services Inc.**
7231 Forest Ave., No. 100
Richmond, VA 23226-3796
Phone: (804)673-3810
Products: Steel. **SIC:** 5051 (Metals Service Centers & Offices). **Est:** 1945. **Sales:** $20,000,000 (2000). **Emp:** 100. **Officers:** Thomas J. Stark IV, Chairman of the Board; Lacy Slone, CFO; Eric Hammond, Information Systems Mgr.

■ **20400** ■ **Steel Suppliers Inc.**
PO Box 1185
Elkhart, IN 46515
Phone: (219)264-7561 **Fax:** (219)262-3002
Products: Hot rolled sheet and strip, including tin plate, black plate, terne plate, and tin free steel; Steel. **SIC:** 5051 (Metals Service Centers & Offices). **Est:** 1963. **Emp:** 20. **Officers:** Kevin J. Culp, President.

■ **20401** ■ **Steel Supply Co.**
PO Box 82579
Oklahoma City, OK 73148
Phone: (405)631-1551
Products: Steel; Pipes; Plates; Beams. **SICs:** 5051 (Metals Service Centers & Offices); 5039 (Construction Materials Nec). **Est:** 1952. **Sales:** $2,000,000 (2000). **Emp:** 15. **Officers:** Bob Rice, President; Betty Rice, VP & Treasurer.

■ **20402** ■ **Steel Supply Co. (Rolling Meadows, Illinois)**
5105 Newport Dr.
Rolling Meadows, IL 60008
Phone: (847)255-2460 **Fax:** (847)255-2463
Products: General and CNC machining, drilling, boring, cutting, lathe and mill work. **SIC:** 5051 (Metals Service Centers & Offices). **Sales:** $42,000,000 (2000). **Emp:** 35. **Officers:** Don Hjortland, President; Kathy McCraren, CFO.

■ **20403** ■ **Steel Warehouse Company Inc.**
PO Box 1377
South Bend, IN 46624
Phone: (219)236-5100 **Fax:** (219)236-5154
Products: Hot-rolled steel. **SIC:** 5051 (Metals Service Centers & Offices). **Est:** 1948. **Sales:** $95,000,000 (2000). **Emp:** 315. **Officers:** D. Lerman, President; G. Lerman, VP of Finance; Michael Lerman, VP of Marketing; David Samber, Dir. of Data Processing; Joe Holmes, Dir of Human Resources.

■ **20404** ■ **Steel Yard Inc.**
PO Box 4828
Portland, OR 97208
Phone: (503)282-9273
Free: (800)280-9273 **Fax:** (503)282-7490
Products: Metals. **SIC:** 5051 (Metals Service Centers & Offices). **Sales:** $6,000,000 (1999). **Emp:** 30. **Officers:** Leleand Waltuck, President; Thai Nguyen, Controller.

■ **20405** ■ **Steelco Inc.**
PO Box 3335
Salem, OR 97302
Phone: (503)581-2516
Free: (800)452-0344 **Fax:** (503)581-2521
E-mail: steel@goldcom.com
Products: Raw steel. **SIC:** 5051 (Metals Service

Centers & Offices). **Est:** 1960. **Sales:** $13,000,000 (2000). **Emp:** 24. **Officers:** Tim Woock, President.

■ **20406** ■ **Stock Steel**
PO Box 2610
Spokane, WA 99220
Phone: (509)535-6363 **Fax:** (509)536-5415
Products: Steel service center. **SIC:** 5051 (Metals Service Centers & Offices). **Officers:** Marilyn Schroeder, CFO & Treasurer.

■ **20407** ■ **Stone Steel Corp.**
PO Box 2893
Baltimore, MD 21225
Phone: (410)355-4140
Free: (800)624-4599 **Fax:** (410)355-4883
E-mail: stonesteel@interinc.com
Products: Steel. **SIC:** 5051 (Metals Service Centers & Offices). **Est:** 1971. **Sales:** $9,000,000 (2000). **Emp:** 15. **Officers:** V. Pappas, Vice President; T. Motsco, President.

■ **20408** ■ **Stripco Sales Inc.**
PO Box 248
Osceola, IN 46561
Phone: (219)256-7800 **Fax:** (219)256-7813
Products: Metals service center: narrow coil slitting, edging and annealing. **SIC:** 5051 (Metals Service Centers & Offices). **Officers:** Jack Hiler, President; Chuck Nightingale, CFO.

■ **20409** ■ **Stulz-Sickles Steel Co.**
929 Julia St.
Elizabeth, NJ 07201
Phone: (908)351-1776
Free: (800)351-1776 **Fax:** (908)351-8231
URL: http://www.stulzsicklessteel.com
Products: Manganese and steel products, including welding electrodes. **SIC:** 5051 (Metals Service Centers & Offices). **Est:** 1916. **Sales:** $7,000,000 (1999). **Emp:** 30. **Officers:** E. Chapin, Chairman of the Board; P. De Stasio, President; R. Farina, Dir. of Marketing.

■ **20410** ■ **Style Master**
5020 Lincolnway E
PO Box 1330
Mishawaka, IN 46546
Phone: (219)255-9692 **Fax:** (219)256-6577
Products: Aluminum extruded products; Diamond plate running boards and accessories. **SICs:** 5051 (Metals Service Centers & Offices); 5013 (Motor Vehicle Supplies & New Parts). **Est:** 1965.

■ **20411** ■ **Sumitomo Corporation of America**
345 Park Ave.
New York, NY 10154
Phone: (212)207-0700 **Fax:** (212)207-0813
Products: Steel. **SIC:** 5051 (Metals Service Centers & Offices). **Est:** 1952. **Sales:** $10,000,000,000 (2000). **Emp:** 1,400. **Officers:** Kenji Miyahara, CEO & President; Tadasu Takagi, Exec. VP; Masahiko Yamane, Dir of Personnel.

■ **20412** ■ **Sunland Steel Inc.**
1004 N Hwy. 51
Truth Or Consequences, NM 87901
Phone: (505)894-7017
Products: Steel. **SIC:** 5051 (Metals Service Centers & Offices).

■ **20413** ■ **Sunshine Steel Enterprises Corp.**
8265 Belvedere Ave.
Sacramento, CA 95826
Phone: (916)451-7031
Products: Aluminum; Brass; Copper; Steel. **SIC:** 5051 (Metals Service Centers & Offices). **Est:** 1975. **Sales:** $5,000,000 (2000). **Emp:** 10. **Officers:** Ping Mao, President.

■ **20414** ■ **Supra Alloys Inc.**
351 Cortez Cir
Camarillo, CA 93012
Phone: (805)388-2138 **Fax:** (805)987-6492
Products: Metals. **SIC:** 5051 (Metals Service Centers & Offices). **Officers:** George Esseff, President.

■ **20415** ■ **Synergy Steel Inc.**
1450 Rochester Rd.
Troy, MI 48083
Phone: (248)583-9740 **Fax:** (248)583-9746
Products: Metals service centers: sawing and flame cutting, shearing, heat treating, blanchard and mattison grinding. **SIC:** 5051 (Metals Service Centers & Offices). **Sales:** $6,000,000 (1999). **Emp:** 25. **Officers:** Andrew A. Mair, President; Edmond M. Groos, Vice President.

■ **20416** ■ **Tang Industries Inc.**
1965 Pratt Blvd.
Elk Grove Village, IL 60007
Phone: (708)806-7200 **Fax:** (708)806-7220
Products: Steel service center. **SIC:** 5051 (Metals Service Centers & Offices). **Sales:** $1,560,000,000 (1993). **Emp:** 2,100. **Officers:** Cyrus Tang, CEO.

■ **20417** ■ **TCI Aluminum**
PO Box 2069
Gardena, CA 90247
Phone: (310)323-5613
Free: (800)234-5613 **Fax:** (310)323-1255
Products: Aluminum sheets, plates, bar, and rod; Precision machining. **SIC:** 5051 (Metals Service Centers & Offices). **Est:** 1956. **Sales:** $17,000,000 (2000). **Emp:** 104. **Officers:** B.E. Belzer, CEO.

■ **20418** ■ **Techno Steel Corp.**
1207 Riverside Blvd.
Memphis, TN 38106
Phone: (901)942-3770 **Fax:** (901)942-3791
E-mail: tscmem@aol.com
Products: Steel processing. **SIC:** 5051 (Metals Service Centers & Offices). **Est:** 1990. **Sales:** $8,000,000 (2000). **Emp:** 14. **Officers:** Kenji Yamazaki, President.

■ **20419** ■ **Tex Isle Supply Inc.**
10830 Old Katy Rd.
Houston, TX 77043
Phones: (713)461-1012 (713)461-5168
Products: Drill pipes and line pipes. **SIC:** 5051 (Metals Service Centers & Offices). **Est:** 1959. **Sales:** $36,000,000 (2000). **Emp:** 10. **Officers:** Hans Kayem, CEO & Chairman of the Board; Lee Kayem, Treasurer & Secty.; Curtis Kayem, President.

■ **20420** ■ **Texas Pipe and Supply Company Inc.**
2330 Holmes Rd.
Houston, TX 77051-1098
Phone: (713)799-9235 **Fax:** (713)799-8701
E-mail: tps@texaspipe.com
URL: http://www.texaspipe.com
Products: Carbon and stainless steel pipes. **SIC:** 5051 (Metals Service Centers & Offices). **Est:** 1918. **Sales:** $139,000,000 (2000). **Emp:** 130. **Officers:** Jerry R. Rubenstein, Co-Chairman of the Board & COO; James R. Dunn, Sr. VP & CFO; Maury Rubenstein, Co-Chairman of the Board & COO; James A. Fitzgerald, President.

■ **20421** ■ **Thypin Stainless Steel**
125 Carson Rd.
Birmingham, AL 35215
Phone: (205)663-1100
Products: Steel. **SIC:** 5051 (Metals Service Centers & Offices).

■ **20422** ■ **Thypin Steel Co.**
49-49 30th St.
Long Island City, NY 11101
Phone: (718)937-2700 **Fax:** (718)706-4533
Products: Carbon and steel beams, strips, and coils; Stainless steel. **SIC:** 5051 (Metals Service Centers & Offices). **Est:** 1910. **Sales:** $260,000,000 (2000). **Emp:** 550. **Officers:** Larry Gilbert, Exec. VP; James Reynolds, VP of Finance; Christopher Hall, VP of Marketing; David Simmons, Dir. of Information Systems; Rita Herman, Dir of Human Resources.

■ **20423** ■ **Thyssen Incorporated N.A.**
400 Renaissance Ctr.
Detroit, MI 48243
Phone: (313)567-5600 **Fax:** (313)567-5667
Products: Carbon steel, copper, brass, and aluminum; Plastics. **SICs:** 5051 (Metals Service Centers & Offices); 5162 (Plastics Materials & Basic Shapes). **Sales:** $2,500,000,000 (2000). **Emp:** 3,500. **Officers:**

Kenneth Graham, CEO & President; Walter J. Oehler, Exec. VP & CFO.

■ 20424 ■ **Tiernay Metals Inc.**
2600 Marine Ave.
Redondo Beach, CA 90278
Phone: (310)676-0184 **Fax:** (310)679-0223
Products: Aluminum extrusions. **SIC:** 5051 (Metals Service Centers & Offices). **Est:** 1954. **Sales:** $50,000,000 (2000). **Emp:** 120. **Officers:** Robert Stoltz, President; Thomas Rasmussen, Treasurer; Gene Gambill, Sr. VP; Dan Prines, Dir. of Marketing.

■ 20425 ■ **Titan Industrial Corp.**
555 Madison Ave.
New York, NY 10022
Phone: (212)421-6700 **Fax:** (212)421-6708
Products: Steel. **SIC:** 5051 (Metals Service Centers & Offices). **Est:** 1946. **Sales:** $450,000,000 (2000). **Emp:** 150. **Officers:** Michael S. Levin, President; Richard Blumberg, Controller; Stephen A. Levy, Exec. VP of Marketing & Sales; Craig Morritt, Information Systems Mgr.; Thomas A. Potter, Vice President.

■ 20426 ■ **Titan Steel Co.**
322 Miami St.
Tiffin, OH 44883
Phone: (419)447-0442
Products: Steel. **SIC:** 5051 (Metals Service Centers & Offices).

■ 20427 ■ **TMX**
12817 NE Airport Way
Portland, OR 97230
Phone: (503)254-2600 **Fax:** (503)254-4181
Products: Metals service center. **SIC:** 5051 (Metals Service Centers & Offices).

■ 20428 ■ **Toledo Pickling and Steel Inc.**
1149 Campbell St.
PO Box 3395
Toledo, OH 43607
Phone: (419)255-1570
Free: (800)537-8695 **Fax:** (419)255-2243
Products: Steel; Steel processing, including pickling, slitting, leveling, and shearing. **SIC:** 5051 (Metals Service Centers & Offices). **Est:** 1984. **Sales:** $75,000,000 (2000). **Emp:** 100. **Officers:** Robert Mary, President; Paul Eagle, Vice President; Ross Keller, Chairman of the Board.

■ 20429 ■ **Toledo Pickling and Steel Sales Inc.**
PO Box 3395
Toledo, OH 43607
Phone: (419)255-1570
Free: (800)537-8695 **Fax:** (419)255-2243
Products: Steel. **SIC:** 5051 (Metals Service Centers & Offices). **Sales:** $87,000,000 (2000). **Emp:** 909. **Officers:** Robert G. Mang, CEO & President; Ross Keller, CFO.

■ 20430 ■ **Tomen America Inc.**
1285 Ave. of the Amer.
New York, NY 10019
Phone: (212)397-4600 **Fax:** (212)582-2007
Products: Metals; Chemicals; Minerals; Machinery; Food. **SICs:** 5051 (Metals Service Centers & Offices); 5169 (Chemicals & Allied Products Nec); 5141 (Groceries—General Line); 5153 (Grain & Field Beans). **Est:** 1951. **Sales:** $2,645,000,000 (2000). **Emp:** 850. **Officers:** Hajime Kawamura, President; Hideki Mushika, Treasurer; J. Farley, Vice President.

■ 20431 ■ **Tool King Inc.**
PO Box 366
Wheeling, IL 60090
Phone: (847)537-2881 **Fax:** (847)537-6937
Products: Steel service center: flat rolled coiled, high and low carbon annealed, tempered spring, edge conditioning, galvanized, aluminized and stainless steel. **SIC:** 5051 (Metals Service Centers & Offices).

■ 20432 ■ **Tool Steel Service Inc.**
7333 S 76th Ave.
Bridgeview, IL 60455
Phone: (708)458-7878 **Fax:** (708)458-3778
Products: Metals service center: cutting, grinding and drilling. **SIC:** 5051 (Metals Service Centers & Offices).

■ 20433 ■ **Totten Tubes Inc.**
500 Danlee St.
Azusa, CA 91702
Phone: (626)812-0220
Free: (800)882-3748 **Fax:** (626)812-0413
Products: Steel tubing. **SIC:** 5051 (Metals Service Centers & Offices). **Est:** 1955. **Sales:** $24,000,000 (1999). **Emp:** 50. **Officers:** Dave M. Totten, President; Jeff Totten, CFO.

■ 20434 ■ **Toyota Tsusho America Inc.**
437 Madison Ave.
New York, NY 10022
Phone: (212)418-0100 **Fax:** (212)752-3914
Products: Steel; Textiles; Chemicals. **SICs:** 5051 (Metals Service Centers & Offices); 5084 (Industrial Machinery & Equipment); 5169 (Chemicals & Allied Products Nec). **Est:** 1961. **Sales:** $160,000,000 (2000). **Emp:** 40. **Officers:** Senji Fujita, President; Yuji Noda, Treasurer.

■ 20435 ■ **Tradearbed Inc.**
825 3rd Ave.
New York, NY 10022
Phone: (212)486-9890 **Fax:** (212)355-2159
Products: Imported steel. **SIC:** 5051 (Metals Service Centers & Offices). **Est:** 1926. **Sales:** $1,000,000,000 (2000). **Emp:** 300. **Officers:** F. Lamesch, CEO; Gilles Feider, VP of Finance; Robert Bortz, President; Mary Pisacane, Dir of Human Resources.

■ 20436 ■ **Tradex International Corp.**
505 Northern Blvd.
Great Neck, NY 11021
Phone: (516)829-3855 **Fax:** (516)829-8390
Products: Steel pipes and tubes; Hot-rolled steel shapes and plates; Industrial pumps, compressors and parts; Construction plastic pipes and fittings; Metal valves and fittings. **SICs:** 5051 (Metals Service Centers & Offices); 5084 (Industrial Machinery & Equipment); 5085 (Industrial Supplies). **Officers:** M. Salis, President.

■ 20437 ■ **Transfer Print Foils**
1787 Pomona Rd., Ste. B
Corona, CA 91718
Phone: (949)753-1135
Free: (800)268-1414 **Fax:** (949)753-1430
Products: Hot stamping foil; Holographic foils and images; Woodgrain, marble, and granite foils. **SIC:** 5051 (Metals Service Centers & Offices). **Est:** 1961. **Sales:** $3,000,000 (2000). **Emp:** 3. **Officers:** Charles Motola, General Mgr.

■ 20438 ■ **Transit Mix Concrete Co.**
PO Box 1030
Colorado Springs, CO 80901
Phone: (719)475-0700 **Fax:** (719)475-0226
Products: Ready-mixed concrete, metal frames, sand and gravel. **SICs:** 5051 (Metals Service Centers & Offices); 5032 (Brick, Stone & Related Materials). **Sales:** $28,000,000 (2000). **Emp:** 186. **Officers:** Carl Herskind, President.

■ 20439 ■ **Transworld Alloys Inc.**
334 E Gardena Blvd.
Gardena, CA 90248
Phone: (310)217-8777 **Fax:** (310)217-0066
Products: Stocks and sells metals in sheet, plate, tube and bar—aluminum, titanium, all metals. **SIC:** 5051 (Metals Service Centers & Offices). **Officers:** Robert Katz, President.

■ 20440 ■ **Transworld Metal USA Ltd.**
335 Madison Ave., Rm 815
New York, NY 10017-4605
Phone: (212)750-8600
Products: Aluminum; Tin and tin base metals, shapes, forms, etc. **SIC:** 5051 (Metals Service Centers & Offices). **Est:** 1969. **Sales:** $4,000,000 (2000). **Emp:** 7. **Officers:** Edward Mear, President.

■ 20441 ■ **Trenton Iron and Metal Corp.**
301 Enterprise Ave.
Trenton, NJ 08638
Phone: (609)396-2250
Products: Iron, copper, and metal. **SIC:** 5051 (Metals Service Centers & Offices). **Sales:** $7,000,000 (2000). **Emp:** 19. **Officers:** Joseph Lonchar, President.

■ 20442 ■ **Tri-State Aluminum**
PO Box 504
Toledo, OH 43697
Phone: (419)666-0100 **Fax:** (419)666-2285
Products: Aluminum and stainless steel service center: cutting, shearing and sawing. **SIC:** 5051 (Metals Service Centers & Offices). **Officers:** Jerry Wright, Director.

■ 20443 ■ **Nathan Trotter and Company Inc.**
PO Box 1066
Exton, PA 19341
Phone: (610)524-1440
Products: Nonferrous metals. **SIC:** 5051 (Metals Service Centers & Offices). **Sales:** $13,000,000 (2000). **Emp:** 9. **Officers:** Russell Etherington, President; Peter Morris, VP & CFO.

■ 20444 ■ **Tube Service Co.**
9351 S Norwalk Blvd.
Santa Fe Springs, CA 90670
Phone: (213)728-9105
Free: (800)776-8823 **Fax:** (310)695-4027
Products: Carbon, stainless, and alloy tubing; Aluminum pipe. **SIC:** 5051 (Metals Service Centers & Offices). **Est:** 1976. **Sales:** $25,000,000 (2000). **Emp:** 100. **Officers:** Dan Hollar, Group Mgr.; Paul Ragsdale, Sales Mgr., e-mail: pragsdale@tubeservice.com.

■ 20445 ■ **Tubesales**
175 Tubeway
Forest Park, GA 30297
Phone: (404)361-5050 **Fax:** (404)728-5310
Products: Steel tubing. **SIC:** 5051 (Metals Service Centers & Offices). **Est:** 1946. **Sales:** $220,000,000 (2000). **Emp:** 550. **Officers:** James F. Cameron, President; Richard Hilseberg, VP of Finance; George Supko, VP of Marketing; Carol Madsen, Dir. of Information Systems; Sue Potter, Dir of Human Resources.

■ 20446 ■ **Tubular Steel Inc.**
1031 Executive Pkwy.
St. Louis, MO 63141
Phone: (314)851-9200 **Fax:** (314)851-9336
E-mail: http://www.tubularsteel.com
Products: Carbon; Steel; Piping; Tubing; Metal bars. **SIC:** 5051 (Metals Service Centers & Offices). **Est:** 1953. **Sales:** $185,000,000 (1999). **Emp:** 320. **Officers:** John C. Hauck, President; Jim Morgan, VP of Finance; Stan Mueller, Dir. of Systems.

■ 20447 ■ **J.M. Tull Metals Company Inc.**
PO Box 4725
Norcross, GA 30091
Phone: (404)368-4311 **Fax:** (404)368-4305
Products: Metal. **SIC:** 5051 (Metals Service Centers & Offices). **Est:** 1926. **Sales:** $540,000,000 (2000). **Emp:** 730. **Officers:** Stephen E. Makarewicz, President; Chris Tarquinio, Controller; Joseph Moyer, VP of Marketing; J.T. Morris, Dir. of Information Systems; Ed Gossage, Dir of Human Resources.

■ 20448 ■ **Tulsa Metal Processing Co.**
PO Box 4676
Tulsa, OK 74159
Phone: (918)584-3354
Products: Metals. **SIC:** 5051 (Metals Service Centers & Offices). **Est:** 1969. **Sales:** $15,000,000 (2000). **Emp:** 55. **Officers:** Jerry D. Smithey, President; Sarah E. Smithey, Treasurer & Secty.; Valerie J. Koeninger, Office Mgr.

■ 20449 ■ **TW Metals Co.**
946 Kane
Toledo, OH 43612-1246
Phone: (419)476-7805
Free: (800)895-9591 **Fax:** (419)470-5996
Products: Metals. **SIC:** 5051 (Metals Service Centers & Offices). **Officers:** Joe Darmofal, General Mgr. **Alternate Name:** Williams Metals Company.

■ 20450 ■ T.W.P. Inc.
2831 10th St.
Berkeley, CA 94710
Phone: (510)548-4434
Free: (800)227-1570 **Fax:** (510)548-3073
E-mail: sales@twpinc.com
URL: http://www.buymesh.com
Products: Wire mesh and cloth; Galvanized hardware.
SICs: 5051 (Metals Service Centers & Offices); 5072 (Hardware). **Est:** 1969. **Sales:** $5,000,000 (2000). **Emp:** 50.

■ 20451 ■ Uddeholm Corp.
4902 Tollview Dr.
Rolling Meadows, IL 60008-3713
Phone: (708)577-2220 **Fax:** (708)577-8028
Products: Steel for tools. **SIC:** 5051 (Metals Service Centers & Offices). **Est:** 1923. **Sales:** $60,000,000 (2000). **Emp:** 195. **Officers:** E. Svendsen, CEO; S. Koelsch, Dir. of Data Processing; N. Wolowicki, Dir of Human Resources.

■ 20452 ■ Uddeholm Steel Corp.
9331 Santa Fe Springs Rd.
Santa Fe Springs, CA 90670
Phone: (562)946-6503 **Fax:** (562)946-4274
Products: Tool steel bars and forgings; Ground die steel and drill rods. **SIC:** 5051 (Metals Service Centers & Offices).

■ 20453 ■ Ulbrich of California Inc.
5455 Home Ave.
Fresno, CA 93727
Phone: (209)456-2310
Products: Steel. **SIC:** 5051 (Metals Service Centers & Offices). **Sales:** $18,000,000 (2000). **Emp:** 25. **Officers:** Gregg Boucher, General Mgr.

■ 20454 ■ Ulbrich of Illinois Inc.
12340 S Laramie Ave.
Alsip, IL 60803
Phone: (773)568-7500 **Fax:** (773)371-1802
Products: Stainless steel. **SIC:** 5051 (Metals Service Centers & Offices). **Est:** 1924. **Sales:** $8,000,000 (2000). **Emp:** 80. **Officers:** Chris Ulbrich, President; Tom Niemiera, Controller; Dale Blouin, General Mgr.

■ 20455 ■ Uni-Steel Inc.
G St. & Lexington St.
Muskogee, OK 74403
Phone: (918)682-7833
Products: Steel. **SIC:** 5051 (Metals Service Centers & Offices).

■ 20456 ■ Uni-Steel Inc.
PO Box 3528
Enid, OK 73702
Phone: (580)233-0411 **Fax:** (580)230-9844
Products: Steel. **SIC:** 5051 (Metals Service Centers & Offices). **Sales:** $152,000,000 (2000). **Emp:** 130. **Officers:** Richard Singer, CEO.

■ 20457 ■ Unico Alloys Inc.
1555 Joyce Ave.
Columbus, OH 43219
Phone: (614)299-0545
Products: High temperature alloys. **SIC:** 5051 (Metals Service Centers & Offices).

■ 20458 ■ Unimast Inc.
9595 Grand Ave.
Franklin Park, IL 60131
Phone: (708)451-1410
Products: Steel. **SIC:** 5032 (Brick, Stone & Related Materials). **Sales:** $40,000,000 (2000). **Emp:** 400. **Officers:** Garen W. Smith, President; A. Whittman, CFO.

■ 20459 ■ Unisteel Inc.
PO Box 1090
Sterling Heights, MI 48311
Phone: (810)826-8040
Products: Steel service center: steel cutting. **SIC:** 5051 (Metals Service Centers & Offices).

■ 20460 ■ Unistrut Detroit Service Co.
4045 2nd St.
Wayne, MI 48184
Phone: (734)722-1400 **Fax:** (734)722-6843
Products: Steel framing. **SIC:** 5051 (Metals Service Centers & Offices). **Est:** 1946. **Sales:** $3,500,000 (2000). **Emp:** 15. **Officers:** W.F. Snure, Owner; L.D. Kilgore, Controller; M. Eleski, Secretary.

■ 20461 ■ Unistrut Los Angeles
PO Box 3545
Santa Fe Springs, CA 90670
Phone: (562)404-9966 **Fax:** (562)404-9053
Products: Metal service center and specialty contractors. **SIC:** 5051 (Metals Service Centers & Offices).

■ 20462 ■ Unistrut Northern California
2057 West Ave. 140th
San Leandro, CA 94577
Phone: (510)351-4200
Free: (800)351-8623 **Fax:** (510)351-0174
Products: Metals. **SIC:** 5051 (Metals Service Centers & Offices). **Sales:** $10,000,000 (2000). **Emp:** 20.

■ 20463 ■ United Alloys Inc.
PO Box 514599
Los Angeles, CA 90051
Phone: (323)264-5101
Products: Metals; Metal service center for aircraft titanium. **SIC:** 5051 (Metals Service Centers & Offices).

■ 20464 ■ U.S. Metal Service Inc.
20900 Saint Clair Ave.
Euclid, OH 44117
Phone: (216)692-3800 **Fax:** (216)692-3803
Products: Steel service center: metal slitting and shearing. **SIC:** 5051 (Metals Service Centers & Offices). **Officers:** Mort Kaufman, President.

■ 20465 ■ United Steel Associates Inc.
4501 Curtis Ave.
Baltimore, MD 21226
Phone: (410)355-8980 **Fax:** (410)355-6618
Products: Steel. **SIC:** 5051 (Metals Service Centers & Offices). **Est:** 1961. **Sales:** $6,000,000 (2000). **Emp:** 13. **Officers:** Joseph A. Dillon, President; M.C. Butler, Vice President.

■ 20466 ■ United Steel Service Inc.
PO Box 149
Brookfield, OH 44403
Phone: (330)448-4057 **Fax:** (330)448-1304
Products: Split steel coils. **SIC:** 5051 (Metals Service Centers & Offices). **Sales:** $16,000,000 (1993). **Emp:** 110. **Officers:** Steven Friedman, President; R. Joel Miller, Treasurer.

■ 20467 ■ Universal Metal Services Corp.
16655 S Canal St.
South Holland, IL 60473
Phone: (708)596-2700
Free: (800)323-7667 **Fax:** (708)596-7262
URL: http://www.universalmetal.net
Products: Steel. **SIC:** 5051 (Metals Service Centers & Offices). **Est:** 1967. **Emp:** 100. **Officers:** Mark Ruder, Exec. VP; Dave Chess, Controller; Bob Daffron, VP of Sales.

■ 20468 ■ Universal Steel Co.
6600 Grant Ave.
Cleveland, OH 44105
Phone: (216)883-4972
Free: (800)669-2645 **Fax:** (216)341-0421
URL: http://www.univsteel.com
Products: Steel and metals. **SIC:** 5051 (Metals Service Centers & Offices). **Est:** 1926. **Sales:** $74,000,000 (1999). **Emp:** 100. **Officers:** David Miller, President; Steve Ruscher, CFO.

■ 20469 ■ Value Added Distribution Inc.
5458 Steubenville Pike, No. 1st Fl.
Mc Kees Rocks, PA 15136-1412
Phone: (412)695-1180 **Fax:** (412)695-1183
Products: Aluminum plates. **SIC:** 5051 (Metals Service Centers & Offices). **Sales:** $4,000,000 (2000). **Emp:** 6. **Officers:** Scott L. Davidson, President.

■ 20470 ■ Van Bebber Brothers Inc.
PO Box 760
Petaluma, CA 94953
Phone: (707)762-4528
Products: Steel. **SIC:** 5051 (Metals Service Centers & Offices). **Est:** 1901. **Sales:** $4,000,000 (2000). **Emp:** 28. **Officers:** Royce L. Van Bebber, President; Lois Roberts, Treasurer & Secty.; Helen Finley, Dir. of Marketing.

■ 20471 ■ Vanadium Pacific Steel Co.
707 W Olympic Blvd.
Montebello, CA 90640
Phone: (213)723-5331 **Fax:** (213)725-6381
Products: Aerospace quality steel. **SIC:** 5051 (Metals Service Centers & Offices). **Est:** 1954. **Sales:** $5,000,000 (2000). **Emp:** 20. **Officers:** R.P. Stemmler, Chairman of the Board; Anita Seitz, CFO; John M. Heberling, VP, Treasurer & Chief Acct. Officer.

■ 20472 ■ Viking Materials Inc.
3225 Como Ave. SE
Minneapolis, MN 55414
Phone: (612)617-5800 **Fax:** (612)623-9070
URL: http://www.vikingmaterials.com
Products: Carbon sheet and coil. **SIC:** 5051 (Metals Service Centers & Offices). **Est:** 1973. **Sales:** $80,000,000 (2000). **Emp:** 105. **Officers:** Allen Applegate, President; Doug Lilyquist, CFO.

■ 20473 ■ Vincent Metal Goods
455 85th Ave. NW
Minneapolis, MN 55433
Phone: (612)717-9000 **Fax:** (612)717-7168
URL: http://www.vincentmetalgoods.com
Products: Metals. **SIC:** 5051 (Metals Service Centers & Offices). **Est:** 1936. **Sales:** $560,000,000 (2000). **Emp:** 900. **Officers:** Harrison P. Jones, President & CEO; Mike Goldberg, Exec. VP & COO; Dave Cagle, CFO; Thomas J. O'Hara, Sr. VP of Sales & Marketing; Mike Pionk, Information Systems Mgr.; John Oldendorf, Human Resources Mgr.

■ 20474 ■ Vitco Steel Supply Corp.
PO Box 220
Posen, IL 60469
Phone: (708)388-8300 **Fax:** (708)385-2645
Products: Cut steel. **SIC:** 5051 (Metals Service Centers & Offices). **Est:** 1971. **Sales:** $12,000,000 (2000). **Emp:** 20. **Officers:** Dominic Vitucci Sr., President; William M. Vitucci, Treasurer; Dominic Vitucci Jr., Vice President.

■ 20475 ■ Nicholas Vitto Sheet Metal Inc.
3426 Burnet Ave.
Syracuse, NY 13206
Phone: (315)463-5550
Products: Sheet metal. **SIC:** 5051 (Metals Service Centers & Offices). **Est:** 1951. **Sales:** $500,000 (2000). **Emp:** 6. **Officers:** Nicholas Vitto Sr., President.

■ 20476 ■ Vorberger Group Ltd.
409 Broad St.
Sewickley, PA 15143
Phone: (412)741-1634 **Fax:** (412)741-1980
Products: Metals, including base metals, nickel, and aluminum. **SIC:** 5051 (Metals Service Centers & Offices). **Est:** 1984. **Sales:** $100,000,000 (2000). **Emp:** 5. **Officers:** John Vorberger, President; Keith W. Koebley, Controller.

■ 20477 ■ Waco Inc.
PO Box 836
Sandston, VA 23150-0836
Phone: (804)222-8440
Products: Sheet metal; Adhesive products. **SICs:** 5039 (Construction Materials Nec); 5169 (Chemicals & Allied Products Nec). **Est:** 1963. **Sales:** $35,000,000 (2000). **Emp:** 500. **Officers:** Daniel Walker, President; James Foegoe, Treasurer & Secty.; Dan Hemp, Dir. of Marketing.

■ 20478 ■ Ward Manufacturing Inc.
115 Gulick St.
Blossburg, PA 16912
Phone: (717)638-2131
Products: Stainless steel tubing. **SIC:** 5051 (Metals Service Centers & Offices). **Sales:** $57,000,000 (1992).

Emp: 700. **Officers:** Doyne Chartran, COO; David Smith, CFO.

■ 20479 ■ **Waukegan Steel Sales Inc.**
1201 Belvidere Rd.
Waukegan, IL 60085
Phone: (847)662-2810   **Fax:** (847)662-2818
Products: Aluminum and stainless steel; Structural steel and miscellaneous metals. **SIC:** 5051 (Metals Service Centers & Offices). **Est:** 1929. **Sales:** $13,477,017 (2000). **Emp:** 60. **Officers:** C.A. Kropp, Chairman of the Board; L. Simmons, CFO; Donald Robison, President; Wayne Griesbaum, VP of Operations; Mike Engels, Dir. of Data Processing; Jeff Goldewski, Customer Service Contact.

■ 20480 ■ **Waukegan Steel Sales Inc.**
1201 Belvidere Rd.
Waukegan, IL 60085
Phone: (847)662-2810   **Fax:** (847)662-2818
Products: Metals. **SIC:** 5051 (Metals Service Centers & Offices). **Sales:** $1,200,000 (2000). **Emp:** 60.

■ 20481 ■ **Wayne Steel Co.**
PO Box 460
Elizabeth, NJ 07207
Phone: (908)354-7300   **Fax:** (908)354-9187
Products: Cold-rolled carbon steel bars, sheets, and strips. **SIC:** 5051 (Metals Service Centers & Offices). **Sales:** $20,000,000 (1994). **Emp:** 60. **Officers:** Robert W. Hagelin, President; Evelyn Mossey, Treasurer.

■ 20482 ■ **Wayne Steel Co., Ray H. Morris Div.**
30 Precision Ct.
New Britain, CT 06051
Phone: (860)224-2678
Free: (800)243-0662   **Fax:** 800-628-5176
E-mail: info@rhmorris.com
URL: http://www.rhmorris.com
Products: Steel. **SIC:** 5051 (Metals Service Centers & Offices). **Est:** 1954. **Emp:** 25. **Officers:** Robert W. Hagelin, President, e-mail: bobh@rhmorris.com.

■ 20483 ■ **Weiner Steel Corp.**
8200 E Slauson Ave.
Pico Rivera, CA 90660-4321
Phone: (213)723-8327   **Fax:** (213)726-1988
Products: Steel recyclers. **SIC:** 5093 (Scrap & Waste Materials). **Sales:** $75,000,000 (1992). **Emp:** 200. **Officers:** Herman L. Weiner, President.

■ 20484 ■ **Henry Weingartner Company Inc.**
111 Brook St.
Scarsdale, NY 10583
Phone: (914)472-6464   **Fax:** (914)472-1846
Products: Metals and chemical products. **SICs:** 5051 (Metals Service Centers & Offices); 5169 (Chemicals & Allied Products Nec). **Sales:** $4,000,000 (2000). **Emp:** 5. **Officers:** Henry Weingartner, President; Marilyn Weingartner, CFO.

■ 20485 ■ **Welded Products Inc.**
1030 N Merrifield
Mishawaka, IN 46545
Phone: (219)255-9689   **Fax:** (219)256-1885
Products: Fabricated steel plate (stacks and weldments). **SIC:** 5051 (Metals Service Centers & Offices). **Sales:** $1,500,000 (2000). **Emp:** 25. **Officers:** Jack E. Coleman, President; Roger L. Coleman, Vice President.

■ 20486 ■ **Weldtube Inc.**
5000 Stecker Ave.
Dearborn, MI 48126
Phone: (313)584-6500   **Fax:** (313)584-6250
Products: Square and rectangular structural steel tubing. **SIC:** 5051 (Metals Service Centers & Offices). **Est:** 1964. **Sales:** $6,000,000 (2000). **Emp:** 24. **Officers:** Kenneth Di Laura, CEO; Carole Campbell, Controller; Kathy Miller, Sales & Marketing Contact.

■ 20487 ■ **Wesco Financial Corp.**
301 E Colorado Blvd., Ste. 300
Pasadena, CA 91101-1901
Phone: (626)585-6700
Products: Steel. **SIC:** 5051 (Metals Service Centers &

Offices). **Sales:** $2,588,100,000 (2000). **Emp:** 271. **Officers:** Robert H. Bird, President; Jeffrey L. Jacobson, VP & CFO.

■ 20488 ■ **West Central Steel Inc.**
PO Box 1178
Willmar, MN 56201
Phone: (612)235-4070   **Fax:** (612)235-4070
Products: Steel. **SIC:** 5051 (Metals Service Centers & Offices). **Est:** 1949. **Sales:** $81,000,000 (2000). **Emp:** 130. **Officers:** Orvis Pattison, President; Jeff Pattison, Treasurer; Jeff Allinder, Dir. of Marketing.

■ 20489 ■ **West Coast Wire and Steel**
1027 Palmyrita Ave.
Riverside, CA 92507-1701
Phone: (909)683-7252
Free: (800)428-4977   **Fax:** (909)275-0113
Products: Flat steel; Welded wire; Roof panels. **SIC:** 5051 (Metals Service Centers & Offices). **Est:** 1913. **Sales:** $10,000,000 (2000). **Emp:** 45. **Officers:** William C. Stalberger, President.

■ 20490 ■ **Western Flat Rolled Steel**
141 S Western Coil Rd.
Lindon, UT 84042
Phone: (801)785-8600   **Fax:** (801)785-8627
Products: Steel service center; slit steel; distributes steel; steel tubing. **SIC:** 5051 (Metals Service Centers & Offices). **Officers:** George Schaeffer, CEO & President; Daniel Goodsell, CFO.

■ 20491 ■ **Wilkof Morris Steel Corp.**
PO Box 3095
North Canton, OH 44720
Phone: (330)456-3401   **Fax:** (330)456-3409
Products: Steel. **SIC:** 5051 (Metals Service Centers & Offices). **Est:** 1937. **Sales:** $31,000,000 (2000). **Emp:** 50. **Officers:** Todd Wilkof, President; Nancy Welch, Comptroller.

■ 20492 ■ **Williams and Company Inc.**
901 Pennsylvania Ave.
Pittsburgh, PA 15233
Phone: (412)237-2211   **Fax:** (412)237-3727
Products: Metal. **SIC:** 5051 (Metals Service Centers & Offices). **Est:** 1907. **Sales:** $140,000,000 (2000). **Emp:** 600. **Officers:** Roger Gaillard, CEO & President; Scott Schaffner, VP of Finance; Richard Finley, VP of Marketing & Sales; Frank W. Miller, Dir. of Information Systems; Hugh Beswick, Dir of Human Resources.

■ 20493 ■ **Williams Steel and Supply Company Inc.**
999 W Armour Ave.
Milwaukee, WI 53221
Phone: (414)481-7100
Products: Steel. **SIC:** 5051 (Metals Service Centers & Offices). **Est:** 1944. **Sales:** $20,000,000 (2000). **Emp:** 60. **Officers:** Lester G. Peterson, President.

■ 20494 ■ **Willis Steel Corp.**
PO Drawer 149
Galesburg, IL 61401
Phone: (309)342-0135   **Fax:** (309)342-0136
E-mail: info@willissteel.com
URL: http://www.willissteel.com
Products: Heating sheet metal. **SICs:** 5051 (Metals Service Centers & Offices); 5031 (Lumber, Plywood & Millwork). **Est:** 1891. **Sales:** $600,000 (2000). **Emp:** 3. **Officers:** M.J. Near, President, e-mail: willissteel@misslink.net; Robert B. Near, Vice President, e-mail: rbnear@willissteel.com.

■ 20495 ■ **Winograd's Steel and Supply**
PO Box 1765
Greeley, CO 80632-1765
Phone: (970)352-6722   **Fax:** (970)352-8745
E-mail: winograd@cros.com
Products: Steel and steel supplies, including steel beams and flat core valves. **SICs:** 5051 (Metals Service Centers & Offices); 5085 (Industrial Supplies). **Est:** 1917. **Sales:** $20,000,000 (2000). **Emp:** 80. **Officers:** Ronald Wildeman, General Mgr.; Roger Belleau, Controller; C. Deckard, Sales Mgr. **Alternate Name:** WINOCO Inc.

■ 20496 ■ **Winter Wolff Inc.**
131 Jericho Tpk.
Jericho, NY 11753
Phone: (516)997-3300   **Fax:** (516)997-3016
Products: Aluminum foil. **SIC:** 5051 (Metals Centers & Offices). **Est:** 1926. **Sales:** $17,500,000 (2000). **Emp:** 10. **Officers:** F. Weil, President.

■ 20497 ■ **Wisconsin Steel and Tube Corp.**
PO Box 26365
Milwaukee, WI 53226
Phone: (414)453-4441   **Fax:** (414)453-0789
Products: Steel. **SIC:** 5051 (Metals Service Centers & Offices). **Sales:** $20,000,000 (1992). **Emp:** 45. **Officers:** Mike Poelman, President; R.B. Kappel, VP of Finance.

■ 20498 ■ **Wolverine Metal Company Inc.**
21870 Hoover Rd.
Warren, MI 48089
Phone: (734)758-6100
Products: Stainless steel. **SIC:** 5051 (Metals Service Centers & Offices).

■ 20499 ■ **Worthington Industries Inc.**
1205 Dearborn Dr.
Columbus, OH 43085
Phone: (614)438-3210   **Fax:** (614)438-7948
Products: Steel service center: steel processing, slitting, cold rolling and strip. **SIC:** 5051 (Metals Service Centers & Offices). **Sales:** $1,763,000,000 (1999). **Emp:** 7,500. **Officers:** John P. McConnell, CEO & Chairman of the Board; John Baldwin, VP & CFO.

■ 20500 ■ **Worthington Steel Co.**
1127 Dearborn Dr.
Columbus, OH 43085
Phone: (614)438-3205   **Fax:** (614)438-7380
Products: Steel service center: steel processing, slitting, cold rolling and strip. **SIC:** 5051 (Metals Service Centers & Offices). **Sales:** $254,000,000 (2000). **Emp:** 1,000. **Officers:** Ralph Roberts, President.

■ 20501 ■ **Yaffe Iron and Metal Company Inc.**
PO Box 916
Muskogee, OK 74401
Phone: (918)687-7543
Products: Iron and metal. **SICs:** 5093 (Scrap & Waste Materials); 5051 (Metals Service Centers & Offices). **Est:** 1961. **Sales:** $50,000,000 (2000). **Emp:** 400. **Officers:** Robert Yaffe, President.

■ 20502 ■ **Yarde Metals Inc.**
71 Horizon Dr.
Bristol, CT 06010
Phone: (860)589-2386   **Fax:** (860)584-0670
Products: Metals service center: metal slitting, cutting and shearing. **SIC:** 5051 (Metals Service Centers & Offices). **Officers:** Jack Nicklis, CFO.

■ 20503 ■ **Yen Enterprises Inc.**
1360 W 9th St.
Cleveland, OH 44113-1254
Phone: (216)621-5115   **Fax:** (216)621-0557
Products: Stamping metal; Metalworking machinery; Carbon steel castings. **SICs:** 5051 (Metals Service Centers & Offices); 5084 (Industrial Machinery & Equipment). **Officers:** David Yen, Director.

■ 20504 ■ **Young Steel Products Co.**
17819 Foxborough Ln.
Boca Raton, FL 33496
Phone: (330)759-3911   **Fax:** (330)759-3914
Products: Steel products, including flat rolled, galvanized, galvalume and aluminized. **SIC:** 5051 (Metals Service Centers & Offices). **Est:** 1950. **Sales:** $6,000,000 (2000). **Emp:** 3. **Officers:** M.A. Young, CEO & President; B.S. Young, CFO.

■ 20505 ■ **Zuckerman, Charles and Son Inc.**
PO Box 2037
Winchester, VA 22604
Phone: (540)667-9000   **Fax:** (540)665-2979
Products: Steel service center: cutting, shearing, and braking. **SIC:** 5051 (Metals Service Centers & Offices). **Officers:** Dave Brill, Director.

(36) Minerals and Ores

Entries in this section are arranged alphabetically by company name. When the company name is a personal name, the company name is alphabetized by the surname unless the first name or initial(s) are part of a trade name. See the User's Guide at the front of this directory for additional information.

■ 20506 ■ **Addwest Mining, Inc.**
313 Frederica St.
Owensboro, KY 42301
Phone: (502)684-2490 **Fax:** (502)684-0363
Products: Coal. **SIC:** 5052 (Coal, Other Minerals & Ores).

■ 20507 ■ **AJ Coal Co.**
PO Box 387
Meriden, CT 06450-0387
Phone: (203)235-6358 **Fax:** (203)630-1471
Products: Coal. **SIC:** 5052 (Coal, Other Minerals & Ores).

■ 20508 ■ **Alabama Coal Cooperative**
2870 Old Rocky Ridge Dr.
Birmingham, AL 35243
Phone: (205)979-5963
Products: Coal. **SIC:** 5052 (Coal, Other Minerals & Ores). **Sales:** $45,000,000 (2000). **Emp:** 450. **Officers:** Randy C. Johnson, General Mgr.

■ 20509 ■ **Allegheny Mining Corp.**
321 N Jefferson St.
Lewisburg, WV 24901-1116
Phone: (304)693-7621 **Fax:** (304)693-7743
Products: Coal. **SIC:** 5052 (Coal, Other Minerals & Ores).

■ 20510 ■ **Alley-Cassetty Coal Co.**
PO Box 23305
Nashville, TN 37202
Phone: (615)244-7077 **Fax:** (615)254-4280
Products: Coal; Brick; Roofing; Block; Truck sales and service. **SICs:** 5052 (Coal, Other Minerals & Ores); 5032 (Brick, Stone & Related Materials); 5033 (Roofing, Siding & Insulation). **Est:** 1964. **Sales:** $70,000,000 (2000). **Emp:** 200. **Officers:** Fred Cassetty, President; Jimmy Alley, Vice President; Randy West, Sec. & Treas.; Jeff Oliver, VP of Operations; Chester Schmidt, Sales/Marketing Contact. **Alternate Name:** Alley-Cassetty-Building Supplies. **Alternate Name:** Custom Truck Sales and Service.

■ 20511 ■ **Ambrose Branch Coal Co. Inc.**
PO Box 806
Pound, VA 24279
Phone: (540)796-4941 **Fax:** (540)796-4977
Products: Coal. **SIC:** 5052 (Coal, Other Minerals & Ores).

■ 20512 ■ **American Carbon Corporation**
PO Box 837
Grundy, VA 24614
Phone: (540)531-8626
Products: Coal. **SIC:** 5052 (Coal, Other Minerals & Ores).

■ 20513 ■ **American Resources Inc.**
PO Box 592
Evansville, IN 47704
Phone: (812)424-9000 **Fax:** (812)424-6551
Products: Coal. **SIC:** 5052 (Coal, Other Minerals & Ores). **Est:** 1975. **Sales:** $153,000,000 (2000). **Emp:** 500. **Officers:** Steven E. Chancellor, CEO; Daniel S. Hermann, Exec. VP of Finance.

■ 20514 ■ **Amvest Coal Sales Inc.**
PO Box 5347
Charlottesville, VA 22905
Phone: (804)977-3350 **Fax:** (804)295-3203
Products: Coal. **SIC:** 5052 (Coal, Other Minerals & Ores). **Sales:** $5,000,000 (1994). **Emp:** 10. **Officers:** William H. Dickey Jr., President.

■ 20515 ■ **Andalex Resources, Inc.**
PO Box 902
Price, UT 84501
Phone: (435)637-5385 **Fax:** (435)637-8860
Products: Coal. **SIC:** 5052 (Coal, Other Minerals & Ores).

■ 20516 ■ **Anker Energy Corp.**
2708 Cranberry Sq.
Morgantown, WV 26505
Phone: (304)594-1616 **Fax:** (304)594-3695
Products: Coal. **SIC:** 5052 (Coal, Other Minerals & Ores). **Sales:** $240,000,000 (2000). **Emp:** 60. **Officers:** Bruce Sparks, President.

■ 20517 ■ **ANR Coal Company L.L.C.**
PO Box 1871
Roanoke, VA 24008-1871
Phone: (540)983-0222 **Fax:** (540)983-0267
Products: Coal. **SIC:** 5052 (Coal, Other Minerals & Ores). **Sales:** $854,000,000 (2000). **Emp:** 800. **Officers:** James Van Lanen, President.

■ 20518 ■ **Anthony Mining, Inc.**
State Rt. 43
Richmond, OH 43944
Phone: (740)765-4185 **Fax:** (740)765-4777
Products: Coal products. **SIC:** 5052 (Coal, Other Minerals & Ores).

■ 20519 ■ **Arch Coal Sales Company Inc.**
City Place 1, Ste. 300
St. Louis, MO 63141
Phone: (314)994-2700
Free: (800)238-7398 **Fax:** (314)994-2719
E-mail: postmaster@archcoal.com
URL: http://www.archcoal.com
Products: Coal. **SIC:** 5052 (Coal, Other Minerals & Ores). **Est:** 1997. **Sales:** $1,500,000,000 (2000). **Emp:** 28. **Officers:** John Eaves, President.

■ 20520 ■ **Arch of West Virginia Inc.**
PO Box 156
Yolyn, WV 25654-0156
Phone: (304)792-8200 **Fax:** (304)792-8250
Products: Coal. **SIC:** 5052 (Coal, Other Minerals & Ores).

■ 20521 ■ **Bitor America Corp.**
5200 Town Center Cir., Ste. 301
Boca Raton, FL 33486
Phone: (561)392-0026 **Fax:** (561)392-0490
URL: http://www.orimulsionfuel.com
Products: Orimulsion for power generation. **SIC:** 5052 (Coal, Other Minerals & Ores). **Est:** 1989. **Sales:** $35,000,000 (2000). **Emp:** 6. **Officers:** Nelson Garcia-Tavel, VP of Operations & Environmental Affairs;

Eduardo Hernandez-Carstens, VP of Marketing & Sales, e-mail: hernandeze@pdvsa.com.

■ 20522 ■ **Black Beauty Coal Co.**
PO Box 312
Evansville, IN 47702
Phone: (812)424-9000 **Fax:** (812)424-6551
Products: Coal. **SIC:** 5052 (Coal, Other Minerals & Ores). **Est:** 1974. **Sales:** $350,000,000 (2000). **Emp:** 1,000. **Officers:** Steve Chancellor, CEO; Daniel S. Hermann, President; Gene Almone, Sr. VP of Marketing.

■ 20523 ■ **Black Gold Sales Inc.**
PO Box 1097
Hazard, KY 41701
Phone: (606)439-4559
Products: Coal. **SIC:** 5052 (Coal, Other Minerals & Ores).

■ 20524 ■ **The Bradenton Financial Ctr.**
1401 Manatee Ave. W, Ste 520
Bradenton, FL 34205
Phone: (941)747-2630 **Fax:** (941)747-8081
E-mail: fjm@energyweb.com
URL: http://www.energyweb.com
Products: Coal. **SIC:** 5052 (Coal, Other Minerals & Ores). **Est:** 1987. **Emp:** 3. **Officers:** Frederick J. Murrell, President; Anita E. Lambert, Vice President; Anita E. Lambert, Sales/Marketing Contact. **Alternate Name:** Adaro Envirocoal Americas. **Alternate Name:** Carbon Resources of Florida. **Former Name:** Phoenix Coal Sales of Florida Inc.

■ 20525 ■ **C/C Chemical and Coal Co.**
2321 Fortune Dr.
Lexington, KY 40505
Phone: (606)299-0026
Products: Coal. **SIC:** 5052 (Coal, Other Minerals & Ores). **Sales:** $100,000 (2000). **Emp:** 3. **Officers:** Don Cain, President.

■ 20526 ■ **Caemi International Inc.**
100 1st Stamford Pl.
Stamford, CT 06902-6732
Phone: (203)969-1442 **Fax:** (203)358-8281
Products: Iron ore. **SIC:** 5052 (Coal, Other Minerals & Ores). **Sales:** $10,000,000 (2000). **Emp:** 17. **Officers:** James Ramming, President; Syng Paik, Controller; Morgan M. Wynkoop Jr., Vice President.

■ 20527 ■ **Candlewax Smokeless Fuel Company Inc.**
PO Box 29
Tazewell, VA 24651
Phone: (540)988-2591
Products: Coal. **SIC:** 5052 (Coal, Other Minerals & Ores). **Est:** 1947. **Sales:** $3,000,000 (2000). **Emp:** 4. **Officers:** Claude H. Van Dyke, President.

■ 20528 ■ **Carbon Resources of Florida**
1111 Third Ave. W, Ste. 140
Bradenton, FL 34205
Phone: (941)747-2630 **Fax:** (941)747-8081
Products: Minerals and ores. **SIC:** 5052 (Coal, Other Minerals & Ores).

■ **20529** ■ **Coal Bunkers**
270 Illinois St.
Fairbanks, AK 99701
Phone: (907)456-5005 **Fax:** (907)451-6188
Products: Coal. **SIC:** 5052 (Coal, Other Minerals & Ores).

■ **20530** ■ **Coal Hill Mining Co.**
405 Virginia Ave.
Pittsburgh, PA 15215
Phone: (412)782-1814 **Fax:** (412)782-1869
Products: Coal. **SIC:** 5052 (Coal, Other Minerals & Ores). **Est:** 1921. **Sales:** $15,000,000 (2000). **Emp:** 3. **Officers:** Lex R. Winans, Owner, e-mail: lex@sgi.net.

■ **20531** ■ **CoalARBED International Trading Co.**
210 E Lombard St.
Baltimore, MD 21202
Phone: (410)727-4600
Products: Coal. **SIC:** 5052 (Coal, Other Minerals & Ores).

■ **20532** ■ **Coors Energy Co.**
PO Box 467
Golden, CO 80402
Phone: (303)277-6042
Products: Coal; Oil and natural gas. **SICs:** 5052 (Coal, Other Minerals & Ores); 5171 (Petroleum Bulk Stations & Terminals). **Sales:** $1,000,000 (2000). **Emp:** 7. **Officers:** Donald W. MacDonald, Operations Mgr.

■ **20533** ■ **D.J. Enterprises, Inc.**
PO Box 31366
Cleveland, OH 44131
Phone: (216)524-3879
Products: Ground or treated minerals; Industrial foundry equipment; Non-clay refractories; Industrial inorganic chemicals. **SICs:** 5052 (Coal, Other Minerals & Ores); 5169 (Chemicals & Allied Products Nec); 5084 (Industrial Machinery & Equipment). **Officers:** Donald J. Shuki, President.

■ **20534** ■ **Downing Coal Co.**
13 Pepperwood Ln.
Cleveland, OH 44124-4701
Phone: (216)831-6750
Products: Coal. **SIC:** 5052 (Coal, Other Minerals & Ores). **Sales:** $6,000,000 (2000). **Emp:** 3. **Officers:** Thurman Downing, President & Treasurer.

■ **20535** ■ **Draper Energy Co. Inc.**
PO Box 419
Wilton, NH 03086-0419
Phone: (603)654-6400
Products: Coal; Coke; Minerals and earths; Metallic ores. **SIC:** 5052 (Coal, Other Minerals & Ores). **Officers:** Stuart Draper, President.

■ **20536** ■ **DuCoa**
115 Executive Dr.
Highland, IL 62249
Phone: (618)654-2070 **Fax:** (618)654-1818
E-mail: DuCoa@DuCoa.com
URL: http://www.ducoa.com
Products: Mineral mixes and base mixes, including mold inhibitors, antioxidants, vitamin premixes, and others. **SIC:** 5122 (Drugs, Proprietaries & Sundries). **Emp:** 320. **Officers:** Dan Rose, President; Dean Barker, President of Nutrition & Blending; Ike Isaacson, VP of Sales. **Former Name:** DuCoa-Technical Products Group.

■ **20537** ■ **Electric Fuels Corp.**
PO Box 15208
St. Petersburg, FL 33733
Phone: (727)824-6600 **Fax:** (727)824-6601
Products: Coal and minerals. **SIC:** 5052 (Coal, Other Minerals & Ores). **Est:** 1976. **Sales:** $643,000,000 (2000). **Emp:** 1,400. **Officers:** Richard D. Keller, CEO & President; Samuel Hopkins II, Controller.

■ **20538** ■ **Emerald International Corp.**
7310 Turfway Rd., No. 330
Florence, KY 41042
Phone: (606)525-2522 **Fax:** (606)525-4052
Products: Minerals. **SIC:** 5052 (Coal, Other Minerals & Ores). **Est:** 1991. **Sales:** $26,000,000 (2000). **Emp:** 6.

Officers: Jack J. Wells Jr., Partner; Aidan C. Bowles, Partner; Micheal E. Allen, Dir. of Marketing & Sales.

■ **20539** ■ **Energy Group P.L.C.**
701 Market St., Ste. 750
St. Louis, MO 63101
Phone: (314)342-7590
Products: I. **SIC:** 5052 (Coal, Other Minerals & Ores). **Officers:** Derek Bonham, Chairman of the Board; Eric Anstee, Finance Officer.

■ **20540** ■ **Farmers Investment Company Inc.**
PO Box 316
Horse Cave, KY 42749
Phone: (502)786-2124 **Fax:** (502)786-2120
Products: Coal. **SIC:** 5052 (Coal, Other Minerals & Ores). **Est:** 1961. **Sales:** $45,000,000 (2000). **Emp:** 300. **Officers:** James K. Bale, President.

■ **20541** ■ **Foreign Exchange Ltd.**
429 Stockton St.
San Francisco, CA 94108
Phone: (415)677-5100
Free: (800)274-1108 **Fax:** (415)788-8834
URL: http://www.forexUSA.com
Products: Foreign currencies; Foreign and domestic travelers checks; Wire and draft funds transfer. **SIC:** 5094 (Jewelry & Precious Stones). **Est:** 1958. **Sales:** $11,000,000 (2000). **Emp:** 4. **Officers:** Stephanie Gouw, Manager.

■ **20542** ■ **Gassmon Coal and Oil Company Inc.**
Bronx Pl. & E 132nd St.
Bronx, NY 10454
Phone: (212)369-7700
Products: Coal and oil. **SICs:** 5052 (Coal, Other Minerals & Ores); 5172 (Petroleum Products Nec).

■ **20543** ■ **Gulf Reduction Div.**
PO Box 611
Houston, TX 77001
Phone: (713)926-1705
Products: Zinc dust; Oxide; Scrap metal. **SICs:** 5051 (Metals Service Centers & Offices); 5093 (Scrap & Waste Materials). **Est:** 1951. **Sales:** $7,000,000 (2000). **Emp:** 80. **Officers:** Howard Robinson, President; Edwin Schlotzhauer, VP of Marketing & Sales; Carl Lenz, Dir. of Data Processing; Steve Brown, Vice President.

■ **20544** ■ **Hammill and Gillespie Inc.**
PO Box 104
Livingston, NJ 07039
Phone: (201)994-3650
Free: (800)454-8846 **Fax:** (201)994-3847
E-mail: hamgilinc@aol.com
URL: http://www.hamgil.com
Products: Clay and minerals. **SIC:** 5052 (Coal, Other Minerals & Ores). **Est:** 1848. **Sales:** $3,000,000 (2000). **Emp:** 8. **Officers:** Patricia B. Isaacs, President; Dorna L. Isaacs, Vice President.

■ **20545** ■ **Hill and Griffith Co.**
1262 State Ave.
Cincinnati, OH 45204
Phone: (513)921-1075 **Fax:** (513)244-4199
Products: Coal; Liquid partings; Bentonites; Foundry supplies. **SICs:** 5052 (Coal, Other Minerals & Ores); 5082 (Construction & Mining Machinery); 5051 (Metals Service Centers & Offices). **Est:** 1896. **Sales:** $28,000,000 (2000). **Emp:** 150. **Officers:** Gary Follmer, VP of Finance; Rolland Tibbits, VP of Marketing & Sales; Shirley Mote, Personnel Mgr.; David N. Greek, CEO & President.

■ **20546** ■ **Holmes Limestone Co.**
PO Box 295
Berlin, OH 44610
Phone: (216)893-2721
Products: Coal. **SICs:** 5052 (Coal, Other Minerals & Ores); 5032 (Brick, Stone & Related Materials). **Sales:** $80,000,000 (2000). **Emp:** 100. **Officers:** Merle Mulet, President.

■ **20547** ■ **Horsehead Resource Development Company Inc.**
110 East 59th St.
New York, NY 10022
Phone: (212)527-3003 **Fax:** (212)826-8911
Products: Zinc oxide; Iron material for cement making. **SICs:** 5093 (Scrap & Waste Materials); 5051 (Metals Service Centers & Offices). **Est:** 1986. **Sales:** $98,200,000 (2000). **Officers:** William M. Quirk, CEO & President; William A. Smelas, Exec. VP; Daniel R. Brenden, VP of Human Resources.

■ **20548** ■ **James River Coal Sales, Inc.**
701 E Byrd St., Ste. 1100
Richmond, VA 23219
Phone: (804)780-3003 **Fax:** (804)649-9319
Products: Coal. **SIC:** 5052 (Coal, Other Minerals & Ores). **Sales:** $80,000,000 (2000). **Emp:** 14. **Officers:** John R. Pellmann, President; W.R. Beasley, Sr. VP; Mark W. Dooley, Vice President; Ken C. Eastwood, Sales Mgr.

■ **20549** ■ **Kiewit Mining Group, Inc.**
1000 Kiewit Plaza
Omaha, NE 68131
Phone: (402)342-2052 **Fax:** (402)271-2908
Products: Coal. **SIC:** 5052 (Coal, Other Minerals & Ores). **Est:** 1884. **Sales:** $200,000,000 (2000). **Emp:** 500. **Officers:** Chris Murphy, President; Linden S. Swensen, Marketing/Sales Contact, e-mail: linden.swensen@kiewit.com. **Former Name:** Rosebud Coal Sales Co.

■ **20550** ■ **Elmer Kincaid Coal Co. Inc.**
Off Hwy. 25 E
Thorn Hill, TN 37881
Phone: (423)767-2600 **Fax:** (423)767-2045
Products: Coal. **SIC:** 5052 (Coal, Other Minerals & Ores). **Est:** 1947. **Sales:** $5,000,000 (2000). **Emp:** 13. **Officers:** E. Kincaid Sr., President.

■ **20551** ■ **Lakeland Sand and Gravel Inc.**
PO Box 137
Hartstown, PA 16131
Phone: (814)382-8178
Products: Sand and gravel. **SIC:** 5032 (Brick, Stone & Related Materials).

■ **20552** ■ **A.T. Massey Coal Company Inc.**
PO Box 26765
Richmond, VA 23261
Phone: (804)788-1800
Products: Coal. **SIC:** 5052 (Coal, Other Minerals & Ores). **Est:** 1916. **Sales:** $850,000,000 (1999). **Emp:** 2,000. **Officers:** Don L. Blankenship, CEO & Chairman of the Board; Bennett K. Hatfield, Exec. VP & COO.

■ **20553** ■ **J.S. McCormick Co.**
650 Smiriges St., Ste. 1050
Pittsburgh, PA 15222-3907
Phone: (412)471-7246 **Fax:** (412)471-7247
Products: Foundry coatings and binders; Industrial carbons; Refractories; Trough blackings; Sand additives. **SICs:** 5052 (Coal, Other Minerals & Ores); 5085 (Industrial Supplies). **Est:** 1989. **Sales:** $8,000,000 (2000). **Emp:** 50. **Officers:** J.B. Snyder, President; L. J. Spernak, Exec. VP of Operations, e-mail: lspernak@jsmccormick.com; R. W. Dorves, Operations Mgr.

■ **20554** ■ **Northmont Sand and Gravel Co.**
PO Box 185
Englewood, OH 45322
Phone: (937)836-1998
Products: Sand and gravel. **SIC:** 5032 (Brick, Stone & Related Materials).

■ **20555** ■ **Oremco Inc.**
261 Madison Ave.
New York, NY 10016
Phone: (212)867-4400
Products: Coal; Machinery. **SICs:** 5052 (Coal, Other Minerals & Ores); 5084 (Industrial Machinery & Equipment). **Est:** 1971. **Sales:** $6,000,000 (2000). **Emp:** 10. **Officers:** R.J. Hiemstra, President; Gary Schachen, Controller.

■ 20556 ■ **Oxbow Carbon International Inc.**
1601 Forum Pl.
West Palm Beach, FL 33401
Phone: (561)697-4300
Products: Solid fuel. **SIC:** 5052 (Coal, Other Minerals & Ores). **Sales:** $8,000,000 (2000). **Emp:** 10. **Officers:** William Koch, President.

■ 20557 ■ **Peabody COALSALES Co.**
701 Market St.
St. Louis, MO 63101-1826
Phone: (314)342-7600 **Fax:** (314)342-7609
E-mail: publicrelations@peabodygroup.com
URL: http://www.peabodygroup.com
Products: Coal. **SIC:** 5052 (Coal, Other Minerals & Ores). **Est:** 1983. **Sales:** $2,610,991,000 (2000). **Emp:** 57. **Officers:** Paul J. Vining, President.

■ 20558 ■ **Peabody Group**
701 Market St.
St. Louis, MO 63101-1826
Phone: (314)342-3400 **Fax:** (314)342-7799
E-mail: publicrelations@peabodygroup.com
URL: http://www.peabodygroup.com
Products: Coal. **SIC:** 5052 (Coal, Other Minerals & Ores). **Est:** 1997. **Sales:** $2,610,991,000 (1999). **Emp:** 7,200. **Officers:** Irl F. Engelhardt, CEO & Chairman of the Board, e-mail: iengelha@peabodygroup.com; Richard M. Whiting, President & COO, e-mail: rwhiting@peabodygroup.com; Richard A. Navarre, CFO, e-mail: rnavarre@peabodygroup.com.

■ 20559 ■ **People's Coal Co.**
75 Mill St.
Cumberland, RI 02864
Phone: (401)725-2700 **Fax:** (401)421-5120
Products: Coal products; Grilling supplies. **SICs:** 5052 (Coal, Other Minerals & Ores); 5199 (Nondurable Goods Nec).

■ 20560 ■ **Prospect Energy Inc.**
PO Box 112
Mt. Sterling, IL 62353
Phone: (217)773-3969
Products: Coal. **SIC:** 5052 (Coal, Other Minerals & Ores). **Est:** 1989. **Sales:** $800,000 (2000). **Emp:** 2. **Officers:** Dave Clinard, President.

■ 20561 ■ **C. Reiss Coal Co.**
PO Box 688
Sheboygan, WI 53082-0688
Phone: (920)457-4411
Products: Coal. **SIC:** 5052 (Coal, Other Minerals &

Ores). **Est:** 1880. **Sales:** $90,000,000 (2000). **Emp:** 21. **Officers:** William Reiss, President; Dan Legge, Controller.

■ 20562 ■ **Ring's Coal Co.**
51 Main St.
Yarmouth, ME 04096
Phone: (207)846-5503
Products: Coal. **SIC:** 5052 (Coal, Other Minerals & Ores).

■ 20563 ■ **River Trading Co.**
3300 Bass Lake Rd., No. 220
Brooklyn Center, MN 55429
Phone: (612)561-9206
Products: Coal. **SIC:** 5052 (Coal, Other Minerals & Ores). **Sales:** $11,000,000 (2000). **Emp:** 14. **Officers:** Tom Conlan, President.

■ 20564 ■ **Riverton Coal Co.**
1520 Kanawha Blvd.
Charleston, WV 25311
Phone: (304)739-4136
Products: Coal. **SIC:** 5032 (Brick, Stone & Related Materials). **Sales:** $20,000,000 (1993). **Emp:** 34. **Officers:** Steve Issacs, Vice President.

■ 20565 ■ **Royal Fuel Co.**
PO Drawer 517
Oneida, TN 37841
Phone: (423)569-8900
Products: Coal. **SIC:** 5052 (Coal, Other Minerals & Ores).

■ 20566 ■ **H.M. Royal Inc.**
PO Box 28
Trenton, NJ 08601
Phone: (609)396-9176 **Fax:** (609)396-3185
Products: Processed minerals. **SIC:** 5052 (Coal, Other Minerals & Ores). **Sales:** $80,000,000 (1999). **Emp:** 40. **Officers:** Toms B. Royal, President.

■ 20567 ■ **Samuel-Whittar Inc.**
20001 Sherwood Ave.
Detroit, MI 48234
Phone: (313)893-5000 **Fax:** (313)893-8422
Products: Carbon. **SIC:** 5052 (Coal, Other Minerals & Ores).

■ 20568 ■ **Smoky Mountain Coal Corp.**
9040 Executive Park Dr.
Knoxville, TN 37923
Phone: (423)694-8222
Products: Coal. **SIC:** 5052 (Coal, Other Minerals &

Ores). **Est:** 1986. **Sales:** $3,000,000 (2000). **Emp:** 7. **Officers:** Henny Weissinger, President; Tim Patterson, Treasurer & Secty.

■ 20569 ■ **Stinnes Intercoal Inc.**
605 3rd Ave.
New York, NY 10158-0180
Phone: (212)986-1515
Products: Coal. **SIC:** 5052 (Coal, Other Minerals & Ores). **Sales:** $4,000,000 (2000). **Emp:** 6. **Officers:** Jurgen Lorenz, President.

■ 20570 ■ **Stratcor Technical Sales Inc.**
4955 Steubenville Pike
Pittsburgh, PA 15205
Phone: (412)787-4700
Products: Alloys; Silicone; Magnesium; Chemicals; Vanadium. **SICs:** 5052 (Coal, Other Minerals & Ores); 5169 (Chemicals & Allied Products Nec); 5051 (Metals Service Centers & Offices).

■ 20571 ■ **Summers Fuel Inc.**
28 Allegheny Ave., Ste. 1201
Baltimore, MD 21204
Phone: (410)825-8555 **Fax:** (410)828-8657
Products: Coal. **SIC:** 5052 (Coal, Other Minerals & Ores). **Est:** 1962. **Sales:** $10,000,000 (2000). **Emp:** 2. **Officers:** William N. Clements III, CEO & President; Jean Alger, Treasurer & Secty.

■ 20572 ■ **Suneel Alaska Corp.**
PO Box 1789
Seward, AK 99664-1789
Phone: (907)224-3120
Products: Coal. **SIC:** 5052 (Coal, Other Minerals & Ores). **Officers:** M. Chung, Chairman of the Board.

■ 20573 ■ **Tejas Resources Inc.**
105 Tejas Dr.
Terrell, TX 75160
Phone: (972)563-1220
Products: Lead and lead oxide. **SIC:** 5052 (Coal, Other Minerals & Ores). **Est:** 1991. **Sales:** $28,000,000 (2000). **Emp:** 75. **Officers:** Don Rabon, President.

■ 20574 ■ **Transocean Coal Company L.P.**
599 Lexington Ave., No. 2300
New York, NY 10022
Phone: (212)370-3600 **Fax:** (212)836-4909
Products: Coal. **SIC:** 5052 (Coal, Other Minerals & Ores). **Est:** 1992. **Sales:** $50,000,000 (2000). **Emp:** 6. **Officers:** Lawrence Perlstein, President.

(37) Motorized Vehicles

Entries in this section are arranged alphabetically by company name. When the company name is a personal name, the company name is alphabetized by the surname unless the first name or initial(s) are part of a trade name. See the User's Guide at the front of this directory for additional information.

■ **20575** ■ **AAA Manufacturing Inc.**
5055 Convair Dr.
Carson City, NV 89706
Phone: (775)883-6901
Products: Tanks; Steel. **SICs:** 5088 (Transportation Equipment & Supplies); 5051 (Metals Service Centers & Offices).

■ **20576** ■ **Action Chevrolet-Subaru-Geo**
795 Hoosick Rd.
Troy, NY 12180
Phone: (518)279-1741
Products: Automobiles and trucks. **SIC:** 5012 (Automobiles & Other Motor Vehicles).

■ **20577** ■ **ADESA Auctions of Birmingham**
PO Box 130
Moody, AL 35004
Phone: (205)640-1010   **Fax:** (205)640-1024
Products: Auctioned automobiles. **SIC:** 5012 (Automobiles & Other Motor Vehicles). **Est:** 1987. **Sales:** $73,000,000 (2000). **Emp:** 200. **Officers:** Billy Noles, General Mgr.; Susan Landrum, Controller; Marie Flynt, Dir. of Marketing.

■ **20578** ■ **ADESA Indianapolis Inc.**
2950 E Main St.
Plainfield, IN 46168-2723
Phones: (317)298-9700   (317)838-8000
Free: (800)531-2960   **Fax:** (317)838-8081
URL: http://www.adesaauctions.com
Products: Automobiles. **SIC:** 5012 (Automobiles & Other Motor Vehicles). **Est:** 1995. **Former Name:** Indianapolis Auto Auctions Inc.

■ **20579** ■ **Air Combat Exchange Ltd.**
2533 N Carson St.
Carson City, NV 89706
Phone: (775)841-4015
Products: Aircraft. **SIC:** 5088 (Transportation Equipment & Supplies).

■ **20580** ■ **Akron Auto Auction Inc.**
2471 Ley Dr.
Akron, OH 44319
Phone: (216)773-8245
Products: Auctioned automobiles. **SIC:** 5012 (Automobiles & Other Motor Vehicles).

■ **20581** ■ **Alfa Romeo Distributors of North America**
PO Box 598026
Orlando, FL 32859-8026
Phone: (407)856-5000   **Fax:** (407)856-5075
Products: Cars. **SICs:** 5012 (Automobiles & Other Motor Vehicles); 5013 (Motor Vehicle Supplies & New Parts). **Est:** 1960. **Sales:** $30,000,000 (2000). **Emp:** 9. **Officers:** Franco Forhasari, CEO & President; Tana Seibert, Accounting Manager; Bernie Harak, Dir. of Information Systems; Barbara Gingold, Dir of Human Resources.

■ **20582** ■ **Allison Inc.**
114 W Bland
Roswell, NM 88201
Phone: (505)624-0151
Products: Motorcycles. **SIC:** 5012 (Automobiles & Other Motor Vehicles). **Est:** 1980. **Sales:** $1,500,000 (2000). **Emp:** 15. **Officers:** Jimmy W. Allison, President.

■ **20583** ■ **Allstate Sales and Leasing Corp.**
558 E Villaume Ave.
South St. Paul, MN 55075
Phone: (612)455-6500
Free: (800)328-0104   **Fax:** (612)450-8176
URL: http://www.wdlarson.com
Products: Diesel trucks; Utility trailers. **SICs:** 5012 (Automobiles & Other Motor Vehicles); 5084 (Industrial Machinery & Equipment). **Est:** 1971. **Sales:** $100,000,000 (2000). **Emp:** 120. **Officers:** W.D. Larson, President.

■ **20584** ■ **Altec Industries Inc. Eastern Div.**
250 Laird St.
Plains, PA 18705
Phone: (717)822-3104
Products: Utility trucks and parts. **SICs:** 5012 (Automobiles & Other Motor Vehicles); 5082 (Construction & Mining Machinery). **Est:** 1947. **Sales:** $45,000,000 (2000). **Emp:** 154. **Officers:** Jerry Eisenhart, Vice President; Ted Meadows, Mgr. of Finance & Admin.; Bob Ginn, Dir. of Sales.

■ **20585** ■ **American Carrier Equipment Inc.**
2285 East Date Ave.
Fresno, CA 93745-2615
Phone: (559)442-1500
Free: (800)344-2174   **Fax:** (559)442-3618
E-mail: trailerl@thegrid.net
URL: http://www.trailerl.com
Products: Truck trailers, chassis, and bodies. **SIC:** 5012 (Automobiles & Other Motor Vehicles). **Est:** 1968. **Sales:** $6,000,000 (2000). **Emp:** 60. **Officers:** Philip Sweet, General Mgr.; Ed Hollingshead, Sales Mgr.; Bob Peerson.

■ **20586** ■ **American Emergency Vehicles**
165 American Way
Jefferson, NC 28640
E-mail: aev@ambulance.com
URL: http://www.ambulance.com
Products: Ambulances. **SIC:** 5012 (Automobiles & Other Motor Vehicles). **Est:** 1990. **Sales:** $25,000,000 (2000). **Emp:** 190. **Officers:** Mark Van Arnam, President & CEO; Greg Warmuth; Dennis Hamby, VP of Sales; Randy Hanson, VP of Manufacturing.

■ **20587** ■ **American Honda Motor Company Inc.**
1919 Torrance Blvd.
Torrance, CA 90504-2746
Phone: (310)783-2000   **Fax:** (310)783-3900
Products: Automobiles. **SIC:** 5012 (Automobiles & Other Motor Vehicles). **Est:** 1959. **Sales:** $3,970,000,000 (2000). **Emp:** 2,500. **Officers:** Koichi Amemiya, President; LLewellyn King, Vice President;

Thomas Elliott, Exec. VP of Operations; Tom Ross, Dir. of Information Systems.

■ **20588** ■ **American Honda Motor Co. Inc. Acura Div.**
1919 Torrance Blvd.
Torrance, CA 90501-2746
Phone: (310)783-2000
Products: Autos and motorcycles. **SIC:** 5012 (Automobiles & Other Motor Vehicles).

■ **20589** ■ **American Isuzu Motors Inc.**
13340 183rd St.
Cerritas, CA 90703
Phone: (562)229-5000
Free: (800)255-6727   **Fax:** (562)926-5174
URL: http://www.isuzu.com
Products: Motor vehicles. **SIC:** 5012 (Automobiles & Other Motor Vehicles). **Est:** 1980. **Sales:** $500,000,000 (1999). **Emp:** 480. **Officers:** Yasuyuki Sudo, President.

■ **20590** ■ **American Lease Co.**
PO Box 27069
Seattle, WA 98125
Phone: (206)367-3300   **Fax:** (206)363-0591
Products: Trucks and cars. **SIC:** 5012 (Automobiles & Other Motor Vehicles). **Sales:** $3,100,000 (2000). **Emp:** 10. **Officers:** Jamie Pierre, President; Donald S. Cooley, Finance Officer; Danial C. Glaefke, Dir. of Marketing & Sales.

■ **20591** ■ **American Suzuki Motor Corp.**
PO Box 1100
Brea, CA 92822-1100
Phone: (714)996-7040   **Fax:** (714)970-6005
Products: Automobile, motorcycle, and outboard engines. **SIC:** 5013 (Motor Vehicle Supplies & New Parts). **Est:** 1963. **Sales:** $1,000,000,000 (2000). **Emp:** 450. **Officers:** Ryosaku Suzuki, President; Kenichi Ayukawa, Treasurer; Gary Anderson, Vice President; Melvin Harris, Vice President; Hideaki Tanaka, Vice President.

■ **20592** ■ **ASC International Inc.**
PO Box 5068
Arlington, TX 76006
Phone: (817)640-1300
Products: Transportation equipment and supplies. **SIC:** 5088 (Transportation Equipment & Supplies). **Sales:** $14,000,000 (1994). **Emp:** 50. **Officers:** Ollin Taylor, President; Delores Barton, Accountant.

■ **20593** ■ **Atlantic International Corp.**
PO Box 1657
Framingham, MA 01701
Phone: (508)875-6286
Products: Tires and tubes; New and used automobiles. **SICs:** 5012 (Automobiles & Other Motor Vehicles); 5014 (Tires & Tubes). **Officers:** Joseph Carter, Export Manager.

■ **20594** ■ **Audi of America Inc.**
3800 Hamlin Rd.
Auburn Hills, MI 48326
Phone: (313)340-5000
Products: Automobiles. **SIC:** 5012 (Automobiles &

Other Motor Vehicles). **Sales:** $220,000,000 (1999). **Emp:** 24. **Officers:** Len Hunt, Vice President; Kevin Kelly, Controller; Walter Hanek, Dir. of Marketing; Russell R. Hall, Dir. of Sales.

■ **20595** ■ **Auto Dealers Exchange of Illinois**
43363 Old Hwy. 41
Russell, IL 60075
Phone: (847)395-7570
Products: Used automobiles and parts. **SICs:** 5012 (Automobiles & Other Motor Vehicles); 5015 (Motor Vehicle Parts—Used).

■ **20596** ■ **Badger Truck Center Inc.**
2326 W St. Paul Ave.
Milwaukee, WI 53201-1530
Phone: (414)344-9500
Free: (800)537-7183 **Fax:** (414)344-4323
E-mail: Fordsale@execpc.com
URL: http://www.Badgertruck.com
Products: Trucks. **SIC:** 5012 (Automobiles & Other Motor Vehicles). **Est:** 1965. **Sales:** $44,000,000 (2000). **Emp:** 120. **Officers:** Paul Schlagenhauf, President; John Schlagenhauf, Chairman of the Board & CFO.

■ **20597** ■ **Baer Sport Center**
Rte. 6 E
Honesdale, PA 18431
Phone: (570)253-2000
Free: (800)BAE-RINC **Fax:** (570)253-9490
E-mail: baer@baer-inc.com
URL: http://www.baer-inc.com
Products: Motorcycles; Snowmobiles, self-propelled and parts; Recreational vehicles; ATVs. **SIC:** 5012 (Automobiles & Other Motor Vehicles). **Est:** 1958. **Emp:** 19.

■ **20598** ■ **Carl Beasley Ford Inc.**
PO Box 3115
York, PA 17402-3115
Phone: (717)755-2911 **Fax:** (717)755-5714
Products: Cars and trucks. **SICs:** 5012 (Automobiles & Other Motor Vehicles); 5012 (Automobiles & Other Motor Vehicles). **Est:** 1958. **Sales:** $41,800,000 (2000). **Emp:** 95. **Officers:** Gary E. Jay, President.

■ **20599** ■ **Berge Ford Inc.**
PO Box 4008
Mesa, AZ 85211
Phone: (602)497-1111 **Fax:** (602)497-7576
Products: Cars and trucks. **SIC:** 5012 (Automobiles & Other Motor Vehicles). **Est:** 1950. **Sales:** $91,000,000 (2000). **Emp:** 250. **Officers:** Craig Berge, President; Scott Elsworth, Manager; Angelo Santoni, General Mgr.

■ **20600** ■ **Big-2 Oldsmobile Inc.**
PO Box 4007
Mesa, AZ 85211
Phone: (602)898-6000 **Fax:** (602)827-0963
Products: Cars and trucks. **SIC:** 5012 (Automobiles & Other Motor Vehicles). **Est:** 1940. **Sales:** $87,000,000 (2000). **Emp:** 160. **Officers:** R.W. Henkel, General Mgr.; Teresa Toslin, Finance Officer.

■ **20601** ■ **Big Sky Auto Auction Inc.**
1236 Cordova St.
Billings, MT 59101
Phone: (406)259-5999
Free: (800)726-6786 **Fax:** (406)259-2776
E-mail: bigsky@wtp.net
URL: http://www.bigskyauction.com
Products: Automobiles. **SIC:** 5012 (Automobiles & Other Motor Vehicles). **Est:** 1997. **Sales:** $80,000,000 (1999). **Emp:** 100. **Officers:** Theodore Becker, President.

■ **20602** ■ **Billings Truck Center**
PO Box 30236
Billings, MT 59107
Phone: (406)252-5121 **Fax:** (406)252-5910
Products: Semi-trucks and parts and accessories. **SICs:** 5012 (Automobiles & Other Motor Vehicles); 5013 (Motor Vehicle Supplies & New Parts). **Est:** 1947. **Sales:** $12,000,000 (2000). **Emp:** 35. **Officers:** B.A. Fisher, President; Cliff Hanson, Exec. VP of Finance; Maralyn Gangstad, Dir. of Marketing.

■ **20603** ■ **BMW of North America Inc.**
PO Box 1227
Westwood, NJ 07675-1227
Phone: (201)307-4000
Products: Automobiles. **SIC:** 5012 (Automobiles & Other Motor Vehicles). **Est:** 1975. **Sales:** $2,500,000,000 (2000). **Emp:** 929. **Officers:** Karl Gerlinger, CEO & President; Wolfgang Stofer, Exec. VP & CFO; Carl Flesher, VP of Marketing; Ken Barile, Information Systems Mgr.; John Cagnina, Human Resources Mgr.

■ **20604** ■ **Bond Equipment Company Inc.**
2946 Irving Blvd.
Dallas, TX 75247
Phone: (214)637-0760 **Fax:** (214)637-4731
Products: Diesel trucks and equipment. **SICs:** 5012 (Automobiles & Other Motor Vehicles); 5013 (Motor Vehicle Supplies & New Parts). **Est:** 1951. **Sales:** $15,000,000 (2000). **Emp:** 19. **Officers:** J.A. Bond, President.

■ **20605** ■ **Brennan Industrial Truck Co.**
3409 South Ave.
Toledo, OH 43609
Phone: (419)385-4601 **Fax:** (419)385-4609
Products: Industrial trucks and parts. **SIC:** 5084 (Industrial Machinery & Equipment). **Est:** 1957. **Sales:** $3,000,000 (2000). **Emp:** 25. **Officers:** James H. Brennan, President & Chairman of the Board; James Brennan Jr., Controller; Thomas J. Backoff, Dir. of Marketing.

■ **20606** ■ **C. Earl Brown Inc.**
PO Box 420
Chambersburg, PA 17201
Phone: (717)264-6151 **Fax:** (717)264-4229
Products: Trucks and freight trucks. **SIC:** 5012 (Automobiles & Other Motor Vehicles). **Est:** 1920. **Sales:** $20,800,000 (2000). **Emp:** 56. **Officers:** John W. Brown, President; Mildred L. Brown, Treasurer & Secty.; David H. Lent, Dir. of Systems.

■ **20607** ■ **Buffalo White GMC Inc.**
271 Dingens St.
Buffalo, NY 14206
Phone: (716)821-9911 **Free:** (800)933-9462
Products: Trucks, tractors, and trailers. **SICs:** 5012 (Automobiles & Other Motor Vehicles); 5083 (Farm & Garden Machinery). **Est:** 1946. **Sales:** $15,000,000 (2000). **Emp:** 55. **Officers:** Henry T. Dutson, President.

■ **20608** ■ **Geo. Byers Sons Inc.**
PO Box 16513
Columbus, OH 43216
Phone: (614)228-5111 **Fax:** (614)228-1227
Products: Automobiles; Auto parts. **SICs:** 5012 (Automobiles & Other Motor Vehicles); 5013 (Motor Vehicle Supplies & New Parts). **Est:** 1897. **Sales:** $236,700,000 (2000). **Emp:** 452. **Officers:** George W. Byers III, President; Donald Grant, Treasurer.

■ **20609** ■ **Capitol Chevrolet Inc.**
711 Eastern Blvd.
Montgomery, AL 36117
Phone: (205)272-8700 **Fax:** (205)270-9313
Products: Automobiles. **SIC:** 5013 (Motor Vehicle Supplies & New Parts). **Est:** 1948. **Sales:** $80,000,000 (2000). **Emp:** 204. **Officers:** Frank E. McGough Jr., President.

■ **20610** ■ **Carlsbad Volvo**
6830 Avenida Encinas
Carlsbad, CA 92009
Phone: (760)931-7100
Free: (800)338-6586 **Fax:** (760)931-1618
Products: Automobiles; Automotive parts. **SICs:** 5012 (Automobiles & Other Motor Vehicles); 5013 (Motor Vehicle Supplies & New Parts). **Emp:** 40. **Officers:** Moe Singh, e-mail: mjsinghji@yahoo.com; Bobby Askari, Sales/Marketing Contact; Don Bishop, Customer Service Contact.

■ **20611** ■ **Charles Clark Chevrolet Co.**
PO Box 938
McAllen, TX 78502
Phone: (956)686-5441 **Fax:** (956)686-1623
Products: Automobiles and trucks. **SIC:** 5012 (Automobiles & Other Motor Vehicles). **Est:** 1936.

Sales: $60,000,000 (2000). **Emp:** 150. **Officers:** Kirk A. Clark, CEO; Rick Carter, Manager.

■ **20612** ■ **Coachmen Industries Inc.**
  Coachmen Vans Div.
PO Box 50
Elkhart, IN 46515
Phone: (219)262-3474
Products: Converted vans not qualifying as van campers; Recreational vehicles. **SIC:** 5012 (Automobiles & Other Motor Vehicles).

■ **20613** ■ **Colorado Kenworth Inc.**
4901 York St.
Denver, CO 80216
Phone: (303)292-0833
Products: Trucks. **SIC:** 5084 (Industrial Machinery & Equipment). **Sales:** $25,000,000 (2000). **Emp:** 125. **Officers:** Timothy R. Murphy, President.

■ **20614** ■ **Columbus Fair Auto Auction Inc.**
PO Box 32490
Columbus, OH 43232
Phone: (614)497-2000
Products: Automobiles. **SIC:** 5012 (Automobiles & Other Motor Vehicles).

■ **20615** ■ **Commercial Motor Co.**
160 S Commercial St.
Aransas Pass, TX 78336
Phone: (512)758-5361 **Fax:** (512)758-5364
Products: Automobiles. **SIC:** 5012 (Automobiles & Other Motor Vehicles). **Est:** 1939. **Sales:** $14,900,000 (2000). **Emp:** 47. **Officers:** Gary Boehnke, President; Debi Seale, Comptroller.

■ **20616** ■ **Cornhusker International**
3131 Cornhusker Hwy.
Lincoln, NE 68504
Phone: (402)466-8461
Products: Trucks; Buses. **SIC:** 5012 (Automobiles & Other Motor Vehicles).

■ **20617** ■ **Cunill Motors Inc.**
PO Box 10189
Houston, TX 77206
Phone: (713)695-2981
Products: Cars and trucks. **SIC:** 5012 (Automobiles & Other Motor Vehicles). **Est:** 1954. **Sales:** $4,000,000 (2000). **Emp:** 8. **Officers:** Fred F. Cunill, President; Vivian Jefcoat, Manager.

■ **20618** ■ **Custom Car Center**
10541 Independence Ave.
Independence, MO 64053
Phone: (816)254-1177
Products: Used automobiles. **SIC:** 5012 (Automobiles & Other Motor Vehicles).

■ **20619** ■ **Dal-Kawa Hijet**
312 Kanuga St.
Hendersonville, NC 28739
Phone: (704)692-7519 **Fax:** (704)697-2234
Products: Motorcycles; Farm machinery. **SICs:** 5012 (Automobiles & Other Motor Vehicles); 5083 (Farm & Garden Machinery).

■ **20620** ■ **Dallas Auto Auction Inc.**
5333 W Keist Blvd.
Dallas, TX 75236
Phone: (214)330-1800
Products: Automobiles. **SIC:** 5012 (Automobiles & Other Motor Vehicles). **Sales:** $170,000,000 (2000). **Emp:** 325. **Officers:** Barry Roop, General Mgr.; David Robertson, Dir. of Sales; Jan Marrs, Dir of Personnel.

■ **20621** ■ **Darlings**
153 Perry Rd.
Bangor, ME 04401
Phone: (207)941-1240
URL: http://www.darlings.com
Products: Automobiles and automotive parts. **SICs:** 5012 (Automobiles & Other Motor Vehicles); 5013 (Motor Vehicle Supplies & New Parts). **Est:** 1937. **Sales:** $60,000,000 (2000). **Emp:** 155. **Officers:** J.B. Darling, President; C.G. Rohn, VP of Finance.

■ **20622** ■ **Detroit Auto Auction**
20911 Gladwin Rd.
Taylor, MI 48180
Phone: (734)285-7300 **Fax:** (734)285-2025
Products: Automobiles. **SIC:** 5012 (Automobiles &
Other Motor Vehicles). **Sales:** $70,000,000 (2000).
Emp: 252. **Officers:** Charles L. Hudgins, General Mgr.;
Pamela Pejman, Business Mgr.

■ **20623** ■ **Dixie Auto Auction Inc.**
PO Box 1271
Grenada, MS 38901
Phone: (601)226-5637 **Fax:** (601)227-9060
E-mail: dixmsauc@dixie-net.com
Products: Auctioned automobiles. **SIC:** 5012
(Automobiles & Other Motor Vehicles). **Est:** 1981.
Sales: $4,000,000 (2000). **Emp:** 7. **Officers:** Jimmy
Boling, President.

■ **20624** ■ **Doonan Truck and Equipment Inc.**
PO Box 1286
Great Bend, KS 67530
Phone: (316)792-2491 **Fax:** (316)792-4653
Products: Trucks and trailers. **SICs:** 5012
(Automobiles & Other Motor Vehicles); 5013 (Motor
Vehicle Supplies & New Parts). **Est:** 1948. **Sales:**
$20,000,000 (1999). **Emp:** 80. **Officers:** W. Doonan,
CEO; Steve Dellinger, CFO; Mike McCarty, Dir. of Data
Processing; Jeff Dalley, Human Resources Contact.

■ **20625** ■ **Dothan Auto Auction Inc.**
3664 S Oates St.
Dothan, AL 36301
Phone: (334)792-1115
Products: Auctioned automobiles. **SIC:** 5012
(Automobiles & Other Motor Vehicles). **Sales:**
$150,000,000 (2000). **Emp:** 100.

■ **20626** ■ **DSW Inc.**
PO Box 3817
Wilson, NC 27893
Phone: (919)291-0131 **Fax:** (919)291-7745
Products: Trucks; Farm equipment. **SICs:** 5012
(Automobiles & Other Motor Vehicles); 5083 (Farm &
Garden Machinery). **Est:** 1987. **Sales:** $25,000,000
(2000). **Emp:** 100. **Officers:** D. Stephen White,
President; Sandra Pridgen, Treasurer & Secty.; Edwin
Ellis, General Mgr.

■ **20627** ■ **Duckett Truck Center Inc.**
Rte. 6, Box 580
Poplar Bluff, MO 63901-9806
Phone: (314)785-0193 **Fax:** (314)785-2450
Products: Freight-liner trucks. **SIC:** 5012 (Automobiles
& Other Motor Vehicles). **Est:** 1964. **Sales:**
$27,000,000 (2000). **Emp:** 100. **Officers:** Paul
Duckett, President.

■ **20628** ■ **Dunlap and Kyle Company Inc.**
PO Box 720
Batesville, MS 38606
Phone: (601)563-7601 **Fax:** (601)563-0019
Products: Tires, tubes, and wheels for automobiles,
trucks, and farm equipment. **SICs:** 5014 (Tires &
Tubes); 5014 (Tires & Tubes). **Est:** 1956. **Sales:**
$280,000,000 (2000). **Emp:** 650. **Officers:** Robert H.
Dunlap, Chairman of the Board; Richard Dunlap, Vice
President; Danny Jones, Dir. of Mktg. & Sales; Stan
Johnson, Dir. of Information Systems.

■ **20629** ■ **Dyer Auto Auction Inc.**
PO Box 115
Dyer, IN 46311
Phone: (219)865-2361
Products: Automobiles. **SIC:** 5012 (Automobiles &
Other Motor Vehicles).

■ **20630** ■ **Dyer Motor Co.**
PO Box 246
Dyer, TN 38330-0246
Phone: (901)692-2266
Products: Automobiles and trucks. **SIC:** 5012
(Automobiles & Other Motor Vehicles). **Est:** 1936.
Sales: $10,000,000 (2000). **Emp:** 25. **Officers:** G.B.
Robinson Jr., President; Richard Parks, VP of
Marketing; Norman Robinson, Dir. of Marketing &
Sales.

■ **20631** ■ **Dynacraft Co.**
650 Milwaukee Ave.
Algona, WA 98001
Phone: (253)351-3000 **Fax:** (253)351-3041
Products: Trucks. **SIC:** 5012 (Automobiles & Other
Motor Vehicles). **Est:** 1967. **Sales:** $105,500,000
(2000). **Emp:** 170. **Officers:** Everrett Seymoure,
General Mgr.; Don Rudell, Controller.

■ **20632** ■ **Elliott Equipment Company Inc.**
PO Box 401
Easton, MD 21601
Phone: (410)822-0066 **Fax:** (410)820-7792
Products: Trucks. **SIC:** 5012 (Automobiles & Other
Motor Vehicles). **Est:** 1941. **Sales:** $16,000,000
(2000). **Emp:** 55. **Officers:** George H. Wilson Jr.,
President; Ernest Fuchs, CFO.

■ **20633** ■ **Engs Motor Truck Co.**
8830 E Slauson Ave.
Pico Rivera, CA 90660
Phone: (213)685-9910 **Fax:** (213)942-8760
Products: Trucks and truck parts. **SICs:** 5012
(Automobiles & Other Motor Vehicles); 5013 (Motor
Vehicle Supplies & New Parts). **Est:** 1945. **Sales:**
$85,000,000 (2000). **Emp:** 300. **Officers:** Edward W.
Engs III, President; Stuart R. Engs, Treasurer & Secty.;
Thomas Shank, General Mgr.

■ **20634** ■ **Farnsworth Armored Inc.**
2077 Kirby Pkwy.
Memphis, TN 38119-5534
Phone: (901)753-4232 **Fax:** (901)753-4124
Products: Armored trucks. **SIC:** 5012 (Automobiles &
Other Motor Vehicles). **Est:** 1993. **Officers:** Hal
Farnsworth, President.

■ **20635** ■ **Ford Body Company Inc.**
1218 Battleground Ave.
PO Box 9354
Greensboro, NC 27429-0354
Phone: (336)272-1131 **Fax:** (336)272-7766
E-mail: sales@fordbody.com
URL: http://www.fordbody.com
Products: New truck bodies and truck equipment. **SIC:**
5012 (Automobiles & Other Motor Vehicles). **Est:** 1917.
Emp: 25. **Officers:** Mr. Lynn R. Ford, President, e-
mail: lford@fordbody.com.

■ **20636** ■ **Fresno Truck Center**
2727 E Central Ave.
Fresno, CA 93725-2425
Phone: (209)486-4310 **Fax:** (209)233-2785
Products: Large trucks. **SIC:** 5012 (Automobiles &
Other Motor Vehicles). **Est:** 1935. **Sales:** $120,000,000
(2000). **Emp:** 485. **Officers:** Gary Howard, President;
Brian Nicholson, VP of Finance; D. Howard, VP of
Marketing.

■ **20637** ■ **Fruehauf Trailer Services, Inc.**
38600 Ford Rd.
Westland, MI 48185
Phone: (734)729-6767 **Fax:** (734)729-5682
Products: Truck trailers and chassis; Motor vehicle
parts and accessories. **SICs:** 5012 (Automobiles &
Other Motor Vehicles); 5013 (Motor Vehicle Supplies &
New Parts). **Former Name:** Fruehauf Trailer Corp.

■ **20638** ■ **Full Bore - Cycle Lines USA**
9515 51st Ave., Unit 12
College Park, MD 20740
Phone: (301)474-9119
Free: (800)333-9119 **Fax:** (301)345-3231
E-mail: full_bore@compuserve.com
Products: Motor oil; Motorcycle parts; Bearings; Light
bulbs; Specialty transmission and gear lubricants; Two
cycle lubes. **SIC:** 5013 (Motor Vehicle Supplies & New
Parts). **Est:** 1981. **Emp:** 7. **Officers:** Ralph Flanagan,
CEO. **Alternate Name:** Cycle Lines USA - Full Bore.

■ **20639** ■ **Fyda Freightliner Inc.**
1250 Walcutt Rd.
Columbus, OH 43228
Phone: (614)851-0002 **Fax:** (614)851-0011
Products: Freight trucks. **SIC:** 5012 (Automobiles &
Other Motor Vehicles). **Sales:** $150,000,000 (2000).
Emp: 110. **Officers:** Walter Fyda, President; Patty
DePaula, Controller.

■ **20640** ■ **G and S Motors Inc.**
211 N I-70 Service Rd.
St. Peters, MO 63376
Phone: (314)258-3298
Products: Motorcycles. **SIC:** 5012 (Automobiles &
Other Motor Vehicles).

■ **20641** ■ **Garden Island Motors Ltd.**
3050 Hoolako St.
Lihue, HI 96766
Phone: (808)245-6711
Products: Automobiles. **SIC:** 5013 (Motor Vehicle
Supplies & New Parts). **Est:** 1918. **Sales:** $12,000,000
(2000). **Emp:** 39. **Officers:** David W. Goodnbe,
President; Toni Ortiz, Controller; Doug Domen, Sales
Mgr.

■ **20642** ■ **General Truck Sales Corp.**
PO Box 8557
South Charleston, WV 25303
Phone: (304)744-1321
Products: Trucks and truck parts. **SICs:** 5012
(Automobiles & Other Motor Vehicles); 5013 (Motor
Vehicle Supplies & New Parts). **Est:** 1937. **Sales:**
$10,000,000 (2000). **Emp:** 45. **Officers:** Charles H.
Haden III, President; Orual D. Bush, Vice President.

■ **20643** ■ **Great Lakes Peterbilt Inc.**
5900 Southport Rd.
Portage, IN 46368-6407
Phone: (219)763-7227 **Fax:** (219)762-7974
Products: Used trucks. **SIC:** 5012 (Automobiles &
Other Motor Vehicles). **Est:** 1960. **Sales:** $25,000,000
(2000). **Emp:** 73. **Officers:** Steve Buha, President;
Diana Bunton, Controller; Robert Buha, Vice President.

■ **20644** ■ **Greater Lansing Auto Auction Inc.**
PO Box 359
Dimondale, MI 48821-0359
Phone: (517)322-2444
Products: Auctioned automobiles. **SIC:** 5012
(Automobiles & Other Motor Vehicles).

■ **20645** ■ **Gulf Coast Auto Auction Inc.**
6005 24th St. E
Bradenton, FL 34203
Phone: (941)756-8478
Products: Automobiles. **SIC:** 5012 (Automobiles &
Other Motor Vehicles).

■ **20646** ■ **Jay Dee Harris Truck Equipment
Co.**
PO Box 189
Tremonton, UT 84337
Phone: (801)257-3333
Products: Trucks and equipment. **SICs:** 5082
(Construction & Mining Machinery); 5084 (Industrial
Machinery & Equipment). **Est:** 1933. **Sales:**
$20,000,000 (2000). **Emp:** 20. **Officers:** Jay D. Harris,
Owner; E. Johnson, Treasurer.

■ **20647** ■ **Heidema Brothers Inc.**
A-5496 144th Ave.
Holland, MI 49423
Phone: (616)396-6551 **Fax:** (616)396-9499
Products: Trucks and truck parts. **SICs:** 5149
(Groceries & Related Products Nec); 5013 (Motor
Vehicle Supplies & New Parts). **Est:** 1946. **Sales:**
$8,300,000 (2000). **Emp:** 42. **Officers:** John Heidema,
President; George J. Heidema, CFO.

■ **20648** ■ **Hibbard Aviation**
1825 Karin Dr.
Carson City, NV 89706
Phones: (775)884-3555 (775)884-3796
URL: http://www.hibbardaviation.com
Products: Aircraft; Commercial, corporate, and
general aviation. **SIC:** 5088 (Transportation Equipment
& Supplies). **Est:** 1966. **Emp:** 2. **Officers:** Norm
Hibbard, Owner, e-mail: norm@hibbardaviation.com.

■ **20649** ■ **O.S. Hill and Co., Inc.**
PO Box 2170
East Liverpool, OH 43920
Phone: (330)386-6440 **Free:** (800)837-3000
URL: http://www.osh.u.com
Products: Semi-trucks. **SICs:** 5012 (Automobiles &
Other Motor Vehicles); 5013 (Motor Vehicle Supplies &
New Parts). **Est:** 1890. **Sales:** $22,700,000 (1999).

Emp: 70. Officers: Jack Hill, Chairman of the Board; Mike Fisher, President; Len Yanni, Vice President.

■ 20650 ■ HT & T Co.
PO Box 4190
Hilo, HI 96720-0190
Phone: (808)933-7700 Fax: (808)933-7768
Products: Trucks. SIC: 5012 (Automobiles & Other Motor Vehicles). Est: 1946. Sales: $20,000,000 (2000). Emp: 146. Officers: Richard Hill, President; Charles Haneberg, Sales/Marketing Contact; Kai Torngren, Dir. of Marketing.

■ 20651 ■ Hyundai Motor America
PO Box 20850
Fountain Valley, CA 92728-0850
Phone: (714)965-3000 Fax: (714)965-3816
Products: Automobiles. SIC: 5012 (Automobiles & Other Motor Vehicles). Est: 1985. Sales: $1,400,000,000 (2000). Emp: 578. Officers: M.H. Juhn, CEO & President; Jim Hannefield, VP & CFO; Doug Mazza, VP of Marketing; Fred Sipes, Dir. of Information Systems; Keith Duckworth, Dir. of Admin.

■ 20652 ■ Indiana Auto Auction Inc.
PO Box 8039
Ft. Wayne, IN 46898
Phone: (219)489-2776
Products: Automobiles. SIC: 5012 (Automobiles & Other Motor Vehicles).

■ 20653 ■ Intermountain Wholesale Hardware Inc.
4990 Dahlia St.
Denver, CO 80216
Phone: (303)288-4040 Fax: (303)322-1121
Products: Semi-trailers; Hydraulic parts. SICs: 5012 (Automobiles & Other Motor Vehicles); 5084 (Industrial Machinery & Equipment). Sales: $3,000,000 (2000). Emp: 25. Officers: Mark Moskowitz, President.

■ 20654 ■ Island Classic Automotive Inc.
750 E Sample Rd., Bldg. 7, Bay 4
Pompano Beach, FL 33064
Phone: (954)941-0400 Fax: (954)941-4998
Products: Used automobiles, trucks, pickups, and vans. SIC: 5012 (Automobiles & Other Motor Vehicles). Officers: Arthur Freiberg, President.

■ 20655 ■ Isuzu Motors America Inc.
13340 183rd St., #6007
Cerritos, CA 90703-8748
Products: Automobiles. SIC: 5012 (Automobiles & Other Motor Vehicles). Est: 1980. Sales: $150,000,000 (2000). Emp: 300. Officers: Kazuo Okasaka, President; Fumitaka Nishiura, VP of Finance; N. Oda, VP of Business Development; Thomas Weaver, Dir of Human Resources.

■ 20656 ■ JM Family Enterprises Inc.
100 Northwest 12th Ave.
Deerfield Beach, FL 33442
Phone: (954)429-2000 Fax: (954)429-2244
Products: Automobiles. SIC: 5012 (Automobiles & Other Motor Vehicles). Est: 1968. Sales: $5,200,000,000 (2000). Emp: 2,800. Officers: Patricia Moran, President; James R. Foster, Exec. VP & CFO; E.D. Machek, Vice President; Wayne McClain, Exec. VP of Human Resources.

■ 20657 ■ Joyserv Company Ltd.
1751 Talleyrand Ave.
Jacksonville, FL 32206
Phone: (904)358-4400 Fax: (904)358-4415
Products: Automobiles. SIC: 5012 (Automobiles & Other Motor Vehicles). Emp: 550. Officers: Robert A. Moore, VP & General Merchandising Mgr.

■ 20658 ■ Kansas City Auto Auction Inc.
3901 N Great Midwest
Kansas City, MO 64161
Phone: (816)452-4084 Fax: (816)459-4711
Products: Automobiles. SIC: 5012 (Automobiles & Other Motor Vehicles). Sales: $54,000,000 (2000). Emp: 100. Officers: Jim Orr, General Mgr.

■ 20659 ■ Kawasaki Motors Corporation U.S.A.
PO Box 25252
Santa Ana, CA 92799-5252
Phone: (714)770-0400 Fax: (714)460-5600
Products: Motorcycles; Jet skis; Generators. SICs: 5012 (Automobiles & Other Motor Vehicles); 5063 (Electrical Apparatus & Equipment); 5091 (Sporting & Recreational Goods). Est: 1966. Sales: $830,000,000 (2000). Emp: 425. Officers: Masatoshi Tsurutami, President; Terry Kitajima, VP of Finance; Robert Moffitt, VP of Sales; Robert Shepard, VP of Information Systems; James Klein, Dir of Personnel.

■ 20660 ■ Kenworth Sales Company Inc.
PO Box 65829
Salt Lake City, UT 84165-0829
Phone: (801)487-4161 Fax: (801)467-3820
E-mail: kenworthsalesco.com
Products: Trucks. SIC: 5012 (Automobiles & Other Motor Vehicles). Est: 1954. Sales: $39,000,000 (2000). Emp: 75. Officers: R. Kyle Treadway, President; Kip Ekker, VP of Operations; Charles Knorr, General Mgr.

■ 20661 ■ Kesler-Schaefer Auto Auction Inc.
PO Box 53203
Indianapolis, IN 46253
Phone: (317)297-2300
Products: Automobiles. SIC: 5012 (Automobiles & Other Motor Vehicles).

■ 20662 ■ Kia Motors America Inc.
PO Box 52410
Irvine, CA 92619-2410
Phone: (714)470-7000 Fax: (714)470-2801
Products: Automobiles. SIC: 5012 (Automobiles & Other Motor Vehicles). Est: 1992. Sales: $240,000,000 (2000). Emp: 200. Officers: W. K. Kim, CEO & President; Dick Macedo, Dir. of Marketing; G.A. Stacey, Dir. of Information Systems; Terri Miller, Human Resources Mgr.

■ 20663 ■ King Fleet Group
1406 Sand Lake Rd.
Orlando, FL 32809
Phone: (407)858-4822
Free: (800)444-8701 Fax: (407)851-6618
Products: New and used automobiles. SIC: 5012 (Automobiles & Other Motor Vehicles). Officers: Peter Popiel, Sales/Marketing Contact, e-mail: peteelmago@aol.com. Former Name: Fountain Hijet.

■ 20664 ■ Walter A. Kohl Sales
4022 Lake Ave.
Lockport, NY 14094-1116
Phone: (716)433-3903
Products: Motorcycles and motorcycles parts. SICs: 5013 (Motor Vehicle Supplies & New Parts); 5012 (Automobiles & Other Motor Vehicles). Sales: $200,000 (2000). Emp: 2. Officers: Walter A. Kohl, Owner.

■ 20665 ■ Kolstad Company Inc.
8501 Naples St. NE
Blaine, MN 55449-6702
Phone: (612)633-8451 Fax: (612)379-8980
Products: Truck, bus, and other vehicle bodies; Motor vehicles. SICs: 5012 (Automobiles & Other Motor Vehicles); 5013 (Motor Vehicle Supplies & New Parts). Est: 1947. Sales: $13,000,000 (2000). Emp: 100. Officers: Robert Crosson, CEO; Paul O'Brien, President.

■ 20666 ■ Kruse Inc.
104 Gallagherville Rd.
PO Box 245
Downingtown, PA 19335
Phone: (610)925-5600
Products: Classic cars. SIC: 5012 (Automobiles & Other Motor Vehicles). Sales: $7,500,000 (2000). Emp: 30. Officers: Mitchell Kruse, President; Renee Morland, President & Dir. of Research.

■ 20667 ■ La Beau Brothers Inc.
295 N Harrison Ave.
Kankakee, IL 60901
Phone: (815)933-5519
Free: (800)747-9519 Fax: (815)933-4366
Products: Trucks. SIC: 5012 (Automobiles & Other Motor Vehicles). Est: 1950. Sales: $24,000,000 (2000). Emp: 30. Officers: W. Hove, President; Bruce Hove, CFO.

■ 20668 ■ La Crosse Truck Center Inc.
205 Causeway Blvd.
PO Box 1176
La Crosse, WI 54602-1176
Phone: (608)785-0800
Free: (800)236-0800 Fax: (608)784-2533
E-mail: webmaster@lacrossetruck.com
URL: http://www.lacrossetruck.com
Products: Trucks and parts. SICs: 5012 (Automobiles & Other Motor Vehicles); 5013 (Motor Vehicle Supplies & New Parts). Est: 1953. Sales: $13,100,000 (2000). Emp: 35. Officers: Stephen T. Heustein, President.

■ 20669 ■ Lakeland Auto Auction Inc.
PO Box 90007
Lakeland, FL 33804
Phone: (941)984-1551
Products: Automobiles. SIC: 5012 (Automobiles & Other Motor Vehicles).

■ 20670 ■ Langer Equipment Company Inc.
1400 W Chestnut St.
Virginia, MN 55792
Phone: (218)749-4700
Products: Trucks; Pumps; Wrenches. SICs: 5012 (Automobiles & Other Motor Vehicles); 5084 (Industrial Machinery & Equipment). Est: 1963. Sales: $6,000,000 (2000). Emp: 17. Officers: W. Bart Berg Jr., President; Jerry Brien, CFO; Michael Murray, Sales Mgr.

■ 20671 ■ LDI, Ltd.
54 Monument Cir., Ste. 800
Indianapolis, IN 46204
Phone: (317)237-5400 Fax: (317)237-2329
Products: Motorcycle parts, video cassettes and auto refinishing supplies. SIC: 5013 (Motor Vehicle Supplies & New Parts). Est: 1912. Sales: $855,400,000 (2000). Emp: 2,900. Officers: Andre Lacy, CEO; Michael P. Hutson, VP of Finance; David N. Shane, Exec. VP. Former Name: Lacy Diversified Industries.

■ 20672 ■ LeMans Corp.
PO Box 5222
Janesville, WI 53547-5222
Phone: (608)758-1111
Products: Motorcycle and snowmobile parts and accessories. SICs: 5013 (Motor Vehicle Supplies & New Parts); 5014 (Tires & Tubes). Sales: $195,000,000 (2000). Emp: 800. Officers: Fred Fox, Owner; Mark Scharenbrouch, VP of Finance.

■ 20673 ■ Los Angeles Freightliner
1031 E Holt Ave.
Ontario, CA 91761
Phone: (909)988-5511
Free: (800)673-0500 Fax: (909)391-1695
Products: Trucks and truck parts. SICs: 5012 (Automobiles & Other Motor Vehicles); 5013 (Motor Vehicle Supplies & New Parts). Est: 1918. Sales: $7,300,000 (2000). Emp: 33. Officers: William J. Scully Jr., President; Michael J. McRoberts, CFO.

■ 20674 ■ Devan Lowe Inc.
1151 Gault Ave. S
Ft. Payne, AL 35967
Phone: (205)845-0922 Fax: (205)845-0142
Products: Automobiles. SIC: 5012 (Automobiles & Other Motor Vehicles). Est: 1965. Sales: $31,000,000 (2000). Emp: 90. Officers: W.D. Lowe, President & Treasurer; Larry Gray, CFO; Ron Sparks, General Mgr.

■ 20675 ■ Mazda Motor of America Inc.
PO Box 19734
Irvine, CA 92623
Phone: (714)727-1990 Fax: (714)727-6101
Products: Automobile parts and engines. SICs: 5012 (Automobiles & Other Motor Vehicles); 5015 (Motor Vehicle Parts—Used). Est: 1920. Sales:

$1,230,000,000 (2000). **Emp:** 780. **Officers:** George Toyama, President; Jeff Badrtalei, VP of Finance; Jan Thompson, VP of Sales; Michael Anzis, VP of Information Systems; Herb Clark, VP of Human Resources.

■ **20676** ■ **Mazda North American Operations**
7755 Irvine Center Dr.
Irvine, CA 92618
Phone: (714)727-1990 **Fax:** (714)727-6101
Products: Automobiles. **SIC:** 5012 (Automobiles & Other Motor Vehicles). **Emp:** 1,350. **Officers:** Richard Beattie, CEO & President; Charles Woolard, CFO.

■ **20677** ■ **McLean County Truck Company Inc.**
PO Box 102
Bloomington, IL 61702-0102
Phone: (309)662-1331
Products: Trucks. **SIC:** 5012 (Automobiles & Other Motor Vehicles). **Est:** 1945. **Sales:** $16,500,000 (2000). **Emp:** 64. **Officers:** N.R. Stahly, President; Lyle Leesman, Controller.

■ **20678** ■ **Mel Farr Automotive Group Inc.**
24750 Greenfield Rd.
Oak Park, MI 48237
Phone: (248)967-3700 **Fax:** (248)967-0703
URL: http://www.melfarrford.com
Products: Automobiles. **SIC:** 5012 (Automobiles & Other Motor Vehicles). **Est:** 1975. **Sales:** $535,000,000 (2000). **Emp:** 862. **Officers:** Mel Farr Sr. Sr., Owner; Derrik Mayes, CFO; Mary Farr, Human Resources Mgr.

■ **20679** ■ **Mercedes-Benz of North America Inc.**
1 Mercedes Dr.
Montvale, NJ 07645
Phone: (201)573-0600 **Fax:** (201)573-6780
Products: Automobiles. **SIC:** 5012 (Automobiles & Other Motor Vehicles). **Est:** 1965. **Sales:** $1,730,000,000 (2000). **Emp:** 1,100. **Officers:** Michael Bassermann, CEO & Chairman of the Board; Wilfried Steffen, VP of Finance; Michael Jackson, Exec. VP; Vincent Morrotti, Information Systems Mgr.; Robert Erzen, VP of Human Resources.

■ **20680** ■ **Mid-America Auto Auction**
3515 Newburg Rd.
Louisville, KY 40218
Phone: (502)454-6666
Products: Automobiles. **SIC:** 5012 (Automobiles & Other Motor Vehicles).

■ **20681** ■ **Midwest Action Cycle**
251 Host Dr.
Lake Geneva, WI 53147-4607
Phone: (262)249-0600
Free: (800)343-9065 **Fax:** (262)249-0608
E-mail: macycle@execpc.com
URL: http://www.execpc.com/macycle/
Products: Motorcycle parts. **SICs:** 5012 (Automobiles & Other Motor Vehicles); 5091 (Sporting & Recreational Goods). **Est:** 1971. **Emp:** 20. **Officers:** John B. Lindsey, President.

■ **20682** ■ **Midwest Truck Equipment Inc.**
825 N Main
Paris, IL 61944
Phone: (217)465-8785 **Fax:** (217)463-1236
Products: Truck equipment. **SIC:** 5012 (Automobiles & Other Motor Vehicles). **Est:** 1993. **Sales:** $750,000 (2000). **Emp:** 3. **Officers:** Fredric Alwardt, CEO & President; Jenia Kennedy, Controller & Office Mgr.; Fredric Alwardt, Sales Mgr.

■ **20683** ■ **Minneapolis Northstar Auto Auction Inc.**
4908 Valley Industl Blvd. N
Shakopee, MN 55379
Phone: (612)445-5544
Free: (888)445-2277 **Fax:** (612)445-6773
URL: http://www.adtauto.com
Products: Motor vehicles. **SIC:** 5012 (Automobiles & Other Motor Vehicles). **Est:** 1971. **Emp:** 225. **Officers:** Jerry Aman, General Mgr.

■ **20684** ■ **Mitsubishi Motor Sales of America Inc.**
6400 Katella Ave.
Cypress, CA 90630-5208
Phone: (714)372-6000 **Fax:** (714)373-1020
Products: Automobiles; Automobile parts and equipment. **SICs:** 5012 (Automobiles & Other Motor Vehicles); 5013 (Motor Vehicle Supplies & New Parts). **Est:** 1981. **Sales:** $3,691,000,000 (2000). **Emp:** 2,000. **Officers:** Takashi Sonobe, CEO & President; Masaki Takahashi, Exec. VP of Finance; Garrett J. Nash, VP of Marketing; Richard D. Recchia, COO & Exec. VP; Daniel McNamara, Sr. VP.

■ **20685** ■ **Monroe Tractor and Implement Company Inc.**
PO Box 370
Henrietta, NY 14467
Phone: (716)334-3867 **Fax:** (716)334-0001
URL: http://www.monroetractor.com
Products: Construction equipment and related attachments; Trailer line. **SICs:** 5082 (Construction & Mining Machinery); 5083 (Farm & Garden Machinery). **Est:** 1951. **Sales:** $60,000,000 (2000). **Emp:** 150. **Officers:** Janet E. Felosky, President, e-mail: jfelosky@ monroetractor.com.

■ **20686** ■ **Montgomery GMC Trucks Inc.**
PO Box 8187
Springfield, MO 65801
Phone: (417)869-0990 **Fax:** (417)869-0882
E-mail: mont_truck_trailer@yahoo.com
URL: http://www.truckpaper.com/montgomery
Products: Used trucks and trailers. **SIC:** 5012 (Automobiles & Other Motor Vehicles). **Est:** 1951. **Sales:** $6,000,000 (2000). **Emp:** 5. **Officers:** Hershel P. Montgomery Sr., President; H.P. Montgomery Jr., General Mgr.; John Montgomery, Sales/Marketing Contact, e-mail: hnoj99@yahoo.com; Monty Montgomery, Customer Service Contact, e-mail: mont_truck_trailer@yahoo.com; Gabe Montgomery, Human Resources Contact, e-mail: hpg142s@bearmail.edu. **Doing Business As:** Montgomery Truck and Trailer Sales.

■ **20687** ■ **Moto America Inc.**
613 Lillington St. E
Angier, NC 27501-9661
Phone: (919)893-6647 **Fax:** (919)893-8087
Products: Motorcycles. **SIC:** 5012 (Automobiles & Other Motor Vehicles). **Est:** 1991. **Sales:** $3,000,000 (2000). **Emp:** 9. **Officers:** Fran Contaldi, President.

■ **20688** ■ **Muscle Shoals Mack Sales Inc.**
PO Box 535
Tuscumbia, AL 35674
Phone: (205)383-9546 **Fax:** (205)383-9546
Products: Trucks. **SIC:** 5012 (Automobiles & Other Motor Vehicles). **Est:** 1958. **Sales:** $12,000,000 (2000). **Emp:** 53. **Officers:** Morris Britton, President; R.C. King, Vice President.

■ **20689** ■ **Nashville Auto Auction Inc.**
1450 Lebanon Rd.
Nashville, TN 37210
Phone: (615)244-2140 **Fax:** (615)255-2047
Products: Automobiles. **SIC:** 5012 (Automobiles & Other Motor Vehicles). **Sales:** $160,000,000 (2000). **Emp:** 300. **Officers:** Nick Snow, General Mgr.; Clint Green, Business Mgr.; Doug Jones, Sales Mgr.

■ **20690** ■ **Natchez Equipment Company Inc.**
PO Drawer A
Natchez, MS 39121
Phone: (601)445-9097
Products: Trucks; Tractors, including garden tractors. **SICs:** 5012 (Automobiles & Other Motor Vehicles); 5083 (Farm & Garden Machinery). **Est:** 1941. **Sales:** $7,000,000 (2000). **Emp:** 44. **Officers:** W.O. Womack, President.

■ **20691** ■ **Neely Coble Company Inc.**
PO Box 100347
Nashville, TN 37224
Phone: (615)244-8900
Free: (800)367-7712 **Fax:** (615)726-2411
Products: Trucks and truck parts. **SIC:** 5013 (Motor Vehicle Supplies & New Parts). **Est:** 1951. **Sales:**

$160,000,000 (2000). **Emp:** 182. **Officers:** Neely Coble III, President; William Foster, Exec. VP & CFO.

■ **20692** ■ **New York Motorcycle, Ltd.**
222-02 Jamaica Ave.
Queens Village, NY 11428
Phone: (718)479-7777
Free: (800)527-2727 **Fax:** (718)740-4887
Products: Motorcycles and motorcycle parts. **SICs:** 5012 (Automobiles & Other Motor Vehicles); 5013 (Motor Vehicle Supplies & New Parts).

■ **20693** ■ **NHK Intex Corp.**
1325 Remington Rd.
Schaumburg, IL 60173
Phone: (708)843-7277 **Fax:** (708)843-7329
Products: Automobiles. **SIC:** 5012 (Automobiles & Other Motor Vehicles). **Est:** 1993. **Sales:** $6,000,000 (2000). **Emp:** 4. **Officers:** Kazuaki Matsuzaki, President; Ken Matsubara, CFO.

■ **20694** ■ **Nichols Motorcycle Supply, Inc.**
4135 W 126th St.
Alsip, IL 60803
Phone: (708)597-3346
Products: Automobiles. **SIC:** 5012 (Automobiles & Other Motor Vehicles).

■ **20695** ■ **Nissan Motor Corporation U.S.A.**
PO Box 191
Gardena, CA 90248-0191
Phone: (310)532-3111 **Fax:** (310)719-3343
Products: Automobiles; Auto parts. **SICs:** 5012 (Automobiles & Other Motor Vehicles); 5013 (Motor Vehicle Supplies & New Parts). **Est:** 1960. **Sales:** $1,740,000,000 (2000). **Emp:** 2,300. **Officers:** Minoru Nakamura, CEO & President; Stephen A. Welsh, CFO; Jerry Florence, VP of Marketing; Evan L. Wride, Dir. of Information Systems; Robert M. Paskie, Dir of Human Resources.

■ **20696** ■ **Nissan Motor Corporation U.S.A. Infiniti Div.**
PO Box 191
Gardena, CA 90248
Phone: (310)719-5253 **Fax:** (310)719-5661
Products: Cars and trucks. **SIC:** 5012 (Automobiles & Other Motor Vehicles). **Est:** 1988. **Sales:** $330,000,000 (2000). **Emp:** 175. **Officers:** William Bruce, General Mgr.; Robert M. Paske, Marketing Mgr.

■ **20697** ■ **North East Auto-Marine Terminal Inc.**
403 Port Jersey Blvd.
Jersey City, NJ 07305
Phone: (201)432-7335
Products: Automobile imports and exports. **SIC:** 5012 (Automobiles & Other Motor Vehicles). **Sales:** $65,000,000 (2000). **Emp:** 120. **Officers:** David Husak, President.

■ **20698** ■ **Northern Truck Equip. Corp.**
47213 Schweigers Cir.
PO Box 1104
Sioux Falls, SD 57101-1104
Phone: (605)543-5206 **Fax:** (605)543-5219
URL: http://www.ntecorp.com
Products: Truck and trailer equipment. **SICs:** 5084 (Industrial Machinery & Equipment); 5083 (Farm & Garden Machinery). **Est:** 1934. **Sales:** $4,000,000 (1999). **Emp:** 30. **Officers:** Dean R. Wartenbee, President, e-mail: dean@ntecorp.com; Liz Navratil, Treasurer & Secty.; John Wartenbee, Vice President; Steve Bentele, Sales/Marketing Contact; Liz Navratil, Human Resources Contact. **Former Name:** Schweigers, Inc.

■ **20699** ■ **Northland Industrial Truck Company Inc.**
6 Jonspin Rd.
Wilmington, MA 01887
Phone: (978)658-5900 **Fax:** (978)658-8837
Products: Industrial trucks; Material handling products. **SICs:** 5084 (Industrial Machinery & Equipment); 5012 (Automobiles & Other Motor Vehicles). **Est:** 1969. **Sales:** $30,000,000 (2000). **Emp:** 100. **Officers:** Stephen O'Leary, CEO; Robert Bolduc, CFO.

■ 20700 ■ **Northwest Truck and Trailer Sales Inc.**
PO Drawer 2511
Billings, MT 59103
Phone: (406)252-5667 **Fax:** (406)252-9749
Products: Large industrial trucks. **SICs:** 5012 (Automobiles & Other Motor Vehicles); 5084 (Industrial Machinery & Equipment). **Est:** 1961. **Sales:** $19,000,000 (2000). **Emp:** 50. **Officers:** David Griffiths, Vice President; Gene Godfrey, CFO.

■ 20701 ■ **Orlando Yamaha**
9334 E Colonial Dr.
Orlando, FL 32817-4130
Phone: (407)273-3579 **Fax:** (407)275-3189
Products: ATV and personal water vehicles; Motorcycles and motorcycle parts. **SICs:** 5013 (Motor Vehicle Supplies & New Parts); 5091 (Sporting & Recreational Goods). **Emp:** 9. **Officers:** Vincent Rutigliano.

■ 20702 ■ **Pak-Mor Manufacturing Co.**
PO Box 14147
San Antonio, TX 78214
Phone: (210)923-4317 **Fax:** (210)922-7782
Products: Truck bodies for trash, recycling, and leaves. **SIC:** 5012 (Automobiles & Other Motor Vehicles). **Est:** 1947. **Sales:** $22,000,000 (2000). **Emp:** 60. **Officers:** J.V. Thurmond Jr., President.

■ 20703 ■ **Peck Road Ford Truck Sales Inc.**
2450 Kella Ave.
Whittier, CA 90601
Phone: (310)692-7267 **Fax:** (310)692-8390
Products: Light and heavy duty trucks and truck parts. **SICs:** 5012 (Automobiles & Other Motor Vehicles); 5013 (Motor Vehicle Supplies & New Parts). **Est:** 1970. **Sales:** $35,000,000 (2000). **Emp:** 100. **Officers:** A.W. Fraser, President; Sam Treynor, CFO; Weaver Jackson, Dir. of Marketing.

■ 20704 ■ **Perfection Equipment Co.**
5100 W Reno
Oklahoma City, OK 73127
Phone: (405)947-6603
Free: (800)888-7326 **Fax:** (405)948-1859
Products: Heavy trucks, parts, and equipment; Auto cranes; Truck platform beds. **SICs:** 5012 (Automobiles & Other Motor Vehicles); 5013 (Motor Vehicle Supplies & New Parts). **Est:** 1946. **Sales:** $14,000,000 (2000). **Emp:** 55. **Officers:** Chris Simpson, President; Maura Berney, VP of Finance; P. Voogt, VP of Sales; Bridget Fuchs, Dir of Human Resources.

■ 20705 ■ **Phoenix Manufacturing Incorporated**
PO Box 97
Nanticoke, PA 18634
Phone: (717)735-1800 **Fax:** (717)735-4228
Products: Ambulances and hearses; Truck mounted cranes; Truck bodies; Van tank and platform trailers. **SICs:** 5012 (Automobiles & Other Motor Vehicles); 5013 (Motor Vehicle Supplies & New Parts). **Officers:** Joseph A. Dougherty, COO.

■ 20706 ■ **C.E. Pollard Co.**
13575 Auburn
Detroit, MI 48223
Phone: (313)837-6776 **Fax:** (313)837-5374
E-mail: cep1934@aol.com
URL: http://www.members.aol.com/cep1934
Products: Truck and trailer equipment; Airport ground support equipment; Mobile municipal equipment. **SICs:** 5012 (Automobiles & Other Motor Vehicles); 5013 (Motor Vehicle Supplies & New Parts); 5083 (Farm & Garden Machinery). **Est:** 1934. **Sales:** $4,000,000 (2000). **Emp:** 8. **Officers:** Timothy C. Pollard, President; Terrence E. Pollard, Vice President; Dennis R. Pollard, Treasurer & Secty.; Paul Vitale, Marketing & Sales Mgr.

■ 20707 ■ **Pottstown Truck Sales Inc.**
1402 W High St.
Pottstown, PA 19464
Phone: (215)323-8100
Products: Trucks. **SIC:** 5012 (Automobiles & Other Motor Vehicles). **Est:** 1985. **Sales:** $7,000,000 (2000). **Emp:** 23. **Officers:** Lawrence O'Connor, President; Jack Hipple, Controller.

■ 20708 ■ **Power Motive Corp.**
5000 Vasquez Blvd.
Denver, CO 80216
Phone: (303)355-5900 **Fax:** (303)388-9328
Products: Construction and mining equipment. **SIC:** 5082 (Construction & Mining Machinery). **Est:** 1959. **Sales:** $21,000,000 (1999). **Emp:** 65. **Officers:** W.H. Blount Jr., CEO; J.D. Paranto, CFO; Ron Haraldson, President & COO; Paul Valdez, Information Systems Mgr.; Paul Valdez, Information Systems Mgr.

■ 20709 ■ **R & F Auto Sales**
Rd. 3, Box 331
Seaford, DE 19973
Phone: (302)629-2587 **Fax:** (302)628-3155
Products: Used automobiles. **SIC:** 5012 (Automobiles & Other Motor Vehicles).

■ 20710 ■ **Reliable Chevrolet Inc.**
3655 S Campbell St.
Springfield, MO 65807
Phone: (417)887-5800 **Fax:** (417)887-5754
Products: New and used automobiles. **SIC:** 5012 (Automobiles & Other Motor Vehicles). **Est:** 1967. **Sales:** $125,000,000 (2000). **Emp:** 275. **Officers:** Ceacil Van Tuyl, President; Mike Reynolds, General Mgr.

■ 20711 ■ **Reliance Trailer Manufacturing Inc.**
7911 Redwood Dr.
Cotati, CA 94931
Phone: (707)795-0081
Free: (800)339-7911 **Fax:** (707)795-9305
Products: Industrial truck trailers. **SIC:** 5012 (Automobiles & Other Motor Vehicles). **Est:** 1964. **Sales:** $16,000,000 (2000). **Emp:** 120. **Officers:** Brian Ling, President; James H. Coops, CFO; Lynn Meister, Sales Mgr.; Paul S. Winkler, Dir. of Systems; Donald Ling, CEO.

■ 20712 ■ **Rihm Motor Co.**
2108 University Ave.
St. Paul, MN 55114
Phone: (612)646-7833
Products: Trucks. **SIC:** 5084 (Industrial Machinery & Equipment). **Est:** 1934. **Sales:** $35,000,000 (2000). **Emp:** 63. **Officers:** Walter Rihm, President & Treasurer.

■ 20713 ■ **Roberts Motor Co.**
550 NE Columbia Blvd.
Portland, OR 97211
Phone: (503)240-6282
Products: Trucks and tractor trailers. **SIC:** 5012 (Automobiles & Other Motor Vehicles). **Est:** 1911. **Sales:** $53,000,000 (2000). **Emp:** 170. **Officers:** Vittz J. Ramsdell, President; Patrick Howard, Treasurer & Secty.; Ron DeVolder, Vice President.

■ 20714 ■ **Rocket Supply Corp.**
Hwy. 115 & Hwy. 54
Roberts, IL 60962
Phone: (217)395-2281
Products: Trucks, tanks, and parts. **SICs:** 5012 (Automobiles & Other Motor Vehicles); 5013 (Motor Vehicle Supplies & New Parts). **Sales:** $48,000,000 (2000). **Emp:** 75. **Officers:** Todd Coady, President.

■ 20715 ■ **Ruxer Ford, Lincoln, Mercury Inc.**
123 Place Rd.
Jasper, IN 47546
Phone: (812)482-1200 **Fax:** (812)634-2119
Products: Automobiles; Motor vehicles. **SIC:** 5012 (Automobiles & Other Motor Vehicles). **Est:** 1932. **Sales:** $30,000,000 (2000). **Emp:** 81. **Officers:** W. Weinzapfel, President.

■ 20716 ■ **Saab Cars USA Inc.**
4405-A International Blvd.
Norcross, GA 30093
Phone: (770)279-0100 **Fax:** (770)279-6582
Products: Automobiles. **SIC:** 5012 (Automobiles & Other Motor Vehicles). **Est:** 1956. **Sales:** $600,000,000 (2000). **Emp:** 188. **Officers:** Joel Manby, President; Kenneth Adams, VP of Finance & Admin.; John C. Kramer, VP of Marketing & Sales; Thomas Reis, VP of Human Resources & Admin.

■ 20717 ■ **St. Pete Auto Auction Inc.**
14950 Roosevelt Blvd.
Clearwater, FL 33762-3501
Phone: (813)531-7717
Products: Used automobiles. **SIC:** 5012 (Automobiles & Other Motor Vehicles).

■ 20718 ■ **Savage Inc.**
2968 Niagara Falls Blvd.
North Tonawanda, NY 14120
Phone: (716)692-2208 **Fax:** (716)692-2208
Products: Motor homes. **SIC:** 5012 (Automobiles & Other Motor Vehicles). **Est:** 1975. **Sales:** $200,000 (2000). **Emp:** 6. **Officers:** Claudia Savage, President.

■ 20719 ■ **Schetky Northwest Sales Inc.**
PO Box 20041
Portland, OR 97220-0041
Phone: (503)287-4141
Products: School buses. **SIC:** 5012 (Automobiles & Other Motor Vehicles). **Est:** 1945. **Sales:** $15,000,000 (2000). **Emp:** 35. **Officers:** John R. Schetky, President; John L. Schetky, CEO.

■ 20720 ■ **Don Schmid Motor Inc.**
PO Box 789762
Wichita, KS 67278-9762
Phone: (316)522-2253
Products: Cars and trucks. **SIC:** 5012 (Automobiles & Other Motor Vehicles). **Est:** 1938. **Sales:** $11,000,000 (2000). **Emp:** 50. **Officers:** Don Schmid, President; Frankie Schmid, Treasurer & Secty.

■ 20721 ■ **Simpson Buick Co.**
8400 E Firestone Blvd
Downey, CA 90241
Phone: (310)861-1261
Products: Cars. **SIC:** 5012 (Automobiles & Other Motor Vehicles). **Est:** 1950. **Sales:** $26,000,000 (2000). **Emp:** 74. **Officers:** Gary Simpson, CEO; David A. Simpson, Vice President.

■ 20722 ■ **Sonnen Mill Valley BMW**
1599 Francisco Blvd. E
San Rafael, CA 94901-5503
Phone: (415)388-2750
Free: (800)243-2269 **Fax:** (415)388-6264
Products: Automobiles, auto service. **SIC:** 5012 (Automobiles & Other Motor Vehicles). **Emp:** 49. **Officers:** Lise L. Sonnen. **Former Name:** Ervin Supply Corp. (Knoxville, Tennessee).

■ 20723 ■ **Sound Ford Inc.**
750 S Rainier Ave.
Renton, WA 98055
Phone: (425)235-1000 **Fax:** (425)277-1322
Products: Automobiles. **SIC:** 5012 (Automobiles & Other Motor Vehicles). **Est:** 1973. **Sales:** $90,000,000 (2000). **Emp:** 190. **Officers:** Richard Snyder, President; David Burgess, Information Systems Mgr.

■ 20724 ■ **Southeast Toyota Distributors Inc.**
100 NW 12th Ave.
Deerfield Beach, FL 33442
Phone: (305)429-2000 **Fax:** (305)429-2685
Products: Cars; Trucks. **SICs:** 5012 (Automobiles & Other Motor Vehicles); 5013 (Motor Vehicle Supplies & New Parts). **Est:** 1969. **Sales:** $4,500,000,000 (2000). **Emp:** 802. **Officers:** Pat Moran, President; Casey Gunnell, Exec. VP & CFO; John William, VP of Sales.

■ 20725 ■ **Southside Ford Truck Sales Inc.**
810 W Pershing Rd.
Chicago, IL 60609
Phone: (312)247-4000 **Fax:** (312)247-7152
Products: Trucks. **SIC:** 5012 (Automobiles & Other Motor Vehicles). **Sales:** $41,000,000 (2000). **Emp:** 80. **Officers:** Carl E. Statham, President.

■ 20726 ■ **Southwest Florida Auction Inc.**
PO Box 1646
Ft. Myers, FL 33902
Phone: (941)337-5141
Products: Cars. **SIC:** 5012 (Automobiles & Other Motor Vehicles).

■ 20727 ■ **Specialty Hearse and Ambulance Sales Corp.**
180 Dupont St.
Plainview, NY 11803
Phone: (516)349-7700 **Fax:** (516)349-0482
Products: Ambulances; Hearses; Limousines. **SIC:** 5012 (Automobiles & Other Motor Vehicles). **Est:** 1960. **Sales:** $14,000,000 (2000). **Emp:** 16. **Officers:** Terence J. O'Neill, President; Scott O'Neill, Vice President; Jim O'Neill, Sales Manager. **Alternate Name:** Specialty Vehicles Inc.

■ 20728 ■ **Specialty Vehicles, Inc.**
16351 Gothard St., Ste. C.
Huntington Beach, CA 92647
Phone: (714)848-8455
Free: (800)784-8726 **Fax:** (714)848-2114
E-mail: svi1@ix.netcom.com
URL: http://www.specialtyvehicles.com
Products: Trolleys; Trams; Used vehicles; Alternate fueled vehicles; Parts. **SIC:** 5012 (Automobiles & Other Motor Vehicles). **Est:** 1982. **Emp:** 10. **Officers:** Nancy C. Munoz, President; Dale R. DeLine, Sales Coordinator; Dennene Shephard, Parts and Service Manager; Rachel Munoz, Marketing Coordinator; David Smith, Admin. Asst.

■ 20729 ■ **Spong Trade Co.**
4125 Landing Dr.
Aurora, IL 60504
Phone: (630)851-1753 **Fax:** (630)851-1797
Products: New and used automobiles. **SIC:** 5012 (Automobiles & Other Motor Vehicles). **Officers:** Lee Spong, President.

■ 20730 ■ **Stag/Parkway Inc.**
PO Box 43463
Atlanta, GA 30336
Phone: (404)349-1918 **Fax:** (404)349-6869
Products: Recreational vehicles and supplies. **SIC:** 5013 (Motor Vehicle Supplies & New Parts). **Est:** 1968. **Sales:** $60,800,000 (2000). **Emp:** 250. **Officers:** Stan Sunshine, President; Michael Kantor, Controller; Mike McKay, Dir. of Marketing & Sales.

■ 20731 ■ **Subaru of America Inc.**
PO Box 6000
Cherry Hill, NJ 08034-6000
Phone: (609)488-8500 **Fax:** (609)488-0485
Products: Automobiles. **SIC:** 5012 (Automobiles & Other Motor Vehicles). **Est:** 1968. **Sales:** $1,500,000,000 (2000). **Emp:** 668. **Officers:** George Muller, President & COO; Joe Scharff, Treasurer; Chuck Worrell, Exec. VP; Monica Haley, VP of Human Resources.

■ 20732 ■ **Sunderland Motor Company Inc.**
PO Box 429
Jerseyville, IL 62052-0429
Phone: (618)498-2123
Products: Cars; Trucks. **SIC:** 5012 (Automobiles & Other Motor Vehicles). **Sales:** $7,500,000 (2000). **Emp:** 30. **Officers:** L.W. Sunderland, President; John P. Sunderland, General Mgr.

■ 20733 ■ **Superior Auto Sales Inc.**
5201 Camp Rd.
Hamburg, NY 14075
Phone: (716)649-6695
Free: (800)732-3275 **Fax:** (716)649-2375
E-mail: superior@cidcorp.com
Products: Automobiles. **SIC:** 5012 (Automobiles & Other Motor Vehicles). **Sales:** $30,000,000 (2000). **Emp:** 14. **Officers:** Richard J. Izzo, President; John LaVigne, Controller.

■ 20734 ■ **Susquehanna Motor Company Inc.**
PO Box 55
West Milton, PA 17886
Phone: (717)568-6941 **Fax:** (717)568-0987
Products: Trucks and truck parts. **SICs:** 5012 (Automobiles & Other Motor Vehicles); 5013 (Motor Vehicle Supplies & New Parts). **Est:** 1940. **Sales:** $7,000,000 (2000). **Emp:** 24. **Officers:** Harvey C. Follmer Jr., CEO; David G. Wagner, Vice President; Harvey C. Follmer III, President.

■ 20735 ■ **Jim Tate Jr.'s Murray Auto Auction Inc.**
Rte. 1
Almo, KY 42020
Phone: (502)753-8300
Products: Used automobiles, including parts. **SICs:** 5012 (Automobiles & Other Motor Vehicles); 5015 (Motor Vehicle Parts—Used).

■ 20736 ■ **Tate-Reynolds Company Inc.**
27 Commercial Blvd.
Novato, CA 94949
Phone: (415)883-3591
Products: Moving equipment; Vans. **SIC:** 5012 (Automobiles & Other Motor Vehicles). **Est:** 1966. **Sales:** $3,000,000 (2000). **Emp:** 10. **Officers:** John M. Tate Jr., President; Susan Rice, Controller.

■ 20737 ■ **Toyota Motor Sales U.S.A. Inc.**
19001 S Western Ave.
Torrance, CA 90509
Phone: (310)618-4000 **Fax:** (310)618-7801
Products: Cars and trucks. **SIC:** 5012 (Automobiles & Other Motor Vehicles). **Est:** 1957. **Sales:** $25,030,000,000 (2000). **Emp:** 15,748. **Officers:** Shinji Sakai, CEO & President; Robert Pitts, VP of Finance & Admin.; Yale Gieszl, Exec. VP; Doug Plescio, Dir. of Information Systems; Jim Lacy, VP of Human Resources.

■ 20738 ■ **Transnational Motors Inc.**
PO Box 2008
Grand Rapids, MI 49501
Phone: (616)949-7570 **Fax:** (616)949-7828
Products: Automobiles and automobile parts. **SICs:** 5012 (Automobiles & Other Motor Vehicles); 5013 (Motor Vehicle Supplies & New Parts). **Est:** 1977. **Sales:** $500,000,000 (2000). **Emp:** 105. **Officers:** Tom Claus, VP of Finance & Treasurer; David S. Hooker, President; James Fouts, Human Resources Mgr.

■ 20739 ■ **Truck Enterprises Inc.**
PO Box 472
Harrisonburg, VA 22801
Phone: (540)433-2631 **Fax:** (540)433-0460
Products: Trucks; Truck parts. **SICs:** 5012 (Automobiles & Other Motor Vehicles); 5013 (Motor Vehicle Supplies & New Parts). **Est:** 1962. **Sales:** $280,000,000 (2000). **Emp:** 180. **Officers:** Dwight Hartman, CEO; John Harter, Controller; M. Ritchie, Dir. of Data Processing; Karl Waizecker, Dir of Human Resources.

■ 20740 ■ **United Export Import, Inc.**
4113 Telegraph Rd., Ste. 227D
Bloomfield Hills, MI 48302
Phone: (248)644-6623 **Fax:** (248)258-8809
Products: Automobiles; Confections; Appliances. **SICs:** 5012 (Automobiles & Other Motor Vehicles); 5145 (Confectionery); 5064 (Electrical Appliances—Television & Radio). **Officers:** Rafael Hassan, President.

■ 20741 ■ **United States Export Co.**
1693 Merchant St.
Ambridge, PA 15003
Phone: (412)266-9300 **Fax:** (412)266-9109
Products: Motor vehicle supplies and parts; Automobiles and motor vehicles. **SICs:** 5012 (Automobiles & Other Motor Vehicles); 5013 (Motor Vehicle Supplies & New Parts). **Officers:** A.N. Gidwani, President.

■ 20742 ■ **Utility Trailer Sales of Oregon Inc.**
PO Box 1190
Clackamas, OR 97015
Phone: (503)653-8686
Products: Utility and semi-trailers. **SIC:** 5012 (Automobiles & Other Motor Vehicles). **Est:** 1985. **Sales:** $7,000,000 (2000). **Emp:** 27. **Officers:** Pat Hilsinger, President; Chris Graham, Accountant; Cliff Armstrong, Dir. of Marketing & Sales.

■ 20743 ■ **Volkswagen of America Inc.**
3800 Hamlin Rd.
Auburn Hills, MI 48326
Phone: (313)340-5000
Products: Automobiles. **SIC:** 5012 (Automobiles & Other Motor Vehicles). **Est:** 1955. **Sales:**

$1,930,000,000 (2000). **Emp:** 1,217. **Officers:** Clive Warrillow, CEO & President; John Vermeulen, VP of Finance; Urlich Fahrun, Vice President; H. William Lytle, VP of Human Resources.

■ 20744 ■ **Volkswagen of America Inc. Industrial Engine Div.**
420 Barclay Blvd.
Lincolnshire, IL 60069
Phone: (847)634-6000 **Fax:** (847)634-5295
Products: Cars. **SIC:** 5012 (Automobiles & Other Motor Vehicles). **Sales:** $50,000,000 (2000). **Emp:** 230. **Officers:** N. Phillips, President.

■ 20745 ■ **Volvo Cars of North America Inc.**
PO Box 913
Rockleigh, NJ 07647
Phone: (201)768-7300 **Fax:** (201)767-4835
Products: Automobiles. **SIC:** 5012 (Automobiles & Other Motor Vehicles). **Est:** 1956. **Sales:** $1,740,000,000 (2000). **Emp:** 620. **Officers:** Helge Alten, CEO & President; David Korpics, Sr. VP & CFO; William J. Hoover, Sr. VP; Michael Forbes, Dir. of Information Systems; Keld D. Alstrup, VP of Human Resources.

■ 20746 ■ **Von Housen Motors Inc.**
1810 Howe Ave.
Sacramento, CA 95825
Phone: (916)924-8000
Products: Automobiles. **SIC:** 5013 (Motor Vehicle Supplies & New Parts). **Est:** 1964. **Sales:** $27,000,000 (2000). **Emp:** 144. **Officers:** G. Grinzewitsch, President & Chairman of the Board; J. Pomares, CFO.

■ 20747 ■ **W.W. Wallwork Inc.**
PO Box 1819
Fargo, ND 58107
Phone: (701)476-7000
URL: http://www.wallworktrucks.com
Products: Commercial trucks. **SICs:** 5013 (Motor Vehicle Supplies & New Parts); 5013 (Motor Vehicle Supplies & New Parts); 5012 (Automobiles & Other Motor Vehicles). **Est:** 1921. **Sales:** $80,000,000 (2000). **Emp:** 125. **Officers:** William W. Wallwork III, President.

■ 20748 ■ **Dave Walters Inc.**
PO Box 946
Bemidji, MN 56601
Phone: (218)751-5655
Products: Mobile homes; Automobiles. **SIC:** 5084 (Industrial Machinery & Equipment). **Est:** 1953. **Sales:** $12,000,000 (2000). **Emp:** 24. **Officers:** W.R. Fankhanel, President.

■ 20749 ■ **Weed Chevrolet Company Inc.**
Rte. 413, Box 227
Bristol, PA 19007
Phone: (215)788-5511
Products: Automobiles. **SICs:** 5012 (Automobiles & Other Motor Vehicles); 5012 (Automobiles & Other Motor Vehicles); 5013 (Motor Vehicle Supplies & New Parts). **Est:** 1927. **Sales:** $20,000,000 (2000). **Emp:** 60. **Officers:** E.V. Weed, President; H. Weed, CFO; Bruce Weed, Dir. of Marketing.

■ 20750 ■ **Elliot Wilson Capital Truck L.L.C.**
8300 Ardwick-Ardmore Rd.
Landover, MD 20785
Phone: (301)341-5500
Products: Trucks, truck tractors, and truck chassis; Truck trailers. **SIC:** 5012 (Automobiles & Other Motor Vehicles). **Est:** 1986. **Sales:** $27,000,000 (2000). **Emp:** 50. **Officers:** Jr., George Wilson, President.

■ 20751 ■ **Wolfe's Terre Haute Auto Auction Inc.**
1601 Margaret Ave.
Terre Haute, IN 47802
Phone: (812)238-1431
Products: Automobiles. **SIC:** 5012 (Automobiles & Other Motor Vehicles).

■ 20752 ■ **Wolfington Body Company Inc.**
PO Box 218
Exton, PA 19341
Phone: (610)458-8501 **Fax:** (610)458-0293
Products: Motor vehicles, including school buses,

hearses, limousines, and ambulances. SIC: 5012 (Automobiles & Other Motor Vehicles). Est: 1932. Sales: $40,000,000 (2000). Emp: 100. Officers: Richard I. Wolfington, President.

■ 20753 ■ **Woodpecker Truck and Equipment Inc.**
PO Box 1306
Pendleton, OR 97801
Phone: (503)276-5515
Products: Large, heavy duty trucks. SIC: 5012 (Automobiles & Other Motor Vehicles). Est: 1960. Sales: $20,000,000 (2000). Emp: 100. Officers: Woody Clark, President; Lanny Cooper, VP & Controller.

■ 20754 ■ **World Wide Equipment Inc.**
PO Box 71
Prestonsburg, KY 41653
Phone: (606)874-2172   Fax: (606)874-2025
Products: Trucks. SIC: 5012 (Automobiles & Other

Motor Vehicles). Est: 1967. Sales: $100,000,000 (2000). Emp: 358. Officers: Terry L. Dotson, President; Randy Polk, CFO; John Mullins, Data Processing Mgr.

■ 20755 ■ **Yamaha Motor Corporation USA**
PO Box 6555
Cypress, CA 90630
Phone: (714)761-7300   Fax: (714)761-7302
Products: Transportation parts and equipment, including water vehicles, motorcycles, and snowmobiles. SICs: 5012 (Automobiles & Other Motor Vehicles); 5091 (Sporting & Recreational Goods). Sales: $870,000,000 (2000). Emp: 550. Officers: Mike Shibuya, President; Tom Ishiwaka, VP of Finance; Bob Starr, VP of Marketing; Phillip Wendel, VP of Human Resources.

■ 20756 ■ **York Truck Center Inc.**
55 S Fayette St.
York, PA 17404
Phone: (717)792-2636
Products: Trucks. SIC: 5012 (Automobiles & Other Motor Vehicles). Est: 1945. Sales: $6,000,000 (2000). Emp: 38. Officers: Barry L. Trattner, President; Kay Fry, Treasurer & Secty.

■ 20757 ■ **Zappia Enterprises Inc.**
173 Dingens St.
Buffalo, NY 14206
Phone: (716)822-6850
Products: Semi-trailers. SIC: 5012 (Automobiles & Other Motor Vehicles). Sales: $1,000,000 (2000). Emp: 20. Officers: Tony Zappia Jr., President.

(38) Office Equipment and Supplies

Entries in this section are arranged alphabetically by company name. When the company name is a personal name, the company name is alphabetized by the surname unless the first name or initial(s) are part of a trade name. See the User's Guide at the front of this directory for additional information.

■ **20758** ■ **A-1 Lock & Safe Co.**
8485 Overland Rd.
Boise, ID 83709-1642
Phone: (208)377-4500
Products: Office equipment; Vaults and safes. **SIC:** 5044 (Office Equipment). **Officers:** John Mussell, Owner.

■ **20759** ■ **A & B Business Equipment Inc.**
2904 W Russell St.
Sioux Falls, SD 57107-0706
Phone: (605)335-8520 **Fax:** (605)335-8942
Products: Office equipment. **SIC:** 5044 (Office Equipment). **Officers:** Dennis Aanenson, President.

■ **20760** ■ **A & B Electronic Systems Inc.**
612 Main Ave. N
Twin Falls, ID 83301-5740
Phone: (208)734-1740
Products: Office equipment. **SIC:** 5044 (Office Equipment). **Officers:** Alger Todd, President.

■ **20761** ■ **A-Copy Inc.**
7551 Winding Brook Dr.
Glastonbury, CT 06033
Phone: (860)633-6070
Products: Photocopiers and facsimile machines. **SIC:** 5044 (Office Equipment). **Sales:** $90,000,000 (2000). **Emp:** 900. **Officers:** P.W. Shoemaker, President.

■ **20762** ■ **A Timely Tech Services**
10301 Comanche Rd. NE
Albuquerque, NM 87111-3602
Phone: (505)296-6331 **Fax:** (505)296-6673
Products: Office equipment. **SIC:** 5044 (Office Equipment). **Officers:** Charlene Baehr, Owner.

■ **20763** ■ **AAA Distributors Inc.**
PO Box 415
Braddock Heights, MD 21714-0415
Phone: (301)428-0330
Free: (800)426-9967 **Fax:** (301)698-0146
E-mail: info@aaadist.com
URL: http://www.aaadist.com
Products: Overhead projectors and transparencies; Ink jet printer supplies; Report covers, sleeves, and frames. **SIC:** 5064 (Electrical Appliances—Television & Radio). **Est:** 1983. **Sales:** $2,000,000 (2000). **Emp:** 5. **Officers:** Ronald Martin, President, e-mail: ronm@aaadist.com.

■ **20764** ■ **Abacus**
PO Box 1242
Rapid City, SD 57709-1242
Phone: (605)343-3726
Products: Office equipment, including cash registers, scales, and calculators. **SIC:** 5044 (Office Equipment). **Officers:** D. Jacobi, Owner.

■ **20765** ■ **Able Steel Equipment Co. Inc.**
50-02 23rd St.
Long Island City, NY 11101
Phone: (718)361-9240 **Fax:** (718)937-5742
Products: Components for stationary buildings including wall, partition, floor, ceiling panels, etc.; Shelving and lockers; Office machines; Office supplies.

SICs: 5044 (Office Equipment); 5112 (Stationery & Office Supplies). **Sales:** $1,000,000 (2000). **Emp:** 49. **Officers:** Harris Singer.

■ **20766** ■ **ABM of Bismarck Inc.**
PO Box 2658
Bismarck, ND 58502-2658
Phone: (701)258-0210 **Fax:** (701)258-5572
Products: Office equipment. **SIC:** 5044 (Office Equipment). **Officers:** Ray Schuh, President.

■ **20767** ■ **A.C. Supply**
21160 Drake Rd.
Strongsville, OH 44136
Phone: (440)238-9150 **Free:** (800)321-1494
Products: Lead pencils, crayons, and artists' materials. **SICs:** 5112 (Stationery & Office Supplies); 5049 (Professional Equipment Nec).

■ **20768** ■ **Accent Business Products**
PO Box 1310
Fargo, ND 58107-1310
Phone: (701)236-6702 **Free:** (800)333-6132
Products: Office equipment. **SIC:** 5044 (Office Equipment). **Est:** 1982. **Sales:** $25,000 (2000). **Emp:** 2. **Officers:** Esther Schreiner, Partner.

■ **20769** ■ **Accurate Office Machines Inc.**
246 Federal Rd.
Brookfield, CT 06804-2647
Phone: (203)775-9668 **Fax:** (203)775-2459
Products: Electronic systems and equipment; Electronic parts; Computers; Computers; Fax machines; Computer printers. **SICs:** 5065 (Electronic Parts & Equipment Nec); 5045 (Computers, Peripherals & Software); 5044 (Office Equipment). **Officers:** Fred Pokrinchak, President.

■ **20770** ■ **ACS Digital Solutions**
PO Box 2163
Buena Park, CA 90621
Phone: (714)999-7733
Free: (800)491-2679 **Fax:** (714)999-7732
Products: Copying machines; Fax machines; Printers; Digital equipment. **SIC:** 5044 (Office Equipment). **Sales:** $2,000,000 (1999). **Emp:** 12. **Officers:** Tooraj Bakhtiari, President. **Former Name:** Alltech Business Solutions Inc.

■ **20771** ■ **Ada Copy Supplies Inc.**
8361 W State St.
Boise, ID 83703-6071
Phone: (208)853-2026 **Fax:** (208)853-2026
Products: Office equipment; Calculating machines; Cash registers. **SIC:** 5044 (Office Equipment). **Officers:** Don Grandmason, President.

■ **20772** ■ **S.G. Adams Printing and Stationery Co.**
1611 Locust St.
St. Louis, MO 63103
Phone: (314)621-2213 **Fax:** (314)241-6994
Products: Office supplies, including furniture, printed goods, and interior design products. **SICs:** 5112 (Stationery & Office Supplies); 5021 (Furniture). **Est:** 1890. **Sales:** $7,600,000 (2000). **Emp:** 100. **Officers:**

Hartley B. Comfort, President, Chairman of the Board & Treasurer.

■ **20773** ■ **Adirondack Chair Company Inc.**
31-01 Vernon Blvd.
Long Island City, NY 11106
Phones: 800-221-2444 (718)204-4555
Free: (800)221-2444 **Fax:** 800-477-1330
E-mail: info@adirondackdirect.com
URL: http://www.adirondackdirect.com
Products: Office furniture. **SIC:** 5021 (Furniture). **Est:** 1926. **Sales:** $20,000,000 (2000). **Emp:** 98. **Officers:** A. Siegel, President; Charles Endy, Treasurer; Marianna Lokis, Dir. of Advertising; Syl Cangero, Dir. of Marketing; Andrea Ross, Sales Mgr.

■ **20774** ■ **Adkins Printing Company Inc.**
PO Box 2440
New Britain, CT 06050
Phone: (203)229-1673 **Fax:** (203)229-1815
Products: Commercial office supplies. **SIC:** 5112 (Stationery & Office Supplies). **Sales:** $3,000,000 (1994). **Emp:** 35. **Officers:** Scott Pechout, President.

■ **20775** ■ **Advance Business Systems and Supply Co.**
PO Box 627
Cockeysville, MD 21030
Phone: (410)252-4800 **Fax:** (410)683-6691
Products: Office equipment. **SIC:** 5044 (Office Equipment). **Est:** 1964. **Sales:** $22,000,000 (2000). **Emp:** 140. **Officers:** Alan I. Elkin, President.

■ **20776** ■ **Advanced Financial Systems**
6827 Valley View Pl.
Cheyenne, WY 82009-2558
Phone: (307)634-7402
Products: Office equipment; Bank automatic teller machines. **SIC:** 5044 (Office Equipment). **Officers:** Gary Moore, President.

■ **20777** ■ **Advanced Office Systems Inc.**
2744 E Kemper Rd.
Cincinnati, OH 45241-1818
Phone: (513)771-1200
Free: (800)229-4267 **Fax:** (513)771-1285
Products: Ofice equipment, including fax machines, copiers, and shredders. **SIC:** 5044 (Office Equipment). **Est:** 1987. **Sales:** $6,000,000 (2000). **Emp:** 47. **Officers:** Ronald E. McCann, CEO; Delores J. McCann, President.

■ **20778** ■ **Advocate Publishing Co.**
214 Knox St.
Barbourville, KY 40906-1428
Phone: (606)546-9225 **Fax:** (606)546-3175
Products: Newspapers; Office equipment, including photocopy machines, cash registers, fax machines, and calculators. **SICs:** 5044 (Office Equipment); 5192 (Books, Periodicals & Newspapers). **Est:** 1938. **Sales:** $2,000,000 (2000). **Emp:** 25. **Officers:** Viola Wilson.

■ 20779 ■ Alabama Art Supply
2229 Magnolia Ave. S
Birmingham, AL 35205
Phone: (205)326-2132
Products: Lead pencils, crayons, and artists' materials.
SICs: 5112 (Stationery & Office Supplies); 5049
(Professional Equipment Nec).

■ 20780 ■ Alan Desk Business Interiors
8575 Washington Blvd.
Culver City, CA 90232
Phone: (323)655-6655
Free: (800)966-4337 **Fax:** (310)836-3748
E-mail: alaninc@aol.com
URL: http://www.alandesk.com
Products: Wood office furniture; Desks; High end
custom and standard products. **SIC:** 5021 (Furniture).
Est: 1941. **Sales:** $5,000,000 (2000). **Emp:** 21.
Officers: Ron Tucker, President; Frank Tucker, CEO;
Rosalie Tucker, Treasurer.

■ 20781 ■ Alaska Education & Recreational
Products
3520 B Balchen
PO Box 190333
Anchorage, AK 99519-0333
Phone: (907)243-8773
Free: (800)478-8773 **Fax:** (907)243-3243
Products: School supplies. **SIC:** 5112 (Stationery &
Office Supplies). **Est:** 1990. **Sales:** $250,000 (2000).
Emp: 1. **Officers:** Kit Wilson.

■ 20782 ■ Henry Alders Wholesale
Egbertson Rd.
Campbell Hall, NY 10916
Phone: (914)496-9191
Products: Lead pencils, crayons, and artists' materials.
SICs: 5112 (Stationery & Office Supplies); 5049
(Professional Equipment Nec).

■ 20783 ■ All About Offices Inc.
PO Box 7826
Boise, ID 83707-1826
Phone: (208)336-4700 **Fax:** (208)336-9887
Products: Office supplies, machines, and furniture.
SICs: 5044 (Office Equipment); 5021 (Furniture); 5112
(Stationery & Office Supplies). **Officers:** Paul
Shepherd, President.

■ 20784 ■ All Makes Office Machine Company
Inc.
150 W 24th St.
Los Angeles, CA 90007
Phone: (213)749-7483 **Fax:** (213)746-2905
URL: http://www.all-makes.com
Products: Office equipment sales and on-site service.
SIC: 5044 (Office Equipment). **Est:** 1945. **Sales:**
$3,000,000 (2000). **Emp:** 28. **Officers:** Joan
Degelsmith, President.

■ 20785 ■ Allied School and Office Products
PO Box 92677
Albuquerque, NM 87199-2677
Phone: (505)884-4900
Products: School and office products, including desks,
file cabinets, book cases and tables. **SICs:** 5112
(Stationery & Office Supplies); 5021 (Furniture). **Sales:**
$4,000,000 (2000). **Emp:** 25. **Officers:** A. Westfall,
President.

■ 20786 ■ Alling and Cory Co.
PO Box 20403
Rochester, NY 14602-0403
Phone: (716)581-4100
Free: (800)255-4642 **Fax:** (716)581-4708
URL: http://www.allingandcory.com
Products: Business products; Computer supplies.
SICs: 5111 (Printing & Writing Paper); 5112 (Stationery
& Office Supplies); 5113 (Industrial & Personal Service
Paper). **Est:** 1819. **Sales:** $750,000,000 (2000). **Emp:**
1,200. **Officers:** Arthur J. Dourville, President; James
W. Stenger, Treasurer; Thomas C. Drechsler, VP of
Marketing & Sales, e-mail: tdrechsler@
allingandcory.com; Margaret Supinski, VP of Human
Resources.

■ 20787 ■ Allstate Office Products Inc.
1605 E Hillsborough Ave.
Tampa, FL 33610
Phone: (813)238-9571 **Fax:** (813)237-1253
Products: Office supplies. **SIC:** 5112 (Stationery &
Office Supplies). **Est:** 1976. **Sales:** $25,000,000
(1993). **Emp:** 90. **Officers:** Larry Butler, Treasurer.

■ 20788 ■ Amcraft, Inc.
4348 S 90th St.
Omaha, NE 68127
Phone: (402)339-7950 **Free:** (800)AMC-RAFT
Products: Lead pencils, crayons, and artists' materials.
SICs: 5112 (Stationery & Office Supplies); 5049
(Professional Equipment Nec).

■ 20789 ■ American Business Concepts
2800 Gallows Rd., Ste. C
Vienna, VA 22180
Phone: (703)573-9313 **Fax:** (703)573-9317
E-mail: abc@vais.net
Products: Photocopying equipment and supplies; Fax
machines. **SIC:** 5044 (Office Equipment). **Officers:**
Bashar Islam, President.

■ 20790 ■ American Business International
Inc.
7860 Estancia Way
Sarasota, FL 34238
Phone: (941)921-1201 **Fax:** (941)921-1201
Products: Office supplies. **SIC:** 5112 (Stationery &
Office Supplies). **Officers:** Bill Crossley, President.

■ 20791 ■ American Business Machines
3475 Forest Lake Dr.
Uniontown, OH 44685-8105
Phone: (330)699-9912 **Fax:** (330)494-3239
Products: Copiers, faxes, and typewriters. **SIC:** 5044
(Office Equipment). **Est:** 1969. **Sales:** $38,000,000
(2000). **Emp:** 275. **Officers:** Mathew Blakney,
President; Dave Foltz, VP of Finance & Admin.; Dale
Highsmith, Sales Mgr.

■ 20792 ■ American Copy Inc.
PO Box 777
Merrimack, NH 03054-0777
Phone: (603)424-4771 **Fax:** (603)424-5917
Products: Electronic systems and equipment;
Electronic parts; Communication systems and
equipment; Fax machines. **SICs:** 5065 (Electronic
Parts & Equipment Nec); 5044 (Office Equipment).
Officers: Anthony Vilela, President.

■ 20793 ■ American Loose Leaf Business
Products Inc.
4015 Papin St.
St. Louis, MO 63110
Phone: (314)535-1414 **Fax:** (314)535-1905
Products: Office equipment and supplies. **SICs:** 5112
(Stationery & Office Supplies); 5044 (Office
Equipment). **Est:** 1920. **Sales:** $70,000,000 (2000).
Emp: 394. **Officers:** Gerald Holschen, President; Doug
Short, CFO.

■ 20794 ■ American Mailing Systems Inc.
PO Box 6808
Albuquerque, NM 87197-6808
Phone: (505)344-8704 **Fax:** (505)345-7683
Products: Office equipment; Addressing and mailing
machines; Shredders. **SIC:** 5044 (Office Equipment).
Officers: Steve Randall, President.

■ 20795 ■ American Office Machines Inc.
PO Box 9429
Metairie, LA 70055
Phone: (504)833-1964
Products: Office supplies and equipment. **SICs:** 5112
(Stationery & Office Supplies); 5044 (Office
Equipment).

■ 20796 ■ American Office Systems
1089 Wyoming Ave.
Exeter, PA 18643-1915
Phone: (717)655-4587 **Fax:** (717)655-4599
E-mail: apecoman@aol.com
URL: http://www.americanofficesystems.net
Products: Photocopy machines. **SIC:** 5044 (Office
Equipment). **Est:** 1977. **Emp:** 13. **Officers:** L. Jones,
President.

■ 20797 ■ American Photocopy Equipment Co.
9349 China Grove Church Rd.
Pineville, NC 28134
Phone: (704)551-8640
Free: (800)868-6482 **Fax:** (704)551-8659
Products: Copiers; Fax machines and accessories.
SIC: 5044 (Office Equipment). **Est:** 1977. **Sales:**
$4,000,000 (2000). **Emp:** 36. **Officers:** Ken Desio,
President, e-mail: kdesio@aol.com.

■ 20798 ■ American Safe and Lock Co.
117 N Main St.
Providence, RI 02903-1309
Phone: (401)331-3013
Products: Office equipment; Vaults and safes. **SIC:**
5044 (Office Equipment). **Officers:** Milton Wolferseder,
Owner.

■ 20799 ■ American Systems of the Southeast
Inc.
999 Harbor Dr.
West Columbia, SC 29169-3608
Phone: (803)796-9790
Free: (800)845-9895 **Fax:** (803)796-6322
Products: Printing and filing systems. **SICs:** 5045
(Computers, Peripherals & Software); 5021 (Furniture).
Est: 1972. **Sales:** $3,250,000 (2000). **Emp:** 41.
Officers: Billy Neese.

■ 20800 ■ Ameritrend Corp.
3710 Park Central Blvd.
Pompano Beach, FL 33064
Phone: (954)970-4900
Free: (800)940-2252 **Fax:** (954)970-9099
URL: http://www.ameritrend.com
Products: Fax machine systems and supplies; Voice
mail; Telephones; Computers. **SICs:** 5044 (Office
Equipment); 5065 (Electronic Parts & Equipment Nec);
5045 (Computers, Peripherals & Software). **Sales:**
$2,500,000 (2000). **Emp:** 50. **Officers:** Jeffrey Kline,
President.

■ 20801 ■ Ames Industries Inc.
2537 Curtiss St.
Downers Grove, IL 60515
Phone: (630)964-2440 **Fax:** (630)964-0497
Products: Office machines, parts and accessories,
including print wheels and drums. **SIC:** 5044 (Office
Equipment). **Est:** 1902. **Sales:** $15,000,000 (2000).
Emp: 75. **Officers:** R.C. Hilderbrandt, President; E.
Imredy, Treasurer & Secty.; R. Slager, Vice President.

■ 20802 ■ Ames Supply Co.
2537 Curtiss St.
Downers Grove, IL 60515
Phone: (630)964-2440
Free: (800)323-3856 **Fax:** (630)964-0497
URL: http://www.amessupply.com
Products: Tools, parts, and supplies for servicing
industry. **SIC:** 5112 (Stationery & Office Supplies). **Est:**
1902. **Sales:** $8,000,000 (1999). **Emp:** 45. **Officers:**
R.C. Hildebrandt, President; R. Slager, Vice President.

■ 20803 ■ Anacomp Inc. International Div.
PO Box 509005
San Diego, CA 92150
Phone: (619)679-9797 **Fax:** (619)748-8030
Products: Microfiche. **SIC:** 5044 (Office Equipment).
Sales: $180,000,000 (2000). **Emp:** 500. **Officers:** P.
Fred Walz, Vice President.

■ 20804 ■ Anchorage Reprographics Center
851 SW 6th Ave., Ste. 625
Portland, OR 97204-1343
Products: Office supplies; Drafting supplies. **SICs:**
5112 (Stationery & Office Supplies); 5049 (Professional
Equipment Nec).

■ 20805 ■ Anders Office Equipment Co.
1525 S Russell St.
Missoula, MT 59801
Phone: (406)549-4143
E-mail: aoecspro@aol.com
Products: Office machines, including printers, copiers,
and faxes. **SIC:** 5044 (Office Equipment). **Est:** 1960.
Officers: J. Davenport, Owner.

■ **20806** ■ **Andover Communications Inc.**
500 W Cummings Park
Woburn, MA 01801-6503
Phone: (781)932-3400
Free: (800)922-5604 **Fax:** (781)932-3648
Products: Fax machines; Photocopying equipment
and supplies. **SIC:** 5044 (Office Equipment). **Officers:**
James Dalis, President.

■ **20807** ■ **L'Anse Sentinel Co.**
PO Box 7
L' Anse, MI 49946
Phone: (906)524-6194 **Fax:** (906)524-6197
Products: Office supplies; Sports cards. **SIC:** 5112
(Stationery & Office Supplies). **Sales:** $1,000,000
(2000). **Emp:** 11. **Officers:** Edward Danner, Owner;
Lucille Conley, Bookkeeper.

■ **20808** ■ **Apgar Office Systems Inc.**
PO Box 2207
Manchester, ME 04351
Phone: (207)623-2674 **Fax:** (207)623-4535
E-mail: apgar@miut.net
URL: http://www.apgarofficesystems.com
Products: Office equipment including copiers,
furniture, fax machines, and multifunctional products;
Ergonomic seating; Color laser printers. **SICs:** 5044
(Office Equipment); 5021 (Furniture). **Est:** 1990.
Officers: Samuel W. Apgar, President.

■ **20809** ■ **Arbee Associates**
15890 Gaither Dr.
Gaithersburg, MD 20877-1404
Phone: (301)963-3900 **Fax:** (301)977-1734
Products: Contract office furniture. **SIC:** 5021
(Furniture). **Emp:** 150.

■ **20810** ■ **Arnold Pen Co. Inc.**
PO Box 791
Petersburg, VA 23804
Phone: (804)733-6612
Free: (800)296-6612 **Fax:** (804)862-3889
Products: Writing instruments, including pens and
markers. **SIC:** 5112 (Stationery & Office Supplies). **Est:**
1917. **Sales:** $1,750,000 (2000). **Emp:** 15. **Officers:**
Christopher Shepherd, Owner.

■ **20811** ■ **Arrow Business Products Inc.**
3770 S Perkins Rd.
Memphis, TN 38118
Phone: (901)362-8355 **Fax:** (901)362-7770
Products: Office machine fillers, including toners and
ribbons. **SIC:** 5112 (Stationery & Office Supplies).
Sales: $16,000,000 (2000). **Emp:** 80. **Officers:** Don
Nichleson, VP of Operations.

■ **20812** ■ **Arrow Sales Inc.**
1215 17th St.
Monroe, WI 53566-2403
Phone: (608)325-4260
Products: Janitors' supplies; Metal office furniture;
Wood office furniture. **SICs:** 5021 (Furniture); 5087
(Service Establishment Equipment). **Emp:** 31.
Officers: Thomas R. Smith.

■ **20813** ■ **Art Essentials**
PO Box 148
Alpha, OH 45301-0148
Phone: (937)426-3503
Free: (800)543-3465 **Fax:** (937)426-9726
E-mail: hollinsent@aol.com
Products: Artists' materials and craft supplies. **SICs:**
5099 (Durable Goods Nec); 5049 (Professional
Equipment Nec). **Est:** 1973. **Sales:** $200,000 (2000).
Emp: 3. **Officers:** Debra Fitzpatrick, President; James
Fitzpatrick, Sec. & Treas. **Former Name:** Hollins
Enterprises.

■ **20814** ■ **Artist Brush & Color Dist.**
Hofcraft Catalog
1730-B Air Park Dr.
Grand Haven, MI 49417
Phone: (616)847-8989 **Free:** (800)828-0359
Products: Lead pencils, crayons, and artists' materials.
SICs: 5112 (Stationery & Office Supplies); 5049
(Professional Equipment Nec).

■ **20815** ■ **Associated Business Products Inc.**
Scanning Systems
11413 Valley View Rd.
Eden Prairie, MN 55344
Phone: (612)941-2585
Free: (800)776-6688 **Fax:** (612)941-2996
URL: http://www.scansys.com
Products: Optic mark read and bar code scanners.
SIC: 5045 (Computers, Peripherals & Software). **Est:**
1992. **Sales:** $8,000,000 (2000). **Emp:** 25. **Officers:**
Richard Kleindl, VP of Operations.

■ **20816** ■ **Astro Business Solutions Inc.**
110 W Walnut St.
Gardena, CA 90248
Phone: (310)217-3000
Free: (888)OK-ASTRO **Fax:** (310)715-7050
URL: http://www.astro.canon.com
Products: Copiers and fax machines; Color graphic
systems; Image filing; Facilities management; Supplies;
Systems support. **SICs:** 5044 (Office Equipment); 5045
(Computers, Peripherals & Software). **Est:** 1974.
Sales: $140,000,000 (1999). **Emp:** 650. **Officers:** Ollie
Hatch Jr., President.

■ **20817** ■ **Astro Office Products Inc.**
110 Walnut St.
Gardena, CA 90248
Phone: (310)217-3000 **Fax:** (310)217-7050
Products: Copiers, facsimile, and information
management systems. **SIC:** 5044 (Office Equipment).
Sales: $180,000,000 (2000). **Emp:** 650. **Officers:** Ollie
Hatch, President; Ken Echizen, Exec. VP & Treasurer.

■ **20818** ■ **ATC Computer and Business**
Machines Inc.
15703 E Valley Blvd.
La Puente, CA 91744-3932
Phone: (626)333-0193
Products: Office machines; Computers. **SICs:** 5044
(Office Equipment); 5045 (Computers, Peripherals &
Software).

■ **20819** ■ **Atlantic Microsystems Inc.**
585 Grove St.
Herndon, VA 20170
Phone: (703)478-2764 **Fax:** (703)478-2721
Products: Work stations. **SIC:** 5021 (Furniture). **Est:**
1988. **Sales:** $5,500,000 (2000). **Emp:** 15. **Officers:**
Sanjay K. Puri, President.

■ **20820** ■ **Atlas Reproduction Inc.**
PO Box 2901
Casper, WY 82602-2901
Phone: (307)237-9523
Free: (800)372-3837 **Fax:** (307)237-4014
E-mail: atlas@trib.com
URL: http://www.atlasreproduction.com
Products: Office equipment. **SIC:** 5044 (Office
Equipment). **Est:** 1955. **Sales:** $1,500,000 (2000).
Emp: 12. **Officers:** James Mc Kenna, President, e-
mail: jim@atlasreproduction.com.

■ **20821** ■ **Audria's Crafts**
6821 McCart
Ft. Worth, TX 76133
Phone: (817)346-2494
Products: Lead pencils, crayons, and artists' materials.
SICs: 5112 (Stationery & Office Supplies); 5049
(Professional Equipment Nec).

■ **20822** ■ **Automated Business Systems**
2332 N Wingate Pl.
Meridian, ID 83642-7337
Phone: (208)344-8442
Products: Office equipment, including telephones.
SICs: 5044 (Office Equipment); 5065 (Electronic Parts
& Equipment Nec). **Officers:** Wayne Ball, President.

■ **20823** ■ **Automated Office Products Inc.**
9700A M.L. King Jr.
Lanham Seabrook, MD 20706
Phone: (301)731-4000 **Fax:** (301)459-2783
Products: Office equipment and supplies. **SIC:** 5112
(Stationery & Office Supplies). **Sales:** $3,500,000
(2000). **Emp:** 35.

■ **20824** ■ **Automated Office Systems Inc.**
6th Ave. N
PO Box 2404
Billings, MT 59105-0208
Phone: (406)245-3171 **Fax:** (406)245-9296
Products: Photocopying equipment and supplies. **SIC:**
5044 (Office Equipment). **Officers:** Jack Lutgen,
President.

■ **20825** ■ **Axis Communications Inc.**
4 Constitution Way, No. G
Woburn, MA 01801-1042
Phone: (781)938-1188
Free: (800)444-2947 **Fax:** (781)938-6161
Products: Copiers. **SIC:** 5045 (Computers, Peripherals
& Software). **Est:** 1989. **Sales:** $25,000,000 (2000).
Emp: 62. **Officers:** Les Yetton, President; Maura
Sheilds, Mgr. of Finance.

■ **20826** ■ **Aztec Business Machines Inc.**
3663 Via Mercado
La Mesa, CA 91941
Phone: (619)660-1300
E-mail: sales@aztecbm.com
URL: http://www.aztecbm.com
Products: Copiers, fax machines, shredders, printers,
multifunctional office machines, and typewriters;
Document imaging systems; Document management;
Electronic imaging. **SICs:** 5044 (Office Equipment);
5045 (Computers, Peripherals & Software). **Est:** 1969.
Sales: $10,000,000 (2000). **Emp:** 60.

■ **20827** ■ **B & B Office Supply Inc.**
3923 Garth Rd.
Baytown, TX 77521-3105
Phone: (281)422-8151 **Fax:** (281)427-7092
Products: Office supplies, including machines and
paper. **SICs:** 5044 (Office Equipment); 5112
(Stationery & Office Supplies). **Sales:** $1,000,000
(2000). **Emp:** 19. **Officers:** J. S. Blackburn.

■ **20828** ■ **Balfour Printing Company Inc.**
320 W 7th
Little Rock, AR 72201-4210
Phone: (501)374-2363 **Fax:** (501)371-9029
Products: Custom continuous forms; Stationary;
Brochures; Newsletters. **SIC:** 5112 (Stationery & Office
Supplies). **Est:** 1950. **Sales:** $1,250,000 (2000). **Emp:**
12. **Officers:** Linda Bell Stanford; Ray Bell.

■ **20829** ■ **Ball Stalker Co.**
1636 Northeast Expwy.
Atlanta, GA 30318
Phone: (404)679-8999 **Fax:** (404)679-8950
Products: Office furniture, including desks, chairs, and
file cabinets. **SIC:** 5021 (Furniture). **Est:** 1953. **Sales:**
$12,500,000 (2000). **Emp:** 54. **Officers:** Richard
Davenport, President.

■ **20830** ■ **Banking Forms Supply Company**
Inc.
PO Box 210
Marysville, MI 48040
Phone: (810)364-5000 **Free:** (800)446-6655
Products: Mortgage forms. **SIC:** 5112 (Stationery &
Office Supplies). **Sales:** $800,000 (2000). **Emp:** 20.
Officers: Steve Caverly, President; Sharon E. Caverly,
Treasurer & Secty.

■ **20831** ■ **Barnaby Inc.**
1620 De Kalb Ave.
Sycamore, IL 60178
Phone: (815)895-6555 **Fax:** (815)895-3617
Products: Office supplies, including paper, staples,
and paper clips. **SICs:** 5112 (Stationery & Office
Supplies); 5111 (Printing & Writing Paper). **Est:** 1963.
Sales: $2,000,000 (2000). **Emp:** 25. **Officers:** Paul
Barnaby Sr., Chairman of the Board; Paul Barnaby Jr.,
President; Steve Barnaby, Vice President.

■ **20832** ■ **Barry's Office Service Inc.**
1370 University Ave.
Morgantown, WV 26505-5518
Phone: (304)296-2594 **Fax:** (304)296-4014
Products: Office supplies; Artists' equipment;
Engineering and scientific instruments. **SICs:** 5112
(Stationery & Office Supplies); 5199 (Nondurable
Goods Nec); 5049 (Professional Equipment Nec).
Emp: 20. **Officers:** James D. Barry.

■ 20833 ■ Bates Manufacturing Co.
36 Newburgh Rd.
Hackettstown, NJ 07840
Phone: (908)852-9300 **Fax:** (908)852-7837
Products: Office supplies. **SIC:** 5112 (Stationery & Office Supplies). **Officers:** G.E. Mahon, Vice Pres./Intl.

■ 20834 ■ Batty & Hoyt Inc.
1444 Emerson St.
Rochester, NY 14606-3086
Phone: (716)647-9400
Free: (800)558-7874 **Fax:** (716)458-4790
E-mail: solutions@battyhoyt.com
URL: http://www.battyhoyt.com
Products: Office furniture; Material handling products. **SICs:** 5021 (Furniture); 5084 (Industrial Machinery & Equipment). **Est:** 1946. **Sales:** $15,000,000 (2000). **Emp:** 49. **Officers:** Gary Albanese; Stephen Platner; Dan Foster.

■ 20835 ■ Bay Area Data Supply Inc.
1282 Hammerwood Ave.
Sunnyvale, CA 94089
Phone: (408)745-6435 **Fax:** (408)745-7061
E-mail: mail@badsi.com
Products: Computer ribbon; Laser printer cartridges. **SIC:** 5113 (Industrial & Personal Service Paper). **Est:** 1969. **Sales:** $2,000,000 (2000). **Emp:** 15. **Officers:** Tom Barrett, President.

■ 20836 ■ Bay Microfilm Inc. Library Microfilms
1115 E Arques Ave.
Sunnyvale, CA 94086
Phone: (408)736-7444 **Fax:** (408)736-4397
E-mail: info@bmiimaging.com
URL: http://www.bmiimaging.com
Products: Micrographic equipment. **SIC:** 5044 (Office Equipment). **Est:** 1952. **Sales:** $10,000,000 (1999). **Emp:** 120. **Officers:** William D. Whitney, President.

■ 20837 ■ Bay Paper Co. Inc.
1 Bay Paper Dr.
Mobile, AL 36607
Phone: (205)476-9791 **Fax:** (205)476-9898
Products: Janitors' supplies; Paper cups; Laundry soap, chips, and powder; Soaps and detergents; Paper dishes; Paper and allied products. **SICs:** 5113 (Industrial & Personal Service Paper); 5087 (Service Establishment Equipment); 5169 (Chemicals & Allied Products Nec). **Est:** 1952. **Sales:** $3,000,000 (2000). **Emp:** 23. **Officers:** Violet Hirsch, President; Alan V. Hirsch, Exec. VP; M. Richard Hirsch, Treasurer.

■ 20838 ■ Beckley-Cardy, Inc.
100 Paragon Pky.
Mansfield, OH 44903
Phone: (419)589-1900
Free: (800)637-0955 **Fax:** (419)589-1522
Products: School supplies. **SIC:** 5112 (Stationery & Office Supplies). **Est:** 1932. **Sales:** $180,000,000 (2000). **Emp:** 800. **Officers:** James D. Miller, President. **Former Name:** Pyramid Art Supply.

■ 20839 ■ Russell Belden Electric Co.
PO Box 167
Joplin, MO 64802
Phone: (417)624-5650 **Fax:** (417)624-2756
URL: http://www.beldenelectric.com
Products: Electric equipment and supplies; Indoor and outdoor commercial and industrial lighting. **SIC:** 5063 (Electrical Apparatus & Equipment). **Est:** 1929. **Sales:** $6,000,000 (2000). **Emp:** 24. **Officers:** Jack M. Belden, CFO; Scott Belden, President.

■ 20840 ■ Bernstein Office Machine Co.
389 W Lincoln Hwy.
Penndel, PA 19047
Phone: (215)750-8740 **Fax:** (215)750-8754
Products: Office machines. **SIC:** 5044 (Office Equipment). **Emp:** 10. **Officers:** Meyer J. Bernstein.

■ 20841 ■ Best Business Products Inc.
PO Box 749
Sioux Falls, SD 57101-0749
Phone: (605)336-1484
Products: Office equipment. **SIC:** 5044 (Office Equipment). **Officers:** Betty Best, Chairman of the Board.

■ 20842 ■ BEST Cash Registers
418 W 5th St.
Reno, NV 89503-4412
Phone: (702)322-7054 **Fax:** (702)322-7055
Products: Office equipment, including calculating machines and cash registers. **SIC:** 5044 (Office Equipment). **Officers:** Jay Mowbray, President.

■ 20843 ■ Big Sky Office Products Inc.
501 N 23rd St.
Billings, MT 59101
Phone: (406)252-9210 **Fax:** (406)252-9718
Products: Furniture, including office and public building furniture. **SIC:** 5021 (Furniture). **Officers:** Dan Muller, President.

■ 20844 ■ BKM Total Office
340 Woodmont Rd.
Milford, CT 06460
Phone: (203)324-3138
Products: Commercial furniture. **SIC:** 5021 (Furniture). **Sales:** $350,000,000 (2000). **Emp:** 2,000. **Officers:** Don Northrop, President.

■ 20845 ■ Block and Company Inc.
1111 S Wheeling Rd.
Wheeling, IL 60090
Phone: (847)537-7200
Free: (800)323-7556 **Fax:** (847)537-1120
Products: Banking and cashier supplies. **SICs:** 5044 (Office Equipment); 5112 (Stationery & Office Supplies). **Est:** 1948. **Sales:** $9,000,000 (2000). **Emp:** 216. **Officers:** Mitchell Block, Chairman of the Board; Val Burlini, President; Judith Barsy, VP & Treasurer; Kenneth Block, Exec. VP; Barbara Cole, VP of Merchandising.

■ 20846 ■ Blue Ribbon Business Products Co.
930 SE Sherman St.
Portland, OR 97214-4655
Phone: (503)233-7288
Products: Copier toner; Typewriter ribbons. **SIC:** 5044 (Office Equipment). **Est:** 1984. **Sales:** $2,000,000 (2000). **Emp:** 9. **Officers:** Scott Kessler, President.

■ 20847 ■ Boise Cascade
800 W Bryn Mawr Ave.
Itasca, IL 60143
Phone: (708)773-5000 **Fax:** (708)773-6708
Products: Office supplies, including paper clips and furniture. **SIC:** 5112 (Stationery & Office Supplies).

■ 20848 ■ Boise Cascade Office Products Corp.
3025 Powers Ave.
Jacksonville, FL 32207-8011
Phone: (904)773-5000
Products: Office furniture; Copiers; Paper. **SICs:** 5112 (Stationery & Office Supplies); 5044 (Office Equipment); 5113 (Industrial & Personal Service Paper). **Sales:** $1,985,600,000 (2000). **Emp:** 8,500. **Officers:** Peter G. Danis Jr., CEO & President; Carol B. Moerdyk, Sr. VP & CFO.

■ 20849 ■ T. Talbott Bond Co.
7138 Windsor Blvd.
Baltimore, MD 21244
Phone: (410)265-8600
Products: Office equipment. **SIC:** 5044 (Office Equipment). **Sales:** $86,000,000 (2000). **Emp:** 540. **Officers:** Henry Bond, President; Mike Gomsac, Controller.

■ 20850 ■ Bottman Design Inc.
340 Whitney Ave.
Salt Lake City, UT 84115-5120
Phone: (801)973-5410 **Fax:** (801)973-0511
Products: Greeting cards. **SIC:** 5112 (Stationery & Office Supplies). **Officers:** Thomas Bottman, President.

■ 20851 ■ Boutique Trim
21200 Pontiac Trl.
South Lyon, MI 48178
Phone: (248)437-2017
Free: (888)437-3888 **Fax:** (248)437-9463
E-mail: info@btcrafts.com
URL: http://www.btcrafts.com
Products: Jewelry findings; Silk flowers; Craft supplies, including paints. **SICs:** 5112 (Stationery & Office Supplies); 5193 (Flowers & Florists' Supplies); 5092 (Toys & Hobby Goods & Supplies); 5094 (Jewelry & Precious Stones); 5049 (Professional Equipment Nec). **Est:** 1969. **Emp:** 17. **Officers:** Lois Heerema, President, e-mail: lheerema@btcrafts.com; Kevin Williams, VP of Operations.

■ 20852 ■ Bowlus School Supply Inc.
PO Box 1349
Pittsburg, KS 66762
Phone: (316)231-3450 **Fax:** (316)231-7351
Products: School and office supplies. **SIC:** 5112 (Stationery & Office Supplies). **Sales:** $25,000,000 (2000). **Emp:** 85. **Officers:** Rudy Simoncic, Owner.

■ 20853 ■ Brain Corp.
HC 66 Box 94A
Wilmot, NH 03287-9617
Phone: (603)668-3325 **Fax:** (603)668-3680
Products: Office equipment; Calculating machines; Cash registers; Computers. **SICs:** 5044 (Office Equipment); 5045 (Computers, Peripherals & Software). **Officers:** Richard Dumais, President.

■ 20854 ■ Don Brann Associates Inc.
21840 Wyoming Pl.
Oak Park, MI 48237
Phone: (248)543-1950 **Fax:** (248)543-1368
Products: Office storage units, files, and tables, except wood; Floorcoverings; Panel and modular systems furniture and all other nonwood office furniture; Wood office furniture. **SICs:** 5021 (Furniture); 5023 (Homefurnishings); 5046 (Commercial Equipment Nec). **Est:** 1967. **Sales:** $1,200,000 (2000). **Emp:** 4. **Officers:** Donald T. Brann, President; Nancy Bonar, Exec. VP.

■ 20855 ■ Bristol Retail Solutions Inc.
3760 Kilroy Airport Way, Ste. 450
Long Beach, CA 90806-2484
Phone: (562)988-3660
Free: (888)449-4012 **Fax:** (562)988-7911
URL: http://www.bristolpos.com
Products: Point of sale systems. **SIC:** 5087 (Service Establishment Equipment). **Est:** 1996. **Sales:** $21,100,000 (2000). **Emp:** 262. **Officers:** David Kaye, CEO & President; Bill Kerechek, CFO; Michael Pollastro, COO.

■ 20856 ■ Broadway Office Interiors
2115 Locust St.
St. Louis, MO 63103
Phone: (314)421-0753 **Fax:** (314)421-5437
E-mail: boi@boffice.com
Products: Office furniture. **SICs:** 5021 (Furniture); 5044 (Office Equipment). **Est:** 1934. **Emp:** 45. **Officers:** Paul Friedman, President.

■ 20857 ■ Brooks Duplicator Co.
10402 Rockley Rd.
Houston, TX 77099
Phone: (281)568-9787
Products: Office machines. **SIC:** 5044 (Office Equipment).

■ 20858 ■ Brother International Corp.
100 Somerset Corporate Blvd.
Bridgewater, NJ 08807
Phone: (908)704-1700 **Fax:** (908)704-8235
Products: Office equipment parts. **SICs:** 5044 (Office Equipment); 5064 (Electrical Appliances—Television & Radio). **Sales:** $1,000,000,000 (2000). **Emp:** 725. **Officers:** Hiromi Gunji, CEO, President & Chairman of the Board.

■ 20859 ■ Brothers Office Supply Inc.
901 Hilliard Rome Rd.
Columbus, OH 43228
Phone: (614)870-6414
Products: Office supplies; Office furniture. **SICs:** 5044 (Office Equipment); 5021 (Furniture).

■ 20860 ■ Stan Brown Arts & Crafts
13435 Whitaker Way
Portland, OR 97230
Phone: (503)257-0559
Products: Lead pencils, crayons, and artists' materials.

SICs: 5112 (Stationery & Office Supplies); 5049 (Professional Equipment Nec).

■ 20861 ■ BT Office Products International Inc. Detroit Div.
28241 Mound Rd.
Warren, MI 48092
Phone: (810)573-8877
Free: (888)982-8674   Fax: (810)573-8469
URL: http://www.btopi.com
Products: Office furniture and supplies. SICs: 5021 (Furniture); 5044 (Office Equipment). Sales: $30,000,000 (2000). Emp: 110. Officers: David Londal, General Mgr.

■ 20862 ■ BT Office Products USA
6 Parkway N
Deerfield, IL 60015-2544
Phone: (708)808-3000
Products: Office supplies, including desks, chairs, and file cabinets. SICs: 5112 (Stationery & Office Supplies); 5021 (Furniture).

■ 20863 ■ BT Summit Office Products Inc.
303 W 10th St.
New York, NY 10014
Phone: (914)997-9400
Products: Office supplies. SIC: 5112 (Stationery & Office Supplies).

■ 20864 ■ Buffalo Office Interiors Inc.
1418 Niagra St.
Buffalo, NY 14213
Phone: (716)883-8222
Products: Office furniture, including chairs, desks, and tables. SIC: 5021 (Furniture). Sales: $4,000,000 (2000). Emp: 25. Officers: James Stano, President; Jane Greenslade, Controller.

■ 20865 ■ Buschart Office Products Inc.
1834 Walton Rd.
St. Louis, MO 63114
Phone: (314)426-7222
Products: Office products, including pens and folders; Furniture. SICs: 5112 (Stationery & Office Supplies); 5021 (Furniture). Est: 1896. Sales: $33,000,000 (2000). Emp: 125. Officers: Richard C. Dubin, President; Ted Scheff, CFO; Paul Stuart, VP of Marketing & Sales.

■ 20866 ■ Business Data Systems Inc.
1 Swords Ln.
Billings, MT 59105-3029
Phone: (406)256-3782
Products: Office equipment; Calculating machines; Cash registers. SIC: 5044 (Office Equipment). Officers: Doug Heine, President.

■ 20867 ■ Business Express of Boulder Inc.
1904 Pearl St.
Boulder, CO 80302
Phone: (303)443-9300
Products: Office and business furnishings, including cabinets and table lamps; Paper and writing pads. SIC: 5112 (Stationery & Office Supplies). Est: 1985. Sales: $3,000,000 (2000). Emp: 25. Officers: Pavel Bouska, President; Chelli Smith, Secretary; Beth Byerlein, Dir. of Marketing & Sales.

■ 20868 ■ Business Office Supply Co.
816 E Broadway St.
Louisville, KY 40204
Phone: (502)589-8400   Fax: (502)589-8488
Products: Office supplies; Wood office furniture. SIC: 5112 (Stationery & Office Supplies). Est: 1966. Sales: $40,000,000 (2000). Emp: 200. Officers: Stephen Zink, President; Joyce Marcell, Controller.

■ 20869 ■ Business Support Services
1810 49th St. S, Apt. 206
Fargo, ND 58103-7705
Phone: (701)232-8221   Fax: (701)232-6737
Products: Office equipment. SIC: 5044 (Office Equipment). Officers: Larry Jensen, President.

■ 20870 ■ Business With Pleasure
PO Box 309
Thermopolis, WY 82443-0309
Phone: (307)864-2385
Products: Office supplies. SIC: 5112 (Stationery & Office Supplies). Officers: Barbara Campbell, Partner.

■ 20871 ■ Business World Inc.
PO Box 624
Manchester Center, VT 05255
Phone: (802)362-3318   Fax: (802)362-3841
Products: Office equipment. SIC: 5044 (Office Equipment). Officers: Edmund Lauzon, President.

■ 20872 ■ Cabin-Craft Southwest
1500 Westpark Way
Euless, TX 76040
Phone: (817)571-4925
Products: Lead pencils, crayons, and artists' materials. SICs: 5112 (Stationery & Office Supplies); 5049 (Professional Equipment Nec).

■ 20873 ■ Camilo Office Furniture, Inc.
4110 Laguna St.
Coral Gables, FL 33146
Phone: (305)445-3505   Fax: (305)447-8566
E-mail: info@camilo.com
URL: http://www.camilo.com
Products: Chairs; Desks; Metal office furniture; Wood office furniture. SIC: 5021 (Furniture). Est: 1963. Sales: $7,500,000 (2000). Emp: 105. Officers: Camilo Lopez Jr., President; Jose Lopez, Secretary; Luis Lopez, Treasurer; Ricardo Lopez, Vice President; Camilo Lopez III, Vice President.

■ 20874 ■ Cano Corp.
225 Industrial Rd.
Fitchburg, MA 01420-4603
Phone: (978)342-0953   Fax: (978)342-5082
Products: Office furniture. SIC: 5021 (Furniture). Est: 1971. Sales: $16,000,000 (1999). Emp: 99. Officers: Jan Kapstad, Sales & Marketing Contact, e-mail: jan@canocorp.com.

■ 20875 ■ Canon U.S.A. Inc., Office Products Div.
PO Box 1000
Jamesburg, NJ 08831
Phone: (732)521-7000
Products: Copiers and copier cartridges; Calculators; Digital cameras. SIC: 5044 (Office Equipment).

■ 20876 ■ Capital Stationery Corp.
PO Box 230
Mineola, NY 11501-0230
Phone: (516)248-3700   Fax: (516)248-3760
Products: Panel and modular systems furniture and all other nonwood office furniture; Wood office furniture; Stationery and office supplies; Printing; Rubber stamps; Office machine sales and repairs. SICs: 5044 (Office Equipment); 5112 (Stationery & Office Supplies). Est: 1886. Sales: $1,000,000 (2000). Emp: 5. Officers: Jack I. Baker.

■ 20877 ■ Capitol Copy Products Inc.
12000 Old Baltimore Pike
Beltsville, MD 20705
Phone: (301)937-5030   Fax: (301)937-6031
Products: Copier and facsimile equipment and supplies. SIC: 5044 (Office Equipment). Sales: $20,200,000 (2000). Emp: 99. Officers: Armen A. Manoogian, President; Doris Green, CFO.

■ 20878 ■ Capri Arts & Crafts
06864 McGlincey Ln.
Campbell, CA 95008
Phone: (408)377-3833
Products: Lead pencils, crayons, and artists' materials. SICs: 5112 (Stationery & Office Supplies); 5049 (Professional Equipment Nec).

■ 20879 ■ Cardamation Company Inc.
PO Box 329
Phoenixville, PA 19460
Phone: (610)935-9700
Free: (800)848-1718   Fax: (610)935-7340
Products: Card sorters, aperture card and page scanners. SIC: 5044 (Office Equipment). Sales:

$1,500,000 (2000). Emp: 12. Officers: Robert Swartz, President; Mary Lou Francesco, Finance Officer.

■ 20880 ■ Cardinal Office Systems
101 Bradley Dr.
Nicholasville, KY 40356
Phone: (606)885-6161
Free: (800)766-0963   Fax: (606)885-9610
Products: Office furniture and supplies. SICs: 5021 (Furniture); 5112 (Stationery & Office Supplies). Est: 1956. Sales: $6,000,000 (2000). Emp: 49. Officers: Jim Gray Jr.

■ 20881 ■ Carolina Office Equipment Co.
1030 2nd Ave. NW
PO Box 2145
Hickory, NC 28601
Phone: (704)322-6190   Fax: (704)327-4148
Products: Office machines and supplies. SICs: 5044 (Office Equipment); 5112 (Stationery & Office Supplies). Emp: 51. Officers: Byron Logan.

■ 20882 ■ Carolina Office Equipment Co.
PO Box 1888
Rocky Mount, NC 27801
Phone: (919)977-1121   Fax: (919)985-1564
Products: Office machines, including copiers, typewriters, and facsimile machines. SIC: 5044 (Office Equipment). Est: 1921. Sales: $17,000,000 (2000). Emp: 175. Officers: C.A. Robbins Sr., Chairman of the Board; David Manus, Controller; M.C. Culpepper, Dir. of Marketing & Sales.

■ 20883 ■ Casas Office Machines Inc.
PO Box 13666
Santurce, PR 00908
Phone: (787)781-0040
Products: Office machines. SIC: 5044 (Office Equipment).

■ 20884 ■ Cash Register Sales Inc.
2909 Anthony Ln. NE
Minneapolis, MN 55418
Phone: (612)781-3474
Free: (800)333-4949   Fax: (612)781-9418
E-mail: moreinfo@crs-usa.com
URL: http://www.crs-usa.com
Products: Cash registers. SICs: 5044 (Office Equipment); 5045 (Computers, Peripherals & Software). Est: 1927. Sales: $20,000,000 (2000). Emp: 58. Officers: David Sanders, President; William Oas, Controller; Craig Fuss, Sales Mgr.

■ 20885 ■ Cash Register Sales & Service
2080 Dimond Dr.
Anchorage, AK 99507-1359
Phone: (907)563-0761   Fax: (907)563-2898
Products: Office equipment. SIC: 5044 (Office Equipment). Officers: Don Nusbaum, Partner.

■ 20886 ■ Cash Register Systems Inc.
60110 Constitution NE
Albuquerque, NM 87110
Phone: (505)265-5979   Fax: (505)265-5979
Products: Cash registers. SIC: 5044 (Office Equipment). Officers: Ken Boyd, Chairman of the Board.

■ 20887 ■ Castle Copiers & More Inc.
23 Austin Rd.
North Kingstown, RI 02852-1313
Phone: (401)884-1180   Fax: (401)884-7838
Products: Office equipment. SIC: 5044 (Office Equipment). Officers: Daniel Porter, President.

■ 20888 ■ Centercore New England Inc.
23 Lincoln St.
Biddeford, ME 04005-2019
Phone: (207)283-0147
Products: Office and public building furniture. SIC: 5021 (Furniture). Officers: Wayne Sharkey, President.

■ 20889 ■ Central Business Supply Inc.
PO Box 807
Brookings, SD 57006-0807
Phone: (605)692-6363
Products: Office equipment. SIC: 5044 (Office Equipment). Officers: Alan Rogers, President.

■ 20890 ■ Central Business Systems Inc.
2514 Hwy. 281 S
Jamestown, ND 58401-6606
Phone: (701)252-7474 **Fax:** (701)252-7477
E-mail: cbsi1@daktel.com
Products: Office equipment, including calculating machines and copiers; Computers and computer software. **SIC:** 5044 (Office Equipment). **Est:** 1974. **Sales:** $25,000,000 (2000). **Emp:** 23. **Officers:** Lloyd Kuhlmann, President; William Bader, Vice President.

■ 20891 ■ Central Maine Business Machines
84 Western Ave.
Augusta, ME 04330-7225
Phone: (207)622-6100 **Fax:** (207)622-6100
Products: Office equipment. **SIC:** 5044 (Office Equipment). **Officers:** Clifton Smith, Owner.

■ 20892 ■ Central Office Supply Co.
1408 Bunton Rd.
Louisville, KY 40213-1857
Phone: (502)456-4080 **Fax:** (502)454-6972
Products: Office equipment and supplies. **SIC:** 5112 (Stationery & Office Supplies). **Sales:** $1,300,000 (2000). **Emp:** 10.

■ 20893 ■ Century Business Equipment Inc.
1080 W Sam Houston Pkwy. N
Houston, TX 77043
Phone: (713)973-6147 **Fax:** (713)973-6141
Products: Office equipment. **SIC:** 5044 (Office Equipment). **Sales:** $4,800,000 (2000). **Emp:** 30. **Officers:** T.C. Huguley, President; B.P. Drawbaugh, Secretary.

■ 20894 ■ CERBCO Inc.
3421 Pennsy Dr.
Landover, MD 20785
Phone: (301)773-1784 **Fax:** (301)322-3041
Products: Sewer reconstruction; Facsimile and copier equipment and supplies. **SIC:** 5044 (Office Equipment). **Sales:** $23,300,000 (1999). **Emp:** 204. **Officers:** Robert W. Erickson, President; Robert F. Hartman, VP & Treasurer.

■ 20895 ■ Champion Industries Inc. (Huntington, West Virginia)
PO Box 2968
Huntington, WV 25728
Phone: (304)528-2791
Products: Office products and furniture. **SICs:** 5112 (Stationery & Office Supplies); 5021 (Furniture). **Sales:** $108,400,000 (2000). **Emp:** 897. **Officers:** Marshall T. Reynolds, CEO, President & Chairman of the Board; Joseph C. Worth III, VP & CFO.

■ 20896 ■ Charlotte Copy Data Inc.
4404-A Stuart Andrew Blvd.
Charlotte, NC 28217
Phone: (704)523-3333
Products: Photocopying equipment and supplies; Fax machines. **SICs:** 5045 (Computers, Peripherals & Software); 5044 (Office Equipment). **Est:** 1988. **Sales:** $11,700,000 (2000). **Emp:** 100. **Officers:** Kal Kardous, Owner; Maryanne Walker, CFO & Treasurer.

■ 20897 ■ Chemicraft Corp.
351 W 35th St.
New York, NY 10001
Phone: (212)563-5278 **Fax:** (212)967-5875
Products: Computer ribbons; Ink; Ink powder. **SIC:** 5113 (Industrial & Personal Service Paper). **Est:** 1915. **Sales:** $29,000,000 (2000). **Emp:** 100. **Officers:** A. Sharkey, President; S. Stevens, Exec. VP of Finance; J. Weston, Dir. of Marketing; S. Klein, Dir. of Systems; R. Scott, Dir of Human Resources.

■ 20898 ■ Chip & Wafer Office Automation
PO Box 17290
Honolulu, HI 96817-0290
Phone: (808)842-5146 **Fax:** (808)842-7402
Products: Electronic parts and equipment; Communication equipment; Facsimile equipment; Copiers. **SICs:** 5044 (Office Equipment); 5065 (Electronic Parts & Equipment Nec). **Est:** 1986. **Officers:** Linda Eto, President.

■ 20899 ■ Church Business Machines
7901 Earhart Blvd., Ste. F
New Orleans, LA 70125
Phone: (504)488-8763
Products: Office equipment. **SIC:** 5044 (Office Equipment).

■ 20900 ■ Citifax Corp.
28427 N Ballard Dr.
Lake Forest, IL 60045
Phone: (847)362-3300 **Fax:** (847)362-3050
Products: Fax paper. **SIC:** 5111 (Printing & Writing Paper). **Sales:** $4,000,000 (2000). **Emp:** 40. **Officers:** Doug Doyle, CFO.

■ 20901 ■ City Business Machines Inc.
2201 Brockwood Dr., Ste. 112
Little Rock, AR 72202
Phone: (501)663-4044
Products: Copiers and fax machines. **SIC:** 5044 (Office Equipment).

■ 20902 ■ E.H. Clarke and Bro. Inc.
3272 Winbrook Dr.
Memphis, TN 38116
Phone: (901)398-5700 **Fax:** (901)398-9696
Products: Office supplies and furniture. **SICs:** 5112 (Stationery & Office Supplies); 5021 (Furniture). **Est:** 1897. **Sales:** $4,000,000 (2000). **Emp:** 19. **Officers:** Larry W. Miller, President; John D. Ivy Jr., Treasurer.

■ 20903 ■ Clute Office Equipment Inc.
PO Box 1745
Minot, ND 58702-1745
Phone: (701)838-8624 **Fax:** (701)852-9384
Products: Office equipment. **SIC:** 5044 (Office Equipment). **Officers:** James Clute, President.

■ 20904 ■ COE Distributing, Inc.
Franklin Commercial Park
Rte. 51 N
Uniontown, PA 15401
Phone: (724)437-8202
Free: (800)388-8202 **Fax:** (724)437-6037
E-mail: coedist@hhs.net
URL: http://www.coedist.com
Products: Office furniture; Ergonomic accessories; Installation. **SIC:** 5021 (Furniture). **Est:** 1986. **Emp:** 33. **Officers:** J.D. Ewing, President, e-mail: jcoedist@coedist.com; Melanie Ewing, Dir. of Merchandising, e-mail: coedist@hhs.net; Karen Rahl, Customer Service Manager, e-mail: kcoedist@coedist.com.

■ 20905 ■ Colonial Office Supplies Inc.
21710 Great Mills Rd.
PO Box 250
Lexington Park, MD 20653-0250
Phone: (301)862-2760 **Fax:** (301)862-4819
Products: Office supplies. **SIC:** 5112 (Stationery & Office Supplies). **Officers:** Shirley Colleary, President.

■ 20906 ■ Colorcon
Moyer Blvd.
West Point, PA 19486
Phone: (215)699-7733 **Fax:** (215)661-2605
Products: Pharmaceutical coating systems, colorants, excipients, monogramming inks, and non-toxic printing inks. **SIC:** 5122 (Drugs, Proprietaries & Sundries). **Sales:** $50,000,000 (1994). **Emp:** 320. **Officers:** M.B. McLelland, CEO; W.R. Motzer, CFO.

■ 20907 ■ Commercial Office Supply Inc.
11822 N Creek Pkwy. N, Ste. 109
Bothell, WA 98011
Phone: (425)485-6900
Products: Office supplies. **SIC:** 5112 (Stationery & Office Supplies).

■ 20908 ■ Comtech Inc.
2001 Hammond St.
Bangor, ME 04401-5725
Phone: (207)848-2801 **Fax:** (207)848-2877
Products: Office equipment, including copying equipment and duplicating machines. **SIC:** 5044 (Office Equipment). **Officers:** James Batey, President.

■ 20909 ■ Connecticut Valley Paper & Envelope Co. Inc.
239 Lindbergh Place
Paterson, NJ 07503
Phone: (973)278-4004
Free: (800)922-0591 **Fax:** (973)278-4040
Products: Envelopes; Business letter-heads; Stationery. **SIC:** 5112 (Stationery & Office Supplies). **Est:** 1867. **Sales:** $12,000,000 (2000). **Emp:** 50. **Officers:** Roy Ward, President; Gary Rygh, Sr. VP; Charles Baron, Sales Mgr.

■ 20910 ■ Contemporary Office Products Inc.
3904 St. Clair Ave.
Cleveland, OH 44114
Phone: (216)391-5555 **Fax:** (216)391-3311
Products: Office products. **SICs:** 5112 (Stationery & Office Supplies); 5044 (Office Equipment). **Est:** 1981. **Sales:** $4,500,000 (2000). **Emp:** 30. **Officers:** Donald N. Thies, President; Ken Mastilak, Vice President.

■ 20911 ■ Continental Craft Distributors
PO Box 3373
South Attleboro, MA 02703-0933
Phone: (617)726-9091
Products: Artist's materials, including lead pencils and crayons. **SICs:** 5112 (Stationery & Office Supplies); 5049 (Professional Equipment Nec).

■ 20912 ■ Contract Associates Inc.
4545 McLeod Rd. NE, Ste. B
Albuquerque, NM 87109-2202
Phone: (505)888-7536
Products: Office and public building furniture. **SIC:** 5021 (Furniture). **Officers:** Maria Raby-Mondragon, President.

■ 20913 ■ Cook's Inc.
807 S Broadway St.
Watertown, SD 57201
Phone: (605)886-5892 **Fax:** (605)886-6353
Products: Office equipment and supplies. **SICs:** 5044 (Office Equipment); 5112 (Stationery & Office Supplies). **Officers:** Merlin Jeitz, President.

■ 20914 ■ Copy Center Inc.
PO Box 2428
Farmingdale, NJ 07727
Phone: (908)280-1333 **Fax:** (908)280-8268
Products: Photocopiers. **SICs:** 5044 (Office Equipment); 5112 (Stationery & Office Supplies). **Est:** 1980. **Sales:** $2,000,000 (2000). **Emp:** 20. **Officers:** George A. Krebs, President; Linda H. Mushock, Treasurer & Secty.; Jeffrey D. Pruden, Vice President.

■ 20915 ■ Copy Center Inc.
PO Box 2428
Farmingdale, NJ 07727
Phone: (908)280-1333 **Fax:** (908)280-8268
Products: Office equipment and supplies. **SIC:** 5044 (Office Equipment). **Sales:** $2,000,000 (2000). **Emp:** 20.

■ 20916 ■ Copy-Co Inc.
10014 Monroe Dr.
Dallas, TX 75229
Phone: (972)699-9911
Products: Copy machines. **SIC:** 5044 (Office Equipment). **Sales:** $4,000,000 (1993). **Emp:** 53. **Officers:** Guy Shaw, President.

■ 20917 ■ Copy Plus Inc.
7100 W Good Hope Rd.
Milwaukee, WI 53223-4611
Phone: (414)353-2704
Products: Photocopying equipment and supplies; Office machines, including typewriters, dictating, transcribing, and recording machines. **SIC:** 5044 (Office Equipment). **Est:** 1947. **Sales:** $3,500,000 (1999). **Emp:** 33. **Officers:** Bob Feutz.

■ 20918 ■ Copy Sales Inc.
4950 E Evans Ave.
Denver, CO 80222-5209
Phone: (303)758-0797 **Fax:** (303)758-1162
Products: Duplicating machines. **SIC:** 5044 (Office Equipment). **Officers:** Nick Kuchurka, President.

■ **20919** ■ **Copyline Corp.**
PO Box 880367
San Diego, CA 92111
Phone: (619)220-0500 **Fax:** (619)565-8752
Products: Copiers. **SIC:** 5044 (Office Equipment). **Est:** 1963. **Sales:** $24,000,000 (2000). **Emp:** 239. **Officers:** Dennis Farrell, President; Randy Lydy, VP of Finance & Admin.; Michael Sherman, VP of Sales; Tom Goulet, Dir. of Information Systems; Sherry French, Dir of Human Resources.

■ **20920** ■ **Copytronics Inc.**
2461 Rolac Rd.
Jacksonville, FL 32207
Phone: (904)731-5100
Products: Office copiers. **SIC:** 5044 (Office Equipment). **Sales:** $20,000,000 (2000). **Emp:** 230. **Officers:** Paul Shields, President; Bob Shields, COO & Exec. VP.

■ **20921** ■ **Cornelius Systems Inc.**
3966 11 Mile Rd., No. 1A
Berkley, MI 48072-1005
Phone: (248)545-5558 **Fax:** (248)545-5557
E-mail: csi@wwnet.com
Products: Financial and legal printing(lithographic); Printing trade machinery, equipment, and supplies. **SICs:** 5044 (Office Equipment); 5112 (Stationery & Office Supplies). **Est:** 1973. **Emp:** 16. **Officers:** Michael Cornelius, President.

■ **20922** ■ **Corporate Copy Inc.**
3967 Hickory Hill
Memphis, TN 38115
Phone: (901)367-9500 **Free:** (800)289-7524
URL: http://www.corporatecopy.com
Products: Copying and facsimile machines. **SIC:** 5044 (Office Equipment). **Sales:** $6,000,000 (2000). **Emp:** 37. **Officers:** Tom Pease, President; Cindy McLarty, Treasurer.

■ **20923** ■ **Corporate Data Products**
PO Box 7148
Charlotte, NC 28241
Phone: (704)522-1234
Free: (800)476-2234 **Fax:** (704)522-1235
Products: Shredders, mailing equipment, and folding machines; Computer supplies; Custom forms; Promotional products. **SICs:** 5044 (Office Equipment); 5112 (Stationery & Office Supplies). **Sales:** $5,000,000 (2000). **Emp:** 26. **Officers:** Max Daniel, President.

■ **20924** ■ **Corporate Environments of Georgia Inc.**
PO Box 29725
Atlanta, GA 30359-0725
Phone: (404)679-8999
Products: Office furniture. **SIC:** 5021 (Furniture). **Est:** 1986. **Sales:** $41,000,000 (2000). **Emp:** 95. **Officers:** John R. Harris, President; Karen Hughes, VP of Finance; John Harris, President.

■ **20925** ■ **Corporate Express**
PO Box 9339
Pittsburgh, PA 15225
Phone: (412)741-6494 **Fax:** (412)749-8808
URL: http://www.corporateexpress.com
Products: Office products, including interior design, office furniture, and supplies; Promotional products; Printing materials; Janitorial supplies. **SICs:** 5112 (Stationery & Office Supplies); 5021 (Furniture). **Est:** 1933. **Sales:** $60,000,000 (2000). **Emp:** 160. **Officers:** John R. Kennedy, Regional President Central Region; Joe Barch, VP of Marketing & Sales; Tony Matteo, VP of Operations. **Former Name:** BT Office Products.

■ **20926** ■ **Corporate Express**
35 Melanie Ln.
Whippany, NJ 07981
Phone: (973)386-8900 **Fax:** (973)515-0698
Products: Office supplies, including furniture, computers, pens, and paper. **SICs:** 5112 (Stationery & Office Supplies); 5045 (Computers, Peripherals & Software); 5021 (Furniture); 5044 (Office Equipment). **Sales:** $150,000,000 (2000). **Emp:** 745. **Officers:** Robert Kroll, President; Frank Marx, CFO; Roger Post, VP of Sales; Jack Cotroneo, VP of Operations; Frank Bimonte, Dir of Personnel.

■ **20927** ■ **Corporate Express**
2655 W Georgia Ave.
Phoenix, AZ 85017-2728
Phone: (602)242-2200 **Fax:** (602)242-3620
Products: Office products, including desks, chairs, paper, and pens. **SICs:** 5112 (Stationery & Office Supplies); 5021 (Furniture). **Est:** 1986. **Sales:** $58,000,000 (2000). **Emp:** 250. **Officers:** Steve Casselman, President; George Neal, VP of Operations; J.B. Drake, VP of Sales. **Former Name:** City-Wide Discount Office Supply, Inc.

■ **20928** ■ **Corporate Express of the East Inc.**
160 Avon St.
Stratford, CT 06615
Phone: (203)383-6300
Free: (800)972-9781 **Fax:** (203)378-3648
Products: Stationery and office supplies. **SIC:** 5112 (Stationery & Office Supplies). **Sales:** $21,000,000 (2000). **Emp:** 140. **Officers:** Robert Wood, President.

■ **20929** ■ **Corporate Express Inc.**
1 Environmental Way
Broomfield, CO 80021-3416
Phone: (303)664-2000
Free: (800)677-8750 **Fax:** (303)664-3474
Products: Office supplies and furniture; Computers. **SICs:** 5112 (Stationery & Office Supplies); 5021 (Furniture). **Est:** 1986. **Sales:** $3,196,000,000 (2000). **Emp:** 25,000. **Officers:** Robert L. King, President & CEO; Gary Jacobs, Exec. VP & CFO.

■ **20930** ■ **Corporate Express of the MidAtlantic Inc.**
7700 Port Capital Dr.
Baltimore, MD 21227
Phone: (410)799-7700 **Fax:** (410)799-7144
Products: Office furniture. **SIC:** 5021 (Furniture). **Sales:** $64,000,000 (2000). **Emp:** 400. **Officers:** Rick Nelson, President; Randall Jenkins, VP of Finance.

■ **20931** ■ **Corporate Express of Northern California Inc.**
2010 North 1st St., Ste. 530
San Jose, CA 95131-2040
Phone: (408)000-0000
Free: (800)695-9732 **Fax:** (408)428-0350
Products: Office supplies, including pens, paper pads, and desks. **SICs:** 5112 (Stationery & Office Supplies); 5021 (Furniture). **Est:** 1925. **Sales:** $70,000,000 (2000). **Emp:** 300. **Officers:** Steve Van Guelpen, President; Brad Carson, CFO; Bill Buckhout, Dir. of Sales; Steve Spanos, Dir. of Data Processing; Julie Jarvis, Dir of Human Resources.

■ **20932** ■ **Corporate Interiors Inc.**
318 W Depot Ave.
Knoxville, TN 37917-7522
Phone: (865)637-3214 **Fax:** (865)637-4377
URL: http://www.corporateinteriors.net
Products: Systems and cubicle furniture; Panels. **SICs:** 5021 (Furniture); 5046 (Commercial Equipment Nec). **Est:** 1983. **Sales:** $6,000,000 (2000). **Emp:** 28. **Officers:** Sandra Fitzgerald, President, e-mail: sfitzgerald@mindspring.com; Mary Frances Tucker, Vice President.

■ **20933** ■ **Cosons Inc.**
12115 Parklawn
Rockville, MD 20852
Phone: (301)816-6900 **Fax:** (301)816-0010
Products: Office supplies. **SIC:** 5112 (Stationery & Office Supplies). **Sales:** $1,000,000 (2000). **Emp:** 14. **Officers:** S. Robert Cohen, President.

■ **20934** ■ **Craft & Hobby Supplies**
118 Edwardia Dr.
Greensboro, NC 27409
Phone: (910)855-8880
Free: (800)438-1024 **Fax:** (910)547-0431
Products: Lead pencils, crayons, and artists' materials. **SICs:** 5112 (Stationery & Office Supplies); 5049 (Professional Equipment Nec). **Est:** 1965. **Emp:** 23. **Officers:** Larry B. Shook, President; Kathy B. Staley, Vice President.

■ **20935** ■ **Craft King**
5675 N Tampa Hwy.
PO Box 90637
Lakeland, FL 33801
Phone: (941)680-1313
Products: Lead pencils, crayons, and artists' materials. **SICs:** 5112 (Stationery & Office Supplies); 5049 (Professional Equipment Nec).

■ **20936** ■ **Craft Wholesalers**
77 Cypress St. SW
Reynoldsburg, OH 43068-9673
Phone: (740)964-6210
Free: (800)666-5858 **Fax:** (740)964-6212
URL: http://www.craftwholesalers.com
Products: Craft supplies; Country gifts; Crayons and artist's supplies. **SICs:** 5112 (Stationery & Office Supplies); 5049 (Professional Equipment Nec); 5092 (Toys & Hobby Goods & Supplies). **Est:** 1980. **Sales:** $6,000,000 (2000). **Emp:** 60. **Officers:** Farley Piper, President, e-mail: farley@craftwholesaler.com; Ohma Willette, Sales Mgr., e-mail: ohma@craftwholesalers.com; Linda Reck, Customer Service Contact, e-mail: sales@craftwholesalers.com; Aileen Roberts, e-mail: aileen@craftwholesalers.com; Karen Piper, Corp. Secty., e-mail: karen@craftwholesalers.com.

■ **20937** ■ **Crawfords Office Furniture & Supplies**
435 Westlake N
Seattle, WA 98109-5221
Phone: (206)682-1757 **Fax:** (206)682-6939
Products: Office furniture and supplies, including desks and paper clips. **SICs:** 5021 (Furniture); 5112 (Stationery & Office Supplies). **Est:** 1923. **Emp:** 34. **Officers:** Edward Webb.

■ **20938** ■ **Creative Business Concepts**
PO Box 2354
Twin Falls, ID 83303-2354
Phone: (208)734-9988 **Fax:** (208)734-9989
Products: Office equipment, including copiers. **SIC:** 5044 (Office Equipment). **Officers:** Mike Frazier, President.

■ **20939** ■ **Creative Craft Distributors**
PO Box 134
Manville, RI 02838
Phone: (401)769-4010
Products: Lead pencils, crayons, and artists' materials. **SICs:** 5112 (Stationery & Office Supplies); 5049 (Professional Equipment Nec).

■ **20940** ■ **A.T. Cross Co.**
One Albion Rd.
Lincoln, RI 02865
Phone: (401)333-1200 **Fax:** (401)333-9759
Products: Writing instruments. **SIC:** 5112 (Stationery & Office Supplies). **Est:** 1846. **Sales:** $154,700,000 (2000). **Emp:** 800. **Officers:** Bradford R. Boss, Chairman of the Board; Russell A. Boss, CEO & President; John E. Buckley, Exec. VP & COO; John T. Ruggieri, Sr. VP, Treasurer & CFO; Joseph V. Bassi, Dir. of Finance; Tina C. Benik, VP, Legal Counsel & Secty.; Joseph F. Eastman, VP of Human Resources.

■ **20941** ■ **CRS Business Products**
142 N Kimball St.
Casper, WY 82601-2028
Phone: (307)235-8822
Products: Office equipment; Cash registers. **SIC:** 5044 (Office Equipment). **Officers:** Gene Theriault, President.

■ **20942** ■ **Cuna Strategic Services, Inc.**
PO Box 431
Madison, WI 53701
Phone: (608)231-4000 **Fax:** (608)231-4370
URL: http://www.cuna.org
Products: Stationery and office supplies. **SIC:** 5112 (Stationery & Office Supplies). **Est:** 1999. **Sales:** $10,000,000 (2000). **Officers:** Daniel Mica, President; Mary Wolfenberger, CFO. **Former Name:** Cuna Service Group Inc.

■ **20943** ■ **C.W. Mills**
2900 Dixie Ave.
Grandville, MI 49418-1159
Phone: (616)538-4009
Free: (800)748-0004 **Fax:** (616)538-9799
Products: Office products; Fine paper. **SICs:** 5113 (Industrial & Personal Service Paper); 5112 (Stationery & Office Supplies). **Est:** 1903. **Sales:** $17,400,000 (2000). **Emp:** 75. **Officers:** David C. Gezon, President; Garry L. Overbeek, Controller; William R. Gezon, Dir. of Marketing & Sales.

■ **20944** ■ **Dale Office Plus**
31938 Groesbeck
Fraser, MI 48026-3914
Phone: (810)296-2340 **Fax:** (810)296-9769
Products: Office furniture and equipment; Office supplies. **SICs:** 5021 (Furniture); 5044 (Office Equipment); 5112 (Stationery & Office Supplies). **Emp:** 30. **Officers:** Dale Madison; John Madison.

■ **20945** ■ **Dancker, Sellew and Douglas Inc.**
53 Park Pl.
New York, NY 10007
Phone: (212)619-7171 **Fax:** (212)349-0695
Products: Office furniture. **SIC:** 5021 (Furniture). **Sales:** $55,000,000 (2000). **Emp:** 150. **Officers:** J. Scott Douglas, President; Gerard Kehoe, VP & Treasurer; Dennis J. Doherty, VP of Sales.

■ **20946** ■ **Danka Business Systems PLC**
11201 Danka Cir. N
St. Petersburg, FL 33716
Phone: (813)576-6003
Products: Photocopy machines. **SIC:** 5044 (Office Equipment). **Sales:** $2,101,000,000 (2000). **Emp:** 21,800. **Officers:** Daniel Doyle, CEO; David Snell, Chief Accounting Officer.

■ **20947** ■ **Danka Industries Inc.**
11201 Danka Cir. N
St. Petersburg, FL 33716-3712
Phone: (813)579-2300
Free: (800)833-2652 **Fax:** (813)579-2775
URL: http://www.dankawholesale.com
Products: Office equipment, including facsimile, photocopying machines, printers, supplies, and multifunctional equipment. **SIC:** 5044 (Office Equipment). **Est:** 1977. **Sales:** $3,500,000,000 (2000). **Emp:** 20,000. **Officers:** Dan Doyle, President; Art Richardson, Sr. VP; Will Arthur, VP of Sales; Gary Buhler, Natl. Marketing Mgr.

■ **20948** ■ **Danka Inwood Business Systems Inc.**
10280 Miller Rd.
Dallas, TX 75238
Phone: (214)484-7720 **Fax:** (214)241-9548
Products: Photocopying equipment and supplies. **SICs:** 5044 (Office Equipment); 5045 (Computers, Peripherals & Software). **Sales:** $12,000,000 (2000). **Emp:** 80. **Officers:** David Rivera, President; Gregg Watson, Data Processing Mgr.; Marlene Adair, Dir of Human Resources.

■ **20949** ■ **Data Information Service**
13 Partridge Rd.
Concord, NH 03301-7886
Phone: (603)228-3549
Products: Office equipment. **SIC:** 5044 (Office Equipment). **Officers:** Robert Anderson, President.

■ **20950** ■ **Data Management Corp.**
PO Box 70
Butler, WI 53007
Phone: (414)783-6910 **Fax:** (414)783-6910
Products: Inked ribbons; Diskettes; Custom continuous forms. **SIC:** 5112 (Stationery & Office Supplies). **Est:** 1969. **Sales:** $2,000,000 (2000). **Emp:** 14. **Officers:** Barry Klass, President; Thom Hahn, CFO.

■ **20951** ■ **DEA Specialties Co.**
6874 Alamo Downs Pkwy.
San Antonio, TX 78238
Phone: (210)523-1073 **Fax:** (210)523-1544
E-mail: sales@deaspecialties.com
URL: http://www.deaspecialties.com
Products: Folding walls; Accordion doors; Toilet partitions; Toilet accessories; Lockers; Corner and wall guards; Coiling doors and grilles. **SIC:** 5021 (Furniture). **Est:** 1984. **Sales:** $4,500,000 (2000). **Emp:** 18. **Officers:** Diane E. Alberthal, President, e-mail: diane@deaspecialties.com; David E. Alberthal, Vice President, e-mail: dave@deaspecialties.com; Peter Mills, Vice President, e-mail: peter@deaspecialties.com; Jill Sulak, Secretary, e-mail: jill@mail.deaspecialties.com; Susan Moore, Treasurer, e-mail: susan@mail.deaspecialties.com.

■ **20952** ■ **Dealer's Discount Crafts**
8199 10 Mile Rd.
Center Line, MI 48015
Phone: (810)757-2690
Products: Lead pencils, crayons, and artists' materials. **SICs:** 5112 (Stationery & Office Supplies); 5049 (Professional Equipment Nec).

■ **20953** ■ **Decorator & Craft Corp.**
428 S Zelta
Wichita, KS 67207
Phone: (316)685-6265
Products: Lead pencils, crayons, and artists' materials. **SICs:** 5112 (Stationery & Office Supplies); 5049 (Professional Equipment Nec).

■ **20954** ■ **Demco Inc.**
PO Box 7488
Madison, WI 53707
Phone: (608)241-1201
Free: (800)356-1200 **Fax:** (608)241-1799
E-mail: info@demco.com
URL: http://www.demco.com
Products: Library and office supplies and equipment; Audio-visual supplies and equipment; Computer supplies, including furniture. **SICs:** 5044 (Office Equipment); 5021 (Furniture). **Est:** 1905. **Sales:** $40,000,000 (2000). **Emp:** 250. **Officers:** John E. Wall, Chairman of the Board; Donald Rogers, VP of Finance; Edward Muir, President; Michael Snapper, VP of Marketing; Susan Sippola, Dir of Human Resources.

■ **20955** ■ **Dependable Business Machines**
2521 Railroad Ave.
Bismarck, ND 58501-5072
Phone: (701)258-7676
Products: Office equipment; Cash registers. **SIC:** 5044 (Office Equipment). **Officers:** Gene Kurtz, President.

■ **20956** ■ **Desert Stationers**
212 E Main St.
Barstow, CA 92311-2324
Phone: (760)256-2161 **Fax:** (760)256-7119
Products: Office supplies; Wood office furniture; Office machines. **SICs:** 5112 (Stationery & Office Supplies); 5044 (Office Equipment); 5021 (Furniture). **Emp:** 49. **Officers:** Margie Gilbert, Manager; Ed Freifoff, Dir. of Sales; Jim Barcus, Technical Dir.

■ **20957** ■ **Desk Concepts**
3670 NW 76th St.
Miami, FL 33147
Phone: (305)696-3376 **Fax:** (305)835-0478
Products: Office furniture, including desks, wall units, and tables. **SIC:** 5021 (Furniture). **Sales:** $3,000,000 (2000). **Emp:** 15. **Officers:** Sheldon Jaffee, President.

■ **20958** ■ **Desk-Mate Products Inc.**
7492 Chancellor Dr.
Orlando, FL 32809-6242
Phone: (407)826-0600
Free: (800)330-0015 **Fax:** (407)826-0504
Products: Panel and modular systems furniture and all other nonwood office furniture; Wood office furniture. **SIC:** 5021 (Furniture). **Emp:** 49. **Officers:** Roger R. Tetu, Manager.

■ **20959** ■ **Desks Inc. (Chicago, Illinois)**
2323 W Pershing Rd.
Chicago, IL 60609
Phone: (312)664-8500
Products: Office furniture. **SIC:** 5021 (Furniture). **Sales:** $50,000,000 (2000). **Emp:** 95. **Officers:** Robert A. Stacey, President; Greg Erazmus, CFO.

■ **20960** ■ **Diane Ribbon Wholesale**
2319 W Holly
Phoenix, AZ 85009
Phone: (602)271-9273
Free: (800)622-7263 **Fax:** (602)271-4011
Products: Art and craft materials. **SICs:** 5112 (Stationery & Office Supplies); 5049 (Professional Equipment Nec). **Est:** 1946. **Officers:** Jeff Rust, Vice President.

■ **20961** ■ **A.B. Dick Co.**
5700 W Touhy Ave.
Niles, IL 60714
Phone: (847)779-1900
Free: (800)422-3616 **Fax:** (847)647-6940
Products: Printing presses and printing equipment; Copiers and printing supplies. **SICs:** 5044 (Office Equipment); 5084 (Industrial Machinery & Equipment). **Sales:** $36,000,000 (2000). **Emp:** 189. **Officers:** Gerald McConnell, President; James Bryom, CFO.

■ **20962** ■ **A.B. Dick Products of Albuquerque**
1430 Girard Blvd. NE
Albuquerque, NM 87106-1821
Phone: (505)265-1212 **Fax:** (505)265-3970
Products: Office equipment; Copying equipment; Duplicating machines. **SIC:** 5044 (Office Equipment). **Officers:** Richard Gilenfelt, President.

■ **20963** ■ **Digital Business Automation**
15121 Graham, Unit 101
Huntington Beach, CA 92649
Phone: (714)379-9300
Products: Copying machines. **SIC:** 5044 (Office Equipment). **Sales:** $8,000,000 (1994). **Emp:** 50. **Officers:** Richard Gomez, President.

■ **20964** ■ **Direct Office Furniture Outlet**
2525 Paxton St.
Harrisburg, PA 17111
Phone: (717)236-7200 **Fax:** (717)236-8913
Products: Office furniture. **SIC:** 5021 (Furniture). **Emp:** 4.

■ **20965** ■ **Discount Desk Etc., Inc.**
955 S McCarrah
Sparks, NV 89431-5815
Phone: (702)359-4440 **Fax:** (702)359-3378
E-mail: riplon@aol.com
Products: Furniture, including office and public building furniture; Shelving; Lockers. **SICs:** 5021 (Furniture); 5046 (Commercial Equipment Nec). **Est:** 1979. **Sales:** $1,000,000 (2000). **Emp:** 4. **Officers:** Rip Lonergan, President.

■ **20966** ■ **Discount Office Equipment Inc.**
1991 Coolidge Hwy.
Berkley, MI 48072
Phone: (248)548-6900
Free: (800)900-9333 **Fax:** (248)548-6905
URL: http://www.discountoffice.com
Products: Office furniture. **SIC:** 5021 (Furniture). **Est:** 1948. **Sales:** $2,500,000 (2000). **Emp:** 15. **Officers:** Mitchell Merzin, President, e-mail: mmerzin@aol.com; Neil Merzin, Vice President; Jeffrey Merzin, Treasurer.

■ **20967** ■ **Distinctive Business Products Inc.**
5328 W 123rd Pl.
Alsip, IL 60803-3203
Phone: (708)371-6700 **Fax:** (708)371-6744
Products: Copiers and fax machines. **SIC:** 5044 (Office Equipment). **Est:** 1982. **Sales:** $16,000,000 (2000). **Emp:** 100. **Officers:** John Cosich, President; Joe Mokszyski, Exec. VP.

■ **20968** ■ **Dittos**
1 5th St. E
Kalispell, MT 59901-4947
Phone: (406)752-7110 **Fax:** (406)752-2166
Products: Office supplies; Greeting cards. **SIC:** 5112 (Stationery & Office Supplies). **Officers:** Edgar Trippet, Owner.

■ **20969** ■ **Diversified Copier Products Inc.**
9765 Clairemont Mesa Blvd., Ste. C
San Diego, CA 92124
Phone: (619)565-2737
Products: Copiers and fax machines. **SIC:** 5044 (Office Equipment).

■ **20970** ■ **Dixie Art Supplies Inc.**
PO Box 30650
New Orleans, LA 70190
Phone: (504)522-5308
Products: Office supplies and equipment. **SICs:** 5112 (Stationery & Office Supplies); 5044 (Office Equipment).

■ **20971** ■ **Dixie Craft & Floral Wholesale**
9070 McLaurin St.
Bay St. Louis, MS 39520
Phone: (228)467-7261   **Fax:** (228)467-7261
E-mail: yrprsnltch@aol.com
Products: Artist materials, including lead pencils; Craft supplies; Floral supplies. **SICs:** 5112 (Stationery & Office Supplies); 5049 (Professional Equipment Nec); 5193 (Flowers & Florists' Supplies). **Est:** 1985. **Sales:** $500,000 (2000). **Emp:** 4. **Officers:** Marlene Ladner.

■ **20972** ■ **Document Solutions Inc.**
500 Garden City Dr.
Monroeville, PA 15146-1111
Phone: (412)373-6500
Free: (800)662-9022   **Fax:** (412)810-1111
URL: http://www.docsolinc.com
Products: Photocopying machines; Printers; Fax machines. **SICs:** 5044 (Office Equipment); 5045 (Computers, Peripherals & Software). **Est:** 1994. **Sales:** $7,000,000 (2000). **Emp:** 20. **Officers:** Ken Holes, President.

■ **20973** ■ **DocuSource Inc.**
9346 DeSoto Ave.
Chatsworth, CA 91311
Phone: (818)717-9790
Free: (800)711-2815   **Fax:** (818)717-0367
Products: Used photocopiers and duplicators. **SIC:** 5044 (Office Equipment). **Sales:** $27,000,000 (2000). **Emp:** 100. **Officers:** Lester Walker, CEO; Lester Walker, CFO.

■ **20974** ■ **Doubleday Brothers and Co.**
1919 E Kilgore Rd.
Kalamazoo, MI 49002
Phone: (616)381-1040
Free: (800)248-0888   **Fax:** (616)381-4306
Products: Office furniture and supplies. **SICs:** 5112 (Stationery & Office Supplies); 5021 (Furniture). **Est:** 1898. **Sales:** $20,000,000 (2000). **Emp:** 140. **Officers:** Paul G. Lenke, Vice President; Jerry Krizan, Controller.

■ **20975** ■ **Dupli-Fax Inc.**
300 Commerce Sq. Blvd.
Burlington, NJ 08016
Phone: (609)387-8700
Products: Copiers and facsimile machines. **SIC:** 5044 (Office Equipment). **Sales:** $140,000,000 (2000). **Emp:** 300. **Officers:** Ed McLaughlin, President.

■ **20976** ■ **Earthworm Inc.**
35 Medford St.
Somerville, MA 02143-4211
Phone: (617)628-1844   **Fax:** (617)628-2773
Products: Office supplies. **SIC:** 5112 (Stationery & Office Supplies). **Est:** 1970. **Sales:** $300,000 (2000). **Emp:** 7. **Officers:** Jeffrey Coyne, President; Robin Inganthron, VP & CFO.

■ **20977** ■ **Eastern Data Paper**
135 Stevens Ave.
Little Falls, NJ 07424
Phone: (973)256-4600   **Fax:** (973)256-3608
Products: Office supplies; Telecommunications equipment. **SICs:** 5112 (Stationery & Office Supplies); 5065 (Electronic Parts & Equipment Nec).

■ **20978** ■ **Eaton Office Supply Company Inc.**
180 John Glenn Dr.
Amherst, NY 14226
Phone: (716)691-6100
Products: Office supplies; Office furniture. **SICs:** 5112 (Stationery & Office Supplies); 5021 (Furniture).

■ **20979** ■ **Ecco Corp.**
625 Spice Islands Dr., Ste. F
Sparks, NV 89431-7122
Phone: (702)329-9505   **Fax:** (702)329-7747
Products: Office equipment, including calculating machines. **SIC:** 5044 (Office Equipment). **Officers:** Joseph Wilson, President.

■ **20980** ■ **Economy Office Furniture**
6300 N Sepulveda Blvd.
Van Nuys, CA 91411-1112
Phone: (818)781-5552   **Fax:** (818)786-5192
Products: Office furniture. **SIC:** 5021 (Furniture). **Emp:** 49.

■ **20981** ■ **EcoTech Recycled Products**
14241 60th St. N
Clearwater, FL 33760-2706
Phone: (813)531-5353
Products: Office and industrial supplies made from recycled materials, including desks, paper, and paper clips. **SICs:** 5112 (Stationery & Office Supplies); 5021 (Furniture); 5084 (Industrial Machinery & Equipment). **Sales:** $600,000 (2000). **Emp:** 3. **Officers:** Audrey Bell, President.

■ **20982** ■ **ECR Sales & Service Inc.**
1515 Western Ave.
Las Vegas, NV 89102-2601
Phone: (702)385-0706   **Fax:** (702)385-9553
Products: Office equipment, including calculating machines and cash registers. **SIC:** 5044 (Office Equipment). **Officers:** Richard Valdez, President.

■ **20983** ■ **EDM Business Interiors Inc.**
7575 Empire Dr., No. 2
Florence, KY 41042
Phone: (606)371-0444   **Fax:** (606)371-0637
Products: Office products and furniture. **SICs:** 5021 (Furniture); 5112 (Stationery & Office Supplies). **Est:** 1984. **Sales:** $850,000 (1999). **Emp:** 5. **Officers:** Edward Moore, Owner; Terri Moore, Owner.

■ **20984** ■ **Educators Resource, Inc.**
2575 Schillinger Rd.
Semmes, AL 36575
Phone: (205)666-1537
Products: Teachers suppliers. **SICs:** 5112 (Stationery & Office Supplies); 5044 (Office Equipment). **Emp:** 30. **Officers:** Frank H. Summersell, President. **Former Name:** Mobile Pen Company Inc.

■ **20985** ■ **Edward Business Machines Inc.**
524 Penn Ave.
West Reading, PA 19611
Phone: (215)372-8414
Products: Business machines. **SIC:** 5044 (Office Equipment).

■ **20986** ■ **EGP Inc.**
2715 Hwy. 44 W
Inverness, FL 34453
Phones: (352)344-1200   (352)799-1804
Free: (800)432-4731   **Fax:** (352)344-0421
Products: Copiers, fax machines, and supplies. **SICs:** 5044 (Office Equipment); 5112 (Stationery & Office Supplies). **Emp:** 49.

■ **20987** ■ **Eldon Rubbermaid Office Products**
1427 William Blount Dr.
Maryville, TN 37801-8249
Phone: (423)518-1600
Free: (800)827-5060   **Fax:** 800-733-5366
Products: Desk accessories. **SIC:** 5099 (Durable Goods Nec). **Sales:** $175,000,000 (2000). **Emp:** 300. **Officers:** Robert Silverstein.

■ **20988** ■ **Electronic Bus Systems of Nevada**
PO Box 6150
Reno, NV 89513-6150
Phone: (702)746-3600   **Fax:** (702)746-3603
Products: Office equipment, including calculating machines and cash registers. **SIC:** 5044 (Office Equipment). **Officers:** Richard Cieri, President.

■ **20989** ■ **Electronic Office Systems**
107 Fairfield Ave.
Fairfield, NJ 07004-2402
Phone: (973)808-0100   **Fax:** (973)882-2882
Products: Office equipment. **SIC:** 5044 (Office Equipment). **Sales:** $7,000,000 (2000). **Emp:** 48. **Officers:** Andrew Ritschel, President.

■ **20990** ■ **Elliott Office Products Inc.**
PO Box 235
Gardiner, ME 04345-0235
Phone: (207)582-4625
Free: (800)218-0774   **Fax:** (207)582-8298
E-mail: eop@mint.net
Products: Office equipment. **SIC:** 5044 (Office Equipment). **Est:** 1985. **Sales:** $1,500,000 (2000). **Emp:** 12. **Officers:** Charles Elliott, President; Bernadette Elliott, Sales/Marketing Contact; Charles H. Elliott IV, Sales/Marketing Contact.

■ **20991** ■ **Eltrex Industries Inc.**
65 Sullivan St.
Rochester, NY 14605
Phone: (716)454-6100   **Fax:** (716)263-7766
Products: Office products; Industrial vacuum cleaners. **SIC:** 5044 (Office Equipment). **Est:** 1968. **Sales:** $14,000,000 (2000). **Emp:** 100. **Officers:** Matthew Augustine, President; Ronald Augustine, Sr. VP.

■ **20992** ■ **Empire Office Machines Inc.**
821 N Main St.
Helena, MT 59601-3352
Phone: (406)442-8890   **Fax:** (406)442-3665
E-mail: empire@initco.net
Products: Office equipment. **SIC:** 5044 (Office Equipment). **Est:** 1967. **Sales:** $2,000,000 (2000). **Emp:** 11. **Officers:** Kelley Patzer, President.

■ **20993** ■ **Environmental Interiors**
2595 Interstate Dr.
Harrisburg, PA 17110-9602
Phone: (717)652-6060   **Fax:** (717)652-2617
Products: Office panel systems. **SIC:** 5046 (Commercial Equipment Nec). **Emp:** 20. **Officers:** Charles Miller.

■ **20994** ■ **Ergonomic Design Inc.**
10650 Irma Dr Ste. 33
Northglenn, CO 80233
Phone: (303)452-8006   **Fax:** (303)452-2296
Products: Ergonomic office accessories, including wrist savers, footrests, articulating keyboard arms and document holders. **SIC:** 5199 (Nondurable Goods Nec). **Officers:** Jack Hicks, President.

■ **20995** ■ **Executive Converting Corp.**
4750 Simonton Rd.
Dallas, TX 75244
Phone: (972)387-0500
Free: (800)992-0997   **Fax:** (972)387-0516
Products: Stationery, copy and industrial paper. **SICs:** 5112 (Stationery & Office Supplies); 5111 (Printing & Writing Paper); 5113 (Industrial & Personal Service Paper). **Sales:** $20,000,000 (2000). **Emp:** 82. **Officers:** Greg Wilemon, President; Lorena Pohl, Controller.

■ **20996** ■ **Executive Office Furniture Outlet**
1352 Reber St.
Green Bay, WI 54301
Phone: (920)436-6820   **Fax:** (920)436-6830
Products: New and used office furniture. **SIC:** 5021 (Furniture). **Emp:** 29. **Officers:** Doug La Violette. **Former Name:** As Is Office Furniture.

■ **20997** ■ **Expressive Art & Craft**
12455 Branford St., Unit 6
Arleta, CA 91331
Phone: (818)834-4640
Free: (800)747-6880   **Fax:** (818)897-0148
E-mail: exprart@smartlink.net
URL: http://www.expressivearts.net
Products: Lead pencils, crayons, and artists' materials. **SICs:** 5112 (Stationery & Office Supplies); 5049 (Professional Equipment Nec). **Est:** 1980. **Sales:** $4,000,000 (2000). **Emp:** 6. **Officers:** Charles G. Yacoobian, President.

■ **20998** ■ **F-D-C Corp.**
PO Box 1047
Elk Grove Village, IL 60009-1047
Phone: (847)437-3990
Free: (800)848-5622   **Fax:** (847)437-3995
URL: http://www.fdccorp.com
Products: CAD plotters; Engineering copiers; Wide-format color graphics; Digital printers. **SICs:** 5049 (Professional Equipment Nec); 5112 (Stationery &

Office Supplies). **Est:** 1961. **Sales:** $7,000,000 (1999).
Emp: 28. **Officers:** R.I. Hawley, CEO & Chairman of
the Board; R. B. Wright, President.

■ **20999** ■ **F & E Check Protector Co. Inc.**
20 Rolfe Square
Cranston, RI 02910-2810
Phone: (401)738-9444   **Fax:** (401)781-6667
Products: Office equipment. **SIC:** 5044 (Office
Equipment). **Officers:** Edward Mc Donough, President.

■ **21000** ■ **Farmer Office Products Inc.**
3725 Reveille
Houston, TX 77087
Phone: (713)645-5666
Products: Office machines. **SIC:** 5044 (Office
Equipment).

■ **21001** ■ **Fas-Co Coders Inc.orporated**
500 E Comstock Dr.
Chandler, AZ 85225
Phone: (480)545-7500   **Fax:** (480)545-1998
Products: Data coding equipment. **SIC:** 5044 (Office
Equipment). **Officers:** Roger Vansteenkiste, CEO.

■ **21002** ■ **Michael Ferro Co.**
RR 1, Box 301
South Royalton, VT 05068-0301
Phone: (802)763-8575
Products: Office equipment. **SIC:** 5044 (Office
Equipment). **Officers:** Michael Ferro, Owner.

■ **21003** ■ **Finch-Brown Company Inc.**
PO Box 915
Boise, ID 83701-0915
Phone: (208)342-9345   **Fax:** (208)342-6762
Products: Office equipment. **SIC:** 5044 (Office
Equipment). **Officers:** David Burpee, President.

■ **21004** ■ **Fineline Products, Inc.**
1616 Grand Ave.
Kansas City, MO 64108
Phone: (816)474-4593   **Fax:** (816)474-4593
Products: Fixtures for stores, banks, offices; Office
supplies; Office machines. **SICs:** 5044 (Office
Equipment); 5112 (Stationery & Office Supplies); 5046
(Commercial Equipment Nec).

■ **21005** ■ **Flower Factory**
5655 Whipple Ave. NW
North Canton, OH 44720
Phone: (216)494-7978
Products: Artist supplies, including pencils, crayons,
craft supplies, and hobby goods; Floral supplies; Office
supplies; Gifts; Toys. **SICs:** 5112 (Stationery & Office
Supplies); 5049 (Professional Equipment Nec); 5092
(Toys & Hobby Goods & Supplies); 5193 (Flowers &
Florists' Supplies).

■ **21006** ■ **FMC Resource Management Corp.**
14640 172nd Dr.SE
Monroe, WA 98272
Phone: (360)794-3157
Products: Provides and prints complete range of
business products—forms, labels, commercial printing,
packaging, promotional, uniforms, plastic molded and
injected products; Expertise in complex distribution.
SICs: 5112 (Stationery & Office Supplies); 5099
(Durable Goods Nec). **Sales:** $18,000,000 (2000).
Emp: 100. **Officers:** Mark Trumper, CEO; Bill Smith,
CFO.

■ **21007** ■ **Forms and Supplies Inc.**
PO Box 18694
Memphis, TN 38181-0694
Phone: (901)365-1249
Products: Computer and office supplies, including
copy paper, pens, pencils, and furniture. **SICs:** 5112
(Stationery & Office Supplies); 5044 (Office
Equipment); 5021 (Furniture). **Est:** 1974. **Sales:**
$22,000,000 (2000). **Emp:** 112. **Officers:** Richard
Mason, President; Terri Vaughan, CFO.

■ **21008** ■ **Fuchs Copy Systems Inc.**
12200 W Adler Ln.
West Allis, WI 53214
Phone: (414)778-0210   **Fax:** (414)778-2018
Products: Copiers and fax machines. **SIC:** 5044
(Office Equipment). **Est:** 1990. **Sales:** $7,000,000

(2000). **Emp:** 60. **Officers:** Jim Fuchs, President; Craig
Scherbarth, Controller.

■ **21009** ■ **Furniture Consultants Inc.**
11 W 19th St.
New York, NY 10011
Phone: (212)229-4500
Products: Office furniture, new and used. **SIC:** 5021
(Furniture). **Est:** 1975. **Sales:** $60,000,000 (2000).
Emp: 150. **Officers:** John Varacchi, President;
Lawrence Itkin, Treasurer; Crans Baldwin, Dir. of
Marketing.

■ **21010** ■ **General Business Machines Inc.**
PO Box 637
Brunswick, ME 04011-0637
Phone: (207)725-6333   **Fax:** (207)725-9756
Products: Office equipment and supplies. **SICs:** 5044
(Office Equipment); 5112 (Stationery & Office
Supplies). **Officers:** William Crocker, President.

■ **21011** ■ **General Office Products Co.**
2050 Old Hwy. 8
New Brighton, MN 55112
Phone: (612)639-4700
Free: (800)279-3839   **Fax:** (612)697-6061
Products: Office supplies. **SICs:** 5112 (Stationery &
Office Supplies); 5021 (Furniture). **Est:** 1963. **Sales:**
$50,000,000 (2000). **Emp:** 270. **Officers:** Thomas J.
Reaser, President; Mark Grina, Controller; Reed
Tropht, Vice President.

■ **21012** ■ **Gestetner Corp.**
PO Box 10270
Stamford, CT 06904-2270
Phone: (203)625-7600   **Fax:** (203)863-5540
Products: Fax machines, copiers, and duplicators.
SIC: 5044 (Office Equipment). **Est:** 1881. **Sales:**
$130,000,000 (2000). **Emp:** 600. **Officers:** C.
Rajaratnarm, President; Rick DeVincenzo, Vice
President; Marie Yenni, VP of Marketing; George
Carmichael, Dir. of Data Processing; Dennis Murphy,
Dir of Human Resources.

■ **21013** ■ **GF Office Furniture Ltd.**
916 Merchandise Mart
Chicago, IL 60654
Phone: (312)836-1750   **Fax:** (312)836-0449
Products: Office and contract furniture. **SIC:** 5021
(Furniture). **Emp:** 49.

■ **21014** ■ **Give Something Back Inc.**
7303 Edgewater Dr.
Oakland, CA 94621
Phone: (510)635-5500
Free: (800)635-4677   **Fax:** (510)635-4677
Products: Office supplies. **SIC:** 5112 (Stationery &
Office Supplies). **Sales:** $7,500,000 (2000). **Emp:** 7.
Officers: Mike Hannigan, President.

■ **21015** ■ **Globe Business Furniture Inc.**
520 Royal Pky.
Nashville, TN 37214-3645
Phone: (615)889-4722   **Free:** (800)995-4562
Products: Panel and modular systems furniture and all
other nonwood office furniture; Wood office furniture;
Metal office furniture. **SIC:** 5021 (Furniture). **Sales:**
$30,000,000 (2000). **Emp:** 499. **Officers:** John Park.

■ **21016** ■ **Goldsmiths Inc.**
151 N Main St.
Wichita, KS 67202
Phone: (316)263-0131   **Fax:** (316)263-6679
E-mail: info@goldsmithsinc.com
URL: http://www.goldsmithsinc.com
Products: Office furnishings. **SIC:** 5021 (Furniture).
Est: 1893. **Sales:** $60,000,000 (2000). **Emp:** 170.
Officers: Rodger M. Arst, CEO; Michael Arst,
President; Matt Arst, President; Kim Roark, Human
Resources Contact, e-mail: kimr@goldsmithsinc.com.

■ **21017** ■ **Goodmans Design Interior**
4860 Pan American Fwy. NE
Albuquerque, NM 87107
Phone: (505)889-0195   **Fax:** (505)889-8698
Products: Office furniture. **SIC:** 5021 (Furniture). **Emp:**
17. **Officers:** Murray Goodman.

■ **21018** ■ **Granite State Office Supplies, Inc.**
6 Augusta National Ctr.
Bedford, NH 03110-6132
Phone: (603)669-8179   **Fax:** (603)669-0754
Products: Office equipment. **SIC:** 5044 (Office
Equipment). **Est:** 1995. **Sales:** $600,000 (2000). **Emp:**
5. **Officers:** Richard Simard, President.

■ **21019** ■ **Graphic Systems Inc. (Memphis,
Tennessee)**
2127 Thomas Rd.
Memphis, TN 38134-5615
Phone: (901)372-3762
Products: Business forms. **SIC:** 5112 (Stationery &
Office Supplies). **Sales:** $12,000,000 (1994). **Emp:** 25.
Officers: C.T. Mitchell Jr., CEO; Dennis B. Kopcial,
CFO.

■ **21020** ■ **Great Falls Business Services**
9514 Georgetown Pike
Great Falls, VA 22066-2616
Phone: (703)759-3024   **Fax:** (703)759-3024
Products: Duplicating machines. **SIC:** 5044 (Office
Equipment). **Officers:** Nancy Markowitz, President.

■ **21021** ■ **GSI Corp.**
6399 Amp Dr.
Clemmons, NC 27012
Phone: (336)766-7070
Free: (800)334-1990   **Fax:** (336)766-0884
Products: Printing equipment and supplies. **SICs:**
5084 (Industrial Machinery & Equipment); 5043
(Photographic Equipment & Supplies). **Est:** 1954.
Sales: $150,000,000 (2000). **Emp:** 150. **Officers:** Jon
Wright, President; Jim Clark, Controller. **Former Name:**
Young-Phillip Corporation.

■ **21022** ■ **Hadley Office Products Inc.**
399 S River Dr.
Wausau, WI 54402-1326
Phone: (715)842-5651   **Fax:** (715)845-6063
E-mail: mhadley@hadleyofficeproducts
URL: http://www.hadleyofficeproducts.com
Products: Office machines; Office furniture; Office
supplies. **SICs:** 5044 (Office Equipment); 5112
(Stationery & Office Supplies); 5021 (Furniture). **Est:**
1965. **Sales:** $5,000,000 (1999). **Emp:** 45. **Officers:**
Mark Hadley.

■ **21023** ■ **Hallmarkets International Ltd.**
1415 Midway Dr.
Alpine, CA 91901
Phone: (619)445-1999   **Fax:** (619)445-6600
Products: Computer peripherals and software;
Electronic parts and equipment; Hardware; Office
equipment. **SICs:** 5044 (Office Equipment); 5045
(Computers, Peripherals & Software); 5065 (Electronic
Parts & Equipment Nec); 5072 (Hardware). **Officers:**
David D. Hall, President.

■ **21024** ■ **J.L. Hammett Co.**
PO Box 9057
Braintree, MA 02184
Phone: (781)848-1000   **Fax:** (781)843-4901
Products: School supplies. **SIC:** 5112 (Stationery &
Office Supplies). **Est:** 1863. **Sales:** $65,000,000
(2000). **Emp:** 500. **Officers:** Richmond Y. Holden,
President & Treasurer.

■ **21025** ■ **Hampton-Haddon Marketing Corp.**
230 2nd Ave.
Waltham, MA 02454
Phone: (781)290-4700
Free: (800)275-3820   **Fax:** (781)890-1751
Products: Electric razors and dry shavers; Pens and
mechanical pencils; Wood-cased pencils, crayons, and
chalk; Coats. **SICs:** 5112 (Stationery & Office
Supplies); 5136 (Men's/Boys' Clothing); 5064
(Electrical Appliances—Television & Radio); 5137
(Women's/Children's Clothing). **Officers:** David Peters,
President.

■ **21026** ■ **Harbor Packaging Inc.**
13100 Danielson St.
Poway, CA 92064
Phone: (858)513-1800   **Fax:** (858)513-0800
Products: Corrugated boxes and packaging materials.
SIC: 5112 (Stationery & Office Supplies). **Sales:**
$29,000,000 (1999). **Emp:** 150.

■ 21027 ■ Harpel's Inc.
701 Cumberland
Lebanon, PA 17042
Phone: (717)272-6687
Products: Office supplies. **SIC:** 5112 (Stationery & Office Supplies).

■ 21028 ■ Dub Harris Corp.
2301 Tubeway Ave.
City of Commerce, CA 90040
Phone: (213)722-3344 **Fax:** (213)722-3311
Products: Banking products, including bags for armored trucks. **SICs:** 5044 (Office Equipment); 5113 (Industrial & Personal Service Paper). **Est:** 1966. **Sales:** $3,000,000 (2000). **Emp:** 50. **Officers:** Maurice Harris, CEO.

■ 21029 ■ Hendrix Technologies Inc.
20 Gilbert Ave., Ste. 101
Smithtown, NY 11787
Phone: (516)361-5021 **Fax:** (516)361-4955
Products: Integrity systems for laser printers and inserters. **SICs:** 5045 (Computers, Peripherals & Software); 5085 (Industrial Supplies); 5169 (Chemicals & Allied Products Nec). **Est:** 1983. **Sales:** $2,600,000 (2000). **Emp:** 3. **Officers:** John F. Harvey, President & Treasurer.

■ 21030 ■ Hermann Associates Inc.
1405 Indiana St.
San Francisco, CA 94107
Phone: (415)285-8486
Free: (800)799-1738 **Fax:** (415)826-3118
Products: Safes, vaults and safety-deposit boxes. **SICs:** 5044 (Office Equipment); 5046 (Commercial Equipment Nec). **Sales:** $3,000,000 (2000). **Emp:** 6. **Officers:** James Nuss, President; Christine Nuss, Treasurer & Secty.

■ 21031 ■ Hesters/McGlaun Office Supply Co.
PO Box 3098
Lubbock, TX 79452
Phone: (806)766-8888 **Fax:** (806)747-7067
Products: Office furniture and supplies. **SICs:** 5021 (Furniture); 5112 (Stationery & Office Supplies). **Est:** 1956. **Emp:** 25. **Officers:** Ronald Edmondson, CEO. **Former Name:** Frank #McGlaun Office Supply Co.

■ 21032 ■ H.H. West Co.
505 N 22nd St.
Milwaukee, WI 53233
Phone: (414)344-1000
Free: (800)242-7225 **Fax:** (414)344-1974
Products: Office supplies, office furniture and computer equipment. **SICs:** 5112 (Stationery & Office Supplies); 5045 (Computers, Peripherals & Software). **Sales:** $54,000,000 (2000). **Emp:** 280. **Officers:** Craig Cooper, President.

■ 21033 ■ Hickson's Office Supplies Co.
17 E Wheeling St.
Washington, PA 15301
Phone: (412)222-0140 **Fax:** (412)222-6108
Products: Office supplies, including cabinets, desks, files, pens, and erasers. **SIC:** 5112 (Stationery & Office Supplies). **Sales:** $300,000 (2000). **Emp:** 6. **Officers:** Alice Montgomery, President.

■ 21034 ■ Hills Office Supply Co. Inc.
490 Main St.
Pawtucket, RI 02860-2914
Phone: (401)723-1240 **Fax:** (401)724-8920
Products: Office and public building furniture. **SIC:** 5021 (Furniture). **Officers:** William Whalen, President.

■ 21035 ■ C.F. Hoeckel Co.
PO Box 11519
Denver, CO 80211-0519
Phone: (303)433-7481 **Fax:** (303)433-7487
Products: Office supplies. **SIC:** 5112 (Stationery & Office Supplies). **Sales:** $4,000,000 (2000). **Emp:** 23. **Officers:** Susan Dawson, President.

■ 21036 ■ Holcomb's Education Resource
PO Box 94636
Cleveland, OH 44101-4636
Phone: (216)341-3000 **Fax:** (216)341-5151
E-mail: holcombs.com
URL: http://www.holcombs.com
Products: Educational materials, including supplies and teaching aids; Furniture. **SICs:** 5112 (Stationery & Office Supplies); 5045 (Computers, Peripherals & Software); 5021 (Furniture). **Est:** 1872. **Sales:** $30,000,000 (2000). **Emp:** 170. **Officers:** Paul F. Culler, President; Don McKinnie, VP ofSchool Supplies; Mo Beck, Marketing Mgr.; Tony Hess, Dir. of Data Processing.

■ 21037 ■ Holcomb's Education Resource
PO Box 94636
Cleveland, OH 44101-4636
Phone: (216)341-3000 **Fax:** (216)341-5151
Products: Office equipment and supplies. **SIC:** 5112 (Stationery & Office Supplies). **Sales:** $30,000,000 (2000). **Emp:** 170.

■ 21038 ■ Holga Inc.
7901 Woodley Ave.
Van Nuys, CA 91406
Phone: (818)782-0600
Free: (800)544-4623 **Fax:** (818)374-5544
URL: http://www.holga.com
Products: Metal office furniture; Steel shelving; Mobile filing systems. **SICs:** 5021 (Furniture); 5046 (Commercial Equipment Nec). **Est:** 1947. **Sales:** $10,000,000 (2000). **Emp:** 110. **Officers:** Brian Oken; Brian Eustace.

■ 21039 ■ Holtzman Office Furniture Co.
2155 E 7th St.
Los Angeles, CA 90023
Phone: (323)266-5700
Products: Office furniture, including desks and chairs. **SIC:** 5021 (Furniture). **Est:** 1962. **Sales:** $3,000,000 (1999). **Emp:** 20. **Officers:** Susan Petlik, CEO & President; Sandra Manning, Controller.

■ 21040 ■ HPS Inc.
8020 Zionsville Rd.
Indianapolis, IN 46268
Phone: (317)875-9000 **Fax:** (317)471-4126
Products: Photocopying equipment and supplies including printing presses. **SICs:** 5044 (Office Equipment); 5084 (Industrial Machinery & Equipment). **Sales:** $40,000,000 (2000). **Emp:** 280. **Officers:** William A. Boncosky, President; Harry Montgomery, Vice President.

■ 21041 ■ HPS Office Systems
8020 Zionsville Rd.
Indianapolis, IN 46268
Phone: (317)875-9000 **Fax:** (317)471-4126
Products: Office equipment including copiers, fax machines and telephone systems. **SICs:** 5044 (Office Equipment); 5065 (Electronic Parts & Equipment Nec). **Sales:** $15,000,000 (2000). **Emp:** 90. **Officers:** William A. Boncosky, President.

■ 21042 ■ HPS Printing Products
8020 Zionsville Rd.
Indianapolis, IN 46268
Phone: (317)875-9000
Free: (800)732-1467 **Fax:** (317)471-4128
Products: Printing equipment including copiers. **SIC:** 5044 (Office Equipment). **Sales:** $64,000,000 (2000). **Emp:** 400. **Officers:** William A. Boncosky, CEO & President; Harry Montgomery, Vice President.

■ 21043 ■ Hughes-Calihan Corp.
4730 N 16th St.
Phoenix, AZ 85016
Phone: (602)264-9631 **Fax:** (602)234-2406
Products: Copying and microphone products. **SIC:** 5044 (Office Equipment). **Est:** 1917. **Sales:** $12,000,000 (2000). **Emp:** 140. **Officers:** P.E. Calihan, President; Lee Kirtley, Controller; P.J. Calihan, VP of Sales.

■ 21044 ■ Hunter The Typewriter Man
314 S Federal Blvd.
Riverton, WY 82501-4730
Phone: (307)856-3240
Products: Office equipment. **SIC:** 5044 (Office Equipment). **Est:** 1959. **Emp:** 1. **Officers:** Jay Hunter, President.

■ 21045 ■ Hunters Inc.
PO Box 17508
Honolulu, HI 96817
Phone: (808)841-8002 **Fax:** (808)847-7301
Products: Office furniture, including desks, chairs, and file cabinets. **SIC:** 5021 (Furniture). **Est:** 1960. **Sales:** $2,800,000 (2000). **Emp:** 10. **Officers:** Howard H. Yoshinobu, President & General Mgr.

■ 21046 ■ Hurst Office Suppliers Inc.
257 E Short St.
Lexington, KY 40507
Phone: (606)255-4422 **Fax:** (606)255-4471
Products: Metal office furniture; Wood office furniture. **SIC:** 5021 (Furniture). **Est:** 1923. **Sales:** $6,000,000 (2000). **Emp:** 49. **Officers:** R.L. Hurst, President; Tom Gormley, Vice President.

■ 21047 ■ Icon Office Solutions
PO Box 649
Exton, PA 19341-0649
Phone: (215)296-8600 **Fax:** (215)296-8604
Products: Copiers; Fax machines. **SIC:** 5044 (Office Equipment). **Est:** 1982. **Sales:** $2,560,000,000 (2000). **Emp:** 16,000. **Officers:** Kurt E. Dinkelacker, President; Robert Kearns, VP of Finance; Donna Unger, Information Systems Mgr.; Larry Kludt.

■ 21048 ■ IDEAL Scanners & Systems, Inc.
11810 Parklawn Dr.
Rockville, MD 20852
Phone: (301)468-0123
Free: (800)764-3325 **Fax:** (301)230-0813
E-mail: sales@ideal.com
URL: http://www.ideal.com
Products: Scanners; Conversion and indexing software. **SICs:** 5044 (Office Equipment); 5045 (Computers, Peripherals & Software). **Est:** 1978. **Sales:** $5,000,000 (2000). **Emp:** 25. **Officers:** Jay Magenheim, CEO; Philip G. Magenheim, COO.

■ 21049 ■ Ikon Office Solutions
PO Box 5615
Greenville, SC 29606
Phone: (864)281-5400
Products: Office equipment, including copying machines and facsimile machines; Graphics equipment. **SIC:** 5044 (Office Equipment). **Est:** 1954. **Sales:** $35,000,000 (2000). **Emp:** 350. **Officers:** Tee Hooper, President; Marty Harrison, CFO. **Alternate Name:** MOM/Modern Office Machines.

■ 21050 ■ Ikon Office Solutions
12100 SW Garden Pl.
Portland, OR 97223
Phone: (503)620-2800 **Fax:** (503)620-3500
URL: http://www.ikon.com
Products: Copiers; Fax machines; One source outsourcing for copy and mail services; Technology training. **SIC:** 5044 (Office Equipment). **Est:** 1980. **Sales:** $71,000,000 (2000). **Emp:** 420. **Officers:** Jim Forese, CEO; Mike Royce, VP of Finance; Tom Deveral, Northwest District Mgr.; Ernie White, Oregon Marketplace Pres. **Former Name:** Automated Office Systems, Inc.

■ 21051 ■ IKON Office Solutions Inc.
PO Box 834
Valley Forge, PA 19482-0834
Phone: (610)296-8000 **Fax:** (610)408-7025
Products: Photocopiers, facsimile machines, and other office equipment. **SIC:** 5044 (Office Equipment). **Sales:** $5,629,000,000 (2000). **Emp:** 42,600. **Officers:** James J. Forese, CEO & President; Kurt F. Dinkelacker, Exec. VP & CFO.

■ 21052 ■ Imagetech RICOH Corp.
192 Nickerson St., No. 200
Seattle, WA 98109
Phone: (206)298-1600
Products: Photocopying machines; Facsimile

machines. **SIC:** 5044 (Office Equipment). **Est:** 1907. **Sales:** $30,000,000 (2000). **Emp:** 190. **Officers:** Warren White, President; Ralph Pride, CFO.

■ **21053** ■ **Imaging Technologies**
2120 Rittenhouse
Des Moines, IA 50321
Phone: (515)953-7306 **Fax:** (515)953-7312
Products: Copiers and fax machines. **SIC:** 5044 (Office Equipment). **Sales:** $1,000,000 (2000). **Emp:** 7. **Officers:** Tom Miner, President; Larry Perry, Dir. of Marketing & Sales.

■ **21054** ■ **Import Export Management Service Inc.**
2205 Royal Lane
Dallas, TX 75229
Phone: (972)620-9545 **Fax:** (972)243-4627
E-mail: klaus@mexusa.com
URL: http://www.imexusa.com
Products: Computer and office supplies; Art goods; Ceramic hobby supplies and materials; Drafting and engineering supplies; Stationery; School supplies. **SICs:** 5112 (Stationery & Office Supplies); 5045 (Computers, Peripherals & Software); 5199 (Nondurable Goods Nec); 5092 (Toys & Hobby Goods & Supplies); 5049 (Professional Equipment Nec). **Est:** 1967. **Sales:** $15,000,000 (1999). **Emp:** 12. **Officers:** Klaus Engels, President; Klaus Engels Jr., Vice President; Jeffrey Lamb, Sales/Marketing Contact, e-mail: jeffrey@mexusa.com.

■ **21055** ■ **Independent Photocopy Inc.**
14455 Jefferson Davis Hwy.
Woodbridge, VA 22191
Phone: (703)494-5356 **Fax:** (703)494-0862
Products: Photocopying equipment and supplies; Fax machines. **SIC:** 5044 (Office Equipment). **Est:** 1985. **Sales:** $1,500,000 (2000). **Emp:** 15. **Officers:** B. Mendell.

■ **21056** ■ **Indiana Carbon Company Inc.**
3164 N Shadeland Ave.
Indianapolis, IN 46226
Phone: (317)547-9621
URL: http://www.iccbpi.com
Products: Inked ribbons; Computer and office system supplies. **SICs:** 5045 (Computers, Peripherals & Software); 5044 (Office Equipment). **Sales:** $11,000,000 (2000). **Emp:** 32. **Officers:** Quinn Ray, President.

■ **21057** ■ **Infincom Inc.**
1702 W 3rd St.
Tempe, AZ 85281
Phone: (602)894-6200 **Fax:** (602)966-2789
Products: Photocopiers. **SIC:** 5044 (Office Equipment).

■ **21058** ■ **Information Processing Center**
454 N Phillippi St.
Boise, ID 83706-1426
Phone: (208)377-3256 **Fax:** (208)377-3261
Products: Microfiche readers; Copiers. **SIC:** 5044 (Office Equipment). **Officers:** David Miller, President.

■ **21059** ■ **Inland NW Services Inc.**
PO Box 1101
Lewiston, ID 83501-1101
Phone: (208)746-2557 **Fax:** (208)746-3216
Products: Office equipment. **SIC:** 5044 (Office Equipment). **Officers:** Cheryl Crouse, President.

■ **21060** ■ **Input Automation Inc.**
3155 Fujita St.
Torrance, CA 90505
Phone: (310)539-3598
Products: Bar coding equipment. **SIC:** 5045 (Computers, Peripherals & Software). **Sales:** $2,000,000 (2000). **Emp:** 6. **Officers:** Jay O'Donnell, President.

■ **21061** ■ **Interior Enterprises Inc.**
101 W Grand Ave.
Chicago, IL 60610
Phone: (312)527-3636
Products: Office furniture. **SIC:** 5021 (Furniture). **Est:** 1943. **Sales:** $700,000 (1999). **Emp:** 5. **Officers:** David Masur, President.

■ **21062** ■ **Interior Services Inc.**
1360 Kemper Meadow Dr.
Cincinnati, OH 45240
Phone: (513)851-0933 **Fax:** (513)742-6415
Products: Office furniture. **SIC:** 5021 (Furniture). **Est:** 1982. **Emp:** 22. **Officers:** Michael Schwartzman, President; Dawn Schwartzman, Vice President.

■ **21063** ■ **International Business Equipment**
1402 S Minnesota Ave.
Sioux Falls, SD 57105-1716
Phone: (605)335-1050 **Fax:** (605)335-0714
Products: Office machines, including typewriters, dictating, transcribing, fax, and recording machines; Computers; Printers. **SIC:** 5044 (Office Equipment). **Est:** 1984. **Emp:** 8. **Officers:** Brian Feit, President.

■ **21064** ■ **International Office Systems Inc.**
2740 W 80th St.
Minneapolis, MN 55431
Phone: (612)456-9999 **Fax:** (612)885-7999
Products: Fax machines; Photocopying equipment and supplies. **SIC:** 5044 (Office Equipment). **Sales:** $35,000,000 (2000). **Emp:** 140. **Officers:** John Hey, President.

■ **21065** ■ **International Tape Products Co.**
901 Murray Rd.
East Hanover, NJ 07936
Phone: (973)748-7870
Free: (800)423-0138 **Fax:** (973)748-0408
Products: Printing materials; Labels; Carton sealing equipment. **SICs:** 5044 (Office Equipment); 5085 (Industrial Supplies); 5113 (Industrial & Personal Service Paper). **Est:** 1965. **Sales:** $6,000,000 (2000). **Emp:** 17. **Officers:** Pierre Guariglia, President; Gary Guariglia, Vice President; David Guariglia, Manager.

■ **21066** ■ **International Typewriter Exchange**
1229 W Washington
Chicago, IL 60607
Phone: (312)733-1200 **Fax:** (312)733-8241
Products: Typewriters, photocopying machines, and paper shredders. **SIC:** 5044 (Office Equipment). **Est:** 1915. **Sales:** $5,000,000 (2000). **Emp:** 40. **Officers:** W. Nelson, CEO; Ralph Projahn, CFO.

■ **21067** ■ **Interstate Companies of Louisiana**
PO Box 3358
Baton Rouge, LA 70821
Phone: (504)387-5131
Free: (800)272-9800 **Fax:** (504)336-1419
Products: School equipment, including cafeteria tables and seating, desks, tables, and bleachers. **SIC:** 5021 (Furniture). **Sales:** $8,000,000 (2000). **Emp:** 10. **Officers:** John Pace, President.

■ **21068** ■ **Interstate Copy Shop**
1516 N Bennett St.
Silver City, NM 88061-6522
Phone: (505)538-9530 **Fax:** (505)388-3836
Products: Office equipment, including copying equipment and photocopy machines. **SIC:** 5044 (Office Equipment). **Officers:** Bevan Barney, Owner.

■ **21069** ■ **Iowa Office Supplies Inc.**
PO Box 1386
Storm Lake, IA 50588
Phone: (712)732-4801 **Fax:** (712)732-4426
Products: Office supplies. **SIC:** 5112 (Stationery & Office Supplies). **Sales:** $12,000,000 (2000). **Emp:** 91. **Officers:** Kirby Roberts, President.

■ **21070** ■ **Iowa Office Supply Inc.**
PO Box 1386
Storm Lake, IA 50588
Phone: (712)732-4801 **Fax:** (712)732-4426
URL: http://www.iowaofficesupply.com
Products: Office equipment and supplies, including photocopying machines and facsimile machines; Furniture. **SIC:** 5112 (Stationery & Office Supplies). **Est:** 1967. **Sales:** $15,000,000 (2000). **Emp:** 100. **Officers:** Kirby Roberts, President.

■ **21071** ■ **ITE Distributing**
1229 W Washington Blvd.
Chicago, IL 60607
Phone: (312)733-1200
Products: Typewriters, facsimile and photocopy

machines. **SIC:** 5044 (Office Equipment). **Sales:** $4,000,000 (2000). **Emp:** 25. **Officers:** William Nelson, CEO; Richard Nelson, VP of Finance.

■ **21072** ■ **ITP Business Communications**
PO Box 866
Hickory, NC 28603-0866
Phone: (704)322-6261 **Fax:** (704)322-6267
E-mail: itp@twave.net
Products: Bar code equipment; Time and attendance systems. **SIC:** 5044 (Office Equipment). **Est:** 1979. **Sales:** $2,000,000 (2000). **Emp:** 24. **Officers:** Mike Filip, President.

■ **21073** ■ **Ives Business Forms Inc.**
1009 Camp St.
New Orleans, LA 70130
Phone: (504)561-8811 **Fax:** (504)581-4837
Products: Office supplies; Printing and engraving equipment and supplies. **SICs:** 5112 (Stationery & Office Supplies); 5084 (Industrial Machinery & Equipment); 5199 (Nondurable Goods Nec). **Sales:** $6,500,000 (2000). **Emp:** 70. **Officers:** Charles M. Ives Jr.

■ **21074** ■ **J-Snell & Co., Inc.**
156 Mendell St.
San Francisco, CA 94124
Phone: (415)206-7700 **Fax:** (415)550-8326
E-mail: sales@jsnell.com
URL: http://www.jsnell.com
Products: Office equipment; Office supplies, including folders. **SICs:** 5044 (Office Equipment); 5112 (Stationery & Office Supplies). **Est:** 1971. **Sales:** $1,500,000 (2000). **Emp:** 15. **Officers:** Helen Snell, President; J. Snell, Vice President; Anthony Groshong, Manager.

■ **21075** ■ **Jax International**
40 E Verdugo Ave.
Burbank, CA 91502-1931
Phone: (707)584-7360
Free: (800)800-5699 **Fax:** (707)585-0553
Products: Office furniture. **SIC:** 5021 (Furniture). **Sales:** $5,000,000 (2000). **Emp:** 70.

■ **21076** ■ **Jeter Systems Corp.**
1560 Firestone Pkwy.
Akron, OH 44301
Phone: (330)773-8971
Free: (800)321-8261 **Fax:** (330)773-7402
Products: Office storage units, files, and tables, except wood. **SIC:** 5021 (Furniture). **Emp:** 175.

■ **21077** ■ **Jewel Paula-Ronn Records**
PO Box 1125
Shreveport, LA 71163
Phone: (318)865-5318
Products: Labels. **SIC:** 5112 (Stationery & Office Supplies).

■ **21078** ■ **J.J.R. Enterprises Inc.**
10491 Old Placerville Rd., No. 150
Sacramento, CA 95827
Phone: (916)363-2666 **Fax:** (916)361-1829
URL: http://www.caltronics.net
Products: Copying machines and facsimile machines. **SIC:** 5044 (Office Equipment). **Est:** 1975. **Sales:** $27,000,000 (1999). **Emp:** 150. **Officers:** John Reilly, President; Carl J. Jantz, CFO; Daniel Reilly, Sales Mgr. **Doing Business As:** Caltronics Business Systems.

■ **21079** ■ **Al Jones Office Equipment**
8636 Highacre Dr.
Las Vegas, NV 89128-4808
Phone: (702)623-2003
Products: Office and public building furniture. **SIC:** 5021 (Furniture). **Officers:** Alvin Jones, Partner.

■ **21080** ■ **JOS Projection Systems Inc.**
180 S Prospect Ave.
Tustin, CA 92780-3617
Phone: (714)476-2222 **Fax:** (310)769-1177
Products: Overhead projectors. **SIC:** 5043 (Photographic Equipment & Supplies). **Est:** 1981. **Sales:** $6,000,000 (2000). **Emp:** 16. **Officers:** Alice Schellin, President; Martin Wood, Controller.

■ 21081 ■ **Joyce International Inc.**
156 W 56th St., Ste. 1604
New York, NY 10019-3800
Phone: (212)463-9044 **Fax:** (212)638-8920
Products: Office supplies, including furniture, copiers, and paper. **SICs:** 5112 (Stationery & Office Supplies); 5021 (Furniture). **Est:** 1984. **Sales:** $540,000,000 (2000). **Emp:** 3,000. **Officers:** G. Lynn Schostack, CEO; Peter Tracy, CFO.

■ 21082 ■ **J.R.M. Inc.**
523 E Malone St.
Sikeston, MO 63801
Phone: (314)471-9111
Products: Copiers. **SIC:** 5044 (Office Equipment). **Est:** 1969. **Sales:** $3,500,000 (2000). **Emp:** 35. **Officers:** Henry Dirnberger, President; Pam Dirnberger, Treasurer & Secty.; Don Miller, Sales Mgr.

■ 21083 ■ **K & S Tole & Craft Supply**
1556 Florence
Aurora, CO 80010
Phone: (303)364-3031
Products: Lead pencils, crayons, and artists' materials. **SICs:** 5112 (Stationery & Office Supplies); 5049 (Professional Equipment Nec).

■ 21084 ■ **Kalbus Office Supply**
PO Box 800
Nampa, ID 83653-0800
Phone: (208)466-4653
Products: Office and public building furniture; Office supplies. **SICs:** 5021 (Furniture); 5112 (Stationery & Office Supplies). **Officers:** Burke Jones, President.

■ 21085 ■ **Kaneka Far West, Inc.**
2290 Nugget Way
Eugene, OR 97403-2472
Phone: (541)687-8374
Products: Lead pencils, crayons, and artists' materials. **SICs:** 5112 (Stationery & Office Supplies); 5049 (Professional Equipment Nec).

■ 21086 ■ **Kardex Systems Inc.**
PO Box 171
Marietta, OH 45750
Phone: (740)374-9300
Free: (800)234-3654 **Fax:** (740)374-9953
E-mail: sales@kardex.com
URL: http://www.kardex.com
Products: Information management systems. **SIC:** 5044 (Office Equipment). **Est:** 1978. **Sales:** $40,000,000 (2000). **Emp:** 200. **Officers:** Ronald J. Nienhuis, President; Ron Williams, Vice President, e-mail: freeman@kardex.com.

■ 21087 ■ **Ken's Craft Supply**
54 Ashman Cir.
Midland, MI 48640
Phone: (517)835-8401
Free: (800)835-8854 **Fax:** (517)855-6861
Products: Craft supplies, including flowers and art supplies; Gifts. **SICs:** 5112 (Stationery & Office Supplies); 5049 (Professional Equipment Nec); 5193 (Flowers & Florists' Supplies); 5092 (Toys & Hobby Goods & Supplies). **Est:** 1974. **Sales:** $2,000,000 (2000). **Emp:** 15. **Officers:** Chris Colvin, CEO & President; Ken Colvin, Vice President; V.K. Colvin, Sec. & Treas.

■ 21088 ■ **Keystone Office Supply Co. Inc.**
52 Olneyville Sq.
Providence, RI 02909
Phone: (401)421-7872 **Fax:** (401)421-7872
Products: Office and printing supplies; Office furniture. **SICs:** 5044 (Office Equipment); 5021 (Furniture); 5112 (Stationery & Office Supplies). **Officers:** John Laurito, President.

■ 21089 ■ **Kiddie Academy International Inc.**
108 Wheel Rd.
Bel Air, MD 21015-6198
Phone: (410)515-0788
Products: School supplies and equipment. **SIC:** 5021 (Furniture). **Sales:** $4,800,000 (2000). **Emp:** 238. **Officers:** George Miller, CEO & Chairman of the Board; Guy A. Matta, CFO.

■ 21090 ■ **Kielty and Dayton Co.**
23125 Bernhard St.
Hayward, CA 94545
Phone: (510)732-9200
Products: Office supplies. **SIC:** 5112 (Stationery & Office Supplies).

■ 21091 ■ **Kights' Printing and Office Products**
8505 Baymeadows Rd.
Jacksonville, FL 32256
Phone: (904)731-7990 **Fax:** (904)448-7127
Products: Office equipment, including photocopiers; Office furniture and supplies. **SICs:** 5044 (Office Equipment); 5021 (Furniture). **Est:** 1968. **Sales:** $14,400,000 (2000). **Emp:** 30. **Officers:** David E. Kight, President; Sue Harms, Controller.

■ 21092 ■ **Kilpatrick Equipment Co.**
PO Box 35786
Dallas, TX 75235
Phone: (214)358-4346 **Fax:** (214)358-3723
Products: Office equipment. **SIC:** 5044 (Office Equipment). **Sales:** $1,000,000 (2000). **Emp:** 10. **Officers:** Steve Kilpatrick, President.

■ 21093 ■ **Kimsco Supply Co.**
PO Box 307
Hancock, ME 04640-0307
Phone: (207)422-3363 **Fax:** (207)422-3703
Products: School equipment; Office equipment. **SIC:** 5044 (Office Equipment). **Officers:** Bruce Morrison, President.

■ 21094 ■ **Konica Business Technologies, Inc.**
500 Day Hill Rd.
Windsor, CT 06095
Phone: (860)683-2222 **Fax:** (860)285-0858
URL: http://www.konicabt.com
Products: Digital photocopying machines, facsimile machines, and laser printers. **SIC:** 5044 (Office Equipment). **Est:** 1979. **Sales:** $668,000,000 (1999). **Emp:** 2,000. **Officers:** Teruo Nakazawa, CEO & President; Michael Lecnczyk, CFO; Jun Haraguchi, Exec. VP of Marketing; Donald Warwick, VP of Human Resources. **Former Name:** Konica Business Machines U.S.A. Inc.

■ 21095 ■ **Lad Enterprises, Ltd.**
1906 Great Falls Hwy.
Lancaster, SC 29720
Phone: (803)285-2800 **Fax:** (803)286-4400
E-mail: ladent@infoave.net
Products: Artist supplies; Pencils; Paints, including oils, acrylics, watercolors, and mediums; Brushes; Canvases; Decorative supplies. **SICs:** 5199 (Nondurable Goods Nec); 5049 (Professional Equipment Nec). **Est:** 1983. **Sales:** $627,849 (2000). **Emp:** 5. **Officers:** Linda DeBruycker, President.

■ 21096 ■ **Lake Business Products**
38322 Apollo Pkwy.
Willoughby, OH 44094
Phone: (440)953-1199
Products: Business machines. **SIC:** 5044 (Office Equipment).

■ 21097 ■ **Lake County Office Equipment Inc.**
1428 Glen Flora Ave.
Waukegan, IL 60085
Phone: (708)662-5393
Free: (800)468-8104 **Fax:** (708)662-8761
Products: Office products, furniture, and business machines. **SICs:** 5044 (Office Equipment); 5112 (Stationery & Office Supplies); 5021 (Furniture). **Est:** 1945. **Sales:** $4,000,000 (2000). **Emp:** 32. **Officers:** Wes T. Trombino Jr., President; Donna Trombino, Treasurer; W.T. Trombino, President; Sandy Trombino, VP of Marketing.

■ 21098 ■ **Lamb's Office Products**
PO Box 191
Beaumont, TX 77703-5256
Phone: (409)838-3703 **Fax:** (409)838-2950
Products: Office supplies. **SIC:** 5112 (Stationery & Office Supplies). **Sales:** $6,000,000 (2000). **Emp:** 66. **Officers:** Tom Lamb.

■ 21099 ■ **Lane Office Furniture Inc.**
116 John St.
New York, NY 10038
Phone: (212)233-4100 **Fax:** (212)693-2124
E-mail: office@laneofficefurniture.com
URL: http://www.laneofficefurniture.com
Products: Office furniture. **SIC:** 5021 (Furniture). **Est:** 1921. **Emp:** 35. **Officers:** Raymond G. Niessing, Chairman of the Board, e-mail: ray@laneofficefurniture.com.

■ 21100 ■ **Lanier Worldwide Inc.**
2300 Parklake Dr. NE
Atlanta, GA 30345
Phone: (404)496-9500
Free: (800)708-7088 **Fax:** (404)621-1062
Products: Photocopying machines and facsimile machines. **SICs:** 5044 (Office Equipment); 5045 (Computers, Peripherals & Software). **Est:** 1934. **Sales:** $1,270,000,000 (2000). **Emp:** 7,000. **Officers:** Wesley E. Cantrell, CEO & President; Joe Payne, CFO; Charles Cobb, VP of Sales; Buddy Harrell, Dir. of Data Processing; Harley Ostis, Dir of Human Resources.

■ 21101 ■ **Laser Logic Inc.**
2190 Paragon Dr.
San Jose, CA 95131
Phone: (408)452-1284 **Free:** (800)638-2292
Products: Laser printer and copier supplies. **SIC:** 5044 (Office Equipment). **Sales:** $3,000,000 (2000). **Emp:** 18. **Officers:** Ronald K. Paul, President; Katie Paul, VP & CFO.

■ 21102 ■ **Laser Magnetic Storage International Co.**
4425 Arrowswest Dr.
Colorado Springs, CO 80907
Phone: (719)593-7900 **Fax:** (719)593-8713
Products: Office desks. **SIC:** 5021 (Furniture). **Est:** 1963. **Sales:** $100,000,000 (2000). **Emp:** 475. **Officers:** Willem Andersen, President; Bob Biemesderfer, VP & CFO; Roy Roque, VP of Marketing.

■ 21103 ■ **Laser Technologies and Services Inc.**
1155 Phenixville Pike, No. 106
West Chester, PA 19380
Phone: (215)692-9756 **Fax:** (215)430-2008
Products: Printer and copier parts and supplies. **SICs:** 5044 (Office Equipment); 5045 (Computers, Peripherals & Software). **Est:** 1988. **Sales:** $5,000,000 (2000). **Emp:** 40. **Officers:** Robert W. Falcone, President; C. Roper, CFO; D. Weaver, Dir. of Marketing & Sales.

■ 21104 ■ **Lees Office Equipment & Supplies**
170 W Granite St.
Butte, MT 59701-9216
Phone: (406)782-8355 **Free:** (800)823-5337
Products: Office supplies. **SIC:** 5044 (Office Equipment). **Officers:** William Lee, Owner.

■ 21105 ■ **Leland Paper Company Inc.**
PO Box 2148
Glens Falls, NY 12801-2148
Phone: (518)792-0949
Free: (800)825-3526 **Fax:** (518)792-7966
Products: Paper goods or products, including book mailers; Stationery and office supplies; Janitors' supplies; Packaging. **SICs:** 5112 (Stationery & Office Supplies); 5087 (Service Establishment Equipment); 5113 (Industrial & Personal Service Paper). **Est:** 1951. **Sales:** $4,500,000 (2000). **Emp:** 25. **Officers:** Richard D. Leland, President; Darwin E. Leland, CEO & Treasurer; John Jenkins, Purchasing Agent.

■ 21106 ■ **Lessco Products Inc.**
529 Railroad Ave.
South San Francisco, CA 94080
Phone: (650)873-8700
Products: Binders, business forms, office supply, furniture, and commercial lithographic printing. **SICs:** 5112 (Stationery & Office Supplies); 5021 (Furniture). **Sales:** $4,000,000 (2000). **Emp:** 30. **Officers:** Richard Koss, President.

■ 21107 ■ Lewan and Associates Inc.
PO Box 22855
Denver, CO 80222
Phone: (303)759-5440 **Fax:** (303)758-7563
URL: http://www.lewan.com
Products: Fax machines; Computers; Networks. **SICs:** 5065 (Electronic Parts & Equipment Nec); 5045 (Computers, Peripherals & Software). **Est:** 1972. **Sales:** $100,000,000 (2000). **Emp:** 450. **Officers:** Paul R. Lewan, Founder; James Arnold, CEO; Fred Cannataro, President; Sue Clifford, Customer Service Contact, e-mail: scliffor@lewan.com; Nancy Stenberg, Human Resources Contact, e-mail: stenberg@lewan.com.

■ 21108 ■ Liberty Business Systems Inc.
PO Box 9887
Fargo, ND 58106-9887
Phone: (701)241-8504
Free: (800)998-7519 **Fax:** (701)241-8541
Products: Photocopier and facsimile machines; Repair and maintenance of photocopier and facsimile machines. **SIC:** 5044 (Office Equipment). **Sales:** $6,000,000 (2000). **Emp:** 21. **Officers:** Ron Fuhrman, CEO & President; Pam Fuhrman, Controller.

■ 21109 ■ Lincoln Office Equipment Co.
2535 O St.
Lincoln, NE 68510
Phone: (402)476-8833
Products: Office supplies; Desks; Pens. **SIC:** 5044 (Office Equipment). **Est:** 1937. **Sales:** $6,000,000 (2000). **Emp:** 45. **Officers:** John Kuchta, President; Keith Schneider, Treasurer & Secty.

■ 21110 ■ Michael Little & Son
191 Silk Farm Rd.
Concord, NH 03302-1455
Phone: (603)225-6066
Products: Office equipment. **SIC:** 5044 (Office Equipment). **Officers:** Michael Little, Owner.

■ 21111 ■ LogEtronics Corp.
7001 Loisdale Rd.
Springfield, VA 22150
Phone: (703)971-1400 **Fax:** (703)971-9325
Products: Photocopying equipment and supplies. **SIC:** 5044 (Office Equipment). **Sales:** $8,000,000 (2000). **Emp:** 30. **Officers:** Ray Luca, President; Al Royston; Gary Aheimer; Dick Uchic; Dick Uchic, Sales Dir.; Al Royston, Engineering Dir.; Maria Alvarez, International Sales Mgr.; Michael Bugge, Marketing Support Mgr.

■ 21112 ■ Duncan Long Inc.
2152 44th Dr.
Long Island City, NY 11101-4710
Phone: (718)937-0701 **Fax:** (718)392-7750
Products: Office machines; Metal office furniture; Partitions and fixtures; Carpets, rugs, and mats. **SICs:** 5021 (Furniture); 5046 (Commercial Equipment Nec); 5044 (Office Equipment); 5023 (Homefurnishings). **Est:** 1967. **Sales:** $2,000,000 (2000). **Emp:** 14. **Officers:** Donald Long.

■ 21113 ■ Los Alamos Stationers
PO Box 620
Los Alamos, NM 87544-0620
Phone: (505)662-4229 **Fax:** (505)662-4287
Products: Office supplies. **SIC:** 5112 (Stationery & Office Supplies). **Officers:** C Robertson, Owner.

■ 21114 ■ Louisiana Office Products
PO Box 23851
New Orleans, LA 70183-0851
Phone: (504)733-9650
Products: Office supplies and equipment. **SICs:** 5112 (Stationery & Office Supplies); 5044 (Office Equipment).

■ 21115 ■ Lucas Brothers Inc.
7700 Port Capital Dr.
Baltimore, MD 21227
Phone: (410)799-7700 **Fax:** (410)799-7144
Products: Office furniture; Office supplies. **SICs:** 5021 (Furniture); 5112 (Stationery & Office Supplies). **Est:** 1804. **Sales:** $55,000,000 (2000). **Emp:** 350. **Officers:** Neil Dvores, President; Randall Jenkins, VP of Finance; Mark Daliesera, Sales Mgr.; Ray Kostkowsky, Vice President; Diane McCloskey, Personnel Mgr.

■ 21116 ■ Luther's Creative Craft Studios
65 Innsbruck Dr.
Buffalo, NY 14227-2703
Phone: (716)632-4741
Products: Lead pencils, crayons, and artists' materials. **SICs:** 5112 (Stationery & Office Supplies); 5049 (Professional Equipment Nec).

■ 21117 ■ Lynde-Ordway Company Inc.
PO Box 8709
Fountain Valley, CA 92728
Phone: (714)957-1311 **Fax:** (714)433-2166
Products: Money-handling equipment; Graphics and form handling equipment. **SIC:** 5044 (Office Equipment).

■ 21118 ■ Mac Thrift Clearance Center
1201 S Holden
Greensboro, NC 27407
Phone: (919)852-1727 **Fax:** (919)852-1531
Products: Office furniture, new and used, including computer desks and chairs. **SIC:** 5021 (Furniture). **Emp:** 49. **Officers:** Andy McKinney.

■ 21119 ■ Maine Office Supply Co. Inc.
48 Quimby St.
Biddeford, ME 04005-2308
Phone: (207)284-7782
Products: Office equipment. **SIC:** 5044 (Office Equipment). **Officers:** Helga Sheltra, President.

■ 21120 ■ Majestic Penn State Inc.
Comly & Caroline Rd.
Philadelphia, PA 19154
Phone: (215)676-7600 **Fax:** (215)676-7603
Products: Office supplies. **SIC:** 5112 (Stationery & Office Supplies). **Est:** 1938. **Sales:** $500,000 (2000). **Emp:** 2. **Officers:** Benjamin Levy, President; Bernard Levy, Treasurer & Secty.; Herbert Greenberg, Controller.

■ 21121 ■ Mankato Business Products
1715 Commerce Dr.
North Mankato, MN 56003
Phone: (507)625-7440 **Fax:** (507)625-4101
Products: Typewriters; Photocopying equipment and supplies; Fax machines; Computers. **SICs:** 5044 (Office Equipment); 5045 (Computers, Peripherals & Software); 5112 (Stationery & Office Supplies). **Sales:** $2,000,000 (2000). **Emp:** 99. **Officers:** Jeannie Thompson.

■ 21122 ■ Mansfield Typewriter Co.
1150 National Pkwy.
Mansfield, OH 44906-1911
Phone: (419)529-6100 **Fax:** (419)529-3903
Products: Typewriters; Fax machines. **SIC:** 5044 (Office Equipment). **Sales:** $10,000,000 (2000). **Emp:** 100. **Officers:** John Fernyak.

■ 21123 ■ Marimon Business Machines Inc.
1500 N Post Oak, Ste. 100
Houston, TX 77055
Phone: (713)868-1262
Products: Office machines. **SIC:** 5044 (Office Equipment).

■ 21124 ■ Marion Office Products Inc.
18 Airport Rd.
Nashua, NH 03063-1714
Phone: (603)886-2760 **Fax:** (603)886-2769
Products: Office equipment. **SIC:** 5044 (Office Equipment). **Officers:** Paul Arruda, President.

■ 21125 ■ Mark-Rite Distributing Corp.
4045 Vincennes Rd.
Indianapolis, IN 46268
Free: (800)848-7279 **Fax:** 800-362-3651
URL: http://www.mark-rite.com
Products: Labels for hand guns, bar coding, table top machines, fasteners, and bags; Hangers. **SIC:** 5112 (Stationery & Office Supplies). **Est:** 1985. **Sales:** $4,000,000 (2000). **Emp:** 27. **Officers:** Robert Copeland, President.

■ 21126 ■ Marks Paper Co.
1801 L and A Rd.
Metairie, LA 70001
Phone: (504)832-1801
Free: (800)345-1801 **Fax:** (504)835-3413
Products: Office equipment and supplies. **SIC:** 5112 (Stationery & Office Supplies). **Sales:** $15,000,000 (2000). **Emp:** 49.

■ 21127 ■ Marks Paper Co., Inc.
1801 L & A Rd.
Metairie, LA 70001
Phone: (504)832-1801
Free: (800)345-1801 **Fax:** (504)835-3413
E-mail: markspaper@ibm.net
Products: Printing, computer, digital and copy paper. **SIC:** 5112 (Stationery & Office Supplies). **Est:** 1948. **Sales:** $15,000,000 (2000). **Emp:** 49. **Officers:** Sam Marks, Chairman of the Board; Alan Rosenbloom, President; Allen Marks, Exec. VP.

■ 21128 ■ Marni International
105 Campbell, No. 88
Kerrville, TX 78028
Phone: (512)895-1483 **Fax:** (512)895-1483
Products: Handbags; Cosmetics and perfumes; Pens and mechanical pencils. **SICs:** 5112 (Stationery & Office Supplies); 5137 (Women's/Children's Clothing); 5122 (Drugs, Proprietaries & Sundries). **Officers:** Eugene E. Roberts, President.

■ 21129 ■ John A. Marshall Co.
10930 Lackman Rd.
Lenexa, KS 66219-1232
Phone: (913)842-5368 **Fax:** (913)842-1310
Products: Metal office furniture; Wood office furniture; Desks. **SIC:** 5021 (Furniture). **Est:** 1923. **Sales:** $15,000,000 (2000). **Emp:** 49. **Officers:** John S. Marshall; John E. Marshall; William C. Marshall.

■ 21130 ■ Martin Stationers
PO Box 3007
Idaho Falls, ID 83403
Phone: (208)529-0510
Free: (800)433-2748 **Fax:** (208)524-3920
Products: Office supplies; Metal office furniture; Wood office furniture. **SICs:** 5112 (Stationery & Office Supplies); 5021 (Furniture). **Sales:** $20,000,000 (2000). **Emp:** 160. **Officers:** Jeff Martin.

■ 21131 ■ Gus Martinez
205 W 3rd St.
Roswell, NM 88201-4623
Phone: (505)623-4987
Products: Office equipment, including dictation equipment, typewriters, copiers, and facsimile machines. **SIC:** 5044 (Office Equipment). **Officers:** Augustine Martinez, Owner.

■ 21132 ■ Marvel Group Inc.
3843 W 43rd St.
Chicago, IL 60632
Phone: (773)523-4804
Free: (800)621-8846 **Fax:** 800-237-0358
Products: Metal office furniture; Panel and modular systems furniture and all other nonwood office furniture; Wood office furniture. **SICs:** 5021 (Furniture); 5046 (Commercial Equipment Nec). **Sales:** $30,000,000 (2000). **Emp:** 499. **Officers:** Vernon S. Schroeder, President; Roger E. Hayes, Exec. VP.

■ 21133 ■ Marysville Office Center
116 S Main St.
Marysville, OH 43040
Phone: (937)642-8893
Products: Office supplies; Office furniture. **SICs:** 5112 (Stationery & Office Supplies); 5021 (Furniture).

■ 21134 ■ McQuiddy Office Designers Inc.
110 7th Ave. N
Nashville, TN 37203
Phone: (615)256-5643 **Fax:** (615)256-7765
Products: Panel and modular systems furniture and all other nonwood office furniture; Office supplies; Wood office furniture. **SICs:** 5021 (Furniture); 5046 (Commercial Equipment Nec). **Est:** 1966. **Sales:** $37,000,000 (2000). **Emp:** 200. **Officers:** Ray Jones, President; Jack Scott, Exec. VP; Caren Shaffer, Exec.

VP of Marketing; Randy Downing, VP of Sales; Harold Rideout, Dir of Human Resources.

■ 21135 ■ **McRae Industries Inc.**
402 N Main St.
Mt. Gilead, NC 27306
Phone: (910)439-6147 **Fax:** (252)439-9596
Products: Photocopier and facsimile machines. **SIC:** 5044 (Office Equipment). **Sales:** $48,700,000 (2000).
Emp: 850. **Officers:** Branson J. McRae, CEO, President & Chairman of the Board; D. Gary McRae, VP & Treasurer.

■ 21136 ■ **MDR Corp.**
101 Parsons Ave.
Endicott, NY 13760
Phone: (607)754-2393 **Fax:** (607)754-4984
Products: Furniture; Electrical apparatus and equipment; Medical and dental equipment and supplies; Laboratory apparatus; Stationery and office supplies. **SICs:** 5112 (Stationery & Office Supplies); 5021 (Furniture); 5063 (Electrical Apparatus & Equipment); 5047 (Medical & Hospital Equipment); 5049 (Professional Equipment Nec). **Officers:** Diana Ramsey, President & CEO.

■ 21137 ■ **Merchants Cash Register Co.**
4422 Roosevelt Rd.
Hillside, IL 60162
Phone: (708)449-6650
Products: Cash registers. **SIC:** 5044 (Office Equipment). **Est:** 1934. **Sales:** $5,000,000 (2000).
Emp: 35. **Officers:** Gary Hornstra, President; Paul Hornstra, Treasurer & Secty.

■ 21138 ■ **Merchants Information Solutions Inc.**
415 S Brandon St.
Seattle, WA 98108
Phone: (206)763-1010
Products: Cash registers. **SIC:** 5044 (Office Equipment).

■ 21139 ■ **Merkel Donohue Inc.**
200 South Ave.
Rochester, NY 14604-1807
Phone: (716)325-7696 **Fax:** (716)325-3065
Products: Office furniture. **SIC:** 5021 (Furniture). **Est:** 1962. **Sales:** $20,000,000 (2000). **Emp:** 66. **Officers:** Thomas J. Merkel; John M. Donohue III; John M. Hedges III.

■ 21140 ■ **Microform Systems Inc.**
16803 Industrial Pkwy.
Lansing, MI 48906
Phone: (517)323-3231
Free: (800)968-6818 **Fax:** (517)323-9674
Products: Document conversion services and retrieval systems; CD-ROM and micrographics equipment and supplies. **SICs:** 5044 (Office Equipment); 5045 (Computers, Peripherals & Software). **Est:** 1983.
Sales: $2,000,000 (2000). **Emp:** 49. **Officers:** Dale Bussa.

■ 21141 ■ **Micropoint Inc.**
1280 L'Avinda Ave.
Mountain View, CA 94043
Phone: (650)968-5511 **Fax:** (650)968-5513
Products: Ballpoint pens; Office furniture. **SICs:** 5112 (Stationery & Office Supplies); 5021 (Furniture). **Est:** 1953. **Sales:** $1,200,000 (2000). **Emp:** 8. **Officers:** Rod T. Geiman, President.

■ 21142 ■ **Micros of South Florida Inc.**
852 S Military Trail
Deerfield Beach, FL 33442
Phone: (954)421-3184
Products: Cash registers. **SIC:** 5044 (Office Equipment).

■ 21143 ■ **Midwest Office Furniture and Supply Company Inc.**
987 SW Temple
Salt Lake City, UT 84101
Phone: (801)359-7681 **Fax:** (801)355-2713
E-mail: midwestoffice.com
Products: Office furniture; Floor coverings; Carpet. **SICs:** 5021 (Furniture); 5044 (Office Equipment); 5112 (Stationery & Office Supplies). **Est:** 1938. **Sales:**

$14,000,000 (2000). **Emp:** 80. **Officers:** M.S. Lake, President; Lindsay Jones, CFO; John Christofferson, Dir. of Marketing & Sales; Jo Anne Thompson, Dir. of Data Processing.

■ 21144 ■ **Mifax-New Hampshire**
30 Liscette Dr.
Salem, NH 03079
Phone: (603)898-5631 **Fax:** (603)898-8167
Products: Office equipment; Calculating machines; Accounting machines, excluding machine program readable type; Checks and ledger cards. **SIC:** 5044 (Office Equipment). **Officers:** Nick Czifrik.

■ 21145 ■ **Herman Miller Workplace Resources**
2900 E Robinson St.
Orlando, FL 32803
Phone: (407)895-5159 **Fax:** (407)895-5371
Products: Office furniture. **SIC:** 5021 (Furniture). **Est:** 1983. **Sales:** $12,000,000 (2000). **Emp:** 35. **Officers:** Jack Howard, President; Tom Brown, VP of Sales, e-mail: tom_brown@hermanmiller.com; Rick Bodah, Customer Service Contact, e-mail: rick_bodah@hermanmiller.com; Mike Duffey, General Mgr.; Cynthia Guarino, Human Resources Contact, e-mail: cynthia_johnson@hermanmiller.com. **Former Name:** Herman #Miller Office Pavillion.

■ 21146 ■ **Milner Document Products Inc.**
5125 Peachtree Industrial Blvd.
Norcross, GA 30092-3027
Phone: (770)263-5300
Products: Copiers; Fax machines. **SIC:** 5044 (Office Equipment). **Sales:** $24,000,000 (2000). **Emp:** 150.
Officers: Gene Milner, President; Robbie Haverstick, CFO; Wendy Harrah, Human Resources Mgr.

■ 21147 ■ **Minnesota Mining & Manufacturing Co.**
3M Center
St. Paul, MN 55144-1000
Phone: (612)737-6501
Free: (800)364-3577 **Fax:** 800-713-6329
E-mail: innovation@mmm.com
URL: http://www.mmm.com
Products: Adhesives; Electronic equipment; Telecommunications components; Pharmaceuticals; Healthcare products; Automotive components; Post-it notes. **SICs:** 5112 (Stationery & Office Supplies); 5065 (Electronic Parts & Equipment Nec); 5122 (Drugs, Proprietaries & Sundries); 5013 (Motor Vehicle Supplies & New Parts); 5169 (Chemicals & Allied Products Nec). **Est:** 1902. **Sales:** $15,000,000,000 (2000). **Emp:** 70,000. **Alternate Name:** 3M.

■ 21148 ■ **Mississippi School Supply Co./MISSCO Corp.**
2510 Lakeland Ter., No. 100
Jackson, MS 39216
Phone: (601)987-8600
Free: (800)647-5333 **Fax:** (601)987-3038
URL: www.missco.com
Products: School furniture and equipment; Laboratory casework and equipment. **SIC:** 5021 (Furniture). **Est:** 1919. **Sales:** $27,000,000 (2000). **Emp:** 125. **Officers:** Victor L. Smith, President; Mark Sorgenfrei, CFO; Randy Peets, Exec. VP; Mel Edmonds, Vice President. **Former Name:** Mississippi School Supply Co.

■ 21149 ■ **Modern Business Machines Inc.**
505 N 22nd St.
Milwaukee, WI 53233
Phone: (414)344-1000 **Fax:** (414)344-1974
Products: Office supplies, office furniture and computer equipment. **SICs:** 5112 (Stationery & Office Supplies); 5021 (Furniture); 5045 (Computers, Peripherals & Software). **Sales:** $57,600,000 (2000).
Emp: 300. **Officers:** Marvin Cooper, CEO & Chairman of the Board; Craig Cooper, CFO.

■ 21150 ■ **Modern Information Systems**
PO Box 5479
Grand Forks, ND 58206-5479
Phone: (701)772-4844 **Fax:** (701)772-1266
Products: Office equipment; Optical disks; Microfilm equipment. **SIC:** 5044 (Office Equipment). **Officers:** K. Inman, President.

■ 21151 ■ **Morse Typewriter Company Inc.**
131 Eileen Way
Syosset, NY 11791-5302
Phone: (516)364-1616 **Fax:** (516)364-9553
Products: Typewriters. **SIC:** 5044 (Office Equipment).
Est: 1931. **Sales:** $5,000,000 (2000). **Emp:** 9.
Officers: Marvin W. Morse, President; Marguret Reikon, Controller; Stuart Ebner, Dir. of Marketing & Sales.

■ 21152 ■ **Mountain States Microfilm Inc.**
PO Box 8304
Boise, ID 83707-2304
Phone: (208)336-2720
Products: Office equipment; Copying equipment; Microfilm equipment. **SIC:** 5044 (Office Equipment).
Officers: Roger Brazier, President.

■ 21153 ■ **Multigraphics Inc.**
431 Lakeview Ct.
Mt. Prospect, IL 60056-6048
Phone: (847)375-1700
Free: (800)323-6053 **Fax:** (847)375-1810
Products: Offset printers, duplicating machines and supplies. **SIC:** 5044 (Office Equipment). **Sales:** $107,300,000 (1999). **Emp:** 614. **Officers:** Steven R. Andrews, Vice President; Gregory T. Knipp, CFO & Treasurer.

■ 21154 ■ **Murata Business Systems Inc.**
6400 International Pkwy., Ste. 1500
Plano, TX 75093-8213
Phone: (972)403-3300 **Fax:** (972)403-3460
Products: Fax machines; Cellular telephones. **SIC:** 5044 (Office Equipment). **Sales:** $200,000,000 (2000).
Emp: 200. **Officers:** R. Michael Franz, CEO & President; Michael Duchin, VP of Finance; Michael Pocock, VP of Marketing; Michael A. Norris, Exec. VP; Elizabeth Garmon, Dir of Human Resources.

■ 21155 ■ **Nashua Corp.**
11 Trafalgar Sq., 2nd Fl.
Nashua, NH 03063-1995
Phone: (603)880-2323 **Fax:** (603)880-5671
Products: Computer supplies, including copy supplies, tapes and labels. **SIC:** 5112 (Stationery & Office Supplies). **Est:** 1904. **Sales:** $389,700,000 (2000).
Emp: 2,398. **Officers:** Gerald G. Garbacz, CEO & President; Daniel M. Junius, VP, CFO & Treasurer.

■ 21156 ■ **National Trading Co. Inc.**
PO Box 2773
Providence, RI 02907-0773
Phone: (401)861-1660
Free: (800)861-1660 **Fax:** (401)861-2980
Products: Cash registers; Computers. **SICs:** 5044 (Office Equipment); 5045 (Computers, Peripherals & Software). **Officers:** Richard Levitt, President.

■ 21157 ■ **Netherland Typewriter**
51 North St.
Presque Isle, ME 04769
Phone: (207)769-2691 **Fax:** (207)764-7125
Products: Office equipment. **SIC:** 5044 (Office Equipment). **Officers:** Beverly Guiggey, President.

■ 21158 ■ **Nevada Business Systems Inc.**
4041 S Industrial Rd.
Las Vegas, NV 89103
Phone: (702)733-4008 **Fax:** (702)733-4948
Products: Office equipment, including facsimile and photocopy machines. **SIC:** 5044 (Office Equipment).
Est: 1962. **Sales:** $4,000,000 (2000). **Emp:** 24.
Officers: Gary A. Martin, President.

■ 21159 ■ **Nevada Cash Register Inc.**
PO Box 1566
Las Vegas, NV 89101-1566
Phone: (702)382-9200
Products: Computers; Facsimile machines; Calculating machines; Cash registers. **SIC:** 5044 (Office Equipment). **Officers:** Roberta Taylor, Chairman of the Board.

■ 21160 ■ **Nevada Office Machines Inc.**
1072 Matley Ln.
Reno, NV 89502-2177
Phone: (702)329-2870   **Fax:** (702)329-9605
Products: Office equipment. **SIC:** 5044 (Office Equipment). **Officers:** Jim Pilzner, President.

■ 21161 ■ **New Mexico International Trade & Development**
4007 Comanche NE
Albuquerque, NM 87110
Phone: (505)264-1995   **Fax:** (505)881-2682
Products: Office machines and equipment. **SIC:** 5044 (Office Equipment). **Officers:** Jess Hernandez Jr., President.

■ 21162 ■ **New Mexico School Products Co.**
PO Box 2126
Albuquerque, NM 87103-2126
Phone: (505)884-1426   **Fax:** (505)884-0319
Products: Office, school, and public building furniture. **SIC:** 5021 (Furniture). **Officers:** Pete Moore, President.

■ 21163 ■ **Newell Office Products**
2514 Fish Hatchery Rd.
Madison, WI 53713-2407
Phone: (608)257-2227
Free: (800)362-8349   **Fax:** 800-537-0287
Products: Office supplies. **SIC:** 5112 (Stationery & Office Supplies). **Sales:** $85,000,000 (2000). **Emp:** 280. **Officers:** Jim Purdin, President; Norma Connors, Vice President; Karl Adrian, Vice President; Bob McCormick, Controller.

■ 21164 ■ **Northcoast Business Systems Inc.**
8000 Hub Park
Cleveland, OH 44125
Phone: (216)642-7555   **Fax:** (216)642-6046
Products: Color copiers. **SIC:** 5044 (Office Equipment). **Est:** 1985. **Sales:** $6,200,000 (2000). **Emp:** 75. **Officers:** Sonny Kumar, President.

■ 21165 ■ **Northway Acres Craft Supply**
9198 Brewerton Rd.
PO Box 709
Brewerton, NY 13029
Phone: (315)699-5931
E-mail: ljrnwa@dreamscape.com
URL: http://www.Northwayacres.com
Products: Beads, silk flowers, general craft supplies, wedding supplies, dolls, miniatures, baskets, glassware, ribbons, laces, paints, brushes, glues, varnishes, and jewelry suppliess. **SICs:** 5112 (Stationery & Office Supplies); 5049 (Professional Equipment Nec). **Former Name:** Sunshine Craft Supply.

■ 21166 ■ **Northway Acres Craft Supply**
9198 Brewerton Rd.
Brewerton, NY 13029
Phone: (315)699-5931
Products: Office equipment and supplies. **SIC:** 5112 (Stationery & Office Supplies).

■ 21167 ■ **NSC International**
PO Box 21370
Hot Springs, AR 71902
Phone: (501)525-0133
Free: (800)643-1520   **Fax:** (501)525-1527
Products: Industrial office and roll feed laminators, binding equipment and supplies. **SICs:** 5084 (Industrial Machinery & Equipment); 5113 (Industrial & Personal Service Paper). **Sales:** $15,000,000 (2000). **Emp:** 50. **Officers:** Bill Hall, General Mgr.; Diane McCaslin, Accountant.

■ 21168 ■ **O Henry Inc.**
6920 W Market St.
Greensboro, NC 27419-1805
Phone: (910)294-0630
Free: (800)972-4930   **Fax:** 800-972-4930
Products: Office supplies. **SIC:** 5112 (Stationery & Office Supplies). **Sales:** $25,000,000 (2000). **Emp:** 130.

■ 21169 ■ **OCE-USA Inc.**
5450 N Cumberland Ave.
Chicago, IL 60656
Phone: (773)714-8500   **Fax:** (773)714-0544
Products: Photocopying machines; Design engineering equipment. **SICs:** 5044 (Office Equipment); 5049 (Professional Equipment Nec). **Est:** 1963. **Sales:** $430,000,000 (2000). **Emp:** 1,700. **Officers:** Jan Dix, President; Taj Dharamshi, CFO; Larry Kleuser, Dir. of Marketing; Dan Krzesinski, VP of Operations; William Mayer.

■ 21170 ■ **O'Connor and Raque Office Products Co.**
PO Box 1689
Louisville, KY 40201
Phone: (502)589-5900   **Fax:** (502)589-6578
Products: Office equipment, including furniture. **SICs:** 5021 (Furniture); 5044 (Office Equipment); 5112 (Stationery & Office Supplies). **Est:** 1948. **Sales:** $20,000,000 (2000). **Emp:** 150. **Officers:** E.J. Raque Jr., President; Belva Ollis, CFO; N.A. Carswell Jr., Dir. of Marketing & Sales; William E. Palmer, Data Processing Mgr.; Pat Magruder, Dir of Human Resources.

■ 21171 ■ **Office America Inc.**
PO Box 2430
Glen Allen, VA 23058-2430
Phone: (804)747-9964   **Fax:** (804)747-9425
Products: Office furniture and supplies, including desks, chairs, and file cabinets. **SICs:** 5112 (Stationery & Office Supplies); 5021 (Furniture). **Est:** 1987. **Sales:** $52,900,000 (2000). **Emp:** 650. **Officers:** Allan Werner, President; Clay Stiles, VP & Controller; Robert A. Kendig, VP of Marketing; Donald E. Jones Jr., VP of Information Systems; James K. Mayo, VP of Admin.

■ 21172 ■ **Office Club Inc.**
1631 Challenge Dr.
Concord, CA 94520
Phones: (510)689-2582   (510)682-2582
Fax: (510)689-0179
Products: Fax machines; Office desks and extensions, except wood; Wood office furniture; Office machines; Typewriters; Standard typewriters, dictating, transcribing, and recording machines and all other office machines. **SICs:** 5044 (Office Equipment); 5021 (Furniture). **Sales:** $280,500,000 (2000). **Emp:** 1,117. **Officers:** Mark D. Begelman, CEO & President; Barry Goldstein, Exec. VP & CFO; Gary Foss, Exec. VP of Marketing.

■ 21173 ■ **Office Depot Inc.**
2200 Old GermanTown Rd.
Delray Beach, FL 33445
Phone: (561)278-4800   **Fax:** (561)265-4401
Products: Office supplies and furniture. **SICs:** 5112 (Stationery & Office Supplies); 5021 (Furniture); 5044 (Office Equipment). **Est:** 1986. **Sales:** $5,300,000,000 (2000). **Emp:** 30,000. **Officers:** David I. Fuente, CEO & Chairman of the Board; Barry J. Goldstein, VP & CFO; Harry Brown, Exec. VP; Bill Seltzer, VP of Information Systems; David Pile.

■ 21174 ■ **Office Depot Inc. Business Services Div.**
3366 E Willow St.
Signal Hill, CA 90806
Phone: (562)490-1000
Products: Furniture. **SICs:** 5021 (Furniture); 5112 (Stationery & Office Supplies). **Est:** 1948. **Sales:** $350,000,000 (1999). **Emp:** 2,000. **Officers:** John Maloney, Exec. VP; Benton Melbourne, Dir of Human Resources.

■ 21175 ■ **Office Environments Inc.**
11415 Granite St.
PO Box 411248
Charlotte, NC 28241
Phone: (704)714-7200   **Fax:** (704)714-7400
URL: http://www.office-environments.com
Products: Office furniture, including desks, chairs, file cabinets; Systems furniture. **SIC:** 5021 (Furniture). **Est:** 1984. **Sales:** $45,000,000 (2000). **Emp:** 180. **Officers:** Thomas McAnallen, President; VP ofFinance and Operations.

■ 21176 ■ **Office Equipment Co.**
200 2nd St.
Havre, MT 59501-3415
Phone: (406)265-9611
Free: (800)371-9611   **Fax:** (406)265-8573
Products: Office equipment. **SIC:** 5044 (Office Equipment). **Est:** 1968. **Sales:** $1,200,000 (2000). **Emp:** 13. **Officers:** Ray Edmonds, President; Harry Spangler, Vice President; Garrett Edmonds, Sales Mgr.; Susie Leonard, Comptroller.

■ 21177 ■ **Office Equipment Sales**
5319 W 25th St.
Cicero, IL 60804
Phone: (708)652-1222   **Fax:** (708)652-4528
E-mail: o.e.s.officeplus@att.net
Products: Office supplies, including fax machines and office furniture. **SICs:** 5044 (Office Equipment); 5112 (Stationery & Office Supplies). **Est:** 1954. **Emp:** 15. **Officers:** Linda Mack-Casey, Sales/Marketing Contact; Jim Kozel, Customer Service Contact; Joann Hovorka, Human Resources Contact.

■ 21178 ■ **Office Equipment Service**
PO Box 16
Huron, SD 57350-0016
Phone: (605)352-8243
Free: (800)658-4732   **Fax:** (605)352-9280
E-mail: officeequip@basec.net
URL: http://www.basec.net/~officeequip
Products: Office equipment. **SIC:** 5044 (Office Equipment). **Est:** 1987. **Emp:** 8. **Officers:** Darwin Peterson, President. **Alternate Name:** Darwin W. #Peterson Inc.

■ 21179 ■ **Office Equipment Service Inc.**
5520 Shelby Oaks Dr.
Memphis, TN 38134
Phone: (901)388-4637   **Fax:** (901)382-5717
Products: Copiers; Fax machines; Computers; Calculators. **SIC:** 5045 (Computers, Peripherals & Software). **Officers:** Darren Meetze, President.

■ 21180 ■ **Office Express**
164 Mushroom Boulevard
Rochester, NY 14623-6462
Phone: (716)424-1500
Free: (800)266-6462   **Fax:** (716)424-3275
Products: Office supplies; Hand stamps, type holders, and dies, custom and stock; Office machines; Wood office furniture. **SICs:** 5112 (Stationery & Office Supplies); 5044 (Office Equipment); 5021 (Furniture). **Est:** 1904. **Sales:** $4,000,000 (2000). **Emp:** 49. **Officers:** Albert A. Yahn.

■ 21181 ■ **Office Furniture & Design Center Inc.**
2323 Cleveland Ave.
Ft. Myers, FL 33901-3541
Phone: (941)337-1212   **Fax:** (941)337-4910
Products: Office furniture. **SIC:** 5021 (Furniture). **Emp:** 31. **Officers:** David W. Black; John K. Willis.

■ 21182 ■ **Office Interiors Inc.**
33 Chubb Way
Branchburg, NJ 08876
Phone: (908)231-1600   **Fax:** (908)231-0469
Products: Office furniture. **SICs:** 5021 (Furniture); 5023 (Homefurnishings). **Est:** 1961. **Sales:** $25,000,000 (2000). **Emp:** 70. **Officers:** J. Scott Douglas, President; Lawrence Katz, VP of Finance; Thomas D. White, VP of Sales; Laurette Padfield, Dir. of Information Systems; Mary Snyder, Dir of Human Resources.

■ 21183 ■ **Office Machine & Furniture Inc.**
PO Box 2881
Fargo, ND 58108-2881
Phone: (701)223-6250
Free: (800)472-2198   **Fax:** (701)223-9257
Products: Office supplies, machines, furniture, phone systems, and dictation systems. **SICs:** 5112 (Stationery & Office Supplies); 5021 (Furniture); 5044 (Office Equipment); 5065 (Electronic Parts & Equipment Nec). **Sales:** $11,000,000 (2000). **Emp:** 100. **Officers:** Mark Jantzer.

■ **21184** ■ **Office to Office Inc.**
1474 Alameda St.
St. Paul, MN 55117
Phone: (612)489-6113
Products: Panel and modular systems furniture and all other nonwood office furniture; Wood office furniture. **SIC:** 5021 (Furniture). **Sales:** $700,000 (2000). **Emp:** 4. **Officers:** Denise Dian, President.

■ **21185** ■ **Office Pavillion/National Systems Inc.**
6315 McDonough Dr.
Norcross, GA 30093-1208
Phone: (404)447-6650   **Fax:** (404)448-3138
Products: Office furniture. **SIC:** 5021 (Furniture). **Est:** 1970. **Emp:** 52. **Officers:** W. T. Caiaccio.

■ **21186** ■ **Office Planning Group Inc.**
1809 S Eastern Ave.
Las Vegas, NV 89104-3933
Phone: (702)798-5000   **Fax:** (702)431-1727
Products: Office equipment. **SIC:** 5044 (Office Equipment). **Officers:** Steen Hedegaard, President.

■ **21187** ■ **Office Resources Inc.**
PO Box 1689
Louisville, KY 40201
Phone: (502)589-5900   **Fax:** (502)589-6578
Products: Stationery and office supplies. **SIC:** 5021 (Furniture). **Est:** 1945. **Sales:** $40,000,000 (2000). **Emp:** 200. **Officers:** Stephen Zink, President; R. Raque, Treasurer; Cam Willis, Marketing Mgr.; Fred Hale, Sales Mgr.; Marvena Smith, Dir of Human Resources.

■ **21188** ■ **Office Stop Inc.**
55 E Galena
Butte, MT 59701
Phone: (406)782-2334
Products: Office supplies. **SIC:** 5112 (Stationery & Office Supplies).

■ **21189** ■ **Office System Inc.**
PO Box 977
Bismarck, ND 58502-0977
Phone: (701)223-6033   **Fax:** (701)223-2009
Products: Photocopying equipment and supplies; Fax machines; Microfilming equipment. **SIC:** 5044 (Office Equipment). **Officers:** Bill Huschka, President.

■ **21190** ■ **Office Systems Co.**
PO Box 9000
Sioux City, IA 51102
Phone: (712)277-7000   **Fax:** (712)277-7048
Products: Office equipment and supplies, including typewriters, copiers, and facsimile machines. **SICs:** 5112 (Stationery & Office Supplies); 5021 (Furniture). **Est:** 1893. **Sales:** $4,500,000 (2000). **Emp:** 50. **Officers:** R.H. Wolfe, President; C. Wolfe, Controller.

■ **21191** ■ **Office Systems of Texas**
104 Lockhaven Dr.
Houston, TX 77073
Phone: (281)443-2996
Products: Office machines. **SIC:** 5044 (Office Equipment).

■ **21192** ■ **Officeland of the N.H. Seacoast**
180 Lafayette Rd.
North Hampton, NH 03862-0541
Phone: (603)964-1115   **Fax:** (603)964-7292
Products: Office equipment and supplies. **SIC:** 5044 (Office Equipment).

■ **21193** ■ **OfficeScapes & Scott Rice**
9900 E 51st Ave.
Denver, CO 80238
Phone: (303)574-1115   **Fax:** (303)574-1116
E-mail: info@officescapes.com
URL: http://www.officescapes.com
Products: Office furniture and accessories, including desks. **SIC:** 5021 (Furniture). **Est:** 1950. **Sales:** $80,000,000 (2000). **Emp:** 230. **Officers:** James A. Perry, CEO; Bob Deibel, President. **Former Name:** OfficeScapes Business Furniture.

■ **21194** ■ **OffiSource**
PO Box 258
Jackson, MS 39205
Phone: (601)352-9000
Free: (800)467-5399   **Fax:** (601)352-8683
URL: http://www.offisource.com
Products: Office supplies; Office furniture. **SICs:** 5112 (Stationery & Office Supplies); 5021 (Furniture). **Est:** 1928. **Sales:** $8,800,000 (1999). **Emp:** 34. **Officers:** Charles H. Hooker Jr., CEO.

■ **21195** ■ **Ohio Business Machines Inc.**
1728 St. Claire Ave.
Cleveland, OH 44114
Phones: (216)579-1300   (216)579-1300
Fax: (216)579-4017
Products: Typewriters; Fax machines; Photocopying equipment and supplies. **SIC:** 5044 (Office Equipment).
Former Name: Point Business Machines Inc.

■ **21196** ■ **Ohio Calculating Inc.**
20160 Center Ridge Rd.
Cleveland, OH 44116
Phone: (216)333-7310
Products: Typewriters and word processors. **SIC:** 5044 (Office Equipment). **Est:** 1962. **Sales:** $2,000,000 (2000). **Emp:** 30. **Officers:** Carl Eichler, President; Harlow Eichler, Vice President.

■ **21197** ■ **Ohio Desk Co.**
1122 Prospect Ave.
Cleveland, OH 44115
Phone: (216)623-0600   **Fax:** (216)623-0611
Products: Office furniture. **SIC:** 5021 (Furniture). **Est:** 1908. **Sales:** $36,000,000 (2000). **Emp:** 125. **Officers:** David B. Humphrey, President; Mike Stepanek, Controller.

■ **21198** ■ **Okhai-Moyer Inc.**
PO Box 2668
Huntington, WV 25726
Phone: (304)523-9433   **Fax:** (304)525-5038
Products: Educational products; School supplies; Textbooks, including teachers' editions; Scissors and shears. **SICs:** 5112 (Stationery & Office Supplies); 5199 (Nondurable Goods Nec). **Est:** 1913. **Sales:** $15,000,000 (2000). **Emp:** 55. **Officers:** A. George Okhai, CEO & President; Joe Bickar, Bookkeeper; A.George Okhai, CEO & President.

■ **21199** ■ **Olivetti Office USA Inc.**
PO Box 6945
Bridgewater, NJ 08807
Phone: (908)526-8200   **Fax:** (908)526-8405
Products: Typewriters, fax machines, and calculators. **SICs:** 5044 (Office Equipment); 5063 (Electrical Apparatus & Equipment). **Sales:** $56,000,000 (2000). **Emp:** 200. **Officers:** Solomon Suwalsky, President; David Fraser, CFO.

■ **21200** ■ **OmniFax**
PO Box 80709
Austin, TX 78708-0709
Phone: (512)719-5566   **Fax:** (512)670-8578
Products: Fax machines. **SIC:** 5044 (Office Equipment). **Est:** 1888. **Sales:** $35,500,000 (2000). **Emp:** 280. **Officers:** Paul Umberg, President; Dennis Gilmour, Controller.

■ **21201** ■ **Omnifax Danka Co.**
449 S 48th St., Ste. 103
Tempe, AZ 85281
Phone: (602)894-6688   **Fax:** (602)894-6699
Products: Fax machines. **SIC:** 5044 (Office Equipment). **Est:** 1888. **Sales:** $500,000,000 (2000). **Emp:** 49. **Officers:** Lori Kling.

■ **21202** ■ **Panasonic Copier Co.**
1510 S Lewis St.
Anaheim, CA 92805
Phone: (714)999-2500   **Fax:** (714)999-2525
Products: Copiers and facsimile machines. **SIC:** 5044 (Office Equipment). **Sales:** $4,000,000 (2000). **Emp:** 26. **Officers:** Frank Grillo, General Mgr.; Paul Clapp, CFO.

■ **21203** ■ **Paoletti and Urriola Inc.**
397 Court St.
Elko, NV 89801-3157
Phone: (702)738-6005   **Fax:** (702)738-9650
Products: Office equipment. **SIC:** 5044 (Office Equipment). **Officers:** Floyd Hibdon, President.

■ **21204** ■ **Papercraft Inc.**
3710 N Richards St.
PO Box 12615
Milwaukee, WI 53212
Phone: (414)332-5092   **Fax:** (414)332-9714
Products: Embossing seals; Envelopes; Paper and allied products. **SICs:** 5112 (Stationery & Office Supplies); 5111 (Printing & Writing Paper). **Est:** 1939. **Emp:** 20. **Officers:** Carl E. Buege, President; Joseph F. Depan, Vice President.

■ **21205** ■ **Paperwork Products Co.**
5 Eversley Ave.
Norwalk, CT 06851
Phone: (203)866-2852
Products: Folders; Printing supplies. **SIC:** 5112 (Stationery & Office Supplies). **Sales:** $1,000,000 (2000). **Emp:** 6. **Officers:** Pat Gribbon, President.

■ **21206** ■ **Peabody Office Furniture Corp.**
234 Congress St.
Boston, MA 02110
Phone: (617)542-1902   **Fax:** (617)542-6950
URL: http://www.peabodyoffice.com
Products: Used and new office furniture. **SIC:** 5021 (Furniture). **Est:** 1899. **Sales:** $25,000,000 (2000). **Emp:** 85. **Officers:** Jonathan C. Peabody, President & Treasurer; Don Brooks, Controller; Mark Anderson, CFO.

■ **21207** ■ **Peak Technologies Inc. (Columbia, Maryland)**
9200 Berger Rd.
Columbia, MD 21046
Phone: (410)312-6000
Free: (800)950-6372   **Fax:** (410)312-6171
Products: Bar code systems. **SIC:** 5065 (Electronic Parts & Equipment Nec). **Sales:** $205,000,000 (2000). **Emp:** 900. **Officers:** Jim Wyner, CEO, President & Chairman of the Board; Andy Cutten, Sr. VP & Finance Officer.

■ **21208** ■ **Perdue Inc.**
8443 Baymeadows Rd.
Jacksonville, FL 32256-7440
Phone: (904)737-5858
Products: Office furniture, including desks, chairs, and file cabinets. **SIC:** 5021 (Furniture). **Est:** 1916. **Sales:** $23,000,000 (2000). **Emp:** 95. **Officers:** Richard Moore, President.

■ **21209** ■ **Perkins Stationery**
PO Box 3776
Sioux City, IA 51102-3776
Phone: (712)255-8892   **Fax:** (712)255-3122
Products: Office equipment, furniture, and supplies. **SICs:** 5044 (Office Equipment); 5021 (Furniture); 5112 (Stationery & Office Supplies). **Sales:** $4,000,000 (2000). **Emp:** 32.

■ **21210** ■ **Peters Office Equipment**
4124 Broadway
PO Box 1078
Galveston, TX 77553
Phone: (409)765-9403   **Fax:** (409)765-7194
Products: Stationery and office supplies; Metal office furniture; Wood office furniture. **SICs:** 5112 (Stationery & Office Supplies); 5021 (Furniture). **Emp:** 12. **Officers:** Richard F. Peters.

■ **21211** ■ **Petersen-Arne**
3690 W 1st Ave.
Eugene, OR 97402
Phone: (541)485-1406
Free: (800)547-2509   **Fax:** 800-285-3549
Products: Lead pencils, crayons, and artists' materials. **SICs:** 5112 (Stationery & Office Supplies); 5049 (Professional Equipment Nec).

■ 21212 ■ Peterson Business Systems Inc.
938 S Highway Dr.
Fenton, MO 63026-2040
Phone: (314)343-1515 **Fax:** (314)326-3419
Products: Office storage units, files, and tables, except wood; Stationery and office supplies; File folders; Metal office furniture; Wood office furniture. **SICs:** 5021 (Furniture); 5112 (Stationery & Office Supplies). **Emp:** 10.

■ 21213 ■ Peterson Spacecrafters
938 S Hwy. Dr.
Fenton, MO 63026
Phone: (314)343-7910 **Fax:** (314)326-3419
Products: Office storage units, files, and tables, except wood. **SICs:** 5021 (Furniture); 5169 (Chemicals & Allied Products Nec).

■ 21214 ■ Pickens Electronics
PO Box 1178
Pocatello, ID 83204-1178
Phone: (208)233-1191 **Fax:** (208)233-1191
Products: Office equipment; Cash registers. **SIC:** 5044 (Office Equipment). **Officers:** Harvey Pickens, Owner.

■ 21215 ■ Pilot Corporation of America
60 Commerce Dr.
Trumbull, CT 06611
Phone: (203)377-8800 **Fax:** (203)377-4024
Products: Writing instruments. **SIC:** 5112 (Stationery & Office Supplies). **Est:** 1970. **Sales:** $135,000,000 (2000). **Emp:** 220. **Officers:** Ronald Shaw, President; Larry Silberman, CFO; Thomas Restivo, VP of Sales; Jozef Kiewlen, Dir. of Information Systems.

■ 21216 ■ Plaza Stationery & Printing Inc.
29-42 Northern Blvd.
Long Island City, NY 11101
Phone: (718)784-7980 **Fax:** (718)784-7214
Products: Panel and modular systems furniture and all other nonwood office furniture; Wood office furniture; Computers. **SICs:** 5021 (Furniture); 5045 (Computers, Peripherals & Software). **Est:** 1896. **Emp:** 49. **Officers:** Mr. Greenwald.

■ 21217 ■ Plus Corporation of America
80 Commerce Dr.
Allendale, NJ 07401
Phone: (201)818-2700
Products: Office supplies. **SIC:** 5112 (Stationery & Office Supplies).

■ 21218 ■ PMC of Indiana
PO Box 33803
Indianapolis, IN 46203
Phone: (317)353-6209
Products: Computer forms. **SIC:** 5112 (Stationery & Office Supplies). **Est:** 1979. **Sales:** $2,000,000 (2000). **Emp:** 23. **Officers:** John Cornelius, President.

■ 21219 ■ Porter Office Machine Corp.
PO Box 119
North Conway, NH 03860-0119
Phone: (603)356-2222
Products: Office equipment. **SIC:** 5044 (Office Equipment). **Officers:** Robert Porter, President.

■ 21220 ■ Postalia Inc.
1980 University Ln.
Lisle, IL 60532-2152
Phone: (708)241-9090 **Fax:** (708)241-9091
Products: Postage meters. **SIC:** 5044 (Office Equipment). **Est:** 1963. **Sales:** $8,000,000 (2000). **Emp:** 60. **Officers:** George Gelfer, President; Peter Landwehr, CFO; Sandi Urig, Dir. of Data Processing.

■ 21221 ■ Precept Business Products Inc.
1050 Northfield Ct., Ste. 400
Roswell, GA 30076
Phone: (404)410-4080
Products: Business forms. **SIC:** 5112 (Stationery & Office Supplies).

■ 21222 ■ Precise Industries, Inc.
PO Box 10
Ardara, PA 15615-0010
Phone: (412)864-3900
Free: (800)279-3901 **Fax:** (412)864-3737
Products: Office supplies and used furniture. **SICs:**

5112 (Stationery & Office Supplies); 5021 (Furniture).
Emp: 49. **Officers:** Ken Ross.

■ 21223 ■ Pro Form and File
PO Box 1370
Bucksport, ME 04416-1370
Phone: (207)469-2401
Free: (800)696-2626 **Fax:** (207)469-3069
Products: Furniture, including office and public building furniture; Filing units and filing accessories; Forms. **SICs:** 5021 (Furniture); 5112 (Stationery & Office Supplies). **Est:** 1985. **Officers:** Kim Delbridge, Owner; Lindy Delbridge, Owner.

■ 21224 ■ Promicro Systems
229 Broadway
Yankton, SD 57078-4211
Phone: (605)665-4448
Products: Office equipment; Copying equipment; Microfilm equipment. **SIC:** 5044 (Office Equipment). **Officers:** Terry Bochman, President.

■ 21225 ■ Publix Office Supplies, Inc.
1301 International Pky.
Woodridge, IL 60517-4956
Phone: (312)226-1000
Free: (800)678-2549 **Fax:** (312)226-8140
Products: Office supplies. **SIC:** 5112 (Stationery & Office Supplies). **Est:** 1941. **Sales:** $91,000,000 (2000). **Emp:** 400. **Officers:** Norman Labusky, VP & Treasurer; Nathan Gold, Chairman of the Board; David Kirshner, President; Edward Wellman, Secretary.

■ 21226 ■ Purchasing Support Services
1 Town Ctr.
West Amherst, NY 14228
Phone: (716)688-1994
Products: Office supplies. **SIC:** 5112 (Stationery & Office Supplies).

■ 21227 ■ Quality Art
200 E 52nd St.
Boise, ID 83714
Phone: (208)672-0530
Free: (800)311-7707 **Fax:** (208)672-1196
URL: http://www.quality-art.com
Products: Artists' materials, including lead pencils, crayons, and picture frames. **SICs:** 5112 (Stationery & Office Supplies); 5049 (Professional Equipment Nec). **Est:** 1981. **Emp:** 17. **Officers:** Brett Stigile, President.

■ 21228 ■ Quality Business Forms Inc.
5097 Nathan Ln.
Minneapolis, MN 55442
Phone: (612)559-4330
Products: Custom business forms. **SIC:** 5112 (Stationery & Office Supplies). **Sales:** $8,500,000 (2000). **Emp:** 50. **Officers:** Thomas Hoerr, President.

■ 21229 ■ Quill Corp.
100 Shelter Rd.
Lincolnshire, IL 60069
Phone: (847)634-6690
Free: (800)789-8965 **Fax:** (847)634-6697
E-mail: info@quillcorp.com
URL: http://www.quillcorp.com
Products: Office supplies. **SIC:** 5044 (Office Equipment). **Est:** 1956. **Sales:** $600,000,000 (2000). **Emp:** 1,250. **Officers:** Jack Miller, President.

■ 21230 ■ Edward H. Quimby Co. Inc.
PO Box 918
Dover, NH 03820-0918
Phone: (603)742-3515 **Fax:** (603)742-2617
Products: Office furniture. **SIC:** 5021 (Furniture).
Officers: William Quimby, President.

■ 21231 ■ Quorum Corp.
PO Box 510
Hurricane, WV 25526
Phone: (304)743-9699 **Fax:** (304)562-3932
Products: Copiers. **SIC:** 5044 (Office Equipment). **Est:** 1956. **Sales:** $6,000,000 (2000). **Emp:** 70. **Officers:** R.O. Robertson Jr., President; Brenda Keyser, Mgr. of Admin.; Dick Jennings, Sales Mgr.

■ 21232 ■ RABCO Equipment Corp.
1145 State Hwy. 33
Farmingdale, NJ 07727
Phone: (732)938-7200 **Fax:** (732)938-4257
Products: Storage systems; Office furniture. **SIC:** 5021 (Furniture). **Sales:** $1,000,000 (2000). **Emp:** 6. **Officers:** Ralph Devito, President.

■ 21233 ■ Raster Graphics Inc.
3025 Orchard Pkwy.
San Jose, CA 95134
Phone: (408)232-4000
Free: (800)441-4788 **Fax:** (408)232-4100
Products: Printing systems, printers and image processing software. **SIC:** 5045 (Computers, Peripherals & Software). **Sales:** $39,400,000 (2000). **Emp:** 155. **Officers:** Rakesh Kumar, CEO, President & Chairman of the Board; Dennis R. Mahoney, VP & CFO.

■ 21234 ■ RCP Inc.
813 Virginia St. E
Charleston, WV 25301
Phone: (304)343-5135 **Fax:** (304)343-5854
Products: Office furniture. **SIC:** 5021 (Furniture). **Sales:** $3,300,000 (2000). **Emp:** 31. **Officers:** Ron Hayes, President & Treasurer.

■ 21235 ■ Reds Office Supply
PO Box 1131
Hamilton, MT 59840-1131
Phone: (406)363-2242 **Fax:** (406)363-2245
Products: Office storage units, files, and tables, except wood. **SIC:** 5044 (Office Equipment). **Officers:** Betty Krueger, Owner.

■ 21236 ■ R.E.I. Glitter
21851 Sherman Way
Canoga Park, CA 91303-1941
Phone: (818)887-9300
Products: Lead pencils, crayons, and artists' materials. **SICs:** 5112 (Stationery & Office Supplies); 5049 (Professional Equipment Nec).

■ 21237 ■ Remco Business Systems Inc.
3000 Parston Dr.
Forestville, MD 20747
Phone: (301)420-0800 **Fax:** (301)735-8931
Products: Office filing systems, including office and systems furniture. **SIC:** 5021 (Furniture). **Emp:** 29. **Officers:** Thomas Povey.

■ 21238 ■ Rheas Crafts
1914 111th St.
Lubbock, TX 79423-7203
Phone: (806)795-2655
Products: Lead pencils, crayons, and artists' materials. **SICs:** 5112 (Stationery & Office Supplies); 5049 (Professional Equipment Nec).

■ 21239 ■ RI Business Equipment Co. Inc.
1021 Waterman Ave.
East Providence, RI 02914-1314
Phone: (401)438-9593 **Fax:** (401)438-6479
Products: Mailing equipment; Card personalization systems; Scales; Photo ID systems; Shredders. **SIC:** 5044 (Office Equipment). **Est:** 1955. **Emp:** 7. **Officers:** Anne Smith, President.

■ 21240 ■ Scott Rice of Kansas City Inc.
PO Box 412027
Kansas City, MO 64141
Phone: (816)221-6025
Free: (800)877-1167 **Fax:** (816)221-7520
URL: http://www.scottrice.com
Products: Commercial office furniture. **SIC:** 5021 (Furniture). **Est:** 1925. **Sales:** $15,000,000 (1999). **Emp:** 110. **Officers:** Aubrey Richardson, Chairman of the Board; John Clinger, General Mgr.; Fran Molley, Sales Mgr.; Dave Ronnau, Dir. of Data Processing; Laurie Evans, Mgr. of Admin.

■ 21241 ■ S.P. Richards Co.
1012 McDermott Rd.
Metairie, LA 70001-6226
Phone: (504)834-3540 **Fax:** (504)834-9404
Products: Office supplies. **SIC:** 5112 (Stationery & Office Supplies). **Emp:** 49. **Officers:** Earl V. McNeal.

■ 21242 ■ **S.P. Richards Co.**
PO Box 1266
Smyrna, GA 30081
Phone: (770)436-6881 **Fax:** (770)333-7663
Products: Office supplies, including writing pens, staples, pencils, and pens. **SICs:** 5112 (Stationery & Office Supplies); 5021 (Furniture). **Sales:** $1,000,000,000 (1999). **Emp:** 2,100. **Officers:** Robert L. Fitts, President; Philip Welch, VP of Finance & Controller; William Hurley, Sr. VP of Sales & Marketing; Bill Hurley, Sales/Marketing Contact, e-mail: Bhurley@sprich.com.

■ 21243 ■ **Richmond Office Supply**
816 E Main St.
Richmond, VA 23219-3306
Phone: (804)644-4025 **Fax:** (804)343-1662
Products: Office supplies. **SIC:** 5112 (Stationery & Office Supplies). **Sales:** $2,000,000 (2000). **Emp:** 18. **Officers:** William D. Johnson III.

■ 21244 ■ **Roatan International Corporation**
20 West 38th St., 4th Floor
New York, NY 10018
Phone: (212)768-7538 **Fax:** (212)768-7679
E-mail: sales@roatanint.com
Products: Stationery and office supplies, including pens, mechanical pencils, advertising specialties, and gifts. **SIC:** 5112 (Stationery & Office Supplies). **Est:** 1973. **Officers:** Everett Murray, President; Wanda Almada, Operations Mgr.

■ 21245 ■ **Robinson's Woods**
1057 Trumbull Ave., Unit N
Girard, OH 44420
Phone: (330)759-3843
Products: Lead pencils, crayons, and artists' materials. **SICs:** 5112 (Stationery & Office Supplies); 5049 (Professional Equipment Nec).

■ 21246 ■ **Rons Office Equipment Inc.**
127 W 4th St.
Roswell, NM 88201-4709
Phone: (505)622-0756 **Fax:** (505)622-0756
Products: Furniture for offices and other public buildings. **SIC:** 5021 (Furniture). **Officers:** Ron Milota, President.

■ 21247 ■ **Rosedale Fabricators/Ampco**
Hwy. 1 N
Rosedale, MS 38769-0608
Phone: (601)759-3521
Free: (800)289-2672 **Fax:** (601)759-3721
Products: Copier cabinets; Institutional furniture; Kitchen cabinets. **SIC:** 5021 (Furniture). **Est:** 1946. **Sales:** $5,000,000 (2000). **Emp:** 100. **Officers:** Pete Perry.

■ 21248 ■ **Rosemount Office Systems, Inc.**
21785 Hamburg Ave.
Lakeville, MN 55044-9035
Phone: (612)469-4416
Free: (800)328-6446 **Fax:** (612)469-5981
Products: Office furniture. **SIC:** 5021 (Furniture). **Sales:** $17,000,000 (1999). **Emp:** 145. **Officers:** Thomas Canfield.

■ 21249 ■ **Rowley-Schlimgen Inc.**
1020 John Nolen Dr.
Madison, WI 53713-1428
Phone: (608)257-0521 **Fax:** (608)257-1859
E-mail: solutions@rschlinger.com
URL: http://www.rowley.schlinger.com
Products: Office furniture. **SIC:** 5021 (Furniture). **Est:** 1949. **Sales:** $25,000,000 (2000). **Emp:** 65. **Officers:** Melissa Novinski, CFO.

■ 21250 ■ **Royce, Inc.**
723 Hickory Ln.
Berwyn, PA 19312-1438
Phone: (215)873-9444
Products: Lead pencils, crayons, and artists' materials. **SICs:** 5112 (Stationery & Office Supplies); 5049 (Professional Equipment Nec).

■ 21251 ■ **RST Reclaiming Co. Inc.**
66 River Rd. B
Hudson, NH 03051-5225
Phone: (603)595-8708 **Fax:** (603)889-3230
Products: Office and computer equipment. **SIC:** 5044 (Office Equipment). **Officers:** Lucille Tranni, President.

■ 21252 ■ **Thomas W. Ruff and Company of Florida Inc.**
3201 Commerce Pkwy.
Miramar, FL 33025
Phone: (954)435-7300
Free: (800)985-5858 **Fax:** (954)435-7212
Products: Office furniture. **SIC:** 5021 (Furniture). **Sales:** $27,000,000 (2000). **Emp:** 110. **Officers:** Jack Gorman, CEO & Chairman of the Board.

■ 21253 ■ **Thomas W. Ruff and Co.**
1114 Dublin Rd.
Columbus, OH 43215
Phone: (614)487-4000 **Fax:** (614)487-4306
URL: http://www.thomasruff.com
Products: Office systems and furniture; Carpet and wallcoverings. **SICs:** 5021 (Furniture); 5023 (Homefurnishings). **Est:** 1936. **Sales:** $65,000,000 (2000). **Emp:** 245. **Officers:** Michael Gorman, President; John Crane, CFO; John Cleland, Dir. of Marketing; Jack Reau, Dir. of Data Processing; Mary Jayne Fox, Dir of Human Resources.

■ 21254 ■ **S & R Inc.**
PO Box 9275
Fargo, ND 58106-9275
Phone: (701)241-7960 **Fax:** (701)241-7972
Products: Office equipment. **SIC:** 5044 (Office Equipment). **Officers:** Rhonda Anderson, President.

■ 21255 ■ **Safina Office Products**
5803 Sovereign, Ste. 214
Houston, TX 77036
Phone: (713)981-6153
Free: (800)247-2344 **Fax:** (713)981-7217
E-mail: safina@safinaoffice.com
URL: http://www.safinaoffice.com
Products: Office supplies. **SIC:** 5112 (Stationery & Office Supplies). **Est:** 1982. **Sales:** $3,000,000 (2000). **Emp:** 8. **Officers:** Robert Lee, President, e-mail: rlee@safinaoffice.com; Edward M. Wilder, Customer Service Contact, e-mail: edwilder@safinaoffice.com; Lily Lee, Human Resources Contact, e-mail: info@safinaoffice.com.

■ 21256 ■ **St. Louis Business Forms Inc.**
1571 Senpark Dr.
Fenton, MO 63026
Phone: (314)343-6860
Products: Business forms, including invoices and stationery. **SIC:** 5112 (Stationery & Office Supplies). **Est:** 1968. **Sales:** $2,500,000 (2000). **Emp:** 10. **Officers:** Joseph Raible, President.

■ 21257 ■ **William B. Sambito**
179 Main St.
Colebrook, NH 03576-1216
Phone: (603)237-5705 **Fax:** (603)234-8452
Products: Office equipment. **SIC:** 5044 (Office Equipment). **Officers:** William Sambito, Owner.

■ 21258 ■ **Savin Corp.**
PO Box 10270
Stamford, CT 06904-2270
Phone: (203)967-5000 **Fax:** (203)967-5348
Products: Photocopy and facsimile machines. **SIC:** 5044 (Office Equipment). **Est:** 1959. **Sales:** $228,100,000 (2000). **Emp:** 920. **Officers:** William R. Krehbiel, CEO; Thomas L. Salierno Jr., VP, Treasurer & Controller; John Breiten, VP of Sales; Rudy Szuch, Dir. of Information Systems; Robert V. Riley, VP of Human Resources.

■ 21259 ■ **School Specialty Inc.**
5800 NE Hassalo St.
Portland, OR 97213
Phone: (503)281-1193 **Fax:** (503)281-1198
URL: http://www.schoolspecialty.com
Products: School and office supplies and equipment. **SICs:** 5021 (Furniture); 5049 (Professional Equipment Nec); 5044 (Office Equipment); 5046 (Commercial Equipment Nec). **Est:** 1960. **Sales:** $7,000,000 (2000).

Emp: 32. **Officers:** Dan Spalding, President; Deborah Schunk, Treasurer & Secty.

■ 21260 ■ **Schwarz Paper Co.**
PO Box 82266
Lincoln, NE 68501
Phone: (402)477-1202
Free: (800)742-0024 **Fax:** (402)477-1204
E-mail: schwarz@navix.net
Products: Paper products; Office supplies; Janitorial supplies. **SICs:** 5112 (Stationery & Office Supplies); 5113 (Industrial & Personal Service Paper). **Est:** 1899. **Sales:** $2,000,000 (1999). **Emp:** 12. **Officers:** David K. Jones, President; Knox F. Jones, Dir. of Sales; Julie A. Jones, Treasurer.

■ 21261 ■ **Scope Office Services Inc.**
1510 S Lewis St.
Anaheim, CA 92805
Phone: (714)999-2500
Products: Office equipment, including photocopiers and fax machines. **SIC:** 5044 (Office Equipment).

■ 21262 ■ **Scriptex Enterprises Ltd.**
575 Corporate Dr.
Mahwah, NJ 07430
Phone: (201)825-1100
Products: Copiers; Fax machines. **SIC:** 5044 (Office Equipment). **Sales:** $27,000,000 (2000). **Emp:** 170. **Officers:** Anthony Pavoni, President.

■ 21263 ■ **Second City Systems Inc.**
28427 N Ballard Dr. No. D
Lake Forest, IL 60045
Phone: (847)362-2700
Products: Office products. **SICs:** 5112 (Stationery & Office Supplies); 5044 (Office Equipment). **Est:** 1979. **Sales:** $4,000,000 (2000). **Emp:** 40. **Officers:** Michael Einarsen, CEO; Douglas Doyle, VP of Finance.

■ 21264 ■ **Select Copy Systems of Southern California Inc.**
6229 Santos Diaz St.
Irwindale, CA 91706
Phone: (626)334-0383 **Fax:** (626)969-4421
Products: Copy machines. **SIC:** 5044 (Office Equipment). **Sales:** $32,000,000 (2000). **Emp:** 150. **Officers:** Frank Mendicina, President.

■ 21265 ■ **Service Office Supply Corp.**
PO Box 2
Getzville, NY 14068
Phone: (716)691-3511 **Fax:** (716)691-8726
Products: Office equipment and supplies, including file cabinets, desks, and printing paper. **SIC:** 5112 (Stationery & Office Supplies). **Est:** 1861. **Sales:** $5,000,000 (2000). **Emp:** 42. **Officers:** Howard Hutton Jr., President; Paul Bedworth, Controller.

■ 21266 ■ **Shachihata Incorporated USA**
3305 Kashiwa St.
Torrance, CA 90505
Phone: (310)530-4445
Free: (800)851-2686 **Fax:** (310)530-2892
URL: http://www.xstamper.com
Products: X-stampers; Self-inking and traditional rubber stampers; Signs; Name badges; Plaques; Embossers; Awards. **SIC:** 5112 (Stationery & Office Supplies). **Est:** 1968. **Sales:** $40,000,000 (1999). **Emp:** 200. **Officers:** S. Asano, President, e-mail: sasano@xstamper.com; Dennis Thomas, VP of Marketing & Sales, e-mail: dthomas@xstamper.com; Jerry C. Hutchins, Asst. VP of Sales, e-mail: jhutchins@xstamper.com.

■ 21267 ■ **Sherman Business Forms Inc.**
55 Tanners Rd.
Great Neck, NY 11020-1628
Phone: (516)773-0142
Products: Paper and paper products. **SIC:** 5112 (Stationery & Office Supplies). **Sales:** $400,000 (2000). **Emp:** 2.

■ 21268 ■ **Sheyenne Publishing Co.**
PO Box 449
Valley City, ND 58072-0449
Phone: (701)845-0275 **Fax:** (701)845-8004
Products: Office and public building furniture. **SIC:** 5021 (Furniture). **Officers:** Steven Hoss, President.

■ 21269 ■ Shredex Inc.
49 Natcon Dr.
Shirley, NY 11967
Phone: (516)345-0300 **Fax:** (516)345-0791
E-mail: shredex@northeast.net
URL: http://www.shredex.net
Products: Shredders for business and office. **SIC:**
5044 (Office Equipment). **Est:** 1982. **Sales:**
$27,000,000 (2000). **Emp:** 20. **Officers:** Michael J.
Falco Jr., President; Al Kizelewicz, CFO.

■ 21270 ■ Singing Poppe's, Inc.
8055 N 24th Ave., No. 104-105
Phoenix, AZ 85021-4865
Phone: (602)249-2617
Products: Lead pencils, crayons, and artists' materials.
SICs: 5112 (Stationery & Office Supplies); 5049
(Professional Equipment Nec).

■ 21271 ■ Siri Office Equipment Inc.
PO Box 2555
Reno, NV 89505-2555
Phone: (702)323-2776 **Fax:** (702)323-7066
Products: Office equipment; Furniture; Typewriter
repair. **SICs:** 5044 (Office Equipment); 5021
(Furniture). **Est:** 1952. **Sales:** $1,250,000 (2000).
Emp: 10. **Officers:** Carolyn Hursh, President.

■ 21272 ■ Skyline Supply Company Inc.
71 Park Ln.
Brisbane, CA 94005
Phone: (415)468-4200 **Fax:** (415)468-0187
Products: Office supplies. **SICs:** 5044 (Office
Equipment); 5045 (Computers, Peripherals &
Software); 5111 (Printing & Writing Paper); 5085
(Industrial Supplies). **Est:** 1963. **Sales:** $3,300,000
(2000). **Emp:** 19. **Officers:** Frank Simoni, Mng.
Partner; Judith Ann Simoni, Dir. of Data Processing;
Michael P. Scolieri, Dir of Human Resources.

**■ 21273 ■ Smith Brothers Office Environments
Inc.**
PO Box 2719
Portland, OR 97208
Phone: (503)226-4151
Free: (800)556-4255 **Fax:** (503)226-9233
E-mail: info@sboe.com
URL: http://www.sboe.com
Products: Office furniture. **SIC:** 5021 (Furniture). **Est:**
1941. **Sales:** $30,000,000 (2000). **Emp:** 60. **Officers:**
Richard Hass, President; Brad Stoffer, Vice President.

■ 21274 ■ Source Management Inc.
2460 W 26th Ave., Ste. 370-C
Denver, CO 80211
Phone: (303)964-8100 **Fax:** (303)964-8010
Products: General office supplies, including computer
supplies and laser cartridges. **SICs:** 5045 (Computers,
Peripherals & Software); 5112 (Stationery & Office
Supplies). **Sales:** $22,000,000 (2000). **Emp:** 45.
Officers: John Givens, President & General Mgr.; Rod
Johnson, CFO.

■ 21275 ■ Source Technologies Inc.
2910 Whitehall Park Dr.
Charlotte, NC 28273
Phone: (704)969-7500
Free: (800)922-8501 **Fax:** (704)969-7595
URL: http://www.sourcetech.com
Products: Printers; E-forms software. **SIC:** 5045
(Computers, Peripherals & Software). **Est:** 1986.
Sales: $52,000,000 (2000). **Emp:** 85. **Officers:** Miles
Busby, President; Gordon W. Friedrich, VP &
Treasurer.

■ 21276 ■ Southern Business Systems Inc.
4945 American Way
Memphis, TN 38118
Phone: (901)368-0044
Free: (800)365-8973 **Fax:** (901)332-6663
Products: Office equipment and supplies; Furniture.
SICs: 5044 (Office Equipment); 5021 (Furniture); 5112
(Stationery & Office Supplies). **Sales:** $1,500,000
(2000). **Emp:** 9. **Officers:** Dennis Howell, President;
Virginia Howelll, Treasurer.

■ 21277 ■ Southern Copy Machines
495 Hawthorne Ave., Ste. 106
Athens, GA 30606-2503
Phones: (706)353-0229 (706)535-0810
Fax: (706)353-0501
Products: Copiers. **SIC:** 5044 (Office Equipment).
Emp: 49.

**■ 21278 ■ Southern New Mexico Office
Machines**
PO Box 940
Mesilla Park, NM 88047-0940
Phone: (505)525-1322 **Fax:** (505)525-8611
Products: Office equipment. **SIC:** 5044 (Office
Equipment). **Officers:** Orlando Benividez, Owner.

**■ 21279 ■ Southern Office Furniture
Distributors Inc.**
PO Box 49009
Greensboro, NC 27419
Phone: (919)668-4195 **Fax:** (919)668-2076
Products: Office furniture. **SIC:** 5021 (Furniture). **Est:**
1980. **Sales:** $26,000,000 (2000). **Emp:** 110. **Officers:**
Frank Biggerstaff, President; Brenda Rivenbark,
Manager; Amelia Hicks, Sales Mgr.

■ 21280 ■ Specialized Marketing
138 West St.
Annapolis, MD 21401-2802
Phone: (410)267-0545 **Fax:** (410)267-7576
Products: Office furniture. **SIC:** 5021 (Furniture). **Est:**
1980. **Sales:** $6,000,000 (1999). **Emp:** 8. **Officers:**
Cris Buck, e-mail: cris@smarketltd.com.

■ 21281 ■ Spectrum Financial System Inc.
163 McKenzie Rd.
Mooresville, NC 28115
Phone: (704)663-4466
E-mail: admin@spectrumfinancialinc.com
URL: http://www.spectrumfinancialinc.com
Products: Bank equipment. **SIC:** 5044 (Office
Equipment). **Est:** 1987. **Sales:** $18,000,000 (1999).
Emp: 110. **Officers:** Vennie A. Pent, President;
Rosemary G. Macri, Vice President; Charles K.
Hatcher, Sr. VP.

■ 21282 ■ Spiral Binding Company Inc.
PO Box 286
Totowa, NJ 07511
Phone: (973)256-0666
Free: (800)631-3572 **Fax:** (973)256-5981
Products: Binding, laminating and presentation
products. **SIC:** 5131 (Piece Goods & Notions). **Sales:**
$20,000,000 (2000). **Emp:** 300. **Officers:** Robert M.
Roth, President; Pete Coletto, VP of Finance.

■ 21283 ■ Splash Technology Inc.
555 Del Rey Ave.
Sunnyvale, CA 94085
Phone: (408)328-6300 **Fax:** (408)328-6400
URL: http://www.splashtech.com
Products: Office supplies. **SIC:** 5112 (Stationery &
Office Supplies). **Sales:** $5,000,000 (2000). **Emp:** 40.
Officers: John Farina; President; Richard Hoff,
Controller.

**■ 21284 ■ Standard Duplicating Machines
Corp.**
10 Connector Rd.
Andover, MA 01810
Phone: (508)470-1920 **Fax:** (508)470-2771
Products: Digital duplicators; Document finishing
products. **SIC:** 5044 (Office Equipment). **Est:** 1910.
Sales: $27,000,000 (2000). **Emp:** 55. **Officers:** L. Guy
Reny, President; Mike Hegerfeld, Controller.

■ 21285 ■ The Standard Register Co
5743 Rostrata Ave.
Buena Park, CA 90621
Phone: (714)521-0232 **Fax:** (714)521-0782
Products: Manifold and continuous business forms.
SIC: 5112 (Stationery & Office Supplies).

■ 21286 ■ Stanfields Inc.
PO Box 245
Cheyenne, WY 82003-0245
Phone: (307)634-6921
Products: Furniture for offices and public buildings.

SIC: 5021 (Furniture). **Officers:** Lucille Stanfield,
President.

■ 21287 ■ Staples Business Advantage
5399 Lancaster Dr.
Cleveland, OH 44131
Phone: (216)351-5200
Free: (800)235-3116 **Fax:** (216)351-1885
Products: Office and computer supplies. **SIC:** 5112
(Stationery & Office Supplies). **Est:** 1986. **Officers:** Jay
Slaukovsky, Operations Mgr.

■ 21288 ■ Staples Business Advantage
41554 Koppernick
Canton, MI 48187
Phone: (734)454-9292
Free: (800)968-9750 **Fax:** (734)416-6487
Products: Office supplies; Computers. **SICs:** 5112
(Stationery & Office Supplies); 5045 (Computers,
Peripherals & Software). **Est:** 1869. **Emp:** 210. **Former
Name:** Macauley's, Inc.

■ 21289 ■ Staples Business Advantage
125 Mushroom Blvd.
Rochester, NY 14692
Phone: (716)424-3600 **Fax:** (716)424-3639
Products: Office supplies, including paper products
and furniture. **SICs:** 5112 (Stationery & Office
Supplies); 5021 (Furniture). **Est:** 1975. **Sales:**
$63,000,000 (2000). **Emp:** 315. **Officers:** Joe Doody,
President. **Former Name:** Spectrum Office Products
Inc.

■ 21290 ■ Staples Office Products Inc.
100 Pennsylvania Ave.
Framingham, MA 01701
Phone: (508)370-8500
Products: Office supplies. **SIC:** 5112 (Stationery &
Office Supplies).

■ 21291 ■ Staples, The Office Superstore Inc.
18300 Euclid St.
Fountain Valley, CA 92708
Phone: (714)668-9523
Products: Office supplies, including business
machines and office furniture. **SIC:** 5112 (Stationery &
Office Supplies).

■ 21292 ■ Star Office Machines
PO Box 20215
Billings, MT 59104-0215
Phone: (406)259-0429 **Fax:** (406)259-1937
Products: Office equipment. **SIC:** 5044 (Office
Equipment). **Officers:** Diane Reiss, President.

■ 21293 ■ Stargel Office Systems Inc.
1220 Blalock Rd., Ste. 100
Houston, TX 77055
Phone: (713)461-5382 **Fax:** (713)461-6450
E-mail: stargel@fyi.toshiba.com
URL: http://www.stargel.com
Products: Office equipment, copiers, facsimilie
machines, printers, document shredders, and
multifunction network connections. **SIC:** 5044 (Office
Equipment). **Est:** 1987. **Sales:** $8,000,000 (2000).
Emp: 55. **Officers:** Jack Stargel, President.

**■ 21294 ■ Stationers' Corporation of Hawaii
Ltd.**
708 Kanoelehua Ave.
Hilo, HI 96720
Phone: (808)935-5477 **Fax:** (808)935-2161
Products: Stationery; Office equipment, including
photocopiers and calculators; Computers. **SICs:** 5112
(Stationery & Office Supplies); 5044 (Office
Equipment); 5045 (Computers, Peripherals &
Software). **Est:** 1938. **Sales:** $3,000,000 (2000). **Emp:**
32. **Officers:** Thomas Hirano, President.

**■ 21295 ■ Stationers Inc. (Huntington, West
Virginia)**
PO Box 2167
Huntington, WV 25722
Phone: (304)528-2780 **Fax:** (304)528-2795
Products: Office supplies. **SIC:** 5112 (Stationery &
Office Supplies). **Est:** 1916. **Sales:** $12,700,000
(2000). **Emp:** 60. **Officers:** J.M. Aldridge, President.

■ 21296 ■ Stationers Inc. (Indianapolis, Indiana)
5656 W 74th St.
Indianapolis, IN 46278
Phone: (317)298-0808 **Fax:** (317)298-8811
Products: Commercial office supplies. **SIC:** 5112 (Stationery & Office Supplies). **Sales:** $11,000,000 (1994). **Emp:** 100. **Officers:** W.J. Wills, President; Debbie Kelb, VP of Finance.

■ 21297 ■ Steel Partners L.P.
750 Lexington Ave.
New York, NY 10022
Phone: (212)446-5217
Products: Office machines; Parts for computers and peripheral equipment. **SICs:** 5045 (Computers, Peripherals & Software); 5044 (Office Equipment).

■ 21298 ■ Steinhardt & Hanson, Inc.
217-219 E Main St.
PO Box 386
Madison, IN 47250
Phone: (812)265-4131 **Fax:** (812)265-3235
Products: Office supplies. **SIC:** 5112 (Stationery & Office Supplies).

■ 21299 ■ Story Wright Printing
Shepherd & 3rd
Lufkin, TX 75901
Phone: (409)632-7727 **Fax:** (409)632-7633
Products: Office supplies. **SIC:** 5112 (Stationery & Office Supplies). **Emp:** 40.

■ 21300 ■ Strayer Products
PO Box 284
New Brighton, PA 15066-2020
Phone: (412)846-2600
Products: Fixtures for stores, banks, and offices. **SIC:** 5046 (Commercial Equipment Nec). **Sales:** $2,000,000 (2000). **Emp:** 49. **Officers:** Cletus Bonner.

■ 21301 ■ J. Edward Stromberg
6275 Harrison Dr., Ste. 6
Las Vegas, NV 89120-4022
Phone: (702)798-8970
Products: Replacement parts for blueprinting equipment. **SIC:** 5049 (Professional Equipment Nec). **Officers:** J. Stromberg, Owner.

■ 21302 ■ Adolph Sufrin Inc.
5770 Baum Blvd.
Pittsburgh, PA 15206
Phone: (412)363-8000
Products: Office supplies; Paper; Cups; Mini-refrigerators; Desks; Chairs. **SIC:** 5112 (Stationery & Office Supplies).

■ 21303 ■ Sukut Office Equipment Co.
PO Box 1405
Williston, ND 58802-1405
Phone: (701)572-7676 **Fax:** (701)572-7678
Products: Office equipment. **SIC:** 5044 (Office Equipment). **Officers:** Gary Sukut, President.

■ 21304 ■ Summervilles Inc.
PO Box 2094
Akron, OH 44309-2094
Phone: (330)535-3163 **Fax:** (330)762-9144
URL: http://www.summervilles.com
Products: Office supplies; Mid-market and contract furniture. **SICs:** 5112 (Stationery & Office Supplies); 5021 (Furniture). **Est:** 1941. **Sales:** $7,000,000 (2000). **Emp:** 30. **Officers:** John C. Summerville, President; Paul Reich, Vice President.

■ 21305 ■ The Supply Room Companies, Inc.
4103 W Clay St.
Richmond, VA 23230-3307
Phone: (804)342-6060
Free: (800)849-7239 **Fax:** (804)342-6070
E-mail: sales@thesupplyroom.com
URL: http://www.thesupplyroom.com
Products: Office machines. **SIC:** 5044 (Office Equipment). **Est:** 1986. **Sales:** $50,000,000 (1999). **Emp:** 340. **Officers:** Yancey Jones, President; Addison Jones, Exec. VP; Jim Bowman, Regional Sales Manager; Diane Childress, Customer Service Mgr.; John Nicar, Human Resources Contact; Bud Rand, VP of Sales; Becky Via, Customer Service Mgr.

■ 21306 ■ SupplySource Inc.
PO Box 3553
Williamsport, PA 17701
Phone: (717)327-1500
Free: (800)633-8753 **Fax:** (717)327-1244
URL: http://www.officesupplysource.com
Products: Office furniture and supplies. **SICs:** 5112 (Stationery & Office Supplies); 5021 (Furniture). **Est:** 1984. **Sales:** $12,284,000 (2000). **Emp:** 40. **Officers:** Ray Thompson, President; Sid Furst, Sales/Marketing Contact, e-mail: sidf@supplysourceinc.com; Lisa Baxter, Customer Service Contact, e-mail: lisab@supplysourceinc.com; Lou Anne Bastian, Human Resources Contact, e-mail: louanne@supplysourceinc.com.

■ 21307 ■ Surplus Office Equipment Inc.
295 Lincoln St.
Manchester, NH 03103-3655
Phone: (603)668-9230 **Fax:** (603)668-4432
Products: Panel and modular systems furniture and all other nonwood office furniture; Wood office furniture. **SIC:** 5021 (Furniture). **Officers:** Jeff Marion, President; Jay Galnon, Sales/Marketing Contact; Dan McCain, Customer Service Contact; Deb Marion, Human Resources Contact.

■ 21308 ■ Swanson, Inc.
1200 Park Ave.
Murfreesboro, TN 37133
Phone: (615)896-4114
Free: (800)251-1402 **Fax:** (615)898-1313
Products: Lead pencils, crayons, and artists' materials; Christian and church supplies; Custom engraving; Industrial vacuum formed plastic molding. **SICs:** 5112 (Stationery & Office Supplies); 5199 (Nondurable Goods Nec); 5049 (Professional Equipment Nec). **Est:** 1935. **Emp:** 50. **Officers:** Joseph Swanson.

■ 21309 ■ Swanson Sales and Service
402 Main St.
Truth or Consequences, NM 87901-2843
Phone: (505)894-7517
Products: Office equipment, including calculating machines and cash registers; Vaccuum cleaners; Sewing machines. **SICs:** 5044 (Office Equipment); 5084 (Industrial Machinery & Equipment); 5064 (Electrical Appliances—Television & Radio). **Est:** 1976. **Sales:** $130,000 (2000). **Officers:** Ted Swanson, Owner.

■ 21310 ■ Systel Business Equipment Inc.
PO Box 35910
Fayetteville, NC 28303
Phone: (910)483-7114 **Fax:** (910)483-2846
Products: Digital office equipment, including copiers, fax machines, and multifunctional machines. **SIC:** 5044 (Office Equipment). **Est:** 1981. **Sales:** $22,000,000 (2000). **Emp:** 175. **Officers:** Keith Allison, President; Tim Teasley, Controller; Tracy L. Call, Dir. of Marketing.

■ 21311 ■ Systems Inc.
PO Box 9713
New Haven, CT 06536-0713
Phone: (203)624-8600
Free: (800)922-2679 **Fax:** (203)772-3318
Products: Office equipment, including copiers, facsimile machines, typewriters, and shredders. **SIC:** 5044 (Office Equipment). **Est:** 1979. **Sales:** $11,000,000 (2000). **Emp:** 100. **Officers:** William Palumbo, President; Anthony Maturo, CFO.

■ 21312 ■ Systems Unlimited Inc.
3920 S Willow Ave.
Sioux Falls, SD 57105
Phone: (605)334-8588 **Fax:** (605)334-8664
E-mail: systemsunltd@systemsunltd.com
Products: Plastic cards; Office equipment; Addressing and mailing machines. **SIC:** 5044 (Office Equipment). **Est:** 1982. **Emp:** 14. **Officers:** Jeffrey Krell, President.

■ 21313 ■ Tab Business Systems Inc.
11960 Menaul Blvd. NE
Albuquerque, NM 87112-2422
Phone: (505)292-7887 **Fax:** (505)296-6312
Products: Office equipment, including supplies. **SIC:** 5044 (Office Equipment). **Officers:** Jim Bell, President.

■ 21314 ■ Tab of Northern New England
133 Spur Rd.
Dover, NH 03820-9110
Phone: (603)749-4042 **Fax:** (603)749-6416
Products: Color-coded filing systems. **SIC:** 5112 (Stationery & Office Supplies). **Officers:** William Wilson, President.

■ 21315 ■ Tatung Science and Technology Inc.
1840 McCarthy Blvd.
Milpitas, CA 95035
Phone: (408)383-0988
Free: (800)659-5902 **Fax:** (408)383-0886
Products: Office furniture and equipment; Work stations. **SICs:** 5045 (Computers, Peripherals & Software); 5044 (Office Equipment); 5021 (Furniture). **Est:** 1983. **Sales:** $30,000,000 (2000). **Emp:** 60. **Officers:** Kam H. Chan, President; Stella Zhou, Mgr. of Finance.

■ 21316 ■ Taylor-Made Office Systems Inc.
PO Box 8026
Walnut Creek, CA 94596
Phone: (510)988-4000 **Fax:** (510)988-4200
Products: Office equipment, including fax machines, overhead projectors, and coffee machines; Cameras. **SIC:** 5044 (Office Equipment). **Est:** 1972. **Sales:** $130,000,000 (2000). **Emp:** 1,400. **Officers:** John Kaminski, President; Jay Fischer, Exec. VP & CFO; W. Scott Osterman, Sr. VP; Michael Tritch, Dir. of Information Systems; Joe Bankston, Sr. VP.

■ 21317 ■ Techmart Computer Products
1424 Odenton Rd.
Odenton, MD 21113-0370
Phone: (410)674-8202
Free: (800)247-3053 **Fax:** (410)674-3071
E-mail: sales@techmartinc.com
URL: http://www.techmartinc.com
Products: Computers; Computer software; Peripheral computer equipment; Fax machines; Photocopying equipment and supplies. **SIC:** 5044 (Office Equipment). **Est:** 1986. **Emp:** 15. **Officers:** Marc A. Resnick, President.

■ 21318 ■ Thompson Office Equipment Company Inc.
5301 NW 9th Ave.
Ft. Lauderdale, FL 33309-3119
Phone: (954)491-4500 **Fax:** (954)491-2956
Products: Office supplies and office furniture. **SICs:** 5112 (Stationery & Office Supplies); 5021 (Furniture). **Emp:** 22.

■ 21319 ■ Tibbet Inc.
PO Box 2266
Toledo, OH 43603
Phone: (419)244-9558
Free: (800)DIV-IDER **Fax:** (419)244-2654
E-mail: tibbet@glasscity.net
URL: http://www.glasscity.net/users/tibbet/index.html
Products: Custom office furniture. **SIC:** 5021 (Furniture). **Est:** 1981. **Sales:** $6,000,000 (2000). **Emp:** 99. **Officers:** Theodore H. Kunkel Jr., President; Ellen Jenne, Treasurer.

■ 21320 ■ Time Products Inc.
701 Park Ave.
Cranston, RI 02910-2104
Phone: (401)941-9100
Products: Time recorders; Labor management systems. **SIC:** 5044 (Office Equipment). **Officers:** Francis Cardarella, President.

■ 21321 ■ Transco South Inc.
418 Lafayette Rd.
Hampton, NH 03842-2222
Phone: (603)926-6240 **Fax:** (603)926-2603
Products: Photocopying equipment and supplies. **SIC:** 5044 (Office Equipment). **Officers:** Alfio Graceffa, President.

■ 21322 ■ Tri-Quality Business Forms Inc.
PO Box 2529
Eugene, OR 97402
Phone: (541)343-5755 **Fax:** (541)343-4894
Products: Business forms. **SIC:** 5112 (Stationery & Office Supplies).

■ 21323 ■ Trick and Murray Inc.
300 W Lake Ave. N
Seattle, WA 98109
Phone: (206)628-0059
Products: Office supplies; Office storage units, files, and tables, except wood; Desks. **SICs:** 5112 (Stationery & Office Supplies); 5021 (Furniture). **Est:** 1905. **Sales:** $2,000,000 (2000). **Emp:** 30. **Officers:** Julie Harrison, President; Brenda Hansen, Vice President.

■ 21324 ■ TRM Copy Centers Corp.
5208 NE 122nd Ave.
Portland, OR 97230-1074
Phone: (503)257-8766 **Fax:** (503)251-5473
Products: Commercial printing; Copying services; Copy equipment. **SIC:** 5044 (Office Equipment). **Sales:** $68,400,000 (2000). **Emp:** 593. **Officers:** Frederic P. Stockton, CEO & President; Shami Patel, VP & CFO.

■ 21325 ■ Unisource International
International Plz., Ste. 2
Philadelphia, PA 19113
Phone: (610)521-3300 **Fax:** (610)521-3304
Products: Printing paper. **SIC:** 5113 (Industrial & Personal Service Paper). **Sales:** $230,000,000 (2000). **Emp:** 50. **Officers:** John R. Buchanan III, President; Richard Bonkoski, CFO.

■ 21326 ■ Unitech Inc.
PO Box 20639
Jackson, MS 39289-1639
Phone: (601)922-3911
Products: Fax machines; Typewriters; Copiers; Computers. **SICs:** 5044 (Office Equipment); 5046 (Commercial Equipment Nec). **Sales:** $20,000,000 (2000). **Emp:** 130. **Officers:** Glen Holmes, President; Virginia Henderson, Controller.

■ 21327 ■ United Business Machines Inc.
91 Plaistow Rd.
Plaistow, NH 03865
Phone: (603)382-3300 **Fax:** (603)382-9448
Products: Copiers and fax machines. **SIC:** 5044 (Office Equipment). **Est:** 1988. **Sales:** $3,500,000 (2000). **Emp:** 26. **Officers:** Paul N. LaMalfa, President; Ken M. LaMaifa, Vice President.

■ 21328 ■ United States Check Book Co.
PO Box 3644
Omaha, NE 68103
Phone: (402)345-3162
Free: (800)383-3162 **Fax:** (402)345-6679
E-mail: ucheckbook@aol.com
URL: http://www.uscheckbook.com; www.uscheckbook.net
Products: Promotional products; Office products; Financial and commercial printing/forms. **SICs:** 5044 (Office Equipment); 5044 (Office Equipment); 5199 (Nondurable Goods Nec). **Est:** 1872. **Sales:** $6,500,000 (2000). **Emp:** 65. **Officers:** E. Batchelder, President; Dan Kraft, VP & Controller; Richard Yopp, VP of Production.

■ 21329 ■ U.S. Office Products Co.
1025 Thomas Jefferson St. NW, Ste. 600E
Washington, DC 20007
Phone: (202)339-6700 **Fax:** (202)339-6733
Products: Office products: binders, folders and furniture. **SIC:** 5112 (Stationery & Office Supplies). **Sales:** $2,664,600,000 (1999). **Emp:** 14,700. **Officers:** Chuck Pieper, Chairman of the Board; Joseph T. Doyle, Exec. VP & CFO.

■ 21330 ■ U.S. Ring Binder Corp.
6800 Arsenal St.
St. Louis, MO 63139
Phone: (314)645-7880
Free: (800)888-8772 **Fax:** (314)645-7239
Products: Metal binder rings. **SIC:** 5112 (Stationery & Office Supplies). **Sales:** $3,000,000 (2000). **Emp:** 75. **Officers:** Eugene J. Angel, CEO & President.

■ 21331 ■ US Office Products, Midwest District Inc.
4015 Papin St.
St. Louis, MO 63110
Phone: (314)535-1414 **Fax:** (314)535-5613
Products: Office supplies. **SICs:** 5112 (Stationery & Office Supplies); 5112 (Stationery & Office Supplies); 5044 (Office Equipment). **Est:** 1920. **Sales:** $85,000,000 (2000). **Emp:** 250. **Officers:** Robert Rouegno, President; Dennis Shaw, Dir. of Finance; Mike Jakubik, VP of Operations; Ted Michael, VP of Human Resources; Ed Gruener, Vice President.
Alternate Name: American Loose Leaf Business Products Inc.

■ 21332 ■ USA Datafax Inc.
1819 Firman Dr., Ste. 115
Richardson, TX 75081
Phone: (972)437-4791 **Fax:** (972)437-5215
Products: Facsimile machines. **SIC:** 5044 (Office Equipment). **Sales:** $3,500,000 (2000). **Emp:** 12. **Officers:** Jerry Ezelle, President; Elizabeth Ezelle, CFO.

■ 21333 ■ USI Inc.
98 Fort Path Rd.
Madison, CT 06443
Phone: (203)245-8586
Free: (800)243-4565 **Fax:** (203)245-7845
Products: Overhead projectors, laminators, punchers for laminators, and transparencies. **SICs:** 5044 (Office Equipment); 5043 (Photographic Equipment & Supplies). **Est:** 1975. **Sales:** $13,000,000 (2000). **Emp:** 60. **Officers:** David R. Polastri, President; Jack Bowser, CFO; David R. Polastri, VP of Sales; George Olt, VP of Operations; Sandra Eagan, Dir of Human Resources.

■ 21334 ■ Valley Office Products Inc.
110 S Main St.
Milbank, SD 57252-1807
Phone: (605)432-5536
Free: (800)336-2298 **Fax:** (605)432-5575
Products: Office equipment. **SIC:** 5044 (Office Equipment). **Officers:** Larry Cantine, President.

■ 21335 ■ Van Ausdall and Farrar Inc.
1214 N Meridian St.
Indianapolis, IN 46204
Phone: (317)634-2913 **Fax:** (317)638-1843
URL: http://www.VanAusdall.com
Products: Office equipment, including copiers, shredders, fax machines, and dictation equipment; Optical imaging; WAN and LAN networks; Telephone systems; Web site development. **SIC:** 5044 (Office Equipment). **Est:** 1914. **Sales:** $30,000,000 (2000). **Emp:** 225. **Officers:** Clyde vonGrimmenstein, Chairman of the Board; Michael J. Wolanin Jr., CFO; Eric vonGrimmenstein, President.

■ 21336 ■ Variety Distributors Inc.
702 Spring St.
Harlan, IA 51537
Phone: (712)755-2184 **Fax:** (712)755-5041
Products: Stationery, gifts and toys. **SICs:** 5112 (Stationery & Office Supplies); 5092 (Toys & Hobby Goods & Supplies). **Sales:** $60,000,000 (2000). **Emp:** 300. **Officers:** Paul Mahler, President.

■ 21337 ■ Victor Business Systems Inc.
5300 E Raines Rd.
Memphis, TN 38118
Phone: (901)363-6201 **Fax:** (901)363-1566
Products: Office furniture; Interior design accessories. **SICs:** 5021 (Furniture); 5023 (Homefurnishings). **Est:** 1985. **Sales:** $3,000,000 (2000). **Emp:** 26. **Officers:** Lawrence E. Victor Jr., President & Chairman of the Board; Kathy C. Victor, CFO.

■ 21338 ■ Viking Acoustical Corp.
21480 Heath Ave.
Lakeville, MN 55044-9105
Phone: (612)469-3405
Free: (800)328-8385 **Fax:** (612)469-4503
Products: Panel and modular systems furniture and all other nonwood office furniture; Wood office furniture. **SICs:** 5021 (Furniture); 5046 (Commercial Equipment Nec). **Sales:** $9,000,000 (2000). **Emp:** 99. **Officers:** Bret Starkweather.

■ 21339 ■ Viking Office Products Inc.
950 W 190th St.
Gardena, CA 90248
Phone: (310)225-4500 **Fax:** (310)327-2376
Products: Office supplies. **SIC:** 5112 (Stationery & Office Supplies). **Sales:** $1,286,300,000 (2000). **Emp:** 2,826. **Officers:** Irwin Helford, CEO & Chairman of the Board; Frank R. Jarc, Exec. VP & CFO.

■ 21340 ■ Vitra Seating Inc.
6560 Stonegate Dr.
Allentown, PA 18106-9242
Phone: (215)391-9780 **Fax:** (215)391-9816
Products: Office seating, including chairs; Desks. **SIC:** 5021 (Furniture). **Emp:** 49.

■ 21341 ■ Vogann Business Machines
907 Willow Way
Deming, NM 88030-4446
Phone: (505)546-9183
Products: Office equipment. **SIC:** 5044 (Office Equipment). **Officers:** James Vogann, Owner.

■ 21342 ■ Wahl and Wahl of Iowa Inc.
2711 Grand Ave.
Des Moines, IA 50312
Phone: (515)244-5545
Free: (800)995-9245 **Fax:** (515)244-5572
URL: http://www.wahltek.com
Products: Computer hardware and software. **SIC:** 5046 (Commercial Equipment Nec). **Est:** 1990. **Sales:** $3,000,000 (2000). **Emp:** 17. **Officers:** Bruce Fagerstrom, President, e-mail: Bruce@wahltek.com; Lisa Donnelly, Controller, e-mail: Brent@wahltek.com; e-mail: randy@wahltek.com **Former Name:** Wahl & Wahl of Iowa, Inc.

■ 21343 ■ D. Waldner Company Inc.
125 Rte. 110
Farmingdale, NY 11735
Phone: (631)844-9300 **Fax:** (631)694-3503
URL: http://www.waldners.com
Products: Office furniture. **SIC:** 5021 (Furniture). **Est:** 1939. **Sales:** $108,000,000 (2000). **Emp:** 200. **Officers:** John P. Gallivan, CEO & President; John A. Marsicano, CFO.

■ 21344 ■ Walsh Bros.
PO Box 1711
Phoenix, AZ 85001
Phone: (602)252-6971 **Fax:** (602)252-8222
Products: Office furniture, including chairs and desks. **SIC:** 5021 (Furniture). **Est:** 1919. **Sales:** $35,000,000 (2000). **Emp:** 210. **Officers:** Timothy J. Walsh, President; Douglas Thomey, Treasurer; Donald J. Myers, VP of Marketing.

■ 21345 ■ Wang's International, Inc.
4250 E Shelby Dr.
Memphis, TN 38118-7721
Free: (800)443-6579
Products: Lead pencils, crayons, and artists' materials. **SICs:** 5112 (Stationery & Office Supplies); 5049 (Professional Equipment Nec).

■ 21346 ■ Wang's International, Inc.
6135-A Northbelt Dr.
Norcross, GA 30071
Phone: (404)622-0787
Products: Lead pencils, crayons, and artists' materials. **SICs:** 5112 (Stationery & Office Supplies); 5049 (Professional Equipment Nec).

■ 21347 ■ Ward Thompson Paper Inc.
PO Box 3839
Butte, MT 59702
Phone: (406)494-2777
Free: (800)823-1237 **Fax:** (406)494-2676
Products: Paper and paper products. **SIC:** 5112 (Stationery & Office Supplies).

■ 21348 ■ Wasserstrom Co.
477 S Front St.
Columbus, OH 43215
Phone: (614)228-6525 **Fax:** (614)228-2165
URL: http://www.wasserstrom.com
Products: Office furniture and supplies; Restaurant supplies. **SICs:** 5021 (Furniture); 5046 (Commercial Equipment Nec). **Est:** 1902. **Sales:** $100,000,000 (1999). **Emp:** 300. **Officers:** Rodney Wasserstrom, President; Dean R. Blank, CFO; Ursula Vermillion, Dir. of Marketing & Sales; Tom Rush, CIO; Shelly Myers, Human Resources Contact, e-mail: shellym@wasserstorm.com; Ursula Vermillion, Sales/Marketing

Contact, e-mail: ursulav@wassterstorm.com; Brenda Wagner, Customer Service Contact, e-mail: brendawagner@wassterstorm.com.

■ 21349 ■ Weber Office Supply Inc.
412 E Main St.
Riverton, WY 82501-4439
Phone: (307)856-4228
Products: Office equipment. SIC: 5044 (Office Equipment). Officers: James Weber, President.

■ 21350 ■ Weber and Sons Inc.
PO Box 104
Adelphia, NJ 07710
Phone: (908)431-1128   Fax: (908)431-9578
Products: Office supplies, including time card files, computer disk storage systems, and identification file systems. SIC: 5044 (Office Equipment). Est: 1940. Sales: $100,000 (2000). Emp: 2. Officers: Terry Weber, President; Doris Weber, Secretary.

■ 21351 ■ Websource
161 Ave. of the Americas
New York, NY 10013
Phone: (212)255-1600   Fax: (212)463-7095
Products: Printing and writing paper. SIC: 5111 (Printing & Writing Paper). Sales: $43,600,000 (2000). Emp: 87. Officers: Donald J. Heller, President; James DiMauro, VP of Finance.

■ 21352 ■ Cliff Weil Inc.
PO Box 427
Mechanicsville, VA 23116
Phone: (804)746-1321   Fax: (804)746-2595
Products: Office supplies. SICs: 5112 (Stationery & Office Supplies); 5094 (Jewelry & Precious Stones). Est: 1905. Sales: $13,900,000 (2000). Emp: 65. Officers: A.B. Hutzler II, President; Jerry E. Schwartzlow, VP of Operations; Thomas E. Siceloff, VP of Sales; Renaldo Meli, VP of Merchandising.

■ 21353 ■ Wescosa Inc.
PO Box 66626
Scotts Valley, CA 95066
Phone: (831)438-4600
Free: (800)367-4003   Fax: (831)438-8613
E-mail: wescosa@wescosainc.com
URL: http://www.wescosainc.com
Products: Office supplies and accessories; Toy glow balls. SIC: 5112 (Stationery & Office Supplies). Est: 1954. Sales: $2,000,000 (2000). Emp: 8. Officers: T. H. Ramsey; S.G. Vallys.

■ 21354 ■ Western Office Equipment
PO Box 1822
Billings, MT 59103-1822
Phone: (406)245-3029   Fax: (406)245-3020
Products: Office equipment. SIC: 5044 (Office Equipment). Officers: Greg Erickson, President.

■ 21355 ■ J.C. White Office Furniture and Interiors
200 SW 12th Ave.
Pompano Beach, FL 33069-3224
Phone: (305)785-3212
Products: Office furniture, including desks, chairs, and cabinets. SIC: 5021 (Furniture).

■ 21356 ■ Gary Williamson
PO Box 2800
Great Falls, MT 59401-3141
Phone: (406)761-0373   Fax: (406)454-0772
Products: Office equipment. SIC: 5044 (Office Equipment). Officers: Gary Williamson, Owner.

■ 21357 ■ Wisconsin Office Systems
6531 N Sidney Place
Milwaukee, WI 53209-3215
Phone: (414)352-9700   Fax: (414)352-4361
Products: Office systems. SIC: 5044 (Office Equipment). Emp: 49.

■ 21358 ■ Wittigs Office Interiors
2013 Broadway
San Antonio, TX 78215-1117
Phone: (512)270-0100   Fax: (210)270-0126
E-mail: mwittig@wittigsoi.com
Products: Office furniture. SIC: 5021 (Furniture). Est: 1951. Sales: $15,000,000 (2000). Emp: 75. Officers: Mark Wittig, President.

■ 21359 ■ WJS Enterprises Inc.
PO Box 6620
Metairie, LA 70009
Phone: (504)837-5666
Products: Photocopiers and facsimile machines. SIC: 5044 (Office Equipment). Est: 1968. Sales: $12,000,000 (2000). Emp: 75. Officers: Cy Hosch, President; Susan Hedrick, Dir. of Admin.

■ 21360 ■ W.B. Wood Co.
150 Floral Ave.
New Providence, NJ 07974
Phone: (908)771-9000
Products: Office furniture. SIC: 5021 (Furniture). Est: 1905. Sales: $35,000,000 (2000). Emp: 200. Officers: Willard Wood III III, President; Stewart Bradway, VP of Finance.

■ 21361 ■ Woodmansee Inc.
PO Box 798
Bismarck, ND 58502-0798
Phone: (701)223-9595   Fax: (701)223-8428
Products: Furniture, including chairs; Office supplies. SICs: 5021 (Furniture); 5112 (Stationery & Office Supplies). Officers: Joe Woodmansee, President.

■ 21362 ■ Word Systems Inc.
4181 E 96th St., Ste. 100
Indianapolis, IN 46240
Phone: (317)574-0499
Free: (800)425-7637   Fax: (317)574-4717
Products: Office equipment. SIC: 5044 (Office Equipment). Sales: $2,000,000 (2000). Emp: 13. Officers: Richard Baretto, President.

■ 21363 ■ Word Technology Systems Inc.
12046 Lackland Rd.
St. Louis, MO 63129
Phone: (314)434-9999
Products: Office equipment. SIC: 5044 (Office Equipment).

■ 21364 ■ Wyoming Stationery Company of Casper
PO Box 19
Casper, WY 82602-0019
Phone: (307)234-2145   Fax: (307)234-7133
Products: Office supplies. SIC: 5112 (Stationery & Office Supplies).

■ 21365 ■ Xerographic Copier Services Inc.
231 E Rhapsody
San Antonio, TX 78216
Phone: (210)341-4431   Fax: (210)341-5124
Products: Copiers. SIC: 5044 (Office Equipment). Sales: $4,000,000 (2000). Emp: 50. Officers: Vick Meredith, President; Tedra Fricks, Controller.

■ 21366 ■ Yankton Office Equipment
PO Box 604
Yankton, SD 57078-0604
Phone: (605)665-2289
Products: Office supplies and machines. SIC: 5112 (Stationery & Office Supplies). Est: 1980. Officers: Ellis Bliley, Owner.

■ 21367 ■ Yorktown Industries Inc.
330 Factory Rd.
Addison, IL 60101
Phone: (630)543-6110   Fax: (630)543-9864
Products: Copy machine and facsimile supplies. SICs: 5044 (Office Equipment); 5112 (Stationery & Office Supplies). Est: 1965. Sales: $8,000,000 (2000). Emp: 35. Officers: Kenneth W. Reick, President.

■ 21368 ■ Yost Office Systems, Inc.
675 E Anderson
Idaho Falls, ID 83401
Phone: (208)523-3549   Fax: (208)524-7216
Products: Photocopying equipment and supplies; Office supplies. SICs: 5044 (Office Equipment); 5112 (Stationery & Office Supplies). Sales: $30,000,000 (2000). Emp: 135. Officers: S. Bruce Jones, President; Jack Larsen, VP of Sales; Bruce Newbold, VP of Sales; Wayne Griffin, Controller.

■ 21369 ■ Robert Zakion
PO Box 677
Amesbury, MA 01913-0677
Phones: (978)388-0021   (978)363-4332
Free: (800)852-2357   Fax: (978)388-9592
E-mail: sales@labelsinc.com
URL: http://www.labelsinc.com
Products: Labels and decals; Flexographic and silk screen printing. SIC: 5112 (Stationery & Office Supplies). Est: 1976. Sales: $4,000,000 (2000). Emp: 50. Officers: Robert Zakian, President; Robert Dion, Treasurer.

■ 21370 ■ Zebra Pen Corp.
105 Northfield Ave.
Edison, NJ 08837
Phone: (732)225-6310
Free: (800)247-7170   Fax: (732)494-0919
Products: Writing instruments, including pens. SIC: 5112 (Stationery & Office Supplies). Est: 1982. Sales: $40,000,000 (2000). Emp: 50. Officers: Akihiko Tanigawa, President; Clem Restaino, Sales/Marketing Contact, e-mail: clem@zebrapen.com; Linda Stern, Customer Service Contact, e-mail: lindas@zebrapen.com.

■ 21371 ■ Zero US Corp.
Industrial Cir.
Lincoln, RI 02865-2600
Phone: (401)724-4470   Fax: (401)724-1190
Products: Office and public building furniture. SIC: 5021 (Furniture). Officers: Alfredo Brancucci, President.

■ 21372 ■ Zeroid and Company Inc.
5500 Cherokee Ave., No. 120
Alexandria, VA 22312
Phone: (703)461-8383   Fax: (703)461-0292
Products: Electronic office equipment. SIC: 5044 (Office Equipment). Est: 1986. Sales: $4,000,000 (2000). Emp: 31. Officers: Dan Gallagher, President; VP of Service Operations.

(39) Paints and Varnishes

Entries in this section are arranged alphabetically by company name. When the company name is a personal name, the company name is alphabetized by the surname unless the first name or initial(s) are part of a trade name. See the User's Guide at the front of this directory for additional information.

■ 21373 ■ **ABC Auto Paint Supply**
3099 South 300 West
Salt Lake City, UT 84115
Phone: (801)466-9195 **Fax:** (801)466-9217
Products: Automotive paint and supplies. **SIC:** 5198 (Paints, Varnishes & Supplies).

■ 21374 ■ **Advanced Color Coatings Inc.**
806 Jackman St.
El Cajon, CA 92020
Phone: (619)447-1400 **Fax:** (619)447-2017
Products: Automotive paint. **SIC:** 5198 (Paints, Varnishes & Supplies). **Est:** 1991. **Sales:** $1,000,000 (2000). **Emp:** 16. **Officers:** Dave Romero; John Romero.

■ 21375 ■ **Akers & Chrysler Inc.**
PO Box 1050
Auburn, ME 04211-1050
Phone: (207)764-1511 **Fax:** (207)764-3624
Products: Floor coverings and supplies; Wallcoverings and supplies. **SICs:** 5198 (Paints, Varnishes & Supplies); 5023 (Homefurnishings). **Est:** 1946. **Emp:** 14. **Officers:** Ronald R. Akers, President.

■ 21376 ■ **Akzo Coatings**
5555 Spalding Dr.
Norcross, GA 30092
Phone: (404)662-8464 **Fax:** 800-888-8464
Products: Paint and acrylic coatings. **SIC:** 5198 (Paints, Varnishes & Supplies).

■ 21377 ■ **Alaskan Paint Manufacturing Company Inc.**
2040 Spar Ave.
Anchorage, AK 99501
Phone: (907)272-2942 **Fax:** (907)272-4556
Products: Primers; Paints and allied products. **SIC:** 5198 (Paints, Varnishes & Supplies). **Est:** 1971.

■ 21378 ■ **All Paint Supply Co.**
325 W Main St.
Farmington, NM 87401-8422
Phone: (505)327-2468 **Fax:** (505)327-0939
Products: Paints and allied products; Varnishes. **SIC:** 5198 (Paints, Varnishes & Supplies). **Officers:** Roger Buffington, President.

■ 21379 ■ **Allpro Corp.**
2310 E Douglas
Wichita, KS 67214
Phone: (316)267-3329 **Fax:** (316)267-1379
Products: Paint. **SIC:** 5198 (Paints, Varnishes & Supplies).

■ 21380 ■ **Allpro Corp.**
1373 Ingleside Rd.
Norfolk, VA 23502
Phone: (757)853-4371
Free: (800)766-0540 **Fax:** (757)853-6838
Products: Paints and sprayers. **SIC:** 5198 (Paints, Varnishes & Supplies). **Alternate Name:** Norfolk Paint.

■ 21381 ■ **Allpro Corp.**
Sixth Industrial Park Dr.
Wheeling, WV 26003
Phone: (304)232-2200 **Fax:** (304)332-6413
Products: Paint and glass for windshields. **SICs:** 5198 (Paints, Varnishes & Supplies); 5013 (Motor Vehicle Supplies & New Parts).

■ 21382 ■ **Almar, Ltd.**
607 Ala Moana Blvd.
Honolulu, HI 96813
Phone: (808)521-7566 **Fax:** (808)531-5043
Products: Paint and other coatings. **SIC:** 5198 (Paints, Varnishes & Supplies).

■ 21383 ■ **Alta Paint & Coatings**
136 West 3300 South
Salt Lake City, UT 84115
Phone: (801)466-9625
Free: (800)400-0427 **Fax:** (801)466-9470
Products: Industrial coatings. **SICs:** 5198 (Paints, Varnishes & Supplies); 5169 (Chemicals & Allied Products Nec).

■ 21384 ■ **Aluma Panel, Inc.**
2410 Oak St. W
Cumming, GA 30041-6456
Phone: (404)889-3996
Free: (800)258-3003 **Fax:** (404)889-8972
Products: Corrugated plastic; Paints; Wood products; Banners; Alum sheets and blanks; Pressure sensitive vinyls; Plastic sheets. **SICs:** 5198 (Paints, Varnishes & Supplies); 5031 (Lumber, Plywood & Millwork); 5162 (Plastics Materials & Basic Shapes). **Est:** 1972. **Sales:** $5,500,000 (2000). **Emp:** 30. **Officers:** Carter F. Barnes.

■ 21385 ■ **Ameritone Devoe Paints**
18 Pohaku St., No. A
Hilo, HI 96720
Phone: (808)935-2011 **Fax:** (808)935-5936
Products: Paint. **SIC:** 5198 (Paints, Varnishes & Supplies).

■ 21386 ■ **Ameritone Paint Corp.**
1353 Dillingham Blvd.
Honolulu, HI 96817
Phone: (808)841-3693 **Fax:** (808)847-0093
Products: Paint. **SIC:** 5198 (Paints, Varnishes & Supplies).

■ 21387 ■ **Amsterdam Brush Corp.**
PO Box 71
Amsterdam, NY 12010
Phone: (518)842-2470 **Fax:** (518)842-3315
Products: Paint; Brushes; Paint sundries. **SIC:** 5198 (Paints, Varnishes & Supplies). **Est:** 1884. **Sales:** $4,000,000 (2000). **Emp:** 6. **Officers:** S. Edelson, CEO & Chairman of the Board.

■ 21388 ■ **Anatech Ltd.**
1020 Harts Lake Rd.
Battle Creek, MI 49015
Phone: (616)964-6450 **Fax:** (616)964-8084
E-mail: email@anatechltdusa.com
URL: http://www.anatechltdusa.com
Products: Histology stains and reagents. **SICs:** 5198 (Paints, Varnishes & Supplies); 5169 (Chemicals & Allied Products Nec). **Est:** 1984. **Sales:** $1,300,000 (2000). **Emp:** 10. **Officers:** Richard Dapson, President; Elizabeth K. Dapson, Treasurer; Ada Feldman, Secretary.

■ 21389 ■ **Apollo Colors Inc.**
3000 Dundee Rd., No. 415
Northbrook, IL 60062
Phone: (847)564-9190 **Fax:** (847)564-9296
Products: Organic printing pigments. **SIC:** 5198 (Paints, Varnishes & Supplies). **Est:** 1969. **Sales:** $50,000,000 (2000). **Emp:** 200. **Officers:** Thomas W. Rogers, CEO & President; Jesse M. Wilson Sr. Sr., Treasurer & Secty.; L.D. Bykerk, VP of Marketing & Sales; John Ott, Human Resources Mgr.

■ 21390 ■ **Approved Color Corp.**
PO Box 413
Greenville, NH 03048-0413
Phone: (603)878-1470
Products: Paints and allied products; Varnishes; Colors and pigments. **SIC:** 5198 (Paints, Varnishes & Supplies). **Officers:** Hans Chemello, President.

■ 21391 ■ **A.T. Supply**
PO Box 663
Amherst, NY 14228
Phone: (716)691-3331
Free: (800)724-4109 **Fax:** (716)641-3837
Products: Paints; Coolants; Lubricants; Tools. **SICs:** 5198 (Paints, Varnishes & Supplies); 5172 (Petroleum Products Nec); 5169 (Chemicals & Allied Products Nec).

■ 21392 ■ **Aucutt's General Store**
2600 Mabry Dr.
Clovis, NM 88101-8372
Phone: (505)762-3333
Free: (800)769-2181 **Fax:** (505)762-8288
E-mail: aucutts@3lefties.com
URL: http://www.aucuttsgeneralstore.com
Products: Paint and paint equipment. **SIC:** 5198 (Paints, Varnishes & Supplies). **Sales:** $4,000,000 (2000). **Emp:** 22. **Officers:** Bob Aucutt. **Former Name:** Aucutt's Paint Store.

■ 21393 ■ **Auto Body Paint and Supply**
339 4th Ave. W
Twin Falls, ID 83301-5816
Phone: (208)733-5731
Free: (800)255-8978 **Fax:** (208)733-5732
Products: Automotive paints. **SIC:** 5198 (Paints, Varnishes & Supplies). **Est:** 1976. **Sales:** $90,000 (2000). **Emp:** 3. **Officers:** Bruce Cameron, President; Joe D. Mabey, Vice President.

■ 21394 ■ Auto Body Supply of Orem
115 North 1200 West
Orem, UT 84057
Phone: (801)225-1155 **Fax:** (801)225-0149
Products: Automotive paint supplies. **SICs:** 5013
(Motor Vehicle Supplies & New Parts); 5198 (Paints, Varnishes & Supplies).

■ 21395 ■ Auto Wholesale and Hartsville Paint Store
1525 S 5th St.
Hartsville, SC 29550
Phone: (803)332-8586 **Fax:** (803)332-3196
Products: Automotive paints. **SIC:** 5198 (Paints, Varnishes & Supplies). **Sales:** $1,000,000 (2000).
Emp: 2. **Officers:** John Houck, President.

■ 21396 ■ B & A Paint Co.
287 Neil Ave.
Columbus, OH 43215
Phone: (614)224-6161 **Fax:** (614)227-6191
Products: Paint; Wall coverings. **SIC:** 5198 (Paints, Varnishes & Supplies).

■ 21397 ■ Barry Sales Inc.
1155 Park Ave.
Cranston, RI 02910-3145
Phone: (401)943-0090 **Fax:** (401)943-2790
Products: Paints and allied products. **SIC:** 5198
(Paints, Varnishes & Supplies). **Officers:** Rita Di Capiro, President.

■ 21398 ■ A.G. Barstow Company Inc.
1211 Madera Way
Riverside, CA 92503
Phone: (909)372-2900 **Fax:** (909)340-4171
Products: Sprayers. **SIC:** 5046 (Commercial Equipment Nec). **Est:** 1945. **Sales:** $1,500,000 (2000).
Emp: 5. **Officers:** Robert Zimel, President.

■ 21399 ■ Bennetts East Side Paint & Gloss
PO Box 1605
Idaho Falls, ID 83403-1605
Phone: (208)522-5630
Products: Paints, varnishes, gloss, and supplies. **SIC:** 5198 (Paints, Varnishes & Supplies). **Officers:** David Rhoades, President.

■ 21400 ■ Big Sky Paint Co., Heating & Air Conditioning
505 Main St. SW
Ronan, MT 59864
Phones: (406)676-0700 (406)676-3399
Fax: (406)676-3398
Products: Paint and log oil sealer; Heating, air conditioning, and refrigeration installation and parts.
SICs: 5198 (Paints, Varnishes & Supplies); 5074 (Plumbing & Hydronic Heating Supplies); 5075 (Warm Air Heating & Air-Conditioning). **Est:** 1990.

■ 21401 ■ Blaine's Paint Store, Inc.
360 E International Airport Rd.
Anchorage, AK 99518
Phone: (907)563-3412 **Fax:** (907)562-5988
Products: Paint and supplies. **SIC:** 5198 (Paints, Varnishes & Supplies).

■ 21402 ■ Boise Paint & Glass Inc.
410 N Orchard St.
Boise, ID 83706-1977
Phone: (208)343-4811 **Fax:** (208)343-4293
Products: Paints, varnishes, wallpaper, and supplies; Window treatments. **SICs:** 5198 (Paints, Varnishes & Supplies); 5023 (Homefurnishings). **Est:** 1949. **Emp:** 6.
Officers: Brice Katula, President.

■ 21403 ■ Bond Paint Co.
1802 San Juan Blvd.
Farmington, NM 87401
Phone: (505)326-3368 **Fax:** (505)326-4843
Products: Automotive paint products. **SIC:** 5198 (Paints, Varnishes & Supplies).

■ 21404 ■ Bond Paint Co.
2512 Graceland Dr. NE
Albuquerque, NM 87110-3802
Phone: (505)888-3737 **Fax:** (505)881-6697
Products: Automotive painting supplies. **SIC:** 5198

(Paints, Varnishes & Supplies). **Officers:** Jean Bond, Chairman of the Board.

■ 21405 ■ Bridges Smith & Co.
118-122 E Main St.
Louisville, KY 40202
Phone: (502)584-4173 **Fax:** (502)581-0390
Products: Paint and allied products; Window glass.
SIC: 5198 (Paints, Varnishes & Supplies). **Est:** 1875.
Emp: 26. **Officers:** Paul J. Schmidt.

■ 21406 ■ Broadway Industries Corp.
2066 W Broadway
South Portland, ME 04106-3223
Phone: (207)774-7707
Free: (800)559-1254 **Fax:** (207)775-3613
Products: Paints and allied products; Varnishes. **SIC:** 5198 (Paints, Varnishes & Supplies). **Est:** 1960. **Sales:** $5,000,000 (2000). **Emp:** 24. **Officers:** Ronald F. Blanchard, President.

■ 21407 ■ Brod-Dugan Co./Sherwin Williams Co.
2145 Schuetz Rd.
St. Louis, MO 63146
Phone: (314)567-1111 **Fax:** (314)997-1603
Products: Paint; Wallpaper. **SIC:** 5198 (Paints, Varnishes & Supplies). **Est:** 1947. **Sales:** $20,000,000 (2000). **Emp:** 220. **Officers:** Doug Henson, District Mgr.

■ 21408 ■ M.A. Bruder and Sons Inc.
PO Box 600
Broomall, PA 19008
Phone: (215)353-5100 **Fax:** (215)353-8189
Products: Paint. **SIC:** 5198 (Paints, Varnishes & Supplies).

■ 21409 ■ Budeke's Paint
418 S Broadway
Baltimore, MD 21231
Phone: (410)732-4354 **Fax:** (410)732-3299
Products: Painting supplies, including paints and brushes. **SIC:** 5198 (Paints, Varnishes & Supplies).

■ 21410 ■ Capital Carousel Inc.
520 Hampton Park Blvd.
Capitol Heights, MD 20743
Phones: (301)350-5400 (301)795-0852
Free: (800)795-0852 **Fax:** (301)350-7361
Products: Wallpaper. **SIC:** 5198 (Paints, Varnishes & Supplies).

■ 21411 ■ Capital Paint & Glass Inc.
PO Box 8287
Boise, ID 83707-2287
Phone: (208)342-5656 **Fax:** (208)342-5658
Products: Paints and allied products; Varnishes; Floorcoverings. **SICs:** 5198 (Paints, Varnishes & Supplies); 5023 (Homefurnishings). **Officers:** Mike Thacker, President.

■ 21412 ■ Cappel Distributing Co.
116 Chestnut St.
Atlantic, IA 50022
Phone: (712)243-4712
Products: Home and farm store supplies, including paint, clothes, and toys. **SICs:** 5198 (Paints, Varnishes & Supplies); 5136 (Men's/Boys' Clothing); 5137 (Women's/Children's Clothing); 5092 (Toys & Hobby Goods & Supplies). **Sales:** $3,000,000 (2000). **Emp:** 21. **Officers:** Dick Cappel, President.

■ 21413 ■ Clamyer International Corp.
55 Northern Blvd.
Great Neck, NY 11021
Phone: (516)504-9292 **Fax:** (516)504-1155
E-mail: clamyer@aol.com
Products: Aerosol paints; Pressure sensitive tape; Hospital equipment; Construction adhesive products; Office supplies and equipment. **SICs:** 5198 (Paints, Varnishes & Supplies); 5113 (Industrial & Personal Service Paper); 5112 (Stationery & Office Supplies); 5047 (Medical & Hospital Equipment); 5085 (Industrial Supplies). **Est:** 1949. **Officers:** J.W. Schlesinger, Exec. VP.

■ 21414 ■ Clarence House Imports Ltd.
211 E 58th St.
New York, NY 10021
Phone: (212)752-2890
Products: Fabric wallcoverings and trimmings. **SIC:** 5198 (Paints, Varnishes & Supplies). **Sales:** $40,000,000 (2000). **Emp:** 88. **Officers:** Robin Roberts, CEO & Chairman of the Board; JoAnne Platarote, Controller.

■ 21415 ■ Columbia Paint & Coatings
9275 South 700 East
Sandy, UT 84070
Phone: (801)561-7117 **Fax:** (801)561-7422
Products: Paints and coatings. **SIC:** 5198 (Paints, Varnishes & Supplies).

■ 21416 ■ Columbia Paint Co.
641 Jackson Ave.
Huntington, WV 25728
Phone: (304)529-8070 **Fax:** (304)525-2921
Products: Paint, including water resistant and industrial. **SIC:** 5198 (Paints, Varnishes & Supplies).

■ 21417 ■ Consolidated Coatings Corp.
3735 Green Rd.
Beachwood, OH 44122
Phone: (216)514-7596
Free: (800)321-7886 **Fax:** (216)514-7532
E-mail: info@consolidated-coatings.com
URL: http://www.consolidated-coatings.com
Products: Protective coatings and liquid products for roofing applications, maintenance and repair of interior and exterior walls, concrete flooring, and blacktop surfaces. **SICs:** 5169 (Chemicals & Allied Products Nec); 5198 (Paints, Varnishes & Supplies). **Est:** 1904.
Sales: $10,000,000 (2000). **Emp:** 100. **Officers:** J.K. Milliken, General Mgr.

■ 21418 ■ Cook and Dunn Paint Corp. Adelphi Coating
700 Gotham Pkwy.
Carlstadt, NJ 07072
Phone: (201)935-4900
Products: Paint. **SIC:** 5198 (Paints, Varnishes & Supplies). **Sales:** $3,000,000 (2000). **Emp:** 100.
Officers: W.G. Parker, CEO.

■ 21419 ■ Courtaulds Coatings Inc. Southeast Div.
3658 Lawrenceville Hwy.
Tucker, GA 30084
Phone: (404)938-4600
Products: Paint and varnish. **SIC:** 5198 (Paints, Varnishes & Supplies). **Sales:** $38,000,000 (2000).
Emp: 150. **Officers:** Mike Bura, Vice President.

■ 21420 ■ Creative Paint & Glass Inc.
1204 Strand Ave.
Missoula, MT 59801-5609
Phone: (406)543-7158 **Fax:** (406)549-2363
Products: Paints and allied products; Varnishes. **SIC:** 5198 (Paints, Varnishes & Supplies). **Officers:** Ray Burns, President.

■ 21421 ■ Crittenden Paint and Glass
248 24th St.
Ogden, UT 84401
Phone: (801)394-4643 **Fax:** (801)394-5966
URL: http://www.browz.com/ut-crittendenpaintandglass
Products: Paints; Glass products. **SICs:** 5198 (Paints, Varnishes & Supplies); 5039 (Construction Materials Nec). **Est:** 1958. **Sales:** $1,700,000 (2000). **Emp:** 15.
Officers: C. Lee Crittenden, President.

■ 21422 ■ Curtis & Campbell Inc.
6239 B St., No. 102
Anchorage, AK 99518-1728
Phone: (907)561-6011 **Fax:** (907)563-5670
E-mail: curtisandcampbell@alaska.com
URL: http://curtisandcampbell.com
Products: Paints, varnishes, and supplies; Window coverings; Carpets. **SICs:** 5198 (Paints, Varnishes & Supplies); 5023 (Homefurnishings). **Est:** 1966.
Officers: Dale Campbell, President.

■ **21423** ■ **Curtis Paint**
751 S 200 W
Salt Lake City, UT 84101-2708
Phone: (801)364-1933
E-mail: info@curtispaint.com
URL: http://www.curtispaint.com
Products: Paint. **SIC:** 5198 (Paints, Varnishes &
Supplies). **Est:** 1951. **Sales:** $500,000 (1999). **Emp:** 2.

■ **21424** ■ **Dale's Auto Paints & Supplies**
1101 W Broadway St.
Hobbs, NM 88240-5501
Phone: (505)393-1541   **Fax:** (505)393-2920
Products: Automotive and industrial paints. **SIC:** 5198
(Paints, Varnishes & Supplies). **Officers:** Dale
McDonald, Owner.

■ **21425** ■ **Daret Inc.**
33 Daret Dr.
Ringwood, NJ 07456
Phone: (973)962-6001   **Fax:** (973)962-6091
Products: Wallpaper sample books. **SIC:** 5198
(Paints, Varnishes & Supplies). **Est:** 1974. **Sales:**
$13,200,000 (2000). **Emp:** 200. **Officers:** B. Cowan,
President; Martin R. Pitts, Dir. of Marketing & Sales.

■ **21426** ■ **Davis Paint Co.**
PO Box 7589
North Kansas City, MO 64116
Phone: (816)471-4447
Free: (800)821-2029   **Fax:** (816)471-1460
E-mail: davispaint@aol.com
Products: Paint and brushes. **SIC:** 5198 (Paints,
Varnishes & Supplies). **Est:** 1921. **Sales:** $13,000,000
(2000). **Emp:** 95. **Officers:** Kevin C. Ostby, CEO;
Gladys Rains, CFO.

■ **21427** ■ **Design Impressions Inc.**
PO Box 2149
Hudson, OH 44236
Phone: (330)425-8011   **Fax:** (330)425-2607
Products: Vinyl; Paints; Papers; Cloth; Foils; Films;
Tape; Liners; Sign supplies. **SICs:** 5198 (Paints,
Varnishes & Supplies); 5113 (Industrial & Personal
Service Paper); 5199 (Nondurable Goods Nec). **Est:**
1978. **Officers:** Mark T. Seryak, President.

■ **21428** ■ **Devoe Paint**
2179 South 300 West, No. 1
South Salt Lake, UT 84115
Phone: (801)486-2211   **Fax:** (801)486-2286
Products: Paint products. **SIC:** 5198 (Paints,
Varnishes & Supplies).

■ **21429** ■ **Dial Battery Paint & Auto Supply**
414 Taunton Ave.
East Providence, RI 02914-2646
Phone: (401)434-2770   **Fax:** (401)434-4790
Products: Automotive paints, batteries, and parts.
SICs: 5198 (Paints, Varnishes & Supplies); 5013
(Motor Vehicle Supplies & New Parts). **Officers:**
Richard Acciardo, President.

■ **21430** ■ **Diamond Vogel Inc.**
4500 E 48th Ave.
Denver, CO 80216
Phone: (303)333-4499   **Fax:** (303)333-3499
Products: Paint. **SIC:** 5198 (Paints, Varnishes &
Supplies). **Est:** 1898. **Sales:** $6,000,000 (2000). **Emp:**
100. **Officers:** Frank Vogel, President; Robert V.
Lyons, Dir. of Marketing & Sales.

■ **21431** ■ **Diamond Vogel Paint Center**
119 Cole Shopping Ctr.
Cheyenne, WY 82001
Phone: (307)635-6803
Products: Wall coverings, including paint. **SIC:** 5198
(Paints, Varnishes & Supplies).

■ **21432** ■ **Diamond Vogel Paint Center**
1700 W 1st
Casper, WY 82604
Phone: (307)577-0172   **Fax:** (307)577-0173
Products: Paint. **SIC:** 5198 (Paints, Varnishes &
Supplies).

■ **21433** ■ **Diamond Vogel Paint Center**
215 W Broadway
Farmington, NM 87401
Phone: (505)325-9851   **Fax:** (505)325-7837
Products: Paint and paint equipment; Wallpaper. **SIC:**
5198 (Paints, Varnishes & Supplies).

■ **21434** ■ **Dremont-Levy Co.**
365 Albany St.
Boston, MA 02118
Phone: (617)423-5580
Products: Paint; Glass; Sponges. **SICs:** 5198 (Paints,
Varnishes & Supplies); 5039 (Construction Materials
Nec).

■ **21435** ■ **Du Pont Co.**
2929 Koapaka St.
Honolulu, HI 96819
Phone: (808)833-4117   **Fax:** (808)833-0535
Products: Automotive paints; Medical supplies;
Herbicides; Insecticides. **SICs:** 5198 (Paints, Varnishes
& Supplies); 5047 (Medical & Hospital Equipment);
5169 (Chemicals & Allied Products Nec).

■ **21436** ■ **Eco Design Co.**
1365 Rufina Circle
Santa Fe, NM 87502-2964
Phone: (505)438-3448
Free: (800)621-2591   **Fax:** (505)438-0199
URL: http://www.bioshieldpaint.com
Products: Paints and allied products; Varnishes. **SIC:**
5198 (Paints, Varnishes & Supplies). **Officers:** Rudolf
Reitz, President.

■ **21437** ■ **Ellis Paint Co.**
3150 E Pico Blvd.
Los Angeles, CA 90023
Phone: (213)261-9071   **Fax:** (213)780-9940
Products: Paints and allied products. **SIC:** 5198
(Paints, Varnishes & Supplies).

■ **21438** ■ **Elmwood Paint Center**
249 Academy Ave.
Providence, RI 02908
Phone: (401)351-7200   **Fax:** (401)351-8117
Products: Paints. **SIC:** 5198 (Paints, Varnishes &
Supplies). **Officers:** Marc Gillson, Vice President.

■ **21439** ■ **Erickson's Decorating Products,
Inc.**
6040 N Pulaski Rd.
Chicago, IL 60646
Phone: (773)539-7555   **Fax:** (773)539-9698
Products: Paint; Industrial coatings; Hardwood floor
equipment and finishes. **SIC:** 5198 (Paints, Varnishes
& Supplies).

■ **21440** ■ **Fargo Glass and Paint Co.**
1801 7th Ave. N
Fargo, ND 58102
Phone: (701)235-4441   **Fax:** (701)235-3435
Products: Paints; Windows; Glass. **SICs:** 5039
(Construction Materials Nec); 5198 (Paints, Varnishes
& Supplies); 5023 (Homefurnishings). **Est:** 1917.
Sales: $20,000,000 (2000). **Emp:** 120. **Officers:**
Gerald Lovell, President; Dan Martinson, Controller;
Gerald Hendricks, VP of Marketing.

■ **21441** ■ **Fisher's Incorporated Painting Co.**
2409 E 15th St.
Cheyenne, WY 82001
Phone: (307)632-5096   **Fax:** (307)634-3593
Products: Paint products. **SIC:** 5198 (Paints,
Varnishes & Supplies).

■ **21442** ■ **Flamemaster Corp.**
PO Box 1458
Sun Valley, CA 91353
Phone: (818)982-1650   **Fax:** (818)765-5603
Products: sealants, adhesives, fire-retardants and
high heat-resistant coatings. **SIC:** 5198 (Paints,
Varnishes & Supplies). **Sales:** $4,300,000 (1999).
Emp: 28. **Officers:** Joseph Mazin, CEO, President &
Chairman of the Board; Barbara E. Waite, CFO.

■ **21443** ■ **Florida Protective Coatings
Consultants Inc.**
250 Waymont Ct., Ste. 120
Lake Mary, FL 32746-6024
Phone: (407)322-1243   **Fax:** (407)322-1245
Products: Industrial and commercial coatings; Floor
coatings and waterproofing materials. **SIC:** 5198
(Paints, Varnishes & Supplies). **Est:** 1988. **Sales:**
$3,000,000 (1999). **Emp:** 5. **Officers:** Michael R.
Kendig, President; Michael Stensrud, VP of Sales; Mike
Kendig, Sales/Marketing Contact.

■ **21444** ■ **Forbo Wallcoverings Inc.**
3 Killdeer Ct.
Bridgeport, NJ 08014
Phone: (609)467-3800   **Fax:** (609)467-4880
Products: Household items. **SIC:** 5198 (Paints,
Varnishes & Supplies). **Sales:** $8,000,000 (2000).
Emp: 3.

■ **21445** ■ **Fortman's Paint & Glass**
1355 N 4th St.
Laramie, WY 82072
Phone: (307)745-9469   **Fax:** (307)745-3056
Products: Paint; Carpeting; Blinds; Vinyl flooring;
Glass. **SICs:** 5198 (Paints, Varnishes & Supplies);
5023 (Homefurnishings); 5039 (Construction Materials
Nec). **Est:** 1961. **Emp:** 6. **Officers:** Mike Fortman,
President.

■ **21446** ■ **Fuller Color Center Inc.**
75 S Wells Ave.
Reno, NV 89502-1334
Phone: (702)329-4478   **Fax:** (702)329-4492
Products: Paint. **SIC:** 5198 (Paints, Varnishes &
Supplies). **Est:** 1967. **Emp:** 10. **Officers:** John Carter,
President.

■ **21447** ■ **Fuller-O'Brien Paint Stores**
4500 Lois Dr.
Anchorage, AK 99501
Phone: (907)261-9186   **Fax:** (907)201-9193
Products: Paints. **SIC:** 5198 (Paints, Varnishes &
Supplies).

■ **21448** ■ **Fuller-O'Brien Paint Stores**
4042 Pacific Ave.
Ogden, UT 84405
Phone: (801)621-4633   **Fax:** (801)621-2939
Products: Paint. **SIC:** 5198 (Paints, Varnishes &
Supplies).

■ **21449** ■ **GCM Corp.**
1329 Warwick Ave.
Warwick, RI 02888-5030
Phone: (401)463-5262
Products: Paints and allied products; Varnishes. **SIC:**
5198 (Paints, Varnishes & Supplies). **Officers:** John
Mc Kenna, President.

■ **21450** ■ **Gehlhausen Paint Wholesalers**
520 N Main St.
Evansville, IN 47711
Phone: (812)428-5444   **Fax:** (812)428-5446
Products: Interior and exterior paint. **SIC:** 5198
(Paints, Varnishes & Supplies).

■ **21451** ■ **Glidden Paint & Wallcovering**
4900 Jefferson St. NE, No. B
Albuquerque, NM 87109
Phone: (505)883-7339
Products: Paint; Wallpaper. **SIC:** 5198 (Paints,
Varnishes & Supplies).

■ **21452** ■ **Griggs Paint Co.**
3635 S 16th St.
Phoenix, AZ 85040-1319
Phone: (602)243-3293
Free: (888)947-4444   **Fax:** (602)268-6801
E-mail: info@griggspaint.com
URL: http://www.griggspaint.com
Products: Paint and Coatings, including epoxies,
polyeurethanes, acrylics, and elastomerics. **SIC:** 5198
(Paints, Varnishes & Supplies). **Est:** 1972. **Sales:**
$5,000,000 (2000). **Emp:** 30. **Officers:** Dominic
Commisso; Ed Lind, Sales & Marketing Contact, e-
mail: ed@griggspaint.com; Jim Kleen, Customer
Service Contact, e-mail: angelo@griggspaint.com;

Robert Commisso, Human Resources Contact, e-mail: bob@griggspaint.com.

■ **21453** ■ **H & R General Painting**
PO Box 90570
Anchorage, AK 99509
Phone: (907)243-0728
Products: Wallpaper, paint, and supplies. **SIC:** 5198 (Paints, Varnishes & Supplies).

■ **21454** ■ **Hadlock Paint Co.**
7273 Victor-Pittsford Rd.
PO Box 376
Victor, NY 14564
Phone: (716)924-8420   **Fax:** (716)924-8843
Products: Household and industrial paint and supplies. **SICs:** 5198 (Paints, Varnishes & Supplies); 5085 (Industrial Supplies). **Est:** 1922.

■ **21455** ■ **Hansen-Kinney Company Inc.**
PO Box 1203
Great Falls, MT 59403-1203
Phone: (406)727-6660   **Free:** (800)634-2707
Products: Paints; Chemicals and sundries. **SIC:** 5198 (Paints, Varnishes & Supplies). **Est:** 1948. **Sales:** $500,000 (1999). **Emp:** 3. **Officers:** Donald Richcreek, President.

■ **21456** ■ **Hirshfield's, Inc.**
725 2nd Ave. N
Minneapolis, MN 55405
Phone: (612)377-3910   **Fax:** (612)377-2734
E-mail: hirshfield@hirshfields.com
URL: http://www.hirshfields.com
Products: Paints and allied products; Wallcoverings, wallpaper. **SIC:** 5198 (Paints, Varnishes & Supplies). **Est:** 1894. **Sales:** $40,000,000 (2000). **Emp:** 200. **Officers:** Hans Hirshfield, CEO.

■ **21457** ■ **Holladay Color Center**
2291 E Murray-Holladay Rd.
Holladay, UT 84117
Phone: (801)277-2604   **Fax:** (801)277-2625
Products: Paint and wallpaper; Picture frames; Furniture. **SICs:** 5198 (Paints, Varnishes & Supplies); 5023 (Homefurnishings); 5021 (Furniture).

■ **21458** ■ **House of Glass Inc.**
PO Box 228
Aberdeen, SD 57402-0228
Phone: (605)225-2010   **Fax:** (605)225-7454
E-mail: housglas@nvc.net
Products: Paints, varnishes, and supplies; Cabinets; Glass work; Door frames. **SICs:** 5198 (Paints, Varnishes & Supplies); 5031 (Lumber, Plywood & Millwork); 5039 (Construction Materials Nec). **Est:** 1960. **Emp:** 22. **Officers:** Stanley Albrecht, President.

■ **21459** ■ **Hubbard Paint and Wallpaper**
Rte. 28
Hyannis, MA 02601
Phone: (508)775-1568
Products: Paints; Wallpaper. **SIC:** 5198 (Paints, Varnishes & Supplies).

■ **21460** ■ **ICI Dulux Paint Centers**
74-5599 Alapa St.
Kailua Kona, HI 96740
Phone: (808)329-2766   **Fax:** (808)329-2768
Products: Commercial and industrial paints. **SIC:** 5198 (Paints, Varnishes & Supplies).

■ **21461** ■ **ICI Dulux Paints**
404-406 S Adams St.
Peoria, IL 61602
Phone: (309)673-3761   **Fax:** (309)673-2529
Products: Paint products. **SIC:** 5198 (Paints, Varnishes & Supplies). **Officers:** Mike Howard, Customer Service Contact, e-mail: paintrep@ntslink.net.

■ **21462** ■ **ICI Dulux Paints**
6100 Garfield Ave.
Commerce, CA 90040
Phone: (323)727-2000   **Fax:** (323)728-3834
Products: Paints, varnishes, architectural and baking enamels; Wallcoverings; Fabric; Paints. **SIC:** 5198 (Paints, Varnishes & Supplies).

■ **21463** ■ **ICI Paints**
925 Euclid Ave.
Cleveland, OH 44115
Phone: (216)344-8000
Free: (800)984-5444   **Fax:** (216)344-8900
URL: http://www.icipaintstores.com
Products: Paint products, including paint, paint brushes, thinner, mixers, and turpentine. **SIC:** 5198 (Paints, Varnishes & Supplies). **Est:** 1875. **Sales:** $900,000,000 (2000). **Emp:** 5,000. **Officers:** Thomas C. Osborne, CEO; Robert McCauley, Exec. VP; Robert J. Koch, Exec. VP of Marketing; Robert T. Crumling.

■ **21464** ■ **Indurall Coatings Inc.**
PO Box 2371
Birmingham, AL 35201
Phone: (205)324-9588   **Fax:** (205)324-6942
Products: Paint. **SIC:** 5198 (Paints, Varnishes & Supplies). **Est:** 1947. **Sales:** $10,100,000 (2000). **Emp:** 70. **Officers:** David D. Hood, President; Donald R. Matthews, Controller.

■ **21465** ■ **Intermountain Specialty Coatings**
1021 W 24th St.
Ogden, UT 84401
Phone: (801)394-3489
Products: Paints and varnishes; Ceramic tile. **SICs:** 5198 (Paints, Varnishes & Supplies); 5032 (Brick, Stone & Related Materials). **Est:** 1980. **Sales:** $5,000 (2000). **Emp:** 3. **Officers:** Lyle Karras.

■ **21466** ■ **Iowa Paint Manufacturing Company Inc.**
PO Box 1417
Des Moines, IA 50305
Phone: (515)283-1501   **Fax:** (515)283-1470
Products: Paint and wallpaper. **SIC:** 5198 (Paints, Varnishes & Supplies). **Est:** 1933. **Sales:** $15,000,000 (2000). **Emp:** 160. **Officers:** Thomas Goldman, President; Marty Hermann, Controller; Michael Scharferberg, Dir. of Sales; Kirk McCombs, Dir. of Systems.

■ **21467** ■ **J & J Supply, Inc.**
2510 White Settlement Rd.
Ft. Worth, TX 76107
Phone: (817)335-5536
Free: (800)792-2212   **Fax:** (817)877-3316
Products: Automotive paint; Boat and camper upholstery. **SIC:** 5013 (Motor Vehicle Supplies & New Parts). **Est:** 1961. **Emp:** 19.

■ **21468** ■ **J & R Industries Inc.**
PO Box 4221
Shawnee Mission, KS 66204-0221
Phone: (913)362-6667
Free: (800)999-9513   **Fax:** (913)362-7421
Products: Paint; Paintable surfaces and finishes; Tin products. **SICs:** 5198 (Paints, Varnishes & Supplies); 5198 (Paints, Varnishes & Supplies). **Est:** 1972. **Emp:** 3. **Officers:** Kathy Whalen, President, e-mail: kamawha@hotmail.com.

■ **21469** ■ **Jones Blair Co.**
PO Box 35286
Dallas, TX 75235
Phone: (214)353-1600   **Fax:** (214)350-7624
Products: Paint. **SIC:** 5198 (Paints, Varnishes & Supplies). **Est:** 1928. **Sales:** $98,000 (2000). **Emp:** 480. **Officers:** P.D. Dague, CEO; Tom Wagner, President.

■ **21470** ■ **Kauai Paint & Jalousie**
3196 Akahi St.
Lihue, HI 96766
Phone: (808)245-6181
Products: Paint; Screens; Glass figurines. **SICs:** 5198 (Paints, Varnishes & Supplies); 5023 (Homefurnishings).

■ **21471** ■ **Keith-Sinclair Company Inc.**
PO Box 24770
Nashville, TN 37202-4770
Phone: (615)259-3601   **Fax:** (615)726-3564
Products: Paints and allied products; Abrasive products. **SIC:** 5198 (Paints, Varnishes & Supplies). **Est:** 1936. **Sales:** $5,500,000 (2000). **Emp:** 15. **Officers:** Jere C. Sinclair, President.

■ **21472** ■ **S. Klenosky Co.**
543 Metropolitan Ave.
Brooklyn, NY 11211
Phone: (718)782-7142   **Fax:** (718)387-0452
Products: Paints. **SIC:** 5198 (Paints, Varnishes & Supplies).

■ **21473** ■ **Klinger Paint Co., Inc.**
333 5th SE
PO Box 1945
Cedar Rapids, IA 52406
Phone: (319)366-7165   **Fax:** (319)366-4996
URL: http://www.klingerpaint.com
Products: Interior and exterior paint, including industrial maintenance coatings, urethanes, epoxies, and tank paints. **SIC:** 5198 (Paints, Varnishes & Supplies). **Est:** 1900. **Emp:** 34.

■ **21474** ■ **Komac Paint Center**
119 Cole Shopping Ctr.
Cheyenne, WY 82001
Phone: (307)635-5714
Products: Wall covering, including wallpaper and paint. **SIC:** 5198 (Paints, Varnishes & Supplies).

■ **21475** ■ **Komac Paint Center**
215 W Broadway
Farmington, NM 87401
Phone: (505)325-7837   **Fax:** (505)325-7837
Products: Paint and paint equipment; Wallpaper. **SIC:** 5198 (Paints, Varnishes & Supplies).

■ **21476** ■ **Komer and Co.**
2528 W Pembroke Ave.
Hampton, VA 23661
Phone: (757)247-6651
Products: Paints. **SIC:** 5198 (Paints, Varnishes & Supplies).

■ **21477** ■ **Kraft Chemical Co.**
1975 N Hawthorne Ave.
Melrose Park, IL 60160
Phone: (708)345-5200
Free: (800)345-5200   **Fax:** (708)345-4005
URL: http://www.kraftchemical.com
Products: Chemicals; Metals. **SICs:** 5169 (Chemicals & Allied Products Nec); 5169 (Chemicals & Allied Products Nec); 5141 (Groceries—General Line); 5122 (Drugs, Proprietaries & Sundries). **Est:** 1934. **Sales:** $30,000,000 (2000). **Emp:** 30. **Officers:** Gerald G. Kraft, President, e-mail: gkraft@kraftchemical.com; Richard Pollina, Finance Officer.

■ **21478** ■ **KR's Paint Shop**
One Alii Molokai
Kaunakakai, HI 96748
Phone: (808)553-3744
Products: House paint. **SIC:** 5198 (Paints, Varnishes & Supplies).

■ **21479** ■ **Kwal-Hanley Paint Co.**
1400 N Solano Dr.
Las Cruces, NM 88001
Phone: (505)527-0482   **Fax:** (505)527-0483
Products: Paint and paint supplies. **SIC:** 5198 (Paints, Varnishes & Supplies). **Former Name:** Hanley Paint Company Inc.

■ **21480** ■ **Kwal-Howells Inc.**
PO Box 39-R
Denver, CO 80239
Phone: (303)371-5600   **Fax:** (303)373-5688
Products: Paint. **SIC:** 5198 (Paints, Varnishes & Supplies). **Sales:** $82,000,000 (1999). **Emp:** 400. **Officers:** Kent Child, President; Miles Tunns, VP - General Manager.

■ **21481** ■ **Kwal-Howells Paint & Wallcovering**
390 N State St.
Orem, UT 84057
Phone: (801)225-6630   **Fax:** (801)226-0349
Products: Paint and wallcoverings. **SIC:** 5198 (Paints, Varnishes & Supplies).

■ 21482 ■ **Kwal-Howells Paint & Wallcovering**
4285 S State St.
Murray, UT 84107
Phone: (801)262-8466 **Fax:** (801)263-1294
Products: Paint and wallpaper products and accessories. **SIC:** 5198 (Paints, Varnishes & Supplies).

■ 21483 ■ **Kwal-Howells Paint & Wallcovering**
5640 S Redwood Rd.
Salt Lake City, UT 84123
Phone: (801)967-8213 **Fax:** (801)967-3713
Products: Paint and wall coverings. **SIC:** 5198 (Paints, Varnishes & Supplies).

■ 21484 ■ **Laagco Sales**
2930 N San Fernando
Burbank, CA 91504
Phone: (818)843-2382
Products: Paint; Varnish. **SIC:** 5198 (Paints, Varnishes & Supplies). **Est:** 1893. **Sales:** $16,000,000 (2000). **Emp:** 70. **Officers:** William Izakowitz, CEO; A. Shaker, VP of Finance; J. Auerbach, Dir. of Marketing.

■ 21485 ■ **Landers-Segal Color Co.**
305 W Grand Ave.
Montvale, NJ 07645
Phone: (973)779-5001
Free: (888)452-6426 **Fax:** (201)307-5855
Products: Color pigments, fillers, and extenders; Minerals; Specialty chemicals. **SIC:** 5198 (Paints, Varnishes & Supplies). **Sales:** $23,000,000 (2000). **Emp:** 25. **Officers:** Donald Greenwald, President.

■ 21486 ■ **Lannans Paint & Decorating Ctr.**
184 E Burkitt St.
Sheridan, WY 82801
Phone: (307)674-8491 **Fax:** (307)672-0105
Products: Paint and painting supplies; Engineering supplies; Architecture supplies; Framing supplies. **SICs:** 5198 (Paints, Varnishes & Supplies); 5023 (Homefurnishings); 5049 (Professional Equipment Nec).

■ 21487 ■ **Bill Lapierre**
924 E Main St.
Newport, VT 05855-1812
Phone: (802)334-8878
Products: Paints and allied products; Varnishes. **SIC:** 5198 (Paints, Varnishes & Supplies). **Officers:** Bill Lapierre, Owner.

■ 21488 ■ **Layton Marketing Group Inc.**
1845 Buerkle Rd.
St. Paul, MN 55110-5246
Phone: (612)490-5000 **Fax:** (612)490-9409
Products: t-lt notes; Anti-tarnish and anti-corrosion products; Safety vests. **SICs:** 5112 (Stationery & Office Supplies); 5169 (Chemicals & Allied Products Nec). **Sales:** $2,000,000 (2000). **Emp:** 17. **Officers:** Les Layton, President; Jenine Pierce, Accountant.

■ 21489 ■ **LBI Wallcovering**
3950 South 500 West
Murray, UT 84123
Phone: (801)262-6618 **Fax:** (801)263-3404
Products: Wallcoverings. **SIC:** 5198 (Paints, Varnishes & Supplies).

■ 21490 ■ **W.W. Leach Company Inc.**
196 Bedford St.
Fall River, MA 02720
Phone: (508)678-5238 **Fax:** (508)679-8988
Products: Automotive paints. **SIC:** 5198 (Paints, Varnishes & Supplies). **Est:** 1927. **Sales:** $1,900,000 (2000). **Emp:** 15. **Officers:** L. Viveiros, President.

■ 21491 ■ **Lehman Paint Co. Inc.**
112 S Canyon St.
Carlsbad, NM 88220
Phone: (505)885-5330 **Fax:** (505)887-9587
Products: Paints, varnishes, and supplies. **SIC:** 5198 (Paints, Varnishes & Supplies). **Officers:** Patricia Younger, President.

■ 21492 ■ **J.C. Licht Company Inc.**
45 N Brandon Dr.
Glendale Heights, IL 60139-2091
Phone: (630)351-0400 **Fax:** (630)351-4144
E-mail: jclicht@jclicht.com
URL: http://www.jclicht.com
Products: Paint and allied products; Paint and varnish brushes, rollers, and pads; Wallcoverings, wallpaper; Carpeting; Window blinds and related products. **SIC:** 5198 (Paints, Varnishes & Supplies). **Est:** 1907. **Sales:** $48,000,000 (1999). **Emp:** 400. **Officers:** Gregory Licht, CEO; Mark S. Licht, President; Maria D. Eriksen, Dir. of Marketing; Steve Miller, Dir of Human Resources.

■ 21493 ■ **Reston Lloyd Ltd.**
PO Box 2302
Reston, VA 20195
Phone: (703)437-0003
Free: (800)394-5693 **Fax:** (703)437-3041
E-mail: restonloyd@aol.com
Products: Enamel for kitchen items such as tea kettles, colanders and bowl sets. **SIC:** 5198 (Paints, Varnishes & Supplies). **Est:** 1971. **Emp:** 14. **Officers:** Rita Bolle, President.

■ 21494 ■ **Loomis Paint & Wallpaper Ctr**
35 Main St.
Poultney, VT 05764-1106
Phone: (802)287-4009
Products: Paints and allied products; Varnishes; Rubber floor and wall coverings; Carpets. **SICs:** 5198 (Paints, Varnishes & Supplies); 5023 (Homefurnishings). **Officers:** Lawrence Loomis, President.

■ 21495 ■ **Mantrose-Haeuser Company Inc.**
1175 Post Rd. E
Westport, CT 06880
Phone: (203)454-1800
Free: (800)344-4229 **Fax:** (203)227-0558
URL: http://www.mbzgroup.com
Products: Shellacs; Glazes. **SIC:** 5198 (Paints, Varnishes & Supplies). **Sales:** $20,000,000 (1999). **Emp:** 90. **Officers:** William Barrie, President; Dan Connors, Industrial Prod. Mgr., e-mail: dan.connors@zinsser.com.

■ 21496 ■ **Masterchem Industries Inc.**
PO Box 368
Barnhart, MO 63012
Phone: (314)942-2510
Free: (800)325-3552 **Fax:** (314)942-3663
E-mail: custservice@masterchem.com
URL: http://www.masterchem.com
Products: Stain sealing primers. **SIC:** 5198 (Paints, Varnishes & Supplies). **Est:** 1959. **Emp:** 109. **Officers:** Robert Caldwell, President; Stan Korte, Controller.

■ 21497 ■ **Matthews Paint Co.**
8201 100th St.
Kenosha, WI 53142-7739
Phone: (262)947-0700 **Fax:** (262)947-0444
URL: http://www.signpaint.com
Products: Paint; Paint mixing systems. **SIC:** 5198 (Paints, Varnishes & Supplies).

■ 21498 ■ **Mattos Inc.**
4501 Beech Rd.
Camp Springs, MD 20748
Phone: (301)423-1142
Free: (800)423-2338 **Fax:** (301)423-2338
Products: Automotive paint. **SICs:** 5198 (Paints, Varnishes & Supplies); 5013 (Motor Vehicle Supplies & New Parts). **Est:** 1928. **Sales:** $20,000,000 (1999). **Emp:** 104. **Officers:** Joseph G. Mattos, Exec. VP; Jeffrey Whipple, VP of Finance; Joe Mattos, Exec. VP.

■ 21499 ■ **Mautz Paint Co.**
PO Box 7068
Madison, WI 53707-7068
Phone: (608)255-1661 **Fax:** (608)255-4342
Products: Paint. **SIC:** 5198 (Paints, Varnishes & Supplies). **Est:** 1922. **Sales:** $40,000,000 (2000). **Emp:** 250. **Officers:** B.F. Mautz Jr., Chairman of the Board; Dan Drury, President.

■ 21500 ■ **Mercantile Buyer's Service Inc.**
4715 N 32nd St.
PO Box 090528
Milwaukee, WI 53209-0528
Phone: (414)445-4440
Free: (800)752-7874 **Fax:** (414)445-9656
E-mail: l.pon-r.franklin@worldnet.att.net
Products: Paint accessories, including paint brushes, roller covers, closeouts, casters, wheels, pan and roller sets, knives, and masks. **SICs:** 5198 (Paints, Varnishes & Supplies); 5072 (Hardware). **Est:** 1961. **Sales:** $2,000,000 (2000). **Emp:** 12. **Officers:** Robert A. Franklin, President.

■ 21501 ■ **Mid-South Supply Corp.**
2417 S Wabash
Chicago, IL 60616-2306
Phone: (312)842-8282
Free: (800)842-8201 **Fax:** (312)842-7222
E-mail: midsou@aol.com
Products: Industrial Supplies; Paint; Fastenings; Tools; Lubricants; Cleaning supplies. **SICs:** 5198 (Paints, Varnishes & Supplies); 5172 (Petroleum Products Nec); 5085 (Industrial Supplies); 5169 (Chemicals & Allied Products Nec). **Est:** 1932. **Sales:** $5,000,000 (2000). **Emp:** 14. **Officers:** Ross Fienberg, CEO; Josh Fienberg, COO.

■ 21502 ■ **Midwest Industrial Coatings Inc.**
6667 W Old Shakopee Rd., Ste. 101
Bloomington, MN 55438
Phone: (612)942-1840 **Fax:** (612)942-1830
Products: Paints and allied products. **SIC:** 5198 (Paints, Varnishes & Supplies). **Est:** 1985. **Officers:** Dan Seeler, President.

■ 21503 ■ **Mission Paint & Glass**
PO Box 4665
Missoula, MT 59806-4665
Phone: (406)549-7802
Products: Paint and varnish brushes, rollers, and pads. **SIC:** 5198 (Paints, Varnishes & Supplies). **Officers:** Bruce Serviss, President.

■ 21504 ■ **Mobile Paint Distributors**
4775 Hamilton Blvd.
PO Box 717
Theodore, AL 36582
Phone: (205)443-6110
Free: (800)621-6952 **Fax:** (205)443-7313
Products: Paints and allied products. **SIC:** 5198 (Paints, Varnishes & Supplies).

■ 21505 ■ **Modern Paint & Wallpaper Inc.**
899 Brighton Ave.
Portland, ME 04102-1005
Phone: (207)772-4431 **Fax:** (207)772-7261
Products: Paints and stains. **SIC:** 5198 (Paints, Varnishes & Supplies). **Officers:** Jeanne Mullen, President.

■ 21506 ■ **Mohawk Finishing Products Inc.**
4715 State Hwy. 30
Amsterdam, NY 12010-7417
Phone: (518)843-1380
Free: (800)545-0047 **Fax:** 800-721-1545
E-mail: Mohawkfin@aol.com
Products: Finishing products, including stains and varnishes. **SIC:** 5198 (Paints, Varnishes & Supplies). **Est:** 1948. **Sales:** $35,000,000 (2000). **Emp:** 200. **Officers:** Richard Loomis, President; Kathleen Cetnar, VP of Finance; Robert Clusker, VP of Marketing & Sales; Brian D. Jackson, VP, General Mgr.

■ 21507 ■ **Motif Designs, Inc.**
20 Jones St.
New Rochelle, NY 10801
Phone: (914)633-1170 **Fax:** (914)633-1176
Products: Wallpaper and borders; Fabric. **SICs:** 5198 (Paints, Varnishes & Supplies); 5131 (Piece Goods & Notions).

■ 21508 ■ **Mount Pleasant Hardware Inc.**
249 Academy Ave.
Providence, RI 02908-4144
Phone: (401)351-7200 **Fax:** (401)351-8117
Products: Plumbing supplies; Electrical supplies; Paints. **SICs:** 5198 (Paints, Varnishes & Supplies);

5072 (Hardware); 5074 (Plumbing & Hydronic Heating Supplies). **Officers:** Paul Gillson, President.

■ **21509** ■ **Mountain West Paint Distributor**
5080 S 1600 W
Ogden, UT 84405
Phone: (801)393-3333
Products: Paint and wallpaper. **SIC:** 5198 (Paints, Varnishes & Supplies).

■ **21510** ■ **Muralo Company Inc.**
PO Box 455
Bayonne, NJ 07002
Phone: (201)437-0770   **Fax:** (201)437-2316
Products: Paint and painting supplies, including brushes and rollers; Spackle; Wallcovering adhesives. **SIC:** 5198 (Paints, Varnishes & Supplies). **Est:** 1894. **Sales:** $42,000,000 (1999). **Emp:** 400. **Officers:** James S. Norton, President; Chuck Lee, CFO; Lee Flemming, VP of Marketing; Don Everett, Sales/Marketing Contacct; Jen Sakowski, Customer Service Contact; Helen Owens, Human Resources Contact.

■ **21511** ■ **MVR Auto Refinishing Supplies**
891 Alua, No. B3
Wailuku, HI 96793
Phones: (808)242-8175   (808)244-1440
Fax: (808)242-7488
Products: Automobile paints. **SICs:** 5013 (Motor Vehicle Supplies & New Parts); 5198 (Paints, Varnishes & Supplies). **Est:** 1987. **Sales:** $400,000 (2000). **Emp:** 4. **Officers:** Melvin Ahyou, President; Dennis Tamanaha, General Mgr.; Geane Figueiroa, Office Mgr.

■ **21512** ■ **James Nakagawa Painting, Inc.**
Waialo Rd.
Hanapepe, HI 96716
Phone: (808)335-6412   **Fax:** (808)335-3420
Products: Paint. **SIC:** 5198 (Paints, Varnishes & Supplies).

■ **21513** ■ **Nashua Wallpaper & Paint Co.**
129 W Pearl St.
Nashua, NH 03060-3304
Phone: (603)882-9491   **Fax:** (603)880-0367
Products: Paints and allied products; Varnishes; Wallcoverings, wallpaper. **SIC:** 5198 (Paints, Varnishes & Supplies). **Officers:** Spiro Linatsas, Owner.

■ **21514** ■ **Nason Automotive**
1007 Market St.
Wilmington, DE 19898
Phone: (302)774-6950   **Fax:** (302)774-6655
Products: Paint. **SIC:** 5198 (Paints, Varnishes & Supplies). **Est:** 1849. **Sales:** $25,000,000 (2000). **Emp:** 100. **Officers:** Jon D. Owen, General Mgr.; John McMenamin, Operations Mgr.; Jerry Cassidy, Dir. of Sales.

■ **21515** ■ **National Paint Distributors**
25822 Schoolcraft
Detroit, MI 48239
Phone: (313)537-4500   **Fax:** (313)537-2827
Products: Interior and exterior paint. **SIC:** 5198 (Paints, Varnishes & Supplies).

■ **21516** ■ **National Paint Distributors**
6280 Broad St.
Pittsburgh, PA 15206
Phone: (412)361-8770   **Fax:** (412)361-2555
Products: Industrial and commercial paint. **SIC:** 5198 (Paints, Varnishes & Supplies). **Est:** 1940. **Emp:** 98.

■ **21517** ■ **National Patent Development Corp.**
9 West 57th St.
New York, NY 10019
Phone: (212)826-8500   **Fax:** (212)230-9545
Products: Paint, stain, and sundry items. **SIC:** 5198 (Paints, Varnishes & Supplies). **Sales:** $234,800,000 (2000). **Emp:** 2,000. **Officers:** Jerome I. Feldman, CEO & President; Scott N. Greenberg, VP & CFO.

■ **21518** ■ **New United Distributors**
6917 Carnegie Ave.
Cleveland, OH 44103
Phone: (216)881-4070
Free: (800)800-7343   **Fax:** (216)881-4073
Products: Paints and allied products. **SIC:** 5198 (Paints, Varnishes & Supplies). **Est:** 1926. **Sales:** $2,000,000 (2000). **Emp:** 9. **Officers:** Erik Silverman, Sales/Marketing Contact; Herb Jaffe, Human Resources Contact.

■ **21519** ■ **Niles Color Center**
7652 Milwaukee Ave.
Niles, IL 60714
Phone: (847)967-9585   **Fax:** (847)967-9571
Products: Paint, wallpaper, and decorating products; Floor sanding products. **SICs:** 5198 (Paints, Varnishes & Supplies); 5023 (Homefurnishings). **Est:** 1985.

■ **21520** ■ **Otto's Paint & Supply Co.**
917 E 16th St.
Cheyenne, WY 82001
Phone: (307)634-3549   **Fax:** (307)638-4506
Products: Paints and painting supplies. **SIC:** 5198 (Paints, Varnishes & Supplies).

■ **21521** ■ **Pacific Coast Chemical Co.**
2424 4th St.
Berkeley, CA 94710
Phone: (510)549-3535   **Fax:** (510)549-0890
Products: Paint coatings. **SIC:** 5198 (Paints, Varnishes & Supplies). **Sales:** $20,000,000 (2000). **Emp:** 40. **Officers:** Haxom K. Stull, President; Dan V. Stull, CFO.

■ **21522** ■ **Pacific Paint Center, Inc.**
2865 Ualena St.
Honolulu, HI 96819
Phone: (808)836-3142   **Fax:** (808)839-9894
Products: Household paint. **SIC:** 5198 (Paints, Varnishes & Supplies).

■ **21523** ■ **Padco Inc.**
2220 Elm St. SE
Minneapolis, MN 55414
Phone: (612)378-7270   **Fax:** (612)378-9388
E-mail: padco@uswest.net
Products: Paint and varnish brushes, rollers, and pads. **SIC:** 5198 (Paints, Varnishes & Supplies). **Officers:** Robert Janssen, CEO; David Bergeson, Vice President; Ed Gokdstein, President; Chandra Meka, VP & Treasurer; Dean Cowdery, Vice President. **Former Name:** Padco Companies, Inc.

■ **21524** ■ **The Paint Bucket**
1051 W Holt Blvd.
Ontario, CA 91762
Phone: (714)983-2664   **Fax:** (714)988-3336
Products: Paint. **SIC:** 5198 (Paints, Varnishes & Supplies).

■ **21525** ■ **Paint Dept.**
PO Box 22737
Billings, MT 59104-2737
Phone: (406)245-5585
Products: Paint and varnish brushes, rollers, and pads. **SIC:** 5198 (Paints, Varnishes & Supplies). **Officers:** Robert Craig, Owner.

■ **21526** ■ **Paint & Equipment Supply**
3400 Hwy. 30 W
Pocatello, ID 83201-6071
Phone: (208)232-8665   **Fax:** (208)234-0985
Products: Paints and allied products; Automotive paints. **SIC:** 5198 (Paints, Varnishes & Supplies). **Officers:** David Guissi. **Former Name:** Bradys Industrial Tool & Supplies.

■ **21527** ■ **Paint & Glass Supply Company Inc.**
301 4th St.
Devils Lake, ND 58301-2411
Phone: (701)662-4976   **Fax:** (701)662-6752
Products: Paints, varnishes, and supplies; Furniture; Floor coverings. **SICs:** 5198 (Paints, Varnishes & Supplies); 5021 (Furniture); 5023 (Homefurnishings). **Officers:** Thomas Lamotte, President.

■ **21528** ■ **The Paint Store**
PO Box 1365
Casper, WY 82602-1365
Phone: (307)234-6454
Products: Paints and allied products; Varnishes. **SIC:** 5198 (Paints, Varnishes & Supplies). **Officers:** William Stapert, President.

■ **21529** ■ **Paint Supply Co.**
3504 S Grand Ave.
St. Louis, MO 63118
Phone: (314)773-3223   **Fax:** (314)773-1944
Products: Paint. **SIC:** 5198 (Paints, Varnishes & Supplies). **Est:** 1950. **Sales:** $150,000,000 (2000). **Emp:** 5.

■ **21530** ■ **Paint West Decor Center**
1606 West 3500 South
West Valley City, UT 84119
Phone: (801)972-9380
Products: Paint and wallcoverings; Windows. **SICs:** 5198 (Paints, Varnishes & Supplies); 5039 (Construction Materials Nec).

■ **21531** ■ **Painter's Choice**
43 North 700 East
St. George, UT 84770
Phone: (435)673-6222
Products: Paint and wallcoverings; Professional painting equipment. **SIC:** 5198 (Paints, Varnishes & Supplies).

■ **21532** ■ **Parks Corp.**
One West St.
Fall River, MA 02720
Phone: (508)679-5938   **Fax:** (508)674-8404
URL: http://www.parkscorp.com
Products: Solvents; Paint removers; Clear finishes; Wood stains. **SIC:** 5198 (Paints, Varnishes & Supplies). **Est:** 1899. **Sales:** $40,000,000 (1999). **Emp:** 130. **Officers:** F. Lee Davidson, President; Dennis Dessault, Treasurer.

■ **21533** ■ **Passonno Paints**
500 Broadway
Watervliet, NY 12189
Phone: (518)273-3822
Products: Paint and paint supplies. **SIC:** 5198 (Paints, Varnishes & Supplies). **Est:** 1947. **Sales:** $8,000,000 (2000). **Emp:** 50. **Officers:** Richard B. Cunningham, President.

■ **21534** ■ **Pearl Paint Co., Inc.**
2411 Hempstead Turnpike
East Meadow, NY 11554
Phone: (516)731-3700   **Fax:** (516)731-3721
Products: Paint and paint supplies. **SIC:** 5198 (Paints, Varnishes & Supplies).

■ **21535** ■ **Penn Color Inc.**
400 Old Dublin Pike
Doylestown, PA 18901
Phone: (215)345-6550   **Fax:** (215)345-0270
Products: Color concentrates for printing inks, paints, vinyl siding, and vehicle paints and interiors. **SIC:** 5198 (Paints, Varnishes & Supplies). **Est:** 1948. **Sales:** $100,000,000 (2000). **Emp:** 500. **Officers:** K. Putman, President; David B. Hill III, CFO; David M. McGarrity, VP of Marketing & Sales; Barbara Hampel, Dir. of Information Systems; Jeff Parris, Dir of Human Resources.

■ **21536** ■ **Penobscot Paint Products Co.**
31 Washington St.
Bangor, ME 04401-6518
Phone: (207)945-3171
Products: Paints, varnishes, and supplies; Artist supplies. **SICs:** 5198 (Paints, Varnishes & Supplies); 5199 (Nondurable Goods Nec). **Officers:** Anthony D Amico, President.

■ **21537** ■ **Perschon Paint & Wallcovering**
2468 S State St.
South Salt Lake, UT 84115
Phone: (801)487-1061   **Fax:** (801)467-0313
Products: Paint, wallcoverings, and supplies. **SIC:** 5198 (Paints, Varnishes & Supplies).

■ 21538 ■ **Perspectives**
352 Longview Dr.
Lexington, KY 40503
Phone: (606)277-0521 **Fax:** (606)278-4441
Products: Paint; Wallpaper. **SIC:** 5198 (Paints, Varnishes & Supplies).

■ 21539 ■ **Pioneer Coatings Inc.**
7265 Bethel St.
Boise, ID 83704-9226
Phone: (208)377-0112 **Fax:** (208)376-7906
Products: Paints and allied products; Varnishes. **SIC:** 5198 (Paints, Varnishes & Supplies). **Officers:** Daniel Morgan, President.

■ 21540 ■ **Pioneer Manufacturing Co.**
4529 Industrial Pkwy.
Cleveland, OH 44135
Phone: (216)671-5500 **Fax:** (216)671-5502
Products: Paint and paint supplies; Sterilization equipment; Coatings. **SICs:** 5198 (Paints, Varnishes & Supplies); 5169 (Chemicals & Allied Products Nec); 5172 (Petroleum Products Nec).

■ 21541 ■ **Plaza Paint Co.**
771 Roosevelt Ave.
Carteret, NJ 07008
Phone: (732)969-8818 **Fax:** (732)969-8923
Products: Hardware; Paint. **SICs:** 5198 (Paints, Varnishes & Supplies); 5072 (Hardware).

■ 21542 ■ **Polar Supply Company Inc.**
300 E 54th Ave.
Anchorage, AK 99518-1230
Phone: (907)563-5000 **Fax:** (907)562-7001
Products: Paints, varnishes, industrial coatings, and supplies; Construction supplies. **SICs:** 5198 (Paints, Varnishes & Supplies); 5039 (Construction Materials Nec). **Officers:** Don Dunavant, President.

■ 21543 ■ **Ponderosa Paint Stores**
3040 West 3500 South
West Valley City, UT 84119
Phone: (801)966-1491 **Fax:** (801)966-1492
Products: Paint and wallcoverings. **SIC:** 5198 (Paints, Varnishes & Supplies).

■ 21544 ■ **PPG Industries, Inc.**
500 Oakridge Turnpike
Oak Ridge, TN 37830
Phone: (423)483-3524 **Fax:** (423)483-3525
Products: Paint and supplies. **SIC:** 5198 (Paints, Varnishes & Supplies).

■ 21545 ■ **Preservative Paint Company Inc.**
5410 Airport Way S
Seattle, WA 98108
Phone: (206)763-0300 **Fax:** (206)767-2251
Products: Paint and supplies. **SIC:** 5198 (Paints, Varnishes & Supplies).

■ 21546 ■ **Prime Coatings**
875 West 2600 South
Salt Lake City, UT 84119
Phone: (801)972-1436
Free: (800)851-9693 **Fax:** (801)972-1680
E-mail: primeslc@msn.com
URL: http://www.PrimeCoatings.com
Products: Paint and supplies; Automobile refinishing products. **SIC:** 5198 (Paints, Varnishes & Supplies). **Est:** 1991. **Emp:** 12. **Officers:** Byron Lee Bowman, President.

■ 21547 ■ **Pritchard Paint and Glass Co.**
PO Box 30547
Charlotte, NC 28230
Phone: (704)376-8561 **Fax:** (704)342-3185
Products: Window glass; Automobile glass; Paints and allied products. **SICs:** 5039 (Construction Materials Nec); 5013 (Motor Vehicle Supplies & New Parts). **Est:** 1904. **Sales:** $39,000,000 (2000). **Emp:** 150. **Officers:** Donald R. Beard, Chairman of the Board; Gerald Beiersdorf, Finance Officer; Tony Brklacich, Exec. VP; Ken Roughen, Dir. of Data Processing.

■ 21548 ■ **Professional Paint Supply**
5610 Singer Blvd. NE
Albuquerque, NM 87109
Phone: (505)344-0000 **Fax:** (505)344-4753
Products: Paint. **SIC:** 5198 (Paints, Varnishes & Supplies).

■ 21549 ■ **Quill, Hair & Ferrule**
1 Greengate Park Rd.
Columbia, SC 29223
Phone: (803)788-4499 **Fax:** (803)736-4731
Products: Paint, strippers, and brushes. **SIC:** 5198 (Paints, Varnishes & Supplies).

■ 21550 ■ **Ray's Workshop**
1750 E 27th Ave.
Anchorage, AK 99508-4017
Phone: (907)277-2101 **Fax:** (907)277-9463
Products: Paint spray equipment. **SIC:** 5198 (Paints, Varnishes & Supplies). **Est:** 1971. **Sales:** $100,000 (2000). **Emp:** 2. **Officers:** Marcelle Phillips.

■ 21551 ■ **Re-Neva Inc.**
935 S Rock Blvd.
Sparks, NV 89431
Phone: (775)352-2510 **Fax:** (775)331-8172
Products: Automotive paints and allied products. **SIC:** 5198 (Paints, Varnishes & Supplies). **Est:** 1956. **Sales:** $2,000,000 (2000). **Emp:** 7. **Officers:** Don Ellis, President.

■ 21552 ■ **Red Spot Paint Varnish Co.**
PO Box 418
Evansville, IN 47703-0418
Phone: (812)428-9100 **Fax:** (812)428-9167
Products: Automotive paint. **SIC:** 5198 (Paints, Varnishes & Supplies). **Est:** 1903. **Sales:** $56,000,000 (2000). **Emp:** 450. **Officers:** C.D. Storms, President; Steve Halling, CFO; M. Rhiver, Dir. of Marketing; M. Murphy, Dir. of Systems; Don Johnson, Dir of Human Resources.

■ 21553 ■ **Relco Engineers**
13303 E Rosecrans Ave.
Santa Fe Springs, CA 90670
Phone: (562)404-7574 **Fax:** (562)404-1451
Products: Spray paint equipment. **SIC:** 5198 (Paints, Varnishes & Supplies). **Est:** 1972. **Sales:** $4,000,000 (2000). **Emp:** 10. **Officers:** Robert S. Smith, President & CFO; Fabian Cardenas, Dir. of Marketing & Sales.

■ 21554 ■ **Reno Brake Inc.**
PO Box 7452
Reno, NV 89510-7452
Phone: (702)322-8635 **Fax:** (702)322-2351
Products: Paints and allied products. **SIC:** 5198 (Paints, Varnishes & Supplies). **Officers:** Mike Evasovic, President.

■ 21555 ■ **Ren's Clearfield Paint & Glass**
426 N Main St.
Clearfield, UT 84015
Phone: (801)776-2190 **Fax:** (801)825-5479
Products: Paint; Glass. **SICs:** 5198 (Paints, Varnishes & Supplies); 5039 (Construction Materials Nec).

■ 21556 ■ **Reston Lloyd Ltd.**
PO Box 2302
Reston, VA 20195
Phone: (703)437-0003
Free: (800)394-5693 **Fax:** (703)437-3041
Products: Paints and varnishes. **SIC:** 5198 (Paints, Varnishes & Supplies).

■ 21557 ■ **Rodda Paint Co.**
12000 SW Garden Pl.
Portland, OR 97223
Phone: (503)521-4300 **Fax:** (503)521-4400
URL: http://www.roddapaint.com
Products: Factory paints; Sundries; Wall coverings; Window coverings. **SIC:** 5198 (Paints, Varnishes & Supplies). **Est:** 1932. **Sales:** $70,000,000 (2000). **Emp:** 400.

■ 21558 ■ **Ruidoso Paint Center Inc.**
PO Box 848
Ruidoso, NM 88355-0848
Phone: (505)257-7447
Products: Paints and allied products; Varnishes. **SIC:** 5198 (Paints, Varnishes & Supplies). **Officers:** Jerry Holder, President.

■ 21559 ■ **Sanborn's Paint Spot Inc.**
12 Terrill St.
Rutland, VT 05701-4155
Phone: (802)775-7159 **Fax:** (802)775-0799
E-mail: jjpaint16@aol.com
Products: Paint; Wall and floor coverings. **SICs:** 5198 (Paints, Varnishes & Supplies); 5023 (Homefurnishings). **Est:** 1974. **Sales:** $675,000 (2000). **Emp:** 4. **Officers:** John J. Magro, President.

■ 21560 ■ **Schulte Paint**
PO Box 461
Florissant, MO 63032-0461
Phone: (314)381-3830
Free: (800)325-8010 **Fax:** (314)261-3160
Products: Paint and roof coatings. **SIC:** 5198 (Paints, Varnishes & Supplies). **Est:** 1923. **Emp:** 25. **Officers:** Francis T. Schulte Jr., President. **Alternate Name:** Wear-Rite.

■ 21561 ■ **Sequence (USA) Co. Ltd.**
151 E Rosemary St., Ste. 240
Chapel Hill, NC 27514
Phone: (919)918-7990 **Fax:** (919)918-7993
Products: Decorative paper wall appliques; Wallpaper; Paint brushes and rollers; Computer parts and attachments. **SICs:** 5198 (Paints, Varnishes & Supplies); 5199 (Nondurable Goods Nec); 5045 (Computers, Peripherals & Software). **Officers:** Neil E. Bolick, President.

■ 21562 ■ **Sequoia Paint**
700 Baker St.
Bakersfield, CA 93305
Phone: (805)323-7948 **Fax:** (805)323-7973
Products: Paint and paint supplies. **SIC:** 5198 (Paints, Varnishes & Supplies).

■ 21563 ■ **Service Central, Inc.**
1629 Palolo Ave.
Honolulu, HI 96816
Phone: (808)735-9575 **Fax:** (808)735-1697
Products: Paint Colorant Dispensers, paint shakers, mixers, compressors, sprayers, and pressure washers. **SIC:** 5198 (Paints, Varnishes & Supplies). **Est:** 1986. **Sales:** $100,000 (1999). **Emp:** 3. **Officers:** Albert K. Machida Sr., President & General Mgr.

■ 21564 ■ **John Seven Paint and Wallpaper Co.**
3070 29th St. SE
Grand Rapids, MI 49512
Phone: (616)942-2020 **Fax:** (616)942-1883
Products: Paint and wallpaper. **SIC:** 5198 (Paints, Varnishes & Supplies). **Est:** 1889. **Sales:** $13,000,000 (2000). **Emp:** 80. **Officers:** Charles K. Seven, President.

■ 21565 ■ **Seymour of Sycamore Inc.**
917 Crosby Ave.
Sycamore, IL 60178
Phone: (815)895-9101
Free: (800)435-4482 **Fax:** (815)895-8475
E-mail: seymour_syc@earthlink.net
URL: http://www.seymourpaint.com
Products: Paints and allied products; Miscellaneous end-use chemicals and chemical products. **SICs:** 5198 (Paints, Varnishes & Supplies); 5169 (Chemicals & Allied Products Nec). **Est:** 1949. **Emp:** 120. **Officers:** Nancy Heatley, CEO.

■ 21566 ■ **Shaheen Paint and Decorating Company, Inc.**
1400 St. Paul St.
Rochester, NY 14621
Phone: (716)266-1500 **Fax:** (716)544-7832
E-mail: paint@shaheenmgt.com
Products: Paint and wall coverings; Carpeting; Window blinds; Industrial epoxies. **SICs:** 5198 (Paints, Varnishes & Supplies); 5023 (Homefurnishings); 5085 (Industrial Supplies). **Est:** 1948. **Sales:** $6,000,000 (2000). **Emp:** 51. **Officers:** David V. Shaheen, President; Jeff Coleman, General Mgr.; Pat Shaheen, Vice President.

■ 21567 ■ Sherwin Williams Paint Co.
1604 S Commerce St.
Las Vegas, NV 89102
Phone: (702)382-4994 **Fax:** (702)382-6489
Products: Paint. **SIC:** 5198 (Paints, Varnishes & Supplies).

■ 21568 ■ Sherwin Williams Paint Co.
3905 E 2nd St.
Casper, WY 82609
Phone: (307)235-0106 **Fax:** (307)237-9612
Products: Paints; Carpeting; Blinds; Wallpaper. **SICs:** 5198 (Paints, Varnishes & Supplies); 5023 (Homefurnishings).

■ 21569 ■ Sherwin Williams Paint Co.
1706 Stillwater Ave.
Cheyenne, WY 82009-7361
Phone: (307)638-8781
Products: Paints. **SIC:** 5198 (Paints, Varnishes & Supplies).

■ 21570 ■ Sherwin Williams Paint Co.
1281 Coffeen Ave.
Sheridan, WY 82801
Phone: (307)672-5821
Products: Paint; Painting supplies. **SIC:** 5198 (Paints, Varnishes & Supplies).

■ 21571 ■ Sherwin Williams Paint Co.
929 Grand Ave.
Billings, MT 59102
Phone: (406)245-7155 **Fax:** (406)245-3077
URL: http://www.sherwin-Williams.com
Products: Paint and paint products. **SIC:** 5198 (Paints, Varnishes & Supplies). **Est:** 1868. **Emp:** 5.

■ 21572 ■ Sherwin Williams Paint Co.
1920 Harrison Ave.
Butte, MT 59701
Phone: (406)782-0491 **Fax:** (406)782-0495
Products: Paint and painting supplies. **SIC:** 5198 (Paints, Varnishes & Supplies).

■ 21573 ■ Sherwin Williams Paint Co.
1700 N Montana Ave.
Helena, MT 59601
Phone: (406)442-2300 **Fax:** (406)442-2553
Products: Paint and painting supplies; Drywall products. **SICs:** 5198 (Paints, Varnishes & Supplies); 5039 (Construction Materials Nec).

■ 21574 ■ Sherwin Williams Paint Co.
405 W Idaho St.
Kalispell, MT 59901
Phone: (406)752-5588
Products: Paint and painting supplies. **SIC:** 5198 (Paints, Varnishes & Supplies).

■ 21575 ■ Sherwin Williams Paint Co.
601 Main St.
MiLes City, MT 59301
Phone: (406)232-3267 **Fax:** (406)232-5238
Products: Paint and paint products. **SIC:** 5198 (Paints, Varnishes & Supplies).

■ 21576 ■ Sherwin Williams Paint Co.
1428 S Reserve St.
Missoula, MT 59801-4758
Phone: (406)543-5970
Products: Paint and painting supplies. **SIC:** 5198 (Paints, Varnishes & Supplies).

■ 21577 ■ Shur-Line Inc.
PO Box 285
Lancaster, NY 14086
Phone: (716)683-2500 **Fax:** (716)683-0188
Products: Paint and varnish brushes, rollers, and pads; Miscellaneous allied paint products. **SIC:** 5198 (Paints, Varnishes & Supplies).

■ 21578 ■ Siperstein Freehold Paint
PO Box 298A, Rd. 1
Englishtown, NJ 07726
Phone: (732)780-2000 **Fax:** (732)409-2771
Products: Paint and wallpaper; Ladders. **SICs:** 5198 (Paints, Varnishes & Supplies); 5084 (Industrial Machinery & Equipment).

■ 21579 ■ N. Siperstein, Inc.
326 S Washington Ave.
Bergenfield, NJ 07621
Phone: (201)385-4800 **Fax:** (201)385-1366
Products: Paints. **SIC:** 5198 (Paints, Varnishes & Supplies).

■ 21580 ■ N. Siperstein, Inc.
372 New Brunswick Ave.
Fords, NJ 08863
Phone: (732)738-8300
Free: (800)618-7246 **Fax:** (732)738-8720
E-mail: sipspaint@aol.com
Products: Paint supplies, including sprayers. **SIC:** 5198 (Paints, Varnishes & Supplies). **Est:** 1977.

■ 21581 ■ N. Siperstein, Inc.
119 Rte. 46 West
Lodi, NJ 07644
Phone: (973)777-7100 **Fax:** (973)773-8610
Products: Paints. **SIC:** 5198 (Paints, Varnishes & Supplies).

■ 21582 ■ N. Siperstein, Inc.
415 Montgomery St.
Jersey City, NJ 07302
Phone: (201)867-0336 **Fax:** (201)333-2299
Products: Paint products; Wood coverings. **SIC:** 5198 (Paints, Varnishes & Supplies).

■ 21583 ■ Siperstein MK Paint
935 Rte. 22 West
North Plainfield, NJ 07060
Phone: (908)756-0089 **Fax:** (908)756-9690
URL: http://www.siperstein.com
Products: Wallpaper and paint; Window treatments. **SIC:** 5198 (Paints, Varnishes & Supplies). **Est:** 1905.

■ 21584 ■ Siperstein West End
128 Broadway
Long Branch, NJ 07740
Phone: (732)542-6142 **Fax:** (732)571-1249
Products: Paint. **SIC:** 5198 (Paints, Varnishes & Supplies).

■ 21585 ■ Siperstein's Middletown
549 Highway 35
Red Bank, NJ 07701
Phone: (732)842-6000 **Fax:** (732)727-6659
Products: Paints. **SIC:** 5198 (Paints, Varnishes & Supplies).

■ 21586 ■ Skips Ameritone Paint Center
512 S Boulder Hwy.
Henderson, NV 89015-7512
Phone: (702)565-9591
Products: Paints, varnishes, and supplies. **SIC:** 5198 (Paints, Varnishes & Supplies). **Officers:** Gordon Kline, Partner.

■ 21587 ■ SmithChem Div.
84 Dayton Ave.
Passaic, NJ 07055
Phone: (201)779-5001 **Fax:** (973)779-8948
Products: Pigments. **SIC:** 5198 (Paints, Varnishes & Supplies). **Sales:** $13,000,000 (2000). **Emp:** 60.
Officers: Warren Klugman, President.

■ 21588 ■ Stein Paint Co.
545 W Flagler St.
Miami, FL 33130
Phone: (305)545-8700 **Fax:** (305)545-5688
Products: Paint. **SIC:** 5198 (Paints, Varnishes & Supplies). **Est:** 1940. **Sales:** $2,500,000 (1999). **Emp:** 8. **Officers:** Lance Turner, President; Fernin Garcia, Sales & Marketing Contact.

■ 21589 ■ Steven Industries, Inc.
39 Avenue C
PO Box 8
Bayonne, NJ 07002
Phone: (201)437-6500 **Fax:** (201)437-0366
E-mail: stevenindustries@mindspring.com
Products: Paint adhesives; Sealing compound; Lubricants; Corrosion preventatives; Coatings. **SICs:** 5198 (Paints, Varnishes & Supplies); 5039 (Construction Materials Nec); 5169 (Chemicals & Allied Products Nec). **Est:** 1965. **Sales:** $3,000,000 (2000).

Emp: 20. **Officers:** Steven Rubenstein, President; William Rubenstein, Exec. VP.

■ 21590 ■ Stratham Hardware & Lumber Co.
17 Portsmouth Ave.
Stratham, NH 03885-2520
Phone: (603)772-3031 **Fax:** (603)778-7055
Products: Building materials and hardware. **SICs:** 5039 (Construction Materials Nec); 5072 (Hardware).
Officers: Lionel La Bonte, President.

■ 21591 ■ Street Art Supply Dallas
2270 Manana
Dallas, TX 75220
Phone: (972)432-0030
Free: (800)880-9774 **Fax:** (972)432-8138
URL: http://www.streetart.com
Products: Plywood; Paints, including fluorescent; Computer vinyls; Sign making systems. **SICs:** 5198 (Paints, Varnishes & Supplies); 5031 (Lumber, Plywood & Millwork).

■ 21592 ■ Thompson Lacquer Company Inc.
2324 S Grand Ave.
Los Angeles, CA 90007
Phone: (213)746-2290
Products: Automotive paint. **SIC:** 5198 (Paints, Varnishes & Supplies). **Est:** 1935. **Sales:** $24,000,000 (2000). **Emp:** 300. **Officers:** Mort Kline, President; David Martin, VP & Controller; S. Moore, Dir. of Marketing.

■ 21593 ■ Thybony Wallcoverings Co.
3720 N Kedzie Ave.
Chicago, IL 60618
Phone: (773)463-3005
Free: (800)289-3000 **Fax:** (773)463-8988
Products: Wall coverings. **SIC:** 5198 (Paints, Varnishes & Supplies). **Est:** 1886. **Officers:** James Thybony, President; Bo Pruski, Vice President; Robin Thybony, Vice President; Matthew White, Vice President.

■ 21594 ■ Tower Paint Manufacturing
620 W 27th St.
Hialeah, FL 33010
Phone: (305)887-9583 **Fax:** (305)883-4692
E-mail: towerpaint@bellsouth.net
URL: http://www.towerpaintmfg.com
Products: House paint. **SIC:** 5198 (Paints, Varnishes & Supplies). **Est:** 1945. **Sales:** $4,000,000 (1999). **Emp:** 40. **Officers:** Muriel Tower, President; Ernesto Rodriguez, Controller; John M. Duty, Dir. of Marketing; Douglas A. Seda, Dir. of Systems.

■ 21595 ■ Triangle Coatings, Inc.
1930 Fairway Dr.
San Leandro, CA 94577
Phone: (510)895-8000
Free: (800)895-8000 **Fax:** (510)895-8800
E-mail: info@tricoat.com
URL: http://www.tricoat.com
Products: Specialty paints, coatings, and inks. **SIC:** 5198 (Paints, Varnishes & Supplies). **Est:** 1932. **Sales:** $9,000,000 (1999). **Emp:** 48. **Officers:** Ned B. Kisner, President, e-mail: nkisner@tricoat.com; Brad Kisner, VP of Sales & Mktg., e-mail: bkisner@tricoat.com; Connie Kelly, Customer Relations, e-mail: ckelly@tricoat.com; Lily Kessler, CFO, e-mail: lkessler@tricoat.com; Ken Kisner, VP of Operations, e-mail: kkisner@tricoat.com. **Alternate Name:** Triangle Paint. **Alternate Name:** Danacolors. **Alternate Name:** Modern Options. **Alternate Name:** White Mountain.

■ 21596 ■ Tsigonia Paint Sales
4117 Broadway
Astoria, NY 11103
Phone: (718)932-3664 **Fax:** (718)545-0331
Products: House and metal paints. **SIC:** 5198 (Paints, Varnishes & Supplies).

■ 21597 ■ Valdes Paint & Glass
1008 Marquez Pl.
Santa Fe, NM 87501
Phone: (505)982-4661
Products: Paint and stain; Mirrors; Shower doors. **SICs:** 5198 (Paints, Varnishes & Supplies); 5023 (Homefurnishings).

■ **21598** ■ **Valley Paint**
629 S State St.
Salt Lake City, UT 84111
Phone: (801)595-1819 **Fax:** (801)298-4582
Products: Paint. **SIC:** 5198 (Paints, Varnishes &
Supplies).

■ **21599** ■ **Viking Woodcrafts, Inc.**
1317 8th St. SE
Waseca, MN 56093
Phone: (507)835-8043
Free: (800)328-0116 **Fax:** (507)835-3895
E-mail: viking@vikingwoodcrafts.com
URL: http://www.vikingwoodcrafts.com
Products: Woodcrafts; Instructional painting material;
Paint; Brushes; Painting supplies. **SICs:** 5198 (Paints,
Varnishes & Supplies); 5049 (Professional Equipment
Nec). **Est:** 1980. **Sales:** $2,000,000 (1999). **Emp:** 14.

■ **21600** ■ **Wallcoverings, Ltd.**
3654 Waialae Ave.
Honolulu, HI 96816
Phone: (808)734-2177 **Fax:** (808)737-9480
Products: Wallpaper. **SIC:** 5198 (Paints, Varnishes &
Supplies).

■ **21601** ■ **Wallpaper Hawaii, Ltd.**
3160 Waialae Ave.
Honolulu, HI 96816
Phone: (808)735-2861 **Fax:** (808)734-8351
Products: Wallcoverings. **SIC:** 5198 (Paints,
Varnishes & Supplies). **Est:** 1959. **Emp:** 3. **Officers:**
Audrey Tanaka, President; Corinne Kwock, Customer
Service Contact.

■ **21602** ■ **Warner Manufacturing Co.**
13435 Industrial Park Blvd.
Minneapolis, MN 55441
Phone: (763)559-4740
Free: (800)444-0606 **Fax:** (763)559-0613
E-mail: gmueller@warnertool.com
URL: http://www.warnertool.com
Products: Knives; Paint scrapers; Wallpapering tools;
Drywall tools. **SICs:** 5198 (Paints, Varnishes &
Supplies); 5084 (Industrial Machinery & Equipment);
5072 (Hardware). **Est:** 1927.

■ **21603** ■ **Warwick Auto Parts Inc.**
641 Warwick Ave.
Warwick, RI 02888-2602
Phone: (401)781-2525
Free: (800)551-2523 **Fax:** (401)781-5340
Products: Paints; Varnishes; Auto parts, marine. **SIC:**
5198 (Paints, Varnishes & Supplies). **Est:** 1977. **Sales:**
$1,000,000 (1999). **Emp:** 5. **Officers:** Lionel Verrier,
President.

■ **21604** ■ **Carl Weissman & Sons Inc.**
PO Box 1609
Great Falls, MT 59403-1609
Phone: (406)761-4848
Free: (800)334-5964 **Fax:** (406)791-6731
E-mail: sales@weissman.com
URL: http://www.sales.weissman.com
Products: Paint and allied products; Varnishes;
Hardware; Steel; Plumbing fittings and brass goods;
Industrial supplies; PWF; Machinery. **SICs:** 5198
(Paints, Varnishes & Supplies); 5072 (Hardware); 5051
(Metals Service Centers & Offices). **Est:** 1915.
Officers: Jerrold Weissman, President.

■ **21605** ■ **Wellborn Paint Manufacturing Co.**
215 Rossmoor Rd. SW
Albuquerque, NM 87105
Phone: (505)877-5050 **Fax:** (505)982-3560
Products: Paint and paint equipment. **SIC:** 5198
(Paints, Varnishes & Supplies).

■ **21606** ■ **West Carpenter Paint & Flooring**
124 Hall St.
Concord, NH 03301-3442
Phone: (603)225-2832 **Fax:** (603)225-6590
Products: Paints; Floor coverings. **SIC:** 5198 (Paints,
Varnishes & Supplies). **Est:** 1870. **Sales:** $1,000,000
(2000). **Emp:** 6. **Officers:** George Katis, President.
Alternate Name: Carpenter & Wither Inc.

■ **21607** ■ **Westgate Fabrics Inc.**
PO Box 539503
Grand Prairie, TX 75050-9503
Phone: (972)647-2323
Free: (800)527-2517 **Fax:** (972)660-7096
Products: Full line of exclusive and open-line fabrics,
hand-screened wallpapers, exclusive trimmings,
furniture, and finials. **SICs:** 5198 (Paints, Varnishes &
Supplies); 5021 (Furniture); 5023 (Homefurnishings).
Sales: $20,000,000 (2000). **Emp:** 100. **Officers:** J. Jay
Cassen, President & COO; Chuck VanCleave, CFO.

■ **21608** ■ **Whisler Bearing Co.**
PO Box 1336
Rapid City, SD 57709-1336
Phone: (605)342-8822
Free: (800)843-4006 **Fax:** (605)342-5804
Products: Paints, varnishes, and supplies; Industrial
power transmissions. **SICs:** 5198 (Paints, Varnishes &
Supplies); 5084 (Industrial Machinery & Equipment).
Est: 1956. **Sales:** $5,000,000 (2000). **Emp:** 19.
Officers: Charles Whisler, Chairman of the Board.

■ **21609** ■ **Wholesale Paint Center, Inc.**
PO Box 1526
Rocky Mount, NC 27802-1526
Phone: (919)446-6045 **Fax:** (919)972-4724
Products: Paint and wallpaper. **SIC:** 5198 (Paints,
Varnishes & Supplies).

■ **21610** ■ **Williams Paint & Coatings**
7680 N Government Way
Coeur D Alene, ID 83814-8753
Phone: (208)772-6243 **Fax:** (208)772-9132
Products: Paints and allied products; Varnishes. **SIC:**
5198 (Paints, Varnishes & Supplies). **Officers:** Dennis
Williams, Owner.

■ **21611** ■ **Wiltech Corp.**
PO Box 517
Longview, WA 98632
Phone: (425)423-4990 **Fax:** (425)423-4730
Products: Paints and supplies. **SIC:** 5198 (Paints,
Varnishes & Supplies).

■ **21612** ■ **Young's: The Paint Place**
1421 W 2nd St.
Roswell, NM 88201
Phone: (505)622-3251
Products: Paint and paint supplies. **SIC:** 5198 (Paints,
Varnishes & Supplies).

■ **21613** ■ **William Zinsser & Co., Inc.**
173 Belmont Dr.
Somerset, NJ 08875-1218
Phone: (732)469-8100 **Fax:** (732)469-4539
Products: Paints and allied products. **SIC:** 5198
(Paints, Varnishes & Supplies). **Est:** 1849. **Emp:** 100.
Officers: Tom McNicholas, Sales/Marketing Contact;
Kevin Harrington, Customer Service Contact; Richard
Fulton, Human Resources Contact.

(40) Paper and Paper Products

Entries in this section are arranged alphabetically by company name. When the company name is a personal name, the company name is alphabetized by the surname unless the first name or initial(s) are part of a trade name. See the User's Guide at the front of this directory for additional information.

■ 21614 ■ **Ace Advance Paper Co.**
46 St. Claire Ave.
New Britain, CT 06051
Phone: (860)224-2485 **Fax:** (860)223-0678
Products: Paper and allied products; Paper towels; Paper cups; Napkins; Janitor's supplies. **SICs:** 5113 (Industrial & Personal Service Paper); 5087 (Service Establishment Equipment). **Est:** 1948. **Sales:** $1,500,000 (2000). **Emp:** 12. **Officers:** Zdenka Chrapek, President.

■ 21615 ■ **Acme Paper and Supply Company Inc.**
PO Box 422
Savage, MD 20763-0422
Phone: (410)792-2333
Products: Paper products for food service industry; Janitorial supplies. **SICs:** 5113 (Industrial & Personal Service Paper); 5087 (Service Establishment Equipment). **Sales:** $67,000,000 (2000). **Emp:** 125. **Officers:** Edward Attman, President.

■ 21616 ■ **Acorn Distributors Inc.**
5820 Fortune Cir. W
Indianapolis, IN 46241-5503
Phone: (317)924-6345
Free: (800)783-2446 **Fax:** (317)924-7946
Products: Paper and allied products; Janitors' supplies. **SICs:** 5113 (Industrial & Personal Service Paper); 5111 (Printing & Writing Paper); 5112 (Stationery & Office Supplies); 5087 (Service Establishment Equipment). **Est:** 1976.

■ 21617 ■ **Alaska Paper Co. Inc.**
PO Box 101977
Anchorage, AK 99510-1977
Phone: (907)274-6681 **Fax:** (907)258-4246
Products: Printing and writing paper; Industrial and janitorial supplies. **SICs:** 5111 (Printing & Writing Paper); 5085 (Industrial Supplies); 5087 (Service Establishment Equipment). **Officers:** Jim Wagner, President.

■ 21618 ■ **Albert Paper Co.**
PO Box 8630
Stockton, CA 95208
Phone: (209)466-7931
Free: (800)366-7931 **Fax:** (209)466-6516
Products: Paper products; Packaging materials; Janitorial products. **SICs:** 5113 (Industrial & Personal Service Paper); 5112 (Stationery & Office Supplies); 5111 (Printing & Writing Paper). **Est:** 1933. **Sales:** $6,000,000 (2000). **Emp:** 22. **Officers:** Peter G. Schmitz, President; Norm Gorley, Controller.

■ 21619 ■ **Albright Paper & Box Corp.**
14 Robison St.
Pottstown, PA 19464
Phone: (610)327-4990 **Fax:** (610)327-9480
Products: Paperboard boxes; Packaging. **SIC:** 5113 (Industrial & Personal Service Paper). **Est:** 1947. **Sales:** $2,500,000 (2000). **Emp:** 25. **Officers:** Gary R. Gross, President.

■ 21620 ■ **Alco Standard Corp.**
PO Box 834
Valley Forge, PA 19482-0834
Phone: (610)296-8000 **Fax:** (610)296-8419
Products: Paper office products and supplies; Industrial and fine printing paper. **SIC:** 5111 (Printing & Writing Paper). **Est:** 1952. **Sales:** $9,892,000,000 (2000). **Emp:** 36,500. **Officers:** John E. Stuart, CEO, President & Chairman of the Board; O. Gordon Brewer Jr., VP of Finance; David B. Kirkland, VP of Corp. Communications; Elisabeth H. Barrett, Dir. of Information Systems; Hugh G. Moulton, Exec. VP of Admin.

■ 21621 ■ **Aldine Technologies Industries, Inc.**
585 Industrial Rd.
Carlstadt, NJ 07072
Phone: (201)935-1110
Free: (888)820-8400 **Fax:** (201)935-5695
Products: Paper products, including specialty paper, industrial paper, lens tissue, wipers, filter media, and art restoration papers. **SIC:** 5113 (Industrial & Personal Service Paper). **Est:** 1937. **Emp:** 100. **Officers:** Peter J. Gould, President; Keith Schonbrun, Sales/Marketing Contact; Sylvia Attanasio, Customer Service Contact.

■ 21622 ■ **Alles Corp.**
177 Wells Ave.
Newton, MA 02459
Phone: (617)965-1800
Products: Packaging supplies, including staples and tape. **SIC:** 5113 (Industrial & Personal Service Paper). **Est:** 1940. **Sales:** $9,000,000 (2000). **Emp:** 49. **Officers:** Steve Berman, President; John N. Hynes, VP of Operations; Howard Snyder, VP of Sales.

■ 21623 ■ **Allied Boise Cascade**
1100 International Plz. S
Chesapeake, VA 23323
Phone: (757)485-1500
Products: Stationery. **SIC:** 5112 (Stationery & Office Supplies).

■ 21624 ■ **Allied Box Co.**
1931 Stout Field West Dr.
Indianapolis, IN 46241-4020
Phone: (317)352-0083
Products: Packing supplies, including corrugated boxes, packing paper, and tape. **SIC:** 5113 (Industrial & Personal Service Paper). **Est:** 1988. **Sales:** $2,000,000 (2000). **Emp:** 8. **Officers:** Sandy Hott, President.

■ 21625 ■ **Allied Container Corp.**
435 E Hedding St.
San Jose, CA 95112
Phone: (408)293-3628 **Fax:** (408)293-2014
Products: Packaging materials; Janitorial supplies. **SICs:** 5113 (Industrial & Personal Service Paper); 5169 (Chemicals & Allied Products Nec). **Est:** 1963. **Sales:** $5,000,000 (2000). **Emp:** 10. **Officers:** Evelynn Johnson, President.

■ 21626 ■ **Alpina International Inc.**
102 Madison Ave.
New York, NY 10016-7318
Phone: (212)683-3511 **Fax:** (212)683-3965
E-mail: info@alpina.net
URL: http://www.alpina.net
Products: Office equipment; Printing and writing paper; Printing machinery; Books. **SICs:** 5111 (Printing & Writing Paper); 5044 (Office Equipment); 5149 (Groceries & Related Products Nec). **Est:** 1981. **Emp:** 6. **Officers:** Harish Sawhney, President; Nev Sawhney, VP of Sales, e-mail: nev@alpina.net.

■ 21627 ■ **American Fibre Supplies, Inc.**
PO Box 4345
Portland, OR 97208
Phone: (503)292-1908 **Fax:** (503)292-2106
Products: Paper kraft linerboard. **SIC:** 5113 (Industrial & Personal Service Paper). **Est:** 1982. **Sales:** $40,000,000 (2000). **Emp:** 4. **Officers:** John C. Braestrup, President, e-mail: john@amfibre.com.

■ 21628 ■ **American Mail-Well Co.**
25 Linden Ave. E
Jersey City, NJ 07305
Phone: (201)434-2100 **Fax:** (201)434-8431
Products: Envelopes. **SIC:** 5112 (Stationery & Office Supplies). **Est:** 1907. **Sales:** $17,000,000 (2000). **Emp:** 160. **Officers:** Donald E. Riga, General Mgr.; Ernest Bassil, Controller; Warren Minsky, Dir. of Marketing.

■ 21629 ■ **American Paper Products Co.**
2113 E Rush St.
Philadelphia, PA 19134
Phone: (215)739-5718 **Fax:** (215)739-3019
Products: Paper tubes and cores. **SIC:** 5113 (Industrial & Personal Service Paper). **Est:** 1929. **Sales:** $10,000,000 (2000). **Emp:** 100. **Officers:** David Perelman, President; Ramon Gerber, Secretary.

■ 21630 ■ **American Paper Towel Co.**
145 Meyer St.
Hackensack, NJ 07602
Phone: (201)487-2500
Products: Paper towels, toilet tissue, soap, cleaning chemicals, plastic bags, and janitorial supplies. **SICs:** 5113 (Industrial & Personal Service Paper); 5122 (Drugs, Proprietaries & Sundries); 5087 (Service Establishment Equipment). **Sales:** $10,000,000 (2000). **Emp:** 45. **Officers:** Larry Shapiro, General Mgr.

■ 21631 ■ **American Paper and Twine Co.**
7400 Cockrill Bend Blvd.
Nashville, TN 37209-1047
Phone: (615)350-9000
Products: Office supplies, including fax paper; Packaging material, including freezer paper, boxes, and twine; Janitorial supplies. **SICs:** 5112 (Stationery & Office Supplies); 5113 (Industrial & Personal Service Paper); 5087 (Service Establishment Equipment); 5169 (Chemicals & Allied Products Nec). **Est:** 1926. **Sales:** $27,000,000 (2000). **Emp:** 81. **Officers:** R.S. Doochin, President; W.D. Morris, Treasurer.

■ 21632 ■ **American Renaissance Paper Corp.**
33 Rock Hill Rd.
BaLa Cynwyd, PA 19004
Phone: (610)668-7200
Free: (800)961-3388 **Fax:** (610)668-0719
Products: Fine recycled office paper and collector of paper for recycling. **SICs:** 5112 (Stationery & Office Supplies); 5093 (Scrap & Waste Materials). **Sales:** $7,000,000 (2000). **Emp:** 10. **Officers:** Peter McGrath, President; Robert Gruchacz, VP of Finance.

■ 21633 ■ **Anchor Paper Co.**
480 Broadway St.
St. Paul, MN 55101
Phone: (612)298-1311 **Fax:** (612)298-0060
Products: Paper products, including printing paper, cover stock, wrapping paper, envelopes, and photocopy paper; Tape. **SICs:** 5111 (Printing & Writing Paper); 5113 (Industrial & Personal Service Paper). **Est:** 1925. **Sales:** $38,000,000 (2000). **Emp:** 100. **Officers:** Hamel Hartinger, Owner; James P. Kemmer, CFO; Linda Hartinger, VP of Sales; Mike Hateletach.

■ 21634 ■ **Andrews Paper House of York Inc.**
351 East St.
PO Box 1227
York, PA 17405-1227
Phone: (717)846-8816
Free: (800)848-8816 **Fax:** (717)852-0078
E-mail: andrews@andrewspaper.com
URL: http://www.andrewspaper.com
Products: Stationary and office supplies; Computer paper; Paper and allied products. **SICs:** 5113 (Industrial & Personal Service Paper); 5111 (Printing & Writing Paper). **Est:** 1916. **Sales:** $3,000,000 (2000). **Emp:** 9. **Officers:** Kevin M. Gable, President, e-mail: kgable@andrewspaper.com; Patricia K. Strayer, Vice President; Amy S. Holland, Vice President, e-mail: aholand@andrewspaper.com; Stacy S. Myers, VP of Human Resources, e-mail: smyers@andrewspaper.com; T. Smith, Sales/Marketing Contact, e-mail: tsmith@andrewspaper.com.

■ 21635 ■ **A.W. Archer Company Inc.**
185 Glen Cove Ave.
Sea Cliff, NY 11579
Phone: (516)671-4100 **Fax:** (516)676-0567
Products: Packaging materials. **SIC:** 5113 (Industrial & Personal Service Paper). **Est:** 1923. **Sales:** $2,000,000 (2000). **Emp:** 3. **Officers:** Melvin E. Seddon, President.

■ 21636 ■ **Asbury Syrup and Paper Company Inc.**
904 Sunset Ave.
Asbury Park, NJ 07712
Phone: (732)774-5746
Products: Paper cups and dishes. **SIC:** 5113 (Industrial & Personal Service Paper). **Sales:** $800,000 (2000). **Emp:** 12. **Officers:** Kevin Latosky, President.

■ 21637 ■ **A.T. Clayton and Company Inc.**
2 Pickwick Plz.
Greenwich, CT 06830
Phone: (203)861-1190 **Fax:** (203)861-1170
Products: Printing paper used in magazines, catalogs, inserts, mailers and advertising. **SIC:** 5111 (Printing & Writing Paper). **Sales:** $300,000,000 (2000). **Emp:** 57. **Officers:** Mark Vallely Jr., President; Michael J. McLaughlin, CFO.

■ 21638 ■ **Atlanta Broom Company Inc.**
4750 Bakers Ferry Rd. SW
Atlanta, GA 30336
Phone: (404)696-4600
Free: (800)696-6919 **Fax:** (404)691-3183
Products: Paper and plastic products. **SICs:** 5113 (Industrial & Personal Service Paper); 5162 (Plastics Materials & Basic Shapes). **Est:** 1919. **Sales:** $20,000,000 (1999). **Emp:** 65. **Officers:** Herman Fishman, President; Steve Mote, General Mgr.; Brian Minnick, Sales Mgr.; David Spain, Corp. Secty.; Ella Raiden, Controller; Nina Whitfield, Credit Mgr.

■ 21639 ■ **Atlantic Corp.**
8400 Triad Dr.
Greensboro, NC 27409
Phone: (919)668-0081
Products: Packaging supplies, packaging equipment, industrial paperboard, SBS paperboard for packaging.

SICs: 5113 (Industrial & Personal Service Paper); 5111 (Printing & Writing Paper); 5112 (Stationery & Office Supplies). **Est:** 1946. **Sales:** $150,000,000 (2000). **Emp:** 350. **Officers:** Rusty Carter, CEO & President.
Former Name: Henley Paper Co.

■ 21640 ■ **Atlantic Paper & Twine Co. Inc.**
85 York Ave.
PO Box 443
Pawtucket, RI 02862
Phone: (401)725-0950
Free: (800)613-0950 **Fax:** (401)724-7840
E-mail: info@atlanticpaper.com
URL: http://www.atlanticpaper.com
Products: Special industrial paper; Twine; Maintenance brushes, including floor, scrub, dusting, and window; Janitorial supplies and equipment; Packaging and shipping room supplies; Printed boxes. **SIC:** 5113 (Industrial & Personal Service Paper). **Est:** 1948. **Emp:** 12. **Officers:** David Spencer Jr., President.

■ 21641 ■ **Autron Inc.**
5 Appleton St.
Holyoke, MA 01040
Phone: (413)535-4200
Free: (800)628-8812 **Fax:** (413)533-0513
URL: http://www.Autron.com
Products: Cash register rolls; ATM rolls; Fax rolls; Plotter and wide format rolls; Custom roll products. **SICs:** 5113 (Industrial & Personal Service Paper); 5112 (Stationery & Office Supplies); 5111 (Printing & Writing Paper). **Est:** 1924. **Emp:** 80. **Officers:** Dennis Pocius, Sales/Marketing Contact.

■ 21642 ■ **Autron Inc. Precision Rolls Division**
4205 McEwen Rd.
Farmers Branch, TX 75234
Phone: (214)630-1210
Free: (800)628-8812 **Fax:** (972)386-6411
URL: http://www.autron.com
Products: Paper and allied products; Paper business machine supplies; Computer paper; Stationery and office supplies. **SICs:** 5113 (Industrial & Personal Service Paper); 5112 (Stationery & Office Supplies); 5111 (Printing & Writing Paper).

■ 21643 ■ **B and B Paper Converters Inc.**
12500 Elmwood Ave.
Cleveland, OH 44111-5987
Phone: (216)941-8100 **Fax:** (216)941-8174
Products: Paperboard products. **SIC:** 5113 (Industrial & Personal Service Paper). **Sales:** $12,000,000 (1992). **Emp:** 23. **Officers:** J. Jazwa, President.

■ 21644 ■ **B & G Export Management Associates**
300 High St.
PO Box 71
Holyoke, MA 01041
Phone: (413)536-4565 **Fax:** (413)536-5249
Products: Converted paper; Stationery and office supplies. **SICs:** 5112 (Stationery & Office Supplies); 5113 (Industrial & Personal Service Paper). **Est:** 1974. **Emp:** 3. **Officers:** Gerry Grant, President; Tammy J. Tetreault, Office Mgr.

■ 21645 ■ **Baldwin Paper Co.**
161 Ave. of the Americas
New York, NY 10013
Phone: (212)255-1600 **Fax:** (212)463-7095
Products: Fine paper products. **SIC:** 5111 (Printing & Writing Paper). **Est:** 1921. **Sales:** $10,000,000 (2000). **Emp:** 65. **Officers:** Donald J. Heller, President; D. Romano, VP of Finance; John R. Buchanan III, Exec. VP.

■ 21646 ■ **Batliner Paper Stock Co.**
2501 Front St.
Kansas City, MO 64120
Phone: (816)483-3343
Products: Paper, including packaging and fine paper. **SICs:** 5093 (Scrap & Waste Materials); 5112 (Stationery & Office Supplies); 5113 (Industrial & Personal Service Paper). **Est:** 1920. **Sales:** $20,000,000 (2000). **Emp:** 55. **Officers:** William J. Batliner, CEO, President & Chairman of the Board; Rod Graves, Controller.

■ 21647 ■ **Baumann Paper Company Inc.**
PO Box 13022
Lexington, KY 40512
Phone: (859)252-8891
Free: (800)860-8891 **Fax:** (859)254-0578
URL: http://www.baumannpaper.com
Products: Industrial paper goods and janitorial chemicals. **SICs:** 5113 (Industrial & Personal Service Paper); 5087 (Service Establishment Equipment). **Est:** 1950. **Sales:** $14,000,000 (2000). **Emp:** 49. **Officers:** F.W. Baumann Jr., President, e-mail: fbaumann@mis.net.

■ 21648 ■ **BCT International Inc.**
3000 Northeast 30th Place, 5th Fl.
Ft. Lauderdale, FL 33306
Phone: (954)563-1224 **Fax:** (954)565-0742
Products: Printing paper. **SIC:** 5111 (Printing & Writing Paper). **Sales:** $17,800,000 (2000). **Emp:** 90. **Officers:** James H. Kaufenberg, CEO & President; Michael R. Hull, CFO & Treasurer.

■ 21649 ■ **Beck Packaging Corp.**
PO Box 20250
Lehigh Valley, PA 18002-0250
Phone: (610)264-0551
Free: (800)722-2325 **Fax:** (610)264-7465
E-mail: priority@backpack.com
Products: Industrial packaging material and equipment, including cartons, tape, strapping, stretch film, poly bags and tubes, shipping room supplies, foam cushioning, void fill, clipboard, and tissue. **SIC:** 5113 (Industrial & Personal Service Paper). **Est:** 1970. **Sales:** $6,000,000 (2000). **Emp:** 30. **Officers:** David E. Friedrich, President.

■ 21650 ■ **Beisler Weidmann Company Inc.**
233 Cortlandt St.
Belleville, NJ 07109
Phone: (973)759-5020 **Fax:** (973)759-2754
Products: Corrugated paper; Janitorial supplies. **SICs:** 5113 (Industrial & Personal Service Paper); 5087 (Service Establishment Equipment). **Est:** 1921. **Sales:** $4,000,000 (2000). **Emp:** 14. **Officers:** Warren E. Beisler, President; John H. Weidmann, Vice President.

■ 21651 ■ **Bell Paper Products Co.**
1001 D Nicholas Blvd.
Elk Grove Village, IL 60007-2581
Phone: (847)640-1310 **Fax:** (847)640-1325
Products: Paper goods or products, including book mailers. **SICs:** 5113 (Industrial & Personal Service Paper); 5112 (Stationery & Office Supplies); 5111 (Printing & Writing Paper). **Est:** 1945. **Emp:** 2. **Officers:** James R. Glass III.

■ 21652 ■ **Ben-Mar Paper Co. Inc.**
PO Box 250304
Montgomery, AL 36125
Phone: (205)263-4448 **Fax:** (205)263-4860
Products: Paper products, including napkins, paper towels, craft paper, and copy paper; Janitorial supplies. **SICs:** 5113 (Industrial & Personal Service Paper); 5087 (Service Establishment Equipment). **Est:** 1959. **Sales:** $5,000,000 (2000). **Emp:** 30. **Officers:** Michael A. Greenblatt, President; Richard Kennedy, Sales Mgr.; Velma Bailey, Manager; Henry Williams, Dir of Human Resources.

■ 21653 ■ **H.T. Berry Company Inc.**
50 North St.
Canton, MA 02021-3356
Phone: (781)828-6000 **Fax:** (781)828-9788
Products: Paper and allied products; Plastics. **SICs:** 5113 (Industrial & Personal Service Paper); 5111 (Printing & Writing Paper). **Est:** 1964. **Sales:** $12,000,000 (2000). **Emp:** 40. **Officers:** Henry T. Berry, President.

■ 21654 ■ **Borden & Riley Paper Co.**
184-10 Jamaica Ave.
Hollis, NY 11423
Phone: (718)454-0791
Free: (800)221-1416 **Fax:** (718)454-9494
E-mail: woodward4@aol.com
URL: http://www.artproducts.com/borden
Products: Paper. **SICs:** 5113 (Industrial & Personal Service Paper); 5111 (Printing & Writing Paper); 5112 (Stationery & Office Supplies). **Est:** 1910. **Sales:**

$3,000,000 (2000). **Emp:** 15. **Officers:** Zoila P. Woodward, President; Juan Guerra, Vice President; Juan Guerra, Vice President; Nick Cedeno, Sales and Marketing.

■ 21655 ■ **The Box Maker**
6412 S 190th St.
Kent, WA 98032
Phone: (425)251-9892
Free: (800)443-5431 **Fax:** (425)251-1484
Products: Packaging; Boxes and crates. **SIC:** 5113 (Industrial & Personal Service Paper). **Est:** 1980. **Emp:** 140. **Officers:** David Hill, President; Tom Bareuther, Sales/Marketing Contact; Mary Harper, Customer Service Contact. **Former Name:** Todd-Zenner Packaging.

■ 21656 ■ **Bradner Central Co.**
333 S Des Plaines St.
Chicago, IL 60661-5596
Phone: (312)454-1852 **Fax:** (312)454-0783
Products: Writing paper and printing paper. **SIC:** 5111 (Printing & Writing Paper). **Est:** 1852. **Sales:** $400,000,000 (2000). **Emp:** 194. **Officers:** Harry C. Bull, CEO & Chairman of the Board; Bernard Tarte Jr., VP & Treasurer.

■ 21657 ■ **Bro Tex Company Inc., Wiping Cloth Div.**
800 Hampden Ave.
St. Paul, MN 55114
Phone: (651)645-5721
Free: (800)328-2282 **Fax:** (651)646-1876
E-mail: info@brotex.com
URL: http://www.brotex.com
Products: Paper goods and products; Wiping rags and cloths, including washing and conditioning; Janitorial and industrial sorbents. **SICs:** 5113 (Industrial & Personal Service Paper); 5131 (Piece Goods & Notions). **Est:** 1923. **Emp:** 90. **Officers:** Roger Greenberg, President; Edwin Freeman, General Mgr.; Erwin Rendall, Dir. of Marketing; Arlys Freeman, Vice President.

■ 21658 ■ **Bunzl Distribution Inc.**
701 Emerson Rd., No. 500
St. Louis, MO 63141
Phone: (314)997-5959
Free: (800)997-4515 **Fax:** (314)997-0247
E-mail: marketingservices@bunzlusa.com
URL: http://www.bunzldistribution.com
Products: Paper products, including towels, tissue, plates, and cups; Foil pans. **SIC:** 5113 (Industrial & Personal Service Paper). **Est:** 1932. **Sales:** $1,950,000,000 (1999). **Emp:** 2,500. **Officers:** Paul Lorenzini, President & COO; Pat Larmon, VP of Finance & Admin.; Pat Oliverio, Exec. VP; Paul Scotti, VP of Marketing, e-mail: pscotti@bunzlusa.com; Bob Cauffman, Exec. VP, National Accounts; Mark Brasher, President, East Div.; Jeff Earnhart, President, Central Div.; Terry Frack, President, West Div. **Former Name:** Bunzl Distribution USA.

■ 21659 ■ **Bunzl New Jersey Inc.**
PO Box 668
Dayton, NJ 08810-0668
Phone: (732)821-7000
Products: Folding paperboard boxes. **SIC:** 5113 (Industrial & Personal Service Paper). **Sales:** $80,000,000 (2000). **Emp:** 250. **Officers:** Mark Brasher, Manager; Dennis Mette, Controller.

■ 21660 ■ **Business Cards Tomorrow Inc.**
3000 NE 30th Pl., 5th Fl.
Ft. Lauderdale, FL 33306
Phone: (954)563-1224
Free: (800)627-9998 **Fax:** (954)565-0742
E-mail: info@bctonline.com
URL: http://www.bctonline.com
Products: Stationary; Thermography; Stamps; Labels; Internet ordering solutions. **SIC:** 5111 (Printing & Writing Paper). **Est:** 1975. **Sales:** $110,000,000 (2000). **Emp:** 1,500. **Officers:** Peter Gaughn, President & COO; Michael R. Hull, CFO & Treasurer.

■ 21661 ■ **Butler-Dearden Paper Service Inc.**
80 Shrewsbury St.
Boylston, MA 01505
Phone: (508)869-9000
Free: (800)662-1989 **Fax:** (508)869-0211
E-mail: bdpaper@ma.ultranet.com
URL: http://www.bdpaper.com
Products: Industrial cleaning chemicals; Paper and allied products. **SICs:** 5111 (Printing & Writing Paper); 5169 (Chemicals & Allied Products Nec); 5112 (Stationery & Office Supplies); 5113 (Industrial & Personal Service Paper). **Est:** 1882. **Sales:** $8,500,000 (2000). **Emp:** 26. **Officers:** George S. Butler, President; David S. Butler, Vice President; Austin L. Brainerd, Vice President.

■ 21662 ■ **Butler Paper Co.**
12601 E 38th Ave.
Denver, CO 80239-3408
Phone: (303)790-8343 **Fax:** (303)799-7493
Products: Paper, including writing and toilet paper. **SICs:** 5111 (Printing & Writing Paper); 5112 (Stationery & Office Supplies); 5113 (Industrial & Personal Service Paper). **Est:** 1980. **Sales:** $1,200,000,000 (2000). **Emp:** 6,000. **Officers:** Bruce Williams, President; Ken Siefken, Exec. VP & CFO; Glenn Barton, VP of Marketing; Bill Weart, Dir. of Systems; Timothy Sparks, Dir of Human Resources.

■ 21663 ■ **C-N Corrugated and Sheeting Inc.**
PO Box 23570
Louisville, KY 40223
Phone: (502)244-5333
Products: Cardboard and corrugated cardboard. **SIC:** 5113 (Industrial & Personal Service Paper). **Est:** 1981. **Sales:** $2,500,000 (2000). **Emp:** 10. **Officers:** Matt Kousmeier, President.

■ 21664 ■ **Cady Industries Inc.**
PO Box 15085
Tampa, FL 33684
Phone: (813)876-2474 **Fax:** (813)870-3968
Products: Multiwall paper bags, woven polypropylene bags, and burlap bags; Wire baskets; Nursery supplies. **SICs:** 5113 (Industrial & Personal Service Paper); 5199 (Nondurable Goods Nec). **Officers:** Dee Sanders, Manager. **Former Name:** Ricketts Bag Corporation.

■ 21665 ■ **Camden Bag and Paper Company, Inc.**
114 Gaither Dr.
Mt. Laurel, NJ 08054-1702
Phone: (856)727-3313 **Fax:** (856)727-4110
E-mail: cambag@visi-net.com
Products: Paper goods; Industrial packaging; Janitorial supplies; Food service disposables; Bakery supplies. **SIC:** 5113 (Industrial & Personal Service Paper). **Est:** 1932. **Sales:** $7,000,000 (2000). **Emp:** 30. **Officers:** R Gerber, Owner.

■ 21666 ■ **Capital Paper Company Div.**
315 Park Ave. S, 18th Fl.
New York, NY 10010-3607
Phone: (212)505-1000 **Fax:** (212)505-7559
Products: Printing and copying paper. **SIC:** 5111 (Printing & Writing Paper). **Est:** 1919. **Sales:** $18,000,000 (2000). **Emp:** 10. **Officers:** Carl R. Meisel, President; Harry Clark, Controller.

■ 21667 ■ **Capstone Paper Co.**
1464 Old Country Rd.
Plainview, NY 11803
Phone: (516)752-4242 **Fax:** (516)752-4245
Products: Printing paper. **SICs:** 5111 (Printing & Writing Paper); 5112 (Stationery & Office Supplies). **Est:** 1952. **Sales:** $600,000,000 (2000). **Emp:** 5. **Officers:** Arnold Colton, Owner.

■ 21668 ■ **Carleton Oil Company Inc.**
PO Box 220
Union, MS 39365
Phone: (601)774-9205
Products: Packaging products. **SIC:** 5172 (Petroleum Products Nec). **Est:** 1940. **Sales:** $2,000,000 (2000). **Emp:** 10. **Officers:** Harold G. Carleton, President.

■ 21669 ■ **Carolina Pad and Paper Co.**
PO Box 7525
Charlotte, NC 28241
Phone: (704)588-3190 **Fax:** (704)588-1123
URL: http://www.carolinapad.com
Products: Writing paper. **SIC:** 5111 (Printing & Writing Paper). **Est:** 1945. **Sales:** $30,000 (2000). **Emp:** 100. **Officers:** Joseph K. Hall III, Chairman of the Board; Mark W. Howell, CFO; W. Clay Presley, President.

■ 21670 ■ **Carolina Retail Packaging Inc.**
138 Zenker Rd.
Lexington, SC 29072
Phone: (803)359-0036
Free: (800)868-5878 **Fax:** (803)359-7746
URL: http://www.carolinaretail.com
Products: Gift wrap paper; Ribbons for gifts; Packaging; Bags; Boxes; Store fixtures. **SIC:** 5113 (Industrial & Personal Service Paper). **Est:** 1973. **Sales:** $6,600,000 (2000). **Emp:** 49. **Officers:** Dennis Egan, Vice President; Tom Burbage, President, e-mail: tburbage@carolinaretail.com.

■ 21671 ■ **Carpenter Paper Co.**
PO Box 2709
Grand Rapids, MI 49501
Phone: (616)452-9741 **Fax:** (616)452-3740
Products: Paper. **SICs:** 5111 (Printing & Writing Paper); 5112 (Stationery & Office Supplies). **Est:** 1909. **Sales:** $50,000,000 (2000). **Emp:** 115. **Officers:** James Holtsclaw, President; Frank Geary, CFO.

■ 21672 ■ **Carter Paper Co.**
136 Wayside Ave.
PO Box 315
West Springfield, MA 01090-0315
Phone: (413)785-1961 **Fax:** (413)731-9960
Products: Paper; Packaging products, including corrugated supplies, steel and plastic strapping, tapes, and bubble-wrap. **SICs:** 5113 (Industrial & Personal Service Paper); 5111 (Printing & Writing Paper); 5112 (Stationery & Office Supplies). **Est:** 1937. **Sales:** $4,000,000 (2000). **Emp:** 15. **Officers:** Barry M. Beckwith, President & Chairman; Raymond H. Roy, Vice President; David A. Bennett, Assistant Treasurer.

■ 21673 ■ **Carter Paper and Packaging Inc.**
PO Box 1349
Peoria, IL 61654-1349
Phone: (309)637-7711 **Fax:** (309)637-7748
E-mail: carter2@mail.iaonline.com
Products: Paper products, including toilet paper and paper towels; Packaging materials. **SICs:** 5112 (Stationery & Office Supplies); 5113 (Industrial & Personal Service Paper). **Est:** 1954. **Sales:** $11,000,000 (2000). **Emp:** 18. **Officers:** Billie H. Carter, President; Michael C. Rettke, Treasurer & Secty.; Roger L. Knaggs, Exec. VP of Marketing.

■ 21674 ■ **Case Paper Co.**
23-30 Borden Ave.
Long Island City, NY 11101
Phone: (718)361-9000 **Fax:** (718)361-9068
Products: Paper for printers. **SIC:** 5111 (Printing & Writing Paper). **Est:** 1945. **Sales:** $15,000,000 (2000). **Emp:** 175. **Officers:** Peter Schaffer, President; Frank Sabino, CFO; Eugene Goldberg, VP of Sales; Joseph Lepore, VP of Data Processing.

■ 21675 ■ **Central National-Gottesman Inc.**
3 Manhattanville Rd.
Purchase, NY 10577-2110
Phone: (914)696-9000 **Fax:** (914)696-1066
Products: Industrial and personal service paper. **SIC:** 5113 (Industrial & Personal Service Paper). **Sales:** $2,000,000,000 (2000). **Emp:** 900. **Officers:** Kenneth L. Wallach, CEO & President; Joshua Eisenstein, Treasurer.

■ 21676 ■ **Central Paper Products Co. Inc.**
Brown Ave. Industrial Park
PO Box 4480
Manchester, NH 03108
Phone: (603)624-4064
Free: (800)339-4065 **Fax:** (603)624-8795
URL: http://www.centralpaper.com
Products: Paper products; Plastics; Janitorial supplies. **SICs:** 5113 (Industrial & Personal Service Paper); 5087 (Service Establishment Equipment). **Est:** 1948. **Emp:**

45. **Officers:** Fred B. Kfoury Jr., President; Edmund A. Bednarowski, VP of Marketing & Sales, e-mail: ebed@centralpaper.com; David Martineau, Sales Mgr.; Matt Kfoury, Operations Mgr., e-mail: mkfoury@centralpaper.com; Frank Albrizio, Human Resources Contact, e-mail: falbrizio@centralpaper.com.

■ 21677 ■ **Chess Business Forms Co.**
25 Burnside St.
PO Box 436
Nashua, NH 03061-0436
Phone: (603)889-1786 **Fax:** (603)889-1786
Products: Printed forms; Office supplies. **SIC:** 5111 (Printing & Writing Paper). **Est:** 1978. **Sales:** $80,000 (2000). **Emp:** 2. **Officers:** Chesley Layne, Partner, e-mail: chetlayne@aol.com; Geraldine Layne, President.

■ 21678 ■ **Chris Cam Corp.**
808 W Cherokee St.
Sioux Falls, SD 57104
Phone: (605)336-1190 **Fax:** (605)332-8378
Products: Paper products. **SICs:** 5111 (Printing & Writing Paper); 5113 (Industrial & Personal Service Paper). **Sales:** $32,000,000 (1994). **Emp:** 145. **Officers:** Dempster Christenson, CEO; Bryan Thill, Accountant.

■ 21679 ■ **Cincinnati Cordage and Paper Co.**
PO Box 17125
800 E Ross Ave.
Cincinnati, OH 45217
Phone: (513)242-3600
Free: (800)331-0263 **Fax:** (513)242-0836
URL: http://www.cordage.com
Products: Paper products, including paper towel and toilet paper; Industrial packaging. **SICs:** 5113 (Industrial & Personal Service Paper); 5111 (Printing & Writing Paper). **Est:** 1892. **Sales:** $150,000,000 (2000). **Emp:** 210. **Officers:** Lawrence A. Bresko, President; Chuck Johansen, VP of Operations.

■ 21680 ■ **Cincinnati Cordage and Paper Co. Cordage Papers Cleveland Div.**
5370 Naiman Pkwy.
Solon, OH 44139-1086
Phone: (216)349-1231 **Fax:** (216)349-3367
Products: Fine and printing paper and paper products. **SIC:** 5111 (Printing & Writing Paper). **Est:** 1892. **Sales:** $25,000,000 (2000). **Emp:** 40. **Officers:** Daniel T. Mooers, General Mgr.

■ 21681 ■ **Clampitt Paper Co.**
9207 Ambassador Row
Dallas, TX 75247
Phone: (214)638-3300
Products: Printing paper. **SIC:** 5111 (Printing & Writing Paper). **Est:** 1940. **Emp:** 78. **Officers:** Don Clampitt, President; Gary Martin, CFO; Don Clampitt, VP of Marketing.

■ 21682 ■ **C.M. Paula Co.**
6049 HiTech Ct.
Mason, OH 45040
Phone: (513)336-3100
Products: Stationery and giftware. **SICs:** 5112 (Stationery & Office Supplies); 5199 (Nondurable Goods Nec). **Sales:** $55,000,000 (2000). **Emp:** 200. **Officers:** Charles W. McCullough, President; Richard Dickerson, Treasurer.

■ 21683 ■ **Coast Paper Box Co.**
4650 Ardine St.
Cudahy, CA 90201
Phone: (213)771-8772 **Fax:** (213)771-1671
Products: Boxes and crates; Paperboard boxes; Corrugated and solid fiber boxes. **SIC:** 5113 (Industrial & Personal Service Paper). **Est:** 1920. **Sales:** $2,500,000 (2000). **Emp:** 44. **Officers:** Chester Marcell Jr., President; Carl A. Lorenzen, Secretary; Mary Marcell, Treasurer.

■ 21684 ■ **Cocoa Brevard Paper Co.**
105 Forrest Ave.
Cocoa, FL 32922
Phone: (407)632-8200 **Fax:** (407)632-0420
Products: Paper products; Janitorial supplies. **SIC:** 5113 (Industrial & Personal Service Paper). **Est:** 1960. **Sales:** $4,900,000 (2000). **Emp:** 25. **Officers:** V.H. Davis, President; Jack E. Sampley, Vice President.

■ 21685 ■ **Cole Papers Inc.**
PO Box 2967
1300 38th St NW
Fargo, ND 58108-2967
Phone: (701)282-5311
Free: (800)800-8090 **Fax:** (701)282-5513
URL: http://www.colepapers.com
Products: Printing and writing paper; Industrial papers and packaging; Janitorial supplies and equipment; Floor covering products. **SIC:** 5111 (Printing & Writing Paper). **Est:** 1918. **Emp:** 160. **Officers:** Chuck Perkins, President.

■ 21686 ■ **Colony Papers Inc.**
1776 Stanley Dr.
York, PA 17404
Phone: (717)764-5088 **Fax:** (717)764-5567
Products: Paper products; Packaging. **SIC:** 5113 (Industrial & Personal Service Paper). **Est:** 1964. **Emp:** 41. **Officers:** N.M. Callahan Jr., CEO; F.B. Callahan; Richard J. Manning, Vice President; Thomas S. Corse.

■ 21687 ■ **Columbia Jobbing Co. Inc.**
1702 5th Ave.
Tampa, FL 33605-5116
Phone: (813)248-4142 **Fax:** (813)247-7526
Products: Paper products. **SIC:** 5112 (Stationery & Office Supplies). **Est:** 1941. **Emp:** 19. **Officers:** Nelson Lazzara.

■ 21688 ■ **Commerce Packaging Corp.**
850 Canal St.
Stamford, CT 06904
Phone: (203)327-4200 **Fax:** (203)327-4711
Products: Packaging materials; Wood crates. **SIC:** 5113 (Industrial & Personal Service Paper). **Est:** 1954. **Sales:** $6,000,000 (1999). **Emp:** 50. **Officers:** Stuart Alexander, President.

■ 21689 ■ **M. Conley Company Inc.**
1312 4th St. SE
Canton, OH 44701
Phone: (216)456-8243
Products: Paper and packaging products. **SIC:** 5113 (Industrial & Personal Service Paper). **Est:** 1910. **Sales:** $40,000,000 (2000). **Emp:** 100. **Officers:** Richard D. Conley, President; Doug Marianek, Controller; Jim Haupt, Dir. of Marketing & Sales.

■ 21690 ■ **Convermat Corp.**
45 N Station Plz, Ste. 400
Great Neck, NY 11021-5011
Phone: (516)487-7100 **Fax:** (516)487-7170
E-mail: convermat@convermat.com
URL: http://www.convermat.com
Products: Jumbo roll tissue. **SIC:** 5113 (Industrial & Personal Service Paper). **Est:** 1976. **Sales:** $116,000,000 (2000). **Emp:** 22. **Officers:** Shaw Shahery, President; Frank Shahery, Vice President.

■ 21691 ■ **Cornelius Printed Products**
2700 E 55th Pl.
Indianapolis, IN 46220-3545
Phone: (317)251-8990 **Fax:** (317)251-8992
E-mail: cpp@corneliusprint.com
Products: Business forms, ad specialities, labels. **SIC:** 5112 (Stationery & Office Supplies). **Sales:** $1,000,000 (2000). **Emp:** 4. **Officers:** D.J. Cornelius, President. **Former Name:** Cornelius Business Forms, Inc.

■ 21692 ■ **Coronet Paper Corp.**
484 Washington Ave.
Carlstadt, NJ 07072
Phone: (201)933-5400
Free: (800)526-9028 **Fax:** (201)933-0645
Products: Paper. **SIC:** 5111 (Printing & Writing Paper). **Est:** 1951. **Emp:** 20. **Officers:** A. A. Sobel, President; S. C. Sobel, Vice President.

■ 21693 ■ **Coronet Paper Products**
3200 NW 119th St.
Miami, FL 33167-2925
Phone: (305)688-6601 **Fax:** (305)688-7228
Products: Printing paper. **SIC:** 5111 (Printing & Writing Paper).

■ 21694 ■ **Cottingham Paper Co.**
PO Box 163579
Columbus, OH 43216
Phone: (614)294-6444 **Fax:** (614)294-5785
Products: Disposable paper; Janitorial products, including cleaning agents and floor machines. **SIC:** 5113 (Industrial & Personal Service Paper). **Est:** 1932. **Sales:** $30,000,000 (2000). **Emp:** 90. **Officers:** Richard S. Cottingham, President; Marybeth Willis, CFO; Shelia Cottingham, Dir of Human Resources; Craig Cottingham, VP of Sales; John Shalvoy, Sales Mgr.

■ 21695 ■ **Cox Paper & Printing Co.**
1160 Carter Rd.
Owensboro, KY 42301
Phone: (270)684-1436
Free: (800)467-0436 **Fax:** (270)684-2750
E-mail: jimg@coxpaper.com
URL: http://www.coxpaper.com
Products: Paper and allied products. **SICs:** 5113 (Industrial & Personal Service Paper); 5111 (Printing & Writing Paper); 5112 (Stationery & Office Supplies). **Est:** 1946. **Sales:** $2,750,000 (2000). **Emp:** 30. **Officers:** Robert Gant, President; Mary Gant, CEO.

■ 21696 ■ **Crescent Paper Co.**
1940 W Oliver Ave.
PO Box 1983
Indianapolis, IN 46221
Phone: (317)236-6900
Free: (800)669-9986 **Fax:** (317)236-6911
Products: Paper and allied products. **SICs:** 5113 (Industrial & Personal Service Paper); 5111 (Printing & Writing Paper); 5112 (Stationery & Office Supplies). **Est:** 1896. **Sales:** $40,000,000 (2000). **Emp:** 60. **Officers:** Jack Bryant, President.

■ 21697 ■ **Crest Paper Products Inc.**
457 Mulberry St.
Trenton, NJ 08638
Phone: (609)394-5357 **Fax:** (609)394-3046
E-mail: crestapc@crestpaper.com
URL: http://www.crestpaper.com
Products: Food service and custodial paper products. **SIC:** 5113 (Industrial & Personal Service Paper). **Est:** 1953. **Sales:** $11,000,000 (1999). **Emp:** 45. **Officers:** Paul F. DiManno, President; F. P. DiManno, VP & Treasurer; M. L. DiManno, Secretary.

■ 21698 ■ **Crown Products Co.**
450 Nepperhan Ave.
Yonkers, NY 10701
Phone: (914)968-2222
Free: (800)431-1745 **Fax:** (914)968-0029
E-mail: info@crownproducts.com
URL: http://www.crownproducts.com
Products: Packaging, janitorial, and material handling supplies, systems, equipment, and repair service. **SIC:** 5113 (Industrial & Personal Service Paper). **Est:** 1919. **Sales:** $11,000,000 (1999). **Emp:** 40. **Officers:** Peter Mollo, President; Dave Isaacs, Sales Mgr.; Ainsworth McFarlane, Dir. of Operations; David Isaacs, Sales/Marketing Contact, e-mail: David@crownproducts.com; Elias Maksoud, Human Resources Contact, e-mail: Elias@crownproducts.com.

■ 21699 ■ **Dacotah Paper Co.**
3940 15th NW
Fargo, ND 58108
Phone: (701)281-1730
Free: (800)323-7583 **Fax:** (701)281-0446
E-mail: dacotah@rrnet.com
URL: http://www.dacotahpaper.com
Products: Cleaning solvents; Toilet paper, paper towels, and tissues; Waxes. **SICs:** 5113 (Industrial & Personal Service Paper); 5169 (Chemicals & Allied Products Nec). **Est:** 1906. **Emp:** 115.

■ 21700 ■ **Danforth International Trade Associates, Inc.**
3156 Route 88
Point Pleasant, NJ 08742
Phone: (732)892-4454 **Fax:** (732)892-1421
E-mail: danforth@mail.monmouth.com
Products: Specialty paper; Printing paper. **SICs:** 5111 (Printing & Writing Paper); 5113 (Industrial & Personal Service Paper). **Officers:** Frank Riccio Jr., President.

■ 21701 ■   J.L. Darling Corp.
2614 Pacific Hwy. E
Tacoma, WA 98424-1017
Phone: (253)922-5000   **Fax:** (253)922-5300
E-mail: sales@riteintherain.com
URL: http://www.riteintherain.com
Products: Printing and all-weather paper; Field books.
SICs: 5111 (Printing & Writing Paper); 5112 (Stationery & Office Supplies). **Est:** 1955. **Sales:** $3,600,000 (2000). **Emp:** 24. **Officers:** Scott E. Silver, President; Linda Crain, Finance Officer; Todd Silver, VP of Marketing. **Alternate Name:** Rite in the Rain Paper. **Alternate Name:** Polytag Paper.

■ 21702 ■   Data Forms Inc.
PO Box 1050
Fayetteville, AR 72701
Phone: (501)443-0099   **Fax:** (501)443-1418
Products: Business forms. **SICs:** 5112 (Stationery & Office Supplies); 5045 (Computers, Peripherals & Software); 5065 (Electronic Parts & Equipment Nec). **Est:** 1982. **Sales:** $4,000,000 (2000). **Emp:** 20. **Officers:** Michael Emis, President.

■ 21703 ■   Data Papers Inc.
PO Box 149
Muncy, PA 17756
Phone: (717)546-2201   **Fax:** 888-546-2366
Products: Business forms. **SIC:** 5112 (Stationery & Office Supplies). **Est:** 1969. **Sales:** $25,000,000 (2000). **Emp:** 150. **Officers:** Gene Crawford, President; Rodger L. Melvin, VP of Finance; Nelson Crawford, VP of Marketing.

■ 21704 ■   Data Print Inc.
4810 N Lagoon Ave., Ste. 300
Portland, OR 97217-7665
Products: Business forms, including inventory lists and sales slips. **SIC:** 5112 (Stationery & Office Supplies). **Est:** 1971. **Sales:** $5,000,000 (2000). **Emp:** 25. **Officers:** Anne Marie Zinzer, President.

■ 21705 ■   DeHater
3201 N Main
East Peoria, IL 61611-1718
Phone: (309)694-2083   **Free:** (800)322-2624
Products: Paper towels; Paper dishes; Paper cups; Tissue paper and other machine creped paper. **SIC:** 5113 (Industrial & Personal Service Paper). **Emp:** 49.

■ 21706 ■   Dennis Paper Co. Inc.
1940 Elm Tree Dr.
Nashville, TN 37210
Phone: (615)883-9010
Products: Fine paper. **SIC:** 5111 (Printing & Writing Paper). **Est:** 1969. **Emp:** 41. **Officers:** M. Dennis, President.

■ 21707 ■   Diamond Paper Corp.
PO Box 7000
Sterling, VA 20167-1049
Phone: (703)450-0000   **Fax:** (703)450-0001
Products: Copying and fax paper. **SICs:** 5111 (Printing & Writing Paper); 5112 (Stationery & Office Supplies). **Est:** 1971. **Sales:** $15,000,000 (2000). **Emp:** 70. **Officers:** Alison D. Diamond, President; Paul Diamond, CFO.

■ 21708 ■   Dibs Chemical & Supply Co. Inc.
205 Courthouse Rd.
Gulfport, MS 39507-1215
Phone: (228)896-7811   **Fax:** (228)896-1550
Products: Paper goods and products; Janitor's supplies; Chemical preparations; Cups; Disinfection equipment; Paper towels; Pool equipment and supplies; Sanitary femenine products; Toilet paper and sanitary tissue products; Soaps and detergents. **SICs:** 5113 (Industrial & Personal Service Paper); 5169 (Chemicals & Allied Products Nec); 5087 (Service Establishment Equipment); 5085 (Industrial Supplies); 5091 (Sporting & Recreational Goods). **Est:** 1969. **Sales:** $1,400,000 (2000). **Emp:** 18. **Officers:** Irene Audenaert.

■ 21709 ■   Dillard Paper Co. Birmingham Div.
PO Box 11367
Birmingham, AL 35202
Phone: (205)798-8380   **Fax:** (205)791-2661
Products: Industrial paper and printing paper. **SICs:**
5113 (Industrial & Personal Service Paper); 5111 (Printing & Writing Paper). **Sales:** $10,000,000 (2000). **Emp:** 47. **Officers:** Bill Gravely, General Mgr.

■ 21710 ■   Dillard Paper Co. Chattanooga Div.
PO Box 1567
Chattanooga, TN 37401-1567
Phone: (615)698-8111
Products: Paper products and janitors' supplies. **SICs:** 5111 (Printing & Writing Paper); 5113 (Industrial & Personal Service Paper); 5087 (Service Establishment Equipment). **Sales:** $16,000,000 (2000). **Emp:** 45. **Officers:** Steve Broughman, VP & General Merchandising Mgr.; Margaret Manning, Bookkeeper.

■ 21711 ■   Dillard Paper Co. Knoxville Div.
PO Box 50008
Knoxville, TN 37950-0008
Phone: (615)584-5741
Products: Paper, including toilet paper. **SIC:** 5113 (Industrial & Personal Service Paper). **Est:** 1950. **Sales:** $15,000,000 (2000). **Emp:** 61. **Officers:** Gene Russell, VP & General Merchandising Mgr.; Dorothy Davis, Manager; Judy Westenhaver, Dir. of Sales; Sherry Townsend, Dir. of Data Processing; Miranda B. Rogers, Dir of Human Resources.

■ 21712 ■   Dillard Paper Co. Macon Div.
3115 Hillcrest Ave.
Macon, GA 31204
Phone: (912)746-8501   **Fax:** (912)743-2174
Products: Paper and janitorial products. **SIC:** 5113 (Industrial & Personal Service Paper). **Sales:** $10,000,000 (2000). **Emp:** 31. **Officers:** Michael W. Hildebrand, General Mgr.

■ 21713 ■   Direct Way Distributors Inc.
12 Acme Rd., No. 215
Brewer, ME 04412
Phone: (207)989-2162
Products: Paper products. **SIC:** 5111 (Printing & Writing Paper).

■ 21714 ■   Douron Inc.
30 New Plant Ct.
Owings Mills, MD 21117
Phone: (410)363-2600
Free: (800)533-1296   **Fax:** (410)363-1659
E-mail: solutions@douron.com
URL: http://www.douron.com
Products: Stationery and office furniture. **SICs:** 5112 (Stationery & Office Supplies); 5021 (Furniture). **Est:** 1969. **Sales:** $30,000,000 (1999). **Emp:** 102. **Officers:** Eugene L. Hux, CEO; Ronald W. Hux, President; Bryan Simmons, Exec. VP; Frank Clark, VP of Sales.

■ 21715 ■   The Dowd Co.
Tonkin-Symons Paper Div.
167 Klondike Ave.
Fitchburg, MA 01420
Phone: (978)343-4861   **Fax:** (978)345-2813
Products: Paper products; Chemicals. **SICs:** 5113 (Industrial & Personal Service Paper); 5169 (Chemicals & Allied Products Nec). **Est:** 1825. **Emp:** 25. **Officers:** Michael C. Feenan, Manager.

■ 21716 ■   Duradex Inc.
202 Main Ave.
PO Box 1050
Clifton, NJ 07014
Phone: (973)773-0660
Free: (800)524-0518   **Fax:** (973)778-3005
Products: Record management systems; Filing supplies. **SIC:** 5112 (Stationery & Office Supplies). **Est:** 1928. **Sales:** $6,000,000 (2000). **Emp:** 46. **Officers:** Gerarda Fisher, Chairman of the Board; Thomas H. Fisher, President.

■ 21717 ■   Eagle of Cody Printing
PO Box 522
Cody, WY 82414-0522
Phone: (307)527-7523
Products: Printing and writing paper. **SIC:** 5111 (Printing & Writing Paper). **Officers:** Wesley Huber, Owner.

■ 21718 ■   EcoCycle Inc.
PO Box 19006
Boulder, CO 80308
Phone: (303)444-6634   **Fax:** (303)444-6647
E-mail: recycle@ecocycle.org
URL: http://www.ecocycle.org
Products: Paper products; Glass; Auto batteries; Aluminum steel; Plastic. **SICs:** 5111 (Printing & Writing Paper); 5112 (Stationery & Office Supplies); 5113 (Industrial & Personal Service Paper); 5039 (Construction Materials Nec); 5063 (Electrical Apparatus & Equipment). **Est:** 1976. **Sales:** $4,000,000 (1999). **Emp:** 60. **Officers:** Eric Lombardi, Executive Director.

■ 21719 ■   Economy Paper Company Inc.
1175 E Main St.
PO Box 90420
Rochester, NY 14609
Phone: (716)482-5340   **Fax:** (716)482-2089
E-mail: info@economypaper.com
URL: http://www.economypaper.com
Products: Paper items, including industrial, packaging, and printing paper; Janitorial supplies. **SICs:** 5113 (Industrial & Personal Service Paper); 5111 (Printing & Writing Paper); 5112 (Stationery & Office Supplies). **Est:** 1936. **Sales:** $10,000,000 (2000). **Emp:** 43. **Officers:** Robert Cherry, CEO; Sheldon R. Shear, CEO.

■ 21720 ■   Eisenberg Brothers Inc.
PO Box 169
Camden, NJ 08101-0169
Phone: (609)964-5552   **Fax:** (609)964-3377
Products: Paper goods or products, including book mailers. **SIC:** 5113 (Industrial & Personal Service Paper). **Est:** 1913. **Officers:** Samuel Kleinburd, President; James Kleinburd, Vice President; Adele Kleinburd, Treasurer & Secty.

■ 21721 ■   Elgin Paper Co.
1025 N McLean Blvd.
Elgin, IL 60120
Phone: (708)741-0137   **Fax:** (708)741-0293
Products: Paper products, including computer paper, paper towels, and paper plates. **SIC:** 5113 (Industrial & Personal Service Paper). **Est:** 1929. **Sales:** $6,000,000 (2000). **Emp:** 30. **Officers:** Arthur W. Funk, President & Treasurer; Patrick Funk, Vice President; Michael Funk, Sales Mgr.; Dolores Davie, Dir. of Data Processing.

■ 21722 ■   Harry Elish Paper Company Inc.
407 Sette Dr.
Paramus, NJ 07652
Phone: (201)262-1300
Free: (800)473-5474   **Fax:** (201)265-3330
E-mail: elishpaper@aol.com
URL: http://www.elishpaper.com
Products: Paper and allied products. **SIC:** 5111 (Printing & Writing Paper). **Est:** 1917. **Sales:** $6,000,000 (2000). **Emp:** 8. **Officers:** Lawrence Elish, President; James Payne, Vice President.

■ 21723 ■   Empire Paper Co.
PO Box 479
Wichita Falls, TX 76307
Phone: (940)766-3216
Free: (800)299-9626   **Fax:** (940)766-3867
E-mail: empirepaper@worldnet.att.net
Products: Paper; Janitorial supplies; Office supplies. **SICs:** 5113 (Industrial & Personal Service Paper); 5087 (Service Establishment Equipment); 5112 (Stationery & Office Supplies). **Est:** 1926. **Sales:** $12,000,000 (1999). **Emp:** 31. **Officers:** John M. Estes, President; Ron Wright, Vice President; Edward C. Naylon, Purchasing.

■ 21724 ■   Ernest Paper Products
2727 Vernon Ave.
Vernon, CA 90058
Phone: (213)583-6561
Products: Packaging products, including cardboard boxes and tape. **SIC:** 5113 (Industrial & Personal Service Paper). **Est:** 1946. **Sales:** $50,000,000 (2000). **Emp:** 100. **Officers:** Timothy G. Wilson, President; Ben Alhadeff, VP of Finance; Warren Pazolt, VP of Marketing & Sales.

■ **21725** ■ **Fidelity Paper Supply Inc.**
901 Murray Rd.
East Hanover, NJ 07936-2200
Phone: (973)748-3475
Free: (800)762-1931 **Fax:** (973)748-0408
Products: Paper products including tapes, strapping, and corrugated cartons; Cushioning materials, including bubble wrap, wadding, and foam. **SICs:** 5113 (Industrial & Personal Service Paper); 5111 (Printing & Writing Paper). **Est:** 1957. **Sales:** $18,000,000 (2000). **Emp:** 35. **Officers:** Pierre Guariglia, President; David Guariglia, Vice President; Gary Guariglia, Treasurer & Secty.

■ **21726** ■ **First State Paper, Inc.**
100 Paper Pl.
New Castle, DE 19720
Phone: (302)656-6546
Free: (800)736-0635 **Fax:** (302)656-5740
Products: Fine paper. **SIC:** 5111 (Printing & Writing Paper).

■ **21727** ■ **Fisher Paper**
PO Box 1720
Ft. Wayne, IN 46801
Phone: (219)747-7442 **Fax:** (219)747-1358
Products: Industrial and janitorial paper; Packaging equipment and supplies, including paper, tape, strapping, and wrapping machines. **SICs:** 5113 (Industrial & Personal Service Paper); 5087 (Service Establishment Equipment); 5112 (Stationery & Office Supplies). **Est:** 1882. **Sales:** $87,000,000 (2000). **Emp:** 160. **Officers:** Floyd Sims, General Mgr.; Brian Witt, Accounting Manager. **Former Name:** Fisher Paper.

■ **21728** ■ **Fleetwood Paper Co.**
2222 Windsor Ct.
Addison, IL 60101
Phone: (630)268-9999 **Fax:** (630)268-9919
Products: Packaging; Packaging and industrial converting paper. **SIC:** 5113 (Industrial & Personal Service Paper). **Emp:** 27. **Officers:** Francis Houlihan, President.

■ **21729** ■ **Fotofolio Inc.**
561 Broadway
New York, NY 10012
Phone: (212)226-0923
Free: (800)955-3686 **Fax:** (212)226-0072
E-mail: fotofolio@aol.com
URL: http://www.fotofolio.com
Products: Photography and art supplies; Paper products, including postcards, note cards, posters, holiday cards, and calendars; Books; T-shirts. **SICs:** 5112 (Stationery & Office Supplies); 5199 (Nondurable Goods Nec). **Est:** 1975. **Emp:** 40. **Officers:** Juliette Galant, President; Martin Bondell, Vice President; Susan Fields, Sales/Marketing Contact. **Former Name:** Artpost.

■ **21730** ■ **S. Freedman and Sons Inc.**
3322 Pennsy Dr.
Landover, MD 20785
Phone: (301)322-5000 **Fax:** (301)322-1447
E-mail: info@sfreedman.com
Products: Paper products, including paper towels and facial tissues; Straws. **SIC:** 5113 (Industrial & Personal Service Paper). **Est:** 1907. **Sales:** $40,000,000 (2000). **Emp:** 115. **Officers:** Mark S. Freedman, President; Barry R. Perlis, Exec. VP; Joyce Tschudy, Dir. of Marketing & Sales; Robert Brown, Dir. of Data Processing; Steve O'Neill, Dir of Human Resources.

■ **21731** ■ **Fuller Paper Company Inc.**
3700 Wm. Penn Hwy.
Easton, PA 18042
Phone: (215)253-3591 **Fax:** (215)253-9870
Products: Toilet paper and sanitary tissue products; Napkins; Janitors' supplies. **SIC:** 5113 (Industrial & Personal Service Paper). **Sales:** $3,000,000 (2000). **Emp:** 12.

■ **21732** ■ **Fulton Paper Co.**
334 Surburban Dr.
Newark, DE 19711
Phone: (302)368-1440 **Fax:** (302)368-2277
Products: Paper products, including party supplies and paper products. **SICs:** 5113 (Industrial & Personal Service Paper); 5111 (Printing & Writing Paper).

■ **21733** ■ **Fulton Paper Co.**
1006 W 27th St.
Wilmington, DE 19802
Phone: (302)594-0400
Free: (800)327-0210 **Fax:** (302)594-0644
Products: Paper products. **SIC:** 5113 (Industrial & Personal Service Paper).

■ **21734** ■ **Fulton Paper Company Inc.**
PO Box 43884
Atlanta, GA 30336-0884
Phone: (404)691-4070 **Fax:** (404)629-4700
Products: Packaging supplies, including boxes, tape, and strapping; Foodservice disposables; Janitorial supplies. **SIC:** 5113 (Industrial & Personal Service Paper). **Est:** 1919. **Sales:** $30,000,000 (2000). **Emp:** 85. **Officers:** William N. Hirsch, President; A.W. Lamb, VP & Treasurer; Scott Bradway, Dir. of Mktg. & Sales; Richard Smith, Controller.

■ **21735** ■ **G & O Paper & Supplies**
PO Box 367
Lemmon, SD 57638-0367
Phone: (605)374-3697
Products: Paper and allied products. **SIC:** 5113 (Industrial & Personal Service Paper). **Officers:** Marvin Haase, Partner.

■ **21736** ■ **GBS Corp.**
PO Box 2340
North Canton, OH 44720
Phone: (330)494-5330
Products: Business forms. **SIC:** 5112 (Stationery & Office Supplies). **Sales:** $40,000,000 (1994). **Emp:** 120. **Officers:** Skip Dragoiu, President; Mike Merriman, VP of Finance.

■ **21737** ■ **Gem State Paper and Supply Co.**
PO Box 469
Twin Falls, ID 83303-0469
Phone: (208)733-6081
Products: Toilet tissue; Paper towels; Facial tissues; Fax paper. **SIC:** 5113 (Industrial & Personal Service Paper). **Est:** 1946. **Sales:** $8,000,000 (2000). **Emp:** 72. **Officers:** John C. Anderson, President & General Mgr.; Armour Anderson, CFO; Larry Amen, Dir. of Sales.

■ **21738** ■ **General Supply and Paper Co.**
1 George Ave.
Wilkes Barre, PA 18705-2511
Phone: (717)823-1194 **Fax:** (717)822-6065
Products: Industrial supplies, including packaging films and equipment. **SICs:** 5084 (Industrial Machinery & Equipment); 5113 (Industrial & Personal Service Paper). **Est:** 1921. **Sales:** $4,000,000 (2000). **Emp:** 15. **Officers:** Gil Helmick, General Mgr.; Ken Bailey, Sales Mgr.

■ **21739** ■ **Gibson Group Inc.**
PO Box 8028
Cincinnati, OH 45208
Phone: (513)871-9966
Products: Paperboard. **SIC:** 5113 (Industrial & Personal Service Paper). **Est:** 1981. **Sales:** $37,000,000 (2000). **Emp:** 4. **Officers:** Joseph G. Donohoo, President; William G. Donohoo, VP of Finance; Richard G. Donohoo, VP of Marketing.

■ **21740** ■ **GKR Industries, Inc.**
13653 S Kenton Ave.
Crestwood, IL 60445
Phone: (708)389-2003
Free: (800)526-7879 **Fax:** (708)389-3267
Products: Specialty bags and liners. **SIC:** 5113 (Industrial & Personal Service Paper). **Est:** 1986. **Officers:** Richard Fleury, President.

■ **21741** ■ **Glendale Envelope Co.**
807 Air Way
Glendale, CA 91201
Phone: (818)243-2127
Free: (800)451-8173 **Fax:** (818)547-9911
URL: http://www.glendaleenvelope.com
Products: Printed & custom envelopes. **SIC:** 5112 (Stationery & Office Supplies). **Est:** 1981. **Sales:** $1,000,000 (2000). **Emp:** 9. **Officers:** Michael T. Fullerton, President.

■ **21742** ■ **Goes Lithographing Co.**
42 W 61st St.
Chicago, IL 60621-3999
Phone: (773)684-6700
Free: (800)730-4637 **Fax:** (773)684-2065
E-mail: goeslitho@ameritech.net
URL: http://www.goeslitho.com
Products: Calendars and calendar pads; Awards, certificates, and plaques; Holiday stationery; Invitations, florist enclosure cards; Record books. **SIC:** 5111 (Printing & Writing Paper). **Est:** 1879. **Sales:** $4,000,000 (2000). **Emp:** 55. **Officers:** Charles B. Goes IV, President; Lawrence Bieneck, Vice President; Cynthia Thompson, Dir. of Marketing; Wayne Anderson, Dir. of Systems. **Alternate Name:** Falls Enterprises. **Alternate Name:** Rocketline.

■ **21743** ■ **G.B. Goldman Paper Co.**
2201 E Allegheny Ave.
Philadelphia, PA 19134
Phone: (215)423-8600
Products: Paper. **SIC:** 5113 (Industrial & Personal Service Paper). **Est:** 1950. **Sales:** $80,000,000 (2000). **Emp:** 250. **Officers:** Mervin M. Golder, President; Richard F. Doyle, VP of Marketing; Joseph J. Wrobel, VP of Data Processing.

■ **21744** ■ **Harry Goodman Inc.**
203 Tremont St.
Springfield, MA 01101
Phone: (413)785-5331 **Fax:** (413)734-1540
Products: Paper recycling. **SIC:** 5093 (Scrap & Waste Materials). **Sales:** $17,000,000 (1994). **Emp:** 30. **Officers:** Danny Goodman, President.

■ **21745** ■ **Gould Paper Corp.**
11 Madison Ave.
New York, NY 10010
Phone: (212)301-0000
Free: (800)ASK-GOULD **Fax:** (212)320-4333
URL: http://www.gouldpaper.com
Products: Fine printing paper. **SIC:** 5111 (Printing & Writing Paper). **Est:** 1943. **Sales:** $350,000,000 (2000). **Officers:** Harry E. Gould Jr., CEO & President; Dan J. Lala, VP & CFO; Robert Anderson, Exec. VP of Sales; Joe Bergman, VP & Controller; Michael Pearl, VP of Admin.

■ **21746** ■ **R.B. Grant & Associates, LLC**
30 Lower College Rd.
Kingston, RI 02881-1316
Phone: (401)782-8077 **Fax:** (401)789-1920
E-mail: sales@rbgrant.com
URL: http://www.rbgrant.com
Products: Cardboard printing; Specialty plastic printing; Display printing; Book, catalog, folder, and package printing; CD replication; Packaging; Folding plastic. **SIC:** 5111 (Printing & Writing Paper). **Est:** 1971. **Sales:** $5,000,000 (2000). **Emp:** 3. **Officers:** Richard Grant, Manager.

■ **21747** ■ **Graphic Controls**
189 Van Rensselaer St.
PO Box 1271
Buffalo, NY 14240-1271
Phone: (716)853-7500 **Free:** (800)628-8812
E-mail: autronweb@graphiccontrols.com
URL: http://www.autron.com/
Products: Paper and allied products; Paper business machine supplies; Computer paper; Stationery and office supplies. **SICs:** 5113 (Industrial & Personal Service Paper); 5112 (Stationery & Office Supplies); 5111 (Printing & Writing Paper). **Former Name:** Autron Inc. Z Paper Div.

■ **21748** ■ **Graphic Papers Inc.**
2070 Poydras St.
New Orleans, LA 70112
Phone: (504)525-5686
Free: (800)966-2165 **Fax:** (504)525-1162
Products: Paper. **SICs:** 5113 (Industrial & Personal Service Paper); 5111 (Printing & Writing Paper); 5112 (Stationery & Office Supplies). **Est:** 1975. **Emp:** 25. **Officers:** Earl A. Spindel, CEO; Craig M. Spindel, President; Elizabeth G. Spindel, Treasurer & Secty.; Elizabeth Spindel, Treasurer & Secty.

■ **21749** ■ **Great Bay Paper Co.**
1900 Monkton Rd.
Monkton, MD 21111
Phone: (410)329-3808
Products: Paper goods or products, including book mailers. **SIC:** 5113 (Industrial & Personal Service Paper). **Sales:** $1,000,000 (2000). **Emp:** 3. **Officers:** William Bridges, President.

■ **21750** ■ **Great Falls Paper Co.**
600 2nd St. S
PO Box 269
Great Falls, MT 59405
Phone: (406)453-7671
Free: (800)992-7671   **Fax:** (406)453-7673
Products: Paper bags; Paperboard boxes; Paper towels; Paper dishes; Paper cups; Toilet paper and sanitary tissue products. **SIC:** 5113 (Industrial & Personal Service Paper). **Est:** 1913. **Sales:** $990,000 (2000). **Emp:** 8. **Officers:** James J. Flaherty, CEO; Helen F. Flaherty, Secretary; Michael J. Flaherty, President.

■ **21751** ■ **Great Scott Services Ltd.**
36 S College St.
PO Box 1414
Danville, IL 61834-1414
Phone: (217)442-1143
Free: (800)343-1182   **Fax:** (217)442-1182
Products: Paper products; Janitorial supplies; Coffee service. **SICs:** 5113 (Industrial & Personal Service Paper); 5087 (Service Establishment Equipment). **Est:** 1950. **Officers:** Glen D. Scott, President; Lou Hinkle, Sales & Marketing Contact; Mary Gilbert, Customer Service Contact.

■ **21752** ■ **Great Southern Industries Inc.**
PO Box 5325
Jackson, MS 39216
Phone: (601)948-5700   **Fax:** (601)355-3214
Products: Corrugated cardboard boxes. **SIC:** 5113 (Industrial & Personal Service Paper). **Sales:** $8,800,000 (2000). **Emp:** 100. **Officers:** W.F. Barnett, President; Joe Russel, Controller; Bob Lee, Sales Mgr.

■ **21753** ■ **Griffin Container and Supply Co.**
PO Box 916
Salinas, CA 93902
Phone: (408)422-6458
Products: Cardboard boxes. **SIC:** 5113 (Industrial & Personal Service Paper). **Est:** 1927. **Sales:** $1,000,000 (2000). **Emp:** 5. **Officers:** Hubert E. Jackson, General Mgr.

■ **21754** ■ **Albert Guarnieri Co.**
1133-71 E Market St.
Warren, OH 44483
Phone: (216)394-5636   **Fax:** (216)395-2200
Products: Foodservice; Candy; Tobacco; Snacks; Beverages; Grocery; Equipment; Concessions; Paper; General merchandise. **SICs:** 5194 (Tobacco & Tobacco Products); 5145 (Confectionery); 5141 (Groceries—General Line); 5122 (Drugs, Proprietaries & Sundries). **Est:** 1888. **Sales:** $15,000,000 (2000). **Emp:** 40. **Officers:** A. Guarnieri III, President; John Guarnieri, Vice President; Rob Guarnieri, Vice President.

■ **21755** ■ **Harder Paper and Packaging Inc.**
5301 Verona Rd.
Madison, WI 53711
Phone: (608)271-5127   **Fax:** (608)271-4677
Products: Paper and plastic tapes; Bandings; Chemicals. **SICs:** 5113 (Industrial & Personal Service Paper); 5169 (Chemicals & Allied Products Nec). **Est:** 1947. **Sales:** $7,000,000 (2000). **Emp:** 30. **Officers:** Richard Zimmerman, CEO & President.

■ **21756** ■ **Hathaway Paper Co.**
S Oak Ln.
PO Box 1618
Waynesboro, VA 22980
Phone: (540)949-8285   **Fax:** (540)943-7619
Products: Industrial paper and packaging products and equipment; Janitorial equipment and supplies; Pressure-sensitive tape. **SICs:** 5113 (Industrial & Personal Service Paper); 5112 (Stationery & Office Supplies); 5087 (Service Establishment Equipment).

Est: 1981. **Sales:** $12,000,000 (2000). **Emp:** 38. **Officers:** Curtis Hathaway Jr.

■ **21757** ■ **Hearn Paper Company Inc.**
556 N Merdian Rd.
Youngstown, OH 44509
Phone: (330)792-6533
Free: (800)225-2989   **Fax:** (330)792-4762
Products: Paper and allied products; Toilet paper and sanitary tissue products; Packaging; Molded packings and seals. **SICs:** 5113 (Industrial & Personal Service Paper); 5087 (Service Establishment Equipment); 5112 (Stationery & Office Supplies). **Est:** 1924. **Sales:** $5,000,000 (2000). **Emp:** 28. **Officers:** Bryan K. Reed, President & Treasurer; Robert F. Bakalik, VP & Secty.

■ **21758** ■ **Heartland Paper Co.**
808 W Cherokee St.
Sioux Falls, SD 57104
Phone: (605)336-1190   **Fax:** (605)332-8378
Products: Paper products, including plates, napkins, and boxes; Chemicals; Equipment. **SICs:** 5111 (Printing & Writing Paper); 5085 (Industrial Supplies). **Est:** 1894. **Emp:** 180. **Officers:** Sandra Christenson, President.

■ **21759** ■ **Heritage Paper Company Inc.**
4011 Morton St.
Jacksonville, FL 32217
Phone: (904)737-6603   **Fax:** (904)737-4902
Products: Paper products, including paper towel, toilet paper, and tissues; Janitorial supplies; Food service disposable packaging supplies. **SICs:** 5113 (Industrial & Personal Service Paper); 5111 (Printing & Writing Paper). **Est:** 1972. **Sales:** $17,200,000 (2000). **Emp:** 110. **Officers:** Robert F. Purser Sr. Sr., CEO & President; Robert F. Purser Jr., Marketing Mgr.

■ **21760** ■ **Hill City Wholesale Company Inc.**
PO Box 10245
Birmingham, AL 35202
Phone: (804)847-6641   **Fax:** (804)847-0807
Products: Paper products, including grocery bags, table cloths, paper towels, plates, cups, and toilet tissue; Tobacco and cigarettes; School supplies; Groceries; Candies; Institutional foods. **SICs:** 5194 (Tobacco & Tobacco Products); 5145 (Confectionery); 5141 (Groceries—General Line); 5113 (Industrial & Personal Service Paper). **Est:** 1920. **Sales:** $10,000,000 (1999). **Emp:** 20. **Officers:** W.S. Thomasson, President; Butch Scott, Sales Mgr.

■ **21761** ■ **The Hillcraft Group**
6800 Grant Ave.
Cleveland, OH 44105
Phone: (216)441-5500   **Fax:** (216)641-2610
Products: Paper and paper products. **SIC:** 5111 (Printing & Writing Paper). **Sales:** $200,000,000 (2000). **Emp:** 300.

■ **21762** ■ **Hillcrest Food Service Co.**
2695 E 40th St.
Cleveland, OH 44115
Phone: (216)361-4625
Free: (800)952-4344   **Fax:** (216)361-0764
URL: http://www.hillcrestfoods.com
Products: Groceries, including coffee, meats, seafood, and poultry; Paper products; Chemicals. **SIC:** 5141 (Groceries—General Line). **Est:** 1974. **Sales:** $29,000,000 (1999). **Emp:** 73. **Officers:** Armin Abraham, President.

■ **21763** ■ **Hillsdale Paper Co.**
4880 Hills & Dales Rd. NW
Canton, OH 44708
Phone: (330)477-3411   **Fax:** (330)477-2669
Products: Fine paper products. **SIC:** 5111 (Printing & Writing Paper). **Est:** 1981. **Emp:** 8. **Officers:** Ronald D. Cullen, Pres. & Treas.; Joseph R. Cullen, Vice President; Jeanne M. Cullen, Secretary.

■ **21764** ■ **Hollinger Corp.**
PO Box 8360
Fredericksburg, VA 22404-8360
Products: Cardboard boxes for packaging. **SIC:** 5113 (Industrial & Personal Service Paper). **Est:** 1945. **Sales:** $5,000,000 (2000). **Emp:** 44. **Officers:** Mary H. Hollinger, President; Mary Lou Hollinger, Controller.

■ **21765** ■ **Holstein Paper & Janitorial Supply**
12 Music Fair Rd.
Owings Mills, MD 21117
Phone: (410)363-0400   **Fax:** (410)581-1327
Products: Paper and allied products; Janitors' supplies. **SICs:** 5113 (Industrial & Personal Service Paper); 5087 (Service Establishment Equipment); 5111 (Printing & Writing Paper); 5112 (Stationery & Office Supplies). **Est:** 1916. **Emp:** 30. **Officers:** Randy Moss, President; Ellen Moss, Vice President.

■ **21766** ■ **Holt Distributors, Inc.**
865 E Loockerman St.
Dover, DE 19901-7419
Phone: (302)674-0666   **Fax:** (302)674-0674
Products: Paper products; Chemicals; Machinery. **SICs:** 5113 (Industrial & Personal Service Paper); 5169 (Chemicals & Allied Products Nec); 5084 (Industrial Machinery & Equipment).

■ **21767** ■ **Howard Invitations and Cards**
PO Box 2009
Hazleton, PA 18201-0675
Phone: (717)875-3571   **Fax:** 800-777-1810
Products: Wedding invitations. **SIC:** 5112 (Stationery & Office Supplies). **Est:** 1932. **Sales:** $1,000,000 (2000). **Emp:** 20. **Officers:** M.R. Lewis, President; George Helenbrook, General Mgr.

■ **21768** ■ **Howard Sales Inc.**
5742 W 79th St.
Indianapolis, IN 46278
Phone: (317)872-8300   **Fax:** (317)872-8964
Products: Paper and disposable plastic shipping supplies; Boxes and crates; Adhesives and sealants. **SICs:** 5113 (Industrial & Personal Service Paper); 5169 (Chemicals & Allied Products Nec). **Est:** 1946. **Sales:** $4,000,000 (2000). **Emp:** 25. **Officers:** James E. Schram, President; Nina B. Turner, Treasurer & Secty.

■ **21769** ■ **Hudson Paper Co.**
1341 W Broad St.
Stratford, CT 06497
Phone: (203)378-0123   **Fax:** (203)378-7109
Products: Packaging products. **SIC:** 5113 (Industrial & Personal Service Paper). **Est:** 1908. **Sales:** $10,000,000 (2000). **Emp:** 70. **Officers:** R.W. Wilk, President; Bill Botte, VP of Finance; Richard J. Boucher, VP of Marketing.

■ **21770** ■ **Hudson Valley Paper Co.**
PO Box 1988
Albany, NY 12201
Phone: (518)471-5111
Free: (800)497-5111   **Fax:** (518)455-8803
Products: Paper; Envelopes; Fax paper. **SICs:** 5111 (Printing & Writing Paper); 5112 (Stationery & Office Supplies); 5113 (Industrial & Personal Service Paper). **Est:** 1875. **Sales:** $40,000,000 (2000). **Emp:** 85. **Officers:** S.T. Jones III, President; Lisa Gunderman, Controller; Kurt Van Steemburg, VP of Marketing; Karen McCabe, Dir of Human Resources.

■ **21771** ■ **Huff Paper Co.**
Rte. 322 & Creek Pkwy.
Boothwyn, PA 19061
Phone: (610)497-5100   **Fax:** (215)497-6255
URL: http://www.huffpaper.com
Products: Food service disposableS; Janitorial maintenance products. **SICs:** 5113 (Industrial & Personal Service Paper); 5169 (Chemicals & Allied Products Nec). **Est:** 1890. **Sales:** $25,000,000 (1999). **Emp:** 45. **Officers:** Paul Burns, President; Fred Hilbert, Exec. VP, e-mail: fredhilbert@huffunitedpaper.com; Terry Ward, Dir. of Information Systems.

■ **21772** ■ **Huntsville/Redstone Paper Co.**
PO Box 3368
Huntsville, AL 35810
Phone: (256)851-2100
Free: (800)444-7452   **Fax:** (256)851-2115
Products: Paper supplies; Janitorial supplies; Shipping supplies. **SICs:** 5113 (Industrial & Personal Service Paper); 5087 (Service Establishment Equipment). **Est:** 1962. **Sales:** $6,500,000 (2000). **Emp:** 25. **Officers:** Gary Drake, General Mgr.

■ 21773 ■ Industrial Paper Corp.
300 Villanova Dr. SW
Atlanta, GA 30336
Phone: (404)346-5800 **Fax:** (404)346-5811
Products: Packaging and industrial converting paper;
Folding paperboard boxes; Disposable plastic bags;
Paper and allied products. **SICs:** 5113 (Industrial &
Personal Service Paper); 5111 (Printing & Writing
Paper); 5112 (Stationery & Office Supplies). **Est:** 1950.
Sales: $28,000,000 (2000). **Emp:** 65. **Officers:** Mark
Lichtenstein, President; Will Trantham, Dir. of Mktg. &
Sales.

■ 21774 ■ Industrial Paper & Plastic Products Company Inc.
240 Austin Rd.
Waterbury, CT 06705
Phone: (203)753-2196 **Fax:** (203)755-9095
URL: http://www.industrialpaper.com
Products: Bags; Can liners; Chipboard; Coil wrapping;
Corner boards; Cushioning materials; Cutters;
Desiccant; Die cuts; Envelopes; Films; Gloves;
Gummed tapes; Industrial wipers; Interleaving paper;
Mailing tubes; Military packaging; Sanitary napkins;
Soaps; Strapping; Stretch wrap; Tapes; Ties; Towels;
Toilet tissue; Twine; Waterproof papers; Waxed
papers. **SIC:** 5113 (Industrial & Personal Service
Paper). **Est:** 1955. **Emp:** 7. **Officers:** Thomas F.
Moran III, e-mail: tmoran@industrialpaper.com.

■ 21775 ■ Industrial Wiper & Paper
200 Spruce St.
PO Box 505679
Chelsea, MA 02150
Phone: (617)884-5550
Free: (800)649-1709 **Fax:** (617)884-5115
URL: http://www.indwip.com
Products: Paper and allied products; Janitors'
supplies; Odor control materials. **SICs:** 5113 (Industrial
& Personal Service Paper); 5087 (Service
Establishment Equipment); 5111 (Printing & Writing
Paper); 5112 (Stationery & Office Supplies). **Est:** 1981.
Emp: 40. **Officers:** Dennis McGurk, President; Owen
Clark, General Mgr., e-mail: oclarke@indwip.com;
Steven Bergholtz, Vice President.

■ 21776 ■ Infinity Paper Inc.
51 Haddonfield Rd., Ste. 120
Cherry Hill, NJ 08002-4801
Phone: (856)665-5500 **Fax:** (856)665-1119
E-mail: cb@infinitypaper.com
Products: Paper and allied products. **SICs:** 5111
(Printing & Writing Paper); 5111 (Printing & Writing
Paper); 5112 (Stationery & Office Supplies). **Est:** 1990.
Sales: $5,000,000 (2000). **Emp:** 8. **Officers:** Clifford I.
Barnett, President; Raymond G. Wall, Vice President.

■ 21777 ■ Ingram Paper Co.
PO Box 60003
City of Industry, CA 91716
Phone: (818)854-5400 **Fax:** (818)854-5449
Products: Paper products, including cups, plates, and
typing paper. **SICs:** 5111 (Printing & Writing Paper);
5113 (Industrial & Personal Service Paper). **Est:** 1923.
Sales: $150,000,000 (2000). **Emp:** 250. **Officers:**
Larry Stillman, President; Erik Odeen, CFO.

■ 21778 ■ Inter-City Paper Co.
PO Box 1401
Minneapolis, MN 55440
Phone: (612)228-1234
Products: Printing paper. **SIC:** 5111 (Printing & Writing
Paper). **Sales:** $19,000,000 (1994). **Emp:** 79.
Officers: James D. Wilson, President; Charles A.
Belland, VP of Finance.

■ 21779 ■ International Forest Products Corp.
1 Boston Pl., 35th Fl.
Boston, MA 02108
Phone: (617)723-3455 **Fax:** (617)723-3458
Products: Corrugated materials, including cardboard
boxes. **SIC:** 5113 (Industrial & Personal Service
Paper). **Est:** 1972. **Sales:** $47,000,000 (2000). **Emp:**
145. **Officers:** Robert Kraft, President; Dan Moore,
Treasurer.

■ 21780 ■ ITC Inc.
6 N Park Dr., Ste. 105
Hunt Valley, MD 21030
Phone: (410)825-2920 **Fax:** (410)333-2997
E-mail: info@itcglobal.com
URL: http://www.itcglobal.com
Products: Industrial minerals and chemicals. **SIC:**
5052 (Coal, Other Minerals & Ores). **Est:** 1964. **Sales:**
$60,000,000 (2000). **Emp:** 60. **Officers:** Dennis C.
Parker, President; Robert Purcell, Vice President, e-
mail: rjpurcell@itcglobal.com.

■ 21781 ■ Jackson Paper Company Inc.
197 N Gallatin St.
Jackson, MS 39207
Phone: (601)360-9620
Free: (800)844-5449 **Fax:** (601)360-9634
Products: Paper and allied products. **SICs:** 5111
(Printing & Writing Paper); 5113 (Industrial & Personal
Service Paper). **Est:** 1921. **Sales:** $37,000,000 (2000).
Emp: 130. **Officers:** Jim P. Archer, CEO & Chairman
of the Board; B.J. Graves, President.

■ 21782 ■ James River Corporation of Connecticut
PO Box 6000
Norwalk, CT 06856
Phone: (203)854-2000
Products: Paper cups, napkins, plates, and tissue.
SIC: 5113 (Industrial & Personal Service Paper).

■ 21783 ■ JC Paper
650 Brennan St.
PO Box 610460
San Jose, CA 95161-0460
Phone: (408)435-2700 **Fax:** (408)435-2703
Products: Paper and allied products; Toilet paper and
sanitary tissue products. **SIC:** 5113 (Industrial &
Personal Service Paper). **Est:** 1956.

■ 21784 ■ Joiner Foodservice, Inc.
PO Drawer 2547
Harlingen, TX 78550
Phone: (956)423-2003 **Fax:** (956)421-2025
Products: Paper products, including paper towel, toilet
paper, and paper plates; Food. **SICs:** 5113 (Industrial &
Personal Service Paper); 5141 (Groceries—General
Line). **Est:** 1960. **Sales:** $11,500,000 (2000). **Emp:** 30.
Officers: Andy Joiner, General Mgr.

■ 21785 ■ Jordan Graphics
PO Box 668306
Charlotte, NC 28266
Phone: (704)394-2121 **Fax:** (704)394-9338
Products: Business labels. **SIC:** 5112 (Stationery &
Office Supplies). **Est:** 1955. **Sales:** $58,500,000
(2000). **Emp:** 377. **Officers:** John L. Chanon,
President; Ned Meier, Vice President; Rick Segers, VP
of Sales; Jim Huff, Dir. of Data Processing; Ron
Russell.

■ 21786 ■ George F. Joseph Orchard Siding Inc.
PO Box 158
Wapato, WA 98951-0158
Phone: (509)966-2130 **Fax:** (509)966-2512
Products: Fruit packaging. **SIC:** 5113 (Industrial &
Personal Service Paper). **Est:** 1950. **Sales:** $2,000,000
(2000). **Emp:** 200. **Officers:** Gary N. Bailey, CEO.

■ 21787 ■ Judd Paper Co.
PO Box 669
Holyoke, MA 01041
Phone: (413)534-5661
E-mail: jpco@fiam.net
Products: Specialty packaging supplies; Bonded
paper; Soft wrap tissue; Roll-edge protectors. **SIC:**
5113 (Industrial & Personal Service Paper). **Est:** 1883.
Sales: $3,000,000 (1999). **Emp:** 12. **Officers:** W.C.
Jolicoeur, President & Treasurer; Steve Stanford, VP of
Marketing.

■ 21788 ■ Katz Paper, Foil & Cordage Corp.
2900 1st Ave. S
Seattle, WA 98134
Phone: (206)624-2494 **Fax:** (206)382-9315
Products: Giftwrap, paper, and foil. **SIC:** 5113
(Industrial & Personal Service Paper). **Est:** 1940. **Emp:**
6. **Officers:** Thomas J. Weingarten, President.

■ 21789 ■ Kayboys Empire Paper Company Inc.
11 Azar Ct.
Benson Business Ctr.
Baltimore, MD 21227
Phone: (410)247-5000 **Fax:** (410)247-7665
Products: Paper products. **SICs:** 5113 (Industrial &
Personal Service Paper); 5111 (Printing & Writing
Paper); 5112 (Stationery & Office Supplies). **Est:** 1954.
Emp: 44. **Officers:** Myron Kreitzer, President; Albert
Kreitzer, Vice President.

■ 21790 ■ Kelly Paper Co.
1441 E 16th St.
Los Angeles, CA 90021
Phone: (213)749-1311
Free: (800)675-3559 **Fax:** (213)749-3637
URL: http://www.kellypaper.com
Products: Printing supplies, including paper. **SIC:**
5111 (Printing & Writing Paper). **Est:** 1936. **Sales:**
$87,000,000 (2000). **Emp:** 280. **Officers:** Ed Pearson,
President; Don Hart, Merchandising Mgr.; Rob
Witherby, Marketing Mgr., e-mail: rob4kelly@aol.com;
Jackie DiFranco, Dir of Human Resources; Norman
Cole, Treasurer; Rod Schuar, Operations Mgr.

■ 21791 ■ Kenzacki Specialty Papers Inc.
1500 Main St.
Springfield, MA 01115
Phone: (413)736-3216 **Fax:** (413)734-5101
Products: Paper, including fax and pressure-sensitive
paper. **SICs:** 5113 (Industrial & Personal Service
Paper); 5111 (Printing & Writing Paper); 5112
(Stationery & Office Supplies). **Est:** 1948. **Sales:**
$5,000,000 (2000). **Emp:** 270. **Officers:** Kazuhiko
Watanabe, President; H. Fukuda, CFO.

■ 21792 ■ Kirk Paper Co.
7500 Amigos Ave.
Downey, CA 90242
Phone: (562)803-0550
Products: Fine paper. **SIC:** 5111 (Printing & Writing
Paper).

■ 21793 ■ Leon Korol Co.
2050 E Devon Ave.
Elk Grove Village, IL 60007
Phone: (708)956-1616
Products: Paper goods, including paper plates and
cups. **SIC:** 5113 (Industrial & Personal Service Paper).
Est: 1960. **Sales:** $11,000,000 (2000). **Emp:** 55.
Officers: Leon Korol, President; James F. Olesuk, VP
of Finance.

■ 21794 ■ Kozak Distributors
520 E Hunting Park Ave.
Philadelphia, PA 19124-6009
Phone: (215)426-1870 **Fax:** (215)426-3548
Products: Household paper goods. **SIC:** 5113
(Industrial & Personal Service Paper). **Emp:** 49.

■ 21795 ■ La Boiteaux Co.
PO Box 175708
Covington, KY 41017-5708
Phone: (606)578-0400
Products: Paper, including draft paper and liner board.
SIC: 5113 (Industrial & Personal Service Paper). **Est:**
1896. **Sales:** $40,000,000 (2000). **Emp:** 38. **Officers:**
John Nakaoka, President; Jane Dennig, Controller.

■ 21796 ■ Kent H. Landsberg Co.
1640 S Greenwood Ave.
Montebello, CA 90640
Phone: (213)726-7776 **Fax:** (213)725-0775
Products: Corrugated shipping containers and
packaging. **SICs:** 5113 (Industrial & Personal Service
Paper); 5087 (Service Establishment Equipment). **Est:**
1947. **Sales:** $65,000,000 (1991). **Emp:** 450. **Officers:**
Gene Shelton, President & Chairman of the Board;
Darryl Abotomey, CFO.

■ 21797 ■ LaSalle Paper and Packaging Inc.
105 S 41st Ave., No. 2
Phoenix, AZ 85009-4627
Phone: (602)484-7337
Products: Fine paper and packaging paper. **SICs:**
5111 (Printing & Writing Paper); 5113 (Industrial &
Personal Service Paper). **Sales:** $25,000,000 (2000).
Emp: 30. **Officers:** Thomas P. Hayes III, Manager.

■ 21798 ■ Leavenworth Paper Supply Co.
521 S 2nd St.
Leavenworth, KS 66048
Phone: (913)682-3861   Fax: (913)682-3854
Products: Janitorial supplies; Paper products. SICs: 5113 (Industrial & Personal Service Paper); 5087 (Service Establishment Equipment); 5111 (Printing & Writing Paper); 5112 (Stationery & Office Supplies). Emp: 10. Officers: Don Briggs, Owner.

■ 21799 ■ Leonard Paper Company Inc.
725 N Haven St.
Baltimore, MD 21205
Phone: (410)563-0800
Free: (800)327-5547   Fax: (410)563-0249
URL: http://www.LeonardPaper.com
Products: Paper and janitorial supplies. SICs: 5113 (Industrial & Personal Service Paper); 5087 (Service Establishment Equipment); 5111 (Printing & Writing Paper); 5112 (Stationery & Office Supplies). Est: 1940. Sales: $45,000,000 (2000). Emp: 98. Officers: Charles B. Leonard, Chairman of the Board; Daniel D. Leonard, President; L. Gene Crocetti, Vice President; Michael Leonard, Vice President; Elizabeth L. Carroll, Treasurer & Secty.

■ 21800 ■ Leslie Paper Co. Chicago Div.
775 Belden Ave.
Addison, IL 60101
Phone: (630)628-0400   Fax: (630)628-0422
Products: Printing paper. SICs: 5111 (Printing & Writing Paper); 5112 (Stationery & Office Supplies). Est: 1882. Sales: $140,000,000 (2000). Emp: 130. Officers: Bill Blocker, Vice President; Carol Graham, Operations Mgr. Alternate Name: xpedx.

■ 21801 ■ J.J. Levis Paper Company Inc.
12-18 Methuen
Lawrence, MA 01840
Phone: (978)682-0712   Fax: (978)688-7778
Products: Paper, including recycled kraft, natural kraft, butchers, bogus, and newsprint. SIC: 5113 (Industrial & Personal Service Paper). Est: 1944. Sales: $4,200,000 (2000). Emp: 20. Officers: J.R. Levis, President.

■ 21802 ■ Lindenmeyer Munroe
240 Forbes Blvd.
Mansfield, MA 02048
Phone: (508)339-6161
Free: (800)343-7782   Fax: (508)339-1996
Products: Paper and allied products. SIC: 5111 (Printing & Writing Paper). Officers: David Manning, General Mgr.

■ 21803 ■ Lindenmeyer Munroe
468 Pepsi Rd.
Manchester, NH 03109
Phone: (603)627-1320
Free: (800)462-1911   Fax: (603)627-4816
Products: Printing paper. SIC: 5112 (Stationery & Office Supplies). Officers: Edwin Berns, General Mgr.

■ 21804 ■ Lindenmeyer Munroe
301 Veterans Blvd.
Rutherford, NJ 07070-2706
Phone: (201)935-2900
Free: (800)631-0193   Fax: (201)935-5264
Products: Paper and allied products. SIC: 5113 (Industrial & Personal Service Paper). Officers: Anthony W. Sorge Jr., Senior VP.

■ 21805 ■ Lindenmeyer Munroe
921 Riverside St.
Portland, ME 04103
Phone: (207)878-0007   Free: (800)342-2215
Products: Paper business machine supplies. SIC: 5112 (Stationery & Office Supplies). Officers: James W. Barrett, General Mgr.

■ 21806 ■ Lindenmeyer Munroe
3041 Industry Dr.
Lancaster, PA 17603-4025
Phone: (717)393-2111
Free: (800)222-4908   Fax: (717)393-0948
Products: Paper business machine supplies. SIC: 5112 (Stationery & Office Supplies). Officers: Dale Rohrer, General Mgr.

■ 21807 ■ Lindenmeyer Munroe
921 Riverside St.
Portland, ME 04103
Phone: (207)878-0007
Free: (800)442-1390   Fax: (207)874-0653
URL: http://www.lindenmeyer.com
Products: Paper. SIC: 5113 (Industrial & Personal Service Paper). Officers: Mike Gibson, General Mgr.

■ 21808 ■ Lindenmeyr Munroe
200 Riverpark Dr.
Box 0129
North Reading, MA 01864-0129
Phone: (978)276-2300
Free: (800)237-2737   Fax: (978)276-2301
Products: Paper and allied products. SICs: 5111 (Printing & Writing Paper); 5113 (Industrial & Personal Service Paper). Est: 1859. Emp: 80. Officers: David Manning, VP & Mgr.

■ 21809 ■ Lindenmeyr Munroe
PO Box 6033
Farmingdale, NY 11735
Phone: (718)520-1586   Fax: (718)482-9526
Products: Paper for industrial, commercial and stationery use. SICs: 5112 (Stationery & Office Supplies); 5113 (Industrial & Personal Service Paper). Sales: $150,000,000 (1993). Emp: 70. Officers: Kenneth Obletz, Vice President.

■ 21810 ■ Loftin Web Graphics
789 Gateway Center Way
San Diego, CA 92102
Phone: (619)262-0200   Fax: (619)262-0390
Products: Commercial color web printing. SIC: 5112 (Stationery & Office Supplies). Est: 1957. Sales: $7,500,000 (2000). Emp: 55. Officers: Bill Loftin, President. Former Name: Loftin Business Forms Inc.

■ 21811 ■ Lord Brothers & Higgins
PO Box 390
Seaford, DE 19973
Phone: (302)629-7093
Products: Paper products; Candy; Tobacco. SICs: 5111 (Printing & Writing Paper); 5194 (Tobacco & Tobacco Products); 5145 (Confectionery). Est: 1920. Emp: 5.

■ 21812 ■ Lorel Co.
PO Box 570211
Houston, TX 77257
Phone: (713)464-0670
Products: Greeting cards; Travel kits (fitted and unfitted); Blankets; Rugs; Paper goods or products, including book mailers; Paper bags. SICs: 5113 (Industrial & Personal Service Paper); 5199 (Nondurable Goods Nec); 5023 (Homefurnishings); 5122 (Drugs, Proprietaries & Sundries). Officers: Lore Martin, President.

■ 21813 ■ Los Angeles Carton Co.
5100 S Santa Fe Ave.
Vernon, CA 90058
Phone: (213)587-1500
Products: Corrugated cartons for shipping and packaging. SIC: 5113 (Industrial & Personal Service Paper). Est: 1974. Sales: $6,000,000 (2000). Emp: 12. Officers: Leonard Subotnick, President.

■ 21814 ■ F.W. Lotz Paper and Fixture Co.
9710 Glenfield Ct.
Dayton, OH 45458-9173
Phone: (937)223-7223
Products: Restaurant paper; Commercial silverware and dishes; Commercial freezers. SICs: 5113 (Industrial & Personal Service Paper); 5085 (Industrial Supplies). Est: 1913. Sales: $3,250,000 (2000). Emp: 19. Officers: Frank E. Gebhart, President; Jill Gebhart, Vice President.

■ 21815 ■ M and R International Inc.
15 Valley Dr.
Greenwich, CT 06831
Phone: (203)625-0500   Fax: (203)625-0440
E-mail: m-r-international@mcimail.com
Products: Special industrial paper; Paper goods or products, including book mailers. SIC: 5113 (Industrial & Personal Service Paper). Est: 1942. Sales: $40,000,000 (2000). Emp: 12. Officers: B.E. Olrik,

President; D. Stillman, VP of Finance; P. Schuler, Exec. VP of Marketing; P. Velez, Export Director.

■ 21816 ■ Mac Papers Inc.
PO Box 5369
Jacksonville, FL 32247
Phone: (904)348-3300   Fax: (904)348-3340
URL: http://www.macpapers.com
Products: Fine paper. SIC: 5111 (Printing & Writing Paper). Est: 1964. Sales: $391,000,000 (1999). Emp: 950. Officers: F. Sutton McGehee Jr., President; John Brent, VP of Finance; Thomas R. McGehee Jr., VP & Secty.; Pat Patterson, VP of Finance.

■ 21817 ■ Mack-Chicago Corp.
2445 S Rockwell St.
Chicago, IL 60608
Phone: (773)376-8100   Fax: (773)650-5745
Products: Corrugated and solid fiber boxes; Packaging. SIC: 5113 (Industrial & Personal Service Paper). Est: 1955. Emp: 191. Officers: William Swisshelm, President; Don Farnsworth, Exec. VP; George Pluta, Sales Mgr.

■ 21818 ■ MacKinnon Paper Company Inc.
PO Box 12
Mobile, AL 36601-0012
Phone: (205)666-8175   Fax: (205)666-8179
Products: Fine paper products. SICs: 5112 (Stationery & Office Supplies); 5111 (Printing & Writing Paper). Est: 1973. Emp: 15. Officers: Thopmas B. MacKinnen, President; Charleston Harfour, Vice President.

■ 21819 ■ Macy Associates Inc.
Mountain Rd.
PO Box 40
Jaffrey, NH 03452
Phone: (603)532-7490   Fax: (603)532-4556
Products: Writing paper. SIC: 5111 (Printing & Writing Paper). Officers: Susan Macy, President.

■ 21820 ■ Mansfield Bag & Paper Company Inc.
441 N Main St.
PO Box 1414
Mansfield, OH 44902
Phone: (419)525-2814
Free: (800)654-8654   Fax: (419)522-6942
Products: Packaging equipment and supplies, including bags. SIC: 5113 (Industrial & Personal Service Paper). Est: 1931. Sales: $3,000,000 (2000). Emp: 25. Officers: Bruce Goldman, CEO; Michael Lawrentz, General Mgr., e-mail: morkand4@bright.net; Paul Goldman, President.

■ 21821 ■ Mansfield Paper Company Inc.
PO Box 1070
West Springfield, MA 01089
Phone: (413)781-2000
Free: (800)225-4641   Fax: (413)734-9666
Products: Paper cups, plates, and napkins; Disposable food service packaging; Janitorial supplies; Cleaners and equipment. SICs: 5113 (Industrial & Personal Service Paper); 5087 (Service Establishment Equipment); 5169 (Chemicals & Allied Products Nec). Est: 1946. Sales: $21,000,000 (2000). Emp: 75. Officers: Michael Shapiro, CFO; Scott Parent, President; Carol Teixera, General Mgr.

■ 21822 ■ Mark-Pack Inc.
PO Box 305
Coopersville, MI 49404-0305
Phone: (616)698-0033
Free: (800)333-9389   Fax: (616)698-0750
Products: Paper and disposable plastic shipping supplies. SICs: 5113 (Industrial & Personal Service Paper); 5112 (Stationery & Office Supplies). Est: 1946. Emp: 22.

■ 21823 ■ Marquardt and Company Inc.
161 6th Ave.
New York, NY 10013
Phone: (212)645-7200   Fax: (212)536-0282
Products: Paper for printers and publishers. SIC: 5111 (Printing & Writing Paper). Est: 1918. Sales: $100,000,000 (2000). Emp: 82. Officers: John Cooper, President; Elvin Bartholomew, Controller; Steve Varvaro, Vice President.

■ 21824 ■ **Massena Paper Company Inc.**
345 E Orvis St.
PO Box 28
Massena, NY 13662
Phone: (315)769-2433
Free: (800)479-7774 **Fax:** (315)769-2629
Products: Toilet paper and sanitary tissue products; Paper towels; Janitors' supplies; Specialty cleaning and sanitation products. **SICs:** 5113 (Industrial & Personal Service Paper); 5169 (Chemicals & Allied Products Nec); 5046 (Commercial Equipment Nec); 5087 (Service Establishment Equipment). **Est:** 1957. **Sales:** $1,400,000 (2000). **Emp:** 15. **Officers:** Wm. Reid, President.

■ 21825 ■ **Matz Paper Company, Inc.**
14122 Aetna St.
PO Box 195
Van Nuys, CA 91408-0195
Phone: (818)786-4153
Free: (800)776-4153 **Fax:** (818)901-8270
E-mail: matzpaper@msn.com
Products: Paper supplies; Printing paper. **SICs:** 5113 (Industrial & Personal Service Paper); 5111 (Printing & Writing Paper); 5112 (Stationery & Office Supplies). **Est:** 1924. **Sales:** $4,000,000 (2000). **Emp:** 20. **Officers:** Kenneth Matz, President; Larry Matz, Vice President; Fred Matz, Treasurer.

■ 21826 ■ **Mayer Myers Paper Co.**
1769 Latham St.
Memphis, TN 38106
Phone: (901)948-5631
Free: (800)766-1466 **Fax:** (901)774-7482
URL: http://www.mayermyerspaper.com
Products: Paper and allied products; Packaging and industrial converting paper; Industrial and heavy chemicals; Restaurant supplies. **SICs:** 5113 (Industrial & Personal Service Paper); 5169 (Chemicals & Allied Products Nec); 5141 (Groceries—General Line). **Est:** 1919. **Sales:** $13,000,000 (2000). **Emp:** 45. **Officers:** M. Levi Jr., Chairman of the Board; Steve Phillips, President; Bobby Benefield, Dir. of Purchasing; Harry Scott.

■ 21827 ■ **McComb Wholesale Paper Co.**
PO Box 463
McComb, MS 39649
Phone: (601)684-5521
Products: Paper; Restaurant supplies; School supplies. **SICs:** 5113 (Industrial & Personal Service Paper); 5111 (Printing & Writing Paper); 5112 (Stationery & Office Supplies). **Est:** 1947. **Sales:** $600,000 (2000). **Emp:** 7. **Officers:** Emmit Johnston Jr., President; Clara Johnston, Vice President.

■ 21828 ■ **J.B. McCoy and Son Inc.**
PO Box 9256
Canton, OH 44711
Phone: (330)456-8261
Free: (800)838-9883 **Fax:** (330)456-8265
Products: Food service; Disposables; Janitorial and cleaning supplies; Candy; Non food products; Fountain supplies; Coffee; Coke. **SICs:** 5085 (Industrial Supplies); 5046 (Commercial Equipment Nec). **Est:** 1893. **Sales:** $5,000,000 (2000). **Emp:** 25. **Officers:** Rick McCoy, President.

■ 21829 ■ **McMahon Paper Company Inc.**
PO Box 10162
Ft. Wayne, IN 46805
Phone: (219)422-3491 **Fax:** (219)422-3493
Products: Industrial paper supplies, including bathroom tissue and butcher's paper. **SIC:** 5113 (Industrial & Personal Service Paper). **Est:** 1950. **Sales:** $3,000,000 (2000). **Emp:** 10. **Officers:** Daniel F. Fulkerson, President; Max Baughman, CFO.

■ 21830 ■ **Mead Corp. Zellerbach Paper Co.**
50 E Rivercenter Blvd., Ste. 700
Covington, KY 41011-1626
Products: Paper products, including writing and copier paper; Packaging supplies. **SICs:** 5111 (Printing & Writing Paper); 5113 (Industrial & Personal Service Paper). **Est:** 1870. **Sales:** $800,000,000 (2000). **Emp:** 3,600. **Officers:** John Franz, President; Kurt Renick, VP of Admin.; Dale Simonsen, VP of Marketing; Mike Light, VP of Operations; Phil Morris.

■ 21831 ■ **Mead Pulp Sales Inc.**
Courthouse Plz. NE
Dayton, OH 45463
Phone: (937)222-6323 **Fax:** (937)495-4402
Products: Paper including filter, writing, carbon, and toilet paper. **SIC:** 5113 (Industrial & Personal Service Paper). **Sales:** $11,000,000 (2000). **Emp:** 20. **Officers:** J.H. Stausboll, President; M.E. McIntyre, Controller; Richard N. Platt, VP of Sales.

■ 21832 ■ **Melo Envelope Company Inc.**
525 W 52nd St.
New York, NY 10019
Phone: (212)315-4700 **Fax:** (212)974-0449
Products: Envelopes. **SIC:** 5112 (Stationery & Office Supplies). **Est:** 1932. **Sales:** $33,000,000 (2000). **Emp:** 125. **Officers:** Harry Fishbein, President; Robert M. Fishbein, Exec. VP of Finance.

■ 21833 ■ **Metro Recycling Co.**
2424 Beekman St.
Cincinnati, OH 45214
Phone: (513)251-1800
Products: Scrap paper. **SIC:** 5093 (Scrap & Waste Materials). **Sales:** $9,000,000 (1993). **Emp:** 25. **Officers:** Chuck Francis, Owner.

■ 21834 ■ **Michigan Retail Packaging**
1688 Gover Pky.
Mt. Pleasant, MI 48858
Phone: (517)772-9416
Free: (800)292-0420 **Fax:** (517)772-9417
E-mail: michretailpkg@journey.com
Products: Plastic and paper merchandise; Shopping bags; Apparel; Gift boxes, gift wrap, bows and ribbons; Tissue paper. **SICs:** 5113 (Industrial & Personal Service Paper); 5131 (Piece Goods & Notions). **Est:** 1972. **Officers:** Arlen Van Den Bos.

■ 21835 ■ **Mid-West Paper Products Co.**
1237 S 11th St.
Louisville, KY 40210
Phone: (502)636-2741
Products: Industrial paper products. **SIC:** 5113 (Industrial & Personal Service Paper). **Sales:** $20,000,000 (1992). **Emp:** 65. **Officers:** Howard McFarland, CFO.

■ 21836 ■ **Midwest Greeting Card Distributor**
2443 Burl Ct.
Mc Farland, WI 53558
Phone: (608)838-6018
Products: Greeting cards. **SIC:** 5112 (Stationery & Office Supplies).

■ 21837 ■ **The Millcraft Group**
6800 Grant Ave.
Cleveland, OH 44105
Phone: (216)441-5500 **Fax:** (216)641-2610
Products: Fine paper. **SIC:** 5111 (Printing & Writing Paper). **Est:** 1920. **Sales:** $200,000,000 (2000). **Emp:** 300. **Officers:** Charles L. Mlakar Jr.; Joe Maslowski; John Shoup; Larry Koverman; Debbie Bahr, Human Resources Contact. **Former Name:** Millcraft Paper Co.

■ 21838 ■ **Millcraft Paper Co.**
6800 Grant Ave.
Cleveland, OH 44105
Phone: (216)441-5505 **Fax:** (216)641-2610
Products: Paper and paper products. **SIC:** 5111 (Printing & Writing Paper). **Sales:** $200,000,000 (2000). **Emp:** 300.

■ 21839 ■ **Simon Miller Sales Co.**
1218 Chestnut St.
Philadelphia, PA 19107
Phone: (215)923-3600 **Fax:** (215)923-1173
URL: http://www.simonmiller.com
Products: Single web paper, coated rolls and sheets, including waxed packaging paper; Recycled paper products; Allied products; Paper bags; Paper towels; Printing trades; ECF certified paper. **SIC:** 5113 (Industrial & Personal Service Paper). **Est:** 1926. **Emp:** 50. **Officers:** Joseph Levit, President; Henri C. Levit, Vice President, e-mail: Henri.Levit@simonmiller.com.

■ 21840 ■ **Mobile Data Shred Inc.**
1744 W Burnett Ave.
Louisville, KY 40210-1740
Phone: (502)778-8266
Products: Recycled paper. **SIC:** 5093 (Scrap & Waste Materials). **Sales:** $1,000,000 (2000). **Emp:** 5. **Officers:** Roy Foster, Owner.

■ 21841 ■ **Monahan Paper Co.**
175 2nd St.
Oakland, CA 94607
Phone: (510)835-4670 **Fax:** (510)273-4585
E-mail: mpaper@pacbell.net
Products: Paper; Packaging; Janitorial chemicals; Sanitary papers. **SICs:** 5113 (Industrial & Personal Service Paper); 5087 (Service Establishment Equipment); 5169 (Chemicals & Allied Products Nec). **Est:** 1902. **Sales:** $7,000,000 (2000). **Emp:** 30. **Officers:** James E. Croft, Chairman of the Board; James M. Croft, President; Daniel Croft, Vice President; Dan Croft.

■ 21842 ■ **Monumental Paper Co.**
8261 Preston Ct
Jessup, MD 20794-9681
Phone: (410)945-1370 **Fax:** (410)947-0092
Products: Janitors' supplies; Paper and allied products. **SICs:** 5113 (Industrial & Personal Service Paper); 5087 (Service Establishment Equipment); 5111 (Printing & Writing Paper); 5112 (Stationery & Office Supplies). **Est:** 1925. **Emp:** 50. **Officers:** Soll L. Selko, President; Brad C. Selko, Vice President; J. Leo Levy, Vice President; Alan S. Dorenfeld, Vice President.

■ 21843 ■ **Mooney General Paper Co.**
1451 Chestnut Ave.
Hillside, NJ 07205
Phone: (973)926-3800 **Fax:** (973)926-0425
Products: Paper and allied products; Janitors' supplies; Packaging. **SICs:** 5113 (Industrial & Personal Service Paper); 5111 (Printing & Writing Paper); 5112 (Stationery & Office Supplies). **Est:** 1917. **Sales:** $18,000,000 (2000). **Emp:** 70.

■ 21844 ■ **Morse Wholesale Paper Company Inc.**
3302 Canal St.
Houston, TX 77003
Phone: (713)223-8361
Products: Paper products, including paper bags and plates, janitorial items, and freezer and butcher paper. **SICs:** 5113 (Industrial & Personal Service Paper); 5087 (Service Establishment Equipment). **Est:** 1928. **Sales:** $6,200,000 (2000). **Emp:** 45. **Officers:** Alice Morse, CEO & President; Earl Morse, Treasurer & Secty; Jerry Morse, VP of Marketing.

■ 21845 ■ **Mt. Ellis Paper Company Inc.**
Gateway International Park
Wembly Rd.
Box 4083
New Windsor, NY 12553
Phone: (914)567-1100 **Fax:** (914)567-1146
E-mail: jim1it@aol.com
Products: Paper and plastic disposables; Maintenance products. **SICs:** 5113 (Industrial & Personal Service Paper); 5087 (Service Establishment Equipment). **Est:** 1954. **Sales:** $27,000,000 (2000). **Emp:** 59. **Officers:** Seymour Kaplowitz, President; Clifford Kaplan, VP, Treasurer & Secty.

■ 21846 ■ **Nagel Paper & Box Co.**
1900 E Holland Ave.
PO Box 1567
Saginaw, MI 48605-1567
Phone: (517)753-4405 **Fax:** (517)753-2493
E-mail: npbc@worldnet.att.net
URL: http://www.npbc.com
Products: Packaging products. **SIC:** 5113 (Industrial & Personal Service Paper). **Est:** 1924. **Emp:** 16. **Officers:** James L. Baker, President; Linda E. Baker, Vice President; Linda Baker, Human Resources Contact; Melinda Lentner, Customer Service Contact. **Doing Business As:** MC Industries.

■ 21847 ■ **Nation Wide Paper Co.**
6901 Scott Hamilton Dr.
Little Rock, AR 72209
Phone: (501)565-8421
Free: (800)228-3321 **Fax:** (501)565-2426
Products: Janitorial supplies; Printing paper supplies; Food service items; Data communications equipment. **SICs:** 5113 (Industrial & Personal Service Paper); 5087 (Service Establishment Equipment). **Est:** 1938. **Sales:** $10,000,000 (2000). **Emp:** 60. **Officers:** Doug Foster, General Mgr.; Joan Ward, Admin. Mgr.; Terri Boatman, Merchandising Mgr.

■ 21848 ■ **Nationwide Papers Div.**
1 Champion Plz.
Stamford, CT 06921
Phone: (203)358-7000 **Fax:** (203)358-7495
Products: Paper. **SIC:** 5113 (Industrial & Personal Service Paper). **Est:** 1937. **Sales:** $1,340,000,000 (2000). **Emp:** 200. **Officers:** Thomas V. Zeuthen, President; Galen D. Todd, VP of Admin.; Greg Wilson, Sales Mgr.; Mel Kubiak, Dir. of Admin.

■ 21849 ■ **Neece Paper Company Inc.**
1307 Hadtner St.
Williamsport, PA 17701
Phone: (717)323-4679
Products: Paper and allied products, including napkins, paper towels, toilet paper, and sanitary tissue. **SIC:** 5113 (Industrial & Personal Service Paper). **Est:** 1880. **Emp:** 25. **Officers:** Fred Neece, President.

■ 21850 ■ **New England Industrial Supply Company Inc.**
210 Broadway
Everett, MA 02149
Phone: (617)389-2888
Free: (800)225-3496 **Fax:** (617)381-9280
URL: http://www.xygraphix.com
Products: Packaging supplies, including tapes; Shipping supplies, pallet wrap, stencil machines and tape dispensing machines. **SIC:** 5113 (Industrial & Personal Service Paper). **Est:** 1957. **Sales:** $5,000,000 (2000). **Emp:** 52. **Officers:** Mike Karess, President.

■ 21851 ■ **Newell Paper Co.**
PO Box 631
Meridian, MS 39301
Phone: (601)693-1783
Free: (800)844-8894 **Fax:** (601)483-4900
Products: Printing paper; Sanitary chemicals; Paper towels. **SICs:** 5111 (Printing & Writing Paper); 5113 (Industrial & Personal Service Paper); 5169 (Chemicals & Allied Products Nec). **Est:** 1945. **Sales:** $15,000,000 (2000). **Emp:** 70. **Officers:** Tommy Galyean, CEO; Oscar Burt, President & General Mgr.; Bill Allen, VP of Sales.

■ 21852 ■ **Garland C. Norris Co.**
PO Box 28
Apex, NC 27502
Phone: (919)387-1059
Free: (800)654-4875 **Fax:** (919)387-1325
URL: http://www.gcnorris.com
Products: Paper and allied products; Plastics; Industrial and heavy chemicals. **SICs:** 5113 (Industrial & Personal Service Paper); 5162 (Plastics Materials & Basic Shapes); 5169 (Chemicals & Allied Products Nec). **Est:** 1904. **Sales:** $23,000,000 (2000). **Emp:** 43. **Officers:** James A. King, President; James A. King II, Treasurer; Charles King, V.P. of Sales and Secty., e-mail: charles@gcnorris.com; Emma Gilliam, Customer Service Contact, e-mail: emma@gcnorris.com; Jean Council, Human Resources Contact, e-mail: jean@gcnorris.com.

■ 21853 ■ **Oak Paper Products Company Inc.**
3686 E Olympic Blvd.
Los Angeles, CA 90023
Phone: (213)268-0507
Free: (800)522-2676 **Fax:** (213)262-8517
Products: Boxes; Paper-based packaging supplies. **SIC:** 5113 (Industrial & Personal Service Paper). **Est:** 1945. **Sales:** $30,000,000 (2000). **Emp:** 150. **Officers:** Max Weissberg, President; Richard C. Seff, CFO; David Weissberg, Dir. of Marketing; Bernard Singer, Controller.

■ 21854 ■ **Jack Opler Sales Company Inc.**
2715 Avalon Ave.
Muscle Shoals, AL 35661
Phone: (205)381-3242 **Fax:** (205)381-5163
Products: Stationery and office supplies. **SIC:** 5112 (Stationery & Office Supplies). **Est:** 1967. **Emp:** 9. **Officers:** Jack Opler, President.

■ 21855 ■ **Orange Distributors Inc.**
4573 Dardanelle Dr.
Orlando, FL 32808
Phone: (407)295-2217
Free: (800)777-6012 **Fax:** (407)291-6455
Products: Paper and disposable plastic shipping supplies; Flat metal strapping; Packaging. **SICs:** 5113 (Industrial & Personal Service Paper); 5051 (Metals Service Centers & Offices). **Est:** 1971. **Sales:** $3,100,000 (1999). **Emp:** 17. **Officers:** W. R. Cornett, President.

■ 21856 ■ **Pacific Packaging Products Inc.**
PO Box 697
Wilmington, MA 01887
Phone: (978)657-9100
Free: (800)777-0300 **Fax:** (978)658-4933
URL: http://www.pacific@packagingproducts.com
Products: Packaging products, including boxes, printed tape, and labels; Packaging equipment; Die cutting. **SIC:** 5113 (Industrial & Personal Service Paper). **Est:** 1952. **Sales:** $60,000,000 (1999). **Emp:** 170. **Officers:** Robert Goldstein, Treasurer; John Leydon, CFO; Frank D. Goldstein, President.

■ 21857 ■ **Packaging Concepts and Design**
800 E Mandoline
Madison Heights, MI 48071
Phone: (248)585-3200 **Fax:** (248)585-2124
Products: Industrial packaging, including returnables and full service programs. **SIC:** 5085 (Industrial Supplies). **Est:** 1914. **Sales:** $20,000,000 (2000). **Emp:** 27. **Officers:** Richard Kaspers, President.

■ 21858 ■ **Pan American Papers Inc.**
5101 NW 37th Ave.
Miami, FL 33142
Phone: (305)635-2534 **Fax:** (305)635-2538
E-mail: panampap@bellsouth.net
Products: Paper and allied products. **SICs:** 5111 (Printing & Writing Paper); 5112 (Stationery & Office Supplies). **Est:** 1969. **Sales:** $10,000,000 (1999). **Emp:** 25. **Officers:** Jesus F. Valdes, President; Jesus A. Roca, Sr. VP; Francisco A. Valdes, Exec. VP.

■ 21859 ■ **Paper Center Inc.**
154 Saint John St.
Portland, ME 04102-3021
Phone: (207)774-3971 **Fax:** (207)879-7155
Products: Printing and writing paper. **SIC:** 5111 (Printing & Writing Paper). **Officers:** Richard Halloran, President.

■ 21860 ■ **Paper Corp.**
1865 NE 58th Ave.
PO Box 599
Des Moines, IA 50302
Phone: (515)262-9776
Free: (800)369-TREE **Fax:** (515)263-1641
Products: Computer paper; Paper business machine supplies. **SICs:** 5111 (Printing & Writing Paper); 5112 (Stationery & Office Supplies). **Est:** 1968. **Officers:** Dean Nims, President & Owner.

■ 21861 ■ **Paper Corporation of the United States**
161 Ave. of the Amer.
New York, NY 10013
Phone: (212)645-5900 **Fax:** (212)645-5908
Products: Paper and paper products, including writing paper and paper bags. **SIC:** 5111 (Printing & Writing Paper). **Est:** 1908. **Sales:** $150,000,000 (2000). **Emp:** 28. **Officers:** Daniel D. Romanaux, General Mgr.; James DiMauro, CFO.

■ 21862 ■ **Paper Mart**
5631 Alexander
Commerce, CA 90040
Phone: (323)726-8200
Free: (800)745-8800 **Fax:** (323)837-2242
E-mail: sales@papermart.com
URL: http://www.papermart.com
Products: Industrial and retail packaging products. **SICs:** 5113 (Industrial & Personal Service Paper); 5112 (Stationery & Office Supplies); 5087 (Service Establishment Equipment). **Est:** 1921. **Sales:** $16,000,000 (2000). **Emp:** 75. **Officers:** Tom Flick, CEO.

■ 21863 ■ **Paper Products Company Inc.**
36 Terminal Way
Pittsburgh, PA 15219
Phone: (412)481-6200 **Fax:** (412)481-4787
Products: Paper towels; Computer and facsimile paper; Adhesive tape. **SICs:** 5113 (Industrial & Personal Service Paper); 5162 (Plastics Materials & Basic Shapes). **Est:** 1913. **Sales:** $24,000,000 (2000). **Emp:** 65. **Officers:** D.R. Lackner, President; Paul F. Lackner, CFO; Douglas Townshend, Dir. of Marketing & Sales.

■ 21864 ■ **Paper Sales Corp.**
4 Testa Pl.
PO Box 1055
Norwalk, CT 06856
Phone: (203)866-5500
Products: Paper and allied products. **SICs:** 5113 (Industrial & Personal Service Paper); 5111 (Printing & Writing Paper); 5112 (Stationery & Office Supplies). **Est:** 1939. **Sales:** $2,000,000 (2000). **Emp:** 5. **Officers:** James O. Bamman, CEO & President.

■ 21865 ■ **Paper Service Company Inc.**
PO Box 970
1419 N Riverfront Dr.
Mankato, MN 56002
Phone: (507)625-7931
Free: (800)933-7931 **Fax:** (507)388-8266
Products: Paper products; Janitorial products; Food service products. **SICs:** 5113 (Industrial & Personal Service Paper); 5087 (Service Establishment Equipment); 5046 (Commercial Equipment Nec).

■ 21866 ■ **Paper Stock of Iowa**
PO Box 1284
Des Moines, IA 50305
Phone: (515)243-3156 **Fax:** (515)243-1741
Products: Corrugated products. **SIC:** 5111 (Printing & Writing Paper). **Est:** 1965. **Sales:** $800,000 (2000). **Emp:** 10. **Officers:** Bruce Sherman, President; David Smith, Controller.

■ 21867 ■ **Paragon Packaging Products Inc.**
625 Beaver Rd.
Girard, PA 16417
Phone: (814)774-9621
Free: (800)458-0425 **Fax:** (814)774-3689
E-mail: buyit@parapack.com
URL: http://www.parapack.com
Products: Corrugated Boxes. **SIC:** 5113 (Industrial & Personal Service Paper). **Est:** 1970. **Sales:** $3,500,000 (2000). **Emp:** 26. **Officers:** D.E. Wingerter, President; Linda Susko, Sales/Marketing Contact, e-mail: lsusko@parapack.com.

■ 21868 ■ **Frank Parsons Paper Co.**
2270 Beaver Rd.
Landover, MD 20785
Phone: (301)386-4700 **Fax:** (301)773-7864
Products: Paper and allied products. **SICs:** 5111 (Printing & Writing Paper); 5112 (Stationery & Office Supplies). **Est:** 1938. **Sales:** $80,000,000 (2000). **Emp:** 200. **Officers:** Douglas T. Parsons, CEO.

■ 21869 ■ **Patrick and Co.**
560 Market St.
San Francisco, CA 94104
Phone: (415)392-2640
Products: Stationery supplies. **SIC:** 5112 (Stationery & Office Supplies). **Est:** 1873. **Sales:** $5,000,000 (2000). **Emp:** 130. **Officers:** J.M. Patrick, President; Anita White, Controller; Mark Rodby, Dir. of Marketing.

■ 21870 ■ Patterson Sales Associates
PO Box 13156
Savannah, GA 31416-0156
Phone: (912)598-0086 **Fax:** (912)598-0174
Products: Paper products; Microfilm packaging; Paper bags for mailing and storing blue prints and drawings. **SIC:** 5113 (Industrial & Personal Service Paper). **Est:** 1956. **Sales:** $1,000,000 (2000). **Emp:** 2. **Officers:** Edward N. Patterson.

■ 21871 ■ Walter D. Peek Inc.
8 Wilson Dr.
Rye, NY 10580-1216
Phone: (914)835-5945 **Fax:** (914)835-5945
Products: Paper. **SIC:** 5111 (Printing & Writing Paper). **Est:** 1931. **Sales:** $5,000,000 (2000). **Emp:** 15. **Officers:** Walter D. Peek, President; Anthony V. Chiofolo, Treasurer & Secty.

■ 21872 ■ Pelican Paper Products Div.
3000 NE 30th Pl., 5th Fl.
Ft. Lauderdale, FL 33306
Phone: (954)563-1224
E-mail: pelican@bctonline.net
Products: Paper. **SIC:** 5111 (Printing & Writing Paper). **Est:** 1984. **Sales:** $14,000,000 (2000). **Emp:** 20. **Officers:** Gene Ebel, Vice President, e-mail: pelican@bctonline.com.

■ 21873 ■ Peninsular Paper Company Inc.
5101 E Hanna Ave.
Tampa, FL 33610
Phone: (813)621-3091 **Fax:** (813)623-1380
Products: Paper goods or products, including book mailers; Packaging; Paper and disposable plastic shipping supplies. **SICs:** 5113 (Industrial & Personal Service Paper); 5169 (Chemicals & Allied Products Nec). **Est:** 1911. **Sales:** $16,000,000 (2000). **Emp:** 25. **Officers:** R.S. Clarke Sr., President.

■ 21874 ■ Penmar Industries Inc.
1 Bates Ct.
Norwalk, CT 06854
Phone: (203)853-4868 **Fax:** (203)855-8136
E-mail: penmarct@aol.com
URL: http://www.penmar-industries.com
Products: Packaging supplies, including tape and bubble wrap; Boxes; Tapes; Industrial supplies; Shipping room supplies. **SIC:** 5113 (Industrial & Personal Service Paper). **Est:** 1967. **Sales:** $3,000,000 (1999). **Emp:** 15. **Officers:** Tony Soegaard, President; Rick Cipot; Nick Esposito, Sales/Marketing Contact; Laila Rudinas, Customer Service Contact.

■ 21875 ■ Penn-Jersey Paper Co.
2801 Red Lion Rd.
Philadelphia, PA 19154
Phone: (215)671-9800
Free: (800)992-3430 **Fax:** (215)673-8760
Products: Food service products; Sanitary paper products. **SIC:** 5113 (Industrial & Personal Service Paper). **Emp:** 140.

■ 21876 ■ Pennsylvania Paper & Supply Co.
215 Vine St.
PO Box 511
Scranton, PA 18501
Phone: (717)343-1112
Free: (800)982-4022 **Fax:** (717)343-1175
Products: Janitors' supplies; Paper towels; Toilet paper and sanitary tissue products. **SIC:** 5113 (Industrial & Personal Service Paper). **Est:** 1922. **Emp:** 35. **Officers:** Jerry Fink, President; Doug Fink, Vice President.

■ 21877 ■ Perez Trading Company Inc.
3490 NW 125th St.
Miami, FL 33167
Phone: (305)769-0761 **Fax:** (305)681-7963
Products: Printing paper. **SIC:** 5111 (Printing & Writing Paper). **Est:** 1947. **Sales:** $139,000,000 (2000). **Emp:** 170. **Officers:** J. Perez, Chairman of the Board; Carl A. Perez, CFO.

■ 21878 ■ Perkins-Goodwin Company Inc.
300 Atlantic St., 5th Fl.
Stamford, CT 06901-3522
Phone: (203)363-7800 **Fax:** (203)363-7809
Products: Printing, writing, industrial and personal service paper. **SICs:** 5111 (Printing & Writing Paper); 5113 (Industrial & Personal Service Paper). **Est:** 1846. **Sales:** $300,000,000 (1994). **Emp:** 75. **Officers:** Robert T. O'Hara, COO & Exec. VP; Cheryl Sadlon, Mgr. of Finance.

■ 21879 ■ Permalin Products Co.
109 W 26th St.
New York, NY 10001-6806
Phone: (212)627-7750 **Fax:** (212)463-9812
E-mail: permalin@aop.com
URL: http://www.booksatoz.com/permalin
Products: Book cover material. **SIC:** 5113 (Industrial & Personal Service Paper). **Est:** 1958. **Sales:** $18,000,000 (2000). **Emp:** 80. **Officers:** A. Shapiro, President; Jerry Molin, VP of Finance; Brice Draper, Vice President.

■ 21880 ■ Peterson Paper Co.
PO Box 254
Davenport, IA 52805-0254
Phone: (319)323-9946 **Fax:** (319)323-4625
Products: Paper and allied products. **SICs:** 5113 (Industrial & Personal Service Paper); 5111 (Printing & Writing Paper); 5112 (Stationery & Office Supplies). **Est:** 1891.

■ 21881 ■ Peyton's
PO Box 34250
Louisville, KY 40232
Phone: (502)429-4800 **Fax:** (502)429-4834
Products: Non-food supplies for grocery stores. **SICs:** 5113 (Industrial & Personal Service Paper); 5122 (Drugs, Proprietaries & Sundries). **Sales:** $210,000,000 (2000). **Emp:** 1,200. **Officers:** Robert Rice, President; Robert G. Welty, Controller.

■ 21882 ■ Piedmont National Corp.
PO Box 20118
Atlanta, GA 30325
Phone: (404)351-6130 **Fax:** (404)350-8383
Products: Packaging materials and industrial supplies. **SICs:** 5113 (Industrial & Personal Service Paper); 5085 (Industrial Supplies). **Est:** 1950. **Sales:** $45,000,000 (2000). **Emp:** 125. **Officers:** Albert Marx, CEO; Gary Mave, President.

■ 21883 ■ Piedmont Paper Company Inc.
PO Box 5413
Asheville, NC 28813-5413
Phone: (704)253-8721
Products: Coarse paper. **SIC:** 5113 (Industrial & Personal Service Paper). **Est:** 1944. **Sales:** $6,000,000 (2000). **Emp:** 19. **Officers:** Edward N. Dalton, President.

■ 21884 ■ Pierce Box & Paper Corp.
1505 Kishwaukee St.
Rockford, IL 61104
Phone: (815)963-1505 **Fax:** (815)963-0792
Products: Boxes and crates; Paper and allied products. **SICs:** 5113 (Industrial & Personal Service Paper); 5111 (Printing & Writing Paper); 5112 (Stationery & Office Supplies). **Est:** 1953. **Sales:** $4,500,000 (2000). **Emp:** 14. **Officers:** Lou Franchini, President.

■ 21885 ■ Plymouth Paper Company Inc.
PO Box 188
Holyoke, MA 01041
Phone: (413)536-2810
Free: (800)776-8433 **Fax:** (413)532-9134
Products: Stationery, paper, pads, and recycled printing and copying paper. **SICs:** 5111 (Printing & Writing Paper); 5093 (Scrap & Waste Materials); 5112 (Stationery & Office Supplies). **Est:** 1888.

■ 21886 ■ Pollock Paper Distributors
PO Box 660005
Dallas, TX 75266-0005
Phone: (214)263-2126
Free: (800)843-7320 **Fax:** (972)262-4737
URL: http://www.pollockpaper.com
Products: Paper products, including wrapping and cardboard. **SIC:** 5113 (Industrial & Personal Service Paper). **Est:** 1918. **Sales:** $52,000,000 (1999). **Emp:** 300. **Officers:** L. Pollock III, President; Kenneth Schroeder, Controller; David Berman, Marketing Mgr.; Charles Overstreet, Dir of Personnel.

■ 21887 ■ Pomerantz Diversified Services Inc.
PO Box 1284
Des Moines, IA 50305
Phone: (515)243-3156 **Fax:** (515)243-1741
Products: Corrugated boxes and containers. **SIC:** 5113 (Industrial & Personal Service Paper). **Est:** 1963. **Sales:** $6,800,000 (2000). **Emp:** 30. **Officers:** David Lettween, CEO; Rick Dobesh, CFO; Bruce Sherman, President.

■ 21888 ■ S. Posner Sons Inc.
950 3rd Ave.
New York, NY 10022
Phone: (212)486-1360 **Fax:** (212)593-3092
Products: Paper bags. **SIC:** 5113 (Industrial & Personal Service Paper). **Est:** 1889. **Officers:** Joel Busel, President; Samuel Posner, Treasurer & Secty.; Joyce Mintzer, Exec. VP.

■ 21889 ■ Presto Paper Company Inc.
292 5th Ave., No. 501
New York, NY 10001-4513
Phone: (212)243-3350 **Fax:** (212)613-2267
Products: Corrugated and solid fiber boxes; Packaging and industrial converting paper. **SIC:** 5113 (Industrial & Personal Service Paper). **Est:** 1941. **Officers:** T. M. Rosenthal, Chairman of the Board; B. H. Rosenthal, President; N. A. Rosenthal, Treasurer.

■ 21890 ■ Price and Pierce International Inc.
PO Box 971
Stamford, CT 06904-0971
Phone: (203)328-2000 **Fax:** (203)967-3651
Products: Paper; Pulp. **SICs:** 5099 (Durable Goods Nec); 5111 (Printing & Writing Paper). **Sales:** $200,000,000 (2000). **Emp:** 44. **Officers:** Peter J. Napoli, Exec. VP & CFO.

■ 21891 ■ Quaker City Paper & Chemical
Rte. 26
Ocean View, DE 19970
Phone: (302)539-4373 **Fax:** (302)539-4880
Products: Paper; Chemicals; Party supplies, including plates, napkins, and balloons. **SICs:** 5111 (Printing & Writing Paper); 5199 (Nondurable Goods Nec); 5169 (Chemicals & Allied Products Nec). **Est:** 1979. **Sales:** $1,000,000 (2000). **Emp:** 6. **Officers:** Sue Stauffer; Joe Stauffer.

■ 21892 ■ Quaker City Paper and Chemical
Rte. 26
Ocean View, DE 19970
Phone: (302)539-4373 **Fax:** (302)539-4880
Products: Paper and paper products. **SIC:** 5111 (Printing & Writing Paper). **Sales:** $1,000,000 (2000). **Emp:** 6.

■ 21893 ■ Quaker City Paper Co.
300 N Sherman St.
PO Box 2677
York, PA 17405
Phone: (717)843-9061
Free: (800)533-2553 **Fax:** (717)843-7850
E-mail: qsales@quakercitypaper.com
URL: http://www.quakercitypaper.com
Products: Paper and allied products. **SICs:** 5113 (Industrial & Personal Service Paper); 5199 (Nondurable Goods Nec). **Est:** 1946. **Sales:** $12,000,000 (2000). **Emp:** 67. **Officers:** Paul E. Newcomer, Chairman of the Board; Mike Leas, VP of Operations; David Newcomer, President. **Alternate Name:** Paper Plus.

■ 21894 ■ Quality First Greetings Corp.
10500 American Rd.
Cleveland, OH 44144
Phone: (216)252-7300 **Fax:** (216)252-4495
Products: Greeting cards; Gift wrap and accessories. **SIC:** 5112 (Stationery & Office Supplies).

■ 21895 ■ Quimby-Walstrom Paper Co.
PO Box 1806
Grand Rapids, MI 49501
Phone: (616)784-4700 **Fax:** (616)784-7813
Products: Printer paper. **SIC:** 5111 (Printing & Writing Paper). **Sales:** $21,000,000 (2000). **Emp:** 38. **Officers:** Richard Tietema, President; James C. De Vries, Exec. VP; Bob Vos, VP of Marketing.

■ 21896 ■ Rainbow Paper Company, Inc.
2404 Hwy.14
PO Box 9985
New Iberia, LA 70562-9985
Phone: (318)369-9007
Free: (888)858-4334 **Fax:** (318)369-9009
Products: Janitors' supplies; Restaurant supplies; Paper and allied products. **SICs:** 5113 (Industrial & Personal Service Paper); 5087 (Service Establishment Equipment); 5111 (Printing & Writing Paper); 5112 (Stationery & Office Supplies). **Est:** 1952. **Sales:** $5,000,000 (2000). **Emp:** 7. **Officers:** Willis P. Gachassin.

■ 21897 ■ Range Paper Corp.
PO Box 970
Virginia, MN 55792
Phone: (218)741-7644 **Fax:** (218)741-7647
Products: Paper products. **SICs:** 5113 (Industrial & Personal Service Paper); 5111 (Printing & Writing Paper); 5112 (Stationery & Office Supplies). **Est:** 1921. **Sales:** $1,500,000 (2000). **Emp:** 12. **Officers:** Bruce Nevala, President.

■ 21898 ■ Regal Supply & Chemical Co.
1801 Texas Ave.
PO Box 1955
El Paso, TX 79950
Phone: (915)542-1831 **Fax:** (915)542-1839
Products: Janitors' supplies; Paper and allied products; Specialty cleaning and sanitation products. **SICs:** 5113 (Industrial & Personal Service Paper); 5169 (Chemicals & Allied Products Nec). **Est:** 1953. **Sales:** $4,000,000 (2000). **Emp:** 45. **Officers:** H. Ettinger, President.

■ 21899 ■ Reliable Paper & Supply Company Inc.
13 Water St.
PO Box 666
Claremont, NH 03743-0666
Phone: (603)542-2161 **Fax:** (603)543-3053
E-mail: rosenpl@cyberportal.net
Products: Paper products; Restaurant supplies and equipment. **SICs:** 5113 (Industrial & Personal Service Paper); 5111 (Printing & Writing Paper); 5112 (Stationery & Office Supplies); 5046 (Commercial Equipment Nec). **Est:** 1947. **Sales:** $450,000 (1999). **Emp:** 4. **Officers:** Lewis H. Rosen, President, e-mail: rosenpl@cyberportal.net.

■ 21900 ■ Reliance Group of Michigan
23920 Freeway Park Dr.
Farmington Hills, MI 48335
Phone: (248)478-6620 **Fax:** (248)478-0032
URL: http://www.proforma.com
Products: Commercial printers; Business forms; Advertising. **SIC:** 5112 (Stationery & Office Supplies). **Est:** 1980. **Sales:** $3,000,000 (2000). **Emp:** 13. **Officers:** Jonathan Grant, President; Richard Stemple, Vice President.

■ 21901 ■ Reliance Paper Co.
1404 W 12th St.
Kansas City, MO 64101
Phone: (816)471-8338 **Fax:** (816)471-8338
E-mail: ReliancePaper@aol.com
Products: Corrugated boxes, tape, and packaging materials. **SIC:** 5113 (Industrial & Personal Service Paper). **Est:** 1959. **Officers:** Richard P. Rielley, Owner.

■ 21902 ■ Resource Net International
PO Box 2967
Shawnee Mission, KS 66201
Phone: (913)451-1213 **Fax:** (913)451-2824
Products: Fine paper, including printing and writing. **SIC:** 5111 (Printing & Writing Paper). **Est:** 1865. **Sales:** $320,000,000 (2000). **Emp:** 1,000. **Officers:** David Gruenewald, President; Jerry Bax, Controller.

■ 21903 ■ Resource Net International
PO Box 1337
Harrisburg, PA 17105
Phone: (717)564-9761 **Fax:** (717)561-3180
Products: Industrial service paper and food service. **SICs:** 5113 (Industrial & Personal Service Paper); 5142 (Packaged Frozen Foods). **Sales:** $120,000,000 (2000). **Emp:** 250. **Officers:** Tony Myers, President; Jeanette Malinoski, CFO.

■ 21904 ■ ResourceNet International (Shawnee Mission, Kansas)
50 E River Center Blvd., Ste. 700
Covington, KY 41011
Phone: (606)655-2000 **Fax:** (606)655-6846
Products: Printing papers, industrial paper and plastics, food service disposable products, sanitary maintenance products, packaging equipment and supplies, and printing equipment and supplies. **SICs:** 5111 (Printing & Writing Paper); 5113 (Industrial & Personal Service Paper); 5084 (Industrial Machinery & Equipment). **Sales:** $320,000,000 (2000). **Emp:** 1,000. **Officers:** Thomas E. Costello, President; Jerry Bax, Controller.

■ 21905 ■ Retailers Supply Co.
380 Freeport Blvd., No. 22
Sparks, NV 89431-6263
Phone: (775)356-8156
Free: (800)621-2241 **Fax:** (775)356-8161
E-mail: retailsupply@powernet.net
Products: Retail packaging and display equipment; Paper and plastic products. **SICs:** 5113 (Industrial & Personal Service Paper); 5162 (Plastics Materials & Basic Shapes). **Est:** 1974. **Emp:** 3. **Officers:** Michael Edwardson, Owner.

■ 21906 ■ Ris Paper Company Inc.
7300 Turfway Rd., Ste. 540
Florence, KY 41042
Phone: (606)746-8700 **Fax:** (606)746-0050
Products: Printing and writing paper. **SIC:** 5111 (Printing & Writing Paper). **Sales:** $525,000,000 (2000). **Emp:** 700. **Officers:** Mark Griffin, CEO, President & Chairman of the Board; Peter Strople, CFO.

■ 21907 ■ Riverside Paper Company Inc.
5770 NW 36th Ave.
Miami, FL 33142
Phone: (305)633-5221 **Fax:** (305)638-4167
Products: Paper and allied products; Paper and disposable plastic shipping supplies; Packaging. **SICs:** 5113 (Industrial & Personal Service Paper); 5111 (Printing & Writing Paper); 5112 (Stationery & Office Supplies). **Officers:** Marshall Steirn, President; Howard Steirn, Secretary.

■ 21908 ■ Roa Distributors
341 E Liberty St.
Lancaster, PA 17603
Phone: (717)295-9023
Products: Paper products. **SIC:** 5111 (Printing & Writing Paper).

■ 21909 ■ Roberts Paper Co.
PO Box 1029
100-104 Lincoln
Amarillo, TX 79105
Phone: (806)376-9814 **Fax:** (806)376-1974
Products: Paper and allied products; Janitors' supplies. **SIC:** 5113 (Industrial & Personal Service Paper). **Est:** 1942. **Sales:** $3,500,000 (2000). **Emp:** 29. **Officers:** Richard E. Roberts, President; Jim Roberts, Vice President; Joy Lacy, Vice President.

■ 21910 ■ Rome Paper Co.
1 E 16th St.
PO Box 313
Rome, GA 30161
Phone: (706)234-8208
Free: (800)342-6434 **Fax:** (706)234-9572
Products: Paper products. **SIC:** 5113 (Industrial & Personal Service Paper). **Est:** 1947. **Sales:** $5,000,000 (2000). **Emp:** 15. **Officers:** Wilson Burgess, President.

■ 21911 ■ Roosevelt Paper Co.
One Roosevelt Dr.
Mt. Laurel, NJ 08054
Phone: (856)303-3470
Free: (800)523-3470 **Fax:** (856)303-4100
E-mail: info@rooseveltpaper.com
URL: http://www.rooseveltpaper.com
Products: Printing paper. **SIC:** 5111 (Printing & Writing Paper). **Est:** 1932. **Sales:** $190,000,000 (2000). **Emp:** 500. **Officers:** Ted Kosloff, President; Tom Salvato, CFO.

■ 21912 ■ Roto-Litho Inc.
1827 E 16th St.
Los Angeles, CA 90021
Phone: (213)749-7551
Products: Printing paper. **SICs:** 5112 (Stationery & Office Supplies); 5111 (Printing & Writing Paper). **Est:** 1958. **Sales:** $25,000,000 (2000). **Emp:** 15. **Officers:** R.E. Burkett III., President; Richard Burkett, Dir. of Sales.

■ 21913 ■ Royal Industries
538 N Milwaukee Ave.
Chicago, IL 60622
Phone: (312)733-4920 **Fax:** (312)733-9774
Products: Disposable plastic goods, including eating utensils, cups, and dishes; Paper cups and dishes; Food service products; Housewares; Furniture table bases; Baby chairs; Stainless steel flatware; Holloware; Aluminum stockpots; Skillets; Dinnerware; Glassware. **SIC:** 5113 (Industrial & Personal Service Paper). **Est:** 1944. **Sales:** $15,000,000 (2000). **Emp:** 50.

■ 21914 ■ Royal Paper Corp.
185 Madison Ave.
New York, NY 10016
Phone: (212)684-1200
Products: Paper. **SIC:** 5111 (Printing & Writing Paper). **Sales:** $60,000,000 (2000). **Emp:** 100. **Officers:** Edward Furlong, President; S.Y. Sehonfeld, VP of Sales.

■ 21915 ■ Runge Paper Co., Inc.
2201 Arthur Ave.
Elk Grove Village, IL 60007
Phone: (708)593-1788 **Fax:** (847)228-6827
E-mail: info@rungepaper.com
URL: http://www.rungepaper.com
Products: Paper products; Packaging; Disposables; Janitorial and maintenance supplies. **SIC:** 5113 (Industrial & Personal Service Paper). **Est:** 1940. **Sales:** $18,000,000 (2000). **Emp:** 49. **Officers:** Richard Benhart, President; Robert O'Day, VP of Operations; Stan Bensen, General Mgr.; Hans Albers, Controller.

■ 21916 ■ S.E. Rykoff & Co.
PO Box 10007
Portland, OR 97210
Phone: (503)224-3553 **Fax:** (503)224-0429
Products: Paper for food service and janitorial needs. **SICs:** 5113 (Industrial & Personal Service Paper); 5087 (Service Establishment Equipment).

■ 21917 ■ S and S Inc.
21300 St. Clair Ave.
Cleveland, OH 44117
Phone: (216)383-1880 **Fax:** (216)383-9597
Products: Packaging. **SIC:** 5113 (Industrial & Personal Service Paper). **Est:** 1965. **Sales:** $5,000,000 (2000). **Emp:** 30. **Officers:** Daniel J. Kunes, President; Paul Nared, Sales Mgr.; Tim Spicer, Operations Mgr.

■ 21918 ■ Sabin Robbins Paper Co.
106 Circle Freeway Dr.
Cincinnati, OH 45246
Phone: (513)874-5270 **Fax:** (513)874-5785
Products: Fine printing paper. **SIC:** 5111 (Printing & Writing Paper). **Est:** 1884. **Sales:** $74,600,000 (2000). **Emp:** 200. **Officers:** Thomas P. Price Jr., President; Peter Countryman, Treasurer.

■ 21919 ■ Sacramento Bag Manufacturing Co.
PO Box 1563
Sacramento, CA 95812
Phone: (916)441-6121 **Fax:** (916)448-3141
Products: Bags. **SIC:** 5199 (Nondurable Goods Nec). **Est:** 1923. **Sales:** $4,500,000 (2000). **Emp:** 45. **Officers:** Alex Fahn, President; David Rosenberg, Dir. of Marketing & Sales.

■ 21920 ■ Safeguard Abacus
226 Mary St.
Reno, NV 89509-2719
Phone: (702)323-3592 **Fax:** (702)348-8361
Products: Computer forms; Printing and writing paper. **SIC:** 5111 (Printing & Writing Paper). **Officers:** Richard Wilkins, Owner.

■ 21921 ■ **St. Louis Paper and Box Co.**
PO Box 8260
St. Louis, MO 63156-8260
Phone: (314)531-7900
Free: (800)779-7901 **Fax:** (314)531-0968
Products: Packaging materials, supplies, and equipment. **SIC:** 5113 (Industrial & Personal Service Paper). **Est:** 1960. **Emp:** 33. **Officers:** William M. Livingston Jr., CEO; Robert Mayer, President.

■ 21922 ■ **Saxon Paper Co.**
3005 Review Ave.
Long Island City, NY 11101-3239
Phone: (718)937-6622
Products: Paper and allied products; Envelopes; Computer paper; Special industrial paper. **SICs:** 5113 (Industrial & Personal Service Paper); 5112 (Stationery & Office Supplies); 5111 (Printing & Writing Paper). **Est:** 1935. **Emp:** 78. **Officers:** Michael J. Mazo, President; John F. Mancl, VP & General Mgr.; Robert F. Luongo, VP of Marketing.

■ 21923 ■ **Schilling Paper Co.**
1500 Opportunity Rd. NW
Rochester, MN 55901
Phone: (507)288-8940
Free: (800)888-1885 **Fax:** (507)781-2344
Products: Disposable paper products, including paper plates, toilet paper, napkins and paper towels; Hand soap, laundry soap, washer supplies, and janitorial supplies. **SICs:** 5113 (Industrial & Personal Service Paper); 5122 (Drugs, Proprietaries & Sundries); 5169 (Chemicals & Allied Products Nec); 5087 (Service Establishment Equipment).

■ 21924 ■ **A.D. Schinner Co.**
4901 W State St.
Milwaukee, WI 53208
Phone: (414)771-4300 **Fax:** (414)771-7450
Products: Disposable goods, including tissue products, paper bags, cups, plates, and foil products. **SIC:** 5113 (Industrial & Personal Service Paper). **Est:** 1912. **Sales:** $17,000,000 (2000). **Emp:** 32. **Officers:** R. Kutalek, President; Nancy Osterman, President.

■ 21925 ■ **School Stationers Corp.**
1641 S Main St.
Oshkosh, WI 54901
Phone: (920)426-1300 **Fax:** (920)233-3755
Products: School supplies, including drawing paper, construction paper, theme paper, and newsprint paper. **SICs:** 5111 (Printing & Writing Paper); 5112 (Stationery & Office Supplies). **Est:** 1910. **Sales:** $1,200,000 (2000). **Emp:** 11. **Officers:** Robert Stauffer Jr., President; Robert Stauffer Sr., CFO; Karen Stauffer, Dir. of Marketing.

■ 21926 ■ **Schorin Company Inc.**
1800 Penn Ave.
Pittsburgh, PA 15222
Phone: (412)281-0650 **Fax:** (412)281-2880
Products: Paper and party supplies. **SIC:** 5113 (Industrial & Personal Service Paper). **Est:** 1952. **Emp:** 11. **Officers:** Daniel Bendas, Vice President; Neila Bendas, Asst. Treasurer & Sec.; Ruth B. Hecht, Treasurer & Secty.; Neila Bendas, Asst. Treasurer & Secty.

■ 21927 ■ **A.J. Schrafel Paper Corp.**
PO Box 788
Floral Park, NY 11002-0788
Phone: (516)437-1700
Free: (800)727-3723 **Fax:** (516)437-1702
E-mail: schrafelpaper@msn.com
URL: http://www.schrafelpaper.com
Products: Paperboard for boxes and packaging. **SIC:** 5113 (Industrial & Personal Service Paper). **Est:** 1946. **Sales:** $18,000,000 (2000). **Emp:** 49. **Officers:** Alfred J. Schrafel, President; Richard Schrafel, Exec. VP; Robert A. Schrafel, Dir. of Marketing & Sales.

■ 21928 ■ **Scott Paper, Inc.**
Hazlettville Rd.
PO Box 7010 C
Dover, DE 19903
Phone: (302)678-2600 **Fax:** (302)678-2600
Products: Paper products, including wet wipes. **SICs:** 5113 (Industrial & Personal Service Paper); 5111 (Printing & Writing Paper).

■ 21929 ■ **Sealed Air Corp.**
Park 80 E
Saddle Brook, NJ 07663
Phone: (201)791-7600 **Fax:** (201)703-4205
URL: http://www.cfonews.com/see
Products: Packaging. **SIC:** 5113 (Industrial & Personal Service Paper). **Officers:** T.J. Dermot Dunphy, CEO & Chairman of the Board; Elmer N. Funkhouser III, Sr. VP; William V. Hickey, COO & President; Dale Wormwood, Sr. VP; James A. Bixby, Vice President; Bruce A. Cruikshank, Vice President; Warren H. McCandless, Vice President; Ross G. Morrison, Vice President; Robert A. Pesci, Vice President; Horst Tebbe, Vice President; Robert M. Grace Jr., General Counsel & Secty.

■ 21930 ■ **Patrick Seaman Paper Co.**
2000 Howard St.
Detroit, MI 48216
Phone: (313)496-3131
Free: (800)477-0050 **Fax:** (313)965-5284
Products: Paper and allied products. **SICs:** 5111 (Printing & Writing Paper); 5112 (Stationery & Office Supplies); 5113 (Industrial & Personal Service Paper). **Est:** 1906. **Emp:** 110. **Officers:** F. Michael Starling, Chairman of the Board; W. John Wickett, President; Rick Akkashian, VP of Sales; George H. Ashley, VP of Finance; William Cartwright, VP of Purchasing; David M. LaMothe, VP of Operations; Ellen E. Shook, VP of Creative Services.

■ 21931 ■ **Seaman-Patrick Paper Co.**
2000 Howard St.
Detroit, MI 48216
Phone: (313)496-3131 **Fax:** (313)965-5284
Products: Printing and writing paper. **SIC:** 5111 (Printing & Writing Paper). **Sales:** $100,000,000 (2000). **Emp:** 140. **Officers:** Michael Starling, CEO & Chairman of the Board; George Ashley, VP of Finance.

■ 21932 ■ **Select Robinson Paper Co.**
160 Fox St.
Portland, ME 04101
Phone: (207)773-2973 **Fax:** (207)773-0142
Products: Printing paper. **SICs:** 5111 (Printing & Writing Paper); 5113 (Industrial & Personal Service Paper). **Est:** 1886. **Sales:** $26,000,000 (2000). **Emp:** 45. **Officers:** David H. Drake, VP & General Merchandising Mgr.; Keith P. Malone, Controller; David A. Oleson, Marketing Mgr.

■ 21933 ■ **Seneca Paper**
5786 Collett Rd.
Farmington, NY 14425-9536
Phone: (716)424-1600 **Fax:** (716)424-3192
Products: Paper products. **SICs:** 5113 (Industrial & Personal Service Paper); 5111 (Printing & Writing Paper). **Est:** 1944. **Sales:** $5,000,000 (2000). **Emp:** 35. **Officers:** Robert S. Adams, President.

■ 21934 ■ **Servall Products Inc.**
199-205 Westwood Ave.
Long Branch, NJ 07740
Phone: (732)222-0083 **Fax:** (732)870-1668
URL: http://www.servallproducts.com
Products: Paper; Janitorial supplies. **SICs:** 5113 (Industrial & Personal Service Paper); 5087 (Service Establishment Equipment); 5111 (Printing & Writing Paper); 5112 (Stationery & Office Supplies). **Est:** 1931. **Emp:** 15. **Officers:** Shamus J. Dunn, President; Robert R. Franco, Vice President; Robert R. Franco, Sales/Marketing Contact; Christine Rodriguez, Human Resources Contact.

■ 21935 ■ **Service Packaging Corp.**
3701 Highland Park NW
North Canton, OH 44720-4535
Phone: (330)499-0872
Products: Personal paper products and supplies. **SIC:** 5112 (Stationery & Office Supplies).

■ 21936 ■ **Seventh Generation, Inc.**
1 Mill St.
Box A26
Burlington, VT 05401-1530
Phone: (802)658-3773
Free: (800)456-1191 **Fax:** (802)658-1771
E-mail: recycle@seventhgen.com
URL: http://www.seventhgen.com
Products: Environmentally safe household products. **SICs:** 5113 (Industrial & Personal Service Paper); 5169 (Chemicals & Allied Products Nec). **Est:** 1989. **Sales:** $13,000,000 (2000). **Emp:** 13. **Officers:** Jeffrey Hollender, CEO & President; Jeffrey Phillips, VP of Sales. **Former Name:** Seventh Generation Wholesale, Inc.

■ 21937 ■ **Sherman Business Forms, Inc.**
55 Tanners Rd.
Great Neck, NY 11020-1628
Phone: (516)773-0142 **Fax:** (516)773-0144
Products: Business forms. **SIC:** 5112 (Stationery & Office Supplies). **Est:** 1922. **Sales:** $400,000 (2000). **Emp:** 2. **Officers:** Sol Sherman, President.

■ 21938 ■ **Shipman Printing Industries Inc.**
PO Box 157
Niagara Falls, NY 14302
Phone: (716)731-3281
Free: (800)462-2114 **Fax:** (716)731-9620
E-mail: printing@spiprint.com
Products: Envelopes; Letterhead; Commercial printing. **SICs:** 5112 (Stationery & Office Supplies); 5113 (Industrial & Personal Service Paper). **Est:** 1966. **Sales:** $5,000,000 (1999). **Emp:** 41. **Officers:** Gary Blum, President; Michael A. Fiore, VP of Sales, e-mail: Mfiore@spiprint.com; Richard Faiola, Vice President; Frank Shipman, Chairman.

■ 21939 ■ **Shorewood Packaging of California Inc.**
5900 Wilshire Blvd., No. 530
Los Angeles, CA 90036-5013
Phone: (213)463-3000 **Fax:** (213)465-4300
E-mail: jpalmer@shorepak.com
Products: Packaging for compact discs, games, software, and videos; Cardboard packaging. **SIC:** 5085 (Industrial Supplies). **Est:** 1962. **Sales:** $600,000 (2000). **Emp:** 3. **Officers:** Marc Shore, President.

■ 21940 ■ **Shorewood Packaging Company of Illinois Inc.**
1300 W Belmont Ave., Ste. 504
Chicago, IL 60657-3242
Phone: (847)934-5579
Products: Commercial packaging. **SIC:** 5085 (Industrial Supplies). **Sales:** $600,000 (1999). **Emp:** 3. **Officers:** Timothy A. Klewicki, Sales Mgr.

■ 21941 ■ **Shorr Paper Products Inc.**
PO Box 6800
Aurora, IL 60504
Phone: (630)978-1000 **Fax:** (630)978-1300
Products: Paper and allied products. **SIC:** 5113 (Industrial & Personal Service Paper). **Est:** 1922. **Sales:** $60,000,000 (2000). **Emp:** 200. **Officers:** K. Shorr, Chairman of the Board; R. Shorr, President; L.A. Dieter, CFO.

■ 21942 ■ **Snyder Paper Corp.**
PO Box 758
Hickory, NC 28603
Phone: (828)328-2501
Products: Furniture cushions. **SICs:** 5111 (Printing & Writing Paper); 5085 (Industrial Supplies). **Est:** 1946. **Sales:** $100,000,000 (2000). **Emp:** 280. **Officers:** Roger McGuire, President.

■ 21943 ■ **Southeastern Paper Group**
Wadsworth Industrial Pk.
PO Box 6220
Spartanburg, SC 29304
Phone: (864)574-0440
Free: (800)858-7230 **Fax:** (864)576-3828
E-mail: sepaper@att.net
Products: Paper and allied products; Packaging; Chemical preparations. **SICs:** 5113 (Industrial & Personal Service Paper); 5169 (Chemicals & Allied Products Nec). **Est:** 1969. **Sales:** $40,000,000 (2000). **Emp:** 105. **Officers:** E. Lewis Miller Jr., President;

Jimey High, Sales/Marketing Contact; Linda Garner, VP of Finance.

■ 21944 ■ **Southwest Paper Company Inc.**
PO Box 21270
Wichita, KS 67208-7270
Phone: (316)838-7755
Free: (800)657-6046 **Fax:** (316)838-7864
E-mail: swpaper@swpaper.com
URL: http://www.swpaper.com
Products: Packaging and industrial converting paper; Food service disposables; Janitor's supplies and equipment. **SICs:** 5113 (Industrial & Personal Service Paper); 5087 (Service Establishment Equipment). **Est:** 1938. **Sales:** $33,000,000 (1999). **Emp:** 96. **Officers:** John Tangeman, CEO; Eric Tangeman, President.

■ 21945 ■ **Specialty Box and Packaging Co.**
1040 Broadway
Albany, NY 12204
Phone: (518)465-7344
Products: Gift boxes, including cardboard. **SIC:** 5113 (Industrial & Personal Service Paper). **Est:** 1963. **Sales:** $1,000,000 (2000). **Emp:** 10. **Officers:** D. Fialkoff, President; Pauline Garisia, Bookkeeper.

■ 21946 ■ **Spicers Paper Inc.**
12310 E Slauson Ave.
Santa Fe Springs, CA 90670
Phone: (562)698-1199
Free: (800)422-4120 **Fax:** (562)945-2597
E-mail: www.spicers.com
Products: Printing and writing paper. **SIC:** 5111 (Printing & Writing Paper). **Est:** 1987. **Sales:** $277,000,000 (2000). **Emp:** 340. **Officers:** Chris Creighton, President; Anthony J. Kennedy, VP of Finance & Admin.

■ 21947 ■ **Springfield Paper Co.**
PO Box 3336
Springfield, MO 65808
Phone: (417)862-5061
Products: Paper packaging supplies; Janitorial supplies; Gift wrap; Food service supplies. **SIC:** 5113 (Industrial & Personal Service Paper). **Sales:** $2,800,000 (2000). **Emp:** 18. **Officers:** Keith G. Wells, President; J. Paul Todd, Vice President.

■ 21948 ■ **Springfield Paper Specialties, Inc.**
1754 Limekiln Pke.
Ft. Washington, PA 19034
Phone: (215)643-2800 **Fax:** (215)643-0639
Products: Industrial supplies; Janitors' supplies; Paper and allied products. **SICs:** 5113 (Industrial & Personal Service Paper); 5085 (Industrial Supplies); 5111 (Printing & Writing Paper). **Est:** 1963. **Sales:** $7,000,000 (2000). **Emp:** 25. **Officers:** Ralph N. Jennings Jr., President.

■ 21949 ■ **Stanford Paper Co.**
1901 Stanford Ct.
Landover, MD 20785
Phone: (410)772-1900 **Fax:** (410)386-4364
Products: Paper products. **SICs:** 5113 (Industrial & Personal Service Paper); 5111 (Printing & Writing Paper); 5112 (Stationery & Office Supplies). **Est:** 1925. **Emp:** 100. **Officers:** Samuel J. Nutwell, President; Carter Leach, Sales Mgr.

■ 21950 ■ **Stark Co.**
432 W Allegheny Arms
Philadelphia, PA 19133
Phone: (215)425-2222 **Fax:** (215)425-3560
E-mail: sales@starkcompany.com
Products: Packaging supplies, including tape; Mailroom equipment and supplies. **SIC:** 5113 (Industrial & Personal Service Paper). **Est:** 1935. **Sales:** $4,000,000 (2000). **Emp:** 21. **Officers:** N. Marucci, President.

■ 21951 ■ **SWM Inc.**
1978 Innerbelt Business Center Dr.
St. Louis, MO 63114
Phone: (314)426-6677
Free: (800)844-8243 **Fax:** (314)426-6679
Products: Business forms. **SIC:** 5112 (Stationery & Office Supplies). **Est:** 1981. **Sales:** $6,000,000 (2000). **Emp:** 23. **Officers:** John Sanders, President; Barbara Barbarash, Chairman of the Board, Secty. & Treasurer.

■ 21952 ■ **Tayloe Paper Co.**
PO Box 580880
Tulsa, OK 74158
Phone: (918)835-6911
Free: (800)825-6911 **Fax:** (918)935-7255
URL: http://www.TaylorPaper.com
Products: Paper products, including copy and office paper; Janitorial equipment and supplies; Packaging equipment and supplies. **SICs:** 5113 (Industrial & Personal Service Paper); 5111 (Printing & Writing Paper). **Est:** 1923. **Sales:** $24,000,000 (2000). **Emp:** 73. **Officers:** David L. Bayles, President & Treasurer.

■ 21953 ■ **Todd-Zenner Packaging**
20803 SW 105th St.
Tualatin, OR 97062
Phone: (503)692-6992 **Fax:** (503)692-6627
Products: Packaging. **SIC:** 5113 (Industrial & Personal Service Paper).

■ 21954 ■ **Total Office Interiors**
PO Box 16010
Baltimore, MD 21218
Phone: (410)366-6000
URL: http://www.totalofficeint.com
Products: Office furniture. **SICs:** 5021 (Furniture); 5112 (Stationery & Office Supplies). **Est:** 1930. **Sales:** $42,000,000 (2000). **Emp:** 78. **Officers:** William W. Jones Jr., President; Alan McCracken, CFO; Joanne Gleason, Director of Corporate Services. **Former Name:** Baltimore Stationery Co.

■ 21955 ■ **Trade Supplies**
3188 E Slauson Ave.
Vernon, CA 90058
Phone: (213)581-3250
Products: Plastic and paper cups, plates, napkins, and straws for restaurants. **SICs:** 5113 (Industrial & Personal Service Paper); 5162 (Plastics Materials & Basic Shapes). **Sales:** $13,000,000 (2000). **Emp:** 25. **Officers:** Martin Sanders, President.

■ 21956 ■ **Trails West Publishing**
PO Box 1483
Great Falls, MT 59403
Phone: (406)453-6453
Products: Christmas cards. **SIC:** 5112 (Stationery & Office Supplies). **Officers:** Frank Flaherty, Partner.

■ 21957 ■ **Tyco Adhesives**
1400 Providence Hwy.
Norwood, MA 02062
Phone: (781)440-6200
Free: (800)248-7659 **Fax:** (781)440-6276
URL: http://www.tycoadhesives.com
Products: Pressure sensitive products, including tape. **SIC:** 5113 (Industrial & Personal Service Paper). **Est:** 1950. **Sales:** $30,000,000,000 (2000). **Emp:** 30,000. **Former Name:** Kendall-Polyken.

■ 21958 ■ **Unger Co.**
12401 Berea Rd.
Cleveland, OH 44111
Phone: (216)252-1400
Free: (800)321-1418 **Fax:** (216)252-1427
E-mail: ungerco@aol.com
Products: Bakery and deli packaging. **SIC:** 5113 (Industrial & Personal Service Paper). **Est:** 1920. **Sales:** $20,000,000 (2000). **Emp:** 32. **Officers:** Gerald Unger, CEO & Chairman of the Board; Brenda K. Roby, Finance Officer.

■ 21959 ■ **Unijax Div.**
815 S Main St.
Jacksonville, FL 32207-8140
Phone: (904)783-0550
Products: Paper products, including janitorial, business, and packaging supplies; Corrugated containers; Food packaging equipment; Shipping room supplies. **SICs:** 5113 (Industrial & Personal Service Paper); 5087 (Service Establishment Equipment). **Est:** 1968. **Sales:** $600,000,000 (2000). **Emp:** 1,700. **Officers:** Charles F. White, President; Michael R. Simpson, VP & CFO; E. Charles Walter, VP of Marketing; Cecil A. McClary, Dir of Human Resources. **Former Name:** Unijax Div.

■ 21960 ■ **Union Paper Company Div.**
10 Admiral St.
Providence, RI 02908
Phone: (401)274-7000
Free: (800)556-6454 **Fax:** (401)331-1910
E-mail: mary_anne_ferreira@unionind.com
URL: http://www.unionind.com
Products: Flexible paper packaging. **SIC:** 5113 (Industrial & Personal Service Paper). **Est:** 1898. **Sales:** $25,000,000 (1999). **Emp:** 165. **Officers:** Harley A. Frank, President; John Wilbur, CFO; Tony Abreu, VP of Operations; Eric Blackwell, Dir of Human Resources. **Former Name:** Union Paper Company Inc.

■ 21961 ■ **Unisource Paper Co.**
PO Box 37190
Louisville, KY 40233-7190
Phone: (502)636-1341 **Fax:** (502)637-3675
Products: Paper; Industrial items, including janitorial supplies. **SICs:** 5111 (Printing & Writing Paper); 5085 (Industrial Supplies); 5087 (Service Establishment Equipment). **Est:** 1897. **Sales:** $50,000,000 (2000). **Emp:** 47. **Officers:** Jim Leopold; David Baumann; Rick Weppler; Jim Flautt.

■ 21962 ■ **Unisource**
109 Lincoln Ave.
PO Box 3395
Evansville, IN 47732
Phone: (812)422-1184 **Fax:** (812)429-2585
Products: Paper and allied products; Toilet paper and sanitary tissue products; Paper towels. **SICs:** 5113 (Industrial & Personal Service Paper); 5111 (Printing & Writing Paper); 5112 (Stationery & Office Supplies). **Est:** 1960. **Officers:** Nelson Heimicks, President.

■ 21963 ■ **Unisource**
2737 S Adams Rd.
Rochester Hills, MI 48309
Phone: (248)853-9111 **Fax:** (248)853-9871
Products: Fine paper, including writing paper; Industrial supplies. **SICs:** 5111 (Printing & Writing Paper); 5112 (Stationery & Office Supplies); 5085 (Industrial Supplies). **Est:** 1860. **Sales:** $50,000,000 (2000). **Emp:** 90. **Officers:** John P. Taylor; Tom Donnellon, VP of Marketing & Sales.

■ 21964 ■ **Unisource**
4700 S Palisade
Wichita, KS 67217
Phone: (316)522-3494 **Fax:** (316)522-2245
Products: Printing papers; Business imaging papers; Packaging equipment and products; Sanitary maintenance equipment products. **SICs:** 5111 (Printing & Writing Paper); 5113 (Industrial & Personal Service Paper). **Sales:** $30,000,000 (2000). **Emp:** 36. **Officers:** J. Robinson, Sales Mgr. **Former Name:** Mid-Continent Paper Co.

■ 21965 ■ **Unisource**
3587 Oakcliff Rd.
Atlanta, GA 30340
Phone: (404)447-9000 **Fax:** (404)840-9810
Products: Fine printing papers; Industrial products. **SICs:** 5111 (Printing & Writing Paper); 5113 (Industrial & Personal Service Paper); 5112 (Stationery & Office Supplies); 5085 (Industrial Supplies). **Est:** 1918. **Sales:** $110,000,000 (2000). **Emp:** 400. **Officers:** Coley Evans, CEO; James Vansant, CFO; E. Charles Walton, Exec. VP; James Escarius, Dir of Human Resources.

■ 21966 ■ **Unisource-Central Region Div.**
1015 Corporate Square Dr.
St. Louis, MO 63132
Phone: (314)919-1800
Free: (800)775-3952 **Fax:** (314)919-3899
Products: Packaging materials, including styrofoam, paper, cardboard, and plastic. **SICs:** 5111 (Printing & Writing Paper); 5113 (Industrial & Personal Service Paper). **Est:** 1963. **Sales:** $265,000,000 (2000). **Emp:** 400. **Officers:** Steve Olroyd, President; Richard Frizzell, VP of Finance; Tom Ransone, Dir. of Marketing; Karl Bruce, Dir. of Information Systems.

■ 21967 ■ **Unisource Midwest Inc.**
PO Box 308001
Gahanna, OH 43230-8001
Phone: (614)251-7000 **Fax:** (614)251-7054
Products: Paper. **SICs:** 5111 (Printing & Writing

Paper); 5087 (Service Establishment Equipment). **Est:** 1875. **Sales:** $230,000,000 (2000). **Emp:** 460. **Officers:** Jack Bryant, President; Robert Noble, VP of Admin.

■ 21968 ■ **Unisource Worldwide**
510 E Courtland St.
Morton, IL 61550-9042
Phone: (309)263-6834
Free: (800)767-1531 **Fax:** (309)263-3140
Products: Packaging; Sanitary food trays, plates, and dishes; Printing paper; Chemicals. **SIC:** 5113 (Industrial & Personal Service Paper). **Est:** 1935. **Emp:** 46. **Officers:** Jon Montgomery, Operations Mgr.; Soren Olesen, Fine Papers Sales Mgr.; Jim Burgerer, Suppy Systems Sales Mgr.

■ 21969 ■ **Unisource Worldwide Inc.**
7575 Brewster Ave.
Philadelphia, PA 19153
Phone: (215)492-1776
Free: (800)222-2757 **Fax:** (215)365-8121
E-mail: unisourcelink.com
Products: Paper, including fine textured and writing paper. **SIC:** 5111 (Printing & Writing Paper). **Est:** 1865. **Sales:** $110,000,000 (2000). **Emp:** 70. **Officers:** Raymond Radomicki.

■ 21970 ■ **Unisource Worldwide Inc.**
PO Box 649
Exton, PA 19341-0649
Phone: (610)296-4470 **Fax:** (610)722-3400
Products: Paper products; Industrial products. **SICs:** 5111 (Printing & Writing Paper); 5113 (Industrial & Personal Service Paper); 5084 (Industrial Machinery & Equipment); 5087 (Service Establishment Equipment). **Est:** 1968. **Sales:** $7,108,400,000 (2000). **Emp:** 14,200. **Officers:** Ray B. Mundt, CEO & Chairman of the Board; Richard H. Bogan, Sr. VP & CFO; Medio Waldt, Dir. of Marketing; Richard Hrapczynski, Information Systems Mgr.; William Kirby, VP of Human Resources.

■ 21971 ■ **Unisource Worldwide Inc. Denver Div.**
12601 E 38th Ave.
Denver, CO 80239
Phone: (303)371-4260 **Fax:** (303)371-5467
Products: Printing paper; Plastic bags; Styrofoam. **SICs:** 5113 (Industrial & Personal Service Paper); 5111 (Printing & Writing Paper). **Est:** 1969. **Sales:** $33,000,000 (2000). **Emp:** 80. **Officers:** Robert Keating, General Mgr.; Robert Keating, Dir. of Marketing & Sales; Eric Boshart, Dir. of Information Systems.

■ 21972 ■ **Unisource Worldwide Inc. (Southborough, Massachusetts)**
9 Crystal Pond Rd.
Southborough, MA 01772
Phone: (508)480-6000 **Fax:** (508)480-6299
Products: Industrial paper products, including paper towels, cups, and napkins; Packaging machinery and supplies. **SIC:** 5113 (Industrial & Personal Service Paper). **Est:** 1972. **Sales:** $200,000,000 (1999). **Emp:** 150. **Officers:** Michael Connelly, VP & General Mgr.

■ 21973 ■ **Unisource Worldwide Inc. West**
17011 Beach Blvd.
Huntington Beach, CA 92647
Phone: (714)375-1650 **Fax:** (310)432-4061
Products: Boxes, paper towels, envelopes, and printing paper. **SIC:** 5111 (Printing & Writing Paper). **Est:** 1985. **Sales:** $750,000,000 (2000). **Emp:** 1,500. **Officers:** James Swearingen, President; Robert Di Mascio, Exec. VP of Finance; Frank Andruss, VP of Marketing; Steven Becker.

■ 21974 ■ **United Container Corp.**
1350 N Elston Ave.
Chicago, IL 60622
Phone: (773)342-2200 **Fax:** (773)342-4231
Products: Corrugated packaging. **SIC:** 5113 (Industrial & Personal Service Paper). **Est:** 1963. **Sales:** $3,500,000 (2000). **Emp:** 25. **Officers:** P.P. Heymann, President & Chairman of the Board; B. Heymann, VP of Finance; Florian Seidel, Dir. of Marketing; Wayne Meyers, Dir. of Systems.

■ 21975 ■ **United Envelope Co.**
525 W 52nd St. 2nd Fl.
New York, NY 10019
Phone: (212)315-4700
Products: Envelopes. **SIC:** 5112 (Stationery & Office Supplies).

■ 21976 ■ **United Paper Company Inc.**
4101 Sarellen Rd.
Richmond, VA 23231
Phone: (804)226-1936
Free: (800)347-1936 **Fax:** (804)226-4030
Products: Paper supplies; Chemicals. **SICs:** 5113 (Industrial & Personal Service Paper); 5169 (Chemicals & Allied Products Nec). **Est:** 1906. **Emp:** 28. **Officers:** Paul Burns, President; Herman Clarke, Vice President.

■ 21977 ■ **United Stationers Inc.**
2200 E Golf Rd.
Des Plaines, IL 60016-1267
Phone: (847)699-5000
Free: (800)424-4003 **Fax:** (847)699-4716
E-mail: kdvorak@ussco.com
URL: http://www.unitedstationers.com
Products: Computer office products, consumables, furniture and facilities supplies. **SICs:** 5112 (Stationery & Office Supplies); 5021 (Furniture); 5044 (Office Equipment). **Est:** 1921. **Sales:** $3,400,000,000 (1999). **Emp:** 6,400. **Officers:** Randall W. Larrimore, CEO & President; Steven R. Schwarz, Exec. VP & President, United Supply Div.; Tom Helton, VP of Human Resources.

■ 21978 ■ **United Systems Software Inc.**
955 E Javelina Ave Ste 106
Mesa, AZ 85204
Phone: (480)545-5100 **Fax:** (480)892-9877
Products: Develops real estate and appraisal software; Develops electronic forms. **SIC:** 5111 (Printing & Writing Paper). **Officers:** Michael Schafer, Owner.

■ 21979 ■ **Universal Blueprint Paper**
730 Great SW Pkwy.
Atlanta, GA 30336-2338
Phone: (404)349-0600
Free: (800)241-1498 **Fax:** (404)349-7334
Products: Paper and allied products. **SIC:** 5111 (Printing & Writing Paper). **Emp:** 20. **Officers:** A.L. Hill, Branch Manager.

■ 21980 ■ **Universal Forms, Labels, and Systems, Inc.**
2020 S Eastwood
Santa Ana, CA 92705
Phone: (714)540-8025
Free: (800)559-8404 **Fax:** (714)540-3279
Products: Business forms; Labels; Custom combinations of forms, labels, cards, laminates, barcodes, and die-cutting. **SIC:** 5112 (Stationery & Office Supplies). **Est:** 1967. **Sales:** $900,000 (2000). **Emp:** 55. **Officers:** Joel Van Boom, President.

■ 21981 ■ **Universal Paper Goods Co.**
7171 Telegraph Rd.
Los Angeles, CA 90040-3227
Phone: (213)685-6220
Products: Paper and allied products. **SICs:** 5113 (Industrial & Personal Service Paper); 5112 (Stationery & Office Supplies). **Sales:** $30,000,000 (2000). **Emp:** 499. **Officers:** Paul Herzbrun, VP & General Mgr.

■ 21982 ■ **Universal Paper and Packaging**
PO Box 537
Appleton, WI 54912-0537
Phone: (920)731-4171 **Fax:** (920)731-7185
Products: Industrial packing products; Fine paper products. **SICs:** 5111 (Printing & Writing Paper); 5113 (Industrial & Personal Service Paper). **Est:** 1890. **Sales:** $20,000,000 (2000). **Emp:** 180. **Officers:** Edward H. Strand, President; Richard S. Frizzell, Finance Officer; Larry A. Spaeth, Dir. of Marketing; Roger C. Kusserow, Controller.

■ 21983 ■ **Valley Wholesalers Inc.**
RR 5, Box 39
Winona, MN 55987-9700
Phone: (507)454-1556
Free: (800)657-4592 **Fax:** (507)454-6507
Products: Towels and napkins; Cleaning supplies. **SICs:** 5113 (Industrial & Personal Service Paper); 5169 (Chemicals & Allied Products Nec). **Emp:** 23. **Officers:** James W. Bushard, General Mgr.; Dennis E. Neville.

■ 21984 ■ **Van Paper Co.**
2107 Stewart Ave.
St. Paul, MN 55116
Phone: (612)690-1751
Products: Paper products, including tissue, trash liners, and towels. **SIC:** 5113 (Industrial & Personal Service Paper). **Est:** 1916. **Sales:** $10,000,000 (2000). **Emp:** 34. **Officers:** Mark Van, President.

■ 21985 ■ **Victory Packaging**
800 Junction Ave.
Plymouth, MI 48170
Phone: (734)459-2000
Free: (800)331-2089 **Fax:** (734)459-3833
Products: Packaging supplies, including tape, boxes, and Styrofoam. **SICs:** 5113 (Industrial & Personal Service Paper); 5085 (Industrial Supplies). **Est:** 1971. **Sales:** $15,000,000 (2000). **Emp:** 30. **Officers:** Ray Stachura, General Mgr.

■ 21986 ■ **Joseph Weil and Sons, Inc.**
825 E 26th St.
La Grange Park, IL 60526
Phone: (708)579-9595 **Fax:** (708)579-9897
URL: http://www.josephweil.com
Products: Janitorial equipment and supplies; Industrial packaging equipment and supplies. **SICs:** 5113 (Industrial & Personal Service Paper); 5112 (Stationery & Office Supplies); 5078 (Refrigeration Equipment & Supplies). **Est:** 1893. **Sales:** $40,000,000 (2000). **Emp:** 80. **Officers:** Joseph P. Weil, CEO & President; Michael G. Burchinal, Dir. of Operations; Kenneth Finfer, CFO; Chip Auerbach, Dir. of Packaging Sales; J. Tom Keller, Dir. of Chemical Sales; Clayton L. Mark, Distribution Mgr.; Thomas R. Beggan, Purchasing Mgr.

■ 21987 ■ **Werts Novelty Co.**
1520 W 5th
Muncie, IN 47302-2103
Phone: (765)288-8825
Free: (800)428-8602 **Fax:** (765)741-3009
Products: Tickets. **SIC:** 5113 (Industrial & Personal Service Paper). **Est:** 1932. **Sales:** $30,000,000 (2000). **Emp:** 499. **Officers:** Joe Wilner; Robert W. Harvey, General Mgr.

■ 21988 ■ **West Coast Paper Co.**
23200 64th Ave. S
Kent, WA 98032
Phone: (206)623-1850 **Fax:** (206)623-6082
Products: Printing paper. **SICs:** 5111 (Printing & Writing Paper); 5113 (Industrial & Personal Service Paper). **Est:** 1930. **Sales:** $76,000,000 (2000). **Emp:** 230. **Officers:** Frederick J. Stabbert, President; David Yonce, CFO; Richard D. Smith, Dir. of Marketing & Sales; Michael Hasbrook, Dir. of Data Processing; Nancy Schroeder, Dir of Human Resources.

■ 21989 ■ **Western Printing Co.**
PO Box 1555
Aberdeen, SD 57401
Phone: (605)229-1480 **Fax:** (605)229-2147
Products: Stationery. **SIC:** 5112 (Stationery & Office Supplies). **Est:** 1929. **Sales:** $3,000,000 (2000). **Emp:** 45. **Officers:** Steven Pfeiffer, President & CFO.

■ 21990 ■ **Westvaco Worldwide**
299 Park Ave.
New York, NY 10171
Phone: (212)688-5000
Products: Printing and writing paper; Lumber and millwork; Industrial inorganic chemicals; Wood pulp. **SICs:** 5111 (Printing & Writing Paper); 5099 (Durable Goods Nec); 5031 (Lumber, Plywood & Millwork); 5169 (Chemicals & Allied Products Nec). **Officers:** James L. Martin, VP & Gen. Mgr.

■ 21991 ■ White River Paper Company Inc.
PO Box 455
White River Junction, VT 05001-0455
Phone: (802)295-3188
Free: (800)639-7226   Fax: (802)295-5494
E-mail: wrpaper@valley.net
URL: http://www.wrpaper.com
Products: Janitorial supplies; Packaging supplies; Foodservice disposables; Office supplies. SICs: 5113 (Industrial & Personal Service Paper); 5087 (Service Establishment Equipment). Est: 1881. Sales: $12,000,000 (2000). Emp: 45. Officers: Michael Lyford, President; Bill Ladd, Controller; James Keighley, Sales Mgr.; Jeffrey Lyford, Secretary; Gary Gervais, Purchasing Manager.

■ 21992 ■ White Rose Paper Co.
4665 Hollins Ferry Rd.
Baltimore, MD 21227
Phone: (410)247-1900
Products: Printing paper. SIC: 5111 (Printing & Writing Paper). Sales: $22,000,000 (2000). Emp: 60. Officers: Theodore A. Imbach, President; Robert S. Barber, CFO; Frank E. Curran, Dir. of Marketing & Sales; Elizabeth Horseman, Dir. of Information Systems.

■ 21993 ■ Wilcox Paper Co.
5916 Court St. Rd.
PO Box 378
Syracuse, NY 13206-0378
Phone: (315)437-1496   Fax: (315)463-9645
E-mail: sparks-dave@msn.com
Products: Janitorial and Packaging products. SICs: 5113 (Industrial & Personal Service Paper); 5111 (Printing & Writing Paper); 5169 (Chemicals & Allied Products Nec); 5087 (Service Establishment Equipment). Est: 1927. Emp: 17. Officers: David Sparks, President; Brian Sparks, Vice President; Sam Bovalino, Controller.

■ 21994 ■ Wilson Paper Co.
363 S Kellogg St.
Galesburg, IL 61401
Phone: (309)342-0168   Fax: (309)342-0362
Products: Packaging; Janitors' supplies; Paper and disposable plastic shipping supplies; Paper and allied products; Specialty cleaning and sanitation products. SICs: 5113 (Industrial & Personal Service Paper); 5087 (Service Establishment Equipment); 5169 (Chemicals & Allied Products Nec); 5111 (Printing & Writing Paper); 5112 (Stationery & Office Supplies). Est: 1934. Sales: $2,000,000 (2000). Emp: 14. Officers: C.D. Guenther, President; Estelle Sopher, Vice President.

■ 21995 ■ Wisconsin Paper and Products Co.
PO Box 13455
Milwaukee, WI 53213-0455
Phone: (414)771-3771
Products: Paper products, including printing paper and toilet paper. SICs: 5111 (Printing & Writing Paper); 5113 (Industrial & Personal Service Paper). Est: 1921. Sales: $10,000,000 (2000). Emp: 35. Officers: Thomas C. Boyce, CEO.

■ 21996 ■ Wolcotts Forms Inc.
15124 Downey Ave.
Paramount, CA 90723
Phone: (310)630-0911   Fax: (310)630-4180
Products: Legal forms. SIC: 5112 (Stationery & Office Supplies). Est: 1893. Sales: $2,000,000 (2000). Emp: 18. Officers: E.C. Hughes Jr., President.

■ 21997 ■ Wurzburg Inc.
PO Box 710
Memphis, TN 38101
Phone: (901)525-1441
Products: Packaging supplies. SIC: 5113 (Industrial & Personal Service Paper). Est: 1908. Sales: $95,000,000 (2000). Emp: 380. Officers: Reginald Wurzburg, CEO; Bernard Lapides, Exec. VP of Marketing.

■ 21998 ■ WWF Paper Corp.
2 Bala Plz., Ste.200
Bala Cynwyd, PA 19004
Phone: (610)667-9210
Free: (800)345-1305   Fax: (610)667-1663
E-mail: info@wwfpaper.com
URL: http://www.wwfpaper.com
Products: Fine paper. SIC: 5111 (Printing & Writing Paper). Est: 1922. Sales: $800,000,000 (2000). Emp: 380. Officers: Edward V. Furlong Jr., President; George D. Sergio, Exec. VP & CFO; Donald H. Palmer, Sr. VP; James Adelsberger, Information Systems Mgr.; Peter K. Wittman, Exec. VP of Distribution; Morris C. Swope, VP of Employee Development.

■ 21999 ■ WWF Paper Corp.
1150 Lively Blvd.
Elk Grove Village, IL 60007
Phone: (847)593-7500
Free: (800)942-8817   Fax: (847)593-7956
Products: Paper and paper products. SIC: 5111 (Printing & Writing Paper). Est: 1948. Sales: $70,000,000 (2000). Emp: 50.

■ 22000 ■ Xpedx
PO Box 1567
Chattanooga, TN 37401-1567
Phone: (423)698-8111
Products: Printing paper; Janitorial supplies, including cleaning solutions; Packaging products; Graphic supplies; Food service supplies; Sanitary paper products. SICs: 5111 (Printing & Writing Paper); 5113 (Industrial & Personal Service Paper); 5045 (Computers, Peripherals & Software). Est: 1919. Sales: $10,000,000 (2000). Emp: 42. Officers: Keith Earle, VP & General Mgr. Former Name: Dillard Paper Co.

■ 22001 ■ Xpedx
3940 Olympic Blvd., No. 250
Erlanger, KY 41018
Phone: (859)282-5600
URL: http://www.xpedx.com
Products: Writing paper, drawing paper, construction paper, printing paper, industrial supplies, packaging equipment and supplies, and graphics equipment and supplies. SIC: 5113 (Industrial & Personal Service Paper). Est: 1976. Sales: $7,000,000,000 (2000). Emp: 10,000. Officers: Tom Costello, President; Paul Quinn, VP of Operations. Former Name: International Paper Co. CDA Distributors Div.

■ 22002 ■ xpedx
PO Box 21767
Greensboro, NC 27420
Phone: (336)299-1211   Fax: (336)852-8925
Products: Paper products, including bathroom tissue and fine writing paper. SIC: 5111 (Printing & Writing Paper). Est: 1926. Sales: $560,000,000 (2000). Emp: 1,800. Officers: Robert Grillet, President; Gary De Villers, VP of Admin.; John Patrick, Dir. of Systems; Thomas E. Trivett, Dir of Human Resources. Former Name: Dillard.

■ 22003 ■ XPEDX
W 232 N 2950 Roundy Cir. E
PO Box 550
Pewaukee, WI 53072-4034
Phone: (262)549-9400
Free: (800)242-2139   Fax: (262)549-3422
E-mail: http://www.xpedx.com
Products: Paper and paper products, including packaging papers and equipment; Graphic supplies. SICs: 5111 (Printing & Writing Paper); 5113 (Industrial & Personal Service Paper). Est: 1952. Sales: $200,000,000 (2000). Emp: 180. Officers: David Watson, General Mgr.; Renee Albrecht, CFO; John Dillon, CEO. Former Name: ResourceNet International.

■ 22004 ■ xpedx
4510 Reading Rd.
Cincinnati, OH 45229
Phone: (513)641-5000
Free: (800)669-7102   Fax: (513)641-5003
Products: Industrial and personal service paper; Food service disposables; Janitorial chemicals and equipment. SIC: 5113 (Industrial & Personal Service Paper). Est: 1919. Emp: 300. Officers: Gordon L. Eanes, VP & General Mgr. Former Name: ResourceNet International (Cincinnati, Ohio).

■ 22005 ■ Xpedx/Carpenter Group
PO Box 2709
Grand Rapids, MI 49548
Phone: (616)452-9741   Fax: (616)452-3740
Products: Fine paper; Book publishing; Imaging; Graphic and industrial supplies. SICs: 5111 (Printing & Writing Paper); 5112 (Stationery & Office Supplies). Est: 1909. Sales: $50,000,000 (2000). Emp: 130. Officers: Steven DeKruyter, President; James Fraher, VP of Sales; Randy Riemersma, Admin. Mgr.; John Idema, Operations Mgr.; Doug Kroll, Data Processing Mgr.

■ 22006 ■ Xpedx-Carpenter Group
401 Fernhill Ave.
Ft. Wayne, IN 46805
Phone: (219)482-4686   Fax: (219)484-2619
Products: Fine printing paper; Industrial and graphic paper. SIC: 5111 (Printing & Writing Paper). Est: 1980. Sales: $6,000,000 (2000). Emp: 34. Officers: Rick Waggoner, General Mgr.; Tom Yaggy, Sales Mgr. Former Name: Carpenter Paper of Indiana.

■ 22007 ■ Xpedx/Carpenter Group
PO Box 2709
Grand Rapids, MI 49548
Phone: (616)452-9741   Fax: (616)452-3740
Products: Paper and paper products. SIC: 5111 (Printing & Writing Paper). Sales: $50,000,000 (2000). Emp: 130.

■ 22008 ■ xpedx West Region
55 Madison Ave., Ste. 800
Denver, CO 80206
Phone: (303)329-6644   Fax: (303)355-7506
Products: Office paper and supplies; Janitorial supplies; Graphics and industrial supplies. SICs: 5112 (Stationery & Office Supplies); 5087 (Service Establishment Equipment). Est: 1911. Sales: $260,000,000 (2000). Emp: 1,200. Officers: Richard B. Lowe, President; Charles R. Donnelly, VP of Operations; Jim Elder, VP of Marketing; Ray France, Information Technology Mgr.; Kenneth Siefken, VP of Finance. Former Name: Dixon Paper Co.

■ 22009 ■ Yasutomo and Company Inc.
490 Eccles Ave.
South San Francisco, CA 94080
Phone: (415)737-8888
Free: (800)262-6454   Fax: (415)737-8877
E-mail: yandc@aol.com
URL: http://www.yasutomo.com
Products: Stationery; Arts and crafts supplies. SIC: 5112 (Stationery & Office Supplies). Est: 1954. Sales: $12,000,000 (2000). Emp: 30. Officers: Daniel H. Egusa, President; Wayne Barringer, Vice President. Former Name: Yasutomo and Company Inc.

■ 22010 ■ Yellowstone Paper Co.
PO Box 1557
Billings, MT 59103-1557
Phone: (406)252-3488   Fax: (406)252-3489
Products: Paper and paper products. SIC: 5111 (Printing & Writing Paper). Est: 1946. Sales: $3,000,000 (2000). Emp: 6.

■ 22011 ■ York Tape and Label Co.
PO Box 1309
York, PA 17405
Phone: (717)846-4840   Fax: (717)845-5372
Products: Labels; Label applicator equipment. SIC: 5113 (Industrial & Personal Service Paper). Est: 1947. Sales: $50,000,000 (2000). Emp: 300. Officers: Timothy Hue, President; Dennis Cole, Comptroller; John Attagel, Dir. of Sales; Diedra A. McMeans, Dir of Personnel.

■ 22012 ■ Zellerbach Co.
3131 New Mark Dr.
Miamisburg, OH 45342
Phone: (937)495-6000   Fax: (937)495-6010
Products: Paper packaging. SIC: 5113 (Industrial & Personal Service Paper). Sales: $685,000,000 (2000). Emp: 2,200. Officers: Peter H. Vogel, President; Ed Herzog, Controller.

(41) Petroleum, Fuels, and Related Equipment

Entries in this section are arranged alphabetically by company name. When the company name is a personal name, the company name is alphabetized by the surname unless the first name or initial(s) are part of a trade name. See the User's Guide at the front of this directory for additional information.

■ **22013** ■ **3-D Energy Inc.**
Pierce Rd.
Buxton, ME 04093
Phone: (207)929-8804
Products: Gasoline additive. **SIC:** 5172 (Petroleum Products Nec).

■ **22014** ■ **A and A Pump Co.**
1119 Camden St.
San Antonio, TX 78215
Phone: (210)226-1191
Products: Service station equipment, including hoses, nozzles and pumps. **SIC:** 5013 (Motor Vehicle Supplies & New Parts). **Est:** 1950. **Sales:** $3,000,000 (2000). **Emp:** 30. **Officers:** C.J. Kuenstler, Owner.

■ **22015** ■ **A-Doc Oil Co.**
1617 N Garden Ave.
Roswell, NM 88201
Phone: (505)622-4210
Products: Oil. **SIC:** 5172 (Petroleum Products Nec).

■ **22016** ■ **A and W Oil Company Inc.**
PO Box 6608
Ft. Smith, AR 72906
Phone: (501)646-0595 **Fax:** (501)646-0597
Products: Gasoline, fuel oil, and diesel fuel. **SIC:** 5172 (Petroleum Products Nec). **Est:** 1966. **Sales:** $5,000,000 (2000). **Emp:** 7. **Officers:** A.B. Littlefield, President & CFO.

■ **22017** ■ **A-X Propane Co.**
300 Airport Rd.
Milan, NM 87021
Phone: (505)287-4346
Products: Propane. **SIC:** 5072 (Hardware).

■ **22018** ■ **Abel's Quik Shops**
PO Box 532
Louisiana, MO 63353
Phone: (314)754-5595
Products: Fuel. **SIC:** 5172 (Petroleum Products Nec). **Est:** 1952. **Sales:** $15,000,000 (2000). **Emp:** 130. **Officers:** James H. Redhage, President; Randall Anderson, Controller; Mark Abel, Vice President.

■ **22019** ■ **AC and T Company Inc.**
PO Box 4217
Hagerstown, MD 21740
Phone: (301)582-2700
Products: Petroleum, including fuel oil, gasoline, and diesel. **SIC:** 5172 (Petroleum Products Nec). **Est:** 1959. **Sales:** $45,000,000 (1999). **Emp:** 66. **Officers:** A.B. Fulton, President; W.E. Wamsley, Controller; C. Goodie, Dir. of Marketing.

■ **22020** ■ **Acorn Petroleum Inc.**
PO Box 112
Walsenburg, CO 81089
Phone: (719)738-1966 **Fax:** (719)738-3950
Products: Petroleum bulk station. **SIC:** 5171 (Petroleum Bulk Stations & Terminals). **Sales:** $16,000,000 (2000). **Emp:** 24. **Officers:** Mark McKinney, General Mgr.

■ **22021** ■ **Addington Oil Co.**
PO Box 125
Gate City, VA 24251
Phone: (703)386-3961 **Fax:** (540)386-9105
E-mail: addco@mounet.com
Products: Petroleum. **SIC:** 5172 (Petroleum Products Nec). **Est:** 1932. **Sales:** $6,500,000 (2000). **Emp:** 28. **Officers:** James H. Addington, President; B.J. Addington, Vice President.

■ **22022** ■ **Advance Petroleum Distributing Company Inc.**
2451 Great Southwest Pkwy.
Ft. Worth, TX 76106
Phone: (817)626-5458 **Fax:** (817)624-3102
Products: Gasoline; Diesel fuel. **SIC:** 5172 (Petroleum Products Nec). **Est:** 1967. **Sales:** $20,000,000 (1999). **Emp:** 16. **Officers:** Royce H. Kirby, President; Carolyn Stevens, Treasurer & Secty.; Fred Shaw, VP of Marketing & Sales.

■ **22023** ■ **Advance Petroleum Inc.**
700 S Royal Poinciana Blvd., Ste. 800
Miami Springs, FL 33166
Phone: (305)883-8554 **Fax:** (305)887-2642
Products: Fuel oil and petroleum products. **SIC:** 5172 (Petroleum Products Nec). **Sales:** $241,000,000 (1993). **Emp:** 125. **Officers:** Ralph R. Weiser, CEO; Robert S. Tocci, CFO.

■ **22024** ■ **Advanced Petroleum Recycling Inc.**
PO Box 16747
Salt Lake City, UT 84116-0747
Phone: (801)364-9444
Products: Recycled oil, fuels, filters, and antifreeze. **SIC:** 5093 (Scrap & Waste Materials).

■ **22025** ■ **AgBest Cooperative Inc.**
PO Box 392
Muncie, IN 47305
Phone: (317)288-5001 **Fax:** (317)282-4006
Products: Petroleum and its products; Grain. **SICs:** 5191 (Farm Supplies); 5172 (Petroleum Products Nec). **Est:** 1930. **Sales:** $20,000,000 (2000). **Emp:** 52. **Officers:** D.P. Wright, President; Charles Kerber, General Mgr.

■ **22026** ■ **Agland Cooperative**
PO Box 777
Gaylord, MN 55334
Phone: (507)237-2210
Products: Petroleum and farm supplies. **SICs:** 5172 (Petroleum Products Nec); 5191 (Farm Supplies). **Sales:** $8,300,000 (2000). **Emp:** 18. **Officers:** Jeff Polivka, Finance General Manager.

■ **22027** ■ **Agriland F.S. Inc.**
PO Box 680
Harlan, IA 51537
Phone: (712)755-5141
Products: Petroleum. **SIC:** 5172 (Petroleum Products Nec). **Sales:** $40,000,000 (2000). **Emp:** 45. **Officers:** Lud Buman, President; Bill Ridgely, General Manager, Finance.

■ **22028** ■ **Agway Energy Products**
PO Box 4852
Syracuse, NY 13221-4852
Phone: (315)449-7380 **Fax:** (315)449-6213
Products: Petroleum. **SIC:** 5172 (Petroleum Products Nec). **Est:** 1972. **Sales:** $720,000,000 (2000). **Emp:** 1,450. **Officers:** Michael Hopsicker, President; Karen Zasadny, Finance Officer; Joseph Cunningham, Dir. of Marketing & Sales; Joseph McGraw, Dir of Human Resources.

■ **22029** ■ **Allen Petroleum Corp.**
PO Box 210
Seaford, DE 19973
Phone: (302)629-9428 **Fax:** (302)629-9018
Products: Gasoline, including diesel. **SIC:** 5172 (Petroleum Products Nec). **Est:** 1950. **Sales:** $18,000,000 (2000). **Emp:** 28. **Officers:** Robert W. Allen, President; Ralph Graves, Controller.

■ **22030** ■ **Alliance Maintenance and Services Inc.**
3355 W 11th St.
Houston, TX 77008
Phone: (713)863-0000 **Fax:** (713)863-1004
Products: Fueling equipment. **SIC:** 5084 (Industrial Machinery & Equipment). **Sales:** $5,000,000 (2000). **Emp:** 45. **Officers:** Patrick Reynolds, CEO; John Reynolds, Treasurer & Secty.

■ **22031** ■ **Allied Oil and Supply Inc.**
PO Box 3687
Omaha, NE 68103
Phone: (402)344-4343 **Fax:** (402)344-4360
Products: Oil and lubricants. **SICs:** 5172 (Petroleum Products Nec); 5014 (Tires & Tubes). **Est:** 1957. **Sales:** $60,000,000 (2000). **Emp:** 200. **Officers:** R.C. Heinson, President; Richard Sherburne, Controller; Debra Thiesfeld, Dir. of Marketing; K. Anderson, Dir. of Systems.

■ **22032** ■ **Almena Cooperative Association**
PO Box 118
Almena, WI 54805
Phone: (715)357-3650
Products: Gasoline; Convenience items. **SICs:** 5172 (Petroleum Products Nec); 5141 (Groceries—General Line). **Est:** 1930. **Sales:** $3,000,000 (2000). **Emp:** 25. **Officers:** Wayne Jansen, President; Garry Hoff, Controller.

■ **22033** ■ **Almena Cooperative Association**
PO Box 118
Almena, WI 54805
Phone: (715)357-3650
Products: Gasoline, diesel fuel, liquid propane gas and fuel oil. **SIC:** 5172 (Petroleum Products Nec). **Est:** 1930. **Sales:** $10,000,000 (2000). **Emp:** 70. **Officers:** Alfred Thil, President.

■ **22034** ■ **Alpena Oil Company Inc.**
235 Water St.
Alpena, MI 49707
Phone: (517)356-1098
Products: Diesel fuel, including mid-grade and no-grade fuel. **SICs:** 5171 (Petroleum Bulk Stations &

Terminals); 5172 (Petroleum Products Nec). **Est:** 1926. **Sales:** $24,000,000 (2000). **Emp:** 50. **Officers:** Jerry Jereston, President.

■ 22035 ■ **Amerada Hess Corp.**
1185 Ave. of the Amer.
New York, NY 10036
Phone: (212)997-8500
Products: Refined oil. **SIC:** 5171 (Petroleum Bulk Stations & Terminals). **Est:** 1920. **Sales:** $8,929,700,000 (2000). **Emp:** 9,085. **Officers:** John B. Hess, CEO & Chairman of the Board; John Y. Schreyer, Exec. VP & CFO; Robert F. Wright, President & COO; Neal Gelfand, Sr. VP of Human Resources.

■ 22036 ■ **AmeriGas Propane Inc.**
PO Box 965
Valley Forge, PA 19482
Phone: (610)337-7000
Products: Propane and butane. **SIC:** 5171 (Petroleum Bulk Stations & Terminals). **Sales:** $512,000,000 (2000). **Emp:** 5,000. **Officers:** Lon Greenberg, President.

■ 22037 ■ **Amoco Energy Trading Corp.**
PO Box 3092
Houston, TX 77253
Phone: (281)556-3338
Products: Natural gas. **SIC:** 5172 (Petroleum Products Nec).

■ 22038 ■ **Ampride**
2075 Dakota S
Huron, SD 57350
Phone: (605)352-6493   **Fax:** (605)352-6516
Products: Petroleum and its products; Field, garden, and flower seeds. **SICs:** 5171 (Petroleum Bulk Stations & Terminals); 5085 (Industrial Supplies). **Est:** 1940. **Sales:** $45,000,000 (2000). **Emp:** 19. **Officers:** Lori Ogden, Manager.

■ 22039 ■ **Apex Oil Co.**
8182 Maryland Ave.
St. Louis, MO 63105
Phone: (314)889-9600   **Fax:** (314)854-8539
Products: Gasoline; Fuel. **SIC:** 5172 (Petroleum Products Nec). **Est:** 1932. **Sales:** $310,000,000 (2000). **Emp:** 400. **Officers:** P.A. Novelly, President; John L. Hank Jr., CFO; Tom Clapper, Dir. of Marketing; John Diderrich, Controller; Jody A. McMahon, Dir of Human Resources.

■ 22040 ■ **Apollo Oil LLC**
1175 Early Dr.
PO Box 4040
Winchester, KY 40392-4040
Phone: (606)744-5444
Free: (800)473-5823   **Fax:** (606)745-5823
URL: http://www.apollooil.com
Products: Motor oil; Industrial and commercial oils; Antifreeze; Chemicals; Filters. **SIC:** 5172 (Petroleum Products Nec). **Est:** 1972. **Sales:** $70,000,000 (2000). **Emp:** 85. **Officers:** Ed Dotson, CFO; Phil Holley, President; Skip Holley, Purchasing Mgr.; Bill Whitaker, Sales Mgr.; Judy Watts, Human Resources Contact. **Former Name:** Apollo Oil and Warehouse Distributors, Inc.

■ 22041 ■ **Aranosian Oil Co. Inc.**
557 N State St.
Concord, NH 03301
Phone: (603)224-7500
Products: Gasoline. **SIC:** 5172 (Petroleum Products Nec). **Est:** 1933. **Sales:** $12,000,000 (2000). **Emp:** 25. **Officers:** Isabelle E. Hodgison, President.

■ 22042 ■ **ARB Inc. (Franklinton, Louisiana)**
PO Box 625
Franklinton, LA 70438
Phone: (504)839-4494
Products: Petroleum bulk stations and terminals. **SIC:** 5171 (Petroleum Bulk Stations & Terminals). **Officers:** James R. Morgan III., President.

■ 22043 ■ **Ard Oil Co. Inc.**
PO Box 100
Summerdale, AL 36580
Phone: (205)947-2302
Products: Gasoline; Diesel fuels. **SIC:** 5172 (Petroleum Products Nec). **Est:** 1947. **Sales:** $100,000 (2000). **Emp:** 12. **Officers:** Herbert Russell, President; Earl Cauthers, Dir. of Marketing.

■ 22044 ■ **Arkansas Valley Companies**
8316 E 73rd St.
Tulsa, OK 74133
Phone: (918)252-0508   **Fax:** (918)250-4921
Products: Gasoline and diesel fuel. **SIC:** 5172 (Petroleum Products Nec). **Est:** 1971. **Sales:** $100,000,000 (1999). **Emp:** 15. **Officers:** W.O. Smith, President.

■ 22045 ■ **Arkla Chemical Corp.**
PO Box 21734
Shreveport, LA 71151
Phone: (318)429-2700   **Fax:** (318)429-5323
Products: Natural gas. **SICs:** 5171 (Petroleum Bulk Stations & Terminals); 5171 (Petroleum Bulk Stations & Terminals); 5172 (Petroleum Products Nec). **Est:** 1958. **Sales:** $26,000,000 (2000). **Emp:** 23. **Officers:** Harry R. Shobe, Vice President; William H. May Jr., CFO; Steven L. Huie, Dir. of Marketing.

■ 22046 ■ **Atlanta Fuel Company Inc.**
PO Box 93586
Atlanta, GA 30377
Phone: (404)792-9888   **Fax:** (404)792-2202
Products: Gasoline; Motor oil. **SIC:** 5172 (Petroleum Products Nec). **Est:** 1962. **Sales:** $13,000,000 (2000). **Emp:** 28. **Officers:** Gail E. Waters, President; Carolyn Waters, Treasurer; J. Boyles, Vice President.

■ 22047 ■ **Atlantic Aviation Service Inc.**
Philadelphia International Airport, H1
Philadelphia, PA 19153
Phone: (215)492-2970
Products: Aircraft refueling. **SIC:** 5172 (Petroleum Products Nec). **Sales:** $39,000,000 (1994). **Emp:** 80. **Officers:** S.N. Smith, President; Frank Zirnilkton, Treasurer.

■ 22048 ■ **Atlantic Trading Company Ltd.**
225 W 34th St., Ste. 2015
New York, NY 10122
Phone: (212)268-4487
Free: (888)482-2725   **Fax:** (212)268-4487
E-mail: 101332.1630@compuserve.com
Products: Gas and oil dispensing nozzles and pumps; Industrial metering pumps for chemical fluids. **SICs:** 5084 (Industrial Machinery & Equipment); 5048 (Ophthalmic Goods). **Est:** 1988. **Sales:** $5,000,000 (2000). **Emp:** 4. **Officers:** Walter Luysterborg, President.

■ 22049 ■ **Atlantis International, Inc.**
4744 Kawanee Ave.
Metairie, LA 70006
Phone: (504)455-6509   **Fax:** (504)885-3879
E-mail: 103040.315@compuserve.com
URL: http://www.atlantis-usa.com
Products: Anti-freeze and brake fluids; Lubricating oils and greases. **SICs:** 5172 (Petroleum Products Nec); 5169 (Chemicals & Allied Products Nec). **Est:** 1977. **Sales:** $3,500,000 (2000). **Emp:** 5. **Officers:** Manuel F. Blanco, President.

■ 22050 ■ **Atlas Fuel Oil Co.**
1110 Bronx River Ave.
Bronx, NY 10472
Phones: (718)893-4400   (718)893-1122
Fax: (718)893-4939
Products: Fuel oil. **SIC:** 5172 (Petroleum Products Nec). **Est:** 1952. **Sales:** $16,000,000 (1999). **Emp:** 25. **Officers:** James Coretti, President.

■ 22051 ■ **Automotive Service Inc.**
Box 2157
Reading, PA 19608
Phone: (215)678-3421   **Fax:** (215)678-3515
Products: Heating oil; Bulk oil. **SIC:** 5171 (Petroleum Bulk Stations & Terminals). **Est:** 1954. **Sales:** $20,000,000 (2000). **Emp:** 60. **Officers:** John K. Palmer, President.

■ 22052 ■ **Avfuel Corp.**
47 W Ellesworth Rd.
Ann Arbor, MI 48108
Phone: (734)663-6466   **Fax:** (734)663-1681
URL: http://www.avfuel.com
Products: Aviation fuel. **SIC:** 5172 (Petroleum Products Nec). **Sales:** $39,000,000 (2000). **Emp:** 130. **Officers:** Craig Sincock, President.

■ 22053 ■ **AWC Propane Co.**
813 N Virginia Ave.
Roswell, NM 88201
Phone: (505)622-1130
Products: Propane. **SIC:** 5172 (Petroleum Products Nec).

■ 22054 ■ **Ayers Oil Company Inc.**
PO Box 229
Canton, MO 63435
Phone: (314)288-4466
Products: Lubricants, including motor oil. **SICs:** 5171 (Petroleum Bulk Stations & Terminals); 5172 (Petroleum Products Nec). **Est:** 1965. **Sales:** $110,000,000 (2000). **Emp:** 240. **Officers:** Steve Ayers, President; Jim Crane, Treasurer.

■ 22055 ■ **B & J Oil Co.**
402 S B St.
Muskogee, OK 74403
Phone: (918)687-4181   **Fax:** (918)687-5629
Products: Oil; Fuel. **SIC:** 5172 (Petroleum Products Nec). **Est:** 1967. **Emp:** 4. **Officers:** Buddy Forbes; Barbara Rhodes.

■ 22056 ■ **B.A. Box Tank and Supply Inc.**
PO Box 547
Beeville, TX 78104
Phone: (512)358-1984
Products: Oil fill tanks and supplies. **SIC:** 5084 (Industrial Machinery & Equipment). **Est:** 1951. **Sales:** $3,000,000 (2000). **Emp:** 10. **Officers:** M. Box, CEO & President.

■ 22057 ■ **E.M. Bailey Distributing Co.**
1000 S 8th St.
Paducah, KY 42001
Phone: (502)442-4306
Products: Oil; Gasoline. **SICs:** 5171 (Petroleum Bulk Stations & Terminals); 5172 (Petroleum Products Nec). **Est:** 1953. **Sales:** $60,000,000 (2000). **Emp:** 100. **Officers:** E.M. Bailey Sr., President & Treasurer; Edward Bailey Jr., VP & Secty.

■ 22058 ■ **Bardahl Manufacturing Corp.**
PO Box 70607
Seattle, WA 98107
Phone: (206)783-4851
Free: (888)227-3245   **Fax:** (206)784-3219
E-mail: customersupport@bardahl.com
URL: http://www.bardahl.com
Products: Lubricating oils; Fuel additives. **SICs:** 5169 (Chemicals & Allied Products Nec); 5172 (Petroleum Products Nec). **Est:** 1939. **Emp:** 35. **Officers:** Evelyn McNeil, President; Eric Bardahl-Manchester, Vice President.

■ 22059 ■ **Bayside Fuel Oil Depot Corp.**
1776 Shore Pkwy.
Brooklyn, NY 11214
Phone: (718)372-9800   **Fax:** (718)266-3744
Products: Fuel oil. **SICs:** 5171 (Petroleum Bulk Stations & Terminals); 5172 (Petroleum Products Nec). **Est:** 1943. **Sales:** $125,000,000 (2000). **Emp:** 250. **Officers:** Alfred Allegretti, President.

■ 22060 ■ **Beach Supply Co.**
19061 Crystal St.
Huntington Beach, CA 92648
Phone: (714)847-7144
Products: Oil well supplies; Pipe fittings; Pumps. **SICs:** 5082 (Construction & Mining Machinery); 5084 (Industrial Machinery & Equipment). **Est:** 1957. **Sales:** $600,000 (2000). **Emp:** 4. **Officers:** Carl Weaver, President.

■ **22061** ■ **Beard Oil Pipeline Supply Inc.**
PO Box 485
Mt. Pleasant, MI 48804-0485
Phone: (517)773-9957
Products: Petroleum products. **SIC:** 5172 (Petroleum Products Nec). **Sales:** $5,600,000 (2000). **Emp:** 6.
Officers: Leo Beard, President & Treasurer.

■ **22062** ■ **Beck Suppliers Inc.**
PO Box 808
Fremont, OH 43420
Phone: (419)332-5527   **Fax:** (419)332-5614
Products: Oil; Fuel oil; Gasoline; Diesel; Car washes.
SICs: 5171 (Petroleum Bulk Stations & Terminals);
5172 (Petroleum Products Nec). **Est:** 1950. **Sales:**
$14,000,000 (2000). **Emp:** 25. **Officers:** Douglas L.
Beck, President.

■ **22063** ■ **Bedford Valley Petroleum Corp.**
PO Box 120
Everett, PA 15537
Phone: (814)623-5151   **Fax:** (814)623-6352
Products: Gasoline; Diesel fuel; Petroleum. **SIC:** 5172
(Petroleum Products Nec). **Est:** 1947. **Sales:**
$24,000,000 (2000). **Emp:** 80. **Officers:** R.G. Salathe
Jr., Chairman of the Board; Robert G. Salathe III,
President; K.P. Steinbrunner, Dir. of Marketing; Duane
S. Morgret, Dir. of Admin.

■ **22064** ■ **Bell Additives Inc.**
1340 Bennett Dr.
Longwood, FL 32750
Phone: (407)831-5021
Free: (800)659-2355   **Fax:** (407)831-9667
E-mail: bai@belladditives.com
URL: http://www.belladditives.com
Products: Gas, diesel, fuel, engine additives, and
lubricants. **SICs:** 5169 (Chemicals & Allied Products
Nec); 5172 (Petroleum Products Nec). **Est:** 1909.
Sales: $10,000,000 (2000). **Emp:** 15. **Officers:**
Charles G. Williams, President; Ola R. Williams, Vice
President; Richard Wolfe, VP of Marketing; Roberta
Cira, Controller; James Powell, Dir of Human
Resources; Stan Whitelatch, Sales/Marketing Contact.

■ **22065** ■ **Bell Gas Inc.**
PO Box 490
Roswell, NM 88202
Phone: (505)622-4800   **Fax:** (505)622-4710
Products: Petroleum bulk, petroleum products; Gas
service station. **SICs:** 5171 (Petroleum Bulk Stations &
Terminals); 5172 (Petroleum Products Nec). **Est:** 1984.
Sales: $50,000,000 (2000). **Emp:** 460. **Officers:**
Eugene Bell, President; Tom Lancaster, CFO.

■ **22066** ■ **Bemidji Cooperative Association**
PO Box 980
Bemidji, MN 56601
Phone: (218)751-4260   **Fax:** (218)751-1976
Products: Fuel, including diesel and propane;
Batteries; Tires. **SICs:** 5172 (Petroleum Products Nec);
5014 (Tires & Tubes). **Est:** 1933. **Sales:** $8,000,000
(2000). **Emp:** 70. **Officers:** R. Lewis, President &
Chairman of the Board; Roy E. Mills, CFO.

■ **22067** ■ **Benton Oil Co.**
PO Box 31
Lubbock, TX 79408
Phone: (806)763-5301
Products: Gasoline; Diesel; Fuel oil. **SIC:** 5172
(Petroleum Products Nec). **Est:** 1945. **Sales:**
$12,000,000 (2000). **Emp:** 15. **Officers:** Giles M.
Forbess, President & CFO.

■ **22068** ■ **Benz Oil Inc.**
2724 W Hampton Ave.
Milwaukee, WI 53209
Phone: (414)442-2900
Products: Oil. **SIC:** 5172 (Petroleum Products Nec).
Est: 1898. **Sales:** $20,000,000 (2000). **Emp:** 50.
Officers: D.W. Benz, President; John Graff, VP of
Finance; Lee Konkel, VP of Marketing.

■ **22069** ■ **Berreth Oil Company Inc.**
1301 W 6th St.
Mishawaka, IN 46544
Phone: (219)255-1255   **Fax:** (219)255-1264
Products: Oil. **SIC:** 5172 (Petroleum Products Nec).
Est: 1975. **Sales:** $38,000,000 (2000). **Emp:** 77.

Officers: Dennis Berreth, President; Margaret Berreth,
Treasurer & Secty.; Jack Nederhood, General Mgr.

■ **22070** ■ **Berry-Hinkley Terminal Inc.**
147 S Stanford Way
Sparks, NV 89431
Phone: (702)359-3778
Products: Gasoline and diesel fuel. **SIC:** 5171
(Petroleum Bulk Stations & Terminals). **Sales:**
$7,000,000 (2000). **Emp:** 15. **Officers:** Mike Berry,
President.

■ **22071** ■ **Besche Oil Co. Inc.**
PO Box 277
Waldorf, MD 20604
Phone: (301)645-7061
Products: Petroleum products, including gasoline,
diesel, and kerosene. **SIC:** 5172 (Petroleum Products
Nec). **Est:** 1948. **Sales:** $30,000,000 (2000). **Emp:**
200. **Officers:** M.A. Besche, President; Melvin G.
Williams, CFO; Robert Parlett, Dir. of Marketing &
Sales; John Hartline, Dir. of Information Systems.

■ **22072** ■ **Big/Little Stores Inc.**
PO Box 1236
Enterprise, AL 36331
Phone: (334)347-9546   **Fax:** (334)393-1477
Products: Oil. **SIC:** 5172 (Petroleum Products Nec).
Sales: $32,000,000 (2000). **Emp:** 285. **Officers:** A.R.
McCreary Jr., President; Curtis Edwards, Controller;
Toby Rankin, Vice President, e-mail: Trankin@
snowhill.com.

■ **22073** ■ **Big Saver Inc.**
PO Box 198
Montgomery, NY 12549
Phone: (914)457-9622
Products: Home heating oil. **SIC:** 5172 (Petroleum
Products Nec).

■ **22074** ■ **Biltmore Oil Co. Inc.**
191 Amboy Rd.
Asheville, NC 28806
Phone: (828)253-4591   **Fax:** (828)254-7064
E-mail: eblengo@aol.com
Products: Heating oil; Fuel oil; Gasoline; Diesel fuel.
SIC: 5172 (Petroleum Products Nec). **Est:** 1925.
Sales: $17,000,000 (2000). **Emp:** 20. **Officers:** Joe P.
Eblen, President.

■ **22075** ■ **Bison Oil**
PO Box 807
Sheridan, WY 82801
Phones: (307)672-2363   (307)674-4522
Fax: (307)672-6757
Products: Petroleum products, including oil and
grease. **SIC:** 5172 (Petroleum Products Nec).

■ **22076** ■ **Black Oil Company Inc.**
PO Box 159
Monticello, UT 84535-0159
Phone: (435)587-2215   **Fax:** (435)587-2863
Products: Gasoline, diesel, fuel, and oil. **SICs:** 5171
(Petroleum Bulk Stations & Terminals); 5014 (Tires &
Tubes). **Est:** 1953. **Sales:** $14,100,000 (2000). **Emp:**
57. **Officers:** J. Burton Black, CEO & President, e-mail:
bblack@sisna.com. **Former Name:** Parkway Texaco.
Former Name: Thompson Texaco.

■ **22077** ■ **Blackburn Oil Co. Inc.**
PO Box 430
Opelika, AL 36803-0430
Phone: (334)745-2951   **Fax:** (334)742-0799
E-mail: jbstok@opel.mindspring.com
Products: Fuel; Petroleum products. **SIC:** 5172
(Petroleum Products Nec). **Est:** 1934. **Sales:**
$9,000,000 (2000). **Emp:** 8. **Officers:** J.B. Stokley,
President & CFO; Charles Maddox Jr., Vice President.

■ **22078** ■ **Blalock Oil Company Inc.**
PO Box 775
Jonesboro, GA 30236
Phone: (770)478-8888
Products: Fuel oil. **SICs:** 5171 (Petroleum Bulk
Stations & Terminals); 5172 (Petroleum Products Nec).
Est: 1939. **Sales:** $4,000,000 (2000). **Emp:** 9.
Officers: Edgar Blalock Jr., President; Sandy Blalock,
Treasurer & Secty.

■ **22079** ■ **Blanchardville Cooperative Oil
Association**
401 S Main St., Box 88
Blanchardville, WI 53516
Phone: (608)523-4294
Products: Fuel, oil, and petroleum products. **SIC:** 5172
(Petroleum Products Nec). **Est:** 1935. **Sales:**
$6,000,000 (2000). **Emp:** 25. **Officers:** David Erickson,
President, Steven Stangeland, Treasurer & Secty.;
Donald R. Rufenacht, General Mgr.

■ **22080** ■ **Blarney Castle Oil Co.**
PO Box 246
Bear Lake, MI 49614
Phone: (616)864-3111   **Fax:** (616)864-3516
Products: Oil. **SICs:** 5171 (Petroleum Bulk Stations &
Terminals); 5172 (Petroleum Products Nec). **Est:** 1933.
Sales: $220,000,000 (2000). **Emp:** 400. **Officers:**
Dennis E. McCarthy, President.

■ **22081** ■ **Blue Flame Div.**
6502 Dixie Hwy., Ste. 240
Fairfield, OH 45014
Phone: (513)247-0660
Products: Liquid petroleum gas and oil. **SIC:** 5172
(Petroleum Products Nec). **Sales:** $50,000,000 (1994).
Emp: 300. **Officers:** Paul Baker, Vice President.

■ **22082** ■ **Boeing Petroleum Services Inc.**
850 S Clearview Pkwy.
New Orleans, LA 70123
Phone: (504)734-4200
Products: Oil reserves. **SIC:** 5172 (Petroleum
Products Nec). **Est:** 1984.

■ **22083** ■ **Joseph F. Boente Sons Inc.**
543 W Main St.
Carlinville, IL 62626-0288
Phone: (217)854-3164
Products: Gasoline. **SIC:** 5172 (Petroleum Products
Nec). **Est:** 1925. **Sales:** $15,000,000 (2000). **Emp:** 85.
Officers: Larry Boente, President; Rebecca Salskey,
Treasurer & Secty.

■ **22084** ■ **Boncosky Oil Co.**
739 N State St.
Elgin, IL 60123
Phone: (847)741-2577   **Fax:** (847)741-2590
Products: Petroleum and petroleum products. **SICs:**
5171 (Petroleum Bulk Stations & Terminals); 5172
(Petroleum Products Nec). **Sales:** $52,000,000 (2000).
Emp: 110. **Officers:** Kevin McCarter, Owner; Phil
Lindsey, CFO.

■ **22085** ■ **Bonfield Brothers, Inc.**
Calk Ave.
Box 450
Mt. Sterling, KY 40353
Phone: (606)498-1993
Free: (800)928-1993   **Fax:** (606)498-5083
Products: Petroleum-based products; Filter racing
products. **SICs:** 5172 (Petroleum Products Nec); 5013
(Motor Vehicle Supplies & New Parts). **Officers:**
Dennis Bonfield.

■ **22086** ■ **Boone County Farm Bureau
Cooperative Inc.**
PO Box 626
Lebanon, IN 46052
Phone: (765)482-5600
Products: Petroleum products; Plant food. **SICs:** 5172
(Petroleum Products Nec); 5191 (Farm Supplies). **Est:**
1930. **Sales:** $17,000,000 (2000). **Emp:** 50. **Officers:**
Ronald W. Hysong, President; Ronald L. Sibert, CFO.

■ **22087** ■ **Bowen-Hall Petroleum Inc.**
PO Box 2012
Pocatello, ID 83201
Phone: (208)233-2794   **Fax:** (208)232-1276
Products: Gas and diesel fuel. **SIC:** 5171 (Petroleum
Bulk Stations & Terminals). **Est:** 1977. **Sales:**
$52,000,000 (2000). **Emp:** 80. **Officers:** E. Daniel
Bowen, President, Chairman of the Board & Finance
Officer.

■ 22088 ■ Bowen Petroleum
PO Box 2012
Pocatello, ID 83206
Phone: (208)233-2794
Products: Crude petroleum bulk stations. **SIC:** 5171 (Petroleum Bulk Stations & Terminals). **Sales:** $40,000,000 (2000). **Emp:** 60. **Officers:** Clair Bowen, President, Chairman of the Board & Finance Officer.

■ 22089 ■ BP Oil Co.
200 Public Sq.
Cleveland, OH 44114
Phone: (216)586-4141   **Fax:** (216)586-5593
Products: Jet and marine fuel. **SIC:** 5172 (Petroleum Products Nec). **Sales:** $10,525,000,000 (2000). **Emp:** 11,850. **Officers:** Steve Percy, CEO & President; William E. Boswell, Controller.

■ 22090 ■ Bradford Supply Co.
PO Box 246
Robinson, IL 62454
Phone: (618)544-3171   **Fax:** (618)546-0181
Products: Oil field supplies. **SIC:** 5084 (Industrial Machinery & Equipment). **Est:** 1961. **Sales:** $16,000,000 (2000). **Emp:** 85. **Officers:** W.J. Chamblin, President & Treasurer.

■ 22091 ■ Brentari Oil Co.
661 E Hwy. 66
Gallup, NM 87301
Phone: (505)863-4562
Products: Oil. **SIC:** 5172 (Petroleum Products Nec).

■ 22092 ■ R.E. Breon and Sons Inc.
PO Box 27
Rebersburg, PA 16872
Phone: (814)349-5681
Products: Petroleum products, including gases and fuels. **SIC:** 5172 (Petroleum Products Nec). **Sales:** $8,000,000 (2000). **Emp:** 13. **Officers:** Larry R. Breon, President.

■ 22093 ■ Brewer Oil Co.
PO Box 1347
Artesia, NM 88210
Phone: (505)748-1248
Products: Gasoline and diesel fuel. **SIC:** 5172 (Petroleum Products Nec). **Est:** 1957. **Sales:** $120,000,000 (2000). **Emp:** 250. **Officers:** Don Brewer, President; Stan Brewer, Treasurer.

■ 22094 ■ Don Brewer Oil Co.
300 E 2nd St.
Roswell, NM 88201
Phone: (505)622-8560
Products: Oil. **SIC:** 5172 (Petroleum Products Nec).

■ 22095 ■ Broad Street Oil & Gas Co.
125 Dillmont Dr.
Columbus, OH 43085
Phone: (614)786-1801
Products: Gas and oil. **SIC:** 5172 (Petroleum Products Nec).

■ 22096 ■ Brown Evans Distributing Co.
PO Box 5840
Mesa, AZ 85211
Phone: (602)962-6111   **Fax:** (602)827-8712
Products: Fuel oils and lubricants. **SIC:** 5172 (Petroleum Products Nec). **Sales:** $49,000,000 (2000). **Emp:** 62. **Officers:** Kathye W. Brown, CEO & President; Steve Walters, CFO.

■ 22097 ■ Bryant and Blount Oil Co.
1200 E Woodhurst Dr., Ste. G-200
Springfield, MO 65804-3776
Phone: (417)883-1611
Products: Motor oil, lubricants, and fuel. **SIC:** 5172 (Petroleum Products Nec). **Est:** 1956. **Sales:** $7,000,000 (2000). **Emp:** 16. **Officers:** William Blount, President.

■ 22098 ■ Bud's Service Inc.
5148 N Meridian St.
Indianapolis, IN 46208-2626
Phone: (317)781-5600
Products: Petroleum products. **SIC:** 5172 (Petroleum Products Nec). **Est:** 1931. **Sales:** $12,000,000 (2000). **Emp:** 25. **Officers:** S.B. Vickery, Partner.

■ 22099 ■ Buy-Rite Petroleum Ltd.
11724 Parkshire Dr.
St. Louis, MO 63126
Phone: (314)421-1100
Products: Gasoline and diesel fuel. **SIC:** 5172 (Petroleum Products Nec).

■ 22100 ■ C and J Service Co.
PO Box 178
De Witt, IA 52742
Phone: (319)659-5145
Products: Petroleum products, including propane; Agricultural supplies, including fertilizer and feed. **SICs:** 5172 (Petroleum Products Nec); 5191 (Farm Supplies). **Est:** 1946. **Sales:** $28,000,000 (2000). **Emp:** 60. **Officers:** Jim Nelson, CEO & President.

■ 22101 ■ C and P Oil Inc.
PO Box 157
Millersburg, IN 46543
Phone: (219)642-3823
Products: Petroleum products. **SIC:** 5172 (Petroleum Products Nec). **Sales:** $1,900,000 (2000). **Emp:** 4. **Officers:** Larry Hartzler, President; Ted Groff, CFO.

■ 22102 ■ C and S Inc.
PO Box 388
Portales, NM 88130
Phone: (505)356-4496
Products: Fuel oil; Pneumatic tires. **SIC:** 5171 (Petroleum Bulk Stations & Terminals). **Est:** 1937. **Sales:** $7,000,000 (2000). **Emp:** 35. **Officers:** W. Stratton, President; Bill Jones, Controller.

■ 22103 ■ C and W Enterprises Inc.
317 N Farr St.
San Angelo, TX 76903
Phone: (915)655-5795   **Fax:** (915)658-2762
Products: Fuel; Wire cable systems. **SICs:** 5171 (Petroleum Bulk Stations & Terminals); 5063 (Electrical Apparatus & Equipment); 5172 (Petroleum Products Nec). **Est:** 1972. **Sales:** $25,000,000 (2000). **Emp:** 85. **Officers:** John W. Jones Jr., President; W.J. Leach, VP of Finance; L Luce, VP of Marketing.

■ 22104 ■ Cactus Pipe and Supply Co.
1 Greenway Plz., Ste. 450
Houston, TX 77046
Phone: (713)877-1948   **Fax:** (713)877-8204
Products: Oil field pipes. **SIC:** 5051 (Metals Service Centers & Offices). **Sales:** $15,000,000 (1993). **Emp:** 8. **Officers:** Jack J. Bender, President; Ray E. Kliesing, Controller.

■ 22105 ■ Campbell Oil Co.
PO Box 907
Massillon, OH 44648-0907
Phone: (330)833-8555   **Fax:** (330)833-1043
Products: Gas, motor oil, and lubricants; Convenience stores. **SIC:** 5172 (Petroleum Products Nec). **Est:** 1939. **Sales:** $106,000,000 (1999). **Emp:** 64. **Officers:** Brian D. Burrow, President; Douglas A. Donavan, Treasurer & Secty.; Robert D. Engel, VP of Operations.

■ 22106 ■ CAP Propane Plus Inc.
PO Box 38
Kettle River, MN 55757
Phone: (218)273-4850
Free: (800)262-6605   **Fax:** (218)273-6130
Products: Propane gas. **SIC:** 5172 (Petroleum Products Nec). **Est:** 1929. **Sales:** $5,000,000 (2000). **Emp:** 27. **Officers:** Mike Wayrynen, CEO; James J. Sanders, General Mgr.

■ 22107 ■ Capital City Companies Inc.
1295 Johnson St. NE
Salem, OR 97303
Phone: (503)362-5558   **Fax:** (503)581-4576
Products: Petroleum. **SIC:** 5172 (Petroleum Products Nec). **Sales:** $37,000,000 (2000). **Emp:** 165. **Officers:** W.B. Loch, CEO & President.

■ 22108 ■ Cargill Inc. Northeast Petroleum Div.
72 Cherry Hill Dr.
Beverly, MA 01915
Phone: (978)524-1500   **Fax:** (978)524-1691
Products: Petroleum and its products; Gasoline. **SIC:** 5172 (Petroleum Products Nec). **Est:** 1958. **Sales:** $675,000,000 (2000). **Emp:** 180. **Officers:** Yannick Lecamp, General Mgr.; James White, Controller; Robert Takvorian, Marketing Mgr.

■ 22109 ■ Carr Oil Inc.
1001 W Bankhead St.
New Albany, MS 38652
Phone: (601)534-6314
Products: Gas and diesel oil. **SIC:** 5172 (Petroleum Products Nec). **Est:** 1984. **Sales:** $4,000,000 (2000). **Emp:** 10. **Officers:** Charlie E. Carr, President.

■ 22110 ■ Carse Oil Company Inc.
1700 S Bumby Ave.
Orlando, FL 32806
Phone: (407)898-9494   **Fax:** (407)894-0755
Products: Diesel fuel and gasoline. **SIC:** 5172 (Petroleum Products Nec). **Est:** 1966. **Sales:** $3,000,000 (2000). **Emp:** 6. **Officers:** Wayne L. Carse, President.

■ 22111 ■ Carson Co. Tri-County Oil Div.
101 Summit St.
Spruce Pine, NC 28777
Phone: (704)765-6171   **Fax:** (704)765-1316
Products: Heating fuel; Kerosene. **SIC:** 5172 (Petroleum Products Nec). **Sales:** $5,000,000 (2000). **Emp:** 10. **Officers:** David C. Reevs, President.

■ 22112 ■ Carson Oil Company Inc.
PO Box 10948
Portland, OR 97296-0948
Phone: (503)224-8500
Free: (800)998-7767   **Fax:** (503)222-0186
E-mail: info@carsonoil.com
URL: http://www.carsonoil.com
Products: Diesel and gasoline; Asphalt; Retail stations; HVAC; Home heating oil; Lubricating oils and greases. **SIC:** 5172 (Petroleum Products Nec). **Est:** 1938. **Sales:** $75,000,000 (2000). **Emp:** 195. **Officers:** J.A. Carson, CEO, e-mail: jarmand@carsonoil.com; Terry Mohr, CFO, e-mail: tmohr@carsonoil.com; Lance C. Woodbury, Vice President, e-mail: woodbury@carsonoil.com; Sandra Gaylord, Vice President, e-mail: gaylord@carsonoil.com.

■ 22113 ■ Jerry C. Carter Inc.
PO Box 18
Gainesville, GA 30503
Phone: (770)534-5129   **Fax:** (770)532-9263
Products: Gasoline and petroleum products. **SIC:** 5172 (Petroleum Products Nec). **Sales:** $1,000,000 (2000). **Emp:** 1. **Officers:** Bill Jones, President; Cary Pope, Controller.

■ 22114 ■ Carver's Oil Co.
304 Uranium Ave.
Milan, NM 87021
Phone: (505)287-4291
Products: Oil. **SIC:** 5172 (Petroleum Products Nec).

■ 22115 ■ Castle Oil Corp.
500 Mamaroneck Ave.
Harrison, NY 10528
Phone: (914)381-6500
Products: Oil. **SIC:** 5172 (Petroleum Products Nec). **Est:** 1928. **Sales:** $130,000,000 (2000). **Emp:** 275. **Officers:** Mauro C. Romita, President.

■ 22116 ■ Castrol North America Holdings Inc.
1500 Valley Rd.
Wayne, NJ 07470
Phone: (201)633-2200   **Fax:** (201)633-0039
Products: Oil, lubricants, and motor oil. **SIC:** 5172 (Petroleum Products Nec). **Est:** 1954. **Sales:** $1,160,000,000 (2000). **Emp:** 2,000. **Officers:** Thomas R. Crane Jr., CEO; Michael D. Miller, Sr. VP & Finance Officer; Peter J. Meola, VP of Marketing; Michael Studney, Dir. of Information Systems; Jeffrey T. Farley, VP of Human Resources.

■ 22117 ■ Celeron Trading and Transportation Co.
PO Box 40160
Bakersfield, CA 93384
Phone: (805)664-5300
Products: Crude oil. **SIC:** 5171 (Petroleum Bulk Stations & Terminals).

■ **22118** ■ **Cen-Tex AG Supply**
201 W 4th St.
McGregor, TX 76657
Phone: (254)840-3288
Products: Diesel and no-lead fuel; Oil; Grease. **SIC:** 5172 (Petroleum Products Nec). **Est:** 1989. **Sales:** $6,000,000 (2000). **Emp:** 11. **Officers:** Roy Westerfeld, President; Kathy Hale, General Mgr.

■ **22119** ■ **CENCO Refining Co.**
PO Box 2108
Santa Fe Springs, CA 90670-9883
Phone: (562)944-6111 **Fax:** (562)944-8522
URL: http://www.cencorefining.com
Products: Gasoline and diesel fuel. **SIC:** 5172 (Petroleum Products Nec). **Est:** 1998. **Sales:** $42,000,000 (2000). **Emp:** 42. **Officers:** Geoff Soares, President; Mike Egner, Controller; Bob Turner, Dir of Human Resources. **Former Name:** Powerline Oil Co.

■ **22120** ■ **Cenex-Harvest States Cooperative**
PO Box 190
Tyler, MN 56178
Phone: (507)247-5586
Free: (888)468-5586 **Fax:** (507)247-5198
Products: Petroleum products, including oil and gasoline. **SICs:** 5171 (Petroleum Bulk Stations & Terminals); 5172 (Petroleum Products Nec). **Est:** 1935. **Sales:** $2,000,000 (2000). **Emp:** 13. **Officers:** Todd Reif, General Mgr. **Former Name:** Lincoln County Cooperative Oil Co.

■ **22121** ■ **Center Oil Co.**
600 Mason Ridge Center Dr.
St. Louis, MO 63141
Phone: (314)682-3500 **Fax:** (314)682-3599
E-mail: info@centeroil.com
URL: http://www.centeroil.com
Products: Petroleum refined products. **SIC:** 5172 (Petroleum Products Nec). **Est:** 1986. **Sales:** $1,600,000,000 (2000). **Emp:** 37. **Officers:** Gary R. Parker, President; Richard I. Powers, CFO & Treasurer.

■ **22122** ■ **Center Valley Cooperative Association**
PO Box 158
Seymour, WI 54165-0156
Phone: (920)734-1409
Products: Fuel oil, gasoline and farm supplies. **SICs:** 5172 (Petroleum Products Nec); 5191 (Farm Supplies). **Sales:** $7,400,000 (1994). **Emp:** 25. **Officers:** Bruce Mlsna, CEO; Robert Van De Loo, President.

■ **22123** ■ **Central Cooperative Oil Association**
712 N Cedar St.
Owatonna, MN 55060
Phone: (507)451-1230
Products: Petroleum bulk stations and petroleum products. **SICs:** 5171 (Petroleum Bulk Stations & Terminals); 5172 (Petroleum Products Nec). **Sales:** $10,000,000 (1993). **Emp:** 35. **Officers:** Chuck D. Hosfield, President.

■ **22124** ■ **Central Illinois Enterprises Ltd.**
707 E Fayette Ave.
Effingham, IL 62401
Phone: (217)342-9755
Products: Petroleum products; Tires; Dry cleaning supplies. **SICs:** 5172 (Petroleum Products Nec); 5014 (Tires & Tubes). **Sales:** $10,000,000 (1991). **Emp:** 45. **Officers:** John H. Bredenkamp Jr., President & Chairman of the Board; Charles W. Gebben, Treasurer.

■ **22125** ■ **Central Motive Power Inc.**
6301 Broadway
Denver, CO 80216
Phone: (303)428-3611 **Fax:** (303)428-6785
Products: Petroleum, fuels, and related equipment. **SIC:** 5172 (Petroleum Products Nec). **Est:** 1926. **Sales:** $7,500,000 (2000). **Emp:** 60.

■ **22126** ■ **Central Oil Company Inc.**
1001 McCloskey Blvd.
Tampa, FL 33605
Phone: (813)248-2105 **Fax:** (813)248-2105
E-mail: cofuels@aol.com
URL: http://www.centraloil.com
Products: Oil. **SIC:** 5172 (Petroleum Products Nec).

Est: 1936. **Sales:** $60,000,000 (2000). **Emp:** 35. **Officers:** Ruben Martin, Chairman of the Board; J.E. McIntyre, President.

■ **22127** ■ **Central Oil of Virginia Corp.**
PO Box 587
Rocky Mount, VA 24151
Phone: (703)483-5342
Free: (800)294-5026 **Fax:** (703)483-0477
E-mail: centoil@cablenet-va.com
Products: Gasolines; Heating fuel; Diesel fuel; Kerosene. **SIC:** 5172 (Petroleum Products Nec). **Sales:** $11,000,000 (2000). **Emp:** 17. **Officers:** Don Thacker, VP & General Merchandising Mgr.; Launa Turner, Treasurer; Terry Taft, Manager; Danny Smith, Sales & Marketing Contact.

■ **22128** ■ **Centre Oil and Gas Co. Inc.**
206 S Potter St.
Bellefonte, PA 16823
Phone: (814)355-4749
Products: Oils; Greases. **SIC:** 5172 (Petroleum Products Nec). **Est:** 1924. **Sales:** $8,400,000 (2000). **Emp:** 30. **Officers:** Frank Hartranft, President; John Hartranft, Vice President.

■ **22129** ■ **Chapin Co.**
PO Box 2568
Myrtle Beach, SC 29578-2568
Phone: (803)448-6955 **Fax:** (803)448-5554
Products: Oil; Lumber; Furniture; Building supplies. **SICs:** 5172 (Petroleum Products Nec); 5021 (Furniture); 5031 (Lumber, Plywood & Millwork). **Est:** 1928. **Sales:** $6,000,000 (2000). **Emp:** 40. **Officers:** Harold Clardy, President.

■ **22130** ■ **Chapman Inc.**
PO Box 1298
Sherman, TX 75091
Phone: (903)893-8106
Free: (800)899-8106 **Fax:** (903)893-6731
Products: Gasoline and petroleum products. **SIC:** 5172 (Petroleum Products Nec). **Est:** 1956. **Sales:** $35,000,000 (1999). **Emp:** 40. **Officers:** Ellis Olmstead, President; Andrew W. Olmstead, VP of Operations.

■ **22131** ■ **Chase Oil Co. Inc.**
PO Box 1599
Florence, SC 29503
Phone: (803)662-1594
Products: Fuels and gasoline. **SIC:** 5172 (Petroleum Products Nec). **Est:** 1948. **Sales:** $24,000,000 (1999). **Emp:** 65. **Officers:** Charles G. Howard, President.

■ **22132** ■ **Chemoil Corp.**
4 Embarcadero Ctr., Ste. 1800
San Francisco, CA 94111-5951
Phone: (415)268-2700 **Fax:** (415)268-2701
URL: http://www.chemoil.com
Products: Marine fuel. **SIC:** 5172 (Petroleum Products Nec). **Est:** 1981. **Sales:** $502,473,000 (2000). **Emp:** 70. **Officers:** Robert V. Chandran, President, e-mail: rvc@chemoil.com; Adrian Tolson, VP of Marketing, e-mail: adriant@chemoil.com.

■ **22133** ■ **Chesapeake Utilities Corp.**
909 Silver Lake Blvd.
Dover, DE 19904
Phone: (302)734-6799
Products: Liquefied petroleum gas. **SIC:** 5172 (Petroleum Products Nec). **Sales:** $137,400,000 (2000). **Emp:** 397. **Officers:** Ralph J. Adkins, CEO; Michael P. McMasters, VP, CFO & Treasurer.

■ **22134** ■ **Chevron Industries**
PO Box 7643
San Francisco, CA 94104
Phone: (415)894-7700 **Fax:** (415)894-8897
Products: Oil and Gas. **SIC:** 5172 (Petroleum Products Nec). **Emp:** 272. **Officers:** Hilmare P. Walker, General Mgr.

■ **22135** ■ **Chickasaw Distributors Inc.**
800 Bering Dr., Ste. 330
Houston, TX 77057
Phone: (713)974-2905
Products: Oilfield equipment. **SIC:** 5084 (Industrial Machinery & Equipment).

■ **22136** ■ **W.R. Childress Oil Co.**
2729 NE 28th St.
Ft. Worth, TX 76111
Phone: (817)834-1901
Products: Petroleum products. **SIC:** 5172 (Petroleum Products Nec). **Sales:** $2,000,000 (1994). **Emp:** 4. **Officers:** A. Childress, CEO; R. Childress, VP of Finance.

■ **22137** ■ **Childs Oil Company Inc.**
PO Box 1417
Arcadia, FL 34265
Phone: (941)494-2605 **Fax:** (941)494-6781
Products: Bulk petroleum products. **SIC:** 5171 (Petroleum Bulk Stations & Terminals). **Sales:** $5,000,000 (2000). **Emp:** 10. **Officers:** Martha Childs Hoover, President.

■ **22138** ■ **Christensen Oil Co.**
200 East 600 South
Provo, UT 84606
Phone: (801)373-7970
Products: Gasoline; Oil. **SIC:** 5172 (Petroleum Products Nec).

■ **22139** ■ **Chronister Oil Co.**
2026 Republic Ave.
Springfield, IL 62702
Phone: (217)523-5050
Free: (800)238-4912 **Fax:** (217)523-5001
Products: Gas station supplies; Convenience store supplies. **SIC:** 5172 (Petroleum Products Nec). **Est:** 1968. **Sales:** $30,000,000 (1999). **Emp:** 97. **Officers:** Grady Chronister, CEO & Chairman of the Board; Linda Chronister, VP of Finance; Roger Harney, Sales Mgr.; Victoria Jacob, General Mgr.; Tom Clemens, Marketing Mgr.

■ **22140** ■ **Circleville Oil Co.**
PO Box 189
Circleville, OH 43113
Phone: (614)474-7544
Products: Fuel oil; Heating oil; Kerosene. **SICs:** 5171 (Petroleum Bulk Stations & Terminals); 5172 (Petroleum Products Nec). **Est:** 1924. **Sales:** $22,000,000 (2000). **Emp:** 70. **Officers:** Norman W. Wilson, President; Joseph Reis, CFO; Rex Riddle, Sales Mgr.

■ **22141** ■ **Citrus Trading Inc.**
1400 Smith St., Ste. 3902
Houston, TX 77002
Phone: (713)853-6569
Products: Natural gas. **SIC:** 5172 (Petroleum Products Nec). **Sales:** $20,000,000 (2000). **Officers:** Terence H. Thorn, Chairman of the Board; Robert Butts, VP & Controller.

■ **22142** ■ **City Coal of New London Inc.**
410 Bank St.
New London, CT 06320
Phone: (860)442-4321
Products: Petroleum, fuels, and related equipment. **SIC:** 5172 (Petroleum Products Nec). **Sales:** $6,000,000 (2000). **Emp:** 35.

■ **22143** ■ **Clarks Petroleum Service Inc.**
7846 Oxbow Rd.
Canastota, NY 13032
Phone: (315)697-2278
Products: Gas. **SIC:** 5172 (Petroleum Products Nec). **Sales:** $36,000,000 (1994). **Emp:** 60. **Officers:** R.K. Clark, President; S. Tornabene, VP & Controller.

■ **22144** ■ **Coastal Engineering Equipment Sales LLC**
PO Box 23526
New Orleans, LA 70183-0526
Phone: (504)733-8511 **Fax:** (504)733-8516
URL: http://www.coastaleng.com
Products: Oil field equipment, including regulators and water treating chemicals. **SICs:** 5084 (Industrial Machinery & Equipment); 5169 (Chemicals & Allied Products Nec). **Est:** 1939. **Sales:** $11,000,000 (2000). **Emp:** 23. **Officers:** Howard F. Allbritton, President, e-mail: howardf@gs.verio.net; Faith Sheldon, Finance Officer; Jeff Mcauliffe, Sr. VP; David Carley Jr., Vice President; Barbara Allbritton, VP of Admin. **Former Name:** Coastal Engineering Corp.

■ 22145 ■ Coastal Fuels Marketing Inc.
PO Box 025500
Miami, FL 33102-5500
Phone: (305)551-5200 **Fax:** (305)551-5366
Products: Gasoline, oil, and diesel fuel. **SIC:** 5172
(Petroleum Products Nec). **Est:** 1915. **Sales:**
$600,000,000 (2000). **Emp:** 82. **Officers:** Dan Hill,
CEO & President; Roger Childers, CFO; Paul Stanton,
Sr. VP; Jorge Gabaldon, Dir. of Information Systems.

■ 22146 ■ Coastal Gas Services Co.
Nine Greenway Plz.
Houston, TX 77046
Phone: (713)877-1400
Products: Gas products. **SIC:** 5171 (Petroleum Bulk
Stations & Terminals). **Officers:** James R. Storfer, Sr.
VP of Finance & Admin.

■ 22147 ■ Coastal Oil New York Inc.
PO Box 818
Hasbrouck Heights, NJ 07604
Phone: (201)393-9494 **Fax:** (201)393-4565
Products: Petroleum products, including gasoline, fuel
oil, motor oil, and diesel fuel. **SIC:** 5172 (Petroleum
Products Nec). **Est:** 1986. **Sales:** $1,600,000,000
(2000). **Emp:** 200. **Officers:** Steven C, Boyd, Exec.
VP; Sanford Riesenfeld, Controller; Sam Farooki, Sr.
VP of Marketing.

■ 22148 ■ Coastal States Trading
9 E Greenway Plz
Houston, TX 77046
Phone: (713)877-1400 **Fax:** (713)877-3299
Products: Ammonia. **SICs:** 5172 (Petroleum Products
Nec); 5169 (Chemicals & Allied Products Nec). **Est:**
1975. **Sales:** $970,000,000 (2000). **Emp:** 1,500.

■ 22149 ■ Coen Oil Co. Inc.
1100 W Chestnut St.
Washington, PA 15301
Phone: (412)225-1300
Products: Oil. **SIC:** 5172 (Petroleum Products Nec).
Est: 1928. **Sales:** $23,000,000 (2000). **Emp:** 38.
Officers: Charles R. Coen, President; Larry Withum,
VP & Controller.

■ 22150 ■ COFSCO Inc.
291 Branstetter St.
Wooster, OH 44691
Phone: (216)264-2131
Products: Oil drill fittings. **SIC:** 5084 (Industrial
Machinery & Equipment). **Est:** 1955. **Sales:**
$12,000,000 (2000). **Emp:** 30. **Officers:** Jeff E. Smith,
CEO.

■ 22151 ■ Coleman Oil Co. Inc.
PO Box 2009
Pikeville, KY 41502
Phone: (606)432-1476 **Fax:** (606)432-0447
Products: Gasoline and diesel fuel. **SICs:** 5171
(Petroleum Bulk Stations & Terminals); 5172
(Petroleum Products Nec). **Est:** 1948. **Sales:**
$19,000,000 (2000). **Emp:** 25. **Officers:** Terrell
Coleman, President; Doug Charles, Vice President.

■ 22152 ■ Colonial Oil Industries Inc.
PO Box 576
Savannah, GA 31402
Phone: (912)236-1331 **Fax:** (912)236-3868
Products: Oil; Petroleum products; Diesel feul. **SICs:**
5171 (Petroleum Bulk Stations & Terminals); 5172
(Petroleum Products Nec). **Est:** 1921. **Sales:**
$450,000,000 (2000). **Emp:** 350. **Officers:** Robert
Demere Jr., President; Francis Brown, VP of Finance;
Schaeffer Wimbish Jr., VP of Marketing; William A.
Baker, VP of Operations; E.M. Almeida, Dir of
Personnel.

■ 22153 ■ Colvard Oil Company Inc.
317 S Jefferson Ave.
West Jefferson, NC 28694
Phone: (919)246-4231
Products: Petroleum products, including gasoline,
diesel, and kerosene. **SIC:** 5172 (Petroleum Products
Nec). **Est:** 1924. **Sales:** $25,000,000 (2000). **Emp:** 98.
Officers: Larry Dollar, President.

■ 22154 ■ Commerce Consultants Inc.
6815 Bradley Ave.
Cleveland, OH 44129
Phone: (440)845-5682 **Fax:** (440)845-3857
Products: Cement; Rice; Chemicals, including
ammonium nitrate; Industrial machine lathe bits;
Petroleum crude. **SICs:** 5172 (Petroleum Products
Nec); 5032 (Brick, Stone & Related Materials); 5153
(Grain & Field Beans); 5169 (Chemicals & Allied
Products Nec); 5085 (Industrial Supplies). **Officers:**
Mila Templeton, President.

■ 22155 ■ Commonwealth Oil Co. Inc.
2328 Lakeside Dr.
Lynchburg, VA 24501
Phone: (804)385-5140
Products: Oil. **SIC:** 5171 (Petroleum Bulk Stations &
Terminals). **Sales:** $9,000,000 (2000). **Emp:** 20.
Officers: Bruce C. Harvey, President & CFO.

**■ 22156 ■ Community Cooperative Oil
Association**
PO Box 665
Essig, MN 56030
Phone: (507)354-5490
Free: (800)281-8643 **Fax:** (507)354-6822
Products: Petroleum; Propane; Oil; Tires. **SIC:** 5172
(Petroleum Products Nec). **Est:** 1937. **Sales:**
$6,500,000 (2000). **Emp:** 19. **Officers:** Fred Juni,
President; Doug Lund, General Mgr.

■ 22157 ■ Community Oil Company Inc.
PO Box 400
Charles Town, WV 25414
Phone: (304)725-7021
Products: Petroleum products, including oil and gas.
SIC: 5171 (Petroleum Bulk Stations & Terminals). **Est:**
1931. **Sales:** $6,500,000 (2000). **Emp:** 34. **Officers:**
W. Edward Morgan, Owner; Heather L. Walters, Vice
President.

■ 22158 ■ Condon Oil Company Inc.
PO Box 184
Ripon, WI 54971-0184
Phone: (920)748-3186
Products: Petroleum; Tires. **SICs:** 5172 (Petroleum
Products Nec); 5014 (Tires & Tubes). **Est:** 1928.
Sales: $95,000,000 (2000). **Emp:** 250. **Officers:** Kent
B. Bauman, President; Leigh Fennedale, Treasurer;
Glenn Muenster, Dir. of Marketing & Sales.

■ 22159 ■ Connie's Enterprise
PO Box 11238
Jacksonville, FL 32239
Phone: (904)353-0604 **Fax:** (904)355-1525
E-mail: capital1@leading.net
Products: Gas pumps and valves; Pipes and fittings;
Meters; Tanks. **SIC:** 5084 (Industrial Machinery &
Equipment). **Est:** 1977. **Sales:** $7,000,000 (2000).
Emp: 35. **Officers:** Clifford E. Carter, President;
Richard Carter, Vice President; Tom McClean; Janet
Smith, Office Mgr. **Alternate Name:** Capital Petroleum
Equipment Co.

■ 22160 ■ Consolidated Fuel Oil Co. Inc.
PO Box 7226
Shawnee Mission, KS 66207
Phone: (913)451-3764
Products: Fuel. **SIC:** 5172 (Petroleum Products Nec).
Sales: $20,000,000 (2000). **Emp:** 4. **Officers:** Norman
L. Leblond, CEO.

■ 22161 ■ Consumer Cooperative Oil Co.
PO Box 668
Sauk City, WI 53583
Phone: (608)643-3301 **Free:** (800)446-3301
Products: Petroleum products. **SIC:** 5172 (Petroleum
Products Nec). **Sales:** $13,600,000 (2000). **Emp:** 85.
Officers: Gary Schlender, Controller.

■ 22162 ■ Consumer Oil Company of Meridian
PO Box 950
Meridian, MS 39301
Phone: (601)693-3933
Products: Oil. **SICs:** 5171 (Petroleum Bulk Stations &
Terminals); 5172 (Petroleum Products Nec). **Est:** 1930.
Sales: $7,000,000 (2000). **Emp:** 7. **Officers:** William
McWilliams, President & CFO.

■ 22163 ■ Consumers Cooperative Oil Co.
PO Box 76
Rosholt, SD 57260
Phone: (605)537-4216
Products: Gas and oil. **SIC:** 5171 (Petroleum Bulk
Stations & Terminals). **Est:** 1928. **Sales:** $2,000,000
(2000). **Emp:** 9. **Officers:** Devon Hanson, President.

■ 22164 ■ Consumers Petroleum Co.
13507 Auburn Ave.
Detroit, MI 48223
Phone: (313)272-3800
Products: Oil; Gasoline. **SIC:** 5172 (Petroleum
Products Nec). **Est:** 1947. **Sales:** $10,000,000 (2000).
Emp: 15. **Officers:** Roger Albertie, President; Jerry
Feltman, Vice President.

■ 22165 ■ Continental Ozark Corp.
PO Box 1503
Fayetteville, AR 72702
Phone: (501)521-5565 **Fax:** (501)442-4650
Products: Petroleum. **SIC:** 5172 (Petroleum Products
Nec). **Est:** 1977. **Sales:** $500,000,000 (2000). **Emp:**
75. **Officers:** E.G. Bradberry, President; Wayne Story,
VP of Finance; Keith Davis, Marketing Mgr.

**■ 22166 ■ Cooperative Gas and Oil Co.
(Geneseo, Illinois)**
324 E Exchange St.
Geneseo, IL 61254
Phone: (309)944-4616 **Fax:** (309)944-4087
Products: Petroleum products. **SIC:** 5172 (Petroleum
Products Nec). **Sales:** $15,000,000 (2000). **Emp:** 45.
Officers: Larry Wenthold, General Mgr.; Jerry Lee,
Controller.

**■ 22167 ■ Cooperative Gas and Oil Company
Inc.**
PO Box 117
Sioux Center, IA 51250
Phone: (712)722-2501
Products: Petroleum. **SIC:** 5171 (Petroleum Bulk
Stations & Terminals). **Sales:** $7,700,000 (1993). **Emp:**
25. **Officers:** Roger Bomgaars, President; Jim
Harskamp, Finance General Manager.

■ 22168 ■ Cooperative Oil Association
1110 3rd Ave.
Mountain Lake, MN 56159
Phone: (507)427-2333
Products: Petroleum, fertilizer and lumber. **SICs:** 5171
(Petroleum Bulk Stations & Terminals); 5191 (Farm
Supplies); 5031 (Lumber, Plywood & Millwork). **Sales:**
$6,000,000 (1994). **Emp:** 40. **Officers:** Gary Mohr,
Finance General Manager.

■ 22169 ■ Cooperative Oil Co.
PO Box 30
Osage, IA 50461
Phone: (515)732-3716 **Fax:** (515)732-3718
Products: Oil, petroleum, diesel, and gasoline. **SICs:**
5171 (Petroleum Bulk Stations & Terminals); 5172
(Petroleum Products Nec). **Est:** 1929. **Sales:**
$8,000,000 (2000). **Emp:** 50. **Officers:** George Taets,
President; David J. Low, General Mgr.

■ 22170 ■ Copeland Oil Co.
Hwy. 259
Idabel, OK 74745
Phone: (580)286-3272
Products: Oil. **SIC:** 5172 (Petroleum Products Nec).

■ 22171 ■ Cornerstone Propane G.P. Inc.
432 Westridge Dr.
Watsonville, CA 95076
Phone: (408)724-1921
Products: Liquid propane. **SIC:** 5172 (Petroleum
Products Nec). **Sales:** $595,800,000 (2000). **Emp:**
1,685. **Officers:** Keith G. Baxter, CEO & President;
Ronald J. Goedde, Exec. VP & CFO.

■ 22172 ■ Cornerstone Propane Partners L.P.
432 Westridge Dr.
Watsonville, CA 95076
Phone: (831)724-1921 **Fax:** (831)724-2799
Products: Liquid propane. **SIC:** 5172 (Petroleum
Products Nec). **Sales:** $768,100,000 (2000). **Emp:**
2,503. **Officers:** Keith G. Baxter, CEO & President;
Ronald J. Goedde, Exec. VP & CFO.

■ 22173 ■ Cosbel Petroleum Corp.
9 Greenway Plz.
Houston, TX 77046-0995
Phone: (713)877-1400 **Free:** (800)788-2500
Products: Fuel oil and refined products. **SICs:** 5171 (Petroleum Bulk Stations & Terminals); 5172 (Petroleum Products Nec).

■ 22174 ■ Cota and Cota Inc.
4 Green St.
Bellows Falls, VT 05101
Phone: (802)463-4150
Products: Fuel and kerosene. **SIC:** 5172 (Petroleum Products Nec).

■ 22175 ■ Cottonwood Cooperative Oil Co.
Hwy. 23 S
Cottonwood, MN 56229
Phone: (507)423-6282
Products: Fertilizer; Chemicals; Petroleum. **SICs:** 5172 (Petroleum Products Nec); 5191 (Farm Supplies); 5169 (Chemicals & Allied Products Nec). **Est:** 1921. **Sales:** $6,800,000 (2000). **Emp:** 25. **Officers:** M. Fischer, General Mgr.

■ 22176 ■ Cowboy Oil Co.
PO Box L
Pocatello, ID 83201
Phone: (208)232-7814 **Fax:** (208)234-7245
Products: Motor oil and fuel. **SIC:** 5171 (Petroleum Bulk Stations & Terminals). **Sales:** $10,000,000 (2000). **Emp:** 35. **Officers:** D.G. Geisler, President & Chairman of the Board; Alan Barnes, Controller.

■ 22177 ■ Craft Oil Corp.
837 Cherry St.
Avoca, PA 18641
Phone: (717)457-5485 **Fax:** (717)451-0700
Products: Motor oil. **SIC:** 5172 (Petroleum Products Nec). **Est:** 1925. **Sales:** $2,000,000 (2000). **Emp:** 15. **Officers:** Richard K. Mangan, President & Treasurer.

■ 22178 ■ Crest Distributing Co.
PO Box 818
Provo, UT 84603
Phone: (801)373-7970
Products: Oil. **SIC:** 5172 (Petroleum Products Nec). **Est:** 1976. **Sales:** $31,000,000 (2000). **Emp:** 15. **Officers:** Todd Christensen, President; Lou Strasburg, Controller.

■ 22179 ■ Cronin Asphalt Corp.
PO Box 4257
East Providence, RI 02914-4257
Phone: (401)434-5252 **Fax:** (401)336-3892
Products: Products of petroleum refining. **SIC:** 5172 (Petroleum Products Nec). **Officers:** Richard Cronin, President.

■ 22180 ■ Crus Oil Inc.
2260 SW Temple
Salt Lake City, UT 84115
Phone: (801)466-8783
Products: Oils. **SIC:** 5172 (Petroleum Products Nec). **Est:** 1947. **Sales:** $12,000,000 (2000). **Emp:** 31. **Officers:** Anthony J. Crus, President.

■ 22181 ■ Crystal Flash Petroleum Corp.
PO Box 684
Indianapolis, IN 46206
Phone: (317)879-2849
Free: (800)886-3835 **Fax:** (317)879-2855
Products: Gasoline, fuel and lubricants at convenience stores. Gasoline, fuel and lubricants at convenience stores. **SICs:** 5172 (Petroleum Products Nec); 5171 (Petroleum Bulk Stations & Terminals). **Sales:** $75,000,000 (2000). **Emp:** 300. **Officers:** Mac Fehsenfeld, CEO; Toni Neimann, Controller.

■ 22182 ■ Cumberland Oil Co. Inc.
7260 Centennial Blvd.
Nashville, TN 37209
Phone: (615)350-7333
URL: http://www.cumberlandoil.com
Products: Fuel. **SIC:** 5172 (Petroleum Products Nec). **Est:** 1939. **Sales:** $6,000,000 (1999). **Emp:** 10. **Officers:** R.F. Cummins, CEO.

■ 22183 ■ Curry Oil Company Inc.
1450 S Main St.
London, KY 40741
Phone: (606)864-5119
Products: Gasoline and fuel. **SICs:** 5171 (Petroleum Bulk Stations & Terminals); 5172 (Petroleum Products Nec). **Est:** 1932. **Sales:** $31,000,000 (2000). **Emp:** 180. **Officers:** Joe Curry, President; Nanette Jensen, Treasurer & Secty.; Rick Curry, Vice President.

■ 22184 ■ Curt's Oil Co.
2220 E Shawnee Rd.
Muskogee, OK 74403
Phone: (918)682-7888
Products: Oil. **SIC:** 5172 (Petroleum Products Nec).

■ 22185 ■ Cuyahoga Landmark Inc.
PO Box 361189
Strongsville, OH 44136
Phone: (440)238-6600
Products: Petroleum, including diesel fuel and gasoline. **SIC:** 5172 (Petroleum Products Nec). **Est:** 1935. **Sales:** $26,000,000 (2000). **Emp:** 40. **Officers:** Gary Smith, President.

■ 22186 ■ CY Hart Distributig Co.
433 Atlas Dr.
Nashville, TN 37211
Phone: (615)834-1652
Products: Oil additives. **SIC:** 5172 (Petroleum Products Nec).

■ 22187 ■ Dakota Pride Cooperative
648 W 2nd St.
Winner, SD 57580
Phone: (605)842-2711 **Fax:** (605)842-2715
Products: Petroleum products and farm supplies. **SICs:** 5172 (Petroleum Products Nec); 5191 (Farm Supplies). **Sales:** $31,200,000 (1999). **Emp:** 125. **Officers:** Mike Barfuss, General Mgr.; Miger Rofell, Controller.

■ 22188 ■ Danville Gasoline and Oil Company Inc.
201 W Main St.
Danville, IL 61832-5709
Phone: (217)446-8500
Free: (800)779-1077 **Fax:** (217)442-0052
Products: Oil and lubricants; Auto and truck parts. **SICs:** 5172 (Petroleum Products Nec); 5015 (Motor Vehicle Parts—Used). **Sales:** $3,000,000 (2000). **Emp:** 14. **Officers:** W.T. Leverenz IV, President.

■ 22189 ■ Daubert Oil & Gas Co.
110 E 1st St.
Dexter, NM 88230
Phone: (505)734-6001
Products: Oil and gas. **SIC:** 5172 (Petroleum Products Nec).

■ 22190 ■ Dead River Co.
PO Box 1427
Bangor, ME 04401
Phone: (207)947-8641 **Fax:** (207)990-0828
Products: Petroleum products. **SIC:** 5172 (Petroleum Products Nec). **Sales:** $450,000,000 (2000). **Emp:** 900. **Officers:** P. Andrews Nixon, President; Richard M. Roderick, VP of Finance.

■ 22191 ■ Dean Oil Co.
PO Box 9
Cullman, AL 35055
Phone: (256)734-6831
Products: Petroleum storage. **SIC:** 5171 (Petroleum Bulk Stations & Terminals). **Est:** 1957. **Sales:** $8,000,000 (2000). **Emp:** 9. **Officers:** Gary Dean, President; Marlene Dean, Treasurer & Secty.

■ 22192 ■ Delaware Storage Co.
PO Box 313
Dover, DE 19903
Phone: (302)736-1774 **Fax:** (302)734-2749
Products: Jet fuel. **SIC:** 5172 (Petroleum Products Nec).

■ 22193 ■ Delgasco Inc.
3617 Lexington Rd.
Winchester, KY 40391
Phone: (606)744-6171
Products: Petroleum. **SIC:** 5172 (Petroleum Products Nec).

■ 22194 ■ Delta Oil Company Inc.
PO Box 829
Petersburg, VA 23803
Phone: (804)733-3582 **Fax:** (804)732-2135
Products: Fuels, including gasoline, kerosene, and diesel. **SICs:** 5171 (Petroleum Bulk Stations & Terminals); 5172 (Petroleum Products Nec). **Est:** 1921. **Sales:** $4,300,000 (2000). **Emp:** 55. **Officers:** Mark E. Holt III, CEO & President; Ricky L. Shull, VP of Finance; Patsy Mann, Dir. of Marketing.

■ 22195 ■ Delta Resources Inc.
3617 Lexington Rd.
Winchester, KY 40391
Phone: (606)744-6171
Products: Petroleum. **SIC:** 5172 (Petroleum Products Nec).

■ 22196 ■ Denatec Distributors
5254 S Saginaw Rd., No. 200
Flint, MI 48507
Phone: (810)694-3300
Products: Lubricating oils. **SIC:** 5172 (Petroleum Products Nec).

■ 22197 ■ Denton Petroleum Co.
PO Box 360
Driscoll, TX 78351
Phone: (512)387-0592 **Fax:** (512)387-3769
Products: Petroleum. Gasoline service stations. **SIC:** 5172 (Petroleum Products Nec). **Est:** 1946. **Sales:** $7,000,000 (2000). **Emp:** 25. **Officers:** Claude Denton Jr., Owner; Carolyn Miller, CFO.

■ 22198 ■ Detlefsen Oil Inc.
PO Box 728
North Platte, NE 69103-0728
Phone: (308)532-8780 **Fax:** (308)532-8790
Products: Petroleum products. **SIC:** 5172 (Petroleum Products Nec). **Est:** 1951. **Sales:** $14,000,000 (2000). **Emp:** 52. **Officers:** Ron Detlefsen, President.

■ 22199 ■ Deuel County Farmers Union Oil Co.
PO Box 430
Toronto, SD 57268
Phone: (605)794-4861
Products: Fertilizers and chemicals; Batteries; Oil. **SICs:** 5172 (Petroleum Products Nec); 5063 (Electrical Apparatus & Equipment); 5191 (Farm Supplies); 5169 (Chemicals & Allied Products Nec). **Est:** 1936. **Sales:** $5,000,000 (2000). **Emp:** 26. **Officers:** Eugene Lorenzen, President; Gary French, General Mgr.

■ 22200 ■ Dickey Oil Corp.
PO Box 809
Packwood, IA 52580
Phone: (319)695-3601
Products: Petroleum products. **SIC:** 5172 (Petroleum Products Nec). **Sales:** $12,000,000 (2000). **Emp:** 30. **Officers:** Dave Dickey, President.

■ 22201 ■ Dilmar Oil Company Inc.
PO Box 5629
Florence, SC 29502-5629
Phone: (803)752-5611
Products: Heating oil, gas, diesel fuel, and motor oil. **SICs:** 5171 (Petroleum Bulk Stations & Terminals); 5172 (Petroleum Products Nec). **Est:** 1932. **Sales:** $38,300,000 (2000). **Emp:** 230. **Officers:** D.J. Lane, President; Vicki Jackson, Controller.

■ 22202 ■ M.O. Dion and Sons Inc.
1543 W 16th St.
Long Beach, CA 90813
Phone: (562)432-3949
Products: Petroleum products including fuels, lubricants and solvents. **SIC:** 5172 (Petroleum Products Nec). **Sales:** $12,000,000 (1994). **Emp:** 25. **Officers:** Pat Cullen, President.

■ **22203** ■ **Distributors Oil Co. Inc.**
11441 Industriplex Blvd., Ste. 100
Baton Rouge, LA 70809-4268
Phone: (504)344-3314 **Fax:** (504)338-9714
Products: Oil and gasoline. **SICs:** 5171 (Petroleum Bulk Stations & Terminals); 5172 (Petroleum Products Nec). **Est:** 1949. **Sales:** $38,000,000 (2000). **Emp:** 21. **Officers:** W.J. Chadwick, President; B.A. Lax, Dir. of Marketing.

■ **22204** ■ **District Petroleum Products Inc.**
1832 Milan Ave.
Sandusky, OH 44870
Phone: (419)625-8373
Products: Oil. **SICs:** 5171 (Petroleum Bulk Stations & Terminals); 5172 (Petroleum Products Nec). **Est:** 1951. **Sales:** $120,000,000 (2000). **Emp:** 250. **Officers:** Scott Stipp, President; T.J. Donnelly, CFO.

■ **22205** ■ **Dixie Oil Co. Inc.**
PO Box 1007
Tifton, GA 31793
Phone: (912)382-2700
Products: Oil. **SIC:** 5172 (Petroleum Products Nec). **Est:** 1946. **Sales:** $64,000,000 (2000). **Emp:** 3,500. **Officers:** William F. Lindsey, Chairman of the Board; Robert B. Lindsey, CFO.

■ **22206** ■ **D.O. Inc.**
PO Box 1065
Gillette, WY 82716
Phone: (307)682-9049 **Fax:** (307)686-0867
Products: Oil; Gasoline; Gasoline pumps. **SICs:** 5172 (Petroleum Products Nec); 5084 (Industrial Machinery & Equipment).

■ **22207** ■ **Dooley Oil Company, Inc.**
PO Box 189
E Yellowstone Hwy.
Evansville, WY 82636
Phone: (307)234-9812 **Fax:** (307)234-9813
Products: Gas and oil. **SIC:** 5172 (Petroleum Products Nec).

■ **22208** ■ **Dooley Oil Company, Inc.**
PO Box 370
Laramie, WY 82070
Phone: (307)742-5667 **Fax:** (307)742-9044
Products: Fuel. **SIC:** 5172 (Petroleum Products Nec).

■ **22209** ■ **B.A. Dorsey Oil Co.**
PO Box 786
Nashville, GA 31639-0786
Phone: (912)686-3751
Products: Propane. **SIC:** 5172 (Petroleum Products Nec). **Est:** 1956. **Sales:** $5,000,000 (2000). **Emp:** 7. **Officers:** B.A. Dorsey, President; Dee Dorsey, Vice President.

■ **22210** ■ **Bill L. Dover Company Inc.**
PO Box 600
Jasper, TX 75951
Phone: (409)384-2441
Products: Fuel oil, including gasoline and diesel. **SIC:** 5172 (Petroleum Products Nec). **Est:** 1967. **Sales:** $12,000,000 (2000). **Emp:** 40. **Officers:** Wade Dover, President.

■ **22211** ■ **Drake Petroleum Company Inc.**
PO Box 72616, Elmwood Sta.
Providence, RI 02907
Phone: (401)781-9900 **Fax:** (401)941-2050
Products: Petroleum products. **SIC:** 5172 (Petroleum Products Nec). **Sales:** $51,800,000 (2000). **Emp:** 25. **Officers:** Warren Alpert, Chairman of the Board; Amato DiBiasio, Treasurer.

■ **22212** ■ **Duke Energy Field Services Inc.**
370 17th St Ste. 900
Denver, CO 80202
Phone: (303)595-3331 **Fax:** (303)595-0480
Products: Processes crude petroleum and natural gas. **SIC:** 5172 (Petroleum Products Nec). **Officers:** Jim Mogg, President.

■ **22213** ■ **Dumas Oil Co.**
PO Box 1296
Goldsboro, NC 27533-1296
Phone: (919)735-0571
Products: Gasoline; Fuel oil; Kerosene. **SIC:** 5172 (Petroleum Products Nec). **Sales:** $48,000,000 (2000). **Emp:** 75. **Officers:** W.L. Joiner, President.

■ **22214** ■ **Dunlap Oil Company Inc.**
759 S Haskell Ave.
Willcox, AZ 85643
Phone: (602)384-2248
Products: Automotive oil. **SIC:** 5172 (Petroleum Products Nec). **Est:** 1959. **Sales:** $8,000,000 (2000). **Emp:** 40. **Officers:** Kenneth T. Dunlap, President.

■ **22215** ■ **Dyna-Lube**
1056 E 425 N
Ogden, UT 84404
Phone: (801)782-0400
Products: Oil. **SIC:** 5172 (Petroleum Products Nec).

■ **22216** ■ **DynAir Fueling Inc.**
2000 Edmund Halley Dr.
Reston, VA 20190
Phone: (703)264-9500 **Fax:** (703)264-9593
Products: Aircraft fuel. **SIC:** 5172 (Petroleum Products Nec). **Sales:** $240,000,000 (1993). **Emp:** 500. **Officers:** Hal Watson, President.

■ **22217** ■ **E-Z Serve Petroleum Marketing Co.**
1824 Hillandale Rd.
Durham, NC 27705-2650
Products: Gasoline. **SIC:** 5172 (Petroleum Products Nec). **Sales:** $86,200,000 (2000). **Emp:** 4,845. **Officers:** Neil McLaurin, CEO & Chairman of the Board; Liz Marshall, Controller.

■ **22218** ■ **East Jordan Cooperative Co.**
PO Box 377
East Jordan, MI 49727
Phone: (231)536-2275 **Fax:** (231)536-2277
Products: Bulk petroleum and farm supplies. **SICs:** 5171 (Petroleum Bulk Stations & Terminals); 5191 (Farm Supplies). **Sales:** $13,000,000 (2000). **Emp:** 20. **Officers:** D. Graham, President.

■ **22219** ■ **East Texas Gas Co.**
PO Box 660
Mineola, TX 75773
Phone: (903)592-3809
Products: Propane. **SIC:** 5172 (Petroleum Products Nec). **Sales:** $5,000,000 (2000). **Emp:** 8. **Officers:** Stan Mallory, President.

■ **22220** ■ **Eastern Fuels Inc.**
Hwy. 42 W
Ahoskie, NC 27910
Phone: (919)332-2037 **Fax:** (919)332-8161
Products: Petroleum products, including gasoline and kerosene. **SIC:** 5172 (Petroleum Products Nec). **Est:** 1925. **Sales:** $60,000,000 (2000). **Emp:** 400. **Officers:** C. Wood Beasley, CEO.

■ **22221** ■ **Eastern Petroleum Corp.**
PO Box 398
Enfield, NC 27823
Phone: (252)445-5131 **Fax:** (252)445-3634
Products: Petroleum; Gasoline; Diesel fuel. **SICs:** 5171 (Petroleum Bulk Stations & Terminals); 5172 (Petroleum Products Nec). **Est:** 1956. **Sales:** $12,000,000 (2000). **Emp:** 120. **Officers:** Audrey L. Shearin, President & CEO.

■ **22222** ■ **Eaton Metal Products Co.**
920 E C St.
Casper, WY 82601
Phone: (307)234-0870 **Fax:** (307)577-1974
Products: Petroleum tanks and equipment. **SIC:** 5084 (Industrial Machinery & Equipment). **Est:** 1919. **Emp:** 4. **Officers:** Gerald Morietta, Division Manager; Clayton Winn, Service Manager.

■ **22223** ■ **Eden Oil Company Inc.**
PO Box 1375
Reidsville, NC 27323
Phone: (336)349-8228
Free: (800)437-8852 **Fax:** (336)634-1744
Products: Gasoline, petroleum, and oil. **SIC:** 5172

(Petroleum Products Nec). **Est:** 1941. **Sales:** $32,000,000 (2000). **Emp:** 16. **Officers:** E. Reid Teague Jr., President; Cynthia F. Teague, Sec.-Treas. & VP.

■ **22224** ■ **Edgewood Oil Inc.**
PO Box 188
Edgewood, IA 52042-0188
Phone: (319)928-6437
Free: (800)634-3379 **Fax:** (319)928-6438
Products: Lubricants. **SIC:** 5172 (Petroleum Products Nec). **Est:** 1923. **Sales:** $900,000 (2000). **Emp:** 5. **Officers:** Paul F. Ruba, Owner. **Former Name:** Edgewood Oil Co.

■ **22225** ■ **Elkhart County Farm Cooperative**
806 Logan St.
Goshen, IN 46526-0076
Phone: (219)533-4131 **Fax:** (219)534-4162
Products: Petroleum and its products; Liquefied petroleum gases. **SIC:** 5172 (Petroleum Products Nec). **Est:** 1927. **Sales:** $15,000,000 (2000). **Emp:** 55. **Officers:** Dee Byerly, General Mgr.; Doug Bible, CFO.

■ **22226** ■ **Ellenbecker Oil Co.**
1514 Russell Ave.
Cheyenne, WY 82001
Phone: (307)632-5151
Products: Petroleum, including oil, gasoline, and diesel. **SIC:** 5172 (Petroleum Products Nec).

■ **22227** ■ **Elser Oil Co.**
461 Middle Rd.
Sheridan, MT 59749
Phone: (406)842-5478
Products: Oil. **SIC:** 5172 (Petroleum Products Nec).

■ **22228** ■ **Empire Petroleum Inc.**
PO Box 4036
Toledo, OH 43609
Phone: (419)534-6025
Products: Fuel oil. **SICs:** 5171 (Petroleum Bulk Stations & Terminals); 5172 (Petroleum Products Nec). **Est:** 1922. **Sales:** $21,000,000 (2000). **Emp:** 35. **Officers:** R. Mallendick, President & Treasurer.

■ **22229** ■ **Empiregas Trucking Corp.**
R.R. 2, Box 80
Carthage, MO 64836-9617
Phone: (417)394-2670
Products: Petroleum products. **SIC:** 5172 (Petroleum Products Nec). **Sales:** $4,000,000 (2000). **Emp:** 11. **Officers:** Earl Noe, Finance General Manager.

■ **22230** ■ **Energy Buyers Service Corp.**
PO Box 79265
Houston, TX 77279-9265
Phone: (713)464-5335
Products: Natural gas. **SIC:** 5172 (Petroleum Products Nec). **Sales:** $900,000 (1993). **Emp:** 2. **Officers:** Robert Silverthorn, President.

■ **22231** ■ **EnergyNorth Propane Inc.**
75 Regional Dr.
Concord, NH 03301
Phone: (603)225-6660
Products: Propane gas. **SIC:** 5172 (Petroleum Products Nec).

■ **22232** ■ **Englefield Oil Co.**
447 James Pkwy.
Newark, OH 43055
Phone: (614)522-1310 **Fax:** (614)928-3844
Products: Oil; Gas. **SIC:** 5171 (Petroleum Bulk Stations & Terminals). **Est:** 1961. **Sales:** $210,000,000 (2000). **Emp:** 1,200. **Officers:** Frederick W. Englefield III, CEO & Chairman of the Board; Fred Kaseman, Controller; Edward Stevens, VP of Operations; Ben Englefield, VP of Human Resources.

■ **22233** ■ **Enron Liquid Fuels Co.**
1400 Smith St.
Houston, TX 77002
Phone: (713)654-6161
Products: Oil, natural gas, and propane. **SICs:** 5171 (Petroleum Bulk Stations & Terminals); 5172 (Petroleum Products Nec). **Est:** 1985. **Sales:** $2,200,000,000 (2000). **Emp:** 1,400. **Officers:** John M.

Muckleroy, President; Geroge Fastuca, Sr. VP & Finance Officer.

■ 22234 ■ Enron Power Services
PO Box 1188
Houston, TX 77251-1188
Phone: (713)853-6161   Fax: (713)646-7040
Products: Oil; Gas. SICs: 5171 (Petroleum Bulk Stations & Terminals); 5172 (Petroleum Products Nec).

■ 22235 ■ Enterprise Oil Co.
PO Box 366
Cartersville, GA 30120
Phone: (770)382-4804   Fax: (770)382-4824
Products: Oil. SIC: 5172 (Petroleum Products Nec). Sales: $26,000,000 (2000). Emp: 100. Officers: Dennis W. Collier, President; Brad Cagle, Vice President.

■ 22236 ■ EOTT Energy Operating L.P.
PO Box 4666
Houston, TX 77210-4666
Phone: (713)993-5200   Fax: (713)993-5821
Products: Natural gas liquids. SIC: 5172 (Petroleum Products Nec). Sales: $1,000,000,000 (2000). Emp: 710. Officers: Gary W. Luce, Exec. VP; Lori Maddox, Accounting Manager.

■ 22237 ■ EOTT Energy Partners L.P.
1330 Post Oak Blvd., Ste. 2700
Houston, TX 77056
Phone: (713)993-5200
Products: Crude oil. SIC: 5171 (Petroleum Bulk Stations & Terminals). Sales: $5,294,700,000 (2000). Officers: Michael D. Burke, President; Lori L. Maddox, Controller.

■ 22238 ■ Equity Cooperative Association
PO Box 340
Malta, MT 59538-0340
Phone: (406)654-2240
Free: (800)578-2240   Fax: (406)654-2287
Products: Gas; Candy; Feed. SICs: 5172 (Petroleum Products Nec); 5145 (Confectionery); 5194 (Tobacco & Tobacco Products). Est: 1932. Sales: $2,000,000 (2000). Emp: 6. Officers: Larry Olson, President; Orvin Solberg, Treasurer & Secty.

■ 22239 ■ Erie Petroleum Inc.
1502 Greengarden Rd.
Erie, PA 16502
Phone: (814)456-7516
Products: Petroleum; Oil; Gasoline; Kerosene. SICs: 5171 (Petroleum Bulk Stations & Terminals); 5172 (Petroleum Products Nec). Est: 1982. Sales: $20,000,000 (2000). Emp: 100. Officers: Patrick F. Callahan, President; Mike Callahan, Controller.

■ 22240 ■ Etna Oil Company Inc.
PO Box 429
Ottawa, IL 61350
Phone: (815)434-0353   Fax: (815)434-0401
Products: Gasoline and diesel fuel; Convenience store products. SICs: 5171 (Petroleum Bulk Stations & Terminals); 5141 (Groceries—General Line). Est: 1957. Sales: $15,000,000 (2000). Emp: 60. Officers: William H. Hess, CEO & President.

■ 22241 ■ Evans Oil Co.
520 Ave. F North
Bay City, TX 77414
Phone: (409)245-2424   Fax: (409)244-5070
Products: Lubricants; Gasoline; Oil gears. SICs: 5172 (Petroleum Products Nec); 5171 (Petroleum Bulk Stations & Terminals); 5085 (Industrial Supplies). Emp: 49. Officers: Jerriel L. Evans.

■ 22242 ■ Evans Systems Inc.
PO Box 2480
Bay City, TX 77404-2480
Phone: (409)245-2424
Products: Fuel. SIC: 5172 (Petroleum Products Nec). Est: 1968. Sales: $160,000,000 (2000). Emp: 487. Officers: Jerriel L. Evans Sr., CEO & Chairman of the Board; Charles N. Way, VP & CFO.

■ 22243 ■ Ever-Ready Oil Co.
PO Box 25845
Albuquerque, NM 87125
Phone: (505)842-6120   Fax: (505)247-3918
Products: Petroleum products. SIC: 5172 (Petroleum Products Nec). Est: 1929. Sales: $85,000,000 (2000). Emp: 200. Officers: Charles Ochs, President; Robert Shepherd, Vice President.

■ 22244 ■ Export Oil Field Supply Company Inc.
PO Box 770
Garden City, NY 11530
Phone: (516)227-2500   Fax: (516)222-0339
Products: Oil field equipment. SICs: 5082 (Construction & Mining Machinery); 5084 (Industrial Machinery & Equipment). Est: 1963. Sales: $25,000,000 (2000). Emp: 50. Officers: M.P. Carney, President; Frank Smith, Controller; E.J. Carney, VP of Sales.

■ 22245 ■ Exxon Company USA
17 Miles NW
La Barge, WY 83123
Phones: (307)276-6200   (307)276-6300
Fax: (307)276-6458
Products: Petroleum and its products; Carbon dioxide; Liquefied petroleum gases; Elemental, compressed, and liquefied gases. SICs: 5172 (Petroleum Products Nec); 5169 (Chemicals & Allied Products Nec).

■ 22246 ■ Exxon Company U.S.A. Santa Ynez Unit
PO Box 5025
Westlake Village, CA 91359
Phone: (805)494-2000
Products: Crude petroleum and natural gas. SIC: 5172 (Petroleum Products Nec). Sales: $44,000,000 (2000). Emp: 275.

■ 22247 ■ F and R International
14611 Cypress Meadow Dr.
Cypress, TX 77429
Phone: (281)251-4746
Products: Oilfield equipment. SIC: 5084 (Industrial Machinery & Equipment).

■ 22248 ■ F and R Oil Company Inc.
PO Box 32756
Charlotte, NC 28232-2756
Phone: (704)333-6177   Fax: (704)333-2701
E-mail: info@froil.com
URL: http://www.froil.com
Products: Lubricants, heating oil and fuel, motor oils, greases, solvents, and oil absorbents. SIC: 5172 (Petroleum Products Nec). Est: 1922. Sales: $5,000,000 (2000). Emp: 12. Officers: Leigh K. Black, President; Leigh K. Black, President.

■ 22249 ■ Fair City Oil
PO Box 625
Franklinton, LA 70438
Phone: (504)839-4753
Products: Petroleum bulk station. SIC: 5171 (Petroleum Bulk Stations & Terminals). Sales: $1,000,000 (1994). Emp: 2. Officers: Jim Morgan, Controller.

■ 22250 ■ N.B. Fairclough and Sons Inc.
PO Box 69
Paterson, NJ 07513
Phone: (973)742-6412
Products: Oil, gasoline, and diesel fuel. SIC: 5172 (Petroleum Products Nec).

■ 22251 ■ Fannon Petroleum Services Inc.
PO Box 989
Alexandria, VA 22313
Phone: (703)836-1133   Fax: (703)836-4398
Products: Petroleum broker. SIC: 5172 (Petroleum Products Nec). Emp: 25. Officers: Carolyn Simpson, Bookkeeper.

■ 22252 ■ Far-Mor Cooperative
1433 Illinois St.
Sidney, NE 69162
Phone: (308)254-5541
Free: (800)383-5541   Fax: (308)254-6389
Products: Petroleum products. SICs: 5171 (Petroleum

Bulk Stations & Terminals); 5191 (Farm Supplies). Est: 1928. Sales: $7,100,000 (2000). Emp: 25. Officers: Randy Miller, CEO.

■ 22253 ■ Farmers Cooperative Association
PO Box 149
Canby, MN 56220
Phone: (507)223-7241
Products: Petroleum and farm supply. SIC: 5172 (Petroleum Products Nec). Est: 1930. Sales: $6,000,000 (2000). Emp: 25. Officers: P. Schmitz, General Mgr.

■ 22254 ■ Farmers Cooperative Association
808 Railroad St.
Boyden, IA 51234
Phone: (712)725-2331
Products: Petroleum; Lumber; Grain elevators. SICs: 5153 (Grain & Field Beans); 5031 (Lumber, Plywood & Millwork); 5084 (Industrial Machinery & Equipment). Est: 1907. Sales: $16,000,000 (2000). Emp: 30. Officers: Ronald Smith, President.

■ 22255 ■ Farmers Cooperative Oil Co.
Rte. 1
Parkin, AR 72373
Phone: (870)755-5418
Products: Oil; Chemicals. SICs: 5172 (Petroleum Products Nec); 5169 (Chemicals & Allied Products Nec). Est: 1940. Sales: $6,000,000 (2000). Emp: 25. Officers: Donald McKnight, President; Dennis Wood, Dir. of Marketing.

■ 22256 ■ Farmers Cooperative Oil Company of Clara City
PO Box 717
Clara City, MN 56222
Phone: (320)847-2318
Products: Oil; Gasoline. SIC: 5172 (Petroleum Products Nec). Est: 1955. Sales: $7,300,000 (2000). Emp: 14. Officers: Erv Ahrenholz, CEO.

■ 22257 ■ Farmers Petroleum Cooperative Inc.
7373 W Saginaw Hwy.
Lansing, MI 48909
Phone: (517)323-7000
Products: Petroleum products, including liquid fuel and motor oil; Tires; Batteries. SICs: 5172 (Petroleum Products Nec); 5063 (Electrical Apparatus & Equipment); 5014 (Tires & Tubes). Est: 1948. Sales: $23,600,000 (2000). Emp: 44. Officers: John G. Laurie, President; Thomas J. Parker, Treasurer; Tim Underwood, Marketing Mgr.

■ 22258 ■ Farmers Union Cooperative
PO Box 729
Adams, WI 53910
Phone: (608)339-3394   Fax: (608)339-7068
Products: Fuel; Oil; Fertilizer; Hardware. SICs: 5171 (Petroleum Bulk Stations & Terminals); 5191 (Farm Supplies); 5072 (Hardware). Est: 1947. Sales: $13,000,000 (2000). Emp: 50. Officers: Robert Grabarski, President; Gerald Cardo, Treasurer & Secty.; Timothy Diemert, General Mgr.

■ 22259 ■ Farmers Union Cooperative Association of Alcester and Beresford South Dakota
Rte. 3, Box 10-A
Beresford, SD 57004
Phone: (605)957-4141
Products: Petroleum products. SIC: 5172 (Petroleum Products Nec). Sales: $9,000,000 (1994). Emp: 60. Officers: Dan Pomranke, General Mgr.

■ 22260 ■ Farmers Union Oil Co.
PO Box 398
Crookston, MN 56716-0398
Phone: (320)235-3700   Fax: (320)235-7651
Products: Fuel, including propane, gas, and oil. SIC: 5172 (Petroleum Products Nec). Est: 1931. Sales: $3,000,000 (2000). Emp: 20. Officers: Lynn Dokkebakken, General Mgr.

■ 22261 ■ Farmers Union Oil Co.
PO Box 129
Lake Bronson, MN 56734
Phone: (218)754-4300
Products: Gas; Diesel fuel; Fertilizer. SICs: 5191

(Farm Supplies); 5172 (Petroleum Products Nec). **Est:** 1935. **Sales:** $5,000,000 (2000). **Emp:** 14. **Officers:** Rick Sele, General Mgr.

■ 22262 ■ Farmers Union Oil Co.
PO Box 219
Ellendale, ND 58436
Phone: (701)349-3280
Free: (800)528-3280 **Fax:** (701)349-3280
Products: Petroleum; Fertilizer. **SICs:** 5171 (Petroleum Bulk Stations & Terminals); 5172 (Petroleum Products Nec). **Est:** 1930. **Sales:** $4,000,000 (2000). **Emp:** 21. **Officers:** Kevin Brokaw, President.

■ 22263 ■ Farmers Union Oil Co.
PO Box 67
Harvey, ND 58341
Phone: (701)324-2231 **Fax:** (701)324-2250
Products: Fuel. **SICs:** 5172 (Petroleum Products Nec); 5072 (Hardware). **Est:** 1941. **Sales:** $8,000,000 (2000). **Emp:** 18. **Officers:** Lloyd Bredine, General Mgr.

■ 22264 ■ Farmers Union Oil Co.
Hwy. 2 and 19 W
Devils Lake, ND 58301
Phone: (701)662-4014
Products: Fuel oil. **SIC:** 5172 (Petroleum Products Nec). **Est:** 1931. **Sales:** $12,000,000 (2000). **Emp:** 25. **Officers:** Francis Liephon, President; Emil Gregory, CFO.

■ 22265 ■ Farmers Union Oil Co.
151 9th Ave. NW
Valley City, ND 58072
Phone: (701)845-0812
Products: Petroleum; Plant food; Crop protection; Hardware; Tires; Batteries; Propane. **SICs:** 5172 (Petroleum Products Nec); 5014 (Tires & Tubes); 5072 (Hardware); 5063 (Electrical Apparatus & Equipment). **Est:** 1929. **Sales:** $10,500,000 (2000). **Emp:** 25. **Officers:** Gene Lueb, Manager.

■ 22266 ■ Farmers Union Oil Co.
PO Box 70
Climax, MN 56523
Phone: (218)857-2165 **Fax:** (218)857-2115
Products: Plant food; Crop protection; Petroleum; Hardware. **SICs:** 5171 (Petroleum Bulk Stations & Terminals); 5171 (Petroleum Bulk Stations & Terminals); 5191 (Farm Supplies); 5172 (Petroleum Products Nec). **Est:** 1934. **Sales:** $5,600,000 (1999). **Emp:** 12. **Officers:** Robert Burner, General Mgr.

■ 22267 ■ Farmers Union Oil Co.
PO Box U
Napoleon, ND 58561
Phone: (701)754-2252
Products: Petroleum products. **SIC:** 5171 (Petroleum Bulk Stations & Terminals). **Est:** 1945. **Sales:** $5,000,000 (2000). **Emp:** 18. **Officers:** Leonard Bitz, President; Glen Mormon, Vice President.

■ 22268 ■ Farmers Union Oil Co.
PO Box 219
Ellendale, ND 58436
Phone: (701)349-3280
Free: (800)528-3280 **Fax:** (701)349-3280
Products: Petroleum, fuels, and related equipment. **SIC:** 5171 (Petroleum Bulk Stations & Terminals). **Sales:** $4,000,000 (2000). **Emp:** 21.

■ 22269 ■ Farmers Union Oil Co. (Napoleon, North Dakota)
PO Box U
Napoleon, ND 58561
Phone: (701)754-2252 **Fax:** (701)754-2703
Products: Hardware; Fuel; Gas; Chemicals; Tires. **SICs:** 5171 (Petroleum Bulk Stations & Terminals); 5172 (Petroleum Products Nec); 5072 (Hardware); 5014 (Tires & Tubes); 5169 (Chemicals & Allied Products Nec). **Est:** 1945. **Sales:** $5,000,000 (2000). **Emp:** 18. **Officers:** Leonard Bitz, President; Frank Wangler, Vice President; Paul Doll, Dir. of Marketing; Violet Hilzendeger, Office Mgr.

■ 22270 ■ Farmers Union Oil Co. (Rolla, North Dakota)
104 W Main Ave.
Rolla, ND 58367
Phone: (701)852-2501 **Fax:** (701)852-4794
Products: Fertilizer, agricultural chemicals and bulk petroleum. Gas stations and convenience store. **SIC:** 5172 (Petroleum Products Nec). **Sales:** $35,000,000 (2000). **Emp:** 150. **Officers:** Art Perdue, General Mgr.

■ 22271 ■ Farmers Union Oil Cooperative
2006 E Broadway Ave.
Bismarck, ND 58501
Phone: (701)223-8707 **Fax:** (701)663-6402
Products: Gasoline; Diesel fuel; Oil; Heating fuel. **SIC:** 5172 (Petroleum Products Nec). **Est:** 1934. **Sales:** $14,000,000 (2000). **Emp:** 55. **Officers:** Rick Schlosser, President; Michael T. Frantes, CFO.

■ 22272 ■ Federal Heating and Engineering Company Inc.
160 Cross St.
Winchester, MA 01890
Phone: (781)721-2468
Products: Fuel oil; Heating systems; Air-conditioning equipment. **SICs:** 5172 (Petroleum Products Nec); 5075 (Warm Air Heating & Air-Conditioning). **Est:** 1943. **Sales:** $1,000,000 (2000). **Emp:** 15. **Officers:** Alfred La Pointe, President.

■ 22273 ■ Fegley Oil Company Inc.
PO Drawer A
Tamaqua, PA 18252
Phone: (717)386-4151
Products: Kerosene; Heating oil; Gasoline; Diesel; Lubricating oil. **SIC:** 5172 (Petroleum Products Nec). **Est:** 1955. **Sales:** $20,000,000 (2000). **Emp:** 64. **Officers:** William H. Fegley, President.

■ 22274 ■ Ferrellgas Partners L.P.
1 Liberty Plz.
Liberty, MO 64068
Phone: (816)792-1600 **Fax:** (816)792-7985
Products: Liquid propane. **SIC:** 5172 (Petroleum Products Nec). **Sales:** $1,200,000,000 (2000). **Emp:** 3,370. **Officers:** James E. Ferrell, CEO & Chairman of the Board; Danley K. Sheldon, Sr. VP & CFO.

■ 22275 ■ FFP Operating Partners L.P.
2801 Glenda Ave.
Ft. Worth, TX 76117-4391
Phone: (817)838-4700
Products: Gasoline. **SIC:** 5172 (Petroleum Products Nec). **Sales:** $371,000,000 (2000). **Emp:** 1,330. **Officers:** John H. Harvison, CEO & Chairman of the Board; Steven Hawkins, VP & CFO.

■ 22276 ■ FFP Partners L.P.
2801 Glenda Ave.
Ft. Worth, TX 76117-4391
Phone: (817)838-4700 **Fax:** (817)838-4799
Products: Gasoline. **SIC:** 5172 (Petroleum Products Nec). **Sales:** $311,400,000 (2000). **Emp:** 1,688. **Officers:** John H. Harvison, CEO, President & Chairman of the Board; Steven B. Hawkins, VP, CFO & Treasurer.

■ 22277 ■ Field Oil Inc.
136 W Rushton St.
Ogden, UT 84401
Phone: (801)394-5551
Products: Oil. **SIC:** 5172 (Petroleum Products Nec).

■ 22278 ■ First State Petroleum Services
RR 3 Box 156
Harrington, DE 19952
Phone: (302)398-9704 **Fax:** (302)398-4631
Products: Petroleum and its products; Automobile service station equipment. **SICs:** 5172 (Petroleum Products Nec); 5013 (Motor Vehicle Supplies & New Parts).

■ 22279 ■ Fleischli Oil Company Inc.
PO Box 487
Cheyenne, WY 82003
Phone: (307)634-4466 **Fax:** (307)778-8036
Products: Oil; Fueling stations. **SICs:** 5171 (Petroleum Bulk Stations & Terminals); 5172 (Petroleum Products Nec). **Est:** 1955. **Sales:** $75,000,000 (2000). **Emp:** 95.

Officers: J. John, Rocky Mtn. Regional Mgr.; K. Henry, Dir. of Data Processing.

■ 22280 ■ Fleischli Oil Company Inc.
PO Box 158
Rock Springs, WY 82902
Phone: (307)362-6611 **Fax:** (307)362-3945
Products: Oil; Petroleum products. **SIC:** 5172 (Petroleum Products Nec).

■ 22281 ■ Fleischli Oil Company Inc.
PO Box 50097
Casper, WY 82605
Phone: (307)265-3300 **Fax:** (307)265-3303
Products: Fuels; Lubricants. **SIC:** 5172 (Petroleum Products Nec). **Est:** 1958.

■ 22282 ■ Flintex Marketing, Inc.
16420 Park Ten Pl., Ste. 540
Houston, TX 77084-5052
Phone: (281)578-0529 **Fax:** (281)578-0845
E-mail: mfaircloth@flintex.com
Products: Oil, petroleum, and gasoline. **SIC:** 5172 (Petroleum Products Nec). **Est:** 1965. **Sales:** $6,000,000 (2000). **Emp:** 11. **Officers:** Tom Zatopek, President; S.A. Flint Jr., CEO.

■ 22283 ■ Flitz International Ltd.
821 Mohr Ave.
Waterford, WI 53185
Phone: (414)534-5898
Free: (800)558-8611 **Fax:** (414)534-2991
E-mail: info@flitz.com
URL: http://www.flitz.com
Products: Metal polish; Waxes. **SIC:** 5172 (Petroleum Products Nec). **Est:** 1979. **Sales:** $2,500,000 (2000). **Emp:** 12. **Officers:** Peter Jentzsch, CEO; Ulrich Jentzsch, President; Angie Hensley, Human Resources Contact.

■ 22284 ■ Flying J Inc.
PO Box 678
Brigham City, UT 84302
Phone: (435)734-6400 **Fax:** (435)734-6556
Products: Diesel fuel. **SIC:** 5172 (Petroleum Products Nec). **Est:** 1968. **Sales:** $1,600,000,000 (2000). **Emp:** 8,000.

■ 22285 ■ Flying J Travel Plaza
1920 Harrison Dr.
Evanston, WY 82930
Phones: (307)789-9129 (307)789-5461
Fax: (307)789-5461
Products: Oil; Snacks; Ice cream; Tools. **SICs:** 5172 (Petroleum Products Nec); 5145 (Confectionery); 5143 (Dairy Products Except Dried or Canned); 5072 (Hardware).

■ 22286 ■ FMI Hydrocarbon Co.
1615 Poydras St.
New Orleans, LA 70112
Phone: (504)582-4899
Products: Petroleum products. **SIC:** 5172 (Petroleum Products Nec). **Sales:** $4,000,000 (1993). **Emp:** 10. **Officers:** James Glanzer, President.

■ 22287 ■ FOF Inc.
471 N Curtis Rd.
Boise, ID 83706
Phone: (208)377-0024
Products: Petroleum. **SIC:** 5171 (Petroleum Bulk Stations & Terminals).

■ 22288 ■ Leid Ford Distributing Co.
948 May Ave.
WalLa Walla, WA 99362
Phone: (509)525-8180
Products: Gas; Oil. **SIC:** 5172 (Petroleum Products Nec).

■ 22289 ■ Fort Worth Jet Center
4201 N Main St.
Ft. Worth, TX 76106
Phone: (817)625-4012
Products: Aircraft fuel. **SIC:** 5172 (Petroleum Products Nec).

■ **22290** ■ **Fortmeyer's Inc.**
4151 Goshen Rd.
Ft. Wayne, IN 46818
Phone: (219)489-3511 **Fax:** (219)489-8931
Products: Motor oil; Distillates; Diesel fuel. **SICs:** 5171 (Petroleum Bulk Stations & Terminals); 5172 (Petroleum Products Nec). **Est:** 1930. **Sales:** $9,000,000 (2000). **Emp:** 60. **Officers:** H. Fortmeyer, President.

■ **22291** ■ **M.M. Fowler Inc.**
4220 Neal Rd.
Durham, NC 27705-2322
Phone: (919)596-8246
Products: Fuel; Convenience store products. **SIC:** 5172 (Petroleum Products Nec). **Est:** 1937. **Sales:** $50,000,000 (2000). **Emp:** 18. **Officers:** M.L. Barnes, President.

■ **22292** ■ **Frank Carroll Oil Co.**
2957 Royal Palm Ave.
Ft. Myers, FL 33901-6323
Phone: (941)334-2345 **Fax:** (941)334-0737
Products: Bulk petroleum products. **SIC:** 5171 (Petroleum Bulk Stations & Terminals). **Sales:** $15,600,000 (2000). **Emp:** 50. **Officers:** Martha R. Childs-Hoover, President; Vernon Wolf, Controller.

■ **22293** ■ **Fredericksen Tank Lines**
850 Delta Ln.
West Sacramento, CA 95691
Phone: (916)371-4655
Products: Discard fuel. **SIC:** 5172 (Petroleum Products Nec). **Est:** 1940. **Sales:** $6,000,000 (2000). **Emp:** 100. **Officers:** Len Robinson, President; Leonard Robinson, Controller.

■ **22294** ■ **Freeborn County Cooperative Oil Co.**
226 E Clark St.
Albert Lea, MN 56007
Phone: (507)373-3991 **Fax:** (507)373-6324
Products: Fuel, including gas. **SIC:** 5172 (Petroleum Products Nec). **Est:** 1925. **Sales:** $14,000,000 (2000). **Emp:** 45. **Officers:** Robert Johnson, President; Marlyn Mostrom, General Mgr.

■ **22295** ■ **Frontier Texaco**
580 W Broadway
PO Box 1771
Jackson, WY 83001
Phone: (307)733-2168
Products: Oil; Petroleum products. **SIC:** 5172 (Petroleum Products Nec).

■ **22296** ■ **Fuel South Company Inc.**
PO Box 572
Hazlehurst, GA 31539
Phone: (912)285-4011 **Fax:** (912)375-2703
Products: Petroleum, including gasoline, oil, and diesel fuel. **SIC:** 5172 (Petroleum Products Nec). **Est:** 1964. **Sales:** $34,000,000 (2000). **Emp:** 53. **Officers:** Jimmy Walker, President; Phil Wysong, Treasurer; Patrick Jones, VP of Marketing.

■ **22297** ■ **Fuller Oil Company Inc.**
PO Box 605
Fayetteville, NC 28302
Phone: (919)488-2815
Products: Fuel oil and kerosene. **SIC:** 5172 (Petroleum Products Nec). **Sales:** $4,000,000 (2000). **Emp:** 7. **Officers:** Charles Fuller, President.

■ **22298** ■ **G and B Oil Company Inc.**
PO Box 811
Elkin, NC 28621
Phone: (336)835-3607
Products: Petroleum terminals and coal products. **SICs:** 5171 (Petroleum Bulk Stations & Terminals); 5052 (Coal, Other Minerals & Ores). **Sales:** $30,000,000 (2000). **Emp:** 105. **Officers:** Jeffery C. Eidson, President.

■ **22299** ■ **G and M Oil Company Inc.**
HC 84
PO Box 6
Barbourville, KY 40906
Phone: (606)546-3909 **Fax:** (606)546-4044
Products: Gas; Oil. **SICs:** 5171 (Petroleum Bulk

Stations & Terminals); 5172 (Petroleum Products Nec). **Est:** 1961. **Sales:** $43,000,000 (2000). **Emp:** 115. **Officers:** Beckham Garland, President; Tony Todd, Controller.

■ **22300** ■ **Galvin Flying Service Inc.**
7149 Perimeter Rd.
Seattle, WA 98108
Phone: (206)763-0350 **Fax:** (206)767-9333
Products: Aircraft; Aircraft fuel. **SIC:** 5172 (Petroleum Products Nec). **Sales:** $12,000,000 (1994). **Emp:** 100. **Officers:** Peter G. Anderson, President; Gina Haggerty, Controller.

■ **22301** ■ **Gant Oil Co.**
PO Box 68
Walkertown, NC 27051
Phone: (336)595-2151 **Free:** (800)932-3087
Products: Petroleum. **SIC:** 5171 (Petroleum Bulk Stations & Terminals). **Est:** 1918. **Sales:** $44,000,000 (2000). **Emp:** 150. **Officers:** Annie H. Gant, Chairman of the Board; Marshall M. Wilson, Controller.

■ **22302** ■ **Gas Equipment Supply Co.**
1125 Satellite Blvd., Ste. 112
Suwanee, GA 30024
Phone: (770)813-1199
Free: (800)241-4155 **Fax:** (770)813-1008
E-mail: gesco@mindspring.com
URL: http://www.gasequipmentsupplyco.com
Products: Liquid propane gas equipment and supplies. **SIC:** 5084 (Industrial Machinery & Equipment). **Est:** 1947. **Sales:** $14,000,000 (2000). **Emp:** 45.

■ **22303** ■ **Gate City Equipment Company Inc.**
2000 Northfield Ct.
Roswell, GA 30076-3825
Phone: (404)475-1900 **Fax:** (404)475-1717
Products: Blending injection systems for oil, gasoline, and petroleum mixing. **SIC:** 5172 (Petroleum Products Nec). **Est:** 1951. **Sales:** $18,000,000 (2000). **Emp:** 40. **Officers:** L.W. Silzle, CEO & President.

■ **22304** ■ **GATX Terminals Corp.**
500 W Monroe
Chicago, IL 60661
Phone: (312)621-6200 **Fax:** (312)621-8110
Products: Petroleum products. **SICs:** 5171 (Petroleum Bulk Stations & Terminals); 5169 (Chemicals & Allied Products Nec). **Sales:** $293,000,000 (2000). **Emp:** 1,110. **Officers:** Anthony J Anprukaitis, President; Joseph McNeely, Controller.

■ **22305** ■ **Gayle Oil Company Inc.**
PO Drawer 100
Gueydan, LA 70542
Phone: (318)536-6738
Products: Petroleum products, including gasoline and diesel. **SIC:** 5172 (Petroleum Products Nec). **Sales:** $20,000,000 (2000). **Emp:** 65. **Officers:** T.J. Fontenot, President.

■ **22306** ■ **Geer Tank Trucks Inc.**
PO Drawer J
Jacksboro, TX 76458
Phone: (940)567-2677 **Fax:** (940)567-3634
Products: Crude oil. **SIC:** 5172 (Petroleum Products Nec). **Sales:** $24,000,000 (2000). **Emp:** 50. **Officers:** Johnny Geer, Treasurer & Secty.

■ **22307** ■ **Gemini Enterprises Inc.**
16920 Kuykendahl, Ste. 228
Houston, TX 77068
Phone: (281)583-2900
Products: Oilfield equipment. **SIC:** 5084 (Industrial Machinery & Equipment).

■ **22308** ■ **Gerlach Oil Company Inc.**
PO Box 364
Abilene, TX 79604
Phone: (915)692-1293
Products: Fuel; Motor oil. **SICs:** 5171 (Petroleum Bulk Stations & Terminals); 5172 (Petroleum Products Nec); 5199 (Nondurable Goods Nec). **Est:** 1938. **Sales:** $10,000,000 (2000). **Emp:** 30. **Officers:** Fred Gerlach, President; George Swinney, CFO.

■ **22309** ■ **Getty Petroleum Marketing Inc.**
125 Jericho Tpke.
Jericho, NY 11753
Phone: (516)338-6000
Products: Petroluem products. **SIC:** 5172 (Petroleum Products Nec). **Sales:** $900,000,000 (2000). **Officers:** Vincent J. DeLaurentis, President.

■ **22310** ■ **Getty Realty Corp.**
125 Jericho Tpke.
Jericho, NY 11753
Phone: (516)338-6000 **Fax:** (516)338-6062
Products: Petroleum products. **SICs:** 5172 (Petroleum Products Nec); 5171 (Petroleum Bulk Stations & Terminals). **Est:** 1971. **Sales:** $920,000,000 (2000). **Emp:** 673. **Officers:** Leo Liebowitz, CEO & President; John J. Fitteron, Sr. VP & CFO; James R. Craig, Vice President; Alvin A. Smith, Sr. VP of Operations; Stephen P. Salzman, Sr. VP.

■ **22311** ■ **Giant Refining Co.**
Interstate 40, Exit 39
Jamestown, NM 87347
Phone: (505)722-3833
Products: Petroleum. **SIC:** 5172 (Petroleum Products Nec).

■ **22312** ■ **Gibble Oil Company Inc.**
PO Box 1270
Cushing, OK 74023
Phone: (918)225-0189
Products: Gasoline. **SIC:** 5171 (Petroleum Bulk Stations & Terminals). **Sales:** $15,000,000 (1994). **Emp:** 21. **Officers:** Earl Gibble, President; Betty Whalen, Treasurer & Secty.

■ **22313** ■ **Gibbons and LeFort Inc.**
PO Box 758
Thibodaux, LA 70302
Phone: (504)447-9338
Products: Petroleum products. **SIC:** 5172 (Petroleum Products Nec). **Est:** 1949. **Sales:** $6,000,000 (2000). **Emp:** 10. **Officers:** Paul W. LeFort Jr., President; Robert Orgeron, Treasurer & Secty.

■ **22314** ■ **Global Petroleum Corp.**
800 South St.
Waltham, MA 02454
Phone: (617)894-8800 **Fax:** (617)893-7642
Products: Home heating oil; Industrial heating oil; Gasoline. **SIC:** 5172 (Petroleum Products Nec). **Est:** 1950. **Sales:** $86,000,000 (2000). **Emp:** 175. **Officers:** Alfred Slifka, President; Richard Slifka, Treasurer; Joe DeStefano, Marketing Mgr.; James Shelton, Data Processing Mgr.; Barbara Rosenbloom, Dir of Personnel.

■ **22315** ■ **Glover Oil Company Inc.**
3109 S Main St.
Melbourne, FL 32902-0790
Phone: (407)723-7461
Free: (800)342-7121 **Fax:** (407)727-2309
Products: Motor oil. **SICs:** 5171 (Petroleum Bulk Stations & Terminals); 5172 (Petroleum Products Nec). **Est:** 1947. **Sales:** $6,500,000 (2000). **Emp:** 15. **Officers:** J.H. Glover, President; Trina Downey, CFO; Laco Rhodes, Sales Mgr.; Shirley McGrath, Dir. of Data Processing; Ann Suhl, Manager.

■ **22316** ■ **Godwin Oil Company Inc.**
PO Box 150
Wilmington, NC 28402
Phone: (910)762-0312 **Free:** (800)489-4626
E-mail: goco@isaac.net
Products: Lubricants, including motor oil and grease. **SIC:** 5172 (Petroleum Products Nec). **Est:** 1944. **Sales:** $5,000,000 (2000). **Emp:** 25. **Officers:** Charles M. Godwin, President; William C. Godwin II II, Treasurer & Secty.; Ronnie Ottaway, VP of Marketing.

■ **22317** ■ **Goetz Energy Corp.**
PO Box A
Buffalo, NY 14217
Phone: (716)876-4324
E-mail: goetzen@localnet.com
Products: Fuel, including diesel and gasoline. **SIC:** 5172 (Petroleum Products Nec). **Est:** 1954. **Sales:** $75,000,000 (2000). **Emp:** 50. **Officers:** Stephen

Schintzius, President; Kathy Wilder, Controller; Roger Schintius, Vice President.

■ **22318** ■   **GOEX International Inc.**
423 Vaughn Rd. W
Cleburne, TX 76031
Phone: (817)641-2261   **Fax:** (817)556-0657
Products: Oil field explosive and non-explosive equipment. **SIC:** 5084 (Industrial Machinery & Equipment). **Sales:** $12,600,000 (1994). **Emp:** 100. **Officers:** Claude E. Badgett, CEO.

■ **22319** ■   **Gothic Energy Corp.**
6120 S Yale Ave., No. 1200
Tulsa, OK 74136-4241
Phone: (918)749-5666
Products: Petroleum and petroleum products. **SIC:** 5172 (Petroleum Products Nec).

■ **22320** ■   **Grays Petroleum Inc.**
PO Box 1010
De Queen, AR 71832
Phone: (870)642-2234
Products: Petroleum products. **SIC:** 5172 (Petroleum Products Nec). **Sales:** $39,000,000 (2000). **Emp:** 80. **Officers:** Ron Moore, President.

■ **22321** ■   **Gresham Petroleum Co.**
PO Box 690
Indianola, MS 38751
Phone: (662)887-2160   **Fax:** (662)887-6873
E-mail: wgresham@doublequick.com
Products: Gasoline; Diesel fuel; Propane; Lubricants. **SIC:** 5172 (Petroleum Products Nec). **Est:** 1920. **Sales:** $14,000,000 (2000). **Emp:** 30. **Officers:** W.W. Gresham Jr., President; W.W. Gresham III, Treasurer & Secty.; Allen Holloway, Comptroller.

■ **22322** ■   **Jack Griggs Inc.**
PO Box 547
Exeter, CA 93221
Phone: (209)592-3154   **Fax:** (209)592-3583
Products: Gas, diesel, and propane. **SIC:** 5172 (Petroleum Products Nec). **Est:** 1933. **Sales:** $12,000,000 (2000). **Emp:** 34. **Officers:** Dave W. Griggs, President.

■ **22323** ■   **Grimes Oil Company Inc.**
165 Norfolk St.
Boston, MA 02124
Phone: (617)825-1200   **Fax:** (617)265-0255
Products: Heavy oil; Wool; Residual fuels. **SICs:** 5172 (Petroleum Products Nec); 5159 (Farm-Product Raw Materials Nec). **Est:** 1940. **Sales:** $24,000,000 (2000). **Emp:** 5. **Officers:** Calvin M. Grimes Jr., President.

■ **22324** ■   **Grimsley Oil Company Inc.**
PO Box 520
Avon Park, FL 33825
Phone: (941)453-3550   **Fax:** (941)453-6649
Products: Products of petroleum refining. **SICs:** 5171 (Petroleum Bulk Stations & Terminals); 5172 (Petroleum Products Nec). **Sales:** $15,000,000 (2000). **Emp:** 15. **Officers:** Joseph M. Adams III, CEO.

■ **22325** ■   **GTA Aviation Inc.**
2730 E Sky Harbor Blvd.
Phoenix, AZ 85034
Phone: (602)273-7704   **Fax:** (602)231-9087
Products: Aircraft fuel. **SIC:** 5172 (Petroleum Products Nec). **Sales:** $22,000,000 (1993). **Emp:** 47. **Officers:** Giselle Strandquest, President & General Mgr.; Mary Crane, Chairman of the Board & Finance Officer.

■ **22326** ■   **Guard All Chemical Company Inc.**
PO Box 445
Norwalk, CT 06856
Phone: (203)838-5515   **Fax:** (203)854-6789
Products: Petroleum, fuels, and related equipment. **SIC:** 5172 (Petroleum Products Nec). **Est:** 1952. **Sales:** $10,000,000 (2000). **Emp:** 20.

■ **22327** ■   **Gulf Oil L.P.**
PO Box 9151
Chelsea, MA 02150-2337
Phone: (617)889-9000
Products: Oil and gasoline. **SIC:** 5172 (Petroleum Products Nec). **Sales:** $99,300,000 (2000). **Emp:** 200. **Officers:** Gary Kaneb, President; Alice Kuhune, CFO.

■ **22328** ■   **Gull Industries Inc.**
PO Box 24687
Seattle, WA 98124
Phone: (206)624-5900   **Fax:** (425)866-4855
Products: Petroleum products. **SIC:** 5172 (Petroleum Products Nec). **Sales:** $99,000,000 (2000). **Emp:** 201. **Officers:** Dougals L. True, President; Roger Masauda, CFO.

■ **22329** ■   **Gunderson Oil Co.**
6339 Hwy. 44
Cuba, NM 87013
Phone: (505)289-4040
Products: Oil. **SIC:** 5172 (Petroleum Products Nec).

■ **22330** ■   **Guttman Oil Co.**
Speers Rd.
Belle Vernon, PA 15012
Phone: (724)483-3533
Products: Oil. **SIC:** 5172 (Petroleum Products Nec). **Officers:** A. Guttman, CEO; A. Melick, VP of Finance.

■ **22331** ■   **E.O. Habhegger Company Inc.**
460 Penn St.
Yeadon, PA 19050-3017
Phone: (610)622-1977   **Fax:** (610)622-5889
URL: http://www.habhegger.com
Products: Petroleum equipment. **SIC:** 5171 (Petroleum Bulk Stations & Terminals). **Est:** 1927. **Sales:** $8,000,000 (1993). **Emp:** 29. **Officers:** Kenneth T. Hagman, President; James E. Duck, General Mgr.; James J. Porter, Sales Mgr.; Caroline Hagman, Controller.

■ **22332** ■   **Halron Oil Company Inc.**
PO Box 2188
Green Bay, WI 54306
Phone: (414)437-0466   **Fax:** (920)437-2037
E-mail: halron@halron.com
Products: Fuels, including oil and diesel; Motor oils; Industrial lubricants; Marine diesel fuel. **SIC:** 5172 (Petroleum Products Nec). **Est:** 1918. **Sales:** $65,000,000 (2000). **Emp:** 70. **Officers:** James Halron, President; Joseph Vandenhouten, CFO; Michael Halron, Vice President.

■ **22333** ■   **Hanover Compression**
12001 N Houston Rosslyn
Houston, TX 77086
Phone: (281)447-8787   **Fax:** (214)528-5151
Products: Gas compressors. **SIC:** 5084 (Industrial Machinery & Equipment). **Sales:** $74,000,000 (1994). **Emp:** 386. **Officers:** Michael J. McGhan, CEO & President; Curtis Bedrich, CFO.

■ **22334** ■   **Harbor Enterprises Inc.**
PO Box 389
Seward, AK 99664
Phone: (907)224-3190
Products: Petroleum. **SIC:** 5172 (Petroleum Products Nec). **Sales:** $100,000,000 (2000). **Emp:** 65. **Officers:** Dale Lindsey, President; Carol Lindsey, Treasurer & Secty.

■ **22335** ■   **Harbor Fuel Company Inc.**
PO Box 270
Oyster Bay, NY 11771-0270
Phone: (516)676-2500
Products: Home heating oils. **SIC:** 5172 (Petroleum Products Nec). **Sales:** $5,000,000 (2000). **Emp:** 40. **Officers:** Donald C. Death Jr., President & Chairman of the Board; Ronald Shield, Exec. VP.

■ **22336** ■   **Harper Distributing Company Inc.**
PO Box 6325
Florence, KY 41022
Phone: (606)283-1001
Products: Gas and oil. **SIC:** 5172 (Petroleum Products Nec).

■ **22337** ■   **Harris County Oil Company Inc.**
3325 W 11th St.
Houston, TX 77008
Phone: (713)861-8115   **Fax:** (713)861-6986
Products: Fuel oil. **SIC:** 5172 (Petroleum Products Nec). **Est:** 1933. **Sales:** $12,000,000 (2000). **Emp:** 17. **Officers:** George Francklow Jr., CEO; Stephen D. Francklow, President.

■ **22338** ■   **Bob Harris Oil Co.**
PO Box 691
Cleburne, TX 76031
Phone: (817)641-9749   **Fax:** (817)641-3074
Products: Fuel. **SIC:** 5172 (Petroleum Products Nec). **Est:** 1971. **Sales:** $15,000,000 (1999). **Emp:** 50. **Officers:** David Harris, CEO & President; M. Harris, Controller; Bob J. Harris, Vice President.

■ **22339** ■   **Harrison Oil Co.**
16 E Martin Luther King St.
Muskogee, OK 74403
Phone: (918)682-8861
Products: Oil. **SIC:** 5172 (Petroleum Products Nec).

■ **22340** ■   **Hartsook Equipment & Pump Services**
1640 W 18th St.
Cheyenne, WY 82001
Phone: (307)634-4489   **Fax:** (307)635-5072
Products: Service station equipment, including tanks. **SICs:** 5087 (Service Establishment Equipment); 5013 (Motor Vehicle Supplies & New Parts).

■ **22341** ■   **Heating Oil Partners**
PO Box 431
Norwich, CT 06360
Phone: (860)887-3525
Free: (888)225-5540   **Fax:** (860)886-2183
Products: Petroleum and petroleum products. **SIC:** 5172 (Petroleum Products Nec). **Sales:** $19,000,000 (2000). **Emp:** 40. **Officers:** Chris Johnson, General Manager, Finance.

■ **22342** ■   **Heetco Inc.**
PO Box 188
Lewistown, MO 63452
Phone: (573)497-2295   **Fax:** (573)497-2357
Products: Propane. **SIC:** 5172 (Petroleum Products Nec). **Sales:** $8,000,000 (2000). **Emp:** 100. **Officers:** D. Phillips, President; Jim Behn, Controller.

■ **22343** ■   **Heetco Inc. Kansas Div.**
1853 E 1450 Rd.
PO Box 886
Lawrence, KS 66044
Phone: (785)843-4655   **Fax:** (785)749-1146
Products: Propane. **SIC:** 5172 (Petroleum Products Nec). **Est:** 1962. **Sales:** $3,000,000 (2000). **Emp:** 20. **Officers:** D. Phillips, President; Monte Milstead, VP & General Merchandising Mgr.

■ **22344** ■   **Heffner Brothers Co.**
PO Box 226
Hawthorn, PA 16230
Phone: (814)365-5311
Products: Gasoline; Diesel fuel. **SIC:** 5172 (Petroleum Products Nec). **Est:** 1937. **Sales:** $3,000,000 (2000). **Emp:** 5. **Officers:** Harold J. Heffner Jr., President.

■ **22345** ■   **Henry Service Co.**
PO Box 79
Cambridge, IL 61238
Phone: (309)937-3369
Products: Petroleum; Fertilizers. **SICs:** 5172 (Petroleum Products Nec); 5191 (Farm Supplies). **Est:** 1927. **Sales:** $64,000,000 (2000). **Emp:** 55. **Officers:** Dick Anderson, President; Dan Nolan, Controller; Dave Vandevelde, Dir. of Sales.

■ **22346** ■   **Heritage F.S. Inc.**
PO Box 339
Gilman, IL 60938
Phone: (815)265-4751   **Fax:** (815)265-4769
Products: Petroleum products and farm supplies. **SICs:** 5172 (Petroleum Products Nec); 5191 (Farm Supplies). **Sales:** $20,000,000 (2000). **Emp:** 62. **Officers:** Charles Yhonka, President; Mark Weilbacher, CFO.

■ **22347** ■   **Heritage Propane Partners, L.P.**
8801 S Yale Ave., Ste. 310
Tulsa, OK 74137
Phone: (918)492-7272   **Fax:** (918)493-7290
Products: Propane. **SIC:** 5172 (Petroleum Products Nec). **Est:** 1989. **Sales:** $200,000,000 (2000). **Emp:** 950. **Officers:** James E. Bertelsmayer, CEO & Chairman of the Board; Mike Krimbill, CFO; R.C. Mills, COO; Al Darr, VP of Corp. Development.

■ **22348** ■ **Hermes Consolidated Inc.**
1600 Broadway Ste. 2300
Denver, CO 80202
Phone: (303)894-9966
Products: Petroleum refining. **SIC:** 5172 (Petroleum Products Nec). **Sales:** $78,000,000 (2000). **Emp:** 100. **Officers:** Dennis McCormick, President.

■ **22349** ■ **Hickman & Willey, Inc.**
PO Box 146
Selbyville, DE 19975
Phone: (302)436-8533
Products: Heating fuel. **SIC:** 5172 (Petroleum Products Nec).

■ **22350** ■ **Hicks Oil and Hicks Gas Inc.**
PO Box 98
202 N Rte. 54
Roberts, IL 60962
Phones: (217)395-2281   (217)947-0103
Free: (800)227-0023   **Fax:** (217)724-0224
Products: Oil and gas. **SICs:** 5171 (Petroleum Bulk Stations & Terminals); 5172 (Petroleum Products Nec). **Est:** 1946. **Sales:** $70,000,000 (1999). **Emp:** 450. **Officers:** Todd M. Coady, President; Randy J. Spitz, CFO; J.C. Flessner, Dir. of Marketing; Mark McLaughlin, Dir. of Operations.

■ **22351** ■ **High Point Oil Co.**
3520 E 96th St., Ste. 11
Indianapolis, IN 46240-3734
Phone: (317)844-8886
Products: Petroleum and its products; Gasoline. **SICs:** 5171 (Petroleum Bulk Stations & Terminals); 5172 (Petroleum Products Nec). **Sales:** $9,000,000 (2000). **Emp:** 11. **Officers:** Karl N. Kelb, President; Don E. Kelb, Vice President.

■ **22352** ■ **Hightower Oil and Petroleum Company Inc.**
PO Box 36
Plumerville, AR 72127
Phone: (501)354-4780
Products: Motor oil. **SICs:** 5171 (Petroleum Bulk Stations & Terminals); 5172 (Petroleum Products Nec). **Est:** 1953. **Sales:** $5,000,000 (2000). **Emp:** 13. **Officers:** Kenny Shipp, President; Patti Shipp, CFO; Leon Whittaker, Dir. of Sales.

■ **22353** ■ **Hillger Oil Company Inc.**
PO Box 1989
Las Cruces, NM 88005
Phone: (505)526-8481
Products: Gas. **SICs:** 5171 (Petroleum Bulk Stations & Terminals); 5172 (Petroleum Products Nec). **Est:** 1931. **Sales:** $42,000,000 (2000). **Emp:** 85. **Officers:** Marvin Hillger, CEO; Carol Glenn, CFO; Scott Hillger, VP of Marketing & Sales.

■ **22354** ■ **Angus I. Hines Inc.**
1426 Holland Rd.
Suffolk, VA 23434
Phone: (757)539-2358
Products: Oil. **SIC:** 5172 (Petroleum Products Nec). **Est:** 1923. **Sales:** $90,000,000 (2000). **Emp:** 400. **Officers:** Angus I. Hines Jr., President; L.L. Felton, Treasurer & Secty.; Robert L. Story, Vice President.

■ **22355** ■ **Hollar Company Inc.**
PO Box 407
Gadsden, AL 35902
Phone: (205)547-1644
Products: Gasoline. **SIC:** 5172 (Petroleum Products Nec). **Est:** 1976. **Sales:** $27,000,000 (2000). **Emp:** 110. **Officers:** Wayne A. Hollar, President; Don F. Hollar, Treasurer; Chester Berry, Dir. of Marketing.

■ **22356** ■ **Holston Gases Inc.**
PO Box 27248
Knoxville, TN 37927
Phone: (423)573-1917   **Fax:** (423)573-0063
Products: Gas, propane, acetylene, and oxygen. **SICs:** 5084 (Industrial Machinery & Equipment); 5169 (Chemicals & Allied Products Nec). **Est:** 1960. **Sales:** $23,000,000 (2000). **Emp:** 130. **Officers:** William W. Baxter, CEO; Robert Anders, VP & CFO; W.W. Baxter, President.

■ **22357** ■ **Homax Oil**
605 S Poplar St.
Casper, WY 82601
Phone: (307)237-5800   **Fax:** (307)237-6144
Products: Oil products. **SIC:** 5172 (Petroleum Products Nec).

■ **22358** ■ **Home Oil Co.**
PO Box 608
Osceola, AR 72370
Phone: (870)563-6573   **Fax:** (870)563-3621
Products: Gasoline and diesel fuels; Petroleum. **SICs:** 5171 (Petroleum Bulk Stations & Terminals); 5191 (Farm Supplies). **Est:** 1946. **Sales:** $20,000,000 (2000). **Emp:** 30. **Officers:** Bill DeLine, General Mgr.

■ **22359** ■ **Home Oil Company of Sikeston Inc.**
PO Box 810
Sikeston, MO 63801
Phone: (314)471-5141
Products: Gasoline, diesel, and propane. **SIC:** 5172 (Petroleum Products Nec). **Est:** 1937. **Sales:** $10,000,000 (2000). **Emp:** 13. **Officers:** J.F. Cox III, President.

■ **22360** ■ **Home Oil and Gas Company Inc.**
PO Box 397
Henderson, KY 42419-0397
Phone: (502)826-3925   **Fax:** (502)826-2566
Products: Oil, gas, and lubricants for industrial use. **SIC:** 5172 (Petroleum Products Nec). **Est:** 1925. **Sales:** $14,500,000 (2000). **Emp:** 28. **Officers:** James M. Crafton Jr., President; James M. Crafton Sr., Secretary.

■ **22361** ■ **Home Service Oil Company Inc.**
6910 Front St.
Barnhart, MO 63012
Phone: (314)464-5266
Free: (800)467-5044   **Fax:** (314)464-6936
URL: http://www.homeserviceoil.com
Products: Fuels; Lubricating oils. **SIC:** 5172 (Petroleum Products Nec). **Est:** 1930. **Sales:** $32,000,000 (1999). **Emp:** 140. **Officers:** D. Mangelsdorf, President; V. Boxdorfer, Human Resources Contact; S. Overberg, Sec. & Treas.

■ **22362** ■ **Hone Oil Co.**
2004 Wall Ave.
Ogden, UT 84401
Phone: (801)394-2649
Products: Oil. **SIC:** 5172 (Petroleum Products Nec).

■ **22363** ■ **Hoosier Oil Inc.**
PO Box 458
Jasper, IN 47547
Phone: (812)482-3191   **Fax:** (812)634-2000
Products: Petroleum products. **SIC:** 5172 (Petroleum Products Nec). **Sales:** $12,000,000 (1993). **Emp:** 50. **Officers:** Larry Haas, President; Pat Haas, Treasurer & Secty.

■ **22364** ■ **Hopkins-Gowen Oil Company Inc.**
402 W Main St.
Folkston, GA 31537
Phone: (912)496-2331
Products: Petroleum. **SIC:** 5171 (Petroleum Bulk Stations & Terminals).

■ **22365** ■ **Harry Houston Texaco Oil Co.**
215 NW Texas St.
Idabel, OK 74745
Phone: (580)286-3066
Products: Oil. **SIC:** 5172 (Petroleum Products Nec).

■ **22366** ■ **Howell Corp.**
1500 Howell Buliding 1111 Fanni
Houston, TX 77002-6923
Phone: (713)658-4000   **Fax:** (713)658-4007
Products: Oil and gas. **SIC:** 5171 (Petroleum Bulk Stations & Terminals). **Est:** 1955. **Sales:** $684,500,000 (2000). **Emp:** 103. **Officers:** Donald W. Clayton, CEO & Chairman of the Board; J. Richard Lisenby, VP & CFO.

■ **22367** ■ **Howell Petroleum Products Inc.**
499 Van Brunt St.
Brooklyn, NY 11231
Phone: (718)855-4400   **Fax:** (718)855-0595
URL: http://www.howellpetroleum.com
Products: Industrial lubricants, including oil and anti-freeze. **SICs:** 5172 (Petroleum Products Nec); 5169 (Chemicals & Allied Products Nec). **Est:** 1985. **Sales:** $1,000,000 (2000). **Emp:** 10. **Officers:** Bill Howell, President, e-mail: bill@howellpetroleum.com.

■ **22368** ■ **Humboldt Petroleum Inc.**
PO Box 131
Eureka, CA 95502
Phone: (707)443-3069   **Fax:** (707)445-4433
Products: Petroleum products; Gasoline station chain. **SIC:** 5172 (Petroleum Products Nec). **Sales:** $60,000,000 (2000). **Emp:** 150. **Officers:** Robert Wotherspoon, President; Rick Dearns, President.

■ **22369** ■ **Hunt and Sons Inc.**
5750 S Watt Ave.
Sacramento, CA 95829
Phone: (916)363-5555
Products: Petroleum products. **SIC:** 5172 (Petroleum Products Nec).

■ **22370** ■ **IGI Div.**
85 Old Eagle School Rd.
PO Box 383
Wayne, PA 19087
Phone: (610)687-9030   **Fax:** (610)254-8548
E-mail: igiwax@msn.com
URL: http://www.igiwax.xom
Products: Petroleum based waxes. **SIC:** 5172 (Petroleum Products Nec). **Est:** 1928. **Sales:** $14,000,000 (2000). **Emp:** 29. **Officers:** Ross Reucassel, President; Anthony Adley, Finance Officer; Sherry Everett, Marketing Mgr. **Also Known by This Acronym:** IGI.

■ **22371** ■ **Illini F.S. Inc.**
1509 E University St.
Urbana, IL 61802
Phone: (217)384-8300   **Fax:** (217)384-6317
Products: Petroleum bulk station and farm supplies. **SICs:** 5171 (Petroleum Bulk Stations & Terminals); 5191 (Farm Supplies). **Est:** 1972. **Sales:** $47,000,000 (1999). **Emp:** 130. **Officers:** Steve Wattnem, General Mgr.; Darrell Trouth, Controller.

■ **22372** ■ **Illinois Oil Products Inc.**
321 24th St.
Rock Island, IL 61201
Phone: (309)786-4474
Free: (800)289-5827   **Fax:** (309)786-4472
URL: http://www.illinoisoilproducts.com
Products: Anti-freeze, oils, and greases. **SIC:** 5172 (Petroleum Products Nec). **Est:** 1945. **Sales:** $5,500,000 (1999). **Emp:** 40. **Officers:** R.A. Jackson, President, e-mail: rjackson@illinoisoilproducts.com; Douglas Schott, Controller; John Bickett, Marketing Mgr., e-mail: jbickett@illinoisoilproducts.com; Carol Jackson, Human Resources Contact, e-mail: cjackson@illinoisoilproducts.com. **Alternate Name:** Supreme.

■ **22373** ■ **Imlay City Total Oil Inc.**
15750 N East St.
Lansing, MI 48906
Phone: (517)372-2220   **Fax:** (517)372-5811
Products: Fuel oil. **SIC:** 5172 (Petroleum Products Nec). **Est:** 1983. **Sales:** $48,000,000 (2000). **Emp:** 75. **Officers:** Dennis Pappas, Manager.

■ **22374** ■ **Industrial Fuel Co.**
25 1st Ave., NE
Hickory, NC 28601
Phone: (828)324-7887   **Fax:** (828)324-8488
Products: Industrial fuels. **SIC:** 5172 (Petroleum Products Nec). **Sales:** $1,000,000 (2000). **Emp:** 5. **Officers:** Ross Rogers, President.

■ **22375** ■ **Interior Fuels Co.**
PO Box 70199
Fairbanks, AK 99707
Phone: (907)456-1312   **Fax:** (907)456-1659
Products: Heating oil; Lube oils; Gasoline. **SIC:** 5172 (Petroleum Products Nec). **Sales:** $5,000,000 (2000).

Emp: 12. Officers: Andrew Kjera, Operations Mgr., e-mail: akjera@serviceoil.com; Marc Wery, Sales Mgr., e-mail: mwery@serviceoil.com.

■ 22376 ■   International Marine Fuels Inc.
2121 3rd St.
San Francisco, CA 94107
Phone: (415)552-9340
Products: Marine fuels. SIC: 5172 (Petroleum Products Nec).

■ 22377 ■   Interstate Petroleum Products Inc.
3635 Dunbury Rd.
Brewster, NY 10509
Phone: (914)279-5625
Free: (800)876-6457   Fax: (914)279-7763
Products: Lubricating oils. SIC: 5172 (Petroleum Products Nec). Sales: $2,000,000 (2000). Emp: 5. Officers: Rob Clark, Vice President.

■ 22378 ■   Iowa Oil Co.
PO Box 712
Dubuque, IA 52001
Phone: (319)583-3563   Fax: (319)583-5401
Products: Petroleum products. SIC: 5172 (Petroleum Products Nec). Sales: $100,000,000 (1994). Emp: 212. Officers: Ronald P. Enke, CEO; John Noel, Controller.

■ 22379 ■   J and H Oil Co.
PO Box 9464
Wyoming, MI 49509
Phone: (616)534-2181
Free: (800)442-9110   Fax: (616)534-1663
Products: Gasoline, diesel fuel and motor oil. SIC: 5172 (Petroleum Products Nec). Est: 1970. Sales: $115,000,000 (2000). Emp: 550. Officers: Jerry Hop, President; Mike O'Brien, Controller.

■ 22380 ■   J & J Steel and Supply Co.
PO Box 1886
Odessa, TX 79760
Phone: (915)332-4351   Fax: (915)332-9731
Products: Oil tanks. SIC: 5084 (Industrial Machinery & Equipment). Est: 1947. Sales: $4,200,000 (2000). Emp: 22. Officers: Gene G. Williams, General Mgr.; Kevin Ballard, Sales & Marketing Contact; Jack Whitley, Customer Service Contact.

■ 22381 ■   Jackson-Jennings Farm Bureau Cooperative
PO Box 304
Seymour, IN 47274
Phone: (812)522-4911   Fax: (812)522-3242
Products: Petroleum; Heating gas; Propane; Gasoline. SICs: 5191 (Farm Supplies); 5153 (Grain & Field Beans); 5172 (Petroleum Products Nec). Est: 1928. Sales: $27,000,000 (2000). Emp: 57. Officers: Robert E. Marley, General Mgr.; Jerry H. Wetzel, Finance Officer.

■ 22382 ■   Jacobus Energy
11815 W Bradley Rd.
Milwaukee, WI 53224
Phone: (414)354-0700   Fax: (414)359-1469
E-mail: jacobux@execpc.com
URL: http://www.jacobusenergy.com
Products: Petroleum and its products. SICs: 5171 (Petroleum Bulk Stations & Terminals); 5172 (Petroleum Products Nec). Est: 1919. Sales: $80,000,000 (2000). Emp: 150. Officers: C.D. Jacobus, President & Treasurer; Fred Regenfuss, Controller; Shelley Brannan, Marketing Mgr. Former Name: Jacobus Co.

■ 22383 ■   James Oil Co.
PO Box 328
Carlisle, IA 50047
Phone: (515)989-3314
Products: Petroleum; Petroleum products. SICs: 5171 (Petroleum Bulk Stations & Terminals); 5172 (Petroleum Products Nec). Est: 1947. Sales: $4,000,000 (2000). Emp: 4. Officers: Robert James, Owner.

■ 22384 ■   Jardine Petroleum
814 W 24th St.
Ogden, UT 84401
Phone: (801)393-7930
Products: Oil. SIC: 5172 (Petroleum Products Nec).

■ 22385 ■   Jardine Petroleum Co.
PO Box 510170
Salt Lake City, UT 84151-0170
Phone: (801)532-3211   Fax: (801)531-2280
Products: Gas and oil. SIC: 5171 (Petroleum Bulk Stations & Terminals). Est: 1973. Sales: $80,000,000 (2000). Emp: 50. Officers: S.J. Jardine, CEO; Alan Hansen, VP & CFO.

■ 22386 ■   Jefferson City Oil Company Inc.
PO Box 576
Jefferson City, MO 65102-0576
Phone: (573)634-2025
Products: Gas and oil; Batteries. SICs: 5171 (Petroleum Bulk Stations & Terminals); 5172 (Petroleum Products Nec). Est: 1928. Sales: $50,000,000 (1999). Emp: 60. Officers: Cletus A. Kolb, President; Thomas G. Kolb, Treasurer; John C. Kolb, VP of Marketing.

■ 22387 ■   Jenkel Oil Company Inc.
PO Box 25
Combined Locks, WI 54113
Phone: (920)739-6101
Products: Petroleum products. SIC: 5172 (Petroleum Products Nec). Sales: $2,300,000 (2000). Emp: 70. Officers: Tom Schmidt, President; Paul Bachman, CFO.

■ 22388 ■   Jenkins Gas and Oil Company Inc.
PO Box 156
Pollocksville, NC 28573
Phone: (919)224-8911
Products: Liquid petroleum gas. SIC: 5172 (Petroleum Products Nec). Est: 1953. Sales: $33,400,000 (2000). Emp: 158. Officers: Robert Mattocks II, President; Robert Meadows, CFO; Daniel Brinson, VP of Sales; Ginger Mattocks, Dir of Human Resources.

■ 22389 ■   Johnson Oil Company of Gaylord
507 Otesgo Rd.
Gaylord, MI 49735
Phone: (517)732-2451   Fax: (517)732-1682
Products: Bulk petroleum products. SIC: 5171 (Petroleum Bulk Stations & Terminals). Sales: $44,000,000 (1994). Emp: 85. Officers: Dale E. Johnson, Owner; Don Elgas, Treasurer.

■ 22390 ■   Johnston-Lawrence Co.
PO Box 1759
Kilgore, TX 75663-1759
Phone: (903)984-1591   Fax: (903)984-2541
Products: Oil field machinery. SIC: 5084 (Industrial Machinery & Equipment). Est: 1968. Sales: $1,500,000 (2000). Emp: 9. Officers: Perry Johnston, President; Richard Taliaferro, Treasurer & Secty.; Blake Hightower, Sales Mgr.

■ 22391 ■   John E. Jones Oil Company Inc.
1016 S Cedar St.
Stockton, KS 67669
Phone: (785)425-6746   Fax: (785)425-6323
Products: Petroleum products. SIC: 5172 (Petroleum Products Nec). Est: 1958. Sales: $20,000,000 (2000). Emp: 20. Officers: Eugene Westhusing, President.

■ 22392 ■   N.E. Jones Oil Company Inc.
PO Box 5070
Texarkana, TX 75505
Phone: (903)838-8541   Fax: (903)832-6081
Products: Gasoline; Diesel fuel. SIC: 5172 (Petroleum Products Nec). Est: 1945. Sales: $17,000,000 (2000). Emp: 57. Officers: Gary Jones, CEO; Mike Cherry, Comptroller.

■ 22393 ■   JV Inc.
PO Box 628
Clearfield, PA 16830
Phone: (814)765-7511   Fax: (814)765-6839
Products: Motor oil; Heating fuels. SIC: 5172 (Petroleum Products Nec). Est: 1961. Sales: $14,000,000 (2000). Emp: 25. Officers: Thomas Misuira, President; Bob Hileman, CFO.

■ 22394 ■   Kanabec Cooperative Association
206 S Union St.
Mora, MN 55051
Phone: (320)679-2682
Products: Petroleum and its products; Fertilizer and fertilizer materials; Field, garden, and flower seeds. SICs: 5172 (Petroleum Products Nec); 5191 (Farm Supplies). Est: 1926. Sales: $3,000,000 (2000). Emp: 20. Officers: Loren Barnick, President; Tim Faust, Controller.

■ 22395 ■   Kanematsu U.S.A. Inc.
114 W 47th St.
New York, NY 10036
Phone: (212)704-9400   Fax: (212)704-9483
Products: Petroleum; Electronics. SICs: 5172 (Petroleum Products Nec); 5065 (Electronic Parts & Equipment Nec); 5063 (Electrical Apparatus & Equipment). Est: 1951. Sales: $2,250,000,000 (2000). Emp: 1,005. Officers: Minoru Inoue, President; Keiji Uemuru, Treasurer; Ikuro Yasui, Exec. VP of Marketing.

■ 22396 ■   Kansas Propane
707 N Main St.
South Hutchinson, KS 67505
Phone: (316)663-3338   Fax: (316)663-2751
Products: Petroleum products. SIC: 5172 (Petroleum Products Nec). Sales: $2,000,000 (2000). Emp: 2. Officers: Martin M. Burke, President.

■ 22397 ■   Keller Oil Inc.
PO Box 147
St. Marys, PA 15857
Phone: (814)781-1507   Fax: (814)781-3715
Products: Oil; Greases; Gasoline; Kerosene; Diesel fuel. SIC: 5172 (Petroleum Products Nec). Est: 1935. Sales: $10,000,000 (2000). Emp: 75. Officers: Mary Keller, CEO; Steven Frank, Secretary.

■ 22398 ■   Kellerstrass Oil Co.
2450 Wall Ave.
Ogden, UT 84401
Phone: (801)392-9516
Products: Oil. SIC: 5172 (Petroleum Products Nec).

■ 22399 ■   Jack B. Kelley Inc.
8101 SW 34th Ave.
Amarillo, TX 79121
Phone: (806)353-3553
Free: (800)225-5525   Fax: (806)353-9611
Products: Liquefied petroleum gases; Transportation equipment. SICs: 5172 (Petroleum Products Nec); 5012 (Automobiles & Other Motor Vehicles). Est: 1946. Sales: $50,100,000 (2000). Emp: 750. Officers: Ken Kelley, President; Robert Smith, Finance Officer.

■ 22400 ■   Kennedy Oil Company Inc.
1203 Courtesy Rd.
High Point, NC 27260
Phone: (910)885-5184   Fax: (919)885-5162
Products: Petroleum and its products. SIC: 5172 (Petroleum Products Nec). Est: 1934. Sales: $5,500,000 (2000). Emp: 15. Officers: Harold R. Ridge, President; Kay K. More, VP & Secty.

■ 22401 ■   Kent Distribution Inc.
PO Box 908001
Midland, TX 79708
Phone: (915)563-1620
Products: Petroleum. SIC: 5171 (Petroleum Bulk Stations & Terminals). Sales: $36,000,000 (1993). Emp: 200. Officers: William B. Kent, President; Bennett Robb, VP of Finance.

■ 22402 ■   Keystops Inc.
PO Box 2809
Franklin, KY 42135
Phone: (502)586-8283   Fax: (502)586-3112
Products: Diesel fuels and gasoline. SIC: 5172 (Petroleum Products Nec). Est: 1967. Sales: $218,000,000 (2000). Emp: 200. Officers: Lester Key, President; Richard Shephard, Treasurer & Secty.; Rex Hazelip, VP of Marketing.

■ **22403** ■ **Kiel Brothers Oil Company Inc.**
PO Box 344
Columbus, IN 47202
Phone: (812)372-3751
Products: Heating fuel and gasoline. **SIC:** 5172 (Petroleum Products Nec). **Est:** 1941. **Sales:** $640,000,000 (2000). **Emp:** 1,300. **Officers:** T. Kiel, President; D. Roll, CFO; T. Kiel, VP of Marketing.

■ **22404** ■ **J.C. Kilburn and Company Inc.**
501 E Cedar St.
Rawlins, WY 82301
Phone: (307)324-2721
Products: Gasoline; Petroleum and its products. **SIC:** 5172 (Petroleum Products Nec). **Est:** 1928. **Sales:** $2,000,000 (2000). **Emp:** 11. **Officers:** K.W. Keldsen, President; Pam Keldsen, Treasurer & Secty.

■ **22405** ■ **Kimber Petroleum Corp.**
545 Martinsville Rd.
PO Box 860
Liberty Corner, NJ 07938
Phone: (908)903-9600   **Fax:** (908)903-1830
Products: Gasoline. **SIC:** 5172 (Petroleum Products Nec). **Est:** 1938. **Sales:** $105,000,000 (1999). **Emp:** 250. **Officers:** Warren S. Kimber III, President; Kathryn Kimber, Treasurer.

■ **22406** ■ **Kingman Aero Services Inc.**
5070 Flightline Dr.
Kingman, AZ 86401
Phone: (520)757-1335
Products: Aircraft fuel. **SIC:** 5172 (Petroleum Products Nec).

■ **22407** ■ **Kingston Oil Supply Corp.**
Foot of N Broadway
Port Ewen, NY 12466
Phone: (914)331-0770
Products: Fuel oil; Gasoline; Kerosene. **SIC:** 5172 (Petroleum Products Nec). **Sales:** $60,000,000 (2000). **Emp:** 150. **Officers:** Leo Lebowitz, President; Barry Motzin, Controller.

■ **22408** ■ **Kirby Oil Co.**
2026 E Front St.
Tyler, TX 75702
Phone: (903)592-3841   **Fax:** (903)592-3383
Products: Gasoline. **SIC:** 5172 (Petroleum Products Nec). **Sales:** $73,000,000 (2000). **Emp:** 85. **Officers:** Caroline Kirby, President; Edwin D. Kirby, Vice President.

■ **22409** ■ **Koenig Fuel & Supply Co.**
500 East Seven Mile Rd.
Detroit, MI 48203
Phone: (313)368-1870   **Fax:** (313)368-3040
Products: Ready mixed concrete; Fuel oil. **SICs:** 5172 (Petroleum Products Nec); 5032 (Brick, Stone & Related Materials). **Est:** 1870. **Sales:** $30,000,000 (2000). **Emp:** 100. **Officers:** Peter G. Fredericks Jr., President.

■ **22410** ■ **Kohler Oil and Propane Co.**
8956 Burnside Rd.
Brown City, MI 48416
Phone: (810)346-2606
Products: Petroleum and related products. **SICs:** 5171 (Petroleum Bulk Stations & Terminals); 5172 (Petroleum Products Nec). **Sales:** $1,000,000 (1993). **Emp:** 4. **Officers:** Robert Kohler, Owner.

■ **22411** ■ **Kunz Oil Company Inc.**
7900 Excelsior Blvd.
Hopkins, MN 55343-3423
Phone: (612)920-9373
Products: Oil; Automotive parts. **SICs:** 5172 (Petroleum Products Nec); 5013 (Motor Vehicle Supplies & New Parts). **Sales:** $19,000,000 (2000). **Emp:** 30. **Officers:** Mary Kunz, President.

■ **22412** ■ **L-K Industries Inc.**
PO Box 230305
Houston, TX 77223-0305
Phone: (713)926-2623   **Fax:** (713)926-7736
E-mail: lkind@lk-ind.com
URL: http://www.lk-ind.com
Products: Oil field equipment. **SIC:** 5084 (Industrial Machinery & Equipment). **Est:** 1930. **Sales:**

$3,000,000 (2000). **Emp:** 25. **Officers:** J.H. Hugghins, Chairman of the Board & President; Bill Hugghins, VP of Purchasing; R. Hugghins, VP of Sales; Kennon H. Hugghins, Exec. VP.

■ **22413** ■ **L & L Gas & Oil Inc.**
PO Box 754
Socorro, NM 87801
Phone: (505)835-1127
Products: Gas and oil. **SIC:** 5172 (Petroleum Products Nec).

■ **22414** ■ **L & L Oil and Gas Service LLC**
PO Box 6984
Metairie, LA 70009-6984
Phone: (504)832-8600   **Fax:** (504)832-8620
E-mail: admin@lloilco.com
URL: http://www.lloil.com
Products: Diesel fuel and lubricants. **SIC:** 5172 (Petroleum Products Nec). **Est:** 1956. **Sales:** $200,000,000 (2000). **Emp:** 245. **Officers:** Jim Newlin, President; Dave Sellers, VP of Sales; Brian F. LeBourgeois, CFO; Danny M. Brown, Exec. VP.

■ **22415** ■ **Lake County Farm Bureau Cooperative Association Inc.**
PO Box C
Crown Point, IN 46307-0975
Phone: (219)663-0018   **Fax:** (219)662-7453
Products: Fuel oil and farm supplies. **SIC:** 5191 (Farm Supplies). **Sales:** $5,000,000 (1994). **Emp:** 18. **Officers:** Carl Supper Jr., Comptroller; Don Harrell, Finance General Manager.

■ **22416** ■ **Lake Region Cooperative Oil Association**
PO Box 728
Maple Lake, MN 55358
Phone: (320)963-3137   **Fax:** (320)454-0486
E-mail: marketing@wpds.com
URL: http://www.wpds.com
Products: Software. **SICs:** 5153 (Grain & Field Beans); 5191 (Farm Supplies). **Est:** 1931. **Sales:** $10,500,000 (1999). **Emp:** 200. **Officers:** Mike Richardson, President; Terry Lubenow, VP of Sales & Merchandising.

■ **22417** ■ **Lakeside Oil Company Inc.**
PO Box 23440
Milwaukee, WI 53223-0440
Phone: (414)445-6464   **Fax:** (414)445-6616
Products: Gasoline; Petroleum and its products. **SICs:** 5171 (Petroleum Bulk Stations & Terminals); 5172 (Petroleum Products Nec). **Est:** 1933. **Sales:** $210,000,000 (2000). **Emp:** 20. **Officers:** Herbert H. Elliott, President; William S. Elliott, VP of Finance; Jack Sobczak, Dir. of Marketing; Gregory Panell, Operations Mgr.

■ **22418** ■ **Laurel Valley Oil Co.**
State Rte. 800
Stillwater, OH 44679
Phone: (740)922-2312   **Fax:** (740)922-2313
Products: Home heating oil. **SIC:** 5172 (Petroleum Products Nec). **Est:** 1926. **Sales:** $10,000,000 (2000). **Emp:** 16. **Officers:** K.O. Marstrell, President; Crystal Marstrow, VP of Finance.

■ **22419** ■ **Laurel Valley Oil Co.**
State Rte. 800
Stillwater, OH 44679
Phone: (740)922-2312   **Fax:** (740)922-2313
Products: Petroleum products. **SIC:** 5172 (Petroleum Products Nec). **Sales:** $10,000,000 (2000). **Emp:** 20. **Officers:** Crystal Marstrell, Treasurer & Secty.

■ **22420** ■ **E.T. Lawson and Son**
PO Box 249
Hampton, VA 23669
Phone: (757)722-1928   **Fax:** (757)722-3490
Products: Fuel oil and gasoline. **SIC:** 5172 (Petroleum Products Nec). **Sales:** $34,000,000 (1994). **Emp:** 52. **Officers:** Donald B. Allen Jr., President; D.J. Boester, CFO.

■ **22421** ■ **Leahy's Fuels Inc.**
PO Box 130
Danbury, CT 06813
Phone: (203)866-0738
Products: Fuel oil. **SIC:** 5172 (Petroleum Products Nec).

■ **22422** ■ **Leemon Oil Company Inc.**
13507 Auburn Dr.
Detroit, MI 48223
Phone: (313)272-6700
Products: Petroleum products. **SIC:** 5172 (Petroleum Products Nec). **Est:** 1951. **Sales:** $70,000,000 (2000). **Emp:** 70. **Officers:** Roger K. Albertie, President; Janice Doyle, Controller.

■ **22423** ■ **Leemon Shores Oil**
13507 Auburn St.
Detroit, MI 48223-3414
Phone: (313)776-2670
Products: Petroleum products, including oil and gasoline. **SIC:** 5172 (Petroleum Products Nec). **Est:** 1846. **Sales:** $3,000,000 (2000). **Emp:** 8. **Officers:** Deanna Livingston, General Mgr.

■ **22424** ■ **Carlos R. Leffler Inc.**
PO Box 278
Richland, PA 17087
Phone: (717)866-2105   **Fax:** (717)866-9361
URL: http://www.leffler.com
Products: Oil; Gasoline; Petroleum products; Heating and air conditioning equipment. **SICs:** 5171 (Petroleum Bulk Stations & Terminals); 5172 (Petroleum Products Nec). **Est:** 1941. **Emp:** 950. **Officers:** Patrick Castagna, President; Carla O'Neill, Sales/Marketing Contact, e-mail: coneill@leffler.com; Tim Steinrock, Human Resources Contact, e-mail: snagle@leffler.com; John Byler, Exec. VP.

■ **22425** ■ **Lehigh Gas and Oil Co.**
80-82 Broad St.
Beaver Meadows, PA 18216
Phone: (717)455-5828   **Fax:** (717)455-9590
Products: Home heating oil. **SIC:** 5172 (Petroleum Products Nec). **Est:** 1929. **Sales:** $22,000,000 (2000). **Emp:** 30. **Officers:** Roman Baran, President; Victor G. Baran, Treasurer & Secty.

■ **22426** ■ **Lehigh Oil Co.**
1 Terminal Way
Norwich, CT 06360
Phone: (860)889-1311
Products: Diesel fuel; Home heating oil; Kerosene. **SICs:** 5171 (Petroleum Bulk Stations & Terminals); 5172 (Petroleum Products Nec). **Est:** 1934. **Sales:** $22,000,000 (2000). **Emp:** 40. **Officers:** Tom Castle, President; Peter Castle, CFO.

■ **22427** ■ **Lemmen Oil Co.**
13 E Randall St.
Coopersville, MI 49404
Phone: (616)837-6531
Products: Petroleum, including gas and diesel. **SIC:** 5171 (Petroleum Bulk Stations & Terminals). **Est:** 1946. **Sales:** $30,000,000 (2000). **Emp:** 75. **Officers:** Wayne Lemmen, President; Doug Lemmen, Secretary.

■ **22428** ■ **H.C. Lewis Oil Co.**
PO Box 649
Welch, WV 24801-0649
Phone: (304)436-2148
Products: Gasoline, diesel fuel, and petroleum. **SICs:** 5171 (Petroleum Bulk Stations & Terminals); 5014 (Tires & Tubes); 5015 (Motor Vehicle Parts—Used). **Sales:** $28,000,000 (2000). **Emp:** 60. **Officers:** H.C. Lewis Jr., CEO; H.C. Lewis III, VP & General Merchandising Mgr.

■ **22429** ■ **Lexington Cooperative Oil Co.**
PO Box A
Lexington, NE 68850
Phone: (308)324-5539   **Fax:** (308)324-3459
E-mail: lexcorp@alltel.net
URL: http://www.lexcoop.com
Products: Petroleum and its products; Fertilizer and fertilizer materials; Agricultural chemicals. **SICs:** 5172 (Petroleum Products Nec); 5169 (Chemicals & Allied Products Nec); 5191 (Farm Supplies). **Est:** 1926.

Sales: $19,000,000 (2000). **Emp:** 75. **Officers:** Donald Swanson, CEO, President & General Mgr.

■ 22430 ■ **Liberal Hull Co.**
1600 W Pancake Blvd.
Liberal, KS 67901
Phone: (316)624-2211
Products: Cottonseed oil hulls for use in oil well drilling. **SIC:** 5159 (Farm-Product Raw Materials Nec). **Sales:** $500,000 (2000). **Emp:** 6. **Officers:** Thomas Manning, President; Suzanne Crisp, Controller.

■ 22431 ■ **Liberty Oil Company Inc.**
2 Main St.
Port Carbon, PA 17965
Phone: (717)622-3595
Free: (800)220-3595 **Fax:** (717)622-3412
Products: Fuel and heating oil; Petroleum; Industrial and commercial lubricants. **SIC:** 5172 (Petroleum Products Nec). **Est:** 1925. **Sales:** $19,000,000 (2000). **Emp:** 40. **Officers:** Darryl D. Klotz, President; Norwood E. Klotz, Treasurer; Todd Wagner, Dir. of Marketing.

■ 22432 ■ **Lightening Oil Co.**
Philipsburg, MT 59858
Phone: (406)859-3164
Products: Oil. **SIC:** 5172 (Petroleum Products Nec).

■ 22433 ■ **Lilyblad Petroleum Inc.**
PO Box 1556
Tacoma, WA 98401
Phone: (206)572-4402
Products: Oil; Gasoline; Chemicals, including thinners. **SICs:** 5172 (Petroleum Products Nec); 5169 (Chemicals & Allied Products Nec). **Est:** 1963. **Sales:** $9,000,000 (2000). **Emp:** 40. **Officers:** Glenn Tegen, President; Brian Tegen, Controller.

■ 22434 ■ **Linn Cooperative Oil Co.**
325 35th St.
Marion, IA 52302
Phone: (319)377-4881 **Fax:** (319)377-8953
Products: Petroleum and its products; Agricultural chemicals; Fertilizer and fertilizer materials. **SICs:** 5172 (Petroleum Products Nec); 5191 (Farm Supplies). **Est:** 1930. **Sales:** $29,000,000 (2000). **Emp:** 60. **Officers:** James Fisher, General Mgr.

■ 22435 ■ **Local Oil Company of Anoka Inc.**
2015 7th Ave. N
Anoka, MN 55303
Phone: (612)421-4923
Products: Petroleum bulk station. **SIC:** 5171 (Petroleum Bulk Stations & Terminals). **Sales:** $15,000,000 (1994). **Emp:** 120. **Officers:** Leonard Dehn, President; Herbert Perry, Controller.

■ 22436 ■ **Lone Star Company Inc.**
PO Box 2067
Jonesboro, AR 72402
Phone: (501)932-6679 **Fax:** (501)932-2925
Products: Petroleum products, including gasoline, diesel fuel, and oil. **SICs:** 5171 (Petroleum Bulk Stations & Terminals); 5172 (Petroleum Products Nec). **Est:** 1940. **Sales:** $12,000,000 (2000). **Emp:** 65. **Officers:** A.M. Heringer, President; Ed Gibson, Controller.

■ 22437 ■ **Lord Equipment Co.**
1147 E C St.
Casper, WY 82601
Phone: (307)265-4430
Products: Petroleum-based drilling products. **SICs:** 5084 (Industrial Machinery & Equipment); 5172 (Petroleum Products Nec).

■ 22438 ■ **Lotepro Corp.**
115 Stevens Ave.
Valhalla, NY 10595
Phone: (914)747-3500 **Fax:** (914)747-3422
Products: Gas, atmospheric gas, liquified natural gases, hydrogen, carbon monoxide and waste water purifications. **SIC:** 5169 (Chemicals & Allied Products Nec). **Sales:** $67,000,000 (2000). **Emp:** 123. **Officers:** Dr. Hans Kistenmacher, President; William DuRie, VP of Finance.

■ 22439 ■ **Bob Loyd LP Gas Co.**
PO Box 367
Winters, TX 79567
Phone: (915)754-4555 **Fax:** (915)754-5691
Products: Fuels, including gasoline, propane, and diesel fuel; Lubricants. **SICs:** 5171 (Petroleum Bulk Stations & Terminals); 5172 (Petroleum Products Nec). **Sales:** $4,000,000 (2000). **Emp:** 15. **Officers:** Gene Wheat, President.

■ 22440 ■ **LTV Corp.**
PO Box 6778
Cleveland, OH 44101
Phone: (216)622-5000 **Fax:** (216)622-1066
Products: Oilfield equipment; Seamless tubular products. **SIC:** 5084 (Industrial Machinery & Equipment). **Sales:** $4,446,000,000 (2000). **Emp:** 15,500. **Officers:** David H. Hoag, CEO, President & Chairman of the Board; Arthur W. Huge, Sr. VP & CFO.

■ 22441 ■ **Lubrichem Environmental Inc.**
206 Valley Creek Rd.
Elizabethtown, KY 42701
Phone: (502)491-6100
Free: (800)456-4330 **Fax:** (502)491-8686
E-mail: sales@lubrichem.com
URL: http://www.lubrichem.com
Products: Lubricants; Cleaners; Solvent blends. **SIC:** 5172 (Petroleum Products Nec). **Est:** 1985. **Sales:** $6,000,000 (2000). **Emp:** 18. **Officers:** Jerry T. McAdams, President.

■ 22442 ■ **Lyden Co.**
PO Box 1854
Youngstown, OH 44501
Phone: (330)744-3118 **Fax:** (330)792-1462
Products: Gasoline, oil, and diesel fuel. **SIC:** 5172 (Petroleum Products Nec). **Est:** 1919. **Sales:** $290,000,000 (2000). **Emp:** 450. **Officers:** William G. Lyden Jr., Chairman of the Board; Gary L. Steib, Treasurer; Mark Lyden, VP of Marketing.

■ 22443 ■ **Lyon County Cooperative Oil Co.**
1100 E Main St.
Marshall, MN 56258
Phone: (507)532-9686
Free: (888)532-9686 **Fax:** (507)532-4394
Products: Petroleum. **SIC:** 5171 (Petroleum Bulk Stations & Terminals). **Est:** 1924. **Sales:** $15,000,000 (2000). **Emp:** 85. **Officers:** Merle Lyons, General Mgr.; Kathy C. Pollock, Treasurer.

■ 22444 ■ **M and M Supply Co.**
PO Box 548
Duncan, OK 73534-0548
Phone: (580)252-7879 **Fax:** (580)252-7708
E-mail: info@mmsupply.com
URL: http://www.mmsupply.com
Products: Oil well machinery and equipment. **SIC:** 5084 (Industrial Machinery & Equipment). **Est:** 1948. **Sales:** $15,000,000 (2000). **Emp:** 60. **Officers:** James P. Garis, President; T. H. McCasland Jr., Exec. VP; James E. Tow, VP of Operations; H. E. Foreman Jr., VP of Admin.; J. R. Braught, Secretary; Noble Means, Treasurer.

■ 22445 ■ **Maine Propane Distributors Inc.**
1625 Hammond St.
Bangor, ME 04401
Phone: (207)848-2456
Products: Liquid gases. **SIC:** 5172 (Petroleum Products Nec).

■ 22446 ■ **Major Oil Inc.**
3423 Money Rd.
Montgomery, AL 36108
Phone: (205)263-5401 **Fax:** (205)263-9113
Products: Motor oil. **SIC:** 5172 (Petroleum Products Nec). **Est:** 1934. **Sales:** $25,000,000 (2000). **Emp:** 50. **Officers:** Ben McNiel, President.

■ 22447 ■ **Mallard Oil Co.**
PO Box 1008
Kinston, NC 28503-1008
Phone: (919)393-8153
Products: Fuels, including propane, oil, and gasoline. **SIC:** 5172 (Petroleum Products Nec). **Sales:** $65,000,000 (2000). **Emp:** 100. **Officers:** Frank Famulard, President.

■ 22448 ■ **Manley Oil Co.**
410 N Center St.
Los Angeles, CA 90012
Phone: (213)628-5674
Products: Crude oil. **SIC:** 5171 (Petroleum Bulk Stations & Terminals).

■ 22449 ■ **Mansfield Oil Company of Gainesville Inc.**
1025 Airport Pkwy. SW
Gainesville, GA 30506
Phone: (404)532-7571
Products: Petroleum and its products; Gasoline; Kerosene. **SIC:** 5172 (Petroleum Products Nec). **Sales:** $32,000,000 (2000). **Emp:** 50. **Officers:** Michael Mansfield, President.

■ 22450 ■ **Marathon Ashland Petroleum L.L.C.**
539 S Main St.
Findlay, OH 45840
Phone: (419)422-2121 **Fax:** (419)421-2540
Products: Petroleum products. **SIC:** 5172 (Petroleum Products Nec). **Sales:** $2,000,000,000 (2000). **Emp:** 30,000. **Officers:** J.L. Frank, President; Garry L. Pifer, Sr. VP & Finance Officer.

■ 22451 ■ **Marcley Oil Inc.**
614 Prairie St.
Aurora, IL 60506
Phone: (708)892-3832
Products: Petroleum products. **SIC:** 5172 (Petroleum Products Nec). **Sales:** $6,000,000 (1994). **Emp:** 25. **Officers:** Robert D. Marcley, President.

■ 22452 ■ **Mark Oil Company Inc.**
PO Box 32064
Charlotte, NC 28232
Phone: (704)375-4249
Products: Gasoline. **SIC:** 5172 (Petroleum Products Nec). **Est:** 1907. **Sales:** $7,000,000 (2000). **Emp:** 13. **Officers:** Mark P. Johnson Jr., President & Chairman of the Board; M. Rollins, Comptroller; Bill Tome, Dir. of Marketing & Sales.

■ 22453 ■ **Marshall County Cooperative Association**
PO Box 82
Warren, MN 56762
Phone: (218)745-5323
Products: Petroleum products. **SIC:** 5172 (Petroleum Products Nec). **Est:** 1935. **Sales:** $600,000 (2000). **Emp:** 2. **Officers:** Terry Potuceh, President; Julie Tydlocka, Bookkeeper; Leonard Novak, Manager.

■ 22454 ■ **Martin Oil Co.**
528 N First St.
Bellwood, PA 16617
Phone: (814)742-8438
Free: (800)252-3868 **Fax:** (814)742-8458
URL: http://www.martinoil.com
Products: Petroleum and its products, including gasoline, diesel fuel, and kerosene; Convenience stores; Fleet fueling system. **SIC:** 5172 (Petroleum Products Nec). **Est:** 1963. **Sales:** $27,000,000 (1999). **Emp:** 180. **Officers:** Thos. C. Martin, Chairman of the Board; Janice Martin, General Mgr.; Thos. G. Martin, President.

■ 22455 ■ **Massey Wood and West Inc.**
PO Box 5008
Richmond, VA 23220
Phone: (804)355-1721
Products: Fuel oil; Gasoline; Kerosene; Propane. **SIC:** 5172 (Petroleum Products Nec). **Est:** 1923. **Sales:** $20,000,000 (2000). **Emp:** 100. **Officers:** Gerard W. Bradley, President; Tom Meyers, Accountant.

■ 22456 ■ **Matthews Brothers Wholesale Inc.**
PO Box 1186
Clarksburg, WV 26301
Phone: (304)624-7601
Products: Gas, fuels, and motor oils. **SIC:** 5172 (Petroleum Products Nec). **Est:** 1924. **Sales:** $30,000,000 (2000). **Emp:** 250. **Officers:** Nelson E. Matthews Jr., CEO.

■ **22457** ■ **Maugansville Elevator and Lumber Company Inc.**
PO Box 278
Maugansville, MD 21767
Phone: (301)739-4220   **Fax:** (301)739-4220
Products: Fuel oil. **SIC:** 5172 (Petroleum Products Nec). **Sales:** $2,000,000 (1994). **Emp:** 20. **Officers:** James S. Martin, President; Ethel P. Martin, CFO.

■ **22458** ■ **Maxam Corp.**
1117 Maurice Rd.
Broussard, LA 70518
Phone: (318)364-5536   **Fax:** (318)365-0811
Products: Oil and gas field drilling machinery and equipment; Well points, (drilling equipment). **SIC:** 5084 (Industrial Machinery & Equipment). **Est:** 1979. **Sales:** $800,000 (2000). **Emp:** 3. **Officers:** W.A. Waters Jr., CEO.

■ **22459** ■ **Mayes County Petroleum Products**
1600 N 11th St.
Muskogee, OK 74401
Phone: (918)682-9924
Products: Petroleum products. **SIC:** 5172 (Petroleum Products Nec).

■ **22460** ■ **Maytag Aircraft Corp.**
6145 Lehman Dr., Ste. 300
Colorado Springs, CO 80918
Phone: (719)593-1600   **Fax:** (719)593-8518
Products: Refueling for military aircraft. **SIC:** 5172 (Petroleum Products Nec). **Sales:** $15,000,000 (2000). **Emp:** 350. **Officers:** William L. Silva, Exec. VP; Katherine Pleshek, Treasurer & Secty.

■ **22461** ■ **McAdams Pipe and Supply Co.**
PO Box 428
Muskogee, OK 74402
Phone: (918)682-1323   **Fax:** (918)682-8521
Products: Industrial supplies. **SICs:** 5085 (Industrial Supplies); 5084 (Industrial Machinery & Equipment). **Est:** 1947. **Sales:** $1,200,000 (2000). **Emp:** 5. **Officers:** William B. Reaves III, President.

■ **22462** ■ **McBax Ltd.**
3501 Pearl St.
Boulder, CO 80301
Phone: (303)442-6000
Products: Lubricants, including grease; Chemicals; Hydraulic fluids. **SICs:** 5171 (Petroleum Bulk Stations & Terminals); 5172 (Petroleum Products Nec); 5169 (Chemicals & Allied Products Nec). **Est:** 1946. **Sales:** $3,500,000 (1999). **Emp:** 10. **Officers:** Frank D. Baxley, President. **Doing Business As:** Bartkus Oil Co.

■ **22463** ■ **J.B. McBride Distributing Inc.**
760 Iron St.
Butte, MT 59701
Phone: (406)782-3034   **Free:** (800)287-3034
Products: Gas; Diesels. **SIC:** 5172 (Petroleum Products Nec). **Est:** 1967. **Sales:** $5,000,000 (2000). **Emp:** 2. **Officers:** John Fagan, President.

■ **22464** ■ **McCall Oil and Chemical Co.**
826 SW 15th Ave.
Portland, OR 97205
Phone: (503)228-2600
Free: (800)622-2558   **Fax:** (503)221-5752
Products: Fuels, including diesel and gasoline. **SIC:** 5172 (Petroleum Products Nec). **Est:** 1939. **Sales:** $38,000,000 (2000). **Emp:** 80. **Officers:** Bob McCall, President; Doug Kieffer, Exec. VP; Rob Abbott, Dir of Human Resources.

■ **22465** ■ **McGuirk Oil Company Inc.**
PO Box 2010
Bowling Green, KY 42101
Phone: (502)842-2188   **Fax:** (502)782-1646
Products: Gasoline. **SIC:** 5172 (Petroleum Products Nec). **Est:** 1955. **Sales:** $2,500,000 (2000). **Emp:** 10. **Officers:** J.W. McGuirk, President; Mike McGuirk, Treasurer & Secty.

■ **22466** ■ **McJunkin Appalachian Oil Field Supply Co.**
PO Box 513
Charleston, WV 25322
Phone: (304)348-5847   **Fax:** (304)348-1529
Products: Oil; Gasoline. **SIC:** 5072 (Hardware). **Est:** 1989. **Sales:** $29,000,000 (2000). **Emp:** 93. **Officers:** Bernard Wehrle, President; Michael Wehrle, President; William Board, Dir of Personnel.

■ **22467** ■ **McLain Oil Company Inc.**
PO Box 1393
Lubbock, TX 79408
Phone: (806)762-0432   **Fax:** (806)762-2805
E-mail: McLainOil@aol.com
Products: Gasoline; Diesel fuel. **SIC:** 5172 (Petroleum Products Nec). **Est:** 1945. **Sales:** $16,000,000 (2000). **Emp:** 70. **Officers:** T.J. Womack Jr., President; Janie Dillard, Chairman of the Board.

■ **22468** ■ **McLeieer Oil Inc.**
PO Box 2977
Kalamazoo, MI 49003-2977
Phone: (616)343-7677   **Fax:** (616)341-4880
Products: Oil and gas. **SICs:** 5171 (Petroleum Bulk Stations & Terminals); 5172 (Petroleum Products Nec). **Est:** 1939. **Sales:** $26,600,000 (2000). **Emp:** 50. **Officers:** Michael O. McLeieer, President.

■ **22469** ■ **McLeod Merchantile Inc.**
Hwy. 287
Alder, MT 59710
Phone: (406)842-5495
Products: Oil; Gas. **SIC:** 5172 (Petroleum Products Nec).

■ **22470** ■ **McLeod Merchantile Inc. Conoco**
Jct. 84 and Hwy. 287
Norris, MT 59745
Phone: (406)685-3379
Products: Gas; Oil. **SIC:** 5172 (Petroleum Products Nec).

■ **22471** ■ **McMillan-Shuller Oil Company Inc.**
PO Box 590
Fayetteville, NC 28302
Phone: (910)484-7196
Products: Fuel; Diesel oil. **SIC:** 5172 (Petroleum Products Nec). **Est:** 1932. **Sales:** $1,000,000 (2000). **Emp:** 12. **Officers:** Allen B. McMillan, CEO.

■ **22472** ■ **Meeder Equipment Co.**
PO Box 3459
Alhambra, CA 91803
Phone: (818)289-3746   **Fax:** (818)289-4730
Products: Liquid propane gas and industrial equipment. **SICs:** 5084 (Industrial Machinery & Equipment); 5172 (Petroleum Products Nec). **Est:** 1955. **Sales:** $14,000,000 (2000). **Emp:** 90. **Officers:** Jeffrey Vertz, President; Martin Koers, Controller.

■ **22473** ■ **Meenan Oil Company L.P.**
6900 Jericho Tpke., Ste. 310
Syosset, NY 11791
Phone: (516)364-9030   **Fax:** (516)364-9171
Products: Fuel and home heating oil. **SIC:** 5171 (Petroleum Bulk Stations & Terminals). **Est:** 1933. **Sales:** $180,000,000 (2000). **Emp:** 750. **Officers:** Paul A. Vermylen Jr. Jr., President; Richard Oakley, Controller; Richard Okaley, Dir. of Data Processing.

■ **22474** ■ **Mercury Air Center**
655 S Rock Blvd.
Reno, NV 89502
Phone: (775)858-7300   **Fax:** (775)858-7334
E-mail: macrnogm@aol.com
Products: Fuel for private planes, commercial jets, and military. **SIC:** 5172 (Petroleum Products Nec). **Est:** 1972. **Sales:** $5,500,000 (2000). **Emp:** 84. **Officers:** Wes Daniels, General Mgr., e-mail: wdaniels@mercuryair.com. **Former Name:** Reno Jet Center.

■ **22475** ■ **Mercury Air Group Inc.**
5456 McConnell Ave.
Los Angeles, CA 90066
Phone: (310)827-2737   **Fax:** (310)215-5794
Products: Aviation fuel, including diesel and gasoline. **SIC:** 5172 (Petroleum Products Nec). **Est:** 1956. **Sales:** $279,300,000 (2000). **Emp:** 1,130. **Officers:**

Seymour Kahn, CEO & Chairman of the Board; Joseph Czyzyk, President; Randolph E. Ajer, Exec. VP & Treasurer; Eric Beelar, VP of Sales; Steve Antonoff, Dir of Personnel.

■ **22476** ■ **Merrimac Petroleum Inc.**
444 W Ocean Blvd., Ste. 1106
Long Beach, CA 90802-4519
Phone: (562)983-9350
Products: Petroleum products. **SIC:** 5172 (Petroleum Products Nec). **Sales:** $8,500,000 (1993). **Emp:** 4. **Officers:** Mary Hazelrigg, President.

■ **22477** ■ **Methanex Methanol Co.**
1237 Merrit Dr., Ste. 1237
Dallas, TX 75240
Phone: (972)702-0909
Products: Methanol fuel. **SIC:** 5169 (Chemicals & Allied Products Nec). **Sales:** $4,000,000 (1992). **Emp:** 10. **Officers:** Charles Senn, President; Robert Smith, CFO.

■ **22478** ■ **Meyer Oil Co.**
PO Box 2004
Cleona, PA 17042
Phone: (717)273-8544
Products: Oil; Kerosene; Gasoline. **SICs:** 5171 (Petroleum Bulk Stations & Terminals); 5172 (Petroleum Products Nec). **Sales:** $16,000,000 (2000). **Emp:** 25. **Officers:** Donald H. Dreibelbis, CEO.

■ **22479** ■ **M.F.A. Oil Co.**
Box 774
Lees Summit, MO 64063
Phone: (816)524-3466
Products: Petroleum products. **SIC:** 5172 (Petroleum Products Nec).

■ **22480** ■ **Mid West Oil Ltd.**
PO Box 1681
Enid, OK 73702
Phone: (580)237-0299
Products: Oil. **SICs:** 5171 (Petroleum Bulk Stations & Terminals); 5172 (Petroleum Products Nec). **Est:** 1969. **Sales:** $25,000,000 (2000). **Emp:** 100. **Officers:** Don Stehr, President & Chairman of the Board.

■ **22481** ■ **Midland 66 Oil Company Inc.**
1612 Garden City Hwy.
Midland, TX 79701
Phone: (915)682-9404
Products: Propane; Diesel; Gasoline. **SICs:** 5171 (Petroleum Bulk Stations & Terminals); 5172 (Petroleum Products Nec). **Est:** 1951. **Sales:** $9,000,000 (2000). **Emp:** 17. **Officers:** Kenneth A. Peeler, President.

■ **22482** ■ **Midway Oil Co.**
PO Box 4540
Rock Island, IL 61204
Phone: (309)788-4549
Products: Gasoline; Motor oil. **SICs:** 5171 (Petroleum Bulk Stations & Terminals); 5172 (Petroleum Products Nec). **Est:** 1920. **Sales:** $35,000,000 (2000). **Emp:** 70. **Officers:** David Requet, President.

■ **22483** ■ **Midwest Oil Co.**
615 E 8th St.
Sioux Falls, SD 57103
Phone: (605)336-3337   **Fax:** (605)336-3338
Products: Petroleum products. **SIC:** 5171 (Petroleum Bulk Stations & Terminals). **Sales:** $18,000,000 (2000). **Emp:** 35. **Officers:** Brad Dyar, CEO; Joe van Holland, Treasurer & Secty.

■ **22484** ■ **Miller Distributing**
43 E 5th St.
Yuma, AZ 85364
Phone: (520)783-2136
Products: Gasoline; Lubricating oils. **SIC:** 5172 (Petroleum Products Nec).

■ **22485** ■ **Luther P. Miller Inc.**
PO Box 714
Somerset, PA 15501
Phone: (814)445-6569   **Fax:** (814)443-4329
Products: Oil, propane, and motor oil. **SIC:** 5172 (Petroleum Products Nec). **Est:** 1952. **Sales:**

$32,000,000 (2000). **Emp:** 50. **Officers:** Alan Miller, CEO.

■ 22486 ■ **Miller Oil Co.**
1000 E City Hall Ave.
Norfolk, VA 23504
Phone: (757)623-1682 **Fax:** (757)640-2175
Products: Motor oils, solvents, and gas products. **SIC:** 5172 (Petroleum Products Nec). **Est:** 1977. **Sales:** $78,000,000 (2000). **Emp:** 200. **Officers:** Augustus C. Miller, President; Michael Miller, Controller.

■ 22487 ■ **Misco Industries Inc.**
155 N Market St., Ste. 125
Wichita, KS 67202-1802
Phone: (316)265-6641
Products: Natural gas. **SIC:** 5172 (Petroleum Products Nec). **Est:** 1985. **Sales:** $12,000,000 (2000). **Emp:** 25. **Officers:** Stanley O. Beren, President; V. Dale Shelley, Treasurer.

■ 22488 ■ **Missouri Petroleum Products**
1620 Woodson Rd.
St. Louis, MO 63114
Phone: (314)991-2180 **Free:** (800)392-4295
Products: Petroleum products, including driveway sealers, crack fillers, and roof coating. **SICs:** 5172 (Petroleum Products Nec); 5169 (Chemicals & Allied Products Nec). **Est:** 1932. **Sales:** $18,000,000 (2000). **Emp:** 200. **Officers:** Gene R. Allen, President; Thomas Feldmann, CFO.

■ 22489 ■ **Mitchell Supreme Fuel Co.**
532 Freeman St.
Orange, NJ 07050
Phone: (201)678-1800 **Free:** (800)832-7090
E-mail: info@mitchellsupreme.com
URL: http://www.mitchellsupreme.com
Products: Home heating oil; Natural gas. **SIC:** 5172 (Petroleum Products Nec). **Est:** 1921. **Sales:** $6,500,000 (1999). **Emp:** 130. **Officers:** J. Bozik, President; D. Owens, Treasurer; R. Schanz, Sales Mgr.

■ 22490 ■ **Moffitt Oil Company Inc.**
9000 Emmott, Ste. A
Houston, TX 77040
Phone: (713)896-4300
Free: (800)406-FUEL **Fax:** (713)937-9118
Products: Petroleum products including, diesel fuel, gasoline, and lubricating oils; Filters. **SIC:** 5172 (Petroleum Products Nec). **Est:** 1960. **Sales:** $70,000,000 (2000). **Emp:** 72. **Officers:** Andy Hansen, President; Johnny Cline, General Mgr.

■ 22491 ■ **Molo Oil Co.**
PO Box 719
Dubuque, IA 52004
Phone: (319)557-7540 **Fax:** (319)557-9632
Products: Oil; Gasoline; Fuel oil; Lubricants; Water softeners. **SIC:** 5172 (Petroleum Products Nec). **Est:** 1870. **Officers:** Mark Molo, CEO; Mark Hoffmann; Larry Snyder.

■ 22492 ■ **Mon Valley Petroleum Inc.**
5515 W Smithfield Rd.
Mc Keesport, PA 15135
Phone: (412)751-5210
Products: Heating oil; Diesel fuel; Gasoline. **SIC:** 5172 (Petroleum Products Nec). **Est:** 1928. **Sales:** $40,000,000 (2000). **Emp:** 100. **Officers:** H.C. King, President; David Chetsko, CFO. **Former Name:** King and Keeney Inc.

■ 22493 ■ **Monroe Oil Company Inc.**
PO Box 1109
Monroe, NC 28111
Phone: (704)289-5438
Products: Oil, gasoline, and diesel fuel. **SICs:** 5171 (Petroleum Bulk Stations & Terminals); 5172 (Petroleum Products Nec). **Sales:** $9,000,000 (2000). **Emp:** 20. **Officers:** Mary Hargette, President.

■ 22494 ■ **Montgomery Div.**
17191 Chrysler Fwy.
Detroit, MI 48203
Phone: (313)891-3700
Products: Metal lubricants. **SIC:** 5169 (Chemicals & Allied Products Nec). **Est:** 1924. **Sales:** $8,000,000 (2000). **Emp:** 20. **Officers:** David Sobaleski, Manager.

■ 22495 ■ **Montour Oil Service Co.**
112 Broad St.
Montoursville, PA 17754
Phone: (717)368-8611
Products: Petroleum products. **SIC:** 5172 (Petroleum Products Nec). **Sales:** $60,000,000 (1994). **Emp:** 280. **Officers:** Richard W. DeWald, President; Richard Haas, Controller.

■ 22496 ■ **Moore Drums Inc.**
2819 Industrial Ave.
Charleston, SC 29405
Phone: (803)744-7448 **Fax:** (803)744-2740
URL: http://www.mooredrums.com
Products: Steel and poly drums. **SIC:** 5085 (Industrial Supplies). **Est:** 1882. **Sales:** $8,000,000 (2000). **Emp:** 100. **Officers:** J.H. Moore Jr., President; J. Denning, Vice President.

■ 22497 ■ **Moore Oil Company Inc.**
PO Box 460
Manning, SC 29102
Phone: (803)435-4376 **Fax:** (803)435-2186
Products: Gasoline. **SIC:** 5172 (Petroleum Products Nec). **Est:** 1958. **Sales:** $63,000,000 (1999). **Emp:** 97. **Officers:** Larry Bryant, President; Jackie Cutter; Sale.

■ 22498 ■ **Lee Moore Oil Company Inc.**
PO Box 9
Sanford, NC 27331
Phone: (919)775-2301
Products: Petroleum. **SIC:** 5172 (Petroleum Products Nec). **Sales:** $55,000,000 (2000). **Emp:** 20. **Officers:** Kirk Bradley, President; Pat Gaster, VP of Finance; Linda G. Harris, Dir. of Marketing.

■ 22499 ■ **Morris Oil Inc.**
409 S High School Ave.
Columbia, MS 39429
Phone: (601)736-2634
Products: Gasoline. **SICs:** 5171 (Petroleum Bulk Stations & Terminals); 5172 (Petroleum Products Nec). **Est:** 1953. **Sales:** $10,000,000 (2000). **Emp:** 7. **Officers:** Bradley Morris, President; Steve Morris, Treasurer & Secty.

■ 22500 ■ **Morrison Petroleum Company Inc.**
2600 S & 1710 W St.
Woods Cross, UT 84087
Phone: (801)295-5591
Products: Petroleum and its products; Gasoline. **SIC:** 5172 (Petroleum Products Nec). **Est:** 1975. **Sales:** $2,000,000 (2000). **Emp:** 6. **Officers:** Dick Giesler, President.

■ 22501 ■ **Mulgrew Oil Co.**
85 Terminal
Dubuque, IA 52001
Phone: (319)583-7386 **Fax:** (319)583-7389
Products: Lube oil; Tires and car batteries. **SICs:** 5172 (Petroleum Products Nec); 5013 (Motor Vehicle Supplies & New Parts); 5014 (Tires & Tubes). **Est:** 1893. **Sales:** $12,000,000 (2000). **Emp:** 39. **Officers:** J.P. Mulgrew, President.

■ 22502 ■ **Mullis Petroleum Co.**
PO Box 517
Bedford, IN 47421
Phone: (812)275-5981 **Fax:** (812)275-2822
Products: Petroleum; Auto parts. **SICs:** 5172 (Petroleum Products Nec); 5013 (Motor Vehicle Supplies & New Parts). **Est:** 1954. **Sales:** $18,000,000 (2000). **Emp:** 22. **Officers:** P.E. Mullis, Owner.

■ 22503 ■ **Mustang Fuel Corp.**
2000 Classen Ctr No. 800
Oklahoma City, OK 73106
Phone: (405)557-9400 **Fax:** (405)557-9550
Products: Petroleum and its products. **SIC:** 5172 (Petroleum Products Nec). **Est:** 1950. **Sales:** $25,000,000 (2000). **Emp:** 120. **Officers:** E.C. Joullian III, CEO & President; Scott Chapline, VP of Finance & Admin.; Thomas C. Bennett, VP of Operations.

■ 22504 ■ **Nana Development Corp.**
1001 E Benson Blvd.
Anchorage, AK 99508
Phone: (907)265-4100
Products: Petroleum products; Arts and crafts,

including indigenous crafts. **SICs:** 5171 (Petroleum Bulk Stations & Terminals); 5172 (Petroleum Products Nec); 5092 (Toys & Hobby Goods & Supplies). **Est:** 1974. **Sales:** $24,000,000 (2000). **Emp:** 75. **Officers:** Charlie A. Curtis, CEO; J. Shelby Stastny, CFO; John Shively, CEO.

■ 22505 ■ **National Oil and Gas Inc.**
PO Box 476
Bluffton, IN 46714
Phone: (219)824-2220 **Fax:** (219)824-2223
Products: Fuel; Lubricants. **SICs:** 5171 (Petroleum Bulk Stations & Terminals); 5172 (Petroleum Products Nec). **Est:** 1941. **Sales:** $125,000,000 (2000). **Emp:** 35. **Officers:** Gene Moser, President; J.D. Kipfer, Controller; Edward Alberding, Sales Mgr.; Craig Baumgartner, Dir. of Data Processing.

■ 22506 ■ **National Propane Corp.**
PO Box 35800
Richmond, VA 23235-0800
Products: Propane gas; Gasoline; LP gas. **SIC:** 5172 (Petroleum Products Nec). **Est:** 1953. **Sales:** $149,000,000 (2000). **Emp:** 1,007. **Officers:** Ronald D. Paliughi, CEO & President; Ronald R. Rominiecki, Sr. VP & CFO; Ross Boyle, VP of Marketing & Sales; Kathy Agosti, Dir of Personnel.

■ 22507 ■ **National Propane SGP Inc.**
PO Box 35800
Richmond, VA 23235-0800
Products: Petroleum and petroleum products. **SIC:** 5172 (Petroleum Products Nec).

■ 22508 ■ **Nebraska Iowa Supply Co.**
1160 Lincoln St.
Blair, NE 68008
Phone: (402)426-2171
Products: Petroleum products, including fuel oil, lube oil, and gasoline. **SIC:** 5172 (Petroleum Products Nec). **Est:** 1947. **Sales:** $40,000,000 (2000). **Emp:** 75. **Officers:** Thomas J. Lippincott, President.

■ 22509 ■ **New Horizon FS Inc.**
655 Liberty Way
Anamosa, IA 52205
Phone: (319)462-3563 **Fax:** (319)626-8570
Products: Fuel; Gasoline; Oil; Propane. **SIC:** 5172 (Petroleum Products Nec). **Est:** 1946. **Sales:** $9,700,000 (2000). **Emp:** 40. **Officers:** Allen Rush, CEO.

■ 22510 ■ **New Horizons FS Inc.**
PO Box 447
North Liberty, IA 52317
Phone: (319)626-8555
Free: (800)362-6437 **Fax:** (319)626-8570
Products: Petroleum and farm supplies. **SICs:** 5172 (Petroleum Products Nec); 5191 (Farm Supplies). **Sales:** $17,000,000 (2000). **Emp:** 40. **Officers:** Kendall Miller, General Mgr.; David Summers, Controller.

■ 22511 ■ **New Richmond Farmers Union Cooperative Oil Co.**
PO Box 188
New Richmond, WI 54017
Phone: (715)246-2125
Products: Petroleum products and farm supplies. **SICs:** 5172 (Petroleum Products Nec); 5191 (Farm Supplies). **Sales:** $6,000,000 (1992). **Emp:** 25. **Officers:** Fred Ball, CEO; Jim Dittman, Treasurer & Secty.

■ 22512 ■ **New World Acquisition Inc.**
PO Box 731
Jackson, MI 49204
Phone: (517)787-1350
Products: Equipment for the oil and gas industry. **SIC:** 5084 (Industrial Machinery & Equipment). **Sales:** $30,000,000 (1992). **Emp:** 71. **Officers:** Michael J. Cetro, President; Tom Norton, Controller.

■ 22513 ■ **Newcomer Oil Corp.**
101 E Cherry St.
Elizabethtown, PA 17022
Phone: (717)367-1138
Products: Gasoline; Petroleum and its products. **SIC:** 5172 (Petroleum Products Nec). **Est:** 1926. **Sales:**

$7,300,000 (2000). **Emp:** 27. **Officers:** David K. Newcomer, President.

■ **22514** ■ **Newell Oil Company Inc.**
PO Box 390
Alpine, TX 79831-0390
Phone: (915)837-3322 **Fax:** (915)837-1250
Products: Gasoline; Oils and greases. **SICs:** 5171 (Petroleum Bulk Stations & Terminals); 5172 (Petroleum Products Nec). **Est:** 1939. **Sales:** $3,300,000 (2000). **Emp:** 8. **Officers:** L. Cowell, CEO; D. Asgeirsson, Controller.

■ **22515** ■ **Newsom Oil Company Inc.**
1503 W 10th St.
Roanoke Rapids, NC 27870
Phone: (919)537-3587 **Fax:** (919)537-8124
Products: Petroleum and its products. **SIC:** 5172 (Petroleum Products Nec). **Est:** 1928. **Sales:** $24,800,000 (2000). **Emp:** 130. **Officers:** David J. Newsom, President; Thurman Askew, Treasurer & Secty.; Bernard Robertson, Sales Mgr.; David J. Newsom, President.

■ **22516** ■ **Nezperce Rochdale Company Inc.**
PO Box 160
Nezperce, ID 83543
Phone: (208)937-2411
Products: Automotive greases and oils. **SIC:** 5172 (Petroleum Products Nec). **Est:** 1909. **Sales:** $13,000,000 (2000). **Emp:** 10. **Officers:** Dave Kuther, President; Andrew D. Leitch, CFO.

■ **22517** ■ **NHC Inc.**
1503 W 10th St.
Roanoke Rapids, NC 27870
Phone: (252)537-3587 **Fax:** (252)537-8124
Products: Petroleum and petroleum products. **SIC:** 5172 (Petroleum Products Nec). **Sales:** $21,000,000 (2000). **Emp:** 110. **Officers:** David J. Newsom, President; Thurman Askew, Treasurer & Secty.

■ **22518** ■ **Nielsen Oil and Propane Inc.**
660 S Main St.
West Point, NE 68788
Phone: (402)372-5485 **Fax:** (402)372-3878
Products: Fuels, including oil, propane, gasoline, and diesel; Food; Grain; Fertilizer; Chemicals; Livestock. **SICs:** 5172 (Petroleum Products Nec); 5013 (Motor Vehicle Supplies & New Parts); 5191 (Farm Supplies). **Est:** 1953. **Sales:** $13,000,000 (2000). **Emp:** 60. **Officers:** Donald E. Nielsen, President.

■ **22519** ■ **Nisbet Oil Co.**
PO Box 35367
Charlotte, NC 28235
Phone: (704)332-7755 **Fax:** (704)377-1607
Products: Petroleum and its products. **SIC:** 5172 (Petroleum Products Nec). **Est:** 1927. **Sales:** $65,000,000 (2000). **Emp:** 39. **Officers:** James J. White III, President; James J. White II, Vice President; William S. Johns Jr., CFO. **Former Name:** E.P. #Nisbet Co.

■ **22520** ■ **Nittany Oil Co.**
321 N Front St.
Philipsburg, PA 16866
Phone: (814)342-0210
Free: (800)252-3882 **Fax:** (814)342-5865
URL: http://www.nittanyoil.com
Products: Petroleum products. **SICs:** 5171 (Petroleum Bulk Stations & Terminals); 5172 (Petroleum Products Nec). **Sales:** $24,000,000 (2000). **Emp:** 121. **Officers:** James O. Martin, President; James W. Scott, Finance General Manager.

■ **22521** ■ **Nobles County Cooperative Oil Co.**
PO Box 278
Worthington, MN 56187-0278
Phone: (507)376-3104 **Fax:** (507)376-9696
E-mail: ncco@rconnect.com
Products: Gasoline; Diesel; Oil; Tires. **SICs:** 5172 (Petroleum Products Nec); 5014 (Tires & Tubes). **Est:** 1926. **Sales:** $7,200,000 (2000). **Emp:** 35. **Officers:** Leonard Reusch, President.

■ **22522** ■ **NOCO Energy Corp.**
2440 Sheridan Dr.
Tonawanda, NY 14150
Phone: (716)614-6226
Free: (800)500-6626 **Fax:** (716)832-1312
URL: http://www.noco.com
Products: Petroleum. **SIC:** 5172 (Petroleum Products Nec). **Est:** 1933. **Sales:** $200,000,000 (1999). **Emp:** 700. **Officers:** Denise Hauser, Human Resources Contact; John T. Brodfueher, Treasurer; Reginald B. Newman II, President; James D. Newman, Exec. VP; Robert Kelley, Sales/Marketing Contact; Jack Welch, Customer Service Contact.

■ **22523** ■ **Norrick Petroleum**
3919 E McGalliard Rd.
Muncie, IN 47303
Phone: (765)284-7374
Products: Oil; Fuel. **SIC:** 5172 (Petroleum Products Nec).

■ **22524** ■ **North Central Cooperative Association**
825 E 250 N
Warsaw, IN 46580-7869
Phone: (219)267-5101
Products: Petroleum and its products; Pumps and pumping equipment; Tanks and parts. **SICs:** 5153 (Grain & Field Beans); 5191 (Farm Supplies); 5172 (Petroleum Products Nec). **Sales:** $21,000,000 (2000). **Emp:** 95. **Officers:** Dee Byerly, CEO.

■ **22525** ■ **Northeast Cooperative**
PO Box 160
Wisner, NE 68791
Phone: (402)529-3538
Products: Gas; Oil. **SIC:** 5172 (Petroleum Products Nec).

■ **22526** ■ **Northern Coop Services (Lake Mills, Iowa)**
107 W Main St.
Lake Mills, IA 50450
Phone: (515)592-0011 **Fax:** (515)592-0017
Products: Petroleum bulk station and gasoline. **SICs:** 5171 (Petroleum Bulk Stations & Terminals); 5172 (Petroleum Products Nec). **Sales:** $28,000,000 (2000). **Emp:** 42. **Officers:** Laverne Lee, President; Lef Hobert, General Manager, Finance.

■ **22527** ■ **Northville Industries Corp.**
25 Melville Park Rd.
Melville, NY 11747
Phone: (516)293-4700 **Fax:** (516)293-4780
Products: Gasoline; Heating oil; Kerosene; Jet fuel. **SIC:** 5172 (Petroleum Products Nec). **Est:** 1956. **Sales:** $42,000,000 (2000). **Emp:** 85. **Officers:** Jay Bernstein, Chairman of the Board; Peter Ripp, CFO; Gene M. Bernstein, Dir. of Marketing.

■ **22528** ■ **Northwest Oil Company Inc.**
PO Box 1505
Fayetteville, AR 72702
Phone: (501)521-1573
Products: Petroleum by-products. **SIC:** 5172 (Petroleum Products Nec). **Est:** 1972. **Sales:** $18,800,000 (2000). **Emp:** 12. **Officers:** George T. Williams, President; L. Leen Threet, Treasurer & Secty.; E. Lamar Pettus, Secretary.

■ **22529** ■ **Norton Petroleum Corp.**
290 Possum Park Rd.
Newark, DE 19711
Phone: (302)731-8220 **Fax:** (302)737-6479
Products: Petroleum products, including lubricating oils. **SIC:** 5172 (Petroleum Products Nec).

■ **22530** ■ **Nova Vista Industries Inc.**
PO Box 731
Jackson, MI 49204
Phone: (517)787-1350
Products: Pipes, valves, and fittings for the oil industry. **SIC:** 5084 (Industrial Machinery & Equipment). **Est:** 1980. **Sales:** $30,000,000 (2000). **Emp:** 70. **Officers:** Michael J. Cetro, President; Thomas W. Norton, Controller.

■ **22531** ■ **Novakovich Enterprises**
3940 Alitak
Anchorage, AK 99515
Phone: (907)344-3230
Products: Industrial lubricants; Roofing material. **SICs:** 5172 (Petroleum Products Nec); 5033 (Roofing, Siding & Insulation).

■ **22532** ■ **Oakes Oil Co.**
PO Box 160
Laceys Spring, AL 35754
Phone: (205)881-3310
Products: Motor oil; Hydraulic fuel. **SIC:** 5172 (Petroleum Products Nec). **Sales:** $4,000,000 (2000). **Emp:** 10. **Officers:** Billy Oakes, President.

■ **22533** ■ **Oceanex Services International, Inc.**
16115 Park Row, Ste. 120
Houston, TX 77084
Phone: (281)579-0808 **Fax:** (281)579-0802
E-mail: oceanex@oceanexservices.com
Products: Industrial and oil field machinery equipment. **SIC:** 5084 (Industrial Machinery & Equipment). **Est:** 1981. **Sales:** $12,000,000 (1999). **Emp:** 11. **Officers:** Bernard Crouhade, CEO, e-mail: bernardc@oceanexservices.com; Lucio Solis, President; Kevin Dornak, Sales Contact, e-mail: kevind@oceanexservices.com; Irma Bein, Human Resources Contact.

■ **22534** ■ **O'Day Equipment Inc.**
PO Box 2706
Fargo, ND 58108
Phone: (701)282-9260 **Fax:** (701)281-9770
E-mail: sales@odayeqipment.com
URL: http://www.odayequipment.com
Products: Petroleum products; Underground tanks. **SICs:** 5172 (Petroleum Products Nec); 5088 (Transportation Equipment & Supplies). **Est:** 1935. **Sales:** $16,000,000 (2000). **Emp:** 96. **Officers:** J. O'Day, President; Lee Holschuh, Vice President; Al Peach, Vice President.

■ **22535** ■ **Ogden Services Corp.**
2 Penn Plz.
New York, NY 10121
Phone: (212)868-6000 **Fax:** (212)868-5714
Products: Fuel oils. **SIC:** 5172 (Petroleum Products Nec). **Sales:** $1,749,700,000 (2000). **Emp:** 39,000. **Officers:** R. Richard Ablon, CEO; Phil Husby, CFO.

■ **22536** ■ **Oil-Dri Corp.**
PO Box 200-A
Ochlocknee, GA 31773
Phone: (912)574-5131
Products: Oil and industrial absorbents, special cleaning agents, and cat litter. **SIC:** 5199 (Nondurable Goods Nec). **Sales:** $50,000,000 (2000). **Emp:** 300. **Officers:** Richard M. Jaffee, CEO & Chairman of the Board.

■ **22537** ■ **Oil Equipment Supply Corp.**
3120 W Morris St.
Indianapolis, IN 46241
Phone: (317)243-3120
Free: (800)792-3120 **Fax:** (317)243-1615
Products: Measuring and dispensing pumps for gasoline and oil. **SIC:** 5084 (Industrial Machinery & Equipment). **Est:** 1956. **Sales:** $20,000,000 (2000). **Emp:** 40. **Officers:** Robert Wright, President; Jan A. Forslund, Treasurer & Secty.; Monti Harris, Dir. of Marketing.

■ **22538** ■ **Oil Marketing Company Inc.**
PO Box 1709
Tahlequah, OK 74465
Phone: (918)456-9805
E-mail: conoco@ipa.net
Products: Gasoline; Convenience store items. **SICs:** 5171 (Petroleum Bulk Stations & Terminals); 5172 (Petroleum Products Nec); 5141 (Groceries—General Line). **Est:** 1955. **Sales:** $15,000,000 (2000). **Emp:** 48. **Officers:** Jim D. Hopkins, President.

■ **22539** ■ **Oilworld Supply Co.**
PO Box 55301
Houston, TX 77255
Phone: (713)681-9777 **Fax:** (713)939-8462
Products: Oil field machinery. **SIC:** 5084 (Industrial

Machinery & Equipment). **Est:** 1973. **Sales:** $12,000,000 (2000). **Emp:** 20. **Officers:** Ed Carney, CEO; Frank Smith, CFO; Ken Griffin, Dir. of Marketing & Sales; Susan Buckley, VP of Human Resources.

■ **22540** ■ **Olympian Oil Co.**
260 Michele Ct.
South San Francisco, CA 94080
Phone: (415)873-8200   **Fax:** (650)873-3327
URL: http://www.oly.com
Products: Fuel, including oil, gasoline, and diesel; Lube equipment; Tanks; Chemicals. **SICs:** 5171 (Petroleum Bulk Stations & Terminals); 5169 (Chemicals & Allied Products Nec). **Sales:** $52,000,000 (2000). **Emp:** 250. **Officers:** Fred Bertetta, President; George Shammas, Sr. VP & Finance Officer.

■ **22541** ■ **Onyx Petroleum Inc.**
441 EE Butler Pkwy.
Gainesville, GA 30506
Phone: (770)536-0068
Free: (800)843-0134   **Fax:** (770)536-1017
URL: http://www.onyx-petro.com
Products: Oil; Gasoline; Diesel fuel. **SIC:** 5172 (Petroleum Products Nec). **Est:** 1986.

■ **22542** ■ **Orca Oil Company, Inc.**
100 Ocean Dock Rd.
Cordova, AK 99574
Phone: (907)424-3264   **Fax:** (907)424-3294
Products: Engine and hydraulic oils; Marine-related petroleum products; Roofing products. **SICs:** 5172 (Petroleum Products Nec); 5033 (Roofing, Siding & Insulation).

■ **22543** ■ **Arnold Owens Inc.**
PO Box 3697
Bloomington, IL 61702-3697
Phone: (309)828-7750   **Fax:** (309)829-3813
Products: Gasoline and diesel fuels. **SIC:** 5172 (Petroleum Products Nec). **Est:** 1958. **Sales:** $53,000,000 (2000). **Emp:** 250. **Officers:** Michael Koenig, President.

■ **22544** ■ **Ownbey Enterprises Inc.**
PO Box 1146
Dalton, GA 30722
Phone: (706)278-3019
Products: Oil, gasoline, and diesel fuel; Lubricants. **SIC:** 5172 (Petroleum Products Nec). **Sales:** $35,000,000 (2000). **Emp:** 50. **Officers:** Rodney Ownbey, President; Jerry Nolan, Comptroller; Jack Martin, General Mgr.

■ **22545** ■ **Oxbow Corp.**
1601 Forum Pl.
West Palm Beach, FL 33401
Phone: (561)697-4300
Products: Petroleum products. **SIC:** 5171 (Petroleum Bulk Stations & Terminals). **Sales:** $50,000,000 (2000). **Emp:** 75. **Officers:** William Koch, President; Zachary Shipley, VP of Finance.

■ **22546** ■ **Pace Oil Company Inc.**
PO Box 827
Magee, MS 39111
Phone: (601)849-2492   **Fax:** (601)849-5022
Products: Gasoline and petroleum products. **SIC:** 5172 (Petroleum Products Nec). **Emp:** 60. **Officers:** Alfred Pace, President.

■ **22547** ■ **Pacific Northern**
100 W Harrison St.
Seattle, WA 98119
Phone: (206)282-4421   **Fax:** (206)282-6574
Products: Petroleum, fuels, and related equipment. **SIC:** 5172 (Petroleum Products Nec). **Est:** 1973. **Sales:** $90,000,000 (2000). **Emp:** 50.

■ **22548** ■ **Pam Oil Inc.**
PO Box 5200
Sioux Falls, SD 57117
Phone: (605)336-1788
Free: (800)456-2660   **Fax:** (605)339-9909
URL: http://www.pam-companies.com
Products: Oil. **SIC:** 5172 (Petroleum Products Nec). **Est:** 1963. **Sales:** $100,000,000 (2000). **Emp:** 360. **Officers:** William G. Peterson, CFO; A.S. Peterson,

President; Dan Dressen, Dir. of Marketing & Sales; Mike Hase, General Mgr.; Scott Scofield, Marketing & Sales Mgr.; Carol Nickles, Human Resources Mgr.

■ **22549** ■ **Panhandle Trading Co.**
5718 Westheimer Rd.
Houston, TX 77057
Phone: (713)627-5400
Products: Gasoline. **SIC:** 5172 (Petroleum Products Nec).

■ **22550** ■ **Paraco Gas Corp.**
2975 W Chester Ave.
Purchase, NY 10577
Phone: (914)696-4427
Products: Propane gas. **SIC:** 5172 (Petroleum Products Nec).

■ **22551** ■ **Parker Oil Company Inc.**
PO Box 120
South Hill, VA 23970
Phone: (804)447-3146   **Fax:** (804)447-2646
Products: Petroleum and its products. **SIC:** 5172 (Petroleum Products Nec). **Est:** 1935. **Sales:** $60,000,000 (2000). **Emp:** 160. **Officers:** Lewis W. Parker Jr., President; Charles F. Parker, CFO; Loften D. Allen, Vice President.

■ **22552** ■ **Patterson Brothers Oil and Gas Inc.**
141 S Pine St.
Williamsville, IL 62693
Phone: (217)566-3328
Products: Gasoline, propane, and diesel fuel. **SICs:** 5171 (Petroleum Bulk Stations & Terminals); 5172 (Petroleum Products Nec); 5169 (Chemicals & Allied Products Nec). **Est:** 1926. **Sales:** $6,000,000 (2000). **Emp:** 9. **Officers:** George W. Patterson, President; Robert Barbee, Treasurer & Secty.

■ **22553** ■ **Patterson Oil Co.**
PO Box 898
Torrington, CT 06790
Phone: (860)489-1198
Products: Gasoline; Propane; Fuel oil. **SICs:** 5172 (Petroleum Products Nec); 5169 (Chemicals & Allied Products Nec). **Est:** 1922. **Sales:** $44,000,000 (2000). **Emp:** 90. **Officers:** Barry Patterson, President; Ronald Martin, Treasurer; Robert Mueller, Vice President.

■ **22554** ■ **Paynesville Farmers Union Cooperative Oil Co.**
419 E Hoffman St.
PO Box 53
Paynesville, MN 56362-0053
Phone: (320)243-3751   **Fax:** (320)243-3865
Products: Petroleum, including fuel, gas, and oil; Fertilizer. **SICs:** 5172 (Petroleum Products Nec); 5191 (Farm Supplies). **Est:** 1953. **Sales:** $3,000,000 (2000). **Emp:** 15. **Officers:** Paul Evans, General Mgr.

■ **22555** ■ **PDQ Air Service Inc.**
3939 International
Columbus, OH 43219
Phone: (614)238-1912   **Fax:** (614)338-2035
E-mail: airnetFBO.com
Products: Aircraft fuel. **SIC:** 5172 (Petroleum Products Nec). **Est:** 1974. **Sales:** $60,000,000 (2000). **Emp:** 1,000. **Officers:** G.G. Mercer, Chairman of the Board; Joel Biggerstaff, President & CEO; Bill Sumser, CFO.

■ **22556** ■ **Peck's Petroleum Inc.**
PO Box 540
Boaz, AL 35957
Phone: (205)593-4286
Products: Petroleum and gasoline. **SIC:** 5172 (Petroleum Products Nec). **Est:** 1961. **Sales:** $27,000,000 (2000). **Emp:** 23. **Officers:** Peggy Conn, President; Sandra Hyatt, Controller; Morris Hyatt, Dir. of Marketing & Sales.

■ **22557** ■ **Pedroni Fuel Co.**
385 E Wheat Rd.
Vineland, NJ 08360
Phone: (609)691-4855
Products: Fuel; Lubricants; Motor oils. **SIC:** 5172 (Petroleum Products Nec). **Est:** 1952. **Sales:** $12,000,000 (2000). **Emp:** 42. **Officers:** Richard Pedroni, President.

■ **22558** ■ **Peerless Distributing Co.**
21700 Northwestern Hwy.
Southfield, MI 48075
Phone: (313)559-1800
Products: Fuel oils, including gasoline. **SIC:** 5172 (Petroleum Products Nec). **Est:** 1934. **Sales:** $57,000,000 (2000). **Emp:** 16. **Officers:** Marvin Fleischman, President; Steven Robinson, Secretary; Jeff Fleischman, Dir. of Marketing; Naweed A. Rana, Controller.

■ **22559** ■ **Pen-Fern Oil Co.**
640 Main Rd.
Dallas, PA 18612
Phone: (717)675-5731
Products: Gasoline; Kerosene; Petroleum and its products. **SIC:** 5172 (Petroleum Products Nec). **Est:** 1944. **Sales:** $9,000,000 (2000). **Emp:** 20. **Officers:** Jay H. May, President.

■ **22560** ■ **Penco Corp.**
PO Box 690
Seaford, DE 19973
Phone: (302)629-7911
Products: Pipe; Values; Fittings. **SIC:** 5085 (Industrial Supplies). **Est:** 1949. **Sales:** $19,000,000 (2000). **Emp:** 175. **Officers:** William C. Robertson Jr., Sec. & Treas.; George H. Sapna II, President; Kent T. Peterson, Vice President.

■ **22561** ■ **Penfield Petroleum Products**
147 Peconic Ave.
Medford, NY 11763
Phone: (516)758-3838   **Fax:** (516)758-7566
Products: Fuel oil, gasoline, and diesel. **SIC:** 5172 (Petroleum Products Nec). **Est:** 1948. **Sales:** $55,000,000 (2000). **Emp:** 85. **Officers:** George Rice, CEO.

■ **22562** ■ **Peoples Communitive Oil Cooperative**
211 Main St.
Darlington, WI 53530
Phone: (608)776-4437
Products: Petroleum products and fertilizers. **SICs:** 5172 (Petroleum Products Nec); 5191 (Farm Supplies). **Sales:** $4,500,000 (2000). **Emp:** 25. **Officers:** Craig Hillery, President; Paul John, Treasurer & Secty.

■ **22563** ■ **Peoples Gas and Oil Company Inc.**
PO Drawer 8
Maxton, NC 28364
Phone: (910)844-3124
Products: Liquid propane. **SIC:** 5172 (Petroleum Products Nec). **Est:** 1952. **Sales:** $2,000,000 (2000). **Emp:** 8. **Officers:** Joe B. Clark III III, Vice President.

■ **22564** ■ **Julian W. Perkins Inc.**
40657 Butternut Ridge
Elyria, OH 44035
Phone: (216)458-5125
Products: Fuel oil. **SIC:** 5171 (Petroleum Bulk Stations & Terminals). **Est:** 1936. **Sales:** $5,000,000 (2000). **Emp:** 10. **Officers:** M.P. Brine, Owner; E. Brine, President; Hill Hutchins, VP of Marketing.

■ **22565** ■ **Peterson Oil Co.**
55 East 680 South
Provo, UT 84606
Phone: (801)373-8620
Products: Gasoline; Oil. **SIC:** 5172 (Petroleum Products Nec).

■ **22566** ■ **Petrofina Delaware Inc.**
PO Box 2159
Dallas, TX 75201
Phone: (214)750-2400
Products: Mining: Oil exploration; Gasoline, diesel, and asphalt. **SICs:** 5172 (Petroleum Products Nec); 5032 (Brick, Stone & Related Materials). **Est:** 1977. **Sales:** $4,081,200,000 (2000). **Emp:** 2,664. **Officers:** Ron W. Haddock, CEO & President; Jeoffroy Petit, VP & CFO.

■ **22567** ■ **Petrolec Inc.**
PO Box 727
Clearfield, PA 16830-0727
Phone: (814)765-9603
Products: Oil; Gasoline; Diesel fuel. **SIC:** 5172

(Petroleum Products Nec). **Est:** 1938. **Sales:** $15,000,000 (2000). **Emp:** 100. **Officers:** Yvonne Cook, President.

■ **22568** ■ **Petroleum Marketers Inc.**
PO Box 12203
Roanoke, VA 24023
Phone: (703)362-4900 **Fax:** (703)366-2820
Products: Petroleum products, including lubricants, oil, and gasoline. **SIC:** 5172 (Petroleum Products Nec). **Est:** 1950. **Sales:** $151,000,000 (2000). **Emp:** 650. **Officers:** Terry M. Phelps, CEO & President; Roy Fornes, CFO; Scott Blankenship, Exec. VP.

■ **22569** ■ **Petroleum Products Corp.**
PO Box 2621
Harrisburg, PA 17105
Phone: (717)939-0466
Products: Petroleum, fuels, and related equipment. **SIC:** 5172 (Petroleum Products Nec). **Est:** 1961. **Sales:** $200,000,000 (2000). **Emp:** 19.

■ **22570** ■ **Petroleum Products Corporation North**
167 Willow Ave.
Middleburg, PA 17842
Phone: (717)837-1724
Products: Petroleum products, including fuel oil and kerosene. **SIC:** 5172 (Petroleum Products Nec). **Sales:** $17,000,000 (2000). **Emp:** 100. **Officers:** Wallace Rohrbach, President.

■ **22571** ■ **Petroleum Sales and Service Inc.**
300 Ohio St.
Buffalo, NY 14204
Phone: (716)856-8675
Products: Petroleum. **SIC:** 5172 (Petroleum Products Nec). **Est:** 1930. **Sales:** $88,000,000 (1999). **Emp:** 80. **Officers:** Bernard Kieffer, President; James M. Broardt, Treasurer.

■ **22572** ■ **Petroleum Service Company Inc.**
PO Box 454
Wilkes Barre, PA 18703
Phone: (570)822-1151 **Fax:** (570)823-1910
E-mail: pscinc@epix.net
Products: Lubricating oils and greases; Petroleum and its products; Industrial paints; Protective coatings. **SIC:** 5172 (Petroleum Products Nec). **Est:** 1930. **Sales:** $20,000,000 (2000). **Emp:** 100. **Officers:** R.W. Simms, CEO; Richard Rose, President. **Former Name:** Petroleum Service Co.

■ **22573** ■ **Petroleum World Inc.**
PO Box 307
Cliffside, NC 28024
Phone: (704)482-0438 **Fax:** (704)453-0165
Products: Petroleum products, including motor oil and fuels. **SICs:** 5171 (Petroleum Bulk Stations & Terminals); 5172 (Petroleum Products Nec). **Est:** 1972. **Sales:** $200,000,000 (2000). **Emp:** 350. **Officers:** Michael J. Frost, President; Hampton Hager, Exec. VP & CFO.

■ **22574** ■ **Petron Oil Corp.**
180 Gordon Dr.
Lionville, PA 19353
Phone: (215)524-1700 **Fax:** (215)524-1572
Products: Diesel, gasoline, heating oil, and kerosene. **SIC:** 5171 (Petroleum Bulk Stations & Terminals). **Est:** 1980. **Sales:** $7,000,000 (2000). **Emp:** 15. **Officers:** Charles Hurchalla, President.

■ **22575** ■ **Petrotank Equipment Inc.**
10709 E Ute St.
Tulsa, OK 74116
Phone: (918)838-0781 **Fax:** (918)838-0428
Products: Tank parts and accessories and floating roof seals for storage tanks. **SIC:** 5039 (Construction Materials Nec). **Officers:** Terry Clark, Manager.

■ **22576** ■ **Phibro Inc.**
500 Nyala Farms
Westport, CT 06880-6262
Phone: (203)221-5800 **Fax:** (203)625-6970
Products: Oil. **SICs:** 5171 (Petroleum Bulk Stations & Terminals); 5172 (Petroleum Products Nec). **Est:** 1902. **Sales:** $46,000,000 (2000). **Emp:** 170. **Officers:**

Andrew J. Hall, President; William J. Cronin, VP & Treasurer; Joe Licata, Dir of Human Resources.

■ **22577** ■ **Phillips 66 Propane Co.**
756 Adams Bldg.
Bartlesville, OK 74004
Phone: (918)661-3207
Free: (800)662-6033 **Fax:** (918)662-2178
E-mail: jrfouts@ppeo.com
Products: Propane gas. **SIC:** 5171 (Petroleum Bulk Stations & Terminals). **Emp:** 7.

■ **22578** ■ **Tom M. Phillips Company Inc.**
PO Box 207
Jasper, GA 30143
Phone: (706)692-2012
Products: Fuels, including gasoline, oil, and diesel. **SIC:** 5172 (Petroleum Products Nec). **Est:** 1966. **Sales:** $25,000,000 (2000). **Emp:** 12. **Officers:** Tom Phillips, Owner.

■ **22579** ■ **Phillips Hardware Co.**
PO Box 279
Cambridge, MD 21613
Phone: (410)228-4900
Products: General line of petroleum products. **SIC:** 5172 (Petroleum Products Nec). **Sales:** $3,000,000 (1993). **Emp:** 11. **Officers:** Edward H. Mowbray, President; Betty Hollerman, Treasurer & Secty.

■ **22580** ■ **Ira Phillips Inc.**
310 N 3rd St.
Gadsden, AL 35901
Phone: (256)547-0591 **Fax:** (256)547-0516
Products: Petrolem and its products. **SIC:** 5172 (Petroleum Products Nec). **Est:** 1938. **Sales:** $4,000,000 (2000). **Emp:** 9. **Officers:** Ira Phillips Jr., President.

■ **22581** ■ **Phillipsburg Cooperative Association**
PO Box 624
Phillipsburg, KS 67661
Phone: (785)543-2114
Products: Fuel, including oil, gasoline, and diesel. **SIC:** 5172 (Petroleum Products Nec). **Est:** 1942. **Sales:** $4,000,000 (2000). **Emp:** 15. **Officers:** Calvin Schemper, President; Richard Osterhaus, General Mgr.

■ **22582** ■ **Phoenix Fuel Company Inc.**
2343 N 27th Ave.
Phoenix, AZ 85009
Phone: (602)278-6271 **Fax:** (602)278-7196
Products: Unleaded, super-unleaded gasoline. **SICs:** 5171 (Petroleum Bulk Stations & Terminals); 5172 (Petroleum Products Nec). **Est:** 1927. **Sales:** $91,000,000 (2000). **Emp:** 110. **Officers:** Joseph W. Wilhoit, President.

■ **22583** ■ **Piasa Motor Fuels Inc.**
PO Box 484
Alton, IL 62002
Phone: (618)254-7341
Products: Gasoline; Diesel fuel. **SICs:** 5171 (Petroleum Bulk Stations & Terminals); 5013 (Motor Vehicle Supplies & New Parts). **Est:** 1932. **Sales:** $165,000,000 (2000). **Emp:** 100. **Officers:** R. William Schrimpf, President; Drexine Bade, Accountant.

■ **22584** ■ **Piedmont Propane Co.**
100 Forsyth Hall Dr., Ste. E
Charlotte, NC 28273
Phone: (704)588-9215 **Fax:** (704)588-9217
Products: Propane. **SIC:** 5172 (Petroleum Products Nec). **Sales:** $32,000,000 (1999). **Emp:** 237. **Officers:** Jane Sullivan, President; Gregg Winchester, VP of Admin.

■ **22585** ■ **J.W. Pierson Co.**
89 Dodd St.
East Orange, NJ 07019
Phone: (201)673-5000
Products: Fuel oil. **SIC:** 5074 (Plumbing & Hydronic Heating Supplies). **Est:** 1888. **Sales:** $15,000,000 (2000). **Emp:** 50. **Officers:** James Pierson, President.

■ **22586** ■ **Pipeline Oil Sales Inc.**
744 E South St.
Jackson, MI 49203
Phone: (517)782-0467
Products: Oil. **SIC:** 5171 (Petroleum Bulk Stations & Terminals). **Sales:** $4,000,000 (2000). **Emp:** 10. **Officers:** James Ahern, President.

■ **22587** ■ **A.J. Ploch Co.**
PO Box 200658
San Antonio, TX 78220-0658
Phone: (210)661-2344
Products: Oil, fuel, and kerosene; Lubricants. **SIC:** 5172 (Petroleum Products Nec). **Sales:** $7,000,000 (2000). **Emp:** 11. **Officers:** E. Ploch, President.

■ **22588** ■ **Pollard-Swain Inc.**
218 E Meats Ave.
Orange, CA 92856
Phone: (714)637-1531
Products: Motor oil; Engine degreaser; Carburetor cleaner. **SIC:** 5172 (Petroleum Products Nec). **Est:** 1983. **Sales:** $7,000,000 (2000). **Emp:** 15. **Officers:** Dale Swain, President.

■ **22589** ■ **Porter Oil Company Inc.**
306 S Motel Blvd.
Las Cruces, NM 88005
Phone: (505)524-8666 **Fax:** (505)523-2998
Products: Gasoline. **SICs:** 5171 (Petroleum Bulk Stations & Terminals); 5013 (Motor Vehicle Supplies & New Parts). **Est:** 1953. **Sales:** $13,400,000 (2000). **Emp:** 75. **Officers:** Martin Porter, President; Darren Davis, CFO; Louise Porter, Vice President.

■ **22590** ■ **Powell Distributing Company Inc.**
PO Box 17160
Portland, OR 97217-0160
Phone: (503)289-5558 **Fax:** (503)735-0100
E-mail: aero180@aol.com
Products: Gasoline; Diesel. **SICs:** 5171 (Petroleum Bulk Stations & Terminals); 5172 (Petroleum Products Nec). **Est:** 1945. **Sales:** $17,000,000 (2000). **Emp:** 8. **Officers:** Jason Powell, Secretary; Sondra K. Powell, Vice President; Marilyn Meek, Comptroller.

■ **22591** ■ **Power Products Service**
465 Hwy. 182
Morgan City, LA 70380-5107
Phone: (504)395-5224 **Fax:** (504)395-2903
Products: Off-shore drilling pumps and compressors. **SIC:** 5084 (Industrial Machinery & Equipment). **Est:** 1964. **Sales:** $2,500,000 (2000). **Emp:** 15. **Officers:** Emmett Hardaway, President; Tom Forgey, Dir. of Marketing.

■ **22592** ■ **Praxah Gas Tech Inc.**
12000 Roosevelt Rd.
Hillside, IL 60162
Phone: (708)449-9300 **Fax:** (708)449-0345
Products: Gases and welding equipment supplies. **SICs:** 5169 (Chemicals & Allied Products Nec); 5084 (Industrial Machinery & Equipment). **Officers:** Ron Castle, Division General Mgr. **Former Name:** Linox Gas Tech Inc.

■ **22593** ■ **Premium Oil Co.**
2005 S 300 W
Salt Lake City, UT 84115
Phone: (801)487-4721
Products: Gasoline; Automotive oil. **SIC:** 5172 (Petroleum Products Nec). **Est:** 1933. **Sales:** $32,200,000 (2000). **Emp:** 168. **Officers:** Paul S. Callister, President; Donald M. Murphy, Treasurer & Secty.; Rulon Hymas, Vice President.

■ **22594** ■ **Primrose Oil Company Inc.**
PO Box 29665
Dallas, TX 75229
Phone: (972)241-1100
Free: (800)275-2772 **Fax:** (972)241-4188
URL: http://www.primrose.com
Products: Industrial oils, greases, and fuel additives. **SICs:** 5172 (Petroleum Products Nec); 5169 (Chemicals & Allied Products Nec). **Est:** 1916. **Sales:** $11,000,000 (2000). **Emp:** 50. **Officers:** Randy Bacon, Vice President.

■ 22595 ■ Progas Service Inc.
PO Box 278
Ft. Madison, IA 52627
Phone: (319)372-1062
Products: Propane gas. **SIC:** 5169 (Chemicals & Allied Products Nec). **Sales:** $5,000,000 (2000). **Emp:** 10. **Officers:** James B. Winke, President.

■ 22596 ■ Propane Equipment Corp.
11 Apple St.
Tinton Falls, NJ 07724
Phone: (908)747-3795   **Fax:** (908)219-0161
Products: Propane gas; Tanks; Pumps. **SICs:** 5172 (Petroleum Products Nec); 5084 (Industrial Machinery & Equipment). **Est:** 1963. **Sales:** $3,000,000 (2000). **Emp:** 17. **Officers:** M.J. Vranken, President; Joan Vranken, CFO; Ronald Cassell, VP of Marketing.

■ 22597 ■ Propane/One Inc.
PO Box 38
Oakland City, IN 47660
Phone: (812)749-4411
Products: Propane. **SIC:** 5172 (Petroleum Products Nec). **Est:** 1925. **Sales:** $5,500,000 (2000). **Emp:** 15. **Officers:** Donald K. Wilder, President; Richard Wilder, Vice President.

■ 22598 ■ P.S. Energy Group Inc.
PO Box 29399
Atlanta, GA 30359
Phone: (404)321-5711
Free: (800)334-7548   **Fax:** (404)321-3938
Products: Liquid fuels; Natural gas; Coal; Propane fleet fuel management. **SIC:** 5172 (Petroleum Products Nec). **Est:** 1985. **Emp:** 30. **Officers:** Livia Whisenhunt, President; Deedie Golden, CFO; Roger W. Murray, COO, e-mail: coo@psenergy.com; Tom Fowler, Dir. of Marketing, e-mail: tom@psenergy.com; Chris Curro, Project Director, Fuel Management, e-mail: chriscurro@psenergy.com. **Former Name:** Petroleum Source and Systems Group Inc.

■ 22599 ■ PSNC Propane Corp.
PO Box 1398
Gastonia, NC 28053
Phone: (704)864-6731
Products: tled propane gas; Propane gas appliances. **SIC:** 5172 (Petroleum Products Nec).

■ 22600 ■ Quality Oil Company L.P.
PO Box 2736
Winston-Salem, NC 27102
Phone: (919)722-3441
Products: Fuel oil, kerosene, and lubricants. **SIC:** 5172 (Petroleum Products Nec). **Est:** 1929. **Sales:** $80,000,000 (2000). **Emp:** 300. **Officers:** James K. Glenn Jr., President; Rocky Nolen, VP of Finance; Andy Sayles, Dir. of Marketing.

■ 22601 ■ Quality Oil Company L.P.
PO Box 2736
Winston-Salem, NC 27102
Phone: (336)722-3441
Products: Petroleum products. **SIC:** 5172 (Petroleum Products Nec). **Sales:** $143,000,000 (2000). **Emp:** 300. **Officers:** James K. Glenn Jr., President; Rocky Nolen, VP of Finance.

■ 22602 ■ Quality Petroleum Corp.
PO Box 3889
Lakeland, FL 33802-3889
Phone: (941)687-2682   **Fax:** (941)688-1613
Products: Petroleum products. **SIC:** 5172 (Petroleum Products Nec). **Sales:** $49,000,000 (2000). **Emp:** 200. **Officers:** Ralph W. Weeks, President; Jim Thompson, Controller.

■ 22603 ■ Queen Oil & Gas
Mayhill 66, Hwy. 82
Mayhill, NM 88339
Phone: (505)687-3605
Products: Oil; Gas. **SIC:** 5172 (Petroleum Products Nec).

■ 22604 ■ Quogue Sinclair Fuel Inc.
PO Box 760
Hampton Bays, NY 11946
Phone: (516)726-4700   **Fax:** (516)728-1233
Products: Fuel oil, diesel and kerosene. **SIC:** 5172

(Petroleum Products Nec). **Emp:** 25. **Officers:** Chester Sinclair, President; Charlotte Sinclair, Treasurer.

■ 22605 ■ Racetrac Petroleum Inc.
300 Technology Ct.
Smyrna, GA 30082
Phone: (770)431-7600   **Fax:** (770)431-7612
Products: Gas; Oil; Antifreeze. **SIC:** 5172 (Petroleum Products Nec). **Est:** 1934. **Sales:** $1,600,000,000 (2000). **Emp:** 3,000. **Officers:** Carl E. Bolch Jr. Jr., CEO & Chairman of the Board; Robert J. Dumbacher, CFO; Ben Tyon, VP of Operations; Bob Stier.

■ 22606 ■ Racine Elevator Co.
PO Box 37
Racine, MN 55967
Phone: (507)378-2121   **Fax:** (507)378-2131
Products: Natural gas. **SIC:** 5172 (Petroleum Products Nec). **Est:** 1950. **Sales:** $2,000,000 (2000). **Emp:** 12. **Officers:** Lloyd V. Crum, Owner.

■ 22607 ■ Rad Oil Company Inc.
287 Bowman Ave.
Purchase, NY 10577-2517
Phone: (914)253-8945
Products: Petroleum. **SIC:** 5171 (Petroleum Bulk Stations & Terminals). **Sales:** $100,000,000 (2000). **Emp:** 225. **Officers:** Donald Draizin, President; Gerald Maughan, CFO.

■ 22608 ■ Raymond Oil Co.
PO Box 142
Huron, SD 57350
Phone: (605)352-8711
Products: Propane. **SIC:** 5171 (Petroleum Bulk Stations & Terminals). **Est:** 1938. **Sales:** $1,800,000 (2000). **Emp:** 8. **Officers:** Carol Erling, Partner; Ernest Erling, Partner.

■ 22609 ■ Raymond Oil Company Inc.
1 Main Pl., No. 900
Wichita, KS 67202
Phone: (316)267-4214   **Fax:** (316)267-4218
Products: Oil and gasoline. **SIC:** 5084 (Industrial Machinery & Equipment). **Est:** 1956. **Sales:** $13,000,000 (2000). **Emp:** 25. **Officers:** William S. Raymond, President; Charles Roach, Treasurer.

■ 22610 ■ RBM Company Inc.
PO Box 12
Knoxville, TN 37901
Phone: (423)524-8621
Products: Petroleum handling equipment, including metal shelving and air compressors. **SIC:** 5084 (Industrial Machinery & Equipment). **Est:** 1945. **Sales:** $5,000,000 (2000). **Emp:** 27. **Officers:** W.D. Bruce, President.

■ 22611 ■ Rebel Oil Company Inc.
1900 W Sahara Ave.
Las Vegas, NV 89102
Phone: (702)382-5866
Products: Petroleum. **SIC:** 5171 (Petroleum Bulk Stations & Terminals).

■ 22612 ■ Red Giant Oil Co.
PO Box 247
Council Bluffs, IA 51502
Phone: (712)323-2441   **Fax:** (712)323-1493
Products: Petroleum and its products; Waste oil. **SICs:** 5093 (Scrap & Waste Materials); 5172 (Petroleum Products Nec). **Est:** 1941. **Sales:** $11,000,000 (2000). **Emp:** 30. **Officers:** Fred Galvani, President.

■ 22613 ■ Red-Kap Sales Inc.
PO Box 1078
Schenectady, NY 12301
Phone: (518)377-6431   **Fax:** (518)377-4529
Products: Gasoline; Diesel fuel. **SIC:** 5172 (Petroleum Products Nec). **Est:** 1933. **Sales:** $7,000,000 (2000). **Emp:** 16. **Officers:** F.R. Kaplan, President; H.V. Kaplan, Chairman of the Board & Treasurer; Anthony Famiano, Dir. of Marketing.

■ 22614 ■ Red Rock Distributing Co.
PO Box 82336
Oklahoma City, OK 73148
Phone: (405)677-3371
Products: Fuel. **SIC:** 5172 (Petroleum Products Nec).

Sales: $25,000,000 (1994). **Emp:** 11. **Officers:** Steven M. Brown, President; Barney Brown, Vice President.

■ 22615 ■ Redlake County Co-op
PO Box 37
Brooks, MN 56715
Phone: (218)698-4271
Products: Petroleum; Fertilizer; Gas. **SICs:** 5172 (Petroleum Products Nec); 5191 (Farm Supplies). **Est:** 1943. **Sales:** $5,000,000 (2000). **Emp:** 35. **Officers:** Robert Solein, General Mgr.

■ 22616 ■ Reece Oil Co.
PO Box 3195
Terre Haute, IN 47803-0195
Phone: (812)232-6621
Products: Gasoline, diesel, kerosene, and petroleum. **SICs:** 5171 (Petroleum Bulk Stations & Terminals); 5172 (Petroleum Products Nec). **Est:** 1954. **Sales:** $7,000,000 (2000). **Emp:** 7. **Officers:** Jack Reece, President.

■ 22617 ■ Reeder Distributors Inc.
PO Box 8237
Ft. Worth, TX 76124-0237
Phone: (817)429-5957   **Fax:** (817)429-9052
Products: Fuel and oil. **SIC:** 5171 (Petroleum Bulk Stations & Terminals). **Est:** 1973. **Sales:** $36,000,000 (2000). **Emp:** 37. **Officers:** Gary M. Reeder, President; Grace Reeder, CFO; Jimmy D. Norman, General Mgr.

■ 22618 ■ Reeled Tubing Inc.
206 Gunther Ln.
Belle Chasse, LA 70037
Phone: (504)393-7880
Products: Petroleum products. **SIC:** 5172 (Petroleum Products Nec).

■ 22619 ■ Region Oil Div.
PO Box 828
Dover, NJ 07802-0828
Phone: (973)366-3100   **Fax:** (908)328-4738
Products: Fuel oil. **SIC:** 5172 (Petroleum Products Nec). **Sales:** $49,000,000 (1994). **Emp:** 100. **Officers:** Bill Oliver, Manager; Richard Oakley, Controller.

■ 22620 ■ Reif Oil Co.
911 Osborn St.
Burlington, IA 52601-5023
Phone: (319)752-9809
Free: (800)582-5673   **Fax:** (319)753-6624
Products: Fuel oil; C-stores. **SICs:** 5172 (Petroleum Products Nec); 5172 (Petroleum Products Nec). **Est:** 1978. **Sales:** $5,000,000 (2000). **Emp:** 96. **Officers:** Clifford Reif, e-mail: cliff@reifoil.com; Robert Walters; Doug Stewart; Harry Zippe.

■ 22621 ■ Reinauer Petroleum Co.
3 University Plz., #606
Hackensack, NJ 07601
Phone: (201)489-9700   **Fax:** (201)489-0097
Products: Petroleum products. **SIC:** 5172 (Petroleum Products Nec). **Sales:** $5,000,000 (2000). **Emp:** 7. **Officers:** B.F. Reinauer III, President & Treasurer; J. Adams, Controller.

■ 22622 ■ Republic Supply Co. (Dallas, Texas)
5646 Milton St., Ste. 800
Dallas, TX 75206
Phone: (214)987-9868   **Fax:** (214)692-7700
Products: Oil field supplies. **SIC:** 5084 (Industrial Machinery & Equipment). **Sales:** $75,000,000 (1992). **Emp:** 240. **Officers:** Frank M. Late, President; Victor Heffesse, Treasurer & Secty.

■ 22623 ■ Retif Oil and Fuel Inc.
PO Box 58349
New Orleans, LA 70158-8349
Phone: (504)349-9000
Products: Petroleum products. **SIC:** 5172 (Petroleum Products Nec).

■ 22624 ■ Rex Oil Company Inc.
PO Box 1050
Thomasville, NC 27360
Phone: (919)472-3000   **Fax:** (919)472-3368
Products: Industrial lubricants. **SIC:** 5172 (Petroleum Products Nec). **Est:** 1933. **Sales:** $14,000,000 (2000).

Emp: 30. **Officers:** H.S. Kennedy, President; Jim F. Patton, Comptroller.

■ **22625** ■ **Reynolds Industries Inc.**
(Watertown, Massachusetts)
33 Mount Auburn St.
Watertown, MA 02472
Phone: (617)924-4650 **Fax:** (617)923-9019
Products: Fuel. **SIC:** 5172 (Petroleum Products Nec).
Est: 1945. **Sales:** $12,000,000 (2000). **Emp:** 40.
Officers: Philip Reynolds, CEO & President.

■ **22626** ■ **Rhodes Oil Co.**
PO Box 557
Cape Girardeau, MO 63701
Phone: (573)334-7733 **Fax:** (573)334-2578
Products: Gas and oil. **SIC:** 5172 (Petroleum Products Nec). **Est:** 1955. **Sales:** $50,000,000 (2000). **Emp:** 150. **Officers:** Francis E. Rhodes, President; Jim Mauerer, General Mgr.; Paul Dirberger, Dir. of Marketing.

■ **22627** ■ **Rice Oil Company Inc.**
34 Montague City Rd.
Greenfield, MA 01302
Phone: (413)772-0227
Products: Gasoline and oil; Ice. **SICs:** 5172 (Petroleum Products Nec); 5199 (Nondurable Goods Nec). **Sales:** $24,000,000 (2000). **Emp:** 180. **Officers:** Timothy Rice, President; R. Krietz, Controller.

■ **22628** ■ **L.S. Riggins Oil Co.**
3938 S Main Rd.
Vineland, NJ 08360
Phone: (609)825-7600
Products: Gasoline, kerosene, and fuel oil. **SIC:** 5172 (Petroleum Products Nec). **Est:** 1925. **Sales:** $34,000,000 (2000). **Emp:** 50. **Officers:** R. Paul Riggins, President.

■ **22629** ■ **W.H. Riley and Son Inc.**
PO Box 910
North Attleboro, MA 02761
Phone: (508)699-4651
Products: Fuel; Oil. **SIC:** 5172 (Petroleum Products Nec). **Est:** 1873. **Sales:** $10,600,000 (2000). **Emp:** 25. **Officers:** Warren B. Allen, President; Jean Pasquantonio, Treasurer.

■ **22630** ■ **Risser Oil Corp.**
2865 Executive Dr.
Clearwater, FL 33762
Phone: (813)573-4000 **Free:** (800)572-0075
E-mail: kristend@heronholdings.com
Products: Petroleum, including oil and gasoline. **SIC:** 5172 (Petroleum Products Nec). **Est:** 1960. **Sales:** $62,000,000 (1999). **Officers:** P.N. Risser III, President; Sharon Harrison, CFO.

■ **22631** ■ **Rite Way Oil and Gas Company Inc.**
PO Box 27049
Omaha, NE 68127-0049
Phone: (402)331-6400 **Fax:** (402)331-7408
Products: Gasoline. **SIC:** 5172 (Petroleum Products Nec). **Est:** 1965. **Sales:** $52,000,000 (2000). **Emp:** 135. **Officers:** Rex E. Ekwall, President; John D. Carpenter, Treasurer & Secty.

■ **22632** ■ **River City Petroleum Inc.**
840 Delta Ln.
West Sacramento, CA 95691
Phone: (916)371-4960
Products: Petroleum. **SIC:** 5172 (Petroleum Products Nec). **Est:** 1984. **Sales:** $180,000,000 (2000). **Emp:** 150. **Officers:** Leonard D. Robinson, CEO & President; David Ward, Controller.

■ **22633** ■ **James River Petroleum Inc.**
PO Box 7200
Richmond, VA 23221
Phone: (804)358-9000 **Fax:** (804)359-6307
Products: Petroleum. **SIC:** 5172 (Petroleum Products Nec). **Est:** 1985. **Sales:** $4,000,000 (2000). **Emp:** 20. **Officers:** Lloyd T. Little, CEO; Lewis R. Little, CFO.

■ **22634** ■ **RKA Petroleum Companies, L.L.C.**
29120 Wick Rd.
Romulus, MI 48174
Phone: (734)947-1811
Free: (800)922-9911 **Fax:** (734)946-1920
E-mail: info@rkapetroleum.com
URL: http://www.rkapetroleum.com
Products: Petroleum products, including gasoline and oil; Aviation fuel; Diesel Work clothing. **SIC:** 5172 (Petroleum Products Nec). **Est:** 1951. **Sales:** $50,000,000 (2000). **Emp:** 70. **Officers:** Roger K. Albertie, President; Keith Albertie, e-mail: Kelliott@rkapetroleum.com; Kari Elliott, Controller, e-mail: Pvanleuven@rkapetroleum.com; Patty Van Leuven, Human Resources Contact, e-mail: Kelliott@rkapetroleum.com; Patty Van Leuven, Human Resources Contact, e-mail: Pvanleuven@rkapetroleum.com. **Former Name:** Leemon Oil Company Inc. **Former Name:** Marathon Fuels. **Former Name:** Shores Oil. **Former Name:** Rex Carriers. **Former Name:** Express Fueling.

■ **22635** ■ **Roland J. Robert Distributors Inc.**
PO Box 70
Burnside, LA 70738
Phone: (504)644-4886 **Fax:** (504)473-1197
Products: Petroleum products, including gasoline, oil, and diesel fuel; Lubricants. **SIC:** 5172 (Petroleum Products Nec). **Est:** 1924. **Sales:** $30,000,000 (2000). **Emp:** 30. **Officers:** Gayle T. Robert, President; Peter M. Graffaginno, Controller; Harold Higgins, Dir. of Sales.

■ **22636** ■ **F.L. Roberts and Company Inc.**
93 W Broad St.
Springfield, MA 01105
Phone: (413)781-7444 **Fax:** (413)781-4328
Products: Gasoline; Fuel oil. **SIC:** 5172 (Petroleum Products Nec). **Sales:** $32,000,000 (2000). **Emp:** 50. **Officers:** Steven Roberts, President.

■ **22637** ■ **Rock Valley Oil and Chemical Company Inc.**
1911 Windsor Rd.
Loves Park, IL 61111
Phone: (815)654-2400 **Fax:** (815)654-2428
URL: http://www.rockvalleyoil.com
Products: Lubricating and motor oils; Chemicals. **SICs:** 5169 (Chemicals & Allied Products Nec); 5172 (Petroleum Products Nec). **Est:** 1971. **Sales:** $12,800,000 (2000). **Emp:** 37. **Officers:** J. Moberg, General Mgr.; R.L. Schramm, President; James C. Lang, Marketing Mgr., e-mail: jlang@rockvalleyoil.com.

■ **22638** ■ **Romanelli and Son Inc.**
PO Box 544
Lindenhurst, NY 11757
Phone: (516)454-7500
Products: Fuel oil. **SIC:** 5172 (Petroleum Products Nec).

■ **22639** ■ **Rosebud Farmers Union Cooperative Associates Inc.**
PO Box 24 A, RR 2
Gregory, SD 57533
Phone: (605)835-9656
Products: Petroleum products and farm supplies.oline station. **SICs:** 5172 (Petroleum Products Nec); 5191 (Farm Supplies). **Sales:** $19,000,000 (2000). **Emp:** 22. **Officers:** Robert Sperl Sr., President; Jerone Frasch, General Manager, Finance.

■ **22640** ■ **Rosetta Oil Inc.**
Rockledge & Robbins
Rockledge, PA 19046
Phone: (215)379-4400 **Fax:** (215)279-4574
Products: Fuel oil. **SIC:** 5171 (Petroleum Bulk Stations & Terminals). **Sales:** $29,000,000 (2000). **Emp:** 45. **Officers:** Don Waldman, President.

■ **22641** ■ **Rosetta Oil Inc.**
1463 Lamberton Rd.
Trenton, NJ 08611
Phone: (609)393-6899
Products: Petroleum. **SIC:** 5171 (Petroleum Bulk Stations & Terminals). **Sales:** $29,000,000 (1991). **Emp:** 45. **Officers:** Don Waldman, President.

■ **22642** ■ **Rosetta Oil Inc. Duck Island Terminal**
1463 Lamberton Rd.
Trenton, NJ 08611
Phone: (609)393-6899 **Fax:** (609)695-2104
Products: Petroleum products, including, fuel oil, diesel fuel, and kerosene. **SICs:** 5171 (Petroleum Bulk Stations & Terminals); 5172 (Petroleum Products Nec). **Sales:** $3,000,000 (2000). **Emp:** 8. **Officers:** Howard Waldman, Manager.

■ **22643** ■ **Royal Fuel Corp.**
101 Lions Dr.
Barrington, IL 60010
Phone: (708)304-4330
Products: Coal and petroleum products. **SICs:** 5052 (Coal, Other Minerals & Ores); 5172 (Petroleum Products Nec). **Sales:** $18,000,000 (1993). **Emp:** 15. **Officers:** Tom F. Murphy, CEO; Patricia Grimes, Accountant.

■ **22644** ■ **Rupp Oil Company Inc.**
PO Box 457
Bay City, MI 48707
Phone: (517)684-5993 **Fax:** (517)684-5995
Products: Gasoline. **SIC:** 5172 (Petroleum Products Nec). **Est:** 1958. **Sales:** $28,000,000 (2000). **Emp:** 5. **Officers:** H.M. Rupp, President; E. Legner, Finance Officer.

■ **22645** ■ **Russell Petroleum Corp.**
PO Box 250330
Montgomery, AL 36125
Phone: (334)834-3750 **Fax:** (334)834-3755
Products: Petroleum products. **SIC:** 5172 (Petroleum Products Nec). **Sales:** $65,000,000 (2000). **Emp:** 100. **Officers:** Wayne Russell, President; Gerry Wood, Controller.

■ **22646** ■ **G.A. Sadowsky and Son Inc.**
PO Drawer D
Dickinson, ND 58601
Phone: (701)225-2713
Products: Petroleum. **SIC:** 5172 (Petroleum Products Nec). **Est:** 1950. **Sales:** $4,000,000 (2000). **Emp:** 5. **Officers:** A.G. Sadowsky, President.

■ **22647** ■ **Sage Creek Refining Co.**
339 Carmon Ave.
Lovell, WY 82431-1603
Products: Gasoline; Convenience store supplies. **SIC:** 5172 (Petroleum Products Nec). **Est:** 1958. **Sales:** $1,250,000 (2000). **Emp:** 13. **Officers:** R.N. Baird, President.

■ **22648** ■ **St. Martin Oil and Gas Inc.**
2040 Terrace Hwy.
St. Martinville, LA 70582
Phone: (318)394-3163 **Fax:** (318)394-7365
E-mail: stmartinoi@aol.com
Products: Fuel; Petroleum products; Batteries; Tires; Hydraulic hoses. **SIC:** 5171 (Petroleum Bulk Stations & Terminals). **Est:** 1925. **Sales:** $5,600,000 (2000). **Emp:** 15. **Officers:** Margaret L. Poirier, CEO; Jimmy Poirier, President.

■ **22649** ■ **Sampson-Bladen Oil Co.**
PO Box 367
Elizabethtown, NC 28337
Phone: (919)862-3197 **Fax:** (919)862-8475
Products: Gasoline and motor oil. **SIC:** 5172 (Petroleum Products Nec). **Est:** 1936. **Sales:** $23,000,000 (2000). **Emp:** 130. **Officers:** R.H. Clark, President; D.R. Clark, Treasurer & Secty.

■ **22650** ■ **Sandy Supply Co.**
PO Box 299
Wooster, OH 44691
Phone: (330)262-1730 **Fax:** (330)262-0635
Products: Oil field supply products. **SIC:** 5084 (Industrial Machinery & Equipment). **Est:** 1949. **Sales:** $3,500,000 (2000). **Emp:** 19. **Officers:** Charles R. Yenne, President; Rick Yenne, VP of Finance; B. Hesser, Dir. of Marketing.

■ 22651 ■ **Santa Fuel Inc.**
154 Admiral St.
PO Box 1141
Bridgeport, CT 06601-1141
Phone: (203)367-3661
Free: (800)93S-ANTA **Fax:** (203)367-2412
Products: Fuels, including oil, gasoline, and diesel.
SIC: 5172 (Petroleum Products Nec). **Sales:**
$97,000,000 (2000). **Emp:** 150. **Officers:** John S.
Santa, President; Kevin Lloyd, CFO.

■ 22652 ■ **Sapp Brothers Petroleum Inc.**
PO Box 37305
Omaha, NE 68137
Phone: (402)895-1380
Products: Petroleum products, including fuel and oil.
SIC: 5172 (Petroleum Products Nec). **Est:** 1971.
Sales: $68,000,000 (2000). **Emp:** 33. **Officers:** William
D. Sapp, President.

■ 22653 ■ **Sawyer Gas Co.**
7162 Phillips Hwy.
Jacksonville, FL 32256
Phone: (904)296-8600
Products: Propane. **SIC:** 5172 (Petroleum Products
Nec).

■ 22654 ■ **Saybeck Inc.**
1045 Airport Blvd.
South San Francisco, CA 94080
Phone: (415)588-3088
Products: Petroleum. **SIC:** 5171 (Petroleum Bulk
Stations & Terminals).

■ 22655 ■ **SBM Drilling Fluids**
15810 Park Ten Pl., Ste. 300
Houston, TX 77084
Phone: (281)578-2919
Products: Drilling fluids for the petroleum industry.
SIC: 5172 (Petroleum Products Nec). **Sales:**
$9,000,000 (1993). **Emp:** 20. **Officers:** Jim Sampey,
President.

■ 22656 ■ **Scana Propane Supply Inc.**
PO Box 640
Sumter, SC 29151-0640
Phone: (803)778-1981 **Fax:** (803)773-9832
Products: Petroleum, fuels, and related equipment.
SIC: 5172 (Petroleum Products Nec). **Sales:**
$40,000,000 (2000). **Emp:** 220.

■ 22657 ■ **Fred M. Schildwachter and Sons
Inc.**
1400 Ferris Pl.
Bronx, NY 10461
Phone: (212)828-2500 **Fax:** (212)828-3661
Products: Fuel oil. **SIC:** 5172 (Petroleum Products
Nec). **Sales:** $57,000,000 (2000). **Emp:** 80. **Officers:**
Daniel A. Schildwacter Jr., CEO.

■ 22658 ■ **Schmuckal Oil Co.**
1516 Barlow
Traverse City, MI 49686
Phone: (231)946-2800 **Fax:** (231)941-7435
URL: http://www.schmuckaloil.com
Products: Petroleum products. **SIC:** 5172 (Petroleum
Products Nec). **Est:** 1945. **Sales:** $50,000,000 (1999).
Emp: 300. **Officers:** Arthur Schmuckal, Chairman of
the Board; Paul Schmuckal, President; Barbara
Benson, Vice President.

■ 22659 ■ **Scullin Oil Co.**
PO Box 350
Sunbury, PA 17801
Phone: (717)286-4519
Products: Fuel oil, including home heating, gasoline,
and diesel. **SIC:** 5172 (Petroleum Products Nec). **Est:**
1939. **Sales:** $14,000,000 (2000). **Emp:** 96. **Officers:**
R.K. Scullin, President.

■ 22660 ■ **Sellers Oil Co.**
PO Box 1907
Bainbridge, GA 31717
Phone: (912)246-0646
Products: Gasoline, oil, and diesel fuel. **SIC:** 5172
(Petroleum Products Nec).

■ 22661 ■ **September Enterprises Inc.**
PO Box 980804
Houston, TX 77098
Phone: (713)520-0359 **Fax:** (713)520-8751
Products: Drilling equipment; Alloys, including metal
tubing; Truck parts; Oil field equipment. **SICs:** 5084
(Industrial Machinery & Equipment); 5051 (Metals
Service Centers & Offices); 5013 (Motor Vehicle
Supplies & New Parts). **Officers:** A.F. Vazquez,
Contact.

■ 22662 ■ **Service Oil Company Inc.**
PO Box 446
Colby, KS 67701
Phone: (785)462-3441 **Fax:** (785)462-3153
Products: Petroleum products, including diesel and
gasoline. **SIC:** 5172 (Petroleum Products Nec). **Est:**
1924. **Sales:** $8,000,000 (2000). **Emp:** 45. **Officers:**
R.W. Edgar, President.

■ 22663 ■ **Service Oil Inc.**
1718 E Main
West Fargo, ND 58078
Phone: (701)277-1050
Products: Petroleum gas. **SIC:** 5171 (Petroleum Bulk
Stations & Terminals). **Sales:** $43,000,000 (1994).
Emp: 150. **Officers:** Steven D. Lenthe, President;
Cindy Keller, Finance General Manager.

■ 22664 ■ **Sharp Oil Company Inc.**
PO Box 2645
Anthony, NM 88021
Phone: (505)882-2512
Products: Petroleum. **SIC:** 5172 (Petroleum Products
Nec). **Sales:** $6,000,000 (1994). **Emp:** 25. **Officers:**
Jack B. Sharp, Owner.

■ 22665 ■ **Shelby Industries Inc.**
PO Box 88
La Follette, TN 37766
Phone: (423)562-3361 **Fax:** (423)562-3182
Products: Petroleum products, including gasoline and
diesel fuel. **SIC:** 5172 (Petroleum Products Nec). **Est:**
1959. **Sales:** $12,000,000 (2000). **Emp:** 70. **Officers:**
Patricia A. Shelby, President; Floyd O. Burris, Vice
President.

■ 22666 ■ **Shell Lake Cooperative**
331 Hwy. 63
Shell Lake, WI 54871
Phone: (715)468-2302
Products: Petroleum products, crop protection
supplies including pesticides and herbicides. **SICs:**
5172 (Petroleum Products Nec); 5191 (Farm Supplies).
Est: 1934. **Sales:** $10,000,000 (2000). **Emp:** 35.
Officers: Gary Sutherland, President & General Mgr.

■ 22667 ■ **Shields Harper and Co.**
5107 Broadway
Oakland, CA 94611
Phone: (510)653-9119
Products: Petroleum tanks and pumps. **SICs:** 5039
(Construction Materials Nec); 5088 (Transportation
Equipment & Supplies). **Est:** 1917. **Sales:** $20,000,000
(2000). **Emp:** 48. **Officers:** N.I. Kemsley, President; J.
Fuchs, VP of Finance; B. Scowley, VP of Marketing;
William Leyva, Dir. of Information Systems.

■ 22668 ■ **Shipley Oil Co.**
550 E King St.
York, PA 17405
Phone: (717)848-4100 **Fax:** (717)853-5496
Products: Home heating oil; Home heaters and air
conditioners. **SICs:** 5172 (Petroleum Products Nec);
5074 (Plumbing & Hydronic Heating Supplies); 5075
(Warm Air Heating & Air-Conditioning). **Est:** 1929.
Sales: $80,000,000 (2000). **Emp:** 350. **Officers:** W.S.
Shipley III, President & Chairman of the Board; D.
Wilson, Exec. VP & CFO; R.C. Borden Jr., VP of
Marketing.

■ 22669 ■ **Shipley-Phillips Inc.**
PO Box 1047
Tucumcari, NM 88401
Phone: (505)461-1730 **Fax:** (505)461-2877
Products: Gas and fuel. **SIC:** 5172 (Petroleum
Products Nec). **Est:** 1959. **Sales:** $35,100,000 (2000).
Emp: 120. **Officers:** M.E. Phillips, President; Edgar H.

Shipley Jr., VP & Secty.; Donald Shipley, Vice
President.

■ 22670 ■ **Sico Co.**
15 Mount Joy St.
Mt. Joy, PA 17552
Phone: (717)653-1411 **Fax:** (717)653-2302
Products: Petroleum products, including gasoline,
diesel, kerosene, fuel oil, and lubricants. **SIC:** 5172
(Petroleum Products Nec). **Est:** 1876. **Sales:**
$190,000,000 (2000). **Emp:** 400. **Officers:** Franklin R.
Eichler, President; Harrison Diehl; Michael Reese, VP
of Marketing; Charles Ricedorf, VP of Operations;
Thomas Ruffner, Dir of Human Resources.

■ 22671 ■ **Siegel Oil Co.**
1380 Zuni St.
Denver, CO 80204
Phone: (303)893-3211 **Fax:** (303)595-8741
Products: Industrial lubricants. **SICs:** 5171 (Petroleum
Bulk Stations & Terminals); 5172 (Petroleum Products
Nec). **Est:** 1927. **Sales:** $22,000,000 (2000). **Emp:** 58.
Officers: Larry Siegel, President; Lynn Byrd, CFO;
Donald Siegel, General Mgr.

■ 22672 ■ **Sierra Airgas Inc.**
PO Box 19252
Sacramento, CA 95819
Phone: (916)454-9353
Products: Industrial gases. **SIC:** 5169 (Chemicals &
Allied Products Nec). **Sales:** $43,000,000 (2000).
Emp: 235. **Officers:** K. John Nacey, CEO.

■ 22673 ■ **Sinclair Oil Corp.**
PO Box 30825
Salt Lake City, UT 84130
Phone: (801)524-2700 **Fax:** (801)322-2762
Products: Gasoline. **SIC:** 5172 (Petroleum Products
Nec). **Sales:** $1,930,000,000 (2000). **Emp:** 3,900.
Officers: Peter Johnson, President; Charles Barlow,
VP of Finance.

■ 22674 ■ **Sinclair Oil Corp. Eastern Region**
3401 Fairbanks Ave.
Kansas City, KS 66106
Phone: (913)321-3700
Products: Crude oil. **SIC:** 5172 (Petroleum Products
Nec). **Est:** 1916. **Sales:** $12,000,000 (2000). **Emp:** 25.
Officers: R.S. Helton, Manager.

■ 22675 ■ **Sioux Valley Cooperative**
PO Box 965
Watertown, SD 57201
Phone: (605)886-5829
Products: Fuels, including gas, diesel, and kerosene.
SIC: 5172 (Petroleum Products Nec). **Est:** 1956.
Sales: $7,000,000 (2000). **Emp:** 23. **Officers:** Jim
Comes, President; Vincent Rics, Treasurer & Secty.;
Dale Zirbel, President.

■ 22676 ■ **Slick 50 Corp.**
1187 Brittmoore Rd.
Houston, TX 77043
Phone: (713)932-9954 **Fax:** (713)932-0853
Products: Petroleum, fuels, and related equipment.
SIC: 5172 (Petroleum Products Nec). **Sales:**
$110,000,000 (2000). **Emp:** 80.

■ 22677 ■ **Smith Brothers of Dudley Inc.**
PO Box 10
Dudley, NC 28333
Phone: (919)735-2764
Products: Fuel oil. **SIC:** 5172 (Petroleum Products
Nec). **Sales:** $15,000,000 (2000). **Emp:** 25. **Officers:**
William H. Smith, President.

■ 22678 ■ **Glenn Smith Oil Co.**
4 W Martin Luther King St.
Muskogee, OK 74401
Phone: (918)682-2212
Products: Oil. **SIC:** 5172 (Petroleum Products Nec).

■ 22679 ■ **Smith Oil Company Inc.**
PO Box 1719
Clinton, OK 73601
Phone: (580)323-2929
Products: Petroleum products, including gasoline,
diesel, and kerosene. **SIC:** 5172 (Petroleum Products
Nec). **Est:** 1955. **Sales:** $25,400,000 (2000). **Emp:** 95.

Officers: Elmer M. Smith, President; Kaylon Smith, CFO.

■ 22680 ■ SMO Inc.
6355 Crain Hwy.
La Plata, MD 20646
Phone: (301)934-8101
Products: Fuel oil. **SIC:** 5172 (Petroleum Products Nec). **Est:** 1926. **Sales:** $99,000,000 (2000). **Emp:** 200. **Officers:** Lock Wills Jr., President & COO; Charles Boyers, VP of Finance.

■ 22681 ■ Sooner Pipe Inc.
PO Box 1530
Tulsa, OK 74101
Phone: (918)587-3391 **Fax:** (918)587-0863
URL: http://www.soonerpipe.com
Products: Oilfield tubular products. **SIC:** 5084 (Industrial Machinery & Equipment). **Est:** 1937. **Emp:** 100. **Officers:** Mike Chaddick, COO, e-mail: mike_chaddick@soonerpipe.com;Chris Cragg, CFO, e-mail: chris_cragg@soonerpipe.com. **Former Name:** Sooner Pipe and Supply Corp.

■ 22682 ■ Southern Company Inc.
PO Box 343
Williamsburg, VA 23187-0343
Phone: (757)229-2311
Products: Gasoline and petroleum equipment. **SIC:** 5084 (Industrial Machinery & Equipment). **Est:** 1944. **Sales:** $9,000,000 (2000). **Emp:** 65. **Officers:** Pete Shearon, President; Julie Milborne, Vice President; Todd Shearon, VP of Sales.

■ 22683 ■ Southern LNG Inc.
PO Box 2563
Birmingham, AL 35202
Phone: (205)325-7410
Products: Liquefied natural gas. **SIC:** 5172 (Petroleum Products Nec). **Sales:** $10,000,000 (2000). **Emp:** 35. **Officers:** William Smith, President; Tom W. Barker Jr., Treasurer.

■ 22684 ■ Southern Valley Co-op
301 W Mabel St.
Mankato, MN 56001
Phone: (507)625-7077 **Fax:** (507)388-6731
Products: Petroleum. **SIC:** 5172 (Petroleum Products Nec). **Est:** 1935. **Sales:** $17,000,000 (2000). **Emp:** 39. **Officers:** Doug Fitsky, President; Donald Peterson, General Mgr.

■ 22685 ■ Southwest Energy Distributors Inc.
415 N Grant Ave.
Odessa, TX 79760
Phone: (915)332-1301
Products: Fuel. **SIC:** 5172 (Petroleum Products Nec). **Est:** 1982. **Sales:** $32,000,000 (2000). **Emp:** 110. **Officers:** Clay Wood, President; Donald Wood, Treasurer & Secty.

■ 22686 ■ Southwest Grain Farm Marketing and Supply Div.
PO Box 239
Lemmon, SD 57638
Phone: (605)374-3301
Products: Fuel, including gasoline; Batteries; Grain; Feed; Chemicals. **SICs:** 5153 (Grain & Field Beans); 5171 (Petroleum Bulk Stations & Terminals). **Est:** 1914. **Sales:** $17,000,000 (2000). **Emp:** 16. **Officers:** Bob Stevens, General Mgr.

■ 22687 ■ Spartan Oil Co.
PO Box 710
Dover, NJ 07802-0710
Phone: (973)328-3434
Free: (800)246-4942 **Fax:** (908)328-4783
E-mail: sales@spartanonline.com
URL: http://www.spartanonline.com
Products: Motor fuels; Automotive and industrial lubricants. **SIC:** 5172 (Petroleum Products Nec). **Est:** 1940. **Sales:** $30,000,000 (2000). **Emp:** 60. **Officers:** D.J. Gilbride, CEO; J. Squeri, VP & General Mgr.

■ 22688 ■ Spartan Petroleum Company Inc.
PO Box 307
Cliffside, NC 28024-0307
Phone: (704)453-7351 **Fax:** (704)453-0165
Products: Gas and motor oil. **SICs:** 5171 (Petroleum

Bulk Stations & Terminals); 5172 (Petroleum Products Nec). **Est:** 1938. **Sales:** $1,000,000 (2000). **Emp:** 2. **Officers:** Michael J. Frost, CEO; Hampton Hager, Sr. VP & CFO; John Thornton, General Mgr.

■ 22689 ■ Speaks Oil Company Inc.
PO Box 68
Camden, SC 29020
Phone: (803)432-3501
Products: Gasoline; Fuel; Motor oil. **SIC:** 5172 (Petroleum Products Nec). **Est:** 1936. **Sales:** $9,000,000 (2000). **Emp:** 23. **Officers:** J.R. Speaks, President; Joe B. McCarley, Controller.

■ 22690 ■ Spear Oil Co.
PO Box 128
Lapine, AL 36046
Phone: (205)537-4334
Products: Oil and gasoline. **SIC:** 5172 (Petroleum Products Nec). **Sales:** $3,000,000 (2000). **Emp:** 5. **Officers:** Dee Hawk, President & CFO.

■ 22691 ■ Spencer Companies Inc. (Huntsville, Alabama)
PO Box 18128
Huntsville, AL 35804
Phone: (256)533-1150 **Fax:** (256)535-2910
Products: Petroleum products. **SIC:** 5172 (Petroleum Products Nec). **Sales:** $58,000,000 (2000). **Emp:** 150. **Officers:** Guy J. Spencer Jr., CEO & President; Randall G. Birdsong, CFO.

■ 22692 ■ M. Spiegel and Sons Oil Corp.
10 E Village Rd.
Tuxedo, NY 10987
Phone: (914)351-4701 **Fax:** (914)351-4694
Products: Fuels, including oil, gasoline, and diesel fuel; Heating equipment. **SICs:** 5172 (Petroleum Products Nec); 5084 (Industrial Machinery & Equipment). **Est:** 1964. **Sales:** $18,500,000 (2000). **Emp:** 25. **Officers:** Richard Spiegel, President; Linda Wilkinson, Comptroller; Robert Spiegel, Secretary.

■ 22693 ■ Sprague Energy Corp.
195 Hanover St., Ste. 1
Portsmouth, NH 03801-3771
Phone: (603)431-1000 **Fax:** (603)431-6371
Products: Distillate and residual fuels, including natural gas and coal; liquid and solid bulk material handling. **SICs:** 5172 (Petroleum Products Nec); 5052 (Coal, Other Minerals & Ores); 5084 (Industrial Machinery & Equipment). **Est:** 1876. **Sales:** $500,000,000 (2000). **Emp:** 200. **Officers:** James M. Kantelis, CEO & President.

■ 22694 ■ Sprague Energy Corp.
195 Hanover St., Ste. 1
Portsmouth, NH 03801-3771
Phone: (603)431-1000 **Fax:** (603)431-6371
Products: Petroleum, fuels, and related equipment. **SIC:** 5172 (Petroleum Products Nec). **Sales:** $500,000,000 (2000). **Emp:** 200.

■ 22695 ■ Spruill Oil Company Inc.
310 U.S Hwy. 13-17 S
Windsor, NC 27983
Phone: (252)794-4027
Products: Petroleum products. **SIC:** 5172 (Petroleum Products Nec). **Sales:** $36,000,000 (1994). **Emp:** 75. **Officers:** Charles T. Spruill, President; Charles Whitehead, Finance General Manager.

■ 22696 ■ Squibb-Taylor Inc.
10480 Shady Trail, No. 106
Dallas, TX 75220-2533
Phone: (214)357-4591
Products: Propane equipment, including pumps, valves, and gauges. **SICs:** 5084 (Industrial Machinery & Equipment); 5085 (Industrial Supplies). **Est:** 1947. **Sales:** $12,000,000 (2000). **Emp:** 24. **Officers:** Milford Therrell, President; Jack Potts, Controller.

■ 22697 ■ S.T. and H. Oil Company Inc.
101 W Huron Ave.
Bad Axe, MI 48413
Phone: (517)269-6447 **Fax:** (517)269-6448
Products: Gasoline, fuel oil and diesel oil. **SIC:** 5171 (Petroleum Bulk Stations & Terminals). **Est:** 1925. **Sales:** $2,000,000 (2000). **Emp:** 6. **Officers:** Gib

Rooney, President; Jerome Bouverette, Treasurer & Secty.

■ 22698 ■ Stahl Oil Company Inc.
PO Box 773
Somerset, PA 15501
Phone: (814)443-2615
Products: Oil, petroleum, and gasoline. **SIC:** 5172 (Petroleum Products Nec). **Est:** 1976. **Sales:** $10,000,000 (2000). **Emp:** 17. **Officers:** Ernest E. Stahl, President.

■ 22699 ■ Standard Cycle and Auto Supply Co.
22 Rowley St.
Winsted, CT 06098
Phone: (860)489-4183 **Fax:** (203)738-0945
Products: Home heating oil; Gasoline. **SIC:** 5172 (Petroleum Products Nec). **Est:** 1915. **Sales:** $30,000,000 (2000). **Emp:** 65. **Officers:** David Dolinsky, CEO & President; Candice Campetti, Controller.

■ 22700 ■ Standish Oil Co.
PO Box 457
Bay City, MI 48707-0457
Phone: (517)846-6961
Products: Gasoline; Fuel oil. **SICs:** 5171 (Petroleum Bulk Stations & Terminals); 5172 (Petroleum Products Nec). **Est:** 1930. **Sales:** $6,000,000 (2000). **Emp:** 9. **Officers:** Robert M. Neering, President; Edward C. Legner, CFO.

■ 22701 ■ Star Oil Company Inc.
PO Box 610867
Port Huron, MI 48061-0867
Phone: (810)985-9586 **Fax:** (810)985-7134
Products: Gasoline and motor oil. **SICs:** 5171 (Petroleum Bulk Stations & Terminals); 5172 (Petroleum Products Nec). **Est:** 1920. **Sales:** $16,000,000 (2000). **Emp:** 17. **Officers:** C.A. Kellerman, President; Ruth E. Piechowiak, Controller.

■ 22702 ■ State Gas and Oil Co.
110 Village Dr.
State College, PA 16803
Phone: (814)237-4355
Products: Heating oil; Kerosene. **SIC:** 5172 (Petroleum Products Nec). **Est:** 1924. **Emp:** 10. **Officers:** Charles R. Markham, President & COO; J. Kirk Gallaher, Exec. VP & CFO; Chuck Bower, Vice President.

■ 22703 ■ Stein Distributing
1013 Express Dr.
Belleville, IL 62223
Phone: (618)398-2902 **Fax:** (618)398-0810
Products: Motor oil; Oil filters. **SICs:** 5013 (Motor Vehicle Supplies & New Parts); 5172 (Petroleum Products Nec). **Est:** 1954. **Sales:** $10,000,000 (2000). **Emp:** 6. **Officers:** Frederick A. Stein, Owner.

■ 22704 ■ Stem Brothers Inc.
PO Box T
Milford, NJ 08848
Phone: (908)995-4825 **Fax:** (908)996-3508
Products: Oil. **SIC:** 5172 (Petroleum Products Nec). **Est:** 1960. **Sales:** $4,500,000 (2000). **Emp:** 33. **Officers:** Richard Stem, President; Craig Stem, Treasurer.

■ 22705 ■ Steuart Petroleum Co.
4646 40th NW
Washington, DC 20016
Phone: (202)537-8900 **Fax:** (202)364-0829
Products: Fuels, including gasoline, home heating, diesel, and motor oil. **SIC:** 5172 (Petroleum Products Nec). **Est:** 1905. **Sales:** $910,000,000 (2000). **Emp:** 1,400. **Officers:** John C. Johnson, CEO; Melody Barackman, Controller; Harold G. Youngling, VP of Marketing; Michael Woodruff.

■ 22706 ■ Stinnes Corp.
120 White Plains Rd., 6th Fl.
Tarrytown, NY 10591-5522
Phone: (914)366-7200 **Fax:** (914)366-8226
Products: Oil; Coal. **SICs:** 5169 (Chemicals & Allied Products Nec); 5052 (Coal, Other Minerals & Ores). **Sales:** $430,000,000 (2000). **Emp:** 1,200. **Officers:**

Henning Maier, President; Joseph Groneman, Controller.

■ **22707** ■ **Stockton Oil Co.**
PO Box 1756
Billings, MT 59103
Phone: (406)245-6376
Products: Fuel oil; Gasoline; Diesel fuel; Grease. **SIC:** 5172 (Petroleum Products Nec). **Sales:** $22,000,000 (2000). **Emp:** 17. **Officers:** Dan Stockton, President.

■ **22708** ■ **Stockton Service Corp.**
PO Box 508
Stockton, CA 95201-0508
Phone: (209)464-8333
Products: Service station equipment. **SICs:** 5087 (Service Establishment Equipment); 5013 (Motor Vehicle Supplies & New Parts).

■ **22709** ■ **Stone County Oil Company Inc.**
101 N Commerce St.
Crane, MO 65633
Phone: (417)723-5201 **Fax:** (417)723-8353
Products: Gasoline. **SICs:** 5171 (Petroleum Bulk Stations & Terminals); 5172 (Petroleum Products Nec). **Est:** 1926. **Sales:** $1,000,000 (2000). **Emp:** 2. **Officers:** Robert E. Wilson Sr., President; Robert E. Wilson Jr., VP & Treasurer.

■ **22710** ■ **J.D. Streett and Company Inc.**
144 Weldon Pkwy.
Maryland Heights, MO 63043
Phone: (314)432-6600 **Fax:** (314)567-4182
Products: Oil; Gasoline. **SIC:** 5172 (Petroleum Products Nec). **Est:** 1884. **Sales:** $120,000,000 (2000). **Emp:** 180. **Officers:** Newell A. Baker, Chairman of the Board; Darrell Huisinga, CEO & President.

■ **22711** ■ **Streicher Mobile Fueling Inc.**
2720 NW 55th Ct.
Ft. Lauderdale, FL 33309
Phone: (954)739-3880 **Fax:** (954)739-3842
URL: http://www.mobilefueling.com
Products: Fleet vehicle fuel and fueling. **SIC:** 5172 (Petroleum Products Nec). **Est:** 1996. **Sales:** $74,171,000 (2000). **Emp:** 250. **Officers:** Stanley H. Streicher, CEO & President; Walter B. Barrett, VP of Finance; Steven M. Alford, VP of Operations; Timothy W. Kosholek, VP of Marketing.

■ **22712** ■ **Struthers Industries Inc.**
7633 East 63rd Plaza, Ste. 220
Tulsa, OK 74133
Phone: (918)582-1788
Products: Cottonseed hulls for use in oil drilling. **SIC:** 5159 (Farm-Product Raw Materials Nec). **Sales:** $1,600,000 (2000). **Emp:** 2. **Officers:** G. David Gordon, President & CFO.

■ **22713** ■ **Stuarts' Petroleum Co.**
11 E 4th St.
Bakersfield, CA 93307
Phone: (805)325-6320
Products: Gasoline. **SIC:** 5172 (Petroleum Products Nec).

■ **22714** ■ **Sun Company Inc.**
1801 Market St., 10 Penn Ctr.
Philadelphia, PA 19103-1699
Phone: (215)977-3000 **Fax:** (215)977-3409
Products: Gasoline. **SIC:** 5172 (Petroleum Products Nec). **Sales:** $10,464,000,000 (2000). **Emp:** 10,900. **Officers:** Robert H. Campbell, CEO & Chairman of the Board; Robert M. Aiken Jr., Exec. VP & CFO.

■ **22715** ■ **Supreme Oil Company Inc.**
PO Box 62
New Albany, IN 47151
Phone: (812)945-5266
Products: Fuel, including gasoline and diesel fuel. **SIC:** 5172 (Petroleum Products Nec). **Est:** 1937. **Sales:** $7,000,000 (2000). **Emp:** 17. **Officers:** Lillian B. Sexton, President; Suzy Sexton, Vice President; Ray L. Sexton, President.

■ **22716** ■ **Surner Heating Company Inc.**
60 Shumway St.
Amherst, MA 01002
Phone: (413)253-5999
Products: Diesel and kerosene oil. **SIC:** 5172 (Petroleum Products Nec).

■ **22717** ■ **Sutey Oil CO.**
2000 Holmes Ave.
Butte, MT 59701
Phone: (406)494-2305
Products: Oil. **SIC:** 5172 (Petroleum Products Nec).

■ **22718** ■ **Swifty Oil Company Inc.**
PO Box 1002
Seymour, IN 47274
Phone: (812)522-1640 **Fax:** (812)522-8554
Products: Fuel, including gasoline and diesel fuel. **SIC:** 5172 (Petroleum Products Nec). **Est:** 1963. **Sales:** $200,000,000 (2000). **Emp:** 800. **Officers:** Donald W. Myers Jr., President; Bill Klinger, Controller; Don Marcum, Dir. of Marketing; Tom Bullaud, Dir. of Data Processing; Paul Ertel, Controller.

■ **22719** ■ **Switzer Petroleum Products**
PO Box 860343
Plano, TX 75086
Phone: (972)423-0173 **Fax:** (972)423-8171
Products: Gasoline; Lubricating oils and greases. **SIC:** 5172 (Petroleum Products Nec). **Est:** 1968. **Sales:** $4,000,000 (2000). **Emp:** 10. **Officers:** E.W. Switzer, President.

■ **22720** ■ **Taconite Oil Company Inc.**
810 Hoover Rd.
Virginia, MN 55792
Phone: (218)741-3350
Products: Oil. **SIC:** 5171 (Petroleum Bulk Stations & Terminals). **Est:** 1946. **Sales:** $4,000,000 (2000). **Emp:** 10. **Officers:** John C. Carlsen, President.

■ **22721** ■ **Tauber Oil Co.**
PO Box 4645
Houston, TX 77210
Phone: (713)869-8700 **Fax:** (713)869-8069
E-mail: tauber@tauberoil.com
Products: Gasoline; Petroleum; LPG. **SIC:** 5172 (Petroleum Products Nec). **Est:** 1953. **Sales:** $901,000,000 (1999). **Emp:** 52. **Officers:** David W. Tauber, Principal; Stephen E. Hamlin, VP of Finance; Richard F. Tauber, Principal.

■ **22722** ■ **Teeco Products Inc.**
16881 Armstrong Ave.
Irvine, CA 92614
Phone: (714)261-6295
Products: Propane fittings, valves. **SIC:** 5074 (Plumbing & Hydronic Heating Supplies). **Est:** 1948. **Sales:** $12,000,000 (2000). **Emp:** 100. **Officers:** D.M. Etter, President; Gary Childress, CFO; Michael Parkinson, Marketing Mgr.

■ **22723** ■ **TENGASCO Inc.**
4928 Humberg Dr., Ste. B-3
Knoxville, TN 37902-2609
Phone: (423)523-1124
Products: Oil and gas. **SIC:** 5149 (Groceries & Related Products Nec). **Sales:** $13,000,000 (2000). **Emp:** 25. **Officers:** Ted Scallan, President.

■ **22724** ■ **Tenneco Energy Resources Corp.**
PO Box 2511
Houston, TX 77252
Phone: (713)757-2131
Products: Gasoline. **SIC:** 5172 (Petroleum Products Nec).

■ **22725** ■ **Tenneco Gas Marketing Co.**
PO Box 2511
Houston, TX 77252-2511
Phone: (713)757-2131
Products: Gasoline. **SIC:** 5172 (Petroleum Products Nec).

■ **22726** ■ **Tesoro Petroleum Corp.**
PO Box 17536
San Antonio, TX 78217
Phone: (210)828-8484 **Fax:** (210)828-8600
Products: Fuel and lubricants. **SIC:** 5172 (Petroleum

Products Nec). **Sales:** $943,400,000 (2000). **Emp:** 1,000. **Officers:** Bruce A. Smith, CEO & President; James C. Reed Jr., Exec. VP of Finance.

■ **22727** ■ **Tesoro Petroleum Distributing Co.**
PO Box 23278
New Orleans, LA 70183
Phone: (504)733-6700 **Fax:** (504)734-8216
Products: Petroleum-based lubricants. **SIC:** 5172 (Petroleum Products Nec). **Est:** 1968. **Sales:** $49,000,000 (2000). **Emp:** 100. **Officers:** George Dogen, Exec. VP; Jerry C. Jotzur, Controller.

■ **22728** ■ **Tesoro Petroleum Distributing Co.**
PO Box 23278
New Orleans, LA 70183
Phone: (504)733-6700 **Fax:** (504)734-8216
Products: Petroleum, fuels, and related equipment. **SIC:** 5172 (Petroleum Products Nec). **Sales:** $49,000,000 (2000). **Emp:** 100.

■ **22729** ■ **Texaco Internatinal Trader, Inc.**
2000 Westchester Ave.
White Plains, NY 10650
Phone: (914)253-4000 **Fax:** (914)253-6266
Products: Fuel oil, including diesel and gasoline; Lubricants. **SIC:** 5172 (Petroleum Products Nec). **Est:** 1905. **Sales:** $6,000,000,000 (2000). **Emp:** 150. **Officers:** R.C. OElkers, President. **Former Name:** Texaco Oil Trading and Supply Co.

■ **22730** ■ **Texaco Oil Co.**
3511 NW Texas
Idabel, OK 74745
Phone: (580)286-3066
Products: Oil. **SIC:** 5172 (Petroleum Products Nec).

■ **22731** ■ **Texaco Trading and Transportation Inc.**
PO Box 5568
Denver, CO 80217
Phone: (303)861-4475 **Fax:** (303)860-3210
Products: Oil. **SIC:** 5172 (Petroleum Products Nec). **Sales:** $470,000,000 (2000). **Emp:** 500. **Officers:** J.E. Shamas, President; Felix C. Spizale, VP of Finance & Admin.; R.G. Lawrence, VP of Marketing; John D. Williamson, Dir. of Information Systems; John C. Fischer, Human Resources Mgr.

■ **22732** ■ **Thaler Oil Company Inc.**
310 S Main St.
Chippewa Falls, WI 54729
Phone: (715)723-2822
Products: Gasoline and motor oil. **SIC:** 5171 (Petroleum Bulk Stations & Terminals). **Est:** 1955. **Sales:** $4,000,000 (2000). **Emp:** 10. **Officers:** G.W. Thaler, President.

■ **22733** ■ **Thibaut Oil Company Inc.**
PO Box 270
Donaldsonville, LA 70346
Phone: (504)473-1300 **Fax:** (504)473-4973
Products: Oil and gas. **SIC:** 5172 (Petroleum Products Nec). **Est:** 1974. **Sales:** $4,000,000 (2000). **Emp:** 9. **Officers:** Thomas A. Thibaut, President.

■ **22734** ■ **Thompson Oil Co.**
PO Box 589
Waynesboro, PA 17268
Phone: (717)762-3011
Products: Fuel oil, including kerosene. **SICs:** 5171 (Petroleum Bulk Stations & Terminals); 5172 (Petroleum Products Nec). **Est:** 1928. **Sales:** $3,000,000 (2000). **Emp:** 7. **Officers:** Alfred S. Bendell, Owner.

■ **22735** ■ **Thornhill Oil Company Inc.**
2920 Connett Ave.
Ft. Wayne, IN 46802
Phone: (219)432-9407
Products: Oil. **SIC:** 5172 (Petroleum Products Nec). **Est:** 1953. **Sales:** $50,000,000 (2000). **Emp:** 100. **Officers:** Amie J. Klimczak, President; Stan Jay, General Mgr.

■ 22736 ■ **Time Oil Co.**
PO Box 24447
Seattle, WA 98124
Phone: (206)285-2400 **Fax:** (206)283-8036
Products: Gasoline. **SIC:** 5171 (Petroleum Bulk
Stations & Terminals). **Est:** 1941. **Sales:** $270,000,000
(2000). **Emp:** 200. **Officers:** H. Roger Holliday,
President; Dave Rietmann, CFO; Lynn C. Tierney,
Terminal Marketing Contact.

■ 22737 ■ **Tippins Oil and Gas Company Inc.**
PO Box 98
Richmond, MO 64085
Phone: (816)776-5558 **Fax:** (816)781-5082
Products: Fuel, including diesel and gasoline. **SICs:**
5171 (Petroleum Bulk Stations & Terminals); 5172
(Petroleum Products Nec). **Est:** 1961. **Sales:**
$18,000,000 (2000). **Emp:** 7. **Officers:** Benny Tippins,
President.

■ 22738 ■ **Toms Sierra Company Inc.**
PO Box 759
Colfax, CA 95713
Phone: (530)346-2264
Products: Petroleum products. **SIC:** 5171 (Petroleum
Bulk Stations & Terminals). **Sales:** $117,000,000
(2000). **Emp:** 350. **Officers:** Nick Toms, President;
Claudette Fletcher, Controller.

■ 22739 ■ **Toney Petroleum Inc.**
508 S John St.
Crawfordsville, IN 47933
Phone: (765)362-1800
Free: (800)346-2103 **Fax:** (765)364-4551
Products: Petroleum products, including oil, gasoline,
diesel fuel, and kerosene. **SIC:** 5172 (Petroleum
Products Nec). **Sales:** $14,000,000 (2000). **Emp:** 30.
Officers: Steven Smith, President.

■ 22740 ■ **Toney Petroleum Inc.**
508 S John St.
Crawfordsville, IN 47933
Phone: (765)362-1800
Free: (800)346-2103 **Fax:** (765)364-4551
Products: Petroleum, fuels, and related equipment.
SIC: 5172 (Petroleum Products Nec). **Sales:**
$14,000,000 (2000). **Emp:** 30.

■ 22741 ■ **TOSCO Marketing Co.**
1500 Priest Dr.
Tempe, AZ 85281
Phone: (602)728-8000 **Fax:** (602)728-5234
Products: Oil refining, distribution and retail sales. **SIC:**
5172 (Petroleum Products Nec). **Officers:** Robert
Lavinia, CEO.

■ 22742 ■ **Tower Oil and Technology Co.**
205 W Randolph St.
Chicago, IL 60606
Phone: (312)346-0562 **Fax:** (312)346-6873
Products: Oil. **SIC:** 5172 (Petroleum Products Nec).
Est: 1933. **Sales:** $8,000,000 (2000). **Emp:** 37.
Officers: Al Simon, President; Harry Simon, VP of
Operations; Joseph Hough, Dir. of Marketing & Sales.

■ 22743 ■ **Town Pump Inc.**
600 S Main St.
Butte, MT 59701
Phone: (406)782-9121
Products: Gas; Oil. **SIC:** 5172 (Petroleum Products
Nec).

■ 22744 ■ **Townsend-Strong Inc.**
PO Box 2802
Lubbock, TX 79401
Phone: (806)763-0491
Products: Fuel, including gasoline and kerosene. **SIC:**
5172 (Petroleum Products Nec). **Est:** 1942. **Sales:**
$4,000,000 (2000). **Emp:** 6. **Officers:** Patrick Strong,
President.

■ 22745 ■ **Toyo USA Inc.**
1155 Dairy Ashford, Ste. 805
Houston, TX 77079
Phone: (281)496-4448
Products: Petrochemical industry equipment. **SIC:**
5085 (Industrial Supplies).

■ 22746 ■ **Trans-Tec Services Inc.**
500 Frank W Burr Blvd.
Teaneck, NJ 07666
Phone: (201)692-9292 **Fax:** (201)692-1786
Products: Marine fuel. **SIC:** 5172 (Petroleum Products
Nec). **Sales:** $321,100,000 (2000). **Emp:** 67. **Officers:**
Michael Kasbar, CEO & Chairman of the Board; Paul
Stebbins, President & COO.

■ 22747 ■ **TransMontaigne Product Services
Inc.**
PO Box 1503
Fayetteville, AR 72702
Phone: (501)521-5565 **Fax:** (501)442-4650
Products: Petroleum products. **SIC:** 5172 (Petroleum
Products Nec). **Sales:** $80,000,000 (2000). **Emp:** 120.
Officers: Richard Gathright, President; Rodney Pless,
VP of Finance.

■ 22748 ■ **Dan Trease Distributing Co.**
5600 S 5900 W
Hooper, UT 84315
Phone: (801)773-0450 **Fax:** (801)773-0458
Products: Diesel and gas. **SIC:** 5172 (Petroleum
Products Nec). **Est:** 1959. **Sales:** $6,000,000 (2000).
Emp: 3. **Officers:** Dan Trease, Owner.

■ 22749 ■ **Tri Lakes Petroleum**
E 76 Mt. Branson
Branson, MO 65616
Phone: (417)334-3940
Products: Petroleum products. **SIC:** 5172 (Petroleum
Products Nec).

■ 22750 ■ **Triton Marketing Inc.**
8255 Dunwoody Pl., Bldg. 17, Ste. 100
Atlanta, GA 30350
Phone: (770)992-7088 **Fax:** (770)457-0652
Products: Petroleum products. **SIC:** 5172 (Petroleum
Products Nec). **Sales:** $45,000,000 (2000). **Emp:** 160.
Officers: James Patton, President; Mark Bevill,
Controller. **Former Name:** Triton Inc.

■ 22751 ■ **Troutman Brothers**
PO Box 73
Klingerstown, PA 17941
Phone: (717)425-2341
Products: Petroleum products. **SIC:** 5172 (Petroleum
Products Nec). **Est:** 1931. **Sales:** $10,100,000 (2000).
Emp: 30. **Officers:** Glenn Troutman, Office Mgr.

■ 22752 ■ **Truman Arnold Co.**
PO Box 1481
Texarkana, TX 75504
Phone: (903)794-3835
Products: Petroleum. **SIC:** 5171 (Petroleum Bulk
Stations & Terminals). **Sales:** $500,000,000 (2000).
Emp: 300. **Officers:** Truman Arnold, CEO; Larry
Fincher, Exec. VP & CFO.

■ 22753 ■ **Tulco Oils Inc.**
5240 E Pine St.
Tulsa, OK 74115
Phone: (918)838-3354
Products: Petroleum products. **SIC:** 5172 (Petroleum
Products Nec). **Sales:** $35,000,000 (1993). **Emp:** 60.
Officers: Jeff Cope, CEO; Mike Friedmann, Treasurer.

■ 22754 ■ **Turner Marine Bulk Inc.**
1 Elaine St.
New Orleans, LA 70126-7100
Phone: (504)245-1089
Products: Petroleum. **SIC:** 5171 (Petroleum Bulk
Stations & Terminals). **Sales:** $39,000,000 (1993).
Emp: 130. **Officers:** William Turner, President.

■ 22755 ■ **UCG Energy Corp.**
150 South East Pkwy., PO Box 682028
Franklin, TN 37068
Phone: (615)591-6200
Products: Propane gas. **SIC:** 5172 (Petroleum
Products Nec). **Sales:** $38,400,000 (1994). **Emp:** 128.
Officers: Gene C. Koonce, CEO & President; James
B. Ford, Sr. VP & Treasurer.

■ 22756 ■ **Ultramar Diamond Shamrock Corp.**
6000 N Loop 1604, W
San Antonio, TX 78249-1112
Phone: (210)592-2000 **Fax:** (210)592-2064
Products: Gasoline and other refined petroleum
products. **SIC:** 5172 (Petroleum Products Nec). **Sales:**
$11,134,600,000 (2000). **Emp:** 24,000. **Officers:** Jean
Gaulin, CEO & Chairman of the Board; H. Pete Smith,
Exec. VP & CFO.

■ 22757 ■ **Union Distributing Co.**
4000 E Michigan St.
Tucson, AZ 85714
Phone: (520)571-7600 **Fax:** (520)571-8722
Products: Bulk fuel and oil. **SIC:** 5172 (Petroleum
Products Nec). **Est:** 1986. **Sales:** $20,000,000 (2000).
Emp: 30. **Officers:** David Lueth, President; J. Warren
Lueth, CFO.

■ 22758 ■ **Union Oil Company of Maine**
PO Box 2528
South Portland, ME 04106
Phone: (207)799-1521
Products: Fuel oil. **SIC:** 5172 (Petroleum Products
Nec). **Est:** 1921. **Sales:** $45,000,000 (2000). **Emp:** 65.
Officers: Bernard D. Shapiro, President; Vince
Bouvier, COO.

■ 22759 ■ **UniSource Energy Inc.**
245 W Rosevelt Rd., Bldg. 15
West Chicago, IL 60185
Phone: (630)231-7990 **Fax:** (630)231-8036
Products: Specialty petroleum products. **SIC:** 5172
(Petroleum Products Nec). **Sales:** $3,000,000 (2000).
Emp: 3.

■ 22760 ■ **United Distributing Co.**
101 N Kings Hwy.
Cape Girardeau, MO 63701
Phone: (314)335-3341
Products: Fuel, including motor oil, gasoline and
diesel. **SIC:** 5172 (Petroleum Products Nec). **Est:**
1951. **Sales:** $16,000,000 (2000). **Emp:** 35. **Officers:**
Fred R. Wilferth, President; Jim Wilferth, CFO.

■ 22761 ■ **United Oil of the Carolinas, Inc.**
PO Box 68
Gastonia, NC 28053
Phone: (704)824-3561
Free: (800)277-8541 **Fax:** (704)824-8567
Products: Gasoline; Diesel fuel. **SIC:** 5172 (Petroleum
Products Nec). **Est:** 1938. **Sales:** $38,000,000 (2000).
Emp: 22. **Officers:** D.L. Efird, President; Dick J.
Bedgood, CFO; Tom Glover, Dir. of Marketing.

■ 22762 ■ **United Pride Inc.**
PO Box 84107
Sioux Falls, SD 57118-4707
Phone: (605)336-1558 **Fax:** (605)336-3381
Products: Gasoline; Petroleum and its products. **SICs:**
5171 (Petroleum Bulk Stations & Terminals); 5172
(Petroleum Products Nec). **Est:** 1925. **Sales:**
$7,000,000 (2000). **Emp:** 36. **Officers:** Wayne
Krumvieda, President; Robert C. Johnson, General
Mgr.

■ 22763 ■ **United States Exploration Inc.**
1560 Broadway, Ste. 1900
Denver, CO 80202
Phone: (303)863-3550
Products: Petroleum and gas products. **SIC:** 5172
(Petroleum Products Nec). **Sales:** $17,100,000 (2000).
Emp: 26. **Officers:** Bruce D. Benson, CEO &
Chairman of the Board.

■ 22764 ■ **Universal Companies Inc. (Wichita,
Kansas)**
PO Box 2920
Wichita, KS 67201
Phone: (316)832-0151
Products: Gasoline. **SIC:** 5172 (Petroleum Products
Nec). **Sales:** $25,000,000 (1994). **Emp:** 105.

■ 22765 ■ **Universal Lubricants Inc.**
PO Box 2920
Wichita, KS 67201-2920
Phone: (316)832-0151 **Fax:** (316)832-0301
URL: http://www.universallubes.com
Products: Automotive and industrial lubricants;

Grease; Antifreeze; Hydraulic oils; Gear lubricants; Transmission oils; Engine oils. **SIC:** 5172 (Petroleum Products Nec). **Est:** 1929. **Emp:** 68. **Officers:** Mike Maloney, President; Tim Crowley, Comptroller; Terry Maloney, VP of Marketing; Conald Serrel, Dir. of Data Processing; Josie Salinas, Dir of Human Resources.

■ 22766 ■ **Valley National Gases Inc.**
PO Box 6628
Wheeling, WV 26003-0900
Phone: (304)232-1541   **Fax:** (304)233-2812
Products: Industrial and specialty gases, including propane gas; Welding equipment and supplies. **SICs:** 5169 (Chemicals & Allied Products Nec); 5084 (Industrial Machinery & Equipment). **Sales:** $73,900,000 (2000). **Emp:** 462. **Officers:** Lawrence E. Bandi, CEO & President; Robert D. Scherich, CFO.

■ 22767 ■ **Valley Oil Co.**
PO Box 12249
Salem, OR 97309
Phone: (503)362-3633
Free: (800)322-3233   **Fax:** (503)362-9954
E-mail: webmaster@valleyoilco.com
URL: http://www.valeyoilco.com
Products: Aviation and home heating fuels; Aviation refueler trucks. **SIC:** 5172 (Petroleum Products Nec). **Est:** 1939. **Sales:** $85,000,000 (2000). **Emp:** 75. **Officers:** Mike Delk, President; Jim Green, CFO.

■ 22768 ■ **Van Waters and Rogers Inc.**
3002 F St.
Omaha, NE 68107
Phone: (402)733-3266   **Free:** (800)325-5147
Products: Industrial chemicals. **SIC:** 5169 (Chemicals & Allied Products Nec). **Sales:** $26,000,000 (2000). **Emp:** 35. **Officers:** Barry Kopf, Finance General Manager.

■ 22769 ■ **Van Zeeland Oil Company Inc.**
PO Box 208
Little Chute, WI 54140
Phone: (920)788-7980   **Fax:** (920)788-7983
Products: Gasoline and diesel fuel. **SIC:** 5172 (Petroleum Products Nec). **Est:** 1936. **Sales:** $30,000,000 (2000). **Emp:** 250. **Officers:** Chuck Van Zeeland, President; Gary Strick, Controller.

■ 22770 ■ **Vanguard Petroleum Corp.**
1111 N Loop W, Ste. 1100
Houston, TX 77008
Phone: (713)802-4242   **Fax:** (713)802-4250
Products: Petroleum and liquid petroleum gases. **SIC:** 5172 (Petroleum Products Nec). **Sales:** $300,000,000 (2000). **Emp:** 15. **Officers:** Tom Garner, President; Jack Faubion, CFO.

■ 22771 ■ **Veach Oil Co.**
Hwy. 37 & 146 W
Vienna, IL 62995
Phone: (618)658-2581
Products: Gasoline; Diesel fuel. **SICs:** 5171 (Petroleum Bulk Stations & Terminals); 5172 (Petroleum Products Nec). **Est:** 1925. **Sales:** $16,000,000 (2000). **Emp:** 60. **Officers:** Alan Veach, President; Jesse Veach, Controller.

■ 22772 ■ **Vesco Oil Corp.**
PO Box 525
Southfield, MI 48037-0525
Phone: (810)557-1600
Products: Industrial and automotive oils. **SIC:** 5172 (Petroleum Products Nec). **Est:** 1947. **Sales:** $100,000,000 (2000). **Emp:** 215. **Officers:** Donald Epstein, CEO; Cheryl Reitzloff, CFO.

■ 22773 ■ **Vintage Petroleum Inc.**
110 W 7th St., #2300
Tulsa, OK 74119-1029
Phone: (918)592-0101
Products: Oil and gas. **SIC:** 5172 (Petroleum Products Nec). **Est:** 1983. **Sales:** $311,700,000 (2000). **Emp:** 500. **Officers:** Jo Bob Hille, CEO; William C. Barnes, Exec. VP & CFO; Patrick I. Chapman, VP of Marketing; S. Craig George, COO & Exec. VP.

■ 22774 ■ **Vista Oil Co.**
PO Box 5127
McAllen, TX 78502
Phone: (210)381-0976   **Fax:** (210)383-1744
Products: Oil, gasoline, diesel, and propane gas. **SIC:** 5172 (Petroleum Products Nec). **Est:** 1966. **Sales:** $13,000,000 (2000). **Emp:** 27. **Officers:** Gus E. Clemons Jr., President; Gary Clemons, Treasurer.

■ 22775 ■ **V.T. Petroleum**
412 Metz Rd.
King City, CA 93930
Phone: (408)385-4872
Products: Gas. **SICs:** 5171 (Petroleum Bulk Stations & Terminals); 5172 (Petroleum Products Nec). **Est:** 1970. **Sales:** $3,000,000 (2000). **Emp:** 6. **Officers:** Ron Loudermilk, Manager.

■ 22776 ■ **W-B Supply Co.**
PO Drawer 2479
Pampa, TX 79066-2479
Phone: (806)669-1103   **Fax:** (806)669-0369
Products: Oil field supplies and equipment and oil country tubular goods. **SIC:** 5084 (Industrial Machinery & Equipment). **Sales:** $13,000,000 (2000). **Emp:** 41. **Officers:** Ron Hess, President.

■ 22777 ■ **Wabash Power Equipment Co.**
444 Carpenter
Wheeling, IL 60090
Phone: (847)541-5600
Products: Oilers and oil. **SICs:** 5084 (Industrial Machinery & Equipment); 5171 (Petroleum Bulk Stations & Terminals). **Sales:** $5,000,000 (2000). **Emp:** 24. **Officers:** Severin Caitung, President.

■ 22778 ■ **Wainoco Oil Corp.**
10000 Memorial Dr., No. 600
Houston, TX 77024-3411
Phone: (713)688-9600   **Fax:** (713)688-0616
Products: Petroleum, fuels, and related equipment. **SIC:** 5172 (Petroleum Products Nec). **Est:** 1949. **Sales:** $374,100,000 (2000). **Emp:** 291.

■ 22779 ■ **Wakefield Oil Co.**
311 S Virginia Ave.
Roswell, NM 88201
Phone: (505)622-4160
Products: Oil. **SIC:** 5172 (Petroleum Products Nec).

■ 22780 ■ **Wallace Oil Co.**
5370 Oakdale Rd.
Smyrna, GA 30082
Phone: (404)799-9400
Products: Gasoline. **SIC:** 5172 (Petroleum Products Nec). **Est:** 1950. **Sales:** $19,000,000 (2000). **Emp:** 25. **Officers:** James C. Wallace, CEO & President; Jim Phillips, Controller; Hubert Brooks, VP of Marketing.

■ 22781 ■ **Wareco Service Inc.**
400 W State St.
Jacksonville, IL 62650
Phone: (217)245-9528
Products: Petroleum bulk station. **SIC:** 5171 (Petroleum Bulk Stations & Terminals). **Sales:** $10,000,000 (2000). **Emp:** 100. **Officers:** Richard Ware, President; Mark Scobbie, CFO.

■ 22782 ■ **E.R. Warren Co. Inc.**
PO Box 949
Kennebunk, ME 04043
Phone: (207)985-3154   **Fax:** (207)985-1178
Products: Fuel oil; Propane; Gasoline. **SIC:** 5172 (Petroleum Products Nec). **Sales:** $32,000,000 (2000). **Emp:** 50. **Officers:** Prayson Perkins, President.

■ 22783 ■ **George E. Warren Corp.**
605 17th St.
Vero Beach, FL 32960
Phone: (561)778-7100
Products: Petroleum and its products. **SIC:** 5172 (Petroleum Products Nec). **Sales:** $14,000,000 (2000). **Emp:** 22. **Officers:** Thomas Carr, President; Martin Paris, Dir of Personnel.

■ 22784 ■ **Waste Recovery Inc.**
309 S Pearl Expwy.
Dallas, TX 75201
Phone: (214)741-3865   **Fax:** (214)745-8945
Products: Refined fuel supplement made from scrapped tires. **SIC:** 5093 (Scrap & Waste Materials). **Sales:** $10,700,000 (2000). **Emp:** 200. **Officers:** Thomas L. Earnshaw, CEO, President & Treasurer; John E. Cockrum, Controller.

■ 22785 ■ **Waterloo Service Company Inc.**
PO Box 300
Waterloo, IA 50704
Phone: (319)233-4232   **Fax:** (319)233-5134
Products: Petroleum and petroleum products. **SIC:** 5172 (Petroleum Products Nec). **Est:** 1935. **Sales:** $30,000,000 (2000). **Emp:** 25. **Officers:** Stephen Hinman, President; Don Kohagen, General Mgr.; David Krueger, Manager.

■ 22786 ■ **WD-40 Co.**
1061 Cudahy Pl.
San Diego, CA 92110
Phone: (619)275-1400   **Fax:** (619)275-5823
URL: http://www.wd40.com
Products: Multipurpose and heavy-duty lubricants; Water displacement; Hand cleaner. **SIC:** 5172 (Petroleum Products Nec). **Est:** 1953. **Sales:** $144,000,000 (1999). **Emp:** 167.

■ 22787 ■ **Webber Oil Co.**
PO Box 929
Bangor, ME 04402-0929
Phone: (207)942-5501   **Fax:** (207)947-6522
Products: Heating oil and gas. **SIC:** 5172 (Petroleum Products Nec). **Est:** 1935. **Sales:** $390,000,000 (2000). **Emp:** 800. **Officers:** Larry Mahaney, President; Andy Pease Jr., VP of Finance.

■ 22788 ■ **Webb's Oil Corp.**
8223 Resevoir Rd.
Roanoke, VA 24019-6939
Phone: (703)362-3796
Products: Gas and home heating oil. **SICs:** 5171 (Petroleum Bulk Stations & Terminals); 5172 (Petroleum Products Nec). **Est:** 1961. **Sales:** $35,000,000 (2000). **Emp:** 35. **Officers:** Harry W. Webb, President; Janice Webb, Controller.

■ 22789 ■ **Wehman Inc.**
PO Drawer W
Pleasanton, TX 78064
Phone: (210)569-2181   **Fax:** (210)281-2181
Products: Gasoline; Fuel. **SIC:** 5172 (Petroleum Products Nec). **Est:** 1976. **Sales:** $24,000,000 (2000). **Emp:** 50. **Officers:** E.W. Wehman Jr., President; Staci Jones, VP & Comptroller.

■ 22790 ■ **Weil Service Products Corp.**
PO Box 6127
Bloomingdale, IL 60108-6127
Phone: (773)528-6800   **Fax:** (773)528-9925
Products: Petroleum dispensing and transport equipment. **SICs:** 5088 (Transportation Equipment & Supplies); 5172 (Petroleum Products Nec). **Est:** 1948. **Sales:** $6,000,000 (2000). **Emp:** 20. **Officers:** Rich Schult; Al Mazzocchi.

■ 22791 ■ **Wesson, Inc.**
PO Box 2127
Waterbury, CT 06722-2127
Phone: (203)757-7950   **Fax:** (203)754-6664
Products: Heating oil and gasoline. **SIC:** 5172 (Petroleum Products Nec). **Sales:** $42,000,000 (2000). **Emp:** 100. **Officers:** Robert Wesson, President; William Derwin, Controller.

■ 22792 ■ **West Liberty Oil Co.**
PO Box 147
MoscoW, IA 52760-0147
Phone: (319)627-2113
Products: Petroleum products. **SIC:** 5172 (Petroleum Products Nec). **Est:** 1924. **Sales:** $27,000,000 (2000). **Emp:** 85. **Officers:** Tom Brooke, President; Darren Brooke, Treasurer; Bruce Brooke, VP of Marketing.

■ **22793** ■ **West Minerals Inc.**
101 Tidewater Rd. NE
Warren, OH 44483
Phone: (330)372-1781
Products: Chemicals; Fuel. **SICs:** 5172 (Petroleum Products Nec); 5169 (Chemicals & Allied Products Nec). **Sales:** $9,000,000 (2000). **Emp:** 35. **Officers:** William J. West, President.

■ **22794** ■ **Western Petroleum Co.**
9531 W 78th St.
Eden Prairie, MN 55344
Phone: (612)941-9090   **Fax:** (612)941-7470
Products: Petroleum; Gasoline. **SIC:** 5172 (Petroleum Products Nec). **Est:** 1969. **Sales:** $328,000,000 (2000). **Emp:** 50. **Officers:** James W. Emison, President; Lee Granlund, VP of Finance; Richard Neville, VP of Marketing.

■ **22795** ■ **Western Pioneer Inc.**
PO Box 70438
Seattle, WA 98107
Phone: (206)789-1930   **Fax:** (206)789-1717
Products: Fuel barges and tank farms. **SIC:** 5169 (Chemicals & Allied Products Nec). **Sales:** $150,000,000 (2000). **Emp:** 450. **Officers:** Larry Soriano, Mgr. of Admin.; Vicki Crouch, Finance Officer.

■ **22796** ■ **Western States Oil Company Inc.**
1790 S 10th St.
San Jose, CA 95112
Phone: (408)292-1041
Free: (800)743-6950   **Fax:** (408)293-2093
URL: http://www.lubeoil.com
Products: Fuel and oil; Specialty lubricants. **SIC:** 5172 (Petroleum Products Nec). **Est:** 1962. **Sales:** $35,000,000 (2000). **Emp:** 42. **Officers:** Stephen T. Lopes, CEO & President; Jeffrey M. Lopes, Vice President, e-mail: jlopes@lubeoil.com.

■ **22797** ■ **Western States Petroleum Inc.**
450 S 15th Ave.
Phoenix, AZ 85007
Phone: (602)252-4011   **Fax:** (602)340-9621
Products: Gasoline, diesel, fuel oil. **SIC:** 5172 (Petroleum Products Nec). **Est:** 1974. **Sales:** $12,000,000 (2000). **Emp:** 25. **Officers:** Robert F. Kec, President; Janet Kec, Treasurer & Secty.

■ **22798** ■ **Western Stations Co.**
2929 NW 29th
Portland, OR 97210
Phone: (503)243-2929   **Fax:** (503)243-7874
Products: Gasoline; Cigarettes. **SICs:** 5172 (Petroleum Products Nec); 5194 (Tobacco & Tobacco Products). **Est:** 1970. **Sales:** $150,000,000 (2000). **Emp:** 225. **Officers:** Richard W. Dyke, President; Al Stickel, CFO; Glenn Zirkle, Vice President.

■ **22799** ■ **Whitaker Oil Co.**
PO Box 93487
Atlanta, GA 30377
Phone: (404)355-8220
Free: (800)221-0521   **Fax:** (404)355-8217
Products: Petroleum solvents. **SIC:** 5172 (Petroleum Products Nec). **Est:** 1928. **Sales:** $35,000,000 (2000). **Emp:** 52. **Officers:** Bart Whitaker III, President; Bob Ward, CFO; Dick Mackey, VP of Sales.

■ **22800** ■ **Whiteside F.S. Inc.**
PO Box 79
Cambridge, IL 61238-0079
Phone: (815)772-2155
Products: Petroleum; Grain; Fertilizer. **SICs:** 5191 (Farm Supplies); 5172 (Petroleum Products Nec); 5153 (Grain & Field Beans). **Est:** 1931. **Sales:** $23,000,000 (2000). **Emp:** 45. **Officers:** Daniel Witmer, President; Stephen Swanstrom, General Mgr.

■ **22801** ■ **Whiteville Oil Company Inc.**
PO Box 689
Whiteville, NC 28472
Phone: (919)642-3188
Products: Fuel, including gasoline and diesel. **SIC:** 5172 (Petroleum Products Nec). **Est:** 1946. **Sales:** $11,000,000 (2000). **Emp:** 10. **Officers:** W. D. Black, CEO; P. Sellers, Treasurer & Secty.

■ **22802** ■ **Wilbanks Oil Company Inc.**
110 Maple St.
Cleburne, TX 76031
Phone: (817)645-2701
Products: Diesel fuel. **SIC:** 5172 (Petroleum Products Nec). **Est:** 1957. **Sales:** $8,000,000 (2000). **Emp:** 6. **Officers:** David Wilbanks, President.

■ **22803** ■ **Wilkerson Fuel Company Inc.**
PO Box 2835
Rock Hill, SC 29731
Phone: (803)324-4080   **Fax:** (803)328-8700
Products: Gasoline, diesel, motor oil, and kerosene. **SICs:** 5171 (Petroleum Bulk Stations & Terminals); 5172 (Petroleum Products Nec). **Est:** 1981. **Sales:** $20,000,000 (2000). **Emp:** 35. **Officers:** David Bratton, CEO; Frank M. Wilkerson, CFO; George Booth, Dir. of Marketing & Sales; Kim Gwinn, Dir. of Information Systems.

■ **22804** ■ **Williams Oil Co.**
PO Box 220
Bridgeport, AL 35740
Phone: (205)495-2413
Products: Gasoline. **SICs:** 5171 (Petroleum Bulk Stations & Terminals); 5172 (Petroleum Products Nec). **Est:** 1955. **Sales:** $4,500,000 (2000). **Emp:** 13. **Officers:** J.J. Williams, Owner.

■ **22805** ■ **A.T. Williams Oil Co.**
PO Box 7287
Winston-Salem, NC 27109
Phone: (910)767-6280   **Fax:** (910)767-6283
Products: Petroleum products, including gas. **SICs:** 5172 (Petroleum Products Nec); 5171 (Petroleum Bulk Stations & Terminals). **Est:** 1950. **Sales:** $320,000,000 (2000). **Emp:** 1,450. **Officers:** Arthur T. Williams Jr., Chairman of the Board; Ron Padgett, CFO; Steve Williams, VP of Marketing.

■ **22806** ■ **J.H. Williams Oil Company Inc.**
PO Box 439
Tampa, FL 33601
Phone: (813)228-7776   **Fax:** (813)224-9413
Products: Petroleum products. **SICs:** 5171 (Petroleum Bulk Stations & Terminals); 5172 (Petroleum Products Nec). **Sales:** $85,800,000 (2000). **Emp:** 220. **Officers:** J. Hulon Williams III, President; L. Darlene Sanders, Controller.

■ **22807** ■ **Williston Industrial Supply Corp.**
PO Box 2477
Williston, ND 58801
Phone: (701)572-2135   **Fax:** (701)572-0664
Products: Used oil field equipment. **SIC:** 5084 (Industrial Machinery & Equipment). **Sales:** $15,000,000 (1994). **Emp:** 50. **Officers:** James R. Scheele, President.

■ **22808** ■ **Wilson Industries Inc.**
PO Box 1492
Houston, TX 77251
Phone: (713)237-3700
Products: Oil field supplies. **SIC:** 5084 (Industrial Machinery & Equipment). **Est:** 1921. **Sales:** $450,000,000 (2000). **Emp:** 1,100. **Officers:** W.S. Wilson, Chairman of the Board; Robert Brown Jr., VP of Finance; Rupert W. Barefield, Sr. VP of Marketing; Walter Lueck, Dir. of Data Processing; Anne Gray, Dir of Personnel.

■ **22809** ■ **Wilson Supply Co.**
PO Box 94100
Oklahoma City, OK 73143
Phone: (405)677-3382
Products: Oil field supplies. **SIC:** 5084 (Industrial Machinery & Equipment). **Est:** 1921. **Sales:** $100,000,000 (2000). **Emp:** 250. **Officers:** Mark Gwynn, General Mgr.

■ **22810** ■ **Winnco Inc.**
PO Box 688
Weatherford, OK 73096
Phone: (580)772-3448
Products: Gas and oil. **SIC:** 5172 (Petroleum Products Nec). **Est:** 1970. **Sales:** $15,000,000 (2000). **Emp:** 5. **Officers:** John Winn, Owner.

■ **22811** ■ **Winters Oil Co.**
PO Box 1637
Corsicana, TX 75151
Phone: (903)872-4166   **Fax:** (903)872-2020
Products: Oil and gasoline. **SIC:** 5172 (Petroleum Products Nec). **Est:** 1972. **Sales:** $18,000,000 (2000). **Emp:** 28. **Officers:** Willy H. Winters, President.

■ **22812** ■ **Wixson Brothers Equipment Co.**
PO Box 205
Fisher, AR 72429
Phone: (870)328-7251
Products: Oil. **SIC:** 5172 (Petroleum Products Nec). **Est:** 1925. **Sales:** $4,000,000 (2000). **Emp:** 54. **Officers:** Charles H. Wixson, President.

■ **22813** ■ **R.W. Wogaman Oil Co.**
425 S Barron St.
Eaton, OH 45320
Phone: (513)456-4882   **Fax:** (513)839-4154
Products: Gasoline. **SIC:** 5172 (Petroleum Products Nec). **Est:** 1946. **Sales:** $2,000,000 (2000). **Emp:** 4. **Officers:** Joyce Etsinger, President.

■ **22814** ■ **Wolfriver Country Cooperative**
PO Box 320
Weyauwega, WI 54983
Phone: (414)867-2176
Products: Gas and fuel. **SIC:** 5172 (Petroleum Products Nec). **Est:** 1934. **Sales:** $6,000,000 (2000). **Emp:** 30. **Officers:** Dean Clark, General Mgr.; Tim Wenzeo, CFO.

■ **22815** ■ **Wooten Oil Co.**
PO Box 1277
Goldsboro, NC 27533
Phone: (919)734-1357   **Fax:** (919)735-4677
Products: Bulk petroleum products; Convenience store. **SIC:** 5171 (Petroleum Bulk Stations & Terminals). **Sales:** $10,000,000 (2000). **Emp:** 15. **Officers:** S.D. Wooten Jr., CEO & President; Brian McNeese, CFO.

■ **22816** ■ **World Fuel Services Corp.**
700 S Royal Poinciana Blvd., St
Miami Springs, FL 33166
Phone: (305)884-2001   **Fax:** (305)883-0186
Products: Oil and fuel. **SIC:** 5172 (Petroleum Products Nec). **Est:** 1984. **Sales:** $7,726,000,000 (2000). **Emp:** 246. **Officers:** Jerrold Blair, President; Carlos A. Abaunza, CFO & Treasurer; Howard A. Goldman, Dir. of Marketing.

■ **22817** ■ **Worsley Oil Company of Wallace Inc.**
Hwy. 117 N
Wallace, NC 28466
Phone: (919)285-7125
Products: Petroleum products, including gasoline, diesel, propane, and kerosene. **SIC:** 5172 (Petroleum Products Nec). **Est:** 1941. **Sales:** $5,000,000 (2000). **Emp:** 15. **Officers:** Cecil Worsley, CEO.

■ **22818** ■ **Yoder Oil Company Inc.**
PO Box 10
Elkhart, IN 46515
Phone: (219)264-2170   **Fax:** (219)264-1475
Products: Gasoline, diesel fuel, lubricants, and related equipment. **SICs:** 5171 (Petroleum Bulk Stations & Terminals); 5084 (Industrial Machinery & Equipment). **Est:** 1937. **Sales:** $85,000,000 (2000). **Emp:** 180. **Officers:** Kent J. Yoder, President; Thomas M. Rowlen, Controller; Al Miller, VP of Sales.

■ **22819** ■ **Young Oil CO.**
1010 S Central Ave.
Idabel, OK 74745
Phone: (580)286-5693
Products: Oil. **SIC:** 5172 (Petroleum Products Nec).

■ **22820** ■ **Youngblood Oil Company Inc.**
PO Box 2590
Hendersonville, NC 28793
Phone: (704)693-6219
Products: Gasoline, diesel, fuel oil, and kerosene. **SIC:** 5172 (Petroleum Products Nec). **Est:** 1942. **Sales:** $11,000,000 (2000). **Emp:** 50. **Officers:** Victor B. Jones, President; Joe Youngblood, Treasurer & Secty.; David Parris, Dir. of Sales.

■ **22821** ■ **Zuni Investment Co.**
1380 Zuni St.
Denver, CO 80204

Phone: (303)893-3211   **Fax:** (303)595-8741
Products: Petroleum bulk station. **SIC:** 5171
(Petroleum Bulk Stations & Terminals). **Sales:**

$22,000,000 (2000). **Emp:** 58. **Officers:** Larry Siegel,
President.

(42) Photographic Equipment and Supplies

Entries in this section are arranged alphabetically by company name. When the company name is a personal name, the company name is alphabetized by the surname unless the first name or initial(s) are part of a trade name. See the User's Guide at the front of this directory for additional information.

■ 22822 ■ **Acfer International Inc.**
4218 Center Gate
San Antonio, TX 78217
Phone: (210)653-6800 **Fax:** (210)653-6226
Products: Commercial equipment; Industrial machinery and equipment; Industrial supplies; Micrographic equipment and supplies. **SICs:** 5084 (Industrial Machinery & Equipment); 5046 (Commercial Equipment Nec); 5084 (Industrial Machinery & Equipment); 5085 (Industrial Supplies); 5139 (Footwear). **Est:** 1979. **Officers:** Mario A. Ray, President.

■ 22823 ■ **AGFA Corp.**
1801 Century Park E, Ste. 110
Century City, CA 90067-2302
Phone: (310)552-9622 **Fax:** (310)203-9672
Products: Film. **SIC:** 5043 (Photographic Equipment & Supplies). **Emp:** 52. **Officers:** Pieter Bulcke.

■ 22824 ■ **Albums Inc.**
11422 Grissom
Dallas, TX 75229-2352
Phone: (972)247-0677
Free: (800)662-1000 **Fax:** (972)243-0874
Products: Photographic equipment and supplies. **SIC:** 5043 (Photographic Equipment & Supplies). **Emp:** 49.
Alternate Name: ProCraft.

■ 22825 ■ **Amcam International Inc.**
601 Academy Dr.
Northbrook, IL 60062-1915
Phone: (847)291-1560 **Fax:** (847)291-2261
Products: Video accessories; Photographic accessories. **SIC:** 5043 (Photographic Equipment & Supplies). **Emp:** 49. **Officers:** Don Colby, Vice President; Mark Klitzky, President.

■ 22826 ■ **Apollo Space Systems Inc.**
60 Trade Zone Ct.
Ronkonkoma, NY 11779
Phone: (516)467-8033 **Fax:** (516)467-8996
Products: Overhead projectors, films, and projection screens. **SIC:** 5043 (Photographic Equipment & Supplies). **Est:** 1981. **Sales:** $58,000,000 (2000).
Emp: 150. **Officers:** Harry G. Charlston, President; Skip Show, Controller; Eric Milburn, VP of Sales.

■ 22827 ■ **Arriflex Corp.**
617 Rte. 303
Blauvelt, NY 10913
Phone: (845)353-1200 **Fax:** (845)425-1250
E-mail: arriflex@arri.com
URL: http://www.arri.com
Products: Motion picture cameras and lighting equipment. **SIC:** 5043 (Photographic Equipment & Supplies). **Est:** 1970. **Sales:** $48,000,000 (2000).
Emp: 50. **Officers:** Volker Bahnemann, President.

■ 22828 ■ **Attraction Services Corp.**
PO Box 176
North Woodstock, NH 03262-0176
Phone: (603)745-8720 **Fax:** (603)745-6765
Products: Photographic equipment and supplies. **SIC:** 5043 (Photographic Equipment & Supplies). **Officers:** Richard Hamilton, Vice President.

■ 22829 ■ **Beattie Systems Inc.**
2407 Guthrie Ave. NW
Cleveland, TN 37311-3651
Phone: (423)479-8566
Free: (800)251-6333 **Fax:** (423)476-6171
Products: Photographic equipment and supplies. **SIC:** 5043 (Photographic Equipment & Supplies). **Sales:** $2,000,000 (2000). **Emp:** 21. **Officers:** Anthony G. Fox.

■ 22830 ■ **Bel Trade USA Corp.**
55 W 47th St.
New York, NY 10036
Phone: (212)840-3920 **Fax:** (718)746-5160
Products: Stationery and office supplies; Jewelry; Precious stones (gems); Photographic equipment and supplies. **SICs:** 5043 (Photographic Equipment & Supplies); 5112 (Stationery & Office Supplies); 5094 (Jewelry & Precious Stones). **Officers:** Helen Sy Choi, Manager.

■ 22831 ■ **Birns & Sawyer Inc.**
1026 N Highland Ave.
Hollywood, CA 90038-2407
Phone: (213)466-8211 **Fax:** (213)466-7049
Products: Motion picture equipment. **SIC:** 5043 (Photographic Equipment & Supplies). **Est:** 1955.
Emp: 49. **Officers:** Marvin Stern, President; Mark Schweickart, Rental Manager; Peter Anway, Sales Mgr.; Marianne Exbrayat, Marketing Mgr.

■ 22832 ■ **Bogen Photo Corp.**
565 E Crescent Ave.
PO Box 506
Ramsey, NJ 07446-0506
Phone: (201)818-9500 **Fax:** (201)818-9177
E-mail: info@bogenphoto.com
URL: http://www.bogenphoto.com
Products: Photographic equipment. **SIC:** 5043 (Photographic Equipment & Supplies). **Officers:** Susan Bogen, Pres.; Bruce Landau, VP, Sales & Mktg.; Bob Rose.

■ 22833 ■ **Boston Electronics Corporation**
91 Boylston St.
Brookline, MA 02445-7602
Phone: (617)566-3821
Free: (800)347-5445 **Fax:** (617)731-0935
E-mail: boselec@world.std.com
URL: http://www.boselec.com
Products: Photo detectors; Infrared sources; Oxide electrodes. **SIC:** 5043 (Photographic Equipment & Supplies). **Est:** 1977. **Sales:** $2,000,000 (2000). **Emp:** 4. **Officers:** F.S. Perry, President.

■ 22834 ■ **Boston Productions Inc.**
648 Beacon St., No. 2
Boston, MA 02215
Phone: (617)236-1180
Products: Film. **SIC:** 5043 (Photographic Equipment & Supplies).

■ 22835 ■ **Brandons Camera**
1819 Kings Ave.
Jacksonville, FL 32207-8787
Phone: (904)398-1591
Free: (800)874-5273 **Fax:** (904)396-5271
Products: Cameras; Photographic equipment and supplies. **SIC:** 5043 (Photographic Equipment & Supplies). **Est:** 1945. **Sales:** $100,000 (2000). **Emp:** 28. **Officers:** George W. Breslin.

■ 22836 ■ **CAI Div.**
550 W Northwest Hwy.
Barrington, IL 60010
Phone: (847)381-2400 **Fax:** (847)381-4987
Products: Reconnaissance cameras and sighting systems for military and nonmilitary applications. **SIC:** 5043 (Photographic Equipment & Supplies). **Sales:** $50,000,000 (2000). **Emp:** 300. **Officers:** William Owens.

■ 22837 ■ **Camera Corner Inc.**
PO Box 1899
Burlington, NC 27216-1899
Phone: (919)228-0251 **Fax:** (919)222-8011
Products: Cameras, including 35mm and video; Camera supplies. **SIC:** 5043 (Photographic Equipment & Supplies). **Est:** 1949. **Sales:** $18,000,000 (2000).
Emp: 60. **Officers:** Ray Bailey, CEO.

■ 22838 ■ **Camera Service Center of Maine**
40 Lisbon St.
Lewiston, ME 04240-7116
Phone: (207)784-1509 **Fax:** (207)777-5973
E-mail: slmmlm@aol.com
Products: Photographic equipment and supplies. **SIC:** 5043 (Photographic Equipment & Supplies). **Est:** 1948.
Emp: 11. **Officers:** Susan Mitchell; Michael Mitchell.

■ 22839 ■ **Capitol Entertainment & Home**
6205 Adelaide Dr.
Bethesda, MD 20817
Phone: (301)564-9700
Products: Film. **SIC:** 5043 (Photographic Equipment & Supplies).

■ 22840 ■ **Cash Indiana**
387 Melton Rd.
Burns Harbor, IN 46304
Phone: (219)787-8311 **Fax:** (219)787-8316
Products: Jewelry; Cameras; Coins; Televisions; Guns. **SICs:** 5043 (Photographic Equipment & Supplies); 5091 (Sporting & Recreational Goods); 5094 (Jewelry & Precious Stones). **Est:** 1966. **Emp:** 4. **Officers:** Jack Batz, President.

■ 22841 ■ **Veronica Cass Inc.**
PO Box 5519
Hudson, FL 34674
Phone: (727)863-2738
Free: (800)472-9336 **Fax:** (813)727-3567
E-mail: veronicacassinc@worldnet.att.net
URL: http://www.veronicacass.com
Products: Photographic art retouching supplies. **SIC:** 5043 (Photographic Equipment & Supplies). **Est:** 1975.
Emp: 4. **Officers:** Veronica Cass Weiss, CEO; Veronica Cass Weiss, CEO.

■ 22842 ■ **Celestron International**
2835 Columbia St.
Torrance, CA 90503
Phone: (310)328-9560 **Fax:** (310)212-5835
Products: Telescopes; Binoculars, microscopes and lenses. **SIC:** 5043 (Photographic Equipment & Supplies). **Officers:** Joe Lupica, VP of Finance.

■ 22843 ■ **Central Audio Visual Equipment Inc.**
271 E Helen Rd.
Palatine, IL 60067-6954
Phone: (847)776-9200
Free: (800)323-4239 **Fax:** (847)776-9240
E-mail: JenniferBashir@aol.com
URL: http://www.cavinc.com
Products: Audio visual equipment; Batteries; Projector lamps; Overhead projectors; Video projectors; Polaroid film; Audio-video tapes; A/V screens. **SICs:** 5043 (Photographic Equipment & Supplies); 5064 (Electrical Appliances—Television & Radio); 5044 (Office Equipment). **Est:** 1958. **Sales:** $1,000,000 (2000). **Emp:** 5. **Officers:** Michael Bashir, President.

■ 22844 ■ **Chilcote Co.**
2160 Superior Ave.
Cleveland, OH 44114
Phone: (216)781-6000
Free: (800)227-5679 **Fax:** (216)771-2572
E-mail: dhein@concentric.net
URL: http://www.tap-usa.com
Products: Photographic equipment and supplies. **SIC:** 5043 (Photographic Equipment & Supplies). **Est:** 1906. **Sales:** $50,000,000 (2000). **Emp:** 450. **Officers:** D. Hein, CEO & Chairman of the Board; R. Marn, CFO; D. Chilcote, President.

■ 22845 ■ **Chimera Co**
1812 Valtec Ln.
Boulder, CO 80301
Phone: (303)444-8000 **Fax:** (303)444-8303
Products: Photographic equipment and supplies, including hand-sewn light diffusion devices for TV, film and studio use. **SIC:** 5043 (Photographic Equipment & Supplies).

■ 22846 ■ **Chromaline Corp.**
4832 Grand Ave.
Duluth, MN 55807
Phone: (218)628-2217 **Fax:** (218)628-3245
E-mail: chromali@chromaline.com
URL: http://www.chromaline.com
Products: Photo stencil products for screen printing. **SIC:** 5043 (Photographic Equipment & Supplies). **Est:** 1952. **Sales:** $8,900,000 (2000). **Emp:** 70. **Officers:** William Ulland, CEO & President; Jeff Laabs, VP of Finance; Claude Piguet, Dir. of Operations.

■ 22847 ■ **Comprehensive Video Group**
55 Ruta Ct.
South Hackensack, NJ 07606
Phone: (201)229-0025
Free: (800)526-0242 **Fax:** (201)814-0510
Products: Video production supplies and equipment. **SICs:** 5043 (Photographic Equipment & Supplies); 5045 (Computers, Peripherals & Software). **Sales:** $19,600,000 (2000). **Emp:** 50. **Officers:** Shelly Goldstein, President.

■ 22848 ■ **Computer Optics Inc.**
PO Box 7
Hudson, NH 03051
Phone: (603)889-2116 **Fax:** (603)889-2393
E-mail: coi@jlc.net
Products: Industrial optics and machine vision systems. **SICs:** 5043 (Photographic Equipment & Supplies); 5085 (Industrial Supplies). **Est:** 1985. **Emp:** 20. **Officers:** H. Harry Spinakis, President. **Also Known by This Acronym:** COI.

■ 22849 ■ **CPAC Inc.**
2364 Leicester Rd.
Leicester, NY 14481
Phone: (716)382-3223
Free: (800)878-6011 **Fax:** (716)382-3031
URL: http://www.cpac-fuller.com
Products: Silver recovery units; Fuller brush cleaning supplies and products. **SICs:** 5043 (Photographic Equipment & Supplies); 5085 (Industrial Supplies). **Est:**

1969. **Sales:** $110,000,000 (2000). **Emp:** 600. **Officers:** Thomas N. Hendrickson, CEO, President & Treasurer; Thomas Weldgen, CFO; Robert C. Isaacs, Vice President; Robert Oppenheimer, Secretary.

■ 22850 ■ **Custom Photo Manufacturing**
10830 Sanden Dr.
Dallas, TX 75238-1337
Phone: (214)349-9779
Free: (800)627-0252 **Fax:** (214)503-1557
SIC: 5043 (Photographic Equipment & Supplies). **Est:** 1971. **Sales:** $8,000,000 (2000). **Emp:** 49.

■ 22851 ■ **Dot Line**
9420 Eton Ave.
Chatsworth, CA 91311-5295
Phone: (818)631-9730
Products: Photographic equipment and wood cabinets. **SICs:** 5043 (Photographic Equipment & Supplies); 5021 (Furniture). **Sales:** $3,000,000 (1994). **Emp:** 20. **Officers:** Walter A. Reeves Jr., CEO.

■ 22852 ■ **Eye Communication Systems Inc.**
455 E Industrial Dr.
Hartland, WI 53029
Phone: (414)367-1360 **Fax:** (414)367-1362
Products: Photographic equipment; Microfiche readers, printers and computers. **SICs:** 5043 (Photographic Equipment & Supplies); 5044 (Office Equipment); 5045 (Computers, Peripherals & Software). **Sales:** $12,000,000 (2000). **Emp:** 100. **Officers:** John Bessent, President; Jeanne Sutter, Controller.

■ 22853 ■ **Film Technologies International, Inc.**
2544 Terminal Dr. S
St. Petersburg, FL 33712
Phone: (727)327-2544
Free: (800)777-1770 **Fax:** (727)327-7132
E-mail: info@filmtechnologies.com
URL: http://www.filmtechnologies.com
Products: Solar film; Safety film; Security film; Sun guard; Glass guard. **SIC:** 5043 (Photographic Equipment & Supplies). **Est:** 1970. **Sales:** $25,000 (2000). **Emp:** 135. **Officers:** Donald Wheeler, President; Steve Michaud, VP of Marketing & Sales; Stephanie Knapp, Advertising and Communications Manager.

■ 22854 ■ **Fuji Medical Systems USA Inc.**
419 West Ave.
Stamford, CT 06902
Phone: (203)353-0300 **Fax:** (203)353-0926
Products: X-ray and industrial film. **SIC:** 5043 (Photographic Equipment & Supplies). **Sales:** $200,000,000 (2000). **Emp:** 300. **Officers:** Takushi Nasu, President; John J. Weber, CFO.

■ 22855 ■ **Gate Group USA, Inc.**
75 Varick St.
New York, NY 10013
Phone: (212)966-8995
Free: (800)966-9889 **Fax:** (212)966-8996
Products: Printing dyes, ink, and paper; Photographic printing equipment and trades machinery. **SICs:** 5043 (Photographic Equipment & Supplies); 5099 (Durable Goods Nec). **Officers:** Isaac M. Savitt, President.

■ 22856 ■ **GKM Enterprises Inc.**
5059 Lankershi Blvd.
North Hollywood, CA 91601-4224
Phone: (818)762-2846 **Fax:** (818)766-9436
Products: Photo and photo finishing equipment and supplies; Digital equipment and supplies; Industrial products. **SICs:** 5043 (Photographic Equipment & Supplies); 5085 (Industrial Supplies). **Est:** 1952. **Emp:** 70. **Officers:** Jack M. Williams, President; Gary A. Williams, Vice President.

■ 22857 ■ **Glacier Studio**
PO Box J
Browning, MT 59417
Phone: (406)338-2100
Products: Photographic equipment and supplies; Cameras; Projectors. **SIC:** 5043 (Photographic Equipment & Supplies). **Officers:** Edward Aubert, Owner.

■ 22858 ■ **GMI Photographic Inc.**
125 Schmitt Blvd.
Farmingdale, NY 11735
Phone: (516)752-0066
Products: Cameras. **SIC:** 5043 (Photographic Equipment & Supplies). **Sales:** $13,000,000 (1993). **Emp:** 35. **Officers:** Joseph Gallen, President.

■ 22859 ■ **Great Lakes Technologies Corp.**
PO Box 51415
Kalamazoo, MI 49005-1415
Phone: (616)385-2200
Free: (800)289-4582 **Fax:** (616)385-4684
Products: Film and photographic equipment. **SIC:** 5043 (Photographic Equipment & Supplies). **Est:** 1977. **Sales:** $9,000,000 (2000). **Emp:** 45. **Officers:** Robin L. Marshall, President.

■ 22860 ■ **Greentree Productions Inc.**
200 Lake St.
Burlington, VT 05401
Phone: (802)865-0502
Products: Films. **SIC:** 5043 (Photographic Equipment & Supplies).

■ 22861 ■ **Gross-Medick-Barrows Inc.**
PO Box 12727
El Paso, TX 79913
Phone: (915)584-8133
Free: (800)777-1565 **Fax:** (915)584-9779
E-mail: gmbco@g-m-b.com
URL: http://www.g-m-b.com
Products: Photo mounts; Folios; Wedding albums; Mounting boards. **SIC:** 5043 (Photographic Equipment & Supplies). **Est:** 1906. **Sales:** $7,000,000 (2000). **Emp:** 100. **Officers:** Tom Kanouse, President; Ed Maestas, Treasurer.

■ 22862 ■ **Hamamatsu Photonic Systems**
PO Box 6910
Bridgewater, NJ 08807
Phone: (908)231-0960 **Fax:** (908)231-1539
Products: Photo-sensitive devices. **SIC:** 5043 (Photographic Equipment & Supplies).

■ 22863 ■ **Heitz Service Corp.**
34-11 62nd St.
Woodside, NY 11377
Phone: (718)565-0004 **Fax:** (718)565-2582
E-mail: karlheitz@compuserve.com
URL: http://www.karlheitz.com
Products: Photographic and cinema equipment. **SIC:** 5043 (Photographic Equipment & Supplies). **Est:** 1947. **Sales:** $400,000 (2000). **Emp:** 3. **Officers:** Karl Heitz, President, e-mail: karlheitz@compuserve.com; Loretta Rosas, Vice President.

■ 22864 ■ **Helix Ltd.**
310 S Racine St.
Chicago, IL 60607
Phone: (312)421-6000 **Fax:** (312)421-5723
Products: Audio visual equipment; Underwater video equipment. **SIC:** 5043 (Photographic Equipment & Supplies). **Est:** 1963. **Sales:** $25,000,000 (2000). **Emp:** 200. **Officers:** P.L. Schutt, President.

■ 22865 ■ **Hoag Enterprises, Inc.**
PO Box 4406
Springfield, MO 65807
Phone: (417)883-8300 **Fax:** (417)883-8305
URL: http://www.lawrencephotovideo.com
Products: Cameras and camcorders; Photo supplies. **SIC:** 5043 (Photographic Equipment & Supplies). **Est:** 1986. **Sales:** $3,500,000 (1999). **Emp:** 16. **Officers:** Charles Hoag, President, e-mail: choag@ lawrencephotovideo.com. **Doing Business As:** Lawrence Photo & Video.

■ 22866 ■ **HPS, Inc.**
8020 Zionsville Rd.
PO Box 68536
Indianapolis, IN 46268-0536
Phone: (317)875-9000 **Fax:** (317)471-4126
URL: http://www.hpsinc.com
Products: Cameras and industrial photographic equipment; Office products, including copiers, phones, computers, and faxes; Printing products. **SICs:** 5043 (Photographic Equipment & Supplies); 5044 (Office Equipment); 5045 (Computers, Peripherals &

Software). **Est:** 1939. **Sales:** $125,000 (2000). **Emp:** 360. **Officers:** William Boncosky, President; Ronald Sharpe, Treasurer & Secty. **Former Name:** HPS Printing Products.

■ **22867** ■ **Industrial Service Co.**
PO Box 2164
Providence, RI 02905-0164
Phone: (401)467-6454
Products: Photographic equipment and supplies. **SIC:** 5043 (Photographic Equipment & Supplies). **Officers:** Helmut Thielsch, Owner.

■ **22868** ■ **Hal Kaufman Co. Inc.**
2545 Jackson Ave.
Memphis, TN 38108
Phone: (901)458-3143 **Fax:** (901)324-2185
E-mail: hkauf46743@aol.com
Products: Photographic equipment and supplies; Small electrical appliances; Sporting and athletic goods; Lawn and garden equipment. **SICs:** 5064 (Electrical Appliances—Television & Radio); 5083 (Farm & Garden Machinery); 5091 (Sporting & Recreational Goods); 5043 (Photographic Equipment & Supplies). **Est:** 1971. **Emp:** 7. **Officers:** Herb Kaufman, President.

■ **22869** ■ **Kinetronics Corp.**
1778 Main St.
Sarasota, FL 34236
Phone: (813)388-2432
Products: Photo finishing equipment. **SIC:** 5043 (Photographic Equipment & Supplies). **Sales:** $1,000,000 (1993). **Emp:** 5. **Officers:** Bill Stelcher, President.

■ **22870** ■ **Konica Quality Photo East**
PO Box 2011
Portland, ME 04104-5008
Phone: (207)883-7200 **Fax:** (207)883-7255
Products: Photographic equipment and supplies. **SIC:** 5043 (Photographic Equipment & Supplies). **Officers:** Margaret Weston, President.

■ **22871** ■ **Konica U.S.A. Inc.**
440 Silvan Ave.
Englewood Cliffs, NJ 07632
Phone: (201)568-3100 **Fax:** (201)569-2167
Products: Photographic supplies. **SIC:** 5043 (Photographic Equipment & Supplies). **Est:** 1956. **Sales:** $58,000,000 (2000). **Emp:** 150. **Officers:** Richard Carter, President; Frank Shapiro, Exec. VP & Treasurer; Paul Gordon, Marketing Mgr.

■ **22872** ■ **Lawrence Photo-Graphic Inc.**
1211 Cambridge Cir. Dr.
Kansas City, KS 66103
Phone: (913)621-1211
Products: Photographic equipment, including film, cameras, and batteries. **SIC:** 5043 (Photographic Equipment & Supplies). **Est:** 1888. **Sales:** $35,000,000 (2000). **Emp:** 83. **Officers:** Robert Gorley, Owner; Tom Prater, CFO; Walter Stolarski, Sales Mgr.

■ **22873** ■ **Leedal Inc.**
4025 S Western Blvd.
Chicago, IL 60609
Phone: (773)376-5900 **Fax:** (773)376-7844
Products: Photographic equipment; Dental equipment and supplies; Food service equipment. **SICs:** 5043 (Photographic Equipment & Supplies); 5047 (Medical & Hospital Equipment); 5087 (Service Establishment Equipment). **Sales:** $6,000,000 (2000). **Emp:** 99. **Officers:** S.L. Levin.

■ **22874** ■ **Light Creations**
260 S Main St.
Fallon, NV 89406-3312
Phone: (702)423-8060 **Fax:** (702)423-0628
Products: Photocopying equipment and supplies; Cameras; Projectors; Mirror and picture frames. **SIC:** 5043 (Photographic Equipment & Supplies). **Officers:** Fred Olson, Partner.

■ **22875** ■ **Mamiya America Corp.**
8 Westchester Plz.
Elmsford, NY 10523
Phone: (914)347-3300
Products: Cameras. **SIC:** 5043 (Photographic

Equipment & Supplies). **Sales:** $19,000,000 (2000). **Emp:** 55. **Officers:** Henry Froehlich, President.

■ **22876** ■ **Don McAlister Camera Co.**
1454 W Lane Ave.
Columbus, OH 43221
Phone: (614)488-1865 **Fax:** (614)488-3292
Products: Photographic equipment. **SICs:** 5043 (Photographic Equipment & Supplies); 5099 (Durable Goods Nec). **Sales:** $10,000,000 (2000). **Emp:** 125. **Officers:** R.E. Longenbaker, President; John Lange, CFO; Rick Pisauro, General Mgr.

■ **22877** ■ **Media Communications Corp.**
3251 Old Lee Hwy., No. 412
Fairfax, VA 22030
Phone: (703)385-3430
Products: Films. **SIC:** 5043 (Photographic Equipment & Supplies).

■ **22878** ■ **Minolta Corp.**
101 Williams Dr.
Ramsey, NJ 07446
Phone: (201)825-4000
Free: (800)646-6582 **Fax:** (201)825-0870
Products: Photographic equipment, including cameras and document imaging systems. **SICs:** 5043 (Photographic Equipment & Supplies); 5044 (Office Equipment). **Est:** 1959. **Sales:** $1,150,000,000 (2000). **Emp:** 3,000. **Officers:** Hiroshi Fujii, CEO & President; H. Kocmond, Controller.

■ **22879** ■ **Minolta Corp.**
11150 Hope St.
Cypress, CA 90630
Phone: (714)895-6633 **Fax:** (714)894-1695
Products: Camera and photocopier manufacturing; Microfilm readers. **SIC:** 5043 (Photographic Equipment & Supplies).

■ **22880** ■ **Moviola/J & R Film Company, Inc.**
1135 N Mansfield Ave.
Hollywood, CA 90038
Phone: (213)467-3107
Free: (800)366-3564 **Fax:** (213)466-2201
Products: Film supplies and equipment. **SIC:** 5043 (Photographic Equipment & Supplies). **Officers:** Joe Paskal, Pres.; Jim Reichow, V.P.; Ron Powell, V.P., Sales.

■ **22881** ■ **Murphy Co.**
455 W Broad St.
Columbus, OH 43215-2795
Phone: (614)221-7731
Free: (800)282-9598 **Fax:** (614)221-6991
URL: http://www.murphycompany.com
Products: Printing trades machinery, equipment, and supplies; Prepared photographic chemicals. **SICs:** 5043 (Photographic Equipment & Supplies); 5099 (Durable Goods Nec); 5169 (Chemicals & Allied Products Nec). **Est:** 1947. **Sales:** $13,000,000 (2000). **Emp:** 28. **Officers:** John L. Murphy, President; Richard J. Murphy, Treasurer; Gary A. Jewell, VP of Sales; James D. Murphy, VP, Service & Delivery.

■ **22882** ■ **New Era Media Supply**
4440-A Commerce Cir.
Atlanta, GA 30336
Phone: (404)691-4260
Free: (800)363-9372 **Fax:** (404)691-8719
E-mail: roadman@sprintmail.com
Products: Audio visual equipment and supplies. **SIC:** 5043 (Photographic Equipment & Supplies). **Est:** 1996. **Officers:** Walter A. Reeves Jr., Owner. **Former Name:** Reeves Photo Sales Inc.

■ **22883** ■ **Nikon Inc.**
1300 Walt Whitman Rd.
Melville, NY 11747
Phone: (631)547-4200 **Fax:** (631)547-0299
Products: Photographic equipment, including cameras; Rifle scopes; Sunglasses. **SICs:** 5043 (Photographic Equipment & Supplies); 5048 (Ophthalmic Goods). **Est:** 1960. **Sales:** $290,000,000 (2000). **Emp:** 490. **Officers:** Hideo Fukuchi, President; Peter Molseki Jr., VP & Controller; Richard LoPinto, VP of Marketing; Jim Ritsch, Dir. of Systems; C. Estrada, Dir of Human Resources.

■ **22884** ■ **Noodle Head Network**
107 Intervale Ave.
Burlington, VT 05401
Phone: (802)862-8675
Products: Films. **SIC:** 5040 (Professional & Commercial Equipment).

■ **22885** ■ **Noritsu America Corp.**
PO Box 5039
Buena Park, CA 90622
Phone: (714)521-9040 **Fax:** (714)670-2049
Products: Photographic finishing equipment and supplies; sales and service. **SIC:** 5043 (Photographic Equipment & Supplies). **Officers:** Osame Miki, CEO & President.

■ **22886** ■ **O'Connor Engineering Laboratories**
100 Kalmus Dr.
Costa Mesa, CA 92626
Phone: (714)979-3993 **Fax:** (714)957-8138
E-mail: sales@ocon.com
URL: http://www.ocon.com
Products: Tripods and camera heads. **SIC:** 5043 (Photographic Equipment & Supplies). **Officers:** Joel Johnson, General Mgr.

■ **22887** ■ **Olympus America Inc.**
2 Corporate Center Dr.
Melville, NY 11747-3157
Phone: (516)844-5000 **Fax:** (516)844-5930
Products: Cameras, microscopes, medical instruments and industrial equipment. **SICs:** 5043 (Photographic Equipment & Supplies); 5049 (Professional Equipment Nec); 5047 (Medical & Hospital Equipment); 5084 (Industrial Machinery & Equipment). **Sales:** $800,000,000 (2000). **Emp:** 1,500. **Officers:** Sidney Braginsky, President; Yasou Takeuchi, CFO.

■ **22888** ■ **Paulist Productions**
17575 Pacific Coast Hwy.
Pacific Palisades, CA 90272
Phone: (310)454-0688 **Fax:** (310)459-6549
E-mail: paulistpro@aol.com
Products: Films and videocassettes. **SICs:** 5043 (Photographic Equipment & Supplies); 5099 (Durable Goods Nec). **Est:** 1968. **Emp:** 8.

■ **22889** ■ **Pentax Corp.**
35 Inverness Dr. E
Englewood, CO 80112
Phone: (303)799-8000 **Fax:** (303)790-1131
Products: Cameras and supplies. **SIC:** 5043 (Photographic Equipment & Supplies). **Est:** 1976. **Sales:** $97,000,000 (2000). **Emp:** 250. **Officers:** Mafa Tanaka, CEO; Ken Okushi, Treasurer; Joe Graham, VP of Marketing & Sales; Jim Hill, Dir. of Data Processing; Ann Welch, Dir of Human Resources.

■ **22890** ■ **Photo-Cine Labs**
123 Grand Ave.
Billings, MT 59101-6020
Phone: (406)252-3077
URL: http://www.idbadge.com
Products: Photographic equipment and supplies. **SIC:** 5043 (Photographic Equipment & Supplies). **Est:** 1965. **Officers:** Peter Schmidt, Owner.

■ **22891** ■ **Photo Control Corp.**
4800 Quebec Ave. N
Minneapolis, MN 55428
Phone: (612)537-3601 **Fax:** (612)537-2852
E-mail: pcc-info@photo-control.com
URL: http://www.photo-control.com
Products: Professional photographic equipment. **SIC:** 5043 (Photographic Equipment & Supplies). **Est:** 1959. **Sales:** $13,000,000 (2000). **Emp:** 110. **Officers:** Jack R. Helmen.

■ **22892** ■ **Prepress Supply**
18433 Amistad St.
Fountain Valley, CA 92708
Phone: (714)965-9542 **Fax:** (714)965-9546
E-mail: ijsupply@aol.com
Products: Darkroom supplies, including film, paper, and chemicals; Laser supplies and printers, large format ink jet printers, and media scanners. **SIC:** 5043 (Photographic Equipment & Supplies). **Est:** 1991.

Sales: $5,000,000 (2000). Emp: 7. Officers: Mark Bitzer, President.

■ 22893 ■ Primesource
1650 Magnolia Dr.
Cincinnati, OH 45215
Phone: (513)563-6700
Free: (800)582-7406 Fax: (513)563-0377
Products: specialty equipment and products. SIC: 5043 (Photographic Equipment & Supplies). Sales: $27,000,000 (2000). Emp: 45.

■ 22894 ■ Production Services Atlanta Inc.
2000 Lakewood Way Bldg. 4
Atlanta, GA 30315
Phone: (404)622-1311
Free: (800)669-9407 Fax: (404)622-1691
Products: Motion picture equipment. SIC: 5043 (Photographic Equipment & Supplies). Emp: 49. Officers: Jerry Crowder.

■ 22895 ■ Quintana Sales
2411 Camino De Vida
Santa Fe, NM 87505-6428
Phone: (505)471-1053
Products: Photographic equipment and supplies; Cameras. SIC: 5043 (Photographic Equipment & Supplies). Officers: Nancy Quintana, Owner.

■ 22896 ■ Rainbow Photography
213 E Grand Ave.
Laramie, WY 82070-3639
Phone: (307)742-7597
Products: Photographic equipment and supplies; Photographic cameras; Photographic projectors. SIC: 5043 (Photographic Equipment & Supplies). Officers: George Burnette, Owner.

■ 22897 ■ Really Right Stuff Co.
PO Box 6531
Los Osos, CA 93412
Phone: (805)528-6321
Products: Quick release mounting plates for cameras. SIC: 5043 (Photographic Equipment & Supplies). Emp: 2.

■ 22898 ■ Redlake Imaging Corp.
18450 Technology Dr., Ste A
Morgan Hill, CA 95037-5450
Phone: (408)779-6464
Free: (800)453-1223 Fax: (408)778-6256
E-mail: sales@redlake.com
URL: http://www.redlake.com
Products: High speed video equipment. SIC: 5043 (Photographic Equipment & Supplies). Est: 1961. Sales: $6,500,000 (1999). Emp: 30. Officers: Stephen W. Ferrell, Pres. & Treas.; Galen Collins, Secretary; John Foley, Sales/Marketing Contact, e-mail: John.Foley@worldnet.att.net; Tara Corona, Customer Service Contact, e-mail: Tarac@redlake.com; Jeannie Clayton, Human Resources Contact, e-mail: Jclayton@redlake.com.

■ 22899 ■ RPL Supplies Inc.
280 Midland Ave.
Saddle Brook, NJ 07663
Phone: (201)794-8400
Free: (800)524-0914 Fax: (201)794-8458
Products: Computer portrait machines; Ceramic photo mug systems and supplies. SICs: 5045 (Computers, Peripherals & Software); 5099 (Durable Goods Nec). Sales: $8,000,000 (2000). Emp: 18. Officers: Larry Milazzo, President.

■ 22900 ■ Samsung Opto-Electronics America Inc.
40 Seaview Dr.
Secaucus, NJ 07094
Phone: (201)902-0347
Products: Cameras. SIC: 5043 (Photographic Equipment & Supplies). Sales: $60,000,000 (2000). Emp: 30. Officers: Steve Lee, President.

■ 22901 ■ Santa Barbara Instrument Group Corp.
147 Castilian Dr., Ste. A
Goleta, CA 93117-5598
Phone: (805)969-1851
Products: Imaging cameras for telescopes. SICs: 5049 (Professional Equipment Nec); 5043 (Photographic Equipment & Supplies). Sales: $3,000,000 (2000). Emp: 11. Officers: Richard Schwartz, President.

■ 22902 ■ Savage Universal Corp.
550 E Elliot Rd.
Chandler, AZ 85225
Phone: (480)632-1320
Free: (800)624-8891 Fax: (480)632-1322
E-mail: info@savagepaper.com
URL: http://www.savagepaper.com
Products: Photographic supplies; Matboards and mountboards. SICs: 5043 (Photographic Equipment & Supplies); 5112 (Stationery & Office Supplies). Est: 1937. Sales: $10,000,000 (2000). Emp: 50. Officers: Richard Pressman, President; Sylvester Hank, Vice President; Paul G. Poulos, Chairman of the Board & CFO.

■ 22903 ■ Schillers Photo Graphics
9420 Manchester Rd.
St. Louis, MO 63144-2678
Phone: (314)968-3650
Free: (800)366-7244 Fax: (314)968-1184
Products: Photographic supplies, including electronic imaging, televisions, video recorders, graphic art supplies, cameras, and film. SICs: 5043 (Photographic Equipment & Supplies); 5064 (Electrical Appliances—Television & Radio); 5199 (Nondurable Goods Nec). Sales: $14,000,000 (2000). Emp: 58. Officers: William Schiller; Edwin O. Miller.

■ 22904 ■ Sigma Corporation of America
15 Fleetwood Ct.
Ronkonkoma, NY 11779
Phone: (516)585-1144
Free: (800)874-4621 Fax: (516)585-1895
E-mail: sca@mail.com
URL: http://www.signmaphoto.com
Products: Cameras and camera equipment, including lenses and flash units. SIC: 5043 (Photographic Equipment & Supplies). Est: 1985. Sales: $35,200,000 (2000). Emp: 22. Officers: Yoshio Yamaki, President; Vicky Schwarting, Manager; Mark Amirhamzeh, Sales Mgr.

■ 22905 ■ Sinar-Bron Inc.
17 Progress St.
Edison, NJ 08820
Phone: (908)754-5800 Fax: (908)754-5807
Products: Large cameras; Studio lighting equipment. SIC: 5043 (Photographic Equipment & Supplies). Est: 1980. Sales: $24,000,000 (2000). Emp: 37. Officers: Jim Bellina, President.

■ 22906 ■ Southwestern Camera
500 N Shepard
Houston, TX 77007
Phone: (713)880-0121 Fax: (713)880-0356
Products: Cameras; Bags; Tripods; Chemicals. SICs: 5043 (Photographic Equipment & Supplies); 5169 (Chemicals & Allied Products Nec). Sales: $18,000,000 (2000). Emp: 72. Officers: Calvin Jones.

■ 22907 ■ John Stimpson Productions
11 California Ave.
Framingham, MA 01701-8801
Phone: (508)626-0522
Products: Films. SIC: 5043 (Photographic Equipment & Supplies).

■ 22908 ■ Studio Film & Tape Inc.
630 9th Ave., 8th Fl.
New York, NY 10036
Phone: (212)977-9330
Free: (800)444-9330 Fax: (212)586-2420
URL: http://www.sftweb.com
Products: Video tapes and film. SICs: 5043 (Photographic Equipment & Supplies); 5099 (Durable Goods Nec). Est: 1970. Sales: $2,000,000 (2000).

Emp: 20. Officers: Henry Royal; Drew Figuerda, Sec. & Treas.; Dallas Crumley, Customer Service Contact; Olga Castilla, Human Resources Contact.

■ 22909 ■ Supercircuits Inc.
1 Supercircuits Plz.
Leander, TX 78645
Phone: (512)260-0333 Free: (800)335-9777
Products: Micro cameras and equipment. SIC: 5043 (Photographic Equipment & Supplies). Sales: $6,000,000 (2000). Emp: 6. Officers: Steve Klindworth, Owner.

■ 22910 ■ Taskforce Batteries
3596 Moline St., Ste. 101
Aurora, CO 80010-1422
Phone: (303)340-2727
E-mail: task@wswest.net
URL: http://www.taskforcebatteries.com
Products: Batteries for motion picture and video cameras, lights, and telescope equipment. SIC: 5043 (Photographic Equipment & Supplies). Est: 1989. Sales: $900,000 (2000). Emp: 3. Officers: Matt King, President. Former Name: Task-Force Batteries.

■ 22911 ■ Transoceanic Trade, Inc.
2250 N Druid Hills Rd., Ste. 238
Atlanta, GA 30329
Phone: (404)633-8912 Fax: (404)633-3858
Products: Office equipment; Computers; Medical equipment; Electrical appliances, including televisions and radios; Photographic equipment. SICs: 5043 (Photographic Equipment & Supplies); 5044 (Office Equipment); 5045 (Computers, Peripherals & Software); 5047 (Medical & Hospital Equipment); 5064 (Electrical Appliances—Television & Radio). Officers: Samuel Bettsak, President.

■ 22912 ■ UMI
300 N Zeeb Rd.
Ann Arbor, MI 48103
Phone: (734)761-4700
Free: (800)521-0600 Fax: (734)761-3940
Products: Microfilm. SIC: 5043 (Photographic Equipment & Supplies). Est: 1938. Alternate Name: University Microfilms Inc.

■ 22913 ■ Vision Broadcasting Network
1017 New York Ave.
Alamogordo, NM 88310-6921
Phone: (505)437-6363 Fax: (505)437-6363
Products: Photographic equipment and supplies; Cameras; Projectors; Motion picture cameras. SIC: 5043 (Photographic Equipment & Supplies). Officers: William Oechsner, General Manager.

■ 22914 ■ Vivitar Corp.
PO Box 2559
Newbury Park, CA 91319-8559
Phone: (805)498-7008 Fax: (818)700-9862
Products: Cameras and accessories. SIC: 5043 (Photographic Equipment & Supplies). Est: 1938. Sales: $110,000,000 (2000). Emp: 102. Officers: Victor Chernick, CEO; Mark Latt, CFO; Chuck Peralta, Exec. VP of Marketing; Jon Zegan, Dir. of Data Processing; Cathy Pericone, Human Resources Mgr.

■ 22915 ■ Western Photo Packaging
3100 NW Industrial St., Ste. 4
PO Box 10285
Portland, OR 97210-0285
Phone: (503)226-0369 Fax: (503)226-1655
E-mail: wphoto@worldstar.com
Products: Paperboard photo mounts; Presentation folders; Report covers. SIC: 5043 (Photographic Equipment & Supplies). Sales: $550,000 (1999). Emp: 6. Officers: William Dailey. Former Name: Western Photo Mount. Former Name: Photo Packaging West.

■ 22916 ■ Yankee Photo Products Inc.
4024 E Broadway, Ste. 1002
Phoenix, AZ 85040-8823
Phone: (602)437-8200 Fax: (602)437-8978
Products: Camera equipment. SIC: 5043 (Photographic Equipment & Supplies). Sales: $2,000,000 (2000). Emp: 49.

(43) Plastics

Entries in this section are arranged alphabetically by company name. When the company name is a personal name, the company name is alphabetized by the surname unless the first name or initial(s) are part of a trade name. See the User's Guide at the front of this directory for additional information.

■ 22917 ■ **A-Top Polymers Inc.**
47 Rockingham Rd.
Windham, NH 03087-1307
Phone: (603)893-4366 **Fax:** (603)898-5937
URL: http://www.a-toppolymers.com
Products: Resins, including polypropylene and polyetheylene. **SIC:** 5162 (Plastics Materials & Basic Shapes). **Est:** 1978. **Emp:** 8. **Officers:** Peter Krippendorf, President.

■ 22918 ■ **Advanced Plastics Inc.**
7360 Cockrill Bend Blvd.
Nashville, TN 37209-1024
Phone: (615)350-6500
Products: Fiberglass; Sheet plastic; Liquid plastic. **SICs:** 5162 (Plastics Materials & Basic Shapes); 5169 (Chemicals & Allied Products Nec). **Est:** 1959. **Sales:** $15,000,000 (2000). **Emp:** 30. **Officers:** Roy Abner, President; Keith Abner, CFO.

■ 22919 ■ **Aetna Plastics Corp.**
1702 St. Clair Ave.
Cleveland, OH 44114
Phone: (216)781-4421
Free: (800)321-7004 **Fax:** (216)781-4474
E-mail: sales@aetnaplastic.com
URL: http://www.aetnaplastic.com
Products: Industual plastic and plastic piping products. **SIC:** 5162 (Plastics Materials & Basic Shapes). **Est:** 1946. **Sales:** $7,600,000 (2000). **Emp:** 30. **Officers:** Gary P. Davis, President; Alicia Cornelius, Sales/Marketing Contact; Chuck Ogrin, Customer Service Contact.

■ 22920 ■ **AIA Plastics Inc.**
290 E 56th Ave.
Denver, CO 80216
Phone: (303)296-9696
Free: (800)748-2036 **Fax:** (303)296-2146
Products: Plastic fabrication and vacuum forming; Flat glass and plastic skylights; Full line of plastics. **SIC:** 5162 (Plastics Materials & Basic Shapes). **Sales:** $6,000,000 (1999). **Emp:** 30. **Officers:** James W. Donaldson, President.

■ 22921 ■ **AIN Plastics Inc.**
PO Box 151
Mt. Vernon, NY 10551-0151
Phone: (914)668-6800 **Fax:** (914)668-8820
Products: Plastic materials. **SIC:** 5162 (Plastics Materials & Basic Shapes). **Est:** 1970. **Sales:** $30,000,000 (2000). **Emp:** 185. **Officers:** N. Drucker, President; Alex Gabay, CFO.

■ 22922 ■ **AIN Plastics of Michigan Inc.**
PO Box 102
Southfield, MI 48037-0102
Phone: (810)356-4000
Free: (800)521-1757 **Fax:** (810)356-4745
Products: Plastic. **SIC:** 5162 (Plastics Materials & Basic Shapes). **Est:** 1977. **Sales:** $8,000,000 (2000). **Emp:** 35. **Officers:** M.W. Ettenson, President; I. Thompson, Controller; T. Cassani, Sales Mgr.

■ 22923 ■ **American Commodities Inc.**
2945 Davison Rd.
Flint, MI 48506
Phone: (810)767-3800 **Fax:** (810)767-3883
Products: Recycled plastic resins. **SICs:** 5162 (Plastics Materials & Basic Shapes); 5093 (Scrap & Waste Materials). **Est:** 1984. **Emp:** 75. **Officers:** Mark Lieberman, President; Jon Whitlock, Vice President.

■ 22924 ■ **American Renolit Corp.**
135 Algonquin Pkwy.
Whippany, NJ 07981
Phone: (973)386-9200 **Fax:** (973)386-0271
Products: Vinyl sheetings. **SIC:** 5162 (Plastics Materials & Basic Shapes). **Sales:** $10,000,000 (2000). **Emp:** 34. **Officers:** Peter Lowenstein, President.

■ 22925 ■ **American Trade Co.**
1314 Texas Ave., No. 1419
Houston, TX 77002-3515
Phone: (713)229-8602 **Fax:** (713)227-0313
Products: Plastic films. **SIC:** 5162 (Plastics Materials & Basic Shapes). **Est:** 1980. **Sales:** $1,000,000 (2000). **Emp:** 4. **Officers:** Don Dykstra, Managing Director, e-mail: dykstra@hal-pc.org.

■ 22926 ■ **Anaheim Custom Extruders, Inc.**
4640 E La Palma Ave.
Anaheim, CA 92807-1910
Phone: (714)693-8508
Free: (800)229-2760 **Fax:** (714)693-9531
E-mail: info@acextrusions.com
URL: http://www.acextrusions.com
Products: Plastic, including tubing and extruded shapes. **SIC:** 5162 (Plastics Materials & Basic Shapes). **Est:** 1977. **Sales:** $4,800,000 (2000). **Emp:** 47. **Officers:** William A. Czapar; Ron Cooper, Customer Service Contact.

■ 22927 ■ **Angus-Campbell Inc.**
4417 S Soto St.
Vernon, CA 90058
Phone: (213)587-1236 **Fax:** (213)588-7816
Products: Industrial plastics. **SIC:** 5162 (Plastics Materials & Basic Shapes). **Sales:** $1,000,000 (1994). **Emp:** 10. **Officers:** K. Campbell, President.

■ 22928 ■ **Apex Plastic Industries Inc.**
155 Marcus Blvd.
Hauppauge, NY 11788
Phone: (516)231-8888
Free: (800)APEX-INC **Fax:** (516)231-8890
E-mail: apex@webspan.net
URL: http://www.apexplastic.com
Products: PVC films, sheetings, rigid and prismatic sheets and rolls; Holographic effects; Decorative and display products. **SICs:** 5162 (Plastics Materials & Basic Shapes); 5199 (Nondurable Goods Nec). **Est:** 1926. **Emp:** 29. **Officers:** Jon F. Weinstein, President & CEO; Jerome Weinstein, Chairman of the Board; Marjorie Weinstein, Vice President; Michael Rosenthal, Sales & Marketing Contact.

■ 22929 ■ **Artform Industries Inc.**
3310 Towanda Ave.
Baltimore, MD 21215
Phone: (410)664-2800 **Fax:** (410)664-5048
Products: Thermo-formed plastics. **SIC:** 5162 (Plastics Materials & Basic Shapes). **Sales:** $7,000,000 (2000). **Emp:** 100. **Officers:** Arnold Bereson, CEO; Steven Wasserman, President; Scott Macdonald, VP of Admin.

■ 22930 ■ **Atlantis Plastics, Inc.**
PO Box 2118
Elkhart, IN 46515
Phone: (219)294-6502 **Fax:** (219)294-3214
Products: Extruded PVC. **SICs:** 5162 (Plastics Materials & Basic Shapes); 5093 (Scrap & Waste Materials). **Est:** 1957. **Emp:** 100.

■ 22931 ■ **Auburn Plastics and Rubber Inc.**
PO Box 19871
Indianapolis, IN 46219
Phone: (317)352-1565 **Fax:** (317)351-2752
Products: Plastic parts. **SIC:** 5162 (Plastics Materials & Basic Shapes). **Est:** 1967. **Sales:** $5,000,000 (2000). **Emp:** 15. **Officers:** Paul E. Lewis, President.

■ 22932 ■ **Aztec Supply Co.**
954 N Batavia St.
Orange, CA 92867
Phone: (714)771-6580 **Fax:** (714)771-3013
Products: Plastic storage bins, steel shelving, mezzanines, and modular offices. **SICs:** 5162 (Plastics Materials & Basic Shapes); 5046 (Commercial Equipment Nec). **Sales:** $1,800,000 (2000). **Emp:** 9. **Officers:** Eric Berge, Partner; Alex Yakutis, Partner, Finance.

■ 22933 ■ **Bags Direct, Inc.**
3482 Oakcliff Rd., Ste. B-2
Atlanta, GA 30340
Phone: (770)454-7276 **Fax:** (770)455-1446
E-mail: sales@bagsdirectusa.com
URL: http://www.bagsdirectusa.com
Products: Disposable paper and plastic bags; Plastic film and sheet. **SIC:** 5162 (Plastics Materials & Basic Shapes). **Est:** 1995. **Sales:** $6,000,000 (1999). **Emp:** 10. **Officers:** Ike Maya, e-mail: ike@bagsrus.com; Sid Maya. **Former Name:** Bags R Us, Inc.

■ 22934 ■ **Robert A. Beard and Associates Inc.**
4918 70th St.
Kenosha, WI 53142-1626
Phone: (414)658-1778 **Fax:** (414)658-3478
Products: New product research, design, and development of plastic devices and packaging. **SIC:** 5162 (Plastics Materials & Basic Shapes).

■ 22935 ■ **B.E.B. Ltd.**
5970 River Chase Cir.
Atlanta, GA 30328
Phone: (404)850-0795 **Fax:** (404)850-0895
Products: Plastic materials and supplies. **SIC:** 5162 (Plastics Materials & Basic Shapes).

■ 22936 ■ **Bevco Inc.**
PO Box 3494
Billings, MT 59103-3494
Phone: (406)248-2670   **Fax:** (406)248-5645
Products: Laminated plastics; Plastic materials, including countertops and room dividers. **SIC:** 5162 (Plastics Materials & Basic Shapes). **Officers:** Scott Lay, President.

■ 22937 ■ **Big Valley Plastics Inc.**
PO Box 1690
Sumner, WA 98390
Phone: (253)863-8111   **Fax:** (253)863-5833
Products: Plastic flower pots and nursery containers; Custom injection molding; Water systems; Horticultural supplies. **SIC:** 5199 (Nondurable Goods Nec). **Sales:** $31,200,000 (2000). **Emp:** 150.

■ 22938 ■ **Business Development International**
45 E End Ave., Ste. 11D
New York, NY 10028
Phone: (212)650-1689   **Fax:** (212)650-1689
Products: Specializing in the business side of chemical, plastics and related industries-international technology transfer, licensing, acquisitions, divestitures, mergers, joint ventures, evaluating, due diligence, trouble-shooting, marketing research, plastics flame retardance and recycling. **SIC:** 5162 (Plastics Materials & Basic Shapes).

■ 22939 ■ **Cadillac Plastic and Chemical Div.**
2855 Coolidge Hwy., Ste. 300
Troy, MI 48084-3217
Phone: (810)583-1200   **Fax:** (810)583-4715
Products: Plastic rods and tubes. **SIC:** 5162 (Plastics Materials & Basic Shapes). **Est:** 1945. **Sales:** $170,000,000 (2000). **Emp:** 1,000. **Officers:** Kent Darragh, President; Steve Augustyn, VP & CFO; Thomas Taylor, VP of Marketing; William Watson, Dir of Human Resources.

■ 22940 ■ **Cadillac Plastic Group Inc.**
2855 Coolidge Hwy., Ste. 300
Troy, MI 48084
Phone: (248)205-3100   **Fax:** (248)205-3187
Products: Plastic sheets, tubes, film and rods. **SIC:** 5162 (Plastics Materials & Basic Shapes). **Sales:** $270,000,000 (2000). **Emp:** 1,549. **Officers:** Kent Darragh, President; Steve Augustyn, Vice President.

■ 22941 ■ **Capital Design Inc.**
860 a Waterman Ave.
East Providence, RI 02914
Phone: (401)431-2150   **Fax:** (401)438-9360
E-mail: info@freemiums.com
URL: http://www.freemiums.com
Products: Metal stampings; Promotional items. **SICs:** 5162 (Plastics Materials & Basic Shapes); 5051 (Metals Service Centers & Offices). **Est:** 1987. **Officers:** Judith Mann, President.

■ 22942 ■ **Carson Industries LLC**
1160 Nicole Ct
Glendora, CA 91740-5386
Phone: (909)592-6272
Free: (800)735-5566   **Fax:** (909)592-7971
E-mail: customerservice@carsonind.com
URL: http://www.carsonind.com
Products: Plastics. **SIC:** 5162 (Plastics Materials & Basic Shapes). **Est:** 1969. **Former Name:** Carson-Brooks Plastics, Inc. **Former Name:** Carson Industries, Inc.

■ 22943 ■ **Clark-Schwebel Distribution Corp.**
PO Box 3448
Santa Fe Springs, CA 90670
Phone: (562)921-9926
Products: Plastics materials. **SIC:** 5162 (Plastics Materials & Basic Shapes). **Sales:** $16,000,000 (1991). **Emp:** 80. **Officers:** Marvin B. Fuller, President.

■ 22944 ■ **Cloutier Supply Co.**
445 W Main St.
Hyannis, MA 02601
Phone: (508)775-6100
Products: Plastics; Ceramic tile. **SICs:** 5162 (Plastics Materials & Basic Shapes); 5032 (Brick, Stone & Related Materials).

■ 22945 ■ **Dr. Ernest A. Coleman**
293 Janes Ln.
Stamford, CT 06903-4822
Phone: (203)329-3693   **Fax:** (203)595-0833
Products: Supplies expert knowledge of plastics, plastics additives, plastic compounding, formulation, and processing. **SIC:** 5162 (Plastics Materials & Basic Shapes).

■ 22946 ■ **Commercial Plastics and Supply Corp.**
543 NW 77th St.
Boca Raton, FL 33487
Phone: (561)994-0076
Free: (800)635-0880   **Fax:** (561)994-9050
E-mail: http://www.complas.com
Products: Plastic sheets, rods, tubes, film and resins. **SIC:** 5162 (Plastics Materials & Basic Shapes). **Est:** 1945. **Sales:** $113,000,000 (2000). **Emp:** 800. **Officers:** M.R. French Sr., CEO.

■ 22947 ■ **Commercial Plastics and Supply Inc.**
9831 Jamaica Ave.
Richmond Hill, NY 11418
Phone: (718)849-9000   **Fax:** (718)847-1656
Products: Plastics, including plexiglass. **SIC:** 5162 (Plastics Materials & Basic Shapes). **Est:** 1946. **Sales:** $13,000,000 (2000). **Emp:** 155. **Officers:** M.R. French Sr., CEO; Richard Bilello, VP of Sales.

■ 22948 ■ **Conprotec Inc.**
6 Raymond Ave.
Salem, NH 03079-2945
Phone: (603)893-2727   **Fax:** (603)893-3737
Products: Plastics materials and resins; Plastics basic shapes. **SIC:** 5162 (Plastics Materials & Basic Shapes). **Officers:** S. Chen, President.

■ 22949 ■ **Corr Tech Inc.**
4545 Homestead Rd.
Houston, TX 77028
Phone: (713)674-7887   **Fax:** (713)674-7242
Products: Corrosion resistant and high purity fluid and air handling products. **SICs:** 5162 (Plastics Materials & Basic Shapes); 5074 (Plumbing & Hydronic Heating Supplies); 5049 (Professional Equipment Nec). **Sales:** $30,000,000 (2000). **Emp:** 95. **Officers:** Doris Gottesman, President.

■ 22950 ■ **Curbell Inc.**
7 Cobham Dr.
Orchard Park, NY 14127-4180
Phone: (716)667-3377
Free: (888)287-2355   **Fax:** (716)667-3702
E-mail: plastics@curbell.com
URL: http://www.curbell.com
Products: Plastic sheets, rods, tubes, adhesives, and sealants. **SICs:** 5162 (Plastics Materials & Basic Shapes); 5169 (Chemicals & Allied Products Nec). **Est:** 1942. **Sales:** $32,000,000 (2000). **Emp:** 135. **Officers:** Tom Leone, President; Steve Whitehead, Mgr. of Finance; Art Weibel, GM of Finance; Sandy Kutch, Marketing & Sales Mgr.; Susan Schubbe, Dir of Human Resources; Larry Thomas, Customer Service Contact.

■ 22951 ■ **Currie Industries Inc.**
PO Box 567
Old Saybrook, CT 06475
Phone: (203)388-4638
Products: Plastic and metal components. **SICs:** 5162 (Plastics Materials & Basic Shapes); 5085 (Industrial Supplies). **Sales:** $1,000,000 (1993). **Emp:** 5. **Officers:** James A. Currie, President.

■ 22952 ■ **Darant Distribution**
1832 E 68th Ave.
Denver, CO 80229
Phone: (303)289-2220   **Fax:** (303)289-2225
Products: Plastics; Adhesives; Hinges; Slides. **SIC:** 5031 (Lumber, Plywood & Millwork). **Est:** 1985. **Emp:** 50. **Officers:** Robert Grant, President.

■ 22953 ■ **Depco Inc.**
PO Box 486
Contoocook, NH 03229-0486
Phone: (603)226-4393
Products: Plastics materials and basic shapes. **SIC:**

5162 (Plastics Materials & Basic Shapes). **Officers:** R. Howard, President.

■ 22954 ■ **Dielectric Corp.**
N 83 W 13330 Leon Rd.
Menomonee Falls, WI 53051
Phone: (414)255-2600   **Fax:** (414)255-2761
Products: Plastics materials. **SIC:** 5162 (Plastics Materials & Basic Shapes). **Sales:** $12,500,000 (1992). **Emp:** 100. **Officers:** Raymond Esser, CEO; Carl Mikowitz, CFO.

■ 22955 ■ **Discas Inc.**
567-1 S Leonard St., Bldg. 1
Waterbury, CT 06708
Phone: (203)753-5147
Products: Thermoplastic resin custom molding and extrusion; Recycling of TPE compounds. **SIC:** 5093 (Scrap & Waste Materials). **Sales:** $3,000,000 (2000). **Emp:** 23. **Officers:** Patrick A. DePaolo, President.

■ 22956 ■ **Diversified Foam Products Inc.**
5117 Central Hwy.
Pennsauken, NJ 08109
Phone: (609)662-1981   **Fax:** (609)662-2273
Products: Plastics foam products; Sponge, expanded and foam rubber products. **SICs:** 5199 (Nondurable Goods Nec); 5162 (Plastics Materials & Basic Shapes). **Est:** 1982. **Sales:** $5,000,000 (2000). **Emp:** 35. **Officers:** Matthew Harris, President; Conrad Ambrette, Vice President.

■ 22957 ■ **Eager Plastics Inc.**
3350 W 48th Pl.
Chicago, IL 60632-3000
Phone: (773)927-3484   **Fax:** (773)650-5853
Products: Silicone, epoxy, polyester, and polyurethane products. **SICs:** 5162 (Plastics Materials & Basic Shapes); 5169 (Chemicals & Allied Products Nec). **Est:** 1977. **Sales:** $1,000,000 (1999). **Emp:** 5. **Officers:** Peter Cumerford, President, e-mail: petercumerford@msn.com.

■ 22958 ■ **Engineered Plastics Inc.**
211 Chase St.
PO Box 227
Gibsonville, NC 27249-0227
Phone: (336)449-4121   **Fax:** (336)449-6352
E-mail: epi@netpath.net
Products: Plastic products; Custom fabricated components/assemblies. **SIC:** 5162 (Plastics Materials & Basic Shapes). **Est:** 1947. **Sales:** $3,000,000 (2000). **Emp:** 30. **Officers:** Dwight M. Davidson III, President; Robert C. Ratliff, Dir. of Marketing.

■ 22959 ■ **Fabricated Plastics Inc.**
PO Box 1907
Morristown, NJ 07960-1907
Phone: (973)539-4200
Free: (800)932-0715   **Fax:** (973)539-1317
Products: Custom mold plastic items. **SIC:** 5162 (Plastics Materials & Basic Shapes). **Est:** 1947. **Sales:** $15,000,000 (2000). **Emp:** 150. **Officers:** Sebastian Murray, CEO & President; Samuel Murray, Vice President; Jay Disler, CFO & VP of Finance & Admin.

■ 22960 ■ **Federal Plastics Corp.**
715 South Ave.
Cranford, NJ 07016
Phone: (908)272-5800   **Fax:** (908)272-9021
Products: Plastic pellets. **SIC:** 5162 (Plastics Materials & Basic Shapes). **Est:** 1960. **Sales:** $10,000,000 (2000). **Emp:** 33. **Officers:** Peter T. Triano, President; Michael A. Triano, Treasurer & Secty.

■ 22961 ■ **Fiberglass Hawaii, Inc.**
1377 Colburn St.
Honolulu, HI 96817
Phone: (808)847-3951   **Fax:** (808)841-2108
Products: Fiberglass resin and accessories. **SIC:** 5162 (Plastics Materials & Basic Shapes).

■ 22962 ■ **FIC International Corp.**
556 Commercial St.
San Francisco, CA 94111
Phone: (510)463-1073   **Fax:** (510)463-2937
Products: Acrylic sheet. **SIC:** 5162 (Plastics Materials & Basic Shapes). **Est:** 1976. **Sales:** $2,500,000 (2000). **Emp:** 3. **Officers:** Walter Mossner, General Mgr.

■ 22963 ■ First Phillips Marketing Company Inc.
1 Acton Pl.
Acton, MA 01720
Phone: (508)264-9034 Fax: (508)264-4715
Products: Plastic goods, including bowls and trays; Chrome. SICs: 5162 (Plastics Materials & Basic Shapes); 5085 (Industrial Supplies). Est: 1984. Sales: $4,000,000 (2000). Emp: 4. Officers: Samuel T. Phillips, President; Chuck Piper, VP of Finance; Paul Kaminker, Dir. of Marketing.

■ 22964 ■ Foam Factory and Upholstery Inc.
7777 Sixteen Mile Rd.
Sterling Heights, MI 48312
Phone: (810)795-3626
Products: Foam products. SIC: 5199 (Nondurable Goods Nec).

■ 22965 ■ Foam Products of San Antonio Inc.
1119 N Mesquite
San Antonio, TX 78202-1120
Phone: (210)228-0033
Products: Foam products. SIC: 5199 (Nondurable Goods Nec).

■ 22966 ■ Galaxy Liner Company Inc.
7546 W McNab Rd.
North Lauderdale, FL 33068
Phone: (954)720-5384
Free: (800)940-6067 Fax: (954)721-0157
Products: Plastic bags, sheeting, and tubing. SIC: 5162 (Plastics Materials & Basic Shapes).

■ 22967 ■ Gar-Ron Plastics Corp.
5424 Pulaski Hwy.
Baltimore, MD 21205
Phone: (410)483-1122
Products: Plastic products, including tubing. SIC: 5162 (Plastics Materials & Basic Shapes). Est: 1967. Sales: $4,000,000 (2000). Emp: 35. Officers: R.M. Ruane, President.

■ 22968 ■ General Polymers Div.
12001 Toepfer Rd.
Warren, MI 48089
Phone: (810)755-1100 Fax: (810)755-2727
Products: Plastic, including resins. SIC: 5162 (Plastics Materials & Basic Shapes). Est: 1973. Sales: $650,000,000 (2000). Emp: 270. Officers: Daniel W. McGuire, VP & General Merchandising Mgr.; Bob Sparks, CFO.

■ 22969 ■ GeoCHEM Inc.
PO Box 838
Renton, WA 98057-0838
Phone: (425)227-9312 Fax: (425)227-8797
URL: http://www.geocheminc.com
Products: Specialty plastic products for civil construction, land protection, and bioremediation. SIC: 5162 (Plastics Materials & Basic Shapes). Est: 1982. Sales: $1,000,000 (2000). Emp: 6. Officers: David Neubauer, Vice President, e-mail: davneub@geocheminc.com; Joe Neubauer, President, e-mail: joeneub1@geocheminc.com.

■ 22970 ■ GLS Thermoplastic Elastomers Div.
833 Ridgeview Dr.
McHenry, IL 60050
Phone: (815)385-8500 Fax: (815)385-8533
E-mail: info@glscorp.com
URL: http://www.glscorporation.com
Products: Thermoplastic elastomers. SICs: 5162 (Plastics Materials & Basic Shapes); 5169 (Chemicals & Allied Products Nec). Est: 1940. Emp: 60. Officers: Daniel V. Dague, General Mgr.

■ 22971 ■ Goldmark Plastic Co.
Nassau Terminal Rd.
New Hyde Park, NY 11040
Phone: (516)352-4373 Fax: (516)352-4364
Products: Plastic raw materials and resins. SIC: 5162 (Plastics Materials & Basic Shapes). Est: 1957. Sales: $75,000,000 (2000). Emp: 50. Officers: Kenneth Gross, Treasurer & Secty.; Stanley Goldmack, Sales/Marketing Contact.

■ 22972 ■ Len Gordon Co.
7215 Bermuda Rd.
Las Vegas, NV 89119-4304
Phone: (702)361-0600
Free: (800)237-9937 Fax: (702)361-0613
E-mail: lgordon@lengordon.com
URL: http://www.lengordon.com
Products: Pneumatic and electronic controls and components; Plastic injection molding. SICs: 5162 (Plastics Materials & Basic Shapes); 5063 (Electrical Apparatus & Equipment). Emp: 99. Officers: Judge Gordon, CEO; Marie Levesque, VP of Sales; Carla Cannon, VP of Finance.

■ 22973 ■ Grafix Plastic
19499 Miles Rd.
Cleveland, OH 44128
Phone: (216)581-9050 Fax: (216)581-9041
E-mail: info@grafixplastics.com
URL: http://www.grafixplastics.com
Products: Plastic film and sheets. SIC: 5162 (Plastics Materials & Basic Shapes). Est: 1963. Sales: $4,000,000 (2000). Emp: 22. Officers: Jordan Katz, President, e-mail: jordan@grafixplastics.com; Roger Baden, Sales/Marketing Contact; Amy Middock, Customer Service Contact; Gary Sloan, Human Resources Contact. Former Name: Graphic Arts Systems Inc.

■ 22974 ■ Graphic Arts Systems Inc.
19499 Miles Rd.
Cleveland, OH 44128
Phone: (216)581-9050 Fax: (216)581-9041
Products: Plasticss. SIC: 5162 (Plastics Materials & Basic Shapes). Sales: $4,000,000 (2000). Emp: 22.

■ 22975 ■ Greenstreak Inc.
PO Box 7139
St. Louis, MO 63177
Phone: (636)225-9400
Free: (800)325-9504 Fax: (636)225-2049
E-mail: info@greenstreak.com
URL: http://www.greenstreak.com
Products: Water stops. SIC: 5162 (Plastics Materials & Basic Shapes). Sales: $11,000,000 (1999). Emp: 11. Officers: Mark England, President; Anna Craven, Admin. Mgr. Former Name: Greenstreak Plastic Products.

■ 22976 ■ Greenstreak Plastic Products
PO Box 7139
St. Louis, MO 63177
Phone: (314)225-9400
Products: Plastics. SIC: 5162 (Plastics Materials & Basic Shapes). Sales: $11,000,000 (2000). Emp: 60. Officers: Charlie Van Dyke, President; Gary Williams, CFO.

■ 22977 ■ M.A. Hanna Resin Distribution Inc.
PO Box 428
Lemont, IL 60439
Phone: (708)972-0505 Fax: (708)972-0520
Products: Nylon; Polyurethane. SIC: 5162 (Plastics Materials & Basic Shapes). Est: 1965. Sales: $200,000,000 (2000). Emp: 90. Officers: Richard Anderson, President; David Knowles, Exec. VP; Jack Klingenmeier, VP & General Merchandising Mgr.; Larry Cobden, Controller.

■ 22978 ■ Harrington Industrial Plastics Inc.
14480 Yorba Ave.
Chino, CA 91710
Phone: (909)597-8641
Products: Plastic piping products. SIC: 5162 (Plastics Materials & Basic Shapes). Est: 1960. Sales: $81,000,000 (2000). Emp: 275. Officers: William McCollum, CEO & President; Neville G. Alexander, CFO; Paul E. Crist, VP & General Merchandising Mgr.; Donald Chioda, Dir. of Data Processing.

■ 22979 ■ HBG Export Corp.
454 S Anderson Rd., B.T.C. 506
Rock Hill, SC 29730
Phone: (803)329-2128 Fax: (803)329-2129
E-mail: hbgexpor@cetlink.net
Products: Thermoplastic resins, including inks; Textile finishing agents; Paper chemical additives. SICs: 5162 (Plastics Materials & Basic Shapes); 5099 (Durable Goods Nec); 5169 (Chemicals & Allied Products Nec).

Est: 1986. Sales: $3,000,000 (2000). Emp: 5. Officers: Jack Dodd, President.

■ 22980 ■ Ryan Herco Products Corp.
PO Box 588
Burbank, CA 91503
Phone: (818)841-1141 Fax: (818)842-4488
Products: Industrial plastics. SICs: 5162 (Plastics Materials & Basic Shapes); 5085 (Industrial Supplies). Est: 1948. Sales: $60,000,000 (2000). Emp: 160. Officers: Frank Gibbs, President; Brian Bowman, Chairman of the Board & CFO; Larry King, VP of Marketing & Sales; Natalee Pucher, Dir. of Data Processing; Linda Kass, Treasurer & Secty.

■ 22981 ■ M. Holland Co.
400 Skokie Blvd.
Northbrook, IL 60062
Phone: (847)272-7370
Free: (800)872-7370 Fax: (847)272-0525
Products: Thermoplastic resins. SIC: 5162 (Plastics Materials & Basic Shapes). Est: 1950. Sales: $110,000,000 (2000). Emp: 62. Officers: Edward Holland, President; Barbara Martin-Wyatt, Exec. VP & CFO; Philip Holland, Vice President.

■ 22982 ■ Horn Plastics Inc.
4207 12th Ave. NW
PO Box 5312
Fargo, ND 58105-5312
Phone: (701)282-7447
Free: (800)373-7448 Fax: (701)281-0439
E-mail: plastics@rrnet.com
URL: http://www.superslide.com
Products: Plastic truck box liner systems; Plastic parts. SICs: 5162 (Plastics Materials & Basic Shapes); 5013 (Motor Vehicle Supplies & New Parts). Est: 1983. Sales: $5,000,000 (2000). Emp: 26. Officers: Phil Horn, President; Ilene Osten, Sales/Marketing Contact.

■ 22983 ■ Industrial Plastics Inc.
740 S 28th St.
Washougal, WA 98671
Phone: (253)835-2129 Fax: (253)835-3521
Products: Plastic pipes and fittings. SIC: 5162 (Plastics Materials & Basic Shapes). Est: 1972. Sales: $5,000,000 (2000). Emp: 35. Officers: Jayne K. Salsberry, President; Rolland E. Salsberry, Exec. VP; Gordon M. Ochs, Dir. of Marketing.

■ 22984 ■ Intersystems of Delaware
93 Mason St.
Greenwich, CT 06830
Phone: (203)629-1400
Products: Thermoplastic resins. SIC: 5162 (Plastics Materials & Basic Shapes). Sales: $15,000,000 (1993). Emp: 328. Officers: Herbert M. Pearlman, CEO & President; Daniel T. Murphy, VP & CFO.

■ 22985 ■ JATCO Inc.
725 Zwissig Way
Union City, CA 94587
Phone: (510)487-0888 Fax: (510)487-1880
Products: Custom plastic injection molding, finishing and assembly; Contract manufacturing and distribution. SIC: 5162 (Plastics Materials & Basic Shapes). Officers: Paul Appelblom, President.

■ 22986 ■ Kerr Group Inc.
500 New Holland Ave.
Lancaster, PA 17602-2104
Phone: (717)299-6511
Free: (800)367-1877 Fax: (717)299-5844
URL: http://www.kerrgroup.com
Products: Plastic caps and containers. SIC: 5162 (Plastics Materials & Basic Shapes). Est: 1903. Sales: $140,000,000 (2000). Emp: 800. Officers: Richard Hofman, CEO & President; Larry Caldwell, CFO.

■ 22987 ■ Labinal, Inc.
881 Parkview Blvd.
Lombard, IL 60148
Phone: (630)705-5700 Fax: (630)705-5704
Products: Nonferrous, die and plaster castings. SIC: 5088 (Transportation Equipment & Supplies). Sales: $200,000,000 (2000). Emp: 2,500. Officers: Amaury Du Fretay, President.

■ 22988 ■ Lainiere De Picardie Inc.
180 Wheeler Ct., Ste. 4
Langhorne, PA 19047
Phone: (215)702-9090 **Fax:** (215)702-9040
Products: Plastic clips for the textile industry. **SIC:** 5162 (Plastics Materials & Basic Shapes). **Sales:** $6,000,000 (2000). **Emp:** 15. **Officers:** John Huss, President; Joyce Duffy, Controller.

■ 22989 ■ Laird Plastics Inc.
1400 Centrepark, Ste. 500
West Palm Beach, FL 33401
Phone: (561)684-7000
Free: (800)610-1016 **Fax:** (561)684-7088
E-mail: feedback@lairdplastics.com
URL: http://www.lairdplastics.com
Products: Semi-finished plastic sheets, rods, tubes, films, and other specialized plastics. **SIC:** 5162 (Plastics Materials & Basic Shapes). **Sales:** $61,000,000 (2000). **Emp:** 500. **Officers:** John W. Perdiue, CEO & President.

■ 22990 ■ Lake Crescent Inc.
33-00 Broadway, Ste. 202
Fair Lawn, NJ 07410
Phone: (201)794-3500
Free: (800)252-7735 **Fax:** (201)794-8090
E-mail: ici@kasselsales.com
Products: Plastic film. **SIC:** 5162 (Plastics Materials & Basic Shapes). **Est:** 1988. **Sales:** $20,000,000 (2000). **Emp:** 8. **Officers:** Jack Kassel, President. **Alternate Name:** Bestmark International.

■ 22991 ■ Laminates Unlimited Inc.
PO Box 25036
Oklahoma City, OK 73125-0036
Phone: (405)239-2646
Products: Plastics materials such as formica. **SIC:** 5162 (Plastics Materials & Basic Shapes). **Sales:** $5,000,000 (1994). **Emp:** 19. **Officers:** Richard Clements, President & CFO.

■ 22992 ■ Lavanture Plastic Extrusion Technologies
PO Box 2088
Elkhart, IN 46515
Phone: (219)264-0658
Free: (800)348-7625 **Fax:** (219)264-6601
Products: Plastic profile extrusions. **SIC:** 5162 (Plastics Materials & Basic Shapes). **Sales:** $32,000,000 (2000). **Emp:** 163. **Officers:** Richard Lavanture, President; Steve Fulton, Treasurer.

■ 22993 ■ Leathertone Inc.
PO Box 247
153 Hamlet Ave.
Woonsocket, RI 02895-0781
Phone: (401)765-2450 **Fax:** (401)769-8246
E-mail: Leathertone@EZGRAV.com
Products: Plastic materials; Engraving materials. **SICs:** 5162 (Plastics Materials & Basic Shapes); 5049 (Professional Equipment Nec). **Officers:** James Rubenstein, President; Robbie Robidona, Sales/Marketing Contact.

■ 22994 ■ Leed Plastics Corp.
793 E Pico Blvd.
Los Angeles, CA 90021-2105
Phone: (213)746-5984
Free: (800)421-9880 **Fax:** (213)746-5991
Products: Miscellaneous plastics products; machined plastic parts. **SIC:** 5162 (Plastics Materials & Basic Shapes). **Est:** 1945. **Sales:** $1,000,000 (2000). **Emp:** 17. **Officers:** I. Sankey, President; Gary A. Tomsik, Dir. of Marketing; Damian Lopez.

■ 22995 ■ Marval Industries Inc.
315 Hoyt Ave.
Mamaroneck, NY 10543
Phone: (914)381-2400 **Fax:** (914)381-2259
Products: Plastics; Color concentrates. **SICs:** 5169 (Chemicals & Allied Products Nec); 5162 (Plastics Materials & Basic Shapes). **Est:** 1956. **Sales:** $15,000,000 (2000). **Emp:** 65. **Officers:** Alan K. Zimmerman, President; Tom Zimmerman, Exec. VP; Harold A. Holz, VP of Sales.

■ 22996 ■ Matthews and Associates Inc.
16000 Dallas Pwky., No. 235
Dallas, TX 75248-1145
Phone: (972)385-3773 **Fax:** (972)385-3737
E-mail: ma2dal@airmail.net
URL: http://www.matthews-associates.com
Products: Plastics; Oscillators; Motors; Injection molding; Structural foam molding; Stepper motors; Metal cabinets and sheet metal; Plastic extrusions; Vacuum and pressure forming; Aluminum diecasting. **SICs:** 5162 (Plastics Materials & Basic Shapes); 5065 (Electronic Parts & Equipment Nec). **Est:** 1980. **Sales:** $30,000,000 (2000). **Emp:** 7. **Officers:** R. Matthews, President; George Fink, CFO.

■ 22997 ■ Meyer Plastics Inc.
PO Box 20902
Indianapolis, IN 46220-4816
Phone: (317)259-4131 **Fax:** (317)252-4687
Products: Plastics. **SIC:** 5162 (Plastics Materials & Basic Shapes). **Est:** 1926. **Emp:** 100. **Officers:** Ralph R. Meyer, President; Michael O'Connell, CFO; Michael W. Hill, VP of Sales; Thomas G. Weesner, Strategic Planning/Marketing, e-mail: weesner@ meyerplastics.com.

■ 22998 ■ Midwest Plastics Supply Inc.
2248 S Mead
Wichita, KS 67211
Phone: (316)267-7511 **Fax:** (316)267-0928
Products: Plastic sheets and rods. **SIC:** 5162 (Plastics Materials & Basic Shapes). **Est:** 1961. **Sales:** $6,000,000 (2000). **Emp:** 8. **Officers:** Skip Smith, President and owner; Myrtle Dewey, Vice President.

■ 22999 ■ Milvan Packaging Company Inc.
31090 San Antonio St.
Hayward, CA 94544-7904
Phone: (510)793-7918 **Fax:** (510)793-7684
Products: Plastics packaging products. **SIC:** 5162 (Plastics Materials & Basic Shapes). **Sales:** $3,000,000 (2000). **Emp:** 10. **Officers:** Michael P. Keenan, President & Treasurer.

■ 23000 ■ MTH Corp.
5 Northern Blvd.
Amherst, NH 03031-2302
Phone: (603)886-0011 **Fax:** (603)886-7244
Products: Plastics materials and resins; Plastics basic shapes. **SIC:** 5162 (Plastics Materials & Basic Shapes). **Officers:** O. Hodges, President.

■ 23001 ■ H. Muehlstein and Company Inc.
PO Box 5445
Norwalk, CT 06856-5445
Phone: (203)855-6000 **Fax:** (203)855-6222
Products: Commodity, specialty, and engineering plastic and rubber polymers. **SICs:** 5162 (Plastics Materials & Basic Shapes); 5085 (Industrial Supplies). **Est:** 1911. **Sales:** $700,000,000 (2000). **Emp:** 280. **Officers:** J. Kevin Donohue, CEO & President; Ron Restivo, Controller; Damian Mullin, North American Sales Mgr.; Mark Lux, VP & Commercial Dir.

■ 23002 ■ Multi-Craft Plastics, Inc.
240 N Broadway
Portland, OR 97227
Phone: (503)288-5131 **Fax:** (503)282-5696
Products: Fabricated plastic. **SIC:** 5162 (Plastics Materials & Basic Shapes).

■ 23003 ■ Northern Laminate Sales Inc.
11 Industrial Way
Atkinson, NH 03811-2194
Phone: (603)894-5804 **Fax:** (603)894-5537
Products: Plastic laminates. **SIC:** 5162 (Plastics Materials & Basic Shapes). **Officers:** Derek Russell, President.

■ 23004 ■ Olympic Industries Inc.
PO Box 1832
Hobbs, NM 88241-1832
Phone: (505)393-8048
Products: Plastics; Plastics basic shapes. **SIC:** 5162 (Plastics Materials & Basic Shapes). **Officers:** Kenneth Marsh, President.

■ 23005 ■ Percura Inc.
19142 Mesa Dr.
Villa Park, CA 92861-1319
Fax: (714)998-3146
Products: Provides technical assistance in biomedical materials and processes. Materials include polyurethanes, silicones, thermosets, thermoplastics, and adhesive. Processes include dip molding, foam molding, casting, extrusion, injection molding, welding, and prototyping. **SIC:** 5162 (Plastics Materials & Basic Shapes). **Emp:** 2.

■ 23006 ■ Plascom Trading Company
2155 US Highway 1
Trenton, NJ 08648-4407
Phone: (609)587-9522 **Fax:** (609)587-3328
Products: Plastics, including polystyrene thermoplastics, polycarbonate thermoplastics, polyethylene thermoplastics, and polypropylene thermoplastics. **SIC:** 5162 (Plastics Materials & Basic Shapes). **Officers:** Michael D. Domino, Director.

■ 23007 ■ Plastic Distributing Corp.
Molumco Industrial Pk
Ayer, MA 01432
Phone: (508)772-0764 **Fax:** (508)772-4624
Products: Plastic. **SIC:** 5162 (Plastics Materials & Basic Shapes). **Sales:** $65,000,000 (2000). **Emp:** 150. **Officers:** Regis Magnus, President; Chuck Walkovich, CFO; David E. Hazel, Dir. of Marketing & Sales; Bob Murphy, Dir of Human Resources.

■ 23008 ■ Plastic Fabricators Inc.
555 Sherman Ave.
Hamden, CT 06514
Phone: (203)288-2303
Products: Plastic materials. **SIC:** 5162 (Plastics Materials & Basic Shapes). **Sales:** $1,000,000 (1993). **Emp:** 2. **Officers:** Burt Firtel, President.

■ 23009 ■ The Plastic Man Inc.
3919 Renate Dr.
Las Vegas, NV 89103-1804
Phone: (702)362-2113 **Fax:** (702)362-3584
Products: Plastics materials; Plastics basic shapes; Plastics sheet and rods; Custom fabrication. **SIC:** 5162 (Plastics Materials & Basic Shapes). **Est:** 1985. **Sales:** $1,000,000 (2000). **Officers:** Art Roehl, President. **Former Name:** A.M. Roehl Sales Inc.

■ 23010 ■ Plastic Piping Systems Inc.
3601 Tryclan Dr.
Charlotte, NC 28217
Phone: (704)527-6494 **Fax:** (704)527-6497
Products: Molded plastics products; Plastics basic shapes. **SIC:** 5162 (Plastics Materials & Basic Shapes). **Est:** 1969. **Sales:** $23,000,000 (2000). **Emp:** 85. **Officers:** L.G. Arnold, President; C.D. Wendroff, VP of Operations; Betty Whitrhead, Dir of Personnel.

■ 23011 ■ Plastic Sales Southern Inc.
6490 Fleet St.
Los Angeles, CA 90040
Phone: (323)728-8309 **Fax:** (323)722-4221
Products: Raw plastic material, including sheets and tubing. **SIC:** 5162 (Plastics Materials & Basic Shapes). **Est:** 1958. **Sales:** $6,000,000 (2000). **Emp:** 25. **Officers:** Eugene M. Quinn, President & CFO.

■ 23012 ■ Plastic Supply Inc.
735 E Industrial Park Dr.
Manchester, NH 03109-5640
Phone: (603)669-2727
Free: (800)752-7759 **Fax:** (603)668-1691
Products: Plastics materials and basic shapes; Plastic products. **SIC:** 5162 (Plastics Materials & Basic Shapes). **Est:** 1972. **Sales:** $5,000,000 (2000). **Emp:** 25. **Officers:** Richard Dutile, President; Bill Johnson, Manager.

■ 23013 ■ Plastic Supply Inc.
3448 Girard Ave.
Albuquerque, NM 87107
Phone: (505)884-0507 **Fax:** (505)884-0525
Products: Plastics materials and basic shapes. **SIC:** 5162 (Plastics Materials & Basic Shapes). **Est:** 1976. **Officers:** Ronald Montoya, President; Victor Padilla, General Mgr.

■ 23014 ■ Polymer Plastics Corp.
645 National Ave.
Mountain View, CA 94043
Phone: (650)968-2212 Fax: (650)968-2218
Products: Plastics sheet and rods. SIC: 5162 (Plastics Materials & Basic Shapes). Est: 1975. Sales: $3,000,000 (2000). Emp: 22. Officers: L.A. Stock, CEO.

■ 23015 ■ Port Plastics Inc.
16750 Chestnut St.
La Puente, CA 91747
Phone: (626)333-7678 Fax: (626)336-3780
URL: http://www.portplastics.com
Products: Plastics, including heat treated plastics; PVC sheets and acrylic; Cable ties. SICs: 5162 (Plastics Materials & Basic Shapes); 5065 (Electronic Parts & Equipment Nec). Est: 1961. Sales: $32,000,000 (2000). Emp: 100. Officers: Keith Piggot, President; Keith Eitzen, VP & CFO; T.R. Eckroth, Branch Mgr.

■ 23016 ■ Power Plastics Inc.
2031 Karbach
Houston, TX 77092
Phone: (713)957-3695 Fax: (713)957-1248
Products: Provide a full range of custom molding, prototypes, and manufacturing of plastic products for medical and pharmaceutical devices, assembly, and hand fabrication. Our plant is FDA registered and inspected and GMP compliant. SIC: 5162 (Plastics Materials & Basic Shapes). Emp: 22.

■ 23017 ■ Prestige Packaging Inc.
6190 Regency Pkwy No. 312
Norcross, GA 30071-2345
Phone: (404)448-1422
Products: Disposable plastic products, including garbage bags and shrink films. SIC: 5162 (Plastics Materials & Basic Shapes). Est: 1986. Sales: $2,000,000 (2000). Emp: 8. Officers: Michael A. Griffin, President.

■ 23018 ■ Prime Alliance Inc.
1803 Hull Ave.
Des Moines, IA 50309
Phone: (515)264-4110 Fax: (515)264-4167
URL: http://www.primealliance.com
Products: Plastic pellets. SIC: 5162 (Plastics Materials & Basic Shapes). Sales: $60,000,000 (2000). Emp: 55. Officers: Tom Irvine, President; Al Whitlow, Controller.

■ 23019 ■ Pro Plastics Inc.
1190 Sylvan St.
Linden, NJ 07036
Phone: (908)925-5555 Fax: (908)862-8364
Products: Plastic bulk sheets. SIC: 5162 (Plastics Materials & Basic Shapes). Sales: $3,500,000 (1993). Emp: 35. Officers: G. Sievewright, Partner; Denis Krokosz, Partner.

■ 23020 ■ Quality Paper & Plastic Corp.
PO Box 8981
Albuquerque, NM 87108-8981
Phone: (505)262-1722 Fax: (505)262-1783
Products: Plastics materials and resins; Plastics basic shapes. SIC: 5162 (Plastics Materials & Basic Shapes). Officers: Gene Ayala, President.

■ 23021 ■ Rapid Industrial Plastics Co.
13 Linden Ave. E
Jersey City, NJ 07305
Phone: (201)433-5500 Fax: (201)433-4941
Products: Raw plastic. SIC: 5162 (Plastics Materials & Basic Shapes). Est: 1956. Sales: $100,000,000 (2000). Emp: 150. Officers: Martin Sirotkin, President.

■ 23022 ■ Regal Plastic Supply Co.
111 E 10th Ave.
North Kansas City, MO 64116
Phone: (816)421-6290
Free: (800)627-2101 Fax: (816)421-0445
URL: http://www.regalplastic.com
Products: Plastic sheets and rods. SIC: 5162 (Plastics Materials & Basic Shapes). Est: 1954. Sales: $25,000,000 (2000). Emp: 186. Officers: R. Cull, President; Robert McFarlane, Vice President.

■ 23023 ■ Regal Plastic Supply Co. Kansas City Div.
1500 Burlington
Kansas City, MO 64116-3815
Phone: (816)471-6390 Fax: (816)221-5822
Products: Plexiglass; Silicone; Prismatic light lenses. SIC: 5162 (Plastics Materials & Basic Shapes). Est: 1954. Sales: $2,000,000 (2000). Emp: 20. Officers: Jerrod Montgomery, Manager; R.E. McFarlane, CFO; Richard Cull, Dir. of Marketing.

■ 23024 ■ Regal Plastic Supply Inc.
PO Box 59977
Dallas, TX 75229
Phone: (972)484-0741
Free: (800)441-1553 Fax: (972)484-0746
Products: Plastic sheets. SIC: 5162 (Plastics Materials & Basic Shapes). Sales: $15,000,000 (2000). Emp: 85. Officers: Don Walker, President; Wayne Gono, Treasurer.

■ 23025 ■ Regional Supply Inc.
3571 S 300 W
Salt Lake City, UT 84115
Phone: (801)262-6451
Free: (800)365-8920 Fax: (801)261-5658
E-mail: regional@regionalsupply.net
URL: http://www.regionalsupply.citysearch.com
Products: Plastics. SIC: 5162 (Plastics Materials & Basic Shapes). Est: 1951. Sales: $10,000,000 (2000). Emp: 80. Officers: D.C. Mendenhall, President; D. Whitehead, Controller; C. Birkeland, Dir. of Marketing.

■ 23026 ■ Resyn Corp.
1540 W Blanke St.
Linden, NJ 07036
Phone: (908)862-8787 Fax: (908)862-8537
Products: Resin and resin raw matrials. SIC: 5162 (Plastics Materials & Basic Shapes). Est: 1952. Sales: $2,000,000 (2000). Emp: 7. Officers: Leo N. Levitt, President.

■ 23027 ■ Ridout Plastics Inc.
5535 Ruffin Rd.
San Diego, CA 92123
Phone: (619)560-1551
Products: Fabricates custom plastic products; Industrial and architectural plastics; Skateboards. SIC: 5162 (Plastics Materials & Basic Shapes). Officers: Elliott Rabin, President.

■ 23028 ■ Riley and Geehr Inc.
2205 Lee St.
Evanston, IL 60202-1597
Phone: (847)869-8100 Fax: (847)869-4765
Products: Plastic stand-up pouches. SIC: 5162 (Plastics Materials & Basic Shapes). Est: 1944. Sales: $6,500,000 (2000). Emp: 73. Officers: T.E. Riley Jr., President, e-mail: triley@rileyflex.com; Lisa Sacasa, CFO; Diane Riley, VP of Sales, e-mail: Driley@rileyflex.com; Nancy Malicki, Human Resources Contact, e-mail: Nmalicki@rileyflex.com.

■ 23029 ■ River City Enterprises
PO Box 9365
Peoria, IL 61612
Phone: (309)688-3223 Fax: (309)688-3258
E-mail: sales@pistontech.com
URL: http://www.pistontech.com
Products: Plastic and steel containers; Reusable bulk containers. SIC: 5162 (Plastics Materials & Basic Shapes). Est: 1986. Sales: $1,200,000 (2000). Emp: 3. Officers: Stewart Boal Jr., VP & General Mgr.

■ 23030 ■ Roberts Colonial House Inc.
570 W armory Dr.
PO Box 308
South Holland, IL 60473
Phone: (708)331-6233
Free: (800)234-0537 Fax: (708)331-0538
Products: Plexiglass. SIC: 5162 (Plastics Materials & Basic Shapes). Est: 1941. Sales: $3,850,000 (2000). Emp: 45. Officers: Anita Keller, Vice President.

■ 23031 ■ Rue Plastics Inc.
2999 Yorkton Blvd.
St. Paul, MN 55117
Phone: (612)481-9000
Products: Film for envelope windows. SIC: 5162

(Plastics Materials & Basic Shapes). Est: 1952. Sales: $2,000,000 (2000). Emp: 5. Officers: Curtis Rue, President.

■ 23032 ■ Joseph T. Ryerson and Son Inc., Ryerson Plastics Div.
PO Box 8000
Chicago, IL 60680
Phone: (773)762-2121
Products: Plastics; Steel tubing; Nickel. SICs: 5051 (Metals Service Centers & Offices); 5162 (Plastics Materials & Basic Shapes).

■ 23033 ■ Shepherd Products Co.
8080 Moors Bridge Rd., No. 103
Portage, MI 49024-4074
Phone: (616)324-3017
Products: Tarps; Vinyl coverings; Pan liners; Animal bedding. SICs: 5131 (Piece Goods & Notions); 5031 (Lumber, Plywood & Millwork); 5199 (Nondurable Goods Nec). Est: 1961. Sales: $17,000,000 (2000). Emp: 22. Officers: Joel M. Shepherd Jr., CEO; W. David Griffith, President; James H. Field, Sales Mgr.

■ 23034 ■ Signcaster Corp.
9240 Grand Ave. S
Minneapolis, MN 55420
Phone: (952)888-9507
Free: (800)869-7800 Fax: (952)888-4997
E-mail: service@johnsonplastics.com
URL: http://www.johnsonplastics.com
Products: Plastic sign supplies and engraving materials. SIC: 5162 (Plastics Materials & Basic Shapes). Est: 1970. Sales: $9,000,000 (2000). Emp: 60. Officers: Tom Johnson, President.

■ 23035 ■ Southeastern Adhesive Co.
PO Box 2070
Lenoir, NC 28645
Phone: (704)754-3493 Fax: (704)754-0052
Products: Hot melds; Polyurethane. SICs: 5162 (Plastics Materials & Basic Shapes); 5169 (Chemicals & Allied Products Nec). Est: 1968. Sales: $14,000,000 (2000). Emp: 50. Officers: F. Fulmer, President.

■ 23036 ■ Stopol Inc.
31875 Solon Rd.
Solon, OH 44139-3533
Phone: (440)498-4000
Products: Used plastics industry equipment. SIC: 5084 (Industrial Machinery & Equipment).

■ 23037 ■ Sumitomo Plastics America Inc.
900 Lafayette St., Ste. 510
Santa Clara, CA 95050-4967
Phone: (408)243-8402 Fax: (408)243-8405
Products: Raw plastics materials. SIC: 5162 (Plastics Materials & Basic Shapes). Sales: $5,000,000 (2000). Emp: 13. Officers: Yoshiaki Suzuki, President.

■ 23038 ■ Suntuf USA
2558 E 2980 S
Salt Lake City, UT 84109
Phone: (801)466-6919
Products: Plastics. SIC: 5162 (Plastics Materials & Basic Shapes). Sales: $900,000 (1994). Emp: 3. Officers: Amos Netzer, President.

■ 23039 ■ Targun Plastics Co.
899 Skokie Blvd.
Northbrook, IL 60062
Phone: (708)272-0869
Products: Plastics. SIC: 5162 (Plastics Materials & Basic Shapes). Sales: $12,000,000 (1994). Emp: 5. Officers: Jerome Targun, Owner; Gloria Targun, VP & Treasurer.

■ 23040 ■ Tay/Chem L.L.C.
3624 Melrose Dr.
Raleigh, NC 27604-3815
Phone: (919)231-6668 Fax: (919)231-6668
Products: Expertise includes polymeric materials synthesis and compounding, materials selection and development, product and process development, surface chemistry and modification, molding, and sterilization effects on polymers. SIC: 5162 (Plastics Materials & Basic Shapes). Emp: 3.

■ **23041** ■ **Tekra Corp.**
16700 W Lincoln Ave.
New Berlin, WI 53151
Phone: (414)784-5533
Free: (800)448-3572 **Fax:** (414)797-3276
Products: Plastic film for graphic arts. **SIC:** 5162 (Plastics Materials & Basic Shapes). **Est:** 1938. **Sales:** $65,000,000 (2000). **Emp:** 205. **Officers:** W.G. Godfrey, President & CEO; Harry Whelpley, CFO; Richard Grzenia, President.

■ **23042** ■ **Texatek International**
7100 Regency Square Blvd., Ste. 168
Houston, TX 77036
Phone: (713)977-7200 **Fax:** (281)493-5165
Products: Plastic raw materials. **SIC:** 5162 (Plastics Materials & Basic Shapes). **Est:** 1978. **Emp:** 10. **Officers:** Clement Chang, President.

■ **23043** ■ **Texberry Container Corp.**
1701 Crosspoint Ave.
Houston, TX 77233
Phone: (713)796-8800
Products: Plastic Containers. **SIC:** 5162 (Plastics Materials & Basic Shapes). **Sales:** $12,500,000 (2000). **Emp:** 11. **Officers:** Michael Vaughn, General Mgr.; Cheri Hutchison, Dir. of Operations.

■ **23044** ■ **Tomchuck Insulators**
262 Old Hwy. 93
Ronan, MT 59864-9508
Phone: (406)676-3641
Products: Plastic materials and basic shapes; Plastic insulation. **SIC:** 5162 (Plastics Materials & Basic Shapes). **Officers:** Tom Walchuk, Partner.

■ **23045** ■ **United Packaging Corp.**
1136 Samuelson St.
City of Industry, CA 91748
Phone: (626)968-0791
Products: Plastic bags. **SIC:** 5113 (Industrial & Personal Service Paper). **Sales:** $54,000,000 (1993).

Emp: 100. **Officers:** Gene Raper, President; Cheryl Hanson, VP of Finance.

■ **23046** ■ **Veb Plastics Inc.**
10748-A Tucker St.
Beltsville, MD 20705
Phone: (301)937-5530 **Fax:** (301)595-9205
Products: Disposable plastic bags; Vinyl coated fabrics (including expanded vinyl coated fabrics). **SIC:** 5162 (Plastics Materials & Basic Shapes). **Est:** 1949. **Sales:** $1,500,000 (2000). **Emp:** 13. **Officers:** N. Barman, President; Leon Barman, VP of Marketing.

■ **23047** ■ **Werner and Pfleiderer Corp.**
663 E Crescent Ave.
Ramsey, NJ 07446
Phone: (201)327-6300 **Fax:** (201)825-6494
Products: Plastics and plastic products. **SIC:** 5084 (Industrial Machinery & Equipment). **Est:** 1959. **Sales:** $78,000,000 (2000). **Emp:** 250. **Officers:** Dieter Gras, CEO; Ron Rubin, CFO; Asmut Kahns, Dir. of Marketing & Sales; Dieter Ohl, Dir. of Data Processing; Greg Chaberski, Dir of Human Resources.

(44) Plumbing Materials and Fixtures

Entries in this section are arranged alphabetically by company name. When the company name is a personal name, the company name is alphabetized by the surname unless the first name or initial(s) are part of a trade name. See the User's Guide at the front of this directory for additional information.

■ 23048 ■ **A-1 Plumbers Supply**
994 20th St.
Chico, CA 95928
Phone: (530)891-6428   **Fax:** (530)891-0654
Products: Plumbing supplies, including pipe fittings and tools. **SICs:** 5074 (Plumbing & Hydronic Heating Supplies); 5072 (Hardware). **Est:** 1977. **Emp:** 13. **Officers:** Vic Makau; Mike Palmer.

■ 23049 ■ **ABM Distributors Inc.**
3316 Lincoln Way E
Massillon, OH 44646
Phone: (330)833-2661   **Fax:** (330)833-4153
Products: Kitchen and plumbing supplies; Heating and electrical supplies. **SIC:** 5074 (Plumbing & Hydronic Heating Supplies). **Est:** 1960. **Sales:** $3,000,000 (1999). **Emp:** 16. **Officers:** Tom Porter, Vice President.

■ 23050 ■ **Ace Plumbing and Electrical Supply, Inc.**
601 S Delsea Dr.
Vineland, NJ 08360-4458
Phone: (856)692-9374
Free: (800)TEAM-ACE   **Fax:** (856)696-8678
Products: Plumbing and heating equipment, including pipe, fixtures, and furnaces; Electrical equipment. **SICs:** 5074 (Plumbing & Hydronic Heating Supplies); 5063 (Electrical Apparatus & Equipment); 5075 (Warm Air Heating & Air-Conditioning). **Est:** 1950. **Emp:** 25. **Officers:** Larry Berman.

■ 23051 ■ **Active Carb Ltd.**
PO Box 238
Gardena, CA 90248
Phone: (310)366-7663
Free: (800)424-2049   **Fax:** (310)366-7867
Products: specialty equipment and products. **SIC:** 5074 (Plumbing & Hydronic Heating Supplies). **Sales:** $1,000,000 (2000). **Emp:** 6.

■ 23052 ■ **Active Plumbing Supply Co.**
216 Richmond St.
Painesville, OH 44077
Phone: (440)352-4411   **Fax:** (440)352-0096
Products: Plumbing fittings and brass goods; Plumbing fixtures, equipment, and supplies. **SIC:** 5074 (Plumbing & Hydronic Heating Supplies). **Est:** 1956. **Sales:** $24,000,000 (1999). **Emp:** 80. **Officers:** Chuck Rathburn, President; Cindy Barber, CEO; Denny Johnson, Sales Mgr.

■ 23053 ■ **Adel Wholesalers Inc.**
PO Box B
Bettendorf, IA 52722
Phone: (319)355-4734
Free: (800)747-7586   **Fax:** (319)355-0923
URL: http://www.adel-wholesalers-inc.com
Products: Plumbing supplies; HVAC. **SIC:** 5074 (Plumbing & Hydronic Heating Supplies). **Est:** 1952. **Sales:** $17,200,000 (2000). **Emp:** 58. **Officers:** Ralph Gibson, President, e-mail: rgibson@adel-wholesalers-inc.com.

■ 23054 ■ **Ahrens and McCarron Inc.**
4621 Beck Ave.
St. Louis, MO 63116
Phone: (314)772-8400   **Fax:** (314)772-7185
Products: Plumbing equipment and supplies, including boilers and faucets; Electrical products, including fans and fixtures; Kitchen and bath products, including countertops and cabinets. **SICs:** 5074 (Plumbing & Hydronic Heating Supplies); 5065 (Electronic Parts & Equipment Nec). **Est:** 1946. **Sales:** $15,000,000 (2000). **Emp:** 100. **Officers:** Shirley L. Ahrens, Chairman of the Board; Thomas Zakibe, President; Earline McCubbin, Controller.

■ 23055 ■ **J and H Aitcheson Inc.**
100 Dove St.
Alexandria, VA 22314
Phone: (703)548-7600
Products: Plumbing supplies. **SIC:** 5074 (Plumbing & Hydronic Heating Supplies). **Est:** 1896. **Sales:** $14,700,000 (2000). **Emp:** 70. **Officers:** John K. Aitcheson Jr., President; George W. Atwood III, VP & Treasurer; T. Warren Brown, Vice President.

■ 23056 ■ **Albuquerque Winnelson Co.**
3545 Princeton NE
Albuquerque, NM 87107
Phone: (505)884-1553   **Fax:** (505)884-1558
Products: Plumbing supplies, including sinks, faucets, and tubs. **SIC:** 5074 (Plumbing & Hydronic Heating Supplies). **Est:** 1968. **Sales:** $7,000,000 (2000). **Emp:** 18. **Officers:** Greg Hoffman, President.

■ 23057 ■ **Allied Supply Inc.**
6300 Murray St.
Little Rock, AR 72209-8532
Phone: (501)562-6180
Free: (800)482-5652   **Fax:** (501)562-8874
E-mail: sales@alliedsupplylr.com
URL: http://www.homestead.com/alliedsupply
Products: Pipes, valves, and fittings. **SICs:** 5074 (Plumbing & Hydronic Heating Supplies); 5051 (Metals Service Centers & Offices). **Est:** 1973. **Sales:** $4,500,000 (2000). **Emp:** 19. **Officers:** C.W. Trent, President; Larry Gray, General Mgr.; Bryan Trent, Controller; Linda Follett, Office Mgr., e-mail: lfollett@alliedsupplylr.com.

■ 23058 ■ **Alloy Piping Products Inc.**
PO Box 7368
Shreveport, LA 71137
Phone: (318)226-9851
Products: Pipe, flanges, and fittings. **SIC:** 5085 (Industrial Supplies). **Sales:** $22,100,000 (2000). **Emp:** 300. **Officers:** Ron D. Brown, President; Jerry Formby, Accounting Manager.

■ 23059 ■ **Almerica Overseas Inc.**
PO Box 2188
Tuscaloosa, AL 35403
Phone: (205)758-1311   **Fax:** (205)759-1962
Products: specialty equipment and products. **SIC:** 5074 (Plumbing & Hydronic Heating Supplies). **Sales:** $2,000,000 (2000). **Emp:** 5.

■ 23060 ■ **Amarillo Winnelson Co.**
PO Box 1306
Amarillo, TX 79105
Phone: (806)372-2259
Products: Plumbing supplies. **SIC:** 5074 (Plumbing & Hydronic Heating Supplies).

■ 23061 ■ **AMC Industries Inc.**
PO Box 171290
San Antonio, TX 78217-8290
Phone: (210)226-8218   **Fax:** (210)223-5351
Products: Irrigation and plumbing supplies. **SIC:** 5074 (Plumbing & Hydronic Heating Supplies). **Est:** 1924. **Sales:** $9,000,000 (2000). **Emp:** 40. **Officers:** Patrick Morgan, President; Robert Buchek, CFO; Monroe Jackson, VP of Sales.

■ 23062 ■ **American Environmental Systems Inc.**
2840 Wilderness Pl Ste. C
Boulder, CO 80301
Phone: (303)449-3670   **Fax:** (303)449-3669
Products: Air cleaning and water purification systems for high-tech industries and cleanrooms. **SICs:** 5074 (Plumbing & Hydronic Heating Supplies); 5075 (Warm Air Heating & Air-Conditioning). **Sales:** $3,000,000 (2000). **Emp:** 20. **Officers:** James Yehl, President.

■ 23063 ■ **American Foundry and Manufacturing Co.**
920 Palm St.
St. Louis, MO 63147
Phone: (314)231-6114   **Fax:** (314)231-6117
Products: Plumbing supplies; Fire hydrants; Grates; Cast iron and brass castings. **SICs:** 5074 (Plumbing & Hydronic Heating Supplies); 5051 (Metals Service Centers & Offices). **Est:** 1888. **Sales:** $1,500,000 (2000). **Emp:** 12. **Officers:** Don J. Costello, CEO; Michael Costello, Vice President; Dan Costello, President.

■ 23064 ■ **Americo Wholesale Plumbing Supply Co.**
3500 Woodland Ave.
Cleveland, OH 44115
Phone: (216)696-1910
Products: Plumbing and bathroom supplies; Appliances, including stoves. **SICs:** 5074 (Plumbing & Hydronic Heating Supplies); 5064 (Electrical Appliances—Television & Radio). **Est:** 1936. **Sales:** $11,000,000 (2000). **Emp:** 50. **Officers:** Floyd Goldberg, CEO & President; Jim Buckley, Controller.

■ 23065 ■ **W.T. Andrew Co.**
15815 Hamilton Ave.
Detroit, MI 48203
Phone: (313)883-2000   **Fax:** (313)883-2834
Products: Pipe valves and fixtures; Heating equipment. **SICs:** 5074 (Plumbing & Hydronic Heating Supplies); 5075 (Warm Air Heating & Air-Conditioning). **Est:** 1932. **Sales:** $5,000,000 (2000). **Emp:** 18. **Officers:** Kathleen Kalt, President; Christine Kraushaar, Controller; Judith Andrew, Vice President.

■ 23066 ■ A.P. Supply Co.
PO Box 1927
Texarkana, AR 71854
Phone: (870)773-6586 **Fax:** (870)773-6585
Products: Pipes, valves, and fittings. **SIC:** 5074
(Plumbing & Hydronic Heating Supplies). **Est:** 1960.
Sales: $6,000,000 (2000). **Emp:** 21. **Officers:** A.P.
Legrand Jr., President.

■ 23067 ■ APR Supply Co.
305 N 5th St.
Lebanon, PA 17046
Phone: (717)273-9375 **Fax:** (717)273-2150
Products: Plumbing and heating equipment. **SIC:**
5074 (Plumbing & Hydronic Heating Supplies). **Sales:**
$16,000,000 (2000). **Emp:** 65. **Officers:** M.R. Tice,
CEO; Sarah Tice, Secretary.

■ 23068 ■ Aqua Magnetics International
915-B Harbor Lake Dr.
Safety Harbor, FL 34695
Phone: (813)447-2575
Free: (800)328-2843 **Fax:** (813)726-8888
Products: specialty equipment and products. **SIC:**
5074 (Plumbing & Hydronic Heating Supplies).

■ 23069 ■ Aqua Systems International, Inc.
4627 Bay Crest Dr.
Tampa, FL 33615-4901
Phone: (813)287-8802 **Fax:** (813)287-8848
E-mail: aqua@pipeline.com
URL: http://www.aquasystemsintl.com
Products: Industrial and munincipal water products.
SICs: 5074 (Plumbing & Hydronic Heating Supplies);
5084 (Industrial Machinery & Equipment). **Est:** 1980.
Sales: $2,000,000 (2000). **Emp:** 5. **Officers:** Julio E.
Moisa, President.

■ 23070 ■ Aquanetics Systems
5252 Lovelock St.
San Diego, CA 92110
Phone: (619)291-8444 **Fax:** (619)291-8335
Products: Titanium chillers and heaters; Filtration
equipment and ultraviolet sterilizers for ponds and
aquariums; Pumping and filtration equipment. **SIC:**
5074 (Plumbing & Hydronic Heating Supplies).

■ 23071 ■ Aquatec Water Systems Inc.
17422 Pullman St.
Irvine, CA 92614
Phone: (714)535-8300 **Fax:** (714)535-7867
Products: Pumps. **SIC:** 5074 (Plumbing & Hydronic
Heating Supplies). **Officers:** Mike Pennington.

■ 23072 ■ Arizona Water Works Supply Inc.
PO Box 219
Tempe, AZ 85280
Phone: (602)966-5804 **Fax:** (602)967-7857
Products: Water meters, pipes, and fittings. **SICs:**
5074 (Plumbing & Hydronic Heating Supplies); 5085
(Industrial Supplies). **Est:** 1969. **Sales:** $3,300,000
(2000). **Emp:** 7. **Officers:** Neil Folkman, President.

■ 23073 ■ Arrow Precision Products Inc.
5026 E Slauson Ave.
Maywood, CA 90270
Phone: (213)562-3300 **Fax:** (213)562-3173
Products: Electrical supplies; Plumbing items,
including faucets, pipes, valves, connectors, chords,
and plugs. **SICs:** 5074 (Plumbing & Hydronic Heating
Supplies); 5063 (Electrical Apparatus & Equipment).
Est: 1931. **Sales:** $5,000,000 (2000). **Emp:** 70.
Officers: John Ridgely, President; Jeff Mills, Sales
Mgr.

■ 23074 ■ Atlantic Plumbing Supply Co. Inc.
807 V St. NW
Washington, DC 20001
Phone: (202)667-6500
Products: Plumbing and heating supplies. **SIC:** 5074
(Plumbing & Hydronic Heating Supplies). **Sales:**
$15,000,000 (2000). **Emp:** 40. **Officers:** Edward
Needle, President; Malcolm Jacobs, Controller.

■ 23075 ■ B & K Industries Inc.
2600 Elmhurst Rd.
Elk Grove Village, IL 60007
Phone: (708)773-8585
Free: (800)782-2385 **Fax:** (708)773-0330
Products: Plumbing supplies, including plungers. **SIC:**
5074 (Plumbing & Hydronic Heating Supplies). **Est:**
1969. **Emp:** 60. **Officers:** Richard Kuhlman, President;
Jeffrey Berkman, Exec. VP.

■ 23076 ■ Leif Ball Pipe & Supply
31240 W Cedar Valley Dr.
Westlake Village, CA 91362-4035
Phone: (805)495-8458 **Fax:** (818)991-0138
Products: Plumbing and heating valves and
specialties. **SICs:** 5074 (Plumbing & Hydronic Heating
Supplies); 5075 (Warm Air Heating & Air-Conditioning).
Emp: 25. **Officers:** Leif Ball.

■ 23077 ■ Barnett Brass and Copper Inc.
PO Box 2317
Rt. 3333 Lenox Ave.
Jacksonville, FL 32203-2317
Phone: (904)384-6530 **Fax:** (904)388-2635
Products: Plumbing supplies, including copper tubing;
Electrical supplies, including outlets and wiring. **SICs:**
5063 (Electrical Apparatus & Equipment); 5051 (Metals
Service Centers & Offices); 5074 (Plumbing & Hydronic
Heating Supplies). **Sales:** $60,000,000 (2000). **Emp:**
220.

■ 23078 ■ Barnett Inc.
PO Box 2317
Jacksonville, FL 32203-2317
Phone: (904)384-6530
Free: (800)288-2000 **Fax:** (904)388-2723
E-mail: jjarrett@bntt.com
URL: http://www.bntt.com
Products: Plumbing, electrical and hardware products;
HVAC; MRO. **SICs:** 5074 (Plumbing & Hydronic
Heating Supplies); 5072 (Hardware). **Est:** 1948. **Sales:**
$300,000 (2000). **Emp:** 564. **Officers:** William R. Pray,
CEO & President; Andrea M. Luiga, VP & CFO.

■ 23079 ■ Barneys Pumps Inc.
PO Box 3529
Lakeland, FL 33802-3529
Phone: (941)665-8500 **Fax:** (941)666-3858
Products: Pumps, including sump pumps. **SICs:** 5074
(Plumbing & Hydronic Heating Supplies); 5084
(Industrial Machinery & Equipment). **Est:** 1950. **Sales:**
$18,000,000 (2000). **Emp:** 100. **Officers:** John Curls,
Chairman of the Board; Greg Riching, President; Chris
White, Purchasing Mgr.

■ 23080 ■ Beckman Brothers Inc.
320 SE 6th St.
Des Moines, IA 50309
Phone: (515)244-2233
Free: (800)532-1244 **Fax:** (515)244-4628
Products: Plumbing, heating, and cooling equipment
and supplies. **SICs:** 5074 (Plumbing & Hydronic
Heating Supplies); 5075 (Warm Air Heating & Air-
Conditioning). **Est:** 1883. **Sales:** $3,000,000 (2000).
Emp: 15. **Officers:** C.D. Vande Krol V; Jim Wilhite,
President.

■ 23081 ■ Bell Supply Company Inc.
262 Fortner St.
Dothan, AL 36302
Phone: (205)793-4500 **Fax:** (205)677-6641
Products: Plumbing supplies. **SIC:** 5074 (Plumbing &
Hydronic Heating Supplies). **Est:** 1961. **Sales:**
$5,000,000 (2000). **Emp:** 30. **Officers:** Phillip Bell,
President.

■ 23082 ■ Bells Supply Co.
718 Stanton Christiana Rd.
Newark, DE 19713
Phone: (302)998-0800
Free: (800)284-4601 **Fax:** (302)998-0400
Products: Plumbing, heating, and air conditioning
supplies. **SICs:** 5074 (Plumbing & Hydronic Heating
Supplies); 5075 (Warm Air Heating & Air-Conditioning).
Est: 1932. **Sales:** $5,000,000 (2000). **Emp:** 17.
Officers: Raymond Kursh, President; Jack Conner,
Vice President; David Kursh, Treasurer.

■ 23083 ■ Berg-Dorf Pipe & Supply Co. Inc.
3300 South High
PO Box 95638
Oklahoma City, OK 73143
Phone: (405)672-3381 **Fax:** (405)672-4624
E-mail: Bergdorf@Berg-Dorf.com
URL: http://www.Berg-Dorf.com
Products: Pipes, valves, and fittings. **SIC:** 5074
(Plumbing & Hydronic Heating Supplies). **Est:** 1936.
Sales: $3,000,000 (2000). **Emp:** 16. **Officers:** Jerry
Bendorf, President; Lavern Humann, Vice President;
Jackie Bendorf, Sec. & Treas.

■ 23084 ■ Best Plumbing Supply Inc.
3333-1 Crompond Rd.
Yorktown Heights, NY 10598
Phone: (914)736-2468
Products: Plumbing supplies. **SIC:** 5074 (Plumbing &
Hydronic Heating Supplies).

■ 23085 ■ Big Inch Marine Systems Inc.
12235 FM 529
Houston, TX 77041-2805
Phone: (713)896-1501 **Fax:** (713)446-1283
Products: Pipe line connectors and flanges. **SIC:** 5084
(Industrial Machinery & Equipment). **Est:** 1977. **Sales:**
$11,000,000 (2000). **Emp:** 35. **Officers:** Lee Avery,
President, e-mail: flavery@big-inch.com; B. E. Morris,
Sr. VP, e-mail: bemorris@big-inch.com.

■ 23086 ■ Biggs Pump and Supply Inc.
PO Box 7208
Lafayette, IN 47903
Phone: (765)447-1141 **Fax:** (765)448-4460
Products: Heating and plumbing supplies. **SICs:** 5074
(Plumbing & Hydronic Heating Supplies); 5075 (Warm
Air Heating & Air-Conditioning). **Est:** 1868. **Sales:**
$10,000,000 (2000). **Emp:** 40. **Officers:** G. Ronald
Needham, President.

■ 23087 ■ Bion Environmental Technologies Inc.
555 17th St.
Denver, CO 80202
Phone: (303)294-0750 **Fax:** (303)298-8251
Products: Designs and installs wastewater and storm
water treatment systems and wetlands structures.
SICs: 5074 (Plumbing & Hydronic Heating Supplies);
5191 (Farm Supplies). **Sales:** $1,300,000 (1999).
Emp: 26. **Officers:** Jon Northrop, CEO; M. Duane
Stutzman, CFO & Treasurer.

■ 23088 ■ W.A. Birdsall and Company Inc.
1819 W Elizabeth Ave.
Linden, NJ 07036
Phone: (908)862-4455 **Fax:** (908)862-3106
Products: Plumbing and heating supplies. **SICs:** 5074
(Plumbing & Hydronic Heating Supplies); 5075 (Warm
Air Heating & Air-Conditioning). **Est:** 1911. **Sales:**
$5,600,000 (2000). **Emp:** 17. **Officers:** H. Ball Jr.,
President.

■ 23089 ■ Blackman Medford Corp.
2700 Rte. 112
Medford, NY 11763-2553
Phone: (516)475-3170 **Fax:** (516)475-3986
Products: Plumbing supplies. **SIC:** 5074 (Plumbing &
Hydronic Heating Supplies). **Emp:** 49.

■ 23090 ■ Bluffs Budget Plumbing
PO Box 255
Pine Bluffs, WY 82082-0255
Phone: (307)245-9224
Products: Plumbing fixtures, equipment, and supplies.
SIC: 5074 (Plumbing & Hydronic Heating Supplies).
Officers: Jerry Sanders, Owner.

■ 23091 ■ Boiler and Heat Exchange Systems Inc.
PO Box 23566
Chattanooga, TN 37422
Phone: (423)899-6600
Free: (800)243-7424 **Fax:** (423)899-6759
E-mail: mail@bhes.com
URL: http://www.bhes.com
Products: Boilers, heat exchangers, and valves. **SICs:**
5074 (Plumbing & Hydronic Heating Supplies); 5075
(Warm Air Heating & Air-Conditioning). **Est:** 1977.
Sales: $7,000,000 (2000). **Emp:** 60. **Officers:** Richard

W. Key, President; Tom Roberts, Operations Mgr.; Stan Wagner, General Mgr.; Sharon Newby, Dir of Human Resources; Nick LeJeune, Manager.

■ 23092 ■ I.D. Booth Inc.
PO Box 579
Elmira, NY 14902
Phone: (607)733-9121
Products: Plumbing and heating supplies. **SICs:** 5074 (Plumbing & Hydronic Heating Supplies); 5065 (Electronic Parts & Equipment Nec). **Est:** 1875. **Sales:** $20,000,000 (1999). **Emp:** 110. **Officers:** J.S. Booth Jr., President & Treasurer; Dan Murphy, Dir. of Marketing.

■ 23093 ■ Boston Pipe and Fittings Company Inc.
171 Sidney St.
Cambridge, MA 02139
Phone: (617)876-7800
Products: Pipes and fittings. **SICs:** 5051 (Metals Service Centers & Offices); 5074 (Plumbing & Hydronic Heating Supplies). **Est:** 1932. **Sales:** $6,000,000 (2000). **Emp:** 27. **Officers:** William B. Carstensenn, President; Ellen J. Carstensen-Caywood, Treasurer.

■ 23094 ■ Bradley Supply Co.
PO Box 29096
Chicago, IL 60629
Phone: (773)434-7400   **Fax:** (773)434-6289
Products: Pipe valves; Fittings. **SICs:** 5085 (Industrial Supplies); 5074 (Plumbing & Hydronic Heating Supplies). **Est:** 1924. **Sales:** $8,000,000 (2000). **Emp:** 31. **Officers:** Edward M. Lewis, President; Bob Reitz, CFO; Roger A. Norkus, VP of Marketing.

■ 23095 ■ Briggs Incorporated of Omaha
113 S 10th St.
Omaha, NE 68102
Phone: (402)342-0778   **Fax:** (402)342-2989
Products: Plumbing supplies; Heating and cooling systems. **SICs:** 5074 (Plumbing & Hydronic Heating Supplies); 5075 (Warm Air Heating & Air-Conditioning). **Est:** 1906. **Sales:** $12,300,000 (2000). **Emp:** 89. **Officers:** D.C. Dickinson, President; Jed Brown, CFO; G.R. Averill, Dir. of Marketing.

■ 23096 ■ Brill Hygenic Products Inc.
2905 S Congress Ave., Ste. E
Delray Beach, FL 33445-7337
Phone: (561)278-5600
Products: Toilet seats. **SIC:** 5074 (Plumbing & Hydronic Heating Supplies). **Sales:** $3,000,000 (2000). **Emp:** 6. **Officers:** Alan Brill, President.

■ 23097 ■ Broadway Collection
PO Box 1210
Olathe, KS 66051-1210
Phone: (913)782-6244
Products: Faucets; Door hardware. **SICs:** 5074 (Plumbing & Hydronic Heating Supplies); 5072 (Hardware). **Est:** 1972. **Sales:** $15,000,000 (2000). **Emp:** 170. **Officers:** Charles D. Miller, Exec. VP.

■ 23098 ■ Broedell Plumbing Supply Inc.
19686 U.S Hwy. 1
Tequesta, FL 33469
Phone: (561)747-8000   **Fax:** (561)747-8007
URL: http://www.broedell.com
Products: Plumbing supplies. **SIC:** 5074 (Plumbing & Hydronic Heating Supplies). **Est:** 1987. **Sales:** $20,000,000 (2000). **Emp:** 50. **Officers:** John Broedell, President; Miriam Mears, Controller.

■ 23099 ■ Bruce-Rogers Company Inc.
PO Box 879
Ft. Smith, AR 72902-0879
Phone: (501)782-7901   **Fax:** (501)785-3857
Products: Plumbing, heating, and air-conditioning equipment. **SICs:** 5074 (Plumbing & Hydronic Heating Supplies); 5075 (Warm Air Heating & Air-Conditioning). **Est:** 1922. **Sales:** $8,000,000 (1999). **Emp:** 57. **Officers:** D.G. Rogers III, CEO; Dan Mills, Sales Mgr.; Bradford Sharpe, Dir. of Systems.

■ 23100 ■ Buderus Hydronic Systems Inc.
PO Box 647
Salem, NH 03079
Phone: (603)898-0505
Products: Boilers; Panel radiators; Residential and commercial hot water tanks. **SICs:** 5074 (Plumbing & Hydronic Heating Supplies); 5084 (Industrial Machinery & Equipment). **Est:** 1991. **Sales:** $4,000,000 (2000). **Emp:** 10. **Officers:** Peter Deltorn, VP of Marketing & Sales; Chris Hoff, VP of Marketing and Administration.

■ 23101 ■ I. Burack Inc.
59 Kenilworth Rd.
Rye, NY 10580-1910
Phone: (914)968-8100   **Fax:** (914)968-8007
Products: Plumbing equipment and supplies, including pipes. **SIC:** 5074 (Plumbing & Hydronic Heating Supplies). **Emp:** 49.

■ 23102 ■ Burns Brothers Contractors
400 Leavenworth Ave.
Syracuse, NY 13204
Phone: (315)422-0261
Products: I-beams; Plumbing supplies. **SIC:** 5074 (Plumbing & Hydronic Heating Supplies). **Est:** 1948. **Sales:** $20,000,000 (2000). **Emp:** 300. **Officers:** D.S. Burns, President; R. Granozio, Controller.

■ 23103 ■ Burns Supply/Great Lakes Inc.
760 W Genesee St.
Syracuse, NY 13204
Phone: (315)474-7471   **Fax:** (315)474-7478
Products: Plumbing and heating supplies. **SICs:** 5074 (Plumbing & Hydronic Heating Supplies); 5075 (Warm Air Heating & Air-Conditioning). **Est:** 1904. **Sales:** $3,000,000 (2000). **Emp:** 30. **Officers:** Chuck Kiner, President.

■ 23104 ■ Capitol Plumbing and Heating Supply Co.
1900 S 8th St.
Springfield, IL 62703
Phone: (217)753-6900
Products: Plumbing and heating equipment, including fixtures, valves, coders, and heaters. **SICs:** 5074 (Plumbing & Hydronic Heating Supplies); 5075 (Warm Air Heating & Air-Conditioning). **Est:** 1942. **Sales:** $35,000,000 (2000). **Emp:** 150. **Officers:** Eugene Drendel, President & Chairman of the Board; Jan Smith, Comptroller; T. Lonson, VP of Marketing.

■ 23105 ■ Capitol Plumbing and Heating Supply Company Inc.
6 Storrs St.
Concord, NH 03301
Phone: (603)224-1901
Products: Plumbing and heating supplies. **SICs:** 5074 (Plumbing & Hydronic Heating Supplies); 5075 (Warm Air Heating & Air-Conditioning). **Est:** 1936. **Sales:** $22,000,000 (2000). **Emp:** 96. **Officers:** Robert A. Hill, President; Elaine McMahon, Controller.

■ 23106 ■ Carolina Plastics Supply Inc.
100 D Forsyth Hall Dr.
Charlotte, NC 28273
Phone: (704)588-0541   **Fax:** (704)588-5742
Products: Valves and pipe fittings; Plastics piping. **SICs:** 5162 (Plastics Materials & Basic Shapes); 5074 (Plumbing & Hydronic Heating Supplies). **Est:** 1987. **Sales:** $5,000,000 (2000). **Emp:** 18. **Officers:** Kenneth Pollack, President.

■ 23107 ■ Carr Co.
6000 Park of Commerce Blvd.
Boca Raton, FL 33487
Phone: (407)997-0999   **Fax:** (407)997-2633
Products: Valves and pipe fittings. **SIC:** 5074 (Plumbing & Hydronic Heating Supplies). **Est:** 1967. **Sales:** $50,000,000 (2000). **Emp:** 35. **Officers:** James M. Gizzie, e-mail: jgizzie@gate.net; Larry M. Hobbs.

■ 23108 ■ Cast Products Corp.
PO Box 1368
Elkhart, IN 46515
Phone: (219)294-2684   **Fax:** (219)295-6921
Products: Bathroom supplies for the recreation vehicle industry. **SIC:** 5074 (Plumbing & Hydronic Heating Supplies). **Est:** 1956. **Sales:** $8,000,000 (2000). **Emp:** 35. **Officers:** Bruce McKibbin, President; Brian Conwell, Controller.

■ 23109 ■ Cedar Builders Supply Company Inc.
309 N 200 W
Cedar City, UT 84720
Phone: (801)586-9424   **Fax:** (801)586-4622
E-mail: cbs@netutah.com
URL: http://www.netutah.com/cbs
Products: Plumbing fixtures, including toilets and sinks; Electrical supplies. **SICs:** 5063 (Electrical Apparatus & Equipment); 5063 (Electrical Apparatus & Equipment). **Est:** 1947. **Sales:** $2,000,000 (2000). **Emp:** 13. **Officers:** Jeff Marchant, President; E.T. Marchant, CFO; Don Marchant, Dir. of Marketing.

■ 23110 ■ Central Supply Co.
701 E Wallace
Ft. Wayne, IN 46803
Phone: (219)745-4961   **Fax:** 800-589-4972
Products: Plumbing supplies; Electrical supplies; Industrial supplies. **SICs:** 5074 (Plumbing & Hydronic Heating Supplies); 5063 (Electrical Apparatus & Equipment); 5085 (Industrial Supplies).

■ 23111 ■ Central Supply Co.
PO Box 337
Worcester, MA 01613
Phone: (508)755-6121   **Fax:** (508)755-6127
Products: Plumbing equipment. **SIC:** 5074 (Plumbing & Hydronic Heating Supplies). **Sales:** $28,000,000 (1992). **Emp:** 120. **Officers:** P. Kevin Condron, President; Joseph Goff, VP of Finance.

■ 23112 ■ Century Plumbing Wholesale
901 SW 69th Ave.
Miami, FL 33144
Phone: (305)261-4731   **Fax:** (305)261-0635
Products: Plumbing equipment and supplies. **SIC:** 5074 (Plumbing & Hydronic Heating Supplies). **Est:** 1977. **Sales:** $20,000,000 (2000). **Emp:** 50. **Officers:** Sergio Pino, President; Carlos Pino, General Mgr.; Jose J. Davila Jr., Sales Mgr.

■ 23113 ■ Champion Furnace Pipe Co.
6021 N Galena Rd.
Peoria, IL 61614-3603
Phone: (309)685-1031   **Fax:** (309)685-1088
Products: Pipes. **SIC:** 5074 (Plumbing & Hydronic Heating Supplies). **Est:** 1886. **Sales:** $12,000,000 (2000). **Emp:** 104. **Officers:** R.J. Lax, President.

■ 23114 ■ Champlain Winair Co.
921 Hercules Dr., Ste. 1
Colchester, VT 05446
Phone: 800-343-1350
Products: Plumbing and heating supplies. **SICs:** 5074 (Plumbing & Hydronic Heating Supplies); 5075 (Warm Air Heating & Air-Conditioning).

■ 23115 ■ Cities Supply Company Inc.
PO Box 309
Sumter, SC 29151
Phone: (803)775-7355   **Fax:** (803)775-7358
Products: Waterworks supplies; Water meters; Piping. **SIC:** 5074 (Plumbing & Hydronic Heating Supplies). **Sales:** $12,000,000 (2000). **Emp:** 30. **Officers:** A.J. Bynum, CEO.

■ 23116 ■ H.L. Claeys and Co.
31239 Mound Rd.
Warren, MI 48090
Phone: (810)264-2561   **Fax:** (810)264-4250
E-mail: hlclaeys@usol.com
Products: Plumbing fixtures; Water heaters; Boilers. **SIC:** 5074 (Plumbing & Hydronic Heating Supplies). **Est:** 1922. **Sales:** $9,000,000 (2000). **Emp:** 32. **Officers:** Henrietta C. Busch, President; John Gideon, CFO; John M. Stevens, General Mgr.; Tom Rinke, Sales/Marketing Contact. **Alternate Name:** Luxury Bath Showrooms.

■ 23117 ■ Coastal Industries Inc.
3700 St. Johns Industrial Pkwy. W
PO Box 16091
Jacksonville, FL 32245
Phones: (904)642-3970   800-342-6013
Free: (800)874-8601   Fax: (904)641-1697
URL: http://www.coastalind.com
Products: Shower doors. SIC: 5074 (Plumbing & Hydronic Heating Supplies). Est: 1972. Sales: $20,000,000 (2000). Emp: 140. Officers: William M. Cobb, President; David L. Herbert, VP of Marketing & Sales; Bartley Rainey, CFO; William Palmer, VP of Production; Robert Zvacik, Dir of Human Resources.

■ 23118 ■ Coburn Supply Co. Inc.
PO Box 2177
Beaumont, TX 77704
Phones: (409)838-6363   (409)835-1447
Fax: (409)838-1920
Products: Plumbing equipment. SIC: 5074 (Plumbing & Hydronic Heating Supplies). Est: 1934. Sales: $77,000,000 (2000). Emp: 330. Officers: Don Maloney, President; Jay Shah, Controller.

■ 23119 ■ Colladay Hardware Co.
PO Box 766
Hutchinson, KS 67504
Phone: (316)663-4477   Fax: (316)663-5390
Products: Plumbing supplies; Electrical supplies; Garden tools. SICs: 5074 (Plumbing & Hydronic Heating Supplies); 5072 (Hardware); 5063 (Electrical Apparatus & Equipment). Est: 1885. Sales: $5,000,000 (2000). Emp: 20. Officers: H. Duane Banning, President & General Mgr.

■ 23120 ■ Columbus Pipe and Equipment Co.
773 E Markison Ave.
Columbus, OH 43207
Phone: (614)444-7871
Products: Plumbing fixtures, equipment, and supplies. SICs: 5051 (Metals Service Centers & Offices); 5074 (Plumbing & Hydronic Heating Supplies). Est: 1934. Sales: $15,000,000 (2000). Emp: 39. Officers: Bruce J. Silberstein, President; John Silberstein, VP of Finance; Jim Brushia, Dir. of Marketing & Sales.

■ 23121 ■ Conestoga Heating and Plumbing Supply Inc.
340 W Roseville Rd.
Lancaster, PA 17601
Phone: (717)569-3246   Fax: (717)569-4021
Products: Plumbing and heating supplies. SICs: 5074 (Plumbing & Hydronic Heating Supplies); 5075 (Warm Air Heating & Air-Conditioning). Est: 1961. Sales: $4,000,000 (2000). Emp: 20. Officers: Kenneth Shoemaker, President.

■ 23122 ■ Connor Co.
2800 NE Adams St.
PO Box 5007
Peoria, IL 61601-5007
Phone: (309)688-1068   Fax: (309)688-4120
E-mail: Connorco@worldnet.att.com
URL: http://www.Connorco.com
Products: Plumbing and heating equipment. SIC: 5074 (Plumbing & Hydronic Heating Supplies). Est: 1884. Sales: $73,000,000 (2000). Emp: 190. Officers: W.P. Collins, Treasurer; D.M. Ludolph, Chairman of the Board & CFO; S.D. Collins, President; J.E. Bulger, General Mgr.

■ 23123 ■ Consolidated Pipe and Supply Company Inc.
PO Box 2472
Birmingham, AL 35201
Phone: (205)323-7261   Fax: (205)251-7838
Products: Steel and plastics. SIC: 5074 (Plumbing & Hydronic Heating Supplies). Est: 1960. Sales: $250,000,000 (2000). Emp: 497. Officers: Howard Kerr, President; C. Gene Estill, VP of Finance.

■ 23124 ■ Consolidated Supply Co.
PO Box 3183
Spokane, WA 99220-3183
Phone: (509)535-0896
Products: Heating and plumbing supplies. SIC: 5074 (Plumbing & Hydronic Heating Supplies). Est: 1948. Sales: $3,500,000 (2000). Emp: 10. Officers: Thomas B. Neupert, President.

■ 23125 ■ Consumers Plumbing Heating Supply
23233 Aurora Rd.
Cleveland, OH 44146-1704
Phone: (440)232-8400   Fax: (440)232-1165
Products: Plumbing supplies. SIC: 5074 (Plumbing & Hydronic Heating Supplies). Emp: 49. Officers: James R. Friedman.

■ 23126 ■ Cook Brothers Manufacturing and Supply Co.
1030 Calle Recodo
San Clemente, CA 92672
Phone: (949)361-8767   Fax: (949)361-3157
E-mail: cookbro@aol.com
Products: Pipe fittings and valves. SICs: 5085 (Industrial Supplies); 5074 (Plumbing & Hydronic Heating Supplies). Est: 1953. Sales: $3,000,000 (2000). Emp: 7. Officers: Doug Cook, President; Jerry Langner, Sales Mgr.

■ 23127 ■ P.S. Cook Co.
400 W 15th St.
Cheyenne, WY 82001
Phone: (307)634-4481   Fax: (307)635-3638
Products: Plumbing supplies, including tubing and pipes; Hardware. SICs: 5074 (Plumbing & Hydronic Heating Supplies); 5072 (Hardware). Est: 1883. Sales: $2,000,000 (2000). Emp: 50. Officers: Scot S. Cook, President.

■ 23128 ■ CORR TECH, Inc.
4545 Homestead Rd.
Houston, TX 77028
Phone: (713)674-7887
Free: (800)752-7054   Fax: (713)674-7242
E-mail: corrtech@ix.netcom.com
URL: http://www.corr-tech.com
Products: Thermoplastic pipe systems, valves, pumps, tanks, accessories, and other plastic systems. SICs: 5074 (Plumbing & Hydronic Heating Supplies); 5162 (Plastics Materials & Basic Shapes). Est: 1969. Sales: $20,000,000 (2000). Emp: 70. Officers: Doris Gottesman, President; Michael Spiess, Exec. VP & General Mgr., e-mail: corrtech@ix.netcom.com.

■ 23129 ■ Cowan Supply Co.
485 Bishop St.
Atlanta, GA 30361
Phone: (404)351-6351
Products: Plumbing supplies; Hardware supplies. SICs: 5074 (Plumbing & Hydronic Heating Supplies); 5072 (Hardware). Est: 1946. Sales: $2,000,000 (2000). Emp: 18. Officers: Joe Albright, President.

■ 23130 ■ Dahl
1000 Siler Park Ln.
Santa Fe, NM 87505-3116
Phone: (505)471-1968   Fax: (505)473-2005
Products: Plumbing and heating equipment, including tools and utilities. SIC: 5074 (Plumbing & Hydronic Heating Supplies). Est: 1988. Sales: $180,000,000 (2000). Emp: 392. Officers: David Alexander, President.

■ 23131 ■ M.J. Daly and Sons Inc.
110 Mattheuck
Waterbury, CT 06705
Phone: (203)753-5131   Fax: (203)597-0227
Products: Construction: Mechanical contractors for the plumbing indusry. Plumbing supplies. SIC: 5074 (Plumbing & Hydronic Heating Supplies). Sales: $23,000,000 (2000). Emp: 200. Officers: Jan A. Dembinski, President; George Stitchalk, Controller.

■ 23132 ■ Dana Kepner Co.
700 Alcott
Denver, CO 80204
Phone: (303)623-6161
Products: Water and sewer materials. SICs: 5074 (Plumbing & Hydronic Heating Supplies); 5039 (Construction Materials Nec). Sales: $60,000,000 (2000). Emp: 85. Officers: Wayne E. Johnson, President.

■ 23133 ■ Davidson Pipe Supply Company Inc.
5002 2nd Ave.
Brooklyn, NY 11232
Phone: (718)439-6300   Fax: (718)438-8078
E-mail: sales@davidsonpipe.com
URL: http://www.davidsonpipe.com
Products: Pipes and piping accessories. SICs: 5074 (Plumbing & Hydronic Heating Supplies); 5051 (Metals Service Centers & Offices). Est: 1904. Sales: $30,000,000 (2000). Emp: 60. Officers: J. Klausner, President; Stewart Krueger, Treasurer; Peter Davidson, CFO.

■ 23134 ■ Davis Supply Co.
PO Box 22189
Savannah, GA 31403-2189
Phone: (770)449-7000
Free: (800)395-2739   Fax: (770)263-4834
Products: Plumbing, electrical appliances and industrial supplies. SICs: 5074 (Plumbing & Hydronic Heating Supplies); 5064 (Electrical Appliances—Television & Radio); 5085 (Industrial Supplies). Sales: $53,000,000 (2000). Emp: 200. Officers: Clyde Rodbell, President.

■ 23135 ■ De Best Manufacturing Company Inc.
PO Box 2002
Gardena, CA 90247
Phone: (310)352-3030
Free: (800)421-5588   Fax: (310)327-1921
E-mail: debest@debestmfg.com
URL: http://www.debestmfg.com
Products: Plumbing and heating valves and specialties. SIC: 5074 (Plumbing & Hydronic Heating Supplies). Est: 1956. Sales: $2,500,000 (2000). Emp: 21. Officers: Jim Turner, President; Shamy Turner, Vice President; Debra Shaul, Office Mgr.

■ 23136 ■ Delaware Plumbing Supply Co.
2309 N Dupont Hwy.
New Castle, DE 19720-6300
Phone: (302)656-5437   Fax: (302)656-4309
Products: Plumbing and heating supplies. SIC: 5074 (Plumbing & Hydronic Heating Supplies). Est: 1928. Emp: 12.

■ 23137 ■ Detroit Pump and Manufacturing Co.
18943 John R.
Detroit, MI 48203-2090
Phone: (313)893-4242   Fax: (313)893-7139
URL: http://www.detroitpump.com
Products: General line of pumps. SICs: 5084 (Industrial Machinery & Equipment); 5013 (Motor Vehicle Supplies & New Parts). Est: 1926. Sales: $15,000,000 (1999). Emp: 45. Officers: Paul M. Horvath, CEO & President, e-mail: paul.horvath@detroitpump.com.

■ 23138 ■ Diller Tile Company Inc.
PO Box 727
Chatsworth, IL 60921
Phone: (815)635-3131   Fax: (815)635-3133
Products: Plastic drainage tubing and accessories; Clay drain tiles and accessories. SICs: 5074 (Plumbing & Hydronic Heating Supplies); 5032 (Brick, Stone & Related Materials). Est: 1946. Sales: $5,000,000 (2000). Emp: 30. Officers: William Diller, President; Allen E. Diller, Treasurer & Secty.; Dale E. Diller, Secretary.

■ 23139 ■ Duhig and Co.
14275 Wicks Blvd.
San Leandro, CA 94577
Phone: (510)352-6460   Fax: (510)352-1042
Products: Stainless steel pipe valves; Fittings. SICs: 5051 (Metals Service Centers & Offices); 5074 (Plumbing & Hydronic Heating Supplies). Est: 1943. Sales: $16,000,000 (2000). Emp: 48. Officers: Rich Hernandez, President.

■ 23140 ■ Duluth Plumbing Supply Co.
PO Box 16329
Duluth, MN 55816-0329
Phone: (218)722-3393   Fax: (218)722-3163
Products: Plumbing and heating supplies. SICs: 5074 (Plumbing & Hydronic Heating Supplies); 5051 (Metals

Service Centers & Offices). **Est:** 1889. **Sales:** $4,000,000 (2000). **Emp:** 17. **Officers:** Greg Anderson, President; Craig A. Guzzo, Treasurer & Secty.; John Amundsen, VP of Sales.

■ 23141 ■ **Duro Supply Co.**
801 S Henry St.
PO Box 188
Bay City, MI 48706
Phone: (517)894-2811 **Fax:** (517)894-2817
Products: Plumbing and HVAC supplies, equipment, and tools. **SIC:** 5074 (Plumbing & Hydronic Heating Supplies). **Est:** 1945. **Sales:** $5,000,000 (2000). **Emp:** 25. **Officers:** Lee Haddix, CEO, e-mail: lhaddix@ a1access.net.

■ 23142 ■ **Durst Corp.**
PO Box 1252
Mountainside, NJ 07092-0252
Phone: (908)789-2880 **Fax:** (908)789-2911
Products: Plumbing supplies. **SIC:** 5074 (Plumbing & Hydronic Heating Supplies). **Est:** 1902. **Emp:** 23. **Officers:** Dana Egert, Chairman of the Board; Lawrence Brodey, President.

■ 23143 ■ **H.G. Dyer Co.**
19 Old Bliss St.
Rehoboth, MA 02769
Phone: (508)621-1622
Products: Heating equipment; Plumbing fixtures, equipment, and supplies. **SIC:** 5074 (Plumbing & Hydronic Heating Supplies). **Officers:** Robert Morse, Owner.

■ 23144 ■ **Eastern Penn Supply Co.**
700 Scott St.
Wilkes Barre, PA 18705
Phone: (570)823-1181 **Fax:** (570)824-2514
E-mail: sales@easternpenn.com
URL: http://www.easternpenn.com
Products: Plumbing, heating, and industrial supplies; Building materials; Electric pumps. **SICs:** 5074 (Plumbing & Hydronic Heating Supplies); 5085 (Industrial Supplies); 5039 (Construction Materials Nec). **Est:** 1889. **Sales:** $32,000,000 (2000). **Emp:** 129. **Officers:** Guthrie G. Conyngham, CEO; Joseph D. Kerestes, CFO; Donald Conyngham, Vice President; George G. Conyngham Jr., VP of Sales; R. Schuler, VP of Operations. **Former Name:** Conyngham and Company Inc.

■ 23145 ■ **Eau Claire Plumbing Supply Co.**
PO Box 166
Eau Claire, WI 54702-0166
Phone: (715)832-6638 **Fax:** (715)832-0561
Products: Plumbing supplies; Heating supplies. **SICs:** 5074 (Plumbing & Hydronic Heating Supplies); 5075 (Warm Air Heating & Air-Conditioning). **Est:** 1951. **Sales:** $12,000,000 (2000). **Emp:** 50. **Officers:** Michael D. Hickok, President.

■ 23146 ■ **Electrical Materials Co.**
1236 1st Ave.
Ft. Dodge, IA 50501-4834
Phone: (515)573-7166
Free: (800)697-3137 **Fax:** (515)573-7168
Products: Plumbing equipment; Electrical supplies. **SICs:** 5074 (Plumbing & Hydronic Heating Supplies); 5063 (Electrical Apparatus & Equipment). **Est:** 1960. **Sales:** $7,000,000 (2000). **Emp:** 28.

■ 23147 ■ **Elite Consumer Products**
65 Grove St.
Watertown, MA 02472
Phone: 800-457-4449
Free: (888)ELI-TECP **Fax:** (617)923-3486
E-mail: elite@ionics.com
URL: http://www.elitecp.com
Products: Cleaners, automotive, pool. **SIC:** 5074 (Plumbing & Hydronic Heating Supplies). **Est:** 1948. **Sales:** $25,000,000 (1999). **Emp:** 150. **Officers:** Alan M. Crosby, VP & General Mgr.; David A. Gunning, Business Mgr.; William J. Iaconelli, Sales/Marketing Contact, e-mail: wiaconellijr@ionics.com; Joanne M. Bernier, Customer Service Contact, e-mail: jbernier@ ionics.com; David A. Gunning, Human Resources Contact, e-mail: dgunning@ionics.com.

■ 23148 ■ **Emerson-Swan Inc.**
PO Box 783
Randolph, MA 02368
Phone: (781)986-2000
Free: (800)346-9215 **Fax:** (781)986-2028
Products: Plumbing supplies; Heating supplies. **SICs:** 5074 (Plumbing & Hydronic Heating Supplies); 5075 (Warm Air Heating & Air-Conditioning). **Est:** 1932. **Sales:** $47,000,000 (2000). **Emp:** 200. **Officers:** Joseph E. Swan, President; Anne Kelley, VP of Operations.

■ 23149 ■ **Engineering and Equipment Co.**
PO Box 588
Albany, GA 31702
Phone: (912)435-5601
Products: Plumbing, heating, and air-conditioning supplies. **SICs:** 5074 (Plumbing & Hydronic Heating Supplies); 5075 (Warm Air Heating & Air-Conditioning). **Est:** 1946. **Sales:** $25,500,000 (2000). **Emp:** 100. **Officers:** Collins Knight III, President.

■ 23150 ■ **Equipment Valve and Supply Inc.**
PO Box 722155
Houston, TX 77272-2155
Phone: (281)498-6600
Free: (800)882-5838 **Fax:** (281)498-8293
E-mail: equip.valve@prodigy.net
Products: Valves; Fittings; Flanges. **SIC:** 5085 (Industrial Supplies). **Est:** 1944. **Sales:** $13,000,000 (2000). **Emp:** 15. **Officers:** John Nicholas, President & Chairman of the Board; Bob Moore.

■ 23151 ■ **Ermco Inc.**
2122 Kratky Rd.
St. Louis, MO 63114-1704
Phone: (314)241-3334 **Fax:** (314)241-4137
Products: Water conditioning equipment. **SIC:** 5074 (Plumbing & Hydronic Heating Supplies). **Officers:** Dr. M.J. Bellavance, Vice President.

■ 23152 ■ **Esco Supply Company Inc.**
1234 San Francisco St.
San Antonio, TX 78201
Phone: (210)736-4205 **Fax:** (210)736-4372
E-mail: esco@escosupply.com
URL: http://www.escosupply.com
Products: Valves; Fitting; Piping. **SICs:** 5074 (Plumbing & Hydronic Heating Supplies); 5085 (Industrial Supplies). **Est:** 1969. **Sales:** $19,000,000 (2000). **Emp:** 85. **Officers:** Randolph Dent, President; John Carner, Controller; Kevin Bowman, Vice President.

■ 23153 ■ **E.W.C. Supply Inc.**
2336 S Main St.
Elkhart, IN 46517
Phone: (219)293-9211 **Fax:** (219)293-8432
Products: Fabricated pipe and fittings. **SICs:** 5074 (Plumbing & Hydronic Heating Supplies); 5085 (Industrial Supplies). **Officers:** Raoul H. "Bud" Peeters, President.

■ 23154 ■ **R.F. Fager Company Inc.**
2058 State Rd.
Camp Hill, PA 17011
Phone: (717)761-0660
Products: Plumbing and heating equipment, and roofing material. **SICs:** 5074 (Plumbing & Hydronic Heating Supplies); 5039 (Construction Materials Nec). **Sales:** $16,000,000 (1993). **Emp:** 70. **Officers:** Richard Fager Sr., President; Richard Fager Jr., Controller.

■ 23155 ■ **Fairbury Winnelson Co.**
PO Box 419
Fairbury, NE 68352
Phone: (402)729-2215 **Fax:** (402)729-2574
Products: Plumbing fixtures, equipment, and supplies; Air-conditioning equipment; Heating equipment. **SICs:** 5074 (Plumbing & Hydronic Heating Supplies); 5075 (Warm Air Heating & Air-Conditioning). **Est:** 1991. **Sales:** $1,800,000 (1999). **Emp:** 7. **Officers:** Karen Banahan, President.

■ 23156 ■ **Falcon Plumbing Inc.**
2414 N Gilbert Rd.
Mesa, AZ 85203-1302
Phone: (602)964-6622 **Fax:** (602)898-0445
Products: Plumbing supplies. **SIC:** 5074 (Plumbing & Hydronic Heating Supplies). **Emp:** 49. **Officers:** Jerry Newsome.

■ 23157 ■ **Falk Supply Co.**
PO Box 1329
Hot Springs, AR 71902
Phone: (501)321-1231
Free: (800)844-3255 **Fax:** (501)321-4015
E-mail: info@falksupply.com
URL: http://www.falksupply.com
Products: Plumbing supplies, including pipes, fixtures, and fittings. **SIC:** 5074 (Plumbing & Hydronic Heating Supplies). **Est:** 1937. **Sales:** $7,200,000 (2000). **Emp:** 46. **Officers:** Louis F. Kleinman, President, e-mail: louis@falksupply.com.

■ 23158 ■ **Familian Northwest Inc.**
PO Box 17098
Portland, OR 97217
Phone: (503)283-4444 **Fax:** (503)978-2273
URL: http://www.familiannw.com
Products: Plumbing and piping equipment; HVAC; Waterworks. **SICs:** 5074 (Plumbing & Hydronic Heating Supplies); 5051 (Metals Service Centers & Offices). **Est:** 1969. **Sales:** $650,000,000 (2000). **Emp:** 2,000. **Officers:** Bob Johnson, CEO; Ron Saltmarsh, CFO.

■ 23159 ■ **Familian Pipe and Supply**
7651 Woodman Ave.
Van Nuys, CA 91402
Phone: (818)786-9720
Products: Plumbing supplies. **SIC:** 5074 (Plumbing & Hydronic Heating Supplies). **Est:** 1926. **Sales:** $300,000,000 (2000). **Emp:** 1,300. **Officers:** David Shapiro, President; Leonard Gross, Exec. VP of Finance; Jerry Grosslight, VP of Marketing; Steven Dunn, Dir. of Systems; Karen Gorham, Personnel Mgr.

■ 23160 ■ **Familiar Northwest**
PO Box 220
Minot, ND 58702-0220
Phone: (701)852-4411
Free: (800)755-4559 **Fax:** (701)839-7813
Products: Plumbing supplies; Heating supplies. **SICs:** 5074 (Plumbing & Hydronic Heating Supplies); 5075 (Warm Air Heating & Air-Conditioning). **Est:** 1961. **Sales:** $5,000,000 (2000). **Emp:** 10. **Officers:** Tom Stern, President.

■ 23161 ■ **Famous Industries**
PO Box 1420
Akron, OH 44309-1420
Phone: (216)535-1811
Products: Heating, plumbing, and cooling equipment and supplies. **SICs:** 5085 (Industrial Supplies); 5075 (Warm Air Heating & Air-Conditioning). **Est:** 1933. **Sales:** $16,000,000 (2000). **Emp:** 75. **Officers:** David C. Ross, CEO & President; Craig Raub, Finance Officer; James Remarks, Dir. of Sales; Norman Lawson, Dir of Human Resources.

■ 23162 ■ **Ferguson Enterprises**
4505 Triangle St.
Mc Farland, WI 53558
Phone: (608)257-3755
Free: (800)236-1255 **Fax:** (608)838-9387
Products: Plumbing equipment, industrial pipes, valves and fittings. **SIC:** 5074 (Plumbing & Hydronic Heating Supplies). **Sales:** $11,000,000 (2000). **Emp:** 55. **Officers:** John Mcdaniel, President; Tom Lorrig, Controller.

■ 23163 ■ **Ferguson Enterprises Inc.**
2700-A Yonkers Rd.
Raleigh, NC 27604
Phone: (919)828-7300 **Fax:** (919)872-6383
Products: Pumps; Valves and pipe fittings; Plumbing fixtures, equipment, and supplies. **SICs:** 5074 (Plumbing & Hydronic Heating Supplies); 5085 (Industrial Supplies). **Est:** 1955. **Sales:** $10,000,000 (2000). **Emp:** 50. **Officers:** John L. Wilcox, President & General Mgr.; Wayne Stevens, Controller; Bruce Ford, Operations Mgr.

■ 23164 ■ Ferguson Enterprises Inc.
PO Box 2778
Newport News, VA 23609-0778
Phone: (804)874-7795 **Fax:** (804)877-3954
Products: Heating and cooling equipment and supplies. **SIC:** 5074 (Plumbing & Hydronic Heating Supplies). **Sales:** $1,000,000,000 (2000). **Emp:** 3,000.

■ 23165 ■ Ferguson Supply Co.
345 Pleasant St. SW
Grand Rapids, MI 49503
Phone: (616)456-1688 **Fax:** (616)456-7615
Products: Fixtures; Plumbing and heating supplies. **SICs:** 5074 (Plumbing & Hydronic Heating Supplies); 5075 (Warm Air Heating & Air-Conditioning). **Est:** 1901. **Sales:** $4,200,000 (2000). **Emp:** 27. **Officers:** Craig Hecker, President.

■ 23166 ■ Fiberglass Representatives Inc.
PO Box 1109
Antioch, CA 94509
Phone: (510)778-2200 **Fax:** (510)778-9233
E-mail: fbrglass@aol.com
Products: Fiberglass pipes, tanks, grating, stairtreads, plates, decking, and platforms. **SICs:** 5074 (Plumbing & Hydronic Heating Supplies); 5039 (Construction Materials Nec). **Est:** 1971. **Sales:** $2,000,000 (2000). **Emp:** 25. **Officers:** Jim Barrett, President.

■ 23167 ■ Fibredyne Inc.
47 Crosby Rd.
Dover, NH 03820
Phone: (603)749-1610 **Fax:** (603)749-2699
Products: Filtration equipment. **SIC:** 5074 (Plumbing & Hydronic Heating Supplies). **Officers:** Robert Long, Marketing Mgr.

■ 23168 ■ Fields and Company of Lubbock Inc.
1610 5th. St.
Lubbock, TX 79408
Phone: (806)762-0241
Products: Plumbing heating supplies; Appliances. **SICs:** 5074 (Plumbing & Hydronic Heating Supplies); 5063 (Electrical Apparatus & Equipment). **Sales:** $59,000,000 (2000). **Emp:** 250. **Officers:** Dan Law, President; Dennis Johnnston, Treasurer & Secty.; Norman Gooch, Vice President.

■ 23169 ■ First Supply Group
6800 Gisholt Dr.
Madison, WI 53708
Phone: (608)222-7799 **Fax:** (608)223-6664
URL: http://www.1supply.com
Products: Plumbing fixtures, equipment, and supplies; Heating equipment; Warm air heating and cooling equipment; Pump products. **SICs:** 5074 (Plumbing & Hydronic Heating Supplies); 5075 (Warm Air Heating & Air-Conditioning). **Est:** 1898. **Sales:** $200,000,000 (2000). **Emp:** 725. **Officers:** Joseph S. Poehling, President; Thomas J. Golden, CFO; David Prahler, Chief Investment Officer; Elliot Collier, VP of Contractor Sales; Tim Sawyer, Dir of Human Resources; Mike Hickok, VP of Purchasing. **Former Name:** La Crosse Plumbing Supply Co.

■ 23170 ■ Flotec-Town and Country
293 Wright St.
Delavan, WI 53115
Phone: (414)728-1543
Free: (800)365-6832 **Fax:** 800-526-3757
Products: Industrial water pumps. **SIC:** 5074 (Plumbing & Hydronic Heating Supplies). **Est:** 1933. **Sales:** $4,000,000 (2000). **Emp:** 30. **Officers:** Doug Jackson, General Mgr.; James J. Monnat, Treasurer; D. Ellis, Dir. of Marketing.

■ 23171 ■ Fluid-O-Tech International, Inc.
161 Atwater St.
Plantsville, CT 06479
Phone: (860)620-0393 **Fax:** (860)620-0193
Products: Pumps; Filters. **SICs:** 5084 (Industrial Machinery & Equipment); 5074 (Plumbing & Hydronic Heating Supplies). **Officers:** Raymond M. Petrucci, President.

■ 23172 ■ Forgy Process Instruments Inc.
10785 Indian Head Industrial Blv
St. Louis, MO 63132
Phone: (314)423-6262 **Fax:** (314)423-8673
Products: Steam traps, valves, and fittings; Musical instrument parts. **SICs:** 5065 (Electronic Parts & Equipment Nec); 5099 (Durable Goods Nec). **Est:** 1988. **Sales:** $3,600,000 (2000). **Emp:** 13. **Officers:** Randall Forgy, President.

■ 23173 ■ Forrer Supply Company Inc.
PO Box 220
Germantown, WI 53022-0220
Phone: (414)255-3030 **Fax:** (414)255-4064
Products: Pipe. **SIC:** 5074 (Plumbing & Hydronic Heating Supplies). **Est:** 1982. **Sales:** $8,000,000 (2000). **Emp:** 18. **Officers:** Stephen Forrer, President; Connie Forrer, CFO.

■ 23174 ■ Fort Collins Winnelson Co.
1616 Riverside Ave.
Ft. Collins, CO 80524
Phone: (970)484-8161
Products: Plumbing supplies. **SIC:** 5074 (Plumbing & Hydronic Heating Supplies). **Est:** 1968. **Sales:** $3,000,000 (2000). **Emp:** 6. **Officers:** Mike Bopp, CEO.

■ 23175 ■ Fort Smith Winnelson Co.
1700 Towson Ave.
PO Box 1299
Ft. Smith, AR 72902-1299
Phone: (501)783-5177
Free: (800)775-1453 **Fax:** (501)783-0541
E-mail: ftsmithwne@earthlink.net
Products: Plumbing equipment and supplies. **SIC:** 5074 (Plumbing & Hydronic Heating Supplies). **Est:** 1955. **Sales:** $2,000,000 (2000). **Emp:** 6. **Officers:** Ron Bohannon, President.

■ 23176 ■ Frakco Inc.
PO Box 566
Luverne, MN 56156
Phone: (507)283-4416 **Fax:** (507)283-4417
Products: Plumbing supplies, including water softeners. **SIC:** 5074 (Plumbing & Hydronic Heating Supplies). **Est:** 1949. **Sales:** $1,300,000 (2000). **Emp:** 5. **Officers:** Annabelle Frakes, President; Dawn Frakes, CFO; Bob Frakes, VP of Marketing.

■ 23177 ■ Frischkorn Distributors Inc.
PO Box 1547
Washington, NC 27889-1547
Phone: (919)537-4169 **Fax:** (919)537-1122
Products: Valves and pipe fittings. **SIC:** 5074 (Plumbing & Hydronic Heating Supplies). **Est:** 1954. **Sales:** $8,000,000 (2000). **Emp:** 100. **Officers:** H. Harding, President.

■ 23178 ■ Frontier Water and Steam Supply Co.
366 Oak St.
Buffalo, NY 14203
Phone: (716)853-4400 **Fax:** (716)855-0993
Products: Plumbing and heating supplies. **SICs:** 5074 (Plumbing & Hydronic Heating Supplies); 5075 (Warm Air Heating & Air-Conditioning). **Est:** 1905. **Sales:** $400,000 (2000). **Emp:** 4. **Officers:** Peter Seiffert, President; Joe Caparco, General Mgr.

■ 23179 ■ Fuller Supply Co.
1958 Turner NW
Grand Rapids, MI 49504
Phone: (616)364-8455
Free: (800)292-8768 **Fax:** (616)364-4817
Products: Water well supplies; Water treatment systems; Pipes, valves, and fittings. **SIC:** 5074 (Plumbing & Hydronic Heating Supplies). **Est:** 1933. **Emp:** 9. **Officers:** Phillip G. Bednarek, President, e-mail: phil@fullersupplycompany.com; Dee Carrow, Sales/Marketing Contact, e-mail: sales@fullersupplycompany.com.

■ 23180 ■ The Gage Co.
815 Main Ave.
Hagerstown, MD 21740
Phone: (301)739-7474 **Fax:** (301)733-3753
E-mail: gagehagerstown@NFIS.com
Products: Plumbing and heating supplies. **SICs:** 5074

(Plumbing & Hydronic Heating Supplies); 5075 (Warm Air Heating & Air-Conditioning). **Est:** 1993. **Sales:** $5,000,000 (2000). **Emp:** 17. **Officers:** Jim Weller, Manager.

■ 23181 ■ Gage Co. Redlon and Johnson Plumbing Supply Div.
PO Box 3554
Portland, ME 04104
Phone: (207)773-4755
Products: Plumbing, heating, and well supplies. **SIC:** 5074 (Plumbing & Hydronic Heating Supplies).

■ 23182 ■ J.O. Galloup Co.
130 N Helmer Rd.
Battle Creek, MI 49015
Phone: (616)965-2303 **Fax:** (616)965-2393
Products: Industrial pipes, valves, and fittings. **SIC:** 5074 (Plumbing & Hydronic Heating Supplies). **Est:** 1886. **Sales:** $28,000,000 (2000). **Emp:** 110. **Officers:** Bruce Shurtz, President; Gary Longman, Controller; Carl Bolles, Inventory Control.

■ 23183 ■ B. Gates Co. Inc.
1010 Pamela Dr.
Euless, TX 76040
Phone: (817)267-8755 **Fax:** (817)545-8454
URL: http://www.bgatesco.com
Products: Plumbing and heating valves and specialties. **SICs:** 5074 (Plumbing & Hydronic Heating Supplies); 5072 (Hardware). **Est:** 1981. **Sales:** $10,000,000 (1999). **Emp:** 7. **Officers:** Mitch Gates, Sales/Marketing Contact; Helen Gates, Customer Service Contact, e-mail: heleng1@bgatesco.com

■ 23184 ■ Gateway Supply Co.
1401 E Higgins Rd.
Elk Grove Village, IL 60007
Phone: (847)956-1560
Products: Toilets; Faucets; Sinks; Tubs. **SIC:** 5074 (Plumbing & Hydronic Heating Supplies). **Est:** 1969. **Sales:** $2,000,000 (2000). **Emp:** 10. **Officers:** Shirley Burkhart, President; Kevin Buckhart, Vice President.

■ 23185 ■ Gateway Supply Company Inc.
PO Box 56
Columbia, SC 29202
Phone: (803)771-7160 **Fax:** (803)376-5600
Products: Heating and air-conditioning equipment; Plumbing equipment, including pipes and fittings, faucets, sinks, and tubs. **SICs:** 5074 (Plumbing & Hydronic Heating Supplies); 5075 (Warm Air Heating & Air-Conditioning). **Est:** 1964. **Sales:** $23,000,000 (2000). **Emp:** 108. **Officers:** S.P. Williams Jr., President; D. Marsha, Comptroller; Leonard Moore, Manager.

■ 23186 ■ General Mill Supplies Inc.
PO Box 23587
New Orleans, LA 70183
Phone: (504)736-0404 **Fax:** (504)736-0006
E-mail: genmill@bellsouth.net
URL: http://www.generalmill.com
Products: Industrial supplies, including pipes, pipe fittings, and valves. **SIC:** 5074 (Plumbing & Hydronic Heating Supplies). **Est:** 1945. **Sales:** $10,000,000 (1999). **Emp:** 49. **Officers:** Bernard Morvant, Chairman of the Board; Mike Rittler; Clarence Steeg, Dir. of Marketing; Connie Durel, Dir. of Systems.

■ 23187 ■ General Pipe and Supply Company Inc.
PO Box 13185
Memphis, TN 38113
Phone: (901)774-7000
Free: (800)727-6062 **Fax:** (901)774-7006
Products: Pipes; Valves; Fittings. **SICs:** 5074 (Plumbing & Hydronic Heating Supplies); 5051 (Metals Service Centers & Offices); 5085 (Industrial Supplies). **Est:** 1955. **Sales:** $4,000,000 (2000). **Emp:** 10. **Officers:** W. Quinn, President & CFO; James Quinn, Vice President.

■ 23188 ■ General Plumbing Supply Company of Maryland Inc.
1829 Edison Hwy.
Baltimore, MD 21213
Phone: (410)276-5200 **Fax:** (410)327-8198
Products: Sinks, toilets, and tubs. **SIC:** 5074

(Plumbing & Hydronic Heating Supplies). **Est:** 1943. **Sales:** $5,000,000 (2000). **Emp:** 40. **Officers:** Leon Waclawski, President.

■ **23189** ■ **Max Gerber Inc.**
2293 N Milwaukee Ave.
Chicago, IL 60647
Phone: (773)342-7600 **Fax:** (773)342-2051
E-mail: lmoscovic@ameritech.net
Products: Kitchen and bathroom fixtures. **SIC:** 5074 (Plumbing & Hydronic Heating Supplies). **Est:** 1919. **Sales:** $6,500,000 (1999). **Emp:** 28. **Officers:** Josef Moskovic, President.

■ **23190** ■ **Gerber Plumbing Fixtures Corp.**
4600 W Touhy Ave.
Lincolnwood, IL 60712
Phone: (847)675-6570
URL: http://www.gerberonline.com
Products: Plumbing fixtures, including sinks and toilets. **SIC:** 5074 (Plumbing & Hydronic Heating Supplies). **Est:** 1932. **Sales:** $115,000,000 (2000). **Emp:** 900. **Officers:** Harriet G. Lewis, Chairman of the Board; Jon Deiter, President; Ron Grabski, Sr. VP of Sales & Marketing.

■ **23191** ■ **A.A. Gilbert Pipe and Supply Co.**
4037 Mansfield Rd.
Shreveport, LA 71103
Phone: (318)425-2447
Products: Pipe and pipe supplies. **SICs:** 5051 (Metals Service Centers & Offices); 5074 (Plumbing & Hydronic Heating Supplies). **Est:** 1939. **Sales:** $1,400,000 (2000). **Emp:** 10. **Officers:** Pauline G. Murov, Partner; William M. Braunig, Manager; Ronald G. Nierman, Manager; Neal H. Nierman, Partner.

■ **23192** ■ **Global Exports, Inc.**
11 Orchard Hill Dr.
Manalapan, NJ 07726
Phone: (732)308-0767
Free: (800)724-5505 **Fax:** (732)303-8128
E-mail: howarda780@aol.com
URL: http://www.globalexports.com
Products: Plumbing fixtures and fittings; Commercial foodservice equipment and parts. **SICs:** 5074 (Plumbing & Hydronic Heating Supplies); 5046 (Commercial Equipment Nec). **Est:** 1990. **Sales:** $3,000,000 (2000). **Officers:** Robyn L. Allen, President.

■ **23193** ■ **Globe Inc.**
6363 Hwy. 7
St. Louis Park, MN 55416
Phone: (612)929-1377
Free: (800)456-2346 **Fax:** (612)928-7372
Products: Heating, plumbing, and air-conditioning equipment and supplies. **SICs:** 5074 (Plumbing & Hydronic Heating Supplies); 5075 (Warm Air Heating & Air-Conditioning). **Est:** 1996. **Sales:** $20,000,000 (2000). **Emp:** 72. **Officers:** Michael J. Goldstein, President.

■ **23194** ■ **Golden West Pipe & Supply Co.**
11700 S Woodruff Ave.
Downey, CA 90241-5630
Phone: (562)803-4321 **Fax:** (562)803-6226
Products: Plumbing supplies. **SIC:** 5074 (Plumbing & Hydronic Heating Supplies). **Est:** 1957. **Sales:** $14,000,000 (2000). **Emp:** 49. **Officers:** Shirley Lutgen, President; Michael Lutgen, Vice President; Jim McGough.

■ **23195** ■ **Herman Goldner Company Inc.**
7777 Brewster Ave.
Philadelphia, PA 19153
Phone: (215)365-5400
Free: (888)GOL-DNER **Fax:** (215)365-8550
E-mail: webmaster@goldner.com
URL: http://www.goldner.com
Products: Pipe, valves, fittings, engineering and steam products, and valve actuation products. **SICs:** 5074 (Plumbing & Hydronic Heating Supplies); 5039 (Construction Materials Nec). **Est:** 1887. **Sales:** $25,000,000 (2000). **Emp:** 65. **Officers:** H.E. Goldner, CEO & Chairman of the Board; J.D. Goldner, Treasurer & Secty., e-mail: jdgoldner@goldner.com; G.C. Goldner, President, e-mail: ggoldner@goldner.com; H.W. Goldner, Exec. VP, e-mail: hgoldner@goldner.com;

Emma Anello, Human Resources Contact, e-mail: eanello@goldner.com; Gregory Goldner, General Mgr.

■ **23196** ■ **Goodin Co.**
2700 N 2nd St.
Minneapolis, MN 55411
Phone: (612)588-7811 **Fax:** (612)588-7820
Products: Plumbing, heating, and air-conditioning supplies. **SICs:** 5074 (Plumbing & Hydronic Heating Supplies); 5075 (Warm Air Heating & Air-Conditioning). **Est:** 1943. **Sales:** $47,000,000 (2000). **Emp:** 200. **Officers:** B.D. Reisberg, President.

■ **23197** ■ **Goulet Supply Company Inc.**
381 Elm St.
Manchester, NH 03101
Phone: (603)669-2170
Products: Plumbing supplies. **SIC:** 5074 (Plumbing & Hydronic Heating Supplies). **Est:** 1952. **Sales:** $16,000,000 (2000). **Emp:** 100. **Officers:** Kevin Condron, CEO; Joe Goff, CFO; William T. Hilfinger, VP of Operations.

■ **23198** ■ **Graybow-Daniels Co.**
205 10th Ave. N
Plymouth, MN 55441
Phone: (612)797-7000 **Fax:** (612)797-7012
Products: Plumbing and heating equipment. **SICs:** 5074 (Plumbing & Hydronic Heating Supplies); 5075 (Warm Air Heating & Air-Conditioning). **Est:** 1955. **Sales:** $75,000,000 (2000). **Emp:** 247. **Officers:** Marvin Graybow, CEO & President; Bob Carter, Controller; Bruce Graybow, Exec. VP.

■ **23199** ■ **Grinnell Supply Sales Co.**
1930 Warren St.
North Kansas City, MO 64116
Phone: (816)474-0500
Products: Sprinkler systems; Pipes; Fittings; Valves. **SICs:** 5074 (Plumbing & Hydronic Heating Supplies); 5085 (Industrial Supplies). **Sales:** $3,000,000 (2000). **Emp:** 13. **Officers:** L. Dennis Kozowski, President.

■ **23200** ■ **Hahn Supply Inc.**
2101 Main St.
Lewiston, ID 83501
Phone: (208)743-1577 **Fax:** (208)743-2938
E-mail: hahn@lewiston.com
Products: Plumbing and heating equipment; Industrial equipment. **SICs:** 5074 (Plumbing & Hydronic Heating Supplies); 5084 (Industrial Machinery & Equipment). **Est:** 1898. **Sales:** $5,000,000 (1999). **Emp:** 40. **Officers:** Keith Church, President; A.L. Alford Jr., Treasurer & Secty.; Skip Olson, Operations Mgr.; Marie Butler, Controller; Larry Bean, Vice President.

■ **23201** ■ **Hajoca Corp.**
127 Coulter Ave.
Ardmore, PA 19003
Phone: (215)649-1430
Products: Industrial plumbing and heating supplies. **SICs:** 5074 (Plumbing & Hydronic Heating Supplies); 5075 (Warm Air Heating & Air-Conditioning). **Est:** 1911. **Sales:** $300,000,000 (2000). **Emp:** 1,300. **Officers:** R.F. Parsons, President; T. Callahan, VP of Finance.

■ **23202** ■ **Ham and McCreight Inc.**
PO Box 1046
Temple, TX 76503-1046
Phone: (254)778-4747 **Fax:** (254)778-4798
Products: Plumbing supplies. **SIC:** 5074 (Plumbing & Hydronic Heating Supplies). **Est:** 1968. **Sales:** $6,000,000 (2000). **Emp:** 18. **Officers:** Pat Ham, CEO; Bill Tse, Controller; David Ham, President.

■ **23203** ■ **Harrington Corp.**
PO Box 10335
Lynchburg, VA 24506
Phone: (804)845-7094 **Fax:** (804)845-8562
E-mail: sales@harcofittings.com
Products: PVC and ductile iron pipe fittings. **SIC:** 5074 (Plumbing & Hydronic Heating Supplies). **Est:** 1966. **Sales:** $10,000,000 (2000). **Emp:** 100. **Officers:** Michael Harrington, President; Steven Harrington, Controller.

■ **23204** ■ **Harris Supply Company Inc.**
36 Central Pl.
Wellsville, NY 14895
Phone: (716)593-5811
Free: (800)626-1660 **Fax:** (716)593-5184
Products: Industrial supplies. **SIC:** 5074 (Plumbing & Hydronic Heating Supplies). **Sales:** $10,000,000 (2000). **Emp:** 55.

■ **23205** ■ **Harrison Piping Supply Co.**
38777 Schoolcraft Rd.
Livonia, MI 48150
Phone: (734)464-4400 **Fax:** (734)464-6488
Products: Pipe, valves, and fittings; Instrumentation; HVAC boilers; Water heaters and controls. **SICs:** 5051 (Metals Service Centers & Offices); 5074 (Plumbing & Hydronic Heating Supplies); 5084 (Industrial Machinery & Equipment). **Est:** 1959. **Sales:** $32,700,000 (2000). **Emp:** 100. **Officers:** Jeffrey D. Harrison, CEO & President; Ray Debo, CFO; Jeffrey D. Harrison, Marketing Mgr.; Bob Bush, Sales/Marketing Contact, e-mail: bbush@harrisonco.com.

■ **23206** ■ **L.A. Hazard and Sons Inc.**
1695 Overhead Rd.
Derby, NY 14047
Phone: (716)627-2364 **Fax:** (716)627-0237
Products: Heating, plumbing, and electrical supplies. **SICs:** 5074 (Plumbing & Hydronic Heating Supplies); 5063 (Electrical Apparatus & Equipment); 5075 (Warm Air Heating & Air-Conditioning). **Est:** 1912. **Sales:** $9,000,000 (2000). **Emp:** 55. **Officers:** Robert Hazard, President; Dennis Potozniak, Controller.

■ **23207** ■ **Heatwave Supply Inc.**
6529 E 14th St.
Tulsa, OK 74112
Phone: (918)838-9841
Products: Plumbing supplies. **SIC:** 5074 (Plumbing & Hydronic Heating Supplies). **Est:** 1948. **Sales:** $4,000,000 (2000). **Emp:** 25. **Officers:** R. Rice, President.

■ **23208** ■ **C. Herzog Supply Inc.**
1915 Main St.
East Worcester, NY 12064
Phone: (607)397-8292 **Fax:** (607)397-8742
Products: Plumbing, heating, industrial and electrical supplies. **SICs:** 5074 (Plumbing & Hydronic Heating Supplies); 5063 (Electrical Apparatus & Equipment). **Est:** 1946. **Sales:** $8,000,000 (2000). **Emp:** 100. **Officers:** C. Herzog, President.

■ **23209** ■ **Hirsch Pipe & Supply Co.**
32107 Alipaz
San Juan Capistrano, CA 92675-3616
Phone: (949)493-4591 **Fax:** (949)496-7348
E-mail: sales@hirsch.com
URL: http://www.hirsch.com
Products: Plumbing and heating valves and specialties. **SIC:** 5074 (Plumbing & Hydronic Heating Supplies). **Est:** 1933. **Emp:** 12. **Officers:** Jim Russell, e-mail: jrussell@hirsch.com.

■ **23210** ■ **Holloway Corp.**
2501 Front St.
Philadelphia, PA 19148
Phone: (215)879-9550
Products: Plumbing equipment and supplies. **SIC:** 5074 (Plumbing & Hydronic Heating Supplies).

■ **23211** ■ **Holmes Plumbing and Heating Supply Inc.**
PO Box 460
Kearney, NE 68848-0460
Phone: (308)234-1922 **Fax:** (308)237-5381
Products: Plumbing and heating supplies. **SIC:** 5074 (Plumbing & Hydronic Heating Supplies). **Est:** 1968. **Sales:** $5,000,000 (2000). **Emp:** 16. **Officers:** C. Prochaska, General Mgr.

■ **23212** ■ **Home Reverse Osmosis Systems**
RR 1
Peru, IL 61354
Phone: (815)339-6300 **Fax:** (815)339-6350
E-mail: h2robill@aol.com
URL: http://www.h2ro.com
Products: Water purification equipment. **SIC:** 5074 (Plumbing & Hydronic Heating Supplies). **Est:** 1977.

Sales: $300,000 (2000). Emp: 1. Officers: Nick Pasulka, Owner.

■ 23213 ■ Hotsy Corp.
PO Box 3867
Englewood, CO 80155
Phone: (303)792-5200
Free: (800)525-1976   Fax: (303)792-0547
Products: hot and cold pressure water washers and water recycling systems; Detergents. SIC: 5074 (Plumbing & Hydronic Heating Supplies). Sales: $20,400,000 (2000). Emp: 200. Officers: Larry Cohen, President; Lloyd Rizer, CFO.

■ 23214 ■ Hubbard Pipe and Supply Inc.
PO Drawer 1570
Fayetteville, NC 28302
Phone: (910)484-0187
Products: Plumbing supplies. SIC: 5074 (Plumbing & Hydronic Heating Supplies).

■ 23215 ■ Hughes Supply Inc.
4915 Commercial Dr.
Huntsville, AL 35816
Phone: (205)830-6986   Fax: (205)722-0528
Products: Plumbing supplies. SIC: 5074 (Plumbing & Hydronic Heating Supplies). Emp: 15.

■ 23216 ■ Hughes Supply Inc.
PO Box 2273
Orlando, FL 32802
Phone: (407)841-4755   Fax: (407)426-9173
E-mail: mharrison@hughessupply.com
URL: http://www.hughessupply.com
Products: Building materials; Electrical supplies and utilities; Heating and air conditioning units; Plumbing equipment; Pools; Spas; Water and sewer equipment. SICs: 5063 (Electrical Apparatus & Equipment); 5074 (Plumbing & Hydronic Heating Supplies); 5075 (Warm Air Heating & Air-Conditioning); 5091 (Sporting & Recreational Goods). Est: 1928. Sales: $1,082,200,000 (2000). Emp: 3,350. Officers: David H. Hughes, CEO & Chairman of the Board; J. Stephen Zepf, CFO & Treasurer; A. Stewart Hall, President & COO.

■ 23217 ■ ICS Intercounty Supply
255 S Regent St.
Port Chester, NY 10573
Phone: (914)939-4350
Free: (800)836-0781   Fax: (914)939-4734
E-mail: intercountysupply.com
URL: http://www.intercountysupply.com
Products: Plumbing and heating supplies. SICs: 5074 (Plumbing & Hydronic Heating Supplies); 5075 (Warm Air Heating & Air-Conditioning). Est: 1955. Sales: $20,000,000 (2000). Emp: 70. Officers: Bill Owen, President. Former Name: Border Sales Inc.

■ 23218 ■ Ideal Supply Co.
445 Communipaw Ave.
Jersey City, NJ 07304
Phone: (201)333-2600
Products: Sinks; Pipes. SIC: 5074 (Plumbing & Hydronic Heating Supplies). Est: 1930. Sales: $14,000,000 (2000). Emp: 47. Officers: Don Strittmatter, President.

■ 23219 ■ Industrial Sales Company Inc.
PO Box 2148
Wilmington, NC 28402
Phone: (919)763-5126   Fax: (919)762-2149
Products: Pipes and fittings. SIC: 5074 (Plumbing & Hydronic Heating Supplies). Est: 1966. Sales: $6,000,000 (2000). Emp: 25. Officers: George W. Jones Jr., President.

■ 23220 ■ Inland Supply Inc.
109 Plum St.
Syracuse, NY 13204
Phone: (315)471-6171   Fax: (315)471-2481
Products: Plumbing equipment and supplies, including pumps; Heating equipment and supplies; Tools. SICs: 5074 (Plumbing & Hydronic Heating Supplies); 5075 (Warm Air Heating & Air-Conditioning); 5072 (Hardware).

■ 23221 ■ Intermountain Irrigation
350 N Interchange
Dillon, MT 59725
Phone: (406)683-6571
Products: Irrigation systems; Pumps. SIC: 5074 (Plumbing & Hydronic Heating Supplies).

■ 23222 ■ Irr Supply Centers Inc.
908 Niagra Falls Blvd.
North Tonawanda, NY 14120
Phone: (716)692-1600
Products: Plumbing, heating, and air-conditioning supplies. SICs: 5074 (Plumbing & Hydronic Heating Supplies); 5075 (Warm Air Heating & Air-Conditioning). Est: 1896. Sales: $41,000,000 (2000). Emp: 175. Officers: William R. Irr Sr., President; Bob Hendricks, Treasurer.

■ 23223 ■ Jabo Supply Corp.
PO Box 238
Huntington, WV 25707
Phone: (304)736-8333   Fax: (304)736-8551
Products: Pipe valves; Fittings. SICs: 5051 (Metals Service Centers & Offices); 5085 (Industrial Supplies). Est: 1964. Sales: $19,400,000 (2000). Emp: 93. Officers: J.G. Bazemore, President; Joe Holley, VP of Finance; Bob Bailey, Sales Mgr.; Carl Waddle, Data Processing Mgr.

■ 23224 ■ Jensen Bridge and Supply Co.
PO Box 151
Sandusky, MI 48471
Phone: (810)648-3000   Fax: (810)648-3549
Products: Corrugated steel pipe; Steel roofing and siding. SICs: 5074 (Plumbing & Hydronic Heating Supplies); 5039 (Construction Materials Nec). Est: 1931. Sales: $9,000,000 (2000). Emp: 40. Officers: Roger Loding, President; Marcie Kolakovich, Controller; Dale Chambers, Sales Mgr.

■ 23225 ■ Johnson Pipe and Supply Co.
999 W 37th St.
Chicago, IL 60609
Phone: (773)927-2427   Fax: (773)927-6784
Products: Pipes and fittings for faucets. SIC: 5074 (Plumbing & Hydronic Heating Supplies). Est: 1923. Sales: $7,000,000 (2000). Emp: 18. Officers: Edward Marco, President.

■ 23226 ■ Kamen Supply Company Inc.
4705 Nome St.
Denver, CO 80239
Phone: (303)371-1700
Free: (800)864-4337   Fax: (303)371-1742
Products: Plumbing supplies. SIC: 5074 (Plumbing & Hydronic Heating Supplies). Est: 1896. Sales: $52,000,000 (2000). Emp: 184. Officers: Harlan R. Kamen, District Mgr.; Keith A. Alter, District Mgr.

■ 23227 ■ Kansas City Winnelson Co.
1529 Lake Ave.
Kansas City, KS 66103
Phone: (913)262-6868   Fax: (913)262-6843
Products: Plumbing and water works supplies. SIC: 5074 (Plumbing & Hydronic Heating Supplies). Est: 1967. Sales: $5,400,000 (1999). Emp: 11. Officers: A. Kent Best, President.

■ 23228 ■ Keidel Supply Co.
2026 Delaware Ave.
Cincinnati, OH 45212
Phone: (513)351-1600
Products: Plumbing supplies. SIC: 5074 (Plumbing & Hydronic Heating Supplies). Sales: $18,000,000 (2000). Emp: 90. Officers: Barry Keidel, President & Treasurer.

■ 23229 ■ Keller Supply Co.
3209 17th Ave. W
Seattle, WA 98119
Phone: (206)285-3300
URL: http://www.kellersupply.com
Products: Plumbing supplies, including kitchen fixtures, meters, and pipes. SIC: 5074 (Plumbing & Hydronic Heating Supplies). Est: 1945. Officers: Nick Keller, CEO; Mike Murphy, President.

■ 23230 ■ Kelly's Pipe and Supply Co.
PO Box 14750
Las Vegas, NV 89114
Phone: (702)382-4957
Free: (888)382-4954   Fax: (702)382-4879
URL: http://www.kellyspipe.com
Products: Plumbing supplies, including faucets. SIC: 5074 (Plumbing & Hydronic Heating Supplies). Est: 1961. Sales: $56,000,000 (2000). Emp: 40. Officers: Brad Shoen, CEO & President.

■ 23231 ■ Keltech, Inc.
9285 N 32nd St.
PO Box 405
Richland, MI 49083
Phone: (616)629-4814
Free: (800)999-4320   Fax: (616)629-4853
E-mail: hotwater12@aol.com
URL: http://www.keltech.thomasregister.com
Products: Water heaters (excluding boilers). SIC: 5074 (Plumbing & Hydronic Heating Supplies). Est: 1987. Officers: Melody Lutz, Vice President.

■ 23232 ■ Keltech Inc.
9285 N 32nd St.
Richland, MI 49083
Phone: (616)629-4814
Free: (800)999-4320   Fax: (616)629-4853
Products: Plumbing Materials and fixtures. SIC: 5074 (Plumbing & Hydronic Heating Supplies).

■ 23233 ■ Kessler Industries Inc.
40 Warren St.
Paterson, NJ 07524
Phone: (201)684-2130
Products: Plumbing supplies. SIC: 5074 (Plumbing & Hydronic Heating Supplies). Est: 1925. Sales: $40,000,000 (2000). Emp: 56. Officers: Neil Kessler, President; Julius Levine, Treasurer & Secty.

■ 23234 ■ Keystone Plumbing Sales Co.
225 W 7th Ave.
Homestead, PA 15120
Phone: (412)462-8600
Products: Plumbing supplies. SIC: 5074 (Plumbing & Hydronic Heating Supplies). Est: 1933. Sales: $6,500,000 (2000). Emp: 65. Officers: M.J. Collura, President.

■ 23235 ■ W.H. Kiefaber Co.
PO Box 681188
Indianapolis, IN 46268-7188
Products: Heating and plumbing supplies. SIC: 5074 (Plumbing & Hydronic Heating Supplies). Est: 1920. Sales: $20,000,000 (2000). Emp: 90. Officers: W.H. Kiefaber III, President; Nancy Stringer, Treasurer; Lee Mossman, Dir. of Marketing.

■ 23236 ■ KII, Inc.
2429 Vauxhall Rd.
Union, NJ 07083
Phone: (908)964-4040   Fax: (908)688-6668
E-mail: export@cs123.com
Products: Heating equipment, including oil burners, gas burners, and furnaces; Water heaters; Steel power boilers. SICs: 5074 (Plumbing & Hydronic Heating Supplies); 5064 (Electrical Appliances—Television & Radio); 5075 (Warm Air Heating & Air-Conditioning). Officers: Robert Leiz, President.

■ 23237 ■ Knapp Supply Company Inc.
PO Box 2488
Muncie, IN 47307-0488
Phone: (765)288-1893   Fax: (765)288-0610
URL: http://www.knappsupply.com
Products: Plumbing; Kitchen cabinets. SICs: 5074 (Plumbing & Hydronic Heating Supplies); 5031 (Lumber, Plywood & Millwork). Est: 1874. Officers: Jim Feick, President; Jeff Kessler, VP of Marketing & Sales; Mike Mcdonald, VP of Finance; Sam Herwehg, VP of Operations.

■ 23238 ■ Koremen Ltd.
2146 U.S 41
Schererville, IN 46375
Phone: (219)865-1455
Products: Kitchen and bath products, including sinks. SIC: 5074 (Plumbing & Hydronic Heating Supplies). Est: 1956. Sales: $5,000,000 (2000). Emp: 10.

Officers: Jerry Hughes, President; Carol Hughes, Vice President.

■ **23239** ■ **Lakeside Supply Company Inc.**
3000 W 117th St.
Cleveland, OH 44111
Phone: (216)941-6800 **Fax:** (216)941-8408
Products: Plumbing supplies. **SIC:** 5074 (Plumbing & Hydronic Heating Supplies). **Est:** 1932. **Sales:** $6,500,000 (2000). **Emp:** 30. **Officers:** Kenneth J. Mathews, Co-Pres. & CEO; Lawrence G. Mathews, Co-Pres. & COO.

■ **23240** ■ **Frank P. Langley Company Inc.**
PO Box 744
Buffalo, NY 14226-0744
Phone: (716)691-7575 **Fax:** (716)691-7347
Products: Industrial plumbing equipment. **SIC:** 5074 (Plumbing & Hydronic Heating Supplies). **Est:** 1938. **Emp:** 19. **Officers:** Frank P. Langley Jr., CEO; Scott A. Crego, President.

■ **23241** ■ **Lawson-Yates Inc.**
PO Box 65278
Salt Lake City, UT 84165-0278
Phone: (801)467-5491 **Fax:** (801)487-4477
Products: Sinks, toilets, tubs, and faucets. **SIC:** 5074 (Plumbing & Hydronic Heating Supplies). **Est:** 1947. **Sales:** $12,000,000 (2000). **Emp:** 52. **Officers:** Tom Stern, CEO; Bud White, General Mgr.

■ **23242** ■ **LCR Corp.**
6232 Siegen Ln.
Baton Rouge, LA 70809
Phone: (504)292-9915 **Fax:** (504)292-7572
Products: Plumbing supplies and fixtures. **SIC:** 5074 (Plumbing & Hydronic Heating Supplies). **Emp:** 175.

■ **23243** ■ **A.L. Lease Wholesale Plumbing Supply**
PO Box 1600
Watsonville, CA 95077-1600
Phone: (831)724-1044 **Fax:** (831)724-1183
E-mail: allease@bigfoot.com
Products: Plumbing and heating products. **SICs:** 5074 (Plumbing & Hydronic Heating Supplies); 5075 (Warm Air Heating & Air-Conditioning). **Est:** 1959. **Emp:** 20. **Officers:** Lawrence Lease.

■ **23244** ■ **George G. Lee Company Inc.**
210 E 22nd St.
PO Box 11105
Norfolk, VA 23517
Phone: (757)622-5733
Free: (888)295-1907 **Fax:** (757)622-4055
Products: Plumbing and heating equipment; Insect screens; Maintenance supplies; Water heaters. **SIC:** 5074 (Plumbing & Hydronic Heating Supplies). **Est:** 1923. **Sales:** $4,000,000 (2000). **Emp:** 14. **Officers:** E. Ottinger, President; George W. Worley III, General Mgr.; Hershel Norton, Sales/Marketing Contact.

■ **23245** ■ **Lee Supply Corp.**
6610 Guion Rd.
Indianapolis, IN 46268
Phone: (317)290-2500
Products: Plumbing and electrical supplies. **SICs:** 5074 (Plumbing & Hydronic Heating Supplies); 5063 (Electrical Apparatus & Equipment). **Est:** 1949. **Sales:** $31,000,000 (2000). **Emp:** 131. **Officers:** Thomas D. Lee, President; Robert T. Lee, Exec. VP.

■ **23246** ■ **Lewis Supply Company Inc.**
PO Box 24268
Richmond, VA 23224
Phone: (804)232-7801
Products: Plumbing and heating supplies. **SIC:** 5074 (Plumbing & Hydronic Heating Supplies). **Est:** 1954. **Sales:** $6,000,000 (2000). **Emp:** 29. **Officers:** B.A. Ackman, President & Treasurer.

■ **23247** ■ **Longley Supply Company Inc.**
2018 Oleander Dr.
Wilmington, NC 28406
Phones: (919)762-7793 (919)762-9178
(919)762-0379 **Fax:** (919)799-7312
Products: Plumbing, heating, and electrical supplies. **SICs:** 5074 (Plumbing & Hydronic Heating Supplies); 5075 (Warm Air Heating & Air-Conditioning). **Est:** 1936.

Sales: $35,000,000 (2000). **Emp:** 150. **Officers:** Henry Longley Jr., President; Victor Hall, Controller; Scott McKennan, Vice President.

■ **23248** ■ **Management Supply Co.**
2395 Research Dr.
Farmington Hills, MI 48335-2630
Phone: (248)471-5500
Products: Plumbing equipment and supplies; electrical equipment and supplies; Janitorial equipment and supplies; Hardware equipment and supplies. **SICs:** 5074 (Plumbing & Hydronic Heating Supplies); 5169 (Chemicals & Allied Products Nec); 5072 (Hardware); 5198 (Paints, Varnishes & Supplies). **Sales:** $21,300,000 (2000). **Emp:** 90. **Officers:** Fred Blechman, General Mgr.

■ **23249** ■ **Manchester Wholesale Supply Inc.**
Hwy. 55E
PO Box 570
Manchester, TN 37355
Phones: (931)728-4011 (931)473-6525
Free: (800)726-1265 **Fax:** (931)723-0253
Products: Plumbing supplies; Electrical appliances. **SICs:** 5074 (Plumbing & Hydronic Heating Supplies); 5064 (Electrical Appliances—Television & Radio). **Emp:** 49. **Officers:** James H. Walker, Sales Mgr.

■ **23250** ■ **Charles Manoog Inc.**
9 Piedmont St.
Worcester, MA 01610
Phone: (508)756-5783 **Fax:** (508)756-0165
E-mail: manoogwork@aol.com
Products: Heating equipment; Plumbing and heating valves and specialties. **SICs:** 5074 (Plumbing & Hydronic Heating Supplies); 5075 (Warm Air Heating & Air-Conditioning). **Sales:** $5,000,000 (2000). **Emp:** 25. **Officers:** Russell Manoog, President; Philip Mastorson, Vice President; Timothy Marsdon, Sales/Marketing Contact; Paul Gilchrist, Human Resources Contact.

■ **23251** ■ **Marine Specialty Company Inc.**
PO Box 1388
Mobile, AL 36633
Phone: (205)432-0581 **Fax:** (205)432-0589
Products: Fabricated pipe and fittings. **SIC:** 5074 (Plumbing & Hydronic Heating Supplies). **Est:** 1923. **Sales:** $8,000,000 (2000). **Emp:** 33. **Officers:** Thomas L. Kelly III, President; Sam Box, VP of Operations.

■ **23252** ■ **Marus and Weimer, Inc.**
PO Box 749
Chagrin Falls, OH 44022
Phone: (440)247-3570 **Fax:** (440)247-2132
Products: Plumbing fittings and brass goods; Plumbing and heating valves; Blowers and fans; High pressure cleaning and blasting machinery; Metal doors and frames; Enameled iron and metal plumbing fixtures, including portable chemical toilets, and flush tanks; Bath tub and shower fittings; Water treatment systems. **SICs:** 5074 (Plumbing & Hydronic Heating Supplies); 5039 (Construction Materials Nec); 5075 (Warm Air Heating & Air-Conditioning); 5085 (Industrial Supplies). **Officers:** Kevin Parker, Export Mgr.

■ **23253** ■ **Maryville Wholesale Supply Inc.**
1513 Monroe Ave.
Maryville, TN 37802
Phone: (423)982-3630
Free: (800)451-6896 **Fax:** (423)982-0184
Products: Plumbing Materials and fixtures. **SIC:** 5074 (Plumbing & Hydronic Heating Supplies). **Sales:** $4,900,000 (2000). **Emp:** 25.

■ **23254** ■ **Masters Supply Inc.**
PO Box 34337
Louisville, KY 40232
Phone: (502)459-2900
Products: Plumbing supplies and equipment. **SIC:** 5074 (Plumbing & Hydronic Heating Supplies). **Est:** 1939. **Sales:** $13,000,000 (2000). **Emp:** 60. **Officers:** C.J. Zoeller, President; R.B. Carr, CFO; S. Reider, Dir. of Marketing; D. Steinke, Dir. of Data Processing.

■ **23255** ■ **Matt-Son Inc.**
28W005 Industrial Ave.
Barrington, IL 60010
Phone: (847)382-7810 **Fax:** (847)382-5814
E-mail: intl@matt-son.com
URL: http://www.matt-son.com
Products: Plastic components for water treatment equipment. **SIC:** 5074 (Plumbing & Hydronic Heating Supplies). **Est:** 1957. **Emp:** 55. **Officers:** Robert Oleskow, President & CEO; Greg Maguire, Sales Mgr.; Michael Green, Intl. Sales Mgr.; Joyce Sierzega, Office Mgr.

■ **23256** ■ **A.I. McDermott Co. Inc.**
2009 Jackson St.
Oshkosh, WI 54901
Phone: (920)231-7080 **Fax:** (920)231-6041
Products: Plumbing fixtures and supplies; Water well and environmental pumps; Drilling supplies. **SICs:** 5074 (Plumbing & Hydronic Heating Supplies); 5084 (Industrial Machinery & Equipment). **Officers:** Thomas McDermott Jr., President.

■ **23257** ■ **A.Y. McDonald Supply Company Inc.**
PO Box 708
Dubuque, IA 52004-0708
Phone: (319)583-2558 **Fax:** (319)583-0031
Products: Plumbing equipment; Lighting fixtures; Woodencabinets. **SICs:** 5074 (Plumbing & Hydronic Heating Supplies); 5063 (Electrical Apparatus & Equipment); 5021 (Furniture). **Sales:** $38,000,000 (2000). **Emp:** 225. **Officers:** John McDonald III, CEO; Scott Zartman, VP of Finance.

■ **23258** ■ **McMillan Sales Corp.**
4801 E 46th
Denver, CO 80216
Phone: (303)399-8500
Free: (800)248-6655 **Fax:** (303)399-0303
Products: Plumbing fixtures, equipment, and supplies. **SIC:** 5074 (Plumbing & Hydronic Heating Supplies). **Est:** 1960. **Sales:** $8,000,000 (2000). **Emp:** 49. **Officers:** Harold Maslanik.

■ **23259** ■ **N. Merfish Supply Co.**
PO Box 1937
Houston, TX 77251-1937
Phone: (713)869-5731 **Fax:** (713)867-0759
URL: http://www.merfish.com
Products: Carbon steel pipe; Weld fittings and flanges. **SICs:** 5074 (Plumbing & Hydronic Heating Supplies); 5050 (Metals & Minerals Except Petroleum); 5051 (Metals Service Centers & Offices). **Est:** 1920. **Emp:** 85. **Officers:** Rochelle Merfish Jacobson, President, e-mail: rjacobson@merfish.com; Gerald Merfish, Vice President; Abe Merfish, C.O.B.; Ida K. Merfish, Sec. & Treas.; Cole Artzer, Sales/Marketing Contact, e-mail: cartzer@merfish.com; Barbara Whitaker, Human Resources Contact, e-mail: bbaldwin@merfish.com. **Former Name:** N. #Merfish Plumbing Supply Co.

■ **23260** ■ **Merit Metal Products Corp.**
242 Valley Rd.
Warrington, PA 18976
Phone: (215)343-2500 **Fax:** (215)343-4839
URL: http://www.meritmetal.com
Products: Plumbing fittings; Brass goods, including hardware. **SIC:** 5074 (Plumbing & Hydronic Heating Supplies). **Est:** 1876. **Emp:** 48. **Officers:** A. Richard Stefanowicz; Daryl T. Schaefer, Marketing Contact.

■ **23261** ■ **William F. Meyer Company Inc.**
PO Box 37
Aurora, IL 60507-0037
Phone: (630)851-4441
Products: Plumbing supplies; Painting materials. **SICs:** 5074 (Plumbing & Hydronic Heating Supplies); 5198 (Paints, Varnishes & Supplies). **Est:** 1952. **Sales:** $8,000,000 (2000). **Emp:** 38. **Officers:** William J. Meyer, President; Thomas Kieso, VP & Treasurer.

■ **23262** ■ **Michigan Industrial Piping Supply Company Inc.**
PO Box 282
Wyandotte, MI 48192
Phone: (313)285-2161 **Fax:** (313)285-3936
Products: Industrial piping. **SICs:** 5074 (Plumbing & Hydronic Heating Supplies); 5085 (Industrial Supplies).

Est: 1958. **Sales:** $6,000,000 (2000). **Emp:** 21. **Officers:** John Felder, President; Pete Kluender, Treasurer; Bruce W. Dawson, Dir. of Marketing.

■ 23263 ■ **Michigan Supply Co.**
PO Box 17069
Lansing, MI 48901
Phone: (517)484-6444 **Fax:** (517)484-3837
E-mail: misupply@voyager.net
Products: Plumbing and heating equipment, including valve fittings and pipes. **SICs:** 5074 (Plumbing & Hydronic Heating Supplies); 5075 (Warm Air Heating & Air-Conditioning). **Est:** 1872. **Sales:** $5,000,000 (2000). **Emp:** 17. **Officers:** Steven P. Reader, General Mgr.; Richard Bordayo, Sales Mgr.

■ 23264 ■ **Microphor**
452 E Hill Rd.
Willits, CA 95490
Phone: (707)459-5563
Free: (800)358-8280 **Fax:** (707)459-6617
E-mail: info@microphor.com
URL: http://www.microphor.com
Products: Plumbing products, including half-gallon flush toilets and self-cleaning and slow-closing faucets. **SIC:** 5074 (Plumbing & Hydronic Heating Supplies). **Est:** 1963. **Emp:** 75. **Officers:** Ted Mayfield, VP & General Mgr.; Walt Hess, Sales Mgr.; Maynard Stubberfield, Human Resources Contact.

■ 23265 ■ **Mid Pac Lumber**
PO Box 31267
Honolulu, HI 96820-1267
Phone: (808)836-8111 **Fax:** (808)836-8297
Products: Plumbing equipment and supplies; Appliances; Lumber. **SICs:** 5074 (Plumbing & Hydronic Heating Supplies); 5064 (Electrical Appliances—Television & Radio); 5031 (Lumber, Plywood & Millwork). **Est:** 1956. **Sales:** $40,000,000 (2000). **Emp:** 160. **Officers:** Michael K. Yoshida, Chairman of the Board; Dennis K. Hironaka, COO; Wayne K. Lincoln, Exec. VP of Marketing.

■ 23266 ■ **Mid-States Industrial Div.**
907 S Main St.
Rockford, IL 61105
Phone: (815)962-8841 **Fax:** (815)962-1051
Products: Industrial heating and plumbing products. **SICs:** 5085 (Industrial Supplies); 5074 (Plumbing & Hydronic Heating Supplies); 5075 (Warm Air Heating & Air-Conditioning). **Est:** 1911. **Sales:** $4,000,000 (2000). **Emp:** 18. **Officers:** Thomas E. Mott, President; Michael A. Moore, CFO; Doug Long, General Mgr.; Tim Anderson, Dir. of Data Processing.

■ 23267 ■ **Mid-States Supply Company Inc.**
1716 Guinotte Ave.
Kansas City, MO 64120
Phone: (816)842-4290
Products: Plumbing supplies, including fixtures, pipes, and fittings. **SICs:** 5085 (Industrial Supplies); 5074 (Plumbing & Hydronic Heating Supplies). **Est:** 1970. **Sales:** $33,000,000 (2000). **Emp:** 59. **Officers:** Milton Brown, President; Robert Brown, Finance Officer.

■ 23268 ■ **Miller's Supply**
PO Box 938
Anniston, AL 36202
Phone: (205)237-5415 **Fax:** (205)237-5418
Products: Plumbing supplies; Steel; Office furniture. **SICs:** 5074 (Plumbing & Hydronic Heating Supplies); 5021 (Furniture); 5051 (Metals Service Centers & Offices). **Sales:** $3,000,000 (2000). **Emp:** 32.

■ 23269 ■ **Missouri Pipe Fittings Co.**
400 Withers Ave.
St. Louis, MO 63147
Phone: (314)421-0790 **Fax:** (314)421-5347
Products: Valves and pipe fittings. **SIC:** 5074 (Plumbing & Hydronic Heating Supplies). **Est:** 1934. **Sales:** $7,500,000 (2000). **Emp:** 47. **Officers:** William A. Roewe, CEO; Daniel T. Roewe, General Mgr.

■ 23270 ■ **Mitchell Hardware Co.**
Rte. 47, Delsea Dr.
PO Box 96
Hurffville, NJ 08080
Phone: (856)589-1135 **Fax:** (856)582-6118
URL: http://www.mitchellhardware.com
Products: Decorative plumbing and hardware; Commercial hardware; Commercial arts and frames; Fireplaces. **SICs:** 5074 (Plumbing & Hydronic Heating Supplies); 5072 (Hardware). **Est:** 1949. **Emp:** 21. **Officers:** Michael Greenberg, President. **Former Name:** Mitchell's Decorative Hardware.

■ 23271 ■ **Modern Supply Company Inc.**
1202 W Summit St.
Ponca City, OK 74601
Phone: (405)765-2524
Products: Valves. **SICs:** 5085 (Industrial Supplies); 5074 (Plumbing & Hydronic Heating Supplies). **Est:** 1960. **Sales:** $17,000,000 (2000). **Emp:** 80. **Officers:** Rick T. Brewer, President; Joe Coleby, Controller.

■ 23272 ■ **Modern Supply Company Inc.**
(Knoxville, Tennessee)
PO Box 22997
Knoxville, TN 37933-0997
Phone: (615)966-4567 **Fax:** (615)675-5711
Products: Plumbing, heating, warm air heating, and air-conditioning equipment and supplies. **SICs:** 5074 (Plumbing & Hydronic Heating Supplies); 5075 (Warm Air Heating & Air-Conditioning). **Sales:** $16,000,000 (1994). **Emp:** 125. **Officers:** Jackie Jenkins, CFO.

■ 23273 ■ **Monogram Sanitation Co.**
800 W Artesia Blvd.
PO Box 9057
Compton, CA 90224
Phone: (310)638-8445 **Fax:** (310)638-8458
Products: Enameled iron and metal plumbing fixtures, including portable chemical toilets, and flush tanks; Household and industrial chemicals. **SICs:** 5074 (Plumbing & Hydronic Heating Supplies); 5169 (Chemicals & Allied Products Nec). **Est:** 1958. **Emp:** 160. **Officers:** Ron Balsden, Sales/Marketing Contact, e-mail: rbalsden@monsan.com.

■ 23274 ■ **Monumental Supply Company Inc.**
401 S Haven St.
Baltimore, MD 21224
Phone: (410)732-9300 **Fax:** (410)675-3220
URL: http://www.monumentalpvf.com
Products: Pipe valves and fittings. **SICs:** 5085 (Industrial Supplies); 5074 (Plumbing & Hydronic Heating Supplies). **Est:** 1950. **Sales:** $18,000,000 (2000). **Emp:** 65. **Officers:** M. Kirchner, Chairman of the Board; Edward Zimmerman, President, e-mail: jbelzner@aol; J. Joiner, VP of Marketing.

■ 23275 ■ **Mooney Process Equipment Co.**
3000 E 14th Ave.
Columbus, OH 43219-2355
Products: Cast iron pipe; Valves. **SICs:** 5084 (Industrial Machinery & Equipment); 5074 (Plumbing & Hydronic Heating Supplies). **Est:** 1964. **Sales:** $20,000,000 (2000). **Emp:** 55. **Officers:** Paul Mooney, President; Phillip Szurek, Controller; Harry Wertman, Dir. of Marketing.

■ 23276 ■ **Moore Supply Co.**
PO Box 448
Conroe, TX 77305
Phone: (409)756-4445
E-mail: sgmsc@lcc.net
Products: Plumbing equipment, including sinks, toilets, and fixtures. **SIC:** 5074 (Plumbing & Hydronic Heating Supplies). **Est:** 1953. **Emp:** 225. **Officers:** Mark Hanley, President; Steven Glaeser, VP of Marketing & Sales.

■ 23277 ■ **Walter F. Morris Co.**
425 Turnpike St.
Canton, MA 02021
Phone: (617)828-5300 **Fax:** 800-888-1972
Products: Plumbing and heating supplies. **SIC:** 5074 (Plumbing & Hydronic Heating Supplies). **Est:** 1923. **Sales:** $20,000,000 (2000). **Emp:** 100. **Officers:** David L. Hickerson, President, e-mail: dhickerson@valleyresources.com; Rosemary Platt, Controller; Richard C. Hadfield, Exec. VP.

■ 23278 ■ **Morrison Supply Co.**
PO Box 70
Ft. Worth, TX 76101
Phone: (817)870-2227 **Fax:** (817)877-4942
Products: Plumbing supplies. **SIC:** 5074 (Plumbing & Hydronic Heating Supplies). **Est:** 1917. **Sales:** $200,000,000 (1999). **Emp:** 400. **Officers:** Scott Sangalli, CEO; Darrell Hawkins, President.

■ 23279 ■ **Mountain States Pipe and Supply Co.**
PO Box 698
Colorado Springs, CO 80903
Phone: (719)634-5555
Free: (800)777-7173 **Fax:** (719)634-5551
E-mail: pcarroll@msps.com
URL: http://www.msps.com
Products: Plumbing and heating supplies; Water and gas meters; Meter reading systems. **SIC:** 5074 (Plumbing & Hydronic Heating Supplies). **Est:** 1955. **Sales:** $30,000,000 (2000). **Emp:** 59. **Officers:** Paul Carroll, CEO; Christine Newkirk, CFO; Elizabeth L. Carroll, President; Janet T. Wilcox, Chairman of the Board.

■ 23280 ■ **Mountain States Supply Inc.**
184 W 3300 S
Salt Lake City, UT 84115
Phone: (801)484-8885
Products: Plumbing supplies. **SIC:** 5074 (Plumbing & Hydronic Heating Supplies). **Est:** 1956. **Sales:** $9,000,000 (2000). **Emp:** 35. **Officers:** Dee F. Johnson, President; John Heslop, Controller.

■ 23281 ■ **Mountain Supply Co.**
2101 Mullan Rd.
Missoula, MT 59801
Phone: (406)543-8255
Products: Plumbing supplies. **SIC:** 5074 (Plumbing & Hydronic Heating Supplies). **Est:** 1961. **Sales:** $6,000,000 (2000). **Emp:** 50. **Officers:** Mike Ruby, President.

■ 23282 ■ **Mountainland Supply Co.**
1505 W 130 S
Orem, UT 84058
Phone: (801)224-6050 **Fax:** (801)224-6058
Products: Plumbing fixtures, equipment, and supplies; Hardware; Whirlpool baths. **SICs:** 5074 (Plumbing & Hydronic Heating Supplies); 5072 (Hardware). **Est:** 1972. **Sales:** $27,500,000 (2000). **Emp:** 48. **Officers:** R.J. Rasmussen, President.

■ 23283 ■ **Mueller Sales Inc.**
PO Box 930323
Wixom, MI 48393-0323
Phone: (248)348-2942
Products: Pumps, valves, and spray nozzles. **SICs:** 5085 (Industrial Supplies); 5074 (Plumbing & Hydronic Heating Supplies). **Est:** 1937. **Sales:** $1,000,000 (2000). **Emp:** 4. **Officers:** Robert Mueller, President.

■ 23284 ■ **G.A. Murdock, Inc.**
1200 Division Ave. S
PO Box 465
Madison, SD 57042-0465
Phone: (605)256-9632
Free: (800)568-7565 **Fax:** (605)256-9682
E-mail: sales@gamurdock.com
URL: http://www.gamurdock.com
Products: Plumbing and heating valves and specialties; Hydraulic valves. **SIC:** 5074 (Plumbing & Hydronic Heating Supplies). **Est:** 1987. **Officers:** Gene Appelwick, President, e-mail: gene@gamurdock.com; Brian Appelwick, Vice President, e-mail: brian@gamurdock.com; Paul Schamber, Customer Service Contact, e-mail: paul@gamurdock.com; Jenny Weatherill, Human Resources Contact, e-mail: jenny@gamurdock.com.

■ 23285 ■ **Mutual Pipe and Supply Inc.**
PO Box 55627
Indianapolis, IN 46205
Phone: (317)923-2581
Free: (800)772-7346 **Fax:** (317)923-4819
Products: Valves, pipes, and fittings; Plumbing fixtures and faucets; Heating equipment; Pumps and water regulating equipment. **SICs:** 5074 (Plumbing & Hydronic Heating Supplies); 5075 (Warm Air Heating &

Air-Conditioning). **Est:** 1959. **Sales:** $12,000,000 (2000). **Emp:** 25. **Officers:** William S. Hague Jr., President & Chairman of the Board; Randy L. Pittman, Treasurer & Secty.; Mark S. Hague, Vice President.

■ **23286** ■ **National Safety Associates Inc.**
PO Box 18603
Memphis, TN 38181
Phone: (901)366-9288 **Fax:** (901)795-2726
Products: Water purifying equipment, air filtration devices and nutritional food supplements. **SICs:** 5074 (Plumbing & Hydronic Heating Supplies); 5149 (Groceries & Related Products Nec). **Sales:** $115,000,000 (2000). **Emp:** 110. **Officers:** Jay Martin, President.

■ **23287** ■ **Naughton Plumbing Sales, Inc.**
1140 W Prince Rd.
Tucson, AZ 85705
Phone: (602)293-2220 **Fax:** (602)888-8233
E-mail: info@naughton's.com
URL: http://www.naughton's.com
Products: Plumbing supplies. **SIC:** 5074 (Plumbing & Hydronic Heating Supplies). **Est:** 1951.

■ **23288** ■ **Naughton Plumbing Sales Inc.**
1140 W Prince Rd.
Tucson, AZ 85705
Phone: (602)293-2220 **Fax:** (602)888-8233
Products: Plumbing Materials and fixtures. **SIC:** 5074 (Plumbing & Hydronic Heating Supplies).

■ **23289** ■ **New Energy Distributors**
PO Box 87
Dyersville, IA 52040
Phone: (319)875-2445
Free: (800)852-1224 **Fax:** (319)875-2023
Products: Heating and cooling equipment and supplies. **SIC:** 5074 (Plumbing & Hydronic Heating Supplies). **Sales:** $8,000,000 (2000). **Emp:** 10.

■ **23290** ■ **Noland Co.**
80 29th St.
Newport News, VA 23607
Phone: (757)928-9000 **Fax:** (757)245-6532
URL: http://www.noland.com
Products: Plumbing; Air Conditioning; Electrical; Industrial supplies, including pipe, wire, and cable. **SICs:** 5074 (Plumbing & Hydronic Heating Supplies); 5075 (Warm Air Heating & Air-Conditioning); 5084 (Industrial Machinery & Equipment); 5078 (Refrigeration Equipment & Supplies). **Est:** 1915. **Sales:** $482,830 (1999). **Emp:** 1,450. **Officers:** Lloyd U. Noland III, President & Chairman of the Board; Arthur P. Henderson Jr., VP of Finance; Kenneth King, VP of Marketing & Operations; Rhonda L. Binger, Dir of Human Resources; John Gullett, VP of Corporate Communications; Jean Preston, VP Corporate Data.

■ **23291** ■ **Noland Co.**
4700 Zenilworth Ave.
Hyattsville, MD 20781
Phone: (301)779-8282 **Fax:** (301)779-5710
Products: Plumbing, piping, and fixtures. **SIC:** 5074 (Plumbing & Hydronic Heating Supplies).

■ **23292** ■ **Noland Co.**
Hwy. 5
Mechanicsville, MD 20659
Phone: (301)884-8141 **Fax:** (301)884-2130
Products: Plumbing, piping, and fixtures. **SIC:** 5074 (Plumbing & Hydronic Heating Supplies).

■ **23293** ■ **Noland Co.**
5511 Nicholson Ln.
Rockville, MD 20852
Phone: (301)881-4225 **Fax:** (301)881-6446
Products: Plumbing, piping, and fixtures. **SIC:** 5074 (Plumbing & Hydronic Heating Supplies).

■ **23294** ■ **Noland Co.**
8849 Brookville Rd.
Silver Spring, MD 20910
Phone: (301)588-0223 **Fax:** (301)588-7032
Products: Plumbing, piping, and fixtures. **SIC:** 5074 (Plumbing & Hydronic Heating Supplies).

■ **23295** ■ **Norman Supply**
PO Box 1811
Idaho Falls, ID 83403
Phone: (208)522-6994
Products: Plumbing fixtures, including toilets, sinks, faucets, and bath tubs. **SIC:** 5074 (Plumbing & Hydronic Heating Supplies). **Est:** 1955. **Sales:** $5,000,000 (2000). **Emp:** 19. **Officers:** Craig Norby, General Mgr.

■ **23296** ■ **Norman Supply Co.**
PO Box 26048
Oklahoma City, OK 73126
Phone: (405)235-9511
Products: Hoses; Toilets. **SIC:** 5074 (Plumbing & Hydronic Heating Supplies). **Est:** 1949. **Sales:** $15,000,000 (2000). **Emp:** 35. **Officers:** J. Richard Kunkel, President; Joy Burnett, Treasurer & Secty.

■ **23297** ■ **North Star Water Conditioning**
1890 Woodlane Dr.
Woodbury, MN 55125
Phone: (612)738-5839
Free: (800)972-0135 **Fax:** (612)739-5293
Products: specialty equipment and products. **SIC:** 5074 (Plumbing & Hydronic Heating Supplies).

■ **23298** ■ **Northern Plumbing & Heating Supply**
404 Stephenson Ave.
Escanaba, MI 49829-2734
Phone: (906)786-5252 **Fax:** (906)786-5511
Products: Plumbing and heating valves and specialties; Electrical equipment and supplies. **SICs:** 5074 (Plumbing & Hydronic Heating Supplies); 5063 (Electrical Apparatus & Equipment). **Est:** 1940. **Emp:** 14.

■ **23299** ■ **Northwest Pipe Fittings Inc.**
33 S 8th St. W
Billings, MT 59103
Phone: (406)252-0142 **Fax:** (406)248-8072
Products: Plumbing fixtures, equipment, and supplies. **SIC:** 5074 (Plumbing & Hydronic Heating Supplies). **Est:** 1957. **Sales:** $18,000,000 (2000). **Emp:** 70. **Officers:** Jerry Evenson, CEO & President; Henry Mellgren, CFO.

■ **23300** ■ **N.R.G. Enterprises Inc.**
22 42nd St. NW, Ste. A
Auburn, WA 98001
Phone: (253)852-3111
Free: (800)264-7872 **Fax:** (253)852-3222
Products: specialty equipment and products. **SIC:** 5074 (Plumbing & Hydronic Heating Supplies).

■ **23301** ■ **Nu-Way Supply Company Inc.**
PO Box 182600
Utica, MI 48318-9004
Phone: (810)731-4000
Products: Plumbing, heating and air conditioning equipment. **SICs:** 5074 (Plumbing & Hydronic Heating Supplies); 5075 (Warm Air Heating & Air-Conditioning). **Sales:** $23,000,000 (1994). **Emp:** 100. **Officers:** Larry Merritt, President.

■ **23302** ■ **Ohio Pipe and Supply Company Inc.**
14615 Lorain Ave.
Cleveland, OH 44111
Phone: (216)251-2345 **Fax:** (440)251-2352
Products: Pipe valves; Fittings. **SIC:** 5074 (Plumbing & Hydronic Heating Supplies). **Est:** 1915. **Sales:** $10,000,000 (2000). **Emp:** 50. **Officers:** James W. Irwin, CEO, e-mail: jirwin@hotmail.com; Alice W. Irwin, Treasurer; David W. Wade, Sales Mgr.

■ **23303** ■ **Osmonics, Aquamatic**
2412 Grant Ave.
Rockford, IL 61103
Phone: (815)964-9421
Free: (800)245-9421 **Fax:** (815)964-4449
URL: http://www.osmonics.com
Products: Valves and controls. **SIC:** 5074 (Plumbing & Hydronic Heating Supplies). **Est:** 1932. **Sales:** $12,000,000 (1999). **Emp:** 75. **Officers:** Ed Fierko, President; Guy Jang, Sales/Marketing Contact; Sheila McCartan, Customer Service Contact; Gloralee Dixon, Human Resource Contact.

■ **23304** ■ **H.C. Oswald Supply Company Inc.**
120 E 124th St.
New York, NY 10035
Phone: (212)722-7000 **Fax:** (212)860-2843
Products: Boilers; Plumbing repair parts and controls; Manhole plates. **SICs:** 5074 (Plumbing & Hydronic Heating Supplies); 5099 (Durable Goods Nec). **Est:** 1923. **Sales:** $3,000,000 (1999). **Emp:** 14. **Officers:** Robert Oswald, President; Richard Oswald, Vice President.

■ **23305** ■ **Packing Seals and Engineering Company Inc.**
3507 N Kenton Ave.
Chicago, IL 60641
Phone: (773)725-3810
Free: (800)PSE-RING **Fax:** (773)725-1333
E-mail: pse-ring@worldnet.att.net
URL: http://www.psering.com
Products: Rubber seals, o-rings, oil seals, special molded rubber, and urethane u-cups; Wipers. **SICs:** 5074 (Plumbing & Hydronic Heating Supplies); 5085 (Industrial Supplies). **Est:** 1959. **Sales:** $2,000,000 (2000). **Emp:** 11. **Officers:** Donald W. Dooley, Chairman of the Board & President; Stephen P. Baas, General Mgr.

■ **23306** ■ **Palermo Supply Company Inc.**
71 N Washington Ave.
Bergenfield, NJ 07621
Phone: (201)387-1141 **Fax:** (201)387-6771
Products: Plumbing supplies; Pipes; Fixtures; Pipe fittings. **SIC:** 5074 (Plumbing & Hydronic Heating Supplies). **Est:** 1926. **Sales:** $27,000,000 (2000). **Emp:** 125. **Officers:** Thomas Palermo, CEO; Frank Palermo, Treasurer; Carl Palermo, VP of Marketing; Jim McMorrow, Dir. of Data Processing; John Horsman, Dir of Human Resources.

■ **23307** ■ **Paragon Supply Co.**
1180 Dundee Ave.
Elgin, IL 60120
Phone: (708)742-8760 **Fax:** (708)742-0154
URL: http://www.crawfordsupply.com
Products: Plumbing and heating supplies, including sinks, faucets, tubes, and heaters. **SICs:** 5074 (Plumbing & Hydronic Heating Supplies); 5075 (Warm Air Heating & Air-Conditioning). **Est:** 1949. **Sales:** $6,000,000 (2000). **Emp:** 15. **Officers:** Steven Feiger, Vice President; Charles Schwartz, General Mgr.

■ **23308** ■ **Parkset Supply Ltd.**
1499 Atlantic Ave.
Brooklyn, NY 11213
Phone: (718)774-0600 **Fax:** (718)953-0206
Products: Plumbing supplies. **SIC:** 5074 (Plumbing & Hydronic Heating Supplies). **Est:** 1959. **Sales:** $4,000,000 (2000). **Emp:** 15. **Officers:** Bruce Wolk, President; Mitchell Racker, VP & Treasurer.

■ **23309** ■ **Parnell-Martin Co.**
PO Box 30067
Charlotte, NC 28230
Phone: (704)375-8651
Products: Pumps and pumping equipment; Valves and pipe fittings; Plumbing fixtures, equipment, and supplies. **SICs:** 5074 (Plumbing & Hydronic Heating Supplies); 5085 (Industrial Supplies). **Est:** 1942. **Sales:** $42,000,000 (2000). **Emp:** 180. **Officers:** F.A. Cash, Chairman of the Board; J.L. George, Exec. VP of Finance.

■ **23310** ■ **Peebles Supply Div.**
618 Bland Blvd.
Newport News, VA 23602
Phone: (757)874-7400 **Fax:** (757)877-3767
Products: Plumbing fixtures, equipment, and supplies; Heating and air conditioning equipment; Electrical products. **SICs:** 5074 (Plumbing & Hydronic Heating Supplies); 5063 (Electrical Apparatus & Equipment). **Est:** 1953. **Sales:** $10,000,000 (2000). **Emp:** 46. **Officers:** Larry Topping, President; Mark Stough, Controller.

■ **23311** ■ **Penco Corp.**
PO Box 690
Seaford, DE 19973
Phone: (302)629-7911 **Fax:** (302)629-2601
Products: Plumbing, heating and air conditioning

equipment. **SICs:** 5074 (Plumbing & Hydronic Heating Supplies); 5075 (Warm Air Heating & Air-Conditioning). **Sales:** $42,000,000 (2000). **Emp:** 160. **Officers:** Kent Peterson, President; Bill Robertson, Comptroller.

■ 23312 ■ **Penstan Supply**
850 Horner St.
Johnstown, PA 15902
Fax: (814)539-2808
Products: Industrial and commercial plumbing and heating supplies. **SICs:** 5074 (Plumbing & Hydronic Heating Supplies); 5063 (Electrical Apparatus & Equipment); 5085 (Industrial Supplies); 5075 (Warm Air Heating & Air-Conditioning).

■ 23313 ■ **Perrigo Inc.**
204-216 Chapel St.
New Haven, CT 06513
Phone: (203)787-0236
Products: Industrial plumbing supplies, including pipes and fittings. **SICs:** 5074 (Plumbing & Hydronic Heating Supplies); 5085 (Industrial Supplies). **Est:** 1920. **Sales:** $6,000,000 (2000). **Emp:** 15. **Officers:** Grant Nelson, President; George Franco, CFO.

■ 23314 ■ **Petersen Products Co.**
421 Wheeler
PO Box 340
Fredonia, WI 53021-0340
Phone: (414)692-2416
Free: (800)926-1926   **Fax:** (414)692-2418
E-mail: mail@petersen.cc
URL: http://www.petersen.cc
Products: Plumbing supplies. **SIC:** 5074 (Plumbing & Hydronic Heating Supplies). **Est:** 1916. **Officers:** Philip L. Lundman, President, e-mail: mail@Petersen.cc.

■ 23315 ■ **Pickrel Brothers Inc.**
901 S Perry St.
Dayton, OH 45402
Phone: (937)461-5960
Products: Heating and plumbing supplies. **SIC:** 5074 (Plumbing & Hydronic Heating Supplies). **Est:** 1953. **Sales:** $10,000,000 (2000). **Emp:** 52. **Officers:** Thomas R. Pickrel, President.

■ 23316 ■ **Pittsburgh Plug and Products**
PO Box H
Evans City, PA 16033
Phone: (412)538-4022   **Fax:** (412)538-4105
E-mail: pppc@nauticom.net
URL: http://www.nauticom.net/www/pppc
Products: Pipe plugs, cold formed from steel, brass, and aluminum. **SIC:** 5074 (Plumbing & Hydronic Heating Supplies). **Est:** 1942. **Sales:** $7,800,000 (2000). **Emp:** 30. **Officers:** Thomas D. Williams, President.

■ 23317 ■ **Plant and Flanged Equipment**
4000 85th Ave. N
Minneapolis, MN 55443
Phone: (612)424-8400   **Fax:** (612)424-1141
Products: Pipes and fittings. **SICs:** 5051 (Metals Service Centers & Offices); 5074 (Plumbing & Hydronic Heating Supplies). **Est:** 1965. **Sales:** $3,000,000 (2000). **Emp:** 10. **Officers:** W.D. Goodman, President; J.W. Ackerman, Vice President.

■ 23318 ■ **Plotts Brothers**
462 Main St.
PO Box 130
Royersford, PA 19468
Phone: (215)948-7220
Products: Plumbing equipment; Heating equipment. **SICs:** 5074 (Plumbing & Hydronic Heating Supplies); 5075 (Warm Air Heating & Air-Conditioning).

■ 23319 ■ **Plumb Supply Co.**
PO Box 4558
Des Moines, IA 50306
Phone: (515)262-9511
Free: (800)483-9511   **Fax:** (515)262-5893
Products: Heating and air conditioning equipment. **SICs:** 5074 (Plumbing & Hydronic Heating Supplies); 5075 (Warm Air Heating & Air-Conditioning). **Est:** 1946. **Sales:** $33,000,000 (2000). **Emp:** 125. **Officers:** John Templeton, President; D.J. Gebhardt, Finance Officer.

■ 23320 ■ **Plumbers Supply Co.**
PO Box 33519
Indianapolis, IN 46203
Phone: (317)783-2981
Free: (800)886-2981   **Fax:** (317)783-2987
E-mail: psc1921@aol.com
Products: Plumbing fixtures, equipment, and supplies. **SICs:** 5074 (Plumbing & Hydronic Heating Supplies); 5085 (Industrial Supplies). **Est:** 1921. **Sales:** $10,000,000 (2000). **Emp:** 40. **Officers:** John Werst, President; Gene Hobbs, Sales Mgr.; Jay Werst, VP & Secty.; Bruce Madison, Vice President; David Pappas, Branch Mgr.

■ 23321 ■ **Plumbers Supply Co.**
PO Box 65987
Salt Lake City, UT 84165-0987
Phone: (801)261-1144
Free: (800)657-0598   **Fax:** (801)265-3993
E-mail: ronz@plumbersupply.com
URL: http://www.plumbersupply.com
Products: Toilets; Fire hydrants; Roof drains; Tubs; Plumbing supplies; Water works supplies. **SICs:** 5074 (Plumbing & Hydronic Heating Supplies); 5085 (Industrial Supplies). **Est:** 1955. **Sales:** $55,000,000 (2000). **Emp:** 110. **Officers:** Earl Zarbock, President.

■ 23322 ■ **Plumber's Supply Company Inc.**
1000 E Main St.
Louisville, KY 40206
Phone: (502)582-2261   **Fax:** (502)581-1255
Products: Plumbing fixtures, equipment, and supplies. **SIC:** 5074 (Plumbing & Hydronic Heating Supplies). **Est:** 1921. **Sales:** $16,000,000 (2000). **Emp:** 300. **Officers:** John Werst Jr., President; Dick Wagner, Controller.

■ 23323 ■ **Plumbing Distributors Inc.**
PO Box 1167
Lawrenceville, GA 30046-1167
Phone: (404)963-9231   **Fax:** (404)822-9509
Products: Plumbing fixtures and supplies, including sinks, faucets, and bath tubs. **SIC:** 5074 (Plumbing & Hydronic Heating Supplies). **Est:** 1973. **Sales:** $16,500,000 (2000). **Emp:** 50. **Officers:** Gladston Mealor, President; Janie Clower, Controller; Sidney Mealor, Vice President.

■ 23324 ■ **PMI Sales and Marketing Services Inc.**
8967 Market St.
Houston, TX 77029
Phone: (713)674-8735   **Fax:** (713)672-6000
Products: Pipes, fittings, and valves. **SICs:** 5074 (Plumbing & Hydronic Heating Supplies); 5085 (Industrial Supplies). **Sales:** $4,000,000 (2000). **Emp:** 20. **Officers:** Dick Fogenhagen, President.

■ 23325 ■ **Precision Fitting & Gauge Co.**
1001 Enterprise Ave., Ste. 14
Oklahoma City, OK 73128
Phone: (405)943-4786   **Fax:** (405)943-2742
Products: Tubing fittings. **SIC:** 5074 (Plumbing & Hydronic Heating Supplies).

■ 23326 ■ **Precision Fitting & Gauge Co.**
1214 S Joplin
Tulsa, OK 74112
Phone: (918)834-5011   **Fax:** (918)834-5961
Products: Tube fittings. **SIC:** 5074 (Plumbing & Hydronic Heating Supplies).

■ 23327 ■ **Premier Manufactured Systems**
17431 N 25th Ave.
Phoenix, AZ 85023
Phone: (602)931-1977
Free: (800)752-5582   **Fax:** (602)931-0191
Products: specialty equipment and products. **SIC:** 5074 (Plumbing & Hydronic Heating Supplies).

■ 23328 ■ **Everett J. Prescott Inc.**
191 Central St.
Gardiner, ME 04345
Phone: (207)582-1851   **Fax:** (207)582-5637
E-mail: ejp@ejprescott.com
URL: http://www.ejprescott.com
Products: Water, sewer, drain, and gas products and services. **SIC:** 5074 (Plumbing & Hydronic Heating Supplies). **Est:** 1955. **Sales:** $110,000,000 (2000).

Emp: 210. **Officers:** Peter E. Prescott, President; Ed Boudreau, CFO; David G. Gardner, Sr. VP.

■ 23329 ■ **Primus Inc.**
3110 Kettering Blvd.
Dayton, OH 45439
Phone: (937)294-6878   **Fax:** (937)293-9591
E-mail: wallen@dapsoo.com
Products: Plumbing, heating, air conditioning and electrical supplies. **SICs:** 5074 (Plumbing & Hydronic Heating Supplies); 5075 (Warm Air Heating & Air-Conditioning); 5063 (Electrical Apparatus & Equipment); 5065 (Electronic Parts & Equipment Nec). **Est:** 1958. **Sales:** $900,000,000 (1999). **Emp:** 2,700. **Officers:** Richard F. Schiewetz, Chairman of the Board, e-mail: dschiewetz@primusinc.com; Richard Schwartz, President, e-mail: rschwartz@primusinc.com.

■ 23330 ■ **Pro-Flo Products**
30 Commerce Rd.
Cedar Grove, NJ 07009
Phone: (973)239-2400
Free: (800)325-1057   **Fax:** (973)239-5817
E-mail: pro-flo@worldnet.att.net
URL: http://www.launchsite.com/proflo
Products: Water coolers and filters; Reverse osmosis systems; Faucets. **SIC:** 5074 (Plumbing & Hydronic Heating Supplies). **Est:** 1985. **Sales:** $1,600,000 (2000). **Emp:** 8. **Officers:** Richard Smith, Sales/Marketing Contact.

■ 23331 ■ **Probst Supply Co.**
366 W Center St.
Marion, OH 43302
Phone: (614)383-6071
Free: (800)776-2783   **Fax:** (614)383-2497
Products: Industrial and plumbing supplies; Fixtures. **SICs:** 5074 (Plumbing & Hydronic Heating Supplies); 5085 (Industrial Supplies). **Est:** 1905. **Sales:** $6,000,000 (2000). **Emp:** 30. **Officers:** Richard E. Probst, President; John Probst III, Vice President; Dave Everson.

■ 23332 ■ **Pureflow Ultraviolet, Inc.**
1750 Spectrum Dr.
Lawrenceville, GA 30043-5744
Phone: (770)277-6330   **Fax:** (770)277-6344
Products: Ultraviolet disinfection equipment. **SIC:** 5074 (Plumbing & Hydronic Heating Supplies). **Est:** 1978. **Sales:** $5,000,000 (1999). **Emp:** 9. **Officers:** Richard Combs, President.

■ 23333 ■ **R and R Plumbing Supply Corp.**
170 Chandler St.
Worcester, MA 01609-2924
Phone: (508)757-4543   **Fax:** (508)755-9369
E-mail: jritzIII@worldnet.att.net
URL: http://www.randrplumbing.com
Products: Plumbing supplies, including pipes and tubes; Heating and industrial supplies. **SICs:** 5074 (Plumbing & Hydronic Heating Supplies); 5075 (Warm Air Heating & Air-Conditioning); 5085 (Industrial Supplies). **Est:** 1905. **Sales:** $4,000,000 (2000). **Emp:** 18. **Officers:** Jesse Ritz, President, e-mail: jritzIII@worldnet.att.net.

■ 23334 ■ **RAL Corp.**
24 Dunning Rd.
Middletown, NY 10940-1819
Phone: (914)343-1456
Products: Plumbing and ventilation components. **SICs:** 5074 (Plumbing & Hydronic Heating Supplies); 5075 (Warm Air Heating & Air-Conditioning). **Sales:** $15,000,000 (1990). **Emp:** 101. **Officers:** David E. Berman, CEO & President; Murray J. Zucker, VP of Finance.

■ 23335 ■ **Raritan Supply Co.**
301 Meadow Rd.
Edison, NJ 08817-6082
Phone: (732)985-5000   **Fax:** (732)985-5002
E-mail: raritansupply@worldnet.att.net
URL: http://www.raritansupply.com
Products: Pipes; Valves; Fittings; Waterworks; Utility piping. **SIC:** 5074 (Plumbing & Hydronic Heating Supplies). **Est:** 1943. **Sales:** $2,500,000 (2000). **Emp:** 7. **Officers:** William Richardson, President & Chairman

of the Board; James Richardson, Sales/Marketing Contact.

■ **23336** ■ **RB Royal Industries Inc.**
442 Arlington Ave.
Fond du Lac, WI 54935
Phone: (920)921-1550
Products: Brass fittings; Hydraulics equipment. **SICs:** 5074 (Plumbing & Hydronic Heating Supplies); 5085 (Industrial Supplies). **Est:** 1940. **Sales:** $10,000,000 (2000). **Emp:** 120. **Officers:** J.W. Neumann Jr., President; James Neumann, Manager; Daniel May, Marketing Mgr.; Vickie Huck, Data Processing Mgr.; Wayne Techyn, Dir of Human Resources.

■ **23337** ■ **Reeves-Wiedeman Co.**
14861 W 100 St.
Lenexa, KS 66215
Phone: (913)492-7100   **Fax:** (913)492-6961
E-mail: mail@rwco.com
URL: http://www.rwco.com
Products: Plumbing supplies. **SIC:** 5074 (Plumbing & Hydronic Heating Supplies). **Est:** 1887. **Sales:** $21,500,000 (2000). **Emp:** 55. **Officers:** Ted G. Wiedeman, President; Kurt A. Wiedeman, Treasurer & Secty.

■ **23338** ■ **Reiner Enterprises**
9683 Sycamore Trace Ct.
Cincinnati, OH 45242
Phone: (513)527-4949   **Fax:** (513)527-4848
Products: Electronic sanitary toilet seats. **SIC:** 5046 (Commercial Equipment Nec). **Sales:** $1,000,000 (2000). **Emp:** 3. **Officers:** Robert L. Reiner, Owner.

■ **23339** ■ **D.W. Rhoads Co.**
133 Cannell Dr.
Somerset, PA 15501
Phone: (814)445-6531
Products: Plumbing equipment, including sinks and faucets; Heating and air-conditioning equipment. **SICs:** 5074 (Plumbing & Hydronic Heating Supplies); 5063 (Electrical Apparatus & Equipment). **Est:** 1903. **Sales:** $3,500,000 (2000). **Emp:** 22. **Officers:** Thomas Simmons, Partner; Perry S. Kreger, Partner.

■ **23340** ■ **Riback Supply Company Inc.**
2412 Business Loop 70 E
Columbia, MO 65201
Phone: (573)875-3131   **Fax:** (573)449-8738
Products: Plumbing supplies; Heating and air conditioning supplies. **SICs:** 5074 (Plumbing & Hydronic Heating Supplies); 5075 (Warm Air Heating & Air-Conditioning). **Est:** 1934. **Sales:** $30,000,000 (2000). **Emp:** 160. **Officers:** Marty Riback, President; Ernie Gaeth, Exec. VP; Teresa Heim, Dir. of Merchandising; Cherie Karl, Dir. of Admin.

■ **23341** ■ **Richards Manufacturing Company Inc.**
725 Ionia SW
Grand Rapids, MI 49503
Phone: (616)247-0965
Free: (800)968-1200   **Fax:** (616)247-8721
URL: http://www.richardsplumbing.com
Products: Plumbing supplies; Heating supplies. **SICs:** 5074 (Plumbing & Hydronic Heating Supplies); 5075 (Warm Air Heating & Air-Conditioning). **Est:** 1920. **Sales:** $18,000,000 (2000). **Emp:** 54. **Officers:** T.C. Evert, President; J. Potter, CFO, e-mail: judypotter@richardsplumbing.com.

■ **23342** ■ **Richmond Foundry Inc.**
8500 Sanford Dr.
Richmond, VA 23228
Phone: (804)266-4244   **Fax:** (804)266-4246
Products: Plumbing equipment and supplies. **SIC:** 5074 (Plumbing & Hydronic Heating Supplies). **Sales:** $1,600,000 (2000). **Emp:** 8. **Officers:** Steve Holloway, Vice President.

■ **23343** ■ **Ridgewood Corp.**
PO Box 716
Mahwah, NJ 07430
Phone: (201)529-5500   **Fax:** (201)529-4834
Products: Plumbing and air-conditioning equipment. **SICs:** 5074 (Plumbing & Hydronic Heating Supplies); 5075 (Warm Air Heating & Air-Conditioning). **Sales:**

$10,000,000 (2000). **Emp:** 40. **Officers:** Jules Weinstein, President; Stan Harris, Treasurer.

■ **23344** ■ **Ritter Engineering Co.**
100 Williams Dr.
Zelienople, PA 16063
Phone: (724)452-6000   **Fax:** (724)452-0766
Products: Tube fittings and cylinders. **SIC:** 5085 (Industrial Supplies). **Sales:** $53,000,000 (2000). **Emp:** 210. **Officers:** H. Jay Williams, President; Andy Chomos, Controller.

■ **23345** ■ **RKB Enterprises Inc.**
PO Box 659
Portland, ME 04104-5020
Products: Plumbing supplies, including sinks, tubs, and faucets; Lightbulbs; Paints; Electrical equipment. **SICs:** 5074 (Plumbing & Hydronic Heating Supplies); 5063 (Electrical Apparatus & Equipment); 5198 (Paints, Varnishes & Supplies). **Est:** 1864. **Sales:** $55,000,000 (2000). **Emp:** 240. **Officers:** Richard Kimball, President; Robert W. Anderson, CFO; G. Dene Kimball, Dir. of Marketing; Charles Suermann, Dir. of Information Systems; Ellen Corradene, Dir of Human Resources.

■ **23346** ■ **RMC Inc.**
PO Box 1109
Harrisonburg, VA 22801
Phone: (540)434-5333   **Fax:** (540)434-7090
Products: Plumbing supplies; Hardware; Feed. **SICs:** 5074 (Plumbing & Hydronic Heating Supplies); 5072 (Hardware); 5191 (Farm Supplies). **Est:** 1919. **Sales:** $21,000,000 (2000). **Emp:** 85. **Officers:** Jack Reich, President.

■ **23347** ■ **Roberts-Hamilton Co., Div. of Hajoca Corp.**
800 Turners Crossroads S
Golden Valley, MN 55416
Phone: (612)544-1234   **Fax:** (612)544-1812
Products: Plumbing supplies. **SIC:** 5074 (Plumbing & Hydronic Heating Supplies). **Est:** 1898. **Officers:** David Maiers, Branch Mgr. **Former Name:** Roberts-Hamilton Co.

■ **23348** ■ **Robertson Heating Supply Co.**
500 W Main St.
Alliance, OH 44601
Phone: (330)821-9180   **Fax:** (330)821-8251
E-mail: postmaster1@robertsonheatingsupply.com
URL: http://www.robertsonheatingsupply.com
Products: Plumbing and heating supplies. **SICs:** 5074 (Plumbing & Hydronic Heating Supplies); 5075 (Warm Air Heating & Air-Conditioning). **Est:** 1934. **Sales:** $73,351,000 (2000). **Emp:** 230. **Officers:** Scott Robertson, President.

■ **23349** ■ **Robertson Supply Inc.**
PO Box R
Nampa, ID 83653-0057
Phone: (208)466-8907   **Fax:** (208)466-8900
E-mail: michels@robertsonsupply.com
URL: http://www.robertsonsupply.com
Products: Plumbing and agricultural supplies. **SICs:** 5074 (Plumbing & Hydronic Heating Supplies); 5191 (Farm Supplies). **Est:** 1948. **Sales:** $20,000,000 (2000). **Emp:** 68. **Officers:** Thomas W. Malson, President; Thomas M. Malson, Vice President.

■ **23350** ■ **Rocamar Services Inc.**
12764 NW 9th Terrace
Miami, FL 33182
Phone: (305)221-7121   **Fax:** (305)221-6385
Products: Mechanical and plumbing systems. **SIC:** 5074 (Plumbing & Hydronic Heating Supplies). **Est:** 1986. **Officers:** Bernardo Cardenal, President.

■ **23351** ■ **Roekel Co.**
PO Box 2220
Zanesville, OH 43702
Phone: (740)452-5421   **Fax:** (740)452-6508
Products: Plumbing and electrical supplies. **SICs:** 5074 (Plumbing & Hydronic Heating Supplies); 5063 (Electrical Apparatus & Equipment). **Est:** 1876. **Sales:** $10,000,000 (2000). **Emp:** 50. **Officers:** Thomas Arnold, President; Bob Werner, CFO.

■ **23352** ■ **Ross Supply Company Inc.**
3015 S Valley Ave.
PO Box 1087
Marion, IN 46952
Phone: (765)664-2384   **Fax:** (765)664-9098
E-mail: cw@rosssupply.com
URL: http://www.rosssupply.com
Products: Plumbing and heating supplies; Kitchen and bathroom cabinets. **SICs:** 5074 (Plumbing & Hydronic Heating Supplies); 5031 (Lumber, Plywood & Millwork). **Est:** 1950. **Sales:** $5,000,000 (2000). **Emp:** 23. **Officers:** Charles Wallace, President.

■ **23353** ■ **Rubenstein Supply Co.**
2800 San Pablo Ave.
Oakland, CA 94608-4529
Phone: (510)444-6614
Free: (800)TRY-RUBE   **Fax:** (510)444-2518
E-mail: rubysup@aol.com
URL: http://www.rubensteinsupply.com
Products: Plumbing equipment; Heating, ventilating, and air conditioning equipment. **SICs:** 5074 (Plumbing & Hydronic Heating Supplies); 5075 (Warm Air Heating & Air-Conditioning). **Est:** 1939. **Emp:** 24. **Officers:** Craig Rubenstein; Bob Rubenstein.

■ **23354** ■ **Rubenstein Supply Co.**
96 Woodland Ave.
San Rafael, CA 94901
Phone: (415)454-1174
Free: (800)622-7433   **Fax:** (415)454-9879
Products: Plumbing and heating supplies; Sheet metal. **SICs:** 5074 (Plumbing & Hydronic Heating Supplies); 5051 (Metals Service Centers & Offices). **Est:** 1995. **Sales:** $2,000,000 (2000). **Emp:** 6. **Officers:** Lucy A. Lantz, Branch Mgr.

■ **23355** ■ **Rundle-Spence Manufacturing Co.**
PO Box 510008
New Berlin, WI 53151
Phone: (414)782-3000
Products: Plumbing, heating and industrial equipment. **SICs:** 5074 (Plumbing & Hydronic Heating Supplies); 5075 (Warm Air Heating & Air-Conditioning); 5084 (Industrial Machinery & Equipment). **Sales:** $13,000,000 (1994). **Emp:** 60. **Officers:** M.R. Spence Jr., CEO & President; Marie Spence, Controller.

■ **23356** ■ **St. Louis Screw and Bolt Co.**
6900 N Broadway
St. Louis, MO 63147
Phone: (314)389-7500
Products: Water and sewer pipes; Fire hydrants. **SICs:** 5074 (Plumbing & Hydronic Heating Supplies); 5085 (Industrial Supplies). **Est:** 1887. **Sales:** $6,500,000 (2000). **Emp:** 35. **Officers:** James E. Schiele, President; Lloyd Watson, Controller.

■ **23357** ■ **Salina Supply Co.**
302 N Santa Fe
Salina, KS 67401
Phone: (785)823-2221
Free: (800)288-1231   **Fax:** (785)823-3532
Products: Plumbing supplies; Heating and cooling supplies; Pumps; Waterworks supplies. **SICs:** 5074 (Plumbing & Hydronic Heating Supplies); 5075 (Warm Air Heating & Air-Conditioning); 5085 (Industrial Supplies). **Est:** 1919. **Sales:** $9,000,000 (2000). **Emp:** 37. **Officers:** John L. Zimmerman, Chairman of the Board; Mark A. Zimmerman, President.

■ **23358** ■ **George T. Sanders Company Inc.**
10201 W 49th Ave.
Wheat Ridge, CO 80033
Phone: (303)423-9660
Free: (800)284-0400   **Fax:** (303)420-8737
Products: Plumbing and heating equipment. **SIC:** 5074 (Plumbing & Hydronic Heating Supplies). **Est:** 1950. **Sales:** $40,000,000 (2000). **Emp:** 110. **Officers:** Gary T. Sanders, President; Thomas C. Tooley, VP of Admin.; Matthew Sanders, VP of Marketing; Michael Raisch, VP of Finance; Beverly Sanders, Secretary.

■ **23359** ■ **Satterlund Supply Co.**
26277 Sherwood Ave.
Warren, MI 48091
Phone: (810)755-9700
URL: http://www.satterlund.com
Products: Pipes, valves, and fittings. **SIC:** 5074

(Plumbing & Hydronic Heating Supplies). **Est:** 1964. **Sales:** $15,000,000 (2000). **Emp:** 46. **Officers:** Fred Satterlund, CEO; Tim Quinn, Vice President.

■ **23360** ■ **SB Developments Inc.**
PO Box 205
Milan, MI 48160-0205
Phone: (734)439-1231 **Fax:** (734)439-0190
Products: Prefabricated fireplaces; Whirlpool baths; Fireplaces; Woodburning stoves; Central vacuum systems; Saunas and spas. **SICs:** 5074 (Plumbing & Hydronic Heating Supplies); 5091 (Sporting & Recreational Goods). **Est:** 1975. **Sales:** $1,000,000 (2000). **Officers:** Morton Leonard, President; Marlenes Leonard, Secretary.

■ **23361** ■ **Schumacher and Seiler Inc.**
15 W Aylesbury Rd.
Timonium, MD 21093-4142
Phone: (410)561-2461 **Fax:** (410)561-0285
Products: Plumbing and heating supplies. **SICs:** 5074 (Plumbing & Hydronic Heating Supplies); 5075 (Warm Air Heating & Air-Conditioning). **Est:** 1978. **Sales:** $7,000,000 (2000). **Emp:** 32. **Officers:** Russell C. Trout, CEO & President; Sara Derman, Controller.

■ **23362** ■ **Scottco Service Co.**
PO Box 7729
Amarillo, TX 79114
Phone: (806)355-8251 **Fax:** (806)359-8507
Products: Plumbing, heating, and air conditioner supplies. **SICs:** 5074 (Plumbing & Hydronic Heating Supplies); 5075 (Warm Air Heating & Air-Conditioning). **Est:** 1972. **Sales:** $5,000,000 (2000). **Emp:** 75. **Officers:** William B. Martin, President; Robert Vanderford, Bookkeeper; Bill Hunt, Sales Mgr.

■ **23363** ■ **Scotts Inc.**
100 W Main St.
Fair Bluff, NC 28439
Phone: (910)649-7581 **Fax:** (910)649-7376
Products: Plumbing and electrical supplies. **SICs:** 5074 (Plumbing & Hydronic Heating Supplies); 5063 (Electrical Apparatus & Equipment). **Est:** 1936. **Sales:** $3,000,000 (2000). **Emp:** 25. **Officers:** I. M. Scott, President; D. Scott, VP of Finance; Frank Elvington, Dir. of Marketing; Gayle Brown, Dir. of Systems. **Alternate Name:** Scott Water Treatment.

■ **23364** ■ **Scranton Sales Co.**
1027 Jefferson Ave.
Scranton, PA 18510
Phone: (717)346-0718
Products: Plumbing and heating equipment. **SICs:** 5074 (Plumbing & Hydronic Heating Supplies); 5075 (Warm Air Heating & Air-Conditioning). **Est:** 1946. **Sales:** $4,000,000 (2000). **Emp:** 20. **Officers:** Steve Brickell, President & Treasurer.

■ **23365** ■ **Sea Recovery**
PO Box 2560
Gardena, CA 90247
Phone: (310)327-4000 **Fax:** (310)327-4350
Products: Water treatment systems. **SIC:** 5074 (Plumbing & Hydronic Heating Supplies).

■ **23366** ■ **Seashore Supply Company Inc.**
PO Box 1286
Ocean City, NJ 08226-7286
Products: Plumbing supplies. **SIC:** 5074 (Plumbing & Hydronic Heating Supplies). **Est:** 1919. **Sales:** $5,000,000 (2000). **Emp:** 37. **Officers:** Fred Raring, CEO.

■ **23367** ■ **Security Supply Corp.**
Maple Ave.
Selkirk, NY 12158
Phone: (518)767-2226 **Fax:** (518)767-2065
URL: http://www.secsupply.com
Products: Plumbing and heating supplies. **SIC:** 5074 (Plumbing & Hydronic Heating Supplies). **Est:** 1934. **Sales:** $25,000,000 (1999). **Emp:** 94. **Officers:** Keith Bennett, President; David Willey, Controller; Kevin Williams, Treasurer; Kim Willey, Secretary; Brian Fowler, Marketing & Sales Mgr., e-mail: bdf@secsupply.com.

■ **23368** ■ **Seneca Plumbing and Heating Supply Company Inc.**
192-196 Seneca St.
Buffalo, NY 14204
Phone: (716)852-4744 **Fax:** (716)856-3276
E-mail: plumbingdept@netzero.com
URL: http://www.plumbingdept.com
Products: Plumbing and heating supplies; Kitchen and bathroom products; Drain parts, including faucet, toilet, and tub parts. **SICs:** 5074 (Plumbing & Hydronic Heating Supplies); 5075 (Warm Air Heating & Air-Conditioning). **Est:** 1932. **Sales:** $1,500,000 (2000). **Emp:** 10. **Officers:** Alan B. Linsky, President; Louis Linsky, General Mgr.

■ **23369** ■ **Service Supply Systems Inc.**
PO Box 749
Cordele, GA 31015
Phone: (912)273-1112
Products: Plumbing products; Faucets; Bathtubs; Sinks. **SIC:** 5074 (Plumbing & Hydronic Heating Supplies). **Est:** 1972. **Sales:** $70,000,000 (2000). **Emp:** 240. **Officers:** C.M. Hunt, President; J. Zolkowski, Treasurer & Secty.; Fred Brown, Dir. of Marketing.

■ **23370** ■ **J.A. Sexauer Inc.**
531 Central Park Ave.
Scarsdale, NY 10583
Phone: (914)472-7500 **Fax:** (914)472-3774
Products: plumbing supplies. **SIC:** 5074 (Plumbing & Hydronic Heating Supplies). **Est:** 1921. **Sales:** $46,000,000 (1999). **Emp:** 350. **Officers:** G.V. Silva, President; V. Pescasolido, VP of Finance; C. Sbezzi, VP of Marketing; A. Maya, Dir. of Systems.

■ **23371** ■ **SG Supply Co.**
12900 S Throop St.
Calumet Park, IL 60643
Phone: (708)371-8800 **Fax:** (708)371-2752
Products: Plumbing and piping supplies. **SIC:** 5074 (Plumbing & Hydronic Heating Supplies). **Est:** 1959. **Sales:** $20,000,000 (2000). **Emp:** 75. **Officers:** Norman E. Weiss, President; Robert M. Aldrich, Controller; James Schuller, Sales Mgr.

■ **23372** ■ **Charles D. Sheehy Inc.**
PO Box 105
Avon, MA 02322
Phone: (508)583-7612 **Fax:** (508)586-2312
Products: Pipe valves and fittings. **SIC:** 5074 (Plumbing & Hydronic Heating Supplies). **Est:** 1951. **Sales:** $16,500,000 (2000). **Emp:** 22. **Officers:** Arthur R. Sheehy, President & Treasurer; Patricia H. Sheehy, CFO; Kevin R. Sheehy, VP of Marketing; Craig Camuso, Dir. of Systems.

■ **23373** ■ **Showcase Kitchens and Baths Inc.**
222 S Central Ave., Ste. 800
St. Louis, MO 63105-3509
Phone: (314)644-3105
Products: Kitchen and bathroom fixtures. **SICs:** 5023 (Homefurnishings); 5074 (Plumbing & Hydronic Heating Supplies).

■ **23374** ■ **Sierra Craft Inc.**
18825 E San Jose Ave.
City of Industry, CA 91748
Phone: (626)964-2395
Free: (800)735-4503 **Fax:** (626)964-1471
Products: Plumbing fixtures, equipment, and supplies; Sighting, tracking, and fire control equipment. **SICs:** 5074 (Plumbing & Hydronic Heating Supplies); 5087 (Service Establishment Equipment). **Est:** 1974. **Sales:** $37,000,000 (2000). **Emp:** 160. **Officers:** Lee Klein, President; Lou Razza, VP of Operations; Lynn Homertgen, VP of Sales.

■ **23375** ■ **Sig Cox Inc.**
1431 Greene St.
Augusta, GA 30901
Phone: (706)722-5304
Products: Plumbing supplies; Electrical supplies; Air conditioning supplies. **SICs:** 5074 (Plumbing & Hydronic Heating Supplies); 5063 (Electrical Apparatus & Equipment); 5075 (Warm Air Heating & Air-Conditioning). **Est:** 1926. **Sales:** $10,000,000 (2000). **Emp:** 90. **Officers:** R.S. Haynie, President & Chairman of the Board.

■ **23376** ■ **Sign of the Crab Ltd.**
3756 Omec Cir.
Rancho Cordova, CA 95742
Phone: (916)638-2722
Free: (800)843-2722 **Fax:** (916)638-2725
URL: http://www.signofthecrab.com
Products: Plumbing fixtures. **SIC:** 5074 (Plumbing & Hydronic Heating Supplies). **Est:** 1972. **Sales:** $5,000,000 (2000). **Emp:** 30. **Officers:** Frank Strom, President; Larry H. Jacobs, Pres. of Ashley Harris.

■ **23377** ■ **Simmons-Huggins Supply Co.**
425 M.L. King
San Angelo, TX 76902
Phone: (915)655-9163
Products: Plumbing and hydronic heating supplies. **SICs:** 5074 (Plumbing & Hydronic Heating Supplies); 5063 (Electrical Apparatus & Equipment). **Sales:** $4,000,000 (1992). **Emp:** 19. **Officers:** D.R. Shahan, President.

■ **23378** ■ **Siroflex of America Inc.**
14658 Plummer
Van Nuys, CA 91402
Phone: (818)892-8382 **Fax:** (818)894-6828
Products: Plumbing fixtures, equipment, and supplies. **SIC:** 5074 (Plumbing & Hydronic Heating Supplies).

■ **23379** ■ **Sloan and Company Inc.**
15 Tobey Village
Pittsford, NY 14534-1727
Phone: (716)385-4004
Products: Plumbing equipment, including faucets, sinks, and tubs. **SIC:** 5074 (Plumbing & Hydronic Heating Supplies). **Est:** 1860. **Sales:** $3,000,000 (2000). **Emp:** 10. **Officers:** William L. Ely, President; Jim Ryan, Controller.

■ **23380** ■ **Thomas Somerville Co.**
4900 Sixth St. NE
Washington, DC 20017
Phone: (202)635-4321 **Fax:** (202)635-4151
Products: Plumbing supplies. **SIC:** 5074 (Plumbing & Hydronic Heating Supplies).

■ **23381** ■ **Thomas Somerville Co.**
25 Gwynns Mill Ct.
Owings Mills, MD 21117
Phone: (410)363-1322 **Fax:** (410)363-2016
Products: Plumbing; Piping; Fixtures; Copper. **SICs:** 5074 (Plumbing & Hydronic Heating Supplies); 5051 (Metals Service Centers & Offices).

■ **23382** ■ **Thomas Somerville Co.**
15901 Somerville Dr.
Rockville, MD 20855
Phone: (301)948-8650 **Fax:** (301)948-4091
Products: Plumbing; Piping; Fixtures; Copper. **SICs:** 5074 (Plumbing & Hydronic Heating Supplies); 5051 (Metals Service Centers & Offices).

■ **23383** ■ **Thomas Somerville, Co.**
1300 Continental Dr.
Abingdon, MD 21009-2334
Phone: (410)676-6400 **Fax:** (410)676-6656
Products: Plumbing; Piping; Fixtures; Copper. **SICs:** 5074 (Plumbing & Hydronic Heating Supplies); 5051 (Metals Service Centers & Offices).

■ **23384** ■ **Thomas Somerville Co.**
2349 Solomon's Island Rd.
Annapolis, MD 21401
Phone: (410)266-6022 **Fax:** (410)266-9158
Products: Plumbing; Piping; Fixtures; Copper. **SICs:** 5074 (Plumbing & Hydronic Heating Supplies); 5051 (Metals Service Centers & Offices).

■ **23385** ■ **Thomas Somerville Co.**
11002 Cathal Rd.
Berlin, MD 21811
Phone: (410)641-5020 **Fax:** (410)641-5041
Products: Plumbing; Piping; Fixtures; Copper. **SICs:** 5074 (Plumbing & Hydronic Heating Supplies); 5051 (Metals Service Centers & Offices).

■ 23386 ■ Thomas Somerville Co.
PO Box 2247
York, PA 17405
Phone: (717)848-1545 **Fax:** (717)843-4953
Products: Heating, cooling, and plumbing supplies.
SICs: 5074 (Plumbing & Hydronic Heating Supplies);
5075 (Warm Air Heating & Air-Conditioning).

■ 23387 ■ Thomas Somerville Co.
425 Nelson St.
Chambersburg, PA 17201
Phone: (717)264-9300 **Fax:** (717)264-3316
Products: Plumbing and heating supplies. **SICs:** 5074
(Plumbing & Hydronic Heating Supplies); 5075 (Warm
Air Heating & Air-Conditioning).

■ 23388 ■ Thomas Somerville Co.
9825 Lee Hwy.
Fairfax, VA 22030
Phone: (703)273-4900 **Fax:** (703)385-3743
Products: Plumbing equipment; Heating equipment.
SICs: 5074 (Plumbing & Hydronic Heating Supplies);
5075 (Warm Air Heating & Air-Conditioning).

■ 23389 ■ Thomas Somerville Co.
3703 Price Club Blvd.
Midlothian, VA 23112
Phone: (804)745-6400 **Fax:** (804)745-6478
Products: Plumbing equipment; Heating equipment.
SICs: 5074 (Plumbing & Hydronic Heating Supplies);
5075 (Warm Air Heating & Air-Conditioning).

■ 23390 ■ Thomas Somerville Co.
824 Professional Place W
Chesapeake, VA 23320
Phone: (757)436-2323 **Fax:** (757)547-2703
Products: Plumbing equipment; Heating equipment.
SICs: 5074 (Plumbing & Hydronic Heating Supplies);
5075 (Warm Air Heating & Air-Conditioning).

■ 23391 ■ South Central Company Inc.
2685 N National
Columbus, IN 47201
Phone: (812)376-3343
Free: (800)832-5440 **Fax:** (812)376-0556
Products: Heating equipment; Plumbing fixtures,
equipment, and supplies; Air-conditioning equipment;
Paints and allied products. **SICs:** 5074 (Plumbing &
Hydronic Heating Supplies); 5075 (Warm Air Heating &
Air-Conditioning); 5198 (Paints, Varnishes & Supplies).
Est: 1953. **Sales:** $10,000,000 (2000). **Emp:** 49.
Officers: Bill Sasse.

■ 23392 ■ Southard Supply Inc.
234-6 N 3rd St.
Columbus, OH 43215
Phone: (614)221-3323
Products: Plumbing supplies, including pipes. **SIC:**
5074 (Plumbing & Hydronic Heating Supplies). **Est:**
1931. **Sales:** $7,000,000 (2000). **Emp:** 17. **Officers:**
E.S. Eastman, President; Barbara Blaschke, Treasurer
& Secty.

■ 23393 ■ Southern Wholesalers Inc.
418 S Glenwood Ave.
Dalton, GA 30720
Phone: (706)278-1583 **Fax:** (706)272-4713
Products: Electrical and plumbing supplies. **SICs:**
5074 (Plumbing & Hydronic Heating Supplies); 5063
(Electrical Apparatus & Equipment). **Est:** 1945. **Sales:**
$7,900,000 (2000). **Emp:** 49. **Officers:** James H.
Adams, President.

■ 23394 ■ Sprite Industries
1827 Capital St.
Corona, CA 91718
Phone: (909)735-1015
Free: (800)327-9137 **Fax:** (909)735-1016
E-mail: solutions@spritewater.com
URL: http://www.spritewater.com
Products: Shower filters; Drinking water filters; Sports
bottle filters. **SIC:** 5074 (Plumbing & Hydronic Heating
Supplies). **Est:** 1974. **Sales:** $2,500,000 (2000). **Emp:**
25. **Officers:** David Farley, President; Scott Crawford,
Sales & Marketing Contact; Paula Van Dusen,
Customer Service; Carol Worth, Human Resources.

■ 23395 ■ SPS Company Inc.
6363 Hwy. 7
Minneapolis, MN 55416
Phone: (612)929-1377
Free: (800)346-5877 **Fax:** (612)929-8979
Products: Plumbing supplies. **SIC:** 5074 (Plumbing &
Hydronic Heating Supplies). **Est:** 1951. **Sales:**
$100,000,000 (2000). **Emp:** 300. **Officers:** Ralph
Gross, President.

■ 23396 ■ Standard Plumbing Supply
Company Inc.
2100 W Cold Spring Ln.
Baltimore, MD 21209
Phone: (410)466-3500
Free: (800)439-3512 **Fax:** (410)466-8715
URL: http://www.dopkin.com
Products: Plumbing and fixtures, including faucets,
tubs, and toilet bowls; Water heaters. **SIC:** 5074
(Plumbing & Hydronic Heating Supplies). **Est:** 1945.
Sales: $11,000,000 (2000). **Emp:** 34. **Officers:** Burton
H. Gold, President; Richard M. Gold, Vice President;
Jeffrey Raugh, Dir. of Marketing; Nancy Joy, Dir. of
Information Systems. **Alternate Name:** Lee L.
#Dopkin.

■ 23397 ■ Star Tubular Products Co.
4747 S Richmond St.
Chicago, IL 60632
Phone: (773)523-8445
Products: Plumbing, including metal tubes. **SICs:**
5074 (Plumbing & Hydronic Heating Supplies); 5051
(Metals Service Centers & Offices). **Est:** 1948. **Sales:**
$5,000,000 (2000). **Emp:** 40. **Officers:** W.D. Reed,
President; D.R. Kopp, VP & Treasurer.

■ 23398 ■ State Supply Co.
597 E 7th St.
St. Paul, MN 55101
Phone: (612)774-5985
Products: Industrial plumbing supplies; Heating
supplies. **SICs:** 5074 (Plumbing & Hydronic Heating
Supplies); 5075 (Warm Air Heating & Air-Conditioning).

■ 23399 ■ Summit Wholesale
38 Ganson Ave.
Batavia, NY 14021
Phone: (716)343-7022 **Fax:** (716)343-5562
Products: Heating and Cooling equipment and
supplies. **SIC:** 5074 (Plumbing & Hydronic Heating
Supplies). **Sales:** $6,000,000 (2000). **Emp:** 15.

■ 23400 ■ Supply One Corp.
2601 W Dorothy Ln.
Dayton, OH 45439
Phone: (937)297-1111
Free: (800)875-1111 **Fax:** (937)299-9740
URL: http://www.supplyonedayton.com
Products: Kitchen and bathroom fixtures, including
tubs and sinks; Doors; Windows. **SICs:** 5074
(Plumbing & Hydronic Heating Supplies); 5031
(Lumber, Plywood & Millwork). **Est:** 1940. **Emp:** 66.
Officers: R.T. Flaute, President; R.T. Flaute Jr., Vice
President; Steve Dennis, Sales/Marketing Contact;
Nicholas Weidner, Customer Service Contact; Fred
Poland, Human Resources Contact.

■ 23401 ■ Swaim Supply Company Inc.
PO Box 2406
High Point, NC 27261
Phone: (919)883-7161 **Fax:** (919)883-6477
Products: Plumbing, heating, and air-conditioning
supplies. **SICs:** 5074 (Plumbing & Hydronic Heating
Supplies); 5075 (Warm Air Heating & Air-Conditioning).
Est: 1945. **Sales:** $12,000,000 (2000). **Emp:** 70.
Officers: J.B. Sloan, President; C.L. Nichols,
Controller.

■ 23402 ■ Swartz Supply Company Inc.
5550 Allentown Blvd.
Harrisburg, PA 17112
Phone: (717)652-7111 **Fax:** (717)652-7077
Products: Faucets; Kitchen sinks; Counter tops. **SICs:**
5074 (Plumbing & Hydronic Heating Supplies); 5031
(Lumber, Plywood & Millwork). **Est:** 1930. **Sales:**
$7,000,000 (2000). **Emp:** 25. **Officers:** Robert E.
Swartz, President.

■ 23403 ■ Sydney Supply Co.
176 Union Ave.
Providence, RI 02909
Phone: (401)944-0200 **Fax:** (401)944-2595
Products: Plumbing supplies, including pipes and
sinks; Heating supplies; Boilers. **SICs:** 5074 (Plumbing
& Hydronic Heating Supplies); 5075 (Warm Air Heating
& Air-Conditioning). **Est:** 1934. **Sales:** $4,000,000
(2000). **Emp:** 25. **Officers:** Allan Sydney, President.

■ 23404 ■ T and L Supply Inc.
112 19th St.
Wheeling, WV 26003
Phone: (304)233-3340 **Fax:** (304)232-2397
Products: Plumbing equipment, including piping and
bathroom fixtures. **SIC:** 5074 (Plumbing & Hydronic
Heating Supplies). **Est:** 1907. **Sales:** $6,000,000
(1999). **Emp:** 18. **Officers:** Tim Williams, President;
Ray Johnson, Vice President.

■ 23405 ■ Tallman Company Inc.
8642 Pardee Ln.
Crestwood, MO 63126
Phone: (314)843-9119 **Fax:** (314)843-7226
E-mail: tallmanco@aol.com
Products: Plumbing, heating, and cooling fixtures and
supplies, including upscale fixtures and faucets; Tile.
SICs: 5074 (Plumbing & Hydronic Heating Supplies);
5075 (Warm Air Heating & Air-Conditioning); 5032
(Brick, Stone & Related Materials). **Est:** 1926. **Sales:**
$5,000,000 (2000). **Emp:** 35. **Officers:** Roscoe
Tallman Jr., CEO; Kathie Tallman, CFO.

■ 23406 ■ Taylor Supply Co.
6530 Beaubien
Detroit, MI 48202
Phone: (313)872-0400 **Fax:** (313)872-0970
Products: Pipes, valves, and fittings. **SIC:** 5074
(Plumbing & Hydronic Heating Supplies). **Est:** 1910.
Sales: $500,000 (2000). **Emp:** 10. **Officers:** Richard
Larsen, President; Andy Lucus, CFO; Michael Larsen,
Dir. of Marketing & Sales.

■ 23407 ■ Jesse E. Terry Inc.
PO Box 67
Levittown, PA 19059-0067
Phone: (215)355-1000 **Fax:** (215)943-9837
Products: Plumbing, heating and air conditioning
equipment. **SICs:** 5074 (Plumbing & Hydronic Heating
Supplies); 5075 (Warm Air Heating & Air-Conditioning).
Sales: $11,000,000 (2000). **Emp:** 100. **Officers:** John
Kuebler, Finance General Manager.

■ 23408 ■ H.W. Theis Company Inc.
PO Box 325
Brookfield, WI 53008-0325
Phone: (414)783-0500 **Fax:** (414)783-0513
E-mail: hwt@hwtheis.com
Products: Plumbing supplies and equipment. **SIC:**
5074 (Plumbing & Hydronic Heating Supplies). **Est:**
1928. **Sales:** $12,000,000 (1999). **Emp:** 41. **Officers:**
Jeffrey W. Theis, CEO, e-mail: jwt@hwtheis.com;
Gregory Theis, Treasurer.

■ 23409 ■ C.I. Thornburg Co. Inc.
PO Box 2163
Huntington, WV 25722
Phone: (304)523-3484 **Fax:** (304)523-0510
Products: Pipes; Valves; Fittings. **SIC:** 5074 (Plumbing
& Hydronic Heating Supplies). **Est:** 1958. **Sales:**
$8,000,000 (2000). **Emp:** 40. **Officers:** Edward
Morrison Jr., President; Alan S. Morrison, Vice
President.

■ 23410 ■ B.K. Thorpe Co.
PO Box 2547
Long Beach, CA 90806
Phone: (562)595-1811 **Fax:** (562)426-6016
Products: Pipes, valves, and fittings. **SICs:** 5085
(Industrial Supplies); 5074 (Plumbing & Hydronic
Heating Supplies). **Est:** 1965. **Sales:** $5,000,000
(2000). **Emp:** 8. **Officers:** Gary K. Dohman, CEO.

■ 23411 ■ Toole and Company Inc.
PO Box 21322
Houston, TX 77226-1322
Phone: (713)691-2011 **Fax:** (713)691-5821
Products: Plumbing supplies, including pipes, fittings,
valves, faucets, sinks, and tubs. **SIC:** 5074 (Plumbing &

Hydronic Heating Supplies). **Est:** 1948. **Sales:** $6,000,000 (2000). **Emp:** 10. **Officers:** Doug Toole Jr., President.

■ 23412 ■ **Torrington Supply Company Inc.**
PO Box 2838
Waterbury, CT 06723-2838
Phone: (203)756-3641
Free: (800)552-7437 **Fax:** (203)753-4317
Products: Plumbing supplies; Heating supplies; Pumps. **SICs:** 5074 (Plumbing & Hydronic Heating Supplies); 5075 (Warm Air Heating & Air-Conditioning); 5085 (Industrial Supplies). **Est:** 1917. **Sales:** $18,000,000 (2000). **Emp:** 80. **Officers:** Joel S. Becker, CEO; David C. Petitti, Controller; Fred Stein, President.

■ 23413 ■ **Touch Flo Manufacturing**
75 E Palm Ave.
Burbank, CA 91502
Phone: (818)843-8117
Free: (800)223-0490 **Fax:** (818)842-4893
Products: Water purification and plumbing products. **SIC:** 5074 (Plumbing & Hydronic Heating Supplies). **Emp:** 100.

■ 23414 ■ **Trayco Inc.**
PO Box 950
Florence, SC 29503
Phone: (803)669-5462 **Fax:** (803)679-3856
Products: Plumbing supplies, including pipes and tools. **SIC:** 5074 (Plumbing & Hydronic Heating Supplies). **Est:** 1967. **Sales:** $12,000,000 (2000). **Emp:** 100. **Officers:** Jim Hulsman, President; Erich Grotti, CFO; Judy Mills, Dir of Human Resources.

■ 23415 ■ **Treaty Co.**
PO Box 40
Greenville, OH 45331
Phone: (513)548-2181 **Fax:** (513)547-0124
Products: Plumbing supplies; Heating systems. **SICs:** 5074 (Plumbing & Hydronic Heating Supplies); 5075 (Warm Air Heating & Air-Conditioning). **Est:** 1908. **Sales:** $50,000,000 (2000). **Emp:** 800. **Officers:** M. Mead Montgomery, Chairman of the Board; Mike Tinka, CFO; Ron Puterbaugh, Territory Mgr.

■ 23416 ■ **Tri-Bro Supply Co.**
232 Vestal Parkway W
Vestal, NY 13850
Phone: (607)748-8144 **Fax:** (607)748-2937
Products: Plumbing and heating supplies. **SICs:** 5074 (Plumbing & Hydronic Heating Supplies); 5075 (Warm Air Heating & Air-Conditioning).

■ 23417 ■ **Triangle Supply Company Inc.**
12705 Bee St.
Dallas, TX 75234
Phone: (972)620-1661
Products: Plumbing products, including sinks, faucets, and tubs; Electrical products, including lighting. **SICs:** 5074 (Plumbing & Hydronic Heating Supplies); 5063 (Electrical Apparatus & Equipment). **Est:** 1957. **Sales:** $9,000,000 (2000). **Emp:** 33. **Officers:** John Flavin, President; Jo Sparling, Controller; William Mannes, Sales Mgr.

■ 23418 ■ **Trumbull Industries Inc.**
PO Box 30
Warren, OH 44482-0030
Phone: (216)393-6624 **Fax:** (216)399-4421
Products: Plumbing supplies, including fiberglass, china, and brass; Shower doors. **SIC:** 5074 (Plumbing & Hydronic Heating Supplies). **Est:** 1922. **Sales:** $70,000,000 (2000). **Emp:** 330. **Officers:** Richard C. Mueller, CEO; Julian Lehman, Comptroller; Samuel M. Miller, Vice President.

■ 23419 ■ **Turtle Island Herbs Inc.**
1705 14th St. Ste. 172
Boulder, CO 80302
Phone: (303)442-2215
Free: (800)684-4060 **Fax:** (303)442-7722
Products: Hrbal extracts; Processes organic herbs. **SIC:** 5074 (Plumbing & Hydronic Heating Supplies). **Sales:** $700,000 (2000). **Emp:** 19. **Officers:** Feather Jones, President.

■ 23420 ■ **Uni-Flange Corp.**
5285 Ramona Blvd.
Jacksonville, FL 32205
Phone: (904)781-3628 **Fax:** (904)781-3835
Products: Flanges; Pipe fittings and restraints. **SIC:** 5074 (Plumbing & Hydronic Heating Supplies). **Est:** 1977. **Sales:** $6,000,000 (2000). **Emp:** 15. **Officers:** Patrick H. Gray, CEO; Ricardo Salas, CFO; Steve McDonald, Dir. of Marketing & Sales.

■ 23421 ■ **Union Supply Co.**
3001 N Big Spring St., Ste. 200
Midland, TX 79705-5372
Phone: (915)684-8841 **Fax:** (915)684-3972
Products: Plumbing parts, including valves and fitting pipes; Oil field supplies. **SICs:** 5084 (Industrial Machinery & Equipment); 5085 (Industrial Supplies). **Est:** 1939. **Sales:** $24,200,000 (2000). **Emp:** 80. **Officers:** Eddie L. Nowell, President & COO; Robert L. Brewington, VP of Admin.; John E. Scott, Vice President.

■ 23422 ■ **United Pipe and Supply Company Inc.**
PO Box 2220
Eugene, OR 97402
Phone: (503)688-6511 **Fax:** (503)688-5988
Products: Pumps and irrigation products; Water tanks; Valves; Steel pipes. **SICs:** 5074 (Plumbing & Hydronic Heating Supplies); 5085 (Industrial Supplies). **Est:** 1953. **Sales:** $50,000,000 (2000). **Emp:** 200. **Officers:** Taylor Ramsey, Chairman of the Board; Bev Williams, CFO; Dave Ramsey, CEO; Norm Kopp, Dir. of Data Processing; Steve Ramsey, President.

■ 23423 ■ **United Plumbing and Heating Supply Co.**
9947 W Carmen Ave.
Milwaukee, WI 53225
Phone: (414)464-5100
Free: (800)242-5454 **Fax:** (414)464-0238
Products: Pipe, valves, and fittings. **SICs:** 5074 (Plumbing & Hydronic Heating Supplies); 5085 (Industrial Supplies). **Est:** 1922. **Sales:** $11,000,000 (2000). **Emp:** 32. **Officers:** Michael Steil, Corp. Secty.; Chip Roska, President & General Mgr., e-mail: chiproska@msn.com; Paul T. Roska, VP of Operations & Treas. **Alternate Name:** United Technical Products.

■ 23424 ■ **Universal Supply Company Inc.**
515 33rd St.
Parkersburg, WV 26101
Phone: (304)422-3533
Products: Plumbing, heating, and electrical supplies; Industrial products; Bathroom and kitchen cabinets. **SICs:** 5074 (Plumbing & Hydronic Heating Supplies); 5063 (Electrical Apparatus & Equipment). **Est:** 1925. **Sales:** $3,000,000 (2000). **Emp:** 23. **Officers:** S. Clay Van Voorhis, President.

■ 23425 ■ **Usco Inc.**
PO Box 1160
Monroe, NC 28111
Phone: (704)289-5406
Products: Plumbing equipment, including pipes and tools. **SIC:** 5074 (Plumbing & Hydronic Heating Supplies). **Est:** 1949. **Sales:** $32,000,000 (2000). **Emp:** 147. **Officers:** James C. Plyler Jr., President; Alex Sutherland, Accountant; Kent Lee, Dir. of Marketing.

■ 23426 ■ **Utica Plumbing Supply Co.**
332 Lafayette St.
Utica, NY 13502
Phone: (315)735-9555
Free: (800)871-9555 **Fax:** (315)735-9558
URL: http://www.howlandpump.com
Products: Plumbing and heating supplies. **SICs:** 5074 (Plumbing & Hydronic Heating Supplies); 5075 (Warm Air Heating & Air-Conditioning). **Est:** 1914. **Sales:** $3,000,000 (2000). **Emp:** 10. **Officers:** Ken McDonald, CEO; Tim Sherry, Manager, e-mail: tsherry@howlandpump.com.

■ 23427 ■ **Vail Enterprises Inc.**
PO Box 765
New Castle, DE 19720
Phone: (302)322-5411 **Fax:** (302)322-3493
Products: Commercial and industrial plumbing supplies. **SIC:** 5074 (Plumbing & Hydronic Heating Supplies). **Est:** 1908. **Sales:** $12,000,000 (2000). **Emp:** 35. **Officers:** William S. Vail, President; Joseph J. Pendrak Jr., Controller; A.J. Wright, VP of Sales.

■ 23428 ■ **Valley Cities Supply Co.**
9510 Rush St.
South el Monte, CA 91733
Phone: (626)453-0020 **Fax:** (626)448-0620
Products: Plastic and steel pipes. **SIC:** 5074 (Plumbing & Hydronic Heating Supplies). **Est:** 1946. **Sales:** $5,000,000 (1999). **Emp:** 16. **Officers:** Dennis Bright, Dir. of Sales; Dennis Bright, Dir. of Sales.

■ 23429 ■ **Valley Supply Co.**
S Railroad & 11th St.
Elkins, WV 26241
Phone: (304)636-4015 **Fax:** (304)636-4064
Products: Plumbing supplies; Air conditioning and heating equipment. **SICs:** 5074 (Plumbing & Hydronic Heating Supplies); 5075 (Warm Air Heating & Air-Conditioning). **Est:** 1905. **Sales:** $8,400,000 (2000). **Emp:** 55. **Officers:** Pat Lafayette, President; Nancy Ramsey, CFO; H.K. Pritt, Dir. of Marketing; Delano Chewning, Dir. of Purchasing.

■ 23430 ■ **Vamac Inc.**
PO Box 11225
Richmond, VA 23230
Phone: (804)353-7996 **Fax:** (804)358-7855
URL: http://www.vamac.com
Products: Plumbing supplies, including pipes, water heaters, faucets, and bath tubs. **SIC:** 5074 (Plumbing & Hydronic Heating Supplies). **Est:** 1915. **Sales:** $26,000,000 (2000). **Emp:** 98. **Officers:** Kenneth Perry, Chairman of the Board; Christopher Perry, Comptroller.

■ 23431 ■ **Van Leeuwen Pipe and Tube Corp.**
PO Box 40904
Houston, TX 77240
Phone: (713)466-9966 **Fax:** (713)466-7423
URL: http://www.vanleeuwen.com
Products: Pipes, valves, flanges, and fittings. **SICs:** 5051 (Metals Service Centers & Offices); 5085 (Industrial Supplies). **Est:** 1924. **Sales:** $200,000,000 (2000). **Emp:** 350. **Officers:** Charles S. Wolley, CEO; Roland Balkenende, President; M. Colleen Estes, CFO.

■ 23432 ■ **Vierk Industrial Products**
3521 Coleman Ct.
PO Box 1668
Lafayette, IN 47902
Phone: (765)447-0458
Free: (800)428-7548 **Fax:** (765)449-9830
E-mail: vipvalves@aol.com
URL: http://www.vipvalves.com
Products: Plumbing and heating equipment and supplies; Valves and regulators; Faucets; Pipes and fittings. **SICs:** 5074 (Plumbing & Hydronic Heating Supplies); 5075 (Warm Air Heating & Air-Conditioning). **Est:** 1949. **Sales:** $3,200,000 (2000). **Emp:** 15. **Officers:** Marlow Miller, Chairman of the Board; Kenneth Sponagle, President; Jeff Sugarman, Vice President.

■ 23433 ■ **Vinson Supply Co.**
PO Box 702440
Tulsa, OK 74170-2440
Phone: (918)481-8770 **Fax:** (918)481-8664
Products: Pipes; Valves; Fittings. **SICs:** 5074 (Plumbing & Hydronic Heating Supplies); 5085 (Industrial Supplies). **Est:** 1937. **Sales:** $300,000,000 (2000). **Emp:** 475. **Officers:** Robert C. Mellor, CEO & President; A. Lee Mulkey, CFO; RichArd Stewart, Vice President; Russ Staurovsky, Manager; Bob Kendall, VP of Human Resources.

■ 23434 ■ **Waldor Pump and Equipment**
9700 Humboldt Ave. S
Minneapolis, MN 55431
Phone: (612)884-5394
Free: (800)536-5394 **Fax:** (612)884-3239
Products: specialty equipment and products. **SIC:** 5074 (Plumbing & Hydronic Heating Supplies). **Sales:** $8,000,000 (2000). **Emp:** 30.

■ 23435 ■ Wallace Company Inc.
PO Box 1492
Houston, TX 77251-1492
Phone: (713)675-2661 **Fax:** (713)672-5848
Products: Pipes, valves, and fittings. **SICs:** 5074 (Plumbing & Hydronic Heating Supplies); 5085 (Industrial Supplies). **Est:** 1942. **Sales:** $88,000,000 (2000). **Emp:** 280. **Officers:** John Wallace, President; Carl Anderson, Dir. of Data Processing; Barbara Lane, Dir of Human Resources.

■ 23436 ■ Wallace Pump and Supply Company Inc.
PO Box 157
Brundidge, AL 36010
Phone: (205)735-2338 **Fax:** (205)735-2339
Products: Plumbing supplies. **SIC:** 5074 (Plumbing & Hydronic Heating Supplies). **Est:** 1946. **Sales:** $3,000,000 (2000). **Emp:** 16. **Officers:** R.E. Wallace Jr., President.

■ 23437 ■ Wallace Supply Co.
PO Box 829
Vineland, NJ 08360
Phone: (609)692-4800 **Fax:** (609)692-8674
Products: Plumbing and heating equipment and industrial supplies. **SICs:** 5074 (Plumbing & Hydronic Heating Supplies); 5085 (Industrial Supplies). **Sales:** $11,000,000 (1993). **Emp:** 50. **Officers:** G.A. Wallace, President; Thomas Peters, Vice President.

■ 23438 ■ Washburn-Garfield Corp.
100 Prescott St.
Worcester, MA 01605
Phone: (508)753-7225 **Fax:** (508)797-4248
E-mail: info@washgar.com
URL: http://www.washgar.com
Products: Plumbing and industrial supplies. **SIC:** 5074 (Plumbing & Hydronic Heating Supplies). **Est:** 1872. **Sales:** $8,000,000 (1999). **Emp:** 22. **Officers:** Richard F. O'Hearn Jr., President & Treasurer; David Smith, CFO; Emile St. Pierre, General Mgr.; Fred Meyer, Manufacturing Mgr.

■ 23439 ■ Water and Waste Water Equipment Co.
PO Box 9405
Boise, ID 83707
Phone: (208)377-0440 **Fax:** (208)377-0493
Products: Water equipment, including pipes, fire hydrants, and chlorination equipment. **SICs:** 5074 (Plumbing & Hydronic Heating Supplies); 5085 (Industrial Supplies). **Est:** 1975. **Sales:** $13,500,000 (2000). **Emp:** 26. **Officers:** Roy L. Phillips, President; Charlie Zupsic, Treasurer; Chris Oakes, Dir. of Marketing; Randy Phillips, Dir. of Data Processing.

■ 23440 ■ WaterPro Supplies Inc.
220 S Westgate Dr.
Carol Stream, IL 60188
Phone: (708)665-1800
Products: Water and sewer supplies. **SIC:** 5084 (Industrial Machinery & Equipment). **Sales:** $72,100,000 (1994). **Emp:** 330. **Officers:** Richard J. Klau, President; Christopher Pappo, VP of Finance & Admin.

■ 23441 ■ Watts Regulator Co.
Rte. 114 & Chestnut St.
North Andover, MA 01845
Phone: (978)688-1811 **Fax:** (978)794-1848
Products: Miniature regulators; Backflow prevention equipment. **SIC:** 5074 (Plumbing & Hydronic Heating Supplies).

■ 23442 ■ Watts/Taras Valve Corp.
815 Chestnut St.
North Andover, MA 01845
Phone: (978)689-6157
Free: (800)233-2054 **Fax:** (978)689-2457
Products: Plumbing materials and fixtures. **SIC:** 5074 (Plumbing & Hydronic Heating Supplies). **Sales:** $800,000 (2000). **Emp:** 150.

■ 23443 ■ Waxman Industries Inc.
24460 Aurora Rd.
Bedford Heights, OH 44146
Phone: (216)439-1830 **Fax:** (216)439-1262
Products: Plumbing supplies. **SIC:** 5074 (Plumbing & Hydronic Heating Supplies). **Est:** 1934. **Sales:** $266,400,000 (2000). **Emp:** 770. **Officers:** Armond Waxman, CEO & President; Mark W. Wester, VP & CFO; John S. Peters, Sr. VP of Operations.

■ 23444 ■ Wayne Pipe and Supply Inc.
PO Box 2201
Ft. Wayne, IN 46801
Phone: (219)423-9577
Products: Plumbing supplies. **SIC:** 5074 (Plumbing & Hydronic Heating Supplies). **Est:** 1896. **Sales:** $13,000,000 (2000). **Emp:** 65. **Officers:** Thomas Lapp, President; George Kistler, Treasurer & Secty.; James Wilson, VP of Marketing.

■ 23445 ■ Wayne Pipe and Supply Inc.
PO Box 2201
Ft. Wayne, IN 46801
Phone: (219)423-9577 **Fax:** (219)422-7794
Products: Plumbing supplies including valves and fittings. **SIC:** 5074 (Plumbing & Hydronic Heating Supplies). **Sales:** $19,000,000 (2000). **Emp:** 70. **Officers:** Thomas Lapp, President; Janice Ball, Treasurer & Secty.

■ 23446 ■ F.W. Webb Co.
200 Middlesex Tpk.
Burlington, MA 01803
Phone: (617)272-6600 **Fax:** (617)272-7790
Products: Industrial heating, cooling, and plumbing supplies. **SICs:** 5074 (Plumbing & Hydronic Heating Supplies); 5075 (Warm Air Heating & Air-Conditioning); 5085 (Industrial Supplies). **Est:** 1866. **Sales:** $180,000,000 (2000). **Emp:** 600. **Officers:** John Pope, CEO; Robert Mucciarone, Treasurer; Ernest R. Coutermarsh, Sales Mgr.; Larry Moore, Dir. of Systems.

■ 23447 ■ Webstone Company Inc.
703 Plantation St.
Worcester, MA 01605
Phone: (508)852-5700
Free: (800)225-9529 **Fax:** 800-336-5133
E-mail: service@webstonevalves.com
URL: http://www.webstonevalves.com
Products: Brass, stainless steel, and plastic plumbing valves for the residential, commercial and industrial markets; Faucets and plumbing specialties for residential use. **SIC:** 5074 (Plumbing & Hydronic Heating Supplies). **Est:** 1954. **Emp:** 20. **Officers:** Michael Reck, President, e-mail: michael@webstonevalves.com.

■ 23448 ■ Weinstein Supply Corp.
Davisville & Moreland
Willow Grove, PA 19090
Phone: (215)657-0700 **Fax:** (215)657-0180
Products: Plumbing supplies; Heating and air conditioning units. **SICs:** 5074 (Plumbing & Hydronic Heating Supplies); 5075 (Warm Air Heating & Air-Conditioning). **Sales:** $30,300,000 (2000). **Emp:** 225. **Officers:** Howard Weinstein, President.

■ 23449 ■ Welker-McKee Supply Co. Division of Hajoca
6606 Granger Rd.
Cleveland, OH 44131
Phone: (216)447-0050
Free: (800)522-2284 **Fax:** (216)447-3005
URL: http://www.welkermckee.com
Products: Plumbing supplies; Heating supplies. **SICs:** 5074 (Plumbing & Hydronic Heating Supplies); 5075 (Warm Air Heating & Air-Conditioning). **Est:** 1909. **Sales:** $13,000,000 (2000). **Emp:** 43. **Officers:** Gene Strine, General Mgr.

■ 23450 ■ West Texas Wholesale Supply Co.
PO Box 1020
Abilene, TX 79604
Phone: (915)677-2851 **Fax:** (915)677-1360
Products: Plumbing; Pipes; Batteries. **SIC:** 5074 (Plumbing & Hydronic Heating Supplies). **Est:** 1944. **Sales:** $20,000,000 (2000). **Emp:** 70. **Officers:** M. Kellar, Chairman of the Board; Steven Kellar, President; Randy Anderson, Marketing & Sales Mgr.; Jeff Wyatt, Data Processing Mgr.

■ 23451 ■ Westburne Supply Inc.
PO Box 65013
Anaheim, CA 92815
Phone: (714)590-3000 **Fax:** (714)590-3018
Products: Plumbing fixtures, equipment, and supplies; Heating equipment. **SICs:** 5074 (Plumbing & Hydronic Heating Supplies); 5075 (Warm Air Heating & Air-Conditioning). **Est:** 1965. **Sales:** $245,000,000 (1999). **Emp:** 530. **Officers:** Lynn Tossell, General Mgr.

■ 23452 ■ Western Nevada Supply Co.
PO Box 1576
Sparks, NV 89432
Phone: (775)359-5800
Free: (800)648-1230 **Fax:** (775)359-4649
Products: Plumbing, irrigation and waterworks supplies. **SICs:** 5074 (Plumbing & Hydronic Heating Supplies); 5075 (Warm Air Heating & Air-Conditioning). **Est:** 1964. **Sales:** $30,000,000 (2000). **Emp:** 150. **Officers:** J.T. Reviglio, President; Tom Reviglio, Vice President.

■ 23453 ■ Western Purifier Water Purifier Co.
PO Box 688
Woodland Hills, CA 91365-0688
Phone: (818)703-0444
Free: (800)55-WATER **Fax:** (818)992-8170
Products: Drinking water systems and parts; Faucets. **SIC:** 5074 (Plumbing & Hydronic Heating Supplies). **Est:** 1971. **Sales:** $1,150,000 (2000). **Emp:** 4. **Officers:** R. Baker, President.

■ 23454 ■ Western Steel and Plumbing Inc.
PO Box 774
Bismarck, ND 58502-0774
Phone: (701)223-3130 **Fax:** (701)222-1734
Products: Plumbing and heating supplies. **SIC:** 5074 (Plumbing & Hydronic Heating Supplies). **Est:** 1949.

■ 23455 ■ Wholesale Distributors of Alaska
2548 N Post Rd.
Anchorage, AK 99501-1757
Phone: (907)277-8584 **Fax:** (907)277-5707
Products: Baths, whirlpools, spas, and saunas; Plumbing fixtures; Wood and gas stoves and fireplaces; Chimneys. **SICs:** 5074 (Plumbing & Hydronic Heating Supplies); 5075 (Warm Air Heating & Air-Conditioning). **Est:** 1967. **Sales:** $3,000,000 (2000). **Emp:** 15. **Officers:** Robert Carlson Sr., President; Robert Carlson Jr., Vice President.

■ 23456 ■ Wholesale Distributors of Alaska
2548 N Post Rd.
Anchorage, AK 99501-1757
Phone: (907)277-8584 **Fax:** (907)277-5707
Products: Plumbing materials and fixtures. **SIC:** 5074 (Plumbing & Hydronic Heating Supplies). **Sales:** $3,000,000 (2000). **Emp:** 15.

■ 23457 ■ Wholesale Supply Group Inc.
PO Box 4080
Cleveland, TN 37320-4080
Phone: (423)478-1191 **Fax:** (423)479-2644
URL: http://www.wsginc.com
Products: Plumbing and electrical supplies. **SICs:** 5074 (Plumbing & Hydronic Heating Supplies); 5063 (Electrical Apparatus & Equipment). **Est:** 1953. **Sales:** $30,600,000 (2000). **Emp:** 185. **Officers:** Lloyd D. Rogers, President; Reggie Bishop, VP of Finance; Ronny Guthric, VP of Operations; Gary Millaway, VP of Inventory.

■ 23458 ■ Wholesale Supply Group, Inc. Maryville Division
1513 Monroe Ave.
PO Box 4216
Maryville, TN 37802
Phone: (423)982-3630 **Fax:** (423)982-0184
Products: Plumbing supplies, including faucets; Tubs, whirlpools, and sinks; Electrical supplies; Cabinets; Countertops; Appliances; Doors and windows. **SICs:** 5074 (Plumbing & Hydronic Heating Supplies); 5063 (Electrical Apparatus & Equipment); 5031 (Lumber, Plywood & Millwork); 5064 (Electrical Appliances—Television & Radio). **Emp:** 14. **Officers:** Andy Frogg, Manager; Johnny Settlemyre, Assistant Manager. **Former Name:** Maryville Wholesale Supply Inc.

■ **23459** ■ **M.P. Wilkins Supply Co.**
PO Box 352918
Toledo, OH 43635-2918
Phone: (419)531-5574
Products: Pipes, valves, and fittings. **SICs:** 5085 (Industrial Supplies); 5074 (Plumbing & Hydronic Heating Supplies). **Est:** 1947. **Sales:** $10,000,000 (2000). **Emp:** 30. **Officers:** Robert W. Wilkins, President; Chuck Beyer, CFO.

■ **23460** ■ **Wilkinson Supply Inc.**
PO Box 6066
Raleigh, NC 27628
Phone: (919)834-0395
E-mail: wilksup@intrex.net
Products: Plumbing supplies; Pipe; Toilets. **SIC:** 5074 (Plumbing & Hydronic Heating Supplies). **Est:** 1965. **Sales:** $18,000,000 (1999). **Emp:** 53. **Officers:** Andrew Wilkinson, President.

■ **23461** ■ **Wilmar Industries Inc.**
303 Harper Dr.
Moorestown, NJ 08057
Phone: (609)439-1222   **Fax:** (609)439-1333
Products: Plumbing equipment and supplies; Electrical equipment and supplies; Janitorial equipment and supplies; Hardware. **SICs:** 5074 (Plumbing & Hydronic Heating Supplies); 5169 (Chemicals & Allied Products Nec); 5072 (Hardware); 5198 (Paints, Varnishes & Supplies). **Sales:** $150,800,000 (2000). **Emp:** 764. **Officers:** William S. Green, CEO, President & Chairman of the Board; Michael T. Toomey, CFO & Treasurer.

■ **23462** ■ **Win Nelson Inc.**
420 Byrd St.
Little Rock, AR 72203
Phone: (501)376-1327
Products: Faucets; Sinks; Bathtubs. **SIC:** 5074 (Plumbing & Hydronic Heating Supplies). **Est:** 1884. **Sales:** $6,000,000 (2000). **Emp:** 17. **Officers:** B. Kim Emerson, President.

■ **23463** ■ **Winnelson Inc.**
3110 Kettering Blvd.
Dayton, OH 45439
Phone: (937)294-7242   **Fax:** (937)294-6921
Products: Plumbing supplies. **SIC:** 5074 (Plumbing &

Hydronic Heating Supplies). **Est:** 1958. **Sales:** $500,000,000 (2000). **Emp:** 1,050. **Officers:** Jack D. Osenbaugh, President; Michael L. Creech, Vice President; John C. Lapour, Secretary; Jack W. Johnston, Treasurer. **Former Name:** Win Nelson Inc.

■ **23464** ■ **Wisconsin Supply Corp.**
PO Box 8124
Madison, WI 53708-8124
Phone: (608)222-7799
Free: (800)236-9795   **Fax:** (608)223-6621
Products: Furnaces, air conditioners, heaters, kitchen cabinets and plumbing products; Home furnishings and floor coverings. **SICs:** 5074 (Plumbing & Hydronic Heating Supplies); 5075 (Warm Air Heating & Air-Conditioning). **Sales:** $40,000,000 (2000). **Emp:** 150. **Officers:** Phil Durst, President; Mike Reilly, CFO.

■ **23465** ■ **Wittock Supply Co.**
2201 E Industrial Dr.
Iron Mountain, MI 49801-1466
Phone: (906)774-4455
Products: Plumbing products; Electrical products. **SICs:** 5074 (Plumbing & Hydronic Heating Supplies); 5063 (Electrical Apparatus & Equipment). **Est:** 1950. **Sales:** $24,000,000 (2000). **Emp:** 80. **Officers:** D.E. Duff, President; G.E. Anderson, Treasurer.

■ **23466** ■ **Wolff Brothers Supply Inc.**
6078 Wolff Rd.
Medina, OH 44256
Phone: (330)725-3451
Free: (800)879-6533   **Fax:** (330)723-3721
E-mail: wolffbros@wolffbros.com
URL: http://www.wolffbros.com
Products: Plumbing equipment; Electrical and lightning; HVAC equipment; Tools and fasteners; Cabinets. **SICs:** 5074 (Plumbing & Hydronic Heating Supplies); 5063 (Electrical Apparatus & Equipment); 5075 (Warm Air Heating & Air-Conditioning). **Est:** 1965. **Sales:** $80,000,000 (2000). **Emp:** 250. **Officers:** Howard Wolff, CEO; George Wolff, President of Sales; Ken Wolff, President of Purchasing; Jeff Wolff, President of Accounts Receivable; Irene Hill, Sec. & Treas.; Mike Huttinger, President.

■ **23467** ■ **World Wide Metric, Inc.**
67 Veronica Ave.
Somerset, NJ 08873
Phone: (732)247-2300   **Fax:** (732)247-7258
E-mail: info@worldwidemetric.com
URL: http://www.worldwidemetric.com
Products: Valves, tubing, and fittings. **SIC:** 5074 (Plumbing & Hydronic Heating Supplies). **Sales:** $7,000,000 (2000). **Emp:** 19.

■ **23468** ■ **Yaun Company Inc.**
17 Commercial Rd.
Albany, NY 12205
Phone: (518)438-6433   **Fax:** (518)438-6435
E-mail: yaunco@yaunco.com
URL: http://www.yaunco.com
Products: Plumbing supplies, including sinks, faucets, and steel pipes; Electrical supplies; Air conditioning supplies; Heating supplies; Sheet metal; Radiant heating. **SICs:** 5074 (Plumbing & Hydronic Heating Supplies); 5063 (Electrical Apparatus & Equipment); 5075 (Warm Air Heating & Air-Conditioning); 5085 (Industrial Supplies). **Est:** 1923. **Sales:** $8,000,000 (2000). **Emp:** 43. **Officers:** Richard Yaun Jr., CEO; D. Yaun, Controller; A. Willi, President; Larry Richardson, VP of Sales & Service.

■ **23469** ■ **York Corrugating Co.**
PO Box 1192
York, PA 17405
Phone: (717)845-3511   **Fax:** (717)854-0193
Products: Stampings; Fenders; Plumbing and heating supplies. **SICs:** 5074 (Plumbing & Hydronic Heating Supplies); 5013 (Motor Vehicle Supplies & New Parts); 5075 (Warm Air Heating & Air-Conditioning). **Est:** 1902. **Sales:** $18,000,000 (2000). **Emp:** 150. **Officers:** Kim P. Raub, President; Thomas R. Miller, Vice President.

■ **23470** ■ **Yuma Winnelson Co.**
PO Box 709
Yuma, AZ 85365
Phone: (520)341-1993   **Fax:** (520)782-3221
Products: Industrial plumbing, including plumbing supplies and water works. **SIC:** 5074 (Plumbing & Hydronic Heating Supplies).

(45) Railroad Equipment and Supplies

Entries in this section are arranged alphabetically by company name. When the company name is a personal name, the company name is alphabetized by the surname unless the first name or initial(s) are part of a trade name. See the User's Guide at the front of this directory for additional information.

■ 23471 ■ **A and K Railroad Materials Inc.**
PO Box 30076
Salt Lake City, UT 84130
Phone: (801)974-5484
Free: (800)453-8812 **Fax:** (801)972-2041
URL: http://www.akrailroad.com
Products: New and used railroad materials and supplies. **SIC:** 5088 (Transportation Equipment & Supplies). **Est:** 1966. **Sales:** $100,000,000 (1999). **Emp:** 480. **Officers:** Kern Schumacher, Chairman of the Board; Ray Yamasaki, CFO; David E. Muirbrook, VP of Marketing, e-mail: dmuirbro@akrailroad.com; Bruce Skousen, Asst. Controller, e-mail: bskousen@akrailroad.com; Morris Kulmer, President; John L. Boisdore, VP of Sales.

■ 23472 ■ **Atlantic Track and Turnout Co.**
PO Box 1589
Bloomfield, NJ 07003
Phone: (973)748-5885
Free: (800)631-1274 **Fax:** (973)748-4520
E-mail: info@atlantictrack.com
URL: http://www.atlantictrack.com
Products: Train track; Crane rail and accessories. **SICs:** 5088 (Transportation Equipment & Supplies); 5051 (Metals Service Centers & Offices). **Sales:** $15,000,000 (2000). **Emp:** 45. **Officers:** Peter Hughes, President, e-mail: peterh@atlantictrack.com.

■ 23473 ■ **Atlas Railroad Construction Co.**
PO Box 8
Eighty Four, PA 15330
Phone: (724)228-4500 **Fax:** (724)228-3183
URL: http://www.atlasrailroad.com
Products: Railroad equipment. **SIC:** 5088 (Transportation Equipment & Supplies). **Est:** 1954. **Sales:** $20,000,000 (2000). **Emp:** 250. **Officers:** William M. Stout, President; William Kerns, CFO.

■ 23474 ■ **Birmingham Rail Locomotive Company Inc.**
PO Box 530157
Birmingham, AL 35253
Phone: (205)424-7245
Free: (800)241-2260 **Fax:** (205)424-7436
URL: http://www.bhamrail.com
Products: Railroad materials, including rails, track spikes, and fastenings; Rebuilt locomotives; New and reconditioned locomotive parts; Locomotive maintenance. **SIC:** 5088 (Transportation Equipment & Supplies). **Est:** 1899. **Sales:** $25,000,000 (2000). **Emp:** 75. **Officers:** Monroe Jones, President; Carlisle Jones Jr., Sales/Marketing Contact; Jane Tingle, Customer Service Contact; Johanna Dunn, Human Resources Contact; Joann Cary, General Mgr.

■ 23475 ■ **Burningtons, Inc.**
824 Laramie Ave.
Alliance, NE 69301-2952
Phone: (308)762-8716 **Fax:** (308)762-8717
E-mail: burningt@btigate.com
URL: http://www.burningtons.com
Products: Parts for railroad, locomotive, and mining equipment. **SICs:** 5088 (Transportation Equipment & Supplies); 5082 (Construction & Mining Machinery).

Est: 1982. **Sales:** $3,000,000 (2000). **Emp:** 6. **Officers:** David T. Burnett, President.

■ 23476 ■ **Consolidated Asset Management Company Inc.**
PO Box 600
Grain Valley, MO 64029-0600
Phone: (660)226-8985
Products: Railroad signal and crossing components. **SIC:** 5088 (Transportation Equipment & Supplies). **Sales:** $17,700,000 (1993). **Emp:** 20. **Officers:** J. Randall John, President; Rebecca Davis, Accountant.

■ 23477 ■ **DIFCO Inc.**
PO Box 238
Findlay, OH 45839-0238
Phone: (419)422-0525 **Fax:** (419)422-1275
Products: Railroad cars and parts. **SIC:** 5088 (Transportation Equipment & Supplies). **Est:** 1915. **Sales:** $38,000,000 (2000). **Emp:** 130. **Officers:** Wayne Westlake, CEO; John Murray, Exec. VP; Robert Ward, Exec. VP of Sales.

■ 23478 ■ **GATX Corp.**
500 W Monroe St.
Chicago, IL 60661-3676
Phone: (312)621-6200
Free: (800)428-8161 **Fax:** (312)621-6698
URL: http://www.gatx.com
Products: Railroad tank cars. **SIC:** 5088 (Transportation Equipment & Supplies). **Est:** 1898. **Sales:** $17,000,000,000 (2000). **Emp:** 5,999. **Officers:** Ronald H. Zech, CEO, President & Chairman of the Board; David M. Edwards, VP & CFO; William L. Chambers, VP of Human Resources.

■ 23479 ■ **Gregg Company Ltd.**
15 Dyatt Pl.
Hackensack, NJ 07601
Phone: (201)489-2440 **Fax:** (201)592-0282
Products: Passenger and freight train cars and components, including wheels, axles, and hand brakes. **SIC:** 5088 (Transportation Equipment & Supplies). **Officers:** Richard T. Gregg, Chairman of the Board.

■ 23480 ■ **Gross and Janes Co.**
PO Box 26113
Fenton, MO 63026
Phone: (314)241-9170
Products: Railroad ties. **SIC:** 5088 (Transportation Equipment & Supplies). **Est:** 1938. **Sales:** $8,000,000 (2000). **Emp:** 25. **Officers:** John Sexton, President; R.S. McBride, Controller.

■ 23481 ■ **Industry-Railway Suppliers Inc.**
811 Golf Ln.
Bensenville, IL 60106
Phone: (630)766-5708 **Fax:** (630)766-0017
E-mail: sales@industryrailway.com
Products: Railroad equipment and supplies; Hand tools. **SICs:** 5088 (Transportation Equipment & Supplies); 5072 (Hardware). **Est:** 1988. **Sales:** $20,000,000 (2000). **Emp:** 30. **Officers:** Ron Hobbs, President; Bob Holden, Treasurer.

■ 23482 ■ **ITG, Inc.**
PO Box 1777
Victoria, TX 77902
Phone: (512)573-4378 **Fax:** (512)573-6452
Products: Locomotives and parts; Railroad freight cars. **SIC:** 5088 (Transportation Equipment & Supplies). **Officers:** Michael Sagebiel, President.

■ 23483 ■ **Landis Rail Fastening Systems Inc.**
PO Box 638
Los Altos, CA 94022
Phone: (650)948-3557 **Fax:** (650)941-0369
Products: Rails and accessories; Railroad equipment and supplies. **SIC:** 5088 (Transportation Equipment & Supplies). **Est:** 1975. **Sales:** $2,000,000 (2000). **Emp:** 7. **Officers:** R.J. Quigley, President.

■ 23484 ■ **Midland Reclamation Co.**
RR 2 Box 100
Dow, IL 62022-9613
Phone: (618)885-5494 **Fax:** (618)885-5346
URL: http://www.midlandrailway.com
Products: Railroad freight car parts. **SIC:** 5088 (Transportation Equipment & Supplies). **Est:** 1925. **Sales:** $1,000,000 (2000). **Emp:** 15. **Officers:** John Ferenbach, President.

■ 23485 ■ **Molly Corp.**
103 N Village Rd.
Ogunquit, ME 03907
Phone: (207)646-5908
Products: Buses and railroad cars. **SIC:** 5088 (Transportation Equipment & Supplies).

■ 23486 ■ **Rails Co.**
101 Newark Way
Maplewood, NJ 07040
Phone: (201)763-4320 **Fax:** (201)763-2585
Products: Railroad maintenance equipment, including switch heaters, snow detectors, and de-icers. **SICs:** 5088 (Transportation Equipment & Supplies); 5063 (Electrical Apparatus & Equipment). **Est:** 1932. **Sales:** $4,700,000 (2000). **Emp:** 35. **Officers:** G.N. Burwell, President; M. Kinda, Treasurer; Todd Burwell, Dir. of Information Systems.

■ 23487 ■ **Railway Services International**
38 Sheffield Rd.
Gansevoort, NY 12831
Phone: (518)584-9407 **Fax:** (518)484-9241
E-mail: alcospares@hotmail.com
Products: Locomotive and marine diesel engine parts. **SIC:** 5088 (Transportation Equipment & Supplies). **Est:** 1978. **Sales:** $500,000 (2000). **Emp:** 3. **Officers:** Paul Legac, President.

■ 23488 ■ **Transco Products Inc.**
55 E Jackson Blvd.
Chicago, IL 60604
Phone: (312)427-2818 **Fax:** (312)427-4975
Products: Railroad car parts. **SIC:** 5088 (Transportation Equipment & Supplies). **Est:** 1936. **Sales:** $11,000,000 (2000). **Emp:** 230. **Officers:** Robert M. Goss, President; Ellen Smith, Controller; Jim Coonan, Dir. of Marketing & Sales.

(46) Recreational and Sporting Goods

Entries in this section are arranged alphabetically by company name. When the company name is a personal name, the company name is alphabetized by the surname unless the first name or initial(s) are part of a trade name. See the User's Guide at the front of this directory for additional information.

■ **23489** ■ **3 GI Athletics Inc.**
9037 14th Ave. NW
Seattle, WA 98117
Phone: (206)782-5860 **Fax:** (206)783-0888
Products: Team sporting goods, including football and baseball. **SIC:** 5091 (Sporting & Recreational Goods). **Est:** 1946. **Sales:** $1,200,000 (2000). **Emp:** 19. **Officers:** George LaMaine Sr., President; K. Cope, Controller.

■ **23490** ■ **ABA Enterprise Inc.**
PO Box 3424
Bartlesville, OK 74006-3424
Phone: (918)333-0941
Products: Sporting and recreation goods, including fitness and exercise equipment and supplies. **SIC:** 5091 (Sporting & Recreational Goods). **Officers:** John Anthony, President.

■ **23491** ■ **Access Bicycle Components Inc.**
3838 N 36th Ave.
Phoenix, AZ 85019-3214
Phone: (602)278-5506 **Fax:** (602)278-5507
Products: Sporting and athletic goods; Bicycle parts; Bicycle tires and tubes. **SICs:** 5091 (Sporting & Recreational Goods); 5014 (Tires & Tubes). **Officers:** Robert Hinkle, President.

■ **23492** ■ **Accu-Care Supply, Inc.**
95 Hathaway Ctr., H-36
Providence, RI 02907
Phone: (401)785-9577 **Fax:** (401)785-9577
Products: Pool equipment and supplies. **SIC:** 5091 (Sporting & Recreational Goods).

■ **23493** ■ **Action Sports of Edmond**
1601 S Broadway St.
Edmond, OK 73013-4037
Phone: (405)340-1680 **Fax:** (405)340-1681
Products: Sporting and athletic goods. **SIC:** 5091 (Sporting & Recreational Goods). **Est:** 1981. **Officers:** Janice Dove, President; Alan Dove, Treasurer & Secty.

■ **23494** ■ **AcuSport Corp.**
One Hunter Pl.
Bellefontaine, OH 43311-3001
Phone: (937)593-7010 **Fax:** (937)592-2595
E-mail: acusport@acusport.com
URL: http://www.acusport.com
Products: Outdoor and shooting sports products. **SIC:** 5091 (Sporting & Recreational Goods). **Est:** 1965. **Sales:** $204,000,000 (2000). **Emp:** 166. **Officers:** William L. Fraim, President; David K. Ray, VP of Finance & Admin.; F. Hewitt Grant, VP of Operations; Hewitt Grant, VP of Operations.

■ **23495** ■ **Adams & Durvin Marine Inc.**
5607 Mechanicsville Pke.
Mechanicsville, VA 23111-1218
Phone: (804)746-5930 **Fax:** (804)746-8576
Products: Sporting and recreational goods, including boats, canoes, watercrafts, and equipment. **SIC:** 5091 (Sporting & Recreational Goods). **Officers:** A. Godsey, President.

■ **23496** ■ **Agee's Sporting Goods**
PO Box 755
Murfreesboro, TN 37133-0755
Phone: (615)896-1272
Products: Sporting and athletic goods. **SIC:** 5091 (Sporting & Recreational Goods). **Officers:** L. Agee, Owner.

■ **23497** ■ **Agri Volt & Cabinet Co.**
PO Box 767
Carroll, IA 51401-0767
Phone: (712)792-3376
Free: (800)369-2580 **Fax:** (712)792-2427
Products: Sporting and recreational goods; Fitness equipment and supplies; Hot tubs. **SIC:** 5091 (Sporting & Recreational Goods). **Officers:** Paul Schaben, Owner.

■ **23498** ■ **Ajay Leisure Products Inc.**
1501 E Wisconsin St.
Delavan, WI 53115
Phone: (414)728-5521 **Fax:** (414)728-8119
URL: http://www.usgolfshop.com
Products: Golf bags; Golf carts; Golf accessories, including gloves. **SIC:** 5091 (Sporting & Recreational Goods). **Est:** 1989. **Sales:** $25,000,000 (2000). **Emp:** 200. **Officers:** Chuck Yahn; Duane Stiverson; Rob Appel, Sales/Marketing Contact, e-mail: rfa-ajay@pensys.com; Jackie Sargent, Customer Service Contact; Bettie Peters, Human Resources Contact.

■ **23499** ■ **Albany Bowling Supply Inc.**
PO Box 3346
Albany, GA 31706-3346
Phone: (912)435-8751
Products: Sporting and athletic goods; Bowling equipment. **SIC:** 5091 (Sporting & Recreational Goods). **Officers:** Lawrence Simpson, Treasurer.

■ **23500** ■ **Albuquerque Balloon Center**
523 Rankin Rd. NE
Albuquerque, NM 87107-2238
Phone: (505)344-5844 **Fax:** (505)344-9716
E-mail: aerco@rt66.com
URL: http://www.rt66.com/~aerco
Products: Hot air balloons; Banners; Contract fabric piece sewing; Upholstery; Parachutes. **SICs:** 5091 (Sporting & Recreational Goods); 5131 (Piece Goods & Notions). **Est:** 1983. **Sales:** $1,000,000 (2000). **Emp:** 11. **Officers:** George Hahn, President.

■ **23501** ■ **Alexander & Townsend**
507 N Mur Len Rd., Ste. A
Olathe, KS 66062-1267
Phone: (913)829-3266 **Fax:** (913)829-3285
Products: Sporting and athletic goods. **SIC:** 5091 (Sporting & Recreational Goods). **Officers:** James Townsend, Owner.

■ **23502** ■ **Algoma Net Co.**
1525 Mueller St.
Algoma, WI 54201
Phone: (920)487-5577 **Fax:** (920)487-2852
E-mail: algomanet@itol.com
Products: Cast and wrought iron hammocks; Sporting and athletic goods. **SICs:** 5091 (Sporting &

Recreational Goods); 5021 (Furniture). **Est:** 1902. **Sales:** $10,000,000 (2000). **Emp:** 150. **Officers:** A.L. Kotler, President; James Westrich, General Mgr.

■ **23503** ■ **All American Pool N Patio**
2021 Curry Ford Rd.
Orlando, FL 32806-2419
Phone: (407)898-8722 **Fax:** (407)898-8743
Products: Pools, patios, and supplies. **SICs:** 5091 (Sporting & Recreational Goods); 5031 (Lumber, Plywood & Millwork). **Emp:** 23. **Officers:** Robert Ewald; Robin Ewald Joyner; Patricia Ewald.

■ **23504** ■ **All Quality Builders**
47-237 Kam Hwy.
Kaneohe, HI 96744
Phone: (808)247-4245 **Fax:** (808)239-4321
Products: Sporting and athletic goods. **SIC:** 5091 (Sporting & Recreational Goods).

■ **23505** ■ **All Star Sports Inc.**
7321 42nd Ave. N
Minneapolis, MN 55427-1317
Phone: (612)535-3312 **Fax:** (612)535-4984
Products: Sporting and athletic goods. **SIC:** 5091 (Sporting & Recreational Goods). **Officers:** Jerry Norman, President; Mark Norman, Vice President.

■ **23506** ■ **Allied Cycle Distributors Inc.**
PO Box 430
Waltham, MA 02454-0430
Phone: (781)899-3571
Free: (800)233-2453 **Fax:** (781)647-7876
Products: Sporting and athletic goods; Bicycles and parts. **SIC:** 5091 (Sporting & Recreational Goods). **Officers:** Guy Tropeano, President.

■ **23507** ■ **Alpine Slide of Jackson Hole**
PO Box SKI
Jackson, WY 83001-1846
Phone: (307)733-7680 **Fax:** (307)733-0345
Products: Sporting and recreation goods; Watersports equipment and supplies; Water slides for recreational parks. **SIC:** 5091 (Sporting & Recreational Goods). **Officers:** James Peck, Manager.

■ **23508** ■ **American Camper**
14760 Santa Fe Tr. Dr.
Lenexa, KS 66215
Phones: (913)492-3200 800-255-6061
Fax: (913)492-8749
Products: Camping equipment. **SIC:** 5091 (Sporting & Recreational Goods). **Est:** 1946. **Sales:** $60,000,000 (2000). **Emp:** 130. **Officers:** Dave Kern, CEO; Bryan Sanderlin, VP of Finance.

■ **23509** ■ **American Exercise & Fitness Equipment Co.**
23966 Freeway Park Dr.
Farmington Hills, MI 48335-2816
Phone: (248)476-4017
Free: (800)929-1260 **Fax:** (248)476-2450
Products: Fitness equipment and supplies. **SIC:** 5091 (Sporting & Recreational Goods). **Est:** 1977. **Officers:** Bob Montgomery, President.

■ 23510 ■ American Fitness Products Inc.
623 Shallcross Lake Rd.
Middletown, DE 19709-9440
Phone: (302)378-2997
Free: (800)333-1255 **Fax:** (302)378-8136
Products: Sporting and recreational goods; Fitness equipment and supplies; Exercise equipment. **SIC:** 5091 (Sporting & Recreational Goods). **Officers:** Kenneth Billings, President.

■ 23511 ■ American Outdoor Sports
2040 Broad Hollow Rd.
Farmingdale, NY 11735
Phone: (516)249-1832 **Fax:** (516)249-3045
Products: Sports equipment. **SIC:** 5091 (Sporting & Recreational Goods). **Est:** 1971. **Emp:** 15.

■ 23512 ■ American Pool Supply Inc.
4195 Pioneer Ave.
Las Vegas, NV 89102-8225
Phone: (702)876-1634 **Fax:** (702)877-1468
Products: Watersports equipment and supplies; Swimming pool equipment and supplies. **SIC:** 5091 (Sporting & Recreational Goods). **Est:** 1970. **Sales:** $6,000,000 (2000). **Emp:** 10. **Officers:** Richard Crockett, President. **Former Name:** APF Inc.

■ 23513 ■ American Recreation Products Inc.
1224 Fern Ridge Park Way
St. Louis, MO 63141
Phone: (314)576-8000
Free: (800)325-4121 **Fax:** (314)576-8072
Products: Sporting goods. **SIC:** 5091 (Sporting & Recreational Goods). **Sales:** $160,000,000 (2000). **Emp:** 600. **Officers:** George J. Grabner Jr., President; Allen Good, VP of Finance.

■ 23514 ■ American Tennis Courts Inc.
163 N Florida St.
Mobile, AL 36607-3009
Phone: (205)476-4714 **Fax:** (205)476-4723
Products: Tennis and racquet ball equipment. **SIC:** 5091 (Sporting & Recreational Goods). **Officers:** James Hasser, President.

■ 23515 ■ Anazeh Sands
1339 28th St. SW
Grand Rapids, MI 49509-2703
Phone: (616)538-0810
Products: Sporting and recreational goods, including billiard equipment and supplies. **SIC:** 5091 (Sporting & Recreational Goods). **Officers:** Scott Wellman, Owner.

■ 23516 ■ Earl F. Andersen Inc.
9808 James Cir.
Bloomington, MN 55431
Phone: (612)884-7300
Free: (800)862-6026 **Fax:** (612)884-5619
Products: Playground equipment; Traffic equipment, including signs, cones, flashers, and sandbags. **SICs:** 5046 (Commercial Equipment Nec); 5099 (Durable Goods Nec). **Est:** 1971. **Sales:** $4,000,000 (2000). **Emp:** 22. **Officers:** Ross Johnson, President.

■ 23517 ■ Anderson Bait Distributors
4569 Hwy. 120
Duluth, GA 30026
Phone: (404)476-2461 **Fax:** (404)497-1796
Products: Sporting and athletic goods; Fishing tackle and equipment. **SIC:** 5091 (Sporting & Recreational Goods). **Officers:** Jimmy Anderson, President.

■ 23518 ■ Anderson Recreational Design, Inc.
PO Box 465
Medina, OH 44258
Phone: (330)722-8804
Free: (800)232-7529 **Fax:** (330)723-2356
E-mail: info@ar-design.com
URL: http://www.ar-design.com
Products: Sporting and athletic goods; Playground equipment, including waterslides; scoreboards, shelters, bleachers, site amenities, and safety surfacing. **SIC:** 5091 (Sporting & Recreational Goods).

■ 23519 ■ R.E. Anson & Co.
484 Westfield Rd.
Alpine, UT 84004-1501
Phone: (801)756-5221
Products: Sporting and athletic goods. **SIC:** 5091 (Sporting & Recreational Goods). **Officers:** R. Anson, Owner.

■ 23520 ■ Aqua Dream Pools Inc.
7 Main St.
Plaistow, NH 03865-3002
Phone: (603)382-4900
Products: Sporting and recreation goods, including watersports equipment and supplies and swimming pools, equipment, and supplies. **SIC:** 5091 (Sporting & Recreational Goods). **Officers:** Ronald Charette, President.

■ 23521 ■ Aquajogger
PO Box 1453
Eugene, OR 97440
Phone: (541)484-2454
Free: (800)922-9544 **Fax:** (541)484-0501
E-mail: info@aquajogger.com
URL: http://www.aquajogger.com
Products: Aquatic exercise equipment; Nutritional supplements. **SICs:** 5091 (Sporting & Recreational Goods); 5122 (Drugs, Proprietaries & Sundries). **Est:** 1984. **Sales:** $2,000,000 (1999). **Emp:** 15. **Officers:** Roger Langenberg, President; Jim Spencer, Controller; Linda Gosch, East Coast Sales Director; Steve Bergstrom, West Coast Sales Director & Intl. Sales; Niki Howard, Asst. to the President & Dir. of PR. **Former Name:** Excel Sports Science Inc.

■ 23522 ■ Arcadia Merchandising Corp.
PO Box 140
Millburn, NJ 07041
Phone: (973)467-2856 **Fax:** (973)912-0636
Products: Swimming pool float pads and kick boards; Pool safety markers; Stadium seating; Floats and buoys. **SICs:** 5091 (Sporting & Recreational Goods); 5021 (Furniture). **Officers:** Wes Elsawi, President.

■ 23523 ■ Arkansas Import & Distributing Co.
702 SW 8th St.
Bentonville, AR 72712-6299
Phone: (501)273-4173
Products: Sporting and recreation goods. **SIC:** 5091 (Sporting & Recreational Goods). **Officers:** David Glass, President.

■ 23524 ■ Artomate Co.
PO Box 172
Cockeysville, MD 21030-0172
Phone: (410)666-9429
Products: Sporting and athletic goods. **SIC:** 5091 (Sporting & Recreational Goods). **Officers:** John Critcher, Owner.

■ 23525 ■ Asian World of Martial Arts Inc.
917-21 Arch St.
Philadelphia, PA 19107-2477
Phone: (215)925-1161
Free: (800)345-AWMA **Fax:** (215)925-1194
Products: Martial art and boxing supplies; Books; Videos. **SICs:** 5091 (Sporting & Recreational Goods); 5192 (Books, Periodicals & Newspapers).

■ 23526 ■ Atlantic Fitness Products Co.
PO Box 300
Linthicum Heights, MD 21090-0300
Phone: (410)488-2020 **Fax:** (410)488-3059
Products: Fitness products. **SIC:** 5091 (Sporting & Recreational Goods). **Emp:** 49.

■ 23527 ■ Atlantic Pump and Equipment Co.
3055 NW 84th Ave.
Miami, FL 33122
Phone: (305)597-8300
Products: Pool pumps and supplies. **SIC:** 5084 (Industrial Machinery & Equipment).

■ 23528 ■ Atlantic Skates Inc.
12632 Sunset Ave.
Ocean City, MD 21842-9662
Phone: (410)213-0680
Free: (800)638-5562 **Fax:** (410)213-0468
Products: Sporting and athletic goods. **SIC:** 5091 (Sporting & Recreational Goods). **Officers:** Dorsey Truitt, President.

■ 23529 ■ AutoBike Inc.
108 Black Brook Rd.
South Easton, MA 02375
Phone: (508)238-9651 **Fax:** (508)238-4101
Products: Bicycles and automatic shifting bicycles. **SICs:** 5091 (Sporting & Recreational Goods); 5012 (Automobiles & Other Motor Vehicles).

■ 23530 ■ Avis Enterprises Inc.
900 Avis Dr.
Ann Arbor, MI 48108
Phone: (313)761-2800 **Fax:** (313)996-4440
Products: Sporting goods. **SIC:** 5091 (Sporting & Recreational Goods). **Est:** 1966. **Sales:** $25,000,000 (2000). **Emp:** 50. **Officers:** Patricia Kalmbach, CEO; Pam Totten, Controller.

■ 23531 ■ Avon North America Inc.
805 W 13th St.
Cadillac, MI 49601-9281
Phone: (616)775-1345 **Fax:** (616)775-7304
Products: Sporting and recreational goods, including boats, canoes, watercrafts, and equipment. **SIC:** 5091 (Sporting & Recreational Goods). **Officers:** Donald Samardich, President.

■ 23532 ■ Babco International Inc.
PO Box 27187
Tucson, AZ 85726-7187
Phone: (520)628-7596 **Fax:** (520)628-9622
Products: Sporting and recreational goods; Military supplies; Household supplies. **SICs:** 5091 (Sporting & Recreational Goods); 5023 (Homefurnishings). **Officers:** Patrick Brodecky, President.

■ 23533 ■ Bacharach-Rasin Co.
802 Gleneagles Ct.
Towson, MD 21204
Phone: (410)825-6747 **Fax:** (410)321-0720
Products: Sporting goods, including clothing and protective equipment. **SIC:** 5091 (Sporting & Recreational Goods). **Est:** 1917. **Sales:** $2,500,000 (2000). **Emp:** 30. **Officers:** Christopher Hutchins, President; Priscilla Broccalo, Secretary.

■ 23534 ■ Bacon Creek Gun Shop
1205 Cumberland Falls Hwy.
Corbin, KY 40701-2718
Phone: (606)528-4860 **Fax:** (606)523-0620
Products: Hunting equipment; Firearms. **SIC:** 5091 (Sporting & Recreational Goods). **Officers:** Thomas Elliott, Partner.

■ 23535 ■ Badger Shooters Supply Inc.
PO Box 397
Owen, WI 54460
Phone: (715)229-2101
Free: (800)424-9069 **Fax:** (715)229-2332
Products: Sporting goods, including hunting supplies. **SIC:** 5091 (Sporting & Recreational Goods). **Est:** 1935. **Sales:** $3,000,000 (2000). **Emp:** 7. **Officers:** Tim L. Bulgrin, President.

■ 23536 ■ Baja Products Ltd.
515 Airport Rd.
Salisbury, NC 28144-8446
Phone: (704)633-0498 **Fax:** (704)633-5058
Products: Hot tubs. **SIC:** 5091 (Sporting & Recreational Goods). **Sales:** $1,000,000 (2000). **Emp:** 49. **Officers:** Bruce Kolkebeck.

■ 23537 ■ Baker Hydro Inc.
1812 Tobacco Rd.
Augusta, GA 30906
Phone: (706)793-7291 **Fax:** (706)796-3776
Products: Pool filters. **SIC:** 5091 (Sporting & Recreational Goods). **Sales:** $5,500,000 (2000). **Emp:** 49. **Officers:** T. E. Peckel.

■ 23538 ■ Barker & Co.
7745 E Redfield, Ste. 100
Scottsdale, AZ 85260
Phone: (602)483-0780 **Fax:** (602)483-0780
Products: Sporting and recreational goods, including golf and skiing equipment and supplies. **SIC:** 5091 (Sporting & Recreational Goods). **Officers:** Robert Barker, President.

■ **23539** ■ **Bauer Cycle Supply Inc.**
404 3rd Ave. N
Minneapolis, MN 55401
Phone: (612)333-2581
Free: (800)328-8320 **Fax:** (612)333-1738
Products: Bicycles and parts. **SIC:** 5091 (Sporting & Recreational Goods). **Est:** 1976. **Emp:** 8. **Officers:** Lowell J. Osterbauer, President.

■ **23540** ■ **Beacon Sporting Goods Inc.**
1240 Furnace Brook Pkwy.
Quincy, MA 02169-4718
Phone: (617)479-8537 **Fax:** (617)376-0655
Products: Sporting and athletic goods. **SIC:** 5091 (Sporting & Recreational Goods). **Officers:** Robert Beniers, President.

■ **23541** ■ **Beauty Pools Inc.**
2700 Transit Rd.
West Seneca, NY 14224-2523
Phone: (716)674-3500 **Fax:** (716)674-9198
Products: Swimming pools. **SIC:** 5091 (Sporting & Recreational Goods). **Emp:** 99. **Officers:** James Metz; Steven Metz; Michelle Metz; David Thill.

■ **23542** ■ **Bel-Aqua Pool Supply Inc.**
750 Main St.
New Rochelle, NY 10805
Phone: (914)235-2200
Products: Swimming pool supplies. **SIC:** 5091 (Sporting & Recreational Goods).

■ **23543** ■ **Benson Pool Systems**
800 Central Ave.
University Park, IL 60466
Phone: (708)534-0505 **Fax:** (708)534-5540
Products: Pool equipment and supplies. **SIC:** 5091 (Sporting & Recreational Goods). **Former Name:** Benson Pump Co.

■ **23544** ■ **Benson Pool Systems**
14535 Grover St.
Omaha, NE 68144
Phone: (402)330-8424 **Fax:** (402)330-8426
Products: Pool equipment and supplies. **SIC:** 5091 (Sporting & Recreational Goods).

■ **23545** ■ **Benson Pump Co.**
5390 E 39th Ave.
Denver, CO 80207
Phone: (303)322-8978 **Fax:** (303)322-5884
Products: Pool equipment and supplies. **SIC:** 5091 (Sporting & Recreational Goods).

■ **23546** ■ **Benson Pump Co.**
150 Millwell Dr.
Maryland Heights, MO 63043
Phone: (314)344-9991 **Fax:** (314)344-8121
Products: Swimming pools; Spas. **SIC:** 5091 (Sporting & Recreational Goods).

■ **23547** ■ **Benson Pump Co.**
1936 11th St.
Rockford, IL 61104
Phone: (815)964-9000 **Fax:** (815)966-3506
Products: Pool equipment and supplies. **SIC:** 5091 (Sporting & Recreational Goods).

■ **23548** ■ **Benson Pump Co.**
6885 E 34th St.
Indianapolis, IN 46226
Phone: (317)542-1091 **Fax:** (317)542-9724
Products: Pool equipment and supplies. **SIC:** 5091 (Sporting & Recreational Goods).

■ **23549** ■ **Benson Pump Co.**
13345 Merriman Rd.
Livonia, MI 48150-1815
Phone: (517)548-1010 **Fax:** (517)548-1055
Products: Pool equipment and supplies. **SIC:** 5091 (Sporting & Recreational Goods).

■ **23550** ■ **Benson Pump Co.**
2468 Louisiana Ave., N
Minneapolis, MN 55427
Phone: (612)545-5606 **Fax:** (612)545-2650
Products: Pool equipment and supplies. **SIC:** 5091 (Sporting & Recreational Goods).

■ **23551** ■ **Benson Pump Co.**
4505 McEwen
Farmers Branch, TX 75244
Phone: (972)490-3367 **Fax:** (972)490-6783
Products: Pool equipment and supplies. **SIC:** 5091 (Sporting & Recreational Goods).

■ **23552** ■ **Bicknell Distributors Inc.**
12 Parkwood Dr.
Hopkinton, MA 01748-1660
Phone: (508)435-2321 **Fax:** (508)435-4127
Products: Swimming pool products and supplies. **SIC:** 5091 (Sporting & Recreational Goods). **Est:** 1957. **Sales:** $60,000,000 (2000). **Emp:** 200. **Officers:** Jon Hulme, President; Jay Forte, Controller; Brad Smith, Marketing Mgr.

■ **23553** ■ **Bicknell Distributors, Inc.**
45 Industrial Park Rd.
Albany, NY 12206-2021
Phone: (518)489-4401 **Fax:** (518)489-5448
Products: Pool equipment and supplies. **SIC:** 5091 (Sporting & Recreational Goods).

■ **23554** ■ **Bicknell Huston Distributors**
6E Easy St.
PO Box 391
Bound Brook, NJ 08805
Phone: (732)271-1177 **Fax:** (732)271-4631
Products: Swimming pools and swimming pool equipment and supplies. **SIC:** 5091 (Sporting & Recreational Goods).

■ **23555** ■ **Bicknell Huston Distributors, Inc.**
436 Hayden Station Rd.
Windsor, CT 06095
Phone: (860)687-1437 **Fax:** (860)687-1746
Products: Pool equipment and supplies. **SIC:** 5091 (Sporting & Recreational Goods).

■ **23556** ■ **Bicknell Huston Distributors, Inc.**
520 Riverside Industrial Pky.
Portland, ME 04103
Phone: (207)878-3888 **Fax:** (207)878-3909
Products: Pool equipment and supplies. **SIC:** 5091 (Sporting & Recreational Goods).

■ **23557** ■ **Bicknell-Tidewater Inc.**
707 Industry Dr.
Hampton, VA 23661-1002
Phone: (804)826-4001
Free: (800)360-5885 **Fax:** (804)826-0240
Products: Swimming pool equipment; Gas stoves. **SIC:** 5091 (Sporting & Recreational Goods). **Est:** 1982. **Sales:** $3,000,000 (2000). **Emp:** 9. **Officers:** Vera Small, President.

■ **23558** ■ **Big Rock Sports Inc.**
Hwy. 24 W Hankinson Dr., PO Drawer 1107
Morehead City, NC 28557
Phone: (252)726-6186
Products: Sporting goods. **SIC:** 5091 (Sporting & Recreational Goods).

■ **23559** ■ **Bio-Tech Maintenance Products**
2635 S Santa Fe Dr., Unit 2A
Denver, CO 80223
Phone: (970)774-8285 **Fax:** (303)744-8336
Products: Swimming pool supplies, including maintenance products. **SIC:** 5091 (Sporting & Recreational Goods). **Officers:** Donald Bondi, President.

■ **23560** ■ **Blue Mount Quarry**
17701 Big Falls Rd.
White Hall, MD 21161-9208
Phone: (410)343-0500 **Fax:** (410)343-0524
Products: Sporting and recreational goods; Landscape products, including topsoil and compost. **SICs:** 5091 (Sporting & Recreational Goods); 5193 (Flowers & Florists' Supplies). **Officers:** Donald Matthews, President.

■ **23561** ■ **Blue Ridge Sporting Supplies**
PO Box 1537
Salem, VA 24153-0019
Phone: (540)389-1368
Free: (800)669-2471 **Fax:** (540)389-1368
Products: Sporting and athletic goods; Hunting equipment; Sporting firearms. **SIC:** 5091 (Sporting & Recreational Goods). **Officers:** Leonard Wright, Manager.

■ **23562** ■ **Bob's Business Inc.**
PO Box 35
Red Wing, MN 55066-0035
Phone: (612)388-4742 **Fax:** (612)388-4739
Products: Sporting and athletic goods; Bowling equipment. **SIC:** 5091 (Sporting & Recreational Goods). **Officers:** Robert Rehder, President.

■ **23563** ■ **Bocock-Stroud Co.**
PO Box 25746
Winston-Salem, NC 27114
Phone: (919)724-2421
Products: Sporting equipment. **SIC:** 5091 (Sporting & Recreational Goods). **Sales:** $5,000,000 (2000). **Emp:** 100. **Officers:** J.C. Wilson, President.

■ **23564** ■ **Bonitz Brothers Inc.**
931 Dana Dr.
Harrisburg, PA 17109-5937
Phone: (717)545-3754
Products: Hunting and fishing equipment. **SIC:** 5091 (Sporting & Recreational Goods). **Est:** 1968. **Sales:** $12,000,000 (2000). **Emp:** 50. **Officers:** Byer Ziomek, President.

■ **23565** ■ **Boss Hawaii Inc.**
3210 F. Koapaka St.
Honolulu, HI 96819
Phone: (808)839-1057 **Fax:** (808)839-1071
Products: Bowling equipment and supplies. **SIC:** 5091 (Sporting & Recreational Goods). **Est:** 1996. **Emp:** 8. **Officers:** Sos Tabieros, President.

■ **23566** ■ **Boswell Golf Cars, Inc.**
401 Fesslers Ln.
Nashville, TN 37210
Phone: (615)256-0737 **Fax:** (615)242-7282
Products: Golf carts. **SIC:** 5091 (Sporting & Recreational Goods).

■ **23567** ■ **Brine Inc.**
47 Sumner St.
Milford, MA 01757
Phone: (508)478-3250 **Fax:** (508)478-2430
URL: http://www.brine.com
Products: Soccer and lacrosse equipment and apparel. **SIC:** 5091 (Sporting & Recreational Goods). **Est:** 1922. **Emp:** 90. **Officers:** Bill McLean, President; Tom Pelletier, Chairman of the Board & Finance Officer; Nelson Clement, Dir. of Operations.

■ **23568** ■ **Brookfield Athletic Company**
13 Centennial Dr.
Peabody, MA 01960
Phone: (978)532-9000
Free: (800)477-6553 **Fax:** (978)532-6105
Products: In-line and roller skates; Protective gear; Licensed products. **SIC:** 5091 (Sporting & Recreational Goods). **Officers:** James Buchanan, President.

■ **23569** ■ **Brown Bear Sporting**
46853 Gratiot Ave.
Chesterfield, MI 48051
Phone: (810)949-5348 **Fax:** (810)949-3917
Products: Hunting equipment. **SIC:** 5091 (Sporting & Recreational Goods).

■ **23570** ■ **E. Arthur Brown Co.**
3404 Pawnee Dr. SE
Alexandria, MN 56308-8984
Phone: (320)762-8847 **Fax:** (320)763-4310
E-mail: orders@eabco.com
URL: http://www.eabco.com
Products: Handgun hunting equipment; Competition shooting equipment. **SIC:** 5091 (Sporting & Recreational Goods). **Est:** 1981. **Officers:** Eben Brown, Owner.

■ **23571** ■ **BSE Engineering Corp.**
986-998 Cherry St.
Fall River, MA 02720
Phone: (508)678-4419 **Fax:** (508)673-1544
Products: Sailboats; Hardware; Rigging and masts. **SICs:** 5091 (Sporting & Recreational Goods); 5072 (Hardware). **Officers:** Francis Colaneri, Treasurer.

■ 23572 ■ Buck & Bass Shop
905 Azalea Dr.
Waynesboro, MS 39367-2501
Phone: (601)735-4867
Products: Sporting and athletic goods. **SIC:** 5091 (Sporting & Recreational Goods). **Officers:** Fred Stanley, Owner.

■ 23573 ■ Buck Rub Archery Inc.
157 Bank St.
Waukesha, WI 53188
Phone: (414)547-0535
Products: Archery products, including bows and arrows. **SIC:** 5091 (Sporting & Recreational Goods). **Sales:** $2,000,000 (2000). **Emp:** 40. **Officers:** Greg Kazmierski, President.

■ 23574 ■ Buck's War Surplus
45 Lailani St.
Las Vegas, NV 89110-5110
Phone: (702)452-8076   **Fax:** (702)438-2266
Products: Army and navy surplus; Nets, including fishnetting and shade netting. **SICs:** 5091 (Sporting & Recreational Goods); 5099 (Durable Goods Nec); 5199 (Nondurable Goods Nec). **Est:** 1946. **Sales:** $400,000 (1999). **Emp:** 3. **Officers:** Harold W. Buck, Owner; Karen Luckett, Dir. of Marketing.

■ 23575 ■ Bumble Bee Wholesale
12521 Oxnard St.
North Hollywood, CA 91606
Phone: (818)985-2939   **Fax:** (818)985-6914
Products: Sporting goods. **SIC:** 5091 (Sporting & Recreational Goods). **Est:** 1968. **Sales:** $4,000,000 (2000). **Emp:** 6. **Officers:** Robert Kahn, CEO; Keith Phillips, Sales & Marketing Contact, e-mail: depart1@bnbsales.com. **Former Name:** B and B Group Inc.

■ 23576 ■ Philip Burgess
300 Union St.
Randolph, MA 02368-4930
Phone: (781)963-1710
Products: Sporting and athletic goods; Fishing tackle and equipment. **SIC:** 5091 (Sporting & Recreational Goods). **Officers:** Philip Burgess, Owner.

■ 23577 ■ Burts Sports Specialty Inc.
850 Main St.
Falmouth, MA 02540-3656
Phone: (508)540-0644   **Fax:** (508)540-6654
Products: Sporting and athletic goods. **SIC:** 5091 (Sporting & Recreational Goods). **Officers:** Jeff Burton, President.

■ 23578 ■ A. Buttross Wholesale Co.
Drawer 1206
Natchez, MS 39121-1206
Phone: (601)445-4112   **Fax:** (601)445-4277
Products: Military supplies. **SIC:** 5099 (Durable Goods Nec). **Est:** 1948. **Officers:** Alphonse Buttross, Owner.

■ 23579 ■ C & J Bait Co.
PO Box 251
Purcell, OK 73080-0251
Phone: (405)527-2586
Products: Fishing tackle and equipment; Sporting and athletic goods. **SIC:** 5091 (Sporting & Recreational Goods). **Est:** 1976. **Officers:** John Buterbaugh, Owner.

■ 23580 ■ Callaway Golf Co
2285 Rutherford Rd.
Carlsbad, CA 92008-8815
Phone: (760)931-1771   **Fax:** (760)930-5015
Products: Designs, develops and innovative golf clubs; Golf related equipment and supplies. **SIC:** 5091 (Sporting & Recreational Goods). **Sales:** $714,500,000 (1999). **Emp:** 2,252. **Officers:** Ely Callaway, CEO, President & Chairman of the Board; David Rane, CFO.

■ 23581 ■ Camfour Inc.
65 Westfield Industrial Park
Westfield, MA 01085
Phone: (413)568-3371   **Fax:** (413)568-9663
Products: Sporting goods. **SIC:** 5091 (Sporting & Recreational Goods). **Sales:** $25,000,000 (2000). **Emp:** 26. **Officers:** A.F. Ferst, President & Treasurer.

■ 23582 ■ Cariddi Sales Co.
508 State Rd.
North Adams, MA 01247-3045
Phone: (413)663-3722
Free: (800)628-0375   **Fax:** (413)663-9098
Products: Toys; Sporting and athletic goods. **SICs:** 5091 (Sporting & Recreational Goods); 5092 (Toys & Hobby Goods & Supplies). **Est:** 1936. **Sales:** $3,000,000 (2000). **Emp:** 49.

■ 23583 ■ Carolina Fisherman Supply Inc.
2507 NC Hwy. 172
Sneads Ferry, NC 28460-6637
Phone: (910)327-2560
Free: (800)682-2005   **Fax:** (910)327-2608
Products: Sports nets; Commercial fishing netting and supplies; Knives; Raingear; Twine. **SIC:** 5091 (Sporting & Recreational Goods). **Est:** 1984. **Emp:** 3. **Officers:** William Shepard, President.

■ 23584 ■ Carolina Pools & Patios
1312 W 2nd Ave.
Gastonia, NC 28052-3773
Phone: (704)865-9586   **Fax:** (704)868-3000
Products: Swimming pools and equipment; Hot tubs. **SIC:** 5091 (Sporting & Recreational Goods). **Emp:** 49. **Officers:** Dan Mitchem.

■ 23585 ■ Cassemco Sporting Goods
728 E 15th St.
PO Box 1495
Cookeville, TN 38503-1495
Phone: (931)528-6588
Free: (800)844-3626   **Fax:** (931)528-2290
E-mail: cassemco@tnaccess.com
URL: http://www.cassenco.com
Products: Automotive and commercial packaging; Chin straps. **SIC:** 5091 (Sporting & Recreational Goods). **Est:** 1975. **Sales:** $2,500,000 (1999). **Emp:** 65. **Officers:** Barbara G. Nipper; Scott Ward, Sales & Marketing Contact; Gloria J. Breen, Human Resources Contact.

■ 23586 ■ Century Sports Inc.
1995 Rutgers University Blvd.
PO Box 2035
Lakewood, NJ 08701-8035
Phone: (908)905-4422
Free: (800)526-7548   **Fax:** (908)901-7766
E-mail: centurysports@compuserve.com
Products: Tennis, racquetball, and squash equipment. **SIC:** 5091 (Sporting & Recreational Goods). **Est:** 1972. **Sales:** $15,000,000 (2000). **Emp:** 24. **Officers:** Robert Hellerson, CEO; C. Noonan, Controller; Joanne D'Angelo, Customer Service Contact.

■ 23587 ■ Champion Athletic Supply Inc.
14806 Pacific Ave. S
Tacoma, WA 98444-4655
Phone: (253)537-4204   **Fax:** (253)536-9113
Products: Sporting and athletic goods. **SIC:** 5091 (Sporting & Recreational Goods). **Est:** 1976. **Sales:** $1,000,000 (2000). **Emp:** 8. **Officers:** Scott Webster, President.

■ 23588 ■ Chattanooga Shooting Supplies
2600 Walker Rd.
Chattanooga, TN 37421
Phone: (423)894-3007   **Fax:** (423)855-5513
Products: Hunting equipment. **SIC:** 5091 (Sporting & Recreational Goods). **Officers:** John Hamn, President. **Former Name:** Spartan Supply Company Inc.

■ 23589 ■ Cheerleader Supply Co.
2010 Merritt Dr.
Garland, TX 75041
Phone: (972)840-1233   **Fax:** (972)840-4007
Products: Cheerleading supplies. **SIC:** 5091 (Sporting & Recreational Goods). **Est:** 1948. **Sales:** $25,000,000 (2000). **Emp:** 300. **Officers:** L.R. Herkimer, President; Jim Varnon, VP of Operations.

■ 23590 ■ Chesal Industries
6702 N Lake Dr.
Milwaukee, WI 53217-3620
Phone: (414)228-7920   **Fax:** (414)228-7940
Products: Golf accessories. **SIC:** 5091 (Sporting & Recreational Goods). **Sales:** $1,500,000 (2000). **Emp:** 29. **Officers:** C Pasternak.

■ 23591 ■ Chesapeake Gun Works
6644 Indian River Rd.
Virginia Beach, VA 23464
Phone: (757)420-1712
Products: Hunting equipment; Fishing tackle and equipment; Archery equipment; Sporting firearms. **SIC:** 5091 (Sporting & Recreational Goods). **Est:** 1963.

■ 23592 ■ Ely Churchich & Associates
11818 Oakair Plz.
Omaha, NE 68137-3509
Phone: (402)861-8880
Free: (888)758-8100   **Fax:** (402)861-8881
Products: Equipment for parks, playgrounds, and athletic fields. **SIC:** 5091 (Sporting & Recreational Goods). **Est:** 1966. **Emp:** 4. **Officers:** Ely Churchich, e-mail: echurchich@aol.com; Jeff Churchich.

■ 23593 ■ Churchich Recreation
7174 Four Rivers Rd.
Boulder, CO 80301
Phone: (303)530-4414
Free: (800)729-7529   **Fax:** (303)530-9239
Products: Sporting and athletic goods. **SIC:** 5091 (Sporting & Recreational Goods).

■ 23594 ■ Cinderella Inc.
1215 S Jefferson St.
Saginaw, MI 48601
Phone: (517)755-7741
Products: Pool equipment and supplies. **SIC:** 5091 (Sporting & Recreational Goods).

■ 23595 ■ Cissna's Sporting Goods Inc.
1026 Clarks Ln.
PO Box 17051
Louisville, KY 40217-0051
Phone: (502)636-1885   **Fax:** (502)636-1857
Products: Sporting and athletic goods; Trophies. **SIC:** 5091 (Sporting & Recreational Goods). **Officers:** Carl Cissna, President.

■ 23596 ■ CMT Sporting Goods Co.
3475 Brandon Ave. SW
Roanoke, VA 24018-1521
Phone: (540)343-5533
Products: Sporting goods, including clothing and equipment. **SICs:** 5091 (Sporting & Recreational Goods); 5136 (Men's/Boys' Clothing); 5137 (Women's/Children's Clothing). **Est:** 1970. **Sales:** $10,600,000 (2000). **Emp:** 158. **Officers:** B.H. Conner, President.

■ 23597 ■ Coach's Connection Inc.
PO Box 1123
Huntington, IN 46750-4138
Phone: (219)356-0400
Products: Sporting and athletic goods; Printed garments and accessories. **SICs:** 5091 (Sporting & Recreational Goods); 5136 (Men's/Boys' Clothing); 5137 (Women's/Children's Clothing). **Officers:** Janice Cunningham, President.

■ 23598 ■ Coastal Net Marine Co.
23 Battle Rd.
Brunswick, ME 04011
Phone: (207)725-1052   **Free:** (800)262-1889
Products: Boating and fishing equipment. **SIC:** 5091 (Sporting & Recreational Goods). **Est:** 1992. **Sales:** $2,000,000 (2000). **Emp:** 6. **Officers:** Ken Gray; Chris Gray.

■ 23599 ■ Collins Landing
10 Miles SW
Dent, MN 56528
Phone: (218)758-2697
Products: Sporting and athletic goods; Fishing tackle and equipment. **SIC:** 5091 (Sporting & Recreational Goods). **Officers:** Steve Collins, Partner.

■ 23600 ■ Competition Karting Inc.
PO Box 1777
Welcome, NC 27374-1777
Phone: (336)731-6111   **Fax:** (336)731-3750
Products: Sporting and athletic goods; Gocarts. **SIC:** 5091 (Sporting & Recreational Goods). **Officers:** Paul Klutz, President.

■ 23601 ■ Complete Golf Services Co.
2410 W Evans Dr.
Phoenix, AZ 85023
Phone: (602)863-1233
Free: (800)949-1109 **Fax:** (602)993-4635
Products: Golf accessories; Computer hardware and software for golf courses. **SICs:** 5091 (Sporting & Recreational Goods); 5045 (Computers, Peripherals & Software). **Est:** 1988. **Sales:** $400,000 (2000). **Emp:** 5. **Officers:** Ron J. Turk, President.

■ 23602 ■ Compool Corp.
599 Fairchild Dr.
Mountain View, CA 94043
Phone: (650)964-2201 **Fax:** (650)964-5429
Products: Pool equipment and supplies; Special purpose computers. **SICs:** 5091 (Sporting & Recreational Goods); 5045 (Computers, Peripherals & Software). **Sales:** $4,000,000 (2000). **Emp:** 25. **Officers:** Peter Bajka.

■ 23603 ■ Consumer Direct Inc.
1375 Raff Rd. SW
Canton, OH 44750
Phone: (330)478-0755
Products: Exercise equipment. **SIC:** 5091 (Sporting & Recreational Goods).

■ 23604 ■ Continental Sports Supply Inc.
PO Box 1251
Englewood, CO 80150
Phone: (303)934-5657 **Fax:** (303)934-5725
Products: Inflatable athletic balls; Athletic footwear; Athletic goods; Team uniforms. **SICs:** 5091 (Sporting & Recreational Goods); 5139 (Footwear). **Est:** 1977. **Emp:** 23. **Officers:** David Banning, President.

■ 23605 ■ Coosa Co. Inc.
PO Box 367
Rome, GA 30162-0367
Phone: (706)291-0199
Products: Sporting and athletic goods; Fishing tackle and equipment. **SIC:** 5091 (Sporting & Recreational Goods). **Officers:** J. Nichols, President.

■ 23606 ■ Cormans Sporting Goods
PO Box 144
Stanford, KY 40484-0144
Phone: (606)365-2463
Products: Sporting and athletic goods; Black powder. **SIC:** 5091 (Sporting & Recreational Goods). **Est:** 1981. **Sales:** $500,000 (1999). **Emp:** 5. **Officers:** Shannon Corman, Owner.

■ 23607 ■ Cortland Line Company Inc.
3736 Kellogg
Cortland, NY 13045
Phone: (607)756-2851 **Fax:** (607)753-8835
E-mail: info@cortlandline.com
URL: http://www.cortland.com
Products: Fishing lines; Braided and extruded industrial lines. **SICs:** 5091 (Sporting & Recreational Goods); 5091 (Sporting & Recreational Goods). **Est:** 1915. **Sales:** $9,000,000 (2000). **Emp:** 100. **Officers:** Brian P. Ward, CEO; Paul G. Corriveau, VP of Business Development.

■ 23608 ■ Counter Assault
120 Industry Ct.
Kalispell, MT 59901
Phone: (406)257-4740
Free: (800)695-3394 **Fax:** (406)257-6674
E-mail: counter@bigsky.net
URL: http://www.counterassault.com
Products: Self-defense pepper spray; Grizzly bear deterrent. **SICs:** 5091 (Sporting & Recreational Goods); 5169 (Chemicals & Allied Products Nec). **Est:** 1986. **Emp:** 6. **Officers:** Kirsten Johnson, CFO; Pride Johnson, President.

■ 23609 ■ Coyote Engineering, Inc.
11555 27th Ave. NE
Seattle, WA 98125-5341
Phone: (206)363-5047 **Fax:** (206)361-2353
Products: Sporting goods. **SIC:** 5091 (Sporting & Recreational Goods). **Officers:** Val Albert Kiefer, President.

■ 23610 ■ Cressi-Sub USA Inc.
10 Reuten Dr.
Closter, NJ 07624
Phone: (201)784-1005
Products: Scuba diving wet suits and equipment. **SIC:** 5091 (Sporting & Recreational Goods).

■ 23611 ■ CSI Sports, LLC
360 Industrial Blvd.
Sauk Rapids, MN 56379
Phone: (320)252-4193
Free: (800)328-7087 **Fax:** (320)252-7177
Products: Sporting and athletic goods. **SIC:** 5091 (Sporting & Recreational Goods). **Est:** 1963. **Sales:** $50,000,000 (2000). **Emp:** 125. **Officers:** Al Dehler, General Mgr.

■ 23612 ■ Custom Design Play Structures Inc.
444 Winnebago Dr.
Lake Winnebago, MO 64034
Phone: (816)537-7171 **Fax:** (816)537-8088
Products: Park and playground equipment. **SIC:** 5091 (Sporting & Recreational Goods). **Est:** 1962. **Sales:** $2,000,000 (2000). **Emp:** 2. **Officers:** Craig L. Freerksen, e-mail: craig.l.f.@worldnet.att.net.

■ 23613 ■ Daiwa Corp.
PO Box 6031
Artesia, CA 90702-6031
Phone: (562)802-9589 **Fax:** (562)404-6212
Products: Fishing equipment. **SIC:** 5091 (Sporting & Recreational Goods). **Former Name:** Daiwa Golf Co.

■ 23614 ■ Darton Archery
3540 Darton Dr.
Hale, MI 48739-9003
Phone: (517)728-4231 **Fax:** (517)728-2410
E-mail: darton@centuryinter.net
URL: http://www.dartonarchery.com
Products: Bows and archery accessories, including compound bows, traditional bows, and crossbows. **SIC:** 5091 (Sporting & Recreational Goods). **Est:** 1950. **Sales:** $6,000,000 (2000). **Emp:** 50. **Officers:** Rex F. Darlington, VP & General Mgr.; Bruce Plude, Director of Purchasing; Ron Pittsley, Sales Mgr.

■ 23615 ■ Dave's Sport Shop
23701 Nantocoke Rd.
Quantico, MD 21856
Phone: (410)742-2454 **Fax:** (410)742-0158
Products: Hunting equipment; Fishing tackle and equipment. **SIC:** 5091 (Sporting & Recreational Goods).

■ 23616 ■ Dayman USA Inc.
1111 Service Ave. SE
Roanoke, VA 24013-2923
Phone: (540)586-2803
Free: (800)334-1928 **Fax:** (540)586-6481
Products: Military surplus goods. **SICs:** 5091 (Sporting & Recreational Goods); 5139 (Footwear); 5136 (Men's/Boys' Clothing); 5137 (Women's/Children's Clothing). **Est:** 1987. **Sales:** $15,000,000 (2000). **Emp:** 10. **Officers:** John Tolliday, President.

■ 23617 ■ Deep See Products Inc.
18935 59th Ave. NE
Arlington, WA 98223-8763
Phone: (253)435-6696
Free: (800)367-2626 **Fax:** (253)435-4314
Products: Sporting and athletic goods. **SIC:** 5091 (Sporting & Recreational Goods). **Officers:** Sheryl Williams, President.

■ 23618 ■ Del Mar Distributing Company Inc.
PO Box 270300
Corpus Christi, TX 78427-0300
Phone: (361)992-8901 **Fax:** (361)993-9260
Products: Fishing products. **SIC:** 5091 (Sporting & Recreational Goods). **Est:** 1953. **Sales:** $8,000,000 (2000). **Emp:** 50. **Officers:** William B. Miller Jr., President; David Wilson, Treasurer; Jack Rohde, Vice President.

■ 23619 ■ Joan Denzak & Associates, Inc.
PO Box 176
Buffalo, NY 14217
Phone: (716)876-0752
Free: (800)925-1545 **Fax:** (716)877-3004
Products: Playground, gymnasium, and exercise equipment. **SIC:** 5091 (Sporting & Recreational Goods).

■ 23620 ■ Derby Cycle
22710 72nd Ave. S
Kent, WA 98032-1926
Products: Bicycles and parts. **SIC:** 5091 (Sporting & Recreational Goods).

■ 23621 ■ Developed Technology Resource Inc.
7300 Metro Blvd., Ste. 550
Edina, MN 55439
Phone: (612)820-0022 **Fax:** (612)820-0011
Products: Fitness equipment. **SIC:** 5091 (Sporting & Recreational Goods). **Sales:** $1,800,000 (2000). **Emp:** 11. **Officers:** John P. Hupp, CEO & President; LeAnn Davis, CFO.

■ 23622 ■ Dia-Compe Inc.
PO Box 798
Fletcher, NC 28732
Phone: (828)684-3551
Products: Bicycle brake systems. **SIC:** 5091 (Sporting & Recreational Goods). **Sales:** $17,000,000 (1994). **Emp:** 30. **Officers:** Brad Thorn, President; Jack McCurry, Controller.

■ 23623 ■ Dimmer-Warren Enterprises
1470 Mitchell Lake Rd.
Attica, MI 48412-9217
Phone: (810)724-0228 **Fax:** (810)724-8971
Products: Sporting and athletic goods. **SIC:** 5091 (Sporting & Recreational Goods). **Officers:** Albert Dimmer, President.

■ 23624 ■ Discount Fishing Tackle
203 S Union St.
Shawnee, OK 74801-7942
Phone: (405)275-8151
Products: Fishing equipment and supplies, including fishing tackle. **SIC:** 5091 (Sporting & Recreational Goods). **Officers:** Fred McDuff, Owner.

■ 23625 ■ Diversified Investments Inc.
4311 Triangle St.
Mc Farland, WI 53558
Phone: (608)838-8813 **Fax:** (608)838-8825
Products: Fitness equipment. **SIC:** 5091 (Sporting & Recreational Goods). **Sales:** $13,000,000 (2000). **Emp:** 12. **Officers:** Chris Hornung, President; Robert Gooze, CFO; Daniel Gillette, Dir. of Marketing.

■ 23626 ■ Dixons Bicycling Center Inc.
257 W Broad St.
Athens, GA 30601-2810
Phone: (706)549-2453
Free: (800)462-4531 **Fax:** (706)549-8600
Products: Sporting and athletic goods; Bicycles and parts. **SIC:** 5091 (Sporting & Recreational Goods). **Officers:** E. Dixon, President.

■ 23627 ■ Do-It Corp.
501 N State St.
Denver, IA 50622-0612
Phone: (319)984-6055 **Fax:** (319)984-6403
Products: Fishing tacklee. **SIC:** 5091 (Sporting & Recreational Goods). **Officers:** Jerry Bond, President.

■ 23628 ■ Dolphin Pools Inc.
6219 E 11th St.
Tulsa, OK 74112-3121
Phone: (918)838-7670
Free: (800)879-1422 **Fax:** (918)838-2859
Products: Sporting and athletic goods; Swimming pools and equipment. **SIC:** 5091 (Sporting & Recreational Goods). **Officers:** Douglas Hoehn, President.

■ 23629 ■ Down River Equipment Co.
12100 W 52nd Ave.
Wheat Ridge, CO 80033-2000
Phone: (303)467-9489 **Fax:** (303)940-8812
URL: http://www.downriverequip.com
Products: Inflatable rafts, kayaks, and sport boats; Whitewater frames; Float fishing rigs; Boating accessories. **SIC:** 5091 (Sporting & Recreational Goods). **Emp:** 15. **Officers:** Christine Wolfe, President.

■ 23630 ■ Drayton Swimming Pool Supply
4763 Dixie Hwy.
Waterford, MI 48329-3523
Phone: (248)673-6734 **Fax:** (248)673-0847
Products: Swimming pools, equipment, and supplies. **SIC:** 5091 (Sporting & Recreational Goods). **Est:** 1955. **Emp:** 10. **Officers:** Craig M. Remington, President.

■ 23631 ■ Drybranch Inc.
1 Commercial Ct.
Plainview, NY 11803-1600
Phone: (516)576-7000 **Fax:** (516)576-7008
Products: Sporting and athletic goods; Nonelectronic games; Gifts and novelties. **SICs:** 5091 (Sporting & Recreational Goods); 5199 (Nondurable Goods Nec); 5092 (Toys & Hobby Goods & Supplies). **Est:** 1975. **Emp:** 49. **Alternate Name:** Sport Design.

■ 23632 ■ Duck Commander Company, Inc.
538 Mouth of Cypress Rd.
West Monroe, LA 71291
Phone: (318)325-1189
Free: (800)234-1595 **Fax:** (318)387-9322
E-mail: dccom2@iamerica.com
URL: http://www.duckcommander.com
Products: Sporting goods. **SIC:** 5091 (Sporting & Recreational Goods). **Est:** 1972. **Sales:** $900,000 (1999). **Emp:** 7. **Officers:** Phil Robertson, Owner; Kay Robertson, Owner.

■ 23633 ■ Dugans Inc.
7841 S 180th St.
PO Box 220
Kent, WA 98032
Phone: (425)251-9000 **Fax:** (425)251-0457
Products: Sportswear; Trophies and awards; Promotional products. **SICs:** 5091 (Sporting & Recreational Goods); 5094 (Jewelry & Precious Stones). **Est:** 1983. **Sales:** $2,000,000 (2000). **Emp:** 10. **Officers:** Kelly Dugan, President.

■ 23634 ■ Dunns Sporting Goods Co. Inc.
PO Box 631
Pevely, MO 63070
Phone: (314)479-4240 **Fax:** (314)479-7140
Products: Hunting and fishing equipment. **SIC:** 5091 (Sporting & Recreational Goods). **Est:** 1958. **Sales:** $5,000,000 (2000). **Emp:** 30. **Officers:** G. Dunn, President; Mary Dunn, Secretary; Steven Dunn, Dir. of Marketing & Sales.

■ 23635 ■ Durham Boat Co. Inc.
220 Newmarket Rd.
Durham, NH 03824-4203
Phone: (603)659-2548 **Fax:** (603)659-2548
Products: Rowing oars and shells. **SIC:** 5091 (Sporting & Recreational Goods). **Officers:** James Dreher, Vice President.

■ 23636 ■ Dyna Group International Inc.
1801 W 16th St.
Broadview, IL 60153
Phone: (708)450-9200
Free: (800)341-4436 **Fax:** (708)450-9273
Products: Gifts and novelties. **SIC:** 5091 (Sporting & Recreational Goods). **Sales:** $10,000,000 (2000). **Emp:** 221.

■ 23637 ■ Dynacraft Golf Products, Inc.
71 Malholm St.
Newark, OH 43055
Phone: (740)344-1191
Free: (800)321-4833 **Fax:** (740)344-6174
E-mail: dynacraft@nextek.net
URL: http://www.dynacraftgolf.com
Products: Golf products. **SIC:** 5091 (Sporting & Recreational Goods). **Est:** 1980. **Emp:** 150. **Officers:** Jeff Jackson, President; Joseph Altomonte Sr.,

Chairman of the Board; Joseph Altomonte Jr., CEO; Duane Egeland, CFO.

■ 23638 ■ Dynamic Classics Ltd.
230 5th Ave.
New York, NY 10001
Phone: (212)571-0267 **Fax:** (212)213-0390
Products: Excercise equipment and luggage. **SICs:** 5091 (Sporting & Recreational Goods); 5099 (Durable Goods Nec). **Est:** 1964. **Sales:** $29,500,000 (2000). **Emp:** 64. **Officers:** Marvin Cooper, President; William P. Dolan, Treasurer & Secty.

■ 23639 ■ Eagle Claw Fishing Tackle
4245 E 46th Ave.
Denver, CO 80216-3262
Phone: (303)321-1481 **Fax:** (303)321-4750
E-mail: custsvc@eagleclaw.com
Products: Fishing tackle, fishhooks, rods, and reels. **SIC:** 5091 (Sporting & Recreational Goods). **Est:** 1925. **Officers:** Lee McGill, Owner, e-mail: lmcgill@eagleclaw.com; Bill Miller, Vice Chairman of the Board, e-mail: bmiller@eagleclaw.com; John Jilling, President, e-mail: jjilling@eagleclaw.com; Tenny Mount, Sr. VP of Marketing, e-mail: tmount@eagleclaw.com; Paul Kirley, Customer Service Contact. **Alternate Name:** Wright & McGill Co.

■ 23640 ■ Eagle River Corp.
320 W 4th Ave.
Anchorage, AK 99501-2321
Phone: (907)279-2401 **Fax:** (907)278-7174
Products: Sporting goods. **SIC:** 5091 (Sporting & Recreational Goods). **Officers:** Michael Miller, President.

■ 23641 ■ East Providence Cycle Co. Inc.
414 Warren Ave.
East Providence, RI 02914-3842
Phone: (401)434-3838 **Free:** (800)235-BIKE
Products: Sporting and recreation goods; Fitness equipment and supplies; Exercise equipment. **SIC:** 5091 (Sporting & Recreational Goods). **Officers:** Robert Foulkes, President.

■ 23642 ■ East Side Sporting Goods Co.
27427 Schoenherr Rd.
Warren, MI 48093-6639
Phone: (810)755-5520 **Fax:** (810)755-2898
Products: Sporting and athletic goods. **SIC:** 5091 (Sporting & Recreational Goods). **Officers:** Gerald Phillips, President.

■ 23643 ■ East West Trading Co.
PO Box 19188
Irvine, CA 92623-9188
Phone: (949)660-0888 **Fax:** (949)660-0611
Products: Sporting and athletic goods. **SIC:** 5091 (Sporting & Recreational Goods). **Est:** 1974. **Emp:** 5. **Officers:** James Park, Sales Mgr.

■ 23644 ■ Eaton Corp. Golf Grip Div.
PO Box 1848
Laurinburg, NC 28353
Phone: (919)276-6901 **Fax:** (919)277-3700
Products: Golf grips. **SIC:** 5091 (Sporting & Recreational Goods). **Emp:** 700. **Officers:** Bill Hill.

■ 23645 ■ Ebisuzaki Fishing Supply
92 Kalanianaole Ave.
Hilo, HI 96720
Phone: (808)935-8081 **Fax:** (808)969-1823
Products: Fishing supplies. **SIC:** 5091 (Sporting & Recreational Goods).

■ 23646 ■ John Edwards & Associates
1 Loma Ln.
Carmel Valley, CA 93924-9543
Phone: (408)659-7212
Free: (800)303-7529 **Fax:** (408)659-7226
Products: Sporting and athletic goods. **SIC:** 5091 (Sporting & Recreational Goods).

■ 23647 ■ Efinger Sporting Goods Inc.
513 W Union Ave.
Bound Brook, NJ 08805
Phone: (732)356-0604 **Fax:** (732)805-9860
E-mail: efingerspt@aol.com
Products: Sporting goods, including fishing, camping,

hunting, and athletics. **SIC:** 5091 (Sporting & Recreational Goods). **Est:** 1909. **Sales:** $11,300,000 (1999). **Emp:** 45. **Officers:** T.P. Hoey, President; Murray Greenberg, Vice President; Ed Schafer, Customer Service Contact; George Fazan, Human Resources Contact.

■ 23648 ■ Electric Car Distributors
71415 Highway 111
Rancho Mirage, CA 92270
Phone: (760)346-5661 **Fax:** (760)346-7006
Products: Golf carts. **SICs:** 5088 (Transportation Equipment & Supplies); 5091 (Sporting & Recreational Goods).

■ 23649 ■ Elliott Sales Corp.
2502 S 12th St.
Tacoma, WA 98405
Phone: (253)383-3883
Free: (800)576-3945 **Fax:** (253)383-3130
Products: Custom-imprinted fishing related promotional products. **SIC:** 5099 (Durable Goods Nec). **Sales:** $4,200,000 (2000). **Emp:** 9. **Officers:** Frank Elliott, President & CFO.

■ 23650 ■ EMSCO
22350 Royalton Rd.
PO Box 360660
Strongsville, OH 44136
Phone: (440)238-2100 **Fax:** (440)238-4839
E-mail: emscocorp.com
Products: Pool equipment and supplies. **SIC:** 5091 (Sporting & Recreational Goods). **Emp:** 35. **Officers:** Mark Stoyanoff, President; Richard Laneve, Vice President.

■ 23651 ■ EMSCO
12861 Rte. 30
North Huntingdon, PA 15642
Phone: (412)863-9480 **Fax:** (412)863-9596
Products: Pool equipment and supplies. **SIC:** 5091 (Sporting & Recreational Goods).

■ 23652 ■ Engan-Tooley-Doyle & Associates Inc.
PO Box 829
Okemos, MI 48805-0829
Phone: (517)347-7970
Free: (800)722-8546 **Fax:** (517)349-1911
E-mail: etdinc@acd.net
URL: http://www.etdred.com
Products: Playground equipment; Site amenities; Shelters and gazebos; Safety surfacing; Drinking fountains; Athletic equipment; Water slides. **SICs:** 5091 (Sporting & Recreational Goods); 5078 (Refrigeration Equipment & Supplies). **Est:** 1986. **Sales:** $4,000,000 (2000). **Emp:** 8. **Officers:** Robert W. Tooley, President; Timothy J. Doyle, Vice President; Michael R. Engan, CEO.

■ 23653 ■ Eppinger Manufacturing Co.
6340 Schaefer Rd.
Dearborn, MI 48126
Phone: (313)582-3205 **Fax:** (313)582-0110
E-mail: Dardevle1@aol.com
URL: http://www.eppinger.net
Products: Fishing lures. **SIC:** 5091 (Sporting & Recreational Goods). **Est:** 1906. **Sales:** $2,000,000 (2000). **Emp:** 22. **Officers:** Karen Eppinger.

■ 23654 ■ Vic Ericksons Super-Pros, Inc.
1295 Ada Ave.
Idaho Falls, ID 83402-2148
Phone: (208)524-6457
Free: (800)669-6457 **Fax:** (208)525-4707
Products: Arrow shafts; Arrow shaft selection tool. **SIC:** 5091 (Sporting & Recreational Goods). **Est:** 1971. **Emp:** 4. **Officers:** Vic Erickson, President.

■ 23655 ■ Esneault Inc.
3018 Galleria Dr.
Metairie, LA 70001-2969
Phone: (504)833-6602
Products: Sporting and athletic goods. **SIC:** 5091 (Sporting & Recreational Goods). **Officers:** James Esneault, President.

■ 23656 ■ Everett Square Sporting Goods
427 Broadway
Everett, MA 02149-3435
Phone: (617)387-6530
Products: Sporting and recreation goods. **SIC:** 5091 (Sporting & Recreational Goods). **Officers:** Anthony Ventura, President.

■ 23657 ■ Ewing Aquatech Pools Inc.
11414 Industriplex Blvd.
Baton Rouge, LA 70809
Phone: (225)751-7946
Free: (800)673-1504 **Fax:** (225)752-6361
E-mail: info@ewingaquatech.com
URL: http://www.ewingaquatech.com
Products: Swimming pools and equipment; Pool chemicals; Lawn furniture. **SICs:** 5091 (Sporting & Recreational Goods); 5021 (Furniture); 5169 (Chemicals & Allied Products Nec). **Emp:** 35.

■ 23658 ■ Exsaco Corp.
PO Drawer 328
Alvarado, TX 76009
Phone: (817)783-2265 **Fax:** (817)783-3355
Products: Amusement and carnival rides. **SIC:** 5087 (Service Establishment Equipment). **Sales:** $6,000,000 (2000). **Emp:** 30. **Officers:** John J. Casoli, President.

■ 23659 ■ Extex Co.
2363 Boulevard Cir., Ste. 104
Walnut Creek, CA 94595
Phone: (510)988-1090 **Fax:** (510)988-1092
Products: Sport fishing tackle. **SIC:** 5091 (Sporting & Recreational Goods). **Officers:** Ted Bamberger, President.

■ 23660 ■ Exxersource
15000 Calvert St.
Van Nuys, CA 91411
Phone: (818)787-6460
Products: Excercise equipment. **SIC:** 5091 (Sporting & Recreational Goods). **Est:** 1973. **Sales:** $2,000,000 (2000). **Emp:** 9. **Officers:** Alf Pemme, President.

■ 23661 ■ F & E Sportswear Inc.
1230 Newell Pkwy.
Montgomery, AL 36110-3212
Phone: (205)244-6477
Free: (800)523-7762 **Fax:** (205)277-2543
E-mail: fande1****.com
URL: http://www.FandEsportswear.com
Products: Sporting and athletic goods. **SIC:** 5091 (Sporting & Recreational Goods). **Est:** 1978. **Emp:** 25. **Officers:** Tom Chapman, President; Richard Patino, Vice President.

■ 23662 ■ Faber Brothers Inc.
4141 S Pulaski
Chicago, IL 60632
Phone: (773)376-9300
Free: (800)366-2000 **Fax:** (773)376-0732
Products: Sporting goods. **SIC:** 5091 (Sporting & Recreational Goods). **Est:** 1929. **Sales:** $75,000,000 (1999). **Emp:** 145. **Officers:** A. Shapiro, Chairman of the Board; Wayne Kozlowski, President; M. Snowsky, Treasurer; Richard Niziolek, Finance Officer; Jim Danielson, Sales/Marketing Contact, e-mail: jdanielson@faberbrothers.com; Calvin Connors, Customer Service Contact, e-mail: cconnors@faberbrothers.com; Leslie Lanza, Human Resources Contact, e-mail: jlenza@faberbrothers.com.

■ 23663 ■ Gary Fain & Associates
PO Box 1370
Sand Springs, OK 74063
Free: (800)933-6484 **Fax:** (918)245-5466
Products: Sporting and athletic goods; Playground, gymnasium, and exercise equipment. **SIC:** 5091 (Sporting & Recreational Goods).

■ 23664 ■ FEMCO Corp.
235 Arcadia St.
Richmond, VA 23225-5611
Phone: (804)276-0011
Free: (800)476-5432 **Fax:** (804)276-0557
E-mail: advantagetennis.supply@cwix.com
Products: Sporting goods; Tennis equipment. **SIC:** 5091 (Sporting & Recreational Goods). **Est:** 1977. **Emp:** 4. **Officers:** Frank McDavid, President; Shayne McDavid, Sales/Marketing Contact; Joanne Faney, Customer Service Contact. **Former Name:** Advantage Tennis Supply.

■ 23665 ■ R.J. Filut & Associates Inc.
667 Old Shakopee Rd., Ste. 105
Minneapolis, MN 55438-5815
Phone: (612)942-6576
Free: (800)322-4440 **Fax:** (612)942-6615
Products: Sporting and athletic goods. **SIC:** 5091 (Sporting & Recreational Goods). **Officers:** Richard Filut, President.

■ 23666 ■ First Service, Div. of Straightline Enterprises, Inc.
737 Southpoint Blvd., Ste. D
Petaluma, CA 94954
Free: (800)227-1742 **Fax:** 800-809-9172
E-mail: firstservice@clubstuff.com
URL: http://www.clubstuff.com
Products: Sporting and athletic goods, including basketball equipment, volleyball equipment, scoreboards, bleachers, outdoor equipment, lockers, and benches. **SIC:** 5091 (Sporting & Recreational Goods). **Est:** 1974. **Sales:** $4,000,000 (2000). **Emp:** 6. **Officers:** Mel Goldblatt, President; Dan Goldblatt, Vice President.

■ 23667 ■ Fish Net Co.
PO Box 462
Jonesville, LA 71343-0462
Phone: (318)339-9655
Products: Sporting and athletic goods; Fishing tackle and equipment. **SIC:** 5091 (Sporting & Recreational Goods). **Officers:** Benny Champlin, Owner.

■ 23668 ■ Fisher Enterprises Inc.
2191 Hwy. 105
Boone, NC 28607-9210
Phone: (704)264-8827
Products: Sporting and recreational goods; Fitness equipment and supplies; Hot tubs. **SIC:** 5091 (Sporting & Recreational Goods). **Officers:** John Fisher, President.

■ 23669 ■ Fishermans Factory Outlet
701 Dakota Ave.
South Sioux City, NE 68776-2058
Phone: (402)494-6930
Products: Fishing tackle and equipment. **SIC:** 5091 (Sporting & Recreational Goods). **Est:** 1947. **Sales:** $500,000 (1999). **Emp:** 6. **Officers:** Morey Wheeler, President.

■ 23670 ■ Fitness Corporation of America
PO Box 300
Linthicum Heights, MD 21090-0300
Phone: (410)859-3538
Free: (800)445-1855 **Fax:** (410)859-3907
E-mail: atlantic@atlantic-fitness.com
URL: http://www.atlantic-fitness.com
Products: Sporting and recreational goods; Fitness equipment and supplies. **SIC:** 5091 (Sporting & Recreational Goods). **Est:** 1966. **Sales:** $2,800,000 (2000). **Emp:** 3. **Officers:** Warren Miller, President. **Doing Business As:** Atlantic Fitness Products.

■ 23671 ■ Fitness Expo Inc.
4124 Vetarnes
Metairie, LA 70006
Phone: (504)887-0880
Free: (800)323-1831 **Fax:** (504)888-7090
Products: Sporting and recreational goods; Fitness equipment and supplies; Exercise equipment. **SIC:** 5091 (Sporting & Recreational Goods). **Officers:** Rodney Rice, President.

■ 23672 ■ Fitness Shop
12012 SW Canyon Rd.
Beaverton, OR 97005-2150
Phone: (503)641-8892 **Fax:** (503)626-2765
Products: Sporting and recreational goods; Fitness equipment and supplies. **SIC:** 5091 (Sporting & Recreational Goods). **Officers:** John Potts, Owner.

■ 23673 ■ Fitness Systems Inc.
7101 Sharondale Ct.
PO Box 1544
Brentwood, TN 37024-1544
Phone: (615)661-5858 **Fax:** (615)661-6618
Products: Fitness equipment and exercise supplies. **SIC:** 5091 (Sporting & Recreational Goods). **Est:** 1985. **Officers:** Rodney Freeman, President.

■ 23674 ■ Fitness Systems Inc.
5566 N Academy Blvd.
Colorado Springs, CO 80918-3682
Phone: (719)594-6969
Free: (800)735-6290 **Fax:** (719)594-6912
Products: Sporting and recreational goods; Exercise equipment and supplies. **SIC:** 5091 (Sporting & Recreational Goods). **Officers:** Jay Huey, President.

■ 23675 ■ Folsom Corp.
43 McKee Dr.
Mahwah, NJ 07430
Phone: (201)529-3550 **Fax:** (201)529-0291
Products: Fishing and tackle equipment and related accessories. **SIC:** 5091 (Sporting & Recreational Goods). **Sales:** $65,000,000 (2000). **Emp:** 150. **Officers:** L. Feldsott, President & Treasurer; Robert Feldsott, President & Treasurer.

■ 23676 ■ Franklin Sports Industries Inc.
PO Box 508
Stoughton, MA 02072
Phone: (781)344-1111
Products: Sporting and athletic goods. **SIC:** 5091 (Sporting & Recreational Goods). **Est:** 1946. **Sales:** $32,000,000 (2000). **Emp:** 225. **Officers:** Larry Franklin, President; George Small, CFO; Charles Quinn, Dir. of Marketing; Michael Kirby, Dir. of Systems; Jack Cassidy, Dir of Human Resources.

■ 23677 ■ French's Athletics Inc.
1543 Harrison St.
Batesville, AR 72501-7222
Phone: (870)793-8205 **Fax:** (870)793-8062
Products: Sporting and athletic goods. **SIC:** 5091 (Sporting & Recreational Goods). **Officers:** Edward French, President.

■ 23678 ■ FTG Manufacturing
4251 NE Port Dr.
PO Box 266
Lees Summit, MO 64064
Phone: (816)795-7171 **Fax:** (816)795-2481
Products: Exercise equipment; Suntanning equipment. **SIC:** 5091 (Sporting & Recreational Goods). **Est:** 1985. **Sales:** $3,000,000 (2000). **Emp:** 12. **Officers:** Brad Henson, President.

■ 23679 ■ Fuji America Inc.
118 Bauer Dr.
Oakland, NJ 07436
Phone: (201)337-1700 **Fax:** (201)337-1762
Products: Bicycles. **SIC:** 5091 (Sporting & Recreational Goods). **Est:** 1966. **Sales:** $20,000,000 (2000). **Emp:** 20. **Officers:** Ken Moriya, President; Karen Warren, Treasurer; Joan Quigley, Dir. of Marketing; Mike Smith, Dir. of Information Systems.

■ 23680 ■ Funco Inc.
PO Box 241824
Omaha, NE 68124-5824
Phone: (402)734-0989 **Fax:** (402)397-8581
Products: Spas; Pools. **SIC:** 5091 (Sporting & Recreational Goods). **Est:** 1990. **Sales:** $3,000,000 (2000). **Emp:** 25. **Officers:** Steve Chelin, President & Treasurer.

■ 23681 ■ Future Pro Inc.
PO Box 486
Inman, KS 67546
Phone: (316)585-6405
Free: (800)328-4625 **Fax:** (316)585-6799
E-mail: futurepro@futureproinc.com
URL: http://www.futureproinc.com
Products: Sporting and athletic goods. **SIC:** 5091 (Sporting & Recreational Goods). **Est:** 1988. **Emp:** 5. **Officers:** Ron Ensz, CEO.

■ 23682 ■ Gander Mountain Inc.
PO Box 1224
Minneapolis, MN 55440-1224
Phone: (612)862-2331 **Fax:** (612)862-2330
Products: Hunting, boating, and fishing equipment and supplies. **SIC:** 5091 (Sporting & Recreational Goods).

■ 23683 ■ Gared Sports Inc.
1107 Mullanphy St.
St. Louis, MO 63106
Phone: (314)421-0044
Free: (800)325-2682 **Fax:** (314)421-6014
Products: Sporting and athletic goods. **SIC:** 5091 (Sporting & Recreational Goods). **Est:** 1922. **Sales:** $12,000,000 (2000). **Emp:** 60. **Officers:** C.J. Engle, President; Ralph Miller, National Sales Mgr.

■ 23684 ■ Garrett & Co., Inc.
PO Box 57426
Murray, UT 84157
Free: (800)748-4608 **Fax:** (801)263-1254
Products: Sporting and athletic goods. **SIC:** 5091 (Sporting & Recreational Goods).

■ 23685 ■ J.W. Garrett III & Co. Inc.
156 N Main St.
Chase City, VA 23924-1610
Phone: (804)372-4555
Free: (800)237-5608 **Fax:** (804)372-2105
E-mail: garrettco@kerrlakil.com
Products: Fishing, hunting, and convenience store items. **SIC:** 5091 (Sporting & Recreational Goods). **Est:** 1932. **Sales:** $1,000,000 (2000). **Emp:** 13. **Officers:** J. Garrett, President; Wanda Garrett, Vice President; Sarah Caknipe, VP, Treasurer & Secty.

■ 23686 ■ Jerry Gazaway & Associates
1703 S 6th St.
Marshalltown, IA 50158
Phone: (515)752-7589
Free: (800)798-7589 **Fax:** (515)752-6604
Products: Sporting and athletic goods. **SIC:** 5091 (Sporting & Recreational Goods).

■ 23687 ■ Gazelle Athletics
PO Box 1011
The Dalles, OR 97058-9011
Phone: (541)298-4277
Products: Sporting and athletic goods; Zippered hand luggage. **SIC:** 5091 (Sporting & Recreational Goods). **Officers:** Joe Martin, Partner.

■ 23688 ■ Gemini Manufacturing Inc.
Hwy. 67 N
Walnut Ridge, AR 72476
Phone: (870)886-5512 **Fax:** (870)886-7140
Products: Golf equipment. **SIC:** 5091 (Sporting & Recreational Goods). **Est:** 1973. **Sales:** $1,250,000 (2000). **Emp:** 65. **Officers:** Donald L. Walzer; Kurt L. Walzer.

■ 23689 ■ Gleeson Inc.
PO Box 7449
Louisville, KY 40257-0449
Phone: (502)895-4880 **Fax:** (502)895-5734
Products: Sporting and athletic goods. **SIC:** 5091 (Sporting & Recreational Goods). **Officers:** James Roth, President.

■ 23690 ■ Hank Gnieweks Trophies Inc.
21925 Michigan Ave.
Dearborn, MI 48124-2379
Phone: (313)278-1130
Free: (800)594-5158 **Fax:** (313)278-1787
Products: Sporting and athletic goods. **SIC:** 5091 (Sporting & Recreational Goods). **Officers:** Henry Gniewek, President.

■ 23691 ■ Go/Sportsmen's Supply Inc.
1535 Industrial Ave.
Billings, MT 59104
Phone: (406)252-2109 **Fax:** (406)248-7767
Products: Fishing and camping products; Firearms. **SIC:** 5091 (Sporting & Recreational Goods). **Est:** 1957. **Sales:** $25,000,000 (2000). **Emp:** 62. **Officers:** Duane Grasulak, Dir. of Operations; Mark Beadle, Controller; Steve Edwards, Sales Mgr.; Lisa Reid, Office Mgr.

■ 23692 ■ Golf Training Systems Inc.
3400 Corporate Way, Ste. G
Duluth, GA 30096
Phone: (404)623-6400
Products: Golf training equipment. **SIC:** 5091 (Sporting & Recreational Goods).

■ 23693 ■ Golf Ventures
2101 E Edgewood Dr.
Lakeland, FL 33803
Phone: (941)665-5800 **Fax:** (941)667-0888
Products: Golf course maintenance equipment and supplies. **SICs:** 5091 (Sporting & Recreational Goods); 5083 (Farm & Garden Machinery).

■ 23694 ■ Gould Athletic Supply
3156 N 96th St.
Milwaukee, WI 53222-3499
Phone: (414)871-3943
Products: Physical education equipment. **SIC:** 5091 (Sporting & Recreational Goods). **Est:** 1950. **Emp:** 2. **Officers:** James W. Gould, Owner; M.D. Gould, Owner.

■ 23695 ■ Grafalloy Corp.
1020 N Marshall Ave.
El Cajon, CA 92020
Phone: (619)562-1020
Free: (800)727-3241 **Fax:** (619)562-4695
Products: Golf equipment. **SIC:** 5091 (Sporting & Recreational Goods). **Est:** 1970. **Emp:** 40. **Officers:** William M. Gerhart, President.

■ 23696 ■ Grandoe Corp.
PO Box 713
Gloversville, NY 12078
Phone: (518)725-8641 **Fax:** (518)725-9088
Products: Ski, golf, outdoor and fashion gloves. **SICs:** 5136 (Men's/Boys' Clothing); 5137 (Women's/Children's Clothing). **Sales:** $45,000,000 (2000). **Emp:** 250. **Officers:** Richard J. Zuckerwar, CEO & President; Keith Lajole, CFO.

■ 23697 ■ Great Northwest Bicycle Supply
2335 NW Savier St.
Portland, OR 97210-2513
Phone: (503)226-0696
Free: (800)927-9242 **Fax:** (503)226-0824
E-mail: gnwbs@transport.com
Products: Sporting and athletic goods; Bicycles and parts. **SIC:** 5091 (Sporting & Recreational Goods). **Est:** 1983. **Emp:** 12. **Officers:** Robert Mandelson, Owner.

■ 23698 ■ Dale Green Associates
PO Box 263
Alamo, CA 94507-0263
Phone: (510)837-0355
Free: (800)879-7730 **Fax:** (510)837-6782
Products: Sporting and athletic goods; Playground, gymnasium, and exercise equipment. **SIC:** 5091 (Sporting & Recreational Goods). **Officers:** Dale Green.

■ 23699 ■ Green Top Sporting Goods Inc.
PO Box 1015
Glen Allen, VA 23060
Phone: (804)550-2188 **Fax:** (804)550-2693
Products: Guns; Fishing rods and lures. **SIC:** 5091 (Sporting & Recreational Goods). **Est:** 1947. **Sales:** $2,000,000 (2000). **Emp:** 31. **Officers:** Patrick R. Hopkins, President; Barry Hopkins, VP of Finance; Vance Hopkins, VP of Sales.

■ 23700 ■ Gregco Inc.
PO Box 810
Powell, TN 37849
Phone: (423)947-7500 **Fax:** (423)938-4140
Products: Camping equipment and supplies. **SIC:** 5091 (Sporting & Recreational Goods). **Officers:** Jim Gregg, President.

■ 23701 ■ Gulbenkian Swim Inc.
70 Memorial Plz.
Pleasantville, NY 10570
Phone: (914)747-3240
Free: (800)431-2586 **Fax:** (914)747-3243
Products: Aquatic equipment and swimwear. **SICs:** 5091 (Sporting & Recreational Goods); 5136 (Men's/Boys' Clothing); 5137 (Women's/Children's Clothing). **Est:** 1961. **Sales:** $1,500,000 (2000). **Emp:** 17. **Officers:** Ed Gulbenkian, CEO; Brian Ickes, Operations Mgr.; Ed Gulbenkian III, Vice President; Scott Bernard, Operations Mgr.

■ 23702 ■ Gulf Pool Equipment Co.
PO Box 790462
San Antonio, TX 78279-0462
Phone: (210)341-9103
Free: (800)383-4853 **Fax:** (210)341-7689
Products: Pool products and equipment. **SIC:** 5091 (Sporting & Recreational Goods). **Sales:** $5,000,000 (2000). **Emp:** 25. **Officers:** D. E. Tottenham.

■ 23703 ■ Gun Traders Inc.
512 Muldoon Rd.
Anchorage, AK 99504-1508
Phone: (907)337-6522 **Fax:** (907)337-1628
Products: Sporting and athletic goods; Hunting equipment; Firearms. **SIC:** 5091 (Sporting & Recreational Goods). **Officers:** Judith Hart, President.

■ 23704 ■ Guptons Sporting Goods Inc.
324 S Garnett St.
Henderson, NC 27536-4538
Phone: (919)492-2311 **Fax:** (919)492-7121
Products: Sporting and athletic goods; Hunting equipment; Sporting firearms. **SIC:** 5091 (Sporting & Recreational Goods). **Officers:** Betty Furniss, President.

■ 23705 ■ Guterman International Inc.
603 Pleasant St.
Paxton, MA 01612-1305
Phone: (508)852-8206
Free: (800)343-6096 **Fax:** (508)856-0632
Products: Tennis and racquet ball equipment. **SIC:** 5091 (Sporting & Recreational Goods). **Est:** 1976. **Emp:** 15. **Officers:** Peter S. Guterman, President.

■ 23706 ■ Gym Source
40 E 52nd St.
New York, NY 10022
Phone: (212)688-4222 **Fax:** (212)688-6933
URL: http://www.gymsource.com
Products: Gym equipment. **SIC:** 5091 (Sporting & Recreational Goods). **Est:** 1938. **Sales:** $40,000,000 (1999). **Emp:** 62. **Officers:** Richard Miller, President; Lars Rhode, Sales Mgr.; Bill Kemnitzer, Sales Mgr.

■ 23707 ■ H & W Sport Monticello Inc.
1500 N Main St., No. 104
Monticello, KY 42633-2046
Phone: (606)348-6259
Free: (800)323-6469 **Fax:** (606)348-6259
Products: Team sporting goods. **SIC:** 5091 (Sporting & Recreational Goods). **Officers:** Sherman York, President.

■ 23708 ■ H2O
3000 South 300 West
Salt Lake City, UT 84115-3407
Phone: (801)486-9388
Products: Sporting and recreational goods; Fitness equipment and supplies; Hot tubs. **SIC:** 5091 (Sporting & Recreational Goods). **Officers:** Joel Johnson, Partner.

■ 23709 ■ Hachik Distributors Inc.
2300 Island Ave.
Philadelphia, PA 19142
Phone: (215)365-8500
Free: (800)365-4224 **Fax:** (215)365-4550
URL: http://www.hachik.com
Products: Swimming pool products. **SIC:** 5091 (Sporting & Recreational Goods). **Est:** 1923. **Sales:** $10,000,000 (2000). **Emp:** 30. **Officers:** Nanette Zakian, CEO & President; Robert Lawson, General Mgr., e-mail: rl@hachik.com.

■ 23710 ■ Hadfield Sport Shops Inc.
96 Webster Square Rd.
Berlin, CT 06037-2327
Phone: (860)828-6391 **Fax:** (860)828-6395
Products: Sporting and athletic goods. **SIC:** 5091 (Sporting & Recreational Goods). **Officers:** Richard Schaller, Secretary.

■ **23711** ■ **Halbro America**
885 Warren Ave.
East Providence, RI 02914
Phone: (401)438-2727 **Fax:** (401)438-8260
URL: http://www.rugbyimports.com
Products: Rugby jerseys. **SIC:** 5091 (Sporting & Recreational Goods). **Est:** 1982. **Sales:** $500,000 (2000). **Emp:** 6. **Officers:** Robert J. Hoder, President.

■ **23712** ■ **Hansen & Co.**
244-246 Old Post Rd.
Southport, CT 06490
Phone: (203)259-7337 **Fax:** (203)254-3832
Products: Sporting and athletic goods; Hunting equipment; Sporting firearms. **SIC:** 5091 (Sporting & Recreational Goods). **Officers:** John Hansen, President.

■ **23713** ■ **Har-Tru Corp.**
12932 Salem Ave.
Hagerstown, MD 21740
Phone: (301)739-3077
Free: (800)842-7878 **Fax:** (301)739-6104
E-mail: mail@har-tru.com
URL: http://www.har-tru.com
Products: Sporting and athletic goods; Tennis and racquet ball equipment. **SIC:** 5091 (Sporting & Recreational Goods). **Est:** 1932. **Officers:** Richard Funkhouser, President; Skip Fielden, Vice President.

■ **23714** ■ **Hard Hat Inc.**
711 Leitchfield Rd.
Owensboro, KY 42303-0350
Phone: (502)926-7000 **Fax:** (502)683-1234
URL: http://www.hardhatusa.com
Products: Belt buckles; Hunting and pocket knives; Lapel pins. **SICs:** 5091 (Sporting & Recreational Goods); 5094 (Jewelry & Precious Stones); 5072 (Hardware). **Est:** 1976. **Sales:** $9,250,000 (2000). **Emp:** 91. **Officers:** Kaye Clark, President.

■ **23715** ■ **Harper & Associates**
PO Box 838
Allen, TX 75002
Phone: (972)727-6283
Free: (800)982-8973 **Fax:** (972)727-7357
Products: Sporting and athletic goods; Playground, gymnasium, and exercise equipment. **SIC:** 5091 (Sporting & Recreational Goods).

■ **23716** ■ **Hasley Recreation and Design Inc.**
PO Box 936
Greensboro, GA 30642
Phone: (706)467-3328
Free: (800)685-2063 **Fax:** (706)467-3304
E-mail: hasleyrec@plantationcable.net
Products: Playground equipment site furnishings, shelters, basketball goals. **SIC:** 5091 (Sporting & Recreational Goods). **Est:** 1981. **Sales:** $2,000,000 (2000). **Emp:** 3. **Officers:** Norvel Hasley. **Former Name:** Norvel #Hasley & Associates.

■ **23717** ■ **Hauff Sporting Goods Co. Inc.**
1120 Capitol Ave.
Omaha, NE 68102-1113
Phone: (402)341-7011
Free: (800)642-8423 **Fax:** (402)341-1410
Products: Sporting and athletic goods. **SIC:** 5091 (Sporting & Recreational Goods). **Officers:** Dwight Hauff, Chairman of the Board.

■ **23718** ■ **Hawaii Martial Art Supply**
1041 Maunakea St.
Honolulu, HI 96817-5130
Phone: (808)536-5402 **Fax:** (808)523-5489
E-mail: hmas1041@aol.com
URL: http://www.sceneamerica.com/hawaiimartialarts
Products: Martial arts equipment and uniforms. **SICs:** 5091 (Sporting & Recreational Goods); 5136 (Men's/Boys' Clothing); 5137 (Women's/Children's Clothing). **Est:** 1981. **Emp:** 3. **Officers:** Ramona Fukumoto, President.

■ **23719** ■ **Health and Leisure Mart Inc.**
1516 W Mound St.
Columbus, OH 43223
Phone: (614)274-3640 **Fax:** (614)464-1120
Products: Exercise equipment, hot tubs, and therapeutic equipment. **SIC:** 5091 (Sporting &

Recreational Goods). **Est:** 1952. **Sales:** $1,000,000 (2000). **Emp:** 3. **Officers:** Louis May, Owner.

■ **23720** ■ **HealthTech International Inc.**
1237 S Val Vista Dr.
Mesa, AZ 85204
Phone: (602)396-0660
Products: Health fitness machines. **SIC:** 5099 (Durable Goods Nec). **Sales:** $5,600,000 (2000). **Emp:** 140. **Officers:** Gordon L. Hall, CEO & Chairman of the Board; Stephen Smith, VP & CFO.

■ **23721** ■ **Helmet House Inc.**
26855 Malibu Hills Rd.
Calabasas Hills, CA 91301
Phone: (818)880-0000
Free: (800)421-7247 **Fax:** (818)880-4550
URL: http://www.helmethouse.com
Products: Motorcycle helmets, luggage, gloves, and apparel; Off-road apparel and boots. **SICs:** 5091 (Sporting & Recreational Goods); 5136 (Men's/Boys' Clothing). **Est:** 1969. **Sales:** $40,000,000 (2000). **Emp:** 60. **Officers:** Bob Miller, President; Phil Bellomy, Vice President.

■ **23722** ■ **Jen Henbest & Associates, Inc.**
PO Box 459
Oconomowoc, WI 53066
Free: (800)688-6504 **Fax:** (414)567-6500
Products: Sporting and athletic goods; Playground, gymnasium, and exercise equipment. **SIC:** 5091 (Sporting & Recreational Goods).

■ **23723** ■ **Henry's Tackle L.L.C.**
PO Drawer 1107
Morehead City, NC 28557
Phone: (252)726-6186 **Fax:** (252)726-7599
Products: Fishing tackle, shooting sports and marine goods. **SIC:** 5091 (Sporting & Recreational Goods). **Sales:** $80,000,000 (2000). **Emp:** 270. **Officers:** Mark Suber, General Mgr.; Dan Reitz, CFO.

■ **23724** ■ **Here's Fred Golf Co.**
13627 Beach Blvd.
Jacksonville, FL 32246
Phone: (919)223-3136
Free: (800)874-7395 **Fax:** 800-438-7691
Products: Licensed products, including hats and shirts; Custom logo products; Golf course and range equipment and supplies. **SICs:** 5091 (Sporting & Recreational Goods); 5136 (Men's/Boys' Clothing); 5137 (Women's/Children's Clothing). **Est:** 1978. **Emp:** 27. **Officers:** Fred Akel, President.

■ **23725** ■ **HG International Corporation**
PO Box 51513
Durham, NC 27717
Phone: (919)489-4840 **Fax:** (919)489-0982
Products: Sporting goods, including soccer and volleyball equipment; Processed food products; Industrial textiles and yarns. **SICs:** 5091 (Sporting & Recreational Goods); 5149 (Groceries & Related Products Nec); 5131 (Piece Goods & Notions). **Officers:** Robert B. Green, Director of Mktg.

■ **23726** ■ **Hicks Inc.**
PO Box 232
Luverne, AL 36049
Phone: (205)335-3311 **Fax:** (205)335-6243
Products: Sporting goods. **SIC:** 5091 (Sporting & Recreational Goods). **Emp:** 49. **Officers:** John M. Wise.

■ **23727** ■ **Hike A Bike**
621 Loma Prieta Dr.
Aptos, CA 95003
Phone: (408)688-5411
Free: (800)541-4453 **Fax:** (408)688-4949
Products: Bike and ski racks. **SIC:** 5091 (Sporting & Recreational Goods). **Est:** 1987. **Sales:** $50,000 (2000). **Emp:** 2. **Officers:** Carolyn Frentz; Austin Frentz.

■ **23728** ■ **Hiltons Tent City Inc.**
272 Friend St.
Boston, MA 02114-1801
Phone: (617)227-9104
Free: (800)277-9242 **Fax:** (617)227-9543
Products: Sporting and recreational goods and

supplies. **SIC:** 5091 (Sporting & Recreational Goods). **Officers:** Irving Liss, President.

■ **23729** ■ **Hopkins Sporting Goods Inc.**
10000 Hickman Rd.
Des Moines, IA 50325-5326
Phone: (515)270-0132
Free: (800)362-2937 **Fax:** (515)270-0413
Products: Sporting and athletic goods. **SIC:** 5091 (Sporting & Recreational Goods). **Officers:** John McClintock, President.

■ **23730** ■ **Horner Equipment of Florida Inc.**
5755 Power Line Rd.
Ft. Lauderdale, FL 33309
Phone: (305)944-3851
Products: Swimming pool equipment and supplies. **SIC:** 5091 (Sporting & Recreational Goods). **Sales:** $18,000,000 (2000). **Emp:** 75. **Officers:** Bill Kent, President.

■ **23731** ■ **Hornung's Pro Golf Sales Inc.**
PO Box 1078
Fond du Lac, WI 54935
Phone: (920)922-2640
Free: (800)323-3569 **Fax:** (920)922-4986
E-mail: info@hornungs.com
URL: http://www.hornungs.com
Products: Golf equipment; Import and export. **SIC:** 5091 (Sporting & Recreational Goods). **Est:** 1936. **Emp:** 40.

■ **23732** ■ **Lew Horton Distributing Co.**
PO Box 5023
Westborough, MA 01581
Phone: (508)366-7400 **Fax:** (508)366-5332
URL: http://www.lewhorton.com
Products: Hunting supplies. **SIC:** 5091 (Sporting & Recreational Goods). **Est:** 1977. **Sales:** $30,000,000 (2000). **Emp:** 35. **Officers:** Lew Horton, President.

■ **23733** ■ **House For Sports Inc.**
4411 Common St.
Lake Charles, LA 70605-4507
Phone: (318)477-0348 **Fax:** (318)477-0372
Products: Sporting and athletic goods. **SIC:** 5091 (Sporting & Recreational Goods). **Officers:** T. Miller, President.

■ **23734** ■ **Pat Huet & Associates**
15657 Marble Rd.
Northport, AL 35475
Phone: (205)339-5518 **Fax:** (205)339-5096
E-mail: pbhuet@dbtech.net
Products: Scoreboard equipment; Message centers. **SIC:** 5091 (Sporting & Recreational Goods). **Est:** 1980. **Sales:** $200,000 (2000). **Officers:** Pat Huet; Bette Huet.

■ **23735** ■ **Art Hughes Golf Inc.**
1044 Ruritan Blvd.
Chesapeake, VA 23324-3646
Phone: (804)443-5820 **Fax:** (804)443-1087
Products: Golf equipment. **SIC:** 5091 (Sporting & Recreational Goods). **Officers:** Arthur Hughes, President.

■ **23736** ■ **Huston Distributors Inc.**
Coopertown Rd.
Delanco, NJ 08075
Phone: (609)764-1500 **Fax:** (609)461-8271
Products: Pool equipment and supplies. **SIC:** 5091 (Sporting & Recreational Goods).

■ **23737** ■ **Roger J. Hutchinson & Associates, Inc.**
PO Box 194
Troy, MO 63379
Free: (800)848-5616 **Fax:** (314)528-8413
Products: Sporting and athletic goods; Playground, gymnasium, and exercise equipment. **SIC:** 5091 (Sporting & Recreational Goods).

■ **23738** ■ **D.H. Hutson Enterprises, Inc.**
PO Box 429
Waxhaw, NC 28173-0429
Phone: (704)843-2251
Products: Sporting and athletic goods; Golf

equipment; Skiing equipment. **SIC:** 5091 (Sporting & Recreational Goods). **Officers:** Dan Hutson, President.

■ **23739** ■ **Hyperox Technologies**
2180 Garnet Ave., Ste. 2-G5
San Diego, CA 92109
Phone: (619)490-0193
Products: Diving equipment. **SIC:** 5091 (Sporting & Recreational Goods). **Sales:** $700,000 (1993). **Emp:** 3.
Officers: Clifton Fitzhugh, President.

■ **23740** ■ **Imperial Pools Inc.**
Cornfield Rd.
Buxton, ME 04093
Phone: (207)929-4800
Products: Swimming pools. **SIC:** 5091 (Sporting & Recreational Goods).

■ **23741** ■ **Imperial Wax and Chemical Company Inc.**
2065 Robb Rd.
Walnut Creek, CA 94596-6246
Phone: (925)825-9121   **Fax:** (925)825-9121
Products: Swimming pool supplies such as thermal pool blanket covers and chlorine producing systems.
SIC: 5091 (Sporting & Recreational Goods). **Sales:** $1,000,000 (1992). **Emp:** 15. **Officers:** William C. Vernon, President.

■ **23742** ■ **Indian Industries Inc.**
PO Box 889
Evansville, IN 47706
Phone: (812)467-1200
Free: (800)457-3373   **Fax:** (812)467-1300
Products: Recreational goods, including basketball backboards, goals and poles, archery equipment, table tennis equipment, dart boards, and game tables; Billiard equipment, tables. **SIC:** 5091 (Sporting & Recreational Goods). **Est:** 1927. **Sales:** $60,000,000 (2000). **Emp:** 300. **Officers:** Daniel A. Messmer.
Doing Business As: Escalade Sports.

■ **23743** ■ **Indiana Recreation Equipment & Design, Inc.**
127 S Main St.
PO Box 510
Monticello, IN 47960
Phone: (219)583-6483
Free: (800)583-6483   **Fax:** (219)583-6793
Products: Park and playground equipment including waterslides, bleachers, gazebos, and picnic shelters.
SIC: 5091 (Sporting & Recreational Goods). **Est:** 1994.
Sales: $1,700,000 (2000). **Emp:** 3. **Officers:** Daniel J. Downey, President.

■ **23744** ■ **Institutional Equipment Inc.**
4557 W 100 S
New Palestine, IN 46163-9624
Phone: (317)541-0021   **Fax:** (317)541-0024
Products: Sporting and athletic goods. **SIC:** 5091 (Sporting & Recreational Goods). **Officers:** James Sheridan, President.

■ **23745** ■ **Intermountain Resources**
3856 Hwy. 88 East
Mena, AR 71953
Phone: (501)394-7893   **Fax:** (501)394-7893
Products: Exports outdoor recreation equipment for U.S. and foreign manufacturers of these goods. **SIC:** 5091 (Sporting & Recreational Goods). **Emp:** 1.

■ **23746** ■ **International Marine Industries**
PO Box 3609
221 Third St.
Newport, RI 02840-0990
Phone: (401)849-4982   **Fax:** (401)847-9966
E-mail: bill@wrpimi.com
Products: Fishing boats; Frozen bait products, frozen fish. **SIC:** 5091 (Sporting & Recreational Goods). **Est:** 1977. **Sales:** $5,000,000 (1999). **Emp:** 12. **Officers:** William Palombo, President; Chuck Paina, P Fish Division, e-mail: chuck@wrpimi.com; Chris Patso, General Mgr.

■ **23747** ■ **International Projects Inc.**
PO Box 397
Holland, OH 43528
Phone: (419)865-6201   **Fax:** (419)865-0954
Products: Biological indicators; Log cabin kits;

Refrigeration and air conditioning repair equipment.
SICs: 5075 (Warm Air Heating & Air-Conditioning); 5075 (Warm Air Heating & Air-Conditioning); 5047 (Medical & Hospital Equipment). **Est:** 1976. **Sales:** $2,000,000 (2000). **Emp:** 4. **Officers:** Frank J. Reynolds, President, e-mail: fjr424@aol.com.

■ **23748** ■ **Island Cycle Supply Co.**
425 Washington Ave. N
Minneapolis, MN 55401-1316
Phone: (612)333-7771   **Fax:** (612)338-6650
E-mail: info@islandcycle.com
URL: http://www.islandcycle.com
Products: Bicycle parts, accessories and tools. **SIC:** 5091 (Sporting & Recreational Goods). **Est:** 1898.
Emp: 10. **Officers:** Thomas Kieffer, President.

■ **23749** ■ **Island Style**
PO Box 50458
Jacksonville Beach, FL 32240
Phone: (904)246-7182
Free: (800)957-8953   **Fax:** (904)241-5204
Products: Surfing supplies, including boards, leashes, and sunscreen. **SICs:** 5091 (Sporting & Recreational Goods); 5122 (Drugs, Proprietaries & Sundries).

■ **23750** ■ **Izuo Brothers Ltd.**
PO Box 1197
Honolulu, HI 96807-1197
Phone: (808)591-8488   **Fax:** (808)591-9387
E-mail: izuo@lava.net
Products: Sporting goods, including fishing, camping, and outdoor recreational equipment. **SIC:** 5091 (Sporting & Recreational Goods). **Est:** 1949. **Emp:** 28.
Officers: Randall Izuo, President; Rodney Izuo, Exec. VP; Darrell Okamato, Sales/Marketing Contact; Lisa Saito, Customer Service Contact; Raylene Izuo, Human Resources Contact.

■ **23751** ■ **J and B Foam Fabricators Inc.**
PO Box 144
Ludington, MI 49431-0144
Phone: (616)843-2448
Free: (800)621-3626   **Fax:** (616)843-8723
Products: Recreational and sporting goods. **SIC:** 5091 (Sporting & Recreational Goods). **Sales:** $600,000 (2000). **Emp:** 4.

■ **23752** ■ **J & B Importers Inc.**
11925 SW 128th St.
Miami, FL 33186-5207
Phone: (305)238-1866   **Fax:** (305)235-8056
URL: http://www.jbimporters.com
Products: Bicycles, including parts and accessories; Helmets; Adult tricycles. Recumbent bicycles; Tandems. **SIC:** 5091 (Sporting & Recreational Goods).
Est: 1971. **Emp:** 200. **Officers:** Ben Joannou Jr., Sales/Marketing Contact.

■ **23753** ■ **J & B Tackle Company Inc.**
25 Smith Ave.
Niantic, CT 06357-3229
Phone: (860)739-7419   **Fax:** (860)739-4999
Products: Sporting and athletic goods; Fishing tackle and equipment. **SIC:** 5091 (Sporting & Recreational Goods). **Officers:** John Douton, President.

■ **23754** ■ **J & E Fishing Supplies Inc.**
2295 N King St.
Honolulu, HI 96819-4505
Phone: (808)847-4327
Products: Sporting and athletic goods; Fishing tackle and equipment. **SIC:** 5091 (Sporting & Recreational Goods). **Officers:** Janet Oasa, President.

■ **23755** ■ **JBM Associates Inc.**
PO Box 188
Foxboro, MA 02035-0188
Phone: (508)543-3611   **Fax:** (508)543-8178
Products: Sporting and athletic goods. **SIC:** 5091 (Sporting & Recreational Goods). **Officers:** Gerald Mintz, President.

■ **23756** ■ **Jerry's Sport Center Inc.**
PO Box 121
Forest City, PA 18421-0121
Phone: (570)785-9400
Free: (800)234-2612   **Fax:** (570)785-9505
Products: Guns. **SIC:** 5091 (Sporting & Recreational

Goods). **Sales:** $98,000,000 (2000). **Emp:** 225.
Officers: Bernard Ziomek, President; Andrew Kupchick, Controller.

■ **23757** ■ **Jewel Box Inc.**
601 N Central Ave.
Phoenix, AZ 85004-2126
Phone: (602)252-5777   **Fax:** (602)252-5770
Products: Sporting and recreation goods, including hunting equipment, supplies, and firearms. **SIC:** 5091 (Sporting & Recreational Goods). **Officers:** Morris Reznik, President.

■ **23758** ■ **G. Joannou Cycle Company Inc.**
151 Ludlow Ave.
Northvale, NJ 07647
Phone: (201)768-9050
Products: Bicycles. **SIC:** 5091 (Sporting & Recreational Goods). **Sales:** $24,000,000 (2000).
Emp: 100. **Officers:** Madeline Joannou, CEO.

■ **23759** ■ **Jog-A-Lite Inc.**
18 High St.
PO Box 125
Silver Lake, NH 03875
Phone: (603)367-4741
Free: (800)258-8974   **Fax:** (603)367-8098
E-mail: jogalite@landmarknet.net
Products: Reflective sporting gear; Highway vests.
SIC: 5091 (Sporting & Recreational Goods). **Est:** 1977.
Sales: $2,000,000 (2000). **Emp:** 9. **Officers:** Peter Lang, President; Hunt Barclay, CEO; Tammy Flanagin, Customer Service Contact. **Alternate Name:** Nitefighter International. **Doing Business As:** American Custom Safety.

■ **23760** ■ **Johnny's Crab Traps Inc.**
10410 Chef Menteur Hwy.
New Orleans, LA 70127-4216
Phone: (504)246-2325
Products: Sporting and athletic goods; Fishing tackle and equipment. **SIC:** 5091 (Sporting & Recreational Goods). **Officers:** Johnny Russo, President.

■ **23761** ■ **Hans Johnsen Co.**
8901 Chancellor Row
Dallas, TX 75247
Phone: (214)879-1515   **Fax:** (214)879-1520
Products: Locks; Bicycle Equipment. **SICs:** 5091 (Sporting & Recreational Goods); 5072 (Hardware).
Est: 1901. **Sales:** $11,000,000 (2000). **Emp:** 39.
Officers: Howard H. Johnsen, President.

■ **23762** ■ **Johnson Camping Inc.**
PO Box 966
Binghamton, NY 13902
Phone: (607)779-2200
Free: (800)847-1460   **Fax:** (607)779-2293
Products: Backpacks, tents, and sleeping bags. **SIC:** 5091 (Sporting & Recreational Goods).

■ **23763** ■ **Jack Jolly & Sons, Inc.**
513 Pleasant Valley Ave.
Moorestown, NJ 08057
Phone: (609)234-4448
Products: Golf equipment. **SIC:** 5091 (Sporting & Recreational Goods).

■ **23764** ■ **Joseph's Clothing & Sporting Goods**
PO Box 180
Fairfield, ME 04937-0180
Phone: (207)453-9756   **Fax:** (207)453-6736
Products: Sporting and recreational goods, including golf and skiing equipment and supplies. **SIC:** 5091 (Sporting & Recreational Goods). **Officers:** Jon Eustis, President.

■ **23765** ■ **JP International Imports & Exports**
PO Box 68
Marysville, MI 48040-0068
Phone: (810)364-9300
Products: Sporting and recreational goods. **SIC:** 5091 (Sporting & Recreational Goods). **Officers:** Peter Kim, Partner.

■ **23766** ■ **K & P Manufacturing**
950 W Foothill Blvd.
Azusa, CA 91702
Phone: (626)334-0334 **Fax:** (626)334-0333
E-mail: kartsparts91702@aol.com
URL: http://www.kpmfg.com
Products: Go-carts. **SIC:** 5091 (Sporting & Recreational Goods). **Est:** 1957. **Sales:** $1,000,000 (2000). **Emp:** 7. **Officers:** T.J. Pierson, Vice President, e-mail: tom91722@aol.com; Jon Pierson, President; Faye Pierson, Dir. of Marketing.

■ **23767** ■ **K-Swiss Inc.**
31248 Oak Crest Dr.
Westlake Village, CA 91361
Free: (800)297-1919
Products: Gym shoes; Athletic clothing; Backpacks; Jackets. **SICs:** 5091 (Sporting & Recreational Goods); 5139 (Footwear); 5099 (Durable Goods Nec). **Est:** 1966. **Sales:** $96,000,000 (2000). **Emp:** 265. **Officers:** Steven Nichols, President.

■ **23768** ■ **K2 Corp.**
19215 Vashon Hwy. SW
Vashon, WA 98070
Phone: (206)463-3631 **Fax:** (206)463-2861
Products: Fiberglass snow skis, snow boards, in-line skates and mountain bikes; Skiing-related accessories, gloves and hats. **SIC:** 5091 (Sporting & Recreational Goods). **Sales:** $547,500,000 (2000). **Emp:** 3,200. **Officers:** Richard M. Rodstein, CEO & President; John J. Rangel, Sr. VP & Finance Officer.

■ **23769** ■ **Karhu USA Inc.**
550 Hinesburg Rd., Ste. 200
South Burlington, VT 05403-6542
Phone: (802)864-4519
Products: Ice Hockey equipment. **SIC:** 5091 (Sporting & Recreational Goods). **Sales:** $18,000,000 (2000). **Emp:** 20. **Officers:** Dave Smallwood, Vice President.

■ **23770** ■ **Keller Supply Co.**
21017 77th Ave., S
Kent, WA 98032
Phone: (253)872-7575 **Fax:** (253)872-6525
URL: http://www.kellersupply.com
Products: Pool equipment and supplies. **SIC:** 5091 (Sporting & Recreational Goods).

■ **23771** ■ **A.C. Kerman, Inc.**
1308-K N Magnolia Ave.
El Cajon, CA 92020-1646
Phone: (619)440-4470 **Fax:** (619)440-4478
E-mail: sales@ackinc.com
Products: Fishing tackle and accessories, including rods, reels, bait, lures, tackle boxes, and nets; camping equipment, including tents, sleeping bags, and laterns. **SIC:** 5091 (Sporting & Recreational Goods). **Est:** 1986. **Emp:** 12. **Officers:** Claire Ackerman, President.

■ **23772** ■ **Keys Fitness Products Inc.**
11220 Petal St.
Dallas, TX 75238
Phone: (214)340-8888
Products: Exercise equipment. **SIC:** 5091 (Sporting & Recreational Goods). **Sales:** $15,200,000 (1994). **Emp:** 32. **Officers:** Tim W. Chen, President; H. Dale Hawes, Controller.

■ **23773** ■ **Keystone Cue & Cushion Inc.**
2800 Dickerson Rd.
Reno, NV 89503-4313
Phone: (702)329-5718 **Fax:** (702)329-8816
Products: Sporting and athletic goods; Billiard tables and supplies. **SIC:** 5091 (Sporting & Recreational Goods). **Officers:** Michael Peel, President.

■ **23774** ■ **Martin Kilpatrick Table Tennis Co.**
PO Box 157
Wilson, NC 27894-0157
Phone: (919)291-8202
Free: (800)334-8315 **Fax:** (919)291-8203
Products: Table tennis equipment and accessories. **SIC:** 5091 (Sporting & Recreational Goods). **Est:** 1960. **Sales:** $2,500,000 (2000). **Emp:** 10. **Officers:** Bowie Martin Jr., President. **Former Name:** Bowmar Productions Inc. **Former Name:** Martin #Kilpatrick Co.

■ **23775** ■ **E.F. King Co. Inc.**
640 Pleasant St.
Norwood, MA 02062
Phone: (617)762-3113 **Fax:** (617)762-7743
Products: Pool chemicals. **SIC:** 5169 (Chemicals & Allied Products Nec). **Est:** 1834. **Sales:** $6,000,000 (2000). **Emp:** 15. **Officers:** Eric Landau, President & CFO.

■ **23776** ■ **Klein's Allsports Distributors**
1 Crossgates Mall Rd.
Albany, NY 12203
Phone: (518)464-1495
Products: Sporting goods. **SIC:** 5091 (Sporting & Recreational Goods).

■ **23777** ■ **Kryptonics Inc.**
740 S Pierce Ave.
Louisville, CO 80027
Phone: (303)665-5353 **Fax:** (303)665-7395
Products: Roller skate, in-line skate and skateboard wheels. **SIC:** 5091 (Sporting & Recreational Goods).

■ **23778** ■ **Kwik Ski Products**
PO Box 465
Mercer Island, WA 98040
Phone: (425)228-4480
Free: (800)426-4250 **Fax:** (425)228-4102
URL: http://www.kwikski.com
Products: Repair and tuning equipment for skis and snowboards, including waxing equipment, wax, boot dryers, and boot fittings. **SIC:** 5091 (Sporting & Recreational Goods). **Est:** 1976. **Emp:** 6. **Officers:** Randy Mintz, President, e-mail: randy@kwikski.com.

■ **23779** ■ **Paul Labieniec & Associates**
28 Organ Hill Rd.
Poughkeepsie, NY 12603
Phone: (914)462-1860
Free: (800)365-3339 **Fax:** (914)462-1853
Products: Sporting and athletic goods; Playground, gymnasium, and exercise equipment. **SIC:** 5091 (Sporting & Recreational Goods).

■ **23780** ■ **Las Vegas Discount Golf and Tennis Inc.**
2701 Crimson Canyon Dr.
Las Vegas, NV 89128-0803
Products: Golf and tennis equipment and accessories. **SIC:** 5091 (Sporting & Recreational Goods). **Est:** 1974. **Sales:** $13,200,000 (2000). **Emp:** 29. **Officers:** Kim A. Stevenson, CFO; Ronald Boreta, President.

■ **23781** ■ **Lavro Inc.**
16311 177th Ave. SE
Monroe, WA 98272-1942
Phone: (206)794-5525
Free: (888)337-2980 **Fax:** (360)805-9277
Products: River boats and related equipment. **SIC:** 5091 (Sporting & Recreational Goods). **Est:** 1973. **Officers:** Ronald Lavigueure, President.

■ **23782** ■ **LBK Distributors**
1710 S Wabash St.
Wabash, IN 46992-4118
Phone: (219)563-3372 **Fax:** (219)563-3372
Products: Sporting and athletic goods. **SIC:** 5091 (Sporting & Recreational Goods). **Officers:** Larry Keffaber, Owner.

■ **23783** ■ **Lee Tennis, LLC**
2975 Ivy Rd.
Charlottesville, VA 22903
Phone: (804)295-6167
Free: (800)327-8379 **Fax:** (804)971-6995
E-mail: hartru@hartru.com
URL: http://www.hartru.com
Products: Tennis and racquet ball equipment; Floorcoverings; Surfacing. **SICs:** 5091 (Sporting & Recreational Goods); 5023 (Homefurnishings). **Est:** 1964. **Sales:** $9,000,000 (2000). **Emp:** 45. **Officers:** John Welborn, Manager. **Former Name:** Lee Tennis Products.

■ **23784** ■ **Leisurelife USA Inc.**
5232 Buckhead Trail
Knoxville, TN 37919-8903
Phone: (865)558-6302 **Fax:** (865)558-6303
E-mail: trektrentgg@mindspring.com
Products: Camping products, including tents and jungle and combat boots. **SICs:** 5091 (Sporting & Recreational Goods); 5139 (Footwear). **Est:** 1989. **Officers:** George Smith, President.

■ **23785** ■ **Leland Limited Inc.**
PO Box 382
Bedminster, NJ 07921
Phone: (908)668-1008
Free: (800)984-9793 **Fax:** (908)668-7716
Products: Recreational and sporting goods. **SIC:** 5091 (Sporting & Recreational Goods). **Sales:** $5,000,000 (2000). **Emp:** 12.

■ **23786** ■ **Jerry Lenz Sports**
PO Box 4466
Victoria, TX 77903
Phone: (512)575-2378 **Fax:** (512)575-8219
Products: Sporting and athletic goods. **SIC:** 5091 (Sporting & Recreational Goods). **Sales:** $1,500,000 (2000). **Emp:** 21. **Officers:** Jerry Lenz.

■ **23787** ■ **Life-Link International**
PO Box 2913
Jackson, WY 83001
Phone: (307)733-2266
Free: (800)443-8620 **Fax:** (307)733-8469
E-mail: life-link@life-link.com
URL: http://www.life-link.com
Products: Sporting and athletic goods. **SIC:** 5091 (Sporting & Recreational Goods). **Est:** 1978. **Sales:** $10,000,000 (2000). **Emp:** 130. **Officers:** John Krisik, President; John Scott, Vice President.

■ **23788** ■ **Lightnin Fiberglass Co.**
PO Box 268
Kilauea, HI 96754
Phone: (808)828-1583 **Fax:** (808)828-1583
Products: Fiberglass boats, including power catamarans. **SIC:** 5091 (Sporting & Recreational Goods). **Sales:** $500,000 (2000). **Emp:** 3.

■ **23789** ■ **Lisk Lures**
915 Onslow Dr.
Greensboro, NC 27408-7709
Phone: (336)299-7787 **Fax:** (336)851-5864
Products: Fishing tackle and equipment; Lures. **SIC:** 5091 (Sporting & Recreational Goods). **Est:** 1954. **Sales:** $1,000,000 (2000). **Emp:** 9. **Officers:** Eva Lisk, Owner; Terry Lisk, Sales; Van Lisk, Customer Service Contact.

■ **23790** ■ **Lob-Ster Inc.**
PO Box 2865
Plainfield, NJ 07062
Phone: (908)668-1900
Free: (800)526-4041 **Fax:** (908)668-0436
Products: Tennis and racquet ball equipment. **SIC:** 5091 (Sporting & Recreational Goods). **Est:** 1975. **Sales:** $1,200,000 (2000). **Emp:** 12. **Officers:** Harry A. Giuditta, President.

■ **23791** ■ **Lolo Sporting Goods Inc.**
1026 Main St.
Lewiston, ID 83501-1842
Phone: (208)743-1031
Products: Sporting and athletic goods. **SIC:** 5091 (Sporting & Recreational Goods). **Officers:** John Nolt, President.

■ **23792** ■ **London Bridge Trading Company Ltd.**
3509 Virginia Beach Blvd.
Virginia Beach, VA 23452-4421
Phone: (757)498-0207
Free: (800)229-0207 **Fax:** (757)498-0059
E-mail: lbt@visi.net
URL: http://www.londonbridgetrading.com
Products: Footwear, including boots; Backpacks and belt pouches; Weight-bearing equipment; Special military equipment. **SICs:** 5091 (Sporting & Recreational Goods); 5139 (Footwear). **Est:** 1985. **Sales:** $1,250,000 (2000). **Emp:** 35. **Officers:** Doug McDougal, President.

■ 23793 ■ **Longnecker Inc.**
3707 Pacific Ave. SE
Olympia, WA 98501-2124
Phone: (360)459-3226 **Fax:** (360)459-1315
E-mail: vlongnecker@prodigy.net
URL: http://www.longnecker.uswestdex.com
Products: Spas, bathtubs, whirlpools, and swimming pools. **SIC:** 5091 (Sporting & Recreational Goods). **Est:** 1979. **Sales:** $2,000,000 (2000). **Emp:** 10. **Officers:** Mark Longnecker, President.

■ 23794 ■ **M & M Vehicle Co.**
530 N Jefferson
Mexico, MO 65265
Phone: (573)581-8188 **Fax:** (573)581-7267
Products: Golf carts and supplies. **SICs:** 5091 (Sporting & Recreational Goods); 5088 (Transportation Equipment & Supplies).

■ 23795 ■ **MacGregor Sports and Fitness Inc.**
8100 White Horse Rd.
Greenville, SC 29611-1836
Phone: (864)294-5230
Products: Inflatable sports equipment; Baseballs, softballs and baseball gloves. **SIC:** 5091 (Sporting & Recreational Goods).

■ 23796 ■ **Magic Distributing**
1001 Orchard Lake Rd.
Pontiac, MI 48341
Phone: (248)334-1730
Free: (800)783-5859 **Fax:** (248)332-9410
Products: Dirt bike accessories. **SIC:** 5091 (Sporting & Recreational Goods).

■ 23797 ■ **Maine Battery Distributors**
261 Black Point Rd.
Scarborough, ME 04074
Products: Recreational vehicles and equipment including snowmobiles. **SIC:** 5091 (Sporting & Recreational Goods).

■ 23798 ■ **Ralph Maltby's Golfworks**
4820 Jacksontown Rd.
Newark, OH 43056
Phone: (740)328-4193
Free: (800)848-8358 **Fax:** 800-800-3290
E-mail: golfwork@golfworks.com
URL: http://www.golfworks.com
Products: Golf equipment. **SIC:** 5091 (Sporting & Recreational Goods). **Est:** 1977. **Emp:** 150.

■ 23799 ■ **Marine Electric Co.**
9804 James Cir. S
Minneapolis, MN 55431-2919
Phone: (612)881-0077
Products: Sporting and recreational goods, including boats, canoes, watercrafts, and equipment. **SIC:** 5091 (Sporting & Recreational Goods). **Officers:** Daniel Chesky, President.

■ 23800 ■ **Mark-It of Colorado LLC**
233 Milwaukee St.
Denver, CO 80206
Phone: (303)377-9110
Free: (800)878-5256 **Fax:** (303)333-1905
Products: Golf accessories. **SIC:** 5091 (Sporting & Recreational Goods). **Emp:** 12. **Officers:** John Gart, President.

■ 23801 ■ **Marker USA**
PO Box 26548
Salt Lake City, UT 84126-0548
Phone: (801)972-2100
Free: (800)453-3862 **Fax:** (801)973-7241
Products: Sporting and recreation goods. **SIC:** 5091 (Sporting & Recreational Goods). **Officers:** Hank Tauber, President.

■ 23802 ■ **Mike Marks Pro Shop**
141 28th St. SE
Grand Rapids, MI 49548-1103
Phone: (616)245-7503 **Free:** ((61))752-4102
Products: Bowling equipment; Men's clothing and uniforms. **SICs:** 5091 (Sporting & Recreational Goods); 5136 (Men's/Boys' Clothing). **Officers:** William Reiffer, Sole Proprietor.

■ 23803 ■ **Markwort Sporting Goods Co.**
4300 Forest Park Ave.
St. Louis, MO 63108-2884
Phone: (314)652-8935
Free: (800)280-5555 **Fax:** (314)652-6241
E-mail: sales@markwort.com
URL: http://www.markwort.com
Products: Sporting and athletic goods. **SIC:** 5091 (Sporting & Recreational Goods). **Est:** 1931. **Emp:** 60. **Officers:** Herb Markwort Jr., President; Glenn Markwort, Vice President; Dorothy Rhodes, Chairman of the Board.

■ 23804 ■ **Marquis Corp.**
596 Hoffman Rd.
Independence, OR 97351-9601
Phone: (503)838-0888 **Fax:** (503)838-3849
Products: Whirlpool baths. **SIC:** 5091 (Sporting & Recreational Goods). **Sales:** $12,000,000 (2000). **Emp:** 99. **Officers:** M. C. Bickest; Jeffery C. Kurth.

■ 23805 ■ **Masek Sports Inc.**
PO Box 1089
Mills, WY 82644
Phone: (307)237-9566 **Fax:** (307)237-9567
Products: Sporting and recreational goods, including canoes, watercrafts, motorboats, and equipment. **SIC:** 5091 (Sporting & Recreational Goods). **Officers:** Lee Underbrink, President.

■ 23806 ■ **Master Cartridge Corp.**
PO Box 238
VilLa Rica, GA 30180-0238
Phone: (404)459-5116 **Fax:** (404)459-1904
Products: Sporting and athletic goods; Hunting equipment; Sporting ammunition. **SIC:** 5091 (Sporting & Recreational Goods). **Officers:** L. Shipley, President.

■ 23807 ■ **Master Industries Inc.**
PO Box 17808
Irvine, CA 92623-7808
Phone: (949)660-0644 **Fax:** (949)660-1678
E-mail: info@masterindustries.com
Products: Bowling accessories, including gloves and bags. **SIC:** 5091 (Sporting & Recreational Goods). **Est:** 1967. **Emp:** 50. **Officers:** Steve Norman.

■ 23808 ■ **Maumee Co.**
PO Box 621
Adrian, MI 49221-0621
Phone: (517)263-6791
Free: (800)837-7767 **Fax:** (517)263-8552
Products: Team goods; Corporate logo merchandise. **SIC:** 5091 (Sporting & Recreational Goods). **Est:** 1946. **Sales:** $1,500,000 (1999). **Emp:** 6. **Officers:** Rick A. Baker, President, e-mail: rabaker@dmcl.net.

■ 23809 ■ **Maurice Sporting Goods**
1825 Shermer Rd.
Northbrook, IL 60065
Phone: (847)480-7900
Free: (800)477-3474 **Fax:** (847)480-1704
Products: Fishing and hunting equipment. **SIC:** 5091 (Sporting & Recreational Goods).

■ 23810 ■ **Mayfield & Co. Inc.**
3101 W Clearwater Ave.
Kennewick, WA 99336-2738
Phone: (509)735-8525
Free: (800)827-8157 **Fax:** (509)783-8672
Products: Sporting and recreational goods, including fitness equipment and supplies. **SIC:** 5091 (Sporting & Recreational Goods). **Est:** 1948. **Officers:** John Mayfield, President.

■ 23811 ■ **Mayfield Pool Supply L.L.C.**
PO Box 148
El Paso, TX 79942
Phone: (915)532-1483 **Fax:** (915)532-5838
Products: Swimming pool supplies, including chemicals, hoses, nets, pumps, and covers. **SICs:** 5091 (Sporting & Recreational Goods); 5169 (Chemicals & Allied Products Nec). **Est:** 1924. **Sales:** $3,500,000 (2000). **Emp:** 14. **Officers:** Carson Hatfied, President; Gay Thompson, Vice President; Alex Garrio, General Mgr. **Former Name:** Mayfield Lumber and Container Corp.

■ 23812 ■ **Mc-U Sports**
822 W Jefferson St.
Boise, ID 83702-5826
Phone: (208)342-7734
Free: (800)632-6651 **Fax:** (208)342-8348
Products: Sporting and athletic goods. **SIC:** 5091 (Sporting & Recreational Goods). **Officers:** Richard Urresti, President.

■ 23813 ■ **McBroom Pool Products Inc.**
2025 George Washington Memorial Hwy.
Yorktown, VA 23692-4222
Phone: (757)874-1699
Free: (800)277-9461 **Fax:** (757)595-0432
Products: Pool equipment and supplies; Wood porch, lawn, beach, and similar furniture, including gliders, swings, folding cots, tables, and picnic table sets. **SICs:** 5091 (Sporting & Recreational Goods); 5021 (Furniture). **Est:** 1980. **Emp:** 20. **Officers:** James B. Garrison.

■ 23814 ■ **McCabe Bait Company Inc.**
PO Box 190
Kennebunkport, ME 04046-0190
Phone: (207)967-2409
Products: Sporting and athletic goods; Fishing tackle and equipment; Fresh fish. **SICs:** 5091 (Sporting & Recreational Goods); 5146 (Fish & Seafoods). **Officers:** F. Mc Cabe, President.

■ 23815 ■ **McCorkle Cricket Farm Inc.**
PO Box 285
Metter, GA 30439-0285
Phone: (912)685-2677
Free: (888)333-2677 **Fax:** (912)685-3927
Products: Sporting and recreation goods, including fishing equipment and supplies. **SIC:** 5091 (Sporting & Recreational Goods). **Est:** 1936. **Sales:** $2,000,000 (2000). **Emp:** 17. **Officers:** Oliff Mc Elveen, President.

■ 23816 ■ **McGuire Sun and Fitness Inc.**
770 Tyvola Rd.
Charlotte, NC 28217-3508
Phone: (704)523-2401 **Fax:** (704)523-0155
Products: Recreational and sporting goods. **SIC:** 5091 (Sporting & Recreational Goods).

■ 23817 ■ **M.E. O'Brien and Sons Inc.**
93 West St.
Medfield, MA 02052-2043
Phone: (508)359-4200
Free: (800)835-0056 **Fax:** (508)359-2817
Products: Recreational and sporting goods. **SIC:** 5091 (Sporting & Recreational Goods).

■ 23818 ■ **Mel Pinto Imports Inc.**
2860 Annandale Rd.
Falls Church, VA 22042-2149
Phone: (703)237-4686
Free: (800)336-3721 **Fax:** (703)534-9518
Products: Recreational and sporting goods. **SIC:** 5091 (Sporting & Recreational Goods). **Sales:** $2,000,000 (2000). **Emp:** 15.

■ 23819 ■ **Gregory N. Melges**
8640 Riverwood Cir.
New London, MN 56273-9710
Phone: (320)796-2421
Products: Sporting and athletic goods; Fishing tackle and equipment. **SIC:** 5091 (Sporting & Recreational Goods). **Officers:** Gregory Melges, Owner.

■ 23820 ■ **Memphis Import Company Inc.**
648 Riverside Dr.
Memphis, TN 38103
Phone: (901)526-4185 **Fax:** (901)525-3233
Products: Tools; Fishing tackle. **SICs:** 5091 (Sporting & Recreational Goods); 5072 (Hardware). **Est:** 1964. **Sales:** $6,000,000 (2000). **Emp:** 11. **Officers:** Mary Jo McMillian, President; Jo Ellen Hoy, Treasurer.

■ 23821 ■ **Memphis Pool Supply Co. Inc.**
2762 Getwell Rd.
Memphis, TN 38118-1846
Phone: (901)365-2480 **Fax:** (901)365-4089
E-mail: infomps@memphispool.com
URL: http://www.memphispool.com
Products: Swimming pool, spa, and water feature equipment, parts, and supplies. **SIC:** 5091 (Sporting &

Recreational Goods). **Est:** 1952. **Emp:** 31. **Officers:** Roy Reed, President.

■ **23822** ■ **Mercantile Sales Company Inc.**
1141 S 7th St.
St. Louis, MO 63104
Phone: (314)421-1676
Free: (800)421-1676 **Fax:** (314)421-3732
URL: http://www.campersoutdooroutlet.com
Products: Camping supplies, including sleeping bags, tents, and canteens. **SIC:** 5091 (Sporting & Recreational Goods). **Est:** 1947. **Sales:** $2,000,000 (2000). **Emp:** 10. **Officers:** R.J. Faeth, President.

■ **23823** ■ **Merrymeeting Corp.**
US Rte. 1
PO Box 372
Woolwich, ME 04579-0372
Phone: (207)442-7002 **Fax:** (207)442-0936
E-mail: bikeman@bikeman.com
URL: http://www.bikeman.com
Products: Sporting and recreational goods, including bicycle equipment and supplies, skis, and rollerblades. **SIC:** 5091 (Sporting & Recreational Goods). **Est:** 1976. **Sales:** $1,300,000 (2000). **Emp:** 10. **Officers:** Davis Carver, President.

■ **23824** ■ **MH Associates Ltd.**
712 38th St. N
Fargo, ND 58102-2961
Phone: (701)282-7877 **Fax:** (701)282-7779
Products: Coin-operated game machines. **SIC:** 5087 (Service Establishment Equipment). **Officers:** Vicky Sieben, President.

■ **23825** ■ **Mickeys Sales Co.**
2601-09 Strong
Kansas City, KS 66106
Phone: (913)831-1493
Products: Sporting and athletic goods; Army surplus goods; Work clothes and boots. **SIC:** 5091 (Sporting & Recreational Goods). **Est:** 1957. **Sales:** $5,000,000 (2000). **Emp:** 15. **Officers:** Major Goldstein, President.

■ **23826** ■ **Mid-Atlantic Park & Playground Concepts**
PO Box 710
Tunkhannock, PA 18657-0710
Phone: (570)836-8037
Free: (800)392-8736 **Fax:** (570)836-6597
Products: Sporting and athletic goods; Playground, gymnasium, and exercise equipment. **SIC:** 5091 (Sporting & Recreational Goods). **Est:** 1990. **Sales:** $1,500,000 (2000). **Emp:** 2. **Officers:** William J. Gibbons, President.

■ **23827** ■ **Mid-Atlantic Spa Distributors**
2611 Philmont Ave.
Huntingdon Valley, PA 19006-5301
Phone: (215)947-8644 **Fax:** (215)947-7256
Products: Spas and hot tubs; Pond and water garden products. **SIC:** 5091 (Sporting & Recreational Goods). **Est:** 1980. **Sales:** $3,000,000 (2000). **Emp:** 49.

■ **23828** ■ **Middleground Golf Inc.**
PO Box 612
Leitchfield, KY 42755-0612
Phone: (270)259-5510
Free: (800)635-3098 **Fax:** (270)259-4160
Products: Sporting and recreational goods, including golf equipment, supplies, and custom golf clubs. **SIC:** 5091 (Sporting & Recreational Goods). **Officers:** Jerry Childress, President.

■ **23829** ■ **Midwest Pool Distributors Inc.**
7607 Murphy Dr.
Middleton, WI 53562
Phone: (608)831-5957
Products: Swimming pools. **SIC:** 5091 (Sporting & Recreational Goods).

■ **23830** ■ **Miracle Playground Sales**
27537 Commerce Ctr., Ste. 105
Temecula, CA 92590
Phone: (909)695-4515
Free: (800)264-7225 **Fax:** (909)676-8706
E-mail: sales@miracleplayground.com
Products: Sporting and athletic goods. **SIC:** 5091 (Sporting & Recreational Goods). **Est:** 1996. **Emp:** 6.

■ **23831** ■ **Miracle Recreation of Minnesota Inc.**
2175 Brooke Ln.
Hastings, MN 55033
Phone: (612)438-3630
Free: (800)677-5153 **Fax:** (612)438-3939
Products: Playground, gymnasium, and exercise equipment. **SIC:** 5091 (Sporting & Recreational Goods).

■ **23832** ■ **Mitchell Manufacturing, Hagens Division**
3150 W Havens
Box 82
Mitchell, SD 57301
Phone: (605)996-1891
Free: (800)541-4586 **Fax:** (605)996-8946
URL: http://www.hagensfish.com
Products: Fishing components. **SIC:** 5091 (Sporting & Recreational Goods). **Est:** 1976.

■ **23833** ■ **Mobile Cycle Center**
5373 Halls Mill Rd.
Mobile, AL 36619
Phone: (205)666-2650 **Fax:** (205)660-0986
Products: Motorcycles, jet skis, and gocarts. **SICs:** 5091 (Sporting & Recreational Goods); 5012 (Automobiles & Other Motor Vehicles).

■ **23834** ■ **Monticello Sports Inc.**
100 W 1st St.
Monticello, IA 52310-1519
Phone: (319)465-5429 **Fax:** (319)465-5587
Products: Sporting and athletic goods. **SIC:** 5091 (Sporting & Recreational Goods). **Est:** 1977. **Emp:** 25. **Officers:** Dan Read, President.

■ **23835** ■ **Moore-Sigler Sports World Inc.**
PO Box 6612
Shreveport, LA 71136-6612
Phone: (318)686-1880
Products: Sporting and athletic goods. **SIC:** 5091 (Sporting & Recreational Goods). **Officers:** Randall Moore, Chairman of the Board.

■ **23836** ■ **Morris Rothenberg and Son Inc.**
25 Ranick Rd.
Smithtown, NY 11788
Phone: (631)234-8000
Free: (800)645-5195 **Fax:** (631)234-8772
E-mail: bdus@rothco.com
URL: http://www.rothco.com
Products: Sporting goods and army surplus; Camping supplies; Outerwear; Law enforcement equipment. **SICs:** 5091 (Sporting & Recreational Goods); 5199 (Nondurable Goods Nec). **Est:** 1943. **Sales:** $38,000,000 (2000). **Emp:** 62. **Officers:** Howard Somberg, President; Richard Fleishman, Controller.

■ **23837** ■ **Morrow Snowboards Inc.**
599 Menlo Dr., No. 200
Rocklin, CA 95765-3708
Products: Snow boarding boots and related accessories. **SICs:** 5091 (Sporting & Recreational Goods); 5136 (Men's/Boys' Clothing); 5137 (Women's/Children's Clothing). **Sales:** $20,300,000 (2000). **Emp:** 284. **Officers:** David Calapp, CEO & Chairman of the Board; P. Blair Mullin, CFO.

■ **23838** ■ **Mountain Shades Distributing Co.**
PO Box 609
Vail, CO 81658-0609
Phone: (970)949-6301
Free: (800)234-0735 **Fax:** (970)949-4993
Products: Sporting and athletic goods; Eye and face protection devices. **SIC:** 5091 (Sporting & Recreational Goods). **Officers:** Ken Fox, President.

■ **23839** ■ **Mountain States Sporting Goods**
PO Box 25863
Albuquerque, NM 87125-0863
Phone: (505)243-5515 **Fax:** (505)243-5938
Products: Sporting and recreation goods, including camping equipment. **SIC:** 5091 (Sporting & Recreational Goods). **Officers:** Raymond Garcia, President.

■ **23840** ■ **Multisports Inc.**
4660 Pine Timbers St.
Houston, TX 77041
Phone: (713)460-8188
Products: Exercise equipment, including weights, steppers, skiers, and home gyms. **SIC:** 5091 (Sporting & Recreational Goods). **Est:** 1986. **Sales:** $2,000,000 (2000). **Emp:** 10. **Officers:** Brucie Chen, President & CFO.

■ **23841** ■ **O. Mustad and Son Inc.**
PO Box 838
Auburn, NY 13021
Phone: (315)253-2793
Products: Sporting goods. **SIC:** 5091 (Sporting & Recreational Goods). **Est:** 1969. **Sales:** $12,000,000 (2000). **Emp:** 50. **Officers:** Arne Forsberg, President; Robert Hoerger, Controller.

■ **23842** ■ **N Pool Patio Ltd.**
PO Box 495
North Chatham, MA 02650-0495
Phone: (508)945-1540
Products: Casual furniture; Spas; Pool chemicals and supplies. **SICs:** 5091 (Sporting & Recreational Goods); 5021 (Furniture); 5169 (Chemicals & Allied Products Nec). **Officers:** Marshall Caron, Owner.

■ **23843** ■ **Nashville Sporting Goods Co.**
169 8th Ave. N
Nashville, TN 37203-3717
Phone: (615)259-4241
Products: Sporting and athletic goods. **SIC:** 5091 (Sporting & Recreational Goods). **Officers:** Walter Nipper, President.

■ **23844** ■ **Nebraska Golf Discount Inc.**
724 N 109th Ct.
Omaha, NE 68154-1718
Phone: (402)493-5656
Products: Golf equipment. **SIC:** 5091 (Sporting & Recreational Goods). **Officers:** Craig Reitz, President.

■ **23845** ■ **Nefouse Brothers Distributing Co.**
4320 Delemere Ct.
Royal Oak, MI 48073-1810
Phone: (248)549-5554
Products: Sporting and athletic goods; Golf equipment. **SIC:** 5091 (Sporting & Recreational Goods). **Officers:** Paul Nefouse, Owner.

■ **23846** ■ **Tim J. Noland & Associates, Inc.**
10005 Trailridge Dr.
Shreveport, LA 71106
Free: (800)733-2022 **Fax:** (318)797-0465
Products: Sporting and athletic goods. **SIC:** 5091 (Sporting & Recreational Goods).

■ **23847** ■ **Nordica USA Inc.**
1 Sportsystem Plz.
Bordentown, NJ 08505
Phone: (609)291-5800 **Free:** (800)892-2668
Products: Ski boots, men's and women's ski suits. **SIC:** 5091 (Sporting & Recreational Goods). **Sales:** $26,000,000 (2000). **Emp:** 30. **Officers:** Charles Peifer, CEO & President; Brian Kovalchuk, CFO.

■ **23848** ■ **Normark Corp.**
10395 Yellow Circle Dr.
Minnetonka, MN 55343
Phone: (612)933-7060
Products: Fishing lures. **SIC:** 5091 (Sporting & Recreational Goods). **Est:** 1960. **Sales:** $30,000,000 (2000). **Emp:** 30. **Officers:** Ronald W. Weber, President; Robert A. Miller, CFO; Warren Reader, Dir. of Sales.

■ **23849** ■ **North American Parts Inc.**
10589 Main St.
PO Box 392
Clarence, NY 14031
Phone: (716)759-8351 **Fax:** (716)759-8195
URL: http://www.nap-inc.com
Products: Amusement park rides and spare parts. **SICs:** 5087 (Service Establishment Equipment); 5091 (Sporting & Recreational Goods). **Est:** 1981. **Emp:** 3. **Officers:** Louis P. Butenschoen, President; Margi Butenschoen, Vice President; Don Hereth, Parts Mgr., e-mail: parts@naparinc.com; Tanya Wiener, Sales.

■ 23850 ■ North Auburn Cash Market
584 N Auburn Rd.
Auburn, ME 04210-9803
Phone: (207)783-7378
Products: Sporting and athletic goods; Fishing tackle and equipment. **SIC:** 5091 (Sporting & Recreational Goods). **Officers:** Annette Breton, Owner.

■ 23851 ■ North Country Marketing Ltd.
9915 N 170th Ave.
Hugo, MN 55038
Phones: (612)433-4600   (612)433-4600
Fax: (612)433-4800
Products: Sporting and athletic goods. **SIC:** 5091 (Sporting & Recreational Goods). **Officers:** Michael Schuett, President.

■ 23852 ■ Northland Sports Inc.
PO Box 5009
Minot, ND 58702-5009
Phone: (701)857-1187   **Fax:** (701)857-1188
Products: Sporting and athletic goods. **SIC:** 5091 (Sporting & Recreational Goods). **Officers:** Richard Saunders, President.

■ 23853 ■ Northwest Coast Trading Company
1546 NE 89th St.
Seattle, WA 98115
Phone: (206)524-2307   **Fax:** (206)524-6137
Products: Sporting goods, including hiking and climbing equipment. **SIC:** 5091 (Sporting & Recreational Goods). **Officers:** Scott Ernest, President.

■ 23854 ■ Norvel Hasley and Associates
PO Box 936
Greensboro, GA 30642
Phone: (706)467-3328
Free: (800)685-2063
Products: Recreational and sporting goods. **SIC:** 5091 (Sporting & Recreational Goods). **Sales:** $1,500,000 (2000). **Emp:** 2.

■ 23855 ■ Norwood Products Co.
3202 Railroad
Oscoda, MI 48750-0333
Phone: (517)739-9852   **Fax:** (517)739-0811
Products: Pool tables. **SIC:** 5091 (Sporting & Recreational Goods). **Est:** 1932. **Sales:** $1,000,000 (2000). **Emp:** 35. **Officers:** R.L. Wassmann, President; M.L. Wassmann, Sec. & Treas.; Steve Mallak, Sales Mgr.

■ 23856 ■ M.E. O'Brien & Sons Inc.
93 West St.
Medfield, MA 02052-2043
Phone: (508)359-4200
Free: (800)835-0056   **Fax:** (508)359-2817
E-mail: meobrien@worldnet.att.net
URL: http://www.obrienandsons.com
Products: Playground equipment; Site furnishings; Surfacing; Waterplay; Planters; Shelters and buildings; Tree grates; Bollards; Track and field equipment. **SIC:** 5091 (Sporting & Recreational Goods). **Est:** 1930. **Sales:** $13,000,000 (2000). **Emp:** 15. **Officers:** Eric O'Brien, President.

■ 23857 ■ Ohio Pool Equipment Supply Co.
22350 Royalton Rd.
PO Box 360660
Strongsville, OH 44136-3826
Phone: (440)238-2800
Free: (800)541-4806   **Fax:** (440)238-4839
Products: Swimming pool supplies and equipment. **SIC:** 5091 (Sporting & Recreational Goods). **Est:** 1969. **Emp:** 14. **Officers:** Mark Stoyanoff, Owner; John Justice, Marketing & Sales Mgr.

■ 23858 ■ Olhausen Billiard Manufacturing, Inc.
12460 Kirkham Ct.
Poway, CA 92064
Phone: (858)486-0761
Free: (800)866-4606   **Fax:** (858)486-0713
E-mail: dsimms@olhausenbilliards.com
URL: http://www.olhausenbilliards.com
Products: Pool tables and accessories, including cue racks. **SIC:** 5091 (Sporting & Recreational Goods). **Est:** 1972. **Sales:** $30,000,000 (2000). **Emp:** 170. **Officers:** William Olhausen, President, e-mail: bolhausen@olhausenbilliards.com; Don Olhausen, Vice President, e-mail: dolhausen@olhausenbilliards.com. **Former Name:** Olhausen Pool Table Manufacturing.

■ 23859 ■ Olympia Sports
745 State Circle
PO Box 1941
Ann Arbor, MI 48106-1941
Phone: (734)761-5135
Free: (800)521-2832   **Fax:** (734)761-8711
E-mail: service@school-tech.com
URL: http://www.olympiasports.com
Products: Recreational sporting goods. **SIC:** 5091 (Sporting & Recreational Goods). **Est:** 1955. **Sales:** $3,000,000 (2000). **Emp:** 70. **Officers:** Don N. Canham.

■ 23860 ■ Orbex Inc.
4444 Ball Rd. NE
Circle Pines, MN 55014-1820
Phone: (612)333-1208   **Fax:** (612)333-9043
Products: Sports equipment; Replacement lawn mower blades. **SICs:** 5091 (Sporting & Recreational Goods); 5083 (Farm & Garden Machinery). **Sales:** $4,000,000 (2000). **Emp:** 49. **Officers:** Don E. Wintz.

■ 23861 ■ Orcal Inc.
701 N Hariton Ave.
Orange, CA 92856
Phone: (714)997-4780
Products: Pools and spas. **SIC:** 5091 (Sporting & Recreational Goods). **Est:** 1976. **Sales:** $39,000,000 (2000). **Emp:** 160. **Officers:** Ron Heffner, President.

■ 23862 ■ Oshman's Sporting Goods Inc.
2302 Maxwell Ln.
Houston, TX 77023
Phone: (713)928-3171   **Fax:** (713)967-8276
Products: Sporting goods. **SIC:** 5091 (Sporting & Recreational Goods). **Est:** 1970. **Sales:** $318,100,000 (2000). **Emp:** 3,200. **Officers:** Alvin N. Lubetkin, CEO & President; Edward R. Carlin, Exec. VP & CFO; Will A. Clark, Dir of Human Resources.

■ 23863 ■ Outdoor Research Inc.
2203 1st Ave. S
Seattle, WA 98134-1424
Phone: (206)467-8197   **Fax:** (206)467-0374
Products: Outdoor accessories, including first aid kits, hiking apparel, and boots. **SICs:** 5091 (Sporting & Recreational Goods); 5137 (Women's/Children's Clothing); 5122 (Drugs, Proprietaries & Sundries); 5136 (Men's/Boys' Clothing). **Est:** 1981. **Sales:** $2,000,000 (2000). **Emp:** 230. **Officers:** Ron Gregg, President; DeNova Chung, Vice President; Randall W. King, Vice President; Kirsten Elmore, Dir of Human Resources.

■ 23864 ■ Outdoor Sports Headquarters Inc.
967 Watertower Ln.
Dayton, OH 45449
Phone: (937)865-5855
Free: (800)234-6744   **Fax:** (937)865-0002
Products: Camping tents and equipment; Fishing tackle and equipment; Hunting equipment. **SIC:** 5091 (Sporting & Recreational Goods). **Est:** 1960. **Sales:** $70,000,000 (2000). **Emp:** 200. **Officers:** Martin Altman, President; Roger Vignolo, VP of Operations; Robert B. Barnard, VP of Finance.

■ 23865 ■ P & B Enterprises Inc.
PO Box 887
Mt. Holly, NC 28120-0887
Phone: (704)827-8406
Free: (800)926-3006   **Fax:** (704)827-4060
Products: Sporting and athletic goods; Hunting equipment; Sporting firearms. **SIC:** 5091 (Sporting & Recreational Goods). **Est:** 1980. **Sales:** $5,000,000 (2000). **Emp:** 15. **Officers:** Martha Paxton, President.

■ 23866 ■ P & K Athletics Inc.
Hwy. 2
Cut Bank, MT 59427
Phone: (406)873-5242   **Fax:** (406)873-5260
Products: Sporting and athletic goods. **SIC:** 5091 (Sporting & Recreational Goods). **Officers:** Patrick Winterrowd, President.

■ 23867 ■ Pacific International Marketing Co.
1300 W Olympic Blvd., No. 307
Los Angeles, CA 90015
Phone: (213)381-2826   **Fax:** (213)381-2826
Products: Sporting and recreational goods. **SIC:** 5091 (Sporting & Recreational Goods). **Officers:** Deborah Luna, Export Manager.

■ 23868 ■ Paddock Swimming Pool Co.
15120 Southlawn Ln., No. C
Rockville, MD 20850-1323
Phone: (301)424-0790   **Fax:** (301)424-0556
Products: Sporting and athletic goods; Swimming pools and equipment. **SIC:** 5091 (Sporting & Recreational Goods). **Officers:** Mark Wilkinson, President.

■ 23869 ■ Palm Pool Products Inc.
32620 Dequindre Rd.
Warren, MI 48092-1062
Phone: (313)537-5550   **Fax:** (313)533-7664
Products: Watersports equipment and supplies. **SIC:** 5091 (Sporting & Recreational Goods). **Officers:** Graham Clements, Chairman of the Board.

■ 23870 ■ Pana Bait Co.
284 N 2600 E Rd.
Pana, IL 62557
Phone: (217)562-4122   **Fax:** (217)562-4146
Products: Fishing tackle; Live bait. **SICs:** 5091 (Sporting & Recreational Goods); 5199 (Nondurable Goods Nec). **Est:** 1976. **Emp:** 10. **Officers:** John Downs.

■ 23871 ■ Pape's Archery Inc.
250 Terry Blvd.
PO Box 19889
Louisville, KY 40259-0889
Phone: (502)955-8118
Free: (800)727-3462   **Fax:** (502)955-7863
E-mail: papesinc@aol.com
URL: http://www.papesinc.com
Products: Sporting goods. **SIC:** 5091 (Sporting & Recreational Goods). **Est:** 1946. **Emp:** 65. **Officers:** Fred J. Pape Jr.; Malcolm Snyder, Sales/Marketing Contact; Rick Bagley, Human Resources Contact; Joyce Abner, Customer Service Contact.

■ 23872 ■ Park Place Recreation Designs Inc.
4225 Woodburn Dr.
San Antonio, TX 78218
Phone: (210)599-4899
Free: (800)626-0238   **Fax:** (210)599-6515
E-mail: parkplace@flash.net
Products: Sporting and athletic goods; Playground, gymnasium, and exercise equipment. **SIC:** 5091 (Sporting & Recreational Goods). **Est:** 1980. **Sales:** $1,000,000 (2000). **Emp:** 3. **Officers:** Robert Ahrens; Marilyn Ahrens.

■ 23873 ■ Parr Golf Car Company, Inc.
100 N Rockwell No. 76
Oklahoma City, OK 73127
Phone: (405)495-0585   **Fax:** (405)495-2278
Products: Golf carts and parts; Off road. **SICs:** 5088 (Transportation Equipment & Supplies); 5091 (Sporting & Recreational Goods).

■ 23874 ■ Party Kits Unlimited Inc.
PO Box 7831
Louisville, KY 40257-0831
Phone: (502)425-2126
Free: (800)993-3729   **Fax:** (502)425-5230
E-mail: info@partykits.com
URL: http://www.equinegifts.com
Products: Equestrian goods; Horse racing party supplies; Gourmet food products; Recipe books; Horse prints; Jewelry and watches, including children's gifts and decorator accent pieces. **SICs:** 5199 (Nondurable Goods Nec); 5149 (Groceries & Related Products Nec); 5192 (Books, Periodicals & Newspapers); 5094 (Jewelry & Precious Stones). **Est:** 1979. **Emp:** 6. **Officers:** Becky Biesel, President, e-mail: beckyb@partykits.com.

■ 23875 ■ **Paul Company Inc.**
27385 Pressonville Rd.
Wellsville, KS 66092-9119
Phone: (785)883-4444 **Fax:** (785)883-2525
Products: Sporting and athletic goods; Hunting equipment; Sporting ammunition. **SIC:** 5091 (Sporting & Recreational Goods). **Officers:** Terry Paul, President.

■ 23876 ■ **Jack Pearl's Sports Center**
26 W Michigan
Battle Creek, MI 49017
Phone: (616)964-9476
Free: (800)652-7724 **Fax:** (616)964-7082
Products: Sporting and athletic goods. **SIC:** 5091 (Sporting & Recreational Goods). **Officers:** Jack Pearl, President.

■ 23877 ■ **Pedersen's Ski and Sport**
1976 Candleridge Dr.
Twin Falls, ID 83301-8304
Phone: (208)733-0367
Products: Sporting goods and equipment. **SIC:** 5091 (Sporting & Recreational Goods). **Est:** 1935. **Sales:** $2,600,000 (2000). **Emp:** 115. **Officers:** E.F. Pedersen Jr., President; D. Pedersen, Dir. of Marketing.

■ 23878 ■ **Pettit and Sons**
Box 22
Gays Mills, WI 54631
Phone: (608)735-4470
Free: (800)873-2413 **Fax:** (608)735-4469
E-mail: apland@mwt.net
Products: Hunting and fishing equipment. **SIC:** 5091 (Sporting & Recreational Goods). **Est:** 1975. **Sales:** $3,500,000 (2000). **Emp:** 14. **Officers:** Michael Pettit, President; Robert Pettit, Vice President.

■ 23879 ■ **Phillips Energy Inc.**
989 S Airport Rd. W
Traverse City, MI 49684
Phone: (616)929-1396
Products: Gas and wood stoves and fireplaces; Furnaces; Spa equipment and supplies. **SICs:** 5091 (Sporting & Recreational Goods); 5075 (Warm Air Heating & Air-Conditioning). **Officers:** Richard Phillips, President.

■ 23880 ■ **Phoenix Wholesale Sporting Supplies Inc.**
3500 E Lincoln Dr., No. 35
Phoenix, AZ 85018-1010
Phone: (602)620-3194 **Fax:** (602)667-5867
E-mail: phoenixwholesale@home.com
Products: Hunting supplies, including rifles, ammunition, and vests. **SIC:** 5091 (Sporting & Recreational Goods). **Est:** 1976. **Sales:** $2,000,000 (1999). **Emp:** 10. **Officers:** Dennis Toy, President.

■ 23881 ■ **Pifer, Inc.**
1350 Indiantown Rd.
Jupiter, FL 33458
Phone: (561)746-5321 **Fax:** (561)746-5510
Products: Golf, turf, resort, and hotel equipment and supplies. **SIC:** 5087 (Service Establishment Equipment). **Est:** 1972. **Sales:** $5,000,000 (2000). **Emp:** 10. **Officers:** Rick Pifer, President; Scott C. Jones, Exec. VP; Eric Burk, VP of Finance; Ruth Pifer, Secretary.

■ 23882 ■ **Pinch a Penny Pool Patio**
32350 US 19 N
Palm Harbor, FL 34684
Phone: (813)785-8841 **Fax:** (813)461-0360
Products: Pool supplies, including hoses, chlorine, chemicals, nets, and brushes. **SICs:** 5091 (Sporting & Recreational Goods); 5169 (Chemicals & Allied Products Nec). **Emp:** 49. **Officers:** Vic Tetreault.

■ 23883 ■ **Mel Pinto Imports Inc.**
2860 Annandale Rd.
Falls Church, VA 22042-2149
Phone: (703)237-4686
Free: (800)336-3721 **Fax:** (703)534-9518
Products: Bicycle parts and accessories. **SIC:** 5091 (Sporting & Recreational Goods). **Est:** 1958. **Sales:** $2,000,000 (2000). **Emp:** 15. **Officers:** Nadine Pinto, President.

■ 23884 ■ **Piper Sport Racks Inc.**
1160 Industrial Rd., Ste. 8
San Carlos, CA 94070
Phone: (650)598-0858 **Fax:** (650)598-0859
URL: http://www.PiperSportRacks.com
Products: Bike, ski, and snowboard carriers. **SIC:** 5091 (Sporting & Recreational Goods). **Est:** 1973. **Officers:** Paul Piper, President.

■ 23885 ■ **Playfield Industries Inc.**
Murray Industrial Blvd.
PO Box 8
Chatsworth, GA 30705-0008
Phone: (404)695-4581
Free: (800)221-7449 **Fax:** (404)695-4755
Products: Synthetic turf. **SIC:** 5091 (Sporting & Recreational Goods). **Sales:** $2,000,000 (2000). **Emp:** 49. **Officers:** Steve Linville, President; George Chadwick, Vice President.

■ 23886 ■ **Playsafe Playground Systems of N.Y.**
135 Freeman St.
Brooklyn, NY 11222
Phones: (718)383-0791 800-523-4202
Free: (800)454-0008 **Fax:** (718)383-2788
E-mail: playgroundman@msn.com
Products: Playground equipment. **SIC:** 5091 (Sporting & Recreational Goods). **Est:** 1988. **Sales:** $2,000,000 (2000). **Emp:** 15.

■ 23887 ■ **Pocket Pool & Patio**
6220 Belleau Wood Ln.
Sacramento, CA 95822-5922
Phone: (916)429-7145 **Fax:** (916)429-8452
Products: Swimming pools and equipment; Lawn furniture. **SICs:** 5091 (Sporting & Recreational Goods); 5021 (Furniture). **Est:** 1987. **Emp:** 5. **Officers:** Jerry Sylvia.

■ 23888 ■ **Pohle NV Center Inc.**
9922 W Santa Fe Dr.
Sun City, AZ 85351
Phone: (602)974-5859 **Fax:** (602)974-8395
URL: http://www.pohlenv.com
Products: Golf carts. **SICs:** 5088 (Transportation Equipment & Supplies); 5091 (Sporting & Recreational Goods). **Est:** 1983. **Sales:** $3,000,000 (2000). **Emp:** 22. **Officers:** Steve Pohle, President; Doug Pohle, VP of Finance.

■ 23889 ■ **Point Sporting Goods Inc.**
2925 Welsby Ave.
Stevens Point, WI 54481
Phone: (715)344-4620
Free: (800)222-4600 **Fax:** (715)344-6487
E-mail: psg@wctc.net
Products: Fishing tackle; Hunting goods, including guns; Archery equipment; Marine equipment. **SIC:** 5091 (Sporting & Recreational Goods). **Est:** 1923. **Emp:** 120. **Officers:** Tom Siegmund, President; Brian Eick, Exec. VP; Greg Roe, VP of Sales & Merchandising; Sheila Fugate, VP & Controller.

■ 23890 ■ **Pool Doctor**
101 E Linden
Burbank, CA 91502
Phone: (818)841-6161
Free: (800)535-7665 **Fax:** (818)841-1161
E-mail: pooldr1@aol.com
URL: http://www.pooldoctrs.com
Products: Swimming pool products, including automatic pool cleaners and spiral plastic hoses. **SICs:** 5091 (Sporting & Recreational Goods); 5169 (Chemicals & Allied Products Nec). **Est:** 1962. **Sales:** $8,500,000 (2000). **Emp:** 99. **Officers:** Sam Nazaryan, President.

■ 23891 ■ **Pool Fact, Inc.**
PO Box 816639
Hollywood, FL 33081-0639
Free: (800)330-3228 **Fax:** (954)923-3944
Products: Pool equipment and supplies. **SIC:** 5091 (Sporting & Recreational Goods).

■ 23892 ■ **Pool Water Products**
2334 Havenhurst
Dallas, TX 75234
Phone: (972)243-6006
Free: (800)545-1987 **Fax:** (972)484-0346
Products: Swimming pools and equipment. **SIC:** 5091 (Sporting & Recreational Goods).

■ 23893 ■ **Pool Water Products**
17872 Mitchell Ave., Ste. 250
Irvine, CA 92614
Phone: (949)756-1666 **Fax:** (949)474-1973
Products: Swimming pools and equipment. **SIC:** 5091 (Sporting & Recreational Goods). **Sales:** $73,000,000 (2000). **Emp:** 300. **Officers:** Dean C. Allred, President; Zelma Allred, CEO; James R. Bledsoe, VP of Operations.

■ 23894 ■ **Pool Water Products**
12849 Windfern
Houston, TX 77064
Phone: (281)894-7071
Free: (800)247-9466 **Fax:** (281)894-5379
Products: Pool equipment and supplies. **SIC:** 5091 (Sporting & Recreational Goods).

■ 23895 ■ **Poolmaster Inc.**
770 W Del Paso Rd.
Sacramento, CA 95834
Phone: (916)567-9800 **Fax:** (916)567-9880
E-mail: customerservice@poolmaster.net
URL: http://www.poolmaster.net
Products: Swimming pool maintenance supplies. **SIC:** 5099 (Durable Goods Nec). **Est:** 1959. **Sales:** $17,000,000 (2000). **Emp:** 125. **Officers:** L.H. Tager, President; Bernadette Munroe, Customer Service Contact, e-mail: cservice@poolmaster.net.

■ 23896 ■ **Poseidon Adventure Inc.**
3301 Lancaster Pike, Ste. 5A
Wilmington, DE 19805-1436
Phone: (302)656-2326 **Fax:** (302)656-9324
E-mail: poseidon@dpnet.net
URL: http://www.delanet.com/~poseidon
Products: Watersports equipment and supplies; Diving equipment and supplies. **SIC:** 5091 (Sporting & Recreational Goods). **Est:** 1987. **Sales:** $500,000 (2000). **Emp:** 7. **Officers:** Scott Jenkins, President.

■ 23897 ■ **Precision Sports Surfaces Inc.**
PO Box 55
Charlottesville, VA 22902-0055
Phone: (804)971-9628
Free: (800)488-9628 **Fax:** (804)971-1131
Products: Athletic surfaces, including running tracks. **SIC:** 5091 (Sporting & Recreational Goods). **Est:** 1987. **Officers:** Richard Hord, President.

■ 23898 ■ **PRO Sports Products**
2438 W Anderson Ln.
Austin, TX 78757
Phone: (512)451-7141
Free: (800)444-1158 **Fax:** (512)451-7141
Products: Baseball pants; Protective gear. **SIC:** 5091 (Sporting & Recreational Goods). **Emp:** 49.

■ 23899 ■ **Putt-Putt Golf & Games**
2280 Lakeland Dr.
Flowood, MS 39208-9592
Products: Miniature golf equipment. **SIC:** 5091 (Sporting & Recreational Goods). **Emp:** 30. **Officers:** Allen Smith, Manager.

■ 23900 ■ **Queens City Distributing Co.**
PO Box 186
Bridgeville, PA 15017-0186
Phone: (412)257-4120
Products: Athletic uniforms and equipmentt. **SICs:** 5136 (Men's/Boys' Clothing); 5137 (Women's/Children's Clothing); 5091 (Sporting & Recreational Goods). **Est:** 1931. **Sales:** $17,200,000 (1994). **Emp:** 46. **Officers:** David Neft, President.

■ 23901 ■ **R & T Enterprises Inc.**
PO Box 727
Bridgeport, WV 26330-0727
Phone: (304)622-5546 **Fax:** (304)662-5546
Products: Sporting and athletic goods; Wholesale electrical products. **SIC:** 5091 (Sporting & Recreational

Goods). **Est:** 1977. **Sales:** $1,000,000 (2000). **Emp:** 7. **Officers:** Adam Rohrig, President.

■ **23902** ■ **Raco Manufacturing Inc.**
61 E Longden Ave.
Arcadia, CA 91006-5170
Phone: (213)723-9955
Products: Golf putters. **SIC:** 5084 (Industrial Machinery & Equipment). **Est:** 1971. **Sales:** $600,000 (2000). **Emp:** 2. **Officers:** Roman L. Anyzeski, President & Chairman of the Board.

■ **23903** ■ **Rainbow Sports**
610 Cave Mill Rd.
Bowling Green, KY 42104-4682
Phone: (502)782-5411 **Fax:** (502)782-5411
Products: Sporting and athletic goods. **SIC:** 5091 (Sporting & Recreational Goods). **Officers:** Phillip Carr, Owner.

■ **23904** ■ **Raleigh Cycle of America**
22710 72nd S
Kent, WA 98032-1926
Phone: (425)656-0126
Free: (800)222-5527 **Fax:** (425)251-8069
Products: Bicycles. **SIC:** 5091 (Sporting & Recreational Goods). **Sales:** $40,000,000 (2000). **Emp:** 200.

■ **23905** ■ **Rand International Leisure Products Ltd.**
51 Executive Blvd.
Farmingdale, NY 11735
Phone: (516)249-6000
Products: Bicycles. **SIC:** 5091 (Sporting & Recreational Goods). **Sales:** $65,000,000 (2000). **Emp:** 60. **Officers:** Larry Goldmeier, President; Elizabeth Tangent, Vice President.

■ **23906** ■ **Rax Works Inc.**
PO Box 2078
Del Mar, CA 92014-1378
Phone: (619)578-4430
Products: Skateboards; Volleyballs and volleyball nets. **SIC:** 5091 (Sporting & Recreational Goods). **Est:** 1974. **Sales:** $4,000,000 (2000). **Emp:** 8. **Officers:** Brandon Wander, President.

■ **23907** ■ **RC Sports Inc.**
9910 Lakeview Ave.
Lenexa, KS 66219-2502
Phone: (913)894-6040
Free: (800)255-6588 **Fax:** (913)894-5179
E-mail: info@rcsportsinc.com
URL: http://www.rcsportsinc.com
Products: Roller, inline, and hockey skates. **SIC:** 5091 (Sporting & Recreational Goods). **Est:** 1958. **Emp:** 20. **Officers:** Ronald Creten, Chairman of the Board; Dale Hanson, President.

■ **23908** ■ **Recreation Supply Co.**
Box 2757
Bismarck, ND 58502-2757
Phone: (701)222-4860
Free: (800)437-8072 **Fax:** (701)255-7895
Products: Pool equipment and supplies. **SIC:** 5091 (Sporting & Recreational Goods). **Est:** 1979. **Emp:** 19. **Officers:** Erling Haugland.

■ **23909** ■ **Reda Sports Express**
PO Box 68
Easton, PA 18044
Phone: (215)258-5271 **Fax:** (215)220-7332
Products: Sporting goods, including baseball bats, gloves, balls, and soccer balls. **SIC:** 5091 (Sporting & Recreational Goods). **Est:** 1985. **Sales:** $15,000,000 (2000). **Emp:** 25. **Officers:** Scott L. Reda, President; Isidore H. Dethomas, Finance Officer; Sal Matteis, VP of Marketing & Sales; David Fisher, Information Systems Mgr.; Carol Klus, Dir. of Operations.

■ **23910** ■ **Regent Sports Corp.**
45 Ranick Rd.
Hauppauge, NY 11788-4208
Phone: (516)234-2800
Free: (800)645-5190 **Fax:** (516)234-2948
Products: Baseball equipment; Football protective equipment (helmets, shoulder, hip, kidney, thigh pads, etc.); Sporting and athletic goods. **SIC:** 5091 (Sporting

& Recreational Goods). **Sales:** $30,000,000 (2000). **Emp:** 95. **Officers:** Irving Lawner; Jay Lipman.

■ **23911** ■ **Resilite Sports Products Inc.**
PO Box 764
Sunbury, PA 17801
Phone: (570)473-3529
Free: (800)326-9307 **Fax:** (570)473-8988
E-mail: resilite@ptd.net
URL: http://www.resilite.com
Products: Wall padding; Athletic wrestling mats. **SIC:** 5091 (Sporting & Recreational Goods). **Est:** 1959. **Sales:** $10,000,000 (2000). **Emp:** 60. **Officers:** Warren F. Tischler.

■ **23912** ■ **Rex International**
815 Western Ave. No. 2 & 3
Glendale, CA 91201
Phone: (818)242-2899
Free: (800)237-7640 **Fax:** (818)242-6371
Products: Sporting goods and knives. **SICs:** 5091 (Sporting & Recreational Goods); 5072 (Hardware).

■ **23913** ■ **Rex Playground Equipment Inc.**
PO Box 75141
Oklahoma City, OK 73147-0141
Phone: (405)942-2880
Free: (800)243-7412 **Fax:** (405)946-5799
E-mail: requipment@worldnet.att.net
URL: http://www.rexplayground.com
Products: Sporting and athletic goods; Playground, gymnasium, and exercise equipment. **SIC:** 5091 (Sporting & Recreational Goods). **Est:** 1947. **Emp:** 10. **Officers:** John Walters, President.

■ **23914** ■ **Reynolds & Sons Inc.**
12 Monroe Ctr.
Grand Rapids, MI 49503
Phone: (616)456-7161
Products: Sporting and athletic goods. **SIC:** 5091 (Sporting & Recreational Goods). **Emp:** 10. **Officers:** Jeffrey Reynolds, President.

■ **23915** ■ **Richardson Sports Inc.**
3490 W 1st Ave.
Eugene, OR 97402
Phone: (541)687-1818
Free: (800)545-8686 **Fax:** (541)687-1130
E-mail: sales@Richardsonsports.com
Products: Sporting and athletic goods, including caps. **SIC:** 5091 (Sporting & Recreational Goods). **Est:** 1973. **Sales:** $16,000,000 (2000). **Emp:** 65. **Officers:** Neil Richardson, CEO; Donna Richardson, Vice President; Kelly Richardson, President.

■ **23916** ■ **Robco Corp.**
4842 Park Glen Rd.
Minneapolis, MN 55416-5702
Phone: (612)920-8966 **Fax:** (612)920-1879
Products: Sporting and athletic goods; Lawn furniture. **SICs:** 5091 (Sporting & Recreational Goods); 5021 (Furniture). **Officers:** Phillip Marks, President.

■ **23917** ■ **Robinson Wholesale Inc.**
PO Box 338
Genoa City, WI 53128-0338
Phone: (414)279-2320
Free: (800)457-2248 **Fax:** (414)279-6408
Products: Live bait and tackle. **SIC:** 5091 (Sporting & Recreational Goods).

■ **23918** ■ **Jerry Robison & Associates**
PO Box 17509
Fountain Hills, AZ 85269
Phone: (602)471-1411
Free: (800)905-1411 **Fax:** (602)471-1318
Products: Sporting and athletic goods. **SIC:** 5091 (Sporting & Recreational Goods).

■ **23919** ■ **Rockys II Inc.**
615 N Wenatchee Ave.
Wenatchee, WA 98801-2059
Phone: (509)663-7973 **Fax:** (509)663-6106
Products: Sporting and athletic goods; Hunting equipment; Firearms. **SIC:** 5091 (Sporting & Recreational Goods). **Officers:** Rocky Crocker, President.

■ **23920** ■ **Rogers Pool Supply, Inc.**
1826 Brooks Rd. E
Memphis, TN 38116-3608
Phone: (901)345-1470
Free: (888)345-1470 **Fax:** (901)345-1472
URL: http://www.rpspool.com
Products: Pool equipment, supplies, and chemicals. **SICs:** 5091 (Sporting & Recreational Goods); 5169 (Chemicals & Allied Products Nec). **Est:** 1953. **Emp:** 7.

■ **23921** ■ **Roller Derby Skate Corp.**
311 W Edwards St.
Litchfield, IL 62056
Phone: (217)324-3961
Products: Roller skates. **SIC:** 5091 (Sporting & Recreational Goods). **Est:** 1936. **Sales:** $30,000,000 (2000). **Emp:** 50. **Officers:** Edwin Seltzer, President; Walter Frazier, Vice President.

■ **23922** ■ **The John Rouzee Green Company Inc.**
65 N Congress St.
PO Box 379
York, SC 29745
Phone: (803)684-6853
Free: (800)332-6853 **Fax:** (803)684-6077
E-mail: oldmaster@infoave.net
Products: Golf products, including putters and putter grips. **SIC:** 5091 (Sporting & Recreational Goods). **Est:** 1974. **Sales:** $1,000,000 (2000). **Emp:** 11. **Officers:** John R. Green, President; Lisa L. Taylor, Treasurer; Roger Pierson, Sales & Marketing Contact; Pat Burns, Customer Service Contact. **Alternate Name:** Old Master.

■ **23923** ■ **Royal Golf, Inc.**
32 Garvies Point Rd.
Glen Cove, NY 11542
Phone: (516)671-8200
Free: (800)221-2022 **Fax:** (516)671-8264
E-mail: royalbags@aol.com
Products: Golf bags and components. **SIC:** 5091 (Sporting & Recreational Goods). **Est:** 1973. **Emp:** 20. **Officers:** JoAnn Suk, General Mgr. **Former Name:** Exim Manufacturers Inc.

■ **23924** ■ **Royal Golf Inc.**
32 Garvies Point Rd.
Glen Cove, NY 11542
Phone: (516)671-8200
Free: (800)221-2022 **Fax:** (516)671-8264
Products: Recreational and sporting goods. **SIC:** 5091 (Sporting & Recreational Goods).

■ **23925** ■ **RSR Wholesale Guns Midwest Inc.**
8817 W Lynx Ave.
Milwaukee, WI 53225
Phone: (414)461-1111
Free: (800)832-4867 **Fax:** (414)461-9836
Products: Guns and weapons. **SIC:** 5091 (Sporting & Recreational Goods).

■ **23926** ■ **Rubin Inc.**
120 25th St.
Ogden, UT 84401-1302
Phone: (801)394-8946
Products: Sporting and recreation goods; Hunting equipment and supplies. **SIC:** 5091 (Sporting & Recreational Goods). **Officers:** Scott Vanleewen, President.

■ **23927** ■ **S & F Associates Inc.**
PO Box 5996
Portland, OR 97228-5996
Phone: (503)288-6876
Free: (800)547-6258 **Fax:** (503)287-5078
E-mail: info@sfassoc.com
Products: Sporting and recreational goods. **SIC:** 5091 (Sporting & Recreational Goods). **Est:** 1952. **Emp:** 14. **Officers:** Glen Simons, President.

■ **23928** ■ **Safesport Manufacturing Co.**
1100 W 45th Ave.
Denver, CO 80211
Phone: (303)433-6506 **Fax:** (303)433-4112
Products: Sporting goods, including tarps, rain slickers, and fur parkas. **SICs:** 5091 (Sporting & Recreational Goods); 5136 (Men's/Boys' Clothing); 5137 (Women's/Children's Clothing). **Est:** 1948. **Sales:**

$6,000,000 (2000). **Emp:** 30. **Officers:** Allan Striker, President; Judy Striker, VP of Marketing.

■ **23929** ■ **Salomon North America Inc.**
9401 SW Nimbus Ave.
Beaverton, OR 97008-7145
Phone: (503)548-7001
Free: (800)225-6850   **Fax:** (503)906-4583
URL: http://www.salomonsports.com
Products: Ski equipment, including skis, boots, bindings, and poles; Snowboards and snowblades; Hiking boots. **SICs:** 5091 (Sporting & Recreational Goods); 5139 (Footwear). **Est:** 1972. **Sales:** $19,000,000 (2000). **Emp:** 80. **Officers:** Tom Wright.

■ **23930** ■ **Saunier-Wilhelm Co.**
3216 5th Ave.
Pittsburgh, PA 15213-3026
Phone: (412)621-4350
Products: Bowling equipment; Billiard tables and supplies; Bowling alleys and bowling pin setters. **SIC:** 5091 (Sporting & Recreational Goods). **Est:** 1988. **Sales:** $2,000,000 (2000). **Emp:** 31. **Officers:** M. G. Wilhelm, President; James F. Wilhelm, VP & Treasurer; Thomas H. Boyle, Dir. of Sales.

■ **23931** ■ **Mike Schram & Associates**
PO Box 201
Geneva, IL 60134
Free: (800)952-0962   **Fax:** (630)513-1947
Products: Sporting and athletic goods. **SIC:** 5091 (Sporting & Recreational Goods).

■ **23932** ■ **Schwinn Cycling and Fitness**
340 W Crossroads Pky., Ste. B
Bolingbrook, IL 60440-4939
Phone: (630)231-5340   **Fax:** (630)231-1845
Products: Bicycles and fitness equipment. **SIC:** 5091 (Sporting & Recreational Goods). **Emp:** 999.

■ **23933** ■ **Scientific Anglers**
3M Ctr., Bldg. 223-4NE-513
St. Paul, MN 55144-1000
Phone: (651)733-4751   **Fax:** (651)737-7429
URL: http://www.scientificanglers.com
Products: Fishing equipment, including fly fish lines, reels, rodtubes, outfitters packs and personal floatation devices, flies and fly tying and fly fishing videos and accessories. **SICs:** 5091 (Sporting & Recreational Goods); 5099 (Durable Goods Nec). **Est:** 1946. **Emp:** 40. **Officers:** Ken Prchal, Project Mgr.; George Dierberger. **Alternate Name:** 3M.

■ **23934** ■ **Second Chance Golf Ball Recyclers Inc.**
1943 SE Airport Rd.
Stuart, FL 34996-4016
Phone: (561)223-3730
Free: (800)366-4876   **Fax:** (561)223-3750
URL: http://wwww.nitrogolf.com
Products: Recycled golf balls. **SIC:** 5091 (Sporting & Recreational Goods). **Est:** 1997. **Sales:** $9,000,000 (2000). **Emp:** 63. **Officers:** Amin Khoury, President; Paul Kaneb, Vice President.

■ **23935** ■ **Sheldons', Inc.**
626 Center St.
Antigo, WI 54409-2496
Phone: (715)623-2382   **Fax:** (715)623-3001
E-mail: shep@mepps.com
URL: http://www.mepps.com
Products: Fishing tackle. **SIC:** 5091 (Sporting & Recreational Goods). **Est:** 1955. **Sales:** $17,000,000 (2000). **Emp:** 200. **Officers:** J.M. Sheldon, President; Robert Bender, Controller; Jim Martinsen, Dir. of Marketing; Robert Bender, Dir. of Systems.

■ **23936** ■ **Shimano American Corp.**
1 Holland Dr.
Irvine, CA 92618
Phone: (949)951-5003
Products: Bike parts. **SIC:** 5091 (Sporting & Recreational Goods). **Sales:** $45,000,000 (2000). **Emp:** 100. **Officers:** Hiro Hirata, Chairman of the Board.

■ **23937** ■ **Shimano American Corp. Fishing Tackle Div.**
1 Holland Dr.
Irvine, CA 92618
Phone: (949)951-5003   **Fax:** (949)951-5071
Products: Bicycle components; Fishing tackle and equipment. **SIC:** 5091 (Sporting & Recreational Goods). **Est:** 1980. **Sales:** $400,000 (2000). **Emp:** 100. **Officers:** Yoshi Shimano, President; Ray Privette, VP & CFO; Kozo Shimano, Vice President; Dave Pfeitter, Vice President; Ward Lennon, Sales/Marketing Contact, e-mail: wlennon@shimano.com; Kevin Dart, Customer Service Contact, e-mail: kdart@shimano.com; Suzanne Ramet, Human Resources Contact, e-mail: sramet@shimano.com.

■ **23938** ■ **Sierra Pacific**
510 Salmar Ave.
Campbell, CA 95008
Phone: (408)374-4700   **Fax:** (408)374-4773
Products: Golf equipment; Landscaping equipment. **SICs:** 5091 (Sporting & Recreational Goods); 5083 (Farm & Garden Machinery).

■ **23939** ■ **Bill Simione and Associates, Inc.**
5 Krey Blvd.
Rensselaer, NY 12144
Phone: (518)283-0126
Free: (800)PLA-YPRO   **Fax:** (518)283-0046
Products: Playground equipment; Outdoor shelters; Bleachers; Lighting. **SICs:** 5091 (Sporting & Recreational Goods); 5063 (Electrical Apparatus & Equipment); 5039 (Construction Materials Nec). **Est:** 1976. **Emp:** 5. **Officers:** William M. Simione, President.

■ **23940** ■ **Simmons Sporting Goods Company Inc.**
2001 2nd Ave. N
Bessemer, AL 35020-4948
Phones: (205)425-4720   (205)426-0490
Fax: (205)425-4740
Products: Firearms; Hunting equipment; Fishing tackle and equipment. **SIC:** 5091 (Sporting & Recreational Goods). **Emp:** 15. **Officers:** Clay Simmons, President.

■ **23941** ■ **Sinclair Imports Inc.**
2775 W Hwy. 40
PO Box 707
Verdi, NV 89439
Phone: (702)345-0600
Free: (800)654-8052   **Fax:** (702)345-6013
E-mail: info@sinclairimports.com
URL: http://www.sinclairimports.com
Products: Cycling products, including shoes, frames, small parts, clothing, tires, rims, and bars. **SIC:** 5091 (Sporting & Recreational Goods). **Est:** 1986. **Emp:** 10. **Officers:** Glenn S. Spiller, Pres. and Partner; Jim Mitchell, V.P. and Partner; Lance Donnell, Sales/Marketing Manager and Partner, e-mail: ldonnell@sinclairimports.com.

■ **23942** ■ **Sinclair & Rush, Inc.**
13515 Barrett Pkwy. Dr., Ste. 155
Ballwin, MO 63021-5870
Free: (800)827-2277
Products: Golf equipment. **SIC:** 5091 (Sporting & Recreational Goods).

■ **23943** ■ **Site Concepts**
PO Box 9309
Chesapeake, VA 23321-9309
Phone: (757)547-3553
Free: (800)568-8396   **Fax:** (757)436-0081
Products: Sporting and athletic goods; Playground, gymnasium, and exercise equipment. **SIC:** 5091 (Sporting & Recreational Goods).

■ **23944** ■ **Skipper Bills Inc.**
E7915 E Sprague Ave.
Spokane, WA 99212-2938
Phone: (509)928-1000   **Fax:** (509)924-2529
Products: Sporting and recreational goods, including boats, and watercrafts. . **SIC:** 5091 (Sporting & Recreational Goods). **Officers:** Bill Bongers, President.

■ **23945** ■ **Skis Dynastar Inc.**
Hercules Dr.
PO Box 25
Colchester, VT 05446-0025
Phone: (802)655-2400   **Fax:** (802)655-4329
E-mail: info@gynastar.net
URL: http://www.dynastar.com
Products: Skiing equipment. **SIC:** 5091 (Sporting & Recreational Goods). **Est:** 1977. **Sales:** $35,000,000 (1999). **Emp:** 40. **Officers:** David J. Provost; Charles K. Adams; Michael Solimano; Mark Gonsalves.

■ **23946** ■ **Smith Distributing Co.**
PO Box 252
Anniston, AL 36202-0252
Phone: (205)237-2895
Products: Sporting and athletic goods. **SIC:** 5091 (Sporting & Recreational Goods). **Est:** 1946. **Emp:** 5. **Officers:** Hester L. Smith, Owner.

■ **23947** ■ **P. Smith Enterprises Inc.**
PO Box 3162
West Columbia, SC 29171-3162
Phone: (803)791-5155
Products: Sporting and athletic goods. **SIC:** 5091 (Sporting & Recreational Goods). **Officers:** William Smith, President.

■ **23948** ■ **Kenneth Smith Inc.**
12931 W 71st St.
Shawnee, KS 66216-2640
Phone: (913)631-5100
Free: (800)234-8968   **Fax:** (913)631-4065
Products: Golf clubs, bags, and balls; Scales, including swinging; Measuring devices, including rulers and protractors. **SICs:** 5091 (Sporting & Recreational Goods); 5046 (Commercial Equipment Nec); 5049 (Professional Equipment Nec); 5199 (Nondurable Goods Nec). **Est:** 1919. **Emp:** 35. **Officers:** Patrick J. McMahon, President & Chairman of the Board. **Former Name:** The Kenneth Smith Golf Club Co.

■ **23949** ■ **L.L. Smith Sporting Goods Inc.**
2328 W Royal Palm Rd.
Phoenix, AZ 85021-4937
Phone: (602)995-2424   **Fax:** (602)995-2075
Products: Sporting and recreational goods for teams and schools. **SIC:** 5091 (Sporting & Recreational Goods). **Officers:** Don Smith, President.

■ **23950** ■ **Soccer House Inc.**
803 W Coliseum Blvd.
Ft. Wayne, IN 46808-3611
Phone: (219)482-3919   **Fax:** (219)484-2568
Products: Sporting and athletic goods, including soccer equipment. **SIC:** 5091 (Sporting & Recreational Goods). **Est:** 1987. **Sales:** $1,000,000 (2000). **Emp:** 15. **Officers:** Roger Bartholow, President.

■ **23951** ■ **Soccer Plus Inc.**
161 Main St.
Wethersfield, CT 06109-2339
Phone: (860)563-6263   **Fax:** (860)721-8619
Products: Sporting and athletic goods. **SIC:** 5091 (Sporting & Recreational Goods). **Officers:** Anthony Dicicco, President.

■ **23952** ■ **M.J. Soffe**
919 Filley St.
Lansing, MI 48906
Phone: (517)321-4220
Free: (800)453-6610   **Fax:** (517)321-4384
Products: Sports clothing. **SICs:** 5136 (Men's/Boys' Clothing); 5137 (Women's/Children's Clothing). **Officers:** Coanne Knuth, President.

■ **23953** ■ **Sorcerer Lures**
822 E 2nd St.
Duluth, MN 55805
Phone: (218)723-8130   **Fax:** (218)723-4046
Products: Fish and tackle equipment. **SIC:** 5091 (Sporting & Recreational Goods).

■ **23954** ■ **South Central Pool Supply, Inc.**
4310 Hessmer Blvd.
Metairie, LA 70002
Phone: (504)887-2240
Free: (800)883-7665   **Fax:** (504)888-1683
Products: Pool equipment and supplies. **SIC:** 5091

(Sporting & Recreational Goods). **Emp:** 1,000. **Officers:** Frank St. Romain.

■ **23955** ■ **South Central Pool Supply, Inc.**
149 Distribution Dr.
Birmingham, AL 35209
Phone: (205)945-9110
Free: (800)969-5059 **Fax:** (205)945-1169
Products: Pool equipment and supplies. **SIC:** 5091 (Sporting & Recreational Goods).

■ **23956** ■ **South Central Pool Supply, Inc.**
4800 Southridge, No. 20
Memphis, TN 38141
Phone: (901)367-4884
Free: (800)883-2850 **Fax:** (901)367-2582
Products: Pool equipment and supplies. **SIC:** 5091 (Sporting & Recreational Goods).

■ **23957** ■ **South Central Pool Supply, Inc.**
1305 N Hills Blvd., No. 105/106
North Little Rock, AR 72114
Phone: (501)771-1422
Free: (800)394-1153 **Fax:** (501)771-4721
Products: Pool equipment and supplies. **SIC:** 5091 (Sporting & Recreational Goods).

■ **23958** ■ **South Central Pool Supply, Inc.**
9802 Widmer
Lenexa, KS 66215
Phone: (913)888-6633
Free: (800)825-0366 **Fax:** (913)888-2575
Products: Pool equipment and supplies. **SIC:** 5091 (Sporting & Recreational Goods).

■ **23959** ■ **South Central Pool Supply, Inc.**
10801 Millington Ct.
Cincinnati, OH 45242
Phone: (513)891-6977
Free: (800)394-6977 **Fax:** (513)891-7017
Products: Pool equipment and supplies. **SIC:** 5091 (Sporting & Recreational Goods).

■ **23960** ■ **South Central Pool Supply, Inc.**
2469 Bransford Ave.
Nashville, TN 37204
Phone: (615)297-1616
Free: (800)966-7277 **Fax:** (615)297-0347
Products: Pool equipment and supplies. **SIC:** 5091 (Sporting & Recreational Goods).

■ **23961** ■ **South Central Pool Supply, Inc.**
2235-39 Hwy. 80, W
Jackson, MS 39204
Phone: (601)948-7277
Free: (800)989-7277 **Fax:** (601)948-2931
Products: Pool equipment and supplies. **SIC:** 5091 (Sporting & Recreational Goods).

■ **23962** ■ **South Central Pool Supply, Inc.**
320 Quapah Ave., N
Oklahoma City, OK 73107
Phone: (405)943-1700
Free: (800)394-1397 **Fax:** (405)943-3837
Products: Pool equipment and supplies. **SIC:** 5091 (Sporting & Recreational Goods).

■ **23963** ■ **South Central Pool Supply, Inc.**
3691 S 73rd Ave.
Tulsa, OK 74145
Phone: (918)663-9101
Free: (800)554-9101 **Fax:** (918)663-9105
Products: Pool equipment and supplies. **SIC:** 5091 (Sporting & Recreational Goods).

■ **23964** ■ **South Central Pool Supply, Inc.**
4460 South Blvd.
Charlotte, NC 28209
Phone: (704)522-7946
Free: (800)883-7946 **Fax:** (704)522-7846
Products: Pool equipment and supplies. **SIC:** 5091 (Sporting & Recreational Goods).

■ **23965** ■ **South Central Pool Supply, Inc.**
5821A Midway Park, NE
Albuquerque, NM 87109
Phone: (505)345-3535
Free: (800)486-3535 **Fax:** (505)343-8535
Products: Pool equipment and supplies. **SIC:** 5091

(Sporting & Recreational Goods). **Officers:** Mike Huppert, Branch Manager.

■ **23966** ■ **South Central Pool Supply, Inc.**
9230 Neils Thompson Dr., Ste. 108
Austin, TX 78758-7647
Phone: (512)835-4200
Free: (800)883-4200 **Fax:** (512)835-9245
Products: Pool equipment and supplies. **SIC:** 5091 (Sporting & Recreational Goods).

■ **23967** ■ **South Central Pool Supply, Inc.**
9307 Millsview Rd.
Houston, TX 77070
Phone: (281)469-9696
Free: (800)969-2056 **Fax:** (281)897-0534
Products: Pool equipment and supplies. **SIC:** 5091 (Sporting & Recreational Goods).

■ **23968** ■ **South Central Pool Supply, Inc.**
11225 Gordon Rd., No. 102
San Antonio, TX 78216
Phone: (210)545-6161
Free: (800)545-0129 **Fax:** (210)545-6165
Products: Pool equipment and supplies. **SIC:** 5091 (Sporting & Recreational Goods).

■ **23969** ■ **South Central Pool Supply, Inc.**
11140 Leadbetter Rd.
Ashland, VA 23005
Phone: (804)798-2507
Free: (800)685-1553 **Fax:** (804)798-2599
Products: Pool equipment and supplies. **SIC:** 5091 (Sporting & Recreational Goods).

■ **23970** ■ **South Central Pool Supply, Inc.**
12 Parkwood Dr.
Hopkinton, MA 01748-1660
Phone: (508)435-2321 **Fax:** (508)435-4127
Products: Pool equipment and supplies. **SIC:** 5091 (Sporting & Recreational Goods). **Est:** 1957. **Emp:** 200. **Officers:** Jon Hulme, General Mgr.

■ **23971** ■ **Southeastern Skate Supply of Virginia Inc.**
PO Box 12448
Roanoke, VA 24025
Phone: (540)342-7871 **Fax:** (540)342-7873
E-mail: seskate@aol.com
URL: http://www.seskate.com
Products: Skates, including in-line and roller skates; Novelty and carnival supplies. **SICs:** 5091 (Sporting & Recreational Goods); 5099 (Durable Goods Nec). **Est:** 1949. **Sales:** $5,500,000 (2000). **Emp:** 14. **Officers:** Glenn Ramsey Jr., President.

■ **23972** ■ **Southwest Sporting Goods Co.**
PO Box 471
Arkadelphia, AR 71923-0471
Phone: (870)246-2311 **Fax:** (870)246-3932
Products: Sporting and athletic goods. **SIC:** 5091 (Sporting & Recreational Goods). **Officers:** Robert Nelson, President.

■ **23973** ■ **Spartan Sporting Goods Inc.**
113 Appalachian Dr.
Beckley, WV 25801-2201
Phone: (304)255-1434
Products: Sporting and athletic goods. **SIC:** 5091 (Sporting & Recreational Goods). **Officers:** William Baker, President.

■ **23974** ■ **Spas Unlimited**
209 Mobile Ave.
Trussville, AL 35173-1955
Products: Sporting and athletic goods; Playground, gymnasium, and exercise equipment. **SIC:** 5091 (Sporting & Recreational Goods). **Officers:** Pat Roll, Owner.

■ **23975** ■ **Sport Obermeyer Ltd.**
115 AABC
Aspen, CO 81611
Phone: (970)925-5060 **Fax:** (970)925-9203
Products: Skiwear. **SICs:** 5136 (Men's/Boys' Clothing); 5137 (Women's/Children's Clothing). **Est:** 1952. **Sales:** $30,000,000 (2000). **Emp:** 60. **Officers:** Klaus Obermeyer, President; Tim Belinski, CFO.

■ **23976** ■ **Sport Shop Inc.**
8055 Airline Hwy.
Baton Rouge, LA 70815-8108
Phone: (504)927-2600 **Fax:** (504)925-9952
Products: Recreational products, including hunting, fishing and boating goods. **SIC:** 5091 (Sporting & Recreational Goods). **Officers:** Fred Parnell, President.

■ **23977** ■ **The Sporting House**
PO Box 468
Vashon Island, WA 98070
Phone: (206)463-2563 **Fax:** (206)463-5599
Products: Women's sportswear; Men's and boys' sportswear; Sporting and athletic goods. **SICs:** 5091 (Sporting & Recreational Goods); 5136 (Men's/Boys' Clothing); 5137 (Women's/Children's Clothing). **Est:** 1979. **Officers:** Jeanne Wright, President; Bill Wright, VP of Marketing; Lillian Rielly, Treasurer.

■ **23978** ■ **Sportmaster Inc.**
521 Madison Ave.
Covington, KY 41011-1505
Phone: (606)431-3555 **Fax:** (606)431-3556
Products: Tennis and racquet ball equipment. **SIC:** 5091 (Sporting & Recreational Goods). **Officers:** Mark Wheatley, President.

■ **23979** ■ **Sports Cellar**
402 Sherman Ave.
Coeur D Alene, ID 83814
Phone: (208)664-9464 **Fax:** (208)664-2014
Products: Sporting and athletic goods; Athletic uniforms. **SICs:** 5091 (Sporting & Recreational Goods); 5136 (Men's/Boys' Clothing); 5137 (Women's/Children's Clothing). **Est:** 1912. **Sales:** $1,000,000 (2000). **Emp:** 8. **Officers:** Greg Crimp, President.

■ **23980** ■ **Sports Specialist Inc.**
9559 Foley Ln.
Foley, AL 36535-3723
Phone: (205)943-1901 **Fax:** (205)943-1999
Products: Sporting and athletic goods. **SIC:** 5091 (Sporting & Recreational Goods).

■ **23981** ■ **Sportsmans Inc.**
414 Pierce St.
Sioux City, IA 51101-1414
Phone: (712)255-0125
Free: (800)352-4665 **Fax:** (712)255-0640
Products: Sporting and athletic goods. **SIC:** 5091 (Sporting & Recreational Goods). **Officers:** Robert Rogers, President.

■ **23982** ■ **Sportsware West**
415 E Figueroa St., Ste. A
Santa Barbara, CA 93101-1444
Phone: (805)962-7454
E-mail: cryocup@aol.com
Products: Sports equipment; Sports medicine products. **SIC:** 5091 (Sporting & Recreational Goods). **Est:** 1988. **Emp:** 4.

■ **23983** ■ **Stano Components**
PO Box 2048
Carson City, NV 89702-2048
Phone: (702)246-5281 **Fax:** (702)246-5211
Products: Sporting and recreational goods; Hunting equipment and supplies; Night opti.cs. **SIC:** 5091 (Sporting & Recreational Goods). **Officers:** Allen Glanze, Owner.

■ **23984** ■ **Starks Sport Shop**
108 W Blackhawk
Prairie du Chien, WI 53821
Phone: (608)326-2478
Products: Sporting goods; Marine gear. **SIC:** 5091 (Sporting & Recreational Goods).

■ **23985** ■ **Starlight Archery Inc.**
21570 Groesbeck Hwy.
Warren, MI 48089
Phone: (313)771-1580
Products: Archery supplies, including bows, arrows, and targets. **SIC:** 5091 (Sporting & Recreational Goods). **Est:** 1955. **Sales:** $500,000 (2000). **Emp:** 3. **Officers:** Charlie Nicholas, President; Marilyn Nicholas, Treasurer.

■ 23986 ■ Stateline Sports
PO Box 5511
West Lebanon, NH 03784-5511
Phone: (603)298-7078 **Fax:** (603)298-7078
Products: Sporting and athletic goods. **SIC:** 5091 (Sporting & Recreational Goods). **Officers:** Jon Damren, Partner.

■ 23987 ■ Steamboat International LLC
7215 Bermuda Rd.
Las Vegas, NV 89119
Phone: (702)361-0600
Free: (800)237-9937 **Fax:** (702)361-0613
E-mail: sales@lengordon.com
URL: http://www.gordon-aqualine.com
Products: Spa equipment packages; Spa equipment/control modules; Heaters; Electronic controls/components. **SIC:** 5091 (Sporting & Recreational Goods). **Emp:** 75. **Officers:** Judith A. Gordon, CEO; Marie Levesque, VP of Marketing & Sales. **Former Name:** Brett Aqualine Inc.

■ 23988 ■ Steele's Sports Co.
5223 W 137th St.
Brook Park, OH 44142
Phone: (216)267-5300
Free: (800)367-7114 **Fax:** (216)267-5304
Products: Baseball bats, including softball bats; Baseball mitts and gloves, including softball; Baseballs and softballs. **SIC:** 5091 (Sporting & Recreational Goods). **Officers:** Raymond C. Whitaker Jr., President.

■ 23989 ■ Stream & Lake Tackle
3305 Remembrance NW
Grand Rapids, MI 49544-2203
Phones: (616)791-2311 800-442-3620
Free: (800)632-8770 **Fax:** (616)791-9752
Products: Outdoor sports equipment, including archery and fishing. **SIC:** 5091 (Sporting & Recreational Goods). **Est:** 1967. **Sales:** $1,000,000 (2000). **Emp:** 49. **Officers:** Bill Gonom; Frank Grodick; Al Peck.

■ 23990 ■ Striplings Tackle Co.
PO Box 811
Waycross, GA 31502-0811
Phone: (912)283-8370
Products: Fishing tackle and equipment. **SIC:** 5091 (Sporting & Recreational Goods). **Officers:** R. Stripling, Owner.

■ 23991 ■ Sues Young and Brown Inc.
5151 Commerce Dr.
Baldwin Park, CA 91706-7890
Phone: (818)338-3800
Products: Jacuzzis. **SIC:** 5091 (Sporting & Recreational Goods). **Est:** 1946. **Sales:** $17,000,000 (2000). **Emp:** 45. **Officers:** Richard F. Young, President; Jeanette Roe, Secretary.

■ 23992 ■ Sun America Corp.
770 Tyvola Rd.
Charlotte, NC 28217-3508
Phone: (704)522-9219
Free: (800)367-7973 **Fax:** (704)522-9219
E-mail: sunamerica770@netscape
Products: Electric sun tanning beds and sunal beds. **SIC:** 5091 (Sporting & Recreational Goods). **Est:** 1998. **Emp:** 20. **Officers:** Kent McGuire, President. **Former Name:** McGuire Sun & Fitness Inc.

■ 23993 ■ Sunny's Great Outdoors Inc.
7540 Washington Blvd., Ste. SS
Elkridge, MD 21075
Phone: (410)799-4900 **Fax:** (410)799-8267
Products: Camping, hunting, and fishing equipment; Men's and women's clothing; Kayaks; Golf and paintball equipment; Footwear; Military clothing; Travel accessories. **SICs:** 5091 (Sporting & Recreational Goods); 5136 (Men's/Boys' Clothing); 5137 (Women's/Children's Clothing). **Est:** 1948. **Sales:** $30,000,000 (2000). **Emp:** 320. **Officers:** John D. Reier, CEO & President; Eric Meyer, VP Store Operations; Loralea Sanderson, Controller; Cathie DeGonia, Dir. of Advertising.

■ 23994 ■ Sunshine Golf, Inc.
13835 SW 77th Ave.
Miami, FL 33158
Phone: (305)234-4448
Products: Golf equipment. **SIC:** 5091 (Sporting & Recreational Goods).

■ 23995 ■ Superb Cooking Products Co./Empire Comfort Systems, Inc.
918 Freeburg Ave.
Belleville, IL 62222
Phone: (618)233-7420
Free: (800)851-3153 **Fax:** (618)233-7097
URL: http://www.empirecomfort.com
Products: Portable gas stoves. **SIC:** 5091 (Sporting & Recreational Goods). **Est:** 1959. **Sales:** $990,000 (2000). **Emp:** 200. **Officers:** Marisa Lucash, Sales Mgr.; Betty Senulis, Human Resources.

■ 23996 ■ Superior Pool Products Inc.
4900 E Landon Dr.
Anaheim, CA 92807
Phone: (714)693-8035 **Fax:** (714)693-8048
Products: Pool products, including chemicals, cleaning tools, and toys. **SICs:** 5091 (Sporting & Recreational Goods); 5169 (Chemicals & Allied Products Nec). **Sales:** $36,000,000 (2000). **Emp:** 180. **Officers:** Dave Chess, President; Randy Williams, Controller; Larry Lamers, Dir. of Marketing & Sales.

■ 23997 ■ Superior Turf Equipment
13212 E Indiana
Spokane, WA 99216
Phone: (509)926-8974 **Fax:** (509)927-8974
Products: Golf course maintenance equipment. **SICs:** 5091 (Sporting & Recreational Goods); 5083 (Farm & Garden Machinery).

■ 23998 ■ Surfco Hawaii Inc.
98-723 Kuahao Pl.
Pearl City, HI 96782
Phone: (808)488-5996
Free: (800)755-9283 **Fax:** (808)488-8338
E-mail: surfcohi@aol.com
URL: http://www.surfcohawaii.com
Products: Sporting and recreational goods; Watersports equipment and supplies, including noseguards, surfing equipment, and supplies. **SIC:** 5091 (Sporting & Recreational Goods). **Est:** 1986. **Sales:** $1,000,000 (2000). **Emp:** 10. **Officers:** David Skedeleski, President.

■ 23999 ■ Surplus City USA Inc.
PO Box 20425
Jackson, MS 39209-1425
Phone: (601)922-5120
Products: Sporting and athletic goods; Hunting equipment. **SIC:** 5091 (Sporting & Recreational Goods). **Officers:** Carl Thomas, President.

■ 24000 ■ Swimming Pool Supply Co.
5292 NW 111th Dr.
Grimes, IA 50111-8731
Phone: (515)986-3931
Free: (800)798-7946 **Fax:** (515)986-3805
Products: Sporting and recreational goods, including watersports equipment and supplies; Swimming pool equipment and supplies. **SIC:** 5091 (Sporting & Recreational Goods). **Officers:** Thor Iverson, President.

■ 24001 ■ T & D Sporting Goods
PO Box 837
Pikeville, KY 41502-0837
Phone: (606)432-2153
Products: Sporting and athletic goods. **SIC:** 5091 (Sporting & Recreational Goods). **Officers:** David Collier, President.

■ 24002 ■ Tackle Craft
1440 Kennedy Rd.
Chippewa Falls, WI 54729
Phone: (715)723-3645 **Fax:** (715)723-2489
Products: Recreational and sporting goods. **SIC:** 5091 (Sporting & Recreational Goods).

■ 24003 ■ Tackle Service Center
246 E Washington St.
Mooresville, IN 46158-1459
Phones: (317)831-2400 (317)831-3737
Fax: (317)831-8500
Products: Sporting and recreational goods; Fishing equipment and supplies, including fishing tackle; Hunting equipment. **SIC:** 5091 (Sporting & Recreational Goods). **Est:** 1970. **Emp:** 6. **Officers:** Robert Matt, Partner.

■ 24004 ■ Taylor Sports & Recreation Inc.
136 Warm Springs Ave.
Martinsburg, WV 25401
Phone: (304)263-7857
Free: (800)286-9693 **Fax:** (304)263-9392
Products: Playground and athletic equipment. **SIC:** 5091 (Sporting & Recreational Goods). **Est:** 1977. **Sales:** $3,000,000 (2000). **Emp:** 10. **Officers:** Steven C. Taylor, President.

■ 24005 ■ Team Distributors Inc.
PO Box 6069
Annapolis, MD 21401-0069
Phone: (410)263-0668 **Fax:** (410)263-7489
Products: Sporting and athletic goods. **SIC:** 5091 (Sporting & Recreational Goods). **Officers:** Norman Phillips, President.

■ 24006 ■ Team Sporting Goods Inc.
2614 SW 17th St.
Topeka, KS 66604-2670
Phone: (785)354-1794 **Fax:** (785)354-1795
Products: Sporting and athletic goods. **SIC:** 5091 (Sporting & Recreational Goods). **Officers:** Ronald Miller, President.

■ 24007 ■ Tennis Factory
2500 Wilson Blvd., Ste. 100
Arlington, VA 22201-3834
Phone: (703)522-2700 **Fax:** (703)522-7490
Products: Sporting and recreational goods, including racquet sports equipment and supplies. **SIC:** 5091 (Sporting & Recreational Goods).

■ 24008 ■ Texas Recreation Corp.
PO Box 539
Wichita Falls, TX 76307
Phone: (940)322-4463
Free: (800)433-0956 **Fax:** (940)723-8505
Products: Sponge, expanded and foam rubber products; Plastics foam products; Beverage cooler. **SICs:** 5091 (Sporting & Recreational Goods); 5199 (Nondurable Goods Nec). **Est:** 1956. **Sales:** $10,000,000 (2000). **Emp:** 100. **Officers:** Jim Lollar, Sales Mgr.

■ 24009 ■ Three Epsilon Inc.
6753 Jones Mill Ct, Ste. A
Norcross, GA 30092-4379
Phone: (404)452-7519
Free: (800)343-2652 **Fax:** (404)452-7537
Products: Sporting and athletic goods. **SIC:** 5091 (Sporting & Recreational Goods). **Officers:** George Theodoridis, President.

■ 24010 ■ Three M Leisure Time
4100 James Savage
Midland, MI 48642-5887
Phone: (517)496-3401 **Fax:** (517)496-3374
Products: Fly-fishing lines. **SIC:** 5091 (Sporting & Recreational Goods). **Emp:** 49. **Officers:** Arden L. Freeman.

■ 24011 ■ Titleist Golf
2819 Loker Ave. E
Carlsbad, CA 92008-6626
Phone: (760)745-1000
Products: Golf equipment. **SICs:** 5091 (Sporting & Recreational Goods); 5099 (Durable Goods Nec). **Sales:** $12,500,000 (2000). **Emp:** 102. **Officers:** John Worster.

■ 24012 ■ Toner Sales Inc.
4290 Freeman Rd.
Marietta, GA 30062-5640
Phone: (404)993-8805 **Fax:** (404)998-5692
Products: Swimming pools and equipment. **SIC:** 5091

(Sporting & Recreational Goods). **Officers:** Robert Toner, President.

■ **24013** ■ **Trans-Global Sports Co.**
13104 S Avalon Blvd.
Los Angeles, CA 90061
Phone: (213)321-9714
Free: (800)776-7884 **Fax:** (310)327-6465
Products: Sporting and athletic goods. **SIC:** 5091 (Sporting & Recreational Goods). **Emp:** 10. **Officers:** J. A. Soloman, CEO; E. Soloman, Vice President; M. Soloman, President. **Alternate Name:** T.G. Sports Co.

■ **24014** ■ **Tri-Color International**
9197 El Cortez Ave.
Fountain Valley, CA 92708
Phone: (714)847-2191 **Fax:** (714)847-3031
Products: Bicycles and parts. **SIC:** 5091 (Sporting & Recreational Goods). **Officers:** Charles W. Bolin, President.

■ **24015** ■ **Trojan Pools**
25 Tivoli
Albany, NY 12207-1304
Phone: (518)434-4161 **Fax:** (518)432-6554
Products: Swimming pools. **SIC:** 5091 (Sporting & Recreational Goods). **Sales:** $2,000,000 (2000). **Emp:** 99. **Officers:** Henry S. Mantell Sr.

■ **24016** ■ **T.T.S. Distributors**
116 Riveria St.
San Marcos, TX 78666
Phone: (512)353-8725
Products: Bicycle frames. **SIC:** 5091 (Sporting & Recreational Goods). **Officers:** Mark Turcotte, Customer Service Contact.

■ **24017** ■ **Tulsa Bowling Supply Co.**
3121 S Sheridan Rd.
Tulsa, OK 74145-1102
Phone: (918)627-2728
Free: (800)331-5509 **Fax:** (918)627-2767
Products: Bowling equipment. **SIC:** 5091 (Sporting & Recreational Goods). **Officers:** Theodore Sieler, President.

■ **24018** ■ **Tulsa Firearms Training Academy**
5949 S Garnett Rd.
Tulsa, OK 74146-6825
Phone: (918)250-4867 **Fax:** (918)250-3845
Products: Sporting and athletic goods; Hunting equipment; Firearms. **SIC:** 5091 (Sporting & Recreational Goods). **Officers:** W. Gilmore, President.

■ **24019** ■ **Turbo Link International Inc.**
1452 Crestview St.
Clearwater, FL 33755
Phone: (813)442-2570
Free: (800)462-3993 **Fax:** (813)443-5462
Products: Sport turf, flooring, and related products. **SIC:** 5091 (Sporting & Recreational Goods). **Emp:** 49. **Officers:** Charles A. Meeks, President, e-mail: cmeeks1eb3@tampabay.rr.com.

■ **24020** ■ **Tuscarora Corp.**
PO Box 912
Rocky Mount, NC 27802-0912
Phone: (252)443-7041
Products: Sporting goods. **SIC:** 5091 (Sporting & Recreational Goods). **Sales:** $100,000,000 (1990). **Emp:** 800. **Officers:** Robert D. Gorham Jr., President; E. Wayne Gibson, CFO.

■ **24021** ■ **United Industries Inc.**
PO Box 58
Sterling, KS 67579
Phone: (316)278-3160
Free: (800)835-3272 **Fax:** 800-500-3115
E-mail: jack@swimtime.com
URL: http://www.swimtime.com
Products: Sporting and athletic goods; Swimming pools and equipment. **SIC:** 5091 (Sporting & Recreational Goods). **Est:** 1954. **Sales:** $5,000,000 (2000). **Emp:** 20. **Officers:** Wallace Stromberg, President, e-mail: mac@swimtime.com. **Alternate Name:** Tower-Flo.

■ **24022** ■ **U.S. Line Co.**
16 Union Ave.
Westfield, MA 01085-2497
Phone: (413)562-3629
Free: (800)456-4665 **Fax:** (413)562-7328
Products: Fishing tackle. **SIC:** 5091 (Sporting & Recreational Goods). **Sales:** $2,000,000 (2000). **Emp:** 24. **Officers:** Chester E. Cook; Bradlee E. Gage, Sales/Marketing Contact.

■ **24023** ■ **Universal Bowling and Golf Co.**
619 S Wabash
Chicago, IL 60605
Phone: (312)922-5255 **Fax:** (312)922-5321
Products: Bowling equipment, including balls, bags, and shoes. **SIC:** 5091 (Sporting & Recreational Goods). **Est:** 1939. **Sales:** $3,000,000 (2000). **Emp:** 25. **Officers:** Lawrence C. Weinstein, President; Sanford S. Weinstein, Dir. of Systems.

■ **24024** ■ **Utikem Products**
225 Passaic St.
Passaic, NJ 07055
Phone: (973)473-1222 **Fax:** (973)473-0535
Products: Swimming pool equipment, including chlorine, kits, hoses and nets. **SIC:** 5091 (Sporting & Recreational Goods). **Est:** 1986. **Sales:** $4,500,000 (2000). **Emp:** 25. **Officers:** John Ferentinos, President; Thomas Ferentinos, Vice President.

■ **24025** ■ **Vans Pro Shop**
10001 W Bell Rd., Ste. 118
Sun City, AZ 85351-1284
Phone: (602)972-0171 **Fax:** (602)972-9803
Products: Sporting and recreational goods, including golf equipment and supplies. **SIC:** 5091 (Sporting & Recreational Goods). **Officers:** Frank Bocchini, Owner.

■ **24026** ■ **Vantage Pools Inc.**
1098 S 5th St.
San Jose, CA 95112-3926
Phone: (408)275-6217
Products: Above ground swimming pools. **SIC:** 5091 (Sporting & Recreational Goods). **Sales:** $500,000 (2000). **Emp:** 6.

■ **24027** ■ **Varsity Sports Center Inc.**
415 W Wall St.
Griffin, GA 30223-2860
Phone: (404)228-2738 **Fax:** (404)228-0035
Products: Sporting and athletic goods. **SIC:** 5091 (Sporting & Recreational Goods). **Officers:** Edward Duke, President.

■ **24028** ■ **Vectra Fitness Inc.**
15135 NE 90th St.
Redmond, WA 98052
Phone: (425)867-1500 **Fax:** (425)861-0506
Products: Home gym systems. **SIC:** 5091 (Sporting & Recreational Goods). **Officers:** Doug MacLean, President.

■ **24029** ■ **Venture Vehicles Inc.**
205 Pine St.
Contoocook, NH 03229-2602
Phone: (603)746-6406 **Free:** (800)521-3703
Products: Golf carts. **SICs:** 5091 (Sporting & Recreational Goods); 5088 (Transportation Equipment & Supplies). **Officers:** Robert Polish, President.

■ **24030** ■ **Venus Knitting Mills Inc.**
140 Spring St.
Murray Hill, NJ 07974
Phone: (908)464-2400
Free: (800)955-4200 **Fax:** (908)464-5108
Products: Sporting and athletic goods. **SIC:** 5091 (Sporting & Recreational Goods). **Est:** 1917. **Sales:** $20,000,000 (2000). **Emp:** 50.

■ **24031** ■ **Versatile Vehicles Inc.**
12461 Rhode Island Ave.
Savage, MN 55378
Phone: (952)894-1123
Free: (800)678-1123 **Fax:** (952)894-9670
E-mail: info@versatilevehicles.com
URL: http://www.versatilevehicles.com
Products: Golf carts; Utility vehicles and parts. **SICs:** 5088 (Transportation Equipment & Supplies); 5091 (Sporting & Recreational Goods); 5012 (Automobiles &

Other Motor Vehicles). **Est:** 1985. **Sales:** $1,500,000 (2000). **Emp:** 8. **Officers:** Gaby Accad. **Former Name:** Versatile Vehicles.

■ **24032** ■ **Victor Sports**
PO Box 208
Hinsdale, IL 60522
Phone: (708)352-1580 **Fax:** (708)352-1581
Products: Racket sports equipment for tennis, squash, badminton, and racquetball. **SIC:** 5091 (Sporting & Recreational Goods). **Est:** 1947. **Officers:** Glenn A. Bjorkman, President.

■ **24033** ■ **Viking Cue Manufacturing, Inc.**
2710 Syene Rd.
Madison, WI 53713-3202
Phone: (608)271-5155
Free: (800)397-0122 **Fax:** (608)271-5157
E-mail: info@vikingcue.com
URL: http://www.vikingcue.com
Products: Billiard two-piece cues and supplies. **SIC:** 5091 (Sporting & Recreational Goods). **Est:** 1965. **Officers:** Gordon Hart, President; Nancy Hart, Vice President, e-mail: joel@vikingcue.com.

■ **24034** ■ **Keith Vint & Associates**
15585 Graham St.
Huntington Beach, CA 92649
Phone: (714)898-2318
Free: (800)541-8897 **Fax:** (714)898-6969
Products: Sporting and athletic goods. **SIC:** 5091 (Sporting & Recreational Goods).

■ **24035** ■ **VMC Inc.**
1901 Oakcrest Ave., Ste. 10
St. Paul, MN 55113-2617
Phone: (612)636-9649
Free: (800)999-4665 **Fax:** (612)636-7053
URL: http://www.vmchooks.com
Products: Fishing products, including hooks, lines, and floats. **SIC:** 5091 (Sporting & Recreational Goods). **Est:** 1980. **Emp:** 8. **Officers:** Christophe Viellard, President; Jackie Kiklas, Vice President.

■ **24036** ■ **Volunteer Janitorial Supply Co.**
2136 Hollywood Dr.
Jackson, TN 38305-4323
Phone: (901)668-4005
Free: (800)722-8618 **Fax:** (901)668-4070
Products: Sporting and recreational goods, including watersport and swimming pool equipment and supplies; Cleaning and sanitary supplies; Paper products. **SICs:** 5091 (Sporting & Recreational Goods); 5113 (Industrial & Personal Service Paper). **Est:** 1966. **Sales:** $3,000,000 (2000). **Emp:** 20. **Officers:** Jerry Wood, President.

■ **24037** ■ **Waco Sales Inc.**
3603 N Main St.
Wayland, MI 49348-1001
Phone: (616)792-2291 **Fax:** (616)792-2361
Products: Sporting and athletic goods. **SIC:** 5091 (Sporting & Recreational Goods). **Officers:** Robert Swainston, President.

■ **24038** ■ **Wallace & Associates**
20 Fieldwood Pl.
Newnan, GA 30263-1364
Phone: (404)251-5281 **Fax:** (404)251-9909
Products: Sporting and athletic goods. **SIC:** 5091 (Sporting & Recreational Goods). **Officers:** Henry Wallace, Owner.

■ **24039** ■ **Walmsley Marine Inc.**
656 Metacom Ave.
Warren, RI 02885-2316
Phone: (401)245-9069
Products: Sporting and recreation goods; Boats, canoes, and equipment. **SIC:** 5091 (Sporting & Recreational Goods). **Officers:** Arthur Walmsley, President.

■ **24040** ■ **Washington Tysons Golf Center**
PO Box 9025
West McLean, VA 22102-0025
Phone: (703)790-8844 **Fax:** (703)790-8871
Products: Golf equipment. **SIC:** 5091 (Sporting & Recreational Goods). **Officers:** Joseph Chang, President.

■ **24041** ■ **Waters Edge Distributors Inc.**
PO Box 384
Ceda Indus
Charlestown, NH 03603
Phone: (603)826-3702 **Fax:** (603)826-3742
Products: Spa equipment and supplies. **SIC:** 5091 (Sporting & Recreational Goods). **Officers:** William Austin, President.

■ **24042** ■ **Wenger N.A.**
15 Corporate Dr.
Orangeburg, NY 10962
Phone: (914)365-3500 **Fax:** (914)425-4700
URL: http://www.wengerna.com
Products: Knives; Promotional Productss; Watches; Fragrances. **SICs:** 5091 (Sporting & Recreational Goods); 5094 (Jewelry & Precious Stones). **Est:** 1954. **Sales:** $60,000,000 (2000). **Emp:** 95. **Officers:** D. Thomas Abbott, Chairman of the Board; Kennith C. Johnson, VP & CFO; Dennis Piretra, Contact; Peter Policastro, Contact; Lauren Ponce, Contact. **Alternate Name:** Swiss Army Parfum. **Alternate Name:** Wenger. **Former Name:** Precise International/Wenger.

■ **24043** ■ **West Virginia Archery Supply**
PO Box 9216
Charleston, WV 25309-0216
Phone: (304)768-6091
Products: Archery equipment. **SIC:** 5091 (Sporting & Recreational Goods). **Officers:** Katherine Tucci, Owner.

■ **24044** ■ **Westar Inc.**
6031 S 58th St. C
Lincoln, NE 68516-3645
Phone: (402)421-2100 **Fax:** (402)421-6101
Products: Sporting and athletic goods; Lumber and wood products; Adhesives and sealants. **SICs:** 5091 (Sporting & Recreational Goods); 5031 (Lumber, Plywood & Millwork); 5169 (Chemicals & Allied Products Nec). **Officers:** Johna Kipper, President.

■ **24045** ■ **Western Golf Inc.**
PO Box 970
Thousand Palms, CA 92276-0970
Phone: (760)343-1050
Free: (800)443-4350 **Fax:** (760)343-2834
E-mail: info@westerngolf.com
URL: http://www.westerngolf.com
Products: Golf equipment. **SIC:** 5091 (Sporting & Recreational Goods). **Est:** 1956. **Sales:** $4,500,000 (2000). **Emp:** 17. **Officers:** Robert Wagner, President; Aaron R. Montano, Vice President; Lyn Montano, Treasurer.

■ **24046** ■ **Jim Williams Sales & Service**
PO Box 873
New Town, ND 58763-0873
Phone: (701)627-3212
Products: Fishing tackle and equipment. **SIC:** 5091 (Sporting & Recreational Goods). **Officers:** Jim Williams, Owner.

■ **24047** ■ **John Wilson Wholesale Sporting Goods**
3710 Liberty Dr. 1
Iowa City, IA 52240-1800
Phone: (319)338-6352
Products: Sporting and athletic goods. **SIC:** 5091 (Sporting & Recreational Goods). **Officers:** J. Wilson, President.

■ **24048** ■ **Winn Inc.**
PO Box 1936
Huntington Beach, CA 92647
Phone: (714)842-1301
Free: (800)854-7676 **Fax:** (714)848-3894
E-mail: custsvc@winngrips.com
URL: http://www.winngrips.com
Products: Golf club grips. **SIC:** 5091 (Sporting &

Recreational Goods). **Est:** 1977. **Sales:** $25,000,000 (2000). **Emp:** 13. **Officers:** Ben Huang, President; Mavis Huang, Vice President.

■ **24049** ■ **Wittek Golf Supply Co., Inc.**
3650 N Avondale
Chicago, IL 60618
Phone: (773)463-2636
Free: (800)869-1800 **Fax:** (773)463-2150
E-mail: info@weittekgolf.com
URL: http://www.wittekgolf.com
Products: Golf equipment, including driving range equipment, golf course accessories, miniature golf supplies, and golf shop display fixtures. **SIC:** 5091 (Sporting & Recreational Goods). **Est:** 1946. **Officers:** Robert Wittek Sr., Chairman of the Board; Ron Dudzik, Exec. VP.

■ **24050** ■ **Woodshill Pool**
PO Box 843
Swanton, VT 05488
Phone: (802)868-7057
Products: Sporting and athletic goods; Swimming pools and equipment. **SIC:** 5091 (Sporting & Recreational Goods). **Officers:** Harry Richard.

■ **24051** ■ **Wuu Jau Company Inc.**
PO Box 5062
Edmond, OK 73083
Phone: (405)359-5031
Free: (800)772-5760 **Fax:** (405)340-5965
URL: http://www.wuujau.com
Products: Hunting and pocket knives; Crossbows; Swords; Personal safety devices. **SICs:** 5091 (Sporting & Recreational Goods); 5072 (Hardware). **Est:** 1981. **Sales:** $5,000,000 (2000). **Emp:** 14.

(47) Restaurant and Commercial Foodservice Equipment and Supplies

Entries in this section are arranged alphabetically by company name. When the company name is a personal name, the company name is alphabetized by the surname unless the first name or initial(s) are part of a trade name. See the User's Guide at the front of this directory for additional information.

■ **24052** ■ **4 BS Wholesale Supply Inc.**
PO Box 7369
Missoula, MT 59807-7369
Phone: (406)543-8265
Products: Commercial cooking equipment; Restaurant supplies. **SIC:** 5046 (Commercial Equipment Nec).
Officers: Wilbur Hainline, President.

■ **24053** ■ **Abbott Foods Inc.**
2400 Harrison Rd.
Columbus, OH 43204
Phone: (614)272-0658   **Fax:** (614)272-7095
Products: Food for restaurants; Cleaning supplies for restaurants. **SICs:** 5141 (Groceries—General Line); 5046 (Commercial Equipment Nec); 5169 (Chemicals & Allied Products Nec). **Est:** 1940. **Sales:** $185,000,000 (1999). **Emp:** 450. **Officers:** Larry Abbott, President; Gordon J. Jablonka, VP of Purchasing.

■ **24054** ■ **Accurate Partitions Corp.**
PO Box 287
Lyons, IL 60534
Phone: (708)442-6801   **Fax:** (708)442-7439
Products: Furniture and fixtures. **SIC:** 5046 (Commercial Equipment Nec). **Sales:** $10,000,000 (2000). **Emp:** 99.

■ **24055** ■ **Ad Art Electronic Sign Corp.**
19603 Figueroa St.
Carson, CA 90745
Phone: (310)523-9500   **Fax:** (310)538-1215
Products: Electrical and electronic signs and message centers. **SIC:** 5046 (Commercial Equipment Nec).

■ **24056** ■ **Adams-Burch Inc.**
5556 Tuxedo Rd.
Hyattsville, MD 20781
Phone: (301)341-1600
Products: Restaurant and hotel supplies. **SIC:** 5087 (Service Establishment Equipment). **Sales:** $22,600,000 (2000). **Emp:** 110. **Officers:** Dan W. Blaylock, President; D.M. Blaylock, CFO.

■ **24057** ■ **Alfredos Restaurant Equipment**
801 Delaware Ave.
Alamogordo, NM 88310-7103
Phone: (505)437-1745
Products: Commercial cooking and food warming equipment; Restaurant supplies. **SIC:** 5046 (Commercial Equipment Nec). **Officers:** Alfredo Paz, Owner.

■ **24058** ■ **All American Food Group Inc.**
4475 S Clinton Ave.
South Plainfield, NJ 07080
Phone: (908)757-3022   **Free:** (800)922-4350
Products: Bagel bakery equipment. **SIC:** 5084 (Industrial Machinery & Equipment). **Sales:** $2,400,000 (2000). **Emp:** 61. **Officers:** Andrew Thorburn, CEO; Chris R. Decker, Exec. VP & CFO.

■ **24059** ■ **Alliant FoodService Inc.**
One Parkway North Ctr.
Deerfield, IL 60015
Phone: (847)405-8500   **Fax:** (847)405-8980
Products: Groceries and food service products. **SIC:** 5149 (Groceries & Related Products Nec). **Sales:** $6,100,000,000 (2000). **Emp:** 12,000. **Officers:** James A. Miller, CEO & President.

■ **24060** ■ **Allstate Restaurant Equipment Inc.**
125 Esten Ave.
Pawtucket, RI 02860-4877
Phone: (401)727-0880   **Fax:** (401)727-0930
Products: Commercial cooking and food service equipment, including restaurant equipment and supplies. **SIC:** 5046 (Commercial Equipment Nec). **Est:** 1977. **Emp:** 7. **Officers:** Giacomo Meo, President.

■ **24061** ■ **Alpine Restaurant Equipment**
1661 Lonsdale Ave.
Lincoln, RI 02865-1707
Phone: (401)723-1300
Products: Commercial cooking and food service equipment; Restaurant equipment and supplies. **SIC:** 5046 (Commercial Equipment Nec). **Officers:** Alfred Pine, President.

■ **24062** ■ **American Coffee Co. Inc.**
PO Box 4789
Rumford, RI 02916-0789
Phone: (401)438-8666
Products: Commercial equipment, including cooking and food service equipment, coffee brewing equipment, and supplies. **SIC:** 5046 (Commercial Equipment Nec).
Officers: Salvatore Guglielmo, President.

■ **24063** ■ **AmeriServe**
PO Box 9016
Addison, TX 75001
Phone: (972)338-7000
Products: Restaurant food. **SICs:** 5141 (Groceries—General Line); 5149 (Groceries & Related Products Nec). **Sales:** $850,000,000 (2000). **Emp:** 700. **Officers:** Raymond Marshall, Vice Chairman of the Board; Diana Moog, CFO.

■ **24064** ■ **AMJ Inc.**
25 Precourt St.
Biddeford, ME 04005-4315
Phone: (207)284-5731   **Fax:** (207)282-4759
Products: Cleaning and janitorial supplies. **SIC:** 5087 (Service Establishment Equipment). **Sales:** $3,000,000 (2000). **Emp:** 10.

■ **24065** ■ **Anchorage Restaurant Supply**
PO Box 10399
Anchorage, AK 99510
Phone: (907)276-7044   **Fax:** (907)276-6875
Products: Commercial cooking equipment; Restaurant supplies. **SIC:** 5046 (Commercial Equipment Nec).
Officers: Robert Richard, Owner.

■ **24066** ■ **Earl F. Anderson Associates Inc.**
9808 James Cir.
Bloomington, MN 55431
Phone: (612)884-7300
Products: Foodservice equipment. **SICs:** 5046 (Commercial Equipment Nec); 5099 (Durable Goods Nec). **Sales:** $4,000,000 (2000). **Emp:** 22. **Officers:** Warren Anondson, President; Jack Ashmore, Vice President.

■ **24067** ■ **Arbuckle Coffee Roasters Inc.**
3498 S Dodge Blvd Ste 100
Tucson, AZ 85713
Phone: (520)790-5282   **Fax:** (520)748-7910
Products: Coffee roasting; Coffee brewing equipment. **SICs:** 5087 (Service Establishment Equipment); 5149 (Groceries & Related Products Nec). **Officers:** Denney Willis, CEO.

■ **24068** ■ **Asbury Worldwide Inc.**
10011 Pines Blvd., Ste. 101
Pembroke Pines, FL 33024-6167
Phone: (954)438-4381
Products: Food service equipment. **SIC:** 5046 (Commercial Equipment Nec).

■ **24069** ■ **Associated Building Specialties**
20 Frankford Ave.
Blackwood, NJ 08012-2850
Phone: (609)227-3900   **Fax:** (609)227-9307
Products: Furniture and fixtures. **SIC:** 5046 (Commercial Equipment Nec). **Sales:** $3,000,000 (2000). **Emp:** 25.

■ **24070** ■ **Atlanta Fixture and Sails Co.**
3185 NE Expressway
Atlanta, GA 30341
Phone: (404)455-8844
Products: Restaurant equipment and supplies. **SICs:** 5046 (Commercial Equipment Nec); 5021 (Furniture).
Est: 1927. **Sales:** $19,000,000 (2000). **Emp:** 100.
Officers: Paul Klein, CEO.

■ **24071** ■ **Atlantis Restaurant Equipment**
27 Industrial Park Rd.
Saco, ME 04072
Phone: (207)284-7394   **Fax:** (207)282-9742
URL: http://www.atlantisrestauranteqcom
Products: Food service equipment and supplies. **SIC:** 5046 (Commercial Equipment Nec). **Est:** 1976. **Sales:** $3,000,000 (1999). **Emp:** 11. **Officers:** Peter Zafirson, Chairman of the Board, e-mail: peterz@fccosuseq.com; Steve Zafirson, President; Lea Zafirson, Vice President; Carol Zafirson, Vice President.

■ **24072** ■ **Atlas Merchandising Co.**
138-142 McKean Ave.
Charleroi, PA 15022
Phone: (412)489-9561   **Fax:** (412)489-9563
Products: Bar supplies; Janitorial supplies; Candy. **SICs:** 5046 (Commercial Equipment Nec); 5145 (Confectionery). **Est:** 1935. **Sales:** $13,000,000 (2000). **Emp:** 20. **Officers:** Rose Kiski, President.

■ **24073** ■ **AVK II Inc.**
PO Box 310
Lyndonville, VT 05851-0310
Phone: (802)626-9274
Products: Service establishment equipment, including restaurant supplies. **SICs:** 5087 (Service Establishment Equipment); 5046 (Commercial Equipment Nec).
Officers: Ashley Gray, President.

■ **24074** ■ **B-J Pac-A-Part**
410 25th Ave. S
Great Falls, MT 59405-7147
Phone: (406)761-4487
Free: (800)462-3543   **Fax:** (406)761-5725
Products: Cleaning and janitorial supplies. **SIC:** 5087 (Service Establishment Equipment). **Sales:** $100,000 (2000). **Emp:** 3.

■ **24075** ■ **Baker's Kneads**
5598 E 10 Mile Rd.
Warren, MI 48091
Phone: (734)758-4440
Products: Cooking equipment and parts. **SIC:** 5046 (Commercial Equipment Nec).

■ **24076** ■ **Bintz Distributing Co.**
1855 S 300 W
Salt Lake City, UT 84115
Phone: (801)463-1515
Free: (800)443-4746   **Fax:** (801)463-1693
URL: http://www.bintzsupply.com
Products: Restaurant equipment and supplies including china, flatware, and glasses. **SIC:** 5046 (Commercial Equipment Nec). **Est:** 1891. **Sales:** $20,000,000 (1999). **Emp:** 40. **Officers:** B. Williams, President, e-mail: bwilliams@bintzsupply.com; Larry Glauser, Vice President, e-mail: lglauser@ bintzsupply.com.

■ **24077** ■ **G.S. Blodgett International Sales**
PO Box 586
Burlington, VT 05402-0586
Phone: (802)658-6600   **Fax:** (802)860-3732
Products: Ovens. **SIC:** 5046 (Commercial Equipment Nec). **Officers:** J. Johnson, President.

■ **24078** ■ **Blue Cold Distributors**
323 Pine Point Rd.
Scarborough, ME 04074
Phone: (207)885-0107
Products: Restaurant equipment and supplies. **SIC:** 5087 (Service Establishment Equipment).

■ **24079** ■ **Boelter Companies Inc.**
11100 W Silver Spr Rd
Milwaukee, WI 53225
Phone: (414)461-3400
Products: Restaurant supplies, including pots, pans, fryers, and coolers. **SIC:** 5046 (Commercial Equipment Nec). **Est:** 1929. **Sales:** $25,000,000 (2000). **Emp:** 150. **Officers:** F.W. Boelter, President; Dave Schulz, VP of Finance.

■ **24080** ■ **Boelter Co.**
7370 N Lincoln Ave.
Lincolnwood, IL 60646
Phone: (773)267-0505   **Fax:** (312)708-0507
Products: Restaurant supplies. **SIC:** 5087 (Service Establishment Equipment). **Est:** 1919. **Sales:** $2,200,000 (2000). **Emp:** 30. **Officers:** Donald Prince, President; Richard Bowman, Treasurer & Secty.

■ **24081** ■ **Bolton and Hay Inc.**
PO Box 3247
Des Moines, IA 50316
Phone: (515)265-2554
Free: (800)362-1861   **Fax:** (515)265-6090
E-mail: boltonhay@worldnet.att.net
URL: http://www.boltonhay.com
Products: Restaurant supplies, including silverware, glasses, plates, walk-in coolers, and commercial ovens. **SIC:** 5046 (Commercial Equipment Nec). **Est:** 1920. **Sales:** $4,000,000 (2000). **Emp:** 22. **Officers:** Lew Bolton, President; John Speicher, Vice President.

■ **24082** ■ **Boyer Printing Co.**
PO Box 509
Lebanon, PA 17042-0509
Phone: (717)272-5691
Free: (800)860-5691   **Fax:** (717)272-9698
Products: specialty equipment and products. **SIC:** 5046 (Commercial Equipment Nec). **Sales:** $6,000,000 (2000). **Emp:** 57.

■ **24083** ■ **Budd Mayer Co.**
3444 Memorial Hwy.
Tampa, FL 33607
Phone: (813)282-6900   **Fax:** (813)286-3030
Products: Food services. **SICs:** 5141 (Groceries— General Line); 5149 (Groceries & Related Products Nec). **Sales:** $156,000,000 (2000). **Emp:** 1,200. **Officers:** Mike Sunderland, CEO & President; Robert Erger, CFO.

■ **24084** ■ **Budget Sales Inc.**
1534 1st Ave. S
Seattle, WA 98134
Phone: (206)621-9500   **Fax:** (206)621-0648
Products: Used restaurant equipment. **SIC:** 5046 (Commercial Equipment Nec). **Est:** 1986. **Sales:** $2,000,000 (2000). **Emp:** 7. **Officers:** John Kazdal, President.

■ **24085** ■ **Butler Wholesale Products**
37 Pleasant St.
PO Box 308
Adams, MA 01220
Phone: (413)743-3885
Free: (800)233-0717   **Fax:** (413)743-3887
Products: Food and supplies for restaurants. **SICs:** 5046 (Commercial Equipment Nec); 5141 (Groceries— General Line); 5149 (Groceries & Related Products Nec). **Est:** 1915. **Sales:** $16,000,000 (2000). **Emp:** 45. **Officers:** George Apkin, Treasurer; Michael Richardello, President.

■ **24086** ■ **Byczek Enterprises**
3924 W Devon Ave.
Lincolnwood, IL 60659
Phone: (847)673-6050   **Fax:** (847)673-6085
Products: Food service equipment. **SIC:** 5046 (Commercial Equipment Nec). **Est:** 1952. **Sales:** $30,000,000 (2000). **Emp:** 50. **Officers:** J.L. Byczek, President; David Koder, Controller; Ralph Aylward, Vice President; Eric Chaplick, Dir. of Sales.

■ **24087** ■ **D. Canale Food Services Inc.**
PO Box 1739
Memphis, TN 38101-1739
Phone: (901)525-6811
Products: Institutional food products. **SICs:** 5141 (Groceries—General Line); 5142 (Packaged Frozen Foods). **Sales:** $40,000,000 (2000). **Emp:** 175. **Officers:** John D. Canale III, President; Donald L. Jordan, Comptroller.

■ **24088** ■ **Canton China and Equipment Co.**
6309 Mack Ave.
Detroit, MI 48207
Phone: (313)925-3100   **Fax:** (313)925-8341
Products: Electric ranges and ovens; Commercial reach-in and walk-in refrigerators; Restaurant, cafeteria, and bar furniture and fixtures. **SICs:** 5046 (Commercial Equipment Nec); 5064 (Electrical Appliances—Television & Radio). **Est:** 1927. **Sales:** $10,000,000 (2000). **Emp:** 20. **Officers:** Meyer Pearlman, President; Allan J. Pearlman, Corporate Secty.; Sheldon Pearlman, Vice President.

■ **24089** ■ **Capital City Restaurant Supply Co.**
321 S 1st St.
PO Box 721
Bismarck, ND 58502-0721
Phone: (701)255-4576
Free: (800)279-4576   **Fax:** (701)255-4651
Products: Commercial cooking and food warming equipment; Restaurant supplies. **SIC:** 5046 (Commercial Equipment Nec). **Est:** 1970. **Emp:** 3. **Officers:** Alfred Lang, President.

■ **24090** ■ **Capresso Inc.**
39 Rugen Dr.
Harrington Park, NJ 07640
Phone: (201)767-3999
Products: European-manufactured espresso and coffee machines. **SIC:** 5064 (Electrical Appliances— Television & Radio).

■ **24091** ■ **Central Procurement Inc.**
1 Kingfisher Dr.
Coventry, RI 02816-6826
Phone: (401)823-8600
Free: (800)370-8601   **Fax:** (401)823-8639
Products: Restaurant and hotel equipment and supplies. **SIC:** 5046 (Commercial Equipment Nec). **Est:** 1974. **Sales:** $300,000 (2000). **Emp:** 2. **Officers:** Jordan Liner, President, e-mail: jordliner@aol.com.

■ **24092** ■ **Cirelli Foods Inc.**
970 W Chestnut St.
Brockton, MA 02301
Phone: (508)584-6700   **Fax:** (508)559-0729
Products: Food and cleaning supplies for restaurants. **SICs:** 5141 (Groceries—General Line); 5169 (Chemicals & Allied Products Nec). **Est:** 1946. **Sales:** $45,000,000 (1999). **Emp:** 140. **Officers:** Chuck Dillon, President & CEO; Leon Tarentino, VP of Marketing & Sales; Bruce Taylor, Dir. of Sales; Ray LeBlanc, CFO.

■ **24093** ■ **Clark County Bar & Restaurant Supply**
1117 S Commerce St.
Las Vegas, NV 89102-2526
Phone: (702)382-6762
Free: (888)382-9767   **Fax:** (702)382-7582
E-mail: vegaskitchens@earthlink.net
URL: http://www.vegaskitchens.com
Products: Commercial equipment; Cooking and food service equipment; Restaurant equipment and supplies. **SIC:** 5046 (Commercial Equipment Nec). **Officers:** Loren Horten, President.

■ **24094** ■ **Clark Food Service Inc. South Bend Div.**
1901 Bendix Dr.
South Bend, IN 46628
Phone: (219)234-5011   **Fax:** (219)232-4515
Products: Food service supplies. **SICs:** 5141 (Groceries—General Line); 5046 (Commercial Equipment Nec); 5113 (Industrial & Personal Service Paper). **Est:** 1911. **Sales:** $60,000,000 (1999). **Emp:** 210. **Officers:** Tom Ruszkowski, President; Jeff Ireland, VP of Sales; Bob Hoffer, VP of Marketing/Purchasing.

■ **24095** ■ **Classic Beauty Supply and Service Center**
Glenmont Shopping Ctr.
Wheaton, MD 20906
Phone: (301)946-2223
Products: Health and beauty aids. **SIC:** 5087 (Service Establishment Equipment).

■ **24096** ■ **CMC America Corp.**
210 S Center St.
Joliet, IL 60436
Phone: (815)726-4336   **Fax:** (815)726-7138
Products: specialty equipment and products. **SIC:** 5046 (Commercial Equipment Nec). **Sales:** $2,000,000 (2000). **Emp:** 15.

■ **24097** ■ **Crisci Food Equipment Co.**
1103 Croton Ave.
PO Box 8327
New Castle, PA 16107
Phone: (412)654-6609
Free: (800)245-8110   **Fax:** (412)654-9266
Products: Food products machinery; Household and industrial chemicals; Paper dishes; Janitors' supplies. **SICs:** 5046 (Commercial Equipment Nec); 5169 (Chemicals & Allied Products Nec); 5113 (Industrial & Personal Service Paper). **Emp:** 20.

■ **24098** ■ **Cromers Inc.**
PO Box 163
Columbia, SC 29202
Phone: (803)779-1147
Free: (800)322-7688   **Fax:** (803)779-4743
Products: Concession equipment and supplies;

Novelties and party items, including bingo supplies, flags, banners, and advertising specialties. **SICs:** 5046 (Commercial Equipment Nec); 5092 (Toys & Hobby Goods & Supplies). **Sales:** $3,000,000 (2000). **Emp:** 37. **Officers:** Barry D. Cromer, CEO & President.

■ **24099** ■ **D and M Distributors Inc.**
273 Presumpscot St.
Portland, ME 04103-5226
Phone: (207)772-4796 **Fax:** (207)772-7159
Products: specialty equipment and products. **SIC:** 5087 (Service Establishment Equipment). **Sales:** $800,000 (2000). **Emp:** 4.

■ **24100** ■ **D & P Enterprises Inc.**
960 S Virginia St.
Reno, NV 89502-2416
Phone: (702)786-6565 **Fax:** (702)786-1952
Products: Commercial cooking and food warming equipment; Restaurant supplies. **SIC:** 5046 (Commercial Equipment Nec). **Officers:** Paul Oelsner, President.

■ **24101** ■ **Daffin Mercantile Company Inc.**
PO Box 779
Marianna, FL 32447
Phone: (850)482-4026
Products: Restaurant food. **SIC:** 5141 (Groceries—General Line). **Sales:** $25,000,000 (1994). **Emp:** 49. **Officers:** Ralph H. Daffin Jr., President; Brian Milton, Treasurer.

■ **24102** ■ **Dakota Food Equipment Inc.**
PO Box 2925
Fargo, ND 58108-2925
Phone: (701)232-4428
Free: (800)437-4076 **Fax:** (701)232-1323
Products: Commercial cooking and food service equipment. **SIC:** 5046 (Commercial Equipment Nec). **Est:** 1947. **Sales:** $11,000,000 (2000). **Emp:** 54. **Officers:** Darrel Nelson, President.

■ **24103** ■ **Dana-Lu Imports Inc.**
280 Midland Ave.
Bldg. M-1
Saddle Brook, NJ 07663
Phone: (201)791-2244 **Fax:** (201)791-2288
Products: Espresso machines; granita machines; cappucino steamers. **SIC:** 5046 (Commercial Equipment Nec). **Est:** 1988. **Sales:** $4,000,000 (2000). **Emp:** 10. **Officers:** Dana M. Rafferty, President. **Former Name:** Saeco USA. **Former Name:** Blickman Supply.

■ **24104** ■ **Deuster Co.**
N57 W13636 Carman Ave.
Menomonee Falls, WI 53051
Phone: (414)783-4140
Products: Bar and restaurant supplies; Janitorial supplies. **SICs:** 5084 (Industrial Machinery & Equipment); 5078 (Refrigeration Equipment & Supplies); 5087 (Service Establishment Equipment).

■ **24105** ■ **Dorian International Inc.**
2 Gannett Dr.
White Plains, NY 10604
Phone: (914)697-9800 **Fax:** (914)697-9190
Products: Restaurant supplies; Auto parts; Industrial, lawn, and garden hardware. **SICs:** 5013 (Motor Vehicle Supplies & New Parts); 5083 (Farm & Garden Machinery); 5072 (Hardware); 5046 (Commercial Equipment Nec). **Est:** 1946. **Sales:** $35,000,000 (2000). **Emp:** 63. **Officers:** Edward S. Dorian Jr., President; John Mott, Controller; Rudy Bruckenthal, Dir. of Marketing.

■ **24106** ■ **E and B Beauty and Barber Supply**
1811 E Thayer Ave.
Bismarck, ND 58501-4780
Phone: (701)223-7408 **Free:** (888)258-4707
Products: Health and beauty aids. **SIC:** 5087 (Service Establishment Equipment). **Sales:** $200,000 (2000). **Emp:** 3.

■ **24107** ■ **Electric Motor Repair Co.**
700 E 25th St.
Baltimore, MD 21218
Phone: (410)467-8080
Free: (800)879-4994 **Fax:** (410)467-4191
E-mail: emr@emtco.com
URL: http://www.emrco.com
Products: Restaurant equipment, including ovens, fryers, and slicers. **SIC:** 5046 (Commercial Equipment Nec). **Est:** 1928. **Sales:** $11,000,000 (2000). **Emp:** 128. **Officers:** H. Roger Kauffman, President & Treasurer; Randy Bear, Controller; Janet Pope, Personnel Mgr.

■ **24108** ■ **Elliott Manufacturing Company Inc.**
PO Box 11277
Fresno, CA 93772
Phone: (559)233-6235 **Fax:** (559)233-9833
E-mail: elliottmfg@elliott.mfg.com
URL: http://www.elliott-mfg.com
Products: Food processing machinery. **SIC:** 5046 (Commercial Equipment Nec). **Est:** 1929. **Sales:** $5,000,000 (2000). **Emp:** 50. **Officers:** Thomas E. Cole, President; Richard Allbritton, VP of Marketing & Sales.

■ **24109** ■ **Epicurean International Inc.**
229 Castro St.
Oakland, CA 94607
Phone: (510)268-0209
Free: (800)967-8424 **Fax:** (510)834-3102
Products: Groceries, specializing in Thai products, food service, and private labels. **SIC:** 5141 (Groceries—General Line). **Sales:** $21,000,000 (2000). **Emp:** 40. **Officers:** Seth Jacobson, President.

■ **24110** ■ **Erika-Record Inc.**
20 Vanderhoof Ave.
Rockaway, NJ 07866
Phone: (973)664-1750
Free: (800)682-8203 **Fax:** (973)664-1752
E-mail: max@erikarecord.com
Products: Bakery equipment and parts. **SIC:** 5046 (Commercial Equipment Nec). **Est:** 1991. **Sales:** $2,000,000 (2000). **Emp:** 4. **Officers:** Max Oehler, President.

■ **24111** ■ **Euroven Corp.**
225 Industrial
Fredericksburg, VA 22408
Phone: (540)891-2481 **Fax:** (540)891-2826
Products: Commercial cooking equipment. **SIC:** 5046 (Commercial Equipment Nec). **Officers:** Jean-Franc Villard, Vice President.

■ **24112** ■ **Exmart International, Inc.**
PO Box 408
Succasunna, NJ 07876-0408
Phone: (973)402-8600 **Fax:** (973)402-8444
Products: Refrigeration and ice making equipment; Food whippers, mixers, and blenders; Commercial kitchen tableware; Furniture, including restaurant, cafeteria, and bar furniture; Commercial cooking and food warming equipment. **SICs:** 5046 (Commercial Equipment Nec); 5078 (Refrigeration Equipment & Supplies); 5021 (Furniture). **Officers:** Jack Mcgrath, President.

■ **24113** ■ **Export Contract Corp.**
PO Box 380039
Jacksonville, FL 32205-0539
Products: Commercial food slicers; Food processing machinery. **SICs:** 5084 (Industrial Machinery & Equipment); 5046 (Commercial Equipment Nec). **Officers:** Kenneth Taylor, President. **Former Name:** Calico Trading Private Ltd. Co.

■ **24114** ■ **Far East Restaurant Equipment Mfg. Co.**
306 S Maple Ave.
South San Francisco, CA 94080
Phone: (650)872-6585
Free: (800)488-3888 **Fax:** (650)872-0848
E-mail: fareast8@spacbell.net
URL: http://www.fareast88.com
Products: Wok ranges; Restarant equipment. **SIC:** 5046 (Commercial Equipment Nec). **Est:** 1982. **Emp:** 49. **Officers:** Johhny Fong.

■ **24115** ■ **Federated Foodservice**
3025 W Salt Creek Ln.
Arlington Heights, IL 60005
Phone: (708)577-1200
Products: Food services products. **SIC:** 5141 (Groceries—General Line).

■ **24116** ■ **FES**
PO Box 2306
York, PA 17405
Phone: (717)767-6411 **Fax:** (717)764-3627
URL: http://www.fessystems.com
Products: Industrial refrigeration. **SICs:** 5078 (Refrigeration Equipment & Supplies); 5084 (Industrial Machinery & Equipment). **Est:** 1949. **Sales:** $66,000,000 (2000). **Emp:** 250. **Officers:** Jeffrey Graby, President; John C. Lutz, CFO; John Miranda, Natl. Sales Mgr.; John Hall, Dir of Human Resources.

■ **24117** ■ **Fetzer Company-Restaurateurs**
209 E Main St.
Louisville, KY 40202
Phone: (502)583-2744
Products: Food service equipment. **SICs:** 5078 (Refrigeration Equipment & Supplies); 5046 (Commercial Equipment Nec). **Sales:** $2,000,000 (2000). **Emp:** 12. **Officers:** Keith Fetzer, President.

■ **24118** ■ **Filbert Refrigeration**
PO Box 161909
Altamonte Springs, FL 32716-1909
Phone: (407)862-1011 **Fax:** (407)862-9189
Products: Industrial refrigeration equipment and parts. **SIC:** 5078 (Refrigeration Equipment & Supplies). **Est:** 1867. **Sales:** $6,000,000 (2000). **Emp:** 17. **Officers:** Mark Lowery, VP & Mgr. **Former Name:** Filbert Corp.

■ **24119** ■ **Fire Fighters Equipment Co.**
3038 Lemox Ave.
Jacksonville, FL 32254
Phone: (904)388-8542
Free: (800)488-8542 **Fax:** (904)384-2610
Products: Security and safety equipment. **SIC:** 5087 (Service Establishment Equipment). **Sales:** $1,000,000 (2000). **Emp:** 12.

■ **24120** ■ **Fitch Dustdown Co.**
2201 Russell St.
Baltimore, MD 21230
Phone: (410)539-1953
Products: Cleaning and janitorial supplies. **SIC:** 5087 (Service Establishment Equipment). **Sales:** $9,000,000 (2000). **Emp:** 50.

■ **24121** ■ **Fixture-World, Inc.**
1555 Interstate Dr.
Cookeville, TN 38501
Phones: (931)528-7259 800-251-6871
Free: (800)634-9887 **Fax:** (931)528-9214
URL: http://www.fixturworld.com
Products: Vending and food service cabinetry. **SIC:** 5046 (Commercial Equipment Nec). **Est:** 1979. **Sales:** $15,000,000 (2000). **Emp:** 125. **Officers:** Horace Burks, President; Al Parker, General Mgr.

■ **24122** ■ **R.M. Flagg Co.**
PO Box 617
Bangor, ME 04401-0617
Phone: (207)945-9463 **Fax:** (207)945-0956
Products: Commercial cooking and food service equipment, including restaurant equipment and supplies. **SIC:** 5046 (Commercial Equipment Nec). **Officers:** Jerry Whitehouse, President.

■ **24123** ■ **Joseph Flihan Co.**
PO Box 4039
Utica, NY 13504
Phone: (315)452-5886
Products: Food service equipment, including ranges, refrigerators, mixers, and kettles. **SICs:** 5078 (Refrigeration Equipment & Supplies); 5046 (Commercial Equipment Nec).

■ **24124** ■ **Food Equipment Specialists**
8181 Commerce Pk., Ste. 708
Houston, TX 77036-7403
Phone: (713)988-8700 **Fax:** (713)988-5129
Products: Food products machinery; Electric and microwave ranges and ovens; Restaurant supplies.

SICs: 5064 (Electrical Appliances—Television & Radio); 5046 (Commercial Equipment Nec). **Est:** 1981. **Emp:** 18. **Officers:** Stephen Schmitt, President; Sanford Manning, Vice President; William Bley Jr., Vice President.

■ 24125 ■ G & C Restaurant Equipment
359 Elm St.
Manchester, NH 03101
Phone: (603)627-1221
Products: Commercial cooking and food warming equipment. **SIC:** 5046 (Commercial Equipment Nec). **Officers:** George Zioze, President.

■ 24126 ■ Gardner and Benoit Inc.
PO Box 30005
Charlotte, NC 28230
Phone: (704)332-5086
Free: (800)467-6676 **Fax:** (704)343-9144
Products: Restaurant equipment, including silverware, china, dishwashers, and ice makers. **SICs:** 5046 (Commercial Equipment Nec); 5078 (Refrigeration Equipment & Supplies). **Est:** 1953. **Sales:** $6,000,000 (2000). **Emp:** 23. **Officers:** H.B. Benoit Jr., President; Karlo D. Waataja, Treasurer & Secty.; Jack W. Mock, Vice President.

■ 24127 ■ David Gering
2020 3rd St. N
Nampa, ID 83687-4425
Phone: (208)466-9003 **Fax:** (208)466-9003
Products: Commercial cooking and food service equipment, including restaurant equipment and supplies. **SIC:** 5046 (Commercial Equipment Nec). **Officers:** David Gering, Owner.

■ 24128 ■ Glacier Water Services Inc.
2261 Cosmos Ct.
Carlsbad, CA 92009
Phone: (760)930-2420 **Fax:** (760)930-1206
Products: Coin vending machines. **SIC:** 5046 (Commercial Equipment Nec). **Sales:** $56,300,000 (2000). **Emp:** 372. **Officers:** Jerry Gordon, President; William Walter, VP & CFO.

■ 24129 ■ Golden Light Equipment Co.
PO Box 9005
Amarillo, TX 79105
Phone: (806)373-4277
Products: Restaurant and cafeteria equipment. **SIC:** 5046 (Commercial Equipment Nec). **Est:** 1930. **Sales:** $6,000,000 (2000). **Emp:** 54. **Officers:** K.J. Poole, President & CFO.

■ 24130 ■ Guest Supply Inc.
PO Box 902, 720 U.S Hwy. 1
Monmouth Junction, NJ 08852-0902
Phone: (908)246-3011 **Fax:** (732)828-2342
Products: Restaurant and hotel food service equipment. **SIC:** 5046 (Commercial Equipment Nec). **Est:** 1979. **Sales:** $144,500,000 (2000). **Emp:** 980. **Officers:** Clifford W. Stanley, CEO & President; Paul T. Xenis, VP of Finance; Teri E. Unsworth, VP of Marketing; James H. Reisenberg, VP of Operations.

■ 24131 ■ H A Foodservice-HAFSCO
47 Railroad Ave.
West Haven, CT 06516
Phone: (203)933-5636 **Fax:** (203)934-5633
Products: Food service equipment. **SIC:** 5046 (Commercial Equipment Nec). **Est:** 1934. **Sales:** $2,800,000 (2000). **Emp:** 17. **Officers:** Thomas Capobianco, CEO; John Roche, Equipment Purchasing/Sales; Carol Skeens, Purchasing & Sales. **Former Name:** Howard-Arnold Inc.

■ 24132 ■ HALCO
600 Green Ln.
Union, NJ 07083
Phone: (908)289-1000
Free: (888)289-1005 **Fax:** (908)289-3186
URL: http://www.halco.com
Products: Restaurant supplies, including spoons, mixers, and pots. **SIC:** 5046 (Commercial Equipment Nec). **Est:** 1938. **Emp:** 70. **Officers:** Carl Marcus, President. **Former Name:** Harold #Leonard Southwest Corp.

■ 24133 ■ Hale Industries Inc.
2038 S Cole Rd.
Boise, ID 83709-2815
Phone: (208)322-0203
Free: (800)633-7337 **Fax:** (208)322-2894
E-mail: HaleInd@HaleInd.com
Products: Food equipment, including scales. **SIC:** 5046 (Commercial Equipment Nec). **Est:** 1981. **Sales:** $2,900,000 (2000). **Emp:** 16. **Officers:** Doug Hale, President; Dwight Eck, Vice President.

■ 24134 ■ Hampshire Furniture Co.
673 Black Brook Rd.
Goffstown, NH 03045-2911
Phone: (603)774-5120
Free: (800)774-5120 **Fax:** (603)774-5123
Products: specialty equipment and products. **SIC:** 5087 (Service Establishment Equipment).

■ 24135 ■ Hard Times Vending Inc.
RR, Box 59
Tripp, SD 57376-0059
Phone: (605)935-6251
Products: Commercial cooking and food service equipment and supplies. **SIC:** 5046 (Commercial Equipment Nec). **Officers:** Pete Klein, President.

■ 24136 ■ Harrington Co.
PO Box 3178
Butte, MT 59702-3178
Phone: (406)494-3200 **Fax:** (406)494-5355
Products: Commercial cooking equipment; Restaurant supplies. **SIC:** 5046 (Commercial Equipment Nec). **Officers:** Donald Harrington, President.

■ 24137 ■ Henderson Auctions Inc.
PO Box 336
Livingston, LA 70754
Phone: (225)686-2252 **Fax:** (225)686-7658
Products: Auctioneer of general commercial equipment and automobiles. **SICs:** 5046 (Commercial Equipment Nec); 5012 (Automobiles & Other Motor Vehicles). **Sales:** $20,000,000 (2000). **Emp:** 15. **Officers:** Jeffrey Henderson, President.

■ 24138 ■ Hockenberg Equipment Co.
2611 Sunset Rd.
Des Moines, IA 50321-1146
Phone: (515)255-5774 **Fax:** (515)244-8522
Products: Commercial reach-in and walk-in refrigerators; Stoves. **SICs:** 5046 (Commercial Equipment Nec); 5078 (Refrigeration Equipment & Supplies). **Est:** 1986. **Sales:** $800,000 (2000). **Emp:** 3. **Officers:** Betty Sue Halferty, CEO.

■ 24139 ■ Hughes Company Inc. of Columbus
PO Box 280
1200 W James St.
Columbus, WI 53925
Phone: (920)623-2000 **Fax:** (920)623-4098
E-mail: hughes@powerweb.net
URL: http://www.thehughesco.com
Products: Industrial food products machinery; Commercial food products machinery. **SIC:** 5046 (Commercial Equipment Nec). **Est:** 1961. **Sales:** $6,000,000 (2000). **Emp:** 44. **Officers:** D.O. Mietzel, President; Mike Harper, Exec. VP & General Mgr.; William Butch, Dir. of Sales & Marketing; William Butch, Sales/Marketing Contact.

■ 24140 ■ Ifeco Inc.
1776 Commerce Ave.
Boise, ID 83705-5309
Phone: (208)344-3574 **Fax:** (208)344-3642
Products: Restaurant equipment and supplies. **SIC:** 5046 (Commercial Equipment Nec). **Officers:** Brad Elg, President.

■ 24141 ■ Independent Distributors of America Inc.
100 1st St.
Lemont, IL 60439
Phone: (708)972-1919
Products: Dried food products for fast food restaurants. **SIC:** 5149 (Groceries & Related Products Nec). **Sales:** $7,000,000 (1993). **Emp:** 15. **Officers:** Bill Woodall, President.

■ 24142 ■ Intedge Industries Inc.
1875 Chumley Rd.
Woodruff, SC 29388
Phone: (864)969-9601 **Fax:** (864)969-3246
E-mail: intedge1@bellsouth.net
URL: http://www.intedge.com
Products: Commercial cooking and foodwarming equipment; Dishwashing machines; Foodservice equipment; Kitchen textiles. **SIC:** 5046 (Commercial Equipment Nec). **Est:** 1914. **Sales:** $9,000,000 (2000). **Emp:** 75. **Officers:** R.S. Beltram, CEO & Finance Officer; Debi Collier, Customer Service Contact; Terry Lawing, Human Resources Contact; Jackie Beltram, Dir of Human Resources.

■ 24143 ■ International Dairy Queen Inc.
7505 Metro Blvd.
Minneapolis, MN 55439
Phone: (612)830-0200 **Fax:** (612)830-0270
Products: Restaurant equipment. **SIC:** 5046 (Commercial Equipment Nec). **Sales:** $425,000,000 (2000). **Emp:** 750. **Officers:** Michael P. Sullivan, CEO & President; Charles W. Mooty, Exec. VP & CFO.

■ 24144 ■ International Restaurant Equipment Company Inc.
PO Box 35497
Los Angeles, CA 90035
Phone: (323)933-1896 **Fax:** (323)933-4710
URL: http://www.irekitchen.com
Products: Restaurant equipment, supplies, and furnishings. **SIC:** 5046 (Commercial Equipment Nec). **Est:** 1979. **Sales:** $2,000,000 (2000). **Emp:** 3. **Officers:** Arlette Cohen, President; Albert Cohen, Vice President, e-mail: albert@irekitchen.com; Brian Cohen, Customer Service Contact.

■ 24145 ■ Interstate Distributors Inc.
4101 Blue Ridge
Norcross, GA 30071
Phone: (404)476-0103 **Fax:** (404)497-1681
Products: Restaurant supplies; Food. **SICs:** 5087 (Service Establishment Equipment); 5141 (Groceries—General Line). **Est:** 1972. **Sales:** $330,000,000 (2000). **Emp:** 550. **Officers:** Thomas Willingham, President; William Bartels, VP of Finance; A. Nelson Gale, VP of Sales; Dave Kuntz, VP, CFO & Chief Acct. Officer; Rebecca Watson-Pufresne, Dir of Personnel.

■ 24146 ■ Interstate Restaurant Equipment Corp.
37 Amoskeag St.
Manchester, NH 03102
Phone: (603)669-3400 **Fax:** (603)641-6140
Products: Commercial cooking equipment; Restaurant supplies. **SIC:** 5046 (Commercial Equipment Nec). **Officers:** Scott Robinson, President.

■ 24147 ■ Jackson Supply Co.
1012 NE 3rd
Amarillo, TX 79107
Phone: (806)373-1888
Free: (800)288-9126 **Fax:** (806)373-5621
Products: Cleaning and janitorial supplies. **SIC:** 5087 (Service Establishment Equipment). **Sales:** $3,500,000 (2000). **Emp:** 22.

■ 24148 ■ Jacobi-Lewis Co.
622 S Front St.
PO Box 1289
Wilmington, NC 28402
Phone: (910)763-6201
Free: (800)763-2433 **Fax:** (910)763-5610
E-mail: jl@Jacobi-Lewis.com
URL: http://www.jacobi-lewis.com
Products: Restaurant, cafeteria, and bar furniture and fixtures; Commercial cooking and food warming equipment; Janitors' supplies; Paper goods or products. **SICs:** 5046 (Commercial Equipment Nec); 5113 (Industrial & Personal Service Paper). **Est:** 1940. **Sales:** $7,500,000 (2000). **Emp:** 30. **Officers:** French Lewis, Chairman of the Board; Greg Lewis, President; Gloria Ludewig, Exec. VP.

■ **24149** ■ **Janitor Supply Co.**
1100 S Main St.
Aberdeen, SD 57401-7030
Phone: (605)225-0444
Free: (800)225-6444 **Fax:** (605)225-0444
Products: Cleaning and janitorial supplies. **SIC:** 5087 (Service Establishment Equipment). **Sales:** $100,000 (2000). **Emp:** 1.

■ **24150** ■ **Josephson's Smokehouse and Dock**
PO Box 412
Astoria, OR 97103
Phone: (503)325-2190
Free: (800)772-3474 **Fax:** (503)325-4075
E-mail: smokey@aone.com
URL: http://www.josephsons.com
Products: Restaurants and gourmet food store; Specialty seafood products. **SIC:** 5146 (Fish & Seafoods). **Est:** 1920. **Sales:** $1,000,000 (1999). **Emp:** 12. **Officers:** Michael Josephson, Owner; Linda Josephson, Owner.

■ **24151** ■ **JS Enterprises Inc.**
1905 Main St.
MiLes City, MT 59301-3724
Phone: (406)232-6662 **Fax:** (406)232-5315
Products: Service industry machinery and parts; Restaurant supplies. **SICs:** 5087 (Service Establishment Equipment); 5046 (Commercial Equipment Nec). **Officers:** Gerald Schlepp, President.

■ **24152** ■ **Jurins Distributing Co.**
200 N 16th St.
PO Box 19476
Sacramento, CA 95819
Phone: (916)448-2052 **Fax:** (916)448-2076
Products: Full service bar and restaurant supplies. **SIC:** 5046 (Commercial Equipment Nec). **Est:** 1972. **Sales:** $2,000,000 (2000). **Emp:** 6. **Officers:** Thomas Jurin; Michael Jurin, Sales/Marketing Contact.

■ **24153** ■ **JVLNET By Electrolarm**
1220 W Court St.
Janesville, WI 53545-3537
Phone: (608)758-8750 **Fax:** (608)754-0015
Products: Computers and software. **SIC:** 5087 (Service Establishment Equipment). **Sales:** $1,500,000 (2000). **Emp:** 29.

■ **24154** ■ **Keefe Supply Co.**
10950 Lin Page Rd.
St. Louis, MO 63132
Phone: (314)423-4343
Products: Groceries for food commissaries. **SIC:** 5141 (Groceries—General Line).

■ **24155** ■ **J.F. Kenney Distributors**
37 Beach St.
Westerly, RI 02891-0471
Phone: (401)596-6760
Free: (800)967-6760 **Fax:** (401)596-4709
Products: Vending machines; Restaurant supplies. **SIC:** 5046 (Commercial Equipment Nec). **Est:** 1977. **Sales:** $600,000 (2000). **Emp:** 8. **Officers:** James Kenney, Owner.

■ **24156** ■ **Kesterson Food Company Inc.**
PO Box 87
Paris, TN 38242
Phone: (901)642-5031 **Fax:** (901)642-7804
Products: Commercial machines; Coffee makers; Dishwashers; Silverware for restaurants. **SICs:** 5141 (Groceries—General Line); 5149 (Groceries & Related Products Nec). **Est:** 1963. **Sales:** $64,800,000 (2000). **Emp:** 190. **Officers:** Thomas M. Kesterson, President; Jimmy Kiser, VP of Finance; Danny Kesterson, Exec. VP of Marketing; Anita Peale, Dir. of Data Processing; Mark Thompson, Dir of Human Resources.

■ **24157** ■ **Key Sales Inc.**
820 Packer Way
Sparks, NV 89431-6445
Phone: (702)359-3535
Products: Bar supplies; Paper products; Popcorn; Popcorn machines. **SICs:** 5046 (Commercial Equipment Nec); 5145 (Confectionery); 5113 (Industrial & Personal Service Paper). **Officers:** Robert Taylor, President.

■ **24158** ■ **Kitcor Corp.**
9959 Glenoaks Blvd.
Sun Valley, CA 91352
Phone: (818)767-4800 **Fax:** (818)767-4658
Products: Commercial kitchen equipment; Microwaves; Refrigerators. **SICs:** 5046 (Commercial Equipment Nec); 5064 (Electrical Appliances—Television & Radio). **Est:** 1942. **Sales:** $4,000,000 (1999). **Emp:** 27. **Officers:** William Kitchen, Owner & Pres.; Kent Kitchen, Sales/Marketing Contact; Sharon Brady, Human Resources Contact.

■ **24159** ■ **Kittredge Equipment Co.**
2155 Columbus Ave.
Springfield, MA 01104
Phone: (413)788-6101
Free: (800)423-7082 **Fax:** (413)781-3352
Products: Restaurant supplies; Commercial food products machinery. **SIC:** 5046 (Commercial Equipment Nec). **Est:** 1920. **Sales:** $11,500,000 (2000). **Emp:** 27. **Officers:** Ralph Webber, President; G. Kittredge, Vice President; Sid Kittredge, Treasurer.

■ **24160** ■ **Knapp Supply & Equipment Co.**
PO Box 99
Casper, WY 82602-0099
Phone: (307)234-7323 **Fax:** (307)235-7902
Products: Service industry machinery; Restaurant supplies; Janitorial equipment and supplies. **SICs:** 5087 (Service Establishment Equipment); 5046 (Commercial Equipment Nec). **Est:** 1946. **Emp:** 9. **Officers:** Dave Kurtenbach, President.

■ **24161** ■ **L & M Food Service**
PO Box 2277
Laughlin, NV 89029-2277
Phone: (702)754-3241 **Fax:** (702)754-2241
Products: Service establishment equipment, including cleaning and maintenance equipment and supplies; Bar products. **SIC:** 5046 (Commercial Equipment Nec). **Officers:** Ronald Laughlin, Partner.

■ **24162** ■ **Lane and McClain Distributors Inc.**
2062 Irving Blvd.
Dallas, TX 75207
Phone: (214)748-7669 **Fax:** (214)748-7888
Products: Food service equipment. **SIC:** 5087 (Service Establishment Equipment). **Est:** 1946. **Sales:** $10,000,000 (2000). **Emp:** 17. **Officers:** Bruce R. Lane Sr., President; Virginia Dugger, Controller.

■ **24163** ■ **A. R. Larsen Co., Inc.**
15040 NE 95th St.
Redmond, WA 98073-0088
Phone: (425)861-8868
Free: (800)735-7286 **Fax:** (425)861-8668
Products: Food service equipment. **SIC:** 5046 (Commercial Equipment Nec). **Est:** 1985. **Sales:** $3,000,000 (2000). **Emp:** 7. **Officers:** Andrea Larsen, President.

■ **24164** ■ **Ledyard Company Inc.**
1005 17th Ave.
Santa Cruz, CA 95062
Phone: (408)462-4400
Free: (800)487-3259 **Fax:** (408)479-1596
Products: Paper and allied products; Janitors' supplies; Commercial cooking and food warming equipment. **SICs:** 5046 (Commercial Equipment Nec); 5142 (Packaged Frozen Foods); 5113 (Industrial & Personal Service Paper). **Est:** 1929. **Emp:** 110.

■ **24165** ■ **Kenneth O. Lester Company Inc.**
PO Box 340
Lebanon, TN 37087
Phone: (615)444-2963
Products: Commercial equipment. **SICs:** 5046 (Commercial Equipment Nec); 5169 (Chemicals & Allied Products Nec). **Est:** 1931. **Sales:** $98,000,000 (2000). **Emp:** 180. **Officers:** Thomas Hoffman, President.

■ **24166** ■ **Lindox Equipment Corp.**
108 Randolph Rd.
Newport News, VA 23601-4222
Phone: (757)599-4500 **Fax:** (757)595-5904
Products: Commercial reach-in and walk-in refrigerators; Commercial cooking equipment. **SICs:** 5078 (Refrigeration Equipment & Supplies); 5046

(Commercial Equipment Nec). **Officers:** Neal Knemeyer.

■ **24167** ■ **Linvar Inc.**
237 Hamilton St.
Hartford, CT 06106
Phone: (860)951-3818
Free: (800)282-5288 **Fax:** (860)951-4512
Products: Storage equipment and containers. **SIC:** 5046 (Commercial Equipment Nec). **Sales:** $5,000,000 (2000). **Emp:** 11.

■ **24168** ■ **LKS International Inc.**
4001 W Devon Ave.
Chicago, IL 60646
Phone: (773)283-6601 **Fax:** (773)283-6710
E-mail: lksintl@ameritech.net
Products: Commercial refrigerators, including reach-in and walk-in; Commercial cooking, frying, broiling and food warming equipment; Commercial food products machinery; Ice cream and slush machines; Coffee machines. **SICs:** 5078 (Refrigeration Equipment & Supplies); 5046 (Commercial Equipment Nec). **Est:** 1984. **Sales:** $4,000,000 (2000). **Emp:** 6. **Officers:** Walter P. Lehmann, President; John M. Kulinski, Vice President.

■ **24169** ■ **LRP Enterprises**
1275 Colusa Hwy., Ste. C
Yuba City, CA 95991
Phone: (530)743-4288 **Fax:** (530)742-5824
Products: Health and beauty aids. **SIC:** 5046 (Commercial Equipment Nec). **Sales:** $400,000 (2000). **Emp:** 2.

■ **24170** ■ **LTD Dozier Inc.**
869 Pickens Industrial Dr.
Marietta, GA 30062-3100
Phone: (404)419-1920 **Fax:** (404)419-9779
Products: Beverage vending machines. **SIC:** 5046 (Commercial Equipment Nec). **Officers:** David Enser, President.

■ **24171** ■ **Luzo Food Service Inc.**
PO Box 50370
New Bedford, MA 02745
Phone: (508)993-9976
Free: (800)225-8169 **Fax:** (508)997-8357
URL: http://www.luzo.com
Products: Food service. **SIC:** 5141 (Groceries—General Line). **Est:** 1936. **Sales:** $25,000,000 (2000). **Emp:** 75. **Officers:** Mark Champagne, Controller, e-mail: marh@famousfoods.com; Carl Ribeiro, Human Resource Contact, e-mail: carl@luzo.com.

■ **24172** ■ **M & M Distributors**
431 W 121st St.
Anchorage, AK 99515-3364
Phone: (907)349-5941 **Fax:** (907)344-0125
Products: Commercial equipment; Cooking and food service equipment; Bakery equipment and supplies. **SIC:** 5046 (Commercial Equipment Nec). **Officers:** Jerry Miller, Partner.

■ **24173** ■ **Scottie MacBean Inc.**
660 High St.
Worthington, OH 43085
Phone: (614)888-3494 **Fax:** (614)888-7961
E-mail: roaster@aol.com
URL: http://www.scottiemacbean.com
Products: Coffee roasters; Teas. **SICs:** 5046 (Commercial Equipment Nec); 5149 (Groceries & Related Products Nec). **Est:** 1910. **Sales:** $1,000,000 (2000). **Emp:** 12. **Officers:** Robert Han, Sales/Marketing Contact.

■ **24174** ■ **Magnolia Casket Co.**
PO Box 40105
Jacksonville, FL 32203
Phone: (904)384-0015
Free: (800)881-4461 **Fax:** (904)384-8997
Products: specialty equipment and products. **SIC:** 5087 (Service Establishment Equipment). **Sales:** $600,000 (2000). **Emp:** 2.

■ 24175 ■ **Main Street and Main Inc.**
5050 N 40th St., No. 200
Phoenix, AZ 85018-2163
Phone: (602)852-9000
Products: Restaurant equipment and supplies. **SICs:** 5087 (Service Establishment Equipment); 5149 (Groceries & Related Products Nec); 5046 (Commercial Equipment Nec). **Est:** 1983. **Sales:** $119,500,000 (2000). **Emp:** 4,010. **Officers:** Joe W. Panter, CEO & President; Mark C. Walker, VP, CFO & Treasurer; Robert McGeorge, VP of Business Development.

■ 24176 ■ **Major Appliances Inc.**
8687 SW 178th St.
Miami, FL 33157-6031
Phone: (954)777-0079
Products: Commercial appliances, including microwaves and refrigerators. **SICs:** 5078 (Refrigeration Equipment & Supplies); 5046 (Commercial Equipment Nec); 5064 (Electrical Appliances—Television & Radio). **Est:** 1936. **Sales:** $2,000,000 (2000). **Emp:** 9. **Officers:** Doug Rowlands, President.

■ 24177 ■ **Mark VII Equipment Inc.**
5981 Tennyson St.
Arvada, CO 80003
Phone: (303)423-4910 **Fax:** (303)430-0139
Products: Carwash equipment. **SIC:** 5087 (Service Establishment Equipment). **Officers:** Phil Mercorella, President; Tammy McGee, CFO.

■ 24178 ■ **Marstan Industries Inc.**
10814 Northeast Ave.
Philadelphia, PA 19116
Phone: (215)969-0600
Products: Food service equipment for restaurants. **SIC:** 5087 (Service Establishment Equipment). **Sales:** $75,000,000 (1992). **Emp:** 490. **Officers:** Mark Levin, President.

■ 24179 ■ **May Engineering Company Inc.**
51 Washington Ave.
Cranston, RI 02920-7828
Phone: (401)942-4221 **Fax:** (401)942-2470
Products: Commercial cooking and food warming equipment; Restaurant supplies. **SIC:** 5046 (Commercial Equipment Nec). **Officers:** James Maintanis, President.

■ 24180 ■ **McComas Sales Co. Inc.**
2315 4th St. NW
Albuquerque, NM 87102
Phone: (505)243-5263 **Fax:** (505)243-4880
Products: Service industry machinery; Restaurant supplies. **SIC:** 5046 (Commercial Equipment Nec). **Est:** 1950. **Officers:** Jack McComas, President.

■ 24181 ■ **MD Foods Ingredients Inc.**
2840 Morris Ave.
Union, NJ 07083
Phone: (908)964-4420
Free: (800)972-2096 **Fax:** (908)964-6270
Products: Milk protein emulsifiers. **SIC:** 5122 (Drugs, Proprietaries & Sundries). **Sales:** $30,000,000 (2000). **Emp:** 10. **Officers:** Torben Lange, President; Claus Sorensen, Mgr. of Finance & Admin.

■ 24182 ■ **MDG Inc.**
PO Box 17387
Denver, CO 80217
Phone: (303)662-7100
Free: (800)880-9900 **Fax:** (303)662-7565
URL: http://www.mfdg.com; http://www.vsalink.com
Products: Food service distribution, vending, office coffee service, specialty distribution, such as pizza products, sub shop products, and theater and fund raising products. **SIC:** 5141 (Groceries—General Line). **Est:** 1970. **Sales:** $1,900,000,000 (1999). **Emp:** 2,200. **Officers:** Jeff Boies, President; Patrick Hagerty, VP of Merchandising; Richard Weil, VP of Marketing & Sales. **Former Name:** International MultiFoods Corp.

■ 24183 ■ **Medley Hotel and Restaurant Supply Co.**
PO Box 328
Albany, GA 31702
Phone: (912)432-5116 **Fax:** (912)432-6894
Products: Restaurant supplies, including ovens, spoons, and forks. **SIC:** 5046 (Commercial Equipment Nec). **Est:** 1963. **Sales:** $29,000,000 (2000). **Emp:** 82. **Officers:** William D. Campbell, President.

■ 24184 ■ **H.E. Meidlinger Inc.**
18 14th St. S
Fargo, ND 58103-1620
Phone: (701)237-5240
Products: Commercial cooking and food warming equipment; Restaurant supplies. **SIC:** 5046 (Commercial Equipment Nec). **Officers:** Harold Meidlinger, President.

■ 24185 ■ **Mikara Corp.**
3109 Louisiana Ave.
Minneapolis, MN 55427
Phone: (612)546-9500
Free: (800)682-6622 **Fax:** (612)546-5212
Products: Professional beauty supplies. **SICs:** 5087 (Service Establishment Equipment); 5122 (Drugs, Proprietaries & Sundries). **Sales:** $65,000,000 (2000). **Emp:** 185. **Officers:** Michael P. Hicks, President; Kevin Sathre, CFO.

■ 24186 ■ **Mile High Equipment Co.**
11100 E 45th Ave.
Denver, CO 80239
Phone: (303)371-3737
Products: commercial ice making equipment and storage bins. **SIC:** 5046 (Commercial Equipment Nec). **Sales:** $26,000,000 (2000). **Emp:** 200. **Officers:** Jim Grob, President; Bob Landis, VP of Finance.

■ 24187 ■ **Miller Machinery and Supply Co.**
127 NE 27th St.
Miami, FL 33137
Phone: (305)573-1300 **Fax:** (305)576-9535
Products: Food industry machines, including soft drink and ice cream machines. **SIC:** 5046 (Commercial Equipment Nec). **Est:** 1918. **Sales:** $5,000,000 (2000). **Emp:** 25. **Officers:** Robert W. Decker, CEO & President; Peter Hale, Finance Officer.

■ 24188 ■ **Montana Scale Company Inc.**
1207 13th Ave. E
Polson, MT 59860-3620
Phone: (406)883-4697 **Fax:** (406)883-9248
Products: Scientific and measurement devices. **SIC:** 5046 (Commercial Equipment Nec). **Sales:** $300,000 (2000). **Emp:** 2.

■ 24189 ■ **Mountain View Supply Inc.**
PO Box 252
Billings, MT 59103-0252
Phone: (406)259-4493 **Fax:** (406)259-7511
Products: Commercial cooking and food warming equipment. **SIC:** 5046 (Commercial Equipment Nec). **Officers:** Stan Wilson, President.

■ 24190 ■ **MTS Wireless Components**
562 Captain Nevelle Dr.
Waterbury, CT 06705
Phone: (203)759-1234
Free: (888)687-2569 **Fax:** (203)759-0034
Products: Wireless communication hardware components. **SIC:** 5046 (Commercial Equipment Nec).

■ 24191 ■ **Nelson Wholesale Corp.**
PO Box 16348
Mobile, AL 36616-0348
Phone: (334)479-1471
E-mail: nelsonw@mobileinterlink.net
Products: Commercial refrigeration; Microwaves; Kitchen appliances. **SICs:** 5046 (Commercial Equipment Nec); 5064 (Electrical Appliances—Television & Radio). **Est:** 1923. **Sales:** $3,500,000 (2000). **Emp:** 17. **Officers:** James C. Nelson, President.

■ 24192 ■ **Newells Bar & Restaurant Supply, Inc.**
3110 Railroad Ave.
Redding, CA 96001
Phone: (530)244-3980 **Fax:** (530)244-1675
Products: Bar and restaurant supplies. **SICs:** 5046 (Commercial Equipment Nec); 5113 (Industrial & Personal Service Paper). **Est:** 1966. **Sales:** $100,000 (2000). **Emp:** 5. **Officers:** James L. Newell, President; Jeanne Newell, Vice President.

■ 24193 ■ **Nicewonger Co.**
901 W Evergreen Blvd.
Vancouver, WA 98660-3034
Phone: (206)699-4747
Free: (800)426-5972 **Fax:** (206)699-4753
Products: Restaurant equipment, including fryers, ice cream machines, espresso machines, and broilers. **SIC:** 5046 (Commercial Equipment Nec). **Emp:** 70. **Officers:** Paul Nicewonger.

■ 24194 ■ **NJCT Corp.**
775 Passaic Ave.
West Caldwell, NJ 07006
Phone: (973)575-7500
Free: (800)631-1132 **Fax:** (973)575-6195
Products: Commercial kitchen and laundry equipment; Refrigeration equipment; Cooking, baking, and serving equipment. **SICs:** 5046 (Commercial Equipment Nec); 5087 (Service Establishment Equipment); 5078 (Refrigeration Equipment & Supplies). **Officers:** Daniel M. Spritzer, President.

■ 24195 ■ **Northern Chemical/Janitor Sply**
6110 NW Grand Ave.
Glendale, AZ 85301
Phone: (623)937-1668 **Fax:** (623)435-8574
Products: Janitorial supplies; Assembles chemical cleaner products. **SIC:** 5087 (Service Establishment Equipment).

■ 24196 ■ **Northwest Distribution Services Inc.**
PO Box 277
Emmett, ID 83617
Phone: (208)365-1445
Products: Food service products and services. **SIC:** 5149 (Groceries & Related Products Nec).

■ 24197 ■ **Ogden Aviation Services**
Philadelphia Airport, TWA Hangar
Philadelphia, PA 19153
Phone: (215)492-2880
Products: Airline food and beveragess. **SIC:** 5172 (Petroleum Products Nec).

■ 24198 ■ **Oliver Supply Co.**
PO Box 430297
Pontiac, MI 48343-0297
Phone: (248)682-7222 **Fax:** (248)682-1786
Products: Cleaning and janitorial supplies. **SIC:** 5087 (Service Establishment Equipment). **Sales:** $1,500,000 (2000). **Emp:** 9.

■ 24199 ■ **Robert Orr-Sysco Food Services Co.**
PO Box 305137
Nashville, TN 37230-5137
Phone: (615)350-7100 **Fax:** (615)350-9715
Products: Full line of food, non-food, and related items. **SICs:** 5046 (Commercial Equipment Nec); 5141 (Groceries—General Line). **Est:** 1859. **Emp:** 780. **Officers:** Nick K. Taras, President & Chairman of the Board; Cameron Blakely, VP of Finance & CFO; David Snyder, Exec. VP; Bar Ivy, Sr. VP of Merchandising and Marketing; Donna Hensley, Dir of Human Resources.

■ 24200 ■ **Otis Distributors**
4224 Airport Rd.
Cincinnati, OH 45226
Phone: (513)321-6847
Products: Restaurant equipment and supplies, including ice cream makers and store fixtures. **SIC:** 5046 (Commercial Equipment Nec).

■ **24201** ■ **Palm Brothers Inc.**
2727 Nicollet Ave.
Minneapolis, MN 55408
Phone: (612)871-2727
Products: Restaurant equipment. **SIC:** 5046
(Commercial Equipment Nec). **Sales:** $29,000,000
(2000). **Emp:** 150. **Officers:** Reuben Palm, President.

■ **24202** ■ **Par-Way/Tryson Co.**
107 Bolte Ln.
St. Clair, MO 63077
Phone: (636)629-4545
Free: (800)844-4554   **Fax:** (636)629-1330
Products: Cooking oils. **SIC:** 5046 (Commercial
Equipment Nec). **Est:** 1948. **Emp:** 50. **Officers:**
Dennis Norton, COO; Brad Channing, Sales/Marketing
Contact. **Former Name:** Par-Way Group.

■ **24203** ■ **H.I. Patten Inc.**
168 Eastern Ave.
Lynn, MA 01902-1310
Phone: (781)592-4621   **Fax:** (781)592-4622
Products: Refrigeration equipment and supplies;
Commercial refrigeration equipment, including reach-in
and walk-in refrigerators. **SIC:** 5078 (Refrigeration
Equipment & Supplies). **Est:** 1921. **Officers:** Lloyd
Patten, President.

■ **24204** ■ **Pop's E-Z Popcorn & Supply Co.**
17151 SE Petrovitsky Rd.
Renton, WA 98058-9610
Phone: (425)255-4545
Free: (800)244-7830   **Fax:** (425)255-8181
URL: http://www.popsezpopcorn.com
Products: Concession equipment and supplies. **SIC:**
5046 (Commercial Equipment Nec). **Est:** 1986. **Sales:**
$1,750,000 (1999). **Emp:** 8. **Officers:** David Vreeken,
President, e-mail: dkvreeken@msn.com. **Alternate
Name:** E-Z Popcorn & Supply. **Alternate Name:**
Vreeken Enterprises Inc.

■ **24205** ■ **Prairie Farms Dairy Supply Inc.**
1800 Adams St.
Granite City, IL 62040
Phone: (618)451-5600
Products: Food and nonfood product supplies for the
fast food industry. **SICs:** 5141 (Groceries—General
Line); 5149 (Groceries & Related Products Nec); 5113
(Industrial & Personal Service Paper). **Sales:**
$130,000,000 (2000). **Emp:** 250. **Officers:** Alan
Thomas, Comptroller.

■ **24206** ■ **Professional Salon Services**
16 Stafford Ct.
Cranston, RI 02920-4464
Phone: (401)463-5353
Free: (800)666-2580   **Fax:** (401)463-5807
Products: Health and beauty aids. **SIC:** 5087 (Service
Establishment Equipment). **Sales:** $3,500,000 (2000).
Emp: 30.

■ **24207** ■ **Proficient Food Co.**
9408 Richmond Pl.
Rancho Cucamonga, CA 91730
Phone: (909)484-6100   **Fax:** (909)466-6107
Products: Food for restaurants and vending operators.
SIC: 5142 (Packaged Frozen Foods). **Sales:**
$485,000,000 (1994). **Emp:** 510. **Officers:** Brock
Partin, President; Michael LeMaster, VP of Finance.

■ **24208** ■ **ProSource Inc.**
1550 San Remo Ave.
Miami, FL 33136
Phone: (305)740-1000   **Fax:** (305)740-1010
Products: Foodservice items to restaurant chains.
SIC: 5149 (Groceries & Related Products Nec). **Sales:**
$3,901,200,000 (2000). **Emp:** 3,400. **Officers:** Thomas
C. Highland, CEO & President; William F. Evans, Exec.
VP & CFO.

■ **24209** ■ **J. Red Gaskins and Co.**
357 W Main St.
Lake City, SC 29560-2315
Phone: (803)394-8830   **Fax:** (803)289-2778
Products: Restaurant and store supplies, including
coolers, ice machines, and scales. **SICs:** 5078
(Refrigeration Equipment & Supplies); 5046
(Commercial Equipment Nec). **Est:** 1963. **Sales:**

$1,200,000 (2000). **Emp:** 8. **Officers:** Carlton Gaskins,
President.

■ **24210** ■ **Robert Ricci**
30 Roosevelt Trail
Windham, ME 04062-4350
Phone: (207)892-2635
Products: Commercial cooking and food service
equiment, including restaurant equipment and supplies.
SIC: 5046 (Commercial Equipment Nec). **Officers:**
Robert Ricci, Owner.

■ **24211** ■ **A.K. Robins L.L.C.**
4030 Benson Ave.
Baltimore, MD 21227
Phone: (410)247-4000
Free: (800)486-9656   **Fax:** (410)247-9165
Products: Food processing machinery. **SIC:** 5046
(Commercial Equipment Nec). **Est:** 1855. **Sales:**
$5,000,000 (2000). **Emp:** 20. **Officers:** Sheila Canelos,
President.

■ **24212** ■ **Rykoff-Sexton Inc.**
11711 N Creek Pkwy. S, No. D107
Bothell, WA 98011-8808
Phone: (206)281-4900   **Fax:** (206)284-5988
Products: Restaurant and institutional supplies. **SIC:**
5046 (Commercial Equipment Nec).

■ **24213** ■ **St. Paul Bar/Restaurant Equipment**
655 Payne Ave.
St. Paul, MN 55101
Phone: (612)774-0361
Free: (800)840-2286   **Fax:** (612)381-3191
E-mail: admin@palmbrothers.com
URL: http://www.commkitchen.com
Products: Industrial food service equipment and
supplies, including glassware, refrigerators,
dishwashers, ranges, kitchen untensils, pots, and pans.
SICs: 5046 (Commercial Equipment Nec); 5087
(Service Establishment Equipment); 5084 (Industrial
Machinery & Equipment). **Est:** 1950. **Sales:**
$6,000,000 (2000). **Emp:** 10. **Officers:** Ryan Vroman,
General Mgr.

■ **24214** ■ **Sandler Foods**
1224 Diamond Spring Rd
Virginia Beach, VA 23455
Phone: (804)464-3551   **Fax:** (804)464-5515
Products: Restaurant supplies, including food and
food preparation equipment. **SIC:** 5141 (Groceries—
General Line). **Est:** 1929. **Sales:** $230,000,000 (2000).
Emp: 439. **Officers:** Tom Giancoli, President; Greg
Lee, Finance Officer; Roger Martin, VP of Marketing;
Debra Bunch, Personnel Mgr.

■ **24215** ■ **Sarco Inc.**
1402 Auburn Way N
PMB 393
Auburn, WA 98002-3309
Phone: (206)441-5977   **Fax:** (206)441-4162
E-mail: sarcoinc@aol.com
Products: Restaurant equipment repair, parts, sales,
and service. **SICs:** 5064 (Electrical Appliances—
Television & Radio); 5046 (Commercial Equipment
Nec). **Est:** 1968. **Sales:** $250,000 (2000). **Emp:** 4.
Officers: Troy W. Rose, Vice President.

■ **24216** ■ **Schlueter Company Inc.**
PO Box 548
Janesville, WI 53547
Phone: (608)755-5455   **Fax:** (608)755-0332
Products: Processing and sanitation equipment for the
food industry, including mix tanks. **SIC:** 5046
(Commercial Equipment Nec). **Est:** 1919. **Sales:**
$16,000,000 (2000). **Emp:** 70. **Officers:** Bradley
Losching, President; Bernard Losching, VP & CFO;
Chas Benskin, Marketing Mgr.; Ken Algrim, Office Mgr.

■ **24217** ■ **H.D. Sheldon and Company Inc.**
19 Union Sq. W
New York, NY 10003
Phone: (212)924-6920   **Fax:** (212)627-1759
Products: Fast food service equipment. **SIC:** 5046
(Commercial Equipment Nec). **Est:** 1944. **Sales:**
$20,000,000 (2000). **Emp:** 32. **Officers:** Robert
Metros, President; Mohammad Moulabi, Controller.

■ **24218** ■ **Shelving Inc.**
PO Box 215050
Auburn Hills, MI 48321-5050
Phone: (248)852-8600
Free: (800)637-9508   **Fax:** (248)852-0904
Products: Storage equipment and containers. **SIC:**
5046 (Commercial Equipment Nec). **Sales:** $3,500,000
(2000). **Emp:** 10.

■ **24219** ■ **Jim L. Shetakis Distributing Co.**
PO Box 14987
Las Vegas, NV 89114-4987
Phone: (702)735-8985   **Fax:** (702)735-0136
Products: Commercial equipment, including cooking
and food service equipment, restaurant equipment, and
supplies; Food. **SIC:** 5046 (Commercial Equipment
Nec). **Officers:** Bruno Campo, President; Anthony
DeGravina, Vice President.

■ **24220** ■ **Singer Equipment Company Inc.**
PO Box 13668
Reading, PA 19612
Phone: (610)929-8000
Free: (800)422-8126   **Fax:** (610)929-3060
E-mail: singereq@epix.net
Products: Restaurant supplies and equipment. **SICs:**
5046 (Commercial Equipment Nec); 5087 (Service
Establishment Equipment). **Est:** 1918. **Sales:**
$50,000,000 (2000). **Emp:** 135. **Officers:** H.D. Singer,
CEO; John Vozzo, COO; Fred Singer, President.

■ **24221** ■ **Skip Dunn Sales**
162 Washington Ave.
New Rochelle, NY 10801
Phone: (914)636-2200
Free: (800)624-9720   **Fax:** (914)636-1535
Products: specialty equipment and products. **SIC:**
5046 (Commercial Equipment Nec).

■ **24222** ■ **Skyline Designs**
1090 John Stark Hwy.
Newport, NH 03773
Phone: (603)542-6649
Free: (800)775-1478   **Fax:** (603)542-8854
Products: Furniture and fixtures. **SIC:** 5046
(Commercial Equipment Nec). **Sales:** $1,000,000
(2000). **Emp:** 17.

■ **24223** ■ **Smellkinson Sysco Food Services
Inc.**
8000 Dorsey Run Rd.
Jessup, MD 20794
Phone: (410)799-7000   **Fax:** (410)799-2445
Products: Food service equipment and supplies. **SIC:**
5046 (Commercial Equipment Nec). **Est:** 1917. **Sales:**
$330,000,000 (2000). **Emp:** 850. **Officers:** G. Kent
Humphries, President; Larry G. Pulliam, Exec. VP; Jack
Trutt, Dir. of Marketing; Ed Howard, Dir. of Data
Processing; Kathleen Klein, VP of Human Resources.

■ **24224** ■ **Solutions and Cleaning Products**
208 W Brundage St.
Sheridan, WY 82801
Phone: (307)672-1846
Free: (888)672-1846   **Fax:** (307)672-0883
Products: Cleaning and janitorial supplies. **SIC:** 5087
(Service Establishment Equipment).

■ **24225** ■ **Southern Industrial Corp.**
9009 Regency Square Blvd.
Jacksonville, FL 32211
Phone: (904)725-4122   **Fax:** (904)723-3498
Products: Frozen food; Restaurant equipment and
supplies. **SICs:** 5046 (Commercial Equipment Nec);
5142 (Packaged Frozen Foods). **Est:** 1954. **Sales:**
$120,000,000 (2000). **Emp:** 240. **Officers:** David A.
Stein, President; Edward F. Hicks, Exec. VP of
Finance; Beverly N. Jelinek, VP of Marketing.

■ **24226** ■ **State Restaurant Equipment Inc.**
3163 S Highland Dr.
Las Vegas, NV 89109-1010
Phone: (702)733-1515   **Fax:** (702)733-0814
URL: http://www.staterestaurant.net
Products: Restaurant equipment and supplies. **SIC:**
5046 (Commercial Equipment Nec). **Est:** 1967. **Emp:**
28. **Officers:** Edmond Haddad, President; Scott Miller,
Vice President.

■ 24227 ■ Steam Way International Inc.
4550 Jackson St.
Denver, CO 80216
Phone: (303)355-3566 **Fax:** (303)355-3516
Products: Professional carpet steam cleaning equipment; Carpet and upholstery cleaning accessories and equipment; parts and cleaning chemicals. **SICs:** 5087 (Service Establishment Equipment); 5169 (Chemicals & Allied Products Nec). **Officers:** R Doyle Bloss, CEO.

■ 24228 ■ F.D. Stella Products Co.
7000 Fenkell Ave.
Detroit, MI 48238
Phone: (313)341-6400
Free: (800)447-7356 **Fax:** (313)342-8398
Products: Commercial food products machinery; Restaurant, cafeteria, and bar furniture and fixtures. **SIC:** 5046 (Commercial Equipment Nec). **Est:** 1946. **Sales:** $7,500,000 (2000). **Emp:** 35. **Officers:** Frank D. Stella, President; David G. Kingwill; Andrew J. Stella; James C. Stella.

■ 24229 ■ Storage Equipment Company Inc.
1258 Titan Ave.
Dallas, TX 75247
Phone: (214)630-9221
Free: (800)443-1791 **Fax:** (214)637-6340
Products: Storage Equipment and Containerss. **SIC:** 5046 (Commercial Equipment Nec). **Sales:** $9,000,000 (2000). **Emp:** 35.

■ 24230 ■ Storage Solutions Inc.
12342 Hancock St.
Carmel, IN 46032
Phone: (317)848-2001 **Fax:** (317)575-0306
Products: Storage Equipment and Containerss. **SIC:** 5046 (Commercial Equipment Nec). **Sales:** $1,000,000 (2000). **Emp:** 10.

■ 24231 ■ Structural Concepts Corp.
888 Porter Rd.
Muskegon, MI 49441-5895
Phone: (616)846-3300
Free: (800)433-9489 **Fax:** (616)846-7460
Products: Refrigerated display cases. **SIC:** 5078 (Refrigeration Equipment & Supplies). **Sales:** $10,000,000 (2000). **Emp:** 230. **Officers:** James A Doss; Pat Pyman.

■ 24232 ■ Struve Distributing Company Inc.
276 W 1st St.
Salt Lake City, UT 84101
Phone: (801)328-1636
Free: (800)252-1177 **Fax:** (801)328-1641
Products: Video games, phonographs and vending machines. **SIC:** 5046 (Commercial Equipment Nec). **Sales:** $4,000,000 (2000). **Emp:** 12. **Officers:** Sandy Wright, Controller.

■ 24233 ■ Sunlow Inc.
1071 Howell Mill Rd.
Atlanta, GA 30318
Phone: (404)872-8135
Products: Food equipment. **SIC:** 5046 (Commercial Equipment Nec). **Est:** 1954. **Sales:** $4,500,000 (2000). **Emp:** 18. **Officers:** Dan Graham, President.

■ 24234 ■ Superior Products
PO Box 64177
St. Paul, MN 55164
Phone: (651)636-1110
Free: (800)328-9800 **Fax:** (651)636-3671
E-mail: comments@superprod.com
URL: http://www.superprod.com
Products: Commercial food products machinery; Restaurant, cafeteria, and bar furniture and fixtures. **SICs:** 5046 (Commercial Equipment Nec); 5078 (Refrigeration Equipment & Supplies). **Est:** 1933. **Sales:** $150,000,000 (2000). **Emp:** 275. **Former Name:** Superior Products Manufacturing Company Hospitality Supply.

■ 24235 ■ Superior Products Manufacturing Co.
510 West County Rd. D
St. Paul, MN 55112
Phone: (651)636-1110
Free: (800)328-9800 **Fax:** (651)636-3671
E-mail: comments@superprod.com
URL: http://www.superprod.com
Products: Restaurant and bar equipment. **SICs:** 5078 (Refrigeration Equipment & Supplies); 5046 (Commercial Equipment Nec). **Est:** 1933. **Sales:** $120,000,000 (2000). **Emp:** 275. **Officers:** Robert M. Kurek, President; J. Cox, VP of Finance.

■ 24236 ■ Surfas Inc.
8825 National Blvd.
Culver City, CA 90232
Phone: (310)559-4770
Products: Restaurant equipment and supplies. **SIC:** 5046 (Commercial Equipment Nec). **Sales:** $5,000,000 (1993). **Emp:** 30. **Officers:** L.O. Surfas, CEO.

■ 24237 ■ SYSCO Food Services of Arkansas, Inc.
PO Box 194060
Little Rock, AR 72219
Phone: (501)562-4111
Free: (800)827-3411 **Fax:** (501)562-1092
Products: Food service supplies. **SIC:** 5046 (Commercial Equipment Nec). **Emp:** 210.

■ 24238 ■ Sysco Food Services of Idaho Inc.
5710 Pan Am Ave.
Boise, ID 83705
Phone: (208)345-9500 **Fax:** (208)387-2499
Products: Restaurant equipment. **SIC:** 5046 (Commercial Equipment Nec). **Emp:** 210. **Officers:** Thomas Morgan, Chairman of the Board; Renee LoveJoy, President.

■ 24239 ■ T & R Beverage Control
6680 N Government Way, Ste. 3
Coeur D Alene, ID 83815-7708
Phone: (208)667-2468
Products: Service establishment equipment; Liquor dispensing equipment and systems; Restaurant, cafeteria, and bar furniture and fixtures. **SIC:** 5046 (Commercial Equipment Nec). **Est:** 1972. **Sales:** $35,000 (2000). **Emp:** 1. **Officers:** Andrew Netzel. **Former Name:** T & R Dispensing Inc.

■ 24240 ■ Table Supply Co.
1513 Broadway NE
Albuquerque, NM 87102-1547
Phone: (505)224-9833 **Fax:** (505)224-9829
Products: Restaurant and commercial foodservice equipment and supplies. **SIC:** 5046 (Commercial Equipment Nec).

■ 24241 ■ Taylor Restaurant Equipment
8307 Central Ave. NE
Albuquerque, NM 87108-2409
Phone: (505)255-9898 **Fax:** (505)255-3279
Products: Commercial cooking and food service equipment, including restaurant equipment and supplies. **SIC:** 5046 (Commercial Equipment Nec). **Officers:** Barry Lane, Partner.

■ 24242 ■ TEC America Inc.
4401-A Bankers Cir.
Atlanta, GA 30360
Phone: (770)449-3040 **Fax:** (770)449-1152
Products: Scales and balances; Printers. **SIC:** 5046 (Commercial Equipment Nec). **Sales:** $29,000,000 (2000). **Emp:** 100. **Officers:** N. Kuramochi, President; Jeff Warren, Comptroller.

■ 24243 ■ Tech Fire and Safety Co.
514 4th St.
Watervliet, NY 12189
Phone: (518)274-7599 **Fax:** (518)274-7899
Products: Security and safety equipment. **SIC:** 5087 (Service Establishment Equipment). **Sales:** $2,800,000 (2000). **Emp:** 10.

■ 24244 ■ Tetra Laval Convenience Food Inc.
PO Box 358
Avon, MA 02322
Phone: (508)588-2600 **Fax:** (508)588-1791
Products: Food products machinery. **SIC:** 5084 (Industrial Machinery & Equipment). **Est:** 1973. **Sales:** $200,000,000 (2000). **Emp:** 150. **Officers:** Paul Lyqum, President; Henning Fink-Jensen, Finance Officer; Ronald E. Merrill, Dir. of Marketing & Sales.

■ 24245 ■ Thayer Inc.
225 5th St.
Benton Harbor, MI 49023-0867
Phone: (616)925-0633
Free: (800)870-0009 **Fax:** (616)925-0639
Products: Cleaning and janitorial supplies. **SIC:** 5087 (Service Establishment Equipment). **Sales:** $4,000,000 (2000). **Emp:** 17.

■ 24246 ■ Thoms-Proestler Co.
8001 TPC Rd.
PO Box 7210
Rock Island, IL 61204-7210
Phone: (309)787-1234 **Fax:** (309)787-1254
URL: http://www.tpcinfo.com
Products: Foodservice items, including fresh, frozen, and dry food, equipment, and disposables. **SICs:** 5141 (Groceries—General Line); 5046 (Commercial Equipment Nec). **Est:** 1885. **Sales:** $206,000,000 (2000). **Emp:** 440. **Officers:** Stuart Thoms, Chairman of the Board, e-mail: thomss@tpcinfo.com; Thomas Thoms, CEO; Michael Thoms, COO; Jim Hendrickson, VP of Marketing & Sales, e-mail: hendricksonj@tpcinfo.com; Bill Brownson, Customer Service Contact, e-mail: brownsonb@tpcinfo.com; Sally Benson, Human Resources Contact, e-mail: bensons@tpcinfo.com.

■ 24247 ■ Trak-Air/Rair
7006-B S Alton Way
Englewood, CO 80112
Phone: (303)779-9888
Free: (800)688-TRAK **Fax:** (303)694-3575
E-mail: sales@trak-air.com
URL: http://www.trak-air.com
Products: Ovens; Greaseless fryers; Snack bar and deli equipment. **SIC:** 5046 (Commercial Equipment Nec). **Est:** 1988. **Sales:** $1,200,000 (2000). **Emp:** 7. **Officers:** Dale Terry, President. **Alternate Name:** Rair Systems.

■ 24248 ■ Transmedia Restaurant Company Inc.
750 Lexington Ave., 16th Fl.
New York, NY 10022
Products: Foods for restaurants. **SIC:** 5141 (Groceries—General Line). **Officers:** James M. Callaghan, President.

■ 24249 ■ Tri-State
3 S Bedford St.
Manchester, NH 03101-1111
Phone: (603)668-4840
Products: Commercial equipment, including commercial cooking and food service equipment. **SIC:** 5046 (Commercial Equipment Nec). **Officers:** Nick Bonardi, Owner.

■ 24250 ■ M. Tucker Company Inc.
900 S 2nd St.
Harrison, NJ 07029
Phone: (973)484-1200
Free: (800)338-8397 **Fax:** (973)484-8112
URL: http://www.mtucker.com
Products: Non-food items for the foodservice industry, including dishes, dishwashers, napkins, and silverware. **SICs:** 5046 (Commercial Equipment Nec); 5113 (Industrial & Personal Service Paper). **Est:** 1956. **Sales:** $60,000,000 (2000). **Emp:** 95. **Officers:** Stephen Tucker, President, e-mail: stucker@mtucker.com; Marc Fuchs, Exec. VP, e-mail: mfuchs@mtucker.com.

■ 24251 ■ M. Tucker Company Inc.
900 S 2nd St.
Harrison, NJ 07029
Phone: (973)484-1200
Free: (800)338-8397 **Fax:** (973)484-8112
Products: Food service equipment. **SIC:** 5046 (Commercial Equipment Nec). **Sales:** $28,000,000

(2000). **Emp:** 100. **Officers:** Stephen Tucker, President.

■ **24252** ■ **Unarco Commercial Products**
8470 Belvedere Ave Ste. C
Sacramento, CA 95826
Phone: (916)381-7373 **Fax:** (916)381-4919
Products: Shopping carts, stock handling and food handling equipment. **SIC:** 5046 (Commercial Equipment Nec).

■ **24253** ■ **United Beauty Equipment Co.**
91 N Lowell Rd.
Windham, NH 03087-1669
Phone: (603)434-8039
Products: Health and beauty aids. **SIC:** 5087 (Service Establishment Equipment). **Sales:** $900,000 (2000). **Emp:** 2.

■ **24254** ■ **United East Foodservice Supply Co.**
PO Box 1460
Woonsocket, RI 02895-0847
Phone: (401)769-1000
Free: (800)556-7338 **Fax:** (401)769-7056
E-mail: sales@unitedeast.com
URL: http://www.unitedeast.com
Products: Commercial cooking and food warming equipment; Foodservice equipment; Kitchen supplies; Buffet/catering supplies; Interior design; Furniture; Janitorial and sanitary maintenance; Warewashing supplies. **SIC:** 5046 (Commercial Equipment Nec). **Est:** 1947. **Sales:** $50,000,000 (2000). **Emp:** 145. **Officers:** Jerry Hyman, President, e-mail: jhyman@unitedeast.com; Bob Meyer, VP of Purchasing; Gary Halpern, VP of Marketing, e-mail: ghalpern@unitedeast.com; Jeff Oppenheim, VP of National Accounts. **Former Name:** United Restaurant Equipment Co.

■ **24255** ■ **United Fire Equipment Co.**
335 N 4th Ave.
Tucson, AZ 85745
Phone: (520)622-3639
Free: (800)362-0150 **Fax:** (520)882-3991
Products: Security and safety equipment. **SIC:** 5087 (Service Establishment Equipment). **Sales:** $7,000,000 (2000). **Emp:** 55.

■ **24256** ■ **United Restaurant Equipment**
2980 Jefferson St.
PO Box 2223
Harrisburg, PA 17105-2223
Phone: (717)238-1214 **Fax:** (717)238-3756
Products: Food service equipment and supplies; Paper and janitorial products. **SICs:** 5046 (Commercial Equipment Nec); 5078 (Refrigeration Equipment & Supplies). **Est:** 1933. **Emp:** 50. **Officers:** Joseph Weiss; Michael Weiss.

■ **24257** ■ **U.S. Foodservice Inc.**
9830 Patuxent Woods Dr.
Columbia, MD 21046
Phone: (410)312-7100 **Fax:** (410)312-7597
Products: Groceries; Commercial food service equipment. **SICs:** 5141 (Groceries—General Line); 5046 (Commercial Equipment Nec). **Sales:** $6,000,000,000 (2000). **Emp:** 12,000. **Officers:** James L. Miller, CEO, President & Chairman of the Board; Lewis Hay III, Sr. VP & CFO.

■ **24258** ■ **Vreeken Enterprises Inc.**
17151 SE Petrovitsky Rd.
Renton, WA 98058-9610
Phone: (425)255-4545
Free: (800)244-7830 **Fax:** (425)255-8181
Products: Restaurant and commercial foodservice equipment and supplies. **SIC:** 5046 (Commercial Equipment Nec). **Sales:** $1,800,000 (2000). **Emp:** 8.

■ **24259** ■ **Warren Equipment Co.**
PO Box 2872
Beaumont, TX 77704
Phone: (409)838-3791 **Fax:** (409)838-5047
Products: Hotel and restaurant equipment. **SIC:** 5046 (Commercial Equipment Nec). **Est:** 1989. **Sales:** $1,000,000 (2000). **Emp:** 5. **Officers:** Marvin W. Hall, President & CFO.

■ **24260** ■ **Weigh-Tronix Inc.**
19821 Cabot Blvd.
Hayward, CA 94545
Phone: (510)264-1692 **Fax:** (510)264-1697
Products: scales. **SIC:** 5046 (Commercial Equipment Nec).

■ **24261** ■ **Western Facilities Supply Inc.**
PO Box 928
Everett, WA 98206-0928
Phone: (425)252-2105
Free: (800)448-9314 **Fax:** (425)259-5130
Products: Cleaning and janitorial supplies. **SIC:** 5087 (Service Establishment Equipment).

■ **24262** ■ **Bob White Fountain Supply Co.**
2211 S Saginaw St.
Flint, MI 48503
Phone: (810)238-1231
Products: Restaurant equipment and supplies, including ice cream. **SICs:** 5141 (Groceries—General Line); 5143 (Dairy Products Except Dried or Canned).

■ **24263** ■ **World Wide Distributors Inc.**
2730 W Fullerton
Chicago, IL 60647-3089
Phone: (773)384-2300 **Fax:** (773)384-0639
Products: Specialty equipment and products. **SIC:** 5046 (Commercial Equipment Nec).

(48) Rubber

Entries in this section are arranged alphabetically by company name. When the company name is a personal name, the company name is alphabetized by the surname unless the first name or initial(s) are part of a trade name. See the User's Guide at the front of this directory for additional information.

■ **24264** ■ **Acme Machell Company Inc.**
PO Box 1617
Waukesha, WI 53187
Phone: (262)521-2870 **Fax:** (262)521-2894
Products: Rubber; Hydraulics. **SIC:** 5199 (Nondurable Goods Nec). **Est:** 1954. **Sales:** $11,000,000 (2000). **Emp:** 145. **Officers:** J.C. Riebe, President; Anne Wallis, Controller; Ron Schweitser, Sales/Marketing Contact, e-mail: rshweitzer@acmemachell.com; Al Hansen, Customer Service Contact, e-mail: ahansen@acmemachell.com; Anne Wallis, Human Resources Contact, e-mail: awallis@acmemachell.com.

■ **24265** ■ **Adams Foam Rubber Co.**
4737 S Christiana Ave.
Chicago, IL 60632
Phone: (312)523-5252
Products: Foam rubber. **SIC:** 5199 (Nondurable Goods Nec). **Est:** 1950. **Sales:** $4,000,000 (2000). **Emp:** 40. **Officers:** Lonny G. Gold, CEO; James Tarmichael, Vice President.

■ **24266** ■ **Akrochem Corp.**
255 Fountain St.
Akron, OH 44304
Phone: (330)535-2108
Products: Rubber and plastics products. **SICs:** 5199 (Nondurable Goods Nec); 5162 (Plastics Materials & Basic Shapes). **Sales:** $19,000,000 (1993). **Emp:** 44. **Officers:** Walton A. Silver, President; R.L. Silver, Chairman of the Board & Finance Officer.

■ **24267** ■ **Atlantic India Rubber Co.**
1425 Lake Ave.
Woodstock, IL 60098-7419
Phone: (815)334-9230
Free: (800)GRO-MMET **Fax:** (815)334-9422
E-mail: info@atlanticindia.com
URL: http://www.atlanticindia.com
Products: Mechanical rubber goods. **SIC:** 5085 (Industrial Supplies). **Est:** 1919. **Emp:** 120.

■ **24268** ■ **Baker Rubber Inc.**
PO Box 2438
South Bend, IN 46680
Phone: (219)237-6200 **Fax:** (219)237-6293
Products: Ground rubber material for asphalt, tires, and molded plastics. **SIC:** 5093 (Scrap & Waste Materials). **Est:** 1934. **Sales:** $9,000,000 (2000). **Emp:** 115. **Officers:** Tim Baker, President; Jim Dincolo, VP of Finance; Brian Jacobson, Dir. of Marketing & Sales; Cheryl Stordahl, Dir. of Information Systems; Susan Chell, Human Resources Mgr.

■ **24269** ■ **Bay Rubber Co.**
404 Pendleton Way
Oakland, CA 94621
Phone: (510)635-9151
Free: (800)229-7822 **Fax:** (510)430-9815
E-mail: tmbrco@bay-rubber.company.com
Products: Industrial rubber. **SIC:** 5085 (Industrial Supplies). **Est:** 1950. **Sales:** $2,500,000 (2000). **Emp:** 10. **Officers:** D.J. Higgins, Chairman of the Board; Dora Werner, Treasurer; Tom MacKenzie, President.

■ **24270** ■ **Big River Rubber & Gasket**
214 W 10th St.
Owensboro, KY 42303
Phone: (270)926-0241
Free: (800)626-7030 **Fax:** (270)686-7327
E-mail: connect@bigriver.com
URL: http://www.bigriver.com/
Products: Hoses, belting, couplings, v-belts, and gaskets. **SIC:** 5085 (Industrial Supplies).

■ **24271** ■ **Brost International Trading Co.**
222 W 33rd St.
Chicago, IL 60616-3700
Phone: (312)225-4900
Products: Rubber tires, seals, and latex gloves; Snack foods, including potato chips and nuts; Motor vehicle parts and supplies. **SICs:** 5064 (Electrical Appliances—Television & Radio); 5072 (Hardware); 5013 (Motor Vehicle Supplies & New Parts); 5145 (Confectionery). **Sales:** $2,000,000 (2000). **Emp:** 5. **Officers:** David Brost, President; Elaine Brost, Vice President.

■ **24272** ■ **California Industrial Rubber Co.**
Yuba City Branch
1690 Sierra Ave.
Yuba City, CA 95993
Phone: (530)674-2444 **Fax:** (530)674-1645
E-mail: http://www.cir.net/
Products: Industrial rubber; Plastic products. **SIC:** 5085 (Industrial Supplies).

■ **24273** ■ **Chicago Industrial Rubber**
862 Industrial Blvd.
Elmhurst, IL 60126
Phone: (708)834-2950
Products: Rubber products. **SIC:** 5085 (Industrial Supplies). **Sales:** $3,000,000 (1990). **Emp:** 7. **Officers:** W Nissen, President; R Heacock, CFO.

■ **24274** ■ **Curtis TradeGroup Inc.**
PO Box 17575
Sarasota, FL 34276-0575
Phone: (941)927-2333 **Fax:** (941)927-1332
Products: Reclaimed rubber, scrap rubber, electronics parts. **SICs:** 5093 (Scrap & Waste Materials); 5065 (Electronic Parts & Equipment Nec). **Sales:** $1,900,000 (2000). **Emp:** 3. **Officers:** James M. Haberman, President.

■ **24275** ■ **H.C. Gabler Inc.**
PO Box 220
Chambersburg, PA 17201
Phone: (717)264-4184 **Fax:** (717)264-8967
Products: Truck tires and tubes. **SIC:** 5014 (Tires & Tubes). **Sales:** $9,000,000 (2000). **Emp:** 65. **Officers:** Harold C. Gabler Jr., President; Harold Gabler III, VP of Marketing & Sales.

■ **24276** ■ **Gateway Tire Company Inc.**
4 W Crescentville Rd.
Cincinnati, OH 45246
Phone: (513)874-2500
Free: (800)837-1405 **Fax:** (513)874-7412
Products: Tires and tubes. **SIC:** 5014 (Tires & Tubes). **Sales:** $20,000,000 (2000). **Emp:** 32. **Officers:** William A. Patton, President; Brent A. Benson, Accountant.

■ **24277** ■ **Gooding and Shields Rubber Co.**
4915 Campbell's Run Rd.
Pittsburgh, PA 15205-1320
Phone: (412)257-5880 **Fax:** (412)257-5895
Products: Rubber and plastic hose; Rubber and plastic belts and belting, flat. **SIC:** 5085 (Industrial Supplies). **Est:** 1935. **Sales:** $8,000,000 (2000). **Emp:** 43. **Officers:** Andrew B. Lewis, CEO; David R. Goetz, CFO; Karen Hignett, Dir. of Information Systems.

■ **24278** ■ **Gordon Rubber and Packing Company Inc.**
PO Box 298
Derby, CT 06418
Phone: (203)735-7441 **Fax:** (203)734-7152
Products: Custom molded rubber products, including tubing and hoses. **SICs:** 5199 (Nondurable Goods Nec); 5085 (Industrial Supplies). **Est:** 1950. **Sales:** $3,000,000 (2000). **Emp:** 40. **Officers:** S.R. Nichols, President; Jay Mazur, CFO.

■ **24279** ■ **Greene Rubber Company Inc.**
20 Cross St.
Woburn, MA 01801-5606
Phone: (781)937-9909 **Fax:** (781)937-9739
Products: Rubber products. **SICs:** 5085 (Industrial Supplies); 5122 (Drugs, Proprietaries & Sundries). **Sales:** $12,000,000 (1994). **Emp:** 60. **Officers:** John Connors, President.

■ **24280** ■ **Hanna Rubber Co.**
1511 Baltimore Ave.
Kansas City, MO 64108
Phone: (816)221-9600
Free: (800)591-3035 **Fax:** (816)421-0583
Products: Molded and extruded rubber. **SIC:** 5199 (Nondurable Goods Nec). **Sales:** $22,000,000 (2000). **Emp:** 40. **Officers:** J.T. Vandergrift, President; Debbie Ward, Controller.

■ **24281** ■ **Hercules Tire and Rubber Co.**
1300 Morrical Blvd.
Findlay, OH 45840
Phone: (419)425-6400
Free: (800)677-9535 **Fax:** (419)425-6403
Products: Tread rubber. **SIC:** 5014 (Tires & Tubes). **Est:** 1952. **Sales:** $246,000,000 (2000). **Emp:** 325. **Officers:** Craig E. Anderson, President; Larry Seawell, Controller; Mel Baddorf, Dir. of Marketing; Barb Huth, Dir. of Data Processing; Ruth Carr, Dir of Human Resources.

■ **24282** ■ **Industrial Rubber Products Co.**
PO Box 2348
Charleston, WV 25328
Phone: (304)344-1791
Products: Rubber products. **SIC:** 5085 (Industrial Supplies). **Est:** 1937. **Sales:** $20,000,000 (2000). **Emp:** 100. **Officers:** R.C. White, President.

■ **24283** ■ **Kansas City Rubber and Belting Co.**
1815 Prospect Ave.
Kansas City, MO 64127
Phone: (816)483-8580 **Fax:** (816)483-8583
Products: Industrial rubber product; Hose; Belting; V

belts; Power transmission; Rubber lining. **SIC:** 5085 (Industrial Supplies). **Est:** 1906. **Sales:** $2,000,000 (2000). **Emp:** 15. **Officers:** Tom Skates, President; S. Skates, Treasurer & Secty.; Mike Vickers, Marketing Mgr.; Joe Skates, Vice President.

■ **24284** ■ **Lewis-Goetz and Company Inc.**
650 Washington Rd., No. 310
Pittsburgh, PA 15228
Phone: (412)341-7100
Free: (800)289-1236 **Fax:** (412)341-7192
URL: http://www.lewis-goetz.com
Products: Rubber goods, including hoses, conveyor belting, gaskets, and seals. **SIC:** 5085 (Industrial Supplies). **Est:** 1935. **Sales:** $75,000,000 (2000). **Emp:** 260. **Officers:** Andrew B. Lewis, CEO & Chairman of the Board; David R. Goetz, President & COO; Jay Shar, Dir. of Information Systems; Kelly Garvey, Dir of Human Resources.

■ **24285** ■ **Los Angeles Rubber Co.**
PO Box 23910
Los Angeles, CA 90023-0910
Phone: (213)263-4131 **Fax:** (213)269-2033
Products: Rubber products; Conveyor belts. **SIC:** 5085 (Industrial Supplies).

■ **24286** ■ **MBL USA Corp.**
601 Dayton Rd.
Ottawa, IL 61350
Phone: (815)434-1282 **Fax:** (815)434-2763
Products: Rubber belts. **SICs:** 5085 (Industrial Supplies); 5013 (Motor Vehicle Supplies & New Parts). **Est:** 1973. **Sales:** $30,000,000 (2000). **Emp:** 290. **Officers:** Keiji Murata, President; Rich Ott, Controller; Ains E. Hanson, VP of Marketing.

■ **24287** ■ **Mohawk Rubber Sales of N.E. Inc.**
65A Industrial Park Rd.
Hingham, MA 02043
Phone: (781)741-6000
Free: (800)242-1446 **Fax:** 800-982-9556
E-mail: c.service@mohawkrubber.com
URL: http://www.mohawkrubber.com/
Products: Retread tires. **SICs:** 5085 (Industrial Supplies); 5014 (Tires & Tubes).

■ **24288** ■ **Frank Murken Products Inc.**
PO Box 1083
Schenectady, NY 12301
Phone: (518)381-4270 **Fax:** (518)381-4351
E-mail: fmproducts@fmproducts.com
Products: Industrial rubber parts; Gaskets; Hydraulic hoses; Adhesives; Silicones. **SIC:** 5085 (Industrial Supplies). **Est:** 1963. **Sales:** $3,000,000 (2000). **Emp:** 18. **Officers:** J. Murray, CEO.

■ **24289** ■ **Potomac Rubber Company Inc.**
9011 Hampton Overlook
Capitol Heights, MD 20743
Phone: (301)336-7400
Free: (800)WORKS-4-U **Fax:** (301)350-6543
E-mail: info@potomacrubber.com
URL: http://www.jg209@aol.com
Products: Industrial rubber products and related items. **SIC:** 5085 (Industrial Supplies). **Est:** 1921. **Sales:** $1,500,000 (2000). **Emp:** 13. **Officers:** Sharon Ogle, President; Karen Brand, Secretary.

■ **24290** ■ **Reliable Tire Distributors Inc.**
PO Box 560
Camden, NJ 08101
Phone: (609)365-6500
Free: (800)342-3426 **Fax:** (609)365-8717
Products: Automobile tires. **SIC:** 5014 (Tires & Tubes).

Sales: $69,000,000 (2000). **Emp:** 110. **Officers:** Richard Betz, CEO.

■ **24291** ■ **Rosebar Tire Shredding Inc.**
PO Box 924
Cedar Rapids, IA 52406-0924
Phone: (319)472-5271
Products: Shredded rubber; Tire derived fuel. **SIC:** 5093 (Scrap & Waste Materials). **Est:** 1989. **Sales:** $7,000,000 (2000). **Emp:** 20. **Officers:** Eleanor J. Kaiser, President.

■ **24292** ■ **Rubber Plus Inc.**
PO Box 50430
Knoxville, TN 37950-0430
Phone: (865)588-2981
Free: (800)251-9138 **Fax:** (865)588-6984
E-mail: csrpi@aol.com
URL: http://www.rubberplusinc.com
Products: Industrial rubber. **SICs:** 5085 (Industrial Supplies); 5084 (Industrial Machinery & Equipment). **Est:** 1976. **Sales:** $5,000,000 (2000). **Emp:** 15. **Officers:** Charles A. Snow, CEO; Charles A. Snow, CEO.

■ **24293** ■ **M. Sacks International Inc.**
PO Box 1048
Akron, OH 44309-1048
Phone: (330)762-9385 **Fax:** (330)762-4832
E-mail: email@msacks.com
Products: Tire and paper mill industry products. **SICs:** 5014 (Tires & Tubes); 5113 (Industrial & Personal Service Paper); 5199 (Nondurable Goods Nec). **Est:** 1979. **Officers:** Michael B. Sacks, President.

■ **24294** ■ **SerVaas Inc.**
1000 Waterway Blvd.
Indianapolis, IN 46202
Phone: (317)636-1000 **Fax:** (317)634-1791
Products: Scrap rubber. **SIC:** 5093 (Scrap & Waste Materials). **Sales:** $71,000,000 (2000). **Emp:** 550. **Officers:** Beurt Servaas, Chairman of the Board.

■ **24295** ■ **Specialties Co.**
PO Box 266084
Houston, TX 77207
Phone: (713)644-1491 **Fax:** (713)644-9830
Products: Rubber hose. **SIC:** 5085 (Industrial Supplies). **Est:** 1957. **Sales:** $6,000,000 (2000). **Emp:** 50. **Officers:** Ray Love, President; Clif Love, VP of Sales.

■ **24296** ■ **Sterling Rubber and Plastics**
3190 Kettering Blvd.
Dayton, OH 45439-1924
Phone: (937)298-0241 **Fax:** (937)298-6086
E-mail: sales@sterlingrubber.com
URL: http://www.sterlingrubber.com
Products: Rubber industrial supplies, including sheet rubber, hoses, and conveyor belts, gaskets, plastics, and rubber specialties. **SICs:** 5085 (Industrial Supplies); 5162 (Plastics Materials & Basic Shapes). **Est:** 1929. **Officers:** Rodney R. Yarger, President; John F. Bramlage, Sales Mgr.; Cheryl L. Bailey, Human Resources Contact.

■ **24297** ■ **Superior Tire Inc.**
8577 Haven Ave.
Rancho Cucamonga, CA 91730
Phone: (909)484-9497 **Fax:** (909)484-1870
Products: Tires and accessories. **SIC:** 5014 (Tires & Tubes). **Sales:** $7,000,000 (2000). **Emp:** 12. **Officers:** Nick Mitsos, President; Armando Maliglig, Treasurer & Secty.

■ **24298** ■ **Tampa Rubber & Gasket Co., Inc.**
22nd St. & Causeway Blvd.
Tampa, FL
Phone: (813)247-3647
Free: (800)940-4673 **Fax:** (813)247-3180
URL: http://www.tamparubber.com/
Products: Sheet rubber, gaskets, hoses and belts. **SIC:** 5085 (Industrial Supplies). **Officers:** Carlton Marshall, President, e-mail: CMarshall@TampaRubber.com; Tony Marshall, Office Mgr., e-mail: TMarshall@TampaRubber.com; Mike Torres, Sales Mgr., e-mail: MTorres@TampaRubber.com.

■ **24299** ■ **TBC Corp.**
PO Box 18342
Memphis, TN 38181-0342
Phone: (901)363-8030 **Fax:** (901)541-3625
Products: Tires; Tubes; Batteries; Custom wheels; Filters; Brake parts and chassis parts. **SICs:** 5014 (Tires & Tubes); 5013 (Motor Vehicle Supplies & New Parts). **Sales:** $646,100,000 (2000). **Emp:** 780. **Officers:** Lawrence C. Day, CEO & President; Ronald E. McCollough, Exec. VP & CFO.

■ **24300** ■ **Teknor Apex Co.**
505 Central Ave.
PO Box 2290
Pawtucket, RI 02861
Phone: (401)725-8000
Free: (800)556-3864 **Fax:** (401)725-8095
Products: Rubber floor and wall coverings; Tread rubber, tire sundries, and repair materials; Rubber and plastic hose and belting. **SICs:** 5013 (Motor Vehicle Supplies & New Parts); 5199 (Nondurable Goods Nec).

■ **24301** ■ **Texas Rubber Supply Inc.**
2436 Irving Blvd.
Dallas, TX 75207
Phone: (214)631-3143
Free: (800)366-2904 **Fax:** (214)631-3651
Products: Industrial rubber products, including hoses, fittings, and sheet rubber; Hydraulic hose and fillings; Boots and gloves; Metal base assemblies; Mats and matting; PVC pipe and fittings. **SIC:** 5085 (Industrial Supplies). **Est:** 1952. **Sales:** $7,500,000 (2000). **Emp:** 50. **Officers:** E.O. Johnson, CEO.

■ **24302** ■ **TRC Industries Inc.**
1777 Commerce Dr.
Stow, OH 44224
Phone: (330)688-1583 **Fax:** (330)688-6561
Products: Silicone rubber; Scrap silicone. **SIC:** 5093 (Scrap & Waste Materials). **Est:** 1979. **Sales:** $5,000,000 (2000). **Emp:** 32. **Officers:** Bruce Bowers, President; R. James Regueiro, Sales/Marketing Contact; Darlene Minne, Customer Service Contact.

■ **24303** ■ **Trelltex Inc.**
5520 Armour Dr.
Houston, TX 77020
Phone: (713)675-8590
Free: (800)231-7116 **Fax:** (713)678-4757
URL: http://www.texcelrubber.com
Products: Rubber products. **SIC:** 5085 (Industrial Supplies). **Est:** 1981. **Emp:** 30. **Officers:** Edward Loke, Chairman of the Board; Linda Gibson, Dir. of Admin.; Ed Nasta, President.

(49) Scientific and Measurement Devices

Entries in this section are arranged alphabetically by company name. When the company name is a personal name, the company name is alphabetized by the surname unless the first name or initial(s) are part of a trade name. See the User's Guide at the front of this directory for additional information.

■ **24304** ■ **Aardvark Controls Equipment**
19571 Progress Dr.
Strongsville, OH 44136
Phone: (440)572-1368 **Fax:** (440)572-5613
Products: Control equipment, including pressure gauges, switches, and thermometers. **SICs:** 5049 (Professional Equipment Nec); 5084 (Industrial Machinery & Equipment).

■ **24305** ■ **ACI Controls**
295 Main St.
West Seneca, NY 14224
Phone: (716)675-9450 **Fax:** (716)675-1906
Products: Technical instrumentation. **SIC:** 5049 (Professional Equipment Nec).

■ **24306** ■ **Acme Vial and Glass Co. Inc.**
1601 Commerce Way
Paso Robles, CA 93446-3644
Phone: (805)239-2666 **Fax:** (805)239-9406
E-mail: acmevial@thegrid.net
URL: http://www.acmevial.com
Products: Glass vials and tubeware. **SIC:** 5049 (Professional Equipment Nec). **Est:** 1942. **Sales:** $2,500,000 (2000). **Emp:** 30. **Officers:** D.C. Knowles, President; Kay Anderson, Vice President; Kiki Anderson, Human Resources Contact.

■ **24307** ■ **Advanced Research Instruments Corp.**
2434 30th St.
Boulder, CO 80301
Phone: (303)449-2288 **Fax:** (303)449-9376
Products: Pre-amplifier rate meters; Image X-ray analyzers for scanning electron microscopes. **SIC:** 5049 (Professional Equipment Nec). **Sales:** $400,000 (2000). **Emp:** 4. **Officers:** Jozef Lebiedzik, President.

■ **24308** ■ **Alaska Instrument Company Inc.**
PO Box 230087
Anchorage, AK 99523-0087
Phone: (907)561-7511
Products: Thermometers; Pipes; Gauges. **SIC:** 5065 (Electronic Parts & Equipment Nec). **Est:** 1967. **Sales:** $2,000,000 (2000). **Emp:** 7. **Officers:** Dan Conrad, President; Sherrie Bancroft, CFO.

■ **24309** ■ **Alexon Trend Inc.**
14000 Unity St. NW
Ramsey, MN 55303
Phone: (612)323-7800
Products: Laboratory supplies. **SIC:** 5049 (Professional Equipment Nec). **Sales:** $9,000,000 (2000). **Emp:** 34. **Officers:** David Taus, President.

■ **24310** ■ **Alvin and Company Inc.**
PO Box 188
Windsor, CT 06095
Phone: (860)243-8991
Free: (800)444-2584 **Fax:** (860)242-8037
Products: Drafting, engineering and graphic arts supplies. **SICs:** 5049 (Professional Equipment Nec); 5199 (Nondurable Goods Nec). **Sales:** $38,000,000 (2000). **Emp:** 150. **Officers:** Joe Miller, CEO; Diane Gale, Controller.

■ **24311** ■ **Amics International Inc.**
2430 Pagehurst Dr.
PO Box 1027
Midlothian, VA 23113
Phone: (804)379-2305 **Fax:** (804)379-3520
Products: Aircraft instruments; Medical instruments; Sporting goods; Industrial measuring devices; Women's embroidered clothing. **SICs:** 5084 (Industrial Machinery & Equipment); 5049 (Professional Equipment Nec); 5047 (Medical & Hospital Equipment); 5091 (Sporting & Recreational Goods); 5137 (Women's/Children's Clothing). **Officers:** Nicholas J. Maiolo Jr., VP of Intl. Trade.

■ **24312** ■ **Anderson Machinery Co.**
PO Box 245
Stratford, CT 06615
Phone: (203)375-4481 **Fax:** (203)375-0195
E-mail: andmy@aol.com
Products: New and used optical and video comparators, and microscopes; Tool room machines. **SIC:** 5049 (Professional Equipment Nec). **Est:** 1973. **Sales:** $1,500,000 (2000). **Emp:** 4. **Officers:** Stuart C. Anderson, President.

■ **24313** ■ **Ando Corp. Measuring Instruments Div.**
7617 Standish Pl.
Rockville, MD 20855
Phone: (301)294-3365
Free: (800)367-2636 **Fax:** (301)294-3359
Products: Fiber optic automatic test equipment for the telecommunications industry. **SIC:** 5065 (Electronic Parts & Equipment Nec). **Sales:** $1,000,000 (2000). **Emp:** 10.

■ **24314** ■ **Anritsu Co.**
1155 E Collins Blvd.
Richardson, TX 75081
Phone: (972)644-1777
Free: (800)ANR-ITSU **Fax:** (972)671-1877
E-mail: moreinfo@anritsu.com
URL: http://www.us.anritsu.com
Products: Microwave, RF, and optical testing and measurement equipment, components, and devices. **SIC:** 5065 (Electronic Parts & Equipment Nec). **Est:** 1895. **Sales:** $1,200,000,000 (2000). **Emp:** 1,100. **Officers:** Mark Guans, President. **Former Name:** Anritsu Wiltron Sales Co.

■ **24315** ■ **Applied Chemical Solutions Inc.**
307 Fallon Rd.
Hollister, CA 95023
Phone: (408)637-0969
Products: Pressure gage. **SIC:** 5084 (Industrial Machinery & Equipment).

■ **24316** ■ **Aristo Import Company Inc.**
15 Hunt Rd.
Orangeburg, NY 10962
Phone: (914)359-0720 **Fax:** (914)359-0020
Products: Stop watches. **SIC:** 5049 (Professional Equipment Nec). **Est:** 1920. **Sales:** $1,000,000 (2000). **Emp:** 5. **Officers:** N. Baumann, CEO; R. Baumann, CEO.

■ **24317** ■ **Arun Technology Inc.**
PO Box 2947
Dearborn, MI 48123-2947
Phone: (313)277-8186
Free: (800)355-2786 **Fax:** (313)277-8360
URL: http://www.aruntechnology.com
Products: Optical emission spectrometers. **SIC:** 5049 (Professional Equipment Nec). **Est:** 1988. **Sales:** $2,300,000 (2000). **Emp:** 10. **Officers:** Paul K. Penney, President; Richard Milns, Finance Officer; Deborah Freer, Dir. of Marketing & Sales; Cindy Hyuck, Dir of Human Resources.

■ **24318** ■ **Atec, Inc.**
12600 Executive Dr.
Stafford, TX 77477-3064
Phone: (281)276-2700 **Fax:** (281)240-2682
E-mail: atecsale@atec.com
URL: http://www.atec.com
Products: Aerospace components; Electronic testing equipment; Oil field equipment; Power generation systems. **SICs:** 5084 (Industrial Machinery & Equipment); 5049 (Professional Equipment Nec); 5065 (Electronic Parts & Equipment Nec). **Est:** 1956. **Sales:** $12,500,000 (1999). **Emp:** 100. **Officers:** Howard Lederer, President; Paul Fenley, Vice President; Ken Neef, Vice President; Brair Durbie, Project Development.

■ **24319** ■ **AWC, Inc.**
6655 Exchequer Dr.
Baton Rouge, LA 70809
Phone: (504)752-1100
Free: (800)364-0292 **Fax:** (504)755-6723
URL: http://www.awc-inc.com
Products: Instrumentation products. **SIC:** 5049 (Professional Equipment Nec). **Est:** 1965. **Sales:** $80,000,000 (2000). **Emp:** 160.

■ **24320** ■ **B & L Scales**
503 Wicks Ln.
Billings, MT 59105-4444
Phone: (406)248-4531 **Fax:** (406)259-9948
Products: Commercial equipment; Scales, except laboratory. **SIC:** 5046 (Commercial Equipment Nec). **Officers:** Leroy Mc Bride, Owner.

■ **24321** ■ **Basic Service Corp.**
2525 Imlay City Rd.
Lapeer, MI 48446-3215
Phone: (810)667-1800
Free: (800)258-8320 **Fax:** (810)667-4542
E-mail: basic@tir.com
URL: http://www.basicservice.com
Products: Measuring and controlling devices. **SIC:** 5049 (Professional Equipment Nec). **Est:** 1946. **Sales:** $750,000 (2000). **Emp:** 6. **Officers:** Jeff Doerr, Sales & Marketing Contact; Loraine Hoxie, Human Resources Contact; Lorraine Hoxie, Human Resources Contact.

■ **24322** ■ **Baxter Scientific Products**
1430 Waukegan Rd.
Mc Gaw Park, IL 60085
Phone: (847)689-8410
Free: (800)964-5227 **Fax:** (847)473-2114
Products: Laboratory supplies. **SIC:** 5049 (Professional Equipment Nec).

■ **24323** ■ **A. Biederman Inc.**
1425 Grand Central Ave.
Glendale, CA 91201-3095
Phone: (818)246-8431
Free: (800)525-6696 **Fax:** (818)244-2189
E-mail: indsales@abiederman.com
URL: http://www.abiederman.com
Products: Gauges; Valves; Safety and air quality instruments. **SIC:** 5063 (Electrical Apparatus & Equipment). **Est:** 1933. **Sales:** $16,000,000 (2000). **Emp:** 79. **Officers:** R. Rockwood, President; Bill Reis, Vice President.

■ **24324** ■ **Blue White Industries Limited Inc.**
14931 Chestnut St.
Westminster, CA 92683
Phone: (714)893-8529 **Fax:** (714)894-0149
Products: Measuring and dispensing pumps; Electromagnetic, flow meters (flow tubes). **SICs:** 5084 (Industrial Machinery & Equipment); 5049 (Professional Equipment Nec). **Officers:** Selma Ponsell, Sales and Marketing Coordinator.

■ **24325** ■ **George E. Booth Co.**
800 Cawthon St., Ste. 100
Louisville, KY 40203
Phone: (502)589-1056 **Fax:** (502)589-1169
Products: Level controls, including valves and gauges. **SIC:** 5049 (Professional Equipment Nec).

■ **24326** ■ **Branom Instrument Company Inc.**
PO Box 80307
Seattle, WA 98108-0307
Phone: (206)762-6050
Free: (800)767-6051 **Fax:** (206)767-5669
E-mail: sales@branom.com
URL: http://www.branom.com
Products: Process control instruments; Electrical and electronic test and measurement equipment. **SICs:** 5049 (Professional Equipment Nec); 5065 (Electronic Parts & Equipment Nec); 5063 (Electrical Apparatus & Equipment). **Est:** 1947. **Sales:** $12,000,000 (1999). **Emp:** 80. **Officers:** William W. Branom, CEO; Ray H. Branom, President; John Schneider, Inside Sales Mgr., e-mail: jschneider@branom.com.

■ **24327** ■ **Branom Instrument Company Inc.**
626 N Helena
Spokane, WA 99202
Phone: (509)534-9395 **Fax:** (509)534-9397
Products: Process control instruments. **SIC:** 5049 (Professional Equipment Nec).

■ **24328** ■ **Brinkmann Instruments, Inc.**
1 Cantiague Rd.
PO Box 1019
Westbury, NY 11590-0207
Phone: (516)334-7500
Free: (800)645-3050 **Fax:** (516)334-7506
E-mail: info@brinkmann.com
URL: http://www.brinkman.com
Products: Centrifuges; Dispensers; Circulators; Pipettes; Titrators; Homogenizers; Auto claves; Fat analyzers; Tensiometers. **SICs:** 5047 (Medical & Hospital Equipment); 5049 (Professional Equipment Nec); 5084 (Industrial Machinery & Equipment). **Est:** 1941. **Sales:** $72,000,000 (2000). **Emp:** 253. **Officers:** Joseph Milack.

■ **24329** ■ **Bruwiler Precise Sales Company, Inc.**
4308 Burns Ave.
Los Angeles, CA 90029
Phone: (323)666-4551
Free: (800)272-4499 **Fax:** (323)668-0183
Products: Precision measuring tools. **SIC:** 5084 (Industrial Machinery & Equipment). **Est:** 1962. **Emp:** 12. **Officers:** E. Mike Bruhwiler, President; Remo Buhlmann, General Mgr.; Rudi Buergi, Sales Mgr.; Fred Soriano, Sales.

■ **24330** ■ **Buffalo Scale and Supply Co. Inc.**
PO Box 140
Buffalo, NY 14205
Phone: (716)847-2880
Products: Scales. **SIC:** 5046 (Commercial Equipment Nec).

■ **24331** ■ **Burton-Rogers Co. Inc.**
220 Grove St.
Waltham, MA 02453
Phone: (781)894-6440
Free: (800)225-4678 **Fax:** (781)893-8393
E-mail: sales@calibroninst.com
URL: http://www.calibroninst.com
Products: Analytical and scientific instruments; Gauges. **SIC:** 5049 (Professional Equipment Nec). **Est:** 1919. **Sales:** $1,800,000 (1999). **Emp:** 10. **Officers:** William Burton, President & Treasurer; Helen Adelman, Sales/Marketing Contact. **Alternate Name:** Calibron Instruments Div.

■ **24332** ■ **Butler National Services Inc.**
2772 NW 31st Ave.
Ft. Lauderdale, FL 33311
Phone: (954)733-7511
Products: Monitoring systems for remote waste water pumping stations. **SIC:** 5084 (Industrial Machinery & Equipment). **Sales:** $2,000,000 (1993). **Emp:** 8. **Officers:** Clark Stewart, President.

■ **24333** ■ **California Surveying and Drafting Supply Inc.**
4733 Auburn Blvd.
Sacramento, CA 95841
Phone: (916)344-0232 **Fax:** (913)344-2998
Products: Surveying and drafting instruments, laboratory furniture. **SICs:** 5049 (Professional Equipment Nec); 5021 (Furniture). **Est:** 1986. **Sales:** $3,000,000 (2000). **Emp:** 15. **Officers:** Tom Kubo, President; Bruce Gandelman, CFO.

■ **24334** ■ **Cameca Instruments Inc.**
204 Spring Hill Rd.
Trumbull, CT 06611
Phone: (203)459-0623 **Fax:** (203)348-5516
Products: Scientific instruments, including electron probe micro analyzers and secondary ion mass spectrometers. **SIC:** 5049 (Professional Equipment Nec). **Est:** 1971. **Sales:** $8,000,000 (2000). **Emp:** 23. **Officers:** Claude Conty, President; Robert Merritt, Controller; Florence Pindrys, Dir. of Sales.

■ **24335** ■ **Capital Scale**
PO Box 2021
Bismarck, ND 58502-2021
Phone: (701)255-1556 **Fax:** (701)255-3512
Products: Commercial equipment; Scales, including laboratory scales. **SICs:** 5049 (Professional Equipment Nec); 5046 (Commercial Equipment Nec). **Officers:** Michael Kennedy, Owner.

■ **24336** ■ **Centro, Inc.**
7600 Hardin Dr.
PO Box 6248
Sherwood, AR 72117
Phone: (501)835-2193 **Fax:** (501)835-2277
URL: http://www.centromemphis.com
Products: Controls and ball valves; Fitting and tubings; Metering pumps; Level and flow controls; Gauges; Temperature indicators; Industrial process systems. **SICs:** 5049 (Professional Equipment Nec); 5084 (Industrial Machinery & Equipment). **Est:** 1974. **Sales:** $4,000,000 (2000). **Emp:** 10. **Officers:** Greg Stanseu, Branch Mgr.

■ **24337** ■ **Centro, Inc.**
321 Hill Ave.
Nashville, TN 37210-4711
Phone: (615)255-2220 **Fax:** (615)225-2212
Products: Industrial products, including gauges and control valves. **SICs:** 5049 (Professional Equipment Nec); 5085 (Industrial Supplies).

■ **24338** ■ **Chiral Technologies Inc.**
PO Box 564
Exton, PA 19341
Phone: (610)594-2100 **Fax:** (610)594-2325
Products: Analytical instruments used in liquid chromatography. **SIC:** 5049 (Professional Equipment

Nec). **Sales:** $4,000,000 (1994). **Emp:** 15. **Officers:** Thomas B. Lewis, CEO & President.

■ **24339** ■ **Chronomix Corp.**
650F Vaqueros Ave.
Sunnyvale, CA 94086-3580
Phone: (408)737-1920
Free: (800)538-1548 **Fax:** (408)737-0160
E-mail: anyone@chronomix.com
URL: http://www.chronomix.com
Products: Timing equipment, including sports and industry. **SIC:** 5049 (Professional Equipment Nec). **Est:** 1975. **Emp:** 12. **Officers:** D.P. Baxter.

■ **24340** ■ **CILCORP Energy Services Inc.**
300 Liberty St.
Peoria, IL 61602
Phone: (309)672-5271
Products: Carbon monoxide sensors. **SIC:** 5084 (Industrial Machinery & Equipment).

■ **24341** ■ **Cole-Parmer Instrument Co.**
625 E Bunker Ct.
Vernon Hills, IL 60061-1844
Phone: (847)647-7600
Products: Laboratory equipment, including testing. **SIC:** 5049 (Professional Equipment Nec). **Est:** 1959. **Sales:** $94,000,000 (2000). **Emp:** 300. **Officers:** J.C. Parmer, President.

■ **24342** ■ **Cream City Scale Company Inc.**
PO Box 749
Menomonee Falls, WI 53051
Phone: (414)255-5640
Products: Scales, including industrial and home scales. **SICs:** 5046 (Commercial Equipment Nec); 5047 (Medical & Hospital Equipment). **Est:** 1921. **Sales:** $4,000,000 (2000). **Emp:** 30. **Officers:** Judson C. Higgins Jr., President.

■ **24343** ■ **Crouch Supply Company Inc.**
PO Box 163829
Ft. Worth, TX 76161-3829
Phone: (817)332-2118
Free: (800)825-1110 **Fax:** (817)332-6511
URL: http://www.crouchinc.com
Products: Chemical cleaners; Lab ware; Glassware; Sanitary pumps, valves and fittings for food, dairy beverage and pharmaceutical processing plants. **SICs:** 5084 (Industrial Machinery & Equipment); 5169 (Chemicals & Allied Products Nec). **Est:** 1914. **Sales:** $14,000,000 (2000). **Emp:** 45. **Officers:** Glen D. Woodson Jr., President; Michael L. Davis, Treasurer & Secty.; Bradford S. Barnes, Chairman of the Board; Bradford S. Barnes, Sales/Marketing Contact, e-mail: bbarnes@crouchinc.com; Travis Hopkins, Customer Service Contact, e-mail: thopkins@crunchinc.com; Michael Davis, Human Resources Contact, e-mail: mdavis@crunchinc.com.

■ **24344** ■ **A. Daigger and Co. Inc.**
620 Lakeview Pkwy.
Vernon Hills, IL 60061
Free: (800)621-7193 **Fax:** 800-320-7200
E-mail: daigger@daigger.com
URL: http://www.daigger.com
Products: Laboratory apparatus and supplies, including glassware and plasticware; Scientific instruments. **SIC:** 5049 (Professional Equipment Nec). **Est:** 1894. **Emp:** 65. **Officers:** Mike Gogoel, Vice President.

■ **24345** ■ **Ed Deveault**
PO Box 932
Portland, ME 04104-0932
Phone: (207)772-3451 **Fax:** (207)772-6932
Products: Commercial equipment, including scales. **SIC:** 5046 (Commercial Equipment Nec). **Officers:** Ed Deveault, Owner.

■ **24346** ■ **Displaytech Inc.**
2602 Clover Basin Dr.
Longmont, CO 80503
Phone: (303)772-2191 **Fax:** (303)772-2193
Products: Electro-optical devices. **SIC:** 5049 (Professional Equipment Nec). **Officers:** Haviland Wright, CEO.

■ 24347 ■ J.R. Douglass Co.
PO Box 31075
Cincinnati, OH 45231
Phone: (513)931-4986 Fax: (513)931-4924
Products: Valves; Tube fittings; Pressure regulators.
SIC: 5049 (Professional Equipment Nec).

■ 24348 ■ Dresco Reproduction Inc.
12603 Allard St.
Santa Fe Springs, CA 90670
Phone: (562)863-6677
Free: (800)423-5834 Fax: (562)868-9757
Products: Full line architectural and engineering
supply company specializing in large document
machines. SICs: 5049 (Professional Equipment Nec);
5044 (Office Equipment). Sales: $3,000,000 (2000).
Emp: 13. Officers: Stanley P. Taylor, President;
Shirley A. Taylor, CFO.

■ 24349 ■ Duke Scientific Corp.
PO Box 50005
Palo Alto, CA 94303
Phone: (650)424-1177 Fax: (650)424-1158
Products: particle size standards for calibration of
scientific instruments. SIC: 5049 (Professional
Equipment Nec). Officers: Stanley Duke, President.

■ 24350 ■ DW Enterprises
510 W 41st Ave., No. C
Anchorage, AK 99503
Phone: (907)561-8363 Fax: (907)561-8843
Products: Drafting supplies. SIC: 5049 (Professional
Equipment Nec).

■ 24351 ■ Dynamic Reprographics Inc.
1002 W 12th St.
Austin, TX 78703
Phone: (512)474-8842 Fax: (512)474-9133
Products: Engineering equipment; Plotters and
copiers. SIC: 5049 (Professional Equipment Nec).
Sales: $1,000,000 (2000). Emp: 25. Officers: Lisa
Tipps, Owner.

■ 24352 ■ Edmund Scientific Co., Industrial
Optics Div.
101 E Gloucester Pike
Barrington, NJ 08007
Phones: (609)547-3488 (609)573-6250
Free: (800)363-1992 Fax: (609)573-6295
E-mail: industrialsales@edsci.com
URL: http://www.edmundoptics.com
Products: Optics and optical instruments; Binoculars
and telescopes; Imaging systems; Machine vision
equipment. SICs: 5049 (Professional Equipment Nec);
5084 (Industrial Machinery & Equipment). Est: 1952.
Emp: 150. Officers: Robert Edmund, CEO; Frank
DiMinno, President.

■ 24353 ■ Elan Technical Corp.
35 Kings Hwy. E
Fairfield, CT 06432
Phone: (203)335-2115
Free: (888)840-2011 Fax: (203)335-2723
E-mail: rb/etc@usa.net
URL: http://www.elan.thomosregister.com
Products: Environmental control instruments. SIC:
5049 (Professional Equipment Nec). Est: 1988. Sales:
$1,500,000 (2000). Emp: 11. Officers: Randolph C.
Bush, President.

■ 24354 ■ Engineered Systems & Designs,
Inc.
119A Sandy Dr.
Newark, DE 19713
Phone: (302)456-0446 Fax: (302)456-0441
E-mail: esd@esdinc.com
URL: http://www.esdinc.com
Products: PH, conductivity, turbidity, and oxygen
meters and controllers; X-ray pulse counters. SICs:
5084 (Industrial Machinery & Equipment); 5049
(Professional Equipment Nec). Est: 1974. Sales:
$1,000,000 (2000). Emp: 10. Officers: Dolores Raker,
Dir. of Marketing; Robert Spring, President.

■ 24355 ■ Environetics
1 Idexx
Westbrook, ME 04092
Phone: (207)856-0300 Fax: (207)481-6358
Products: Water-testing products. SIC: 5049

(Professional Equipment Nec). Est: 1986. Sales:
$3,000,000 (2000). Emp: 20. Officers: J. Larry
Cohoon, CEO; Bernard F. Denoyer, CFO; Dean
Layton, VP of Marketing & Sales; Jacquie Pickering,
Dir. of Data Processing; Alliette P. Laughran, Dir of
Human Resources.

■ 24356 ■ Epic Inc.
150 Nassau St.
New York, NY 10038
Phone: (212)308-7039 Fax: (212)308-7266
Products: Scientific and measurement devices. SIC:
5049 (Professional Equipment Nec). Sales: $1,000,000
(2000). Emp: 15.

■ 24357 ■ Evergreen Scientific Inc.
PO Box 58248
Los Angeles, CA 90058
Phone: (213)583-1331 Fax: (213)581-2503
Products: Disposable laboratory products. SIC: 5049
(Professional Equipment Nec). Est: 1969. Sales:
$5,000,000 (2000). Emp: 100. Officers: Johnson
Wong, President; Doris McAmis, Controller.

■ 24358 ■ Export Consultant Service
108 S Patton Dr.
Coraopolis, PA 15108
Phone: (412)264-7877 Fax: (412)264-4543
E-mail: exportpit@aol.com
Products: Laboratory and scientific glassware;
Measuring and testing instruments; Pumps, cylinders,
compressors, and thermocouples; Spare parts. SICs:
5049 (Professional Equipment Nec); 5199 (Nondurable
Goods Nec); 5065 (Electronic Parts & Equipment Nec).
Est: 1965. Emp: 5. Officers: Gerard F. Schweiger,
President.

■ 24359 ■ Fisher Healthcare
9999 Veterans Memorial Dr.
Houston, TX 77038-2499
Phone: 800-640-0640 Fax: 800-290-0290
E-mail: fhc@gcs.fishersci.com
URL: http://www.fishersci.com
Products: Clinical laboratory supplies, including
diagnostic tests, equipment, and services. SICs: 5047
(Medical & Hospital Equipment); 5049 (Professional
Equipment Nec). Est: 1995. Sales: $500,000,000
(2000). Emp: 350. Officers: Dan A. Eckert, President;
Jack Daniels, Sales/Marketing Contact, e-mail:
jack.daniels@gcs.fishersci.com; Jeff Gleason,
Customer Service Contact, e-mail: jeff.gleason@
gcs.fishersci.com; Jena Abernathy, Human Resources
Contact, e-mail: jena.abernathy@gcs.fishersci.com.
Former Name: Curtin Matheson Scientific Inc.

■ 24360 ■ Fisher Scientific Co.
2000 Park Lane Dr.
Pittsburgh, PA 15275-1126
Phone: (412)562-8300
Free: (800)766-7000 Fax: (412)562-5344
Products: Chemicals; Centrifuges; Hospital and lab
supplies; Glassware; Biotech; Safety products. SICs:
5049 (Professional Equipment Nec); 5047 (Medical &
Hospital Equipment); 5169 (Chemicals & Allied
Products Nec).

■ 24361 ■ Flinn Scientific, Inc.
PO Box 219
Batavia, IL 60510-0219
Phone: (630)879-6962
Free: (800)452-1261 Fax: (630)879-6962
Products: Chemistry supplies. SICs: 5049
(Professional Equipment Nec); 5047 (Medical &
Hospital Equipment).

■ 24362 ■ Fred V. Fowler Company Inc.
PO Box 66299
Newton, MA 02466
Phone: (617)332-7004
Free: (800)788-2353 Fax: (617)332-4137
E-mail: sales@fvfowler.com
URL: http://www.fvfowler.com
Products: Precision, optical, and electronic measuring
instruments. SIC: 5084 (Industrial Machinery &
Equipment). Est: 1946. Sales: $21,000,000 (1999).
Emp: 53. Officers: Fred V. Fowler, President; William
Ozolins, Exec. VP of Finance; Fred V. Fowler III, VP of
Marketing; Marshal Rakusin, VP Automotive Product
Division.

■ 24363 ■ Frey Scientific
100 Paragon Pky.
Mansfield, OH 44903
Phone: (419)589-2100 Fax: (419)589-1522
Products: Scientific materials. SIC: 5049 (Professional
Equipment Nec).

■ 24364 ■ Geotronics of North America Inc.
911 Hawthorn Dr.
Itasca, IL 60143
Phone: (708)285-1400 Fax: (708)285-1410
Products: Surveying equipment, including global
positioning systems. SIC: 5049 (Professional
Equipment Nec). Sales: $7,000,000 (2000). Emp: 25.
Officers: Frank Larsson, President; Hakan Orvell,
Controller.

■ 24365 ■ Gilman Industrial Exports, Inc.
98A Fairport Village Landing
Fairport, NY 14450
Phone: (716)425-0310 Fax: (716)425-0304
E-mail: gilmanexprots@cs.com
Products: Industrial process analyzers; Software; Data
loggers; Calibrators; Flow meters; Controllers;
Recorders; Valves. SICs: 5084 (Industrial Machinery &
Equipment); 5049 (Professional Equipment Nec); 5045
(Computers, Peripherals & Software). Est: 1974.
Officers: Danny Covill, President.

■ 24366 ■ Glen Mills Inc.
395 Allwood Rd.
Clifton, NJ 07012-1704
Phone: (973)777-0777 Fax: (973)777-0070
E-mail: staff@glenmills.com
URL: http://www.glenmills.com
Products: Mills for laboratories; Steel balls; Blenders.
SICs: 5084 (Industrial Machinery & Equipment); 5049
(Professional Equipment Nec). Est: 1980. Sales:
$3,000,000 (2000). Emp: 12. Officers: Peter Kendall,
President; Stanley Goldberg, Director, e-mail:
Stanley@glenmills.com; Anita Ahrens, Office Mgr.

■ 24367 ■ HAAKE
53 W Century Rd.
Paramus, NJ 07652
Phone: (201)265-7865 Free: (800)631-1369
URL: http://www.haake-usa.com
Products: Viscometers; Rheometers; Circulators;
Thermal analysis. SIC: 5049 (Professional Equipment
Nec). Sales: $7,000,000 (1999). Emp: 25. Officers:
Randy Byrne, Vice President; John Quigley, Vice
President.

■ 24368 ■ HAZCO Services Inc.
PO Box 2635
Dayton, OH 45401
Phone: (513)293-2700 Fax: (513)293-9227
Products: Products for the environment; Protective
clothing; Air quality measuring instruments. SICs: 5049
(Professional Equipment Nec); 5046 (Commercial
Equipment Nec). Est: 1986. Sales: $45,000,000
(2000). Emp: 180. Officers: Philip J. Sheridan,
President.

■ 24369 ■ HB Instruments Inc.
53 W Century Rd.
Paramus, NJ 07652
Phone: (201)265-7865 Fax: (201)265-1977
Products: Analytical instruments. SIC: 5049
(Professional Equipment Nec). Sales: $12,000,000
(2000). Emp: 35. Officers: Chip Ganz, General Mgr.;
Cheryl Mullane, Accounting Manager.

■ 24370 ■ Heights Pump & Supply
1359 Clarhill Rd.
Laurel, MT 59044
Phone: (406)628-4755 Fax: (406)628-4755
Products: Service establishment equipment;
Firefighting equipment; Sprinkler systems supplies;
Water well supplies. SICs: 5046 (Commercial
Equipment Nec); 5074 (Plumbing & Hydronic Heating
Supplies); 5049 (Professional Equipment Nec).
Officers: David M. Carpenter.

■ 24371 ■ Hoover Instrument Service Inc.
401 N Home Rd.
Mansfield, OH 44906
Phone: (419)529-3226
Products: Industrial controls. SIC: 5063 (Electrical Apparatus & Equipment).

■ 24372 ■ Instrument Engineers
12335 World Trade Dr., Ste. 7A
San Diego, CA 92128-3783
Phone: (858)673-3644
Free: (800)444-6106 Fax: (858)673-3643
E-mail: answers@ie2000.com
URL: http://www.ie2000.com
Products: Electrical testing equipment and instruments; Microscopes; Furniture; Material handling equipment; Color LCDs; Solder-desolder stations; Industrial PCs. SICs: 5065 (Electronic Parts & Equipment Nec); 5065 (Electronic Parts & Equipment Nec). Est: 1971. Sales: $2,400,000 (1999). Emp: 4. Officers: Jimm Hoffmann, Partner, e-mail: Jimm@ie2000.com; Richard Hoffmann, Mng. Partner.

■ 24373 ■ Instrument Sales-East
24037 Acacia
Redford, MI 48239
Phone: (313)535-5252
Free: (800)821-1954 Fax: (313)535-4411
E-mail: sales@instrumentsales1com
URL: http://www.instrumentsales1com
Products: Surveying equipment; Measuring equipment (devices); Laser levels. SIC: 5049 (Professional Equipment Nec). Est: 1997. Sales: $4,700,000 (1999). Emp: 17. Officers: Milad Zohrob, President; Sherry Meyers, Customer Service Contact.

■ 24374 ■ Intermountain Scientific Corp.
PO Box 380
Kaysville, UT 84037-0380
Phone: (801)547-5047
Products: Laboratory supplies; Scientific instruments. SICs: 5122 (Drugs, Proprietaries & Sundries); 5049 (Professional Equipment Nec). Sales: $15,000,000 (2000). Emp: 53. Officers: Cynthia A. Lindberg, President; Rob Crouch, Controller.

■ 24375 ■ inTEST Corp.
2 Pin Oak Ln.
Cherry Hill, NJ 08003
Phone: (609)424-6886
Products: Docking hardware, test head manipulators, and related automatic test equipment interface products. SIC: 5065 (Electronic Parts & Equipment Nec). Sales: $18,600,000 (2000). Emp: 61. Officers: Robert E. Matthiessen, President & COO; Hugh T. Regan Jr., CFO & Treasurer.

■ 24376 ■ Intoximeters Inc.
8110 Lackland Rd.
St. Louis, MO 63114
Phone: (314)429-4000
Free: (800)451-8639 Fax: (314)429-4170
E-mail: sales@intox.com
URL: http://www.intox.com
Products: Breath alcohol testing instruments. SIC: 5049 (Professional Equipment Nec). Est: 1945. Sales: $15,000,000 (2000). Emp: 40. Officers: M.R. Forrester, CEO; C.H. Dalton, President.

■ 24377 ■ J & H Berge, Inc.
4111 S Clinton Ave.
South Plainfield, NJ 07080
Phone: (908)561-1234
Free: (800)684-1234 Fax: (908)561-3002
E-mail: sales@labmartexpress.com
URL: http://www.labmartexpress.com
Products: Laboratory equipment and supplies. SIC: 5049 (Professional Equipment Nec). Est: 1850. Sales: $6,000,000 (2000). Emp: 30. Officers: Steven N. Krupp, President; Charles Feldman, Vice President; Rob Gardner, Dir. of Materials; Pam Van Horn, Human Resources Contact; Pam Van Horn, Human Resources Contact.

■ 24378 ■ JEOL U.S.A. Inc.
11 Dearborn Rd.
Peabody, MA 01960
Phone: (978)535-5900 Fax: (978)536-2205
Products: Scanning and electron microscopes. SIC:

5065 (Electronic Parts & Equipment Nec). Est: 1962. Sales: $96,000,000 (2000). Emp: 300. Officers: Kazuyoshi Yasutalle, President; Robert Santorelli, VP of Marketing & Sales.

■ 24379 ■ Jim Sales & Service
804 S B St.
Grangeville, ID 83530-1510
Phone: (208)983-1442
Products: Commercial equipment, including scales. SIC: 5046 (Commercial Equipment Nec). Officers: Jim Frei, Owner.

■ 24380 ■ Shelby Jones Co.
8800 Westchester Pike
Upper Darby, PA 19082
Phones: (610)446-6600 (610)528-5885
Free: (800)346-4620 Fax: (215)449-7010
E-mail: info@instrumentation.com
URL: http://www.instrumentation.com
Products: Pressure and temperature instruments. SIC: 5049 (Professional Equipment Nec). Est: 1950. Sales: $4,100,000 (2000). Emp: 14. Officers: Michael R. Murray, e-mail: mmurray@instrumentation.com; Christina Murray.

■ 24381 ■ K & R Instruments Inc.
4315-B SW 34th St.
Orlando, FL 32811-6419
Phone: (407)859-7740 Fax: (407)855-3560
Products: Pedometers. SIC: 5049 (Professional Equipment Nec). Sales: $4,800,000 (2000). Emp: 49. Officers: H. Werner Korten.

■ 24382 ■ Kanawha Scales and Systems
Rte. 1, Box 254A
Parkersburg, WV 26101
Phone: (304)344-5925 Fax: (304)464-5300
Products: Scales. SIC: 5046 (Commercial Equipment Nec). Sales: $7,000,000 (1990). Emp: 100. Officers: Jim Bradbury, President.

■ 24383 ■ Kitrick Management Company, Ltd.
175 Novner Dr.
PO Box 15523
Cincinnati, OH 45215
Phone: (513)782-2930 Fax: (513)782-2936
E-mail: bachb@aol.com
Products: Biomedical equipment and supplies; Chemicals; Books; Industrial air control clutches; Aluminum extrusions; Leather laces; Air pollution testing equipment; Gas Diffusers for wastewater and water treatment. SICs: 5047 (Medical & Hospital Equipment); 5169 (Chemicals & Allied Products Nec); 5049 (Professional Equipment Nec); 5192 (Books, Periodicals & Newspapers). Est: 1964. Sales: $1,000,000 (2000). Emp: 8. Officers: Howard Johnson, Export Dept. Mgr.; Bernard F. Kitrick, General Mgr.; Betty J. Kitrick, Sales Mgr.; Anne-Marie Nightingale.

■ 24384 ■ R.S. Knapp Company Inc.
PO Box 234
Lyndhurst, NJ 07071
Phone: (201)438-1500 Fax: (201)438-5852
E-mail: sales@napconet.com
URL: http://www.napconet.com
Products: Engineering copiers, plotters, and related supplies. SIC: 5045 (Computers, Peripherals & Software). Est: 1946. Sales: $17,000,000 (2000). Emp: 100. Officers: James O'Keefe, President; Dianne Murray, Accounting Manager.

■ 24385 ■ KOBOLD Instruments Inc.
1801 Parkway View Dr.
Pittsburgh, PA 15205
Phone: (412)788-2830
Free: (800)998-1020 Fax: (412)788-4890
E-mail: info@koboldusa.com
URL: http://www.koboldusa.com
Products: Meters, switches, and transmitters for flow, pressure, level and temperature measurement and control. SIC: 5063 (Electrical Apparatus & Equipment). Est: 1990. Sales: $5,000,000 (2000). Emp: 24.

■ 24386 ■ Laser Resale Inc.
54 Balcom Rd.
Sudbury, MA 01776
Phone: (978)443-8484 Fax: (978)443-7620
E-mail: laseresale@aol.com
URL: http://www.laserresale.com
Products: Industrial, scientific, and light-show lasers. SICs: 5049 (Professional Equipment Nec); 5084 (Industrial Machinery & Equipment). Est: 1984. Sales: $2,500,000 (2000). Emp: 4. Officers: Tom Van Duyne, President; David J. Jacobson.

■ 24387 ■ Leica Inc.
111 Deer Lake Rd.
Deerfield, IL 60015
Phone: (847)405-0123 Fax: (847)405-0147
Products: Microscopes; Optical instruments and lenses. SIC: 5047 (Medical & Hospital Equipment). Sales: $76,000,000 (2000). Emp: 264. Officers: Henry B. Smith III, President; Al Szklany, Controller; Larry Bruder, VP of Marketing; Chuck Bolton, VP of Human Resources.

■ 24388 ■ Lesman Instrument Co.
215 Wrightwood Ave.
Elmhurst, IL 60126
Phone: (630)834-2200
Free: (800)953-7626 Fax: (630)834-2386
E-mail: sales@lesman.com
URL: http://www.lesman.com
SICs: 5049 (Professional Equipment Nec); 5084 (Industrial Machinery & Equipment). Est: 1962. Emp: 36.

■ 24389 ■ Lewiston Rubber and Supply Inc.
PO Box 139
Lewiston, ME 04240-0139
Phone: (207)784-6985 Fax: (207)786-3961
Products: specialty equipment and products. SIC: 5049 (Professional Equipment Nec).

■ 24390 ■ M & E Sales - A Honeywell Business
3303 Chestnut Ave.
Baltimore, MD 21211
Phone: (410)889-2070 Fax: (410)889-2106
E-mail: info@mesales.com
URL: http://www.mesales.com
Products: Temperature controls. SIC: 5075 (Warm Air Heating & Air-Conditioning). Est: 1932. Sales: $10,000,000,000 (2000). Emp: 57,000. Officers: James Husband, President; Ron Mitchem, General Mgr. Former Name: Machinery and Equipment Sales, Inc.

■ 24391 ■ MacAlaster Bicknell Company Inc.
181 Henry St.
New Haven, CT 06510
Phone: (203)624-4191
Free: (800)468-6226 Fax: (203)624-6308
E-mail: mbcoct@mbcoct.com
URL: http://www.mbcoct.com
Products: Laboratory supplies. SIC: 5049 (Professional Equipment Nec). Est: 1932. Sales: $6,000,000 (2000). Emp: 23. Officers: John M. Bee Jr. Jr., President & Treasurer.

■ 24392 ■ Macalaster Bicknell Company of NJ, Inc.
Depot & North Sts.
PO Box 109
Millville, NJ 08332
Phone: (856)825-3222
Free: (800)257-8405 Fax: (856)825-3375
E-mail: macbicnj@eticomm.net
URL: http://www.macbicnj.com
Products: Glass tubing and rod, lab supplies, chemicals and equipment. SIC: 5049 (Professional Equipment Nec). Est: 1950. Sales: $3,500,000 (2000). Emp: 9. Officers: Karen Barsuglia, President; Kathleen Greenfield, Treasurer & Secty.

■ 24393 ■ **Mager Scientific Inc.**
1100 Baker Rd.
PO Box 160
Dexter, MI 48130
Phone: (734)426-3885 **Fax:** (734)426-3987
E-mail: sales@magersci.com
URL: http://www.magersci.com
Products: Microscopes; Instruments and supplies for material science and metallurgy. **SICs:** 5049 (Professional Equipment Nec); 5047 (Medical & Hospital Equipment). **Est:** 1961.

■ 24394 ■ **Martin Instrument Co. (Burnsville, Minnesota)**
11965 12th Ave. S
Burnsville, MN 55337-1404
Phone: (952)882-8222 **Fax:** (952)882-8223
E-mail: sales@martininstrument.com
URL: http://www.martininstrument.com
Products: Inspection gauging, industrial tools and equipment. **SIC:** 5084 (Industrial Machinery & Equipment). **Est:** 1980. **Sales:** $3,500,000 (2000). **Emp:** 25. **Officers:** William R. Martin, CEO & President.

■ 24395 ■ **McBain Instruments**
9601 Variel Ave.
Chatsworth, CA 91311
Phone: (818)998-2702
Products: Microscopes. **SIC:** 5047 (Medical & Hospital Equipment).

■ 24396 ■ **McCauley's Reprographics, Inc.**
721 Gaffney Rd.
Fairbanks, AK 99701
Phone: (907)452-8141 **Fax:** (907)456-5170
Products: Engineering and architectural supplies. **SIC:** 5049 (Professional Equipment Nec).

■ 24397 ■ **Miller Mechanical Specialties**
PO Box 1613
Des Moines, IA 50306
Phone: (515)243-4287 **Fax:** (515)243-7313
Products: Control valves; Meters; Regulators; Pipe motion equipment. **SICs:** 5084 (Industrial Machinery & Equipment); 5049 (Professional Equipment Nec).

■ 24398 ■ **Mississippi Tool Supply Co.**
Hwy. 25 S
Golden, MS 38847
Phone: (601)454-9245
Free: (800)647-8168 **Fax:** (601)454-9385
Products: Security and safety equipment. **SIC:** 5049 (Professional Equipment Nec). **Sales:** $4,000,000 (2000). **Emp:** 54.

■ 24399 ■ **Mitcham Industries Inc.**
PO Box 1175
Huntsville, TX 77342
Phone: (409)291-2277 **Fax:** (409)295-1922
Products: Geometric instruments. **SIC:** 5084 (Industrial Machinery & Equipment). **Sales:** $5,000,000 (1994). **Emp:** 10. **Officers:** Billy F. Mitcham Jr., CEO, President & Chairman of the Board; Roberto Rios, VP of Finance.

■ 24400 ■ **Mitutoyo/MTI Corp.**
965 Corporate Blvd.
Aurora, IL 60504
Phone: (630)978-5385 **Fax:** (630)820-7403
Products: Precision measuring devices. **SIC:** 5049 (Professional Equipment Nec). **Est:** 1963. **Sales:** $100,000,000 (2000). **Emp:** 402. **Officers:** K. Nakanishi, President; A. Morishita; M. Nonaka, Dir. of Marketing and Advertising; Noel Ryan, Exec. VP.

■ 24401 ■ **MMC Metrology Lab Inc.**
4989 Cleveland St.
Virginia Beach, VA 23462
Phone: (804)456-2220 **Fax:** (804)473-2204
Products: Gauges and meters. **SIC:** 5065 (Electronic Parts & Equipment Nec). **Sales:** $3,000,000 (2000). **Emp:** 14. **Officers:** William Marcum, President.

■ 24402 ■ **Montana Scale Co. Inc.**
1207 13th Ave. E
Polson, MT 59860-3620
Phone: (406)883-4697 **Fax:** (406)883-9248
Products: Scales; Weighing equipment. **SICs:** 5046 (Commercial Equipment Nec); 5091 (Sporting & Recreational Goods). **Est:** 1937. **Sales:** $300,000 (2000). **Emp:** 2. **Officers:** Ed Clark, President. **Former Name:** Western Montana Scale Co. Inc.

■ 24403 ■ **Moonlight Products Inc.**
PMB 392
5663 Balboa Ave.
San Diego, CA 92111-2705
Phone: (619)625-0300 **Fax:** (619)625-0199
Products: Imaging products, including night vision lens devices. **SIC:** 5048 (Ophthalmic Goods). **Sales:** $20,000,000 (2000). **Emp:** 25. **Officers:** David W. Knight, President; Murray Palmer, Controller.

■ 24404 ■ **Mosier Fluid Power of Indiana Inc.**
9851 Park Davis Dr.
Indianapolis, IN 46236-2393
Phone: (317)895-6200
Products: Timing mechanisms; Counting devices; Electronic systems and equipment. **SICs:** 5049 (Professional Equipment Nec); 5065 (Electronic Parts & Equipment Nec). **Sales:** $7,000,000 (2000). **Emp:** 30. **Officers:** Mike South, President.

■ 24405 ■ **MTI Corp.**
965 Corporate Blvd.
Aurora, IL 60504
Phone: (630)978-5390 **Fax:** (630)820-7403
Products: Precision measuring equipment. **SIC:** 5049 (Professional Equipment Nec). **Sales:** $170,000,000 (2000). **Emp:** 300. **Officers:** K. Nakanishi, President; A. Morishita, VP of Finance.

■ 24406 ■ **Myron L Co.**
6115 Corte del Cedro
Carlsbad, 24895, 92009-1516
Phone: (760)438-2021 **Fax:** (760)931-9189
URL: http://www.myron1.com
Products: Water quality test instruments. **SIC:** 5049 (Professional Equipment Nec). **Est:** 1957. **Emp:** 59. **Officers:** Carol Solinger, VP of Marketing, e-mail: csolinger@myron1.com; Dan Trybulski, Customer Service Contact, e-mail: dtrybulski@myron1.com.

■ 24407 ■ **N Squared Inc.**
4003D Green Briar Dr.
Stafford, TX 77477
Phone: (281)240-3322
Free: (800)966-3636 **Fax:** (281)240-3344
Products: Graphics supplies, including paper, films, toners, and ink; Computer media and supplies, including CDs, tape, and optical disks. **SICs:** 5049 (Professional Equipment Nec); 5199 (Nondurable Goods Nec). **Est:** 1978. **Sales:** $5,000,000 (2000). **Emp:** 12. **Officers:** David Norton, President; Terri Smith, Manager. **Doing Business As:** Spectrum Data Products.

■ 24408 ■ **Newcomb Company Inc. Newcomb Associates**
6438 University Dr.
Huntsville, AL 35806
Phone: (256)837-3233
Products: Analytical instruments and other related lab instruments. **SIC:** 5049 (Professional Equipment Nec).

■ 24409 ■ **Northeast Engineering Inc.**
124 Trumbull Rd.
Manhasset, NY 11030
Phone: (516)365-9633
Products: Measurement and control instrumentation. **SIC:** 5084 (Industrial Machinery & Equipment).

■ 24410 ■ **Northeast Scale Company Inc.**
2 Priscilla Ln.
Auburn, NH 03032-1739
Phone: (603)622-0080 **Fax:** (603)622-4561
Products: Commercial equipment; Scales. **SIC:** 5046 (Commercial Equipment Nec). **Officers:** Paul Parodi, President.

■ 24411 ■ **Nurnberg Thermometer Co.**
PO Box 590
Rockville Centre, NY 11571
Phone: (516)766-7619 **Fax:** (516)536-3225
Products: Scientific thermometers. **SICs:** 5047 (Medical & Hospital Equipment); 5047 (Medical & Hospital Equipment). **Est:** 1895. **Sales:** $5,000,000

(2000). **Emp:** 40. **Officers:** Jack Friedland, CEO; Philip Friedland, CFO.

■ 24412 ■ **Outdoor Outfitters of Wisconsin Inc.**
705 Elm St.
Waukesha, WI 53186
Phone: (414)542-7772 **Fax:** (414)542-4435
Products: Metal detectors. **SIC:** 5065 (Electronic Parts & Equipment Nec). **Est:** 1972. **Sales:** $2,400,000 (2000). **Emp:** 4. **Officers:** Gary Bischke, President.

■ 24413 ■ **Pacific Combustion Engineering Inc.**
5520 Alhambra Ave.
Los Angeles, CA 90032
Phone: (323)225-6191
Free: (800)342-4442 **Fax:** (323)225-1441
Products: Microscopes; Ovens; Furnaces. **SICs:** 5049 (Professional Equipment Nec); 5064 (Electrical Appliances—Television & Radio); 5075 (Warm Air Heating & Air-Conditioning). **Est:** 1950. **Sales:** $1,000,000 (2000). **Emp:** 10. **Officers:** Henry Posner, President.

■ 24414 ■ **Pacific Exports**
PO Box 3113
San Dimas, CA 91773
Phone: (949)599-4424 **Fax:** (949)599-8309
Products: Industrial soil moisture measuring equipment. **SICs:** 5084 (Industrial Machinery & Equipment); 5049 (Professional Equipment Nec). **Officers:** Karl J. Ruzicka, Managing Director.

■ 24415 ■ **Particle Measuring Systems Inc.**
5475 Airport Blvd.
Boulder, CO 80301-2339
Phone: (303)547-7300
Free: (800)238-1801 **Fax:** (303)449-6870
Products: Laser particle counters. **SIC:** 5049 (Professional Equipment Nec). **Sales:** $40,000,000 (2000). **Emp:** 232. **Officers:** Paul Kelly, President.

■ 24416 ■ **Perfect Measuring Tape Co.**
1116 Summit St.
Toledo, OH 43604
Phone: (419)243-6811 **Fax:** (419)243-8298
Products: Textile measurement systems. **SIC:** 5049 (Professional Equipment Nec). **Est:** 1912. **Emp:** 7. **Officers:** A. L. Bohnengez, President.

■ 24417 ■ **Perstorp Analytical Inc.**
12101 Tech Rd.
Silver Spring, MD 20904
Phone: (301)680-0001
Products: Analytical equipment; Farm seeds. **SICs:** 5049 (Professional Equipment Nec); 5153 (Grain & Field Beans). **Sales:** $10,000,000 (2000). **Emp:** 41. **Officers:** David Patteson, President.

■ 24418 ■ **Philips Electronic Instruments Co.**
85 McKee Dr.
Mahwah, NJ 07430
Phone: (201)529-3800 **Fax:** (201)529-2252
Products: Electrical microscopes; Analytical x-ray equipment. **SIC:** 5049 (Professional Equipment Nec). **Est:** 1933. **Sales:** $80,000,000 (2000). **Emp:** 400. **Officers:** William A. Enser, CEO & President.

■ 24419 ■ **Preiser Scientific**
94 Oliver St.
PO Box 1330
St. Albans, WV 25177-1330
Phone: (304)727-2902
Free: (800)624-8285 **Fax:** (304)727-2932
Products: Laboratory supplies and equipment; Coal testing equipment. **SIC:** 5049 (Professional Equipment Nec). **Est:** 1924. **Sales:** $8,000,000 (2000). **Emp:** 42. **Officers:** A.E. Preiser, President; J. Gatens, Vice President; G. Preiser, Secretary; J. Khuri, Human Resources Mgr.; Don Meddings, Customer Service Contact.

■ 24420 ■ **Priz Co.**
4032 Transport St.
Palo Alto, CA 94303
Phone: (650)493-8600 **Fax:** (650)493-8522
Products: Automatic controls for food and power

industries. **SICs:** 5084 (Industrial Machinery & Equipment); 5049 (Professional Equipment Nec).

■ **24421** ■ **Protein Databases Inc.**
405 Oakwood Rd.
Huntington Station, NY 11746
Phone: (516)673-3939
Products: Densitometers. **SIC:** 5049 (Professional Equipment Nec). **Sales:** $2,700,000 (2000). **Emp:** 19. **Officers:** Stephen H. Blose, CEO & President; Alan P. Chodosh, VP of Finance.

■ **24422** ■ **Rawson and Company Inc.**
PO Box 924288
Houston, TX 77292-4288
Phone: (713)684-1400 **Fax:** (713)684-1407
Products: Instruments and control valves. **SIC:** 5065 (Electronic Parts & Equipment Nec). **Sales:** $50,000,000 (2000). **Emp:** 179. **Officers:** W. Earl Phillips, CEO & President; Micheal B. Parson, Controller.

■ **24423** ■ **Rocky Mountain Lasers and Instruments Inc.**
3975 E 56th Ave., Ste. A-1
Commerce City, CO 80022-3662
Phone: (303)898-5277 **Fax:** (303)298-0079
E-mail: rockymountainlasers@uswest.net
Products: Lasers; Surveying instruments. **SIC:** 5049 (Professional Equipment Nec). **Sales:** $1,000,000 (2000). **Emp:** 10. **Officers:** Brad Neeley, President.

■ **24424** ■ **Saber Enterprises Inc.**
9520 Padgett St., Ste. 216
San Diego, CA 92126-4452
Phone: (619)271-1523 **Fax:** (619)586-0529
Products: Physical measurement instrumentation. **SIC:** 5063 (Electrical Apparatus & Equipment). **Sales:** $10,000,000 (2000). **Emp:** 10. **Officers:** Robert E. Benn, CEO & President; Makihito Omata, CFO.

■ **24425** ■ **Sargent-Welch Scientific Co.**
911 Commerce Ct.
Buffalo Grove, IL 60089-2362
Phone: (708)459-6625 **Fax:** (708)459-6889
Products: Scientific supplies, including microscopes and lab coats. **SICs:** 5049 (Professional Equipment Nec); 5169 (Chemicals & Allied Products Nec). **Est:** 1852. **Sales:** $23,000,000 (2000). **Emp:** 85. **Officers:** Jerrold Harrold, CEO & President; Walter Sobon, CFO; Ben Crum, VP of Marketing.

■ **24426** ■ **Scantek Inc.**
916 Gist Ave.
Silver Spring, MD 20910
Phone: (301)495-7738 **Fax:** (301)495-7739
Products: Portable sound and vibration test and measurement instrumentation. **SIC:** 5065 (Electronic Parts & Equipment Nec). **Sales:** $1,000,000 (2000). **Emp:** 4. **Officers:** Svein Nordby, President.

■ **24427** ■ **Schenck Trebel Corp.**
535 Acorn St.
Deer Park, NY 11729
Phone: (631)242-4010
Free: (800)873-2352 **Fax:** (631)242-4147
E-mail: sales@schenck-usa.com
URL: http://www.schenck-usa.com
Products: Balancing machines. **SICs:** 5084 (Industrial Machinery & Equipment); 5049 (Professional Equipment Nec). **Est:** 1964. **Sales:** $10,000,000 (1999). **Emp:** 70. **Officers:** Bertram Dittmar, Exec. VP; Willi Burkert, Dir. of Sales; Ron Kapps, Dir. of Information Systems; Rich Idtensohn, Marketing Mgr.

■ **24428** ■ **Schleicher and Schuell Inc.**
10 Optical Ave.
Keene, NH 03431
Phone: (603)352-3810
Free: (800)245-4042 **Fax:** (603)357-3627
E-mail: techserv@s-and-s.com
URL: http://www.s-and-s.com
Products: Products for life science research; Diagnostic test kit components. **SIC:** 5049 (Professional Equipment Nec). **Est:** 1923. **Emp:** 110. **Officers:** David L. Bacon, President.

■ **24429** ■ **Scientific Equipment Co.**
15 Kent Rd.
Aston, PA 19014
Phone: (610)358-2855
Free: (800)770-7326 **Fax:** (610)558-1475
Products: Lab supplies, including glass flasks, breakers, and tubes; Lab furniture; Lab equipment and instrumentation; Chemicals. **SICs:** 5049 (Professional Equipment Nec); 5169 (Chemicals & Allied Products Nec). **Est:** 1933. **Sales:** $10,000,000 (2000). **Emp:** 25.

■ **24430** ■ **Selsi Company Inc.**
PO Box 10
Midland Park, NJ 07432-0010
Phone: (201)612-9200 **Fax:** (201)612-9548
E-mail: info@selsioptics.com
URL: http://www.selsioptics.com
Products: Binoculars; Magnifiers; Telescopes; Microscopes; Compasses; Opera and sport glasses; Magnets; Low vision products; and other optical products. **SICs:** 5049 (Professional Equipment Nec); 5048 (Ophthalmic Goods). **Emp:** 10. **Officers:** Walter Silbernagel Sr., CEO & President; Walter Silbernagel Jr., Treasurer.

■ **24431** ■ **Semi Systems Inc.**
7949 E Tacoma Dr., Ste. 101
Scottsdale, AZ 85260
Phone: (602)922-0040
Products: Wheel monitoring system. **SIC:** 5084 (Industrial Machinery & Equipment).

■ **24432** ■ **Sierra Scales**
539 Ideal Ct.
Reno, NV 89506-9604
Phone: (702)972-3760
Free: (800)SCALES-5 **Fax:** (702)972-3760
URL: http://www.sierrasc.nvbell.net
Products: Scales. **SIC:** 5046 (Commercial Equipment Nec). **Est:** 1981. **Sales:** $200,000 (2000). **Officers:** Tony Hart, Owner.

■ **24433** ■ **A and B Smith Co.**
PO Box 1776
Pittsburgh, PA 15230
Phone: (412)858-5400 **Fax:** (412)372-3734
Products: Art, engineering and drafting supplies. **SIC:** 5049 (Professional Equipment Nec). **Sales:** $2,000,000 (2000). **Emp:** 20. **Officers:** Stuart Smith, CEO; Alan Smith, CFO.

■ **24434** ■ **Sony Precision Technology**
20381 Hermana Cir.
Lake Forest, CA 92630
Phone: (949)770-8400 **Fax:** (949)770-8408
E-mail: marketing @sonypt.com
URL: http://www.sonyprecision.com
Products: Digital read-out systems. **SIC:** 5049 (Professional Equipment Nec). **Est:** 1969. **Emp:** 40. **Officers:** Larry Sato, President; Tak Tanaka, CFO; Jackie Rieck, e-mail: rieck@sonypt.com; Mike Avey, e-mail: avey@sonypt.com. **Former Name:** Sony Magnescale America Inc.

■ **24435** ■ **Guy Speaker Company, Inc.**
14620 Martin Dr.
Eden Prairie, MN 55344
Phone: (612)937-8705 **Fax:** (612)937-9726
Products: Thermometers and scaling equipment; Pressure regulators. **SICs:** 5049 (Professional Equipment Nec); 5084 (Industrial Machinery & Equipment).

■ **24436** ■ **Spectronic Instruments Inc.**
820 Linden Ave.
Rochester, NY 14625
Phone: (716)248-4000
Free: (800)654-9955 **Fax:** (716)248-4014
Products: Analytical and scientific instruments. **SIC:** 5049 (Professional Equipment Nec).

■ **24437** ■ **A.W. Sperry Instruments Inc.**
PO Box 9300
Smithtown, NY 11787
Phone: (631)231-7050
Free: (800)645-5398 **Fax:** (631)434-3128
E-mail: cat@awsperry.com
URL: http://www.awsperry.com
Products: Electrical and electronic testing equipment.

SIC: 5065 (Electronic Parts & Equipment Nec). **Est:** 1966. **Emp:** 50. **Officers:** F. Malawista, President; David Lay, Controller; D.W. Carroll, VP of Marketing; Sherry Mullins, Systems Mgr.; Fran D'Amore, Exec. Asst.

■ **24438** ■ **State Scale Co., Inc.**
155 Bemis Rd., RFD No. 12
Manchester, NH 03102
Phone: (603)625-8274
Free: (800)734-3747 **Fax:** (603)625-5387
Products: Retail and commercial scales. **SIC:** 5046 (Commercial Equipment Nec). **Officers:** Bruce Pratico, Owner.

■ **24439** ■ **Herman H. Sticht Company Inc.**
57 Front St.
Brooklyn, NY 11201-1038
Phone: (718)852-7602
Free: (800)221-3203 **Fax:** (718)852-7915
E-mail: stichtco@aol.com
URL: http://www.stichtco.thomasregister.com
Products: Speed measuring instruments, including speedometers; Electrical products. **SICs:** 5063 (Electrical Apparatus & Equipment); 5049 (Professional Equipment Nec). **Est:** 1917. **Sales:** $2,500,000 (2000). **Emp:** 12. **Officers:** Paul H. Plotkin, President.

■ **24440** ■ **Sun International**
3700 Hwy. 421 N
Wilmington, NC 28401
Phone: (910)762-0278
Free: (800)522-8425 **Fax:** 800-231-7861
E-mail: labrial@sun-intl.com
URL: http://www.sun-intl.com
Products: Scientific lab wear; Specialty glass. **SICs:** 5049 (Professional Equipment Nec); 5199 (Nondurable Goods Nec). **Est:** 1988. **Emp:** 60. **Officers:** Jane Fliesbach, Intl. Trade Specialist. **Former Name:** Sun International Trading Ltd.

■ **24441** ■ **S.W. Controls, Inc.**
9200 Market Place
Cleveland, OH 44147
Phone: (440)838-4444 **Fax:** (440)838-5852
Products: Process control equipment. **SICs:** 5049 (Professional Equipment Nec); 5084 (Industrial Machinery & Equipment).

■ **24442** ■ **Techmark Corporation**
PO Box 375
Cheshire, CT 06410
Phone: (203)272-3559 **Fax:** (203)272-2053
Products: Fluid meters; Measuring and controlling devices; Industrial valves; Process control instruments. **SICs:** 5049 (Professional Equipment Nec); 5084 (Industrial Machinery & Equipment); 5085 (Industrial Supplies). **Officers:** James Spacek Jr., VP of Marketing & International Sales.

■ **24443** ■ **Telogy Inc.**
3885 Bohannon Dr.
Menlo Park, CA 94025
Phone: (650)462-9000
Free: (800)835-6494 **Fax:** (650)462-5152
Products: General purpose testing equipment. **SIC:** 5065 (Electronic Parts & Equipment Nec). **Sales:** $141,000,000 (2000). **Emp:** 500. **Officers:** Anthony Schiavo, CEO & Chairman of the Board; Steve Jacobson, Sr. VP of Finance & Admin.

■ **24444** ■ **The Test Connection Inc.**
25 D Main St.
Reisterstown, MD 21136
Phone: (410)526-2800 **Fax:** (410)526-3547
E-mail: info@ttci.com
URL: http://www.ttci.com
Products: Printed circuit boards for test engineering. **SIC:** 5049 (Professional Equipment Nec). **Est:** 1980. **Sales:** $2,000,000 (2000). **Emp:** 15. **Officers:** Wilbert Horner, President.

■ **24445** ■ **Test Equipment Distributors**
1370 Piedmont
Troy, MI 48083
Phone: (734)524-1900 **Fax:** (313)689-3779
Products: Non-destructive testing equipment. **SIC:** 5049 (Professional Equipment Nec). **Sales:** $7,000,000

(2000). **Emp:** 30. **Officers:** Scott W. Thams, President; Kurt Andrews, CFO; David E. Ostergaard, Sales Mgr.

■ **24446** ■ **Thomas Scientific**
PO Box 99
Swedesboro, NJ 08085
Phone: (856)467-2000
Free: (800)345-2100 **Fax:** (856)467-3087
E-mail: value@thomassci.com
URL: http://www.thomassci.com
Products: Research and scientific equipment. **SICs:** 5049 (Professional Equipment Nec); 5169 (Chemicals & Allied Products Nec). **Est:** 1900. **Sales:** $76,000,000 (2000). **Emp:** 300. **Officers:** G. Wesner, President; E.L. Sudnick, CFO; E.J. Pierzynski, Vice President.

■ **24447** ■ **Timberline Instruments Inc.**
PO Box 20356
Boulder, CO 80308
Phone: (303)440-8779 **Fax:** (303)440-8786
Products: Laboratory and analytical instruments. **SIC:** 5049 (Professional Equipment Nec).

■ **24448** ■ **Transit Services Inc.**
69 McAdenville Rd.
Belmont, NC 28012
Phone: (704)825-8146
Free: (800)848-9865 **Fax:** (704)825-4498
Products: Transit and cold-chain monitoring products. **SIC:** 5084 (Industrial Machinery & Equipment). **Sales:** $10,000,000 (2000). **Emp:** 100. **Officers:** James L. Cox, President; Trudy Marvin, Controller.

■ **24449** ■ **United Pacific Corp.**
245 Roosevelt Rd.
West Chicago, IL 60185
Phone: (630)231-6030 **Fax:** (630)231-2888
Products: Process control instruments; Automotive parts; Computer boards. **SICs:** 5049 (Professional Equipment Nec); 5045 (Computers, Peripherals & Software); 5013 (Motor Vehicle Supplies & New Parts). **Officers:** Harold C. Wu, President.

■ **24450** ■ **United Scale and Engr. Corp.**
1322 Russett Ct.
Green Bay, WI 54313
Phone: (414)434-2737
Free: (800)236-2737 **Fax:** (414)434-9605
Products: Truck, mill, and grain scales; Laboratory balances; Industrial scales and weighing systems. **SICs:** 5046 (Commercial Equipment Nec); 5049 (Professional Equipment Nec). **Est:** 1962. **Sales:** $5,000,000 (2000). **Emp:** 30. **Officers:** J.A. Trunec, President.

■ **24451** ■ **Vector Engineering Inc.**
12438 Loma Rica Dr., Ste. C
Grass Valley, CA 95945
Phone: (530)272-2448 **Fax:** (530)272-8533
E-mail: vector@vectoreng.com
URL: http://www.vectoreng.com
Products: Soil testing equipment. **SIC:** 5049 (Professional Equipment Nec). **Est:** 1986. **Sales:** $5,000,000 (2000). **Emp:** 80. **Officers:** Scott Purdy, President; Vince Suryasasmita, Exec. VP.

■ **24452** ■ **Vermont Optechs**
PO Box 69
Charlotte, VT 05445-0069
Phone: (802)425-2040 **Fax:** (802)425-2074
Products: Microscopes. **SIC:** 5049 (Professional

Equipment Nec). **Est:** 1986. **Emp:** 1. **Officers:** John Oren, Owner.

■ **24453** ■ **VWR Scientific Products**
3745 Bayshore Blvd.
Brisbane, CA 94005
Phone: (415)468-7150
Products: Laboratory and scientific equipment. **SIC:** 5049 (Professional Equipment Nec). **Sales:** $1,244,700,000 (2000). **Emp:** 2,097. **Officers:** Gerrold Harris, President; David M. Bronson, Sr. VP & CFO.

■ **24454** ■ **VWR Scientific Products Corp.**
1310 Goshen Pkwy.
West Chester, PA 19380
Phone: (610)431-1700
Free: (800)932-5000 **Fax:** (610)429-9340
E-mail: solutions@vwrsp.com
URL: http://www.vwrsp.com
Products: Scientific supplies, including microscopes, beakers, test tubes, chemicals, and laboratory equipment. **SICs:** 5049 (Professional Equipment Nec); 5169 (Chemicals & Allied Products Nec). **Est:** 1853. **Sales:** $1,349,000,000 (2000). **Emp:** 3,024. **Officers:** Paul Nowak, President & CEO; Pete Forrest, Exec. VP; Hal Nichter, Exec. VP; John Griffith, Sr. VP of Finance & CFO; Matt Malenfant, Sr. VP of Marketing & Sales; Kevin Leak, VP of Marketing.

■ **24455** ■ **Webster Scale Inc.**
PO Box 127
Webster, SD 57274-0127
Phone: (605)345-3881 **Fax:** (605)345-3405
Products: Commercial equipment; Scales, except laboratory. **SIC:** 5046 (Commercial Equipment Nec). **Officers:** Roger Shoemaker, President.

■ **24456** ■ **Westberg Manufacturing Inc.**
3400 Westach Way
Sonoma, CA 95476
Phone: (707)938-2121
Free: (800)400-7024 **Fax:** (707)938-4968
E-mail: westach@juno.com
URL: http://www.westach.com
Products: Electric tachometers and engine instruments. **SICs:** 5049 (Professional Equipment Nec); 5084 (Industrial Machinery & Equipment). **Est:** 1944. **Sales:** $1,500,000 (2000). **Emp:** 20. **Officers:** G.L. Westberg, President; R.R. Westberg, VP of Sales.

■ **24457** ■ **Wilkens-Anderson Co.**
4525 W Division St.
Chicago, IL 60651
Phone: (773)384-4433
Free: (800)847-2222 **Fax:** (773)384-6260
Products: Laboratory instruments and supplies. **SIC:** 5049 (Professional Equipment Nec). **Sales:** $7,000,000 (1999). **Emp:** 26. **Officers:** Bruce Wilkens, President; Tad Rock, Controller.

■ **24458** ■ **X-Ray Industrial Distributor Corp.**
338 Delawanna Ave.
Clifton, NJ 07014
Phone: (201)773-9400 **Fax:** (201)773-1864
Products: Metal detectors; Explosives detectors. **SICs:** 5047 (Medical & Hospital Equipment); 5065 (Electronic Parts & Equipment Nec). **Est:** 1960. **Sales:** $1,000,000 (2000). **Emp:** 4. **Officers:** Philip Cogan, President; Maria Malaszuk, Office Mgr.

■ **24459** ■ **Yamato Corp.**
PO Box 15070
Colorado Springs, CO 80935-5070
Phone: (719)591-1500
Free: (800)538-1762 **Fax:** (719)591-1045
E-mail: scales@yamatocorp.com
URL: http://www.yamatocorp.com
Products: Scales and balances. **SIC:** 5046 (Commercial Equipment Nec). **Est:** 1993. **Sales:** $8,500,000 (2000). **Emp:** 25. **Officers:** Shozo Kawanishi, CEO; Mr. Irahara, President; Liliane Okamoto, Office Mgr.

■ **24460** ■ **Z-Weigh Inc.**
26469 Northline Rd.
Taylor, MI 48180-4479
Phone: (313)846-2550
Free: (800)252-9712 **Fax:** (313)846-3932
Products: Scales. **SIC:** 5084 (Industrial Machinery & Equipment). **Est:** 1979. **Sales:** $7,000,000 (2000). **Emp:** 23. **Officers:** - James A. Bradbury, CEO & President.

■ **24461** ■ **Carl Zeiss Inc.**
1 Zeiss Dr.
Thornwood, NY 10594
Phone: (914)747-1800
Free: (800)442-4020 **Fax:** (914)682-8296
Products: Medical microscopes. **SICs:** 5049 (Professional Equipment Nec); 5047 (Medical & Hospital Equipment); 5084 (Industrial Machinery & Equipment); 5048 (Ophthalmic Goods). **Est:** 1925. **Sales:** $300,000,000 (2000). **Emp:** 350. **Officers:** Thomas J. Miller, President; Wolfgang Senne, CFO; James Bucher, Dir. of Marketing & Sales; John Tiglias, VP of Operations; Larry Hart, VP of Planning.

■ **24462** ■ **Zeuschel Equipment Co.**
2717 Breckenridge
St. Louis, MO 63144
Products: Industrial instrumentation, including gauges, fittings, valves, controllers, and pumps. **SICs:** 5049 (Professional Equipment Nec); 5084 (Industrial Machinery & Equipment).

■ **24463** ■ **Zeuschel Equipment Co.**
7824 Barton
Lenexa, KS 66214
Phone: (913)631-4747 **Fax:** (913)631-1454
Products: Industrial instrumentation, including gauges, fittings, valves, controllers, and pumps. **SICs:** 5049 (Professional Equipment Nec); 5084 (Industrial Machinery & Equipment).

■ **24464** ■ **Zeuschel Equipment Co.**
2717 Breckenridge Industrial Ct.
St. Louis, MO 63144
Phone: (314)645-5003 **Fax:** (314)645-8833
Products: Industrial controls. **SICs:** 5049 (Professional Equipment Nec); 5084 (Industrial Machinery & Equipment).

■ **24465** ■ **Zonic A and D Co.**
50 W TechneCenter Dr.
Milford, OH 45150
Phone: (513)248-1911 **Fax:** (513)248-1589
Products: Computerized test equipment. **SIC:** 5065 (Electronic Parts & Equipment Nec). **Est:** 1988. **Sales:** $2,800,000 (2000). **Emp:** 12. **Officers:** Gerald J. Zobrist, CEO; Cliff Reed, CFO; William J. Ashton, General Mgr.

(50) Security and Safety Equipment

Entries in this section are arranged alphabetically by company name. When the company name is a personal name, the company name is alphabetized by the surname unless the first name or initial(s) are part of a trade name. See the User's Guide at the front of this directory for additional information.

■ **24466** ■ **AAA Fire & Safety Inc.**
3013 3rd Ave. N
Seattle, WA 98109-1602
Phone: (206)284-1721 **Fax:** (206)284-1769
Products: Fire extinguishers. **SIC:** 5099 (Durable Goods Nec). **Sales:** $3,000,000 (2000). **Emp:** 40.
Officers: Brian Krinbring.

■ **24467** ■ **Abatix Environmental Corp.**
8311 Eastpoint Dr., Ste. 400
Dallas, TX 75227
Phone: (214)381-1146 **Fax:** (214)381-9513
Products: Industrial safety products. **SICs:** 5084 (Industrial Machinery & Equipment); 5085 (Industrial Supplies). **Est:** 1983. **Sales:** $33,100,000 (2000).
Emp: 83. **Officers:** Terry W. Shaver, CEO & President; Frank J. Cinatl IV, VP & CFO; Gary L. Cox, VP, CFO & Chief Acct. Officer.

■ **24468** ■ **ADEMCO/ADI**
5300 D. Fulton Industrial Blvd.
Atlanta, GA 30336
Phone: (404)346-7800 **Fax:** (404)346-3740
Products: Security equipment; Sound systems; Vacuum systems. **SICs:** 5063 (Electrical Apparatus & Equipment); 5087 (Service Establishment Equipment).

■ **24469** ■ **ADEMCO/ADI**
5300 Old Pineville Rd., Ste. 152
Charlotte, NC 28217
Phone: (704)525-8899
Free: (800)438-1107 **Fax:** (704)523-2078
Products: Security devices. **SIC:** 5063 (Electrical Apparatus & Equipment).

■ **24470** ■ **ADEMCO/ADI**
1801 Shelby Oaks Dr. N, Ste. 16
Memphis, TN 38134
Phone: (901)377-0033
Free: (800)233-6261 **Fax:** (901)377-0095
URL: http://www.adilink.com
Products: Security products; including alarms; Voice and data cabling solutions. **SIC:** 5063 (Electrical Apparatus & Equipment). **Est:** 1985. **Emp:** 1,000.

■ **24471** ■ **ADEMCO/ADI**
Beacon Centre, Bldg. 10
1910 NW 84th Ave.
Miami, FL 33126
Phone: (305)477-5504 **Fax:** (305)477-7120
Products: Alarms; Security products. **SIC:** 5063 (Electrical Apparatus & Equipment).

■ **24472** ■ **ADEMCO/ADI**
1410 Donelson Pike Ste. A3
Nashville, TN 37217
Phone: (615)361-5254 **Fax:** (615)361-5354
Products: Security systems and alarms. **SIC:** 5063 (Electrical Apparatus & Equipment).

■ **24473** ■ **ADEMCO/ADI**
7260 Radford Ave.
North Hollywood, CA 91605
Phone: (818)764-4202 **Fax:** (818)765-4005
Products: Security systems and alarms. **SIC:** 5063 (Electrical Apparatus & Equipment).

■ **24474** ■ **ADEMCO/ADI**
3140 N 35th Ave., Ste. 4 & 5
Phoenix, AZ 85017
Phone: (602)484-7484 **Fax:** (602)484-0836
Products: Security systems, alarms, intercoms, and fire alarms. **SIC:** 5063 (Electrical Apparatus & Equipment).

■ **24475** ■ **ADEMCO/ADI**
22121 17th Ave. SE, Ste. 103
Bothell, WA 98021
Phone: (425)485-3938 **Fax:** (425)488-0279
Products: Alarms; Security systems. **SIC:** 5063 (Electrical Apparatus & Equipment).

■ **24476** ■ **ADEMCO/ADI**
304 N Meridian Ave., Ste. 7
Oklahoma City, OK 73107
Phone: (405)946-2177
Free: (800)233-6261 **Fax:** (405)946-2179
Products: Alarm systems. **SIC:** 5063 (Electrical Apparatus & Equipment).

■ **24477** ■ **ADEMCO/ADI**
811 S Orlando Ave., Ste A
Winter Park, FL 32789
Phone: (407)740-5622
Free: (800)522-2390 **Fax:** (407)740-5942
Products: Security systems and alarms; Closed circuit television equipment. **SIC:** 5063 (Electrical Apparatus & Equipment).

■ **24478** ■ **ADEMCO/ADI**
2833 Banksville Rd.
Pittsburgh, PA 15216-2815
Phone: (412)928-0100
Free: (800)ADEMCO-1 **Fax:** (412)928-0123
Products: Security systems and alarms. **SIC:** 5063 (Electrical Apparatus & Equipment).

■ **24479** ■ **ADEMCO/ADI**
2755 NW 153RD Ave.
Beaverton, OR 97006-5365
Free: (800)644-5241
Products: Alarm systems and security systems. **SIC:** 5063 (Electrical Apparatus & Equipment).

■ **24480** ■ **ADEMCO/ADI**
235 Elm St.
Warwick, RI 02888
Phone: (401)781-2190
Products: Electronic security products. **SICs:** 5065 (Electronic Parts & Equipment Nec); 5063 (Electrical Apparatus & Equipment).

■ **24481** ■ **ADEMCO/ADI**
3902 Corporex Park Dr.
Tampa, FL 33619
Phone: (813)623-1269 **Fax:** (813)623-3590
Products: Alarms; Electronic supplies. **SIC:** 5063 (Electrical Apparatus & Equipment).

■ **24482** ■ **Ademco Distribution Inc.**
165 Eileen Way
Syosset, NY 11791
Phone: (516)921-6700
Products: Electric alarms and signaling equipment.
SIC: 5063 (Electrical Apparatus & Equipment).

■ **24483** ■ **ADI**
307 Cayuga Rd., Ste. 160
Buffalo, NY 14225
Phone: (716)631-2197 **Fax:** (716)631-9006
Products: Security equipment. **SIC:** 5063 (Electrical Apparatus & Equipment). **Also Known by This Acronym:** ADEMCO.

■ **24484** ■ **ADI**
13190 56th Ct., Ste. 401-404
Clearwater, FL 33760
Phone: (813)573-1166
Free: (800)233-6261 **Fax:** (813)572-0652
Products: Security systems; Sound equipment; Structured cable access control; Telephone systems; Fire control systems. **SICs:** 5063 (Electrical Apparatus & Equipment); 5065 (Electronic Parts & Equipment Nec).

■ **24485** ■ **ADI**
West Valley Business Center
7112 S 212th St.
Kent, WA 98032
Phone: (253)872-7128
Free: (800)233-6261 **Fax:** (253)872-7119
URL: http://www.adilink.com
Products: Alarm systems. **SIC:** 5063 (Electrical Apparatus & Equipment).

■ **24486** ■ **ADT Ltd.**
PO Box 5035
Boca Raton, FL 33431-0835
Phone: (561)988-3600 **Fax:** (561)241-1923
Products: Automobile security systems. **SIC:** 5012 (Automobiles & Other Motor Vehicles). **Est:** 1984.
Sales: $1,704,000,000 (2000). **Emp:** 16,000. **Officers:** Michael A. Ashcroft, CEO & Chairman of the Board; Stephen J. Ruzika, Exec. VP & CFO.

■ **24487** ■ **ADT Security Systems**
315 Hamilton St.
Worcester, MA 01604
Phone: (508)791-6265 **Fax:** (508)791-0407
Products: Alarm systems. **SIC:** 5063 (Electrical Apparatus & Equipment). **Est:** 1874. **Emp:** 49.
Officers: Jack Bollus, Manager, e-mail: jbollus@adt.com; Liss Cloutier, Sales/Marketing Contact, e-mail: lcloutier@adt.com.

■ **24488** ■ **ADT Security Systems**
2032 E Pleasant Valley Blvd.
Altoona, PA 16602
Phone: (814)946-4389 **Fax:** (814)942-6015
Products: Security systems for home and commercial use. **SIC:** 5063 (Electrical Apparatus & Equipment).
Emp: 49. **Officers:** R Terry.

■ **24489** ■ **ADT Security Systems**
231 Harbor Cir.
New Orleans, LA 70126-1103
Phone: (504)246-7800   **Fax:** (504)246-8996
Products: Alarm systems. **SIC:** 5063 (Electrical Apparatus & Equipment). **Emp:** 49.

■ **24490** ■ **ADT Security Systems, Mid-South Inc.**
5590 Lauby Rd. NW
North Canton, OH 44720
Phones: (330)497-5325   (216)526-0450
Fax: (330)494-3684
Products: Alarm systems. **SIC:** 5063 (Electrical Apparatus & Equipment). **Sales:** $10,000,000 (2000). **Emp:** 499. **Officers:** Barry P. Kinney.

■ **24491** ■ **Advance Glove & Safety Co.**
1008 Terminal Rd.
Lansing, MI 48906
Phone: (517)323-8400
Free: (800)322-4048   **Fax:** (517)323-7595
Products: Industrial safety equipment, including gloves and devices. **SICs:** 5085 (Industrial Supplies); 5047 (Medical & Hospital Equipment). **Est:** 1984. **Emp:** 18.

■ **24492** ■ **Advance Glove & Safety Co.**
3638 S Saginaw
Flint, MI 48503
Phone: (810)235-3000
Free: (800)323-1223   **Fax:** (810)235-3115
E-mail: agsco@juno.com
Products: Industrial safety equipment, including gloves and devices. **SIC:** 5085 (Industrial Supplies). **Est:** 1984. **Emp:** 16.

■ **24493** ■ **Advanced Federated Protection Inc.**
2108 Payne Ave., Ste. 714
Cleveland, OH 44114-4440
Phones: (216)696-8739   (216)696-6664
Fax: (216)696-5135
Products: Alarm systems, including medical alerts, card access, and closed circuit television. **SIC:** 5063 (Electrical Apparatus & Equipment). **Est:** 1984. **Emp:** 49. **Officers:** Al S. Lewis, General Mgr.

■ **24494** ■ **Advantor Corp.**
6101 Lake Ellenor Dr.
Orlando, FL 32809
Phone: (407)859-3350   **Fax:** 800-523-1921
E-mail: sales@advantor.com
URL: http://www.advantor.com
Products: Electronic security systems. **SIC:** 5063 (Electrical Apparatus & Equipment). **Est:** 1960. **Sales:** $37,000,000 (2000). **Emp:** 150. **Officers:** Harry S. Flemming, CEO; Chris Cobb, CFO.

■ **24495** ■ **AFA Protective Systems Inc.**
155 Michael Dr.
Syosset, NY 11791
Phone: (516)496-2322   **Fax:** (516)496-2848
Products: Alarm systems, including fire, burglar, home, and business. **SIC:** 5063 (Electrical Apparatus & Equipment). **Est:** 1873. **Sales:** $25,800,000 (2000). **Emp:** 270. **Officers:** Philip Kleinman, CEO, President & Chairman of the Board; Raymond S. Greenberger, Treasurer; Richard Kleinman, VP, CFO & Chief Acct. Officer.

■ **24496** ■ **Afy Security Distributros**
1548 Bristol Pke.
Bensalem, PA 19020
Phone: (215)638-3880
Products: Security equipment. **SIC:** 5046 (Commercial Equipment Nec).

■ **24497** ■ **AHM Security Inc.**
23 Orinda Way
Orinda, CA 94563-2520
Phone: (510)254-2566   **Fax:** (510)254-6752
Products: Security systems. **SIC:** 5063 (Electrical Apparatus & Equipment). **Emp:** 49.

■ **24498** ■ **Alarm Controls Corp.**
19 Brandywine Dr.
Deer Park, NY 11729-5721
Phone: (516)586-4220
Free: (800)645-5538   **Fax:** (516)586-6500
E-mail: info@alarmcontrols.com
URL: http://www.alarmcontrols.com
Products: Electronic security equipment. **SIC:** 5063 (Electrical Apparatus & Equipment). **Est:** 1971. **Emp:** 49. **Officers:** John Behedeito, Marketing & Sales Mgr.

■ **24499** ■ **Alarm-It Distributors Inc.**
1930 19th Avenue Dr. NE
Hickory, NC 28601
Phone: (828)328-2074
Products: Burglar alarm systems. **SIC:** 5046 (Commercial Equipment Nec).

■ **24500** ■ **Alarm Services Inc.**
204 N Magnolia St.
Albany, GA 31707-4223
Phone: (912)436-7000
Products: Alarm systems. **SIC:** 5063 (Electrical Apparatus & Equipment). **Emp:** 15. **Officers:** Ernest Smith.

■ **24501** ■ **Alaska Fire & Safety Equipment**
416 Shoreline Dr.
Thorne Bay, AK 99919
Phone: (907)828-3346
Products: Fire extinguishers; Smoke detectors. **SICs:** 5099 (Durable Goods Nec); 5063 (Electrical Apparatus & Equipment).

■ **24502** ■ **Alaska General Alarm Inc.**
405 W 27th Ave.
Anchorage, AK 99503-2612
Phone: (907)279-8511
Free: (800)770-8511   **Fax:** (907)279-9319
URL: http://www.27alarm.com
Products: Alarm systems; Video systems. **SIC:** 5063 (Electrical Apparatus & Equipment). **Est:** 1953. **Sales:** $3,000,000 (2000). **Emp:** 49. **Officers:** James Wong; Mike Rink, Dir. of Marketing, e-mail: mrink@ 27alarm.com.

■ **24503** ■ **William B. Allen Supply Company, Inc.**
301 N Rampart
New Orleans, LA 70112-3015
Phone: (504)525-8222
Free: (800)535-9593   **Fax:** (504)525-6361
Products: Electronic systems and equipment; Alarm systems; Batteries; Video surveillance equipment. **SICs:** 5065 (Electronic Parts & Equipment Nec); 5063 (Electrical Apparatus & Equipment). **Est:** 1940. **Emp:** 50. **Officers:** Joe Labadie, Vice President.

■ **24504** ■ **Ally Industries Inc.**
30-A Progress Ave.
Seymour, CT 06483
Phone: (203)366-5410   **Fax:** (203)368-4834
Products: Industrial safety equipment. **SICs:** 5085 (Industrial Supplies); 5049 (Professional Equipment Nec). **Est:** 1974. **Sales:** $7,000,000 (2000). **Emp:** 18. **Officers:** James Bebrin, President; Ron Brauer, Controller; Charles Hoxley, Dir. of Marketing & Sales.

■ **24505** ■ **American Convenience Inc.**
5625 N Academy Blvd.
Colorado Springs, CO 80918-3658
Phone: (719)548-9500   **Fax:** (719)548-9533
Products: Alarm systems. **SIC:** 5063 (Electrical Apparatus & Equipment). **Officers:** Craig Ward, President.

■ **24506** ■ **American Lock and Supply Company Inc.**
PO Box 8500
Van Nuys, CA 91409-8500
Phone: (714)996-8882   **Fax:** (714)579-6625
Products: Security devices and related hardware. **SIC:** 5072 (Hardware). **Sales:** $85,000,000 (1993). **Emp:** 261. **Officers:** Sean DeForrest, President.

■ **24507** ■ **Arctic Fire Equipment**
702 30th Ave.
Fairbanks, AK 99701
Phone: (907)452-7806   **Fax:** (907)452-7876
Products: Fire safety equipment; First aid equipment. **SICs:** 5099 (Durable Goods Nec); 5047 (Medical & Hospital Equipment).

■ **24508** ■ **Armstrong's Lock & Supply, Inc.**
1440 Dutch Valley Pl. NE
Atlanta, GA 30324-5302
Phone: (404)875-0136
Free: (800)726-3332   **Fax:** 800-998-1733
Products: Lock supplies. **SIC:** 5072 (Hardware). **Sales:** $11,000,000 (2000). **Emp:** 56. **Officers:** Virl Mullins.

■ **24509** ■ **Artesia Fire Equipment Inc.**
PO Box 1367
Artesia, NM 88211-1367
Phone: (505)746-6111
Free: (800)748-2076   **Fax:** (505)748-1128
Products: Service establishment equipment; Firefighting equipment. **SIC:** 5087 (Service Establishment Equipment). **Officers:** Steve Davis, President.

■ **24510** ■ **Autco**
10900 Midwest
St. Louis, MO 63132-1631
Phone: (314)426-6524   **Fax:** (314)426-7378
Products: Electronics, including automotive radios and alarms. **SICs:** 5065 (Electronic Parts & Equipment Nec); 5063 (Electrical Apparatus & Equipment); 5013 (Motor Vehicle Supplies & New Parts). **Est:** 1970. **Emp:** 80. **Officers:** M. F. Hennessey; Bruce S. Dole.

■ **24511** ■ **Barco Municipal Products Inc.**
PO Box 45507
Omaha, NE 68145-0507
Phone: (402)334-8000   **Fax:** (402)334-8002
Products: Industrial personal safety devices, including first aid kits and masks; Traffic signs, signposts, and paints. **SICs:** 5039 (Construction Materials Nec); 5047 (Medical & Hospital Equipment); 5099 (Durable Goods Nec). **Officers:** Edward Jukes, President.

■ **24512** ■ **D.D. Bean and Sons Co.**
PO Box 348
207 Peterborough St.
Jaffrey, NH 03452
Phone: (603)532-8311
Free: (800)326-8311   **Fax:** (603)532-6001
E-mail: support@ddbean.com
URL: http://www.ddbean.com
Products: Matches. **SIC:** 5087 (Service Establishment Equipment). **Est:** 1938. **Sales:** $30,000,000 (1999). **Emp:** 250. **Officers:** Delcie D. Bean, Chairman of the Board; Mark C. Bean, President; Peter Leach, VP of Marketing & Sales; Julia Bartlett, VP of Distribution Center; Susan Peterson, Human Resources; Terry Fecto, Sales/Marketing Contact, e-mail: tfecto@ ddbean.com; Kane Lane, Customer Service Contact, e-mail: k_lane@ddbean.com; Susan Peterson, Human Resources Contact, e-mail: speterson@ddbean.com.

■ **24513** ■ **Best Locking Systems of Georgia Inc.**
1901 Montreal Rd., Ste. 122
Tucker, GA 30084
Phone: (770)491-3101   **Fax:** (770)491-7445
Products: Locks and related materials; Electronic systems and equipment. **SICs:** 5072 (Hardware); 5063 (Electrical Apparatus & Equipment). **Est:** 1976. **Sales:** $4,500,000 (2000). **Emp:** 26. **Officers:** Robert Powell, President.

■ **24514** ■ **Best Locking Systems of Wisconsin Inc.**
N45 W33490 Wisconsin Ave.
Nashotah, WI 53058
Phone: (414)367-8316   **Fax:** (414)367-2898
Products: Security systems and locks. **SICs:** 5072 (Hardware); 5063 (Electrical Apparatus & Equipment). **Est:** 1984. **Sales:** $1,000,000 (2000). **Emp:** 18. **Officers:** Rod Barnett, President.

■ 24515 ■ **Bestex Company Inc.**
3368 San Fernando Rd., Unit 110
Los Angeles, CA 90065
Phone: (323)255-4477 **Fax:** (323)255-4542
E-mail: sales@bestexcompany.com
URL: http://www.bestexcompany.com
Products: Stun guns; Flashlights; Walking alarms;
Backpacks. **SICs:** 5063 (Electrical Apparatus &
Equipment); 5091 (Sporting & Recreational Goods).
Est: 1981. **Emp:** 6.

■ 24516 ■ **M.C. Blais Enterprises**
RR 1 Box 19
Mt. Holly, VT 05758-9703
Phone: (802)259-2213 **Fax:** (802)259-9309
Products: Security equipment. **SIC:** 5087 (Service
Establishment Equipment). **Officers:** Michael Blais,
Owner.

■ 24517 ■ **Bobs Fire Extinguisher**
1033 N Polk Ext.
Moscow, ID 83843-9271
Phone: (208)882-3693
Products: Fire extinguishers. **SIC:** 5099 (Durable
Goods Nec). **Officers:** Robert Mc Gahan, Owner.

■ 24518 ■ **Bozeman Safe & Lock**
2304F N 7th Ave.
Bozeman, MT 59715
Phone: (406)587-8911 **Fax:** (406)587-9120
Products: Alarm systems; Hardware; Vaults and
safes. **SICs:** 5063 (Electrical Apparatus & Equipment);
5072 (Hardware). **Officers:** Casey Camper, Owner.

■ 24519 ■ **Broward Fire Equipment and
Service Inc.**
101 SW 6th St.
Ft. Lauderdale, FL 33301
Phone: (954)467-6625 **Fax:** (954)463-9750
Products: Fire extinguishers and safety supplies,
including smoke alarms. **SIC:** 5099 (Durable Goods
Nec). **Est:** 1950. **Sales:** $1,500,000 (2000). **Emp:** 17.
Officers: John A. Gioseffi, President & CFO.

■ 24520 ■ **Buckeye Fire Equipment Co. Sales
Div.**
110 Kings Rd.
Kings Mountain, NC 28086
Phone: (704)739-7415 **Fax:** (704)739-7418
Products: Fire equipment. **SIC:** 5099 (Durable
Goods Nec). **Est:** 1969. **Sales:** $20,000,000 (1999).
Emp: 190. **Officers:** Tom Bower, President; Bill
Cowley, CFO; Bryan Bower, Vice President; Kevin
Bower, Vice President.

■ 24521 ■ **Bushwacker Inc.**
9200 N Decatur
Portland, OR 97203-2819
Phone: (503)283-4335
Free: (800)234-8920 **Fax:** (503)283-3007
Products: Safety products. **SIC:** 5047 (Medical &
Hospital Equipment). **Emp:** 49. **Officers:** Jerry Logan.

■ 24522 ■ **C & S Specialty Inc.**
1181 Old Smithfield Rd.
North Smithfield, RI 02896
Phone: (401)769-2260 **Fax:** (401)769-2270
Products: Service industry machinery; Firefighting
equipment. **SIC:** 5087 (Service Establishment
Equipment). **Officers:** Henry Heroux, President.

■ 24523 ■ **Calolympic Glove and Safety Co.
Inc.**
PO Box 2323
Riverside, CA 92516-2323
Phone: (909)369-0165
Free: (800)421-6630 **Fax:** (909)369-0950
E-mail: calo@caloly-safety.com
URL: http://www.caloly-safety.com
Products: Safety products, including protective
clothing, gloves, eye and ear protection, and first aid
kits. **SICs:** 5085 (Industrial Supplies); 5136
(Men's/Boys' Clothing); 5137 (Women's/Children's
Clothing); 5099 (Durable Goods Nec). **Est:** 1958.
Sales: $10,200,000 (2000). **Emp:** 30. **Officers:** Dale
Bermond, President.

■ 24524 ■ **Carey Machinery & Supply Co.**
9108 Yellow Brick Rd., No. B
Baltimore, MD 21237-4701
Phone: (410)485-2323 **Fax:** (410)488-2914
Products: Safety products, compressors, and wheels.
SICs: 5085 (Industrial Supplies); 5084 (Industrial
Machinery & Equipment); 5047 (Medical & Hospital
Equipment). **Est:** 1870. **Sales:** $6,500,000 (2000).
Emp: 29. **Officers:** David M. Kelly.

■ 24525 ■ **Carolina FireMasters Inc.**
PO Box 1116
Bennettsville, SC 29512
Phone: (803)479-3871
Products: Fire trucks and equipment. **SICs:** 5087
(Service Establishment Equipment); 5012 (Automobiles
& Other Motor Vehicles). **Sales:** $4,000,000 (2000).
Emp: 30. **Officers:** Julian Drake, President.

■ 24526 ■ **Chubb Security Systems Inc.**
903 N Bowser, No. 250
Richardson, TX 75081
Phone: (972)690-4691 **Fax:** (972)644-1735
URL: http://www.chubbops.com
Products: Security systems. **SIC:** 5063 (Electrical
Apparatus & Equipment). **Emp:** 58. **Former Name:**
Racal-Chubb Security Systems Inc.

■ 24527 ■ **Conney Safety Products Co.**
3202 Latham Dr.
Madison, WI 53713-4614
Free: (800)356-9100 **Fax:** 800-845-9095
E-mail: safety@conney.com
URL: http://www.conney.com
Products: Safety and first aid products. **SICs:** 5047
(Medical & Hospital Equipment); 5122 (Drugs,
Proprietaries & Sundries). **Sales:** $50,000,000 (2000).
Emp: 150. **Officers:** Mike Stamn, President.

■ 24528 ■ **Corkey Control Systems Inc.**
846 Mahler Rd.
Burlingame, CA 94010-1604
Phone: (510)786-4241 **Fax:** (510)786-2090
Products: Locks and related materials. **SIC:** 5072
(Hardware).

■ 24529 ■ **L.N. Curtis and Sons**
1800 Peralta St.
Oakland, CA 94607
Phone: (510)839-5111 **Fax:** (510)839-5325
Products: Fire safety equipment. **SIC:** 5099 (Durable
Goods Nec). **Est:** 1929. **Sales:** $24,000,000 (2000).
Emp: 65. **Officers:** Paul F. Curtis, President; Larry
Shields, Dir. of Data Processing.

■ 24530 ■ **Custom Design Security & Sound**
33305 W 7 Mile
Livonia, MI 48152
Phone: (248)442-2233 **Fax:** (248)442-7140
Products: Security systems; Video surveillance
systems; Asset management systems. **SIC:** 5064
(Electrical Appliances—Television & Radio). **Officers:**
Dale Pacynski, President. **Former Name:** Navatron
Communications, Inc.

■ 24531 ■ **D/A Mid South Inc.**
9000 Jameel, No. 100
Houston, TX 77040
Phone: (713)895-0090
URL: http://www.damidsouth.com
Products: Security cameras; Access control
equipment. **SIC:** 5043 (Photographic Equipment &
Supplies). **Est:** 1982. **Sales:** $25,000,000 (2000).
Emp: 15. **Officers:** Richard J. Gunn, President, e-mail:
dgunn@damidsouth.com.

■ 24532 ■ **R.E. Davison Co.**
170 Green St.
Vergennes, VT 05491-8656
Phone: (802)877-3469 **Fax:** (802)877-3970
Products: Firefighting manuals and videos. **SIC:** 5087
(Service Establishment Equipment). **Est:** 1970. **Emp:**
1. **Officers:** Ray Davison, Owner.

■ 24533 ■ **DEI Inc.**
900 N Lehigh St.
Baltimore, MD 21205
Phone: (410)522-3700 **Fax:** (410)522-3728
Products: Commercial and residential alarms.s. **SICs:**

5065 (Electronic Parts & Equipment Nec); 5063
(Electrical Apparatus & Equipment). **Est:** 1964. **Sales:**
$18,000,000 (2000). **Emp:** 64. **Officers:** Thomas Steg,
President.

■ 24534 ■ **Diamond Electronics, Inc.**
4445 Coonpath Rd.
Carroll, OH 43112
Phone: (740)756-9222
Free: (800)443-6680 **Fax:** (740)756-4237
Products: Closed camera security systems. **SIC:** 5063
(Electrical Apparatus & Equipment). **Est:** 1946. **Sales:**
$15,000,000 (2000). **Emp:** 95. **Officers:** Richard
Tompkins, Pres.; Jerry Zielinski, V.P., Manufacturing;
Gene McKenzie, V.P., Engineering; Norman Pritchard,
V.P., Mktg.; Perry Wolse, Nat. Sales Mgr.

■ 24535 ■ **Electronic Security Integration, Inc.**
68-46 Selfridge St.
Forest Hills, NY 11375
Phone: (718)575-9493
Free: (888)798-2690 **Fax:** (718)268-4030
E-mail: information@esi-systems.com
URL: http://www.esi-systems.com
Products: Electronic security systems; Access control
systems; Closed circuit television systems. **SIC:** 5065
(Electronic Parts & Equipment Nec). **Est:** 1988. **Sales:**
$1,000,000 (2000). **Emp:** 2. **Officers:** Steve
Schuchman, President, e-mail: schuchman@esi-
systems.com. **Former Name:** SMS International
Marketing Co.

■ 24536 ■ **Electronic Security Services**
15050 Buck Ln.
Upper Marlboro, MD 20772-7821
Phone: (301)449-3850 **Fax:** (301)449-1016
Products: Alarm systems. **SIC:** 5063 (Electrical
Apparatus & Equipment). **Emp:** 99. **Officers:** Samuel
Alexander.

■ 24537 ■ **Engineering Equipment Co.**
1020 W 31st St.
Downers Grove, IL 60515-5501
Phone: (630)963-7800 **Fax:** (630)963-7123
Products: Firefighting and construction equipment.
SICs: 5099 (Durable Goods Nec); 5082 (Construction
& Mining Machinery). **Sales:** $10,000,000 (1999).
Emp: 12. **Officers:** Frank J. Cullen, Vice President;
Susan Stock, Secretary.

■ 24538 ■ **Epley Sales Co.**
324 Murfreesboro Rd.
Nashville, TN 37210
Phone: (615)254-7254
Products: Safety equipment, including clothing and
gloves; Metal tubing; Abrasives; Steel. **SIC:** 5085
(Industrial Supplies).

■ 24539 ■ **Financial Commercial Security**
3655 Walnut St.
Denver, CO 80205
Phone: (303)295-1066
Free: (800)843-4810 **Fax:** (303)295-1073
Products: Security equipment, including alarms and
surveillance systems. **SICs:** 5065 (Electronic Parts &
Equipment Nec); 5065 (Electronic Parts & Equipment
Nec). **Est:** 1962. **Sales:** $5,000,000 (2000). **Emp:** 35.
Officers: Bob Gregory, President; Sue Ellyne Holmes,
Controller. **Former Name:** Pike Safe Co.

■ 24540 ■ **Fire Alarm Service Corp.**
12226 Hazen Ave.
Thonotosassa, FL 33592-9398
Phone: (813)986-5400 **Fax:** (813)986-1316
Products: Fire alarms. **SIC:** 5063 (Electrical Apparatus
& Equipment). **Emp:** 49. **Officers:** Edward Reid; Paul
Fraleigh.

■ 24541 ■ **Fire Appliance & Safety Co.**
Drawer 3648
Little Rock, AR 72203-3648
Phone: (501)455-2430 **Fax:** (501)455-2509
Products: Safety equipment and supplies. **SICs:** 5099
(Durable Goods Nec); 5047 (Medical & Hospital
Equipment). **Officers:** David Baumgardner, President.

■ 24542 ■ Fire Boss of Louisiana Inc.
7905 Hwy. 90 W
New Iberia, LA 70560-7651
Phone: (318)365-6729
Products: Fire extinguishers. **SIC:** 5087 (Service Establishment Equipment). **Est:** 1976. **Sales:** $3,000,000 (2000). **Emp:** 25. **Officers:** Henry T. Porter Jr., President; Debbie Sellers, Vice President.

■ 24543 ■ Fire Command Company Inc.
475 Long Beach Blvd.
Long Beach, NY 11561-2233
Phone: (516)889-1111   **Fax:** (516)431-0502
Products: Alarm systems; Safety products; Sighting, tracking, and fire control equipment. **SICs:** 5063 (Electrical Apparatus & Equipment); 5099 (Durable Goods Nec). **Sales:** $2,500,000 (2000). **Emp:** 25. **Officers:** Michael J. Kerr.

■ 24544 ■ Fire Equipment Inc.
88 Hicks Ave.
Medford, MA 02155
Phone: (781)391-8050   **Fax:** (781)391-8835
Products: Fire equipment, including fire extinguishers. **SICs:** 5087 (Service Establishment Equipment); 5099 (Durable Goods Nec). **Est:** 1927. **Sales:** $3,000,000 (2000). **Emp:** 30. **Officers:** Russell Murphy, President.

■ 24545 ■ Fire Fighters Equipment Co.
3038 Lenox Ave.
Jacksonville, FL 32254
Phone: (904)388-8542
Free: (800)488-8542   **Fax:** (904)384-2610
Products: Fire fighting equipment, including extinguishers, hoses, nozzles, fittings; Safety products. **SICs:** 5087 (Service Establishment Equipment); 5047 (Medical & Hospital Equipment). **Est:** 1949. **Sales:** $1,000,000 (1999). **Emp:** 12. **Officers:** Alex Stuckey, President; Nancy Nelson, Sales/Marketing Contact; Bob Hess, Customer Service Contact.

■ 24546 ■ Fire Spec Inc.
PO Box 296
Raynham, MA 02767-0500
Phone: (508)279-0058   **Fax:** (508)279-0288
E-mail: firespec@ici.net
URL: http://www.firespec.home.ici.net
Products: Fire sprinkler equipment; Earthquake bracing; Fasteners; Backflow preventers. **SIC:** 5087 (Service Establishment Equipment). **Est:** 1983. **Sales:** $500,000 (1999). **Emp:** 3. **Officers:** Christopher Gray, President.

■ 24547 ■ Fire Systems Unlimited Inc.
PO Box 190739
Hungry Horse, MT 59919-0739
Phone: (406)755-3473   **Free:** (800)839-3473
Products: Sighting, tracking, and fire control equipment. **SIC:** 5087 (Service Establishment Equipment). **Officers:** Earl Pruitt, President.

■ 24548 ■ Fire-Tec Inc.
89 Prospect St.
Manville, RI 02838-1013
Phone: (401)765-0213   **Fax:** (401)762-5406
Products: Service establishment equipment; Firefighting equipment and fire extinguishers. **SIC:** 5087 (Service Establishment Equipment). **Officers:** Harlan Lunt, President.

■ 24549 ■ Fire Tech & Safety of Neng
PO Box 435
Winthrop, ME 04364-0435
Phone: (207)377-2800   **Fax:** (207)377-6260
Products: Service industry machinery; Firefighting equipment; Safety products. **SIC:** 5087 (Service Establishment Equipment). **Officers:** Lawrence Guerette, President.

■ 24550 ■ Firecom Inc.
39-27 59th St.
Woodside, NY 11377
Phone: (718)899-6100
Products: Life, safety, and other electronic building systems. **SIC:** 5065 (Electronic Parts & Equipment Nec). **Sales:** $14,100,000 (2000). **Emp:** 123. **Officers:** Paul Mendez, CEO, President & Chairman of the Board; Jeffrey Cohen, VP of Finance.

■ 24551 ■ Fireman's Supply Inc.
6123 Airport Rd.
Nampa, ID 83687-8567
Phone: (208)467-6729
Free: (800)727-9972   **Fax:** (208)467-2979
Products: Service establishment equipment; Firefighting equipment; Industrial supplies. **SICs:** 5099 (Durable Goods Nec); 5085 (Industrial Supplies); 5087 (Service Establishment Equipment). **Officers:** Margaret Zeal, President.

■ 24552 ■ Fisher Scientific International Inc.
Liberty Ln.
Hampton, NH 03842
Phone: (603)929-2650   **Fax:** (603)929-1940
URL: http://www.fishersci.com
Products: Safety products; Laboratory equipment and supplies; Organic and inorganic chemicals. **SICs:** 5047 (Medical & Hospital Equipment); 5049 (Professional Equipment Nec). **Est:** 1991. **Sales:** $2,250,000,000 (2000). **Emp:** 8,000. **Officers:** Paul M. Montrone, CEO & Chairman of the Board; Paul M. Meister, Vice Chairman and CFO; David Della Penta, COO & President.

■ 24553 ■ Fredriksen and Sons Fire Equipment Company Inc.
760 Thomas Dr.
Bensenville, IL 60106
Phone: (708)595-9500
Products: Fire equipment, including hoses, extinguishers, and alarms. **SICs:** 5099 (Durable Goods Nec); 5087 (Service Establishment Equipment). **Est:** 1947. **Sales:** $2,000,000 (2000). **Emp:** 36.

■ 24554 ■ Fyr Fyter Inc.
10905-1 Gladiolus Dr.
Ft. Myers, FL 33908
Phone: (941)481-5737
Free: (877)481-5737   **Fax:** (941)481-8231
Products: Fire fighting equipment. **SIC:** 5099 (Durable Goods Nec). **Est:** 1962. **Emp:** 18. **Officers:** Greg Miller, President.

■ 24555 ■ Genesis Safety Systems Inc.
7 Doig Rd.
Wayne, NJ 07470
Phone: (973)696-9400
Products: Industrial safety equipment. **SICs:** 5085 (Industrial Supplies); 5047 (Medical & Hospital Equipment). **Sales:** $500,000 (2000). **Emp:** 6. **Officers:** Sam Di Giralomo, President.

■ 24556 ■ Gillmore Security Systems Inc.
26165 Broadway Ave.
Cleveland, OH 44146-6519
Phone: (440)232-1000   **Fax:** (440)232-3040
Products: Burlary and fire alarm systems. **SIC:** 5063 (Electrical Apparatus & Equipment). **Est:** 1971. **Emp:** 40. **Officers:** A. Gillmore.

■ 24557 ■ Graves Fire Protection
PO Box 451
Lunenburg, MA 01462
Phone: (978)345-0165   **Free:** (800)214-1456
Products: Fire extinguishers; Firefighting equipment. **SICs:** 5169 (Chemicals & Allied Products Nec); 5085 (Industrial Supplies); 5087 (Service Establishment Equipment); 5099 (Durable Goods Nec). **Emp:** 6. **Officers:** Donald P. Caron, President.

■ 24558 ■ Janis Gyles
PO Box 1827
Pueblo, CO 81002-1827
Phone: (719)542-4325
Free: (800)759-2852   **Fax:** (719)542-8537
Products: Electrical appliances and equipment, including home and automotive security systems. **SIC:** 5064 (Electrical Appliances—Television & Radio). **Officers:** Janis Gyles, Owner.

■ 24559 ■ Hart Equipment Company Inc.
PO Box 1187
Madisonville, KY 42431
Phone: (502)821-4645   **Fax:** (502)821-4818
E-mail: hartequip@vci.net
Products: Industrial supplies. **SIC:** 5047 (Medical & Hospital Equipment). **Est:** 1957. **Sales:** $3,000,000 (2000). **Emp:** 12. **Officers:** B.W. Asher, President; Martha Lewis, VP of Finance.

■ 24560 ■ Hawaii Instrumentation, Inc.
822 Halekauwila St.
Honolulu, HI 96813
Phone: (808)531-3595   **Fax:** (808)591-2508
Products: Fire alarm equipment. **SIC:** 5063 (Electrical Apparatus & Equipment).

■ 24561 ■ Hermann Associates Inc.
1405 Indiana St.
San Francisco, CA 94107
Phone: (415)285-8486   **Fax:** (415)826-3118
Products: Safes and vaults; Metal doors and frames. **SICs:** 5044 (Office Equipment); 5031 (Lumber, Plywood & Millwork). **Sales:** $3,000,000 (2000). **Emp:** 15. **Officers:** James Nuss, President.

■ 24562 ■ Herbert S. Hiller Corp.
401 Commerce Pt.
Harahan, LA 70123
Phone: (504)736-0008
Products: Fire safety equipment. **SIC:** 5099 (Durable Goods Nec).

■ 24563 ■ Hiller Investments Inc.
PO Box 91508
Mobile, AL 36691-1508
Phone: (334)432-5570
URL: http://www.hillercompanies.com
Products: Fire suppression and detection equipment. **SIC:** 5087 (Service Establishment Equipment). **Est:** 1919. **Sales:** $50,000,000 (2000). **Emp:** 450. **Officers:** Lucien D. Greenwood, CEO; J. Robert Copeland, CFO.

■ 24564 ■ Hintz Fire Equipment Inc.
PO Box 2492
Fargo, ND 58108-2492
Phone: (701)237-6006   **Fax:** (701)237-4051
Products: Service establishment equipment; Firefighting equipment. **SIC:** 5087 (Service Establishment Equipment). **Officers:** Bradley Olslund, President.

■ 24565 ■ H. Hoffman Co.
7330 W Montrose Ave.
Chicago, IL 60634
Phone: (708)456-9600
Products: Locks, including dead bolts, key, and combination pad locks. **SICs:** 5063 (Electrical Apparatus & Equipment); 5072 (Hardware). **Sales:** $16,000,000 (2000). **Emp:** 55. **Officers:** Al Hoffman, President; Karen Hoffman, Vice President; Dan Young, Operations Mgr.

■ 24566 ■ Holmes Protection Inc.
701 Callowhill
Philadelphia, PA 19123
Phone: (215)923-1500
Free: (800)440-5637   **Fax:** (215)923-5450
Products: Alarm systems. **SIC:** 5063 (Electrical Apparatus & Equipment). **Est:** 1867. **Emp:** 99. **Officers:** Joe Riggio.

■ 24567 ■ Honeywell Protection Services
6707 Carnegie
Cleveland, OH 44103
Phone: (216)361-6585   **Fax:** (216)881-2009
Products: Security systems for commercial and residential use. **SICs:** 5063 (Electrical Apparatus & Equipment); 5065 (Electronic Parts & Equipment Nec). **Emp:** 50. **Officers:** Frank Feleppelle.

■ 24568 ■ R.S. Hughes Company Inc.
PO Box 25061
Sunnyvale, CA 94086
Phone: (408)739-3211   **Fax:** (408)739-5889
Products: Safety products; Abrasives; Adhesives, including tapes and shipping and packaging materials; Electrical insulation products. **SICs:** 5047 (Medical & Hospital Equipment); 5099 (Durable Goods Nec); 5085 (Industrial Supplies); 5063 (Electrical Apparatus & Equipment); 5169 (Chemicals & Allied Products Nec). **Est:** 1954. **Sales:** $160,000,000 (2000). **Emp:** 375. **Officers:** R.H. McCollum, President & CEO.

■ 24569 ■ **IBA Protection Services**
701 E Hyde Park Blvd.
Inglewood, CA 90302-2507
Phone: (310)674-7000 **Fax:** (310)674-3333
Products: Alarm systems. **SIC:** 5063 (Electrical
Apparatus & Equipment). **Est:** 1956. **Sales:**
$1,000,000 (2000). **Emp:** 20. **Officers:** David M.
Conlon, President.

■ 24570 ■ **IDN-ACME, Inc.**
PO Drawer 13748
New Orleans, LA 70185
Phone: (504)837-7315
Free: (800)788-2263 **Fax:** (504)837-7321
Products: Security and door hardware. **SIC:** 5072
(Hardware).

■ 24571 ■ **Industrial Safety Supply Co. Interex
Div.**
176 Newington Rd.
West Hartford, CT 06110
Phone: (860)233-9881
Free: (800)243-2316 **Fax:** (860)236-7603
E-mail: ssco@industrialsafety.com
URL: http://www.industrialsafety.com
Products: Safety supplies; Plastics; Maintenance
products; Fasteners; Tools; Material handling
equipment; Fire/rescue. **SICs:** 5085 (Industrial
Supplies); 5162 (Plastics Materials & Basic Shapes);
5099 (Durable Goods Nec). **Est:** 1944. **Emp:** 90.
Officers: Henry F. Bonk, CEO.

■ 24572 ■ **Intec Video Systems Inc.**
23301 Vista Grande
Laguna Hills, CA 92653
Phone: (949)859-3800
Free: (800)468-3254 **Fax:** (949)859-3178
E-mail: info@intecvideo.com
URL: http://www.intecvideo.com
Products: Camera equipment, rear vision, and back-
up safety cameras. **SIC:** 5065 (Electronic Parts &
Equipment Nec). **Est:** 1970. **Emp:** 25. **Officers:**
Donald Nama II, President; Dino Nama, Sr. VP of
Technical Services.

■ 24573 ■ **Interwest Safety Supply Inc.**
PO Box 31
Provo, UT 84603
Phone: (801)375-6321 **Fax:** (801)377-2739
Products: Highway signs and highway safety devices.
SIC: 5099 (Durable Goods Nec). **Officers:** Bryce
Sorenson, President.

■ 24574 ■ **Intruder Alert Security**
410 E Kennedy
Lakewood, NJ 08701
Phone: (732)363-4105 **Fax:** (732)905-9437
Products: Security and alarm systems. **SIC:** 5063
(Electrical Apparatus & Equipment). **Emp:** 49.
Officers: Mark Exler.

■ 24575 ■ **Island Pacific Distributors, Inc.**
PO Box 22189
Honolulu, HI 96826
Phone: (808)955-1126 **Fax:** (808)946-6480
Products: Security products, including lock sets. **SIC:**
5072 (Hardware).

■ 24576 ■ **J & J Distributors**
1028 Donaldson
San Antonio, TX 78228
Phone: (210)734-6165 **Fax:** (210)735-2248
Products: Locksmith supplies and equipment. **SICs:**
5072 (Hardware); 5049 (Professional Equipment Nec).

■ 24577 ■ **JLJ Inc.**
2538 Addison Ave., No. E-1
Twin Falls, ID 83301-6749
Phone: (208)734-9089 **Fax:** (208)734-2644
Products: Service establishment equipment; Sprinkler
systems. **SIC:** 5087 (Service Establishment
Equipment). **Officers:** Jerry Boesel, President.

■ 24578 ■ **Jonas Aircraft and Arms Company
Inc.**
225 Broadway
New York, NY 10005
Phone: (212)619-0330 **Fax:** (212)619-2743
Products: Police equipment including armament and

aircraftparts. **SICs:** 5099 (Durable Goods Nec); 5088
(Transportation Equipment & Supplies). **Sales:**
$5,000,000 (2000). **Emp:** 10. **Officers:** G.S.
Steinemann, President & Treasurer.

■ 24579 ■ **Julius Kraft Company Inc.**
7 Pulaski St.
Auburn, NY 13021
Phone: (315)252-7251
Free: (800)557-2381 **Fax:** (315)252-6386
URL: http://www.jkraft.com
Products: Industrial gloves; Safety equipment; Clean
room supplies. **SICs:** 5136 (Men's/Boys' Clothing);
5099 (Durable Goods Nec); 5199 (Nondurable Goods
Nec). **Est:** 1868. **Sales:** $11,000,000 (2000). **Emp:** 30.
Officers: Kim Vorreuter, President; Cathy Fronczek,
CFO.

■ 24580 ■ **Kidde Safety**
1394 S 3rd St.
Mebane, NC 27302
Phone: (919)563-5911 **Fax:** (919)563-3954
Products: Fire extinguishers; Smoke and carbon
monoxide detectors; Escape ladders. **SIC:** 5099
(Durable Goods Nec).

■ 24581 ■ **King Safe and Lock Company Inc.**
8429 Katy Fwy.
Houston, TX 77024
Phone: (713)465-2500
Free: (800)546-4565 **Fax:** (713)465-0824
E-mail: kinglok@kinglok.com
URL: http://www.kinglok.com
Products: Safes; Locks; Access control products.
SICs: 5072 (Hardware); 5046 (Commercial Equipment
Nec). **Est:** 1972. **Sales:** $2,200,000 (2000). **Emp:** 16.
Officers: Carl King, President; Jerry King, Vice
President.

■ 24582 ■ **La Grand Industrial Supply Co.**
PO Box 1959
Portland, OR 97207-1959
Phone: (503)224-5800 **Fax:** (503)224-0639
E-mail: lagrand@teleport.com
Products: Foundry equipment, including first aid kits
and masks; Sandblast equipment and supplies;
Industrial safety supplies. **SICs:** 5047 (Medical &
Hospital Equipment); 5085 (Industrial Supplies); 5087
(Service Establishment Equipment); 5099 (Durable
Goods Nec). **Officers:** Louis La Grand, President;
Lawrence Schick, Sales/Mktg.

■ 24583 ■ **LaFrance Equipment Corp.**
PO Box 333
Elmira, NY 14902
Phone: (607)733-5511 **Fax:** (607)733-0482
Products: Fire fighting clothing and equipment;
Chemical fire extinguishing equipment; Personal
industrial safety devices; Fire department vehicles.
SICs: 5087 (Service Establishment Equipment); 5012
(Automobiles & Other Motor Vehicles); 5099 (Durable
Goods Nec); 5047 (Medical & Hospital Equipment).
Officers: T.D. Morse, President.

■ 24584 ■ **Donald Lane Fire Service**
230 Dolloff Ave.
Peru, ME 04290
Phone: (207)562-4268
Products: Firefighting equipment. **SIC:** 5087 (Service
Establishment Equipment). **Officers:** Donald Lane,
Owner.

■ 24585 ■ **Locks Co.**
2050 NE 151st St.
North Miami, FL 33162
Phone: (305)949-0700
Free: (800)288-0801 **Fax:** (305)949-3619
E-mail: locksco@gate.net
Products: Locks and related materials; Safes and
vaults; Professional and edge hand tools. **SICs:** 5072
(Hardware); 5044 (Office Equipment). **Est:** 1954.
Sales: $7,000,000 (2000). **Emp:** 25. **Officers:** Mark
Dorn; Milton Dorn; Michael Dorn.

■ 24586 ■ **LoJack of New Jersey Corp.**
12 Rte. 17 N
Paramus, NJ 07652
Phone: (201)368-8716 **Fax:** (201)368-1915
Products: Automobile theft prevention devices. **SIC:**

5013 (Motor Vehicle Supplies & New Parts). **Sales:**
$10,000,000 (2000). **Emp:** 20. **Officers:** Michael Perry,
President; Mary Jane Deletto, Marketing Mgr.

■ 24587 ■ **Marshall and Johnson**
1146 N Central Ave., No. 396
Glendale, CA 91202
Phone: (818)243-5424
Free: (800)613-2511 **Fax:** (818)243-0480
E-mail: raffi@ogtl.com
URL: http://www.stun-gun.com
Products: Stun guns. **SIC:** 5099 (Durable Goods Nec).
Est: 1987.

■ 24588 ■ **Julian A. McDermott Corp.**
1639 Stephen St.
Flushing, NY 11385-5345
Phone: (718)456-3606
Free: (800)842-5708 **Fax:** (718)381-0229
URL: http://www.mcdermottlight.com
Products: Emergency warning lights. **SIC:** 5063
(Electrical Apparatus & Equipment). **Est:** 1943. **Sales:**
$2,000,000 (2000). **Emp:** 38. **Officers:** M. McDermott;
Charles Vernon, Marketing Contact, e-mail: Vernon@
mcdermottlight.com; John Boc, Customer Service
Contact.

■ 24589 ■ **McLean International Marketing Inc.**
PO Box 535
Mequon, WI 53092
Phone: (262)242-0958 **Fax:** (262)242-6644
E-mail: mcleanex@execpc.com
URL: http://www.execpc.commcleanex
Products: Safety apparel and devices, including
devices for hearing and respiratory, eye, head, feet,
hand, and face protection. **SICs:** 5085 (Industrial
Supplies); 5047 (Medical & Hospital Equipment). **Est:**
1979. **Sales:** $1,000,000 (2000). **Emp:** 3. **Officers:**
Samuel E. Greeley, President; Jack Greeley, Vice
President; Jack Greeley, Sales/Marketing Contact, e-
mail: jgrel266@aol.com.

■ 24590 ■ **Meridian International Co.**
PO Box 6224
Libertyville, IL 60048
Phone: (847)362-3325 **Fax:** (847)362-3325
Products: Traffic safety flashing lights, plastic cones,
safety fences, and traffic safety barricades. **SIC:** 5099
(Durable Goods Nec). **Officers:** Laurence L. Prince,
President.

■ 24591 ■ **Mid-Continent Fire & Safety, Inc.**
2909 S Spruce St.
PO Box 16689
Wichita, KS 67216-6689
Phone: (316)522-0900 **Fax:** (316)522-0956
E-mail: wichita@midsafe.com
URL: http://www.midsafe.com
Products: Safety equipment. **SIC:** 5099 (Durable
Goods Nec). **Est:** 1938. **Sales:** $10,000,000 (2000).
Emp: 25. **Officers:** Bob Dool; Ken Watts, General
Mgr.; Pete Williams, Marketing & Sales Mgr.

■ 24592 ■ **Midland Lock & Safe Service**
1408 N Big Spring
Midland, TX 79701-2754
Phone: (915)682-4202
Products: Locks; Safes. **SICs:** 5072 (Hardware); 5044
(Office Equipment). **Emp:** 6. **Officers:** John Proctor,
President; Phil McKown, Vice President.

■ 24593 ■ **Minnesota Conway**
4565 W 77th St.
Edina, MN 55435-5009
Phone: (612)893-0798 **Fax:** (612)893-9301
Products: Fire safety equipment, including fire
extinguishers. **SIC:** 5099 (Durable Goods Nec). **Sales:**
$2,000,000 (2000). **Emp:** 38. **Officers:** Richard H.
Burt.

■ 24594 ■ **Mississippi Safety Services Inc.**
PO Box 1379
Clinton, MS 39060
Phone: (601)924-7815
Products: Safety education and awareness materials.
SIC: 5192 (Books, Periodicals & Newspapers). **Sales:**
$100,000 (1994). **Emp:** 2. **Officers:** John Brodbeck,
President.

■ 24595 ■ Mississippi Tool Supply Co.
Hwy. 25 S
PO Box 204
Golden, MS 38847
Phone: (601)454-9245
Free: (800)647-8168 **Fax:** (601)454-9385
Products: Safety supplies and equipment. **SICs:** 5049 (Professional Equipment Nec); 5099 (Durable Goods Nec). **Est:** 1977. **Sales:** $4,000,000 (2000). **Emp:** 54. **Officers:** Eddie Hall; Peggy Hall.

■ 24596 ■ Moniteq Research Labs, Inc.
7640 Fulerton Rd.
Springfield, VA 22153-2814
Phone: (703)569-0195
Free: (800)989-9891 **Fax:** (703)569-0196
E-mail: zachmagw@ix.netcom.com
URL: http://www.moniteq.com
Products: Access control systems. **SIC:** 5063 (Electrical Apparatus & Equipment). **Est:** 1997. **Sales:** $1,000,000 (2000). **Emp:** 10. **Officers:** G. Zachmann. **Alternate Name:** MRL, Inc.

■ 24597 ■ Tom Nagy Sales Corp.
PO Box 464
Goshen, IN 46527
Phone: (219)262-4479 **Fax:** (219)264-0140
Products: Alarm systems; Electronic systems and equipment; Speaker systems, microphones, home type electronic kits, and commercial sound equipment, including public address systems. **SICs:** 5065 (Electronic Parts & Equipment Nec); 5063 (Electrical Apparatus & Equipment). **Sales:** $1,000,000 (2000). **Emp:** 8. **Officers:** Tom Nagy, President; Pat Stover.

■ 24598 ■ Nardini Fire Equipment Company of North Dakota
PO Box 9707
Fargo, ND 58106-9707
Phone: (701)235-4224
Free: (800)950-1139 **Fax:** (701)235-5089
Products: Service industry machinery; Firefighting equipment. **SIC:** 5087 (Service Establishment Equipment). **Est:** 1980. **Emp:** 12. **Officers:** Ralph Nardini, President.

■ 24599 ■ National Mine Service Inc.
PO Box 310
Indiana, PA 15701
Phone: (724)349-7100
Free: (800)848-6672 **Fax:** (724)463-4040
Products: Safety products; Mining equipment and replacement parts for mining machinery. **SIC:** 5082 (Construction & Mining Machinery). **Sales:** $65,000,000 (2000). **Emp:** 220. **Officers:** William S. Tate, President; Mark F. Fornari, Controller.

■ 24600 ■ National Safety Apparel Inc.
3865 W 150th St.
Cleveland, OH 44111
Phone: (216)941-1111
Free: (800)553-0672 **Fax:** (216)941-1130
E-mail: nsaservice@safety-apparel.com
URL: http://www.safety-apparel.com
Products: Industrial safety clothing, including gloves, leggings, and hoods. **SICs:** 5099 (Durable Goods Nec); 5136 (Men's/Boys' Clothing). **Est:** 1984. **Sales:** $12,000,000 (2000). **Emp:** 90. **Officers:** Charles Grossman, President; Richard Papa, Finance Officer; Chuck Grossman Jr., Dir. of Sales; Sal Geraci, VP of Operations; Annette Klein, Customer Service Contact. **Former Name:** Q.P.C., Inc.

■ 24601 ■ Nelson Holland Inc.
5330 N 16th St.
Phoenix, AZ 85016-3204
Phone: (602)264-1841
Free: (800)224-5625 **Fax:** (602)230-0906
Products: Architectural hardware; Doors , including metal and wood, and frames; Access control systems. **SIC:** 5063 (Electrical Apparatus & Equipment). **Est:** 1956. **Sales:** $5,000,000 (1999). **Emp:** 30. **Officers:** Dan Heinz; Joann Colan, Customer Service Contact.

■ 24602 ■ Nicolet Imaging Systems
8221 Arjons Dr., Ste. F
San Diego, CA 92126-4394
Phone: (619)635-8600
Free: (800)228-1147 **Fax:** (619)695-9902
Products: Real-time, non-destructive X-ray imaging and inspection systems and air bag inspection and monitoring systems. **SIC:** 5013 (Motor Vehicle Supplies & New Parts). **Officers:** Ronald Lindell, President.

■ 24603 ■ Night Owl Security Inc.
855 Brightseat Rd.
Landover, MD 20785
Phone: (410)461-6300
Free: (800)688-0150 **Fax:** (301)808-1473
Products: Alarm systems, including fire, intercom, and camera systems. **SIC:** 5063 (Electrical Apparatus & Equipment). **Emp:** 70. **Officers:** Barry R. Sisson, President; Coleman Raphael, Chairman of the Board; Asa Beck, CFO.

■ 24604 ■ North American Security
4138 E Ponce De Leon Ave.
Clarkston, GA 30021-1818
Phone: (404)294-7222
Free: (800)625-6251 **Fax:** (404)294-0242
E-mail: sales@nasecurity.com
URL: http://www.northamericansecurity.com
Products: Alarm and fire systems; CCTV; Access control; and Gates. **SIC:** 5063 (Electrical Apparatus & Equipment). **Est:** 1971. **Sales:** $1,000,000 (2000). **Emp:** 30. **Officers:** George Tanguay; Helene Tanguay.

■ 24605 ■ Omni Group Inc.
PO Box 398
Timonium, MD 21094
Phone: (410)296-0113
E-mail: b.dennis410@aol.com
Products: Home, business and personal security systems; Closed-circuit televisions. **SICs:** 5065 (Electronic Parts & Equipment Nec); 5063 (Electrical Apparatus & Equipment). **Est:** 1985. **Sales:** $800,000 (1999). **Emp:** 11. **Officers:** B. Dennis, President.

■ 24606 ■ OPTEX Morse, Inc.
12960 Bradley Ave.
Sylmar, CA 91342-3829
Phone: (818)367-5951 **Fax:** (818)367-6884
Products: Electrical products, including security systems. **SIC:** 5063 (Electrical Apparatus & Equipment). **Est:** 1971. **Sales:** $6,000,000 (2000). **Emp:** 50. **Former Name:** Morse Products Mfg.

■ 24607 ■ Optex USA Inc.
365 Van Ness Way, Ste. 510
Torrance, CA 90501
Phone: (310)212-7271
Products: Electronic security systems. **SIC:** 5063 (Electrical Apparatus & Equipment). **Sales:** $7,600,000 (1993). **Emp:** 16. **Officers:** Sean Izu, President.

■ 24608 ■ Orr Safety Corp.
PO Box 16326
Louisville, KY 40256-0326
Phone: (502)774-5791
Free: (800)669-1677 **Fax:** (502)776-8030
E-mail: custserv@orrcorp.com
URL: http://www.orrsafety.com
Products: Personal protective and safety-related supplies and equipment; Fire protection equipment; First aid and medical supplies. **SICs:** 5099 (Durable Goods Nec); 5047 (Medical & Hospital Equipment). **Est:** 1948. **Sales:** $72,000,000 (2000). **Emp:** 240. **Officers:** Clark Orr, President; Bob Ash, Controller.

■ 24609 ■ OST Inc. (Fremont, California)
41786 Christy St.
Fremont, CA 94538
Phone: (510)440-0841
Products: Car alarms. **SIC:** 5063 (Electrical Apparatus & Equipment). **Sales:** $5,000,000 (2000). **Emp:** 25. **Officers:** Harold Jang, President.

■ 24610 ■ Pagel Safety Inc.
N51 W13251 Brahm Ct.
Menomonee Falls, WI 53051
Phone: (414)783-3595 **Fax:** (414)783-3577
Products: OSHA-approved safety products. **SIC:** 5047 (Medical & Hospital Equipment).

■ 24611 ■ Pagel Safety Inc.
W229N1687 Westwood Dr., Ste. E
Waukesha, WI 53186-1174
Phone: (414)544-8060 **Fax:** (414)783-3577
Products: Hard hats, safety gloves, and safety goggles. **SICs:** 5085 (Industrial Supplies); 5049 (Professional Equipment Nec). **Sales:** $4,000,000 (1994). **Emp:** 12. **Officers:** Bruce S. Pagel, President.

■ 24612 ■ P.K. Safety Supply
7303E Edgewater Dr.
Oakland, CA 94621
Phone: (415)821-9580 **Fax:** (415)821-2211
Products: Safety equipment, including respirators, gloves, glasses, and signs. **SICs:** 5047 (Medical & Hospital Equipment); 5099 (Durable Goods Nec). **Est:** 1947. **Sales:** $5,000,000 (2000). **Emp:** 20. **Officers:** E.A. Pedley, President. **Former Name:** Pedley-Knowles and Co.

■ 24613 ■ Plastic Safety Systems, Inc.
2444 Baldwin Rd.
Cleveland, OH 44120
Phone: (216)231-8590
Free: (800)662-6338 **Fax:** (216)231-2702
E-mail: sales@plasticsafety.com
URL: http://www.plasticsafety.com
Products: Traffic and construction safety products, including highway barricades. **SICs:** 5099 (Durable Goods Nec); 5087 (Service Establishment Equipment). **Est:** 1961. **Sales:** $5,000,000 (2000). **Emp:** 28. **Officers:** D.E. Cowan, President; Chuck Bailey, Sales/Marketing Contact.

■ 24614 ■ Potter-Roemer
3100 S Susan St.
Santa Ana, CA 92704
Phone: (714)430-5300
Free: (800)366-3473 **Fax:** 888-404-7960
Products: Fire extinguishers; Fire proof cabinets. **SIC:** 5099 (Durable Goods Nec). **Est:** 1937. **Sales:** $6,600,000 (2000). **Emp:** 55. **Officers:** Lance McCabe, President.

■ 24615 ■ Protech Safety Equipment
PO Box 400128
Cambridge, MA 02140-0002
Phone: (908)862-1550 **Fax:** (908)862-4436
Products: Safety equipment. **SIC:** 5099 (Durable Goods Nec). **Est:** 1960. **Sales:** $4,200,000 (2000). **Emp:** 10. **Officers:** T.M. Brickley, President; Edward G. Krusman, Sales Mgr.; Patricia Sunderlin, Operations Mgr.

■ 24616 ■ R & H Wholesale Supply, Inc.
1655 Folsom St.
San Francisco, CA 94103
Phone: (415)863-0404 **Fax:** (415)863-7046
Products: Locksmith equipment and supplies. **SICs:** 5072 (Hardware); 5049 (Professional Equipment Nec).

■ 24617 ■ Reis Environmental Inc.
11022 Linpage Pl.
St. Louis, MO 63132
Phone: (314)426-5603 **Free:** (800)777-7347
Products: Safety equipment, including asbestos and lead abatement and environmental cleanup products. **SIC:** 5099 (Durable Goods Nec). **Sales:** $52,000,000 (2000). **Emp:** 103. **Officers:** Rudolph L. Wise, President; Michael Milne, Controller.

■ 24618 ■ Reliable Fire Equipment Co.
12845 S Cicero Ave.
Alsip, IL 60803
Phone: (708)597-4600 **Fax:** (708)389-1150
E-mail: fire@reliablefire.com
URL: http://www.reliablefire.com
Products: Fire equipment, including fire extinguishers and hoses; Security systems including alarms. **SICs:** 5063 (Electrical Apparatus & Equipment); 5087 (Service Establishment Equipment); 5099 (Durable Goods Nec). **Est:** 1955. **Sales:** $14,200,000 (2000). **Emp:** 100. **Officers:** Ernest E. Horvath, Chairman of the Board; Debra Horvath, President; Robert Pikula, Marketing & Sales Mgr.; Tina Studzinski, Controller.

■ 24619 ■ Rutherford Controls Int'l.
2697 International Pkwy., Ste. 100
Virginia Beach, VA 23452
Phone: (757)427-1230
Free: (800)899-5625 **Fax:** (757)427-9549
E-mail: rutherford@rutherfordusa.com
URL: http://www.rutherfordcontrols.com
Products: Electric locking products. **SIC:** 5065
(Electronic Parts & Equipment Nec). **Est:** 1990. **Emp:**
15. **Officers:** Tracy Rutherford, VP of Operations;
David Halls, VP of Sales; Trisha Rohr, Sales/Marketing
Contact, e-mail: trisha@rutherfordusa.com; Jeff
Jeffries, Customer Service Contact, e-mail: jeff@
rutherfordusa.com. **Alternate Name:** Rutherford
Controls Inc.

■ 24620 ■ SA-SO
1025 Post and Paddock Rd.
Grand Prairie, TX 75050
Phone: (214)647-1525 **Fax:** (903)988-6202
Products: Traffic and OSHA signs; Police equipment,
including badges; Safety equipment, including flags
and emergency eye wash stations. **SICs:** 5099
(Durable Goods Nec); 5047 (Medical & Hospital
Equipment); 5087 (Service Establishment Equipment).
Est: 1948. **Officers:** Parker Fanning, President.
Former Name: Sargent-Sowell Co.

■ 24621 ■ Safeguard International, Inc.
PO Box 884
Chester, PA 19016
Phone: (215)876-2800
Free: (800)334-9893 **Fax:** (215)876-2849
Products: Chemical metal working compounds;
Specialty envelopes; Check signing and certifying
machinery; Check protecting machinery; Check
handling bank perforators; Film and TV lighting
equipment. **SICs:** 5044 (Office Equipment); 5169
(Chemicals & Allied Products Nec); 5112 (Stationery &
Office Supplies); 5065 (Electronic Parts & Equipment
Nec). **Officers:** Laura Royce, President.

■ 24622 ■ Safety Flare Inc.
2803 Richmond Dr. NE
Albuquerque, NM 87107
Phone: (505)884-2274 **Fax:** (505)884-0721
E-mail: safetyplus@lobo.net
Products: Safety products. **SICs:** 5099 (Durable
Goods Nec); 5047 (Medical & Hospital Equipment).
Est: 1966. **Emp:** 6. **Officers:** Rhonda K. Maxfield,
President.

■ 24623 ■ Safety Flare Inc.
2803 Richmond Dr. NE
Albuquerque, NM 87107
Phone: (505)884-2274 **Fax:** (505)884-0721
Products: Security and safety equipment. **SIC:** 5099
(Durable Goods Nec).

■ 24624 ■ Sanderson Safety Supply Co.
1101 SE 3rd Ave.
Portland, OR 97214
Phone: (503)238-5700
Free: (800)547-0927 **Fax:** (503)238-6443
E-mail: sandersonsafety@sansafe.com
Products: Industrial safety equipment. **SICs:** 5087
(Service Establishment Equipment); 5099 (Durable
Goods Nec). **Est:** 1916. **Emp:** 110. **Officers:** Stephen
Spahr, President; Jerry Griffin, VP of Finance & Admin.;
Dave Soyster, Sales/Marketing Contact; Mike Harris,
Customer Service Contact.

■ 24625 ■ Leslie Schiffer Wholesale Hardware
34 Ludlow St.
New York, NY 10002
Phone: (212)677-7530 **Fax:** (212)353-8529
Products: Locks and keys. **SIC:** 5072 (Hardware).

■ 24626 ■ SDA Security Systems, Inc.
2054 State St.
San Diego, CA 92101
Phone: (619)239-3473
Free: (800)624-8305 **Fax:** (619)237-0131
E-mail: reales@sdasecurity.com
URL: http://www.sdasecurity.com
Products: Alarm systems, including commercial and
residential alarms. **SIC:** 5063 (Electrical Apparatus &
Equipment). **Est:** 1930. **Sales:** $8,000,000 (2000).
Emp: 94. **Officers:** Rodney Eales, President.

■ 24627 ■ Seatronics Inc.
PO Box 1138
Auburn, WA 98071
Phone: (253)939-6060 **Fax:** (253)735-3540
Products: Fire protection systems. **SIC:** 5087 (Service
Establishment Equipment). **Sales:** $2,000,000 (2000).
Emp: 7. **Officers:** J.K. Deonigi, President.

■ 24628 ■ Securaplane Technologies L.L.C.
10800 N Mavinee Dr.
Tucson, AZ 85737
Phone: (520)297-0844 **Fax:** (520)498-4924
Products: Security systems; Battery packs; Main ship
battery chargers and wireless smoke detectors for
airlines and business aviation. **SIC:** 5088
(Transportation Equipment & Supplies). **Sales:**
$7,000,000 (2000). **Emp:** 100. **Officers:** Richard
Lukso, Owner; Joe Stucky, Finance Officer.

■ 24629 ■ Security Data Group
6726 Arlington
Jacksonville, FL 32211
Phone: (904)724-2740 **Fax:** (904)721-6116
Products: Alarm systems. **SIC:** 5063 (Electrical
Apparatus & Equipment). **Est:** 1929. **Emp:** 49.
Officers: Tim Carny. **Alternate Name:** Security
Consultants. **Former Name:** Sentinel Alarm Service.

■ 24630 ■ Security Engineers Systems Inc.
8403 Benjamin Rd., Ste. C
Tampa, FL 33634-1204
Phone: (813)854-2078 **Fax:** (813)855-2505
Products: Alarm systems. **SIC:** 5063 (Electrical
Apparatus & Equipment). **Est:** 1982. **Sales:**
$8,000,000 (2000). **Emp:** 115. **Officers:** Walter
Wiseman, President; Candace J. Wiseman, Treasurer
& Secty.; Mark Taylor, Vice President. **Alternate
Name:** Security Engineers.

■ 24631 ■ SecurityLink Corp.
125 Frontage Rd.
Orange, CT 06477
Phone: (203)795-9000
Products: Alarm systems. **SIC:** 5063 (Electrical
Apparatus & Equipment).

■ 24632 ■ Select Security Inc.
800 Seahawk Cir., Ste. 134
Virginia Beach, VA 23452-7814
Phone: (757)468-3700 **Fax:** (757)468-0428
Products: Electronic parts and equipment; Security
control equipment and systems. **SICs:** 5065 (Electronic
Parts & Equipment Nec); 5063 (Electrical Apparatus &
Equipment). **Officers:** Mark Wilging, President.

■ 24633 ■ Sentry Alarm, Inc.
707 Hickory Farm Ln.
Appleton, WI 54914-3032
Phone: (920)739-9559 **Fax:** (920)739-8603
Products: Security alarms, including fire alarms, card
access and closed circuit cameras. **SIC:** 5063
(Electrical Apparatus & Equipment). **Emp:** 7. **Officers:**
Guy Smith.

■ 24634 ■ Sentry Group
900 Linden Ave.
Rochester, NY 14625
Phone: (716)381-4900
Free: (800)828-1438 **Fax:** (716)381-8559
URL: http://www.sentry-grp.com
Products: Safes and chests; Files. **SIC:** 5044 (Office
Equipment).

■ 24635 ■ Sentry Technology Corp.
350 Wireless Blvd.
Hauppauge, NY 11788
Phone: (516)232-2100 **Fax:** (516)232-2124
Products: Security systems. **SICs:** 5064 (Electrical
Appliances—Television & Radio); 5064 (Electrical
Appliances—Television & Radio); 5045 (Computers,
Peripherals & Software). **Est:** 1966. **Sales:**
$37,500,000 (2000). **Emp:** 251. **Officers:** Thomas A.
Nicolette, CEO & President; Peter J. Mundy, VP &
CFO.

■ 24636 ■ Sentry Watch Inc.
1705 Holbrook
Greensboro, NC 27404
Phone: (919)273-8103 **Fax:** (919)299-5862
Products: Burglar and fire alarms. **SIC:** 5063
(Electrical Apparatus & Equipment). **Emp:** 49.
Officers: Gene Loye.

■ 24637 ■ SLC Technologies Inc.
12345 S Leventon Dr.
Tualatin, OR 97062
Phone: (503)691-7270
Products: Security, life, and safety and
communications products. **SIC:** 5199 (Nondurable
Goods Nec). **Sales:** $1,107,000,000 (2000). **Emp:**
2,000. **Officers:** Kenneth L. Boyda, CEO; John Logan,
VP of Finance.

■ 24638 ■ Smarter Security Systems, Inc.
5825 Glenridge Dr., Ste. 1-126
Atlanta, GA 30328
Phone: (404)256-4244 **Fax:** (404)252-1340
E-mail: info@smartersecurity.com
URL: http://www.smartesecurity.com
Products: Security systems; Access control systems;
Optical Turnstiles; Perimeter security systems. **SIC:**
5065 (Electronic Parts & Equipment Nec). **Est:** 1992.
Emp: 2. **Officers:** John E. Forbat, President, e-mail:
johneforbat@msn.com. **Alternate Name:** International
Market Entry Management Co.

■ 24639 ■ SOS Alarm
3273 Bittle Rd.
Medford, OR 97504
Phone: (541)772-6668 **Fax:** (541)776-2819
Products: Alarms. **SIC:** 5063 (Electrical Apparatus &
Equipment). **Emp:** 20. **Officers:** Ray Claborn.

■ 24640 ■ Standard Electric Time Corp.
PO Box 320
Tecumseh, MI 49286
Phone: (517)423-8331 **Fax:** (517)423-9486
Products: Fire alarms, clocks, nurse calls and security
card access systems. **SIC:** 5065 (Electronic Parts &
Equipment Nec). **Sales:** $3,000,000 (2000). **Emp:** 43.
Officers: Gilbert E. Pierce, President; James Harkey,
Treasurer.

■ 24641 ■ Sterling Security Services Inc.
1018 S Van Buren St.
Amarillo, TX 79101
Phone: (806)376-1193 **Fax:** (806)374-7527
Products: Guard and alarm systems. **SIC:** 5063
(Electrical Apparatus & Equipment). **Emp:** 250.
Officers: Glen Parkey.

■ 24642 ■ Tech Fire and Safety Co.
514 4th St.
Watervliet, NY 12189
Phone: (518)274-7599 **Fax:** (518)274-7899
Products: Fire hoses and extinguishers; Safety
equipment. **SICs:** 5087 (Service Establishment
Equipment); 5099 (Durable Goods Nec). **Est:** 1938.
Sales: $2,800,000 (2000). **Emp:** 10. **Officers:** Don
Smith, CEO; T. Lane, CFO; Jeff Montross, Dir. of
Marketing.

■ 24643 ■ Total Recall Corp.
50A S Main St.
Spring Valley, NY 10977
Phone: (914)425-3000
Free: (800)659-7793 **Fax:** (914)425-3097
E-mail: totlrcl@aol.com
URL: http://www.totalrecallcorp.com
Products: Video surveillance equipment. **SIC:** 5064
(Electrical Appliances—Television & Radio). **Est:** 1985.
Sales: $3,000,000 (2000). **Emp:** 8. **Officers:** Jordan P.
Heilweil, President.

■ 24644 ■ Traffic Control Service Inc.
1881 Betmor Ln.
Anaheim, CA 92805
Phone: (714)937-0422 **Fax:** (714)937-1070
Products: Safety equipment including concrete
barricades, columns and vests. **SICs:** 5032 (Brick,
Stone & Related Materials); 5136 (Men's/Boys'
Clothing); 5137 (Women's/Children's Clothing). **Sales:**
$12,000,000 (2000). **Emp:** 46. **Officers:** James
Westphal, President.

■ 24645 ■ Tri M Specialties
554 Bailey Ln.
Corvallis, MT 59828-9640
Phone: (406)961-4794 **Fax:** (406)961-2460
Products: Service industry machinery; Firefighting equipment. **SIC:** 5087 (Service Establishment Equipment). **Officers:** Marilyn Manny, Owner.

■ 24646 ■ Tri-S Co.
2209 E Main St.
Chattanooga, TN 37404
Phone: (423)698-8821 **Fax:** (423)698-8823
Products: Safety equipment, including fire extinguishers, hard hats, and safety glasses. **SICs:** 5099 (Durable Goods Nec); 5047 (Medical & Hospital Equipment).

■ 24647 ■ Tri-State Police Fire Equipment Inc.
912 Broadway
East Providence, RI 02914-3718
Phone: (401)434-1892 **Fax:** (401)431-2838
Products: Police equipment. **SIC:** 5087 (Service Establishment Equipment). **Officers:** Barry Morrissette, President.

■ 24648 ■ Twyman Templeton Company Inc.
PO Box 44490
Columbus, OH 43204
Phone: (614)272-5623 **Fax:** (614)272-0167
Products: Safety products, including hardhats, coveralls, and boots. **SICs:** 5087 (Service Establishment Equipment); 5136 (Men's/Boys' Clothing); 5139 (Footwear). **Est:** 1946. **Sales:** $45,000,000 (2000). **Emp:** 80. **Officers:** Donald Lewis, President; Tom Campbell, CFO; Walter Dole, COO.

■ 24649 ■ Unistrut Fall Arrest Systems Inc.
3980 Varsity Dr.
Ann Arbor, MI 48108-2226
Phone: (734)677-3380 **Fax:** (734)677-1518
Products: Safety equipment. **SICs:** 5085 (Industrial Supplies); 5047 (Medical & Hospital Equipment). **Est:** 1990. **Sales:** $1,000,000 (2000). **Emp:** 5. **Officers:** Edward C. Cady, President; Paul Chase, VP & General Merchandising Mgr.

■ 24650 ■ United Fire Equipment Co.
335 N 4th Ave.
Tucson, AZ 85745
Phone: (520)622-3639
Free: (800)362-0150 **Fax:** (520)882-3991
URL: http://www.ufec.com
Products: Fire extinguishers; Uniforms; Hoses; Fire suppression systems; Dry chemicals. **SICs:** 5087 (Service Establishment Equipment); 5099 (Durable Goods Nec). **Est:** 1968. **Sales:** $7,000,000 (2000). **Emp:** 55. **Officers:** Stan Matlick, President.

■ 24651 ■ U.S. Lock Corp.
77 Rodeo Dr.
Brentwood, NY 11717
Phone: (631)243-3000
Free: (800)925-5000 **Fax:** 800-338-5625
URL: http://www.uslock.org
Products: Architectural and security hardware. **SIC:** 5072 (Hardware). **Est:** 1988. **Sales:** $32,000,000

(2000). **Emp:** 65. **Officers:** Gene Merber, President; Geoffrey Meyer, Vice President; Geoffrey Meyer, Vice President.

■ 24652 ■ Universal Security Instruments Inc.
7A Gwynns Mill Crt.
Owings Mills, MD 21117
Phone: (410)363-3000 **Fax:** (410)363-2218
E-mail: sales@universalsecurity.com
URL: http://www.smokealarms.com
Products: Security products, including smoke alarms and security lighting; Door chimes. **SICs:** 5063 (Electrical Apparatus & Equipment); 5065 (Electronic Parts & Equipment Nec). **Est:** 1969. **Sales:** $7,668,000 (2000). **Emp:** 17.

■ 24653 ■ Uvex Safety
10 Thurber Blvd.
Smithfield, RI 02917
Phone: (401)232-1200
Free: (800)343-3411 **Fax:** (401)232-1830
E-mail: sales@uvex.com
URL: http://www.uvex.com
Products: Safety eyewear. **SICs:** 5085 (Industrial Supplies); 5048 (Ophthalmic Goods). **Officers:** Jamie Metcalf, Sales/Marketing Contact, e-mail: Jamie_Metcalf@uvex.com; Janice Clark, Customer Service Contact.

■ 24654 ■ F.M. Valenti Inc.
5 Bourbon St.
Peabody, MA 01960-1339
Phone: (978)536-2666 **Fax:** (978)536-2065
E-mail: sean@fmvalenti.com
Products: Audio and video products. **SIC:** 5063 (Electrical Apparatus & Equipment). **Est:** 1967. **Sales:** $20,000,000 (2000). **Emp:** 11. **Officers:** Francis Valenti, President; Sean Valenti, Vice President; Steven Valenti, Vice President; Sarita Valenti, Treasurer.

■ 24655 ■ Vallen Corp.
PO Box 3587
Houston, TX 77253-3587
Phone: (713)462-8700
Free: (800)482-5536 **Fax:** 800-303-8256
Products: Industrial safety equipment; Air pack respirators. **SICs:** 5047 (Medical & Hospital Equipment); 5047 (Medical & Hospital Equipment). **Est:** 1947. **Sales:** $257,800,000 (2000). **Emp:** 982. **Officers:** James W. Thompson, CEO & President; Leighton J. Stephenson, VP of Finance & Treasurer; Robin R. Hutton, Exec. VP of Marketing & Sales; Kent M. Edwards, Dir. of Admin.

■ 24656 ■ Vanguard Distributors Inc.
PO Box 608
Savannah, GA 31402
Phone: (912)236-1766 **Fax:** (912)238-3072
Products: Safety and laboratory supplies, including clothing; Industrial supplies. **SICs:** 5136 (Men's/Boys' Clothing); 5137 (Women's/Children's Clothing); 5139 (Footwear); 5085 (Industrial Supplies). **Est:** 1984. **Officers:** Sylvester Formey, President; Donald Formey, Marketing & Sales Mgr.

■ 24657 ■ Vector Security Systems Inc.
950 Windham Ct., Ste. 1
Boardman, OH 44512
Phone: (330)726-9841 **Fax:** (330)726-9826
Products: Alarm systems. **SIC:** 5063 (Electrical Apparatus & Equipment). **Emp:** 28. **Officers:** Mike Brindley; Mark Russell. **Former Name:** WESTEC/PC Security Systems Inc.

■ 24658 ■ Video Sentry Corp.
350 Wireless Blvd.
Hauppauge, NY 11788
Phone: (516)232-2100 **Fax:** (516)232-2124
Products: Closed circuit video systems; Computer hardware and software packages. **SICs:** 5064 (Electrical Appliances—Television & Radio); 5045 (Computers, Peripherals & Software). **Officers:** Thomas A. Nicolette, CEO & President; Peter J. Mundy, VP & CFO.

■ 24659 ■ W.A. Vorpahl, Inc.
PO Box 12175
Green Bay, WI 54307
Phone: (920)497-7200 **Fax:** (920)497-8388
E-mail: safety@wavsafety.com
URL: http://www.wavsafety.com
Products: Safety equipment. **SICs:** 5099 (Durable Goods Nec); 5047 (Medical & Hospital Equipment). **Est:** 1951. **Emp:** 30. **Officers:** Kent Vorpahl, President; Scott Imig, Sales/Marketing Contact; Craig Vorpahl, Customer Service Contact; Kathy Beyer, Human Resources Contact.

■ 24660 ■ Wells Fargo Alarm Services Inc.
450 S 5th
Reading, PA 19602-2642
Phone: (215)372-8484 **Fax:** (215)372-8605
Products: Alarms. **SIC:** 5063 (Electrical Apparatus & Equipment). **Emp:** 49.

■ 24661 ■ Westguard Inc.
PO Box 616
Twinsburg, OH 44087
Phone: (330)963-5116 **Fax:** (330)425-1834
Products: Alarms; Locks. **SICs:** 5072 (Hardware); 5063 (Electrical Apparatus & Equipment). **Sales:** $1,000,000 (2000). **Emp:** 6. **Officers:** Robert Fox, Chairman of the Board.

■ 24662 ■ Zink Safety of Arkansas Inc.
PO Box 15004
Little Rock, AR 72231-5004
Phone: (501)945-2666
Free: (800)482-6916 **Fax:** (501)945-8869
E-mail: zinkark@concentric.net
Products: Personal safety equipment. **SIC:** 5099 (Durable Goods Nec). **Est:** 1984. **Emp:** 10. **Officers:** James Kaminski, President.

■ 24663 ■ Zink Safety Equipment
15101 W 110th St.
Lenexa, KS 66219
Phone: (913)492-9444
Free: (800)255-1101 **Fax:** (913)492-4327
Products: Safety equipment. **SIC:** 5099 (Durable Goods Nec).

(51) Shoes

Entries in this section are arranged alphabetically by company name. When the company name is a personal name, the company name is alphabetized by the surname unless the first name or initial(s) are part of a trade name. See the User's Guide at the front of this directory for additional information.

■ 24664 ■ **Aerogroup International Inc.**
201 Meadow Rd.
Edison, NJ 08817
Phone: (732)985-6900
Products: Women's casual and comfort-style shoes.
SIC: 5139 (Footwear). **Sales:** $60,500,000 (2000).
Emp: 100. **Officers:** Jules Schneider, President;
Richard Dandilene, Vice President.

■ 24665 ■ **African Export Ltd.**
2401 Sinclair Ln.
Baltimore, MD 21213-1331
Phone: (410)563-9118
Free: (800)876-7559 **Fax:** (410)563-9128
Products: Used footwear; Clothes. **SIC:** 5139
(Footwear). **Est:** 1989. **Officers:** Elowechi Aka, Owner.

■ 24666 ■ **Alec Corp.**
PO Box 15229
Stamford, CT 06901-0229
Phone: (203)327-0922
Free: (800)967-8898 **Fax:** (203)967-4498
Products: Footwear. **SIC:** 5139 (Footwear). **Officers:**
Alexander Pisciella, President.

■ 24667 ■ **Allen Trading Co. Inc.**
275 Dean Rd.
Brookline, MA 02445-4144
Phone: (617)232-7747 **Fax:** (617)232-0640
E-mail: atcoinc@ma.ultranet.com
Products: Footwear components and soles. **SIC:** 5139
(Footwear). **Est:** 1985. **Officers:** Howard Allen,
President.

■ 24668 ■ **Alpina Sports Corp.**
PO Box 23
Hanover, NH 03755-0023
Phone: (603)448-3101 **Fax:** (603)448-1586
Products: Footwear; Athletic footwear. **SIC:** 5139
(Footwear). **Officers:** Rolf Schaer, President.

■ 24669 ■ **AmAsia International Ltd.**
34 3rd Ave.
Burlington, MA 01803-4414
Phone: (781)229-6611 **Fax:** (781)229-9431
Products: Women's shoes. **SIC:** 5139 (Footwear).
Est: 1987.

■ 24670 ■ **American Footwear Corp.**
1 Oak Hill Rd.
Fitchburg, MA 01420-3986
Free: (800)735-6332
Products: Footwear. **SIC:** 5139 (Footwear). **Officers:**
Kenneth Ansin, President.

■ 24671 ■ **Angel-Etts Inc.**
5900 Rodeo Rd.
Los Angeles, CA 90016
Phone: (213)870-4637
Products: Tennis shoes and sandals for women and
children. **SIC:** 5139 (Footwear). **Est:** 1952. **Sales:**
$24,000,000 (2000). **Emp:** 40. **Officers:** Louis
Jackson, President; Rudy Mellow, Controller.

■ 24672 ■ **Annie C.P. Productions Inc.**
PO Box 701287
Tulsa, OK 74170-1287
Phone: (918)298-0770 **Fax:** (918)298-2517
URL: http://www.c.p.annieproductions.com
Products: Footwear; Women's clothing; Swimsuits,
pageant swimwear, jewelry, stage shoes, and
accessories for pageants. **SICs:** 5139 (Footwear);
5137 (Women's/Children's Clothing); 5094 (Jewelry &
Precious Stones). **Est:** 1985. **Officers:** Harry Salem,
President; Cheryl Salem.

■ 24673 ■ **Paul Anthony International Inc.**
5165 N Riley St.
Las Vegas, NV 89129-4136
Phone: (702)645-5751 **Fax:** (702)645-5751
Products: Footwear; Women's handbags and purses.
SICs: 5139 (Footwear); 5137 (Women's/Children's
Clothing). **Officers:** James Cholke, President.

■ 24674 ■ **Apex Foot Health Industries**
170 Wesley St.
South Hackensack, NJ 07606
Phone: (201)487-2739
Free: (800)526-APEX **Fax:** 800-526-0073
E-mail: info@apexfoot.com
URL: http://www.apexfoot.com
Products: Footwear and equipment. **SIC:** 5047
(Medical & Hospital Equipment). **Est:** 1946. **Sales:**
$20,000,000 (2000). **Emp:** 110. **Officers:** R.B.
Schwartz, President.

■ 24675 ■ **Arky House Inc.**
218 E Grand Ave.
Hot Springs, AR 71901-4132
Phone: (501)624-0605 **Fax:** (870)264-0835
Products: Footwear. **SIC:** 5139 (Footwear). **Officers:**
Earl Wells, President.

■ 24676 ■ **Athletic Supply Inc.**
PO Box C19050
Seattle, WA 98109
Phone: (206)623-8972 **Fax:** (206)467-6801
Products: Footwear; Athletic footwear. **SIC:** 5139
(Footwear). **Officers:** Mike Lambert, President.

■ 24677 ■ **Atlas Safety Equipment Co. Inc.**
132 Industrial Dr.
Birmingham, AL 35211-4444
Phone: (205)942-4070 **Fax:** (205)942-6899
Products: Footwear, including safety shoes. **SIC:** 5139
(Footwear). **Officers:** William Yeilding, President.

■ 24678 ■ **Atsco Footwear Inc.**
500 Bodwell St.
Avon, MA 02322-1000
Phone: (508)583-7600 **Fax:** (508)559-7975
Products: Footwear. **SIC:** 5139 (Footwear). **Est:** 1911.
Emp: 24. **Officers:** David Epstein, Chairman of the
Board.

■ 24679 ■ **J. Baker Inc.**
555 Turnpike St.
Canton, MA 02021
Phone: (781)828-9300
Products: Footwear. **SIC:** 5139 (Footwear). **Est:** 1961.

Sales: $592,200,000 (2000). **Emp:** 6,630. **Officers:**
Alan I. Weinstein, CEO & President; Philip G.
Rosenberg, Exec. VP & CFO.

■ 24680 ■ **Baklayan Garbis**
531 S Broadway
Baltimore, MD 21231
Phone: (410)276-2234
Products: Athletic footwear; Footwear. **SIC:** 5139
(Footwear). **Officers:** Garbis Baklayan, Owner.

■ 24681 ■ **Bally Retail Inc.**
1 Bally Pl.
New Rochelle, NY 10801
Phone: (914)632-4444 **Fax:** (914)632-8264
Products: Men's and women's footwear and
accessories. **SIC:** 5139 (Footwear). **Sales:**
$100,000,000 (2000). **Emp:** 400. **Officers:** Susan K.
Sussman, President; Tony Falcone, Finance Officer.

■ 24682 ■ **Barry Manufacturing Company, Inc.**
Bubier St.
Lynn, MA 01901
Phone: (781)598-1055
Free: (800)642-4674 **Fax:** (781)598-9912
Products: Children's footwear. **SIC:** 5139 (Footwear).
Est: 1942. **Sales:** $20,000,000 (2000). **Emp:** 250.
Officers: Robert Rothbard, President.

■ 24683 ■ **Bata Shoe Co. Inc.**
U.S Hwy. 40
4501 Pulaski Hwy.
Belcamp, MD 21017
Phone: (410)272-2000
Free: (800)365-2282 **Fax:** (410)272-3346
E-mail: jdiem@bata-usa.com
URL: http://www.bata-usa.com
Products: Injected industrial footwear and clothing;
Specialty rubber compounds. **SICs:** 5139 (Footwear);
5199 (Nondurable Goods Nec); 5136 (Men's/Boys'
Clothing); 5137 (Women's/Children's Clothing). **Est:**
1939. **Sales:** $28,000,000 (1999). **Emp:** 158. **Officers:**
D.B. Talbot, President; C.C. Maistros, Vice President;
Robin Roberts, VP of Marketing & Sales.

■ 24684 ■ **Battlefield Police Supply Inc.**
7221 Nathan Ct.
Manassas, VA 20109-2436
Phone: (703)330-1902
Products: Footwear. **SIC:** 5139 (Footwear). **Officers:**
Dawn Hazard, President.

■ 24685 ■ **Bay Corp.**
PO Box 124
Colchester, VT 05446-0124
Phone: (802)863-2653 **Fax:** (802)658-5496
Products: Footwear. **SIC:** 5139 (Footwear). **Officers:**
David Bailey, President.

■ 24686 ■ **Bay Merchandising Inc.**
68 Old Mill Bottom Rd. N
Annapolis, MD 21401-5418
Phone: (410)757-5926 **Fax:** (410)757-0928
Products: Footwear. **SIC:** 5139 (Footwear). **Officers:**
Fulvio Alviani, President.

■ 24687 ■ John Baynes Co. Inc.
16234 Sasanoa Dr.
Cornelius, NC 28031-8740
Phone: (704)527-2440 **Fax:** (704)527-2439
Products: Shoe accessories; Women's clothing
accessories. **SICs:** 5139 (Footwear); 5137
(Women's/Children's Clothing). **Officers:** John Baynes,
President.

■ 24688 ■ Beijing Trade Exchange Inc.
701 E St. SE
Washington, DC 20003-2841
Phone: (202)546-5534 **Fax:** (202)543-3288
Products: Footwear; Raincoats and other waterproof
outerwear; Sporting and athletic goods. **SICs:** 5139
(Footwear); 5091 (Sporting & Recreational Goods);
5136 (Men's/Boys' Clothing); 5137
(Women's/Children's Clothing). **Officers:** John
Canellakis, Vice President.

■ 24689 ■ Jim Benge & Co.
927 N Northlake Way
Seattle, WA 98103-8871
Phone: (206)545-4262 **Fax:** (206)632-5268
E-mail: bengelo@accessone.com
Products: Footwear; Athletic footwear. **SIC:** 5139
(Footwear). **Est:** 1979. **Officers:** Jim Benge, Owner;
Bari Clemons, Customer Service Contact.

■ 24690 ■ Bennett Importing Inc.
145 Wells Ave.
Newton, MA 02459
Phone: (617)332-7500 **Fax:** (617)332-1968
Products: Footwear. **SIC:** 5139 (Footwear). **Officers:**
Don Ribatt, CEO.

■ 24691 ■ Birkenstock Footprint Sandals Inc.
PO Box 6140
Novato, CA 94948
Phone: (415)892-4200
Free: (800)487-9255 **Fax:** (415)899-1324
URL: http://www.birkenstock.com
Products: Comfort footwear, including sandals;
Insoles; Socks. **SICs:** 5139 (Footwear); 5136
(Men's/Boys' Clothing); 5137 (Women's/Children's
Clothing). **Sales:** $81,000,000 (2000). **Emp:** 135.
Officers: Margot Fraser, President; Dennis Cutter,
Mgr. of Finance.

■ 24692 ■ Emery Blau
20 Pumpkin Ln.
Norwalk, CT 06851-1421
Phone: (203)846-9606
Products: Footwear; Western hats; Buckles; Bolos.
SICs: 5139 (Footwear); 5137 (Women's/Children's
Clothing); 5136 (Men's/Boys' Clothing). **Officers:**
Emery Blau, Owner.

■ 24693 ■ Bobbett & Associates Inc.
263 N Madison Ave.
Greenwood, IN 46142-3633
Phone: (317)882-6051 **Fax:** (317)882-6085
Products: Footwear. **SIC:** 5139 (Footwear). **Officers:**
Jonathon Bobbett, President.

■ 24694 ■ Mel Boley Co.
1484 S State St.
Salt Lake City, UT 84115-5424
Phone: (801)484-5372 **Fax:** (801)487-1998
Products: Footwear. **SIC:** 5139 (Footwear). **Officers:**
M. Boley, President.

■ 24695 ■ Boot & Shoe Village
5704 Vickie Dr.
Winston Salem, NC 27106-9655
Phone: (910)969-6408
Products: Footwear. **SIC:** 5139 (Footwear). **Officers:**
Wade Boone, Owner.

■ 24696 ■ Bostonian Shoe Co.
520 S Broad St.
Kennett Square, PA 19348
Phone: (215)444-6550 **Fax:** (215)444-4345
Products: Shoes. **SIC:** 5139 (Footwear). **Est:** 1884.
Sales: $70,000,000 (2000). **Emp:** 46. **Officers:** Robert
Landerman, President; R. Trent Sams, Controller;
Jeffrey Staub, VP of Sales.

■ 24697 ■ Brenner Companies Inc.
27-31 Osprey Rd.
Saugus, MA 01906
Phone: (781)231-0555
Products: Footwear. **SIC:** 5139 (Footwear). **Officers:**
Gerald Brenner, President.

■ 24698 ■ Charles Brocato
1618 Stockton Rd.
Joppa, MD 21085-1825
Phone: (410)679-6534 **Free:** (800)354-6534
Products: Footwear. **SIC:** 5139 (Footwear). **Officers:**
Charles Brocato, Owner.

■ 24699 ■ Brown Group Inc.
PO Box 29
St. Louis, MO 63166-0029
Phone: (314)854-4000 **Fax:** (314)854-4274
Products: Men's, women's, and children's footwear.
SIC: 5139 (Footwear). **Sales:** $1,567,200,000 (2000).
Emp: 22,000. **Officers:** Ronald A. Fromm, CEO,
President & Chairman of the Board; Andrew M. Rosen,
CFO and Treasurer.

■ 24700 ■ Brown Shoe Co.
PO Box 29
St. Louis, MO 63166-0029
Phone: (314)854-4000
Free: (800)766-6465 **Fax:** (314)854-4274
E-mail: info@brownshoe.com
URL: http://www.brownshoe.com
Products: Footwear. **SIC:** 5139 (Footwear). **Est:** 1878.
Sales: $1,600,000,000 (2000). **Emp:** 3,000. **Officers:**
Ronald A. Fromm, President; Robert E. Stadler Jr., VP
of Finance.

■ 24701 ■ BTF Inc.
PO Box 408
Westborough, MA 01581-0408
Phone: (508)366-0638 **Fax:** (508)366-3615
Products: Footwear. **SIC:** 5139 (Footwear). **Officers:**
Thomas Sweeney, President.

■ 24702 ■ Buckhead Shoes Corp. II
PO Box 13523
Atlanta, GA 30324
Phones: (404)233-5554 (404)426-5445
Products: Footwear. **SIC:** 5139 (Footwear). **Officers:**
Monik Tannour, President.

■ 24703 ■ Burchs Fine Footwear Inc.
16 Oakway Ctr.
Eugene, OR 97401-5612
Phone: (541)485-2070
Free: (800)201-2070 **Fax:** (541)484-1345
E-mail: raftersrec@aol.com
Products: Sport footwear. **SIC:** 5139 (Footwear). **Est:**
1991. **Sales:** $3,500,000 (2000). **Emp:** 12. **Officers:**
Bill Combs, President; John Hayer, Sales/Marketing
Contact. **Doing Business As:** Rafters Recreational
Footwear.

■ 24704 ■ Cadillac Shoe Products Inc.
50761 W Pontiac Trl.
Wixom, MI 48393
Phone: (248)624-5800 **Fax:** (248)624-4604
Products: Shoe care products, including brushes,
laces, polishes, cleaners, and kits. **SIC:** 5139
(Footwear). **Est:** 1963. **Officers:** Marilyn Beckham,
President.

■ 24705 ■ Candie's Inc.
2975 Westchester Ave.
Purchase, NY 10577
Phone: (914)694-8600
Products: Fashion and leisure footwear. **SIC:** 5139
(Footwear). **Sales:** $45,000,000 (2000). **Emp:** 61.
Officers: Neil Cole, CEO, President & Chairman of the
Board; Gary Klein, VP of Finance.

■ 24706 ■ Caporicci Footwear Ltd.
11325 Lee Hwy. 103
Fairfax, VA 22030-5610
Phone: (703)591-6000 **Fax:** (703)591-3600
Products: Footwear. **SIC:** 5139 (Footwear). **Officers:**
Domenico Caporicci, Chairman of the Board.

■ 24707 ■ Carl's Clogging Supplies
525 Poverty Ln.
Salem, SC 29676-2414
Phone: (864)944-8125
Products: Footwear. **SIC:** 5139 (Footwear). **Officers:**
Carl Blanton, Owner.

■ 24708 ■ Cascade Clothing
1707 NE Woodridge Ln.
Bend, OR 97701-5847
Phone: (541)389-1454 **Fax:** (541)383-3548
Products: Footwear. **SIC:** 5139 (Footwear). **Officers:**
Jack Mc Cleary, Partner.

■ 24709 ■ Cels Enterprises Inc.
3485 S La Cienega
Los Angeles, CA 90016
Phone: (310)838-2103
Products: Women's dress shoes. **SIC:** 5139
(Footwear). **Est:** 1970. **Sales:** $8,000,000 (2000).
Emp: 150. **Officers:** Bob Goldman, President; Ann
Yen, Controller; Mike Parmenter, Vice President.

■ 24710 ■ Chapmans Shoe Repair
110 N Mill St.
Lexington, KY 40507-1207
Phone: (606)231-7463
Products: Footwear; Shoe repair materials. **SICs:**
5139 (Footwear); 5087 (Service Establishment
Equipment). **Officers:** James Chapman, Owner.

■ 24711 ■ Chesapeake Shoe Co. of California
284 Harbor Way
South San Francisco, CA 94080
Phone: (650)873-1434
Products: Athletic shoes. **SIC:** 5139 (Footwear). **Est:**
1946. **Sales:** $10,000,000 (2000). **Emp:** 30. **Officers:**
Daniel Goldfein, President & Treasurer.

■ 24712 ■ Chilis Footwear Inc.
PO Box 1658
Santa Maria, CA 93456
Phone: (805)922-7753
Free: (800)843-5933 **Fax:** (805)925-0450
E-mail: chilis@impo.com
Products: Junior fashion shoes. **SIC:** 5139 (Footwear).
Est: 1985. **Sales:** $5,000,000 (1999). **Emp:** 35.
Officers: Soren Kieler, President.

■ 24713 ■ CK Footwear Inc.
1935 Revere Beach Pky.
Everett, MA 02149-5945
Phone: (781)307-5005
Products: Footwear. **SIC:** 5139 (Footwear). **Officers:**
Joan Helpern, President.

■ 24714 ■ Classic Sales Inc.
1754 Hoe St.
Honolulu, HI 96819-3124
Phone: (808)845-0122 **Fax:** (808)842-5639
Products: Footwear; House slippers. **SIC:** 5139
(Footwear). **Officers:** Carlton Shimomi, President.

■ 24715 ■ Cofish International Inc.
PO Box 242
East Haddam, CT 06423
Phone: (860)873-9500
Free: (800)582-3474 **Fax:** (860)873-9890
Products: Footwear and clothing for commercial
fishermen. **SICs:** 5139 (Footwear); 5136 (Men's/Boys'
Clothing); 5137 (Women's/Children's Clothing). **Est:**
1900. **Sales:** $2,500,000 (2000). **Emp:** 10. **Officers:**
Edward Stolarz, President.

■ 24716 ■ Kenneth Cole Productions Inc.
152 W 57th St.
New York, NY 10019
Phone: (212)265-1500 **Free:** (800)536-2653
Products: Women's and men's footwear, leather
handbags and accessories. **SICs:** 5139 (Footwear);
5137 (Women's/Children's Clothing). **Sales:**
$185,300,000 (2000). **Emp:** 650. **Officers:** Kenneth D.
Cole, CEO & President; Stanley A. Mayer, Exec. VP &
CFO.

■ 24717 ■ Colonial Shoe Co.
PO Box 43001
Atlanta, GA 30336-0001
Phone: (404)691-4141
Free: (800)678-7463 **Fax:** (404)691-7663
E-mail: colonial@mindspring.com
URL: http://www.colonialshoe.com
Products: Footwear. **SIC:** 5139 (Footwear). **Est:** 1960.
Officers: Kevin Jon Moran, President.

■ 24718 ■ Comfort Shoe Corp.
PO Box 1360
Haverhill, MA 01831-1860
Phone: (978)373-0133
Free: (800)234-7463 **Fax:** (978)373-7492
Products: Slip-resistant footwear; Women's leather comfort and orthopedic shoes. **SIC:** 5139 (Footwear).
Est: 1946. **Officers:** William Brindis, President.

■ 24719 ■ Consolidated Shoe Company Inc.
PO Box 10549
Lynchburg, VA 24506-0549
Phone: (804)239-0391 **Fax:** (804)237-3473
Products: Footwear. **SIC:** 5139 (Footwear). **Est:** 1896.
Emp: 150. **Officers:** Richard Carrington, President.

■ 24720 ■ Contour Lynnsoles Inc.
PO Box 20016
Sarasota, FL 34276
Phone: (941)921-0790
Products: Footwear; Shoe accessories. **SIC:** 5139 (Footwear). **Officers:** Kenneth Lynn, President.

■ 24721 ■ Corrective Shoe Repair
1502 21st St. NW
Washington, DC 20036-1008
Phone: (202)232-9749
Products: Footwear. **SIC:** 5139 (Footwear). **Officers:** Nelson Ramos, Owner.

■ 24722 ■ D & D Shoe Company, LLC
200 S 5th St.
Mayfield, KY 42066
Phone: (270)251-2055 **Fax:** (270)251-0054
E-mail: dandd@ldd.net
Products: Footwear, including store returns, closeouts, and factory irregulars. **SIC:** 5139 (Footwear). **Est:** 1985. **Emp:** 38. **Officers:** David Hardin, Owner; Lucy Hardin, Owner.

■ 24723 ■ David Shoe Co.
1201 Edgecliff Pl., Apt. 1051
Cincinnati, OH 45206-2853
Products: Athletic footwear. **SIC:** 5139 (Footwear).
Officers: Mark Levenshus, President.

■ 24724 ■ Davis County Cooperative Society
3500 S West Temple
Salt Lake City, UT 84115-4408
Phone: (801)467-4003
Products: Footwear. **SIC:** 5139 (Footwear). **Officers:** John Kingston, President.

■ 24725 ■ Deckers Outdoor Corp.
495-A S Fairview Ave.
Goleta, CA 93117
Phone: (805)967-7611 **Fax:** (805)967-9722
Products: Sandals; Shoes. **SICs:** 5139 (Footwear); 5136 (Men's/Boys' Clothing); 5137 (Women's/Children's Clothing). **Est:** 1973. **Sales:** $109,000,000 (1999). **Emp:** 100. **Officers:** Doug Otto, CEO; Peter Benjamin, President; Tom Stevenson, Dir. of Information Systems; Bob Beatty, VP & CFO.

■ 24726 ■ Dentex Shoe Corp.
PO Box 1774
Laredo, TX 78041
Phone: (956)727-3591 **Fax:** (956)726-9061
Products: Shoes. **SIC:** 5139 (Footwear). **Emp:** 36.
Officers: James P. Masino.

■ 24727 ■ Driscoll Leather Co. Inc.
714 S 15th St.
Omaha, NE 68102-3103
Phone: (402)341-4307
Free: (800)228-7012 **Fax:** (402)341-2774
E-mail: driscoll75@aol.com
Products: Footwear; Shoe accessories. **SIC:** 5139 (Footwear). **Est:** 1924. **Sales:** $1,600,000 (2000).

Emp: 8. **Officers:** John Vokoun, President; Katie Henningsen, Sales/Marketing Contact; Kevin Henningsen, Customer Service Contact.

■ 24728 ■ Dynamic Foam Products Inc.
PO Box 774942
Steamboat Springs, CO 80477-4942
Phone: (970)879-3631
Free: (800)421-3626 **Fax:** (970)879-3631
Products: Footwear; Shoe accessories. **SIC:** 5139 (Footwear). **Officers:** Keith Liefer, President.

■ 24729 ■ East Coast Connection Inc.
5016 Rte. 130 N
Delran, NJ 08075
Phone: (609)461-8003 **Fax:** (609)461-2702
Products: Athletic footwear. **SIC:** 5139 (Footwear).

■ 24730 ■ Easy Shoe Distributors Inc.
2842 NE 187th St.
Miami, FL 33180
Phone: (305)687-9576
Products: Athletic footwear; Women's dress shoes; Children's shoes; Shoes. **SIC:** 5139 (Footwear).

■ 24731 ■ Eidai International, Inc.
2676 Waiwai Loop
Honolulu, HI 96819-1938
Phone: (808)836-0999 **Fax:** (808)833-3410
Products: Footwear. **SIC:** 5139 (Footwear). **Officers:** Jenter Fan, President.

■ 24732 ■ Elan-Polo Inc.
1699 S Hanley Rd.
St. Louis, MO 63144
Phone: (314)645-3018 **Fax:** (314)645-5601
Products: Shoes, including athletic, dress, children's, men's, and women's shoes. **SIC:** 5139 (Footwear). **Est:** 1965. **Sales:** $100,000,000 (2000). **Emp:** 300.
Officers: Joe Russell, President; Robert Callahan; Paul Cahn.

■ 24733 ■ Elliott Shoe Co.
3911 Western Ave.
Knoxville, TN 37921-4452
Phone: (423)524-1722 **Fax:** (423)637-2455
Products: Footwear. **SIC:** 5139 (Footwear). **Officers:** Jack Elliott, Owner.

■ 24734 ■ Emit International Corp.
PO Box 22238
Minneapolis, MN 55422-0238
Phone: (612)521-2246 **Fax:** (612)521-1677
Products: Footwear; Shoes. **SIC:** 5139 (Footwear).
Officers: Wendy Nego, President.

■ 24735 ■ Ener-Gee Sales Inc.
927 McCully St.
Honolulu, HI 96826-2703
Phone: (808)949-1899 **Fax:** (808)946-3589
Products: Footwear; Athletic footwear. **SIC:** 5139 (Footwear). **Officers:** Valerie Nagatori, President.

■ 24736 ■ Euroimport Co. Inc.
PO Box 80624
Seattle, WA 98108-0624
Phone: (206)763-7303
Free: (800)726-7304 **Fax:** (206)763-7240
Products: Footwear; Shoe accessories. **SIC:** 5139 (Footwear). **Officers:** David Shinder, President.

■ 24737 ■ Eurostar Inc.
13425 S Figueroa St.
Los Angeles, CA 90061
Phone: (310)715-9300 **Fax:** (310)329-0196
Products: Athletic shoes. **SIC:** 5139 (Footwear). **Est:** 1984. **Emp:** 350. **Officers:** Eric Alon, President; Jerrold R. Silva, COO; Helen Tsao, CFO.

■ 24738 ■ Fabiano Shoe Company Inc.
850 Summer St.
Boston, MA 02127-1537
Phone: (617)268-5625 **Fax:** (617)268-2322
Products: Footwear, including hiking boots. **SIC:** 5139 (Footwear). **Officers:** Michael Fabiano, President.

■ 24739 ■ Fair Inc.
2260 Terminal Rd.
Roseville, MN 55113-2516
Phone: (612)379-0110 **Fax:** (612)623-4440
Products: Footwear, including theatrical and dance shoes. **SIC:** 5139 (Footwear). **Officers:** Theodore Schroepfer, President.

■ 24740 ■ Family Shoe Center
PO Box 911
Marion, VA 24354-0911
Phone: (540)783-5061
Free: (800)553-9535 **Fax:** (540)782-9535
Products: Footwear. **SIC:** 5139 (Footwear). **Officers:** Tony Glavocich, Owner.

■ 24741 ■ Fancy Feet Inc.
26650 Harding
Oak Park, MI 48237
Phone: (248)398-8460
Free: (800)858-8460 **Fax:** (248)398-5650
Products: Footwear. **SIC:** 5139 (Footwear). **Est:** 1982.
Officers: Mary Ann Fontana, President.

■ 24742 ■ Fashion Slippers Import USA
PO Box 180
Stamford, CT 06904-0180
Phone: (203)324-2191 **Fax:** (203)324-6651
Products: Footwear. **SIC:** 5139 (Footwear). **Officers:** Joseph Maxner, President.

■ 24743 ■ FE. MA. Inc.
12 W 57th St., Ste. 1001
New York, NY 10019-3900
Phone: (212)438-8353
Products: Men's shoes. **SIC:** 5139 (Footwear). **Est:** 1987. **Sales:** $6,000,000 (2000). **Emp:** 10. **Officers:** Fernando Strappa, President; Tony Enea, Sales Mgr.

■ 24744 ■ First Native American Corp.
7828 N 19th Ave., No. 11-12
Phoenix, AZ 85021-7029
Phone: (602)266-9889 **Fax:** (602)266-9880
Products: Athletic footwear. **SIC:** 5139 (Footwear).
Officers: Harry Sloan, President.

■ 24745 ■ Flexible Feat Sandals
2344 County Rd. 225
Durango, CO 81301-7034
Phone: (970)247-4628
E-mail: flex@bwn.net
URL: http://www.durango.com/flyers
Products: Footwear. **SIC:** 5139 (Footwear). **Est:** 1985.
Sales: $5,000 (2000). **Emp:** 2. **Officers:** Robin Fritch, Partner.

■ 24746 ■ Foot Loose Inc.
PO Box 598
Irmo, SC 29063-0598
Phone: (803)772-3485 **Fax:** (803)772-7754
Products: Footwear. **SIC:** 5139 (Footwear). **Officers:** Michael Long, President.

■ 24747 ■ Free Shoe Shop
217 W Main St.
Union, SC 29379-2214
Phone: (864)427-3103
Products: Footwear; Shoes. **SIC:** 5139 (Footwear).
Officers: Howard Free, Owner.

■ 24748 ■ French Dressing Inc.
PO Box 971
Williston, VT 05495-0971
Phone: (802)658-1434 **Fax:** (802)658-3397
Products: Footwear. **SIC:** 5139 (Footwear). **Officers:** Emmanuel Tissot, President.

■ 24749 ■ Gardners Shoes Inc.
8513 Midlothian Tpke.
Richmond, VA 23235-5123
Phone: (804)323-5979
Products: Footwear; Shoes. **SIC:** 5139 (Footwear).
Officers: John Gardner, President.

■ 24750 ■ Gilbert & Son Shoe Company
149 S Daniel Morgan Ave.
Spartanburg, SC 29306-3211
Phone: (864)582-8049 **Fax:** (864)582-6267
Products: Footwear. **SIC:** 5139 (Footwear). **Officers:** Barbara Gilbert, President.

■ 24751 ■ Gilvins Boots & Shoes
3838 S Madison Ave.
Indianapolis, IN 46227-1310
Phone: (317)783-3210   **Fax:** (317)783-3210
Products: Footwear; Shoes. **SIC:** 5139 (Footwear).
Officers: Dan Gilvin, Partner.

■ 24752 ■ Gita Sporting Goods, Ltd.
12600 Steele Creek Rd.
Charlotte, NC 28273-3770
Phone: (704)588-7550   **Fax:** (704)588-4322
E-mail: gitabike@bellsouth.net
URL: http://www.gitabike.com
Products: Footwear; Clothing; Bikes and cycling accessories. **SIC:** 5139 (Footwear). **Officers:** Giorgio Andretta, President. **Former Name:** Gita Sports Ltd.

■ 24753 ■ Goodwear Shoe Co. Inc.
144 Duane St.
New York, NY 10013-3808
Phone: (212)233-6813
Free: (800)221-5656   **Fax:** (212)349-5862
Products: Children's shoes. **SIC:** 5139 (Footwear).
Est: 1934. **Sales:** $4,000,000 (2000). **Emp:** 12.
Officers: Joe Goldstein, President; Arthur Goldstein, Vice President.

■ 24754 ■ Granton Shoe Imports
524 Riverdale Dr.
Glendale, CA 91204
Phone: (818)507-8449
Free: (800)237-7458   **Fax:** (818)507-6605
E-mail: sales@granton.com
URL: http://www.granton.com
Products: Children's footwear. **SIC:** 5139 (Footwear).
Est: 1982. **Sales:** $5,000,000 (2000). **Emp:** 11.
Officers: Ken Ho, President.

■ 24755 ■ Graves Import Co. Inc.
1911 21st Ave. S
Nashville, TN 37212-3833
Phone: (615)269-3475   **Fax:** (615)269-2654
Products: Footwear. **SIC:** 5139 (Footwear). **Officers:** David Graves, President.

■ 24756 ■ Green Market Services Co.
1105 W Chestnut St.
Brockton, MA 02301
Phone: (508)587-8661   **Fax:** (508)559-9212
Products: Footwear. **SIC:** 5139 (Footwear). **Officers:** Robert Green, President.

■ 24757 ■ Haney Shoe Store Inc.
PO Box 4400
Omaha, NE 68104-0400
Phone: (402)556-2022   **Fax:** (402)556-4205
Products: Footwear. **SIC:** 5139 (Footwear). **Officers:** Don Haney, President.

■ 24758 ■ Happy Feet Plus
18837 U.S 19 N
Clearwater, FL 33764
Phone: (727)538-1111
Free: (800)336-6657   **Fax:** (727)539-8550
E-mail: happy@happyfeet.com
URL: http://www.happyfeet.com
Products: Footwear, including massage sandals. **SIC:** 5139 (Footwear). **Est:** 1985. **Sales:** $6,000,000 (2000). **Emp:** 53. **Officers:** Jane Strong, e-mail: jane@happyfeet.com; Jacob R. Wurtz, e-mail: jacob@happyfeet.com.

■ 24759 ■ William H. Harris & Co.
320 Monroe Ave.
Memphis, TN 38103-2720
Phone: (901)527-2558   **Fax:** (901)527-2578
Products: Footwear; Men's and boy's clothing; Infant clothing; Jewelry; Toys. **SICs:** 5139 (Footwear); 5136 (Men's/Boys' Clothing); 5137 (Women's/Children's Clothing); 5092 (Toys & Hobby Goods & Supplies); 5094 (Jewelry & Precious Stones). **Est:** 1926. **Emp:** 2. **Officers:** Warren Lee, Partner.

■ 24760 ■ Scott Hawaii
1212 Kona
Honolulu, HI 96814-4303
Phone: (808)591-2921
Free: (800)726-8828   **Fax:** (808)597-8101
E-mail: scothi@aloha.net
Products: Sandals. **SIC:** 5139 (Footwear). **Est:** 1932.
Sales: $3,000,000 (2000). **Emp:** 12. **Officers:** Steven Scott, President.

■ 24761 ■ Joan & David Helpern Inc.
1935 Revere Beach Pkwy.
Everett, MA 02149-5945
Phone: (617)387-5005   **Fax:** (617)389-8018
Products: Footwear. **SIC:** 5139 (Footwear). **Officers:** David Helpern, Treasurer.

■ 24762 ■ Henco Inc.
1025 W 25th St.
Norfolk, VA 23517-1014
Phone: (757)625-5361   **Fax:** (757)626-3104
Products: Foot socks. **SICs:** 5139 (Footwear); 5136 (Men's/Boys' Clothing); 5137 (Women's/Children's Clothing). **Officers:** Edward Kesser, President.

■ 24763 ■ Hi-Tec Sports USA Inc.
4801 Stoddard Rd.
Modesto, CA 95356
Phone: (209)545-1111
Free: (800)521-1698   **Fax:** (209)545-2543
URL: http://www.hi-tec.com
Products: Women's, men's, and children's adventure outdoor footwear and occupational footwear. **SIC:** 5139 (Footwear). **Est:** 1979. **Emp:** 80. **Officers:** Jonathan Caplan, President & CEO; Robert Kaiser, CFO; Jeff Bua, Sr. VP of Sales & Marketing; Dawn Standart, Human Resources Dir.; Scott Mikkelsen, Sales Mgr.; Linda Olson, Supervisor of Customer Services.

■ 24764 ■ Himex International Inc.
PO Box 745
Ellicott City, MD 21041-0745
Phone: (410)247-7718   **Fax:** (410)247-7719
Products: Footwear. **SIC:** 5139 (Footwear). **Officers:** Ayub Hira, President.

■ 24765 ■ Hondo Boots
6425 Boeing Dr., Ste. C3
El Paso, TX 79925-1052
Phone: (915)778-9481   **Fax:** (915)779-2274
Products: Cowboy boots. **SIC:** 5139 (Footwear). **Emp:** 49. **Officers:** Filbert Guijarro.

■ 24766 ■ Hush Puppies Co.
9341 Courtland Dr.
Rockford, MI 49351
Phone: (616)866-5500   **Fax:** (616)866-0438
Products: Shoes and boots. **SIC:** 5139 (Footwear). **Est:** 1883. **Officers:** David Bok, President; Nick Ottenwess, CFO.

■ 24767 ■ Ilani Shoes Ltd.
47 W 34th St.
New York, NY 10001
Phone: (212)947-5830   **Fax:** (212)947-2319
Products: Women's shoes, casual, except sandals; Women's dress shoes. **SIC:** 5139 (Footwear). **Est:** 1980. **Sales:** $5,000,000 (2000). **Emp:** 6. **Officers:** Ilian Cohen, President.

■ 24768 ■ IMR Corp.
PO Box 1690
Harvey, LA 70059-1690
Phone: (504)362-9888   **Fax:** (504)362-7000
URL: http://www.imrcorporation.com
Products: Safety footwear, equipment and clothing; Medical and first-aid supplies. **SIC:** 5139 (Footwear). **Est:** 1970. **Sales:** $7,000,000 (1999). **Emp:** 28. **Officers:** G Seamon, President.

■ 24769 ■ Inter-Pacific Corp.
2257 Colby Ave.
Los Angeles, CA 90064
Phone: (310)473-7591
Products: Men's, women's, and childrens' footwear. **SICs:** 5139 (Footwear); 5137 (Women's/Children's Clothing). **Sales:** $120,000,000 (2000). **Emp:** 30. **Officers:** Frank Arnsteine, CEO.

■ 24770 ■ Intermountain Lea Findings Co.
1064 East 300 South
Salt Lake City, UT 84102-2513
Phone: (801)355-3737
Free: (800)658-8798   **Fax:** (801)521-4362
Products: Footwear; Leather; Shoe findings. **SIC:** 5139 (Footwear). **Est:** 1948. **Sales:** $360,000 (2000). **Emp:** 4. **Officers:** Ralph Morris, President.

■ 24771 ■ Iron Age Corp.
Robinson Plz. 3, Ste. 400
Pittsburgh, PA 15205
Phone: (412)787-4100
Free: (800)223-8912   **Fax:** (412)787-8123
E-mail: ironage.shoes@internetmci.com
URL: http://www.ironageshoes.com
Products: Safety boots and shoes, including specialized shoes, non-slip foorwear, and uniform footwear. **SIC:** 5139 (Footwear). **Est:** 1817. **Sales:** $80,000,000 (2000). **Emp:** 800. **Officers:** William J. Mills, CEO & President; Keith McDonough, CFO; Jay Sebes, Exec. VP; Pat Porta, Customer Service Contact.

■ 24772 ■ Island Import and Export Co.
1020 Kristin Ct.
St. Paul, MN 55110
Phone: (612)481-9663   **Fax:** (612)481-0863
Products: Footwear; Men's sportswear; Women's clothing. **SICs:** 5139 (Footwear); 5136 (Men's/Boys' Clothing); 5137 (Women's/Children's Clothing). **Officers:** Richard Leier, Owner.

■ 24773 ■ Items International Airwalk Inc.
PO Box 951
Altoona, PA 16603-0951
Phone: (814)943-6164   **Fax:** (814)943-3921
Products: Footwear. **SIC:** 5139 (Footwear). **Sales:** $236,000,000 (2000). **Emp:** 130. **Officers:** George Yohn, CEO; Robert Fischer, CFO.

■ 24774 ■ Izenco Inc.
501 W 172nd St.
South Holland, IL 60473
Phone: (708)596-3600
Products: Work shoes. **SIC:** 5139 (Footwear). **Est:** 1949. **Sales:** $4,100,000 (2000). **Emp:** 25. **Officers:** Art Eisenberg, President; Jim Manning, General Mgr.; Victor Veguilla, Dir. of Sales.

■ 24775 ■ J & B Import Ltd. Inc.
294 Columbia St.
Fall River, MA 02721-1322
Phone: (508)679-2710
Products: Footwear. **SIC:** 5139 (Footwear). **Officers:** Joao Rodrigues, President.

■ 24776 ■ J & J Shoe Co.
PO Box 792
Brinkley, AR 72021-0792
Phone: (870)734-2360
Products: Footwear. **SIC:** 5139 (Footwear). **Officers:** Jubal Etheridge, Partner.

■ 24777 ■ Jasmine Ltd.
8501 Maple Ave.
Pennsauken, NJ 08109-3337
Phone: (609)665-7117
Products: Women's and children's shoes. **SIC:** 5139 (Footwear). **Est:** 1980. **Sales:** $30,700,000 (2000). **Emp:** 79. **Officers:** Irving M. Mangel, CEO, President & Chairman of the Board; Edward W. Maskaly, CFO; Melvin Twersky, Dir. of Marketing & Sales.

■ 24778 ■ Jeffress Business Services
18834 SE 42nd St.
Issaquah, WA 98027-9366
Phone: (425)643-1917
Free: (800)735-2462   **Fax:** (425)562-2462
Products: Footwear. **SIC:** 5139 (Footwear). **Est:** 1990. **Emp:** 2. **Officers:** Roy Jeffress, Partner. **Doing Business As:** IBS Co.

■ 24779 ■ Jimlar Corp.
160 Great Neck Rd.
Great Neck, NY 11021
Phone: (516)829-1717   **Fax:** (516)829-2970
Products: Shoes. **SIC:** 5139 (Footwear). **Est:** 1958.
Sales: $130,000,000 (2000). **Emp:** 130. **Officers:**

James Tarica, President; Laurence Tarica, Executive VP, Finance and Treasurer; James McCormick, Dir. of Marketing; Ellen Moran, Information Systems Mgr.; John Castella, Dir. of Operations.

■ 24780 ■ Johannsens Inc.
PO Box 23
Augusta, GA 30903-0023
Phone: (706)722-0949 Fax: (706)724-2226
Products: Footwear; Sporting and athletic goods. SICs: 5139 (Footwear); 5091 (Sporting & Recreational Goods).

■ 24781 ■ Kambach & Kettman Inc.
323 N Harrison St.
Davenport, IA 52801-1301
Phone: (319)322-2122
Free: (800)292-6900 Fax: (319)322-2122
Products: Shoe repair materials; Rubber and plastic footwear. SIC: 5139 (Footwear). Officers: G. Kettman, President.

■ 24782 ■ Kearns Associates
2071 N Fairview Ln.
Rochester Hills, MI 48306-3927
Products: Footwear; Shoe accessories. SIC: 5139 (Footwear). Officers: Michael Kearns, Partner.

■ 24783 ■ Eddie Kilpatrick
644 N Blythe St.
Gallatin, TN 37066-2226
Phone: (615)452-5488
Products: Footwear. SIC: 5139 (Footwear). Officers: Eddie Kilpatrick, Owner.

■ 24784 ■ Kims Family Shoes Inc.
132 N Morley Ave.
Nogales, AZ 85621-3116
Phone: (520)287-2249 Fax: (520)287-3022
Products: Footwear. SIC: 5139 (Footwear). Officers: David Kim, President.

■ 24785 ■ Kipling Shoe Company Inc.
PO Box 187
Milton, WV 25541-0187
Phone: (304)743-5721
Free: (800)926-0207 Fax: (304)743-1226
Products: Footwear. SIC: 5139 (Footwear). Officers: Carroll Osburn, President.

■ 24786 ■ B. Klitzner and Son Inc.
PO Box 1357
Rocky Mount, NC 27802
Phone: (252)442-5740 Fax: (252)977-7281
Products: Shoes. SIC: 5139 (Footwear). Sales: $16,000,000 (1992). Emp: 27. Officers: David Jay, President.

■ 24787 ■ Knapp Shoes of Tucson Inc.
1835 S Alvernon Way
Tucson, AZ 85711-7602
Phone: (520)745-4643
Products: Footwear, including safety shoes. SIC: 5139 (Footwear). Officers: Harold Katz, President.

■ 24788 ■ La Crosse Footwear, Inc.
1407 St. Andrew St.
PO Box 1328
La Crosse, WI 54602
Phone: (608)782-3020
Free: (800)323-2668 Fax: (608)782-3025
URL: http://www.lacrosse-outdoors.com
Products: Boots; Clothing. SICs: 5139 (Footwear); 5136 (Men's/Boys' Clothing); 5137 (Women's/Children's Clothing). Est: 1897. Emp: 1,500. Officers: Andrew Kennelly, Sales/Marketing Contact; Jill Coughlin, Customer Service Contact; David Flaschberger, Human Resources Contact.

■ 24789 ■ Lanahan Sales
10325 SW 57th Pl.
Portland, OR 97219-5704
Phone: (503)244-6451 Fax: (503)245-7224
E-mail: lansales@aol.com
Products: Sporting and athletic goods; Footwear. SICs: 5139 (Footwear); 5091 (Sporting & Recreational Goods). Est: 1981. Sales: $1,000,000 (2000). Emp: 2. Officers: Jerry Lanahan, Owner.

■ 24790 ■ Landwerlen Leather Co. Inc.
PO Box 731
Indianapolis, IN 46206-0731
Phone: (317)636-8300
Free: (800)827-9867 Fax: (317)636-7369
Products: Footwear; Shoe accessories; Shoe repair supplies. SIC: 5139 (Footwear). Est: 1908. Officers: Dee Landwerlen, President.

■ 24791 ■ Ralph Lauren Footwear Inc.
120 E 56th St.
New York, NY 10022
Phone: (212)308-3805 Fax: (212)752-5840
Products: Footwear. SIC: 5139 (Footwear). Sales: $68,000,000 (2000). Emp: 100. Officers: Bruce Baker, President.

■ 24792 ■ Left Foot Ltd.
109 Tosca Dr.
Stoughton, MA 02072-1505
Phone: (508)238-4686 Fax: (508)238-9331
Products: Footwear. SIC: 5139 (Footwear). Officers: Robert Oshry, President.

■ 24793 ■ Lehigh Safety Shoe Co.
1100 E Main St.
Endicott, NY 13760
Phone: (607)757-4800 Fax: (607)757-4070
Products: Work boots. SIC: 5139 (Footwear). Sales: $40,000,000 (2000). Emp: 225. Officers: Kieth Johnson, President; David Jones, Controller.

■ 24794 ■ Mitchell Linwood
1249 S Beretania St. B
Honolulu, HI 96814-1822
Phone: (808)539-9358 Fax: (808)593-9354
Products: Footwear. SIC: 5139 (Footwear). Officers: Linwood Mitchell, Owner.

■ 24795 ■ LJO Inc.
401 Hamburg Tpk., Ste. 305
Wayne, NJ 07470
Phone: (973)956-6990
Products: Athletic shoes. SIC: 5139 (Footwear). Sales: $21,000,000 (1992). Emp: 35. Officers: Leif J. Ostberg, President.

■ 24796 ■ Loeffler's Safety Shoes Inc.
959 Payne Ave.
St. Paul, MN 55101-4003
Phone: (612)771-3833 Fax: (612)771-9287
Products: Footwear. SIC: 5139 (Footwear). Officers: James Loeffler, President.

■ 24797 ■ Fred Lurie Associates
777 NW 72nd Ave., Ste. 3AA9
Miami, FL 33126
Phone: (305)261-3682 Fax: (305)261-0244
Products: Shoes; Socks; Women's hosiery; Slippers. SICs: 5139 (Footwear); 5137 (Women's/Children's Clothing).

■ 24798 ■ C.O. Lynch Enterprises Inc.
2655 Fairview Ave. N
Roseville, MN 55113-2616
Phone: (612)331-3000 Fax: (612)331-3138
Products: Footwear. SIC: 5139 (Footwear). Officers: Charles Lynch, President.

■ 24799 ■ Markon Footwear Inc.
350 5th Ave., Ste. 1397
New York, NY 10118-1397
Phone: (212)947-0099 Fax: (212)967-7327
Products: Women's footwear. SIC: 5139 (Footwear). Est: 1981. Emp: 16. Officers: Marvin Guthartz.

■ 24800 ■ Marlboro Footworks Ltd.
60 Austin St.
Newton, MA 02460
Phone: (617)969-7070 Fax: (617)244-7463
E-mail: nancysh@ma.ultranet.com
Products: Footwear. SIC: 5139 (Footwear). Est: 1987. Officers: Laurence Koplan, President; Steve Goldberg, Sales/Mktg.; Don Schwarz, Sales/Mktg.; Judy Maynard, Customer Service.

■ 24801 ■ Marshal Glove & Safety Supply
PO Box 1346
Evansville, IN 47706-1346
Phone: (812)425-5167
Free: (800)457-3033 Fax: (812)428-8791
Products: Footwear; Shoes. SIC: 5139 (Footwear). Officers: Stella Shavitz, CEO.

■ 24802 ■ Maryland Industrial Inc.
28 Alco Pl.
Baltimore, MD 21227-2004
Phone: (410)247-9117 Fax: (410)247-3461
E-mail: skippyshoe@aol.com
Products: Work shoes and boots. SIC: 5139 (Footwear). Est: 1981. Sales: $1,900,000 (2000). Emp: 8. Officers: Philip McManus, President.

■ 24803 ■ Maxwell Shoe Company Inc.
PO Box 37
Readville, MA 02137
Phone: (617)364-5090 Fax: (617)364-9058
Products: Footwear. SIC: 5139 (Footwear). Sales: $150,000,000 (2000). Officers: Mark J. Cocozza, Chairman of the Board.

■ 24804 ■ Maye Hosiery Sales
3408 Eastway Dr.
Charlotte, NC 28205-6269
Phone: (704)537-5141
Products: Footwear; Shoes. SIC: 5139 (Footwear). Officers: Harold Maye, Owner.

■ 24805 ■ Maytown Shoe Manufacturing Company Inc.
1820 8th Ave.
Altoona, PA 16602
Phone: (814)943-5343 Fax: (814)943-0919
Products: Shoes. SIC: 5139 (Footwear). Est: 1948. Emp: 149. Officers: Victor Lombardo.

■ 24806 ■ McClendons Boot Store
217 N Main St.
McAlester, OK 74501-4650
Phone: (918)426-3291
Products: Boots. SIC: 5139 (Footwear). Officers: Bill McClendon, Owner.

■ 24807 ■ McCullar Enterprises Inc.
1850 Gen. George Patton
Franklin, TN 37067
Phone: (615)371-1056
Free: (800)347-7463 Fax: (615)371-1059
E-mail: mccullar@interserv.com
Products: Shoes. SIC: 5139 (Footwear). Est: 1970. Officers: Carrel McCullar, President.

■ 24808 ■ Mercury International Trading Corp.
PO Box 222
North Attleboro, MA 02761-0222
Phone: (508)699-9000 Fax: (508)699-9099
Products: Footwear, including athletic shoes. SIC: 5139 (Footwear). Officers: Irving Wiseman, Chairman of the Board.

■ 24809 ■ Mia Shoes Inc.
258 Chapman Rd., Ste. 100
Newark, DE 19702
Phone: (302)454-8500 Fax: (302)454-1110
Products: Footwear. SIC: 5139 (Footwear). Officers: Richard Strauss, President; Joseph Angelini, Vice President.

■ 24810 ■ Michigan Industrial Shoe Co.
25477 W 8 Mile Rd.
Detroit, MI 48240
Phone: (313)532-0902 Fax: (313)592-0903
Products: Footwear. SIC: 5139 (Footwear). Officers: Victor Girolami, President.

■ 24811 ■ Mid-America Footwear Co.
2700 Purdue Dr.
Oklahoma City, OK 73128-5802
Phone: (405)681-5560 Fax: (405)722-2314
Products: Footwear. SIC: 5139 (Footwear). Officers: Donald Parker, Owner.

■ 24812 ■ Miller Safety Products
1209 Orville Ave.
Kansas City, KS 66102-5114
Phone: (913)321-4955 **Fax:** (913)321-5661
Products: Footwear; Hoses; Safety glasses; First aid supplies. **SICs:** 5139 (Footwear); 5199 (Nondurable Goods Nec). **Est:** 1982. **Sales:** $95,000,000 (2000).
Emp: 7. **Officers:** Joseph Miller, Owner.

■ 24813 ■ Moccasin Tipi
1703 Acacia Dr.
Colorado Springs, CO 80907-4811
Phone: (719)590-7668
Products: Footwear. **SIC:** 5139 (Footwear). **Officers:** Herbert Perry, Partner.

■ 24814 ■ Money Saver
67 Leo Dr.
Gardner, MA 01440-1228
Phone: (978)632-9500 **Fax:** (978)630-3797
Products: Footwear; Shoes. **SIC:** 5139 (Footwear). **Officers:** Joe Kraskouskas, Owner.

■ 24815 ■ Morse Enterprises Inc.
108 S Stanton
El Paso, TX 79901
Phone: (915)533-2746 **Fax:** (915)533-3246
Products: Athletic shoes. **SIC:** 5139 (Footwear). **Officers:** Luanne Morse; Van Tyson Morse.

■ 24816 ■ Munro and Co.
PO Box 1157
Hot Springs, AR 71902
Phone: (501)262-1440 **Fax:** (501)262-6084
Products: Shoes; Children's shoes; Men's dress and casual shoes; Women's shoes, casual, except sandals. **SIC:** 5139 (Footwear). **Sales:** $100,000,000 (2000). **Emp:** 2,000.

■ 24817 ■ D. Myers and Sons Inc.
4311 Erdman Ave.
Baltimore, MD 21213
Phone: (410)522-7500
Free: (800)367-7463 **Fax:** (410)522-7575
E-mail: shoes@dmyers.com
Products: Women's footwear. **SIC:** 5139 (Footwear). **Est:** 1910. **Sales:** $16,000,000 (2000). **Emp:** 48. **Officers:** E. Carey Ries, President; James M Ries, Vice President, e-mail: jries@dmyers.com; E.C. Ries, Dir. of Marketing.

■ 24818 ■ National Rubber Footwear Inc.
310 N Colvin St.
Baltimore, MD 21202-4808
Phone: (410)752-0910
Free: (800)966-7463 **Fax:** (410)332-8145
E-mail: athex@aol.com
Products: Footwear; Shoes. **SIC:** 5139 (Footwear). **Est:** 1972. **Sales:** $2,000,000 (2000). **Emp:** 6. **Officers:** Leon Levy, President.

■ 24819 ■ Naturalizer
PO Box 1749
Ponce, PR 00733-1749
Phone: (787)259-7208
Products: Shoes. **SIC:** 5139 (Footwear).

■ 24820 ■ New City Shoes Inc.
29 W 56th St.
New York, NY 10019
Phone: (212)262-9494
Products: Shoes. **SIC:** 5139 (Footwear).

■ 24821 ■ Nickels Supply
686 Rocky Branch Rd.
Blountville, TN 37617-5636
Phone: (423)323-5738 **Fax:** (423)325-8573
E-mail: nickelsentrp@wireco.net
Products: Footwear. **SIC:** 5139 (Footwear). **Officers:** Garold Nickels, Owner.

■ 24822 ■ Nine West Group
5001 Kingsley Dr.
Cincinnati, OH 45227-1114
Products: Women and men's walking shoes. **SIC:** 5139 (Footwear). **Sales:** $10,000,000 (2000). **Emp:** 325. **Officers:** Tom Crabtree, Plant Mgr.

■ 24823 ■ Norden Inc.
4620 Churchill St.
St. Paul, MN 55126-5829
Phone: (612)481-9092 **Fax:** (612)481-1509
Products: Footwear, including imported clogs. **SIC:** 5139 (Footwear). **Officers:** John Isaksen, President.

■ 24824 ■ North American Shoe Co. Inc.
895 Warren Ave.
East Providence, RI 02914-1423
Phone: (401)434-1177 **Fax:** (401)435-3429
Products: Footwear. **SIC:** 5139 (Footwear). **Officers:** Harriet Myers, President.

■ 24825 ■ North West Quality Innovations
18050 Skyland Cir
Lake Oswego, OR 97034-6452
Phone: (503)636-1887
Products: Footwear. **SIC:** 5139 (Footwear). **Officers:** Julie Lewis, President.

■ 24826 ■ Olathe Boot Co.
705 S Kansas Ave
Olathe, KS 66061
Phone: (913)764-5110
Free: (800)255-6126 **Fax:** (913)764-0950
E-mail: hrsmn@juno.com
URL: http://www.olatheboots.com
Products: Boots, including men's and boys' dress and casual boots, and women's boots. **SIC:** 5139 (Footwear). **Sales:** $3,800,000 (2000). **Emp:** 70. **Officers:** Tom Frey; Suzie Frey.

■ 24827 ■ Oomphies Inc.
5 Franklin St.
Lawrence, MA 01840-1106
Phone: (978)682-5268
Free: (800)227-1370 **Fax:** (978)685-7868
Products: Footwear; House slippers. **SIC:** 5139 (Footwear). **Officers:** James Dizazzo, President.

■ 24828 ■ Pagoda Trading Co.
8300 Maryland Ave.
St. Louis, MO 63105
Phone: (314)854-4000 **Fax:** (314)854-3250
Products: Shoes, including dress, athletic, children's, women's, and men's shoes. **SIC:** 5139 (Footwear). **Est:** 1970. **Sales:** $120,000,000 (2000). **Emp:** 200. **Officers:** Thomas A. William, CEO & Chairman of the Board; Joseph T. Ennenbach, VP of Admin.

■ 24829 ■ Wayne Parnell
1112 S Oak St.
Broken Arrow, OK 74012-4959
Phone: (918)258-6000
Products: Athletic footwear. **SIC:** 5139 (Footwear). **Officers:** Wayne Parnell, Owner.

■ 24830 ■ Pemalot Inc.
1025 NW State Ave.
Chehalis, WA 98532-1826
Phone: (206)748-8387 **Fax:** (206)748-0548
Products: Footwear; Clothing. **SICs:** 5139 (Footwear); 5137 (Women's/Children's Clothing); 5136 (Men's/Boys' Clothing). **Officers:** Neil Pemerl, President.

■ 24831 ■ D.S. Peterman & Company, Inc.
110-114 N George St.
PO Box 1664
York, PA 17401
Phone: (717)846-8823 **Fax:** (717)845-9789
E-mail: dnpeterman@mindspring.com
Products: Shoes. **SIC:** 5139 (Footwear). **Est:** 1988. **Emp:** 14. **Officers:** Daniel Peterman Jr., CEO.

■ 24832 ■ Austin Phillips Shoe Co. Inc.
209 Terminal Ln.
New Haven, CT 06519-1800
Phone: (203)777-5485
Products: Footwear. **SIC:** 5139 (Footwear). **Officers:** James Millen, President.

■ 24833 ■ Phillips Shoes
115 Commercial Ave.
Monterey, TN 38574
Phone: (931)839-3119
Products: Footwear. **SIC:** 5139 (Footwear). **Officers:** Jack Phillips, Owner.

■ 24834 ■ Jack A. Pierce Inc.
3833 N Delaware St.
Indianapolis, IN 46205-2647
Phone: (317)283-8279 **Fax:** (317)283-7205
Products: Footwear; Athletic footwear. **SIC:** 5139 (Footwear). **Officers:** Jack Pierce, President.

■ 24835 ■ Pierre Shoes Inc.
PO Box 2387
Woburn, MA 01888-0687
Phone: (781)933-6900
Free: (800)343-5236 **Fax:** (781)935-7023
Products: Footwear. **SIC:** 5139 (Footwear). **Officers:** Lewis Epstein, President.

■ 24836 ■ Propet USA, Inc.
25612 74th Ave. S
Kent, WA 98032
Phone: (253)854-7600 **Fax:** (253)854-7607
Products: Footwear. **SIC:** 5139 (Footwear). **Officers:** Robert Propet, Chairman of the Board; Jack Hawkins, President & CEO.

■ 24837 ■ Prosper Shevenell and Son Inc.
PO Box 667
Dover, NH 03820
Phone: (603)742-5636
Products: Shoes. **SIC:** 5139 (Footwear). **Est:** 1960. **Sales:** $700,000 (2000). **Emp:** 5. **Officers:** J.P. Shevenell, President & Treasurer.

■ 24838 ■ R & S Sales Co. Inc.
21 Pleasant Valley Ln.
Westport, CT 06880-2731
Phone: (203)226-1709
Products: Footwear. **SIC:** 5139 (Footwear). **Officers:** Alan Rosenberg, President.

■ 24839 ■ Red Wing Shoe Store
1014 Harlow Rd.
Springfield, OR 97477-1141
Phone: (541)344-2323
Products: Footwear. **SIC:** 5139 (Footwear). **Officers:** Kenneth Splinter, Owner.

■ 24840 ■ Reebok International Ltd.
100 Technology Center Dr.
Stoughton, MA 02072
Phone: (781)401-5000
URL: http://www.reebok.com
Products: Shoes; Sportswear. **SICs:** 5139 (Footwear); 5136 (Men's/Boys' Clothing); 5137 (Women's/Children's Clothing). **Est:** 1979. **Sales:** $2,900,000 (2000). **Emp:** 6,100. **Officers:** Paul B. Fireman, CEO, President & Chairman of the Board; Kenneth Watchmaker, Exec. VP & CFO.

■ 24841 ■ Reebok International Ltd. Reebok Metaphors
4 W 58th St.
New York, NY 10019
Phone: (212)755-2610
Products: Athletic shoes; Athletic clothing, including shirts and shorts. **SICs:** 5139 (Footwear); 5136 (Men's/Boys' Clothing); 5137 (Women's/Children's Clothing).

■ 24842 ■ Lyle Richards International
1 Cabot Pl.
Stoughton, MA 02072
Phone: (781)344-1994 **Fax:** (781)344-9002
Products: Mens'/Dress/Casual/sport footwear. **SIC:** 5139 (Footwear). **Sales:** $20,000,000 (2000). **Emp:** 8. **Officers:** Richard Herman, President, e-mail: rherman678@aol.com; Lyle Herman, President; Julie Spinazzola, Vice President; Joe Carter, General Mgr.

■ 24843 ■ Right Stuff Inc.
24 Ray Ave., Ste. 103
Burlington, MA 01803-4760
Products: Footwear. **SIC:** 5139 (Footwear). **Est:** 1982. **Officers:** Robert Isenberg, President.

■ 24844 ■ Rossignol Ski Co.
PO Box 298
Williston, VT 05495
Phone: (802)863-2511
Products: Footwear. **SIC:** 5139 (Footwear). **Officers:** Laurent Vives, Chairman of the Board.

■ **24845** ■ **Royal Alaskan Sales**
3418 W 80th Ave.
Anchorage, AK 99502-4421
Phone: (907)243-2106 **Fax:** (907)243-5532
Products: Footwear. **SIC:** 5139 (Footwear).

■ **24846** ■ **Royce International Inc.**
1 Sound Shore Dr.
Greenwich, CT 06830-7251
Phone: (203)625-2660 **Fax:** (203)625-2694
Products: Footwear. **SIC:** 5139 (Footwear). **Officers:**
Anthony Di Paolo, President.

■ **24847** ■ **S & L International**
875 Waimanu St., No. 610
Honolulu, HI 96813
Phone: (808)591-1336 **Fax:** (808)591-1011
Products: Footwear. **SIC:** 5139 (Footwear). **Officers:**
Sandra Yang, President.

■ **24848** ■ **Sand Mountain Shoe Co.**
PO Box 447
Sharon, TN 38255-0447
Phone: (901)456-2580 **Fax:** (901)456-2580
E-mail: iguana@iswt.com
Products: Footwearr. **SIC:** 5139 (Footwear). **Est:**
1955. **Emp:** 3. **Officers:** Oscar Vickers, Owner.

■ **24849** ■ **Sartorius Sports Ltd.**
175 W Main St.
Avon, CT 06001-3670
Phone: (860)677-5540
Products: Sporting and athletic goods; Athletic
footwear. **SICs:** 5139 (Footwear); 5091 (Sporting &
Recreational Goods). **Officers:** Christophe Stephan,
President.

■ **24850** ■ **SBC/Sporto Corp.**
2 Midway St.
Boston, MA 02210
Phone: (617)345-8800
Free: (888)277-6786 **Fax:** (617)423-4160
E-mail: sportocorp@worldnet.att.net
URL: http://www.sporto.net
Products: Shoes. **SIC:** 5139 (Footwear). **Est:** 1934.
Sales: $30,000,000 (2000). **Emp:** 52. **Officers:** David
Brilliant, CEO.

■ **24851** ■ **Eric Schapero Co. Inc.**
98 Union Park St.
Boston, MA 02118
Phone: (617)423-2842 **Fax:** (617)426-6314
Products: Footwear. **SIC:** 5139 (Footwear). **Officers:**
Eric Schapero, President.

■ **24852** ■ **Arthur Schneider Sales Inc.**
1788 Ellsworth Industrial Blvd.
Atlanta, GA 30318-3748
Phone: (404)350-2550 **Fax:** (404)350-2563
Products: Footwear; Women's handbags and purses;
Jewelry. **SICs:** 5139 (Footwear); 5094 (Jewelry &
Precious Stones); 5137 (Women's/Children's Clothing).
Officers: Arthur Schneider, President.

■ **24853** ■ **Schwartz and Benjamin Inc.**
100 Marine Blvd.
Lynn, MA 01901
Phone: (781)595-5600
Free: (800)937-4637 **Fax:** (781)596-1475
Products: Shoes, including women's imported shoes.
SIC: 5139 (Footwear). **Sales:** $18,000,000 (2000).
Emp: 30. **Officers:** Arthur Schwartz, President.

■ **24854** ■ **Shane's Shoe**
1200 S Charles St.
Baltimore, MD 21230
Phone: (410)539-4709
Free: (800)922-1170 **Fax:** (410)727-4330
Products: Work and safety footwear. **SIC:** 5139
(Footwear). **Est:** 1910. **Officers:** Fredric Sherr, Owner.

■ **24855** ■ **Shoe Barn**
PO Box 92
Cecilia, KY 42724-0092
Phone: (502)862-4482
Products: Footwear. **SIC:** 5139 (Footwear). **Officers:**
John Carothers, Owner.

■ **24856** ■ **Shoe Corporation of Birmingham Inc.**
1415 1st Ave. S
Birmingham, AL 35233
Phone: (205)326-2800 **Fax:** (205)326-2808
E-mail: shoecorp@mindspring.com
URL: http://www.shoecorp.com
Products: Footwear. **SIC:** 5139 (Footwear). **Est:** 1950.
Sales: $2,000,000 (2000). **Emp:** 25. **Officers:** James
Calhoun, President. **Former Name:** Calhoun's Shoes.
Former Name: Shoe Corp. of Birmingham.

■ **24857** ■ **Shoe Flair**
108 Business Cir.
Thomasville, GA 31792-3962
Phone: (912)226-8375
Free: (800)451-3617 **Fax:** (912)226-2519
Products: Footwear. **SIC:** 5139 (Footwear).

■ **24858** ■ **Shoe Shack Inc.**
47 Bridge St.
East Windsor, CT 06088-0472
Phone: (860)623-3279
Products: Footwear. **SIC:** 5139 (Footwear). **Officers:**
Jeanne Katkavich, President.

■ **24859** ■ **Shoes To Boot Inc.**
PO Box 573
Lancaster, KY 40444
Phone: (606)792-4150 **Fax:** (606)792-4142
Products: Footwear. **SIC:** 5139 (Footwear). **Officers:**
James Montgomery, President.

■ **24860** ■ **Shore Imports Inc.**
PO Box 476
Weston, MA 02493-0003
Phone: (781)891-6363
Products: Footwear. **SIC:** 5139 (Footwear). **Officers:**
Bernard Shore, President.

■ **24861** ■ **Shtofman Company Inc.**
PO Box 4758
Tyler, TX 75712
Phone: (903)592-0861 **Fax:** (903)592-8380
Products: Women's, men's, and children's shoes. **SIC:**
5139 (Footwear). **Est:** 1929. **Sales:** $11,000,000
(1999). **Emp:** 190. **Officers:** Norman Shtofman, CEO;
Marvin Krasner, President; Alicia Avery, Dir. of
Systems.

■ **24862** ■ **Skechers U.S.A. Inc.**
228 Manhattan Beach Blvd., Ste. 200
Manhattan Beach, CA 90266
Phone: (310)318-3100 **Fax:** (310)318-5019
Products: Imported footwear. **SIC:** 5139 (Footwear).
Sales: $229,000,000 (2000). **Emp:** 400. **Officers:**
Robert Greenberg, CEO; David Weinberg, CFO.

■ **24863** ■ **Slippers International Inc.**
PO Box 505602
Chelsea, MA 02150-5602
Phone: (617)884-3752
Free: (800)221-0545 **Fax:** (617)884-1093
Products: Footwear. **SIC:** 5139 (Footwear). **Officers:**
Stephen Paratore, President.

■ **24864** ■ **Shirley Smith-Claypool**
PO Box 188
Opp, AL 36467-0188
Phones: (205)493-4551 (205)493-9490
Free: (800)469-1620
Products: Shoes. **SIC:** 5139 (Footwear). **Officers:**
Shirley Smith-Claypool, Owner.

■ **24865** ■ **South China Import Inc.**
42 W 29th St.
New York, NY 10001
Phone: (212)689-3688
Free: (800)235-0020 **Fax:** (212)779-0211
E-mail: sochinany@aol.com
Products: Footwear, including low end sandals,
slippers, and canvas shoes. **SIC:** 5139 (Footwear).
Est: 1979. **Sales:** $5,000,000 (2000). **Emp:** 10.
Officers: Jimmy K.O. Cheung; Joe Lee.

■ **24866** ■ **Southern Leather Co.**
PO Box 6
Memphis, TN 38101
Phone: (901)525-1200 **Fax:** (901)526-5603
Products: Shoes; Shoe repair materials; Leather. **SIC:**
5139 (Footwear). **Est:** 1910. **Sales:** $15,000,000
(2000). **Emp:** 100. **Officers:** William Loewenberg,
Chairman of the Board.

■ **24867** ■ **Speen & Company Inc.**
PO Box 2408
Woburn, MA 01888-0708
Phone: (781)933-8490
Free: (800)225-5746 **Fax:** (781)938-5864
Products: Footwear. **SIC:** 5139 (Footwear). **Officers:**
Claire Speen, President.

■ **24868** ■ **Street Cars Inc.**
7801 Mesquite Bend Dr., Ste. 110
Irving, TX 75063-6043
Phone: (972)230-7256
Free: (800)225-2005 **Fax:** (972)230-7279
Products: Footwear. **SIC:** 5139 (Footwear). **Officers:**
Al Simon, President.

■ **24869** ■ **Sullco Inc.**
40 Beach St., Ste. 105
Manchester, MA 01944
Phone: (978)526-4244 **Fax:** (978)526-1445
Products: Footwear. **SIC:** 5139 (Footwear). **Officers:**
Richard Sullivan, President.

■ **24870** ■ **Sun Pacific Trading Co. Inc.**
3050 Ualena St. B
Honolulu, HI 96819-1914
Phone: (808)836-2168 **Fax:** (808)836-3168
Products: Footwear. **SIC:** 5139 (Footwear). **Officers:**
Peter Chan, President.

■ **24871** ■ **Super Shoe Stores Inc.**
PO Box 239
Cumberland, MD 21502
Phone: (301)759-4300 **Fax:** (301)759-4795
Products: Shoes for men, women, and children,
including dress and casual styles; Nylons. **SICs:** 5139
(Footwear); 5137 (Women's/Children's Clothing). **Est:**
1926. **Sales:** $14,000,000 (2000). **Emp:** 200. **Officers:**
William D. Smith Jr., President; Margaret Lester,
Controller.

■ **24872** ■ **Superfeet In-Shoe Systems Inc.**
1419 Whitehorn St.
Ferndale, WA 98248-8923
Phone: (206)384-1820
Free: (800)634-6618 **Fax:** 800-320-2724
Products: Footwear. **SIC:** 5139 (Footwear). **Officers:**
Dennis Brown, President.

■ **24873** ■ **Sween ID Products Inc.**
PO Box 8300
Mankato, MN 56002-8300
Phone: (507)386-4393
Free: (800)533-8543 **Fax:** 800-533-3026
Products: Footwear; Shoe accessories. **SIC:** 5139
(Footwear). **Officers:** Maurice Sween, President.

■ **24874** ■ **Swenson Imports**
PO Box 70644
Seattle, WA 98107-0644
Phone: (206)784-7558 **Fax:** (206)784-6143
Products: Footwear. **SIC:** 5139 (Footwear). **Officers:**
Tom Swenson, Partner.

■ **24875** ■ **Tecnica USA**
Airport Rd.
West Lebanon, NH 03784
Phone: (603)298-8032
Free: (800)258-3897 **Fax:** (603)298-5790
Products: Footwear. **SIC:** 5139 (Footwear). **Officers:**
John Stahler, President.

■ **24876** ■ **Thomas Industrial Products Company Inc.**
11412 Cronhill Dr.
Owings Mills, MD 21117
Phone: (410)356-0003 **Fax:** 800-395-4545
Products: Footwear; Raincoats and other waterproof
outerwear; Seals, gaskets, and packing. **SICs:** 5139
(Footwear); 5085 (Industrial Supplies); 5136

(Men's/Boys' Clothing); 5137 (Women's/Children's Clothing). **Officers:** Robert Lyons, President.

■ **24877** ■ **Tober Industries Inc.**
1520 Washington Ave.
St. Louis, MO 63103
Phone: (314)421-2030
Products: Shoes. **SIC:** 5139 (Footwear). **Est:** 1904. **Sales:** $20,000,000 (2000). **Emp:** 12. **Officers:** Lester Tober, CEO; Michael Hillis, CFO.

■ **24878** ■ **Topline Corp.**
13150 SE 32nd St.
Bellevue, WA 98005-4436
Phone: (425)643-3003   **Fax:** (425)643-3846
Products: Footwear. **SIC:** 5139 (Footwear). **Officers:** William Snowden, CEO.

■ **24879** ■ **Two Left Feet**
7923 Norton Ave.
West Hollywood, CA 90046
Phone: (415)626-5338
Products: Women's shoes, casual, except sandals. **SIC:** 5139 (Footwear).

■ **24880** ■ **Uman Corp.**
517 6th St. N
Texas City, TX 77590
Phone: (409)945-8353
Products: Shoes. **SIC:** 5139 (Footwear).

■ **24881** ■ **United Shoe Ornament Company Inc.**
35 Tripoli St.
Providence, RI 02909-5418
Phone: (401)944-3060   **Fax:** (401)943-8737
E-mail: Unshoeco@AOL.com
URL: http://www.Unitedshoeornamentcocom
Products: Shoes; Luggage tags. **SIC:** 5139 (Footwear). **Officers:** George Turini, President.

■ **24882** ■ **Universal Athletic Services of Utah**
PO Box 1629
Bozeman, MT 59771-1629
Phone: (406)587-1220   **Fax:** (406)587-0228
Products: Footwear; Athletic goods. **SICs:** 5139 (Footwear); 5091 (Sporting & Recreational Goods). **Officers:** Larry Aasheim, Chairman of the Board.

■ **24883** ■ **Valencia Imports Co.**
1020 Campus Dr. W
Morganville, NJ 07751
Phone: (732)972-7211
Products: Children's shoes. **SIC:** 5139 (Footwear). **Sales:** $4,000,000 (2000). **Emp:** 6. **Officers:** Harry Heitner, President.

■ **24884** ■ **Valley Athletic Supply Co. Inc.**
PO Box 995
Ft. Valley, GA 31030-0995
Phone: (912)825-3306   **Fax:** (912)825-3307
Products: Footwear; Athletic footwear. **SIC:** 5139 (Footwear). **Officers:** Robert Sparks, President.

■ **24885** ■ **Vincent Jobbing Co.**
PO Box 144
Martin, TN 38237-0144
Phone: (901)587-2334
Free: (800)932-3195   **Fax:** (901)587-4224
E-mail: vincents@aeneas.com
URL: http://www.weakley.aeneas.net/~vincents
Products: Shoes. **SIC:** 5139 (Footwear). **Est:** 1952.

Emp: 36. **Officers:** Frank Vincent, Partner; Joe Vincent; Chris Vincent; Matt Vincent.

■ **24886** ■ **Virgs Inc.**
116 S Main St.
Ishpeming, MI 49849-1820
Phone: (906)486-6671
Products: Footwear. **SIC:** 5139 (Footwear). **Officers:** Louis Lattrel, President.

■ **24887** ■ **Benjamin Walk Corp.**
511 Rte. 125
PO Box 627
Barrington, NH 03825-0627
Phone: (603)664-2400
Free: (800)621-0029   **Fax:** (603)664-7544
Products: Bridal footwear. **SIC:** 5139 (Footwear). **Officers:** Ed Rene, President.

■ **24888** ■ **Warrington Group Ltd.**
Greenleaf Woods Dr.
Portsmouth, NH 03801
Phone: (603)431-1515   **Fax:** (603)431-3232
Products: Protective footwear. **SIC:** 5139 (Footwear). **Officers:** Peter Gilson, President.

■ **24889** ■ **Wearhouse**
616 N Chamberlain St.
Terre Haute, IN 47803-9503
Phone: (812)234-1441
Products: Uniforms; Footwear. **SICs:** 5139 (Footwear); 5136 (Men's/Boys' Clothing); 5137 (Women's/Children's Clothing). **Officers:** Betty Swalls, Owner.

■ **24890** ■ **Weintrob Brothers**
2036 11th Ave.
Morgantown, WV 26505-8751
Phone: (304)296-4336
Products: Footwear. **SIC:** 5139 (Footwear). **Officers:** Seymour Bailes, Owner.

■ **24891** ■ **West Coast Shoe Co.**
PO Box 607
Scappoose, OR 97056
Phone: (503)543-7114
Free: (800)326-2711   **Fax:** (503)543-7110
E-mail: boots@westcoastshoe.com
URL: http://www.westcoastshoe.com
Products: Heavy duty boots. **SIC:** 5139 (Footwear). **Est:** 1918. **Sales:** $6,000,000 (2000). **Emp:** 47. **Officers:** Roberta Shoemaker, President.

■ **24892** ■ **Wesvic's Clothing and Shoe Brokers, Inc.**
PO Box 1379
Pembroke, GA 31321-1379
Phone: (912)653-2379   **Fax:** (912)653-3366
Products: Footwear. **SIC:** 5139 (Footwear). **Officers:** Victor Duggar, Owner.

■ **24893** ■ **Whites Shoe Shop Inc.**
4002 E Ferry Ave.
Spokane, WA 99202
Phone: (509)487-7277
Products: Boots. **SIC:** 5139 (Footwear). **Est:** 1909. **Sales:** $6,400,000 (2000). **Emp:** 85. **Officers:** Skip March, President.

■ **24894** ■ **Wigwam Inc.**
PO Box 288
Lake George, MN 56458-0228
Phone: (218)266-3978   **Fax:** (218)266-3978
URL: http://www.2havefun.com/ItoscoMoccasin
Products: Moccasins. **SIC:** 5139 (Footwear). **Est:** 1982. **Sales:** $90,000 (2000). **Emp:** 3. **Officers:** Mardel Bents, President. **Doing Business As:** Itasca Moccasin.

■ **24895** ■ **Willard Safety Shoe Co.**
37455 Rhonswood Dr.
Northville, MI 48167-9748
Phone: (248)471-4944
Products: Footwear. **SIC:** 5139 (Footwear). **Officers:** Eunice Robinson, President.

■ **24896** ■ **Winter Port Boot Shop**
264 State St.
Brewer, ME 04412-1519
Phone: (207)989-6492   **Fax:** (207)989-6496
Products: Footwear. **SIC:** 5139 (Footwear). **Officers:** Michael Allen, President.

■ **24897** ■ **Wolff Shoe Co.**
1705 Larkin Williams Rd.
Fenton, MO 63026
Phone: (314)343-7770   **Fax:** (314)326-4922
Products: Women's shoes. **SIC:** 5139 (Footwear). **Est:** 1918. **Sales:** $30,000,000 (2000). **Emp:** 50. **Officers:** Gary Wolff, President; Dough Bay, Treasurer.

■ **24898** ■ **Wolfpax Inc.**
PO Box 5214
Manchester, NH 03108-5214
Phone: (603)623-3326   **Fax:** (603)647-4175
Products: Footwear. **SIC:** 5139 (Footwear). **Officers:** Martin Wolff, President.

■ **24899** ■ **Work Duds**
5215 S Laburnum Ave.
Richmond, VA 23231-4432
Phone: (804)226-1366
Products: Footwear; Clothing. **SICs:** 5139 (Footwear); 5136 (Men's/Boys' Clothing); 5137 (Women's/Children's Clothing). **Officers:** Frank Di Perna, Owner.

■ **24900** ■ **E.T. Wright and Co.**
1356 Williams St.
Chippewa Falls, WI 54729
Free: (800)934-1022
URL: http://www.etwrightshoe.com
Products: Men's footwear. **SIC:** 5139 (Footwear). **Est:** 1876. **Sales:** $18,000,000 (2000). **Emp:** 30. **Officers:** Mason Shoe.

■ **24901** ■ **Yearwoods Inc.**
PO Box 18350
Shreveport, LA 71138-1350
Phone: (318)688-1844   **Fax:** (318)688-9997
Products: Footwear. **SIC:** 5139 (Footwear). **Officers:** Pat Mc Govern, President.

(52) Soft Drinks

Entries in this section are arranged alphabetically by company name. When the company name is a personal name, the company name is alphabetized by the surname unless the first name or initial(s) are part of a trade name. See the User's Guide at the front of this directory for additional information.

■ 24902 ■ **3 Springs Water Co.**
1800 Pine Run Rd.
Wilkes Barre, PA 18702-9419
Phones: (717)823-7019   (717)823-6446
Fax: (717)822-6177
E-mail: 3springs@microserve.net
URL: http://www.3springs.com
Products: Bottled spring water. **SIC:** 5149 (Groceries & Related Products Nec). **Est:** 1989. **Emp:** 30.

■ 24903 ■ **Abbey Ice Co.**
1 Hoffman St.
Spring Valley, NY 10977
Phone: (914)356-1700
Free: (800)722-2823   **Fax:** (914)356-1767
Products: Ice; Bottled spring water; Rock salt; Calcium chloride. **SICs:** 5199 (Nondurable Goods Nec); 5149 (Groceries & Related Products Nec).

■ 24904 ■ **Abita Water Company Inc.**
101 Airline Hwy.
Metairie, LA 70001
Phone: (504)465-0022
Free: (800)858-8250   **Fax:** (504)465-0030
Products: Bottled water. **SIC:** 5149 (Groceries & Related Products Nec).

■ 24905 ■ **Absolute Bottled Water Co.**
849 Seahawk Circle
Virginia Beach, VA 23452
Phone: (757)468-4426   **Fax:** (757)468-0352
Products: Spring water. **SIC:** 5149 (Groceries & Related Products Nec).

■ 24906 ■ **Absopure Water Co.**
96 84th St. SW
Byron Center, MI 49315
Phone: (616)385-2771
Free: (800)422-7678   **Fax:** (616)455-5201
Products: Bottled water. **SIC:** 5149 (Groceries & Related Products Nec).

■ 24907 ■ **Acadiana Culligan**
708 Eraste Landry
Lafayette, LA 70506
Phone: (318)233-1645
Free: (800)960-1989   **Fax:** (318)233-2595
Products: Bottled water; Water filtration equipment and supplies. **SICs:** 5149 (Groceries & Related Products Nec); 5074 (Plumbing & Hydronic Heating Supplies).

■ 24908 ■ **Agrigold Juice Products**
PO Box 1630
355 N Joy St.
Corona, CA 91718-1630
Phone: (714)272-2600   **Fax:** (714)272-8438
Products: Canned fruit juices, nectars, and concentrates. **SIC:** 5149 (Groceries & Related Products Nec). **Emp:** 99. **Officers:** Arthur J. Martori.

■ 24909 ■ **Ale-8-One Bottling Co. Inc.**
PO Box 645
Winchester, KY 40391
Phone: (606)744-3484   **Fax:** (606)744-7950
Products: Soft drinks. **SIC:** 5149 (Groceries & Related

Products Nec). **Est:** 1902. **Sales:** $9,000,000 (2000). **Emp:** 66. **Officers:** F.A. Rogers III, President; Phil Kearns, VP of Sales; Carolyn A. White, Customer Service and Human Resources Con, e-mail: carolyn@aleeightone.com.

■ 24910 ■ **ARA-Cory Refreshment Services**
750 Nuttman St.
Santa Clara, CA 95054
Phone: (408)988-8211   **Fax:** (408)988-8264
Products: Coffee; Tea; Soft drinks; Fresh fruit juices and nectars. **SIC:** 5149 (Groceries & Related Products Nec).

■ 24911 ■ **ARA Services, Inc.**
1665 Townhurst
Houston, TX 77043
Phone: (713)932-0093   **Fax:** (713)932-1070
Products: Coffees, soft drinks, and juices. **SIC:** 5149 (Groceries & Related Products Nec).

■ 24912 ■ **Atlas Distributing, Inc.**
44 Southbridge St.
Auburn, MA 01501
Phone: (508)791-6221   **Fax:** (508)791-0812
Products: Beer; Soft drinks; Teas. **SICs:** 5149 (Groceries & Related Products Nec); 5182 (Wines & Distilled Beverages); 5181 (Beer & Ale). **Est:** 1933. **Sales:** $35,000,000 (2000). **Emp:** 105. **Officers:** J. Sadowsky, Chairman of the Board; J. Salois, President; K. Sadowsky, VP of Sales; F. Chapman, VP of Sales.

■ 24913 ■ **Beauchamp Distributing Co.**
1911 S Santa Fe Ave.
Compton, CA 90221
Phone: (310)639-5320   **Fax:** (310)537-8641
Products: Beverages. **SIC:** 5149 (Groceries & Related Products Nec). **Sales:** $54,500,000 (2000). **Emp:** 130. **Officers:** Patrick Beauchamp, President; Peter Gumpert, CFO.

■ 24914 ■ **Charles A. Bernick Inc.**
PO Box 7008
St. Cloud, MN 56302
Phone: (320)252-6441
Products: Soft drinks. **SIC:** 5149 (Groceries & Related Products Nec). **Est:** 1915. **Sales:** $20,000,000 (2000). **Emp:** 200. **Officers:** R.J. Bernick, General Mgr.; M Heinen, CFO; J. Marrer, Dir. of Marketing & Sales.

■ 24915 ■ **Big Shot Beverage Inc.**
272 Plauche St.
Harahan, LA 70123
Phone: (504)733-4343   **Fax:** (504)733-4365
Products: Soft drinks. **SIC:** 5149 (Groceries & Related Products Nec). **Sales:** $3,600,000 (2000). **Emp:** 54. **Officers:** R.A. De Tiege, General Mgr.

■ 24916 ■ **Black Mountain Spring Water Inc.**
PO Box 3010
San Carlos, CA 94070-3010
Phone: (650)595-3800   **Fax:** (650)595-0327
E-mail: bmsw@best.com
URL: http://www.bmsw.com
Products: Spring water. **SIC:** 5149 (Groceries & Related Products Nec). **Est:** 1937. **Sales:** $32,000,000

(2000). **Emp:** 250. **Officers:** Marty Ruberry, CEO & President; Shahin Tabrizi, CFO; Roy Christensen, VP of Marketing.

■ 24917 ■ **Bradley Distributing**
1975 W County Rd., B-2
Roseville, MN 55113
Phone: (612)639-0523   **Fax:** (612)639-8309
Products: Bottled water; Snack foods. **SICs:** 5149 (Groceries & Related Products Nec); 5145 (Confectionery).

■ 24918 ■ **Brookfield's Great Water Inc.**
9533 Nall Ave.
Overland Park, KS 66207
Phone: (913)648-1234
Products: Purified water and installation of residential water treatment systems. **SIC:** 5149 (Groceries & Related Products Nec). **Sales:** $200,000 (2000). **Emp:** 2. **Officers:** Arthur D. Brookfield II, President.

■ 24919 ■ **Brother's Gourmet Coffees Inc.**
(Boca Raton, Florida)
2255 Glades Rd.
Boca Raton, FL 33431
Phone: (561)995-2600
Free: (800)808-5282   **Fax:** (561)994-4681
Products: Roasted coffee. **SIC:** 5149 (Groceries & Related Products Nec). **Sales:** $83,000,000 (1994). **Emp:** 120. **Officers:** Donald Breen, President; Barry Bilmes, Exec. VP of Finance.

■ 24920 ■ **Buffalo Don's Artesian Wells Ltd.**
PO Box 2500-C
Plymouth, MI 48170
Phone: (313)455-3600
Products: Bottled water. **SIC:** 5149 (Groceries & Related Products Nec). **Est:** 1982. **Sales:** $7,000,000 (2000). **Emp:** 45. **Officers:** William C. Young, CEO & Chairman of the Board; Mary E. Young, Treasurer & Secty.

■ 24921 ■ **Buffalo Rock Co. Gadsden Div.**
PO Box 2307
Gadsden, AL 35903
Phone: (256)492-8400
Products: Soft drinks. **SIC:** 5149 (Groceries & Related Products Nec). **Sales:** $58,000,000 (1994). **Emp:** 125.

■ 24922 ■ **Canada Dry of Delaware Valley**
8275 Rte. 130
Pennsauken, NJ 08110
Phone: (609)662-6767
Products: Bottled and canned soft drinks. **SIC:** 5149 (Groceries & Related Products Nec). **Sales:** $40,000,000 (2000). **Emp:** 250. **Officers:** Thomas J. Dooley, President; John Dale, VP & CFO.

■ 24923 ■ **A.J. Canfield Co.**
7955 S Cass Ave., No. 201
Darien, IL 60561-5009
Phone: (773)483-7000   **Fax:** (773)483-9312
Products: Soft drinks. **SIC:** 5149 (Groceries & Related Products Nec). **Est:** 1925. **Sales:** $44,000,000 (2000). **Emp:** 300. **Officers:** A.J. Canfield III, President; Allen Addante, VP of Finance.

■ 24924 ■ Central Distributing Co.
695 S 6th
Carrington, ND 58421-2322
Phone: (701)652-2141 **Fax:** (701)652-1887
E-mail: central@daktel.com
Products: Bottled water. **SIC:** 5149 (Groceries & Related Products Nec). **Est:** 1975. **Emp:** 2. **Officers:** Donald Bickett, President.

■ 24925 ■ Central States Coca-Cola Bottling Co.
3495 Sangamon Ave.
Springfield, IL 62707
Phone: (217)544-4891
Products: Soft drinks. **SIC:** 5149 (Groceries & Related Products Nec). **Sales:** $37,000,000 (1993). **Emp:** 80. **Officers:** Jeffrey Richardson, General Mgr.

■ 24926 ■ City Bottling Company Inc.
1820 5th Ave.
Arnold, PA 15068
Phone: (724)335-3350
Products: Soft drinks. **SIC:** 5149 (Groceries & Related Products Nec). **Sales:** $1,000,000 (1993). **Emp:** 6. **Officers:** Louis Lombardo, President; S. Sam Lombardo, Chairman of the Board.

■ 24927 ■ CJW Inc.
2437 Chicory Rd.
Racine, WI 53403
Phone: (414)554-4288
Free: (800)273-5748 **Fax:** (262)554-5748
Products: Beverages. **SIC:** 5149 (Groceries & Related Products Nec). **Est:** 1958. **Sales:** $33,000,000 (2000). **Emp:** 100.

■ 24928 ■ Clermont Inc.
HCO1, Box 117
Hudson, NY 12534
Phone: (518)537-6251 **Fax:** (518)537-6239
Products: Canned fruit juices, nectars, and concentrates; Canned fruits. **SIC:** 5149 (Groceries & Related Products Nec). **Emp:** 49.

■ 24929 ■ Coca-Cola Aberdeen
PO Box 38
Aberdeen, SD 57402-3308
Phone: (605)225-6780 **Fax:** (605)225-8143
Products: Bottled and canned soft drinks. **SIC:** 5149 (Groceries & Related Products Nec). **Sales:** $14,000,000 (2000). **Emp:** 30. **Officers:** Jeff Toupal, General Mgr.

■ 24930 ■ Coca-Cola Bottlers of Detroit Inc.
880 Doris Rd.
Auburn Hills, MI 48326
Phone: (248)373-2653 **Fax:** (248)373-5799
Products: Soft drinks. **SIC:** 5149 (Groceries & Related Products Nec). **Est:** 1916. **Sales:** $32,000,000 (2000). **Emp:** 90. **Officers:** Richard Costs, General Mgr.

■ 24931 ■ Coca-Cola Bottling Co.
69 N Chadbourne St.
San Angelo, TX 76903
Phone: (915)655-6991
Products: Soda pop. **SIC:** 5149 (Groceries & Related Products Nec). **Sales:** $98,000,000 (2000). **Emp:** 210. **Officers:** Richard Burrage, General Mgr.

■ 24932 ■ Coca-Cola Bottling Co. of California
7901 Oakport St.
Oakland, CA 94621
Phone: (510)638-5001
Products: Soft drinks. **SIC:** 5149 (Groceries & Related Products Nec). **Est:** 1922. **Sales:** $46,000,000 (2000). **Emp:** 100. **Officers:** John Schaefer, General Mgr.; John Parent, CFO; Richard D. Bishop, VP of Marketing & Sales.

■ 24933 ■ Coast Coca-Cola Bottling Co.
PO Drawer E
Gulfport, MS 39502
Phone: (228)864-1122 **Fax:** (228)863-8525
Products: Soft drinks. **SIC:** 5149 (Groceries & Related Products Nec). **Est:** 1906. **Sales:** $10,000,000 (2000). **Emp:** 87.

■ 24934 ■ Coca-Cola Bottling Co. Consolidated
PO Box 31487
Charlotte, NC 28231
Phones: (704)551-4400 (704)393-4200
Fax: (704)393-4369
Products: Pop. **SIC:** 5149 (Groceries & Related Products Nec). **Sales:** $650,000,000 (2000). **Emp:** 3,000.

■ 24935 ■ Coca-Cola Bottling Co. of Lincoln
1200 King Bird Rd.
Lincoln, NE 68521-3008
Phone: (402)475-3749
Products: Soft drinks, water, and juices. **SIC:** 5149 (Groceries & Related Products Nec). **Sales:** $21,000,000 (2000). **Emp:** 50. **Officers:** Terry Buntemeyer, Manager.

■ 24936 ■ Coca-Cola Bottling Co. of Manchester
99 Eddy Rd.
Manchester, NH 03102
Phone: (603)623-6033 **Fax:** (603)644-0926
Products: Soft drinks; Water. **SIC:** 5149 (Groceries & Related Products Nec). **Est:** 1974. **Sales:** $13,000,000 (2000). **Emp:** 60. **Officers:** Joseph Pagliuca, General Mgr.

■ 24937 ■ Meridian Coca-Cola Bottling Co.
PO Box 5207
Meridian, MS 39302-5207
Phone: (601)483-5272 **Fax:** (601)483-5272
Products: Soft drinks. **SIC:** 5149 (Groceries & Related Products Nec). **Est:** 1904. **Sales:** $20,000,000 (1999). **Emp:** 175. **Officers:** Hardy P. Graham, President; Richard James, Treasurer & Secty.; Tommy Duncan, Sales Mgr., e-mail: tduncan@mdncoke.net; B. Lee, Human Resources Contact, e-mail: blee@mdncoke.net.

■ 24938 ■ Coca-Cola Bottling Company of Mobile Inc.
PO Box 190129
Mobile, AL 36619
Phone: (205)666-2410 **Fax:** (205)661-8227
Products: Soft drinks. **SIC:** 5149 (Groceries & Related Products Nec). **Est:** 1906. **Sales:** $52,000,000 (2000). **Emp:** 400. **Officers:** Jim R. Jardina, General Mgr.

■ 24939 ■ Coca-Cola Bottling Company of New York Inc.
375 Wireless Blvd.
Smithtown, NY 11787
Phone: (516)849-8200
Products: Soft drinks. **SIC:** 5149 (Groceries & Related Products Nec). **Sales:** $60,000,000 (2000). **Emp:** 90. **Officers:** Mike Harford, Sr. VP.

■ 24940 ■ Coca-Cola Bottling Company of Shreveport
305 Stoner Ave.
Shreveport, LA 71101-4154
Phone: (318)429-0205
Products: Soft drinks. **SIC:** 5149 (Groceries & Related Products Nec). **Sales:** $70,000,000 (1993). **Emp:** 150. **Officers:** Billy Floyd, General Mgr.; Beverly Doughty, Finance Officer.

■ 24941 ■ Coca-Cola Bottling Company of Virginia
832 17th St. N
Virginia, MN 55792
Phone: (218)741-7690
Products: Soft drinks. **SIC:** 5149 (Groceries & Related Products Nec). **Sales:** $10,000,000 (1994). **Emp:** 22. **Officers:** Katherine Ware, President; Robert Bonner, VP of Finance.

■ 24942 ■ Dixie Coca-Cola Bottling
1913 W State St.
Bristol, VA 24201
Phone: (540)669-3124
Products: Soft drinks. **SIC:** 5149 (Groceries & Related Products Nec). **Sales:** $18,000,000 (2000). **Emp:** 50. **Officers:** Wayne Kinley, President.

■ 24943 ■ Valdosta Coca-Cola Bottling Works Inc.
PO Box 189
Valdosta, GA 31603
Phone: (912)242-6325
Products: Soft drinks. **SIC:** 5149 (Groceries & Related Products Nec). **Est:** 1897. **Sales:** $9,000,000 (2000). **Emp:** 20. **Officers:** Don Sayers, General Mgr.

■ 24944 ■ Lexington Coca-Cola Bottling Works
10 Front St.
Lexington, TN 38351
Phone: (901)968-3636
Products: Soft drinks. **SIC:** 5149 (Groceries & Related Products Nec). **Est:** 1912. **Sales:** $6,000,000 (2000). **Emp:** 30. **Officers:** Charles Taylor, General Mgr.

■ 24945 ■ Coca-Cola Co.
PO Box 1500
Cortaro, AZ 85652-0529
Phone: (520)744-1333
Products: Soft drinks, including diet sodas. **SIC:** 5149 (Groceries & Related Products Nec). **Est:** 1906. **Sales:** $6,000,000 (2000). **Emp:** 150. **Officers:** Jimmy Curry, General Mgr.; John Johnson, Controller; William E. Neslage II, Sales Mgr.

■ 24946 ■ Johnston Coca-Cola
PO Box 50338
Knoxville, TN 37950-0338
Products: Soft drinks. **SIC:** 5149 (Groceries & Related Products Nec). **Est:** 1950. **Sales:** $28,000,000 (2000). **Emp:** 60. **Officers:** Ken Jones, Manager.

■ 24947 ■ Coca-Cola of Northern Arizona
PO Box 2848
Flagstaff, AZ 86003-2848
Phone: (520)526-2239
Products: Soft drinks, water, and juices. **SIC:** 5149 (Groceries & Related Products Nec). **Est:** 1985. **Sales:** $54,000,000 (2000). **Emp:** 150. **Officers:** Ivan Luster, Manager; Brad Moore, Controller.

■ 24948 ■ Pacific Coca-Cola
9705 E Montgomery
Spokane, WA 99206
Phone: (509)921-6200 **Fax:** (509)921-6211
Products: Beverages. **SIC:** 5149 (Groceries & Related Products Nec). **Est:** 1963. **Sales:** $23,000,000 (2000). **Emp:** 50. **Officers:** Elvin K. Bonguard, General Mgr.

■ 24949 ■ Pacific Coca-Cola
3333 S 38th St.
Tacoma, WA 98409
Phone: (253)474-9567
Products: Soft drinks. **SIC:** 5149 (Groceries & Related Products Nec). **Sales:** $6,500,000 (2000). **Emp:** 100. **Officers:** Tim Mercurio, General Mgr.

■ 24950 ■ Coca-Cola Pocatello
PO Box 607
Pocatello, ID 83204
Phone: (208)232-0762
Products: Soft drinks. **SIC:** 5149 (Groceries & Related Products Nec). **Est:** 1909. **Sales:** $2,000,000 (1999). **Emp:** 30. **Officers:** Gary Hagler, General Mgr.; Linda Land.

■ 24951 ■ Courtesy Distributors Inc.
PO Box 2217
Glenview, IL 60025-6217
Phone: (708)495-5480
Products: Beverages. **SIC:** 5149 (Groceries & Related Products Nec).

■ 24952 ■ Crystal Bottling Company Inc.
575 Display Way
Sacramento, CA 95838
Phone: (916)568-3300
Products: Spring water. **SIC:** 5149 (Groceries & Related Products Nec).

■ 24953 ■ Decatur Bottling Co.
PO Box 3520
Decatur, IL 62524-3250
Phone: (217)429-5415
Products: Soft drinks. **SIC:** 5149 (Groceries & Related

Products Nec). **Sales:** $23,000,000 (1994). **Emp:** 50. **Officers:** Dave Faulkner, Finance General Manager.

■ 24954 ■ **Eagle Family Foods**
61 Swift St.
Waterloo, NY 13165
Phone: (315)539-9291 **Fax:** (315)539-8677
Products: Lemon and lime juice. **SIC:** 5149 (Groceries & Related Products Nec). **Emp:** 55. **Officers:** Paul Hoffman.

■ 24955 ■ **Eldorado Artesian Springs Inc.**
PO Box 445
Eldorado Springs, CO 80025-0445
Phone: (303)499-1316 **Fax:** (303)499-1339
E-mail: info@eldoradosprings.com
URL: http://www.eldoradosprings.com
Products: Bottled water. **SIC:** 5149 (Groceries & Related Products Nec). **Est:** 1982. **Sales:** $4,000,000 (2000). **Emp:** 47. **Officers:** Kevin M. Sipple, Chairman of the Board; Doug Larson, President; Jeremy Martin, VP of Public Relations, e-mail: jeremy@eldoradosprings.com; Cathleen Collins, CFO; Robert Weidler, Vice President.

■ 24956 ■ **Full Service Beverage Co.**
2900 S Hydraulic St.
Wichita, KS 67216-2403
Phone: (316)529-3777
Products: Beverages, including soft drinks, flavored waters, and iced teas. **SIC:** 5149 (Groceries & Related Products Nec). **Sales:** $55,000,000 (2000). **Emp:** 450. **Officers:** John L.D. Frazier, CEO; R.G. Phipps, CFO.

■ 24957 ■ **Georgia Mountain Water Inc.**
PO Box 1243
Marietta, GA 30061
Phone: (404)928-9971 **Fax:** (404)928-9166
Products: Bottled water. **SIC:** 5149 (Groceries & Related Products Nec). **Est:** 1985. **Sales:** $2,000,000 (2000). **Emp:** 40. **Officers:** Jim Carroll, President; Alisa Batchelor, Controller; Linda Smith, Dir. of Sales.

■ 24958 ■ **Ginseng Up Corp.**
392 5th Ave., Rm. 1004
New York, NY 10018-8114
Phone: (212)696-1930 **Fax:** (212)779-0493
E-mail: mling10@aol.com
URL: http://www.members.aol.com/mling10/gup2.html
Products: Ginseng soda and beverages; Contract packaging. **SIC:** 5149 (Groceries & Related Products Nec). **Est:** 1981. **Sales:** $50,000,000 (2000). **Emp:** 30. **Officers:** Matthew S. Ling; Sang Kil Han.

■ 24959 ■ **Global Beverage Co.**
PO Box 25107
Rochester, NY 14625
Phone: (716)381-3560 **Fax:** (716)381-4025
URL: http://www.joltcola.com
Products: Soft drinks. **SIC:** 5149 (Groceries & Related Products Nec). **Est:** 1985. **Sales:** $10,000,000 (2000). **Emp:** 18. **Officers:** C.J. Rapp, President; David Lyttle, Controller; Brian Creary, VP of International Sales.

■ 24960 ■ **Golden Gem Growers Inc.**
PO Drawer 9
Umatilla, FL 32784
Phone: (352)669-2101 **Fax:** (352)669-7241
Products: Citrus concentrates, including orange and grapefruit concentrate. **SIC:** 5149 (Groceries & Related Products Nec). **Sales:** $125,000,000 (2000). **Emp:** 850. **Officers:** John F. Nelson Jr.

■ 24961 ■ **Golden State Foods Corp.**
18301 Von Karman Ave., No. 1100
Irvine, CA 92612-1009
Phone: (714)252-2000 **Fax:** (714)252-2080
Products: Soft drinks and juices; Dairy products for fast food restaurants. **SICs:** 5199 (Nondurable Goods Nec); 5143 (Dairy Products Except Dried or Canned). **Est:** 1969. **Sales:** $1,000,000,000 (2000). **Emp:** 1,800. **Officers:** James E. Williams, CEO & Chairman of the Board; Gene Olson, Exec. VP & CFO; Ron Childers, Dir of Human Resources.

■ 24962 ■ **Good-O-Beverage Co.**
1801 Boone Ave.
Bronx, NY 10460
Phone: (718)328-6400
Products: Carbonated soft drinks. **SIC:** 5149 (Groceries & Related Products Nec). **Officers:** Roy Kaplan, Sales Mgr.

■ 24963 ■ **GOYA Foods Inc.**
1900 NW 92nd Ave.
Miami, FL 33172
Phone: (305)592-3150 **Fax:** (305)591-8019
Products: Beverages; Fruit drinks, cocktails, and ades. **SIC:** 5149 (Groceries & Related Products Nec). **Emp:** 20.

■ 24964 ■ **Great Bear Spring Co.**
777 W Putnam Ave.
Greenwich, CT 06830
Phone: (203)531-4100
Products: Bottled water. **SIC:** 5149 (Groceries & Related Products Nec). **Est:** 1888. **Sales:** $55,000,000 (2000). **Emp:** 500. **Officers:** Kim Jeffery, General Mgr.; Dennis Crumbine, Controller; Andrew Carter, Dir. of Marketing; Rowan Snyder, Dir. of Data Processing; Jim Rouse, Dir of Human Resources.

■ 24965 ■ **Great Brands of Europe Inc.**
208 Harbor Dr.
Stamford, CT 06902-7441
Phone: (203)425-1700
Free: (800)253-8426 **Fax:** (203)425-1900
URL: http://www.evian.com
Products: Bottled water; Biscuits and crackers; Sauces and condiments. **SIC:** 5149 (Groceries & Related Products Nec). **Est:** 1979. **Sales:** $376,000,000 (1999). **Emp:** 600. **Officers:** Jim Stevens, CEO & President.

■ 24966 ■ **H & H Products Co.**
PO Box 607668
Orlando, FL 32860
Phone: (407)299-5410
Free: (800)678-8448 **Fax:** (407)298-6966
E-mail: hhproducts@aol.com
Products: Juices; Juice and liquid drink mixes; Tea concentrates; Snow cones; Cola syrups; Slush syrups; Frozen carbonated beverages; pancake and waffle syrups; Daiquiris; Imitation flavors; Food colors. **SIC:** 5149 (Groceries & Related Products Nec). **Est:** 1964. **Sales:** $10,000,000 (1999). **Emp:** 35. **Officers:** M. L. Hartley.

■ 24967 ■ **H & M Distributing**
PO Box 1633
Pocatello, ID 83204-1633
Phone: (208)233-6633
Free: (800)826-1156 **Fax:** (208)233-4628
Products: Soft drinks. **SIC:** 5149 (Groceries & Related Products Nec). **Est:** 1916. **Emp:** 9. **Officers:** Edwin Prater; Tom Betty; Ron Nelson. **Former Name:** WAM Company Beverage.

■ 24968 ■ **Hart Beverage Co.**
400 W Colonial Dr.
South Sioux City, NE 68776
Phone: (402)494-3023
Products: Soft drinks. **SIC:** 5149 (Groceries & Related Products Nec). **Est:** 1936. **Sales:** $23,000,000 (2000). **Emp:** 50. **Officers:** Steve Ford, President & CFO; Harvey Steinhoff, Sales Mgr.

■ 24969 ■ **Hawaiian Natural Water Company Inc.**
98-746 Kuahao Pl.
Pearl City, HI 96782-3125
Phone: (808)832-4550 **Fax:** (808)832-4559
Products: Bottled water. **SIC:** 5149 (Groceries & Related Products Nec). **Sales:** $1,000,000 (2000). **Emp:** 27. **Officers:** Marcus Bender, CEO & President; David Laeha, CFO.

■ 24970 ■ **HealthComm Inc.**
5800 Soundview Dr.
PO Box 1729
Gig Harbor, WA 98335
Phone: (253)851-3943
Free: (800)843-9660 **Fax:** (253)851-9749
E-mail: info@healthcomm.com
URL: http://www.healthcomm.com
Products: Powdered drink mixes. **SIC:** 5149 (Groceries & Related Products Nec). **Emp:** 70. **Officers:** Jeffery S. Bland, CEO; Darrell Medcalf, President; Leo Schultz, COO.

■ 24971 ■ **A.D. Huesing Corp.**
PO Box 3880
Rock Island, IL 61204
Phone: (309)788-5652 **Fax:** (309)788-7266
URL: http://www.huesing.com
Products: Soft drinks. **SIC:** 5149 (Groceries & Related Products Nec). **Est:** 1899. **Sales:** $23,000,000 (2000). **Emp:** 80. **Officers:** Franz Helpenstell, Chairman of the Board; Amy Helpenstell, President.

■ 24972 ■ **ICEE-USA Corp.**
4701 Airport Dr.
Ontario, CA 91761-7817
Phone: (909)467-4233 **Fax:** (909)467-4260
Products: Machines; Frozen carbonated beverages. **SICs:** 5149 (Groceries & Related Products Nec); 5142 (Packaged Frozen Foods); 5046 (Commercial Equipment Nec). **Est:** 1967. **Sales:** $23,500,000 (2000). **Emp:** 225. **Officers:** Edward J. Steele, President; Kent Galloway, CFO & Treasurer; Rod Sexton, Exec. VP of Marketing.

■ 24973 ■ **Indianapolis Coca-Cola Bottling Company Inc.**
5000 W 25th St.
Speedway, IN 46224
Phone: (317)243-3771
Products: Soft drinks. **SIC:** 5149 (Groceries & Related Products Nec). **Sales:** $160,000,000 (2000). **Emp:** 350. **Officers:** Anthony Stroinsky, President.

■ 24974 ■ **Indianapolis Coca-Cola Bottling Company Inc./Richmond Div.**
1700 Dana Pkwy.
Richmond, IN 47374
Phone: (765)966-7687
Products: Soft drinks. **SIC:** 5149 (Groceries & Related Products Nec). **Sales:** $16,000,000 (2000). **Emp:** 35. **Officers:** Sam M. Witherby, Finance General Manager.

■ 24975 ■ **J and R Bottling and Distribution Co.**
820 S Vail Ave.
Montebello, CA 90640
Phone: (213)685-8387
Products: Soft drinks and juice. **SIC:** 5149 (Groceries & Related Products Nec). **Est:** 1974. **Sales:** $3,000,000 (2000). **Emp:** 15. **Officers:** Ralph Santora, CEO.

■ 24976 ■ **Jackson Coca-Cola Bottling Co.**
PO Box 2397
Jackson, MS 39225-2397
Phone: (601)355-6487 **Fax:** (601)969-0308
Products: Canned and bottled soft drinks. **SIC:** 5149 (Groceries & Related Products Nec). **Sales:** $45,000,000 (1994). **Emp:** 275. **Officers:** Jerry Staines, General Mgr.; Ran Jones, Controller.

■ 24977 ■ **Jarritos Distributors**
1477 Lomaland Dr., Bldg. E, Ste. 7
El Paso, TX 79935
Phone: (915)594-1618 **Fax:** (915)590-1225
Products: Soft drinks. **SIC:** 5149 (Groceries & Related Products Nec). **Sales:** $7,000,000 (1994). **Emp:** 8. **Officers:** Luis Fernandez, VP & General Merchandising Mgr.; Rossana Salcido, Finance Officer.

■ 24978 ■ **Jeff Bottling Company Inc.**
1035 Bradley St.
Watertown, NY 13601
Phone: (315)788-6751 **Fax:** (315)788-6756
Products: Soft drinks, including soda pop. **SIC:** 5149 (Groceries & Related Products Nec). **Sales:** $10,000,000 (2000). **Emp:** 30. **Officers:** Robert

Murphy, President; Gary Simser, Controller; Joe Fusco Jr., Sales Mgr.

■ 24979 ■ **Jonesboro Coca-Cola**
PO Box 19189
Jonesboro, AR 72402
Phone: (870)932-6601 **Fax:** (870)931-8810
Products: Soft drinks. **SIC:** 5149 (Groceries & Related Products Nec). **Sales:** $30,000,000 (1994). **Emp:** 190. **Officers:** Gary James, Sales Mgr.

■ 24980 ■ **Keystone-Ozone Pure Water Co.**
1075 General Sullivan Rd.
Washington Crossing, PA 18977
Phone: (215)493-2511
Free: (800)235-4860 **Fax:** (215)493-8521
Products: Bottled water; Coffee. **SIC:** 5149 (Groceries & Related Products Nec). **Est:** 1909. **Sales:** $9,500,000 (2000). **Emp:** 83. **Officers:** John Henry, President; Jeffrey C. Keener, Controller; Patrick J. Birmingham, Vice President; Tim Petrosky, Dir. of Information Systems.

■ 24981 ■ **Koldkist-Beverage Ice Company Inc.**
955 N Columbia Blvd., Bldg. C
Portland, OR 97217
Phone: (503)285-2800
Products: Ice. **SIC:** 5199 (Nondurable Goods Nec). **Sales:** $11,000,000 (2000). **Emp:** 25. **Officers:** James Porcelli, President.

■ 24982 ■ **LaCROIX Beverages Inc.**
200 W Adams St., Ste. 2011
Chicago, IL 60606-5230
Phone: (312)683-0100
Products: Bottler of spring water. **SIC:** 5149 (Groceries & Related Products Nec). **Officers:** Jim Harford, CEO.

■ 24983 ■ **Laurel Vending Inc.**
15 Nashua St.
Greensburg, PA 15601
Phone: (412)834-4635 **Fax:** (412)832-9508
Products: Canned soft drinks. **SIC:** 5149 (Groceries & Related Products Nec). **Sales:** $10,000,000 (2000). **Emp:** 299. **Officers:** Jack Robertshaw.

■ 24984 ■ **Love Bottling Co.**
PO Box 625
Muskogee, OK 74402
Phone: (918)682-3434 **Fax:** (918)683-4242
Products: Soda, including cola. **SIC:** 5149 (Groceries & Related Products Nec). **Est:** 1919. **Sales:** $10,000,000 (2000). **Emp:** 110. **Officers:** William B. Love, President.

■ 24985 ■ **Made-Rite Co.**
PO Box 3283
Longview, TX 75606
Phone: (903)753-8604
Products: Soda pop. **SIC:** 5149 (Groceries & Related Products Nec). **Est:** 1925. **Sales:** $13,000,000 (2000). **Emp:** 95. **Officers:** J.M. Mann, President; Carolyn Strickland, Dir. of Marketing; Bob Mann, VP & General Mgr.

■ 24986 ■ **Malolo Beverages & Supplies, Ltd.**
2815 Koapaka St.
Honolulu, HI 96819
Phone: (808)836-2111 **Fax:** (808)833-4809
Products: Soft drinks; Disposable products; Sundae toppings; Industrial paper, including napkins, towels, tissue; Cups and plates; Wax wraps, foil, and film; Containers; Janitorial supplies. **SIC:** 5149 (Groceries & Related Products Nec). **Est:** 1927. **Sales:** $13,000,000 (2000). **Emp:** 40. **Officers:** Sanford K.J. Young, President, e-mail: sanfordy@malolbeverages.com.
Former Name: Malolo Beverages and Supply Co.

■ 24987 ■ **Meadowbrook Distributing Corp.**
550 New Horizons Blvd.
Amityville, NY 11701-1166
Phone: (516)228-8200
Products: Soft drinks. **SIC:** 5149 (Groceries & Related Products Nec). **Sales:** $19,000,000 (2000). **Emp:** 55. **Officers:** Richard Poillon, President.

■ 24988 ■ **Midwest Coca-Cola Bottling Co. Rhinelander**
PO Box 1108
Rhinelander, WI 54501
Phone: (715)362-3131
Products: Soft drinks. **SIC:** 5149 (Groceries & Related Products Nec). **Officers:** Bernie Dart, General Mgr.; Mike Jenkins, Controller.

■ 24989 ■ **Natchez Coca-Cola Bottling Co.**
191 Devereaux Dr.
Natchez, MS 39120
Phone: (601)442-1641 **Fax:** (601)442-2428
Products: Soft drinks. **SIC:** 5149 (Groceries & Related Products Nec). **Est:** 1909. **Sales:** $19,000,000 (2000). **Emp:** 41. **Officers:** Ray George, President; Morris Strickland, VP of Finance; Larry Clarkston, General Mgr.

■ 24990 ■ **National Beverage Corp.**
1 N University Dr., #400A
Plantation, FL 33324
Phone: (954)581-0922
Free: (800)757-7677 **Fax:** (954)473-4710
Products: Spring water. **SIC:** 5149 (Groceries & Related Products Nec). **Sales:** $400,700,000 (2000). **Emp:** 1,200. **Officers:** Nick A. Caporella, CEO & Chairman of the Board; George R. Bracken, VP & Treasurer.

■ 24991 ■ **National Distributors Inc.**
116 Wallace Ave.
South Portland, ME 04106
Phone: (207)773-1719 **Fax:** (207)775-4413
Products: Beverages. **SIC:** 5149 (Groceries & Related Products Nec). **Est:** 1959. **Sales:** $36,000,000 (2000). **Emp:** 100. **Officers:** Jeffery D. Kane, President; Charles Gagnon, CFO.

■ 24992 ■ **New Age Distributing Co.**
1000 E Markham St.
Little Rock, AR 72201
Phone: (501)374-5015
Products: Juice and bottled water. **SICs:** 5149 (Groceries & Related Products Nec); 5141 (Groceries—General Line). **Sales:** $300,000 (2000). **Emp:** 25. **Officers:** Danny Sky-eagle, General Mgr.; Paul Cantrell, CFO.

■ 24993 ■ **New England Variety Distributors**
34 Industrial Park Rd.
Niantic, CT 06357
Phone: (860)739-6291 **Fax:** (860)739-2119
Products: Cigarettes. **SICs:** 5149 (Groceries & Related Products Nec); 5194 (Tobacco & Tobacco Products); 5145 (Confectionery). **Est:** 1933. **Sales:** $250,000 (2000). **Emp:** 3. **Officers:** Bruce Engelman, CEO.

■ 24994 ■ **Niagara Drinking Waters Inc.**
17842 Cowen St.
Irvine, CA 92614
Phone: (949)863-1400 **Fax:** (949)863-9349
Products: Drinking water. **SIC:** 5149 (Groceries & Related Products Nec). **Sales:** $28,000,000 (2000). **Emp:** 60. **Officers:** Andrew Peykoff, President; Max Orta, Accountant.

■ 24995 ■ **Noel Corp.**
1001 S 1st St.
Yakima, WA 98901
Phone: (509)248-4545 **Fax:** (509)248-2843
Products: Soft drinks. **SIC:** 5149 (Groceries & Related Products Nec). **Est:** 1967. **Sales:** $23,200,000 (2000). **Emp:** 135. **Officers:** Rodger Noel, President; Larry Estes, VP & Secty.

■ 24996 ■ **North Star Distributors**
2210 Hewitt Ave.
Everett, WA 98201
Phone: (425)252-9600 **Fax:** (425)252-7598
E-mail: info@northstarinc.com
URL: http://www.northstarinc.com
Products: Espresso drinks. **SIC:** 5149 (Groceries & Related Products Nec). **Officers:** Craig Bunney, President.

■ 24997 ■ **Northeast Mississippi Coca-Cola Bottling Co.**
PO Box 968
Starkville, MS 39760
Phone: (662)323-4150
Free: (800)273-7394 **Fax:** (662)338-3401
Products: Bottled and canned soft drinks, water and sport drinks. **SIC:** 5199 (Nondurable Goods Nec). **Sales:** $50,000,000 (2000). **Emp:** 150. **Officers:** Harold Clark, President; Jimmy Briggs, Controller.

■ 24998 ■ **Northern California Beverage Company Inc.**
2286 Stone Blvd.
West Sacramento, CA 95691-4050
Phone: (916)372-0600 **Fax:** (916)372-1673
Products: Sodas; Juices; Refrigeration equipment. **SICs:** 5149 (Groceries & Related Products Nec); 5078 (Refrigeration Equipment & Supplies). **Sales:** $50,000,000 (2000). **Emp:** 499. **Officers:** Grant Deary.

■ 24999 ■ **Northwest Bottling Co.**
7523 15th Ave. NW
Seattle, WA 98117-5410
Phone: (425)251-0800
Products: Soft drinks. **SIC:** 5149 (Groceries & Related Products Nec). **Est:** 1946. **Sales:** $25,000,000 (2000). **Emp:** 130. **Officers:** S. Sourapas, President; C. McLeod, CFO; George MacKay, Dir. of Marketing.

■ 25000 ■ **Nutri-Fruit Inc.**
PO Box 338
Sumner, WA 98390
Phone: (425)643-4489 **Fax:** (425)641-8567
Products: Fruit juices, including apple, orange, grape, grapefruit, and pineapple juice. **SIC:** 5149 (Groceries & Related Products Nec). **Est:** 1987. **Sales:** $2,000,000 (2000). **Emp:** 18. **Officers:** Charles C. Jarrett, President; Deandra Bishop, Vice President.

■ 25001 ■ **Oasis Drinking Waters Inc.**
1506 N Clinton St.
Santa Ana, CA 92703
Phone: (714)554-6000 **Fax:** (714)554-6131
Products: Bottled water. **SIC:** 5149 (Groceries & Related Products Nec). **Sales:** $10,000,000 (2000). **Emp:** 60. **Officers:** John Shelton, President; Chandler Beach, Controller.

■ 25002 ■ **Pacific Beverage Company Inc.**
5305 Ekwill St.
Santa Barbara, CA 93111
Phone: (805)964-0611
Products: Soda; Plates; Eating utensils; Beer and wine. **SICs:** 5149 (Groceries & Related Products Nec); 5181 (Beer & Ale); 5199 (Nondurable Goods Nec). **Sales:** $60,000,000 (2000). **Emp:** 200. **Officers:** P.C. Jordano, President; M.F. Sieckowski, CFO; G. Johnson, VP of Marketing.

■ 25003 ■ **Peninsula Bottling Company Inc.**
311 S Valley St.
Port Angeles, WA 98362
Phone: (206)457-3383
Products: Soft drinks. **SIC:** 5149 (Groceries & Related Products Nec). **Est:** 1955. **Sales:** $1,000,000 (2000). **Emp:** 22. **Officers:** Jeffrey Hinds, President.

■ 25004 ■ **Buffalo Rock Pepsi**
PO Box 3218
Columbus, GA 31903-0218
Phone: (706)687-1240
Free: (800)868-1240 **Fax:** (706)687-8450
URL: http://www.buffalorock.com
Products: Soft drinks. **SIC:** 5149 (Groceries & Related Products Nec). **Est:** 1985. **Sales:** $24,000,000 (1999). **Emp:** 180. **Officers:** David Hawkins, e-mail: david.hawkins@buffalorock.com.

■ 25005 ■ **Pepsi-Cola Batavia Bottling Corp.**
319 W Main St.
Batavia, NY 14020
Phone: (716)343-7479
Free: (800)462-4800 **Fax:** (716)343-7793
URL: http://www.pepsimart.com
Products: Soft drinks; Teas; Juices; Water. **SIC:** 5149 (Groceries & Related Products Nec). **Est:** 1890. **Sales:** $24,000,000 (2000). **Emp:** 125. **Officers:** Ralph W.

Houseknecht Jr., President, e-mail: bhouseknecht@pepsimart.com.

■ 25006 ■ Pepsi-Cola Bottling Co. of Daytona Beach
860 Bellevue Ave.
Daytona Beach, FL 32114-5106
Phone: (904)252-2507
Products: Bottled and canned soft drinks. SIC: 5149 (Groceries & Related Products Nec). Emp: 60. Officers: Dave Kessler.

■ 25007 ■ Pepsi-Cola Bottling Company of Denver
3801 Brighton Blvd.
Denver, CO 80216-3625
Phone: (303)292-9220   Fax: (303)295-2741
Products: Soft drinks. SIC: 5149 (Groceries & Related Products Nec). Sales: $75,000,000 (2000). Emp: 700.

■ 25008 ■ Pepsi-Cola Bottling Company of Luverne Inc.
PO Box 226
Luverne, AL 36049
Phone: (334)335-6521
Products: Soft drinks. SIC: 5149 (Groceries & Related Products Nec). Sales: $4,000,000 (2000). Emp: 53. Officers: Winston B. Springford, President; Marvin G. Motley Jr., VP of Finance.

■ 25009 ■ Pepsi-Cola Bottling Company of Marysville Inc.
604 Center Dr.
Marysville, KS 66508
Phone: (785)562-5334   Fax: (785)562-5164
Products: Soft drinks. SIC: 5149 (Groceries & Related Products Nec). Sales: $6,000,000 (2000). Emp: 50. Officers: H.G. Wassenberg, President.

■ 25010 ■ Pepsi-Cola Bottling Company of New Bern Inc.
PO Box 12036
New Bern, NC 28561
Phone: (252)637-2193
Products: Bottled and canned soft drinks. SIC: 5149 (Groceries & Related Products Nec). Sales: $29,000,000 (1994). Emp: 64. Officers: Hoyt Minges, President.

■ 25011 ■ Pepsi-Cola Bottling Company of Rochester
1307 Valley High Dr.
Rochester, MN 55901
Phone: (507)288-3772
Products: Soft drinks; Juices. SIC: 5149 (Groceries & Related Products Nec). Est: 1942. Sales: $27,000,000 (2000). Emp: 100. Officers: Norman L. Gillette, President.

■ 25012 ■ Pepsi-Cola Bottling Company of Rockford
4622 Hydraulic Rd.
Rockford, IL 61125
Phone: (815)965-8701   Fax: (815)874-9730
Products: Bottled and canned soft drinks. SIC: 5149 (Groceries & Related Products Nec). Sales: $30,000,000 (1993). Emp: 65. Officers: Richard Anders, Mgr. of Finance.

■ 25013 ■ Pepsi-Cola Bottling Company of Salisbury
PO Box 2138
Salisbury, MD 21801
Phone: (410)546-1136   Fax: (410)742-6020
Products: Soft drinks. SIC: 5149 (Groceries & Related Products Nec). Est: 1915. Sales: $29,000,000 (2000). Emp: 250. Officers: Richard F. Hazel, President; Jay Pierce, Controller; Tony Brocato, Dir. of Marketing & Sales.

■ 25014 ■ Pepsi-Cola Bottling Company of Shreveport
1501 Corporate Dr.
Shreveport, LA 71107
Phone: (318)222-1201   Fax: (318)227-8907
Products: Beverages, including soft drinks and iced tea. SIC: 5149 (Groceries & Related Products Nec). Est: 1980. Sales: $10,000,000 (2000). Emp: 50. Officers: Greg Barrett, General Mgr.

■ 25015 ■ Pepsi-Cola Company of Jonesboro
1301 Aggie Rd.
Jonesboro, AR 72401
Phone: (870)932-6649
Products: Soft drinks. SIC: 5149 (Groceries & Related Products Nec). Officers: Bruce Fritz, CEO.

■ 25016 ■ Pepsi-Cola Company South
4532 Hwy. 67
Mesquite, TX 75150
Phone: (214)324-8500
Products: Soft drinks. SIC: 5149 (Groceries & Related Products Nec). Officers: Mark Higgins, Manager.

■ 25017 ■ Pepsi-Cola General Bottlers of South Bend
PO Box 1596
South Bend, IN 46634
Phone: (219)234-1311   Fax: (219)234-0270
Products: Soft drinks. SIC: 5149 (Groceries & Related Products Nec). Est: 1940. Sales: $15,000,000 (2000). Emp: 77. Officers: R. Rahal, Manager; Art Brown, Controller.

■ 25018 ■ Pepsi-Cola Ogdensburg Inc.
1001 Mansion Ave.
Ogdensburg, NY 13669
Phone: (315)393-1720   Fax: (315)393-2751
Products: Soft drinks; Juices; Tea. SIC: 5149 (Groceries & Related Products Nec). Est: 1940. Sales: $7,000,000 (1999). Emp: 45. Officers: Bonita Wright, President; Michael Looney, VP of Finance; Richard Wright, VP of Sales; Scott Wright, Secretary.

■ 25019 ■ Pepsi-Cola Pittsfield
1 Pepsi Cola Dr.
Latham, NY 12110-2306
Phone: (518)445-4579
Products: Soft drinks. SIC: 5149 (Groceries & Related Products Nec). Sales: $4,000,000 (2000). Emp: 25. Officers: James Sikora, General Mgr.

■ 25020 ■ Pepsi-Cola of Salem
3011 Silverton Rd. NE
Salem, OR 97303
Phone: (503)363-9221   Fax: (503)361-7305
Products: Bottled and canned soft drinks. SIC: 5149 (Groceries & Related Products Nec). Sales: $34,000,000 (2000). Emp: 70. Officers: Tammy Hoogestraat, General Mgr.

■ 25021 ■ Perrier Group of America Inc.
777 W Putnam Ave.
Greenwich, CT 06830
Phone: (203)531-4100   Fax: (203)863-0297
Products: Bottled water. SIC: 5149 (Groceries & Related Products Nec). Sales: $2,000,000,000 (2000). Emp: 4,500. Officers: Kim Jeffery, CEO & President; Rick Croarkin, VP of Finance; Lisa Druker, Dir. of Marketing; Rowan Snyder, Dir. of Information Systems; James Rouse, Dir of Human Resources.

■ 25022 ■ Purity Products Inc. (Baltimore, Maryland)
4001 Washington Blvd.
Baltimore, MD 21227
Phone: (410)242-7200
Free: (800)935-1366   Fax: (410)247-5750
Products: Fruit drink concentrates, cocktail mixes and fruit juices. SIC: 5149 (Groceries & Related Products Nec). Sales: $5,000,000 (2000). Emp: 15. Officers: Ivan Goldstein, President; Scott Goldstein, Treasurer.

■ 25023 ■ Puro Corporation of America
PO Box 10
Maspeth, NY 11378
Phone: (718)326-7000   Fax: (718)894-8357
Products: Bottled water. SIC: 5149 (Groceries & Related Products Nec). Est: 1905. Sales: $23,000,000 (2000). Emp: 50. Officers: Jack C. West, President; David Treidel, Controller.

■ 25024 ■ A.T. Reynolds and Sons Inc.
PO Box K
Kiamesha Lake, NY 12751
Phone: (914)794-7040
Products: Ice; Spring water. SIC: 5149 (Groceries & Related Products Nec). Est: 1884. Sales: $46,000,000

(2000). Emp: 100. Officers: Harold A. Reynolds, President & Treasurer.

■ 25025 ■ Rock Hill Coca-Cola Bottling Co.
PO Box 2555
Rock Hill, SC 29732
Phone: (803)328-2406
Products: Canned and bottled soft drinks. SIC: 5149 (Groceries & Related Products Nec). Sales: $9,000,000 (2000). Emp: 39.

■ 25026 ■ Rock Springs Casper Coca-Cola Bottling Co.
PO Box 939
Rock Springs, WY 82902
Phone: (307)382-2233
Products: Soft drinks. SIC: 5149 (Groceries & Related Products Nec). Est: 1935. Sales: $5,000,000 (2000). Emp: 55. Officers: Joe Decora, President; Kathleen Bottgenbach, Finance Officer; Helmut Wise, Sales Mgr.

■ 25027 ■ Royal Crown Beverage Co.
553 N Fairview Ave.
St. Paul, MN 55104
Phone: (612)645-0501   Fax: (612)645-0247
Products: Soft drinks. SIC: 5149 (Groceries & Related Products Nec). Est: 1933. Sales: $33,500,000 (2000). Emp: 80. Officers: Steve R. Schreiber, President; Scott R. Morris, VP of Marketing; Wanda Knippenberg, Dir. of Admin.

■ 25028 ■ Royal Crown Bottling Company Inc.
2801 W 47th Pl.
Chicago, IL 60632-2035
Phone: (630)229-0101
Products: Flavored water, juice, and soda. SIC: 5149 (Groceries & Related Products Nec). Sales: $15,000,000 (2000). Emp: 100. Officers: Chalker A. Anderson, Vice President; Ray Myers, Dir. of Marketing.

■ 25029 ■ Johnnie Ryan Co.
3084 Niagara St.
Niagara Falls, NY 14303
Phone: (716)282-1606   Fax: (716)282-6737
Products: Bottled soft drinks; Soft drink syrups; Fruit juice concentrates; Bottled spring water. SIC: 5149 (Groceries & Related Products Nec). Est: 1935. Sales: $2,000,000 (2000). Emp: 15. Officers: Paul J. Janik, President.

■ 25030 ■ S & S Variety Beverages Inc.
905 Caldwell Ave.
Tiffin, OH 44883
Products: Beverages. SIC: 5149 (Groceries & Related Products Nec).

■ 25031 ■ Saccani Distributing Co.
2600 5th St.
Sacramento, CA 95818-2899
Phone: (916)441-0213   Fax: (916)441-0806
Products: Beer; Soda; Fine juices. SICs: 5149 (Groceries & Related Products Nec); 5181 (Beer & Ale). Est: 1933. Emp: 70. Officers: Gary Saccani; Roland Saccani; Steve Fishman.

■ 25032 ■ Salem Coca-Cola Bottling Co.
23 S Broadway
Salem, NH 03079
Phone: (603)898-5916
Products: Soft drinks. SIC: 5149 (Groceries & Related Products Nec). Est: 1937. Sales: $46,000,000 (2000). Emp: 100. Officers: James Clougherty, General Mgr.

■ 25033 ■ San Diego Beverage and Cup Inc.
5310 Riley St.
San Diego, CA 92110
Phone: (619)297-2600
Products: Natural beverages. SIC: 5149 (Groceries & Related Products Nec). Sales: $1,500,000 (2000). Emp: 7. Officers: Joe Ferro, President.

■ 25034 ■ Seven-Up Baltimore Inc.
PO Box 244
Gladwyne, PA 19035
Phone: (610)834-6551
Products: Soft drinks. SIC: 5149 (Groceries & Related Products Nec). Est: 1936. Sales: $900,000 (2000).

Emp: 6. **Officers:** Lawrence Imbesi, President; Mark Imbesi, Controller.

■ **25035** ■ **Seven-Up Dayton Div.**
3131 Transportation Rd.
Dayton, OH 45404
Phone: (937)236-0333
Products: Soft drinks. **SIC:** 5149 (Groceries & Related Products Nec). **Sales:** $46,000,000 (2000). **Emp:** 100. **Officers:** Michael Beekman, General Mgr.; Jim Bauer, CFO.

■ **25036** ■ **Seven-Up Royal Crown**
5151 Fischer Ave.
Cincinnati, OH 45217
Phone: (513)242-5151
Products: Soft drinks. **SIC:** 5149 (Groceries & Related Products Nec). **Sales:** $100,000,000 (2000). **Emp:** 175. **Officers:** Mark Wendling, General Mgr.

■ **25037** ■ **Seven-Up Salem**
2561 Pringle Rd. SE
Salem, OR 97302-1531
Phone: (503)585-2822   **Fax:** (503)585-1702
Products: Soft drinks. **SIC:** 5149 (Groceries & Related Products Nec). **Est:** 1945. **Sales:** $3,000,000 (2000). **Emp:** 22. **Officers:** Bob Cole, President; Tim Morgan, Controller; Ron LaLonde, Manager.

■ **25038** ■ **Southern Beverage Company Inc.**
PO Box 1349
Jackson, MS 39215
Phone: (601)969-5550
Products: Beverages. **SIC:** 5149 (Groceries & Related Products Nec).

■ **25039** ■ **Spaz Beverage Co.**
890 S Matlack
West Chester, PA 19382-4956
Phone: (215)696-6320   **Fax:** (215)692-0116
Products: Beverages, including soft drinks, juice, and beer. **SICs:** 5149 (Groceries & Related Products Nec); 5181 (Beer & Ale). **Emp:** 29. **Officers:** R. J. Spaziani.

■ **25040** ■ **Springfield Pepsi-Cola Bottling Co.**
PO Box 4146
Springfield, IL 62708
Phone: (217)522-8841
Products: Soft drinks. **SIC:** 5149 (Groceries & Related Products Nec).

■ **25041** ■ **Sun States Beverage Co.**
2480 Weaver Way
Doraville, GA 30340
Phone: (404)840-7178
Products: Soft drinks. **SIC:** 5149 (Groceries & Related

Products Nec). **Sales:** $1,000,000 (1993). **Emp:** 4. **Officers:** Lawrence Potts, President.

■ **25042** ■ **Sundrop Inc.**
29599 Old Hwy. 20
Madison, AL 35758
Phone: (256)772-8596   **Fax:** (256)772-8598
Products: Canned and bottled soft drinks. **SIC:** 5149 (Groceries & Related Products Nec). **Sales:** $10,000,000 (2000). **Emp:** 22. **Officers:** Jack Bethshares, President; Jim Montgomery, Mgr. of Finance.

■ **25043** ■ **K. Takitani Enterprises Inc.**
1162 Lower Main St.
Wailuku, HI 96793
Phone: (808)244-3777
Products: Beverages, including soft drinks, cranberry juices, and purified water. **SICs:** 5149 (Groceries & Related Products Nec); 5143 (Dairy Products Except Dried or Canned). **Est:** 1913. **Sales:** $4,000,000 (2000). **Emp:** 37. **Officers:** Robert Takitani, President; Susan Duboin, Mgr. of Finance; Garret Abe, VP of Marketing & Sales.

■ **25044** ■ **Tipp Distributors Inc.**
1477 Lomaland Dr., Bldg. E, Ste. 7
El Paso, TX 79935
Phone: (915)594-1618   **Fax:** (915)590-1225
Products: Soft drinks. **SIC:** 5149 (Groceries & Related Products Nec). **Sales:** $15,000,000 (1994). **Emp:** 8. **Officers:** Luis Fernandez, VP & General Merchandising Mgr.

■ **25045** ■ **Trundle and Company Inc.**
155 E 55th St.
New York, NY 10022
Phone: (212)486-1011   **Fax:** (212)486-1304
E-mail: ertrundle@mindspring.com
Products: Beverages, including canned and bottled juices and juice concentrates; Popcorn; Canned vegetables. **SIC:** 5149 (Groceries & Related Products Nec). **Est:** 1985. **Sales:** $10,000,000 (1999). **Emp:** 4. **Officers:** Edward Trundle, President, e-mail: ertrundle@aol.com.

■ **25046** ■ **U.S. Beverage Corp.**
PO Box 3364
Longview, TX 75606
Phone: (903)757-2168
Products: Soft drinks. **SIC:** 5149 (Groceries & Related Products Nec). **Sales:** $20,000,000 (2000). **Emp:** 47. **Officers:** A.T. Burke, President; S.R. Rose, VP of Finance.

■ **25047** ■ **Vermont Pure Holdings Ltd.**
PO Box C
Randolph, VT 05060
Phone: (802)728-3600   **Fax:** (802)728-4614
Products: Bottled spring water. **SIC:** 5149 (Groceries & Related Products Nec). **Sales:** $17,700,000 (2000). **Emp:** 138. **Officers:** Timothy G. Fallon, CEO & President; Bruce MacDonald, Sr. VP & CFO.

■ **25048** ■ **Virginia Beach Beverages**
5700 Ward Ave.
Virginia Beach, VA 23455
Phone: (757)464-1771
Free: (800)777-1771   **Fax:** (757)464-1917
Products: Bottled and canned soft drinks. **SIC:** 5149 (Groceries & Related Products Nec). **Sales:** $13,000,000 (2000). **Emp:** 75. **Officers:** John Kuckinskas, General Mgr.

■ **25049** ■ **Vitality Foodservice Inc.**
400 N Tampa St., Ste. 1700
Tampa, FL 33602-4716
Phone: (813)783-6200
Products: Juices, coffee, and tea. **SIC:** 5149 (Groceries & Related Products Nec). **Sales:** $163,000,000 (2000). **Emp:** 340. **Officers:** Ron Frump, President & COO; Mike Shenefield, VP of Finance & Admin.

■ **25050** ■ **Water Warehouse, Etc.**
PO Box 123
Matawan, NJ 07747
Products: Drinking water, juice, teas, herbal waters and water systems. **SICs:** 5149 (Groceries & Related Products Nec); 5078 (Refrigeration Equipment & Supplies). **Sales:** $2,500,000 (1994). **Emp:** 15. **Officers:** Kenneth Siebenberg, President; Stanley Siebenberg, Chairman of the Board.

■ **25051** ■ **Western Wyoming Beverage Inc.**
PO Box 1336
Rock Springs, WY 82902
Phone: (307)362-6332
Products: Beer and ale; Beverages, including soft drinks and juice. **SICs:** 5149 (Groceries & Related Products Nec); 5181 (Beer & Ale). **Est:** 1970. **Sales:** $9,000,000 (2000). **Emp:** 30. **Officers:** Eldon Spicer, CEO.

(53) Sound and Entertainment Equipment and Supplies

Entries in this section are arranged alphabetically by company name. When the company name is a personal name, the company name is alphabetized by the surname unless the first name or initial(s) are part of a trade name. See the User's Guide at the front of this directory for additional information.

■ 25052 ■ **A and A International Corp.**
1200 1 Tandy Ctr.
Ft. Worth, TX 76102
Phone: (817)390-3011
Products: Radios, calculators, video cassette recorders, and televisions. **SIC:** 5064 (Electrical Appliances—Television & Radio). **Sales:** $100,000,000 (2000). **Emp:** 400. **Officers:** Mark Yamatat, Exec. VP; Mac McClure, VP & Controller.

■ 25053 ■ **A & V TapeHandlers, Inc.**
Bemis Bldg.
55 S Atlantic St., Ste. 1A
Seattle, WA 98134-1217
Phone: (206)621-9222   **Fax:** (206)628-0351
E-mail: avtapehandlers@uswest.net
URL: http://welcome.to/avtapehandlers
Products: Audio-visual supplies. **SIC:** 5064 (Electrical Appliances—Television & Radio). **Est:** 1972. **Sales:** $1,500,000 (2000). **Emp:** 4. **Officers:** George M. Ricci, Vice President; Mary R. Amack, Treasurer and Gen. Mgr.; C.F. O'Reilly Jr., President. **Alternate Name:** AV Tapehandlers.

■ 25054 ■ **AAAA World Import Export Inc.**
11400 NW 32nd Ave.
Miami, FL 33167
Phone: (305)688-1000   **Fax:** (305)688-8220
Products: Consumer electronics and appliances. **SICs:** 5064 (Electrical Appliances—Television & Radio); 5065 (Electronic Parts & Equipment Nec). **Est:** 1978. **Sales:** $200,000,000 (1999). **Emp:** 150.

■ 25055 ■ **AAT Communications Systems Corp.**
1854 Hylan Blvd.
Staten Island, NY 10305
Phone: (718)351-4782
Free: (800)622-6224   **Fax:** (718)351-2525
E-mail: aatcom_ny@compuserve.com
Products: Radios; Satellites; Voice logging recorders; Intercom systems. **SICs:** 5064 (Electrical Appliances—Television & Radio); 5065 (Electronic Parts & Equipment Nec). **Est:** 1950. **Sales:** $8,000,000 (2000). **Emp:** 55. **Officers:** Joseph P. Amodea, President; Jerry Barton, Exec. VP; Joseph P. Amodea III, Secretary.

■ 25056 ■ **ABKCO Music and Records Inc.**
1700 Broadway
New York, NY 10019
Phone: (212)399-0300
Products: Records, tapes, and compact discs. **SIC:** 5099 (Durable Goods Nec). **Sales:** $3,000,000 (2000). **Emp:** 25. **Officers:** Allen Klein, President.

■ 25057 ■ **Acoustical Material Services**
1620 S Maple Ave.
Montebello, CA 90640
Phone: (213)721-9011   **Fax:** (213)721-2476
Products: Acoustical materials for windows, walls, and ceilings. **SIC:** 5039 (Construction Materials Nec). **Sales:** $100,000,000 (2000). **Emp:** 350. **Officers:** Max Gondon, Owner; John Gorey, Controller.

■ 25058 ■ **AIMS Multimedia**
9710 De Soto Ave.
Chatsworth, CA 91311-4409
Phone: (818)773-4300
Free: (800)367-2467   **Fax:** (818)341-6700
E-mail: info@aims-multimedia.com
URL: http://www.aims-multimedia.com
Products: Audiovisual, CD-ROM, and laser disc educational and training programs. **SIC:** 5099 (Durable Goods Nec). **Est:** 1957. **Emp:** 50. **Officers:** Jeffrey M. Sherman; Wynn A. Sherman; David S. Sherman; Michael Wright.

■ 25059 ■ **Aiwa America Inc.**
800 Corporate Dr.
Mahwah, NJ 07430
Phone: (201)512-3600   **Fax:** (201)512-3707
URL: http://www.aiwa.com
Products: Electronic equipment, including radios. **SIC:** 5065 (Electronic Parts & Equipment Nec). **Est:** 1978. **Sales:** $28,200,000 (2000). **Emp:** 170. **Officers:** Hideki Tafuku, President; Jack Cox, Sr. VP & Controller; Ken Fang, Dir. of MIS; Cathie Evanisko, Dir of Human Resources.

■ 25060 ■ **Alaron Inc.**
PO Box 215287
Auburn Hills, MI 48321-5287
Phone: (248)340-7500   **Fax:** (248)340-7555
E-mail: alaronah@aol.com
URL: http://www.alaroninc.com
Products: Home entertainment electronics and musical toys. **SICs:** 5064 (Electrical Appliances—Television & Radio); 5065 (Electronic Parts & Equipment Nec). **Est:** 1959. **Sales:** $30,000,000 (2000). **Emp:** 46. **Officers:** Robert Bourque, President; Jim McAtamney, Controller; James Mulvehill, VP & General Merchandising Mgr.; S. Douglas Stedtefeld, Dir. of Data Processing; Gerald Milkovich, Dir of Human Resources; Lionel Gee, Dir. of Marketing.

■ 25061 ■ **Allegheny Electronics Inc.**
PO Box 1963
Altoona, PA 16603
Phone: (814)946-0871   **Fax:** (814)946-1743
Products: Electronics, including televisions, cable, wire, and radios. **SICs:** 5065 (Electronic Parts & Equipment Nec); 5064 (Electrical Appliances—Television & Radio). **Est:** 1952. **Sales:** $5,000,000 (2000). **Emp:** 30. **Officers:** Kenneth O. McGraw, President; Sheri Ventre, Controller.

■ 25062 ■ **Allied Sound Inc.**
230 Cumberland Bnd
Nashville, TN 37228-1807
Phone: (615)248-2800   **Fax:** (615)248-6226
E-mail: allied@alliedsound.com
URL: http://www.alliedsound.com
Products: Electronic parts and equipment for sound and communication. **SIC:** 5065 (Electronic Parts & Equipment Nec). **Officers:** Larry Link, President.

■ 25063 ■ **Allied-Vaughn Inc.**
11923 Brookfield
Livonia, MI 48150
Phone: (734)462-5543   **Fax:** (734)462-4004
URL: http://www.allied-digital.com
Products: Video reproductions; Custom media packaging. **SIC:** 5099 (Durable Goods Nec). **Former Name:** Allied Film Laboratory, Inc.

■ 25064 ■ **Alpha Video & Electronics Co.**
200 Keystone Dr.
Carnegie, PA 15106
Phone: (412)429-2000   **Fax:** (412)429-2015
Products: Televisions and monitors. **SIC:** 5064 (Electrical Appliances—Television & Radio). **Officers:** Henry B. Lassige, Pres.; Terance M. Lassige, V.P.

■ 25065 ■ **Alpine Electronics of America Inc.**
PO Box 2859
Torrance, CA 90509
Phone: (310)326-8000
Products: Car audio systems. **SIC:** 5064 (Electrical Appliances—Television & Radio).

■ 25066 ■ **Altron International**
314 W Walton Blvd.
Pontiac, MI 48340-1041
Phone: (248)334-2549
Free: (800)922-9078   **Fax:** (248)334-3558
E-mail: call-altron@ic.net
Products: Closed circuit televisions and mobile electronics. **SIC:** 5064 (Electrical Appliances—Television & Radio). **Est:** 1975. **Sales:** $5,000,000 (1999). **Emp:** 20. **Officers:** Robert English, President; Tom Kent, Sales/Marketing Contact, e-mail: call-tom@ic.net. **Alternate Name:** Radios Knobs Speakers & Things.

■ 25067 ■ **Amateur Electronics Supply**
28940 Euclid Ave.
Wickliffe, OH 44092
Phone: (440)585-7388   **Fax:** (440)585-1024
Products: Electronic equipment, including radio equipment. **SIC:** 5064 (Electrical Appliances—Television & Radio).

■ 25068 ■ **Amco-McLean Corp.**
766 McLean Ave.
Yonkers, NY 10704
Phone: (914)237-4000   **Fax:** (914)237-4341
E-mail: amc0766@aol.com
Products: Television sets; Video cassette recorders (VCR's); Vacuums. **SIC:** 5064 (Electrical Appliances—Television & Radio). **Est:** 1960. **Sales:** $19,900,000 (2000). **Emp:** 14. **Officers:** Joseph Bonda.

■ 25069 ■ **American Electronics Supply, Inc.**
1546 N Argyle Ave.
Hollywood, CA 90028
Phones: (323)464-1144   (323)466-4321
              (323)462-1200   **Fax:** (323)871-0127
E-mail: info@ametron.com
URL: http://www.ametron.com
Products: Electronic supplies, including televisions, video cassette recorders, and stereos. **SIC:** 5064

(Electrical Appliances—Television & Radio). **Est:** 1952. **Emp:** 99.

■ **25070** ■ **American Media Inc.**
4900 University Ave., Ste. 100
West Des Moines, IA 50266-6779
Phone: (515)224-0919
Free: (800)262-2557 **Fax:** (515)224-0256
E-mail: ami@ammedia.com
URL: http://www.ammedia.com
Products: How-to training products. **SIC:** 5099 (Durable Goods Nec). **Est:** 1977. **Emp:** 120. **Officers:** Art Bauer, President; John Dieseth, Vice President.

■ **25071** ■ **American Terminal Supply Company, Inc.**
48925 West Rd.
Wixom, MI 48393-3555
Phone: (248)380-8887
Free: (800)826-4697 **Fax:** (248)380-8890
Products: Electronic parts and equipment, including radio and television. **SIC:** 5065 (Electronic Parts & Equipment Nec). **Officers:** Wayne Kidder, President.

■ **25072** ■ **American Video & Audio Corp.**
1567 N Eastman Rd.
Kingsport, TN 37664-0010
Phone: (423)239-4222 **Fax:** (423)246-1223
Products: Cameras and video equipment and accessories. **SIC:** 5043 (Photographic Equipment & Supplies). **Officers:** Gary Alexander, President.

■ **25073** ■ **The Amerling Co.**
PO Box 3028
New Haven, CT 06515-0128
Phone: (203)934-7901 **Fax:** (203)934-7907
Products: Small electrical appliances; Television sets; Radios. **SIC:** 5064 (Electrical Appliances—Television & Radio). **Officers:** Robert Jacobs, President.

■ **25074** ■ **Amway Global Inc.**
7575 E Fulton St.
Ada, MI 49301-9117
Phone: (616)676-6000 **Fax:** (616)676-6177
Products: Electrical appliances, including televisions, radios, and vacuum cleaners. **SIC:** 5064 (Electrical Appliances—Television & Radio). **Officers:** Jay Van Andel, Chairman of the Board.

■ **25075** ■ **Antenna Farms Inc.**
4403 Lomas St.
Farmington, NM 87401-3633
Phone: (505)762-9801 **Fax:** (505)762-9760
Products: Electrical entertainment equipment, including televisions, radios, video cassette recorders, and accessories. **SIC:** 5064 (Electrical Appliances— Television & Radio). **Officers:** Allen Hingle, President.

■ **25076** ■ **Apon Record Company, Inc.**
PO Box 3082, Steinway Sta.
Long Island City, NY 11103
Phone: (718)721-5599 **Fax:** (718)721-5599
Products: Recording cassettes; Audio and video recording tapes; Compact discs. **SIC:** 5065 (Electronic Parts & Equipment Nec). **Est:** 1957. **Emp:** 12.

■ **25077** ■ **Appliance Parts Center Inc.**
501 N Eastern Ave.
Las Vegas, NV 89101-3422
Phone: (702)384-7759 **Fax:** (702)384-6416
Products: Electrical appliances, including television and radio; Parts for electrical appliances. **SICs:** 5064 (Electrical Appliances—Television & Radio); 5065 (Electronic Parts & Equipment Nec). **Officers:** Lina Zozaya, President.

■ **25078** ■ **Appliance Parts Inc.**
5520 Jewella Ave.
Shreveport, LA 71109-7641
Phone: (318)631-9591 **Fax:** (318)631-8147
Products: Television sets; Radio receivers; Parts and attachments for small household appliances. **SIC:** 5064 (Electrical Appliances—Television & Radio). **Officers:** Fred Lambert, President.

■ **25079** ■ **Appliance Service Center Inc.**
700 23rd Ave.
Fairbanks, AK 99701-7026
Phone: (907)452-1000 **Fax:** (907)452-8508
E-mail: apsco@gci.net
Products: Electrical appliances and parts. **SICs:** 5064 (Electrical Appliances—Television & Radio); 5065 (Electronic Parts & Equipment Nec). **Est:** 1974. **Emp:** 9. **Officers:** Tammy Burrow.

■ **25080** ■ **Applied Video Systems Inc.**
5816 Shakespeare Rd. D
Columbia, SC 29223-7233
Phone: (803)735-1120
Free: (800)325-2281 **Fax:** (803)735-1121
Products: Electrical appliances, including television sets and radios; Electrical entertainment equipment; Video camera-audio recorders (camcorders). **SIC:** 5064 (Electrical Appliances—Television & Radio). **Officers:** Joseph Brunson, President.

■ **25081** ■ **A.R. Musical Enterprises Inc.**
9031 Technology Dr.
Fishers, IN 46038
Phone: (317)577-6999 **Fax:** (317)577-7288
Products: Musical instruments and accessories. **SIC:** 5099 (Durable Goods Nec). **Est:** 1973. **Sales:** $6,000,000 (2000). **Emp:** 30. **Officers:** Tony Blair, President; Bill Wissel, Exec. VP.

■ **25082** ■ **Arista Records Inc.**
6 W 57th St.
New York, NY 10019
Phone: (212)489-7400 **Fax:** (212)247-7234
Products: Phonograph records; Prerecorded audio tapes; Video discs prerecorded for home entertainment; Compact discs. **SIC:** 5099 (Durable Goods Nec). **Est:** 1975. **Emp:** 499. **Officers:** Clive Davis, President; Ray Lott, Exec. VP.

■ **25083** ■ **ARS Electronics**
7110 Decelis Pl.
Van Nuys, CA 91406
Phone: (818)997-6279
Free: (800)422-4250 **Fax:** (818)997-6158
E-mail: 4423@worldnet.att.net
Products: Electronic equipment, including electron tubes, capacitors, broadcast, aircraft, and industrial electron components. **SIC:** 5064 (Electrical Appliances—Television & Radio). **Est:** 1947. **Sales:** $1,500,000 (2000). **Emp:** 7. **Officers:** Martin Sanett, President; Anne Sanett, VP & Treasurer; Robert Sanett, Sales/Marketing Contact.

■ **25084** ■ **Artec Distributing Inc.**
1 Pine Haven Shore Rd.
Shelburne, VT 05482
Phone: (802)985-9411 **Fax:** (802)985-3403
Products: Videocassette recorders. **SIC:** 5064 (Electrical Appliances—Television & Radio). **Est:** 1970. **Sales:** $84,000,000 (2000). **Emp:** 298. **Officers:** Martin F. Gold, President; John LeClair, CFO; William Boyle, VP Marketing & Development.

■ **25085** ■ **Atlantic Communications Inc.**
PO Box 596
Bangor, ME 04402-0596
Phone: (207)947-2575
Free: (800)300-2575 **Fax:** (207)947-2859
Products: 2-Way radios; CCTV equipment and supplies. **SIC:** 5064 (Electrical Appliances—Television & Radio). **Est:** 1983. **Sales:** $1,300,000 (2000). **Emp:** 9. **Officers:** Gerard E. Ouellette, President.

■ **25086** ■ **Audio Acoustics**
800 N Cedarbrook Ave.
Springfield, MO 65802
Phone: (417)869-0770
Products: Sound equipment; Telephone equipment. **SIC:** 5065 (Electronic Parts & Equipment Nec).

■ **25087** ■ **Audio Supply Co.**
1416 N Pennsylvania St.
Indianapolis, IN 46202
Phone: (317)634-1016
Products: Audio equipment and supplies. **SICs:** 5064 (Electrical Appliances—Television & Radio); 5099 (Durable Goods Nec).

■ **25088** ■ **Audio-Tech Inc.**
5600 Oakbrook Pky., Ste. 200
Norcross, GA 30093-1843
Phone: (404)448-3988 **Fax:** (404)448-2922
Products: Electronic systems and equipment; Electronic parts; Communication systems and equipment; Consumer high fidelity components. **SIC:** 5065 (Electronic Parts & Equipment Nec). **Officers:** William Anderson, President.

■ **25089** ■ **Audio-Technica U.S., Inc.**
1221 Commerce Dr.
Stow, OH 44224
Phone: (330)686-2600 **Fax:** (330)688-3752
E-mail: pro@atus.com
URL: http://www.audio-technica.com
Products: Audio products. **SIC:** 5064 (Electrical Appliances—Television & Radio). **Est:** 1972. **Emp:** 115. **Officers:** Philip Cajka, President; Fred Nichols, Sr. VP; Paul Hugo.

■ **25090** ■ **Audio-Video Corp.**
213 Broadway
Albany, NY 12204
Phone: (518)449-7213 **Fax:** (518)449-1205
Products: Audio and video equipment. **SIC:** 5064 (Electrical Appliances—Television & Radio). **Est:** 1946. **Sales:** $8,000,000 (2000). **Emp:** 32. **Officers:** Theodore M. Klarsfeld, CEO; Martha Meader, CFO.

■ **25091** ■ **Auto Radio Specialists**
1335 Lincoln Way E
Mishawaka, IN 46544-2713
Phone: (219)255-6434 **Fax:** (219)256-2544
Products: Car stereos and alarms. **SIC:** 5064 (Electrical Appliances—Television & Radio). **Est:** 1959. **Emp:** 7. **Officers:** Larry Davis, Owner.

■ **25092** ■ **AVAS VIP**
55 Ruta Ct.
South Hackensack, NJ 07606
Phone: (201)229-4270
Free: (800)631-0868 **Fax:** (201)229-4280
URL: http://www.avasvip.com
Products: Audio visual, multimedia and video supplies and equipment. **SIC:** 5043 (Photographic Equipment & Supplies). **Officers:** Scott Schaefer, VP of Marketing. **Former Name:** Comprehensive Video Group.

■ **25093** ■ **AVES Audio Visual Systems Inc.**
PO Box 740620
Houston, TX 77274-0620
Phone: (713)783-3440
Free: (800)365-2837 **Fax:** (713)783-6597
E-mail: sales@avesav.com
URL: http://www.avesav.com
Products: Audio and visual equipment, including film projectors, LCD projectors, presentation systems, and VCRs. **SIC:** 5064 (Electrical Appliances—Television & Radio). **Est:** 1967. **Sales:** $15,250,000 (2000). **Emp:** 25. **Officers:** Frank Rabinovitz, President; S. Ramos, Vice President.

■ **25094** ■ **Axxis Inc.**
PO Box 2106
Richmond, IN 47375-2106
Phone: (765)935-1538 **Fax:** (765)966-6485
E-mail: axxis@axxisinc.com
URL: http://www.axxisinc.com
Products: Audio-visual equipment. **SIC:** 5065 (Electronic Parts & Equipment Nec). **Est:** 1986. **Sales:** $20,000,000 (2000). **Emp:** 136. **Officers:** Roy M. Ridge, Chairman of the Board; Todd Schirtzinger; Steve Smith, President; Ken Rousseau, President & Secty., e-mail: krousseau@axxisinc.com; Brian Gipson, Equipment Sales, e-mail: bgipson@ axxisinc.com; Leah Stewart, Human Resources Contact. **Former Name:** Allied Telecommunications Inc.

■ **25095** ■ **Backstage Pass Productions and Distributing Inc.**
6930 Valjean Ave.
Van Nuys, CA 91406-4747
Phone: (818)786-2222 **Fax:** (818)786-5550
Products: Videos providing musical instrument instructions. **SIC:** 5099 (Durable Goods Nec). **Est:** 1976. **Sales:** $1,000,000 (2000). **Emp:** 14. **Officers:** Lawrence Weisberg, President; Stephen Coonry, CFO;

Colin Walkden, Dir. of Marketing; Dorine Standifer, Dir. of Information Systems.

■ **25096** ■ **Bana Parts Inc.**
PO Box 23388
New Orleans, LA 70183-0388
Phone: (504)734-0076 **Fax:** (504)734-8456
Products: Electrical household appliances, including television sets and radios. **SIC:** 5064 (Electrical Appliances—Television & Radio). **Officers:** Joseph Fitzpatrick, Vice President.

■ **25097** ■ **Jerry Bassin Inc.**
4250 Coral Ridge Dr.
Coral Springs, FL 33065
Phone: (954)346-4024
Products: Prerecorded tapes and records. **SIC:** 5099 (Durable Goods Nec). **Sales:** $320,000,000 (2000). **Emp:** 400. **Officers:** Jerry Bassin, President.

■ **25098** ■ **Bay Microfilm Inc.**
1115 E Arques Ave.
Sunnyvale, CA 94086
Phone: (408)736-7444 **Fax:** (415)736-7444
Products: Video equipment, including video cassette recorders; Cameras. **SIC:** 5064 (Electrical Appliances—Television & Radio). **Est:** 1952. **Sales:** $8,500,000 (2000). **Emp:** 85. **Officers:** William D. Whitney, President; Janice Harrison, Controller; Robert Kyhn, Vice President.

■ **25099** ■ **Beach Sales Inc.**
80 VFW Pkwy.
Revere, MA 02151
Phone: (781)284-0130
Free: (800)562-9020 **Fax:** (781)284-9823
URL: http://www.beachsales.com
Products: Audio and visual electronics; Major home appliances. **SIC:** 5064 (Electrical Appliances—Television & Radio). **Est:** 1947. **Emp:** 10. **Officers:** Alan Belinfante, President.

■ **25100** ■ **Bel Air Distributors**
2002 W Pierson Rd.
Flint, MI 48504-1926
Phone: (810)785-0859 **Fax:** (810)785-9256
Products: Electrical appliances, including televisions and radios. **SIC:** 5064 (Electrical Appliances—Television & Radio). **Officers:** Steve Serges, Owner.

■ **25101** ■ **Best Buy Co. Inc.**
PO Box 9312
Minneapolis, MN 55440-9312
Phone: (612)947-2000 **Fax:** (612)947-2422
Products: Electric and electronic equipment; Television sets; Video cassette recorders (VCR's); Compact discs; Household clothes dryers; Tapes audio and video recording; Household appliances; Washing machines. **SICs:** 5064 (Electrical Appliances—Television & Radio); 5045 (Computers, Peripherals & Software); 5065 (Electronic Parts & Equipment Nec). **Est:** 1966. **Sales:** $665,000,000 (2000). **Emp:** 4,300. **Officers:** Richard Schulze, Founder, CEO & Chairman of the Board; Bradbury Anderson, COO & President; Allen U. Lenzmeier, Exec. VP & CFO; Wade R. Fenn.

■ **25102** ■ **BGW Systems Inc.**
13130 Yukon Ave.
Hawthorne, CA 90250
Phone: (310)973-8090
Free: (800)468-2677 **Fax:** (310)676-6713
E-mail: sales@bgw.com
URL: http://www.bgw.com/
Products: Amplifiers; Computers; Self-powered subwoofer speaker systems; Sheet metal accessory products. **SICs:** 5064 (Electrical Appliances—Television & Radio); 5045 (Computers, Peripherals & Software). **Est:** 1971. **Sales:** $10,000,000 (2000). **Emp:** 99. **Officers:** Barbara Jo Wachner; Joe Demeo, Sales/Marketing Contact, e-mail: jdemeo@bgw.com; Indira Suzberic, Customer Service Contact.

■ **25103** ■ **Big State Record Distribution Corp.**
4830 Lakawana, Ste. 121
Dallas, TX 75247
Phone: (214)631-1100
Products: Records, tapes, and compact discs. **SIC:** 5099 (Durable Goods Nec). **Sales:** $76,000,000

(2000). **Emp:** 150. **Officers:** Billy Emerson, President; Gib Dawson, Controller.

■ **25104** ■ **BJ Distributing**
R.R. 1, Box 432
Rockville, IN 47872
Phone: (765)344-1046 **Fax:** (765)344-1052
Products: Car stereo and electronics. **SIC:** 5064 (Electrical Appliances—Television & Radio).

■ **25105** ■ **Blue Birds International Corp.**
6110 Ledwin Dr.
Troy, MI 48098
Phone: (248)828-7972 **Fax:** (248)828-4038
Products: Small electrical appliances; Television sets; Radios. **SIC:** 5064 (Electrical Appliances—Television & Radio). **Officers:** Albert Liu, President.

■ **25106** ■ **BMG Distribution Co.**
974 United Cir.
Sparks, NV 89431
Phone: (702)331-6600
Products: Recording cassettes; Compact discs. **SIC:** 5099 (Durable Goods Nec). **Sales:** $7,000,000 (2000). **Emp:** 15. **Officers:** Michael Dornemann, President.

■ **25107** ■ **Bray and Scarff Inc.**
11950 Baltimore Ave.
Beltsville, MD 20705-1235
Phone: (301)470-3555
Products: Small electrical appliances; Television sets; Radios. **SIC:** 5064 (Electrical Appliances—Television & Radio). **Officers:** Dennis Scarff, President.

■ **25108** ■ **Breezy Ridge Instruments**
PO Box 295
Center Valley, PA 18034
Phone: (610)691-3302
Free: (800)235-3302 **Fax:** (610)691-3304
E-mail: jpinfo@aol.com
URL: http://www.jpstrings.com
Products: Guitar strings. **SIC:** 5099 (Durable Goods Nec). **Est:** 1980. **Officers:** John Pearse, President; Mary Faith Rhoads, VP & Treasurer. **Alternate Name:** John Pearse Strings.

■ **25109** ■ **Brooke Distributors Inc.**
PO Box 4730
Hialeah, FL 33014
Phone: (305)624-9752 **Fax:** (305)620-3988
Products: Electronics, including computers, televisions, VCRs, and CD players. **SICs:** 5064 (Electrical Appliances—Television & Radio); 5065 (Electronic Parts & Equipment Nec). **Est:** 1949. **Sales:** $10,000,000 (2000). **Emp:** 30. **Officers:** David Rutter, President.

■ **25110** ■ **C. Bruno & Son Inc.**
3443 E Commerce St.
San Antonio, TX 78294
Phone: (512)226-6353 **Free:** (800)351-5337
Products: Musical instruments. **SIC:** 5099 (Durable Goods Nec). **Est:** 1834. **Emp:** 60. **Officers:** Michael W. Sails, Vice President & General Manager.

■ **25111** ■ **Budco**
PO Box 3065
Tulsa, OK 74101
Phone: (918)252-3420
Free: (800)331-2246 **Fax:** (918)252-1997
URL: http://www.budcocable.com
Products: Cable television equipment. **SIC:** 5063 (Electrical Apparatus & Equipment). **Est:** 1970. **Emp:** 16. **Officers:** D. Nicholas Allen, Pres.; David L. Allen, Sales Mgr.; Steve Allen, Sales Rep.

■ **25112** ■ **Burlington A/V Recording Media, Inc.**
106 Mott St.
Oceanside, NY 11572
Phone: (516)678-4414
Free: (800)331-3191 **Fax:** (516)678-8959
E-mail: sales@burlington-av.com
URL: http://www.burlington-av.com
Products: Audio and video recording media, recording equipment, and accessories, including reels, splicing tape, and boxes. **SIC:** 5043 (Photographic Equipment & Supplies). **Est:** 1970. **Sales:** $10,000,000 (2000). **Emp:** 20. **Officers:** Ruth Schwartz, President; Rudy

Schwartz, Vice President; Jan Schwartz, Purchasing; Tom Marchetti, Sales.

■ **25113** ■ **Bursma Electronic Distributing Inc.**
2851 Buchanan SW
Grand Rapids, MI 49548
Phone: (616)831-0080
Free: (800)777-2604 **Fax:** (616)831-9400
Products: Electronic parts; Electronic appliances, including televisions and radios. **SICs:** 5064 (Electrical Appliances—Television & Radio); 5064 (Electrical Appliances—Television & Radio). **Est:** 1947. **Sales:** $8,200,000 (2000). **Emp:** 50. **Officers:** David Van Randwyk, President, e-mail: vanran@dzinet.com; Douglas Bandstra, Sales Manager.

■ **25114** ■ **Cable Services Co. Inc.**
2113 Marydale Ave.
Williamsport, PA 17701
Phone: (717)323-8518
Free: (800)326-9444 **Fax:** (717)322-5373
E-mail: cgblserv@csrlink.net
URL: http://www.cable-services.com
Products: Cable television equipment. **SIC:** 5063 (Electrical Apparatus & Equipment). **Est:** 1964. **Officers:** John M. Roskowski, President; Gene Welliver, V; Neal Kimberling, V; Dennis Hume, Vice President.

■ **25115** ■ **Cable Technologies International of New York Inc.**
Rte. 20, Box 278
Esperance, NY 12066-6101
Phone: (518)664-7500 **Fax:** (518)664-4296
E-mail: sales@cabletechnologies.com
URL: http://www.cabletechnologies.com
Products: Cable television equipment and supplies, including remote controls, covers, buttons, face-plates, semi conductors, and drop equipment. **SIC:** 5063 (Electrical Apparatus & Equipment). **Est:** 1986. **Emp:** 17. **Officers:** P.E. Morse Jr., President; James Chamberlain, VP & General Mgr.; Ed Jette, Plant Mgr.; Paula Bever, Human Resources Mgr.; Gene Civitello, Sales Rep.

■ **25116** ■ **Calato USA Div.**
4501 Hyde Park Blvd.
Niagara Falls, NY 14305
Phone: (716)285-3546 **Fax:** (716)285-2710
Products: Wooden drumsticks; Percussion accessories. **SIC:** 5099 (Durable Goods Nec). **Est:** 1956. **Sales:** $15,000,000 (2000). **Emp:** 30. **Officers:** Carol Calato, President; Cathy Calato, CFO; Paul Pinchuk, Sales/Marketing Contact; Maria Knack, Customer Service Contact.

■ **25117** ■ **Canaan Records**
274 Mallory Station Rd.
Franklin, TN 37067-8244
Phone: (615)327-1240 **Fax:** (615)327-1346
Products: Religious tapes and records. **SIC:** 5099 (Durable Goods Nec).

■ **25118** ■ **Capitol Communications**
1247 85th Ave. SE
Olympia, WA 98501
Phone: (206)943-5378 **Fax:** (206)754-1566
Products: Stereo equipment. **SIC:** 5064 (Electrical Appliances—Television & Radio).

■ **25119** ■ **Capitol Motion Picture Corp.**
630 9th Ave.
New York, NY 10036
Phone: (212)757-4510
Products: Motion picture equipment. **SIC:** 5043 (Photographic Equipment & Supplies). **Est:** 1939. **Sales:** $6,000,000 (2000). **Emp:** 40. **Officers:** Ben Perse, President; Angela Knoel, Controller.

■ **25120** ■ **Capitol Sales Company Inc.**
3110 Neil Armstrong Blvd.
St. Paul, MN 55121-2234
Phone: (612)688-6830
Free: (800)447-5196 **Fax:** (612)688-0107
E-mail: info@capitolsales.com
URL: http://www.capitolsales.com
Products: Electrical entertainment equipment, including televisions and audio and video equipment; Telephone equipment. **SIC:** 5064 (Electrical

Appliances—Television & Radio). **Officers:** Curtis Hayes, President.

■ **25121** ■ **Car Tape Distributors Inc.**
PO Box 5122
Ft. Wayne, IN 46895-5122
Phone: (219)484-2556 **Fax:** (219)484-8738
URL: http://www.ctdmarketing.com
Products: Home electronics, including television sets and radios; Motor vehicle radios. **SIC:** 5064 (Electrical Appliances—Television & Radio). **Est:** 1933. **Sales:** $11,000,000 (2000). **Emp:** 21. **Officers:** Pat Brames; Ron Harker, Sales & Marketing Contact.

■ **25122** ■ **Caribiner International**
525 N Washington Ave.
Minneapolis, MN 55401
Phone: (612)333-1271
Free: (800)292-4125 **Fax:** (612)333-0225
Products: Presentation technology. **SICs:** 5043 (Photographic Equipment & Supplies); 5064 (Electrical Appliances—Television & Radio). **Officers:** Al Kelm, Midwest Regional Gen. Mgr.

■ **25123** ■ **Carmichael and Carmichael Inc.**
PO Box 305151
Nashville, TN 37230-5151
Phone: (615)742-3852
Free: (800)876-4332 **Fax:** (615)742-3270
E-mail: info@knowledgeproducts.com
URL: http://www.knowledgeproducts.net
Products: Educational audiotapes. **SIC:** 5099 (Durable Goods Nec). **Est:** 1985. **Emp:** 10. **Officers:** Oliver C. Carmichael, President, e-mail: ccarmichael@isophere.com.

■ **25124** ■ **Carolina C & E, Inc.**
651 Pilot View St.
Winston-Salem, NC 27101-2717
Phone: (336)788-9191
Free: (800)441-9191 **Fax:** (336)650-1124
URL: http://www.rcscom.com
Products: Wireless emergency call boxes. **SIC:** 5064 (Electrical Appliances—Television & Radio). **Est:** 1976. **Sales:** $6,000,000 (2000). **Emp:** 50. **Officers:** Chris McClellan, President. **Alternate Name:** C & E Carolina Inc.

■ **25125** ■ **Casele Associates Inc.**
102 E Main St.
Stevensville, MD 21666-4000
Phone: (410)643-8950 **Fax:** (410)643-8940
Products: Consumer high fidelity components. **SIC:** 5064 (Electrical Appliances—Television & Radio). **Officers:** Mark Sullivan, President.

■ **25126** ■ **Cash & Carry Electronics Inc.**
120 Wyoming Blvd. SE
Albuquerque, NM 87123-3105
Phone: (505)266-2224 **Fax:** (505)256-1514
Products: Automobile stereos. **SIC:** 5064 (Electrical Appliances—Television & Radio). **Officers:** Sharif Rabadi, President.

■ **25127** ■ **Castiglione Accordion**
13300 E 11 Mile, Ste. A
Warren, MI 48089
Phone: (810)755-6050 **Fax:** (810)755-6339
Products: Accordians; Concertinas; Button boxes; Amps. **SIC:** 5099 (Durable Goods Nec). **Emp:** 3. **Officers:** John Castiglione, e-mail: johncast@internetmci.com; Giovanna Castiglione.

■ **25128** ■ **Catskill Electronics**
4050 Rte. 42 N, No. 12
Monticello, NY 12701
Phone: (914)794-6560
Products: Electronic equipment, including TVs, VCRs, and stereos. **SIC:** 5064 (Electrical Appliances—Television & Radio). **Emp:** 9. **Officers:** Harvey Kornblau.

■ **25129** ■ **CBLX Holdings Inc.**
5730 E Otero Ave.
Englewood, CO 80112
Phone: (303)694-6789 **Fax:** (303)290-9810
Products: Cable television remote control devices. **SIC:** 5065 (Electronic Parts & Equipment Nec). **Est:** 1981. **Sales:** $2,400,000 (2000). **Emp:** 11. **Officers:** F.

Terry Hankins, CEO & President; Dennis R. Carson, VP & CFO; Sandra K. Torres, Secretary.

■ **25130** ■ **CD One Stop**
13 Francis J. Clarke Cir.
Bethel, CT 06801
Phone: (203)798-6590 **Fax:** (203)798-8852
Products: Compact discs. **SIC:** 5099 (Durable Goods Nec). **Est:** 1987. **Sales:** $150,000,000 (2000). **Emp:** 350. **Officers:** Allen Tuchman, CEO; Jay Fink, CFO; Ken Alterwitz, VP of Sales; Chris Brown, Dir. of Information Systems; Janet Cottrell, Human Resources Mgr.

■ **25131** ■ **Central Radio and TV Inc.**
1910 Duss Ave.
Ambridge, PA 15003
Phone: (412)266-9100
E-mail: centralr@ccia.com
URL: http://www.centralradio.com
Products: Electronic parts; Car audio accessories. **SICs:** 5064 (Electrical Appliances—Television & Radio); 5065 (Electronic Parts & Equipment Nec). **Est:** 1951.

■ **25132** ■ **Central South Music Inc.**
3730 Vulcan Dr.
Nashville, TN 37211
Phone: (615)833-5960
Products: Records, tapes, and compact discs. **SIC:** 5099 (Durable Goods Nec). **Sales:** $52,000,000 (1992). **Emp:** 500. **Officers:** Randy Davidson, President; Wayne Davidson, Controller.

■ **25133** ■ **Chartier Double Reed Co.**
PO Box 13344
Albuquerque, NM 87192
Phone: (505)881-0843
Free: (800)729-7333 **Fax:** (505)888-1064
URL: http://www.chartierreeds.com
Products: Reeds and supplies. **SIC:** 5099 (Durable Goods Nec). **Est:** 1948. **Officers:** Gregg A. Chartier, Owner, e-mail: gregg@chartierreeds.com.

■ **25134** ■ **Chesbro Music Co.**
PO Box 2009
Idaho Falls, ID 83403
Phone: (208)522-8691
Free: (800)CHE-SBRO **Fax:** (208)522-8712
E-mail: sales@chesbromusic.com
URL: http://www.chesbromusic.com
Products: Musical instruments and accessories, including printed music and music racks; Music gifts; Jewelry. **SIC:** 5099 (Durable Goods Nec). **Est:** 1911. **Emp:** 88. **Officers:** Vanetta Chesbro Wilson, President; Tana Stahn, CFO; Terry L. Orme, Vice President; Michelle Davies, Vice President; Vanetta Chesbro Wilson, VP of Marketing.

■ **25135** ■ **Cheviot Corp.**
PO Box 34485
Los Angeles, CA 90034-0485
Phone: (310)836-4678
Free: (800)544-7244 **Fax:** (310)837-1534
Products: Phonogragh records; Audio tapes; CD recordings; Tapes; Books; Educational products. **SICs:** 5099 (Durable Goods Nec); 5192 (Books, Periodicals & Newspapers). **Est:** 1960. **Emp:** 4. **Officers:** Ruth S. White, President; Lotte Cherin, Vice President.

■ **25136** ■ **Cine 60 Inc.**
630 9th Ave.
New York, NY 10036
Phone: (212)586-8782 **Fax:** (212)459-9556
E-mail: cine60ny@aol.com
Products: Portable battery operated lighting, including rechargeable nickel cadmium battery packs. **SIC:** 5063 (Electrical Apparatus & Equipment). **Est:** 1960. **Emp:** 24. **Officers:** Paul A. Wildum, President; Robert Kabo, Secretary.

■ **25137** ■ **City Animation Co.**
57 Park St.
Troy, MI 48083-2753
Phone: (248)589-0600 **Fax:** (248)589-2020
URL: http://www.cityanimation.com
Products: Audio and visual equipment and supplies. **SICs:** 5064 (Electrical Appliances—Television & Radio); 5065 (Electronic Parts & Equipment Nec). **Est:**

1960. Sales: $12,000,000 (1999). **Emp:** 90. **Officers:** Charles Theis, CEO & President; Gerard Casari, CFO; Don Allen, Sales/Marketing Contact, e-mail: dona@voyager.net; Kathy Halloran, Customer Service Contact, e-mail: kathy@voyager.net; Heidi Hunt, Human Resources Contact, e-mail: heidi@voyager.net.

■ **25138** ■ **City One Stop**
2551 S Alameda
Los Angeles, CA 90058-1309
Phone: (213)234-3336
Free: (800)962-2009 **Fax:** (213)234-4036
Products: Compact discs; Videos. **SIC:** 5099 (Durable Goods Nec). **Emp:** 49.

■ **25139** ■ **City Sound**
4925 E Firestone Blvd.
South Gate, CA 90280
Phone: (213)563-1173 **Fax:** (213)563-0211
Products: Commercial sound products. **SIC:** 5065 (Electronic Parts & Equipment Nec).

■ **25140** ■ **Clydes Corner Electronics**
15796 E 14th St.
San Leandro, CA 94578
Phone: (510)276-8739 **Fax:** (510)276-8739
Products: Compact disc players; Scanners. **SIC:** 5064 (Electrical Appliances—Television & Radio).

■ **25141** ■ **Coast Wholesale Music**
PO Box 5686
Compton, CA 90224-5686
Phone: (310)537-1712
Free: (800)262-7826 **Fax:** (310)632-7463
Products: Musical instruments and accessories. **SIC:** 5099 (Durable Goods Nec). **Sales:** $11,200,000 (2000). **Emp:** 40. **Officers:** John McGraw, Vice President.

■ **25142** ■ **Coast Wholesale Music Co.**
1381 Calais Ave.
Livermore, CA 94550-6019
Phone: (510)796-3487 **Fax:** (510)796-1243
Products: Musical instruments. **SIC:** 5099 (Durable Goods Nec).

■ **25143** ■ **Commonwealth Films Inc.**
223 Commonwealth Ave.
Boston, MA 02116
Phone: (617)262-5634 **Fax:** (617)262-6948
E-mail: info@commonwealthfilms.com
URL: http://www.commonwealthfilms.com
Products: Videos; Educational products. **SIC:** 5043 (Photographic Equipment & Supplies). **Est:** 1978. **Officers:** Thomas P. McCann, President.

■ **25144** ■ **Commtron Corporation**
405 Murray Hill Pkwy., Ste. 2020
East Rutherford, NJ 07073
Phone: (201)933-9797 **Fax:** (201)933-5139
Products: Video tapes and cleaner head tapes. **SIC:** 5065 (Electronic Parts & Equipment Nec).

■ **25145** ■ **Compol Inc.**
415 Campbell Mill Rd.
Mason, NH 03048-4902
Phone: (603)878-3458 **Fax:** (603)878-1275
Products: Electrical entertainment equipment, including television sets and radios. **SIC:** 5064 (Electrical Appliances—Television & Radio). **Officers:** Frank Karkota, President.

■ **25146** ■ **Components Specialties Inc.**
PO Box 726
Amityville, NY 11701-0726
Phone: (516)957-8700 **Fax:** (516)957-9142
Products: Electric and electronic equipment. **SIC:** 5065 (Electronic Parts & Equipment Nec). **Est:** 1960. **Sales:** $12,000,000 (2000). **Emp:** 35. **Officers:** Louis W. Keller, CEO; Eric Forman, Dir. of Marketing & Sales; Jim Ganci, VP & General Mgr.; Todd Keller, Exec. VP.

■ **25147** ■ **Comse Sales/John Weeks Enterprises**
75 Grayson Industrial Pkwy.
Grayson, GA 30017
Phone: (404)963-7870
Free: (800)241-1232 **Fax:** (404)962-7539
Products: Cable television supplies. **SIC:** 5063

(Electrical Apparatus & Equipment). **Officers:** John P. Weeks Jr., Pres.; Sissy W. Routh, V.P.

■ **25148** ■ **Contract Appliance Sales Inc.**
PO Box 1818
Sandy, UT 84091-1818
Phone: (801)569-8850
Products: Electrical appliances, including television sets and radios. **SIC:** 5064 (Electrical Appliances—Television & Radio). **Officers:** George Mellissis, President.

■ **25149** ■ **Cruse Communication Co.**
230 N Higby St.
Jackson, MI 49202-4021
Phone: (517)332-3579 **Fax:** (517)332-7757
E-mail: cruse@cruse.com
URL: http://www.cruse.com
Products: Professional video. **SIC:** 5065 (Electronic Parts & Equipment Nec). **Est:** 1954. **Emp:** 20.
Officers: Renwood Flagg, President.

■ **25150** ■ **Custom Audio**
422 S Broadway St.
McComb, MS 39648-4118
Phone: (601)684-2869 **Fax:** (601)684-2004
Products: Electrical appliances and entertainment equipment, including television sets, radios, pagers, and cellular telephones. **SIC:** 5064 (Electrical Appliances—Television & Radio). **Est:** 1976. **Emp:** 4.
Officers: Bobby McDaniel, Owner.

■ **25151** ■ **Custom Audio Distributors Inc.**
PO Box 327
Bogart, GA 30622-0327
Phone: (706)353-1380 **Fax:** 800-736-3329
Products: Electrical entertainment equipment, including television sets and radios. **SIC:** 5064 (Electrical Appliances—Television & Radio). **Officers:** Benjamin Murray, Chairman of the Board.

■ **25152** ■ **Custom Music Co.**
1930 Hilton
Ferndale, MI 48220
Phone: (248)546-4135
Free: (800)521-6380 **Fax:** (248)546-8296
E-mail: cmctuba@aol.com
URL: http://www.custommusiccorp.com
Products: Musical instruments. **SIC:** 5099 (Durable Goods Nec).

■ **25153** ■ **Custom Sound of Augusta Inc.**
2029 Gordon Hwy.
Augusta, GA 30909
Phone: (706)738-8181 **Fax:** (706)738-8184
Products: Electrical appliances, including television, radio, and electrical entertainment equipment. **SIC:** 5064 (Electrical Appliances—Television & Radio). **Officers:** Benjamin Murray, President.

■ **25154** ■ **Cutting Edge Audio Group L.L.C.**
290 Division St., Ste. 103
San Francisco, CA 94103
Phone: (415)487-2323
Products: Audio production equipment. **SIC:** 5065 (Electronic Parts & Equipment Nec). **Sales:** $800,000 (2000). **Emp:** 5. **Officers:** Thomas Richardson, Mng. Partner.

■ **25155** ■ **DaLite Screen Co.**
3100 N Detroit St.
Warsaw, IN 46580
Phone: (219)267-8101
Free: (800)622-3737 **Fax:** (219)267-7804
E-mail: info@da-lite.com
URL: http://www.da-lite.com
Products: Audio-visual equipment. **SICs:** 5064 (Electrical Appliances—Television & Radio); 5043 (Photographic Equipment & Supplies). **Est:** 1909.
Sales: $50,000,000 (2000). **Emp:** 499. **Officers:** Rich Lundin, President & CEO; Judy Loughran, Sr. VP; Pat Tusing, Human Resources Contact, e-mail: ptusing@da-lite.com; Wendy Long, Internal Sales Manager, e-mail: wlong@da-lite.

■ **25156** ■ **Dauphin Co.**
PO Box 5137
Springfield, IL 62705
Phones: (217)793-2424 800-448-4827
Free: (800)448-4827 **Fax:** (217)793-2429
Products: Classical guitars. **SIC:** 5099 (Durable Goods Nec). **Est:** 1975. **Officers:** George A. Dauphinais, President; Chris Cliburn, General Mgr.

■ **25157** ■ **J.W. Davis Co.**
3030 Canton
Dallas, TX 75226-1605
Phone: (214)651-7341
Free: (800)527-5705 **Fax:** (214)939-0328
E-mail: jwd@jwd.com
URL: http://www.jwd.com
Products: Audio and communication equipment. **SIC:** 5064 (Electrical Appliances—Television & Radio). **Est:** 1933. **Sales:** $3,000,000 (2000). **Emp:** 25. **Officers:** M.H. Earp, President; Jack Tucker, VP of Sales, e-mail: jt@jwd.com; Jo Earp, Customer Service Mgr., e-mail: bke@jwd.com; Eric Simonson, VP of Engineering; Bobby Carnline, Controller.

■ **25158** ■ **Davitt & Hansen West**
1859 Sabre St.
Hayward, CA 94545
Phone: (510)293-0388
Free: (800)999-5558 **Fax:** (510)293-0389
Products: Musical instruments. **SIC:** 5099 (Durable Goods Nec). **Est:** 1919. **Officers:** Kris Teter, General Mgr. **Former Name:** J.M. #Sahlein Music Co.

■ **25159** ■ **Davitt and Hanser Music Co.**
4940 Delhi Ave.
Cincinnati, OH 45238
Phone: (513)451-5000 **Fax:** (513)347-2298
Products: Musical instruments and accessories, including guitar strings. **SIC:** 5099 (Durable Goods Nec). **Est:** 1924. **Sales:** $20,000,000 (2000). **Emp:** 45. **Officers:** John Hanser Jr., President; Tim Hanser, CFO, e-mail: thanser@davitt-hanser.com; Todd Quincy, Sales/Marketing Contact, e-mail: tquincy@davitt-hanser.com.

■ **25160** ■ **Dawdys Inc.**
PO Box 206
Berthoud, CO 80513-0206
Phone: (970)532-3525 **Fax:** (970)532-3525
Products: Electrical appliances, including television and radio. **SIC:** 5064 (Electrical Appliances—Television & Radio). **Officers:** Yvonne Dawdy, President.

■ **25161** ■ **Day Star Productions**
326 S Wille Ave.
Wheeling, IL 60090
Phone: (847)541-5200 **Fax:** (847)541-3566
E-mail: dayst@home.com
Products: Books; Videos; Audiocassettes. **SICs:** 5192 (Books, Periodicals & Newspapers); 5099 (Durable Goods Nec). **Est:** 1978. **Emp:** 3. **Officers:** Fred Heeren, President; Larry Stanek, Chairman of the Board; Stewart Goodpasture, Treasurer.

■ **25162** ■ **dB Sound L.P.**
1219 Rand Rd.
Des Plaines, IL 60016
Phone: (847)299-0357 **Fax:** (847)299-6509
Products: Professional audio equipment. **SIC:** 5065 (Electronic Parts & Equipment Nec). **Sales:** $7,000,000 (2000). **Emp:** 25. **Officers:** Harry Witz, President; Barry Dane, Partner.

■ **25163** ■ **Richard Dean Associates Inc.**
1 Harris St.
Newburyport, MA 01950-2600
Phone: (978)462-1150 **Fax:** (978)462-4431
Products: Electrical entertainment equipment, including television sets. **SIC:** 5064 (Electrical Appliances—Television & Radio). **Officers:** Dick Bazirgan, President.

■ **25164** ■ **Deering Banjo Co.**
7936-D Lester Ave.
Lemon Grove, CA 91945
Phone: (619)464-8252
Free: (800)845-7791 **Fax:** (619)464-0833
E-mail: info@deeringbanjos.com
URL: http://www.DeeringBanjos.com
Products: Banjos. **SIC:** 5099 (Durable Goods Nec).
Est: 1974. **Sales:** $1,500,000 (2000). **Emp:** 30.
Officers: Janet Deering; Greg Deering; Barry Hunn, Sales/Marketing Contact; Carolina Bridges, Customer Service Contact.

■ **25165** ■ **Densons Sound Systems Inc.**
519 N Witchduck Rd.
Virginia Beach, VA 23462-1914
Phone: (757)499-9005
Products: Electric and electronic equipment; Electronic parts; Communication systems and equipment. **SIC:** 5065 (Electronic Parts & Equipment Nec). **Officers:** James Denson, President.

■ **25166** ■ **Depco Inc.**
1637 Mount Vernon Rd.
Atlanta, GA 30338-4205
Phone: (404)394-0643 **Fax:** (404)396-1737
Products: Electrical appliances, including television sets and radios. **SIC:** 5064 (Electrical Appliances—Television & Radio). **Officers:** L. Benjamin, President.

■ **25167** ■ **Discount Store**
64 S Hotel St.
Honolulu, HI 96813-3106
Phone: (808)531-7777 **Fax:** (808)599-3587
Products: Automobile stereos. **SIC:** 5064 (Electrical Appliances—Television & Radio). **Officers:** Mohamed Allwer, Partner.

■ **25168** ■ **Russ Doughten Films, Inc.**
5907 Meredith Dr.
Des Moines, IA 50322
Phone: (515)278-4737
Free: (800)247-3456 **Fax:** (515)278-4738
E-mail: doughten@mustardseed-rdfilms.com
Products: Videos. **SIC:** 5099 (Durable Goods Nec).
Officers: Gene Mckelvey, Marketing & Art Dir.; Carey Jordan, Assistant. **Former Name:** Mark IV Pictures.

■ **25169** ■ **Dusty Strings Co.**
3406 Fremont Ave. N
Seattle, WA 98103
Phone: (206)634-1656 **Fax:** (206)634-0234
Products: Harps and hammer dulcimers. **SIC:** 5099 (Durable Goods Nec). **Emp:** 30. **Officers:** Ray Mooers, President; Sue Mooers, Treasurer & Secty.

■ **25170** ■ **Eagle Distributors Inc.**
2439 Albany St.
Kenner, LA 70062-5243
Phone: (504)464-5991
Free: (800)659-5991 **Fax:** (504)468-9741
Products: Electrical appliances, including television sets and radios. **SIC:** 5064 (Electrical Appliances—Television & Radio). **Est:** 1972. **Emp:** 56. **Officers:** Wayne Messina, President; Mickey Ural, General Mgr.; Leslie Doyle, Customer Service Manager.

■ **25171** ■ **Educational Activities Inc.**
1937 Grand Ave.
Baldwin, NY 11510
Phone: (516)223-4666 **Fax:** (516)623-9282
Products: Early childhood records and cassettes. **SIC:** 5099 (Durable Goods Nec). **Est:** 1953. **Sales:** $7,000,000 (2000). **Officers:** Alfred S. Harris, President.

■ **25172** ■ **Educational Industrial Systems Inc.**
140 E Dana St.
Mountain View, CA 94041
Phone: (415)969-5212
Products: Audio/visual equipment. **SIC:** 5065 (Electronic Parts & Equipment Nec). **Est:** 1976. **Sales:** $14,000,000 (2000). **Emp:** 48. **Officers:** Robert Adams, President.

■ **25173** ■ **Educational Record Sales, Inc.**
132 W 21st St.
New York, NY 10011
Products: Cassettes and recordings on dance,

literature, music, radio dramas, and social studies; Filmstrips; Microcomputer software; Video cassettes. **SICs:** 5099 (Durable Goods Nec); 5045 (Computers, Peripherals & Software).

■ 25174 ■ Educational Record & Tape Distributors of America
61 Bennington Ave.
Freeport, NY 11520
Phone: (516)867-3770 **Fax:** (516)867-3774
Products: Prerecorded audio tapes; Phonograph records; Films; Educational products. **SIC:** 5099 (Durable Goods Nec). **Est:** 1985. **Sales:** $1,000,000 (2000). **Emp:** 15. **Officers:** Lawrence Sonin, President; Jonathan Messeleff, Director.

■ 25175 ■ Elden Enterprises
PO Box 3201
Charleston, WV 25332-3201
Phone: (304)344-2335
Products: Presentation slide systems. **SIC:** 5043 (Photographic Equipment & Supplies).

■ 25176 ■ Electric Sales & Service of Savannah
PO Box 9661
Savannah, GA 31412-9661
Phones: (912)233-9663 (912)232-5445
(912)232-5445 **Free:** (800)868-5846
Products: Electrical appliances, including television and radio. **SIC:** 5064 (Electrical Appliances—Television & Radio). **Officers:** Charles Waggoner, President.

■ 25177 ■ Electrical Distributing Inc.
PO Box 2720
Portland, OR 97208
Phone: (503)226-4044 **Fax:** (503)226-4040
Products: Televisions. **SIC:** 5064 (Electrical Appliances—Television & Radio). **Est:** 1929. **Sales:** $20,000,000 (2000). **Emp:** 50. **Officers:** A.M. Cronin III, President; Lois Stow, Controller; Fred Jensen, Vice President.

■ 25178 ■ Electro Brand Inc.
5410 W Roosevelt
Chicago, IL 60601
Phone: (312)261-5000 **Fax:** (312)261-5091
Products: Audio equipment, including radios and headphones. **SIC:** 5064 (Electrical Appliances—Television & Radio). **Est:** 1961. **Sales:** $23,000,000 (2000). **Emp:** 28. **Officers:** Richard L. Ettelson, President; Kim A. Kehl, Controller; Stephen J. Ettelson, VP of Marketing & Sales.

■ 25179 ■ Electronic World Sales & Service
27 S End Plaza
New Milford, CT 06776-4235
Phone: (860)355-9848 **Fax:** (860)344-0506
Products: Electrical equipment and supplies; Consumer high fidelity components. **SIC:** 5065 (Electronic Parts & Equipment Nec). **Officers:** Daniel Hepp, President.

■ 25180 ■ Electronics 21 Inc.
5 Mall Terrace
Savannah, GA 31406-3602
Phone: (912)352-0585
Free: (800)866-8938 **Fax:** (912)352-7796
Products: Electrical appliances, including television, radio, and high fidelity equipment. **SIC:** 5064 (Electrical Appliances—Television & Radio). **Officers:** Jack Schultz, President.

■ 25181 ■ EME Corp.
10 Central Pkwy., Ste. 312
Stuart, FL 34994-5903
Phone: (561)798-2050
Free: (800)848-2050 **Fax:** (561)798-9930
Products: Computer software, filmstrips, maps, slides, and video cassettes. **SICs:** 5099 (Durable Goods Nec); 5045 (Computers, Peripherals & Software). **Est:** 1955.

■ 25182 ■ J.R. Enright Co.
4618 Leland St.
Bethesda, MD 20815-6010
Phone: (301)654-1700
Products: Electrical appliances, including television sets and radios. **SIC:** 5064 (Electrical Appliances—Television & Radio). **Officers:** James Enright, Partner.

■ 25183 ■ Entertainment Music Marketing Corp.
770-12 Grand Blvd.
Deer Park, NY 11729
Phone: (516)243-0600
Free: (800)345-6013 **Fax:** (516)243-0605
Products: Musical instruments. **SIC:** 5099 (Durable Goods Nec). **Est:** 1985. **Sales:** $1,000,000 (2000). **Emp:** 11. **Officers:** Joseph Saltzman, President; Mark Saltzman, Vice President.

■ 25184 ■ ERS Distributors, Inc.
20 Midland Ave.
Hicksville, NY 11801
Phones: (516)939-0060 (516)939-0764
Fax: (516)939-0765
URL: http://www.ersdistributors.com
Products: Telephones; Answering systems; Portable personal audio products; Video products. **SIC:** 5065 (Electronic Parts & Equipment Nec). **Est:** 1975. **Officers:** David Honlgman, President; Stephen Honlgman, Exec. VP; Robert Sturgic, Dir. of Marketing.

■ 25185 ■ Essex Entertainment Inc.
95 Oser Ave., Ste. E
Hauppauge, NY 11788-3612
Products: Recorded music. **SIC:** 5099 (Durable Goods Nec). **Sales:** $40,000,000 (2000). **Emp:** 50. **Officers:** Richard Greener, Mng. Partner; John Grein, CFO.

■ 25186 ■ European Crafts/USA
3637 Cahuenga Blvd.
Hollywood, CA 90068
Phone: (213)851-4070
Free: (800)851-0750 **Fax:** (213)851-0148
E-mail: ecraft@pacbell.net
URL: http://www.home.pacbell.net/ecraft/
Products: Musical instrument parts, including drum parts and accessories; Electric and acoustic guitars; Microphones and amplifiers. **SICs:** 5099 (Durable Goods Nec); 5065 (Electronic Parts & Equipment Nec). **Est:** 1953. **Emp:** 15. **Officers:** Mirek Strizka, President; George Reichl, Vice President; Joseph Deraad, Sales/Marketing Contact.

■ 25187 ■ Evans Environmental Corp.
99 S East St., 4th Fl.
Miami, FL 33131
Phone: (305)374-8300 **Fax:** (305)374-7555
Products: le television wireless remote controls, transmitters, and receivers. **SICs:** 5063 (Electrical Apparatus & Equipment); 5065 (Electronic Parts & Equipment Nec). **Sales:** $5,700,000 (2000). **Emp:** 78. **Officers:** Enrique A. Tomeu, CEO & President; Scott E. Salpeter, VP & CFO.

■ 25188 ■ Eyemark Video Services
310 Parkway View Dr.
Pittsburgh, PA 15205
Phone: (412)747-4700 **Fax:** (412)747-4726
Products: Duplicate and distributed sydicated television programs. Satellite uplink/downlink. International standards conversion. **SIC:** 5099 (Durable Goods Nec). **Est:** 1965. **Emp:** 75. **Officers:** George Kieffer, VP & General Mgr. **Former Name:** Group W Video Sources.

■ 25189 ■ Don Faella Co. Inc.
1271 Mineral Spring Ave.
North Providence, RI 02904-4604
Free: (800)272-7166
Products: Motor vehicle radios. **SIC:** 5064 (Electrical Appliances—Television & Radio). **Officers:** Donald Faella, President.

■ 25190 ■ Falmouth Supply Co. Inc.
12 Canapitsit Dr.
East Falmouth, MA 02536-6211
Phone: (508)548-6000 **Fax:** (508)548-1811
Products: Electrical appliances, including televisions and radios. **SIC:** 5064 (Electrical Appliances—Television & Radio). **Officers:** John Fay, President.

■ 25191 ■ First Rep Associates
16000 College Blvd.
Lenexa, KS 66219
Phone: (913)599-3111
Products: Consumer electronics, including video games. **SIC:** 5065 (Electronic Parts & Equipment Nec).

Sales: $1,000,000 (2000). **Emp:** 7. **Officers:** Dave Lemon, President.

■ 25192 ■ Flower Films & Video
10341 San Pablo Ave.
El Cerrito, CA 94530
Phone: (510)525-0942 **Fax:** (510)525-1204
E-mail: blankfilm@aol.com
URL: http://www.lesblank.com
Products: Documentary films. **SIC:** 5099 (Durable Goods Nec). **Est:** 1967. **Emp:** 1.

■ 25193 ■ Folkcraft Instruments
High & Wheeler Sts.
PO Box 807
Winsted, CT 06098
Phone: (860)379-9857 **Fax:** (860)379-7685
E-mail: sales@folkcraft.com
URL: http://www.folkcraft.com
Products: Stringed Musical instruments. **SIC:** 5099 (Durable Goods Nec). **Est:** 1974. **Emp:** 9.

■ 25194 ■ Ford Audio-Video Systems Inc.
4800 W Interstate 40
Oklahoma City, OK 73128-1208
Phone: (405)946-9966 **Fax:** (405)946-9991
URL: http://www.fordav.com
Products: Commercial and professional sound equipment. **SIC:** 5064 (Electrical Appliances—Television & Radio). **Est:** 1973. **Emp:** 130. **Officers:** James Ford, President.

■ 25195 ■ Ford and Garland Inc.
1304 Locust St.
Des Moines, IA 50309-2920
Phone: (515)288-6324 **Fax:** (515)288-8830
Products: Electrical appliances, including televisions, radios, and audio equipment. **SIC:** 5064 (Electrical Appliances—Television & Radio). **Officers:** Steven Garland, President.

■ 25196 ■ Four Star Incentives Inc.
5617 Howard St.
Niles, IL 60714
Phone: (847)647-7662 **Fax:** (847)647-7781
E-mail: sales@fourstarincentives.com
URL: http://www.promostore.com/55207
Products: Electronic audio and video equipment. **SIC:** 5065 (Electronic Parts & Equipment Nec). **Est:** 1979. **Emp:** 12. **Officers:** Bruce Schermerhorn, President; Gene Rontanini, Vice President.

■ 25197 ■ T.E. Fox, Inc.
960 Old Mounta
Statesville, NC 28687
Phone: (704)528-9162
Free: (800)701-4069 **Fax:** (704)528-5292
Products: Videos; Fire fighting equipment. **SIC:** 5099 (Durable Goods Nec). **Est:** 1984. **Officers:** Thomas Fox, Owner, e-mail: thomastonfox@worldnet.att.net. **Former Name:** Broadway Movies.

■ 25198 ■ Fredrico Percussion
152 Lancaster Blvd.
Mechanicsburg, PA 17055
Phone: (717)766-1332 **Fax:** (717)766-1332
Products: Musical instruments. **SIC:** 5099 (Durable Goods Nec).

■ 25199 ■ Freeman's Car Stereo Inc.
6150 Brookshire Blvd.
Charlotte, NC 28216-2410
Phone: (704)398-1822 **Fax:** (704)392-7468
Products: Car audio systems. **SIC:** 5064 (Electrical Appliances—Television & Radio). **Est:** 1971. **Emp:** 50. **Officers:** John Freeman, President.

■ 25200 ■ Frontier Network Systems Inc.
95 N Fitzhugh St.
Rochester, NY 14614
Phone: (716)777-2562 **Fax:** (716)777-2538
Products: PBX, data and video equipment. **SIC:** 5065 (Electronic Parts & Equipment Nec). **Sales:** $31,000,000 (2000). **Emp:** 160. **Officers:** James Cuppini, Vice President; Steve Snider, Finance General Manager.

■ 25201 ■ **Full Perspective Videos Services Inc.**
150 S Mountain Ave.
Montclair, NJ 07042
Phone: (973)746-0421 **Fax:** (973)509-1498
URL: http://www.fpvid.com
Products: Tapes audio and video recording; Fulfillment services; Telemarketing services for direct response. **SIC:** 5099 (Durable Goods Nec). **Est:** 1982. **Emp:** 400.
Officers: Charles J. Selden, CEO, e-mail: selden@fpvid.com.

■ 25202 ■ **Arthur Fuller Associates Inc.**
PO Box 66
Newtown, CT 06470-0066
Phone: (203)426-7895 **Fax:** (203)270-7634
Products: Electrical appliances, including television sets, radios, and household appliances. **SIC:** 5064 (Electrical Appliances—Television & Radio). **Officers:** Arthur Fuller, President.

■ 25203 ■ **Funai Corp.**
100 North St.
Teterboro, NJ 07608
Phone: (201)288-2063 **Fax:** (201)288-8019
Products: Televisions, printers, facsimile machines, telephones, and video cassette recorders. **SICs:** 5064 (Electrical Appliances—Television & Radio); 5045 (Computers, Peripherals & Software); 5065 (Electronic Parts & Equipment Nec); 5044 (Office Equipment). **Sales:** $360,000,000 (2000). **Emp:** 54. **Officers:** Masawo Suwa, CEO; Tadaomi Yamada, Sr. VP & Finance Officer.

■ 25204 ■ **G. Leblanc Corp.**
7001 Leblanc Blvd.
Kenosha, WI 53141-1415
Phone: (262)658-1644 **Fax:** (262)658-2824
E-mail: gleblanc@gleblanc.com
URL: http://www.gleblanc.com/
Products: Brass and woodwind instruments and accessories. **SIC:** 5099 (Durable Goods Nec). **Est:** 1946. **Emp:** 500. **Officers:** Vito Pascucci, CEO & Chairman of the Board; Leon Pascucci, President.

■ 25205 ■ **G & S Products Inc.**
PO Box 229
Ligonier, IN 46767-0229
Phone: (219)894-3620
Free: (800)893-8171 **Fax:** (219)894-3628
URL: http://www.dshowcase.com
Products: Marching band accessories. **SIC:** 5099 (Durable Goods Nec). **Est:** 1979. **Officers:** Thomas Herald, President; Carl Kavanaugh, Sales/Marketing Contact; Jeff Scott, Sales/Marketing Contact; Julie Stout, Customer Service Contact; Janice Wright, Human Resources Contact.

■ 25206 ■ **Gas & Electrical Equipment Co.**
PO Box 26763
Oklahoma City, OK 73126-0763
Phone: (405)528-3551 **Fax:** (405)557-1172
Products: Electrical appliances, including television sets and radios. **SIC:** 5064 (Electrical Appliances—Television & Radio). **Officers:** Nelson Keller, Chairman of the Board.

■ 25207 ■ **Gaylord Brothers**
PO Box 4901
Syracuse, NY 13221-4901
Phone: (315)457-5070
Products: Audio-visual, television, photographic, and motion picture equipment. **SIC:** 5065 (Electronic Parts & Equipment Nec).

■ 25208 ■ **Gemini Sound Products Corp.**
8 Germak Dr.
Carteret, NJ 07008-1102
Phone: (732)969-9000
Free: (800)476-8633 **Fax:** (732)969-9090
URL: http://www.geminidj.com
Products: Sound equipment, including speakers, amplifiers, turntables, wireless microphone systems, mixers; Special effects lighting and fog machines; CD players. **SICs:** 5064 (Electrical Appliances—Television & Radio); 5065 (Electronic Parts & Equipment Nec). **Est:** 1974. **Sales:** $60,000,000 (2000). **Emp:** 130. **Officers:** Ike Cabasso, Chairman of the Board; Artie Cabasso, CEO; Alan Cabasso, President.

■ 25209 ■ **General Music Corp.**
1164 Tower Ln.
Bensenville, IL 60106
Phone: (630)766-8230
Free: (800)323-0280 **Fax:** (630)766-8281
E-mail: gmail@generalmusicus.com
URL: http://www.generalmusic.com
Products: Keyboards; Pianos. **SIC:** 5099 (Durable Goods Nec). **Est:** 1975. **Sales:** $5,000,000 (2000). **Emp:** 10. **Officers:** Daniele Galanti, President.

■ 25210 ■ **Getzen Co.**
530 S Highway H
PO Box 440
Elkhorn, WI 53121
Phone: (414)723-4221
Free: (800)366-5584 **Fax:** (414)723-4045
Products: Musical instruments. **SIC:** 5099 (Durable Goods Nec). **Est:** 1939. **Officers:** Edward M. Getzen, President; Thomas R. Getzen, Vice President.

■ 25211 ■ **Gifford-Brown Inc.**
PO Box 698
Des Moines, IA 50303-0698
Phone: (515)243-1257
Free: (800)369-4433 **Fax:** (515)243-6665
Products: Electrical appliances, including televisions and radios. **SIC:** 5064 (Electrical Appliances—Television & Radio). **Officers:** Craig Gifford, Chairman of the Board.

■ 25212 ■ **Glenray Communications**
PO Box 40400
Pasadena, CA 91114-7400
Phone: (626)797-5462
Free: (800)448-3456 **Fax:** (626)797-7524
E-mail: glenray@pacbell.net
URL: http://www.childrensmedia.com
Products: Videos. **SIC:** 5099 (Durable Goods Nec). **Est:** 1980. **Officers:** C. Ray Carlson; Joy D. Carlson. **Former Name:** Children's Media Productions. **Former Name:** Glenray Productions, Inc.

■ 25213 ■ **Global Access Entertainment Inc.**
212 NW 4th Ave.
Hallandale, FL 33009-4015
Phone: (954)458-7505 **Fax:** (954)458-8554
E-mail: mail@gaccess.net
Products: Specialty and promotional videos; Children's videos; Digital conversion for archiving. **SIC:** 5099 (Durable Goods Nec). **Est:** 1998. **Sales:** $5,000,000 (1999). **Emp:** 25. **Officers:** Mike Rubin, President. **Alternate Name:** Parents Approved Video. **Former Name:** DER Duplicating Services, Inc.

■ 25214 ■ **Good News Productions, International**
PO Box 222
Joplin, MO 64802
Phone: (417)782-0060 **Fax:** (417)782-3999
E-mail: gnpi@gnpi.org
URL: http://www.gnpi.org
Products: Religious videos. **SIC:** 5099 (Durable Goods Nec). **Est:** 1976. **Sales:** $80,000 (2000). **Emp:** 15.

■ 25215 ■ **Gotham Distributing Corp.**
2324 Haverford Rd.
Ardmore, PA 19003
Phone: (215)649-7565
Products: Pre-recorded records, tapes, and compact discs. **SIC:** 5099 (Durable Goods Nec). **Sales:** $40,000,000 (1994). **Emp:** 80. **Officers:** Nina Greene, President; Jerry Greene, President.

■ 25216 ■ **Gotham Sales Co.**
150 Morris Ave.
Springfield, NJ 07081
Phone: (973)912-8412 **Fax:** (973)912-0814
Products: Air conditioners and dehumidifiers; Warranties. **SIC:** 5064 (Electrical Appliances—Television & Radio). **Est:** 1990. **Sales:** $38,000,000 (2000). **Emp:** 8. **Officers:** Daniel Schwartzstein, President, e-mail: danny@gothamsales.com; Sam Schwartzstein, Vice President.

■ 25217 ■ **GPrime Ltd.**
1790 Broadway
New York, NY 10019-1412
Phone: (212)765-3415 **Fax:** (212)581-8938
E-mail: info@gprime.com
URL: http://www.gprime.com
Products: Audio equipment. **SIC:** 5065 (Electronic Parts & Equipment Nec). **Sales:** $2,000,000 (2000). **Emp:** 6. **Officers:** R. Hamm, Director.

■ 25218 ■ **GPX Inc. (St. Louis, Missouri)**
108 Madison St.
St. Louis, MO 63102
Phone: (314)621-3314 **Fax:** (314)621-0869
Products: Electronic appliances, including radios, stereos, televisions, telephones, and toys. **SIC:** 5064 (Electrical Appliances—Television & Radio). **Est:** 1973. **Sales:** $200,000,000 (2000). **Emp:** 500. **Officers:** Kenneth J. Berresheim, President; Terry L. Zintel, VP of Finance; Ken Berresheim, President; David Morlen, Human Resources Mgr.

■ 25219 ■ **Graham Radio Inc.**
505 Main St.
Reading, MA 01867
Phone: (781)944-4000 **Fax:** (781)944-6230
Products: Electronic equipment, including radios and antennas. **SIC:** 5064 (Electrical Appliances—Television & Radio). **Est:** 1946.

■ 25220 ■ **Great Northern Video**
31 Industrial Park Dr., Ste. 9
Concord, NH 03301-8522
Phone: (603)228-0412 **Fax:** (603)225-5435
Products: Video equipment and supplies. **SIC:** 5064 (Electrical Appliances—Television & Radio). **Est:** 1978. **Emp:** 10. **Officers:** Harvey Weinstein, Owner.

■ 25221 ■ **Gulbransen Inc. Crystal Products**
2102 Hancock St.
San Diego, CA 92110
Phone: (619)296-5760
Free: (800)677-7374 **Fax:** (619)296-7157
Products: Pianos, keyboards, and organs; Crystal products. **SIC:** 5099 (Durable Goods Nec). **Est:** 1904. **Officers:** Robert L. Hill, President; Curtis R. Carter Jr., Chairman of the Board; Salim Janmohamed, Exec. VP & CFO; John C. Slump, Sr. VP of Financial Services.

■ 25222 ■ **H-A Distributors Inc.**
1942 West St.
Annapolis, MD 21401-3931
Phone: (410)266-0818
Products: Electrical appliances, including television sets and radios. **SIC:** 5064 (Electrical Appliances—Television & Radio). **Officers:** John Poulos, President.

■ 25223 ■ **Robert Hale & Associates**
7523 Avenue J
Norfolk, VA 23513-4638
Phone: (757)583-7001 **Fax:** (757)583-6689
Products: Electrical entertainment equipment, including television sets and radios. **SIC:** 5064 (Electrical Appliances—Television & Radio). **Officers:** Robert Hale, President.

■ 25224 ■ **Hammond Electronics**
1000 Fairway Blvd.
Columbus, OH 43213-2521
Phone: (614)237-2504 **Fax:** (614)237-2678
Products: Audio and visual equipment for homes and automobiles. **SIC:** 5064 (Electrical Appliances—Television & Radio).

■ 25225 ■ **Handleman Co.**
500 Kirts Blvd.
Troy, MI 48084-4142
Phone: (248)362-4400 **Fax:** (248)362-3415
Products: Pre-recorded music; Software; Books and videos. **SICs:** 5099 (Durable Goods Nec); 5045 (Computers, Peripherals & Software); 5192 (Books, Periodicals & Newspapers). **Est:** 1934. **Sales:** $800,000 (2000). **Emp:** 3,000.

■ 25226 ■ **Harmonia Mundi U.S.A. Inc.**
2037 Granville Ave.
Los Angeles, CA 90025
Phone: (310)559-0802 **Fax:** (310)837-4150
Products: Classical compact discs. **SIC:** 5099

(Durable Goods Nec). **Sales:** $2,000,000 (2000). **Emp:** 27. **Officers:** Rene Goiffon, President; Rosa Rodriguez, Finance Officer.

■ **25227** ■ **Lee Hartman & Sons Equipment**
3236 Cove Rd. NW
Roanoke, VA 24017-2804
Phone: (540)366-3493
Free: (800)344-1832 **Fax:** (540)362-4659
URL: http://www.leehartman.com
Products: Video cassette recorders and disc players; Stereo equipment; Professional and commercial video and audio-visual products. **SICs:** 5064 (Electrical Appliances—Television & Radio); 5065 (Electronic Parts & Equipment Nec). **Est:** 1936. **Emp:** 59. **Officers:** Lee Hartman Jr.; Steve Hartman, Sales/Marketing Contact, e-mail: steve82257@aol.com.

■ **25228** ■ **Harvest Productions (E.B.M.)**
PO Box 2225
Kokomo, IN 46904-2225
Phones: (765)455-2112 (765)453-4488
Fax: (765)455-0889
E-mail: harvestproductions@ebm.org
Products: Religious films and videocassettes. **SIC:** 5099 (Durable Goods Nec). **Est:** 1975. **Sales:** $30,000 (2000). **Emp:** 2. **Officers:** Don Ross, Executive Director; Carol Branes, Sales.

■ **25229** ■ **HAVE Inc.**
309 Power Ave.
Hudson, NY 12534
Phone: (518)828-2000 **Fax:** (518)828-2008
E-mail: have@haveinc.com
URL: http://www.haveinc.com
Products: Audio and video cables, connectors and accessories; Custom patch panels and cables. **SIC:** 5065 (Electronic Parts & Equipment Nec). **Est:** 1977. **Sales:** $6,000,000 (2000). **Emp:** 50. **Officers:** Nancy Gordon, President; David Dobson, Controller; Paul Swedenburg, Vice President.

■ **25230** ■ **Henry Radio Inc.**
2050 S Bundy Dr.
Los Angeles, CA 90025
Phones: (310)820-1234 (310)820-4556
Free: (800)877-7979 **Fax:** (310)826-7790
Products: Radio and radio parts. **SIC:** 5065 (Electronic Parts & Equipment Nec). **Est:** 1941. **Sales:** $9,530,000 (2000). **Emp:** 49. **Officers:** James T. Henry, President; Ted S. Henry, Vice President; Meredith Henry, Secretary.

■ **25231** ■ **Alfred Higgins Productions, Inc.**
15500 Hamner Dr.
Los Angeles, CA 90077-1805
Phone: (818)762-3300
Free: (800)766-5353 **Fax:** (818)762-8223
Products: Educational films and videos. **SIC:** 5099 (Durable Goods Nec). **Est:** 1960.

■ **25232** ■ **Highsmith Inc.**
W5527 Hwy. 106
PO Box 800
Ft. Atkinson, WI 53538-0800
Phone: (920)563-9571
Free: (800)558-2110 **Fax:** (920)563-7395
E-mail: service@highsmith.com
URL: http://www.highsmith.com
Products: Computer furniture and supplies; Library supplies and furniture; AV equipment and carts. **SICs:** 5045 (Computers, Peripherals & Software); 5112 (Stationery & Office Supplies); 5045 (Computers, Peripherals & Software). **Est:** 1956. **Sales:** $48,000,000 (1999). **Emp:** 240. **Officers:** Duncan Highsmith, CEO & President; Paul R. Moss, Exec. VP; Steven C. Hudson, VP of Finance & Secty.; William Herman, Human Resources Contact; Hugh Highsmith, Chairman of the Board & Treasurer.

■ **25233** ■ **Hitachi America Ltd.**
50 Prospect Ave.
Tarrytown, NY 10591-4698
Phone: (914)332-5800
Free: (800)448-2244 **Fax:** (914)332-5834
Products: Electronics, including televisions and telephones; Industrial products. **SICs:** 5064 (Electrical Appliances—Television & Radio); 5045 (Computers,

Peripherals & Software); 5085 (Industrial Supplies). **Est:** 1959. **Sales:** $1,530,000,000 (2000). **Emp:** 6,500. **Officers:** Tomoharu Shimayama, President; K. Ueda, VP of Finance.

■ **25234** ■ **Hohner, Inc./HSS**
PO Box 15035
Richmond, VA 23227
Phone: (804)515-1900
Free: (800)446-6010 **Fax:** (804)515-0189
URL: http://www.hohnerusa.com
Products: Musical instruments. **SIC:** 5099 (Durable Goods Nec). **Est:** 1857. **Sales:** $33,000,000 (2000). **Emp:** 65. **Officers:** Horst Mucha, Chairman of the Board; Percy Pickral, CFO; Robert Cotton, President; Claude Merkel, Dir. of Data Processing.

■ **25235** ■ **Home Entertainment Distributors**
250 Turnpike St.
Canton, MA 02021-2747
Phone: (781)821-0087 **Fax:** (781)821-4193
Products: Small electrical appliances; Consumer high fidelity components; Stereo equipment. **SIC:** 5064 (Electrical Appliances—Television & Radio). **Officers:** Nicky Breitstein, President.

■ **25236** ■ **Home Safety Products**
2534 Washington Blvd.
Baltimore, MD 21230-1407
Phone: (410)646-3470
Products: Electrical appliances, including television sets and radios. **SIC:** 5064 (Electrical Appliances—Television & Radio). **Officers:** Leo Vogelsang, Owner.

■ **25237** ■ **Hondo Guitar Co.**
PO Box 30819
Charleston, SC 29417
Phone: (803)763-9083 **Fax:** (803)763-9096
Products: Musical instruments. **SIC:** 5099 (Durable Goods Nec). **Est:** 1969. **Emp:** 100. **Officers:** Eddie Toporek, CEO & President; Don Rhodes, Dir. of Sales & Products; Tom Malm, Dir. of Marketing Operations.

■ **25238** ■ **Hoshino U.S.A. Inc.**
1726 Winchester Rd.
Bensalem, PA 19020
Phone: (215)638-8670 **Fax:** (215)245-8583
E-mail: hoshinousa@aol.com
URL: http://www.ibanez.com
Products: Guitars and percussion instruments. **SIC:** 5099 (Durable Goods Nec). **Est:** 1972. **Sales:** $35,000,000 (1999). **Emp:** 85. **Officers:** Roy Miyahana, President; Jackie Brady, CFO; Bill Reim, VP of Marketing; Mashasi Inoue, VP of Merchandising.

■ **25239** ■ **House of Guitars Corp.**
645 Titus Ave.
Rochester, NY 14617
Phone: (716)544-3500
Products: Instruments, including guitars, banjoes, mandolins, and ukuleles; CDs; Tapes. **SIC:** 5099 (Durable Goods Nec). **Est:** 1964. **Sales:** $6,000,000 (2000). **Emp:** 49. **Officers:** A. Schaubroeck.

■ **25240** ■ **HP Marketing Co.**
7340 S Alton Way, Ste. G
Englewood, CO 80112
Phone: (303)804-9566
Free: (800)999-8849 **Fax:** (303)804-9662
E-mail: hpdenver@att.net
Products: Electrical appliances, including television sets and radios; Professional electronics. **SICs:** 5064 (Electrical Appliances—Television & Radio); 5065 (Electronic Parts & Equipment Nec). **Est:** 1974. **Sales:** $4,000,000 (2000). **Emp:** 6. **Officers:** Steven D. Johnson, CEO & President.

■ **25241** ■ **IMS Systems, Inc.**
12081-B Tech Rd.
Silver Spring, MD 20904
Phone: (301)680-0006 **Fax:** (301)680-0061
E-mail: imss@imss.com
URL: http://www.imss.com
Products: Tape and disk subsystems for data management, back-up, and archiving in the corporate network environment. **SIC:** 5045 (Computers, Peripherals & Software). **Est:** 1981. **Sales:** $8,000,000 (2000). **Emp:** 10. **Officers:** Howard Byron, CEO & Chairman of the Board; Edwin Hartman, CEO &

President. **Former Name:** Byron Systems International Inc.

■ **25242** ■ **Industrial Video Systems Inc.**
PO Box 6083
Ashland, VA 23005-6083
Phone: (804)798-0557 **Fax:** (804)798-6427
Products: Electrical appliances, including television sets and radios. **SIC:** 5064 (Electrical Appliances—Television & Radio). **Officers:** Alfred Taylor, President.

■ **25243** ■ **Ingram Book Co.**
1125 Heil Quaker Blvd.
La Vergne, TN 37086
Phone: (615)793-5000
Free: (800)937-8000 **Fax:** 800-876-0186
Products: Books; Spoken and music audio tapes; Video cassettes; CD ROMs; Special publications; Laserdiscs; Compact discs; Magazines. **SICs:** 5099 (Durable Goods Nec); 5192 (Books, Periodicals & Newspapers); 5045 (Computers, Peripherals & Software). **Est:** 1933. **Emp:** 60. **Officers:** Tom Scott, President; Marlene Tuyay Scott, VP & General Mgr.

■ **25244** ■ **Ingram Entertainment**
30525 Huntwood Ave.
Hayward, CA 94544-7019
Phone: (510)785-3730 **Fax:** (510)785-5407
Products: Pre-recorded videotape. **SIC:** 5099 (Durable Goods Nec).

■ **25245** ■ **Ingram Entertainment**
12600 SE Highway 212 Bldg. B
Clackamas, OR 97015-9081
Phone: (503)281-2673 **Fax:** (503)284-6046
Products: Pre-recorded videotapes. **SIC:** 5099 (Durable Goods Nec). **Former Name:** Commtron Corp.

■ **25246** ■ **Ingram Entertainment**
1430 Bradley Ln., No. 102
Carrollton, TX 75007
Phone: (972)245-6088 **Fax:** (972)323-3899
Products: Electronic equipment and supplies, including video, audio, and laser items. **SICs:** 5065 (Electronic Parts & Equipment Nec); 5064 (Electrical Appliances—Television & Radio).

■ **25247** ■ **Ingram Entertainment**
1224 N Post Oak Rd.
Houston, TX 77055
Phone: (713)681-9951 **Fax:** (713)681-2482
Products: Videos; Electronic items. **SIC:** 5065 (Electronic Parts & Equipment Nec).

■ **25248** ■ **Ingram Entertainment Inc.**
11103 E 53rd Ave.
Denver, CO 80239
Phone: (303)371-8372 **Fax:** (303)373-4583
Products: Movies. **SIC:** 5099 (Durable Goods Nec). **Former Name:** Commtron Corporation.

■ **25249** ■ **Ingram International Films**
7900 Hickman Rd.
Des Moines, IA 50322
Phone: (515)254-7000
Free: (800)621-1333 **Fax:** (515)254-7021
Products: International films. **SIC:** 5099 (Durable Goods Nec). **Est:** 1978. **Officers:** Kelly Adams, Sales/Marketing Contact.

■ **25250** ■ **Ingram Video**
7319 Innovation Blvd.
Ft. Wayne, IN 46818
Phone: (219)489-6046 **Fax:** (219)489-8850
Products: Videos. **SIC:** 5099 (Durable Goods Nec). **Emp:** 17.

■ **25251** ■ **Inter-Act Inc.**
1030 E Baseline Rd., Ste. 148
Tempe, AZ 85283-3717
Phone: (480)730-6688 **Fax:** (480)730-5592
Products: Electrical appliances, including televisions and radios; Electric power convertors. **SIC:** 5064 (Electrical Appliances—Television & Radio). **Officers:** Deborah Watson, President.

■ 25252 ■ International Cultural Enterprises Inc.
1241 Darmouth Ln.
Deerfield, IL 60015
Phone: (847)945-9516 **Fax:** (847)945-9514
Products: Prerecorded audio cassettes. **SIC:** 5099 (Durable Goods Nec). **Est:** 1989. **Sales:** $1,000,000 (2000). **Emp:** 2. **Officers:** Yuri A. Kovalenko, President; Jennifer L. Kovalenko, CEO & CFO.

■ 25253 ■ International Historic Films Inc.
PO Box 29035
Chicago, IL 60609
Phone: (773)927-9091 **Fax:** (773)927-9211
URL: http://www.ihffilm.com
Products: Pre-recorded video cassettes. **SIC:** 5065 (Electronic Parts & Equipment Nec). **Est:** 1977. **Emp:** 6. **Officers:** Peter Bernotas, President.

■ 25254 ■ Interstate Electronics, Inc.
Airport Plz., Hwy. 36
Hazlet, NJ 07730-1701
Phone: (732)264-3900 **Fax:** (732)264-0167
E-mail: iei@interstateelectronics.com
URL: http://www.interstateelectronics.com
Products: Electronic equipment, including video and audio equipment; Car alarms. **SICs:** 5064 (Electrical Appliances—Television & Radio); 5063 (Electrical Apparatus & Equipment). **Est:** 1968. **Sales:** $12,000,000 (2000). **Emp:** 30. **Officers:** Victor V. Scudiery, President; Edward Ketchum, Vice President.

■ 25255 ■ Island Instruments, Inc.
46-444 Kuneki St.
Kaneohe, HI 96744
Phone: (808)235-7544 **Fax:** (808)235-2617
Products: Sound equipment and systems. **SIC:** 5064 (Electrical Appliances—Television & Radio).

■ 25256 ■ Jacksonville Sound and Communications Inc.
5021 Stepp Ave.
Jacksonville, FL 32216
Phone: (904)737-3511 **Fax:** (904)737-8553
Products: Acoustical equipment; Fire and security alarms. **SICs:** 5065 (Electronic Parts & Equipment Nec); 5063 (Electrical Apparatus & Equipment). **Sales:** $6,000,000 (2000). **Emp:** 65. **Officers:** Robert E. Begley Jr., President; Wilson W. Sick Jr.; Steven Hunter.

■ 25257 ■ Jade Electronics Distributors
275 Andrews Rd.
Trevose, PA 19053
Phone: (215)322-7040
Free: (800)355-5233 **Fax:** (215)322-2891
E-mail: jade@jadeelectronics.com
URL: http://www.jadeelectronics.com
Products: Automotive electronic equipment, including stereos, compact disks, radar detectors, CB radios, and scanners; Cellular phones. **SIC:** 5064 (Electrical Appliances—Television & Radio). **Est:** 1975. **Emp:** 25. **Officers:** Larry Feinstein; Jason Feinstein.

■ 25258 ■ Jan-Mar Industries
PO Box 314
Hillsdale, NJ 07642
Phone: (201)664-3930 **Fax:** (201)666-3693
Products: Musical instrument accessories. **SIC:** 5099 (Durable Goods Nec). **Est:** 1965. **Officers:** Mark Biddelman, President.

■ 25259 ■ Jay Mart Wholesale
1568 S Green Rd.
Cleveland, OH 44121
Phone: (216)382-7600
Products: Pianos. **SIC:** 5099 (Durable Goods Nec). **Est:** 1985. **Officers:** Irv Jacoby; Ellen Jacoby.

■ 25260 ■ Jayark Corp.
300 Plaza Dr.
Vestal, NY 13850-3647
Products: Audio, visual, video, presentation, and duplicating equipment and supplies. **SIC:** 5064 (Electrical Appliances—Television & Radio). **Sales:** $27,500,000 (2000). **Emp:** 24. **Officers:** David L. Koffman, CEO & President; Robert C. Nolt, CFO.

■ 25261 ■ JBL Professional
8500 Balboa Blvd.
Northridge, CA 91329
Phone: (818)894-8850
Free: (800)852-5776 **Fax:** (818)830-1220
URL: http://www.jblpro.com
Products: Loudspeaker systems. **SIC:** 5065 (Electronic Parts & Equipment Nec). **Est:** 1946. **Emp:** 465. **Officers:** Mark Terry, CEO; Dennis Barry, VP of Finance; Michael MacDonald, President; Darlene Murray, Human Resources Contact, e-mail: dmurray@harman.com.

■ 25262 ■ JTG of Nashville
PO Box 158116
Nashville, TN 37215
Phone: (615)665-8384 **Fax:** (615)665-9468
Products: Prerecorded audio tapes; Guitars, banjos, mandolins, ukuleles, etc.; Music books. **SIC:** 5099 (Durable Goods Nec). **Est:** 1974. **Emp:** 12. **Officers:** John S. Ellis, President; Toni Ellis, Sales/Marketing Contact.

■ 25263 ■ Jupiter Band Instruments Inc.
PO Box 90249
Austin, TX 78709
Phone: (512)288-7400
Free: (800)283-4676 **Fax:** (512)288-6445
Products: Band instruments. **SIC:** 5099 (Durable Goods Nec).

■ 25264 ■ K-Tel International Inc.
2605 Fernbrook Ln. N
Minneapolis, MN 55447-4736
Phone: (763)559-6800 **Fax:** (763)509-9416
URL: http://www.k-tel.com
Products: Compact discs and cassette tapes; Consumer products. **SIC:** 5099 (Durable Goods Nec). **Est:** 1968. **Sales:** $75,500,000 (1999). **Emp:** 175. **Officers:** Philip Kives, CEO & Chairman of the Board; Steve Kahn, VP, CFO; Ken Onstad, President; Greg Walsh, Information Systems Mgr.; Mary Newman, Dir of Human Resources.

■ 25265 ■ Kaman Music Corp.
20 Old Windsor Rd.
PO Box 507
Bloomfield, CT 06002
Phone: (860)243-8353 **Fax:** (860)243-7102
Products: Musical instruments. **SIC:** 5099 (Durable Goods Nec).

■ 25266 ■ Kaman Music Corp. Los Angeles
1215 W Walnut St.
PO Box 5686
Compton, CA 90224-5686
Phone: (310)537-1712
Free: (800)262-7826 **Fax:** (310)632-7463
E-mail: sales@kamanmusic.com
URL: http://www.kamanmusic.com
Products: Musical instruments and accessories. **SIC:** 5099 (Durable Goods Nec). **Est:** 1905. **Sales:** $30,000,000 (1999). **Emp:** 85. **Officers:** John McGraw, Vice President; Don Talbot, Sales & Operations Mgr.; Robert King, Dir. of Marketing; Bill Lonaker, Dir. of Operations. **Alternate Name:** Coast Wholesale Music.

■ 25267 ■ Kay Guitar Co.
PO Box 26266
Indianapolis, IN 46226
Phone: (317)545-2486 **Fax:** (317)545-2450
Products: Musical instruments, including percussion and guitars. **SIC:** 5099 (Durable Goods Nec). **Sales:** $6,000,000 (2000). **Emp:** 30. **Officers:** Tony Blair, President; Bill Wissel, Exec. VP.

■ 25268 ■ Kent Electronics Inc.
1300 N Larch St.
Lansing, MI 48906-4422
Phone: (517)487-6267
Products: Electrical appliances, including television sets and radios. **SIC:** 5064 (Electrical Appliances—Television & Radio). **Officers:** Kent Verhougstraete, President.

■ 25269 ■ Kentuckyiana Music Supply Inc.
PO Box 14124
Louisville, KY 40214
Phone: (502)361-4697
Products: Violins and cellos. **SIC:** 5099 (Durable Goods Nec).

■ 25270 ■ Kenwood USA Corp.
PO Box 22745
Long Beach, CA 90801-5745
Phone: (310)639-9000 **Fax:** (310)604-4487
Products: Home and car audio equipment. **SIC:** 5064 (Electrical Appliances—Television & Radio). **Sales:** $98,000,000 (2000). **Emp:** 200. **Officers:** Joe Richter, President.

■ 25271 ■ Keyboard Decals
1029 Pennsylvania Ave.
Hagerstown, MD 21742
Phone: (301)791-2880 **Fax:** (301)791-9312
Products: Musical teaching aids. **SIC:** 5099 (Durable Goods Nec). **Est:** 1971. **Sales:** $70,000 (2000). **Emp:** 2. **Officers:** Doris E. Lake, Owner; Doris E. Lake, Owner.

■ 25272 ■ Kimbo Educational
10 N 3rd Ave.
PO Box 477
Long Branch, NJ 07740-0477
Phone: (732)229-4949
Free: (800)631-2187 **Fax:** (732)870-3340
E-mail: kimboed@aol.com
URL: http://www.kimboed.com
Products: Audio cassettes; CDs; Videos. **SIC:** 5099 (Durable Goods Nec). **Est:** 1962. **Emp:** 20. **Officers:** James Kimble, Vice President; Gertrude Kimble, President; Elaine Murphy, Sales & Marketing Contact, e-mail: emurf99@aol.com; Pat Spencer, Customer Service Contact; Kathryn Beckley, Customer Service Contact; Amy Laufer, Catalog Editor.

■ 25273 ■ Kingdom Co.
PO Box 506
Mansfield, PA 16933
Phone: (717)662-7515 **Fax:** (717)662-3875
Products: Bulk cassette tapes; Audio equipment; Tape recorders and players; Computers; Printers. **SICs:** 5099 (Durable Goods Nec); 5099 (Durable Goods Nec); 5045 (Computers, Peripherals & Software). **Est:** 1980. **Sales:** $12,000,000 (2000). **Emp:** 100. **Officers:** Johnny Berguson, President.

■ 25274 ■ Koch International
2 Tri Harbor Ct.
Port Washington, NY 11050-4617
Phone: (516)484-1000 **Fax:** (516)484-4746
E-mail: koch@kochint.com
URL: http://www.kochint.com
Products: Compact discs; Cassettes. **SIC:** 5099 (Durable Goods Nec). **Est:** 1993. **Emp:** 150.

■ 25275 ■ Korg U.S.A. Inc.
316 S Service Rd.
Melville, NY 11747
Phone: (516)333-9100 **Fax:** (516)333-9108
URL: http://www.korgusa.com
Products: Keyboards and amplifiers. **SIC:** 5099 (Durable Goods Nec). **Est:** 1985. **Sales:** $60,000,000 (2000). **Emp:** 90. **Officers:** Michael I. Kovins, President; Joseph Castronovo, Exec. VP of Finance.

■ 25276 ■ Kultur, White Star, Duke International Films Ltd., Inc.
195 Hwy 36
West Long Branch, NJ 07764
Phone: (732)229-2343
Free: (800)458-5887 **Fax:** (732)229-0066
E-mail: kultur@mindspring.com
URL: http://www.kulturvideo.com
Products: Performing arts and fine arts videos; Nintheatrical programs, motorsports films. **SIC:** 5099 (Durable Goods Nec). **Est:** 1980. **Emp:** 17. **Officers:** Dennis M. Hedlund, Chairman of the Board; Pearl Lee, President; Ron Davis, Acquisitions Dir.; Peter Wilson, United Kingdom Dir.

■ 25277 ■ Claude Lakey Mouthpieces
PO Box 2023
Redmond, WA 98073
Phone: (425)861-5920 **Fax:** (425)861-5630
Products: Musical instruments and parts. **SIC:** 5099
(Durable Goods Nec). **Officers:** Nick Bogden, Owner.

■ 25278 ■ Lang Percussion
325 Gold St., Ste. 1
Brooklyn, NY 11201-3040
Phone: (212)228-5213 **Fax:** (212)673-7082
Products: Percussion instruments (cymbals, drums, vibraphones). **SIC:** 5099 (Durable Goods Nec). **Est:** 1974. **Officers:** Morris Lang, President.

■ 25279 ■ Latin Percussion Inc.
160 Belmont Ave.
Garfield, NJ 07026
Phone: (973)478-6903 **Fax:** (973)772-3568
Products: Percussion musical instruments. **SIC:** 5099
(Durable Goods Nec). **Sales:** $12,000,000 (1994).
Emp: 75. **Officers:** Martin Cohen, President; Marilyn Cohen, Treasurer.

■ 25280 ■ Law Office Information Systems Inc.
105 N 28th St.
Van Buren, AR 72956-5005
Phone: (501)471-5581 **Fax:** (501)471-7145
Products: Legal CD-ROMs. **SIC:** 5045 (Computers, Peripherals & Software). **Sales:** $50,000,000 (2000).
Emp: 250. **Officers:** Kyle Parker, President.

■ 25281 ■ Legal Star Communications
10573 W Pico Blvd.
Los Angeles, CA 90064
Phone: (310)275-8867
Products: Videos for legal research. **SIC:** 5099
(Durable Goods Nec). **Est:** 1989. **Sales:** $300,000
(2000). **Emp:** 5. **Officers:** David Feldman, Partner.

■ 25282 ■ L.E.S. Distributing
6015 Commerce Dr. No. 545
Irving, TX 75063-6025
Phone: (972)751-0488 **Fax:** (972)550-8720
Products: Electronic equipment, including antennae, televisions, radios, and compact disk players. **SIC:** 5064 (Electrical Appliances—Television & Radio).

■ 25283 ■ Library Video Co.
PO Box 580
Wynnewood, PA 19096
Phone: (610)645-4000
Free: (800)843-3620 **Fax:** (610)645-4040
E-mail: cs@libraryvideo.com
URL: http://www.LibraryVideo.com
Products: cational videos and CD-ROMs. **SICs:** 5045 (Computers, Peripherals & Software); 5099 (Durable Goods Nec). **Est:** 1985. **Emp:** 126. **Officers:** Andrew Schlessinger, CEO & President; Tony Pettinato, Controller.

■ 25284 ■ Light Impressions
PO Box 22708
Rochester, NY 14692-2708
Free: (800)828-9859
Products: Audio-visual, television, photographic, and motion picture equipment. **SIC:** 5065 (Electronic Parts & Equipment Nec).

■ 25285 ■ Ligonier Ministries, Inc.
400 Technical Park, Ste. 150
Lake Mary, FL 32746
Phone: (407)333-4244
Free: (800)435-4343 **Fax:** (407)333-4233
URL: http://www.ligonier.org
Products: Religious audio/visual and book materials.
SIC: 5099 (Durable Goods Nec). **Est:** 1971. **Sales:**
$2,965,266 (1999). **Emp:** 56. **Officers:** Linda Rowley, Resource Consultant, e-mail: lrowley@ligonier.org.

■ 25286 ■ LIVE Entertainment Inc.
15400 Sherman Way
Van Nuys, CA 91406
Phone: (818)988-5060
Products: Videos. **SIC:** 5099 (Durable Goods Nec).
Est: 1988. **Sales:** $140,100,000 (2000). **Emp:** 125.
Officers: Roger A. Burlage, CEO & President; Ronald

B. Cushey, Exec. VP & CFO; Michael J. White, Exec. VP of Admin.

■ 25287 ■ Lloyd F. McKinney Associates Inc.
25350 Cypress Ave.
Hayward, CA 94544
Phone: (510)783-8043 **Fax:** (510)783-2130
Products: Professional audio equipment. **SIC:** 5065
(Electronic Parts & Equipment Nec). **Sales:** $1,500,000
(2000). **Emp:** 18. **Officers:** Betty Harmoney, President; Robert Harmoney, CFO.

■ 25288 ■ E.W. Long Inc.
1102 Riverdale St.
West Springfield, MA 01089-4607
Phone: (413)733-0808
Products: Electronic parts and equipment, including communication and sound equipment. **SIC:** 5065
(Electronic Parts & Equipment Nec). **Officers:** Walter Mitus, President.

■ 25289 ■ Loveall Music Co.
3033 Kennedy Ln.
Texarkana, TX 75503-2545
Phone: (903)794-3735
Free: (800)467-3730 **Fax:** (903)831-9992
E-mail: lmctex@aol.com
URL: http://www.loveallmusic.com
Products: Musical instruments. **SIC:** 5099 (Durable Goods Nec). **Est:** 1960. **Sales:** $1,000,000 (2000).
Emp: 9. **Officers:** V. K. Caldwell.

■ 25290 ■ Lowes Home Centers Inc.
PO Box 1111
North Wilkesboro, NC 28659-1111
Phone: (910)651-4000 **Fax:** (910)651-4766
Products: Electrical appliances, including television and radio. **SIC:** 5064 (Electrical Appliances—Television & Radio). **Officers:** Robert Strickland, Chairman of the Board.

■ 25291 ■ LP Music Group
160 Belmont Ave.
Garfield, NJ 07026
Phone: (973)478-6903
Free: (800)526-5312 **Fax:** (973)772-3568
Products: Musical instruments. **SIC:** 5099 (Durable Goods Nec). **Est:** 1962. **Sales:** $9,000,000 (2000).
Emp: 60. **Officers:** Martin Cohen, President; Marilyn Cohen, Vice President; Wayne Cohen, Vice President.

■ 25292 ■ LPD Music International
32575 Industrial Dr.
Madison Heights, MI 48071
Phone: (248)585-9630
Free: (800)527-5292 **Fax:** (248)585-7360
E-mail: mail@lpdmusic.com
URL: http://www.lpdmusic.com
Products: Musical instruments and accessories. **SIC:** 5099 (Durable Goods Nec). **Est:** 1963. **Emp:** 37.
Former Name: La Playa Distributing Co.

■ 25293 ■ L.P.S. Records, Inc.
2140 St. Clair St.
Bellingham, WA 98226-4016
Phone: (360)733-3807 **Fax:** (360)779-8204
URL: http://www.silverlink.net/lps/index.htm
Products: Prerecorded music, including compact discs and albums. **SIC:** 5099 (Durable Goods Nec). **Est:**
1970. **Officers:** Renie Peterson, President; Marion Sluys, Vice President; Harold Peterson, Treasurer.

■ 25294 ■ Luthier's Mercantile Int. Inc.
412 Moore Ln.
Healdsburg, CA 95448
Phone: (707)433-1823
Free: (800)477-4437 **Fax:** (707)433-8802
E-mail: lmi@lmii.com
URL: http://www.lmii.com
Products: Exotic musical instruments wood, tools, and parts. **SIC:** 5099 (Durable Goods Nec). **Est:** 1994.
Sales: $2,000,000 (2000). **Emp:** 15. **Officers:** Duane Waterman.

■ 25295 ■ Stewart MacDonald Manufacturing
21 N Shafer St.
Athens, OH 45701
Phone: (740)592-3021
Free: (800)848-2273 **Fax:** (740)593-7922
Products: Musical instruments and parts. **SIC:** 5099
(Durable Goods Nec). **Est:** 1969.

■ 25296 ■ Madison Electric Co.
31855 Van Dyke Ave.
Warren, MI 48093-1047
Phone: (810)825-0200 **Fax:** (810)825-0225
Products: Electrical appliances, including television sets and radios. **SIC:** 5064 (Electrical Appliances—Television & Radio). **Officers:** Joseph Schneider, President.

■ 25297 ■ Madrigal Audio Laboratories Inc.
PO Box 781
Middletown, CT 06457
Phone: (860)346-0896
Products: High-end audio equipment. **SICs:** 5064
(Electrical Appliances—Television & Radio); 5065
(Electronic Parts & Equipment Nec).

■ 25298 ■ Magnamusic Distributors Inc.
PO Box 338
Sharon, CT 06069-0338
Phone: (860)364-5431 **Fax:** (860)364-5168
E-mail: magnamusic@magnamusic.com
URL: http://www.magnamusic.com
Products: Musical instruments, including woodwinds and harpsichords; Sheet music. **SIC:** 5099 (Durable Goods Nec).

■ 25299 ■ Maiden Music
PO Box 777
Trevilians, VA 23170
Phone: (540)967-0077
Products: Recordings of contemporary religious music. **SIC:** 5099 (Durable Goods Nec).

■ 25300 ■ Majega Records
240 E Radcliffe Dr.
Claremont, CA 91711
Phone: (909)624-0677
Products: Pre-recorded audio materials. **SIC:** 5099
(Durable Goods Nec).

■ 25301 ■ Malletech/Marimba Productions Inc.
501 E Main St.
Gurdon, AR 71743
Phone: (870)353-2525 **Fax:** (870)353-2424
Products: Keyboard instruments and publications.
SIC: 5099 (Durable Goods Nec). **Est:** 1982. **Sales:**
$500,000 (2000). **Emp:** 10. **Officers:** Christopher T. Kobonn, Business Manager.

■ 25302 ■ Manu Reps Inc.
4710 W 73rd St.
Indianapolis, IN 46268-2115
Phone: (317)298-0622 **Fax:** (317)298-0625
Products: Stereo Products. **SIC:** 5064 (Electrical Appliances—Television & Radio). **Officers:** Keith Selby, President.

■ 25303 ■ Maranatha Music
PO Box 31050
Laguna Hills, CA 92654
Phone: (714)248-4000 **Free:** (800)245-7664
E-mail: mm@corinthian.com
URL: http://www.maranathamusic.com
Products: Religious music. **SIC:** 5099 (Durable Goods Nec). **Est:** 1971.

■ 25304 ■ Dean Markley Strings, Inc.
3350 Scott Blvd., No. 45
Santa Clara, CA 95054
Phone: (408)988-2456
Free: (800)800-1008 **Fax:** (408)988-0441
E-mail: info@deanmarkley.com
URL: http://www.deanmarkley.com
Products: Guitar strings and accessories. **SIC:** 5099
(Durable Goods Nec). **Est:** 1976. **Emp:** 150. **Officers:**
Dean Markley, Pres., Owner, & CEO; Thomas G. Dreibelbis, VP of Sales.

■ **25305** ■ **Marsch Enterprises**
8133 Old Seward Hwy.
Anchorage, AK 99518
Phone: (907)522-8083 **Fax:** (907)522-8085
Products: Electrical appliances and entertainment equipment, including television, stereo, video, and audio equipment. **SIC:** 5064 (Electrical Appliances—Television & Radio). **Est:** 1988. **Sales:** $3,000,000 (2000). **Emp:** 12. **Officers:** Kurt Marsch, Owner.

■ **25306** ■ **Maxell Corporation of America**
22-08 Rte. 208 S
Fair Lawn, NJ 07410
Phone: (201)794-5900 **Fax:** (201)796-8790
Products: Audio and video tape. **SIC:** 5065 (Electronic Parts & Equipment Nec). **Est:** 1969. **Sales:** $400,000,000 (2000). **Emp:** 130. **Officers:** Atsushi Matsumoto, President; H. Yoshioka, VP of Finance; Michael Golacinski, VP of Marketing; Tom Grieco, Dir. of Systems; Richard Driscoll, Dir of Human Resources.

■ **25307** ■ **MBT International Inc.**
PO Box 30819
Charleston, SC 29417
Phone: (843)763-9083 **Fax:** (843)763-9096
Products: Musical instruments; Lghting effect products. **SIC:** 5099 (Durable Goods Nec). **Sales:** $53,000,000 (2000). **Emp:** 100. **Officers:** Eddie Toporek, President.

■ **25308** ■ **Howard McAuliffe Inc.**
15 Industrial Park Pl.
Middletown, CT 06457-1501
Phone: (860)632-2678 **Fax:** (860)613-0827
Products: Two-way radios; Cellular phones and pagers. **SIC:** 5064 (Electrical Appliances—Television & Radio). **Officers:** Howard McAuliffe, President.

■ **25309** ■ **Media Concepts Inc.**
559 49 St. S
St. Petersburg, FL 33707
Phone: (727)321-2122
Free: (800)330-3893 **Fax:** (727)321-2272
E-mail: cwrs@aol.com
URL: http://www.mediaconceptsflorida.com
Products: Videos; Tapes, including audio and video; Electric and Electronic equipment. **SIC:** 5065 (Electronic Parts & Equipment Nec). **Est:** 1974. **Sales:** $2,500,000 (2000). **Emp:** 11. **Officers:** Bob Skidmore, President; John P. Gallagher, Vice President.

■ **25310** ■ **Mega Hertz**
6940 S Holly Circle, Ste. 200
Englewood, CO 80112
Phone: (303)779-1717
Free: (800)525-8386 **Fax:** (303)779-1749
URL: http://www.megahz.com
Products: Cable television products. **SICs:** 5064 (Electrical Appliances—Television & Radio); 5063 (Electrical Apparatus & Equipment). **Est:** 1975. **Officers:** Steve Grossman, Marketing & Sales Mgr.; Pierre Cubbage, Regional Sales Mgr.; Steve Fox, Regional Sales Mgr.; Rob Donziger, Regional Sales Mgr.

■ **25311** ■ **Meisel Stringed Instruments Inc.**
PO Box 90
Springfield, NJ 07081-0090
Phone: (973)379-5000
Free: (800)634-7356 **Fax:** (973)379-5020
E-mail: meisel@worldnet.att.net
URL: http://www.meiselmusic.com
Products: Musical instruments and parts. **SIC:** 5099 (Durable Goods Nec). **Est:** 1878. **Former Name:** Meisel Music Inc.

■ **25312** ■ **Melrose Appliance Inc.**
424 Main St.
Melrose, MA 02176-3842
Phone: (781)665-5310 **Fax:** (781)662-6705
Products: Household appliances, including television sets and VCRs. **SIC:** 5064 (Electrical Appliances—Television & Radio). **Est:** 1948. **Officers:** Alfred Porcaro, President.

■ **25313** ■ **Memtek Products/Memorex Audio, Video, CDR's, & Computer Peripherals**
10100 Pioneer Blvd., Ste. 110
Santa Fe Springs, CA 90670
Phone: (562)906-2800 **Fax:** (562)906-2877
E-mail: generalinq@memorex.com
URL: http://www.memorex.com
Products: Blank audio and video tapes; Mini discs, CDR's, and CDRW's; Audio cleaner care/maintenance products; Label makers; Media storage, mice, keyboard and ROM drives. **SICs:** 5099 (Durable Goods Nec); 5064 (Electrical Appliances—Television & Radio). **Emp:** 200. **Officers:** M. Golacinski. **Former Name:** Memtek Products/Memorex Audio & Video.

■ **25314** ■ **Microwave Oven Company of Oregon**
2114 SE 9th Ave.
PO Box 14309
Portland, OR 97214-0309
Phone: (503)236-6140 **Fax:** (503)235-0587
Products: Electrical appliances, including television and radio. **SIC:** 5064 (Electrical Appliances—Television & Radio). **Officers:** F. Englehardt, President.

■ **25315** ■ **Mid-America Appliance Center**
2745 Belmont Blvd.
Salina, KS 67401-7600
Phone: (785)825-8925 **Fax:** (785)825-8925
Products: Electrical appliances, including television sets and radios. **SIC:** 5064 (Electrical Appliances—Television & Radio). **Officers:** Norman Fischer, President.

■ **25316** ■ **Mid-Atlantic Marketing Inc.**
966 Hungerford Dr., Ste. 31
Rockville, MD 20850-1714
Phone: (301)738-9270 **Fax:** (301)738-9277
Products: Electrical entertainment equipment, including television sets and radios. **SIC:** 5064 (Electrical Appliances—Television & Radio). **Officers:** Matthew Wolk, President.

■ **25317** ■ **Mid-East Manufacturing Inc.**
7694 Progress Cir.
Melbourne, FL 32904
Phone: (407)724-1477 **Fax:** (407)952-1080
URL: http://www.mid-east.com
Products: Ethnic musical instruments. **SIC:** 5099 (Durable Goods Nec). **Est:** 1979. **Sales:** $2,000,000 (2000). **Emp:** 12. **Officers:** Steven N. Kundrat, President, e-mail: stevek@mid-east.com.

■ **25318** ■ **Mid South Marketing Inc.**
285 German Oak Dr.
Cordova, TN 38018
Phone: (901)755-8488 **Fax:** (901)754-9464
Products: Electrical appliances, including televisions and radios. **SIC:** 5064 (Electrical Appliances—Television & Radio). **Officers:** David Edmondson, President.

■ **25319** ■ **MIDCO International**
908 W Fayette Ave.
PO Box 748
Effingham, IL 62401
Phone: (217)342-9211
Free: (800)637-9705 **Fax:** (217)347-0316
E-mail: midco@xelnet.com
Products: Musical instruments. **SIC:** 5099 (Durable Goods Nec). **Est:** 1952. **Sales:** $23,000,000 (2000). **Emp:** 80. **Officers:** J. David Samuel, President.

■ **25320** ■ **MIDCO International**
1926 Silver St.
Garland, TX 75042
Phone: (972)272-8399 **Fax:** (972)272-8624
Products: Musical accessories and instruments. **SIC:** 5099 (Durable Goods Nec).

■ **25321** ■ **Midsouth Electric Corp.**
PO Box 276
Austell, GA 30168-0276
Phone: (404)941-0110 **Fax:** (404)941-0162
Products: Electrical appliances, including television sets and radios. **SIC:** 5064 (Electrical Appliances—Television & Radio). **Officers:** Harry Bryant, President.

■ **25322** ■ **Midwest Music Distributors**
5024 Montgomery Rd.
Cincinnati, OH 45212
Phone: (513)631-8318
Products: Sound systems and equipment. **SIC:** 5043 (Photographic Equipment & Supplies).

■ **25323** ■ **Midwest Sales and Service Inc.**
917 S Chapin St.
South Bend, IN 46601-2829
Phone: (219)287-3365 **Fax:** (219)287-3429
E-mail: midwestss@aol.com
Products: Appliances, including televisions; Car audio equipment and supplies. **SIC:** 5064 (Electrical Appliances—Television & Radio). **Est:** 1949. **Sales:** $10,000,000 (2000). **Emp:** 15. **Officers:** Trell Wechter, President.

■ **25324** ■ **Midwest Visual Equipment Co.**
6500 N Hamlin Ave.
Chicago, IL 60645
Phone: (312)478-1250
Products: Visual equipment. **SICs:** 5064 (Electrical Appliances—Television & Radio); 5045 (Computers, Peripherals & Software). **Est:** 1939. **Sales:** $30,000,000 (2000). **Emp:** 140. **Officers:** Tom S. Roberts, President.

■ **25325** ■ **Mill City Music Record Distribution, Inc.**
3820 E Lake St.
Minneapolis, MN 55406
Phone: (612)722-6649
E-mail: millcity@millcitymusic.com
Products: Cassettes, books, videotapes, compact discs, and posters. **SIC:** 5099 (Durable Goods Nec). **Est:** 1980. **Sales:** $2,000,000 (2000). **Emp:** 10.

■ **25326** ■ **Minnesota Western Inc.**
921 Parker St.
Berkeley, CA 94710
Phone: (510)848-2600
Products: Meeting and presentation video projection systems. **SIC:** 5043 (Photographic Equipment & Supplies).

■ **25327** ■ **Mission Service Supply**
PO Drawer 2957
West Monroe, LA 71294-2957
Phone: (318)397-2755 **Fax:** (318)397-1958
E-mail: mission@missionservice.com
Products: Audio and video electronics. **SIC:** 5065 (Electronic Parts & Equipment Nec). **Est:** 1984. **Officers:** James Green.

■ **25328** ■ **MITO Corp.**
54905 County Rd. 17
Elkhart, IN 46516
Phone: (219)295-2441
Free: (888)433-6486 **Fax:** (219)522-5480
E-mail: sales@mitocorp.com
URL: http://www.mitocorp.com
Products: Televisions, microwaves and radios; Entertainment equipment; Navigation systems. **SIC:** 5064 (Electrical Appliances—Television & Radio). **Est:** 1974. **Sales:** $15,000,000 (2000). **Emp:** 44. **Officers:** Mike Stock, CEO; Dan Maloney, Sales/Marketing Contact, e-mail: dmaloney@mitocorp.com; Ken Smith, Human Resources Contact, e-mail: ksmith@mitocorp.com; Melissa Myers, Customer Service Contact, e-mail: mmeyers@mitocorp.com.

■ **25329** ■ **Mitsubishi Electronics America Inc.**
PO Box 6007
Cypress, CA 90630
Phone: (714)220-2500 **Fax:** (714)229-3867
Products: Audio and video parts and equipment, including televisions, VCRs and stereos. **SICs:** 5064 (Electrical Appliances—Television & Radio); 5043 (Photographic Equipment & Supplies). **Sales:** $75,000,000 (2000). **Emp:** 400. **Officers:** Tachi Kiuchi, President.

■ **25330** ■ **MMB Music Inc.**
3526 Washington Ave.
St. Louis, MO 63103-1019
Phone: (314)427-5660 **Fax:** (314)426-3590
Products: Music books; Musical instruments. **SICs:**

5099 (Durable Goods Nec); 5192 (Books, Periodicals & Newspapers).

■ 25331 ■ **Modern Mass Media Inc.**
PO Box 950
Chatham, NJ 07928
Phone: (973)635-6000 **Fax:** (973)635-3404
Products: Electric and electronic equipment. **SIC:** 5065 (Electronic Parts & Equipment Nec). **Est:** 1970. **Sales:** $12,000,000 (2000). **Emp:** 48. **Officers:** Chip Del Coro, President; Carl Del Coro, Exec. VP; Donald Maher, VP of Sales.

■ 25332 ■ **Mohawk Marketing Corp.**
PO Box 62229
Virginia Beach, VA 23466-2229
Phone: (757)499-8901 **Fax:** (757)497-6610
Products: Electrical appliances, including television sets and radios. **SIC:** 5064 (Electrical Appliances—Television & Radio). **Officers:** Ed Stowers, President.

■ 25333 ■ **Mole-Richardson Co.**
937 N Sycamore Ave.
Hollywood, CA 90038-2384
Phone: (323)851-0111 **Fax:** (323)851-5593
E-mail: info@mole.com
URL: http://www.mole.com
Products: Lighting equipment; Transformers; Speaker systems, microphones, home type electronic kits, and commercial sound equipment, including public address systems. **SIC:** 5063 (Electrical Apparatus & Equipment). **Est:** 1927. **Sales:** $10,000,000 (2000). **Emp:** 99. **Officers:** Michael C. Parker.

■ 25334 ■ **Monroe Distributing Co.**
3010 University Dr. NW
Huntsville, AL 35816-3134
Phone: (205)536-0622 **Fax:** (205)536-0644
Products: Electrical appliances and entertainment equipment, including television sets, radios, tape players, and recorders. **SIC:** 5064 (Electrical Appliances—Television & Radio). **Officers:** H Monroe, President.

■ 25335 ■ **Moody Institute of Science**
820 N LaSalle Blvd.
Chicago, IL 60610
Phone: (312)329-4000
Free: (800)842-1223 **Fax:** 800-647-6910
Products: Videos. **SIC:** 5099 (Durable Goods Nec).

■ 25336 ■ **Moore Co.**
PO Box 4564
Portland, OR 97214
Phone: (503)234-5000 **Fax:** (503)238-1603
Products: Electrical appliances and entertainment equipment, including televisions, radios, and computer products; Telecommunications. **SIC:** 5064 (Electrical Appliances—Television & Radio). **Est:** 1947. **Sales:** $30,000,000 (2000). **Emp:** 49. **Officers:** Randolph Miller, CEO; Julie Lenoker, VP of Operations; K.C. Rawls, CFO, Treasurer & Secty.

■ 25337 ■ **Robert J. Moore**
2824 Bransford Ave.
Nashville, TN 37204-3102
Phone: (615)297-5745 **Fax:** (615)297-5608
Products: Electrical appliances, including television sets and radios; Audio and video equipment. **SIC:** 5064 (Electrical Appliances—Television & Radio). **Officers:** Robert Moore, Owner.

■ 25338 ■ **Moore Sales Co.**
11 Gilbert Rd.
Burkburnett, TX 76354
Phone: (940)569-1463
Free: (800)527-1616 **Fax:** (940)569-1468
E-mail: deals@mooresalescompany.com
URL: http://www.mooresalescompany.com
Products: Telephones; Batteries; Automotive stereos. **SICs:** 5065 (Electronic Parts & Equipment Nec); 5064 (Electrical Appliances—Television & Radio). **Est:** 1975. **Emp:** 22.

■ 25339 ■ **Motion Pictures Enterprises**
PO Box 276
Tarrytown, NY 10591
Phone: (212)245-0969
Products: Audio-visual, television, photographic, and motion picture equipment. **SIC:** 5065 (Electronic Parts & Equipment Nec).

■ 25340 ■ **Motivaction Inc.**
9800 Shelard Pkwy., Ste. 300
Minneapolis, MN 55441-6453
Phone: (612)544-7200
Free: (800)326-2226 **Fax:** (612)544-2592
Products: Electrical appliances and entertainment equipment, including television sets and radios. **SIC:** 5064 (Electrical Appliances—Television & Radio). **Officers:** William Bryson, President.

■ 25341 ■ **Mountain Marketing**
716 SW 28th St.
Pendleton, OR 97801
Phone: (541)276-7866
Free: (800)338-9555 **Fax:** (541)276-4122
Products: Car audio products. **SIC:** 5064 (Electrical Appliances—Television & Radio).

■ 25342 ■ **MP Productions Co.**
6301 Murray St.
Little Rock, AR 72209
Phone: (501)562-7425 **Fax:** (501)562-7521
Products: Sound and lighting equipment. **SIC:** 5063 (Electrical Apparatus & Equipment). **Sales:** $1,000,000 (1993). **Emp:** 10. **Officers:** Mike Pope, President.

■ 25343 ■ **MPC Educational Systems Inc.**
27 Fulton St.
New Haven, CT 06512
Phone: (203)469-6481
Free: (800)243-2108 **Fax:** (203)467-9659
E-mail: mpc.educations.sys@snet.net
Products: Audio and video equipment and supplies. **SIC:** 5043 (Photographic Equipment & Supplies). **Est:** 1955. **Sales:** $6,000,000 (2000). **Emp:** 45. **Officers:** Herbert D. Friedlander, President; Thomas W. Guercia, Vice President.

■ 25344 ■ **Music City Record Distributors Inc.**
PO Box 22773
Nashville, TN 37202
Phone: (615)255-7315 **Fax:** (615)255-7329
Products: Pre-recorded records, tapes and compact discs. **SIC:** 5099 (Durable Goods Nec). **Sales:** $19,400,000 (2000). **Emp:** 170. **Officers:** Bruce Carlock, President; Carl Hunter, VP of Finance.

■ 25345 ■ **Music Distributors Inc.**
6413 Midway Rd., #B
Haltom City, TX 76117-5347
Phone: (817)831-2982
Free: (800)898-7812 **Fax:** (817)831-3608
Products: Compact discs, cassettes, and albums. **SIC:** 5099 (Durable Goods Nec). **Est:** 1983. **Sales:** $4,000,000 (2000). **Emp:** 15. **Officers:** Nina K. Easton, CEO; Melissa Koran, General Mgr.

■ 25346 ■ **Music Emporium Record Co.**
3100 23rd Ave.
Meridian, MS 39301
Phone: (601)483-5991
Products: Compact discs and cassettes; T-shirts. **SICs:** 5099 (Durable Goods Nec); 5136 (Men's/Boys' Clothing); 5137 (Women's/Children's Clothing). **Est:** 1973. **Sales:** $200,000 (2000). **Emp:** 5. **Officers:** Art Matthews, President.

■ 25347 ■ **Music Industries Inc.**
99 Tulip Ave., Ste. 101
Floral Park, NY 11001
Phone: (516)352-4110
Free: (800)431-6699 **Fax:** (516)352-0754
E-mail: mic@musicindustries.com
URL: http://www.musicindustries.com
Products: Music; Accessories; Instruments. **SIC:** 5099 (Durable Goods Nec). **Est:** 1976. **Sales:** $13,000,000 (2000). **Emp:** 16. **Officers:** D. Briefel, President.

■ 25348 ■ **Music People Inc.**
PO Box 270648
West Hartford, CT 06127-0648
Phones: (860)236-7134 (860)236-7076
Free: (800)289-8889 **Fax:** (860)233-6888
Products: Speaker systems, microphones, home type electronic kits, and commercial sound equipment, including public address systems. **SIC:** 5065 (Electronic Parts & Equipment Nec). **Est:** 1980. **Sales:** $400,000 (1999). **Emp:** 17. **Officers:** James Hennessey, President.

■ 25349 ■ **Music Sales International**
7466 James Dr.
Middleburg Heights, OH 44130
Phone: (440)243-5115 **Fax:** (440)243-9249
Products: Music and musical merchandise. **SIC:** 5099 (Durable Goods Nec).

■ 25350 ■ **Muzak**
383 E Grand Ave.
South San Francisco, CA 94080-1913
Phone: (650)871-1900 **Fax:** (650)873-6213
Products: Business music; Sound systems. **SIC:** 5065 (Electronic Parts & Equipment Nec). **Est:** 1942. **Emp:** 49. **Officers:** Jay Johnson.

■ 25351 ■ **Muzak**
100 Sebethe Dr.
Cromwell, CT 06416-1032
Phone: (860)635-3236
Free: (800)842-0060 **Fax:** (860)635-5354
Products: Sound equipment. **SIC:** 5065 (Electronic Parts & Equipment Nec). **Officers:** Kenneth Lareau, Vice President.

■ 25352 ■ **Nakamichi America Corp.**
955 Francisco St.
Torrance, CA 90502-1202
Phone: (310)538-8150
Free: (800)421-2313 **Fax:** (310)324-7614
Products: Stereo equipment, including cassette and compact disc players. **SIC:** 5064 (Electrical Appliances—Television & Radio). **Est:** 1973. **Sales:** $17,000,000 (2000). **Emp:** 35. **Officers:** Tsuneo Kobayashi, President; Derek Davis, VP of Operations; Jim Murdock, Dir. of Sales.

■ 25353 ■ **National Audio Company Inc.**
PO Box 3657
Springfield, MO 65808
Phone: (417)863-1925 **Fax:** (417)863-7825
E-mail: nac@dialnet.net
Products: Audio and video cassettes; Analog and digital products. **SIC:** 5099 (Durable Goods Nec). **Est:** 1969. **Emp:** 36. **Officers:** Steven L. Stepp, President; V.P. Stepp, Vice President; Maxine Bass, Sec. & Treas.

■ 25354 ■ **National Electronic Service Co.**
6904-06 4th St. NW
Washington, DC 20012
Phone: (202)882-2216 **Fax:** (202)882-2218
Products: Small electrical appliances; Television sets; Radios. **SIC:** 5064 (Electrical Appliances—Television & Radio). **Officers:** Martin Charles, President.

■ 25355 ■ **National Wholesale**
1404 Rome Rd.
Baltimore, MD 21227
Phone: (410)242-8313 **Fax:** (410)536-0776
Products: Musical instruments. **SIC:** 5099 (Durable Goods Nec).

■ 25356 ■ **New Resource Inc.**
106 Longwinter Dr.
Norwell, MA 02061
Phone: (617)871-2020
Free: (800)872-4434 **Fax:** (617)871-9905
Products: Home theater equipment. **SIC:** 5064 (Electrical Appliances—Television & Radio). **Est:** 1986. **Sales:** $7,000,000 (2000). **Emp:** 7. **Officers:** Marston Duffy, President; Chet Flynn, e-mail: chet@newresource.com.

■ 25357 ■ **NewSound, LLC**
81 Demerritt Place
Waterbury, VT 05676
Phone: (802)244-7858 **Fax:** (802)244-1808
E-mail: sales@newsoundmusic.com
Products: Compact discs; Audio and video cassettes. **SIC:** 5099 (Durable Goods Nec). **Est:** 1998. **Emp:** 14. **Officers:** Scott Berry, e-mail: scott@newsoundmusic.com; Laurel Cram, Sales/Marketing Contact, e-mail: Laurel@newsoundmusic.com.

■ 25358 ■ **N.H.F. Musical Merchandise Corp.**
9244 Commerce Hwy.
Pennsauken, NJ 08110
Phone: (609)663-8900 **Fax:** (609)663-0436
Products: Musical instruments. **SIC:** 5099 (Durable Goods Nec).

■ 25359 ■ **NKK Electronics America Inc.**
450 Park Ave.
New York, NY 10022-2605
Products: Auto optical disc changer. **SIC:** 5065 (Electronic Parts & Equipment Nec). **Sales:** $2,000,000 (2000). **Emp:** 8. **Officers:** Yasuaki Katoh, President.

■ 25360 ■ **Noble Distributors Inc.**
251 E University Dr.
Phoenix, AZ 85004
Phone: (602)495-1852
Free: (800)495-6625 **Fax:** (602)495-9928
E-mail: nobledist@cs.com
Products: Consumer electronics, including televisions and VCRS, audio and satellite systems; Appliances, including refrigerators, Cooling products, dishwashers, microwave ovens, and range hoods. **SIC:** 5064 (Electrical Appliances—Television & Radio). **Est:** 1964. **Sales:** $8,000,000 (2000). **Emp:** 12. **Officers:** Les Poulson, President; Denise Simenson, CFO.

■ 25361 ■ **North Pacific Supply Co. Inc.**
16250 SE Evelyn St.
Clackamas, OR 97015-9515
Phone: (503)656-2940 **Fax:** (503)655-7602
URL: http://www.northpacificsupply.com
Products: Electrical appliances, including television sets and radios. **SIC:** 5064 (Electrical Appliances—Television & Radio). **Est:** 1953. **Emp:** 95. **Officers:** Mike Capri, President; Mike Capri, Sales/Marketing Contact; Louann Boyd, Human Resources Contact.

■ 25362 ■ **The Northeast Group, Inc.**
PO Box 127
Westwood, MA 02090-0127
Phone: (781)461-0880 **Fax:** (781)326-4040
URL: http://www.northeastgroup.com
Products: Small electrical appliances and household items. **SIC:** 5064 (Electrical Appliances—Television & Radio). **Est:** 1973. **Sales:** $30,000,000 (2000). **Emp:** 12. **Officers:** Friedman David, President, e-mail: david@northeastgroup.com.

■ 25363 ■ **Northern Plains Distributing**
PO Box 1921
Fargo, ND 58107-1921
Phone: (701)293-6868
Free: (800)755-7508 **Fax:** (701)293-7242
E-mail: npo@uswest.net
Products: Household appliances, including televisions and radios. **SIC:** 5064 (Electrical Appliances—Television & Radio). **Est:** 1973. **Emp:** 16. **Officers:** John Magnotto, CEO.

■ 25364 ■ **Northern Video Systems Inc.**
4465 Granite Dr., Ste. 700
Rocklin, CA 95677
Phone: (916)630-4700 **Fax:** (916)630-4800
Products: Video equipment. **SIC:** 5064 (Electrical Appliances—Television & Radio). **Sales:** $35,000,000 (2000). **Emp:** 50. **Officers:** Mark Haney, President; Paul Haney, CEO.

■ 25365 ■ **Northwest Wholesale**
910 Automation Way
Medford, OR 97504
Phone: (541)779-4313 **Fax:** (541)772-3106
Products: Musical instruments; Musical equipment. **SIC:** 5099 (Durable Goods Nec).

■ 25366 ■ **NYC Liquidators Inc.**
158 W 27th St.
New York, NY 10001-6216
Phone: (212)675-7400
Free: (888)248-1500 **Fax:** (212)243-7870
Products: Videos; CDs; Magazines; Games. **SIC:** 5099 (Durable Goods Nec).

■ 25367 ■ **O'Connor Distributing Company Inc.**
9030 Directors Row
Dallas, TX 75247
Phone: (214)631-0151 **Fax:** (214)631-0154
Products: Entertainment equipment, including video games, pinball games, pool tables, and juke boxes. **SIC:** 5099 (Durable Goods Nec). **Est:** 1958. **Sales:** $1,000,000 (2000). **Emp:** 4. **Officers:** William O'Connor Sr., President & Treasurer; Robert P. O'Connor, VP & Secty.

■ 25368 ■ **One Valley Bank of Huntington**
PO Box 7938
Huntington, WV 25779
Phone: (304)522-8281
Products: Electrical appliances, including televisions and radios. **SIC:** 5064 (Electrical Appliances—Television & Radio). **Officers:** James Call, President.

■ 25369 ■ **Onkyo USA Corp.**
200 Williams Dr.
Ramsey, NJ 07446
Phone: (201)825-7950
Products: Stereos. **SIC:** 5064 (Electrical Appliances—Television & Radio). **Sales:** $19,000,000 (2000). **Emp:** 40. **Officers:** K. Fujuioka, President; O. Koji, Treasurer.

■ 25370 ■ **Options International Inc.**
913 18th Ave. S
Nashville, TN 37212
Phone: (615)327-8090 **Fax:** (615)327-1326
Products: Film and telecine equipment. **SICs:** 5043 (Photographic Equipment & Supplies); 5064 (Electrical Appliances—Television & Radio). **Sales:** $1,500,000 (2000). **Emp:** 10. **Officers:** Donna Reid, Owner.

■ 25371 ■ **Original Marketing Concepts Ltd.**
6955 Washington Ave. S
Minneapolis, MN 55439-1506
Phone: (612)941-2530 **Fax:** (612)941-6566
Products: Electrical appliances, including televisions, radios, and video cassette recorders. **SIC:** 5064 (Electrical Appliances—Television & Radio). **Officers:** John Mc Neill, President.

■ 25372 ■ **Owens Electric Supply Inc.**
PO Box 3427
Wilmington, NC 28406
Phone: (910)791-6058 **Fax:** (910)395-1376
Products: Electronic parts and equipment. **SICs:** 5064 (Electrical Appliances—Television & Radio); 5065 (Electronic Parts & Equipment Nec). **Est:** 1969. **Sales:** $5,000,000 (2000). **Emp:** 12. **Officers:** John F. Owens Jr., President; Gregg Martin, Sales Mgr.; Grant Johnson, Customer Service Contact.

■ 25373 ■ **Pacific Coast One-Stop**
45 W Easy St.
Simi Valley, CA 93065-1601
Phone: (818)709-3640
Products: Prerecorded audio tapes and discs. **SIC:** 5099 (Durable Goods Nec). **Sales:** $38,000,000 (1994). **Emp:** 75. **Officers:** Steven Kall, President.

■ 25374 ■ **Packtronics Inc.**
7200 Huron River Dr.
Dexter, MI 48130-1099
Phone: (734)426-4646 **Fax:** (734)426-3780
Products: Video equipment; Photographic chemicals. **SIC:** 5043 (Photographic Equipment & Supplies). **Officers:** Alan Fischer, President.

■ 25375 ■ **Paragon Music Center Inc.**
2119 W Hillsborough Ave.
Tampa, FL 33603-1050
Phone: (813)876-3459 **Fax:** (813)876-0972
Products: Musical equipment and instruments. **SIC:** 5099 (Durable Goods Nec). **Sales:** $10,000,000 (2000). **Emp:** 49. **Officers:** Dick Rumore.

■ 25376 ■ **Pearl Corp.**
PO Box 1111240
Nashville, TN 37211
Phone: (615)833-4477 **Fax:** (615)833-6242
Products: Musical instruments; Drums. **SIC:** 5099 (Durable Goods Nec). **Emp:** 45.

■ 25377 ■ **Penton Overseas Inc.**
2470 Impala Dr.
Carlsbad, CA 92008-7226
Phone: (760)431-0060
Free: (800)748-5804 **Fax:** (760)431-8110
E-mail: info@pentonoverseas.com
URL: http://www.pentonoverseas.com
Products: Foreign language instruction and general interest audio cassettes; Children's books and toys. **SIC:** 5099 (Durable Goods Nec). **Est:** 1986. **Sales:** $2,500,000 (2000). **Emp:** 20. **Officers:** Hugh V. Penton, President; Robert Marcus, Controller.

■ 25378 ■ **Performance-Plus Distributing**
10651 E Bethany Dr., Ste. 100
Aurora, CO 80014
Phone: (303)671-8900 **Fax:** (303)745-1094
E-mail: mail@perfplusmktg.com
URL: http://www.perfplusmktg.com
Products: Audio and video electronics. **SIC:** 5064 (Electrical Appliances—Television & Radio). **Est:** 1995. **Emp:** 3. **Officers:** Michael Levy, President, e-mail: mlevy@perfplusmktg.com.

■ 25379 ■ **George R. Peters Associates**
PO Box 850
Troy, MI 48099-0850
Phone: (248)524-2211 **Fax:** (248)524-1758
Products: Electronic musical instruments. **SIC:** 5065 (Electronic Parts & Equipment Nec). **Officers:** George Peters, Chairman of the Board.

■ 25380 ■ **Petillo Masterpiece Guitars**
1206 Herbert Ave.
Ocean, NJ 07712
Phones: (732)531-6338 (732)531-6808
Fax: (732)531-3045
E-mail: philluinc@aol.com
URL: http://www.petilloguitars.com
Products: Stringed instruments, including custom and handmade guitars; Acoustic sensors; Strings, polishes, and guitar related products. **SIC:** 5099 (Durable Goods Nec). **Est:** 1966. **Sales:** $250,000 (2000). **Emp:** 4. **Officers:** Phillip Petillo, Luthier-Engineer, Ph.D.; Lucille Petillo, President.

■ 25381 ■ **Phi Technologies Inc.**
4605 N Stiles St.
Oklahoma City, OK 73105
Phone: (405)521-9000 **Fax:** (405)524-4254
E-mail: sales@phi-tech.com
URL: http://www.phi-tech.com
Products: Analog and digital recording systems. **SIC:** 5064 (Electrical Appliances—Television & Radio). **Officers:** William D. Seaman, President.

■ 25382 ■ **Pioneer Laser Optical Products Div.**
600 E Crescent Ave.
Upper Saddle River, NJ 07458
Phone: (201)327-6400
Products: Laser discs; Karaoke machines. **SICs:** 5065 (Electronic Parts & Equipment Nec); 5099 (Durable Goods Nec).

■ 25383 ■ **Pioneer North America Inc.**
2265 E 220th St.
Long Beach, CA 90810
Phone: (310)835-6177
Products: Audio and video equipment. **SIC:** 5064 (Electrical Appliances—Television & Radio). **Sales:** $222,000,000 (2000). **Emp:** 2,000. **Officers:** Kazunori Yamamoto, President.

■ 25384 ■ **Piraeus International**
3909 Eastern Ave.
Baltimore, MD 21224-4224
Phone: (410)675-4696
Free: (800)296-4696 **Fax:** (410)675-7127
Products: Electrical appliances. **SIC:** 5064 (Electrical Appliances—Television & Radio). **Officers:** Nickolas Bouloubassis, President; Maria Gialamas, Sales/Marketing Contact, e-mail: sales@piraeusintl.com; John DiMarino, Customer Service Contact, e-mail: john@piraeusintl.com; Mike Bouloubassis, Human Resource Contact, e-mail: mike@piraeusintl.com.

■ 25385 ■ Platinum Entertainment Inc.
2001 Butterfield Rd., Ste. 1400
Downers Grove, IL 60515
Phone: (630)769-0033 **Fax:** (630)769-0049
Products: Recorded music in a variety of formats. **SIC:** 5099 (Durable Goods Nec). **Sales:** $42,600,000 (2000). **Emp:** 132. **Officers:** Steven Devick, CEO, President & Chairman of the Board; Douglas C. Laux, CFO.

■ 25386 ■ J.B. Player International
PO Box 30819
Charleston, SC 29417
Phone: (803)763-0220
Free: (800)333-9094 **Fax:** (803)763-9096
Products: Musical instruments. **SIC:** 5099 (Durable Goods Nec). **Emp:** 50. **Officers:** Eddie Toporek, President; Tom Malm, Marketing Mgr.; Don Rhodes, Sales Mgr.

■ 25387 ■ Player Piano Company Inc.
704 E Douglas
Wichita, KS 67202
Phone: (316)263-1714 **Fax:** (316)263-5480
Products: Musical instruments; Restoration supplies for player pianos. **SIC:** 5099 (Durable Goods Nec). **Est:** 1951. **Sales:** $700,000 (2000). **Emp:** 6. **Officers:** Durrell Armstrong, President.

■ 25388 ■ Premiere AVD Corp.
274 Jamie Ln.
Wauconda, IL 60084
Phone: (847)526-1800 **Fax:** (847)526-1828
Products: Recording cassettes; Tapes audio and video recording. **SIC:** 5099 (Durable Goods Nec). **Emp:** 49. **Officers:** George Ricci.

■ 25389 ■ Pro-Mark Corp.
10707 Craighead Dr.
Houston, TX 77025
Phones: (713)666-2525 800-822-1492
Free: (800)822-1492 **Fax:** (713)669-8000
E-mail: info@promark-stix.com
URL: http://www.promark-stix.com
Products: Percussion accessories, including drumsticks. **SIC:** 5099 (Durable Goods Nec). **Est:** 1957. **Emp:** 34. **Officers:** Maury L. Brochstein, President.

■ 25390 ■ Professional Media Service Corp.
19122 S Vermont Ave.
Gardena, CA 90248
Phone: (310)532-9024 **Fax:** (310)532-0131
Products: Video cassettes; Compact discs. **SIC:** 5065 (Electronic Parts & Equipment Nec). **Est:** 1982. **Sales:** $23,000,000 (2000). **Emp:** 40. **Officers:** Peter Jacobs, President; Jeanne Nicodemus, VP & Controller.

■ 25391 ■ Projexions Video Supply
1333 Logan Circle
Atlanta, GA 30318
Phone: (404)872-6247 **Fax:** (404)350-8310
Products: Videos. **SIC:** 5099 (Durable Goods Nec). **Emp:** 49.

■ 25392 ■ Proton Corp.
13855 Struikman Rd.
Cerritos, CA 90703
Phone: (562)404-2222 **Fax:** (562)404-2322
Products: Radios and televisions. **SICs:** 5064 (Electrical Appliances—Television & Radio); 5065 (Electronic Parts & Equipment Nec). **Est:** 1981. **Sales:** $20,000,000 (2000). **Emp:** 25. **Officers:** Frankie Hong, CEO; Michael Chen, President; William Tovatt, Dir. of Marketing & Sales.

■ 25393 ■ Puget Sound Audio
5105 N 46th
Tacoma, WA 98407
Phone: (253)759-4701 **Fax:** (253)759-1418
Products: Professional audio equipment. **SIC:** 5064 (Electrical Appliances—Television & Radio).

■ 25394 ■ Puget Sound Instrument Co. Inc.
4611 11th Ave. NW
Seattle, WA 98107-4613
Phone: (206)789-1198 **Fax:** (206)789-7391
Products: Mobile radios. **SIC:** 5064 (Electrical Appliances—Television & Radio). **Officers:** Ann Hart, Treasurer.

■ 25395 ■ QCA Inc.
2832 Spring Grove Ave.
Cincinnati, OH 45225
Phone: (513)681-8400
Free: (800)859-8401 **Fax:** (513)681-3777
E-mail: info@go-QCA.com
URL: http://www.go-QCA.com
Products: Phonograph records, tapes, and compact discs. **SIC:** 5099 (Durable Goods Nec). **Est:** 1950. **Emp:** 11.

■ 25396 ■ QMI Inc.
4133 Pioneer Dr.
Walled Lake, MI 48390
Phone: (248)855-3466 **Fax:** (248)360-3778
Products: Electrical appliances, including televisions and radios; Electrical entertainment equipment. **SIC:** 5064 (Electrical Appliances—Television & Radio). **Officers:** Jeffrey Trauben, President.

■ 25397 ■ QSound Ltd.
875 Stanton Rd.
Burlingame, CA 94010-1403
Phone: (213)876-6137
Products: Three-dimensional sound recording systems for studios. **SIC:** 5065 (Electronic Parts & Equipment Nec). **Sales:** $1,000,000 (1993). **Emp:** 4. **Officers:** David Gallagher, President; Gordon Kitsul, Controller.

■ 25398 ■ Qualiton Imports Ltd.
24-02 40th Ave.
Long Island City, NY 11101
Phone: (718)937-8515
Products: Compact discs; DVD's; Videos. **SIC:** 5065 (Electronic Parts & Equipment Nec). **Est:** 1963. **Sales:** $8,000,000 (2000). **Emp:** 30. **Officers:** Anita Quittner, Vice President; Otto Quittner, CEO & President; Ron Mannarino, VP of Classical; Matilda Lukacs, Dir of Human Resources.

■ 25399 ■ Quality Sound Enterprise Inc.
833 Bragg Blvd.
Fayetteville, NC 28301-4507
Phone: (910)483-1212 **Fax:** (910)483-4083
E-mail: mnlynch@ibm.net
URL: http://www.qualitysoundinc.com
Products: Audio equipment, including professional and automobile sound systems. **SIC:** 5064 (Electrical Appliances—Television & Radio). **Est:** 1966. **Sales:** $2,500,000 (1999). **Emp:** 42. **Officers:** Mark Lynch, President.

■ 25400 ■ R & R CB Distributors Inc.
245 Fletcher Ave.
Waterloo, IA 50701-2304
Phone: (319)232-6282 **Fax:** (319)234-5951
Products: Electrical appliances and entertainment equipment, including television sets, radios, and motor vehicle radios. **SIC:** 5064 (Electrical Appliances—Television & Radio). **Officers:** La Droste, President.

■ 25401 ■ Radio City Automotive
65 Main St.
Lewiston, ME 04240
Phone: (207)782-1705 **Fax:** (207)782-2085
Products: Electronic systems for automobiles, including stereos, CB radios, scanners, radar detectors, alarms, cruise control, and remote car starters. **SICs:** 5064 (Electrical Appliances—Television & Radio); 5063 (Electrical Apparatus & Equipment). **Est:** 1951. **Officers:** Stephen Sylvester, President.

■ 25402 ■ Radio City Inc.
65 Main St.
Lewiston, ME 04240-7738
Phone: (207)782-1705 **Fax:** (207)782-2085
Products: Electrical appliances and entertainment equipment, including television sets and radios. **SIC:** 5064 (Electrical Appliances—Television & Radio). **Officers:** Stephen Sylvester, President.

■ 25403 ■ Radio Communications Co.
PO Box 68
Cary, NC 27512-1328
Phone: (919)467-2421 **Fax:** (919)467-6548
Products: Electronic entertainment devices, including television sets and radios. **SIC:** 5064 (Electrical Appliances—Television & Radio). **Officers:** L. Floyd, President.

■ 25404 ■ Rae Mel Sales Inc.
661 Akoakoa St.
Kailua, HI 96734
Phone: (808)682-4466 **Fax:** (808)261-3851
Products: Electrical appliances; Electrical entertainment equipment; High fidelity equipment. **SIC:** 5064 (Electrical Appliances—Television & Radio). **Officers:** Alan Stock, President.

■ 25405 ■ Rashid Sales Co.
191 Atlantic Ave.
Brooklyn, NY 11201
Phone: (718)852-3295
Free: (800)843-9401 **Fax:** (718)643-9522
URL: http://www.rashid.com
Products: Arabic music. **SIC:** 5099 (Durable Goods Nec). **Est:** 1934. **Sales:** $600,000 (2000). **Emp:** 7. **Officers:** Stanley K. Rashid, President, e-mail: rashid@rashid.com.

■ 25406 ■ Raub Radio and Television Co.
5909 Carrollton Ave.
Indianapolis, IN 46220
Phone: (317)251-1595
Products: Electronic goods, including radios, televisions, VCRs, and stereos. **SIC:** 5064 (Electrical Appliances—Television & Radio). **Est:** 1949. **Sales:** $2,000,000 (2000). **Emp:** 12. **Officers:** Richard D. Raub, Owner; Rory Raub, Dir. of Marketing.

■ 25407 ■ Rayco Car Electronics Inc.
160 Boston Tpke.
Shrewsbury, MA 01545-3601
Phone: (508)757-8388 **Fax:** (508)756-0088
Products: Electrical appliances and entertainment devices, including television sets and radios; Motor vehicle radios. **SIC:** 5064 (Electrical Appliances—Television & Radio). **Officers:** Ronald Zenaro, President.

■ 25408 ■ RCI Custom Products
5615 Fishers Ln.
Rockville, MD 20852-5200
Phone: (301)984-2202
Free: (800)546-4724 **Fax:** (301)984-9473
URL: http://www.rcicusto m.com
Products: Custom wall plates and panels. **SIC:** 5064 (Electrical Appliances—Television & Radio). **Est:** 1972. **Emp:** 70. **Officers:** Doug Macuch, Contact; Nancy Cox, Sales/Marketing Contact, e-mail: nancyc@rcicustom.com. **Former Name:** RCI Systems Inc.

■ 25409 ■ Re-Mark Co.
2444 Cavell Ave. S
Minneapolis, MN 55426-2318
Phone: (612)545-7744
Products: Audio accessories. **SIC:** 5064 (Electrical Appliances—Television & Radio). **Officers:** Jerry Goldstein, Owner.

■ 25410 ■ Paul A. Real Sales
1507 Mission St.
South Pasadena, CA 91030
Phone: 800-722-0558 **Fax:** (626)441-6686
Products: Musical instruments. **SIC:** 5099 (Durable Goods Nec). **Est:** 1984. **Emp:** 10. **Officers:** Paul A. Real, Owner.

■ 25411 ■ Record Technology Inc.
486 S Dawson Dr., No. 45
Camarillo, CA 93012-8049
Phone: (805)484-2747 **Fax:** (805)987-0508
Products: Phonograph records, compact discs, and audio tapes. **SICs:** 5099 (Durable Goods Nec); 5065 (Electronic Parts & Equipment Nec). **Est:** 1972. **Sales:** $4,500,000 (2000). **Emp:** 43. **Officers:** Reid MacInnis; Donald A. MacInnis, Sales Contact; Linda Ferguson, Customer Service Contact. **Alternate Name:** AcousTech Mastering. **Also Known by This Acronym:** RTI.

■ **25412** ■ **Recreational Sports and Imports Inc.**
PO Box 1587
Idaho Falls, ID 83403
Phone: (208)523-5721 **Fax:** (208)523-0207
Products: Satellite television equipment. **SIC:** 5064 (Electrical Appliances—Television & Radio). **Sales:** $31,900,000 (2000). **Emp:** 65. **Officers:** Gary Olsen, President.

■ **25413** ■ **RED Distribution**
79 5th Ave., 15th Fl.
New York, NY 10003-3034
Phone: (718)740-5700
Products: Music products. **SIC:** 5099 (Durable Goods Nec). **Sales:** $110,000,000 (1994). **Emp:** 101. **Officers:** Sal Licata, President; Mitch Wolk, Finance Officer.

■ **25414** ■ **Phil Reddish Supply**
11725 Royalton Rd.
North Royalton, OH 44133
Phone: (440)582-4333 **Fax:** (440)582-2320
Products: Commercial audio electronics products. **SIC:** 5064 (Electrical Appliances—Television & Radio).

■ **25415** ■ **Reeves Audio Visual Systems Inc.**
227 E 45th St., 15th Fl
New York, NY 10017
Phone: (212)573-8652
Free: (800)507-7662 **Fax:** (212)986-3591
E-mail: info@reevesav.com
URL: http://www.reevesav.com
Products: Video and electronic equipment, including non-linear video editing systems, broadcast and industrial video equipment, video test equipment, switchers, DVD authoring units/players, and gas plasma monitors. **SICs:** 5065 (Electronic Parts & Equipment Nec); 5045 (Computers, Peripherals & Software). **Est:** 1973. **Sales:** $12,000,000 (2000). **Emp:** 16. **Officers:** Joan V. Silver, CEO & President; Ely Laba, Treasurer & Secty.; Erik Thielking, VP of Broadcast System Sales; Erik Thielking, VP of Broadcast System Sales.

■ **25416** ■ **Renkus-Heinz Inc.**
17191 Armstrong Ave.
Irvine, CA 92614
Phone: (949)250-0166 **Fax:** (949)250-1035
Products: Audio speakers. **SIC:** 5064 (Electrical Appliances—Television & Radio). **Emp:** 49. **Officers:** Harro K. Heinz.

■ **25417** ■ **Rhapsody Film Inc.**
30 Charlton St.
New York, NY 10014
Phone: (212)243-0152 **Fax:** (212)645-9250
Products: Videos; Music, including jazz, blues, and world music. **SIC:** 5065 (Electronic Parts & Equipment Nec). **Est:** 1982. **Emp:** 3. **Officers:** Bruce Ricker, President.

■ **25418** ■ **Rickwood Radio Service of Tennessee**
1830 Air Lane Dr.
Nashville, TN 37210-3817
Phone: (615)889-3270
Free: (800)423-4142 **Fax:** (615)391-3842
Products: Electrical appliances and entertainment equipment, including television sets and radios. **SIC:** 5064 (Electrical Appliances—Television & Radio). **Officers:** Raymond Vitelli, President.

■ **25419** ■ **River Park, Inc.**
21953 Protecta Dr.
Elkhart, IN 46516
Phone: (219)295-8780
Free: (800)442-7717 **Fax:** (219)295-8780
Products: Mobile electronics. **SIC:** 5065 (Electronic Parts & Equipment Nec). **Est:** 1981. **Sales:** $17,000,000 (2000). **Emp:** 22. **Officers:** Lou Hansell, President & CEO.

■ **25420** ■ **Roland Corporation U.S.**
7200 Dominion Cir.
Los Angeles, CA 90040
Phone: (213)685-5141
Products: Keyboards for musical instruments. **SIC:** 5099 (Durable Goods Nec). **Est:** 1971. **Sales:**

$150,000,000 (2000). **Emp:** 150. **Officers:** Dennis Houlihan, President; Mark Malbon, VP & CFO; Nancy Kewin, Dir. of Marketing & Sales; Anna Foden, Dir of Personnel.

■ **25421** ■ **Roma Enterprises**
3281 Turgot Circle
Cincinnati, OH 45241
Phone: (513)769-5363 **Fax:** (513)769-5363
Products: Video cameras; Electric transformers; Televisions and video cassette recorders. **SICs:** 5064 (Electrical Appliances—Television & Radio); 5043 (Photographic Equipment & Supplies); 5063 (Electrical Apparatus & Equipment). **Officers:** Arun M. Mehta, President.

■ **25422** ■ **Royal Radio Sales & Service**
612 N Main St.
Royal Oak, MI 48067-1834
Phone: (248)548-8711 **Fax:** (248)548-4849
Products: Electrical appliances and entertainment equipment, including television sets, radios, and motor vehicle radios. **SIC:** 5064 (Electrical Appliances—Television & Radio). **Est:** 1946. **Officers:** Harry Showers, President.

■ **25423** ■ **RPC Video Inc.**
384 Route 909
Verona, PA 15147
Phone: (412)828-1414 **Fax:** (412)828-1488
E-mail: rpcvideo@stargate.net
URL: http://www.rpcvideo.com
Products: VCR's; Video disc players. **SIC:** 5064 (Electrical Appliances—Television & Radio). **Est:** 1967. **Emp:** 19. **Officers:** Sam Liptak; John Szwelnis, Sales/Marketing Contact.

■ **25424** ■ **Connor F. Ryan and Co.**
PO Box 818
Southport, CT 06490-0818
Phone: (203)259-5133 **Fax:** (203)255-0470
Products: Electrical appliances, including television sets, radios, and household appliances. **SIC:** 5064 (Electrical Appliances—Television & Radio). **Officers:** Connor Ryan, President.

■ **25425** ■ **St. Louis Music Supply Co.**
1400 Ferguson Ave.
St. Louis, MO 63133
Phone: (314)727-4512
Free: (800)727-4512 **Fax:** (314)727-8929
Products: Musical instruments and parts; Electronic musical instruments; Electric and electronic equipment. **SICs:** 5099 (Durable Goods Nec); 5065 (Electronic Parts & Equipment Nec). **Est:** 1922. **Officers:** Gene Kornblum, President; Don Collins, VP of Finance; Suzanne Wellbaum, Dir. of Advertising; Rick Becker, Sales Mgr.

■ **25426** ■ **Samsung Electronics America Inc.**
105 Challenger Rd.
Ridgefield Park, NJ 07660
Phone: (201)229-4000 **Fax:** (201)229-4029
Products: Televisions, radios, and videocassette recorders; Electronics. **SIC:** 5064 (Electrical Appliances—Television & Radio). **Sales:** $140,000,000 (2000). **Emp:** 300. **Officers:** B.K. Bae, President; J.H. Choy, CFO.

■ **25427** ■ **Sandusco Inc.**
11012 Aurora Hudson Rd.
Streetsboro, OH 44241
Phone: (330)528-0410
Free: (800)227-2424 **Fax:** (330)528-0423
E-mail: info@arrdis.com
Products: CDs and videos. **SIC:** 5099 (Durable Goods Nec). **Est:** 1956. **Sales:** $100,000,000 (2000). **Emp:** 150. **Officers:** Edwin Singer, Chairman of the Board; Harry Singer, President; Phillip Singer, VP of Marketing; Tom Becker. **Doing Business As:** Arrow Distributing Co.

■ **25428** ■ **Sandusky Distributing Co.**
11012 Aurora Hudson Rd.
Streetsboro, OH 44241-1029
Phone: (330)528-0410
Products: Records, CD's, video and audio cassette tapes. **SIC:** 5099 (Durable Goods Nec). **Sales:**

$26,000,000 (1993). **Emp:** 105. **Officers:** Edwin Z. Singer, President; Larry Harris, Controller.

■ **25429** ■ **Santa Fe Communications**
9640 Legler
Lenexa, KS 66219
Phone: (913)492-8288
Free: (800)332-6465 **Fax:** (913)894-2136
Products: Car stereos. **SIC:** 5064 (Electrical Appliances—Television & Radio).

■ **25430** ■ **Sanyo Sales and Supply (USA) Corp.**
900 N Arlington
Itasca, IL 60143-1477
Phone: (630)775-0404 **Fax:** (630)775-0055
Products: Electronic systems and equipment; Television sets; Radios. **SIC:** 5064 (Electrical Appliances—Television & Radio). **Est:** 1960. **Sales:** $5,000,000 (2000). **Emp:** 22. **Officers:** Yoshio Hattori, President.

■ **25431** ■ **John Schadler and Sons Inc.**
PO Box 1068
Clifton, NJ 07014
Phone: (973)777-3600
Free: (800)457-4266 **Fax:** (973)777-0481
E-mail: edapsco@aol.com
Products: Piano and organ parts and supplies. **SIC:** 5099 (Durable Goods Nec). **Est:** 1915. **Sales:** $4,000,000 (2000). **Emp:** 35. **Officers:** E.J. Schadler, President.

■ **25432** ■ **Schilling TV Inc.**
215 4th St.
Pittsfield, MA 01201-4810
Phone: (413)443-9235
Products: Electrical appliances and entertainment equipment, including television sets and radios; Satellites. **SIC:** 5064 (Electrical Appliances—Television & Radio). **Est:** 1952. **Officers:** Donald Nealon, President.

■ **25433** ■ **Scholl Oil & Transport Co.**
PO Box 148
Holyoke, CO 80734-0148
Phone: (970)854-3300
Free: (800)876-0281 **Fax:** (970)854-3304
E-mail: scholl@schollnet.com
Products: Radios; Radio parts and accessories. **SIC:** 5064 (Electrical Appliances—Television & Radio). **Est:** 1932. **Officers:** Arlan Scholl, President.

■ **25434** ■ **Scorpio Music Inc.**
2500 E State St.
Trenton, NJ 08619
Phone: (609)890-6000 **Fax:** (609)890-0247
E-mail: scorpiomus@aol.com
Products: Records. **SIC:** 5099 (Durable Goods Nec). **Est:** 1969. **Emp:** 45. **Officers:** Steven Parelman.

■ **25435** ■ **Seaway Importing Co.**
8800 F St.
Omaha, NE 68127-1507
Phone: (402)339-2400 **Fax:** (402)339-7239
Products: Electrical appliances, including television sets and radios. **SIC:** 5064 (Electrical Appliances—Television & Radio). **Officers:** Steven Fishman, President.

■ **25436** ■ **Segal, Alpert, McPherson & Associates**
28831 Telegraph Rd.
Southfield, MI 48034-1949
Phone: (248)258-6100 **Fax:** (248)258-5484
Products: Electrical appliances, including television sets and radios. **SIC:** 5064 (Electrical Appliances—Television & Radio). **Officers:** Maurice Alpert, President.

■ **25437** ■ **Select-O-Hits Inc.**
1981 Fletcher Creek Dr
Memphis, TN 38133
Phone: (901)388-1190
Products: Tapes, compact discs, and records. **SIC:** 5099 (Durable Goods Nec). **Est:** 1959. **Sales:** $15,000,000 (2000). **Emp:** 30. **Officers:** Sam Phillips, President.

■ 25438 ■ **Serendipity Communications, Inc.**
4703 Rose St.
Houston, TX 77007
Phone: (713)863-9900 **Fax:** (713)863-1414
Products: Educational video cassettes. **SIC:** 5099
(Durable Goods Nec). **Est:** 1985.

■ 25439 ■ **Seven Star Productions**
PO Box 17126
Long Beach, CA 90807
Phone: (562)633-1777
Products: Christian films. **SIC:** 5099 (Durable Goods
Nec).

■ 25440 ■ **Sherwood Corp. (La Mirada,
California)**
2346 E Walnut Ave.
Fullerton, CA 92831
Phone: (714)870-5100
Free: (800)962-3203 **Fax:** (714)870-6300
E-mail: sales@sherwoodusa.com
URL: http://www.sherwoodusa.com
Products: Stereo equipment. **SIC:** 5064 (Electrical
Appliances—Television & Radio). **Est:** 1980. **Sales:**
$60,000,000 (2000). **Emp:** 60. **Officers:** Juck Hur,
President; Youngbae Gu, CFO; Jeffrey Hipps Sr., VP of
Marketing; Al Kovac, VP of Sales.

■ 25441 ■ **Shiflet and Dickson Inc.**
PO Box 815
Gastonia, NC 28053-0815
Phone: (704)867-7284 **Fax:** (704)866-4742
Products: Car stereos. **SIC:** 5064 (Electrical
Appliances—Television & Radio). **Est:** 1955. **Sales:**
$9,000,000 (2000). **Emp:** 25. **Officers:** B. Shiflet,
President; W.L. Absher, VP of Finance; Susan Absher,
Dir. of Marketing.

■ 25442 ■ **Showscan Entertainment Inc.**
3939 Landmark St.
Culver City, CA 90232
Phone: (310)558-0150
Products: Motion simulation equipment. **SIC:** 5043
(Photographic Equipment & Supplies). **Sales:**
$10,400,000 (2000). **Emp:** 29. **Officers:** Kurt C. Hall,
CEO & President; Gregory W. Betz, VP of Finance.

■ 25443 ■ **Siemens Audio Inc.**
450 Lexington Ave.
New York, NY 10017
Phone: (212)949-2324 **Fax:** (212)450-7339
Products: Professional audio equipment. **SIC:** 5049
(Professional Equipment Nec). **Sales:** $2,000,000
(1994). **Emp:** 29. **Officers:** Frank Massam, President.

■ 25444 ■ **Singer Sewing Inc.**
304 Park Ave. S, 11th Fl.
New York, NY 10010-5339
Phone: (212)632-6700
Products: Audiovisual equipment. **SIC:** 5064
(Electrical Appliances—Television & Radio).

■ 25445 ■ **Bernie Smith Associates**
7122 Ambassador Rd.
Baltimore, MD 21244-2715
Phone: (410)298-0100 **Fax:** (410)298-0138
Products: Entertainment equipment, including
television sets and radios; Electrical appliances,
including refrigerators, ranges and air conditioners.
SIC: 5064 (Electrical Appliances—Television & Radio).
Est: 1974. **Sales:** $2,000,000 (2000). **Emp:** 5.
Officers: Bernie Smith, President; Evelyn L. Smith,
Treasurer & Secty.

■ 25446 ■ **Smith Crown Co.**
1993 South 1100 East
Salt Lake City, UT 84106-2316
Phone: (801)484-5259 **Fax:** (801)466-3351
Products: Electrical appliances, including televisions
and radios. **SIC:** 5064 (Electrical Appliances—
Television & Radio). **Officers:** Maurine Smith, Owner.

■ 25447 ■ **Snyder Wholesale Tire Co.**
PO Box 2280
Wintersville, OH 43952-0280
Phone: (740)264-5543
Products: Electronics, including VCRs, televisions,
and stereos. **SIC:** 5064 (Electrical Appliances—
Television & Radio). **Sales:** $14,000,000 (2000). **Emp:**

50. **Officers:** Donald Snyder, President; Laura F.
Snyder, Vice President.

■ 25448 ■ **Sony Corp. Business and
Professional Products Group**
Sony Dr.
Park Ridge, NJ 07656
Phone: (201)930-1000
Products: Television sets; Telephones; Stereo
equipment; Video cassette recorders (VCR's). **SIC:**
5064 (Electrical Appliances—Television & Radio).

■ 25449 ■ **Sony Precision Technology
America, Inc.**
20381 Hermana Cir.
Lake Forest, CA 92630
Phone: (949)770-8400 **Fax:** (949)770-8408
E-mail: sales@sonypt.com
URL: http://www.sonypt.com
Products: Precision measuring equipmen; data
recorders. **SIC:** 5049 (Professional Equipment Nec).
Emp: 19. **Officers:** Larry Sato, President & CEO; Tak
Tanaka, CFO; Bill Holbird, VP of Sales and Marketing,
e-mail: holbird@sonypt.com; Mike Avey, Customer
Service Contact, e-mail: avey@sonypt.com; Masako
Mullen, Human Resources Contact. **Former Name:**
Sony Magnescale America Inc.

■ 25450 ■ **Sound Advice**
1180 Scenic Dr.
Shelby, NC 28150-3239
Phone: (704)482-6456 **Fax:** (704)482-8807
Products: Home theater systems; DSS; Full-view
satellite systems; Projection televisions; Mobile audio
cd systems. **SIC:** 5064 (Electrical Appliances—
Television & Radio). **Officers:** Gregory Horne, Owner.

■ 25451 ■ **Sound Around Inc.**
1600 63rd St.
Brooklyn, NY 11204
Phone: (718)236-8000 **Fax:** (718)236-2400
Products: Car stereos; Alarms. **SICs:** 5064 (Electrical
Appliances—Television & Radio); 5063 (Electrical
Apparatus & Equipment). **Est:** 1978. **Sales:**
$37,000,000 (2000). **Emp:** 150. **Officers:** Sigmund
Brach, President; Gary Wilkerson, Vice President.

■ 25452 ■ **Sound Com Corp.**
227 Depot St.
Berea, OH 44017
Phone: (440)234-2604
Products: Sound and communications equipment.
SICs: 5064 (Electrical Appliances—Television &
Radio); 5065 (Electronic Parts & Equipment Nec).

■ 25453 ■ **Sound Words Communications, Inc.**
1000 S 84th St.
Lincoln, NE 68510
Phone: (402)483-4541 **Fax:** (402)483-6716
Products: Religious materials, including literature, and
audio tapes. **SICs:** 5099 (Durable Goods Nec); 5192
(Books, Periodicals & Newspapers).

■ 25454 ■ **Sounds Write Productions, Inc.**
6685 Norman Ln.
San Diego, CA 92120
Phone: (619)697-6120
Free: (800)9SO-UND9 **Fax:** (619)697-6124
E-mail: soundswrite@aol.com
URL: http://www.soundswrite.com
Products: Tapes audio and video recording;
Phonograph records; Sheet music; Videos. **SIC:** 5099
(Durable Goods Nec). **Est:** 1988.

■ 25455 ■ **Southern Distributing**
3212 Milledgeville Rd.
Augusta, GA 30909
Phone: (706)736-5526 **Fax:** (706)737-2920
Products: Car audio electronics; CD players; Audio
electronics. **SIC:** 5064 (Electrical Appliances—
Television & Radio).

■ 25456 ■ **Southern Highland Accordions &
Dulcimers Ltd.**
1010 S 14th St.
Slaton, TX 79364
Phone: (806)828-5358 **Fax:** (806)828-5177
URL: http://www.netinstruments.com
Products: Musical instruments, including plucked and

hammered dulcimers, banjoes, fiddles, ukelelees,
accordions, tonguedrums, and organ reeds. **SIC:** 5099
(Durable Goods Nec). **Est:** 1951. **Sales:** $9,000
(2000). **Emp:** 1. **Officers:** Stinson R. Behlen, Owner &
Pres.

■ 25457 ■ **Sparkomatic Corp.**
PO Box 277
Milford, PA 18337-0277
Phone: (717)296-6444
Products: Car stereos and speakers. **SIC:** 5064
(Electrical Appliances—Television & Radio). **Est:** 1961.
Sales: $90,000,000 (2000). **Emp:** 400. **Officers:**
Edward Anchel, President & Chairman of the Board;
Ronald Dion, VP of Finance; Andrew Bergsten, Dir. of
Marketing; Brian McHugh, Dir. of Data Processing; Ann
Marie Bray, Dir of Human Resources.

■ 25458 ■ **Spaulding Company Inc.**
80-90 Hawes Way
Stoughton, MA 02072
Phone: (617)828-8090
Products: Audiovisual, microfilm, and engineering
equipment. **SIC:** 5044 (Office Equipment). **Est:** 1886.
Sales: $10,000,000 (2000). **Emp:** 125. **Officers:**
Carmen DiMatteo, President; Ray Alexander, VP &
Treasurer.

■ 25459 ■ **Specialty Marketing Inc.**
PO Box 308
Mechanicsville, VA 23111-0308
Phone: (804)746-9683
Free: (800)446-9820 **Fax:** (804)730-0027
E-mail: specbest@aol.com
URL: http://www.specialtymarketing.com
Products: Audio and video equipment and
accessories; Car stereo equipment and accessories.
SIC: 5065 (Electronic Parts & Equipment Nec). **Est:**
1950. **Emp:** 30. **Officers:** Harvey Diehr, President.

■ 25460 ■ **Spectrum**
1791 Hurstview Dr.
Hurst, TX 76054-3430
Phone: (817)280-9898 **Free:** (800)628-0088
Products: Cable television, audio/video equipment.
SICs: 5063 (Electrical Apparatus & Equipment); 5064
(Electrical Appliances—Television & Radio). **Officers:**
Doug Sherar, President.

■ 25461 ■ **Sprawls Service and Sound**
856 York St. NE
Aiken, SC 29801-4022
Phone: (803)648-5885
Products: Motor vehicle radios. **SIC:** 5064 (Electrical
Appliances—Television & Radio). **Officers:** James
Sprawls, Owner.

■ 25462 ■ **Square Deal Recordings and
Supplies**
303 Higuera
San Luis Obispo, CA 93401-1002
Phone: (805)543-3636
Free: (800)235-4114 **Fax:** (805)543-3938
E-mail: sdrc@adrc-aol.com
Products: Phonograph records; Tapes; Recording
supplies and accessories. **SIC:** 5099 (Durable Goods
Nec). **Est:** 1971. **Emp:** 7. **Officers:** Richard W. Ferris;
Ray Hanson, Vice President; F. Amos, Dir of Human
Resources. **Also Known by This Acronym:** SDRS.

■ 25463 ■ **SR Distributing**
PO Box 25957
Salt Lake City, UT 84125-0957
Phone: (801)973-4343 **Fax:** (801)973-9193
Products: Electrical appliances, including television
sets and radios; Bath tubs. **SICs:** 5064 (Electrical
Appliances—Television & Radio); 5074 (Plumbing &
Hydronic Heating Supplies). **Officers:** George Sabol,
President.

■ 25464 ■ **Standard Supply Co.**
3424 S Main St.
Salt Lake City, UT 84165
Phone: (801)486-3371
Free: (800)453-7036 **Fax:** (801)466-2362
Products: Electronic equipment, including
videocassette recorders, televisions, and microwaves.
SIC: 5065 (Electronic Parts & Equipment Nec). **Est:**

1929. **Sales:** $9,500,000 (2000). **Emp:** 44. **Officers:** C.R. Stillman, President.

■ **25465** ■ **Stelling Banjo Works Ltd.**
7258 Banjo Ln.
Afton, VA 22920
Phone: (804)295-1917
Free: (800)578-7464   **Fax:** (804)971-8309
E-mail: stelling@stellingbanjo.com
URL: http://www.stellingbanjo.com
Products: Musical instruments. **SIC:** 5099 (Durable Goods Nec). **Est:** 1974. **Sales:** $550,000 (2000). **Emp:** 6. **Officers:** Geoffrey H. Stelling, President; Sherry D. Stelling, Treasurer & Secty.

■ **25466** ■ **Steves Electronics Service**
1621 E 11th St.
Tulsa, OK 74120-4803
Phone: (918)582-0594   **Fax:** (918)582-8225
Products: Radios and other electrical entertainment devices. **SIC:** 5064 (Electrical Appliances—Television & Radio). **Officers:** Steve Wade, President.

■ **25467** ■ **Studio Film & Tape Inc.**
1215 N Highland Ave.
Hollywood, CA 90038
Phone: (213)769-0900
Free: (800)444-9330   **Fax:** (213)466-6815
URL: http://www.sftweb.com
Products: Motion picture films; Video equipment and supplies. **SIC:** 5043 (Photographic Equipment & Supplies). **Est:** 1968. **Sales:** $10,000,000 (2000). **Emp:** 49. **Officers:** Carole Dean, Owner & Pres.

■ **25468** ■ **Sugar Records**
PO Box 1181
Florissant, MO 63031
Phone: (314)837-4095
Products: Records. **SIC:** 5099 (Durable Goods Nec).

■ **25469** ■ **Superscope Technologies, Inc./Marantz Professional**
2640 White Oak Cir.
Aurora, IL 60504
Phone: (630)820-4800   **Fax:** (630)820-8103
URL: http://www.superscope-marantzpro.com
Products: Professional audio and video equipment. **SIC:** 5043 (Photographic Equipment & Supplies). **Emp:** 25. **Officers:** Fred Hackendahl, President; M. Mehdi Allister, Sales & Marketing Contact. **Former Name:** Lloyd's Electronics, Inc. **Alternate Name:** Superscope Professional Products. **Alternate Name:** Marantz Professional Products.

■ **25470** ■ **SVI Systems Inc.**
1520 W Altorfer Dr.
Peoria, IL 61615
Phone: (309)692-1023
Free: (800)255-1143   **Fax:** (309)692-1124
Products: VCR parts and supplies. **SIC:** 5065 (Electronic Parts & Equipment Nec). **Est:** 1985. **Sales:** $26,000,000 (2000). **Emp:** 210. **Officers:** Beth Salmon, President; Troy Behnke, Controller; Ty Tongate, VP of Sales; Eric Goldberg, Dir of Human Resources.

■ **25471** ■ **Target Distributing Co.**
11730 Park Lawn Dr.
Rockville, MD 20852
Phone: (301)770-9400
Free: (800)873-5528   **Fax:** (301)881-5463
E-mail: targetdist@aol.com
URL: http://www.targetd.com
Products: Electrical entertainment equipment; Telecommunications equipment and supplies; Office products; Hardware. **SICs:** 5064 (Electrical Appliances—Television & Radio); 5112 (Stationery & Office Supplies). **Est:** 1975. **Sales:** $20,000,000 (2000). **Emp:** 34. **Officers:** Richard Warsaw, President; Dave Sherman, Sales/Marketing Contact; Joey Carter, Human Resources Contact.

■ **25472** ■ **Tarheel Communications**
4611 Kimbro Rd.
Hillsborough, NC 27278-9998
Phone: (919)644-2929   **Fax:** (919)644-8678
Products: Electrical appliances, including televisions and radios. **SIC:** 5064 (Electrical Appliances—Television & Radio). **Officers:** Mark Apple, Owner.

■ **25473** ■ **Tatung Company of America Inc. Marietta Div.**
815 Allgood Rd.
Marietta, GA 30062
Phone: (404)428-9090   **Fax:** (404)428-4625
Products: Televisions; VCRs; Refrigerators; Monitors; Ceiling fans. **SICs:** 5064 (Electrical Appliances—Television & Radio); 5065 (Electronic Parts & Equipment Nec). **Est:** 1980. **Sales:** $15,000,000 (2000). **Emp:** 46. **Officers:** Joseph Chu, General Mgr.; James Chen, Dir. of Marketing.

■ **25474** ■ **TDK Electronics Corp.**
12 Harbor Park Dr.
Port Washington, NY 11050
Phone: (516)625-0100
Free: (800)835-8273   **Fax:** (516)625-0171
Products: Audio tapes, video tapes, and computer discs. **SIC:** 5065 (Electronic Parts & Equipment Nec). **Est:** 1965. **Emp:** 125. **Officers:** Ken Kihara, President; Koyo Yokoi, Exec. VP of Sales; Tim Sullivan, VP of Marketing & Sales.

■ **25475** ■ **Tele-Measurements Inc.**
145 Main Ave.
Clifton, NJ 07014
Phone: (973)473-8822
Free: (800)223-0052   **Fax:** (973)473-0521
E-mail: tmcorp@aol.com
Products: Videocassette recorders and camcorders. **SIC:** 5043 (Photographic Equipment & Supplies). **Est:** 1959. **Sales:** $10,000,000 (2000). **Emp:** 45. **Officers:** W.E. Endres, President & Treasurer; T. Mayes, CFO; D.W. Cook, VP of Marketing.

■ **25476** ■ **Telemusica Co.**
1888 Century Park E
Los Angeles, CA 90067
Phone: (310)284-6808
Products: Music videos. **SIC:** 5099 (Durable Goods Nec).

■ **25477** ■ **R.F. Thistle Co.**
PO Box 115
West Harwich, MA 02671-0115
Phone: (508)432-7133
Products: Electrical appliances, including television sets and radios; Household appliance parts. **SICs:** 5064 (Electrical Appliances—Television & Radio); 5065 (Electronic Parts & Equipment Nec). **Officers:** Ronald Thistle, Owner.

■ **25478** ■ **Thomson Productions**
PO Box 1225
Orem, UT 84059-1225
Phone: (801)226-0155   **Fax:** (801)226-0166
Products: Feature films. **SIC:** 5099 (Durable Goods Nec). **Est:** 1981. **Emp:** 4. **Officers:** Linda H. Thomson, President.

■ **25479** ■ **TIC Industries Co.**
15224 E Stafford St.
City of Industry, CA 91744-4418
Phone: (626)968-0211
Free: (800)779-6664   **Fax:** (626)968-1363
E-mail: tic@deltanet.com
URL: http://www.tic@ticindustries.com
Products: Unique exterior low voltage lighting and audio equipment; Terrace stones and omni speakers. **SIC:** 5065 (Electronic Parts & Equipment Nec). **Est:** 1979. **Sales:** $10,000,000 (2000). **Emp:** 49. **Officers:** Steven L. Robinson, VP of Operations; James Lee, President; Annie Ying, Customer Service Contact; Laura Stafford, Human Resources Contact.

■ **25480** ■ **Toner Cable Equipment, Inc.**
969 Horsham Rd.
Horsham, PA 19044
Phone: (215)675-2053
Free: (800)523-5947   **Fax:** (215)675-7543
E-mail: info@tonercable.com
URL: http://www.tonercable.com
Products: Cable television equipment. **SIC:** 5063 (Electrical Apparatus & Equipment). **Est:** 1971. **Emp:** 34. **Officers:** Robert L. Toner; B.J. Toner, Vice President; Philip Young; B.J. Toner.

■ **25481** ■ **David F. Tonnies Company Inc.**
6520 W 110th St., Ste. 104
Shawnee Mission, KS 66211
Phone: (913)491-6200   **Fax:** (913)491-6395
Products: Electrical appliances, including television sets and radios. **SIC:** 5064 (Electrical Appliances—Television & Radio). **Officers:** David Tonnies, President.

■ **25482** ■ **Transco Inc.**
PO Box 1025
Linden, NJ 07036
Phone: (908)862-0030
Free: (800)876-0039   **Fax:** (908)862-0035
E-mail: info@transcousa.com
URL: http://www.transcousa.com
Products: Audio and video tapes. **SIC:** 5065 (Electronic Parts & Equipment Nec). **Est:** 1947. **Sales:** $8,000,000 (2000). **Emp:** 20. **Officers:** F. L. Buehler, President; Robert Cosulich, VP & Treasurer.

■ **25483** ■ **Trax Distributors**
16851 Vicory Blvd., No. 11
Van Nuys, CA 91406-5560
Phone: (818)902-0619
Free: (800)344-8729   **Fax:** (818)902-2126
E-mail: trax@pacificnet.net
URL: http://www.traxdist.com
Products: Musical instruments. **SICs:** 5099 (Durable Goods Nec); 5065 (Electronic Parts & Equipment Nec). **Est:** 1986. **Sales:** $2,100,000 (2000). **Emp:** 8. **Officers:** Ernie Taylor, CEO & President; Richard Garcia, Vice President.

■ **25484** ■ **Trevose Electronics Inc.**
4033 Brownsville Rd.
Trevose, PA 19053
Phone: (215)357-1400   **Fax:** (215)355-8958
Products: Televisions; Videocassette recorders; Radios. **SIC:** 5064 (Electrical Appliances—Television & Radio). **Est:** 1949. **Sales:** $3,000,000 (2000). **Emp:** 10. **Officers:** Preston D. Funk, President; Michael J. Funk, Dir. of Marketing.

■ **25485** ■ **Tropical Music and Pro Audio**
7091 NW 51st
Miami, FL 33166
Phone: (305)594-3909   **Fax:** (305)594-0786
E-mail: sales@tropicalmusic.com
URL: http://www.tropicalmusic.com
Products: Electronic musical instruments; Musical instruments. **SIC:** 5099 (Durable Goods Nec). **Est:** 1975. **Emp:** 19. **Officers:** Oscar J. Mederos, President. **Doing Business As:** Tropical Music.

■ **25486** ■ **Troxell Communications Inc.**
4830 S 38th St.
Phoenix, AZ 85040-2998
Free: (800)578-8858   **Fax:** 800-589-5939
URL: http://www.trox.com
Products: Audio-visual equipment. **SIC:** 5064 (Electrical Appliances—Television & Radio). **Emp:** 105. **Officers:** James Troxell, President, e-mail: jim.troxell@trox.com; Jack Hazelwood, VP of Marketing & Sales, e-mail: jack.hazelwood@trox.com; Terry Hixson, Sales Mgr., e-mail: terry.hixson@trox.com; Stewart White, Sales Mgr., e-mail: stewart.white@trox.com.

■ **25487** ■ **TVC Technology Group**
130 Industrial Dr.
Chambersburg, PA 17201-0444
Phone: (717)263-8258
Free: (800)233-7600   **Fax:** (717)263-1547
URL: http://www.tvcinc.com
Products: Cable television electronics; Fiber optics; Test equipment and supplies. **SICs:** 5063 (Electrical Apparatus & Equipment); 5064 (Electrical Appliances—Television & Radio). **Officers:** Rick Anderson, VP of Sales, e-mail: randerson@tvcinc.com; Stephanie Musto, Sales/Marketing Contact, e-mail: smusto@tvcinc.com; Sherri Nitterhouse, Customer Service Contact, e-mail: snitterhou@tvcinc.com; Bob Sollenberger, Sales Rep.; Sherri Nitterhouse, Sales Rep.; Mike Harpster, Sales Rep.; John Miller, Sales Rep.; Beth McClelland, Sales Rep.; Robert DeMuth, Sales Rep.; Robin Y. Sayles, Sales Rep.; Linda Zeigler, Sales Rep.; Suzie Dinkler, Purchasing Agent; Susan Zinn, Customer Service, Sales Rep.; Mike Lyons,

Customer Service, Mktg. **Former Name:** Jerry #Conn Associates, Inc. **Former Name:** JCA Technology Group, A TVC Company.

■ 25488 ■ **Tyndale House Publishers**
351 Executive Dr.
PO Box 80
Wheaton, IL 60189
Phone: (630)668-8300
Free: (800)323-9400 **Fax:** (630)668-9092
URL: http://www.tyndale.com
Products: Religious video cassettes and audios, books, bibles, and calendars. **SIC:** 5099 (Durable Goods Nec). **Est:** 1962. **Emp:** 210. **Officers:** Julie VanderArk, Sales Office Manager, e-mail: julie_vanderark@tyndale.com.

■ 25489 ■ **Uni Distribution Co.**
10 Universal City Plz., No. 400
Universal City, CA 91608
Phone: (818)777-1000 **Fax:** (818)777-6420
Products: Videos; Radio and TV communication equipment. **SICs:** 5099 (Durable Goods Nec); 5064 (Electrical Appliances—Television & Radio). **Est:** 1959. **Sales:** $1,000,000,000 (2000). **Emp:** 1,100. **Officers:** Henry Droz, President; Timothy Bixby, VP of Finance; Bob Schnirdans, VP of Sales; Justin Yaros, General Mgr.

■ 25490 ■ **United Learning Inc.**
6633 W Howard St.
Niles, IL 60714
Phone: (847)647-0600
Free: (800)424-0362 **Fax:** (847)647-0918
Products: Educational videos and media. **SICs:** 5065 (Electronic Parts & Equipment Nec); 5192 (Books, Periodicals & Newspapers). **Sales:** $4,500,000 (2000). **Emp:** 40. **Officers:** Ronald E. Reed, President; Frank S. Marquett, CFO.

■ 25491 ■ **U.S. Recording Co.**
9120 E Hampton Dr.
Capitol Heights, MD 20743
Phone: (301)499-6700 **Fax:** (301)499-6704
Products: Professional audio and video equipment, including sound systems; Satellite systems. **SIC:** 5064 (Electrical Appliances—Television & Radio). **Sales:** $500,000 (2000). **Emp:** 5. **Officers:** Thomas C. Williams, President; Josephine Williams, CFO.

■ 25492 ■ **Universal Percussion**
2773 E Midlothian Blvd.
Struthers, OH 44471
Phone: (330)755-6423 **Fax:** (330)755-6400
Products: Percussion instruments. **SIC:** 5099 (Durable Goods Nec).

■ 25493 ■ **University Products, Inc.**
PO Box 101
PO Box 101
Holyoke, MA 01041
Phone: (413)532-3372
Free: (800)628-1912 **Fax:** (413)532-9281
E-mail: info@universityproducts.com
URL: http://www.universityproducts.com
Products: Audio-visual, television, photographic, and motion picture equipment; Library supplies, including labels and cards for card catalogs. **SICs:** 5065 (Electronic Parts & Equipment Nec); 5112 (Stationery & Office Supplies). **Est:** 1969. **Sales:** $13,000,000 (2000). **Emp:** 120.

■ 25494 ■ **USA Test, Inc.**
182 Village Rd.
Roslyn Heights, NY 11577
Phone: (516)621-0012
Free: (800)966-8378 **Fax:** (516)484-8785
E-mail: custsvc@usatest.com
URL: http://www.usatest.com
Products: Educational videocassettes for college entrance exams, college bound series, high equivalency exams, civil service exams, mathematics, writing/library skills, English language development, and teacher training series; CD-ROMs and DVDs. **SIC:** 5099 (Durable Goods Nec). **Est:** 1995. **Emp:** 7. **Officers:** Peter Lanzer, President; Mona E. Lanzer, Vice President. **Former Name:** Video Aided Instruction, Inc.

■ 25495 ■ **Valdez**
7420 Sunset Blvd.
Los Angeles, CA 90046
Phones: (213)874-9998 (213)874-9999
E-mail: valdezguitar@earthlink.net
Products: Musical instruments, including guitars; Guitar instruction books. **SICs:** 5099 (Durable Goods Nec); 5199 (Nondurable Goods Nec). **Est:** 1965. **Sales:** $175,000 (2000). **Emp:** 2. **Officers:** Arturo Valdez, Owner.

■ 25496 ■ **Valley Media Inc.**
PO Box 2057
Woodland, CA 95776
Phone: (530)661-6600 **Fax:** (530)661-5472
Products: Compact discs, video tapes, records, and cassette tapes. **SIC:** 5099 (Durable Goods Nec). **Emp:** 1,000. **Officers:** Robert Cain, President; Randy Cerf, CFO.

■ 25497 ■ **Valley Sales Company Inc.**
PO Box 53
West Springfield, MA 01090-0053
Phone: (413)732-7754 **Fax:** (413)736-1229
E-mail: vaksaco@aol.com
Products: Refrigerators; Washer and dryers; Ranges; Hoods, Cooktops; Wall ovens. **SIC:** 5064 (Electrical Appliances—Television & Radio). **Est:** 1948. **Sales:** $1,800,000 (1999). **Emp:** 8. **Officers:** Charles Durfee, Vice President; James Durfee, President.

■ 25498 ■ **VCI Home Video**
11333 E 60th Pl.
Tulsa, OK 74146
Phone: (918)254-6337
Free: (800)331-4077 **Fax:** (918)254-6117
E-mail: vci@vcihomevideo.com
URL: http://www.vcihomevideo.com
Products: Videocassettes and DVDs. **SIC:** 5099 (Durable Goods Nec). **Est:** 1976. **Officers:** Bob Blair, President; Don Blair, VP of Sales, e-mail: donblair@vcihomevideo.com; Carolyn West, Customer Service Contact. **Alternate Name:** Video Communications, Inc.

■ 25499 ■ **Veazey Suppliers Inc.**
214 Edwards Ave.
Harahan, LA 70123-4215
Phone: (504)733-5234 **Fax:** (504)733-9598
Products: Electrical appliances, including television sets, radios, and other household appliances. **SIC:** 5064 (Electrical Appliances—Television & Radio). **Officers:** Ira Veazey, President.

■ 25500 ■ **Vehicle Vibres Inc.**
528 Barses
Hyannis, MA 02601-2760
Phone: (508)775-3623
Products: Electrical entertainment equipment, including car stereos. **SIC:** 5064 (Electrical Appliances—Television & Radio). **Officers:** Alan Bernard, President.

■ 25501 ■ **Vermont Hardware Company Inc.**
180 Flynn Ave.
PO Box 4509
Burlington, VT 05406-4509
Phone: (802)864-6835
Free: (800)341-0780 **Fax:** (802)864-7029
Products: Major electronic appliances, including televisions and video cassette recorders. **SICs:** 5064 (Electrical Appliances—Television & Radio); 5074 (Plumbing & Hydronic Heating Supplies). **Est:** 1868. **Sales:** $7,000,000 (2000). **Emp:** 4. **Officers:** Manny Gurowski, President.

■ 25502 ■ **Victor's House of Music**
762 Rt. 17 N
Paramus, NJ 07652
Phone: (201)444-9800 **Fax:** (201)689-0220
E-mail: victors@bellstlantic.net
URL: http://www.americanmusical.com
Products: Sheet music; Variety instruments. **SIC:** 5099 (Durable Goods Nec). **Est:** 1955.

■ 25503 ■ **Victory International Productions**
6191 Trinette Ave.
Garden Grove, CA 92845-2744
Phone: (562)598-7208
Products: Religious movies. **SIC:** 5099 (Durable Goods Nec).

■ 25504 ■ **Video Action**
708 W 1st St.
Los Angeles, CA 90012
Phone: (213)687-8262
Free: (800)422-2241 **Fax:** (213)687-8425
E-mail: videoact@pacbell.net
Products: Videos. **SIC:** 5099 (Durable Goods Nec). **Est:** 1981. **Emp:** 4. **Officers:** Gregg S. Yokoyama, Owner.

■ 25505 ■ **Video Hi-Teck Inc.**
303 Sunnyside Blvd.
Plainview, NY 11803
Phone: (516)785-1200 **Fax:** (516)785-1200
Products: Video cassette recorders; Camcorders; Monitors. **SIC:** 5064 (Electrical Appliances—Television & Radio). **Sales:** $2,500,000 (2000). **Emp:** 10. **Officers:** Trudy Adwar, Owner; Tom Miller, Dir. of Sales.

■ 25506 ■ **Videomedia Inc.**
175 Lewis Rd., No. 23
San Jose, CA 95111
Phone: (408)227-9977
Free: (800)937-5526 **Fax:** (408)227-6707
E-mail: sales@videomedia.com
URL: http://www.videomedia.com
Products: Video editing systems; Digital disk recorders. **SIC:** 5049 (Professional Equipment Nec). **Est:** 1976. **Sales:** $13,500,000 (1999). **Emp:** 20. **Officers:** Bill Stickney; Stan Sult; Kevin Illies, Customer Service Contact, e-mail: killies@videomedia.com.

■ 25507 ■ **VideoTape Distributors Inc.**
423 W 55th St., 3rd Fl.
New York, NY 10019
Phone: (212)581-7111
Free: (800)327-3724 **Fax:** (212)581-7977
Products: Video and audio tapes; Data media storage devices. **SICs:** 5065 (Electronic Parts & Equipment Nec); 5045 (Computers, Peripherals & Software). **Sales:** $4,200,000 (2000). **Emp:** 15. **Officers:** Steve Gabrielli, VP & General Merchandising Mgr.

■ 25508 ■ **Village Electronics**
PO Box 153
Southwest Harbor, ME 04679-0153
Phone: (207)244-7227
Products: Electrical appliances, including radios; Electrical entertainment equipment. **SIC:** 5064 (Electrical Appliances—Television & Radio). **Officers:** Michael Yates, President.

■ 25509 ■ **Vision Video**
2030 Wentz Church Rd.
Box 540
Worcester, PA 19490
Phone: (610)584-1893 **Fax:** (610)584-4610
E-mail: info@visionvideo.com
URL: http://www.visionvideo.com
Products: Religious videos. **SIC:** 5099 (Durable Goods Nec). **Est:** 1981.

■ 25510 ■ **Vitali Import Company Inc.**
13020 Whittier Blvd.
PO Box 4218
Whittier, CA 90602-3045
Free: (800)325-8154 **Fax:** (562)698-2429
Products: Stringed instruments and accessories. **SIC:** 5099 (Durable Goods Nec). **Est:** 1959. **Emp:** 4.

■ 25511 ■ **VWS Inc.**
31000 Viking Pky.
Cleveland, OH 44145-1019
Phone: (216)252-3300 **Fax:** (216)252-3311
Products: Electrical appliances. **SIC:** 5064 (Electrical Appliances—Television & Radio). **Est:** 1997. **Sales:** $40,000,000 (2000). **Emp:** 100. **Officers:** Bengt Gerborg, President; Dave Mechenbier, VP of Finance.

■ **25512** ■ **Warner-Elektra-Atlantic Corp.**
111 N Hollywood Way
Burbank, CA 91505
Phone: (818)843-6311   **Fax:** (818)840-6212
Products: Music. **SIC:** 5099 (Durable Goods Nec).
Est: 1971. **Emp:** 1,200. **Officers:** David Mount, CEO;
David Hendler, Exec. VP of Finance; George Rossi,
Exec. VP of Marketing; Larry Weiss, VP of Data
Processing; Mike White, Exec. VP.

■ **25513** ■ **Warner Music Group**
75 Rockefeller Plz.
New York, NY 10019
Phone: (212)484-6653
Products: Compact discs, DVD's, tapes, and records.
SIC: 5099 (Durable Goods Nec). **Officers:** Robert A.
Daly, CEO & Chairman of the Board; Jerome N. Gold,
Exec. VP & CFO.

■ **25514** ■ **Eddie Warner's Parts Co.**
PO Box 110129
Nashville, TN 37222-0129
Phone: (615)254-1224
Free: (800)254-1224   **Fax:** (615)254-1227
Products: Small electrical appliances; Television sets;
Radios. **SIC:** 5064 (Electrical Appliances—Television &
Radio). **Officers:** Edward Warner, President.

■ **25515** ■ **Waxworks Inc.**
325 E 3rd St.
Owensboro, KY 42303
Phone: (270)926-0008
Free: (800)825-8558   **Fax:** (270)685-0563
URL: http://www.waxworksonline.com
Products: VHS, DVD, CD, audio and video
accessories; Entertainment boutique items; Blank tape
and recordable CD's; Wholesale distributor and
fulfillment company. **SIC:** 5099 (Durable Goods Nec).
Est: 1948. **Sales:** $200,000,000 (1999). **Emp:** 1,227.
Officers: Terry Woodward, e-mail: terry.woodward@
wwvw.com; Kirk Kirkpatrick, VP of Marketing, e-mail:
kirk.kirkpatrick@wwvw.com.

■ **25516** ■ **WaxWorks/VideoWorks Inc.**
325 E 3rd St.
Owensboro, KY 42301
Phone: (502)926-0008
Free: (800)825-8558   **Fax:** (502)685-0563
URL: http://www.waxworksonline.com
Products: Video tapes and audio and video
equipment. **SIC:** 5099 (Durable Goods Nec). **Est:**
1949. **Sales:** $120,300,000 (2000). **Emp:** 250.
Officers: Terry Woodward, President; Bill Young, CFO.

■ **25517** ■ **Waymire Drum Company Inc.**
9316 S Atlantic Ave.
South Gate, CA 90280
Phone: (213)566-6103   **Fax:** (213)566-8923
Products: Steel drums. **SIC:** 5085 (Industrial
Supplies). **Sales:** $11,000,000 (1993). **Emp:** 150.
Officers: Edward L. Waymire, President; Gilbert
Moreno, Controller.

■ **25518** ■ **Webbs Appliance Service Ctr.**
1519 Church St.
Nashville, TN 37203-3004
Phone: (615)329-4079
Free: (800)899-4079   **Fax:** (615)329-0666
Products: Electrical appliances, including television
sets and radios. **SIC:** 5064 (Electrical Appliances—
Television & Radio). **Officers:** Webb Weitzel,
President.

■ **25519** ■ **Weber Piano Co.**
40 Seaview Dr.
Secaucus, NJ 07094
Phone: (201)902-0920
Free: (800)346-5351   **Fax:** (201)902-9472
URL: http://www.weberpiano.com
Products: Pianos. **SIC:** 5099 (Durable Goods Nec).
Est: 1987. **Officers:** David Skidmore, National Sales
Mgr., e-mail: co253@microdsi.net.

■ **25520** ■ **Werleins for Music**
3750 Veterans Blvd.
Metairie, LA 70002
Phone: (504)883-5060   **Fax:** (504)883-5079
Products: Instruments; Records, tapes, and compact
discs; Sheet music and music accessories. **SIC:** 5099
(Durable Goods Nec). **Emp:** 30.

■ **25521** ■ **West L.A. Music**
11345 Santa Monica Blvd.
West Los Angeles, CA 90025-3151
Phone: (310)477-1945   **Fax:** (310)477-2476
E-mail: sales@westlamusic.com
URL: http://www.westlamusic.com
Products: Sheet music; Musical instruments and parts.
SIC: 5099 (Durable Goods Nec). **Est:** 1967. **Emp:** 60.
Officers: D.F. Griffin.

■ **25522** ■ **Weston Woods Studio Inc.**
265 Post Rd W
Westport, CT 06880
Phone: (203)226-3355
Free: (800)243-5020   **Fax:** (203)226-3818
E-mail: wstnwoods@aol.com
Products: Audiovisual children's literature. **SIC:** 5099
(Durable Goods Nec). **Est:** 1953. **Emp:** 12. **Officers:**
Linda Lee, Vice President.

■ **25523** ■ **White Star Video**
195 Hwy. 36
West Long Branch, NJ 07764
Phone: (732)229-2343
Free: (800)458-5887   **Fax:** (732)229-0066
E-mail: kultur@mindspring.com
URL: http://www.whitestarvideo.com
Products: Special interest videos, including comedy,
history, children's biographies, documentaries, and
motorcycle racing. **SIC:** 5099 (Durable Goods Nec).
Est: 1980. **Emp:** 17. **Officers:** Dennis M. Hedlund,
President; Pearl Lee, Vice President.

■ **25524** ■ **Wholesale House**
503 W High St.
Hicksville, OH 43526
Phone: (419)542-7739
Free: (800)722-5553   **Fax:** (419)542-6632
Products: Consumer electronic equipment, including
stereos, protable radios, and telephones. **SICs:** 5064
(Electrical Appliances—Television & Radio); 5065
(Electronic Parts & Equipment Nec). **Sales:**
$30,000,000 (1999). **Emp:** 100. **Officers:** Steve
Height, President; Mary Height, Vice President; David
Cox, Sales/Marketing Contact, e-mail: dcox@
twhouse.com; Cindy Shull, Customer Service Contact,
e-mail: order@twhouse.com; Lance Bowsher, Human
Resources Contact, e-mail: bigdog@twhouse.com.

■ **25525** ■ **Wilson Audio Sales**
5972 Asberry Ct.
Nashville, TN 37221
Phone: (615)646-4477   **Fax:** (615)662-2536
Products: Audio equipment. **SIC:** 5064 (Electrical
Appliances—Television & Radio). **Est:** 1974. **Sales:**
$1,000,000 (2000). **Emp:** 4. **Officers:** Wally Wilson,
Owner.

■ **25526** ■ **Wishing Well Video Distributing Co.**
PO Box 1008
Silver Lake, WI 53170
Phone: (414)889-8501
Free: (800)548-3824   **Fax:** (414)889-8591
E-mail: lotuslight@lotuspress.com
Products: Videos on health, wellness, and spirituality.
SIC: 5192 (Books, Periodicals & Newspapers). **Est:**
1978. **Emp:** 75. **Officers:** Theresa A. May, Dir. of Mktg.
& Sales. **Doing Business As:** Lotus Light.

■ **25527** ■ **Wolf Imports**
2700 Woodson Rd., Ste. 202
St. Louis, MO 63114-4828
Phone: (314)429-3439
Free: (800)844-9653   **Fax:** (314)429-3255
Products: Musical instruments and accessories. **SIC:**
5099 (Durable Goods Nec). **Est:** 1974. **Sales:**
$3,000,000 (2000). **Emp:** 8. **Officers:** Mark Ragin,
President.

■ **25528** ■ **Stanley Wood Products Inc.**
15248 Broadmoor
Shawnee Mission, KS 66223-3137
Phone: (913)681-2804   **Fax:** (913)681-2812
Products: Electrical appliances, including television
sets and radios. **SIC:** 5064 (Electrical Appliances—
Television & Radio). **Officers:** David Davis, President.

■ **25529** ■ **Woodson & Bozeman Inc.**
PO Box 18450
Memphis, TN 38181-0450
Phone: (901)362-1500
Free: (800)876-4243   **Fax:** (901)362-1509
Products: Television sets; Video cassette recorders
(VCR's); Radios; Air-conditioning equipment. **SIC:**
5064 (Electrical Appliances—Television & Radio).
Officers: Edwin Bozeman, Chairman of the Board.

■ **25530** ■ **Word Entertainment**
3319 W End, Ste. 200
Nashville, TN 37203
Phone: (615)385-9673   **Fax:** (615)385-9696
E-mail: contactus@wordentertainment.com
URL: http://www.wordentertainment.com
Products: Christian music and videos. **SIC:** 5099
(Durable Goods Nec). **Est:** 1950. **Sales:** $130,000,000
(2000). **Emp:** 150. **Former Name:** Word Records &
Music.

■ **25531** ■ **World Source Trading Inc.**
19 Beale St., Ste. 19A
Quincy, MA 02170-2702
Phone: (617)847-1616   **Fax:** (617)847-1646
Products: Electrical appliances and entertainment
equipment, including television sets and radios. **SIC:**
5064 (Electrical Appliances—Television & Radio).
Officers: Michael Leung, President.

■ **25532** ■ **World Wide Pictures, Inc.**
1201 Hennepin Ave.
Minneapolis, MN 55403
Phone: (612)338-3335
Free: (800)788-0442   **Fax:** (612)338-3029
E-mail: wesscott@uswest.net
URL: http://www.wwp.org
Products: Christian video/DVD movies. **SIC:** 5099
(Durable Goods Nec). **Est:** 1952. **Emp:** 40. **Officers:**
Barry Werner, Dir. of Operations; Tim Hetchler,
Sales/Marketing Contact, e-mail: wesscott@
uswest.ent; Julie Geddes, Accountant, e-mail:
jgeddes@bgea.org; Tim Morgan, Marketing
Coordinator, e-mail: tmorgan@bgea.org.

■ **25533** ■ **WRI Education**
968 Emerald St., No. 6700
PO Box 9359
San Diego, CA 92169-0359
Phone: (619)456-5278
Free: (800)972-3635   **Fax:** (619)456-7957
Products: Educational videos; Instructional guides.
SIC: 5099 (Durable Goods Nec). **Est:** 1969.

■ **25534** ■ **Yaesu U.S.A. Inc.**
17210 Edwards Rd.
Cerritos, CA 90701
Phone: (562)404-2700   **Fax:** (562)404-1210
Products: Hand held and countertop radios. **SIC:** 5064
(Electrical Appliances—Television & Radio). **Est:** 1971.
Sales: $37,000,000 (2000). **Emp:** 78. **Officers:** Jun
Hasegawa, President; Hermia Fama, CFO; Cyndi
Fischer, Dir. of Marketing & Sales.

■ **25535** ■ **Yamaha Corporation of America**
PO Box 6600
Buena Park, CA 90620
Phone: (714)522-9011
Free: (800)333-4442   **Fax:** (714)228-3913
Products: Electronic musical instruments. **SIC:** 5099
(Durable Goods Nec). **Est:** 1981. **Sales:** $500,000,000
(2000). **Emp:** 1,000. **Officers:** Noriyuki Egawa,
President; Ron Raup, Sr. VP; Chris Scharff, Information
Systems Mgr.; Don Patrick, Human Resources Mgr.

■ **25536** ■ **Yamaha Corporation of America**
Band and Orchestral Division
3445 E Paris Ave. SE
Grand Rapids, MI 49512-0899
Phone: (616)940-4900   **Fax:** (616)949-7721
Products: Orchestra and band equipment. **SIC:** 5099
(Durable Goods Nec).

■ **25537** ■ **Yamaha Electronics Corporation**
USA
6660 Orangethorpe Ave.
Buena Park, CA 90620
Phone: (714)522-9105
Products: Electronic musical instruments. **SIC:** 5065

(Electronic Parts & Equipment Nec). **Est:** 1981. **Sales:** $130,000,000 (2000). **Emp:** 80. **Officers:** Don Palmquist, President; Roger Stange, VP of Finance.

■ 25538 ■ **Yorkville Sound Inc.**
4625 Witmer Industrial Estate
Niagara Falls, NY 14305
Phone: (716)297-2920 **Fax:** (716)297-3689
E-mail: ysusa@yorkville.com

URL: http://www.yorkville.com
Products: Professional audio equipment. **SICs:** 5065 (Electronic Parts & Equipment Nec); 5099 (Durable Goods Nec). **Est:** 1965. **Emp:** 12. **Officers:** Steve Long, President; Bud Mayer, Vice President.

(54) Specialty Equipment and Products

Entries in this section are arranged alphabetically by company name. When the company name is a personal name, the company name is alphabetized by the surname unless the first name or initial(s) are part of a trade name. See the User's Guide at the front of this directory for additional information.

■ **25539** ■ **A To Z Vending Service Corp.**
109 Port Jersey Blvd.
Jersey City, NJ 07305
Phone: (201)333-4900   **Fax:** (201)333-2208
Products: Vending machines, including candy, coffee, pop, food, and water dispensers. **SIC:** 5046 (Commercial Equipment Nec).

■ **25540** ■ **ABC Display and Supply Inc.**
100 Cleveland Ave.
Freeport, NY 11520
Phone: (516)867-8400
Products: Display products for showrooms and stores. **SIC:** 5199 (Nondurable Goods Nec). **Sales:** $17,000,000 (2000). **Emp:** 200. **Officers:** Howard Schulman, President.

■ **25541** ■ **Wilbert Aberdeen Vault Inc.**
2422 S Hwy. 281
Aberdeen, SD 57401-8747
Phone: (605)225-5255   **Fax:** (605)225-7562
Products: Concrete burial vaults and boxes. **SICs:** 5087 (Service Establishment Equipment); 5199 (Nondurable Goods Nec). **Officers:** Ronald Angerhofer, President.

■ **25542** ■ **Absolute Aqua Systems**
8811 Woodman Ave., No. 3
Arleta, CA 91331
Phone: (818)891-9207   **Fax:** (818)891-9207
Products: Water filtration equipment and supplies. **SIC:** 5074 (Plumbing & Hydronic Heating Supplies).

■ **25543** ■ **AccuPro Inc.**
1011 Hwy. 22 W, Bldg. C, Box 8
Phillipsburg, NJ 08865
Phone: (908)454-5998   **Fax:** (908)454-1957
Products: Automated drafting equipment and flatbed plotters. **SIC:** 5049 (Professional Equipment Nec). **Sales:** $1,000,000 (2000). **Emp:** 3. **Officers:** Edmund Harthaus, President; Debra Weitzel, VP of Finance.

■ **25544** ■ **Accurate Water**
6601 N Navarro
Victoria, TX 77904
Phone: (512)576-1501
Free: (800)772-1501   **Fax:** (512)576-2558
Products: Water treatment equipment and supplies. **SIC:** 5074 (Plumbing & Hydronic Heating Supplies). **Est:** 1982. **Emp:** 6. **Officers:** Wilber Cleveland, Owner.

■ **25545** ■ **Action Water Treatment Service**
110 W St. Clair St.
Romeo, MI 48065
Phone: (810)752-7600   **Fax:** (810)752-2483
Products: Water conditioning units. **SIC:** 5074 (Plumbing & Hydronic Heating Supplies).

■ **25546** ■ **Addie Water Systems**
1604 Plainfield Ave.
Janesville, WI 53545
Phone: (608)755-5780
Free: (800)982-1652   **Fax:** (608)755-5780
Products: Water treatment products; Water softeners and components. **SIC:** 5074 (Plumbing & Hydronic Heating Supplies). **Est:** 1979.

■ **25547** ■ **Air & Water Purification Inc.**
300 Hwy. 55
Hamel, MN 55340
Phone: (612)478-6050   **Fax:** (612)478-9763
Products: Water conditioning equipment. **SIC:** 5074 (Plumbing & Hydronic Heating Supplies). **Officers:** Jeff Cates, Owner.

■ **25548** ■ **Alvin and Co. Inc.**
PO Box 188
Windsor, CT 06095
Phone: (860)243-8991   **Fax:** 800-777-2896
Products: Art, graphic design, and drafting supplies. **SICs:** 5049 (Professional Equipment Nec); 5199 (Nondurable Goods Nec). **Est:** 1950. **Sales:** $25,000,000 (2000). **Emp:** 200. **Officers:** A.E. Shoham, President; M.L. Shoham, Treasurer & Secty.; D. Gibbins, VP of Marketing.

■ **25549** ■ **American Compressed Steel Corp.**
PO Box 1817
Cincinnati, OH 45201
Phone: (513)948-0300   **Fax:** (513)948-1534
Products: Steel recyclers. **SIC:** 5093 (Scrap & Waste Materials). **Sales:** $16,000,000 (2000). **Emp:** 40. **Officers:** Larry Byers, President.

■ **25550** ■ **American Granby Inc.**
7645 Henry Clay Blvd.
PO Box 7000
Liverpool, NY 13088
Phone: (315)451-1100
Free: (800)278-4115   **Fax:** 800-729-3299
URL: http://www.americangranby.com
Products: Accessories for water well market, pool and spa, plumbing and heating, and irrigation. **SIC:** 5074 (Plumbing & Hydronic Heating Supplies). **Est:** 1962. **Emp:** 45. **Officers:** Joseph Brown, Mgr. of Marketing Support; Mary Lanzafame; Denise Leitgeb.

■ **25551** ■ **American Plumber**
502 Indiana Ave.
Sheboygan, WI 53081
Phone: 800-645-5428
Free: (800)882-6652   **Fax:** (920)457-6652
E-mail: customerservice@plymouthwater.com
URL: http://www.americanplumber.com
Products: Filters. **SIC:** 5074 (Plumbing & Hydronic Heating Supplies). **Est:** 1970. **Officers:** Dick Thornton, Sales/Marketing Contact, e-mail: dthornton; Shelly Johnson, Customer Service Contact. **Former Name:** AMETEK Inc.

■ **25552** ■ **Anacomp Inc.**
12365 Crosthwaite Cir.
Poway, CA 92064
Phone: (619)679-9797
Products: Micrographics supplies. **SIC:** 5049 (Professional Equipment Nec). **Sales:** $499,000,000 (2000). **Emp:** 3,400. **Officers:** Ralph W. Koehrer, CEO & President; Donald L. Viles, Exec. VP & CFO.

■ **25553** ■ **Angus Fire Armour Corp.**
1000 Junny Rd.
PO Box 879
Angier, NC 27501-8974
Phone: (919)639-6151   **Fax:** (919)639-6131
Products: Firefighting equipment. **SIC:** 5087 (Service Establishment Equipment). **Sales:** $19,000,000 (2000). **Emp:** 150. **Officers:** Robert Harcourt, President; Michael Gorman, Finance Officer.

■ **25554** ■ **Apollo Sales Group Inc.**
24 Sand Island Access Rd., No. 17
Honolulu, HI 96819-2221
Phone: (808)841-1679   **Fax:** (808)841-4190
Products: Central vacuum systems. **SIC:** 5087 (Service Establishment Equipment). **Officers:** Robert Harris, President.

■ **25555** ■ **Applied Membranes Inc.**
110 Bosstick Blvd.
San Marcos, CA 92069
Phone: (760)727-3711
Free: (800)321-9321   **Fax:** (760)727-4427
E-mail: sales@appliedmembranes.com
Products: http://www.appliedmembranes.comm.**SICs:** 5074 (Plumbing & Hydronic Heating Supplies); 5075 (Warm Air Heating & Air-Conditioning). **Officers:** Janell Cedarstrom, Dir. of Marketing.

■ **25556** ■ **Aqua Magnetics International**
915-B Harbor Lake Dr.
Safety Harbor, FL 34695
Phone: (813)447-2575
Free: (800)328-2843   **Fax:** (813)726-8888
E-mail: aquamag@msn
Products: Magnetic products for pipes. **SIC:** 5074 (Plumbing & Hydronic Heating Supplies). **Est:** 1978. **Officers:** Roland Carpenter, President; Eileen Mullen, Office Mgr.

■ **25557** ■ **Arctic Clear Products Inc.**
2130 W Wilden Ave.
Goshen, IN 46526
Phone: (219)533-7671   **Fax:** (219)533-7671
Products: Water control systems. **SIC:** 5074 (Plumbing & Hydronic Heating Supplies). **Officers:** Stephan DePue, President.

■ **25558** ■ **Arensberg Sons Inc.**
1428 10th Ave.
Seattle, WA 98122-3805
Phone: (206)323-7111
Free: (800)537-5495   **Fax:** (206)328-1533
Products: Shoe findings. **SIC:** 5087 (Service Establishment Equipment). **Officers:** Richard Arensberg, President.

■ **25559** ■ **Arnessen Corp.**
1100 Walnut St.
Roselle, NJ 07203
Phone: (908)241-3535   **Fax:** (908)353-8090
Products: Rust removal equipment. **SIC:** 5099 (Durable Goods Nec). **Est:** 1910. **Sales:** $3,000,000 (2000). **Emp:** 15. **Officers:** E.A. Arnessen, President.

■ 25560 ■ **Art Barn Enterprises**
366 Paulk Rd.
Ashford, AL 36312
Phone: (334)899-3503
Products: Paint; Brushes; Canvas; Watercolor paper.
SICs: 5199 (Nondurable Goods Nec); 5199 (Nondurable Goods Nec). **Est:** 1978. **Emp:** 6.
Officers: Latrelle B. Wartman, Owner.

■ 25561 ■ **Art Glass House, Inc.**
3445 North Hwy. 1
Cocoa, FL 32926
Phone: (407)631-4477
Free: (800)525-8009 **Fax:** (407)631-9565
Products: Stained glass materials. **SIC:** 5199 (Nondurable Goods Nec).

■ 25562 ■ **Asel Art Supply**
2701 Cedar Springs
Dallas, TX 75201-1384
Phone: (214)871-2425 **Fax:** (214)871-0007
Products: Paints; Paper; Graphic art supplies; Airbrush equipment. **SICs:** 5199 (Nondurable Goods Nec); 5084 (Industrial Machinery & Equipment); 5198 (Paints, Varnishes & Supplies). **Officers:** Bill Cicherski, Contact.

■ 25563 ■ **Frederick Atkins Inc.**
1515 Broadway
New York, NY 10036
Phone: (212)840-7000 **Fax:** (212)536-7467
Products: Nondurable goods for department stores. **SICs:** 5199 (Nondurable Goods Nec); 5023 (Homefurnishings). **Est:** 1944. **Sales:** $450,000,000 (2000). **Emp:** 225. **Officers:** Nancy Marino, President & COO; Ronald Ventricelli, CFO.

■ 25564 ■ **Atlantic Filter Corp.**
3112 45th St.
West Palm Beach, FL 33407
Phone: (561)683-0101 **Fax:** (561)684-1997
E-mail: atlfil19@mail.idt.net
Products: Commercial and industrial water treatment systems, including filters, softeners, and reverse osmosis systems. **SIC:** 5074 (Plumbing & Hydronic Heating Supplies). **Est:** 1955. **Emp:** 25. **Officers:** James W. Wakem, President.

■ 25565 ■ **Atlantic Promotions**
17 Executive Park Dr. NE, Ste. 100
Atlanta, GA 30329-2222
Phone: (404)355-0515
Free: (800)779-8357 **Fax:** (404)355-6070
URL: http://www.atlanticpromotions.com
Products: Advertising products, t-shirts, and pop. **SICs:** 5199 (Nondurable Goods Nec); 5149 (Groceries & Related Products Nec). **Est:** 1989. **Sales:** $1,900,000 (2000). **Emp:** 4. **Officers:** Travis Bond, President.

■ 25566 ■ **Atlas Water Systems Inc.**
86 Los Angeles St.
Newton, MA 02458-1019
Phone: (617)244-8550 **Fax:** (617)244-5141
Products: Water purification systems. **SIC:** 5074 (Plumbing & Hydronic Heating Supplies). **Est:** 1987. **Sales:** $2,000,000 (2000). **Emp:** 28. **Officers:** Simon O'Leary, President; Cindy N. Mealy, Controller; Norm Maruwitz, COO.

■ 25567 ■ **ATS Money Systems Inc.**
25 Rockwood Pl.
Englewood, NJ 07631
Phone: (201)894-1700 **Fax:** (201)894-0958
Products: Currency and coin counting system equipment. **SICs:** 5044 (Office Equipment); 5087 (Service Establishment Equipment). **Est:** 1979. **Sales:** $20,000,000 (2000). **Emp:** 35. **Officers:** Gerard F. Murphy, CEO; Joseph Burke, Controller; James H. Halpin, Exec. VP of Marketing & Sales.

■ 25568 ■ **R.E. Barry Pumps Inc.**
415 Atwood Ave.
Cranston, RI 02920-4358
Phone: (401)942-5300 **Fax:** (401)942-0618
Products: Service establishment equipment; Power equipment; Sprinkler systems; Well pumps; Irrigation equipment; Landscaping supplies. **SICs:** 5087 (Service Establishment Equipment); 5074 (Plumbing & Hydronic

Heating Supplies); 5099 (Durable Goods Nec); 5083 (Farm & Garden Machinery). **Est:** 1975. **Sales:** $1,250,000 (2000). **Emp:** 6. **Officers:** Robert Barry, President.

■ 25569 ■ **Larson Becker Company Inc.**
PO Box 340
Batavia, IL 60510
Phone: (630)879-1316
Free: (888)426-7867 **Fax:** (630)879-1341
Products: Water well supplies, including pumps, tanks, pipes, and fittings. **SICs:** 5084 (Industrial Machinery & Equipment); 5074 (Plumbing & Hydronic Heating Supplies). **Est:** 1945. **Sales:** $7,000,000 (2000). **Emp:** 25. **Officers:** Brett R. Larson, President; Gerald R. Miller, Treasurer; Mark R. Larson, VP & Secty.

■ 25570 ■ **Beckly Cardy Group**
100 Paragon Pky.
Mansfield, OH 44903
Phone: (419)589-2100
Free: (888)222-1332 **Fax:** (419)589-1650
URL: http://www.becklycardy.com
Products: Educational supplies, instructional materials, and teaching aids; Scool furniture. **SICs:** 5049 (Professional Equipment Nec); 5021 (Furniture). **Est:** 1907. **Officers:** Jeffrey Hewson, CEO & President; Dan Mahoney, VP of Marketing.

■ 25571 ■ **Bell Industries Graphic**
4425 Sheila
Los Angeles, CA 90023-4328
Phone: (213)268-9500 **Fax:** (213)268-2370
Products: Graphic art supplies. **SIC:** 5199 (Nondurable Goods Nec). **Sales:** $6,000,000 (2000). **Emp:** 99. **Officers:** Michael Hazen.

■ 25572 ■ **Beta Screen Corp.**
707 Commercial Ave.
Carlstadt, NJ 07072
Phone: (201)939-2400 **Fax:** (201)939-7656
Products: Graphic art supplies. **SIC:** 5043 (Photographic Equipment & Supplies). **Est:** 1968. **Sales:** $4,000,000 (2000). **Emp:** 20. **Officers:** A. Serchuk, President.

■ 25573 ■ **H. Betti Industries Inc.**
303 Paterson Plank Rd.
Carlstadt, NJ 07072
Phone: (201)438-1300
Free: (800)524-2343 **Fax:** (201)438-4925
Products: Vending machines. **SIC:** 5046 (Commercial Equipment Nec). **Est:** 1934. **Sales:** $68,000,000 (2000). **Emp:** 190. **Officers:** Joe Cirillo, President; R. Geschine, Treasurer; Robert Boals, Dir. of Marketing & Sales.

■ 25574 ■ **Black Hills Jewelers Supply**
713 Main St.
Rapid City, SD 57701-2737
Phone: (605)343-5678
Products: Commercial equipment; Lapidary equipment. **SICs:** 5085 (Industrial Supplies); 5049 (Professional Equipment Nec). **Officers:** Kenneth Kingsbury, Owner.

■ 25575 ■ **Blast-Spray Equipment Co.**
1810 Fortune Rd., Ste. G
Salt Lake City, UT 84104-3808
Phone: (801)486-0803 **Fax:** (801)486-0867
Products: Sand-blasting equipment and media; Painting equipment. **SICs:** 5084 (Industrial Machinery & Equipment); 5198 (Paints, Varnishes & Supplies).

■ 25576 ■ **Dick Blick Co.**
PO Box 1267
Galesburg, IL 61401
Phone: (309)343-6181
Free: (800)447-8192 **Fax:** (309)343-5785
Products: Art and school supplies; Lawn supplies; Paint; Canvases. **SICs:** 5199 (Nondurable Goods Nec); 5083 (Farm & Garden Machinery); 5092 (Toys & Hobby Goods & Supplies); 5198 (Paints, Varnishes & Supplies).

■ 25577 ■ **Blue Chip Stamps**
PO Box 831
Pasadena, CA 91102
Phone: (626)585-6714
Products: Property and casualty insurance. **SIC:** 5051 (Metals Service Centers & Offices). **Sales:** $2,588,100,000 (2000). **Emp:** 6. **Officers:** Bob Bird, President; Jeff Jacobson, Vice President.

■ 25578 ■ **Boyer Printing Co.**
PO Box 509
Lebanon, PA 17042-0509
Phone: (717)272-5691
Free: (800)860-5691 **Fax:** (717)272-9698
E-mail: boyerprint@boyerprint.com
URL: http://www.boyerprint.com
Products: Color commercial offset. **SIC:** 5046 (Commercial Equipment Nec). **Est:** 1907. **Sales:** $6,000,000 (2000). **Emp:** 57. **Officers:** Stephan Boyer, President.

■ 25579 ■ **Brady Distributing Co.**
PO Box 19269
Charlotte, NC 28219
Phone: (704)357-6284 **Fax:** (704)357-1243
Products: Vending and coin operated machinery. **SICs:** 5099 (Durable Goods Nec); 5046 (Commercial Equipment Nec). **Est:** 1945. **Sales:** $50,000,000 (2000). **Emp:** 140. **Officers:** Jon P. Brady, President; Roland B. Norris, Vice President; R. Wayne McQuire, Data Processing Mgr.; Susan L. Ballard, Human Resources Mgr.

■ 25580 ■ **Brain Teaser Money Machines**
PO Box 2065
Vista, CA 92085-2065
Phone: (760)630-5300
Free: (800)464-3313 **Fax:** (760)758-9996
Products: Coin operated game machines. **SIC:** 5099 (Durable Goods Nec). **Officers:** Thomas C. Hardwick, President.

■ 25581 ■ **Bramco Inc.**
PO Box 32230
Louisville, KY 40232
Phone: (502)493-4300 **Fax:** (502)499-3180
Products: Heavy industrial mining equipment. **SICs:** 5082 (Construction & Mining Machinery); 5084 (Industrial Machinery & Equipment). **Est:** 1908. **Sales:** $148,400,000 (2000). **Emp:** 240. **Officers:** Charles Leis, President & COO; Michael D. Brennen, VP of Finance; Carla LaRucque, Dir of Human Resources.

■ 25582 ■ **Brandeis Machinery and Supply Corp.**
1801 Watterson Trail
Jeffersontown, KY 40299
Phone: (502)491-4000 **Fax:** (502)499-3180
Products: Construction and mining products. **SIC:** 5082 (Construction & Mining Machinery). **Est:** 1908. **Sales:** $18,000,000 (2000). **Emp:** 40. **Officers:** Charles W. Leis, President; M.D. Brennen, VP of Finance; Tony Estes, VP of Sales.

■ 25583 ■ **Arthur Brown & Bros. Inc.**
2 W 46th St.
New York, NY 10036
Phone: (212)575-5555
Free: (800)772-7367 **Fax:** (212)575-5825
E-mail: penshop@idt.net
URL: http://www.artbrown.com
Products: Art supplies; Fine writing instruments. **SIC:** 5199 (Nondurable Goods Nec). **Est:** 1975.

■ 25584 ■ **Bruner Corp.**
700 W Virginia St.
Milwaukee, WI 53204
Phone: (414)747-3700
Free: (800)5BR-UNER **Fax:** (414)270-3747
Products: Commercial and industrial water treatment equipment. **SIC:** 5074 (Plumbing & Hydronic Heating Supplies). **Est:** 1946. **Sales:** $15,000,000 (2000). **Emp:** 28. **Officers:** Steve Dahlquist, General Mgr.; Doug Dickenson, Sales/Mktg.; Lynn Kazinski, Customer Service.

■ 25585 ■ Buffalo Hotel Supply Company Inc.
PO Box 646
Amherst, NY 14226
Phone: (716)691-8080
Free: (800)333-1678 **Fax:** (716)691-3255
E-mail: info@buffalohotelsply.com
Products: Commercial kitchen equipment, supplies, and linens. **SICs:** 5046 (Commercial Equipment Nec); 5078 (Refrigeration Equipment & Supplies). **Est:** 1938. **Sales:** $14,900,000 (2000). **Emp:** 55. **Officers:** James M. Bedard, President; III; Maurice Malaney, Dir. of Systems.

■ 25586 ■ C & S Distributors
PO Box 471915
Tulsa, OK 74145-1915
Phone: (918)664-6400 **Fax:** (918)628-1175
Products: Art supplies. **SIC:** 5199 (Nondurable Goods Nec).

■ 25587 ■ C and T Design and Equipment Company Inc.
2855 Toby Dr.
Indianapolis, IN 46219
Phone: (317)898-9602
Products: Commercial food service equipment. **SIC:** 5046 (Commercial Equipment Nec).

■ 25588 ■ Cabin Craft Southwest, Inc.
PO Box 876
Bedford, TX 76095
Phone: (817)571-3837
Free: (800)877-1515 **Fax:** (817)571-4925
Products: Artists' equipment; Paints and allied products. **SICs:** 5199 (Nondurable Goods Nec); 5198 (Paints, Varnishes & Supplies). **Est:** 1982. **Emp:** 10. **Officers:** Lynda McElroy.

■ 25589 ■ Calcom Graphic Supply, Inc.
8215 SW Glencreek Ct.
Portland, OR 97223-9330
Products: Screenprinting equipment and supplies, including ink. **SICs:** 5199 (Nondurable Goods Nec); 5085 (Industrial Supplies); 5084 (Industrial Machinery & Equipment).

■ 25590 ■ Calcom Graphic Supply, Inc.
8215 SW Glencreek Ct.
Portland, OR 97223-9330
Products: Screen printing equipment and supplies. **SIC:** 5199 (Nondurable Goods Nec).

■ 25591 ■ Calcom Graphic Supply, Inc.
1822 NE Grand Ave.
Portland, OR 97212-3912
Phone: (503)281-9698 **Fax:** (503)287-3281
Products: Screen printing supplies. **SICs:** 5199 (Nondurable Goods Nec); 5049 (Professional Equipment Nec).

■ 25592 ■ Calhook
6205 S 231st St.
Kent, WA 98032
Phones: (253)749-8822 800-241-4665
Free: (800)422-4665 **Fax:** (253)749-8833
URL: http://www.calhook.com
Products: Fabric display fixtures. **SIC:** 5021 (Furniture). **Est:** 1970. **Sales:** $6,000,000 (2000). **Emp:** 32. **Officers:** Keith Lee.

■ 25593 ■ California Professional Manufacturing Inc.
PO Box 4832
Modesto, CA 95352
Phone: (209)527-2686
Free: (888)263-9224 **Fax:** (209)527-3095
E-mail: cpmbags@cpmbags.com
URL: http://www.cpmbags.com
Products: Funeral home and coroner supplies. **SICs:** 5047 (Medical & Hospital Equipment); 5087 (Service Establishment Equipment). **Est:** 1983. **Sales:** $900,000 (2000). **Emp:** 12. **Officers:** Pam Robison, President; Glenn Robison, Vice President; Eric Robison, Sales/Marketing Contact; Dee Newsome, Customer Service.

■ 25594 ■ Callahan Brothers Supply Inc.
PO Box 493
Lewiston, ME 04243-0493
Phone: (207)784-5897 **Fax:** (207)786-6611
Products: Service industry machinery; Shoe repair materials; Shoe repair findings. **SIC:** 5087 (Service Establishment Equipment). **Officers:** J Callahan, President.

■ 25595 ■ Camomile Enterprises, Inc.
7853 Standish Ave.
Riverside, CA 92509
Phone: (909)685-7540 **Fax:** (909)685-7540
Products: Water filters; Industrial and commercial water equipment. **SICs:** 5074 (Plumbing & Hydronic Heating Supplies); 5084 (Industrial Machinery & Equipment). **Officers:** Jim R. Camomile, President.

■ 25596 ■ Canson Talens, Inc.
PO Box 220
South Hadley, MA 01075
Phone: (413)538-9250 **Fax:** (413)533-6554
Products: Art materials. **SIC:** 5199 (Nondurable Goods Nec).

■ 25597 ■ Catalina Cottage
125 N Aspan, No. 5
Azusa, CA 91702
Phone: (626)969-4001 **Fax:** (626)969-4451
URL: http://www.catalinacottage.com
Products: Artists' materials. **SICs:** 5199 (Nondurable Goods Nec); 5049 (Professional Equipment Nec). **Est:** 1985. **Officers:** Jane D. Bell, Owner, e-mail: jane@catalinacottage.com.

■ 25598 ■ Central Distributing Co.
609 N 108 St.
Omaha, NE 68154
Phone: (402)493-5600 **Fax:** (402)493-4910
Products: Coin-operated mechanisms and parts. **SIC:** 5046 (Commercial Equipment Nec). **Officers:** Lazier Singer, Chairman of the Board.

■ 25599 ■ Challenger Water International Inc.
133 Newport Dr.
San Marcos, CA 92069
Phone: (760)471-2282 **Fax:** (760)471-8981
Products: Water conditioning equipment. **SIC:** 5074 (Plumbing & Hydronic Heating Supplies). **Officers:** Rodney A. Carmer, International Sales Mgr.

■ 25600 ■ Champion America
PO Box 3092
Branford, CT 06405
Phone: (203)315-1181
Free: (800)521-7000 **Fax:** (203)315-1106
URL: http://www.champion-america.com
Products: Marking devices. **SIC:** 5112 (Stationery & Office Supplies). **Est:** 1989. **Sales:** $5,000,000 (2000). **Emp:** 270. **Officers:** Richard L. Fisk, President. **Former Name:** Seton Name Plate Co.

■ 25601 ■ Clack Corp.
PO Box 500
Windsor, WI 53598
Phone: (608)251-3010 **Fax:** (608)846-2586
Products: Water conditioning equipment; Molding. **SICs:** 5074 (Plumbing & Hydronic Heating Supplies); 5031 (Lumber, Plywood & Millwork). **Officers:** Peter Chermack.

■ 25602 ■ Clean Water Systems International
2322 Marina Dr.
Klamath Falls, OR 97601
Phone: (541)882-9993 **Fax:** (541)882-9994
E-mail: cws@cdsnet.net
URL: http://www.cleanwatersysintl.com
Products: UV water treatment equipment; Monitor and control equipment. **SIC:** 5074 (Plumbing & Hydronic Heating Supplies). **Est:** 1970. **Emp:** 4. **Officers:** Charles G. Romary, President.

■ 25603 ■ CMC America Corp.
210 S Center St.
Joliet, IL 60436
Phone: (815)726-4336 **Fax:** (815)726-7138
Products: Bakery machinery. **SIC:** 5046 (Commercial Equipment Nec). **Est:** 1993. **Sales:** $2,000,000 (2000).

Emp: 15. **Officers:** J.R. Fay, Exec. Consultant. **Former Name:** Champion Machinery Co.

■ 25604 ■ Coastal Supply Co., Inc.
8650 Argent St.
Santee, CA 92071
Phone: (619)562-8880 **Fax:** (619)562-2772
Products: Screen printing supplies. **SICs:** 5085 (Industrial Supplies); 5199 (Nondurable Goods Nec).

■ 25605 ■ Color Brite Fabrics and Displays Inc.
212 E 8th St.
Cincinnati, OH 45202
Phone: (513)721-4402 **Fax:** (513)721-5036
Products: Display equipment and supplies including mannequins, showcases, pictures, and racks. **SICs:** 5099 (Durable Goods Nec); 5046 (Commercial Equipment Nec). **Est:** 1935. **Sales:** $2,000,000 (2000). **Emp:** 5. **Officers:** Christine Brinker, Owner.

■ 25606 ■ Commercial Art Supply
935 Erie Blvd. E
Syracuse, NY 13210
Phone: (315)474-1000
Free: (800)669-2787 **Fax:** (315)474-5311
Products: Art supplies, including screen printing supplies. **SIC:** 5199 (Nondurable Goods Nec).

■ 25607 ■ Commercial Interior Decor
3205 W Sencore Dr.
Sioux Falls, SD 57107-0728
Phone: (605)334-9288
Free: (800)568-7135 **Fax:** (605)334-2706
Products: Interior designs for commercial properties. **SIC:** 5046 (Commercial Equipment Nec). **Officers:** Robert Thimjon, President.

■ 25608 ■ Commercial Music Co. Inc.
1550 Edison St.
Dallas, TX 75207
Phone: (214)741-6381
Products: Phonographs and coin operated machines. **SIC:** 5046 (Commercial Equipment Nec). **Est:** 1938. **Sales:** $6,000,000 (2000). **Emp:** 27. **Officers:** B.E. Williams, President.

■ 25609 ■ C.E. Conrad Memorial Cemetary
641 Conrad Dr.
Kalispell, MT 59901-4629
Phone: (406)257-5303
Products: Service establishment equipment, including cemetery and funeral director's equipment and supplies; Concrete burial vaults and boxes. **SIC:** 5087 (Service Establishment Equipment). **Officers:** Clark Spain, Contact.

■ 25610 ■ Continental Sales and Equipment Co.
PO Box 428
Hibbing, MN 55746
Phone: (218)263-6861 **Fax:** (218)262-6373
Products: Mining equipment. **SIC:** 5082 (Construction & Mining Machinery). **Est:** 1958. **Sales:** $1,000,000 (2000). **Emp:** 5. **Officers:** Wayne J. Nordstrom, President; Jean Hedblom, Accountant; Mark McLellan, Sales & Marketing Contact.

■ 25611 ■ Convenience Equipment and Supplies Enterprises Inc.
2300 N Barrington, No. 400
Hoffman Estates, IL 60195-7855
Phone: (708)397-9247 **Fax:** (708)884-9423
Products: Equipment and fixtures for convenience stores and supermarkets. **SIC:** 5087 (Service Establishment Equipment). **Est:** 1987. **Sales:** $1,000,000 (2000). **Emp:** 6. **Officers:** Earl J. Barbin, President.

■ 25612 ■ Country Time Ceramic Supply Inc.
3200 N Haines Ave.
Rapid City, SD 57701-9562
Phone: (605)342-2505 **Fax:** (605)342-2505
E-mail: waynelyn@enetis.net
Products: Ceramic and pottery. **SIC:** 5032 (Brick, Stone & Related Materials). **Est:** 1985. **Sales:** $75,000 (2000). **Emp:** 5. **Officers:** Lynn Lindsay, Owner; Joy Johnson, Owner.

■ 25613 ■ Crafts Etc. Ltd.
7717 SW 44th St.
Oklahoma City, OK 73179-4808
Phone: (405)745-1200
Free: (800)888-0321 **Fax:** (405)745-1225
Products: Artist supplies; Craft supplies; Jewelry making supplies. **SIC:** 5199 (Nondurable Goods Nec). **Est:** 1977. **Emp:** 80. **Officers:** Randy Green, President.

■ 25614 ■ Creative Store Design Inc.
3728 N Fretney St.
Milwaukee, WI 53212
Phone: (414)963-1900
Products: Mannequins. **SIC:** 5046 (Commercial Equipment Nec). **Sales:** $1,000,000 (1993). **Emp:** 7.

■ 25615 ■ Cunningham Distributing Inc.
2015 Mills St.
El Paso, TX 79901
Phone: (915)533-6993
Products: Commercial washers, dryers, refrigerators, and stoves. **SICs:** 5064 (Electrical Appliances—Television & Radio); 5087 (Service Establishment Equipment). **Est:** 1955. **Sales:** $9,000,000 (2000). **Emp:** 21. **Officers:** J.E. Cunningham, CEO & Chairman of the Board.

■ 25616 ■ Cunningham Distributing Inc.
615 Haines Ave. NW
Albuquerque, NM 87102-1225
Phone: (505)247-8838 **Fax:** (505)243-2717
Products: Service establishment equipment, including laundry and dry cleaning equipment and supplies. **SIC:** 5087 (Service Establishment Equipment). **Est:** 1949. **Sales:** $2,300,000 (2000). **Emp:** 6. **Officers:** James Cunningham, Chairman of the Board.

■ 25617 ■ Cushing and Company Inc.
325 W Huron St.
Chicago, IL 60610
Phone: (312)266-8228 **Fax:** (312)266-8059
URL: http://www.cushingco.com
Products: Blueprinting service, blueprint paper, plain paper and vellium. **SICs:** 5043 (Photographic Equipment & Supplies); 5049 (Professional Equipment Nec). **Est:** 1929. **Sales:** $10,000,000 (1999). **Emp:** 90. **Officers:** Cathleen Duff, President; Patricia Cushing, Treasurer; Michael A. Duff, VP of Marketing & Sales; Terry Beynon, Dir. of Data Processing; Nancy A. Sherkey, Dir of Personnel.

■ 25618 ■ Custer Supply & Fixtures
721 Missouri Ave.
MiLes City, MT 59301-4226
Phone: (406)232-7826
Products: Commercial equipment. **SIC:** 5046 (Commercial Equipment Nec). **Officers:** Warner Feuerherm, Owner.

■ 25619 ■ D & L Stained Glass Supply, Inc.
4939 N Broadway
Boulder, CO 80304
Phone: (303)449-8737
Free: (800)525-0940 **Fax:** (303)442-3429
E-mail: info@dlstainedglass.com
URL: http://www.dlstainedglass.com
Products: Art glass supplies; Sheet glass. **SICs:** 5199 (Nondurable Goods Nec); 5039 (Construction Materials Nec). **Est:** 1974. **Emp:** 28. **Officers:** Leslie L. Silverman, President.

■ 25620 ■ D & M Distributors Inc.
273 Presumpscot St.
Portland, ME 04103-5226
Phone: (207)772-4796 **Fax:** (207)772-7159
Products: Service establishment equipment, including upholsterers' equipment and supplies; Marine fabricators supplies. **SICs:** 5087 (Service Establishment Equipment); 5049 (Professional Equipment Nec). **Est:** 1981. **Sales:** $800,000 (2000). **Emp:** 4. **Officers:** Peter F. Morrison, President; H. Timothy O'Neil.

■ 25621 ■ DAC International Inc.
6702 McNeil Dr.
Austin, TX 78729
Phone: (512)331-5323 **Fax:** (512)331-4516
Products: Search and detection, navigation, and guidance equipment. **SIC:** 5088 (Transportation Equipment & Supplies). **Est:** 1981. **Sales:** $14,000,000 (2000). **Emp:** 14. **Officers:** Mike Crouch, President; Lisa Finley, Dir. of Operations; Terry Armstrong, Vice President.

■ 25622 ■ Dahlco Music & Vending
296 N Pascal
St. Paul, MN 55104
Phone: (612)645-1111 **Fax:** (612)645-3416
Products: Vending machines; Electronic games. **SIC:** 5046 (Commercial Equipment Nec). **Emp:** 25. **Officers:** Steve Dahlin; Dan Dahlin.

■ 25623 ■ Dakota Chemical Inc.
PO Box 88111
Sioux Falls, SD 57109-1001
Phone: (605)225-6290
Products: Water and waste-water treatment equipment. **SIC:** 5084 (Industrial Machinery & Equipment). **Sales:** $1,000,000 (2000). **Emp:** 6. **Officers:** Howard J. Hawkins, CEO & Chairman of the Board.

■ 25624 ■ Dalco Athletic
3719 Cavalier
Garland, TX 75042
Phone: (972)494-1455
Free: (800)288-3252 **Fax:** (972)276-9608
E-mail: sales@dalcoathletic.com
URL: http://www.dalcoathletic.com
Products: Football field equipment. **SIC:** 5091 (Sporting & Recreational Goods). **Est:** 1970. **Emp:** 49. **Officers:** Mike Carter, VP of Sales, e-mail: mcarter@dalcoathletic.com.

■ 25625 ■ Dann Dee Display Fixtures Inc.
7555 N Caldwell Ave.
Niles, IL 60714
Phone: (708)588-1600
Free: (800)888-8515 **Fax:** (708)588-1620
Products: Retail store fixtures. **SIC:** 5046 (Commercial Equipment Nec). **Est:** 1945. **Sales:** $40,000,000 (2000). **Emp:** 120. **Officers:** Earl Dann, President; John Vacala, COO; Karen Pryor, Dir. of Marketing; Wendy Kahen, Public Relations Contact.

■ 25626 ■ Dawson Industries Inc.
1627 Marion Ave.
Grand Haven, MI 49417-2365
Phone: (313)771-5200 **Fax:** (313)771-4890
Products: Printing supplies, including dyes, prototypes, and pins. **SIC:** 5085 (Industrial Supplies). **Est:** 1935. **Sales:** $7,000,000 (2000). **Emp:** 100. **Officers:** Neil K. Hitz, CEO; Gerard McMaster, CFO; Denny McCormick, Dir. of Marketing.

■ 25627 ■ Desmond Process Supply Co.
2277 Elliott Ave.
Troy, MI 48083-4502
Phone: (248)589-9100
Free: (800)968-1115 **Fax:** (248)589-0038
Products: Screen printing supplies. **SICs:** 5199 (Nondurable Goods Nec); 5084 (Industrial Machinery & Equipment). **Est:** 1955. **Emp:** 16. **Officers:** Dominic Ciaravino, President.

■ 25628 ■ Diamond Art & Craft
2207 Royal Ln.
Dallas, TX 75229
Phone: (972)620-9653
Free: (800)278-7450 **Fax:** (972)484-3540
Products: Artists' equipment; Artists' brushes and hair pencils. **SICs:** 5199 (Nondurable Goods Nec); 5198 (Paints, Varnishes & Supplies). **Officers:** Klaus Engels, Contact.

■ 25629 ■ Diamond Supply, Inc.
200 Dalton Ave.
PO Box 5115
Charlotte, NC 28225
Phone: (704)376-2125
Free: (800)438-4139 **Fax:** (704)334-0251
E-mail: plastiva@vnet.net
Products: Sign making supplies. **SIC:** 5199 (Nondurable Goods Nec). **Est:** 1971. **Emp:** 22. **Officers:** H. Diamond, President.

■ 25630 ■ Dispenser Services Inc.
117 Beaver St.
Waltham, MA 02454
Phone: (781)891-6595
Free: (800)633-8899 **Fax:** (781)891-7576
Products: Product dispensers. **SIC:** 5046 (Commercial Equipment Nec). **Sales:** $6,000,000 (2000). **Emp:** 27. **Officers:** Steven Harth, President; Rick Fowler, CFO.

■ 25631 ■ Display Technologies
111-01 14th Ave.
College Point, NY 11356
Phone: (718)321-3100 **Fax:** (718)321-7024
URL: http://www.display-technologies.com
Products: In-store, point-of-purchase displays, including floor stands, modular racks, and shelf management systems; Custom items. **SIC:** 5099 (Durable Goods Nec). **Est:** 1960. **Emp:** 100. **Officers:** Richard Jay, President.

■ 25632 ■ D.M.R. Distributors
3500 SR 520 West, Bldg. A
Cocoa, FL 32926
Phone: (407)632-9065
Free: (800)745-0298 **Fax:** (407)639-8948
Products: Fine art supplies. **SIC:** 5199 (Nondurable Goods Nec). **Est:** 1967. **Officers:** Bill Wuisman, Contact.

■ 25633 ■ DMR International
2263 SW 37 Ave.
Miami, FL 33145
Phone: (305)661-8950
Free: (800)273-6251 **Fax:** (305)661-5454
Products: Specialty equipment and products. **SIC:** 5199 (Nondurable Goods Nec). **Est:** 1980. **Sales:** $1,000,000 (2000). **Emp:** 4.

■ 25634 ■ Dodge Company Inc.
165 Cambridge Park Dr.
Cambridge, MA 02140
Phone: (617)661-0500
Free: (800)443-6343 **Fax:** (617)661-1428
Products: Funeral supplies, including urns, gloves, and chemicals. **SICs:** 5169 (Chemicals & Allied Products Nec); 5169 (Chemicals & Allied Products Nec); 5122 (Drugs, Proprietaries & Sundries). **Est:** 1893. **Sales:** $16,000,000 (2000). **Emp:** 100. **Officers:** A.J. Dodge, President; G.B. Dodge Jr., CFO; K.E. Dodge, Vice President.

■ 25635 ■ Dowler Enterprises Inc.
RR 2, Box 226-1
Cole Camp, MO 65325-9803
Phone: (660)331-1744
Products: Ceramics. **SIC:** 5049 (Professional Equipment Nec). **Officers:** Richard Dowler, President.

■ 25636 ■ Dresco Reproduction Inc.
12603 Allard St.
Santa Fe Springs, CA 90670
Phone: (562)863-6677 **Fax:** (562)868-9757
Products: Drafting and architectural engineering supplies. **SIC:** 5049 (Professional Equipment Nec). **Sales:** $3,000,000 (2000). **Emp:** 24.

■ 25637 ■ Drillers Service Inc.
PO Box 1407
Hickory, NC 28603-1407
Phone: (704)322-1100
Products: Water-well drilling equipment. **SICs:** 5084 (Industrial Machinery & Equipment); 5082 (Construction & Mining Machinery). **Est:** 1954. **Sales:** $36,000,000 (2000). **Emp:** 135. **Officers:** Richard A. Redden, President & Treasurer.

■ 25638 ■ Skip Dunn Sales
162 Washington Ave.
New Rochelle, NY 10801
Phone: (914)636-2200
Free: (800)624-9720 **Fax:** (914)636-1535
E-mail: skipdunn@computer.net
Products: TV and AV carts; TV wall and ceiling mounts; Electronic equipment racks; Modular consoles. **SICs:** 5046 (Commercial Equipment Nec); 5021 (Furniture). **Est:** 1981. **Emp:** 10.

■ **25639** ■ **Durastill Inc.**
PO Box 1570
Roswell, GA 30077
Phone: (404)993-7575 **Fax:** (404)992-1841
Products: Water distillation equipment. **SIC:** 5074 (Plumbing & Hydronic Heating Supplies). **Officers:** Horace Mansfield, Director of Sales.

■ **25640** ■ **Eastern Enterprises**
9 Riverside Rd.
Weston, MA 02493
Phone: (781)647-2300 **Fax:** (781)647-2344
Products: Water system components. **SIC:** 5099 (Durable Goods Nec). **Sales:** $1,518,400,000 (2000). **Emp:** 1,400. **Officers:** J. Atwood Ives, CEO & Chairman of the Board; Walter J. Flaherty, Sr. VP & CFO.

■ **25641** ■ **Edmund's Dummy Company Inc.**
362 Lakeside Dr.
Foster City, CA 94404
Phone: (650)378-5159
Products: Mannequins. **SIC:** 5046 (Commercial Equipment Nec). **Sales:** $5,000,000 (2000). **Emp:** 25. **Officers:** David Shelton, CEO & President; Aimee Ratti, VP & CFO.

■ **25642** ■ **Eickoff Corp.**
PO Box 2000
Pittsburgh, PA 15230
Phone: (412)788-1400
Products: Mining equipment. **SIC:** 5082 (Construction & Mining Machinery). **Est:** 1973. **Sales:** $15,000,000 (2000). **Emp:** 40. **Officers:** Monika D. Ludwig, President; Phil Specht, Treasurer; Karl H. Rieser, Dir. of Marketing.

■ **25643** ■ **Engineered Equipment Co.**
PO Box 2707
Corona, CA 91718
Phone: (909)735-3326 **Fax:** (909)734-7085
Products: Mining wear parts. **SIC:** 5082 (Construction & Mining Machinery). **Est:** 1950. **Sales:** $7,000,000 (2000). **Emp:** 15. **Officers:** Linden T. Curtis, President; Tracy T. Curtis, Vice President; Patricia J. Contreras, Treasurer & Secty.

■ **25644** ■ **Envirotechnology Inc.**
PO Box 2681
Colorado Springs, CO 80901-2681
Phone: (719)633-9642 **Fax:** (719)634-5775
Products: Water conditioning equipment. **SIC:** 5074 (Plumbing & Hydronic Heating Supplies). **Officers:** Chris Heiss, President.

■ **25645** ■ **Everpure Inc.**
660 N Blackhawk Dr.
Westmont, IL 60559
Phone: (630)654-4000
Free: (800)323-7873 **Fax:** (630)654-1115
E-mail: info@everpure.com
URL: http://www.everpure.com
Products: Water filtration products. **SIC:** 5099 (Durable Goods Nec).

■ **25646** ■ **Fairmont Supply Co.**
90 W Chestnut St.
Washington, PA 15301
Phones: (724)223-2200 (412)223-2290
Fax: (724)223-2335
E-mail: info@fairmontsupply.com
URL: http://www.fairmontsupply.com
Products: Rubber; Industrial equipment, including mining supplies, safety, electrical and materials handling equipment. **SIC:** 5085 (Industrial Supplies). **Est:** 1921. **Sales:** $278,000,000 (1999). **Emp:** 600. **Officers:** Chuck Whirlow, President & COO; Ronald Rapp, Controller; Thomas Meacham, Exec. VP of Marketing; Tom Carnahan, Dir. of Systems; T. Richard McMillan, Dir of Human Resources.

■ **25647** ■ **Farris Enterprises**
1855 Sampson Ave.
Corona, CA 91718
Phone: (909)272-3919 **Fax:** (909)735-1195
Products: Water purification and reverse osmosis systems and equipment. **SIC:** 5074 (Plumbing & Hydronic Heating Supplies). **Est:** 1983. **Sales:**

$2,000,000 (2000). **Emp:** 10. **Officers:** Mike Furniss, Marketing & Sales Mgr.

■ **25648** ■ **Feed-Rite Controls Inc.**
3100 E Hennepin Ave.
Minneapolis, MN 55413
Phone: (612)331-9100
Products: Water and waste-water treatment equipment. **SIC:** 5084 (Industrial Machinery & Equipment). **Sales:** $8,000,000 (2000). **Emp:** 28. **Officers:** Howard J. Hawkins, CEO & Chairman of the Board.

■ **25649** ■ **FFR Inc.**
28900 Fountain Pkwy.
Cleveland, OH 44139
Phone: (440)505-6919
Free: (800)422-2547 **Fax:** 800-422-2502
E-mail: info@ffr.com
URL: http://www.ffr.com
Products: Display accessories; Ticket molding; Shelf divider systems; Sign holders; Hooks; Ceiling display systems; Literature holders. **SICs:** 5199 (Nondurable Goods Nec); 5162 (Plastics Materials & Basic Shapes). **Est:** 1963. **Sales:** $50,000,000 (2000). **Emp:** 100. **Officers:** Gerald A. Conway, Comptroller; Don Kimmel, Co-President.

■ **25650** ■ **Filtrex Inc.**
1945 Alpine Way
Hayward, CA 94545
Phone: (510)783-3700
URL: http://www.filtrex.com
Products: Filters for gasoline, water, and other liquids. **SIC:** 5084 (Industrial Machinery & Equipment). **Est:** 1969. **Sales:** $8,000,000 (2000). **Emp:** 25. **Officers:** F. Gibson, Owner; Ed Behrendt, VP & General Mgr.; Rick Ryan, General Mgr. and Sales Mgr.

■ **25651** ■ **Fire-Dex Inc.**
780 S Progress Dr.
Medina, OH 44256-1368
Phone: (330)723-0000
Free: (800)241-6563 **Fax:** (330)723-0035
E-mail: firedex@earthlink.com
URL: http://www.firedex.com
Products: Fire-fighting clothing. **SICs:** 5136 (Men's/Boys' Clothing); 5199 (Nondurable Goods Nec); 5137 (Women's/Children's Clothing). **Est:** 1983. **Sales:** $6,000,000 (2000). **Emp:** 65. **Officers:** William M. Burke, President.

■ **25652** ■ **Ted G. Fite**
6 Ardmore Mall
Ardmore, OK 73401-4363
Phone: (580)223-5820
Products: Vacuum cleaning systems. **SIC:** 5087 (Service Establishment Equipment). **Officers:** Ted Fite, Owner.

■ **25653** ■ **Flexo-Printing Equipment Corp.**
416 Hayward Ave. N
Oakdale, MN 55128
Phone: (651)731-9499 **Fax:** (651)731-0525
Products: Tape and printing equipment. **SIC:** 5084 (Industrial Machinery & Equipment). **Est:** 1988. **Sales:** $1,000,000 (2000). **Emp:** 3. **Officers:** Wynn Lidell, President.

■ **25654** ■ **Freeburg Sign & Lighting**
2326 5th Ave. N
Lewiston, ID 83501-1744
Phone: (208)746-0839 **Fax:** (208)746-0839
Products: Signs, including neon signs. **SIC:** 5046 (Commercial Equipment Nec). **Officers:** William Freeburg, Owner.

■ **25655** ■ **Friend Bit Service Inc.**
RD 3
Smithfield, PA 15478
Phone: (412)564-2072
Products: Mining units. **SIC:** 5082 (Construction & Mining Machinery). **Est:** 1976. **Sales:** $600,000 (2000). **Emp:** 2. **Officers:** Jack Friend, Owner.

■ **25656** ■ **J. Gani International Inc.**
PO Box 713
Plaistow, NH 03865-0713
Phone: (603)382-7551 **Fax:** (603)382-3735
Products: Hotel equipment and supplies. **SIC:** 5046 (Commercial Equipment Nec). **Officers:** Joseph Gani, President.

■ **25657** ■ **Garston, Inc.**
8 Parkridge Rd.
Haverhill, MA 01835-6904
Phone: (978)374-0600
Free: (800)328-7775 **Fax:** (978)374-9777
E-mail: garston@worldnet.att.net
Products: Screen printing supplies; Sign supplies; Digital. **SIC:** 5199 (Nondurable Goods Nec). **Est:** 1960. **Emp:** 15.

■ **25658** ■ **Garston Sign Supplies, Inc.**
110 Batson Dr.
Manchester, CT 06040
Phone: (860)649-9626
Free: (800)966-9626 **Fax:** (860)646-8602
Products: Sign and silk screen supplies. **SIC:** 5199 (Nondurable Goods Nec). **Est:** 1960.

■ **25659** ■ **Gauntlett Agency Ltd.**
76 Amaral St.
Riverside, RI 02915-2205
Phone: (401)434-3355
Products: Commercial equipment. **SIC:** 5046 (Commercial Equipment Nec). **Doing Business As:** Hobart Sales & Services.

■ **25660** ■ **Ghia Corp.**
15870 River Rd.
Guerneville, CA 95446-9288
Phone: (415)282-2832
Products: Caskets and urns. **SIC:** 5087 (Service Establishment Equipment). **Est:** 1989. **Sales:** $1,000,000 (2000). **Emp:** 5. **Officers:** Alexander Ghia, President; Ronda Di Sautel, Vice President.

■ **25661** ■ **N. Glantz & Son**
650 Seco Rd.
Monroeville, PA 15146
Phone: (412)372-8110
Free: (800)642-4240 **Fax:** (412)372-8475
Products: Sign construction materials. **SIC:** 5039 (Construction Materials Nec).

■ **25662** ■ **The Godfrey Group Inc.**
PO Box 90008
Raleigh, NC 27675-0008
Phone: (919)544-6504 **Fax:** (919)544-6729
Products: Signs and advertising displays; Booths, bars, and back bars. **SIC:** 5046 (Commercial Equipment Nec). **Sales:** $300,000 (2000). **Emp:** 49. **Officers:** H. Glenn Godfrey, President.

■ **25663** ■ **Gold Medal Products Co.**
10700 Medallion Dr.
Cincinnati, OH 45241-4807
Phone: (513)769-7676
Free: (800)543-0862 **Fax:** (513)769-8500
E-mail: info@gmpopcorn.com
URL: http://www.gmpopcorn.com
Products: Concession and commercial service machines. **SIC:** 5046 (Commercial Equipment Nec). **Est:** 1931. **Sales:** $35,000,000 (2000). **Emp:** 225. **Officers:** D. R. Kroeger, President; J.C. Evans, CEO; John Evans, VP of Sales; Chris Petroff.

■ **25664** ■ **W.R. Grace and Co. Grace Dearborn Div.**
4636 Somerton Rd.
Trevose, PA 19053-6742
Phone: (267)438-1800 **Fax:** (267)540-1588
Products: Water treatment products. **SIC:** 5169 (Chemicals & Allied Products Nec). **Est:** 1887. **Sales:** $200,000,000 (2000). **Emp:** 500. **Officers:** Fred E. Bennett, President; Greg McCoy, VP of Finance; W. Kenneth Costanzo, VP of Business Development; Don Crawford, VP of Sales; Michael Yorke, Dir of Human Resources.

■ 25665 ■ Graham Blue Print Co.
PO Box 1307
Little Rock, AR 72203-1307
Phone: (501)376-3364 **Fax:** (501)376-4322
Products: Drafting engineering supplies, including tables, blueprint machines and pens. **SIC:** 5049 (Professional Equipment Nec). **Sales:** $1,300,000 (2000). **Emp:** 12. **Officers:** James H. Graham.

■ 25666 ■ Grand Stage Co., Inc.
630 W Lake St.
Chicago, IL 60661
Phone: (312)332-5611 **Fax:** (312)332-3655
Products: Theatrical supplies. **SIC:** 5199 (Nondurable Goods Nec).

■ 25667 ■ Graphco
6563 Cochran Rd.
Cleveland, OH 44139-3901
Phone: (440)248-1700 **Fax:** (440)248-1701
Products: Printing equipment. **SIC:** 5084 (Industrial Machinery & Equipment). **Est:** 1976. **Sales:** $1,600,000 (2000). **Emp:** 20. **Officers:** William Manley, President; C.W. Manley, Vice President; Don Mazzolini, Vice President.

■ 25668 ■ Graphic Media
13916 Cordary Ave.
Hawthorne, CA 90250
Phone: (310)679-0653 **Fax:** (310)679-2263
Products: Art and drafting equipment and supplies. **SICs:** 5199 (Nondurable Goods Nec); 5049 (Professional Equipment Nec).

■ 25669 ■ Graphic Systems Inc.
301 Commerce Dr.
Moorestown, NJ 08057-4208
Phone: (609)234-7500
Free: (800)733-1533 **Fax:** (609)234-2944
Products: Graphic art supplies, including plates and film. **SICs:** 5199 (Nondurable Goods Nec); 5084 (Industrial Machinery & Equipment); 5043 (Photographic Equipment & Supplies). **Sales:** $2,000,000 (2000). **Emp:** 49. **Officers:** Jon Wright.

■ 25670 ■ Graphline, Inc.
5701 NW 94th Ave.
Tamarac, FL 33321
Phone: (954)722-3000 **Fax:** (954)724-2313
E-mail: marketing@graphline.com
Products: Graphic arts equipment and supplies. **SIC:** 5049 (Professional Equipment Nec). **Est:** 1994. **Sales:** $130,000,000 (2000). **Emp:** 450. **Officers:** Michael Ostroft, President; Raymond C. Domis, CFO; Ralph Theile, VP of Operations; Debbie Stansel, Human Resources Mgr. **Former Name:** VGC Corp.

■ 25671 ■ Green Mountain Foam Products
RR 1, BOX 8000
Underhill, VT 05489-9801
Phone: (802)899-4668 **Fax:** (802)899-4668
E-mail: uphsupply@aol.com
Products: Upholsterers' equipment and supplies; Internal packaging. **SICs:** 5087 (Service Establishment Equipment); 5049 (Professional Equipment Nec). **Est:** 1967. **Officers:** Thomas Morse, Owner.

■ 25672 ■ Hach Co.
PO Box 389
Loveland, CO 80539
Phone: (970)669-3050
Free: (800)227-4224 **Fax:** (970)669-2932
URL: http://www.hach.com
Products: Analytic instruments and reagents; Process, flow, and sampling systems. **SIC:** 5049 (Professional Equipment Nec). **Est:** 1947.

■ 25673 ■ Hampshire Furniture Co.
673 Black Brook Rd.
Goffstown, NH 03045-2911
Phone: (603)774-5120
Free: (800)774-5120 **Fax:** (603)774-5123
E-mail: awh1@mediaone.net
Products: Service industry machinery. **SIC:** 5087 (Service Establishment Equipment). **Est:** 1977. **Officers:** Ann Haletky, Partner; Gerald Haletky, Partner. **Alternate Name:** Gerald E. #Haletky.

■ 25674 ■ Harf Inc.
31 Church Rd.
Hatfield, PA 19440
Phone: (215)822-0624
Products: Barber and beauty shop furniture, equipment, and accessories; Hair preparations. **SICs:** 5087 (Service Establishment Equipment); 5122 (Drugs, Proprietaries & Sundries). **Est:** 1935. **Emp:** 3. **Officers:** Art Schmell, President.

■ 25675 ■ William Hecht Inc.
508 Bainbridge St.
Philadelphia, PA 19147
Phone: (215)925-6223 **Fax:** (215)923-6798
Products: Store interiors, including counters and galleries. **SIC:** 5046 (Commercial Equipment Nec). **Est:** 1919. **Sales:** $2,500,000 (2000). **Emp:** 46. **Officers:** S. Hecht, President; C. Hecht, Treasurer & Secty.; Neil Hecht, VP of Marketing.

■ 25676 ■ Hellenbrand Water Conditioners Inc.
404 Moravian Valley Rd.
PO Box 187
Waunakee, WI 53597
Phone: (608)849-3050 **Fax:** (608)849-7398
Products: Residential, commercial, and industrial water softening and iron removal systems. **SIC:** 5046 (Commercial Equipment Nec). **Est:** 1967. **Emp:** 35. **Officers:** Jeff Hellenbrand, President.

■ 25677 ■ Jeffrey Herman
PO Box 704
Chepachet, RI 02814
Phone: (401)461-3156
Products: Silversmithing equipment. **SIC:** 5087 (Service Establishment Equipment). **Officers:** Jeffrey Herman, Owner.

■ 25678 ■ Hess Hair Milk Laboratories Inc.
PO Box 17100
St. Paul, MN 55117-0100
Phone: (612)488-7262
Free: (800)328-9653 **Fax:** (612)488-9656
Products: Professional barber and beauty supplies. **SICs:** 5122 (Drugs, Proprietaries & Sundries); 5087 (Service Establishment Equipment). **Est:** 1906. **Sales:** $5,000,000 (2000). **Emp:** 12. **Officers:** Roger B. Hess Sr., President; Roger B. Hess Jr., Vice President.

■ 25679 ■ Hickel Investment Co.
PO Box 101700
Anchorage, AK 99510
Phone: (907)343-2400 **Fax:** (907)343-2211
Products: Service establishment equipment. **SIC:** 5087 (Service Establishment Equipment). **Officers:** Robert Hickel, President.

■ 25680 ■ Hispania Trading Corporation
5715 Manchester Ave.
St. Louis, MO 63110
Phone: (314)781-1500 **Fax:** (314)781-1507
Products: Refrigeration equipment and supplies; Burial garments; Hearses; Material handling equipment. **SICs:** 5078 (Refrigeration Equipment & Supplies); 5087 (Service Establishment Equipment); 5012 (Automobiles & Other Motor Vehicles); 5199 (Nondurable Goods Nec). **Officers:** Jose L. Molina, Export Manager.

■ 25681 ■ Hotsy Cleaning Systems
2428 W Central Ave.
Missoula, MT 59801-6464
Phone: (406)549-5447
Free: (800)879-3502 **Fax:** (406)549-5478
E-mail: hotsy_1@hotmail.com
Products: Service establishment equipment; Industrial cleaning equipment. **SICs:** 5087 (Service Establishment Equipment); 5085 (Industrial Supplies). **Est:** 1980. **Sales:** $350,000 (2000). **Emp:** 3. **Officers:** Wayne Smith, Owner.

■ 25682 ■ Hubbard Printing Equipment
22C Worldfair Dr.
Somerset, NJ 08873
Phone: (732)271-8200
Products: Printing equipment. **SIC:** 5043 (Photographic Equipment & Supplies).

■ 25683 ■ Hurley Chicago Company Inc.
12621 S Laramie Ave.
Alsip, IL 60803-3225
Phone: (708)388-9222 **Fax:** (708)388-9271
URL: http://www.hurleychicago.com
Products: Water filters. **SIC:** 5074 (Plumbing & Hydronic Heating Supplies). **Est:** 1972. **Sales:** $1,300,000 (1999). **Emp:** 9. **Officers:** Gus Losos, President; Sylvia Losos, VP & Treasurer; Jim DeVries, Secretary.

■ 25684 ■ Hyatt's Graphic Supply Company, Inc.
910 Main St.
Buffalo, NY 14202
Phone: (716)884-8900
Free: (800)234-9288 **Fax:** (716)884-3943
E-mail: sales@hyatts.com
URL: http://www.hyatts.com
Products: Graphic arts supplies; Fine art materials; Computer assisted sign equipment and supplies. **SIC:** 5199 (Nondurable Goods Nec). **Est:** 1959. **Former Name:** Hyatt Graphic Supply Co.

■ 25685 ■ Hyde Marine Inc.
28045 Ranney Pkwy.
Westlake, OH 44145-1188
Phone: (440)871-8000 **Fax:** (440)871-1143
E-mail: info@hydeweb.com
URL: http://www.hydeweb.com
Products: Oil spill equipment. **SIC:** 5084 (Industrial Machinery & Equipment). **Est:** 1865. **Sales:** $5,000,000 (1999). **Emp:** 6. **Officers:** Thomas Mackey, President; Jim Mackey, Vice President, e-mail: info@hydeweb.com. **Former Name:** Hyde Products, Inc.

■ 25686 ■ Illinois Blueprint Corp.
800 SW Jefferson Ave.
Peoria, IL 61605
Phone: (309)676-1306 **Fax:** (309)676-1300
Products: Microfilm equipment and duplicating machines for large documents. **SIC:** 5044 (Office Equipment). **Sales:** $3,000,000 (2000). **Emp:** 12. **Officers:** Lynette Smith, President; Lynette Smith, VP of Finance.

■ 25687 ■ Inaqua International
3180 NW 72nd Ave.
Miami, FL 33122-1316
Phone: (941)377-1889
Free: (800)226-2260 **Fax:** (941)378-4518
Products: Water treatment systems. **SIC:** 5074 (Plumbing & Hydronic Heating Supplies). **Officers:** Lawrence Jessup, General Mgr.

■ 25688 ■ Industrial Services of America Inc.
PO Box 32428
Louisville, KY 40232
Phone: (502)368-1661 **Fax:** (502)363-3756
Products: Waste management equipment, including compactors and balers. **SIC:** 5084 (Industrial Machinery & Equipment). **Est:** 1953. **Sales:** $30,500,000 (2000). **Emp:** 78. **Officers:** Harry Kletter, CEO, President & Chairman of the Board; Alan Schroering, Finance Officer.

■ 25689 ■ Inter-American Trading
PO Box 12254
Seattle, WA 98102
Phone: (206)328-2575 **Fax:** (206)328-2887
Products: Industrial equipment; Costume jewelry; Farm equipment; Oil filled repair kits; 3-D and 2-D holograms. **SICs:** 5083 (Farm & Garden Machinery); 5084 (Industrial Machinery & Equipment); 5094 (Jewelry & Precious Stones); 5122 (Drugs, Proprietaries & Sundries); 5199 (Nondurable Goods Nec). **Officers:** Sean Kilgore, General Mgr.

■ 25690 ■ J & J Distributors Inc.
9461 E Washington
Indianapolis, IN 46229-3085
Phone: (317)899-2530 **Fax:** (317)899-6080
Products: Coin-operated machines. **SIC:** 5092 (Toys & Hobby Goods & Supplies). **Emp:** 99. **Officers:** Kelly J. Flynn.

■ **25691** ■ **Jacks Fragrances**
1953 Canterbury Dr.
Las Vegas, NV 89119-6102
Phone: (702)795-0564   **Fax:** (702)795-0574
Products: Commercial car washing machinery and equipment. **SIC:** 5087 (Service Establishment Equipment). **Officers:** Jack Bassoff, Owner.

■ **25692** ■ **James International Trading Company**
3215 Summit Dr.
Birmingham, AL 35243
Phone: (205)879-0516   **Fax:** (205)879-0516
Products: Mining machinery. **SIC:** 5082 (Construction & Mining Machinery). **Officers:** Michael Ray James, President.

■ **25693** ■ **Jawz Inc.**
501 Industrial Way
Fallbrook, CA 92028
Phone: (760)728-8380   **Fax:** (760)723-7861
Products: Water conservation products; Recycling products. **SIC:** 5074 (Plumbing & Hydronic Heating Supplies). **Est:** 1979. **Sales:** $900,000 (2000). **Emp:** 4. **Officers:** Madaline Plueger, President; Mary K. Stanger, Dir. of Marketing.

■ **25694** ■ **Jerry's Artarama Inc.**
5325 Departure Dr.
Raleigh, NC 27616-1835
Phone: (919)878-6782
Free: (800)827-8478   **Fax:** (919)873-9565
E-mail: uartist@aol.com
URL: http://www.jerryscatalog.com
Products: Art supplies. **SIC:** 5199 (Nondurable Goods Nec). **Est:** 1968. **Sales:** $10,000,000 (2000). **Emp:** 50. **Officers:** Ira Goldstein, President; David Goldstein, CEO.

■ **25695** ■ **Jungkind Photo-Graphic Inc.**
PO Box 1509
Little Rock, AR 72203
Phone: (501)376-3481   **Fax:** (501)374-4127
Products: Graphic arts supplies. **SIC:** 5043 (Photographic Equipment & Supplies). **Est:** 1881. **Sales:** $45,000,000 (2000). **Emp:** 175. **Officers:** Robert L. Bumgardner, President; Dale Gordon, Treasurer & Secty.

■ **25696** ■ **Katcef Sales Inc.**
1981 Moreland Pkwy.
Annapolis, MD 21401
Phone: (410)268-7877
Products: Floor machines, including vacuums and extractors. **SIC:** 5087 (Service Establishment Equipment). **Sales:** $3,000,000 (2000). **Emp:** 12. **Officers:** S.J. Katcef, President.

■ **25697** ■ **Kazuhiro Ltd.**
6747 Paper Birch Cove
Memphis, TN 38119
Phone: (901)755-1264
Products: Beauty salon equipment and supplies. **SIC:** 5087 (Service Establishment Equipment). **Officers:** Michael K. Nishiya, Director.

■ **25698** ■ **Kemper Enterprises Inc.**
13595 Twelfth St.
Chino, CA 91710
Phone: (909)627-6191
Free: (800)388-5367   **Fax:** (909)627-4008
E-mail: kempertool@aol.com
Products: Tools for ceramics, sculpting, pottery, and crafts. **SICs:** 5072 (Hardware); 5099 (Durable Goods Nec). **Est:** 1947. **Emp:** 80. **Officers:** Herbert H. Stampfl, President; Katie Munday, Dir. of Sales & Marketing; Steve Erskine, Human Resources Contact.

■ **25699** ■ **KG Engineering Inc.**
7620 Delhi Ave.
Las Vegas, NV 89129
Phone: (702)648-5711   **Fax:** (702)648-0336
Products: Engineering equipment. **SIC:** 5049 (Professional Equipment Nec). **Officers:** Ed Giles, President.

■ **25700** ■ **Kindt Collins Co.**
12651 Elmwood Ave.
Cleveland, OH 44111
Phone: (216)252-4122
Free: (800)321-3170   **Fax:** (216)252-5639
Products: Pattern shop supplies; Aluminum casting; Sheet wax; Jewelry and dental waxes. **SICs:** 5084 (Industrial Machinery & Equipment); 5169 (Chemicals & Allied Products Nec); 5031 (Lumber, Plywood & Millwork). **Est:** 1978. **Sales:** $20,000,000 (2000). **Emp:** 65. **Officers:** Leo Kovachic, President; Ken Hartman, Mgr. of Finance; Leonard Principe, Marketing Mgr.

■ **25701** ■ **Kirby Company of Wichita**
1905 E Central Ave.
Wichita, KS 67214-4304
Phone: (316)683-5673
Products: Vacuum cleaning systems. **SIC:** 5087 (Service Establishment Equipment). **Officers:** Roger G. Snellen, President.

■ **25702** ■ **Kiss International**
965 Park Center Dr.
Vista, CA 92083
Phone: (760)599-0200
Free: (800)527-5477   **Fax:** (760)599-0207
E-mail: info@kissintl.com
Products: Water purification devices. **SIC:** 5074 (Plumbing & Hydronic Heating Supplies). **Est:** 1985. **Emp:** 22. **Officers:** Theresa Hawks; Mike Saffran. **Alternate Name:** Di-Tech Systems, Inc.

■ **25703** ■ **Koch Filter Corp.**
PO Box 3186
Louisville, KY 40201-3186
Phone: (502)634-4796
Products: Air filters. **SIC:** 5075 (Warm Air Heating & Air-Conditioning). **Est:** 1966. **Sales:** $12,000,000 (2000). **Emp:** 70. **Officers:** J.M. Koch Jr., President.

■ **25704** ■ **U. Koen Co.**
3112 Jessica St.
Metairie, LA 70003
Phone: (504)944-2471
Products: Cigarette vending machines. **SIC:** 5046 (Commercial Equipment Nec).

■ **25705** ■ **Kraftbilt Products**
6504 E 44th St.
Tulsa, OK 74145-4614
Fax: (918)627-7138
Products: specialty equipment and products. **SIC:** 5199 (Nondurable Goods Nec). **Est:** 1925. **Sales:** $2,000,000 (2000). **Emp:** 10.

■ **25706** ■ **Krauss-Maffei Corp.**
PO Box 6270
Florence, KY 41022-6270
Phone: (606)283-0200   **Fax:** (606)283-9631
Products: Wastewater treatment equipment; Centrifugals and separators. **SIC:** 5084 (Industrial Machinery & Equipment). **Est:** 1966. **Sales:** $16,500,000 (2000). **Emp:** 130. **Officers:** Sandra K. Winter, CFO.

■ **25707** ■ **J. Krieger Associates**
1006 Sunset Ave.
Clarks Summit, PA 18411
Phone: (570)585-2020   **Fax:** (570)586-9518
E-mail: customerservice@jkrieger.com
URL: http://www.jkriger.com
Products: Advertising specialties. **SIC:** 5199 (Nondurable Goods Nec). **Est:** 1956. **Sales:** $7,900,000 (2000). **Emp:** 55. **Officers:** James Krieger, President. **Former Name:** Leshore Calgift Corp.

■ **25708** ■ **Kryolan Corp.**
132 9th St.
San Francisco, CA 94103
Phone: (415)863-9684   **Fax:** (415)863-9059
E-mail: kryolanusa@worldnet.att.net
Products: Theatrical make-up; Special effects materials. **SICs:** 5122 (Drugs, Proprietaries & Sundries); 5199 (Nondurable Goods Nec). **Est:** 1977.

■ **25709** ■ **K's Distributors**
6801 Lockley Cir.
Plano, TX 75074
Phone: (972)578-9116
Products: Vending machines. **SIC:** 5046 (Commercial Equipment Nec).

■ **25710** ■ **Lawsons Locksmithing**
237 Wilson St.
Brewer, ME 04412-2033
Phone: (207)989-5104   **Fax:** (207)989-1440
Products: Service establishment equipment; Locksmith equipment and supplies. **SICs:** 5087 (Service Establishment Equipment); 5049 (Professional Equipment Nec). **Est:** 1986. **Emp:** 3. **Officers:** Tom Bernardini, President; Michele Vachon; John Henry Lawson, Vice President; Gary Tibbetts.

■ **25711** ■ **Bob Leish**
4225 E Sahara Ave., Ste. 10
Las Vegas, NV 89104-6331
Phone: (702)641-5400
Products: Beauty and barbershop products; Hair accessories. **SICs:** 5131 (Piece Goods & Notions); 5122 (Drugs, Proprietaries & Sundries). **Est:** 1978. **Emp:** 2. **Officers:** Bob Leish, Owner. **Alternate Name:** Belco Beauty and Barber Supply Co. and Salon.

■ **25712** ■ **Leisure Crafts**
PO Box 1650
Rancho Cucamonga, CA 91729
Phone: (909)948-8838   **Fax:** (909)948-8694
Products: Fine art supplies, including clay and brushes. **SIC:** 5199 (Nondurable Goods Nec).

■ **25713** ■ **Leisure Time Products Inc.**
2650 Davisson St.
River Grove, IL 60171
Phone: (708)452-5400   **Fax:** (708)453-7515
E-mail: pyrographer@msn.com
URL: http://www.choicemall.com/fireart
Products: Pyrographic art burning equipment and supplies; Carving supplies. **SIC:** 5199 (Nondurable Goods Nec). **Est:** 1985. **Sales:** $2,000,000 (1999). **Emp:** 15. **Officers:** Robert E. Boyer, President; M. Vanasek, CFO; J.E. Boyer, Vice President; Robert Hansen, Dir. of Marketing; Robert Hansen Jr., Sales Marketing Contact, e-mail: rhan26@aol.com.

■ **25714** ■ **Lesco Corp. (Lansing, Michigan)**
PO Box 23098
Lansing, MI 48909
Phone: (517)394-1440   **Fax:** (517)394-1447
Products: Advertising specialties. **SIC:** 5199 (Nondurable Goods Nec). **Sales:** $24,500,000 (2000). **Emp:** 55. **Officers:** Russell J. Horton, President; Nancy Eldred, Vice President.

■ **25715** ■ **Lewiston Rubber & Supply Inc.**
PO Box 139
Lewiston, ME 04240-0139
Phone: (207)784-6985   **Fax:** (207)786-3961
E-mail: methread@maine.com
URL: http://www.maine.com/methread
Products: Shoe tacks; Hand-sewing thread. **SICs:** 5049 (Professional Equipment Nec); 5131 (Piece Goods & Notions); 5072 (Hardware). **Est:** 1958. **Officers:** Ronald Vallee, President; Rusty Vallee, Vice President.

■ **25716** ■ **Liberty Industries Inc.**
133 Commerce St.
East Berlin, CT 06023
Phone: (860)828-6361
Free: (800)828-5656   **Fax:** (860)828-8879
E-mail: libind@liberty-ind.com
URL: http://www.liberty-ind.com
Products: Contamination control products; Cleanroom/laminatflow. **SIC:** 5199 (Nondurable Goods Nec). **Est:** 1953. **Emp:** 50. **Officers:** Les Goldsmith, Dir. of Mktg. & Sales.

■ **25717** ■ **Limestone Detailers**
616 36th Ave. NE
Great Falls, MT 59404-1122
Phone: (406)453-3443   **Fax:** (406)453-6222
Products: Laboratory casework; Wheelchair lifts; Building specialties. **SICs:** 5046 (Commercial

Equipment Nec); 5047 (Medical & Hospital Equipment). **Est:** 1983. **Officers:** Paul Lott, President.

■ 25718 ■ Lit Refrigeration Co.
309 Union Ave.
Memphis, TN 38103
Phone: (901)527-8445
Products: Refrigeration and restaurant supplies. **SICs:** 5087 (Service Establishment Equipment); 5078 (Refrigeration Equipment & Supplies). **Sales:** $2,000,000 (2000). **Emp:** 9. **Officers:** Jerome Lit, CEO.

■ 25719 ■ Logan Corp.
555 7th Ave.
Huntington, WV 25701
Phone: (304)526-4700 **Fax:** (304)526-4747
Products: Mining equipment, including buckets. **SICs:** 5082 (Construction & Mining Machinery); 5084 (Industrial Machinery & Equipment). **Est:** 1904. **Sales:** $32,000,000 (1999). **Emp:** 122. **Officers:** C.M. England III, Chairman of the Board; C.R. Holbrook, VP of Finance; J.C. Nelson, President; Don E. Moore, Dir. of Information Systems; William Kirkland, Dir of Human Resources.

■ 25720 ■ V. Loria & Sons Westchester Corp.
1876 Central Park Ave.
Yonkers, NY 10710
Phone: (914)779-3377
Free: (800)540-2927 **Fax:** (914)779-3587
E-mail: loriacorp@aol.com
Products: Trophies; Signs and plaques; Engraving. **SICs:** 5199 (Nondurable Goods Nec); 5091 (Sporting & Recreational Goods). **Est:** 1957. **Sales:** $1,300,000 (2000). **Emp:** 17. **Officers:** Roger Loria, President; Vera Loria, Secretary; Marie E. DiPietro, Treasurer.

■ 25721 ■ MacPherson's-Artcraft
1351 Ocean Ave
Emeryville, CA 94608
Phone: (510)428-9011 **Fax:** (510)768-6630
URL: http://www.macphersonart.com
Products: Art supplies, including paint, brushes, and pencils. **SIC:** 5199 (Nondurable Goods Nec). **Est:** 1906. **Sales:** $85,000,000 (2000). **Emp:** 250. **Officers:** Frank Stapleton, President; Stu Beattie, Exec. VP. **Alternate Name:** Art Supply Enterprises Inc. **Former Name:** MacPherson's.

■ 25722 ■ Mahalick Corp.
PO Box 604
Putnam Valley, NY 10579-0604
Phone: (914)963-1100 **Fax:** (914)963-1316
E-mail: nbroberts@aol.com
Products: Printing equipment, including electronic prepress; Graphic arts supplies and equipment. **SICs:** 5043 (Photographic Equipment & Supplies); 5199 (Nondurable Goods Nec). **Sales:** $13,000,000 (2000). **Emp:** 35. **Officers:** Brian Roberts, President.

■ 25723 ■ John G. Mahowald
PO Box 5157
Grand Forks, ND 58206-0157
Phone: (701)775-9231
Products: Service industry machinery; Shoe repair materials; Shoe repair findings; Tailors' supplies. **SIC:** 5087 (Service Establishment Equipment). **Officers:** John Mahowald, Owner.

■ 25724 ■ Mann U.V. Technology, Inc.
3217 Buncombe Rd.
Greenville, SC 29609
Phone: (919)271-4036 **Fax:** (919)271-4441
Products: Suntanning equipment and supplies. **SIC:** 5064 (Electrical Appliances—Television & Radio). **Officers:** Gordon Mann, President.

■ 25725 ■ Marshall and Bruce Co.
689 Davidson St.
Nashville, TN 37213
Phone: (615)256-3661
Products: Commercial printing supplies. **SICs:** 5112 (Stationery & Office Supplies); 5049 (Professional Equipment Nec). **Est:** 1865. **Sales:** $6,000,000 (2000). **Emp:** 60. **Officers:** Robert Smith, President.

■ 25726 ■ Mathias Reprographics
950 Penn Ave.
Pittsburgh, PA 15222-3706
Phone: (412)281-1800 **Fax:** (412)281-8243
Products: Blueprints and photographs. **SICs:** 5049 (Professional Equipment Nec); 5043 (Photographic Equipment & Supplies). **Emp:** 35. **Officers:** Herbert A. Mathias.

■ 25727 ■ Art Mattson Distributing Co.
11711 Fairview Ave.
Boise, ID 83713
Phone: (208)375-4510
Products: Steam cleaners, including degreasers for motors. **SIC:** 5087 (Service Establishment Equipment). **Est:** 1957. **Sales:** $250,000 (2000). **Emp:** 4. **Officers:** Gary Mattson, President.

■ 25728 ■ Mazel Stores Inc.
31000 Aurora Rd.
Solon, OH 44139
Phone: (440)248-5200
Products: General merchandise. **SIC:** 5099 (Durable Goods Nec). **Sales:** $208,300,000 (2000). **Emp:** 1,181. **Officers:** Reuven Dessler, CEO & Chairman of the Board; Susan Atkinson, Sr. VP & CFO.

■ 25729 ■ Lynn McGuffy Company Inc.
18635 Telge Rd.
Cypress, TX 77429-1362
Phone: (281)255-6955
Products: Filters and parts to the energy industry. **SIC:** 5084 (Industrial Machinery & Equipment).

■ 25730 ■ McLogan Supply
711 S East St.
Anaheim, CA 92805
Phone: (714)999-1194 **Fax:** (714)999-0195
Products: Silk screening; Science supplies. **SIC:** 5199 (Nondurable Goods Nec).

■ 25731 ■ McLogan Supply
2010 S Main
Los Angeles, CA 90007
Phone: (213)749-2262 **Fax:** (213)745-6540
Products: Nonelectric signs. **SIC:** 5199 (Nondurable Goods Nec).

■ 25732 ■ McLogan Supply
7609 Convoy Ct.
San Diego, CA 92111
Phone: (619)292-5664 **Fax:** (619)571-7383
Products: Screen printing supplies; Sign supplies. **SIC:** 5199 (Nondurable Goods Nec).

■ 25733 ■ McMurray Printing Co.
175 Main
Brookville, PA 15825-1233
Phone: (814)849-5338
Free: (800)842-8927 **Fax:** (814)849-6327
Products: Printing. **SICs:** 5084 (Industrial Machinery & Equipment); 5111 (Printing & Writing Paper). **Sales:** $500,000 (2000). **Emp:** 10. **Officers:** Donald McMurray, President; Donald E. Wilson, Vice President; Janet Y. Dinger, Treasurer & Secty.; Kaye L. Abbott.

■ 25734 ■ MDI Production
PO Box 61056
Honolulu, HI 96839
Phone: (808)988-6116
Free: (800)988-6117 **Fax:** (808)988-6511
E-mail: mdihawaii@aloha.net
URL: http://www.aloha.net/mdihnl/
Products: Theatrical supplies and lighting equipment. **SICs:** 5063 (Electrical Apparatus & Equipment); 5199 (Nondurable Goods Nec). **Est:** 1988.

■ 25735 ■ Meredith Stained Glass Center, Inc.
1115 E West Hwy.
Silver Spring, MD 20910
Phone: (301)650-8572 **Free:** (800)966-6667
URL: http://www.meredithglass.com
Products: Stained glass supplies, including etching materials and equipment. **SICs:** 5199 (Nondurable Goods Nec); 5049 (Professional Equipment Nec). **Est:** 1978. **Sales:** $600,000 (2000). **Emp:** 10. **Officers:** John Meredith, Vice President; Jane Meredith, President.

■ 25736 ■ Mermaid Water Services
1801 Pewaukee Rd.
Waukesha, WI 53188
Phone: (414)547-1862 **Fax:** (414)547-5728
Products: Water treatment systems. **SIC:** 5074 (Plumbing & Hydronic Heating Supplies).

■ 25737 ■ Midco International Inc. (Effingham, Illinois)
PO Box 748
Effingham, IL 62401
Phone: (217)342-9211 **Fax:** (217)347-0316
Products: Durable goods. **SIC:** 5099 (Durable Goods Nec). **Sales:** $15,000,000 (1993). **Emp:** 80. **Officers:** L.D. Samuel, President; David Samuel, CFO.

■ 25738 ■ Midwest Environmental Safety Supply
1817 Gardner Rd.
Broadview, IL 60153
Phone: (708)343-6766 **Fax:** (708)343-3398
Products: Environmental spill control and wastewater treatment and remediation products. **SIC:** 5169 (Chemicals & Allied Products Nec). **Sales:** $5,000,000 (1994). **Emp:** 12. **Officers:** W. Paul Kyne, COO.

■ 25739 ■ Mikan Theatricals
86 Tide Mill Rd.
Hampton, NH 03842
Phone: (603)926-2744
Free: (800)289-6452 **Fax:** (603)929-0230
Products: Theatrical supplies, including stage curtain tracks. **SICs:** 5049 (Professional Equipment Nec); 5199 (Nondurable Goods Nec). **Est:** 1976.

■ 25740 ■ Milart Ceramics Inc.
26164 Westfield
Redford, MI 48239-1841
Phone: (313)937-2780
Products: Ceramics. **SIC:** 5049 (Professional Equipment Nec). **Officers:** Arthur Blank, President.

■ 25741 ■ Miller Funeral Home Inc.
507 S Main Ave.
Sioux Falls, SD 57104-6813
Phone: (605)336-2640
Products: Service establishment equipment; Cemetery and funeral director's equipment and supplies; Caskets. **SICs:** 5087 (Service Establishment Equipment); 5199 (Nondurable Goods Nec). **Officers:** Ken Koball, President.

■ 25742 ■ Millers Wholesale, Inc.
PO Box 1070
Battle Creek, MI 49016-1070
Phone: (616)965-0518
Free: (800)632-5436 **Fax:** (616)965-4438
Products: Decorative laminates; Ceramic tile; Adhesives; Shower doors; Interior building products. **SICs:** 5199 (Nondurable Goods Nec); 5032 (Brick, Stone & Related Materials); 5039 (Construction Materials Nec); 5169 (Chemicals & Allied Products Nec).

■ 25743 ■ Montana Leather Co. Inc.
PO Box 394
Billings, MT 59103-0394
Phone: (406)245-1660 **Fax:** (406)245-4109
Products: Shoe repair materials; Shoe repair findings. **SIC:** 5087 (Service Establishment Equipment). **Officers:** Douglas Mac Pherson, President.

■ 25744 ■ Montoya/MAS International Inc.
502 Palm St., No. 21
West Palm Beach, FL 33401
Phone: (561)832-4401
Free: (800)682-8665 **Fax:** (561)833-2722
E-mail: montoya-mas@worldnet.att.net
URL: http://www.home.att.net/~montoya-mas./
Products: Sculpture supplies. **SICs:** 5099 (Durable Goods Nec); 5046 (Commercial Equipment Nec). **Est:** 1973. **Sales:** $500,000 (1999). **Emp:** 6. **Officers:** Marsha Montoya, Owner.

■ 25745 ■ Multicraft Inc.
3233 E Van Buren St.
Phoenix, AZ 85008
Phone: (602)244-9444 **Fax:** (602)275-1135
Products: Silkscreen ink; Graphing equipment;

Airbrush equipment; Drafting furniture. **SICs:** 5199 (Nondurable Goods Nec); 5021 (Furniture); 5084 (Industrial Machinery & Equipment). **Emp:** 35.

■ **25746** ■ **Multicraft Inc.**
4701 Lakeside Ave. E
Cleveland, OH 44114-3805
Phone: (216)791-8600 **Fax:** (216)791-1770
Products: Silk-screening and art supplies; T-shirts.
SICs: 5085 (Industrial Supplies); 5199 (Nondurable Goods Nec); 5084 (Industrial Machinery & Equipment).

■ **25747** ■ **Nannicola Wholesale Co., Inc.**
1417 Youngstown Rd. SE
Warren, OH 44484-4247
Phone: (330)393-8888 **Fax:** (330)395-5800
Products: Carnival supplies; Bingo supplies and equipment. **SICs:** 5046 (Commercial Equipment Nec); 5087 (Service Establishment Equipment). **Emp:** 49. **Officers:** Charles Nannicola, Sales/Marketing Contact; Kim Sikora, Customer Service Contact; Chris Sobel, Human Resources Contact.

■ **25748** ■ **National Art Supply**
2021 Forest Ave.
Kansas City, MO 64108
Phone: (816)842-6700
Free: (800)821-5616 **Fax:** (816)842-6730
Products: Artists' supplies. **SICs:** 5092 (Toys & Hobby Goods & Supplies); 5199 (Nondurable Goods Nec). **Est:** 1978. **Emp:** 50. **Officers:** Robert S. Dix.

■ **25749** ■ **National Impressions Corp.**
1450 E Indian School Rd., Ste. 106
Phoenix, AZ 85014-4954
Phone: (602)230-5999 **Fax:** (602)230-5994
Products: Advertising specialties and wearables. **SIC:** 5199 (Nondurable Goods Nec). **Est:** 1990. **Sales:** $1,000,000 (2000). **Emp:** 5. **Officers:** Frank Vasos, President.

■ **25750** ■ **National Stock Sign Co.**
PO Box 5145
Santa Cruz, CA 95063-5145
Phone: (408)476-2020 **Fax:** (408)476-1734
Products: specialty equipment and products. **SIC:** 5099 (Durable Goods Nec). **Est:** 1962. **Sales:** $1,000,000 (2000). **Emp:** 10.

■ **25751** ■ **Naturo Co.**
4250 E Washington
Los Angeles, CA 90023
Phone: (213)268-7291
Products: Funeral supplies, including embalming fluid, clothes, and powder. **SICs:** 5169 (Chemicals & Allied Products Nec); 5049 (Professional Equipment Nec). **Est:** 1916. **Sales:** $300,000 (2000). **Emp:** 5. **Officers:** Warren W. Condreay, General Mgr.

■ **25752** ■ **Naz-Dar Cincinnati**
3905 Port Union Rd.
Fairfield, OH 45014-2203
Phone: (513)870-5706
Free: (800)729-9942 **Fax:** (513)870-5713
Products: Printing ink; Printing trades machinery, equipment, and supplies. **SICs:** 5085 (Industrial Supplies); 5199 (Nondurable Goods Nec); 5084 (Industrial Machinery & Equipment). **Emp:** 30.

■ **25753** ■ **Neon Co.**
858 DeKalb Ave. NE
Atlanta, GA 30307
Phone: (404)873-6366 **Fax:** (404)584-6366
Products: Neon signs. **SIC:** 5046 (Commercial Equipment Nec). **Emp:** 7. **Officers:** Gregg Brenner.

■ **25754** ■ **Neopost**
1345 Valwood Pkwy., Ste. 310
Carrollton, TX 75006
Phone: (972)243-2421 **Fax:** (972)247-1521
Products: Mailing and shipping equipment. **SIC:** 5084 (Industrial Machinery & Equipment). **Emp:** 49. **Officers:** Prithee Persad; Bill Heck.

■ **25755** ■ **Nero Systems, Inc.**
21331 Valley Forge Cir.
King of Prussia, PA 19406
Phone: (610)783-5724 **Fax:** (610)783-5662
E-mail: neroguy@aol.com
URL: http://www.lifeflo-nerosystems.com/
Products: Water treatment systems; Ultra violet systems. **SIC:** 5074 (Plumbing & Hydronic Heating Supplies). **Est:** 1992. **Sales:** $400,000 (2000). **Emp:** 2. **Officers:** Epamin Vastardis, President.

■ **25756** ■ **New Age Water Technology**
4515 N Hallmark Pkwy.
San Bernardino, CA 92407
Phone: (909)384-7111 **Fax:** (909)887-8111
Products: Water treatment systems. **SIC:** 5074 (Plumbing & Hydronic Heating Supplies). **Officers:** Jon Spears, Director of Sales.

■ **25757** ■ **New Jersey Art Drafting**
926 Haddonfield Rd.
Cherry Hill, NJ 08002-2745
Phone: (609)779-7979 **Fax:** (609)665-5611
Products: Lead pencils, crayons, and artists' materials; Artists' equipment. **SIC:** 5199 (Nondurable Goods Nec). **Emp:** 49. **Officers:** Frank Marone.

■ **25758** ■ **Newhouse Printers Supply Inc.**
5737 E Cork St.
Kalamazoo, MI 49001
Phone: (616)381-9500 **Fax:** (616)381-2009
Products: Printing supplies. **SIC:** 5084 (Industrial Machinery & Equipment). **Est:** 1948. **Sales:** $11,000,000 (2000). **Emp:** 37. **Officers:** Gordon J. Newhouse, President & Treasurer.

■ **25759** ■ **Nimbus Water Systems, Inc.**
288 Distribution St.
San Marcos, CA 92069
Phone: (760)591-0211
Free: (800)451-9343 **Fax:** (760)591-0106
E-mail: salesinfo@nimbuswater.com
URL: http://www.nimbus.com
Products: Membrane based purification and filtration systems and supplies. **SIC:** 5074 (Plumbing & Hydronic Heating Supplies). **Est:** 1967. **Emp:** 30. **Officers:** Donald T. Bray, Chairman of the Board; Mike Faulkner, CEO; Adam Robbins, General Mgr.; Charlie Price, President.

■ **25760** ■ **Noble and Associates**
7136 S Yale, Ste. 311
Tulsa, OK 74136
Phone: (918)493-5015 **Fax:** (918)481-5758
Products: Water purification and filter equipment; Odor eliminators. **SIC:** 5074 (Plumbing & Hydronic Heating Supplies). **Officers:** Charles Noble, President.

■ **25761** ■ **Norcostco Inc.**
3203 N Hwy. 100
Minneapolis, MN 55422
Phone: (612)533-2791 **Fax:** (612)533-3718
Products: Theatrical supplies. **SICs:** 5199 (Nondurable Goods Nec); 5049 (Professional Equipment Nec). **Sales:** $10,500,000 (2000). **Emp:** 150. **Officers:** James Scott.

■ **25762** ■ **North American Aqua Inc.**
18008 State St.
Vandalia, MI 49095
Phone: (616)476-2092 **Fax:** (616)476-2251
Products: Water filters. **SIC:** 5074 (Plumbing & Hydronic Heating Supplies). **Est:** 1985. **Sales:** $1,000,000 (2000). **Emp:** 5. **Officers:** Rocco Papandrea, President.

■ **25763** ■ **North Star Water Conditioning**
1890 Woodlane Dr.
Woodbury, MN 55125
Phone: (612)738-5839
Free: (800)972-0135 **Fax:** (612)739-5293
E-mail: schauerl@ecowater.com
URL: http://www.northstar.conditioning.com
Products: Water treatment equipment and supplies. **SIC:** 5074 (Plumbing & Hydronic Heating Supplies). **Est:** 1925. **Officers:** John Scott, Vice President.

■ **25764** ■ **Northwest Graphic Supply Co.**
4200 E Lake St.
Minneapolis, MN 55406-2265
Phone: (612)729-7361
Free: (800)221-4079 **Fax:** (612)729-6647
Products: Artists and screen printing supplies. **SIC:** 5199 (Nondurable Goods Nec). **Est:** 1961. **Emp:** 20. **Officers:** Alan Puder. **Former Name:** Northwest Graphics.

■ **25765** ■ **Northwestern Systems**
PO Box 1701
Great Falls, MT 59403-1701
Phone: (406)727-4881
Products: Coin-operated mechanisms and parts; Vending machines. **SIC:** 5046 (Commercial Equipment Nec). **Officers:** Don Pencoske, Owner.

■ **25766** ■ **N.R.G. Enterprises, Inc.**
22 42nd St. NW, Ste. A
Auburn, WA 98001
Phone: (253)852-3111
Free: (800)264-7872 **Fax:** (253)852-3222
E-mail: nrgmistra@aol.com
URL: http://www.nrgmistra.com
Products: Water filters and shower filters. **SIC:** 5074 (Plumbing & Hydronic Heating Supplies). **Est:** 1988. **Officers:** Al Spokoiny, President. **Alternate Name:** Mistra, Inc.

■ **25767** ■ **Nsa Independent Distributor**
585 Hoy Rd.
Madison, MS 39110
Phone: (601)856-3236
Products: Water purification/filtration. **SIC:** 5074 (Plumbing & Hydronic Heating Supplies).

■ **25768** ■ **Nyle Home Health Supplies Inc.**
72 Center St.
Brewer, ME 04412
Phone: (207)989-4335
Products: Dry kilns. **SIC:** 5046 (Commercial Equipment Nec).

■ **25769** ■ **OASIS Corp.**
265 N Hamilton Rd.
PO Box 13150
Columbus, OH 43213-0150
Phone: (614)861-1350
Free: (800)950-3226 **Fax:** (614)861-5750
URL: http://www.oasiswatercoolers.com
Products: Water coolers. **SIC:** 5074 (Plumbing & Hydronic Heating Supplies). **Est:** 1910. **Officers:** Mark Blackstone, VP of Marketing; John Schenz, Customer Service Contact; Gary Nelson, Human Resources Contact.

■ **25770** ■ **Oasis Imaging Products**
1617 Southwood Dr.
Nashua, NH 03063-1801
Phone: (603)880-3991
Products: Remanufacturing supplies for laser-printer cartridges. **SIC:** 5045 (Computers, Peripherals & Software). **Officers:** Mike VanDalsum, President.

■ **25771** ■ **OCE-Bruning Inc.**
6300 S Syracuse Way, Ste. 350
Englewood, CO 80111-2017
Phone: (303)779-6970
Free: (800)888-4685 **Fax:** (303)741-5217
Products: Engineering blueprint copiers. **SIC:** 5049 (Professional Equipment Nec). **Emp:** 12.

■ **25772** ■ **OCE-USA Inc.**
840 Croskys Office Pk.
Fairport, NY 14450-3513
Phone: (716)425-4330
Free: (800)253-2203 **Fax:** (716)425-2041
Products: Blueprint machines and supplies. **SIC:** 5049 (Professional Equipment Nec). **Emp:** 49.

■ **25773** ■ **Omega Refrigerant Reclamation Corp.**
12504 E Whittier Blvd.
Whittier, CA 90602
Phone: (310)698-0991 **Fax:** (310)696-1908
E-mail: info@refex.com
Products: Refrigerants and fluorocarbons. **SIC:** 5169 (Chemicals & Allied Products Nec). **Est:** 1963. **Sales:**

$8,600,000 (2000). **Emp:** 20. **Officers:** Dennis O'Meara, President.

■ 25774 ■ **Omnichron**
1438 Oxford St.
Berkeley, CA 94709
Phone: (510)540-6455 **Fax:** (510)540-8550
Products: Voice synthesizers for the blind. **SIC:** 5099 (Durable Goods Nec). **Sales:** $500,000 (2000). **Emp:** 4. **Officers:** Cynthia Lowe, Partner; Steven Smith, Partner.

■ 25775 ■ **Ordway Sign Supply**
16540 Gaulet
Van Nuys, CA 91406
Phone: (818)908-9666 **Fax:** (818)908-9673
Products: Sign supplies. **SIC:** 5199 (Nondurable Goods Nec).

■ 25776 ■ **Oreck Floorcare Center**
15261 E Mississippi Ave.
Aurora, CO 80012-3747
Phone: (303)751-7133 **Fax:** (303)368-0260
Products: Vacuum cleaning systems. **SIC:** 5087 (Service Establishment Equipment). **Officers:** Dave Barhite, Owner.

■ 25777 ■ **Osmonics, Inc.**
5951 Clearwater Dr.
Minnetonka, MN 55343-8995
Phone: (612)933-2277
Free: (800)848-1750 **Fax:** (612)933-0141
E-mail: osmonics@worldnet.att.net
URL: http://www.osmonics.com
Products: Water purifiers; Water treatment systems; Ion exchanges; Distillations; Coalescing and ozonation equipment; Pumps; Flow control components. **SIC:** 5074 (Plumbing & Hydronic Heating Supplies). **Est:** 1969. **Sales:** $200,000,000 (1999). **Emp:** 1,400. **Officers:** Ed Fierko, President & CEO; L.L. Runzheimer, CFO; Kenton C. Toomey, VP of Operations; Roger Miller, VP of Marketing & Sales, e-mail: osmonics@worldnet.att.net; Bjarne Nicolaisen, Vice President.

■ 25778 ■ **OUR Designs Inc.**
PO Box 17404
Covington, KY 41017-0404
Phone: (606)282-5500
Products: Custom badges; Collar insignias; Hats for firefighters and EMS professionals. **SIC:** 5087 (Service Establishment Equipment). **Est:** 1981. **Sales:** $3,000,000 (2000). **Emp:** 25. **Officers:** Michael Daugherty, Vice President; Thomas Drury, Accountant.

■ 25779 ■ **Ozotech, Inc.**
2401 Oberlin Rd.
Yreka, CA 96097
Phone: (530)842-4189 **Fax:** (530)842-3238
E-mail: ozotech@ozotech.com
URL: http://www.ozotech.com
Products: Ozone generators; Water treatment systems. **SICs:** 5084 (Industrial Machinery & Equipment); 5074 (Plumbing & Hydronic Heating Supplies). **Est:** 1986. **Sales:** $6,200,000 (2000). **Emp:** 62. **Officers:** Kenneth W. Mouw, President; Ray Condit, VP of Research & Development; Tim Teffeteller, Dir. of Mktg. & Sales, e-mail: sales@ozotech.com; Nancy Mouw, Dir. of Admin.; Aaron Cenia, Director of Engineering, e-mail: engineering@ozotech.com.

■ 25780 ■ **Pan Am Sign Products, Inc.**
2525 NW 75th St.
Miami, FL 33147
Phone: (305)691-0581
Free: (800)466-0581 **Fax:** (305)691-0587
E-mail: panam@bellsouth.net
Products: Neon and electric sign supplies. **SICs:** 5199 (Nondurable Goods Nec); 5084 (Industrial Machinery & Equipment). **Est:** 1947. **Emp:** 7. **Officers:** John Mulligan, Customer Service Contact. **Former Name:** Pan Am Supply Company Inc.

■ 25781 ■ **Perfection Distributing Co.**
616 Lillian Way
Los Angeles, CA 90004-1108
Phone: (213)751-2345
Products: Barber and beauty shop furniture and equipment; Beauty and barber shop accessories; Hydraulic beauty and barber shop chairs. **SICs:** 5087 (Service Establishment Equipment); 5021 (Furniture). **Est:** 1969. **Officers:** Jack Horne, Owner.

■ 25782 ■ **Persinger Supply Co.**
PO Box 188
Prichard, WV 25555
Phone: (304)486-5401 **Fax:** (304)486-5401
Products: Mining supplies. **SIC:** 5082 (Construction & Mining Machinery). **Est:** 1904. **Sales:** $36,000,000 (2000). **Emp:** 85. **Officers:** R. Douglas Francis, President; B. Vernice Deskins, VP & Treasurer; Robert K. Kiser, VP of Sales; Carl Tickle, Dir of Human Resources.

■ 25783 ■ **Philadelphia Sign Company Inc.**
707 W Spring Garden St
Palmyra, NJ 08065
Phone: (609)829-1460
Products: Electric signs. **SIC:** 5099 (Durable Goods Nec). **Est:** 1918. **Sales:** $23,000,000 (2000). **Emp:** 175. **Officers:** W. Trucksess, President.

■ 25784 ■ **Phillips and Jacobs Inc.**
3991 Commerce Pkwy.
Miramar, FL 33025
Phone: (954)432-1000
Products: Printing supplies, including printing plates. **SIC:** 5199 (Nondurable Goods Nec).

■ 25785 ■ **Photocomm Inc.**
7681 E Gray Rd.
Scottsdale, AZ 85260
Phone: (602)948-8003
Free: (800)223-9580 **Fax:** (602)483-6431
Products: Solar equipment. **SIC:** 5099 (Durable Goods Nec). **Est:** 1981. **Sales:** $10,000,000 (2000). **Emp:** 100. **Officers:** Robert Kauffman, President; Tom LaVoy, CFO.

■ 25786 ■ **Harold M. Pitman Co.**
721 Union Blvd.
Totowa, NJ 07512
Phone: (973)812-0400 **Fax:** (973)812-1630
Products: Graphic arts supplies. **SICs:** 5199 (Nondurable Goods Nec); 5043 (Photographic Equipment & Supplies). **Est:** 1906. **Sales:** $500,000,000 (2000). **Emp:** 600. **Officers:** John W. Dreyer, CEO & President; Gerald Knueven, Exec. VP & Treasurer; Frank McCarthy, Data Processing Mgr.; Robert P. Schmidt, Dir of Human Resources.

■ 25787 ■ **Plastruct Inc.**
1020 S Wallace Pl.
La Puente, CA 91748
Phone: (626)912-7017 **Fax:** (626)965-2036
Products: Architectural scale model parts. **SIC:** 5162 (Plastics Materials & Basic Shapes). **Est:** 1968. **Sales:** $3,000,000 (2000). **Emp:** 35. **Officers:** J.J. Wanderman, President.

■ 25788 ■ **Pottery Art Studio Inc.**
4510 Killam Ave.
Norfolk, VA 23508-2047
Phone: (757)489-7417 **Fax:** (757)489-2023
Products: Ceramic supplies. **SIC:** 5049 (Professional Equipment Nec). **Officers:** Robert Soble, President.

■ 25789 ■ **Premier Manufactured Systems**
17431 N 25th Ave.
Phoenix, AZ 85023
Phone: (623)931-1977
Free: (800)752-5582 **Fax:** (623)931-0191
E-mail: insidesales@premierh2o.com
URL: http://www.premierh2o.com
Products: Residential and commercial water filtration and purification systems. **SIC:** 5074 (Plumbing & Hydronic Heating Supplies). **Est:** 1989. **Emp:** 23. **Officers:** Jerry Monroe; William McKiever III; Bob Maisner, Sales/Marketing Contact; Gayle Birmingham, Customer Service Contact.

■ 25790 ■ **Primesource**
1650 Magnolia Dr.
Cincinnati, OH 45215
Phone: (513)563-6700
Free: (800)582-7406 **Fax:** (513)563-0377
URL: http://www.primesource.com
Products: Graphic equipment. **SICs:** 5043 (Photographic Equipment & Supplies); 5199 (Nondurable Goods Nec). **Est:** 1864. **Sales:** $27,000,000 (2000). **Emp:** 45. **Officers:** Ray Rafalowski, Branch Mgr.

■ 25791 ■ **PrimeSource Corp.**
4350 Haddonfield Rd., No. 222
Pennsauken, NJ 08109
Phone: (609)488-4888 **Fax:** (609)488-7255
Products: Graphic arts supplies. **SICs:** 5085 (Industrial Supplies); 5199 (Nondurable Goods Nec). **Est:** 1865. **Sales:** $357,100,000 (2000). **Emp:** 660. **Officers:** James F. Mullan, CEO & President; William A. DeMarco, VP & CFO; Frederick G. Heinkel, VP of Marketing & Sales.

■ 25792 ■ **Providence Casket Co.**
1 Industrial Cir.
Lincoln, RI 02865-2611
Phone: (401)726-1700 **Fax:** (401)726-1702
Products: Service establishment equipment; Cemetery and funeral director's equipment and supplies; Caskets. **SIC:** 5087 (Service Establishment Equipment). **Est:** 1929. **Emp:** 20. **Officers:** Stephen E. Nazareth; Brett P. Nazareth.

■ 25793 ■ **Roger Pryor & Associates**
412 N Berry Pine Rd.
Rapid City, SD 57702-1857
Phone: (605)343-4628
Products: Service industry machinery. **SIC:** 5087 (Service Establishment Equipment). **Officers:** Roger Pryor, Partner.

■ 25794 ■ **Publishers Supply Inc.**
26 Keewaydin Dr., Ste. C
Salem, NH 03079-2898
Phone: (603)898-9898
Products: Commercial equipment. **SIC:** 5046 (Commercial Equipment Nec). **Officers:** Robert Faulkner, President.

■ 25795 ■ **Pure Water International Inc.**
4350 NE 5th Terr.
Oakland Park, FL 33334
Phone: (954)561-3155 **Fax:** (954)561-7307
E-mail: sales@pureh2o.com
Products: Manufacturing and sales of complete line of water purification equipment. **SIC:** 5074 (Plumbing & Hydronic Heating Supplies). **Est:** 1990. **Sales:** $1,000,000 (1999). **Emp:** 6. **Officers:** Craig Mussler, Sales/Marketing Contact.

■ 25796 ■ **Puro Filter Co.**
15151 S Prairie Ave.
Lawndale, CA 90260
Phone: (213)937-1308
Products: Water drinking fountains and filters. **SIC:** 5074 (Plumbing & Hydronic Heating Supplies). **Est:** 1925. **Sales:** $500,000 (2000). **Emp:** 6. **Officers:** Jack West, President.

■ 25797 ■ **Rainsoft Water Conditioning Co.**
2080 Lunt Ave.
Elk Grove Village, IL 60007
Phone: (847)437-9400 **Fax:** (847)437-1594
Products: Water treatment systems. **SIC:** 5074 (Plumbing & Hydronic Heating Supplies).

■ 25798 ■ **Ready Made Sign Co.**
480 Fillmore Ave.
Tonawanda, NY 14150
Phone: (716)695-7300 **Fax:** (716)695-5884
Products: Safety compliance signs, labels, tags, equipment and training material. **SIC:** 5051 (Metals Service Centers & Offices). **Sales:** $6,900,000 (2000). **Emp:** 40. **Officers:** John Greenberger, CEO.

■ **25799** ■ **Recognition Systems Inc.**
30 Harbor Park Dr.
Port Washington, NY 11050
Phone: (516)625-5000
Free: (800)777-4368 **Fax:** (516)625-1507
E-mail: dotworks@hotmail.com
URL: http://www.dotworks.com
Products: Graphic arts film and paper. **SICs:** 5043 (Photographic Equipment & Supplies); 5199 (Nondurable Goods Nec). **Est:** 1968. **Sales:** $23,000,000 (2000). **Emp:** 90. **Officers:** John E. McCusker, CEO & Chairman of the Board; Jeff McCusker, Treasurer.

■ **25800** ■ **Reece Supply Company of Dallas**
3308 Royalty Row
Irving, TX 75062
Phone: (972)438-3131
Free: (800)776-7448 **Fax:** (972)721-1758
URL: http://www.reecesupply.com
Products: Sign supplies, including paints and boards; Silk screening supplies. **SICs:** 5046 (Commercial Equipment Nec); 5198 (Paints, Varnishes & Supplies). **Est:** 1950. **Sales:** $53,000,000 (2000). **Emp:** 40. **Officers:** Richard Reece, President; John Williams, Vice President.

■ **25801** ■ **M. Renken Distributing**
24 Glen Carran Cir.
Sparks, NV 89431-5830
Phone: (702)355-8001 **Fax:** (702)355-8064
Products: Vacuum cleaning systems. **SIC:** 5087 (Service Establishment Equipment). **Officers:** Mike Renken, Owner.

■ **25802** ■ **Repro Technology Inc.**
PO Box 357
Conroe, TX 77305
Phone: (936)539-4419
Free: (800)835-8918 **Fax:** (936)539-4418
E-mail: reprotec@lcc.net
URL: http://www.reprotechnology.com
Products: Blueprinting equipment; Whiteprinting equipment; Laminators; Trimmers/cutters; Material handling carts. **SIC:** 5049 (Professional Equipment Nec). **Est:** 1977. **Sales:** $2,000,000 (2000). **Emp:** 19. **Officers:** Patrick McPherson Sr.; Maggie McPherson, Sales/Marketing Contact; Cheryl Tardiff, Customer Service Contact.

■ **25803** ■ **Rice Lake Products Inc.**
PO Box 146
Minot, ND 58702
Phone: (701)857-6363
Products: Hunting and pest control devices. **SICs:** 5091 (Sporting & Recreational Goods); 5191 (Farm Supplies).

■ **25804** ■ **R.O. Systems International**
1914 W Mission Rd., Ste. H
Escondido, CA 92029
Phone: (760)747-3100
Free: (800)477-6464 **Fax:** (760)747-3221
E-mail: mail4rosi@aol.com
URL: http://www.rosystemsintl.com
Products: Water treatment systems and equipment. **SIC:** 5074 (Plumbing & Hydronic Heating Supplies). **Est:** 1989. **Sales:** $1,500,000 (2000). **Emp:** 8. **Officers:** Brett Rogers, President; Debbie Collier, Vice President.

■ **25805** ■ **Road Machinery Co.**
716 S 7th St. (85034)
PO Box 4425
Phoenix, AZ 85030
Phone: (602)252-7121 **Fax:** (602)253-9690
URL: http://www.roadmachinery.com
Products: 55-320 tons; Crawler dozers, wheel loaders, and excavators; Blasthole drills; Apshalt and concrete paving equipment; Facilities for repair of electric wheel motors, diesel engines and transmissions; Hydraulic components; Compaction equipment. **SIC:** 5082 (Construction & Mining Machinery). **Est:** 1955. **Sales:** $140,000,000 (2000). **Emp:** 350. **Officers:** Michael J. Boze, President; Joe Scalmato, Asst. Controller; Howard Randy Smith, Sr. VP of Sales & Marketing.

■ **25806** ■ **Russell Associates Inc.**
5755 Rio Vista Dr.
Clearwater, FL 33760-3114
Phone: (727)532-4545 **Fax:** (727)532-4731
E-mail: pas_pas@pall.com
URL: http://www.pall.com
Products: Aerospace filtration products. **SIC:** 5085 (Industrial Supplies). **Est:** 1942. **Sales:** $21,000,000 (2000). **Emp:** 55. **Officers:** Richard Haas, President; Terry Sellman, Controller; Michale Woodland, Vice President.

■ **25807** ■ **S and S Worldwide Inc.**
PO Box 513
Colchester, CT 06415-0513
Phone: (860)537-3451 **Fax:** (860)537-2866
Products: Arts and crafts supplies, including paint and brushes; Health care; Recreation. **SIC:** 5199 (Nondurable Goods Nec). **Sales:** $15,000,000 (1999). **Emp:** 275. **Officers:** Stephen Schwartz, President; Michael Pasternak, Exec. VP.

■ **25808** ■ **J.R. Schneider Company Inc.**
849 Jackson St.
Benicia, CA 94510
Phone: (707)745-0404 **Fax:** (707)745-2159
Products: Filtration equipment. **SIC:** 5084 (Industrial Machinery & Equipment). **Est:** 1965. **Sales:** $10,000,000 (2000). **Emp:** 50. **Officers:** J.S. Schneider, President; C. Canada, Controller; Stephen G. Harris, Dir. of Marketing & Sales.

■ **25809** ■ **Schuylkill Haven Casket Co.**
PO Box 179
Schuylkill Haven, PA 17972
Phone: (717)385-0296
Products: Hardwood caskets. **SIC:** 5087 (Service Establishment Equipment). **Est:** 1919. **Sales:** $8,000,000 (2000). **Emp:** 120. **Officers:** D.W. Houck, President; Robert L. Reggio, VP of Marketing.

■ **25810** ■ **Screen (USA)**
5110 Tollview Dr.
Rolling Meadows, IL 60008
Phone: (847)870-7400
Free: (800)372-7737 **Fax:** (847)870-0149
Products: Graphic art pre-press equipment, including scanners, cameras, and pressers. **SIC:** 5084 (Industrial Machinery & Equipment). **Est:** 1964. **Sales:** $30,000,000 (2000). **Emp:** 90. **Officers:** Kenneth D. Newton, CEO & President; Robert Bernstein, VP of Finance.

■ **25811** ■ **Seacoast Gallery**
PO Box 1077
Wells, ME 04090-1077
Phone: (207)646-2359
Products: Custom and stock frames; Arts supplies. **SIC:** 5049 (Professional Equipment Nec). **Officers:** Phyllis Biasin, Owner.

■ **25812** ■ **Semler Industries Inc.**
3800 N Carnation St.
Franklin Park, IL 60131
Phone: (847)671-5650 **Fax:** (847)671-7686
E-mail: semler@semlerindustries.com
URL: http://www.semlerindustries.com
Products: Pumps, filters, and fittings; Water purification units. **SIC:** 5074 (Plumbing & Hydronic Heating Supplies). **Est:** 1905. **Emp:** 35. **Officers:** L.H. Semler, President; Jeffrey K. Semler Jr., CFO; William Schulz, Dir. of Sales; Alan M. Scheufler, VP of Operations; Christine L. Whetstone, Marketing.

■ **25813** ■ **Sherwood Promotions Inc.**
1335 S Chillicothe Rd.
Aurora, OH 44202
Phone: (330)562-9330
Products: Promotional goods. **SIC:** 5199 (Nondurable Goods Nec).

■ **25814** ■ **Showstopper Exhibits Inc.**
17 E Cary St.
Richmond, VA 23219
Phone: (804)643-4011
Products: Exhibit booths. **SIC:** 5099 (Durable Goods Nec). **Sales:** $2,000,000 (2000). **Emp:** 5. **Officers:** James E. Deady, President.

■ **25815** ■ **Sidener Supply Co.**
PO Box 28446
St. Louis, MO 63146
Phone: (314)432-4700 **Fax:** (314)432-4751
Products: Water sewer supplies. **SIC:** 5074 (Plumbing & Hydronic Heating Supplies). **Est:** 1957. **Sales:** $62,000,000 (2000). **Emp:** 182. **Officers:** Lawrence E. Sidener, CEO; J.J. Werner, Treasurer.

■ **25816** ■ **Signature Services Corp.**
2705 Hawes St.
Dallas, TX 75235
Phone: (214)353-2661
Free: (800)929-5520 **Fax:** (214)358-5873
Products: Laundry equipment, parts, services, and sales. **SIC:** 5087 (Service Establishment Equipment). **Est:** 1929. **Sales:** $8,000,000 (2000). **Emp:** 80. **Officers:** Gray R. Brown, President; Gene Yeatts, Controller.

■ **25817** ■ **Signs of All Kinds**
200 W Main St.
Rockville, CT 06066
Phone: (860)875-9293
Free: (800)214-4449 **Fax:** (860)870-1394
Products: Decorative signs and accessories. **SIC:** 5099 (Durable Goods Nec). **Officers:** John Prusak, President; Allison Prusak, President.

■ **25818** ■ **Sloan International, Inc.**
2950 E Flamingo Rd.
Las Vegas, NV 89121
Phone: (702)896-3955 **Fax:** (702)896-2276
Products: Water treatment systems; Water filters. **SIC:** 5074 (Plumbing & Hydronic Heating Supplies).

■ **25819** ■ **SLS Arts, Inc.**
5524 Mounes St.
New Orleans, LA 70123
Phone: (504)733-1104
Free: (800)666-7881 **Fax:** (504)736-9234
Products: Artists' equipment. **SIC:** 5199 (Nondurable Goods Nec). **Officers:** Sam Seelag, Contact.

■ **25820** ■ **R.W. Smith and Co.**
PO Box 26160
San Diego, CA 92196
Phone: (619)530-1800
Free: (800)942-1101 **Fax:** (619)530-0224
E-mail: sales@srwsmithco.com
URL: http://www.rwsmithco.com
Products: Restaurant supplies and equipment. **SICs:** 5087 (Service Establishment Equipment); 5064 (Electrical Appliances—Television & Radio). **Est:** 1935. **Sales:** $42,000,000 (1999). **Emp:** 103. **Officers:** Allan Keck, President.

■ **25821** ■ **Sodak Gaming Inc.**
5301 S Hwy. 16
Rapid City, SD 57701
Phone: (605)341-5400
Free: (800)711-7322 **Fax:** (605)355-5070
Products: Gaming products and services, including slot machines. **SIC:** 5046 (Commercial Equipment Nec). **Est:** 1989. **Sales:** $154,600,000 (2000). **Emp:** 200. **Officers:** Mike Wordeman, CEO & Chairman of the Board; Roland Gentner, COO.

■ **25822** ■ **Solar Pacific Inc.**
PO Box 5475
Kent, WA 98064-5475
Phone: (253)854-8664 **Fax:** (253)854-0205
Products: Tanning beds and supplies. **SIC:** 5064 (Electrical Appliances—Television & Radio). **Officers:** Gail Cosand, President.

■ **25823** ■ **Solomon M. Casket Company of Rhode Island**
31 Slater Rd.
Cranston, RI 02920-4467
Phone: (401)463-5860
Products: Caskets. **SIC:** 5087 (Service Establishment Equipment). **Officers:** William Lewis, President.

■ **25824** ■ **South King Kirby**
635 SW 150th
Seattle, WA 98166
Phone: (206)244-6440
Products: Vacuum cleaning systems. **SIC:** 5087

(Service Establishment Equipment). **Officers:** Raymond Hinkle, Owner.

■ 25825 ■ **Southern Commercial Machines**
2256 N Wakefield St.
Arlington, VA 22207-3529
Phone: (703)528-5202 **Fax:** (703)524-2713
Products: ID badges and equipment; Bar code systems; Imaging systems. **SICs:** 5065 (Electronic Parts & Equipment Nec); 5046 (Commercial Equipment Nec). **Officers:** Roger Marshall, President.

■ 25826 ■ **Southern Pump and Filter Inc.**
2883 Directors Cove
Memphis, TN 38131-0398
Phone: (901)332-4890 **Fax:** (901)346-4350
Products: Water pumps and water treatment filters; Air purifiers. **SICs:** 5084 (Industrial Machinery & Equipment); 5074 (Plumbing & Hydronic Heating Supplies). **Est:** 1968. **Sales:** $1,500,000 (2000). **Emp:** 4. **Officers:** John A. Ward, President, e-mail: wardja@communityisp.com; Allen Ward, Sec. & Treas.

■ 25827 ■ **Spectrum Corp.**
PO Box 57
Rigby, ID 83442-0057
Phone: (208)745-8706
Free: (800)331-6764 **Fax:** (208)745-8708
Products: Vending machines; Medical supplies; Eyeglass cords. **SICs:** 5046 (Commercial Equipment Nec); 5047 (Medical & Hospital Equipment); 5048 (Ophthalmic Goods). **Est:** 1985. **Emp:** 7. **Officers:** Allen Ball, President.

■ 25828 ■ **Spectrum Lighting/Sound & Beyond**
602 W 22nd St.
Tempe, AZ 85282
Phone: (480)968-4334
Free: (888)968-4334 **Fax:** (480)968-4450
URL: http://www.spectrumlighting.com
Products: Theatrical equipment including lighting, drapes, as well as staging and sound equipment. **SICs:** 5099 (Durable Goods Nec); 5046 (Commercial Equipment Nec); 5063 (Electrical Apparatus & Equipment). **Est:** 1985. **Sales:** $1,000,000 (2000). **Emp:** 5. **Officers:** Joseph Lewis, CEO, e-mail: joseph_lewis@spectrumlighting.com. **Former Name:** ABC Theatricals.

■ 25829 ■ **ST Laminating Corp.**
PO Box 1371
Elkhart, IN 46515
Phone: (219)262-4199 **Fax:** (219)262-2066
Products: Custom laminating equipment and supplies. **SIC:** 5049 (Professional Equipment Nec). **Est:** 1979. **Sales:** $2,000,000 (2000). **Emp:** 15. **Officers:** Ron Spain, President; Gary Taska, Vice President.

■ 25830 ■ **Star Beacon Products Co.**
1104 Goodale Blvd.
Columbus, OH 43212-3726
Phone: (614)294-4657
Free: (800)860-4583 **Fax:** (614)294-3970
Products: Toys, hobby goods, and supplies; Arts and crafts equipment and supplies; School supplies. **SICs:** 5199 (Nondurable Goods Nec); 5112 (Stationery & Office Supplies); 5199 (Nondurable Goods Nec). **Officers:** Phillip Schirtzinger, President.

■ 25831 ■ **Steamboat International LLC**
7215 Bermuda Rd.
Las Vegas, NV 89119-4304
Phone: (702)361-0600
Free: (800)237-9937 **Fax:** (702)361-0613
E-mail: sales@lengordon.com
URL: www.brettaqualine.com
Products: Portable spa systems and portable spa deck side controls; In-ground electronic pool and spa controls; Jetted bathtub and spa heaters. **SIC:** 5091 (Sporting & Recreational Goods). **Est:** 1982. **Emp:** 50. **Officers:** Judith Gordon, CEO; Marie Levesque, VP of Sales, e-mail: lgordon@lengordon.com; Charla Cannon, VP of Finance. **Former Name:** Brett Aqualine.

■ 25832 ■ **Struve Distributing Company Inc.**
276 West 100 South
Salt Lake City, UT 84101
Phone: (801)328-1636
Free: (800)252-1177 **Fax:** (801)328-1641
E-mail: info@struve.com
URL: http://www.struve.com
Products: Coin-operated music, game, and vending equipment; Home recreation products. **SICs:** 5046 (Commercial Equipment Nec); 5099 (Durable Goods Nec); 5145 (Confectionery); 5149 (Groceries & Related Products Nec). **Est:** 1959. **Sales:** $4,100,000 (2000). **Emp:** 12. **Officers:** Stan Larsen.

■ 25833 ■ **Sun Appliance Service Inc.**
645 Griswold St., Ste. 3900
Detroit, MI 48226-4221
Phone: (313)531-3636
Products: Barber and beauty shop furniture and equipment. **SIC:** 5087 (Service Establishment Equipment). **Officers:** Richard Luke, President.

■ 25834 ■ **Superior Distributors**
333 N Pennsylvania Ave.
Wilkes Barre, PA 18702
Phone: (717)824-9994
Free: (800)432-8030 **Fax:** (717)829-4441
Products: Vending machines; Coin-operated game machines. **SIC:** 5046 (Commercial Equipment Nec). **Est:** 1934. **Emp:** 37. **Officers:** Donald DeRemer, President; Leonard Lukas, VP of Marketing; Jack D. Kanter, Sales Mgr.; Guy Chiazza, Manager. **Former Name:** Roth Novelty Co.

■ 25835 ■ **Superior Water Systems**
13529 S Normandie Ave.
Gardena, CA 90249
Phone: (310)532-0470 **Fax:** (310)532-2855
Products: Filtration equipment; Water filters. **SIC:** 5074 (Plumbing & Hydronic Heating Supplies).

■ 25836 ■ **Sweeper Corp.**
2919 Mishawaka Ave.
South Bend, IN 46615-2259
Phone: (219)288-1658
Products: Vacuum cleaning systems. **SIC:** 5087 (Service Establishment Equipment). **Officers:** David Geehring, President.

■ 25837 ■ **TEC America Inc.**
4401-A Bankers Cir.
Atlanta, GA 30360
Phone: (770)449-3040
URL: http://www.tecamerica.com
Products: Electronic cash registers; Scales; Barcode printers; Point of sale systems. **SIC:** 5046 (Commercial Equipment Nec). **Est:** 1969. **Sales:** $40,000,000 (2000). **Emp:** 97. **Officers:** Mike Calderwood, General Mgr.

■ 25838 ■ **Teeters Products Inc.**
125 E 2nd St.
Fletcher, OH 45326
Phone: (937)368-2376 **Fax:** (937)368-2479
Products: Coin operated laundry equipment, including washers, dryers, and heaters. **SIC:** 5087 (Service Establishment Equipment). **Est:** 1957. **Sales:** $4,000,000 (2000). **Emp:** 10. **Officers:** Doug Grise, CEO; Linda Grise, Vice President.

■ 25839 ■ **Tempo Glove Manufacturing Inc.**
3820 W Wisconsin Ave.
Milwaukee, WI 53208-3154
Phone: (414)344-1100
Free: (800)558-8500 **Fax:** (414)344-4084
E-mail: info@tempoglove.com
URL: http://www.tempoglove.com
Products: Industrial and firefighting gloves. **SICs:** 5136 (Men's/Boys' Clothing); 5085 (Industrial Supplies). **Est:** 1936. **Sales:** $1,400,000 (2000). **Emp:** 20. **Officers:** Richard Mandlman; Michael Mandlman.

■ 25840 ■ **Texas Art Supply Co.**
PO Box 66328
Houston, TX 77006-6328
Phone: (713)526-5221 **Fax:** (713)524-7474
E-mail: info@texasart.com
URL: http://www.texasart.com
Products: Art and ceramics supplies. **SICs:** 5199

(Nondurable Goods Nec); 5046 (Commercial Equipment Nec). **Est:** 1948. **Sales:** $47,000,000 (2000). **Emp:** 150. **Officers:** Louis K. Adler, President; John Gilbreath, COO.

■ 25841 ■ **Texas Screen Process Supply Co.**
304 N Walton
Dallas, TX 75226
Phone: (214)748-3271
Free: (800)366-1776 **Fax:** (214)741-6527
E-mail: sales@txscreen.com
URL: http://www.txscreen.com
Products: Screen printing supplies and inks; Digital imaging equipment and supplies. **SICs:** 5199 (Nondurable Goods Nec); 5084 (Industrial Machinery & Equipment). **Est:** 1968. **Emp:** 75. **Officers:** Patrick Jackson, Sales/Marketing Contact, e-mail: pjackson@txscreen.com.

■ 25842 ■ **Thompsons Inc.**
1707 Broadway Ave.
Boise, ID 83706-3803
Phone: (208)344-5179 **Fax:** (208)344-5195
Products: Washing equipment. **SIC:** 5087 (Service Establishment Equipment). **Officers:** Tobe Thompson, President.

■ 25843 ■ **Three Sixty Services Inc.**
12623 Newburgh Rd.
Livonia, MI 48150
Phone: (734)591-9360
Free: (800)860-9360 **Fax:** (734)591-7899
Products: Laser printing, letter shop, document storage and retrieval, systems integration equipment. **SIC:** 5111 (Printing & Writing Paper). **Sales:** $6,000,000 (2000). **Emp:** 120. **Officers:** Kenneth Pickl, President.

■ 25844 ■ **Time Emergency Equipment**
2341 Avon Industrial Dr.
Rochester Hills, MI 48309
Phone: (248)852-0939
Free: (800)752-8504 **Fax:** (248)852-1310
E-mail: www.timeemergency.@aol.com
URL: http://www.timeemergency.@aol.com
Products: Fire and EMS equipment and supplies. **SIC:** 5099 (Durable Goods Nec). **Est:** 1969. **Emp:** 8. **Officers:** Bob Edwards, Owner.

■ 25845 ■ **Tomra Maine**
80 Pine Tree Industrial Pkwy.
Portland, ME 04102-1443
Phone: (207)774-7447
Free: (800)942-5866 **Fax:** (207)774-7471
E-mail: tktname@nlis.net
URL: http://www.tomra.com
Products: Reverse vending machines. **SIC:** 5046 (Commercial Equipment Nec). **Officers:** Trish Boutot, General Mgr. **Former Name:** Halton System Inc.

■ 25846 ■ **Total Safety Inc.**
11111 Wilcrest Green., Ste. 425
Houston, TX 77017
Free: (800)231-6578 **Fax:** (713)941-0801
Products: Mining firefighting safety equipment including fire and gas detection. **SIC:** 5087 (Service Establishment Equipment). **Sales:** $69,000,000 (2000). **Emp:** 205. **Officers:** George Fortenberry, COO; Ted Smith, CFO.

■ 25847 ■ **Trans-Cal Industries Inc.**
16141 Cohasset St.
Van Nuys, CA 91406
Phone: (818)787-1221
Free: (800)423-2913 **Fax:** (818)787-8916
E-mail: transcalind@aol.com
URL: http://www.trans-cal.com
Products: Altitude encoders. **SIC:** 5085 (Industrial Supplies). **Est:** 1973. **Sales:** $800,000 (2000). **Emp:** 10. **Officers:** John Ferrero Jr., President; Linda J. Farnsworth, Controller, e-mail: Linda.TransCal@worldnet.att.net; Hugh W. Smith, Production Mgr., e-mail: Hugh.TransCal@worldnet.att.net; John Ferrero, Customer Service Contact, e-mail: john.transcal@worldnet.att.net.

■ **25848** ■ **Tri-County Distributors**
1906 Harrison St.
Evanston, IL 60201
Phone: (773)273-2160 **Fax:** (847)475-0577
Products: Paint and artist supplies. **SICs:** 5199 (Nondurable Goods Nec); 5198 (Paints, Varnishes & Supplies).

■ **25849** ■ **Tubelite Company, Inc.**
102 Semoran Commerce Pl.
Apopka, FL 32703
Phone: (407)884-0477
Free: (800)505-4900 **Fax:** 800-445-8823
E-mail: demar@tubelite.com
URL: http://www.tubelite.com
Products: Sign and screen printing supplies. **SIC:** 5199 (Nondurable Goods Nec). **Est:** 1925.

■ **25850** ■ **TW Graphics Group**
7220 E Slauson Ave.
Commerce, CA 90040
Phone: (323)721-1400
Free: (800)734-1704 **Fax:** (323)724-2105
URL: http://www.twgraphics.com
Products: Graphic supplies and equipment, including inks, screens, raw materials, blades, racks, and film. **SICs:** 5085 (Industrial Supplies); 5199 (Nondurable Goods Nec); 5084 (Industrial Machinery & Equipment). **Est:** 1923. **Emp:** 15.

■ **25851** ■ **Ultrasource Inc.**
PO Box 237
Tallmadge, OH 44278-0237
Phone: (330)677-1929
Free: (800)829-9913 **Fax:** (330)677-0960
E-mail: ultrahealth@cs.com
URL: http://www.drinkcleanwater.com
Products: Pollen extract; Orbil products; Water filters. **SIC:** 5064 (Electrical Appliances—Television & Radio). **Est:** 1993. **Sales:** $250,000 (2000). **Emp:** 1. **Officers:** Lyle Loughry, Owner.

■ **25852** ■ **Unicen Wastewater Treatment Co.**
PO Box 50001
Bellevue, WA 98015
Phone: (425)641-6168 **Fax:** (425)643-7202
Products: Concrete; Maintenance chemicals; Construction chemicals. **SICs:** 5169 (Chemicals & Allied Products Nec); 5074 (Plumbing & Hydronic Heating Supplies). **Emp:** 4. **Officers:** Victor V. Chao, President.

■ **25853** ■ **United Art Distributors**
144 Mason NW
Grand Rapids, MI 49503
Phone: (616)459-6611 **Fax:** (616)459-6420
Products: Art supplies. **SIC:** 5199 (Nondurable Goods Nec). **Officers:** Bill Holland, Contact.

■ **25854** ■ **United Distributors Inc.**
420 S Seneca St.
Wichita, KS 67213
Phone: (316)263-6181
Products: Coin operated video games. **SIC:** 5046 (Commercial Equipment Nec). **Est:** 1948. **Sales:** $3,500,000 (2000). **Emp:** 40. **Officers:** Mark Blum Jr., President & Treasurer.

■ **25855** ■ **United Receptacle, Inc.**
14th St. & Laurel St.
PO Box 870
Pottsville, PA 17901
Phone: (570)622-7715
Free: (800)233-0314 **Fax:** (570)622-3817
E-mail: united@unitedrecept.com
URL: http://www.unitedrecept.com
Products: Waste receptacles, including trash bags and pails; Smokers' urns; Planters. **SICs:** 5085 (Industrial Supplies); 5199 (Nondurable Goods Nec). **Est:** 1919. **Sales:** $10,000,000 (2000). **Emp:** 210. **Officers:** S. Weiss, CEO & Chairman of the Board; J. Minchhoff, Controller; John M. Knaut, Dir. of Marketing & Sales; Greg Bondura, Customer Service Mgr.; June Reedy, Human Resources Contact; Gene Granata, Commercial Sales Mgr.

■ **25856** ■ **United Scale and Engineering Co.**
16725 W Victor Rd.
New Berlin, WI 53151
Phone: (414)785-1733
Free: (800)236-1733 **Fax:** (414)785-9754
E-mail: sales@unitedscale.com
URL: http://www.unitedscale.com
Products: Scales and balances. **SICs:** 5046 (Commercial Equipment Nec); 5169 (Chemicals & Allied Products Nec). **Est:** 1962. **Sales:** $4,000,000 (2000). **Emp:** 32. **Officers:** Amy Bigott, CEO; Judy Trunec, President.

■ **25857** ■ **U.S. Printing Supply Co.**
1618 Forbes Ave.
Pittsburgh, PA 15219
Phone: (412)566-2244 **Fax:** (412)566-2243
Products: Printing and graphic art supplies. **SICs:** 5111 (Printing & Writing Paper); 5169 (Chemicals & Allied Products Nec); 5112 (Stationery & Office Supplies). **Est:** 1929. **Sales:** $1,500,000 (2000). **Emp:** 7. **Officers:** John Micklege, President.

■ **25858** ■ **U.S. Pure Water Corp.**
184 Bon Air Shopping Center
Greenbrae, CA 94904
Phones: (415)461-4040 (415)256-8801
Free: (800)776-7654 **Fax:** (415)461-6408
E-mail: water@wenet.net
URL: http://www.uspurewater.com
Products: Water; Water purification, bottling, and filtering products. **SICs:** 5074 (Plumbing & Hydronic Heating Supplies); 5149 (Groceries & Related Products Nec). **Est:** 1985. **Sales:** $1,500,000 (2000). **Emp:** 18. **Officers:** Michael Davis, President; Carol Davis, Vice President.

■ **25859** ■ **Universal Aqua**
10555 Norwalk Blvd.
Santa Fe Springs, CA 90670
Phone: (562)944-4121 **Fax:** (562)941-9633
Products: Water treatment systems. **SIC:** 5074 (Plumbing & Hydronic Heating Supplies).

■ **25860** ■ **Universal Industries Inc.**
325 E Stahl Rd.
Fremont, OH 43420
Phone: (419)334-9741
Products: Mining and mineral processing equipment. **SIC:** 5082 (Construction & Mining Machinery). **Est:** 1965. **Sales:** $24,000,000 (2000). **Emp:** 30. **Officers:** William Niggemyer, President.

■ **25861** ■ **Utility Supply Co.**
5929 E 15th St.
Tulsa, OK 74112
Phone: (918)836-4645
Products: Waterworks supplies. **SIC:** 5074 (Plumbing & Hydronic Heating Supplies). **Est:** 1960. **Sales:** $2,000,000 (2000). **Emp:** 12. **Officers:** Curtis Porter, President; Larry Osterhout, CFO; Ben Avery, Dir. of Marketing.

■ **25862** ■ **Van Dyke Supply Co.**
PO Box 278
Woonsocket, SD 57385
Phone: (605)796-4425 **Fax:** (605)796-4085
Products: Service establishment equipment; Taxidermist tools and equipment. **SICs:** 5087 (Service Establishment Equipment); 5049 (Professional Equipment Nec). **Officers:** Lambertus Van Dyke, Owner.

■ **25863** ■ **Van Son Holland Corporation of America**
92 Union St.
Mineola, NY 11501
Phone: (516)294-8811
Free: (800)645-4182 **Fax:** (516)294-8608
URL: http://www.vansonink.com
Products: Printing supplies, including ink. **SIC:** 5084 (Industrial Machinery & Equipment). **Est:** 1953. **Sales:** $42,000,000 (2000). **Emp:** 100. **Officers:** Joseph Bendowski, President, e-mail: jbendowski@aol.com; Robert Langer, Vice President; Bruce Oliva; Janie Veroxie, Dir. of Information Systems.

■ **25864** ■ **Varon and Associates Inc.**
31255 Southfield Rd.
Beverly Hills, MI 48025
Phone: (248)645-9730 **Fax:** (248)642-4166
Products: Advertising specialties. **SIC:** 5199 (Nondurable Goods Nec). **Sales:** $915,000,000 (2000). **Emp:** 6. **Officers:** Shaaron R. Varon, CEO; Shaaron Varon, President.

■ **25865** ■ **Vellano Brothers Inc.**
7 Hemlock St.
Latham, NY 12110
Phone: (518)785-5537
Free: (800)342-9855 **Fax:** (518)785-5561
URL: http://www.vellano.com
Products: Underground water and sewer products. **SICs:** 5085 (Industrial Supplies); 5084 (Industrial Machinery & Equipment); 5075 (Warm Air Heating & Air-Conditioning). **Est:** 1946. **Sales:** $27,000,000 (1999). **Emp:** 60. **Officers:** Joseph Vellano, President; James A. Vellano, Vice President; Bill Hopper, VP of Marketing; Susan Vellano, Dir. of Data Processing.

■ **25866** ■ **Vena Tech Corp.**
910 University Pl., Ste. 8204
Evanston, IL 60201-3121
Phone: (847)866-1833
Products: Filter systems. **SICs:** 5075 (Warm Air Heating & Air-Conditioning); 5074 (Plumbing & Hydronic Heating Supplies). **Sales:** $3,500,000 (2000). **Emp:** 4. **Officers:** Allan R. Freedlon, President.

■ **25867** ■ **Vendor's Supply and Service Inc.**
9350 James Ave. S
Bloomington, MN 55431
Phone: (612)881-8770
Free: (800)274-5510 **Fax:** (612)881-6712
E-mail: manager@vendorsupply.com
Products: Vending equipment. **SIC:** 5046 (Commercial Equipment Nec). **Est:** 1980. **Sales:** $3,500,000 (2000). **Emp:** 19. **Officers:** Don Reinking, President.

■ **25868** ■ **Wacom Technology Corp.**
1311 SE Cardinal Ct.
Vancouver, WA 98683
Phone: (360)750-8882
Free: (800)922-6613 **Fax:** (360)896-9724
Products: Graphic tablets. **SIC:** 5045 (Computers, Peripherals & Software). **Sales:** $17,000,000 (2000). **Emp:** 55. **Officers:** Joseph Deal, CEO & President; Mark Avolio, CFO.

■ **25869** ■ **Waldor Pump and Equipment**
9700 Humboldt Ave. S
Minneapolis, MN 55431
Phone: (612)884-5394
Free: (800)536-5394 **Fax:** (612)884-3239
E-mail: admin@waldorpump.com
Products: Waste water pumps. **SIC:** 5074 (Plumbing & Hydronic Heating Supplies). **Est:** 1946. **Sales:** $8,000,000 (2000). **Emp:** 30. **Officers:** M. Waldor, President.

■ **25870** ■ **Gary L. Wallace Inc.**
12012 Manchester Rd.
St. Louis, MO 63131
Phone: (314)822-8420
Products: Vacuum parts and cleaning supplies. **SIC:** 5087 (Service Establishment Equipment). **Sales:** $4,000,000 (2000). **Emp:** 25. **Officers:** Gary Wallace, President; Alan Muench, CFO.

■ **25871** ■ **Ward's**
4507 Davis St.
Long Island City, NY 11101
Phone: (718)784-7632 **Fax:** (718)706-6537
Products: Trade printing and binding. **SICs:** 5111 (Printing & Writing Paper); 5192 (Books, Periodicals & Newspapers). **Est:** 1918. **Sales:** $500,000 (2000). **Emp:** 4. **Officers:** David Eidlisz. **Former Name:** Ward's.

■ **25872** ■ **Warsaw Chemical Company Inc.**
PO Box 858
Warsaw, IN 46581
Phone: (219)267-3251 **Fax:** (219)267-3884
Products: Industrial maintenance and carwash equipment. **SIC:** 5084 (Industrial Machinery &

Equipment). **Est:** 1941. **Sales:** $14,500,000 (2000). **Emp:** 95. **Officers:** Donald A. Sweatland, President.

■ **25873** ■ **Water Products International, Inc.**
6441 Topaz Ct
Ft. Myers, FL 33912-8311
Phone: (941)768-6100 **Fax:** (941)768-6229
Products: Water treatment systems. **SIC:** 5074 (Plumbing & Hydronic Heating Supplies). **Est:** 1989. **Sales:** $1,000,000 (2000). **Emp:** 14. **Officers:** Wayne K. Masur, President.

■ **25874** ■ **Water Safety Corporation of America**
320 Coney Island Dr.
Sparks, NV 89431
Phone: (702)359-9500 **Fax:** (702)359-9191
Products: Filtration equipment; Water filters. **SIC:** 5074 (Plumbing & Hydronic Heating Supplies).

■ **25875** ■ **Water Works**
2513 Neudorf Rd.
Clemmons, NC 27012
Phone: (336)766-3349 **Fax:** (336)766-8904
URL: http://www.thewaterworks.com
Products: Water treatment systems; Water filters. **SIC:** 5074 (Plumbing & Hydronic Heating Supplies). **Est:** 1992. **Emp:** 6. **Officers:** Jay Koontz, e-mail: pkco@aol.com. **Former Name:** The Watersmith Inc.

■ **25876** ■ **West Bend Water Systems**
400 Washington St.
West Bend, WI 53095
Phone: (414)334-6906 **Fax:** (414)334-6964
Products: Water distilling equipment. **SIC:** 5074 (Plumbing & Hydronic Heating Supplies).

■ **25877** ■ **Western Pioneer Sales Co.**
406 E Colorado St.
Glendale, CA 91205
Phone: (213)245-7281 **Fax:** (213)245-7285
Products: Food service equipment; Refrigeration equipment. **SICs:** 5046 (Commercial Equipment Nec);

5078 (Refrigeration Equipment & Supplies). **Est:** 1938. **Sales:** $4,500,000 (2000). **Emp:** 15. **Officers:** J.B. Callahan, President; R.L. Callahan, Vice President.

■ **25878** ■ **Western Water Products, Inc.**
6060 Enterprise Dr.
Diamond Springs, CA 95619
Phone: (530)621-0255
Free: (800)828-2005 **Fax:** (530)626-7178
E-mail: watpro@aol.com
Products: Water filters. **SIC:** 5074 (Plumbing & Hydronic Heating Supplies). **Est:** 1984. **Sales:** $2,700,000 (2000). **Emp:** 8. **Officers:** Daniel Robey, President.

■ **25879** ■ **Wheelabrator Air Pollution Control**
441 Smithfield St.
Pittsburgh, PA 15222
Phone: (412)562-7300 **Fax:** (412)562-7254
Products: Air pollution control products, including cartridges, precipitators, and bag houses. **SICs:** 5075 (Warm Air Heating & Air-Conditioning); 5085 (Industrial Supplies). **Est:** 1913. **Sales:** $37,000,000 (2000). **Emp:** 160. **Officers:** Paul Feira, President; Charles Hardobey, CFO; Delmar Doyle, Dir. of Marketing.

■ **25880** ■ **Wilbert Vault of Aroostook**
PO Box 127
Houlton, ME 04730
Phone: (207)532-6858 **Fax:** (207)532-9425
Products: Service establishment equipment; Cemetery and funeral director's equipment and supplies; Concrete burial vaults and boxes. **SICs:** 5087 (Service Establishment Equipment); 5199 (Nondurable Goods Nec); 5049 (Professional Equipment Nec). **Officers:** George Bates, Owner.

■ **25881** ■ **Willco Sales and Services Inc.**
PO Box 320003
Fairfield, CT 06432
Phone: (203)366-3895
Products: Partitions, trash compactors and linen chutes. **SICs:** 5046 (Commercial Equipment Nec);

5084 (Industrial Machinery & Equipment). **Sales:** $3,000,000 (1993). **Emp:** 15. **Officers:** D.W. Tague, President & Treasurer.

■ **25882** ■ **William/Reid Ltd.**
PO Box 397
Germantown, WI 53022
Phone: (414)255-5420 **Fax:** (414)255-7495
Products: Water and waste treatment screens; Clarifiers; Remediation equipment. **SICs:** 5169 (Chemicals & Allied Products Nec); 5074 (Plumbing & Hydronic Heating Supplies). **Sales:** $3,000,000 (2000). **Emp:** 7. **Officers:** Reid Shedaker, President.

■ **25883** ■ **World Wide Distributors Inc.**
2730 W Fullerton
Chicago, IL 60647-3089
Phone: (773)384-2300 **Fax:** (773)384-0639
E-mail: wwdi@ix.netcom.com
URL: http://www.inter-mall.com/vendgames/wwdi
Products: Coin-operated amusement games, phonographs, and vending machines. **SIC:** 5046 (Commercial Equipment Nec). **Est:** 1943. **Emp:** 30. **Officers:** Fred Skor, President; Doug Skor, Vice President; Kitty Skor, Secretary; Lorraine Hagen, Treasurer.

■ **25884** ■ **Young-Phillips Sales Co.**
6399 Amp Dr.
Clemmons, NC 27012
Phone: (910)766-7070 **Fax:** (919)765-7866
Products: Graphic arts equipment and supplies. **SICs:** 5044 (Office Equipment); 5043 (Photographic Equipment & Supplies). **Est:** 1954. **Sales:** $72,000,000 (2000). **Emp:** 200. **Officers:** Richard Blair, President; Mark Reese, Controller; Bill O'Day, Exec. VP of Marketing.

(55) Storage Equipment and Containers

Entries in this section are arranged alphabetically by company name. When the company name is a personal name, the company name is alphabetized by the surname unless the first name or initial(s) are part of a trade name. See the User's Guide at the front of this directory for additional information.

■ 25885 ■ **Ace Tank and Equipment Co.**
PO Box 9039
Seattle, WA 98109
Phone: (206)281-5000
Free: (800)426-2880 **Fax:** (206)281-5030
Products: Storage tanks. **SIC:** 5084 (Industrial Machinery & Equipment). **Est:** 1937. **Sales:** $30,000,000 (2000). **Emp:** 190. **Officers:** R. Allan Reese, President; Steve Welsh, Controller.

■ 25886 ■ **Akro-Mils Inc.**
PO Box 989
Akron, OH 44309
Phone: (216)253-5592 **Fax:** (330)761-6348
E-mail: sales@akro-mils.com
URL: http://www.akro-mils.com
Products: Plastic storage cabinets; Plastic tool boxes; Storage bins and boxes; Planters. **SIC:** 5046 (Commercial Equipment Nec). **Officers:** Gary McDonald, General Mgr.; Linda Carter, Marketing Mgr.

■ 25887 ■ **Allpak Co.**
1010 Lake St.
Oak Park, IL 60301
Phone: (708)383-7200
Products: Plastic bags. **SIC:** 5162 (Plastics Materials & Basic Shapes). **Sales:** $1,000,000 (1994). **Emp:** 3. **Officers:** Karen Miller, Vice President.

■ 25888 ■ **Aztec Supply Co.**
954 N Batavia St.
Orange, CA 92867-5502
Phone: (714)771-6580
Products: Shelving and racking. **SIC:** 5046 (Commercial Equipment Nec). **Est:** 1979. **Sales:** $2,800,000 (2000). **Emp:** 20. **Officers:** Eric Berge, CEO; Bob Berdelman, Dir. of Marketing & Sales.

■ 25889 ■ **Davis Bacon Material Handling**
5000 Valley Blvd.
Los Angeles, CA 90032
Phone: (323)227-1921
Free: (800)932-1921 **Fax:** (323)227-1928
E-mail: davisbacon@earthlink.net
Products: Racks and shelving; Loading dock equipment. **SICs:** 5046 (Commercial Equipment Nec); 5046 (Commercial Equipment Nec); 5113 (Industrial & Personal Service Paper); 5084 (Industrial Machinery & Equipment). **Est:** 1952. **Sales:** $5,000,000 (2000). **Emp:** 15. **Officers:** Judy Davis, President; B.G. Davis, Vice President; Dave Adams, Order Desk.

■ 25890 ■ **George Bassi Distributing Co.**
PO Box 1169
Watsonville, CA 95077
Phone: (408)724-1028 **Fax:** (408)724-1482
Products: Wooden pallets. **SIC:** 5031 (Lumber, Plywood & Millwork). **Est:** 1940. **Sales:** $10,000,000 (2000). **Emp:** 75. **Officers:** George Bassi Sr., President.

■ 25891 ■ **Berg Bag Co.**
410 3rd Ave. N
Minneapolis, MN 55401
Phone: (612)332-8845
Products: Bags, including produce bags, paper bags,

mesh bags, and sandbags. **SIC:** 5113 (Industrial & Personal Service Paper). **Est:** 1946. **Sales:** $5,000,000 (2000). **Emp:** 10. **Officers:** R. Berg, President.

■ 25892 ■ **O. Berk Co.**
3 Milltown Crt.
PO Box 1690
Union, NJ 07083
Phone: (908)851-9500
Free: (800)631-7392 **Fax:** (908)851-9367
E-mail: obc@oberk.com
URL: http://www.OBerk.com
Products: Bottles; Closures. **SIC:** 5085 (Industrial Supplies). **Est:** 1910. **Sales:** $40,000,000 (2000). **Emp:** 75. **Officers:** Norbert Gaelen, Chairman of the Board; Marc M. Gaelen, CEO & President; Roy S. Allan, VP of Finance; Steven Nussbaum, Dir. of Marketing.

■ 25893 ■ **Berlin Packaging Inc.**
111 N Canal St.
Chicago, IL 60606
Phone: (847)640-4790
Free: (800)423-7545 **Fax:** 800-423-7545
Products: Glass, metal, and plastic containers. **SIC:** 5113 (Industrial & Personal Service Paper). **Est:** 1898. **Sales:** $140,000,000 (2000). **Emp:** 183. **Officers:** Andrew T. Berlin, President; David Verbeten, VP of Marketing & Sales; Julie Cichon, Personnel Mgr.

■ 25894 ■ **Beynon Farm Products Corp.**
PO Box 82226
Lincoln, NE 68501
Phone: (402)476-2100
Products: Grain storage bins. **SIC:** 5039 (Construction Materials Nec). **Sales:** $23,500,000 (2000). **Emp:** 126. **Officers:** David J. Beynon, President.

■ 25895 ■ **Bowline Family Products Inc.**
1564 Elmira St.
Aurora, CO 80010
Phone: (303)340-4500
Free: (800)366-2287 **Fax:** (303)340-1999
Products: Plastic bottles; Insulated nylon carriers. **SIC:** 5199 (Nondurable Goods Nec). **Sales:** $3,000,000 (2000). **Emp:** 12. **Officers:** Doug Adams, President; Peter Doane, CFO.

■ 25896 ■ **A.D. Bowman Associates Inc.**
PO Box 770
Melrose, MA 02176
Phone: (781)662-7411
Products: Storage equipment including heavy-duty shelves. **SIC:** 5046 (Commercial Equipment Nec). **Est:** 1953. **Sales:** $2,000,000 (2000). **Emp:** 5. **Officers:** Joseph Willwerth, President.

■ 25897 ■ **Calpine Containers Inc.**
PO Box 5050
Walnut Creek, CA 94596
Phone: (510)798-3010 **Fax:** (510)686-0152
Products: Agricultural packaging products, including corrugated and plastic boxes, wooden bins, and pallets. **SIC:** 5113 (Industrial & Personal Service Paper). **Est:** 1895. **Sales:** $63,500,000 (2000). **Emp:** 200. **Officers:** Ted Rathbun, President; Jim Paetz, VP of Finance; Ali

Pervez, Dir. of Marketing; Joe Hester, Controller; Darryl Skiles, VP of Sales.

■ 25898 ■ **W.W. Cannon Inc.**
10323 Harry Hines Blvd.
Dallas, TX 75220
Phone: (214)357-2846
Free: (800)442-3061 **Fax:** (214)357-4576
E-mail: wwcannon@flash.net
URL: http://www.wwcannon.com
Products: Steel shelving and storage equipment; Pallet racks; Mezzanines; Conveyors; Casters; Carts; Dollies; Stretch film; Automotive bins; Partitions. **SIC:** 5046 (Commercial Equipment Nec). **Est:** 1938. **Sales:** $5,500,000 (1999). **Emp:** 20. **Officers:** Greg Brown, President; Ricky Johnson, Sales/Marketing Contact; Dave Wilson, Sales/Marketing Contact; Jim Heiler, Customer Service Contact; Jerry Lawrence, Customer Service Contact.

■ 25899 ■ **Champlin Co.**
236 Hamilton St.
Hartford, CT 06106-2910
Phone: (860)951-9217 **Fax:** (860)951-3464
Products: Wooden corrugated boxes. **SIC:** 5031 (Lumber, Plywood & Millwork). **Est:** 1931. **Sales:** $3,000,000 (2000). **Emp:** 35. **Officers:** Rolland S. Champlin, President.

■ 25900 ■ **Cheatwood Oil Co.**
PO Box 208
Paden, OK 74860
Phone: (405)932-4455
Products: Petroleum storage. **SIC:** 5171 (Petroleum Bulk Stations & Terminals). **Sales:** $900,000 (1994). **Emp:** 2.

■ 25901 ■ **Cincinnati Container Co.**
5060 Duff Dr.
Cincinnati, OH 45246
Phone: (513)874-6874
Free: (800)745-6874 **Fax:** (513)874-7178
E-mail: cincycontainer@juno.com
URL: http://www.cincinatticontainerco.com
Products: Glass, metal, and plastic containers. **SICs:** 5085 (Industrial Supplies); 5162 (Plastics Materials & Basic Shapes). **Est:** 1932. **Emp:** 34. **Officers:** Paul Johnson, President; Ernst Gebhardt, Treasurer; Ralph Piper, VP of Sales.

■ 25902 ■ **Cisco-Eagle, Inc.**
2120 Valley View Ln.
Farmers Branch, TX 75234-8911
Phone: (972)406-9330
Free: (800)441-1162 **Fax:** (972)406-9577
URL: http://www.cisco-eagle.com
Products: Shelving and storage racks; System integration; Conveyor, carousels, RF technology, AS/RS systems; Engineering consulting. **SIC:** 5046 (Commercial Equipment Nec). **Est:** 1961. **Sales:** $46,000,000 (2000). **Emp:** 150. **Officers:** Warren Gandall, CEO; Williams Cupps, Vice President; Steve Strifler, President; Chris Doyle, Dir. of Marketing; Dan Harrison, Sales Mgr. **Former Name:** Cisco Material Handling Inc.

■ 25903 ■ **Clean Green Packing Company of Minnesota**
720 Florida Ave.
Golden Valley, MN 55426-1704
Phone: (612)545-5400 **Fax:** (612)789-5980
Products: Packaging materials. **SIC:** 5113 (Industrial & Personal Service Paper). **Sales:** $3,000,000 (2000).
Emp: 7. **Officers:** Ed Boehmer, CEO & President.

■ 25904 ■ **Columbus Steel Drum Co.**
1385 Blatt Blvd.
Blacklick, OH 43004
Phone: (614)864-1900 **Fax:** (614)860-0028
Products: Steel drums. **SIC:** 5085 (Industrial Supplies). **Est:** 1955. **Sales:** $21,000,000 (2000).
Emp: 150. **Officers:** Sidney I. Blatt, President & Treasurer; John Waddell, Controller; Elliot Bank, VP of Marketing & Sales; John Wadell, Dir. of Data Processing.

■ 25905 ■ **Commercial Shelving**
2835 Ualena St.
Honolulu, HI 96819-1911
Phone: (808)836-3811 **Fax:** (808)839-4946
Products: Material handling equipment; Shelving. **SIC:** 5046 (Commercial Equipment Nec). **Est:** 1983. **Sales:** $11,000,000 (2000). **Emp:** 65. **Officers:** Ralph Cherry.

■ 25906 ■ **Consumer Products Co.**
PO Box 2729
Muncie, IN 47305-2398
Phone: (765)281-5019
Products: Home canning supplies. **SIC:** 5199 (Nondurable Goods Nec). **Sales:** $65,000,000 (2000).
Emp: 115. **Officers:** Jack Metz, President.

■ 25907 ■ **Container Industries Inc.**
4401 W 62nd St.
Indianapolis, IN 46268
Phone: (317)299-5000
Products: Bottles; Glass containers. **SIC:** 5085 (Industrial Supplies). **Est:** 1952. **Sales:** $4,500,000 (2000). **Emp:** 50. **Officers:** Steven K. Heidt, President; Al Habeney, CFO.

■ 25908 ■ **Continental Glass and Plastic Inc.**
841 W Cermak Rd.
Chicago, IL 60608
Phone: (312)666-2050 **Fax:** (312)666-7501
Products: Plastic and glass containers. **SIC:** 5085 (Industrial Supplies). **Est:** 1936. **Sales:** $65,000,000 (2000). **Emp:** 100. **Officers:** Richard A. Giesen, CEO & President; Mark Giesen, e-mail: mark-giesen@cgppkg.com.

■ 25909 ■ **Crown Glass Corp.**
2345 W Hubbard St.
Chicago, IL 60612
Phone: (312)666-2000 **Fax:** (312)666-1505
Products: Glass and plastic containers. **SICs:** 5085 (Industrial Supplies); 5162 (Plastics Materials & Basic Shapes). **Est:** 1947. **Sales:** $60,000,000 (2000). **Emp:** 200. **Officers:** Berle Blitstein, President; Jerry Arp, CFO; Kevin Kerrigan, Sales Mgr.

■ 25910 ■ **Edwards Wood Products Inc.**
(Portola Valley, California)
14425 Liddicoat Dr.
Los Altos Hills, CA 94022-1806
Phone: (650)493-6232 **Fax:** (650)493-6232
Products: Wooden pallets, shelves and decking for storage. **SIC:** 5046 (Commercial Equipment Nec). **Sales:** $500,000 (2000). **Emp:** 2. **Officers:** Thomas F. Turner, President; Gayle C. Turner, VP of Finance.

■ 25911 ■ **Empire/EMCO Inc.**
4043 Maple Rd.
Buffalo, NY 14226-1057
Phone: (716)832-5555 **Fax:** (716)832-7042
E-mail: info@empireemco.com
URL: http://www.empireemco.com
Products: Plastic and glass bottles and custom packaging. **SIC:** 5085 (Industrial Supplies). **Est:** 1911. **Emp:** 26. **Officers:** Joel N. Lippman, President; Bruce Wischerath, Controller; Gary M. Burns, VP of Sales.
Former Name: Empire Bottle Company Inc.

■ 25912 ■ **Enraf Inc.**
500 Century Plz. Dr.
Houston, TX 77073
Phone: (281)443-4291
Free: (800)443-1029 **Fax:** (281)443-6776
E-mail: enrafinc@enrafinc.com
Products: Liquid inventory management systems for storage tanks. **SIC:** 5084 (Industrial Machinery & Equipment). **Est:** 1989. **Sales:** $9,000,000 (2000).
Emp: 25. **Officers:** Steve Yon, President, e-mail: syon@enrafinc.com.

■ 25913 ■ **Eskay Corp.**
5245 Yeager Rd.
Salt Lake City, UT 84116
Phone: (801)359-9900
Products: Warehouse automation systems. **SIC:** 5084 (Industrial Machinery & Equipment). **Emp:** 12.
Officers: James K. Allred, President; Ken Brewster, Mgr. of Admin.

■ 25914 ■ **Carl F. Ewig Inc.**
910 Oak Tree Rd.
South Plainfield, NJ 07080
Phone: (908)756-3944
Products: Marine shipping containers. **SIC:** 5088 (Transportation Equipment & Supplies).

■ 25915 ■ **Feldman Glass Co.**
PO Box 406, Fair Haven Station
New Haven, CT 06513
Phone: (203)624-3113 **Fax:** (203)787-9237
Products: Glass bottles and jars. **SICs:** 5085 (Industrial Supplies); 5162 (Plastics Materials & Basic Shapes). **Est:** 1895. **Sales:** $7,500,000 (2000). **Emp:** 60. **Officers:** Michael Feldman, President; Irwin Feldman, Treasurer & Secty.; Paul Hillegas, VP of Marketing; Lauri Engleman, Dir. of Systems.

■ 25916 ■ **Freund Can Co.**
155 W 84th St.
Chicago, IL 60620-1298
Phone: (312)224-4230
Products: Containers, including boxes and cans; Plastic. **SICs:** 5085 (Industrial Supplies); 5162 (Plastics Materials & Basic Shapes); 5113 (Industrial & Personal Service Paper). **Est:** 1936. **Sales:** $9,000,000 (2000).
Emp: 42. **Officers:** Kenneth G. Freund, President; Eileen Kedzierski, Mgr. of Admin.

■ 25917 ■ **Gilbert Lumber/IFCO Systems**
PO Box 216
Smithville, OH 44677
Phone: (330)669-2726 **Fax:** (330)669-3886
Products: Pallets; crates. **SIC:** 5031 (Lumber, Plywood & Millwork). **Est:** 1867. **Sales:** $8,000,000 (2000). **Emp:** 97. **Officers:** Patrick Lorson, General Mgr. **Former Name:** Palex.

■ 25918 ■ **Golden State Containers Inc.**
6817 E Acco St.
Los Angeles, CA 90040-1901
Phone: (213)887-4266
Products: Cardboard containers, boxes, and packaging. **SIC:** 5113 (Industrial & Personal Service Paper). **Sales:** $190,000,000 (2000). **Emp:** 350.
Officers: Dave Oliver, General Mgr.; John Toot, Controller.

■ 25919 ■ **T.V. Guilfoil and Associates Inc.**
333 Pulaski St.
Syracuse, NY 13204
Phone: (315)474-8771 **Fax:** (315)474-8776
Products: Glass containers for candle making. **SIC:** 5085 (Industrial Supplies). **Est:** 1955. **Sales:** $7,000,000 (2000). **Emp:** 4. **Officers:** P.H. Allen, President; Joanne Brown, Controller.

■ 25920 ■ **J & K Distributors**
512 E Kirby Ave.
Muncie, IN 47303
Phone: (765)289-0722
Products: Metal tanks. **SIC:** 5051 (Metals Service Centers & Offices).

■ 25921 ■ **M. Jacob and Sons**
PO Box 9069
Farmington Hills, MI 48333
Phone: (313)737-9440 **Fax:** (313)737-2151
Products: Plastic and glass bottles and caps. **SICs:** 5113 (Industrial & Personal Service Paper); 5085 (Industrial Supplies). **Est:** 1885. **Sales:** $13,000,000 (2000). **Emp:** 27. **Officers:** Joel Jacob, President; David Lubin, CFO.

■ 25922 ■ **Keene Div.**
10100 East Rd.
Potter Valley, CA 95469
Phone: (707)743-1154
Free: (800)750-1154 **Fax:** (707)743-1159
Products: Softwood pallets; Bins; Cut stock. **SIC:** 5031 (Lumber, Plywood & Millwork). **Est:** 1960. **Sales:** $9,000,000 (2000). **Emp:** 75. **Officers:** Dan Gamble, Manager; Gary Stanton, Controller; John Colesen, Sales Contact; Les Robison, Sales Contact.

■ 25923 ■ **Kranson Industries**
460 N Lindbergh Blvd.
St. Louis, MO 63141-7808
Phone: (314)569-3633
Free: (800)325-7782 **Fax:** (314)569-5087
URL: http://www.tricorbraun.com
Products: Rigid plastic packaging. **SIC:** 5162 (Plastics Materials & Basic Shapes). **Est:** 1902. **Sales:** $300,000,000 (2000). **Emp:** 300. **Officers:** Kenneth Kranzberg, CEO & Chairman of the Board; Richard Glassman, President.

■ 25924 ■ **La Cie. Ltd.**
22985 NW Evergreen Pkwy.
Hillsboro, OR 97124
Phone: (503)844-4500 **Fax:** (503)844-4508
Products: Storage peripherals for micro-computers and workstations. **SIC:** 5045 (Computers, Peripherals & Software). **Sales:** $100,000,000 (2000). **Emp:** 900.
Officers: Philippe Sprueh, President; Lyman Potts, CFO.

■ 25925 ■ **LaGrange Products Inc.**
5656N Wayne St.
PO Box 658
Fremont, IN 46737
Phone: (219)495-3025
Free: (800)369-6978 **Fax:** (219)495-7771
URL: http://www.lagrangeproducts.com
Products: Pressure vessels. **SIC:** 5084 (Industrial Machinery & Equipment). **Est:** 1962. **Sales:** $13,000,000 (2000). **Emp:** 120. **Officers:** Michael D. Poling, President; Lynn Blue, Plant Manager.

■ 25926 ■ **Land & Sea Products**
3106 NW 3 Mile Rd.
Grand Rapids, MI 49544
Phone: (616)791-0331
Free: (800)321-1548 **Fax:** (616)791-1017
Products: Chemical holding tanks for recreational vehicles. **SIC:** 5084 (Industrial Machinery & Equipment). **Est:** 1980. **Sales:** $1,500,000 (2000).
Emp: 12. **Officers:** Jack LaFontaine, President; Betty Tindle, Treasurer & Secty.

■ 25927 ■ **Lee-Rowan Co.**
900 S Highway Dr.
Fenton, MO 63026
Phone: (314)343-0070
Free: (800)325-6150 **Fax:** (314)349-9618
URL: http://www.leerowan.com
Products: Storage products; Shelving. **SIC:** 5046 (Commercial Equipment Nec). **Est:** 1938. **Emp:** 1,200.
Officers: Dave Gereans, VP of Sales.

■ 25928 ■ **Lincoln Office Supply Company Inc.**
7707 N Knoxville Ave.
Peoria, IL 61614
Phone: (309)693-2444 **Fax:** (309)692-1018
Products: Steel cases only. **SIC:** 5051 (Metals Service Centers & Offices). **Est:** 1935. **Sales:** $40,000,000 (2000). **Emp:** 150. **Officers:** Thomas E. Spuegeon, President; John S. Wieland, CFO; Tom Munson, VP of Sales; Judi Gentry, Dir of Human Resources.

■ 25929 ■ Linvar LLC
245 Hamilton St.
Hartford, CT 06106
Phone: (860)951-3818
Free: (800)282-5288 Fax: (860)951-4512
Products: Plastic storage bins and steel racking. SIC: 5046 (Commercial Equipment Nec). Est: 1980. Sales: $5,000,000 (1999). Emp: 15. Officers: Joseph Ramondetta, President; John Ahern, Sales Mgr. Former Name: Linvar Inc.

■ 25930 ■ Martec International
910 Oak Tree Rd.
South Plainfield, NJ 07080
Phone: (908)756-6222
Free: (800)862-7832 Fax: (908)756-2575
E-mail: info@martecintl.com
URL: http://www.martecintl.com
Products: Container components; Chassis components; Vessel spares; Storage equipment; Used and new ISO containers; Cargo securing equipment; Roll trailer leasing. SIC: 5088 (Transportation Equipment & Supplies). Est: 1957. Sales: $7,000,000 (2000). Emp: 40. Officers: Alex Ewig, Vice President; Joern Schmey, General Mgr.; Henry Poorten, Controller. Former Name: Martec International Trading.

■ 25931 ■ Pallet Recycling Center Inc.
PO Box 19638
Indianapolis, IN 46219
Phone: (317)351-2204
Products: Wood pallets. SIC: 5031 (Lumber, Plywood & Millwork). Sales: $5,000,000 (2000). Emp: 10. Officers: Charles Mong, President.

■ 25932 ■ Ply-Gem Manufacturing Co.
PO Box 189
Gloucester City, NJ 08030-0189
Phone: (609)546-0704
Free: (800)752-1478 Fax: (609)546-0539
Products: Shelving and storage imports and distribute ceramic, porcelain and marble tile. SIC: 5032 (Brick, Stone & Related Materials). Sales: $13,000,000 (2000). Emp: 75. Officers: Howard Steinberg, President.

■ 25933 ■ Poly Processing Co.
PO Box 4150
Monroe, LA 71211
Phone: (318)343-7565 Fax: (318)343-8795
Products: Polyethylene storage tanks. SIC: 5088 (Transportation Equipment & Supplies).

■ 25934 ■ Rodico Inc.
18 Park Way
Upper Saddle River, NJ 07458
Phone: (201)327-6303
Products: Packaging equipment. SIC: 5084 (Industrial Machinery & Equipment).

■ 25935 ■ Schermerhorn Brothers Co.
PO Box 668
Lombard, IL 60148
Phone: (630)627-9860
Free: (800)323-9627 Fax: (630)627-1178
E-mail: sbclombard@aol.com
Products: Newspaper bags, rubberbands and twine. SIC: 5085 (Industrial Supplies). Est: 1893. Sales: $22,000,000 (2000). Emp: 40. Officers: T. Duff, Treasurer & Secty.; Wayne W. Rycski, President; Patrick V. O'Brien, Vice President.

■ 25936 ■ SCS Cases Inc.
7420 Unity Ave. N, Ste. 210
Brooklyn Park, MN 55443
Phone: (612)391-7600
Free: (800)544-5395 Fax: (612)391-7602
URL: http://www.caseshow.com
Products: Shipping and custom cases. SIC: 5088 (Transportation Equipment & Supplies). Officers: Jeff walter, President; Tim Jennings, Vice President.

■ 25937 ■ Seattle Box Co.
23400 71st Pl. S
Kent, WA 98032-2994
Phone: (206)854-9700 Fax: (206)852-0891
Products: Wood boxes. SIC: 5088 (Industrial Supplies). Est: 1889. Sales: $20,000,000 (2000). Emp: 100. Officers: F.J. Nist, President & Treasurer

■ 25938 ■ Shelving Inc.
PO Box 215050
Auburn Hills, MI 48321-5050
Phone: (248)852-8600
Free: (800)637-9508 Fax: (248)852-0904
E-mail: storage@shelving.com
URL: http://www.shelving.com
Products: Storage equipment and related material handling equipment. SIC: 5046 (Commercial Equipment Nec). Est: 1960. Sales: $3,500,000 (1999). Emp: 10. Officers: Helen E. Schodowski, CEO; John J. Schodowski, Treasurer; Joseph H. Schodowski, President; Michael Schodowski, Sales/Marketing Contact; Jenifer Woody, Customer Service Contact; Helen Schodowski, Human Resources Contact.

■ 25939 ■ Shurflo
12650 Westminster Ave.
Santa Ana, CA 92706-2100
Phone: (714)554-7709 Fax: (714)554-4721
Products: Pumps; Undergound storage tanks. SIC: 5084 (Industrial Machinery & Equipment).

■ 25940 ■ StarchTech Inc.
720 Florida Ave.
Golden Valley, MN 55426-1704
Phone: (612)545-5400
Products: Packaging materials. SIC: 5113 (Industrial & Personal Service Paper).

■ 25941 ■ Storage Equipment Company Inc.
1258 Titan Ave.
Dallas, TX 75247
Phone: (214)630-9221
Free: (800)443-1791 Fax: (214)637-6340
URL: http://www.storagequip.com
Products: Material handling equipment, including shelving, lockers, wire partitions, racks, and vertical storage carousels. SIC: 5046 (Commercial Equipment Nec). Est: 1955. Sales: $9,000,000 (2000). Emp: 35. Officers: Jim Brown, CEO; Sharon Pults, Controller.

■ 25942 ■ Sun Pacific Industries
15136 Valley Blvd., Ste. C
City of Industry, CA 91744
Phone: (626)855-9048 Fax: (626)855-9047
Products: Plastic water containers and ceramic crocks. SIC: 5162 (Plastics Materials & Basic Shapes). Sales: $1,800,000 (2000). Emp: 8. Officers: Selina Sun, Finance General Manager.

■ 25943 ■ Tapesolutions
649 S Vermont St.
Palatine, IL 60067
Phone: (847)776-8880 Fax: (847)776-8890
Products: Packaging tape. SIC: 5113 (Industrial & Personal Service Paper). Sales: $5,000,000 (2000). Emp: 50. Officers: Jon Knipfer, President.

■ 25944 ■ TCB Inc.
1227 E Hennepin Ave.
Minneapolis, MN 55414
Phone: (612)331-8880
Free: (800)697-0607 Fax: (612)379-5118
E-mail: sales@twincitybottle.com
URL: http://www.twincitybottle.com
Products: Plastic and glass containers; Closures and screen printing. SIC: 5162 (Plastics Materials & Basic Shapes). Est: 1904. Emp: 80. Officers: K. Slater, President, e-mail: kslater@kccbottle.com.

■ 25945 ■ Tricor Braun - Div. of Kranson
460 N Lindbergh Blvd.
St. Louis, MO 63141-7808
Phone: (314)569-3633
Free: (800)325-7782 Fax: (314)569-5087
URL: http://www.tricorbraun.com
Products: Rigid containers, including bottles, plastics, and glass. SIC: 5162 (Plastics Materials & Basic Shapes). Est: 1902. Sales: $300,000,000 (1999). Emp: 300. Officers: Kenneth Kranzberg, CEO & Chairman of the Board; Richard Glassman, President; Keith Strope, COO. Former Name: Northwestern Bottle Co.

■ 25946 ■ Unirak Storage Systems
26051 Michigan Ave.
Inkster, MI 48141
Phone: (313)278-7600
Free: (800)348-7225 Fax: (313)278-6833
E-mail: info@unirak.com
URL: http://www.unirak.com
Products: Storage racks and accessories; Storage equipment; Pallet racks, drivein racks, galvanized racks and selective racks. SIC: 5046 (Commercial Equipment Nec). Est: 1983.

■ 25947 ■ W.S. Westeel Inc.
803 25th St. N
Fargo, ND 58102
Phone: (701)232-3201
Products: Grain bins. SIC: 5039 (Construction Materials Nec). Sales: $1,400,000 (2000). Emp: 2. Officers: Fraser Harrison, Sales Mgr.; Don Bengon, Office Mgr.

■ 25948 ■ Wood Brothers and Halstead Lumber
4098 N 35th Ave.
Phoenix, AZ 85017
Phone: (602)269-3255 Fax: (602)272-1087
Products: Cable reels; Wood boxes; Pallets. SICs: 5085 (Industrial Supplies); 5031 (Lumber, Plywood & Millwork). Est: 1962. Sales: $5,000,000 (2000). Emp: 80. Officers: Harry Wood, President.

■ 25949 ■ K. Yamada Distributors Ltd.
2949 Koapaka St.
Honolulu, HI 96819
Phone: (808)836-3221
Products: Packaging material. SIC: 5113 (Industrial & Personal Service Paper). Sales: $54,000,000 (1994). Emp: 100. Officers: Gil Yamada, President.

■ 25950 ■ Zuckerman-Honickman Inc.
191 S Gulph Rd.
King of Prussia, PA 19406
Phone: (610)962-0100
Free: (800)523-1475 Fax: (610)962-1080
Products: Plastic and glass containers and closures. SIC: 5085 (Industrial Supplies). Est: 1934. Sales: $26,000,000 (2000). Emp: 35. Officers: Benjamin Zuckerman, President; Bruce Rosenberg, VP of Finance.

(56) Textiles and Notions

Entries in this section are arranged alphabetically by company name. When the company name is a personal name, the company name is alphabetized by the surname unless the first name or initial(s) are part of a trade name. See the User's Guide at the front of this directory for additional information.

■ **25951** ■ **3A Products**
1006 S San Pedro St.
Los Angeles, CA 90015
Phone: (213)747-6090 **Fax:** (213)748-6447
E-mail: us3athread@aol.com
Products: Sewing supplies, including threads. **SICs:** 5131 (Piece Goods & Notions); 5199 (Nondurable Goods Nec). **Est:** 1984. **Emp:** 25. **Officers:** Wayne Jung, President; Hugh Quan, Vice President.

■ **25952** ■ **Ace Bag and Burlap Co. Inc.**
205 Water St.
Brooklyn, NY 11201
Phone: (718)852-4705 **Fax:** (718)237-0292
Products: Textile bags. **SIC:** 5199 (Nondurable Goods Nec). **Est:** 1941. **Sales:** $4,000,000 (2000). **Emp:** 12. **Officers:** H. Rochman, President; I.A. Sindell, Manager.

■ **25953** ■ **Acme Linen Co.**
5136 E Triggs St.
Los Angeles, CA 90022
Phone: (213)266-4000 **Fax:** (213)267-5771
Products: Linen, including towels and muslins. **SIC:** 5131 (Piece Goods & Notions). **Est:** 1938. **Sales:** $16,000,000 (2000). **Emp:** 18. **Officers:** Sam Benzonsky, President; Syd Benzonsky, Controller; Luz Pailliotet, Dir of Personnel.

■ **25954** ■ **Aetna Felt Corp. Mechanical Felt and Textile Div.**
2401 W Emaus Ave.
Allentown, PA 18103
Phone: (215)791-0900
Free: (800)526-4451 **Fax:** (215)791-5791
E-mail: info@aetnafelt.com
URL: http://www.aetnafelt.com
Products: Felt; Die cut and roll goods; Die cut cork; Rubber gaskets; Stripping; Wool; SAE; Needled and synthetic felts. **SICs:** 5199 (Nondurable Goods Nec); 5113 (Industrial & Personal Service Paper); 5169 (Chemicals & Allied Products Nec); 5199 (Nondurable Goods Nec). **Est:** 1933. **Sales:** $6,000,000 (1999). **Emp:** 58. **Officers:** W. W. Weppler, President; J. F. Weppler, Vice President; J. Calvache, Secretary.

■ **25955** ■ **Allen Brown Industries Inc.**
1720 Watterson Tr.
Louisville, KY 40299-2430
Phone: (502)499-0628
Free: (800)231-8383 **Fax:** (502)491-0628
Products: Drapery material and accessories. **SIC:** 5131 (Piece Goods & Notions). **Sales:** $40,000,000 (2000). **Emp:** 23. **Officers:** Reynold Engdahl, President; Roland Engdahl, Vice President.

■ **25956** ■ **Robert Allen**
55 Cabot Blvd.
Mansfield, MA 02048
Phone: (508)333-9151 **Fax:** (508)339-8256
Products: Fabrics. **SIC:** 5131 (Piece Goods & Notions). **Est:** 1938. **Emp:** 750. **Officers:** Ronald Kass, CEO; William Goodlatte, Human Resources Contact.

■ **25957** ■ **American Byproducts Inc.**
5601 Paschall Ave.
Philadelphia, PA 19143
Phone: (215)533-4660 **Fax:** (215)724-9983
Products: Textile scraps and rags. **SIC:** 5093 (Scrap & Waste Materials). **Sales:** $45,000,000 (1994). **Emp:** 120. **Officers:** Florre Usatch, President; Mark Burt, Controller.

■ **25958** ■ **American Cord and Webbing Inc.**
88 Century Dr.
Woonsocket, RI 02895
Phone: (401)762-5500 **Fax:** (401)762-5514
E-mail: acwco@ids.net
Products: Webbing; Cord; Plastic and metal buckles. **SICs:** 5131 (Piece Goods & Notions); 5199 (Nondurable Goods Nec). **Est:** 1918. **Sales:** $5,000,000 (2000). **Emp:** 75. **Officers:** M. Krauss, President; Dennis Smith, Sales/Marketing Contact.

■ **25959** ■ **American Fast Print**
PO Box 5765
Spartanburg, SC 29304
Phone: (803)578-2020 **Fax:** (803)578-8593
Products: Custom-print fabric. **SIC:** 5131 (Piece Goods & Notions). **Est:** 1968. **Sales:** $40,000,000 (2000). **Emp:** 700. **Officers:** Jaroslav S. Fryml, President; W.W. Hodge, CFO.

■ **25960** ■ **American Textile Export Co.**
PO Box 66
Gastonia, NC 28053
Phone: (704)824-7803 **Fax:** (704)824-5358
E-mail: amtecexpt@aol.com
Products: Textile yarns. **SIC:** 5199 (Nondurable Goods Nec). **Est:** 1988. **Officers:** Peter J. Hegarty, President. **Also Known by This Acronym:** AMTEC.

■ **25961** ■ **American Textile and Trim Company Inc.**
3830 Euphrosine St.
New Orleans, LA 70125-1427
Phone: (504)821-0452
Products: Fabrics. **SIC:** 5131 (Piece Goods & Notions). **Est:** 1954. **Sales:** $6,000,000 (2000). **Emp:** 30. **Officers:** Paul Seidman, President; George Seidman, CFO; Helen Everhardt, Dir. of Operations.

■ **25962** ■ **Amfib Fibers Ltd.**
740 Edson Hill Rd.
Stowe, VT 05672-4175
Phone: (802)253-9732
Products: Manmade fibers. **SIC:** 5131 (Piece Goods & Notions). **Officers:** Leonard Mandelcorn, President.

■ **25963** ■ **Amicale Mongolia Inc.**
1375 Broadway
New York, NY 10018
Phone: (212)398-0300
Products: Fabrics, including cashmere, wool, and angora. **SIC:** 5131 (Piece Goods & Notions). **Est:** 1990. **Sales:** $100,000 (2000). **Emp:** 2. **Officers:** Boris Shlomm, Chairman of the Board; V. Gongor, President.

■ **25964** ■ **Anchor Specialties Co.**
205 Hallene Rd.
Warwick, RI 02886
Phone: (401)738-1510
Products: Belt buckles; Leather belts; Costume jewellery. **SIC:** 5131 (Piece Goods & Notions). **Est:** 1972. **Officers:** Frank Barbato, President.

■ **25965** ■ **Anichini Inc.**
Rte. 110
PO Box 67
Tunbridge, VT 05077
Phone: (802)889-9430
Free: (800)553-5309 **Fax:** (802)889-9482
E-mail: showe@anichini.com
Products: Luxury textiles, linens, and decorative accessories. **SIC:** 5131 (Piece Goods & Notions). **Est:** 1986. **Sales:** $7,000,000 (2000). **Emp:** 35. **Officers:** Susan Dollenmaier, President; Martha Dollenmaier, Vice President.

■ **25966** ■ **Arbill Inc.**
10450 Drummond Rd.
Philadelphia, PA 19132
Phone: (215)228-4011 **Fax:** (215)426-5808
Products: Industrial supplies; Dyeing and finishing textiles. **SIC:** 5085 (Industrial Supplies). **Sales:** $25,000,000 (1993). **Emp:** 100. **Officers:** Barry Bickman, President; Ronald Borofsky, CFO.

■ **25967** ■ **ARC Mills Corp.**
221 W 37th St.
New York, NY 10018
Phone: (212)221-8400 **Fax:** (212)944-8468
Products: Fabric, including jacket linings. **SIC:** 5131 (Piece Goods & Notions). **Est:** 1979. **Sales:** $70,000,000 (2000). **Emp:** 75. **Officers:** Robert Bender, President; Andrew Klein, CFO.

■ **25968** ■ **Arkansas Sock & Wiping Rag Co.**
PO Box 457
Hughes, AR 72348-0457
Phone: (870)633-0691
Products: Fabrics. **SIC:** 5131 (Piece Goods & Notions). **Officers:** David Feltman, Partner.

■ **25969** ■ **Associated Fabrics Corp.**
104 E 25th St.
New York, NY 10010
Phone: (212)689-7186 **Fax:** (212)260-3531
E-mail: info@afcnewyork.com
URL: http://www.afcnewyork.com
Products: Fabrics, including textiles. **SIC:** 5131 (Piece Goods & Notions). **Est:** 1928. **Sales:** $10,000,000 (2000). **Emp:** 25. **Officers:** I.H. Stevens, President; Bruce Nocera, Dir. of Sales.

■ **25970** ■ **Astrup Co.**
2937 W 25th St.
Cleveland, OH 44113
Phone: (216)696-2820 **Fax:** (216)696-0977
URL: http://www.astrup.com
Products: Fabrics, hardware and finishing supplies for awning, marine, casual furniture, leisure and industrial markets. **SICs:** 5039 (Construction Materials Nec); 5131 (Piece Goods & Notions); 5021 (Furniture). **Est:**

1876. **Emp:** 300. **Officers:** J.H. Kirk, CEO & Chairman of the Board; J.W. Kirk, President; J.S. Szabo, Treasurer.

■ 25971 ■ **ATD-American Co.**
135 Greenwood Ave.
Wyncote, PA 19095
Phone: (215)576-1000
Free: (800)523-2300 **Fax:** (215)576-1827
E-mail: american@atd.com
Products: Textiles; Furniture; Law enforcement equipment; Food service equipment; Medical surgical disposables; Personal care items. **SICs:** 5131 (Piece Goods & Notions); 5021 (Furniture); 5047 (Medical & Hospital Equipment); 5045 (Computers, Peripherals & Software). **Est:** 1931. **Sales:** $59,000,000 (2000). **Emp:** 100. **Officers:** Jerome Zaslow, President; Bruce Rappaport, CFO; Spencer Zaslow, Exec. VP & Secty.; Arnold Zaslow, Exec. VP & Treasurer.

■ 25972 ■ **Joshua L. Baily and Company Inc.**
PO Box 9501
Hoboken, NJ 07030-9501
Phone: (201)656-7777
Products: Textiles. **SIC:** 5131 (Piece Goods & Notions). **Est:** 1876. **Sales:** $87,000,000 (2000). **Emp:** 45. **Officers:** R.I. Bonsal, President; R. Kingman, Treasurer; H. Neal Day, VP of Marketing.

■ 25973 ■ **Barb's Knitting Machines & Supplies**
870 West 100 South
Blackfoot, ID 83221-2016
Phone: (208)684-4391
Products: Knitting machines, yarn, and accessories. **SICs:** 5131 (Piece Goods & Notions); 5084 (Industrial Machinery & Equipment). **Officers:** Barb Anderson, Owner.

■ 25974 ■ **Barrow Industries Inc.**
5 Dan Rd.
Canton, MA 02021
Phone: (617)828-6750 **Fax:** (617)828-5055
Products: Fabric, including upholstery material. **SIC:** 5131 (Piece Goods & Notions). **Est:** 1946. **Sales:** $720,000,000 (2000). **Emp:** 375. **Officers:** Stephen Y. Barrow, President; Daniel J. Harper, CFO; Jeffrey Barrow, Exec. VP; Janet Higgins.

■ 25975 ■ **Barrow Industries Inc.**
75 Crestridge Dr.
Suwanee, GA 30024-3573
Free: (800)332-2776 **Fax:** (404)271-1663
Products: Upholstery and drapery fabric.c. **SIC:** 5131 (Piece Goods & Notions).

■ 25976 ■ **Barrow Industries Inc. Merrimac Textile**
3 Edgewater Dr.
Norwood, MA 02062
Phone: (781)440-2666
Free: (800)225-9954 **Fax:** (781)440-2667
Products: Textiles. **SIC:** 5131 (Piece Goods & Notions). **Sales:** $670,000,000 (2000). **Emp:** 350. **Officers:** Stephen Y. Barrow, President; Daniel F. Harper, CFO.

■ 25977 ■ **Beaulieu of America Inc.**
PO Box 4539
Dalton, GA 30721
Phone: (706)278-6666 **Fax:** (706)278-4961
Products: Yarns and rugs. **SICs:** 5199 (Nondurable Goods Nec); 5023 (Homefurnishings). **Sales:** $30,000,000 (2000). **Emp:** 499. **Officers:** Carl M. Bouckaert.

■ 25978 ■ **Beckenstein Men's Fabrics Inc.**
133 Orchard St.
New York, NY 10002-3103
Phone: (212)475-6666
Products: Fabric for men's suits. **SIC:** 5131 (Piece Goods & Notions). **Sales:** $29,000,000 (2000). **Emp:** 15. **Officers:** Neal Boyarsky, President; Gordon Goldstein, Controller.

■ 25979 ■ **Frank Bella & Co.**
48517 S Broadway
Hicksville, NY 11801
Phone: (516)932-3838
Free: (800)645-7560 **Fax:** (516)932-7347
Products: Fabric. **SIC:** 5131 (Piece Goods & Notions).

■ 25980 ■ **Belwool Corp.**
855 Avenue of the Americas
New York, NY 10001
Phone: (212)594-7195 **Fax:** (212)594-4576
Products: Yarns; Polyamide nylon fibers; Noncellulosic organic fibers; Thermoplastic resins; Processed textile waste. **SICs:** 5131 (Piece Goods & Notions); 5093 (Scrap & Waste Materials); 5162 (Plastics Materials & Basic Shapes); 5199 (Nondurable Goods Nec). **Officers:** Stephen E. Adler, President.

■ 25981 ■ **B. Berger Co.**
PO Box 8009
Macedonia, OH 44056
Phone: (330)425-3838 **Fax:** (216)241-3904
Products: Fabrics. **SIC:** 5131 (Piece Goods & Notions). **Est:** 1924. **Sales:** $10,000,000 (2000). **Emp:** 46. **Officers:** Stuart Giller, President; Michael Neumann, VP of Finance; Lee Giller, VP of Sales.

■ 25982 ■ **Bishops Inc.**
112 Lincoln Ave.
Pittsburgh, PA 15209-2620
Phone: (412)821-3333
Free: (888)4BI-SHOP **Fax:** (412)821-7467
Products: Drapery fabrics and linings. **SICs:** 5131 (Piece Goods & Notions); 5023 (Homefurnishings). **Est:** 1961. **Emp:** 11. **Officers:** Sam Nicotra, President; Rhea Nicotra, Vice President.

■ 25983 ■ **Blumenthal-Lansing Co.**
1 Palmer Ter.
Carlstadt, NJ 07072
Phone: (201)935-6220
Free: (800)448-9749 **Fax:** (201)460-1135
E-mail: sales@blulaw.com
URL: http://www.buttonsplus.com
Products: Buttons; Crafts; Decorative embellishments; Fashion accessories. **SICs:** 5131 (Piece Goods & Notions); 5199 (Nondurable Goods Nec). **Est:** 1877. **Sales:** $68,000,000 (2000). **Emp:** 100. **Officers:** Ed Cooke, President; Kevin Hansey, Controller; Gayle Decker, Exec. VP.

■ 25984 ■ **Philip F. Bogatin, Inc.**
2011 Walnut St.
Philadelphia, PA 19103
Phone: (215)568-1464 **Fax:** (215)568-4275
Products: Plastics; Textile fibers and by-products. **SICs:** 5131 (Piece Goods & Notions); 5162 (Plastics Materials & Basic Shapes). **Officers:** Philip F. Bogatin, President; John H. Wigton, Sales/Marketing Contact, e-mail: jwigton@juno.com.

■ 25985 ■ **Bond Supply Co.**
147 W 35th St.
New York, NY 10001
Phone: (212)695-2672 **Fax:** (212)695-1706
E-mail: bondsupply@aol.com
Products: Fabrics. **SIC:** 5131 (Piece Goods & Notions). **Est:** 1936. **Sales:** $1,000,000 (2000). **Emp:** 3. **Officers:** Louis Gutlaizer, Partner; Evelyn Gutlaizer, Partner; Carl Gutlaizer, Partner.

■ 25986 ■ **Bonded Fibers and Quilting**
1720 Fuller Rd.
West Des Moines, IA 50265
Phone: (515)223-5668
Free: (800)755-6783 **Fax:** (515)223-2276
Products: Textiles and notions. **SIC:** 5131 (Piece Goods & Notions). **Sales:** $8,000,000 (2000). **Emp:** 51.

■ 25987 ■ **Gay Bowles Sales**
3930 Enterprise Dr.
PO Box 1060
Janesville, WI 53547
Phone: (608)754-9466
Free: (800)356-9438 **Fax:** (608)754-0665
Products: Needlecraft supplies. **SIC:** 5131 (Piece Goods & Notions). **Est:** 1981.

■ 25988 ■ **Brewer Sewing Supplies**
3800 W 42nd St.
Chicago, IL 60632
Phone: (773)247-2121
Free: (800)444-3111 **Fax:** 800-999-9639
E-mail: brewer@brewersewing.com
URL: http://www.brewersewing.com
Products: Craft kits; Sewing notions and accessories; Fabric. **SICs:** 5131 (Piece Goods & Notions); 5092 (Toys & Hobby Goods & Supplies). **Est:** 1913. **Emp:** 50. **Officers:** Dennis J. Bromberek, VP of Operations, e-mail: denny@brewersewing.com.

■ 25989 ■ **Brittany Fabrics Inc.**
8 W 40th St.
New York, NY 10018
Phone: (212)391-1250
Products: Fabrics and linens. **SIC:** 5131 (Piece Goods & Notions). **Sales:** $11,000,000 (1992). **Emp:** 13. **Officers:** E.I. Freidenberg, President.

■ 25990 ■ **Brookwood Companies Inc.**
232 Madison Ave., 10th Fl.
New York, NY 10016
Phone: (212)551-0100 **Fax:** (212)725-7311
Products: Woven nylons. **SIC:** 5131 (Piece Goods & Notions). **Sales:** $93,500 (2000). **Emp:** 389. **Officers:** Amber M. Brookman, President.

■ 25991 ■ **Brownstone Gallery Ltd.**
295 5th Ave., Ste. 1618
New York, NY 10016
Phone: (212)696-4663
Products: Table linens. **SIC:** 5023 (Homefurnishings).

■ 25992 ■ **Burlington Industries Equity Inc. Knitted Fabrics Div.**
1345 Ave. of the Americas
New York, NY 10105
Phone: (212)621-3000
Products: Textiles. **SIC:** 5131 (Piece Goods & Notions). **Officers:** Jon Weingarten, President.

■ 25993 ■ **C and F Enterprises**
819 Blue Crab Rd.
Newport News, VA 23606
Phone: (757)873-0410
Products: Home textiles. **SIC:** 5131 (Piece Goods & Notions). **Sales:** $26,000,000 (1993). **Emp:** 100. **Officers:** Carol S Fang, President; Ching S. Fang, Treasurer.

■ 25994 ■ **Canvas Specialty**
PO Box 22268
Los Angeles, CA 90022
Phone: (323)723-8311
Free: (800)423-4082 **Fax:** (323)724-3848
Products: Custom canvas work, tarpaulins, truck covers, straps, bags, covers; Fabric tension structures. **SIC:** 5199 (Nondurable Goods Nec). **Est:** 1943.

■ 25995 ■ **Carhartt Inc.**
3 Parklane Blvd.
PO Box 600
Dearborn, MI 48121
Phone: (313)271-8460 **Fax:** (313)271-3455
Products: Material. **SIC:** 5131 (Piece Goods & Notions). **Sales:** $92,000,000 (2000). **Emp:** 1,400. **Officers:** R.C. Valade.

■ 25996 ■ **Carlyle Industries Inc.**
1 Palmer Terr.
Carlstadt, NJ 07072
Phone: (201)935-6220 **Fax:** (201)507-9060
E-mail: blumenthal@blulan.com
URL: http://www.buttonsplus.com
Products: Home sewing products; Crafts. **SIC:** 5131 (Piece Goods & Notions). **Est:** 1877. **Sales:** $30,000,000 (2000). **Emp:** 225. **Officers:** Robert Levinson, CEO & President; Edward Cooke, VP & CFO.

■ **25997** ■ **Carolyn Fabrics Inc.**
PO Box 2758
1948 W Green Dr.
High Point, NC 27261
Phone: (919)887-3101
Free: (800)333-8400 **Fax:** (919)887-2895
E-mail: customerservice@carolynfabrics.com
URL: http://www.carolynfabrics.com
Products: Upholstery and drapery fabric. **SIC:** 5131
(Piece Goods & Notions). **Est:** 1932. **Emp:** 45.

■ **25998** ■ **Cavalier Fabrics, Ltd./Redrum**
4716 Richneil Rd.
Richmond, VA 23231
Phone: (804)222-5730
Free: (800)552-3841 **Fax:** (804)222-3941
Products: Fabric. **SIC:** 5131 (Piece Goods & Notions).

■ **25999** ■ **Central Textile Co.**
12900 W Sunset Blvd.
Los Angeles, CA 90049-2644
Phone: (213)748-8782 **Fax:** (213)747-5229
Products: Cotton print fabrics. **SIC:** 5131 (Piece
Goods & Notions). **Est:** 1942. **Sales:** $10,000,000
(2000). **Emp:** 15. **Officers:** J.S. Lauterbach, Partner;
Alexander Lauterbach, Dir. of Marketing & Sales.

■ **26000** ■ **Cetex Trading Corp.**
385 Broadway
New York, NY 10013
Phone: (212)925-6774 **Fax:** (212)925-6600
Products: Fabric. **SIC:** 5131 (Piece Goods & Notions).
Officers: C. Theophilos, President.

■ **26001** ■ **Charter Fabrics Inc.**
1430 Broadway
New York, NY 10018
Phone: (212)391-8110
Free: (800)275-5950 **Fax:** (212)944-9095
E-mail: charter143@aol.com
Products: Apparel fabric, including woven, knits,
prints, blends, and cottons. **SIC:** 5131 (Piece Goods &
Notions). **Est:** 1962. **Sales:** $49,500,000 (2000). **Emp:**
35. **Officers:** Robert Murello, President; Kenneth
Winkler, VP of Finance.

■ **26002** ■ **Checker Distributors**
400-B W Dussel Dr.
Maumee, OH 43537
Phone: (419)893-3636
Free: (800)537-1060 **Fax:** 800-258-6416
URL: http://www.checker.com
Products: Sewing and quilting products. **SIC:** 5131
(Piece Goods & Notions). **Est:** 1948. **Officers:** Rob
Krieger, President.

■ **26003** ■ **Eugene Chernin Co.**
1401 Germantown Ave.
Philadelphia, PA 19122-3799
Phone: (215)235-2700 **Fax:** (215)236-1290
E-mail: echernin@aol.com
Products: Sewing notions, art needlework, and craft
supplies. **SICs:** 5131 (Piece Goods & Notions); 5092
(Toys & Hobby Goods & Supplies). **Est:** 1925.

■ **26004** ■ **Chinatex America Inc.**
209 W 40th St. 4th Fl.
New York, NY 10018
Phone: (212)719-3250
Products: Textiles. **SIC:** 5131 (Piece Goods &
Notions).

■ **26005** ■ **Chori America Inc.**
1180 Ave. of the Americas
New York, NY 10036
Phone: (212)563-3264 **Fax:** (212)736-6392
Products: Textiles; Chemicals; Yarn. **SICs:** 5131
(Piece Goods & Notions); 5169 (Chemicals & Allied
Products Nec). **Est:** 1957. **Sales:** $70,000,000 (2000).
Emp: 40. **Officers:** Y. Horiuchi, President.

■ **26006** ■ **Claesson Co.**
PO Box 326
Union, SC 29379-0326
Phone: (864)363-5059
Free: (800)344-9128 **Fax:** (864)363-8250
Products: Drapery hardware and accessories. **SICs:**
5131 (Piece Goods & Notions); 5072 (Hardware). **Est:**

1976. **Emp:** 13. **Officers:** Margacita Claesson,
President.

■ **26007** ■ **Herman Cohen and Company Inc.**
401 Broadway, Ste. 7048
New York, NY 10013
Phone: (212)925-0613 **Fax:** (212)925-0615
Products: Textiles, including unbleached. **SIC:** 5131
(Piece Goods & Notions). **Est:** 1918. **Sales:**
$1,500,000 (2000). **Emp:** 3. **Officers:** Arthur Cohen,
President; Gertrude Cohen, Vice President.

■ **26008** ■ **Consolidated Textiles, Inc.**
PO Box 240416
Charlotte, NC 28224
Phone: (704)554-8621 **Fax:** (704)554-7782
Products: Synthetic textile fibers. **SIC:** 5131 (Piece
Goods & Notions). **Officers:** W.C. Burke, President.

■ **26009** ■ **Culp Inc.**
PO Box 2686
High Point, NC 27261-2686
Phone: (910)889-5161 **Fax:** (910)887-7089
Products: Upholstery fabric. **SIC:** 5131 (Piece Goods
& Notions). **Est:** 1972. **Sales:** $398,900,000 (2000).
Emp: 3,146. **Officers:** Robert G. Culp III, CEO &
Chairman of the Board; Franklin N. Saxon, Sr. VP &
CFO; Andrew W. Adams, VP of Marketing; Thomas K.
Shade, VP of Information Systems; Kenneth M.
Ludwig, VP of Human Resources.

■ **26010** ■ **Custom Laminations Inc.**
932 Market St.
Paterson, NJ 07509
Phone: (973)279-9174 **Fax:** (973)279-6916
Products: Textiles and notions. **SIC:** 5131 (Piece
Goods & Notions). **Est:** 1969.

■ **26011** ■ **Daewoo International (America)**
14848 Northam St.
La Mirada, CA 90638
Phone: (714)228-8800 **Fax:** (714)228-8884
Products: Steel products; Textiles; Shoes; Electronics;
Auto parts and general commodities. **SICs:** 5051
(Metals Service Centers & Offices); 5065 (Electronic
Parts & Equipment Nec); 5136 (Men's/Boys' Clothing);
5137 (Women's/Children's Clothing); 5139 (Footwear).

■ **26012** ■ **Dakota Flags and Banner**
308 LA Plata Rd. NW
Albuquerque, NM 87107-5429
Phone: (505)345-7882 **Fax:** (505)345-3202
Products: Piece goods and notions; Flags and
banners. **SIC:** 5131 (Piece Goods & Notions). **Officers:**
Sally Marjon, Owner.

■ **26013** ■ **David-Martin Co. Inc.**
29 W 34th St.
New York, NY 10001
Phone: (212)947-8452
Products: Textile converters. **SIC:** 5131 (Piece Goods
& Notions). **Est:** 1960. **Sales:** $8,000,000 (2000). **Emp:**
10. **Officers:** M. Schechter, President; David Kimmel,
Vice President.

■ **26014** ■ **Louis De Poortere of America Inc.**
185 Rus Dr.
Calhoun, GA 30701
Phone: (706)624-3110
Free: (800)451-5376 **Fax:** (706)624-3114
URL: http://www.louisdepoortere.com
Products: High-end wool broadloom, runners, and
area rugs. **SIC:** 5131 (Piece Goods & Notions). **Est:**
1985. **Sales:** $20,000,000 (2000). **Emp:** 25. **Officers:**
David Duncan, Exec. VP.

■ **26015** ■ **DeBois Textiles Inc.**
1835 Washington Blvd.
Baltimore, MD 21230
Phone: (410)837-8081 **Fax:** (410)837-6459
E-mail: debtex@ix.netcom.com
Products: Textiles. **SIC:** 5131 (Piece Goods &
Notions). **Sales:** $4,000,000 (2000). **Emp:** 20.
Officers: Theodore DeBois, Chairman of the Board;
June Jacobs, Controller; Robert Jacobs, President.

■ **26016** ■ **Decorator & Upholstery Supply, Inc.**
501 McNeilly Rd.
Pittsburgh, PA 15226
Phone: (412)561-3770
Free: (800)242-0219 **Fax:** (412)561-1105
Products: Fabrics and upholstery supplies. **SIC:** 5131
(Piece Goods & Notions).

■ **26017** ■ **Delaware Dry Goods**
PO Box 10424
Wilmington, DE 19850
Phone: (302)731-0500
Free: (800)441-7300 **Fax:** (302)731-0573
Products: Craft kits; Sewing accessories. **SICs:** 5131
(Piece Goods & Notions); 5092 (Toys & Hobby Goods
& Supplies).

■ **26018** ■ **Derby Fabrics, Inc.**
630 Industry Rd.
PO Box 2556
Louisville, KY 40201
Phone: (502)637-1466
Free: (800)626-3500 **Fax:** (502)636-5721
Products: Fabric. **SIC:** 5131 (Piece Goods & Notions).

■ **26019** ■ **Doral Fabrics Inc.**
191 Central Ave.
East Farmingdale, NY 11735
Phone: (516)694-1570 **Fax:** (516)694-1575
Products: Fabrics. **SIC:** 5131 (Piece Goods &
Notions). **Est:** 1940. **Sales:** $3,000,000 (2000). **Emp:**
20. **Officers:** Eugene Gold, President; Kenneth A.
Gold, Chairman of the Board; Bruce Mailings, Dir. of
Information Systems.

■ **26020** ■ **Dorell Fabrics Co.**
4900 District Blvd.
Los Angeles, CA 90058
Phone: (213)585-5861
Products: Upholstery fabric. **SIC:** 5131 (Piece Goods
& Notions). **Est:** 1959. **Sales:** $4,000,000 (2000). **Emp:**
11. **Officers:** Barry Chasen, President; Rose
Hackman, Secretary.

■ **26021** ■ **Dorr Fabrics Inc.**
PO Box 88
Guild, NH 03754-0088
Phone: (603)863-1197
Free: (800)846-3677 **Fax:** (603)863-7458
Products: Piece goods; Notions; Fabrics. **SIC:** 5131
(Piece Goods & Notions). **Officers:** George Dorr,
Treasurer.

■ **26022** ■ **Down East Wholesalers Inc.**
1 School St.
Damariscotta, ME 04543
Phone: (207)563-3178 **Fax:** (207)563-5681
Products: Piece goods and notions. **SIC:** 5131 (Piece
Goods & Notions). **Officers:** Robert Reny, President.

■ **26023** ■ **DuBois Fabrics**
5520 W 111th St.
Oak Lawn, IL 60453
Phone: (708)499-2040
Free: (800)458-3500 **Fax:** (708)499-2967
E-mail: info@duboisfabrics.com
URL: http://www.duboisfabrics.com
Products: Upholstery and vinyl fabric. **SIC:** 5131
(Piece Goods & Notions). **Est:** 1935. **Emp:** 22.
Officers: Ronald F. Aumueller.

■ **26024** ■ **Duke Sports**
PO Box 5355
Stateline, NV 89449-5355
Phone: (702)588-5052
Products: Piece goods and notions, including fabrics.
SIC: 5131 (Piece Goods & Notions). **Officers:** Peter
Duke, Owner.

■ **26025** ■ **Duplex Novelty Corp.**
575 8th Ave.
New York, NY 10018-3086
Phone: (212)564-1352 **Fax:** (212)465-0549
E-mail: buttonking@aol.com
URL: http://www.virtualforum.com/duplex/
Products: Wood and casein buttons, toggles, belt
buckles, and beads. **SIC:** 5131 (Piece Goods &
Notions). **Est:** 1951. **Sales:** $1,500,000 (2000). **Emp:**
25. **Officers:** Dennis Hoffman; S.B. Hoffman, Mgr. Dir.

■ 26026 ■ Daniel A. Eaton
1 Sheddhill Rd.
Stoddard, NH 03464
Phone: (603)446-3535 **Fax:** (603)446-3535
Products: Piece goods and notions; Groceries; Hardware; Clothing; Gifts; Sporting goods. **SICs:** 5131 (Piece Goods & Notions); 5141 (Groceries—General Line); 5072 (Hardware); 5091 (Sporting & Recreational Goods); 5137 (Women's/Children's Clothing). **Est:** 1951. **Emp:** 5. **Officers:** Daniel Eaton, Owner.

■ 26027 ■ Edgars Fabrics Inc.
261 5th Ave.
New York, NY 10016
Phone: (212)686-2952
Products: Textiles. **SIC:** 5131 (Piece Goods & Notions). **Est:** 1948. **Sales:** $58,000,000 (2000). **Emp:** 30. **Officers:** Albert Rubin, President; Brett Rubin, Treasurer.

■ 26028 ■ Elna Inc.
8220 Commonwealth Dr., Ste.202A
Eden Prairie, MN 55344
Phone: (612)941-5519
Products: Household sewing machines and clothes press equipment; Sewing notions and accessories. **SICs:** 5064 (Electrical Appliances—Television & Radio); 5131 (Piece Goods & Notions). **Sales:** $17,000,000 (1994). **Emp:** 40. **Officers:** Curt Arvidson, President; Jerald J. Rezac, VP of Finance.

■ 26029 ■ W. S. Emerson Company Inc.
PO Box 10
Brewer, ME 04412-0010
Phone: (207)989-3410 **Fax:** (207)989-8540
Products: Piece goods; Footwear. **SICs:** 5131 (Piece Goods & Notions); 5139 (Footwear). **Officers:** John Vickery, President.

■ 26030 ■ Euro-Knit Corp.
1 Junius St.
PO Box 179
Brooklyn, NY 11212
Phone: (718)498-0820 **Fax:** (718)498-0471
Products: Textiles. **SIC:** 5131 (Piece Goods & Notions). **Emp:** 99. **Officers:** Walter Plieninger.

■ 26031 ■ Fabricut Inc.
PO Box 470490
Tulsa, OK 74147
Phone: (918)622-7700 **Fax:** (918)664-8919
Products: Fabric, including cotton, polyester, silk, nylon, and acrylics. **SIC:** 5131 (Piece Goods & Notions). **Est:** 1954. **Sales:** $75,000,000 (2000). **Emp:** 375. **Officers:** Harvey Nudelman, President; Ron Graham, VP of Finance; Sharon Bickle, Dir. of Marketing & Sales.

■ 26032 ■ Falcon Industries Inc.
PO Box 1971
Burlington, NC 27216
Phone: (336)229-1048 **Fax:** (336)229-9273
Products: Yarn. **SIC:** 5199 (Nondurable Goods Nec). **Est:** 1983. **Sales:** $12,000,000 (2000). **Emp:** 5. **Officers:** R.W. Miller, President; W. Hawks, CFO.

■ 26033 ■ Ferman Fabrics Centers
43 W Hollis St.
Nashua, NH 03060-3338
Phone: (603)889-0069 **Fax:** (603)889-8048
Products: Upholstery fabrics; Drapery material. **SIC:** 5131 (Piece Goods & Notions). **Officers:** Louis Ferman, President.

■ 26034 ■ Fisher Bag Company Inc.
2301 S 200th St.
Seattle, WA 98198-5571
Phone: (206)623-1966
Products: Textiles; Agricultural bags. **SIC:** 5131 (Piece Goods & Notions). **Est:** 1923. **Sales:** $200,000 (2000). **Emp:** 3. **Officers:** David Gardner, General Mgr.

■ 26035 ■ Marc J. Fisher, Inc.
391 Broadway, 2nd Fl.
New York, NY 10013-3510
Phone: (212)966-2534
Products: Broad woven wool fabric. **SIC:** 5131 (Piece Goods & Notions). **Officers:** Donald Fink, Vice President.

■ 26036 ■ Fleur de Paris
5835 Washington Blvd.
Culver City, CA 90232
Phone: (213)857-0704
Free: (800)221-6453 **Fax:** (213)857-0708
Products: Craft kits; Sewing accessories. **SICs:** 5131 (Piece Goods & Notions); 5092 (Toys & Hobby Goods & Supplies).

■ 26037 ■ Forte Dupee Sawyer Co.
4 Mechanic St., Ste. 203
Natick, MA 01760-3460
Phone: (617)482-8434 **Fax:** (617)482-1277
E-mail: wool@fortewool.com
Products: Wool; Mohair. **SIC:** 5131 (Piece Goods & Notions). **Est:** 1921. **Sales:** $10,000,000 (1999). **Emp:** 12. **Officers:** Donald Forte Jr. Jr., President.

■ 26038 ■ A. Frank and Sons Inc.
1501 Guilford Ave.
Baltimore, MD 21202
Phone: (410)727-6260 **Fax:** (410)685-2461
E-mail: frankling@aol.com
URL: http://www.afrank.com
Products: Textiles. **SIC:** 5131 (Piece Goods & Notions). **Est:** 1865. **Sales:** $14,000,000 (2000). **Emp:** 20. **Officers:** Samuel L. Frank, President.

■ 26039 ■ Frank Winne and Son Inc.
44 N Front St.
Philadelphia, PA 19106
Phone: (215)627-8080
Products: Cordage. **SIC:** 5085 (Industrial Supplies).

■ 26040 ■ Frankel Associates Inc.
1948 Troutman St.
Ridgewood, NY 11385
Phone: (718)386-2455 **Fax:** (718)386-3186
Products: Textiles. **SIC:** 5131 (Piece Goods & Notions). **Est:** 1943. **Sales:** $6,000,000 (2000). **Emp:** 20. **Officers:** J. Frankel, President.

■ 26041 ■ General Fabrics Co.
PO Box 6084
Providence, RI 02940-6084
Phone: (401)728-4200
Free: (800)745-1611 **Fax:** (401)728-2580
Products: Fabrics. **SIC:** 5131 (Piece Goods & Notions). **Est:** 1954. **Emp:** 45. **Officers:** Edward Odessa, President. **Former Name:** Front Street Fabrics Inc.

■ 26042 ■ Geo-Synthetics Inc.
428 N Pewaukee Rd.
Waukesha, WI 53188
Phone: (414)524-7979 **Fax:** (414)524-7961
URL: http://www.geo-synthetics.com
Products: Textiles; Erosion control geomembranes. **SIC:** 5131 (Piece Goods & Notions). **Est:** 1980. **Sales:** $35,000,000 (2000). **Emp:** 150. **Officers:** Robert F. Groh, President; Scott Nelson, Vice President; Robin O'Brain, Dir of Human Resources.

■ 26043 ■ Georgia Fabrics Inc.
1430 Broadway
New York, NY 10018
Phone: (212)391-2550 **Fax:** (212)391-2584
Products: Polyester. **SIC:** 5131 (Piece Goods & Notions). **Est:** 1915. **Sales:** $5,200,000 (2000). **Emp:** 6. **Officers:** Irwin Levine, President & Chairman of the Board; Margaret Levine, CFO; Murray Miller, Dir. of Marketing & Sales; John Held, Dir. of Information Systems.

■ 26044 ■ C. Goodman and Co. Inc.
75 Spruce St.
PO Box 2777
Paterson, NJ 07509
Phone: (973)278-1303 **Fax:** (973)278-5721
URL: http://www.cgoodman.com
Products: Filter fabrics and fabricated filter cloths for industrial wet filtration; Converted industrial leisure fabrics. **SIC:** 5131 (Piece Goods & Notions). **Est:** 1927. **Sales:** $3,500,000 (1999). **Emp:** 50. **Officers:** A.H. Goodman, President & Treasurer; J.D. Goodman, Vice President; Gene Mearon, Sales/Marketing Contact, e-mail: sales@cgoodman.com; Paul Holmes, Customer Service Contact; Leona Patmos; Gene Gilligan.

■ 26045 ■ Greeff Fabrics Inc.
261 5th Ave.
New York, NY 10016
Phone: (212)683-4800
Products: Cotton and cotton blend fabrics. **SIC:** 5131 (Piece Goods & Notions). **Sales:** $10,000,000 (1994). **Emp:** 20. **Officers:** Richard Downing, President; Bob Johnson, Controller.

■ 26046 ■ Greenburg & Hammer
24 W 57th St.
New York, NY 10019
Phone: (212)246-2836 **Fax:** (212)765-8475
Products: Sewing supplies. **SIC:** 5131 (Piece Goods & Notions).

■ 26047 ■ Greenwood Mills Marketing Co.
111 W 40th St.
New York, NY 10018
Phone: (212)398-9200
Products: Finished denim and chambray. **SIC:** 5131 (Piece Goods & Notions). **Est:** 1949. **Sales:** $97,000,000 (2000). **Emp:** 50. **Officers:** Robert E. Kaplan, President; Leonard Bagwell, Treasurer.

■ 26048 ■ Grover Industries Inc.
PO Box 79
Grover, NC 28073
Phone: (704)937-7434 **Fax:** (704)937-7507
Products: Yarn. **SIC:** 5199 (Nondurable Goods Nec). **Est:** 1965. **Sales:** $40,000,000 (2000). **Emp:** 300. **Officers:** Charles F. Harry III, CEO; Greg Blalock, Controller; R.W. Hewett, VP of Marketing; Dean Ledford, Dir. of Systems; Randy Patterson, Dir of Human Resources.

■ 26049 ■ Guilford of Maine Textile Resources
5300 Corporate Grove Dr. SE, No.
Grand Rapids, MI 49512-5512
Phone: (616)554-2250 **Fax:** (616)554-2255
Products: Commercial fabric. **SIC:** 5131 (Piece Goods & Notions). **Sales:** $33,800,000 (2000). **Emp:** 50. **Officers:** Brian De Moura, President; Ben Dever, Treasurer; Mark Lacroix, VP of Sales.

■ 26050 ■ Victor Guttmann Corp.
95 Madison Ave.
New York, NY 10016
Phone: (212)689-1899 **Fax:** (212)545-1052
Products: Fabric; Textiles. **SIC:** 5131 (Piece Goods & Notions).

■ 26051 ■ Haber Fabrics Corp.
1720 E Hwy. 356
Irving, TX 75060
Phone: (972)579-7451
Free: (800)527-1980 **Fax:** (972)721-1640
E-mail: habfab2@airmail.net
Products: Textile goods. **SIC:** 5131 (Piece Goods & Notions). **Est:** 1967. **Sales:** $30,000,000 (2000). **Emp:** 185. **Officers:** Albert Robbins, President; Murray Colton, Controller; Larry Robbins, Vice President.

■ 26052 ■ Haik's Inc.
1240 E Trafficway
PO Box 709
Springfield, MO 65801-0709
Phone: (417)866-4391
Free: (800)234-4245 **Fax:** (417)863-6620
E-mail: haiks@haiks-inc.com
URL: http://www.haik-inc.com
Products: Cotton broad woven fabrics; Fine cotton fabrics. **SIC:** 5131 (Piece Goods & Notions). **Est:** 1926. **Emp:** 19. **Officers:** James J. Haik Sr.

■ 26053 ■ Hallwood Group Inc.
3710 Rawlans St., Ste. 1500
Dallas, TX 75219
Phone: (214)528-5588
Products: Nylon textiles. **SIC:** 5131 (Piece Goods & Notions). **Sales:** $210,400,000 (2000). **Emp:** 1,020. **Officers:** Anthony J. Gumbiner, Chairman of the Board; Melvin J. Melle, VP & CFO.

■ **26054** ■ **Hancock Fabrics Inc.**
PO Box 2400
Tupelo, MS 38803-2400
Phone: (662)842-2834 **Fax:** (662)842-2834
URL: http://www.hancockfabrics.com
Products: Fabrics, crafts and related home sewing and home decorating accessories. **SIC:** 5131 (Piece Goods & Notions). **Est:** 1957. **Sales:** $381,572,000 (2000). **Emp:** 6,500. **Officers:** Larry G. Kirk, CEO & President; Bruce Smith, Sr. VP & CFO; Jack W. Busby Jr., President & COO.

■ **26055** ■ **Hanes Converting Co.**
500 N McLin Creek Rd.
Conover, NC 28613
Phone: (828)464-4673
Products: Fabrics. **SIC:** 5131 (Piece Goods & Notions). **Sales:** $676,600,000 (2000). **Emp:** 350. **Officers:** Mike Walters, President.

■ **26056** ■ **Hanes Fabrics Co.**
PO Box 457
Conover, NC 28613
Phone: (704)464-4673 **Fax:** (704)464-0459
Products: Drapery linings. **SIC:** 5131 (Piece Goods & Notions). **Est:** 1934. **Sales:** $29,000,000 (2000). **Emp:** 15. **Officers:** Jerry Greene Jr., President; Kim Howard, Controller; Bret Graff, Marketing Contact; Chris Carter, Dir. of Information Systems; Delores Buchanan, Dir of Human Resources.

■ **26057** ■ **Harris & Stearns**
910 W Cass St.
PO Box 2459
Tampa, FL 33601
Phone: (813)253-0111
Free: (800)282-2794 **Fax:** (813)251-4367
E-mail: harris.stearns@gte.net
URL: http://www.harrisstearns.com
Products: Fabric; Upholstery fabrics; Vinyl coated fabrics, including expanded vinyl coated fabrics; Wholesale upholstery fabrics; Vinyls; Supplies for auto, marine, industrial, residential, and commercial. **SIC:** 5131 (Piece Goods & Notions). **Est:** 1928. **Emp:** 9. **Officers:** Steve Harris, Vice President; Tom Harris Jr., President.

■ **26058** ■ **Harwell Fabrics, Inc.**
2030 W Quail Ave.
Phoenix, AZ 85027-2610
Phone: (602)271-0045 **Fax:** (602)271-0066
Products: Fabric. **SIC:** 5131 (Piece Goods & Notions).

■ **26059** ■ **S. Hata Company Ltd.**
938 Austin Ln.
Honolulu, HI 96817-4532
Phone: (808)841-0941
Products: Fabrics. **SIC:** 5131 (Piece Goods & Notions). **Est:** 1948. **Sales:** $100,000 (2000). **Emp:** 2. **Officers:** O. Nakamura, President.

■ **26060** ■ **Hawaii Plastics Corp.**
570 Dillingham Blvd.
Honolulu, HI 96817
Phone: (808)841-3358 **Fax:** (808)841-2345
Products: Acrylic Fabrication and PVC sheet material and supplies. **SIC:** 5162 (Plastics Materials & Basic Shapes). **Sales:** $1,000,000 (2000). **Emp:** 10. **Officers:** Fulton Seto, President.

■ **26061** ■ **Hedlund Fabrics and Supply Co.**
1710 E Washington St.
Phoenix, AZ 85034
Phone: (602)252-6058
Products: Fabric. **SIC:** 5131 (Piece Goods & Notions).

■ **26062** ■ **Hemisphere International**
3415 Eastern Ave.
Grand Rapids, MI 49508
Phone: (616)247-1444
Free: (800)713-0278 **Fax:** (616)452-8452
Products: Leather; Aircraft leather and fabric; Faux leather and suede; Leather supplies. **SICs:** 5199 (Nondurable Goods Nec); 5131 (Piece Goods & Notions). **Est:** 1994. **Emp:** 20. **Officers:** Robert Wood.

■ **26063** ■ **Herr's Inc.**
70 Eastgate Dr.
Danville, IL 61832
Phone: (217)442-4121
Free: (800)637-2647 **Fax:** (217)442-4191
E-mail: herrs@herrsinc.com
URL: http://www.herrsinc.com
Products: Craft and fine art products. **SICs:** 5131 (Piece Goods & Notions); 5092 (Toys & Hobby Goods & Supplies). **Est:** 1974. **Officers:** Hugh Ewing, Sales/Marketing Contact, e-mail: hewing@herrsinc.com; Stephanie Musson, Customer Service Contact, e-mail: custsrv@herrsinc.com; Diana Swartz, Human Resources Contact.

■ **26064** ■ **Hoch & Selby Company, Inc.**
809 NE 25th Ave.
Portland, OR 97232
Phone: (503)234-6476 **Fax:** (503)234-4874
Products: Upholstery fabrics and supplies. **SIC:** 5131 (Piece Goods & Notions).

■ **26065** ■ **Rube P. Hoffman Company Inc.**
25792 Obero Dr.
Mission Viejo, CA 92691
Phone: (714)770-2922
Products: Import and retail clothing fabrics. **SIC:** 5131 (Piece Goods & Notions). **Est:** 1924. **Sales:** $42,500,000 (2000). **Emp:** 80. **Officers:** Philip Hoffman, Chairman of the Board; Walter Hoffman, CFO.

■ **26066** ■ **Hoffman Distributing Co.**
2100 Resource Dr.
Birmingham, AL 35242-2940
Phone: (205)991-3599
Free: (800)624-8866 **Fax:** (205)991-6036
E-mail: info@hoffmandis.com
URL: http://www.hoffmandis.com
Products: Cross-stitch and needlework supplies. **SIC:** 5131 (Piece Goods & Notions). **Est:** 1985.

■ **26067** ■ **Houles USA Inc.**
8584 Melrose Ave.
Los Angeles, CA 90069
Phone: (310)652-6171 **Fax:** (310)652-8370
Products: Upholstery trimmings and accessories for the interior design industry. **SIC:** 5131 (Piece Goods & Notions). **Sales:** $10,000,000 (2000). **Emp:** 20. **Officers:** Pierre Houles, President; Sylvestre Bono, Exec. VP of Finance.

■ **26068** ■ **Gabe Humphries Decorative Fabrics**
330 N Neil St.
Champaign, IL 61820
Phone: (217)352-5318
Free: (800)637-4885 **Fax:** (217)352-5615
Products: Drapery material; Finished cotton fabrics (flame-, mildew-proofed). **SIC:** 5131 (Piece Goods & Notions).

■ **26069** ■ **Hunter and Company Inc.**
1734 Tully Circle NE
Atlanta, GA 30329
Phone: (404)633-2661
Products: Upholstery and drapery products and fabrics. **SICs:** 5131 (Piece Goods & Notions); 5023 (Homefurnishings). **Est:** 1945. **Sales:** $6,000,000 (2000). **Emp:** 45. **Officers:** W.K. McInnis Jr., President; H.R. Pickens, Controller.

■ **26070** ■ **Idaho Outdoor Equipment**
PO Box 8005
Boise, ID 83707-2005
Phone: (208)342-3063
Products: Baseball caps; Printed shirts; Mugs; Shorts; Souvenir pins. **SICs:** 5131 (Piece Goods & Notions); 5199 (Nondurable Goods Nec). **Officers:** David Ogburn, Owner.

■ **26071** ■ **IKO Notions**
4945 Lima St.
Denver, CO 80239
Phone: (303)371-0660
Products: Notions. **SICs:** 5131 (Piece Goods & Notions); 5023 (Homefurnishings). **Officers:** Albert W. Triplett Jr., CEO.

■ **26072** ■ **Institutional Linen Supply**
367 Simmonsville Ave., Apt. 3310
Johnston, RI 02919-6041
Phone: (401)233-2144 **Fax:** (401)232-7272
Products: Health care textiles; Restaurant linen; Chef uniforms; Custom draperies. **SICs:** 5131 (Piece Goods & Notions); 5136 (Men's/Boys' Clothing); 5137 (Women's/Children's Clothing); 5023 (Homefurnishings). **Officers:** Louis Montecalvo, Owner.

■ **26073** ■ **Interiors By Loette**
409 S 8th St. 101
Boise, ID 83702-7136
Phone: (208)345-8598
Products: Piece goods, notions, and other fabrics, including woven silk piece goods. **SIC:** 5131 (Piece Goods & Notions). **Officers:** Loette Miller, Owner.

■ **26074** ■ **Intertech Services**
200 E 57th St., Apt. 5L
New York, NY 10022
Phone: (718)260-3715 **Fax:** (718)260-3136
Products: Flame retardancy of plastic and textiles, consulting research project facilities, chemistry of phosphorus, sulfur and chlorine, research program planning and evaluation, specialty chemical processes, patent strategy, product development strategy. **SIC:** 5162 (Plastics Materials & Basic Shapes).

■ **26075** ■ **Irvin-Alan Fabrics**
PO Box 2248
Grand Rapids, MI 49501-2248
Phone: (616)459-4600
Free: (800)253-8358 **Fax:** (616)459-6843
Products: Upholstery fabrics and vinyls. **SIC:** 5131 (Piece Goods & Notions). **Est:** 1950. **Emp:** 40.

■ **26076** ■ **Irvin-Alan Fabrics**
11875 Kemper Springs Dr.
Forest Park, OH 45240
Phone: (513)825-8866 **Fax:** (513)825-8884
Products: Fabric. **SIC:** 5131 (Piece Goods & Notions).

■ **26077** ■ **Irwin Sales**
PO Box 2096
Baytown, TX 77522-2096
Phone: (281)424-7651 **Fax:** (281)424-7676
Products: Embroidery patches. **SIC:** 5131 (Piece Goods & Notions). **Est:** 1989. **Sales:** $100,000 (2000). **Emp:** 1. **Officers:** Wayne Irwin, e-mail: wirwin7418@aol.com.

■ **26078** ■ **Jacobson Capital Services Inc.**
150 Croton Ave.
Peekskill, NY 10566
Phone: (914)736-0600
Free: (888)JAI-TRIM **Fax:** (914)736-2914
URL: http://www.AJacob7686.com
Products: Garment accessories, including ribbon and tassels. **SIC:** 5131 (Piece Goods & Notions). **Est:** 1946. **Sales:** $16,000,000 (2000). **Emp:** 90. **Officers:** Alvin Jacobson, President; Nancy Kleinberger, CFO; Seth Jacobson, Dir. of Marketing & Sales.

■ **26079** ■ **Jaftex Corp.**
11 E 36th St.
New York, NY 10016
Phone: (212)686-5194 **Fax:** (212)545-0058
Products: Fabrics, including cotton, linen, and wool. **SIC:** 5131 (Piece Goods & Notions). **Est:** 1930. **Sales:** $60,000,000 (2000). **Emp:** 120. **Officers:** Everett Fortunoff, President & CFO.

■ **26080** ■ **JBM Sales**
36 Moreau St.
Stoughton, MA 02072-4022
Phone: (781)344-0573 **Fax:** (781)344-4758
Products: Trimmings for clothing, including velvet, lace, and ribbon. **SIC:** 5131 (Piece Goods & Notions). **Officers:** Richard Hertig, Owner.

■ **26081** ■ **JHB International Inc.**
1955 S Quince St.
Denver, CO 80231
Phone: (303)751-8100 **Fax:** (303)752-0608
Products: Textiles and notions. **SIC:** 5131 (Piece Goods & Notions). **Est:** 1969. **Sales:** $10,000,000 (2000). **Emp:** 155.

■ **26082** ■ **Josin Fabrics**
2501 N 85th St.
Omaha, NE 68134
Phone: (402)393-5677
Free: (800)228-9568 **Fax:** (402)393-0864
Products: Upholstery fabrics. **SIC:** 5131 (Piece Goods & Notions). **Est:** 1967. **Emp:** 15.

■ **26083** ■ **Kabat Textile Corp.**
247 W 37th St., 10th Fl.
New York, NY 10018
Phone: (212)398-0011 **Fax:** (212)719-9706
Products: Fabrics, including chiffon, georgettes, crepes, and stretch fabrics. **SICs:** 5131 (Piece Goods & Notions); 5136 (Men's/Boys' Clothing); 5137 (Women's/Children's Clothing). **Est:** 1935. **Sales:** $10,900,000 (1999). **Emp:** 13. **Officers:** Milton J. Adelman, President Emeritus; Arthur Adelman, President; Steven Stigland, Vice President; Neal Ganzer, Sales/MarketingContact.

■ **26084** ■ **Kagedo Inc.**
520 1st Ave. S
Seattle, WA 98104-2804
Phone: (206)467-9077
Products: Japanese textiles. **SIC:** 5131 (Piece Goods & Notions). **Officers:** Jeffrey Cline, President.

■ **26085** ■ **John Kaldor Fabricmaker USA Ltd.**
500 7th Ave.
New York, NY 10018
Phone: (212)221-8270
Products: Fabric. **SIC:** 5131 (Piece Goods & Notions). **Sales:** $67,000,000 (2000). **Emp:** 35. **Officers:** Rick Wolf, President.

■ **26086** ■ **Kanematsu U.S.A. Inc.**
114 W 47th St.
New York, NY 10036
Phone: (212)704-9400 **Fax:** (212)704-9483
Products: Metal service center, coal, electronic parts and chemical textiles. **SICs:** 5051 (Metals Service Centers & Offices); 5052 (Coal, Other Minerals & Ores); 5065 (Electronic Parts & Equipment Nec); 5169 (Chemicals & Allied Products Nec). **Sales:** $871,000,000 (2000). **Emp:** 1,000. **Officers:** S. Yamanaka, President; Asao Asao, Treasurer.

■ **26087** ■ **Kaplan-Simon Co.**
115 Messina Dr.
Braintree, MA 02184
Phone: (781)848-6500
Products: Textile convertors, except knit goods. **SIC:** 5131 (Piece Goods & Notions). **Est:** 1900. **Sales:** $10,000,000 (2000). **Emp:** 14. **Officers:** Joe Kaplan, President; Peter Kaplan, Dir. of Marketing.

■ **26088** ■ **Karystal International Inc.**
322 Market St.
Warren, RI 02885-2609
Phone: (401)245-8766
Products: Piece goods and notions; Broadwoven fabrics. **SIC:** 5131 (Piece Goods & Notions). **Officers:** Karen Fisher, President.

■ **26089** ■ **KasLen Textiles**
5899 Downey Rd.
Vernon, CA 90058-3701
Phone: (323)588-7700
Free: (800)777-5789 **Fax:** (323)588-7799
E-mail: kaslen@att.net
Products: Drapery material; Upholstery fabrics; Decorative accessories. **SIC:** 5131 (Piece Goods & Notions). **Est:** 1959. **Sales:** $15,000,000 (1999). **Emp:** 53. **Officers:** Jack Cook, Owner; Karin deRiszner, Controller; Marcel Einhorn, VP Marketing & Development. **Former Name:** Kas-Tex Corp.

■ **26090** ■ **Kast Fabrics Inc.**
540 Preston Rd.
PO Box 1660
Pasadena, TX 77501-1660
Phone: (713)473-4848
Free: (800)733-5278 **Fax:** (713)473-3130
URL: http://www.kastfabrics.com
Products: Upholstery; Drapery. **SICs:** 5131 (Piece Goods & Notions); 5023 (Homefurnishings). **Est:** 1952. **Sales:** $1,999 (1999). **Emp:** 30. **Officers:** Sigrid Baugh, President; Sharron Mc Culley, Sales/Marketing Contact, e-mail: info@kastfabrics.com.

■ **26091** ■ **P. Kaufman Inc.**
153 E 53rd St., 42nd Fl.
New York, NY 10022
Phone: (212)292-2200 **Fax:** (212)292-2280
Products: Decorative textiles. **SIC:** 5131 (Piece Goods & Notions). **Sales:** $150,000,000 (2000). **Emp:** 200. **Officers:** Ronald Kaufman, President; Peter Katzburg, CFO.

■ **26092** ■ **Keeton Sales Agency Inc.**
6908 Woodway Dr.
Waco, TX 76712-6196
Phone: (254)776-6011
Free: (800)455-2701 **Fax:** (254)776-6068
Products: Sample book rings and handles; Burlap goods. **SIC:** 5199 (Nondurable Goods Nec). **Sales:** $550,000 (2000).

■ **26093** ■ **Keyston Brothers**
3929 S 500 W
Salt Lake City, UT 84123
Phone: (801)264-8282
Products: Upholstery; Body cloths. **SIC:** 5131 (Piece Goods & Notions).

■ **26094** ■ **Keyston Brothers**
2381 E Winston Rd.
Anaheim, CA 92806
Phone: (714)774-9110 **Fax:** (714)774-0838
Products: Fabric; Upholstery fabrics. **SIC:** 5131 (Piece Goods & Notions). **Emp:** 7.

■ **26095** ■ **Keyston Brothers**
2801 Academy Way
Sacramento, CA 95815
Phone: (916)927-5851 **Fax:** (916)921-9123
Products: Fabric; Upholstery fabrics. **SIC:** 5131 (Piece Goods & Notions). **Emp:** 12.

■ **26096** ■ **Keyston Brothers**
9669 Aero Dr.
San Diego, CA 92123
Phone: (619)277-7770 **Fax:** (619)277-4524
Products: Fabric; Upholstery fabrics. **SIC:** 5131 (Piece Goods & Notions). **Emp:** 19.

■ **26097** ■ **Keyston Brothers**
476 Hester St.
San Leandro, CA 94577
Phone: (510)430-2771
Products: Fabric; Upholstery fabrics. **SIC:** 5131 (Piece Goods & Notions). **Emp:** 9.

■ **26098** ■ **Keyston Brothers**
3012 W Windsor Ave.
Phoenix, AZ 85009-1604
Phone: (602)233-2233 **Fax:** (602)233-3392
Products: Fabric and upholstery goods. **SIC:** 5131 (Piece Goods & Notions).

■ **26099** ■ **Keyston Brothers**
1100 Scott Rd.
Burbank, CA 91504-4237
Phone: (818)841-6015 **Fax:** (818)841-2801
Products: Fabric and upholstery goods. **SIC:** 5131 (Piece Goods & Notions).

■ **26100** ■ **Keyston Brothers**
5252 E Home Ave.
Fresno, CA 93727
Phone: (209)255-0435 **Fax:** (209)255-1889
Products: Fabric and upholstery goods. **SIC:** 5131 (Piece Goods & Notions).

■ **26101** ■ **Keyston Brothers**
1833 Riverview Dr., Ste. B
San Bernardino, CA 92408-3035
Phone: (909)796-5391 **Fax:** (909)799-7520
Products: Fabric and upholstery goods. **SIC:** 5131 (Piece Goods & Notions).

■ **26102** ■ **Keyston Brothers**
1501 Custer Ave.
San Francisco, CA 94124
Phone: (415)285-5050 **Fax:** (415)285-6542
Products: Upholstery goods. **SIC:** 5131 (Piece Goods & Notions).

■ **26103** ■ **Keyston Brothers**
3275 Edward Ave.
Santa Clara, CA 95054
Phone: (408)988-8811 **Fax:** (408)492-9343
Products: Fabric and upholstery goods. **SIC:** 5131 (Piece Goods & Notions).

■ **26104** ■ **Keyston Brothers**
1601 N California, Ste. 350
Walnut Creek, CA 94596-4115
Phone: (925)945-4949 **Fax:** (925)937-7590
E-mail: info@keystonbros.com
URL: http://www.keystonbros.com
Products: Upholstery vinyls, leather, fabrics, and supplies. **SIC:** 5131 (Piece Goods & Notions). **Est:** 1868. **Sales:** $38,000,000 (2000). **Emp:** 170. **Officers:** James R. Mitchell, President; Emily Szeto, CFO.

■ **26105** ■ **Keyston Brothers**
222 Bryant St.
Denver, CO 80219-1637
Phone: (303)935-6795 **Fax:** (303)935-5107
Products: Fabric and upholstery supplies. **SIC:** 5131 (Piece Goods & Notions).

■ **26106** ■ **Keyston Brothers**
690-A Kakoi St.
Honolulu, HI 96819-2014
Phone: (808)836-1941 **Fax:** (808)833-2248
Products: Fabric and upholstery supplies. **SIC:** 5131 (Piece Goods & Notions).

■ **26107** ■ **Keyston Brothers**
920 Avenue N
Grand Prairie, TX 75050-1918
Phone: (214)742-1875 **Fax:** (214)761-9133
Products: Fabric and upholstery supplies. **SIC:** 5131 (Piece Goods & Notions).

■ **26108** ■ **Keyston Brothers**
6823 Fulton St.
Houston, TX 77022-4832
Phone: (713)692-2132 **Fax:** (713)692-7201
Products: Fabric and upholstery supplies. **SIC:** 5131 (Piece Goods & Notions).

■ **26109** ■ **Keyston Brothers**
1601 N California Blvd., Ste. 350
Walnut Creek, CA 94596-4115
Phone: (925)945-4949 **Fax:** (925)937-7590
Products: Upholstery fabrics, supples for automotive, furniture, marine, aircraft, foam rubber and leather goods. **SICs:** 5087 (Service Establishment Equipment); 5199 (Nondurable Goods Nec). **Sales:** $38,000,000 (2000). **Emp:** 225. **Officers:** Jim Mitchell, CEO, President & Chairman of the Board; Emily Szeto, Sr. VP & CFO.

■ **26110** ■ **Kirsch Fabric Corp.**
830 Decatur Avenue North
Minneapolis, MN 55427
Phone: (612)544-9111
Free: (800)328-8626 **Fax:** (612)542-9481
Products: Upholstery, drapery, and naugahyde fabrics. **SIC:** 5131 (Piece Goods & Notions). **Est:** 1953. **Emp:** 50. **Officers:** Clyde Hill, President; Gary Horstman, Vice President.

■ **26111** ■ **Kirsch Fabrics Corp.**
830 Decatur Ave. N
Minneapolis, MN 55427
Free: (800)328-8626
Products: Upholstery and drapery products. **SICs:** 5131 (Piece Goods & Notions); 5023 (Homefurnishings).

■ **26112** ■ **Klemer and Wiseman**
2301 S Broadway
Los Angeles, CA 90007
Phone: (213)747-0307 **Fax:** (213)747-6642
Products: Drapery fabrics. **SIC:** 5131 (Piece Goods & Notions). **Est:** 1946. **Sales:** $2,000,000 (2000). **Emp:** 10. **Officers:** H. Klemer, Owner.

■ **26113** ■ **Kmart Trading Services, Inc.**
3100 W Big Beaver Rd.
Troy, MI 48084
Phone: (248)643-1733
Products: Footwear, except rubber; Motor vehicle

parts and accessories; Fabricated textile products. SICs: 5131 (Piece Goods & Notions); 5139 (Footwear); 5013 (Motor Vehicle Supplies & New Parts). Officers: G.E. Issler, Export Dir.

■ 26114 ■ L.C. Kramer
2525 E Burnside St.
Portland, OR 97214
Phone: (503)236-1207 Fax: (503)239-8907
Products: Craft kits; Sewing accessories. SICs: 5131 (Piece Goods & Notions); 5092 (Toys & Hobby Goods & Supplies).

■ 26115 ■ Kravet Fabrics Inc.
225 Central Ave. S
Bethpage, NY 11714
Phone: (516)293-2000
Products: Fabrics. SIC: 5099 (Durable Goods Nec).

■ 26116 ■ Kreinik Manufacturing Company Inc.
3106 Timanus Ln., No. 101
Baltimore, MD 21241
Phone: (410)281-0040
Free: (800)624-1928 Fax: (410)281-0987
Products: Thread; Lace, embroidery, braiding, tufting; Manmade fiber thread and other thread. SIC: 5131 (Piece Goods & Notions). Est: 1971. Emp: 40.
Officers: Douglas Kreinik, COO; Andrew Kreinik, CFO.

■ 26117 ■ Kwik Sew Pattern Company Inc.
3000 N Washington Ave.
Minneapolis, MN 55411
Phone: (612)521-7651
Free: (888)594-5739 Fax: (612)521-1662
E-mail: info@kwiksew.com
URL: http://www.kwiksew.com
Products: Sewing patterns and instruction books. SIC: 5131 (Piece Goods & Notions). Est: 1967. Emp: 46.
Officers: K. Martensson, President.

■ 26118 ■ Patricia Arscott La Farge
PO Box 762
Santa Fe, NM 87504-0762
Phones: (505)982-2912 (505)983-2358
Fax: (505)988-5196
E-mail: buenamano@cybermesa.com
URL: http://www.collectorsguide.com/buenamano
Products: Religious folk art; Old textiles; Latin American jewelry. SICs: 5131 (Piece Goods & Notions); 5094 (Jewelry & Precious Stones). Est: 1969. Emp: 2. Officers: Patricia La Farge, Owner. Doing Business As: Que Tenga Buena Mano.

■ 26119 ■ Alexander Lamport and Brother
7346 Creek View Ct.
West Bloomfield, MI 48322-3515
Phone: (313)962-5303 Fax: (313)962-2617
Products: Textiles; Linens; Kitchen clothing and chef uniforms.s. SICs: 5131 (Piece Goods & Notions); 5136 (Men's/Boys' Clothing); 5137 (Women's/Children's Clothing). Est: 1912. Sales: $2,900,000 (2000). Emp: 9. Officers: Graham Landau, Partner.

■ 26120 ■ Lansing Company Inc.
36 E Platt Dr.
Lansing, IA 52151
Phone: (319)538-4211 Fax: (319)538-4574
Products: Yarn. SIC: 5199 (Nondurable Goods Nec). Sales: $21,000,000 (2000). Emp: 100. Officers: Gayle Decker, CEO.

■ 26121 ■ Larson Fabrics, Inc.
11820 Mayfield
PO Box 51384
Livonia, MI 48151
Phone: (734)522-1080
Free: (800)521-3811 Fax: (734)522-6525
Products: Upholstery fabrics; Vinyl coated fabrics;. SIC: 5131 (Piece Goods & Notions). Est: 1946. Emp: 8. Officers: Roy Larson, President.

■ 26122 ■ Laundry Textile Co.
2450 Ave. E SW
Winter Haven, FL 33880-0841
Phone: (941)294-2718
Free: (800)829-9853 Fax: (941)299-4763
Products: Industrial fabrics. SIC: 5131 (Piece Goods & Notions). Sales: $19,000,000 (2000). Emp: 10.

■ 26123 ■ Lenzip Manufacturing Corp.
1900 W Kinzie St.
Chicago, IL 60622
Phone: (312)829-1865 Fax: (312)829-1515
E-mail: info@lenzip.com
URL: http://www.lenzip.com
Products: Zippers and slide fasteners. SIC: 5131 (Piece Goods & Notions). Est: 1946.

■ 26124 ■ Level Export Corp.
1411 Broadway, RM 485
New York, NY 10018-3402
Phone: (212)354-2600 Fax: (212)302-8421
E-mail: leveltwo@worldnet.att.net
Products: Denim; Clothing; Canvas; Cotton; Fleece. SICs: 5131 (Piece Goods & Notions); 5137 (Women's/Children's Clothing); 5136 (Men's/Boys' Clothing). Est: 1945. Sales: $50,000,000 (2000). Emp: 10. Officers: Alan Levys, President.

■ 26125 ■ Lion Notions Inc.
222 Harris Ct.
PO Box 2468
South San Francisco, CA 94083-2468
Phone: (650)873-4692
Free: (800)227-6022 Fax: (650)873-0617
Products: Craft kits; Sewing accessories. SICs: 5131 (Piece Goods & Notions); 5092 (Toys & Hobby Goods & Supplies).

■ 26126 ■ Lion Ribbon Company Inc.
Rte. 24, Box 601
Chester, NJ 07930
Phone: (908)879-4700
Free: (800)OFFRAY-7 Fax: (908)879-8588
URL: http://www.offray.com
Products: Ribbons and lace. SIC: 5131 (Piece Goods & Notions). Est: 1906. Sales: $25,000,000 (2000). Emp: 260. Officers: Claude V. Offray Jr., Chairman of the Board, e-mail: offrat@offray.com; Barry Sokol, Exec. VP of Corp. Retail Sales.

■ 26127 ■ Logantex Inc.
1460 Broadway
New York, NY 10036
Phone: (212)221-3900 Fax: (212)398-9817
Products: Fabric. SIC: 5131 (Piece Goods & Notions). Est: 1933. Sales: $15,000,000 (2000). Emp: 30. Officers: Armand J. Vella, President.

■ 26128 ■ Lucerne Textiles Inc.
519 8th Ave.
New York, NY 10018
Phone: (212)563-7800 Fax: (212)563-7937
Products: Fabrics for apparel and non-apparel markets. SIC: 5131 (Piece Goods & Notions). Est: 1921. Sales: $75,000,000 (2000). Emp: 50. Officers: Douglas Rimsky, President; Jerry Burkhof, CFO.

■ 26129 ■ M & R Sales & Service Inc.
1 N 372 Main St.
Glen Ellyn, IL 60137
Phone: (630)858-6101 Fax: (630)858-6134
URL: http://www.mprint.com
Products: Sewing accessories; Machine tools for home workshops, laboratories, garages. SICs: 5131 (Piece Goods & Notions); 5084 (Industrial Machinery & Equipment). Est: 1986. Emp: 4. Officers: Marilyn Perlman, President; Harold Perlman, Vice President. Former Name: M & R Sales & Supply Company Inc.

■ 26130 ■ Maco Vinyl Products Corp.
2900 Westchester Ave.
Purchase, NY 10577-2551
Phone: (914)337-1600 Fax: (914)337-1346
Products: Vinyl coated fabrics (including expanded vinyl coated fabrics); Polyester fabric. SIC: 5131 (Piece Goods & Notions). Est: 1972. Sales: $2,999,815 (2000). Emp: 11. Officers: Joel Neiterman, President.

■ 26131 ■ Maharam Fabric Corp.
PO Box 6900
Hauppauge, NY 11788
Phone: (516)582-3434 Fax: (516)582-1026
Products: Upholstery, drapery, cubicle and panel fabrics, wallcoverings. SICs: 5131 (Piece Goods & Notions); 5198 (Paints, Varnishes & Supplies). Sales: $70,000,000 (1992). Emp: 260. Officers: Donald H. Maharam, President; Michael Belasky, Exec. VP of Finance.

■ 26132 ■ Majilite Corp.
1530 Broadway Rd.
Dracut, MA 01826
Phone: (508)441-6800
Products: Material for shoes, wallcoverings, and upholstery. SIC: 5131 (Piece Goods & Notions). Est: 1962. Sales: $190,000,000 (2000). Emp: 100. Officers: Norm Lowe, President.

■ 26133 ■ Mannix World Imports Inc.
130 Commerce Way
Woburn, MA 01801
Phone: (781)935-4389 Fax: (781)933-2731
Products: Textiles; Men's and boy's sportswear. SICs: 5131 (Piece Goods & Notions); 5136 (Men's/Boys' Clothing). Est: 1972. Sales: $8,000,000 (2000). Emp: 10. Officers: Sandy K. Ganglani, President, e-mail: sganglani@aol.com; Hiro K. Ganglani, Vice President; Sam K. Ganglani, Treasurer.

■ 26134 ■ Marion Fabrics Inc.
PO Box 71
Burbank, CA 91503-0071
Phone: (818)567-0909
Free: (800)321-1041 Fax: (818)567-1422
E-mail: marionfabs@aol.com
URL: http://www.marionaircraft.com
Products: Aircraft interior fabric. SIC: 5131 (Piece Goods & Notions). Est: 1940. Sales: $2,000,000 (2000). Emp: 5. Officers: Julie Tauvaga, President; Garth Sawyer, Sales/Marketing Contact; Carolyn Salazar, Sales/Marketing Contact.

■ 26135 ■ Martinson-Nicholls
4910 E 345th St.
Willoughby, OH 44094-4609
Phone: (440)951-1312
Products: Nonwoven fabrics. SIC: 5099 (Durable Goods Nec).

■ 26136 ■ Marubeni America Corp.
450 Lexington Ave.
New York, NY 10017
Phone: (212)450-0100 Fax: (212)450-0700
Products: Textiles; Metals, except precious; Chemical preparations; Plastics; Electric and electronic equipment; Lumber and wood products. SICs: 5131 (Piece Goods & Notions); 5051 (Metals Service Centers & Offices); 5169 (Chemicals & Allied Products Nec); 5162 (Plastics Materials & Basic Shapes); 5065 (Electronic Parts & Equipment Nec). Est: 1951. Sales: $167,600,000,000 (2000). Emp: 2,196. Officers: Katsuo Koh; Yuichi Ishimaru; Shinichi Saito.

■ 26137 ■ Masco Fabrics Inc.
202 S 12th St.
Birmingham, AL 35233
Phone: (205)322-3476
Free: (800)326-2726 Fax: (205)322-3484
Products: Textiles and notions. SIC: 5131 (Piece Goods & Notions). Est: 1965.

■ 26138 ■ Matthews Hinsman Co.
3821 Olive St.
St. Louis, MO 63108-3488
Phone: (314)531-6554
Free: (800)321-3131 Fax: (314)531-1166
Products: Upholstery fabrics, vinyls, and supplies; Panel fabrics and leathers. SIC: 5131 (Piece Goods & Notions). Est: 1889. Emp: 14. Officers: W. Bogert Kiplinger, CEO & President; Don Martini, Sales/Marketing Contact; Peter Kiplinger, Human Resources Contact.

■ 26139 ■ Mayar Silk Inc.
15 W 36th St.
New York, NY 10018
Phone: (212)564-1380 Fax: (212)564-2329
Products: Cotton shirting; Prints; Silk for homefurnishings. SIC: 5131 (Piece Goods & Notions). Est: 1969. Sales: $19,000,000 (2000). Emp: 25. Officers: Albert E. Berizzi, President.

■ 26140 ■ **Memphis Furniture Manufacturing Co.**
3119 S Perkins Rd.
Memphis, TN 38118-3239
Phone: (901)525-3765
Products: Draperies; Upholstery fabrics. **SICs:** 5023 (Homefurnishings); 5131 (Piece Goods & Notions). **Est:** 1892. **Officers:** Ray Hearn.

■ 26141 ■ **Merrimac Boyce Fabrics**
1303 Corporate Dr.
High Point, NC 27263
Phone: (336)434-6060
Free: (800)339-0020 **Fax:** (336)434-6133
E-mail: hptshipping@barrowindustries.com
URL: http://www.barrowindustries.com
Products: Textiles. **SIC:** 5131 (Piece Goods & Notions). **Est:** 1945. **Sales:** $21,000,000 (2000). **Emp:** 4. **Officers:** Keith Marsh; Beth Myers.

■ 26142 ■ **Meskin and Davis Inc.**
14400 Woodrow Wilson
Detroit, MI 48238
Phone: (313)869-4006
Products: Fabric, including cotton and cotton polyester blends. **SIC:** 5131 (Piece Goods & Notions). **Est:** 1947. **Sales:** $29,100,000 (2000). **Emp:** 15. **Officers:** Julius S. Meskin, President; Russell Meskin, Treasurer.

■ 26143 ■ **MH World Trade Corp.**
140 E 45th St., 23rd Fl.
New York, NY 10017
Phone: (212)808-0810
Products: Men's and boy's suits and coats; Petroleum products; Lumber and plywood; Power and distribution transformers; Cotton textiles. **SICs:** 5131 (Piece Goods & Notions); 5136 (Men's/Boys' Clothing); 5172 (Petroleum Products Nec); 5031 (Lumber, Plywood & Millwork); 5063 (Electrical Apparatus & Equipment). **Officers:** Michael F.J. Mccabe, President.

■ 26144 ■ **Michelle Textile Corp.**
7523 Little Ave., Ste. 210
Charlotte, NC 28226-8170
Phone: (704)544-5520 **Fax:** (704)544-5524
Products: Textiles and notions. **SIC:** 5199 (Nondurable Goods Nec). **Est:** 1976. **Sales:** $900,000 (2000). **Emp:** 3.

■ 26145 ■ **Microfibres Inc.**
1 Moshassuck St.
Pawtucket, RI 02860
Phone: (401)725-4883 **Fax:** (401)722-8520
Products: Piece goods and notions, upholstery fabrics, and other woven fabrics. **SIC:** 5131 (Piece Goods & Notions). **Officers:** James McCulloch, President.

■ 26146 ■ **Mid Mountain Wholesale**
1308 1/2 Boulder Ave.
Helena, MT 59601-3569
Phone: (406)449-7080 **Fax:** (406)449-6517
Products: Piece goods, notions, and other fabrics; Upholstery supplies. **SIC:** 5131 (Piece Goods & Notions). **Officers:** Gary Coopersmith, Partner.

■ 26147 ■ **Miltan Export Corp.**
47 Walker St.
New York, NY 10013
Phone: (212)334-0202 **Fax:** (212)334-0204
Products: Nonwoven fabrics and related products. **SIC:** 5131 (Piece Goods & Notions). **Officers:** David Zolondek, President.

■ 26148 ■ **Miltex International Inc.**
7012 Union Ave.
Cleveland, OH 44105-1330
Phone: (216)645-8390
Free: (888)645-8390 **Fax:** (216)883-8508
Products: Textiles and notions. **SIC:** 5131 (Piece Goods & Notions).

■ 26149 ■ **Minnetonka Mills Inc.**
810 1st St. S
Hopkins, MN 55343
Phone: (612)935-2663
Free: (800)328-4443 **Fax:** (612)935-3444
Products: Textiles. **SIC:** 5131 (Piece Goods & Notions). **Est:** 1962. **Sales:** $4,000,000 (2000). **Emp:** 27. **Officers:** Craig Anderson, President.

■ 26150 ■ **Miroglio Textiles U.S.A. Inc.**
1430 Broadway
New York, NY 10018
Phone: (212)382-2020 **Fax:** (212)382-2609
Products: Fabric; Rayon and/or acetate; Linen thread, fabric, and other linen goods. **SIC:** 5131 (Piece Goods & Notions). **Est:** 1975. **Sales:** $40,000,000 (2000). **Emp:** 25. **Officers:** Frank Iovino, President.

■ 26151 ■ **Mitsubishi International Corp.**
520 Madison Ave.
New York, NY 10022
Phone: (212)605-2000 **Fax:** (212)605-2597
Products: Foods, chemicals, textiles, transportation equipment and general merchandise. **SICs:** 5141 (Groceries—General Line); 5131 (Piece Goods & Notions); 5052 (Coal, Other Minerals & Ores); 5088 (Transportation Equipment & Supplies). **Sales:** $7,143,000,000 (2000). **Emp:** 500. **Officers:** Hiroaki Yano, CEO & President; Hidetoshi Kamezaki, Sr. VP & CFO.

■ 26152 ■ **Florence Moore**
PO Box 31151
Billings, MT 59107-1151
Phone: (406)652-1585
Free: (800)352-4748 **Fax:** (406)656-4147
Products: Flags, flagpoles, and related products. **SIC:** 5131 (Piece Goods & Notions). **Est:** 1989. **Officers:** Florence Moore, Owner; H.L. Moore, General Mgr. **Doing Business As:** Western Flag & Banner.

■ 26153 ■ **Mosehart-Schleeter Company, Inc.**
4404 Directors Row
PO Box 8
Houston, TX 77092
Phone: (713)686-8601
Free: (800)392-3581 **Fax:** (713)686-9578
Products: Upholstery products and supplies. **SIC:** 5131 (Piece Goods & Notions).

■ 26154 ■ **L.P. Muller and Company Inc.**
1 S Executive Pk.
Charlotte, NC 28287
Phone: (704)552-5204
Free: (800)284-9276 **Fax:** (704)552-5203
Products: Textiles. **SIC:** 5131 (Piece Goods & Notions). **Est:** 1907. **Sales:** $125,000,000 (2000). **Emp:** 15. **Officers:** R.W. Hallman, President.

■ 26155 ■ **Neo Fabrics, Inc.**
5650 Hayne Blvd.
PO Box 26789
New Orleans, LA 70126
Phone: (504)241-4020
Free: (800)442-8610 **Fax:** (504)241-4738
URL: http://www.NeoFabrics.com
Products: Upholstery, drapery, and marine fabric. **SIC:** 5131 (Piece Goods & Notions). **Est:** 1934. **Emp:** 30.

■ 26156 ■ **Neo Fabrics, Inc.**
1506 Corporate Dr.
Shreveport, LA 71107
Phone: (318)424-4129
Free: (800)282-8830 **Fax:** (318)424-0160
Products: Upholstery, drapery, and marine fabric. **SIC:** 5131 (Piece Goods & Notions). **Est:** 1934.

■ 26157 ■ **Nomura America Corp.**
60 E 42nd St.
New York, NY 10165
Phone: (212)867-6684 **Fax:** (212)697-3202
Products: Sewing machines; Seafood; Textiles. **SICs:** 5064 (Electrical Appliances—Television & Radio); 5131 (Piece Goods & Notions); 5146 (Fish & Seafoods). **Est:** 1960. **Sales:** $422,000,000 (2000). **Emp:** 21. **Officers:** Masami Ikeuchi, President; Masaru Yamamoto, Treasurer; Shozo Ohnishi, Exec. VP of Marketing.

■ 26158 ■ **Nordic Needle, Inc.**
1314 Gateway Dr. SW
Fargo, ND 58103
Phone: (701)235-5231
Free: (800)433-4321 **Fax:** (701)235-0952
E-mail: info@nordicneedle.com
URL: http://www.nordicneedle.com
Products: Embroidery and needlework supplies and accessories, including thread and fabric; Books. **SICs:** 5131 (Piece Goods & Notions); 5192 (Books,

Periodicals & Newspapers). **Est:** 1975. **Emp:** 26. **Officers:** Susan Meier; Rosalyn Watnemo.

■ 26159 ■ **Notions Marketing Corp.**
PO Box 7392
Grand Rapids, MI 49510
Phone: (616)243-8424
Free: (800)748-0250 **Fax:** (616)243-8055
Products: Sewing, knitting, and craft supplies. **SIC:** 5131 (Piece Goods & Notions).

■ 26160 ■ **Oklahoma Upholstery Supply Co.**
706 N Villa
Oklahoma City, OK 73107
Phone: (405)235-2597
Products: Upholstering materials. **SIC:** 5131 (Piece Goods & Notions).

■ 26161 ■ **Oklahoma Upholstery Supply Co.**
1427 E 4th St.
PO Box 50186
Tulsa, OK 74120
Phone: (918)585-5727
Free: (800)331-3746 **Fax:** (918)585-5722
Products: Upholstery fabrics. **SIC:** 5131 (Piece Goods & Notions).

■ 26162 ■ **O'Neill Div.**
PO Box 758
VilLa Rica, GA 30180
Phone: (770)459-1800 **Fax:** (404)459-1531
Products: Textile goods and industrial wiping cloths. **SIC:** 5093 (Scrap & Waste Materials). **Sales:** $10,000,000 (1993). **Emp:** 100. **Officers:** Robert K. Pease, President; Chuck Wood, Controller.

■ 26163 ■ **Orchard Yarn and Thread Company Inc./Lion Brand Yarn Co.**
34 W 15th St.
New York, NY 10011
Phone: (212)243-8995
Free: (800)795-5466 **Fax:** (212)627-8154
E-mail: http://www.lionbrand.com
Products: Hand knitting yarns; Thread. **SICs:** 5131 (Piece Goods & Notions); 5199 (Nondurable Goods Nec). **Est:** 1878. **Sales:** $10,000,000 (2000). **Emp:** 20. **Officers:** Isidor Blumenthal, President.

■ 26164 ■ **Original Design Silk Screen Co.**
RR 1, Box 89
North Woodstock, NH 03262-9710
Phone: (603)745-6277
Free: (800)421-3345 **Fax:** (603)745-8053
E-mail: odsilk@together.net
URL: http://www.odimprintedwear.com
Products: Screen printed and embroidered apparel. **SIC:** 5131 (Piece Goods & Notions). **Est:** 1974. **Sales:** $4,500,000 (2000). **Emp:** 45. **Officers:** Jeff Martel, President; Karin Martel, Vice President; Holly Boyd, Customer Service Contact; Jeff Martel, Sales/Marketing Contact.

■ 26165 ■ **Oved Corp.**
4143 NW 132nd St.
Miami, FL 33054
Phone: (305)688-5865
Free: (800)332-6833 **Fax:** (305)685-2988
Products: Toys and hobby goods. **SIC:** 5131 (Piece Goods & Notions). **Sales:** $5,000,000 (2000). **Emp:** 6.

■ 26166 ■ **Paragon Fabrics Company Inc.**
441 Broadway
New York, NY 10013
Phone: (212)226-8100
Free: (800)221-7932 **Fax:** (212)226-1249
E-mail: paragonfabrics@aol.com
Products: Decorative fabrics. **SIC:** 5131 (Piece Goods & Notions). **Est:** 1946. **Sales:** $1,500,000 (2000). **Emp:** 10. **Officers:** V. Macaluso, President.

■ 26167 ■ **Peter Patchis Yarn Shop**
174 Cross St.
Central Falls, RI 02863-2907
Phone: (401)723-3116
Products: Yarns and threads. **SIC:** 5131 (Piece Goods & Notions). **Officers:** Peter Patchis, Partner.

■ **26168** ■ **Patrick Dry Goods Company Inc.**
163 W 2nd S
Salt Lake City, UT 84101
Phone: (801)363-5895 **Fax:** (801)363-5898
Products: Fabrics and sewing notions: Quilting batting.
SIC: 5131 (Piece Goods & Notions). **Est:** 1909.

■ **26169** ■ **The Pawley Co.**
PO Box 480585
Denver, CO 80248
Phone: (303)294-0115
Products: Fabric; Upholstery fabrics; Drapery material.
SIC: 5131 (Piece Goods & Notions). **Emp:** 8.

■ **26170** ■ **Peachtree Fabrics Inc.**
1400 English St.
Atlanta, GA 30318
Phone: (404)351-5400
Free: (800)PEA-CHES **Fax:** (404)351-5270
Products: Furniture cloth. **SIC:** 5131 (Piece Goods &
Notions). **Est:** 1947. **Sales:** $330,000,000 (2000).
Emp: 170. **Officers:** D.L. Dutson Jr., CEO; Ron
Crumbley, VP of Admin.

■ **26171** ■ **Peachtree Fabrics Inc.**
1480 Whipple Rd.
Union City, CA 94587
Phone: (510)487-7799 **Fax:** (510)487-5746
Products: Fabric. **SIC:** 5131 (Piece Goods & Notions).
Emp: 4.

■ **26172** ■ **Peachtree Fabrics Inc.**
18 Conneticut Dr. S
East Granby, CT 06026
Phone: (860)653-2188
Free: (800)732-2437 **Fax:** (860)653-3951
Products: Fabric. **SIC:** 5131 (Piece Goods & Notions).

■ **26173** ■ **J.J. Peiger Co.**
101-103 Market St.
Pittsburgh, PA 15222
Phone: (412)281-3133
Free: (800)245-2012 **Fax:** 800-648-1525
Products: Fabric. **SIC:** 5131 (Piece Goods & Notions).

■ **26174** ■ **Personally Yours**
3475 Nowlin Ln.
Sparks, NV 89431-1371
Phone: (702)356-7001 **Fax:** (702)358-7001
Products: Piece goods; Sewing accessories. **SIC:**
5131 (Piece Goods & Notions). **Officers:** Roberta
Copeland, President.

■ **26175** ■ **Phillips Industries Inc.**
PO Box 1350
High Point, NC 27261
Phone: (910)882-3301
Products: Upholstery fabrics. **SIC:** 5131 (Piece Goods
& Notions). **Sales:** $52,000,000 (2000). **Emp:** 500.
Officers: S. Dave Phillips, President; Larry Lewis,
Controller.

■ **26176** ■ **Phoenix Textile Corp.**
13652 Lakefront Dr.
Earth City, MO 63045
Phone: (314)291-2151
Free: (800)325-1440 **Fax:** (314)291-7169
E-mail: generalinfo@PhoenixTextile.com
URL: http://www.PhoenixTile.com
Products: Linens, towels, sheets, curtains and drapes
to hospital and nursing homes; Floor coverings. **SIC:**
5023 (Homefurnishings). **Est:** 1983. **Sales:**
$54,000,000 (2000). **Emp:** 125. **Officers:** Pam
Reynolds, President; Dennis McDonough, VP of
Finance.

■ **26177** ■ **Pinetex**
108 W 39th St., Ste. 500
New York, NY 10018
Phone: (212)719-4999 **Fax:** (212)944-7227
Products: Textiles and notions. **SIC:** 5131 (Piece
Goods & Notions). **Est:** 1976. **Sales:** $24,000,000
(2000). **Emp:** 12.

■ **26178** ■ **PL Preferred Products**
PO Box 477
Ossipee, NH 03864-0477
Phone: (603)539-8013
Products: Piece goods; Notions. **SIC:** 5131 (Piece
Goods & Notions). **Officers:** Pamela Cotton, Owner.

■ **26179** ■ **Plezall Wipers Inc.**
9869 NW 79th Ave.
Hialeah Gardens, FL 33016
Phone: (305)556-3744
Free: (800)237-8724 **Fax:** (305)825-4938
Products: Industrial textiles. **SIC:** 5131 (Piece Goods
& Notions). **Sales:** $67,000,000 (2000). **Emp:** 35.
Officers: Brian Markowitz, President.

■ **26180** ■ **Promotional Sales Co.**
2301 S Broadway
Los Angeles, CA 90007-2715
Phone: (213)749-5015 **Fax:** (213)747-6642
Products: Drapery fabrics. **SIC:** 5131 (Piece Goods &
Notions). **Est:** 1963. **Sales:** $2,000,000 (2000). **Emp:**
10. **Officers:** Harold Klemer, Owner; Ben Z. Porat,
CEO.

■ **26181** ■ **Provo Craft Inc.**
285 East 900 South
Provo, UT 84606
Phone: (801)377-4311
Free: (800)937-7686 **Fax:** (801)373-1901
URL: http://www.provocraft.com
Products: General craft painting supplies; General
scrapbooking and memorabilia supplies; Unfinished
home decor wood products; Craft books and wooden
shapes; Rub-ons; Stencils and templates; Glass
containers and craft metal containers; Template cutting
systems. **SICs:** 5199 (Nondurable Goods Nec); 5092
(Toys & Hobby Goods & Supplies). **Est:** 1960. **Emp:**
600. **Officers:** Robert Workman, President & CEO;
Eric Larsen, CFO; Darwin Russon, Exec. VP of Sales;
Kevin Buckner, VP of Retail.

■ **26182** ■ **Quiltworks**
1055 E 79th St.
Bloomington, MN 55420-1417
Phone: (612)854-1460
Free: (800)328-1850 **Fax:** (612)854-7254
E-mail: hbornstein@r-and-z.com
URL: http://www.r-and-z.com
Products: Quilting books; Quilting fabric and supplies;
Sewing accessories. **SICs:** 5131 (Piece Goods &
Notions); 5092 (Toys & Hobby Goods & Supplies). **Est:**
1968. **Sales:** $8,000,000 (2000). **Emp:** 40.

■ **26183** ■ **Raytex Fabrics Inc.**
469 7th Ave.
New York, NY 10018
Phone: (212)268-6001 **Fax:** (212)736-8835
Products: Nylon and cotton fabrics. **SIC:** 5131 (Piece
Goods & Notions). **Est:** 1899. **Sales:** $60,000,000
(2000). **Emp:** 50. **Officers:** Dan Reich, President;
William Litsky, Controller; Allen Maybloom, Dir. of
Marketing; Tony Falasco, Dir. of Merchandising.

■ **26184** ■ **Representative Sales Co.**
6111 S Sayre Ave.
Chicago, IL 60638
Phone: (773)586-2030
Free: (800)621-1661 **Fax:** (773)586-2783
E-mail: faersc@earthlink.net
URL: http://www.faersc.com
Products: Quilting products; Needlecrafts; Magnifiers;
Wood products; Plastic bubbles. **SICs:** 5131 (Piece
Goods & Notions); 5092 (Toys & Hobby Goods &
Supplies); 5199 (Nondurable Goods Nec). **Est:** 1940.
Sales: $1,000,000 (2000). **Emp:** 14. **Officers:** James
Mann; Dennis Clegg; Nancy Brendel, Customer
Service Contact. **Former Name:** F.A. #Edmunds & Co.

■ **26185** ■ **Richard The Thread**
8320 Melrose
West Hollywood, CA 90069
Phone: (213)852-4997 **Fax:** (213)852-1604
Products: Sewing supplies; Dress forms. **SIC:** 5131
(Piece Goods & Notions). **Est:** 1951. **Sales:**
$1,000,000 (2000). **Emp:** 6.

■ **26186** ■ **Rivertex Company, Inc.**
401 Broadway
New York, NY 10013
Phone: (212)925-1410 **Fax:** (212)925-1411
Products: Textile piece goods. **SIC:** 5131 (Piece
Goods & Notions). **Officers:** Norbert Schoenbach,
President.

■ **26187** ■ **Robert Allen Fabrics Inc.**
55 Cabot Blvd.
Mansfield, MA 02048
Phone: (508)339-9151
Free: (800)333-3776 **Fax:** (508)339-8256
Products: Decorative cotton fabrics. **SIC:** 5131 (Piece
Goods & Notions). **Sales:** $1,260,000,000 (2000).
Emp: 850. **Officers:** Ronald Kass, CEO; Paul Luba,
Chairman of the Board & Finance Officer.

■ **26188** ■ **Rockland Industries Inc.**
1601 Edison Hwy.
Baltimore, MD 21213
Phone: (410)522-2505
Free: (800)876-2566 **Fax:** (410)522-2545
E-mail: rfugate@roc-lon.com
URL: http://www.roc-lon.com
Products: Wide sheeting. **SIC:** 5131 (Piece Goods &
Notions). **Est:** 1832. **Officers:** Rose Fugate, Vice
President, e-mail: cslywczuk@roc-lon.com.

■ **26189** ■ **Rockville Fabrics Corp.**
225 W 34th St., No. 1509
New York, NY 10122
Phone: (212)563-2050 **Fax:** (212)629-0840
E-mail: service@rockvillefabrics.com
URL: http://rockvillefabrics.com
Products: Fabric, including cotton and nylon. **SIC:**
5131 (Piece Goods & Notions). **Est:** 1947. **Sales:**
$12,000,000 (2000). **Emp:** 60. **Officers:** Peter Levy,
President.

■ **26190** ■ **Miles Rogers Decorative Fabrics**
690 Miami Cir., Ste. 500
Atlanta, GA 30324
Free: (800)732-2437 **Fax:** (404)262-2872
Products: Fabric. **SIC:** 5131 (Piece Goods & Notions).

■ **26191** ■ **Rose Brand-Theatrical Fabrics
Fabrications and Supplies**
75 9th Ave.
New York, NY 10011
Phone: (212)242-7554
Free: (800)223-1624 **Fax:** (212)242-7565
E-mail: info@rosebrand.com
URL: http://www.rosebrand.com
Products: Textiles and fabrics. **SIC:** 5131 (Piece
Goods & Notions). **Est:** 1922. **Emp:** 100. **Officers:**
George Jacobstein; Peter Finder, Sales/Marketing
Contact. **Former Name:** Rose Brand Textile Fabrics.

■ **26192** ■ **Rose City Awning Co.**
1638 NW Overton St.
Portland, OR 97209
Phone: (503)226-2761 **Fax:** (503)222-5060
Products: Canvas products; sells flags and flag poles,
vinyl strip doors, solar shades, transparent moving
pads and polyethylene film. **SIC:** 5199 (Nondurable
Goods Nec). **Sales:** $1,500,000 (2000). **Emp:** 15.
Officers: Jack Neustadter, President.

■ **26193** ■ **Rosenstein and Co.**
413 N Cedar St.
Mishawaka, IN 46545
Phone: (219)255-9639 **Fax:** (219)255-9727
Products: Textiles and notions. **SIC:** 5131 (Piece
Goods & Notions). **Sales:** $500,000 (2000). **Emp:** 6.

■ **26194** ■ **Rubenstein & Ziff Inc.**
1055 E 79th St.
Minneapolis, MN 55420-1460
Phone: (612)854-1460
Free: (800)328-1850 **Fax:** (612)854-7254
URL: http://www.r-and-z.com
Products: Craft kits; Sewing accessories; Notions.
SICs: 5131 (Piece Goods & Notions); 5092 (Toys &
Hobby Goods & Supplies). **Est:** 1920.

■ **26195** ■ **Rushin Upholstery Supply, Inc.**
2600 Welch
Little Rock, AR 72206
Phone: (501)376-3194
Free: (800)482-5664 **Fax:** (501)376-1815
URL: http://www.rushin@aol.com
Products: Upholstery supplies and fabric. **SIC:** 5131 (Piece Goods & Notions). **Est:** 1962. **Sales:** $1,200,000 (2000). **Emp:** 9. **Officers:** Stan A. Rushin, Owner; Norma J. Rushin, Owner & Pres.; Scott Rushin, Vice President.

■ **26196** ■ **S & O Industries Inc.**
PO Box 3466
New Hyde Park, NY 11040
Phone: (516)487-9070 **Fax:** (212)228-1721
Products: Yarns. **SIC:** 5199 (Nondurable Goods Nec). **Est:** 1990. **Officers:** Alvin Flaster, President; Richard Flaster, Vice President.

■ **26197** ■ **St. Louis Trimming**
9601-03 Dielman Rock Island Dr.
St. Louis, MO 63132
Phone: (314)432-1131
Free: (800)325-7144 **Fax:** (314)432-7114
E-mail: stljns@aol.com
Products: Lace; Home furnishings; Ribbons. **SIC:** 5131 (Piece Goods & Notions). **Sales:** $13,000,000 (2000). **Emp:** 100. **Officers:** Nell Schneider, President; Robert Herz, Exec. VP.

■ **26198** ■ **E.E. Schenck Co.**
2204 N Clark St.
Portland, OR 97227
Phone: (503)284-4124
Free: (800)433-0723 **Fax:** (503)288-4475
E-mail: info@eeschenck.com
URL: http://www.eeschenck.com
Products: Fabric. **SIC:** 5131 (Piece Goods & Notions). **Est:** 1921. **Sales:** $20,000,000 (2000). **Emp:** 56. **Officers:** S.G. Gray, President; Keith Wernli, Controller; K. Soderling, Dir. of Marketing.

■ **26199** ■ **Schoeller Textil USA Inc.**
RR 3 Box 9D
Newport, VT 05855
Phone: (802)334-5081 **Fax:** (802)334-5000
Products: Fabrics for skiing and cycling apparel. **SIC:** 5131 (Piece Goods & Notions). **Sales:** $1,000,000 (2000). **Emp:** 6. **Officers:** Tom Weinbender, President.

■ **26200** ■ **Scott Foam & Fabrics, Inc.**
2790 Broad
PO Box 820371
Memphis, TN 38112
Phone: (901)324-3800
Free: (800)238-7466 **Fax:** (901)324-3809
Products: Wholesale fabrics for upholstering and drapery; Foam products and upholstery supplies. **SICs:** 5131 (Piece Goods & Notions); 5087 (Service Establishment Equipment). **Officers:** Thomas H. Scott Jr., President; Joel H. Scott, Vice President; Nellie Medlin, Customer Service Contact; Susan Hughes, Human Resources Contact.

■ **26201** ■ **S. Shamash and Sons**
42 W 39th St., 12th Fl.
New York, NY 10018
Phone: (212)840-3111
Products: Silk, rayon and fabric. **SIC:** 5159 (Farm-Product Raw Materials Nec). **Sales:** $100,000,000 (2000). **Emp:** 95. **Officers:** Jeff White, President; Brad Gero, Controller.

■ **26202** ■ **Sher and Mishkin Inc.**
PO Box 430
Phoenixville, PA 19460-0430
Phone: (215)683-8771 **Fax:** (215)683-8773
Products: Textile yarn. **SIC:** 5199 (Nondurable Goods Nec). **Est:** 1959. **Sales:** $10,000,000 (2000). **Emp:** 25. **Officers:** R. Sher, President; Sander Mishkin, Treasurer & Secty.

■ **26203** ■ **Sherri-Li Textile Inc.**
PO Box 6471
Providence, RI 02940-6471
Phone: (401)831-9742
Products: TexTile machinery, knitted elastic, and nylon cord. **SICs:** 5131 (Piece Goods & Notions); 5084

(Industrial Machinery & Equipment). **Officers:** Joyce Pannone, President.

■ **26204** ■ **The Showroom**
331 Rio Grande St., Ste. 101
Salt Lake City, UT 84101-3802
Phone: (801)467-1213 **Fax:** (801)485-7906
Products: Fabrics; Window furnishings. **SICs:** 5131 (Piece Goods & Notions); 5023 (Homefurnishings).

■ **26205** ■ **Singer Textiles Inc.**
55 Delancy St.
New York, NY 10002
Phone: (212)925-4109
Products: Fine wool material for men's wear and theatrical productions. **SIC:** 5131 (Piece Goods & Notions). **Est:** 1953. **Sales:** $600,000 (2000). **Emp:** 2. **Officers:** Edith Singer, President.

■ **26206** ■ **SKF Textile Products Inc.**
PO Box 977
Gastonia, NC 28053
Phone: (704)864-2691
Products: Textile products. **SIC:** 5131 (Piece Goods & Notions). **Est:** 1975. **Sales:** $1,000,000 (2000). **Emp:** 5. **Officers:** Gordon Summey, President.

■ **26207** ■ **The Slosman Corp.**
PO Box 3019
Asheville, NC 28802
Phone: (828)274-2100
Free: (800)544-9387 **Fax:** (828)274-0000
E-mail: info@slosman.com
URL: http://www.slosman.com
Products: Nonwoven fabrics; Wiping cloths; Converters; Disposable garments; Perf rolls; Piece goods, remnants; Exports. **SICs:** 5131 (Piece Goods & Notions); 5131 (Piece Goods & Notions). **Est:** 1902. **Emp:** 70. **Officers:** Fred N. Slosman, CEO & Chairman of the Board, e-mail: fred@slosman.com; Jerry L. Gaddy, President & COO, e-mail: jerry@slosman.com.

■ **26208** ■ **Soltex International Inc.**
50 Commerce Ctr.
Greenville, SC 29615-5814
Phone: (864)234-0322
Products: Mattress ticking. **SIC:** 5131 (Piece Goods & Notions). **Est:** 1985. **Sales:** $29,000,000 (2000). **Emp:** 15. **Officers:** Bernard M. Lenes, President.

■ **26209** ■ **Soviet American Woolens**
475 Porterfield Rd.
Porter, ME 04068
Products: Wool; Wool clothing; Knitting needles. **SIC:** 5199 (Nondurable Goods Nec).

■ **26210** ■ **Spola Fibres International Inc.**
PO Box 1958
Passaic, NJ 07055
Phone: (973)471-7330 **Fax:** (973)777-0250
Products: Yarn; Acrylic. **SIC:** 5199 (Nondurable Goods Nec). **Est:** 1984. **Sales:** $7,000,000 (2000). **Emp:** 4. **Officers:** John Spola, President.

■ **26211** ■ **Springs Industries Inc. Chesterfield Div.**
PO Box 111
Lancaster, SC 29721
Phone: (803)286-2491
Products: Fabric and linens. **SIC:** 5131 (Piece Goods & Notions). **Sales:** $970,000,000 (2000). **Emp:** 500. **Officers:** Larry Ostrower, Controller.

■ **26212** ■ **Staflex/Harotex Co.**
PO Box 1106
Taylors, SC 29687-1106
Phone: (864)268-0613 **Fax:** (864)268-1051
Products: Interfacing and lining materials. **SIC:** 5131 (Piece Goods & Notions). **Est:** 1980. **Sales:** $1,000,000 (2000). **Emp:** 49. **Officers:** Thomas Bridges, General Mgr.

■ **26213** ■ **Star Sales Company of Knoxville**
PO Box 1502
Lake Oswego, OR 97035
Phone: (865)524-0771 **Fax:** (865)524-4889
Products: Computer peripheral equipment, primarily flat panel display monitors. **SICs:** 5131 (Piece Goods &

Notions); 5122 (Drugs, Proprietaries & Sundries). **Sales:** $15,000,000 (2000). **Emp:** 90. **Officers:** Brian Dolinar, President.

■ **26214** ■ **Paul N. Stern Corp.**
1 Market St., Bldg. 25
Passaic, NJ 07055
Phone: (973)777-9422
Free: (800)836-0336 **Fax:** (973)777-3001
Products: Vinyl film; Imitation leather. **SIC:** 5131 (Piece Goods & Notions). **Est:** 1941. **Sales:** $3,000,000 (2000). **Emp:** 9. **Officers:** A. Stylman, President.

■ **26215** ■ **C.F. Stinson, Inc.**
2849 Product Drive
Rochester Hills, MI 48309
Phones: (248)299-3800 800-482-3401
Free: (800)841-6279 **Fax:** (248)299-3884
Products: Upholstery fabric; Panel fabrics; Upholstery vinyl. **SIC:** 5131 (Piece Goods & Notions). **Est:** 1952. **Officers:** Bill Diedrich, Sales/Marketing Contact, e-mail: rollman@cfstinson.com; Pam Harris, Human Resources Contact.

■ **26216** ■ **Stretch and Sew Inc.**
PO Box 25306
Tempe, AZ 85285-5306
Phone: (602)966-1462
Free: (800)547-7717 **Fax:** (602)966-1914
Products: Textiles and notions. **SIC:** 5113 (Industrial & Personal Service Paper). **Est:** 1968. **Sales:** $2,000,000 (2000). **Emp:** 22.

■ **26217** ■ **Stroheim & Romann Inc.**
31-11 Thomson Ave.
Long Island City, NY 11101
Phone: (718)706-7000 **Fax:** (718)361-0159
Products: Decorative fabrics; Wallpaper. **SICs:** 5131 (Piece Goods & Notions); 5023 (Homefurnishings). **Est:** 1865. **Sales:** $100,000,000 (2000). **Emp:** 150. **Officers:** Julian W. Grauer, President.

■ **26218** ■ **Sun Coast Imports**
PO Box 559
Moose Lake, MN 55767
Phone: (218)485-4200
Free: (800)462-6969 **Fax:** (218)485-4200
Products: Imports from Mexico and Guatemala, including textiles and leather goods. **SICs:** 5131 (Piece Goods & Notions); 5199 (Nondurable Goods Nec).

■ **26219** ■ **Symphony Fabrics Corp.**
229 W 36th St.
New York, NY 10018
Phone: (212)244-6700 **Fax:** (212)736-0123
E-mail: sales@symphonyfabrics.com
URL: http://www.symphonyfabrics.com
Products: Apparel fabrics. **SIC:** 5131 (Piece Goods & Notions). **Est:** 1950. **Sales:** $100,000,000 (2000). **Emp:** 80. **Officers:** Seymour D. Schneiderman, President; Haig Schneiderman, Exec. VP of Marketing & Sales; Steven Fried, Data Processing Mgr.; Doris Fried, Human Resources Mgr.

■ **26220** ■ **Talladega Machinery and Supply Co.**
301 N Johnson Ave.
Talladega, AL 35160
Phone: (205)362-4124
Products: Textiles; Wood products. **SICs:** 5131 (Piece Goods & Notions); 5031 (Lumber, Plywood & Millwork). **Est:** 1975. **Sales:** $31,000,000 (2000). **Emp:** 100. **Officers:** Gary Heacock, President.

■ **26221** ■ **Tapetex Inc.**
240 Commerce Dr.
Rochester, NY 14623
Phone: (716)334-0480
Products: Textiles. **SIC:** 5131 (Piece Goods & Notions). **Sales:** $45,000,000 (1993). **Emp:** 25. **Officers:** J. Goodman, President; Doug Evans, CFO.

■ **26222** ■ **Tech Aerofoam Products, Inc.**
5242 Shawland
Jacksonville, FL 32254
Phone: (904)786-3840
Free: (800)940-3840 **Fax:** (904)786-7548
Products: Fabric; Upholstery fabrics; Automotive parts

and supplies, New. **SICs:** 5131 (Piece Goods & Notions); 5013 (Motor Vehicle Supplies & New Parts).

■ **26223** ■ **Tedco Indus Inc.**
3901 Washington Blvd.
Baltimore, MD 21227
Phone: (410)247-0399
Free: (800)638-3814   **Fax:** (410)247-0561
E-mail: tedco@erols.com
Products: Upholstery materials and supplies; Cotton batting. **SIC:** 5131 (Piece Goods & Notions).

■ **26224** ■ **TETKO Inc.**
333 S Highland Ave.
Briarcliff Manor, NY 10510
Phone: (914)941-7767   **Fax:** (914)762-8599
Products: Precision woven materials, including polyester, silk, and nylon. **SIC:** 5131 (Piece Goods & Notions). **Est:** 1929. **Sales:** $45,000,000 (2000). **Emp:** 150. **Officers:** Peter Lohaus, President; Peter Callaghan, Vice President; Paul Vaccare, Dir. of Marketing; Jerry Kehoe, Dir. of Data Processing; Amy Russo, Dir of Human Resources.

■ **26225** ■ **Texstyles Group Inc.**
499 7th Ave.
New York, NY 10018
Phone: (212)967-5113   **Fax:** (212)967-1253
Products: Textiles; Imported fabrics. **SIC:** 5131 (Piece Goods & Notions). **Est:** 1981. **Officers:** George Fox, President, e-mail: gfox@mciworld.com.

■ **26226** ■ **Textile Import Corp.**
135 W 50th St., No. 1910
New York, NY 10020
Phone: (212)581-2840   **Fax:** (212)245-4689
E-mail: textile@ix.netcom.com
Products: Silk; Rayon and/or acetate; Natural fibers (cotton and/or wool, etc.). **SIC:** 5131 (Piece Goods & Notions). **Est:** 1964. **Emp:** 30. **Officers:** David Tell, President.

■ **26227** ■ **Jim Thompson Silk Co.**
2100 Faulkner Rd.
Atlanta, GA 30324
Phone: (404)325-5004
Products: Silk fabric. **SIC:** 5131 (Piece Goods & Notions). **Sales:** $15,000,000 (1993). **Emp:** 8. **Officers:** Mavis Cahoon, President.

■ **26228** ■ **Threadtex Inc.**
1350 Ave. of the Americas
New York, NY 10019
Phone: (212)713-1800   **Fax:** (212)977-4480
Products: Fabrics, including cotton and nylon. **SIC:** 5131 (Piece Goods & Notions). **Sales:** $20,000,000 (2000). **Emp:** 60. **Officers:** Bernard Richman, President; Frank Thomas, Controller.

■ **26229** ■ **Tillinghast-Stiles Co.**
850 Watermen Ave.
East Providence, RI 02914
Phone: (401)434-2100   **Fax:** (401)438-9694
Products: Natural and synthetic spun yarn including, cotton, wool, acrylic, worsted, rayon, textured, nylon, textralized, acetate, polyester, and polypropylene blends. **SIC:** 5131 (Piece Goods & Notions). **Est:** 1892. **Emp:** 3. **Officers:** Stuart W. Eddy, President; Pauline G. Palmisciano, Customer Service Mgr.

■ **26230** ■ **Tingue Brown and Company Inc.**
535 N Midland Ave.
Saddle Brook, NJ 07663-5521
Phone: (201)796-4490   **Fax:** (201)796-5820
Products: Industrial fabrics. **SIC:** 5131 (Piece Goods & Notions). **Est:** 1902. **Sales:** $580,000,000 (2000). **Emp:** 300. **Officers:** William J. Tingue, CEO & President; Ronald Midili, Exec. VP.

■ **26231** ■ **Joan Toggitt Ltd.**
140 Pleasant Hill Rd.
Chester, NJ 07930-2136
Phone: (732)271-1949   **Fax:** (732)271-0758
E-mail: info@zweigart.com
URL: http://www.zweigart.com
Products: Fabric for needlework and hotel and restaurant linens; Home decor. **SICs:** 5131 (Piece Goods & Notions); 5023 (Homefurnishings). **Est:** 1946.

Emp: 15. **Officers:** Rudy H. Heukels, President & CEO; Jim Kornecki, VP of Sales.

■ **26232** ■ **Toray Industries Inc.**
600 3rd Ave.
New York, NY 10016-1902
Phone: (212)697-8150   **Fax:** (212)972-4279
URL: http://www.toray.com
Products: Textiles. **SIC:** 5131 (Piece Goods & Notions). **Est:** 1965. **Sales:** $5,500,000 (2000). **Emp:** 50. **Officers:** Yoshiomi Onishi, President.

■ **26233** ■ **Trim-Pak Inc.**
4135 Southstream Blvd.
Charlotte, NC 28217-4523
Products: Trim for apparel. **SIC:** 5131 (Piece Goods & Notions). **Est:** 1988. **Sales:** $4,000,000 (2000). **Emp:** 18. **Officers:** Thomas Jackson, President; Virginia Jackson, Treasurer & Secty.; Hank Williams Jr., Vice President; Frederick R. Francis, Dir. of Data Processing.

■ **26234** ■ **United Fabrics, Inc.**
9115 Pennsauken Hwy.
Pennsauken, NJ 08110
Phone: (856)665-2040
Free: (800)347-8344   **Fax:** (856)665-5761
E-mail: ufabrics@aol.com
URL: http://www.unitedfabrics.com
Products: Fabric; Vinyl; Leather. **SIC:** 5131 (Piece Goods & Notions). **Est:** 1953. **Sales:** $13,000,000 (2000). **Emp:** 49.

■ **26235** ■ **United Notions**
PO Box 39486
Denver, CO 80239
Phone: (303)371-0660
Free: (800)843-1236   **Fax:** 800-525-0109
Products: Craft kits; Sewing accessories. **SICs:** 5131 (Piece Goods & Notions); 5092 (Toys & Hobby Goods & Supplies).

■ **26236** ■ **United Notions**
PO Box 814490
Dallas, TX 75381-4490
Phone: (972)484-8901
Free: (800)527-9447   **Fax:** 800-468-4209
Products: Craft kits; Sewing accessories. **SICs:** 5131 (Piece Goods & Notions); 5092 (Toys & Hobby Goods & Supplies).

■ **26237** ■ **United Notions & Fabrics**
13795 Hutton Dr.
Dallas, TX 75234
Phone: (972)484-8901   **Free:** (800)527-9447
URL: http://www.unitednotionsfabric.com
Products: Craft kits; Sewing accessories. **SICs:** 5131 (Piece Goods & Notions); 5092 (Toys & Hobby Goods & Supplies). **Former Name:** United Notions.

■ **26238** ■ **United Thread Mills Corp.**
250 Maple Ave.
Rockville Centre, NY 11570
Phone: (516)536-3900   **Fax:** (516)536-3547
Products: Sewing threads; Yarns; Embroidery thread. **SIC:** 5131 (Piece Goods & Notions). **Est:** 1942. **Sales:** $6,500,000 (2000). **Emp:** 20. **Officers:** Ira Henkus, President; Olga Brown, Customer Service Contact; Terri Bree, Human Resources Contact.

■ **26239** ■ **Unitex Inc.**
5175 Commerce Dr.
Baldwin Park, CA 91706
Free: (800)456-6282   **Fax:** (626)814-0027
E-mail: jcworkman@earthlink.net
Products: Industrial fabrics, including boat covers, pool covers, and luggage; Industrial trimmings, including velcro, webbing, buckles, fasteners, and thread. **SIC:** 5131 (Piece Goods & Notions). **Est:** 1912. **Sales:** $15,000,000 (2000). **Officers:** Greg Goulette, President & CEO.

■ **26240** ■ **The Upholstery Supply Co.**
12530 W Burleigh Rd.
Brookfield, WI 53005
Phone: (414)781-7490   **Free:** (800)558-2120
Products: Fabric and upholstery supplies. **SIC:** 5131 (Piece Goods & Notions).

■ **26241** ■ **Viking Sewing Machines Inc.**
31000 Viking Pkwy.
Westlake, OH 44145
Phone: (440)808-6550   **Fax:** (440)847-0001
URL: http://www.husqvarnaviking.com
Products: Sewing machines; Sewing notions and supplies. **SICs:** 5064 (Electrical Appliances—Television & Radio); 5131 (Piece Goods & Notions). **Est:** 1998. **Emp:** 200. **Officers:** Bengt Gerborg, President; Dave Mechenbier, VP of Finance; Stan Ingraham, Sr. VP; Pat Tocarsick, Human Resources Contact. **Former Name:** VWS Inc.

■ **26242** ■ **VWR Scientific Products Corp.**
1310 Goshen Pkwy.
West Chester, PA 19380
Phone: (610)431-1700   **Fax:** (610)436-1763
Products: Laboratory equipment and supplies; Photographic and art supplies; Construction textiles and supplies; Covering fabrics and leathers. **SICs:** 5049 (Professional Equipment Nec); 5043 (Photographic Equipment & Supplies). **Sales:** $1,349,900,000 (2000). **Emp:** 2,725. **Officers:** Jerrold B. Harris, CEO & President; David M. Bronson, Sr. VP & CFO.

■ **26243** ■ **Warren of Stafford Corp. Fabric Merchandising Div.**
46 E 61st St.
New York, NY 10021-8008
Phone: (212)980-7960
Products: Fabric. **SIC:** 5131 (Piece Goods & Notions). **Sales:** $58,000,000 (2000). **Emp:** 30. **Officers:** Pier Guerci, President.

■ **26244** ■ **Wasser Morton Co.**
1450 Broadway, Ste. 1000
New York, NY 10018
Phone: (212)391-6669   **Fax:** (212)391-9384
Products: Fabrics-woolens and blends, cottons, and synthetics. **SIC:** 5131 (Piece Goods & Notions). **Est:** 1945. **Sales:** $4,000,000 (2000). **Emp:** 15. **Officers:** Terry Troy, President.

■ **26245** ■ **Elizabeth Webbing Mills Co.**
PO Box 1168
Pawtucket, RI 02862-1168
Phone: (401)723-0500
Products: Piece goods and notions, including narrow fabrics. **SIC:** 5131 (Piece Goods & Notions). **Officers:** Eliot Lifland, President.

■ **26246** ■ **Westgate Fabrics Inc.**
1000 Fountain Pkwy.
Grand Prairie, TX 75050
Phone: (972)647-2323
Free: (800)527-2517   **Fax:** (972)660-7096
E-mail: webmaster@westgatefabrics.com
URL: http://www.westgatefabrics.com
Products: Draperies; Upholstery fabric. **SICs:** 5131 (Piece Goods & Notions); 5023 (Homefurnishings). **Est:** 1945. **Sales:** $35,000,000 (2000). **Emp:** 130. **Officers:** Jay Cassen, President.

■ **26247** ■ **N.A. Whittenburg, Inc.**
80 NE 13th St.
Miami, FL 33132
Phone: (305)373-7566   **Fax:** (305)379-4432
Products: Textiles and notions. **SIC:** 5131 (Piece Goods & Notions).

■ **26248** ■ **Wichelt Imports Inc.**
N162 Hwy. 35
Stoddard, WI 54658
Phone: (608)788-4600
Free: (800)356-9516   **Fax:** (608)788-6040
E-mail: wichelt@wichelt.com
URL: http://www.wichelt.com
Products: Craft kits; Embroidery and cross-stitch products. **SIC:** 5131 (Piece Goods & Notions). **Est:** 1970. **Emp:** 24.

■ **26249** ■ **Windsor Rhodes Co.**
593 Mineral Spring Ave.
Pawtucket, RI 02860-3408
Phone: (401)722-9500   **Fax:** (401)722-9584
Products: Piece goods and notions. **SIC:** 5131 (Piece Goods & Notions). **Officers:** Linda Blazer, President.

■ 26250 ■ Wonalancet Co.
1711 Tulle Cir. NE, No. 104
Atlanta, GA 30329-2391
Phone: (404)633-4551   Fax: (404)634-2513
Products: Textile fibers. SIC: 5159 (Farm-Product Raw Materials Nec). Est: 1976. Sales: $14,400,000 (2000). Emp: 11. Officers: James J. Dunn, President; J.M. Reichard Jr., Treasurer & Secty.

■ 26251 ■ Wynn and Graff Inc.
2613 Grandview Ave
Nashville, TN 37211
Phone: (615)255-0477
Free: (800)251-1048   Fax: (615)244-4787
Products: Upholstery fabrics and supplies; Quilting products. SIC: 5131 (Piece Goods & Notions). Est: 1946. Sales: $3,000,000 (1999). Emp: 30. Officers: Gary Wynn, President.

■ 26252 ■ Wynn and Graff Inc.
2401 Dutch Valley Rd.
Knoxville, TN 37918
Phone: (423)688-3100   Fax: (423)687-6208
Products: Upholstery fabric and supplies. SIC: 5131 (Piece Goods & Notions).

■ 26253 ■ Yarn Tree Designs
PO Box 724
Ames, IA 50010
Phone: (515)232-3121
Free: (800)247-3952   Fax: (515)232-0789
E-mail: info@yarntree.com
URL: http://www.yarntree.com
Products: Cross-stitch supplies, including floss, needles, and fabric; Mugs; Cards; Books. SICs: 5131 (Piece Goods & Notions); 5112 (Stationery & Office Supplies); 5192 (Books, Periodicals & Newspapers).

■ 26254 ■ Zabin Industries Inc.
3957 S Hill St.
Los Angeles, CA 90037
Phone: (213)749-1215   Fax: (213)747-6162
Products: Closures and identification products for apparel and accessories. SIC: 5131 (Piece Goods & Notions). Est: 1976. Sales: $25,000,000 (2000). Emp: 85. Officers: Alan Faiola, President; Virginia Acosta, VP & CFO; Calvin Au, Sales Mgr.; David Frank, Operations Mgr.

(57) Tobacco Products

Entries in this section are arranged alphabetically by company name. When the company name is a personal name, the company name is alphabetized by the surname unless the first name or initial(s) are part of a trade name. See the User's Guide at the front of this directory for additional information.

■ **26255** ■ **4th Street Tobacco Warehouse**
551 W 4th St.
Lexington, KY 40508
Phones: (606)744-3191   (606)254-1710
Fax: (606)255-2966
Products: Tobacco. **SIC:** 5194 (Tobacco & Tobacco Products). **Officers:** Ben Crain.

■ **26256** ■ **800 JR Cigar Inc.**
301 Rt. 10, E
Whippany, NJ 07981
Phone: (973)884-9555
Products: Brand name premium cigars, mass market cigars, and cigarettes. **SIC:** 5194 (Tobacco & Tobacco Products). **Sales:** $192,000,000 (2000). **Emp:** 564. **Officers:** Lew Rothman, CEO & President; Timothy P. Shannon, CFO.

■ **26257** ■ **S. Abraham and Sons Inc.**
PO Box 1768
Grand Rapids, MI 49501
Phone: (616)453-6358   **Fax:** (616)247-3708
Products: Tobacco; Candy. **SICs:** 5194 (Tobacco & Tobacco Products); 5145 (Confectionery). **Est:** 1952. **Sales:** $300,000,000 (2000). **Emp:** 400. **Officers:** Abe Abraham, CEO; Jim Leonard, Controller; Pat McLaughlin, Dir. of Marketing; Keith Anderson, Dir of Human Resources.

■ **26258** ■ **Alternative Cigarettes Inc.**
PO Box 678
Buffalo, NY 14207
Phone: (716)877-2983
Free: (800)225-1838   **Fax:** (716)877-3064
E-mail: smokin@altcigs.com
Products: Cigarettes. **SIC:** 5194 (Tobacco & Tobacco Products). **Est:** 1992. **Former Name:** Tobacco Alternative Inc.

■ **26259** ■ **Amcon Distributing Co.**
10223 L St.
Omaha, NE 68127
Phone: (402)331-3727   **Fax:** (402)331-4834
E-mail: corporate@amcon-dist.com
URL: http://www.amcon-dist.com
Products: Candy; Tobacco; Manufactured tobacco products. **SICs:** 5194 (Tobacco & Tobacco Products); 5145 (Confectionery). **Emp:** 12. **Officers:** Carl Ward.

■ **26260** ■ **Aquafilter Corp.**
4880 Havana St.
Denver, CO 80239-2416
Phone: (954)491-2200   **Fax:** (954)771-4105
Products: Disposable cigarette filters. **SIC:** 5194 (Tobacco & Tobacco Products). **Sales:** $1,400,000 (2000). **Emp:** 15. **Officers:** Dennis Donohue, General Mgr.

■ **26261** ■ **Automatic Vendors Inc.**
2695 Hwy. 14A
Sturgis, SD 57785
Phone: (605)578-8500   **Fax:** (605)347-5442
Products: Tobacco products. **SIC:** 5194 (Tobacco & Tobacco Products). **Est:** 1962. **Sales:** $1,000,000 (2000). **Emp:** 10.

■ **26262** ■ **Axton Candy and Tobacco Co.**
PO Box 32219
Louisville, KY 40232
Phone: (502)634-8000
Products: Tobacco; Candy. **SICs:** 5194 (Tobacco & Tobacco Products); 5145 (Confectionery). **Sales:** $48,000,000 (2000). **Emp:** 70. **Officers:** Tommy Chappell, President; Lynne Schabel, Controller.

■ **26263** ■ **Edward Badeaux Co.**
311 Jackson
PO Box 710
Thibodaux, LA 70302
Phone: (504)447-3338   **Fax:** (504)447-1598
Products: Candy; Tobacco. **SICs:** 5194 (Tobacco & Tobacco Products); 5145 (Confectionery). **Est:** 1890. **Emp:** 20. **Officers:** Manuel Rodrigue, President; Lorraine Rodrigue; Clark Rodrigue.

■ **26264** ■ **Barentsen Candy Co.**
PO Box 686
Benton Harbor, MI 49023-0686
Phone: (616)927-3171
Free: (800)491-0005   **Fax:** (616)925-4570
Products: Cigarettes; Tobacco; Cigars; Confections. **SICs:** 5145 (Confectionery); 5194 (Tobacco & Tobacco Products). **Est:** 1900. **Sales:** $11,000,000 (2000). **Emp:** 25. **Officers:** Grant W. Derfelt, President.

■ **26265** ■ **Birmingham Tobacco Co.**
PO Box 11021
Birmingham, AL 35202
Phone: (205)324-2581
Products: Tobacco products. **SIC:** 5194 (Tobacco & Tobacco Products). **Sales:** $57,000,000 (1994). **Emp:** 82. **Officers:** Frank P. Damico Jr., President & CFO.

■ **26266** ■ **Bond Wholesale, Inc.**
3025 Mable
Trenton, MO 64683
Phone: (660)359-3710
Free: (800)530-5030   **Fax:** (660)359-5347
E-mail: bondwhol@classicnet.net
Products: Tobacco;Candy. **SICs:** 5194 (Tobacco & Tobacco Products); 5145 (Confectionery). **Est:** 1935. **Emp:** 49. **Officers:** David L. Bain, President; Jerry Stottlemyre, Vice President.

■ **26267** ■ **Briggs Inc.**
504 S Cass St.
PO Box 455
Corinth, MS 38835-0455
Phone: (601)286-3312   **Fax:** (601)286-3311
E-mail: briggs@tsixroads.com
Products: Tobacco; Candy; Institutional food, supplies, and equipment. **SICs:** 5194 (Tobacco & Tobacco Products); 5145 (Confectionery); 5141 (Groceries—General Line). **Est:** 1955. **Emp:** 48. **Officers:** Wayne Briggs, President; Larry Briggs, Secretary.

■ **26268** ■ **Burlington Drug Co.**
92 Catamount Dr.
Milton, VT 05468
Phone: (802)893-5105
Free: (800)338-8703   **Fax:** (802)893-5110
Products: Tobacco; Manufactured tobacco products;

General line groceries. **SICs:** 5194 (Tobacco & Tobacco Products); 5141 (Groceries—General Line). **Officers:** David Mitiguy, President.

■ **26269** ■ **Buyers Paper & Specialty Inc.**
510 W Mill St.
Indianapolis, IN 46225-1429
Phone: (317)639-2591
Free: (800)284-6592   **Fax:** (317)684-7509
Products: Cigarettes. **SIC:** 5194 (Tobacco & Tobacco Products). **Emp:** 18.

■ **26270** ■ **Campbell Tobacco Rehandling Company Inc.**
PO Box 678
Mayfield, KY 42066
Phone: (502)247-0991
Products: Tobacco. **SIC:** 5194 (Tobacco & Tobacco Products). **Est:** 1959. **Sales:** $24,000,000 (2000). **Emp:** 75. **Officers:** Robert J. Baker, President & Treasurer; Kimberly Overby, Controller; Stanley Webb, Manager.

■ **26271** ■ **Capital Wholesale Distribution Co.**
1149 S Pennsylvania Ave.
Lansing, MI 48912
Phone: (517)485-7208
Products: Tobacco products, including cigars and cigarettes; Candy and confectionary. **SICs:** 5145 (Confectionery); 5194 (Tobacco & Tobacco Products).

■ **26272** ■ **Capitol Distributing**
3500 Commercial Ct.
Meridian, ID 83642-6006
Phone: (208)888-5112
Free: (800)769-5659   **Fax:** (208)888-5989
E-mail: cptldist@micron.net
Products: Cigarettes; Candy. **SICs:** 5194 (Tobacco & Tobacco Products); 5145 (Confectionery). **Est:** 1983. **Sales:** $50,000,000 (2000). **Emp:** 45. **Officers:** Keith Reynolds, President.

■ **26273** ■ **Casa Export Ltd.**
PO Box 1337
Smithfield, NC 27577
Phone: (919)934-7101
Products: Tobacco. **SIC:** 5159 (Farm-Product Raw Materials Nec). **Sales:** $72,000,000 (2000). **Emp:** 200. **Officers:** Paolo Cavazzuti, President.

■ **26274** ■ **Central District Inc.**
640 S Broadway
Lexington, KY 40508
Phone: (606)255-4453
Products: Tobacco. **SIC:** 5194 (Tobacco & Tobacco Products). **Est:** 1922. **Sales:** $3,000,000 (2000). **Emp:** 6. **Officers:** Edward Wilson, President.

■ **26275** ■ **Centre Jobbing Co.**
223 S Main
Sauk Centre, MN 56378-1346
Phone: (320)352-2009   **Fax:** (320)352-2009
Products: Candy; Tobacco; Groceries; Gambling supplies; Snack foods; Paper supplies. **SICs:** 5194 (Tobacco & Tobacco Products); 5141 (Groceries—General Line); 5113 (Industrial & Personal Service

Paper). **Est:** 1946. **Sales:** $3,000,000 (2000). **Emp:** 9. **Officers:** Rick Kleinschmidt.

■ **26276** ■ **Coclin Tobacco Corp.**
290 Boston Post Rd.
Milford, CT 06460
Phone: (203)877-0341
Products: Candy; Cigarettes; Manufactured tobacco products. **SICs:** 5194 (Tobacco & Tobacco Products); 5145 (Confectionery). **Est:** 1936. **Sales:** $9,000,000 (2000). **Emp:** 13. **Officers:** J.C. Coclin, President; Nicholas Coclin, CFO.

■ **26277** ■ **Cole Brothers and Fox Co.**
252 Yandell Ave.
Canton, MS 39046
Phone: (601)859-1414   **Fax:** (601)859-2739
Products: Cigarettes; Health and beauty aids; Juices; Groceries; Candy. **SICs:** 5194 (Tobacco & Tobacco Products); 5141 (Groceries—General Line); 5142 (Packaged Frozen Foods); 5143 (Dairy Products Except Dried or Canned). **Est:** 1920. **Sales:** $46,000,000 (2000). **Emp:** 80. **Officers:** William E. Fox, CEO & President; Cecil C. Fox Jr., VP of Finance.

■ **26278** ■ **Concord Sales Co.**
7116 20th Ave.
Brooklyn, NY 11204-5320
Phone: (718)331-0135   **Fax:** (718)256-0400
Products: Cigarettes; Chocolate; Hard candy; Paper goods; Sodas. **SICs:** 5194 (Tobacco & Tobacco Products); 5145 (Confectionery); 5113 (Industrial & Personal Service Paper); 5149 (Groceries & Related Products Nec). **Est:** 1945. **Emp:** 2.

■ **26279** ■ **Consolidated Wholesale Co.**
PO Box 26903
Oklahoma City, OK 73126
Phone: (405)232-5593   **Fax:** (405)232-6885
Products: Cigarettes; Candy; Tobacco. **SICs:** 5194 (Tobacco & Tobacco Products); 5145 (Confectionery). **Est:** 1949. **Sales:** $46,000,000 (2000). **Emp:** 74. **Officers:** J.J. Lehman, President; Elmer Wolf, Vice President; Bill Wolf, Dir. of Marketing & Sales; Robert Timmons, Dir. of Systems.

■ **26280** ■ **Core-Mark International Inc.**
395 Oyster Point Blvd., No. 415
South San Francisco, CA 94080
Phone: (650)589-9445   **Fax:** (650)952-4284
Products: Food. **SIC:** 5194 (Tobacco & Tobacco Products). **Sales:** $220,000,000 (2000). **Emp:** 2,200.

■ **26281** ■ **Corr-Williams Co.**
PO Box 2570
Jackson, MS 39207
Phone: (601)353-5871
Free: (800)644-2677   **Fax:** (601)353-5873
Products: Tobacco; Chips and candy. **SICs:** 5194 (Tobacco & Tobacco Products); 5145 (Confectionery). **Est:** 1904. **Sales:** $16,100,000 (2000). **Emp:** 47. **Officers:** Hal Nievanck, President; Lelend Williams, Vice President; Chris Hinton, Sales Mgr.

■ **26282** ■ **Corr-Williams Wholesale Company Inc.**
5173 Pioneer Dr.
Meridian, MS 39303
Phone: (601)693-6081   **Fax:** (601)482-0700
Products: Tobacco products, candies, toiletries, and sundries. **SICs:** 5194 (Tobacco & Tobacco Products); 5145 (Confectionery); 5122 (Drugs, Proprietaries & Sundries). **Sales:** $16,800,000 (2000). **Emp:** 95. **Officers:** Bobby Beasley, General Mgr.

■ **26283** ■ **Frank P. Corso Inc.**
PO Box 488
Biloxi, MS 39533
Phone: (601)436-4697
Free: (800)748-9243   **Fax:** (228)374-8627
E-mail: fpcorso@bellsouth.net
Products: Cigarettes and tobacco; Candy; Health and beauty aid products; Paper products, groceries, drinks, full line vending. **SICs:** 5194 (Tobacco & Tobacco Products); 5122 (Drugs, Proprietaries & Sundries); 5145 (Confectionery). **Est:** 1924. **Sales:** $18,000,000 (2000). **Emp:** 54. **Officers:** Elizabeth Joachim, Owner; John Joachim III, Sales/Marketing Contact, e-mail: fpcorso@bellsouth.net; Wayne Ross, Customer

Service Contact, e-mail: fpcorso@bellsouth.net; Liz Joachim, Human Resources Contact, e-mail: fpcorso@bellsouth.net.

■ **26284** ■ **Cullen Distributors Inc.**
125 S Park St.
Streator, IL 61364
Phone: (815)672-2975
Products: Tobacco products, including cigarettes and cigars; Paper products, including napkins, plates, bags, and toilet paper; Motor oil; Candy; Institutional and frozen food. **SICs:** 5194 (Tobacco & Tobacco Products); 5145 (Confectionery); 5149 (Groceries & Related Products Nec); 5113 (Industrial & Personal Service Paper). **Est:** 1946. **Sales:** $8,000,000 (2000). **Emp:** 25. **Officers:** John Cullen, President & CFO.

■ **26285** ■ **Davis & Butler, Inc.**
1235 E Division St.
Dover, DE 19901
Phone: (302)734-8100   **Fax:** (302)736-1396
Products: Tobacco; Candy. **SICs:** 5194 (Tobacco & Tobacco Products); 5145 (Confectionery).

■ **26286** ■ **F.A. Davis and Sons Inc.**
6610 Cabot Dr.
Baltimore, MD 21226-1754
Phone: (410)360-6000   **Free:** (800)950-1545
Products: Tobacco products; Health and beauty aids; Candy. **SICs:** 5194 (Tobacco & Tobacco Products); 5122 (Drugs, Proprietaries & Sundries); 5145 (Confectionery). **Est:** 1876. **Sales:** $20,000,000 (2000). **Emp:** 225. **Officers:** Louis V. Manzo, CEO; Harry Commarata, CFO.

■ **26287** ■ **Deli Universal Inc.**
PO Box 25099
Richmond, VA 23261
Phone: (804)359-9311
Products: Tobacco; Dried fruits and nuts. **SICs:** 5159 (Farm-Product Raw Materials Nec); 5149 (Groceries & Related Products Nec). **Sales:** $1,952,000,000 (2000). **Emp:** 2,000. **Officers:** Jack van de Winkel, CEO & President; Harmen M. Heslinga, Treasurer.

■ **26288** ■ **Joseph E. Digrazia Wholesale Distributing**
PO Box 458
Wells, NV 89835-0458
Phone: (702)752-3326
Free: (800)992-8002   **Fax:** (702)752-3051
Products: Tobacco; Smoking tobacco; Manufactured tobacco products; Cigarettes. **SIC:** 5194 (Tobacco & Tobacco Products). **Officers:** Joseph Digrazia, President.

■ **26289** ■ **Eby-Brown Company L.P.**
280 Shuman Blvd.
Naperville, IL 60566-7067
Phone: (630)778-2800   **Fax:** (630)778-2830
Products: Full-line distributor of tobacco, confections, groceries, sundries and refrigerated and frozen foods. **SICs:** 5194 (Tobacco & Tobacco Products); 5145 (Confectionery); 5141 (Groceries—General Line); 5122 (Drugs, Proprietaries & Sundries). **Sales:** $1,700,000,000 (2000). **Emp:** 1,450. **Officers:** William S. Wake Jr., Chairman of the Board; Mark Smetana, CFO.

■ **26290** ■ **El Grande Distributors Inc.**
PO Box 1136
Carlsbad, NM 88221-1136
Phone: (505)885-2425   **Fax:** (505)885-0368
Products: Tobacco products. **SIC:** 5194 (Tobacco & Tobacco Products). **Est:** 1977. **Sales:** $2,800,000 (2000). **Emp:** 10.

■ **26291** ■ **Famous Smoke Shop Inc.**
55 W 39th St.
New York, NY 10018
Phone: (212)840-4860   **Fax:** (212)398-9290
Products: Tobacco products. **SIC:** 5194 (Tobacco & Tobacco Products).

■ **26292** ■ **Farner Bocken Co.**
Hwy. 30 E
Carroll, IA 51401
Phone: (712)792-3503
Free: (800)274-8692   **Fax:** (712)792-3513
E-mail: fb@farner-bocken.com
URL: http://www.farner-bocken.com
Products: Cigarettes; Paper; Candy. **SICs:** 5194 (Tobacco & Tobacco Products); 5112 (Stationery & Office Supplies); 5145 (Confectionery). **Est:** 1939. **Emp:** 700.

■ **26293** ■ **Flue-Cured Tobacco Cooperative Stabilization Corp.**
PO Box 12300
Raleigh, NC 27605
Phone: (919)821-4560   **Fax:** (919)821-4564
E-mail: fccoopsales@ipassnet
URL: http://www.ustobaccofarmer
Products: Tobacco. **SIC:** 5194 (Tobacco & Tobacco Products). **Est:** 1946. **Sales:** $420,000,000 (2000). **Emp:** 45. **Officers:** Bruce Flye, President; James Stocks, CFO; Gary Harris, COO.

■ **26294** ■ **S.M. Frank and Company Inc.**
1000 N Division St.
PO Box 789
Peekskill, NY 10566
Phone: (914)739-3100
Free: (800)431-2752   **Fax:** (914)739-3105
E-mail: smokepipes@aol.com
URL: http://www.smfrankcoinc.com
Products: Smoking pipes and accessories. **SIC:** 5194 (Tobacco & Tobacco Products). **Est:** 1922. **Sales:** $1,300,000 (2000). **Emp:** 14. **Officers:** William F. Feuerbach Jr., President; William F. Feuerbach III, VP of Sales & Merchandising.

■ **26295** ■ **Sam Frank, Inc.**
15 Center St.
Rutland, VT 05701
Phone: (802)773-7770   **Fax:** (802)773-6093
Products: Tobacco; Candy. **SICs:** 5194 (Tobacco & Tobacco Products); 5145 (Confectionery).

■ **26296** ■ **Franklin Cigar and Tobacco Company Inc.**
PO Box 1151
Franklin, LA 70538
Phone: (318)828-3208   **Fax:** (318)828-3413
Products: Tobacco products, confectionery products, beer, ale, paper cups and plates. **SICs:** 5194 (Tobacco & Tobacco Products); 5145 (Confectionery); 5181 (Beer & Ale); 5113 (Industrial & Personal Service Paper). **Sales:** $13,000,000 (1994). **Emp:** 32. **Officers:** Keith A. Landen, President.

■ **26297** ■ **Freeman Tobacco Warehouse**
439 E Office St.
Harrodsburg, KY 40330
Phone: (606)734-2833
Products: Tobacco. **SIC:** 5194 (Tobacco & Tobacco Products). **Est:** 1956. **Sales:** $7,000,000 (2000). **Emp:** 20. **Officers:** Edwin Freeman, Owner.

■ **26298** ■ **Gem State Distributors Inc.**
PO Box 2499
Pocatello, ID 83206-2499
Phone: (208)237-5151   **Fax:** (208)237-0802
E-mail: gemstate@srv.net
Products: Candy; Manufactured tobacco products. **SICs:** 5194 (Tobacco & Tobacco Products); 5199 (Nondurable Goods Nec). **Est:** 1954. **Officers:** Paul Noorda, President, e-mail: paul2@srv.net.

■ **26299** ■ **F.D. Grave and Son Inc.**
PO Box 1626
New Haven, CT 06506
Phone: (203)624-9893
Products: Cigars. **SIC:** 5194 (Tobacco & Tobacco Products). **Est:** 1884. **Sales:** $2,000,000 (1999). **Emp:** 6. **Officers:** Richard M. Grave, President & Treasurer; Dorothy Grave Hoyt, VP of Finance; Fred Grave, Dir. of Marketing.

■ 26300 ■ Gray's Wholesale Inc.
513 State
PO Box 466
Clayton, NY 13624
Phone: (315)686-3541
Free: (800)338-1336   Fax: (315)686-3845
Products: Groceries; Candy; Tobacco; Paper products; Juices. SICs: 5194 (Tobacco & Tobacco Products); 5145 (Confectionery); 5113 (Industrial & Personal Service Paper). Est: 1951. Emp: 30. Officers: Francis Gray.

■ 26301 ■ H & M Distributing Inc.
167 Eastland Dr.
PO Box 314
Twin Falls, ID 83303-0314
Phone: (208)733-1145
Free: (800)826-1156   Fax: (208)733-1297
Products: Tobacco and tobacco products; Candy; Beverages, including water and soft drinks; Groceries; Paper products; Health and beauty supplies. SICs: 5194 (Tobacco & Tobacco Products); 5145 (Confectionery); 5141 (Groceries—General Line); 5113 (Industrial & Personal Service Paper). Est: 1985. Emp: 21. Officers: Edwin Prater, Treasurer; Ron Nelson.

■ 26302 ■ Hawaiian Isles Distributors
843 Leilani St. No. A
Hilo, HI 96720
Phone: (808)935-7176   Fax: (808)961-5954
Products: Tobacco and cigars; Coffee. SICs: 5194 (Tobacco & Tobacco Products); 5149 (Groceries & Related Products Nec).

■ 26303 ■ Hawaiian Isles Distributors
851 Eha St.
Wailuku, HI 96793
Phone: (808)244-9019   Fax: (808)242-7719
Products: Manufactured tobacco products; Coffee. SICs: 5194 (Tobacco & Tobacco Products); 5149 (Groceries & Related Products Nec).

■ 26304 ■ Hayward Distribution Center
31300 Medallion Dr.
Hayward, CA 94544
Phone: (510)487-3000   Fax: (510)487-3257
Products: Tobacco products. SIC: 5194 (Tobacco & Tobacco Products). Sales: $250,000,000 (2000). Emp: 190.

■ 26305 ■ Heartland Distributors, Inc.
111 N Telegraph Rd.
Monroe, MI 48162
Phone: (734)241-8565
Products: Tobacco products, including cigars and cigarettes; Candy and confectionary. SICs: 5194 (Tobacco & Tobacco Products); 5145 (Confectionery).

■ 26306 ■ Hettinger-Mobridge Candy & Tobacco
PO Box 549
Hettinger, ND 58639-0549
Phone: (701)567-2440
Free: (800)584-9242   Fax: (701)567-2116
Products: Candy; Manufactured tobacco products; Candy; Paper and allied products; Specialty cleaning and sanitation products. SICs: 5194 (Tobacco & Tobacco Products); 5145 (Confectionery); 5113 (Industrial & Personal Service Paper); 5087 (Service Establishment Equipment). Est: 1946. Sales: $4,000,000 (2000). Emp: 7. Officers: Lauren Miller, President; Tom Dafnis, Vice President.

■ 26307 ■ HI Line Wholesale Co.
80 U.S Hwy. 2 E
Wolf Point, MT 59201-1942
Phone: (406)653-1313   Fax: (406)653-1321
E-mail: hiline@midrivers.com
Products: Tobacco; Manufactured tobacco products; Candy. SICs: 5194 (Tobacco & Tobacco Products); 5145 (Confectionery). Officers: Tom Ault, Partner.

■ 26308 ■ Holiday Wholesale Inc.
PO Box 177
Wisconsin Dells, WI 53965
Phone: (608)254-8321   Fax: 800-377-1980
Products: Manufactured tobacco products; Paper goods or products, including book mailers; Miscellaneous end-use chemicals and chemical products. SICs: 5194 (Tobacco & Tobacco Products); 5113 (Industrial & Personal Service Paper); 5169 (Chemicals & Allied Products Nec). Est: 1940. Sales: $42,000,000 (2000). Emp: 107. Officers: Bud E. Gussel Jr., President.

■ 26309 ■ Huser-Paul Company Inc.
3636 Illinois Rd.
Ft. Wayne, IN 46804
Phone: (219)432-0557   Fax: (219)432-0559
Products: Tobacco; Candy. SICs: 5145 (Confectionery); 5194 (Tobacco & Tobacco Products). Est: 1931. Sales: $10,000,000 (2000). Emp: 20. Officers: Virginia J. Rogers, President & Treasurer.

■ 26310 ■ Imperial Trading Co.
PO Box 23508
New Orleans, LA 70183-0508
Phone: (504)733-1400   Fax: (504)736-4156
Products: Cigarettes; Tobacco; Candy; Groceries. SICs: 5194 (Tobacco & Tobacco Products); 5145 (Confectionery). Est: 1916. Sales: $300,000,000 (2000). Emp: 270. Officers: Robert L. Pierpoint Jr., President & COO; Gilbert Stroud, CFO; Lee Farrell, Sales/Marketing Contact; Cindy Gervais, Customer Service Contact.

■ 26311 ■ J & V Vending Wholesale
RR 155A Lover's Lane
Salmon, ID 83467
Phone: (208)756-3166   Fax: (208)756-3166
E-mail: vpp@dmi.net
Products: Tobacco and tobacco products; Candy; Meats. SICs: 5194 (Tobacco & Tobacco Products); 5145 (Confectionery); 5147 (Meats & Meat Products). Est: 1989. Officers: Virginia Perry, Partner; Jerry Perry.

■ 26312 ■ J and V Vending Wholesale
RR 155A Lover's Ln.
Salmon, ID 83467
Phone: (208)756-3166   Fax: (208)756-3166
Products: Tobacco products. SIC: 5194 (Tobacco & Tobacco Products). Est: 1989.

■ 26313 ■ Jans Distributing Inc.
1807 W 47th Ave.
Anchorage, AK 99517-3164
Phone: (907)243-5267   Fax: (907)243-5744
Products: Tobacco and tobacco products; Candy; Chips. SICs: 5194 (Tobacco & Tobacco Products); 5145 (Confectionery). Officers: Jan Marquiss, President.

■ 26314 ■ Jones-McIntosh Tobacco Company Inc.
PO Box 245
Syracuse, NY 13206
Phone: (315)463-9183   Free: (800)635-2330
Products: Cigarettes; Tobacco; Candy; School supplies; Automotive supplies; Juices; Cookies. SICs: 5194 (Tobacco & Tobacco Products); 5145 (Confectionery); 5149 (Groceries & Related Products Nec); 5013 (Motor Vehicle Supplies & New Parts); 5044 (Office Equipment). Est: 1909. Sales: $40,000,000 (2000). Emp: 40. Officers: William Corringan, President.

■ 26315 ■ Kaiser Wholesale Inc.
PO Box 1115
New Albany, IN 47150
Phone: (812)945-2651
Products: Tobacco and cigarettes; Chocolate candy; Paper towels and napkins. SICs: 5194 (Tobacco & Tobacco Products); 5145 (Confectionery); 5113 (Industrial & Personal Service Paper). Est: 1956. Sales: $20,000,000 (2000). Emp: 30. Officers: J.R. Kaiser, President; William Schad, Controller; Michael Miller, Dir. of Marketing.

■ 26316 ■ Kamaaina Distribution Co.
69 Railroad Ave.
Hilo, HI 96720
Phone: (808)935-3774   Fax: (808)969-9933
Products: Tobacco products; Confectionery items. SICs: 5194 (Tobacco & Tobacco Products); 5145 (Confectionery).

■ 26317 ■ Keilson-Dayton Co.
PO Box 1457
Dayton, OH 45401
Phone: (937)236-1070   Fax: (937)236-2124
Products: Cigarettes and tobacco; Candy. SICs: 5194 (Tobacco & Tobacco Products); 5145 (Confectionery). Est: 1946. Emp: 35. Officers: Greg Wellinghoff, President; Tom Angerer, Vice President.

■ 26318 ■ Harry Kenyon, Inc.
203 N Market St.
Wilmington, DE 19801
Phone: (302)656-8288   Fax: (302)656-1453
Products: Tobacco products, including cigarettes and cigars; Candy. SICs: 5194 (Tobacco & Tobacco Products); 5145 (Confectionery).

■ 26319 ■ Klee Wholesale Company, Inc.
408 Ridgeway Ave.
Falmouth, KY 41040
Phone: (606)654-5744   Fax: (606)654-5755
Products: Cigarettes; Tobacco; Candy; Beverages; Snacks. SICs: 5194 (Tobacco & Tobacco Products); 5145 (Confectionery); 5149 (Groceries & Related Products Nec). Est: 1953. Emp: 24. Officers: Paul V. Klee, Chairman of the Board; Marge Klee, CEO.

■ 26320 ■ John C. Klosterman Company Inc.
901 Portage St.
Kalamazoo, MI 49001
Phone: (616)381-0870   Fax: (616)381-0872
Products: Tobacco and candy. SICs: 5194 (Tobacco & Tobacco Products); 5145 (Confectionery). Sales: $11,000,000 (1994). Emp: 20. Officers: John H. Bartels, President; Evelyn DeKoek, Treasurer.

■ 26321 ■ L and L Jiroch Distributing Co.
1180 58th St.
Grand Rapids, MI 49509-9536
Phone: (616)530-6600   Fax: (616)530-6677
Products: Convenience store items, including tobacco. SICs: 5194 (Tobacco & Tobacco Products); 5145 (Confectionery); 5149 (Groceries & Related Products Nec). Est: 1926. Sales: $330,000,000 (2000). Emp: 350. Officers: Michael Alexander, President; Judy Lammers, Controller.

■ 26322 ■ Lane Ltd.
2280 Mountain Industrial Blvd.
Tucker, GA 30084
Phone: (404)934-8540   Fax: (404)938-9473
Products: Tobacco. SIC: 5194 (Tobacco & Tobacco Products). Est: 1890. Sales: $44,000,000 (2000). Emp: 200. Officers: David H. Michod, CEO & President; George A. McGrath Jr., VP of Finance; Sydney C. Wooten Jr., VP of Marketing & Sales; David White, Dir. of Systems; D. Christopher Martin, Dir of Human Resources.

■ 26323 ■ Harold Levinson Associates Inc.
1 Enterprise Pl.
Hicksville, NY 11801
Phone: (516)822-0068   Fax: (516)822-2182
Products: Cigarettes; Candy; Cigars; Groceries; Coffee. SICs: 5194 (Tobacco & Tobacco Products); 5145 (Confectionery). Est: 1973. Sales: $600,000,000 (1999). Emp: 350. Officers: Ed Berro, CEO.

■ 26324 ■ Linco Distributors
1037 Wray St.
Knoxville, TN 37917-6452
Phone: (423)524-1476   Fax: (423)524-5747
Products: Tobacco products. SIC: 5194 (Tobacco & Tobacco Products). Est: 1947. Sales: $30,000,000 (2000). Emp: 59. Officers: J. Michael Lindsey.

■ 26325 ■ Longo Distributors Inc.
355 Main St.
Whitinsville, MA 01588-1860
Free: (800)445-6646
Products: Tobacco; Manufactured tobacco products. SIC: 5194 (Tobacco & Tobacco Products). Officers: Robert Longo, President.

■ 26326 ■ Luckett Tobaccos Inc.
222 S 1st St.
Louisville, KY 40202
Phone: (502)561-0070   Fax: (502)584-1650
Products: Cigarettes. SIC: 5194 (Tobacco & Tobacco

Products). **Est:** 1902. **Sales:** $10,000,000 (2000). **Emp:** 3. **Officers:** W.R. Meyer, President.

■ **26327** ■ **Martin Brothers International**
PO Box 2230
Jacksonville, FL 32203
Phone: (904)353-4311 **Fax:** 800-628-4675
Products: Cigars; Crackers. **SICs** 5194 (Tobacco & Tobacco Products); 5149 (Groceries & Related Products Nec). **Officers:** Raymond Hayden, Operations Mgr.

■ **26328** ■ **George Melhado Co.**
10 Merchant St.
Sharon, MA 02067
Phone: (781)784-5550
Products: Tobacco; Candy. **SICs:** 5194 (Tobacco & Tobacco Products); 5145 (Confectionery). **Sales:** $88,000,000 (2000). **Emp:** 127. **Officers:** Warren J. Alberts, President; John Little, CFO.

■ **26329** ■ **Attea Milhem & Brothers**
1509 Clinton
Buffalo, NY 14206-3008
Phone: (716)822-1665 **Fax:** (716)822-1669
Products: Cigarettes; Candy; Paper and allied products. **SICs:** 5194 (Tobacco & Tobacco Products); 5145 (Confectionery); 5113 (Industrial & Personal Service Paper). **Est:** 1924. **Emp:** 39. **Officers:** Frank Attea; Theodore Attea; Rosemary Saffire.

■ **26330** ■ **Mountain Service Distributors**
40 Lake St.
PO Box 520
South Fallsburg, NY 12779-0520
Phone: (914)434-5674 **Fax:** (914)434-0059
Products: Tobacco; Food; Confectionary products; Beverages. **SICs:** 5194 (Tobacco & Tobacco Products); 5141 (Groceries—General Line); 5145 (Confectionery); 5149 (Groceries & Related Products Nec). **Est:** 1928. **Sales:** $60,000,000 (2000). **Emp:** 60. **Officers:** Stephen Altman, President; Josh Altman, Treasurer & Secty.; Bill Freeman, Sales/Marketing Contact; Ed Kennady, Customer Service Contact; Michele Elliott, Human Resources Contact; Michele Elliott, Human Resources Contact.

■ **26331** ■ **New Hampshire Tobacco Corp.**
130 Northeastern Blvd.
Nashua, NH 03062
Phone: (603)882-1131 **Fax:** (603)881-3215
E-mail: tabakco@aol.com
Products: Tobacco products; Confectionery; Health and beauty aids; Groceries; Paper products. **SICs:** 5194 (Tobacco & Tobacco Products); 5111 (Printing & Writing Paper); 5141 (Groceries—General Line); 5145 (Confectionery); 5122 (Drugs, Proprietaries & Sundries). **Est:** 1888. **Sales:** $25,000,000 (2000). **Emp:** 25. **Officers:** R.A. Bertrand, President; Kevin Grelnwood, Sales Mgr.; Evelyn Perkins, Customer Service Contact; Louise Bertrand, VP of Operations.

■ **26332** ■ **New Hampshire Tobacco Corp.**
130 Northeastern Blvd.
Nashua, NH 03060
Phone: (603)882-1131 **Fax:** (603)881-3215
Products: Tobacco and confectionery. **SICs:** 5194 (Tobacco & Tobacco Products); 5145 (Confectionery). **Sales:** $20,000,000 (1999). **Emp:** 25. **Officers:** R.A. Bertrand, President.

■ **26333** ■ **North Idaho Distributing Inc.**
PO Box 2530
Hayden, ID 83835-2530
Phone: (208)772-7512 **Fax:** (208)772-6231
Products: Tobacco; Smoking tobacco; Manufactured tobacco products; Cigarettes; Restaurant supplies; Snack foods. **SICs:** 5194 (Tobacco & Tobacco Products); 5145 (Confectionery). **Officers:** Stanley Feist, President. **Doing Business As:** Doyles Wholesale.

■ **26334** ■ **Northwest Tobacco and Candy Inc.**
PO Box 4215
Fayetteville, AR 72702-4215
Phone: (501)442-8121 **Fax:** (501)442-8666
Products: Candy and gum; Cigarettes; Smokeless tobacco. **SICs:** 5194 (Tobacco & Tobacco Products); 5145 (Confectionery). **Est:** 1945. **Sales:** $11,000,000

(1999). **Emp:** 18. **Officers:** Tony Harp, President; Patsy Harpin, Vice President; Mike Stockburger, General Mgr.; Faye Williams, Sec. & Treas.

■ **26335** ■ **Albert H. Notini and Sons Inc.**
PO Box 299
Lowell, MA 01853
Phone: (508)459-7151 **Fax:** (508)458-7692
Products: Paper goods, including bags, tissue, and paper towels; Cigarettes and tobacco products; Candy; Health and beauty aids. **SICs:** 5194 (Tobacco & Tobacco Products); 5113 (Industrial & Personal Service Paper); 5122 (Drugs, Proprietaries & Sundries); 5145 (Confectionery). **Est:** 1890. **Sales:** $130,000,000 (2000). **Emp:** 180. **Officers:** Alex Turchette, CEO; Dick Flanagan, Controller; Chris Vurguropulos, Dir. of Sales.

■ **26336** ■ **O.K. Distributing Company Inc.**
PO Box 1252
Williston, ND 58802-1252
Phone: (701)572-9161 **Fax:** (701)572-9631
Products: Tobacco products. **SIC:** 5194 (Tobacco & Tobacco Products). **Est:** 1955.

■ **26337** ■ **Pablo Don Cigar Co.**
3025 Las Vegas Blvd. S
Las Vegas, NV 89109-1920
Phone: (702)369-1818
Free: (800)557-4957 **Fax:** (702)369-1818
Products: Tobacco; Manufactured tobacco products; Smoking tobacco; Cigars. **SIC:** 5194 (Tobacco & Tobacco Products). **Officers:** Bob Schear, President.

■ **26338** ■ **Parker Tobacco Company**
636 Forest Ave.
Maysville, KY 41056-0428
Phone: (606)564-5571 **Fax:** (606)564-5573
Products: Leaf tobacco; Tobacco products. **SIC:** 5194 (Tobacco & Tobacco Products). **Est:** 1932. **Sales:** $500,000 (2000). **Emp:** 25. **Officers:** Ernest B. Hillenmeyer Jr., President; S. Alex Parker Jr., CEO.

■ **26339** ■ **Philip Morris Products Inc.**
2001 Walmsley Blvd.
Richmond, VA 23234
Phone: (804)274-2605
Products: Cigarettes. **SIC:** 5194 (Tobacco & Tobacco Products).

■ **26340** ■ **Pine Lesser and Sons Inc.**
PO Box 1807
Clifton, NJ 07015
Phone: (973)478-3310 **Fax:** (973)478-3710
Products: Cigarettes and candies. **SICs:** 5194 (Tobacco & Tobacco Products); 5145 (Confectionery). **Est:** 1925. **Sales:** $40,000,000 (2000). **Emp:** 35. **Officers:** Allan G. Lesser, President; Donald Lesser, Treasurer & Secty.

■ **26341** ■ **Pine State Tobacco and Candy Co.**
PO Box 1080
Augusta, ME 04332-1080
Phone: (207)622-3741
Products: Tobacco; Candy; Cigarettes. **SICs:** 5194 (Tobacco & Tobacco Products); 5145 (Confectionery). **Est:** 1940. **Sales:** $90,000,000 (2000). **Emp:** 270. **Officers:** Charles F. Canning Jr., President; Paul W. Cottrell Jr., Controller; John Miller, VP of Sales; Terry Goddard, Manager; Susan A. Reed, Dir of Human Resources.

■ **26342** ■ **J. Polep Distribution Services Inc.**
705 Meadow St.
Chicopee, MA 01013
Phone: (413)592-4141 **Fax:** (413)592-5870
Products: Health and beauty aids; Cigarettes and tobacco products. **SICs:** 5194 (Tobacco & Tobacco Products); 5122 (Drugs, Proprietaries & Sundries). **Est:** 1946. **Sales:** $92,000,000 (2000). **Emp:** 125. **Officers:** Jeffrey Polep, CEO & Treasurer; Steve Martin, VP & Controller; Rich Patruski, Dir. of Marketing.

■ **26343** ■ **Premium Cigars International Ltd.**
15651 N 77th St.
Scottsdale, AZ 85260
Phone: (602)922-8887 **Free:** (888)696-6399
Products: Cigars. **SIC:** 5194 (Tobacco & Tobacco

Products). **Officers:** John E. Greenwell, CEO & President; Karissa B. Nisted, CFO.

■ **26344** ■ **Quaglino Tobacco and Candy Company Inc.**
2400 S Claiborne Ave.
New Orleans, LA 70125
Phone: (504)561-0101
Products: Tobacco; Candy; Snack items; Health products. **SICs:** 5194 (Tobacco & Tobacco Products); 5122 (Drugs, Proprietaries & Sundries); 5145 (Confectionery). **Est:** 1920. **Sales:** $28,000,000 (2000). **Emp:** 70. **Officers:** J.A. Quaglino, President; Karen Quaglino, Dir. of Marketing & Sales; Michelle Troglio, Dir. of Data Processing; Iona Ball, Dir of Human Resources.

■ **26345** ■ **A.E. Raketty Co.**
PO Box 18555
Seattle, WA 98118
Phone: (206)722-5119 **Fax:** (206)722-6474
Products: Tobacco; Cigarettes; Hard and chocolate candy. **SICs:** 5194 (Tobacco & Tobacco Products); 5145 (Confectionery). **Est:** 1931. **Sales:** $20,000,000 (2000). **Emp:** 50. **Officers:** Arlene Krussel, President; Robert Moshell, Dir. of Operations; Mark Hruska, Marketing & Sales Mgr.

■ **26346** ■ **Republic Tobacco L.P.**
2301 Ravine Way
Glenview, IL 60025
Phone: (847)832-9700
Free: (800)288-8888 **Fax:** (847)832-9710
Products: Cigarette paper, tobacco, and accessories. **SIC:** 5194 (Tobacco & Tobacco Products). **Est:** 1974. **Sales:** $50,000,000 (2000). **Emp:** 250. **Officers:** Donald Levin, Chairman of the Board; Allan Kandelman, Sr. VP & Finance Officer; Mary-Beth Glynn, Dir. of Marketing, e-mail: mbglynn@rpbtob.com; James Kelly, Dir. of Data Processing; Warren Schoening, National Sales Manager.

■ **26347** ■ **Republic Tobacco L.P.**
5100 N Ravenswood Ave.
Chicago, IL 60640
Phone: (312)728-1500 **Fax:** (312)275-4307
Products: Tobacco products. **SIC:** 5194 (Tobacco & Tobacco Products). **Sales:** $50,000,000 (2000). **Emp:** 250.

■ **26348** ■ **Rosario Candy Inc.**
1150 Lyon Rd.
Batavia, IL 60510
Phone: (630)584-4677 **Fax:** (630)584-4787
Products: Candy; Cigarettes; Cigar; Tobacco; Juices; Sundries. **SICs:** 5145 (Confectionery); 5194 (Tobacco & Tobacco Products). **Est:** 1975. **Emp:** 12. **Officers:** Rosario J. Sparacio, President; Delores Sparacio, Treasurer & Secty.

■ **26349** ■ **S & H Co.**
101 Kappa Dr.
Pittsburgh, PA 15238-2809
Products: Cigarettes; Tobacco; Spices; Candy. **SICs:** 5194 (Tobacco & Tobacco Products); 5145 (Confectionery); 5149 (Groceries & Related Products Nec). **Est:** 1966. **Sales:** $80,000,000 (2000). **Emp:** 37. **Officers:** David Shapiro, President; N. Monus, VP of Finance; J.W. Armstrong, General Mgr.

■ **26350** ■ **F.X. Smiths Sons Co.**
372-374 North St.
PO Box 38
McSherrystown, PA 17344-0038
Phone: (717)637-5232 **Fax:** (717)637-4092
Products: Cigars. **SIC:** 5194 (Tobacco & Tobacco Products). **Est:** 1863. **Sales:** $1,500,000 (1999). **Emp:** 40. **Officers:** Craig P. Smith.

■ **26351** ■ **Southwestern Tobacco Co.**
201 Price Rd.
Lexington, KY 40511-1995
Phone: (606)253-2401 **Fax:** (606)253-1412
Products: Tobacco. **SIC:** 5194 (Tobacco & Tobacco Products). **Emp:** 49.

■ 26352 ■ Stalling Inc.
PO Box 4169
Lynchburg, VA 24502
Phone: (804)237-5947 **Fax:** (804)239-0438
Products: Smokeless tobacco. **SIC:** 5194 (Tobacco &
Tobacco Products). **Est:** 1971. **Sales:** $2,500,000
(2000). **Emp:** 45. **Officers:** G.H. Stalling III, President;
W.W. Brown, Treasurer & Secty.

■ 26353 ■ Standard Commercial Corp.
PO Box 450
Wilson, NC 27894-0450
Phone: (919)291-5507 **Fax:** (919)237-1109
Products: Tobacco leaves. **SIC:** 5159 (Farm-Product
Raw Materials Nec). **Est:** 1910. **Sales:** $1,354,300,000
(2000). **Emp:** 2,200. **Officers:** J. Alec Murray, CEO &
President; Robert E. Harrison, Sr. VP & CFO.

■ 26354 ■ Sullivan Candy & Supply
1623 E 6th Ave.
Hibbing, MN 55746-1433
Phones: (218)263-6634   (218)263-7871
Free: (800)450-7855 **Fax:** (218)263-7257
Products: Paper and allied products; Candy; Tobacco;
Janitors' supplies; Restaurant supplies. **SICs:** 5194
(Tobacco & Tobacco Products); 5113 (Industrial &
Personal Service Paper); 5087 (Service Establishment
Equipment); 5145 (Confectionery). **Est:** 1938. **Sales:**
$5,000,000 (2000). **Emp:** 19. **Officers:** Tom Sullivan
Jr.

■ 26355 ■ SWD Corp.
PO Box 340
Lima, OH 45802-0340
Phone: (419)227-2436
Products: Cigarettes; Tobacco; Sanitary paper
products; Candy. **SICs:** 5145 (Confectionery); 5194
(Tobacco & Tobacco Products); 5113 (Industrial &
Personal Service Paper). **Est:** 1968. **Sales:**
$35,000,000 (2000). **Emp:** 60. **Officers:** Carl Berger,
President; Ken Simmers, Treasurer & Secty.; David
Cocrerell, VP of Sales.

■ 26356 ■ Thorpe and Ricks Inc.
PO Box 271
Rocky Mount, NC 27802-0271
Phone: (919)977-3151 **Fax:** (919)977-9690
Products: Leaf tobacco. **SIC:** 5159 (Farm-Product
Raw Materials Nec). **Officers:** Robert L. Minor, Sr. VP.

■ 26357 ■ Tobacco Sales Company Inc.
2445 Santa Ana St.
Dallas, TX 75228
Phone: (214)328-2821
Products: Tobacco, including cigarettes and cigars;
Gum; Candy. **SICs:** 5194 (Tobacco & Tobacco
Products); 5145 (Confectionery). **Est:** 1929. **Sales:**
$15,000,000 (2000). **Emp:** 50. **Officers:** Wesley D.
Hirman, President; Norma Hirman, Controller.

■ 26358 ■ Tobacco Shop at Hyatt
2424 Kalakaua Ave.
Honolulu, HI 96815
Phone: (808)923-8109
Products: Tobacco, pipes, cigars, and cigarettes;
Gifts. **SICs:** 5194 (Tobacco & Tobacco Products); 5199
(Nondurable Goods Nec).

■ 26359 ■ Tobacco Supply Company Inc.
PO Box 726
Springfield, TN 37172-0726
Phone: (615)384-2421 **Fax:** (615)384-7767
Products: Leaf tobacco. **SIC:** 5159 (Farm-Product
Raw Materials Nec). **Est:** 1944. **Sales:** $13,000,000
(2000). **Emp:** 67. **Officers:** M.L. Smith Jr., President.

■ 26360 ■ Topicz
2121 Section Rd.
PO Box 37289
Cincinnati, OH 45222
Phone: (513)351-7700
Free: (800)829-8029 **Fax:** (513)351-1906
Products: Tobacco; Confections. **SICs:** 5194
(Tobacco & Tobacco Products); 5122 (Drugs,
Proprietaries & Sundries); 5141 (Groceries—General
Line). **Est:** 1925. **Emp:** 100. **Officers:** Marvin H.
Schwartz, Vice President; Dennis Kramer, General
Mgr.; Charles Eckert, Dir. of Sales.

■ 26361 ■ John F. Trompeter Co.
637 E Main St.
Louisville, KY 40202
Phone: (502)585-5852 **Fax:** (502)583-2524
Products: Cigarettes and cigars; Candy and popcorn
machines. **SICs:** 5194 (Tobacco & Tobacco Products);
5087 (Service Establishment Equipment). **Est:** 1892.
Sales: $11,000,000 (2000). **Emp:** 35. **Officers:** B.A.
Trompeter, Chairman of the Board; Kathy Trompeter,
President.

■ 26362 ■ UETA Inc.
3407 Northeast Pkwy.
San Antonio, TX 78212
Phone: (210)828-8382
Products: Perfumes; Tobacco; Cigarettes; Electronics.
SICs: 5194 (Tobacco & Tobacco Products); 5064
(Electrical Appliances—Television & Radio); 5122
(Drugs, Proprietaries & Sundries). **Est:** 1987. **Sales:**
$144,600,000 (2000). **Emp:** 600. **Officers:** Ramon
Bosquez, President; Robert C. Petka, Treasurer &
Controller; Ramon Bosquez, Exec. VP of Operations;
Bob Brady, Dir. of Information Systems; Mary Ince,
Human Resources Mgr.

■ 26363 ■ United Candy and Tobacco Co.
7408 Tonnelle Ave.
North Bergen, NJ 07047
Phone: (201)943-8675
Products: Tobacco products, including cigarettes;
Candy. **SICs:** 5194 (Tobacco & Tobacco Products);
5145 (Confectionery). **Est:** 1950. **Sales:** $35,000,000
(2000). **Emp:** 10. **Officers:** J. Choi, President;
Raymond Epifano, Manager.

**■ 26364 ■ United States Tobacco Sales and
Marketing Co.**
100 W Putnam Ave.
Greenwich, CT 06830
Phone: (203)661-1100
Products: Smokeless tobacco. **SIC:** 5194 (Tobacco &
Tobacco Products).

■ 26365 ■ Universal Corp.
PO Box 25099
Richmond, VA 23260
Phone: (804)359-9311 **Fax:** (804)254-3584
Products: Tobacco; Lumber and other building
products; Tea; Rubber; Food products, including
sunflower seeds, nuts, dried fruit, canned meats,
spices, and seasonings. **SICs:** 5159 (Farm-Product
Raw Materials Nec); 5031 (Lumber, Plywood &
Millwork); 5149 (Groceries & Related Products Nec);
5199 (Nondurable Goods Nec). **Sales:** $4,287,200,000
(2000). **Emp:** 25,000. **Officers:** Henry H. Harrell, CEO
& Chairman of the Board; Hartwell H. Roper, VP &
CFO.

**■ 26366 ■ Universal Leaf Tobacco Company
Inc.**
PO Box 25099
Richmond, VA 23260
Phone: (804)359-9311 **Fax:** (804)254-3584
Products: Tobacco. **SIC:** 5194 (Tobacco & Tobacco
Products). **Sales:** $12,000,000 (2000). **Emp:** 1,200.
Officers: Henry Harrell, President; William Coronato,
Controller.

■ 26367 ■ Valley Convenience Products
44 Drawbridge Dr.
West Warwick, RI 02893-5580
Phone: (401)821-6073
Products: Tobacco; Manufactured tobacco products;
Candy. **SICs:** 5194 (Tobacco & Tobacco Products);
5145 (Confectionery). **Officers:** Richard De Ciantis,
President.

■ 26368 ■ Valley Vending Service Inc.
PO Box 506
Martins Ferry, OH 43935
Phone: (614)633-3303
Products: Tobacco and tobacco products, including
cigarettes. **SIC:** 5194 (Tobacco & Tobacco Products).
Sales: $3,000,000 (2000). **Emp:** 5. **Officers:** L.T.
George, President & Treasurer.

■ 26369 ■ Vega Enterprises Inc.
PO Box 4247
Las Vegas, NV 89127-0247
Phone: (702)642-8342 **Fax:** (702)642-4515
Products: Tobacco; Manufactured tobacco products.
SIC: 5194 (Tobacco & Tobacco Products). **Officers:**
Rafael Vega, President.

■ 26370 ■ W.C. Distributors Corp.
2887 Koapaka St.
Honolulu, HI 96819
Phone: (808)836-3605 **Fax:** (808)836-7699
Products: Tobacco; Manufactured tobacco products;
Cigarettes; Snuff; Kitchenware. **SICs:** 5194 (Tobacco &
Tobacco Products); 5023 (Homefurnishings).

■ 26371 ■ Weeke Wholesale Company Inc.
1600 N 89th St.
Fairview Heights, IL 62208
Phone: (618)397-1900 **Fax:** (618)397-7041
Products: Cigarettes; Candy; Groceries. **SICs:** 5194
(Tobacco & Tobacco Products); 5145 (Confectionery).
Est: 1913. **Sales:** $20,000,000 (2000). **Emp:** 45.
Officers: Wayne W. Week, Chairman of the Board;
Scott W. Weeke, President; Patrick J. Schweiss, Sr. VP
of Operations; Scott W. Weeke, President.

■ 26372 ■ Wholesale Supply Company Inc.
212 Linn St.
PO Box 143
Yankton, SD 57078-0143
Phone: (605)665-7827
Products: Candy; Tobacco; Chips; Frozen foods;
Paper products; Janitorial supplies. **SICs:** 5194
(Tobacco & Tobacco Products); 5145 (Confectionery);
5113 (Industrial & Personal Service Paper); 5087
(Service Establishment Equipment). **Est:** 1940.
Officers: Rod Pieper, President; Bruce Pieper, Owner.

■ 26373 ■ Wholesale Supply Company Inc.
PO Box 1948
Minot, ND 58702
Phone: (701)852-2753 **Fax:** (701)839-5574
Products: Tobacco; Manufactured tobacco products.
SIC: 5194 (Tobacco & Tobacco Products). **Officers:**
Roger Borkhuis, President.

■ 26374 ■ Wiemuth and Son Company Inc.
PO Box 3128
Terre Haute, IN 47803
Phone: (812)232-3384
Free: (800)742-2277 **Fax:** (812)234-2888
Products: Tobacco; Candy; Groceries. **SIC:** 5194
(Tobacco & Tobacco Products). **Est:** 1952. **Sales:**
$13,000,000 (2000). **Emp:** 25. **Officers:** Robert A.
Wiemuth, President.

■ 26375 ■ Windsor Shade Tobacco Co.
158 Woodland St.
Hartford, CT 06105
Phone: (860)522-1153
Products: Cigar wrappers. **SIC:** 5194 (Tobacco &
Tobacco Products). **Est:** 1937. **Sales:** $4,000,000
(2000). **Emp:** 100. **Officers:** Oliver J. Thrall II,
President; Stanton F. Brown, Treasurer; Andres
Sepulveda, Dir. of Marketing.

■ 26376 ■ Eli Witt Co.
1879 Forest Pkwy.
Lake City, GA 30260-3674
Phone: (404)363-9110 **Fax:** (404)366-5091
Products: Cigarettes. **SIC:** 5194 (Tobacco & Tobacco
Products). **Emp:** 105. **Officers:** Felton Hartley, Vice
President.

■ 26377 ■ L.J. Zucca Inc.
760 S Delsea Dr.
Vineland, NJ 08360-4464
Phone: (609)692-7425
Free: (800)552-2639 **Fax:** (609)696-7112
Products: Cigarettes; Candy; General line groceries;
Personal goods; Automotive accessories. **SICs:** 5194
(Tobacco & Tobacco Products); 5145 (Confectionery);
5149 (Groceries & Related Products Nec); 5122
(Drugs, Proprietaries & Sundries); 5013 (Motor Vehicle
Supplies & New Parts). **Est:** 1947. **Emp:** 49. **Officers:**
Louis J. Zucca.

(58) Toys and Hobby Goods

Entries in this section are arranged alphabetically by company name. When the company name is a personal name, the company name is alphabetized by the surname unless the first name or initial(s) are part of a trade name. See the User's Guide at the front of this directory for additional information.

■ 26378 ■ **AAA-Four Aces**
855 Inca St.
Denver, CO 80204-4342
Phone: (303)595-0237   **Fax:** (303)595-0248
E-mail: four-aces@uswest.net
Products: Role-playing and fantasy games; Models; Toys; Miniatures; Dice; Gaming accessories. **SIC:** 5092 (Toys & Hobby Goods & Supplies). **Est:** 1982. **Emp:** 5. **Officers:** Douglas Cohn, President; Kathy Burton, Buyer.

■ 26379 ■ **ABC International Traders Inc.**
16730 Schoenborn St.
North Hills, CA 91343-6122
Phone: (818)894-2525   **Fax:** (818)894-8094
Products: Toys; Electrical appliances. **SICs:** 5092 (Toys & Hobby Goods & Supplies); 5064 (Electrical Appliances—Television & Radio). **Est:** 1982. **Sales:** $105,000,000 (2000). **Emp:** 35. **Officers:** Isaac Larian, President; Fred Larian, CFO.

■ 26380 ■ **Acclaim Entertainment Inc.**
1 Acclaim Plz.
Glen Cove, NY 11542
Phone: (516)624-8888   **Fax:** (516)624-2885
Products: Video games. **SIC:** 5092 (Toys & Hobby Goods & Supplies). **Sales:** $140,000,000 (2000). **Emp:** 70. **Officers:** Gregory Fishbock.

■ 26381 ■ **Action Products International Inc.**
390 N Orange Ave.
Orlando, FL 32801
Phone: (407)481-8007
Free: (800)772-2846   **Fax:** 800-232-9228
Products: Space and education products such as space shuttle models, toys, posters, books and dinosaur replicas to museums, NASA bases and employee shops; Freeze dried snack foods and educational books. **SICs:** 5092 (Toys & Hobby Goods & Supplies); 5199 (Nondurable Goods Nec); 5192 (Books, Periodicals & Newspapers). **Est:** 1977. **Sales:** $5,900,000 (2000). **Emp:** 36. **Officers:** Ronald S. Kaplan, CEO, President & Chairman of the Board; Delton G. DeArmas, CFO.

■ 26382 ■ **S.S. Adams Co.**
PO Box 850
Neptune, NJ 07754-0850
Phone: (732)774-0570   **Fax:** (732)775-8045
E-mail: ssadams@monmouth.com
Products: Magic and prank items. **SIC:** 5092 (Toys & Hobby Goods & Supplies). **Est:** 1906. **Sales:** $2,000,000 (2000). **Emp:** 42. **Officers:** J.H. Adams, President; C.S. Adams, Vice President.

■ 26383 ■ **Aladdin Distributors Inc.**
1420 Cliff Rd. E
Burnsville, MN 55337-1414
Phone: (612)890-8700
Products: Hobby kits; Nonelectronic games. **SIC:** 5092 (Toys & Hobby Goods & Supplies). **Officers:** Kenneth Storm, President.

■ 26384 ■ **Alamex Crafts Inc.**
118 Old Durham Rd., No. A
Chapel Hill, NC 27514-2293
Phone: (919)479-8795   **Fax:** (919)478-7830
Products: Arts and crafts equipment and supplies; Hand-crafted, imported folk art. **SICs:** 5092 (Toys & Hobby Goods & Supplies); 5199 (Nondurable Goods Nec). **Officers:** Miriam Palacio, Vice President.

■ 26385 ■ **Aluma Flight Co.**
PO Box 5983
Helena, MT 59604-5983
Phone: (406)442-4977
Products: Toys; Hobby kits; Model kits. **SIC:** 5092 (Toys & Hobby Goods & Supplies). **Officers:** Marilyn Briggs, Vice President.

■ 26386 ■ **Amceco International Corp.**
1314 Long St., Ste. 110
High Point, NC 27262-2568
Phone: (910)887-8647   **Fax:** (910)887-5797
Products: Toys and hobby goods. **SIC:** 5092 (Toys & Hobby Goods & Supplies). **Sales:** $10,000,000 (2000). **Emp:** 2.

■ 26387 ■ **American Educational Products Inc.**
6550 Gunpark Dr.Ste. 200
Boulder, CO 80301
Phone: (303)527-3230   **Fax:** (303)527-3235
Products: Multimedia products and children's games; hands-on education materials for schools and parents. **SIC:** 5092 (Toys & Hobby Goods & Supplies). **Sales:** $11,700,000 (2000). **Emp:** 90. **Officers:** Robert Scott, Chairman of the Board; Frank L. Jennings, VP & CFO.

■ 26388 ■ **American Importers of South Carolina**
PO Box 308
Rowesville, SC 29133-0308
Phone: (803)534-8221   **Fax:** (803)536-6356
Products: Fireworks. **SIC:** 5092 (Toys & Hobby Goods & Supplies). **Officers:** Terrence Anderson, President.

■ 26389 ■ **American Promotional Events, Inc.**
4511 Helton Dr. at Rasch Rd.
Florence, AL 35630
Phone: (205)764-6131
Free: (800)243-1189   **Fax:** (205)760-0154
Products: Fireworks. **SIC:** 5092 (Toys & Hobby Goods & Supplies). **Officers:** Terrence Anderson, President.

■ 26390 ■ **American Visual Aids**
1 Hanson Pl.
Brooklyn, NY 11243
Phone: (718)636-9100
Free: (800)777-2675   **Fax:** (718)636-9388
E-mail: hgm50@aol.com
Products: Educational toys and games. **SIC:** 5092 (Toys & Hobby Goods & Supplies). **Est:** 1946. **Sales:** $1,500,000 (1999). **Emp:** 100. **Officers:** L.B. Moss, President & Chairman of the Board; H. Moss, CFO.

■ 26391 ■ **America's Hobby Center Inc.**
146 W 22nd St.
New York, NY 10011-2466
Phone: (212)675-8922   **Fax:** (212)633-2754
Products: Toy trains and cars. **SIC:** 5092 (Toys & Hobby Goods & Supplies). **Est:** 1931. **Sales:** $4,000,000 (2000). **Emp:** 15. **Officers:** Marshall G. Winston, President; Peter R. Winston, Vice President.

■ 26392 ■ **Ammar's Inc.**
S College Ave.
Bluefield, VA 24605
Phone: (540)322-4686
Products: Hobby and hardware goods. **SICs:** 5092 (Toys & Hobby Goods & Supplies); 5072 (Hardware). **Sales:** $75,000,000 (2000). **Emp:** 750. **Officers:** Keleel A. Ammar Jr., President & Chairman of the Board; Richard Ammar, CFO.

■ 26393 ■ **Mike Angel Associates Inc.**
3728 Hampstead Dr.
Sylvania, OH 43560-5503
Phone: (419)841-1862   **Fax:** (419)841-1063
Products: Toys and hobby goods and supplies. **SIC:** 5092 (Toys & Hobby Goods & Supplies). **Officers:** Michael Angel, Chairman of the Board.

■ 26394 ■ **Applause Enterprises Inc.**
PO Box 4183
Woodland Hills, CA 91365-4183
Phone: (818)992-6000   **Free:** (800)777-6990
URL: http://www.applause.com
Products: Plush toys and novelty gifts. **SIC:** 5092 (Toys & Hobby Goods & Supplies). **Est:** 1966. **Sales:** $280,000,000 (2000). **Emp:** 600. **Officers:** Jonathan Mather, President & CEO; Kevin Murray, CFO.

■ 26395 ■ **Applause, Inc.**
6101 Variel Ave.
PO Box 4183
Woodland Hills, CA 91367
Phone: (818)595-2701   **Fax:** (818)887-2121
Products: Dolls and stuffed toy animals. **SIC:** 5092 (Toys & Hobby Goods & Supplies). **Officers:** Barbara S. Willey, Import/Export Mgr.

■ 26396 ■ **Arkin Distributing Co.**
43100 9 Mile
Novi, MI 48375-3113
Phone: (248)349-9300   **Fax:** (248)349-5202
Products: Toys. **SIC:** 5092 (Toys & Hobby Goods & Supplies). **Emp:** 82. **Officers:** Irwin J. Arkin.

■ 26397 ■ **Arrow Wholesale Co. Inc.**
PO Box 108
Worcester, MA 01613-0108
Phone: (508)753-5830   **Fax:** (508)753-5316
Products: Toys; Housewares stationary notions; Fabric dye; Seasonal merchandise. **SICs:** 5092 (Toys & Hobby Goods & Supplies); 5023 (Homefurnishings); 5199 (Nondurable Goods Nec); 5137 (Women's/Children's Clothing). **Est:** 1928. **Emp:** 8. **Officers:** Elliott Ginsburg, President.

■ 26398 ■ Arrowcopter Inc.
Box 6480
San Jose, CA 95150
Phone: (408)978-1771 **Fax:** (408)978-1270
E-mail: info@arrowcopter.com
URL: http://www.arrowcopter.com
Products: Flying toys. **SIC:** 5092 (Toys & Hobby Goods & Supplies).

■ 26399 ■ Arrowhead Fireworks Co.
3400 Republic Ave.
Minneapolis, MN 55426-4133
Phone: (612)929-8255 **Fax:** (612)721-3910
Products: Fireworks; Toys. **SIC:** 5092 (Toys & Hobby Goods & Supplies). **Est:** 1923. **Emp:** 49. **Officers:** Tom Atol.

■ 26400 ■ Arts & Craft Distributors Inc.
6304 Yadkin Rd.
Fayetteville, NC 28303-2647
Phone: (910)867-1050 **Fax:** (910)867-6356
Products: Sporting and athletic goods; Hobby kits; Craft kits. **SICs:** 5092 (Toys & Hobby Goods & Supplies); 5091 (Sporting & Recreational Goods). **Officers:** David Murphy, President.

■ 26401 ■ Aubford Enterprises
9 Saratoga St.
Lewiston, ME 04240-3527
Phone: (207)784-3828 **Fax:** (207)786-4174
Products: Toys; Hobby goods and supplies; Games; Arcade video games. **SICs:** 5092 (Toys & Hobby Goods & Supplies); 5046 (Commercial Equipment Nec). **Officers:** Edmund Burke, President.

■ 26402 ■ Dan Aungst Wholesale
4570 Maple Dr.
Walnutport, PA 18088-9709
Phone: (215)797-9475
Products: Toys; Tools; Gloves; Sunglasses; Air fresheners. **SICs:** 5092 (Toys & Hobby Goods & Supplies); 5122 (Drugs, Proprietaries & Sundries); 5199 (Nondurable Goods Nec); 5099 (Durable Goods Nec).

■ 26403 ■ Ayers Art Co.
2504 Hwy. 30 E
Kearney, NE 68847-9763
Phone: (308)237-3566
Products: Toys; Hobby goods and supplies; Games; Fund-raising products. **SIC:** 5092 (Toys & Hobby Goods & Supplies). **Officers:** Art Ayers, Partner.

■ 26404 ■ Ralph A. Baer Co.
9100 N Vancouver Ave.
Portland, OR 97217-7560
Phone: (503)283-1180 **Fax:** (503)283-2547
Products: Toys, hobby goods, and supplies. **SIC:** 5092 (Toys & Hobby Goods & Supplies). **Officers:** Ralph Baer, President.

■ 26405 ■ Buck Bailes Inc.
PO Box 11172
Charlotte, NC 28220-1172
Phone: (704)342-0650 **Fax:** (704)342-0751
E-mail: bbailes@aol.com
Products: Toys; Hobby kits; Nonelectronic games. **SIC:** 5092 (Toys & Hobby Goods & Supplies). **Officers:** Walter Bailes, President.

■ 26406 ■ Ballard Enterprises Inc.
7 Broadway
Concord, NH 03301-2843
Phone: (603)225-5666
Products: Toys; Hobby kits; Rubber balloons; Gifts and novelties. **SIC:** 5092 (Toys & Hobby Goods & Supplies). **Officers:** Norman Ballard, President.

■ 26407 ■ Balloon Express
2906 Pailersville Rd.
Louisville, KY 40205
Phone: (502)459-6337 **Fax:** (502)459-6337
Products: Toys; Hobby goods and supplies; Toy novelties and amusements; Balloons. **SIC:** 5092 (Toys & Hobby Goods & Supplies). **Officers:** Larry Green, Owner.

■ 26408 ■ Balloon House
3590 Utah Ave. NE
Iowa City, IA 52240-9283
Phone: (319)354-3471
Free: (800)833-9878 **Fax:** (319)354-7007
E-mail: bhzaprint@aol.com
URL: http://www.balloonhouse.com
Products: Toys; Hobby kits; Gifts and novelties; Rubber balloons. **SICs:** 5092 (Toys & Hobby Goods & Supplies); 5199 (Nondurable Goods Nec). **Est:** 1984. **Emp:** 12. **Officers:** Lyne Grievahn, Partner.

■ 26409 ■ Balloonery Inc.
5240 Benson Ave.
Baltimore, MD 21227-2512
Phone: (410)242-6380
Free: (800)776-0405 **Fax:** (410)242-7257
Products: Rubber balloons; Compressed and liquefied gases. **SICs:** 5092 (Toys & Hobby Goods & Supplies); 5169 (Chemicals & Allied Products Nec). **Officers:** Samuel Buckingham, President.

■ 26410 ■ Balloons, Logos & T-Shirts
220 W Perkins Ave.
Sandusky, OH 44870-4707
Phone: (419)625-6968 **Fax:** (419)627-2789
Products: Toys, hobby goods, and supplies, including novelties and balloons. **SIC:** 5092 (Toys & Hobby Goods & Supplies). **Officers:** Tony Mihalic, Owner.

■ 26411 ■ Balloons & Things
993 Waimanu St.
Honolulu, HI 96814
Phone: (808)538-0076 **Fax:** (808)593-2504
Products: Balloons; Stuffed animals. **SIC:** 5092 (Toys & Hobby Goods & Supplies).

■ 26412 ■ Ballpark Inc.
10791 W 107th Cir.
Broomfield, CO 80021-7331
Phone: (303)425-1480
Products: Toys; Hobby kits. **SIC:** 5092 (Toys & Hobby Goods & Supplies). **Officers:** Judy Christmas, President.

■ 26413 ■ Bayer Wood Products
5122 Dorr St.
Toledo, OH 43615-3849
Phone: (419)536-7416
Free: (800)323-0817 **Fax:** (419)536-7117
Products: Arts and crafts equipment and supplies, including lead pencils and crayons. **SIC:** 5092 (Toys & Hobby Goods & Supplies). **Officers:** Michael Bayer, Owner.

■ 26414 ■ Becksmith Co.
5005 Barrow Ave.
PO Box 9068
Cincinnati, OH 45209
Phone: (513)531-4151 **Fax:** (513)366-4019
Products: Toys; Games; Candy. **SICs:** 5092 (Toys & Hobby Goods & Supplies); 5145 (Confectionery). **Est:** 1907. **Emp:** 15. **Officers:** Raymond Becksmith, Chairman of the Board.

■ 26415 ■ Berkley Game Distributors
2950 San Pablo Ave.
Berkeley, CA 94702
Phone: (510)845-9851 **Free:** (800)424-4263
Products: Role-playing and fantasy games. **SIC:** 5092 (Toys & Hobby Goods & Supplies). **Doing Business As:** Evil Empire.

■ 26416 ■ Best Toy Manufacturing Ltd.
43 Hall St.
Brooklyn, NY 11205-1303
Phone: (718)855-9040 **Fax:** (718)875-5934
Products: Stuffed toy animals; Stuffed dolls. **SIC:** 5092 (Toys & Hobby Goods & Supplies). **Emp:** 29. **Officers:** Abe Hammer, President; Gina Schrader, Vice President.

■ 26417 ■ Betty's Doll House
Rte. 82
East Haddam, CT 06423
Phone: (860)434-2086
Products: Dolls. **SIC:** 5092 (Toys & Hobby Goods & Supplies). **Officers:** Betty Johnson, Partner.

■ 26418 ■ The Bingo Company Inc.
700 W Mississippi Ave., Unit 2, Bldg. A
Denver, CO 80223-3172
Phone: (303)744-3332
Free: (800)443-1395 **Fax:** (303)744-1334
Products: Bingo games and supplies. **SIC:** 5092 (Toys & Hobby Goods & Supplies). **Est:** 1984. **Emp:** 30. **Officers:** John Mulligan, President.

■ 26419 ■ Bingo Depot
PO Box 903
Lake Havasu City, AZ 86405-0903
Phone: (907)561-7115 **Fax:** (907)563-4717
Products: Bingo games and supplies. **SIC:** 5092 (Toys & Hobby Goods & Supplies). **Officers:** Pammie Anthony, Owner.

■ 26420 ■ J.D. Bingo Sales Inc.
1500 Kosciuszko Ave.
Bay City, MI 48708-8028
Phone: (517)894-4004
Free: (800)748-0243 **Fax:** (517)894-4896
Products: Bingo games and supplies. **SIC:** 5092 (Toys & Hobby Goods & Supplies). **Est:** 1982. **Emp:** 6. **Officers:** James Dukarski, President.

■ 26421 ■ B.J. Toy Manufacturing Co.
Applegate Ave.
Pen Argyl, PA 18072-1403
Phone: (215)863-9191 **Fax:** (215)863-4847
Products: Stuffed animals. **SIC:** 5092 (Toys & Hobby Goods & Supplies). **Sales:** $1,000,000 (2000). **Emp:** 49. **Officers:** Robert Antonioli.

■ 26422 ■ Blackhawk Distributors
14225 Hansberry Rd.
Rockton, IL 61072
Phone: (815)624-7227
Free: (800)747-4263 **Fax:** (815)624-4701
E-mail: blackhaw@inwave.com
Products: Role-playing and fantasy games. **SIC:** 5092 (Toys & Hobby Goods & Supplies). **Est:** 1978. **Emp:** 4.

■ 26423 ■ Bowser Manufacturing
21 Howard St.
Montoursville, PA 17754
Phone: (717)368-2516 **Fax:** (717)368-5046
Products: Model railroad equipment. **SIC:** 5092 (Toys & Hobby Goods & Supplies).

■ 26424 ■ Bradley Import Co.
1400 N Spring St.
Los Angeles, CA 90012
Phone: (213)221-4162 **Fax:** (213)221-8272
Products: Collectible dolls. **SIC:** 5092 (Toys & Hobby Goods & Supplies). **Est:** 1954. **Sales:** $4,000,000 (2000). **Emp:** 22. **Officers:** Joanne Hartstein, President.

■ 26425 ■ Dan Brechner and Co. Inc.
PO Box 510
Syosset, NY 11791-0510
Phone: (516)437-8400 **Fax:** (516)352-1744
Products: Toys, including stuffed animals; Novelty items; Souvenirs. **SICs:** 5092 (Toys & Hobby Goods & Supplies); 5199 (Nondurable Goods Nec). **Est:** 1935. **Sales:** $8,000,000 (2000). **Emp:** 80. **Officers:** Milton Brechner, President; Clifford Brechner, VP of Marketing.

■ 26426 ■ BRIO Corp.
PO Box 1013
Germantown, WI 53022-8213
Phone: (262)250-3240
Free: (888)274-6869 **Fax:** (262)250-3255
E-mail: info@briotoy.com
URL: http://www.briotoy.com
Products: Toys. **SIC:** 5092 (Toys & Hobby Goods & Supplies). **Est:** 1977. **Sales:** $32,000,000 (1999). **Emp:** 90. **Officers:** Peter F. Reynolds, President; Katrina Dellerti.

■ 26427 ■ Brohman Distributing Co.
333-335 Pam Dr.
Berrien Springs, MI 49103
Phone: (616)471-1111
Free: (800)272-1966 **Fax:** (616)471-7467
Products: Needlework supplies, including punch embroidery, glues, and heat transfer pens. **SIC:** 5092

(Toys & Hobby Goods & Supplies). **Est:** 1976.
Officers: Linda Brohman, Owner.

■ **26428** ■ **J.L. Brown South**
140 Mendel Dr.
Atlanta, GA 30336
Phone: (404)691-9435 **Fax:** (404)699-7771
Products: Plastic and die-cast models, including trains.
SIC: 5092 (Toys & Hobby Goods & Supplies).

■ **26429** ■ **Bud's Hobbies**
2301 N Broadway
Council Bluffs, IA 51503-4333
Phone: (712)322-1378
Products: Toys; Hobby kits; Nonelectronic games.
SIC: 5092 (Toys & Hobby Goods & Supplies).
Officers: Bud Kilnoski, Owner.

■ **26430** ■ **Burda Brothers**
47725 Michigan
Canton, MI 48188
Phone: (734)397-1441 **Free:** (800)548-5683
Products: Toys; Hobby kits; Fireworks. **SIC:** 5092
(Toys & Hobby Goods & Supplies). **Officers:** Efim
Burda.

■ **26431** ■ **William H. Burnham**
1 Main St.
York Beach, ME 03910
Phone: (207)363-4622 **Fax:** (207)363-4622
Products: Toys and hobby goods and supplies; Food;
Recreation goods. **SICs:** 5092 (Toys & Hobby Goods &
Supplies); 5091 (Sporting & Recreational Goods); 5149
(Groceries & Related Products Nec). **Officers:** William
Burnham, Owner.

■ **26432** ■ **C & P Sales Co.**
540 S Main St., Bldg. 121
Akron, OH 44311-1023
Phone: (330)535-1141
Free: (800)252-1293 **Fax:** (330)535-5504
Products: Toys, hobby goods, games, and supplies;
School supplies. **SICs:** 5092 (Toys & Hobby Goods &
Supplies); 5112 (Stationery & Office Supplies). **Est:**
1947. **Sales:** $2,000,000 (2000). **Emp:** 10. **Officers:**
Ronald Piekarski, President.

■ **26433** ■ **California Gift Center Inc.**
1425 S Main St.
Los Angeles, CA 90015
Phone: (213)747-5809 **Fax:** (213)747-0507
Products: Novelty items; Toys; Fashion accessories.
SICs: 5092 (Toys & Hobby Goods & Supplies); 5199
(Nondurable Goods Nec).

■ **26434** ■ **California Hobby Distributors**
415 S Palm Ave.
Alhambra, CA 91803
Phone: (626)289-8857
Free: (800)242-4440 **Fax:** (626)289-3882
Products: Children's toy vehicles. **SIC:** 5092 (Toys &
Hobby Goods & Supplies). **Est:** 1935.

■ **26435** ■ **Calus & CEI Distributors Inc.**
2625 Turf Valley Rd.
Ellicott City, MD 21042
Phone: (410)465-0044 **Fax:** (410)465-0045
Products: Toys; Hobby kits; Electronic games;
Electronic parts. **SICs:** 5092 (Toys & Hobby Goods &
Supplies); 5065 (Electronic Parts & Equipment Nec).
Officers: Karen Nordhoff, President.

■ **26436** ■ **Capcom Entertainment Inc.**
475 Oakmead Pkwy.
Sunnyvale, CA 94086-4709
Phone: (408)774-0500
Products: Video games. **SIC:** 5099 (Durable Goods
Nec). **Officers:** Bill Gardner, President.

■ **26437** ■ **Cardinal Inc.**
1421 Pinewood St.
Rahway, NJ 07065
Phone: (732)388-6160
Free: (800)888-0936 **Fax:** (732)382-8990
E-mail: cardinal.giftware@worldnet.att.net
URL: http://www.cardinal-giftware.com
Products: Minature collectibles, including tabletop,
serveware, decorative accessories, and giftware. **SIC:**
5092 (Toys & Hobby Goods & Supplies). **Est:** 1946.

Sales: $13,000,000 (2000). **Emp:** 28. **Officers:** S.
Darwin, Chairman of the Board; A.C. Darwin,
President; G.R. Darwin, Exec. VP, e-mail: garyd@
cardinal-giftware.com; Nancy Caldwell, Dir. of Data
Processing, e-mail: nancyc@cardinal-giftware.com;
Mike Arlea, Dir of Human Resources; E.S. Cohen, VP
of Sales; R. Skorupski, VP of Merchandise; S.
Sanfillippo, COO & CFO.

■ **26438** ■ **Casper Pay-Less Drug Co.**
PO Box 1252
Casper, WY 82602-1252
Phone: (307)265-1914
Products: Toys; Hobby kits; Nonelectronic games.
SIC: 5092 (Toys & Hobby Goods & Supplies).
Officers: B Mc Manus, President.

■ **26439** ■ **Cee-J Wholesale**
260 E Broadway Ave.
Muskegon Heights, MI 49444-2158
Phones: (616)733-1293 (616)733-1294
Fax: (616)733-1035
Products: Toys and hobby goods and supplies;
General merchandise; Gifts. **SICs:** 5092 (Toys &
Hobby Goods & Supplies); 5199 (Nondurable Goods
Nec). **Est:** 1950. **Officers:** Carl Suchovsky, President.

■ **26440** ■ **Central Valley Oriental Imports**
3209 N Marks
Fresno, CA 93722
Phone: (209)237-7115 **Fax:** (209)237-7115
Products: Toys and hobby goods. **SIC:** 5092 (Toys &
Hobby Goods & Supplies). **Est:** 1983. **Sales:** $400,000
(2000). **Emp:** 5.

■ **26441** ■ **Ceramics By Bob and Hazel**
108 N Saginaw St.
Pontiac, MI 48342-2112
Phone: (248)334-8521
Products: Arts and crafts equipment and supplies.
SICs: 5092 (Toys & Hobby Goods & Supplies); 5199
(Nondurable Goods Nec). **Officers:** Bob Kimpson,
Owner.

■ **26442** ■ **Checkmate International**
1415 E 58th Ave.
Denver, CO 80216
Phone: (303)292-1000 **Fax:** (303)298-8220
Products: Role-playing and fantasy games; Board
games; Puzzles; Casino supplies. **SIC:** 5092 (Toys &
Hobby Goods & Supplies). **Est:** 1986. **Emp:** 4.

■ **26443** ■ **Chulani International**
PO Box 2844
Clifton, NJ 07015
Phone: (973)773-8100
Free: (800)248-5264 **Fax:** (973)777-1018
Products: Electronics and toys. **SIC:** 5092 (Toys &
Hobby Goods & Supplies).

■ **26444** ■ **Cleveland Hobby Supply**
PO Box 33034
Cleveland, OH 44133
Phone: (440)237-3900 **Fax:** (440)237-3902
Products: Model cars, planes, and trains. **SIC:** 5092
(Toys & Hobby Goods & Supplies).

■ **26445** ■ **CM School Supply**
1025 E Orangethorpe Ave.
Anaheim, CA 92801-1135
Phone: (714)680-6681 **Fax:** (714)680-0963
Products: School supplies, including educational
games and activity sets. **SIC:** 5092 (Toys & Hobby
Goods & Supplies). **Officers:** Steve Rajcic, Contact.

■ **26446** ■ **Coins, Cards & Collectibles**
8128 Girard Plz
Omaha, NE 68122-1455
Phone: (402)968-5973 **Fax:** (402)571-1476
E-mail: coindeal@home.net
Products: Collectibles, including comic books, coins,
and stamps; Hobby kits and equipment; Memorabilia.
SIC: 5092 (Toys & Hobby Goods & Supplies). **Est:**
1969. **Sales:** $1,100,000 (2000). **Emp:** 8. **Officers:**
Joanne O'Conner, Owner.

■ **26447** ■ **Combined Sales Co.**
PO Box 3
North Salt Lake, UT 84054
Phone: (801)936-7302 **Fax:** (801)936-7328
Products: Housewares; Toys; Trading cards. **SICs:**
5092 (Toys & Hobby Goods & Supplies); 5023
(Homefurnishings). **Est:** 1982. **Officers:** Tom Philibin,
President.

■ **26448** ■ **Comics Hawaii Distributors**
4420 Lawehana St., Apt. 3
Honolulu, HI 96818
Phone: (808)423-0265
Products: Role-playing and fantasy games. **SIC:** 5092
(Toys & Hobby Goods & Supplies).

■ **26449** ■ **Comics Unlimited**
28 Yacht Club Cv
Staten Island, NY 10308-3531
Phone: (718)948-2223 **Fax:** (718)356-1173
Products: Role-playing and fantasy games; Comic
books. **SIC:** 5092 (Toys & Hobby Goods & Supplies).
Est: 1975.

■ **26450** ■ **Country Decor**
1107 S Military Hwy. B
Chesapeake, VA 23320-2343
Phone: (757)420-8236 **Fax:** (757)523-0065
Products: Toys; Hobby kits; Craft kits. **SIC:** 5092
(Toys & Hobby Goods & Supplies). **Officers:** W
Boyette, Partner.

■ **26451** ■ **Cousin Corporation of America**
12333 Enterprise Blvd.
PO Box 2939
Largo, FL 33779
Phone: (813)536-3568 **Free:** (800)366-2687
Products: Craft kits; Jewelry; Beads. **SICs:** 5199
(Nondurable Goods Nec); 5092 (Toys & Hobby Goods
& Supplies); 5094 (Jewelry & Precious Stones). **Est:**
1975. **Emp:** 155. **Officers:** Michael Cousin.

■ **26452** ■ **Craft Corner**
719 Main St.
Caldwell, ID 83605-3745
Phone: (208)454-2351 **Fax:** (208)459-6897
Products: Toys and hobby goods and supplies; Arts
and crafts equipment and supplies. **SICs:** 5092 (Toys &
Hobby Goods & Supplies); 5199 (Nondurable Goods
Nec). **Officers:** Dave McKay, Owner.

■ **26453** ■ **Craft Enterprises**
810 W Picacho Ave.
Las Cruces, NM 88005-2236
Phone: (505)527-1470 **Fax:** (505)527-1470
Products: Toys and hobby goods and supplies; Arts
and crafts equipment and supplies. **SICs:** 5092 (Toys &
Hobby Goods & Supplies); 5199 (Nondurable Goods
Nec). **Officers:** Carl Erwin, Owner.

■ **26454** ■ **CTT Distributing**
109 Medallion Ctr.
Dallas, TX 75214
Phone: (214)373-9469
Free: (800)462-4902 **Fax:** (214)373-1622
Products: Model trains and toys. **SIC:** 5092 (Toys &
Hobby Goods & Supplies).

■ **26455** ■ **Curtis Associates Inc.**
PO Box 67171
Chestnut Hill, MA 02467-0002
Phone: (781)455-9191
E-mail: info@curtiscorp.com
URL: http://www.curtiscorp.com
Products: Toys; Hobby kits; Nonelectric games; Gifts.
SICs: 5092 (Toys & Hobby Goods & Supplies); 5023
(Homefurnishings). **Est:** 1986. **Officers:** Robert Curtis,
Owner.

■ **26456** ■ **CX Blaster Co. Inc.**
13218 Jessica Dr.
Spring Hill, FL 34609
Phones: (352)683-4862 800-441-1047
Free: (800)441-1047 **Fax:** (352)683-6821
Products: Sling shots for water balloons. **SIC:** 5092
(Toys & Hobby Goods & Supplies).

■ **26457** ■ **D & D Distributing**
14615 C St. S
Tacoma, WA 98444-4571
Phone: (253)536-2236 **Fax:** (253)536-9513
Products: Toys; Earrings; Sunglasses. **SICs:** 5092
(Toys & Hobby Goods & Supplies); 5048 (Ophthalmic
Goods); 5094 (Jewelry & Precious Stones). **Est:** 1982.
Emp: 15. **Officers:** Kevin Damrau, President.

■ **26458** ■ **A. Daigger and Company Inc.**
ETA/Cuisenaire
500 Greenview Ct.
Vernon Hills, IL 60061
Phone: (847)816-5050
Free: (800)445-5985 **Fax:** (847)816-5066
E-mail: mail@etacuisenaire
URL: http://www.etacuisenaire.com
Products: Educational toys. **SIC:** 5092 (Toys & Hobby
Goods & Supplies). **Est:** 1936. **Former Name:** A.
Daigger and Company Inc. Educational Teaching Aids.

■ **26459** ■ **Dakin Inc.**
230 Spring St. NW, Ste. 1810A
Atlanta, GA 30303
Phone: (404)584-7424 **Fax:** (404)681-9373
Products: Stuffed animals. **SIC:** 5092 (Toys & Hobby
Goods & Supplies). **Emp:** 49.

■ **26460** ■ **Dakin Inc.**
6101 Variel Ave.
Woodland Hills, CA 91365
Phone: (818)992-6000 **Free:** (800)777-6990
E-mail: dakin@applause.com
URL: http://www.applause.com
Products: Plush toys; Home decor items; Collectibles.
SIC: 5092 (Toys & Hobby Goods & Supplies). **Est:**
1955. **Sales:** $80,000,000 (2000). **Emp:** 350. **Officers:**
Jonathan Mather, CEO & President; Kevin Murray,
CFO.

■ **26461** ■ **Daylight Distributors**
4411 Sepulveda Blvd.
Culver City, CA 90230
Phone: (310)313-9370 **Fax:** (310)313-9365
Products: Model trains; Toys; Scale models. **SIC:**
5092 (Toys & Hobby Goods & Supplies). **Est:** 1981.
Sales: $4,500,000 (1999). **Emp:** 15. **Officers:** Allen
Drucker, Owner.

■ **26462** ■ **Dearing Wholesale Inc.**
366 Gay Pl.
Jackson, OH 45640
Phone: (740)286-1046
Products: Toys and hobby goods and supplies. **SIC:**
5092 (Toys & Hobby Goods & Supplies). **Officers:**
John Dearing, President.

■ **26463** ■ **Dee's Delights, Inc.**
3150 State Line Rd.
North Bend, OH 45052
Phone: (513)353-3390
Free: (800)543-1834 **Fax:** (513)353-3933
E-mail: dees@one.net
URL: http://www.deesdelights.com
Products: Dollhouses and miniatures. **SIC:** 5092 (Toys
& Hobby Goods & Supplies). **Est:** 1969. **Emp:** 38.
Officers: Jerry W. Hacker, President.

■ **26464** ■ **Delta Technical Coatings Inc.**
2550 Pellissier Pl
Whittier, CA 90601
Phone: (562)695-7969 **Fax:** (562)695-5157
Products: Arts and crafts paints and allied products.
SIC: 5092 (Toys & Hobby Goods & Supplies).
Officers: Ronald LaRosa, President.

■ **26465** ■ **Dentt Inc.**
4171 Marquis Way
Salt Lake City, UT 84124
Phone: (801)277-7056 **Fax:** (801)967-1709
E-mail: hammond@hammondtoy.com
URL: http://www.hammondtoy.com
Products: Toys and hobby supplies; Computer
software; Hats; T-shirts. **SICs:** 5092 (Toys & Hobby
Goods & Supplies); 5045 (Computers, Peripherals &
Software); 5136 (Men's/Boys' Clothing); 5137
(Women's/Children's Clothing). **Est:** 1957. **Sales:**
$1,500,000 (2000). **Emp:** 28. **Officers:** Gale
Hammond, President; Paul Hammond, Dir. of

Marketing & Sales; Paul Hammond, Dir. of Marketing &
Sales.

■ **26466** ■ **Dentt, Inc.**
1088 Fort Union Blvd.
Midvale, UT 84047
Phone: (801)561-3821 **Fax:** (801)967-1709
URL: http://www.hammondtoy.com
Products: Role-playing and fantasy games; Toys and
hobby supplies. **SIC:** 5092 (Toys & Hobby Goods &
Supplies). **Est:** 1957. **Sales:** $1,500,000 (2000). **Emp:**
3. **Officers:** David Hommond, e-mail: davidh@
hammondtoy.com.

■ **26467** ■ **Designers Ltd.**
PO Box 1046
Meredith, NH 03253-1046
Phone: (603)279-8692 **Fax:** (603)279-5470
Products: Toys and hobby goods. **SIC:** 5092 (Toys &
Hobby Goods & Supplies). **Sales:** $100,000 (2000).
Emp: 2.

■ **26468** ■ **Diamond Comic Distributors Inc.**
1966 Greenspring Dr., Ste. 300
Timonium, MD 21093
Phone: (410)560-7100
Free: (800)452-6642 **Fax:** (410)560-7148
E-mail: service@diamondcomics.com
URL: http://www.diamondcomics.com
Products: Books, including trade paperback, graphic
novels, and comics; Trading cards; Role-playing and
fantasy games; Videos; Toys; Apparel; Models. **SICs:**
5092 (Toys & Hobby Goods & Supplies); 5136
(Men's/Boys' Clothing); 5192 (Books, Periodicals &
Newspapers). **Est:** 1982. **Sales:** $220,000,000 (1999).
Emp: 500. **Officers:** Steve Geppi, CEO & President;
Chuck Parker, Exec. VP & COO; Larry Swanson, VP of
Finance; Roger Fletcher, Sales & Marketing Contact, e-
mail: froger@diamondcomics.com; Roger Fletcher, VP
of Marketing; Bill Neuhaus, Customer Service & Sales
Dir.

■ **26469** ■ **Different Drummer**
RR1 Box 3509
Solon, ME 04979
Phone: (207)643-2572 **Fax:** (207)643-2572
E-mail: diffdrum@kynd.net
Products: Toys; Nonelectronic games; Hobby kits.
SIC: 5092 (Toys & Hobby Goods & Supplies). **Est:**
1973. **Sales:** $60,000 (2000). **Emp:** 3. **Officers:**
Marylou Ridley, Owner.

■ **26470** ■ **Direct Connect International Inc.**
266 Harristown Rd., Ste. 108
Glen Rock, NJ 07452
Phone: (201)445-2101
Products: Toys. **SIC:** 5092 (Toys & Hobby Goods &
Supplies). **Sales:** $500,000 (2000). **Emp:** 6. **Officers:**
Peter L. Schneider, President; Barry A. Rosner, VP &
Treasurer.

■ **26471** ■ **Discovery Toys Inc.**
6400 Brisa St.
Livermore, CA 94550
Phone: (925)606-2600 **Fax:** (925)447-0626
URL: http://www.discoverytoysinc.com
Products: Educational toys, books, games, and
puzzles. **SICs:** 5092 (Toys & Hobby Goods &
Supplies); 5192 (Books, Periodicals & Newspapers).
Est: 1978. **Sales:** $93,000,000 (2000). **Emp:** 100.
Officers: Tom Zimmer, President; Juan Santa Cruz,
Controller; Cathy Adams, VP of Marketing; Janice
Mazibrook, VP of Sales; Susan McCarthy, Vice
President.

■ **26472** ■ **Do-My Ceramics**
PO Box 36
North Ferrisburg, VT 05473-0036
Phone: (802)425-2181
Products: Toys; Hobby kits; Craft kits; Ceramics. **SIC:**
5092 (Toys & Hobby Goods & Supplies). **Officers:**
Dorothy Myers, Owner.

■ **26473** ■ **Dolls By Jerri**
651 Anderson St.
Charlotte, NC 28205
Phone: (704)333-3211
Free: (800)248-2188 **Fax:** (704)333-7706
Products: Dolls. **SIC:** 5092 (Toys & Hobby Goods &
Supplies). **Emp:** 30.

■ **26474** ■ **Douglas Model Distributors**
2065 East 3300 South
Salt Lake City, UT 84109-2630
Phone: (801)487-7752
E-mail: douglasmodels@earthlink.net
Products: Radio-control, plastic or wooden model
airplanes, cars, ships, electric trains; flying model
rockets; and mini-tools and paints. **SIC:** 5092 (Toys &
Hobby Goods & Supplies). **Est:** 1934. **Sales:**
$3,000,000 (1999). **Emp:** 12.

■ **26475** ■ **Eaglecrafts Inc.**
168 W 12th St.
Ogden, UT 84404-5501
Phone: (801)393-3991
Free: (800)547-3364 **Fax:** (801)745-0903
E-mail: eglcrafts@aol.com
Products: Beading and Native American craft
supplies; Books and gifts about Native Americans,
Mountain Men, the fur trade, and frontier history. **SICs:**
5092 (Toys & Hobby Goods & Supplies); 5192 (Books,
Periodicals & Newspapers). **Est:** 1977. **Emp:** 8.
Officers: Sue Smith, Sales/Marketing Contact.

■ **26476** ■ **Educational Coin Co.**
PO Box 3815
Kingston, NY 12401
Phone: (914)338-4871
Products: Bank notes and coins. **SICs:** 5199
(Nondurable Goods Nec); 5094 (Jewelry & Precious
Stones). **Est:** 1980. **Sales:** $1,000,000 (2000). **Emp:** 9.
Officers: John Aiello, President; David Waties,
Treasurer.

■ **26477** ■ **Emery Distributors**
3800 Glover Rd.
Easton, PA 18042
Phone: (215)258-3651 **Fax:** (215)258-7736
Products: Hobby products, including model trains.
SIC: 5092 (Toys & Hobby Goods & Supplies).

■ **26478** ■ **Esco Imports of Texas Inc.**
1946 Shipman Dr.
San Antonio, TX 78219
Phone: (210)271-7794
Free: (800)445-3836 **Fax:** (210)223-1547
E-mail: esco@express-news.net
Products: Toys; Novelties. **SIC:** 5092 (Toys & Hobby
Goods & Supplies). **Est:** 1969. **Sales:** $5,000,000
(2000). **Emp:** 12. **Officers:** Robert Steinfeld, President.

■ **26479** ■ **E.T.S. Distributing**
209 Bellefonte Ave.
Lock Haven, PA 17745
Phone: (717)748-8419 **Fax:** (717)748-7532
Products: Electronic toys. **SIC:** 5092 (Toys & Hobby
Goods & Supplies).

■ **26480** ■ **Evers Toy Store Inc.**
204 1st Ave. E, Box 241
Dyersville, IA 52040-0241
Phone: (319)875-2438
Free: (800)962-9481 **Fax:** (319)875-2673
URL: http://www.everstore.com
Products: Toys; Hobby kits; Die cast replicas. **SIC:**
5092 (Toys & Hobby Goods & Supplies). **Est:** 1978.
Officers: Gary Evers, President.

■ **26481** ■ **F & S Co. Inc.**
4500 Tower Rd. SW
Albuquerque, NM 87121-3424
Phone: (505)247-1451 **Fax:** (505)247-1453
Products: Toys; Hobby goods and supplies; Toy
novelties; Fireworks. **SIC:** 5092 (Toys & Hobby Goods
& Supplies). **Officers:** Kenneth Delfeld, President.

■ **26482** ■ **Flash Fireworks**
RR 2, Box 102
St. Francis, KS 67756-9543
Phone: (785)734-2464 **Fax:** (785)734-2772
Products: Gifts and novelties; Fireworks. **SICs:** 5092

(Toys & Hobby Goods & Supplies); 5199 (Nondurable Goods Nec). **Officers:** Gary Lillich, Owner.

■ **26483** ■ **Flexible Flyer Co.**
PO Box 1296
West Point, MS 39773
Phone: (601)494-4732 **Fax:** (601)494-8456
E-mail: postoffice@flexible.flyer.com
Products: Toys; Swing sets; Plastic toys for lawns; Hobby horses; Trampolines; Fitness equipment; Seasonal decorations. **SICs:** 5092 (Toys & Hobby Goods & Supplies); 5199 (Nondurable Goods Nec). **Sales:** $55,000,000 (2000). **Emp:** 300. **Officers:** Timothy Voss, President; Charles Dismuke, CFO; Chuck Bookstaver, VP of Marketing; Mike Whitley, VP of Sales & Fitness.

■ **26484** ■ **Florida Craft Wholesale**
PO Box 3026
Weaverville, CA 96093-3026
Phone: (530)845-1822
Products: Arts and crafts books; Craft kits; Artists' equipment. **SICs:** 5092 (Toys & Hobby Goods & Supplies); 5192 (Books, Periodicals & Newspapers); 5199 (Nondurable Goods Nec).

■ **26485** ■ **Flying Phoenix Corp.**
PO Box 31
Riverton, WY 82501-0031
Phone: (307)856-0778 **Fax:** (307)856-3336
Products: Explosives. **SIC:** 5092 (Toys & Hobby Goods & Supplies). **Sales:** $2,000,000 (2000). **Emp:** 212.

■ **26486** ■ **Franco Distributing Co. Inc.**
PO Box 927
Montgomery, AL 36102-0927
Phone: (205)834-3455 **Fax:** (205)264-9466
Products: Video games. **SIC:** 5092 (Toys & Hobby Goods & Supplies). **Officers:** Rubin Franco, President.

■ **26487** ■ **Ben Franklin Stores Inc.**
PO Box 5938
Chicago, IL 60680
Phone: (630)462-6100 **Fax:** (630)690-1356
Products: Craft supplies; General merchandise. **SICs:** 5199 (Nondurable Goods Nec); 5092 (Toys & Hobby Goods & Supplies). **Est:** 1877. **Sales:** $340,000,000 (2000). **Emp:** 1,000. **Officers:** Dale D. Ward, CEO & President; John B. Menzer, Exec. VP & CFO; William Lorbaski, VP of Admin. & Development; Larry Bonine, Dir. of Data Processing; James Bouley, Human Resources Mgr.

■ **26488** ■ **FVB Enterprises, Inc.**
PO Box 126
Magnolia, NJ 08049
Phone: (609)435-1555
Products: Role-playing and fantasy games. **SIC:** 5092 (Toys & Hobby Goods & Supplies). **Doing Business As:** Stevens International.

■ **26489** ■ **Galan Enterprises, Inc.**
2740 W Windrose Dr.
Phoenix, AZ 85029
Phone: (602)993-3000 **Fax:** (602)993-3377
E-mail: reg@Galan.org
URL: http://www.Galan.org
Products: Toys, gifts, and novelties; Clocks; Lamps. **SICs:** 5092 (Toys & Hobby Goods & Supplies); 5199 (Nondurable Goods Nec). **Est:** 1985. **Emp:** 10. **Officers:** Robert Galan, President.

■ **26490** ■ **Gamblers General Store Inc.**
500 S Main St.
Las Vegas, NV 89101-6369
Phone: (702)382-9903
Free: (800)322-2447 **Fax:** (702)366-0329
E-mail: ggs@fiax.net
URL: http://www.ggss.com
Products: Casino supplies, including slot machines and casino chips. **SIC:** 5092 (Toys & Hobby Goods & Supplies). **Est:** 1937. **Officers:** Don Jarchow, President.

■ **26491** ■ **Games of Tennessee**
1220 W Jackson St.
Shelbyville, TN 37160
Phone: (931)684-0100
Free: (800)456-6882 **Fax:** (931)685-0144
Products: Board games. **SIC:** 5092 (Toys & Hobby Goods & Supplies). **Sales:** $3,000,000 (2000). **Emp:** 49. **Officers:** Leslie Warren.

■ **26492** ■ **Games Unlimited**
2115 Murray Ave.
Pittsburgh, PA 15217
Phone: (412)421-8807
Products: Role-playing and fantasy games. **SIC:** 5092 (Toys & Hobby Goods & Supplies).

■ **26493** ■ **Gametree Inc.**
PO Box 6532
Boise, ID 83707-6532
Phone: (208)342-8281
Products: Toys; Hobby kits; Nonelectronic games. **SIC:** 5092 (Toys & Hobby Goods & Supplies). **Officers:** Mike Flynn, President.

■ **26494** ■ **E.C. Gann Company Inc.**
1621 196th Pl. SW
Lynnwood, WA 98036-7140
Phone: (425)774-4529 **Fax:** (425)774-4529
E-mail: wonderful_whitey@webtv.net
Products: Toys; Groceries; Wheelchairs; Kitchen utensils. **SICs:** 5092 (Toys & Hobby Goods & Supplies); 5047 (Medical & Hospital Equipment); 5141 (Groceries—General Line). **Est:** 1969. **Sales:** $3,000,000 (2000). **Emp:** 2. **Officers:** Frieda Gann, Treasurer; E.C. Gann, Owner.

■ **26495** ■ **Gayla Industries Inc.**
PO Box 920800
Houston, TX 77292
Phone: (713)681-2411
Free: (800)231-7508 **Fax:** (713)682-1357
E-mail: gayla@gaylainc.com
URL: http://www.gaylainc.com
Products: Kites; Balloons. **SIC:** 5092 (Toys & Hobby Goods & Supplies). **Sales:** $6,000,000 (2000). **Emp:** 499. **Officers:** D. Phillips, President.

■ **26496** ■ **General Sales Co.**
15-17-19 E Court St.
Cincinnati, OH 45202
Phone: (513)621-2075 **Fax:** (513)621-2075
Products: Toys, hobby goods, supplies, and games, including Bingo; Advertising specialties. **SICs:** 5092 (Toys & Hobby Goods & Supplies); 5199 (Nondurable Goods Nec). **Officers:** Irvin Solomon, Owner.

■ **26497** ■ **General Toys of Los Angeles**
522 E 4th St.
Los Angeles, CA 90013
Phone: (213)687-4929
Products: Toys. **SIC:** 5092 (Toys & Hobby Goods & Supplies). **Sales:** $4,000,000 (2000). **Emp:** 3. **Officers:** Sandy Lee, President.

■ **26498** ■ **Geo-Hex**
2126 N Lewis Ave. 2
Portland, OR 97227-1708
Phone: (503)288-4805 **Fax:** (503)288-8992
Products: Hobby goods and supplies. **SIC:** 5092 (Toys & Hobby Goods & Supplies). **Officers:** Cieran Bohan, Owner.

■ **26499** ■ **Georgies Ceramic & Clay Co.**
756 NE Lombard St.
Portland, OR 97211-3562
Phone: (503)283-1353 **Fax:** (503)283-1387
Products: Toys, hobby goods, and supplies; Arts and crafts equipment and supplies; Clay and ceramic supplies for air-conditioning systems. **SICs:** 5092 (Toys & Hobby Goods & Supplies); 5032 (Brick, Stone & Related Materials); 5199 (Nondurable Goods Nec). **Officers:** Stanley Tonneson, President.

■ **26500** ■ **Global Products**
PO Box 93
Winterset, IA 50273
Phone: (515)462-3186 **Fax:** (515)462-9871
Products: Craft items. **SIC:** 5199 (Nondurable Goods Nec). **Est:** 1989. **Emp:** 121. **Officers:** Ray Raymond,

President. **Former Name:** Proteus International Trading Co.

■ **26501** ■ **Go Fly A Kite Inc.**
PO Box AA
East Haddam, CT 06423
Phone: (860)873-8675 **Fax:** (860)873-8724
Products: Kites; Wind socks. **SIC:** 5092 (Toys & Hobby Goods & Supplies). **Est:** 1960. **Sales:** $6,000,000 (2000). **Emp:** 82. **Officers:** A. Skwarek, President; M. Skwarek, VP of Finance.

■ **26502** ■ **Carl Goldberg Models Inc.**
4734 W Chicago
Chicago, IL 60651-3322
Phone: (773)626-9550 **Fax:** (773)626-9566
Products: Model airplanes. **SIC:** 5092 (Toys & Hobby Goods & Supplies). **Sales:** $6,000,000 (1999). **Emp:** 65. **Officers:** Miles Thomson.

■ **26503** ■ **Golden State Models**
21050 Questhaven Rd.
Escondido, CA 92029
Phone: (760)744-7523 **Fax:** (760)727-3007
Products: Model trains. **SIC:** 5092 (Toys & Hobby Goods & Supplies).

■ **26504** ■ **Arthur J. Gonsalves Inc.**
165 Main St.
North Reading, MA 01864
Phone: (508)644-1988
Products: Toys and hobby goods. **SIC:** 5092 (Toys & Hobby Goods & Supplies). **Est:** 1929.

■ **26505** ■ **Great Lakes Area Distributing**
PO Box 599
Bay City, MI 48707
Phone: (517)892-9042 **Fax:** (517)892-9142
Products: Toys and hobby goods and supplies; Seasonal novelties. **SICs:** 5092 (Toys & Hobby Goods & Supplies); 5199 (Nondurable Goods Nec). **Est:** 1987. **Sales:** $160,000 (2000). **Emp:** 6. **Officers:** Doug Adams, President, e-mail: dadams6097@aol.com. **Doing Business As:** D-MAR Corp.

■ **26506** ■ **Great Planes Model Distributors Co.**
1608 Interstate Dr.
Champaign, IL 61821
Phone: (217)398-6300
Products: Model airplanes. **SIC:** 5092 (Toys & Hobby Goods & Supplies). **Sales:** $282,000,000 (2000). **Emp:** 750. **Officers:** Wayne Hemming, President.

■ **26507** ■ **H and H Sales Inc.**
RR 4, Box 36
Thief River Falls, MN 56701-9007
Phone: (218)681-1788
Products: Toys; Hobby kits; Nonelectronic games. **SIC:** 5092 (Toys & Hobby Goods & Supplies). **Officers:** Ron Hamre, President.

■ **26508** ■ **Hall Balloon Co.**
2610 W 6th Ave.
Pine Bluff, AR 71601-3796
Phone: (870)535-0426
Products: Hobby kits; Rubber balloons. **SIC:** 5092 (Toys & Hobby Goods & Supplies). **Officers:** Homer Hall, President.

■ **26509** ■ **Robert J. Hall Enterprises**
2881 Heckman Rd.
Uniontown, OH 44685-9003
Phone: (330)699-6155
Products: Toys and hobby goods and supplies, including bingo. **SIC:** 5092 (Toys & Hobby Goods & Supplies). **Officers:** Robert Hall, President.

■ **26510** ■ **Hallmark Models, Inc.**
4822 Bryan St.
Dallas, TX 75204
Phone: (214)821-2550 **Fax:** (214)824-2101
E-mail: bobbyehall@aol.com
URL: http://www.hallmarkmodels.com
Products: Model railroads and airplanes. **SIC:** 5092 (Toys & Hobby Goods & Supplies). **Est:** 1946. **Emp:** 8.

■ **26511** ■ **Hankes Crafts**
215 N Galbraith
Box 6
Blue Earth, MN 56013-1964
Phone: (507)526-3110 **Fax:** (507)526-5969
E-mail: rhanke@bevcomm.net
URL: http://www.netins.net/showcase/novacon/
dollhouse/hankpenk.htm
Products: Craft kits; Arts and crafts books;
Needlework patterns; Miniature flower patterns: Paper
punches. **SICs:** 5092 (Toys & Hobby Goods &
Supplies); 5199 (Nondurable Goods Nec). **Est:** 1979.
Emp: 2. **Officers:** Ruth Hanke.

■ **26512** ■ **Hauler & Wade Associates Inc.**
PO Box 868
Mentor, OH 44061-0868
Phone: (440)951-7155 **Fax:** (440)255-5571
Products: Toys; Hobby kits; Nonelectronic games.
SIC: 5092 (Toys & Hobby Goods & Supplies).
Officers: Jeffrey Wade, President.

■ **26513** ■ **Hays Distributing Corp.**
1461 Elliott Ave. W
Seattle, WA 98119-3176
Phone: (206)284-7004 **Fax:** (206)284-7006
Products: Toys, games, hobby goods, and supplies.
SIC: 5092 (Toys & Hobby Goods & Supplies).
Officers: Arthur Hays, President.

■ **26514** ■ **Herr's and Bernat Inc.**
70 Eastgate Dr.
Danville, IL 61832
Phone: (217)442-4121 **Fax:** (217)442-4191
Products: Arts and crafts material. **SIC:** 5092 (Toys &
Hobby Goods & Supplies). **Est:** 1979. **Sales:**
$32,000,000 (2000). **Emp:** 85. **Officers:** Ken Cutler,
President; Steve Ford, Controller.

■ **26515** ■ **Ho Imports, Inc.**
3663 14 Mile Rd.
Cedar Springs, MI 49319-9418
Phone: (616)696-3080 **Fax:** (616)696-1306
Products: Tarpaulins and other covers; Ceramics.
SICs: 5092 (Toys & Hobby Goods & Supplies); 5085
(Industrial Supplies). **Officers:** Stella Pease, Owner.

■ **26516** ■ **Hobbies of Huntsville**
Book Villa
1207 Countess Rd. NE
Huntsville, AL 35810-6337
Phone: (205)881-3910
Products: Role-playing and fantasy games. **SIC:** 5092
(Toys & Hobby Goods & Supplies).

■ **26517** ■ **Hobby Crafts**
24 Eugene ONeill Dr.
New London, CT 06320
Phone: (860)447-0315 **Fax:** (860)437-3215
Products: Art and craft supplies, including lead pencils
and crayons; artist materials. **SICs:** 5092 (Toys &
Hobby Goods & Supplies); 5199 (Nondurable Goods
Nec). **Est:** 1968. **Emp:** 7. **Officers:** Don Lumadue,
President & Treasurer; Joyce Lumadue, VP & Secty.

■ **26518** ■ **Hobby House Inc.**
7407 Avon Ln.
Chesterland, OH 44026-2901
Phone: (216)781-3210 **Fax:** (216)781-7366
Products: Hobby goods and supplies, including trains
and plastic models. **SIC:** 5092 (Toys & Hobby Goods &
Supplies). **Officers:** Wallace Jeffery, President.

■ **26519** ■ **Hobby Lobby International Inc.**
5614 Franklin Pike Cir.
Brentwood, TN 37027-4324
Phone: (615)373-1444 **Fax:** (615)377-6948
Products: Toys and hobby goods. **SIC:** 5092 (Toys &
Hobby Goods & Supplies). **Est:** 1963.

■ **26520** ■ **Hobby Stores Distributing Inc.**
333 Park Ave.
East Hartford, CT 06108
Phone: (860)282-7080
Free: (800)289-4000 **Fax:** (860)282-1820
Products: Hobby kits. **SIC:** 5092 (Toys & Hobby
Goods & Supplies). **Est:** 1980. **Emp:** 60. **Officers:**
Howard Chaet, President.

■ **26521** ■ **HobbyGame Distributors Inc.**
2433 W Sherwin Ave.
Chicago, IL 60645-1427
Phone: (847)674-5075 **Free:** (800)621-6419
Products: Role-playing and fantasy games. **SIC:** 5092
(Toys & Hobby Goods & Supplies).

■ **26522** ■ **Hobbyquest Marketing**
62 White St.
Red Bank, NJ 07701
Phone: (732)842-6082
Products: Role-playing and fantasy games. **SIC:** 5092
(Toys & Hobby Goods & Supplies).

■ **26523** ■ **Hobbytyme Distributors**
64 C Oakland Ave.
East Hartford, CT 06108
Phone: (860)528-9854 **Fax:** (860)291-9814
Products: Hobby products. **SIC:** 5092 (Toys & Hobby
Goods & Supplies).

■ **26524** ■ **Hollandia Gift and Toy Co.**
PO Box 549
Princess Anne, MD 21853-0340
Phone: (410)651-3818 **Fax:** (410)651-3742
Products: Toys; Gifts and novelties. **SICs:** 5092 (Toys
& Hobby Goods & Supplies); 5199 (Nondurable Goods
Nec). **Officers:** Robert Richardson, President.

■ **26525** ■ **Hot Products, Inc.com**
7625 E Redfield Rd.
Scottsdale, AZ 85260
Phone: (480)368-9490
Free: (888)617-6863 **Fax:** (480)607-6801
E-mail: sales@hotproductsinc.com
URL: http://www.hotproductsinc.com
Products: Interactive nuon game controllers; Road
emergency and outdoor survival products. **SIC:** 5045
(Computers, Peripherals & Software). **Est:** 1992.
Sales: $4,000,000 (2000). **Emp:** 8. **Officers:** James L.
Copland, CEO, President & Treasurer; Ricky S.
Greenberg, Dir. of Finance. **Former Name:** SC and T
International Inc.

■ **26526** ■ **Hoven Inc.**
Thompson Center
6015 Benjamin Rd., 332
Tampa, FL 33634
Phone: (813)886-9328
Free: (800)666-9328 **Fax:** (813)889-9785
Products: Novelties and gift items, including toys.
SICs: 5092 (Toys & Hobby Goods & Supplies); 5199
(Nondurable Goods Nec). **Est:** 1989.

■ **26527** ■ **H.O.W. Train Distribution**
400 Industrial Dr.
Omro, WI 54963
Phone: (920)685-2200 **Fax:** (920)235-6900
Products: Model trains. **SIC:** 5092 (Toys & Hobby
Goods & Supplies). **Est:** 1974. **Emp:** 5. **Officers:**
Dennis F.E. Frey.

■ **26528** ■ **R.B. Howell Co.**
6030 NE 112th Ave.
Portland, OR 97220-1012
Phone: (503)227-3125 **Fax:** (503)227-6959
Products: Craft kits; Home furnishings. **SICs:** 5092
(Toys & Hobby Goods & Supplies); 5023
(Homefurnishings). **Sales:** $5,000,000 (2000). **Emp:**
12. **Officers:** David Howell, President.

■ **26529** ■ **Hungates Inc.**
102 Hungate Dr.
Greenville, NC 27858-8045
Phone: (919)756-9565 **Fax:** (919)756-2397
Products: Toys; Hobby kits; Craft kits. **SIC:** 5092
(Toys & Hobby Goods & Supplies). **Officers:** R.
Hungate, President.

■ **26530** ■ **Hunt Co.**
4883 Powderhorn Ln
Westerville, OH 43081-4427
Phone: (614)891-7089
Products: Toys and hobby goods and supplies; Arts
and crafts equipment and supplies. **SICs:** 5092 (Toys &
Hobby Goods & Supplies); 5199 (Nondurable Goods
Nec). **Officers:** Jane Hunt, Owner.

■ **26531** ■ **Imperial Display Co.**
1049 Main St.
Wheeling, WV 26003-2704
Phone: (304)233-0711
Free: (800)947-9701 **Fax:** (304)233-9424
Products: Toys; Hobby kits; School supplies;
Christmas tree ornaments and decorations. **SICs:** 5092
(Toys & Hobby Goods & Supplies); 5112 (Stationery &
Office Supplies); 5199 (Nondurable Goods Nec). **Est:**
1959. **Sales:** $1,500,000 (2000). **Emp:** 50. **Officers:**
Jack Mendelson, President.

■ **26532** ■ **Imperial Toy Corp.**
2060 E 7th St.
Los Angeles, CA 90021
Phone: (213)489-2100 **Fax:** (213)489-4467
Products: Toys. **SIC:** 5092 (Toys & Hobby Goods &
Supplies). **Est:** 1961. **Sales:** $60,000,000 (2000).
Emp: 135. **Officers:** Fred Kort, CEO & President;
Chuck Augello, VP of Finance; David Kort, Vice
President.

■ **26533** ■ **Innoland Inc.**
11166 Downs Rd.
Pineville, NC 28134-8445
Phone: (704)588-0519 **Fax:** (704)588-0599
E-mail: innoln@aol.com
Products: Toys and games. **SIC:** 5092 (Toys & Hobby
Goods & Supplies). **Est:** 1984. **Sales:** $5,000,000
(2000). **Emp:** 10. **Officers:** Ting Liu, President.

■ **26534** ■ **Institute for Childhood Resources**
268 Bush St.
San Francisco, CA 94104
Phone: (415)864-1169
Free: (800)551-8697 **Fax:** (510)540-0171
Products: Toys and hobby goods. **SIC:** 5092 (Toys &
Hobby Goods & Supplies). **Est:** 1975.

■ **26535** ■ **International Playthings Inc.**
75 Lackawanna Ave.
Parsippany, NJ 07054-1078
Phone: (201)831-1400 **Fax:** (201)831-8643
Products: Magazines; Children's toys. **SICs:** 5092
(Toys & Hobby Goods & Supplies); 5192 (Books,
Periodicals & Newspapers). **Est:** 1968. **Sales:**
$23,000,000 (2000). **Emp:** 40. **Officers:** Ted
Kiesewetter, President.

■ **26536** ■ **Interstate Bingo Supplies Inc.**
RR 1 Box 28
Jamaica, VT 05343-9701
Phone: (802)874-4269
Products: Toys and hobby goods and supplies; Bingo
games and supplies. **SIC:** 5092 (Toys & Hobby Goods
& Supplies). **Officers:** Robert Brown, President.

■ **26537** ■ **Intromark Inc.**
217 9th St.
Pittsburgh, PA 15222
Phone: (412)238-1300
Free: (800)851-6030 **Fax:** (412)338-0497
Products: Toys and hobby goods. **SIC:** 5092 (Toys &
Hobby Goods & Supplies). **Sales:** $100,000 (2000).
Emp: 12.

■ **26538** ■ **J & M Wholesale Distributors**
70 1/2 Commonwealth Ave.
Bristol, VA 24201
Phone: (540)669-4833
Products: Arts and crafts supplies. **SIC:** 5092 (Toys &
Hobby Goods & Supplies).

■ **26539** ■ **Philip Jagoe**
1536 Main Rd.
Tiverton, RI 02878-4417
Phone: (401)624-9792
Products: Toys and hobby goods and supplies. **SIC:**
5092 (Toys & Hobby Goods & Supplies). **Officers:**
Philip Jagoe, Owner.

■ **26540** ■ **James Industries Inc.**
PO Box 407
Hollidaysburg, PA 16648
Phone: (814)695-5681 **Fax:** (814)695-5686
URL: http://www.slinkytoys.com
Products: Toys. **SIC:** 5092 (Toys & Hobby Goods &
Supplies). **Est:** 1945. **Emp:** 60. **Officers:** Ray
Dallanjeccaia Jr.

■ 26541 ■ Jansco Marketing Inc.
769 Plain St.
Marshfield, MA 02050-2118
Phone: (781)837-4300 Fax: (781)837-8815
Products: Home electronics; Toys; Video games.
SICs: 5092 (Toys & Hobby Goods & Supplies); 5064
(Electrical Appliances—Television & Radio). Officers:
Louis Jannetty, President.

■ 26542 ■ C & D Jarnagin
1012 Washington St.
Corinth, MS 38834-4739
Phone: (601)287-4977 Fax: (601)287-6033
Products: Civil war items. SIC: 5092 (Toys & Hobby
Goods & Supplies).

■ 26543 ■ Jay Mar Sales Inc.
176 Chase River Rd.
Waterbury, CT 06704-1408
Phone: (203)753-1815 Fax: (203)753-4806
Products: Toys and hobby goods and supplies. SIC:
5092 (Toys & Hobby Goods & Supplies). Officers:
Edith Margolis, President.

■ 26544 ■ J.C. Sales Company Inc.
PO Box 1300
Anderson, IN 46015-1300
Phone: (765)644-8815 Fax: (765)649-8697
Products: Toys; Hobby goods and supplies; Games,
including board games. SIC: 5092 (Toys & Hobby
Goods & Supplies). Officers: John Christ, President.

■ 26545 ■ Jersey Model Distributors
806 US Rte. 17
Ramsey, NJ 07446
Phone: (201)327-7911
Products: Plastic Models. SIC: 5092 (Toys & Hobby
Goods & Supplies).

■ 26546 ■ Joissu Products Inc.
4627 L B Mcleod Rd.
Orlando, FL 32811-6405
Phone: (407)648-8746
Free: (800)233-1681 Fax: 800-238-1886
Products: Toys; Hair products and accessories. SICs:
5092 (Toys & Hobby Goods & Supplies); 5122 (Drugs,
Proprietaries & Sundries).

■ 26547 ■ K & L Marketing Inc.
RR 1, Box 79B
Cummings, ND 58223-9774
Phone: (701)786-3476 Fax: (701)786-2311
Products: Toys; Hobby kits; Fireworks; Gifts and
novelties. SIC: 5092 (Toys & Hobby Goods &
Supplies). Officers: Margaret Hoff, President.

■ 26548 ■ Kalweit Sales Company Inc.
8100 Wayzata Blvd.
Minneapolis, MN 55426
Phone: (612)595-9933 Fax: (612)595-9929
Products: Toys and hobby goods. SIC: 5092 (Toys &
Hobby Goods & Supplies). Est: 1972.

■ 26549 ■ Karshner Ceramics Inc.
3109 Griggsview Ct.
Columbus, OH 43221-4605
Products: Toys; Hobby kits; Craft kits. SIC: 5092
(Toys & Hobby Goods & Supplies). Officers: Rolland
Karshner, President.

■ 26550 ■ M.W. Kasch Co.
5401 W Donges Bay, 104N
Mequon, WI 53092
Phone: (414)242-5000 Fax: (414)242-9345
Products: Toys; Games; Stationery/office supplies;
Candles; Seasonal promotions and sporting goods.
SIC: 5092 (Toys & Hobby Goods & Supplies). Est:
1934. Sales: $70,000,000 (2000). Emp: 190. Officers:
Kevin Flanagan, COO & VP, e-mail: kflanagan@
mwkasch.com.

■ 26551 ■ K.B. Brothers Inc.
55 Franklin Ave.
Brooklyn, NY 11205-1503
Phone: (212)924-0673 Fax: (212)627-3970
Products: Toys; Stuffed toy animals. SIC: 5092 (Toys
& Hobby Goods & Supplies). Sales: $6,000,000
(2000). Emp: 100. Officers: William A. Devine.

■ 26552 ■ KD Sales Inc.
2039 S Burdick St.
Kalamazoo, MI 49001-3627
Phone: (616)344-2999
Free: (800)878-5376 Fax: (616)344-9815
Products: Toys, hobby goods, supplies, and games,
including Bingo. SIC: 5092 (Toys & Hobby Goods &
Supplies). Officers: Kermit Powers, President.

■ 26553 ■ Kipp Brothers Inc.
240 S Meridian St.
Indianapolis, IN 46225
Phone: (317)634-5507
Free: (800)428-1153 Fax: 800-832-5477
Products: Toys and hobby goods. SIC: 5092 (Toys &
Hobby Goods & Supplies). Est: 1880. Sales:
$12,000,000 (2000). Emp: 44.

■ 26554 ■ KMS Inc.
1135 N Washington St.
Wichita, KS 67214-3058
Phone: (316)634-0441
Free: (800)752-5262 Fax: (316)634-2892
Products: Toys; Hobby kits; Nonelectronic games.
SIC: 5092 (Toys & Hobby Goods & Supplies).
Officers: George Jabara, President.

■ 26555 ■ Koch Resources Inc.
PO Box 176
Crystal Bay, NV 89402-0647
Phone: (702)831-8213 Fax: (702)831-3910
Products: Toys and hobby goods; Collectables. SIC:
5092 (Toys & Hobby Goods & Supplies). Officers:
Joseph Koch, President.

■ 26556 ■ Kraft Korner Inc.
497 Eagle Truce.
Cleveland, OH 44124-6113
Products: Toys; Hobby kits; Paints and allied products;
Organic coatings, enamels, lacquers, including
alkydes, vinyls, acrylics, plastisols, etc. SICs: 5092
(Toys & Hobby Goods & Supplies); 5198 (Paints,
Varnishes & Supplies). Officers: Marguerite
Wennerstrom, President.

■ 26557 ■ L H Ranch Bunk & Bisket &
Hansens Hobby
471 Mullan Tr.
Gold Creek Stage Stop
Gold Creek, MT 59733
Phone: (406)288-3436
Products: Toys; Hobby kits. SIC: 5092 (Toys & Hobby
Goods & Supplies). Est: 1955. Emp: 3. Officers: Patti
Hansen, Partner. Former Name: Hansens Hobbies &
Supplies.

■ 26558 ■ L & L Lace
218 S Binley Mountain Pkwy.
Arab, AL 35016-1251
Phone: (205)586-6738
Free: (800)828-0033 Fax: (205)586-2280
Products: Arts and crafts equipment and supplies.
SICs: 5092 (Toys & Hobby Goods & Supplies); 5199
(Nondurable Goods Nec). Officers: Rickey Lankford,
Owner.

■ 26559 ■ S. Lachman & Son Inc.
PO Box 590
Odenton, MD 21113-0590
Phone: (410)551-2200
Free: (800)638-0144 Fax: (410)551-3376
Products: Toys, games, and hobby goods and
supplies; Bingo games and supplies. SIC: 5092 (Toys
& Hobby Goods & Supplies). Officers: Gary Cooper,
President.

■ 26560 ■ Alice Lacy Ltd.
1 Front St.
Bath, ME 04530
Phone: (207)443-2319 Fax: (207)677-3994
Products: Craft items, including miniature wicker,
miniature quilts, and pillows. SIC: 5092 (Toys & Hobby
Goods & Supplies). Est: 1985. Officers: Alice Lacy,
President; John Lacy, CEO, e-mail: JohnLacy@
midcoast.com; Callie Harper, Dir. of Marketing.

■ 26561 ■ Lake Instruments & Wholesale
Corp.
Box 329
South Haven, MI 49090
Phone: (616)637-3678 Fax: (616)637-5328
Products: Hobby supplies, including magnifiers and
instruments. SIC: 5092 (Toys & Hobby Goods &
Supplies).

■ 26562 ■ Lankhorst Distributors Inc.
11583 K Tel Dr.
Hopkins, MN 55343-8845
Phone: (612)933-4876 Fax: (612)933-8249
Products: Toys and hobby goods and supplies; Arts
and crafts equipment and supplies. SICs: 5092 (Toys &
Hobby Goods & Supplies); 5199 (Nondurable Goods
Nec). Officers: Jay Wood, Exec. Officer.

■ 26563 ■ The Last Straw Inc.
444 Bayview Ave.
Inwood, NY 11096-1702
Phone: (516)371-2727 Fax: (516)371-2442
Products: Toys. SIC: 5092 (Toys & Hobby Goods &
Supplies). Emp: 49. Officers: Sharon Hecht, CEO.

■ 26564 ■ Lean Year Distributing Inc.
775 Milton St. N
St. Paul, MN 55104-1530
Phone: (612)487-3788 Fax: (612)487-9074
Products: Gambling supplies. SIC: 5092 (Toys &
Hobby Goods & Supplies). Officers: Carol Roith,
President.

■ 26565 ■ Learning Materials Workshop
274 N Winooski Ave.
Burlington, VT 05401-3621
Phone: (802)862-8399
E-mail: mail@learningmaterialswork.com
URL: http://www.learningmaterialswork.com
Products: Toys, games, educational toys, and hard
wood construction blocks. SIC: 5092 (Toys & Hobby
Goods & Supplies). Officers: Karen Hewitt, President.

■ 26566 ■ Legends of Racing Inc.
11820 Antebellum Dr.
Charlotte, NC 28273
Phone: (704)543-9540 Fax: (704)543-9415
Products: Toys; Hobby kits. SIC: 5092 (Toys & Hobby
Goods & Supplies). Officers: J. Vandiver, President.

■ 26567 ■ Leisure Learning Products
PO Box 4869
Greenwich, CT 06830-8869
Phone: (203)531-8700 Fax: (203)531-0545
Products: Toys, hobby goods and supplies, and
games, including learning games. SIC: 5092 (Toys &
Hobby Goods & Supplies). Officers: Richard Bendett,
Owner.

■ 26568 ■ Liberty Hobby
PO Box 922
Lakeland, FL 33802-0922
Phone: (941)688-5904
Products: Role-playing and fantasy games. SIC: 5092
(Toys & Hobby Goods & Supplies).

■ 26569 ■ Marlin Distributors Inc.
91-312 Komohana St.
Kapolei, HI 96707-1714
Phone: (808)682-4314 Fax: (808)682-4365
E-mail: Marlindist@aol.com
Products: Toys and hobby goods and supplies. SIC:
5092 (Toys & Hobby Goods & Supplies). Est: 1968.
Officers: A. Jack Woods, President.

■ 26570 ■ Mary Maxim Inc.
PO Box 5019
Port Huron, MI 48061-5019
Phone: (810)987-2000 Fax: (313)987-5056
Products: Craft kits; Stamped art goods and art
needlework; Yarn goods. SICs: 5092 (Toys & Hobby
Goods & Supplies); 5199 (Nondurable Goods Nec).
Est: 1956. Sales: $25,500,000 (2000). Emp: 120.
Officers: W.M. McPhedrain, President; Donna
Hietikko, CFO; Robert McManaman, Dir. of Marketing
& Sales; Orville Smith, Dir. of Data Processing; Donna
Nietikko, Dir of Human Resources.

■ **26571** ■ **MC Sales**
5070 Santa Fe St.
San Diego, CA 92109
Phone: (858)490-5100 **Fax:** (858)490-5101
Products: Sports memorabilia. **SIC:** 5092 (Toys & Hobby Goods & Supplies). **Sales:** $1,000,000 (2000). **Emp:** 15. **Officers:** Matt Wozniak, President; Neil Whitley Ross, CFO.

■ **26572** ■ **McCall Fireworks Inc.**
PO Box 40
McAlester, OK 74502-0040
Phone: (918)423-3343 **Fax:** (918)423-3387
Products: Toys; Hobby kits; Gifts and novelties; Fireworks. **SICs:** 5092 (Toys & Hobby Goods & Supplies); 5199 (Nondurable Goods Nec). **Officers:** Harold Mc Call, President.

■ **26573** ■ **Mellon Patch**
PO Box 414
Mountain View, AR 72560-0414
Phone: (870)269-3354 **Fax:** (870)269-2433
URL: http://www.globalriver.com/mellonpatch
Products: Toys, including wooden toys; Hobby goods and supplies; Games. **SIC:** 5092 (Toys & Hobby Goods & Supplies). **Est:** 1981. **Emp:** 3. **Officers:** Donald Mellon, President.

■ **26574** ■ **Mary Meyer Corp.**
PO Box 275
1 Teddy Bear Lane
Townshend, VT 05353-0275
Phone: (802)365-7793
Free: (800)451-4387 **Fax:** (802)365-4233
Products: Stuffed toys. **SIC:** 5092 (Toys & Hobby Goods & Supplies). **Est:** 1933. **Emp:** 60. **Officers:** Walter Meyer, Chairman of the Board; Robert Zeif, Marketing Contact; David Quimby, Sales Contact; Kevin Meyer.

■ **26575** ■ **MGA Entertainment**
16730 Schoenborn St.
North Hills, CA 91343-6122
Phone: (818)894-2525 **Fax:** (818)894-8094
Products: Handheld games; Toys; Dolls. **SICs:** 5092 (Toys & Hobby Goods & Supplies); 5064 (Electrical Appliances—Television & Radio). **Est:** 1982. **Sales:** $105,000,000 (2000). **Emp:** 95. **Officers:** Isaac Larian, CEO; Fred Larian, Exec. VP; Paul Warner, VP of Sales; Leslie Gross, VP Marketing & Development. **Former Name:** ABC International Traders Inc.

■ **26576** ■ **Micro-Trains Line Co.**
PO Box 1200
Talent, OR 97540-1200
Phone: (541)535-1755 **Fax:** (541)535-1932
E-mail: mtl@micro_trains.com
URL: http://www.micro_trains.com
Products: Model trains. **SIC:** 5092 (Toys & Hobby Goods & Supplies). **Est:** 1945. **Emp:** 87. **Officers:** Eric D. Smith, President.

■ **26577** ■ **Mid-West Crafts Inc.**
PO Box 367
Whitley City, KY 42653-0367
Phone: (606)376-5152
Products: Coal figurines. **SIC:** 5092 (Toys & Hobby Goods & Supplies). **Officers:** John Beams, President.

■ **26578** ■ **Midwest Sports Cards**
7190 University Ave. NE
Minneapolis, MN 55432-3100
Phone: (612)572-1770
Free: (800)886-3978 **Fax:** (612)572-1286
Products: Toys and hobby goods. **SIC:** 5092 (Toys & Hobby Goods & Supplies). **Est:** 1982.

■ **26579** ■ **Minnesota Clay Co. USA**
8001 Grand Ave.
Minneapolis, MN 55420-1128
Phone: (612)884-9101
Free: (800)CLA-YUSA **Fax:** (612)884-1820
E-mail: mnclayus@mm.com
URL: http://www.mm.com/mnclayus/
Products: Pottery equipment and supplies, including clays and glazes. **SICs:** 5092 (Toys & Hobby Goods & Supplies); 5199 (Nondurable Goods Nec). **Emp:** 40. **Officers:** Mike Daly, President.

■ **26580** ■ **Model Rectifier Corp.**
80 Newfieldn Ave.
Edison, NJ 08837
Phone: (732)248-0400
Products: Static plastic model cars, airplanes, and tanks. **SIC:** 5092 (Toys & Hobby Goods & Supplies). **Sales:** $14,100,000 (1993). **Emp:** 30. **Officers:** Roy Gielber, President.

■ **26581** ■ **Morris Novelty Inc.**
523 Main St.
Pawtucket, RI 02860-2944
Phone: (401)728-3810 **Fax:** (401)722-9055
Products: Toys, hobby goods and supplies, and games, including bingo. **SIC:** 5092 (Toys & Hobby Goods & Supplies). **Officers:** Kenneth Stebenne, President.

■ **26582** ■ **J.D. Morse Wholesale Inc.**
6841 Hawthorn Park Dr.
Indianapolis, IN 46220-3908
Phone: (317)849-7815 **Fax:** (317)849-7891
Products: Toys; Hobby kits; Candy; Batteries; Trading cards; Hair accessories. **SICs:** 5092 (Toys & Hobby Goods & Supplies); 5063 (Electrical Apparatus & Equipment); 5145 (Confectionery); 5122 (Drugs, Proprietaries & Sundries). **Officers:** Douglas R. Morse, President.

■ **26583** ■ **Mountain Lakes Distributors**
10 Romaine Rd.
Mountain Lakes, NJ 07046
Phone: (973)263-1979
Products: Model trains. **SIC:** 5092 (Toys & Hobby Goods & Supplies).

■ **26584** ■ **Mountain Service Corp.**
15503 Lee Hwy.
Bristol, VA 24201-8431
Phone: (540)669-9555
Free: (800)782-4106 **Fax:** (540)669-8961
Products: Toys; Hobby kits; Nonelectronic games. **SIC:** 5092 (Toys & Hobby Goods & Supplies). **Officers:** William Mullins, President.

■ **26585** ■ **Patrick J. Mucci**
31902 Groesbeck Hwy.
Fraser, MI 48026-3914
Phone: (810)296-6118
Free: (800)833-3828 **Fax:** (810)296-5642
Products: Toys; Hobby kits; Model kits. **SIC:** 5092 (Toys & Hobby Goods & Supplies). **Officers:** Patrick Mucci, Owner.

■ **26586** ■ **Mutual Sales Inc.**
1650 Turnpike St.
North Andover, MA 01845-6222
Phone: (508)685-7067 **Fax:** (508)689-4016
Products: Toys and hobby goods. **SIC:** 5092 (Toys & Hobby Goods & Supplies). **Est:** 1950. **Sales:** $4,000,000 (2000). **Emp:** 15.

■ **26587** ■ **Milton D. Myer Co.**
Rothesay Ave.
Carnegie, PA 15106
Phone: (412)279-9151 **Fax:** (412)279-8630
Products: Toys. **SIC:** 5092 (Toys & Hobby Goods & Supplies). **Est:** 1920. **Sales:** $29,000,000 (2000). **Emp:** 50. **Officers:** Richard Myer, President.

■ **26588** ■ **Nadel and Sons Toy Corp.**
915 Broadway
New York, NY 10010
Phone: (212)254-1677
Free: (800)234-4697 **Fax:** (212)505-7160
Products: Toys and novelties, including inflatable animals and stuffed toys; Stationery; Giftware; Housewares. **SICs:** 5092 (Toys & Hobby Goods & Supplies); 5112 (Stationery & Office Supplies); 5199 (Nondurable Goods Nec). **Est:** 1904. **Sales:** $10,000,000 (2000). **Emp:** 20. **Officers:** A. Hornsby, President; C. Nadel, CFO.

■ **26589** ■ **Nasco-Catalog**
901 Janesville Ave.
Ft. Atkinson, WI 53538-0901
Phone: (920)563-2446 **Fax:** (920)563-8296
Products: Farm supplies; Arts and crafts; Educational supplies. **SICs:** 5092 (Toys & Hobby Goods & Supplies); 5191 (Farm Supplies); 5199 (Nondurable Goods Nec).

■ **26590** ■ **Neal's Gauging Trains**
86 Tide Mill Rd.
Hampton, NH 03842
Phone: (603)926-9031 **Fax:** (603)929-0230
E-mail: nngt@webtv.net
Products: Model trains and related hobby items. **SIC:** 5092 (Toys & Hobby Goods & Supplies). **Est:** 1988. **Officers:** Neal Carnaby.

■ **26591** ■ **Nesson Sales**
408 E 18th St.
Norfolk, VA 23504
Phone: (757)662-3208 **Fax:** (757)623-1878
Products: Toys and hobby items. **SIC:** 5092 (Toys & Hobby Goods & Supplies).

■ **26592** ■ **New Mexico Fire Works Inc.**
137 Carlito Rd. NW
Albuquerque, NM 87107-6011
Phone: (505)344-5869
Products: Toys and hobby goods and supplies; Fireworks. **SIC:** 5092 (Toys & Hobby Goods & Supplies). **Officers:** John Stueber, President.

■ **26593** ■ **New York Notions/Craft Supply Corp.**
3800 W 42nd St.
Chicago, IL 60632
Phone: (773)247-2121
Free: (800)444-5111 **Fax:** (773)247-6154
URL: http://www.brewersewing.com
Products: Sewing accessories; Craft kits. **SIC:** 5092 (Toys & Hobby Goods & Supplies).

■ **26594** ■ **Nikko America Inc.**
2801 Summit Ave.
Plano, TX 75074
Phone: (972)422-0838
Products: Radio-controlled boats, cars, and planes. **SIC:** 5092 (Toys & Hobby Goods & Supplies).

■ **26595** ■ **Northern League Sportscards**
858 Kirkwood Mall
Bismarck, ND 58504-5752
Phone: (701)223-4672 **Fax:** (701)222-4170
Products: Hobby goods and supplies, including comic books. **SIC:** 5092 (Toys & Hobby Goods & Supplies). **Officers:** Dave Renner, President.

■ **26596** ■ **Novel-Tees Wholesale**
959 East 3300 South
Salt Lake City, UT 84106
Phone: (801)484-6769 **Free:** (800)637-2799
Products: Toys and novelty items. **SIC:** 5092 (Toys & Hobby Goods & Supplies).

■ **26597** ■ **Old Sutler John**
PO BOx 174 Westview Station
Binghamton, NY 13905
Phone: (607)775-4434 **Fax:** (607)775-4434
Products: Civil War reproductions. **SIC:** 5092 (Toys & Hobby Goods & Supplies).

■ **26598** ■ **Original Appalachian Artworks Inc.**
PO Box 714
Cleveland, GA 30528
Phone: (706)865-2171 **Fax:** (706)865-5862
Products: Brand-name dolls, including soft-sculptured dolls. **SIC:** 5092 (Toys & Hobby Goods & Supplies). **Est:** 1978. **Sales:** $10,000,000 (2000). **Emp:** 80. **Officers:** X. Roberts, Chairman of the Board; S.K. Krueger, CFO; Susan Krueger, Vice President.

■ **26599** ■ **Oved Corp.**
4143 NW 132nd St.
Miami, FL 33054
Phone: (305)688-5865
Free: (800)332-6833 **Fax:** (305)685-2988
Products: Nailheads; Rhinestones; Embroidery; Pearls; Fabric paint; Ribbon roses; Shirts. **SIC:** 5131 (Piece Goods & Notions). **Est:** 1987. **Sales:** $5,000,000 (2000). **Emp:** 6.

■ 26600 ■ P & D Hobby Distributors
31902 Groesbeck Hwy.
Fraser, MI 48026
Phone: (810)296-6116   Fax: (810)296-5642
Products: Hobby supplies. SIC: 5092 (Toys & Hobby Goods & Supplies).

■ 26601 ■ Pacific Model Distributing Inc.
7317 Somerset Blvd.
Paramount, CA 90723-0346
Phone: (562)630-5222   Fax: (562)630-1914
Products: Toys and hobby goods. SIC: 5092 (Toys & Hobby Goods & Supplies). Sales: $6,000,000 (2000). Emp: 49.

■ 26602 ■ Pacific Trading
13501 N Railway Dr.
Oklahoma City, OK 73114
Phone: (405)755-6680
Free: (800)806-3940   Fax: (405)334-7042
Products: Doll house accessories; Polyresin figurines. SIC: 5092 (Toys & Hobby Goods & Supplies). Est: 1985. Emp: 8. Officers: Tony Chen, President.

■ 26603 ■ Pal Productions Inc.
1685 Lakewood Dr.
Troy, OH 45373-9508
Phone: (937)890-6200   Fax: (937)339-7773
Products: Toys; Hobby kits; Nonelectronic games; Educational products. SIC: 5092 (Toys & Hobby Goods & Supplies). Officers: Patty Cochran, President.

■ 26604 ■ Pan American International
3615 NW 20th Ave.
Miami, FL 33142
Phone: (305)635-3134   Fax: (305)633-2678
Products: Hobby supplies. SIC: 5092 (Toys & Hobby Goods & Supplies). Est: 1964.

■ 26605 ■ Parris Manufacturing Co.
PO Box 338
Savannah, TN 38372-0338
Phone: (901)925-3918
Free: (800)530-7308   Fax: (901)925-1139
E-mail: parrismfg@centurytel.net
URL: http://www.parrismfg.com
Products: Toy guns; Children's archery equipment; Stick horses; Easels; Bunkbeds. SIC: 5092 (Toys & Hobby Goods & Supplies). Sales: $7,000,000 (1999). Emp: 170. Officers: D. J. Phillips.

■ 26606 ■ Pat's Ceramics Tile Design Center
1567 N Decatur Blvd.
Las Vegas, NV 89108-1204
Phone: (702)646-6011
Products: Craft kits; Artists' equipment; Designer tiles. SICs: 5092 (Toys & Hobby Goods & Supplies); 5049 (Professional Equipment Nec). Est: 1979. Sales: $50,000 (2000). Officers: Pat Gibbons, Owner.

■ 26607 ■ Paul-Son Gaming Supplies, Inc.
1700 Industrial Rd.
Las Vegas, NV 89102
Phone: (702)384-2425
Free: (800)728-5766   Fax: (702)384-1965
Products: Gaming supplies. SIC: 5092 (Toys & Hobby Goods & Supplies). Est: 1963. Sales: $24,000,000 (2000). Emp: 110. Officers: Eric Endy, Exec. VP.

■ 26608 ■ Peacock Alley Needlepoint
650 Croswell Ave. SE
Grand Rapids, MI 49506-3004
Phone: (616)454-9898   Free: (877)550-9898
E-mail: croswellnp@aol.com
Products: Needlepoint canvases and kits; Threads, accessories, classes, and finishing. SIC: 5092 (Toys & Hobby Goods & Supplies). Est: 1966. Emp: 1. Officers: Sandy Rabideau, Co-Owner; Valerie McAleenan, General Mgr. Former Name: Peacock Alley.

■ 26609 ■ Peatfield Industries
11 Cozy Hollow Rd.
Danbury, CT 06811
Phone: (203)743-7976   Fax: (203)790-0331
Products: Hobby and gaming supplies. SIC: 5092 (Toys & Hobby Goods & Supplies). Est: 1976. Officers: Howard Peatfield, Owner.

■ 26610 ■ Peck-Polymers
PO Box 710399
Santee, CA 92072
Phone: (619)448-1818
Free: (800)392-5520   Fax: (619)448-1833
E-mail: ppmodels@aol.com
Products: Model airplanes, kits, plans, books, and accessories, radio controlled and inflatables. SIC: 5092 (Toys & Hobby Goods & Supplies). Est: 1971. Sales: $750,000 (1999). Emp: 5. Officers: Sandra Peck, Owner; Vera Dudley, Sales/Marketing Contact.

■ 26611 ■ Dale Peterson Co.
305 1st Ave.
Milnor, ND 58060-4205
Phone: (701)427-9281
Products: Toys, games, hobby goods, and supplies. SIC: 5092 (Toys & Hobby Goods & Supplies). Officers: Dale Peterson, Owner.

■ 26612 ■ PFM Industries Inc.
PO Box 57
Edmonds, WA 98020-0057
Phone: (425)776-3112   Fax: (425)775-5076
Products: Books; Model trains. SICs: 5092 (Toys & Hobby Goods & Supplies); 5192 (Books, Periodicals & Newspapers). Officers: Donald Drew, President.

■ 26613 ■ Phase II
12410 N 28th Dr.
Phoenix, AZ 85029-2433
Phone: (602)993-1130   Fax: (602)993-1166
Products: Party supplies; Bingo supplies. SIC: 5092 (Toys & Hobby Goods & Supplies). Est: 1982. Emp: 5. Officers: Kenneth Vadnal, President. Alternate Name: Diamond Sun Ltd.

■ 26614 ■ Phase II Distributors Inc.
13024 Chatsworth Rd.
Moss Point, MS 39562-9566
Phone: (601)475-2400
Free: (800)421-4263   Fax: (601)475-3762
Products: Video games. SIC: 5092 (Toys & Hobby Goods & Supplies). Est: 1989. Officers: Rebecca Adams, President, e-mail: badams@datasync.com.

■ 26615 ■ Pierce Enterprises of Eagle Lake, Inc.
PO Box 107
Eagle Lake, MN 56024-0107
Phone: (507)257-3331
Free: (800)369-8227   Fax: (507)257-4080
Products: Bingo and gambling supplies. SIC: 5092 (Toys & Hobby Goods & Supplies). Officers: Robert Pierce, President.

■ 26616 ■ Plakie Inc.
PO Box 3386
Youngstown, OH 44512
Phone: (330)758-3500   Fax: (330)756-3546
Products: Toys for infants. SIC: 5092 (Toys & Hobby Goods & Supplies). Est: 1938. Sales: $3,000,000 (2000). Emp: 5. Officers: Dean R. Hoover, President & Treasurer.

■ 26617 ■ Playmates Toys Inc.
611 Anton Blvd., Ste. 600
Costa Mesa, CA 92626-1904
Phone: (714)428-2000   Fax: (714)428-2200
URL: http://www.playmatestoys.com
Products: Toys; Dolls; Electronics. SIC: 5092 (Toys & Hobby Goods & Supplies). Est: 1982. Sales: $100,000,000 (2000). Emp: 50. Officers: Ron Welch, President.

■ 26618 ■ Pleasant Co.
PO Box 620998
Middleton, WI 53562-0998
Phone: (608)836-4848
Free: (800)845-0005   Fax: (608)836-0761
Products: Dolls; Books. SICs: 5092 (Toys & Hobby Goods & Supplies); 5192 (Books, Periodicals & Newspapers). Est: 1986. Sales: $300,000,000 (2000). Emp: 727. Officers: Pleasant Rowland, President.

■ 26619 ■ Portman Hobby Distributors
851 Washington St.
Peekskill, NY 10566
Phone: (914)737-6633   Fax: (914)737-6984
Products: Model hobby supplies. SIC: 5092 (Toys & Hobby Goods & Supplies).

■ 26620 ■ Preferred Distributors Inc.
PO Box 458
Tewksbury, MA 01876-0458
Phone: (978)851-9900   Fax: (978)851-8388
Products: Toys, hobby goods, and supplies. SIC: 5092 (Toys & Hobby Goods & Supplies). Officers: Arthur Cerullo, President.

■ 26621 ■ The Premier Group
5200 Lawrence Pl.
Hyattsville, MD 20781
Phone: (301)277-3888   Fax: (301)277-3323
Products: Toys; kites. SIC: 5092 (Toys & Hobby Goods & Supplies). Est: 1984. Officers: Albert Lim, Owner.

■ 26622 ■ Processed Plastic Co.
1001 Aucutt Rd.
Montgomery, IL 60538
Phone: (630)892-7981   Fax: (630)892-6056
Products: Plastic toys. SIC: 5092 (Toys & Hobby Goods & Supplies). Sales: $30,000,000 (2000). Emp: 499. Officers: David R. Bergman; Robert S. Bergman.

■ 26623 ■ Punch It Distributing Inc.
2690 Niles Rd.
St. Joseph, MI 49085-3313
Phone: (616)429-9696
Free: (800)878-6593   Fax: (616)429-9761
Products: Arts and crafts equipment and supplies. SICs: 5092 (Toys & Hobby Goods & Supplies); 5199 (Nondurable Goods Nec). Est: 1987. Emp: 5. Officers: Mary Jane Waldenmaier, President.

■ 26624 ■ Q-Snap Corp.
PO Box 68
Parsons, TN 38363-0068
Phone: (901)847-7155   Fax: (901)847-3523
Products: Quilting, cross-stitch, and needlepoint equipment and supplies, including frames, books, and patterns. SIC: 5092 (Toys & Hobby Goods & Supplies). Officers: Perry M. Kiehl, President.

■ 26625 ■ R/C Henry Company Inc.
3600 Chamberlain Ln., Ste. 342
Louisville, KY 40241
Phone: (502)339-0172   Fax: (502)339-1211
Products: Model railroad products. SIC: 5092 (Toys & Hobby Goods & Supplies).

■ 26626 ■ Racing Champions Corp.
800 Roosevelt Rd., Bldg. C., Ste. 320
Glen Ellyn, IL 60137
Phone: (630)790-3507   Fax: (630)790-9474
URL: http://www.racingchampions.com
Products: Collectible scaled die cast vehicle replicas. SIC: 5099 (Durable Goods Nec). Est: 1989. Sales: $231,400,000 (2000). Emp: 519. Officers: Robert E. Dods, CEO; Curtis W. Stoelting, Exec. VP of Finance & Operations.

■ 26627 ■ Rainbow Balloons Inc.
59 Waters Ave.
Everett, MA 02149-2026
Phone: (617)389-1144   Fax: (617)389-1181
Products: Rubber balloons; Gifts and novelties. SIC: 5092 (Toys & Hobby Goods & Supplies). Officers: Bill Giannasca, President.

■ 26628 ■ Random House Inc.
201 E 50th St.
New York, NY 10022
Phone: (212)572-2120
Free: (800)659-2436   Fax: (212)572-6035
Products: Role-playing and fantasy games and books. SIC: 5092 (Toys & Hobby Goods & Supplies).

■ 26629 ■ Rapers of Spencer Inc.
1109 N Salisbury Ave.
Spencer, NC 28159-1832
Phone: (336)760-1512
Products: Crafts; Silk flowers, ribbons, baskets, and

florist supplies. **SIC:** 5193 (Flowers & Florists' Supplies). **Est:** 1938. **Emp:** 21. **Officers:** John Raper, President.

■ **26630** ■ **Rasmark Display Fireworks Inc.**
PO Box 1702
Bozeman, MT 59771-1702
Phone: (406)587-9060
Free: (800)759-9060 **Fax:** (406)565-3078
Products: Fireworks; Toys. **SIC:** 5092 (Toys & Hobby Goods & Supplies). **Officers:** Gary Reid, President.

■ **26631** ■ **Ray's Hobby**
190 Buttonwoods Ave.
Warwick, RI 02886-7541
Phone: (401)738-4908
Products: Hobby goods, including remote control goods. **SIC:** 5092 (Toys & Hobby Goods & Supplies). **Officers:** Raymond Dean, Owner.

■ **26632** ■ **Reichenbach Fireworks**
815 High Ridge Dr.
Billings, MT 59105-5337
Phone: (406)248-1150
Free: (800)767-4068 **Fax:** (406)248-3174
Products: Toys; Hobby kits; Fireworks. **SIC:** 5092 (Toys & Hobby Goods & Supplies). **Est:** 1946. **Officers:** Victor Reichenbach, Owner.

■ **26633** ■ **Reno Game Sales Inc.**
4750 Longley Ln., Ste. 105
Reno, NV 89502
Phone: (702)829-2080 **Fax:** (702)829-2083
Products: Arcade equipment, including video and pinball machines, jukeboxes, dart boards, billiard tables, and air hockey machines. **SIC:** 5092 (Toys & Hobby Goods & Supplies). **Est:** 1984. **Officers:** Martin Shumsky, President; Cindy Bozman, Manager.

■ **26634** ■ **Rich Brothers Co.**
PO Box 1185
Sioux Falls, SD 57101-1185
Phone: (605)336-3344
Free: (800)658-3538 **Fax:** (605)336-1908
Products: Toys and hobby goods. **SIC:** 5092 (Toys & Hobby Goods & Supplies). **Est:** 1947. **Sales:** $5,500,000 (2000). **Emp:** 30.

■ **26635** ■ **Rieger's Ceramics Arts & Crafts**
1321 4th Ave. E
PO Box 572
Mobridge, SD 57601-0572
Phone: (605)845-2995
Products: Ceramics; Arts and crafts supplies; Office equipment and supplies. **SICs:** 5092 (Toys & Hobby Goods & Supplies); 5112 (Stationery & Office Supplies); 5199 (Nondurable Goods Nec); 5044 (Office Equipment). **Est:** 1968. **Officers:** Robert Cripe, Owner.

■ **26636** ■ **Rita Selections Ltd.**
8208 Mt. Nido Rd.
Las Vegas, NV 89117-5224
Phone: (702)364-2284
Products: Toys and hobby goods and supplies, including games and dolls. **SIC:** 5092 (Toys & Hobby Goods & Supplies). **Officers:** Rita Tseng, President.

■ **26637** ■ **Rochester Imports Inc.**
PO Box 1380
Seneca, SC 29679-1380
Phone: (864)882-5642 **Fax:** (864)882-7293
Products: Toys; Hobby kits; Nonelectronic games. **SIC:** 5092 (Toys & Hobby Goods & Supplies). **Officers:** Kenneth Rochester, President.

■ **26638** ■ **Royal Arts & Crafts**
768 James P Brawley Dr. NW
Atlanta, GA 30318-5243
Phone: (404)881-0075 **Fax:** (404)876-6428
Products: Craft kits; Art goods. **SICs:** 5092 (Toys & Hobby Goods & Supplies); 5199 (Nondurable Goods Nec). **Est:** 1970. **Sales:** $3,500,000 (2000). **Emp:** 49. **Officers:** Donald Reisman; Bruce Reisman.

■ **26639** ■ **Royal Products Corp.**
PO Box 5026
Denver, CO 80217-5026
Phone: (303)778-7711 **Fax:** (303)778-7722
Products: Toys and hobby goods and supplies,

including model kits. **SIC:** 5092 (Toys & Hobby Goods & Supplies). **Officers:** Reynold Murray, President.

■ **26640** ■ **Royal Sales**
PO Box 140035
Bath Beach Sta.
Brooklyn, NY 11214-0035
Phone: (718)946-5947 **Fax:** (718)996-9726
E-mail: info@royalsales.com
URL: http://www.royalsales.com
Products: Toys; Children's furniture and accessories; Wrought iron furniture accessories. **SICs:** 5092 (Toys & Hobby Goods & Supplies); 5021 (Furniture). **Est:** 1971. **Sales:** $10,000,000 (2000). **Emp:** 6. **Officers:** Bernard Weisman, President. **Former Name:** Royal Merchandise Corp. Royal Sales Div.

■ **26641** ■ **Royal Toy Distributors Inc.**
PO Box 3202
Stamford, CT 06905-0202
Phone: (203)853-9513 **Fax:** (203)358-0165
Products: Toys; Hobby kits. **SIC:** 5092 (Toys & Hobby Goods & Supplies). **Officers:** Jerome Klein, President.

■ **26642** ■ **RPV Distributors**
580 W Lambert, Ste. K
Brea, CA 92821
Phones: (714)671-1270 (714)870-1855
Products: Role-playing and fantasy games. **SIC:** 5092 (Toys & Hobby Goods & Supplies).

■ **26643** ■ **S and G Trading Co.**
7110 Newberry Dr.
Columbia, MD 21044
Phone: (301)531-3911
Products: Toys; Electric appliances; Water purification equipment; Stationery; Motor vehicle parts and accessories. **SICs:** 5092 (Toys & Hobby Goods & Supplies); 5013 (Motor Vehicle Supplies & New Parts); 5064 (Electrical Appliances—Television & Radio); 5074 (Plumbing & Hydronic Heating Supplies); 5112 (Stationery & Office Supplies). **Officers:** Steven A. Zak, President.

■ **26644** ■ **S & P Whistle Stop**
3216 Spangle St.
Canandaigua, NY 14424
Phone: (716)396-0160
Free: (800)392-0160 **Fax:** (716)396-9930
Products: Toy trains. **SIC:** 5092 (Toys & Hobby Goods & Supplies). **Est:** 1980. **Emp:** 6.

■ **26645** ■ **S and S Worldwide Inc.**
PO Box 513
Colchester, CT 06415
Phone: (860)537-3451 **Fax:** (860)537-2866
Products: Wooden games and components. **SICs:** 5092 (Toys & Hobby Goods & Supplies); 5099 (Durable Goods Nec). **Sales:** $43,000,000 (2000). **Emp:** 325.

■ **26646** ■ **Samson's Novelty Company Inc.**
37 Riverside Dr.
Auburn, ME 04210-6870
Phone: (207)782-2929 **Fax:** (207)782-4062
Products: Games of chance and Bingo supplies. **SIC:** 5092 (Toys & Hobby Goods & Supplies). **Officers:** Mary Samson, President.

■ **26647** ■ **Sbar's, Inc.**
14 Sbar Blvd.
Moorestown, NJ 08057
Phone: (609)234-8220
Free: (800)989-7227 **Fax:** (609)231-4693
Products: Craft kits; Lead pencils, crayons, and artists' materials. **SICs:** 5092 (Toys & Hobby Goods & Supplies); 5199 (Nondurable Goods Nec). **Officers:** Pepe Piperno, Contact.

■ **26648** ■ **Scenery Unlimited**
7236 W Madison St.
Forest Park, IL 60130
Phone: (708)366-7763 **Fax:** (708)366-1973
Products: Model trains. **SIC:** 5092 (Toys & Hobby Goods & Supplies). **Est:** 1962. **Emp:** 7. **Officers:** Don Heimburger, President.

■ **26649** ■ **Sega of America Inc.**
650 Townsend St., Ste. 575
San Francisco, CA 94103-5646
Products: Video game hardware, software, and accessories. **SICs:** 5092 (Toys & Hobby Goods & Supplies); 5045 (Computers, Peripherals & Software). **Emp:** 900.

■ **26650** ■ **Sentai Distributors International**
8839 Shirley Ave.
Northridge, CA 91324
Phone: (818)886-3113 **Fax:** (818)886-2551
E-mail: plasticm@pacbell.net
URL: http://www.plasticmodels.com
Products: Model kits; Books; Decals and related items. **SICs:** 5092 (Toys & Hobby Goods & Supplies); 5192 (Books, Periodicals & Newspapers). **Est:** 1965. **Sales:** $3,500,000 (2000). **Emp:** 15. **Officers:** Rick Watson, CEO.

■ **26651** ■ **Shepher Distributors and Sales Corp.**
2300 Linden Blvd.
Brooklyn, NY 11208
Phone: (718)649-2525 **Fax:** (718)649-1068
URL: http://www.shephertoy.com
Products: Toys. **SIC:** 5092 (Toys & Hobby Goods & Supplies). **Est:** 1945. **Sales:** $32,000,000 (1999). **Emp:** 75. **Officers:** Hal Monchik, President; Rich Monchik, Vice President; Charles Monchik, VP & CFO; James Albanese, Vice President; Ted Paterek, Sales & Marketing Contact, e-mail: tedsheper@aol.com.

■ **26652** ■ **Slusser Wholesale Inc.**
PO Box 2439
Idaho Falls, ID 83403-2439
Phone: (208)523-0775 **Fax:** (208)522-1837
E-mail: swc@pcif.net
Products: Toys; Drug sundries; Housewares; Pet supplies; Film; Candy; Sporting goods. **SICs:** 5092 (Toys & Hobby Goods & Supplies); 5122 (Drugs, Proprietaries & Sundries); 5023 (Homefurnishings); 5091 (Sporting & Recreational Goods); 5145 (Confectionery). **Est:** 1945. **Sales:** $20,000,000 (2000). **Emp:** 80. **Officers:** Russ Bradley, President.

■ **26653** ■ **Small World Toys**
PO Box 3620
Culver City, CA 90231-3620
Phone: (310)645-9680 **Fax:** (310)410-9606
Products: Specialty toys; Imported toys. **SIC:** 5092 (Toys & Hobby Goods & Supplies). **Emp:** 44.

■ **26654** ■ **Smith Ceramics**
268 Main St.
Bangor, ME 04401-6404
Phone: (207)945-3969
Products: Toys, hobby goods, arts and crafts equipment, and supplies. **SIC:** 5092 (Toys & Hobby Goods & Supplies). **Officers:** Irene Smith, Partner.

■ **26655** ■ **Nicholas Smith**
2343 W Chester Pike
Broomall, PA 19008
Phone: (215)353-8585 **Fax:** (215)359-9846
Products: Novelty items, including electric trains, games, and magazines. **SIC:** 5092 (Toys & Hobby Goods & Supplies).

■ **26656** ■ **SMP Enterprises Inc.**
99-1366 Koaha Pl.
Aiea, HI 96701
Phone: (808)487-1129 **Fax:** (808)487-1452
Products: Video games; Toys; Watches and clocks; Audio; Bicycle accessories; Calculators; Inflatables; Sunglasses. **SICs:** 5064 (Electrical Appliances— Television & Radio); 5092 (Toys & Hobby Goods & Supplies); 5043 (Photographic Equipment & Supplies); 5094 (Jewelry & Precious Stones). **Est:** 1985. **Emp:** 20. **Officers:** Peter Stoddard, President, e-mail: pstoddar@smpent.com; Rayma Lee, Sales/Marketing Contact, e-mail: rjlee@smpent.com; Betsy Stoddard, Human Resources Contact, e-mail: estoddar@smpent.com.

■ **26657** ■ **Sorceror Distributors**
10118 Kinross Ave.
Silver Spring, MD 20901
Phone: (301)681-8060
Products: Role-playing and fantasy games. **SIC:** 5092 (Toys & Hobby Goods & Supplies).

■ **26658** ■ **South Atlantic Distributing Co.**
PO Box 1071
Skyland, NC 28776-1071
Phone: (704)665-1832 **Fax:** (704)665-1833
Products: Toys; Hobby kits; Nonelectronic games. **SIC:** 5092 (Toys & Hobby Goods & Supplies). **Officers:** Thomas Hopkins, Owner.

■ **26659** ■ **South Carolina Distributors Inc.**
1406 Cherokee Falls Rd.
Cherokee Falls, SC 29702
Phone: (803)839-2766
Products: Toys and hobby goods. **SIC:** 5092 (Toys & Hobby Goods & Supplies). **Sales:** $47,000,000 (1992). **Emp:** 100. **Officers:** Herbert Livingston, President.

■ **26660** ■ **Southwest Bingo Supply**
2112 2nd St. SW
Albuquerque, NM 87102-4513
Phone: (505)842-0022 **Fax:** (505)842-1160
Products: Toys; Hobby kits; Nonelectronic games. **SIC:** 5092 (Toys & Hobby Goods & Supplies). **Officers:** Odelio Otero, Partner.

■ **26661** ■ **Sparks Game & Toy Co.**
PO Box 2361
Pikeville, KY 41502-2361
Phone: (606)754-8069
Products: Toys; Hobby kits; Nonelectronic games. **SIC:** 5092 (Toys & Hobby Goods & Supplies). **Officers:** Bobby Sparks, Owner.

■ **26662** ■ **Special Promotion Co.**
3655 N 2400 E
Layton, UT 84040
Phone: (801)771-3649 **Fax:** (801)771-3648
Products: Electronic games; Audio and video cassettes; Movies; Games. **SICs:** 5092 (Toys & Hobby Goods & Supplies); 5065 (Electronic Parts & Equipment Nec). **Officers:** John Harris, President.

■ **26663** ■ **Spellbinders Inc.**
257 S Water St.
Kent, OH 44240-3525
Phone: (330)673-2230
Products: Comic books; Collectible games; Toys, hobby goods, and supplies. **SIC:** 5092 (Toys & Hobby Goods & Supplies). **Officers:** Paul Burdick, President.

■ **26664** ■ **Sportscards & Comics Center**
184 Deanna Dr.
Lowell, IN 46356-2403
Phone: (219)696-4323 **Fax:** (219)696-4323
Products: Collectibles, including cards and comics. **SIC:** 5199 (Nondurable Goods Nec). **Est:** 1991. **Officers:** Alfred Barker, Owner. **Former Name:** Shoes To Boot Center.

■ **26665** ■ **Al Stack**
6100 4th Ave. S 281
Seattle, WA 98108-3234
Phone: (206)762-7607
Free: (800)737-7929 **Fax:** (206)762-8731
Products: Toys and hobby goods and supplies, including board games. **SIC:** 5092 (Toys & Hobby Goods & Supplies). **Officers:** Al Stack, President.

■ **26666** ■ **Staff**
116 N Blettner Ave.
Hanover, PA 17331
Phone: (717)632-7455
Free: (800)727-7322 **Fax:** (717)632-4190
Products: Music boxes; Video games. **SIC:** 5092 (Toys & Hobby Goods & Supplies). **Emp:** 10. **Officers:** Clyde Laughman.

■ **26667** ■ **Stanislaus Imports Inc.**
41 14th St.
San Francisco, CA 94103
Phones: (415)431-7122 800-848-1986
Free: (800)227-4376 **Fax:** (415)431-4144
E-mail: LaSioux@aol.com
URL: http://www.lastan.com
Products: Artist's equipment; Craft kits. **SICs:** 5092 (Toys & Hobby Goods & Supplies); 5199 (Nondurable Goods Nec). **Est:** 1963. **Sales:** $3,200,000 (2000). **Emp:** 22. **Officers:** Stanley Siou, President.

■ **26668** ■ **Star Sales Company of Knoxville**
PO Box 1503
Knoxville, TN 37901
Phone: (865)524-0771 **Fax:** (865)524-4889
Products: Toys; Fishing supplies; Novelties; Craft supplies; Pocket knives. **SICs:** 5092 (Toys & Hobby Goods & Supplies); 5091 (Sporting & Recreational Goods); 5199 (Nondurable Goods Nec). **Est:** 1938. **Sales:** $16,000,000 (1999). **Emp:** 100. **Officers:** Neil Foster, CEO & President.

■ **26669** ■ **Starr Display Fireworks Inc.**
3805 52nd Ave. S
Fargo, ND 58104-5402
Phone: (701)469-2421 **Fax:** (701)469-2422
Products: Toys; Hobby kits; Fireworks; Gifts and novelties. **SIC:** 5092 (Toys & Hobby Goods & Supplies). **Officers:** Cameron Starr, President.

■ **26670** ■ **Steven Smith/Stuffed Animals Inc.**
330 E 89th St.
Brooklyn, NY 11236
Phone: (718)272-2500 **Fax:** (718)257-4668
Products: Stuffed animals with logos and custom designs. **SIC:** 5092 (Toys & Hobby Goods & Supplies). **Est:** 1977. **Emp:** 65. **Officers:** Steven Smith, President, e-mail: ssmithstuf@aol.com.

■ **26671** ■ **M.A. Storck & Co.**
PO Box 3758
Portland, ME 04104-3758
Phone: (207)774-7271
Free: (800)734-7271 **Fax:** (207)774-7272
E-mail: mastorck@compuserve.com
URL: http://www.mastorck.com
Products: Stamps and coins. **SIC:** 5092 (Toys & Hobby Goods & Supplies). **Est:** 1970. **Emp:** 3. **Officers:** James Simmons, Owner.

■ **26672** ■ **Strombecker Corp.**
600 N Pulaski Rd.
Chicago, IL 60624
Phone: (773)638-1000
Free: (800)944-8697 **Fax:** (773)638-3679
Products: Toys, including plastic cars, trucks, and guns. **SIC:** 5092 (Toys & Hobby Goods & Supplies). **Est:** 1876. **Sales:** $45,000,000 (2000). **Emp:** 400. **Officers:** Daniel B. Shure, President; James Ramig, CFO; Kevin Alexander, VP of Marketing.

■ **26673** ■ **Bob Sun Inc.**
PO Box 2637
Honolulu, HI 96803-2637
Phone: (808)845-5999 **Fax:** (808)842-7825
Products: Toys, games, hobby goods, and supplies. **SIC:** 5092 (Toys & Hobby Goods & Supplies). **Officers:** Robert Sun, President.

■ **26674** ■ **Sunset Models, Inc.**
138 W Campbell Ave.
Campbell, CA 95008
Phone: (408)866-1727 **Fax:** (408)866-5673
Products: Model trains. **SIC:** 5092 (Toys & Hobby Goods & Supplies).

■ **26675** ■ **Syndee's Crafts Inc.**
PO Box 94978
Las Vegas, NV 89193
Phone: (702)361-7888
Products: Patterns and parts for making dolls. **SIC:** 5092 (Toys & Hobby Goods & Supplies).

■ **26676** ■ **Tari-Tan Ceramic Supply Inc.**
3919 N Greenbrooke Dr. SE
Grand Rapids, MI 49512-5328
Phone: (616)698-2460
Products: Hobby goods and supplies. **SIC:** 5092 (Toys

& Hobby Goods & Supplies). **Officers:** Tana Wessell, President.

■ **26677** ■ **Tee Pee Advertising Co.**
155 Taft Ave.
Pocatello, ID 83201-5108
Phone: (208)233-2388
Free: (800)959-2388 **Fax:** (208)234-2270
Products: Toys and hobby goods. **SIC:** 5092 (Toys & Hobby Goods & Supplies). **Est:** 1954. **Sales:** $1,700,000 (2000). **Emp:** 26.

■ **26678** ■ **Testor Corp.**
620 Buckbee St.
Rockford, IL 61104
Phone: (815)962-6654 **Fax:** (815)962-7401
Products: Plastic model kits. **SIC:** 5092 (Toys & Hobby Goods & Supplies). **Sales:** $43,000,000 (2000). **Emp:** 250. **Officers:** David Miller, President; John Haussner, CFO.

■ **26679** ■ **Texas Hobby Distributors**
1516 Contour Dr.
San Antonio, TX 78212
Phone: (210)824-9688 **Fax:** (210)824-0810
Products: Plastic models, including cars; Remote controls. **SIC:** 5092 (Toys & Hobby Goods & Supplies).

■ **26680** ■ **Thomas Sales Company Inc.**
9050 Hwy. 421
Colfax, NC 27235
Phone: (336)992-3545 **Fax:** (336)992-3544
Products: Gifts and novelties; Hand tools. **SICs:** 5092 (Toys & Hobby Goods & Supplies); 5072 (Hardware); 5199 (Nondurable Goods Nec). **Est:** 1973. **Officers:** Douglas Thomas, President.

■ **26681** ■ **TJ Wholesale Distributor**
310 Wall St.
Las Vegas, NV 89102
Phone: (702)598-1938 **Fax:** (702)598-3951
Products: Cards; Game supplies. **SIC:** 5092 (Toys & Hobby Goods & Supplies).

■ **26682** ■ **Today's Kids Inc.**
Hwy. 10 E
Booneville, AR 72927
Phone: (501)675-2000 **Fax:** (501)675-3918
Products: Toys. **SIC:** 5092 (Toys & Hobby Goods & Supplies). **Est:** 1909. **Sales:** $27,000,000 (2000). **Emp:** 499. **Officers:** Vicky Rath. **Former Name:** Wolverine Toy.

■ **26683** ■ **Totsy Manufacturing Co., Inc.**
1 Bigelow St.
Holyoke, MA 01040
Phone: (413)536-0510
Free: (800)888-6879 **Fax:** (413)532-9804
Products: Dolls; Doll clothes and accessories. **SIC:** 5092 (Toys & Hobby Goods & Supplies). **Est:** 1930. **Sales:** $10,000,000 (2000). **Emp:** 85. **Officers:** Steven M. Feldman, President; Barry Schulman, Vice President.

■ **26684** ■ **Toy Farmer Ltd.**
RR 2, Box 5
Lamoure, ND 58458
Phone: (701)883-4430 **Fax:** (701)883-5204
Products: Toys, hobby goods, and supplies. **SIC:** 5092 (Toys & Hobby Goods & Supplies). **Officers:** Claire Scheibe, President.

■ **26685** ■ **Toy Wonders Inc.**
234 Moonachie Rd.
Moonachie, NJ 07074
Phone: (201)229-1700
Products: Toys. **SIC:** 5092 (Toys & Hobby Goods & Supplies).

■ **26686** ■ **The Toy Works, Inc.**
Fiddler's Elbow Rd.
Middle Falls, NY 12848
Phone: (518)692-9665
Free: (800)237-9526 **Fax:** (518)692-9186
E-mail: info@thetoyworks.com
URL: http://www.thetoyworks.com
Products: Silk screened stuffed animals; Pillows; Area rugs; Doormats; Backpacks; Canvas totes; Cloth books. **SIC:** 5092 (Toys & Hobby Goods & Supplies).

Est: 1974. **Sales:** $2,500,000 (2000). **Emp:** 30. **Officers:** John Gunther, President; Hester Gunther, Sales/Marketing Contact, e-mail: hester@ thetoyworks.com.

■ **26687** ■ **Trags Distributors**
3023 Hancock St., Ste. C
San Diego, CA 92110
Phone: (619)688-1156
Products: Role-paying and fantasy games. **SIC:** 5092 (Toys & Hobby Goods & Supplies).

■ **26688** ■ **Train Center Distributors**
506 S Broadway
Denver, CO 80209
Phone: (303)722-8444 **Fax:** (303)777-0028
Products: Hobby merchandise, including model trains. **SIC:** 5092 (Toys & Hobby Goods & Supplies).

■ **26689** ■ **Tri-State Hobbycraft**
1 Trimont Ln., Apt. 750C
Pittsburgh, PA 15211-1225
Phone: (412)481-2100 **Fax:** (412)481-9555
Products: Plane, car, and train models for hobbyists. **SIC:** 5092 (Toys & Hobby Goods & Supplies).

■ **26690** ■ **Trims II Inc.**
4636 E Elwood St., Ste. 2
Phoenix, AZ 85040-1963
Phone: (480)966-1564
Free: (800)742-6836 **Fax:** (480)966-2977
Products: Arts and crafts equipment and supplies. **SICs:** 5092 (Toys & Hobby Goods & Supplies); 5199 (Nondurable Goods Nec). **Est:** 1981. **Sales:** $250,000 (1999). **Emp:** 3. **Officers:** Emily Heedum, President.

■ **26691** ■ **Trost Modelcraft Hobbies**
3129 W 47th St.
Chicago, IL 60632-2901
Phone: (773)927-1400
Free: (800)367-8624 **Fax:** (773)927-1482
Products: Hobby kits; Craft kits. **SIC:** 5092 (Toys & Hobby Goods & Supplies). **Est:** 1928. **Emp:** 25.

■ **26692** ■ **Tucson Hobby Shop**
5250 E Pima St.
Tucson, AZ 85712-3630
Phone: (520)326-8006 **Fax:** (520)326-1004
Products: Toys and hobby goods. **SIC:** 5092 (Toys & Hobby Goods & Supplies). **Est:** 1949. **Sales:** $300,000 (2000). **Emp:** 5.

■ **26693** ■ **Tujay's Artist Dolls**
73 N Spring St.
Concord, NH 03301-4203
Phone: (603)226-4501
Products: Dolls. **SIC:** 5092 (Toys & Hobby Goods & Supplies). **Officers:** Joyce Miko, Partner.

■ **26694** ■ **Tulsa Automatic Music Co.**
1218 W Archer St.
Tulsa, OK 74127-8604
Phone: (918)584-4775
Products: Coin-operated mechanisms and parts. **SICs:** 5092 (Toys & Hobby Goods & Supplies); 5099 (Durable Goods Nec). **Officers:** Romine Hogard, President.

■ **26695** ■ **Tuttle Enterprises Inc.**
934 N Industrial Park Dr.
Orem, UT 84057-2804
Phone: (801)226-1517
Free: (800)498-1517 **Fax:** (801)226-1559
E-mail: sales@allcoopedup.com
URL: http://www.allcoopedup.com
Products: Craft supplies, including doll hair, resin faces, doll patterns, and kits. **SIC:** 5092 (Toys & Hobby Goods & Supplies). **Est:** 1980. **Emp:** 25. **Officers:** Becky Tuttle, President.

■ **26696** ■ **Twinson Co.**
1289-E Reamwood Ave.
Sunnyvale, CA 94089-2234
Phone: (408)734-9558 **Fax:** (408)734-9432
E-mail: twinsoncl@aol.com
URL: http://www.infolane.com/twinson/
Products: Educational games. **SIC:** 5092 (Toys & Hobby Goods & Supplies). **Est:** 1946. **Officers:** C. LeBaron, President; Mary B. Dancer, Partner.

■ **26697** ■ **Unicover Corp.**
1 Unicover Ctr.
Cheyenne, WY 82008-0001
Phone: (307)771-3000 **Fax:** (307)771-3134
Products: Philatelist stamps; Collectibles. **SIC:** 5092 (Toys & Hobby Goods & Supplies). **Officers:** James Helzer, President.

■ **26698** ■ **Unique Sales, Inc.**
1409 Hwy. 17
SurfsiDe Beach, SC 29575
Phone: (803)650-8989 **Free:** (800)522-6687
Products: Toys; Sunglasses; Hair accessories; Jewelry. **SICs:** 5092 (Toys & Hobby Goods & Supplies); 5094 (Jewelry & Precious Stones).

■ **26699** ■ **United Model Distributors Inc.**
301 Holbrook Dr.
Wheeling, IL 60090
Phone: (847)459-6700
Free: (800)323-1050 **Fax:** (847)459-4834
Products: Hobby supplies, including model trains and plastic models; Paints and cements; Kids activities and crafts. **SIC:** 5092 (Toys & Hobby Goods & Supplies). **Emp:** 30. **Officers:** R. Rovnick; R. Stone; K. Davis; Ranyd Kennie, Sales & Marketing Contact; Sally Meyer, Customer Service Contact.

■ **26700** ■ **U.S. Games Systems Inc.**
179 Ludlow St.
Stamford, CT 06902
Phone: (203)353-8400
Free: (800)544-2637 **Fax:** (203)353-8431
E-mail: usgames@aol.com
Products: Cards, including playing, gaming, and tarot. **SIC:** 5092 (Toys & Hobby Goods & Supplies). **Est:** 1968. **Sales:** $10,000,000 (2000). **Emp:** 38. **Officers:** Stuart R. Kaplan, Chairman of the Board; Granville R. Gargiulo, President; Hector Alfonso, Treasurer.

■ **26701** ■ **Universal Card & Coin Center Inc.**
18 Theresa Ave.
Lewiston, ME 04240-4723
Phone: (207)774-6724 **Fax:** (207)774-6724
Products: Toys; Hobby kits. **SIC:** 5092 (Toys & Hobby Goods & Supplies). **Est:** 1982. **Officers:** Robert Rioux, President.

■ **26702** ■ **Upper Mississippi Valley Mercantile Co.**
1607 Washington St.
Davenport, IA 52804
Phone: (319)322-0896 **Fax:** (319)383-5549
E-mail: umumco@mciworld.com
Products: Civil War costumes and props. **SIC:** 5092 (Toys & Hobby Goods & Supplies). **Est:** 1980. **Emp:** 6.

■ **26703** ■ **William G. Vallery Co.**
209 W Loveland Ave. 102
Loveland, OH 45140-2933
Phone: (513)677-3339
Products: Toys and hobby goods and supplies. **SIC:** 5092 (Toys & Hobby Goods & Supplies). **Officers:** William Vallery, President.

■ **26704** ■ **Victorian Pearl**
1010 Waverly St.
Eugene, OR 97401-5234
Phone: (541)343-1347
Products: Miniatures. **SIC:** 5092 (Toys & Hobby Goods & Supplies). **Est:** 1979. **Officers:** John Elliott.

■ **26705** ■ **Wm. K. Walthers Inc.**
PO Box 3039
Milwaukee, WI 53201
Phone: (414)527-0770 **Fax:** (414)527-4423
URL: http://www.walthers.com
Products: Model trains. **SIC:** 5092 (Toys & Hobby Goods & Supplies). **Est:** 1932. **Sales:** $25,000,000 (2000). **Emp:** 185. **Officers:** Philip Walthers, CEO; Paul Rotzenberg, Controller; John Sanheim, Dir. of Marketing.

■ **26706** ■ **Wang's International Inc.**
4250 E Shelby Dr.
Memphis, TN 38118
Phone: (901)362-2111
Free: (800)633-8094 **Fax:** (901)362-2292
Products: Arts and crafts supplies. **SICs:** 5092 (Toys

& Hobby Goods & Supplies); 5199 (Nondurable Goods Nec). **Sales:** $165,000,000 (2000). **Emp:** 450. **Officers:** Robert Wang, CEO & President; Jerry Shore, CFO.

■ **26707** ■ **Wargames West**
2434 Baylor SE
Albuquerque, NM 87106
Phone: (505)242-1773
Free: (800)SOS-GAME **Fax:** (505)242-3540
Products: Toys and hobby goods. **SIC:** 5092 (Toys & Hobby Goods & Supplies). **Est:** 1979.

■ **26708** ■ **Well Made Toy Manufacturing Co.**
184-10 Jamaica Ave.
Hollis, NY 11423
Phone: (718)454-1326 **Fax:** (718)454-7862
E-mail: WMTNY@aol.com
Products: Stuffed toy animals and dolls; Rag dolls; Vinyl face dolls. **SIC:** 5092 (Toys & Hobby Goods & Supplies). **Est:** 1968. **Sales:** $6,000,000 (1999). **Emp:** 50. **Officers:** Fred F. Catapano; Susan Cook, Sales/Marketing Contact; Amy-Iris Cordero, Customer Service Contact.

■ **26709** ■ **Western Depot**
PO Box 3001
Yuba City, CA 95992-3001
Phone: (530)673-6776 **Fax:** (530)673-5590
E-mail: wdepot@westerndepot.com
URL: http://www.westerndepot.com
Products: Railroad gift items. **SICs:** 5092 (Toys & Hobby Goods & Supplies); 5199 (Nondurable Goods Nec). **Est:** 1978. **Officers:** Robert M. McBratney.

■ **26710** ■ **Western Star Distributors**
325 N 2nd St.
Lompoc, CA 93436
Phone: (805)736-1865
Free: (800)848-8455 **Fax:** (805)736-6203
Products: Toys and hobby goods. **SIC:** 5092 (Toys & Hobby Goods & Supplies). **Est:** 1985. **Sales:** $1,000,000 (2000). **Emp:** 8.

■ **26711** ■ **Western Toy and Hobby Inc.**
160 West 21st South
Salt Lake City, UT 84115-1829
Phone: (801)486-5831 **Fax:** (801)486-5944
Products: Toys; Hobby kits; School supplies; Notions; Yarn. **SIC:** 5092 (Toys & Hobby Goods & Supplies). **Est:** 1952. **Sales:** $3,000,000 (2000). **Emp:** 17. **Officers:** Herald Hammond, President.

■ **26712** ■ **Western Trading Post Inc.**
PO Box 9070
Denver, CO 80209-0070
Phone: (303)777-7750 **Fax:** (303)698-1387
Products: Arts and crafts equipment and supplies. **SICs:** 5092 (Toys & Hobby Goods & Supplies); 5199 (Nondurable Goods Nec). **Officers:** Ronald Eberhart, President.

■ **26713** ■ **Winchester Sutler**
270 Shadow Brook Ln.
Winchester, VA 22603
Phone: (540)888-3595 **Fax:** (540)888-4632
Products: Civil War reproductions. **SIC:** 5092 (Toys & Hobby Goods & Supplies).

■ **26714** ■ **Wisconsin Toy Company Inc.**
1107 Broadway, Ste. 1408
New York, NY 10010
Phone: (212)741-2125 **Fax:** (212)645-7052
E-mail: jmarcus@cnstores.com
Products: Toys. **SIC:** 5092 (Toys & Hobby Goods & Supplies).

■ **26715** ■ **Wood-N-Stuf**
520 W Sunset Rd., Ste. 1
Henderson, NV 89015-4117
Phone: (702)564-0178
Products: Toys and hobby goods and supplies; Arts and crafts equipment and supplies; Custom work. **SICs:** 5092 (Toys & Hobby Goods & Supplies); 5199 (Nondurable Goods Nec). **Officers:** John Burns, Owner.

■ **26716** ■ **The Wright One Enterprises Inc.**
909 SE Everett Mall Way, Ste. B-200
Everett, WA 98208
Phone: (425)355-5005   **Fax:** (425)348-7292
Products: Toys and hobby goods. **SIC:** 5092 (Toys & Hobby Goods & Supplies). **Est:** 1980. **Sales:** $1,500,000 (2000). **Emp:** 4.

■ **26717** ■ **The Yarn Center**
Rte. 2, Box 2691
Chatsworth, GA 30705
Phone: (706)695-3443
Products: Lead pencils, crayons, and artists' materials. **SICs:** 5092 (Toys & Hobby Goods & Supplies); 5199 (Nondurable Goods Nec).

■ **26718** ■ **Yesco Ltd.**
1960 Crossbeam Dr.
Charlotte, NC 28217-2820
Phone: (704)357-6363   **Fax:** (704)357-6369
Products: Toys and hobby goods. **SIC:** 5092 (Toys & Hobby Goods & Supplies). **Est:** 1980. **Sales:** $15,000,000 (2000). **Emp:** 12.

■ **26719** ■ **ZDI Gaming Inc.**
4117 NE Minnehaha St.
Vancouver, WA 98661-1241
Phone: (360)693-6200
Free: (800)456-3973   **Fax:** (360)694-6639
Products: Bingo supplies. **SIC:** 5092 (Toys & Hobby Goods & Supplies). **Est:** 1985. **Sales:** $6,500,000 (2000). **Emp:** 28. **Officers:** Melanie Keser; Curt Grothe; Jay Gerow; Donald Grothe. **Former Name:** Zanotto Distributing Company Inc.

■ **26720** ■ **Zeiger International Inc.**
625 Prospect St.
Trenton, NJ 08618
Phone: (609)394-1000
Products: Russian dolls and craftware; Polish craftware; German nutcrackers. **SICs:** 5092 (Toys & Hobby Goods & Supplies); 5199 (Nondurable Goods Nec). **Sales:** $25,000,000 (2000). **Emp:** 16. **Officers:** Shelly Zeiger, CEO.

■ **26721** ■ **Zims Inc.**
4370 South 300 West
Salt Lake City, UT 84107
Phone: (801)268-2505
Free: (800)453-6420   **Fax:** (801)268-9859
E-mail: zims@zimscrafts.com
URL: http://www.zimscrafts.com
Products: Arts and crafts; Wood products. **SICs:** 5092 (Toys & Hobby Goods & Supplies); 5199 (Nondurable Goods Nec). **Est:** 1932. **Sales:** $5,000,000 (1999). **Emp:** 70. **Officers:** C. Zimmerman, President.

■ **26722** ■ **Zocchi Distributors**
PO Box 5009
Holly Springs, MS 38634-5009
Free: (800)476-0600
Products: Toys and hobby goods. **SIC:** 5092 (Toys & Hobby Goods & Supplies). **Est:** 1976. **Sales:** $1,000,000 (2000). **Emp:** 7.

(59) Used, Scrap, and Recycled Materials

Entries in this section are arranged alphabetically by company name. When the company name is a personal name, the company name is alphabetized by the surname unless the first name or initial(s) are part of a trade name. See the User's Guide at the front of this directory for additional information.

■ 26723 ■ **A and B Wiper Supply Inc.**
116 Fountain St.
Philadelphia, PA 19127
Phone: (215)482-6100 **Fax:** (215)482-6190
Products: Wiping materials, including rags. **SIC:** 5087 (Service Establishment Equipment). **Est:** 1948. **Sales:** $4,500,000 (1999). **Emp:** 60. **Officers:** H. Kanefsky, Vice President; J. Kanefsky, CFO; M. Klausman, Dir. of Marketing.

■ 26724 ■ **Aaron Scrap Metals**
PO Box 607069
Orlando, FL 32860-7069
Phone: (407)293-6584 **Fax:** (407)295-4908
Products: Scrap metal recycling. **SIC:** 5093 (Scrap & Waste Materials). **Sales:** $18,000,000 (2000). **Emp:** 60. **Officers:** Greg Ledet, General Mgr.

■ 26725 ■ **Abbey Metal Corp.**
70 Commercial Ave.
Moonachie, NJ 07074
Phone: (201)438-0330
Products: Scrap metal. **SICs:** 5051 (Metals Service Centers & Offices); 5093 (Scrap & Waste Materials). **Est:** 1947. **Sales:** $6,000,000 (2000). **Emp:** 11. **Officers:** Burton Zuckerman, President; Kenneth Zuckerman, CFO.

■ 26726 ■ **ACC Recycling Corp.**
1190 20th St. N
St. Petersburg, FL 33713
Phone: (813)896-9600 **Fax:** (813)822-4923
Products: Recycled paper products. **SIC:** 5093 (Scrap & Waste Materials). **Sales:** $20,000,000 (2000). **Emp:** 45. **Officers:** Michael Accomando, President.

■ 26727 ■ **Accurate Iron and Metal Co.**
25 Horseshoe Ln.
Lemont, IL 60439-9150
Phone: (773)404-7771
Products: Recycled metals, including iron, steel, and aluminum. **SIC:** 5093 (Scrap & Waste Materials). **Sales:** $3,000,000 (2000). **Emp:** 5. **Officers:** Judy Ferraro, President.

■ 26728 ■ **Adams International Metals Corp.**
3200 E Frontera Rd.
Anaheim, CA 92806
Phone: (714)630-8901 **Fax:** (714)630-8931
Products: Recycled metals. **SIC:** 5093 (Scrap & Waste Materials). **Est:** 1949. **Sales:** $5,400,000 (2000). **Emp:** 59. **Officers:** George Adams Sr., CEO & Chairman of the Board; Wendy Clark, Controller.

■ 26729 ■ **Addington Environmental Inc.**
2343 Alexandria Dr., Ste. 400
Lexington, KY 40504
Phone: (606)223-3824
Products: Metal recycling. **SIC:** 5051 (Metals Service Centers & Offices). **Sales:** $2,000,000 (1994). **Emp:** 30. **Officers:** Jack T. Baker, VP & General Merchandising Mgr.

■ 26730 ■ **Addington Holdings Inc.**
1500 N Big Run
Ashland, KY 41102
Phone: (606)928-3433
Products: Waste recycling. **SIC:** 5093 (Scrap & Waste Materials).

■ 26731 ■ **Addlestone International Corp.**
PO Drawer 979
Charleston, SC 29402
Phone: (803)577-9300 **Fax:** (803)577-9290
Products: Scrap metal. **SIC:** 5093 (Scrap & Waste Materials). **Est:** 1930. **Sales:** $69,000,000 (2000). **Emp:** 60. **Officers:** Nathan Addlestone, President; Keith S. Rosen, Vice President.

■ 26732 ■ **Advanced Environmental Recycling Technologies Inc.**
PO Box 1237
Springdale, AR 72765
Phone: (501)750-1299
Products: Recycled materials. **SIC:** 5093 (Scrap & Waste Materials). **Emp:** 139.

■ 26733 ■ **Aerospace Metals Inc.**
500 Flatbush Ave.
Hartford, CT 06106
Phone: (860)522-3123 **Fax:** (860)724-9245
Products: Aerospace scrap metal. **SIC:** 5093 (Scrap & Waste Materials). **Sales:** $55,000,000 (2000). **Emp:** 120. **Officers:** Paul Haveson, President; Robert Kaseta, VP of Finance.

■ 26734 ■ **Alcan Recycling**
PO Box 127
Shelbyville, TN 37162
Phone: (615)684-0300 **Fax:** (615)684-1234
Products: Recycled aluminum. **SIC:** 5093 (Scrap & Waste Materials). **Est:** 1990. **Sales:** $75,000,000 (2000). **Emp:** 85. **Officers:** David Christoffersen, General Mgr.; Ray Hopkins, Accounting Manager; Robert L. Holden, Sales Mgr.; Stacey Haddock, Personnel Mgr.

■ 26735 ■ **Allan Co.**
14620 Joanbridge St.
Baldwin Park, CA 91706
Phone: (626)962-4047 **Fax:** (626)962-7611
Products: Cans, aluminum, glass and plastic recycling. **SIC:** 5093 (Scrap & Waste Materials). **Sales:** $92,000,000 (2000). **Emp:** 200. **Officers:** Steve Young, President; Joe Peterson, CFO.

■ 26736 ■ **A. Allan Industries Inc.**
PO Box 999
Wilkes Barre, PA 18701
Phone: (717)826-0123 **Fax:** (717)829-4099
Products: Recycled steel, brass, and aluminum. **SIC:** 5093 (Scrap & Waste Materials). **Est:** 1950. **Sales:** $5,000,000 (2000). **Emp:** 25. **Officers:** A.J. Allan, President.

■ 26737 ■ **Alliance Steel Service Co.**
115 31st Ave. N
Minneapolis, MN 55411
Phone: (612)588-2721
Free: (800)246-1269 **Fax:** (612)588-2724
Products: Used, scrap, and recycled materials. **SIC:** 5093 (Scrap & Waste Materials). **Est:** 1957. **Sales:** $7,000,000 (2000). **Emp:** 17.

■ 26738 ■ **Allied Metals Corp.**
320 E Seven Mile Rd.
Detroit, MI 48203
Phone: (313)368-7110
Products: Scrap metals. **SIC:** 5051 (Metals Service Centers & Offices). **Sales:** $14,000,000 (1992). **Emp:** 20. **Officers:** Gary Wasserman, President.

■ 26739 ■ **Allied Scrap Processors Inc.**
PO Box 1585
Lakeland, FL 33802
Phone: (941)665-7157
Products: Scrap metals. **SIC:** 5093 (Scrap & Waste Materials). **Est:** 1968. **Sales:** $5,000,000 (2000). **Emp:** 30. **Officers:** Frank Giglia Sr., President; Brenda Giglia, Treasurer; Frank Giglia Jr., Vice President; Rose Carey, Secretary.

■ 26740 ■ **Allied Vista Inc. Vista Fibers**
PO Box 807
San Antonio, TX 78293
Phone: (210)226-6371
Products: Recycle cardboard and computer paper. **SIC:** 5093 (Scrap & Waste Materials). **Sales:** $5,000,000 (2000). **Emp:** 15.

■ 26741 ■ **Allwaste Inc.**
5151 San Felipe, No. 1600
Houston, TX 77056
Phone: (713)623-8777 **Free:** (800)726-1300
Products: Scrap and waste materials. **SIC:** 5093 (Scrap & Waste Materials). **Est:** 1986. **Sales:** $337,200,000 (2000). **Emp:** 3,772. **Officers:** Robert M. Chiste, CEO & President; T. Wayne Wren Jr., VP & CFO.

■ 26742 ■ **Allwaste Inc. Allwaste Recycling Div.**
4200 Fidelity Rd.
Houston, TX 77029
Phone: (713)676-1500
Products: Recycled glass products. **SIC:** 5093 (Scrap & Waste Materials). **Sales:** $2,000,000 (2000). **Emp:** 10. **Officers:** David Reeves, General Mgr.

■ 26743 ■ **Alma Iron and Metal Company Inc.**
PO Box 729
Alma, MI 48801
Phone: (517)463-2131 **Fax:** (517)463-2135
Products: Scrap metal. **SICs:** 5093 (Scrap & Waste Materials); 5051 (Metals Service Centers & Offices). **Est:** 1974. **Sales:** $5,000,000 (2000). **Emp:** 45. **Officers:** David A. Simon, President; Forrest Herzog, Controller; R.S. Simon, Vice President.

■ **26744** ■ **Alpert and Alpert Iron and Metal Inc.**
1815 S Soto St.
Los Angeles, CA 90023
Phone: (323)265-4040   **Fax:** (323)264-9839
E-mail: scrap@alpertandalpert.com
URL: http://www.alpertandalpert.com
Products: Ferrous and non-ferrous metals. **SIC:** 5051 (Metals Service Centers & Offices). **Est:** 1930. **Sales:** $100,000,000 (1999). **Emp:** 150. **Officers:** Alan Alpert, President; Howard Farber, Pres., Alpert Group; Freddy Cohen, Sales & Marketing Contact, e-mail: scrap@alpertandalpert.com.

■ **26745** ■ **Alter Norfolk Corp.**
500 Washington Ave.
Norfolk, NE 68701
Phone: (402)371-2200
Products: Scrap metal, including iron. **SIC:** 5093 (Scrap & Waste Materials). **Est:** 1990. **Sales:** $4,000,000 (2000). **Emp:** 7. **Officers:** Mark D. McKinley, General Mgr.

■ **26746** ■ **Alter Scrap Processing**
PO Box 220
West Burlington, IA 52655
Phone: (319)752-3643
Products: Scrap and new steel. **SIC:** 5093 (Scrap & Waste Materials). **Est:** 1898. **Sales:** $2,000,000 (2000). **Emp:** 10. **Officers:** Loren Stein, Plant Mgr. **Former Name:** Chanens Scrap and Steel Inc.

■ **26747** ■ **Alter Trading Corp.**
2117 State St.
Bettendorf, IA 52722
Phone: (319)344-5200   **Fax:** (319)344-5204
Products: Scrap metal. **SIC:** 5093 (Scrap & Waste Materials). **Est:** 1898. **Emp:** 250. **Officers:** Robert Goldstein, President; Robert Pezley; Rufus Moore.

■ **26748** ■ **Alter Trading Corp.**
555 N New Ballas Rd.
St. Louis, MO 63141
Phone: (314)872-2400
Free: (800)553-6722   **Fax:** (314)872-2420
Products: Scrap metal. **SIC:** 5093 (Scrap & Waste Materials). **Sales:** $9,000,000 (2000). **Emp:** 20. **Officers:** Keith Rhodes, President & CFO.

■ **26749** ■ **Ambit Pacific Recycling Inc.**
16222 S Figueroa St.
Gardena, CA 90247
Phone: (310)327-2227
Products: Recycled cardboard, newspaper, office paper, and metal. **SIC:** 5093 (Scrap & Waste Materials).

■ **26750** ■ **AMCEP Inc.**
4484 E Tennessee St.
Tucson, AZ 85714
Phone: (520)748-1900
Products: Recycled metals. **SIC:** 5093 (Scrap & Waste Materials). **Est:** 1967. **Sales:** $7,000,000 (2000). **Emp:** 20. **Officers:** Robert Hoover, President.

■ **26751** ■ **American Iron and Supply Co.**
2800 Pacific St. N
Minneapolis, MN 55411
Phone: (612)529-9221   **Fax:** (612)529-2548
E-mail: sales@scrappy.com
URL: http://www.scrappy.com
Products: Scrap metal processing and recycling. **SIC:** 5093 (Scrap & Waste Materials). **Est:** 1885. **Sales:** $18,000,000 (2000). **Emp:** 50. **Officers:** John D. Issacs, CEO; Roger Muritz, Chairman of the Board & Finance Officer; Daryl Parks, VP & General Mgr.

■ **26752** ■ **Annaco Inc.**
PO Box 1148
Akron, OH 44309
Phone: (216)376-1400   **Fax:** (216)376-9696
Products: Scrap metals. **SIC:** 5093 (Scrap & Waste Materials). **Est:** 1929. **Sales:** $28,000,000 (2000). **Emp:** 75. **Officers:** Morris M. Berzon, President; William W. Lowery, Exec. VP of Finance.

■ **26753** ■ **Arizona Recycling Corp.**
400 S 15th Ave.
Phoenix, AZ 85007
Phone: (602)258-5323
Products: Recycled aluminum, iron, tin, and other materials. **SIC:** 5093 (Scrap & Waste Materials).

■ **26754** ■ **Arizona Scrap Iron and Metals Inc.**
433 S 7th Ave.
Phoenix, AZ 85007
Phone: (602)252-8423
Products: Recycled iron and other metals. **SIC:** 5093 (Scrap & Waste Materials).

■ **26755** ■ **Atlas Steel Inc.**
4221 W 700 S
Salt Lake City, UT 84104
Phone: (801)975-9669   **Fax:** (801)973-0065
Products: Recycled metals, including iron, steel, copper, and brass. **SIC:** 5093 (Scrap & Waste Materials). **Est:** 1972. **Sales:** $30,000,000 (2000). **Emp:** 80. **Officers:** John Spiegel, President; Paula George, Controller.

■ **26756** ■ **Auto Shred Recycling L.L.C.**
PO Box 17188
Pensacola, FL 32522
Phone: (904)432-0977   **Fax:** (904)433-4814
Products: Scrap metal. **SIC:** 5093 (Scrap & Waste Materials). **Est:** 1976. **Sales:** $15,000,000 (2000). **Emp:** 65. **Officers:** Dennis Arrubarrena, President; Richard Creele, Controller; B. Fish, Dir. of Marketing.

■ **26757** ■ **C. Bamberger Molding Compounds Inc.**
PO Box 67
Carlstadt, NJ 07072
Phone: (201)933-6262   **Fax:** (201)933-8129
Products: Scrap materials and purging compounds. **SIC:** 5093 (Scrap & Waste Materials). **Est:** 1953. **Sales:** $6,000,000 (2000). **Emp:** 8. **Officers:** Claude P. Bamberger, President.

■ **26758** ■ **B. Barer and Sons**
PO Box 1492
WalLa Walla, WA 99362
Phone: (509)529-3060
Products: Bearings; Scrap metal. **SIC:** 5093 (Scrap & Waste Materials).

■ **26759** ■ **Barry Metals Company Inc.**
3014 N 30th Ave.
Phoenix, AZ 85017
Phone: (602)484-7186
Products: Recycled aluminum and non-ferrous metal. **SIC:** 5093 (Scrap & Waste Materials).

■ **26760** ■ **Basic Fibres Inc.**
6019 S Manhattan Pl.
Los Angeles, CA 90047
Phone: (213)753-3491
Products: Recycled steel cans, aluminum, glass, and paper. **SIC:** 5093 (Scrap & Waste Materials).

■ **26761** ■ **Bay Polymer Corp.**
44530 Grimmer Blvd.
Fremont, CA 94538
Phone: (510)490-1791
Products: Recycled plastic. **SIC:** 5162 (Plastics Materials & Basic Shapes). **Est:** 1978. **Sales:** $3,000,000 (2000). **Emp:** 20. **Officers:** John LaFountain, President; Estraeata Gonzales, Office Mgr.

■ **26762** ■ **Bedford Recycling Inc.**
PO Box 155
Bedford, IN 47421
Phone: (812)275-6883   **Fax:** (812)275-1991
Products: Metal waste and scrap. **SIC:** 5093 (Scrap & Waste Materials). **Sales:** $10,000,000 (2000). **Emp:** 18. **Officers:** Larry Parsons, President.

■ **26763** ■ **Behr Iron and Steel Inc.**
PO Box 740
Rockford, IL 61105
Phone: (815)987-2600
Products: Recycled scrap iron and steel. **SIC:** 5093 (Scrap & Waste Materials).

■ **26764** ■ **Joseph Behr and Sons Inc.**
1100 Seminary St.
Rockford, IL 61108
Phone: (815)987-2600
Products: Scrap metal. **SIC:** 5093 (Scrap & Waste Materials). **Est:** 1906. **Sales:** $70,000,000 (2000). **Emp:** 245. **Officers:** R. Behr, President; William H. Day, Finance Officer.

■ **26765** ■ **Best Disposal Inc.**
PO Box 6644
Phoenix, AZ 85005
Phone: (602)237-2078
Products: Recycled metal products. **SIC:** 5093 (Scrap & Waste Materials).

■ **26766** ■ **BFI/Allied Recyclery Mpls**
725 44th Ave. N
Minneapolis, MN 55412
Phone: (612)522-6558   **Fax:** (612)522-7608
Products: Recyclable paper; Curbside materials. **SIC:** 5093 (Scrap & Waste Materials). **Est:** 1981. **Sales:** $14,000,000 (2000). **Emp:** 40. **Officers:** Charles Auld, Site Mgr. **Former Name:** Recycling Services Inc.

■ **26767** ■ **BFI Waste Systems of North America Inc.**
3840 NW 37th Ct.
Miami, FL 33142
Phone: (305)638-3800   **Fax:** (305)634-4272
Products: Used, scrap, and recycled materials. **SIC:** 5093 (Scrap & Waste Materials). **Est:** 1972. **Sales:** $47,000,000 (2000). **Emp:** 450.

■ **26768** ■ **Bloch Metals Inc.**
PO Box 306
Tyler, TX 75710
Phone: (903)597-4552   **Fax:** (903)597-6242
Products: Scrap metal, including steel and aluminum. **SIC:** 5093 (Scrap & Waste Materials). **Est:** 1958. **Sales:** $1,000,000 (2000). **Emp:** 30. **Officers:** Bruce Bloch, President.

■ **26769** ■ **Bonded Insulation Company Inc.**
PO Box 337
Hagaman, NY 12086
Phone: (518)842-1470
Products: Recycled newspapers. **SIC:** 5093 (Scrap & Waste Materials).

■ **26770** ■ **Bradley Landfill and Recycling Center**
9081 Tujunga Ave., No. 2
Sun Valley, CA 91352-1516
Phone: (818)767-6180   **Fax:** (818)252-3249
Products: Salvage and recycled products. **SIC:** 5093 (Scrap & Waste Materials). **Est:** 1984. **Sales:** $13,000,000 (1999). **Emp:** 84. **Officers:** Scott Tignac, Manager; Greg Golinski, Controller.

■ **26771** ■ **Bristol Metal Co. Inc.**
PO Box 596
Bristol, RI 02809
Phone: (401)253-4070   **Fax:** (401)253-2651
Products: Scrap metal. **SIC:** 5093 (Scrap & Waste Materials). **Sales:** $10,000,000 (2000). **Emp:** 17. **Officers:** Angelo Stanzione, President.

■ **26772** ■ **Browning-Ferris Industries of Michigan Inc.**
5400 Cogswell Rd.
Wayne, MI 48184
Phone: (734)729-8200   **Fax:** (734)729-5102
Products: Recycled scrap and waste materials. **SIC:** 5093 (Scrap & Waste Materials). **Sales:** $11,000,000 (2000). **Emp:** 150. **Officers:** Denise Gretz, Finance General Manager.

■ **26773** ■ **BTM Recycling**
PO Box 641461
Los Angeles, CA 90047
Phone: (310)477-9636
Products: Recycled aluminum, glass, and paper. **SIC:** 5093 (Scrap & Waste Materials).

■ **26774** ■ **Butech Inc.**
777 S Ellsworth Ave.
Salem, OH 44460
Phone: (330)332-9913 **Fax:** (330)337-0800
Products: Scrap metal choppers. **SIC:** 5093 (Scrap & Waste Materials). **Emp:** 38.

■ **26775** ■ **Calbag Metals Co.**
PO Box 10067
Portland, OR 97210
Phone: (503)226-3441
Products: Recycled metals. **SIC:** 5093 (Scrap & Waste Materials). **Est:** 1954. **Sales:** $50,000,000 (2000). **Emp:** 40. **Officers:** Victor A. Rosenfeld, Chairman of the Board; W.J. Rosenfeld, President; Bruce Halperin, Dir. of Operations.

■ **26776** ■ **Can Land Recycling Center Inc.**
6141 N Federal Blvd.
Denver, CO 80221
Phone: (303)426-4141
Products: Scrap aluminum. **SIC:** 5093 (Scrap & Waste Materials). **Est:** 1989. **Sales:** $1,000,000 (2000). **Emp:** 5. **Officers:** Ed Pearman, President.

■ **26777** ■ **Canusa Corp.**
1616 Shakespeare St.
Baltimore, MD 21231
Phone: (410)522-0110 **Fax:** (410)327-4295
Products: Recyclable secondary fiber. **SIC:** 5113 (Industrial & Personal Service Paper). **Est:** 1985. **Sales:** $30,000,000 (2000). **Emp:** 35. **Officers:** Bruce Flemming, President; William Mullen Jr., Controller.

■ **26778** ■ **Chemical Waste Management Inc.**
720 E Butterfield Rd., 2nd Fl.
Lombard, IL 60148-5689
Phone: (630)218-1500
Products: Scrap and waste materials. **SIC:** 5093 (Scrap & Waste Materials). **Est:** 1978. **Emp:** 3,600. **Officers:** Michael J. Cole, President; Jerome D. Girsch, Exec. VP & CFO.

■ **26779** ■ **City Metal Company Inc.**
279 Jenckes Hill Rd.
Smithfield, RI 02917-1905
Products: Scrap and waste materials. **SIC:** 5093 (Scrap & Waste Materials). **Officers:** Greg Cimino, President.

■ **26780** ■ **CMC Secondary Metals Processing Div.**
PO Box 1046
Dallas, TX 75221
Phone: (214)689-4300 **Fax:** (214)689-5835
E-mail: admin@commercialmetals.com
URL: http://www.commercialmetals.com
Products: Metal recycling. **SIC:** 5093 (Scrap & Waste Materials). **Est:** 1915. **Sales:** $2,251,442 (1999). **Emp:** 8,000. **Officers:** Harry J. Heinkele, President. **Former Name:** CMC Recycling Div.

■ **26781** ■ **Commercial Metals Co. Commercial Levin Div.**
PO Box 30
Burlington, NC 27216
Phone: (336)584-0333
Products: Ferrous and nonferrous scrap metal recycling. **SIC:** 5093 (Scrap & Waste Materials). **Sales:** $22,000,000 (2000). **Emp:** 50.

■ **26782** ■ **Commercial Waste Paper Company Inc.**
PO Box 3583
El Monte, CA 91733-0583
Phone: (626)448-6649
Products: Paper recyclers. **SIC:** 5093 (Scrap & Waste Materials). **Sales:** $30,000,000 (1994). **Emp:** 80. **Officers:** John Macardican, President.

■ **26783** ■ **Connell L.P. Luria Brothers Div.**
20521 Chagrin Blvd.
Cleveland, OH 44122
Phone: (216)752-4000 **Fax:** (216)752-4030
Products: Scrap steel; Plate steel. **SICs:** 5093 (Scrap & Waste Materials); 5051 (Metals Service Centers & Offices). **Est:** 1879. **Sales:** $290,000,000 (2000). **Emp:** 500. **Officers:** Robert Hahn, President; Dennis Salo, Dir. of Systems.

■ **26784** ■ **Consolidated Scrap Processing**
23 Perrine St.
Auburn, NY 13021
Phone: (315)253-0373
Products: Scrap metal. **SIC:** 5093 (Scrap & Waste Materials). **Est:** 1948. **Sales:** $4,000,000 (2000). **Emp:** 20. **Officers:** Alan Aroneck, President.

■ **26785** ■ **Consolidated Scrap Resources, Inc.**
PO Box 1761
Harrisburg, PA 17105
Phone: (717)233-7927 **Fax:** (717)233-3567
Products: Scrap steel. **SIC:** 5093 (Scrap & Waste Materials). **Emp:** 35. **Officers:** Richard E. Abrams, Chairman & CEO. **Former Name:** B. Abrams and Sons Inc.

■ **26786** ■ **Container Recycling Alliance**
8770 W Bryn Mawr Ave., No. 10R
Chicago, IL 60631
Phone: (312)399-8400
Products: Recycled glass and metals. **SIC:** 5093 (Scrap & Waste Materials). **Est:** 1991. **Sales:** $25,000,000 (2000). **Emp:** 30. **Officers:** Charles Porta, President; Steven Ryndak, CFO.

■ **26787** ■ **Continental Paper Grading Co.**
1623 S Lumber St.
Chicago, IL 60616
Phone: (312)226-2010
Products: Waste paper. **SIC:** 5093 (Scrap & Waste Materials). **Est:** 1919. **Sales:** $10,000,000 (2000). **Emp:** 19. **Officers:** S. Epstein, President & Treasurer; D. Kessler, CFO.

■ **26788** ■ **Continental Recycling Inc.**
620 Truxton St.
Bronx, NY 10474
Phone: (718)842-2842
Products: Recycled building materials. **SIC:** 5093 (Scrap & Waste Materials).

■ **26789** ■ **Conversion Resources Inc.**
10145 Philipp Pky.
Streetsboro, OH 44241-4706
Phone: (440)786-7700
Products: Scrap metals. **SIC:** 5093 (Scrap & Waste Materials).

■ **26790** ■ **Cozzi Iron and Metal Inc.**
2232 S Blue Island Ave.
Chicago, IL 60608
Phone: (773)254-1200 **Fax:** (773)254-8201
URL: http://www.cimscrap.com
Products: Recycled metal. **SIC:** 5093 (Scrap & Waste Materials). **Est:** 1965. **Sales:** $350,000,000 (2000). **Emp:** 500. **Officers:** Frank Cozzi, President; Mike Mitchell, CFO; Greg Cozzi, VP of Sales; Tom Cohrs, VP of Operations.

■ **26791** ■ **Curcio Scrap Metal Inc.**
416 Lanza Ave.
Saddle Brook, NJ 07663-6405
Phone: (973)478-3133 **Fax:** (973)478-2572
Products: Used, scrap, and recycled materials. **SIC:** 5093 (Scrap & Waste Materials). **Est:** 1964. **Sales:** $5,000,000 (2000). **Emp:** 12.

■ **26792** ■ **Custom-Pak Inc.**
PO Box 3083
Clinton, IA 52732
Phone: (319)242-1801
Products: Plastic recycling. **SIC:** 5093 (Scrap & Waste Materials). **Sales:** $43,000,000 (1992). **Emp:** 600. **Officers:** Richard Olsen, President; L. Laurent, VP of Finance.

■ **26793** ■ **Damille Metal Supply Inc.**
PO Box 2512
Huntington Park, CA 90255
Phone: (213)587-6001
Products: Recycled iron and non-ferrous metal. **SIC:** 5093 (Scrap & Waste Materials).

■ **26794** ■ **D.C. Materials Inc.**
3334 Kenilworth Ave., Ste. B
Hyattsville, MD 20781
Phone: (301)403-0200
Products: Recycled asphalt, concrete, aggregate, and related materials. **SIC:** 5032 (Brick, Stone & Related Materials).

■ **26795** ■ **Delta Poly Plastic Inc.**
PO Box 799
Stuttgart, AR 72160
Phone: (870)673-7458
Products: Recycled plastics. **SIC:** 5093 (Scrap & Waste Materials).

■ **26796** ■ **Dempster Equipment**
PO Box 1388
Toccoa, GA 30577-6388
Phone: (706)886-2327 **Fax:** (706)886-0088
Products: Refuse and recyling. **SIC:** 5093 (Scrap & Waste Materials). **Sales:** $21,000,000 (2000). **Emp:** 120. **Officers:** John Boonstra, President; Jerry Steeber, Controller.

■ **26797** ■ **Denton Plastics Inc.**
4427 NE 158th Ave.
Portland, OR 97230
Phone: (503)257-9945 **Fax:** (503)252-5319
Products: Recycled plastic. **SIC:** 5093 (Scrap & Waste Materials). **Est:** 1983. **Sales:** $4,200,000 (2000). **Emp:** 50. **Officers:** Dennis Denton, President; Richard Winn, CFO; Jeffrey J. Walter, Vice President.

■ **26798** ■ **Dobrow Industries**
PO Box 2188
Muncie, IN 47307-0188
Phone: (765)284-1497
Products: Ferrous and nonferrous scrap materials. **SIC:** 5093 (Scrap & Waste Materials). **Est:** 1924. **Sales:** $9,000,000 (2000). **Emp:** 30. **Officers:** Edward J. Dobrow, President; Catherine Swift, Controller.

■ **26799** ■ **DuBarry International Inc.**
10624 Southeastern, Ste. A-200
Henderson, NV 89052
Fax: (702)616-4049
E-mail: apiduba@aol.com
Products: Wastepaper, including paper recycling. **SIC:** 5093 (Scrap & Waste Materials). **Est:** 1973. **Emp:** 10. **Officers:** Peter Dubarry, President.

■ **26800** ■ **Earth Care Paper Inc.**
PO Box 14140
Madison, WI 53714-0140
Phone: (608)223-4000 **Fax:** (608)223-4040
Products: Recycled paper products. **SICs:** 5093 (Scrap & Waste Materials); 5113 (Industrial & Personal Service Paper). **Est:** 1987. **Sales:** $3,000,000 (2000). **Emp:** 65. **Officers:** John Magee, President; Richard Norgord, Marketing Mgr.

■ **26801** ■ **Earth Waste Systems Inc.**
29 Lund Rd
PO Box 187
Saco, ME 04072
Phone: (207)284-4516 **Fax:** (207)284-9782
Products: Scrap metal. **SIC:** 5093 (Scrap & Waste Materials). **Est:** 1992. **Officers:** Kevin Elnicki, President.

■ **26802** ■ **Easton Iron and Metal Co. Inc.**
1100 Bushkill Dr.
Easton, PA 18042
Phone: (215)250-6300
Products: Scrap iron and metal. **SIC:** 5093 (Scrap & Waste Materials). **Est:** 1935. **Sales:** $3,700,000 (2000). **Emp:** 10. **Officers:** Jack Stein, President.

■ **26803** ■ **EKCO International Metals Inc.**
1700 Perrino Pl.
Los Angeles, CA 90023
Phone: (213)264-1615 **Fax:** (213)264-6910
Products: Scrap metal. **SIC:** 5093 (Scrap & Waste Materials). **Est:** 1973. **Sales:** $17,000,000 (2000). **Emp:** 42. **Officers:** Ely Keenberg, President.

■ **26804** ■ **Elg Metals, Inc.**
PO Box 369
Mc Keesport, PA 15134
Phone: (412)672-9200
Products: Scrap and waste materials. **SIC:** 5093 (Scrap & Waste Materials). **Est:** 1961. **Sales:** $61,000,000 (2000). **Emp:** 100. **Officers:** Simon

Merrills, President; David Reichenecker, Treasurer & Secty. **Former Name:** Steelmet Inc.

■ 26805 ■ ELG Metals Southern, Inc.
PO Box 96166
Houston, TX 77213-6166
Phone: (281)457-2100 **Fax:** (281)457-2500
E-mail: elgsou@yahoo.com
URL: http://www.elgmetals.com
Products: Recycled stainless steel. **SIC:** 5093 (Scrap & Waste Materials). **Sales:** $11,000,000 (2000). **Emp:** 30. **Officers:** Andy Wilk, President; Anna Arias, Controller. **Former Name:** Gulf Materials Recycling Corp.

■ 26806 ■ Elgin Salvage and Supply Company Inc.
464 McBride St.
Elgin, IL 60120
Phone: (708)742-9500 **Fax:** (708)742-2375
Products: Scrap iron and metal; Grain. **SIC:** 5093 (Scrap & Waste Materials). **Est:** 1935. **Sales:** $12,000,000 (2000). **Emp:** 72. **Officers:** Gordon R. Roth, President & Treasurer; William E. Bennett, Controller; DeAnn McGlynn, Office Mgr.

■ 26807 ■ Empire Recycling Inc.
15729 Crabbs Branch Way
Rockville, MD 20855
Phone: (301)921-9202
Products: Recycling scrap and waste materials. **SIC:** 5093 (Scrap & Waste Materials). **Sales:** $56,000,000 (1994). **Emp:** 150. **Officers:** Barclay E. Booth, President.

■ 26808 ■ Encycle/Texas Inc.
5500 UpRiver Rd.
Corpus Christi, TX 78407
Phone: (512)289-0035 **Fax:** (512)289-0300
Products: Hazardous waste materials. **SIC:** 5093 (Scrap & Waste Materials). **Sales:** $110,000,000 (2000). **Emp:** 120. **Officers:** Ray Cardenas, President.

■ 26809 ■ Energy Answers Corp.
79 N Pearl St.
Albany, NY 12207
Phone: (518)434-1227
Products: Recycled goods. **SIC:** 5093 (Scrap & Waste Materials). **Est:** 1981. **Sales:** $98,000,000 (2000). **Emp:** 220. **Officers:** Patrick F. Mahoney, CEO & Chairman of the Board; Ritter Gaylord, CFO; William C. Sheehan, VP of Marketing; Roland Etcheverry, Information Systems Mgr.; MaryAnn Mahoney, Dir of Human Resources.

■ 26810 ■ Environmental Control Inc.
Rte. 20, Box 29-ECI
Santa Fe, NM 87501
Phone: (505)473-0982 **Fax:** (505)438-3801
Products: Recycled products. **SIC:** 5093 (Scrap & Waste Materials). **Sales:** $15,000,000 (1993). **Emp:** 40. **Officers:** Michael Mulcahy, General Mgr.

■ 26811 ■ EPI Technologies, Inc.
2111 Champlain St.
Toledo, OH 43611
Phone: (419)727-0495 **Fax:** (419)729-7644
E-mail: epimaison@solarstop.net
Products: Paint waste recycling material. **SIC:** 5093 (Scrap & Waste Materials). **Est:** 1989. **Sales:** $4,000,000 (2000). **Emp:** 25. **Officers:** Bruce Maison, President.

■ 26812 ■ Fairway Salvage Inc.
12428 Center St.
South Gate, CA 90280-8052
Phone: (562)630-8766
Products: Recycled metal. **SIC:** 5093 (Scrap & Waste Materials). **Sales:** $20,000,000 (2000). **Emp:** 45. **Officers:** Ed Kushins, COO.

■ 26813 ■ Fibres International Inc.
1533 120th Ave. NE
Bellevue, WA 98005-2131
Phone: (206)762-8520
Products: Scrap glass for recycling. **SIC:** 5093 (Scrap & Waste Materials).

■ 26814 ■ Fisher Steel and Supply Co.
259 Ottawa St.
Muskegon, MI 49442-1008
Phone: (616)722-6081 **Fax:** (616)728-3823
Products: Scrap and waste materials. **SIC:** 5093 (Scrap & Waste Materials). **Est:** 1915. **Sales:** $29,000,000 (2000). **Emp:** 50. **Officers:** James A. Fisher, President; Sharon K. Riekki, Controller.

■ 26815 ■ Frankfort Scrap Metal Company Inc.
PO Box 344
Frankfort, KY 40602
Phone: (502)223-7607 **Fax:** (502)223-1494
Products: Scrap iron; Steel; Copper; Brass; Aluminum. **SIC:** 5093 (Scrap & Waste Materials). **Est:** 1955. **Sales:** $7,000,000 (2000). **Emp:** 32. **Officers:** R.R. Ratliff, President; R. Ratliff, CFO.

■ 26816 ■ Franklin Iron and Metal Corp.
PO Box 1857
Richmond, IN 47375
Phone: (765)966-8295
Products: Scrap and waste materials. **SIC:** 5093 (Scrap & Waste Materials). **Sales:** $30,000,000 (1993). **Emp:** 82. **Officers:** Jack Edelman, President; Debra Edelman, VP & Treasurer.

■ 26817 ■ Joseph Freedman Company Inc.
PO Box 3555
Springfield, MA 01101
Phone: (413)781-4444 **Fax:** (413)734-0790
URL: http://www.josephfreedmanco.com
Products: Scrap metal. **SIC:** 5093 (Scrap & Waste Materials). **Est:** 1891. **Sales:** $18,000,000 (2000). **Emp:** 35. **Officers:** John Freedman, President; Michael Freedman, Treasurer; Ernest Gagnon, Dir. of Marketing.

■ 26818 ■ R. Freedman and Son Inc.
PO Box 1533
Green Island, NY 12183
Phone: (518)273-1141 **Fax:** (518)273-7735
Products: Recycled metal products. **SIC:** 5093 (Scrap & Waste Materials). **Sales:** $11,000,000 (2000). **Emp:** 48. **Officers:** Morris Freedman, President; Ann Zimermen, CFO.

■ 26819 ■ G and L Recycling Inc.
222 N Calverton Rd.
Baltimore, MD 21223
Phone: (410)233-1197
Products: Recycled products. **SIC:** 5093 (Scrap & Waste Materials).

■ 26820 ■ Gamtex Industries Inc.
PO Box 308
Ft. Worth, TX 76101
Phone: (817)334-0211 **Fax:** (817)877-1528
Products: Recycled metal and glass. **SIC:** 5093 (Scrap & Waste Materials). **Sales:** $10,000,000 (2000). **Emp:** 45. **Officers:** Arnold G. Gachman, President; Kim Prichard, Mgr. of Finance; Joel M. Selig, Dir. of Marketing & Sales.

■ 26821 ■ Garbose Metal Co.
770 Salisbury St., Apt. 416
Worcester, MA 01609-1167
Products: Scrap metal. **SIC:** 5093 (Scrap & Waste Materials). **Est:** 1904. **Sales:** $2,500,000 (2000). **Emp:** 18. **Officers:** S.B. Garbose, President.

■ 26822 ■ Gardena Recycling Center Inc.
1538 W 134th St.
Gardena, CA 90249
Phone: (310)516-8195
Products: Scrap metal. **SIC:** 5093 (Scrap & Waste Materials). **Est:** 1980. **Sales:** $1,000,000 (2000). **Emp:** 5. **Officers:** Sam Moross, President.

■ 26823 ■ General Iron Industries Inc.
1909 N Clifton Ave.
Chicago, IL 60614
Phone: (773)327-9600 **Fax:** (773)327-8732
Products: Scrap iron processing. **SIC:** 5093 (Scrap & Waste Materials). **Sales:** $31,000,000 (2000). **Emp:** 70. **Officers:** Marilyn Labkohn, CFO.

■ 26824 ■ General Metals of Tacoma Inc.
1902 Marine View Dr.
Tacoma, WA 98422
Phone: (206)572-4000 **Fax:** (206)572-0316
Products: Recycled scrap metal. **SICs:** 5093 (Scrap & Waste Materials); 5051 (Metals Service Centers & Offices). **Est:** 1956. **Sales:** $50,000,000 (2000). **Emp:** 100. **Officers:** Ralph Miller, President; Keith Gross, Controller.

■ 26825 ■ General Waste Products Inc.
PO Box 6690
Evansville, IN 47713-1038
Phone: (812)423-4267 **Fax:** (812)421-4600
Products: Scrap metals, including steel and aluminum. **SIC:** 5093 (Scrap & Waste Materials). **Est:** 1930. **Sales:** $11,000,000 (2000). **Emp:** 30. **Officers:** Allan Trockman, President.

■ 26826 ■ Gerber Metal Supply Co.
40-50 Montgomery St.
Hillside, NJ 07205
Phone: (908)964-1955
Free: (800)836-4672 **Fax:** (908)964-9249
Products: Hot and cold rolled sheet metal and coils. **SIC:** 5051 (Metals Service Centers & Offices). **Est:** 1963. **Sales:** $28,000,000 (2000). **Emp:** 48. **Officers:** G. Gerber, President; Joe Trainor, Controller.

■ 26827 ■ Gershow Recycling
PO Box 526
Medford, NY 11763
Phone: (516)289-6188
Products: Scrap and waste materials, including aluminum cans, metal cans, glass, and plastics. **SIC:** 5093 (Scrap & Waste Materials). **Est:** 1967. **Sales:** $29,000,000 (2000). **Emp:** 50. **Officers:** Sam Gershowitz, President; John Bellittie, Controller.

■ 26828 ■ G.I. Industries
195 W Los Angles Ave.
Simi Valley, CA 93065
Phone: (805)529-5871 **Fax:** (805)581-5407
Products: Recycling. **SIC:** 5093 (Scrap & Waste Materials). **Sales:** $16,000,000 (1993). **Emp:** 103. **Officers:** Mike Smith, CEO & CFO.

■ 26829 ■ Glant Pacific Co.
PO Box C-3637
Seattle, WA 98124
Phone: (206)628-6222
Products: Scrap metal. **SIC:** 5093 (Scrap & Waste Materials). **Sales:** $15,000,000 (2000). **Emp:** 250. **Officers:** Doug Glant, President; Hoon Siew, VP of Finance.

■ 26830 ■ Glant Pacific Iron and Metal Co.
PO Box C-3637
Seattle, WA 98124
Phone: (206)628-6232 **Fax:** (206)628-6252
E-mail: pacimco@aol.com
Products: Scrap metals. **SIC:** 5093 (Scrap & Waste Materials). **Est:** 1917. **Sales:** $15,000,000 (1999). **Emp:** 250. **Officers:** Doug Glant, President & Chairman of the Board; Bruce Glant, Exec. VP & Vice Chairman.

■ 26831 ■ Global Titanium Inc.
19300 Filer Ave.
Detroit, MI 48234
Phone: (313)366-5300
Free: (800)762-7602 **Fax:** (313)366-5305
E-mail: info@globaltitanium.com
URL: http://www.globaltitanium.com
Products: Titanium metallurgical products. **SIC:** 5093 (Scrap & Waste Materials). **Est:** 1984. **Sales:** $15,000,000 (2000). **Emp:** 50. **Officers:** R.L. Swenson, President; W.E. Hake, Controller. **Former Name:** Frankel Metal Co.

■ 26832 ■ Gordon Waste Company Inc.
PO Box 389
Columbia, PA 17512
Phone: (717)684-2201 **Fax:** (717)684-0162
Products: Recycled paper; Stretch wrap; Strapping. **SIC:** 5093 (Scrap & Waste Materials). **Est:** 1949. **Sales:** $12,000,000 (2000). **Emp:** 11. **Officers:** Robert Gordon, President.

■ **26833** ■ **Great Western Recycling Industries Inc.**
521 Barge Channel Rd.
St. Paul, MN 55107
Phone: (651)224-4877 **Fax:** (651)224-4870
Products: Recycled metal products. **SIC:** 5093 (Scrap & Waste Materials). **Sales:** $27,000,000 (2000). **Emp:** 60. **Officers:** Jerry Bader, President.

■ **26834** ■ **Green Team of San Jose**
1333 Oakland Rd.
San Jose, CA 95112-1364
Phone: (408)283-8500
Products: Recycled glass. **SIC:** 5093 (Scrap & Waste Materials).

■ **26835** ■ **Hans Metals, Inc.**
94-170 Leokane St.
Waipahu, HI 96797
Phone: (808)676-4797 **Fax:** (808)671-0729
Products: Scrap metal. **SIC:** 5093 (Scrap & Waste Materials).

■ **26836** ■ **Harding Metals Inc.**
Rte. 4
Northwood, NH 03261
Phone: (603)942-5573
Products: Scrap metal. **SIC:** 5093 (Scrap & Waste Materials). **Est:** 1963. **Sales:** $10,000,000 (2000). **Emp:** 25. **Officers:** J.J. Harding, President.

■ **26837** ■ **Harding Metals Inc.**
Rte. 4
Northwood, NH 03261
Phone: (603)942-5573
Free: (800)370-5865 **Fax:** (603)942-5646
Products: Ferrous and nonferrous metal recyclers. **SIC:** 5093 (Scrap & Waste Materials). **Sales:** $14,000,000 (1999). **Emp:** 30. **Officers:** J.J. Harding, CEO.

■ **26838** ■ **Harley Metals Recycling Co.**
3315 E Washington Blvd.
Los Angeles, CA 90027
Phone: (213)264-0646
Products: Recycled metal and glass. **SIC:** 5093 (Scrap & Waste Materials).

■ **26839** ■ **Hartley Manufacturing Inc.**
PO Box 398
Ravenswood, WV 26164
Phone: (304)273-5931
Products: Recycled fiber. **SIC:** 5093 (Scrap & Waste Materials).

■ **26840** ■ **Heckett Multiserv Div.**
PO Box 1071
Butler, PA 16003
Phone: (724)283-5741 **Fax:** (724)283-2251
Products: Reclaimed metals and pit cleaning by-products. **SIC:** 5093 (Scrap & Waste Materials). **Sales:** $1,310,000,000 (2000). **Emp:** 3,500. **Officers:** K Bruch, President.

■ **26841** ■ **Heckman Metals Co.**
220 Demeter St.
Palo Alto, CA 94303
Phone: (650)324-9666
Products: Scrap metal including steel, aluminum, and copper. **SIC:** 5093 (Scrap & Waste Materials). **Est:** 1981. **Sales:** $4,000,000 (2000). **Emp:** 12. **Officers:** Carl Heckman, President.

■ **26842** ■ **J.E. Herndon Company Inc.**
100 Industrial Dr.
Kings Mountain, NC 28086
Phone: (704)739-4711
Products: Textile waste, including blending, cleaning cotton, and synthetic fibers. **SIC:** 5093 (Scrap & Waste Materials). **Est:** 1928. **Sales:** $6,000,000 (2000). **Emp:** 35. **Officers:** James E. Herndon Jr., President.

■ **26843** ■ **H. Hirschfield Sons Co.**
1414 N Madison St.
Bay City, MI 48708
Phone: (517)895-5571 **Fax:** (517)895-8616
Products: Scrap and waste materials; Automotive wrecking for scrap. **SIC:** 5093 (Scrap & Waste Materials). **Sales:** $15,500,000 (2000). **Emp:** 75. **Officers:** Robert E. Hirschfield, President.

■ **26844** ■ **Houston Wiper and Mill Supply Co.**
PO Box 24962
Houston, TX 77229-4962
Phone: (713)672-0571
Free: (800)633-5968 **Fax:** (713)673-7637
E-mail: howmisco@msn.com
URL: http://www.houstonwiper.com
Products: Wiping cloths; Used clothing. **SIC:** 5093 (Scrap & Waste Materials). **Est:** 1954. **Sales:** $3,900,000 (2000). **Emp:** 85. **Officers:** Michael J. Brown, President; Jay Grossman, Sec. & Treas.; Barry H. Brown, Vice President; Richard J. Capizzi, Sales/Marketing Contact.

■ **26845** ■ **Hugo-Neu-Schnitzen East**
1 Jersey Ave.
Jersey City, NJ 07302
Phone: (201)333-4300 **Fax:** (201)432-5332
Products: Ferrous metal and nickel alloy recycling. **SIC:** 5093 (Scrap & Waste Materials). **Sales:** $108,000,000 (2000). **Emp:** 240.

■ **26846** ■ **Hummelstein Iron and Metal Inc.**
PO Box 1580
Jonesboro, AR 72403
Phone: (870)932-8361 **Fax:** (870)935-4044
Products: Recycled metal products. **SIC:** 5093 (Scrap & Waste Materials). **Sales:** $15,000,000 (1994). **Emp:** 40. **Officers:** Sam Hummelstein, President.

■ **26847** ■ **Image Industries Inc.**
PO Box 5555
Armuchee, GA 30105
Phone: (706)235-8444
Free: (800)722-2504 **Fax:** (706)235-0386
Products: Plastics recycling. **SIC:** 5093 (Scrap & Waste Materials). **Sales:** $161,000,000 (2000). **Emp:** 1,670. **Officers:** H. Stanley Padgett, CEO & President; Steve Coburn, Controller.

■ **26848** ■ **IMCO Recycling Inc.**
5215 N O'Connor Blvd., No. 940
Irving, TX 75039
Phone: (972)869-6575 **Fax:** (972)869-6585
Products: Recycled aluminum. **SIC:** 5093 (Scrap & Waste Materials). **Est:** 1973. **Sales:** $339,400,000 (2000). **Emp:** 1,537. **Officers:** Donald V. Ingram, CEO & Chairman of the Board; Paul V. Dufour, Exec. VP of Finance & Admin.; Thomas W. Rogers, Sr. VP of Marketing & Sales; Richard L. Kerr, COO & Exec. VP.

■ **26849** ■ **Indianapolis Materials Recycling Facility**
832 Langsdale Ave.
Indianapolis, IN 46202
Phone: (317)926-5492
Products: Recycled metals. **SIC:** 5093 (Scrap & Waste Materials).

■ **26850** ■ **Industrial Disposal Co.**
1423 S Jackson St.
Louisville, KY 40208-2777
Phone: (502)638-9000
Products: Scrap metal; Solid waste collection. **SIC:** 5093 (Scrap & Waste Materials). **Emp:** 50.

■ **26851** ■ **International Cellulose Inc.**
3110 W 28th St.
Chicago, IL 60623
Phone: (773)847-8000
Products: Scrap paper. **SIC:** 5093 (Scrap & Waste Materials). **Est:** 1960. **Sales:** $2,000,000 (2000). **Emp:** 45. **Officers:** Eugene Jodlowski, CEO & President.

■ **26852** ■ **International Mill Service Inc.**
1155 Business Center Dr., No. 200
Horsham, PA 19044
Phone: (215)956-5500 **Fax:** (215)963-5593
Products: Recycled slag. **SIC:** 5093 (Scrap & Waste Materials). **Est:** 1937. **Sales:** $480,000,000 (2000). **Emp:** 1,300. **Officers:** Lou Guzzetti, CEO & President; William Maloney, VP of Finance; Lou Decarlo, Dir. of Information Systems; Kenneth McArthur, VP of Human Resources.

■ **26853** ■ **International Petroleum Corp.**
105 S Alexander St.
Plant City, FL 33566
Phone: (813)754-1504 **Fax:** (813)754-3789
Products: Oil recycling. **SIC:** 5093 (Scrap & Waste Materials). **Sales:** $19,000,000 (2000). **Emp:** 120. **Officers:** Garry Allen, President.

■ **26854** ■ **Ireland Alloys Inc.**
PO Box 369
Mc Keesport, PA 15134-0369
Products: Recycled scrap metal. **SIC:** 5093 (Scrap & Waste Materials). **Sales:** $20,000,000 (2000). **Emp:** 40. **Officers:** Dennis W. Oliver, President; John Goodman, Controller.

■ **26855** ■ **Iron and Metals Inc.**
5555 Franklin St.
Denver, CO 80216
Phone: (303)292-5555 **Fax:** (303)292-0513
Products: Recycled iron and metal. **SIC:** 5093 (Scrap & Waste Materials). **Est:** 1951. **Sales:** $29,000,000 (2000). **Emp:** 50. **Officers:** Robert Cohen, Chairman of the Board; Allen Cohen, President.

■ **26856** ■ **Jacobs Iron and Metal Co.**
3330 Pluto St.
Dallas, TX 75212
Phone: (214)631-6740
Products: Metal waste and scrap. **SIC:** 5093 (Scrap & Waste Materials). **Est:** 1954. **Emp:** 23. **Officers:** Andrew S. Jacobs, CEO & President; Reuben Jacobs, Vice President.

■ **26857** ■ **David J. Joseph Co.**
PO Box 1078
Cincinnati, OH 45201
Phone: (513)621-8770 **Fax:** (513)345-4391
URL: http://www.djj.com
Products: Scrap metal. **SIC:** 5093 (Scrap & Waste Materials). **Est:** 1885. **Sales:** $1,500,000,000 (2000). **Emp:** 725. **Officers:** Keith B. Grass, CEO & President; William J. Zeck, Exec. VP & CFO; Melanie S. Toler, Sr. VP of Human Resources.

■ **26858** ■ **David J. Joseph Co., Ferrous Div.**
PO Box 1078
Cincinnati, OH 45201
Phone: (513)621-8770 **Fax:** (513)345-4397
URL: http://www.djj.com
Products: Scrap metals. **SIC:** 5093 (Scrap & Waste Materials). **Est:** 1885. **Sales:** $2,000,000,000 (2000).

■ **26859** ■ **David J. Joseph Co. International Div.**
PO Box 1078
Cincinnati, OH 45201
Phone: (513)621-8770
Products: Metal waste and scrap. **SIC:** 5093 (Scrap & Waste Materials).

■ **26860** ■ **David J. Joseph Co. Municipal Recycling Div.**
PO Box 1078
Cincinnati, OH 45201
Phone: (513)621-8770 **Fax:** (513)381-7071
Products: Metal waste and scrap; Iron; Secondary copper. **SICs:** 5093 (Scrap & Waste Materials); 5051 (Metals Service Centers & Offices). **Est:** 1989. **Sales:** $8,000,000 (2000). **Emp:** 6. **Officers:** Richard R. Jordan, Vice President.

■ **26861** ■ **David J. Joseph Co. Nonferrous Div.**
PO Box 1078
Cincinnati, OH 45201
Phone: (513)621-8770 **Fax:** (513)345-4394
Products: Metal waste and scrap. **SIC:** 5093 (Scrap & Waste Materials). **Sales:** $14,000,000 (2000). **Emp:** 10. **Officers:** Louis F. Terhar, President; William J. Zeck, CFO.

■ **26862** ■ **K and K Recycling Inc.**
PO Box 58055
Fairbanks, AK 99711
Phone: (907)488-1409 **Fax:** (907)488-4058
E-mail: recycle@polarnet.com
URL: http://www2.polarnet.com/~recycle
Products: Recycled metals, including aluminum,

copper, brass, and steel. **SIC:** 5093 (Scrap & Waste Materials). **Est:** 1984. **Sales:** $1,000,000 (2000). **Emp:** 15. **Officers:** Bernie Karl, President.

■ **26863** ■ **Nathan H. Kelman Inc.**
41 Euclid St.
Cohoes, NY 12047
Phone: (518)237-5133
Products: Recycled metal and paper products. **SIC:** 5093 (Scrap & Waste Materials).

■ **26864** ■ **Kendallville Iron and Metal Inc.**
243 E Lisbon Rd.
PO Box 69
Kendallville, IN 46755
Phone: (219)347-1958   **Fax:** (219)347-1966
E-mail: kmetal@noble.cioe.com
Products: Processed scrap metal, including ferrous and nonferrous. **SIC:** 5093 (Scrap & Waste Materials). **Est:** 1964. **Sales:** $5,000,000 (2000). **Emp:** 20. **Officers:** Gary Spidel, President; Susan Norris, Vice President; Lynn Spidel, Vice President.

■ **26865** ■ **Keystone Resources Inc.**
PO Box 807
Mars, PA 16046
Phone: (412)538-3940   **Fax:** (412)789-9600
Products: Diox secondary aluminum. **SIC:** 5093 (Scrap & Waste Materials). **Sales:** $112,300,000 (2000). **Emp:** 500. **Officers:** R. Stephen Somosye, Exec. VP; Gary Mrazek, Controller; Pattrick J. Schipani, VP of Sales; Christopher D. Moore, General Mgr.

■ **26866** ■ **Keywell Corp.**
3075 Lonyo Ave.
Detroit, MI 48209
Phone: (313)841-6800   **Fax:** (313)841-3843
Products: Scrap metal. **SIC:** 5093 (Scrap & Waste Materials). **Sales:** $190,000,000 (2000). **Emp:** 330. **Officers:** Richard Odle, President.

■ **26867** ■ **Klempner Bros. Inc.**
PO Box 4187
Louisville, KY 40204-0187
Phone: (502)585-5331   **Fax:** (502)587-8699
Products: Scrap processors. **SICs:** 5093 (Scrap & Waste Materials); 5084 (Industrial Machinery & Equipment). **Est:** 1905. **Sales:** $41,000,000 (2000). **Emp:** 110. **Officers:** Jay Klempner, President; Mark Elder, CFO; Doug Elder, Dir. of Marketing.

■ **26868** ■ **Perry H. Koplik and Sons Inc.**
505 Park Ave., 3rd Fl.
New York, NY 10022
Phone: (212)752-2288   **Fax:** (212)838-8790
URL: http://www.koplik.com
Products: Woodpulp and recycled fibers; Container board; Newsprint; Printing and writing paper. **SICs:** 5099 (Durable Goods Nec); 5113 (Industrial & Personal Service Paper). **Est:** 1960. **Sales:** $500,000,000 (2000). **Emp:** 150. **Officers:** Michael R. Koplik, President & CEO; Alvin Siegel, Exec. VP & COO; Edward Stein, Exec. VP & CFO.

■ **26869** ■ **Kramer Metals**
1760 E Slauson Ave.
Los Angeles, CA 90058
Phone: (213)587-2277   **Fax:** (213)588-8007
Products: Scrap metal. **SIC:** 5093 (Scrap & Waste Materials). **Est:** 1983. **Sales:** $7,000,000 (2000). **Emp:** 30. **Officers:** Stanely Kramer, President; Douglas Kramer, Vice President.

■ **26870** ■ **Kramer Scrap Inc.**
PO Box 588
Greenfield, MA 01302
Phone: (413)774-3103   **Fax:** (413)774-7369
Products: Recycled metals, including non-ferrous metals and cast iron. **SIC:** 5093 (Scrap & Waste Materials). **Est:** 1921. **Sales:** $17,000,000 (2000). **Emp:** 30. **Officers:** David Spencer, President.

■ **26871** ■ **Joe Krentzman and Son Inc.**
PO Box 508
Lewistown, PA 17044
Phone: (717)543-5635
Products: Scrap metal. **SIC:** 5093 (Scrap & Waste Materials). **Sales:** $20,000,000 (1994). **Emp:** 55. **Officers:** Steve Krentzman, President.

■ **26872** ■ **Krentzman Supply Co.**
Susquehanna St.
Lewistown, PA 17044
Phone: (717)543-5635
Products: Scrap metal, including aluminum, copper, and bronze. **SIC:** 5093 (Scrap & Waste Materials). **Est:** 1903. **Sales:** $5,000,000 (2000). **Emp:** 25. **Officers:** Stephen M. Krentzman, President.

■ **26873** ■ **Kruger Recycling Inc.**
877 S Pearl St.
Albany, NY 12202
Phone: (518)433-0020
Products: Scrap materials. **SICs:** 5093 (Scrap & Waste Materials); 5113 (Industrial & Personal Service Paper). **Sales:** $11,000,000 (2000). **Emp:** 30. **Officers:** Richard Loyst, President.

■ **26874** ■ **Lakeside Nonferrous Metals Co.**
PO Box 957
Oakland, CA 94607
Phone: (510)444-5466
Products: Scrap metal. **SIC:** 5093 (Scrap & Waste Materials). **Est:** 1940. **Sales:** $7,000,000 (2000). **Emp:** 20. **Officers:** Lester Finkle, President.

■ **26875** ■ **Landfill Alternatives Inc.**
PO Box A.H.
Elburn, IL 60119
Phone: (630)365-2480   **Fax:** (630)365-2484
Products: Recycled foam and polystyrene. **SIC:** 5093 (Scrap & Waste Materials). **Est:** 1988. **Sales:** $700,000 (2000). **Emp:** 8. **Officers:** William E. Roberts, President; James R. Frank, CFO.

■ **26876** ■ **William Lans Sons Co.**
201 Wheeler Ave.
South Beloit, IL 61080
Phone: (815)389-2241   **Fax:** (815)389-3999
Products: Scrap recyclers. **SIC:** 5093 (Scrap & Waste Materials). **Est:** 1910. **Sales:** $24,000,000 (1994). **Emp:** 65. **Officers:** Bertram Lans, President; Bruce Lans, Finance General Manager.

■ **26877** ■ **L. Lavetan and Sons Inc.**
PO Box 389
York, PA 17405
Phone: (717)843-0931   **Fax:** (717)854-4008
Products: Recyclable scrap metal. **SIC:** 5093 (Scrap & Waste Materials). **Est:** 1897. **Sales:** $12,000,000 (2000). **Emp:** 60. **Officers:** Phillip Serls, President; Marty Fogle, General Mgr.

■ **26878** ■ **LB Steel Plate Co.**
1207 E 143rd St.
East Chicago, IN 46312
Phone: (219)397-9224   **Fax:** (219)398-7103
Products: Carbon steel plate recycling. **SIC:** 5051 (Metals Service Centers & Offices). **Sales:** $50,000,000 (1994). **Emp:** 150. **Officers:** Robert O. Blackman, President; Brendan Lally, Vice President.

■ **26879** ■ **Lefton Enterprises Inc.**
PO Box 219
East St. Louis, IL 62202
Phone: (618)274-4900
Products: Scrap metal. **SIC:** 5093 (Scrap & Waste Materials). **Sales:** $2,000,000 (1994). **Emp:** 23. **Officers:** Norman Lefton, Comptroller; Robert Tallyn, Controller.

■ **26880** ■ **Lefton Iron and Metal Co.**
205 S 17th St.
East St. Louis, IL 62207
Phone: (618)274-4900
Free: (800)851-3133   **Fax:** (618)274-7308
Products: Scrap metal. **SIC:** 5093 (Scrap & Waste Materials). **Est:** 1928. **Sales:** $1,600,000 (2000). **Emp:** 9. **Officers:** Benjamin B. Lefton, President; Robert D. Tallyn, Controller; Norman Lefton, Vice President.

■ **26881** ■ **Louis Levin and Company of Tonawanda, Inc.**
PO Box 6601
Buffalo, NY 14240-6601
Phone: (716)692-1395   **Fax:** (716)692-7731
Products: Scrap iron and metals. **SIC:** 5093 (Scrap & Waste Materials). **Sales:** $3,000,000 (2000). **Emp:** 20.

Officers: Robert Levin, President; Todd Levin, Vice President.

■ **26882** ■ **R.J. Liberto Inc.**
PO Box 14027
Pittsburgh, PA 15239
Phone: (412)793-9500
Products: Recycling. **SIC:** 5051 (Metals Service Centers & Offices). **Sales:** $1,000,000 (2000). **Emp:** 9. **Officers:** Carmella M. Liberto, President; Patti Liberto, CFO.

■ **26883** ■ **Liberty Iron and Metal Company Inc.**
PO Box 1391
Erie, PA 16503
Phone: (814)453-6758   **Fax:** (814)456-6107
Products: Metal waste and scrap. **SIC:** 5093 (Scrap & Waste Materials). **Est:** 1932. **Sales:** $31,000,000 (2000). **Officers:** Lou Lechtner, Chairman of the Board; Frani Lechtner, CFO; Barry Rider, Dir. of Marketing & Sales; Marc Olgin, President; Dave Hilbert, VP of Human Resources; Joe Plumadore, VP of Operations.

■ **26884** ■ **M. Lipsitz and Company Inc.**
PO Box 1175
Waco, TX 76703
Phone: (254)756-6661   **Fax:** (254)752-0175
Products: Scrap metal recycling. **SIC:** 5093 (Scrap & Waste Materials). **Est:** 1895. **Sales:** $54,000,000 (2000). **Emp:** 120. **Officers:** Thomas G. Salome, President.

■ **26885** ■ **Loef Company Inc.**
Box 80808
Athens, GA 30608-0808
Phone: (706)549-6700   **Fax:** (706)549-6739
Products: Recyclable metal. **SIC:** 5093 (Scrap & Waste Materials). **Est:** 1925. **Sales:** $20,000,000 (2000). **Emp:** 81. **Officers:** Terry L. Nagelvoort, CEO & President; James O. Nathan, Exec. VP; Guy E. Trambaver, Dir. of Operations.

■ **26886** ■ **Loef Company Inc.**
Box 80808
Athens, GA 30608-0808
Phone: (706)549-6700   **Fax:** (706)549-6739
Products: Used, Scrap, and recycled materials. **SIC:** 5093 (Scrap & Waste Materials). **Est:** 1925. **Sales:** $20,000,000 (2000). **Emp:** 81.

■ **26887** ■ **Lorman Iron and Metal Co.**
PO Box 127
Ft. Atkinson, WI 53538
Phone: (920)563-2488   **Fax:** (920)563-2418
Products: Scrap steel, iron, copper, and aluminum. **SIC:** 5093 (Scrap & Waste Materials). **Est:** 1913. **Sales:** $10,000,000 (2000). **Emp:** 40. **Officers:** Bruce Loeb, President; Neal Loeb, Vice President.

■ **26888** ■ **Los Angeles Paper Box and Board Mills. Paper Stock Div.**
PO Box 60830
Los Angeles, CA 90060-0830
Phone: (213)685-8900
Products: Waste paper recycling. **SIC:** 5093 (Scrap & Waste Materials). **Sales:** $3,000,000 (2000). **Emp:** 7. **Officers:** Pat Hickey, Manager.

■ **26889** ■ **Luntz Corp.**
237 E Tuscarawas St.
Canton, OH 44702
Phone: (216)455-0211   **Fax:** (216)455-2801
Products: Recycled metal products. **SIC:** 5093 (Scrap & Waste Materials). **Est:** 1916. **Sales:** $90,000,000 (2000). **Emp:** 250. **Officers:** Andrew Luntz, President; Greg Luntz, Exec. VP & CFO; Dave Valentine, VP of Marketing; Rodger Beitler, Dir of Personnel.

■ **26890** ■ **M and M Metals International Inc.**
840 Dellway Ave.
Cincinnati, OH 45229
Phone: (513)221-4411
Products: Scrap metal, including copper and brass. **SIC:** 5093 (Scrap & Waste Materials). **Est:** 1962. **Sales:** $44,000,000 (2000). **Emp:** 30. **Officers:** Steve Schuler, President.

■ 26891 ■ MacLeod Group
9309 Rayo Ave.
South Gate, CA 90280
Phone: (213)567-7767
Products: Recycled materials. SIC: 5093 (Scrap &
Waste Materials). Sales: $45,000,000 (2000). Emp:
100. Officers: Ellis White, President; Timothy Lai,
CFO.

■ 26892 ■ Macon Iron and Paper Stock
Company Inc.
PO Box 506
Macon, GA 31202
Phone: (912)743-6773   Fax: (912)743-9965
Products: Scrap iron; Recycled paper. SIC: 5093
(Scrap & Waste Materials). Est: 1919. Sales:
$10,000,000 (2000). Emp: 92. Officers: Evan L.
Koplin, President; Henry K. Koplin, Dir. of Marketing &
Sales.

■ 26893 ■ Maine Scrap Metal LLC
PO Box 326
Des Plaines, IL 60016-0326
Phone: (847)824-3175   Fax: (847)824-5981
Products: Metal waste and scrap. SIC: 5093 (Scrap &
Waste Materials). Est: 1975. Sales: $2,500,000
(2000). Emp: 11. Officers: Gene Cohen, President.
Former Name: Maine Scrap Metal Inc.

■ 26894 ■ Mallin Brothers Company Inc.
3211 Gardner Ave.
Kansas City, MO 64120
Phone: (816)483-1800   Fax: (816)483-1812
Products: Metal waste and scrap. SIC: 5093 (Scrap &
Waste Materials). Est: 1928. Sales: $4,000,000
(2000). Emp: 25. Officers: Harry G. Mallin, President;
Larry G. Mallin, Treasurer & Secty.; Jeffrey K. Mallin,
Vice President.

■ 26895 ■ Mankato Iron and Metal Co.
PO Box 3152
Mankato, MN 56002
Phone: (507)625-6489
Products: Recycled copper, brass, aluminum, iron,
and metal. SIC: 5093 (Scrap & Waste Materials). Est:
1972. Sales: $7,000,000 (2000). Emp: 21. Officers:
Greg Pooley, President.

■ 26896 ■ Manufacturing Sciences Corp.
804 Kerr Hollow Rd.
Oak Ridge, TN 37830
Phone: (615)481-0455
Products: Recycled radiated scrap metal. SIC: 5093
(Scrap & Waste Materials).

■ 26897 ■ Marion Iron Co.
PO Box 345
Marion, IA 52302
Phone: (319)377-1529   Fax: (319)377-4610
Products: Recyled ferrous steel and non-ferrous
items. SIC: 5093 (Scrap & Waste Materials). Est: 1941.
Sales: $4,000,000 (2000). Emp: 25. Officers: Peter
Brown, President & CFO.

■ 26898 ■ Marion Steel Co. Scrap Div.
PO Box 1217
Marion, OH 43301-1217
Phone: (740)383-6068   Fax: (740)382-0118
Products: Scrap metals. SIC: 5093 (Scrap & Waste
Materials). Est: 1987. Sales: $9,000,000 (2000). Emp:
25. Officers: Les Joffe, General Mgr.

■ 26899 ■ Matlow Company Inc.
333 Bridge St.
Solvay, NY 13209
Phone: (315)488-3171   Fax: (315)468-1893
E-mail: MatlowCo@Concentric.net
Products: Scrap metal. SIC: 5093 (Scrap & Waste
Materials). Est: 1983. Sales: $5,000,000 (2000). Emp:
18. Officers: Peter Matlow, President.

■ 26900 ■ Max Scrap Metals Inc.
21608 Nordhoff St.
Chatsworth, CA 91311
Phone: (818)709-4100
Products: Recyclable copper, brass, glass, plastic,
stainless steel, and aluminum. SIC: 5093 (Scrap &
Waste Materials).

■ 26901 ■ Mercury Waste Solutions Inc.
302 N Riverfront Dr., Ste. 100A
Mankato, MN 56001
Phone: (507)345-0522   Fax: (507)345-1483
Products: Mercury waste recycling services. SIC:
5093 (Scrap & Waste Materials). Sales: $6,700,000
(2000). Emp: 51. Officers: Bradley J. Buscher, CEO &
Chairman of the Board; Todd J. Anderson, CFO.

■ 26902 ■ Metal Alloy Corp.
PO Box 18060
River Rouge, MI 48218
Phone: (313)843-7700
Products: Scrap metal. SIC: 5093 (Scrap & Waste
Materials). Est: 1961. Sales: $19,000,000 (2000).
Emp: 60. Officers: Robert Schwartz, CEO; Martin
Previtch, Controller.

■ 26903 ■ Metal Management Aerospace, Inc.
500 Flatbush Ave.
Hartford, CT 06106
Phone: (860)522-3123   Fax: (860)724-9245
URL: http://www.mtlm.com
Products: Scrap metal recycling/processing; High
temperature and titanium alloys. SIC: 5093 (Scrap &
Waste Materials). Est: 1899. Sales: $40,000,000
(2000). Emp: 150. Officers: Paul Haveson, President;
James Nathan, VP of Commercial; Harvey Graine, VP
of Metal Purchasing. Former Name: Aerospace Metals
Inc.

■ 26904 ■ Metal Recovery Systems Inc.
665 St. Cyr Rd.
St. Louis, MO 63137
Phone: (314)388-3600
Products: Recycled copper and aluminum. SIC: 5051
(Metals Service Centers & Offices). Est: 1989. Sales:
$22,000,000 (2000). Emp: 30. Officers: Scott Bichal,
General Mgr.

■ 26905 ■ Metalsco Inc.
2388 Schuetz Rd., Ste. A40
St. Louis, MO 63146
Phone: (314)997-5200   Fax: (314)997-5921
Products: Nonferrous metals scrap. SIC: 5093 (Scrap
& Waste Materials). Sales: $100,000,000 (2000). Emp:
14. Officers: Sheldon Tauben, President; Joseph A.
Pagano, Vice President.

■ 26906 ■ Metech International Inc.
120 Mapleville Main St.
Mapleville, RI 02839
Phone: (401)568-0711   Fax: (401)568-6003
E-mail: customerservice@metech-arm.com
Products: Electronic recycling. SIC: 5093 (Scrap &
Waste Materials). Est: 1983. Sales: $56,000,000
(2000). Emp: 150. Officers: John Koskines, President.
Former Name: Boliden Metech Inc.

■ 26907 ■ Metro Group Inc.
401 W 900 S
Salt Lake City, UT 84101
Phone: (801)328-2051   Fax: (801)328-2055
Products: Recycles metals; metal service center;
trucking; steel and transloading. SICs: 5093 (Scrap &
Waste Materials); 5051 (Metals Service Centers &
Offices). Sales: $12,000,000 (1999). Emp: 45.
Officers: Willis Bond, President; Mark D. Bond,
Treasurer & Secty.

■ 26908 ■ Metro Metals Northwest
5611 NE Columbia Blvd.
Portland, OR 97218-1237
Phone: (503)287-8861   Fax: (503)287-5669
Products: Scrap metal dealer. SIC: 5093 (Scrap &
Waste Materials). Est: 1954. Sales: $64,000,000
(1999). Emp: 140. Officers: Victor Winkler, President.

■ 26909 ■ Metro Recycling Co. Imagination
Store Co.
2424 Beekman St.
Cincinnati, OH 45214
Phone: (513)471-6060
Products: Recycled items, including paper and
cardboard. SIC: 5093 (Scrap & Waste Materials).
Sales: $14,000,000 (2000). Emp: 25. Officers: Chuck
Francis, Owner.

■ 26910 ■ Metropolitan Mining Co.
58-30 57th St.
Maspeth, NY 11378
Phone: (718)894-5025   Fax: (718)894-0992
E-mail: mmreserves@aol.com
Products: Recycled bottles and cans. SIC: 5093
(Scrap & Waste Materials). Est: 1983. Sales:
$6,000,000 (2000). Emp: 80. Officers: Henry A.
Waxman, President.

■ 26911 ■ Michigan Paper Recyling Corp.
1440 Oxford Rd.
Grosse Pointe Woods, MI 48236-1818
Phone: (810)468-0600
Products: Wastepaper, including paper recycling. SIC:
5093 (Scrap & Waste Materials). Sales: $1,000,000
(2000). Emp: 4. Officers: Mary Jo Van Natter,
President.

■ 26912 ■ Mid-South Metals Co.
PO Box 96
Greenville, NC 27835
Phone: (919)752-5027
Products: Recycled aluminum, brass, copper, and tin.
SIC: 5093 (Scrap & Waste Materials). Sales:
$5,000,000 (2000). Emp: 15. Officers: Nick
Simonowich, President.

■ 26913 ■ Midland Iron and Steel Co.
3301 4th Ave.
Moline, IL 61265
Phone: (309)764-6723
Products: Scrap iron; Paper products. SICs: 5093
(Scrap & Waste Materials); 5113 (Industrial & Personal
Service Paper). Sales: $9,000,000 (2000). Emp: 55.
Officers: Martin Davis, President; Mitchell Davis, Vice
President; Scott Robinson, Sales Mgr.

■ 26914 ■ Mill Waste Recovery Inc.
PO Box 145
Brokaw, WI 54417
Phone: (715)675-5572
Products: Recycled sludge. SIC: 5093 (Scrap &
Waste Materials).

■ 26915 ■ Mindis Acquisition Corp.
1990 Defor Ave.
Atlanta, GA 30318
Phone: (404)332-1750
Products: Recycled scrap metal and plastic products.
SIC: 5093 (Scrap & Waste Materials).

■ 26916 ■ Minkin Chandler Corp.
13501 Sanders Ave.
Detroit, MI 48217
Phone: (313)843-5900
Free: (800)843-6601   Fax: (313)843-6782
Products: Metal waste and scrap. SIC: 5093 (Scrap &
Waste Materials). Sales: $46,000,000 (2000). Emp:
100. Officers: Maurice Chandler, Treasurer.

■ 26917 ■ Morris Scrap Metal Inc.
PO Box 460
Sherman, MS 38869
Phone: (601)844-6441   Fax: (601)844-1075
Products: Used, scrap, and recycled materials. SIC:
5093 (Scrap & Waste Materials). Est: 1970. Sales:
$9,000,000 (2000). Emp: 53.

■ 26918 ■ Moskowitz Brothers
5300 Vine St.
Cincinnati, OH 45217
Phone: (513)242-2100
Free: (800)969-6002   Fax: (513)242-2107
E-mail: moskbros.@aol.com
Products: Scrap metals and iron. SIC: 5093 (Scrap &
Waste Materials). Est: 1901.

■ 26919 ■ MRC Polymers Inc.
1716 W Webster Ave.
Chicago, IL 60614
Phone: (312)276-6345
Products: Recycled plastics, including compound
polyester, compound polycarbonate, and nylon. SICs:
5162 (Plastics Materials & Basic Shapes); 5093 (Scrap
& Waste Materials). Sales: $14,000,000 (2000). Emp:
76. Officers: Dan Eberhardt, President; Steven Sola,
CFO; Daniel Eberhand, Dir. of Marketing & Sales.

■ 26920 ■ M.R.D. Products Inc.
1415 U.S Hwy. 19
Holiday, FL 34691-5646
Phone: (813)934-3108
Products: Scrap aluminum; Aluminum products; Vinyl siding; Windows. **SICs:** 5039 (Construction Materials Nec); 5093 (Scrap & Waste Materials); 5031 (Lumber, Plywood & Millwork). **Est:** 1957. **Sales:** $1,500,000 (2000). **Emp:** 15. **Officers:** Michael R. Daly, President.

■ 26921 ■ Naporano Iron and Metal Co.
PO Box 5158
Newark, NJ 07105
Phone: (201)344-4570 **Fax:** (201)344-8155
Products: Scrap metal. **SIC:** 5051 (Metals Service Centers & Offices). **Est:** 1907. **Sales:** $220,000,000 (2000). **Emp:** 300. **Officers:** Joseph Naporano, President.

■ 26922 ■ New England CR Inc.
4 Liberty Ln. W
Hampton, NH 03842-1704
Phone: (603)246-4210
Products: Recycler of paper, bottles and glass. **SIC:** 5093 (Scrap & Waste Materials). **Sales:** $25,000,000 (1994). **Emp:** 50. **Officers:** Richard J. Kattar, President; Vernon Balser, CFO.

■ 26923 ■ New England Recycling Company Inc.
36 Garden St.
Stamford, CT 06902
Phone: (203)327-9778
Products: Paper recycling. **SIC:** 5093 (Scrap & Waste Materials). **Sales:** $11,000,000 (1994). **Emp:** 20. **Officers:** Michael Tomasello, President.

■ 26924 ■ Newell Recycling Company Inc.
PO Box 830808
San Antonio, TX 78283-0808
Phone: (210)227-3141 **Fax:** (210)227-8948
Products: Recycled metals. **SIC:** 5093 (Scrap & Waste Materials). **Est:** 1956. **Sales:** $120,000,000 (2000). **Emp:** 330. **Officers:** Alton S. Newell, President; Shirley Canady, Controller; Nancy Perez, Dir of Human Resources.

■ 26925 ■ North Shore Recycled Fibers
53 Jefferson Ave.
Salem, MA 01970
Phone: (978)744-4330 **Fax:** (978)744-8857
Products: Recycled paper products. **SIC:** 5093 (Scrap & Waste Materials). **Sales:** $38,000,000 (1994). **Emp:** 65. **Officers:** John Gold, VP & General Merchandising Mgr.; Frank Vegan, Comptroller.

■ 26926 ■ Northwest Ribbon Recycling and Supplies
8175 SW Nimbus Ave.
Beaverton, OR 97008-6414
Phone: (503)641-5156
Free: (800)648-5156 **Fax:** (503)641-1636
URL: http://www.nwrr.com
Products: Remanufactured computer supplies. **SIC:** 5093 (Scrap & Waste Materials). **Est:** 1979. **Emp:** 25. **Officers:** Frederick Kroon, President; Fred Kroon, Sales/Marketing Contact.

■ 26927 ■ Frank H. Nott Co.
PO Box 27225
Richmond, VA 23261
Phone: (804)644-8501
Products: Recycled scrap metal. **SIC:** 5051 (Metals Service Centers & Offices).

■ 26928 ■ Oil Recycling Inc.
PO Box 46
Rosemount, MN 55068
Phone: (612)480-8825
Products: Recycled oil. **SIC:** 5093 (Scrap & Waste Materials).

■ 26929 ■ OmniSource Corp.
3101 Maumee Ave.
Ft. Wayne, IN 46803
Phone: (219)422-5541 **Fax:** (219)424-0307
Products: Scrap iron, ferrous and nonferrous metal recycling. **SIC:** 5093 (Scrap & Waste Materials). **Est:** 1946. **Sales:** $680,000,000 (2000). **Emp:** 1,150.

■ 26930 ■ OmniSource Lima Div.
PO Box 5248
Lima, OH 45802
Phone: (419)227-3411
Products: Scrap materials. **Est:** 1952. **Sales:** $5,000,000 (2000). **Emp:** 30. **Officers:** Jake Yessenow, President; Paula LaPoint, CFO.

■ 26931 ■ P & W Industries, Inc.
PO Box 1550
Mandeville, LA 70470
Phone: (504)892-2461 **Fax:** (504)892-2618
E-mail: haw@pandwindustries.com
URL: http://www.pandwindustries.com
Products: Used and processed steel pipe. **SIC:** 5093 (Scrap & Waste Materials). **Est:** 1967. **Sales:** $2,500,000 (2000). **Emp:** 25. **Officers:** Harry A. Warner, President; Adrianne L. Wenk, VP of Admin.; Davis Gardner, VP of Sales, e-mail: davis@pandwindustries.com; Glenn P. Warner, Exec. VP; Herman Farrington, Sales Rep.; Wilda Sharp, Sales Rep.

■ 26932 ■ Pacific Steel Inc.
1700 Cleveland Ave.
National City, CA 91950
Phone: (619)474-7081
Products: Scrap metal. **SIC:** 5093 (Scrap & Waste Materials).

■ 26933 ■ Louis Padnos Iron and Metal Co.
PO Box 1979
Holland, MI 49422-1979
Phone: (616)396-6521
Free: (800)442-3905 **Fax:** (616)396-7789
E-mail: www.padnos@padnos.com
URL: http://www.padnos.com
Products: Secondary raw materials of metals; Fibers and plastics for recycling. **SIC:** 5093 (Scrap & Waste Materials). **Est:** 1905. **Sales:** $100,000,000 (2000). **Emp:** 450. **Officers:** Seymour K. Padnos, Chairman of the Board; Jeffrey Padnos, President; Mitchell Padnos, Exec. VP of Marketing & Sales.

■ 26934 ■ Paper Recovery Inc.
5222 Lovelock St.
San Diego, CA 92110
Phone: (619)291-5257 **Fax:** (619)299-3670
Products: Paper scrap. **SIC:** 5093 (Scrap & Waste Materials). **Sales:** $500,000 (2000). **Emp:** 20. **Officers:** Peter Gault, President.

■ 26935 ■ Parkans International L.L.C.
5521 Armour Dr.
Houston, TX 77020
Phone: (713)675-9141 **Fax:** (713)675-4771
Products: Used, scrap, and recycled materials. **SIC:** 5093 (Scrap & Waste Materials). **Est:** 1969. **Sales:** $20,000,000 (2000). **Emp:** 50.

■ 26936 ■ Parts Inc.
101 McNeeley Rd.
PO Box 1119
Piedmont, SC 29673
Phone: (864)269-7278
Free: (800)435-7278 **Fax:** (864)295-5847
URL: http://www.partsinc.com
Products: Refuse parts; Hydraulic cylinders. **SIC:** 5093 (Scrap & Waste Materials). **Est:** 1985. **Emp:** 20. **Officers:** Terri Bryant, Sales/Marketing Contact; John Beckwith, Customer Service Contact, e-mail: Terri@partsinc.com; Billie Sloan, Human Resources Contact, e-mail: Billie@partsinc.com; Juliea Birkey, General Mgr., e-mail: juliea@partsinc.com.

■ 26937 ■ Peck Recycling Co.
3220 Deepwater Terminal Rd.
Richmond, VA 23234
Phone: (804)232-5601 **Fax:** (804)233-6807
Products: Scrap metal. **SICs:** 5093 (Scrap & Waste Materials); 5051 (Metals Service Centers & Offices). **Est:** 1945. **Sales:** $20,000,000 (2000). **Emp:** 120. **Officers:** B. David Peck, President; B. David Peck, VP of Finance; Harold Shultz, Dir. of Marketing; Elaine Hammett, Dir. of Information Systems; Fred Berman, Dir of Human Resources.

■ 26938 ■ Peltz Group Inc.
PO Box 1799
Milwaukee, WI 53217
Phone: (414)449-3900
Products: Recycled paper, metal, glass, and plastic. **SIC:** 5093 (Scrap & Waste Materials). **Est:** 1960. **Sales:** $100,000,000 (2000). **Emp:** 250. **Officers:** H. Peltz, President; John Vosburg, CFO; A. Peltz, Dir. of Marketing; D. Cohen, Dir. of Systems.

■ 26939 ■ Max Phillips and Son Inc.
PO Box 202
Eau Claire, WI 54702-0202
Phone: (715)832-3431
Products: Recyclable wood, metal, and paper. **SIC:** 5093 (Scrap & Waste Materials). **Est:** 1947. **Sales:** $6,000,000 (2000). **Emp:** 38. **Officers:** R.G. Westphal, Vice President.

■ 26940 ■ Plastic Recycling of Iowa Falls, Inc.
10252 Hwy. 65
Iowa Falls, IA 50126-8823
Phone: (515)648-5073
Free: (800)338-1438 **Fax:** (515)648-5074
E-mail: info@hammersplastic.com
URL: http://www.hammersplastic.com
Products: Recycled plastic lumber; Car stops; Speed bumps; Park benches; Picnic tables; Trash receptacles; Custom moldings. **SICs:** 5093 (Scrap & Waste Materials); 5099 (Durable Goods Nec). **Est:** 1986. **Sales:** $3,000,000 (2000). **Emp:** 40. **Officers:** Jerry Jenson, President; James Hoffman, CEO & CFO; Robert Mestdagh, Plant Mgr.; Susan Waters, Sales Mgr., e-mail: info@hammersplastic.com; Sabrina Caruth, Customer Service Contact, e-mail: info@hammersplastic.com. **Former Name:** Hammer's Plastic Recycling Corp.

■ 26941 ■ Plyler Paper Stock Co.
102 Holly Dr.
Hartsville, SC 29550-4912
Phone: (803)537-2921
Products: Recycled aluminum cans and recycled corrugated paper. **SIC:** 5093 (Scrap & Waste Materials). **Est:** 1930. **Sales:** $1,000,000 (2000). **Emp:** 5. **Officers:** Henry Plyler, President.

■ 26942 ■ Pollock Corp.
Industrial Hwy., S Keim St.
Pottstown, PA 19464
Phone: (610)323-5500 **Fax:** (610)323-5506
Products: Scrap metal recycling. **SIC:** 5093 (Scrap & Waste Materials). **Sales:** $16,000,000 (2000). **Emp:** 75. **Officers:** Mayer Pollock, President; D.J. Owens, CFO.

■ 26943 ■ Mayer Pollock Steel Corp.
Industrial Hwy., S Keim St.
Pottstown, PA 19464
Phone: (610)323-5500
Products: Scrap metal. **SIC:** 5093 (Scrap & Waste Materials). **Est:** 1888. **Sales:** $25,000,000 (2000). **Emp:** 100. **Officers:** Mayer Pollock, President; D.J. Owens, CFO.

■ 26944 ■ Potential Industries Inc.
922 E E St.
Wilmington, CA 90744
Phone: (310)549-5901 **Fax:** (310)513-1361
Products: Recycled paper, aluminum cans, and glass. **SIC:** 5093 (Scrap & Waste Materials). **Sales:** $45,000,000 (2000). **Emp:** 100. **Officers:** Tony Fan, President; Jessica Chen, Treasurer & Secty.

■ 26945 ■ Powmet Inc.
2625 Sewell St.
Rockford, IL 61109
Phone: (815)398-6900 **Fax:** (815)398-6907
Products: Scrap metals. **SICs:** 5051 (Metals Service Centers & Offices); 5093 (Scrap & Waste Materials). **Officers:** William C. Thiede, President.

■ 26946 ■ Prins/Basic Waste Systems Inc.
45 Bunker Hill Rd., Industrial Park
Charlestown, MA 02129
Phone: (781)396-1177 **Fax:** (617)241-3806
Products: Recycled paper. **SIC:** 5093 (Scrap & Waste Materials). **Sales:** $2,000,000 (2000). **Emp:** 11. **Officers:** Robert D. Vincent, Vice President.

■ 26947 ■ Proler International Corp.
4265 San Felipe, No. 900
Houston, TX 77027
Phone: (713)675-2281 **Fax:** (713)675-5968
Products: Steel scrap. **SIC:** 5093 (Scrap & Waste Materials). **Est:** 1925. **Sales:** $13,400,000 (2000). **Emp:** 91. **Officers:** Herman Proler, CEO & Chairman of the Board; Michael F. Loy, VP & CFO; Norman Bishop, Technical Dir.

■ 26948 ■ Prolerized Schiabo-Neu Co.
1 Linden Ave., E
Jersey City, NJ 07305
Phone: (201)333-3131 **Fax:** (201)333-5986
Products: Recycled scrap metal. **SIC:** 5093 (Scrap & Waste Materials). **Est:** 1967. **Sales:** $5,000,000 (2000). **Emp:** 100. **Officers:** Jay Zimmern, General Mgr.

■ 26949 ■ R and R Salvage Inc.
1329 William St.
Buffalo, NY 14206
Phone: (716)856-3608
Products: Used metals, including copper, aluminum, steel, and iron. **SIC:** 5093 (Scrap & Waste Materials). **Est:** 1952. **Sales:** $4,000,000 (2000). **Emp:** 25. **Officers:** Robert Redino, President.

■ 26950 ■ Rag Man Inc.
14676 SE 82nd Dr.
Clackamas, OR 97015
Phone: (503)657-5694
Free: (877)572-4626 **Fax:** (503)657-5694
Products: Used and new clothing, including overalls, pants and shirts; Cleaning rags. **SICs:** 5093 (Scrap & Waste Materials); 5099 (Durable Goods Nec). **Est:** 1988. **Sales:** $400,000 (2000). **Emp:** 2. **Officers:** Jim Whitaker, President; Sam Walker, Vice President.

■ 26951 ■ Rapid Disposal Services Inc.
115 Churchill Ave.
Somerset, NJ 08873-3443
Phone: (732)469-3117
Products: Recycled products. **SIC:** 5093 (Scrap & Waste Materials). **Sales:** $6,000,000 (2000). **Emp:** 40. **Officers:** Steve Dinardi, President.

■ 26952 ■ Recycle America Northern California
800 77th Ave.
Oakland, CA 94621
Phone: (510)638-4327
Products: Recycled products. **SIC:** 5093 (Scrap & Waste Materials).

■ 26953 ■ Recycle Metals Corp.
Allenwood Rd.
Conshohocken, PA 19428
Phone: (215)828-5553 **Fax:** (215)828-5390
Products: Scrap materials including steel and aluminum. **SIC:** 5093 (Scrap & Waste Materials). **Est:** 1971. **Sales:** $20,000,000 (2000). **Emp:** 35. **Officers:** Samuel Blumberg, Chairman of the Board.

■ 26954 ■ Recycling Industries Inc.
9780 S Meridian Blvd., Ste. 180
Englewood, CO 80112
Phone: (303)790-7372
Products: Metals recycler. **SIC:** 5093 (Scrap & Waste Materials). **Sales:** $62,400,000 (2000). **Emp:** 271. **Officers:** Thomas J. Wiens, CEO & Chairman of the Board; Brian L. Klemsz, CFO & Treasurer.

■ 26955 ■ William Reisner Corp.
33 Elm St.
Clinton, MA 01510
Phone: (508)365-4585
Products: Scrap metal. **SICs:** 5051 (Metals Service Centers & Offices); 5093 (Scrap & Waste Materials). **Sales:** $29,000,000 (2000). **Emp:** 40. **Officers:** Harold Reisner, President.

■ 26956 ■ Republic Alloys Inc.
419 Atando Ave.
Charlotte, NC 28206
Phone: (704)375-5937
Products: Copper; Steel; Aluminum; Cast iron. **SIC:** 5093 (Scrap & Waste Materials).

■ 26957 ■ Research Environmental Industries
2777 Rockefeller Ave.
Cleveland, OH 44115
Phone: (216)623-8383 **Fax:** (216)623-8393
Products: Recycled oil and liquid waste management. **SIC:** 5093 (Scrap & Waste Materials). **Est:** 1932. **Sales:** $15,000,000 (2000). **Emp:** 120. **Officers:** Alan Gressel, President; Peter Jaboni, Dir. of Marketing & Sales.

■ 26958 ■ Rich Metals Co.
PO Box 3491
Davenport, IA 52802
Phone: (319)322-0975
Products: Scrap metal. **SIC:** 5051 (Metals Service Centers & Offices). **Est:** 1963. **Sales:** $5,500,000 (2000). **Emp:** 35. **Officers:** Richard Porter, President.

■ 26959 ■ S.D. Richman Sons Inc.
2435 Wheatsheaf Ln.
Philadelphia, PA 19137
Phone: (215)535-5100 **Fax:** (215)288-1043
Products: Scrap metal, including iron. **SIC:** 5093 (Scrap & Waste Materials). **Est:** 1901. **Sales:** $12,000,000 (2000). **Emp:** 60. **Officers:** David Richman, President.

■ 26960 ■ River City Steel and Recycling Inc.
PO Box 240580
San Antonio, TX 78224-0580
Phone: (210)924-1254
Free: (800)580-7833 **Fax:** (210)924-1711
Products: Recycled steel, new and used steel products. **SIC:** 5051 (Metals Service Centers & Offices). **Est:** 1982. **Sales:** $4,000,000 (1999). **Emp:** 25. **Officers:** Justin N. Triesch, President.

■ 26961 ■ Riverside Recycling Inc.
PO Box 17166
Louisville, KY 40217
Phone: (502)634-8531
Products: Used, scrap, and recycled materials. **SIC:** 5093 (Scrap & Waste Materials). **Est:** 1976. **Sales:** $17,000,000 (2000). **Emp:** 30.

■ 26962 ■ Riverside Scrap Iron
PO Box 5288
Riverside, CA 92517
Phone: (909)686-2120 **Fax:** (909)686-8933
Products: Recyclables, including metals. **SIC:** 5093 (Scrap & Waste Materials). **Est:** 1954. **Sales:** $8,000,000 (2000). **Emp:** 40. **Officers:** S. Frankel, CEO; D. Frankel, President; Raj Gandhi, Exec. VP.

■ 26963 ■ Robinson Iron and Metal Company Inc.
2735 Brooks St.
Houston, TX 77020
Phone: (713)227-2376 **Fax:** (713)227-2910
Products: Scrap metal processing; Metals, including iron. **SIC:** 5093 (Scrap & Waste Materials). **Est:** 1928. **Emp:** 15. **Officers:** Stephen Robinson, President; Ralph Robinson, Vice President.

■ 26964 ■ Rocky Mountain Recycling
4431 E 64th Ave.
Commerce City, CO 80022
Phone: (303)288-6868 **Fax:** (303)288-0250
E-mail: Bhenesy@mountainrecycling.com
URL: http://www.mountainrecycling.com
Products: Scrap metal. **SIC:** 5093 (Scrap & Waste Materials). **Est:** 1936. **Sales:** $5,000,000 (2000). **Emp:** 30. **Officers:** Larry Odle, President. **Alternate Name:** Gahagen Iron and Metal Co.

■ 26965 ■ Rogers Iron and Metal Corp.
PO Box 1806
Rogers, AR 72757
Phone: (501)636-2666 **Fax:** (501)631-8413
Products: Recycled metals. **SIC:** 5093 (Scrap & Waste Materials). **Sales:** $12,000,000 (1992). **Emp:** 33. **Officers:** Jerry Pittman, President.

■ 26966 ■ Romic Chemical Corp.
2081 Bay Rd.
East Palo Alto, CA 94303
Phone: (415)324-1638
Products: Recycled goods. **SIC:** 5169 (Chemicals & Allied Products Nec). **Est:** 1963. **Sales:** $37,000,000 (2000). **Emp:** 200. **Officers:** H.M. Schneider, Chairman of the Board; Peter Schneider, President; Ron R. Tressen, Dir. of Marketing.

■ 26967 ■ Rose Metal Processing
2902 Center St.
Houston, TX 77007
Phone: (713)880-7000 **Fax:** (713)880-7011
Products: Recycled metal products. **SIC:** 5093 (Scrap & Waste Materials). **Est:** 1947. **Sales:** $21,800,000 (2000). **Emp:** 60. **Officers:** L.J. Black, President; Lloyd Hall, Controller. **Former Name:** Rose Metal Recycling Inc.

■ 26968 ■ RRT Empire Returns Corp.
4545 Morgan Pl.
Liverpool, NY 13090-3521
Phone: (315)455-7080
Products: Recycled materials, including tin, aluminum, glass, plastic, and paper. **SIC:** 5093 (Scrap & Waste Materials). **Est:** 1982. **Sales:** $30,000,000 (2000). **Emp:** 100. **Officers:** Bruce Anderson, President; Mark Roemer, Dir. of Data Processing; Diana Weir, Dir of Human Resources.

■ 26969 ■ Rubino Brothers Inc.
PO Box 1110
Stamford, CT 06904
Phone: (203)323-3195 **Fax:** (203)975-9483
Products: Scrap metal. **SIC:** 5093 (Scrap & Waste Materials). **Est:** 1930. **Sales:** $2,500,000 (1999). **Emp:** 25. **Officers:** Anthony Rubino, President.

■ 26970 ■ Ruby Metal Traders Inc.
12303 Edwina Blvd.
Houston, TX 77045
Phone: (713)433-0044 **Fax:** (713)433-0444
Products: Scrap metal. **SIC:** 5093 (Scrap & Waste Materials). **Sales:** $14,500,000 (2000). **Emp:** 10. **Officers:** Shekhar Agrawal, President; Mukesh Turakhia, CFO.

■ 26971 ■ Sabel Industries Inc.
PO Drawer 4747
Montgomery, AL 36103
Phone: (334)265-6771
Free: (800)392-5754 **Fax:** (334)264-3692
URL: http://www.sabelsteel.com
Products: Recyclable steel; Full line carbon steel service center. **SICs:** 5051 (Metals Service Centers & Offices); 5093 (Scrap & Waste Materials). **Est:** 1869. **Sales:** $40,000,000 (2000). **Emp:** 220. **Officers:** Keith Sabel, President; Phillip Brown, Controller; Fred Callahan, Dir. of Marketing & Sales; Janet Hinton, Dir of Human Resources.

■ 26972 ■ Stanley Sack Company Inc.
30 Barber Pond Rd.
Bloomfield, CT 06002
Phone: (203)242-6228
Products: Scrap recyclers. **SIC:** 5093 (Scrap & Waste Materials). **Sales:** $19,000,000 (1992). **Emp:** 33. **Officers:** Stanely Sack, President & Treasurer; Staley Sack, President & Treasurer.

■ 26973 ■ Saco Steel Company Inc.
PO Box 187
Saco, ME 04072
Phone: (207)284-4516
Free: (800)464-4516 **Fax:** (207)284-9782
Products: Recycled steel, scrapped non-ferrous and ferrous metals; Scrap metal. **SIC:** 5093 (Scrap & Waste Materials). **Est:** 1914. **Sales:** $3,000,000 (2000). **Emp:** 20. **Officers:** M. Zaitlin, President.

■ 26974 ■ Sadoff and Rudoy Industries
PO Box 1138
Fond du Lac, WI 54936
Phone: (920)921-2070 **Fax:** (920)921-1283
URL: http://www.sadoff.com
Products: Ferrous and nonferrous scrap metals. **SICs:** 5093 (Scrap & Waste Materials); 5051 (Metals Service Centers & Offices). **Est:** 1964. **Sales:** $100,000,000 (2000). **Emp:** 304. **Officers:** Sheldon J. Lasky, CEO; Roger H. Gerlach, CFO; Mark Katz, General Mgr.; Aral Eaton, Ferrous VP; Maurice Berglund, Non Ferrous VP; Thomas A. Knippel, Ind. Marketing Mgr.; David Borsuk, Quality Environment Mgr.

■ 26975 ■ **Safety House**
PO Box 1076
Lake Charles, LA 70601
Phone: (318)436-7538 **Fax:** (318)436-3346
Products: Used pipe. **SIC:** 5093 (Scrap & Waste Materials). **Est:** 1916. **Sales:** $1,500,000 (2000). **Emp:** 14. **Officers:** Belin Landry Sr., Partner.

■ 26976 ■ **Safety-Kleen, Southwest**
1340 W Lincoln St.
Phoenix, AZ 85007
Phone: (602)258-6155
Products: Hazardous waste disposal and collection; Chemicals. **SICs:** 5093 (Scrap & Waste Materials); 5169 (Chemicals & Allied Products Nec). **Est:** 1993. **Sales:** $18,000,000 (2000). **Emp:** 45.

■ 26977 ■ **Samuels Recycling Co.**
PO Box 8800
Madison, WI 53708
Phone: (608)241-7191 **Fax:** (608)241-2641
Products: Recycled items. **SIC:** 5093 (Scrap & Waste Materials). **Est:** 1985. **Sales:** $50,000,000 (2000). **Emp:** 200. **Officers:** John Dulin, President; Mike Siehoff, Treasurer; Jim Jensen, Marketing Mgr.; Wayne Daubner, Dir. of Information Systems.

■ 26978 ■ **Samuels Recycling Co. Janesville Div.**
1753 Beloit Ave.
Janesville, WI 53546
Phone: (608)756-2555 **Fax:** (608)756-5528
Products: Recycled materials. **SIC:** 5093 (Scrap & Waste Materials). **Est:** 1984. **Sales:** $1,000,000 (1999). **Emp:** 15. **Officers:** Richard Walker, General Mgr.

■ 26979 ■ **Scepter Industries Inc.**
R.R. 1, Box 551
Bicknell, IN 47512
Phone: (812)735-2500
Products: Aluminum recycling. **SIC:** 5093 (Scrap & Waste Materials). **Sales:** $31,000,000 (1992). **Emp:** 85. **Officers:** Garney Scott, President; Mike Fielding, Controller.

■ 26980 ■ **Michael Schiavone and Sons Inc.**
234 Universal Dr.
North Haven, CT 06473
Phone: (203)777-2591 **Fax:** (203)865-5072
Products: Scrap metal. **SIC:** 5093 (Scrap & Waste Materials). **Est:** 1895. **Sales:** $50,000,000 (2000). **Emp:** 200. **Officers:** Michael Schiavone, Vice President; Ron Sader, Vice President; Bill Polinsky, Vice President; Jim Keach, Dir. of Data Processing.

■ 26981 ■ **Schlafer Iron and Steel Co.**
1950 Medbury Ave.
Detroit, MI 48211
Phone: (313)925-8200
Products: Scrap steel. **SIC:** 5093 (Scrap & Waste Materials). **Est:** 1987. **Sales:** $18,000,000 (2000). **Emp:** 50. **Officers:** Barry Briskin, CEO; Steven Benacquisto, CFO; Anthony Benacquisto, Dir. of Marketing.

■ 26982 ■ **Schnitzer Steel Products**
PO Box 10047
Portland, OR 97296
Phone: (503)286-5771 **Fax:** (503)286-6948
Products: Steel works; Mini mill; Rolling mills; Scrap manufacturing and processing. **SIC:** 5093 (Scrap & Waste Materials).

■ 26983 ■ **Schwartzman Co.**
2905 N Ferry St.
Anoka, MN 55303
Phone: (612)421-1187 **Fax:** (612)421-4704
Products: Recycled aluminum cans. **SIC:** 5093 (Scrap & Waste Materials). **Sales:** $3,000,000 (2000). **Emp:** 25. **Officers:** Ivan Schwartzman, President; David Schwartzman, Controller.

■ 26984 ■ **Scrap Corporation of America**
12901 S Stony Island Ave.
Chicago, IL 60633
Phone: (312)646-1800
Products: Iron and steel scrap. **SIC:** 5093 (Scrap & Waste Materials). **Est:** 1970. **Sales:** $37,000,000

(2000). **Emp:** 100. **Officers:** Howard Foster, President; George Zemenick, Controller.

■ 26985 ■ **Seattle Iron and Metals Corp.**
601 S Myrtle St.
Seattle, WA 98108-3424
Products: Scrap metal. **SIC:** 5093 (Scrap & Waste Materials). **Est:** 1927. **Sales:** $53,000,000 (2000). **Emp:** 90. **Officers:** David Sidell, President; Allan Sidell, Vice President.

■ 26986 ■ **Segel and Son Inc.**
PO Box 276
Warren, PA 16365
Phone: (814)723-4900
Products: Scrap materials, including steel, carbon, and iron. **SIC:** 5093 (Scrap & Waste Materials). **Est:** 1917. **Sales:** $6,000,000 (2000). **Emp:** 43. **Officers:** Harry Segel, President.

■ 26987 ■ **Sessler Inc.**
111 Hwy. 99 N
Eugene, OR 97402
Phone: (503)686-0515
Products: Ferrous and nonferrous scrap. **SIC:** 5093 (Scrap & Waste Materials).

■ 26988 ■ **Shredded Products Corp.**
700 Commerce Rd.
Rocky Mount, VA 24151
Phone: (540)489-7599
Products: Recycled scrap metal products. **SIC:** 5093 (Scrap & Waste Materials). **Sales:** $18,000,000 (2000). **Emp:** 50. **Officers:** Donald G. Smith, President.

■ 26989 ■ **I. Shulman and Son Co.**
197 E Washington Ave.
Elmira, NY 14901
Phone: (607)733-7111
Products: Scrap metal. **SIC:** 5093 (Scrap & Waste Materials). **Sales:** $600,000 (2000). **Emp:** 23. **Officers:** O. Shulman, President; S. Shulman, VP of Finance.

■ 26990 ■ **Simon Resources Inc.**
2525 Trenton Ave.
Williamsport, PA 17701
Phone: (717)326-9041
Products: Scrap metals. **SIC:** 5093 (Scrap & Waste Materials). **Est:** 1970. **Sales:** $29,000,000 (2000). **Emp:** 50. **Officers:** Sam Simon, President.

■ 26991 ■ **Joseph Simon & Sons**
2200 E River St.
Tacoma, WA 98421
Phone: (253)272-9364 **Fax:** (253)838-1998
Products: Scrap metals. **SIC:** 5093 (Scrap & Waste Materials). **Officers:** Phil Simon, President.

■ 26992 ■ **Sims Brothers Inc.**
PO Box 1170
Marion, OH 43301-1170
Phone: (740)387-9041 **Fax:** (740)387-0083
E-mail: simsbros@acc-net.com
Products: Scrap materials, including ores and metals. **SIC:** 5093 (Scrap & Waste Materials). **Est:** 1930. **Sales:** $21,000,000 (2000). **Emp:** 100. **Officers:** Gary K. Sims, President; Stanley E. Casey, Treasurer & Secty.

■ 26993 ■ **Sims Metal America - Structural Steel Div.**
3220 Deepwater Term Rd.
Richmond, VA 23234
Phone: (804)291-3255 **Fax:** (804)291-3273
Products: Recycled metals. **SIC:** 5093 (Scrap & Waste Materials). **Former Name:** Peck Recycling Co. Structural Steel Div.

■ 26994 ■ **Simsmetal USA Corp.**
600 S 4th St.
Richmond, CA 94804
Phone: (510)412-5300 **Fax:** (510)412-5421
Products: Salvage metal. **SICs:** 5093 (Scrap & Waste Materials); 5051 (Metals Service Centers & Offices). **Est:** 1987. **Sales:** $130,000,000 (2000). **Emp:** 350. **Officers:** John J. Mike, President; Myles Partridge, CFO; Allan Raptner, VP of Operations.

■ 26995 ■ **Smithey Recycling Co.**
PO Box 19050
Phoenix, AZ 85005-9050
Phone: (602)252-8125 **Fax:** (602)252-5917
Products: Recycled metal products. **SIC:** 5093 (Scrap & Waste Materials). **Est:** 1936. **Sales:** $11,000,000 (2000). **Emp:** 15. **Officers:** Sarah E. Smithey, President; Valerie J. Koeninger, Secretary.

■ 26996 ■ **Soave Enterprises L.L.C.**
3400 E Lafayette St.
Detroit, MI 48207
Phone: (313)567-7000 **Fax:** (313)567-0966
Products: Scrap metal and waste. **SIC:** 5093 (Scrap & Waste Materials). **Sales:** $535,000,000 (2000). **Emp:** 1,000. **Officers:** Anthony Soave, CEO & President; Michael Piesko, CFO.

■ 26997 ■ **Sol-Pro Inc.**
PO Box 1781
Tacoma, WA 98401-1781
Phone: (253)627-4822 **Fax:** (253)627-4997
URL: http://www.sol-pro.com
Products: Recycled solvents. **SIC:** 5093 (Scrap & Waste Materials). **Est:** 1974. **Sales:** $14,000,000 (2000). **Emp:** 24. **Officers:** Christian P. Jeuris, President, e-mail: cpjeuris@sol-pro.com.

■ 26998 ■ **Soloman Metals Corp.**
Rte. 1-A N
580 Lynnway
Lynn, MA 01905
Phone: (781)581-7000
Free: (800)326-8959 **Fax:** (781)599-6130
Products: Non-ferrous scrap metal. **SIC:** 5093 (Scrap & Waste Materials). **Officers:** Steven Solomon, VP of Sales.

■ 26999 ■ **J. Solotken and Company Inc.**
PO Box 1645
Indianapolis, IN 46206
Phone: (317)638-5566 **Fax:** (317)638-5569
Products: Non-ferrous scrap metals. **SIC:** 5093 (Scrap & Waste Materials). **Est:** 1914. **Sales:** $7,500,000 (2000). **Emp:** 40. **Officers:** Joseph M. Alpert, President; H.A. Alpert, Secretary.

■ 27000 ■ **South Coast Recycling Inc.**
4560 Doran St.
Los Angeles, CA 90039-1006
Phone: (213)245-5133 **Fax:** (818)548-8814
Products: Recycled glass products; Recycled paper products; Recycled metal products. **SIC:** 5093 (Scrap & Waste Materials). **Est:** 1960. **Sales:** $16,000,000 (2000). **Emp:** 45. **Officers:** John R. Gasparian Sr., President.

■ 27001 ■ **Southeastern Industries Inc.**
PO Box 809
Reidsville, NC 27320
Phone: (910)349-6243 **Fax:** (910)349-9048
Products: Recycled plastic and resin. **SIC:** 5162 (Plastics Materials & Basic Shapes). **Est:** 1955. **Sales:** $2,000,000 (2000). **Emp:** 20. **Officers:** L.S. Snyder, President; Steven B. Andrews, CFO.

■ 27002 ■ **Southern Holdings Inc.**
4801 Florida Ave.
New Orleans, LA 70126
Phone: (504)944-3371
Products: Metal waste and scrap materials. **SIC:** 5093 (Scrap & Waste Materials).

■ 27003 ■ **Southern Metals Company Inc.**
PO Box 668923
Charlotte, NC 28266
Phone: (704)394-3161 **Fax:** (704)394-3163
Products: Scrap metals, including iron. **SIC:** 5093 (Scrap & Waste Materials). **Est:** 1940. **Sales:** $30,000,000 (2000). **Emp:** 80. **Officers:** Robert Helbein, Payroll Mgr.

■ 27004 ■ **Southern Scrap Material Company Ltd.**
PO Box 12388
Pensacola, FL 32582
Phone: (850)438-3197
Products: Scrap metal recycling. **SIC:** 5093 (Scrap & Waste Materials). **Est:** 1940. **Sales:** $6,000,000

(2000). **Emp:** 90. **Officers:** Jack Rosenbaum, President; Tony Cofield, VP of Finance.

■ **27005** ■ **Southern Scrap Material Company Ltd.**
PO Box 26087
New Orleans, LA 70186
Phone: (504)942-0340 **Fax:** (504)947-1614
Products: Recycled metal, including aluminum. **SIC:** 5093 (Scrap & Waste Materials). **Est:** 1900. **Sales:** $140,000,000 (2000). **Emp:** 250. **Officers:** Edward L. Diefenthal, President.

■ **27006** ■ **Southside Recycling Inc.**
4076 Bayless Ave.
St. Louis, MO 63125
Phone: (314)631-3400
Products: Recycled aluminum, glass, paper, and cardboard. **SIC:** 5093 (Scrap & Waste Materials). **Sales:** $11,000,000 (2000). **Emp:** 20. **Officers:** Tim Janson, President.

■ **27007** ■ **Spartan Iron Metal Company Inc.**
826 N 3rd St.
Philadelphia, PA 19123
Phone: (215)627-5344
Products: Scrap metal recycling. **SIC:** 5093 (Scrap & Waste Materials). **Sales:** $37,000,000 (1992). **Emp:** 100.

■ **27008** ■ **SPC Corp.**
26th St. & Penrose Ave.
Philadelphia, PA 19145
Phone: (215)952-1501
Products: Scrap and junk automobiles. **SIC:** 5093 (Scrap & Waste Materials).

■ **27009** ■ **State Salvage Company Inc.**
22500 S Alameda St.
Long Beach, CA 90810
Phone: (310)835-3849
Products: Scrap metal. **SICs:** 5051 (Metals Service Centers & Offices); 5093 (Scrap & Waste Materials). **Sales:** $17,000,000 (2000). **Emp:** 30. **Officers:** Hillard Lewison, President.

■ **27010** ■ **Herman Strauss Inc.**
PO Box 6543
Wheeling, WV 26003
Phone: (304)232-8770
Products: Scrap metal. **SIC:** 5093 (Scrap & Waste Materials). **Est:** 1922. **Sales:** $31,000,000 (2000). **Emp:** 50. **Officers:** Carter Strauss, President; Gil Ullom, Treasurer & Secty.; Ken Burns, Vice President.

■ **27011** ■ **Paul Stuck and Associates**
PO Box 378070
Chicago, IL 60637-8070
Phone: (773)890-0700 **Fax:** (773)890-4362
Products: Recycled office furniture and equipment. **SICs:** 5021 (Furniture); 5044 (Office Equipment). **Sales:** $4,000,000 (1994). **Emp:** 80. **Officers:** Paul Stuck, CEO; Ted Dawson, Controller.

■ **27012** ■ **Sturgis Iron and Metal Company Inc.**
PO Box 579
Sturgis, MI 49091
Phone: (616)651-7851
Products: Scrap metal. **SIC:** 5093 (Scrap & Waste Materials). **Est:** 1948. **Sales:** $48,000,000 (2000). **Emp:** 225. **Officers:** Ralph Levin, President; Robert Driver, Controller.

■ **27013** ■ **Sugar Creek Scrap, Inc.**
PO Box 208
West Terre Haute, IN 47885-0208
Phone: (812)533-2147
Free: (800)466-7462 **Fax:** (812)533-2140
E-mail: sugarcreekscrap@mach500.net
Products: Steel and copper scrap products. **SIC:** 5093 (Scrap & Waste Materials). **Est:** 1968. **Sales:** $6,000,000 (2000). **Emp:** 32. **Officers:** S. Levin, President; Carol K. Briggs, Controller; Grant Dailey, General Mgr. **Former Name:** Dumes Salvage Terre Haute Compressed Steel Inc.

■ **27014** ■ **Suisman and Blumenthal Inc.**
500 Flatbush Ave.
Hartford, CT 06106
Phone: (860)522-3123 **Fax:** (860)724-9245
Products: Recycled metal. **SIC:** 5093 (Scrap & Waste Materials). **Est:** 1899. **Emp:** 170. **Officers:** John Lane, President; Richard Dzubin, CFO.

■ **27015** ■ **Sun Valley Paper Stock Inc.**
11166 Pendleton St.
Sun Valley, CA 91352
Phone: (818)767-8984
Products: Recycled paper. **SIC:** 5093 (Scrap & Waste Materials). **Est:** 1985. **Sales:** $5,000,000 (2000). **Emp:** 44. **Officers:** Robert D. Fagan, President.

■ **27016** ■ **Superior Div.**
1610 N Calhoun St.
Ft. Wayne, IN 46808
Phone: (219)422-5541 **Fax:** (219)423-2569
Products: Metal, including scrap iron. **SICs:** 5093 (Scrap & Waste Materials); 5051 (Metals Service Centers & Offices). **Est:** 1943. **Sales:** $350,000,000 (2000). **Emp:** 700. **Officers:** Leonard Rifkin, President; Charles Quimby, CFO; Larry Fishburn, Dir. of Data Processing; Ben Eisbart, Dir of Human Resources.

■ **27017** ■ **Swenson Metal Salvage Inc.**
PO Box 363
Spanish Fork, UT 84660
Phone: (801)798-3548 **Fax:** (801)798-2220
URL: http://www.kjs9wmrecycling.com
Products: Scrap metal. **SIC:** 5093 (Scrap & Waste Materials). **Est:** 1946. **Sales:** $7,000,000 (2000). **Emp:** 20. **Officers:** Ken Swenson, President.

■ **27018** ■ **TALCO Recycling Inc.**
720 S Temescal St.
Corona, CA 91718
Phone: (909)736-7040
Products: Recycled polystyrene. **SIC:** 5093 (Scrap & Waste Materials). **Sales:** $17,000,000 (2000). **Emp:** 30. **Officers:** John Shedd, President.

■ **27019** ■ **Temple Iron and Metal Company Inc.**
PO Box 805
Temple, TX 76503
Phone: (254)773-2700 **Fax:** (254)773-4487
Products: Scrap iron, copper, aluminum, and cardboard. **SIC:** 5093 (Scrap & Waste Materials). **Est:** 1934. **Sales:** $4,500,000 (1999). **Emp:** 35. **Officers:** David Neman, Owner; Abdul Katz, CFO; Jenna Marie, Customer Service Contact; Newt Knumbella, Dir. of Data Processing; Spencer David, Communications and Human Relations Mgr.

■ **27020** ■ **A. Tenenbaum Company Inc.**
PO Box 15128
Little Rock, AR 72231
Phone: (501)945-0881
Products: Scrap metal. **SICs:** 5093 (Scrap & Waste Materials); 5051 (Metals Service Centers & Offices). **Est:** 1890. **Sales:** $43,000,000 (2000). **Emp:** 90. **Officers:** Harold S. Tenenbaum, President; R.J. Wills, Treasurer.

■ **27021** ■ **Terra Haute Recycling**
PO Box 1798
Terre Haute, IN 47808-1798
Phone: (812)232-1537
Products: Recycled paper and metal products. **SIC:** 5093 (Scrap & Waste Materials).

■ **27022** ■ **Tewksbury Industries Inc.**
860 East St.
Tewksbury, MA 01876
Phone: (508)851-5946 **Fax:** (508)851-0791
Products: Scrap metals. **SIC:** 5093 (Scrap & Waste Materials). **Est:** 1957. **Sales:** $42,000,000 (2000). **Emp:** 87. **Officers:** Thomas Bowley, President; William Busby, Controller.

■ **27023** ■ **Texpack USA Inc.**
1001 S Bayshore Dr., Ste. 2402
Miami, FL 33131
Phone: (305)358-9696
Products: Recycled paper products. **SIC:** 5093 (Scrap & Waste Materials). **Sales:** $74,000,000 (2000). **Emp:**

200. **Officers:** Joseph Artiga, President; Joaquin Vinas, VP of Finance.

■ **27024** ■ **Thalheimer Brothers Inc.**
5550 Whitaker Ave.
Philadelphia, PA 19124
Phone: (215)537-5200 **Fax:** (215)533-3993
Products: Nonferrous metal scrap. **SIC:** 5093 (Scrap & Waste Materials). **Est:** 1937. **Sales:** $15,000,000 (2000). **Emp:** 100. **Officers:** John M. Thalheimer, President; Michael Hayman, CFO; Stanley Ziff, Dir. of Marketing.

■ **27025** ■ **T.L.K. Industries Inc.**
902 Ogden Ave.
Superior, WI 54880
Phone: (715)392-6253 **Fax:** (715)392-6256
Products: Industrial supplies. **SIC:** 5093 (Scrap & Waste Materials). **Sales:** $1,300,000 (2000). **Emp:** 10.

■ **27026** ■ **Tri-State Iron and Metal Co.**
PO Box 775
Texarkana, AR 75504
Phone: (870)773-8409
Products: Recycled scrap metal. **SIC:** 5093 (Scrap & Waste Materials). **Sales:** $12,000,000 (1993). **Emp:** 33. **Officers:** Mordecai Glick, President; Howard Glick, Treasurer.

■ **27027** ■ **Tube City Inc.**
PO Box 2000
Glassport, PA 15045
Phone: (412)678-6141
Products: Scrap metal, including iron, steel, aluminum, and copper. **SICs:** 5093 (Scrap & Waste Materials); 5051 (Metals Service Centers & Offices). **Est:** 1930. **Sales:** $320,000,000 (2000). **Emp:** 250. **Officers:** Michael Coslov, CEO; John Lipinski, Sr. VP & CFO; Bob Odle, Sr. VP.

■ **27028** ■ **Tung Tai Trading Corp.**
1325 Howard Ave., No. 611
Burlingame, CA 94010
Phone: (650)573-5705 **Fax:** (650)685-7200
E-mail: sales@tungtai.com
URL: http://www.tungtai.com
Products: Scrap metal. **SICs:** 5093 (Scrap & Waste Materials); 5051 (Metals Service Centers & Offices). **Est:** 1974. **Sales:** $10,000,000 (2000). **Emp:** 5. **Officers:** Joseph Chen, President, e-mail: jc@ricochet.net.

■ **27029** ■ **United Iron and Metal Co.**
2545 Wilkens Ave.
Baltimore, MD 21223
Phone: (410)947-8000
E-mail: mjf@djj.com
Products: Scrap and waste metal, including iron. **SIC:** 5093 (Scrap & Waste Materials). **Est:** 1912. **Sales:** $120,000,000 (2000). **Emp:** 40. **Officers:** Edgar Johnson, General Mgr.; Michael Finn, Commercial Mgr.

■ **27030** ■ **United Recycling Industries Inc.**
1600 Harvester
West Chicago, IL 60185
Phone: (630)231-6060 **Fax:** (630)231-6565
E-mail: sales@unitedrecycling.com
URL: http://www.unitedrecycling.com
Products: Remarketing and recycling of electronics and components. **SIC:** 5093 (Scrap & Waste Materials). **Est:** 1991. **Sales:** $40,000,000 (2000). **Emp:** 115. **Officers:** Robert Glavin, President, e-mail: rglavin@unitedrecycling.com

■ **27031** ■ **U.S. Tire Recycling**
6322 Poplar Tent Rd.
Concord, NC 28027-7580
Phone: (704)784-1210 **Fax:** (704)784-4716
E-mail: ustirehq@hotmail.com
Products: Scrap tire processing for fuel production and drain field aggregate. **SIC:** 5093 (Scrap & Waste Materials). **Former Name:** U.S. Tire Recycling Partners L.P.

■ 27032 ■ Universal Metal and Ore Company Inc.
PO Box 187
Mt. Vernon, NY 10551
Phone: (914)664-0200
Products: Scrap metal, including ore. **SICs:** 5093 (Scrap & Waste Materials); 5051 (Metals Service Centers & Offices). **Sales:** $2,000,000 (2000). **Emp:** 7. **Officers:** Steven V. Vollweiler, President.

■ 27033 ■ Universal Scrap Metals Co.
2500 W Fulton St.
Chicago, IL 60612-2104
Phone: (312)666-0011 **Fax:** (312)666-8515
E-mail: pklein@universalscrap.com
URL: http://www.universalscrap.com
Products: All nonferrous metals and steel. **SIC:** 5093 (Scrap & Waste Materials). **Est:** 1970. **Sales:** $40,000,000 (1999). **Emp:** 60. **Officers:** Philip Zeld, President.

■ 27034 ■ Vincent Metal Goods
PO Box 1165
Pittsburgh, PA 15230
Phone: (412)771-2600 **Fax:** (412)771-2737
Products: Aluminum service center. **SIC:** 5051 (Metals Service Centers & Offices). **Former Name:** Lockhart Co.

■ 27035 ■ Washington Compressed Steel Corp.
271 W Berkes St.
Philadelphia, PA 19122
Phone: (215)427-2231
Products: Scrap steel. **SIC:** 5093 (Scrap & Waste Materials). **Sales:** $8,000,000 (2000). **Emp:** 23.

■ 27036 ■ Waste Management Recycle America
3850 Holcomb Bridge Rd., No. 105
Norcross, GA 30092
Phone: (770)449-8688
Products: Scrap and waste material. **SIC:** 5093 (Scrap & Waste Materials). **Est:** 1991. **Sales:** $92,000,000 (2000). **Emp:** 69. **Officers:** Bill Fowlkes, Dir. of Sales; Emmett Murray, Controller. **Alternate Name:** Paper Recycling International L.P.

■ 27037 ■ Waste Recovery-Illinois
2658 E Highway 6
Marseilles, IL 61341
Phone: (815)795-6676
Products: Scrap tires for fuel production. **SIC:** 5093 (Scrap & Waste Materials).

■ 27038 ■ Waste Reduction Systems Inc.
12621 Featherwood Dr., No. 380
Houston, TX 77034-4902
Phone: (281)922-1000
Products: Scrap and waste materials for recycling. **SIC:** 5093 (Scrap & Waste Materials).

■ 27039 ■ Charles Weinreich Co.
300 S Mission Rd.
Los Angeles, CA 90033
Phone: (213)268-2755 **Fax:** (213)265-2496
Products: Used clothing. **SIC:** 5093 (Scrap & Waste

Materials). **Est:** 1948. **Sales:** $4,000,000 (2000). **Emp:** 48. **Officers:** Stuart Daniels, President.

■ 27040 ■ Wellman Inc.
1040 Broad St., Ste. 302
Shrewsbury, NJ 07702
Phone: (908)542-7300 **Fax:** (908)542-9344
Products: Recycled plastic. **SIC:** 5093 (Scrap & Waste Materials). **Est:** 1927. **Sales:** $1,098,800,000 (2000). **Emp:** 3,200. **Officers:** Thomas M. Duff, CEO & President; Keith R. Phillips, VP, CFO & Treasurer.

■ 27041 ■ West Bay Resources Inc.
250 China Basin St.
San Francisco, CA 94107
Phone: (415)957-9971
Products: Recycled glass and aluminum products. **SIC:** 5093 (Scrap & Waste Materials).

■ 27042 ■ Western Gold Thermoplastics Inc.
1769 Mount Vernon Ave.
Pomona, CA 91768-3330
Phone: (213)235-3387
Products: Recycled plastics; Industrial gases. **SICs:** 5093 (Scrap & Waste Materials); 5169 (Chemicals & Allied Products Nec). **Sales:** $10,000,000 (2000). **Emp:** 28. **Officers:** Daniel Hoyer, President.

■ 27043 ■ Western Pacific Pulp and Paper
PO Box 4279
Downey, CA 90241
Phone: (562)803-4401
Products: Recycled paper. **SIC:** 5093 (Scrap & Waste Materials).

■ 27044 ■ Western Scrap Processing Co.
PO Box 15158
Colorado Springs, CO 80935
Phone: (719)390-7986 **Fax:** (719)390-3852
Products: Recycled copper, lead, brass, plastic, and glass. **SIC:** 5093 (Scrap & Waste Materials). **Est:** 1955. **Sales:** $16,000,000 (2000). **Emp:** 25. **Officers:** Sydney I. Olesky, President & CFO.

■ 27045 ■ Westreet Industries
8901 Kelso Dr.
Baltimore, MD 21221
Phone: (410)686-8400 **Fax:** (410)574-2664
Products: Waste paper. **SIC:** 5093 (Scrap & Waste Materials). **Est:** 1966. **Sales:** $10,200,000 (2000). **Emp:** 50. **Officers:** Chris Mehiel, President; Tina Hager, Controller; Cliff Burkhardt, General Mgr.; Dennis Grabowski, Dir. of Data Processing; Bob Castle, Human Resources Mgr.

■ 27046 ■ Weyerhaeuser Co. Recycling Business Div.
Mail Stop CH CCB438
Tacoma, WA 98477
Phone: (253)924-3342
Products: Recycled paper products. **SIC:** 5093 (Scrap & Waste Materials).

■ 27047 ■ Wichita Recycling
1300 Burk Rd.
Wichita Falls, TX 76305
Phone: (940)322-1720
Products: Recycled metal products. **SIC:** 5093 (Scrap & Waste Materials).

■ 27048 ■ S. Wilkoff and Sons Co.
2700 E 47th St.
Cleveland, OH 44104
Phone: (216)391-6600
Products: High temperature alloys; Scrap metal. **SIC:** 5093 (Scrap & Waste Materials). **Est:** 1924. **Sales:** $20,000,000 (2000). **Emp:** 35. **Officers:** J.L. Wilkoff, President & Chairman of the Board.

■ 27049 ■ Winston Brothers Iron and Metal Inc.
17384 Conant
Detroit, MI 48212
Phone: (313)891-4410
Products: Scrap and waste materials. **SIC:** 5093 (Scrap & Waste Materials).

■ 27050 ■ Wire and Metal Separation Inc.
542 Southbridge St.
Worcester, MA 01610
Phone: (508)752-5070 **Fax:** (508)798-2833
Products: Scrap metal. **SIC:** 5093 (Scrap & Waste Materials). **Est:** 1900. **Sales:** $4,000,000 (2000). **Emp:** 20. **Officers:** David E. Cotton, President; Wallace H. Cotton, Treasurer; Lawrence Cotton, Dir. of Marketing & Sales; Leatrice Cotton, Manager.

■ 27051 ■ wTe Corp.
7 Alfred Cir.
Bedford, MA 01730
Phone: (781)275-6400 **Fax:** (781)275-8612
Products: Plastics and metals recycling. **SIC:** 5093 (Scrap & Waste Materials). **Est:** 1981. **Sales:** $25,000,000 (2000). **Emp:** 92. **Officers:** David B. Spencer, CEO & President; M. Scott Mellen, COO.

■ 27052 ■ WTE Recycling Corp.
7 Alfred Cir.
Bedford, MA 01730
Phone: (781)275-6400
Products: Recycled plastics. **SIC:** 5093 (Scrap & Waste Materials). **Sales:** $22,000,000 (2000). **Emp:** 60. **Officers:** David B. Spencer, President; Betsy Anderson, Controller.

■ 27053 ■ Zanker Road Resource Management Co.
575 Charles St.
San Jose, CA 95112
Phone: (408)263-2385
Products: Recycling products. **SIC:** 5093 (Scrap & Waste Materials). **Sales:** $18,000,000 (1992). **Emp:** 50. **Officers:** Rich Cristina, President.

(60) Veterinary Products

Entries in this section are arranged alphabetically by company name. When the company name is a personal name, the company name is alphabetized by the surname unless the first name or initial(s) are part of a trade name. See the User's Guide at the front of this directory for additional information.

■ 27054 ■ **A-Pet, Inc.**
299 Beeline Dr.
Bensenville, IL 60106
Phone: (708)595-6808 **Fax:** (708)595-0529
Products: Pet supplies. **SIC:** 5199 (Nondurable Goods Nec).

■ 27055 ■ **Abba Products Corp.**
1004 Elizabeth Ave.
Elizabeth, NJ 07201
Phone: (908)353-0669 **Fax:** (908)353-2065
Products: Pet supplies. **SIC:** 5199 (Nondurable Goods Nec).

■ 27056 ■ **Acme Agri Supply Inc.**
1527 E Broadway St.
North Little Rock, AR 72114-5934
Phone: (501)374-0625
Products: Pet supplies; Veterinary instruments; Pharmaceutical preparations for veterinary use. **SICs:** 5047 (Medical & Hospital Equipment); 5199 (Nondurable Goods Nec); 5122 (Drugs, Proprietaries & Sundries). **Officers:** Ed Coffman, Contact.

■ 27057 ■ **Agri Feed & Supply**
5716 Middlebrooke Pike
Knoxville, TN 37921
Phone: (423)584-3959 **Fax:** (423)584-9243
Products: Pet food and supplies. **SICs:** 5199 (Nondurable Goods Nec); 5149 (Groceries & Related Products Nec).

■ 27058 ■ **Agri Supplies**
15001 N Nebraska
Tampa, FL 33613
Phone: (813)977-8500 **Fax:** (813)977-8793
Products: Pet Supplies. **SIC:** 5199 (Nondurable Goods Nec).

■ 27059 ■ **Alaska Garden and Pet Supply**
114 Orca
Anchorage, AK 99510
Phone: (907)279-4519
Products: Dog collars, leashes, and other household pet accessories; Pet supplies. **SIC:** 5199 (Nondurable Goods Nec). **Doing Business As:** Alaska Mill Feed Co.

■ 27060 ■ **All Pet Distributors**
355 Crooked Hill Rd.
Brentwood, NY 11717
Phone: (516)273-6363 **Fax:** (516)273-6513
Products: Pets and pet supplies. **SIC:** 5199 (Nondurable Goods Nec).

■ 27061 ■ **All Star Pet Supply**
19935 W 157th St.
Olathe, KS 66062
Phone: (913)764-4232 **Fax:** (913)780-4617
Products: Pet supplies. **SIC:** 5199 (Nondurable Goods Nec).

■ 27062 ■ **ALR Wholesale**
115 Sylvan Dr.
Independence, KY 41051
Phone: (606)356-7220
Products: Pet supplies; Veterinary instruments; Pharmaceutical preparations for veterinary use. **SICs:** 5047 (Medical & Hospital Equipment); 5199 (Nondurable Goods Nec); 5122 (Drugs, Proprietaries & Sundries). **Officers:** Natalie Flynn, Contact.

■ 27063 ■ **Amber Grout Sales**
6114 Bolamo Ct.
Westerville, OH 43081-4151
Phone: (614)572-5033
Products: Veterinary instruments; Pharmaceutical preparations for veterinary use; Pet supplies. **SICs:** 5047 (Medical & Hospital Equipment); 5199 (Nondurable Goods Nec); 5122 (Drugs, Proprietaries & Sundries). **Officers:** Amber Grout, Contact.

■ 27064 ■ **American Pet Pro**
2313 American Ave.
Hayward, CA 94545
Phone: (510)732-2781
Free: (800)543-9480 **Fax:** (510)732-1261
E-mail: info@americanpetpro.com
URL: http://www.americanpetpro.com
Products: Pet grooming supplies for the pet professional. **SIC:** 5199 (Nondurable Goods Nec). **Est:** 1986. **Emp:** 5. **Officers:** Bill Reinhardt, President. **Former Name:** Pet Pro.

■ 27065 ■ **Anapet**
1431 N Main
Orange, CA 92867
Phone: (714)532-4200 **Fax:** (714)532-4292
Products: Pet supplies, including food, clothes, and equipment. **SICs:** 5199 (Nondurable Goods Nec); 5149 (Groceries & Related Products Nec).

■ 27066 ■ **Animal Emergency Center**
4306 Bishop Ln.
Louisville, KY 40218-4518
Phone: (502)456-4145
Products: Veterinary instruments. **SIC:** 5047 (Medical & Hospital Equipment). **Officers:** Gary Minh, Owner.

■ 27067 ■ **Animal Medic Inc.**
PO Box 575
Manchester, PA 17345
Phone: (717)266-5611
Products: Pharmaceutical preparations for veterinary use; Veterinary instruments; Pet supplies. **SICs:** 5047 (Medical & Hospital Equipment); 5122 (Drugs, Proprietaries & Sundries); 5199 (Nondurable Goods Nec). **Officers:** Larry E. Gladfelter, President.

■ 27068 ■ **Anjo Distributors**
4380 Victory Blvd.
Staten Island, NY 10314
Phone: (718)698-6550 **Fax:** (718)698-0446
Products: Pet food and supplies. **SICs:** 5199 (Nondurable Goods Nec); 5149 (Groceries & Related Products Nec).

■ 27069 ■ **Apollo Pet Supply**
216 SE Washington St.
Portland, OR 97214
Phone: (503)239-5768 **Fax:** (503)239-7243
Products: Pet supplies. **SIC:** 5199 (Nondurable Goods Nec).

■ 27070 ■ **Aqualife**
51800 Laurel Rd.
South Bend, IN 46637
Phone: (219)272-7777 **Fax:** (219)272-7777
Products: Pet supplies. **SIC:** 5199 (Nondurable Goods Nec).

■ 27071 ■ **Aquaperfect**
7889 A Pines Blvd.
Pembroke Pines, FL 33024
Phone: (954)981-5120 **Fax:** (954)966-9316
Products: Pet supplies. **SIC:** 5199 (Nondurable Goods Nec).

■ 27072 ■ **Aquarium Pet Book Distributors**
PO Box 298
Jarrettsville, MD 21084
Phone: (410)557-9173 **Fax:** (410)557-8592
Products: Pet supplies. **SIC:** 5199 (Nondurable Goods Nec).

■ 27073 ■ **Ark Grooming**
3225 Eagle Dr.
Greenwood, AR 72936
Phone: (501)996-0085
Products: Pet supplies, including dog collars, leashes, and accessories; Shampoos; Dips; Flea sprays. **SIC:** 5199 (Nondurable Goods Nec). **Est:** 1986. **Sales:** $1,000,000 (2000). **Emp:** 5. **Officers:** Ed Lord, President. **Former Name:** Ed Wineland's Wholesale Pet Supplies.

■ 27074 ■ **Ark Manufacturing Inc.**
3780 Boone Rd. SE
Salem, OR 97301
Phone: (503)581-6702 **Fax:** (503)363-6789
Products: Pet supplies; Veterinary instruments; Pharmaceutical preparations for veterinarian use. **SICs:** 5047 (Medical & Hospital Equipment); 5122 (Drugs, Proprietaries & Sundries); 5199 (Nondurable Goods Nec). **Est:** 1987. **Emp:** 10. **Officers:** Ray Reid.

■ 27075 ■ **Avian Kingdom Supply Inc.**
6350 LBJ Fwy., Ste. 151
Dallas, TX 75247
Phone: (972)631-2473
Free: (800)256-7265 **Fax:** (972)239-2473
Products: Pet supplies. **SIC:** 5199 (Nondurable Goods Nec). **Est:** 1990. **Emp:** 9.

■ 27076 ■ **AVM Products, Inc.**
PO Box 667
Chester Springs, PA 19425
Phone: (215)827-7039
Products: Equine supplies. **SIC:** 5191 (Farm Supplies).

■ 27077 ■   Award Pet Supply
1610 B, I-70 Dr. SW
Columbia, MO 65203
Phone: (573)445-8249
Products: Veterinary instruments; Pharmaceutical preparations for veterinary use; Pet supplies. **SICs:** 5047 (Medical & Hospital Equipment); 5122 (Drugs, Proprietaries & Sundries); 5199 (Nondurable Goods Nec). **Officers:** John Sutton, Contact.

■ 27078 ■   B Sharp Co.
74 Jennifer Ln.
Effort, PA 18330
Phone: (717)629-3952
Products: Pharmaceutical preparations for veterinary use; Veterinary instruments; Pet supplies. **SICs:** 5047 (Medical & Hospital Equipment); 5122 (Drugs, Proprietaries & Sundries); 5199 (Nondurable Goods Nec). **Officers:** Anna Burns, Contact.

■ 27079 ■   Barr Enterprises Inc.
W 7276 Chickadee Rd.
Greenwood, WI 54437
Phone: (715)267-6335
Free: (800)826-2341   **Fax:** (715)267-7214
Products: Beef material for pet food. **SIC:** 5149 (Groceries & Related Products Nec). **Est:** 1943. **Sales:** $3,000,000 (2000). **Emp:** 20. **Officers:** Steve Denk, President; Patty Denk, Treasurer & Secty.

■ 27080 ■   Bennett's Pet Center
986 Medina Rd.
Medina, OH 44256
Phone: (330)239-1240
Products: Pharmaceutical preparations for veterinary use; Pet supplies. **SICs:** 5199 (Nondurable Goods Nec); 5122 (Drugs, Proprietaries & Sundries). **Officers:** Rick Bennett, Contact.

■ 27081 ■   Best Pet Distributing
3580 S Church St.
Burlington, NC 27215-9100
Phone: (336)366-4456   **Fax:** (336)563-4415
Products: Pet supplies. **SIC:** 5199 (Nondurable Goods Nec).

■ 27082 ■   B.G.B. Pet Supply Inc.
G1234 N Center Rd.
Burton, MI 48509
Phone: (810)742-8760   **Fax:** (810)742-8542
Products: Pet food. **SIC:** 5149 (Groceries & Related Products Nec). **Emp:** 19. **Officers:** Debbie McCord.

■ 27083 ■   Bird Toy Man
197 S Hillside Ave.
Succasunna, NJ 07876
Phone: (973)584-0756   **Fax:** (973)584-0756
URL: http://www.birdtoyman.com
Products: Pet bird toys. **SIC:** 5199 (Nondurable Goods Nec). **Est:** 1989. **Emp:** 1. **Officers:** Henry E. Pedynowski, Owner, e-mail: hank@birdtoyman.com. **Former Name:** Dena Pedynowski Aviaries.

■ 27084 ■   Blackman Industries
1401 Minnesota Ave.
Kansas City, KS 66102-4309
Phone: (913)342-5010   **Free:** (800)842-5090
E-mail: kcbeefhide@worldnet.att.net
URL: rawhidedirect.com
Products: Pet food. **SIC:** 5149 (Groceries & Related Products Nec). **Est:** 1978. **Emp:** 5.

■ 27085 ■   Bloodline Agency
Attn: Terry Boyarsky
101 Hud Rd.
Winchester, KY 40391
Phone: (606)745-6601
Products: Pharmaceutical preparations for veterinary use; Veterinary instruments; Pet supplies. **SICs:** 5047 (Medical & Hospital Equipment); 5122 (Drugs, Proprietaries & Sundries); 5199 (Nondurable Goods Nec). **Officers:** Terry Boyarsky, Contact.

■ 27086 ■   Blue Ridge Fish Wholesale
330 Berry Garden Rd.
Kernersville, NC 27284
Phone: (910)996-3200   **Fax:** (910)996-4211
Products: Pet supplies. **SIC:** 5199 (Nondurable Goods Nec).

■ 27087 ■   Blue Ridge Wholesale
299 Berry Garden Rd.
Kernersville, NC 27284
Phone: (910)996-3200   **Fax:** (910)996-8861
Products: Salt and fresh water fish; Reptiles; Small animals; Dry goods. **SIC:** 5199 (Nondurable Goods Nec).

■ 27088 ■   Boston Pet Supply, Inc.
1341 W McCoy Ln.
Santa Maria, CA 93454
Phone: (805)922-2175
Free: (800)523-8245   **Fax:** 800-675-8483
Products: Pet supplies. **SIC:** 5199 (Nondurable Goods Nec).

■ 27089 ■   Botkin Grain Co. Inc.
PO Box 145
Argonia, KS 67004
Phone: (316)435-6510   **Fax:** (316)435-6390
Products: Animal health care products; Feed and grain; Batteries. **SICs:** 5199 (Nondurable Goods Nec); 5191 (Farm Supplies); 5063 (Electrical Apparatus & Equipment). **Est:** 1923. **Sales:** $3,500,000 (2000). **Emp:** 7. **Officers:** J.W. Botkin, Owner; D.E. Botkin, Owner.

■ 27090 ■   Bowie Manufacturing Inc.
313 S Hancock St.
Lake City, IA 51449
Phone: (712)464-3191
Free: (800)831-0960   **Fax:** (712)464-8601
E-mail: bowiesales@worldnet.att.net
URL: http://www.bowiemfg.com
Products: Mobile veterinarian clinics; Portable veterinarian X-ray machines. **SIC:** 5047 (Medical & Hospital Equipment). **Officers:** Marion Peterson, President.

■ 27091 ■   Joseph M. Brady Co.
PO Box 307
Needham, MA 02492
Phone: (781)444-0781   **Fax:** (781)444-9693
Products: Pet supplies. **SIC:** 5199 (Nondurable Goods Nec).

■ 27092 ■   Breeders Edge
PO Box 16027
Cincinnati, OH 45216-0027
Phone: (513)542-9933
Free: (800)322-5500   **Fax:** (513)542-9935
Products: Pharmaceutical preparations for veterinary use; Pet supplies. **SICs:** 5047 (Medical & Hospital Equipment); 5122 (Drugs, Proprietaries & Sundries); 5199 (Nondurable Goods Nec). **Est:** 1983. **Emp:** 5. **Officers:** Harry Ortego, Contact.

■ 27093 ■   Burkmann Feed
1111 Perryville Rd.
Danville, KY 40422-1306
Phone: (606)336-3400
Products: Veterinary instruments; Pharmaceutical preparations for veterinary use; Pet supplies. **SICs:** 5047 (Medical & Hospital Equipment); 5199 (Nondurable Goods Nec); 5122 (Drugs, Proprietaries & Sundries).

■ 27094 ■   Burkmann Feeds—Glasgow
Attn: Eugene Myatt
100 Georgetown Ln.
Glasgow, KY 42141
Phone: (502)651-8000
Products: Veterinary instruments; Pharmaceutical preparations for veterinary use; Pet supplies. **SICs:** 5047 (Medical & Hospital Equipment); 5199 (Nondurable Goods Nec); 5122 (Drugs, Proprietaries & Sundries). **Officers:** Eugene Myatt, Contact.

■ 27095 ■   Burkmann Feeds—London
Attn: Gary Allen
1115 S Laurel
London, KY 40741
Phone: (606)877-3333
Products: Veterinary instruments; Pharmaceutical preparations for veterinary use; Pet supplies. **SICs:** 5047 (Medical & Hospital Equipment); 5199 (Nondurable Goods Nec); 5122 (Drugs, Proprietaries & Sundries). **Officers:** Gary Allen, Contact.

■ 27096 ■   Burkmann Mills
1111 Perryville Rd.
Danville, KY 40422
Phone: (606)236-0400
Products: Veterinary instruments; Pharmaceutical preparations for veterinary use; Pet supplies. **SICs:** 5047 (Medical & Hospital Equipment); 5199 (Nondurable Goods Nec); 5122 (Drugs, Proprietaries & Sundries). **Officers:** Brooks Peavler, Contact.

■ 27097 ■   C & K Distributors Inc.
8202 Cooper Ave.
Glendale, NY 11385
Phone: (718)894-4302
Free: (800)244-4041   **Fax:** (718)894-0718
Products: Pet supplies, including litter, litter pans, and pads; Pet food; Pet accessories, including dog collars, leashes, toys, bones, rawhide, and treats. **SIC:** 5149 (Groceries & Related Products Nec). **Est:** 1970. **Emp:** 20. **Officers:** Dan Colombi, President; Len Katz, Sec. & Treas.; Peter Katz, Marketing & Sales Mgr.; William Moran, Operations Mgr.

■ 27098 ■   Cajun Sales
Attn: Bruce Perilloux
412 Oak Ln.
Luling, LA 70070
Phone: (504)785-1644
Products: Veterinary instruments; Pharmaceutical preparations for veterinary use; Pet supplies. **SICs:** 5047 (Medical & Hospital Equipment); 5199 (Nondurable Goods Nec); 5122 (Drugs, Proprietaries & Sundries).

■ 27099 ■   Canine Commissary
11504 Garland Rd.
Dallas, TX 75218
Phones: (972)840-2181   (214)320-0995
Fax: (972)840-9455
E-mail: ftmr@aol.com
URL: http://www.caninecom.com
Products: Pet food and supplies. **SICs:** 5199 (Nondurable Goods Nec); 5149 (Groceries & Related Products Nec). **Est:** 1980. **Emp:** 30. **Officers:** F.T. Rapson; L.G. Rapson.

■ 27100 ■   Capital Pet Supply
1200 Newell Pkwy.
Montgomery, AL 36110
Phone: (205)279-0566   **Fax:** (205)279-0732
Products: Pet supplies. **SIC:** 5199 (Nondurable Goods Nec).

■ 27101 ■   Care-A-Lot
1617 Diamond Springs Rd.
Virginia Beach, VA 23455
Phone: (757)460-9771
Free: (800)343-7680   **Fax:** (757)460-0317
URL: http://www.carealotpets.com
Products: Pet supplies; Dry goods. **SIC:** 5199 (Nondurable Goods Nec). **Est:** 1988. **Officers:** Dick Clarke, Owner; Mary Clarke, Owner.

■ 27102 ■   Carolina Vet Supply
PO Box 2812
Shelby, NC 28150
Phone: (704)482-7158   **Free:** (800)209-8101
E-mail: c.v.s.@shelby.comm
URL: http://www.c.v.s.com
Products: Veterinary instruments; Pharmaceutical preparations for veterinary use; Pet supplies. **SICs:** 5047 (Medical & Hospital Equipment); 5122 (Drugs, Proprietaries & Sundries); 5199 (Nondurable Goods Nec). **Est:** 1983. **Sales:** $250,000 (2000). **Emp:** 1. **Officers:** L.B. Allen, Contact.

■ 27103 ■   Cashway Pet Supply
1325 S Cherokee
Denver, CO 80223
Phone: (303)744-6131   **Fax:** (303)777-5762
Products: Pet supplies. **SIC:** 5199 (Nondurable Goods Nec).

■ **27104** ■ **Central Garden and Pet Co. Pet Supplies Div.**
3697 Mt. Diablo Blvd., Ste. 310
Lafayette, CA 94549
Phone: (925)283-4573
Products: Pet supplies. **SIC:** 5199 (Nondurable Goods Nec).

■ **27105** ■ **Central Garden and Pet Supply Inc.**
4601 Florin Perkins Rd., No. 100
Sacramento, CA 95826-4820
Phone: (916)928-1925 **Fax:** (916)928-1924
Products: Pet supplies. **SIC:** 5199 (Nondurable Goods Nec).

■ **27106** ■ **Central Garden & Pet Supply Inc.**
PO Box 655650
Dallas, TX 75265-5650
Phone: (972)466-0069 **Fax:** (972)466-0069
Products: Lawn and garden equipment; Pet supplies. **SIC:** 5199 (Nondurable Goods Nec).

■ **27107** ■ **Central Garden & Pet Supply Inc.**
PO Box 95001
Auburn, WA 98071
Phone: (253)833-7771
Free: (800)777-4833 **Fax:** (253)833-7931
Products: Lawn and garden equipment; Pet supplies. **SICs:** 5199 (Nondurable Goods Nec); 5191 (Farm Supplies).

■ **27108** ■ **Charter Pet Supplies**
634 Medina
Highland Village, TX 75077-7273
Phone: (972)317-3524
Products: Veterinary instruments; Pharmaceutical preparations for veterinary use; Pet supplies. **SICs:** 5047 (Medical & Hospital Equipment); 5199 (Nondurable Goods Nec); 5122 (Drugs, Proprietaries & Sundries). **Officers:** Dorian Bloom, Contact; Alan Bloom, Contact.

■ **27109** ■ **Cherrybrook**
PO Box 15, Rte. 57
Broadway, NJ 08808
Phone: (908)689-7979
Free: (800)524-0820 **Fax:** (908)689-7988
URL: http://www.cherrybrook.com
Products: Dog and cat supplies. **SIC:** 5199 (Nondurable Goods Nec). **Est:** 1969. **Emp:** 45. **Officers:** Wayne E. Ferguson, President; Duke L. Bunce II, Vice President, e-mail: duke.bunce@att.net; Carl Poff, Asst. VP.

■ **27110** ■ **Columbus Serum Co.**
2025 S High St.
Columbus, OH 43207
Phone: (614)444-1155
Products: Serums for veterinarians; Pharmaceuticals for medical supplies. **SICs:** 5122 (Drugs, Proprietaries & Sundries); 5047 (Medical & Hospital Equipment).

■ **27111** ■ **Congress Leather Co.**
Rte. 193
Kingsville, OH 44048
Phone: (440)224-2133
Products: Veterinary instruments; Pharmaceutical preparations for veterinary use; Pet supplies. **SICs:** 5047 (Medical & Hospital Equipment); 5199 (Nondurable Goods Nec); 5122 (Drugs, Proprietaries & Sundries).

■ **27112** ■ **Cornilsen's Backyard Bird**
1514 Pine Valley Cir.
Roseville, CA 95661
Phone: (916)783-2243 **Fax:** (916)783-2243
Products: Pet supplies. **SIC:** 5199 (Nondurable Goods Nec). **Est:** 1990. **Emp:** 2. **Officers:** Robert Cornilsen; Deanna Cornilsen.

■ **27113** ■ **Coyote Pet Products Inc.**
750 Design Port, Ste. 108
ChuLa Vista, CA 91911
Phone: (619)421-5431
Products: Pet supplies. **SIC:** 5199 (Nondurable Goods Nec).

■ **27114** ■ **C.P. Daniels Co.**
PO Box 119
Waynesboro, GA 30830
Phone: (706)554-2446
Products: Veterinary instruments; Pharmaceutical preparations for veterinary use; Pet supplies. **SICs:** 5047 (Medical & Hospital Equipment); 5122 (Drugs, Proprietaries & Sundries); 5199 (Nondurable Goods Nec). **Officers:** Henry Daniels, Contact.

■ **27115** ■ **Delta Veterinary Clinic**
1520 Bluff St.
Delta, CO 81416-2141
Phone: (970)874-4486
Products: Veterinary supplies. **SIC:** 5047 (Medical & Hospital Equipment). **Officers:** Thomas Gore, Owner.

■ **27116** ■ **DL Pet Supply**
2541 Hwy. 250 S
Norwalk, OH 44857
Phone: (419)668-3756 **Fax:** (419)663-4112
Products: Pet supplies. **SIC:** 5199 (Nondurable Goods Nec).

■ **27117** ■ **Dog Outfitters**
Humboldt Industrial Park
1 Maplewood Dr.
PO Box 2010
Hazleton, PA 18201
Phone: (717)384-5555
Free: (800)FOR-DOGS **Fax:** (717)384-2500
Products: Dog collars, leashes, and other household pet accessories; Pet supplies. **SIC:** 5199 (Nondurable Goods Nec).

■ **27118** ■ **Dogloo Inc.**
20455 Somma Dr.
Perris, CA 92570-9567
Phone: (909)279-9500 **Fax:** (714)279-2206
Products: Pet supplies. **SIC:** 5199 (Nondurable Goods Nec).

■ **27119** ■ **Dogroom Products**
368 Hempstead Ave.
Hempstead, NY 11552
Phone: (516)483-8930
Products: Dog collars, leashes, and other household pet accessories; Pet supplies. **SIC:** 5199 (Nondurable Goods Nec).

■ **27120** ■ **Dove Wholesale**
4581 W Picacho
Las Cruces, NM 88005
Phone: (505)523-8668 **Fax:** (505)523-5805
Products: Pet supplies. **SIC:** 5199 (Nondurable Goods Nec).

■ **27121** ■ **Eagle Milling Co.**
PO Box 15007
Casa Grande, AZ 85230-5007
Phone: (520)836-2131 **Fax:** (520)836-2419
Products: Veterinarians' equipment and supplies. **SIC:** 5047 (Medical & Hospital Equipment). **Officers:** William Dickey, President.

■ **27122** ■ **Economy Distributors**
2370 N Flower St.
Santa Ana, CA 92706
Phone: (714)542-2000
Products: Pet supplies; Pet food. **SICs:** 5199 (Nondurable Goods Nec); 5149 (Groceries & Related Products Nec). **Emp:** 3.

■ **27123** ■ **Edco Manufacturing Co.**
PO Box 5204, EK. Sta.
Johnson City, TN 37602-5204
Phone: (423)926-6956
Products: Veterinary instruments; Pharmaceutical preparations for veterinary use; Pet supplies. **SICs:** 5047 (Medical & Hospital Equipment); 5199 (Nondurable Goods Nec); 5122 (Drugs, Proprietaries & Sundries). **Officers:** Ed Essick, Contact.

■ **27124** ■ **Ed's Leather Co.**
2603 S Lafayette St.
Hwy. 18
Shelby, NC 28150
Phone: (704)482-8080
Products: Veterinary instruments; Pharmaceutical

preparations for veterinary use; Pet supplies. **SICs:** 5047 (Medical & Hospital Equipment); 5122 (Drugs, Proprietaries & Sundries); 5199 (Nondurable Goods Nec). **Officers:** Ed Porter, Contact.

■ **27125** ■ **Edward's Pet Supplies Co.**
990 South 700 West
Salt Lake City, UT 84104
Phone: (801)972-3920
Free: (800)864-1656 **Fax:** 800-864-1653
Products: Full line pet products. **SIC:** 5199 (Nondurable Goods Nec). **Est:** 1958.

■ **27126** ■ **Efland Distributing Co.**
PO Box 26, Hwy. 70 W
Efland, NC 27243
Phone: 800-325-6463
Products: Veterinary instruments; Pharmaceutical preparations for veterinary use; Pet supplies. **SICs:** 5047 (Medical & Hospital Equipment); 5199 (Nondurable Goods Nec); 5122 (Drugs, Proprietaries & Sundries).

■ **27127** ■ **Elchar Dog Bows**
5700 Old Heady Rd.
Louisville, KY 40299
Phone: (502)267-5857
Products: Veterinary instruments; Pharmaceutical preparations for veterinary use; Pet supplies. **SICs:** 5047 (Medical & Hospital Equipment); 5122 (Drugs, Proprietaries & Sundries); 5199 (Nondurable Goods Nec). **Officers:** Charles Stoess, Owner; Elenor Stoess, Owner.

■ **27128** ■ **Elmore County Farms Exchange**
355 Queen Ann Rd.
Wetumpka, AL 36092
Phone: (334)567-4321 **Fax:** (334)567-4330
Products: Pet feed, including bird feed. **SIC:** 5191 (Farm Supplies). **Est:** 1930. **Sales:** $1,300,000 (1999). **Emp:** 8. **Officers:** E.C. Mehearg, President.

■ **27129** ■ **Emma Cooperative Elevator Co.**
125 Lexington Ave.
Sweet Springs, MO 65351-1302
Phone: (660)335-6355
Products: Grain; Medication for farm animals. **SICs:** 5153 (Grain & Field Beans); 5191 (Farm Supplies); 5199 (Nondurable Goods Nec). **Est:** 1920. **Sales:** $9,000,000 (2000). **Emp:** 16. **Officers:** Ronald Meyer, President; John Roth, Treasurer.

■ **27130** ■ **Faithway Feed Company Inc.**
PO Box 995
Guntersville, AL 35976
Phone: (205)582-5646
Products: Pet food; Bird seed; Salts. **SICs:** 5191 (Farm Supplies); 5149 (Groceries & Related Products Nec). **Est:** 1965. **Sales:** $5,000,000 (2000). **Emp:** 65. **Officers:** Dale B. Rowe, President & CFO.

■ **27131** ■ **Firey Pet Supplies**
1065 W National, Unit 7
Sacramento, CA 95834
Phone: (916)928-7878 **Fax:** (916)928-1456
Products: Pet supplies. **SIC:** 5199 (Nondurable Goods Nec). **Est:** 1977. **Emp:** 20.

■ **27132** ■ **First Coast Pet Supply**
4549 St. Augustine Rd., No. 22
Jacksonville, FL 32207
Phone: (904)733-6400 **Fax:** (904)733-6474
Products: Pet food and supplies. **SIC:** 5199 (Nondurable Goods Nec). **Est:** 1994. **Emp:** 14.

■ **27133** ■ **Fort Recovery Equity Exchange Co.**
2351 Walbash St.
Ft. Recovery, OH 45846-0307
Phone: (419)375-4119 **Fax:** (419)375-4838
Products: Animal health products, including vitamins and syringes; Boots and gloves. **SICs:** 5153 (Grain & Field Beans); 5191 (Farm Supplies). **Est:** 1919. **Sales:** $40,000,000 (2000). **Emp:** 58. **Officers:** Marvin Muhlenkemp, President; Vic Post, Treasurer.

■ 27134 ■ Fritz Pet Products
324 Towne E Blvd.
Mesquite, TX 75149
Phone: (972)285-0101 **Fax:** (972)289-9534
Products: Pet supplies. **SIC:** 5199 (Nondurable Goods Nec). **Officers:** Fritz Weisano, President; Randy Klemmer, Vice President; Ed Burks, CFO.

■ 27135 ■ Fritz Pet Supply
PO Box 17040
Dallas, TX 75217-0040
Phone: (918)663-5991 **Fax:** (918)663-0846
Products: Pet supplies. **SIC:** 5199 (Nondurable Goods Nec).

■ 27136 ■ Fuller Supply Co.
203 6th St.
Montgomery, AL 36104
Products: Veterinary instruments; Pharmaceutical preparations for veterinary use; Pet supplies. **SICs:** 5047 (Medical & Hospital Equipment); 5122 (Drugs, Proprietaries & Sundries); 5199 (Nondurable Goods Nec). **Officers:** Charles Dean, Contact.

■ 27137 ■ Fuller Supply Co., Inc.
139 Southgate Rd.
Dothan, AL 36301
Phone: (334)794-7812
Free: (800)633-7533 **Fax:** (334)793-2483
Products: Veterinary instruments; Pharmaceutical preparations for veterinary use; Pet supplies; Livestock equipment. **SICs:** 5047 (Medical & Hospital Equipment); 5122 (Drugs, Proprietaries & Sundries); 5199 (Nondurable Goods Nec). **Est:** 1945. **Emp:** 12. **Officers:** Tommy Adams, General Mgr.

■ 27138 ■ Fuller Supply Company Inc.
1010 N 24th St.
Birmingham, AL 35203
Phone: (205)323-4431 **Fax:** (205)323-4435
Products: Veterinary instruments; Pharmaceutical preparations for veterinary use; Pet supplies. **SICs:** 5047 (Medical & Hospital Equipment); 5122 (Drugs, Proprietaries & Sundries); 5199 (Nondurable Goods Nec). **Officers:** Bill Fuller, Contact.

■ 27139 ■ Golden Crown Corp.
PO Box 820
Coeur D Alene, ID 83816-0820
Phone: (208)667-5689
Free: (800)233-8345 **Fax:** (208)667-8360
Products: Veterinary and pet supplies. **SICs:** 5047 (Medical & Hospital Equipment); 5122 (Drugs, Proprietaries & Sundries); 5199 (Nondurable Goods Nec). **Est:** 1985. **Emp:** 35. **Officers:** Jim Corbett.

■ 27140 ■ Great Eastern Pet Supply
1546 Decatur St.
Ridgewood, NY 11385
Phone: (718)381-7300 **Free:** (800)445-6686
Products: Pet supplies. **SIC:** 5199 (Nondurable Goods Nec).

■ 27141 ■ Great Western Pet Supply
2001 N Black Cnyn Hwy.
Phoenix, AZ 85009
Phone: (602)255-0166 **Fax:** (602)255-0841
Products: Veterinary instruments; Pharmaceutical preparations for veterinary use; Pet supplies. **SICs:** 5047 (Medical & Hospital Equipment); 5122 (Drugs, Proprietaries & Sundries); 5199 (Nondurable Goods Nec). **Officers:** Steve Shearer, Contact.

■ 27142 ■ Green Leaf Distributors, Inc.
6500 New Venture Gear Dr.
East Syracuse, NY 13057-1259
Phone: (518)459-3507
Products: Pet supplies. **SIC:** 5199 (Nondurable Goods Nec).

■ 27143 ■ H & H Distributing
5949 Jackson
Ann Arbor, MI 48103
Phone: (734)662-1931 **Fax:** (734)662-2203
Products: Pet supplies. **SIC:** 5199 (Nondurable Goods Nec). **Est:** 1970. **Officers:** Roger Williams, General Mgr.

■ 27144 ■ Happy Acres Pet Supply
41903 Savage Rd.
Belleville, MI 48111
Phone: (734)699-0318
Products: Veterinary instruments; Pharmaceutical preparations for veterinary use; Pet supplies. **SICs:** 5047 (Medical & Hospital Equipment); 5122 (Drugs, Proprietaries & Sundries); 5199 (Nondurable Goods Nec). **Officers:** Carrol Crews, Contact.

■ 27145 ■ Harrison Wholesale Products Inc.
108 Kingswood Ct.
Cherry Hill, NJ 08034-1332
Phone: (609)344-6801
Products: Veterinary instruments; Pharmaceutical preparations for veterinary use; Pet supplies. **SICs:** 5047 (Medical & Hospital Equipment); 5122 (Drugs, Proprietaries & Sundries); 5199 (Nondurable Goods Nec). **Officers:** Vernon Ellis, Contact.

■ 27146 ■ Hartz Group Inc.
667 Madison Ave.
New York, NY 10021
Phone: (212)308-3336 **Fax:** (212)644-5987
Products: Pet supplies. **SIC:** 5199 (Nondurable Goods Nec). **Sales:** $890,000,000 (2000). **Emp:** 2,000. **Officers:** Leonard N. Stern, CEO & President; Curt Schwartz, CFO.

■ 27147 ■ Hawkeye Seed Company Inc.
900 2nd St. SE
Cedar Rapids, IA 52401
Phone: (319)364-7118
Free: (800)332-7919 **Fax:** (319)362-1423
E-mail: hawkseed@inav.net
Products: Pet supplies, including aquariums, dishes, and bowls; Garden supplies, including fertilizers and chemicals. **SICs:** 5191 (Farm Supplies); 5199 (Nondurable Goods Nec). **Est:** 1955. **Sales:** $6,000,000 (2000). **Emp:** 30. **Officers:** Howard L. Dubishar, President; Ronald Kimrodt, Treasurer & Secty.

■ 27148 ■ High Mountain Distributing
801 Ronan St., Ste. 4
Missoula, MT 59801
Phone: (406)721-7704 **Fax:** (406)721-9995
Products: Pet supplies. **SIC:** 5199 (Nondurable Goods Nec).

■ 27149 ■ Hill's Pet Nutrition Inc.
PO Box 148
Topeka, KS 66601
Phone: (913)354-8523 **Fax:** (913)231-5770
Products: Pet foods. **SIC:** 5149 (Groceries & Related Products Nec). **Est:** 1935. **Sales:** $600,300,000 (2000). **Emp:** 2,500. **Officers:** Robert C. Wheeler, President; Richard C. Wienckowski, CFO; Jim Humphrey, VP of Marketing; Dan Pitts, VP of Information Systems; George Behling, VP of Human Resources.

■ 27150 ■ Honolulu Aquarium & Pet Supplies
94-486 Ukee St.
Waipahu, HI 96797
Phone: (808)676-3646 **Fax:** (808)677-7387
Products: Pets; Pet supplies. **SIC:** 5199 (Nondurable Goods Nec). **Officers:** Barbara Matsui, President; Kenneth Matsui, Sales Mgr.

■ 27151 ■ House of Pets Supplies
PO Box 185190
Ft. Worth, TX 76181
Phone: (817)595-0808 **Fax:** (817)595-3475
Products: Dog and cat supplies, including grooming supplies. **SIC:** 5199 (Nondurable Goods Nec). **Est:** 1977. **Emp:** 8. **Officers:** Jane Barber, Customer Service Contact; S. Mulliken.

■ 27152 ■ Hubbard Milling Co.
PO Box 8500
Mankato, MN 56002
Phone: (507)388-9400 **Fax:** (507)388-9427
Products: Pet food. **SIC:** 5149 (Groceries & Related Products Nec). **Sales:** $10,000,000 (2000). **Emp:** 99. **Officers:** Gerald Edwards.

■ 27153 ■ Humboldt Industries, Inc.
Humboldt Industrial Pk.
Hazleton, PA 18201-9798
Phone: (717)384-5555 **Fax:** (717)384-2500
Products: Pet products. **SIC:** 5199 (Nondurable Goods Nec). **Sales:** $33,000,000 (2000). **Emp:** 80. **Officers:** Jack Rosenzweig, CEO; Judith Patterson, VP of Operations.

■ 27154 ■ The Iams Co.
7250 Poe Ave.
Dayton, OH 45414-2572
Phone: (937)898-7387 **Fax:** (937)898-2408
Products: Dog and cat foods. **SIC:** 5149 (Groceries & Related Products Nec). **Sales:** $200,000,000 (2000). **Emp:** 499.

■ 27155 ■ Ideal Pet Supplies
8 Baldorioty St.
PO Box 83
Naguabo, PR 00718
Phone: (787)874-4000 **Fax:** (787)874-2044
Products: Pet supplies. **SIC:** 5199 (Nondurable Goods Nec). **Est:** 1986. **Emp:** 5.

■ 27156 ■ Imperial Pet Products
PO Box 157
Walnutport, PA 18088
Phone: (215)377-8008
Products: Veterinary instruments; Pharmaceutical preparations for veterinary use; Pet supplies. **SICs:** 5047 (Medical & Hospital Equipment); 5122 (Drugs, Proprietaries & Sundries); 5199 (Nondurable Goods Nec). **Officers:** Rose Steigerwalt, Sales Mgr.

■ 27157 ■ Independent Pet Co-op
Attn: Rick Newton
10466 Tomkinson Dr.
Scotts, MI 49088
Phone: (616)327-2257
Products: Veterinary instruments; Pharmaceutical preparations for veterinary use; Pet supplies. **SICs:** 5047 (Medical & Hospital Equipment); 5122 (Drugs, Proprietaries & Sundries); 5199 (Nondurable Goods Nec). **Officers:** Rick Newton, Contact.

■ 27158 ■ Iowa Veterinary Supply Co.
124 Country Club Rd.
PO Box 638
Iowa Falls, IA 50126
Phone: (515)648-2529 **Fax:** (515)648-5994
Products: Veterinary supplies, including animal health supplies. **SICs:** 5122 (Drugs, Proprietaries & Sundries); 5047 (Medical & Hospital Equipment). **Est:** 1966. **Sales:** $120,000 (2000). **Emp:** 208. **Officers:** Thomas Kruse Sr., CEO; John Dolan, General Mgr.; Gary Huffiny, Sales/Marketing Contact, e-mail: gary@iowanet.com.

■ 27159 ■ Japco Exports
2472 SW Falcon Cir.
Port St. Lucie, FL 34953
Phone: (561)878-6084 **Fax:** (561)878-6084
Products: Veterinary instruments; Pharmaceutical preparations for veterinary use; Pet supplies. **SICs:** 5047 (Medical & Hospital Equipment); 5122 (Drugs, Proprietaries & Sundries); 5199 (Nondurable Goods Nec). **Est:** 1980. **Officers:** Jack Pickard, Contact.

■ 27160 ■ J.B. Wholesale
289 Wagaraw Rd.
Hawthorne, NJ 07506
Phone: (973)423-2222 **Fax:** (973)423-1181
Products: Pet supplies. **SIC:** 5199 (Nondurable Goods Nec).

■ 27161 ■ Jeffers Vet Supply
Old Airport Rd.
West Plains, MO 65775
Phone: (417)256-3197
Free: (800)533-3377 **Fax:** (417)256-1550
Products: Veterinary instruments; Pharmaceutical preparations for veterinary use; Pet supplies. **SICs:** 5047 (Medical & Hospital Equipment); 5122 (Drugs, Proprietaries & Sundries); 5199 (Nondurable Goods Nec). **Emp:** 100. **Officers:** Jeff Copwell, Contact.

■ 27162 ■ **Jeffers Vet Supply**
PO Box 100
Dothan, AL 36302
Phone: (334)793-6257
Free: (800)533-3377 **Fax:** (334)793-5179
URL: http://www.Jefferspet.com
Products: Veterinary instruments; Pharmaceutical preparations for veterinary use; Pet supplies. **SICs:** 5047 (Medical & Hospital Equipment); 5122 (Drugs, Proprietaries & Sundries); 5199 (Nondurable Goods Nec). **Est:** 1974. **Emp:** 140. **Officers:** Monica Dennis, Purchasing Agent; Ruth Jeffers, Sales/Marketing Contact; Mindy Zack, Customer Service Contact; Carla Burkett, Human Resources Contact.

■ 27163 ■ **JFK Enterprises**
No. 2 Schenkers Dr.
Suite A
Kenner, LA 70062
Phone: (504)464-1128
Free: (800)738-7535 **Fax:** (504)469-6131
E-mail: JFKpets@bellsouth.net
Products: Pet supplies. **SIC:** 5199 (Nondurable Goods Nec). **Est:** 1980. **Emp:** 31. **Officers:** Debora Beechler, Sales/Marketing Contact.

■ 27164 ■ **Jorgensen Laboratories Inc.**
1450 N Van Buren Ave.
Loveland, CO 80538
Phone: (970)669-2500
Free: (800)525-5614 **Fax:** (970)663-5042
Products: Veterinary equipment. **SIC:** 5047 (Medical & Hospital Equipment). **Sales:** $7,000,000 (2000). **Emp:** 25. **Officers:** Irvin Jorgensen, President; Hans Jorgensen, Exec. VP of Finance.

■ 27165 ■ **K-9 Specialists**
319-36 Mound Rd.
Warren, MI 48092
Phone: (810)939-5960
Products: Dog collars, leashes, and other household pet accessories; Pet supplies. **SIC:** 5199 (Nondurable Goods Nec).

■ 27166 ■ **K & I Transeau Co.**
4518 Hickory Downs Rd.
Houston, TX 77084-3520
Phone: (281)463-7128
Products: Veterinary instruments; Pharmaceutical preparations for veterinary use; Pet supplies. **SICs:** 5047 (Medical & Hospital Equipment); 5122 (Drugs, Proprietaries & Sundries); 5199 (Nondurable Goods Nec). **Officers:** Ken Transeau, Contact; Irene Transeau, Contact.

■ 27167 ■ **K & K Pet Talk**
2901 Bartlett
Tucson, AZ 85741
Phone: (520)887-4926 **Fax:** (520)888-2293
E-mail: krkppets@juno.com
Products: Veterinary instruments; Pharmaceutical preparations for veterinary use; Pet supplies. **SICs:** 5047 (Medical & Hospital Equipment); 5122 (Drugs, Proprietaries & Sundries); 5199 (Nondurable Goods Nec).

■ 27168 ■ **K & K Vet Supply**
3190 A American St.
Springdale, AR 72765-1756
Phone: (501)751-1516 **Fax:** (501)751-1744
E-mail: kkvetkkvet@aol.com
Products: Veterinary instruments; Pharmaceutical preparations for veterinary use; Pet supplies; Large animal antibiotics and vaccines; Equine products; Lawn and garden products. **SICs:** 5047 (Medical & Hospital Equipment); 5122 (Drugs, Proprietaries & Sundries); 5199 (Nondurable Goods Nec); 5083 (Farm & Garden Machinery). **Est:** 1988. **Emp:** 30. **Officers:** Kenny Lipsmeyer, Contact.

■ 27169 ■ **K & R Distributors**
3123 Esch
Warren, MI 48091
Phone: (810)574-9292
Products: Veterinary instruments; Pharmaceutical preparations for veterinary use; Pet supplies. **SICs:** 5047 (Medical & Hospital Equipment); 5122 (Drugs, Proprietaries & Sundries); 5199 (Nondurable Goods Nec).

■ 27170 ■ **Kenlin Pet Supply**
2225 NC152 E
China Grove, NC 28023
Phone: (704)857-8192 **Fax:** (704)857-8820
Products: Pet supplies. **SIC:** 5199 (Nondurable Goods Nec). **Officers:** Nancy M. Wey; Lewis Moose, Human Resources.

■ 27171 ■ **Kenlin Pet Supply Inc.**
301 Island Rd.
Mahwah, NJ 07430
Phone: (201)529-5050 **Fax:** (201)529-1285
Products: Pet supplies and food. **SICs:** 5199 (Nondurable Goods Nec); 5149 (Groceries & Related Products Nec). **Sales:** $100,000,000 (2000). **Emp:** 350. **Officers:** Neill Hines, President; Gregory Sullivan, Controller.

■ 27172 ■ **Kennel-Aire Inc.**
3580 Holly Ln. N, #10
Plymouth, MN 55447-1269
Phone: (612)519-0521 **Fax:** (612)519-0522
Products: Pet supplies. **SIC:** 5199 (Nondurable Goods Nec). **Est:** 1957. **Emp:** 50. **Officers:** Tryg Pederson, CFO; E. Michael Powers, Chairman of the Board; Bob Tyley, Sales/Marketing Contact, e-mail: btyley@excel.net.

■ 27173 ■ **Kimbet Leather**
2090 Chestnut St.
North Dighton, MA 02764
Phone: (508)252-6805
Products: Veterinary instruments; Pharmaceutical preparations for veterinary use; Pet supplies. **SICs:** 5047 (Medical & Hospital Equipment); 5122 (Drugs, Proprietaries & Sundries); 5199 (Nondurable Goods Nec). **Officers:** Zachary Aghkadian, Contact.

■ 27174 ■ **King's Cage**
145 Sherwood Ave.
Farmingdale, NY 11735
Phone: (631)777-7300 **Fax:** (631)777-7302
E-mail: kingscages@msn.com
URL: http://www.kingscages.com
Products: Pet supplies. **SIC:** 5199 (Nondurable Goods Nec). **Est:** 1976. **Emp:** 8. **Officers:** Richard King; Andrew King; Shari Velazquez, Sales & Marketing Contact; Colleenan Close; Stephany Klein.

■ 27175 ■ **M.P. Krause & Sons**
4956 S Monitor Ave.
Chicago, IL 60638
Phone: (708)458-1600 **Fax:** (708)458-9891
Products: Pet products. **SIC:** 5199 (Nondurable Goods Nec).

■ 27176 ■ **L & B Pet Supplies**
c/o Robert Elie
PO Box 738, Hwy. 1062
Loranger, LA 70446
Phone: (504)878-6241
Products: Veterinary instruments; Pharmaceutical preparations for veterinary use; Pet supplies. **SICs:** 5047 (Medical & Hospital Equipment); 5122 (Drugs, Proprietaries & Sundries); 5199 (Nondurable Goods Nec). **Officers:** Robert L. Elie, Contact.

■ 27177 ■ **L & L Pet Center**
14123 W Hardy
Houston, TX 77060
Products: Veterinary instruments; Pharmaceutical preparations for veterinary use; Pet supplies. **SICs:** 5047 (Medical & Hospital Equipment); 5122 (Drugs, Proprietaries & Sundries); 5199 (Nondurable Goods Nec). **Officers:** Sherry Leverett, Contact.

■ 27178 ■ **Lads Pet Supplies**
1701 Eden Evans Center Rd.
Angola, NY 14006-9728
Phone: (716)947-4293 **Fax:** (716)947-4090
Products: Pet supplies. **SIC:** 5199 (Nondurable Goods Nec).

■ 27179 ■ **Lee-Mar Aquarium and Pet Supplies, Inc.**
2459 Dogwood Way
Vista, CA 92083
Phone: (760)727-1300
Free: (800)372-4400 **Fax:** (760)727-4280
Products: Pet supplies, including glass and acrylic aquariums; Cabinetry; Cages; Cat furniture; Custom store fixtures and displays. **SIC:** 5199 (Nondurable Goods Nec). **Est:** 1972. **Emp:** 110. **Officers:** Terry Boyd, President.

■ 27180 ■ **Leone's Animal Supply**
4352 William Penn Hwy.
Rte. 22
Murrysville, PA 15668
Phone: (412)325-3030
Products: Veterinary instruments; Pharmaceutical preparations for veterinary use; Pet supplies. **SICs:** 5047 (Medical & Hospital Equipment); 5122 (Drugs, Proprietaries & Sundries); 5199 (Nondurable Goods Nec). **Officers:** George Leone, Contact.

■ 27181 ■ **Lextron Inc.**
PO Box BB
Greeley, CO 80632
Phone: (970)353-2600 **Fax:** (303)356-4623
Products: Animal health care products, including vaccines and antibiotics. **SIC:** 5191 (Farm Supplies). **Est:** 1967. **Sales:** $350,000,000 (2000). **Emp:** 600. **Officers:** R.C. Hummel, Chairman of the Board; Roy Sommers, VP of Finance; Bonnie Sowder, Corp. Secty.; Frank Sherman, CEO & President.

■ 27182 ■ **Longhorn Pet Supply**
6450 Clara, Ste. 100
Houston, TX 77041
Phone: (713)466-3999 **Fax:** (713)937-3687
Products: Pet supplies; Dry goods. **SIC:** 5199 (Nondurable Goods Nec).

■ 27183 ■ **Mallory Pet Supplies**
740 Rankin Rd. NE
Albuquerque, NM 87107
Phone: (505)836-4033
Free: (800)824-4464 **Fax:** (505)831-0838
Products: All natural concentrate pet shampoos. **SIC:** 5199 (Nondurable Goods Nec). **Est:** 1987. **Sales:** $800,000 (2000). **Emp:** 8. **Officers:** Kevin Mallory, President; Keith Mallory, Vice President.

■ 27184 ■ **Mandala Corp.**
1215 Reservoir Ave.
Cranston, RI 02920-6009
Phone: (401)944-8070 **Fax:** (401)944-8077
Products: Pet pellets; Index film. **SIC:** 5149 (Groceries & Related Products Nec). **Officers:** Jacob Perl, President.

■ 27185 ■ **R.H. McElheney, Inc.**
16975 Westview Ave.
South Holland, IL 60473
Phone: (708)596-3010
Free: (800)323-7084 **Fax:** (708)596-3012
E-mail: mcelheney@prodigy.net
Products: Pet supplies. **SIC:** 5199 (Nondurable Goods Nec). **Est:** 1947. **Emp:** 24.

■ 27186 ■ **Mer-Roc F.S. Inc.**
PO Box 129
Aledo, IL 61231
Phone: (309)582-7271
Free: (800)322-1435 **Fax:** (309)582-2229
Products: Pet food, including wild bird feed. **SICs:** 5191 (Farm Supplies); 5149 (Groceries & Related Products Nec). **Est:** 1935. **Sales:** $15,000,000 (2000). **Emp:** 41. **Officers:** Dana Robinson, President; Mark Hemphill, Controller.

■ 27187 ■ **Meridian Veterinary Products**
PO Box 3593
Chapel Hill, NC 27515
Phone: (919)833-8119
Products: Veterinary instruments; Pharmaceutical preparations for veterinary use; Pet supplies. **SICs:** 5047 (Medical & Hospital Equipment); 5122 (Drugs, Proprietaries & Sundries); 5199 (Nondurable Goods Nec). **Officers:** Jack Schuler DVM, Contact.

■ 27188 ■ **Tom Meyers**
RD 3, Box 316
Ford City, PA 16226
Phone: (412)763-2422
Products: Veterinary instruments; Pharmaceutical preparations for veterinary use; Pet supplies. **SICs:** 5047 (Medical & Hospital Equipment); 5122 (Drugs, Proprietaries & Sundries); 5199 (Nondurable Goods Nec).

■ 27189 ■ **Midwest Veterinary Supply Inc.**
11965 Larc Industrial Blvd.
Burnsville, MN 55337
Phone: (612)894-4350
Products: Veterinary equipment, supplies and drugs. **SICs:** 5047 (Medical & Hospital Equipment); 5122 (Drugs, Proprietaries & Sundries). **Sales:** $47,000,000 (2000). **Emp:** 140. **Officers:** Guy Flickinger, General Mgr.; Scott Davis, Comptroller.

■ 27190 ■ **Mize Farm & Garden Supply**
625 Wesinpar
Johnson City, TN 37604
Phone: (423)928-2188
Products: Veterinary instruments; Pharmaceutical preparations for veterinary use; Pet supplies. **SICs:** 5047 (Medical & Hospital Equipment); 5199 (Nondurable Goods Nec); 5122 (Drugs, Proprietaries & Sundries). **Officers:** Ken Lowe, Contact.

■ 27191 ■ **Montgomery Seed**
255 Dexter Ave.
Montgomery, AL 36104
Phone: (205)265-8241
Products: Veterinary instruments; Pharmaceutical preparations for veterinary use; Pet supplies. **SICs:** 5047 (Medical & Hospital Equipment); 5199 (Nondurable Goods Nec); 5122 (Drugs, Proprietaries & Sundries).

■ 27192 ■ **Nashville Pet Products Center**
2621 Cruzen St.
Nashville, TN 37211
Phone: (615)242-2223
Products: Veterinary instruments; Pharmaceutical preparations for veterinary use; Pet supplies. **SICs:** 5047 (Medical & Hospital Equipment); 5199 (Nondurable Goods Nec). **Officers:** Kathy Rodgers, Manager.

■ 27193 ■ **New England Pet Supply**
3 Ledgeview Dr.
Westbrook, ME 04092
Phone: (207)761-5687
Free: (800)343-2794   **Fax:** (207)761-5943
Products: Pet supplies. **SIC:** 5199 (Nondurable Goods Nec).

■ 27194 ■ **New England Serum Co.**
U.S Rte. 1
PO Box 128
Topsfield, MA 01983
Phone: (978)887-2368
Free: (800)637-3786   **Fax:** (978)887-8499
E-mail: support@neserum.com
URL: http://www.neserum.com
Products: Veterinary instruments; Pharmaceutical preparation for veterinary use; Pet supplies; Supplies and equipment for groomers, veterinarians, kennels, and breeders. **SICs:** 5199 (Nondurable Goods Nec); 5122 (Drugs, Proprietaries & Sundries); 5199 (Nondurable Goods Nec). **Est:** 1956. **Emp:** 300. **Officers:** Andrew Katz, President.

■ 27195 ■ **NLS Animal Health**
11407 Cronhill Dr., Ste. D-W
Owings Mills, MD 21117
Phone: (410)581-1800
Free: (800)638-8672   **Fax:** (410)581-1809
Products: Veterinarian and pet supplies. **SICs:** 5199 (Nondurable Goods Nec); 5122 (Drugs, Proprietaries & Sundries); 5047 (Medical & Hospital Equipment). **Est:** 1937. **Emp:** 215. **Former Name:** A.J. #Buck & Son.

■ 27196 ■ **Nolt's Ponds Inc.**
PO Box 40
Silver Spring, PA 17575
Phone: (717)285-5925   **Fax:** (717)285-3820
Products: Pet supplies. **SIC:** 5199 (Nondurable Goods Nec).

■ 27197 ■ **Northpoint Trading Co. Inc.**
5113 Pacific Hwy. E, No. 11
Tacoma, WA 98424
Phone: (253)922-2020
Products: Veterinary instruments; Pharmaceutical preparations for veterinary use; Pet supplies. **SICs:** 5047 (Medical & Hospital Equipment); 5122 (Drugs, Proprietaries & Sundries); 5199 (Nondurable Goods Nec). **Officers:** Craig Silver, Contact.

■ 27198 ■ **Northwest Farm Food Cooperative**
1370 S Anacortes St.
Burlington, WA 98233-3038
Phone: (360)757-4225   **Fax:** (360)757-8206
Products: Dog and cat food. **SIC:** 5149 (Groceries & Related Products Nec). **Est:** 1946. **Sales:** $3,200,000 (2000). **Emp:** 25. **Officers:** Jeff Craggs, President; Vern Peterson, Treasurer & Secty.

■ 27199 ■ **Northwest Vet Supply Inc.**
PO Box 1841
Enid, OK 73702-1841
Phone: (580)234-5839
Free: (800)522-1351   **Fax:** (580)233-7161
Products: Veterinary instruments. **SIC:** 5047 (Medical & Hospital Equipment). **Officers:** Robert Lohmann, President.

■ 27200 ■ **Now Pet Products**
320 Berkshire Rd.
Vermilion, OH 44089
Phone: (440)967-6560
Free: (800)541-0176   **Fax:** (440)967-7738
Products: Pet supplies. **SIC:** 5199 (Nondurable Goods Nec). **Est:** 1982. **Officers:** Pauline Docy; Stephen Docy, e-mail: stephen@centurytel.net.

■ 27201 ■ **Omaha Vaccine**
PO Box 7228
Omaha, NE 68107
Phone: (402)731-9600
Free: (800)367-4444   **Fax:** (402)731-9829
URL: http://www.omahavaccine.com
Products: Pets, including horses; Pet supplies. **SIC:** 5199 (Nondurable Goods Nec).

■ 27202 ■ **ORRCO, Inc.**
PO Box 147
Orrville, OH 44667
Phone: (330)683-5015   **Fax:** (330)683-0738
E-mail: orrcoinc@aol.com
Products: Pet supplies; Dog collars, leashes, and other household pet accessories. **SIC:** 5199 (Nondurable Goods Nec). **Est:** 1900. **Officers:** G. P. Butcher, President & CEO, e-mail: gbutcher@valkyrie.net. **Former Name:** Orrville Pet Products.

■ 27203 ■ **Patnaude's Aquarium & Pet**
1193 Ashley Blvd.
New Bedford, MA 02745
Phone: (508)995-0214   **Fax:** (508)998-3803
E-mail: pataq1193@aol.com
Products: Pet supplies. **SIC:** 5199 (Nondurable Goods Nec). **Est:** 1946. **Sales:** $2,000,000 (2000). **Emp:** 21. **Officers:** Normand R. Patnaude, President; Jeanne J. Patnaude, Vice President.

■ 27204 ■ **Perz Feed & Delivery**
3607 W 400 N
La Porte, IN 46350
Phone: (219)326-6339
Products: Veterinary instruments; Pharmaceutical preparations for veterinary use; Pet supplies. **SICs:** 5047 (Medical & Hospital Equipment); 5122 (Drugs, Proprietaries & Sundries); 5199 (Nondurable Goods Nec). **Officers:** Jim Perz, Contact.

■ 27205 ■ **Pet Care Wholesale**
2341 Ampere Dr.
Louisville, KY 40299-6411
Phone: (502)262-0220
Free: (800)331-5275   **Fax:** (502)261-0224
Products: Veterinary products. **SIC:** 5199 (Nondurable Goods Nec). **Sales:** $5,000,000 (2000). **Emp:** 25.

■ 27206 ■ **Pet Food Wholesale, Inc.**
3160B Enterprise St.
Brea, CA 92821
Phone: (714)254-1200   **Fax:** (714)572-8265
E-mail: info@pfw411.com
Products: Pet food and supplies, including food, treats, bedding, and litter. **SICs:** 5149 (Groceries & Related Products Nec); 5199 (Nondurable Goods Nec). **Est:** 1990. **Officers:** Bob Johnson, General Mgr.; Ken Bacon, Sales Mgr.

■ 27207 ■ **Pet Life Foods Inc.**
PO Box 218
Hamilton, MI 49419-0218
Phone: (616)751-8277
Free: (800)323-2267   **Fax:** (616)789-5762
Products: Dog, cat, and other pet food. **SIC:** 5149 (Groceries & Related Products Nec). **Sales:** $40,000,000 (2000). **Emp:** 450. **Officers:** John Donahue; Frank Sloup.

■ 27208 ■ **Pet Lift**
1192 Myrtal Ave.
Brooklyn, NY 11221
Phone: (718)455-4907
Products: Dog collars, leashes, and other household pet accessories; Pet supplies. **SIC:** 5199 (Nondurable Goods Nec).

■ 27209 ■ **The Pet Pharmacy Inc.**
1517 E 10th St.
Alamogordo, NM 88310
Phone: (505)434-2556
Free: (800)453-7444   **Fax:** (505)437-2124
E-mail: thepetrx@zianet.com
URL: http://www.zianet.com/thepetrx
Products: Pet supplies and food. **SICs:** 5199 (Nondurable Goods Nec); 5149 (Groceries & Related Products Nec). **Est:** 1991. **Sales:** $1,000,000 (2000). **Emp:** 7.

■ 27210 ■ **Pet Products Associates, Inc.**
PO Box 2558
Guaynabo, PR 00970-2558
Phone: (787)790-7387   **Fax:** (787)790-7378
E-mail: petprod@prtc.net
Products: Pet supplies. **SIC:** 5199 (Nondurable Goods Nec). **Est:** 1976. **Emp:** 23. **Officers:** Eladio Marquetti.

■ 27211 ■ **Pet Supply Warehouse**
Roseytown Rd.
Greensburg, PA 15601
Phone: (412)834-0500
Products: Veterinary instruments; Pharmaceutical preparations for veterinary use; Pet supplies. **SICs:** 5047 (Medical & Hospital Equipment); 5122 (Drugs, Proprietaries & Sundries); 5199 (Nondurable Goods Nec). **Officers:** Gary Fleming, Contact.

■ 27212 ■ **Pet World**
2833 W Ridge Rd.
Rochester, NY 14626
Phone: (716)292-5786   **Fax:** (716)292-5951
Products: Pet supplies. **SICs:** 5047 (Medical & Hospital Equipment); 5122 (Drugs, Proprietaries & Sundries); 5199 (Nondurable Goods Nec). **Est:** 1969. **Emp:** 70. **Officers:** Jim Seidewand, President.

■ 27213 ■ **Pied Piper Mills Inc.**
PO Box 309
Hamlin, TX 79520
Phone: (915)576-3684   **Fax:** (915)576-3460
Products: Dog and cat food. **SICs:** 5153 (Grain & Field Beans); 5153 (Grain & Field Beans); 5191 (Farm Supplies). **Est:** 1916. **Sales:** $6,300,000 (2000). **Emp:** 27. **Officers:** R. Moore, Exec. VP; B. Moore, Exec. VP.

■ **27214** ■ **Pittman International**
1400 N Jefferson St.
Unit A
Anaheim, CA 92807
Phone: (714)572-9195 **Fax:** (714)528-8062
E-mail: pittmanpi@aol.com
Products: Veterinary instruments; Pharmaceutical preparations for veterinary use; Pet supplies; Animal food, including dog, cat, and horse food; Bird supplies. **SICs:** 5047 (Medical & Hospital Equipment); 5199 (Nondurable Goods Nec); 5149 (Groceries & Related Products Nec). **Est:** 1970. **Emp:** 6. **Officers:** Cody Pittman, Partner; Elinor Pittman, Partner. **Alternate Name:** P.I.

■ **27215** ■ **Poultry Health**
PO Box 40028
Jacksonville, FL 32203
Products: Veterinary instruments; Pharmaceutical preparations for veterinary use; Pet supplies. **SICs:** 5047 (Medical & Hospital Equipment); 5122 (Drugs, Proprietaries & Sundries); 5199 (Nondurable Goods Nec).

■ **27216** ■ **Priddy's General Store**
PO Box 1215
Sophia, WV 25921
Phone: (304)683-3906
Products: Veterinary instruments; Pharmaceutical preparations for veterinary use; Pet supplies. **SICs:** 5047 (Medical & Hospital Equipment); 5122 (Drugs, Proprietaries & Sundries); 5199 (Nondurable Goods Nec). **Officers:** Joe McKenny, Contact.

■ **27217** ■ **Pro-Visions Pet Specialty Enterprises Div.**
Checkerboard Sq.
St. Louis, MO 63164
Phone: (314)982-1000
Free: (800)776-7526 **Fax:** (314)982-4274
Products: Cat and dog food; Cereal. **SIC:** 5149 (Groceries & Related Products Nec). **Est:** 1990. **Sales:** $74,400,000 (2000). **Emp:** 160. **Officers:** John McGinty, President; Ann Patzell, Dir. of Data Processing.

■ **27218** ■ **Provico Inc.**
PO Box 579
Botkins, OH 45306
Phone: (513)693-2411 **Fax:** (513)693-2887
Products: Animal health products. **SIC:** 5122 (Drugs, Proprietaries & Sundries). **Est:** 1929. **Sales:** $47,000,000 (2000). **Emp:** 95. **Officers:** Gailyn Thomsen, President; Mike Loy, Treasurer & Secty.

■ **27219** ■ **Quality Pets, Inc.**
1501 S Agnew
Oklahoma City, OK 73108
Phone: (405)272-1091 **Fax:** (405)236-4019
Products: Non-domestic animals; Pet supplies. **SIC:** 5199 (Nondurable Goods Nec).

■ **27220** ■ **R & R Distributors**
2727-7 Clydo Rd.
Jacksonville, FL 32207
Phone: (904)730-7700 **Fax:** (904)730-7700
Products: Pet supplies. **SIC:** 5199 (Nondurable Goods Nec).

■ **27221** ■ **Ralston Purina Co., Golden Products Div.**
300 Airport Rd.
Cape Girardeau, MO 63701
Phone: (573)334-6618 **Fax:** (573)986-0190
Products: Veterinary products. **SIC:** 5199 (Nondurable Goods Nec). **Est:** 1947. **Sales:** $240,000,000 (2000). **Emp:** 350.

■ **27222** ■ **River Springs Cooperative Association**
8419 N State Rte. 19
Green Springs, OH 44836
Phone: (419)639-2242 **Fax:** (419)639-2990
Products: Dog and cat food; Feed for hogs and cattle; Pool supplies; Fertilizer; Chemicals. **SICs:** 5191 (Farm Supplies); 5169 (Chemicals & Allied Products Nec); 5149 (Groceries & Related Products Nec). **Est:** 1984. **Sales:** $12,000,000 (2000). **Emp:** 15. **Officers:** M.J. Myers, General Mgr.

■ **27223** ■ **Road Runner Pet Supplies**
403 Middle San Pedro
Espanola, NM 87532
Phone: (505)753-6196 **Fax:** (505)657-6277
Products: Veterinary products. **SIC:** 5199 (Nondurable Goods Nec). **Est:** 1983. **Sales:** $900,000 (2000). **Emp:** 7.

■ **27224** ■ **Robbinsdale Farm and Garden Pet Supply Inc.**
7301 32nd Ave. N
Minneapolis, MN 55427-2835
Phone: (612)559-7166
Products: Pet supplies, including dog food, cat food, and bird seed. **SICs:** 5199 (Nondurable Goods Nec); 5149 (Groceries & Related Products Nec). **Sales:** $3,000,000 (2000). **Emp:** 35. **Officers:** Craig Thoeny, President.

■ **27225** ■ **Ryan's Pet Supplies**
3411 S Central Ave.
Phoenix, AZ 85040
Phone: (602)276-5267
Free: (800)525-7387 **Fax:** (602)276-2932
Products: Veterinary products. **SIC:** 5199 (Nondurable Goods Nec).

■ **27226** ■ **S & S**
2750 Maxwell Way
Fairfield, CA 94533
Phone: (707)426-6666 **Fax:** (707)426-0102
Products: Pet supplies; Dry food and produce, including pet and animal food. **SICs:** 5199 (Nondurable Goods Nec); 5149 (Groceries & Related Products Nec).

■ **27227** ■ **St. Charles County Cooperative Co.**
5055 N Hwy. 94
St. Charles, MO 63301-6431
Phone: (314)258-3805
Products: Dog and cat food. **SIC:** 5149 (Groceries & Related Products Nec). **Est:** 1943. **Sales:** $2,500,000 (2000). **Emp:** 8. **Officers:** James Leonard, President; David Forley, Treasurer & Secty.

■ **27228** ■ **Santa Fe Pet and Vet Supply**
2801 Cerrillos Rd.
Santa Fe, NM 87505-2311
Phone: (505)988-2237 **Fax:** (505)983-1019
Products: Pet supplies. **SIC:** 5199 (Nondurable Goods Nec). **Officers:** Larry Valadez, Owner.

■ **27229** ■ **Scotland Yard**
1001 Columbia St.
Newport, KY 41071
Phone: (606)581-0140
Free: (800)957-3540 **Fax:** (606)491-2931
E-mail: wessy2.com
URL: http://www.wessy2@aol.com
Products: Veterinary instruments; Pharmaceutical preparations for veterinary use; Pet supplies. **SICs:** 5047 (Medical & Hospital Equipment); 5199 (Nondurable Goods Nec); 5122 (Drugs, Proprietaries & Sundries). **Est:** 1990. **Sales:** $100,000 (2000). **Emp:** 1. **Officers:** Doris Scott, Contact and Owner; Kevin Raike, Manager.

■ **27230** ■ **Sergeant's Pet Products Inc.**
1 Central Park Plz., No. 700
Omaha, NE 68102-1693
Phone: (402)595-7000
Free: (800)228-9031 **Fax:** (402)595-7099
Products: Pet care products. **SICs:** 5199 (Nondurable Goods Nec); 5149 (Groceries & Related Products Nec). **Sales:** $40,000,000 (2000). **Emp:** 60. **Officers:** Robert Scharf, General Mgr.; Bill Myer, Controller.

■ **27231** ■ **SF Services Inc.**
824 N Palm St.
North Little Rock, AR 72114-5134
Phone: (501)945-2371 **Fax:** (501)945-2371
Products: Veterinary instruments; Pharmaceutical preparations for veterinary use; Pet supplies. **SICs:** 5047 (Medical & Hospital Equipment); 5122 (Drugs, Proprietaries & Sundries); 5199 (Nondurable Goods Nec). **Officers:** Mike Wilson, Contact.

■ **27232** ■ **Small Talk Inc.**
10489 St. Rd. 37 N
Elwood, IN 46036
Phone: (765)552-2007 **Fax:** (765)552-1320
Products: Pet supplies. **SIC:** 5199 (Nondurable Goods Nec).

■ **27233** ■ **V.A. Snell**
5620 Snell Dr.
San Antonio, TX 78219
Phone: (210)661-7300
Products: Veterinarian supplies. **SIC:** 5047 (Medical & Hospital Equipment).

■ **27234** ■ **Southeast Pet**
8005 2nd Flags Dr., SW
Austell, GA 30168
Phone: (404)948-7600 **Fax:** (404)948-4466
Products: Pet supplies. **SIC:** 5199 (Nondurable Goods Nec).

■ **27235** ■ **Spartan Pet Supply**
75 Modular Ave.
Commack, NY 11725
Phone: (516)864-3222 **Fax:** (516)864-1291
Products: Pet supplies. **SIC:** 5199 (Nondurable Goods Nec).

■ **27236** ■ **Speiser Pet Supplies**
7040 SW 21st Pl.
Davie, FL 33317
Phones: (954)472-1404 (954)472-1405
Free: (800)940-PETS **Fax:** (954)472-3189
E-mail: speiser@speiserpet.com
URL: http://www.speiserpet.com
Products: Household pet accessories and supplies, including dog collars and leashes. **SIC:** 5199 (Nondurable Goods Nec). **Est:** 1975. **Officers:** Jane Speiser; Norma Sirocco; W. Piechocki, Dir. of Mktg. & Sales.

■ **27237** ■ **Sporting Dog Specialties Inc.**
1989 Transit Way
Brockport, NY 14420-3007
Phone: (716)637-7508
Free: (800)872-3773 **Fax:** (716)352-1272
Products: Pet supplies. **SIC:** 5199 (Nondurable Goods Nec).

■ **27238** ■ **Steuben County Farm Bureau Association Inc.**
610 W Broad St.
Angola, IN 46703
Phone: (219)665-3161
Products: Horse and pet food; Lawn and garden products; Herbicides. **SICs:** 5153 (Grain & Field Beans); 5191 (Farm Supplies). **Est:** 1927. **Sales:** $13,600,000 (2000). **Emp:** 44. **Officers:** Dennis Buell, General Mgr.

■ **27239** ■ **Stockman Supply Inc.**
802 W Main Ave.
West Fargo, ND 58078
Phone: (701)282-3255
Free: (800)437-4064 **Fax:** (701)282-3545
Products: Veterinary instruments; Pharmaceutical preparations for veterinary use; Pet supplies. **SICs:** 5047 (Medical & Hospital Equipment); 5122 (Drugs, Proprietaries & Sundries); 5199 (Nondurable Goods Nec). **Est:** 1956. **Emp:** 20. **Officers:** Robert Jameson, Contact.

■ **27240** ■ **Storm Pet Supply Inc.**
625 Birkhead Ave.
Owensboro, KY 42303
Phone: (502)926-4168
Products: Pet supplies. **SICs:** 5199 (Nondurable Goods Nec); 5149 (Groceries & Related Products Nec). **Est:** 1971. **Emp:** 22. **Officers:** James B. Storm, President.

■ **27241** ■ **Summit Pet Products**
400 Quaint Acres Dr.
Silver Spring, MD 20904
Phone: (301)791-7138 **Fax:** (301)340-3343
Products: Pet supplies. **SIC:** 5199 (Nondurable Goods Nec).

■ 27242 ■ Summit Pet Products
420 Chimney Rock Rd.
Greensboro, NC 27409-9260
Phone: (910)665-0666 **Fax:** (910)665-1571
Products: Pet supplies. **SIC:** 5199 (Nondurable Goods Nec).

■ 27243 ■ T & E Enterprises & Development
PO Box 240188
Anchorage, AK 99524
Phone: (907)563-5939 **Fax:** (907)258-5214
Products: Pet supplies, including fish and bird food; Aquariums. **SIC:** 5199 (Nondurable Goods Nec).

■ 27244 ■ Tasty Foods/VCA
5724 Hillside Ave.
Cincinnati, OH 45233
Phone: (513)941-3342 **Fax:** (513)941-8064
Products: Dog food. **SIC:** 5149 (Groceries & Related Products Nec).

■ 27245 ■ Taylor Feed & Pet Supply
19 Smiley Ingram Rd.
PO Box 1504
Cartersville, GA 30120-1504
Phone: (770)382-9665
Free: (800)882-9407 **Fax:** (770)386-6117
E-mail: taylorfd@bellsouth.net
Products: Animal feed and pet supplies. **SICs:** 5199 (Nondurable Goods Nec); 5191 (Farm Supplies); 5149 (Groceries & Related Products Nec). **Est:** 1948. **Sales:** $11,000,000 (2000). **Emp:** 42. **Officers:** Shannon Taylor, VP & GM.

■ 27246 ■ Thompson's Veterinary Supplies
1340 N 29th Ave.
Phoenix, AZ 85009
Phone: (602)258-8187 **Fax:** (602)278-1512
Products: Pet supplies, including shampoo and horse harnesses. **SICs:** 5199 (Nondurable Goods Nec); 5191 (Farm Supplies).

■ 27247 ■ Thunder Mountain Dog Supplies
1421 N Mullan Rd.
Spokane, WA 99206-4051
Phone: (509)928-3677 **Fax:** (509)928-0714
E-mail: tmds@ix.net.com
Products: Dog and cat supplies, including books, videos, portable pens, collars, and harnesses; Show and obedience supplies; Animal related novelty items, including mugs, notecards, cups, stickers, and stamps. **SIC:** 5199 (Nondurable Goods Nec). **Est:** 1983. **Emp:** 7. **Officers:** Nancy J. Flanary, Owner; Pamela D. Adams, Dir. of Marketing.

■ 27248 ■ Top Dog Ltd.
1510 Roper Mountain Rd.
Greenville, SC 29615
Free: (800)666-1100
Products: Veterinary instruments; Pharmaceutical preparations for veterinary use; Pet supplies. **SICs:** 5047 (Medical & Hospital Equipment); 5122 (Drugs, Proprietaries & Sundries); 5199 (Nondurable Goods Nec). **Officers:** Bill Lee, Owner.

■ 27249 ■ Town & Country Pet Supply Inc.
6314 Arundel Cove Ave.
Baltimore, MD 21226
Phone: (410)355-2400
Products: Pet supplies. **SIC:** 5199 (Nondurable Goods Nec). **Est:** 1979. **Emp:** 5. **Officers:** Loreen P. Peterson, Owner.

■ 27250 ■ Transcon Trading Company, Inc.
121 Dutchman Blvd.
Irmo, SC 29063
Phone: (803)781-7117 **Fax:** (803)781-8545
E-mail: info@transcontrading.com
URL: http://www.transcontrading.com
Products: Pharmaceutical preparations for veterinary use. **SIC:** 5122 (Drugs, Proprietaries & Sundries). **Officers:** Jerry Smith, President.

■ 27251 ■ Tri-Blue Kennel
4013 County Line Rd.
Southington, OH 44470
Phone: (330)889-3377
Products: Veterinary instruments; Pharmaceutical preparations for veterinary use; Pet supplies. **SICs:** 5047 (Medical & Hospital Equipment); 5122 (Drugs, Proprietaries & Sundries); 5199 (Nondurable Goods Nec). **Officers:** Nancy Collier, Contact.

■ 27252 ■ Tri-State Breeders Cooperative
E 10890 Penny Ln.
Baraboo, WI 53913
Phone: (608)356-8357
Free: (800)451-9275 **Fax:** (608)356-4387
Products: Animal breeding products. **SIC:** 5191 (Farm Supplies). **Est:** 1941. **Sales:** $22,000,000 (2000). **Emp:** 275. **Officers:** Roger Ripley, CEO & President; W. Cox, VP of Finance; Robert Holterman, VP of Marketing. **Former Name:** Tri-State Breeders Cooperative.

■ 27253 ■ Tri-State Vet & Pet Supply
3300 Interstate Dr.
Evansville, IN 47715-1781
Phone: (812)477-4793 **Free:** (800)489-9081
Products: Vaccines; Antibiotics; Dewormers; Preparations; Pet supplies. **SICs:** 5199 (Nondurable Goods Nec); 5199 (Nondurable Goods Nec); 5122 (Drugs, Proprietaries & Sundries). **Est:** 1952. **Emp:** 5. **Officers:** Lee Sorrell, Manager. **Alternate Name:** Tri State Veterinary Supply Co.

■ 27254 ■ Triumph Pet Industries, Inc.
7 Lake Station Rd.
Warwick, NY 10990-3426
Phone: (914)469-5125
Free: (800)331-5144 **Fax:** (914)357-6804
Products: Dog, cat, and other pet food. **SIC:** 5149 (Groceries & Related Products Nec). **Est:** 1936. **Sales:** $10,000,000 (2000). **Emp:** 99. **Officers:** Isadore Gittelman.

■ 27255 ■ Tropical Fisheries
1030 Basse Rd.
San Antonio, TX 78212
Phone: (210)733-6258 **Fax:** (210)733-3429
Products: Tropical and domestic fish; Aquarium products and supplies. **SIC:** 5199 (Nondurable Goods Nec).

■ 27256 ■ United Pacific Pet L.L.C.
12060 Cabernet Dr.
Fontana, CA 92337
Phone: (909)360-8550
Free: (800)979-3333 **Fax:** (909)360-8540
E-mail: lisap@uppet.com
Products: Pet food. **SIC:** 5199 (Nondurable Goods Nec). **Est:** 1998. **Emp:** 44. **Officers:** Maureen Costello, President.

■ 27257 ■ United Pharmacal Co.
3705 Pear St.
St. Joseph, MO 64502
Phone: (816)233-8800
Products: Dog collars, leashes, and other household pet accessories; Pet supplies. **SIC:** 5199 (Nondurable Goods Nec).

■ 27258 ■ UPCO Pet Vet Supply
11200 Menaul St.
Albuquerque, NM 87112
Phone: (505)292-6288 **Fax:** (505)296-9460
Products: Pet food and supplies. **SICs:** 5199 (Nondurable Goods Nec); 5149 (Groceries & Related Products Nec).

■ 27259 ■ Valley Pet Supply
1029 Whipple Rd.
Hayward, CA 94544
Phone: (510)489-3311 **Fax:** (510)487-1295
Products: Pet supplies. **SIC:** 5199 (Nondurable Goods Nec).

■ 27260 ■ Valley Vet Supply
PO Box 504
Marysville, KS 66508
Phone: (785)562-5106
Free: (800)468-0059 **Fax:** 800-446-5597
Products: Veterinary products. **SIC:** 5199 (Nondurable Goods Nec). **Est:** 1981.

■ 27261 ■ John A. Van Den Bosch Co.
509 E Washington Ave.
Zeeland, MI 49464
Phone: (616)772-2179
Free: (800)968-6477 **Fax:** (616)772-4533
Products: Pet supplies, including wild bird seed, seed cakes, deer products, outdoor feeding, and animal feed. **SICs:** 5199 (Nondurable Goods Nec); 5149 (Groceries & Related Products Nec). **Est:** 1934. **Sales:** $15,000,000 (2000). **Emp:** 42. **Officers:** William VanDen Bosch, President; Dave VanDen Bosch, General Mgr.; Mark VanDen Bosch, Operations Mgr.; Mike VanDen Bosch; Jim VanDen Bosch.

■ 27262 ■ Hugh Vann Sales Co.
PO Box 806
White Rock, SC 29177
Phone: (803)781-8266 **Fax:** (803)732-5530
Products: Pet supplies. **SIC:** 5199 (Nondurable Goods Nec).

■ 27263 ■ Vermont Pet Food & Supply
2500 Williston Rd.
South Burlington, VT 05403
Phone: (802)863-5597 **Fax:** (802)660-9575
Products: Pet food and supplies. **SICs:** 5199 (Nondurable Goods Nec); 5149 (Groceries & Related Products Nec).

■ 27264 ■ Veterinary Medical Supply
950 Mack Todd Rd.
Zebulon, NC 27597-9555
Phone: (919)772-3278 **Fax:** (919)772-0289
Products: Medical equipment; Hospital equipment; Veterinary instruments. **SIC:** 5047 (Medical & Hospital Equipment). **Officers:** Ben Weathers, President.

■ 27265 ■ Vetline Inc.
425 John Deere Dr.
Ft. Collins, CO 80524
Phone: (970)484-1900 **Free:** (800)962-4554
Products: Medical and hospital equipment; Veterinarians' equipment and supplies. **SIC:** 5047 (Medical & Hospital Equipment). **Officers:** Kenneth Larson, President.

■ 27266 ■ Vets International Inc.
PO Box 8595
Honolulu, HI 96830-0595
Phone: (808)926-2294 **Fax:** (808)924-9645
Products: Veterinarians' equipment and supplies. **SIC:** 5047 (Medical & Hospital Equipment). **Officers:** Asahiko Wagai, President.

■ 27267 ■ Walco International Inc.
520 S Main St.
Grapevine, TX 76051
Phone: (817)601-6000 **Fax:** (817)601-3099
Products: Animal and veterinary supplies. **SICs:** 5122 (Drugs, Proprietaries & Sundries); 5191 (Farm Supplies). **Est:** 1950. **Sales:** $450,000,000 (2000). **Emp:** 800. **Officers:** Jim Robison, CEO, President & Chairman of the Board; Kevin Holt, CFO; Patricia Blair, VP of Marketing; Greg Eveland, COO.

■ 27268 ■ Weatherford Enterprise of Flagstaff
11705 N Hwy. 89
Flagstaff, AZ 86004
Phone: (520)526-3556 **Fax:** (520)526-3551
Products: Saddles; Ropes; Blankets and pads; Bits and spurs. **SIC:** 5199 (Nondurable Goods Nec). **Est:** 1989. **Emp:** 6. **Officers:** David Weatherford, President.

■ 27269 ■ Weisheimer Pet Supply
1015 Taylor Rd.
Blacklick, OH 43004
Phone: (614)864-2100 **Fax:** (614)864-2310
Products: Pet supplies. **SIC:** 5199 (Nondurable Goods Nec).

■ 27270 ■ West Wholesale
800 NW 65th St.
Ft. Lauderdale, FL 33309
Phone: (954)351-1117
Products: Veterinary instruments; Pharmaceutical preparations for veterinary use; Pet supplies. **SICs:** 5047 (Medical & Hospital Equipment); 5122 (Drugs, Proprietaries & Sundries); 5199 (Nondurable Goods Nec). **Officers:** Tammy Raybold, Contact.

■ 27271 ■ **W.L.C. Ltd.**
PO Box 400
Calverton, NY 11933
Phone: (516)727-3535
Products: Veterinary instruments; Pharmaceutical preparations for veterinary use; Pet supplies. **SICs:** 5047 (Medical & Hospital Equipment); 5122 (Drugs, Proprietaries & Sundries); 5199 (Nondurable Goods Nec). **Officers:** Bob Novak, Contact.

■ 27272 ■ **Wolverton Pet Supply**
16020 Lowell Rd.
Lansing, MI 48906
Phone: (517)321-7250   **Fax:** (517)321-8016
Products: Pet supplies. **SIC:** 5199 (Nondurable Goods Nec).

■ 27273 ■ **Zenter Enterprises Ltd.**
53 Middleburg Ln.
Orchard Park, NY 14127
Phone: (716)826-5797
Products: Veterinary instruments; Pharmaceutical preparations for veterinary use; Pet supplies. **SICs:** 5047 (Medical & Hospital Equipment); 5122 (Drugs, Proprietaries & Sundries); 5199 (Nondurable Goods Nec). **Officers:** Charles Coorradt, Vice President. **Doing Business As:** Groomingdales.

(61) Wood and Wood Products

Entries in this section are arranged alphabetically by company name. When the company name is a personal name, the company name is alphabetized by the surname unless the first name or initial(s) are part of a trade name. See the User's Guide at the front of this directory for additional information.

■ **27274** ■ **J.K. Adams Company Inc.**
PO Box 248
Dorset, VT 05251
Phone: (802)362-2303
Products: Wood products. **SIC:** 5031 (Lumber, Plywood & Millwork). **Est:** 1944. **Sales:** $5,000,000 (2000). **Emp:** 50. **Officers:** Malcolm E. Cooper Jr., CEO; Malcolm E. Cooper Sr., President.

■ **27275** ■ **Allied Building Stores Inc.**
PO Box 8030
Monroe, LA 71211
Phone: (318)699-9100
Products: Lumber and building materials. **SIC:** 5031 (Lumber, Plywood & Millwork). **Est:** 1965. **Sales:** $360,000,000 (1999). **Emp:** 90. **Officers:** Laddie Woods, President.

■ **27276** ■ **Allied Distribution Systems**
11852 Alameda St.
Lynwood, CA 90262-4019
Products: Construction materials and machinery. **SIC:** 5031 (Lumber, Plywood & Millwork). **Sales:** $96,000,000 (2000). **Emp:** 207.

■ **27277** ■ **Alpine Evergreen Company Inc.**
7124 State Hwy. 3 SW
Port Orchard, WA 98367
Phone: (360)674-2303 **Fax:** (360)674-2310
Products: Wood and wood products. **SIC:** 5199 (Nondurable Goods Nec). **Sales:** $2,000,000 (2000). **Emp:** 45.

■ **27278** ■ **American Century Pallet Co.**
PO Box 26704
Oklahoma City, OK 73126
Phone: (405)232-9649 **Fax:** (405)232-6030
Products: Wood mulch and filler ground from recycled pallets. **SIC:** 5093 (Scrap & Waste Materials). **Est:** 1981. **Emp:** 22.

■ **27279** ■ **American Mill and Manufacturing Inc.**
676 Moss St.
Chula Vista, CA 91911
Phone: (619)420-7343 **Fax:** (619)420-4829
Products: Fir trees; Redwood. **SICs:** 5031 (Lumber, Plywood & Millwork); 5099 (Durable Goods Nec). **Est:** 1945. **Sales:** $2,000,000 (2000). **Emp:** 12. **Officers:** William F. Evenson, President; Oberlin J. Evenson, Vice President.

■ **27280** ■ **Andalusia Wood Products Inc.**
PO Box 159
River Falls, AL 36476
Phone: (205)222-2224
Products: Wood products. **SICs:** 5031 (Lumber, Plywood & Millwork); 5099 (Durable Goods Nec).

■ **27281** ■ **Arrowhead Timber Co.**
PO Box 85
Carver, OR 97015
Phone: (503)658-5151 **Fax:** (503)658-3156
Products: Timber. **SICs:** 5031 (Lumber, Plywood & Millwork); 5099 (Durable Goods Nec). **Est:** 1961.

Sales: $100,000 (2000). **Emp:** 20. **Officers:** Lowell E. Patton, President.

■ **27282** ■ **J.M. Ash Woodyard Inc.**
PO Box 128
Potts Camp, MS 38659
Phone: (601)252-1777
Products: Hardwood. **SIC:** 5031 (Lumber, Plywood & Millwork). **Est:** 1975. **Sales:** $2,000,000 (2000). **Emp:** 5. **Officers:** J.M. Ash, President.

■ **27283** ■ **Atlantic Veneer Corp.**
PO Box 660
Beaufort, NC 28516
Phone: (919)728-3169 **Fax:** (919)728-4906
Products: Veneers. **SIC:** 5031 (Lumber, Plywood & Millwork). **Est:** 1964. **Sales:** $50,000,000 (2000). **Emp:** 550. **Officers:** K. Heinz Moehring, CEO & President; Greg Lewis, Treasurer; Leslie Calmon, VP of Sales; Doug Dyreng, Manager; Edmund Nelson, Dir of Human Resources.

■ **27284** ■ **Baker Hardwood Lumber Co.**
PO Box 936
National City, CA 91951-0936
Phone: (619)263-8102 **Fax:** (619)477-5690
Products: Construction materials and machinery. **SIC:** 5031 (Lumber, Plywood & Millwork). **Sales:** $9,000,000 (2000). **Emp:** 35.

■ **27285** ■ **Bakersfield Sandstone Brick Company Inc.**
PO Box 866
Bakersfield, CA 93302
Phone: (805)325-5722 **Fax:** (805)325-3626
Products: Trusses; sells brick and general building materials. **SICs:** 5031 (Lumber, Plywood & Millwork); 5072 (Hardware). **Sales:** $20,000,000 (2000). **Emp:** 60. **Officers:** Walter Heisey, President; Bill F. Steele, Treasurer.

■ **27286** ■ **Banks Lumber Company Inc.**
PO Box 2299
Elkhart, IN 46515
Phone: (219)294-5671 **Fax:** (219)294-1032
Products: Wood roof trusses, shims and cut softwood lumber. **SICs:** 5031 (Lumber, Plywood & Millwork); 5013 (Motor Vehicle Supplies & New Parts). **Sales:** $200,000,000 (2000). **Emp:** 1,000. **Officers:** Chris Wynne, VP of Finance.

■ **27287** ■ **Boise Cascade Corp.**
PO Box 50
Boise, ID 83728
Phone: (208)384-6161 **Fax:** (208)384-7189
Products: Office products and building materials; Integrated manufacturer of paper and wood products. **SICs:** 5031 (Lumber, Plywood & Millwork); 5112 (Stationery & Office Supplies). **Sales:** $6,953,000,000 (1999). **Emp:** 23,726. **Officers:** George Harad, CEO & Chairman of the Board; Ted Crumley, Sr. VP & CFO.

■ **27288** ■ **Boise Cascade Corp. Building Materials Distribution Div.**
1111 W Jefferson St.
Boise, ID 83702
Phone: (208)384-6354 **Fax:** (208)384-4811
Products: Building materials, including lumber, panels, roofing materials, insulation, and metal goods; Engineered wood products. **SICs:** 5031 (Lumber, Plywood & Millwork); 5032 (Brick, Stone & Related Materials); 5033 (Roofing, Siding & Insulation); 5039 (Construction Materials Nec). **Est:** 1957. **Sales:** $1,700,000,000 (2000). **Emp:** 1,100. **Officers:** Stan Bell, VP & General Mgr.; Gib Jones, Mgr. of Finance; Nick Stokes, Operations Mgr.; Tom Hogg, Marketing & Sales Mgr.

■ **27289** ■ **Buettner Brothers Lumber Co.**
PO Box 1087
Cullman, AL 35056-1087
Phone: (205)734-4221
Products: Construction materials and machinery. **SIC:** 5031 (Lumber, Plywood & Millwork). **Sales:** $9,000,000 (2000). **Emp:** 70.

■ **27290** ■ **Builders Wholesale Supply Company Inc.**
Forbes Industrial Park
Topeka, KS 66619-1423
Phone: (913)642-4334
Free: (800)224-9996 **Fax:** (913)648-5598
Products: Furniture and fixtures. **SIC:** 5031 (Lumber, Plywood & Millwork). **Sales:** $2,000,000 (2000). **Emp:** 20.

■ **27291** ■ **Cabin Crafters**
1225 W 1st St.
Nevada, IA 50201
Phone: (515)382-5406 **Fax:** (515)382-3106
Products: Wood and Wood Productss. **SIC:** 5099 (Durable Goods Nec). **Est:** 1994.

■ **27292** ■ **Calcasieu Lumber Co.**
PO Box 17097
Austin, TX 78760
Phone: (512)444-3172
Products: Lumber and plywood; Building supplies; Trusses, components, pehung doors and millwork. **SIC:** 5031 (Lumber, Plywood & Millwork). **Sales:** $81,000,000 (2000). **Emp:** 400. **Officers:** Truman N. Morris, CEO & President; Mark Bunker, CFO.

■ **27293** ■ **Canfor U.S.A. Corp.**
PO Box 674
Meridian, ID 83642
Phone: (208)888-2456
Products: Pine boards. **SIC:** 5031 (Lumber, Plywood & Millwork). **Est:** 1958. **Sales:** $61,000,000 (2000). **Emp:** 150. **Officers:** Harold E. Unruh, President; Frank Hasman, Controller.

■ **27294** ■ **Canterbury Enterprises**
PO Box 16369
Irvine, CA 92623-6369
Phone: (949)496-7313 **Fax:** (714)246-9541
Products: Firewood. **SIC:** 5099 (Durable Goods Nec).

Sales: $3,000,000 (2000). **Emp:** 49. **Officers:** Joseph Leighton.

■ **27295** ■ **Carolina Door Controls**
PO Box 15639
Durham, NC 27704
Phone: (919)381-0094   **Fax:** (919)381-4834
Products: Construction materials and machinery. **SIC:** 5031 (Lumber, Plywood & Millwork). **Sales:** $40,000,000 (2000). **Emp:** 270.

■ **27296** ■ **Central Lumber Sales Inc.**
PO Box 22723
Lincoln, NE 68542-2723
Phone: (402)474-4441   **Fax:** (402)474-0595
Products: Construction materials and machinery. **SIC:** 5031 (Lumber, Plywood & Millwork). **Sales:** $8,000,000 (2000). **Emp:** 22.

■ **27297** ■ **Cimarron Lumber and Supply Co.**
4000 Main St.
Kansas City, MO 64111
Phone: (816)756-3000
Products: Construction materials and machinery. **SIC:** 5031 (Lumber, Plywood & Millwork). **Sales:** $56,000,000 (2000). **Emp:** 200.

■ **27298** ■ **Colco Fine Woods and Tools Inc.**
PO Box 820449
Memphis, TN 38182-0449
Phone: (901)452-9663   **Fax:** (901)452-0277
Products: Construction materials and machinery. **SIC:** 5031 (Lumber, Plywood & Millwork). **Sales:** $2,000,000 (2000). **Emp:** 15.

■ **27299** ■ **Continental Wood Preservers Inc.**
7500 E Davison St.
Detroit, MI 48212
Phone: (313)365-4200
Products: Pressure treated and fire retardant plywood and lumber. **SIC:** 5031 (Lumber, Plywood & Millwork). **Sales:** $23,000,000 (2000). **Emp:** 35. **Officers:** Dave Brandenburg, President.

■ **27300** ■ **Cookson Co.**
2417 S 50th Ave.
Phoenix, AZ 85043
Phone: (602)272-4244   **Fax:** (602)233-2132
Products: Metal doors, sashes, frames, molding and trim. **SICs:** 5031 (Lumber, Plywood & Millwork); 5039 (Construction Materials Nec). **Sales:** $26,000,000 (2000). **Emp:** 250. **Officers:** Bob Cookson, President; Blair Sellers, CFO.

■ **27301** ■ **Custom Industries Inc.**
2 S Grove St.
Bradford, MA 01835-7518
Phone: (978)374-6331   **Fax:** (978)373-7829
Products: Custom-made wood products. **SIC:** 5031 (Lumber, Plywood & Millwork). **Est:** 1969. **Sales:** $1,000,000 (2000). **Emp:** 20. **Officers:** L. Frank Sirois, President.

■ **27302** ■ **Dunbar Doors and Millwork**
1316 Bonneville Ave.
Snohomish, WA 98290
Phone: (360)568-0515
Products: Construction materials and machinery. **SIC:** 5031 (Lumber, Plywood & Millwork). **Sales:** $3,000,000 (2000). **Emp:** 30.

■ **27303** ■ **Frank A. Edmunds and Company Inc.**
6111 S Sayre Ave.
Chicago, IL 60638
Phone: (773)586-2772   **Fax:** (773)586-2783
Products: Construction materials and machinery. **SIC:** 5031 (Lumber, Plywood & Millwork). **Sales:** $2,000,000 (2000). **Emp:** 30.

■ **27304** ■ **Erickson Wood Products**
PO Box 61
Belmont, CA 94002
Phone: (415)591-5785
Products: Storage equipment and containers. **SIC:** 5031 (Lumber, Plywood & Millwork). **Sales:** $1,000,000 (2000). **Emp:** 10.

■ **27305** ■ **Forest City Enterprises Inc.**
1100 Terminal Twr., 50 Public Sq.
Cleveland, OH 44113
Phone: (216)267-1200   **Fax:** (216)433-1827
Products: Lumber. **SIC:** 5031 (Lumber, Plywood & Millwork). **Sales:** $632,700,000 (2000). **Emp:** 3,384. **Officers:** Charles A. Ratner, CEO & President; Thomas G. Smith, Sr. VP & CFO.

■ **27306** ■ **Fort Worth Lumber Co.**
PO Box 969
Ft. Worth, TX 76101
Phone: (817)293-5211
Free: (800)372-6467   **Fax:** (817)293-3487
Products: Wood. **SICs:** 5031 (Lumber, Plywood & Millwork); 5039 (Construction Materials Nec). **Est:** 1946. **Sales:** $14,000,000 (2000). **Emp:** 50. **Officers:** Razz Fiesler, CEO; Emily Fiesler, President.

■ **27307** ■ **Frost Hardwood Lumber Co.**
PO Box 919065
San Diego, CA 92191-9065
Phone: (619)455-9060
Products: Construction materials and machinery. **SIC:** 5031 (Lumber, Plywood & Millwork). **Sales:** $10,000,000 (2000). **Emp:** 47.

■ **27308** ■ **Garick Corp.**
13600 Broadway Ave.
Cleveland, OH 44125
Phone: (216)581-0100
Free: (800)242-7425   **Fax:** (216)581-4712
E-mail: garick@garick.com
URL: http://www.garick.com
Products: Bark mulch; Playground surfacing; Golf course sands; Lightweight aggregates; Landscape stone and boulders; Nursery mixes. **SIC:** 5099 (Durable Goods Nec). **Est:** 1980. **Sales:** $18,000,000 (1999). **Emp:** 29. **Officers:** Gary Trinetti, VP & General Mgr.; Rick Mahoney, Procurement Mgr.; Ralf Engelbrecht, Sales/Marketing Contact, e-mail: ralf.engelbrecht@garick.com.

■ **27309** ■ **Global Forestry Management Group**
PO Box 10167
Portland, OR 97296
Phone: (503)228-1950   **Fax:** (503)288-2291
E-mail: gfmg@teleport.com
Products: Logs and timber from Russia; Port opertions in Russia. **SIC:** 5099 (Durable Goods Nec). **Est:** 1994. **Sales:** $2,000,000 (1999). **Emp:** 150. **Officers:** Jeff Fantazia, President.

■ **27310** ■ **Goshen Sash and Door Co.**
PO Box 517
Goshen, IN 46527
Phone: (219)533-1146   **Fax:** (219)533-4017
Products: Molded and lathe cut synthetic and silicone rubber products; O-rings, seals and boots. **SIC:** 5031 (Lumber, Plywood & Millwork). **Sales:** $45,000,000 (2000). **Emp:** 70.

■ **27311** ■ **Graham-Hardison Hardwood Inc.**
PO Box 344
Linden, TN 37096
Phone: (931)589-2143
Products: Cut lumber. **SIC:** 5031 (Lumber, Plywood & Millwork).

■ **27312** ■ **Griffin Wood Company Inc.**
PO Box 669
Marion, AL 36756
Phone: (334)683-9073
Products: Pulpwood; Logs. **SIC:** 5031 (Lumber, Plywood & Millwork). **Est:** 1968. **Sales:** $23,000,000 (2000). **Emp:** 85. **Officers:** Corin Harrison Jr., President.

■ **27313** ■ **Gulf South Forest Products, Inc.**
PO Box 39299
Ft. Lauderdale, FL 33339-9299
Phone: (954)565-8355   **Fax:** (954)565-8497
E-mail: gulfsouth@worldnet.att.net
URL: http://www.lumberexport.com
Products: Western red cedar; Crossties, timbers, and poles; Lumber and plywood; Southern yellow pine. **SICs:** 5031 (Lumber, Plywood & Millwork); 5099 (Durable Goods Nec). **Est:** 1987. **Officers:** Sam Yohanan, President.

■ **27314** ■ **T.W. Hager Lumber Company Inc.**
PO Box 912
Grand Rapids, MI 49509
Phone: (616)452-5151
Products: Particleboard and fence products. **SIC:** 5031 (Lumber, Plywood & Millwork). **Sales:** $88,000,000 (2000). **Emp:** 131.

■ **27315** ■ **Hancock Lumber Inc.**
PO Box 299
Casco, ME 04015
Phone: (207)627-4400
Products: Lumber; Building materials. **SIC:** 5031 (Lumber, Plywood & Millwork).

■ **27316** ■ **Harbor Sales Co.**
1000 Harbor Ct.
Sudlersville, MD 21668-1818
Free: (800)345-1712   **Fax:** 800-868-9257
Products: Construction materials and machinery. **SIC:** 5031 (Lumber, Plywood & Millwork). **Sales:** $6,000,000 (2000). **Emp:** 54.

■ **27317** ■ **J.E. Higgins Lumber Co.**
PO Box 4124
Concord, CA 94524
Phone: (925)674-9300
Free: (877)241-1883   **Fax:** (925)674-9434
Products: Lumber. **SIC:** 5031 (Lumber, Plywood & Millwork). **Sales:** $122,000,000 (2000). **Emp:** 450. **Officers:** Jonathan R. Long, President & Chairman of the Board; Michael Flener, Controller.

■ **27318** ■ **Hillsdale Sash and Door Co**
PO Box 629
Wilsonville, OR 97070
Phone: (503)682-1000   **Fax:** (503)682-2233
Products: Sells windows and wood and metal doors; Custom cutting. **SIC:** 5031 (Lumber, Plywood & Millwork).

■ **27319** ■ **Holmes Timber Company Inc.**
Rte. 2, Box 244
Johnston, SC 29832
Phone: (803)275-4755
Products: Timber. **SIC:** 5099 (Durable Goods Nec). **Est:** 1981. **Sales:** $17,000,000 (2000). **Emp:** 9. **Officers:** Jerry Holmes, President.

■ **27320** ■ **HPM Building Supply**
380 Kanoelehua Ave.
Hilo, HI 96720
Phone: (808)966-5466   **Fax:** (808)966-5673
Products: Wooden roof trusses and roofing. **SICs:** 5031 (Lumber, Plywood & Millwork); 5198 (Paints, Varnishes & Supplies); 5074 (Plumbing & Hydronic Heating Supplies); 5084 (Industrial Machinery & Equipment). **Sales:** $47,000,000 (2000). **Emp:** 235. **Officers:** Robert Fujimoto, CEO.

■ **27321** ■ **A.P. Hubbard Wholesale Lumber Corp.**
PO Box 14100
Greensboro, NC 27415
Phone: (336)275-1343
Free: (800)868-2745   **Fax:** (336)273-8975
E-mail: aphublum@aol.com
Products: Lumber. **SIC:** 5031 (Lumber, Plywood & Millwork). **Est:** 1952. **Emp:** 6.

■ **27322** ■ **Hunter Trading Corporation**
PO Box 166
Westport, CT 06881
Phone: (203)254-7030   **Fax:** (203)259-4480
Products: Wood kitchen cabinets; Lumber and plywood, flooring. **SICs:** 5031 (Lumber, Plywood & Millwork); 5031 (Lumber, Plywood & Millwork); 5169 (Chemicals & Allied Products Nec). **Est:** 1983. **Sales:** $5,000,000 (2000). **Emp:** 5. **Officers:** Stephan Taranko, Vice President; Peter Lawn, General Mgr.

■ **27323** ■ **Intermountain Wood Products**
1948 S West Temple
Salt Lake City, UT 84115
Phone: (801)486-6859   **Fax:** (801)466-0428
Products: Lumber. **SIC:** 5031 (Lumber, Plywood & Millwork). **Sales:** $39,000,000 (2000). **Emp:** 60. **Officers:** Ben E. Banks, President; Scott Miles, Controller.

■ 27324 ■ H.W. Jenkins Co.
PO Box 18347
Memphis, TN 38181-0347
Phone: (901)363-7641 **Fax:** (901)363-1104
Products: Building materials, including wood, roof truss, and millwork. **SICs:** 5031 (Lumber, Plywood & Millwork); 5039 (Construction Materials Nec). **Est:** 1939. **Sales:** $50,000,000 (2000). **Emp:** 130. **Officers:** H.W. Jenkins Jr. Jr., President; John Edwards, CFO.

■ 27325 ■ Judson Lumber Co.
321 W Bigelow Ave.
Plain City, OH 43064
Phone: (614)873-3911
Free: (888)876-2058 **Fax:** (614)873-6920
Products: Custom millwork. **SIC:** 5031 (Lumber, Plywood & Millwork). **Sales:** $15,000,000 (2000). **Emp:** 22. **Officers:** Judson Blaine, Owner.

■ 27326 ■ K and A Lumber Company Inc.
1001 W Mowry Dr.
Homestead, FL 33030
Phone: (305)245-5312
Products: Lumber; Building materials. **SICs:** 5031 (Lumber, Plywood & Millwork); 5039 (Construction Materials Nec).

■ 27327 ■ Keene Div.
10100 East Rd.
Potter Valley, CA 95469
Phone: (707)743-1154
Free: (800)750-1154 **Fax:** (707)743-1159
Products: Storage Equipment and Containerss. **SIC:** 5031 (Lumber, Plywood & Millwork). **Sales:** $9,000,000 (2000). **Emp:** 75.

■ 27328 ■ Ketcham Forest Products Inc.
PO Box 22789
Seattle, WA 98122
Phone: (206)329-2700 **Fax:** (206)324-6301
Products: Lumber. **SIC:** 5031 (Lumber, Plywood & Millwork). **Sales:** $7,000,000 (1994). **Emp:** 20. **Officers:** Gerald Iverson, President.

■ 27329 ■ Kevco Inc.
1300 S University Dr.
Ft. Worth, TX 76107
Phone: (817)332-2758 **Fax:** (817)332-3403
Products: Building products to the manufactured housing and the recreational vehicle industries. **SIC:** 5031 (Lumber, Plywood & Millwork). **Sales:** $897,500,000 (1999). **Emp:** 2,153. **Officers:** Jerry E. Kimmel, CEO, President & Chairman of the Board; Ellis L. McKinley, Jr., CFO & Treasurer.

■ 27330 ■ KIC International
4109 Fruit Valley Rd.
Vancouver, WA 98660
Phone: (206)696-0561 **Fax:** (206)696-3132
Products: Logging wood chip equipment; Motor vehicle off-highway log trailers; Motor vehicle track skidders; Logging equipment, including mobil debarkers; Logging sawmill machinery. **SICs:** 5084 (Industrial Machinery & Equipment); 5012 (Automobiles & Other Motor Vehicles). **Officers:** G.P. Kuzmer, Co-Owner.

■ 27331 ■ Knecht Home Lumber Center Inc.
320 West Blvd.
Rapid City, SD 57701
Phone: (605)342-4840 **Fax:** (605)342-7079
Products: Construction materials and machinery. **SIC:** 5031 (Lumber, Plywood & Millwork). **Sales:** $16,000,000 (2000). **Emp:** 150.

■ 27332 ■ Koncor Forest Products Co.
3501 Denali St.
Anchorage, AK 99503
Phone: (907)562-3335
Products: Timber. **SIC:** 5099 (Durable Goods Nec). **Sales:** $3,000,000 (2000). **Emp:** 18. **Officers:** John Sturgeon, President.

■ 27333 ■ Landew Sawdust Inc.
190 Clifford St.
Newark, NJ 07105
Phone: (973)344-5255
Products: Sawdust. **SIC:** 5199 (Nondurable Goods

Nec). **Sales:** $2,000,000 (2000). **Emp:** 9. **Officers:** Seymour Landew, President.

■ 27334 ■ Liberty Industries Inc.
555 Tibetts Wick Rd.
Girard, OH 44420-1101
Phone: (330)539-4744
Free: (800)860-4744 **Fax:** (330)539-5825
Products: Industrial wood products. **SIC:** 5031 (Lumber, Plywood & Millwork). **Est:** 1964. **Sales:** $20,000,000 (2000). **Emp:** 65. **Officers:** Ronald C. Ringness, President; Keith Countryman, Vice President.

■ 27335 ■ C.J. Link Lumber Co.
PO Box 1085
Warren, MI 48090
Phone: (810)773-1200
Free: (800)462-9716 **Fax:** (313)773-9611
E-mail: otisredn@ix.netcom.com
Products: Cedar and Douglas fir; Plywood and millwork; Deck coatings and cleaners. **SICs:** 5031 (Lumber, Plywood & Millwork); 5099 (Durable Goods Nec). **Est:** 1951. **Sales:** $15,000,000 (2000). **Emp:** 18. **Officers:** John W. Mergel, CEO & President.

■ 27336 ■ Lott Builders Supply Co.
PO Box 439
Douglas, GA 31534
Phone: (912)384-1800 **Fax:** (912)384-5555
Products: Wooden doors and windows, ready-mixed concrete and precast septic tanks. **SIC:** 5031 (Lumber, Plywood & Millwork). **Sales:** $20,000,000 (2000). **Emp:** 60. **Officers:** David Lott, Owner.

■ 27337 ■ Lumber Yards Inc.
PO Box 27046
Tucson, AZ 85726
Phone: (520)747-5440 **Fax:** (520)747-2816
Products: Lumber, plywood, millwork and doors; Roof trusses and flooring. **SIC:** 5031 (Lumber, Plywood & Millwork).

■ 27338 ■ Lyons Sawmill and Logging
Equipment Co.
5445 NYS Route 353
PO Box 107
Little Valley, NY 14755
Phone: (716)938-9175 **Fax:** (716)938-9227
URL: http://www.lyonstimbertalk.com
Products: Sawmill and logging equipment. **SIC:** 5082 (Construction & Mining Machinery). **Est:** 1963. **Sales:** $41,000,000 (2000). **Emp:** 85. **Officers:** John Lyons, President; Robert Tuyn, Controller; Clyde Houser, Vice President.

■ 27339 ■ Manis Lumber Company Inc.
2 Riverside Industrial Park
Rome, GA 30161
Phone: (706)232-2400
Products: Wood doors and window frames. **SICs:** 5031 (Lumber, Plywood & Millwork); 5072 (Hardware). **Est:** 1949. **Sales:** $61,000,000 (1994). **Emp:** 185. **Officers:** W.J. Manis, President.

■ 27340 ■ Mann and Parker Lumber Co.
335 N Constitution Ave.
New Freedom, PA 17349
Phone: (717)235-4834
Free: (800)632-9098 **Fax:** (717)235-5547
E-mail: sales@m-pgoldbrand.com
URL: http://www.m-pgoldbrand.com
Products: Hardwood lumber. **SIC:** 5031 (Lumber, Plywood & Millwork). **Est:** 1902. **Sales:** $26,000,000 (1999). **Emp:** 80. **Officers:** Stephen Bushman, President & CEO; Gary Johnston, VP & Controller; Gregory V. Lutter, Sr. VP & COO; Victoria L. Krotzer, Human Resources Contact.

■ 27341 ■ Mayfield Timber Co.
PO Box 223
Toxey, AL 36921
Phone: (205)843-5543 **Fax:** (205)843-5501
Products: Pine logs. **SIC:** 5099 (Durable Goods Nec). **Est:** 1983. **Sales:** $4,500,000 (2000). **Emp:** 30. **Officers:** Robert A. Mayfield, President.

■ 27342 ■ Lawrence R. McCoy and Company Inc.
100 Front St., No. 700
Worcester, MA 01608-1444
Phone: (508)798-7575
Free: (800)346-2269 **Fax:** (508)798-7515
Products: Lumber, plywood, millwork, and wood products. **SIC:** 5031 (Lumber, Plywood & Millwork). **Sales:** $68,000,000 (2000). **Emp:** 50. **Officers:** H.S. Poler, CEO; Richard K. Dale, VP & CFO.

■ 27343 ■ Geo. McQuesten Company Inc.
600 Iron Horse Park
North Billerica, MA 01862
Phone: (978)663-3435 **Fax:** (978)667-0934
Products: Building products, including lumber. **SIC:** 5031 (Lumber, Plywood & Millwork). **Est:** 1855. **Sales:** $60,000,000 (2000). **Emp:** 90. **Officers:** R. Starrak, President; Paul Snider, Treasurer; J. Gardner, CFO.

■ 27344 ■ Medply
PO Box 2488
White City, OR 97503
Phone: (541)826-3142 **Fax:** (541)826-8022
Products: Plywood. **SIC:** 5031 (Lumber, Plywood & Millwork). **Sales:** $28,000,000 (1999). **Emp:** 175. **Officers:** Clyde Lang, President; Clyde Lang, CFO.

■ 27345 ■ Meyer Laminates Inc.
1264 La Quinta Dr., Rm. 4B
Orlando, FL 32809
Phone: (407)857-6353 **Fax:** (407)856-9452
Products: Laminated particleboard and decorative plywood. **SIC:** 5031 (Lumber, Plywood & Millwork). **Sales:** $200,000,000 (2000). **Emp:** 650. **Officers:** Rocky Johnson, President; David Sullivan, Accountant.

■ 27346 ■ M.L. Sandy Lumber Sales Company Inc.
PO Box 1535
Corinth, MS 38834-1535
Phone: (601)286-6087 **Fax:** (601)287-4187
Products: Construction materials and machinery. **SIC:** 5031 (Lumber, Plywood & Millwork). **Sales:** $10,000,000 (2000). **Emp:** 50.

■ 27347 ■ Modernfold of Florida Inc.
PO Box 451206
Ft. Lauderdale, FL 33345
Phone: (954)747-7400 **Fax:** (954)747-6600
Products: Construction materials and machinery. **SIC:** 5031 (Lumber, Plywood & Millwork).

■ 27348 ■ Thomas Monahan Co.
202 N Oak St.
Arcola, IL 61910
Phone: (217)268-4955
Free: (800)637-7739 **Fax:** (217)268-3113
Products: Broom, mop, and paint brush handles; Miscellaneous wood products. **SICs:** 5159 (Farm-Product Raw Materials Nec); 5099 (Durable Goods Nec); 5199 (Nondurable Goods Nec). **Est:** 1922. **Sales:** $40,000,000 (1999). **Emp:** 175. **Officers:** Thomas F. Monahan Jr., President & Chairman of the Board; Ned Lunt, COO.

■ 27349 ■ Muench Woodwork Company Inc.
2701 Jackson Ave.
South Chicago Heights, IL 60411
Phone: (708)754-2108 **Fax:** (708)754-5562
Products: Wood products. **SIC:** 5031 (Lumber, Plywood & Millwork). **Est:** 1946. **Sales:** $4,000,000 (2000). **Emp:** 50. **Officers:** Kurt W. Muench, President.

■ 27350 ■ Norby Lumber Company Inc.
PO Box 329
Madera, CA 93639
Phone: (209)674-6712
Products: Wood. **SIC:** 5031 (Lumber, Plywood & Millwork).

■ 27351 ■ Northern Ohio Lumber and Timber Co.
1895 Carter Rd.
Cleveland, OH 44113
Phone: (216)771-4080
Free: (800)771-4081 **Fax:** (216)771-4793
Products: Construction materials and machinery. **SIC:**

5031 (Lumber, Plywood & Millwork). **Sales:** $5,000,000 (2000). **Emp:** 16.

■ **27352** ■ **Ocotillo Lumber Sales Inc.**
3121 N 28th Ave.
Phoenix, AZ 85017
Phone: (602)258-6951 **Fax:** (602)258-6172
Products: Construction materials and machinery. **SIC:** 5031 (Lumber, Plywood & Millwork). **Sales:** $10,000,000 (2000). **Emp:** 17.

■ **27353** ■ **Owens Forest Products**
2320 E 1st St.
Duluth, MN 55812
Phone: (218)723-1151
Free: (800)346-1461 **Fax:** (218)724-9486
E-mail: sales@owensforestproducts.com
URL: http://www.owensforestproducts.com
Products: Lumber. **SIC:** 5031 (Lumber, Plywood & Millwork). **Est:** 1974. **Emp:** 250.

■ **27354** ■ **Pacific Lumber and Shipping Co.**
1301 5th Ave. Ste. 3131
Seattle, WA 98101
Phone: (206)682-7262 **Fax:** (206)682-5887
Products: Sells and exports logs and lumber; Logging. **SIC:** 5031 (Lumber, Plywood & Millwork). **Sales:** $151,000,000 (2000). **Emp:** 400. **Officers:** Jerry Weed, President.

■ **27355** ■ **Frank Paxton Co.**
6311 St. John Ave.
Kansas City, MO 64114
Phone: (816)483-3007 **Fax:** (816)361-2086
Products: Construction materials and machinery. **SIC:** 5031 (Lumber, Plywood & Millwork). **Est:** 1914. **Sales:** $110,000,000 (2000). **Emp:** 700.

■ **27356** ■ **Paxton Timber Co.**
PO Box 1227
Paxton, FL 32538
Phone: (850)834-2153
Products: Timber, including whole wood and pine. **SIC:** 5099 (Durable Goods Nec). **Est:** 1970. **Sales:** $4,500,000 (2000). **Emp:** 10. **Officers:** Scott Beck, Owner.

■ **27357** ■ **Pennville Custom Cabinetry for the Home**
600 E Votaw
Portland, IN 47371
Phone: (219)726-9357 **Fax:** (219)726-7044
Products: Construction materials and machinery. **SIC:** 5031 (Lumber, Plywood & Millwork). **Sales:** $3,000,000 (2000). **Emp:** 42.

■ **27358** ■ **Petersburg Box and Lumber Inc.**
1400 Southwest St.
Petersburg, VA 23803
Phone: (804)732-8921
Products: Lumber and wood products; Southern yellow pine. **SICs:** 5031 (Lumber, Plywood & Millwork); 5099 (Durable Goods Nec). **Sales:** $2,000,000 (2000). **Emp:** 30. **Officers:** J.N. Williamson, President; E. Dowdy, Finance Officer.

■ **27359** ■ **Phillips Brothers Lumber Company Inc.**
PO Box 1356
Brookhaven, MS 39601
Phone: (601)833-7461
Products: Pine lumber. **SIC:** 5031 (Lumber, Plywood & Millwork). **Est:** 1953. **Sales:** $11,000,000 (2000). **Emp:** 35. **Officers:** Paul R. Phillips, President.

■ **27360** ■ **Pioneer Machinery**
PO Box 9230
Richmond, VA 23227
Phone: (804)266-4911 **Fax:** (804)262-5726
Products: Logging equipment; Moving and handling equipment. **SIC:** 5082 (Construction & Mining Machinery). **Sales:** $200,000,000 (2000). **Emp:** 550. **Officers:** Gar Scott, CEO.

■ **27361** ■ **Q.E.P. Co. Inc.**
1081 Holland Dr.
Boca Raton, FL 33487
Phone: (561)994-5550
Products: A broad line of specialty tools and related

products for the home improvement market. **SIC:** 5031 (Lumber, Plywood & Millwork). **Sales:** $98,000,000 (1999). **Emp:** 384. **Officers:** Lewis Gould, CEO & Chairman of the Board; Marc P. Applebaum, Sr. VP & CFO.

■ **27362** ■ **Redhawk Industries Inc.**
PO Box 25322
Portland, OR 97298
Phone: (503)297-7072 **Fax:** (503)297-5158
Products: Wood products, including lumber, utility poles, and shingles. **SIC:** 5031 (Lumber, Plywood & Millwork). **Est:** 1978. **Sales:** $1,200,000 (2000). **Emp:** 2. **Officers:** Cheryl Fellers, President; Bennie Norris, Sales/Marketing Contact.

■ **27363** ■ **Ridout Lumber Cos.**
125 Henry Farr Dr.
Searcy, AR 72143
Phone: (501)268-0386
Products: Lumber. **SIC:** 5031 (Lumber, Plywood & Millwork).

■ **27364** ■ **The Roane Co.**
14141 Arbor Pl.
Cerritos, CA 90703
Phone: (562)404-3464
Free: (800)223-6499 **Fax:** (562)404-8028
Products: Floorcovering equipment and supplies. **SIC:** 5031 (Lumber, Plywood & Millwork). **Sales:** $15,000,000 (2000). **Emp:** 60.

■ **27365** ■ **Robinson Lumber Company Inc.**
4000 Tchoupitoulas St.
New Orleans, LA 70115
Phone: (504)895-6377 **Fax:** (504)897-0820
Products: Construction materials and machinery. **SIC:** 5031 (Lumber, Plywood & Millwork). **Sales:** $5,000,000 (2000). **Emp:** 70.

■ **27366** ■ **Rugby Building Products Inc.**
1335 S Main
Greensburg, PA 15601
Phone: (412)834-5706 **Fax:** (412)834-8560
Products: Construction materials and machinery. **SIC:** 5031 (Lumber, Plywood & Millwork). **Sales:** $25,000,000 (2000). **Emp:** 40.

■ **27367** ■ **Rugby USA Inc.**
570 Lake Cook Rd.
Deerfield, IL 60015
Phone: (847)405-0850 **Fax:** (847)405-0860
Products: Construction materials and machinery. **SIC:** 5031 (Lumber, Plywood & Millwork). **Sales:** $500,000,000 (2000). **Emp:** 1,300.

■ **27368** ■ **S and M Lumber Co.**
424 W Main St.
Flushing, MI 48433
Phone: (810)659-5681 **Fax:** (810)659-7408
Products: Lumber. **SIC:** 5031 (Lumber, Plywood & Millwork). **Sales:** $11,000,000 (2000). **Emp:** 30. **Officers:** Lawrence H. Sharp, President; Scott L. Sharp, VP of Finance.

■ **27369** ■ **Schultz Snyder Steele Lumber Co.**
2419 Science Pkwy.
Lansing, MI 48909
Phone: (517)349-8220 **Fax:** (517)349-8377
Products: Construction materials and machinery. **SIC:** 5031 (Lumber, Plywood & Millwork). **Sales:** $150,000,000 (2000). **Emp:** 165.

■ **27370** ■ **Schutte Lumber Company Inc.**
3001 Southwest Blvd.
Kansas City, MO 64108
Phone: (816)753-6262
Free: (800)456-2148 **Fax:** (816)753-7935
Products: Lumber. **SIC:** 5031 (Lumber, Plywood & Millwork). **Sales:** $33,000,000 (2000). **Emp:** 50. **Officers:** Clayton Egner, President & CFO.

■ **27371** ■ **SCR Inc.**
PO Box 1607
Lake Oswego, OR 97035
Phone: (503)968-1300 **Fax:** (503)968-1400
Products: Plywood. **SIC:** 5031 (Lumber, Plywood & Millwork). **Sales:** $31,000,000 (1999). **Emp:** 12.

Officers: Terry Crabtree, President; William Crabtree, Vice President.

■ **27372** ■ **Sealaska Corp.**
1 Sealaska Plz., Ste. 400
Juneau, AK 99801-1276
Phone: (907)586-1512 **Fax:** (907)586-1827
Products: Timber and related products. **SIC:** 5099 (Durable Goods Nec). **Sales:** $237,000,000 (2000). **Emp:** 500. **Officers:** Robert Loesher, CEO & President; Jim Edenso, CFO.

■ **27373** ■ **Sealaska Timber Corp.**
2030 Sea Level Dr., Ste. 202
Ketchikan, AK 99901
Phone: (907)225-9444 **Fax:** (907)225-5736
Products: Softwood rough lumber; Logs, bolts, and pulpwood. **SICs:** 5031 (Lumber, Plywood & Millwork); 5099 (Durable Goods Nec). **Officers:** Leo H. Barlow Jr., President & CEO.

■ **27374** ■ **Seattle Kitchen Design Inc.**
10002 Holman Rd. NW
Seattle, WA 98177-4921
Phone: (206)782-4900 **Fax:** (206)782-4345
Products: Furniture and fixtures. **SIC:** 5031 (Lumber, Plywood & Millwork). **Sales:** $1,000,000 (2000). **Emp:** 10.

■ **27375** ■ **Shehan-Cary Lumber Co.**
PO Box 19770
St. Louis, MO 63144
Phone: (314)968-8600
Products: Construction materials and machinery. **SIC:** 5031 (Lumber, Plywood & Millwork). **Sales:** $4,000,000 (2000). **Emp:** 3.

■ **27376** ■ **Shelter Super Store Corp.**
4100 Dixon St.
Des Moines, IA 50313-3944
Phone: (515)266-2419 **Fax:** (515)266-0833
Products: Wood products. **SIC:** 5031 (Lumber, Plywood & Millwork). **Sales:** $9,000,000 (2000). **Emp:** 75. **Officers:** Sam Carmichael, President; Ted Roberts, Treasurer.

■ **27377** ■ **Sierra Point Lumber and Plywood Co.**
601 Tunnel Ave.
San Francisco, CA 94134
Phone: (415)468-5620
Products: Construction materials and machinery. **SIC:** 5031 (Lumber, Plywood & Millwork). **Sales:** $4,000,000 (2000). **Emp:** 25.

■ **27378** ■ **South Atlantic Forest Products Inc.**
15010 Abercorn Expwy.
Savannah, GA 31419
Phone: (912)925-1100 **Fax:** (912)927-1112
Products: Lumber and building materials. **SIC:** 5031 (Lumber, Plywood & Millwork). **Est:** 1980. **Sales:** $20,000,000 (2000). **Emp:** 100. **Officers:** O. Raymond Gaster Jr., President.

■ **27379** ■ **Squires Timber Co.**
PO Box 549
Elizabethtown, NC 28337
Phone: (919)862-3533
URL: http://www.Squireslumber.com
Products: Timber. **SIC:** 5099 (Durable Goods Nec). **Est:** 1966. **Sales:** $60,000,000 (2000). **Emp:** 70. **Officers:** Nelson Squires, CEO; Joseph Luther, VP & CFO; Tommy Norris, President.

■ **27380** ■ **Starfire Lumber Co.**
PO Box 547
Cottage Grove, OR 97424
Phone: (541)942-0168
Products: General sawmill and planing mill. **SIC:** 5031 (Lumber, Plywood & Millwork). **Sales:** $22,000,000 (2000). **Emp:** 65. **Officers:** Francis Engle, President.

■ **27381** ■ **Steeler Inc.**
10023 Martin Lthr Kng Jr Way S
Seattle, WA 98178
Phone: (206)725-2500 **Fax:** (206)725-9834
Products: Steel studs; Dry wall and construction tools. **SICs:** 5031 (Lumber, Plywood & Millwork); 5082 (Construction & Mining Machinery).

■ **27382** ■ **Stephan Wood Products Inc.**
605 Huron
PO Box 669
Grayling, MI 49738-0669
Phone: (517)348-5496 **Fax:** (517)348-2427
Products: Miscellaneous wood products. **SIC:** 5031 (Lumber, Plywood & Millwork).

■ **27383** ■ **Sun Control Window Tinting and Shades**
4700 Vestal Pky. E
Vestal, NY 13850
Phone: (607)723-3066 **Fax:** (607)766-9795
Products: Construction materials and machinery. **SIC:** 5031 (Lumber, Plywood & Millwork).

■ **27384** ■ **Superior Lumber Co.**
PO Box 250
Glendale, OR 97442
Phone: (503)832-1121 **Fax:** (503)832-1139
Products: General sawmill, planing, soft and hard veneer and plywood. **SIC:** 5031 (Lumber, Plywood & Millwork). **Sales:** $72,000,000 (2000). **Emp:** 370. **Officers:** Rod Swanson, President; S.D. Swanson, CFO.

■ **27385** ■ **Texas Plywood and Lumber Company Inc.**
PO Box 531110
Grand Prairie, TX 75053
Phone: (972)263-1381 **Fax:** (972)262-1339
Products: Prehung doors, panels and millwork. **SICs:** 5031 (Lumber, Plywood & Millwork); 5039 (Construction Materials Nec). **Sales:** $75,000,000 (2000). **Emp:** 120. **Officers:** Geoff Yates, President; Scott Howard, CFO.

■ **27386** ■ **Thompson Mahogany Co.**
7400 Edmund St.
Philadelphia, PA 19136
Phone: (215)624-1866 **Fax:** (215)338-1060
Products: Mahogany wood. **SIC:** 5031 (Lumber, Plywood & Millwork). **Sales:** $13,000,000 (1994). **Emp:** 31. **Officers:** Donald A. Thompson, President; Raymond M. Remar, Controller.

■ **27387** ■ **Tidewater Companies Inc.**
PO Box 1116
Brunswick, GA 31521
Phone: (912)638-7726 **Fax:** (912)638-5907
Products: Timber harvesting equipment. **SIC:** 5082 (Construction & Mining Machinery). **Est:** 1947. **Sales:** $60,000,000 (2000). **Emp:** 175. **Officers:** K.S. Trowbridge Jr., Chairman of the Board; Earl C. Terry Jr., VP & Treasurer; T. Gillis Morgan III, President; K.S. Trowbridge III, VP & Secty.; J. Roger Brown, Vice President.

■ **27388** ■ **Timber Products Co. Medford**
PO Box 1669
Medford, OR 97501
Phone: (541)773-6681 **Fax:** (541)770-1509
Products: Hardwood plywood and particleboard. **SIC:** 5031 (Lumber, Plywood & Millwork). **Sales:** $187,000,000 (2000). **Emp:** 876.

■ **27389** ■ **Timberwork Oregon Inc.**
PO Box 3955
Portland, OR 97208
Phone: (503)492-3089 **Fax:** (503)492-0998
E-mail: timberwk@teleport.com
URL: http://www.timberwork.com
Products: Forest products, including treated lumber. **SIC:** 5031 (Lumber, Plywood & Millwork). **Est:** 1988. **Sales:** $2,000,000 (2000). **Emp:** 3. **Officers:** E.M. Blondheim, President; Connee Aune, Treasurer & Secty.; Howard Aune, Dir. of Marketing; James A. Fielder, Dir of Human Resources; James A. Fielder, Dir of Human Resources.

■ **27390** ■ **W.M. Tinder Inc.**
PO Box 2188
Manassas, VA 20110
Phone: (703)368-9544
Products: Lumber. **SIC:** 5031 (Lumber, Plywood & Millwork).

■ **27391** ■ **Universal Forest Products, Inc.**
2801 E Beltline, NE
Grand Rapids, MI 49505
Phone: (616)364-6161 **Fax:** (616)361-7534
URL: http://www.ufpi.com
Products: Wood, pressure treated lumber; Engineered building components; Roof trusses; Floor systems; Industrial lumber products. **SIC:** 5031 (Lumber, Plywood & Millwork). **Est:** 1955. **Sales:** $1,500,000,000 (1999). **Emp:** 2,400. **Officers:** William G. Currie, CEO & Vice Chairman; Mike Glenn, President.

■ **27392** ■ **Van Arsdale-Harris Lumber**
PO Box 34008
San Francisco, CA 94134
Phone: (415)467-8711 **Fax:** (415)467-8144
Products: Construction materials and machinery. **SIC:** 5031 (Lumber, Plywood & Millwork). **Sales:** $3,600,000 (2000). **Emp:** 12.

■ **27393** ■ **Washington Loggers Corp.**
3949 Iron Gate Rd.
Bellingham, WA 98226
Phone: (206)734-3660
Products: Wood and wood products. **SIC:** 5031 (Lumber, Plywood & Millwork). **Est:** 1948. **Sales:** $1,000,000 (2000). **Emp:** 2.

■ **27394** ■ **Western Home Center Inc.**
7600 Colerain Ave.
Cincinnati, OH 45239
Phone: (513)931-6300 **Fax:** (513)931-1309
Products: Construction materials and machinery. **SIC:** 5031 (Lumber, Plywood & Millwork). **Sales:** $59,000,000 (2000). **Emp:** 325.

■ **27395** ■ **W.N.C. Pallet and Forest Products Company Inc.**
PO Box 38
Candler, NC 28715
Phone: (828)667-5426 **Fax:** (828)665-4759
Products: Construction materials and machinery. **SIC:** 5031 (Lumber, Plywood & Millwork). **Sales:** $10,000,000 (2000). **Emp:** 100.

■ **27396** ■ **Woodworker's Supply Inc.**
1108 N Glenn Rd.
Casper, WY 82601
Phone: (307)237-5528
Free: (800)645-9292 **Fax:** (307)577-5272
Products: Woodworking machinery. **SIC:** 5084 (Industrial Machinery & Equipment). **Sales:** $56,300,000 (2000). **Emp:** 225. **Officers:** John Wirth Jr., CEO & President; Randy Rosalez, Controller.

■ **27397** ■ **Yezbak Enterprises**
108 N Beeson Blvd.
Uniontown, PA 15401
Phone: (724)438-5543 **Fax:** (724)483-1433
Products: Lumber products. **SIC:** 5031 (Lumber, Plywood & Millwork). **Sales:** $22,000,000 (1992). **Emp:** 75. **Officers:** Thomas J. Yezbak, Chairman of the Board & Treasurer.

■ **27398** ■ **J.W. Younce and W.T. Ralph Lumber Company Inc.**
52 Younce Rd.
PO Box 160
Pantego, NC 27860
Phone: (919)943-6166 **Fax:** (919)943-6162
Products: Lumber, including pine boards. **SIC:** 5031 (Lumber, Plywood & Millwork). **Est:** 1962. **Sales:** $5,000,000 (2000). **Emp:** 35. **Officers:** James W. Younce Jr., President.

■ **27399** ■ **Zeager Brothers Inc.**
4000 E Harrisburg Pke.
Middletown, PA 17057
Phone: (717)944-7481
Free: (800)346-8524 **Fax:** (717)944-7681
E-mail: sales@zeager.com
URL: http://www.zeager.com
Products: Landscape mulch and playground surfacing. **SICs:** 5099 (Durable Goods Nec); 5031 (Lumber, Plywood & Millwork). **Est:** 1967. **Sales:** $9,000,000 (1999). **Emp:** 25. **Officers:** Charles B. Zeager, President; Ernie Miller, Vice President; Ted Illjes, Secretary; Matt Jerchau, Sales/Marketing Contact, e-mail: webmaster@zeager.com; Robert Zeager, Customer Service Contact, e-mail: sales@zeager.com.

SIC Index

This section is arranged numerically by Standard Industrial Classification (SIC) codes. Companies are listed alphabetically within both their primary and secondary SIC codes. When the company name is a personal name, the company name is alphabetized by the surname unless the first name or initial(s) are part of a trade name. See the User's Guide at the front of this directory for additional information.

SIC 5012 — Automobiles & Other Motor Vehicles

A & D Enterprises, Import-Export [2156]
ABC Marketing [2163]
Action Chevrolet-Subaru-Geo [20576]
ADESA Auctions of Birmingham [20577]
ADESA Corp. [2181]
ADESA Indianapolis Inc. [20578]
ADT Automotive Inc. [2182]
ADT Ltd. [24486]
Akron Auto Auction Inc. [20580]
Alfa Romeo Distributors of North America [20581]
Allison Inc. [20582]
Allstate Sales and Leasing Corp. [20583]
Allstate Sales and Leasing Corp. [2219]
Altec Industries Inc. Eastern Div. [20584]
Amberstar International Inc. [10390]
American Bus Sales [2227]
American Carrier Equipment Inc. [20585]
American Emergency Vehicles [20586]
American Honda Motor Company Inc. [20587]
American Honda Motor Co. Inc. Acura Div. [20588]
American Isuzu Motors Inc. [20589]
American Lease Co. [20590]
Anderson Brothers Inc. [241]
Asbury Automotive Group [2259]
Atlantic International Corp. [20593]
Audi of America Inc. [20594]
Auto Dealers Exchange of Illinois [20595]
AutoBike Inc. [23529]
Autoxport Inc. [2300]
AWD International Inc. [13028]
B/T Western Corp. [2307]
Badger Body and Truck Equipment Co. [2308]
Badger Truck Center Inc. [20596]
Baer Sport Center [20597]
Beall Transport Equipment Co [2329]
Beasley Ford Inc.; Carl [20598]
Berge Ford Inc. [20599]
Better Buildings, Inc. [7055]
Big-2 Oldsmobile Inc. [20600]
Big Sky Auto Auction Inc. [20601]
Big Sky Auto Auction Inc. [2360]
Billings Truck Center [20602]
BMW of North America Inc. [20603]
Bond Equipment Company Inc. [20604]
Bowen Supply Inc. [15428]
Brown Inc.; C. Earl [20606]
Bruce Vehicle/Equipment Auction Services Inc. [346]
Buffalo White GMC Inc. [20607]
Byers Sons Inc.; Geo. [20608]
Cadillac Motor Car [2407]
Carlsbad Volvo [20610]
Carnegie Body Co. [2425]
Carolina FireMasters Inc. [24525]
Castriota Chevrolet Inc. [2433]
CCC Heavy Duty Trucks Co. [2436]
Central Atlantic Toyota Distributors Inc. [2437]

Clark Chevrolet Co.; Charles [20611]
Coachmen Industries Inc. Coachmen Vans Div. [20612]
Columbus Fair Auto Auction Inc. [20614]
Commercial Motor Co. [20615]
Connell Motor Truck Company Inc. [15908]
Consumers Financial Corp. [2480]
Cornhusker International [20616]
Cox Enterprises Inc. [2490]
Crain M-M Sales Inc. [2492]
Cunill Motors Inc. [20617]
Custom Car Center [20618]
Dal-Kawa Hijet [20619]
Dallas Auto Auction Inc. [20620]
Darlings [20621]
Detroit Auto Auction [20622]
Dixie Auto Auction Inc. [20623]
D.N. Motors Ltd. [2553]
Doonan Truck and Equipment Inc. [20624]
Dothan Auto Auction Inc. [20625]
Dow-Hammond Trucks Co. [2558]
DSW Inc. [20626]
Duckett Truck Center Inc. [20627]
Dyer Auto Auction Inc. [20629]
Dyer Motor Co. [20630]
Dynacraft Co. [20631]
Elliott Equipment Company Inc. [20632]
Engs Motor Truck Co. [20633]
Engs Motor Truck Co. [2592]
Farnsworth Armored Inc. [20634]
Ferrari North America Inc. [2613]
Fontaine Fifth Wheel Co. [2635]
Ford Body Company Inc. [20635]
Fresno Truck Center [20636]
Frontier Inc. [710]
Fruehauf Trailer Services, Inc. [20637]
Fyda Freightliner Inc. [20639]
G and S Motors Inc. [20640]
Generac Inc. [8782]
General Truck Sales Corp. [20642]
Great Lakes Peterbilt Inc. [20643]
Greater Lansing Auto Auction Inc. [20644]
Greater Mobile Auto Auction Div. [2702]
Gross and Hecht Trucking Corp. [2708]
Gulf Coast Auto Auction Inc. [20645]
Gulf States Toyota Inc. [2711]
Hale Trailer Brake & Wheel [2719]
Harvey Chevrolet Corp. [2729]
Henderson Auctions Inc. [24137]
Hews Company Inc. [7468]
Hill and Co., Inc.; O.S. [20649]
Hispania Trading Corporation [25680]
Houston Peterbilt Inc. [2763]
HT & T Co. [20650]
HT and T Company [2765]
Hyundai Motor America [20651]
Indiana Auto Auction Inc. [20652]
Industrial Development & Procurement [16150]
Intermountain Wholesale Hardware Inc. [20653]
International Marketing Systems Ltd. [864]
Iroquois Manufacturing Company, Inc. [2799]
Irv Seaver Motorcycles [2800]
Island Classic Automotive Inc. [20654]

Isuzu Motors America Inc. [20655]
JM Family Enterprises Inc. [20656]
Joyserv Company Ltd. [20657]
Kansas City Auto Auction Inc. [20658]
Kansas City Auto Auction Inc. [2838]
Kawasaki Motors Corporation U.S.A. [20659]
Kelley Inc.; Jack B. [22399]
Kenworth Sales Company Inc. [20660]
Kenworth of Tennessee Inc. [2850]
Kesler-Schaefer Auto Auction Inc. [20661]
Kia Motors America Inc. [20662]
KIC International [27330]
King Fleet Group [20663]
Kohl Sales; Walter A. [20664]
Kolstad Company Inc. [20665]
Kruse Inc. [20666]
La Beau Brothers Inc. [20667]
La Crosse Truck Center Inc. [20668]
Laforza Automobiles Inc. [2869]
LaFrance Equipment Corp. [24583]
Lakeland Auto Auction Inc. [20669]
Land Rover North America Inc. [2872]
Langer Equipment Company Inc. [20670]
Lexus Div. [2880]
Linder Equipment Co. [961]
Los Angeles Freightliner [20673]
Lotus Cars USA Inc. [2893]
Lowe Inc.; Devan [20674]
Masek Distributing Inc. [2921]
Mazda Motor of America Inc. [20675]
Mazda North American Operations [20676]
McLean County Truck Company Inc. [20677]
MCM Enterprise [2935]
Mel Farr Automotive Group Inc. [20678]
Mendon Leasing Corp. [2942]
Mercedes-Benz of North America Inc. [20679]
M.H. Equipment Corp. [16292]
Michelle International, Ltd. [127]
Mid-America Auto Auction [20680]
Mid States Classic Cars [2953]
Midwest Action Cycle [20681]
Midwest Truck Equipment Inc. [20682]
Minneapolis Northstar Auto Auction Inc. [20683]
Mission Valley Ford Trucks Sales Inc. [2974]
Mitsubishi Motor Sales of America Inc. [20684]
Mobile Cycle Center [23833]
Montgomery GMC Trucks Inc. [20686]
Moto America Inc. [20687]
Muscle Shoals Mack Sales Inc. [20688]
Nalley Cos. [3013]
Nashville Auto Auction Inc. [20689]
Natchez Equipment Company Inc. [20690]
Nelson Leasing Inc. [3024]
New York Motorcycle, Ltd. [20692]
NHK Intex Corp. [20693]
Nichols Motorcycle Supply, Inc. [20694]
Nissan Motor Corporation U.S.A. [20695]
Nissan Motor Corporation U.S.A. Infiniti Div. [20696]
Norse Motors Inc. [3039]
North East Auto-Marine Terminal Inc. [20697]
Northland Industrial Truck Company Inc. [20699]
Northwest Truck and Trailer Sales Inc. [20700]

O'Connor Truck Sales Inc. [3053]
Oldsmobile Div. [3062]
PACCAR International [3071]
Paccar Technical Ctr. [3073]
Pak-Mor Manufacturing Co. [20702]
Peach State Truck Centers [3088]
Peck Road Ford Truck Sales Inc. [20703]
Perfection Equipment Co. [20704]
Peterbilt of Knoxville Inc. [3094]
Pfeiffer Hijet [3096]
Phoenix Manufacturing Incorporated [20705]
Pollard Co.; C.E. [20706]
Pollard Co.; C.E. [3101]
Potomac Industrial Trucks Inc. [16411]
Pottstown Truck Sales Inc. [20707]
Putnam Truck Parts [3127]
R & F Auto Sales [20709]
Reliable Chevrolet Inc. [20710]
Reliance Trailer Manufacturing Inc. [20711]
Roberts Motor Co. [20713]
Rocket Supply Corp. [20714]
Rol-Lift Corp. [3173]
Ruxer Ford, Lincoln, Mercury Inc. [20715]
Saab Cars USA Inc. [20716]
Sadisco of Florence [3178]
St. Pete Auto Auction Inc. [20717]
Sam Yanen Ford Sales Inc. [3184]
Savage Inc. [20718]
Schetky Northwest Sales Inc. [20719]
Schmid Motor Inc.; Don [20720]
Service Unlimited [3208]
Silo International Inc. [8020]
Simpson Buick Co. [20721]
Smith Motor Sales [3233]
Sonnen Mill Valley BMW [20722]
Sound Ford Inc. [20723]
Southeast Toyota Distributors Inc. [20724]
Southern Architectural Systems, Inc. [8047]
Southside Ford Truck Sales Inc. [20725]
Southwest Florida Auction Inc. [20726]
Specialty Hearse and Ambulance Sales
    Corp. [20727]
Specialty Hearse and Ambulance Sales
    Corp. [3247]
Specialty Vehicles, Inc. [20728]
Specialty Vehicles Inc. [3248]
Spong Trade Co. [20729]
Stan's Towing & Repair [3261]
Subaru of America Inc. [20731]
Sunderland Motor Company Inc. [20732]
Superior Auto Sales Inc. [20733]
Superior Auto Sales Inc. [3285]
Susquehanna Motor Company Inc. [20734]
Sweeney Brothers Tractor Co. [1308]
Tate Jr.'s Murray Auto Auction Inc.; Jim [20735]
Tate-Reynolds Company Inc. [20736]
Taylor-Dunn Manufacturing Co. [16550]
Toyota Motor Sales U.S.A. Inc. [20737]
Transnational Motors Inc. [20738]
Tri-State Auction Company Inc. [3336]
Triumph Motorcycles America Ltd. [3342]
Truck Enterprises Inc. [20739]
Truck Equipment Inc. [3347]
Truck Equipment Sales Inc. [3348]
United Export Import, Inc. [20740]
United School Bus Seat Services [3369]
United States Export Co. [20741]
University Motors Ltd. [3376]
Utility Trailer Sales of Oregon Inc. [20742]
Versatile Vehicles Inc. [24031]
Volkswagen of America Inc. [20743]
Volkswagen of America Inc. Industrial Engine
    Div. [20744]
Volvo Cars of North America Inc. [20745]
Wallwork Inc.; W.W. [20747]
Waters Truck and Tractor Company Inc. [3402]
Watson Truck and Supply Inc. [3405]
Weed Chevrolet Company Inc. [20749]
Wilson Capital Truck L.L.C.; Elliot [20750]
Wolfe's Terre Haute Auto Auction Inc. [20751]
Wolfington Body Company Inc. [20752]
Woodpecker Truck and Equipment Inc. [20753]
World Wide Equipment Inc. [20754]
Wrangler Power Products Inc. [3447]
Yamaha Motor Corporation USA [20755]
York Truck Center Inc. [20756]

Zappia Enterprises Inc. [20757]

SIC 5013 — Motor Vehicle Supplies & New Parts

4 Wheel Center Inc. [2147]
A-1 Battery Distributors [2149]
A & A Brake Service Co. Inc. [2151]
A and A Pump Co. [22014]
A and D Auto Parts Inc. [2155]
A & D Enterprises, Import-Export [2156]
A & M Trading Company Inc. [2157]
A & P Auto Parts Inc. [2158]
AA & A Enterprises Inc. [19721]
AAA Parts of Biltmore Inc. [2160]
Aamco Transmissions Inc. [2161]
Aargus Truck & Auto [2162]
Abc Mobile Brake [2164]
Able Welding Co. [2165]
AC-Delco/GM Service Parts Operation [2166]
Acarex Inc. [2167]
Accupart International [2168]
Ace Battery Inc. [2170]
Ace Truck Body, Inc. [2171]
Ace Truck Equipment Co. [2172]
Acme Auto Inc. [2173]
ACME Automotive Accessories Group [2174]
Acme Group [2175]
Acra Custom Wheel [2176]
A.C.T. Vehicle Equipment, Inc. [2177]
Action Fabrication & Truck Equipment, Inc. [2179]
Addison Auto Parts Co. [2180]
Advance Stores Company Inc. [2183]
AEA Distributors [2184]
Aeon International Corp. [190]
AER Inc. [2185]
Ag-Land FS Inc. [194]
AG Truck Equipment Co. [2187]
AGR Warehouse Distributors [2188]
AI Automotive Corp. [2189]
AI International Corp. [2190]
Air-Ax Suspension Systems [2191]
Air Flow Systems Inc. [2192]
Aisin World Corporation of America [2193]
AL-KO KOBER Corp. [2194]
Alabama Crankshaft and Engine [2195]
Alabama Crankshaft and Engine Warehouse
    Inc. [2196]
Alabama Truck Body & Equipment, Inc. [2197]
Alban Engine Power Systems [2198]
Alden Autoparts Warehouse Inc. [2202]
Alfa Romeo Distributors of North America [20581]
All-Car Distributors Inc. [2203]
All-Power Inc. [2207]
All Products Automotive Inc. [2208]
Allied Bearing [2209]
Allied Bearings & Supply [2210]
Allied Body Works Inc. [2212]
Allied Inc. [2213]
Allied Truck Equipment Corp. [2215]
AlliedSignal Automotive Aftermarket [2216]
AlliedSignal Automotive Catalyst Co. [2217]
Allparts Inc. [2218]
Allpro Corp. [21381]
Allyn Air Seat Co. [2221]
Alretta Truck Parts Inc. [2222]
Alsdorf International Ltd. [13554]
Aluminum Line Products Co. [2223]
Amalgamated Automotive Industries Inc. [2224]
Amarillo Clutch & Driveshaft Co. [2225]
American Auto Salvage [2226]
American Carrier Systems, Inc. [2228]
American Ladders & Scaffolds, Inc. [2230]
American Marketing International [2231]
American Mobile Home Products Inc. [2232]
American Performance [2233]
American Suzuki Motor Corp. [20591]
American Suzuki Motor Corp. [2234]
American Tire Distributors [2235]
Americas Trade & Supply Co. [2237]
Ample Technology [2238]
Anderson Auto Parts Co. [2239]
Anderson & Spring Firestone [2240]

Antelope Truck Stop [2241]
AP Parts Co. [2243]
APD Transmission Parts [2244]
Applied Industrial Technologies [2246]
A.P.S. Inc. [2248]
Area Distributors, Inc. [2249]
Arnold Inc.; S.M. [2251]
Arnold Motor Supply Co. [2252]
Arrow Safety Device Co. [2254]
Arrow Speed Warehouse [2255]
Arrow Trucks and Parts Co. [2256]
Arvin Industries Inc. [2257]
Arvin Industries Inc. North American Automotive
    Div. [2258]
ASEC Manufacturing [2260]
ASI Erie [2261]
ATC International [2262]
Atlanta Wheels & Accessories, Inc. [2264]
Atlantic Mobile Homes and RV Supplies
    Corp. [2266]
Autco [24510]
Authorized Motor Parts [2268]
Auto Body Supply of Orem [21394]
Auto Clutch/All Brake Inc. [2269]
Auto Collision Inc. [2270]
Auto Components Inc. [2271]
Auto Electric Sales and Service Co. [2272]
Auto Parts Association [2273]
Auto Parts Club Inc. [2274]
Auto Parts Wholesale [2276]
Auto Safety House Inc. [2277]
Auto Trends Inc. [2279]
Auto Truck Inc. [2280]
Auto Wares Inc. [2281]
Auto Wheel Service Inc. [2282]
Autoline Industries Inc. [2283]
Automoco Corp. [2284]
Automotive Diagnostics [2285]
Automotive Dryers Inc. [2287]
Automotive Ignition Company Inc. [2289]
Automotive Importing Manufacturing Inc. [2290]
Automotive Industries Inc. [2291]
Automotive Parts Distributors [2292]
Automotive Parts Headquarters Inc. [2293]
Automotive Parts Wholesaler [2294]
Automotive Sales Co. [2295]
Automotive Supply Associates [2296]
Automotive Supply Co. [2297]
Automotive Trades Div. [2298]
Automotive Wholesalers Co. [2299]
Autoxport Inc. [2300]
Awalt Wholesale Inc. [2301]
B and B Motor and Control Inc. [2303]
B & B Parts Distributing [2304]
B and C Auto Supply [2305]
B & N Industries [13578]
Badger Body and Truck Equipment Co. [2308]
Badger Trailer and Equipment Corp. [2309]
Baker Truck Equipment [2311]
BAL RV Products Group [15799]
Bales & Truitt Company Inc. [14336]
Ballenger Automotive Service [2313]
Baltimore & Washington Truck Equipment,
    Inc. [2314]
Banjo's Performancenter Inc. [2315]
Banks Lumber Company Inc. [27286]
Barjan Products, L.P. [2316]
Barker-Jennings Corp. [2317]
Barnes Motor and Parts Co. [2318]
Baron [2320]
Barron Motor Inc. [2321]
Barstow Truck Parts and Equipment Co. [2324]
Basic Convenience Foods [2325]
Batteries Plus L.P. [2326]
Battery and Tire Warehouse Inc. [2327]
Battery Warehouse [8422]
Beardslee Transmission Equipment Company
    Inc. [2330]
Bearing Distributors [16730]
Bearing Distributors Inc. [2331]
Bearing Distributors Inc. [2332]
Bearing Distributors Inc. [2333]
Bearing Distributors, Inc. [2334]
Bearing Distributors Inc. [2335]
Bearing Distributors Inc. [2336]
Bearing Engineering [2338]

Bearings & Drives, Inc. [2339]
Bearings & Drives, Inc. [2340]
Bearings & Drives, Inc. [2341]
Bearings & Drives, Inc. [2342]
Bearings & Industrial Supply Co., Inc. [16741]
Bearings & Transmission [2343]
Beck-Arnley Worldparts Corp. [2344]
Beckman Co.; C.C. [18457]
Beerman Auto Supply Inc. [2345]
Behrens Supply Co. [2346]
Bennington Co.; J.C. [2348]
Berg Fargo Motor Supply Inc. [2350]
Berint Trading, Ltd. [13593]
Berry Tire Company Inc. [2351]
Best Battery Company Inc. [2352]
Best Bilt Parts [2353]
Best Plastics Inc. [2354]
Bestop Inc. [2355]
Better Brake Parts Inc. [2356]
Big A Auto Parts [2357]
Big B Automotive Warehouse [2358]
Big Boys Toys [2359]
Biglow Industrial Company Inc. [2361]
Billings Truck Center [20602]
Bill's Battery Co. Inc. [2362]
Binghamton Truck Body & Equipment Corp. [2363]
Birmingham Electric Battery Co. [2364]
Bisho Company, Inc.; J.R. [2365]
Bittle American Inc.; J. [2366]
Blanchard Auto Electric Co. [2367]
Blankenship and Company Inc.; E. [2368]
Blue Hen Spring Works, Inc. [2369]
Bond Equipment Company Inc. [20604]
Bonded Motors, Inc. [2371]
Bonfield Brothers, Inc. [22085]
Borg Warner Automotive Friction Products [2372]
Bornell Supply [2373]
Bowes Industries Inc. [2375]
Bowman Distribution [16759]
Bragg and Sons; N.H. [16762]
Brake & Clutch, Inc. [2377]
Brake Sales Co. Inc. [2378]
Brake and Wheel Parts Industries [2379]
Brandywine Auto Parts Inc. [2381]
Brannon Tire Corp. [2382]
Brittain Brothers Inc. [2387]
Brock Supply Co. [2389]
Brocks Auto Supply [2390]
Brookline Machine Co. [2391]
Brookline Machine Co. [2392]
Brookline Machine Co. [2393]
Brookline Machine Company, Inc. [2394]
Brookline Machine Co. Williams Brothers Div. [2395]
Brost International Trading Co. [24271]
Brown Marine Service Inc. [18471]
Brown and Sons Co. Inc. [2397]
Brown & Sons NAPA Auto Parts [2398]
Bullington Lift Trucks [15855]
Burklund Distributors Inc. [10645]
Burnstine's Distributing Corp. [2400]
Burquip Truck Bodies & Equipment [2401]
Burton Auto Supply Inc. [2402]
Butler County Motor Company Inc. [2404]
BWD Automotive Corp. [2405]
Byers Sons Inc.; Geo. [20608]
Cal-North Auto Brokers Inc. [2408]
California Affiliated Representative Inc. [2409]
Callahan Inc.; S.X. [2411]
CalMark Custom Covers [2412]
Calmini Products Inc. [2413]
Calumet Auto Recycling and Sales Inc. [2414]
Cantrell Auto Supply Company Inc. [2415]
Capitol Chevrolet Inc. [20609]
Caple-Shaw Industries Inc. [2418]
Capriotto and Sons Inc. [2420]
Car-Go Battery Co. [2421]
Car Parts Inc. [2422]
Car Quest Auto Parts Co. [2423]
Carnegie Body Co. [2425]
Carolina Rim and Wheel Co. [18475]
Carolina's Auto Supply House, Inc. [2426]
Carquest [2427]
CARQUEST Corp. [2428]
Carquest Distribution Co. [2429]

Carquest Distribution Co. Cleaner and Equipment Div. [2430]
Carrington Distributing Company Inc. [2431]
Casale Engineering Inc. [2432]
Catamount North [2434]
Celestial Mercantile Corporation [14059]
Central Diesel, Inc. [2438]
Centurion Vehicles Inc. [2439]
Century Wheel & Rim Corp. [2440]
Cenweld Corp. [2441]
Certified Automotive Warehouse Inc. [2442]
Certified Parts Corp. [18477]
Champion Auto Stores Inc. [2443]
Chapman Co.; J.T. [2444]
Charleston Auto Parts Company Inc. [2445]
Chesapeake Rim and Wheel Distributors [2446]
Chesapeake Rim & Wheel Distributors Inc. [2447]
Chicago Chain & Transmission [2448]
Churubusco Distribution Service Center [16797]
Cincinnati Belt & Transmission [2449]
Clarion Sales Corp. [2450]
Clark Brothers Instrument Co. [2451]
Clark County Wholesale Inc. [2452]
Clover Auto Supply Inc. [2455]
CNEAD Division [2456]
C.O. Tools Inc. [2457]
Coach House Products [2458]
Coast Counties Truck and Equipment Co. [2459]
Coast Distribution System [2460]
Coil Center Corp. [19880]
Commercial Body Corp. [2462]
Commercial Body Corp. [2463]
Commercial Body Corp. [2464]
Commercial Body Corp. [2465]
Commercial Body Corp. [2466]
Commercial Motors [2467]
Compact Performance Inc. [2469]
Competition Parts Warehouse Inc. [2470]
Complete Auto & Truck Parts [2471]
Connecticut Driveshaft Inc. [2472]
Connecticut Driveshaft Inc. [2473]
Connell Motor Truck Company Inc. [15908]
Consolidated Service Corp. [2475]
Consolidated Truck Parts Inc. [2476]
Consolidated Utility & Equipment Service [2477]
Consulier Engineering Inc. [2479]
Control Associates Inc. [2481]
Conversion Components Inc. [2482]
Coronet Parts Manufacturing Co. Inc. [2485]
Corts Truck Equipment, Inc. [2486]
Cosmos Enterprises, Inc. [2487]
Covington Diesel Inc. [2489]
Crain Automotive Inc. [2491]
Creger Auto Company Inc. [2493]
Crenshaw Corp. [2494]
Crest Truck Equipment Co. Inc. [2495]
Crotty Corp. [2497]
CRW Parts, Inc. [2498]
CS Battery Inc. [2499]
Cummins Cumberland Inc. [2504]
Cummins Gateway Inc. [2505]
Cummins Great Plains Diesel Inc. [2507]
Cummins Intermountain Inc. [2508]
Cummins Michigan Inc. [2509]
Cummins Midstates Power Inc. [2510]
Cummins North Central Inc. [2511]
Cummins Ohio Inc. [2512]
Cummins Rocky Mountain, Inc. [2514]
Cummins Southern Plains Inc. [2515]
Custom Trim of America [2518]
D & A Distributing [2519]
D E B Industries, Inc. [10890]
D & H Tire Service [2520]
D & M Distributing [2521]
D & W Distributing Co. Inc. [2523]
Dallas Peterbilt Inc. [2524]
Dallas Wheels & Accessories, Inc. [2525]
Dana World Trade Div. [2526]
Darlings [20621]
Dave's Used Auto Parts Inc. [2529]
Davey Motor Co. [2530]
Day Manufacturing Co.; S.A. [2532]
Dealer Chemical Corp. [2533]
Defiance Inc. [8620]
Dega Technologies [2536]
Delphi Saginaw Steering Systems [2537]

Denman Tire Corp. [2538]
Dependable Motor Parts [2539]
Detroit Diesel Overseas Corp. [2541]
Detroit Pump and Manufacturing Co. [23137]
Dial Battery Paint & Auto Supply [21429]
Dickinson Supply Inc. [2543]
Diesel Equipment Specialists [2544]
Diesel Power Equipment Co. [2545]
Discount Engine Exchange Inc. [2547]
Distributors Warehouse Inc. [2548]
Dixie Bearings, Inc. [2549]
Dixie International Co. [2551]
Dixie Parts and Equipment Co. [2552]
D.N. Motors Ltd. [2553]
Do It Best Corp. [7275]
Dodge City Cooperative Exchange Inc. [2554]
Domestic & International Technology [2555]
Doonan Truck and Equipment Inc. [20624]
Dorfman Auto Supply Inc. [2556]
Dorian International Inc. [24105]
Dorman Products Div. [2557]
Drake America Div. [2559]
Dreyco Inc. [2561]
Dreyfus & Assoc. [2562]
Drive Train Industries Inc. [2563]
Drive Train Industries Inc. [2564]
Drivetrain Specialists [2565]
Drucker Associates, Inc. [2566]
Duromotive Industries [2568]
DVH Co. [2569]
E & G Auto Parts Inc. [2570]
East Jordan Cooperative Co. [2571]
Eastern Auto Parts Company Inc. [2572]
Eastern Bearings Inc. [2573]
Eastern Tool Warehouse Corp. [2574]
Edgerton Forge Inc. [15977]
Edwards Co.; Frank [2576]
Eggimann Motor and Equipment Sales Inc. [2577]
Electric Garage Supply Co. [2579]
Electric Specialties Inc. [2580]
Elizabethtown Distributing Co. Inc. [2581]
Elliott Auto Supply Company Inc. [2583]
Ellis Inc. [2584]
Emco Inc. [2587]
Engine & Performance Warehouse Inc. [2590]
Engineered Drives [2591]
Engs Motor Truck Co. [20633]
EPR Automotive Warehouse [2593]
Equipment Rental [2595]
Ertel Products Inc. [2596]
ESCO Industries [2597]
Exhaust Specialties II [2599]
Export Division of Gordon E. Hansen Agency Inc. [2600]
Ezon Inc. [2601]
F & W Rallye Engineering [2602]
Fabco Industries, Inc. [2603]
Factory Motor Parts [2604]
Fair Company Inc.; R.E. [2605]
Fairfield Supply Co. [2606]
Fallsway Equipment Company Inc. [16005]
Fayetteville Automotive Warehouse [2608]
Felt Auto Supply [2609]
Fenders and More Inc. [2610]
Ferodo America [2612]
Ferrari North America Inc. [2613]
Fiamm Technologies [2614]
Filter Supply Co. [2615]
Filtran Div. [2616]
First Automotive Inc. [2618]
First State Petroleum Services [22278]
Fisher Auto Parts [2619]
Fisher Auto Parts Inc. [2620]
Fisher Auto Parts Inc. [2621]
Fisher Auto Parts Inc. Manlove Div. [2622]
Fisher Auto Parts Professionals [2623]
Fisheries Supply Co. Industrial Div. [18503]
Flaherty Company Inc.; L.H. [2627]
Fleet Parts Distributor [2628]
Fleet Pride [2629]
Fleet Specialties Div. [2630]
Flex-a-Lite Consolidated [2631]
Florida Detroit Diesel-Allison North Inc. [2632]
Florig Equipment [2633]
Flowers Auto Parts Co. [2634]
Fontaine Modification Co. [2636]

Forbes & Co. [2637]
Foreign Car Parts Inc. [2638]
Forster Co.; John M. [2641]
Fort Wayne Fleet Equipment [2642]
Four M Parts Warehouse [2643]
Freedland Industries Corp. [2646]
Freedman Seating Co. [2647]
Fremont Electric Company Inc. [2648]
Frey the Wheelman Inc. [2649]
Friend Truck Equipment, Inc.; Matt [2651]
Frigi-Cool/RVAC Inc. [2652]
Frontier Truck Equipment and Parts Co. [2653]
Fruehauf Trailer Services, Inc. [20637]
FTC Corp. [2654]
Full Bore - Cycle Lines USA [20638]
Full Bore - Cycle Lines USA [2655]
Fullwell Products Inc. [2656]
Fumoto Engineering of America [2657]
Gainesville Industrial Supply [2658]
Garden Island Motors Ltd. [20641]
Gates InterAmerica [16890]
Gateway Auto Parts [2662]
Gateway Tire Company Inc. [2663]
Gear Clutch & Joint [2667]
Gear & Wheel Corp. [2668]
Generac Corp. [8782]
General Auto Parts Inc. [2669]
General Parts Corp. [2671]
General Parts, Inc. [2672]
General Parts Inc. [2673]
General Truck Body Co. [2675]
General Truck Parts and Equipment Co. [2676]
General Truck Sales Corp. [20642]
Genuine Auto Parts Co. [2677]
Genuine Parts Co. [2678]
Genuine Parts Company of West Virginia
  Inc. [2679]
Gerhardt's Inc. [2680]
Giles and Ransome Inc. [16065]
Gillespie Oil Company Inc. [2681]
Glasparts Inc. [2682]
Glass Specialty Inc. [2683]
Global Metrics Inc. [2684]
Global Motorsport Group Inc. [2685]
Globe Motorist Supply Company Inc. [2686]
GM Service Parts Operations [2687]
Gold Eagle Co. [2688]
Gooch Brake and Equipment Co. [2690]
Gopher Bearing [2692]
Gor-den Industries Inc. [2693]
Gorence Mobile Marketing Distribution [2694]
Grant Manufacturing & Equipment Co. [2695]
Grant Truck Equipment Co. [2696]
Graves Automotive Supply [2697]
Graywell Equipment Corp. [2698]
Great Lakes Power Products [2699]
Great Lakes Power Products [2700]
Green Manufacturing Company Inc. [2703]
Green Meadow Auto Salvage, Inc. [2704]
Green Point Inc. [2705]
Gruener Sales Inc. [2709]
GTR Truck Equipment [2710]
Gulf States Toyota Inc. [2711]
GWS Automotive and Truck Equipment Sales
  Inc. [2712]
H & D Transmission [2713]
H and H Distributors Inc. [2714]
H & H Sales Company, Inc. [2715]
Hadon Security Company Inc. [2716]
Hahn Automotive Warehouse Inc. [2717]
Halasz from Dallas [2718]
Hale Trailer Brake & Wheel [2719]
Halpin Equipment Corp.; Tim [2720]
Hanco Corp. [2721]
Hansen Machine Co. [20027]
Hanson Tire Service Inc. [2724]
Hardlines Marketing Inc. [13735]
Harlow International [2725]
Hartsook Equipment & Pump Services [22340]
Hatch Grinding Co. [2730]
Havice Inc.; James F. [14121]
Hawaiian Housewares, Ltd. [15521]
Hawkins Auto Parts [2731]
Heafner Company Inc.; J.H. [2734]
Heafner Tires & Products [2735]
Heavy Parts International [2736]

Hedahl's Auto Parts [2738]
Hedahl's Automotive Center [2739]
Heidema Brothers Inc. [20647]
Hella Inc. [2740]
Henderson Wheel and Warehouse Supply [2741]
Herzogs Auto Parts Inc. [2744]
Hesco Parts Corp. [2745]
Hibdon Tire Center Inc. [2748]
Hickory Auto Parts Inc. [2749]
High Performance Distributors [2750]
Highland Auto and Truck Inc. [2751]
Highland Auto and Truck Inc. [2752]
Highway Auto Parts Inc. [2753]
Hill and Co., Inc.; O.S. [20649]
Hinojosa Parts Warehouse [2754]
Hitachi America Ltd. [8846]
Hoekstra Truck Equipment Company, Inc. [2758]
Hoffmann Aircraft Inc. [98]
Hoffmeyer Co. [2759]
Hogan and Associates Inc.; T.J. [2760]
Horn Plastics Inc. [22982]
Horsepower Control System [2761]
Howard Tire Service Inc. [2764]
Hunt Co.; C.P. [2766]
Hunt Co.; C.P. [2767]
Ichikoh America Inc. [2769]
Ideal Sales and Distributing Company Inc. [2770]
Impulse Merchandisers Inc. [2772]
Industrial Parts Distributors Inc. [2774]
Industrial Transmission Inc. [2776]
Industrial Transmission Inc. [2777]
Inland Detroit Diesel/Allison [2778]
Inland Detroit Diesel-Allison Inc. [2779]
Inland Truck Parts [2780]
Inland Truck Parts [2781]
Inland Truck Parts [2782]
Inland Truck Parts [2783]
Inland Truck Parts [2784]
Inland Truck Parts [2785]
Inland Truck Parts [2786]
Inland Truck Parts [2787]
Inland Truck Parts [2788]
Interamerican Motor Corp. [2790]
Intercon, Inc. [2791]
International Brake Industries Inc. [2792]
International Consulting & Contracting
  Services [7517]
International Hi-Tech Trading Corp. [2793]
International Trade Group [18860]
International Trade & Telex Corp. [19378]
Interstate Bearing Technologies [2795]
Intertrade, Inc. [13147]
Intraco Corp. [2796]
Iowa Export Import Trading Co. [867]
IPD Co., Inc. [2797]
IQ Holdings Inc. [14133]
IQ Products Co. [2798]
Isspro Inc. [2801]
ITM, Inc. [2804]
ITTCO Sales Co., Inc. [2805]
J & J Supply, Inc. [21467]
J-Mark [2806]
Jaguar Cars [2809]
Jahm Inc. [2810]
Jarvis Supply Co. [16183]
Jarvis Supply Co. [2812]
JBA Headers [2814]
JC Whitney & Co. [2815]
JDB Merchandising [2816]
Jersey Truck Equipment Co. [2818]
Jideco of Bardstown Inc. [2820]
Jiffy Metal Products Co. [2821]
Johnson Distributing, Inc. [2824]
Johnson Motor Sales Inc. [2825]
Johnson and Towers Inc. [2826]
Johnston Distributing Co. [2827]
Johnstown Axle Works Inc. [2828]
Joint Clutch and Gear Service Inc. [2829]
Joint and Clutch Service Inc. [2830]
Joint and Clutch Service Inc. [2831]
Jones Inc.; Charlie C. [2834]
Jones-McIntosh Tobacco Company Inc. [26314]
Jordan Research Corp. [2836]
Kato Radiator Diesel Systems [2839]
Kay Automotive Graphics [2842]
KD Lamp Co. [2843]

Keeter Manufacturing, Inc. [2844]
Keltner Enterprises Inc. [2846]
Kenco [2847]
Kennedy Engine Co. [2848]
Kentucky Bearings Service [2849]
Keystone Automotive Industries Inc. [2851]
Keystone Automotive Operations Inc. [2852]
Keystone Detroit Diesel Allison Inc. [2853]
Kieser and Sons; Ellwood [2854]
KK Motorcycle Supply [2858]
Kmart Trading Services, Inc. [26113]
Kohl Sales; Walter A. [20664]
Kolstad Company Inc. [20665]
Korber and Co.; J. [2859]
Kostelecky's Fiberglass [2860]
KPK Truck Body Manufacturing and Equipment
  Distributing Company Inc. [2861]
Kraco Enterprises Inc. [2862]
Kranz Automotive Supply [2863]
Kunkel Services Co. [2865]
Kunz Oil Company Inc. [22411]
Kustom Fit [2866]
KYB Corporation of America [2867]
L-Z Truck Equipment Co., Inc. [2868]
La Crosse Truck Center Inc. [20668]
Lafayette Auto Electric [8964]
Lahr Co.; W.E. [2870]
Lakeland Enterprises, Inc. [2871]
LaVanture Products Co. [2874]
L.B. Industries Inc. [2875]
LDI, Ltd. [20671]
Leisure Components/SF Technology [2878]
LeMans Corp. [20672]
Lewisohn Sales Company Inc. [7600]
Lightbourn Equipment Co. [2881]
Liland Trade & Radiator Service Inc. [2882]
Lincoln Clutch and Brake Supply [2883]
Lindeco International Corp. [2884]
LoJack of California Corp. [2887]
LoJack of New Jersey Corp. [24586]
LoJack of New Jersey Corp. [2888]
Lombard Management Inc. [2889]
Long Motor Corp. [2890]
Long Trailer & Body Service, Inc. [2891]
Loock & Company Inc.; R.J. [2892]
Los Angeles Freightliner [20673]
Louisiana Lift & Equipment, Inc. [2894]
Lucas Industries Inc. Aftermarket Operations
  Div. [2895]
Lundahl Inc.; Warner T. [2898]
Lynwood Battery Manufacturing Co. [2899]
M & L Motor Supply Co. [2900]
M & R Distributors Inc. [2901]
Maats Enterprises [19421]
Machine Service, Inc. [2902]
Machine Service Inc. [2903]
Machine Service, Inc. [2904]
Magna Automotive Industries [2906]
Magna Graphics [2907]
Maier Manufacturing [2910]
Maine Equipment Company, Inc. [2911]
Maine Ladder & Staging Co., Inc. [2912]
Maldaver Company Inc. [2913]
Manlove Auto Parts [2914]
Mannesmann Corp. [16260]
Manning Equipment Inc. [2915]
Mar and Sons Inc.; J [16263]
Maraj International [6461]
Marietta Ignition Inc. [2916]
Marnal Corp. [2918]
Marvin Land Systems, Inc. [2919]
Marwil Products Co. [2920]
Matco Tools Corp. [2922]
Matheny Motor Truck Co. [2923]
Matheson Trucking Inc.; R.B. [2924]
Mathewson Co.; George A. [2925]
Matt Friend Truck Equipment Inc. [2926]
Mattos Inc. [21498]
Maz Auto [2927]
MBL USA Corp. [24286]
McCallum Motor Supply Co. [2928]
McCullough Distributing Company, Inc. [2931]
McGraw Group Inc. [17022]
McGuire Bearing [2933]
McGuire Bearing [2934]
MCM Enterprise [2935]

Mechanical Drives Co. [2936]
Mechanic's Auto Parts, Inc. [2937]
Medart Inc. [2938]
Mellen Parts Company Inc. [2940]
Menco Corp. [2941]
Merchants Inc. [2943]
Merrill Co. [2944]
Metrix South Inc. [2947]
Metropolitan Diesel Supply Co. [2948]
Mid-City Automotive Warehouse Inc. [2950]
Mid Michigan Trailer & Truck Equipment, Inc. [2951]
Mid-State Automotive [2952]
Midway Trading, Inc. [2958]
Midwest Auto Parts Distributors Inc. [2959]
Midwest Truck and Auto Parts Inc. [2960]
Mighty Distributing System of America Inc. [2962]
Mill Supply Corp. [2963]
Miller Bearings Inc. [2964]
Miller Bearings Inc. [2965]
Miller Bearings Inc. [2966]
Miller Bearings Inc. [2967]
Minnesota Mining & Manufacturing Co. [21147]
Minnesota Mining & Manufacturing Co. Do-It-Yourself Div. [17044]
Mirly Truck Center Inc. [2973]
Missouri Power Transmission [2975]
Missouri Power Transmission [2976]
Mitsubishi Motor Sales of America Inc. [20684]
Mobile Automotive Diagnostic [2978]
Monroe Truck Equipment Inc. [2980]
Moog Louisville Wholesale [2982]
Moonachie Co. [17048]
Morgan's Auto Parts [2985]
Morse Parker Motor Supply [2987]
Moss Dynamics [2988]
Motion Ind. [2989]
Motion Industries [2990]
Motion Industries [2991]
Motion Industries, Inc. [2992]
Motor Master Products [2993]
Motor Parts & Bearing Co. [2994]
Motor Parts and Supply Inc. [2995]
Motor Products Company Inc. [2996]
Motorcycle Stuff Inc. [2997]
Mt. Kisco Truck & Auto Parts [2998]
Mt. Kisco Truck and Fleet Supply [2999]
Mount Vernon Auto Parts [3000]
Mountain Muffler [3001]
Mr. Hub Cap [3002]
Mulgrew Oil Co. [22501]
Mullis Petroleum Co. [22502]
Mundy Enterprises, Inc.; K.C. [3003]
Murdock Companies Inc. [9109]
Murdock Electric and Supply Co. [17063]
Murray; Thomas W. [3004]
Mustang Power Systems [3005]
Mutual Truck Parts Co. [3006]
MVR Auto Refinishing Supplies [21511]
MVR Auto Refinishing Supplies [3008]
Myco Plastics [3009]
Myers Equipment Corp. [3010]
Myers Industries Inc. [3011]
Nankang USA Inc. [3014]
Napa Auto Parts (Burlington, Vermont) [13842]
National Bushing and Parts Company Inc. [3015]
National Impala Association [3016]
Nationwide Ladder & Equipment Company Inc. [7768]
NBC Truck Equipment Inc. [3018]
Neapco Inc. [3019]
Neely Coble Company Inc. [20691]
Neely TBA [3020]
Neil's Automotive Service, Inc. [3022]
Neil's Automotive Service, Inc. [3023]
Nelson Leasing Inc. [3024]
Ness Company Inc. [3025]
Ness Trading Co. [3026]
New Haven Body, Inc. [3027]
New Haven Filter Co. [3028]
New World Research Corp. [3030]
New York Motorcycle, Ltd. [20692]
Nichols Fleet Equipment [3031]
Nicolet Imaging Systems [24602]
Nielsen Oil and Propane Inc. [22518]
Nikzak [3033]

Nippondenso of Los Angeles Inc. [3034]
Nissan Motor Corporation U.S.A. [20695]
Noel's Automotive Warehouse [3036]
Noleen Racing Inc. [3037]
North American Cylinders Inc. [3041]
North Penn Equipment [3042]
North Riverside Venture Inc. [3044]
Northern Auto Supply Co. [3046]
Northland Equipment Company, Inc. [3047]
Norwood Auto Parts Co. [3048]
Nova Clutch Inc. [3049]
Number One International [3050]
Nylen Products Inc. [3051]
Ochterbeck Distributing Company Inc. [3052]
OEM Parts Center Inc. [3054]
Offenhauser Sales Corp. [3056]
Ohio Light Truck Parts Co. [3058]
Ohio Truck Equipment, Inc. [3059]
O.K. Auto Parts [3060]
Orange Motor Company Inc. [3063]
O'Reilly Automotive Inc. [3064]
Orlando Yamaha [20701]
Orscheln Farm and Home Supply Inc. [1109]
Ost and Ost Inc. [3065]
Ozark Automotive Distributors Inc. [3066]
P & B Truck Accessories [3067]
P and E Inc. [3068]
P-G Products Inc. [3069]
PACCAR Inc. Parts Div. [3070]
PACCAR International [3071]
PACCAR Leasing Corp. [3072]
Pacific Dualies, Inc. [3074]
Pacific Supply Co. [3075]
PAFCO Truck Bodies Inc. [3076]
Palmetto Ford Truck Sales Inc. [3077]
Pam Oil Inc. [3078]
Parker Brothers and Company Inc. [3080]
Parkway Automotive Warehouse [3081]
Parts Depot Company L.P. [3082]
Parts Inc. [3083]
Parts Plus of Dearborn [3084]
Parts Warehouse Inc. [3085]
Pasha Group Co. [3086]
Patron Transmission [3087]
Peck Road Ford Truck Sales Inc. [20703]
Penn Detroit Diesel [3089]
Perfection Equipment Co. [20704]
Performance Products [3091]
The Performance Shop Inc. [3092]
Perpall Enterprises; Michael E. [3093]
Peugeot Citroen Engines [3095]
Pfeiffer Hijet [3096]
Phillips and Temro Industries [3097]
Phoenix Manufacturing Incorporated [20705]
Piasa Motor Fuels Inc. [22583]
Pioneer Mercantile Co. [3098]
Plains Auto Refrigeration [14638]
Plaza Fleet Parts [3099]
Point Spring Co. [3100]
Pollard Co.; C.E. [20706]
Popes Parts Inc. [3103]
Porter Oil Company Inc. [22589]
Potter-Webster Co. [3105]
Power Drive & Equipment [3106]
Power Drive, Inc. [3107]
Power Drives, Inc. [3108]
Power Industries [3110]
Power & Pumps Inc. [3111]
Power Torque [3112]
Powertron Battery Co. [3113]
Precision Bearing Co. [3114]
Precision Built Parts [3115]
Prior Inc.; John [3118]
Pritchard Paint and Glass Co. [21547]
PullRite/Pulliam Enterprise Inc. [3123]
Purolator Products [3124]
Purvis Bearing Service [3125]
Purvis Bearing Service [3126]
Quaker City Motor Parts Co. [3128]
Quality Truck Bodies & Repair, Inc. [3129]
Quinsig Automotive Warehouse Inc. [3130]
Rahn Industries, Inc. [3132]
Ram Turbos Inc. [3134]
Rapac Network International [3135]
Rayside Truck & Trailer [3136]
RBI Corp. [3137]

Redlands Auto Parts [3141]
Relco Corp. [3143]
Reliable Automotive of Kansas Inc. [3144]
Reliable Battery Co. [9273]
Reliable Belt & Transmission [3145]
Republic Automotive [3149]
Republic Automotive Parts Inc. [3150]
Revco Products, Inc. [3151]
Rex Auto Parts [3152]
Rheuban Associates [3155]
Rib River Valley Cooperative [1187]
Richland Ltd. [3157]
Ridge Auto Parts Company Inc. [3158]
Ridge Co. [3159]
Rim and Wheel Service Inc. [3160]
Rippey Auto Parts Company Inc. [3161]
Rising Sun Import Parts Inc. [3162]
Rivers Body Co., Inc. [3163]
Riverside Drives Inc. [3164]
Robbins Auto Parts Inc. [3168]
Roberts Auto Parts; Fred [3169]
Rocket Supply Corp. [20714]
Rodefeld Company Inc. [3171]
Rodi Automotive Inc. [3172]
Roppel Industries Inc. [3174]
Rosebud Farmers Union Cooperative Associates Inc. [1211]
Rowland Equipment, Inc. [3176]
Royal Auto Supply Inc. [3177]
RTI Technologies, Inc. [14670]
S and G Trading Co. [26643]
S and S Automotive Inc. [13898]
S & W Supply Company Inc. [1225]
Safety Industries Inc. [3179]
Safety Service Co. [3180]
Safety Truck Equipment Inc. [3181]
Safeway Tire Co. [3182]
St. Francis Mercantile Equity Exchange [1228]
Salazar International, Inc. [3183]
San Antonio Brake and Clutch Service Inc. [3185]
Sandusky Industrial Supply [3186]
Sanel Auto Parts Inc. [3187]
Santa Rosa Bearing [3189]
Saria International Inc. [13903]
Scales Company Inc.; R.H. [3191]
Scherer Truck Equipment, Inc. [3193]
Scherer Truck Equipment, Inc. [3194]
Schmann Auto Parts [3195]
Schukei Chevrolet Inc. [3197]
Scientific Brake and Equipment Co. [3199]
Scientific Brake and Equipment Co. [3200]
Scruggs Equipment Company Inc. [3201]
Seaboard Automotive Inc. [3202]
September Enterprises Inc. [22661]
Servco Pacific Inc. [3205]
Service Motor Parts [3206]
Shamrock Custom Truck Caps, Inc. [3211]
Shankle Co. Inc.; Earle [3212]
Shaub Ellison Co. [3213]
Shelby Industries Inc. [3215]
Shepherd's Auto Supply Inc. [3216]
Sibco Enterprises Incorporated [3217]
Siemens Automotive Corp. [3219]
Sierra Detroit Diesel Allison Inc. [3220]
Siferd-Hossellman Co. [3221]
Simpson Equipment Corp. [3223]
Singer Products Export Company Inc. [16494]
Singer Products Export Company Inc. [3224]
Six States Distributors [3226]
Six States Distributors Inc. [3227]
Skaggs Automotive Inc. [3228]
Slingman Industries [3229]
SLM Power Group Inc. [3230]
Smith Detroit Diesel [3231]
Smith Detroit Diesel Allison Inc. [3232]
Smyrna Truck Body & Equipment, Inc. [3234]
Snap Products Inc. [3235]
Sound Warehouse Inc. [3236]
South Gateway Tire Co. [3237]
South Kentucky Trucks Inc. [3238]
Southeast Toyota Distributors Inc. [20724]
Southern Automotive Inc. [3239]
Southern Motorcycle Supply [3240]
Southern Power Inc. [3243]
Southford Garage Truck Equippers [3244]
SPAP Company LLC [4517]

Special Fleet Service [3245]
Specialized Sales and Service Inc. [3246]
Speed-O-Motive [3249]
Spencer Industries Inc. Chain Gear Div. [3251]
Spitzer Electrical Co. [3252]
Spokane Diesel Inc. [3253]
Spradling Originals [3254]
Sprague Devices Inc. [3255]
SSF Imported Auto Parts Inc. [3256]
Stag/Parkway Inc. [20730]
Standard Automotive Parts Corp. [3258]
Standard Battery and Electric Co. [3259]
Standard Parts Corp. [3260]
Stant Corp. [3262]
Stant Manufacturing Inc. [14697]
State Electric Company Inc. [3263]
Statler Body Works [3264]
Steelfab [3265]
Stein Distributing [22703]
Stewart & Stevenson [3267]
Stewart & Stevenson [3268]
Stewart & Stevenson [3269]
Stockton Service Corp. [22708]
Stone Heavy Vehicle Specialists Inc. [3271]
Strafco Inc. [3272]
Strickland Auto; Jewell [17199]
Stringfellow, Inc. [3275]
STS Truck Equipment and Trailer Sales [3276]
Stull Industries Inc. [3277]
Sturdevant Auto Supply [3278]
Sturdevant Auto Supply [3280]
Style Master [20410]
Suburban Manufacturing Co. [14701]
Summers Induserve Supply [16535]
Sunnyside Auto Finance [3283]
Superior Auto Electric [3284]
Superior Pump Exchange Co. [3286]
Supply Station Inc. [13945]
Susquehanna Motor Company Inc. [20734]
Sussen Inc. [3288]
Sygnet [16543]
T & E Wholesale Outlet [13460]
T & L Industries Co. [3290]
T-W Truck Equippers, Inc. [3291]
Target Tire and Automotive Corp. [3292]
Taser International Inc. [1314]
Taylor Company Inc.; Nelson A. [18623]
TBC Corp. [24299]
Tech Aerofoam Products, Inc. [26222]
Technovance Corp. [3297]
Teknor Apex Co. [24300]
Teleparts Inc. [3298]
Temple Products of Indiana Inc. [3299]
Terrile Export & Import Corp. [9480]
Texas Kenworth Co. [3300]
Textron Automotive [3301]
Thomas Hardware, Parts and Fasteners Inc. [13952]
Thompson Company Inc.; W.B. [3302]
Throwbot Inc. [3303]
Time Equipment [3304]
T.O. Haas Holding Co. [3314]
T.O. Haas Tire Company Inc. [3315]
Tokico (USA) Inc. [3316]
Tomasco Mulciber Inc. [3317]
Tomco Auto Products Inc. [3318]
Top Source Technologies Inc. [3319]
Torello and Son Machine Co.; F. [3320]
Torque Drive [3321]
Townsend Supply Co. [9498]
Toyota Motor Distributors Inc. [3322]
Trace Engineering [3323]
Tracom Inc. [3324]
Tradex Corporation [14734]
Trailer Craft [3325]
Transmission Exchange Co. [3327]
Transnational Motors Inc. [20738]
Transport Equipment, Inc. [3329]
Transtar Industries Inc. [3330]
Transtat Equipment, Inc. [3331]
Tri Citi Auto Warehouse [3333]
Tri-County Truck Tops, Inc. [3334]
Tri-Power, Inc. [3335]
Tri-State Bearing Co. [3337]
Tri-State Ladder & Scaffolding Company, Inc. [3338]

Tri State Warehouse Inc. [3339]
Triangle Inc. [3340]
Tricon Industries Inc. Electromechanical Div. [3341]
Truck Body Manufacturing Company, Inc. [3343]
Truck Enterprises Inc. [20739]
Truck Equipment Boston, Inc. [3344]
Truck Equipment Co. [3345]
Truck Equipment Distributors [3346]
Truck Equipment Inc. [3347]
Truck Equipment Sales Inc. [3348]
Truck Parts and Equipment Inc. [3349]
Truck Pro [3350]
Truckwell of Alaska [3352]
TRW. Inc [3353]
TRW Replacement [3354]
Twinco Romax Inc. [3356]
U-Joints, Inc. [3357]
U-Joints, Inc. [3358]
Ultraseal International Inc. [3359]
Uni Filter Inc. [3360]
Union Bearing & Transmission [3361]
United Auto Parts Inc. [3362]
United Automotive Supply Co. [3363]
United Engines [3364]
United Engines Inc. [3365]
United Engines Inc. [3366]
United Manufacturers Service [3368]
United Pacific Corp. [24449]
United States Export Co. [20741]
U.S. Manufacturing Corp. [3370]
U.S. Oil Company Inc. [3371]
Unity Manufacturing Co. [3373]
Universal Coach Parts Inc. [3374]
Universal Joint Specialists Inc. [3375]
US Farathane Inc. [3377]
US Reflector [3378]
Utility Trailer Sales Company of Arizona [3380]
Utility Truck Equipment Sales [3381]
Valley Auto and Truck Wrecking Inc. [3383]
Valley Detroit Diesel Allison Inc. [3384]
Valley Ford Truck Sales [3385]
Valley Motor Supply Inc. [3386]
VantageParts Inc. [3387]
Vasso Systems, Inc. [3388]
Vehicle Services/Commercial Truck & Van Equipment [3389]
Venturian Corp. [3390]
Vernitron Corp. AST Bearings Div. [3391]
Viam Manufacturing Inc. [3392]
Vie Americas Inc. [4548]
V.I.P. Discount Auto Center [3393]
Volz Truck Equipment, Inc.; L.W. [3394]
Von Housen Motors Inc. [20746]
W & W Body [3395]
Wagner Hardware Co. [13982]
Wahlberg-McCreary Inc. [3396]
Wallwork Inc.; W.W. [20747]
Waltman's Inc. [16613]
Wareheim Air Brakes [3398]
Warehouse Service Co. [3399]
Warner Fruehauf Trailer Co. [3400]
Warren Distributing Inc. [3401]
Watson Company, Inc.; O.J. [3403]
Watson Co.; Ray V. [3404]
WDI United Warehouse Inc. [3406]
Weed Chevrolet Company Inc. [20749]
Weissman and Sons Inc.; Carl [13991]
Wesco Auto Parts [3408]
Wesco Merchandising [14279]
West Side Distributors Ltd. [3409]
West Virginia Ohio Motor Sales Inc. [3410]
Western Power Sports, Inc. [3411]
Western Truck Equipment Company Inc. [3413]
Westex Automotive Corp. [3414]
Westlake Inc. [3415]
Wetherbee and Co.; George C. [3416]
Wetherill Associates Inc. [3417]
Wharton and Barnard Inc. [3419]
Wheel City Inc. [3420]
Wheel Masters Inc. [3421]
Wheeler Brothers Inc. [3422]
White Bear Equipment, Inc. [3423]
White Brothers Inc. [3424]
White Co.; The C.E. [3425]
Wholesale Tire Inc. [3429]
Wilcox Brothers Co. [3430]

Wilks Tire and Battery Service [3431]
Williams Auto Parts [3432]
Williams Detroit Diesel Allison [3433]
Williams Detroit Diesel Allison [3435]
Williams Detroit Diesel Allison [3436]
Williams Detroit Diesel Allison [3437]
Williams Tire Co.; Jack [3438]
Wilson Brothers Co. [3439]
Wilson Co.; Jim [3440]
WirthCo Engineering Inc. [3441]
Wisconsin Bearing [3442]
Wisconsin Brake and Wheel Inc. [3443]
Womack Machine [3444]
World Buying Service Inc. [9605]
Worldwide Environmental Products Inc. [3446]
Wright Supplier [3448]
Wright Tool Co. [3449]
Yankee Custom, Inc. [3450]
York Corrugating Co. [23469]
Young Company Inc.; A.R. [3451]
Young Windows Inc. [3452]
ZEXEL USA Corp. [3454]
ZF Group NAO [18645]
Ziegler Tire and Supply Co. [3455]
Zinc Positive Inc. [3456]
Zilkoski's Auto Electric [9627]
Zucca Inc.; L.J. [26377]

SIC 5014 — Tires & Tubes

A to Z Tire & Battery Inc. [2159]
Access Bicycle Components Inc. [23491]
Acra Custom Wheel [2176]
Adrian Wheat Growers Inc. [189]
Aerospace Tube & Pipe [19733]
Akron Overseas Inc. [15749]
All-Car Distributors Inc. [2203]
Allied Oil and Supply Inc. [22031]
Allied Tire and Auto Services [2214]
American Tire Distributors [2235]
Anderson & Spring Firestone [2240]
Apollo Tire Co. Inc. [2245]
Area Wholesale Tire Co., Inc. [2250]
Aronson Tire Co. Inc. [2253]
Ashby Equity Association [258]
Atlanta Commercial Tire Inc. [2263]
Atlantic International Corp. [20593]
Atlantic Tire Wholesaler [2267]
Auto Service and Tire Supermarts Inc. [2278]
Automotive Industries Inc. [2291]
Axelrods Tire Inc. [2302]
Baker-Stephens Tire Co. [2310]
Ball Tire and Gas Inc. [2312]
Battery and Tire Warehouse Inc. [2327]
Bauer Built Inc. [2328]
Bemidji Cooperative Association [22066]
Bens Inc. [2349]
Berry Tire Company Inc. [2351]
Black Oil Company Inc. [22076]
Bluegrass Bandag, Inc. [2370]
Brand Co. [2380]
Brannon Tire Corp. [2382]
Bridgestone Firestone, Inc. [2384]
Bridgestone/Firestone Tire Sales Co. [2385]
Broadway Tire Inc. [2388]
Bruces Tire Ltd. [2399]
California Tire Co. [2410]
Capital Tire Inc. [2416]
Capitol Tire Shop [2417]
Carolina Rim and Wheel Co. [18475]
Cate-McLaurin Company Inc. [2435]
Central Illinois Enterprises Ltd. [22124]
Clark's Wholesale Tire Co. [2454]
Coastal Energy Co. [2461]
Community Tire Co. Inc. [2468]
Condon Oil Company Inc. [22158]
Consolidated Service Corp. [2475]
Cooper Tire & Rubber Co. [2483]
Costco Companies, Inc. [10850]
Crockett Farmers Cooperative Co. [476]
Cumming-Henderson Inc. [2501]
D & H Tire Service [2520]
D-M Tire Supply [2522]
Danzey Oil and Tire Co. Inc. [2527]

David Tire Co. Inc. [2531]
Deas Tire Co. [2535]
Delta International [17817]
Denman Tire Corp. [2538]
Dunlap and Kyle Company Inc. [20628]
Dunlop Tire Corp. [2567]
Eastern Auto Parts Company Inc. [2572]
Eddie's Tire Service Inc. [2575]
Emanuel Tire Co. [2586]
Equipment and Parts Export Inc. [2594]
E.W. Tire & Service Centers [2598]
Falken Tire Corp. [2607]
Farmers Cooperative Elevator Co. [621]
Farmers Petroleum Cooperative Inc. [22257]
Farmers Union Oil Co. [22265]
Farmers Union Oil Co. (Napoleon, North
    Dakota) [22269]
Ferguson Tire Service Inc. [2611]
Foreign Tire Sales Inc. [2640]
Free Service Tire Company Inc. [2645]
Friend Tire Co. [2650]
Gabler Inc.; H.C. [24275]
Ganin Tire Company Inc. [2659]
Ganin Tire Inc. [2660]
Gans Tire Company Inc. [2661]
Gateway Tire Company Inc. [2663]
Gateway Tire Company Inc. [24276]
Gay Johnson's Inc. [2664]
GCR Rose Truck Tire Center [2665]
GCR Truck Tire Center [2666]
General Tire Inc. [2674]
Goodyear Tire Rubber Co. [16901]
Goodyear Tire & Rubber Co. [2691]
Great West Truck and Auto Inc. [2701]
Greene Farmers Cooperative [767]
Grismer Tire Co. [2707]
Hanson Tire Service Inc. [2724]
Harold's Tire and Auto [2726]
Harris Tire Co. [2727]
Harris Tire Co. [2728]
Heafner Company Inc.; J.H. [2734]
Heafner Tires & Products [2735]
Hercules/CEDCO [2742]
Hercules Tire and Rubber Co. [24281]
Hercules Tire & Rubber Products [2743]
Hesselbein Tire Company Inc. [2747]
Hibdon Tire Center Inc. [2748]
Howard Tire Service Inc. [2764]
Im-Pruv-All [2771]
Itco Tire Co. [2802]
Itco Tire Co. [2803]
ITEC Enterprises Inc. [6398]
Jetzon Tire and Rubber Company Inc. [2819]
Joe's Firestone Co. [2823]
Johnson Cooperative Grain Co. [888]
Joliet Equipment Corp. [2832]
Jones Inc.; Ken [2835]
K & W Tire Co. [2837]
Kauffman Tire Service Inc. [2840]
Kelly Springfield Tire [2845]
Kimmel Automotive Inc. [2855]
Kumho U.S.A. Inc. [2864]
Laramie Tire Distributors [2873]
Lebzelter and Son Co.; Philip [2876]
Lee/Star Tire Co. [2877]
LeMans Corp. [20672]
Lewis Oil Co.; H.C. [22428]
Lisac's Inc. [2885]
Lucas Tire Inc. [2896]
Madisonville Tire and Retreading Inc. [2905]
Magnum Tire Corp. [2909]
McCarthy Tire Service [2929]
McCord Auto Supply Inc. [2930]
Mega Company [2939]
Merchants Inc. [2943]
Mesabi Radial Tire Co. [2946]
Miller Brothers Giant Tire Service Inc. [2968]
Miller Tire Co. Inc. [2969]
Miller Tire Distributors [2970]
Miller Tire Service Inc. [2971]
Millersburg Tire Service Inc. [2972]
Mitchell Industrial Tire Co. [2977]
Modi Rubber Ltd. [2979]
Mohawk Rubber Sales of N.E. Inc. [24287]
Moore's Wholesale Tire Sales [2983]
Morgan Tire and Auto Inc. [2984]

Morgantown Tire Wholesalers [2986]
Moss Dynamics [2988]
Mott Equity Exchange [13839]
Mulgrew Oil Co. [22501]
Myers Industries Inc. Myers Tire Supply [3012]
Nankang USA Inc. [3014]
Nehawka Farmers Cooperative [18127]
Nitto Tires [3035]
Nobles County Cooperative Oil Co. [22521]
Northeast Tire of Maine [3045]
OK Hafens Tire Store Inc. [3061]
Oxford Recycling Inc. [7818]
Paris Tire City of Montbello Inc.; Jim [3079]
Pomps Tire Service Inc. [3102]
Pos-A-Traction Inc. [3104]
Progressive Tire [3121]
Progressive Tire Group [3122]
Ragan Inc.; Brad [3131]
Red Stone Inc. [3139]
Redburn Tire [3140]
Reinalt-Thomas Corp. [3142]
Reliable Tire Co. [3146]
Reliable Tire Distributors Inc. [3147]
Reliable Tire Distributors Inc. [24290]
Reynolds Tire and Rubber Div. [3153]
Rice Tire Co.; Donald B. [3156]
Rim and Wheel Service Inc. [3160]
Road-Runner Tire Service [3166]
Road Tested Recycled Auto Parts Inc. [3167]
Rockland Tire and Service Co. [3170]
Rott-Keller Supply Co. [3175]
Sacks International Inc.; M. [24293]
Safeway Tire Co. [3182]
Santa Maria Tire Inc. [3188]
Schwab Warehouse Center Inc.; Les [3198]
Sehman Tire Service Inc. [3203]
Service Tire Co. [3207]
Setco Solid Tire and Rim [3209]
Shamrock Auto Parts Inc. [3210]
Shaub Ellison Co. [3213]
Six Robblees Inc. [3225]
South Gateway Tire Co. [3237]
Southeastern Colorado Cooperative [1278]
Southern Nevada T.B.A. Supply Inc. [3242]
Steepleton Tire Co. [3266]
Stratham Tire Inc. [3273]
Straus Frank Co. [3274]
Summit of New England [3282]
Sunnyside Auto Finance [3283]
Superior Tire Inc. [3287]
Superior Tire Inc. [24297]
Swansons Tire Company Inc. [3289]
Target Tire and Automotive Corp. [3292]
TBC Corp. [3293]
TBC Corp. [24299]
Tech Distributing/Supply [3294]
Tech Inc. [3295]
Tire Corral Inc. [3305]
The Tire Rack Wholesale [3306]
Tire Welder Inc. [3307]
Tires Inc. [3308]
Tires, Wheels, Etc. Wholesale Inc. [3309]
T.O. Haas Holding Co. [3314]
T.O. Haas Tire Company Inc. [3315]
Trade America [16573]
Treadways Corp. [3332]
Tuckers Tire & Oil Company Inc. [3355]
United Industrial Tire Inc. [3367]
United Tire Distributors Inc. [3372]
Utility Trailer Sales Company of Arizona [3380]
Warren Farmers Cooperative [1413]
Western States Manufacturing Company,
    Inc. [3412]
Whalen Tire [3418]
Wholesale Tire Company Auto Centers [3428]
Wholesale Tire Inc. [3429]
Wilks Tire and Battery Service [3431]
Williams Tire Co.; Jack [3438]
Wilson Co.; Jim [3440]
Womack Machine [3444]
Woody Tire Company Inc. [3445]
Ziegler Tire and Supply Co. [3455]

SIC 5015 — Motor Vehicle Parts— Used

A 1 Accredited Batteries [2148]
A-1 New & Used Auto Parts, Inc. [2150]
A & A Midwest Distributing Inc. [2152]
A C Auto Recycling [2153]
A-City Auto Glass [2154]
Ace Auto Salvage [2169]
Action Auto Parts [2178]
AF & T Salvage [2186]
Albuquerque Foreign Auto Parts [2199]
All Foreign Used Auto Parts [2204]
All Hours Auto Salvage [2205]
All Parts Brokers [2206]
Allston Street Used Auto Parts [2220]
American Auto Salvage [2226]
American Marketing International [2231]
Any & All Auto Parts Inc. [2242]
Auto Collision Inc. [2270]
Auto Dealers Exchange of Illinois [20595]
Auto Parts Club Inc. [2274]
Auto Parts Depot Inc. [2275]
Autoline Industries Inc. [2283]
Automotive Electric and Supply Co. [2288]
B & D Auto Salvage & Repair [2306]
Barker-Jennings Corp. [13584]
Barneys Auto Salvage Inc. [2319]
Barrows Used Auto Parts [2322]
Belmont Automotive Co. [2347]
Bens Inc. [2349]
Brattleboro Auto Parts [2383]
Brown Associates Inc.; Roger G. [2396]
Capos Auto Parts Inc. [2419]
Cardillo Brothers Inc. [2424]
Compact Performance Inc. [2469]
Complete Auto & Truck Parts [2471]
Coronado Auto Recyclers Inc. [2484]
CTR Used Parts & Equipment [2500]
Danville Gasoline and Oil Company Inc. [22188]
Dave's Auto Inc. [2528]
Dave's Used Auto Parts Inc. [2529]
Desert Sky Wrecking [2540]
Diamond Prairie Ranch Company Inc. [2542]
Drake's Salvage; Fred [2560]
El Mexicano Auto Salvage [2578]
Elliff Motors Inc. [2582]
Ely Auto Dismantlers [2585]
Emery; Stuart [2588]
Equipment and Parts Export Inc. [2594]
Five Foreign Auto Salvage [2625]
Five JS Auto Parts Inc. [2626]
Foreign Car Parts Inc. [2639]
Frank's Auto Parts Co.; Johnny [2644]
General Auto Parts Inc. [2669]
General Auto Sales Company Inc. [2670]
Gold Rush Wrecking [2689]
Green Meadow Auto Salvage, Inc. [2704]
Green Point Inc. [2705]
Hanser Automotive Co. [2722]
Hanser's Pick A Part Inc. [2723]
Hebes Motor Co. [2737]
Hess; Charles [2746]
Highway Auto Parts Inc. [2753]
Hiway 30 Auto Salvage [2756]
House of Hubcaps [2762]
I-90 Auto Salvage & Sales [2768]
Jack's Salvage & Auto Parts Inc. [2807]
Jalopy Jungle Inc. [2811]
JB Junk & Salvage Inc. [2813]
Jenik Automotive Distributors Inc. [2817]
Joliet Equipment Corp. [2832]
King Auto Parts Inc. [2856]
Lewis Oil Co.; H.C. [22428]
Lund Truck Parts Inc. [2897]
Mazda Motor of America Inc. [20675]
McDow & Sons Salvage; V.H. [2932]
Merritts Auto Salvage [2945]
MidAmerican Metals Company Inc. [2954]
Midway Motor Supply Core Supplier [2956]
Midway Parts Inc. [2957]
Midwest Wrecking Co. [2961]
Montana Truck Parts [2981]
Neapco Inc. [3019]

Neil Parts Distribution Corp. [3021]
New Mexico Salvage Pool [3029]
Nick's Junk Inc. [3032]
Nordstroms [3038]
North 54 Salvage Yard [3040]
North Providence Auto Salvation [3043]
O'Connor Truck Sales Inc. [3053]
Off Road Specialty [3055]
Ohio Auto Rebuilders Supply, Inc. [3057]
OK Hafens Tire Store Inc. [3061]
Pioneer Mercantile Co. [3098]
Privilege Auto Parts [3119]
Putnam Truck Parts [3127]
Recycled Auto Parts of Brattleboro Inc. [3138]
Red Stone Inc. [3139]
Reno Auto Wrecking Inc. [3148]
RGA Tire Shop [3154]
Road Tested Recycled Auto Parts Inc. [3167]
Saw Mill Auto Wreckers [3190]
Scarborough Auto Parts Inc. [3192]
Shaw Auto Parts Inc. [3214]
Sidney Auto Wrecking Inc. [3218]
Southern Nevada Auto Parts Inc. [3241]
SSR Pump Co. [3257]
Stan's Towing & Repair [3261]
Sturdevant Auto Supply [3279]
Tate Jr.'s Murray Auto Auction Inc.; Jim [20735]
Tires Wholesale Inc. [3310]
Tisdale Used Auto Parts [3311]
TNT Insured Towing Auto Salvage [3313]
Tri-Parish Cooperative Inc. [1354]
Truckways Inc. [3351]
Valley Auto Parts [3382]
Valley Auto and Truck Wrecking Inc. [3383]
Wallock; John M. [3397]
Weekley Auto Parts Inc. [3407]

SIC 5021 — Furniture

A-Dec Inc. [13007]
A Pickle House/Judy Blair's Rustic
 Collectibles [13008]
A.A. Importing Co. Inc. [13009]
Aanns Trading Co. [4309]
Adams Printing and Stationery Co.; S.G. [20772]
Adirondack Chair Company Inc. [20773]
Adirondack Chair Company Inc. [13011]
Airmo Div. [13012]
Alan Desk Business Interiors [20780]
Alden Comfort Mills [13013]
Algoma Net Co. [23502]
All About Offices Inc. [20783]
Allied Fire Lite Fireplace [14314]
Allied Sales Co. [13014]
Allied School and Office Products [20785]
Allison-Erwin Co. [5907]
Alpha Fine Computer Furniture [13015]
Alumacast Inc. [13016]
Amarillo Hardware Co. [13555]
American International Trading Co. [4769]
American Seating Co. [13018]
American Systems of the Southeast Inc. [20799]
Ampco/Rosedale Fabricators [13019]
Amtec International Inc. [13020]
Anderson's Woodwork Inc. [13021]
Apgar Office Systems Inc. [20808]
Arbee Associates [20809]
Arcadia Chair Co. [13022]
Arcadia Merchandising Corp. [23522]
Arrow Sales Inc. [20812]
Artesanos Imports Company Inc. [6993]
Artlite Office Supply and Furniture Co. [13024]
Aspen Furniture Inc. [13025]
Astrup Co. [25970]
ATD-American Co. [25971]
Atlanta Fixture and Sails Co. [24070]
Atlantic Microsystems Inc. [20819]
A.W. Industries [13027]
AWD International Inc. [13028]
B J's Wholesale Club Inc. [13029]
Ball Stalker Co. [20829]
Bank and Office Interiors [13030]
Barclay Dean Interiors [13032]
Bassett Co.; Russ [13033]

Batty & Hoyt Inc. [20834]
Beckly Cardy Group [25570]
Bell; Philip M. [13034]
BenchCraft [13035]
BFI/Specmark [13036]
B.G. Office Products [13037]
Big Reds Antiques [13038]
Big Sky Office Products Inc. [20843]
BKM Total Office [20844]
Bleecker Furniture Inc. [13039]
Bodine Inc. [13040]
Booker-Price Co. [13041]
Bowlus School Supply Inc. [13042]
Braden's Wholesale Furniture Company
 Inc. [13043]
Brann Associates Inc.; Don [20854]
Brennans Ltd. [13045]
Broadway Office Interiors [20856]
Brothers Office Supply Inc. [20859]
Brown Distributing Co. Inc. [13046]
Brueton Industries Inc. [13047]
Brunschwig and Fils Inc. [15430]
BT Office Products International Inc. Detroit
 Div. [20861]
BT Office Products USA [20862]
Buffalo Office Interiors Inc. [20864]
Burcham and McCune Inc. [13049]
Burgess, Anderson and Tate Inc. [13050]
Burkett's Office Supply Inc. [13051]
Burlington House Inc. [13052]
Buschart Office Products Inc. [20865]
Business Concepts Inc. [13053]
Business Environments Inc. [13054]
Business Furnishings Co. [13055]
Business Interiors Inc. (Denver, Colorado) [13056]
Business Interiors Northwest Inc. [13057]
Business Resource Group [13058]
Calhoun [25592]
California School Furnishing Company Inc. [13059]
California Surveying and Drafting Supply
 Inc. [24333]
Camilo Office Furniture, Inc. [20873]
Camilo Office Furniture Inc. [13061]
Cano Corp. [20874]
Cardinal Office Systems [20880]
Cardinal Office Systems [13062]
Carithers-Wallace-Courtenay Inc. [13063]
Carroll Seating Company Inc. [13064]
Carroll's Discount Office Furniture Co. [13065]
Cascade Pacific Lumber Co. [7150]
Castleberry Office Interiors Inc. [13066]
Centercore New England Inc. [20888]
Chair King Furniture Co. [13067]
Chair Place [13068]
Champion Industries Inc. (Huntington, West
 Virginia) [20895]
Chapin Co. [22129]
Clark and Mitchell Inc. [9808]
Clarke and Bro. Inc.; E.H. [20902]
Classic Designs [13070]
Coaster Company of America [13071]
COE Distributing, Inc. [20904]
Colton Piano and Organ [13072]
Comex International [13073]
Commercial Furniture Services Inc. [13074]
Commercial Laminations [13075]
Commercial Office Interiors Inc. [13076]
Complete Office Solutions Inc. [13077]
Connolly & Associates; Barrie [13078]
Continental Office Furniture and Supply
 Corp. [13080]
Contract Associates Inc. [20912]
Contract Interiors [13081]
Contracted Associates Office Interiors Inc. [13082]
Corporate Design Group [13083]
Corporate Environments of Georgia Inc. [20924]
Corporate Express [20925]
Corporate Express [20926]
Corporate Express [20927]
Corporate Express Inc. [20929]
Corporate Express of the MidAtlantic Inc. [20930]
Corporate Express of Northern California
 Inc. [20931]
Corporate Interiors Inc. [20932]
CPS Marketing Corporation [18757]
Crawfords Office Furniture & Supplies [20937]

Dale Office Plus [20944]
Dancker, Sellew and Douglas Inc. [20945]
Davison Inc. [13085]
DEA Specialties Co. [20951]
Demco Inc. [20954]
Denver Merchandise Mart [17391]
Desert Stationers [20956]
Design Finishes Inc. [13087]
Design Marketing Associates [13088]
Design Toscano Inc. [13089]
Desk Concepts [20957]
Desk-Mate Products Inc. [20958]
Desks Inc. (Chicago, Illinois) [20959]
Desks Inc. (Denver, Colorado) [13090]
Direct Office Furniture Outlet [20964]
Discount Desk Etc., Inc. [20965]
Discount Desk Etc. Inc. [13091]
Discount Office Equipment Inc. [20966]
Discount Office Equipment Inc. [13092]
Donie Chair Co. [13093]
Dot Line [22851]
Doubleday Brothers and Co. [20974]
Doughtie's Foods Inc. [10984]
Douron [21714]
Douron Incorporated Corporate Furniture [13094]
Dunn Sales; Skip [25638]
Eads Brothers Wholesale Furniture Co. [13095]
Eastern Butcher Block Corp. [13096]
Eastern Butcher Block Corp. [13097]
Eastern Furniture Distributors [13098]
Eastern Moulding, Inc. [13099]
Eaton Office Supply Company Inc. [20978]
EBSCO Industries Inc. Western Region [4929]
Economy Office Furniture [20980]
EcoTech Recycled Products [20981]
Edelsteins Better Furniture Inc. [13101]
EDM Business Interiors Inc. [20983]
Educational Distributors of America [13102]
El Dorado Furniture Co. [13103]
Elberfeld Company Inc. [13104]
Enfield Industries Inc. [13105]
Environment Ltd. [13106]
Ergonomic Specialties Ltd. [13107]
Ewing Aquatech Pools Inc. [23657]
Executive Office Furniture Outlet [20996]
Exmart International, Inc. [24112]
Facility Resource Inc. (Seattle,
 Washington) [13108]
Falcon Products Inc. [13109]
Farmers Furniture Company Inc. [13110]
Fashion Bed Group [13111]
Finger Office Furniture [13112]
Finn Distributing Co. Inc. [15497]
Flowers School Equipment Company Inc. [13114]
Forms and Supplies Inc. [21007]
Fraenkel Wholesale Furniture Company
 Inc. [13115]
Furniture on Consignment Inc. [13116]
Furniture Consultants Inc. [21009]
Furniture Distributors Inc. [13117]
Gem Furniture Co. Inc. [13119]
General Office Interiors [13120]
General Office Products Co. [21011]
Georgia Impression Products Inc. [13121]
Getz Bros. & Company Inc. [16062]
GF Office Furniture Ltd. [21013]
Globe Business Furniture Inc. [21015]
Globe Business Resources Inc. [13122]
Globe Industrial Supply Inc. [13123]
Glover Equipment Inc. [13124]
Goldsmiths Inc. [21016]
Goldsmiths Inc. [13125]
Goodmans Design Interior [21017]
GTH Holdings, Inc. [7421]
Hadley Office Products Inc. [21022]
Hampton House [13126]
Harris Marcus Group [13127]
Hart Furniture Company Inc. (Siler City, North
 Carolina) [13128]
Hartzell Acquisition Corp. [13129]
Hauser Company; M.L. [16092]
Hermitage Electric Supply Corp. [15167]
Hesters/McGlaun Office Supply Co. [21031]
Hi Lo Table Manufacturing Inc. [13130]
Higgins Purchasing Group [13131]
Hill and Son Co.; Fred [13133]

Hills Office Supply Co. Inc. [21034]
Hilton Equipment Corp. [13134]
Himark Enterprises Inc. [13135]
Holcomb's Education Resource [21036]
Holga Inc. [21038]
Holladay Color Center [21457]
Holtzman Office Furniture Co. [21039]
Horizon Trading Company [13136]
HSO Corp. [18844]
Humac Engineering and Equipment Inc. [7497]
Hunters Inc. [21045]
Huntington Wholesale Furniture Company Inc. [13137]
Hurst Office Suppliers Inc. [21046]
ICF Gropu Showroom [13138]
Imports International [13139]
Incorporated Business Interiors Inc. [13140]
Inside Source [13141]
Institutional Contract Sales [13142]
Interior Enterprises Inc. [21061]
Interior Services Inc. [21062]
Interior Services Inc. [13143]
Interior Systems Contract Group Inc. [13144]
Interior Systems and Installation Inc. [13145]
International Consulting & Contracting Services [7517]
International Trading & Investment [13146]
Interstate Companies of Louisiana [21067]
Intertrade, Inc. [13147]
Intramar Inc. [16169]
IQ2000 [6397]
Jackson Associates Inc.; Bill [13148]
Jacobi and Sons Inc.; Walter [13149]
Jacobi and Sons Inc.; Walter [13150]
Jamesville Office Furnishing [13151]
Jax International [21075]
Jeter Systems Corp. [21076]
Johnson and Associates Business Interiors Inc. [13152]
Jones-Campbell Co. [13153]
Jones Office Equipment; Al [21079]
Joyce International Inc. [21081]
Kalbus Office Supply [21084]
KBM Workspace [13154]
Keller Group [13155]
Kelly Furniture Co.; F.S. [13156]
Keystone Office Supply Co. Inc. [21088]
Kiddie Academy International Inc. [21089]
Kights' Printing and Office Products [21091]
Kindel Co.; J.A. [13157]
Kyle Furniture Co.; R.H. [13158]
L. Powell Co./Generations for the 21st Century [13159]
La Belle Provence Ltd. [13160]
La Plante Gallery Inc. [13161]
Laboratory Design and Equipment [13162]
Lake County Office Equipment Inc. [21097]
Lane Office Furniture Inc. [21099]
Langlois Stores Inc. [15559]
Laser Magnetic Storage International Co. [21102]
Lee Company Inc. [13163]
Lessco Products Inc. [21106]
Lib-Com Ltd. [13390]
Lindsay-Ferrari [13164]
Lintex Corp. [18891]
Lombard Co.; F.W. [13166]
Long Inc.; Duncan [21112]
Lucas Brothers Inc. [21115]
Mac Thrift Clearance Center [21118]
Macke Business Products [13167]
Main Auction [13168]
Maine Cottage Furniture Inc. [13169]
Mantua Manufacturing Co. [13171]
Marco Business Products Inc. [6463]
Marshall Co.; John A. [21129]
Martin and MacArthur [7654]
Martin Stationers [21130]
Martin Universal Design Inc. [13172]
Marvel Group Inc. [21132]
Marysville Office Center [21133]
Masco Corp. Beacon Hill Showroom [13173]
Mastercraft Inc. [13174]
McBroom Pool Products Inc. [23813]
McCall Woodworks Inc. [13175]
McDonald Supply Company Inc.; A.Y. [23257]
McGuire Furniture Co. [13176]

McKenzie Galleries and Commercial [13177]
McQuiddy Office Designers Inc. [21134]
MDR Corp. [21136]
Meridian Mattress Factory Inc. [13178]
Merkel Donohue Inc. [21139]
M.G. West [13179]
Micropoint Inc. [21141]
Midwest Office Furniture and Supply Company Inc. [21143]
Miles Treaster and Associates [13180]
Miller Inc.; Herman [13181]
Miller Workplace Resources; Herman [21145]
Miller's Supply [23268]
Minton-Jones Co. [13182]
Missco Corporation of Jackson [13183]
Mississippi School Supply Co./MISSCO Corp. [21148]
Modern Business Machines Inc. [21149]
Moore Discount Inc. [15241]
Multicraft Inc. [25745]
N Pool Patio Ltd. [23842]
National Business Furniture Inc. [13185]
New Mexico Mattress Co. Inc. [13187]
New Mexico School Products Co. [21162]
Northeast Interior Systems Inc. [13188]
Northwest Futon Co. [13189]
Nova International Inc. [13190]
O'Connor and Raque Office Products Co. [21170]
Office America Inc. [21171]
Office Club Inc. [21172]
Office Depot Inc. [21173]
Office Depot Inc. Business Services Div. [21174]
Office Environments Inc. [21175]
Office Express [21180]
Office Furniture & Design Center Inc. [21181]
Office Furniture Warehouse Inc. [13191]
Office Interiors Inc. [21182]
Office Machine & Furniture Inc. [21183]
Office to Office Inc. [21184]
Office Pavilion/MBI Systems Inc. [18966]
Office Pavillion [13192]
Office Pavillion/National Systems Inc. [21185]
Office Planning Group Inc. [13193]
Office Resources Inc. [21187]
Office Systems Co. [21190]
OfficeScapes & Scott Rice [21193]
OffiSource [21194]
Ohio Desk Co. [21197]
Omnimedical Inc. [18967]
Omnirax [13194]
One Workplace L. Ferrari LLC [13195]
Oriental Furniture Warehouse [13196]
Owen Distributors Inc. [13197]
Oxford Metal Products [13198]
Pacific Design Center [13199]
Paddock Seating Co. [13200]
Page Foam Cushion Products Inc. [13201]
Paint & Glass Supply Company Inc. [21527]
Palmer/Snyder Furniture Co. [13204]
Passport Furniture [13205]
Patio Production Inc. [13206]
Peabody Office Furniture Corp. [21206]
Perdue Inc. [21208]
Perfection Distributing Co. [25781]
Perkins Stationery [21209]
Peters Office Equipment [21210]
Peterson Business Systems Inc. [21212]
Peterson Spacecrafters [21213]
Peysen Inc.; David [13207]
Phelans [15619]
Phifer Wire Products Inc. [13208]
Pink Business Interiors Inc. [10105]
Pivot Interiors [13209]
Plaza Stationery & Printing Inc. [21216]
Pocket Pool & Patio [23887]
Powell Co./Generations for the 21st Century; L. [13211]
Precise Industries, Inc. [21222]
Price Modern Inc. [13212]
Pro Form and File [21223]
Pruitt; Richard [13213]
Quimby Co. Inc.; Edward H. [21230]
R & R Wood Products [13214]
RABCO Equipment Corp. [21232]
Randolph Distributing Corp. [13216]
RCP Inc. [21234]

Reliance Bedding Corp. [13218]
Rembrandt Lamps [15632]
Remco Business Systems Inc. [21237]
Restonic Carolina Inc. [13219]
Rex Mid-South Service [13221]
Rice of Kansas City Inc.; Scott [21240]
Richards Co.; S.P. [21242]
Richards Quality Bedding [13222]
Robco Corp. [23916]
Roberts Manufacturing Inc. [13223]
Rons Office Equipment Inc. [21246]
Rosedale Fabricators/Ampco [21247]
Rosemount Office Systems, Inc. [21248]
Rowley-Schlimgen Inc. [21249]
Royal Sales [26640]
Ruff and Co. Business Furniture Div.; Thomas W. [13225]
Ruff and Company of Florida Inc.; Thomas W. [21252]
Ruff and Co.; Thomas W. [21253]
Ruland's Used Office Furnishings [13226]
Rustic Creations [13227]
Sadco Inc. [15301]
S.A.K. Industries [13228]
Salman [13229]
Sams Inc.; L.L. [13230]
San Francisco Mart [13231]
Sarreid Ltd. [13232]
School Specialties Inc. [13233]
School Specialty Inc. [21259]
Sealy Mattress Georgia [13235]
Seret & Sons Inc. [13237]
S.G. & B. Inc. [13238]
Sharpe; Cliff [13239]
Sharut Furniture Co. [13240]
Sheffield Furniture Corp. [13241]
Shepler International Inc. [8011]
Sheyenne Publishing Co. [21268]
Silvers Inc. [13242]
Simmons Mattress Factory Inc.; W. [13243]
Siri Office Equipment Inc. [21271]
SIS Human Factor Technologies Inc. [13244]
Skinner Corp. [21245]
Skyline Designs [13246]
Sloan Miyasato [13247]
Smith Brothers Office Environments Inc. [21273]
Southern Business Systems Inc. [21276]
Southern Office Furniture Distributors Inc. [21279]
Southwest Business Furniture [13248]
Specialized Marketing [21280]
Specialized Marketing [13249]
Spivack's Antiques [13250]
Stanfields Inc. [21286]
Staples Business Advantage [21289]
Stein World Inc. [13251]
Stuck and Associates; Paul [27011]
Summervilles Inc. [21304]
Sun Hing Trading Company Inc. [13458]
Sundin Rand; Gloria [13252]
SupplySource Inc. [21306]
Surplus Office Equipment Inc. [21307]
Swindal-Powell Co. [13253]
TAB Products Co. [13254]
Tatung Science and Technology Inc. [21315]
TBT Industries Inc. [13256]
Teaneck Graphics Inc. [13257]
Techline Studio Inc. [13258]
Term City Furniture & Appliance [13259]
Thompson Office Equipment Company Inc. [21318]
Tibbet Inc. [21319]
TML Associates Inc. [8138]
Total Office Interiors [21954]
Trade Corporation [8140]
Tradeways Inc. [13260]
Tri E Distributors [13262]
Trick and Murray Inc. [21323]
Tucker Library Interiors LLC [13263]
Unicorn International Inc. [13264]
United Corporate Furnishings Inc. [13265]
United Stationers Inc. [21977]
University Publishing Co. [13266]
Urban Ore Inc. [8162]
Value City Furniture Div. [13267]
Variety Distributors Inc. [15695]
VersaTec [13268]
Victor Business Systems Inc. [21337]

Viking Acoustical Corp. [21338]
Virginia City Furniture Inc. [13269]
Vitra Seating Inc. [21340]
Vogue Bedding Co. [13270]
Waldner Company Inc.; D. [21343]
Walker and Zanger Inc. [13271]
Walsh Bros. [21344]
Walton Manufacturing Co. [13272]
Walton Manufacturing Co. [13273]
Warehouse Home Furnishing Distributors
    Inc. [13274]
Wasserstrom Co. [21348]
Watson Associates Inc.; Vivian [13275]
Watson Lumber Co. [8197]
Wells and Kimich Inc. [13276]
West Coast Industries Inc. [13277]
Western Office Interiors [13278]
Westgate Fabrics Inc. [21607]
White Office Furniture and Interiors; J.C. [21355]
Wholesale Furniture Distributors [13279]
Wholesale and Home Supply Company
    Inc. [13280]
Wittigs Office Interiors [21358]
Wittigs Office Interiors [13282]
Wood Co.; W.B. [21360]
Woodmansee Inc. [21361]
Woodworks [13283]
Worden Co. [13284]
World Traders (USA) Inc. [9607]
Wynne Company Inc.; A.D. [13285]
Young's [13286]
Zero US Corp. [21371]
Zip Dee Inc. [13287]

SIC 5023 — Homefurnishings

A & S Suppliers [15384]
A.A. Importing Co. Inc. [13009]
AAA Glass Corp. [15385]
Abrahams Oriental Rugs [15386]
Accent Lamp and Shade Co. Inc. [15387]
Access International Marketing Inc. [13524]
Adleta Corp. [9646]
Adleta Corp. [15388]
Admiralty Mills Inc. [9647]
ADO Corp. [15389]
Air Flow Shutters Shade [15391]
Airmo Div. [13012]
Akers & Chrysler Inc. [21375]
Alan Inc.; Charles [9649]
Alaska Housewares Inc. [14996]
Albert Trading Co. [14997]
Alco Building Products Co. [6930]
Alden Comfort Mills [13013]
Alicia Comforts [15393]
Allegheny Inc. [9654]
Allegheny Inc. [15394]
Allied Distributors Inc. [9655]
Allied-Eastern Distributors [9656]
Allied-Eastern Distributors [9657]
Allied Eastern Distributors [9658]
Allied Floors, Inc. [9660]
Allou Distributors Inc. [14014]
Allure Home Creation Company Inc. [15395]
American Commercial Inc. [15396]
American Cut Crystal [15397]
American Equipment Marble & Tile, Inc. [9668]
American Hotel Register Co. [15398]
American Pacific Enterprises Inc. [15399]
American Textile Co. [15400]
Ampco Products Inc. [6971]
AMS Enterprises [9680]
AMS Imports Inc. [15401]
Amway Distributors [15402]
Andrea by Sadek [15403]
Arabel Inc. [15404]
Archer Associates; C.F. [15405]
Architectural Floor Systems, Inc. [9684]
Architectural Surfaces, Inc. [15406]
Arizona Mail Order Co. [4782]
Arrow Wholesale Co. Inc. [26397]
Artmark Chicago Ltd. [15407]
Ashbrook & Associates [15408]
Asmara Inc. [15409]

Asmara Oriental Rugs [9689]
Atkins Inc.; Frederick [25563]
Atlas Carpet Mills Inc. [9693]
B and F System Inc. [15411]
Babco International Inc. [23532]
Baby Needs Inc. [4797]
Back to Basics Products Inc. [15412]
Bacon & Co. Inc. [4798]
Baddour International [14034]
Baker Linen Co.; H.W. [15413]
Bakertowne Company, Inc. [15414]
Bastian Inc.; Owen M. [9694]
Bath/Kitchen & Tile Supply Co. [15415]
Bay Colony Mills Inc. [15416]
BDD Inc. [15417]
Beaulieu of America Inc. [25977]
Beaver's Rugs [9697]
Bellini Co. [9721]
Bennett Brothers Inc. [17334]
Benthin Systems, Inc. [15418]
Bentley Mills Inc. [9722]
Bergquists Imports Inc. [15419]
Best Brands Home Products, Inc. [15420]
Bicor Processing Corp. [15421]
Bigelow-Sanford [9726]
Bird and Company Inc.; William M. [9727]
Bishop Distributing Co. [9728]
Bishops Inc. [25982]
Blackton Inc. [9730]
Boise Paint & Glass Inc. [21402]
Bomaine Corp. [15423]
Bon Motif Co. [15424]
Boone-Davis Inc. [15425]
Bornstein and Company Inc.; L. [9731]
Boston Warehouse Trading Corp. [15426]
Boutross Imports Inc. [15427]
Bowen Supply Inc. [15428]
BPI [9735]
BPI Inc. [9737]
BPI Inc. [9738]
Bradshaw International Inc. [13044]
Brann Associates Inc.; Don [20854]
Bretlin Inc. [9739]
Brewster Wallcovering Co. [15429]
The Brightman Co. [15059]
Brinkman and Co.; LD [9740]
Brooks Designer Rugs; J. [9741]
Brownstone Gallery Ltd. [25991]
Brunschwig and Fils Inc. [15430]
Buchanan Industries [9743]
Builder Contract Sales Inc. [15064]
Building Plastics Inc. [9746]
Burgess Lighting and Distributing [15066]
Burlington Futon Co. Inc. [15432]
Butler-Johnson Corp. [9747]
Butler-Johnson Corp. [9748]
C/D/R/ Inc. [15068]
C-Mor Co. [15433]
Cain and Bultman Inc. [15070]
Calhoun Inc.; Nancy [15434]
Capel Rugs Inc. [9754]
Capital Paint & Glass Inc. [21411]
Caravelle Distributing [9758]
Carolina Braided Rug [9760]
Carpet Barn Inc. [9761]
Carpet Cushion Supply [9763]
Carpet Cushion Supply [9764]
Carpet Cushion Supply [9765]
Carpet Cushion Supply [9766]
Carpet Factory Outlet [9768]
Carpet Mart & Wallpaper [9770]
Carpet Mart & Wallpaper Outlet [15435]
Carpet Warehouse Connection [9771]
Carpetland U.S.A. Inc. [9772]
Carroll Distribution Company, Inc. [9773]
Carvel Hall Inc. [15436]
Casa Carpet Wholesale Distributors [9774]
Casa Linda Draperies [15437]
Casella Lighting Co. [8506]
Casella Lighting Co. [15438]
Castec Window Shading Inc. [15439]
Cathey Wholesale Co. [9780]
CDC [9781]
CDC [9782]
Central Distributors Inc. [9783]
Central Tractor Farm & Country, Inc. [400]

Century Tile and Carpet [9784]
Century Tile & Carpet [9785]
Century Tile and Carpet [9787]
Ceramic Tile Distributors, Inc. [9796]
Chantal Cookware Corp. [15441]
Charter Distributing [9803]
Chernov Brothers Inc. [15442]
Chicago Hardwood Flooring [9804]
Childers & Associates [15443]
Cinti Floor Co. [9805]
Cinti Floor Co. [15444]
Citywide Floor Service [9807]
CK Associates [15445]
Clark and Mitchell Inc. [9808]
Clark's Carpet Connection [9809]
Classic Flooring Distributors [9810]
Classic Tile, Inc. [9811]
Closet Centers America [15447]
Closet City Ltd. [15448]
CMH Flooring Products Inc. [9814]
Cole Wholesale Flooring [9816]
Coleman Interior Service Co. [15450]
Colonial Braided Rug Co. [9817]
Colonial Floors Inc. [9818]
Combined Sales Co. [26447]
Conso Products Co. [13079]
Consolidated Tile and Carpet Co. [9822]
Consolidated Tile and Carpet Co. [15452]
Continental Flooring Inc. [9825]
Contract Decor Inc. [15453]
Cook's Mart Ltd. [15454]
Copenhaver Industries Inc.; Laura [15455]
Cornell Trading Inc. [4895]
Corning Inc. [15457]
Couzon USA [15458]
Coyle Inc. [15459]
Coyne Mattress Co. Ltd. [15460]
Coyne's Inc. [15461]
Craftmade International Inc. [15462]
Craftsmen Supply, Inc. [9831]
The Cronin Co. [9834]
Crystal Clear Industries Inc. [15464]
Cubs Distributing Inc. [9836]
Curtis Associates Inc. [26455]
Curtis & Campbell Inc. [21422]
Custom Drapery and Blinds Inc. [15465]
Custom Wholesale Flooring [9837]
Custom Wholesale Flooring [9839]
Dal Tile Corp. [9847]
Dan Communications Inc.; Lee [5586]
Dandee Creations Ltd. [15466]
Davic Drapery Co. [15467]
Davis Rug Co. [9848]
Dealers Supply Co. [9849]
Dealers Supply Co. [9850]
Deaton's Carpet One [9851]
Decorative Aides Co. Inc. [15468]
Decorative Crafts Inc. [13086]
Decorative Products Group [9852]
Decorative Products Group [9853]
Del Sol Tile Co. [9854]
Denver Hardwood Co. [9855]
Derr Flooring Co. [15469]
Design Carpets [9856]
Design Center of the Americas [15471]
Design/Craft Fabric Corp. [15472]
Design Distributing [9857]
Designer's Den Inc. [15473]
Desso USA Inc. [9862]
Diamond W Supply Co. Inc. [9863]
Diamond W Supply Co. Inc. [9864]
Diamond W Supply Co. Inc. [9865]
Dilmaghani and Company Inc. [15474]
Dimock, Gould and Co. [15475]
D.J.H. Inc. [15477]
Dodge & Son Inc.; Herman [15113]
Dolgencorp [10978]
Don and Co.; Edward [15478]
Down Lite International [15479]
Downs Supply Co. [9872]
Drapery Stitch of Delphos [15480]
Drulane/ Palmer Smith [15481]
Duchin Inc.; Gloria [13347]
Duffy and Lee Co. [9873]
Durand International [13348]
Dutton Co.; Andrew [15483]

East Hampton Industries Inc. [15484]
Eastside Wholesale Supply Co. [9880]
Ebbtide & Associates [15485]
Ebling Distribution, Inc. [9881]
EBSCO Industries Inc. Western Region [4929]
E.C.F. Supply [9882]
Ellis Inc.; A.L. [15487]
Emery Waterhouse Co. [13681]
Empress Linen Import Co. [15488]
Emser International [15489]
Equality Trading [15995]
Eskew, Smith & Cannon [9886]
Euro Classic Distributors Inc. [15491]
FABTEX Inc. [15493]
Fallani and Cohn [15494]
Fargo Glass and Paint Co. [21440]
Fashion Bed Group [13111]
Federal Wholesale Company Inc. [15495]
Fetco International Corp. [13357]
First National Trading Company Inc. [15498]
Fitzgerald Inc.; Albert F. [9890]
Fleet Wholesale [11144]
Fleischman Carpet Co. [9891]
Floor Service Supply [9892]
Floor Supply Co. [9894]
Floor Supply Distributing Inc. [9895]
Flooring Distributors Inc. [9896]
Floors Northwest Inc. [9900]
Florida Hardwood Floor Supply [9901]
Florida Tile [9902]
Focus Carpet Corp. [9903]
Foge Jensen Imports [15502]
Forbex Corporation [9904]
Forbo Industries Inc. [9905]
Forbo Wallcoverings Inc. [15504]
Forschner Group Inc. [15505]
Fortman's Paint & Glass [21445]
Framers On Peachtree [15506]
Frank Brothers Flooring Distributors [9906]
Freund, Freund and Company Inc. [15507]
Frieling USA Inc. [15508]
Function Junction Inc. [15509]
Funsten and Co.; B.R. [15510]
Gallagher Industrial Laundry [4974]
Gamma Inc. [13118]
Garci Plastics Industries [15511]
Garpac Corp. [4980]
Gateway Distributors Inc. [9913]
Gateway Seed Co. [729]
Gattas Company Inc.; Fred P. [15512]
Gemmex Intertrade America Inc. [11247]
General Floor [9915]
Genesis Manufacturing, Inc. [15513]
Gibson Overseas Inc. [15514]
Global Tile [9922]
Golden State Flooring [9923]
Grabarczyk Associates [15515]
Great Lakes Sales, Inc. [9925]
Great Lakes Sales, Inc. [9926]
Gregg Manufacturing Co. [15516]
GTH Holdings, Inc. [7421]
Gurley's Georgia Carpet [9929]
Guthrie-Linebaugh-Coffey, Inc. [9930]
Haleyville Drapery Manufacturing [15517]
Handelsman Co.; Hanco M. [15518]
Hardwood Flooring & Finishes [9937]
Hardy and Company Inc.; James G. [15519]
Harold Import Company Inc. [15520]
Hart Co. Inc.; Edward R. [9938]
Hartmann of Florida [8833]
Hawaiian Housewares, Ltd. [15521]
Haywin Textile Products Inc. [15522]
Heines Custom Draperies [15523]
The Helman Group Ltd. [15524]
Henderson and Co.; J.L. [15525]
Herald Wholesalers Inc. [13751]
Hercules Sales, Inc. [15526]
Heritage Lace Inc. [15527]
Herregan Distributors Inc. [9943]
Herregan Distributors, Inc. [9944]
Herregan Distributors Inc. [9945]
Herregan Distributors, Inc. [9946]
Herregan Distributors Inc. [9947]
Hi-Jac Corporation [15528]
Hi Lo Table Manufacturing Inc. [13130]
Higgins Purchasing Group [13131]

Himark Enterprises Inc. [13135]
Hoboken Wood Flooring Corp. [15529]
Hoboken Wood Floors [9949]
Hoboken Wood Floors [9950]
Hockstein Inc.; David [9951]
Holladay Color Center [21457]
Home Fasions Distributor [15530]
Home Interiors and Gifts Inc. [15531]
Horizon West Draperies [15533]
Horn EB Replacement Service [15534]
Houseware Warehouse Inc. [15535]
Howell Co.; R.B. [26528]
Hunter and Company Inc. [26069]
Hunter and Company of North Carolina [15536]
ICF Gropu Showroom [13138]
Ichikoh Manufacturing Inc. [15537]
IKO Notions [26071]
Import Warehouse Inc. [13374]
Import Wholesale Co. [17454]
In Products Inc. [15538]
Indiana Wholesalers Inc. [15540]
Inland Northwest Distributors Inc. [9962]
Institutional Linen Supply [26072]
International Tile & Marble, Ltd. [9967]
Interstate Supply [9969]
Interstate Supply Co. [9970]
Interstate Supply Co. [9971]
Intile Designs Inc. [7524]
Ivystone Group [15542]
Jaeckle Distributors [9977]
Jaeckle Wholesale Inc. [9978]
Jaunty Co., Inc. [15544]
JB Tile Co. [9980]
K & T Lamp & Shade Company Inc. [15546]
Kahn & Son, Inc.; Irvin [9982]
Kahn & Son, Inc.; Irvin [9983]
Kaough Distributing Company, Inc. [9984]
Kast Fabrics Inc. [26090]
Kauai Paint & Jalousie [21470]
Kelaty International Inc. [9986]
Kenco Distributors, Inc. [9987]
Kinder-Harris Inc. [8945]
King Koil Sleep Product [15549]
Kirsch Fabrics Corp. [26111]
Kitchen Specialties Inc. [15550]
Kitchens Inc. of Paducah [15551]
Kittrich Corp. [15552]
Klam International [7561]
Kmart Corp. [15553]
Knobler International Ltd. [13381]
Koch-Bailey Associates [15554]
Koch-Bailey and Associates [15555]
Koval Marketing Inc. [15556]
Kraft Hardware Inc. [15557]
Kwik-Affix Products [15558]
La Belle Provence Ltd. [13160]
Lanham Hardwood Flooring Co. [9990]
Lannans Paint & Decorating Ctr. [21486]
Larson Distributing Company Inc. [9991]
Laughlin China Co.; Homer [15560]
Lawrin Lighting, Inc. [15561]
Lee Jay Bed and Bath [15563]
Lee Tennis, LLC [23783]
Leese Flooring Supply [9994]
Lefton Co.; Geo Zolton [15564]
Lehleitner and Company Inc.; Geo H. [15565]
Leifheit Sales Inc. [15566]
Lensing Wholesale, Inc. [7595]
Levy, Inc.; Harris [15567]
Lifetime Hoan Corp. [15568]
Lipper International Inc. [15569]
Little Rock Drapery Co. [15570]
Loboflor Bonar Flotex [9996]
Long Inc.; Duncan [21112]
Longust Distributing Inc. [9997]
Loomcraft Textiles Inc. [15571]
Loomis Paint & Wallpaper Ctr [21494]
Lorel Co. [21812]
Lowy Group Inc. [10002]
LW Bristol Collection [5147]
Magic Touch Enterprises, Inc. [10003]
Mahne Company Inc.; William P. [15573]
Mainline Supply Corp. [10004]
Malco Industries [13808]
Malik International Enterprises Ltd. [15574]
Maneto Wholesale Flooring, Inc. [10007]

Mannington Wood Floors [10008]
Maran-Wurzell Glass and Mirror Co. [15575]
Marburn Stores Inc. [15576]
Marc Sales Corp.; Ken [9029]
Marcus Brothers [15577]
Markos Wholesale Clothing Distributors [5166]
Markuse Corp. [15578]
Martexport Inc. [15579]
Masterpiece Crystal [15580]
Mautino Distributing Company Inc. [1855]
McArthur Towels, Inc. [15581]
McArthur Towels Inc. [15582]
McCarthy Drapery Company Inc. [15583]
McCartney Carpet [10013]
McCarty & Son; H.J. [15584]
McEllin Company, Inc. [10015]
McKee Enterprises Inc. [10016]
McKee Enterprises Inc. [10017]
McLendon Co. [11837]
Mees Distributors [10022]
Memphis Furniture Manufacturing Co. [26140]
Merit Industries [10026]
Messina and Zucker Inc. [15585]
Metro Marketing Inc. [15586]
Meyda Tiffany [15587]
Miami Robes International [5190]
Michigan Hardwood Distributors [10028]
Mid-America Export Inc. [15588]
Mid-America Tile [10030]
Mid-America Tile L.P. [10032]
Midwest Floors [10033]
Miller's Interiors Inc. [10038]
Milliken & Co. [10039]
Mills, Inc.; Aladin [10040]
Mirage Rug Imports [10041]
Mirror Lite Co. [13405]
Misco Shawnee Inc. [10042]
Misco Shawnee Inc. [15589]
Modern Door and Hardware Inc. [7732]
Mohr Vinyl & Carpet Supplier [10045]
Momeni Inc. [10046]
Monarch Ceramic Tile Inc. [10049]
Morris Tile Distributors Inc. [10061]
Mottahedeh and Co. [15590]
Mr. Hardwoods [15591]
Mr. Hardwoods, Inc. [10068]
Musolf Distributing Inc.; Lon [10071]
Musson Rubber Co. [10072]
National Potteries Corp. [13408]
Nelson-Roanoke Div. [13845]
Neuwirth Inc. [15592]
Newell Company Inc.; C.A. [10077]
Newell P.R. Ltd. [15594]
Niles Color Center [21519]
Nolarec Industries, Inc. [15595]
Noonoo Rug Company Inc. [15596]
Nordic Products Inc. [15597]
Noritake Company Inc. [15598]
North Branch Flooring [10080]
Noury and Sons Ltd. [15599]
Novelty Cord and Tassel Company Inc. [15600]
N.R.F. Distributors, Inc. [10081]
Office Interiors Inc. [21182]
Ohio Kitchen and Bath [15601]
Old Masters Products Inc. [10085]
Old Masters Products Inc. [10086]
Olympic Flooring Distributors Inc. [10087]
Orders Distributing Company Inc. [10088]
Orian Rugs Inc. [10089]
Ornamental Tile and Design Center [10090]
Orrefors Inc. [15602]
Ostrow Textile L.L.C. [15603]
Otagiri Mercantile Company Inc. [15604]
Over and Back Inc. [15605]
Owen Distributors Inc. [13197]
Owen Manufacturing Company Inc.; Charles
    D. [15606]
Pacific Drapery Co. [15607]
Pacific Flooring Supply [10092]
Pacific Flooring Supply [10093]
Pacific Flooring Supply [10095]
Pacific Flooring Supply [10096]
Pacific Flooring Supply [10097]
Pacific Home Furnishings [15608]
Paint & Glass Supply Company Inc. [21527]
Pampered Chef [15609]

Pande Cameron/Fritz and La Rue [15610]
Paradise Manufacturing Company Inc. [15611]
Paragon Interiors Inc. [15612]
Parkway Drapery Co. [15613]
Patented Products Inc. [15614]
Pearson Rug Manufacturing Co.; Billy D. [10102]
Peeler's Rug Co. [10103]
Penthouse Industries Inc. [15616]
Perfection Products Inc. [15617]
Peterson Co.; Robert H. [15618]
Phelans [15619]
Phoenix Textile Corp. [26176]
Piedmont Distribution Centers [15620]
Pink Business Interiors Inc. [10105]
Portmeirion USA [15621]
Pottery Manufacturing and Distributing Inc. [13425]
Pottery Manufacturing and Distributing Inc. [15622]
Powell Co.; L. [15623]
Preferred Carpets [10106]
The Premium Connection [15624]
Primavera Distributing [10108]
Primavera Distributing [10109]
Prince Street Technologies Ltd. [10110]
Princess House Inc. [15625]
R5 Trading International Inc. [19005]
R & R Hardwood Floors [10112]
Rainbow Rug Inc. [10113]
Ramallah Inc. [15629]
RB Rubber Products Inc. [15630]
Readers Wholesale Distributors Inc. [10116]
Reed Export, Inc.; Charles H. [10117]
Reliable Fabrics Inc. [15631]
Rembrandt Lamps [15632]
Rev-A-Shelf, Inc. [15633]
Revere Mills Inc. [15634]
Rhode Island Tile/G & M Co. [10121]
Richard-Ginori 1735, Inc. [15635]
Riedel Crystal of America Inc. [15636]
The Roane Co. [10124]
The Roane Co. [10125]
The Roane Co. [10126]
Roberts International, Inc. [7942]
Robison Distributors Co. [10127]
Roga International Div. Export-Import
    Marketing [15638]
Romac Export Management Corp. [15639]
Romanoff Corp.; Maya [15640]
Rosanna Inc. [15641]
Rose's Stores Inc. [5320]
Roth Distributing Co. [15294]
Roth Distributing Co. [15295]
Royal Carpet Distribution, Inc. [10129]
Royal Doulton USA Inc. [15642]
Royal Floor Mats [10130]
Royal Prestige of Missouri Inc. [15643]
Royalty Carpet Mills Inc. [10131]
RSB Tile, Inc. [10132]
Rubin Brothers Company Inc. [10133]
Ruff and Co.; Thomas W. [21253]
The Rug Barn Inc. [15644]
Sadek Import Company Inc.; Charles [15645]
Saladmaster Inc. [15646]
Salco Inc. [15647]
Salton/Maxium Housewares Inc. [15648]
Sanborn's Paint Spot Inc. [21559]
Sarreid Ltd. [13232]
Schwartz Co.; Louis J. [13234]
Sea-Pac Sales Co. [10140]
Sentry/Liberty Hardware Distributors Inc. [13911]
Seret & Sons Inc. [13237]
Shaheen Carpet Mills [10145]
Shaheen Carpet Mills [15651]
Shaheen Paint and Decorating Company,
    Inc. [21566]
Shapco Inc. [15652]
Sharp Co.; William G. [10147]
Sherwin Williams Paint Co. [21568]
Showcase Kitchens and Baths Inc. [23373]
The Showroom [26204]
Signature Housewares Inc. [15653]
Silver Loom Associates [10148]
Silvestri Corporation Inc.; Fitz and Floyd [15654]
Simmons Yarn & Rug Co. [10149]
Skinner Company Inc.; S.P. [15655]
Skyline Distributing Co. [15656]
Sloan Miyasato [13247]

Slusser Wholesale Inc. [26652]
Smith Distributors; Laurence [15657]
Smith Glass Co.; L.E. [15658]
Smith Hardwood Floors [10154]
Smith Kitchen Specialties; W.H. [15317]
Smith; Merle B. [10155]
Solar Graphic Inc. [15660]
Solinger and Associates [15318]
Sorce, Inc. [10156]
Sorrell Interiors [15661]
Sound Floor Coverings Inc. [10157]
Southern Distributors Inc. [15662]
Southern Flooring Distributors [10160]
Southern Flooring Distributors [10161]
Southern Flooring Distributors [10162]
Southern Flooring Distributors [10163]
Southern Flooring Distributors [10164]
Southern Interiors Inc. [15663]
Southland Carpet Supplies [10167]
Southland Flooring Supplies Inc. [10168]
Southland Flooring Supply [10169]
Southland Floors, Inc. [10170]
Specialty Distribution [10175]
Standard Textile Company Inc. [15666]
Stanley Roberts Inc. [15667]
Stanline Inc. [10176]
Star International Ltd. [10177]
Stark Carpet Corp. [10178]
Stark Carpet Corp. [15668]
Stiller Distributors Inc. [10182]
Stover Broom [15669]
Stroheim & Romann Inc. [26217]
Stroud Braided Rug Co. [10184]
Stuart's Federal Fireplace, Inc. [15670]
Sultan and Sons Inc. [15671]
Summitville Atlanta [10186]
Summitville Baltimore [10187]
Sun Coast Tile Distributors Inc. [10194]
Sun Supply Corp. [9440]
Super Glass Corp. [15672]
Superior Linen Company Inc. [15673]
Superior Products, Inc. [10195]
Surface Technology Corp. [15674]
Swiff-Train Co. [10196]
Swiff-Train Co. [10197]
Swiff-Train Co. [10198]
Swiff-Train Co. [10199]
Swiff-Train Co. [10200]
Swiff-Train Co. [15675]
Syracuse China Corp. [15677]
T & A Supply Co. [10202]
T and A Supply Co. [15679]
T-Fal Corp. [15680]
T & L Distributors Company Inc. [10203]
T & L Distributors Company Inc. [10204]
T & L Distributors Company Inc. [10205]
T & L Distributors Company Inc. [10206]
T & L Distributors Company Inc. [10207]
Takahashi Trading Corp. [15681]
Tasso Wallcovering [15682]
Tech-Aerofoam Products Inc. [8103]
THC Systems Inc. [15683]
Thomas Tile & Carpet Supply Co. Inc. [10212]
Tianjin-Philadelphia Rug Co. [15684]
Tile Distributors Inc. [10232]
Tile Helper Inc. [10238]
Tilers—Pergo Shop; J.R. [10247]
Tiles Plus [10250]
Toggitt Ltd.; Joan [26231]
Toland Enterprises Inc. [10252]
Torosian Brothers [10254]
Towle Manufacturing Co. [15685]
Toyo Trading Co. [15686]
Trade Am International Inc. [10256]
TradeCom International Inc. [13961]
Trans World Investments, Ltd. [15687]
Trend Pacific Inc. [15688]
Tri-Dee Distributors [13261]
Tri State Electric Company Inc. [9505]
Trident Medical International [19663]
TruServ Corp. [13968]
Trym-Tex, Inc. [10259]
Twin City Tile [10261]
Twin Panda Inc./Katha Diddel Home
    Collection [15689]
Ulster Linen Company, Inc. [15691]

UMBRA U.S.A. Inc. [15692]
United Flooring Distributors Inc. [10265]
Universal International Inc. [5454]
Urken Supply Company Inc. [15693]
USA Plastics Inc. [15694]
Valdes Paint & Glass [21597]
Valley-Western Distributors, Inc. [10270]
Valley-Western Distributors, Inc. [10271]
Valley-Western, Inc. [10272]
Valley-Western, Inc. [10273]
Variety Distributors Inc. [15695]
VC Glass Carpet Co. [10275]
Victor Business Systems Inc. [21337]
Viking Distributors Inc. [10276]
Villa Lighting Supply Company Inc. [9540]
VillaWare Manufacturing Co. [15360]
Villeroy and Boch Tableware Ltd. [15696]
Virginia Hardwood Co. [10277]
Virginia Hardwood Co. [10279]
VMC/USA [15697]
Waechtersbach U.S.A. [15699]
Wal-Mart Stores Inc. [15700]
Walton & Post [12873]
Walton Wholesale Corp. [10284]
Wang's International, Inc. [15701]
Wanke Cascade [10286]
Watermark Association of Artisans Inc. [15703]
W.C. Distributors Corp. [26370]
Weber Co.; H.J. [10290]
Wedgwood U.S.A. Inc. [15704]
Wesco Fabrics Inc. [15705]
Western Pacific Interior [10293]
Western Shower Door Inc. [8213]
Westfield Decorator Fashions [15706]
Westgate Fabrics Inc. [26246]
Westgate Fabrics Inc. [21607]
White Inc.; H. Lynn [15707]
Wilf Corp.; Elias [10300]
Wilf Corp.; Elias [10301]
Windows of the World [15709]
The Wine Enthusiast Companies [15710]
Wipeco Corp. [15711]
WMF of America [15712]
WMF Hutschenreuther USA [15713]
Wonderly Company Inc. [15714]
Woodlawn Hardware [17287]
Woolworth Corp. [15379]
World Carpets Inc. [10308]
Worldwide Manufacturing Inc. [15715]
Xcell International Corp. [12989]
Xcell International Corp. [15382]
Yellow River Systems [19113]
Zak Designs Inc. [15716]
Zeroll Co. [15717]

SIC 5031 — Lumber, Plywood & Millwork

84 Lumber Co. [6894]
A and M Supply Inc. [6896]
A and R Lumber Sales Inc. [6897]
Aanns Trading Co. [4309]
ABC Supply Co., Inc. [6899]
Abilene Lumber Inc. [6902]
Adam Wholesalers Inc. [6913]
Adams Company Inc.; J.K. [27274]
Adams Wholesale Co. Inc. [6914]
Addison Corp. [6915]
Adleta Corp. [9646]
Agland Coop [205]
Agland Inc. [209]
Air Flow Shutters Shade [15391]
Alan Inc.; Charles [9649]
Alco Building Products Co. [6930]
Algert Company, Inc. [14998]
All American Pool N Patio [23503]
All Coast Forest Products Inc. [6933]
All Coast Lumber Products Inc. [6934]
All-Right [6935]
Allen and Allen Company Inc. [6936]
Allen Millwork Inc. [6938]
Allied Building Stores Inc. [27275]
Allied Distribution Systems [6944]

Allied Distribution Systems [27276]
Allied Plywood Corp. [6945]
Allied Plywood Corp. [6946]
Almond Brothers Lumber and Supply Inc. [6947]
Alpine Corp. [6948]
Aluma Panel, Inc. [21384]
Aluminum Distributors Inc. [6950]
Aluminum Products Co. [6951]
Amerhart Ltd. [6956]
American Building Supply, Inc. [6960]
American Building Supply, Inc. [6961]
American Distributing Co. [6962]
American Hardwood Co. [6966]
American International Forest Products Inc. [6968]
American Mill and Manufacturing Inc. [27279]
American Millwork & Hardware, Inc. [13560]
Americas Trade & Supply Co. [2237]
Ampco Products Inc. [6971]
Ampco/Rosedale Fabricators [13019]
AMRE Inc. [6972]
Andalusia Wood Products Inc. [27280]
Anderson & Jarvi Lumber [6975]
Anderson Lumber Co. [6976]
Anthony Forest Products Co. [6979]
Arch-I-Tech Doors Inc. [6982]
Architectural Building Supply [13564]
Architectural Surfaces, Inc. [15406]
Architectural Words Inc. [6983]
Arizona Sash and Door Co. [13565]
Arley Wholesale Inc. [9686]
Arling Lumber Inc. [6985]
Armstrong and Dobbs Inc. [6986]
Arnold Lumber Company Inc. [6987]
Arrowhead Timber Co. [27281]
Arthur Lumber Trading Co. [6994]
ASA Builders Supply Inc. [6996]
Ash Woodyard Inc.; J.M. [27282]
Ashe Industries Inc. [6997]
Associated Building Specialties [13026]
Associated Lumber Industries Inc. [6999]
Athens Building Supply [7000]
Atlantic Building Products [7001]
Atlantic Pre-Hung Doors Inc. [7004]
Atlantic Veneer Corp. [27283]
Averitt Lumber Company Inc. [7005]
Bacon Building Materials Inc.; Henry [7008]
Badger Corrugating Co. [7010]
Bailey Lumber Co. [7011]
Baillie Lumber Co. [7012]
Baisley Lumber Corp. [7013]
Baker Hardwood Lumber Co. [7014]
Baker Hardwood Lumber Co. [27284]
Bakersfield Sandstone Brick Co. Inc. [7015]
Bakersfield Sandstone Brick Company Inc. [27285]
Baldridge Lumber Co.; J.C. [7016]
Banks Lumber Company Inc. [7019]
Banks Lumber Company Inc. [27286]
Barber Cabinet Co. Inc. [13031]
Barber and Ross Co. [7020]
Bassi Distributing Co.; George [25890]
Baton Rouge Lumber Company LLC [7031]
Baxter Co.; J.H. [7032]
Bean Lumber Co.; Buddy [7034]
Bear Paw Lumber Corp. [7036]
Beard Hardwood Lumber Inc.; E.N. [7037]
Becker Builders Supply Co. [7039]
Behling Building Products; Gil [7043]
Berks Products Corp. [7050]
Besse Forest Products Group [7052]
Bishop Distributing Co. [9728]
Bison Building Materials Inc. [7060]
Bodden Lumber Company Inc.; R.K. [7065]
Boehm-Madisen Lumber Company Inc. [7066]
Boise Cascade [7067]
Boise Cascade Corp. [27287]
Boise Cascade Corp. Building Materials Distribution
   Div. [27288]
Booker and Company Inc. [7070]
Borkholder and Company Inc.; F.D. [7071]
BPI [9735]
BPI Inc. [9737]
BPI Inc. [9738]
Bradley Co.; E.B. [13605]
Brands Inc. [7076]
Brewster Wallcovering Co. [15429]
Bridgeport Equipment Co. Inc. [336]

Britton Lumber Company Inc. [7081]
Brockway-Smith Co. [7082]
Brookdale Lumber Inc. [7083]
Brookharts Inc. [7084]
Brown-Graves Co. [7086]
Brown Lumber Corp.; Pat [7087]
Brownell & Associates, Inc. [13607]
BSH of Evansvillle [7090]
BSTC Group Inc. [7091]
Buckeye Pacific Corp. [7093]
Budres Lumber Co. [7094]
Buettner Brothers Lumber Co. [7095]
Buettner Brothers Lumber Co. [27289]
Buffington Corp. [7096]
Buford White Lumber Company Inc. [7097]
Builders Center Inc. [7099]
Builders General Supply Co. [7100]
Builders Hardware & Specialties [13611]
Builders Hardware and Supply Co. Inc. [13612]
Builders Specialties Co. [7101]
Builders Warehouse [7102]
Builders Wholesale Supply Company, Inc. [13048]
Builders Wholesale Supply Company Inc. [27290]
Builderway Inc. [15065]
Building and Industrial Wholesale Co. [7103]
Building Materials Distributors Inc. [7104]
Building Products Inc. [7106]
Bun Patch Supply Corp. [7107]
Burnett and Sons Mill and Lumber Co. [7111]
Burt Millwork Corp. [7113]
Burton Lumber Corp. [7115]
Butler-Johnson Corp. [9747]
Butler-Johnson Corp. [9748]
Butterfield Building Supply [7117]
Byrne Plywood Co. [7119]
C & D Hardwoods [7120]
Cabinet & Cupboard Inc. [7121]
Cache Valley Builders Supply [7122]
Caffall Brothers Forest Products Inc. [7124]
Calcasieu Lumber Co. [7125]
Calcasieu Lumber Co. [27292]
California Panel and Veneer Co. [7127]
Calvert & Hoffman [7129]
Cameo Kitchens Inc. [13060]
Cameron Ashley Building Products Inc. [7130]
Campbell-Payne Inc. [7131]
Canal Industries Inc. [7132]
Canfor U.S.A. Corp. [27293]
Capitol Plywood Inc. [7137]
Carolina Building Co. [7142]
Carolina Door Controls [27295]
Carolina Western Inc. [7145]
Carroll Building Specialties [13621]
Carter-Lee Lumber Company Inc. [7147]
Carter Lumber Co. [7148]
Carter-Waters Corp. [7149]
Cascade Pacific Lumber Co. [7150]
Casco Industries Inc. [7151]
Castle Distributors Inc. [15080]
Cathey Wholesale Co. [9780]
Causeway Lumber Co. [7153]
Cedarburg Lumber Company Inc. [7156]
Central Door & Hardware [7158]
Central Farmers Cooperative [390]
Central Indiana Hardware Co. [7159]
Central Lumber Sales Inc. [7160]
Central Lumber Sales Inc. [27296]
Central Valley Builders Supply [7161]
Central Wholesale Supply Corp. [7162]
Century Tile and Supply [9788]
Champlin Co. [25899]
Chapin Co. [22129]
Charlotte Hardwood Center [7168]
Chatfield Lumber Company Inc. [7169]
Chicago Hardwood Flooring [9804]
Christmas Lumber Company Inc. [7170]
Cimarron Lumber and Supply Co. [7172]
Cimarron Lumber and Supply Co. [27297]
Clack Corp. [25601]
Clapper's Building Materials Inc. [13069]
Classic Tile, Inc. [9811]
Clay Ingels Company Inc. [7178]
Clem Lumber Distributing Company Inc. [7180]
Clermont Lumber Co. [7181]
Cleveland Plywood Co. [7183]
CMH Flooring Products Inc. [9814]

Cofil Inc. [7191]
Colco Fine Woods and Tools Inc. [7192]
Colco Fine Woods and Tools Inc. [27298]
Cole Hardwood Inc. [7193]
Coleman Lumber Inc. [7195]
Colony Lumber Co. [7198]
Comanche Lumber Company Inc. [7199]
Comtech [7201]
Continental Wood Preservers Inc. [7210]
Continental Wood Preservers Inc. [27299]
Cookson Co. [27300]
Cooley Forest Products [7215]
Cooley Industries Inc. [7216]
Cooling Tower Resources, Inc. [7217]
Cooperative Oil Association [22168]
Cooperative Reserve Supply Inc. [7218]
Cooperative Supply Inc. [7219]
Copeland Lumber Yard Inc. [13646]
Cover and Son Wholesale Lumber Inc.;
   H.A. [7225]
Cox Industries, Inc. [7227]
Craftwood Lumber Co. [7229]
Cramer Co. Inc. [15097]
Crane Co. [7230]
The Cronin Co. [9834]
Crosslin Supply Company Inc. [7232]
Culp Lumber Co.; H.W. [7235]
Custom Bilt Cabinet and Supply Inc. [7238]
Custom Industries Inc. [27301]
Custom Wholesale Flooring [9837]
Custom Wholesale Flooring [9838]
Custom Wholesale Flooring [9839]
CustomCraft [7239]
D & D Specialties Millwork [7241]
D & J Cabinet Co. Inc. [13084]
D-J, Inc. [7242]
D & M Plywood, Inc. [7243]
D.A. Distributors Inc. [7244]
Darant Distribution [22952]
Davidson Louisiana Inc. [7251]
Davidson Lumber Co.; Howard A. [7252]
Dayton Door Sales Inc. [7253]
Dealers Supply and Lumber Inc. [7256]
Decorative Products Group [9852]
Decorative Products Group [9853]
Delaware County Supply Co. [13658]
Denver Hardwood Co. [9855]
Design Distributing [9857]
Design House Inc. [13664]
Designed Flooring Distributors [9860]
Devlin Lumber and Supply Corp. [7260]
Diamond Hill Plywood Co. [7261]
Diamond Hill Plywood Co. [7262]
Diamond W Supply Co. Inc. [9863]
Diamond W Supply Co. Inc. [9864]
Discount Building Materials [7268]
Dixie Building Supplies Co. [7272]
Dixieline Lumber Co. [7273]
Dixon Lumber Company Inc. [7274]
Do It Best Corp. [7275]
Doctor Ike's Home Center Inc. [7276]
Dodson Wholesale Lumber Company Inc. [7277]
Door Engineering Corp. [7280]
Doortown Inc. [7281]
Dorsey Millwork Inc. [15958]
Double-T Manufacturing Corp. [7283]
Dougherty Hanna Resources Co. [7284]
Dougherty Lumber Co. [7285]
Downs Supply Co. [9872]
DuBell Lumber Co. [7288]
Dunaway Supply Co. [7289]
Dunbar Doors and Millwork [27302]
DW Distribution [7293]
East Alabama Lumber Co. [7298]
East Coast Mill Sales Co. [7299]
East Side Lumberyard Supply [9878]
Eastern Moulding, Inc. [13099]
Eastern Wood Products Company Inc. [9879]
Eastman-Cartwright Lumber Co. [7301]
E.C.F. Supply [9882]
Economy Builders Supply Inc. [7302]
Edmunds and Company Inc.; Frank A. [7303]
Edmunds and Company Inc.; Frank A. [27303]
Elk Supply Company Inc. [7306]
Emerson Hardwood Co. [7309]
The Empire Company, Inc. [7310]

Erb Lumber Co. Materials Distributors Div. [7316]
Erickson Wood Products [27304]
Erickson's Flooring & Supply [9885]
Escondido Lumber & True Value [7319]
Espy Lumber Co. [7320]
Esty and Sons Inc.; Ralph A. [7323]
Exchange Lumber and Manufacturing Div. [7326]
Farmers Cooperative Association [17842]
Farmers Cooperative Association [22254]
Farmers Cooperative Elevator Co. [620]
Farmers Cooperative Exchange (Elgin, Nebraska) [11101]
Fessenden Hall Inc. [7337]
Fingerle Lumber Co. [7341]
Fircrest Pre-Fit Door Co. [7342]
Firestone Plywood [7345]
Fischer Lime and Cement Co. [7346]
Fitzpatrick and Weller Inc. [7348]
Fleischman Carpet Co. [9891]
Floor Service Supply [9893]
Floors, Inc. [9898]
Floors, Inc. [9899]
Floors Northwest Inc. [9900]
Florida Hardwood Floor Supply [9901]
Foothills Mill & Supply Inc. [7354]
For-Tek [7355]
Forest City-Babin Co. [7357]
Forest City Enterprises Inc. [27305]
Forest City-North America Lumber [7358]
Forest City Trading Group Inc. [7359]
Forest Lumber Co. [7360]
Forest Plywood Sales [7361]
Fort Worth Lumber Co. [27306]
Fountain Lumber Co.; Ed [7362]
Franciscan Glass Co. [7366]
Frontier Lumber Co. [7369]
Frontier Wholesale Co. [7370]
Frost Hardwood Lumber Co. [7371]
Frost Hardwood Lumber Co. [27307]
Futter Lumber Corp. [7373]
Galliher and Brother Inc.; W.T. [7374]
Ganahl Lumber Co. [7375]
Gardner Hardware Co. [7378]
Garka Mill Company Inc. [7380]
General Materials Inc. [7385]
Genesee Reserve Supply Inc. [7386]
Geneva Corp. [7387]
Gennett Lumber Co. [7388]
George Co.; Edward [7389]
Georgia Flush Door Sales Inc. [7392]
Georgia-Pacific Corp. Distribution Div. [7394]
Gibson McIlvain Co.; J. [7396]
Gilbert Lumber/IFCO Systems [25917]
Global Marketing Concepts [7399]
Gold & Reiss Corp. [7402]
Golden State Flooring [9923]
Golden State Flooring Sacramento [9924]
Goshen Sash and Door Co. [27310]
Graebers Lumber Co. [7406]
Graham-Hardison Hardwood Inc. [27311]
Grand Rapids Sash and Door [7408]
Granger Lumber-Hardware, Inc. [7409]
Grasmick Lumber Company Inc.; Louis J. [7413]
Great Lakes Sales, Inc. [9926]
The Great Organization Inc. [7414]
Great Plains [7415]
Griffin Wood Company Inc. [27312]
Griffith Inc.; R.C. [7417]
Grinnell Door Inc. (GS & D) [7418]
Gross-Yowell and Company Inc. [7420]
Grove City Farmers Exchange Co. [771]
Guido Inc.; Gino [7422]
Guido Lumber Company Inc. [7423]
Gulf South Forest Products, Inc. [27313]
Gunther and Co.; Albert [7424]
Gunton Corp. [7425]
Guthrie-Linebaugh-Coffey, Inc. [9930]
Gypsum Wholesalers Inc. [7426]
Hager Lumber Company Inc.; T.W. [7428]
Hager Lumber Company Inc.; T.W. [27314]
Haggerty Lumber [7429]
Hammer-Johnson Supply Inc. [7435]
Hammer Lumber Company Inc. [7436]
Hampton Affiliates Inc. [7437]
Hampton Lumber Sales Co. [7438]
Hancock Lumber Inc. [27315]

Hankins Lumber Company, Inc. [7439]
Harbor Sales Company [7441]
Harbor Sales Co. [27316]
Hardie Export; James [7442]
Harding and Lawler Inc. [7443]
Hardware Imagination [7445]
Hardware Imagination [7446]
Hardwoods of Morganton Inc. [7447]
Hardy Corp. [7448]
Harrell Co.; Hollis [13742]
Hartsburg Grain Co. [17979]
Harvey Industries Inc. [7451]
Harvey Lumber Company Inc. [7452]
Hatley Lumber Co. Inc. [7453]
Hattenbach Co. [7454]
Hauser Company; M.L. [16092]
Hawkeye Building Supply Co. [7458]
Heap Lumber Sales Company Inc. [7465]
Herald Wholesalers Inc. [13751]
Hermann Associates Inc. [24561]
Herregan Distributors, Inc. [9944]
Herregan Distributors Inc. [9945]
Herregan Distributors, Inc. [9946]
Hi Lo Table Manufacturing Inc. [13130]
Higginbotham-Bartlett Co. [7469]
Higgins Lumber Co.; J.E. [7470]
Higgins Lumber Co.; J.E. [7471]
Higgins Lumber Co.; J.E. [7472]
Higgins Lumber Co.; J.E. [7473]
Higgins Lumber Co.; J.E. [7474]
Higgins Lumber Co.; J.E. [27317]
Hillsdale Sash and Door Co [27318]
Hoboken Wood Flooring Corp. [15529]
Hoboken Wood Floors [9949]
Hoboken Wood Floors [9950]
Holland Southwest International Inc. [7477]
Holmquist Grain and Lumber Co. [18002]
Holston Builders Supply Company Inc. [7479]
Holt and Bugbee Co. [9952]
Home Lumber Company Inc. [7481]
HomeBase Inc. [15532]
Hommer Lumber Co.; J.H. [7483]
Honsador Inc. [7484]
Hopson Broker Inc.; Thomas R. [7487]
Horner Flooring Company Inc. [9953]
House of Glass Inc. [21458]
Houston-Starr Co. [7491]
HPG Industries Inc. [7492]
HPM Building Supply [27320]
Hubbard Wholesale Lumber Corp.; A.P. [27321]
Humphrey Company Inc.; P.D. [7498]
Hundman Lumber Do-it Center Inc. [7499]
Hunter Trading Corporation [27322]
Hurst Lumber Company Inc. [7500]
Huttig Sash & Door Co. [7502]
Imagination & Co. [7506]
Indiana Wholesalers Inc. [15540]
Industrial and Wholesale Lumber Inc. [7511]
Inland Plywood Co. [7512]
Insular Lumber Sales Corp. [7513]
Interior Supply Inc. [7515]
Intermountain Lumber Co. [7516]
Intermountain Wood Products [27323]
International Industries Inc. [7518]
International Paper Co. McEwen Lumber Co. [7519]
Interstate Supply [9969]
Interstate Supply Co. [9971]
Jaeckle Wholesale Inc. [9978]
Jarvis Steel and Lumber Company Inc. [7531]
Jay-K Independent Lumber Corp. [7532]
Jenkins Co.; H.W. [27324]
Joffe Lumber and Supply Company Inc. [7535]
Johnson-Doppler Lumber Co. [7536]
Jordan Lumber and Supply Inc. [7538]
Judson Lumber Co. [7539]
Judson Lumber Co. [27325]
K and A Lumber Company Inc. [27326]
Kagiya Trading Co. Ltd. of America [13779]
Kaplan Lumber Company Inc. [7542]
Karpen Steel Custom Doors & Frames [7543]
Keene Div. [25922]
Keene Div. [27327]
Kentucky Indiana Lumber Company Inc. [7546]
Kermit Nolan Lumber Sales [7547]
Ketcham Forest Products Inc. [27328]

Ketcham Lumber Company Inc. [7549]
Kevco Inc. [27329]
Key Wholesale Building Products Inc. [7550]
Kimbrell Ruffer Lumber [7555]
Kindt Collins Co. [25700]
King Sash and Door Inc. [7558]
Kirby Forest Products; J. [7559]
Kiri Trading Co. Ltd. [5111]
Kitchen Distributors Maryland [15189]
Knapp Supply Company Inc. [23237]
Knecht Home Lumber Center Inc. [7565]
Knecht Home Lumber Center Inc. [27331]
Lake Erie Supply, Inc. [7577]
Lake States Lumber [7578]
Lake States Lumber [7579]
Lake States Lumber [7580]
Lake States Lumber Inc. [7581]
Lampert Yards Inc. [7583]
Landvest Development Corp. [7585]
Lanham Hardwood Flooring Co. [9990]
Lansing Corp.; Ted [7586]
Le Roy Farmers Cooperative Grain and Stock Co. [947]
Lebanon Building Supply Co. [7590]
Lee Lumber and Building Materials Corp. [7591]
Lee Wholesale Supply Company Inc. [7593]
Leingang Siding and Window [7594]
Lenover & Son Inc.; J.E. [9]
Lensing Wholesale, Inc. [7595]
Leo Distributors Inc. [7596]
Lewis Brothers Lumber Company Inc. [7598]
Lewis Company Inc.; Dwight G. [7599]
Lewisohn Sales Company Inc. [7600]
Liberty Industries Inc. [27334]
Liberty Woods International, Inc. [7603]
Lincoln-Kaltek [7607]
Link Lumber Co.; C.J. [27335]
Locust Lumber Company Inc. [7608]
Loroman Co. [9003]
Lott Builders Supply Co. [7612]
Lott Builders Supply Co. [27336]
Lumber Exchange Terminal Inc. [7616]
Lumber Inc. [7617]
Lumber Yards Inc. [27337]
Lumbermen's Inc. [7619]
Lumbermen's Merchandising Corp. [7620]
Lumbermens Millwork and Supply Co. [7621]
Lumberyard Supply Co. [7622]
Lyman Lumber Co. [7623]
M & N Supply Corp. [7627]
MacDonald and Owen Lumber [7631]
MacMillan Bloedel Building Materials [7633]
Magic Touch Enterprises, Inc. [10003]
Maine Entrepreneurs Group [17508]
Mallco Lumber and Building Materials Inc. [7635]
Manis Lumber Company Inc. [27339]
Mann and Parker Lumber Co. [27340]
Mar Vista Lumber Co. [7639]
Mariotti Building Products Inc. [7641]
Marketor International Corp. [7642]
Marley Mouldings Inc. [7643]
Marquart-Wolfe Lumber Company Inc. [7644]
Marquette Lumbermen's Warehouse Inc. [7645]
Marsh Kitchens Greensboro Inc. [7647]
Marshall Building Specialties Company Inc. [7648]
Martin and MacArthur [7654]
Martin Millwork Inc. [7655]
Massachusetts Lumber Co. [7662]
Massey Builders Supply Corp. [7663]
Master Building Supply and Lumber Co. [7664]
Matheus Lumber Company Inc. [7667]
Matthews and Fields Lumber of Henrietta [7670]
Mayfield Building Supply Co. [7671]
McCall Woodworks Inc. [13175]
McCausey Lumber Co. [7675]
McCoy and Company Inc.; Lawrence R. [7676]
McCoy and Company Inc.; Lawrence R. [27342]
McCray Lumber Co. [7677]
McDaniels Sales Co. [15224]
McDonald Lumber Company Inc. [7679]
McEllin Company, Inc. [10015]
McGinnis Lumber Company Inc. [7681]
McIlvain Co.; Alan [7682]
McIlvain Co.; T. Baird [7683]
McKenzie; C.D. [7685]
McQuesten Company Inc.; Geo. [27343]

Mechanics Building Materials Inc. [7688]
Medply [27344]
Mega Cabinets Inc. [7689]
Mega Company [2939]
Mehrer Drywall Inc. [7690]
Menominee Tribal Enterprises [7692]
Mentor Lumber and Supply Company Inc. [7694]
Mequon Distributors Inc. [7695]
Merrimack Valley Wood Products Inc. [7698]
Metal Industries Inc. [7700]
Meyer Laminates Inc. [27345]
MH World Trade Corp. [26143]
Michigan Hardwood Distributors [10028]
Michigan Industrial Hardwood Co. [7701]
Michigan Lumber Co. [7702]
Mid-AM Building Supply Inc. [7704]
Mid Pac Lumber [23265]
Mid-South Building Supply of Maryland Inc. [7705]
Midpac Lumber Company Ltd. [7707]
Midwest Farmers Cooperative [1037]
Midwest Veneer Company [7709]
Mill Creek Lumber and Supply Co. [7712]
Miller Bros. Lumber Company Inc. [7713]
Miller and Company Inc. [7714]
Miller Lumber Inc.; William T. [7715]
Miller Lumber Industries Inc. [7716]
Millman Lumber Co. [7717]
Minfelt Wholesale Company Inc. [7719]
Minneapolis Rusco Inc. [7722]
Minooka Grain Lumber and Supply Co. [7723]
Minot Builders Supply Association [7724]
Minton's Lumber and Supply Co. [7725]
Mintzer Brothers Inc. [7726]
Misco Shawnee Inc. [10042]
Mission Lumber Co. [7727]
Mitsui & Co. (USA), Inc. Seattle Branch [16312]
MKS Industries Inc. [7731]
M.L. Sandy Lumber Sales Company Inc. [27346]
Modern Door and Hardware Inc. [7732]
Modern Kitchen Center Inc. [7734]
Modern Supply Company Inc. [15238]
Moderne Cabinet Shop [7736]
Modernfold of Florida, Inc. [7737]
Modernfold of Florida Inc. [27347]
Montrose Hardwood Company Inc. [7741]
Morgan Distribution Inc. [7743]
Morgan Forest Products [7745]
Morgan Lumber Company Inc. [7746]
Morgan-Wightman Supply Company [7747]
Morgan-Wightman Supply Inc. Indiana [7748]
Morris Tile Distributors Inc. [10061]
Moser Lumber Inc. [7750]
Moshofsky Enterprises [7751]
Mott Equity Exchange [13839]
Moynihan Lumber [7753]
Mr. Hardwoods, Inc. [10068]
M.R.D. Products Inc. [26920]
Muench Woodwork Company Inc. [27349]
Musolf Distributing Inc.; Lon [10070]
Musolf Distributing Inc.; Lon [10071]
M.W. Manufacturers Inc. [7756]
Myers and Son Inc.; John H. [7757]
Nashville Sash and Door Co. [7763]
Natcom International [19475]
National Industrial Lumber Co. [7764]
National Lumber Co. [7765]
Neita Product Management [16346]
Netterville Lumber; Fred [7771]
Neubert Millwork Co. [7772]
New England Door Corp. [7773]
Newell Company Inc.; C.A. [10077]
Newman Lumber Co. [7775]
Nickerson Lumber and Plywood Inc. [7777]
Niehaus Lumber Co. [7778]
Nielsen Co. Inc.; E.A. [7779]
Nissho Iwai American Corp. [20226]
Norandex, Inc. [7785]
Norandex, Inc. [7786]
Norandex Sales Co. [7789]
Norby Lumber Company Inc. [27350]
Norfield Industries [7790]
North American Plywood Corp. [7791]
North Branch Flooring [10080]
North Pacific Group, Inc. [7794]
Northern Jersey Reserve Supply Co. [7796]
Northern Ohio Lumber and Timber Co. [7797]

Northern Ohio Lumber and Timber Co. [27351]
Northland Corp. [7798]
Northridge Lumber Company Inc. [7799]
Northwest Wood Products Inc. [7800]
N.R.F. Distributors, Inc. [10081]
O'Connell Wholesale Lumber Co.; John J. [7802]
Ocotillo Lumber Sales Inc. [7803]
Ocotillo Lumber Sales Inc. [27352]
Okaw Buildings Inc. [7808]
Old Masters Products Inc. [10085]
Old Masters Products Inc. [10086]
Olympic Flooring Distributors Inc. [10087]
One Source Home and Building Centers [7812]
Orders Distributing Company Inc. [10088]
OREPAC Millwork Products [7814]
Overhead Door Company Inc. [7817]
Owens Forest Products [27353]
Pacific Coast Building Products Inc. [7822]
Pacific Flooring Supply [10094]
Pacific Lumber and Shipping Co. [27354]
Pacific Mutual Door Co. [7825]
Pacific Supply [7828]
Pallet Recycling Center Inc. [25931]
Palmer-Donovan Manufacturing [7831]
Parr Lumber Co. [7835]
Partners 4 Design Inc. [15266]
Patrick Industries Inc. [7839]
Patrick Lumber Company Inc. [7840]
Pauls Tops & Knobs [7842]
Paxton Co.; Frank [27355]
Pella Windows and Doors Inc. [7844]
Penberthy Lumber Co. [7845]
Peninsula Supply Company Inc. [7846]
Pennsylvania Plywood & Lumber [7848]
Pennville Custom Cabinetry for the Home [7849]
Pennville Custom Cabinetry for the Home [27357]
Penrod Co. [7850]
Petersburg Box and Lumber Inc. [27358]
PGL Building Products [7856]
Philadelphia Fire Retardant Company Inc. [7858]
Philadelphia Reserve Supply Co. [7859]
Phillips Brothers Lumber Company Inc. [27359]
Pikesville Lumber Co. [7863]
Pine City Cooperative Association [18166]
Pine Cone Lumber Company Inc. [7864]
Pine Tree Lumber Co. [7865]
Piper Weatherford Co. [13869]
Pittston Lumber and Manufacturing Co. [7867]
Plunkett Webster Inc. [7871]
Pluswood Distributors [7872]
Plywood-Detroit Inc. [7873]
Plywood Discount Center [7874]
Plywood Oshkosh Inc. [13210]
Plywood Supply Inc. [7875]
Plywood Tropics USA Inc. [7876]
Powell Wholesale Lumber Co. [7880]
Prassel Lumber Company Inc. [7884]
Pratt & Dudley Building Materials [7885]
PrimeSource Inc. [7886]
Products Corp. of North America, Inc. [12226]
Prudential Metal Supply Corp. [7888]
Puget Sound Manufacturing Co. [7890]
Q.E.P. Co. Inc. [27361]
Quality Window & Door [7892]
Quigley Sales and Marketing and
    Associates [7893]
Radford Co. [7897]
Rajala Lumber Co. [7898]
Rand & Jones Enterprises Co., Inc. [16437]
Randall Brothers Inc. [7899]
Randall's Lumber [7900]
Redhawk Industries Inc. [27362]
Redwood Empire Inc. [7907]
Reed Export, Inc.; Charles H. [10117]
Reeves Southeastern Corp. [7908]
Refrigeration Supply Inc. [13217]
Reico Distributors Inc. [7909]
Reisen Lumber and Millwork Co. [7910]
Replacement Hardware Manufacturing Inc. [7917]
R.E.S. Associates [7918]
Rev-A-Shelf, Inc. [15633]
Rew Material Inc. [7923]
Rex Lumber Co. (Acton, Massachusetts) [7924]
Rhodes Supply Company Inc. [7927]
Richardson Dana Div. [7929]
Richardson & Sons Distributors [7930]

Ridout Lumber Cos. [27363]
Riemeier Lumber Company Inc. [7933]
Riggs Wholesale Supply [7934]
Rittner Products Inc. [7938]
Riverside Group Inc. [7940]
RJM Sales, Associates, Inc. [13888]
The Roane Co. [10123]
The Roane Co. [27364]
Roberts and Dybdahl Inc. [7941]
Roberts International, Inc. [7942]
Robinson Lumber Company Inc. [7945]
Robinson Lumber Company Inc. [27365]
Rocco Building Supplies Inc. [7946]
Rock Lumber and Supply Co.; Glen [7947]
Rockwell [7949]
Roddis Lumber and Veneer Company Inc. [7951]
Roethele Building Materials Inc. [7952]
Rogers Kitchens Inc. [13224]
Ross Supply Company Inc. [23352]
Royal Carpet Distribution, Inc. [10129]
Rugby Building Products [7967]
Rugby Building Products, Inc. [7968]
Rugby Building Products Inc. [27366]
Rugby USA Inc. [27367]
S & M Lumber Co. [7970]
S and M Lumber Co. [27368]
Sagebrush Sales Inc. [7971]
San Joaquin Lumber Co. [7976]
Sanders Co. [7978]
Sandy Lumber Sales Company Inc.; M.L. [7979]
Saria International Inc. [13903]
Sashco Inc. [7980]
Sasser Lumber Company Inc. [7981]
Saunders Supply Company Inc. [7983]
Saxonville USA [7984]
Scharpfs Twin Oaks Builders Supply Co. [7985]
Scholl Forest Industries [7986]
Scholl Forest Products Inc. [7987]
Schorr Insulated Glass Inc.; Norm [7988]
Schultz Snyder Steele Lumber Co. [7989]
Schultz Snyder Steele Lumber Co. [27369]
Schutte Lumber Company Inc. [7990]
Schutte Lumber Company Inc. [27370]
Scott Lumber Co. [7992]
Scotty's Inc. [7993]
SCR Inc. [7994]
SCR Inc. [27371]
Scranton Equity Exchange Inc. [7995]
Sea-Pac Sales Co. [10140]
Seaford and Sons Lumber; C.A. [7996]
Seago Export [7997]
Sealaska Timber Corp. [27373]
Seattle Kitchen Design Inc. [13236]
Seattle Kitchen Design Inc. [27374]
SERVISTAR Corp. [8002]
Seven D Wholesale [8004]
Shaw Lumber Co. [8006]
Shehan-Cary Lumber Co. [8008]
Shehan-Cary Lumber Co. [27375]
Shelter Super Store Corp. [27376]
Shepherd Products Co. [23033]
Shepler International Inc. [8011]
Shook Builder Supply Co. [13917]
Shuster's Builders Supply Co. [8015]
Shutters Inc. [8016]
Sierra Building Supply, Inc. [8017]
Sierra Point Lumber and Plywood Co. [8018]
Sierra Point Lumber and Plywood Co. [27377]
Simmons Lumber Company Inc. [8022]
Sinclair Lumber Co. [8025]
Sioux Veneer Panel Co. [8026]
Skelton and Skinner Lumber Inc. [8027]
Slaughter Industries [8031]
SM Building Supply Coompany, Inc. [8032]
Smith Hardwood Floors [10154]
Smith Lumber Co.; G.W. [8034]
Smith; Merle B. [10155]
Smith-Sheppard Concrete Company Inc. [8035]
Snavely Forest Products Inc. [8037]
Solar Graphic Inc. [15660]
Somers Lumber and Manufacturing Inc. [8040]
Soult Wholesale Co. [8041]
South Atlantic Forest Products Inc. [27378]
South Texas Lumber Co. [8042]
Southeastern Supply Company Inc. [8046]
Southern Architectural Systems, Inc. [8047]

Southern Cross and O'Fallon Building Products
   Co. [13929]
Southern Flooring Distributors [10160]
Southern Flooring Distributors [10162]
Southern Flooring Distributors [10164]
Southern Illinois Lumber Co. [8050]
Southern Sash Sales and Supply Co. [8051]
Southern Specialty Corp. [8052]
Southern States Lumber Company Inc. [8053]
Southern Store Fixtures Inc. [8054]
Southland Floors, Inc. [10170]
Southwest Plywood and Lumber Corp. [8056]
Spahn and Rose Lumber Co. [8057]
Spellman Hardwoods Inc. [8061]
Stadelman and Co.; Russell [8065]
Standard Supply Company Inc. [8070]
Stanford Lumber Company Inc. [8071]
Stanline Inc. [10176]
Starfire Lumber Co. [27380]
Steeler Inc. [27381]
Stephan Wood Products Inc. [27382]
Stewart Lumber Co. [8075]
Stiller Distributors Inc. [10182]
Stottlemyer and Shoemaker Lumber Co. [8076]
Strait and Lamp Lumber Company Inc. [8079]
Street Art Supply Dallas [21591]
Stringfellow Lumber Co. [8081]
Stripling Blake Lumber Co. [8082]
Sublette Farmers Elevator Co. [18266]
Summitville Baltimore [10187]
Sumter Wood Preserving Company Inc. [8086]
Sun Control Window Tinting and Shades [8087]
Sun Control Window Tinting and Shades [27383]
Sunnyvale Lumber Inc. [8088]
Superior Lumber Co. [27384]
Superior Products, Inc. [10195]
Supply One Corp. [23400]
Surface Technology Corp. [15674]
Swaner Hardwood Company Inc. [8092]
Swartz Supply Company Inc. [23402]
Sweeney Company Inc.; R.E. [8093]
Swiff-Train Co. [10196]
Swiff-Train Co. [10197]
Swiff-Train Co. [10198]
T & A Supply Co. [10202]
T & L Distributors Company Inc. [10204]
T & L Distributors Company Inc. [10206]
T & L Distributors Company Inc. [10207]
Tabor City Lumber Inc. [8096]
Talladega Machinery and Supply Co. [26220]
Tanner Forest Products Inc. [8097]
Taylor Lumber and Treating Inc. [8100]
Tech-Aerofoam Products Inc. [8103]
Tech Products, Inc. [8104]
Temp Glass Southern, Inc. [8106]
Tennessee Building Products Inc. [8108]
Tennessee-Carolina Lumber Company Inc. [8109]
Texas Plywood and Lumber Company Inc. [8116]
Texas Plywood and Lumber Company Inc. [27385]
Thermal Tech, Inc. [8118]
Thomas Kitchens, Inc. [8121]
Thomas and Proetz Lumber Co. [8122]
Thomas Tile & Carpet Supply Co. Inc. [10212]
Thompson Mahogany Co. [27386]
Tile Distributors Inc. [10232]
Tilers—Pergo Shop; J.R. [10247]
Tiles Plus [10250]
Timber Products Co. [8135]
Timber Products Co. Medford [27388]
Timberwork Oregon Inc. [27389]
Tinder Inc.; W.M. [27390]
TML Associates Inc. [8138]
Tradeways Inc. [13260]
Tradewinds International Inc. [8141]
Tri-Parish Cooperative Inc. [1354]
Triangle Pacific Corp. Beltsville Div. [8148]
Trimble Company Inc.; William S. [8149]
Truman Farmers Elevator Co. [1361]
Tulnoy Lumber Inc. [8152]
Tumac Lumber Company Inc. [8153]
United Builders Supply of Jackson Inc. [8156]
United Hardwood, L.L.C. [8157]
United International Inc. [8158]
United Manufacturers Supplies Inc. [13974]
United Plywood and Lumber Inc. [8159]
U.S. World Trade Corp. [18305]

Universal Corp. [26365]
Universal Forest Products, Inc. [27391]
Urban Ore Inc. [8162]
U.S.A. Woods International [8164]
Vaagen Brothers Lumber Inc. [8165]
Valley Best-Way Building Supply [8166]
Valley Fir and Redwood Co. [8167]
Valley Hardwood Inc. [8168]
Valley-Western Distributors, Inc. [10270]
Valley-Western Distributors, Inc. [10271]
Valley-Western, Inc. [10272]
Valley-Western, Inc. [10273]
Van Arsdale-Harris Lumber [8169]
Van Arsdale-Harris Lumber [27392]
Van Hoose and Company Inc.; F.S. [8170]
Vansant Lumber [8172]
Vaughan and Sons Inc. [8174]
Vaughn Lumber Co.; Emmet [8175]
Vaughn Materials Company Inc. [8176]
Vector Industries Inc. [8177]
Venus Manufacturing Co. [8178]
VerHalen Inc. [8180]
Vidalia Naval Stores Co. [8181]
Viking [8182]
Villafane Inc.; Rene Ortiz [8183]
Virginia Hardwood Co. [8186]
Virginia Hardwood Co. [10278]
Virginia Hardwood Co. [10279]
Virginia Hardwood Co. [10280]
Vivian Corp. [8187]
Waggener Lumber Co. [8191]
Walczak Lumber Inc. [8192]
Walston Co.; William H. [8194]
Walton Lumber Company Inc. [8195]
Walton Wholesale Corp. [10284]
Washington Loggers Corp. [27393]
Watson Lumber Co. [8197]
WBH Industries [13987]
Weiler Wilhelm Window and Door Co. [8201]
Westar Inc. [24044]
Western Door and Sash Co. [8206]
Western Home Center Inc. [8207]
Western Home Center Inc. [27394]
Western Shower Door Inc. [8213]
Westgate Building Materials [8215]
Westvaco Worldwide [21990]
Whittier-Ruhle Millwork [8221]
Wholesale Building Materials Co. [8222]
Wholesale Hardwood Interiors Inc. [8223]
Wholesale Supply Group, Inc. Maryville
   Division [23458]
Wilf Corp.; Elias [10300]
Williams Distributing Co. [15373]
Willis Steel Corp. [20494]
Winco Distributors Inc. [8230]
Window Components Manufacturing [8232]
Window Headquarters Inc. [8233]
Wisconsin Drywall Distributors [8234]
W.N.C. Pallet & Forest Products Company
   Inc. [8237]
W.N.C. Pallet and Forest Products Company
   Inc. [27395]
Wolohan Lumber Co. [8238]
Wood Brothers and Halstead Lumber [25948]
Wood Floor Wholesalers [10305]
Wood Floor Wholesalers [10306]
Wood Flooring Distributors [10307]
Wood & Plastics Industries [8240]
Woody's Big Sky Supply, Inc. [8241]
Yardville Supply Co. [8245]
Yeatman Architectural Hardware Inc. [14004]
Yezbak Enterprises [27397]
Yezbak Lumber Inc. [8246]
Yorktowne Inc. [8247]
Yorktowne Kitchens [8248]
Yorktowne Kitchens [8249]
Younce and W.T. Ralph Lumber Company Inc.;
   J.W. [27398]
Young Co.; William M. [8250]
Zeager Brothers Inc. [27399]
Zeeland Lumber and Supply Inc. [8253]

SIC 5032 — Brick, Stone & Related Materials

A & A Ceramic Tile, Inc. [9637]
A and H Building Materials Co. [6895]
ABC Tile Distributors [9638]
ABC Tile Distributors [6900]
Accent On Tile [9639]
Accent Tile [9640]
Acme Brick Co. [6907]
Acme Brick Co. [9641]
Acme Brick Co. [9642]
Acme Brick Co. [9643]
Acme Brick Co. [9644]
Acme Brick & Tile [9645]
Acme Brick, Tile and More [6908]
Action Equipment Company Inc. [6911]
Advanced Ceramics Research Inc. [6917]
Adventure Group, Inc. [9648]
Albany Tile Supply [9650]
Alfredo's Tile Distributors [9651]
All Standard Tile Corp. [9652]
All Tile [9653]
Allen Company Inc. [6937]
Alley-Cassetty Coal Co. [20510]
Allied-Eastern Distributors [9656]
Allied-Eastern Distributors [9657]
Allied Flooring Supply [9659]
Alpha Tile Distributors, Inc. [9661]
Alpha Tile Distributors, Inc. [9662]
Alpha Tile Distributors, Inc. [9663]
Alpha Tile Distributors, Inc. [9664]
Alpha Tile Distributors, Inc. [9665]
Alpha Tile Distributors, Inc. [9666]
Aluma Systems USA Inc. [6949]
Amarillo Building Products Inc. [6953]
AMC Tile Supply [6954]
American Ceramic Tile [9667]
American Equipment Company Inc. [6963]
American Equipment Marble & Tile, Inc. [6968]
American Floor Covering [9669]
American Import Tile [9670]
American Limestone Company Inc. [6969]
American Marazzi Tile, Inc. [9671]
American Tile Co. of Tucson [9672]
American Tile Distributors [9673]
American Tile Supply [9674]
American Tile Supply [9675]
American Tile Supply [9676]
American Tile Supply [9677]
American Tile Supply Company, Inc. [9678]
American Tile Supply Inc. [9679]
Anderson Tile Sales [9681]
Anderson Tile Sales [9682]
Anderson Tile Sales [9683]
Architectural Floor Systems, Inc. [9684]
Architectural Surfaces, Inc. [9685]
Arley Wholesale Inc. [9686]
Armline [9687]
Artesanos Imports Company Inc. [6993]
Artistic Tile Co. Inc. [9688]
Arundel Corp. [6995]
Ashley Aluminum Inc. [6998]
Associated Tile Sales [9690]
Atlanta Tile Supply, Inc. [9691]
Atlantic Ceramic Tile [9692]
Atlantic Construction Fabrics Inc. [7003]
Badger Corrugating Co. [7010]
Bale Ready-Mix Concrete; Gary [7017]
Barco Industries Inc. [13583]
Bardon Trimount Inc. [7021]
Barker Steel Co. Inc. Lebanon Div. [7023]
Bartley Tile Concepts Inc. [7026]
Basins Inc. [7028]
Bath/Kitchen & Tile Supply Co. [15415]
Batts Distributing Co.; James B. [9695]
Batts Distributing Co.; James B. [9696]
Beaver Distributors [7038]
Bedrosian Building Supply [9698]
Bedrosian Building Supply [9699]
Bedrosian Building Supply [9700]
Bedrosian Tile & Marble Supply [9701]
Bedrosian Tile Supply [9702]
Bedrosian Tile Supply [9703]

Bedrosian Tile Supply [9704]
Bedrosian Tile Supply [9705]
Bedrosian Tile Supply [9706]
Bedrosian Tile Supply [9707]
Bedrosian Tile Supply [9708]
Bedrosian Tile Supply [9709]
Bedrosian Tile Supply [9710]
Bedrosian Tile Supply [9711]
Bedrosian Tile Supply [9712]
Bedrosians [9713]
Bedrosians [7041]
Bedrosians Tile & Marble [9714]
Bedrosians Tile & Marble [9715]
Bedrosians Tile & Marble [9716]
Bedrosians Tile & Marble [9717]
Bedrosians Tile & Marble [9718]
Bedrosians Tile and Marble [7042]
Belair Road Supply Company Inc. [7044]
The Belknap White Group [9719]
The Bella Tile Company, Inc. [9720]
Bently Sand & Gravel [7046]
Best Tile Distributors of Albany, Inc. [9723]
Best Tile Distributors of Syracuse, Inc. [9724]
Best Tile Distributors of Wexford, Inc. [9725]
Big River Industries Inc. [7057]
Bing Construction Company of Nevada [7058]
Bird and Company Inc.; William M. [9727]
Bishop Distributing Co. [9728]
B.J.'s Ceramic Tile Distributing Company,
   Inc. [9729]
Black Forest Tile Distributors [7061]
Blue Diamond Materials Co. [7062]
Boise Cascade Corp. Building Materials Distribution
   Div. [27288]
Bonded Materials Co. [7068]
Boston Tile [9732]
Boston Tile Distributors of Shrewsbury [9733]
Boston Tile of Rhode Island [9734]
BPI [9735]
B.P.I. [9736]
BPI Inc. [9737]
BPI Inc. [9738]
Breckenridge Material [7078]
Brunt Tile & Marble [9742]
Buckeye Ceramic Tile [9744]
Buckeye Ceramic Tile [7092]
Buena Tile Supply, Inc. [9745]
Builder Marts of America Inc. [7098]
Builders General Supply Co. [7100]
Building Plastics Inc. [9746]
Bun Patch Supply Corp. [7107]
Burnett Construction Co. [7110]
Butler-Johnson Corp. [9747]
Butler-Johnson Corp. [9748]
Byrne Co. [7118]
C & R Tile [9749]
Cain & Bultman, Inc. [9750]
California Tile Distributors [9751]
California Tile Supply [9752]
Cancos Tile Corp. [9753]
Cancos Tile Corp. [7133]
Cannon and Sons Inc.; C.L. [7134]
Capitol Ceramic Inc. [9755]
Capitol Concrete Products Co. [7136]
Carabel Export & Import [9757]
Carder Inc. [7139]
Caro-Tile Ltd. [9759]
Carpet Cushion Supply [9765]
Carpet Isle Design Center [9769]
Carpet Mart & Wallpaper [9770]
Carroll Distribution Company, Inc. [9773]
Casa Mexicana [9775]
Case Supply, Inc. [9776]
Case Supply, Inc. [9777]
Case Supply, Inc. [9778]
Casey's Tile Supply Co. [9779]
Castillo Ready-Mix Concrete [7152]
Cathey Wholesale Co. [9780]
CDC [9781]
CDC [9782]
Cen-Cal Wallboard Supply Co. [7157]
Central Distributors Inc. [9783]
Century Tile and Carpet [9784]
Century Tile & Carpet [9785]
Century Tile & Carpet [9786]
Century Tile and Carpet [7163]

Century Tile and Supply [9788]
Century Tile and Supply Co. [9789]
Century Tile & Supply Co. [9790]
Ceramic Concept of Martin County [9791]
Ceramic Tile Center [7164]
Ceramic Tile Center Inc. [9792]
Ceramic Tile Center Inc. [9793]
Ceramic Tile Center, Inc. [9794]
Ceramic Tile Distributors [9795]
Ceramic Tile International [9797]
Ceramic Tile International [9798]
Ceramic Tile International [9799]
Ceramic Tile International [7165]
Ceramic Tile Supply Co. [9800]
Ceramic Tile Supply, Inc. [9801]
Charlotte Tile & Stone [9802]
Chase Trade, Inc. [407]
CISU of Dalton, Inc. [9806]
C.L. Industries Inc. [7175]
Classic Flooring Distributors [9810]
Classic Tile, Inc. [9811]
Clay Classics Inc. [7177]
Clay Ingels Company Inc. [7178]
Clay Tile Products; Allen [9812]
Clayton Tile [9813]
Cloutier Supply Co. [22944]
CMH Flooring Products Inc. [9814]
CMH Flooring Products Inc. [7186]
Coastal Tile & Roofing Co., Inc. [9815]
Cobb Rock Div. [7188]
Cobb Rock Inc. [7189]
Colonial Brick Co. [7197]
Commecial de Azulejos [9819]
Commerce Consultants Inc. [22154]
Commercial Plamar [9820]
Compass Concepts [9821]
Concrete Products and Supply Co. Inc. [7203]
Concrete Supply Corp. [7205]
Consolidated Tile and Carpet Co. [9822]
Contempo Ceramic Tile [9823]
Continental Ceramic Tile [9824]
Continental Flooring Inc. [9825]
Contractors Floor Covering [9826]
Cook Concrete Products Inc. [7213]
Copeland Paving Inc. [7220]
Corning-Donohue Inc. [7222]
Corriveau-Routhier, Inc. [9827]
Corriveau-Routhier, Inc. [7223]
Corriveau-Routhier Inc. [9828]
Corriveau-Routhier, Inc. [9829]
Corriveau-Routhier Inc. [7224]
Country Time Ceramic Supply Inc. [25612]
Coyle Inc. [15459]
Craftsmen Supply, Inc. [9830]
Craftsmen Supply, Inc. [9831]
Crest Distributors [9832]
The Cronin Co. [9833]
The Cronin Co. [9834]
Crown Tile & Marble [9835]
Crystal Tile [7234]
Cummings, McGowan and West Inc. [7236]
Curran Contracting Co. [7237]
D & B Tile [9840]
D & B Tile [9841]
D & B Tile [9842]
D & B Tile [9843]
D & B Tile [9844]
D & B Tile [9845]
D & B Tile Distributors [9846]
D and B Tile Distributors [7240]
Dailey Inc.; William E. [7245]
Daltile [7248]
D.C. Materials Inc. [26794]
Dealers Supply Co. [9849]
Decorative Products Group [9852]
Decorative Products Group [9853]
Del Sol Tile Co. [9854]
Delaware Brick Co. [7258]
Design Carpets [9856]
Design Surfaces [9858]
Design Surfaces [9859]
Designer Tile Co. East [9861]
Devine Brothers Inc. [7259]
Diamond W Supply Co. Inc. [9863]
Diamond W Supply Co. Inc. [9865]
Dickey and Son Inc.; D.W. [7263]

Diener Brick Co. [7264]
Diller Tile Company Inc. [23138]
Dimock, Gould and Co. [9866]
Direct Distributors [7267]
DMI Tile & Marble [9867]
Dobkin Company, Inc.; W.W. [9868]
Dobkin Company, Inc.; W.W. [9869]
Domestic Import Tile [9870]
Domus Corp. [9871]
Dowling Inc.; J.H. [7286]
Downs Supply Co. [9872]
Dura Sales Inc. [7290]
Durand Equipment and Manufacturing Co. [7291]
Dutchess Quarry and Supply Company Inc. [7292]
Dynamic International Company Inc. [7295]
East Coast Tile Imports—East [9875]
East Coast Tile/Terrazzo [9876]
East Coast Tile/Terrazzo [9877]
East Coast Tile/Terrazzo [7300]
Economy Builders Supply Inc. [7302]
El Rey Stucco Co. [7305]
Elsinore Ready-Mix Co. [7308]
Empire Sand and Gravel Company Inc. [7311]
Empire State Marble Manufacturing Corp. [9883]
Empire Wholesale Supply [9884]
Emser International [15489]
Enco Materials Inc. [19953]
Erie Sand and Gravel Co. [7317]
Erie Stone Company Inc. [7318]
Eskew, Smith & Cannon [9886]
Esojon International, Inc. [9887]
ESSROC Corp. [7321]
Expert Tile, Inc. [9888]
Explosive Supply Company Inc. [7327]
Expo Industries Inc. [7328]
Fiorano Design Center [9889]
Fire Brick Engineers Co. [7343]
Fischer Lime and Cement Co. [7346]
Fisher Sand and Gravel Co. [7347]
Fitzgerald Inc.; Albert F. [9890]
Flemington Block and Supply Inc. [7349]
Flooring Distributors Inc. [9897]
Floors Northwest Inc. [9900]
Franklin Industries Inc. [7367]
Frey, Inc. [9907]
Garden State Tile Design Center [9908]
Garden State Tile Distributors [9909]
Garden State Tile Distributors [9910]
Garden State Tile Distributors [9911]
Garden State Tile Distributors [7377]
Garden State Tile Distributors, Inc. [9912]
Gardner Inc.; E.L. [7379]
General Distributors Inc. [9914]
Genesee Ceramic Tile Distribution [9916]
Genesee Ceramic Tile Distributors [9917]
Genesee Ceramic Tile Distributors [9918]
Genesee Ceramic Tile Distributors [9919]
Genesee Ceramic Tile Distributors [9920]
Genesee Ceramic Tile Distributors [9921]
George Inc.; Edward [7389]
Georgetown Energy Inc. [7391]
Georgies Ceramic & Clay Co. [26499]
Gerrity Company Inc. [7395]
Global Tile [9922]
Gomoljak Block [7403]
Grabber Southeast [7405]
Grand Blanc Cement Products [7407]
Granite City Ready Mix Inc. [7410]
Granite City Ready Mix Inc. [7411]
Granite Rock Co. [7412]
Great Lakes Sales, Inc. [9925]
Great Lakes Sales, Inc. [9926]
Greenville Tile Distributors [9927]
Griswold and Company Inc.; S.T. [7419]
Gulf Enterprises [9928]
Guthrie-Linebaugh-Coffey, Inc. [9930]
Gypsum Wholesalers Inc. [7426]
Hager Lumber Company Inc.; T.W. [7428]
Haines & Company, Inc.; J.J. [9931]
Haines & Company, Inc.; J.J. [9932]
Haines & Co.; J.J. [9933]
Halebian; Michael [9934]
Halliday Sand and Gravel Co. [7432]
Hamilton-Parker, Co. [9935]
Hanson Aggregates West, Inc. [7440]
Hardco, Inc. [9936]

Hardie Export; James [7442]
Harrison Supply Co. [7450]
Hart Co. Inc.; Edward R. [9938]
Hawaiian Ceramic Tile [9939]
Hawkinson [9940]
HC Supply [7463]
Henry Corp.; E.P. [7467]
Henry Tile Co.; Robert F. [9941]
Henry Tile Co.; Robert F. [9942]
Herregan Distributors, Inc. [9944]
Herregan Distributors Inc. [9945]
Herregan Distributors Inc. [9947]
Hoboken Wood Flooring Corp. [9948]
Hoboken Wood Floors [9950]
Holmes Limestone Co. [20546]
House of Carpets, Inc. [9954]
Hudson Cos. [7494]
Hudson Valley Tile Co. [9955]
Hurst Supply [7501]
Iberia Tile [9956]
Iberia Tile [9957]
Iberia Tiles Inc. [9958]
IDA Inc. [7504]
Ideal Tile Co. [9959]
ImpoGlaztile [9960]
Import Tile Co. [9961]
Integral Kitchens [9963]
Integral Kitchens [7514]
Interceramic Inc. [9964]
Intercoastal Tile [9965]
Interior Specialties of the Ozarks [9966]
Intermountain Specialty Coatings [21465]
International Procurement Services, Inc. [7520]
International Purchasers, Inc. [7521]
International Tile & Marble, Ltd. [9967]
International Tile & Marble Ltd. [9968]
International Tile and Supply Corp. [15541]
Interstate Supply [9969]
Interstate Supply Co. [9970]
Interstate Supply Co. [9971]
Intertile Distributors, Inc. [9972]
Intertile Distributors, Inc. [9973]
Intertile Distributors, Inc. [9974]
Intile Designs, Inc. [9975]
Intile Designs Inc. [7524]
Intrepid Enterprises Inc. [7525]
Island-Northwest Distributing, Inc. [9976]
Jaeckle Wholesale Inc. [9978]
Jasco Tile Company, Inc. [9979]
JTM Tile Distributing, Inc. [9981]
Kahn & Son, Inc.; Irvin [9982]
Kansas Brick and Tile Company Inc. [7540]
Kansas Brick and Tile Company Inc. [7541]
Kaough Distributing Company, Inc. [9984]
Kate-Lo Div. [9985]
Kepcor Inc. [9988]
Kesseli Morse Company Inc. [7548]
Keystone Cement Co. [7553]
Knox Tile & Marble [9989]
Koenig Fuel & Supply Co. [22409]
Kuhlman Corp. [7572]
Lafarge Concrete [7575]
Lafarge Corp. [7576]
Lakeland Sand and Gravel Inc. [20551]
Lance Construction Supplies Inc. [7584]
Larson Distributing Company Inc. [9991]
Laufen International Inc. [9992]
Laurel Center [7587]
L.B.I. Company [9993]
L.B.I. Company [7589]
Lebanon Building Supply Co. [7590]
Lexco Tile [9995]
LI Tinsmith Supply Corp. [7601]
Lofland Co. [7609]
Louisville Tile Distributors [9998]
Louisville Tile Distributors, Inc. [9999]
Louisville Tile Distributors Inc. [10000]
Louisville Tile Distributors, Inc. [10001]
Louisville Tile Distributors Inc. [7614]
Louisville Tile Distributors Inc. [7615]
Maier Inc.; Ernest [7634]
Mainline Supply Corp. [10004]
Malisani, Inc. [10005]
Maly [10006]
Mankato-Kasota Stone [7636]
Manzo Contracting Co. [7638]

Marino Marble & Tile [10009]
Marlin Manufacturing & Distribution Inc.;
    R. [13396]
Marshall Building Specialties Company Inc. [7648]
Marshall Building Supply [7649]
Marshall's Tile Co. [10010]
Marshalltown Trowel Co. [7650]
Marvin Corp. [7657]
Maryland Clay Products [7658]
Maryland Clay Products [7659]
Maryland Tile Distributors [10011]
The Masonry Center [7660]
Masonry Product Sales Inc. [7661]
Master Tile [10012]
Material Service Corp. [7665]
Material Supply Inc. [7666]
Mathie Supply Inc. [7669]
McCullough Ceramic [10014]
McKee Brothers Inc. [7684]
Medallion Carpets [10018]
Medallion Carpets [10019]
Mees Distributors [10020]
Mees Distributors [10021]
Mees Distributors [10022]
Mees Distributors [10023]
Mees Tile and Marble Inc. [10024]
Mellott Estate Inc.; H.B. [7691]
Menchaca Brick & Tile Co. [10025]
Menoni and Mocogni Inc. [7693]
Metro Tile & Marble, Inc. [10027]
Mid-America Tile [10029]
Mid-America Tile [10030]
Mid-America Tile, Inc. [10031]
Mid-America Tile L.P. [10032]
Midwest Tile [10034]
Midwest Tile [10035]
Midwest Tile Supply Co. [10036]
Milford Enterprises, Inc. [10037]
Mill Contractor and Industrial Supplies, Inc. [7711]
Millers Wholesale, Inc. [25742]
Mills, Inc.; Aladin [10040]
Milroy and Company Inc.; W.H. [7718]
Mitchell Inc.; E. Stewart [7730]
Modern Builders Supply [10043]
Modern Builders Supply [10044]
Modern Methods Inc. [7735]
Monarch Ceramic Tile [10047]
Monarch Ceramic Tile [10048]
Monarch Cermaic Tile, Inc. [10050]
Monarch Tile [10051]
Monarch Tile [10052]
Monarch Tile [10053]
Monarch Tile [10054]
Monarch Tile [10055]
Montgomery Building Materials [10056]
Moreira Tile [10057]
Morris Tile Distributors [10058]
Morris Tile Distributors [10059]
Morris Tile Distributors Inc. [10060]
Morris Tile Distributors Inc. [10061]
Morris Tile Distributors of Norfolk, Inc. [10062]
Morris Tile Distributors of Richmond [10063]
Morris Tile Distributors of Roanoke, Inc. [10064]
Mosaic Tile [10065]
Mosaic Tile Co. [10066]
Mountain Tile [10067]
MQ Power Corp. [7754]
Murphy's Tile & Marble [10069]
Mutual Services of Highland Park [13841]
Nally & Haydon Inc. [7761]
Nattinger Materials Co. [7769]
Nemo Tile Company, Inc. [10073]
Nemo Tile Company, Inc. [10074]
Nemo Tile Company, Inc. [10075]
New England Sand and Gravel Co. [7774]
New Hampshire Tile Distributors [10076]
Nezbeda Tile, Inc. [10078]
Nezbeda Tile Inc. [7776]
Nido, Inc.; Rafael J. [10079]
Nitterhouse Concrete Product Inc. [7782]
Northmont Sand and Gravel Co. [20554]
N.R.F. Distributors, Inc. [10081]
Nu-Way Concrete Forms Inc. [7801]
Nueces Tile Sales [10082]
Ohio Tile & Marble Co. [10083]
Ohio Tile and Marble Co. [7806]

Ohio Valley Flooring [10084]
Olympic Flooring Distributors Inc. [10087]
Ontario Stone Corp. [7813]
Ornamental Tile and Design Center [10090]
Ottavino Corp.; A. [7816]
Oxford Recycling Inc. [7818]
Pacific Clay Brick Products Inc. [7821]
Pacific Coast Cement Corp. [7823]
Pacific Supply [7828]
Palmetto Tile Distributor [10098]
Pamas and Company Inc. [7832]
Paracca & Sons; Peter [10099]
Paradise Ceramics [10100]
Parma Tile Mosaic & Marble [10101]
Parson Cos.; Jack B. [7836]
Payne & Dolan Inc. Muskego Site [7843]
Pennsylvania Floor Coverings [10104]
Petrofina Delaware Inc. [22566]
Phelans [15619]
Phoenix Inc. [7862]
Ply-Gem Manufacturing Co. [25932]
Pozzolanic Northwest Inc. [7883]
Pratt & Dudley Building Materials [7885]
Prestige Marble & Tile Co. [10107]
Primavera Distributing [10108]
Primavera Distributing [10109]
Pumilite-Salem Inc. [7891]
Quality Tile Corp. [10111]
Quigley Sales and Marketing and
    Associates [7893]
Radandt Sons Inc.; Fred [7896]
Randall Tile Company, Inc. [10114]
RBC Tile & Stone [10115]
RBC Tile and Stone [7903]
R.C.P. Block and Brick Inc. [7905]
Readers Wholesale Distributors Inc. [10116]
Reco International Corp. [4109]
Rees Ceramic Tile; Cynthia [10118]
Renaissance Ceramic Tile [10119]
Renaissance Stoneworks [7915]
Renfrow Tile Distributing Company, Inc. [10120]
R.E.S. Associates [7918]
Reuther Material Co. [7921]
Revere Products [7922]
Rhode Island Tile/G & M Co. [10121]
Riley-Stuart Supply Co. [7935]
Rio Grande Co. [7936]
Riverside Group Inc. [7940]
Riverton Coal Co. [20564]
Riviera Tile Inc. [10122]
Robinson Brick Co. [7944]
Rocco Building Supplies Inc. [7946]
Rockville Fuel and Feed Company Inc. [7948]
Rogue Aggregates Inc. [7954]
Roma Tile Co., Inc. [10128]
Roofing Supply Inc. [7958]
Royal Carpet Distribution, Inc. [10129]
RSB Tile, Inc. [10132]
RSB Tile Inc. [7963]
Rubin Brothers Company Inc. [10133]
Rugby Building Products Inc. [7967]
Rugby Building Products, Inc. [7968]
Sahuaro Petroleum-Asphalt Company Inc. [7972]
Salinas Tile Sales Co. [10134]
Salinas Tile Sales, Inc. [10135]
Saltillo Tile Co. [7973]
Samuels Tile [10136]
Sand and Gravel Co.; J.P. [7977]
Sanford Tile Co. [10137]
Santa Clara Tile Supply [10138]
Sawtooth Builders [10139]
Scofield Company Inc.; George [7991]
Seatile Distributors [10141]
Self's, Inc. [10142]
Self's, Inc. [10143]
Sellers Tile Distributors [10144]
SG Wholesale Roofing Supply Inc. [8005]
Shannon Brothers Tile [10146]
Sharp Co.; William G. [10147]
Shears Construction L.P. [8007]
Shepler International Inc. [8011]
Shorts Wholesale Supply Co. [8014]
Sita Tile Distributors, Inc. [10150]
Smethurst & Sons; William [10151]
Smith Floor Covering [10152]
Smith Floor Covering Distributors [10153]

Smith-Sheppard Concrete Company Inc. [8035]
Sound Floor Coverings Inc. [10157]
South Alabama Brick [10158]
Southampton Brick & Tile, Inc. [10159]
Southeastern Construction Inc. [8044]
Southern Flooring Distributors [10160]
Southern Flooring Distributors [10161]
Southern Flooring Distributors [10164]
Southern Tile Distributors Inc. [10165]
Southern Tile Distributors Inc. [10166]
Southland Floors, Inc. [10170]
Southwestern Ceramic, Tile & Marble Co. [10171]
Southwestern Ceramic, Tile & Marble Co. [10172]
Sovereign Distributors, Inc. [10173]
Spaulding Brick Company Inc. [8058]
Spaulding Brick Company Inc. [8059]
Specialty Building Products, Inc. [10174]
Specialty Building Products Inc. [8060]
Stancorp Inc. [8066]
State Ceramic Tile, Inc. [10179]
States Distributing [10180]
Stephens; Stanley [10181]
Stiller Distributors Inc. [10182]
Stockdale Ceramic Tile Center, Inc. [10183]
Sullivan Tile Distributors [10185]
Summit Brick and Tile Co. [8085]
Summitville Atlanta [10186]
Summitville Baltimore [10187]
Summitville Boardman [10188]
Summitville Charlotte [10189]
Summitville Fairfax [10190]
Summitville Orlando [10191]
Summitville Pompano [10192]
Summitville, USA [10193]
Sun Coast Tile Distributors Inc. [10194]
Superior Block and Supply Co. [8090]
Superior Products, Inc. [10195]
Surface Sealing Inc. [8091]
Swiff-Train Co. [10196]
Swiff-Train Co. [10198]
Syverson Tile, Inc. [10201]
T & L Distributors Company Inc. [10203]
T & L Distributors Company Inc. [10204]
T & L Distributors Company Inc. [10206]
T & T Tile Distribution Inc. [10208]
Tallman Company Inc. [23405]
Tampa Tile Center [10209]
Tate Builders Supply L.L.C. [8099]
Taylor Distributors [10210]
Tayo's Tile Co. [8101]
Tee Tile Distributors, Inc. [10211]
Terre Hill Concrete Products [8111]
Tex-Mastic International Inc. [8113]
Texas Mining Co. [8115]
Thomas Tile & Carpet Supply Co. Inc. [10212]
Thompson Tile Co., Inc. [10213]
Thompson Tile Co., Inc. [10214]
Thompson Tile Co., Inc. [10215]
Thorpe Products Co. [8126]
Thunderbird Steel Div. [8130]
Tilcon Tomasso Inc. [8132]
Tile America [10216]
The Tile Barn [10217]
The Tile Center, Inc. [10218]
Tile City [10219]
Tile City [10220]
Tile City [10221]
Tile Club [10222]
Tile Club [10223]
Tile Club [10224]
Tile Club [10225]
Tile Club [10226]
Tile Club [8133]
Tile Collection [10227]
The Tile Collection, Inc. [10228]
Tile Country Inc. [10229]
Tile Creations [10230]
Tile Distributor Company Inc. [10231]
Tile Distributor Company Inc. [8134]
Tile Distributors Inc. [10232]
Tile Distributors, Inc. [10233]
Tile Expressions [10234]
Tile For Less [10235]
Tile Gallery Inc. [10236]
Tile Gallery Inc. [10237]
Tile Helper Inc. [10238]

Tile Inc. of Fayetteville [10239]
Tile International [10240]
Tile Mart, Inc. [10241]
The Tile Place [10242]
The Tile Place [10243]
The Tile Place [10244]
Tile Warehouse [10245]
Tile Wholesalers of Rochester [10246]
Tilers—Pergo Shop; J.R. [10247]
Tiles For Less [10248]
Tiles International [10249]
Tiles Plus [10250]
Tileworks [10251]
Toledo Tile [10253]
Townzen Tile & Laminates [10255]
Traffic Control Service Inc. [24644]
Transit Mix Concrete Co. [8142]
Transit Mix Concrete Co. [20438]
Travis Tile Sales [10257]
Travis Tile Sales [10258]
Tri-State Brick and Tile Co. [8144]
Troy Top Soil Company Inc. [8151]
Trym-Tex, Inc. [10259]
Twin City Marble [10260]
Underwood Builders Supply Co. [8155]
Unimast Inc. [20458]
Uniq Distributing Corp. [10262]
Uniq Distributing Group [10263]
United Distributors, Inc. [10264]
United Flooring Distributors Inc. [10265]
United Tile Company, Inc. [10266]
United Tile of LaFayette, LLC [10267]
Universal Marble and Granite Inc. [8161]
Valley Tile Distributors [10268]
Valley Tile & Marble [10269]
Valley-Western Distributors, Inc. [10270]
Valley-Western Distributors, Inc. [10271]
Valley-Western, Inc. [10272]
Valley-Western, Inc. [10273]
Vimco Concrete Accessories Inc. [8184]
Virginia Tile Co. [10281]
Virginia Tile Co. [10282]
Wade Distributors, Inc. [10283]
Wade Distributors Inc. [8190]
Waldo Brothers Co. [8193]
Walker and Zanger Inc. [13271]
Walton Wholesale Corp. [10284]
Wanke Cascade [10285]
Warrior Asphalt Refining Corp. [8196]
Wayne Tile Co. [10287]
Wayne Tile Co. [10288]
Wayne Tile Co. [10289]
W.B.R. Inc. [8199]
Westcott Worldwide [10291]
Western Design Tile [10292]
Western Materials Inc. [8209]
Western Pacific Interior [10293]
Western Tile Design Center [10294]
Western Tile Design Center (Dublin) [10295]
Western Tile Santa Rosa, Inc. [10296]
Westside Tile Co. [10297]
White Co.; Brock [8218]
Wholesale Ceramic Tile [10298]
Wiggins Concrete Products, Inc. [10299]
Wildish Land Co. [8224]
Wildish Sand and Gravel Co. [8225]
Wilf Corp.; Elias [10300]
Willamette Graystone Inc. [8226]
Winburn Tile [10302]
Wisconsin Brick & Block Corp. [10303]
W.N.C. Tile Distributors [10304]
Wolohan Lumber Co. [8238]
Wyo-Ben Inc. [17289]
Yahara Materials Inc. [8244]
Yardville Supply Co. [8245]
Yeager Hardware [10309]
Zumpano Enterprises, Inc. [10310]
Zumpano Enterprises, Inc. [10311]
Zumpano Enterprises, Inc. [10312]
Zumpano Enterprises, Inc. [10313]
Zumpano Enterprises Inc. [8255]

SIC 5033 — Roofing, Siding & Insulation

A and H Building Materials Co. [6895]
ABC Supply Co., Inc. [6899]
Acutron Co. [6912]
Adams Wholesale Co. Inc. [6914]
Akron Overseas Inc. [15749]
Alaska Insulation Supply, Inc. [6928]
Alcoa Authorized Distributing [6931]
Alexander Wholesale Inc.; W.C. [6932]
All-Right [6935]
Alley-Cassetty Coal Co. [20510]
Allied Building Products [6939]
Allied Building Products Corp. [6940]
Allied Building Products Corp. [6941]
Aluminum Distributors Inc. [6950]
Aluminum Products Co. [6951]
American Associated Roofing Distributor [6958]
American Builders and Contractors Supply
   Company Inc. [6959]
American Hydrotech Inc. [6967]
Anderson Lumber Co. [6976]
Applicator Sales & Service [6981]
Ashley Aluminum Inc. [6998]
Atlantic Building Products [7001]
Atlantic Coast Fiberglass Co. [7002]
Bartells Co.; E.J. [7025]
Basnight and Company Inc.; W.H. [7029]
Becker Builders Supply Co. [7039]
Behling Building Products; Gil [7043]
Berger Building Products Corp. [7048]
Bi-State Distributing Co. [7056]
BMI-France Inc. [7063]
Boatwright Insulation Co. [7064]
Boise Cascade Corp. Building Materials Distribution
   Div. [27288]
Bonnette Supply Inc. [7069]
Branton Industries Inc. [7077]
Brauer Supply Co. [14358]
Britton Lumber Company Inc. [7081]
Builders General Supply Co. [7100]
Builders Specialties Co. [7101]
Building and Industrial Wholesale Co. [7103]
Building Materials Wholesale [7105]
Building Products Inc. [7106]
Bun Patch Supply Corp. [7107]
Burton Building Products Inc. [7114]
Byrne Co. [7118]
Cameron Ashley Building Products Inc. [7130]
Cannon and Sons Inc.; C.L. [7134]
Carlson Distributors Inc. [7141]
Central Lumber Sales Inc. [7160]
Christy Refractories Co. L.L.C. [7171]
Clark-Schwebel Distribution Corp. [7176]
Cleasby Manufacturing Company Inc. [7179]
Coastal Tile & Roofing Co., Inc. [9815]
Collins; James [7196]
Con-Mat Supply [7202]
Condeck Corp. [7206]
Convenience Products [7212]
Corken Steel Products Co. [14405]
Cornerstone Group [7221]
Dal CAM Oil Co. Inc. [7247]
Damon Insulation Co. [7249]
Dealers Supply Co. [7254]
Dealers Supply Co. [7255]
Diomede Enterprises, Inc. [7266]
Dixie Building Supplies Co. [7272]
Dowling Inc.; J.H. [7286]
DW Distribution [7293]
Eagle Supply Inc. [7296]
East Side Lumberyard Supply [9878]
Eikenhout and Sons Inc. [7304]
Fairfax Trailer Sales Inc. [14440]
Fiberlay Inc. [7339]
Four States Industrial Distributors [7363]
Fowler and Associates Inc.; R.W. [7364]
Fowler and Peth Inc. [7365]
FRP Supplies Inc. [7372]
General Materials Inc. [7385]
Genesee Reserve Supply Inc. [7386]
George Co.; Edward [7389]
GLS Corp. [7400]

Guido Inc.; Gino [7422]
H & H Distributing Inc. [7427]
Hardie Export; James [7442]
Harvey Industries Inc. [7451]
Hawkeye Building Supply Co. [7458]
Hodgin Supply Company Inc. [7475]
Hudson Liquid Asphalts, Inc. [7496]
Industrial Distributors [7507]
Industrial Products Co. [7510]
International Procurement Services, Inc. [7520]
Irex Corp. [7526]
Jacobson & Company Inc. [7529]
Jay-K Independent Lumber Corp. [7532]
Key Wholesale Building Products Inc. [7550]
Kinetics Inc. [7557]
Kleptz Aluminum Building Supply Co. [7562]
Kramig Company Inc.; R.E. [7571]
L & L Insulation and Supply Co. [7573]
Lampert Yards Inc. [7583]
Lansing Corp.; Ted [7586]
Lee Wholesale Supply Company Inc. [7593]
Leingang Siding and Window [7594]
Lensing Wholesale, Inc. [7595]
MacArthur Co. [7630]
Manufacturers Reserve Supply Inc. [7637]
Marshall Building Supply [7649]
Marvin Corp. [7657]
Mathews; Manfred [7668]
McBride Insulation Co. [7673]
McKenzie; C.D. [7685]
McLaughlin Distributor; J.E. [7686]
Merit Insulation Inc. [7697]
Mid-AM Building Supply Inc. [7704]
Mid-South Building Supply of Maryland Inc. [7705]
Mid-State Industries Ltd. [7706]
Midwest Sales Company of Iowa Inc. [7708]
Miller Bros. Lumber Company Inc. [7713]
Miller Lumber Inc.; William T. [7715]
Monroe Insulation & Gutter Company Inc. [7739]
Montopolis Supply Co. [7740]
N & L Inc. [7759]
Nailite International Inc. [7760]
National Manufacturing, Inc. [7766]
Norandex, Inc. [7785]
Norandex/Reynolds Distribution Co. [7788]
Norandex Sales Co. [7789]
North Brothers Co. [7792]
Northern Jersey Reserve Supply Co. [7796]
Novakovich Enterprises [22531]
Ollesheimer & Son Inc.; Louis T. [7811]
One Source Home and Building Centers [7812]
Orca Oil Company, Inc. [22542]
Pacific Coast Building Products Inc. [7822]
Pacific Supply [7828]
Packings & Insulations Corp. [7829]
Pan Am Distributing Inc. [7833]
Passaic Metal & Building Supplies Co. [7838]
Patrick Industries Inc. [7839]
Pittston Lumber and Manufacturing Co. [7867]
Plant Insulation Co. [7868]
Plaschem Supply & Consulting [7869]
Plaschem Supply & Consulting Inc. [7870]
Plywood Supply Inc. [7875]
Polycoat Systems Inc. [7878]
Powers Products Co. [7882]
Pratt & Dudley Building Materials [7885]
Quigley Sales and Marketing and
    Associates [7893]
R.E.S. Associates [7918]
Reserve Supply of Central New York Inc. [7920]
Revere Products [7922]
Rew Material Inc. [7923]
Reynolds Metals Co. Construction Products
    Div. [7925]
RI Roof Truss Co. Inc. [7928]
Roberts International, Inc. [7942]
Roberts and Sons Inc.; Frank [7943]
Rocco Building Supplies Inc. [7946]
Roofers Supplies Inc. [7956]
Roofing Distributing Company Inc. [7957]
Roofing Supply Inc. [7958]
Roofing Wholesale Company Inc. [7959]
RPM Inc. [7962]
Rugby Building Products [7966]
Rugby Building Products Inc. [7967]
Sedmak; Louie [7998]

SG Wholesale Roofing Supply Inc. [8005]
Shook and Fletcher Insulation Co. [17173]
Shorts Wholesale Supply Co. [8014]
Sierra Roofing Corp. [8019]
Silver State Roofing Materials [8021]
SKR Distributors [8028]
Snowbelt Insulation Company Inc. [8038]
Soult Wholesale Co. [8041]
Southern Sash Sales and Supply Co. [8051]
Southland Distributors [8055]
Standard Building Products [8067]
Standard Roofings Inc. [8068]
Stowers Manufacturing Inc. [8078]
Tasco Insulations Inc. [8098]
Tate Builders Supply L.L.C. [8099]
Tempco Contracting & Supply [8107]
Tennison Brothers Inc. [8110]
Texxon Enterprises Inc. [8117]
Thermal Tech, Inc. [8118]
Thermax Insulation Inc. [8119]
Thorpe Corp. [8124]
Thorpe Insulation Co. [8125]
T.J.T. Inc. [8137]
Tri-State Insulation Co. [8145]
Trym-Tex, Inc. [10259]
United Builders Supply of Jackson Inc. [8156]
Urethane Contractors Supply [8163]
Vansant Lumber [8172]
Variform Inc. [8173]
Verby Company Inc.; H. [8179]
Vidalia Naval Stores Co. [8181]
Viking [8182]
Warrior Asphalt Refining Corp. [8196]
Wausau Supply Co. [8198]
WD Industries Inc. [8200]
Wesco Cedar Inc. [8202]
Wesmac Enterprises [18636]
West Company; William H. [8203]
Western MacArthur Co. [8208]
Western Materials Inc. [8209]
Western Products Inc. [8212]
Wimsatt Brothers Inc. [8229]
Wood Feathers Inc. [8239]
Young Sales Corp. [8251]

SIC 5039 — Construction Materials Nec

84 Lumber Co. [6894]
A and H Building Materials Co. [6895]
ABC Supply Co., Inc. [6899]
Abeita Glass Co. [6901]
Able Enterprises Inc. [6903]
ACI Distribution [6905]
Acmat Corp. [6906]
Acme Brick & Tile [9645]
Acme Coal Co. [6909]
Acoustical Material Services [25057]
Acoustical Solutions, Inc. [6910]
Action Equipment Company Inc. [6911]
Adams Wholesale Co. Inc. [6914]
Addison Corp. [6915]
AFGD [6919]
AFGD [6920]
AFGD [15390]
AFGD [6921]
AFGD [6922]
AFGD [6923]
AFGD [6924]
Airtex Corp. [6926]
AIS Construction Equipment Corp. [6927]
Alexander Wholesale Inc.; W.C. [6932]
Allen Company Inc. [6937]
Allen Millwork Inc. [6938]
Allied Building Products Corp. [6942]
Aluma Systems USA Inc. [6949]
Aluminum Products Co. [6951]
American Associated Roofing Distributor [6958]
American Distributing Co. [6962]
Americas Trade & Supply Co. [2237]
Anderson Lumber Co. [6976]
Apex Supply Company Inc. [14323]
A.P.I. Inc. [6980]

Armstrong and Dobbs Inc. [6986]
Arrow-Master Inc. [6992]
Ashley Aluminum Inc. [6998]
Astrup Co. [25970]
Atlantic Building Products [7001]
Atlantic Construction Fabrics Inc. [7003]
Atlantic Hardware and Supply Corp. [13571]
Bakersfield Sandstone Brick Co. Inc. [7015]
Barco Municipal Products Inc. [24511]
Barker Steel Co. Inc. Lebanon Div. [7023]
Barnett Millworks Inc. [7024]
Barton and Co.; E.C. [7027]
Basnight and Company Inc.; W.H. [7029]
Beal's Royal Glass and Mirror Inc. [7033]
Bedrosians [9713]
Belair Road Supply Company Inc. [7044]
Berkowitz L.P.; J.E. [7049]
Best Glass Co. [7053]
BET Rentokil Plant Services [7054]
Beynon Farm Products Corp. [25894]
Bi-State Distributing Co. [7056]
Binswanger Glass Co. [7059]
Boise Cascade Corp. Building Materials Distribution
    Div. [27288]
Booker and Company Inc. [7070]
Boston Metal Door Company Inc. [7072]
Bradley Supply Company Inc.; R.W. [7075]
Branton Industries Inc. [7077]
Brin-Northwestern Glass Co. [7079]
Broz, Inc.; John V. [7088]
Buffington Corp. [7096]
Builders Center Inc. [7099]
Builders General Supply Co. [7100]
Builders Hardware & Specialties [13611]
Building and Industrial Wholesale Co. [7103]
Building Materials Distributors Inc. [7104]
Bun Patch Supply Corp. [7107]
Burly Corporation of North America [7109]
Burns Industries Inc. [7112]
Burton Lumber Corp. [7115]
Butler-Johnson Corp. [7116]
Butterfield Building Supply [7117]
Cadillac Glass Co. [7123]
California Glass Co. [7126]
California Panel and Veneer Co. [7127]
Calotex Delaware, Inc. [7128]
Calvert & Hoffman [7129]
Cameron Ashley Building Products Inc. [7130]
Cardinal Glass Co. [7140]
Carolina Building Co. [7142]
Carolina Door Controls [7143]
Carotek Inc. [15879]
Carter-Waters Corp. [7149]
Cash Supply Co. [13623]
Caye and Company Inc.; W.C. [7154]
CBS Contractors Supply Co. [7155]
Central Distributors Inc. [9783]
Central Door & Hardware [7158]
Central Wholesale Supply Corp. [7162]
Cimarron Lumber and Supply Co. [7172]
Cimarron Materials Inc. [7173]
Circle Glass Co. [7174]
Clipper Energy Supply Co. [7184]
CMA Incorporated [10779]
Cofer Brothers Inc. [7190]
Colony Lumber Co. [7198]
Compotite Corp. [7200]
Comtech [7201]
Concrete Supply Co. [7204]
Construction Products of Washington [7208]
Cookson Co. [27300]
Cornerstone Group [7221]
Corning-Donohue Inc. [7222]
Crittenden Paint and Glass [21421]
D & L Stained Glass Supply, Inc. [25619]
D.A. Distributors Inc. [7244]
Dairyman's Supply Co. [7246]
Dana Kepner Co. [23132]
Davidson Louisiana Inc. [7251]
Dennis Refrigeration & Electric [14415]
Design House Inc. [13664]
Devlin Lumber and Supply Corp. [7260]
Diomede Enterprises, Inc. [7266]
Discount Building Materials [7268]
Donnybrook Building Supply Inc. [7279]
Dougherty Hanna Resources Co. [7284]

Dowling Inc.; J.H. [7286]
Dremont-Levy Co. [21434]
D.S.A. Materials Inc. [8635]
Dunaway Supply Co. [7289]
Dutchess Quarry and Supply Company Inc. [7292]
DW Distribution [7293]
Dynamic Distributors [7294]
East Coast Mill Sales Co. [7299]
Eastern Penn Supply Co. [23144]
EcoCycle Inc. [21718]
Economy Builders Supply Inc. [7302]
Ellsworth Builders Supply Inc. [7307]
Erb Hardware Co. Ltd. [13688]
Esty and Sons Inc.; Ralph A. [7323]
Everett Anchor and Chain [19959]
Expo Industries Inc. [7328]
Fager Company Inc.; R.F. [23154]
Fairfax Trailer Sales Inc. [14440]
Fargo Glass and Paint Co. [21440]
Farmers Cooperative Co. [17853]
Federal Pipe and Supply Co. [7332]
Federal Pipe and Supply Co. [7333]
Ferguson Electric Construction Company
   Inc. [8737]
Fiberglass Representatives Inc. [23166]
Fiberlay Inc. [7339]
Fields and Co.; J.D. [7340]
Fingerle Lumber Co. [7341]
Firebird International, Inc. [7344]
Fischer Lime and Cement Co. [7346]
Fontaine Industries Inc. [7353]
Forderer Cornice Works Co. [7356]
Fort Worth Lumber Co. [27306]
Fortman's Paint & Glass [21445]
Foster Co.; L.B. [16875]
Franciscan Glass Co. [7366]
General Glass Company Inc. [7384]
Genesee Reserve Supply Inc. [7386]
George Co.; Edward [7389]
George Co.; Edward [7390]
Georgia Marble Co. [7393]
Getz Bros. & Company Inc. [16062]
Glantz & Son; N. [25661]
Glass Depot [7398]
Globe Iron Construction Company Inc. [20009]
Goldner Company Inc.; Herman [23195]
Grinnell Door Inc. (GS & D) [7418]
GTH Holdings, Inc. [7421]
Gypsum Wholesalers Inc. [7426]
Hager Lumber Company Inc.; T.W. [7428]
Hallmark Building Supplies Inc. [7433]
Hammer Lumber Company Inc. [7436]
Hattenbach Co. [7454]
Hawaii Hardware Company Ltd. [13745]
Hawaii Modular Space Inc. [7457]
Haywood Builders Supply Inc. [7461]
HC Supply [7463]
Hi-Way Products Inc. [20035]
High Country Kitchens [15168]
Holmes A-One Inc. [7478]
Holston Builders Supply Company Inc. [7479]
HomeBase Inc. [15532]
Hopper and Son Inc.; Ora B. [7486]
House of Glass Inc. [21458]
Houston Stained Glass Supply [7490]
Hudson Glass Company Inc. [7495]
Humac Engineering and Equipment Inc. [7497]
IDA Inc. [7504]
Import Tile Co. [9961]
Indiana Supply Corp. [16943]
Industrial Motor Supply Inc. [7509]
Industrial Steel Warehouse Inc. [20060]
International Procurement Services, Inc. [7520]
Interstate Glass Distributors [7523]
Intraco Corp. [2796]
Irving Materials Inc. [7527]
Jacksonville Mechanical Supply Inc. [16967]
Jay-K Independent Lumber Corp. [7532]
Jenkins Co.; H.W. [27324]
Jensen Bridge and Supply Inc. [23224]
JETT Supply Company Inc. [7534]
Johnson Hardware Company Inc. [7537]
K and A Lumber Company Inc. [27326]
Kesseli Morse Company Inc. [7548]
Kinast Distributors Inc.; E. [7556]
Kiri Trading Co. Ltd. [5111]

Kiwi Fence Systems Inc. [7560]
Knape and Vogt Manufacturing Co. [7564]
Knecht Home Lumber Center Inc. [7565]
Kobelco Welding of America Inc. [7566]
Kobrin Builders Supply Inc. [7567]
L and W Supply Corp. [7574]
Lafarge Concrete [7575]
Lakeside Harvestore Inc. [7582]
Lampert Yards Inc. [7583]
Lansing Corp.; Ted [7586]
Lawrence Plate Glass Co. [7588]
Leo Distributors Inc. [7596]
LI Tinsmith Supply Corp. [7601]
Libbey Owens Ford Co. [7602]
Lore L. Ltd. [7611]
Louisville Plate Glass Company Inc. [7613]
Lowville Farmers Cooperative Inc. [973]
Loyd's Electric Supply Co. [9005]
Lumberman of Indiana [7618]
Lumbermen's Merchandising Corp. [7620]
Lyman-Richey Corp. [7624]
Mac Supply Co. [7628]
Machine Maintenance Inc. [7632]
Main Auction [13168]
Maran-Wurzell Glass and Mirror Inc. [15575]
Marchand Contractors Specialties Inc.; R.J. [7640]
Marshall Building Specialties Company Inc. [7648]
Martensen Enterprises Inc. [7651]
Marus and Weimer, Inc. [23252]
Marvitec Export Corporation [16268]
Massey Builders Supply Corp. [7663]
McCarthy Steel Inc. [20161]
McCoy and Company Inc.; Lawrence R. [7676]
McDougall Company Inc.; John W. [7680]
Meadow Steel Products Div. [7687]
Mechanics Building Materials Inc. [7688]
Medford Co-operative Inc. [18085]
Melton Steel Corp. [20164]
Mendez & Co. Inc. [1865]
Mentor Lumber and Supply Company Inc. [7694]
Mervis Industries Inc. [20168]
Mid-AM Building Supply Inc. [7704]
Mid-South Building Supply of Maryland Inc. [7705]
Midpac Lumber Company Ltd. [7707]
Millers Wholesale, Inc. [25742]
Milwaukee Stove and Furnace Supply Company
   Inc. [14606]
Minfelt Wholesale Company Inc. [7719]
Minneapolis Glass Co. [7721]
Mintzer Brothers Inc. [7726]
Modern Kitchen Center Inc. [7734]
Monje Forest Products Co. [7738]
Monroe Insulation & Gutter Company Inc. [7739]
Morgan Distribution Inc. [7743]
Moss Co.; Roscoe [7752]
Mr. Hardwoods, Inc. [10068]
M.R.D. Products Inc. [26920]
Murphy Door Specialties Inc.; Don [7755]
Namasco [20212]
Nashville Sash and Door Co. [7763]
Newell Company Inc.; C.A. [10077]
Nippon Electric Glass America Inc. [7780]
Nitterhouse Masonry Products, LLC [7783]
Nolan Scott Chatard L.L.C. [7784]
Norandex Inc. [7787]
Norandex/Reynolds Distribution Co. [7788]
Northern Jersey Reserve Supply Co. [7796]
Nu-Way Concrete Forms Inc. [7801]
Oki Trading, Ltd.; T. [7809]
Oshtemo Hill Inc. [7815]
Pac-West Inc. [7819]
Pacific Flooring Supply [10095]
Pacific Southwest Sales Company Inc. [9172]
Pacor Inc. [7830]
Paint West Decor Center [21530]
Patrick Industries Inc. [7839]
Petrotank Equipment Inc. [22575]
Pfaff and Smith Builders Supply Co. [7854]
PGL Building Products [7856]
Pharis Organization Inc. [7857]
Pine Cone Lumber Company Inc. [7864]
Plant Insulation Co. [7868]
Plunkett Webster Inc. [7871]
Polar Supply Company Inc. [21542]
Powers Products Co. [7882]
Pratt & Dudley Building Materials [7885]

PrimeSource Inc. [7886]
Pritchard Paint and Glass Co. [21547]
Prudential Building Materials [7887]
Prudential Metal Supply Corp. [7888]
Quality Window & Door [7892]
Quigley Sales and Marketing and
   Associates [7893]
R & R Sales Inc. [7894]
R & R Scaffold Erectors, Inc. [7895]
Reeves Southeastern Corp. [7908]
Regal Steel Supply Inc. [20311]
Reliable Architectural Metals Co. [7911]
Reliable Glass Co. [7912]
Renaissance Drywall and Construction Supplies
   Inc. [7914]
Renner & Associates; E.J. [7916]
Ren's Clearfield Paint & Glass [21555]
Replacement Hardware Manufacturing Inc. [7917]
Reserve Industries Corp. [7919]
Reserve Supply of Central New York Inc. [7920]
Riggs Supply Co. [13886]
Riggs Wholesale Supply [7934]
Riley-Stuart Supply Co. [7935]
Rittner Products Inc. [7938]
Rivard International Corp. [7939]
Roberts and Sons Inc.; Frank [7943]
Rocco Building Supplies Inc. [7946]
Roddis Lumber and Veneer Company Inc. [7951]
Rogers Group Inc. Louisville [7953]
Romac Export Management Corp. [15639]
Roofing Distributing Company Inc. [7957]
Ross Island Sand and Gravel Co. [7961]
Roth Distributing Co. [15294]
Rugby Building Products, Inc. [7968]
Samuels Glass Co. [7975]
Saria International Inc. [13903]
Saunders Oil Company Inc. [7982]
Schorr Insulated Glass Inc.; Norm [7988]
Scion Steel [20357]
Sepia Interior Supply [8000]
Service Keystone Supply [8001]
SERVISTAR Corp. [8002]
Shepler International Inc. [8011]
Sherwin Williams Paint Co. [21573]
Shibamoto America, Inc. [16487]
Shields Harper and Co. [22667]
Shorts Wholesale Supply Co. [8014]
Simione and Associates, Inc.; Bill [23939]
Slakey Brothers Inc. [8030]
Soil Stabilization Products Company Inc. [4514]
Sommer and Maca Industries Inc. [16503]
Southeastern Access Control [8043]
Southern California Pipe and Steel Co. [8048]
Southern Cross and O'Fallon Building Products
   Co. [8049]
Southern Electric Service Company, Inc. [9385]
Southern Specialty Corp. [8052]
Southland Distributors [8055]
Spahn and Rose Lumber Co. [8057]
Spaulding Brick Company Inc. [8058]
Spellman Hardwoods Inc. [8061]
Standard Supplies Inc. [8069]
Standard Supply and Hardware Company
   Inc. [17194]
Star Sales and Distributing Co. [8073]
State Line Supply Co. [20390]
Steel Inc. [20395]
Steel Supply Co. [20401]
Steven Industries, Inc. [21589]
Stewart Lumber Co. [8075]
Stottlemyer and Shoemaker Lumber Co. [8076]
Stratham Hardware & Lumber Co. [21590]
Strober Building Supply Center Inc. [8083]
Structural Materials Inc. [8084]
Sun Control Window Tinting and Shades [8087]
Sun Distributors L.P. [16537]
Sunrise Glass Distributors [8089]
Sweetman Construction Co. [8094]
Tate Builders Supply L.L.C. [8099]
TDA Industries Inc. [8102]
Temp Glass [8105]
Temp Glass Southern, Inc. [8106]
Tews Co. [8112]
Tex-Mastic International Inc. [8113]
Texas Plywood and Lumber Company Inc. [27385]
Theisen Farm and Home Stores [1326]

Thermwell Products Co. Inc. [8120]
Three Rivers Aluminum Co. [8128]
Thunander Corp. [8129]
Thunderbird Steel Div. [8130]
Trade Corporation [8140]
Trimble Company Inc.; William S. [8149]
Troy Top Soil Company Inc. [8151]
United Builders Supply of Jackson Inc. [8156]
United International Inc. [8158]
Urban Ore Inc. [8162]
Vansant Lumber [8172]
Venus Manufacturing Co. [8178]
Viking Distributing Company Inc. [17254]
Virginia Construction Supply Inc. [8185]
Virginia Hardwood Co. [10277]
VVP America Inc. [15698]
Waco Inc. [20477]
Waggener Lumber Co. [8191]
Westeel Inc.; W.S. [25947]
Western Home Center Inc. [8207]
Westshore Glass Corp. [8216]
Wholesale Building Materials Co. [8222]
Wildish Sand and Gravel Co. [8225]
Williams Equipment and Supply Company
    Inc. [8227]
Wilson and Sons Inc.; W.A. [15708]
Wimsatt Brothers Inc. [8229]
Wind-Dorf (USA) Inc. [8231]
Wizard Equipment Corp. [8236]
Wolohan Lumber Co. [8238]
Woody's Big Sky Supply, Inc. [8241]
Yardville Supply Co. [8245]
Yezbak Lumber Inc. [8246]

SIC 5040 — Professional & Commercial Equipment

Noodle Head Network [22884]

SIC 5043 — Photographic Equipment & Supplies

AGFA Corp. [22823]
Albums Inc. [22824]
Amcam International Inc. [22825]
American Video & Audio Corp. [25072]
Anderson and Vreeland Inc. [15773]
Apollo Space Systems Inc. [22826]
Arriflex Corp. [22827]
Attraction Services Corp. [22828]
AVAS VIP [25092]
Beattie Systems Inc. [22829]
Bel Trade USA Corp. [22830]
Beta Screen Corp. [25572]
Birns & Sawyer Inc. [22831]
Bodman Chemicals, Inc. [4337]
Bogen Photo Corp. [22832]
Boston Electronics Corporation [22833]
Boston Productions Inc. [22834]
Brandons Camera [22835]
Brauner Export Co. [8466]
Burlington A/V Recording Media, Inc. [25112]
CAI Div. [22836]
Camera Corner Inc. [22837]
Camera Service Center of Maine [22838]
Cantel Medical Corp. [18725]
Capitol Entertainment & Home [22839]
Capitol Motion Picture Corp. [25119]
Caribiner International [25122]
Cash Indiana [22840]
Cass Inc.; Veronica [22841]
Celestron International [22842]
Central Audio Visual Equipment Inc. [22843]
Chilcote Co. [22844]
Chimera Co [22845]
Chromaline Corp. [22846]
Clark Productions Inc.; Dick [8530]
Commonwealth Films Inc. [25143]
Comprehensive Video Group [22847]
Computer Optics Inc. [22848]

CPAC Inc. [22849]
Cushing and Company Inc. [25617]
Custom Photo Manufacturing [22850]
D/A Mid South Inc. [24531]
DaLite Screen Co. [25155]
Dot Line [22851]
Elden Enterprises [25175]
Eye Communication Systems Inc. [22852]
Film Technologies International, Inc. [22853]
Fuji Medical Systems USA Inc. [22854]
Gate Group USA, Inc. [22855]
Gattas Company Inc.; Fred P. [15512]
GKM Enterprises Inc. [22856]
Glacier Studio [22857]
GMI Photographic Inc. [22858]
Graphic Systems Inc. [25669]
Great Lakes Technologies Corp. [22859]
Greentree Productions Inc. [22860]
Gross-Medick-Barrows Inc. [22861]
GSI Corp. [21021]
Gulf Coast Electric Supply Company Inc. [8821]
Haffner X-Ray Company Inc. [18820]
Hamamatsu Photonic Systems [22862]
HD Communications Inc. [5634]
Heitz Service Corp. [22863]
Helix Ltd. [22864]
Hoag Enterprises, Inc. [22865]
HPS, Inc. [22866]
Hubbard Printing Equipment [25682]
Industrial Service Co. [22867]
JOS Projection Systems Inc. [21080]
Jungkind Photo-Graphic Inc. [25695]
Kaufman Co. Inc.; Hal [22868]
Kinetronics Corp. [22869]
Konica Quality Photo East [22870]
Konica U.S.A. Inc. [22871]
Lamination Services Inc. [16227]
Lawrence Photo-Graphic Inc. [22872]
Leedal Inc. [22873]
Light Creations [22874]
London Litho Aluminum Company Inc. [6444]
Mahalick Corp. [25722]
Mamiya America Corp. [22875]
Mathias Reprographics [25726]
McAlister Camera Co.; Don [22876]
Media Communications Corp. [22877]
Medical Imaging Inc. [18916]
Merit Marketing Inc. [5185]
Midwest Music Distributors [25322]
Minnesota Western Inc. [25326]
Minolta Corp. [22878]
Minolta Corp. [22879]
Mitsubishi Electronics America Inc. [25329]
Moviola/J & R Film Company, Inc. [22880]
MPC Educational Systems Inc. [25343]
Murphy Co. [22881]
New Era Media Supply [22882]
Nikon Inc. [22883]
Noritsu America Corp. [22885]
O'Connor Engineering Laboratories [22886]
Olympus America Inc. [22887]
Options International Inc. [25370]
Packtronics Inc. [25374]
Paulist Productions [22888]
Pentax Corp. [22889]
Photo-Cine Labs [22890]
Photo Control Corp. [22891]
Pitman Co.; Harold M. [25786]
Prepress Supply [22892]
Primesource [25790]
Primesource [22893]
Production Services Atlanta Inc. [22894]
Quintana Sales [22895]
Rainbow Photography [22896]
Really Right Stuff Co. [22897]
Recognition Systems Inc. [25799]
Redlake Imaging Corp. [22898]
Ricom Electronics Ltd. [6690]
Roma Enterprises [25421]
Samsung Opto-Electronics America Inc. [22900]
Santa Barbara Instrument Group Corp. [22901]
Savage Universal Corp. [22902]
Schillers Photo Graphics [22903]
Showscan Entertainment Inc. [25442]
Sigma Corporation of America [22904]
Sinar-Bron Inc. [22905]

SMP Enterprises Inc. [26656]
Southwestern Camera [22906]
Stimpson Productions; John [22907]
Studio Film & Tape Inc. [25467]
Studio Film & Tape Inc. [22908]
Supercircuits Inc. [22909]
Superscope Technologies, Inc./Marantz
    Professional [25469]
Taskforce Batteries [22910]
Tele-Measurements Inc. [25475]
Transoceanic Trade, Inc. [22911]
UMI [22912]
USI Inc. [21333]
UV Process Supply Inc. [9529]
Vanguard Imaging Corp. [4546]
Vision Broadcasting Network [22913]
Vivitar Corp. [22914]
VWR Scientific Products Corp. [26242]
Western Photo Packaging [22915]
Yankee Photo Products Inc. [22916]
Young-Phillips Sales Co. [25884]

SIC 5044 — Office Equipment

A-1 Lock & Safe Co. [20758]
A & A Office Systems Inc. [5498]
A & B Business Equipment Inc. [20759]
A & B Electronic Systems Inc. [20760]
A-Copy Inc. [20761]
A Timely Tech Services [20762]
Abacus [20764]
Able Steel Equipment Co. Inc. [20765]
ABM of Bismarck Inc. [20766]
Accent Business Products [20768]
Accurate Office Machines Inc. [20769]
ACS Digital Solutions [20770]
ADA Computer Supplies Inc. [5873]
Ada Copy Supplies Inc. [20771]
Advance Business Systems and Supply
    Co. [20775]
Advanced Financial Systems [20776]
Advanced Office Systems Inc. [20777]
Advocate Publishing Co. [20778]
All About Offices Inc. [20783]
All Makes Office Machine Company Inc. [20784]
Allanson Business Products [5904]
Alpha Source Inc. [8331]
Alpina International Inc. [21626]
American Business Concepts [20789]
American Business Machines [20791]
American Copy Inc. [20792]
American Loose Leaf Business Products
    Inc. [20793]
American Mailing Systems Inc. [20794]
American Office Machines Inc. [20795]
American Office Systems [20796]
American Photocopy Equipment Co. [20797]
American Safe and Lock Co. [20798]
Americas Trade & Supply Co. [2237]
Ameritrend Corp. [20800]
Ames Industries Inc. [20801]
Anacomp Inc. International Div. [20803]
Anders Office Equipment Co. [20805]
Andover Communications Inc. [20806]
Apgar Office Systems Inc. [20808]
Astro Business Solutions Inc. [20816]
Astro Office Products Inc. [20817]
ATC Computer and Business Machines
    Inc. [20818]
Atlas Reproduction Inc. [20820]
ATS Money Systems Inc. [25567]
Automated Business Systems [20822]
Automated Office Systems Inc. [20824]
Aztec Business Machines Inc. [20826]
B & B Office Supply Inc. [20827]
Bay Microfilm Inc. Library Microfilms [20836]
Bernstein Office Machine Co. [20840]
Best Business Products Inc. [20841]
BEST Cash Registers [20842]
Block and Company Inc. [20845]
Blue Ribbon Business Products Co. [20846]
Boise Cascade Office Products Corp. [20848]
Bond Co.; T. Talbott [20849]
Brain Corp. [20853]

Broadway Office Interiors [20856]
Brooks Duplicator Co. [20857]
Brother International Corp. [20858]
Brothers Office Supply Inc. [20859]
BT Office Products International Inc. Detroit Div. [20861]
Burkett's Office Supply Inc. [13051]
Business Data Systems Inc. [20866]
Business Support Services [20869]
Business World Inc. [20871]
Canon U.S.A. Inc., Office Products Div. [20875]
Capital Stationery Corp. [20876]
Capitol Copy Products Inc. [20877]
Cardamation Company Inc. [20879]
Carolina Office Equipment Co. [20881]
Carolina Office Equipment Co. [20882]
Casas Office Machines Inc. [20883]
Cash Register Sales Inc. [20884]
Cash Register Sales & Service [20885]
Cash Register Systems Inc. [20886]
Casio, Inc. [17362]
Castle Copiers & More Inc. [20887]
Central Audio Visual Equipment Inc. [22843]
Central Business Supply Inc. [20889]
Central Business Systems Inc. [20890]
Central Maine Business Machines [20891]
Century Business Equipment Inc. [20893]
CERBCO Inc. [20894]
Charlotte Copy Data Inc. [20896]
Chip & Wafer Office Automation [20898]
Church Business Machines [20899]
City Business Machines Inc. [20901]
Clute Office Equipment Inc. [20903]
Comtech Inc. [20908]
Contemporary Office Products Inc. [20910]
Cook's Inc. [20913]
Copy Center Inc. [20914]
Copy Center Inc. [20915]
Copy-Co Inc. [20916]
Copy Plus Inc. [20917]
Copy Sales Inc. [20918]
Copyline Corp. [20919]
Copytronics Inc. [20920]
Cornelius Systems Inc. [20921]
Corporate Copy Inc. [20922]
Corporate Data Products [20923]
Corporate Express [20926]
Creative Business Concepts [20938]
Croy & Associates Inc.; Ralph [8595]
CRS Business Products [20941]
Dale Office Plus [20944]
Danka Business Systems PLC [20946]
Danka Industries Inc. [20947]
Danka Inwood Business Systems Inc. [20948]
Data Information Service [20949]
Demco Inc. [20954]
Dependable Business Machines [20955]
Desert Stationers [20956]
Dick Co.; A.B. [20961]
Dick Products of Albuquerque; A.B. [20962]
Digital Business Automation [20963]
Distinctive Business Products Inc. [20967]
Diversified Copier Products Inc. [20969]
Dixie Art Supplies Inc. [20970]
Document Solutions Inc. [20972]
DocuSource Inc. [20973]
Dresco Reproduction Inc. [24348]
Dupli-Fax Inc. [20975]
Ecco Corp. [20979]
ECR Sales & Service Inc. [20982]
Educational Distributors of America [13102]
Educators Resource, Inc. [20984]
Edward Business Machines Inc. [20985]
EGP Inc. [20986]
Electronic Bus Systems of Nevada [20988]
Electronic Office Systems [20989]
Elliott Office Products Inc. [20990]
Eltrex Industries Inc. [20991]
Empire Office Machines Inc. [20992]
Equipment and Parts Export Inc. [2594]
Eye Communication Systems Inc. [22852]
F & E Check Protector Co. Inc. [20999]
Farmer Office Products Inc. [21000]
Fas-Co Coders Inc.orporated [21001]
Ferro Co.; Michael [21002]
File TEC [6269]

Finch-Brown Company Inc. [21003]
Fineline Products, Inc. [21004]
Fireside Office Products Inc. [6270]
Forms and Supplies Inc. [21007]
Fuchs Copy Systems Inc. [21008]
Funai Corp. [25203]
General Business Machines Inc. [21010]
Gestetner Corp. [21012]
Global Products Company [16068]
Granite State Office Supplies, Inc. [21018]
Great Falls Business Services [21020]
Hadley Office Products Inc. [21022]
Hadon Security Systems [2716]
Hallmarkets International Ltd. [21023]
Harris Corp.; Dub [21028]
Hermann Associates Inc. [24561]
Hermann Associates Inc. [21030]
HPS, Inc. [22866]
HPS Inc. [21040]
HPS Office Systems [21041]
HPS Printing Products [21042]
Hughes-Calihan Corp. [21043]
Hunter The Typewriter Man [21044]
Icon Office Solutions [21047]
IDEAL Scanners & Systems, Inc. [21048]
Ikon Office Solutions [21049]
Ikon Office Solutions [21050]
IKON Office Solutions Inc. [21051]
Illinois Blueprint Corp. [25686]
Imagetech RICOH Corp. [21052]
Imaging Technologies [21053]
Independent Photocopy Inc. [21055]
Indiana Carbon Company Inc. [21056]
Industrial Development & Procurement [16150]
Infincom Inc. [21057]
Information Processing Center [21058]
Inland NW Services Inc. [21059]
International Business Equipment [21063]
International Office Systems Inc. [21064]
International Tape Products Co. [21065]
International Typewriter Exchange [21066]
Interstate Copy Shop [21068]
ITE Distributing [21071]
ITP Business Communications [21072]
J-Snell & Co., Inc. [21074]
J.J.R. Enterprises Inc. [21078]
Jones-McIntosh Tobacco Company Inc. [26314]
J.R.M. Inc. [21082]
Kardex Systems Inc. [21086]
Kellco & Associates [15185]
Kelly Computer Supplies [6419]
Keystone Office Supply Co. Inc. [21088]
Kights' Printing and Office Products [21091]
Kilpatrick Equipment Co. [21092]
Kimsco Supply Co. [21093]
Konica Business Technologies, Inc. [21094]
Lake Business Products [21096]
Lake County Office Equipment Inc. [21097]
Lanier Worldwide Inc. [21100]
Laser Logic Inc. [21101]
Laser Technologies and Services Inc. [21103]
Lees Office Equipment & Supplies [21104]
Liberty Business Systems Inc. [21108]
Lincoln Office Equipment Co. [21109]
Little & Son; Michael [21110]
Locks Co. [24585]
Loffler Business Systems Inc. [9001]
LogEtronics Corp. [21111]
Long Inc.; Duncan [21112]
Lotus Group [16246]
Louisiana Office Products [21114]
Lynde-Ordway Company Inc. [21117]
Mailers Equipment Co. [6454]
Maine Office Supply Co. Inc. [21119]
Mankato Business Products [21121]
Mansfield Typewriter Co. [21122]
Marco Business Products Inc. [6463]
Marimon Business Machines Inc. [21123]
Marion Office Products Inc. [21124]
Martinez; Gus [21131]
McRae Industries Inc. [21135]
Merchants Cash Register Co. [21137]
Merchants Information Solutions Inc. [21138]
Microform Systems Inc. [21140]
Micros of South Florida Inc. [21142]
Midland Lock & Safe Service [24592]

Midwest Office Furniture and Supply Company Inc. [21143]
Mifax-New Hampshire [21144]
Milner Document Products Inc. [21146]
Minolta Corp. [22878]
Modern Information Systems [21150]
Morse Typewriter Company Inc. [21151]
Mountain States Microfilm Inc. [21152]
Multigraphics Inc. [21153]
Murata Business Systems Inc. [21154]
National Trading Co. Inc. [21156]
Netherland Typewriter [21157]
Nevada Business Systems Inc. [21158]
Nevada Cash Register Inc. [21159]
Nevada Office Machines Inc. [21160]
New Mexico International Trade & Development [21161]
New World Research Corp. [3030]
Northcoast Business Systems Inc. [21164]
OCE-USA Inc. [21169]
O'Connor and Raque Office Products Co. [21170]
Office Club Inc. [21172]
Office Depot Inc. [21173]
Office Equipment Co. [21176]
Office Equipment Sales [21177]
Office Equipment Service [21178]
Office Express [21180]
Office Machine & Furniture Inc. [21183]
Office Planning Group Inc. [21186]
Office System Inc. [21189]
Office Systems of Texas [21191]
Officeland of the N.H. Seacoast [21192]
Ohio Business Machines Inc. [21195]
Ohio Calculating Inc. [21196]
Olivetti Office USA Inc. [21199]
OmniFax [21200]
Omnifax Danka Co. [21201]
Omnium Corp. [6571]
Orbital Trading Co. [16363]
Panasonic Copier Co. [21202]
Paoletti and Urriola Inc. [21203]
Perkins Stationery [21209]
Pickens Electronics [21214]
Porter Office Machine Corp. [21219]
Postalia Inc. [21220]
Promicro Systems [21224]
Quill Corp. [21229]
Quorum Corp. [21231]
Reds Office Supply [21235]
RI Business Equipment Co. Inc. [21239]
Rieger's Ceramics Arts & Crafts [26635]
RST Reclaiming Co. Inc. [21251]
S & R Inc. [21254]
Safeguard International, Inc. [24621]
Sambito; William B. [21257]
Savin Corp. [21258]
School Specialty Inc. [21259]
Scope Office Services Inc. [21261]
Scriptex Enterprises Ltd. [21262]
Second City Systems Inc. [21263]
Select Copy Systems of Southern California Inc. [21264]
Sentry Group [24634]
Shredex Inc. [21269]
Siri Office Equipment Inc. [21271]
Skyline Supply Company Inc. [21272]
Southern Business Systems Inc. [21276]
Southern Copy Machines [21277]
Southern New Mexico Office Machines [21278]
Spaulding Company Inc. [25458]
Spectrum Financial System Inc. [21281]
Standard Duplicating Machines Corp. [21284]
Star Office Machines [21292]
Stargel Office Systems Inc. [21293]
Stationers' Corporation of Hawaii Ltd. [21294]
Steel Partners L.P. [21297]
Stewart Co.; Douglas [6761]
Stuck and Associates; Paul [27011]
Style Asia Inc. [13454]
Sukut Office Equipment Co. [21303]
The Supply Room Companies, Inc. [21305]
Swanson Sales and Service [21309]
Systel Business Equipment Inc. [21310]
Systems Inc. [21311]
Systems Unlimited Inc. [21312]
Tab Business Systems Inc. [21313]

Tatung Science and Technology Inc. [21315]
Taylor-Made Office Systems Inc. [21316]
Techmart Computer Products [21317]
Technical Business Specialists Inc. [6799]
Telecommunications Bank Inc. [5783]
Time Products Inc. [21320]
Transco South Inc. [21321]
Transoceanic Trade, Inc. [22911]
TRM Copy Centers Corp. [21324]
Unitech Inc. [21326]
United Business Machines Inc. [21327]
United States Check Book Co. [21328]
United Stationers Inc. [21977]
US Office Products, Midwest District Inc. [21331]
USA Datafax Inc. [21332]
USI Inc. [21333]
Valley Office Products Inc. [21334]
Van Ausdall and Farrar Inc. [21335]
Vogann Business Machines [21341]
Weber Office Supply Inc. [21349]
Weber and Sons Inc. [21350]
Western Office Equipment [21354]
Williamson; Gary [21356]
Wisconsin Office Systems [21357]
WJS Enterprises Inc. [21359]
Word Systems Inc. [21362]
Word Technology Systems Inc. [21363]
Xerographic Copier Services Inc. [21365]
Yorktown Industries Inc. [21367]
Yost Office Systems, Inc. [21368]
Young-Phillips Sales Co. [25884]
Zeroid and Company Inc. [21372]
Zzyzx Peripherals Inc. [6893]

SIC 5045 — Computers, Peripherals & Software

A and A Technology Inc. [5856]
A C Systems [5857]
A/E MicroSystems Inc. [5858]
A Plus Sales & Service Inc. [5859]
AA Computech Inc. [5860]
Abacus Data Systems Inc. [5861]
ABC Systems and Development Inc. [5862]
Aberdeen L.L.C. [5863]
Academi-Text Medical Wholesalers [3460]
ACBEL Technologies Inc. [5864]
Access Graphics [5865]
Access Graphics Technology Inc. [5866]
Access International Software [5867]
Access Solutions Inc. [5868]
Accurate Office Machines Inc. [20769]
Ace Technical Resources Inc. [5869]
ACMA Computers Inc. [5870]
Acom Computer Inc. [5871]
Action Business Systems [5872]
ADA Computer Supplies Inc. [5873]
Adams Book Company, Inc. [3469]
Adaptive Living [5874]
ADD Enterprises Inc. [5875]
ADI Systems Inc. [5876]
Admark Corp. [5877]
ADP Hollander Inc. [5878]
ADS Inc. [5879]
Adtek Computer Systems Inc. [5880]
ADTRON. Corp [5881]
Advance Computer Systems [5882]
ADVANCED BusinessLink Corp. [5883]
Advanced Communication Design Inc. [5884]
Advanced Computer Distributors Inc. [5885]
Advanced Concepts Inc. [5886]
Advanced Enterprise Solutions [5887]
Advanced Micro Solutions Inc. [5888]
Advanced Tech Distributors [5889]
Advanced Technology Center Inc. [5890]
Advanced Technology Specialist [5891]
AeroSpace Computer Supplies, Inc. [5892]
Affinitec Corp. [5893]
Aftec Inc. [5894]
Agri-Logic Solution Systems [5895]
AIS Computers [5896]
AITech International Corp. [5897]
Alacrity Systems Inc. [5898]

Alaska Micro Systems Inc. [5899]
Algol Consultants Technology [5900]
Alis-USA [5901]
All Computer Warehouse [5902]
All Seas Exporting Inc. [5903]
Allanson Business Products [5904]
Allen Systems Group Inc. [5905]
Alligator Technologies [5906]
Allstar Systems Inc. [5908]
Allview Services Inc. [5909]
Almaly Trading Corp. [5910]
ALMO [5911]
Almo Corp. [5912]
Almo Distributing [5913]
AlphaNet Solutions Inc. [5914]
Alps Electric (USA) Inc. [5915]
Alternative Computer Solutions Ltd. [5916]
Alternative Computer Technology Inc. [5917]
Altura PC Systems Inc. [5918]
Amemco [5919]
American Business Network and Associates Inc. [5920]
American Business Service and Computer Technologies Inc. [5921]
American Business Systems Inc. [5922]
American Computer Hardware [5923]
American Custom Software [5924]
American Data Systems Marketing [5925]
American Digital Cartography Inc. [5926]
American Disc Corp. [5927]
American Education Corp. [5928]
American Educational Services [3500]
American Liquidators [5930]
American Netronic Inc. [5931]
American Overseas Book Company Inc. [3502]
American Pennant Corp. [5932]
American Software & Hardware Distributors, Inc. [5933]
American Systems of the Southeast Inc. [20799]
American Wholesale Book Co. [3504]
Americas Trade & Supply Co. [2237]
AmeriData Inc. [5934]
AmeriQuest Technologies Inc. [5935]
Ameritrend Corp. [20800]
Ames Sciences Inc. [5936]
Amex Inc. [5937]
AMOs Inc. [5938]
Amtron Corp. [5939]
Analytcal Automation Specialists Inc. [5940]
Analytic Associates [5941]
Andromeda Software Inc. [5942]
Apex Data Systems Inc. [5943]
APPIC Inc. [5944]
Apple Computer Inc. Federal Systems Group [5945]
Apple Pacific Div. [5946]
Applied Business Computers Inc. [5947]
Applied Computer Solutions Inc. (New York, New York) [5948]
Applied Computer Technology Inc. [5949]
Applied Educational Systems Inc. [5950]
Applied Information Solutions Inc. [5951]
Applied Microcomputer Solutions [5952]
Applied Systems Technology and Resources [5953]
Applied Technology Ventures Inc. [5954]
Appropriate Solutions [5955]
AR Industries Inc. [5956]
Arch Associates Corp. [5957]
Archway Systems Inc. [5958]
AremisSoft Corp. [5959]
Arends and Sons Inc. [250]
Arista Enterprises Inc. [5960]
Aristo Computers Inc. [5961]
ARM Computer Inc. [5962]
Arraid Inc. [5963]
Arrow Electronics Inc. [5964]
Arrow Electronics Inc. Almac/Arrow Electronics Div. [5965]
A.R.T. Multimedia Systems, Inc. [5966]
ARTiSan Software Tools [5967]
ARvee Systems Inc. [5968]
ASAP Software Express Inc. [5969]
ASCII Group Inc. [5970]
Ashford International Inc. [5971]
Ashwood Computer Co. [5972]

ASNA Inc. [5973]
Aspen Data [5974]
Aspen Imaging International Inc. [5975]
Assi Computers Inc. [5976]
Associated Business Products Inc. Scanning Systems [20815]
Associated Computers Services [5977]
Associated Systems Inc. [5978]
Associates in Software International [5979]
Assorted Book Co. [3528]
Astro Business Solutions Inc. [20816]
ATC Computer and Business Machines Inc. [20818]
ATD-American Co. [25971]
Atlantic Software [5980]
Atlantis Software [5981]
ATS Money Systems Inc. [5982]
Attorney's Briefcase [5983]
Authentica Security Technology [5984]
Auto-trol Technology Corp. [5985]
Automated Data Systems Inc. [5986]
Automated Office Systems of New England [5987]
Automated Register Systems, Inc. [5988]
Automatic Controls Co. [8397]
Automating Peripherals Inc. [5989]
Automation Image Inc. [5990]
Avant Computer Associates Inc. [5991]
Avanti 4 International Corp. [5992]
Avent Inc. [5993]
AVerMedia Technologies Inc. [5994]
Avnet Computer Inc. [5995]
Axis Communications Inc. [20825]
Axon Import Export Corporation [4793]
Azerty Inc. [5996]
Aztec Business Machines Inc. [20826]
Baker & Taylor [5997]
Balno Incorporated [5998]
Banana Educational Software Distributors [5999]
Bangert's Computer Systems [6000]
Baron Services, Inc. [6001]
Bawamba Software Inc. [6002]
Bay State Computer Group Inc. [6003]
Bay State Computer of New Jersey Inc. [6004]
BCS*A [6005]
BCSR Inc. [6006]
BEAR Computers Inc. [6007]
BEK International Inc. [6008]
Bellsonics [5529]
Belmont Systems Inc. [6009]
Benchmark Systems Inc. of Utah [6010]
Benton Ballard Co. [6011]
Benton Electronics Inc. [6012]
Bergano Book Co., Inc. [3551]
Bernoulli Collection Inc. [6013]
Best Buy Co. Inc. [25101]
BGW Systems Inc. [25102]
Bibliographical Center for Research Inc. [6015]
Big Blue Products Inc. [6016]
BL Associates, Inc. [6017]
BMS Inc. - Barcoded Management Systems, Inc. [6018]
Boston Computer Exchange Corp. [6019]
Boxlight Corp. [6020]
Bradford Publishing Co.; William K. [6021]
Brady Corp. [6022]
Brain Corp. [20853]
BrainTree Technology Inc. [6023]
Bridge Technology Inc. [6024]
Brigadoon.Com Inc. [6025]
BRS Software Products [6026]
Business Computer Solutions [6027]
Business Integrators [6028]
Business Machines Inc. [6029]
Business Management Software [6030]
Business Media Inc. [6031]
Business Systems [6032]
C Companies, Inc. [6033]
C S & S Computer Systems Inc. [6034]
Cables & Chips Inc. [6036]
CAD Store Inc. [6037]
CADCentre Inc. [6038]
CADD Microsystems, Inc. [6039]
Cadec Corporation [6040]
Call-A-Tech Inc. [6041]
Callback Software [6042]
Cambridge Development Laboratory [6043]

Cannon Technologies Inc. [6044]
Capital Business Systems Inc. [6045]
Carolina Training Associates [6046]
Carroll Touch Inc. [7146]
Casey-Johnston Sales Inc. [6047]
Cash Register Sales Inc. [20884]
Casio, Inc. [17362]
Caxton Printers Ltd. [3616]
CBS Technologies LLC [5551]
CCI Triad [6048]
Cedar Co. [6049]
Cedar Group US Inc. [6050]
Cenna International Corp. [19223]
Centaurus Systems Inc. [6051]
Centel Information Systems Inc. [6052]
Centenario Technologies, Inc. [6053]
Centerline Software Inc. [6054]
Centerspan Communications Corp. [6055]
Central Computer Systems Inc. [6056]
Central House Technologies [6057]
Certified Data Processing Inc. [6058]
Certified Ribbon Supply Inc. [6059]
Champion Computer Corp. [6060]
Chandler Enterprises [6061]
Charlotte Copy Data Inc. [20896]
Chase Com Corp. [5559]
Checkpoint International [18736]
Chester Technical Services Inc. [6062]
Choice Medical Distribution Inc. [6064]
Chrismann Computer Services Inc. [6065]
Chrismann Computer Services Inc. [6066]
CHS Electronics Inc. [6067]
CIC Systems Inc. [6068]
Cirrus Technology Inc. [6069]
CIS Corp. [6070]
Citizen America Corp. [6071]
Clare Computer Solutions Inc. [6072]
Clark; Frank [6073]
Classic Components Corp. [6074]
CLG Inc. [6075]
CMOV, Inc. [6077]
Coaxis Inc. Insight Distribution Systems [6078]
Color Group [6079]
Comark Inc. [6080]
Comdisco Inc. [6081]
Comet Micro Systems Inc. [6082]
Command Computer Maintenance [6084]
Command Electronics Inc. [6085]
Command Technology Inc. [6086]
Commercial and Industrial Design Co. Inc. [6087]
Compar, Inc. [6088]
Compcom Enterprises Inc. [6089]
Competitive Edge [6090]
Compex Inc. (Anaheim, California) [6091]
Complete Computer Solutions of New England [6092]
Complete Golf Services Co. [23601]
Compool Corp. [23602]
Comprehensive Systems Inc. [6093]
Comprehensive Video Group [22847]
CompuCom Systems Inc. [6094]
CompuData Inc. [6096]
CompuLink Electronic Inc. [8555]
Compusol Inc. [6097]
Compusolve [6098]
Compusystems Inc. South Carolina [6099]
Computalabel International Ltd. [6100]
Computer Banking Inc. [6101]
Computer Brokers of Kentucky [6102]
Computer Clearing House Inc. [6103]
Computer Commodities Inc. [6104]
Computer Concepts Inc. [6105]
Computer Corner Inc. [6106]
Computer Craft Co. [6107]
Computer Data Systems, Inc. [6108]
Computer Discounters [6109]
Computer Enterprises of Grand Rapids [6110]
Computer Equipment Warehouse Inc. [6111]
Computer Graphics Distributing Co. [6112]
Computer Hardware Maintenance Company Inc. [6113]
Computer Lab International Inc. [6114]
Computer Maintenance Service [6115]
Computer Management Systems [6116]
Computer and Networking Services Inc. [6117]
Computer Parts and Services Inc. [6118]

Computer Plus, Inc. [6119]
Computer Products Center Inc. [6120]
Computer Products of Vermont Inc. [6121]
Computer Recyclers Inc. [6122]
Computer Research Inc. [6123]
Computer Sales International Inc. [6124]
Computer Service and Support [6125]
Computer Source Inc. [6126]
Computer Source Inc. [6127]
Computer Sports Systems Inc. [8556]
Computer Systems Inc. [6128]
Computer Systems Supply Corp. [6129]
Computer Talk Inc. [6130]
Computer Trading Co. [6131]
Computer Trends [6132]
Computers & Applications Inc. [6133]
Computers Unlimited Inc. [6134]
Computers of Willmar Inc. [6135]
ComputersAmerica Inc. [6136]
Computing Technology Inc. [6137]
Comsel Corp. [6139]
Comstor [6140]
Comstor Technology Inc. [6141]
Comtech Systems Brokers [6142]
Comtel Corp. [6143]
Comus Computer Corp. [6144]
Comware Business Systems Inc. [6145]
Concord Computing Corp. [6146]
Concord Technologies Inc. [6147]
Conductive Rubber Tech Inc. [6148]
Connecticut Micro Corp. [6149]
Connections USA [6150]
Consan Inc. [6151]
CONTEC Microelectronics USA [6152]
Contemporary Arts Press Distribution [3655]
Contemporary Computer Wear [6153]
Continental Information Systems Corp. [6154]
Continental Resources Inc. (Bedford, Massachusetts) [6155]
CONVEX Computer Corp. [6156]
Cony Computers Systems Inc. [6157]
Cooper Industries Inc. [6158]
Copper Electronics [6159]
Coroant Inc. [6160]
Corporate Computer Inc. [6161]
Corporate Computer Systems Inc. [6162]
Corporate Express [20926]
Corstar Business Computing Inc. [6163]
Cosmi Corp. [6164]
COSMIC [6165]
Costco Companies, Inc. [10850]
Cox Subscriptions, Inc.; W.T. [3664]
CPS Marketing Corporation [18757]
CPS Technologies Inc. [6166]
Cranel Inc. [6167]
CSM International Corp. [6168]
CTN Data Service Inc. [6169]
Cummins Electronics Company Inc. [6170]
Current Software [6171]
Current Works Inc. [6172]
Cutting Edge Technology Inc. [6173]
CWC Group Inc. [6174]
D and H Distributing Co. [6175]
D and H Distributing Co. [15103]
Daisytek Inc. [6176]
Dallas Digital Corp. [6177]
Dalton Computer Services Inc. [6178]
Danka E.B.S. [6179]
Danka Inwood Business Systems Inc. [20948]
Dartek Corp. [6180]
Dash Inc. [6181]
DATA COM [6182]
Data Forms Inc. [21702]
Data Professionals [6183]
Data Source Media Inc. [6184]
Data Tech Services Inc. [6185]
Database Computer Systems Inc. [6186]
DataCal Corp. [6187]
Datalink Corp. [6188]
Datamatics Management Services, Inc. [6189]
Davis Associates Inc. [6190]
Decision Data Service Inc. [6192]
Decision Support Systems Inc. [6193]
Deerfield Data Systems Inc. [6194]
Delker Electronics Inc. [6195]
Dell Computer Corp. Dell Marketing L.P. [6196]

Delta Products Corp. (Nogales, Arizona) [6197]
Dennis and Schwab Inc. [6198]
Dentt Inc. [26465]
Desfosses and Associates; John J. [6199]
Design Data Systems Corp. [6200]
Design Systems Inc. [6201]
Deuteronomy Inc. [6202]
Develcon Electronics Inc. [6203]
Development Through Self-Reliance Inc. [6204]
Deverger Systems Inc. [6205]
Diab Data Inc. [6206]
Diamond Flower Electric Instruments Company (USA) Inc. [6207]
Diamond Systems Corp. [6208]
Dickens Data Systems Inc. [6209]
Digital Storage Inc. [6210]
Dirt Cheap Drives Inc. [6211]
Disc Distributing Corp. [6212]
DistribuPro Inc. [6213]
Diversified Data Products Inc. [6214]
DMACS International Corp. [6215]
DMS Systems Corp. [6216]
Doctor Computerized Systems [6217]
Document Solutions Inc. [20972]
Dollar Computer Corp. [6218]
Dopar Support Systems Inc. [6219]
Douglas Stewart Co. [6220]
DP Equipment Marketing Inc. [6221]
DS Design [6222]
DsgnHaus, Inc. [6223]
DSi [6224]
DTK Computer Inc. [6225]
Dubl-Click Software Corp. [6226]
Durr and Partners [6227]
Dyna Marketing [6228]
Dyna Marketing [6229]
Dynabit USA Inc. [6230]
Dynamic Computer Concepts [6231]
Eakins Associates Inc. [6232]
E.A.P. Co. [6233]
Eastes Distributing [6234]
ECW Enterprises Inc. [6235]
Educational Record Sales, Inc. [25173]
Educational Technology Inc. [6236]
Efficient Computer System [6237]
EIZO Nanao Technologies Inc. [6238]
EKD Computer Sales and Supplies Corp. [6239]
El Camino Resources International Inc. [6240]
Electrograph Systems Inc. [6241]
Electronic Arts Inc. [6242]
Electronics Discount World [6244]
Electronics and Information Systems [6245]
E.L.F. Software Co. [6246]
Elite Computers and Software Inc. [6247]
EME Corp. [25181]
Emulex Corp. [6248]
En Pointe Technologies Inc. [6249]
Engelhart Co.; H.C. [6250]
Engineering Equipment Co. [15992]
Enterprise Computer Systems Inc. [6251]
Entre [6252]
Eritech International [6253]
ERM Recycling Inc./Crazy Bob's [6254]
ESI Computing [6255]
ESI-Technologies Inc. [6256]
Europa Consulting [6257]
Executive Business Machines, Inc. [6258]
Executive Productivity Systems [6259]
Exodus Computers, Inc. [6260]
Exploration Resources Inc. [6261]
Export Services Inc. [6262]
Eye Communication Systems Inc. [22852]
Facit Div. [6263]
Fairview-AFX Inc. [8730]
Fast Multimedia U.S. Inc. [6264]
Fastlink Network Products [6265]
Federal Computer Corp. [6266]
Federal Systems Group Inc. [6267]
FEI America Inc. [6268]
File TEC [6269]
Fireside Office Products Inc. [6270]
First Class Business Systems Inc. [6271]
Fleet Distribution, Inc. [6272]
Flytech Technology (USA) Inc. [6273]
Forcean Inc. [18800]
ForeFront Direct Inc. [6274]

FORMation mg Inc. [6275]
Formtronix Inc. [6276]
Forsythe Technology Inc. [6277]
Four Wheeler Communications [6278]
FOX Systems Inc. [6279]
Fran-TEC Computer [6280]
Franklin Quest Co. [6281]
Fujitsu Computer Products of America Inc. [6282]
Fujitsu Network Switching of America Inc. [6283]
Funai Corp. [25203]
Future Tech International Inc. [6284]
Gagnons Reprographics Co. [6286]
Galaxie Hardware Publishers Inc. [6287]
Gannsoft Publishing Co. [6288]
Ganson Engineering Inc. [6289]
Gardner and Meredith Inc. [16047]
Gates/Arrow Distributing Inc. [6290]
Gates/FA Distributing Inc. [6291]
Gateswood Software Inc. [6292]
Gateway Software Corp. [6293]
GBC Technologies Inc. [6294]
GC Thorsen Inc. [8777]
GE Capital Information Technology
    Solutions [6295]
Gene Labs Inc. [6296]
General Automation Inc. [6297]
General Microsystems Inc. (Bellevue,
    Washington) [6298]
Generic Computer Products Inc. [6299]
Georgia Business Solutions [6300]
Gibb Co.; Clark R. [6301]
Gigatec (U.S.A.) Inc. [6302]
Gilman Industrial Exports, Inc. [24365]
Global Computer Corp. [6303]
Globus Industries [8791]
Golden Bear Services Inc. [6304]
Government Micro Resources Inc. [6305]
Government Technology Services Inc. [6306]
Granite Microsystems, Inc. [6307]
Gray Sales Co. Inc. [6309]
Greenleaf Distribution Inc. [6310]
Greenpages Inc. [6311]
Greenwich Instruments USA [6312]
Greystone Peripherals Inc. [6313]
GT Interactive Software Corp. [6314]
GT Interactive Software Corp. Value Products
    Div. [6315]
GTI [6316]
Guaranteed Business Services Inc. [6317]
Gulf Coast Software & Systems [6318]
H and H Computers [6319]
H & H Equipment Inc. [6320]
Hagerman and Company Inc. [6321]
Hall Group Inc. [6322]
Hall-Mark Electronics Corp. [6323]
Hall Research Technologies [6324]
Hallmarkets International Ltd. [21023]
Hallogram Publishing [6325]
Halted Specialties Co. [6326]
Hammond Computer Inc. [6327]
Handleman Co. [25225]
Handleman Co. [3811]
Harcourt Brace Professional Publishing [3812]
Hardware Knowledge Group Inc. [6328]
Harvard Associates Inc. [6329]
Health Systems Technology Corp. [6330]
Hendrix Technologies Inc. [21029]
Hewlett-Packard Co. International [6331]
H.H. West Co. [21032]
Hickey and Associates [6332]
Highsmith Inc. [25232]
Hitachi America Ltd. [25233]
Hitachi America Ltd. [8846]
Hitachi Data Systems Corp. [6333]
Hitachi Data Systems Corp. [6334]
Hitron Systems Inc. [6336]
HJV Inc. [6337]
HNSX Supercomputers Inc. [6338]
Holcomb's Education Resource [21036]
Hooleon Corp. [6339]
Horizon Business Systems [6340]
Horizon Micro Distributors [6341]
Horizon Trading Company [13136]
Horizon USA Data Supplies Inc. [6342]
Hot Products, Inc.com [26525]
House of Representatives Inc. [6343]

Howard Enterprises Inc. [5640]
Howtek Inc. [6344]
HPG Industries Inc. [7492]
HPS, Inc. [22866]
HSB Computer Laboratories [6345]
Hunt & Associates; Robert W. [6346]
HVL Technical Services Inc. [6347]
HyperGlot Software Company Inc. [6348]
I-O Corp. [6349]
ICG [6350]
ICL Inc. [6351]
Ideal Computer Services Inc. [6352]
IDEAL Scanners & Systems, Inc. [21048]
IEEI [6353]
Iiyama North America, Inc. [6354]
Image Processing Solutions [6355]
Imagex Inc. [6356]
Imge Guided Technologies, Inc. [6357]
Import Export Management Service Inc. [21054]
Impression Technology Inc. [6358]
Imrex Company Inc. [6359]
IMS Systems, Inc. [25241]
InaCom Corp. [6360]
InaCom Information Systems [6361]
InControl Solutions [6362]
Indiana Carbon Company Inc. [21056]
Infinite Solutions Inc. [6363]
Infinity Data Systems [6364]
Info-Mation Services Co. [6365]
Info Systems Inc. [6366]
Infomax Inc. [6367]
Information Analysis Inc. [6368]
Information Management Inc. [6369]
InfoSource Inc. [6370]
Infotel [6371]
Ingram Book Co. [25243]
Ingram Book Group Inc. [3844]
Ingram Industries Inc. [6372]
Ingram Micro Inc. [6373]
Ingram Micro Inc. [6374]
Inland Associates Inc. [6375]
Input Automation Inc. [21060]
Insight Direct [6376]
Intcomex [6377]
Integral Systems Inc. [6378]
Intel Corp. [6379]
Intelligent Computer Networks [6380]
Intelligent Electronics Inc. [6381]
Intelligent Electronics Inc. Advanced Systems
    Div. [6382]
Intelligent Systems Corp. [6383]
InterACT Systems Inc. [6384]
Interatech [6385]
Interface Data Inc. [6386]
Interface Systems Inc. [6387]
International Business Machines Corp.
    EduQuest [6388]
International Computer and Office Products
    Inc. [6389]
International Data Acquisition and Control
    Inc. [6390]
International Parts Inc. [6391]
International Trade Group [18860]
Internet Communication Corp. [6392]
Intrepid Systems Inc. [6393]
Inventory Conversion Inc. [6394]
Investrade Import & Export [16170]
IOA Data Corp. [6395]
IOB Distributors [6396]
IQ2000 [6397]
ITBR, Inc. [5651]
ITEC Enterprises Inc. [6398]
ITM [6399]
Itron Inc. [6400]
Iverson P.C. Warehouse Inc. [6401]
J & J Computer Resources [6402]
J & M Industries Inc. [6403]
Jacobson Computer Inc. [6404]
Jameco Electronics Inc. [8905]
Jane Co. [6405]
JDL Technologies Inc. [6406]
JDM Data Systems Inc. [6407]
JDR Microdevices Inc. [6408]
Jones Business Systems Inc. [6409]
Joshua Distributing Co. [6410]

JRE Computing [6411]
JSB Software Technologies PLC [6412]
JVLNET By Electrolarm [6413]
JWS Corp. [6414]
K Rep Sales [6415]
Kalthoff International [6416]
Kazette Enterprises Inc. [6417]
Keep It Simple Technology Inc. [6418]
Kelly Computer Supplies [6419]
Kenwood Data Systems Inc. [6420]
Key Curriculum Press Inc. [3878]
Key Products Co. [6421]
Kingdom Co. [25273]
Knapp Company Inc.; R.S. [24384]
KNB Computer Werx Inc. [6422]
Knogo North America Inc. [15192]
Knox Computer Systems Inc. [6423]
Kwik Stop Car Wash Supply [4655]
L and L Products [6424]
La Cie. Ltd. [25924]
Langer Inc.; David [6426]
Lanier Worldwide Inc. [21100]
Lansa USA Inc. [6427]
Lantec Inc. [6428]
Larsen Associates Inc. [8972]
Laser-Scan Inc. [6429]
Laser Technologies and Services Inc. [21103]
LaserCard Systems Corp. [6430]
LaserTone Inc. [6431]
Law Cypress Distributing [6432]
Law Office Information Systems Inc. [25280]
LEA Book Distributors [3900]
Leader Technologies Inc. [6433]
Leading Edge Products Inc. [6434]
LeadingSpect Corp. [6435]
Leecom Data Systems [6436]
Legend Computer Inc. [6437]
Lewan and Associates Inc. [21107]
Lex Computing and Management Corp. [6438]
Liberty Publishing Co. Inc. [3910]
Library Corp. [6439]
Library Video Co. [25283]
Liconix Industries Inc. [16999]
Life Unlimited [3913]
Lincoln Trading Co. [116]
Lite-On Inc. [6440]
Liuski International Inc. [8996]
L.J. Technical Systems Inc. [6441]
Logical Choice [6442]
Logon Inc. [6443]
London Litho Aluminum Company Inc. [6444]
Los Altos PC Inc. [6445]
Lowry Computer Products Inc. [6446]
Lucero Computer Products [6447]
MA Laboratories Inc. [6448]
Maats Enterprises [19421]
Mac America [6449]
Macintosh Inc.; Dr. [6450]
Maconomy NE Inc. [6451]
Macro Computer Products Inc. [6452]
MAG Innovision Inc. [6453]
Majors Scientific Books Inc. [3932]
Majure Data Inc. [6455]
Management Computer Systems Inc. [6456]
Management Techniques Inc. [6457]
Manchester Equipment Company Inc. [6458]
Manhattan Office Products Inc. [6459]
Mankato Business Products [21121]
Manugistics Group Inc. [6460]
Maraj International [6461]
Marathon Codestar [6462]
Marco Business Products Inc. [6463]
Marketex Computer Corp. [6464]
Marketware Corp. [6465]
Marsh Inc.; Paul [4452]
Marubeni Solutions USA, Corp. [6467]
Massa Associates; Ronald A. [9043]
Matthews Book Co. [3940]
Maverick.com Inc. [6469]
Maxey System Inc. [6470]
Maxi Switch Inc [6471]
Maximum Performance [6472]
Maxwell Microsystems Inc. [6473]
MBS/Net, Inc. [6474]
McBride and Associates Inc. [6475]
McDATA Corp. [6476]

McGehee & Associates; Thomas [6477]
Medfax Corp. [6478]
Media Recovery Inc. [6479]
Medical Manager Sales and Marketing Inc. [6480]
MEGA HAUS Hard Drives [6481]
Memory Technologies Texas Inc. [6482]
Mercury Computer Systems [6483]
Merisel Inc. [6484]
Merisel Inc. Macamerica Div. [6485]
Merisel Inc. Merisel World Class
    Distribution [6486]
MET International [6487]
Metamorphous Advances Product Services [3949]
Michiana Micro Inc. [6489]
Micro Central Inc. [6490]
Micro Computer Centre [6491]
Micro K Systems Inc. [6493]
Micro-Pace Computers Inc. [6494]
Micro Star [6495]
Micro Symplex Corp. [6496]
Micro-Tron Inc. [6497]
Microage [6498]
MicroAge Inc. [6499]
MicroCAD Technologies Inc. [6500]
Microcomputer Cable Company Inc. [9075]
Microcomputer Company of Maryland Inc. [6501]
Microform Systems Inc. [21140]
Micrographics [6502]
Microhelp Inc. [6503]
Microlink Enterprises Inc. [6504]
Micronetics Inc. Information Management
    Systems [6505]
Micros-to-Mainframes Inc. [6506]
Microsearch Inc. [6507]
Microsoft Corp. [6508]
Microstar Computer Technology Inc. [6509]
MicroTech Conversion Systems [6510]
MICROTECH Systems Inc. [6511]
Microunited [6512]
Microware Inc. [6513]
Mid-America Information Systems Inc. [6514]
Mid America Ribbon & Supply Co. [6515]
Midland Computers [6516]
MidWest Micro [6517]
Midwest Visual Equipment Co. [25324]
Mikes Computerland [6518]
MIMICS Inc. [6519]
MindWorks Corp. [6520]
Mini-Micro Supply Company Inc. [6521]
Miracle Computers Inc. [6522]
Mitsuba Corp. [6523]
Mitsui Comtek Corp. [6524]
Mitsumi Electronics Corp. [6525]
MLH and Associates [6526]
Modern Business Machines Inc. [21149]
Modular Mining Systems Inc. [6527]
Montero International, Inc. [6528]
Moss Enterprises Inc. [6529]
Motor Sound Corp. [5682]
Mountain Cable Industries Inc. [9102]
Mountain High Technology Inc. [6530]
Moustrak Inc. [6532]
MPS Multimedia Inc. [6533]
MRK Technologies Ltd. [6534]
Muncer and Associates Inc.; J.B. [6535]
MuTech Corp. [6536]
Myers Associates Inc.; Vic [6537]
Myers Associates; Vic [6538]
Myers Associates; Vic [6539]
Myers Associates; Vic [6540]
NACSCORP [3978]
Nanbren-Compsol Ltd. [6541]
National Association of College Stores Inc. [3983]
National Equipment Development Corp. [6542]
National Systems Corp. [6543]
National Trading Co. Inc. [21156]
Navarre Corp. [6544]
NCD [6545]
NCS Assessments [6546]
NCUBE [6547]
NEC America Inc. [5687]
NEC America Inc. Data and Video Communications
    Systems Div. [6548]
NEC Technologies Inc. [6549]
NECX Inc. [9119]

Network Access Corp. (Pittsburgh,
    Pennsylvania) [5689]
Networks 2000 [6550]
New DEST Corp. [9126]
New Process Development [6551]
NewSoft America Inc. [6552]
Nice Computer Inc. [6553]
NIDI Northwest Inc. [6554]
NIDI Technologies Inc. [6555]
N.I.E. International Inc. [6556]
NIENEX Inc. [6557]
Nimax Inc. [6558]
Nokia Display Products Inc. [5690]
Nokia Inc. [6559]
Nolo Press/Folklaw Inc. [4005]
Nordic Computers [6560]
Nova Technology Inc. [6561]
NovaQuest InfoSystems [6562]
NPA West Inc. [6563]
Numeridex Inc. [6564]
NYMA Inc. [6565]
O/E Automation Inc. [6566]
Oasis Imaging Products [25770]
Ocean Interface Company Inc. [6567]
Office Equipment Service Inc. [21179]
Office Manager, Inc. [6568]
Olicom USA Inc. [6569]
Omicron Electronics [6570]
Omnium Corp. [6571]
Operator Interface Technology [6572]
Opportunities for Learning, Inc. [4023]
Optical Laser Inc. [6574]
Oracle Corp. USA Div. [6575]
Oregon Educational Technology Consortium [6576]
Organization Systems Inc. [6577]
P-80 Systems [6578]
Pacific Coast Micro Inc. [6579]
Pacific Dataport Inc. [5697]
Pacific Interface [6580]
Pacific Magtron Inc. [9170]
Packaged Software Solutions Inc. [6581]
Packet Engines [6582]
Paige International [6584]
Paoku International Company Ltd. [6585]
Paragram Sales Co. Inc. [6586]
Parallel PCs Inc. [6587]
Paramount International [6588]
Paramount Technology [6589]
Parasoft Corp. [6590]
Pargh Company Inc.; B.A. [6591]
Parks Software Services Inc. [6592]
Parts Now! Inc. [6593]
PartsPort Ltd. [6594]
Pathtrace Systems Inc. [6595]
PC Club Inc. [6596]
PC L.P. [6597]
PC Professional Inc. [6598]
PC Service Source Inc. [6599]
P.C. Solutions Inc., Entre' [6600]
PC Wholesale Inc. [6601]
PCC Group Inc. [6602]
PCI Tech [6603]
PCs Compleat Inc. [6604]
PDP Systems [6605]
Peak Computer Solutions [6606]
Peake Marketing Inc. [6607]
Peakwon International Inc. [18979]
Perfect Solution Multimedia Inc. [6608]
Pericom Inc. [6609]
Peripheral Land Inc. [6610]
Peripheral Resources Inc. [6611]
Perisol Technology Inc. [6612]
Peroni Business Systems Inc. [6613]
Pervone [6614]
PetrolSoft Corp. [6615]
Phoenix Computer Associates Inc. [6616]
Phone Land Inc. [6617]
Physimetrics Inc. [9199]
Pick Systems [6618]
Piedmont Technology Group Inc. [6619]
Pinnacle Business Systems Inc. [6620]
Pinnacle Business Systems, Inc. [6621]
Pinpoint Systems Inc. [9204]
Pioneer Entertainment (USA) L.P. [6622]
Pioneer-Standard Electronics Inc. [9209]
Pixel U.S.A. [6624]

Plaza Stationery & Printing Inc. [21216]
Plymouth Rock Associates [6625]
Point of Sale System Services Inc. [6626]
Poorman-Douglas Corp. [6627]
POS Systems Company Inc. [6628]
POSitive Software Co. [6629]
PowerData Corp. [6630]
PowerSolutions for Business [6631]
Practical Computer Inc. [6632]
Pratt & Co.; L.F. [6633]
Precision Type Inc. [6634]
Prima International [6635]
Primary Image Inc. [6636]
Primax Inc. [6637]
Prime Systems [6638]
Primeon [6639]
The Print Machine Inc. [6640]
Pro Systems, Inc. [6641]
Pro Systems Inc. [6642]
Pro-Tect Computer Products [6643]
Probe Technology Inc. [6644]
Procise Corp. [6645]
Prodata Computer Marketing Corp. [6646]
Prodata Systems Inc. [6647]
PRODUCT4 [6648]
Professional Computer Systems [6649]
Professional Electronics Inc. [6650]
PROFITsystems Inc. [6651]
Programart Corp. [6652]
Programma Incorporated [6653]
PSDI [6654]
PSDI [6655]
PSDI [6656]
PSDI [6657]
PSDI [6658]
PSDI [6659]
PSDI [6660]
PSDI [6661]
Public Software Library [6662]
Puget Sound Data Systems Inc. [6663]
Pulsar Data Systems Inc. [6664]
Purdy Electronics Corp. [9247]
Purple Frog Software [6665]
PWI Technologies [6666]
QA Technologies Inc. [6667]
Q.I.V. Systems Inc. [6668]
Qualitas Trading Co. [6669]
Quickshot Technology Inc. [6670]
Qumax Corp. [6671]
R-Computer [6672]
R and D Industries Inc. [6673]
R and D Industries Inc. [6674]
R & L Data Systems Inc. [6675]
R and W Technical Services Ltd. [6676]
RACER Computer Corp. [6677]
RAD Graphics [6678]
RadioShack Corp. [9259]
Rail Europe Group [6679]
Rail Europe Holding [6680]
Rainbow Raster Graphics [6681]
Ramacom Inc. [6682]
Raritan Computer Inc. [6683]
Raritan Computer Inc. [6684]
Raster Graphics Inc. [21233]
Redington USA Inc. [6686]
Reeves Audio Visual Systems Inc. [25415]
Renick and Company Inc. [6687]
ReproCAD Inc. [6688]
The Reynolds and Reynolds Co. [6689]
Ricom Electronics Ltd. [6690]
Rodan Inc. [6691]
Roland Digital Group [6692]
Rorke Data Inc. [6693]
Rosas Computer Co. [6694]
Rovac Inc. [6695]
RPL Supplies Inc. [22899]
RT Computers Inc. [6696]
RTM Inc. [6697]
Sabus Group [6698]
SAFLINK Corp. [6699]
Sager Midern Computer Inc. [6700]
SalePoint Inc. [6701]
Sampo Corporation of America [6702]
SAP America, Inc. [6703]
SARCOM Inc. [6704]
Satellite Information Systems Co. [6705]

Save On Software [6706]
Savoir Technology Group Inc. [9339]
Sawtooth Technologies Inc. [6707]
Sayers Computer Source [6708]
Scanning Technologies Inc. [6709]
ScanSource Inc. [6710]
Scientific and Business Minicomputers Inc. [6712]
Scruggs & Associates Inc. [6713]
Seagull Software Systems Inc. [6714]
Seattle Orthotics Group [6715]
SEC International [6716]
SED International, Inc. [6717]
See First Technology Inc. [6718]
Sega of America Inc. [26649]
Seikosha America Inc. [6719]
Sejin America Inc. [6720]
Select Sales [6721]
Select Sales Inc. [6722]
Selectware Technologies, Inc. [6723]
Sentry Technology Corp. [24635]
Sequence (USA) Co. Ltd. [21561]
Server Technology Inc. [9356]
Sherron Broom & Associates [6724]
Shuttle Computer International [6725]
Siboney Learning Group [6726]
Siemens Energy and Automation Inc. [9368]
Siemens Energy and Automation Inc. Electrical
    Apparatus Div. [9369]
Sigma Data Inc. [6727]
Silicon Valley Electronics International [6728]
Silicon Valley Technology Inc. [6729]
SilverPlatter Information Inc. [6730]
Simsim Inc. [6731]
Sirsi Corp. [6732]
Sitek Inc. [6733]
Sky Knob Technologies LLC [6734]
Skyline Supply Company Inc. [21272]
Soft Solutions [6735]
Softcell Inc. [6736]
SoftKey International [6737]
SoftKlone Distributing Corp. [6738]
Software Associates Inc. [6739]
Software and Electrical Engineering [6740]
Software Spectrum Inc. [6741]
Software Technology Inc. [6742]
Softworks Development Corp. [6743]
Sokol Electronics Inc. [6744]
Solutions [6745]
Songtech International Inc. [6746]
Source Management Inc. [21274]
Source Technologies Inc. [21275]
Souris River Telephone Mutual Aid
    Cooperative [5762]
Southern Business Communications Inc. [6747]
Southern Contracts [6748]
Southern Data Systems Inc. [6749]
Southern Territory Associates [4174]
Southwest CTI Inc. [6750]
Southwest Modern Data Systems [6751]
Spainhower; Vic [6752]
Special Purpose Systems Inc. [6753]
Spectrum Computer & Business Supplies [6754]
Spectrum Data Systems Inc. [6755]
The Speech Bin, Inc. [4181]
Squirrel Companies Inc. [6756]
Stan Corporation of America [6757]
Staples Business Advantage [21288]
Star Com Computers [6758]
Star Micronics America Inc. [6759]
StarTech International [6760]
Stationers' Corporation of Hawaii Ltd. [21294]
Steel Partners L.P. [21297]
Stewart Co.; Douglas [6761]
Stok Software Inc. [6762]
Storage Technology Corp. [6763]
StorageTek [6764]
Strategic Products and Services Inc. [6765]
Stream International [6766]
Strictly Business Computer Systems Inc. [6767]
STRO-WARE Inc. [6768]
Summation Legal Technologies Inc. [6769]
Sun Data Inc. [6770]
Sun Moon Star [5771]
Sunbelt Data Systems Inc. [6771]
Sundog Technologies [6772]
Sunkyong America Inc. [15323]

Sunny Group Inc. [6773]
Sunnytech Inc. [6774]
SunRace Technology (USA) Corp. [6775]
Superscape Inc. [6776]
Supplyline Inc. [6777]
Support Net Inc. [6778]
Sutmyn America [6779]
Swift Fulfillment Services [4200]
Symantec Corp. Peter Norton Products Div. [6780]
Symco Group Inc. [6781]
Syrex, Inc. [1311]
Syslink Computer Corp. [6782]
System Solutions Technology Inc. [6783]
Systems House Inc. [6784]
Systems Solutions Inc. [6785]
Taft Development Group [6787]
Taneum Computer Products Inc. [6788]
Tatung Company of America Inc. [6789]
Tatung Science and Technology Inc. [21315]
TC Computers Inc. [6790]
Teaching Aids Inc. [6791]
Tech 101 Inc. [6792]
Tech Arts [6793]
Tech Data Corp. [6794]
Techexport, Inc. [6795]
Techfarm Inc. [6796]
Techlink Alaska [6797]
Techmedia Computer Systems Corp. [6798]
Technical Business Specialists Inc. [6799]
Technical and Scientific Application Inc. [6800]
Technoland Inc. [6801]
Technology Specialists Inc. [6802]
TechQuest Inc. [6803]
Tek-Gear LLC [6804]
Tektronix Inc. [6805]
Tektronix Inc. Logic Analyzer Div. [6806]
Tekvisions Inc. [6807]
Tele-Vue Service Company Inc. [6808]
Telecom Solutions Div. [6809]
Telecomputer Inc. [6810]
Telmar Group Inc. [6811]
Tenet Information Service Inc. [6812]
Terco Computer Systems [6813]
Terralink International [5790]
Tesserax Information Systems [6814]
Textronix Inc. Semiconductor Test Div. [6815]
Thinkware [6816]
Thomas; Johnny [6817]
TimeSaving Services Inc. [6818]
TMA Systems L.L.C. [6819]
Tolman Computer Supply Group [6820]
Tomba Communications and Electronics
    Inc. [6821]
Toshiba America Electronic Components Inc.
    Storage Device Div. [6822]
Toshiba America Information Systems Inc. Network
    Products Div. [6823]
Total Concepts Inc. [6824]
Trade Corporation [8140]
Tradequest International USA [6825]
Tradewinds International Inc. [6826]
TransNet Corp. [6827]
Transoceanic Trade, Inc. [22911]
Transparent Technology Inc. [6828]
TransPro Marketing [6829]
Triangle Computer Corp. [6830]
Trident Medical International [19663]
TriGem Corp. [6831]
TriTech Graphics Inc. [6832]
Triton Electronics [6833]
True Comp America Inc. [6834]
Tucson Computer Products [6835]
TurningPoint Systems Inc. [6836]
TVM Professional Monitor Corp. [6837]
Ultima International Corp. [6838]
UMAX Computer Corp. [6839]
Uniplex Software Inc. [6840]
United Pacific Corp. [24449]
U.S. AudioTex L.L.C. [6841]
U.S. Filter/Diversified Engineering [6842]
United Strategies Inc. [6843]
Unizone Inc. [6844]
Upper Access Inc. [4254]
USAP [6845]
User Friendly Software Hardware [6846]
V-Tek Associates [6847]

Van Woerkom; Jan [6848]
Vangard Technology, Inc. [6849]
Via West Interface Inc. [6850]
ViaGrafix Corp. [6851]
Victs Computers Inc. [6852]
Video Sentry Corp. [24658]
VideoTape Distributors Inc. [25507]
Vine Trading Company [6853]
Vital Image Technology Inc. [6854]
Vitech America Inc. [6855]
VMS Inc. [4261]
Voice It Worldwide Inc. [6856]
VoiceWorld Inc. [5807]
VSS Inc. [6857]
Wacom Technology Corp. [25868]
The Wakanta Group [6858]
Wakely; Austin B. [6859]
Watkins & Associates; Steen [6860]
WebAccess [6861]
Wescorp International Ltd. [6862]
Westcon Inc. [6863]
Westech [6864]
Western Graphtec Inc. [6866]
Western Merchandisers Inc. [4278]
Western Micro Technology Inc. [6867]
Western Pacific Data Systems Inc. [6868]
Whitebox Inc. [6869]
Whitlock Group [6870]
Windows Memory Corp. [6871]
Winners Circle Systems [6872]
Wireless Telecom Inc. [6873]
Wiscomp Systems Inc. [6874]
Wolff Corp. [16646]
Wong's Advanced Technologies Inc. [6875]
Wordware Publishing Inc. [4296]
World Class Software Inc. [6876]
World Computer Corp. [6877]
World Computer Inc. [6878]
World Data Products Inc. [6879]
World Data Products Inc. [6880]
World-Net Microsystems Inc. [6881]
World Wen, Inc. [6882]
Wren Electronics, Inc. [9610]
WTI [6883]
Wyle Electronics [9611]
Wyle Systems [6884]
XML Corp. [6885]
Xpedx [22000]
XYZ Electronics Inc. [6886]
Yellow River Systems [19113]
Yosemite Technologies [6887]
Young Journal Inc.; Richard [6888]
Young Minds Inc. [6889]
Zachary Software Inc. [6890]
Zortec International Inc. [6891]
Zytronix Inc. [6892]
Zzyzx Peripherals Inc. [6893]

SIC 5046 — Commercial Equipment Nec

4 BS Wholesale Supply Inc. [24052]
A & D Enterprises, Import-Export [2156]
A To Z Vending Service Corp. [25539]
Abbott Foods Inc. [24053]
Accurate Partitions Corp. [13010]
Accurate Partitions Corp. [24054]
Acfer International Inc. [22822]
Ad Art Electronic Sign Corp. [24055]
Afy Security Distributros [24496]
Akro-Mils Inc. [25886]
Alarm-It Distributors Inc. [24499]
Alfredos Restaurant Equipment [24057]
Allstate Restaurant Equipment Inc. [24060]
Alpine Restaurant Equipment [24061]
Alsdorf International Ltd. [13554]
Ambex Inc. [15006]
American Coffee Co. Inc. [24062]
American Locker Security Systems Inc. [13017]
Anaheim Marketing International [15012]
Anchorage Restaurant Supply [24065]
Andersen Inc.; Earl F. [23516]
Anderson Associates Inc.; Earl F. [24066]

APW/Wyott Food Service Equipment Co. [10426]
Arie Incorporated [8372]
Arranaga and Co.; Robert [10436]
Art Metal Products [13023]
Asbury Worldwide Inc. [24068]
Associated Building Specialties [13026]
Associated Building Specialties [24069]
Atlanta Fixture and Sails Co. [24070]
Atlantis Restaurant Equipment [24071]
Atlas Merchandising Co. [24072]
Aubford Enterprises [26401]
AUDISSEY [8396]
AVK II Inc. [24073]
Aztec Supply Co. [25888]
Aztec Supply Co. [22932]
B & L Scales [24320]
Bacon Material Handling; Davis [25889]
Baker's Kneads [24075]
Barstow Company Inc.; A.G. [21398]
Bensinger's [10537]
Betti Industries Inc.; H. [25573]
Bev-Tech, Inc. [14345]
Bintz Distributing Co. [24076]
Blodgett International Sales; G.S. [24077]
Boelter Companies Inc. [24079]
Bolton and Hay Inc. [24081]
Bowman Associates Inc.; A.D. [25896]
Boyd-Bluford Co. Inc. [10602]
Boyer Printing Co. [25578]
Boyer Printing Co. [24082]
Brady Distributing Co. [25579]
Brann Associates Inc.; Don [20854]
Briel America Inc. [15058]
Bronson Syrup Company Inc. [10619]
Budget Sales Inc. [24084]
Buffalo Hotel Supply Company Inc. [25585]
Buffalo Scale and Supply Co. Inc. [24330]
Burrows Co. [19205]
Butler Wholesale Products [24085]
Byczek Enterprises [24086]
C and T Design and Equipment Company
    Inc. [25587]
Canfield Co.; M.E. [15870]
Cannon Inc.; W.W. [25898]
Canton China and Equipment Co. [24088]
Capital City Restaurant Supply Co. [24089]
Capital Scale [24335]
Carpet Basics [9762]
Central Distributing Co. [25598]
Central Procurement Inc. [24091]
Cisco-Eagle, Inc. [25902]
Clark County Bar & Restaurant Supply [24093]
Clark Food Service Inc. South Bend Div. [24094]
CMC America Corp. [25603]
CMC America Corp. [24096]
Color Brite Fabrics and Displays Inc. [25605]
Commercial Interior Decor [25607]
Commercial Music Co. Inc. [25608]
Commercial Shelving [25905]
Computer Discounters [6109]
Consolidated Utility Equipment Service, Inc. [2478]
Cook's Mart Ltd. [15454]
Corporate Interiors Inc. [20932]
Cream City Scale Company Inc. [24342]
Creative Store Design Inc. [25614]
Crisci Food Equipment Co. [24097]
Cromers Inc. [24098]
Crystal Refrigeration Inc. [14408]
Custer Supply & Fixtures [25618]
D & P Enterprises Inc. [24100]
Dahlco Music & Vending [25622]
Dakota Food Equipment Inc. [24102]
Dana-Lu Imports Inc. [24103]
Dann Dee Display Fixtures Inc. [25625]
Deveault; Ed [24345]
Discount Desk Etc., Inc. [20965]
Dispenser Services Inc. [25630]
Dixie Store Fixtures and Sales Company
    Inc. [15476]
Domestic & International Technology [2555]
Dorian International Inc. [24105]
Double A Provisions Inc. [10983]
Douron Incorporated Corporate Furniture [13094]
Dunken Distributing Inc. [9874]
Dunn Sales; Skip [25638]
Eastman Sign Co. [13100]

Edmund's Dummy Company Inc. [25641]
EDS Refrigeration Inc. [14429]
Edwards Wood Products Inc. (Portola Valley,
    California) [25910]
Electric Motor Repair Co. [24107]
Electronic Label Technology Inc. [6243]
Elliott Manufacturing Company Inc. [24108]
Empire Wholesale Supply [9884]
Environmental Interiors [20993]
Erika-Record Inc. [24110]
Euroven Corp. [24111]
Exmart International, Inc. [24112]
Export Contract Corp. [24113]
F and B Marketing Inc. [8726]
Far East Restaurant Equipment Mfg. Co. [24114]
Farm Boy Meats Inc. [11083]
Fastener Controls Inc. (FASCON) [13697]
Fetzer Company-Restaurateurs [24117]
Filter Fresh of Northern Virginia Inc. [15496]
Fineline Products, Inc. [21004]
Fixture Hardware Co. [13113]
Fixture-World, Inc. [24121]
Flagg Co.; R.M. [24122]
Flihan Co.; Joseph [24123]
Food Equipment Specialists [24124]
Food Services of America [11178]
Freeburg Sign & Lighting [25654]
FWB Inc. [6285]
G & C Restaurant Equipment [24125]
Gani International Inc.; J. [25656]
Gardner and Benoit Inc. [24126]
Gauntlett Agency Ltd. [25659]
Geis Building Products Inc. [7381]
Gering; David [24127]
Glacier Water Services Inc. [24128]
Global Exports, Inc. [23192]
Globe Industrial Supply Inc. [13123]
The Godfrey Group Inc. [25662]
Gold Medal Products Co. [25663]
Golden Light Equipment Co. [24129]
Gordon Food Service Inc. [11293]
Grayco Products [16904]
Guest Supply Inc. [24130]
H A Foodservice-HAFSCO [24131]
H & H Foodservice [11349]
HALCO [24132]
Haldeman-Homme Inc. [16921]
Hale Industries Inc. [24133]
Hallsmith-Sysco Food Services [11366]
Hard Times Vending Inc. [24135]
Harrington Co. [24136]
HAZCO Services Inc. [24368]
Hecht Inc.; William [25675]
Heights Pump & Supply [24370]
Hellenbrand Water Conditioners Inc. [25676]
Henderson Auctions Inc. [24137]
Hermann Associates Inc. [21030]
HIE Holdings, Inc. [11428]
Hill and Son Co.; Fred [13133]
Hilton Equipment Corp. [13134]
Hockenberg Equipment Co. [24138]
Holga Inc. [21038]
Hopewell Valley Specialties [11459]
HRS Corp. [14489]
Hughes Company Inc. of Columbus [24139]
Husky Food Products of Anchorage [11482]
ICEE-USA Corp. [24972]
Ifeco Inc. [24140]
IJ Co. Tri-Cities Div. [11493]
Intedge Industries Inc. [24142]
International Dairy Queen Inc. [24143]
International Restaurant Equipment Company
    Inc. [24144]
Interroyal Hospital Supply Corp. [18861]
Interstate Restaurant Equipment Corp. [24146]
Jacobi-Lewis Co. [24148]
Jim Sales & Service [24379]
JS Enterprises Inc. [24151]
Jurins Distributing Co. [24152]
Kanawha Scales and Systems [24382]
Kenney Distributors; J.F. [24155]
Key Sales Inc. [24157]
King Safe and Lock Company Inc. [24581]
Kitcor Corp. [24158]
Kittredge Equipment Co. [24159]
Knapp Supply & Equipment Co. [24160]

Koen Co.; U. [25704]
K's Distributors [25709]
L & M Food Service [24161]
Lake Tahoe Supplies [4656]
Larsen Co., Inc.; A. R. [24163]
Le Creuset of America Inc. [15562]
Ledyard Company Inc. [24164]
Lee-Rowan Co. [25927]
Lester Company Inc.; Kenneth O. [24165]
Limestone Detailers [25717]
Lindox Equipment Corp. [24166]
Linvar Inc. [24167]
Linvar LLC [25929]
LKS International Inc. [24168]
Logan Inc. [11722]
Lone Elm Sales Inc. [11726]
Long Inc.; Duncan [21112]
LRP Enterprises [14154]
LRP Enterprises [24169]
LTD Dozier Inc. [24170]
M & M Distributors [24172]
MacBean Inc.; Scottie [24173]
Main Street and Main Inc. [24175]
Maines Paper and Food Service Inc. Equipment
    and Supply Div. [14530]
Major Appliances Inc. [24176]
Man-I-Can Store Fixtures, Inc. [13170]
Mark-Costello Co. [16264]
Marvel Group Inc. [21132]
Massena Paper Company Inc. [21824]
May Engineering Company Inc. [24179]
McComas Sales Co. Inc. [24180]
McCoy and Son Inc.; J.B. [21828]
McQuiddy Office Designers Inc. [21134]
Medica International Ltd. [1009]
Medley Hotel and Restaurant Supply Co. [24183]
Meidlinger Inc.; H.E. [24184]
Midamar Corp. [11882]
Midway Trading, Inc. [2958]
Mile High Equipment Co. [24186]
Miller Machinery and Supply Co. [24187]
Millstone Service Div. [11901]
Monarch Toilet Partition [13184]
Montana Scale Co. Inc. [24402]
Montana Scale Company Inc. [24188]
Montoya/MAS International Inc. [25744]
Mountain Ark Trading Co. [11944]
Mountain Sales & Service Inc. [14612]
Mountain View Supply Inc. [24189]
MTS Wireless Components [24190]
Nannicola Wholesale Co., Inc. [25747]
National Equipment Co. [13186]
Nelson Wholesale Corp. [24191]
Neon Co. [25753]
Newells Bar & Restaurant Supply, Inc. [24192]
Nicewonger Co. [24193]
NJCT Corp. [24194]
Northeast Scale Company Inc. [24410]
Northwestern Systems [25765]
Nyle Home Health Supplies Inc. [25768]
Oliver Supply Co. [4680]
Orr-Sysco Food Services Co.; Robert [24199]
Otis Distributors [24200]
Packers Engineering and Equipment Company
    Inc. [17098]
Palay Display Industries Inc. [13202]
Palay Display Industries Inc. [13203]
Palm Brothers Inc. [24201]
Paper Service Company Inc. [21865]
Par-Way/Tryson Co. [24202]
PBI Market Equipment Inc. [16385]
Pegler-Sysco Food Services Co. [12132]
Penguin Point Systems Inc. [12137]
PFG Lester [12161]
Physicians Supply Co. [18989]
Poppers Supply Co. [12194]
Pop's E-Z Popcorn & Supply Co. [24204]
Publishers Supply Inc. [25794]
Quality Foods Inc. [12250]
Quality Foods Inc. [12251]
Queen City Wholesale Inc. [12255]
R & R Mill Company [15287]
Rave Computer Association Inc. [6685]
Red Gaskins and Co.; J. [24209]
Reece Supply Company of Dallas [25800]
Reed Export, Inc.; Charles H. [10117]

Reiner Enterprises [23338]
Reliable Paper & Supply Company Inc. [21899]
Restaurant Design & Development [14662]
Retail Service Company Inc. [13220]
Ricci; Robert [24210]
Robins L.L.C.; A.K. [24211]
Rykoff-Sexton Inc. [24212]
St. Paul Bar/Restaurant Equipment [24213]
Sarco Inc. [24215]
Schlueter Company Inc. [24216]
School Specialty Inc. [21259]
Seika Machinery, Inc. [16481]
Service Engineering Co. [19037]
Sheldon and Company Inc.; H.D. [24217]
Shelmar Food [12476]
Shelving Inc. [25938]
Shelving Inc. [24218]
Shetakis Distributing Co.; Jim L. [24219]
Sierra Scales [24432]
Siggins Co. [16490]
Singer Equipment Company Inc. [24220]
Skip Dunn Sales [24221]
Skyline Designs [13246]
Skyline Designs [24222]
Smellkinson Sysco Food Services Inc. [24223]
Smith Inc.; Kenneth [23948]
Sodak Gaming Inc. [25821]
Southern Commercial Machines [25825]
Southern Industrial Corp. [24225]
Spectrum Corp. [25827]
Spectrum Lighting/Sound & Beyond [25828]
State Restaurant Equipment Inc. [24226]
State Scale Co., Inc. [24438]
Stella Products Co.; F.D. [24228]
Storage Equipment Company Inc. [25941]
Storage Equipment Company Inc. [24229]
Storage Solutions Inc. [24230]
Strayer Products [21300]
Struve Distributing Company Inc. [25832]
Struve Distributing Company Inc. [24232]
Sunflower Restaurant Supply Inc. [12612]
Sunlow Inc. [24233]
Superior Distributors [25834]
Superior Products [24234]
Superior Products Manufacturing Co. [24235]
Surfas Inc. [24236]
SYSCO Food Services of Arkansas, Inc. [24237]
Sysco Food Services of Atlanta Inc. [12674]
Sysco Food Services of Idaho Inc. [24238]
Sysco Food Services of Philadelphia Inc. [12685]
SYSCO Food Services of South Florida [12688]
SYSCO of Louisville [12691]
T & R Beverage Control [24239]
Table Supply Co. [24240]
Tailor-Made Signs [13255]
Taylor Restaurant Equipment [24241]
TEC America Inc. [25837]
TEC America Inc. [24242]
TENBA Quality Cases, Ltd. [18435]
Terrile Export & Import Corp. [9480]
Texas Art Supply Co. [25840]
Thoms-Proestler Co. [24246]
Tomra Maine [25845]
Trak-Air/Rair [24247]
Tri-State [24249]
Tucker Company Inc.; M. [24250]
Tucker Company Inc.; M. [24251]
Tucker Library Interiors LLC [13263]
Unarco Commercial Products [24252]
Unirak Storage Systems [25946]
Unitech Inc. [21326]
United Distributors Inc. [25854]
United East Foodservice Supply Co. [24254]
United Restaurant Equipment [24256]
United Scale and Engineering Co. [25856]
United Scale and Engr. Corp. [24450]
U.S. Foodservice Inc. [24257]
US Food Service-Pittston Division [12807]
US Reflector [3378]
Vendor's Supply and Service Inc. [25867]
Viking Acoustical Corp. [21338]
Vreeken Enterprises Inc. [24258]
Wahl and Wahl of Iowa Inc. [21342]
Warren Equipment Co. [24259]
Wasserstrom Co. [21348]
Webster Scale Inc. [24455]

Weigh-Tronix Inc. [24260]
Welbilt Corp. [15369]
Western Pioneer Sales Co. [25877]
Willco Sales and Services Inc. [25881]
Winkler Store Fixtures Co. [13281]
World Wide Distributors Inc. [25883]
World Wide Distributors Inc. [24263]
Yamato Corp. [24459]

SIC 5047 — Medical & Hospital Equipment

21st Century Holdings Inc. [18650]
A & A Reconditioned Medical [18651]
A-Dec Inc. [13007]
A-Dec International Inc. [18652]
A Plus Medical, Inc. [19117]
A & W Medical & Oxygen Supply [18653]
A-Welders & Medical Supply [18654]
Abbey Home Healthcare [19119]
Abbey Medical Inc. [19120]
Abbey Pharmaceutical Services Inc. [18655]
Accutron Inc. [18656]
Acme Agri Supply Inc. [27056]
Adco Inc. [18657]
ADCO Surgical Supply Inc. [18658]
ADI Medical [19125]
Adtek Co. [18659]
Adtek Co. [19126]
Advance Glove & Safety Co. [24491]
Advanced Imaging Technologies Inc. [18660]
Advanced Medical Systems Inc. [18661]
Advanced Scientific Inc. [18662]
Aero Products Corp. [18663]
Affiliated Medical Research [18664]
Airgas Safety [18665]
AirSep Corporation [15748]
Akin Industries, Inc. [18666]
Akin Medical Equipment International [19128]
AKMS, Inc. [18667]
AKMS Inc. [19129]
Aladdin Synergetics Inc. [18668]
ALARIS Medical Systems Inc. [18669]
Aleutian Pribilof Island Association [18670]
Alfreds Processor Sales & Service [18671]
Allegiance Corp. [19134]
Allegiance Healthcare Corporation Hospital
   Supply/Scientific Products [18672]
Allegiance Healthcare Corporation Hospital
   Supply/Scientific Products [19135]
Allied Medical, Inc. [19137]
Allied Safety Inc. [19138]
ALM Surgical Equipment Inc. [18673]
ALR Wholesale [27062]
Amber Grout Sales [27063]
American Ambulance [18674]
American Health Systems Inc. [18675]
American Homepatient, Inc. [18676]
American Industrial Exports Ltd. [18449]
American Medical Export Inc. [18677]
American Medical Services [19142]
American Plasma Services L.P [19144]
American Respiratory Inc. [18678]
American Scientific Technology, L.L.C. [18679]
Americo International Trading, Ltd. [19145]
AmeriNet/SupportHealth [19146]
Amics International Inc. [24311]
Amigo Mobility International Inc. [18680]
Amtec International Inc. [13020]
Anabolic Laboratories Inc. [18681]
Anderson Home Health Supply [18682]
Anderson Medical Inc. [18683]
Anderson's Wheelchair Therapeutic Supply [18684]
Anesthesia Equipment Supply [18685]
Angeles Medical Supply Inc. [18686]
Animal Emergency Center [27066]
Animal Medic Inc. [27067]
Anodyne Inc. [19154]
Apex Foot Health Industries [24674]
Apex Medical Corp. [18687]
Apothecary Products Inc. [19156]
Apria Healthcare [19157]
Aramsco, Inc. [16707]

Archbold Health Services Inc. [18688]
Arctic Fire Equipment [24507]
Area Access Inc. [18689]
Area Access Inc. [19159]
Arizona Therapy Source [18690]
Ark Manufacturing Inc. [27074]
Armstrong Medical Industries Inc. [18691]
Aseptico, Inc. [18692]
Associated Healthcare Systems Inc. [18693]
Associated Medical [19164]
Associated Medical Supply Inc. [18694]
Associated Services for the Blind [19165]
Associated X-Ray Corp. [18695]
ATD-American Co. [25971]
Atecs Corp. [18696]
Atecs Corp. [19167]
Athmann Industrial Medical Supply [18697]
Attention Medical Co. [18698]
Auto Suture Company U.S.A. [19169]
Avionix Medical Devices [18699]
Avon-Glendale Home Medical Equipment and
   Supplies Inc. [19171]
Award Pet Supply [27077]
B & B Medical Service Inc. [18700]
B C Sales Co., Inc. [18701]
B & J Enterprises Inc. [18702]
B Sharp Co. [27078]
Barco Municipal Products Inc. [24511]
Baxter Healthcare Corp. Converters/Custom Sterile
   Div. [18703]
Baylor Biomedical Services [19178]
Beck-Lee Inc. [18704]
Beck-Lee Inc. [19180]
Bedsole Medical Companies Inc. [18705]
Bellsonics [5529]
Best Labs [18706]
B.G. Industries Inc. [19186]
Big Sky Fire Equipment [18707]
Bingham Enterprises Inc. [19189]
Binson's Hospital Supplies Inc. [18708]
Bio-Dental Technologies Corp. [19190]
Bio Instruments Inc. [19191]
Bio-Medical Imaging Inc. [18709]
Bio Medical Life Systems Inc. [18710]
Bio-Medical Resources Inc. [18711]
Biocoustics Instruments Inc. [18712]
Bioject Medical Technologies Inc. [19192]
Biomedical Research & Development Laboratories,
   Inc. [18713]
Biopool International Inc. [18714]
Biosound Esaote Inc. [18715]
Biotronik Inc. [18716]
Blankenstein Co. Inc.; F.R. [18717]
Bloodline Agency [27085]
Bock Pharmaceutical, Inc.; James A. [19196]
Bodyline Comfort Systems [18718]
Bowie Manufacturing Inc. [27090]
Branches Medical Inc. [18719]
Breeders Edge [27092]
Brentwood Medical Products Inc. [19198]
Briggs Corp. [19199]
Brinkmann Instruments, Inc. [24328]
Brinkmann Instruments Inc. [19200]
Browns Medical Imaging [18720]
BTE Import-Export [19204]
Buhl Animal Clinic [18721]
Burke Inc. [18722]
Burkhart Dental Supply [18723]
Burkmann Feed [27093]
Burkmann Feeds—Glasgow [27094]
Burkmann Feeds—London [27095]
Burkmann Mills [27096]
Burns Industries Inc. [7112]
Burrows Co. [19205]
Bushwacker Inc. [24521]
Butler Co.; W.A. [19206]
Cajun Sales [27098]
Caldwell and Bloor Company Inc. [19208]
California Professional Manufacturing Inc. [25593]
Campagna Inc. [18724]
Camper's Trade Emporium [13618]
Cantel Medical Corp. [18725]
Cardinal Health Inc. [19212]
Care Medical Equipment Inc. [18726]
Caremed [19214]
Carey Machinery & Supply Co. [24524]

Carl Beatty and Associates [19216]
Carlisle Medical Inc. [18727]
Carolina First Aid Inc. [18728]
Carolina Vet Supply [27102]
Carolina Vet Supply [19219]
Carpenter-Dent-Sublett No. 1 [18729]
Catheter Research Inc. [18730]
Caulk Co.; L.D. [18731]
Cenna International Corp. [19223]
Central Medical Inc. [19224]
Central Nebraska Home Care [18732]
Central Virginia Medical Inc. [18733]
Charron Medical Equipment Inc. [18735]
Charter Pet Supplies [27108]
Checkpoint International [18736]
Chelsea Clock Co. Inc. [18737]
Chem-Tronics Inc. [18738]
Cherney & Associates, Inc. [18739]
Chesapeake Medical Systems [18740]
Chicopee Medical Supplies [18741]
Cho-Pat Inc. [18742]
Choice Medical Inc. [18743]
Claflin Co. [19231]
Clamyer International Corp. [21413]
Clarksville Pharmacy Inc. [18744]
Clinical Homecare Corp. Haemotronic Ltd. [19235]
CMP Industries Inc. [18745]
Colonial Hospital Supply Co. Inc. [19239]
Colonial Medical Supplies [18746]
Columbia Diagnostics Inc. [18747]
Columbus Serum Co. [27110]
Commercial/Medical Electronics [18748]
Complete Medical Products Inc. [18749]
Complete Medical Products Inc. [19242]
Complete Medical Supplies Inc. [19243]
Cone Instruments Inc. [18750]
Conger Dental Supply Co. [18751]
Congress Leather Co. [27111]
Connecticut Physicians & Surgeons [18752]
Conney Safety Products Co. [24527]
Consumer Care Products Inc. [18753]
Consumer Care Products Inc. [19246]
Continental Safety Equipment Inc. [19248]
Cooley Medical Equipment Inc. [18754]
Cora Medical Products Inc. [18755]
Corinthian Healthcare Systems [18756]
Cornell Surgical Co. [19253]
CPS Marketing Corporation [18757]
Cream City Scale Company Inc. [24342]
Creative Health Products [19256]
Creative Rehab [19257]
Crescent City Pharmaceutical [18758]
Cressy & Sons Inc.; W. C. [18759]
Crutcher Dental Inc. [19260]
Crystal Home Health Care Inc. [18760]
Crystal Home Health Care Inc. [19261]
CUI Corp. [18761]
Culver Products Co. Inc. [18762]
Custom Healthcare Systems [19264]
Dako Corp. [19271]
Dalco International, Inc. [18763]
Daly Inc.; James W. [18764]
Daniels Co.; C.P. [27114]
Datex-Ohmeda, Inc. [18765]
Datex-Ohmeda Inc. [19272]
Day Corp.; Alan G. [18766]
DE International Inc. [18767]
De-Tec Inc. [18768]
Delta Hi-Tech Inc. [19276]
Delta-Southland International [18769]
Delta Veterinary Clinic [27115]
Dental Enterprises Inc. [18770]
Dentec Corp. [18771]
Derma Sciences Inc. [19277]
Derma-Therm Inc. [18772]
DeRoyal [18773]
Diagnostic Equipment Service Corp. [18774]
Dialysis Clinic Inc. [18775]
Dittmar Inc. [19283]
Dixon Medical Inc. [18776]
Dockters X-Ray Inc. [18777]
Dockters X-Ray Inc. [19286]
Donico & Associates; J.P. [18778]
Donley Medical Supply Co. [19288]
Down River Home Health Supply [18779]
DRG International Inc. [19289]

Drogueria J.M. Blanco [19291]
Du Pont Co. [21435]
Dupont de Nemours and Co.; E.I. [4376]
Dura Med Inc. [18780]
Durr-Fillauer Medical Inc. [18781]
Durr Medical Corp. [19296]
Dyna Corp. [19297]
Dynamic Medical Equipment Ltd. [19298]
Eagle Milling Co. [27121]
Eastern Maine Healthcare [18782]
Econ Equipment & Supplies Inc. [18783]
Edco Manufacturing Co. [27123]
Ed's Leather Co. [27124]
EEV, Inc. [18784]
Efland Distributing Co. [27126]
ELA Medical Inc. [18785]
Elan Pharmaceuticals [18786]
Elchar Dog Bows [27127]
Electro-Med Co. Inc. [18787]
Elevators Etc. [18788]
Elite Denture Center [18789]
EMP International Corp. [18790]
Empire Equities Inc. [19304]
Endolite North America Ltd. [18791]
Enos Home Oxygen Therapy Inc. [18792]
Enos Home Oxygen Therapy Inc. [19305]
ERW International, Inc. [19307]
Etac USA Inc. [18793]
Etac USA Inc. [19308]
Everest and Jennings International Ltd. [19310]
Express International Corp. [19313]
Extech Ltd. [18794]
Extend-A-Life Inc. [19315]
Fadson International Company [14439]
Falls Welding & Fabricating, FWF Medical Products Div. [18795]
Falls Welding and Fabrication, Medical Products Div. [19321]
Fertility Technologies Inc. [18796]
Fillauer Inc. [18797]
Fire Appliance & Safety Co. [24541]
Fire Fighters Equipment Co. [24545]
First Aid Plus Inc. [18798]
Fisher Healthcare [24359]
Fisher Healthcare [19324]
Fisher Scientific Co. [24360]
Fisher Scientific Co. [19325]
Fisher Scientific International Inc. [24552]
Flex-Foot Inc. [18799]
Flinn Scientific, Inc. [24361]
Forcean Inc. [18800]
Forest Medical Products Inc. [19326]
Franklin Medical Products [19330]
Fuji Medical Systems USA Inc. [18801]
Fukuda Denshi USA, Inc. [18802]
Fuller Supply Co. [27136]
Fuller Supply Co., Inc. [27137]
Fuller Supply Company Inc. [27138]
Future Med, Inc. [19332]
Gainor Medical U.S.A. Inc. [18803]
Gann Company Inc.; E.C. [26494]
Gaspro [18804]
Gell and Co.; Jack [19334]
Gemmex Intertrade America Inc. [11247]
General Biomedical Service Inc. [18805]
General Imaging Corp. [18806]
General Injectables and Vaccines Inc. [19337]
General Medical Corp. [18807]
Genesis Medical Equipment [18808]
Genesis Safety Systems Inc. [24555]
Gensia Sicor Inc. [18809]
Geriatric Medical & Surgical [18811]
Giancola Exports, Inc.; D.J. [4628]
Girzen, Res. [19339]
Godbee Medical Distributors [18812]
Godbee Medical Distributors [18813]
Golden Crown Corp. [27139]
Golden State Medical Supply Inc. [19341]
Graeffs Eastside Drugs; Mike [18814]
Great Lakes Orthopedics Inc. [18815]
Great Western Pet Supply [27141]
Grogan's Healthcare Supply Inc. [18817]
Grogan's, Inc. [19343]
GTS Scientific Inc. [18818]
Gulf South Medical Supply Inc. [18819]
H Enterprises International Inc. [19345]

Haffner X-Ray Company Inc. [18820]
Hal-Hen Company Inc. [18821]
Hamilton Medical Inc. [18822]
Hamilton Medical Inc. [19347]
Handicapped Driving Aids of Michigan Inc. [18823]
Handy Care [19349]
Happy Acres Pet Supply [27144]
Happy Harry's Healthcare Inc. [18824]
Harmony Enterprises America [18825]
Harris Discount Supply [18826]
Harris Enterprises Inc. [18827]
Harrison Wholesale Products Inc. [27145]
Hart Equipment Company Inc. [24559]
Hartwell Medical Corp. [19350]
Hartzler's Inc. Exporters [18828]
Harvard Apparatus, Inc. [18829]
Hayes Medical Inc. [19352]
Hazra Associates, Inc. [18830]
HCI Corp./International Marketing Services [18831]
Health Care Services, Inc. [19353]
Healthcare Services International [18832]
Hearing Aid Centers of America [18833]
Henry Schein Inc. Dental Div. [18834]
Hewlett-Packard Co. International [6331]
Hill; Gary A. [18835]
Hirsh Precision Products Inc. [2755]
Hitachi Medical Systems America Inc. [6335]
Holladay Surgical Supply Co. [18836]
Holladay Surgical Supply Co. [19360]
Home-Bound Medical Care Inc. [18837]
Home Diagnostics Inc. [18838]
Home Edco Home Care [18839]
Home Medical Supply Inc. [18840]
HomeReach Inc. [18841]
Horizon Medical Inc. [18842]
Howmedica Mountain States, Inc. [18843]
HSO Corp. [18844]
Hudson Home Health Care Inc. [18845]
Hughes Company Inc.; R.S. [24568]
Huntleigh Technology Inc. [18846]
Huntleigh Technology Inc. [19363]
Hutchinson Health Care Services [18847]
Hyperbaric Oxygen Therapy Systems Inc. [18848]
Imaging Concepts Inc. [18849]
Imperial Pet Products [27156]
Implant Dynamic [18850]
Independent Pet Co-op [27157]
Infolab Inc. [19371]
Information Sales and Marketing Company Inc. [19372]
Ingram Co.; G.A. [18851]
Inmed Corp. [18852]
Integrated Medical Inc. [19373]
Integrated Medical Systems [18853]
Interactive Medical Technologies Ltd. [18854]
Interchange Corp. [860]
Intercontinental Trade Development [18855]
Intermetra Corp. [8891]
International Domestic Development Corp. [18857]
International Healthcare Products [18858]
International Projects Inc. [23747]
International Surgical Systems [18859]
International Trade Group [18860]
International Trade & Telex Corp. [19378]
Interroyal Hospital Supply Corp. [18861]
Interwest Home Medical Inc. [18862]
Interwest Medical Equipment Distributors Inc. [18863]
Iowa Veterinary Supply Co. [27158]
ISC/BioExpress [18864]
ISC/BioExpress [19380]
ITBR, Inc. [5651]
J & J Supply, Inc. [18865]
J & L Medical Supply Corp. [18866]
Jaco Co. [18867]
Japco Exports [27159]
Jeffers Vet Supply [27161]
Jeffers Vet Supply [27162]
Jeffers Vet Supply [19384]
Jensen Lloyd and Willis [18023]
Jorgensen Laboratories Inc. [27164]
Justlin Medical Inc. [18869]
K & I Transeau Co. [27166]
K & K Pet Talk [27167]
K and K Pet Talk [19389]
K & K Vet Supply [27168]

K and K Vet Supply [19390]
K & R Distributors [27169]
K & S Distributors [19391]
Kagiya Trading Co. Ltd. of America [13779]
Kako International Inc. [18870]
Kalamazoo Dental Supply [18871]
Kane X-Ray Company Inc. [18872]
Kendell Co [19394]
Kentec Medical Inc. [18873]
Kentucky Buying Cooperative Int. [19395]
Kentucky Dental Supply Co. Inc. [18874]
Kentucky Home Care Services, Inc. [18875]
Keomed Inc. [18876]
Kimbet Leather [27173]
Kinray, Inc. [14142]
Kitrick Management Company, Ltd. [24383]
Knit-Rite Inc. [18877]
Koley's Medical Supply Company Inc. [19399]
Krieg Consulting and Trading Inc.; A. [16220]
Kuhlman and Co.; A. [18878]
L & B Pet Supplies [27176]
L & L Pet Center [27177]
La Grand Industrial Supply Co. [24582]
La Pointique International [18879]
Lab Safety Supply Inc. [18880]
Labomed, Inc. [18881]
Laboratory & Biomedical Supplies Inc. [19403]
Laboratory Supply Company [18882]
LaFrance Equipment Corp. [24583]
LDC Corporation of America [18883]
Lease Surgical Inc. [18884]
Leasure & Associates Inc.; Ralph [18885]
Leedal Inc. [22873]
Leeward Inc. [18886]
Leica Inc. [24387]
Leich Div.; Charles [19407]
Leisegang Medical Inc. [18887]
Leisure-Lift, Inc. [18888]
Leisure-Lift Inc. [19408]
LeJoy Uniforms Inc. [18889]
LeMare Medical Inc. [18890]
Leone's Animal Supply [27180]
Life-Tech Inc. [19415]
Limestone Detailers [25717]
Lintex Corp. [18891]
Lors Medical Corp. [18892]
Luffeys Medical & Surgical Supplies [19418]
Luxury Liners [18893]
Luxury Liners [19419]
Lynn Medical Instrument Co. [18894]
Lyntech Corp. [18895]
Maats Enterprises [19421]
Mabis Healthcare Inc. [18896]
Mager Scientific Inc. [24393]
Main Line International Inc. [18898]
Major Medical Supply Co. Inc. [18899]
Manchester Medical Supply Inc. [18900]
Master Works International [18901]
Mastermans [18902]
Matthews Book Co. [3940]
Maxcare International Inc. [19426]
MBI Inc. [18903]
MBI Inc. [19428]
M.C. International [19429]
McAbee Medical Inc. [18904]
McBain Instruments [24395]
McKesson General Medical Corp. [18905]
McLean International Marketing Inc. [24589]
MCM Enterprise [2935]
MDR Corp. [21136]
Med Dent Service Corp. [18907]
Med-Lab Supply Company Inc. [18908]
Med-Tech Inc. [18909]
Med-X International, Inc. [19439]
Meddev Corp. [18910]
Medi-Globe Corp. [18911]
Medi Inc. [19441]
Medi Inc. - School Health Div. [18912]
Medica International Ltd. [1009]
Medical Devices Inc. [18913]
Medical Dynamics Inc. [19443]
Medical Electronics Sales and Service [19444]
Medical Equipment Repair Services Inc. [18914]
Medical Equipment Resale, Inc. [18915]
Medical Equipment Resale Inc. [19445]
Medical Imaging Inc. [18916]

Medical Imaging Services Inc. [18917]
Medical International Inc. [18918]
Medical Marketing Inc. [18919]
Medical Mart Inc. [18920]
Medical Procedures Inc. [18921]
Medical Scientific Service [18922]
Medical Specialists Company Inc. [18923]
Medical Specialists Company Inc. [19446]
Medical Specialties Company Inc. [19447]
Medical Supplies Inc. [18924]
MediQuip International [18925]
Melan International Trading [9064]
Memphis Serum Company Inc. [18926]
Menlo Tool Company Inc. [18927]
Mercy National Purchasing Inc. [18928]
Mercy National Purchasing Inc. [19450]
Mercy Resource Management, Inc. [18929]
Meridian Synapse Corporation [18930]
Meridian Veterinary Products [27187]
Merriam-Graves Corp. [18931]
Merriam-Graves Corp. [18932]
Metropolitan Medical Inc. [18933]
Metropolitan X-Ray Sales Inc. [18934]
Meyers Medical Inc. [18935]
Meyers; Tom [27188]
Michelle International, Ltd. [127]
Micro Bio-Medics Inc. [19454]
Micro Ear Technology Inc. [18936]
Mid-Michigan Regional Health Systems [18937]
Midland Hospital Supply Inc. [18938]
Midland Medical Supply Co. [19457]
Midwest Medical Supply Company Inc. [19461]
Midwest Veterinary Supply Inc. [27189]
Miller's Adaptive Technologies [19464]
Millers Rents & Sells [19465]
MIRA Inc. [18940]
Mississippi Serum Distributors [18941]
Missoula Hearing [18942]
Mitchell Home Medical [18943]
Mitchell Orthopedic Supply Inc. [18944]
Mize Farm & Garden Supply [27190]
MKM Inc. [18945]
MLT International Inc. [17045]
MMI Inc. [18946]
Montgomery Seed [27191]
Moore Industries Inc. [19466]
Moore Medical Corp. [19467]
More Mobility [19468]
Morgan Scientific, Inc. [18947]
Morris Associates; William [18948]
Mountain Aire Medical Equipment [18949]
Mountain Imaging Inc. [18950]
Mountain States Medical Inc. [18951]
Mourad & Associated International Trade [18952]
MRS Industries Inc. [18953]
Mundy Enterprises, Inc.; K.C. [3003]
Nada Concepts Inc. [18954]
Nasco West [18955]
Nashville Pet Products Center [27192]
Nassifs Professional Pharmacy [18956]
Natcom International [19475]
National Keystone Mizzy Tridynamics [19476]
National Medical Excess [18957]
National Medical Excess [19477]
NCS Healthcare [18958]
NCS Healthcare [19480]
Nebraska Medical Mart II [18959]
Nelson Laboratories L.P. [1068]
Neuman Distributors Inc. [19485]
Neuman Health Services Inc. [19486]
NeuroCom International Inc. [19487]
New England Serum Co. [19491]
New Mexico Orthopedic Supplies [18960]
New World Research Corp. [3030]
NFZ Products Inc. [13846]
Niagara Medical [19495]
Nightingale Medical Equipment Services
  Inc. [19496]
Nihon Kohden America Inc. [18961]
NLS Animal Health [27195]
Northpoint Trading Co. Inc. [27197]
Northwest Vet Supply Inc. [27199]
Nowak Dental Supplies Inc. [18962]
Nuclear Associates [18963]
Nurnberg Thermometer Co. [24411]
Nyle International Corp. [18964]

O2 Emergency Medical Care Service
  Corp. [18965]
Office Pavilion/MBI Systems Inc. [18966]
Olympus America Inc. [22887]
Omnimedical Inc. [18967]
On-Gard Systems Inc. [18968]
Orr Safety Corp. [24608]
Ortho-Care Southeast Inc. [18969]
Ortho-Tex Inc. [19520]
Otake Instrument Inc. [18970]
Otto Dental Supply Company Inc. [18971]
Owens and Minor Inc. [18972]
Owens and Minor Inc. Augusta Div. [19521]
Oxygen Co. Inc. [18973]
Pacific Criticare Inc. [18974]
Page Inc.; T.H. [18975]
Pagel Safety Inc. [24610]
Panoramic Corp. [18976]
PanVera Corp. [19522]
Para-Pharm Inc. [18977]
Pascal Company Inc. [19527]
Patterson Dental Co. [19529]
Peakwon International Inc. [18979]
Pegler-Sysco Food Services Co. [12132]
Peninsula Laboratories Inc. [19530]
Performance Medical Group, Inc. [18980]
Perfusion Services of Baxter Healthcare
  Corp. [19533]
Perigon Medical Dist. Corp. [19534]
Peripheral Visions Inc. [18981]
Permark, Inc. [18982]
Perry Supply Company Inc.; Roy L. [18983]
Perz Feed & Delivery [27204]
Pet Supply Warehouse [27211]
Pet World [27212]
Pharm-Med Inc. [18984]
Pharmacies In Medisav Homecare [18985]
Philips Key Modules [9196]
Philips Medical Systems North America
  Co. [19539]
Phoenix Group HI-TEC Corp. [18986]
PhotoVision Inc. [18987]
Physician Sales and Service Inc. [18988]
Physicians Supply Co. [18989]
Pittman International [27214]
Pittman International [19542]
P.K. Safety Supply [24612]
PML Inc. [19545]
PML Microbiologicals Inc. [19546]
Polar Electro Inc. [18990]
Polar Electro Inc. [19547]
Porta-Lung Inc. [14641]
Poultry Health [27215]
Praxair Gas Tech [17110]
Precision Instruments Inc. [18991]
Precision Technology Inc. (Norwood, New
  Jersey) [18992]
Premier Medical Supplies Inc. [18993]
Prescotts Inc. [18994]
Preston Corp.; J.A. [18995]
Priddy's General Store [27216]
Prime Care Medical Supplies Inc. [18996]
Pro-Chem Ltd. Inc. [18997]
Pro-Med Supplies Inc. [18998]
Professional Dental Technologies Inc. [19554]
Promatek Medical Systems Inc. [18999]
Protocol Systems Inc. [19559]
PTC International [19000]
Pulmonary Data Service [19561]
Quality Control Consultants [19001]
Quality Monitor Systems [19002]
Quantum Labs Inc. [19003]
Queen City Home Health Care Inc. [19004]
R5 Trading International Inc. [19005]
R & B Orthopedics Inc. [19006]
R-K Market [19007]
Radiology Resources Inc. [19008]
Radiology Services Inc. [19009]
RadServ Inc. [19010]
Rand-Scot Inc. [19567]
Ransdell Surgical Inc. [19012]
Ransdell Surgical Inc. [19568]
Red Ball Medical Supply Inc. [19013]
Redline Healthcare Corp. [19014]
Redline Healthcare Corp. [19570]
Regional Home Care Inc. [19015]

Rehab Equipment Co. [19574]
Rehab Medical Equipment Inc. [19016]
Rehab Specialties [19575]
The Rehab Tech Center [19576]
Rehab Technology of Colorado [19577]
Remedpar Inc. [19017]
Renishaw Inc. [19018]
Respiratory Homecare Inc. [19019]
Respironics Colorado Inc. [19578]
RF Management Corp. [19020]
RGH Enterprises Inc. [19021]
RGH Enterprises Inc. [19580]
Rieger Medical Supply Co. [19022]
Road Rescue Inc. [3165]
Roane-Barker Inc. [19024]
Roberts Oxygen Company Inc. [19025]
Rushmore Health Care Products [19026]
Rx Rocker Corp. [19027]
SA-SO [24620]
Safety Flare Inc. [24622]
St. Jude Medical Inc. [19028]
St. Louis Ostomy Distributors Inc. [19029]
Sales and Marketing Services Inc. [19030]
Sammons Preston [19031]
San Jose Surgical Supply Inc. [19032]
Sandler Medical Services [19033]
Schuco Inc. [19034]
Scotland Yard [27229]
Scotland Yard [19599]
Seattle Orthotics Group [6715]
Sema Inc. [19035]
Service Drug of Brainerd Inc. [19036]
Service Engineering Co. [19037]
SF Services Inc. [27231]
Shared Service Systems Inc. [19605]
Shaws-Healthtick [19606]
Siemens Energy and Automation Inc. Electrical
  Apparatus Div. [9369]
Sietec Inc. [19609]
sjs X-Ray Corp. [19038]
Sklar Instrument Company Inc. [19039]
Skyland Hospital Supply Inc. [19040]
Skytron [19041]
Smith-Holden Inc. [19042]
SNA Inc. [19043]
Snell; V.A. [27233]
Solares Florida Corp. [16501]
Sontek Industries Inc. [19044]
South Jersey X-Ray Supply Co. [19045]
Southern Carbide Specialists Inc. [13928]
Southern Livestock Supply Co. Inc. [1281]
Southern Prosthetic Supply [19046]
Southern Prosthetic Supply Co. [19628]
SpaceLabs Medical Inc. [19630]
Spar Medical Inc. [19047]
Special Care Medical Inc. [19048]
Specialties of Surgery Inc. [19049]
Specialty Surgical Instrumentation Inc. [19050]
Spectranetics Corp. [19631]
Spectrum Corp. [25827]
Spectrum Labs Inc. [19632]
Spinal Analysis Machine [19051]
SPRI Medical Products Corp. Ballert International
  Div. [19633]
Standard Medical Imaging Inc. [19052]
Stanis Trading Corp. [19636]
Starmac Group [5393]
Stat Surgical Center Inc. [19053]
Stemmans Inc. [19054]
Stepic Corp. [19055]
Steri-Systems Corp. [19056]
Stockman Supply Inc. [27239]
Stolls Medical Rentals Inc. [19057]
Stone Medical Supply Corp. [19639]
Stuart Medical Inc. [19058]
Stuart's Hospital Supply Co. [19640]
Suburban Ostomy Supply Company Inc. [19642]
Sullivan Dental Products Inc. [19059]
Summertree Medisales [19060]
Summit Company [4522]
Summit Instruments Corp. [19061]
Summit Trading Co. [19062]
Sun Medical Equipment and Supply Co. [19063]
Surgical Instrument Associates [19064]
Surgitec [19065]
Syncor International Corp. [19066]

Syrvet, Inc. [19067]
SYSCO Food Services of Minnesota Inc. [12684]
Systems Medical Co. Inc. [19068]
Tactilitics Inc. [19647]
Talon Associates International, Inc. [19069]
Tamarack Ltd. [19070]
Tecan US Inc. [19071]
Technical Products Inc. [19072]
Tens of Charlotte Inc. [19073]
Thau-Nolde Inc. [19654]
Theraquip Inc. [19074]
Thermafil/Tulsa Dental Products [19075]
Thigpen Pharmacy Inc. [19076]
Thompson Dental Company Inc. [19077]
Thrifty Medical Supply Inc. [19078]
Timm Medical Systems [19079]
Titus and Sons Inc.; F.D. [19655]
TMC Orthopedic Supplies Inc. [19656]
Toma International [1340]
Top Dog Ltd. [27248]
Toray Marketing and Sales (America) Inc. [19080]
Toshiba America Medical Systems Inc. [19081]
Toshiba America Medical Systems Inc. [19658]
Total Orthopedic Div. [19659]
Trade America [16573]
Trademark Dental Ceramics Inc. [19082]
Tradex International Corp. [19083]
Transoceanic Trade, Inc. [22911]
Treasure Valley X-Ray Inc. [19084]
Tri-Blue Kennel [27251]
Tri-S Co. [24646]
Tri-State Hospital Supply Corp. [19085]
Tri-State Medical Supply Inc. [19086]
Tri-State Surgical Corp. [19087]
Trident Medical International [19663]
Troxler World Trade Corp. [19088]
Troy Biologicals Inc. [19665]
Tru-Care Health Systems Inc. [19089]
Ulster Scientific Inc. [19090]
Uni-Patch [19670]
Uniquity [19673]
Unistrut Fall Arrest Systems Inc. [24649]
United Biomedical Inc. [19091]
United Exporters [19674]
United Medical Supply Company Inc. [19675]
United Pharmaceutical & Medical Supply
  Co. [19092]
United Service Dental Chair [19093]
U.S.-China Industrial Exchange Inc. [19094]
U.S. Clinical Products [19679]
United States Medical Corp. [19095]
United States Medical Corp. [19680]
U.S. Medical Supply Co. [19096]
United States Pharmaceutical Corp. [19681]
Universal Marine Medical Supply Co. [19684]
Up-Rad Inc. [19097]
Vallen Corp. [24655]
Vallen Safety Supply Co. [19688]
Vallen Safety Supply Co. [17248]
Valley Forge Scientific Corp. [19098]
ValuNet Div. [19099]
Venice Convalescent Aids Medical Supply [19100]
Veterinary Medical Supply [27264]
Vetline Inc. [27265]
Vets International Inc. [27266]
VHA Supply Co. [19101]
Viking Traders, Inc. [19102]
Vitramon Inc. [9544]
Vivax Medical Corp. [19103]
VNA of Rhode Island Inc. [19104]
Vorpahl, Inc.; W.A. [24659]
VZ Ltd. [19692]
Wasserott's Medical Services Inc. [19696]
Watkins Pharmaceutical & Surgical Supply [19105]
Welding Equipment & Supply/All State Medical
  Gases [19106]
Wells & Associates; Kenyon [19107]
West Wholesale [27270]
Westbrook Pharmaceutical and Surgical Supply
  Co. [19698]
Western Stockmen's Inc. [19700]
Westmed Specialties Inc. [19108]
Wheelchair Pit-Stop [19701]
Williams Physicians and Surgeons
  Supplies [19706]
Wilmington Hospital Supply [19707]

Winchester Surgical Supply Co. [19712]
WINMED Products Co. [19109]
W.L.C. Ltd. [27271]
Wolverine X-Ray Sales and Service [19110]
Worldwide Medical [19111]
Wuite Traders International [17663]
X-Ray Industrial Distributor Corp. [24458]
Xetal Inc. [19714]
Xport Port Authority Trading Co. [4559]
Yellow River Systems [19113]
Zee Medical Service Co. [19114]
Zee Service Inc. [19718]
Zeiss Inc.; Carl [24461]
Zenter Enterprises Ltd. [27273]
Zimmer & Associates; Jackson [19115]

SIC 5048 — Ophthalmic Goods

3-D Optical Lab Inc. [19116]
Academy Optical Inc. [19121]
Accu Rx Optical [19122]
Alanco Eyewear [19131]
Allentown Optical Corp. [19136]
Allred Optical Laboratory [19139]
American Health Supplies [19140]
Andover Corp. [19153]
Arkansas Optical Co. [19160]
Arndt Optical Supplies; Ray [19161]
Ashmore Optical Co. Inc. [19162]
Asia Pacific Trading Co. [19163]
Atlantic Trading Company Ltd. [22048]
Atlantis Eyewear, Inc. [19168]
B & G Optics [19173]
Barry Optical Co., Inc. [19175]
Bauer Optical Co. [19176]
Benedict Optical [19182]
Bernell Corp. [19185]
Blue Grass Optical Co. [19194]
BNA Optical Supply Inc. [19195]
Brothers' Optical Lab, Inc. [19202]
Canyon State Opthalmaic Lab, Inc. [19210]
Cardinal Optics, Inc. [19213]
Caribe Optical Lab/Lens [19215]
Carlton Optical Distributors [19217]
Cascade Optical Inc. [19220]
C.D.C. Optical Lab Inc. [19221]
Central Optical of Youngstown Inc. [19225]
Centrex Inc. [19226]
Chadwick Optical Inc. [19227]
Charmant Incorporated USA [18734]
City Optical Company Inc./Division of The Tavel
  Optical Group [19230]
Clancy, Jr.; Arthur V. [19232]
Classic Optical Inc. [19233]
Clear Optics Inc. [19234]
Coates Optical Lab Inc. [19237]
Cobb Optical Lab Inc. [19238]
ComoTec [19241]
Connecticut Optical [19244]
Contact Optical Center Inc. [19247]
Continental Sales Co. [19249]
Continental Sales Co. of America [19250]
Continental Trading Co. Inc. [19251]
Copeland Optical Inc. [19252]
County Optical Inc. [19254]
Coyote Vision USA [14075]
Crown Optical Co. Inc. [19258]
Crown Optical Ltd. [19259]
Cumberland Optical Company Inc. [19262]
Cunningham Sales Corp. [19263]
Custom Labs [19265]
Custom Labs [19266]
Custom Vision Optical [19267]
CVK Corp. [19268]
D & D Distributing [26457]
DBL Labs [19273]
Decot Hy-Wyd Sport Glasses, Inc. [19274]
Delta Enterprises Inc. [19275]
Deschutes Optical [19278]
De'Vons Optics Inc. [19279]
Diamond Optical Corp. [19280]
Dispensers Optical Service Corp. [19282]
Diversified Ophthalmics Inc. [19284]
Diversified Ophthalmics, Inc. [19285]

Duffens Optical [19293]
Duffens Optical [19294]
Dunlaw Optical Laboratories [19295]
Eagle Optical [19300]
Eastern Ophthalmic Supply & Repair [19301]
Eclyptic Inc. [19302]
Evans Optical [19309]
Express Optical Lab [19314]
Eye Care Inc. [19316]
Eye Kraft Optical Inc. [19317]
Eyeglass Shoppe [19318]
Fairwind Sunglasses Trading Company
    Inc. [19320]
FEA Industries, Inc. [19323]
Franz Optical Company Inc. [19331]
Future Optics Inc. [19333]
Global Optics Inc. [19340]
Gulf States Optical Labs Inc. [19344]
Hampton Vision Center [19348]
Hawaiian Sunglass Co. [19351]
Healthcare Services International [18832]
Heard Optical Co. [19356]
HI-Tech Optical Inc. [19358]
Holden, Inc.; John W.W. [19359]
Honolulu Optical [19361]
Horn EB Replacement Service [15534]
House of Plastic Inc. [19362]
I See Optical Co. [19364]
Ideal Optics Inc. [19365]
I.F. Optical Co. Inc. [19366]
Illmo Rx Service Inc. [19367]
Impulse Merchandisers Inc. [2772]
Index 53 Optical [19369]
Industrial Vision Corp. [19370]
Integrated Orbital Implants Inc. [19374]
International Eyewear Inc. [19376]
International Optical Supply Co. [19377]
Intraoptics Inc. [19379]
Irwin International Inc. [106]
J.A. Optronics [19383]
Janos Technology Inc. [18868]
Jerry's At Misquamicut Inc. [19385]
Joy Enterprises [13776]
Joy Enterprises [19387]
Joy Optical Co. [19388]
Kamaaina Vision Center Inc. [19392]
Kasperek Optical Inc. [19393]
Keen Jewelers [14141]
Kluyskens Company Inc.; Gerard [19398]
Krall Optometric Professional LLC [19400]
Langley Optical Company Inc. [19404]
Lawrence Eyewear [19405]
Lenco, Inc. [19409]
Lenco Inc. [19410]
Lens Co. [19411]
Lens Express Inc. [19412]
Lensland [19413]
Luzerne Optical Labs, Ltd. [19420]
Magnivision [18897]
Marine Optical Inc. [19422]
Masbeirn Corp. [19424]
McGary Optical Co.; F.H. [19430]
McGee Eye Fashions Inc. [19431]
McLeod Optical Company Inc. [19438]
Medeiros Optical Service [19440]
MELIBRAD [19448]
Mesa Optical [19451]
MGM Optical Laboratory [19452]
Midark Optical [19455]
Middlefield Optical Company, Inc. [19456]
Midwest Labs [19458]
Midwest Labs, Inc. [19459]
Midwest Lens [19460]
Midwest Optical Laboratories, Inc. [19462]
Midwest Vision Distributors Inc. [18939]
Milam Optical Co. Inc.; J.S. [19463]
Moonlight Products Inc. [24403]
Multi Vision Optical [19470]
Multifocal Rx Lens Lab [19471]
N.A. Marketing Inc. [19474]
National Optical Co. Inc. [19478]
Nelson Hawaiian, Ltd. [19481]
Neostyle Eyewear Corp. [19482]
Neptune Polarized Sunglasses [19483]
Nethercott's Optical [19484]
Neville Optical Inc. [19488]

New City Optical Company Inc. [19489]
New City Optical Company Inc. [19490]
New Hampshire Optical Co. [19492]
The Newton Group, Inc. [19493]
The Newton Group, Inc. - Newton Lab [19494]
Nikon Inc. [22883]
North American Vision Services [19497]
North Atlantic Services Inc. [19498]
North Central Optical Co. [19500]
Obrig Hawaii Contact Lens Lab [19504]
Oliver Peoples Inc. [19506]
Omega Optical Co. [19507]
Ophthalmic Instrument Co. Inc. [19508]
Optech Inc. [19509]
Optek Inc. [19510]
Optical Advantage [6573]
Optical Associates [19511]
Optical Center Laboratory Inc. [19512]
Optical Laboratory of New Bedford [19513]
Optical Measurements Inc. [19514]
Optical One, Inc. [19515]
Optical Plastics [19516]
Optical Suppliers Inc. [19517]
Optical Supply [19518]
Optique Paris Miki [19519]
Paradise Optical Co. [18978]
Paradise Optical Co. [19523]
Pasch Optical Lab [19528]
Perferx Optical Co. Inc. [19531]
Physicians Optical Supply Inc. [19540]
Piedmont Optical Co. [19541]
Plastoptics Inc. [19543]
Plunkett Optical Inc. [19544]
Polo-Ray Sunglass, Inc. [19548]
Precision Optical Co. [19549]
Precision Optical Laboratory [19550]
Prescotts Inc. [18994]
Private Eyes Sunglasses Shop [19552]
Professional Ophthalmic Labs Inc. [19556]
Professional Optical [19557]
Professional Optical Supply [19558]
Rally Products, Inc. [19566]
Read Optical Inc. [19569]
Reed Optical Co. Inc.; Fred [19571]
Reverse & Company [5307]
Richmond Optical Co. [19581]
RLI Corp. [19582]
RLP Inc. [19023]
Robertson Optical Labs, Inc. [19583]
Rocky Mountain Instrument Co [19585]
Rota Systems Inc. [19588]
Rozin Optical Export Corp. [19589]
Safety Optical [19591]
Salem Optical Co. Inc. [19592]
Salt Lake Optical Inc. [19593]
Schmidt Laboratories [19596]
Schneider Optics Inc. [19597]
Schroeder Optical Company Inc. [19598]
Sealey Optical Co. [19601]
Selsi Company Inc. [24430]
Sermel Inc. [19604]
Sheridan Optical Co. [19607]
Sierra Optical [19608]
Sigma America [19610]
Silhouette Optical Ltd. [19612]
Silton USA Corp. [19613]
Singer Optical Co. Inc. [19614]
Siouxland Ophthalmics Lab Inc. [19615]
Socoloff Health Supply Inc. [19617]
Soderburg Optical Services [19618]
Sola International Inc. [19619]
Sound Optical [19621]
South Border Imports, Inc. [19622]
Southeastern Optical Corp. [19623]
Southern Micro Instruments [19624]
Southern Optical Co. [19625]
Southern Optical Co. [19626]
Southern Optical, Inc. [19627]
Spectrum Corp. [25827]
State Optical Company, Inc. [19637]
Style Eyes Inc. [19641]
Sun Design Ltd. [19643]
Swift Instruments, Inc. [19645]
Symd Inc. [19646]
Target Industries Inc. [19648]
Taylor Optical Supplies Inc. [19649]

TNT Optical Supply, Inc. [19657]
Tri-Lite Optical [19660]
Tri-State Optical Co. Inc. [19661]
Triconic Labs Inc. [19662]
Trioptics, Inc. [19664]
Tuscaloosa Optical Dispensary [19666]
Twin City Optical Inc. [19667]
Ultra Lens [19669]
United Optical Co. [19676]
United Optical Corp. [19677]
U.S. Safety Corp. [19682]
Universal Case Company Inc./Designer
    Optical [19683]
Universal/Univis Inc. [19686]
Uvex Safety [24653]
Valley Forge Scientific Corp. [19098]
Vision Plastics USA, Inc. [19690]
Vista Laboratories Inc. [19691]
Wallace Opticians Inc. [19693]
Walman Optical Co. [19694]
Walters Optical Inc.; Wendel [19695]
West Penn Optical [19697]
Western Carolina Optical Inc. [19699]
Williams Optical Laboratory Inc. [19705]
Wilson Optical Company Inc. [19708]
Winchester Optical [19709]
Winchester Optical [19710]
Winchester Optical Company Inc. [19711]
WOS Inc. [19713]
Zeiss Inc.; Carl [24461]

SIC 5049 — Professional Equipment Nec

Aardvark Controls Equipment [24304]
A.C. Supply [20767]
AccuPro Inc. [25543]
ACI Controls [24305]
Acme Vial and Glass Co. Inc. [24306]
Advanced Research Instruments Corp. [24307]
A/E Supplies [13295]
Alabama Art Supply [20779]
Alders Wholesale; Henry [20782]
Alexon Trend Inc. [24309]
Ally Industries Inc. [24504]
Alvin and Co. Inc. [25548]
Alvin and Company Inc. [24310]
Amcraft, Inc. [20788]
American Gulf Co. [6965]
Amics International Inc. [24311]
Anacomp Inc. [25552]
Anchorage Reprographics Center [20804]
Anderson Co.; SW [8353]
Anderson Machinery Co. [24312]
Apria Healthcare [19157]
Aristo Import Company Inc. [24316]
Art Essentials [20813]
Artist Brush & Color Dist. [20814]
Arun Technology Inc. [24317]
Asuka Corp. [19166]
Atec, Inc. [24318]
Audria's Crafts [20821]
AWC, Inc. [24319]
Barry's Office Service Inc. [20832]
Basic Service Corp. [24321]
Baxter Scientific Products [24322]
Beckly Cardy Group [25570]
Black Hills Jewelers Supply [25574]
Blue White Industries Limited Inc. [24324]
Booth Co.; George E. [24325]
Boutique Trim [20851]
Branom Instrument Company Inc. [24326]
Branom Instrument Company Inc. [24327]
Briggs-Weaver Inc. [15845]
Brinkmann Instruments, Inc. [24328]
Broadcasters General Store Inc. [5536]
Brown Arts & Crafts; Stan [20860]
Buckeye Sales Inc. [14831]
Burnett Engraving Co. Inc. [15859]
Burton-Rogers Co. Inc. [24331]
Cabin-Craft Southwest [20872]
Calcom Graphic Supply, Inc. [25591]

California Surveying and Drafting Supply
  Inc. [24333]
Cameca Instruments Inc. [24334]
Cantel Medical Corp. [18725]
Capital Scale [24335]
Capri Arts & Crafts [20878]
Catalina Cottage [25597]
Central Scientific Co. [4346]
Centro, Inc. [24336]
Centro, Inc. [24337]
Chiral Technologies Inc. [24338]
Chronomix Corp. [24339]
Cole-Parmer Instrument Co. [24341]
Construction Specialties Inc. [7209]
Continental Craft Distributors [20911]
Corr Tech Inc. [22949]
Craft & Hobby Supplies [20934]
Craft King [20935]
Craft Wholesalers [20936]
Creative Craft Distributors [20939]
Cushing and Company Inc. [25617]
D & M Distributors Inc. [25620]
Daigger and Co. Inc.; A. [24344]
Dealer's Discount Crafts [20952]
Decorator & Craft Corp. [20953]
Diane Ribbon Wholesale [20960]
Displaytech Inc. [24346]
Dixie Craft & Floral Wholesale [20971]
Dosik International [3700]
Douglass Co.; J.R. [24347]
Dowler Enterprises Inc. [25635]
Dresco Reproduction Inc. [25636]
Dresco Reproduction Inc. [24348]
Duke Scientific Corp. [24349]
DW Enterprises [24350]
Dynamic Reprographics Inc. [24351]
Edmund Scientific Co., Industrial Optics
  Div. [24352]
Elan Technical Corp. [24353]
Engineered Systems & Designs, Inc. [24354]
Environetics [24355]
Epic Inc. [24356]
Evergreen Scientific Inc. [24357]
Export Consultant Service [24358]
Expressive Art & Craft [20997]
F-D-C Corp. [20998]
Fiber Optic Center Inc. [5612]
Fisher Healthcare [24359]
Fisher Scientific Co. [24360]
Fisher Scientific Co. [19325]
Fisher Scientific International Inc. [24552]
Flinn Scientific, Inc. [24361]
Flower Factory [21005]
Frey Scientific [24363]
Geotronics of North America Inc. [24364]
Gesswein and Co.; Paul H. [16061]
Gilman Industrial Exports, Inc. [24365]
Glen Mills Inc. [24366]
Graham Blue Print Co. [25665]
Graphic Media [25668]
Graphic Resources Corp. [6308]
Graphline, Inc. [25670]
Green Mountain Foam Products [25671]
HAAKE [24367]
Hach Co. [25672]
HAZCO Services Inc. [24368]
HB Instruments Inc. [24369]
Heights Pump & Supply [24370]
Hockman Lewis Ltd. [16106]
Hydro-Abrasive Machining Inc. [16131]
Import Export Management Service Inc. [21054]
Indusco, Ltd. [8875]
Instrument Sales-East [24373]
Intermetra Corp. [8891]
Intermountain Scientific Corp. [24374]
Intoximeters Inc. [24376]
J & H Berge, Inc. [24377]
J & J Distributors [24576]
Jones Co.; Shelby [24380]
K & R Instruments Inc. [24381]
K & S Tole & Craft Supply [21083]
Kaneka Far West, Inc. [21085]
Ken's Craft Supply [21087]
KG Engineering Inc. [25699]
Kitrick Management Company, Ltd. [24383]
Lad Enterprises, Ltd. [21095]

Lamination Services Inc. [16227]
Lannans Paint & Decorating Ctr. [21486]
Larsen International, Inc. [4438]
Laser Resale Inc. [24386]
Lawsons Locksmithing [25710]
Leathertone Inc. [22993]
Lesman Instrument Co. [24388]
Lewiston Rubber & Supply Inc. [25715]
Lewiston Rubber and Supply Inc. [24389]
Luther's Creative Craft Studios [21116]
MacAlaster Bicknell Company Inc. [24391]
Macalaster Bicknell Company of NJ, Inc. [24392]
Mager Scientific Inc. [24393]
Marshall and Bruce Co. [25725]
Mathias Reprographics [25726]
McCauley's Reprographics, Inc. [24396]
MDR Corp. [21136]
Meadows Company Inc.; Ben [1007]
Meredith Stained Glass Center, Inc. [25735]
Midland Grocery Co. [11885]
Mikan Theatricals [25739]
Milart Ceramics Inc. [25740]
Miller Mechanical Specialties [24397]
Missco Corporation of Jackson [13183]
Mississippi Tool Supply Co. [24595]
Mississippi Tool Supply Co. [24398]
Mitutoyo/MTI Corp. [24400]
Mosier Fluid Power of Indiana Inc. [24404]
MTI Corp. [24405]
Multimedia Pacific Inc. [5686]
Myron L Co. [24406]
N Squared Inc. [24407]
N.A. Marketing Inc. [19473]
Naturo Co. [25751]
Newcomb Company Inc. Newcomb
  Associates [24408]
Norcostco Inc. [25761]
Northway Acres Craft Supply [21165]
OCE-Bruning Inc. [25771]
OCE-USA Inc. [25772]
OCE-USA Inc. [21169]
Olympus America Inc. [22887]
Operations Technology Inc. [9158]
Pacific Combustion Engineering Inc. [24413]
Pacific Exports [24414]
Pagel Safety Inc. [24611]
Particle Measuring Systems Inc. [24415]
Pat's Ceramics Tile Design Center [26606]
Perfect Measuring Tape Co. [24416]
Perstorp Analytical Inc. [24417]
Petersen-Arne [21211]
Philips Electronic Instruments Co. [24418]
Piher International Corporation [9202]
PMH Associates [16404]
PMH Associates [16404]
PMH Associates [16404]
Pottery Art Studio Inc. [25788]
Preiser Scientific [24419]
Priz Co. [24420]
Process Supplies & Accessories, Inc. [17117]
Protein Databases Inc. [24421]
Quality Art [21227]
R & H Wholesale Supply, Inc. [24616]
ReCellular Inc. [5737]
R.E.I. Glitter [21236]
Repro Technology Inc. [25802]
Republic Group [9279]
Revco Products, Inc. [3151]
Rheas Crafts [21238]
Robinson's Woods [21245]
Rocky Mountain Lasers and Instruments
  Inc. [24423]
Royce, Inc. [21250]
Santa Barbara Instrument Group Corp. [22901]
Sargent-Welch Scientific Co. [24425]
Schenck Trebel Corp. [24427]
Schleicher and Schuell Inc. [24428]
School Specialty Inc. [21259]
Scientific Equipment Co. [24429]
Seacoast Gallery [25811]
Selsi Company Inc. [24430]
Siemens Audio Inc. [25443]
Singing Poppe's, Inc. [21270]
Smith Co.; A and B [24433]
Smith Inc.; Kenneth [23948]
Sony Precision Technology [24434]
Sony Precision Technology America, Inc. [25449]
Speaker Company, Inc.; Guy [24435]

Spectronic Instruments Inc. [24436]
ST Laminating Corp. [25829]
Sticht Company Inc.; Herman H. [24439]
Stromberg; J. Edward [21301]
Sun International [24440]
S.W. Controls, Inc. [24441]
Swanson, Inc. [21308]
Techmark Corporation [24442]
The Test Connection Inc. [24444]
Test Equipment Distributors [24445]
Thomas Scientific [24446]
Timberline Instruments Inc. [24447]
Tower Equipment Company Inc. [16570]
Troxler World Trade Corp. [19088]
Tryon Trading, Inc. [17237]
United Pacific Corp. [24449]
United Scale and Engr. Corp. [24450]
U.S.-China Industrial Exchange Inc. [19094]
Van Dyke Supply Co. [25862]
Vector Engineering Inc. [24451]
Vermont Optechs [24452]
Videomedia Inc. [25506]
Viking Woodcrafts, Inc. [21599]
VWR Scientific Products [24453]
VWR Scientific Products Corp. [24454]
VWR Scientific Products Corp. [26242]
Wang's International, Inc. [21345]
Wang's International, Inc. [21346]
Westberg Manufacturing Inc. [24456]
Western Graphtec Inc. [6866]
Wilbert Vault of Aroostook [25880]
Wilkens-Anderson Co. [24457]
Zeiss Inc.; Carl [24461]
Zeuschel Equipment Co. [24462]
Zeuschel Equipment Co. [24463]
Zeuschel Equipment Co. [24464]

SIC 5050 — Metals & Minerals Except Petroleum

Merfish Supply Co.; N. [23259]

SIC 5051 — Metals Service Centers & Offices

A-1 Metal Services Corp. [19719]
AA & A Enterprises Inc. [19721]
AAA Manufacturing Inc. [20575]
Aaron Scrap Metals, Div. of Commercial Metals
  Co. [19722]
Abbey Metal Corp. [26725]
ABC Metals Inc. [19723]
ABM International Corp. [19724]
Actron Steel [19725]
ACuPowder International, LLC [19726]
Ada Iron and Metal Co. [19727]
Addington Environmental Inc. [26729]
Admiral Metals [19728]
Admiral Metals Inc. [19729]
Admiral Steel [19730]
Advance Steel Co. [19731]
Aerodyne Ulbrich Alloys [19732]
Aerospace Tube & Pipe [19733]
AFCO Metals Inc. [19734]
Affiliated Metals [19735]
Affiliated Metals Co. [19736]
Air Engineering Co. Inc. [19737]
Airport Metals [19738]
Aladdin Steel Inc. [19739]
Alamo Iron Works [19740]
Alaskan Copper & Brass Co. [19741]
Alcan Aluminum Corp. Metal Goods Service Center
  Div. [19742]
Alco Iron and Metal Co. [19743]
All American Recycling Div. [19744]
All Foils Inc. [19745]
Allegheny Rodney Strip Svc Ctr [19746]
Allen and Son Inc.; Sam [19747]
Allen Steel Co. [19748]
Alliance Metals Inc. [19749]

Alliance Steel Corp. [19750]
Allied-Crawford Steel [19751]
Allied Metals Corp. [26738]
Allied Metals Inc. [19752]
Allied Supply Inc. [23057]
Alloy Tool Steel Inc. [19753]
Alma Iron and Metal Company Inc. [26743]
Almetals Co. [19754]
Alpert and Alpert Iron and Metal Inc. [26744]
Alpha Steel Corp. [19755]
Alps Wire Rope Corp. [19756]
Alps Wire Rope Corp. [19757]
Alro Metals Service Center [19758]
Alro Steel Corp. [19759]
Alro Steel Corp. [19760]
Alro Steel Corp. [19761]
Alta Industries Ltd. [19762]
Alumax Building Products [19763]
Aluminum Distributors Inc. [19764]
Aluminum and Stainless Inc. [19765]
Amalco Metals Inc. [19766]
Amarillo Building Products Inc. [6953]
AMB Tools & Equipment [13556]
Ambassador Steel Company Inc. [19767]
American Alloy Steel Inc. [19768]
American Foundry and Manufacturing Co. [23063]
American Industries Inc. [19769]
American Metals Corp. [19770]
American Steel Builders International, Corp. &
    Copper Valley Concrete [19771]
American Steel L.L.C. [19772]
American Tank and Fabricating Co [19773]
AMI Metals Inc. [19774]
AMS International Corp. [19775]
Amsco Steel Company Inc. [19776]
Amsco Steel Products Co. [19777]
Amstek Metal [19778]
Amtex Steel Inc. [19779]
Anaheim Extrusion Co. Inc. [19780]
The Anderson Group [19781]
Ansam Metals Corp. [19782]
Arrow Thompson Metals Inc. [19783]
Art Iron Inc. [19784]
Asheville Steel & Salvage Co. [19785]
Asoma Corp. [19786]
Associated Steel Corp. [19787]
AST USA Inc. [19788]
Atlantic Track and Turnout Co. [23472]
Atlas Steel Products Co. [19791]
Austin, D L Steel Supply Corp. [19792]
Austin Metal and Iron Company Inc. [19793]
Auto-Blankers [19794]
Avesta Sheffield—North American Division,
    Inc. [19795]
Azco Steel Co. [19796]
Azcon Corp. [7006]
B and B Surplus Inc. [19797]
Baird Steel Inc. [19798]
Balco Metals Inc. Recycling World [19799]
Baldwin Steel Co. [19800]
Bangor Steel [19802]
Banner Service Corp. [19803]
Barnett Brass and Copper Inc. [23077]
Baron Drawn Steel Corp. [19804]
Basin Pipe & Metal [19805]
Baszile Metals Service Inc. [19806]
Bellesteel Industries Inc. [19807]
Belmont Steel Corp. [19808]
Benco Steel Inc. [19809]
Benedict-Miller Inc. [19810]
Benjamin Metals Co. [19811]
Benjamin Steel Company Inc. [19812]
Berg Steel Corp. [19813]
Berkshire Valley [19814]
Berlin Enterprises Inc. [19815]
Berlin Metals Inc. [19816]
Berwick Steel Co [19817]
Berwick Steel Co. [19818]
Besco Steel Supply, Inc. [19819]
Bethlehem Steel Export Corp. [19820]
BHP Trading Inc. [19822]
BICO Akron Inc. [19823]
Bissett Steel Co [19824]
Bloch Steel Industries [19825]
Block Steel Corp. [19826]
Blue Chip Stamps [25577]

Blue Mountain Steel [19827]
BMG Metals Inc. [19828]
Bobco Metal Co. [19829]
Boman and Kemp Steel and Supply Inc. [19830]
Borg Compressed Steel Corp. [19831]
Boston Pipe and Fittings Company Inc. [23093]
Brainum Junior Inc.; Harry [19832]
Bralco Metals Div. [19833]
Brauner Export Co. [8466]
Breen International [19834]
Bridgeport Steel Co. [19835]
Brina Steel Products Inc. [19836]
Brown-Campbell Co [19838]
Brown Metals Co. [19839]
Brown Steel Div. [19840]
BSTC Group Inc. [7091]
Buffalo Structural Steel [19841]
Bundy Enterprises Inc. [19842]
Burger Iron Co. [19843]
Burgon Tool Steel Company Inc. [19844]
Busby Metals Inc. [19845]
Cactus Pipe and Supply Co. [22104]
Cain Steel and Supply Co. [19846]
California Steel Services Inc. [19847]
Camalloy Inc. [19848]
Cambridge Street Metal Company Inc. [19849]
Camden Iron and Metal Co. [19850]
Cape & Island Steel Co. [19851]
Capital Design Inc. [22941]
Capitol Metals Company Inc. [19852]
Capitol Steel Inc. [19853]
Caravan Trading Corporation [4342]
Carbon and Alloy Metals Inc. [19854]
Cardel Sales Inc. [19855]
Cargill Steel & Wire [19856]
Carlyle Inc. [19857]
Carolina Door Controls [7143]
Carolina Steel Corp. [19858]
Carolina Steel Corp. [19859]
Carpenter Technology/Steel Div [19860]
Carson Masonry and Steel Supply [19861]
Castle and Co.; A.M. [19862]
Castle and Co. Hy-Alloy Steels Div.; A.M. [19863]
Castle Metals Inc. [19864]
Cavexsa USA Inc. [19865]
Caye and Company Inc.; W.C. [7154]
CCC Steel Inc. [19866]
Central Distributors Inc. [9783]
Central Steel Supply Company Inc. [19867]
Central Steel and Wire Co [19868]
Centrotrade Minerals and Metals Inc. [19869]
Century Steel Corp. [19870]
Chapin and Bangs Co. Inc. [19871]
Chapman-Dyer Steel Manufacturing [19872]
Chatham Steel Corp. [19874]
Chemung Supply Corp. [16795]
Chemung Supply Corp. [19875]
Chicago Tube and Iron Co. [19876]
Choice Metals [19877]
Christy Metals Company Inc. [19878]
Cincinnati Steel Products [19879]
Clark's Store Fixtures Inc. [4599]
CMA International [15894]
Cofil Inc. [7191]
Coil Plus Pennsylvania Inc. [19881]
Columbia Iron and Metal Co. [19882]
Columbia Ventures Corp. [19884]
Columbus Metals Supply Inc. [19885]
Columbus Pipe and Equipment Co. [23120]
Combined Metals of Chicago L.P. [19886]
Cometals Inc. [4361]
Commercial Alloys Corp. [19887]
Commercial Metals Co. [19888]
Commodity Steel and Processing Inc. [19889]
Commonwealth Metal Corp. [19890]
Complex Steel Wire Corp. [19891]
Confederate Steel Corp. [19892]
Conklin and Company Inc.; Lyon [14400]
Connell L.P. Luria Brothers Div. [26783]
Consumers Steel Products Co. [19893]
Contractors Steel Co. [19894]
Cooling & Heating Inc. [14404]
Copper and Brass Sales [19895]
Copper and Brass Sales Inc. [19896]
Copper and Brass Sales Inc. [19897]
Copper and Brass Sales Inc. [19898]

Corey Steel Co. [19899]
Corporacion del Cobre U.S.A. Inc. [19900]
Coulter Steel and Forge Co. [19901]
Coutinho Caro and Company Inc. [19902]
Cragin Metals L.L.C. [19903]
Crest Steel Corp. [19904]
The Crispin Co. [19905]
Crown Steel Sales Inc. [19906]
Crucible Service Center [13649]
Crucible Service Center [19907]
Crucible Service Centers [19908]
Crystal Lite Manufacturing Co [19909]
Curtze Steel Inc. [19910]
Cutter Precision Metals Inc. [19911]
Cutter Precision Metals Inc. [19912]
D and B Steel Co. [19913]
Daewoo International (America) [26011]
Dailey Metal Group Inc. [19914]
Dakota Steel and Supply Co. [19915]
Darco Enterprises Inc. [19916]
Dave Steel Co. Inc. [19917]
Davidson Pipe Supply Company Inc. [23133]
Davis Salvage Co. [19918]
Dean's Materials Inc. [7257]
Decker Steel & Supply Co. [19920]
Decker Steel and Supply Inc. [19921]
Del Paso Pipe and Steel Inc. [19922]
Delta Engineering and Manufacturing Co. [19923]
Delta Steel Inc. [19924]
Denman and Davis [19926]
Dennen Steel Corp. [19927]
Dexter Sales Inc. [19928]
Dick Company Inc.; T.W. [19929]
Dick's Superior Metal Sales [19930]
Diehl Steel Co [19931]
Dillon Supply Co. [15951]
Dimco Steel, Inc. [19932]
Diversified Metals Inc. [19933]
Dixie Pipe Sales Inc. [19934]
Doral Steel Inc. [19935]
Dublin Metal Corp. [19937]
DuBose Steel Incorporated of North
    Carolina [19938]
Duferco Trading Corp. [19939]
Duhig and Co. [23139]
Duhig and Co. [19940]
Duluth Plumbing Supply Co. [23140]
Dura Metals Inc. [19941]
Durrett-Sheppard Steel Co. [19942]
E and E Steel Company Inc. [19943]
E & L Steel Co. Inc. [19944]
E. M J Co [19945]
Eastern Europe, Inc. [536]
Eastern Wire Products [19946]
Easton Steel Service Inc. [19947]
Eaton Steel Corp. [19948]
Edgcomb Corp. [19949]
Edgcomb Metals Co. New England Div. [19950]
Egger Steel Co. [19951]
Ellwood Quality Steels Co. [19952]
Enco Materials Inc. [19953]
Energy and Process Corp. [19954]
Engineered Equipment Co. [7313]
Engineering Equipment Co. [15992]
Equality Trading [15995]
Erb Hardware Co. Ltd. [13688]
Erie Concrete Steel [19956]
Erie Concrete and Steel Supply Co. [19957]
Erie Steel Products Inc. [19958]
Everett Anchor and Chain [19959]
Export USA [17411]
Extrusions Inc. [19960]
F and S Alloys and Minerals Corp. [19961]
Fabwel Inc. [19962]
Factory Steel and Metal Supply Co., LLC [19963]
Fagan Inc.; Ed [19964]
Familian Northwest Inc. [23158]
Farwest Steel Corp. [19965]
Fay Industries [19966]
Fedco Steel Corp. [19967]
Federal Pipe and Supply Co. [7332]
Fedor Steel Co. [19968]
Feralloy Corp. [19969]
Feralloy Corp. Birmingham Div. [19970]
Feralloy Corp. Midwest Div. [19971]
Feralloy Corp./Western Div [19972]

Feralloy Processing Co [19973]
Ferer and Sons Co.; Aaron [19974]
Ferguson Metals, Inc. [19975]
Ferguson Steel Co. [19976]
Ferranti Steel and Aluminum Inc. [19977]
Ferro Union Inc. [19978]
Fischer Lime and Cement Co. [7346]
Fisher Brothers Steel Corp. [19979]
Florida Extruders International Inc. [19980]
Foltz Manufacturing and Supply Co. [13714]
Ford Steel Co [19981]
Four Corners Welding & Gas [19982]
Francosteel Corp. [19983]
Fraser Steel Co. [19985]
Frederick Steel Co. [19986]
Freeport Steel Co. [19987]
Frejoth International Corp. [19988]
Friedman Industries Inc. [19989]
Friedman Steel Company Inc. [19990]
Fullerton Metals Co. [19991]
Gallagher Co.; R.J. [19992]
Gallagher Steel Co. [19993]
Gallup Welding Co. [19994]
General Metals of Tacoma Inc. [26824]
General Pipe and Supply Company Inc. [23187]
General Steel Corp. [19996]
General Steel Fabricators [19997]
General Steel Warehouse Inc. [19998]
Gensco, Inc. [14467]
Gensco, Inc. [19999]
Genzink Steel [20000]
Genzink Steel [20001]
Georgetown Unimetal Sales [20002]
Gerber and Company Inc.; J. [20003]
Gerber Metal Supply Co. [26826]
Gerrard Steel of Illinois [20004]
Gibbs Wire and Steel Co. [20005]
Gibraltar Steel Corp. [20006]
Gibraltar Steel Products [20007]
Gilbert Pipe and Supply Co.; A.A. [23191]
Global Steel Trading Inc. [20008]
Globe Iron Construction Company Inc. [20009]
Glosser and Sons Inc.; M. [20010]
GMA Industries Inc. [20011]
Goldin Industries Inc. [20012]
Goldsmith Chemical and Metal Corp.; D.F. [20013]
Goode's Welding Inc. [20014]
Grand Haven Steel Products [20015]
Grayline Housewares [20017]
Great Central Steel Co. [20018]
Great Lakes Forge, Inc. [20019]
Great Plains Stainless Inc. [20020]
Great Western Steel Co. [20021]
Green Bay Supply Company Inc. [20022]
Griswold and Company Inc.; S.T. [7419]
Gulf Reduction Div. [20543]
H and D Steel Service Inc. [20024]
Habot Steel Company Inc. [20025]
Hadro Aluminum & Metal Corp. [20026]
Hagerty Brothers Co. [16919]
Hardie Export; James [7442]
Harrell Co.; Hollis [13742]
Harris Welco [20028]
Harrison Piping Supply Co. [23205]
Harvey Titanium Ltd. [20029]
Hascall Steel Company Inc. [20030]
Hebard and Associates Inc.; R.W. [20031]
Heidtman Steel Products Inc. [20032]
Henderson Steel Corp. [20033]
Hi-Way Products Inc. [20035]
Hickman, Williams and Co., Black Products Div. [20037]
Highway Metal Services Inc. [20038]
Hill and Griffith Co. [20545]
Hill Steel & Builders Supplies [20039]
Hinely Aluminum Inc. [20040]
Hinkle Metals and Supply Company Inc. [20041]
Holland Corp.; J. Henry [20042]
Holston Steel Services [20043]
Hoogovens Aluminium Corp. [20044]
Horsehead Resource Development Company Inc. [20547]
Howard Corp.; H.H. [20045]
Huntco Steel Inc. [20047]
Huntington Steel and Supply Company Inc. [20048]

Huron Steel Company Inc. [20049]
Hurwitz Brothers Iron and Metal Company Inc. [20051]
Hynes Industries Inc. [20052]
IEI Investments Inc. [16938]
IGC Energy Inc. [16939]
Ilva USA Inc. [20053]
Independent Steel Co. [20054]
Indiana Supply Corp. [16943]
Industrial Development & Procurement [16150]
Industrial Material Corp. [20055]
Industrial Metals of the South Inc. [20057]
Industrial Steel and Machine Sales [20058]
Industrial Steel Service Center [20059]
Industrial Steel Warehouse Inc. [20060]
Industrial Steel and Wire Co. [16949]
Industrial Tube & Steel [20061]
Industrial Tube and Steel Corp. [20062]
Infra Metals [20063]
Infra Metals [20064]
Inland Steel Industries Inc. [20065]
Integrity Steel Co [20066]
International Purchasers, Inc. [7521]
Interstate Steel Co. [20067]
Interstate Steel Supply Co [20068]
Interstate Steel Supply Co. [20069]
Investrade Import & Export [16170]
Iron Mike's Welding & Fab [20070]
J & F Steel Corporation [20071]
J and J Steel and Supply Co. [20072]
J & K Distributors [25920]
Jabo Supply Corp. [23223]
Jacklin Steel Supply Co. [20073]
Jarvis Steel and Lumber Company Inc. [7531]
Jeffrey's Steel Company Inc. [20075]
Jemison Investment Company Inc. [7533]
Jim's Supply Company Inc. [20076]
Jonner Steel Industries [20077]
Jordan Brookes Company Inc.; E. [20078]
Jorgensen Co.; Earle M. [20079]
Jorgensen Steel Co. [20080]
Joseph Co. Municipal Recycling Div.; David J. [26860]
K and M Metals Inc. [20082]
Kalamazoo International, Inc. [16196]
Kalamazoo Mill Supply Co. [20083]
Kalamazoo Steel Processing Inc. [20084]
Kane Steel Co. [20086]
Kanematsu U.S.A. Inc. [26086]
Kasle Steel Corp. [20087]
Kataman Metals Inc. [20088]
Katch and Company Inc.; M. [20089]
Kaw River Shredding Inc. [20090]
Kearney's Metals Inc. [20091]
Keelor Steel Inc. [20092]
Keibler-Thompson Corp. [20093]
Kelly Pipe Co. [16982]
Kemeny Overseas Products Corporation [20094]
Kemp Hardware and Supply Co. [13783]
Ken-Mac Metals Inc. [20095]
Kenilworth Steel Co [20096]
Kentucky Mine Supply Co. [16989]
Kenwal Steel Corp. [20097]
Keystone Iron and Metal Company Inc. [20098]
Keystone Steel Sales Inc. [20099]
Keystone Tube Co. [20100]
Keywest Wire Div. [7554]
KG Specialty Steel Inc. [20101]
Kgs Steel, Inc. [20102]
Kivort Steel Inc. [20103]
Klein Steel Service Inc. [20104]
Klockner Namasco Corp. [20105]
Kojemi Corp. [20106]
Koons Steel Inc. [20107]
Kozel and Son Inc.; J. [20108]
Kreher Steel Co. [20109]
Kreher Steel Company Inc. [20110]
Kurtz Steel; James H. [20111]
L and M Shape Burning Inc. [20112]
La Barge Pipe and Steel [20113]
Lafarge Concrete [7575]
Lafayette Steel Co. [20114]
Lake Steel Inc. [20115]
Lapham-Hickey Steel Corp. [20116]
Lapham-Hickey Steel Corp. [20117]
Lapham-Hickey Steel Corp. [20118]

Lapham-Hickey Steel Corp. Clifford Metal Div. [20119]
LB Steel Plate Co. [26878]
Lebanon Building Supply Co. [7590]
Leeco Steel Products Inc. [20120]
Leico Industries Inc. [20121]
Leonard Inc.; Charles [20123]
Levand Steel and Supply Corp. [20124]
Levine & Co.; L [20125]
Levinson Steel Co. [20126]
Lewisohn Sales Company Inc. [7600]
Lexington Steel Corp. [20127]
Liberto Inc.; R.J. [26882]
Liebovich Brothers Inc. [20128]
Lincoln Machine [20129]
Lincoln Office Supply Company Inc. [25928]
Lindquist Steels Inc. [20130]
Line Power Manufacturing Co. [20131]
Liston Brick Company of Corona Inc. [20132]
Lockhart Co. [20133]
Lofland Co. [7609]
Lorbec Metals USA Ltd. [20134]
Loroman Co. [9003]
Louis Steel Co.; Arthur [20135]
Lovejoy Industries, Inc. [20136]
Lovejoy Industries Inc. [20137]
Loveman Steel Corp. [20138]
Lusk Metals and Plastics [20139]
Maas-Hansen Steel Corp. [20140]
Macsteel Service Centers USA - Edgcomb Metals Div. [20141]
Macuch Steel Products Inc. [20142]
Magnum Diversified Industries Inc. [20143]
Maiale Metal Products [20145]
Majestic Steel Service Inc. [20146]
Malco Products Inc. [13809]
Manhattan Brass and Copper Company Inc. [20147]
Mannesmann Pipe and Steel Corp. [20148]
Manufacturers Steel Supply Company Inc. [20149]
Manutec Inc. [20150]
Mapes and Sprowl Steel Ltd. [20151]
Maraj International [6461]
Markle Steel Co. [20152]
Markovits and Fox [20153]
Marlen Trading Company Inc. [20154]
Marmon/Keystone Corp. [20155]
Marubeni America Corp. [26136]
Mascotech Forming Technologies [20156]
Matex Products, Inc. [20157]
Maurice Pincoffs Company Inc. [20158]
Mausner Equipment Company Inc. [16275]
Maxco Inc. [20159]
May Steel Corp. [20160]
McCarthy Steel Inc. [20161]
McMaster-Carr Supply Co. California [13821]
McNichols Co. [20162]
Meier Metal Servicenters Inc. [20163]
Melton Steel Corp. [20164]
Merfish Supply Co.; N. [23259]
Meridian National Corp. [20165]
Merit USA [20166]
Merritt Machine Inc. [20167]
Metal Commodities Inc. [6488]
Metal Recovery Systems Inc. [26904]
Metal Service and Supply Inc. [20170]
The Metal Store [20171]
MetalCenter Inc. [20172]
Metallurg International Resources [20173]
Metalmart Inc. [20174]
Metals Engineering Co. [20175]
Metals USA Inc. [20176]
Metalwest [20177]
Metro Group Inc. [26907]
Metron Steel Corp. [20178]
Metropolis Metal Spinning and Stamping Inc. [13826]
Miami Valley Steel Service Inc. [20179]
Mickey's Mobile Metal Mending [20180]
Mid-East Materials Co. [20182]
Mid-State Industries LLC [20183]
Mid-West Materials Inc. [20184]
Mid-West Steel Supply Co. [20185]
Midland Aluminum Corp. [20186]
Midland Steel [20187]
Midland Steel Warehouse Co. [20188]

Midwest Coil Processing [20189]
Midwest Metals Inc. [20191]
Mill Steel Co. [20192]
Millard Metal Service Center [20193]
Miller Metal Service Corp. [20194]
Miller's Supply [23268]
Millitrade International Inc. [20195]
Mills Alloy Steel Co. [20196]
Misaba Steel Products Inc. [20198]
Mitsui and Company (U.S.A.) Inc. [20199]
Mitsui & Co. (USA), Inc. Seattle Branch [16312]
Momentum Metals Inc. [20200]
Monarch Brass and Copper Corp. [13835]
Monarch Steel Co. [20201]
Monarch Steel Company Inc. [20202]
Monico Alloys Inc. [20203]
Morin Steel [20204]
Morse Distribution Inc. [17053]
Morse Industries Inc. [20205]
Morton Supply Inc. [9098]
Morweco Steel Co. [20206]
Moses Lake Steel Supply Inc. [20207]
Mound Steel Corp. [20208]
MPL Industries, Inc. [20210]
Mulach Steel Corp. [20211]
Namasco [20212]
Namasco Corp. [20213]
Namasco Div. [20214]
NanoMaterials, Inc. [4465]
Napa Pipe Corp. [20215]
Napco Steel Inc. [20216]
Naporano Iron and Metal Co. [26921]
Nashville Steel Corp. [20217]
National Compressed Steel Corp. [20218]
National Manufacturing, Inc. [7766]
National Material L.P. [20219]
National Metal Processing Inc. [20220]
National Titanium Corp. [20221]
National Tube Supply Co [20222]
Neill-LaVielle Supply Co. [13843]
New Process Steel Corp. [20223]
New York Wire Co. [20224]
Newark Wire Cloth Co. [20225]
Nissen and Company Inc. [7781]
Nissho Iwai American Corp. [20226]
Nitek Metal Service Inc. [20227]
Noffsinger Manufacturing Co [20228]
Noftz Sheet Metal [20229]
Norfolk Iron and Metal Co. [20231]
North American Wire Products [20232]
North Shore Supply Company Inc. [20233]
North Star Recycling Co. [20234]
North State Metals Inc. [20235]
North States Steel Corp. [20236]
Northern Industries Inc. [20237]
Northern Ohio Lumber and Timber Co. [7797]
Northern Steel Corp. [20238]
Northstar Steel and Aluminum Inc. [20239]
Norton Metal Products Inc. [20240]
Nott Co.; Frank H. [26927]
Nova Steel Processing Inc. [20241]
O'Brien Steel Service [20242]
Ocotillo Lumber Sales Inc. [7803]
Ohio Alloy Steels Inc. [20243]
Oilfield Pipe and Supply Inc. [20244]
Okaya U.S.A. Inc. [20245]
Olympic Steel Inc. [20246]
Olympic Steel Inc. Chicago Div. [20247]
Olympic Steel Inc. Eastern Steel and Metal Div. [20248]
Olympic Steel Inc. Juster Steel Div. [20249]
O'Neal Metals Co. [20250]
O'Neal Steel Inc. [20251]
O'Neal Steel Inc. Evansville [20252]
O'Neal Steel Inc. (Waterloo, Iowa) [20253]
Orange Distributors Inc. [21855]
Orion Group (USA), Ltd. [20254]
Orleans Materials and Equipment Company Inc. [20255]
Ottawa River Steel Co. [20256]
Otter Recycling [20257]
Outokumpu Metals (USA) Inc. [20258]
Pacesetter Steel Service Inc. [20259]
Pacific Hide and Fur Depot Inc. [20260]
Pacific Industrial Supply Company Inc. [17097]
Pacific Machinery and Tool Steel Co. [20261]

Pacific Metal Co. [20262]
Pacific Steel and Recycling [20263]
Pacific Steel and Supply Corp. [7827]
Pako Steel Inc. [20264]
Parker Steel Co. [20265]
Pasminco Inc. [20266]
Passaic Metal & Building Supplies Co. [7838]
PDM Steel Service Centers Div. [20267]
Pechiney Corp. [20268]
Pechiney World Trade (USA) Inc. [20269]
Peck Recycling Co. [26937]
Penn Stainless Products Inc. [20270]
Pennsylvania Steel Co. [20271]
Perlow Steel Corp. [20272]
Petersen Aluminum Corp. [20273]
Petroleum Pipe and Supply Inc. [20274]
Pickands Mather, Ltd. [20276]
Pierce Aluminum Company Inc. [20278]
Pimalco Inc. [20279]
Pioneer Aluminum Inc. [20280]
Pioneer Steel Corp. [20281]
Pioneer Steel and Tube Distributors [20282]
Pipe Distributors Inc. [20283]
Pipe Valve and Fitting Co. [17106]
Pitt-Des Moines Inc. [20284]
Plant and Flanged Equipment [23317]
Plant and Flanged Equipment [20285]
PMX Industries Inc. [20286]
Pohang Steel America Corp. [20287]
Pollard Company Inc.; Joseph G. [20288]
Port Everglades Steel Corp. [20289]
Potomac Steel and Supply Inc. [20290]
Powmet Inc. [26945]
Precision Aluminum and Sawing Service Inc. [20291]
Precision Metals Inc. [20292]
Precision Steel Warehouse Inc. [20293]
Primary Industries (USA) Inc. [20294]
Primary Steel Inc. [20295]
Pro-Chem Corp. [20296]
ProCoil Corp. [20297]
Production Carbide and Steel [20298]
Production Supply Co. [20299]
Production Supply Co. [20300]
Prosteel Service Centers Inc. [20301]
PTC International [19000]
Puget Sound Pipe and Supply Inc. [20302]
Pusan Pipe America Inc. [20303]
Queensboro Steel Corp. [20304]
Quikservice Steel Co. [20305]
R and S Steel Co. [20306]
Radnor Alloys Inc. [20307]
Rafferty-Brown Steel Co. [20308]
Ready Made Sign Co. [25798]
Rebco West/Vistawall [20309]
Red Bud Industries Inc. [20310]
Regal Steel Supply Inc. [20311]
Reisner Corp.; William [26955]
Reliable Architectural Metals Co. [7911]
Reliance Sheet and Strip Co. [20312]
Reliance Steel and Aluminum Co. [20313]
Reliance Steel Co. [20314]
Renco Corp. [20315]
Reserve Iron and Metal L.P. [20316]
Reynolds Aluminum Supply [20317]
Reynolds Aluminum Supply Co. [20318]
Rhoda Brothers-Steel & Welding [20319]
Rich Metals Co. [26958]
Richards and Conover Steel Co. [20320]
Richardson Trident Co [20321]
Rickard Metals Inc. [20322]
River City Steel and Recycling Inc. [26960]
RKR Corp. [17139]
Robert-James Sales Inc. [20323]
Roberts Industries Inc.; J.H. [20324]
Robinson Steel Company Inc. [20325]
Roll and Hold Warehousing and Distribution [20326]
Rolled Steel Co. [20327]
Rolled Steel Products Corp. [20328]
Ron's Steel Sales [20329]
Rose Metal Products Inc. [20331]
Rotometals Inc. [18596]
Royal Metals Company Inc. [20332]
Roy's Welding & Wrought Iron [20333]
Rubenstein Supply Co. [23354]

Rubin and Co.; J. [20334]
Rubin, Jack and Sons Inc. [20335]
Rubin Steel Co. [20336]
RuMar Manufacturing Corp. [20337]
Rush Company Inc.; J D [20338]
Russel Metals-Bahcall Group [20339]
Ryan Equipment Co., Inc. [20340]
Ryerson Coil Processing Co. [20341]
Ryerson and Son Inc.; Joseph T. [20342]
Ryerson and Son Inc., Ryerson Plastics Div.; Joseph T. [23032]
Ryerson-Thypin - Div. of Ryerson Tull [20343]
Ryerson Tull Inc. [20344]
Ryerson Tull Inc. [20345]
S I Metals [20346]
S and I Steel Supply Div. [20347]
S and R Metals Inc. [20348]
Sabel Industries Inc. [26971]
Sabel Steel Service [20349]
Sadoff and Rudoy Industries [26974]
St. Louis Coke and Foundry [17156]
Sampson Steel Corp. [20350]
Samuel Specialty Metals Inc. [20351]
Samuels Glass Co. [7975]
Savoye Packaging Corp. [20353]
Sawing and Shearing Services Inc. [20354]
ScanSteel Service Center Inc. [20355]
Schorr Insulated Glass Inc.; Norm [7988]
Schroth Inc.; Emil A. [20356]
Scion Steel Co. [20357]
Scott Stainless Steel [20358]
Sennett Steel Corp. [20359]
September Enterprises Inc. [22661]
Service Steel Aerospace Corp. [20360]
Servsteel Inc. [17169]
SFI-Gray Steel Services Inc. [20361]
SFK Steel Inc. [20362]
Sharon Piping and Equipment Inc. [20363]
Shibamoto America, Inc. [16487]
Showa Denko America Inc. [20364]
Sierra Alloys Company Inc. [20365]
Sierra Pacific Steel Inc. [20366]
Simpson Strong-Tie Company Inc. [8023]
Simsmetal USA Corp. [26994]
Simsmetal USA Corp. C and C Metals Div. [20367]
Singer Steel Co. [20368]
Singer Steel Inc. [20369]
Siskin Steel and Supply Company Inc. [20370]
Smith Pipe and Steel Co. [20371]
SOGEM-Afrimet Inc. [20372]
Somerville Co.; Thomas [23381]
Somerville Co.; Thomas [23382]
Somerville, Co.; Thomas [23383]
Somerville Co.; Thomas [23384]
Somerville Co.; Thomas [23385]
South Bay Foundry, Inc. [20373]
South Main Metal Building [20374]
Southwark Metal Manufacturing Co. [20375]
Southwest Stainless Inc. [20376]
Southwest Steel [20377]
Southwest Steel Supply Co. [20378]
Southwest Wire Rope Inc. [17188]
Southwestern Ohio Steel Inc. [20379]
Southwestern Suppliers Inc. [20380]
Specialty Metals Industries [20381]
Specialty Metals and Minerals Inc. [20382]
Specialty Metals Supply Inc. [20383]
Specialty Pipe and Tube Co. [20384]
St Lawrence Steel Corp. [20385]
Standard Metals Inc. [20386]
Standard Steel and Wire Corp. [20387]
Standard Tube Sales Corp. [20388]
Star Tubular Products Co. [23397]
STATCO Engineering and Fabricators Inc. [20389]
State Line Supply Co. [20390]
State Pipe and Supply Inc. [20391]
State Salvage Company Inc. [27009]
Steel City Corp. [20392]
Steel Co. [20393]
Steel Engineers Inc. [20394]
Steel Inc. [20395]
Steel Industries Inc. [16521]
Steel Industries Inc. [20396]
Steel Manufacturing and Warehouse Co. [20397]
Steel and Pipe Supply Co. [20398]

Steel Services Inc. [20399]
Steel Suppliers Inc. [20400]
Steel Supply Co. [20401]
Steel Supply Co. (Rolling Meadows, Illinois) [20402]
Steel Warehouse Company Inc. [20403]
Steel Yard Inc. [20404]
Steelco Inc. [20405]
Stock Steel [20406]
Stone Steel Corp. [20407]
Stratcor Technical Sales Inc. [20570]
Stripco Sales Inc. [20408]
Stulz-Sickles Steel Co. [20409]
Sturdvant Refrigeration/Air-Conditioning [14700]
Style Master [20410]
Sumitomo Corporation of America [20411]
Sunland Steel Inc. [20412]
Sunshine Steel Enterprises Corp. [20413]
Superior Div. [27016]
Superior Group Inc. [17206]
Supra Alloys Inc. [20414]
Swing Machinery and Equipment Company Inc. [17209]
Synergy Steel Inc. [20415]
Tang Industries Inc. [20416]
TCI Aluminum [20417]
TD Materials Inc. [156]
Techno Steel Corp. [20418]
Teknis Corp. [9471]
Tenenbaum Company Inc.; A. [27020]
Tex Isle Supply Inc. [20419]
Texas Pipe and Supply Company Inc. [20420]
Three States Supply Co. [14728]
Thypin Stainless Steel [20421]
Thypin Steel Co. [20422]
Thyssen Incorporated N.A. [20423]
Tiernay Metals Inc. [20424]
Titan Industrial Corp. [20425]
Titan Steel Co. [20426]
TMX [20427]
Toledo Pickling and Steel Inc. [20428]
Toledo Pickling and Steel Sales Inc. [20429]
Tomen America Inc. [20430]
Tool King Inc. [20431]
Tool Steel Service Inc. [20432]
Totten Tubes Inc. [20433]
Toyota Tsusho America Inc. [20434]
Tradearbed Inc. [20435]
Tradex International Corp. [20436]
Transfer Print Foils [20437]
Transit Mix Concrete Co. [20438]
Transworld Alloys Inc. [20439]
Transworld Metal USA Ltd. [20440]
Trenton Iron and Metal Corp. [20441]
Tri-State Aluminum [20442]
Trotter and Company Inc.; Nathan [20443]
Tube City Inc. [27027]
Tube Service Co. [20444]
Tubesales [20445]
Tubular Steel Inc. [20446]
Tull Metals Company Inc.; J.M. [20447]
Tulsa Metal Processing Co. [20448]
Tung Tai Trading Corp. [27028]
TW Metals Co. [20449]
T.W.P. Inc. [20450]
Uddeholm Corp. [20451]
Uddeholm Steel Corp. [20452]
Ulbrich of California Inc. [20453]
Ulbrich of Illinois Inc. [20454]
Uni-Steel Inc. [20455]
Uni-Steel Inc. [20456]
Unichem Industries Inc. [19671]
Unico Alloys Inc. [20457]
Unisteel Inc. [20459]
Unistrut Detroit Service Co. [20460]
Unistrut Los Angeles [20461]
Unistrut Northern California [20462]
United Alloys Inc. [20463]
U.S. Metal Service Inc. [20464]
United Steel Associates Inc. [20465]
United Steel Service Inc. [20466]
Universal Metal and Ore Company Inc. [27032]
Universal Metal Services Corp. [20467]
Universal Steel Co. [20468]
Value Added Distribution Inc. [20469]
Van Bebber Brothers Inc. [20470]

Van Leeuwen Pipe and Tube Corp. [23431]
Vanadium Pacific Steel Co. [20471]
Viking Materials Inc. [20472]
Vincent Metal Goods [20473]
Vincent Metal Goods [27034]
Vitco Steel Supply Corp. [20474]
Vitto Sheet Metal Inc.; Nicholas [20475]
Voorhies Supply Company Inc. [16608]
Vorberger Group Ltd. [20476]
Ward Manufacturing Inc. [20478]
Waukegan Steel Sales Inc. [20479]
Waukegan Steel Sales Inc. [20480]
Wayne Steel Co. [20481]
Wayne Steel Co., Ray H. Morris Div. [20482]
Wedin International Inc., Ball Screw Manufacturing and Repair, Inc. [13989]
Weingartner Company Inc.; Henry [20484]
Weissman & Sons Inc.; Carl [21604]
Weissman and Sons Inc.; Carl [13991]
Welded Products Inc. [20485]
Weldtube Inc. [20486]
Wesco Financial Corp. [20487]
West Central Steel Inc. [20488]
West Coast Wire Rope and Rigging Inc. [17274]
West Coast Wire and Steel [20489]
Western Flat Rolled Steel [20490]
Western MacArthur Co. [8208]
Wichita Sheet Metal Supply Co. [14766]
Wilkof Morris Steel Corp. [20491]
Williams and Company Inc. [20492]
Williams Steel and Supply Company Inc. [20493]
Willis Steel Corp. [20494]
Winograd's Steel and Supply [20495]
Winter Wolff Inc. [20496]
Wisconsin Steel and Tube Corp. [20497]
Wolverine Metal Company Inc. [20498]
Woodlawn Hardware [17287]
Worthington Industries Inc. [20499]
Worthington Steel Co. [20500]
WRG Corp. [177]
Yaffe Iron and Metal Company Inc. [20501]
Yarde Metals Inc. [20502]
Yen Enterprises Inc. [20503]
Young Steel Products Co. [20504]
Ziegler Steel Service Corp. [8254]
Ziegler's Bolt & Nut House [14005]
Zuckerman, Charles and Son Inc. [20505]

SIC 5052 — Coal, Other Minerals & Ores

Addwest Mining, Inc. [20506]
AJ Coal Co. [20507]
Alabama Coal Cooperative [20508]
Allegheny Mining Corp. [20509]
Alley-Cassetty Coal Co. [20510]
Ambrose Branch Coal Co. Inc. [20511]
American Carbon Corporation [20512]
American Resources Inc. [20513]
Amvest Coal Sales Inc. [20514]
Andalex Resources, Inc. [20515]
Anker Energy Corp. [20516]
ANR Coal Company L.L.C. [20517]
Anthony Mining, Inc. [20518]
Arch Coal Sales Company Inc. [20519]
Arch of West Virginia Inc. [20520]
Asoma [19786]
Bitor America Corp. [20521]
Black Beauty Coal Co. [20522]
Black Gold Sales Inc. [20523]
The Bradenton Financial Ctr. [20524]
C/C Chemical and Coal Co. [20525]
Caemi International Inc. [20526]
Candlewax Smokeless Fuel Company Inc. [20527]
Carbon Resources of Florida [20528]
Castle Metals Inc. [19864]
Coal Bunkers [20529]
Coal Hill Mining Co. [20530]
CoalARBED International Trading Co. [20531]
Connell Brothers Company Ltd. [4362]
Coors Energy Co. [20532]
D.J. Enterprises, Inc. [20533]
Downing Coal Co. [20534]

Draper Energy Co. Inc. [20535]
Eastern Europe, Inc. [536]
Electric Fuels Corp. [20537]
Emerald International Corp. [20538]
Energy Group P.L.C. [20539]
F and S Alloys and Minerals Corp. [19961]
Farmers Investment Company Inc. [20540]
G and B Oil Company Inc. [22298]
Gassmon Coal and Oil Company Inc. [20542]
Hammill and Gillespie Inc. [20544]
Hickman, Williams and Co. [20036]
Hill and Griffith Co. [20545]
Holmes Limestone Co. [20546]
ITC Inc. [21780]
James River Coal Sales, Inc. [20548]
Kanematsu U.S.A. Inc. [26086]
Kiewit Mining Group, Inc. [20549]
Kincaid Coal Co. Inc.; Elmer [20550]
Massey Coal Company Inc.; A.T. [20552]
McCormick Co.; J.S. [20553]
Mitsubishi International Corp. [26151]
Oremco Inc. [20555]
Oxbow Carbon International Inc. [20556]
Peabody COALSALES Co. [20557]
Peabody Group [20558]
People's Coal Co. [20559]
Prospect Energy Inc. [20560]
Reiss Coal Co.; C. [20561]
Ring's Coal Co. [20562]
River Trading Co. [20563]
Royal Fuel Co. [20565]
Royal Fuel Corp. [22643]
Royal Inc.; H.M. [20566]
Samuel-Whittar Inc. [20567]
Smoky Mountain Coal Corp. [20568]
Sprague Energy Corp. [22693]
Stinnes Corp. [22706]
Stinnes Intercoal Inc. [20569]
Stratcor Technical Sales Inc. [20570]
Summers Fuel Inc. [20571]
Suneel Alaska Corp. [20572]
Tejas Resources Inc. [20573]
Transocean Coal Company L.P. [20574]

SIC 5060 — Electrical Goods

General Machinery Company Inc. [5842]
International Components Corp. [11520]

SIC 5063 — Electrical Apparatus & Equipment

1st Source Parts Center [14983]
A-C Supply Inc. [16664]
A. Louis Supply Co. [16665]
ABB Pressure Systems Inc. [8260]
Accent Lamp and Shade Co. Inc. [15387]
Accu Tech Cable Inc. [8261]
Ace Electric Supply Co. [8262]
Ace Hardware Corp. [13525]
Ace Plumbing and Electrical Supply, Inc. [23050]
Ackerman Electrical Supply Co. [8265]
Acme Electric Supply Inc. [8267]
ACT Services Inc. [8269]
Action Electric Sales Co. [8271]
Active Electrical Supply Co. [8272]
ADEMCO/ADI [24468]
ADEMCO/ADI [24469]
ADEMCO/ADI [24470]
ADEMCO/ADI [24471]
ADEMCO/ADI [24472]
ADEMCO/ADI [24473]
ADEMCO/ADI [24474]
ADEMCO/ADI [24475]
ADEMCO/ADI [24476]
ADEMCO/ADI [24477]
ADEMCO/ADI [24478]
ADEMCO/ADI [24479]
ADEMCO/ADI [24480]
ADEMCO/ADI [24481]
Ademco Distribution Inc. [24482]

ADI [24483]
ADI [24484]
ADI [24485]
Adirondack Electronics Inc. [8273]
ADT Security Systems [24487]
ADT Security Systems [24488]
ADT Security Systems [24489]
ADT Security Systems, Mid-South Inc. [24490]
Advance Electrical Supply Co. [8274]
Advanced Federated Protection Inc. [24493]
Advantor Corp. [24494]
Adventure Lighting Supply Ltd. [8276]
AEI Electronic Parts [8277]
Aero-K.A.P. Inc. [8278]
AeroSpace Computer Supplies, Inc. [5892]
Aerospace Materials Corp. [8280]
Aerospace Southwest [8281]
AFA Protective Systems Inc. [24495]
AHM Security Inc. [24497]
Alarm Controls Corp. [24498]
Alarm Services Inc. [24500]
Alaska Fire & Safety Equipment [24501]
Alaska General Alarm Inc. [24502]
Alaska General Alarm Inc. [8286]
Albertville Electric Motor [8288]
Alcoa Conductors Products Co. [2201]
Aleph International [8289]
Alexander; Steve [8290]
All Phase Electric Supply [8293]
All Phase Electric Supply [8294]
All Phase Electric Supply Co. [8295]
Allen Electric Supply Co. [8299]
Allen Supply Company, Inc.; William B. [24503]
Allied Bearing Supply [16685]
Allied Belting and Transmission Inc. [2211]
Allied Electronics [8301]
Allied Electronics [8303]
Allied Electronics [8304]
Allied Electronics [8307]
Allied Electronics [8322]
Allied Electronics [8323]
Allied Tools Inc. [16688]
Allison-Erwin Co. [5907]
Allred's Inc. [14315]
ALMO [5911]
Alpha Source Inc. [8331]
Alpha Wire Co. [8332]
Alsdorf International Ltd. [13554]
Amano Partners USA Inc. [8334]
American Appliance Parts Co. Inc. [15008]
American Contex Corp. [8338]
American Convenience Inc. [24505]
American Electric Co. [8339]
American Electric Co. [8340]
American Electric Co. [8341]
American Electric Co. [8342]
American Electric Supply [8343]
American Fluorescent Corp. [8344]
American Industrial Exports Ltd. [18449]
American Millwork & Hardware, Inc. [13560]
Amherst Electrical Supply [8346]
Amida Industries Inc. [15771]
AMP King Battery Company Inc. [8349]
Anderson Co.; S.W. [8352]
Anderson Co.; SW [8353]
Angelo Brothers Co. [8354]
Anicom [8355]
Anicom Inc. [8356]
Anicom Multimedia Wiring Systems [8357]
Anixter Inc. [8358]
Anixter International Inc. [8359]
Antex Incorporated [8361]
Apem Components, Inc. [8363]
Appliance Dealer Supply Co. [15016]
Appliance Parts Co. [15019]
Appliance Parts Warehouse Inc. [15029]
Applied Controls Inc. [8365]
Applied Hydroponics Inc. [246]
Applied Industrial Technologies [16704]
APS Systems [8366]
Aquatronics Inc. [8367]
Arie Incorporated [8372]
Arizona Commercial Lighting Co. [8374]
Armitage Industrial Supply, Inc. [16710]
Arrow Electronics Inc. [8377]
Arrow Precision Products Inc. [23073]

Arthurs Enterprises Inc. [8379]
Artmark Associates Inc. [8380]
Ashland Electric Company Inc. [8383]
Ashland Electric Company Inc. [8384]
Associated of Los Angeles [8386]
Astrex Inc. [8387]
Astro Industries Inc. [8388]
Atlantic Solar Products Inc. [8391]
Atlas Energy Systems Inc. [8392]
Aucoin and Miller Electric Supply Inc. [8393]
Audiovox Corp. [5523]
Autco [24510]
Automatic Firing Inc. [8398]
Avon Electrical Supplies, Inc. [8404]
B & C Distributors [8406]
Babco, Inc. [8407]
Babsco Supply [8408]
Bagoy and Associates Inc.; John P. [8410]
Barber-Nichols Inc. [8415]
Barnett Brass and Copper Inc. [23077]
Basic Wire & Cable Co. [8418]
Batteries Direct [8419]
Battery Products Inc. [8420]
Battery Specialties Inc. [8421]
Battery Warehouse [8422]
Battin Power Service; John [8423]
Baumer Electric Ltd. [15809]
Bearing Distributors Inc. [16731]
Bearings and Drives, Inc. [16737]
Bearings Inc. [16739]
Becker Co.; J.A. [8426]
Becker Electric Supply [8427]
Beeco Motors and Controls Inc. [8428]
Belden Electric Co.; Russell [20839]
Bellsonics [5529]
Benfield Electric Supply Co.; H.H. [8430]
Benson Eyecare Corp. [8431]
Besco Electic Supply Company of Florida
    Inc. [8433]
Best Electric Supply [13595]
Best Labs [18706]
Best Labs [8434]
Best Locking Systems of Georgia Inc. [24513]
Best Locking Systems of Wisconsin Inc. [24514]
Bestex Company Inc. [24515]
Biederman Inc.; A. [24323]
Billows Electric Supply Co. [8439]
Bird-X, Inc. [318]
Bird-X Inc. [8440]
Biscayne Electric and Hardware Distributors
    Inc. [8441]
Black and Decker Corp. Products Service
    Div. [15053]
Blake Wire and Cable Corp. [8444]
Blue Ridge Electric Motor Repair [8446]
Bluff City Electronics [8447]
Bob's Gard Duty [8448]
Bodine Electric of Decatur [8449]
Boettcher Supply Inc. [8450]
Boggis-Johnson Electric Co. [8451]
Boland Electric Supply Inc. [8452]
Border States Electric Supply [8455]
Border States Industries Inc. [8456]
Botkin Grain Co. Inc. [27089]
Boustead Electric and Manufacturing Co. [8457]
Bowling Green Winlectric [8458]
Boyd Lighting Fixture Co [8459]
Bozeman Safe & Lock [24518]
Brady Co. Xymox Div.; W.H. [8460]
Braid Electric Company Inc. [8461]
Brance-Krachy Company Inc. [15840]
Branch Electric Supply Co. [8462]
Brandon and Clark Inc. [8464]
Branom Instrument Company Inc. [24326]
Brehob Corp. [15843]
Brinkmann Corp. [8468]
Brithinee Electric [2386]
Brohl and Appell Inc. [8470]
Brown of Pennsylvania Corp.; D.P. [15848]
Brownstown Electric Supply Inc. [8471]
Bruce and Merrilee's Electric Co. [8472]
BTR Inc. [8473]
Buckles-Smith Electric [8474]
Budco [25111]
Bulbman Inc. [8476]
Bulbtronics [8477]

Burnstine's Distributing Corp. [2400]
Burroughs Communications Inc. [5538]
Bush Supply Co. [8479]
C and L Supply Inc. [15069]
C and W Enterprises Inc. [22103]
Cable Converter Services Corp. [8481]
Cable Services Co. Inc. [25114]
Cable Technologies International of New York
    Inc. [25115]
Cain Electrical Supply Corp. [8483]
California Electric Supply [8485]
Caltemp Instrument Inc. [8489]
Caltrol Inc. [15867]
Calvert Wire and Cable Corp. [8490]
Cambridge Engineering Inc. [8491]
Canare [8494]
Capacitor Associates [8495]
Capital Lighting & Supply - Baltimore/Lee Electric
    Div. [8496]
Capital Lighting & Supply Inc. [8497]
Capitol Light and Supply Co. [8498]
Captre Electrical Supply [8500]
Car-Go Battery Co. [2421]
Cardello Electric Supply Co. [8501]
Carswell Distributing Co. [15077]
Cashway Electrical Supply Co. [8507]
Cayce Mill Supply Co. [8509]
CED Inc. [8513]
CED/Superior Electrical Supply Co. [8514]
Cedar Builders Supply Company Inc. [23109]
Cel Air Corp. [8515]
Cenna International Corp. [19223]
Central Distribution Services, LLC [13626]
Central Electric Supply Co. [8517]
Central Supply Co. [23110]
Central Supply Division of Central Consolidated
    Inc. [15082]
CEO/United Electric Supply Co. [8519]
Certex Gulf Coast [8521]
Chamberlain Group Inc. [13630]
Channer Corp. [8522]
Chapman Marine Supply [18478]
Chicago Electric Co. [8523]
Christensen Electric Motor Inc. [8524]
Chubb Security Systems Inc. [24526]
Cine 60 Inc. [25136]
Cinemills Corp. [8525]
Cisco Electrical Supply Co. [8526]
City Electric Motor Co. [8527]
City Plumbing & Electrical Supply [8528]
Clark Supply Co. [13634]
Classic Components Supply Inc. [8531]
Cleveland Electric Motors [8532]
Clifford of Vermont Inc. [8533]
Clisby Agency Inc. [16802]
CLS [8534]
CLS [8535]
CMA International [15894]
Coast Appliance Parts Co. [15087]
Coast Wire and Plastic Tech Inc. [8536]
Coastline Parts Co. [15088]
Codale Electric Supply Inc. [8538]
Coleman Electric Company Inc. [8539]
Coleman Powermate Inc. [8540]
Colin Electric Motor Services [8541]
Colladay Hardware Co. [23119]
Colombian Development Corp. [8544]
Colonial Electric Supply Company Inc. [8545]
Colorado Electronic Hardware Inc. [8546]
Colorado Wire and Cable Company Inc. [8547]
Commercial Electric Products Corp. [8551]
Communications Products and Services Inc. [8552]
Component Resources Inc. [8554]
Comse Sales/John Weeks Enterprises [25147]
Con Serve Electric Supply [8558]
Conformance Technology Inc. [8559]
Connectronics Corp. [8560]
Conserve-A-Watt Lighting Inc. [8561]
Conserve Electric [8562]
Consolidated Electrical Distributing [8564]
Consolidated Electrical Distributor [8565]
Consolidated Electrical Distributor [8566]
Consolidated Electrical Distributors° [8567]
Consolidated Electrical Distributors [8568]
Consolidated Electrical Distributors Inc. [8569]
Consolidated Electrical Distributors Inc. [8570]

Consolidated Electrical Distributors Inc. [8571]
Consolidated Electrical Distributors Inc. Perry-Mann
Electrical [8572]
Consolidated Electronics Inc. [8573]
Control Sales Inc. [15912]
Control Switches International Inc. [8576]
Cooling & Heating Inc. [14404]
Cooper Electric Supply Co. [8578]
Craftmade International Inc. [15462]
Creative Stage Lighting Company Inc. [8585]
Crescent Electric Supply (Appleton,
Wisconsin) [15099]
Crescent Electric Supply Co. [8587]
Crescent Electric Supply Co. [8588]
Crescent Electric Supply Co. [8589]
Crescent Electric Supply Co. [8590]
Crescent Electric Supply Co. [8591]
Crescent Electric Supply Co. [8592]
Crest Industries Inc. (Alexandria, Louisiana) [8594]
Crum Electrical Supply Inc. [8596]
Crystal Clear Industries Inc. [15464]
Cummins Alabama Inc. [2502]
Cummins Connecticut Inc. [2503]
Cummins Great Lakes Inc. [2506]
Cummins Great Plains Diesel Inc. [2507]
Cummins Utility Supply [13650]
Curtis Co. [15101]
Cushing Inc.; T.F. [8598]
Custom Cable Industries Inc. [8599]
CW Magnet Wire Co. [8602]
D and H Distributing Co. [6175]
Dalis, Inc.; H.L. [5585]
Dallas Aerospace Inc. [79]
Dalton Supply Co. Inc. [14412]
Dandee Creations Ltd. [15466]
Dauphin Electrical Supply Co. [8611]
Davis Electric Supply Company Inc.; W.B. [5590]
Davis Electrical Supply Company Inc. [8614]
De Sisti Lighting Corp. [8615]
Dealers Electric Motor [8616]
Dearborn West L.P. [8618]
Debenham Electric Supply Co. [8619]
DEI Inc. [24533]
Delta Star Inc. [8622]
Desherbinin Products Inc.; W.N. [15470]
Design Marketing Associates [13088]
Detroit Diesel Overseas Corp. [2541]
Deuel County Farmers Union Oil Co. [22199]
Dey Appliance Parts [8625]
Diamond Electronics, Inc. [24534]
Directed Energy Inc. [8628]
DIT-MCO International Corp. [8629]
Dixie Store Fixtures and Sales Company
Inc. [15476]
Do All Foreign Sales Corp. [15956]
Do It Best Corp. [7275]
Domestic & International Technology [2555]
Dominion Electric Supply Co. [8630]
Dover Electric Supply Company Inc. [8632]
Dreisilker Electric Motors Inc. [8634]
DS America Inc. [15965]
D.S.A. Materials Inc. [8635]
Dudek & Company, Inc.; R.C. [8636]
Dudek & Company, Inc.; R.C. [8637]
Duellman Electric Co. [8638]
Duraline [8639]
E and B Electric Supply Co. [8641]
Eagle Electric Manufacturing Co. [8642]
EASI (Electronic Applications Specialists
Inc.) [8644]
Easter-Owens Electric Co [8645]
Eastern Bearings Inc. [2573]
Eastern Bearings Inc. [8646]
Eastern Electric Supply Co. [8647]
Ebbtide & Associates [15485]
Eck Supply Co. [8649]
Eckart Supply Company Inc. [8650]
EcoCycle Inc. [21718]
Economy Electric Company Inc. [8651]
EDCO Electronics Inc. [8653]
EESCO, A Division of WESCO Distribution,
Inc. [8655]
EESCO Inc. Farrell-Argast Div. [8656]
EH Engineering Ltd. [8657]
EIS, Inc. [8658]
Electrex Inc. [8659]

Electric Fixture and Supply Co. [8660]
Electric Motor and Control Corp. [8661]
Electric Motor Engineering Inc. [15979]
Electric Motor Repair & Sales [8662]
Electric Motor Service [8663]
Electric Motor and Supply Inc. [8664]
Electric Motors Unlimited Inc. [8665]
Electric Supply Co. [8666]
Electric Supply Co. (Asheville, North
Carolina) [8667]
Electric Supply Company of Fayetteville
Inc. [8668]
Electric Supply Co. (Raleigh, North
Carolina) [8669]
Electric Supply Co. (Wilson, North Carolina) [8670]
Electric Supply and Equipment Company
Inc. [8671]
Electric Switches Inc. [8672]
Electrical Appliance Service Co. [15120]
Electrical Communications [8673]
Electrical Construction Co. [8674]
Electrical Controller Products Co. [8675]
Electrical Distributors Inc. [8676]
Electrical Engineering and Equipment Co. [8677]
Electrical Equipment Co. [8678]
Electrical Equipment Co. [8679]
Electrical Materials Co. [23146]
Electrical Materials Inc. [8680]
Electrical Wholesale Supply Company Inc. [8682]
Electro-Matic Products Inc. [8684]
Electronic Contracting Co. [8688]
Electronic Lighting Inc. [8692]
Electronic Security Services [24536]
Electrorep Energy Products Inc. [8697]
Elliot Electric Supply [8699]
Empire Generator Corp. [8702]
EMSCO Electric Supply Company Inc. [8704]
Energy International Corp. [14432]
Engine and Equipment Co. Inc. [15989]
Engineered Components Inc. [8707]
Englewood Electrical Supply [8709]
Eoff Electric Co. [8712]
Equipment and Parts Export Inc. [2594]
Esco Electric Supply Co. [8713]
ESD Co. [8714]
Esojon International, Inc. [9887]
Essex Electrical Supply Company Inc. [8715]
ESSROC Corp. [7322]
Evans Environmental Corp. [25187]
Evans Inc. [14436]
Evansville Auto Parts Inc. [16000]
Evergreen Oak Electric Supply & Sales Co. Crest
Lighting Studios Div. [8718]
Evergreen Oak Electric Supply and Sales Co.
Evergreen Oak Div. [8719]
Everpower Co. [8720]
Ex-Eltronics Inc. [8721]
Excel Electric Service Co. [8722]
Excel Specialty Corp. [8723]
F & S Supply Company Inc. [8728]
Fail-Safe Lighting Systems Inc. [8729]
Farmers Petroleum Cooperative Inc. [22257]
Farmers Union Oil Co. [22265]
Fauver Co. [16857]
Fay Electric Wire Corp. [8732]
Fedco Electronics Inc. [8733]
Federal Signal Corp. [8734]
Fenton Brothers Electrical [8736]
Ferguson Electric Construction Company
Inc. [8737]
Fewkes and Co.; Joseph T. [8738]
FIC Corp. [8739]
Fields and Company of Lubbock Inc. [23168]
Fife Electric Co. [8741]
Fire Alarm Service Corp. [24540]
Fire Command Company Inc. [24543]
Fisher Electric Motor Service [2624]
Fitzpatrick Electric Supply Co. [8743]
Flash Clinic Inc. [8744]
Flato Electric Supply Co. [8745]
Fleming Sales Company Inc. [692]
Florig Equipment [8747]
Forbex Corporation [9904]
ForeSight Electronics Inc. [8752]
Forest City Electric Supply [8753]
Foss Co.; W.J. [16874]

F.R. Industries Inc. [8754]
Franklin Electric Company Inc. (Atlantic City, New
Jersey) [8758]
Fravert Services Inc. [8759]
Fresno Distributing Co. [8760]
Friedman Electric Supply [8762]
Fromm Electric Supply Corp. [8764]
Fujitsu Business Communication Systems
Inc. [8766]
Fullwell Products Inc. [2656]
Fulton Radio Supply Co. [8767]
Furbay Electric Supply Co. [8768]
G & N Appliance Parts [15139]
Gaffney-Kroese Electrical Supply Corp. [8770]
Gaines Electric Supply Co. [8771]
Gaylord Manufacturing Co. [8776]
GE Supply [8779]
GEC Alsthom Balteau, Inc. [8780]
Genal Strap Inc. [17429]
Generac Corp. [8782]
General Electric Supply [8783]
General Machinery Company Inc. [5842]
Georgia Lighting Supply Co. [8786]
Gerhardt's International, Inc. [16060]
Gillmore Security Systems Inc. [24556]
Glaze Supply Company Inc. [8788]
Globe Electric Supply Company, Inc. [8789]
Globus Industries [8791]
Goforth Electric Supply Inc. [8793]
Goldfarb Electric Supply Company Inc. [8796]
Gordon Co.; Len [22972]
Grainger, Inc. [8800]
Grainger Inc. [8801]
Grainger Inc.; W.W. [8802]
Grainger Industrial Supply [8803]
Gramex Corp. [5000]
Grand Light and Supply Co. [8805]
Grand Transformers Inc. [8806]
Granite City Electric Supply Co. [8807]
Graybar Electric Company Inc. [8808]
Graybar Electric Company Inc. [8809]
Graybar Electric Company Inc. [8810]
Graybar Electric Company Inc. [8811]
Graybar Electric Company Inc. [8812]
Graybar Electric Company Inc. [8813]
Greenwood Supply Company Inc. [8817]
Greer Industries Inc. [8818]
Gregg Manufacturing Inc. [15516]
Grimstad Inc.; J.M. [16079]
Gross Electric Inc. [8820]
Group One Capital Inc. [14117]
Gulf Coast Electric Supply Company Inc. [8821]
Haig Lighting & Electric [8822]
Hall Inc.; Melville B. [8823]
Hall & Reis, Inc. [7431]
Hamilton Electric Works Inc. [8824]
Hannan Supply Co. [8826]
Hansen Electrical Supply [8827]
Hardie Export; James [7442]
Hardware Distribution Warehouses Inc. [13736]
Hardware Distributors Inc. [13737]
Hardware Specialties Inc. [13739]
Harris Electric Inc. [8830]
Harris Marcus Group [13127]
Hartman-Spreng Co. [8832]
Hartmann of Florida [8833]
Hauser Company; M.L. [16092]
Hawk Electronics Inc. [8834]
Hawthorne Machinery Inc. [2732]
Hayes & Lunsford Motor Repair [8835]
Hazard and Sons Inc.; L.A. [23206]
Helsel-Jepperson Electric Inc. [8837]
Hermitage Electric Supply Corp. [15167]
Herzog Supply Inc.; C. [23208]
Heyboer Transformers Inc. [8839]
Hi-Line Electric Co. [8840]
Hicks Equipment [8841]
Higgins Purchasing Group [13131]
Hilites; K.C. [8842]
Hisco [8843]
Hisco [8844]
Hisco [8845]
Hitachi Inverter [8848]
Hite Co. [8849]
Hite Co. [8850]

Hoffman Co.; H. [24565]
Holmes Distributors Inc. [8852]
Holmes Protection Inc. [24566]
Holt Electric Inc. [8853]
Holt Electric Motor Co. [8854]
Holzmueller Corp. [8855]
Homier Distributing Inc. [13756]
Honeywell Protection Services [24567]
Honeywell Sensing and Control [8856]
Hoover Instrument Service Inc. [24371]
Horner Electric Inc. [16113]
House Of Batteries [8858]
Houston Wire and Cable Co. [8860]
Howard Electric Co. [8861]
Howland Electric Wholesale Co. [8862]
Hub Material Co. [8863]
Hughes Company Inc.; R.S. [24568]
Hughes Supply Inc. [23216]
Hunt Electric Supply Co. [8865]
Hunzicker Brothers Inc. [8866]
HWC Distribution Corp. [8868]
IBA Protection Services [24569]
iGo [8871]
In Products Inc. [15538]
Inca Corp. [8872]
Indus-Tool [8874]
Indus-Tool Inc. [2773]
Indusco, Ltd. [8875]
Industrial Battery Engineering Inc. [8876]
Industrial Development & Procurement [16150]
Industrial Electrics Inc. [8877]
Industrial Electronic Supply Inc. [8878]
Industrial Supply Co. [16953]
Ingraham Corp.; George [8879]
Inlite Corp. [8880]
Insulectro Corp. [8884]
Intech EDM Electrotools [8885]
Interlectric Corp. [16961]
International Components Corp. [8893]
International Trade Group [18860]
Interstate Battery System of Dallas Inc. [8896]
Interstate Electric Supply [8897]
Interstate Electronics, Inc. [25254]
Intruder Alert Security [24574]
Irby Co.; Stuart C. [8900]
Irby Co.; Stuart C. [16964]
ITS/Intertrade Scientific, Inc. [16177]
J and B Supply Inc. [14496]
Jacksonville Sound and Communications
    Inc. [25256]
Jademar Corp. [8904]
Javatec Inc. [8908]
Jenks & Son; W.S. [8911]
Jensen Distribution Services [13773]
J.H. Service Company Inc. [8913]
JH Service Company Inc. [8914]
Jilnance Corp. [2822]
Joe's Firestone Inc. [2823]
Johnson Electric NA Inc. [8915]
Johnson Electric Supply Co. [8916]
Johnson Supply Controls Center [8918]
Johnstone Supply [14503]
Joliet Equipment Corp. [2832]
Jones Electric Company Inc.; G.E. [2833]
Jones & Lee Supply Co. [8919]
Joy Co.; Edward [8920]
Joy Company Inc.; B. Frank [8921]
K & T Lamp & Shade Company Inc. [15546]
Kahant Electrical Supply Co. [8925]
Kaman Industrial Technologies [8926]
Kaman Industrial Technologies [16977]
Kaman Industrial Technology [16198]
Kanematsu U.S.A. Inc. [22395]
Kansas Electric Supply Company Inc. [8928]
Katolight Corp. [8930]
Kawasaki Motors Corporation U.S.A. [20659]
Keathley-Patterson Electric Co. [8933]
Kelly Supply Company of Iowa [16983]
Kenclaire Electrical Agencies Inc. [8934]
Kendall Electric Inc. [8935]
Kennewick Industrial and Electrical Supply
    Inc. [8937]
Keystone Wire & Cable Company Inc. [8942]
Kiemle-Hankins Co. [8943]
Kinder-Harris Inc. [8945]
King Electronics Distributing [8946]

King Wire and Cable Corp. [8947]
King Wire Inc. [8948]
Kinray, Inc. [14142]
Kirby Risk Electrical Supply [8949]
K.J. Electric Inc. [8950]
KLH Industries Inc. [8951]
Knese, Inc.; Henry [16209]
Knopp Inc. [8953]
KOBOLD Instruments Inc. [24385]
Koontz-Wagner Electric Company Inc. [8956]
Kornfeld-Thorp Electric Co. [8957]
Kovalsky-Carr Electric Supply Company Inc. [8958]
The Kruse Company [13789]
Kulwin Electric Supply [8960]
L-com Inc. [8961]
La Plante Gallery Inc. [13161]
Lacey-Harmer Co [8963]
Lafayette Electronics Supply Inc. [15197]
Lakeland Engineer Equipment Co. [8966]
LAM Electrical Supply Company, Inc. [8967]
Lamar Wholesale and Supply Inc. [8968]
Lamp Glow Industries Inc. [8969]
Lang and Washburn Electric Inc. [8970]
Laredo Hardware Co. [13793]
Larsen International, Inc. [4438]
Larson Co.; J.H. [8973]
Lawrence Electric Co.; F.D. [8974]
Lawrin Lighting, Inc. [15561]
L.B. Electric Supply Company Inc. [8975]
Ledu Corp. [8978]
Lee Lumber and Building Materials Corp. [7591]
Lee Supply Corp. [23245]
Leff Electric Co.; H. [8979]
Lehmann Co. Inc.; Chester C. [8981]
Lehmann Company Inc.; Chester C. [8982]
Light House Electrical Suppliers Inc. [8986]
Lighting Parts Inc. [8988]
Lightolier Inc. Norwich Div. [8989]
Lights Etc. Inc. [8990]
Ligon Electric Supply Co. [8991]
Linder Electric Motors Inc. [8993]
Lister-Petter Inc. [2886]
Lite Brite Distributors [8994]
Littelfuse Inc. [8995]
Liuski International Inc. [8996]
Living Systems Instrumentation [8997]
Livingston & Haven, Inc. [16239]
Loeb Electric Co. [9000]
Long Island Transmission Corp. [16244]
Loyd Armature Works Inc. [9004]
Loyd's Electric Supply Co. [9005]
L.S.I. Lectro Science Inc. [9006]
Lubbock Electric Co. [9007]
Lucky Electric Supply [9009]
Lucoral Company Inc. [9010]
Lundahl Inc.; Warner T. [2898]
Lyncole XIT Grounding [9011]
M & G Industries [9013]
M & G Industries Inc. [9014]
M-Tron Components Inc. [9016]
Mackay Industrial Sales Inc. [17010]
Maddux Supply Co. [9017]
Madison Appliance Parts Inc. [15206]
Magnetic Technology [9019]
Main Electric Supply Co. [9021]
Mallory Inc. [9023]
Maltby Electric Supply Company Inc. [9024]
Mania-Testerion [9025]
Mansfield Electric Supply Inc. [9026]
Marathon Electric Manufacturing Corp. [9028]
Marc Sales Corp.; Ken [9029]
Marco Supply Company Inc. [13812]
Marcone Appliance Parts Center [15211]
Martensen Enterprises Inc. [7651]
Martin Co.; E.A. [7652]
Mas-Tech International Inc. [6468]
Massachusetts Gas and Electric Lighting Supply
    Co. [9044]
Matthews Electric Supply Company Inc. [9046]
Maverick Electric Supply Inc. [9047]
Maxima Electrical Sales Company Inc. [9048]
Mayer Electric Supply Co. [9050]
Mayer Electric Supply Co. [9051]
Mayer Electric Supply Company Inc. [9052]
Mayer-Hammant Equipment Inc. [9053]
McCullough Electric Co. [9054]

McDermott Corp.; Julian A. [24588]
McDiarmid Controls Inc. [9055]
McDonald Equipment Co. [9056]
McDonald Supply Company Inc.; A.Y. [23257]
McGowan Electric Supply Inc. [9057]
McGraw Inc.; James [17023]
McGuire Bearing [17024]
McGuire Furniture Co. [13176]
McJunkin Corp. [9058]
McKenney Supply Inc. [14538]
McLane Group Interntional L.P. [11833]
McNaughton-McKay Electric Company [9059]
McNaughton-McKay Electric Company Inc. [9060]
McWong International Inc.; M.W. [9061]
MDI Production [25734]
MDR Corp. [21136]
Mechanical Drives Inc. [16283]
Medler Electric Co. [9062]
Mega Hertz [25310]
Meier Transmission Ltd. [9063]
Melan International Trading [9064]
Mesa Microwave Inc. [9067]
Metrotek Industries Inc. [9070]
Meyda Tiffany [15587]
MH World Trade Corp. [26143]
Micro-Coax, Inc. [9072]
Mid-Carolina Electric Supply Company, Inc. [9076]
Mid-State Distributing [9077]
Midtown Electric Supply [9079]
MIL-Pack Inc. [9080]
Mil-Spec Supply Inc. [9081]
Milano Brothers International Corp. [9082]
Millbrook Sales & Service Co. [5678]
Miller Bearings Inc. [17041]
Miller Electric Co. (Omaha, Nebraska) [9084]
Miller Wholesale Electric Supply Co., Inc.—
    Morristown Division [9085]
Mills and Lupton Supply Co. [9087]
Minami International Corp. [13404]
Minnesota Electrical Supply Co. [9088]
Missouri Valley Electric Co. [9089]
Mitscher Company Inc.; R.W. [9090]
MKM Electronic Components Inc. [9091]
Modern Door and Hardware Inc. [7732]
Modern Supply Company Inc. [15238]
Mole-Richardson Co. [25333]
Monarch Electric Company Inc. [9092]
Moniteq Research Labs, Inc. [24596]
Moniteq Research Labs Inc. [9094]
Morley Murphy Co. [9096]
Morristown Electric Wholesalers Co. [9097]
Morse Wholesale Inc.; J.D. [26582]
Mortemp Inc. [14611]
Mosebach Electric and Supply Co. [9099]
Moser Lumber Inc. [7750]
Motion Industries, Atlantic Tracy Div. [17056]
Motloid Co. [19469]
Motloid Company [9100]
Motorola MIMS. VLSI Tech Center [9101]
Mountain Cable Industries Inc. [9102]
MP Productions Co. [25342]
Muntz Electrical Supply Co.; Jack H. [9107]
Murdock Companies Inc. [9109]
Murphy Door Specialties Inc.; Don [7755]
Murray Lighting Inc. [15243]
Nagy Sales Corp.; Tom [24597]
Nappco Fastener Co. [9111]
Natchez Electric Supply [9112]
National Barricade Co [9113]
National Electrical Supply Corp. [9114]
National Electro Sales Corp. [9115]
National Hardware and Supplies [9116]
National Plastics Corp. [9117]
National Switchgear Systems [9118]
NEDCO Supply [9120]
Nelson Electric Supply Co. [9121]
Nelson Electric Supply Company Inc. [9122]
Nelson Holland Inc. [24601]
Nesco Electrical Distributors Inc. [9123]
Nevada Illumination Inc. [9124]
New American Electric Distributors, Inc. [9125]
New World Research Corp. [3030]
New York Fastener Corp. [9128]
Night Owl Security Inc. [24603]
Nixon Power Services Co. [9130]
Nolarec Industries, Inc. [15595]

Norfolk Wire and Electronics Inc. [5691]
North American Security [24604]
North Atlantic Engineering Co. [9132]
North Coast Electric Co. [9133]
North Electric Supply Inc. [9134]
North Valley Distributing [9135]
Northern Plumbing & Heating Supply [23298]
Northern Power Technologies [9138]
Northland Electric Supply Co. [9140]
Northwest Electrical Supply [9141]
Norvell Electronics Inc. [9143]
Nunn Electric Supply Corp. [9149]
O.K. Electric Supply Co. [9152]
Olflex Wire and Cable Inc. [9154]
Olivetti Office USA Inc. [21199]
Omni Group Inc. [24605]
Omni USA Inc. [1107]
One Source Distributors [9156]
Ontario Supply Corp. [9157]
OPTEX Morse, Inc. [24606]
Optex USA Inc. [24607]
Optical Cable Corp. [9159]
Optronics Inc. [9160]
Osborn Machinery Company Inc. [13856]
OST Inc. (Fremont, California) [24609]
Ottawa Electric Inc. [9162]
Owensboro Electric Supply [9165]
Owsley and Sons Inc. [16366]
Pac States Electric Wholesalers [9167]
Pacific Electrical Supply [9169]
Pacific Radio Exchange Inc. [9171]
Paige Electric Company L.P. [9173]
Palmieri Associates [9177]
Park Corporation [9179]
Park Supply Co. Inc. [15265]
Peebles Supply Div. [23310]
Peer Light Inc. [9185]
Peerless Electric Supply Co. [9186]
PEI Genesis [9187]
Peninsular Electric Distributors Inc. [9188]
Peninsular Electronic Distributors [9189]
Penstan Supply [23312]
Persona Technologies Inc. [9191]
Peters-De Laet Inc. [9193]
Petsche Company Inc.; A.E. [9194]
Phelans [15619]
Philips and Co. [9195]
Picatti Brothers Inc. [9200]
Piher International Corporation [9202]
Pill Electric Supply Co.; Ralph [9203]
Pioneer [9205]
Pioneer Electric Inc. [9206]
Plainsco Inc. [15274]
PlastiCom Industries Inc. [9211]
Platt Electric Supply Inc. [9212]
Poll Electric Co.; H. [9216]
Port Electric Supply Corp. [9219]
Port Huron Electric Motor [9220]
Power Equipment Co. [3109]
Power Equipment Company [15278]
Power Equipment Corp. [9222]
Power Machine Service [9223]
Power/mation Inc. [9224]
Power Solutions [9225]
Power-Sonic Corp. [9226]
Power Supply, Inc. [9227]
Power and Telephone Supply Company
   Inc. [5713]
Power & Telephone Supply Company, Inc. [5715]
Power & Telephone Supply Company, Inc. [5717]
Powr-Lite Electric Supplies [9232]
Precision Bearing Co. [17113]
Priester Supply Company Inc. [9237]
Primus Inc. [23329]
Production Arts Lighting Inc. [9239]
Progress Electrical Supply Co. [9240]
PSI Resources Inc. [9243]
Pyramid Supply Inc. [9248]
QED [9249]
Quick Cable Corporation [9252]
Quick-Rotan Inc. [15286]
Quinn Electric Supply Co. [9253]
Radio City Automotive [25401]
Radio Holland U.S.A. [18590]
Radix Wire Co. [9260]
Rails Co. [23486]

Ram Meter Inc. [9261]
Ram Motors and Controls Inc. [3133]
Raybro Electric Supplies, Inc., Utility Div. [9266]
Rayvern Lighting Supply Company Inc. [9267]
Rea International Corp. [9268]
Red Wing Products Inc. [9269]
Redco Lighting & Maintenance [9270]
Refrigeration and Electric Supply Co. [15288]
Reily Electrical Supply Inc. [9271]
Reinders, Inc. [1181]
Reliable Battery Co. [9273]
Reliable Fire Equipment Co. [24618]
Reliance Electric Co. [9274]
Rembrandt Lamps [15632]
Reptron Electronics Inc. [9276]
The Republic Companies [9278]
Rero Distribution Co., Inc. [9280]
Resource Electronics Inc. [9282]
Revere Electric Supply Co. [9283]
Revere Electrical Supply Co. [9284]
Rexel Glasco [9285]
Rexel-Summers [9288]
Rexel-Summers [9289]
Rexel-Taylor [9290]
Rhoads Co.; D.W. [23339]
Richard Electric Supply Company Inc. [9292]
Richardson Electronics, Ltd. [9293]
Richmond Electric Supply Co. [9296]
Richton International Corp. [1191]
Riley-Stuart Supply Co. [7935]
Riley's Electrical Supply [9297]
RKB Enterprises Inc. [23345]
RMT Engineering, Inc. [9300]
Robco International Corporation/Advanced
   Technology International [17140]
Roberts Co.; D.B. [9301]
Roberts Co.; D.B. [9302]
Roberts Co.; D.B. [9303]
Robroy Industries [9304]
Rochester Instrument Systems Inc. [9306]
Rockingham Electrical Supplies Inc. [9307]
Roden Electrical Supply Co. [9308]
Roekel Co. [23351]
Roga International Div. Export-Import
   Marketing [15638]
Rogers Electric Supply; Chas. [9310]
Roldan Products Corp. [15293]
Rolls Battery Engineering Inc. [18594]
Roma Enterprises [25421]
Rome Cable Corp. [9314]
Ronco Power Systems Inc. [9316]
Roosevelt Co.; W.A. [14667]
Root, Neal and Company Inc. [9318]
Royalite Co. [9319]
Royce Industries Inc. [9320]
R.S.R. Electronics Inc. [9323]
Rueff Lighting Co. [9324]
RW Electronics Inc. [9325]
Ryall Electric Supply Co. [9327]
S and J Chevrolet Inc. [9328]
Saber Enterprises Inc. [24424]
Sacks Electrical Supply Co. [9329]
Safety Signals Systems Inc. [9330]
Saffron Supply Co. [13899]
Sager Electronics Inc. [9331]
Salinger Electric Co. [9333]
Salomon Co.; Paul R. [18600]
Sandusky Electrical Inc. [9335]
Sarreid Ltd. [13232]
SBM Industries Inc. [9340]
Schaedler/Yesco Distribution [9341]
Schuster Electronics Inc. [9343]
Scotts Inc. [23363]
SDA Security Systems, Inc. [24626]
SEA Wire & Cable Inc. [9348]
Seamans Supply Company Inc. [9349]
Security Data Group [24629]
Security Engineers Systems Inc. [24630]
Security Forces Inc. [9350]
SecurityLink Corp. [24631]
Sel-Tronics, Inc. [9351]
Select Security Inc. [24632]
Semix Inc. [3204]
Sentex Corp. [9354]
Sentrol Inc. [9355]
Sentry Alarm, Inc. [24633]

Sentry Watch Inc. [24636]
Sepco Bearing and P.T. Group [17167]
Service Electric Supply Inc. [9357]
Shealy Electrical Wholesalers Incorporated
   Co. [9358]
Shelby Electric Company Inc. [9359]
Shelby Supply Company Inc. [9360]
Shelly Electric Inc. [9361]
Shepherd Electric Company Inc. [9362]
Shepherd Electric Supply Company Inc. [9363]
Sherburn Electronics Corp. [9364]
Shokai Far East Ltd. [9365]
Sibley Industrial Tool Co. [9367]
Siemens Energy and Automation Inc. [9368]
Siemens Energy and Automation Inc. Electrical
   Apparatus Div. [9369]
Sig Cox Inc. [23375]
Signal Equipment Inc. [9371]
Sile Distributors Inc. [13513]
Silliter/Klebes Industrial Supplies Inc. [17175]
Silo International Inc. [8020]
Simione and Associates, Inc.; Bill [23939]
Simmons-Huggins Supply Co. [23377]
Singer Products Export Company Inc. [3224]
Sitler's Electric Supply Inc. [9373]
SJS Products/Jamcor Corp. [9374]
Sloan Electric Co [9376]
Sloan Miyasato [13247]
Smarter Security Systems Inc. [9377]
Solares Florida Corp. [16501]
Sommer Electric Corp. [9380]
SOR Inc. [9381]
SOS Alarm [24639]
Sound Around Inc. [25451]
Southern Automotive Inc. [3239]
Southern Distributors Inc. [15662]
Southern Electric Service Company, Inc. [9385]
Southern Electric Supply Company Inc. [9386]
Southern Electric Supply Company Inc. [9387]
Southern Electronics Supply, Inc. [9388]
Southern Lighting and Supply Company
   Inc. [9389]
Southern Wholesalers Inc. [23393]
Southwest Cooperative Wholesale [18245]
Southwest Electronics Inc. [9390]
Space Page Inc. [5764]
Spatron Inc. [9391]
Special Mine Services Inc. [9392]
Specialty Control Systems Inc. [9393]
Specialty Supply Co. [9394]
Spectrum [25460]
Spectrum Lighting/Sound & Beyond [25828]
Splane Electric Supply [9395]
Spring and Buckley Inc. [9396]
Springfield Electric Supply Co. [9397]
Staab Battery Manufacturing Company Inc. [9399]
Stacoswitch Inc. [9400]
Standard Electric Co. [9401]
Standard Electric Supply Co. [9402]
Standard Motor Products Inc. [9404]
Standard Wire & Cable Co. [9405]
Staneco Corp. [9406]
Stanion Wholesale Electric Company Inc. [9407]
Star Beam/Nightray Div. Gralco Corp. [9408]
Star Electric Supply Company Inc. [9409]
Starbuck Sprague Co. [9410]
Stark Electronics Inc. [9411]
State Electric Company Inc. [3263]
State Electric Supply [9412]
State Electric Supply Co. [9413]
State Electrical Supply Inc. [9414]
Steiner Electric Co. [9415]
Sterett Supply Co. [9416]
Sterling Security Services Inc. [24641]
Stern & Company, Inc.; Henry [9417]
Sticht Company Inc.; Herman H. [24439]
Stokes Electric Co. [9418]
Stoneway Electric Supply Co. [9420]
Stoneway Electric Supply Co. [9421]
Storm Products Co. [9422]
Storm Products Co. [9423]
Stover Smith Electric Supplies Inc. [9425]
Stusser Electric Co. [9428]
Stusser Electric Co. [9429]
Stusser Electric Co. [9430]
Stusser Electric Co. [9431]

Stusser Electric Co. [9432]
Stusser Electric Co. [9433]
Stusser Electric Co. [9434]
Stusser Electric Co. [9435]
Stusser Electric Co. [9436]
Stusser Electric Co. [9437]
Stusser Electric Company [9438]
Summit Electric Supply Inc. [9439]
Sun Supply Corp. [9440]
Sunbelt Transformer Inc. [9441]
Sunray Electric Supply Co. [9442]
Sunseri's Inc. [15324]
Sunseri's Inc. [15325]
SunSource Technology Services [16539]
Superior Electric Supply Co. (Elyria, Ohio) [9443]
Swam Electric Company Inc. [9449]
Swanson-Nunn Electric Co. [9450]
Swift Electric Supply Co. [9451]
T-Electra/TICA of Dallas Inc. [9453]
T-Fal Corp. [15680]
Tab Electric Supply Inc. [9454]
Tailor-Made Signs [13255]
Talays Inc. [9457]
Talcup, Inc. [9458]
Tampa Appliance Parts Corp. [15330]
Tampa Armature Works Inc. [16546]
Tapeswitch Corp. [9459]
Target Electronics Inc. [9460]
TDK Corporation of America [9461]
Teague Industries Inc. [9464]
Teal Electric Company Inc. [9465]
Tech Electro Industries Inc. [9466]
Teche Electric Supply Inc. [9467]
Tecot Electrical Supply Company Inc. [9470]
Teknis Corp. [9471]
Telecom Electric Supply Co. [9473]
Teleparts, Inc. [3298]
Telewire Supply [5788]
Tennessee Electric Motor Co. [9477]
Tennessee Valley Electric Supply Co. [9478]
Tepper Electrical Supply Inc. [9479]
Terrile Export & Import Corp. [9480]
Terry-Durin Company Inc. [9481]
Tescom [9482]
Thermax Wire Corp. [9485]
Thor Electronics Corp. [9487]
Toner Cable Equipment, Inc. [25480]
Topworx [9494]
Torque-A-Matic [17231]
Total Electric Distributors Inc. [9496]
Tower Fasteners Company, Inc. [9497]
Townsend Supply Co. [9498]
Transmission and Fluid Equipment Inc. [9501]
Transmission Products, Inc. [17233]
Transmission Products, Inc. [17234]
Transply Inc. [3328]
Treadway Electric Co. [9502]
Tri City Electrical Supply Co. [9503]
Tri-Power MPT [17235]
Tri-State Armature and Electrical Works Inc. [9504]
Tri State Electric Company Inc. [9505]
Tri State Electrical Supply Inc. [9506]
Tri-State Lighting and Supply Company Inc. [9507]
Triangle Electric Supply Co. [9508]
Triangle Supply Company Inc. [23417]
Trillennium [9509]
Tristate Electrical & Electronics Supply Company Inc./Uagemeyer N.V. [9511]
Tristate Electrical Supply Company Inc. [9512]
Troumbly Brothers Inc. [8150]
Troy Belting Supply Co. [17236]
Tubelite Company, Inc. [9515]
Tulare Pipe and Electric Supply Co. [9516]
Turtle and Hughes Inc. [9517]
TVC Technology Group [25487]
TW Communication Corp. [5798]
Union Carbide Corp., IPX Services [16587]
United Electric Supply Co. [9522]
United Electric Supply Co. (Salt Lake City, Utah) [9523]
United Electric Supply Inc. [9524]
United Engines Inc. [3366]
United Light Co. [9525]
United States Electric Co. [9526]
Universal Management Consultants Inc. [14749]

Universal Security Instruments Inc. [24652]
Universal Supply Company Inc. [23424]
US Lighting & Electrical Supply [9527]
Uspar Enterprises Inc. [9528]
Valenti Inc.; F.M. [24654]
Valley Electric Company Inc. [9532]
Valley Electric Supply Corp. [9533]
Van Sant Equipment Corp. [17251]
Varta Batteries Inc. [9535]
Vector Security Systems Inc. [24657]
Video Products Distributors [9538]
Viking Supply Company Inc. [9539]
Villa Lighting Supply Company Inc. [9540]
Villarreal Electric Company Inc. [9541]
Vineland Electric CED/Supply, Inc. [9542]
Vista Manufacturing [9543]
Vitramon Inc. [9544]
Vitus Electric Supply Co. [9545]
Wabash Power Equipment Co. [9547]
W.A.C. Lighting [9548]
Wagner-Electric of Fort Wayne Inc. [9550]
Walker and Associates Inc. (Welcome, North Carolina) [5808]
Walker Group Inc. [9553]
Walters Wholesale Electric Co. [9554]
Warren Electric Co. [9556]
Washer and Refrigeration Supply Company Inc. [15365]
Washington Belt & Drive [17263]
Washington Belt & Drive [17264]
Washington Belt & Drive [17266]
Watson Electric Supply Co. [9560]
Watson Electric Supply Co. [9561]
Wayne Distributing Inc. [9562]
Waytek Inc. [9563]
Webber Cable and Electronics [9564]
Wedco Inc. [9565]
Wehle Electric Div. [9567]
Weimer Bearing & Transmission Inc. [9568]
Wells Fargo Alarm Services Inc. [24660]
WESCO Distribution Inc. [9569]
West Philadelphia Electric Supply Co. [9570]
Westburgh Electric Inc. [9572]
Western Automation Inc. [14761]
Western Carolina Electrical Supply Co. [9573]
Western Extralite Co. [9575]
Western United Electric Supply Corp. [9577]
Westgate Enterprises Inc. [9578]
Westguard Inc. [24661]
Westinghouse Electical Supply [9579]
Westinghouse Electric Corp. Trading Co. [5812]
White Company Inc.; William D. [9582]
White Electric Supply Co. [9583]
White Electric Supply Co. (Monroe City, Missouri) [9584]
Whitehill Lighting and Supply Inc. [9585]
Whitmor/Wirenetics [9586]
Whitmor/Wirenetics [9587]
Wholesale Electric Supply Company of Houston Inc. [9589]
Wholesale Electric Supply Company Inc. (Bowling Green, Kentucky) [9590]
Wholesale Electric Supply Company Inc. (Texarkana, Texas) [9591]
Wholesale Electronic Supply Inc. [9592]
Wholesale Supply Group Inc. [23457]
Wholesale Supply Group, Inc. Maryville Division [23458]
Wichita Falls Nunn Electrical Supply [9594]
Willcox and Gibbs Inc. Consolidated Electric Supply [9595]
Wille Electric Supply Co. [9596]
Williams Investigation & SEC [5815]
Williams Supply Inc. [9597]
Wilson Electric Supply Co. [9599]
Wilson's Appliance Co.; Charlie [15374]
Windsor Distributors Co. [9600]
Wire Supplies Inc. [9601]
Wittock Supply Co. [23465]
Wolberg Electrical Supply Company Inc. [9603]
Wolff Brothers Supply Inc. [23466]
Woodlawn Hardware [17287]
Woolley Inc.; L.A. [9604]
World Buying Service Inc. [9605]
World Traders (USA) Inc. [9607]
Xport Port Authority Trading Co. [4559]

Yale Electric Supply Company Inc. [9615]
Yates & Bird [19715]
Yates and Bird [9618]
Yaun Company Inc. [23468]
York Electrical Supply Co. [9619]
Zack Electronics Inc. [9620]
Zeller Electric Inc. [3453]
Zentao Corp. [9622]
Zero 88 Inc. [9623]
Zeta Associates Inc. [9624]
Znyx Corp. [9628]
Zytronics Inc. [9629]

SIC 5064 — Electrical Appliances— Television & Radio

2-Way Radio Communications Engineering [5496]
A-1 Janitorial Supply & Equipment [14984]
A-1 Telecom Inc. [14985]
A and A International Corp. [25052]
A-Air Conditioning Contractor [14986]
A and L Distributing Co. [8257]
A & V TapeHandlers, Inc. [25053]
AAA Distributors Inc. [20763]
AAA Distributors Inc. [14988]
AAAA World Import Export Inc. [25054]
AARP Inc. [8258]
AAT Communications Systems Corp. [25055]
AAT Communications Systems Corp. [14989]
AB Wholesale Co. [13521]
ABC International Traders Inc. [26379]
Absolute Appliance Distributors Inc. [14990]
Accardos Appliance Parts & Services [14991]
Ace Appliances Inc. [14992]
ADI Jacksonville [14993]
Advance Refrigeration Co. [14994]
AEI Electronic Parts [8277]
AIMS Multimedia [14995]
Alaron Inc. [25060]
Alaska Housewares Inc. [14996]
Albert Trading Co. [14997]
Algert Company, Inc. [14998]
All Brand Appliance Parts Inc. [14999]
All Brand Appliance Parts of Pennsylvania [15000]
Allegheny Electronics Inc. [25061]
Allen Appliance Distributors [15001]
Allied Electronics [8301]
Allied Telecommunications Inc. [15002]
Allison-Erwin Co. [5907]
Allstate/GES Appliance Inc. [15003]
Allyn International Corp. [15004]
Alpha Video & Electronics Co. [25064]
Alpine Electronics of America Inc. [25065]
Altron International [25066]
Altron International [15005]
Amarillo Hardware Co. [13555]
Amateur Electronics Supply [25067]
Amco-McLean Corp. [25068]
Amco-McLean Corp. [15007]
American Electronics Supply, Inc. [25069]
American International Exports [15009]
American Sewing Machine Distributors [15010]
Americo Wholesale Plumbing Supply Co. [23064]
The Amerling Co. [25073]
Amway Corp. [8350]
Amway Global Inc. [25074]
Anaheim Manufacturing Co. [15011]
Anaheim Marketing International [15012]
Antenna Farms Inc. [25075]
API Appliance Parts Inc. [15015]
Appliance Distributors Unlimited [15017]
Appliance Parts Center Inc. [25077]
Appliance Parts Co. [15020]
Appliance Parts Co. Inc. [15021]
Appliance Parts Distributors Inc. [15022]
Appliance Parts Distributors Inc. [15023]
Appliance Parts Inc. [15024]
Appliance Parts Inc. [15025]
Appliance Parts Inc. [25078]
Appliance Parts Inc. [15026]
Appliance Parts & Supply Co. [15028]
Appliance Parts Warehouse Inc. [15029]

Appliance Recycling Centers of America Inc. [15030]
Appliance Service Center Inc. [25079]
Applied Video Systems Inc. [25080]
Ariz Coin & Commercial Lndry Eq. [8373]
Arizona Appliance Parts [15031]
Arizona Coin & Commercial Laundry Equipment [15032]
Arizona Wholesale Supply Co. [15033]
Arrow-Cold Control Appliance Parts Co. [15035]
Arrowhead Supply Inc. [15036]
ARS Electronics [25083]
Artec Distributing Inc. [25084]
Ashland Electric Company Inc. [8383]
Associated Sales [15037]
AT Products Inc. [5519]
Atlantic Communications Inc. [25085]
Atlantic Communications Inc. [15039]
Audio Supply Co. [25087]
Audio-Technica U.S., Inc. [25089]
Audio-Video Corp. [25090]
Audiovox Corp. [5523]
Audiovox Specialized Applications LLC [8395]
Auto Chlor System Inc. [15040]
Auto Radio Specialists [25091]
AVAC Corp. [15041]
AVES Audio Visual Systems Inc. [25093]
Avon Appliance & Electric Co. Inc. [15042]
Ayre Acoustics Inc. [15043]
B & B Appliance Parts of Mobile [15044]
B J's Wholesale Club Inc. [13029]
Ball Auto Tech Inc. [8412]
Ballanda Corp. [17327]
Bana Parts Inc. [25096]
Baptist Electronics Supply Company Inc. [8413]
Barnsley-Weis Associates Inc. [15045]
Bay Microfilm Inc. [25098]
BB & W Electronics [8424]
Beach Sales Inc. [25099]
Beam of Denver Inc. [15046]
Bel Air Distributors [25100]
Bell Parts Supply Inc. [15048]
Bennies Warehouse Distribution Center [15049]
Bernina of America Inc. [15051]
Best Buy Co. Inc. [25101]
BGW Systems Inc. [25102]
Birnberg & Sons Inc. [15052]
BJ Distributing [25104]
Blodgett Supply Co. Inc. [15054]
Blue Birds International Corp. [25105]
Bluestem Farm and Ranch Supply Inc. [324]
Bondy Export Corp. [8454]
Bose Corp. [15055]
Boyd Distributing Co. Inc. [15056]
Bray and Scarff Inc. [25107]
Brey Appliance Parts Inc. [15057]
The Brightman Co. [15059]
Broich Enterprises Inc. [15060]
Brooke Distributors Inc. [25109]
Brost International Trading Co. [24271]
Brother International Corp. [20858]
Brown Appliance Parts Co. Inc. [15061]
Brown Distributing Co. Inc. [13046]
Brown-Rogers-Dixson Co. [15062]
Buckeye Vacuum Cleaner Supply Co. Inc. [15063]
Builder Contract Sales Inc. [15064]
Builderway Inc. [15065]
Burnstine's Distributing Corp. [2400]
Bursma Electronic Distributing Inc. [25113]
Bursma Electronic Distributing Inc. [8478]
C and L Supply Inc. [15069]
Cain and Bultman Co. [8482]
Cain and Bultman Inc. [15070]
Caloric Corp. [15071]
Camsco Wholesalers Inc. [15072]
Cange & Associates International [15073]
Canton China and Equipment Co. [24088]
Capitol Communications [25118]
Capitol Sales Company Inc. [25120]
Capitol Sales Company Inc. [15074]
Capresso Inc. [24090]
Car Tape Distributors Inc. [25121]
Carbone of America [5548]
Caribiner International [25122]
Caribiner International [15075]
Carolina C & E, Inc. [25124]

Carolina C and E Inc. [15076]
Carswell Distributing Co. [15077]
Casele Associates Inc. [25125]
Cash & Carry Electronics Inc. [25126]
Cash; Jeff [15078]
Cashwell Appliance Parts Inc. [15079]
Castle Distributors Inc. [15080]
Catskill Electronics [25128]
Central Air Conditioning Distributors Inc. [14374]
Central Audio Visual Equipment Inc. [22843]
Central Distributing Co. [15081]
Central Equipment Distributing Co. [14376]
Central Radio and TV Inc. [25131]
Central Vac International [4595]
Charter Distributing Inc. [15083]
Choquette and Company Inc. [15084]
City Animation Co. [25137]
Clarks Distributing Co. [14384]
Clarkson Co. Inc.; R.J. [15085]
Classic Beauty Supply and Service Center [14065]
Climatic Corp. [14387]
Cloud Brothers Inc. [15086]
Clydes Corner Electronics [25140]
Coastline Parts Co. [15088]
Colorado Prime Foods [15090]
Columbia Audio-Video Inc. [8548]
Commercial Dishwashers [15091]
Commercial Washer Dryer Sales Co. [15092]
Compol Inc. [25145]
Comtel Corp. [6143]
Conair Corp.oration [15093]
Connecticut Appliance & Fireplace Distributors, LLC [15094]
Connor and Associates Inc. [13333]
Continental Marketing [8575]
Contract Appliance Sales Inc. [25148]
Contract Kitchen Distributors [15095]
Cook Brothers Inc. [15096]
Cook's Mart Ltd. [15454]
Costco Wholesale [10851]
Cramer Co. Inc. [15097]
Creative Technologies Corp. [15098]
Cruse Communication Co. [15100]
Cunningham Distributing Inc. [25615]
Custom Audio [25150]
Custom Audio Distributors Inc. [25151]
Custom Design Security & Sound [24530]
Custom Radio Corp. [15102]
Custom Sound of Augusta Inc. [25153]
D and H Distributing Co. [15103]
D & L Appliance Parts Company, Inc. [15104]
Dalis, Inc.; H.L. [5585]
DaLite Screen Co. [25155]
D.A.S. Distributors, Inc. [8608]
Davis Co.; J.W. [25157]
Davis Supply Co. [23134]
Davitt and Hanser Music Co. [15105]
Dawdys Inc. [25160]
Dayton Appliance Parts Co. [15106]
Dean Associates Inc.; Richard [25163]
Deering Banjo Co. [15107]
Defreeze Corp. [14413]
D'ELIA Associates of Connecticut Inc. [15108]
DeLonghi America Inc. [15109]
Depco Inc. [25166]
Derby Industries Inc. [15110]
Dey Distributing [14419]
Discount Store [25167]
Distribution Holdings Inc. [15111]
Diversified Distributors [15112]
D.J.H. Inc. [15477]
Donico & Associates; J.P. [18778]
Douglas/Quikut [15114]
Drillot Corporation [15115]
Drug Guild Distributors Inc. [15116]
DSI Distributing, Inc. [15117]
Dukes Car Stereo Inc. [5598]
Durkopp Adler America Inc. [15968]
Eagle Distributors Inc. [25170]
Eastern Electric [15118]
El Rancho Laundry Equipment [15119]
Elberfeld Company Inc. [13104]
Electric Sales & Service of Savannah [25176]
Electrical Distributing Inc. [25177]
Electro Brand Inc. [25178]
Electronic Contracting Co. [8688]

Electronic Supply [15121]
Electronics 21 Inc. [25180]
Elna Inc. [26028]
Elson Import Export; Walter [4935]
Emerson Radio Corp. [8701]
EMT Electronics Inc. [8705]
Enright Co.; J.R. [25182]
European Crafts/USA [15122]
Evansville Appliance Parts [15123]
Export of International Appliances [15124]
Ezcony Interamerica Inc. [8725]
Faella Co. Inc.; Don [25189]
Fallah Enterprises [13354]
Falmouth Supply Co. Inc. [25190]
Familian Corp. [15125]
Fantec Inc. [15126]
Fiedler; John W. [15127]
Filco Inc. [15128]
Finn Distributing Co. Inc. [15497]
Fleming Associates Inc.; J.S. [14450]
Flower Films and Video [15129]
Folkcraft Instruments [15130]
Food Equipment Specialists [24124]
Ford Audio-Video Systems Inc. [25194]
Ford and Garland Inc. [25195]
Fox Appliance Parts of Atlanta Inc. [15131]
Fox Appliance Parts of Augusta Inc. [15132]
Fox Appliance Parts of Columbus Inc. [15133]
Fox Appliance Parts of Macon Inc. [15134]
Freed Appliance Distributing [15135]
Freeman's Car Stereo Inc. [25199]
Fretz Corp. [15136]
Fuller Associates Inc.; Arthur [25202]
Funai Corp. [25203]
G & E Parts Center, Inc. [15137]
G & N Distributors Inc. [15140]
Gaggenau USA Corp. [15141]
Gas & Electrical Equipment Co. [25206]
Gas Equipment Distributors [15142]
Gateway Appliance Distributing Co. [15143]
Gemini Ex-Im [15144]
Gemini Sound Products Corp. [25208]
Gene Schick Co. [15145]
Genes Appliance Parts Inc. [15146]
Genesis Technologies Inc. [15147]
Gifford-Brown Inc. [25211]
Glindmeyer Distributors Co. [15148]
Global Access Entertainment Inc. [15149]
Goldberg Company Inc. [15150]
Gotham Sales Co. [25216]
GPX Inc. [8798]
GPX Inc. [15151]
GPX Inc. (St. Louis, Missouri) [25218]
Graham Radio Inc. [25219]
Great American Floor Care Center [15152]
Great Northern Video [25220]
Greer Appliance Parts Inc. [15153]
Gulf Central Corp. [15154]
Gunter Jr. & Associates; Guy T. [15155]
Gyles; Janis [24558]
H-A Distributors Inc. [25222]
Hadco Inc. [15156]
Hale & Associates; Robert [25223]
Hall Electric Supply Co., Inc. (HESCO) [15157]
Hamburg Brothers [15158]
Hamilton Appliance Parts Inc. [15159]
Hammond Electronics [25224]
Hampton-Haddon Marketing Corp. [21025]
Hanessian Mercantile Co. [15160]
Hansful Trading Company Inc. [8828]
Harman Appliance Sales [15161]
Harmony International Corporation [15162]
Harris Appliance Parts Company Inc. [15163]
Hart-Greer Ltd. [15164]
Hartman & Sons Equipment; Lee [25227]
Helen of Troy Ltd. [14124]
Helen of Troy Texas Corp. [14125]
Henderson and Baird Hardware Company Inc. [15165]
Heral Enterprises Inc. [15166]
Herald Wholesalers Inc. [13751]
Hermitage Electric Supply Corp. [15167]
High Country Kitchens [15168]
Hitachi America Ltd. [25233]
Hitachi Home Electronics (America) Inc. Visual Technologies Div. [15169]

Hite Co. [8850]
HMA/International Business Development Ltd. [11442]
Home Entertainment Distributors [25235]
Home & Farm Center Inc. [15170]
Home Safety Products [25236]
The Hoover Co. [15171]
Hosey and Port Sales Corp. [15172]
Howard Enterprises Inc. [5640]
HP Marketing Co. [25240]
Hutchs TV and Appliance [15173]
Ideal Appliance Parts Inc. [15174]
Incentive Associates Inc. [15539]
Independent Distribution Services Inc. [15175]
Industrial Video Systems Inc. [25242]
Ingram Entertainment [25246]
Inter-Act Inc. [25251]
International Piecework Controls Co. [15177]
Interstate Electronics, Inc. [25254]
Intertrade, Inc. [13147]
Island Instruments, Inc. [25255]
Ivanco Inc. [5652]
Jack Spratt Woodwind Shop [15178]
Jacoby Appliance Parts [15179]
Jade Electronics Distributors [25257]
Jansco Marketing Inc. [26541]
Jarrell Distributors Inc. [15180]
Jayark Corp. [25260]
JCA Technology Group, A TVC Company [15181]
Jetmore Distributing [15182]
Johnson RDO Communications Co. [8917]
K-Tel International (USA) Inc. [15547]
Kaman Music Corp. Los Angeles [15183]
Kash 'N Gold Ltd. [5657]
Kaufman Co. Inc.; Hal [22868]
Kaufman Supply [15184]
Kellco & Associates [15185]
Kennewick Industry & Electric Supply [8938]
Kennewick Industry and Electric Supply [15186]
Kent Electronics Inc. [25268]
Kenwood USA Corp. [25270]
Key Boston Inc. [15187]
KII, Inc. [23236]
King Kitchens Inc. [15188]
Kitchen Distributors Maryland [15189]
Kitcor Corp. [24158]
Klam International [7561]
Klaus Companies [15190]
KLH Research and Development Corp. [15191]
Knogo North America Inc. [15192]
KSC Industries Inc. [15193]
Kultur, White Star, Duke International Films Ltd. Inc. [15194]
L & D Appliance Corp. [15195]
L and W Enterprises Inc. [15196]
Lafayette Auto Electric [8964]
Lafayette Electronics Supply Inc. [15197]
Langlois Stores Inc. [15559]
Lasonic Electronics Corp. [15199]
Lavery Appliance Co.; S.K. [15200]
Ledgerwood-Herwig Associates Ltd. [15202]
Lehrhoff and Company Inc.; I. [15203]
Lello Appliances Corp. [15204]
Leonard Refrigeration & Heating Sales & Service [14523]
L.E.S. Distributing [25282]
LESCO Distributing [5662]
Liberty Distributors Inc. [15205]
Lincoln Part Supply Inc. [8992]
Lite Source Inc. [13165]
Lowes Home Centers Inc. [25290]
LU International [16250]
Luckenbach and Johnson Inc. [9008]
Madison Electric Co. [25296]
Madison Electric Inc. [15207]
Madrigal Audio Laboratories Inc. [25297]
Magna Communications Inc. [5664]
Magnamusic Distributors Inc. [15208]
MagneTek, Inc. [9018]
Major Appliances Inc. [24176]
Manchester Wholesale Supply Inc. [23249]
Mann U.V. Technology, Inc. [25724]
Manu Reps Inc. [25302]
Manufacturing Distributors [15209]
Marcone Appliance Parts [15210]
Marcone Appliance Parts Center [15212]

Marcone Appliance Parts Center Inc. [15213]
Marsch Enterprises [25305]
Marta Cooperative of America [15214]
Martin Industries Inc. [15215]
Masda Corp. New England [15217]
May & Company Inc. [15218]
May Company Inc.; W.L. [15219]
Maytag Corp. [15221]
McAuliffe Inc.; Howard [25308]
McCombs Supply Co. [15222]
McCombs Supply Company Inc. [15223]
McDaniels Sales Co. [15224]
McPhails Inc. [15225]
Meares & Son Inc.; Ellis [15226]
Mega Hertz [25310]
Melan International Trading [9064]
Melrose Appliance Inc. [25312]
Memtek Products/Memorex Audio, Video, CDR's, & Computer Peripherals [25313]
Merchandise International [9066]
Merit Marketing Inc. [5185]
Metro Builders Supply Inc. [15227]
MGA Entertainment [26575]
Michael Supply Company Inc. [15228]
Microwave Oven Company of Oregon [25314]
Mid-America Appliance Center [25315]
Mid-Atlantic Marketing Inc. [25316]
Mid Pac Lumber [23265]
Mid-South Appliance Parts Inc. [15229]
Mid South Marketing Inc. [25318]
Middle Tennessee Utility District [15230]
Midsouth Electric Corp. [25321]
Midwest Electric Inc. [15231]
Midwest Sales and Service Inc. [25323]
Midwest Sales and Service Inc. [15232]
Midwest Visual Equipment Co. [25324]
Millstone Service Div. [11901]
Miracle Exclusives, Inc. [15234]
MITO Corp. [25328]
MITO Corp. [15235]
Mitsubishi Electronics America Inc. [25329]
MKS Industries Inc. [7731]
MMRF Inc. [25236]
Modern Mass Media Inc. [15237]
Modern Supply Company Inc. [15238]
Mohawk Marketing Corp. [25332]
Molay Supply Inc. [15239]
Monroe Distributing Co. [25334]
Montero International, Inc. [6528]
Moore Co. [25336]
MOORE Co. [15240]
Moore Discount Inc. [15241]
Moore; Robert J. [25337]
Moore Sales Co. [25338]
Motivaction Inc. [25340]
Moulinex Appliances Inc. [15242]
Mountain Marketing [25341]
Murray Lighting Inc. [15243]
Music Industries Inc. [15244]
Nakamichi America Corp. [25352]
National Electronic Service Co. [25354]
Nelco Sewing Machine Sales Corp. [15246]
Nelson Wholesale Corp. [24191]
New Resource Inc. [25356]
New Resource Inc. [15247]
NewSound L.L.C. [15248]
Newton Appliance Sales & Service [15249]
Newtown Appliance Sales & Services [15250]
Noble Distributors Inc. [25360]
Nomura America Corp. [26157]
Nor-Mon Distributing Inc. [15252]
North Pacific Supply Co. Inc. [25361]
North Star Sales Co. [15253]
The Northeast Group, Inc. [25362]
Northeast Group Inc. [15254]
Northern Plains Distributing [25363]
Northern Video Systems Inc. [25364]
Northwest Wholesale Distributors [15255]
Nunn Electric Supply Corp. [9149]
Oakton Distributors Inc. [15256]
O'Donnell Co. Inc.; Roy J. [15257]
Ohio Kitchen and Bath [15601]
OK Distributing Company Inc. [15258]
Olsen Audio Group Inc. [15259]
On Spot Janitor Supplies & Repair [4681]
One Valley Bank of Huntington [25368]

Onkyo USA Corp. [25369]
Options International Inc. [25370]
Oregon Equipment Co. Inc. [15260]
Original Marketing Concepts Ltd. [25371]
Owens Electric Supply Companies Inc. [9164]
Owens Electric Supply Inc. [25372]
Owens Electric Supply Inc. [15261]
Pacific Combustion Engineering Inc. [24413]
Pacific Intertrade Corporation [15262]
Palmieri Associates [9177]
Palmieri Associates [15263]
Panasonic Broadcast and Television Systems Co. [15264]
Paramount Sales Co. [14188]
Park Supply Co. Inc. [15265]
Partners 4 Design Inc. [15266]
Patco Inc. [14633]
PD60 Distributors Inc. [15615]
Pearsol Appliance Company [15267]
Pearsol's Parts Center [15268]
Pelican Plumbing Supply Inc. [15269]
Pells Radio Center [15270]
Pennsylvania Sewing Machine Co. [15271]
Performance-Plus Distributing [25378]
Persona Technologies Inc. [9191]
PHD, Inc. [15272]
Phi Technologies Inc. [25381]
Pioneer Electronics (USA) Inc. [15273]
Pioneer Music Company Inc. [9208]
Pioneer North America Inc. [25383]
Piraeus International [25384]
Pollack Enterprises Inc.; Morton [15275]
Polyconcept USA, Inc. [9217]
Postema Sales Co. Inc. [15276]
Potter Distributing Inc. [15277]
Pro-Mark Corp. [15280]
Producers Tape Service-All Media [9238]
Proton Corp. [25392]
Prudential Builders Center [15281]
Prudential Distributors Inc. [15282]
Puget Sound Audio [25393]
Puget Sound Instrument Co. Inc. [25394]
QMI Inc. [25396]
Quality Sew & Vac [15626]
Quality Sew and Vac [25285]
Quality Sound Enterprise Inc. [25399]
R & R CB Distributors Inc. [25400]
R and R Electronic Supply Co. [9254]
R & R Mill Company [15287]
Radio City Automotive [25401]
Radio City Inc. [25402]
Radio Communications Co. [25403]
Radio Communications Company Inc. [5731]
RadioShack Corp. [9259]
Rae Mel Sales Inc. [25404]
Rangel Distributing Co. [5733]
Raub Radio and Television Co. [25406]
Rayco Car Electronics Inc. [25407]
RCI Custom Products [25408]
Re-Mark Co. [25409]
Recreational Sports and Imports Inc. [25412]
Reddish Supply; Phil [25414]
Refrigeration Supply Inc. [13217]
Reiser and Co.; Robert [15289]
Renkus-Heinz Inc. [25416]
Rep Associates Inc. [25290]
Riccar America Co. [15291]
Richlund Enterprises [15292]
Rickwood Radio Service of Tennessee [25418]
Ricom Electronics Ltd. [6690]
Roldan Products Corp. [15293]
Roma Enterprises [25421]
Rose's Stores Inc. [5320]
Roth Distributing Co. [15294]
Roth Distributing Co. [15295]
Rott-Keller Supply Co. [3175]
Rowenta Inc. [15296]
Royal Radio Sales & Service [25422]
RPC Video Inc. [25423]
Rude Corp.; R.T. [15297]
Russ Doughten Films Inc. [15298]
Ryan and Co.; Connor F. [25424]
S and G Trading Co. [26643]
S & S Appliance Service Co. [15299]
S/S Electronics Inc. [15300]
Sadco Inc. [15301]

St. Paul Appliance Center Inc. [15302]
Sakata U.S.A. Corp. [9332]
Samsung Electronics America Inc. [25426]
Santa Fe Communications [25429]
Sanyo Sales and Supply (USA) Corp. [25430]
Sarco Inc. [24215]
Sarco Inc. [15303]
Schawbel Corp. [14230]
Schillers Photo Graphics [22903]
Schilling TV Inc. [25432]
Scholl Oil & Transport Co. [25433]
Scholl Oil and Transport Co. [15304]
Schwarz Service Co. [15306]
SCMS Inc. [9345]
Seaway Importing Co. [25435]
Segal, Alpert, McPherson & Associates [25436]
Sentry Technology Corp. [24635]
Servall Co. [15308]
Servall Co. [15309]
Servco Pacific Inc. [3205]
Sewing Center Supply Co. [15310]
S.G. & B. Inc. [13238]
Sharp Wholesale Corp. [15311]
Sherwood Corp. (La Mirada, California) [25440]
Shiflet and Dickson Inc. [25441]
Siano Appliance Distributors Inc. [15312]
Siemens Energy and Automation Inc. [9368]
Sigma Electronics Inc. [5755]
Singer Sewing Co. [15313]
Singer Sewing Inc. [25444]
SJA Industries Inc. [15314]
Small Appliance Repair Inc. [15315]
Smeed Communication Services [15316]
Smith Associates; Bernie [25445]
Smith and Co.; R.W. [25820]
Smith Crown Co. [25446]
Smith Kitchen Specialties; W.H. [15317]
SMP Enterprises Inc. [26656]
Snyder Wholesale Tire Co. [25447]
Solar Pacific Inc. [25822]
Solinger and Associates [15318]
Solis America Inc. [14242]
Sony Corp. Business and Professional Products
    Group [25448]
Sound Advice [25450]
Sound Around Inc. [25451]
Sound Around Inc. [15319]
Sound Com Corp. [25452]
Southern Distributing [25455]
Southern Electronics Supply, Inc. [9388]
Southern States Industrial Sales [15320]
Sparkomatic Corp. [25457]
Spectrum [25460]
Sprawls Service and Sound [25461]
SR Distributing [25463]
Standard Appliance Parts Corporation [15321]
Starbuck Sprague Co. [9410]
Steves Electronics Service [25466]
Sun Electrical Appliance Sales & Service [15322]
Sundin Rand; Gloria [13252]
Sunkyong America Inc. [15323]
Sunseri's Inc. [15324]
Superior Appliance Service Co. [15326]
Swanson Sales and Service [21309]
Tacony Corp. [15328]
Tadiran Electronic Industries Inc. [15329]
Tampa Appliance Parts Corp. [15330]
Target Appliances [15331]
Target Distributing Co. [25471]
Target Distributing Co. [15332]
Target Premiums Inc. [15333]
Tarheel Communications [25472]
Tatung Company of America Inc. [6789]
Tatung Company of America Inc. Marietta
    Div. [25473]
TDI Air Conditioning Appliances [15334]
TD's Radio & TV [14713]
TEAC America Inc. Data Storage Products
    Div. [15335]
Texas Sales Co. [15336]
Thermo King Atlanta Inc. [15337]
Thistle Co.; R.F. [25477]
TIC Industries Co. [15338]
Tilia, Inc. [16564]
Time Systems Inc. [9489]
Toner Cable Equipment Inc. [15339]

Tonnies Company Inc.; David F. [25481]
Toshiba America Consumer Products Inc. [9495]
Total Recall Corp. [24643]
ToteVision [5795]
TR Systems [15340]
Tradex Corporation [14734]
Transoceanic Trade, Inc. [22911]
Trek Corp. [15341]
Trevarrow Inc. [15342]
Trevose Electronics Inc. [25484]
Tribles of Maryland Inc. [15343]
Troxell Communications Inc. [25486]
Turner Appliance [15344]
Turner Sherwood Corp. [15345]
TVC Technology Group [25487]
Twin City Supply Company [15346]
UETA Inc. [26362]
Ultrasource Inc. [25851]
Uni Distribution Co. [25489]
Uni Distribution Co. [15347]
United Export Import, Inc. [20740]
United Sewing Machine Distributing [15348]
U.S. Recording Co. [25491]
Universal Service and Supply [15349]
Universal Sewing Supply Inc. [15350]
V & V Appliance Parts Inc. [15351]
Vacuum Center Central Michigan [15352]
Valdez [15353]
Valley Appliance Parts Co. [15354]
Valley Sales Company Inc. [25497]
Valley Sales Company Inc. [15355]
Vanderheyden Distributing Inc. [15356]
Veazey Suppliers Inc. [25499]
Vehicle Vibres Inc. [25500]
Vermont Hardware Company Inc. [25501]
Video Aided Instruction Inc. [15357]
Video Hi-Teck Inc. [25505]
Video Sentry Corp. [24658]
Vihon Associates [15358]
Viking Distributing Company Inc. [15359]
Viking Sewing Machines Inc. [26241]
Village Electronics [25508]
Vita-Mix Corp. [15361]
Voorhees Company Inc.; The Bill [14756]
VWS Inc. [25511]
Wagner Appliance Parts Inc. [15362]
Wal-Mart Stores Inc. [15700]
Walker Vacuum Supply [15363]
Warehouse Home Furnishing Distributors
    Inc. [13274]
Warner's Parts Co.; Eddie [25514]
Warren Distributing Corp. [15364]
Warren Supply Co. [9558]
Washington Electric Membership
    Cooperative [15366]
Water-Vac Distributors-Rainbow [15367]
Wayne Distributing Inc. [9562]
WCI International Co. [15368]
Webbs Appliance Service Ctr. [25518]
Welbilt Corp. [15369]
Western Cascade Equipment Co. [15370]
White Sewing Machine Co. [15371]
Wholesale Builder Supply Inc. [15372]
Wholesale Electronic Supply Inc. [9592]
Wholesale House [25524]
Wholesale Supply Group, Inc. Maryville
    Division [23458]
Willar Corp. [14767]
Williams Distributing Co. [15373]
Wilson Audio Sales [25525]
Wilson's Appliance Co.; Charlie [15374]
Wishing Well Video Distributing Co. [15375]
W.L. Roberts Inc. [15376]
Wonderful World of Imports [15377]
Wood Products Inc.; Stanley [25528]
Woodson & Bozeman Inc. [25529]
Woodson and Bozeman Inc. [15378]
Woolworth Corp. [15379]
World Buying Service Inc. [9605]
World Source Trading Inc. [25531]
World Wide Pictures Inc. [15380]
Wren Electronics, Inc. [9610]
Wright and Wilhelmy Co. [15381]
Xcell International Corp. [15382]
Yaesu U.S.A. Inc. [25534]
Zamoiski Company Inc. [15383]

ZEXEL USA Corp. [3454]

SIC 5065 — Electronic Parts & Equipment Nec

1st Source Parts Center [14983]
21st Century Telecom Group [8256]
A and A Connections Inc. [5497]
A & A Office Systems Inc. [5498]
AAAA World Import Export Inc. [25054]
AARP Inc. [8258]
AAT Communications Systems Corp. [25055]
Abacon Electronics Corp. [8259]
ABC Cellular Corp. [5499]
Academi-Text Medical Wholesalers [3460]
Accurate Office Machines Inc. [20769]
ACF Components and Fasteners, Inc. [8263]
Ack Electronics [8264]
Ackerman Electrical Supply Co. [8265]
ACL Inc. [8266]
Acro Electronics Corp. [8268]
ACT Teleconferencing Inc. [5500]
Action Communications Inc. [8270]
Action Page Inc. [5501]
ADEMCO/ADI [24480]
ADI [24484]
Advance Telecommunication Inc. [5502]
AdvanTel Inc. [5503]
Advent Electronics Inc. [8275]
Adventures Unlimited Press [3474]
AEI Electronic Parts [8277]
Affiliated Holdings Inc. [14303]
AGM Electronics Inc. [8282]
Ahrens and McCarron Inc. [23054]
Air Comm Corp. [5504]
Air Electro Inc. [8283]
Air Mobile Systems [5505]
Airline Hydraulics Corp. [16682]
Airtechnics Inc. [8284]
Airtechnics Inc. [8285]
Aiwa America Inc. [25059]
Alaron Inc. [25060]
Alaska Instrument Company Inc. [24308]
Alaska Quality Control Services [8287]
All American Semiconductor Inc. [8291]
All Spec Static Control Inc. [8296]
All Systems Inc. [8297]
Allcomm of Wisconsin [5506]
Allegheny Electronics Inc. [25061]
Allen Avionics, Inc. [8298]
Allen Supply Company, Inc.; William B. [24503]
Allied Electronics [8300]
Allied Electronics [8301]
Allied Electronics [8302]
Allied Electronics [8305]
Allied Electronics [8306]
Allied Electronics [8308]
Allied Electronics [8309]
Allied Electronics [8310]
Allied Electronics [8311]
Allied Electronics [8312]
Allied Electronics [8313]
Allied Electronics [8314]
Allied Electronics [8315]
Allied Electronics [8316]
Allied Electronics [8317]
Allied Electronics [8318]
Allied Electronics [8319]
Allied Electronics [8320]
Allied Electronics [8321]
Allied Electronics [8322]
Allied Electronics [8323]
Allied Electronics [8324]
Allied Electronics [8325]
Allied Electronics [8326]
Allied Electronics Corp. [8327]
Allied Electronics, Inc. [8328]
Allied-National Inc. [8329]
Allied Sound Inc. [25062]
Allstar Systems Inc. [5908]
ALLTEL Corp. [5507]
ALLTEL Supply Inc. [5508]
Ally Press [3493]

Alpha Communications Inc. [5509]
Alpha-Omega Sales Corp. [8330]
Alpha Source Inc. [8331]
Alpine Supply [13553]
Altex-Mar Electronics Inc. [8333]
Amateur Electronics Supply [5510]
Amateur Electronics Supply [8335]
Amcamex Electronics Corp. [5511]
America II Electronics [8336]
American Appliance Parts Co. Inc. [15008]
American Communications Co. [8337]
American Copy Inc. [20792]
American ELTEC Inc. [5929]
American and International Telephone Inc. [5512]
American Telephone Systems [5513]
American Telephone Technology [5514]
American Terminal Supply Company, Inc. [25071]
Ameritrend Corp. [20800]
Ametron [8345]
Amex Inc. [5937]
Amidon Associates Inc. [8347]
Amkor Technology [8348]
Amtel Communications [5515]
Anchor Commerce Trading Corp. [6973]
Ancient Future Music [3508]
Anderson and Associates Inc. [8351]
The Anderson Group [19781]
Ando Corp. Measuring Instruments Div. [24313]
Anritsu Co. [24314]
Antennas America Inc. [8360]
Antex Incorporated [8361]
Antronnix Antenna Co. Inc. [8362]
Apco Inc. [15013]
Apco Inc. [15014]
API Appliance Parts Inc. [15015]
Apon Record Company, Inc. [25076]
Appliance Dealer Supply Co. [15016]
Appliance Parts Center Inc. [15018]
Appliance Parts Center Inc. [25077]
Appliance Parts Center Inc. [8364]
Appliance Parts Co. Inc. [15021]
Appliance Parts Distributors Inc. [15022]
Appliance Parts Distributors Inc. [15023]
Appliance Parts of Lake Charles [15027]
Appliance Service Center Inc. [25079]
Applied Industrial Technologies [5516]
Arcade Electronics Inc. [8368]
Argraph Central [8369]
Argraph Corp. [8370]
Argraph West [8371]
Arista Enterprises Inc. [5960]
Arizona Electrical Prdts Inc. [8375]
Array Microsystems Inc. [8376]
Arrow Electronics Inc. [8377]
Arrow-Kierulff Electronics Group [8378]
ASA Audiovox Specialized Applications [5517]
ASA Audiovox Specialized Applications [8381]
Ascom Timeplex Inc. [8382]
Ashland Electric Company Inc. [8383]
Associated Industries [5518]
Associated Industries [8385]
Astrex Inc. [8387]
Astrokam [8389]
AT Products Inc. [5519]
AT&T Business Markets Group Div. [5520]
ATCOM Inc. [5521]
Atec, Inc. [24318]
ATI Communications [5522]
Atlantic-Pacific Technologies [8390]
Audio Acoustics [25086]
Audio-Tech Inc. [25088]
Audio-Technica U.S. Inc. [8394]
Audiovox Corp. [5523]
AUDISSEY [8396]
Autco [24510]
Auto Comm Engineering Corp. [5524]
Automated Business Systems [20822]
Automatic Controls Co. [8397]
AV Associates Inc. [8399]
Avcom, Inc. [8400]
Avec Electronics Corp. [8401]
AVED Rocky Mountain Inc. [8402]
Avent Inc. [5993]
AVest Inc. [8403]
Axis Electronics Inc. [8405]
Axxis Inc. [25094]

Azimuth Corp. (Orlando, Florida) [54]
Baggs Co.; L R [8409]
BAI Distributors Inc. [8411]
Bar Code Applications Inc. [8414]
Barbey Electronics Corp. [8416]
Barno Electronics Corp. [8417]
Baron Telecommunications [5525]
Batteries Direct [8419]
BB & W Electronics [8424]
Bear Valley Communications Inc. [5526]
Bearings Inc. [16739]
Beaver Creek Cooperative Telephone Co. [8425]
Bell Atlantic Meridian Systems Inc. [5527]
Bell-Haun Systems Inc. [5528]
Bell Microproducts Inc. [8429]
Bellsonics [5529]
BellSouth Communication Systems Inc. [5530]
Bergen Brunswig Corp. [19184]
Bergquist Co. Inc. [8432]
Best Buy Co. Inc. [25101]
Best Data Products Inc. [6014]
Better Telephones and Technology Inc. [5531]
Bevan-Rabell Inc. [8435]
Bext, Inc. [8436]
Beyda & Associates, Inc. [3553]
Beyerdynamic [5532]
BG Electronics Inc. [8437]
BGE and C Inc. [8438]
Bird-X, Inc. [318]
Bird-X Inc. [8440]
Bisco Industries Inc. [8442]
Blackburn and Co.; Don [8443]
BMI Educational Services [3562]
Bolts & Nuts Inc. [8453]
Booklegger [3576]
Booth Inc.; I.D. [23092]
Brady Co. Xymox Div.; W.H. [8460]
Braid Electric Company Inc. [8461]
Brance-Krachy Company Inc. [15840]
Brand-Rex Co. [8463]
Branom Instrument Company Inc. [24326]
Brantley Electrical Supply Inc. [8465]
Brauner Export Co. [8466]
Bridge Publications Inc. [3592]
Brightpoint, Inc. [5533]
Brightpoint Inc. [8467]
Brix Co.; H.G. [5534]
BroadBand Technologies Inc. [8469]
Broadcast Supply Worldwide [5535]
Broadcasters General Store Inc. [5536]
Brooke Distributors Inc. [25109]
Bud Electronic Supply Co. [8475]
Burk Electronics [5537]
Burroughs Communications Inc. [5538]
Bursma Electronic Distributing Inc. [8478]
Burton-Rogers Company Inc. [2403]
Business Communications Inc. [5539]
C & G Electronics Co. [8480]
C and L Communications Inc. [5540]
CableLAN Express Inc. [5541]
California Eastern Laboratories Inc. [8484]
California Micro Devices Inc. [8486]
Call Dynamics Inc. [5542]
Call Management Products Inc. [8487]
Calrad Electronics [8488]
Calus & CEI Distributors Inc. [26435]
Cambridge Communication Inc. (Niles, Illinois) [5543]
Cameo Electronics Company Inc. [8492]
Cameron & Barkley [8493]
Capacitor Associates [8495]
Cape Electronics [5544]
Capital GBS Communications Corp. [5545]
Capital Telephone Co. [5546]
Capitol Electronics Inc. [5547]
Capp Inc. [8499]
Carlberg Warren & Associates [8502]
Carlos Franco [8503]
Carlton-Bates Co. [8504]
Carroll Electronics Inc. [8505]
Cartell Inc. [5549]
Catalyst Telecom [5550]
Cathay International [8508]
CB Distributing [8510]
C.B. Electronic Marketing [8511]
CBLX Holdings Inc. [25129]

CBS Technologies LLC [5551]
CBS WhitCom Technologies Corp. [5552]
CBS WhitCom Technologies Corp. [8512]
CCA Electronics [5553]
Cel Tech Communications Inc. [5554]
CellStar Corp. [5555]
CellStar Ltd. [5556]
Cellular Wholesales [5557]
Central California Electronics Inc. [8516]
Central Radio and TV Inc. [25131]
Central States Electronics [5558]
Century Fasteners Corp. [13627]
Century Wheels Research [8518]
Cerprobe Corp. [8520]
Chicago Communications Service Inc. [5560]
Chip Supply Inc. [6063]
Chip & Wafer Office Automation [20898]
Choquette and Company Inc. [15084]
Christ for the World, Inc. [3634]
Cincinnati Bell Long Distance Inc. [5561]
City Animation Co. [25137]
City Sound [25139]
Claricom Inc. [8529]
Clarion Corporation of America [5562]
Clarion Sales Corp. [2450]
Coast Appliance Parts Co. [15087]
Coastal Electronics Inc. [5564]
Cobra Electronics Corp. [5565]
Cobra Electronics Corp. [8537]
Coil Sales and Manufacturing Co. [5566]
Collins Appliance Parts Inc. [15089]
Collins & Associates; Paul [8542]
Collins Communications Inc. [8543]
Colombian Development Corp. [8544]
Com-Kyl [8549]
Comlink Inc. [6083]
Comlink Inc. (Marlborough, Massachusetts) [5567]
Comlink Inc. (Roseville, California) [8550]
Commerce Overseas Corp. [72]
Commercial Telephone Systems Inc. [5568]
Common Ground Distributors Inc. [3648]
Commtron Corporation [25144]
Communications Electronics Inc. [5569]
Communications Electronics Inc. [5570]
Communications Marketing S.E. Inc. [5571]
Communications Products Inc. [5572]
Communications Wholesale [5573]
Communications World of Costa Mesa [5574]
Communico Inc. [5575]
Communico Inc. Communico Supply Div. [5576]
Compass Technology of Burlington Massachusetts [8553]
Compcom Enterprises Inc. [6089]
Component Resources Inc. [8554]
Components Specialties Inc. [25146]
Compucon Distributors Inc. [6095]
CompuLink Electronic Inc. [8555]
Computer AC [5577]
Computer Sports Systems Inc. [8556]
Computer Support Systems Inc. [8557]
CompuTrend Systems Inc. [6138]
ComTel Industries Inc. [5578]
Conductive Rubber Tech Inc. [6148]
Connor and Associates Inc. [13333]
Consolidated Communications Corp. [8563]
Consolidated Electrical Distributors Inc. [8571]
Contech Instrumentation [8574]
Continental Information Systems Corp. [6154]
Continental Resources Inc. (Bedford, Massachusetts) [6155]
Controls-Instruments-Devices [8577]
Cook Concrete Products Inc. [7213]
Cooper Industries Inc. [6158]
Copier Supply Inc. [5579]
Copy Supply Concepts Inc. [8579]
Coral Sales Co. [8580]
Cordial/Riley Marketing [8581]
Cosmotec Inc. [8583]
Countryman Co.; D.F. [5580]
Coyote Network Systems, Inc. [8584]
CPP-Belwin Inc. [3665]
Creative Joys Inc. [3670]
Creative Source [3671]
CREOS. Technologies LLC [8586]
Crest Audio/Video/Electronics [8593]
Croy & Associates Inc.; Ralph [8595]

Cruse Communication Co. [25149]
CSSI Cellular [5581]
CUI Stack Inc. [8597]
Cumulous Communications Co. [5582]
Curtis Co. [15101]
Curtis TradeGroup Inc. [24274]
Cushing Inc.; T.F. [8598]
Custom Design and Manufacturing [8600]
Custom Phones Inc. [5583]
Custom Supply Inc. [8601]
Cutting Edge Audio Group L.L.C. [25154]
Cyber-Tech Inc. [8603]
Cybernetic Micro Systems Inc. [8604]
D and H Distributing Co. [15103]
D & L Appliance Parts Company, Inc. [15104]
Daewoo International (America) [26011]
Dakota Communications Service [5584]
Dakota Electric Supply Co. [8605]
Dale Electronics Corp. [8606]
Dalis Electronic Supply Inc. [8607]
Dalis, Inc.; H.L. [5585]
Dan Communications Inc.; Lee [5586]
D.A.S. Distributors, Inc. [8608]
Data Forms Inc. [21702]
Data Net Inc. [5587]
Datalink Ready Inc. [8609]
DATAVOX Inc. [5588]
Datel Communications Corp. [5589]
Datex Inc. [8610]
Davies Electric Supply Co. [8612]
Davis Co.; Kriz [8613]
Davis Electric Supply Company Inc.; W.B. [5590]
Dawn Co. [5591]
dB Sound L.P. [25162]
DCE Corp. [6191]
Deanco Inc. [8617]
DEI Inc. [24533]
Delta Materials Inc. [8621]
Delta Products Corp. (Nogales, Arizona) [6197]
Dencor Energy Cost Controls Inc. [8623]
Densons Sound Systems Inc. [25165]
Denton Enterprises Inc. [5592]
Devoe Co.; Leslie M. [8624]
DeVorss & Co. [3691]
DeYoung Mfg Inc. [8626]
Diablo Cellular Phone Stores Inc. [5593]
Dictaphone Corp. [5594]
Digicorp Inc. [5595]
Digitel Corp. [5596]
Diodes Inc. [8627]
Directed Energy Inc. [8628]
Dixie Electronics [5597]
Double O Electronic Distributors [8631]
Dow Electronics Inc. [8633]
Dukes Car Stereo Inc. [5598]
Dupont de Nemours and Co.; E.I. [4376]
Durkin Hayes Publishing [3704]
Dynamic Engineers Inc. [8640]
Eagle Communications Technology [5599]
Eagle Sales Company Inc. [8643]
Easter-Owens Electric Co [8645]
Eastern Data Paper [20977]
Eastern States Components Inc. [8648]
Eclyptic Inc. [19302]
Economy Maintenance Supply Company
  Inc. [8652]
Edcor Electronics [8654]
Educational Industrial Systems Inc. [25172]
EEV, Inc. [18784]
EEV, Inc. [5600]
Elcotel Inc. [5601]
Electrical Appliance Service Co. [15120]
Electrical Materials Inc. [8680]
Electrical Power and Controls Inc. [8681]
Electro-Line Inc. [8683]
Electro Media of Colorado [8685]
Electro Rent Corp. Data Rentals/Sales Div. [8686]
Electroglas Inc. [8687]
Electronic Contracting Co. [8688]
Electronic Equipment Company Inc. [8689]
Electronic Hardware Ltd [8690]
Electronic Hook-up [8691]
Electronic Maintenance Supply Co. [8693]
Electronic Product Tool [15981]
Electronic Security Integration, Inc. [24535]
Electronic Specialties Inc. [8694]

Electronic Surplus Services [8695]
Electronic Tele-Communications Inc. [5602]
Electronic World Sales & Service [25179]
Electronics Supply Co. [8696]
Electrotex Inc. [8698]
Eliza Corporation [5603]
Elmo Semiconductor Corp. [8700]
Emtel Electronics Inc. [8706]
Encore Broadcast Equipment Sales Inc. [5604]
Englewood Electric [8708]
Entrelec Inc. [8710]
Entronic Industries Inc. [8711]
Eoff Electric Co. [8712]
Equipment and Parts Export Inc. [2594]
Ernest Telecom Inc. [5605]
ERS Distributors, Inc. [25184]
Etchomatic Inc. [8716]
ETMA [8717]
European Crafts/USA [25186]
Evans Environmental Corp. [25187]
Ex-Eltronics Inc. [8721]
Excellence Marketing [8724]
Executone of Fort Wayne Inc. [5606]
Executone Systems of St. Paul Inc. [5607]
Export Consultant Service [24358]
Export Consultants Corp. [84]
F & M Electric Supply Co. [8727]
Fadson International Company [14439]
Fairchild Communications Services Co. [5608]
Fairview-AFX Inc. [8730]
Famous Enterprises Inc. [14442]
Famous Telephone Supply Inc. [5609]
Fargo Manufacturing Company Inc. [8731]
Farmstead Telephone Group Inc. [5610]
Fast Track Communications Inc. [5611]
Federated Purchaser Inc. [8735]
FEI America Inc. [6268]
FIC Corp. [8739]
Fidus Instrument Corp. [8740]
Fife Electric Co. [8741]
Filco Inc. [15128]
Financial Commercial Security [24539]
Fine Wire Coil Company [8742]
Firecom Inc. [24550]
First International Trading Company [16863]
First Rep Associates [25191]
Fitzpatrick Electric Supply Co. [8743]
Flannery Co. [3752]
FLEET Specialties Co. [8746]
FM Systems, Inc. [5614]
Fones West [5615]
Forbes & Co. [2637]
Forbes Distributing Co. [8748]
Force Electronics Inc. [8749]
Force Electronics Inc. [8750]
Force Electronics Inc. Texas Div. [8751]
Forcean Inc. [18800]
ForeSight Electronics Inc. [8752]
Forgy Process Instruments Inc. [23172]
Four Star Incentives Inc. [25196]
Franco; Carlos [8755]
Frankel & Company Inc.; Lou [8756]
Franki Sales Co. [8757]
Frezzolini Electronics Inc. [8761]
Friendship Press [3766]
Frigid North Co. [8763]
Frontier Network Systems Inc. [25200]
Frontier Radio Inc. [5616]
Frontier Radio Inc. [8765]
Funai Corp. [25203]
Future Electronics Corporation [8769]
G & E Parts Center, Inc. [15137]
G & N Appliance Parts [15138]
G & N Appliance Parts [15139]
Galco Industrial Electronics [8772]
Gately Communication Company Inc. [5617]
Gately Communications Company Inc. [8773]
Gates Arrow Distributing Inc. [8774]
Gaylon Distributing Inc. [8775]
Gaylord Brothers [25207]
G.D.E., Inc. [8778]
GEM Electronics [8781]
Gemini Sound Products Corp. [25208]
General Communications [5618]
General Tool & Supply Co. [16893]
Generic Systems Inc. [8784]

Genesis Associates Inc. [8785]
Genesis Telecom Inc. [5619]
Gerber Radio Supply Co. [8787]
Glindmeyer Distributors Co. [15148]
Global Fastener Inc. [13724]
Global Telecommunications [5620]
Globe-Hamburg, Import/Export [8790]
Globus Industries [8791]
GMP [5621]
GMP [8792]
Gold Key Electronics Inc. [8794]
Golden Electronics Inc. [8795]
Good Karma Publishing Inc. [3786]
Gopher Electronics Co. [8797]
Gorton Communications Inc. [5622]
Government Electronic Systems Div. [5623]
GPrime Ltd. [25217]
Graham/Davis, Inc. [8799]
Granada Electronics Corp. [8804]
Granada Systems Design Inc. [5624]
Graveline Electronics Inc. [5625]
Graybar Electric Company Inc. [8814]
GRE America Inc. [5626]
Great Lake Distributors [8815]
Great Lakes Electronics Supply Div. [8816]
Greer Appliance Parts Inc. [15153]
Greylock Electronics Distributors [8819]
Group One Ltd. [5627]
GTE Supply [5628]
Haddad Electronic Supply Inc. [5629]
Hall Electric Supply Co., Inc. (HESCO) [15157]
Hall-Mark Electronics Corp. [6323]
Hallmarkets International Ltd. [21023]
Halted Specialties Co. [6326]
Hammond Electronics Inc. [8825]
Harco Electronics Inc. [8829]
Harris Corp. [5630]
Harris Corporation [5631]
Harris Semiconductor [8831]
Harris Supply Company Inc. [16925]
Hartman & Sons Equipment; Lee [25227]
HAVE Inc. [25229]
Hawk Electronics [5632]
Hawk Electronics Inc. [8834]
HB Distributors [5633]
HB Distributors [8836]
HD Communications Inc. [5634]
Hein and Co., Inc.; William S. [3821]
Henry Radio Inc. [25230]
Henry Radio Inc. [8838]
Hi Country Wire and Telephone Ltd. [5635]
Hickory Tech-Enterprise Solutions [5636]
High Frequency Technology Company Inc. [5637]
Hitachi America Ltd. [8846]
Hitachi America Ltd. Electron Tube Div. [8847]
Hite Co. [8850]
Hobgood Electric & Machinery Company,
  Inc. [8851]
Holzberg Communications, Inc. [5638]
Home/Office Communications Supply [5639]
Honeywell Protection Services [24567]
Hooper Electronics Supply [8857]
Houston Wholesale Electronics Inc. [8859]
HP Marketing Co. [25240]
HPG Industries Inc. [7492]
HPS Office Systems [21041]
Hub Material Co. [8863]
Hughes-Peters Inc. [8864]
Hutch & Son Inc. [8867]
Hutton Communications Inc. [5641]
Ico Rally Corp. [8869]
ICS-Executone Telecom Inc. [5642]
Idec [8870]
IDM Satellite Division Inc. [5643]
Inca Corp. [8872]
Ind-Co Cable TV Inc. [8873]
Independent Telephone Network Inc. [5644]
Indus-Tool [8874]
Indus-Tool Inc. [2773]
Industrial Communications Co. [5645]
Industrial Electronic Supply Inc. [8878]
Ingram Entertainment [25246]
Ingram Entertainment [25247]
INOTEK Technologies Corp. [8881]
Inovonics Co [8882]
Insight Electronics Inc. [8883]

Installation Telephone Services Inc. [5646]
Instrument Engineers [24372]
Intec Video Systems Inc. [24572]
Integral Marketing Inc. [8886]
Integrated Sensor Solutions [2789]
Intel Corp. [8887]
Intelligence Technology Corp. [8888]
Intelliphone Inc. [5647]
Inter-Ocean Industries Inc. [5648]
Inter-Tel Integrated Systs Inc. [8889]
Inter-Tel Technologies, Inc. [5649]
Inter-Tel Technologies Inc. [8890]
Interatech [6385]
Intermetra Corp. [8891]
Internal Sound Communications [8892]
International Historic Films Inc. [25253]
International Importers Inc. [8894]
International Telecom Systems Inc. [5650]
International Television Corp. [8895]
Intertrade Ltd. [105]
inTEST Corp. [24375]
Intrade, Inc. [8898]
IPC Information Systems Inc. [8899]
ITBR, Inc. [5651]
ITC Electronics [8901]
ITC International [8902]
Ivanco Inc. [5652]
Jacksonville Sound and Communications
    Inc. [25256]
Jaco Electronics Inc. [8903]
Jacoby Appliance Parts [15179]
Jameco Electronics Inc. [8905]
Jampro Antennas, Inc. [8906]
Janesway Electronic Corp. [8907]
JBL Professional [25261]
J.C. Supply [8910]
Jenne Distributors [5653]
Jensen Tools Inc. [8912]
JEOL U.S.A. Inc. [24378]
Johnson RDO Communications Co. [8917]
Jones & Bartlett Publishers Inc. [3868]
Jones Sales Group [5654]
JPA Electronics Supply Inc. [18530]
JR Electronics and Assembly Inc. [8922]
Just Drop, Inc. [8923]
Just Phones [5655]
JVC Professional Products Co. [8924]
Kanematsu U.S.A. Inc. [22395]
Kanematsu U.S.A. Inc. [26086]
Kansas Communications Inc. [5656]
Kansas Communications Inc. [8927]
Kash 'N Gold Ltd. [5657]
Kass Electronics Distributors Inc. [8929]
Katy Industries Inc. [8931]
KCG Communications Inc. [5658]
KEA Electronics [8932]
Kenkingdon & Associates [8936]
Kern Special Tools Company Inc. [8939]
Key Curriculum Press Inc. [3878]
Key Distribution, Inc. [8940]
Key Electronics Inc. [8941]
Kiesub Corp. [8944]
Knight Electronics Inc. [8952]
KOA Speer Electronics Inc. [8954]
Konex Corp. [8955]
KS. Electronics L.L.C. [8959]
KTS Services Inc. [5659]
L-3 Communications Corp. [5660]
L-com Inc. [8961]
L.A. TRADE [6425]
Labsphere [8962]
Lafayette Auto Electric [8964]
Lafayette Electronics Supply Inc. [8965]
Langstadt Electric Supply Co. [8971]
Larcan TTC [5661]
Latin Trading Corp. [3898]
Laube Technology Inc. [16994]
L.B. Electric Supply Company Inc. [8975]
LCD Systems Corp. [8976]
Leader Instruments Corp. [8977]
The Learning Plant [3902]
Leff Electronics Inc. [8980]
Lemo USA, Inc. [8983]
LESCO Distributing [5662]
Lesco Distributing [8984]
Levy Home Entertainment [3908]

Lewan and Associates Inc. [21107]
Lewis Electronics Co. [8985]
Liconix Industries Inc. [16999]
Light Impressions [25284]
Light Wave Systems [8987]
Linden Tree Children's Records & Books [3915]
Lite-On Inc. [6440]
Littelfuse Inc. [8995]
LKG Industries Inc. [8998]
Lloyd F. McKinney Associates Inc. [25287]
Lodan West Inc. [8999]
Loffler Business Systems Inc. [9001]
Long Inc.; E.W. [25288]
Loppnow & Associates [9002]
Loroman Co. [9003]
Lowrance Electronics Inc. [18551]
Ludlow Telephone Company Inc. [5663]
M & A Sales [9012]
M/M Electronic Products Ltd. [9015]
M-Tron Components Inc. [9016]
Madrigal Audio Laboratories Inc. [25297]
Magtrol Inc. (Tucson, Arizona) [9020]
Main Line Equipment, Inc. [9022]
Main Office Machine Co. [5665]
Majestic Communications [5666]
Mar Electronics Inc. [9027]
Marcom [5667]
Marcone Appliance Parts Center Inc. [15213]
Marinco-AFI [9030]
Marsh Electronics Inc. [9031]
Marshall Industries [9032]
Marshall Industries [9033]
Marshall Industries [9034]
Marshall Industries [9035]
Marshall Industries [9036]
Marshall Industries [9037]
Marshall Industries [9038]
Marshall Industries [9039]
Marshall Industries [9040]
Marshall Industries [9041]
Martindale Electric Co. [9042]
Marubeni America Corp. [26136]
Master International Corp. [9045]
Matthews and Associates Inc. [22996]
Maxell Corporation of America [25306]
Maxtec International Corp. [9049]
May Company Inc.; W.L. [15219]
Maycor Appliance Parts and Service Co. [15220]
Media Concepts Inc. [25309]
Melan International Trading [9064]
Members Service Corp. [5668]
Memphis Communications Corporation [5669]
Menard Electronics Inc. [9065]
Mer Communications Systems Inc. [5670]
Merchandise International [9066]
Mercury Communication Services, Inc. [5671]
Mercury Communication Services, Inc. [5672]
Metalink Corp. [9068]
Metamorphous Advances Product Services [3949]
MetaSystems Design Group Inc. [5673]
Metro/North [9069]
Meunier Electronics Supply Inc. [9071]
Mickler's Floridiana, Inc. [3953]
Micro Comm Inc. [5674]
Micro-Comp Industries Inc. [9073]
Micro Integrated Communications Corp. [6492]
Microchip Technology Inc. [9074]
Microtech-Tel Inc. [5675]
Mid-Plains Communications Systems Inc. [5676]
Mid-South Appliance Parts Inc. [15229]
Midland Suppliers Inc. [9078]
Midwest Telephone Inc. [5677]
Milano Brothers International Corp. [9082]
Milgray Electronics Inc. [9083]
Military Industrial Supply Co. [130]
Millbrook Sales & Service Co. [5678]
Miller-Jackson Co. [5679]
Mills Communication Inc. [9086]
Milwaukee Appliance Parts Company Inc. [15233]
Minnesota Mining & Manufacturing Co. [21147]
Mission Service Supply [25327]
Mix Bookshelf [3964]
MKM Electronic Components Inc. [9091]
MMC Metrology Lab Inc. [24401]
Mobile Communications of Gwinnett [5680]
Modemsplus Inc. [5681]

Modern Mass Media Inc. [25331]
Monfort Electronic Marketing [9093]
Moore-Handley Inc. [11931]
Moore Sales Co. [25338]
Morgan Agency; J.R. [9095]
Morton Supply Inc. [9098]
Mosier Fluid Power of Indiana Inc. [24404]
Motion Pictures Enterprises [25339]
Motor Sound Corp. [5682]
Motorola Communications [5683]
Motorola Inc. Communications and Electronics
    Div. [5684]
Mott Equity Exchange [13839]
Mountain Systems Inc. [6531]
Mouser Electronics [9103]
MRL Industries [9104]
MSIS Semiconductor Inc. [9105]
Mueller Telecommunications Inc. [5685]
Multi Communication Systems [9106]
Multimedia Pacific Inc. [5686]
Murata Erie North America Inc. State College
    Div. [9108]
Music People Inc. [25348]
Music People Inc. [9110]
Muzak [25350]
Muzak [25351]
Nagy Sales Corp.; Tom [24597]
National Electric Supply Co. [15245]
National Electro Sales Corp. [9115]
NEC America Inc. [5687]
NEC America Inc. Data and Video Communications
    Systems Div. [6548]
NEC Business Communication Systems East
    Inc. [5688]
New Concepts Books & Tapes Distributors [3993]
New Jersey Semiconductor Products Inc. [9127]
Newark Electronics Corp. [9129]
Newborn Enterprises Inc. [3999]
Nichol's Farm Supply Inc. [1074]
NKK Electronics America Inc. [25359]
Nokia Inc. [6559]
Nor-Mon Distributing Inc. [15252]
Norstan Inc. [5692]
Nortel Federal Systems [5693]
North Atlantic Communications Inc. [5694]
North Atlantic Communications Inc. [9131]
North Atlantic Engineering Co. [9132]
North Pittsburgh Systems Inc. [5695]
North Valley Distributing [9135]
Northern Electronics Automation [9136]
Northern Electronics Automation [9137]
Northern Telecom Inc. [9139]
Norvac Electronics Inc. [9142]
Norvell Electronics Inc. [9143]
Nova-Net Communications Inc. [9144]
Nova Science Inc. [9145]
Novellus Systems Inc. [9146]
NTE Electronics Inc. [9147]
Nu Horizons Electronics Corp. [9148]
NWCS Inc. [9150]
Office Machine & Furniture Inc. [21183]
Ohio Valley Sound Inc. [9151]
OKI Semiconductor [9153]
Omni Group Inc. [24605]
Operations Technology Inc. [9158]
ORA Electronics [5696]
Organ Literature Foundation [4024]
Orton Industries Inc. [9161]
Outdoor Outfitters of Wisconsin Inc. [24412]
Ouzunoff & Associates [9163]
Owens Electric Supply Companies Inc. [9164]
Owens Electric Supply Inc. [25372]
Pabco Inc. [9166]
Pace Electronics Inc. [9168]
Pacific Dataport Inc. [5697]
Pacific Radio Exchange Inc. [9171]
Pacific Rim Telecommunications Inc. [5698]
Paging Plus Co. [5699]
Paging Products Group [5700]
Paging Wholesalers [5701]
Pair Electronics Inc. [9174]
PairGain Technologies Inc. [9175]
Paladin Press [4036]
Palco Electronics [9176]
Pana Pacific Corp. [5702]
PanAm Sat Corp. [5703]

Panasonic Industrial Co. [9178]
Pargh Company Inc.; B.A. [6591]
Park Corporation [9179]
Path Press Inc. [4043]
Patrick Electric Supply Co. [9180]
Pavarini Business Communications Inc. [5704]
PC Drilling Control Co. [9181]
PCE Inc. [9182]
PCI Rutherford Controls Intl. Corp. [9183]
Peacock Radio & Wilds Computer Services [5705]
Peak Technologies Inc. (Columbia, Maryland) [21207]
Pearson Electronics Inc. [9184]
PEI Genesis [9187]
Peninsula Engineering Group Inc. [5706]
Penn Telecom Inc. [5707]
Penstock [9190]
Perfect Fit Industries, Inc. [16390]
PerTronix Inc. [9192]
Peters Associates; George R. [25379]
Peters-De Laet Inc. [9193]
PhoneAmerica Corp. [5708]
Phoneby [5709]
PHONEXPRESS Inc. [5710]
Photonics Management Corp. [9197]
Phylon Communications Inc. [9198]
Pico Products, Inc. [9201]
Pictorial Histories Publishing Co. [4064]
PicturePhone Direct [5711]
Piher International Corporation [9202]
Pioneer Electronics USA Inc. [9207]
Pioneer Electronics (USA) Inc. [15273]
Pioneer Laser Optical Products Div. [25382]
Pioneer-Standard Electronics Inc. [9209]
Pioneer-Standard Electronics Inc. [6623]
Piper Associates [9210]
Plains Auto Refrigeration [14638]
Platt Hardin Inc. [9213]
Playboy Entertainment Group Inc. [4067]
PLX Technology Inc. [9214]
PM Marketing [9215]
PMH Associates [16404]
Ponto Associates; [9218]
Port Plastics Inc. [23015]
Potomac Adventist Book Center [4075]
Powell Electronics Inc. [9221]
Power & Telephone Supply Company Inc. [5712]
Power and Telephone Supply Company Inc. [5713]
Power & Telephone Supply Company Inc. [5714]
Power & Telephone Supply Company, Inc. [9228]
Power & Telephone Supply Company, Inc. [9229]
Power & Telephone Supply Company, Inc. [5715]
Power & Telephone Supply Company, Inc. [5716]
Power & Telephone Supply Company, Inc. [9230]
Power & Telephone Supply Company, Inc. [5717]
Power & Telephone Supply Company, Inc. [5718]
Powertronics Inc. [9231]
Pratt Audio Visual and Video [9233]
Premier Farnell Corp. [9234]
Premier Industrial Corp. [3117]
Prentke Romich Co. [5719]
Preventive Electrical Maintenance Co. [9235]
PRI Automation Inc. [9236]
Primus Electronics Corp. [5720]
Primus Inc. [23329]
Professional Aviation Associates Inc. [139]
Professional Media Service Corp. [25390]
Professional Telecommunication Services Inc. [5721]
Progressive Concepts Inc. [5722]
Progressive Marketing [9241]
ProMark [9242]
ProNet Inc. [5723]
Protech Communications [5724]
Proton Corp. [25392]
Provident Music Group [4090]
Prudential Builders Center [15281]
Pugh & Associates, Inc.; C.L. [9244]
Pugh & Associates, Inc.; C.L. [9245]
Pugh & Associates, Inc.; C.L. [9246]
Purdy Electronics Corp. [9247]
QSound Ltd. [25397]
Qualiton Imports Ltd. [25398]
Quement Electronics [9250]
R5 Trading International Inc. [19005]

R & L Electronics [5725]
R and R Electronic Supply Co. [9254]
Racom Products Inc. [5726]
Radak Electronics Inc. [5727]
Radar Electric [9255]
Radar, Inc. [9256]
Radar Marine Electronics [18589]
Radcom, Inc. [5728]
Radio Communications Co. [5729]
Radio Communications Co. [5730]
Radio Communications Company Inc. [5731]
Radio Holland U.S.A. [18590]
Radio Research Instrument [9257]
Radio Resources and Services Corp. [5732]
Radio Resources and Services Corp. [9258]
Ram Meter Inc. [9261]
Rancilio Associates [9262]
Randolph, Hale & Matthews [9263]
Randolph & Rice [9264]
Ranger Communications Inc. [5734]
Rasco Supply Company Ltd. [9265]
Rawson and Company Inc. [24422]
Raybro Electric Supplies, Inc., Utility Div. [9266]
Raycomm Telecommunications Inc. [5735]
Rea International Corp. [9268]
RealCom Office Communications Inc. [5736]
Record Technology Inc. [25411]
Reeves Audio Visual Systems Inc. [25415]
Regional Communications Inc. [5738]
Relay Specialties Inc. [9272]
RELM Communications Inc. [5739]
REM Electronics Supply Company Inc. [9275]
Renault Telephone Supplies [5740]
Reptron Electronics Inc. [9276]
Reptron Electronics Inc. [9277]
Republic Group [9279]
Resource Electronics, Inc. [9281]
Resource Electronics Inc. [9282]
Rexel Inc. [9286]
Rexel Inc. (Coral Gables, Florida) [9287]
RF Ltd. Inc. [5741]
RF Power Products Inc. [9291]
RF Technology, Inc. [5742]
Rhapsody Film Inc. [25417]
Rice Electronics LP [5743]
Richardson Electronics, Ltd. [9294]
Richey Electronics Inc. [9295]
River Park, Inc. [25419]
Riverside Communications [5744]
R.J. Marketing, Ltd. [9298]
R.J. Marketing, Ltd. [9299]
RMT Engineering, Inc. [9300]
Rochester Electronics Inc. [9305]
Rochester Instrument Systems Inc. [9306]
RoData Inc. [5745]
Roe-Comm Inc. [9309]
Rogers Electric Supply Co. [9311]
Rohde and Schwarz Inc. [9312]
Romar Industries Inc. [9313]
Ronco Communications and Electronics [9315]
Ronco Communications and Electronics Inc. [5746]
Ronco Specialized Systems Inc. [9317]
Rothenbuhler Engineering [5747]
RP Sales, Inc. [9321]
RSC Electronics Inc. [9322]
R.S.R. Electronics Inc. [9323]
Rude Corp.; R.T. [15297]
Rutherford Controls Int'l. [24619]
RW Electronics Inc. [9325]
R.W. Sales, Inc. [9326]
S & W Distributors Inc. [4133]
Saddle Brook Controls [17152]
Safeguard International, Inc. [24621]
St. Joe Communications Inc. [5748]
St. Louis Music Supply Co. [25425]
Sakata U.S.A. Corp. [9332]
Samson Technologies Inc. [5749]
Sandusco Inc. [9334]
Sat-Pak Inc. [9336]
Saturn Satellite System, Inc. [9337]
Savannah Communications [5750]
Savannah Communications [9338]
Savoir Technology Group Inc. [9339]
Scantek Inc. [24426]
Schelle Cellular Group Inc. [5751]
Schillinger Associates Inc. [9342]

Sci-Rep Inc. [9344]
SCMS Inc. [9345]
Scott Electronics [9346]
SDI Technologies Inc. [9347]
Security Forces Inc. [9350]
SED International, Inc. [6717]
Select Security Inc. [24632]
Semispecialists of America Inc. [9352]
Semispecialists of America Inc. [9353]
Semler Inc.; Arnold A. [5752]
Servall Co. [15307]
Shared Technologies Cellular Inc. [5753]
Sharp Communication [5754]
Sherburn Electronics Corp. [9364]
Si-Tex Marine Electronics Inc. [9366]
Signal Electronic Supply [9370]
Signal Vision, Inc. [9372]
Signalcom Systems Inc. [5756]
Sigo Press/Coventure [4162]
Siliconix Inc. [3222]
Silke Communications Inc. [5757]
Single Point of Contact Inc. [5758]
SKC Communication Products Inc. [9375]
Smarter Security Systems, Inc. [24638]
SMARTEYE Corp. [9378]
SMC Electrical Products Inc. [9379]
Smeed Sound Service Inc. [5759]
Smith Two-Way Radio Inc. [5760]
Sonin Inc. [13927]
Sound Com Corp. [25452]
Sound Engineering [5761]
Sound Limited Inc. [9382]
Sound Marketing Concepts [9383]
Souris River Telephone Mutual Aid Cooperative [5762]
South West New Mexico Communications, Inc. [5763]
Southeastern Communications [9384]
Southern Commercial Machines [25825]
Southern Electronics Supply, Inc. [9388]
Southwest CTI Inc. [6750]
Southwest Electronics Inc. [9390]
SPAP Company LLC [4517]
Sparrow-Star [4179]
Special Promotion Co. [26662]
Specialty Marketing Inc. [25459]
Spectrum Communications Corp. [5765]
Sperry Instruments Inc.; A.W. [24437]
SPOT Image Corp. [5766]
Spring Arbor Distribution Company Inc. [4184]
Sprint North Supply [5767]
SRS International [9398]
ST and T Communications Inc. [5768]
Standard Appliance Parts Corporation [15321]
Standard Electric Time Corp. [24640]
Standard Electronics [9403]
Standard Supply Co. [25464]
Standard Telecommunications Systems Inc. [5769]
Stanis Trading Corp. [19636]
Stark Electronics Inc. [9411]
Stone Electronic [9419]
Storm Products Co. [9422]
Storm Products Company Inc. [9424]
Strata Inc. [5770]
Stratton Electronics Inc. [9426]
Stromberg Sales Company Inc. [9427]
Sumitok America Inc. [3281]
Sunseri's Inc. [15325]
Superior Insulated Wire Corp. [9444]
Superior Manufacturing Co. (Santa Ana, California) [9445]
Supertek [9446]
Surel International, Inc. [9447]
Surge Components Inc. [9448]
SVI Systems Inc. [25470]
Sylvan Ginsbury Ltd. [9452]
T & E Timers Inc. [15327]
T-Electra/TICA of Dallas Inc. [9453]
Tab Electric Supply Inc. [9455]
Tacony Corp. [15328]
Tactical Business Services [6786]
Tadiran Electronic Industries Inc. [15329]
Taitron Components Inc. [9456]
Talays Inc. [9457]
Talcup, Inc. [9458]
Talk-A-Phone Co. [5772]

Talley Communications [5773]
Talley Electronics [5774]
Target Electronics Inc. [9460]
Taser International Inc. [1314]
Tatung Company of America Inc. Marietta
   Div. [25473]
TDK Corporation of America [9461]
TDK Electronics Corp. [25474]
TDK Electronics Corp. [9462]
TDK U.S.A. Corp. [5775]
TEAC America Inc. [9463]
Techcom Systems Inc. [5776]
Technical Advisory Service [9468]
Technical Devices Co. [9469]
Technical Sales Inc. [3296]
Technical Telephone Systems Inc. [5777]
Technicom Corp. [5778]
Teknis Corp. [9471]
Tel-Data Communications Inc. [5779]
Tele Path Corp. [5780]
Telebeep Wireless Inc. [9472]
Teleco Inc. [5781]
Telecom Engineering Consultants Inc. [5782]
Telecommunications Bank Inc. [5783]
Telecommunications Concepts Inc. [5784]
Telectron Inc. [9474]
Teledata Concepts Inc. [9475]
Telelink Communications Co. [5785]
Telephony International Inc. [5786]
Telesensory Corp. [9476]
Telesystems Inc. [5787]
Telewire Supply [5788]
Telogy Inc. [24443]
Telrad Telecommunications Inc. [5789]
Tepco Corp. [17217]
Terralink International [5790]
Tescom [9482]
Tessco Technologies Inc. [5791]
TESSCO Technologies Inc. [5792]
Test Systems Inc. [9483]
Thalner Electronic Labs Inc. [9484]
Thistle Co.; R.F. [25477]
Thomas Nelson Inc. [13463]
Thompson & Son Inc.; Edwin L. [5793]
Thomson-CSF Inc. [9486]
Thor Electronics Corp. [9487]
Throttle Up Corp. [9488]
TIC Industries Co. [25479]
TIE Systems Inc. [5794]
The TK Group, Inc. [9490]
TML Associates Inc. [8138]
TOA Electronics, Inc. [9491]
Tocos America Inc. [9492]
Toppan Printronics (USA) Inc. [9493]
ToteVision [5795]
Tranex Inc. [9499]
Trans West Communication Systems [9500]
Transco Inc. [25482]
Trax Distributors [25483]
TRCA Electronic Division [5796]
Tri-Parish Communications Inc. [5797]
Tribles of Maryland Inc. [15343]
Trident Medical International [19663]
Trinkle Sales Inc. [9510]
TriTech Graphics Inc. [6832]
Troxler World Trade Corp. [19088]
Truex Associates [9513]
Tryon Trading, Inc. [17237]
TTI Inc. [9514]
Tuscaloosa Electrical Supply Inc. [9518]
TW Communication Corp. [5798]
U and S Services Inc. [9519]
Uniden America Corp. [5799]
Unimark Inc. [9520]
Unique Communications Inc. [5800]
United Chemi-Con Inc. [9521]
United Exporters [19674]
United Learning Inc. [25490]
Universal Security Instruments Inc. [24652]
University of Alaska Press [4244]
University Products, Inc. [25493]
US Lighting & Electrical Supply [9527]
US TeleCenters [5801]
V & V Appliance Parts Inc. [15351]
Val-Comm Inc. [9530]
Valhalla Scientific Inc. [9531]

Valley Appliance Parts Co. [15354]
Valley Communications [5802]
Valtronics Engineering and Mfg [9534]
Van Ran Communications Services Inc. [5803]
Varilease Corp. [5804]
Veetronix Inc. [5805]
Venturian Corp. [3390]
VID COM Distributing [9536]
VID COM Distributing [9537]
VideoTape Distributors Inc. [25507]
Visual Aids Electronics [5806]
Vitramon Inc. [9544]
VMS Inc. [4261]
Vodavi Technology Inc. [9546]
VSS Inc. [6857]
Wacker Chemical Corp. [9549]
Walker and Associates Inc. [9551]
Walker Component Group [9552]
Walters Wholesale Electric Co. [9554]
Warehouse Home Furnishing Distributors
   Inc. [13274]
Warren Associates [9555]
Warren Electric Group [9557]
Warren Supply Co. [9558]
Washer and Refrigeration Supply Company
   Inc. [15365]
Watmet Inc. [9559]
Wedemeyer Electronic Supply Co. [9566]
Wegener Communications Inc. [5809]
West Tennessee Communications [5810]
West Tennessee Communications [9571]
Westcon Inc. [5811]
Western DataCom Company Inc. [6865]
Western Fastener Co. [13995]
Western Merchandisers Inc. [4278]
Western Micro Technology Inc. [6867]
Western Radio Electronics Inc. [9576]
Westinghouse Electric Corp. Trading Co. [5812]
Wheat International Communications Corp. [9581]
White Associates; Bob [5813]
Whitson and Co. [9588]
Wholesale Electronic Supply Inc. [9592]
Wholesale Electronics Inc. [9593]
Wholesale House [25524]
Willar Corp. [14767]
Williams Companies Inc. [5814]
Williams Investigation & SEC [5815]
Wilson Co.; H. [9598]
Windows Memory Corp. [6871]
Windsor Distributors Co. [9600]
Wintenna Inc. [5816]
Wire Supplies Inc. [9601]
Wise Wholesale Electronics [9602]
Worad Inc. [5817]
World Access Inc. [5818]
World Buying Service Inc. [9605]
World Communications Inc. [5819]
World Products Inc. [9606]
World Trade Network, Ltd. [18644]
World Traders (USA) Inc. [9607]
WorldCom Network Services Inc. [5820]
Worth Data [9609]
Wyle Electronics [9611]
Wyle Systems [6884]
X-Ray Industrial Distributor Corp. [24458]
Xebec Corp. [9613]
Xilinx Inc. [9614]
Yamaha Electronics Corporation USA [25537]
Yamaha Systems Technology [9616]
Yankee Electronics Inc. [9617]
Yankee Paperback & Textbook Co. [4302]
Yorkville Sound Inc. [25538]
Zack Electronics [5821]
Zapper Inc. [9621]
Zetex Inc. [9625]
Ziegenbein Associates Inc. [9626]
The Zondervan Corp. [4307]
Zonic A and D Co. [24465]

SIC 5072 — Hardware

A-1 Plumbers Supply [23048]
A & H Turf & Specialties Inc. [13519]
A-X Propane Co. [22017]

AA & A Enterprises Inc. [19721]
AAA Supply Corp. [13520]
AB Wholesale Co. [13521]
Ababa - QA [13522]
Abrasive-Tool Corp. [13523]
ABSCOA Industries Inc. [23]
Access International Marketing Inc. [13524]
Ace Hardware Corp. [13525]
Ace Hardware Corp. [13526]
Ace Tool Co. [13527]
ACF Components and Fasteners, Inc. [8263]
Action Equipment Company Inc. [6911]
Action Threaded Products Inc. [13528]
Action Tool Company Inc. [13529]
Active Screw and Fastener [13530]
Adams Supply Co. [13532]
Addkison Hardware Co. Inc. [13533]
Adelman Sales Corp. [13534]
Adjustable Clamp Co. [13535]
Advanced Affiliates Inc. [13536]
Aggregate Equipment and Supply [16673]
Ahlander Wholesale Hardware Co. [13537]
Aimsco Inc. [13538]
Airmatic Inc. [13539]
Ajax Tool Works Inc. [13540]
Alaska Industrial Hardware, Inc. [15750]
Alaska Nut & Bolt [13541]
Alatec Products [13542]
Albany Steel & Brass Corp. [13543]
Albuquerque Bolt & Fastener [13544]
Alco Tool Supply Inc. [13545]
All Fasteners Inc. [13546]
All-Pro Fasteners, Inc. [13547]
All Stainless Inc. [13548]
All State Fastener Corp. [13549]
All Tool Sales Inc. [13550]
Allen and Allen Company Inc. [6936]
Allied Bolt Co. [13551]
Allied Distribution Systems [6944]
Allied Electronics [8322]
Allied Wholesale Inc. [13552]
Aloha Tap & Die Inc. [16690]
Alpine Supply [13553]
Alsdorf International Ltd. [13554]
Amarillo Building Products Inc. [6953]
Amarillo Hardware Co. [13555]
AMB Tools & Equipment [13556]
American Fastener Specialty Company [13557]
American Global Co. [13558]
American Hotel Register Co. [15398]
American Industrial Tool Co. [15767]
American Kal Enterprises Inc. [13559]
American Lock and Supply Company Inc. [24506]
American Millwork & Hardware, Inc. [13560]
American Saw & Manufacturing Co. [13561]
American Tool Companies Inc. [13562]
Ammar's Inc. [26392]
Architects Hardware & Specialty Company
   Inc. [13563]
Architectural Building Supply [13564]
Arizona Sash and Door Co. [13565]
Armitage Industrial Supply, Inc. [16710]
Armstrong's Lock & Supply, Inc. [24508]
Artesanos Imports Company Inc. [6993]
Assembly Component Systems [13566]
Assembly Components Systems Co. [13567]
Assembly Components Systems Inc. [13568]
Associated Springs [13569]
Athens Hardware Co. [13570]
Atlantic Hardware and Supply Corp. [13571]
Atlantic Pacific Industries [13572]
Atlas Copco North America Inc. [13573]
Atlas Copco Tools Inc. [13574]
Atlas Screw and Specialty Co.; L.P. [13575]
Aubuchon Company Inc.; W.E. [13576]
Austinville Elevator [17713]
Auto Bolt & Nut Co. [13577]
B & N Industries [13578]
B & S Bolts Corp. [13579]
B and T Wholesale Distributors Inc. [13580]
Baer Supply Co. [13581]
Bakersfield Sandstone Brick Co. Inc. [7015]
Bakersfield Sandstone Brick Company Inc. [27285]
Bakertowne Company, Inc. [15414]
Baldridge Lumber Co.; J.C. [7016]
Bamal Fastener Corp. [13582]

Barber and Ross Co. [7020]
Barco Industries Inc. [13583]
Barker-Jennings Corp. [2317]
Barker-Jennings Corp. [13584]
Barnett Inc. [23078]
Barrett Hardware and Industrial Supply
    Co. [13585]
Basnight & Sons; S.H. [13586]
Bass Woodworking Machinery, Inc. [15805]
Baxter International Representations Inc. [13587]
BBC Fasteners Inc. [13588]
Becknell Wholesale Co. [13589]
B.E.E. Industrial Supply Inc. [15814]
Beeson Hardware Industrial Sales Co. [13590]
Behling Building Products; Gil [7043]
Belair Road Supply Company Inc. [7044]
The Bell Group [17331]
Belmer Co.; H. [13591]
Bender Wholesale Distributors [3]
Berger and Company Inc.; Howard [13592]
Berint Trading, Ltd. [13593]
Berkman Co.; Louis [15819]
Berube Municipal Supply; Tom [13594]
Best Locking Systems of Georgia Inc. [24513]
Best Locking Systems of Wisconsin Inc. [24514]
Best Way Tools [13596]
Big Blue Store [13597]
Big D Bolt & Screw Co. [13598]
Bild Industries Inc. [13599]
Biscayne Electric and Hardware Distributors
    Inc. [8441]
Black and Decker Corp. Products Service
    Div. [15053]
Black & Decker US Inc. [4582]
Blaine Window Hardware Inc. [13600]
Blish-Mize Co. [13601]
Blount Farmers Cooperative [323]
Boehm-Madisen Lumber Company Inc. [7066]
Bon Tool Co. [13602]
Bonanza Nut and Bolt Inc. [13603]
Bostwick-Braun Co. [13604]
Bowman Distribution [16759]
Bozeman Safe & Lock [24518]
Bradley Co.; E.B. [13605]
Bradley Supply Company Inc.; R.W. [7075]
Bridgeport Equipment Co. Inc. [336]
Brighton-Best Socket Screw Manufacturing
    Inc. [13606]
Broadway Collection [23097]
Brookdale Lumber Inc. [7083]
Brost International Trading Co. [24271]
Brown-Rogers-Dixson Co. [15062]
Brownell & Associates, Inc. [13607]
Bruckner Machine [13608]
Brushtech Inc. [16769]
BSE Engineering Corp. [23571]
BSH of Evansvillle [7090]
Buck Knives Inc. [15431]
Buford White Lumber Company Inc. [7097]
Buhrman-Pharr Hardware Co. [13609]
Builders Brass Works Corp. [13610]
Builders Hardware & Specialties [13611]
Builders Hardware and Supply Co. Inc. [13612]
Builders Warehouse [7102]
Burbank Aircraft Supply Inc. [68]
Buttery Hardware Company Inc. [13613]
C & J Fasteners [13614]
C & J Tool & Gage Co. [15862]
C & R Tile [9749]
C-Tech Systems Div. [16774]
Calcasieu Lumber Co. [7125]
Caldwell Supply Company Inc. [17759]
California Fasteners Inc. [13615]
California Hardware Co. [13616]
Calotex Inc.; D.E. [13617]
Campbell Supply Co. [16777]
Camper's Trade Emporium [13618]
Carapace Corp. [13619]
Carlson Systems Corp. [13620]
Carpet Basics [9762]
Carpet Cushion Supply [9764]
Carpet Cushion Supply [9767]
Carroll Building Specialties [13621]
Cascade Wholesale Hardware, Inc. [13622]
Casey Co.; A.A. [16784]
Cash Supply Co. [13623]

CBS Fasteners Inc. [13624]
Centennial Bolt Inc. [13625]
Central Distribution Services, LLC [13626]
Central Indiana Hardware Co. [7159]
Central Valley Builders Supply [7161]
Century Fasteners, Inc. [13628]
Century Saw and Tool Co. Inc. [13629]
Chamberlain Group Inc. [13630]
Chandler Products Co. [13631]
Channellock Inc. [13632]
Charken Co. Inc. [16792]
Chubbuck Sales Inc. [13633]
Claesson Co. [26006]
Clark Supply Co. [13634]
Clauss Cutlery Co. [15446]
Cleco Industrial Fasteners, Inc. [13636]
Click Bond Inc. [70]
Click Bond Inc. [13637]
Coast Cutlery Co. [15449]
Cold Headers Inc. [13638]
Coleman Industrial Supply Inc. [13639]
Colladay Hardware Co. [23119]
Colombian Development Corp. [8544]
Colonial Hardware Corp. [13640]
Colonial Hardware Corp. [16803]
Columbus Hardware Supplies Inc. [13641]
Com-Kyl [8549]
Components West [13642]
Contico International Inc. [13643]
Continental Midland [13644]
Cook Co.; P.S. [23127]
Cooper Power Tools Division-Apex [75]
Cooperative Elevator Co. [451]
Copeland Lumber Yard Inc. [13646]
Copeland Lumber Yard Inc. [13647]
Corkey Control Systems Inc. [24528]
Cotter and Co. [13648]
County Line Co-op [469]
Cover and Son Wholesale Lumber Inc.;
    H.A. [7225]
Cowan Supply Co. [23129]
Crystal Cooperative Inc. [479]
Cummins Utility Supply [13650]
Cunningham Co.; C.A. [13651]
Cutlery [13652]
Cutting Tools Inc. [13653]
D and T Services Inc. [13654]
Dakota Electric Supply Co. [8605]
Dallas County Farmers Exchange [488]
Danaher Tool Group [13655]
Darling Bolt Co. [13656]
Davis Supply Co. Inc. [16821]
Deanco Inc. [8617]
Decatur Hopkins [13657]
Delaware County Supply Co. [13658]
Delta Fastener Corp. [13659]
Delta Industrial Systems Co. [13660]
Delta Wholesale Hardware Co. [13661]
Denver Hardware Co. [13662]
Denver Hardware Co. [13663]
Denver Hardwood Co. [9855]
Desoto County Cooperative [516]
Devlin Lumber and Supply Corp. [7260]
Dewco Milwaukee Sales [13665]
Diamond Hill Plywood Co. [7261]
Discount Building Materials [7268]
Disston Co. [13666]
Diversified Fastening [13667]
Dixieline Lumber Co. [7273]
Dixon Co.; William [15953]
DJ Associates, Inc. [13668]
Do It Best Corp. [7275]
Dodge City Cooperative Exchange Inc. [2554]
Dorian International Inc. [24105]
Dougherty Lumber Co. [7285]
Douglas/Quikut [15114]
Dowling Inc.; J.H. [7286]
Drago Supply Co. Inc. [13669]
Drapery Hardware of Florida [13670]
Dreyco Inc. [2561]
Dunaway Supply Co. [7289]
Dunken Distributing Inc. [9874]
Duo-Fast Carolinas Inc. [5839]
Duo-Fast Corp. North Central Sales Div. [13671]
Duo-Fast Northeast [13672]
Earnest Machine Products Co. [13673]

East Jordan Cooperative Co. [2571]
Eastman-Cartwright Lumber Co. [7301]
Easy Gardener Inc. [538]
Eaton; Daniel A. [26026]
Eberly Inc.; John A. [13674]
Eckart and Finard Inc. [13675]
Econo Trading Company [13676]
Edgerton Forge Inc. [15977]
E.K. Fasteners Inc. [13677]
El Paso Saw and Belting Supply Co. [13678]
Elberta Farmers Cooperative [544]
Electronic Fasteners Inc. [13679]
Ellsworth Farmers Union Cooperative Oil Co. [549]
Ellsworth Supply Company Inc. [13680]
Emery Waterhouse Co. [13681]
Empire Level Manufacturing Corp. [13682]
Empire Machinery and Supply Co. [13683]
Empire Staple Co. [13684]
Emporium Specialties Company Inc. [8703]
Enderes Tool Co. Inc. [13685]
Engineering Equipment Co. [15992]
Epstein Co.; Harry J. [13686]
Equality Screw Co. Inc. [13687]
Equality Trading [15995]
Erb Hardware Co. Ltd. [13688]
Escondido Lumber & True Value [7319]
Eskew, Smith & Cannon [9886]
Evans Findings Company, Inc. [13689]
Excalibur Cutlery & Gifts [15492]
Fabsco Corp. [13690]
Fairbanks Co. [13691]
Fairmont Tamper [13692]
Fairview True Value Hardware [13693]
Farmers Cooperative [570]
Farmers Cooperative Company Inc. [604]
Farmers Cooperative Elevator Co. [621]
Farmers Cooperative Exchange (Elgin,
    Nebraska) [11101]
Farmers Cooperative Supply and Shipping
    Association [638]
Farmers Exchange [648]
Farmers Union Cooperative [22258]
Farmers Union Oil Co. [22263]
Farmers Union Oil Co. [22265]
Farmers Union Oil Co. (Napoleon, North
    Dakota) [22269]
Fasnap Corp. [13694]
Fastec Industrial [13695]
Fastenal Co. [13696]
Fastener Supply Co. [13698]
Fasteners Inc. [13699]
Fasteners & Metal Products Corp. [13700]
Fastner House [13701]
Faucet-Queens Inc. [13702]
Faucet-Queens Inc. [13703]
Federal Screw Products Inc. [13704]
Fehr Bros. Industries Inc. [13705]
Feldmann Engineering & Manufacturing Company,
    Inc. [678]
First Choice Tool Co. [13706]
Fitchburg Hardware Company Inc. [13707]
Five Star Trading Company [13708]
Fleming Sales Company Inc. [692]
The Fletcher-Terry Company [13709]
Florida Bolt and Nut Co. [13710]
Florida Bolt and Nut Co. [13711]
Florida Hardware Co. [13712]
Florig Equipment [8747]
Flying J Travel Plaza [22285]
Fold-A-Way Corporation [7351]
Foley-Belsaw Co. [13713]
Foltz Manufacturing and Supply Co. [13714]
Forest City-Babin Co. [7357]
Fortune Industries Inc. [89]
Frederick Trading Co. [13715]
Fried Brothers Inc. [13716]
Frontier Fasteners Inc. [13717]
Fullwell Products Inc. [2656]
Fulton Corp. [13718]
Fulton Supply Co. [16883]
Funk Machine and Supply [13719]
Garden Exchange Limited [13720]
Gardner Hardware Co. [7378]
Garka Mill Company Inc. [7380]
Gates Co. Inc.; B. [23183]
General Fasteners Company Inc. [13721]

General Tool and Supply Co. [13722]
George Co.; Edward [7389]
GLF/SAE [13723]
Global Fastener Inc. [13724]
Globemaster Inc. [13725]
GM International Inc. [13726]
GMP [5621]
Goff Custom Spring Inc. [13727]
Grange Supply Company Inc. [757]
Granger Lumber-Hardware, Inc. [7409]
Grattan & Sons Inc.; Dave [13728]
Graybar Electric Company Inc. [8814]
Gross-Yowell and Company Inc. [7420]
Gulf Bolt & Supply [13729]
Gulf Marine and Industrial Supplies [11346]
Gunther and Co.; Albert [7424]
H. and E. Brothers Inc. [13730]
H & H Distributing Inc. [7427]
Hafele America Co. [13731]
Hager Companies [13732]
Hallmarkets International Ltd. [21023]
Handy Hardware Wholesale Inc. [13733]
Harbor Tool Supply Inc. [16088]
Harco [13734]
Hard Hat Inc. [23714]
Hardlines Marketing Inc. [13735]
Hardware Distribution Warehouses Inc. [13736]
Hardware Distributors Inc. [13737]
Hardware Imagination [13738]
Hardware Specialties Co. [13739]
Hardware Specialty Company Inc. [13740]
Hardware Supply Company Inc. [13741]
Harmony Co-op [17976]
Harmony Country Cooperatives [792]
Harrell Co.; Hollis [13742]
Harrington Tools Inc. [13743]
Hasson-Bryan Hardware Co. [13744]
Hawaii Hardware Company Ltd. [13745]
Hawaiian Housewares, Ltd. [15521]
Hawera Inc. [16094]
Hawley Industrial Supplies Inc. [13746]
Hazlett Company Inc.; T.R. [7462]
Heads & Threads Co. [13747]
Heads and Threads Div. [13748]
Heads and Threads International, LLC [13749]
Heart of America Bolt [13750]
Heller Co.; E.P. [16097]
Henderson and Baird Hardware Company Inc. [15165]
Herald Wholesalers Inc. [13751]
Heritage Industries [13752]
Hi-Line Electric Co. [8840]
Hillman Fastener [13753]
Hisco [8844]
Hitachi Power Tools USA Ltd. [13754]
Hoffman Co.; H. [24565]
Holo-Krome Co. [13755]
Homier Distributing Inc. [13756]
Horizon Distribution Inc. [13757]
House-Hasson Hardware Inc. [13758]
HPM Building Supply [13759]
Huffaker's Inc. [13760]
Humke Co.; Ken R. [13761]
Humphrey Company Inc.; P.D. [7498]
Hurst Lumber Company Inc. [7500]
IDA Inc. [7504]
Ideal Division [13762]
IDN-ACME, Inc. [24570]
IMA Tool Distributors [13763]
Independent Rental, Inc. [853]
Indresco, Inc. [16945]
Industrial Fasteners Corp. [13764]
Industrial Power Sales Inc. [13765]
Industrial Tools and Abrasives Inc. [16959]
Industry-Railway Suppliers Inc. [23481]
Inland Northwest Distributors Inc. [9962]
Inland Supply Inc. [23220]
International Screw & Bolt [13766]
Investrade Import & Export [16170]
Island Pacific Distributors, Inc. [24575]
The IXL Group [13767]
J & J Distributors [24576]
Jacob's Store Inc. [877]
Jay-Cee Sales and Rivet Inc. [13769]
Jealco International, Inc. [16185]
Jed Co.; Leonard [13770]

Jenks & Son; W.S. [8911]
Jennison Industrial Supply [13771]
Jensen-Byrd Company Inc. [13772]
Jensen Distribution Services [13773]
Johnsen Co.; Hans [23761]
Johnson Brothers [13774]
Johnston Industrial Supply Co. [16190]
Jones Hardware Company Inc. [13775]
J.S. Screw Manufacturing Co. [13777]
JZ Allied International Holdings Inc. [13778]
Kagiya Trading Co. Ltd. of America [13779]
Kamaaina Distribution [11578]
Kansas City Bolt, Nut and Screw Co. [13780]
Kar Products [13781]
Kass Industrial Supply Corp. [13782]
Katy Industries Inc. [8931]
Kaufman Supply [15184]
Kellco & Associates [15185]
Kemp Grain Company Inc. [18032]
Kemp Hardware and Supply Co. [13783]
Kemper Enterprises Inc. [25698]
Kentec Inc. [13784]
Kett Tool Co. [13785]
Kilgo Co. Inc.; A.L. [13786]
King Safe and Lock Company Inc. [24581]
Kitchens Inc. of Paducah [15551]
Klarman Sales Inc. [13787]
Knecht Home Lumber Center Inc. [7565]
Knox Industrial Supplies Inc. [13788]
Krieg Consulting and Trading Inc.; A. [16220]
The Kruse Company [13789]
Lake Erie Supply, Inc. [7577]
Lakeside Spring Products [13790]
Lamons Beaumont Bolt & Gasket [16993]
Land, Air & Sea Tool Corp. [13791]
Laredo Hardware Co. [13793]
Larsen Cooperative Company Inc. [939]
Laube Technology Inc. [16994]
Leatherman Tool Group Inc. [13794]
Lee Lumber and Building Materials Corp. [7591]
Lehigh-Armstrong Inc. [13795]
Lewiston Rubber & Supply Inc. [25715]
Lifetime Hoan Corp. [15568]
Lilly Fasteners Inc.; Gary Kenneth [13796]
Lipscomb and Co.; H.G. [13797]
Little Rock Drapery Co. [15570]
Little Rock Tool Service, Inc. [13798]
Locks Co. [24585]
Locks Co. [13799]
Lohr Structural Fasteners Inc. [13800]
Long Lewis Inc. [13801]
Long Lewis Inc. [13802]
Lord & Hodge, Inc. [13803]
Lowell Corp. [13804]
Lowville Farmers Cooperative Inc. [973]
Magic Touch Enterprises, Inc. [10003]
Mahar Tool Supply Inc. [13805]
Maintenance Warehouse/America Corp. [13806]
Makita U.S.A. Inc. [13807]
Malco Industries [13808]
Management Supply Co. [23248]
Manis Lumber Company Inc. [27339]
Mann Edge Tool Co. Collins Axe Div. [13810]
Manware Inc. [13811]
Marchand Contractors Specialties Inc.; R.J. [7640]
Marco Supply Company Inc. [13812]
Marmon Group [13813]
Marshalltown Trowel Co. [7650]
Mass Hardware and Supply Inc. [13814]
Massey Builders Supply Corp. [7663]
Matco Tools Corp. [2922]
Mauro Co.; A.G. [13815]
Mauston Farmers Cooperative [993]
Mayes Brothers Tool Manufacturing [13816]
Mayfield Building Supply Co. [7671]
Mayhew Steel Products [13817]
McCarty & Son; H.J. [15584]
McDonald Lumber Company Inc. [7679]
McGraw Inc.; James [17023]
McJunkin Appalachian Oil Field Supply Co. [22466]
McKim Group [13818]
McLaughlin Industrial Distributors Inc. [13819]
McLendon Hardware Inc. [13820]
McMaster-Carr Supply Co. California [13821]
McMurray Co.; Charles [13822]

MEBCO Contractors Supplies [13823]
Medal, Inc. [13824]
Meijer Inc. [11845]
Memphis Import Company Inc. [23820]
Mercantile Buyer's Service Inc. [21500]
Merit Fasteners Corp. [13825]
MFA Agriservice [1023]
Mid-State Bolt and Nut Company Inc. [13827]
Midland Co-Op Inc. [1030]
Midland Lock & Safe Service [24592]
Midwest Bolt and Supply Inc. [13828]
Miller Hardware Co. [13829]
Mimbres Valley Farmers Association Inc. [1042]
Mine and Mill Supply Co. [20197]
Mining Construction Supply [13830]
Minooka Grain Lumber and Supply Co. [7723]
Minton's Lumber and Supply Co. [7725]
Mitchell Hardware Co. [23270]
Mitchell-Powers Hardware [13831]
Mizutani USA [13832]
MNP Fastener Distribution Group [13833]
Molls Inc. [13834]
Monarch Ceramic Tile [10048]
Monarch Machine and Tool Company Inc. [13836]
Mondovi Cooperative Equity Association Inc. [1045]
Monroe Hardware Co. [13837]
Moore-Handley Inc. [11931]
Morgan-Wightman Supply Inc. Indiana [7748]
Morris Co.; The Robert E. [16323]
Morse Co.; M.K. [13838]
Morton Supply Inc. [9098]
Moser Lumber Inc. [7750]
Moses Lake Steel Supply Inc. [20207]
Mott Equity Exchange [13839]
Mount Pleasant Hardware Inc. [21508]
Mountainland Supply Co. [23282]
Moynihan Lumber [7753]
MSC Industrial Supply Co. [13840]
Mutual Services of Highland Park [13841]
M.W. Manufacturers Inc. [7756]
Napa Auto Parts (Burlington, Vermont) [13842]
National Industrial Hardware Inc. [16341]
Nehawka Farmers Cooperative [18127]
Neill-LaVielle Supply Co. [13843]
Nelson Roanoke Corp. [13844]
Nelson-Roanoke Div. [13845]
New World Research Corp. [3030]
New York Twist Drill Inc. [17073]
Newell P.R. Ltd. [15594]
NFZ Products Inc. [13846]
Nichol's Farm Supply Inc. [1074]
NJ Rivet Co. [13847]
NM Bakery Service Co. [12010]
Nor-Mar Sales Company Inc. [13848]
Normad Fastener Company Inc. [13849]
North Branch Flooring [10080]
North Coast Distributing, Inc. [13850]
North Texas Bolt, Nut & Screw, Inc. [13851]
Northridge Lumber Company Inc. [7799]
Nyssa Cooperative Supply Inc. [1095]
Odell Hardware Company Inc. [13852]
Oklahoma Rig and Supply Company Inc. [17088]
Omega Products Corporation [13853]
Opperman Co., Inc.; Matthew [13854]
Orgill Inc. [13855]
Osborn Machinery Company Inc. [13856]
Osborne Distributing Company Inc. [1111]
OxTech Industries Inc. [13857]
Pacific Coast Air Tool and Supply Inc. [135]
Pacific Flooring Supply [10091]
Pacific Handy Cutter Inc. [17096]
Pacific Hardware & Specialties Inc. [13858]
Palmer Pipe and Supply Inc. [13859]
PanaVise Products International [13861]
The Parker Company [13862]
Parker Metal Goods Corp. [13863]
Parrish-Keith-Simmons Inc. [16380]
Parts Associates Inc. [13864]
Pendleton Grain Growers Inc. [18161]
Pennington Seed Inc. [1121]
Pensacola Mill Supply Company Inc. [13865]
Pentacon Inc. [13866]
Perezi & Associates; K.M. [13867]
Perine Co.; John [13868]
Philadelphia Fire Retardant Company Inc. [7858]

Pine Cone Lumber Company Inc. [7864]
Piper Weatherford Co. [13869]
Plant Service Co. [17108]
Plaza Paint Co. [21541]
Pleasants Hardware Co. [13871]
Poe Corp. [13872]
Pope Distributing Co. [5283]
Porteous Fastener Co. [13873]
Porter Cable [13874]
Precision Tool and Supply [16423]
Primark Tool Group [13875]
Primeco Inc. Southeast Div. [13876]
PrimeSource Inc. [7886]
Prince Corp. [1151]
Pro Cooperative [1155]
Prosperity Tool Corp. [13877]
Pulaski Chase Cooperative [1161]
Purchased Parts Group [13878]
QSN Manufacturing Inc. [13879]
Quest Electronic Hardware Inc. [9251]
Quick Cable Corporation [9252]
R & H Wholesale Supply, Inc. [24616]
Rada Manufacturing Co. [15628]
Raleigh Hardware Co. [13880]
Ram Threading Inc. [13881]
Ram Tool and Supply Co. [13882]
RB & W Corp. [13883]
Red Devil Inc. [13884]
Reichman, Crosby, Hays Inc. [17135]
Reliable Fabrics Inc. [15631]
Rex International [23912]
Rhone Company Inc.; George D. [13885]
Rice Aircraft Inc. [142]
Richlund Enterprises [15292]
Ridgeland Chetek Cooperative [1193]
Riggs Supply Co. [13886]
Riggsbee Hardware & Industrial Supply [13887]
Rittner Products Inc. [7938]
RJM Sales, Associates, Inc. [13888]
RMC Inc. [23346]
Robco International Corporation/Advanced
  Technology International [17140]
Roberts and Sons Inc.; Frank [7943]
Robnet Inc. [13889]
Rockford Bolt & Steel Co. [13890]
Rockingham Cooperative Farm Bureau [1205]
Rocknel Fastener Inc. [13891]
Rods Indiana Inc. [13892]
Rooster Products International Inc./McGuire-
  Nicholas [13893]
Rose Caster Co. [13894]
Ross-Frazer Supply Co. [13895]
Royal Brass and Hose [13896]
Rugg Manufacturing Company Inc. [1218]
Ruklic Screw Company Inc.; J.P. [13897]
Rush County Farm Bureau Cooperative [1219]
Rutland Tool and Supply Company Inc. [16465]
Ryobi America Corp. [1222]
Saffron Supply Co. [13899]
Sales Systems Ltd. [13900]
Samson Hardware & Fairbanks [13901]
Sanson and Rowland Inc. [13902]
Saria International Inc. [13903]
Sawyer and Company Inc.; J.E. [13904]
Scheinert & Son Inc.; Sidney [13905]
Schiffer Wholesale Hardware; Leslie [24625]
Schlafer Supply Company Inc. [13906]
Scotty's Hardware Inc. [13907]
Seaboard Industrial Supply [16477]
Seattle Marine Industrial Division [18608]
Seelye Plastics Inc. [17163]
Seibert Equity Cooperative Association [1256]
Selby Furniture Hardware Company Inc. [13908]
Semcor Equipment & Manufacturing Corp. [13909]
Senco of Florida Inc. [13910]
Sentry/Liberty Hardware Distributors Inc. [13911]
Serson Supply Inc. [17168]
Service Plus Distributors Inc. [13912]
SERVISTAR Corp. [8002]
Setko Fasteners Inc. [13913]
Sewell Hardware Company Inc. [13914]
Shank Spring Design Inc. [13915]
Shapco Inc. [15652]
Shepler International Inc. [8011]
Shepler's Equipment Company Inc. [8012]
Shohet Frederick of New Hampshire Inc. [13916]

Shook Builder Supply Co. [13917]
Shop Tools Inc. [13918]
Shur-Lok Corp. [13919]
Sibley Industrial Tool Co. [9367]
SK Hand Tool Corp. [13920]
Skeels and Co.; Robert [13921]
Skelton and Skinner Lumber Inc. [8027]
Smith Abrasives, Inc. [13922]
Smith Associates; Jay [13923]
Smith Hardware Company Inc. [13924]
Smith; Merle B. [10155]
Snap-on Tools Corp. [13925]
Sona Enterprises [13926]
Sonin Inc. [13927]
South Texas Implement Co. [1276]
Southern Architectural Systems, Inc. [8047]
Southern Carbide Specialists Inc. [13928]
Southern Cross and O'Fallon Building Products
  Co. [13929]
Southern Hardware Company Inc. [13930]
Southern Hardware and Supply Company
  Ltd. [17186]
Southwest Cooperative Wholesale [18245]
Southwest DoAll Industrial Supply [16514]
Spartan Tool Supply [13931]
Spaulding Brick Company Inc. [8059]
Special-T-Metals Company Inc. [13932]
Spencer Products Company [13933]
Spokane Hardware Supply Inc. [13934]
Star Sales and Distributing Co. [8073]
Star Stainless Screw Co. [13935]
Stauber Wholesale Hardware; E. [13936]
Stewart Fastener Corp. [13937]
Stewart Supply Inc. [13938]
Stimpson Company Inc. [13939]
Strasser Hardware Co.; A.L. [13940]
Stratham Hardware & Lumber Co. [21590]
Strong Tool Co. [13941]
Suhner Manufacturing, Inc. [16534]
Summers Induserve Supply [16535]
Sunline USA Group Inc. [13942]
Sunny International Inc. [13943]
Sunshine Industries Inc. [13944]
SuperGrind Co. [17205]
Supply Station Inc. [13945]
Surfa-Shield Corp. [13946]
Surpless, Dunn & Co. [13947]
Swiss Army Brands Inc. [15676]
Szco Supplier Inc. [15678]
Taylor Rental Corp. [1316]
Tazewell Farm Bureau Inc. [1318]
Tech-Aerofoam Products Inc. [8103]
Techni-Tool, Inc. [13948]
Texas Contractors Supply Co. [8114]
Texas Mill Inc. [17219]
Texas Mill Supply Inc. [13949]
Texas Staple Company Inc. [13950]
Texhoma Wheat Growers Inc. [1325]
Thackeray Corp. [13951]
Thomas Sales Company Inc. [26680]
Thornton Industries, Inc. [13953]
Threaded Fasteners Inc. [13954]
Thruway Fasteners Inc. [13955]
Time Saver Tool Corp. [13956]
TML Associates Inc. [8138]
Tool House Inc. [13957]
Tool Mart [13958]
Toolman Co. [13960]
Townsend Supply Co. [9498]
TradeCom International Inc. [13961]
Trans-Atlantic Co. [13962]
Transit Mix Concrete Co. [8142]
Travers Tool Co., Inc. [13964]
Triangle Brass Manufacturing Co. [13965]
Trophy Products Inc. [13966]
True Value Regional Distributor [13967]
TruServ Corp. [13968]
Tulnoy Lumber Inc. [8152]
Twin City Hardware Company Inc. [13969]
T.W.P. Inc. [20450]
Ultra Hardware Products LLC [13970]
UMBRA U.S.A. Inc. [15692]
Union Butterfield Corp. [13971]
United Fastener and Supply Co. [13972]
United Hardware Distributing Co. [13973]
United Manufacturers Supplies Inc. [13974]

U.S. Home and Garden Inc. [1383]
U.S. Industrial Products Corp. [13975]
U.S. Industrial Tool Supply [13976]
U.S. Lock Corp. [24651]
U.S. Marketing Services [5451]
U.S. Rigging Supply Corp. [17243]
Universal Cooperative Inc. [1385]
Universal Fastener Co. [13977]
Universal Management Consultants Inc. [14749]
Vaughan and Bushnell Manufacturing [13978]
Vaughan & Bushnell Manufacturing Co. [13979]
Vaughn Materials Company Inc. [8176]
Vermont American Tool Co. [13980]
Virginia Carolina Tools Inc. [16602]
Voorhees Company Inc.; The Bill [14756]
W C L Co. [13981]
Wagner Hardware Co. [13982]
Wahler Brothers [13983]
Wallace Hardware Co. [1409]
Wallbank Springs Inc.; P.J. [13984]
Walton & Post [12873]
Warner Manufacturing Co. [21602]
Washington Chain and Supply Inc. [18634]
Washington Forge Inc. [15702]
Watters and Martin Inc. [13985]
Wayne Fasteners Inc. [13986]
WBH Industries [13987]
Webb Bolt and Nut Co. [13988]
Wedin International Inc., Ball Screw Manufacturing
  and Repair, Inc. [13989]
Weingart & Sons [13990]
Weissman & Sons Inc.; Carl [21604]
Weissman and Sons Inc.; Carl [13991]
Weldon Tool Co. [16620]
Wells and Wade Hardware [13992]
Wesche Co. [13993]
West Union Corp. [13994]
Western Fastener Co. [13995]
Western Pacific Interior [10293]
Western United Electric Supply Corp. [9577]
Westguard Inc. [24661]
Wholesale Hardwood Interiors Inc. [8223]
Wilco Farmers Inc. [1447]
Wilco Supply [13997]
Williams Inc.; Ralph C. [17280]
Williams Industrial Products, Inc.; J.H. [13998]
Wilmar Industries Inc. [23461]
Wilton Corp. [16638]
Wiurth Adams Nut and Bolt [13999]
Wood Supply Co.; Walter A. [17286]
Woodings-Verona Tool Works Inc. [14000]
Woodlawn Hardware [17287]
Woody's Big Sky Supply, Inc. [8241]
Wuu Jau Company Inc. [24051]
Wynn's International Inc. [14001]
Yakima Hardware Co. [14002]
Yarborough and Co. [14003]
Yardville Supply Co. [8245]
Yeatman Architectural Hardware Inc. [14004]
Zeeland Lumber and Supply Inc. [8253]
Zephyr Manufacturing Co., Inc. [179]
Ziegler's Bolt & Nut House [14005]

SIC 5074 — Plumbing & Hydronic Heating Supplies

A-1 Plumbers Supply [23048]
A and A Mechanical Inc. [15720]
AA Water Service [14987]
ABM Distributors Inc. [23049]
Absolute Aqua Systems [25542]
Acadiana Culligan [24907]
Accurate Water [25544]
Ace Hardware Corp. [13525]
Ace Plumbing and Electrical Supply, Inc. [23050]
Action Water Treatment Service [25545]
Active Carb Ltd. [23051]
Active Plumbing Supply Co. [23052]
Addie Water Systems [25546]
Adel Wholesalers Inc. [23053]
Ahrens and McCarron Inc. [23054]
Air & Water Purification Inc. [25547]
Aitcheson Inc.; J and H [23055]

Ajax Supply Co. [14310]
Akin Medical Equipment International [19128]
Albuquerque Winnelson Co. [23056]
Allied Fire Lite Fireplace [14314]
Allied Supply Inc. [23057]
Almerica Overseas Inc. [23059]
Amarillo Hardware Co. [13555]
Amarillo Winnelson Co. [23060]
AMC Industries Inc. [23061]
American Environmental Systems Inc. [23062]
American Filtration Systems Inc. [14317]
American Foundry and Manufacturing Co. [23063]
American Granby Inc. [25550]
American Plumber [25551]
Americo Wholesale Plumbing Supply Co. [23064]
Andrew Co.; W.T. [23065]
A.P. Supply Co. [23066]
Apex Supply Company Inc. [14323]
Applied Membranes Inc. [25555]
Applied Power Corp. [14324]
APR Supply Co. [14325]
APR Supply Co. [23067]
Aqua Magnetics International [25556]
Aqua Magnetics International [23068]
Aqua Systems International, Inc. [23069]
Aquanetics Systems [23070]
Aquatec Water Systems Inc. [23071]
Arctic Clear Products Inc. [25557]
Arizona Water Works Supply Inc. [23072]
Armitage Industrial Supply, Inc. [16710]
Arrow Precision Products Inc. [23073]
Astro-Pure Water Purifiers [15038]
Atlantic Filter Corp. [25564]
Atlantic Plumbing Supply Co. Inc. [23074]
Atlas Water Systems Inc. [25566]
Automatic Equipment Sales of Virginia Inc. [14330]
Automatic Firing Inc. [14331]
B & K Industries Inc. [23075]
Baker Distributing Co. [14334]
Ball Pipe & Supply; Leif [23076]
Barker Pipe Fittings Inc. [16720]
Barnett Brass and Copper Inc. [23077]
Barnett Inc. [23078]
Barneys Pumps Inc. [23079]
Barry Pumps Inc.; R.E. [25568]
Becker Company Inc.; Larson [25569]
Beckman Brothers Inc. [23080]
Belair Road Supply Company Inc. [7044]
Bell Supply Company Inc. [23081]
Bells Supply Co. [23082]
Belmer Co.; H. [13591]
Berg-Dorf Pipe & Supply Co. Inc. [23083]
Best Plumbing Supply Inc. [23084]
Big Blue Store [13597]
Big Sky Paint Co., Heating & Air
  Conditioning [21400]
Biggs Pump and Supply Inc. [23086]
Bion Environmental Technologies Inc. [23087]
Birdsall and Company Inc.; W.A. [23088]
Blackman Medford Corp. [23089]
Bluffs Budget Plumbing [23090]
Boettcher Supply Inc. [8450]
Boiler and Heat Exchange Systems Inc. [23091]
Booth Inc.; I.D. [23092]
Boston Pipe and Fittings Company Inc. [23093]
Boston Stove Co. [14353]
BP Products Inc. [14355]
Bradley Supply Co. [23094]
Briggs Incorporated of Omaha [23095]
The Brightman Co. [15059]
Brill Hygenic Products Inc. [23096]
Broadway Collection [23097]
Broedell Plumbing Supply Inc. [23098]
Broz, Inc.; John V. [7088]
Bruce-Rogers Company Inc. [23099]
Bruner Corp. [25584]
BSW Inc. [14362]
Buderus Hydronic Systems Inc. [23100]
Burack Inc.; I. [23101]
Burns Brothers Contractors [23102]
Burns Supply/Great Lakes Inc. [23103]
C and L Supply Inc. [15069]
Camomile Enterprises, Inc. [25595]
Camper's Trade Emporium [13618]
Capitol Plumbing and Heating Supply Co. [23104]

Capitol Plumbing and Heating Supply Company
  Inc. [23105]
Carolina Plastics Supply Inc. [23106]
Carr Co. [23107]
Cast Products Corp. [23108]
Cayce Mill Supply Co. [8509]
Central Distribution Services, LLC [13626]
Central Jersey Supply Co. [16787]
Central Supply Co. [23110]
Central Supply Co. [23111]
Central VA Chimney [14378]
Century Plumbing Wholesale [23112]
Challenger Water International Inc. [25599]
Champion Furnace Pipe Co. [23113]
Champlain Winair Co. [23114]
Chase Supply Co. [14382]
Chicago Furnace Supply Inc. [14383]
Cities Supply Company Inc. [23115]
City Plumbing & Electrical Supply [8528]
Clack Corp. [25601]
Claeys and Co.; H.L. [23116]
Clark Supply Co. [13634]
Clean Water Systems International [25602]
Climate Technologies [14385]
Coastal Industries Inc. [23117]
Coburn Supply Co. Inc. [23118]
Colladay Hardware Co. [23119]
Columbia Pipe and Supply [14393]
Columbus Pipe and Equipment Co. [23120]
Comfort Supply Inc. [14395]
Conestoga Heating and Plumbing Supply
  Inc. [23121]
Conklin and Company Inc.; Lyon [14400]
Connecticut Appliance & Fireplace Distributors,
  LLC [15094]
Connor Co. [23122]
Consolidated Pipe and Supply Company
  Inc. [23123]
Consolidated Supply Co. [23124]
Consumers Plumbing Heating Supply [23125]
Cook Brothers Manufacturing and Supply
  Co. [23126]
Cook Co.; P.S. [23127]
CORR TECH, Inc. [23128]
Corr Tech Inc. [22949]
Cowan Supply Co. [23129]
Cramer Co. Inc. [15097]
Dahl [23130]
Dales Mechanical Sales & Service [14411]
Dalton Supply Co. Inc. [14412]
Daly and Sons Inc.; M.J. [23131]
Dana Kepner Co. [23132]
Davidson Pipe Supply Company Inc. [23133]
Davis Supply Co. [23134]
De Best Manufacturing Company Inc. [23135]
Delaware Plumbing Supply Co. [23136]
Design Air [14418]
Dickson Co.; C.C. [14422]
Diller Tile Company Inc. [23138]
Double-T Manufacturing Corp. [7283]
D.S.A. Materials Inc. [8635]
Duhig and Co. [23139]
Duluth Plumbing Supply Co. [23140]
Durastill Inc. [25639]
Duro Supply Co. [23141]
Durst Corp. [23142]
Dyer Co.; H.G. [23143]
Dynamic Distributors [7294]
Eastern Penn Supply Co. [23144]
Eau Claire Plumbing Supply Co. [23145]
Eckart Supply Company Inc. [8650]
Electrical Materials Co. [23146]
Elite Consumer Products [23147]
Emerson-Swan Inc. [23148]
Energy International Corp. [14432]
Energy Plus [14433]
Engineering and Equipment Co. [23149]
Envirotechnology Inc. [25644]
EPPSCO Supply [14434]
Ermco Inc. [23151]
Esco Supply Company Inc. [23152]
Esojon International, Inc. [9887]
Evans Inc. [14436]
E.W.C. Supply Inc. [23153]
Excelsior Manufacturing and Supply [14437]
Fager Company Inc.; R.F. [23154]

Fairbury Winnelson Co. [23155]
Fairfax Trailer Sales Inc. [14440]
Falcon Plumbing Inc. [23156]
Falk Supply Co. [23157]
Familian Northwest Inc. [23158]
Familian Pipe and Supply [23159]
Familiar Northwest [23160]
Famous Enterprises Inc. [14442]
Farris Enterprises [25647]
Faucet-Queens Inc. [13702]
Faucet-Queens Inc. [13703]
Federal Corp. [14443]
Federal Pipe and Supply Co. [7332]
Ferguson Enterprises [23162]
Ferguson Enterprises Inc. [14444]
Ferguson Enterprises, Inc. [14445]
Ferguson Enterprises Inc. [23163]
Ferguson Enterprises Inc. [14446]
Ferguson Enterprises Inc. [23164]
Ferguson Supply Co. [23165]
Fiberglass Representatives Inc. [23166]
Fibredyne Inc. [23167]
Fields and Co.; J.D. [7340]
Fields and Company of Lubbock Inc. [23168]
Filtemp Sales, Inc. [16860]
Fireplace Industries Inc. [14447]
Fireside Distributors [14448]
Fireside Distributors of Oregon, Inc. [14449]
First Supply Group [23169]
Flotec-Town and Country [23170]
Fluid-O-Tech International, Inc. [23171]
Forrer Supply Company Inc. [23173]
Fort Collins Winnelson Co. [23174]
Fort Smith Winnelson Co. [23175]
Frakco Inc. [23176]
Frederick Trading Co. [13715]
Frischkorn Distributors Inc. [23177]
Frontier Water and Steam Supply Co. [23178]
Fuller Supply Co. [23179]
Gage Co. [16885]
The Gage Co. [23180]
Gage Co. Redlon and Johnson Plumbing Supply
  Div. [23181]
Galloup Co.; J.O. [23182]
Gates Co. Inc.; B. [23183]
Gateway Appliance Distributing Co. [15143]
Gateway Supply Co. [23184]
Gateway Supply Company Inc. [23185]
General Mill Supplies Inc. [23186]
General Pipe and Supply Company Inc. [23187]
General Plumbing Supply Company of Maryland
  Inc. [23188]
Gensco, Inc. [14467]
Georgetown Energy Inc. [7391]
Gerber Inc.; Max [23189]
Gerber Plumbing Fixtures Corp. [23190]
Gilbert Pipe and Supply Co.; A.A. [23191]
Glaze Supply Company Inc. [8788]
Global Exports, Inc. [23192]
Global Products Company [16068]
Globe Inc. [23193]
Godby Products Inc. [14471]
Goddard Industries Inc. [16898]
Golden West Pipe & Supply Co. [23194]
Goldner Company Inc.; Herman [23195]
Goodin Co. [23196]
Goulet Supply Company Inc. [23197]
Graybow-Daniels Co. [23198]
Greensboro Pipe Company Inc. [16908]
Grinnell Supply Sales Co. [23199]
Hahn Supply Inc. [23200]
Hajoca Corp. [23201]
Ham and McCreight Inc. [23202]
Hardware Distribution Warehouses Inc. [13736]
Hardware Distributors Inc. [13737]
Harmony International Corporation [15162]
Harrington Corp. [23203]
Harris Supply Company Inc. [16925]
Harris Supply Company Inc. [23204]
Harrison Piping Supply Co. [23205]
Hazard and Sons Inc.; L.A. [23206]
Heat-N-Glo Fireplaces [14480]
Heatilator Inc. [7466]
Heatwave Supply Inc. [23207]
Heights Pump & Supply [24370]
The Helman Group Ltd. [15524]

Herald Wholesalers Inc. [13751]
Hercules Industries [20034]
Herzog Supply Inc.; C. [23208]
Hirsch Pipe & Supply Co. [23209]
Holloway Corp. [23210]
Holmes Plumbing and Heating Supply Inc. [23211]
Home Crafts Inc. [14487]
Home Reverse Osmosis Systems [23212]
Hotsy Corp. [23213]
HPM Building Supply [27320]
Hub/Industrial Mill Supply Co. [16934]
Hubbard Pipe and Supply Inc. [23214]
Hubbell Mechanical Supply Co. [14490]
Hughes Supply Inc. [23215]
Hughes Supply Inc. [23216]
Hurley Chicago Company Inc. [25683]
HVAC Sales and Supply Co. [14491]
ICS Intercounty Supply [23217]
Ideal Supply Co. [23218]
Illco Inc. [14494]
Inaqua International [25687]
Indiana Soft Water Service Inc. [15176]
Industrial Sales Company Inc. [23219]
Industrial Supply Co. [16951]
Industrial Supply Co. [16955]
Inland Supply Inc. [23220]
Intermountain Irrigation [23221]
International Consulting & Contracting
    Services [7517]
International Procurement Services, Inc. [7520]
Irr Supply Centers Inc. [23222]
J and B Supply Inc. [14496]
Jawz Inc. [25693]
Jay-K Independent Lumber Corp. [7532]
Jensen Bridge and Supply Co. [23224]
Jensen Distribution Services [13773]
Johnson Heater Corp. [14499]
Johnson Heating Supply [14500]
Johnson Pipe and Supply Co. [23225]
Johnstone Supply [14503]
Jomar Distributors Inc. [14506]
Jonesboro Winnelson Co. [16972]
Kamen Supply Company Inc. [23226]
Kansas City Winnelson Co. [23227]
Kaufman Supply [15184]
Keidel Supply Co. [23228]
Keller Supply Co. [23229]
Kelly Supply Company of Iowa [16983]
Kelly's Pipe and Supply Co. [23230]
Keltech, Inc. [23231]
Keltech Inc. [23232]
Kennewick Industrial and Electrical Supply
    Inc. [8937]
Kennewick Industry & Electric Supply [8938]
Kentucky Mine Supply Co. [16989]
Kessler Industries Inc. [23233]
Keystone Plumbing Sales Co. [23234]
Kiefaber Co.; W.H. [23235]
KII, Inc. [23236]
Kiss International [25702]
Kitchens Inc. of Paducah [15551]
Kleeko Enterprises [14510]
Knapp Supply Company Inc. [23237]
Knecht Home Lumber Center Inc. [7565]
Koremen Ltd. [23238]
Lakeside Supply Company Inc. [23239]
Langley Company Inc.; Frank P. [23240]
Lapure Water Coolers [15198]
Laredo Hardware [13793]
Lawson-Yates Inc. [23241]
Lazy-Man, Inc. [15201]
LCR Corp. [23242]
Lease Wholesale Plumbing Supply; A.L. [23243]
Lee Company Inc.; George G. [23244]
Lee Supply Corp. [23245]
Leonard's Stone & Fireplace [14524]
Lewis Supply Company Inc. [23246]
Lill and Son Inc.; Frank [16235]
Lipscomb and Co.; H.G. [13797]
Lite Brite Distributors [8994]
Longley Supply Company Inc. [23247]
M & L Trading Company, Inc. [11751]
Management Supply Co. [23248]
Manchester Wholesale Supply Inc. [23249]
Manoog Inc.; Charles [23250]
Marine Specialty Company Inc. [23251]

Marus and Weimer, Inc. [23252]
Maryville Wholesale Supply Inc. [23253]
Masda Corp. [15216]
Masda Corp. New England [15217]
Masters Supply Inc. [23254]
Matt-Son Inc. [23255]
Mazzei Injector Corp. [16276]
McDermott Co. Inc.; A.I. [23256]
McDonald Supply Co.; A.Y. [14537]
McDonald Supply Company Inc.; A.Y. [23257]
McKenzie Co.; P.C. [16280]
McMillan Sales Corp. [23258]
Mechanical Equipment Company Inc. [16284]
Merfish Supply Co.; N. [23259]
Merit Metal Products Corp. [23260]
Mermaid Water Services [25736]
Meyer Company Inc.; William F. [23261]
Michael Supply Company Inc. [15228]
Michel Company Inc.; R.E. [14570]
Michel Company Inc.; R.E. [14597]
Michel Company Inc.; R.E. [14598]
Michel Company Inc.; R.E. [14599]
Michel Company Inc.; R.E. [14601]
Michigan Industrial Piping Supply Company
    Inc. [23262]
Michigan Supply Co. [23263]
Microphor [23264]
Mid Pac Lumber [23265]
Mid-States Industrial Div. [23266]
Mid-States Supply Company Inc. [23267]
Middle Tennessee Utility District [15230]
Miller's Supply [23268]
Milwaukee Stove and Furnace Supply Company
    Inc. [14606]
Missouri Pipe Fittings Co. [23269]
Mitchell Hardware Co. [23270]
Modern Supply Company Inc. [23271]
Modern Supply Company Inc. [15238]
Modern Supply Company Inc. (Knoxville,
    Tennessee) [23272]
Moffett Co. Inc.; J.W. [14609]
Monarch Brass and Copper Corp. [13835]
Monogram Sanitation Co. [23273]
Monumental Supply Company Inc. [23274]
Mooney Process Equipment Co. [23275]
Moore-Handley Inc. [11931]
Moore Supply Co. [23276]
Morris Co.; Walter F. [23277]
Morrison Supply Co. [23278]
Mount Pleasant Hardware Inc. [21508]
Mountain States Pipe and Supply Co. [23279]
Mountain States Supply Inc. [23280]
Mountain Supply Co. [23281]
Mountainland Supply Co. [23282]
Mueller Sales Inc. [23283]
Murdock, Inc.; G.A. [23284]
Mutual Manufacturing and Supply Co. [14615]
Mutual Pipe and Supply Inc. [23285]
Mutual Services of Highland Park [13841]
National Safety Associates Inc. [23286]
Naughton Plumbing Sales, Inc. [23287]
Naughton Plumbing Sales Inc. [23288]
Nero Systems, Inc. [25755]
New Age Water Technology [25756]
New Energy Distributing [14618]
New Energy Distributors [23289]
Nikiforov, Inc.; George [14620]
Nimbus Water Systems, Inc. [25759]
Noble and Associates [25760]
Noland Co. [23290]
Noland Co. [23291]
Noland Co. [23292]
Noland Co. [23293]
Noland Co. [23294]
Noland Co. [14622]
Nor-Mar Sales Company Inc. [13848]
Norman Supply [23295]
Norman Supply Co. [23296]
North American Aqua Inc. [25762]
North Star Water Conditioning [25763]
North Star Water Conditioning [23297]
Northern Plumbing & Heating Supply [23298]
Northwest Pipe Fittings Inc. [23299]
N.R.G. Enterprises, Inc. [25766]
N.R.G. Enterprises Inc. [23300]
Nsa Independent Distributor [25767]

Nu-Way Supply Company Inc. [23301]
OASIS Corp. [25769]
Ohio Kitchen and Bath [15601]
Ohio Pipe and Supply Company Inc. [23302]
Ohio Pipe Valves and Fittings Inc. [17087]
One Stop Distributing [14628]
Osborn Machinery Company Inc. [13856]
Osmonics, Aquamatic [23303]
Osmonics, Inc. [25777]
Oswald Supply Company Inc.; H.C. [23304]
Ozotech, Inc. [25779]
Pacific Hardware & Specialties Inc. [13858]
Packing Seals and Engineering Company
    Inc. [23305]
Palermo Supply Company Inc. [23306]
Paragon Supply Co. [23307]
Park Supply Co. Inc. [15265]
Parkset Supply Ltd. [23308]
Parnell-Martin Co. [23309]
Passaic Metal & Building Supplies Co. [7838]
Peebles Supply Div. [23310]
Pelican Plumbing Supply Inc. [15269]
Penco Corp. [23311]
Penstan Supply [23312]
Perrigo Inc. [23313]
Petersen Products Co. [23314]
Pickrel Brothers Inc. [23315]
Picone Building Products [14636]
Pierson Co.; J.W. [22585]
Pittsburgh Plug and Products [23316]
Plainsco Inc. [15274]
Plant and Flanged Equipment [23317]
Plotts Brothers [23318]
Plumb Supply Co. [23319]
Plumbers Supply Co. [23320]
Plumbers Supply Co. [23321]
Plumber's Supply Company Inc. [23322]
Plumbing Distributors Inc. [23323]
PMI Sales and Marketing Services Inc. [23324]
Pomeco Corp. [14640]
Precision Fitting & Gauge Co. [23325]
Precision Fitting & Gauge Co. [23326]
Premier Manufactured Systems [25789]
Premier Manufactured Systems [23327]
Prescott Inc.; Everett J. [23328]
Preston Fuels; John [15279]
Primus Inc. [23329]
Pro-Flo Products [23330]
Probst Supply Co. [23331]
Prybil Enterprises [14645]
Pure Water International Inc. [25795]
Pureflow Ultraviolet, Inc. [23332]
Puro Filter Co. [25796]
R and R Plumbing Supply Corp. [23333]
Rainsoft Water Conditioning Co. [25797]
RAL Corp. [23334]
Ramclif Supply Co. [17128]
Rand & Jones Enterprises Co., Inc. [16437]
Raritan Supply Co. [23335]
RB Royal Industries Inc. [23336]
Reeve's Refrigeration & Heating Supply [14651]
Reeves-Wiedeman Co. [23337]
Rhoads Co.; D.W. [23339]
Riback Supply Company Inc. [23340]
Richards Manufacturing Company Inc. [23341]
Richmond Foundry Inc. [23342]
Ridgewood Corp. [23343]
RKB Enterprises Inc. [23345]
RMC Inc. [23346]
R.O. Systems International [25804]
Roberts-Hamilton Co., Div. of Hajoca
    Corp. [23347]
Robertson Heating Supply Co. [23348]
Robertson Supply Inc. [23349]
Rocamar Services Inc. [23350]
Roekel Co. [23351]
Roldan Products Corp. [15293]
Roosevelt Co.; W.A. [14667]
Ross Supply Company Inc. [23352]
Rubenstein Supply Co. [23353]
Rubenstein Supply Co. [23354]
Rundle-Spence Manufacturing Co. [23355]
S and G Trading Co. [26643]
Saffron Supply Co. [13899]
St. Louis Screw and Bolt Co. [23356]
Salina Supply Co. [23357]

Sanders Company Inc.; George T. [23358]
Satterlund Supply Co. [23359]
Sawyer and Company Inc.; J.E. [13904]
SB Developments Inc. [23360]
Schumacher and Seiler Inc. [23361]
Scottco Service Co. [23362]
Scotts Inc. [23363]
Scotty's Inc. [7993]
Scranton Sales Co. [23364]
Sea Recovery [23365]
Seashore Supply Company Inc. [23366]
Security Supply Corp. [23367]
Seghers Better Technology [16480]
Semler Industries Inc. [25812]
Seneca Plumbing and Heating Supply Company
    Inc. [23368]
Sentry/Liberty Hardware Distributors Inc. [13911]
Service Supply Systems Inc. [23369]
Sexauer Inc.; J.A. [23370]
SG Supply Co. [23371]
Shaklee Corp. [14234]
Sheehy Inc.; Charles D. [23372]
Shelby-Skipwith Inc. [14678]
Shipley Oil Co. [22668]
Shoemaker of Indiana, Inc. [14681]
Shore Distributors Inc. [14683]
Showcase Kitchens and Baths Inc. [23373]
Sidener Supply Co. [25815]
Sierra Craft Inc. [23374]
Sig Cox Inc. [23375]
Sign of the Crab Ltd. [23376]
Simmons-Huggins Supply Co. [23377]
Siroflex of America Inc. [23378]
Skipper Heating, Air Conditioning & Fireplace
    Showroom [14686]
Slakey Brothers Inc. [8030]
Sloan and Company Inc. [23379]
Sloan International, Inc. [25818]
Smith-Thompson Co. [17177]
S.M.S. Distributors [14687]
Smyth-Despard Company Inc. [16500]
Solares Florida Corp. [16501]
Solinger and Associates [15318]
Somerville Co.; Thomas [23380]
Somerville Co.; Thomas [23381]
Somerville Co.; Thomas [23382]
Somerville, Co.; Thomas [23383]
Somerville Co.; Thomas [23384]
Somerville Co.; Thomas [23385]
Somerville Co.; Thomas [23386]
Somerville Co.; Thomas [23387]
Somerville Co.; Thomas [23388]
Somerville Co.; Thomas [23389]
Somerville Co.; Thomas [23390]
Somerville Co.; Thomas [14688]
South Bend Supply Company Inc. [17181]
South Central Company Inc. [23391]
Southard Supply Inc. [23392]
Southern Pump and Filter Inc. [25826]
Southern Wholesalers Inc. [23393]
Southwest Cooperative Wholesale [18245]
Sprite Industries [23394]
SPS Company Inc. [23395]
Squire Supply Corp. [14694]
SR Distributing [25463]
Standard Plumbing Supply Company Inc. [23396]
Star Tubular Products Co. [23397]
State Pipe and Supply Inc. [20391]
State Supply Co. [23398]
Stuart's Federal Fireplace, Inc. [15670]
Summit Wholesale [14702]
Summit Wholesale [23399]
Superior Water Systems [25835]
Supply One Corp. [23400]
Swaim Supply Company Inc. [23401]
Swartz Supply Company Inc. [23402]
Sydney Supply Co. [23403]
Sydnor Hydrodynamics Inc. [16542]
T and L Supply Inc. [23404]
Tallman Company Inc. [23405]
Taylor Supply Co. [23406]
Teeco Products Inc. [22722]
Temperature Equipment Corp. [14717]
Terry Inc.; Jesse E. [23407]
Theis Company Inc.; H.W. [23408]
Thornburg Co. Inc.; C.I. [23409]

Thornton Industries, Inc. [13953]
Thorpe Co.; B.K. [23410]
Toole and Company Inc. [23411]
Torrington Supply Company Inc. [23412]
Touch Flo Manufacturing [23413]
TradeCom International Inc. [13961]
Trayco Inc. [23414]
Treaty Co. [23415]
Tri-Bro Supply Co. [23416]
Tri-City Fuel and Heating Company Inc. [14737]
Tri-State Distributors Inc. [14738]
Triangle Supply Company Inc. [23417]
Trumbull Industries Inc. [23418]
Tulare Pipe and Electric Supply Co. [9516]
Turtle Island Herbs Inc. [23419]
Ultra Hardware Products LLC [13970]
Uni-Flange Corp. [23420]
Unicen Wastewater Treatment Co. [25852]
United Pipe and Supply Company Inc. [23422]
United Plumbing and Heating Supply Co. [23423]
U.S. Pure Water Corp. [25858]
Universal Aqua [25859]
Universal Supply Company Inc. [23424]
Usco Inc. [23425]
Utica Plumbing Supply Co. [23426]
Utility Supply Co. [25861]
Utter Company Inc. [14750]
Vail Enterprises Inc. [23427]
Valley Cities Supply Co. [23428]
Valley Controls & Supply Co. [14753]
Valley Supply Co. [23429]
Vamac Inc. [23430]
Vena Tech Corp. [25866]
Vermont Hardware Company Inc. [25501]
Vierk Industrial Products [23432]
Village Products [14755]
Vinson Supply Co. [23433]
Waldor Pump and Equipment [25869]
Waldor Pump and Equipment [23434]
Wallace Company Inc. [23435]
Wallace Pump and Supply Company Inc. [23436]
Wallace Supply Co. [23437]
Washburn-Garfield Corp. [23438]
Water Products International, Inc. [25873]
Water Safety Corporation of America [25874]
Water and Waste Water Equipment Co. [23439]
Water Works [25875]
Watts Regulator Co. [23441]
Watts/Taras Valve Corp. [23442]
Waxman Industries Inc. [23443]
Wayne Pipe and Supply Inc. [23444]
Wayne Pipe and Supply Inc. [23445]
Webb Co.; F.W. [23446]
Webstone Company Inc. [23447]
Weinstein Supply Corp. [23448]
Welbilt Corp. [15369]
Welker-McKee Supply Co. Division of
    Hajoca [23449]
West Bend Water Systems [25876]
West Texas Wholesale Supply Co. [23450]
Westburne Supply Inc. [23451]
Western Nevada Supply Co. [23452]
Western Purifier Water Purifier Co. [23453]
Western Steel and Plumbing Inc. [23454]
Western Water Products, Inc. [25878]
Wholesale Distributors of Alaska [23455]
Wholesale Distributors of Alaska [23456]
Wholesale Supply Group Inc. [23457]
Wholesale Supply Group, Inc. Maryville
    Division [23458]
Wichita Sheet Metal Supply Co. [14766]
Wilkins Supply Co.; M.P. [23459]
Wilkinson Supply Inc. [23460]
Willar Corp. [14767]
William/Reid Ltd. [25882]
Wilmar Industries Inc. [23461]
Win Nelson Inc. [23462]
Winnelson Inc. [23463]
Wisconsin Supply Corp. [23464]
Wittock Supply Co. [23465]
Wolff Brothers Supply Inc. [23466]
World Wide Metric, Inc. [23467]
Worldwide Manufacturing Inc. [15715]
Yaun Company Inc. [23468]
York Corrugating Co. [23469]
Yuma Winnelson Co. [23470]

Zenith Supply Company Inc. [17295]

SIC 5075 — Warm Air Heating & Air-Conditioning

A-1 Refrigeration Inc. [14286]
A and A Mechanical Inc. [15720]
A & R Supply Co. Inc. [14287]
AARP Inc. [8258]
ABC Appliance Inc. White Automotive Association
    Div. [14288]
ABCO Refrigeration Supply Corp. [14289]
Able Distributors [14290]
ABR Wholesale, Inc. [14291]
AC & R Specialty Supply [14292]
Ace Plumbing and Electrical Supply, Inc. [23050]
Acme Heat & Power [14293]
Acme Manufacturing Co. [14294]
Acme Refrigeration [14295]
Acme Refrigeration of Baton Rouge Inc. [14296]
ACR Group Inc. [14297]
ACR Supply Inc. (Houston, Texas) [14298]
Actrade International Corp. [14299]
AES of Norfolk Inc. [14300]
AES of Oklahoma Inc. [14301]
AES of Roanoke Inc. [14302]
Affiliated Holdings Inc. [14303]
Air Engineering Co. Inc. [19737]
Air O Quip Corp. [14304]
Air Parts Inc. [14305]
Air Rite Filters Inc. [14306]
Air Systems Distributors Inc. [14307]
Air Temperature Inc. [14308]
Airfan Engineered Products Inc. [14309]
Akin Medical Equipment International [19128]
Albany Steel & Brass Corp. [13543]
Algert Company, Inc. [14998]
AllerMed Corp. [14313]
Allred's Inc. [14315]
American Environmental Systems Inc. [23062]
American Filtration Systems Inc. [14317]
American Hermetics, Inc. [14318]
American Metals Supply Co. Inc. [14319]
American Technotherm Corp. [14320]
Anchor Commerce Trading Corp. [6973]
Andrew Co.; W.T. [23065]
Andrews Distributing Company Inc. [14322]
Apco Inc. [15014]
Apex Supply Company Inc. [14323]
API Appliance Parts Inc. [15015]
Appliance Parts Center Inc. [15018]
Appliance Parts Inc. [15026]
Applied Membranes Inc. [25555]
APR Supply Co. [14325]
Arctic Technical Services [14326]
Armstrong International Inc. Three Rivers
    Div. [15034]
Arrow-Cold Control Appliance Parts Co. [15035]
Auer Steel & Heating Supply [14328]
Authorized Refrigeration Parts Co. [14329]
Automatic Equipment Sales of Virginia Inc. [14330]
Automatic Firing Inc. [14331]
Baker Distributing Co. [14333]
Baker Distributing Co. [14334]
Ball Pipe & Supply; Leif [23076]
Barnebey and Sutcliffe Corp. [14338]
Bartells Co.; E. J [16721]
Beckman Brothers Inc. [23080]
Behler-Young Co. [14342]
Bells Supply Co. [23082]
Berkheimer Company Inc.; G.W. [14343]
Berkheimer Company Inc. South Bend;
    G.W. [14344]
Big Sky Paint Co., Heating & Air
    Conditioning [21400]
Biggs Pump and Supply Inc. [23086]
Billings Distributing Corp. [14346]
Birdsall and Company Inc.; W.A. [23088]
Bitzer Company Inc.; R.D. [14348]
Boiler and Heat Exchange Systems Inc. [23091]
Brackett Supply Inc. [14356]
Brehob Corp. [15843]
Briggs Incorporated of Omaha [23095]

Brock-McVey Co. [14359]
Browning Metal Products Co. [14360]
Brown's Heating & Air Conditioning; Bob [14361]
Bruce-Rogers Company Inc. [23099]
Burke Engineering Company Inc. [14363]
Burns Supply/Great Lakes Inc. [23103]
Butcher Air Conditioning Co. [14364]
C and L Supply Inc. [15069]
Cain and Bultman Co. [8482]
Camco Services Inc. [14366]
Capitol Plumbing and Heating Supply Co. [23104]
Capitol Plumbing and Heating Supply Company Inc. [23105]
Carrier Corp./Bldg Sys and Svc Di [14367]
Carrier North Carolina [14368]
Carroll Air Systems Inc. [14369]
Cashwell Appliance Parts Inc. [15079]
Cavallero Heating and Air Conditioning Inc. [14371]
Central Air Conditioning Distributor [14373]
Central Air Conditioning Distributors Inc. [14374]
Central Engineering & Supply Co. [14375]
Central Plains Distributing Inc. [14377]
Century Air Conditioning and Maintenance Supply, Inc. [14379]
Century Air Conditioning Supply Inc. [14380]
Champlain Winair Co. [23114]
Chase Supply Co. [14382]
Checkpoint International [18736]
Chicago Furnace Supply Inc. [14383]
Clarks Distributing Co. [14384]
Climatic Control Company Inc. [14386]
Climatic Corp. [14387]
Coastal Supply Company Inc. [14388]
Coastline Distributing [14389]
Coastline Distribution Inc. [14390]
Cochrane Supply and Engineering, Inc. [14391]
Columbia Pipe and Supply [14393]
Comfort Mart Dist. Inc. [14394]
Comfort Supply Inc. [14395]
Comfort Supply Inc. [14396]
Comfortmaker Distribution [14397]
Conestoga Heating and Plumbing Supply Inc. [23121]
Conklin and Company Inc.; Lyon [14400]
Contractors Heating and Supply Co. [13645]
Cooling & Heating Inc. [14404]
Corken Steel Products Co. [14405]
Cosco Inc. [14407]
D & L Appliance Parts Company, Inc. [15104]
Dales Mechanical Sales & Service [14411]
Dalton Supply Co. Inc. [14412]
Dennis Supply Co. [14416]
DESA International Inc. [14417]
Design Air [14418]
Dey Distributing [14419]
Dickson CC Co. [14420]
Dickson CC Co. [14421]
Dickson Co.; C.C. [14422]
Donico & Associates; J.P. [18778]
Duncan Supply Co. Inc. [14424]
Earth Energy Technology and Supply Inc. [14425]
Eau Claire Plumbing Supply Co. [23145]
ECS Marketing Services Inc. [14428]
Ehrhart Co.; T.F. [14430]
Elixir Industries [14431]
Emerson-Swan Inc. [23148]
Engineering and Equipment Co. [23149]
EPPSCO Supply [14434]
Equipment Sales Corp. [14435]
Evans Inc. [14436]
Excelsior Manufacturing and Supply [14437]
Fabricated Systems of Atlanta [14438]
Fadson International Company [14439]
Fairbury Winnelson Co. [23155]
Fairfax Trailer Sales Inc. [14440]
Familiar Northwest [23160]
Famous Industries [23161]
Famous Manufacturing Co. [16006]
Federal Corp. [14443]
Federal Heating and Engineering Company Inc. [22272]
Ferguson Enterprises Inc. [14444]
Ferguson Enterprises Inc. [14446]
Ferguson Supply Co. [23165]
First Supply Group [23169]

Fleming Associates Inc.; J.S. [14450]
Fox Appliance Parts of Macon Inc. [15134]
Frontier Water and Steam Supply Co. [23178]
Furnace & Duct Supply Co. [14454]
The Gage Co. [23180]
Gateway Supply Company Inc. [23185]
Geary Pacific Corp. [14457]
Gemaire Distributors Inc. [14458]
General Heating and Cooling Co. [14459]
General Motors Corporation - Harrison Div. [14460]
Gensco, Inc. [14461]
Gensco, Inc. [14462]
Gensco, Inc. [14463]
Gensco, Inc. [14464]
Gensco Inc. [14465]
Gensco, Inc. [14466]
Gensco, Inc. [14467]
Gensco, Inc. [14468]
Gensco, Inc. [14469]
Gensco, Inc. [19999]
Globe Inc. [23193]
Goodin Co. [23196]
Graybow-Daniels Co. [23198]
Griffin Refrigeration Inc. [14474]
Habegger Corp. [14476]
Hajoca Corp. [23201]
Hammond Sheet Metal Company Inc. [14477]
Harmony International Corporation [15162]
Hazard and Sons Inc.; L.A. [23206]
Heat Inc. [14479]
Heating-Cooling Distributors Inc. [14481]
Heating and Cooling Supply Inc. [14482]
Heating Specialties of New Hampshire [14483]
HEPA Corp. [14484]
Hercules Industries [20034]
Hewitt Brothers Inc. [817]
Houston Trane [14488]
Hubbell Mechanical Supply Co. [14490]
Hughes Supply Inc. [23216]
HVAC Sales and Supply Co. [14491]
ICS Intercounty Supply [23217]
Indiana Supply Corp. [14495]
Industrial Supply Co. [16951]
Industrial Supply Co. [16955]
Inland Supply Inc. [23220]
Interatech [6385]
International Hi-Tech Trading Corp. [2793]
International Procurement Services, Inc. [7520]
International Projects Inc. [23747]
Intraco Corp. [2796]
Irr Supply Centers Inc. [23222]
J and B Supply Inc. [14496]
Johnson Controls, Inc. [14498]
Johnson Heater Corp. [14499]
Johnson Heating Supply [14500]
Johnson Supply and Equipment Corp. [14501]
Johnston Company Inc.; George L. [14502]
Johnstone Supply [14503]
Johnstone Supply [14504]
Johnstone Supply [14505]
Kauphusman Inc.; F.W. [14507]
Kelmar Corp. [14508]
KII, Inc. [23236]
Kirsch Energy System [14509]
Kleeko Enterprises [14510]
Kleenaire Corp. [14511]
Klinge Corp. [14512]
Koch Filter Corp. [25703]
L & D Appliance Corp. [15195]
Larson Co.; Gustave A. [14516]
Lay International Consulting Services [14517]
LDI MFG Co., Inc. [14518]
Lease Wholesale Plumbing Supply; A.L. [23243]
Lehman's Commercial Service [14521]
Leonard Refrigeration & Heating Sales & Service [14523]
Lomanco Inc. [14527]
Longley Supply Company Inc. [23247]
Lucky Distributing [974]
M & E Sales - A Honeywell Business [24390]
Maines Paper and Food Service Inc. Equipment and Supply Div. [14530]
Manoog Inc.; Charles [23250]
Marco Sales Inc. [14531]
Marus and Weimer, Inc. [23252]

Mason Supply Co. [14533]
McClintock and Bustad Inc. [14534]
McCrudden Heating Supply [14536]
McDonald Supply Co.; A.Y. [14537]
McKenney Supply Inc. [14538]
Mechanical Services of Orlando Inc. [14540]
Metropolitan AC & Refrigeration [14544]
Michel Company Inc.; R.E. [14545]
Michel Company Inc.; R.E. [14546]
Michel Company Inc.; R.E. [14547]
Michel Company Inc.; R.E. [14548]
Michel Company Inc.; R.E. [14549]
Michel Company Inc.; R.E. [14550]
Michel Company Inc.; R.E. [14551]
Michel Company Inc.; R.E. [14552]
Michel Company Inc.; R.E. [14553]
Michel Company Inc.; R.E. [14554]
Michel Company Inc.; R.E. [14555]
Michel Company Inc.; R.E. [14556]
Michel Company Inc.; R.E. [14557]
Michel Company Inc.; R.E. [14558]
Michel Company Inc.; R.E. [14559]
Michel Company Inc.; R.E. [14560]
Michel Company Inc.; R.E. [14561]
Michel Company Inc.; R.E. [14562]
Michel Company Inc.; R.E. [14563]
Michel Company Inc.; R.E. [14564]
Michel Company Inc.; R.E. [14565]
Michel Company Inc.; R.E. [14566]
Michel Company Inc.; R.E. [14567]
Michel Company Inc.; R.E. [14568]
Michel Company Inc.; R.E. [14569]
Michel Company Inc.; R.E. [14571]
Michel Company Inc.; R.E. [14572]
Michel Company. Inc.; R.E. [14573]
Michel Company Inc.; R.E. [14574]
Michel Company Inc.; R.E. [14575]
Michel Company Inc.; R.E. [14576]
Michel Company Inc.; R.E. [14577]
Michel Company Inc.; R.E. [14578]
Michel Company Inc.; R.E. [14579]
Michel Company Inc.; R.E. [14580]
Michel Company Inc.; R.E. [14581]
Michel Company Inc.; R.E. [14582]
Michel Company Inc.; R.E. [14583]
Michel Company Inc.; R.E. [14584]
Michel Company Inc.; R.E. [14585]
Michel Company Inc.; R.E. [14586]
Michel Company Inc.; R.E. [14587]
Michel Company Inc.; R.E. [14588]
Michel Company Inc.; R.E. [14589]
Michel Company Inc.; R.E. [14590]
Michel Company Inc.; R.E. [14591]
Michel Company Inc.; R.E. [14592]
Michel Company Inc.; R.E. [14593]
Michel Company Inc.; R.E. [14594]
Michel Company Inc.; R.E. [14595]
Michel Company Inc.; R.E. [14596]
Michel Company Inc.; R.E. [14597]
Michel Company Inc.; R.E. [14598]
Michel Company Inc.; R.E. [14599]
Michel Company Inc.; R.E. [14600]
Michel Company Inc.; R.E. [14601]
Michigan Supply Co. [23263]
Mid-Lakes Distributing Inc. [14602]
Mid-States Industrial Div. [23266]
Miller Refrigeration Supply Co. [14604]
Mingledorffs Inc. [14607]
Modern Supply Company Inc. (Knoxville, Tennessee) [23272]
Moore Supply Co. [14610]
Mutual Pipe and Supply Inc. [23285]
Myers Group Inc.; J.B. [14616]
National Temperature Control Centers Inc. [14617]
NGE Inc. [14619]
Nikiforov, Inc.; George [14620]
Noland Co. [23290]
Noland Co. [14621]
Noland Co. [14622]
Noland Co. [14623]
North Atlantic Engineering Co. [9132]
Northeast Louisiana Heating & Air Distributing [14624]
Nu-Way Supply Company Inc. [23301]
O'Connor Company, Inc. [14626]
O'Connor Company, Inc. [14627]

Orbilt Compressors, Inc. [14629]
Pacific Combustion Engineering Inc. [24413]
Pameco Corp. [14631]
Paragon Supply Co. [23307]
Passage Supply Co. [14632]
Pelican Plumbing Supply Inc. [15269]
Pells Radio Center [15270]
Penco Corp. [23311]
Penstan Supply [23312]
Phillips Energy Inc. [23879]
Plotts Brothers [23318]
Plumb Supply Co. [23319]
Potter Distributing Inc. [14642]
Primus Inc. [23329]
Pro Air Inc. [14643]
Progressive Wholesale Supply Co. [14644]
Prybil Enterprises [14645]
R and R Plumbing Supply Corp. [23333]
RAL Corp. [23334]
Ramclif Supply Co. [17128]
Recife Importing & Exporting Inc. [14648]
RECO [14649]
Reeve's Refrigeration & Heating Supply [14651]
Refractory Products Co. [14652]
Refrigeration & Air-Conditioning Maintenance
   Co. [14653]
Refrigeration Equipment Co. [14655]
Refrigeration Sales Corp. [14657]
Refron Inc. [14661]
Riback Supply Company Inc. [23340]
Richards Manufacturing Company Inc. [23341]
Ridgewood Corp. [23343]
Robertshaw Uni-Line North America [14664]
Robertson Heating Supply Co. [23348]
Robinson Fin Machines Inc. [14665]
Rood Utilities [14666]
Roosevelt Co.; W.A. [14667]
Royal Sovereign Corp. [14669]
Rubenstein Supply Co. [23353]
Rundle-Spence Manufacturing Co. [23355]
Sabol and Rice Inc. [14671]
Salina Supply Co. [23357]
Saunco Air Technologies [14673]
Schumacher and Seiler Inc. [23361]
Scottco Service Co. [23362]
Scranton Sales Co. [23364]
Seneca Plumbing and Heating Supply Company
   Inc. [23368]
Servall Co. [15309]
Servidyne System [14677]
Shelby-Skipwith Inc. [14678]
Shelton Winair Co. [14679]
Shipley Oil Co. [22668]
Shoemaker of Indiana, Inc. [14681]
Shollmier Distribution Inc. [14682]
Shore Distributors Inc. [14683]
Shurail Supply Inc. [14684]
Sig Cox Inc. [23375]
Skipper Heating, Air Conditioning & Fireplace
   Showroom [14686]
Slakey Brothers Inc. [8030]
Smith Detroit Diesel [3231]
Somerville Co.; Thomas [23386]
Somerville Co.; Thomas [23387]
Somerville Co.; Thomas [23388]
Somerville Co.; Thomas [23389]
Somerville Co.; Thomas [23390]
Somerville Co.; Thomas [14688]
South Central Company Inc. [23391]
Southern California Air-Conditioning
   Distributors [14691]
Southern Filters Inc. [17184]
Southern Refrigeration Corp. [14692]
Squire Supply Corp. [14694]
Standfix Air Distribution Products - ACME [14696]
Star Steel Supply Co. [14699]
State Supply Co. [23398]
Sturdvant Refrigeration/Air-Conditioning [14700]
Suburban Manufacturing Co. [14701]
Superior Supply Co. [14703]
Superior Supply Co. [14704]
Superior Supply Co. [14705]
Superior Supply Co. [14706]
Superior Supply Co. [14707]
Superior Supply Co. [14708]
Superior Supply Company Inc. [14709]

Swaim Supply Company Inc. [23401]
Sydney Supply Co. [23403]
Symbol Inc. [5852]
Tallman Company Inc. [23405]
Tarrant Service Agency, Inc. [14710]
TDI Air Conditioning Appliances [15334]
Teknis Corp. [9471]
Tempaco Inc. [14715]
Temperature Equipment Corp. [14717]
Temperature Systems Inc. [14718]
Terralink International [5790]
Terry Inc.; Jesse E. [23407]
Tesco Distributors Inc. [14719]
Tesdell Refrigeration Supply Inc. [14720]
Thermo King of Chattanooga [14724]
Thorpe Insulation Co. [8125]
Three States [14727]
Three States Supply Co. [14728]
Torrington Supply Company Inc. [23412]
Total Supply [14729]
Total Supply [14730]
Total Supply [14731]
Total Supply Inc. [14732]
Traco Industrial Corp. [14733]
Tradex Corporation [14734]
Trane Co [14735]
Transport Refrigeration of Sioux Falls [14736]
Treaty Co. [23415]
Tri-Bro Supply Co. [23416]
Tri-City Fuel and Heating Company Inc. [14737]
Tri-State Distributors Inc. [14738]
Ultima [14742]
Underwood HVAC, Inc. [14743]
United Automatic Heating Supplies [14744]
United Automatic Heating Supplies [14745]
United Automatic Heating Supplies [14746]
United Automatic Heating Supplies [14747]
United Refrigeration Inc. [14748]
Universal Management Consultants Inc. [14749]
Utica Plumbing Supply Co. [23426]
Utter Company Inc. [14750]
Vair Corp. [14751]
Valley Controls & Supply Co. [14753]
Valley Supply Co. [23429]
Vellano Brothers Inc. [25865]
Vena Tech Corp. [25866]
Vierk Industrial Products [23432]
Vlcek Corp.; Jerry K. [16604]
Voorhees Company Inc.; The Bill [14756]
Vorys Brothers Inc. [14757]
Weathertrol Supply Company Inc. [14759]
Webb Co.; F.W. [23446]
Weinstein Supply Corp. [23448]
Welker-McKee Supply Co. Division of
   Hajoca [23449]
Wesley Electric and Supply Inc. [14760]
Westburne Supply Inc. [23451]
Western MacArthur Co. [8208]
Western Nevada Supply Co. [23452]
Whalen Co. [4731]
Wheelabrator Air Pollution Control [25879]
Wheelock Company Inc.; George F. [14763]
Wholesale Distributors of Alaska [23455]
Wholesale Heating Supply Co. [14765]
Wichita Sheet Metal Supply Co. [14766]
Willar Corp. [14767]
Willco Wholesale Distributors [14768]
Wisconsin Supply Corp. [23464]
Witherspoon Supply; Yandle [14770]
Wittichen Supply Company Inc. [14771]
Wolff Brothers Supply Inc. [23466]
Yaun Company Inc. [23468]
Yeomans Distributing Co. [14774]
York Corrugating Co. [23469]
York International Corp. [14775]
Young Co.; Behler [14777]
Young Co.; Behler [14778]
Young Co.; Behler [14779]
Young Co.; Behler [14780]
Young Co.; Behler [14781]
Young Co.; Behler [14782]
Young Co.; Behler [14783]
Young Co.; Behler [14784]
Young Co.; Behler [14785]
Young Co.; Behler [14786]
Young Supply North; Frank [14788]

Ziegler Repair [14789]

SIC 5078 — Refrigeration Equipment & Supplies

A-1 Refrigeration Inc. [14286]
A & R Supply Co. Inc. [14287]
AA Water Service [14987]
ABCO Refrigeration Supply Corp. [14289]
AC & R Specialty Supply [14292]
Acme Refrigeration [14295]
ACR Supply Inc. (Houston, Texas) [14298]
All City Refrigeration Co. Inc. [14311]
All Seasons Engines Inc. [14312]
Almerica Overseas Inc. [40]
American Excelsior Co. [14316]
Amtrol International Inc. [14321]
Associated Appliance Service [14327]
Authorized Refrigeration Parts Co. [14329]
Automatic Ice & Beverage Inc. [14332]
Baker Distributing Co. [14333]
Baker Distributing Co. [14334]
Baker-Hauser Co. [14335]
Bales & Truitt Company Inc. [14336]
Bar Beverage Control Inc. [14337]
Barnett Supply Co. Inc. [14339]
Bee Jay Refrigeration Inc. [14341]
Bev-Tech, Inc. [14345]
Biloff Manufacturing Co. Inc. [14347]
Blu-Ridge Sales Inc. [14349]
BMI Equipment Dist. [14350]
Boat Electric Co. Inc. [14351]
Boise Refrigeration Service Co. [14352]
Bowman Refrigeration Inc. [14354]
Brannon; Thomas [14357]
Brock-McVey Co. [14359]
Buffalo Hotel Supply Company Inc. [25585]
Burke Engineering Company Inc. [14363]
Butler & Sons Refrigeration [14365]
Camco Services Inc. [14366]
Castor; Stanley [14370]
Celsco Inc. [14372]
Central Engineering & Supply Co. [14375]
Champion Distributors Inc. [14381]
Clark's Store Fixtures Inc. [4599]
Cochrane Supply and Engineering, Inc. [14391]
Colorado Commercial Refrigeration [14392]
Commercial Equipment & Design, Inc. [14398]
Commercial Refrigeration Inc. [14399]
Continental Equipment Co. [14401]
Control-Equip of Tennessee, Inc. [14402]
Convoy Servicing Co. Inc. [14403]
Cooling & Heating Inc. [14404]
Cornforths [14406]
Cosco Inc. [14407]
Crystal Refrigeration Inc. [14408]
Cummins Southwest Inc. [2516]
D & D Transport Refrigeration Services [14409]
Dakota Refrigeration Inc. [14410]
DeMar Inc.; M & T [14414]
Dennis Refrigeration & Electric [14415]
Dennis Supply Co. [14416]
Deuster Co. [24104]
Dickson Co.; C.C. [14422]
Dugan Equipment & Supply Co. [14423]
Eastern Refrigeration Co. [14426]
Ecology Detergents Inc. [14427]
EDS Refrigeration Inc. [14429]
Engan-Tooley-Doyle & Associates Inc. [23652]
Exmart International, Inc. [24112]
Falgouts Refrigeration & Appliance Service [14441]
FES [24116]
Fetzer Company-Restaurateurs [24117]
Filbert Refrigeration [24118]
Flihan Co.; Joseph [24123]
Fountain Dispensers Co. Inc. [14451]
Freeman Corp. [14452]
French Refrigeration Co. [14453]
Gardner and Benoit Inc. [24126]
Gartner Refrigeration Inc. [14455]
Gaskins; Carlton J. [14456]
Gills Automotive Inc. [14470]
Goodell's Refrigeration [14472]

Goodwin Refrigeration Co. Inc. [14473]
Griffin Refrigeration Inc. [14474]
Grover Brothers Equipment Inc. [14475]
Harken Inc. [14478]
Harmony International Corporation [15162]
HIM Mechanical Systems Inc. [14485]
Hinshaw Supply Company of California [14486]
Hispania Trading Corporation [25680]
Hockenberg Equipment Co. [24138]
HRS Corp. [14489]
Ice Systems & Supplies Inc. [14492]
ICEE Distributors Inc. [14493]
Illco Inc. [14494]
Illinois Auto Electric Co. [16142]
International Hi-Tech Trading Corp. [2793]
Jeter Store Equipment, Inc.; Ken [14497]
Johnson Supply and Equipment Corp. [14501]
Johnston Company Inc.; George L. [14502]
Klinge Corp. [14512]
Kold Temp Refigeration Inc. [14513]
Kopecky & Co.; J. M. [14514]
Kru-Kel Co. Inc. [14515]
Lapure Water Coolers [15198]
Larson Co.; Gustave A. [14516]
Lee's Refrigeration [14519]
Lees Refrigeration, Div. of Hussmann
  Corp. [14520]
Lehman's Commercial Service [14521]
Leming Supply Inc. [14522]
Lindox Equipment Corp. [24166]
Lit Refrigeration Co. [25718]
LKS International Inc. [24168]
LKS International Inc. [14525]
Lloyd's Refrigeration Inc. [14526]
Magic Refrigeration Co. [14528]
Magnum Equipment Inc. [14529]
Maines Paper and Food Service Inc. Equipment
  and Supply Div. [14530]
Major Appliances Inc. [24176]
Market Equipment Company Inc. [14532]
Mason Supply Co. [14533]
McCormick Refrigeration [14535]
McKenney Supply Inc. [14538]
Mechanical Refrigeration & AC [14539]
Metro Refrigeration Supply, Inc. [14541]
Metro Refrigeration Supply, Inc. [14542]
Metro Refrigeration Supply, Inc. [14543]
Michel Company Inc.; R.E. [14555]
Michel Company Inc.; R.E. [14557]
Michel Company Inc.; R.E. [14558]
Michel Company Inc.; R.E. [14560]
Michel Company Inc.; R.E. [14561]
Michel Company Inc.; R.E. [14594]
Michel Company Inc.; R.E. [14595]
Michel Company Inc.; R.E. [14596]
Michel Company Inc.; R.E. [14600]
Michel Company Inc.; R.E. [14601]
Mike's Refrigeration Inc. [14603]
Miller Refrigeration Supply Co. [14604]
Miller Supply Inc.; Bud [14605]
Mobile Fleet Service of Spokane [14608]
Moffett Co. Inc.; J.W. [14609]
Mountain Sales & Service Inc. [14612]
MR Supply Inc. [14613]
Mulder Refrigeration [14614]
National Temperature Control Centers Inc. [14617]
NJCT Corp. [24194]
Noland Co. [23290]
Northern California Beverage Company
  Inc. [24998]
Northwest Diesel & Refrigeration Services [14625]
Osgood SM Company Inc. [14630]
Patten Inc.; H.I. [24203]
Pelreco Inc. [14634]
Phillips Ice Service Inc. [14635]
Pilottes Transport Refrigeration [14637]
Plains Auto Refrigeration [14638]
Polar Refrigeration & Restaurant
  Equipment [14639]
Pomeco Corp. [14640]
Prybil Enterprises [14645]
Pure Water Centers [15283]
Pure Water Centers, Inc. [15284]
R & B Service Co. [14646]
R & E Supply Inc. [14647]
RECO [14649]

Red Gaskins and Co.; J. [24209]
Red River Electric & Refrigeration Supply [14650]
Reeve's Refrigeration & Heating Supply [14651]
Refrigeration & Air-Conditioning Maintenance
  Co. [14653]
Refrigeration Contractors Inc. [14654]
Refrigeration and Electric Supply Co. [15288]
Refrigeration Equipment Co. [14655]
Refrigeration Heating Inc. [14656]
Refrigeration Sales Corp. [14657]
Refrigeration Sales Inc. [14658]
Refrigeration Suppliers Inc. [14659]
Refrigeration Supply Co. [14660]
Refron Inc. [14661]
Restaurant Design & Development [14662]
RI Refrigeration Supply Co. [14663]
Richlund Enterprises [15292]
Roosevelt Co.; W.A. [14667]
Roswell Winnelson Co. [14668]
RTI Technologies, Inc. [14670]
Salem Refrigeration Company Inc. [14672]
Sawnee Refrigeration & Welding Supply,
  Inc. [14674]
Scatena York Company [14675]
Scott's Market Equipment Inc. [14676]
Shepler Refrigeration Inc. [14680]
Shoemaker of Indiana, Inc. [14681]
Sisco Products Inc. [14685]
Soukup Brothers Mechanical Inc. [14689]
Southeast Wholesale Equipment Distributors
  Inc. [14690]
Southern Refrigeration Corp. [14692]
SPL Associates Inc. [14693]
Stancil Refrigeration Services Inc.; Bruce [14695]
Star Restaurant Equipment & Supplies [14698]
Stewart and Stevenson Services Inc.
  Texas [16524]
Structural Concepts Corp. [24231]
Superior Products [24234]
Superior Products Manufacturing Co. [24235]
Superior Supply Co. [14703]
Superior Supply Co. [14704]
Superior Supply Co. [14705]
Superior Supply Co. [14706]
Superior Supply Co. [14707]
Superior Supply Co. [14708]
Tarrant Service Agency, Inc. [14710]
Taylor Dakota Distributors [14711]
Taylor Distributors of Indiana [14712]
Teague Refrigeration Service [14714]
Tempco Supplies Inc. [14716]
Temperature Equipment Corp. [14717]
Tesco Distributors Inc. [14719]
Thermal Equipment Company Inc. [14721]
Thermal Supply Inc. [14722]
Thermo King of Baltimore Inc. [14723]
Thermo King of Nashville Inc. [14725]
Thermo King of Sioux Falls [14726]
Traco Industrial Corp. [14733]
Tradex Corporation [14734]
Trane Co [14735]
Transport Refrigeration of Sioux Falls [14736]
Truck Thermo King Inc. [14739]
Twin City ICEE Inc. [14741]
Twin City Supply Company [15346]
Ultima [14742]
United Refrigeration Inc. [14748]
United Restaurant Equipment [24256]
United States Electric Co. [9526]
Vair Corp. [14751]
Val Dere Co.; W.R. [14752]
Valley Controls & Supply Co. [14753]
Valley Controls and Supply Co. [14754]
Washer and Refrigeration Supply Company
  Inc. [15365]
Washita Refrigeration & Equipment Co. [14758]
Water Warehouse, Etc. [25050]
Weathertrol Supply Company Inc. [14759]
Weil and Sons, Inc.; Joseph [21986]
Western Pioneer Sales Co. [25877]
Westside Development Inc. [14762]
White Inc. [14764]
Winterbottom Supply Co. [14769]
Wittichen Supply Company Inc. [14771]
Wolpert Refrigeration Inc. [14772]
Wurzbach Company Inc.; William [14773]

York International Corp. Frick/Reco Div. [14776]
Young Supply Co. [14787]
Ziegler Repair [14789]

SIC 5082 — Construction & Mining
Machinery

Able Equipment Inc. [6904]
Acme Coal Co. [6909]
Action Equipment Company Inc. [6911]
Advance Scaffold of Alaska [6916]
Advanced Equipment Inc. [6918]
Agorra Building Supply Inc. [6925]
Albany Ladder Company Inc. [6929]
Allied Construction Equipment Co. [6943]
Altec Industries Inc. Eastern Div. [20584]
Alvin Equipment Company Inc. [6952]
Amco Equipment and Steel Inc. [6955]
Ameri-Tech Equipment Co. [6957]
American Equipment Company Inc. (Greenville,
  South Carolina) [6964]
American Gulf Co. [6965]
American International Trading Co. [4769]
American Pecco Corp. [6970]
American United Global Inc. [2236]
Anchor Commerce Trading Corp. [6973]
Anderson Equipment Co. [6974]
Anderson Machinery Company Inc. [6977]
Anderson Machinery San Antonio Inc. [6978]
Aring Equipment Company Inc. [6984]
Arnold Machinery Co. [6988]
Arnold Machinery Co. [6989]
Arnold Machinery Co. [6990]
Arnold Machinery Co. [6991]
Arrow-Master Inc. [6992]
Arrow Truck Sales Inc. [256]
Atlas Lift Truck Rentals [15790]
AWD International Inc. [13028]
B & L Equipment [7007]
Bacon Company Inc.; Edward R. [7009]
Bailey Company Inc. [15798]
Balzer Pacific Equipment Co. [7018]
Bark River Culvert and Equipment Co. [7022]
Bat Rentals [7030]
Beach Supply Co. [22060]
Bear Cat Manufacturing Inc. [7035]
Beco/Boyd Equipment Co. [7040]
Bell Company Inc.; James W. [7045]
Belmer Co.; H. [13591]
Berg Equipment and Scaffolding Company
  Inc. [7047]
Berry Companies Inc. [7051]
Berry Tractor and Equipment Co. [303]
Berube Municipal Supply; Tom [13594]
BET Rentokil Plant Services [7054]
Better Buildings, Inc. [7055]
Bisho Company, Inc.; J.R. [2365]
Bostwick-Braun Lorain Div. [15837]
Bowie Industries Inc. [7073]
Boyd Company Inc.; C.L. [7074]
Bramco Inc. [25581]
Brandeis Machinery and Supply Corp. [25582]
Britton Explosive Supply Inc. [7080]
Brown Co.; Herman M. [7085]
Brunner and Lay Inc. [7089]
Bullington Lift Trucks [15855]
Burke Equipment Co. [7108]
Burningtons, Inc. [23475]
Burns Co.; Troy [15860]
Cantwell Machinery Co. [7135]
Capital Ford New Holland Inc. [17763]
The Car Place [7138]
Carolina Tractor/CAT [7144]
Cash Supply Co. [13623]
CBS Contractors Supply Co. [7155]
CESSCO Rental and Sales Inc. [15883]
Chadwick-BaRoss Inc. [7166]
Challenger Ltd. [7167]
Clemons Tractor Co. [425]
Cleveland Brothers Equipment Company
  Inc. [7182]
Clipper Energy Supply Co. [7184]
Cloverdale Equipment Co. [7185]

Coastal Equipment Inc. [7187]
Coleman Equipment Inc. [7194]
Colombian Development Corp. [8544]
Colorado Clarklift Inc. [15898]
Conesco Industries Ltd. [7207]
Continental Sales and Equipment Co. [25610]
Contractors Machinery Co. [7211]
Cooke Sales and Service Company Inc. [7214]
Cowin Equipment Company Inc. [7226]
Coyote Loader Sales Inc. [7228]
Craven Co.; E.F. [7231]
Croushorn Equipment Company Inc. [478]
Crowe and Co.; F.T. [7233]
Cummings, McGowan and West Inc. [7236]
Dallas Ford New Holland Inc. [489]
Danville Gasoline & Oil Co. Inc. Leverenz
    Automotive & Truck Parts [15929]
Darr Equipment Company Inc. [7250]
Davies and Company Ltd.; Theo. H. [15932]
Dealers Truck Equipment Company Inc. [2534]
Diesel Machinery Inc. [7265]
Ditch Witch of Illinois Inc. [7269]
Ditch Witch Sales Inc. [7270]
Ditch Witch Trencher Incorporated of
    Florida [7271]
Dom-Ex Inc. [7278]
Double T Holding Co. [7282]
Doyle Equipment Co. [7287]
Drilex Corporation [15963]
Drillers Service Inc. [25637]
Earthworm Inc. [7297]
Eickoff Corp. [25642]
Elson Import Export; Walter [4935]
Empire Southwest L.L.C. [7312]
Engineered Equipment Co. [25643]
Engineered Equipment Co. [7313]
Engineering Equipment Co. [15992]
Engineering Equipment Co. [24537]
Enumclaw Co.; Garrett [15993]
Equipment Corporation of America [7314]
Erb Equipment Company Inc. [7315]
Evans Inc.; J.D. [7324]
Everett and Co.; R.B. [7325]
Export Oil Field Supply Company Inc. [22244]
Export Services Inc. [6262]
F & W Welding Service Inc. [7329]
FABCO Equipment Inc. [558]
Fabick Tractor Co.; John [7330]
Fairmont Supply Co. Western Operations [16856]
Faris Machinery Co. [7331]
Feenaughty Machinery Co. [7334]
Ferguson Manufacturing and Equipment Co. [7335]
Ferrex International, Inc. [7336]
Fiatallis North America Inc. [7338]
Folcomer Equipment Corporation [7350]
Foley Equipment Co. [696]
Foley Equipment Company Inc. [7352]
Foley Holding Co. [16026]
Frank's Supply Company Inc. [7368]
Friend Bit Service Inc. [25655]
Gale Force Compression Service [5841]
G.A.R. International Corp. [7376]
Genalco Inc. [7382]
General Equipment and Supplies Inc. [7383]
Giles and Ransome Inc. [16065]
GJ Sales Co. [7397]
Global House [16067]
Goedecke Company Inc.; Vernon L. [7401]
Goodwin Machinery Co. [7404]
Gregory and Sons Inc.; J.J. [7416]
Guyan Machinery Company Inc. [16916]
Hagan & Stone Wholesale [780]
Hahn Systems [7430]
Hall & Reis, Inc. [7431]
Halton Co. [7434]
Harding's Inc. [7444]
Hardy & Son; Joseph T. [7449]
Harris Truck Equipment Co.; Jay Dee [20646]
Hauptly Construction and Equipment Company
    Inc. [7455]
Hausman Corp. [7456]
Hawkins Machinery Inc. [7459]
Hayden-Murphy Equipment Co. [7460]
Head and Engguist Equipment L.L.C. [7464]
Heberer Equipment Company Inc. [809]
Hews Company Inc. [7468]

Hill and Griffith Co. [20545]
Hoffman International Inc. [7476]
Holt Company of Texas [7480]
Homelite, Inc. [7482]
Horizon High Reach, Inc. [7488]
Horizon High Reach Inc. [7489]
Hudson Company [7493]
Humac Engineering and Equipment Inc. [7497]
Hydraulic and Air Controls [16129]
ICE Export Sales Corp. [7503]
IHC Services Inc. [7505]
Industrial Management Systems Corp. [7508]
Interchange Corp. [860]
International Consulting & Contracting
    Services [7517]
International Trading & Investment [13146]
Interstate Equipment Co. [7522]
Intramar Inc. [16169]
J & M Industries, Inc. [7528]
J.A.H. Enterprises, Inc. [7530]
Jahn and Son Inc.; Henry R. [16182]
James International Trading Company [25692]
Jarvis Supply Co. [16183]
Johnston Industrial Supply Co. [16190]
Kanawha Steel and Equipment Inc. [20085]
Kelley Manufacturing Corp. [7544]
Keystone Builders Supply Co. [7551]
Keystone Builders Supply Co. [7552]
Klam International [7561]
K.M.H. Equipment Co. [7563]
Koontz Equipment Co.; Don [7569]
Korte Brothers Inc. [7570]
Krieg Consulting and Trading Inc.; A. [16220]
Kubota Tractor Corp. [921]
Langford Tool & Drill [13792]
Lee Tractor Company Inc. [7592]
Leppo Inc. [7597]
Lewis International [953]
Liebherr-America Inc. [7604]
Liebherr Construction Equipment Co. [7605]
Liebherr Mining Equipment Co. [7606]
Logan Corp. [25719]
Lundahl Inc.; Warner T. [2898]
Lynn Ladder and Scaffolding Company Inc. [7625]
Lyons Equipment Co. [7626]
Lyons Sawmill and Logging Equipment
    Co. [27338]
MacAllister Machinery Company Inc. [7629]
Malvese Equipment Company Inc. [983]
Marr Scaffolding Company Inc. [7646]
Martin Co.; E.A. [7652]
Martin Co.; E.A. [7653]
Martin Tractor Company Inc. [7656]
McAllister Equipment Co. [7672]
McCann Industries, Inc. [7674]
McDonald Industries Inc. [7678]
Meadows Company Inc.; Ben [1007]
Mercer's Dix Equipment [7696]
Mestre Equipment Co.; F.W. [7699]
Michigan Tractor and Machinery Co. [7703]
Mine and Mill Supply Co. [20197]
Minneapolis Equipment Co. [7720]
Minnesota Supply Co. [16306]
Mississippi Valley Equipment Co. [7728]
Mitchell Distributing Co. [7729]
Modern Equipment Sales and Rental Co. [7733]
Money Machinery Co.; Joe [16320]
Monroe Tractor and Implement Company
    Inc. [20685]
Moody and Sons Inc.; M.D. [7742]
Morgan Engineering Systems Inc. [7744]
Morgen Manufacturing Co. [7749]
MQ Power Corp. [7754]
Mustang Tractor and Equipment Co. [1058]
Myrmo and Sons Inc. [7758]
Naples Rent-All and Sales Company Inc. [7762]
National Mine Service Co. Mining Safety and
    Supply Div. [7767]
National Mine Service Inc. [24599]
Nebraska Machinery Co. [7770]
North Carolina Equipment Co. [7793]
North Country Equipment Inc. [16350]
Northern Equipment Company Inc. [7795]
OCT Equipment Inc. [7804]
Ohio Machinery Co. [7805]
Oliver Stores Inc. [7810]

PACCAR International [3071]
Pacific American Commercial Co. [7820]
Pacific Machinery Inc. [7824]
Pacific North Equipment Co. [7826]
Pacific Utility Equipment Co. [16377]
Pape Brothers Inc. [7834]
Park Corporation [9179]
Parts Inc. [7837]
Patten Industries Inc. [7841]
Pearce Industries Inc. [16386]
Penn Machinery Company Inc.; H.O. [7847]
Perry Supply Inc. [7851]
Perry Supply Inc. [7852]
Perry Videx, LLC [16392]
Persinger Supply Co. [25782]
Peterson Tractor Co. [7853]
PFT Of America Inc. [7855]
Phillips Co.; Victor L. [7860]
Phillips, Day and Maddock Inc. [7861]
Pioneer Machinery [27360]
Pioneer Machinery [7866]
Pioneer Machinery Inc. [16401]
Pneumatic and Electric Equipment Co. [7877]
Polyphase Corp. [1140]
Poole Equipment Co.; Gregory [7879]
Power Equipment Co. [7881]
Power Motive Corp. [20708]
Price Brothers Equipment Co. [1148]
Puckett Machinery Co. [7889]
R & R Scaffold Erectors, Inc. [7895]
Radandt Sons Inc.; Fred [7896]
Rasmussen Equipment Co. [7901]
Raymond Equipment Company Inc. [7902]
RB & W Corp. [13883]
R.C.A. America [7904]
RCH Distributors Inc. [1170]
RDO Equipment Co. [1171]
Reco Crane Inc. [7906]
Remixer Contracting Inc. [7913]
Richmond Machinery and Equipment Inc. [7931]
Rieke Equipment Co. Inc.; Ernie [7932]
Rish Equipment Co. [7937]
Road Machinery Co. [25805]
Rocky Mountain Machinery Co. [7950]
Roland Machinery Co. [7955]
Ross Corp. [7960]
Rudd Equipment Co. [7964]
Ruffridge Johnson Equipment Company Inc. [7965]
S and M Equipment Company Corp. [7969]
Samsel Supply Co. [7974]
Scott Machinery Co. [16474]
Scott Truck and Tractor Company Inc. [1246]
Sellers Tractor Company Inc. [1258]
Seneca Supply and Equipment Co. [7999]
S.E.S. Inc. [8003]
Shelley Tractor and Equipment Co. [8009]
Shepherd Machinery Co. [8010]
Shook and Fletcher Supply of Alabama
    Inc. [8013]
Silo International Inc. [8020]
Simpson's Inc. [8024]
Sisco Equipment Rental and Sales Inc. [16495]
Sky-Reach Inc. [8029]
SMA Equipment Inc. [8033]
Smith Tractor and Equipment Co. [8036]
Sokkia Corp. [8039]
Southeastern Equipment Company Inc. [8045]
Southern Electric Service Company, Inc. [9385]
Southwestern Suppliers Inc. [20380]
Southworth-Milton Inc. [1285]
SPH Crane and Hoist Div. [8062]
Spokane Machinery Company Inc. [8063]
Spreitzer Inc. [8064]
Stancorp Inc. [8066]
Star Industries Inc. [8072]
Star Middle East USA Inc. [16520]
Steeler Inc. [27381]
Stephenson Equipment Inc. [8074]
Stowers Machinery Corp. [8077]
Strawn Merchandise Inc. [8080]
Stribling Equipment Inc. [1300]
Sumter Machinery Company Inc. [17201]
Syracuse Supply Co. [8095]
Syrex, Inc. [1311]
Teleparts, Inc. [3298]
Texas Contractors Supply Co. [8114]

Thompson Tractor Company Inc. [8123]
Tidewater Companies Inc. [27387]
Tiger Machinery Co. [8131]
Tink Inc. [8136]
Toolpushers Supply Co. [8139]
Trax Inc. [8143]
Tri-State Truck and Equipment Inc. [8146]
Triad Machinery Inc. [8147]
Tyler Equipment Corp. [8154]
U.S.-China Industrial Exchange Inc. [19094]
Universal Industries Inc. [25860]
Universal Industries Inc. [8160]
Van Keppel Co.; G.W. [8171]
VLP Holding Co. [8188]
WACO Scaffolding and Equipment Co. [8189]
West Equipment Company Inc. [8204]
West Side Tractor Sales Inc. [1424]
West Texas Equipment Co. [1425]
West Virginia Tractor Co. [8205]
Western Plains Machinery Co. [8210]
Western Power and Equipment Corp. [8211]
Western States Equipment [8214]
Western Tool Supply Inc. [13996]
White Co.; Brock [8218]
White Star Machinery and Supply Company
    Inc. [8219]
Whiteman Industries [8220]
Williams Industries Inc. [8228]
Witch Equipment Company Inc. [8235]
Wizard Equipment Corp. [8236]
Wolverine Tractor and Equipment [1459]
Wyoming Machinery Co. [8242]
Wyoming Machinery Co. [8243]
Yellow River Systems [19113]
Yukon Equipment [8252]

SIC 5083 — Farm & Garden Machinery

A & D Enterprises, Import-Export [2156]
AA Equipment [180]
Access International Marketing Inc. [13524]
Ada Feed and Seed Inc. [182]
Adams Hard-Facing Company of California [184]
Adams Tractor Company Inc. [186]
Aeon International Corp. [190]
Ag-Industrial Manufacturing [193]
Ag-Land Inc. [195]
Ag-Pro Inc. [198]
AG Systems Inc. [200]
Agri-Sales Associates Inc. [211]
Agriculture Services Inc. [214]
Agway, Inc. [219]
Alban Tractor Company Inc. [15751]
Allamakee Implement Co. [221]
Allerton Implement Co. [224]
Allyn Air Seat Co. [2221]
Amazing Wind Machines Inc. [231]
Ameriglobe Irrigation Distributors [14804]
Anderson Brothers Inc. [241]
Applied Hydroponics Inc. [246]
Arends Brothers Inc. [249]
Arends and Sons Inc. [250]
Arizona Bag Co. LLC [252]
Arizona Machinery Co., Inc. [253]
Arrow Truck Sales Inc. [256]
Atwater Creamery Co. [260]
Authorized Motor Parts [2268]
B-M-B Company Inc. [265]
Baker Implement Co. [272]
Baker Implement Co. [273]
Baltimore Hydraulics Inc. [16719]
Bar-H-Implement Inc. [275]
Barbee-Neuhaus Implement Co. [276]
Barnett Implement Co. Inc. [278]
Barry Pumps Inc.; R.E. [25568]
BE Implemented Partners Ltd. [285]
Beatty Implement Co. [289]
Becknell Wholesale Co. [13589]
Belarus Machinery Inc. [293]
Bellamy's Inc. [294]
Belzoni Tractor Co. Inc. [298]
Berchtold Equipment Company Inc. [301]

Berg Fargo Motor Supply Inc. [2350]
Bethea Distributing Inc. [306]
Bickett Equipment Company Inc. [307]
Big T Pump Company Inc. [311]
Biggs Inc.; K.M. [315]
Bingham Equipment Co. [317]
Bisho Company, Inc.; J.R. [2365]
Black Enterprises Inc. [320]
Blackmon Auctions Inc.; Tom [321]
Blick Co.; Dick [25576]
Boettcher Supply Inc. [8450]
Bowers Implement Co. Inc. [332]
Bowie Industries Inc. [7073]
Braun & Son Implement Inc. [334]
Bretlin Inc. [9739]
Bridgeport Equipment Co. Inc. [336]
Brown Motors Inc. [341]
Brown Tractor and Implement Inc. [342]
Browning Equipment Inc. [343]
Bryan Equipment Sales Inc. [15852]
Bucklin Tractor and Implement [349]
Buffalo White GMC Inc. [20607]
Buhrman and Son Inc. [351]
Bullington Lift Trucks [15855]
Cairo Cooperative Equity Exchange [356]
Cal-Coast Machinery [357]
Caldwell Implement Co. Inc. [360]
Caldwell, Inc.; Bradley [361]
Caldwell Supply Company Inc. [17759]
CalMark Custom Covers [2412]
Campbell Tractor and Equipment Co. [366]
Campbell Tractors and Implements Inc. [367]
Cane Equipment Cooperative Inc. [369]
Capital Ford New Holland Inc. [17763]
Capriotto and Sons Inc. [2420]
Carco International Inc. [372]
Carroll County Equipment Co. [373]
Carswell Distributing Co. [15077]
Casey Implement Company Inc. [377]
Castongia's Inc. [380]
Cenex/Land O'Lakes AG Services [384]
Central Distribution Services, LLC [13626]
Central Farm Supply Inc. [389]
Central Illinois Harvestore Inc. [395]
Central Power Systems [398]
Central Tractor Farm & Country, Inc. [400]
Century Rain Aid [403]
Checkpoint International [18736]
Chesson and Sons Inc.; Mark [413]
Chick Master International Inc. [415]
Chula Farmers Cooperative [417]
Clark Implement Company Inc.; H.C. [422]
Clemons Tractor Co. [425]
Clerf Equipment Inc. [426]
Cocke Farmers Cooperative Inc. [432]
Coffey and Sons Inc.; Bill [433]
Columbus Tractor Machinery Co. [436]
Conrad Implement Co. [439]
Coop Services Inc. [446]
Cooperative Services of Clark County [460]
Cornlea Auction Co. [463]
Countryside Marketing [467]
Crader Distributing Co. [15917]
Cranston International Inc. [470]
Dal-Kawa Hijet [20619]
Dallas Ford New Holland Inc. [489]
Dalton, Cooper Gates Corp. [490]
Day Co.; John [15933]
Day Co.; John [499]
De Mott Tractor Company Inc. [500]
Dean-Henderson Equipment Co. Inc. [501]
Dean Machinery Co. [502]
Decker and Company Inc. [503]
DeLong Company Inc. [506]
Delphi Products Co. [507]
Delta Cotton Cooperative Inc. [509]
Delta Implement Co. [510]
Delta Ridge Implement [512]
Dent and Co. [513]
Des Arc Implement Co. [514]
Desert Design Inc. [515]
Dexter Implement Co. [518]
DJ's Alaska Rentals, Inc. [15954]
Dodge City Implement Inc. [520]
Dokken Implement Co. Inc. [521]
Donnellson Implement Inc. [524]

Dorian International Inc. [24105]
DSW Inc. [20626]
Dubois County Farm Bureau Cooperative [527]
DuBose and Son Co.; W.A. [529]
Duvall Inc.; H.B. [530]
Early Tractor Co. Inc. [533]
East Central Cooperative Inc. [534]
Eaton Equipment Corp. [539]
Ellis and Capp Equipment Co. [547]
Ellis Equipment Co. Inc. [548]
Elmco Distributors Inc. [550]
Emma Cooperative Elevator Co. [551]
Empire N.A. Inc. [552]
Empire Southwest L.L.C. [7312]
Fabel Inc.; Robert A. [559]
Fabick Tractor Co.; John [7330]
Farm Equipment Company of Asheville Inc. [561]
Farm Implement and Supply Company Inc. [562]
Farm-Oyl Company Inc. [563]
Farmers Cooperative Co. [17853]
Farmers Cooperative Elevator [607]
Farmers Gin Co. [650]
Farmers Grain Exchange [656]
Farmers Supply Sales Inc. [659]
Farwest Equipment, Inc. [673]
Feldmann Engineering & Manufacturing Company,
    Inc. [678]
Ferrex International, Inc. [7336]
Ferriday Farm Equipment Company Inc. [679]
Fey Inc. [681]
Fields Equipment Company Inc. [684]
Fiser Tractor and Equipment Co. [687]
Fisher Implement Co. [688]
Fitzgerald Ltd. [690]
Five Star Trading Company [13708]
Fleming Sales Company Inc. [692]
Florie Corporation Turf Irrigation and Water Works
    Supply [694]
Foley Equipment Co. [696]
Foley Equipment Company Inc. [7352]
Forbes Implement Supply Inc.; Keith [697]
Fort Dodge Machine Supply Company Inc. [16031]
Frederick Manufacturing Corp. [704]
French Implement Company Inc. [707]
Frontier Inc. [710]
Frontier Inc. [711]
Frontier Inc. [712]
Frontier Inc. (New Richmond, Wisconsin) [713]
Garden Exchange Limited [13720]
Gardner Distributing Co. [724]
Garton Ford Tractor Inc. [727]
Gass Horse Supply [17935]
Gaston Sealey Company Inc. [728]
Gateway Seed Co. [729]
Gem Equipment Inc. [732]
General Industrial Tool and Supply Inc. [16056]
George H. International Corp. [734]
German Implement Co.; L.E. [735]
German's Outdoor Power Equipment [736]
Gettel and Co. [737]
Giles Farmers Cooperative Inc. [740]
Glade and Grove Supply Inc. [741]
Golden Spike Equipment Co. [745]
Goldthwaites of Texas, Inc. [748]
Goldthwaites of Texas Inc. [749]
Golf Ventures [23693]
Graico International [752]
Grand Forks Equipment Inc. [755]
Grassland Equipment [759]
Green/Line Equipment Inc. [762]
Green Mountain Tractor Inc. [763]
The Greenhouse [14878]
Grossenburg Implement Inc. [769]
Grosz; Leland [770]
Growers Ford Tractor Co. [774]
Gulbranson Equipment Inc. [777]
Hagan & Stone Wholesale [780]
Halferty and Sons Inc.; H.H. [782]
Hamilton Equipment Inc. [785]
Hanley Company Inc. [786]
Harco Distributing Co. [17974]
Harcourt Equipment [789]
Hardlines Marketing Inc. [13735]
Hardware Distributors Inc. [13737]
Harken Inc. [14478]
Harnack Co. [793]

Harney County Farm Supply Co. [794]
Harold Implement Company Inc. [4406]
Harrold Engineering Group [795]
Hassenfritz Equipment Co.; Tom [799]
Hassenfritz Equipment Co.; Tom [800]
Hauff Co.; H.F. [801]
Hauptly Construction and Equipment Company Inc. [7455]
Hawthorne Machinery Inc. Hawthorne Power Systems Div. [803]
Heberer Equipment Company Inc. [809]
Hector Turf [810]
Helland and Long Implement Co. [812]
Hermann Implement Inc. [816]
HGS Power House, Inc. [818]
HIA Inc. [820]
Hillsboro Equipment Inc. [826]
Hobbs Implement Company Inc. [827]
Hocott Implement Company Inc. [828]
Hog Inc. [831]
Hollingsworths' Inc. [834]
Home & Garden Innovations [835]
Hoover Tractor and Engine Co. [836]
Horn Seed Company Inc. [838]
Hoxie Implement Company Inc. [842]
HPG Industries Inc. [7492]
Hubbard Implement Inc. [4421]
Huffman Equipment Co. [843]
Hultgren Implement Inc. [844]
Huntington County Farm Cooperative [846]
Huss Implement Co. [848]
Hydro-Scape Products, Inc. [850]
IDA Inc. [7504]
Implement Sales LLC [852]
Indiana Farm Systems Inc. [854]
Industrial Management Systems Corp. [7508]
Industrial Tractor Co. [857]
Integrated World Enterprises [859]
Inter-American Trading [25689]
Interchange Corp. [860]
Intermountain Farmers Association [861]
International Agricultural Associates, Inc. [862]
International Division, Inc. [863]
International Marketing Systems Ltd. [864]
Iowa Export Import Trading Co. [867]
Iowa Veterinary Supply Co. [869]
IPE Trade Inc. [870]
Irrideco International Corp. [871]
Jacobi Sales Inc. [876]
Jamestown Implement Inc. [879]
Jefferson Farmers Cooperative [882]
Jeffrey's Seed Company Inc. [883]
Jennings Implement Company Inc. [884]
Jensen Distribution Services [13773]
Jerrine Company Inc. [885]
Jess Implements Inc.; Jim [887]
Johnson Inc.; R.N. [889]
Jones Tractor Company Inc. [891]
J.S. Woodhouse Co. [892]
Justin Seed Company Inc. [894]
K & K Vet Supply [27168]
Kamp Implement Co. [896]
Kaser Implement Co. [897]
Kaufman Co. Inc.; Hal [22868]
Kaye Corp. [899]
Kelly Tractor Co. [16202]
Kennedy-Kuhn Inc. [902]
Kennewick Industrial and Electrical Supply Inc. [8937]
Kenney Machinery Corp. [904]
Keystone STIHL, Inc. [16207]
King Co.; R.M. [912]
Kleberg County Farmers Cooperative [913]
Korvan Industries Inc. [918]
The Kruse Company [13789]
Kubota Tractor Corp. [921]
Kunau Implement Co. [922]
L & L Implement Company Inc. [923]
Ladd, Inc.; Bob [927]
Laethem Farm Service Co. [928]
Lampson Tractor and Equipment Company Inc. [933]
Lano Equipment Inc. [937]
Lansdowne-Moody Company Inc. [938]
Latshaw Enterprises Inc. [941]
Lawn and Golf Supply Company Inc. [944]

Le Roy Farmers Cooperative Grain and Stock Co. [947]
Lee Equipment Co.; Ray [948]
Lee F.S. Inc. [949]
Lefeld Implement Inc. [950]
Leffelman and Sons Inc.; W.G. [951]
LESCO Inc. [952]
Lewis International [953]
Liechty Farm Equipment Inc. [956]
Lillegard Inc. [957]
Linder Equipment Co. [961]
Long Equipment Co. [967]
Long Machinery [968]
Long Machinery Inc. [7610]
Long Machinery Inc. Lewiston [969]
LU International [16250]
Lucky Distributing [974]
Lyford Gin Association [18067]
M and L Industries Inc. [978]
Madison County Cooperative Inc. [981]
Maroa Farmers Cooperative Elevator Co. [988]
Martin Tractor Company Inc. [7656]
McCabe Equipment Inc. [997]
McClung Equipment Co. [998]
McConkey and Company Inc.; J.M. [14919]
McCranie Motor and Tractor Inc. [999]
McCranie Motor and Tractor Inc. McCranie Implement Co. [1000]
McNeil Marketing Co. [1006]
Memphis Ford New Holland Inc. [1014]
Mesa Sprinkler Inc. [1017]
Meyer Equipment Inc. [1019]
Meyer West [1022]
MFA Agriservice [1023]
Mid-Atlantic STIHL, Inc. [16296]
Mid State Power and Equipment Inc. [1028]
Midland Co-Op Inc. [1030]
Midland Implement Co. [1032]
Midwest Distributing Inc. [1036]
Miller Sellner Implement Inc. [1040]
Mississippi Valley STIHL, Inc. [16307]
Modern Distributing Co. [1044]
Mondovi Cooperative Equity Association Inc. [1045]
Monroe Tractor and Implement Company Inc. [20685]
Moodie Implement Co. [1050]
Moore Equipment Co.; R.W. [1051]
Moore-Handley Inc. [11931]
Motor Parts & Bearing Co. [2994]
Myer Brothers Implements Inc. [1062]
Nansemond Ford Tractor Inc. [1064]
Natchez Equipment Company Inc. [20690]
Neff Co. [1067]
Neowa F.S. Inc. [18129]
Nichting Company Inc.; J.J. [1075]
Norseworthy and Wofford Inc. [1077]
Northern Truck Equip. Corp. [20698]
Northwestern Supply Co. [1090]
Northwood Equipment Inc. [1091]
Nylander and Sorenson Inc. [1094]
Ochs Inc. [1097]
Odessa Trading Company Inc. [18149]
Odessa Trading Company Inc. [12053]
Offutt Co.; R.D. [1099]
Olds Seed Co.; L.L. [1104]
OPICO [1108]
Orbex Inc. [23860]
Orscheln Farm and Home Supply Inc. [1109]
Outdoor Equipment Co. [1114]
Pacific Intertrade Corporation [15262]
Pacific Machinery Inc. [1115]
Pacific STIHL, Inc. [16376]
Parts Industries Corp. [1119]
Perry and Son Inc.; C.J. [1123]
Piggott Tractor and Equipment Company Inc. [1129]
Pioneer Implement Corp. [1132]
Plasterer Equipment Company Inc. [1134]
Polfus Implement Inc. [1137]
Polk County Farmers Cooperative [1138]
Pollard Co.; C.E. [20706]
Pounds Motor Company Inc. [1143]
Price Brothers Equipment Co. [1148]
Price Turf Equipment Inc.; Howard [1150]
Prince Corp. [1151]

Producers Tractor Co. [1157]
Puck Implement Co. [1160]
Pulaski Chase Cooperative [1161]
Pulaski Equipment Co., Inc. [1163]
R & R Mill Company [15287]
RCH Distributors Inc. [1170]
RDO Equipment Co. [1171]
RDO Equipment Co. [1172]
RedMax Komatsu Zenoah America Inc. [1176]
Reed Equipment Co. [1177]
Reinders, Inc. [1181]
Revels Tractor Company Inc. [1183]
Revels Tractor Company Inc. [1184]
RHS Inc. [1186]
Richton International Corp. [1191]
Rickreall Farms Supply Inc. [1192]
Right of Way Equipment Co. [1194]
Ritter Equipment Co.; E. [1196]
Riverview FS Inc. [1199]
Robstown Hardware Co. [1202]
Rodgers International Trading Inc. [12341]
Roeder Implement Company Inc. [1208]
Roeder Implement Inc. [1209]
Rose Brothers Inc. [1210]
Rosenau Equipment Co. [1212]
Rotary Corp. [1214]
Rugg Manufacturing Company Inc. [1218]
S and H Tractor Co. [1223]
S & W Farm Equipment [1224]
S & W Supply Company Inc. [1225]
St. Clair Service Co. [1227]
Salem Farm Supply Inc. [1231]
Sand Livestock Systems Inc. [1234]
Sauder and Rippel Inc. [1236]
Schilling Brothers Inc. [1237]
Schmidt Machine Co. [1238]
Scott County Cooperative [1241]
Scott-Hourigan Co. [1243]
Scott Truck and Tractor Company Inc. [1246]
Sedalia Implement Company Inc. [1249]
Shelley Tractor and Equipment Co. [8009]
Sierra Pacific [23938]
Simpson Norton Corp. [1268]
Simpson Norton Corp. [1269]
Sloan Implement Company Inc. [1270]
Smith Group Inc.; E.J. [1271]
Smith Hardware Company Inc. [13924]
Smith Turf & Irrigation Co. [1272]
South Texas Implement Co. [1276]
Southeastern Colorado Cooperative [1278]
Southern Livestock Supply Co. Inc. [1281]
Southworth-Milton Inc. [1285]
Sovana, Inc. [1286]
Spartan Distributors Inc. [1288]
Standard Equipment Co. [1292]
Statz and Sons Inc.; Carl F. [1294]
STIHL Northwest [16525]
STIHL Southeast, Inc. [16526]
STIHL Southwest Inc. [16527]
Stratford Farmers Cooperative [18261]
Stull Enterprises Inc. [1301]
Sunbrand Co. [1303]
Superior Turf Equipment [23997]
Syrex, Inc. [1311]
T-Bone's Salvage and Equipment Inc. [1312]
Taser International Inc. [1314]
Tate & Lyle Enterprises, Inc. [16548]
Taylor and Sons Equipment Co. [1317]
Tennessee Farmers Cooperative [1319]
Theisen Farm and Home Stores [1326]
Thigpen Distributing Inc. [1327]
Thompson Implement Co.; Joe [1329]
Thompson Implement Inc. [1330]
Tidewater Companies Inc. [1334]
Timberland Machines [1336]
Todd Tractor Company Inc. [1339]
Toma International [1340]
Torrences Farm Implement [1343]
Tourbillon Farm [18286]
Tractor Place Inc. [1347]
Trade America [16573]
Trans World Investments, Ltd. [15687]
Tricorp, Inc. [1357]
Tru-Part Manufacturing Corp. [1359]
TruServ Corp. [13968]
Tulia Wheat Growers Inc. [1362]

Turf and Industrial Equipment Co. [1363]
Turf Products Corp. [1365]
Twin City Implement Inc. [1367]
Twin Falls Tractor and Implement Inc. [1369]
United Cooperative Farmers Inc. [1375]
United Farmers Cooperative [1377]
United Service and Sales [1380]
U.S. Global Resources [1382]
United World Supply Co. [17244]
Universal Cooperative Inc. [1385]
Unverferth Manufacturing Company Inc. [1386]
U.S.A. Marketing Alliance Inc. [1388]
UTECO Inc. [1389]
Valley Farm Inc. [1391]
Van's Supply and Equipment Inc. [1396]
Vater Implement Inc. [1397]
Vincent Implements Inc. [1399]
Voorhies Supply Company Inc. [16608]
Wabash Valley Service Co. [1402]
Wade and Co.; R.M. [1403]
Wallace Hardware Co. [1409]
Walpeco [1410]
Warren Farmers Cooperative [1413]
Weaks Martin Implement Co. [1419]
Wesco Turf Inc. [1421]
West Implement Company Inc. [1423]
Westbay Equipment Co. [1427]
Western Implement Co. [1432]
Wetsel, Inc. [1435]
Whayne Supply Co. [1436]
Whelchel Co.; Harry J. [1437]
White's Herring Tractor and Truck Inc. [3427]
White's Inc. [1442]
WHO Manufacturing Co [1444]
Williams Ltd.; Ernie [1453]
Wilson Supply Inc. [1454]
WirthCo Engineering Inc. [3441]
Witmer's Inc. [1457]
Woodhouse Co.; J.S. [1463]
Wyatt-Quarles Seed Company Inc. [1464]
Wylie and Son Inc. [1465]
Yakima Hardware Co. [14002]
Zaloudek Co.; Florein W. [1468]
Zamzow's Inc. [1469]

SIC 5084 — Industrial Machinery & Equipment

1st Call McCall Heating and Clng [15718]
A-1 Air Compressor Corp. [15719]
A-C Supply Inc. [16664]
A & D Enterprises, Import-Export [2156]
A To Z Rental Center [6898]
Aardvark Controls Equipment [24304]
Aaron Equipment Co. [15722]
Aaron Scrap Metals, Div. of Commercial Metals Co. [19722]
Abatix Environmental Corp. [24467]
ABB Power Generation [15723]
Abel and Company Inc.; Robert [15724]
Aberdeen Dynamics [15725]
Abrasive Specialists Inc. [15726]
Abrasive-Tool Corp. [15727]
AC Sales Company Ltd. [15728]
Acarex Inc. [2167]
Access International Marketing Inc. [13524]
Accessorie Air Compressor Systems Inc. [5822]
Accessorie Air Compressor Systems Inc. [15729]
Accurate Air Engineering Inc. [5823]
Accurate Air Engineering Inc. [15730]
Ace Tank and Equipment Co. [25885]
Ace Tool Co. [13527]
Acfer International Inc. [22822]
ACI Controls [15731]
ACM Equipment Rental and Sales Co. [15732]
Acme-Danneman Company Inc. [16669]
Acme-Dixie Inc. [15733]
Acro Electronics Corp. [16671]
Acrowood Corp. [15734]
Action Equipment Company Inc. [6911]
Actrade International Corp. [14299]
Adams Tractor Company Inc. [186]
ADCO Equipment Inc. [15735]

Addkison Hardware Co. Inc. [13533]
Advanced Equipment Company Inc. [15736]
Advanced Industrial Products, Inc. [15737]
Advanced Test Equipmnt Rentals [15738]
Adwood Corp. [15739]
Aeon International Corp. [190]
Aerobic Life Industries Inc. [14010]
AEROGO, Inc. [15740]
AGA Welding [15741]
Aggregate Equipment and Supply [16673]
AGL Welding Supply Company Inc. [16675]
Aimtek Inc. Welding Supply Div. [16676]
Air Compressor Engineering Company Inc. [5824]
Air Flow Systems Inc. [2192]
Air & Hydraulic Engineering [15743]
Air & Hydraulic Equipment, Inc. [15744]
Air Power Equipment Corp. [5825]
Air Power Inc. [15745]
Air & Pump Co. [5826]
Air Systems Inc. [5827]
Air Technologies [5828]
Airgas [15746]
Airgas Intermountain [16680]
Airgas-North Central [16681]
Airgas Safety [18665]
Airgas West [15747]
Airmatic Inc. [13539]
AirSep Corporation [15748]
Akron Overseas Inc. [15749]
Alaska Industrial Hardware, Inc. [15750]
Alban Tractor Company Inc. [15751]
Alco Tool Supply Inc. [13545]
Alden Corp. [15752]
Alfa Laval Celleco Inc. [15753]
All American Food Group Inc. [24058]
All American Truck Brokers [15754]
Allan and Co.; G.B. [15755]
Allegheny High Lift Inc. [15756]
Alliance Maintenance and Services Inc. [22030]
Allied Bearing [2209]
Allied Industrial Equipment Corp. [15757]
Allied Tools Inc. [16688]
Allied Trading Companies [15758]
Allied Transmission, Inc. [15759]
Allied Wholesale Inc. [13552]
Allstate Sales and Leasing Corp. [20583]
Allstates Textile Machinery Inc. [15760]
Almerica Overseas Inc. [40]
Aloha Tap & Die Inc. [16690]
Alphatronics Engineering Corp. [15761]
Alta Sales Inc. [16691]
Aluma Systems USA Inc. [6949]
AM-DYN-IC Fluid Power [15762]
Amchem Inc. [15763]
American Barmag Corp. [15764]
American Chemical Works Co. [15765]
American ELTEC Inc. [5929]
American Export Trading Company [15766]
American Industrial Tool Co. [15767]
American Isuzu Motors Inc. [2229]
American Laubscher Corp. [16695]
American Laubscher Corp. [15768]
American Printing Equipment Inc. [15769]
American Rotary Tools Company Inc. [15770]
Americo International Trading, Ltd. [19145]
Amex Inc. [5937]
Amics International Inc. [24311]
Amida Industries Inc. [15771]
Anatel Corp. [15772]
Anchor Sales Associates Inc. [16698]
The Anderson Group [19781]
Applied Chemical Solutions Inc. [24315]
Applied Controls Inc. [8365]
Applied Energy Company Inc. [15774]
Applied Industrial Tech [16701]
Applied Industrial Technologies [16704]
Applied Industrial Technologies [15775]
Applied Industrial Technologies, Inc. [16705]
Aqua Systems International, Inc. [23069]
Arbor Handling Services Inc. [15776]
Area Distributors, Inc. [2249]
Argo International Corp. [18450]
Arizona Welding Equipment Co. [15777]
Armstrong Bros. Tool Co. [15778]
Arnel Compressor Co. [5829]
Aro Corp. [15779]

Aronson-Campbell Industrial Supply Inc. [15780]
Asel Art Supply [25562]
Assembly Automation Industries [15781]
Associated Bearings [15782]
Associated Bearings [15783]
Associated Material Handling Industries Inc. [15784]
Associated Material Handling Industries Inc. [16713]
Astral Precision Equipment Co. [15785]
ATC International [2262]
Atec, Inc. [24318]
Atec Inc. [15786]
Atecs Corp. [18696]
Athens Material Handling Inc. [15787]
Atlantic Detroit Diesel-Allison Inc. [2265]
Atlantic Fluid Power [15788]
Atlantic Pump and Equipment Co. [23527]
Atlantic Trading Company Ltd. [22048]
Atlantic Trading Company Ltd. [15789]
Atlas Copco North America Inc. [13573]
Atlas Lift Truck Rentals [15790]
Atlas Machine and Supply Inc. [15791]
ATS Machinery and Equipment Co. [15792]
Authorized Motor Parts [2268]
Automatic Controls Co. [8397]
Automatic Pump and Equipment Company Inc. [15793]
Aztech Controls Corp. [16717]
B & J Industrial Supply Co. [15794]
B.A. Box Tank and Supply Inc. [22056]
Babco, Inc. [8407]
Babush Conveyor Corp. [15795]
Babush Corp. [15796]
Bacon Material Handling; Davis [25889]
The Bag Connection Inc. [15797]
Bailey Company Inc. [15798]
BAL RV Products Group [15799]
Baltimore Hydraulics Inc. [16719]
Barb's Knitting Machines & Supplies [25973]
Barnes Co.; A.O. [15800]
Barneys Pumps Inc. [23079]
Barone Inc. [15801]
Barton Group Inc. [15802]
Bass Inc.; Rudolf [15803]
Bass Woodworking Machinery [15804]
Bass Woodworking Machinery, Inc. [15805]
Batson Co.; Louis P. [15806]
Battey Machinery Co. [15807]
Batty & Hoyt Inc. [20834]
Baum Iron Co. [15808]
Baumer Electric Ltd. [15809]
Bayou Import-Export Corp. [15810]
BDT Engineering Company Inc. - Industrial Products Div. [14340]
Beach Supply Co. [22060]
Bearing Distributors Inc. [2331]
Bearing Distributors Inc. [15811]
Bearings and Drives, Inc. [16735]
Bearings & Drives Inc. [15812]
Bearings Inc. [16739]
Bearings Incorporated of Kentucky [16740]
Bearings & Industrial Supply Co., Inc. [16741]
Bearings & Transmission [2343]
Beck Packaging Corp. [16744]
Becker Company Inc.; Larson [25569]
Beckwith Kuffel Industries Inc. [15813]
B.E.E. Industrial Supply Inc. [15814]
Behr Machinery and Equipment Corp. [15815]
Behrens Machinery Co.; C. [15816]
Bencruz Enterprises Corporation [15817]
Benz Engineering Inc. [5830]
Berendsen Fluid Power, Inc. [15818]
Berint Trading, Ltd. [15593]
Berkman Co.; Louis [15819]
The Berns Co. [15820]
Berry Bearing Co. [16751]
Bertsch Co. [16752]
Best Label Company Inc./IMS Div. [15821]
BET Plant Services USA Inc. [15822]
Big Inch Marine Systems Inc. [23085]
Big T Pump Company Inc. [311]
Bimex Incorporated [15824]
Bingham Equipment Co. [317]
Binks Manufacturing Co. [15825]
Birmingham Electric Battery Co. [2364]

Bishop Ladder Co. Inc. [15826]
Black Equipment Co. Inc. [15827]
Blankenstein Co. Inc.; F.R. [18717]
Blast-Spray Equipment Co. [25575]
Blue White Industries Limited Inc. [24324]
Bohl Equipment Co. [15828]
Bolliger Corp. [15829]
Bollinger Healthcare [15830]
Bore Technology Inc. [15831]
Bornell Supply [2373]
Bornell Supply Company Inc. [15832]
Bosch Corp. Packaging Machinery Div.;
    Robert [15833]
Bosch Power Tools; Robert [15834]
Boshco Inc. [15835]
Boshco Inc. [15836]
Bostwick-Braun Lorain Div. [15837]
Boulevard Truck Sales and Service Inc. [2374]
BPC Supply Co. [15838]
Bracken Company Inc. [15839]
Bradford Supply Co. [22090]
Bramco Inc. [25581]
Branom Instrument Co. Inc. [16765]
Branom Instrument Company Inc. [15841]
Braymar Precision Inc. [15842]
Brehob Corp. [15843]
Brennan-Hamilton Co. [15844]
Brennan Industrial Truck Co. [20605]
Briggs-Weaver Inc. [15845]
Brinkmann Instruments, Inc. [24328]
Britton Explosive Supply Inc. [7080]
Brodie Inc. [15846]
Brookline Machine Co. [15847]
Brown of Pennsylvania Corp.; D.P. [15848]
Browne Dreyfus International Ltd. [15849]
Bruening Bearings Inc. [15850]
Brungart Equipment Company Inc. [15851]
Bruwiler Precise Sales Company, Inc. [24329]
Bryan Equipment Sales Inc. [15852]
Bryant Corp.; P.R. [15853]
Buckeye Industrial Supply Company [15854]
Buderus Hydronic Systems Inc. [23100]
Buford Brothers Inc. [16772]
Bullington Lift Trucks [15855]
Burch Body Works Inc. [15857]
Burgmaster [15858]
Burns Co.; Troy [15860]
Bussert Industrial Supply Inc. [16773]
Butler National Services Inc. [24332]
Byrne Co. [7118]
Byrne Compressed Air Equipment Company,
    Inc. [5831]
C and B Sales and Service Inc. [5832]
C. Design International Inc. [15861]
C & J Tool & Gage Co. [15862]
Cal-Coast Machinery [357]
Calcom Graphic Supply, Inc. [25589]
Calcom Inc. [15863]
Calkins Fluid Power, Inc. [15864]
Call Associates Inc. [15865]
Callis-Thompson, Inc. [15866]
Caltrol Inc. [15867]
Cam Industries, Inc. [15868]
Camomile Enterprises, Inc. [25595]
Campbell Group [15869]
Campbell Tractor and Equipment Co. [366]
Canfield Co.; M.E. [15870]
Cannon Engineering and Equipment Co.
    LLC [15871]
Cantel Medical Corp. [18725]
Cantwell Machinery Co. [7135]
Carbide Tooling & Design [16780]
Carbro Corp. [15872]
Cardinal Carryor Inc. [15873]
Cardinal Carryor Inc. [15874]
Cardinal State Fasteners [15875]
Carey Machinery & Supply Co. [24524]
Carloss Well Supply Co. [15876]
Carlson and Beauloye [5833]
Carlson Dimond and Wright [15877]
Carolina Handling Inc. [15878]
Carolina Western Inc. [7145]
Cascade Machinery and Electric Inc. [5834]
Casey Co.; A.A. [16784]
Cash Supply Co. [13623]
Catey Controls [15880]

Catey Controls [15881]
CBW Automation Inc. [15882]
Cedar Rapids Welding Supply Inc. [16785]
Cee Kay Supply Co. [16786]
Central Air Compressor Co. [5835]
Central States Airgas Inc. [16788]
Centro, Inc. [24336]
Centro, Inc. [16789]
Century Equipment Inc. [402]
CESSCO Rental and Sales Inc. [15883]
Challenger Ltd. [7167]
Chaneaco Supply Co. [15884]
Chem-Real Investment Corp. [409]
Chew International Bascom Div. [15885]
Chicago Chain & Transmission [2448]
Chicago Electric Co. [8523]
Chicago Machine Tool Co. [15886]
Chickasaw Distributors Inc. [22135]
Choquettes' Used Trucks & Equipment [15887]
CILCORP Energy Services Inc. [24340]
Cimarron Corporation Inc. [15888]
CIMID Corp. [16798]
Cincinnati Belt & Transmission [2449]
Clarke Detroit Diesel-Allison Inc. [2453]
Clarklift Corporation of Indiana [15889]
Clarklift of Dalton Inc. [15890]
Clarklift of Detroit Inc. [15891]
Clarklift of Minnesota Inc. [15892]
Clausing Industrial Inc. [15893]
Clayhill [5836]
Clipper Energy Supply Co. [7184]
CMA International [15894]
Coast Counties Truck and Equipment Co. [2459]
Coastal Engineering Equipment Sales LLC [22144]
Coffin Turbo Pump Inc. [15895]
COFSCO Inc. [22150]
Cognex Corp. [15896]
Coker International Trading Inc. [15897]
Colombian Development Corp. [8544]
Colorado Kenworth Inc. [20613]
Columbine International [15899]
Columbus Hardware Supplies Inc. [13641]
Comer Inc. [15900]
Comet Industries Inc. [15901]
Commercial Body Corp. [15902]
Common Equipment Co. [15903]
Component Technology [15904]
Component Technology [15905]
Component Technology [15906]
Components & Equipment International [15907]
Con-Tech International, Inc. [16805]
Connie's Enterprise [22159]
Connie's Enterprise [15909]
Consolidated Tool Manufacturers Inc. [15910]
Continental Screen Printing Supply [15911]
Contractors Heating and Supply Co. [13645]
Contractors Parts Supply, Inc. [16808]
Control Sales Inc. [15912]
Controltech [15913]
Conveyor & Drive Equipment [15914]
Coordinated Equipment Co. [15915]
Cosmotec Inc. [8583]
Coulter Welding Inc. [16812]
Covington Detroit Diesel Inc. [2488]
CPS Distributors Inc. [15916]
Crader Distributing Co. [15917]
Crane Engineering Sales Inc. [15918]
Creative Engineering and Manufacturing
    Corp. [15919]
Crellin Handling Equipment Inc. [15920]
Cross Co. [2496]
Crouch Supply Company Inc. [24343]
Crowe and Co.; F.T. [7233]
Crucible Service Centers [19908]
Cruzen Equipment Company Inc. [16814]
Cummins Alabama Inc. [2502]
Cummins Connecticut Inc. [2503]
Cummins Cumberland Inc. [2504]
Cummins Diesel Sales Inc. [15922]
Cummins Gateway Inc. [2505]
Cummins Great Lakes Inc. [2506]
Cummins Great Plains Diesel Inc. [2507]
Cummins Great Plains Diesel Inc. [15923]
Cummins Intermountain Inc. [2508]
Cummins Michigan Inc. [2509]
Cummins Mid-South Inc. [15924]

Cummins Midstates Power Inc. [2510]
Cummins North Central Inc. [2511]
Cummins Ohio Inc. [2512]
Cummins Power Systems Inc. [2513]
Cummins Rocky Mountain, Inc. [2514]
Cummins Southern Plains Inc. [2515]
Cummins Southwest Inc. [2516]
Cummins-Wagner Company Inc. [5837]
Cummins West Inc. [2517]
Curtis Fluid Controls, Inc. [16817]
Curtis Toledo Inc. [5838]
Custom Manufacturing Co. [15925]
Cutters Exchange Inc. [15926]
D & F Distributors [15927]
Daewoo Equipment Corp. [15928]
Dakota Chemical Inc. [25623]
Dapra Corp. [15930]
Darr Equipment Company Inc. [7250]
Dashew Inc.; J. [15931]
Day Co.; John [15933]
Dean Supply Inc.; Bob [15934]
Dearborn Fabricating and Engineering
    Corp. [15935]
Decatur Custom Tool Inc. [15936]
Deco Tool Supply Co. [15937]
Decorative Engineering and Supply Inc. [15938]
Dees Fluid Power [16824]
Delta Materials Handling Inc. [15939]
Denver Air Machinery Co. [15940]
Dependable Foundry Equipment Co. [15941]
Derda Inc. [15942]
DESA International Inc. [14417]
Desmond Process Supply Co. [25627]
Desoutter Inc. [15943]
Desselle-Maggard Corp. [16828]
Detroit Air Compressor and Pump Co. [15944]
Detroit Pump and Manufacturing Co. [23137]
Deuer Manufacturing Co. [15945]
Deuster Co. [24104]
Dev-Air Corp. [15946]
DeVlieg-Bullard Services Group [15947]
D.I. Engineering Corp. of America [15948]
Diamond Industrial Tools Inc. [15949]
Dick Co.; A.B. [20961]
Diesel Power Supply Co. [2546]
Dillon Supply Co. [15951]
Divesco Inc. [16833]
Dixie Mill Inc. [15952]
D.J. Enterprises, Inc. [20533]
DJ's Alaska Rentals, Inc. [15954]
DNB Engineering Inc. [15955]
Do All Foreign Sales Corp. [15956]
D.O. Inc. [22206]
DoAll Co. [16836]
Dodge Chicago/IBT [15957]
Domestic & International Technology [2555]
Downard Hydraulics Inc. [15959]
Doyle Equipment Co. [7287]
Dozier Equipment Co. [15960]
Drago Supply Company Inc. [15961]
Dresser Industries Inc. [15962]
Drey and Co. Inc.; S.E. [16839]
Dreyco Inc. [2561]
Drilex Corporation [15963]
Drillers Service Inc. [25637]
Drillers Supply Inc. [15964]
Drucker Associates, Inc. [2566]
DS America Inc. [15965]
DTC Tool Corp. [15966]
Duncan Co. [16840]
Duncan Equipment Co. [16842]
Duo-Fast Carolinas Inc. [5839]
Durable Packaging Corp. [15967]
Durkopp Adler America Inc. [15968]
DXP Enterprises Inc. [15969]
Dynafluid Products, Inc. [15970]
Dynamic Technology [15971]
Dynamic Technology [15972]
Dynamic Technology [16843]
Eagle International, Inc. [15973]
Eastern Lift Truck Co. [15974]
Eaton Equipment Corp. [539]
Eaton Metal Products Co. [22222]
ebm Industries, Inc. [15975]
Economy Electric Company Inc. [8651]
Ecorse Sales and Machinery Inc. [15976]

EcoTech Recycled Products [20981]
Edlo Sales and Engineering Inc. [15978]
Edmund Scientific Co., Industrial Optics Div. [24352]
Electric Motor Engineering Inc. [15979]
Electrical Engineering and Equipment Co. [8677]
Electro-Matic Products Inc. [15980]
Elias Sales & Service, Inc.; T.J. [15982]
Ellsworth Supply Company Inc. [13680]
Emco Inc. [15983]
Emery Waterhouse Co. [13681]
EMP International Corp. [18790]
Empire Airgas [16848]
Empire Power Systems Inc. [2589]
Enco Manufacturing Co. [15985]
Enfield Overseas Trade Co. [15986]
Engine Center Inc. [15987]
Engine Distributors Inc. [15988]
Engine and Equipment Co. Inc. [15989]
Engine Service and Supply Co. [16851]
Engineered Drives [15990]
Engineered Sales Inc. [15991]
Engineered Systems & Designs, Inc. [24354]
Engineering Equipment Co. [15992]
Enraf Inc. [25912]
Envirosystems Equipment Company Inc. [15994]
Equality Trading [15995]
Equipment Inc. [15996]
Equipment and Technology, Inc. [15997]
Erie Industrial Supply Co. [15998]
ERW International, Inc. [19307]
Eskay Corp. [25913]
Evans Hydro [15999]
Evansville Auto Parts Inc. [16000]
Ex-Cell-O North American Sales and Service Inc. [16001]
Export Contract Corp. [24113]
Export Oil Field Supply Company Inc. [22244]
Eyelet Enterprises Inc. [16002]
F and R International [22247]
Fabricating and Production Machinery Inc. [16003]
Fadson International Company [14439]
Fairmont Supply Co. Western Operations [16856]
Falk Corp. [16004]
Farm Equipment Company of Asheville Inc. [561]
Farmers Cooperative Association [22254]
Feed-Rite Controls Inc. [25648]
Ferrex International, Inc. [7336]
FES [24116]
FGH Systems Inc. [16007]
Fibertron Corp. [5613]
Field Tool Supply Co. [16008]
Filtrex Inc. [25650]
First Line Marketing, Inc. [16864]
Flaherty Company Inc.; L.H. [2627]
Flexbar Machine Corp. [16009]
Flexo-Printing Equipment Corp. [25653]
Flexo-Printing Equipment Corp. [16010]
Florida Detroit Diesel-Allison North Inc. [2632]
Florig Equipment [16011]
Florig Equipment [16012]
Florig Equipment [16013]
Florig Equipment [16014]
Florig Equipment of Buffalo, Inc. [16015]
Florig Equipment of Portland, Inc. [16016]
Flowmatic Systems [16017]
Fluid-Dynamic Midwest Inc. [16018]
Fluid Engineering Inc. [5840]
Fluid-O-Tech International, Inc. [23171]
Fluid Power Equipment [16019]
Fluid Power Inc. [16020]
Fluid Power Inc. [16021]
Fluid Power Inc. [16022]
Fluid-Tech, Inc. [16023]
FMH Material Handling Solutions, Inc. [16024]
FMH Material Handling Solutions, Inc. [16025]
Foley Holding Co. [16026]
FORCE America Inc. [16027]
Force America Inc. [16028]
Force Machinery Company Inc. [16029]
Forest City Tool Co. [16030]
Forster Co.; John M. [2641]
Fort Dodge Machine Supply Company Inc. [16031]
Forte Industrial Equipment Systems Inc. [16032]
Forte Industries [16033]
Fortron/Source Corp. [16034]

Fosburg & McLaughlin Inc. [16035]
Foster Company of St. Louis Inc.; John Henry [16036]
Fowler Company Inc.; Fred V. [24362]
Fox Auctioneers Inc.; Michael [16037]
Fox International Inc.; Michael [16038]
Frank & Thomas, Inc. [16039]
Fraza Equipment Inc. [16040]
Frejoth International Corp. [19988]
Fromm, Inc.; R.K. [16041]
Frost Engineering Service Co. [16042]
Fuchs Machinery Inc. [16043]
Fulton Supply Co. [16883]
G-Riffco [16044]
Gaffey Inc. [16045]
Gahr Machine Co. [16046]
Gainesville Industrial Supply [2658]
Gardner Inc. [725]
Gardner and Meredith Inc. [16047]
Gas Equipment Supply Co. [22302]
Gaspro [18804]
Gavlick Machinery Corporation [16048]
Gaylord Manufacturing Co. [8776]
GE Machine Tool Services [16049]
Gehr Industries [16050]
Gelber Industries [16051]
Gemini Enterprises Inc. [22307]
General Air Service and Supply Company Inc. [16052]
General Automation Manufacturing Inc. [16053]
General Electric Co. Marine and Industrial Engines Div. [16054]
General Handling Systems Inc. [16055]
General Industrial Tool and Supply Inc. [16056]
General Steel Fabricators [19997]
General Supply and Paper Co. [21738]
General Supply and Paper Co. [16057]
General Tool & Supply Co. [16893]
Geneva Corp. [7387]
George H. International Corp. [734]
George Inc.; Al [16058]
Geraghty Industrial Equipment Inc. [16059]
Gerhardt's Inc. [2680]
Gerhardt's International, Inc. [16060]
German Implement Co.; L.E. [735]
Gierston Tool Company Inc. [16063]
Gilbert and Richards Inc. [16064]
Giles and Ransome Inc. [16065]
Gilman Industrial Exports, Inc. [24365]
GL&V/Celleco Inc. [16066]
Glass Co., Inc.; The John M. [16895]
Glen Mills Inc. [24366]
Global House [16067]
Global Products Company [16068]
Globe Machinery and Supply Co. [16069]
Godwin Company, Inc. [16070]
GOEX International Inc. [22318]
Gonzalez International Inc. [16071]
Gosiger Inc. [16072]
Grainger, Inc. [16073]
Graphco [25667]
Graphic Systems Inc. [25669]
Gray Machinery Co. [16074]
Grays Harbor Equipment Inc. [16075]
Great Lakes Power Products [18509]
Great Western Airgas Inc. [16906]
Greaves Company Inc. [16076]
Green and Co.; Carl [16907]
GreenTek Inc. [16077]
Greenwood Supply Company Inc. [8817]
Grimstad, Inc.; J.M. [16078]
Grimstad Inc.; J.M. [16079]
Grinders Clearing House Inc. [16080]
GSI Corp. [21021]
Gusmer Co.; A. [16081]
Gusmer Enterprises Inc. [16915]
Haasco Inc. [16918]
Hackett Co.; J. Lee [16082]
Haggard and Stocking Associates Inc. [16920]
Haggard and Stocking Associates Inc. [16083]
Hahn Supply Inc. [23200]
Hahn Systems [7430]
Hall & Reis, Inc. [7431]
Hallidie Machinery Company Inc. [16084]
Handi-Ramp Inc. [16085]
Handling Systems Inc. [16086]

Hanover Compression [22333]
Hansco Technologies, Inc. [16087]
Harbor Tool Supply Inc. [16088]
Harlow International [2725]
Harris Industrial Gases Inc. [16089]
Harris Pump and Supply Co. [16090]
Harris Truck Equipment Co.; Jay Dee [20646]
Harris Welco [20028]
Harrison Piping Supply Co. [23205]
Haskel International, Inc. [16091]
Hatfield and Company Inc. [16926]
Hauser Company; M.L. [16092]
Hawaiian Fluid Power [16093]
Hawera Inc. [16094]
Hawkins Chemical Inc. [16095]
Hawley Industrial Supplies Inc. [13746]
Hawthorne Machinery Inc. [2732]
Hawthorne Machinery Inc. Hawthorne Power Systems Div. [803]
Hayden-Murphy Equipment Co. [7460]
Hazlett Company Inc.; T.R. [7462]
Heatbath Corp. [16928]
Heavy Machines Inc. [16096]
Heller Co.; E.P. [16097]
Herc-U-Lift Inc. [16098]
Hermes Machine Tool Company Inc. [16099]
Hill and Son Co.; Fred [16101]
Hillsboro Equipment Inc. [826]
Hirschmann Corp. [16102]
Hirsh Precision Products Inc. [2755]
Hisco [8843]
Hisco [8844]
Hisco [8845]
Hixon Manufacturing and Supply [16103]
H.L. Gage Sales Inc. [2757]
Hobart Arc Welding Systems [16104]
Hobart Corp. [16105]
Hockman Lewis Ltd. [16106]
Hoffman Brothers [16107]
Hoist Liftruck Manufacturing [16108]
Holloway Brothers Tools Inc. [16109]
Holloway Brothers Tools Inc. [16110]
Holox Ltd. [16111]
Holston Gases Inc. [22356]
Holt Distributors, Inc. [21766]
Hoosier Company Inc. [7485]
Hope Group [16112]
Horner Electric Inc. [16113]
Horrigan & Associates; E.C. [16114]
Horsepower Control System [2761]
Hosokawa Micron International Inc. [16115]
Hougen Manufacturing Inc. [16116]
Howden Fan Co. [16117]
HPG Industries Inc. [7492]
HPM Building Supply [27320]
HPS Inc. [21040]
H.S. Industrial Equipment [16933]
Hub Tool and Supply Inc. [16118]
Hubbard Industrial Supply Co. [16119]
Hudgins Inc.; T.F. [16935]
Hull Lift Truck Inc. [16120]
Hutchins Manufacturing Co. [16121]
Hyde Marine Inc. [25685]
Hydra-Power, Inc. [16122]
Hydra-Power Systems Inc. [16123]
Hydradyene Hydraulics Inc. [16124]
Hydradyne Hydraulics [16125]
Hydraquip Corp. [16126]
Hydraquip Corp. [16127]
Hydraquip Corp. [16128]
Hydraulic Controls Inc. [16130]
Hydro Dyne Inc. [16132]
Hydro-Power Inc. [16133]
Hyster MidEast [16134]
Hyster New England, Inc. [16135]
IBT Inc. [16136]
IBT Inc. [16137]
ICC Instrument Company Inc. [16138]
Ideal Machinery and Supply Co. [16139]
IHC Services Inc. [7505]
IKR Corporation [16140]
Ilapak Inc. [16141]
Illinois Auto Electric Co. [16142]
Illinois Carbide Tool Co. [16143]
IM/EX Port Inc. [16144]
IMA Tool Distributors [13763]

Impex International [16940]
IMT Corp. [16145]
IMT Inc. [16146]
Indeck Power Equipment Co. [16147]
Independent Rental, Inc. [853]
Indiana Oxygen Co. [16942]
Indianapolis Belting & Supply [16148]
Indianapolis Welding Supply Inc. [16944]
Indusco, Ltd. [8875]
Industrial Belting & Transmission, Inc. [16149]
Industrial Development & Procurement [16150]
Industrial Gas and Supply Co. [16947]
Industrial Motor Supply Inc. [7509]
Industrial Municipal Equipment Inc. [16151]
Industrial Pipe & Steel [16152]
Industrial Safety Supply Co. [16948]
Industrial Services of America Inc. [25688]
Industrial Source [16153]
Industrial Steel and Machine Sales [20058]
Industrial Supply Co. [16953]
Industrial Supply Co. [16154]
Industrial Tool Products Inc. [16156]
Inland Empire Equipment Inc. [16157]
Inland Industries Inc. [16158]
Inland Newspaper Machinery Corp. [16159]
Inotek Technologies Corp. [16160]
Integrated Process Equipment Corp. [16161]
Integrated Systems Inc. [16162]
Inter-American Trading [25689]
Interchange Corp. [860]
Intermarket Imports Inc. [16163]
Intermountain Wholesale Hardware Inc. [20653]
International Hi-Tech Trading Corp. [2793]
International Machine Tool Ltd. [16164]
International Marketing Specialists Inc. [16165]
International Marketing Systems Ltd. [864]
International Medcom [16166]
International Trading & Investment [13146]
Interstate Bearing Technologies [2795]
Interstate Co. [16962]
Interstate Detroit Diesel Inc. [16167]
Interstate Welding Sales Corp. [16168]
Intramar Inc. [16169]
Investrade Import & Export [16170]
Ion Tech Inc. [16171]
Ion Technologies Corp. [16172]
Iowa Machinery and Supply Company Inc. [16173]
IPE Trade Inc. [870]
IPS of California [16174]
Ison Equipment Inc. [16175]
Isspro Inc. [2801]
Isspro Inc. [16176]
ITS/Intertrade Scientific, Inc. [16177]
Ives Business Forms Inc. [21073]
IVI Corp. [16178]
Izumi International, Inc. [16179]
J & J Steel and Supply Co. [22380]
J and L Strong Tool Co. [16180]
J & M Industries, Inc. [7528]
Jackson Welding Supply [16181]
Jahn and Son Inc.; Henry R. [16182]
Jarett Industries Inc. [16969]
Jarvis Supply Co. [16183]
Jasper Engineering and Equipment Co. [16970]
Jay Instrument and Specialty Co. [8909]
Jaytow International Inc. [5843]
JC Industrial Motor Service Inc. [16184]
Jealco International, Inc. [16185]
Jefferds Corp. [16186]
Jennison Industrial Supply [13771]
Jensen Tools Inc. [16187]
JLK Direct Distribution Inc. [16188]
J.M. Equipment Co. [16189]
Johnson and Towers Inc. [2826]
Johnston Industrial Supply Co. [16190]
Johnston-Lawrence Co. [22390]
Joint Production Technology Inc. [16191]
Jones Company of Memphis Inc.; Grady
   W. [16192]
Jones of Little Rock Inc.; Grady W. [16193]
Joseph Industries Inc. [16194]
Juno Industries Inc. [16973]
JWS Technologies Inc. [16195]
K-Tel International (USA) Inc. [15547]
Kagiya Trading Co. Ltd. of America [13779]
Kalamazoo International, Inc. [16196]

Kaman Industrial Technology [16198]
Kansas Oxygen Inc. [16979]
Kar Products, Inc. [16980]
Kawasaki Motors Corporation U.S.A. Engine
   Div. [2841]
Keesler Inc.; C.C. and F.F. [16199]
Keizer Associates [16200]
Kelleigh Corporation [16201]
Kelly Supply Company of Iowa [16983]
Kelly Tractor Co. [16202]
Kennametal Inc. Metalworking Systems
   Div. [16203]
Kennedy Engine Co. [2848]
Kentucky Bearings Service [2849]
Kentucky Mine Supply Co. [16989]
Kentucky Welding Supply [16990]
Keo Cutters Inc. [16204]
Kern Special Tools Company Inc. [8939]
Kerr Pump and Supply Inc. [16205]
Key Oil Co. [16206]
Keystone Detroit Diesel Allison Inc. [2853]
Keystone STIHL, Inc. [16207]
KIC International [27330]
Kindt Collins Co. [25700]
Klempner Bros. Inc. [26867]
Klingelhofer Corp. [16208]
Knese, Inc.; Henry [16209]
Knitting Machine and Supply Company
   Inc. [16210]
Knudson Manufacturing Inc. [16211]
Koike America Inc. [16212]
Komatsu America Industries Corp. [16214]
Komerex Industries, Inc. [16215]
Komori America Corp. [16216]
Komp Equipment Company Inc. [16217]
Kona Marine Supply [18537]
Koontz Equipment Co.; Don [7569]
Kornylak Corp. [16218]
Korte Brothers Inc. [7570]
Koyo Corporation of USA [16219]
Krauss-Maffei Corp. [25706]
Krieg Consulting and Trading Inc.; A. [16220]
Kruger Trailer Inc. [16221]
KSB Inc. [16222]
Kuehn Company Inc.; J.W. [16223]
Kustom Tool Works Inc. [16224]
KYB Corporation of America [2867]
L-K Industries Inc. [22412]
L.A. Liquid Handling Systems [16225]
LaGrange Products Inc. [25925]
Lake Welding Supply Co. [16226]
Lamination Services Inc. [16227]
Land & Sea Products [25926]
Langer Equipment Company Inc. [20670]
Lano Equipment Inc. [937]
Laser Resale Inc. [24386]
Latshaw Enterprises Inc. [941]
Laurence Company Inc.; C.R. [16228]
LCI Corp. [16229]
L.C.I. Process Division [16230]
Leamco-Ruthco [16231]
Lee Engineering Supply Company, Inc. [16232]
Leppo Inc. [7597]
Lesman Instrument Co. [24388]
Letts Equipment Div. [2879]
Lift Truck Sales and Service Inc. [16233]
Liftech Handling Inc. [16234]
The Lincoln Electric Co [16236]
Lindsey Completion Systems [16237]
Lister-Petter Inc. [2886]
Litchfield Packaging Machinery Corp. [16238]
Livingston & Haven, Inc. [16239]
Livingston & Haven, Inc. [16240]
Livingston & Haven, Inc. [16241]
Logan Corp. [25719]
Lombardini USA Inc. [16242]
London Litho Aluminum Company Inc. [16243]
Long Machinery Inc. [7610]
LOR Inc. [16245]
Lord Equipment Co. [22437]
Lotus Group [16246]
Louisiana Welding Supply Company Inc. [16248]
Lowe Supply Co.; Bert [17007]
LPKF Laser and Electronics [16249]
LTV Corp. [22440]
LU International [16250]

Lynch Machinery Co. [16251]
Lynwood Battery Manufacturing Co. [2899]
M and L Industries Inc. [978]
M & L Trading Company, Inc. [11751]
M and M Supply Co. [22444]
M and M Supply Co. [16252]
M & R Sales & Service Inc. [26129]
Machine Drive [16253]
Machine Tool and Supply Corp. [16254]
Machine and Welding Supply Co. [16255]
Machinery Sales Co. [16256]
Machinery Systems Inc. [16257]
MacQueen Equipment Inc. [16258]
Magic Touch Enterprises, Inc. [10003]
Magneto Diesel Injector Service Inc. [2908]
Mahar Tool Supply Inc. [13805]
Mahoning Valley Supply Co. [17012]
Malin and Associates Inc.; N.J. [16259]
The Manderscheid Co. [17013]
Manufacturers Supplies Co. [16261]
Mapal Aaro, Inc. [16262]
Marine Systems Inc. [2917]
MarketForce, Ltd. [16265]
Mars Co.; W.P. and R.S. [16266]
Martin Co.; E.A. [7653]
Martin Instrument Co. (Burnsville,
   Minnesota) [24394]
Martin Sons Inc.; Frank [16267]
Marvitec Export Corporation [16268]
Mascon Inc. [16269]
Mascon Inc. [16270]
Mason Co.; F.C. [16271]
Material Handling Services Inc. [16272]
Material Sales Company Inc. [17019]
Materials Handling Equipment Corp. [16273]
Mathewson Co.; George A. [2925]
Matthews International Corp., Marking Systems
   Div. [16274]
Mausner Equipment Company Inc. [16275]
Maxam Corp. [22458]
Mayer-Hammant Equipment Inc. [9053]
Mazzei Injector Corp. [16276]
MBM Corp. (Charleston, South Carolina) [16277]
McAdams Pipe and Supply Co. [22461]
McDermott Co. Inc.; A.I. [23256]
McGraw Group Inc. [17022]
McGraw Inc.; James [17023]
McGraw Inc.; James [16278]
McGuffy Company Inc.; Lynn [25729]
McGuire Bearing [2933]
McKee-Pitts Industrials Inc. [16279]
McKittrick Company Inc.; Frank G.W. [16281]
McMillan Conroy Machinery [16282]
McMurray Printing Co. [25733]
Mechanical Drives Inc. [16283]
Mechanical Equipment Company Inc. [16284]
Mechanical Finishing Co. [16285]
MEE Material Handling Equipment [16286]
Meeder Equipment Co. [22472]
Melco Embroidery Systems [16287]
Melin Tool Company Inc. [16288]
Metaresearch Inc. [16289]
Methods and Equipment Associates [16290]
Metropolis Metal Spinning and Stamping
   Inc. [13826]
Meyer and Son of Sullivan Inc.; L.W. [1021]
M.H. Equipment Corp. [16292]
Micro Metrology Inc. [16293]
Mid-America Airgas Inc. [17034]
Mid-America Industrial Equipment Co. [16294]
Mid-America Power Drives [16295]
Mid-Atlantic STIHL, Inc. [16296]
Midland Implement Co. [1032]
Midvale Industries Inc. [16297]
Midway Inc. [2955]
Midwest Machinery [16298]
Midwest Refrigeration Supply Inc. [5844]
Midwest Refrigeration Supply Inc. [16299]
Mill-Log Equipment Company Inc. [16300]
Mill Supplies Corp. [17038]
Miller Bearings Inc. [17040]
Miller Industrial Tools Inc. [16301]
Miller Machinery Corp. [16302]
Miller Mechanical Specialties [24397]
Miller Welding Supply Company Inc. [16303]
Milligan-Spika Co. [17042]

Mills Inc.; Glen [16304]
Mills Wilson George Inc. [16305]
Milroy and Company Inc.; W.H. [7718]
Minnesota Supply Co. [16306]
Mississippi Valley STIHL, Inc. [16307]
Missouri Export Trading Company [16308]
Missouri Power Transmission [2975]
Missouri Power Transmission [2976]
Mitcham Industries Inc. [24399]
Mitchell-Hughes Co. [16309]
Mitee-Bite Products Inc. [16310]
Mitek Industries Inc. [16311]
Mitsui and Company (U.S.A.) Inc. [20199]
Mitsui & Co. (USA), Inc. Seattle Branch [16312]
Mizen International, Inc. [16313]
MJL Corp. [16314]
MLT International Inc. [17045]
Mobile Power and Hydraulics [16315]
Modec Inc. [16316]
Modern Equipment Sales and Rental Co. [7733]
Modern Group Ltd. [16317]
Mohawk Machinery Inc. [16318]
Monarch Industries Incorporated U.S.A. [16319]
Mooney Process Equipment Co. [23275]
Morgan Engineering Systems Inc. [7744]
Morgan Graphic Supply [16321]
Morpol Industrial Corporation Ltd. [16322]
Morris Co.; The Robert E. [16323]
Morris Co.; S.G. [16324]
Morris Co.; S.G. [16325]
Morris Co.; S.G. [16326]
Morrison Industrial Equipment Co. [16327]
Morrison Industries Inc. [17052]
Morrow Equipment Company L.L.C. [16328]
Motion Industries [2991]
Motion Industries, Atlantic Tracy Div. [17056]
MPBS Industries [16329]
MQ Power Corp. [7754]
MRS Industries Inc. [18953]
MSC Industrial Direct Inc. [17060]
Multicraft Inc. [25745]
Multicraft Inc. [25746]
Mundy Enterprises, Inc.; K.C. [3003]
Murata of America Inc. [16330]
Murdock Electric and Supply Co. [17063]
Murphy Elevator Company Inc. [16331]
Muscle Shoals Mack Sales Inc. [16332]
Mustang Industrial Equipment Co. [16333]
Mutual Sales Corp. [16334]
Mutual Wheel Co. [3007]
Myles Inc.; J.E. [16335]
Nance Corp. [16337]
Nasco Inc. [16338]
Natchez Electric Supply [9112]
Nation Wide Die Steel and Machinery Co. [16339]
National Equipment Corp. [16340]
National Industrial Hardware Inc. [16341]
National Oil Well Inc. [16342]
National Sales Engineering [16343]
National Welders Supply Company Inc. [17067]
National Welding Supply of Algona [17068]
Nationwide Ladder & Equipment Company
   Inc. [7768]
Nationwide Ladder and Equipment Company
   Inc. [16344]
Naz-Dar Cincinnati [25752]
NC Machinery Co. [16345]
Neita Product Management [16346]
Nelson-Jameson Inc. [16347]
Neopost [25754]
Nestor Sales Co. [16348]
New World Acquisition Inc. [22512]
New York Twist Drill Inc. [17073]
Newhouse Printers Supply Inc. [25758]
Nikiforov, Inc.; George [14620]
Noland Co. [23290]
Norfolk Bearing & Supply Co. [17075]
Norman Equipment Company Inc. [16349]
Norris Co.; Walter [17077]
North Carolina Equipment [7793]
North Country Equipment Inc. [16350]
Northeast Airgas Inc. [17078]
Northeast Engineering Inc. [24409]
Northern Machine Tool Co. [16351]
Northern Truck Equip. Corp. [20698]
Northern Truck Equip. Corp. [16352]

Northland Industrial Truck Company Inc. [20699]
Northland Industrial Truck Company Inc. [16353]
Northwest Truck and Trailer Sales Inc. [20700]
Nott-Atwater Co [16355]
Nova Vista Industries Inc. [22530]
Novelty Machine and Supply Company
   Inc. [17083]
NSC International [21167]
Numatics Inc./Microsmith Div [16356]
Number One International [3050]
Oceanex Services International, Inc. [22533]
Ogle & Co.; Jack [16357]
Ohio Belt & Transmission [16358]
Ohio Brake & Clutch [17086]
Ohio Overseas Corp. [16359]
Ohio Transmission Corp. [5845]
Oil Equipment Supply Corp. [22537]
Oilworld Supply Co. [22539]
OKI Systems Ltd. [16360]
Oklahoma Rig and Supply Company Inc. [17088]
Olympus America Inc. [22887]
Omni USA Inc. [1107]
Omni-X Inc. [16361]
Onan Indiana [9155]
Orbit Fluid Power Co. [16362]
Orbital Trading Co. [16363]
Oremco Inc. [20555]
Orenco Systems Inc. [16364]
OSG Tap and Die Inc. [17092]
Osgood Machinery Inc. [16365]
Osterbauer Compressor Services [5846]
Owsley and Sons Inc. [16366]
Ozotech, Inc. [25779]
Pabco Fluid Power Co. [16367]
Pabco Fluid Power Co. [16368]
Pabco Fluid Power Co. [16369]
Pacific Airgas Inc. [16370]
Pacific Coast Air Tool and Supply Inc. [135]
Pacific Detroit Diesel Allison Co. [16371]
Pacific Exports [24414]
Pacific Fibers, Inc. [16372]
Pacific Fluid Systems Corp. [16373]
Pacific Fluids Systems Inc. [16374]
Pacific Machinery Inc. [16375]
Pacific Southwest Sales Company Inc. [9172]
Pacific STIHL, Inc. [16376]
Pacific Utility Equipment Co. [16377]
Pacon Machines Corp. [16378]
PAGG Corp. [6583]
Pan Am Sign Products, Inc. [25780]
Panama Machinery and Equipment Co. [13860]
Pantropic Power Products Inc. [16379]
Park Corporation [9179]
Parrish-Keith-Simmons Inc. [16380]
Parry Corp. [16381]
Parsons Air Gas Inc. (Riverside,
   California) [16382]
Pathon Co. [16383]
Patron Transmission [3087]
Patron Transmission [17100]
Patten Corp. [16384]
Pattons Inc. [5847]
Pearce Industries Inc. [16386]
Pearl Equipment Co. [16387]
Pearse Pearson Co. [16388]
Pederson-Sells Equipment [16389]
Penn Detroit Diesel Allison Inc. [3090]
Penn Machinery Company Inc.; H.O. [7847]
Perfect Fit Industries, Inc. [16390]
Perfection Type Inc. [16391]
Perry Videx, LLC [16392]
Peterson Machine Tool Co. [16393]
Peterson Machinery Company Inc. [5848]
Petro-Chem Equipment Co. [16394]
Pfaff Pegasus of USA Inc. [16395]
Picanol of America Inc. [16396]
PID, Inc. [16397]
Piedmont Clarklift Inc. [16398]
Pilgrim Instrument & Controls [16399]
Pioneer Equipment Inc. [5849]
Pioneer Equipment Inc. [16400]
Pioneer Machinery Inc. [16401]
PMC Machinery, Inc. [16403]
PMH Associates [16404]
PNB Trading, Inc. [16405]
Pneumatrek, Inc. [16406]

PNR International Ltd. [16407]
Pocahontas Welding Supply Co. [16408]
Poclain Hydraulics Inc. [16409]
Podgor Co. Inc.; Joseph E. [16410]
Poole Equipment Co.; Gregory [7879]
Powell Tool Supply Inc. [16412]
Power Drive & Equipment [3106]
Power Drive, Inc. [3107]
Power Drives, Inc. [3108]
Power Equipment Co. [7881]
Power Industries [3110]
Power Lift Corp. [16414]
Power Machinery Center [16415]
Power Products Service [22591]
Power Pumps Inc. [16416]
Power & Pumps, Inc. [16417]
Power Tool & Machinery [16418]
Power Torque [3112]
Prairie Tool Co. [16419]
Praxah Gas Tech Inc. [22592]
Praxair Distribution, Inc. [16420]
Praxair Distribution/W. Div. [16421]
Praxair Gas Tech [17110]
Precision Bearing [17111]
Precision Bearing Co. [3114]
Precision Industries [16422]
Precision Industries [3116]
Precision Tool and Supply [16423]
Pressotechnik Ltd. [16424]
Prime Label Div. [16425]
Primeco Inc. Southeast Div. [13876]
Printers Supply of Indiana Inc. [16426]
Printers Xchange Inc. [16427]
Priz Co. [24420]
Probe Technology Corp. [16428]
Process Equipment Inc. [16429]
Process Supplies & Accessories, Inc. [17117]
Procon Products [16430]
Proctor Co.; Stanley M. [16431]
ProDiesel [3120]
Production Machinery Inc. [16432]
Production Tool Supply [17119]
Products Corp. of North America, Inc. [12226]
Professional Aviation Associates Inc. [139]
Propane Equipment Corp. [22596]
Pump Systems Inc. [17122]
Pumps, Parts and Service Inc. [16433]
Purity Cylinder Gases Inc. [16434]
Purvis Bearing Service [3125]
Purvis Bearing Service [3126]
Quality Mill Supply Company Inc. [17125]
Quimby Corp. [17126]
Quimby Corp. [16435]
Raco Industrial Corp. [16436]
Raco Manufacturing Inc. [23902]
Rainhart Co. [19011]
Rand & Jones Enterprises Co., Inc. [16437]
Randall-Graw Company Inc. [17129]
Rank America Inc. [16438]
Rapid Air Corp. [16439]
Raymond Oil Company Inc. [22609]
Raymond Sales Corp. [16440]
RBM Company Inc. [22610]
RDO Equipment Co. [16441]
Read-Ferry Company Ltd. [16442]
Reading Crane and Engineering Co. [16443]
Rebel and Associates Inc.; Albert [16444]
RedMax Komatsu Zenoah America Inc. [1176]
Reed Equipment Co. [1177]
Refco IDG. [17134]
Reid Tool Supply Co. [17136]
Reif Carbide Tool Company, Inc. [16445]
Reiner & Company, Inc.; John [16446]
Reiser and Co.; Robert [15289]
Reliable Belt & Transmission [3145]
REM Sales Inc. [16447]
Repete Corp. [16448]
Republic Supply Co. (Dallas, Texas) [22622]
Rero Distribution Co., Inc. [9280]
ResourceNet International (Shawnee Mission,
   Kansas) [21904]
Rex Supply Co. [16449]
RHM Fluid Power Inc. [16450]
Richards Machine and Cutting Tools Inc. [16451]
Richards Machinery Company Inc.; L.L. [16452]
Richlund Enterprises [15292]

Riekes Equipment Co. [16453]
Rihm Motor Co. [20712]
Ringhaver Equipment Co. [16454]
Rish Equipment Co. [7937]
Riverside Drives Inc. [3164]
Robco International Corporation/Advanced
    Technology International [17140]
Roberts and Brune Co. [17141]
Roberts Motor Co. [16455]
Rochester Midland Corp. [4698]
Rocket World Trade Enterprise [5850]
Rockford Industrial Welding Supply Inc. [16456]
Rocky Mountain Conveyor and Equipment [16457]
Rodico Inc. [25934]
Rogers Machinery Company Inc. [16458]
Roll-Rite Corp. [16459]
Root, Neal and Company Inc. [9318]
Ross-Willoughby Co. [16460]
RSL Trading Company, Inc. [16462]
Rubber Plus Inc. [24292]
Rudel Machinery Company Inc. [16463]
Rundle-Spence Manufacturing Co. [23355]
Ruth Corp. [16464]
Rutland Tool and Supply Company Inc. [16465]
RVS Controls Co. [17150]
S. and S. Machinery Co. [16466]
Sack Company Inc.; J. R. [17151]
S.A.C.M. Textile Inc. [16467]
St. Louis Paper and Box Co. [17157]
St. Paul Bar/Restaurant Equipment [24213]
Salem Sales Associates [16468]
Sales International [16469]
Sandusky Industrial Supply [3186]
Sandy Supply Co. [22650]
Sanford Process Corp. [16470]
Saurer Textile Systems Charlotte [16471]
Scales Air Compressor Corp. [5851]
Schenck Trebel Corp. [24427]
Schilling Brothers Inc. [1237]
Schmidt Machine Co. [1238]
Schneider Company Inc.; J.R. [25808]
Schoonmaker Service Parts Co. [16472]
Scotsco Inc. [16473]
Scott Industrial Systems Inc. [17161]
Scott Laboratories Inc. [2014]
Scott Machinery Co. [16474]
Screen Industry Art Inc. [16475]
Screen (USA) [25810]
Sea-Pac Inc. [16476]
Seaboard Industrial Supply [16477]
Sees & Faber-Berlin Inc. [16479]
Sellers Process Equipment Co. [16482]
Sellers Tractor Company Inc. [1258]
Semi Systems Inc. [24431]
Semmelmeyer-Corby Co. [17165]
Sepco-Industries Inc. [16483]
September Enterprises Inc. [22661]
Sewing Machines Distributors [16484]
Shearer Industrial Supply Co. [16485]
Sheats Supply Services, Inc. [16486]
Sherri-Li Textile Inc. [26203]
Shibamoto America, Inc. [16487]
Shingle & Gibb Co. [17172]
Shurflo [25939]
Sibco Enterprises Incorporated [3217]
Sibley Industrial Tool Co. [9367]
Sid Tool Company Inc. [16488]
Sierra Concepts Corp. [16489]
Sierra Detroit Diesel Allison Inc. [3220]
Siggins Co. [16490]
Silent Hoist and Crane Co. [16491]
Silo International Inc. [8020]
Silver State Welding Supply Inc. [16492]
Simpson Industries Inc. [16493]
Singer Products Export Company Inc. [16494]
Siperstein Freehold Paint [21578]
Sisco Equipment Rental and Sales Inc. [16495]
Sky-Reach Inc. [8029]
Slife and Associates; Robert M. [16496]
Slingman Industries [3229]
Smith Co.; Harold E. [16497]
Smith Detroit Diesel Allison Inc. [3232]
Smith-Koch Inc. [16498]
Smith Tractor and Equipment Co. [8036]
SMW Systems Inc. [16499]
Smyth-Despard Company Inc. [16500]

Snap-on Tools Corp. [13925]
Solares Florida Corp. [16501]
Soltis & Co., Inc.; A.R. [16502]
Sommer and Maca Industries Inc. [16503]
Sonics and Materials Inc. [16504]
Sooner Airgas Inc. [17180]
Sooner Pipe Inc. [22681]
SOR Inc. [9381]
SOS Gases Inc. [4515]
Soule Steam Feed Works [16505]
Soule Steam Feed Works [16506]
South-Tex Treaters Inc. [16507]
Southern Belting & Transmission [16508]
Southern California Airgas Inc. [17183]
Southern Company Inc. [22682]
Southern Hardware and Supply Company
    Ltd. [17186]
Southern Ice Equipment Distributor [16509]
Southern Machinery Company Inc. [16510]
Southern Minnesota Machinery Sales Inc. [16511]
Southern Pump and Filter Inc. [25826]
Southern Pump and Filter Inc. [16512]
Southern Pump and Tank Co. [16513]
Southwest Hallowell Inc. [16515]
Spar Tek Industries Inc. [16516]
Speaker Company, Inc.; Guy [24435]
Spectronics Inc. [16517]
Spiegel and Sons Oil Corp.; M. [22692]
Spokane Diesel Inc. [3253]
Sprague Energy Corp. [22693]
Sprunger Corp. [17193]
Squibb-Taylor Inc. [22696]
Standard Machine and Equipment Co. [16518]
Standard Supply and Hardware Company
    Inc. [17194]
Star Cutter Co. [16519]
Star Middle East USA Inc. [16520]
Steelhead Inc. [16522]
Stephenson Equipment Inc. [8074]
Stewart & Stevenson [3267]
Stewart & Stevenson [3268]
Stewart & Stevenson [3269]
Stewart & Stevenson [16523]
Stewart and Stevenson Services Inc. [3270]
Stewart and Stevenson Services Inc.
    Texas [16524]
STIHL Northwest [16525]
STIHL Southeast, Inc. [16526]
STIHL Southwest Inc. [16527]
Stiles Machinery Inc. [16528]
Stokes Equipment Co. [16529]
Stopol Inc. [23036]
Strafco Inc. [3272]
Studer Industrial Tool [16531]
Stultz Fluid Power [16532]
Stump & Company Inc.; Weldon F. [16533]
Stuttgart Industrial Service Inc. [18264]
Stutz Co. [17200]
Suhner Manufacturing, Inc. [16534]
Summers Induserve Supply [16535]
Summit Handling Systems Inc. [16536]
Sun Distributors L.P. [16537]
Sundstrand Fluid Handling Corp. [16538]
Sunny International Inc. [13943]
SunSource Technology Services [16539]
Supa Machinery Sales Inc. [16540]
Supply Station Inc. [13945]
S.W. Controls, Inc. [24441]
Swanson Sales and Service [21309]
Swing Machinery and Equipment Company
    Inc. [17209]
Swiss Precision Instruments [16541]
Sydnor Hydrodynamics Inc. [16542]
Sygnet [16543]
Symtech Inc. [16544]
System Brunner USA Inc. [17210]
Talladega Machinery and Supply Company
    Inc. [16545]
Tamrock USA [16547]
Tapco USA, Inc. [17212]
Taser International Inc. [1314]
Tate Engineering Systems, Inc. [5853]
Tate & Lyle Enterprises, Inc. [16548]
Tavdi Company, Inc. [16549]
Taylor-Dunn Manufacturing Co. [16550]
Taylor Simkins Inc. [17214]

Taylor & Sons, Inc.; Robert [16551]
TCI Machinery Inc. [16552]
TEC Industrial [16553]
Techmark Corporation [24442]
TechniStar Corp. [16554]
Tek-Matic, Inc. [17215]
Tekmatex Inc. [16555]
Televan Sales Inc. [16556]
Tempaco Inc. [14715]
Ternes Register System [16557]
Terrile Export & Import Corp. [9480]
TES (USA) Corp. [16558]
Tetra Laval Convenience Food Inc. [24244]
Tetra Laval Convenience Food Inc. [16559]
Texas Mill Inc. [17222]
Texas Mill Supply and Manufacturing Company
    Inc. [17223]
Texas Mining Co. [8115]
Texas Screen Process Supply Co. [25841]
Textiles South Inc. [16560]
Think and Tinker Ltd. [16561]
Thompson and Cooke Inc. [17226]
Thompson and Johnson Equipment Company
    Inc. [16562]
Thomson Company Inc.; Geo. S. [17227]
Thomson National Press Co. [16563]
Thornton Industries, Inc. [13953]
Thrall Distribution Inc. [17229]
Tiger Machinery Co. [8131]
Tool Service Corp. [16565]
Tool World [13959]
Toolkraft Distributing [16566]
Toolman Co. [13960]
Toombs Truck and Equipment Co. [16567]
Tornos Technologies U.S. Corp. [16568]
Torque-A-Matic [17231]
Torque Drive [3321]
Toshiba Tungaloy America Inc. [16569]
Tower Equipment Company Inc. [16570]
Towlift Inc. [16571]
Toyota Tsusho America Inc. [20434]
T.R. Trading Co. [16572]
Tracom Inc. [3324]
Tractor and Equipment Co. [1346]
Trade America [16573]
Trade Development Corporation of
    Chicago [17232]
Tradex International Corp. [20436]
Transco Industries Inc. [16574]
Transit Services Inc. [24448]
TransLogic Corp. [16575]
Transmission Engineering Co. [3326]
Transmission Equipment International Inc. [16576]
Transupport Inc. [16577]
Travers Tool Co. [13963]
Tri Lift [16578]
Tri-Line Corp. [5854]
Tri-Line Corp. [16579]
Tri-Star Industrial Supply Inc. [16580]
Triangle Industrial Sales, Inc. [16581]
Trinet Industries Inc. [16582]
Triumph Twist Drill Co. [16583]
Troy Belting Supply Co. [17236]
Tryon Trading, Inc. [17237]
Turbex Heat Transfer Corp. [14740]
TW Graphics Group [25850]
Tyler Equipment Corp. [8154]
Tynan Equipment Co. [16585]
Udelson Equipment Co. [16586]
Ultra Hydraulics Inc. [17239]
Unibri International [17240]
Union Bearing & Transmission [3361]
Union Carbide Corp., IPX Services [16587]
Union Standard Equipment Co. [19672]
Union Supply Co. [23421]
Unisource Worldwide Inc. [21970]
United Conveyor Corp. [16588]
United Engines Inc. [3366]
United Engines Inc. [16589]
U.S. Amada Ltd. [16590]
U.S. Equipment Co. [16591]
U.S. Equipment Company Inc. [5855]
U.S. Extrusion Tool and Die [16592]
U.S. Industrial Tool Supply [13976]
U.S. International [16593]
U.S. Machinery, Inc. [16594]

U.S. Manufacturing Corp. [3370]
United World Supply Co. [17244]
Universal Process Equipment Inc. [16595]
Universal Process Equipment Inc. [4540]
Universal Sales Engineering Inc. [17245]
Upchurch Co.; Frank J. [17246]
UTECO Inc. [1389]
Utility Trailer Sales Co. [3379]
Vacuum Pump Systems Inc. [16596]
Valley Fertilizer and Chemical Company
  Inc. [1394]
Valley Industrial Trucks Inc. [16597]
Valley National Gases, Inc. [16598]
Valley National Gases Inc. [22766]
Valley Welding Supply Co. [16599]
Valley Welding Supply Inc. [17250]
Van Horn Company Inc.; Oliver H. [16600]
Van Keppel Co.; G.W. [8171]
Van Sant Equipment Corp. [17251]
Van Son Holland Corporation of America [25863]
Veeco Process Metrology [16601]
Vellano Brothers Inc. [25865]
Victor Machinery Exchange Inc. [17252]
Viking Distributing Company Inc. [17254]
Viking Formed Products [17255]
Virginia Carolina Tools Inc. [16602]
Virginia Materials [16603]
Vlcek Corp.; Jerry K. [16604]
Voell Machinery Company Inc. [16605]
Vogel Tool & Die Corp. [16606]
Volland Electric Equipment Corp. [16607]
Voorhies Supply Company Inc. [16608]
Vorys Brothers Inc. [14757]
Voss Equipment Inc. [16609]
W-B Supply Co. [22776]
Wabash Power Equipment Co. [22777]
WAFAB International [16610]
Wagner Hydraulic Equipment Co. [16611]
Wagner-Smith Co. [17259]
Walke Co.; Henry [17260]
Walker Co.; James [17261]
Walker Machinery Co.; Cecil I. [1405]
Wallace Coast Machinery Co. [16612]
Walters Inc.; Dave [20748]
Waltman's Inc. [16613]
Ward Technologies Inc. [16614]
Warehouse Equipment Inc. [16615]
Warner Manufacturing Co. [21602]
Warsaw Chemical Company Inc. [25872]
Washington Belt & Drive [17263]
Washington Belt & Drive [17266]
WaterPro Supplies Inc. [23440]
Watkins System Inc. [169]
Watson Co.; Ray V. [3404]
WEB Machinery Co. [16616]
Weber Industries Inc. [16617]
Weiss Company Inc.; Max [16618]
Welders Equipment Company Inc. [16619]
Welding Equipment & Supply/All State Medical
  Gases [19106]
Weldon Tool Co. [16620]
Welsco Inc. [17272]
Wenger Manufacturing Inc. [16621]
Werner and Pfleiderer Corp. [23047]
Werres Corp. [16622]
WESCO Distribution Inc. [9569]
West Coast Machine Tools [16623]
West Equipment Company Inc. [8204]
Westberg Manufacturing Inc. [24456]
Westco./DoAll Industrial Distribution [16624]
Western Branch Diesel Inc. [16625]
Western Component Sales Div. [9574]
Western Fluid Power [16626]
Western Fluid Power [16627]
Western Fluid Power [16628]
Westland International Corp. [9580]
Westmark Industries Inc. [16629]
Westmoreland Industrial Supply Co. [17277]
Whisler Bearing Co. [21608]
White Inc.; Billy D. [3426]
White's Herring Tractor and Truck Inc. [3427]
Whitten Pumps Inc. [16630]
WHO Manufacturing Co [1444]
Wickman Corp. [16631]
Wigglesworth Machine Co. [16632]
Wilfley and Sons Inc.; A.R. [16633]

Willamette Electric Products Co. [16634]
Willco Sales and Services Inc. [25881]
Williams Co.; W.W. [16635]
Williams Detroit Diesel Allison [3433]
Williams Detroit Diesel Allison [3434]
Williams Detroit Diesel Allison [3435]
Williams Equipment Co. [16636]
Williston Industrial Supply Corp. [22807]
Wilson Co. [16637]
Wilson Industries Inc. [22808]
Wilson Supply Co. [22809]
Wilton Corp. [16638]
Winchester Equipment Co. [16639]
Windmoeller and Hoelscher Corp. [16640]
Windsor Industries Inc. (Englewood,
  Colorado) [16641]
Wisconsin Bearing [16642]
Wisconsin Bearing [17284]
Wisconsin Lift Truck Corp. [16643]
Wisner Manufacturing Inc. [16644]
WMT Machine Tool Company Inc. [16645]
Wolff Corp. [16646]
Womack Machine [3444]
Womack Machine [16647]
Womack Machine [16648]
Womack Machine Supply [16649]
Woodworker's Supply Inc. [27396]
World Wide Laser Service Corp. [16650]
Worldwide Exporters Inc. [9608]
Wrenn Brungart [16651]
Wyoming Machinery Co. [8242]
X-Ray Industries Inc. [9612]
X-Ray Products Corp. [19112]
Xander Co. Inc.; A.L. [16652]
XWW Alloys, Inc. [16653]
Yale/Chase Materials Handling, Inc. [16654]
Yancey Machine Tool Co. [16655]
Yang Machine Tool Co. [16656]
Yecies Inc.; Herman W. [17291]
Yen Enterprises Inc. [20503]
Yoder Oil Company Inc. [22818]
Z-Weigh Inc. [24460]
Zed Group Inc. [16659]
Zeiss Inc.; Carl [24461]
Zeuschel Equipment Co. [24462]
Zeuschel Equipment Co. [24463]
Zeuschel Equipment Co. [24464]
ZEXEL USA Corp. [3454]
Zima Corp. [16660]
Zimmer Machinery Corp. [16661]
Zoeller Co. [16662]
Zonne Industrial Tool Co. [16663]

SIC 5085 — Industrial Supplies

A-C Supply Inc. [16664]
A. Louis Supply Co. [16665]
A & W Bearings & Supply [16666]
A-Welders & Medical Supply [18654]
AA Electric S.E. Inc. [15721]
Ababa - QA [13522]
Abatix Environmental Corp. [24467]
ABCO Welding and Industrial Supply [16667]
Abrasive Products Inc. [16668]
Abrasive Specialists Inc. [15726]
Abrasive-Tool Corp. [15727]
Acfer International Inc. [22822]
Acme-Danneman Company Inc. [16669]
Acme Group [2175]
Acorn Paper Products Co [16670]
Acro Electronics Corp. [16671]
Active Screw and Fastener [13530]
Adams Supply Co. [13532]
Advance Glove & Safety Co. [24491]
Advance Glove & Safety Co. [24492]
Aero-Motive Co. [8279]
Aero Tec Laboratories Inc. [16672]
Aerospace Tube & Pipe [19733]
Aggregate Equipment and Supply [16673]
Aggregate Equipment and Supply [16674]
Aimsco Inc. [13538]
Aimtek Inc. Welding Supply Div. [16676]
Air-Dreco [15742]
Air-Oil Products Corp. [16677]

Airco Gas and Gear [16678]
Airgas Inc. [16679]
Airgas-North Central [16681]
Airgas West [15747]
Airline Hydraulics Corp. [16682]
Airmatic Inc. [13539]
Alamo Iron Works [19740]
Alaska Nut & Bolt [13541]
Alaska Paper Co. Inc. [21617]
All Appliance Parts Inc. [8292]
All Fasteners Inc. [13546]
All Line Inc. [16683]
Allen Refractories Co. [16684]
Allied Bearing Supply [16685]
Allied Purchasing [16687]
Allied Tools Inc. [16688]
AlliedSignal Automotive Catalyst Co. [2217]
AlliedSignal Hardware Product Group [16689]
Alloy Piping Products Inc. [23058]
Ally Industries Inc. [24504]
Aloha Tap & Die Inc. [16690]
Alpine Supply [13553]
Alta Sales Inc. [16691]
AM-DYN-IC Fluid Power [16692]
Ambraco Inc. [16693]
American Export Trading Company [15766]
American Industrial Tool Co. [15767]
American Laubscher Corp. [16695]
American Rotary Tools Company Inc. [15770]
Americo International Trading, Ltd. [19145]
Ameru Trading Co. [16696]
Ames Industries Inc. [16697]
Ampride [22038]
Apache Hose and Belting Inc. [16700]
Applied Industrial Tech [16701]
Applied Industrial Tech, Inc. [16702]
Applied Industrial Technologies [16703]
Applied Industrial Technologies [16704]
Applied Industrial Technologies, Inc. [16705]
Applied Industrial Technologies, Inc. [16706]
Applied Industrial Technologies Inc. [2247]
Aramsco, Inc. [16707]
Arbill Inc. [25966]
Arizona Bag Co. LLC [252]
Arizona Sealing Devices Inc. [16709]
Arizona Water Works Supply Inc. [23072]
Armitage Industrial Supply, Inc. [16710]
Arrow Trucks and Parts Co. [2256]
Artz Inc.; E.G. [16711]
Arvin Industries Inc. [2257]
Associated Bearings [15782]
Associated Bearings [15783]
Associated Industrial Supply Co. [16712]
Atecs Corp. [18696]
Atlantic India Rubber Co. [24267]
Atlas Screw and Specialty Co.; L.P. [13575]
Aztech Controls Corp. [16717]
B & J Industrial Supply Co. [15794]
B & S Bolts Corp. [13579]
Babbitt Steam Specialty Co. [16718]
Bakertowne Company, Inc. [15414]
Bales & Truitt Company Inc. [14336]
Baltimore Hydraulics Inc. [16719]
Barbour Marine Supply [18451]
Barker-Jennings Corp. [2317]
Barker-Jennings Corp. [13584]
Barnes Co.; A.O. [15800]
Barrett Hardware and Industrial Supply
  Co. [13585]
Bartells Co.; E. J [16721]
Bartlett Bearing Co. Inc. [16722]
Barton Truck Center Inc. [16723]
Batson Co.; Louis P. [15806]
Baumbach Manufacturing Co.; E.A. [16724]
Baxter and Co. Inc.; A.J. [16725]
Bay Rubber Co. [24269]
Bay Rubber Co. [16726]
Bearing Belt Chain Co. [16727]
Bearing Belt and Chain Inc. [16728]
Bearing Distributors [16729]
Bearing Distributors [16730]
Bearing Distributors Inc. [2331]
Bearing Distributors Inc. [15811]
Bearing Distributors Inc. [2332]
Bearing Distributors Inc. [16731]
Bearing Distributors, Inc. [2334]

Bearing Distributors Inc. [2335]
Bearing Distributors Inc. [2336]
Bearing and Drivers Inc. [2337]
Bearing Engineering [2338]
Bearing Engineers Inc. [16732]
Bearing Enterprises Inc. [16733]
Bearings and Drives Inc. [16734]
Bearings and Drives, Inc. [16735]
Bearings & Drives, Inc. [2340]
Bearings & Drives, Inc. [2341]
Bearings & Drives, Inc. [2342]
Bearings and Drives, Inc. [16736]
Bearings and Drives, Inc. [16737]
Bearings & Drives Unlimited, Inc. [16738]
Bearings Inc. [16739]
Bearings Incorporated of Kentucky [16740]
Bearings & Industrial Supply Co., Inc. [16741]
Bearings Service & Supply [16742]
Bearings Service & Supply, Inc. [16743]
Bearings & Transmission [2343]
Beckley Equipment Co. [16745]
B.E.E. Industrial Supply Inc. [15814]
Beemer Precision Inc. [16746]
Behrens Supply Co. [2346]
Belting Industry Company Inc. [16747]
Beltservice Corp. [16748]
Benson Company Inc.; L.A. [16749]
Berendsen Fluid Power, Inc. [15818]
Berk Co.; O. [25892]
Berry Bearing Co. [16751]
Bertsch Co. [16752]
Beta Supply Co. [15823]
Big D Bolt & Screw Co. [13598]
Big River Rubber & Gasket [24270]
Black and Co. [16753]
Black Hills Jewelers Supply [25574]
BMT Commodity Corp. [10583]
Bolk Industrial Supply Corp. [16754]
Bon Tool Co. [13602]
Bonneville Industrial [16756]
Boring and Smith Industries Div. [16757]
Bossert Industrial Supply Inc. [16758]
Boustead Electric and Manufacturing Co. [8457]
Bowman Distribution [16759]
Boyer Steel Inc. [16760]
Boyle Machine and Supply Co. [16761]
Bradley Supply Co. [23094]
Bragg and Sons; N.H. [16762]
Brake Systems Inc. [16763]
Brammall Supply Co. [16764]
Braymar Precision Inc. [15842]
Brennan-Hamilton Co. [15844]
Briggs-Weaver Inc. [15845]
Britain's Steel and Supplies [16766]
Bronze and Plastic Specialties Inc. [19837]
Brown Ship Chandlery Inc. [18472]
Bruckner Supply Co. Inc. [16768]
Bruening Bearings Inc. [15850]
Brushtech Inc. [16769]
Buck-Hilkert Inc. [16770]
Buckeye Industrial Supply Company [15854]
Buckeye Rubber and Packing Co. [16771]
Buford Brothers Inc. [16772]
Bunn Co.; B.H. [15856]
Bussert Industrial Supply Inc. [16773]
Byrne Compressed Air Equipment Company, Inc. [5831]
C and B Sales and Service Inc. [5832]
Calcom Graphic Supply, Inc. [25589]
California Industrial Rubber Co. [24272]
California Industrial Rubber Company Inc. [16775]
Calolympic Glove and Safety Co. Inc. [24523]
Calolympic Glove and Safety Company Inc. [16776]
Camalloy Inc. [19848]
Cameron & Barkley [8493]
Campbell Supply Co. [16777]
Cannon Equipment West [16778]
Capitol Corp. [16779]
Carbide Tooling & Design [16780]
Cardinal State Fasteners [15875]
Carey Machinery & Supply Co. [24524]
Carolina Fluid Components [16781]
Carolina Hardware & Supply, Inc. [16782]
Carpenter Brothers Inc. [16783]
Casey Co.; A.A. [16784]

Cayce Mill Supply Co. [8509]
Central Engineering & Supply Co. [14375]
Central Jersey Supply Co. [16787]
Central Supply Co. [23110]
Centro, Inc. [24337]
Centro, Inc. [16789]
Chamberlin Rubber Company Inc. [16790]
Chambers Supply Inc.; Carter [16791]
Chaneaco Supply Co. [15884]
Chapman Marine Supply [18478]
Charken Co. Inc. [16792]
Chase Industries Inc. [16793]
Cheler Corp. [16794]
Chicago Industrial Rubber [24273]
China House Trading Co. [16796]
Churubusco Distribution Service Center [16797]
Cincinnati Container Co. [25901]
Cincinnati Gasket Packing Manufacturing Inc. [16799]
Clamyer International Corp. [21413]
Clayhill [5836]
Clean Seal [16800]
Clemmons Corp. [16801]
Clisby Agency Inc. [16802]
CMA International [15894]
Coastal Supply Co., Inc. [25604]
Coastline Distributing [14389]
Coleman Industrial Supply Inc. [13639]
Colonial Hardware Corp. [16803]
Columbia Pipe and Supply [14393]
Columbus Paper Company Inc. [4601]
Columbus Steel Drum Co. [25904]
Comet Industries Inc. [15901]
Commerce Consultants Inc. [22154]
Commerce Overseas Corp. [72]
Commonwealth Tool Specialty Inc. [16804]
Computer Optics Inc. [22848]
Con-Tech International, Inc. [16805]
Connect Air International Inc. [16806]
Consolidated Bearing Co. [2474]
Container Industries Inc. [25907]
Continental Glass and Plastic Inc. [25908]
Continental International [16807]
Contractors Parts Supply, Inc. [16808]
Control Associates Inc. [2481]
Control Specialties Inc. [16809]
Cook Brothers Manufacturing and Supply Co. [23126]
Cook Iron Store Co. [16810]
Cornerstone Controls Inc. [8582]
Corrosion Fluid Products Corp. [16811]
Coyle Mechanical Supply [16813]
CPAC Inc. [22849]
Cross Co. [2496]
Crown Supply Corp. [25909]
Cruzen Equipment Company Inc. [16814]
CTI Abrasives and Tools [16815]
Cunningham Equipment Inc.; J.A. [16816]
Currie Industries Inc. [22951]
Curtis Fluid Controls, Inc. [16817]
Cushing Inc.; T.F. [8598]
Cutting Tools Inc. [13653]
Dabney-Hoover Supply Company Inc. [16818]
Dallas Aerospace Inc. [79]
Darter Inc. [4610]
Davies Supply Co. [16820]
Davis Supply Co. [23134]
Davis Supply Co. Inc. [16821]
Dawson Industries Inc. [25626]
Day Co.; John [499]
De Lille Oxygen Co. [16822]
Dean Supply Inc.; Bob [15934]
Decker Steel and Supply Inc. [19921]
Dees Corp. [16823]
Dees Fluid Power [16824]
Delaware County Supply Co. [13658]
Delaware Valley Hydraulics [16825]
Denali Industrial Supply Inc. [16826]
Derkin and Wise Inc. [16827]
Detroit Ball Bearing Company Executive Offices [16829]
Detroit Gas Products Co. [16830]
Dewald Fluid Power Company Inc. [16831]
Dewco Milwaukee Sales [13665]
Diagnostic Equipment Service Corp. [18774]
Diamond Industrial Tools Inc. [15949]

Dibs Chemical & Supply Co. Inc. [21708]
Die-A-Matic Corp. [15950]
Dillon Supply Co. [15951]
Dills Supply Co./Division of Dayton Supply and Tool [16832]
Dixie Bearings, Inc. [2549]
Dixie Bearings Inc. [2550]
Dixie Industrial Supply Co. [16834]
Dixie Industrial Supply Div. [16835]
Do All Foreign Sales Corp. [15956]
DoAll Co. [16836]
Dodge Chicago/IBT [15957]
Douglas and Sons, Inc. [16837]
Doussan Inc. [16838]
Drago Supply Co. Inc. [13669]
Drago Supply Company Inc. [15961]
Drey and Co. Inc.; S.E. [16839]
DTC Tool Corp. [15966]
Duncan Co. [16840]
Duncan-Edward Co. [16841]
Duncan Equipment Co. [16842]
Dynamic Technology [16843]
Dynamic Technology [16844]
Eastern Penn Supply Co. [23144]
Eberly Inc.; John A. [13674]
Edgerton Forge Inc. [15977]
Ehrke & Co.; A. [16846]
EIS Com-Kyl [16847]
El Paso Saw and Belting Supply Co. [13678]
Empire Airgas [16848]
Empire/EMCO Inc. [25911]
Empire Machinery and Supply Co. [13683]
Empire Refactory Sales Inc. [16849]
Emuge Corp. [16850]
Enco Manufacturing Co. [15985]
Energy and Process Corp. [19954]
Engine Service and Supply Co. [16851]
Engineered Drives [2591]
Engineered Sales Inc. [15991]
Epley Sales Co. [24538]
Equipment Valve and Supply Inc. [23150]
Esco Supply Company Inc. [23152]
Evans Oil Co. [22241]
Evansville Auto Parts Inc. [16000]
Everitt & Ray Inc. [5]
E.W.C. Supply Inc. [23153]
Exotic Rubber and Plastics Corp. [16852]
Expanko Cork Co. [16853]
Exploration Supplies of Houma Inc. [16854]
Export USA [17411]
Fairmont Supply Co. [25646]
Fairmont Supply Co. (Washington, Pennsylvania) [16855]
Famous Enterprises Inc. [14442]
Famous Industries [23161]
Fasnap Corp. [13694]
Fastener Supply Co. [13698]
Fauver Co. [16857]
Faxon Engineering Company Inc. [16858]
Federal Signal Corp. [8734]
Fegely Inc.; J. [16859]
Fehr Bros. Industries Inc. [13705]
Feldman Glass Co. [25915]
Ferguson Enterprises Inc. [23163]
Fiber Glass West [18502]
Filtemp Sales, Inc. [16860]
Filter Supply Co, [2615]
Findley Welding Supply Inc. [16861]
Fine Organics Corp. [16862]
Fireman's Supply Inc. [24551]
First International Trading Company [16863]
First Line Marketing, Inc. [16864]
First Phillips Marketing Company Inc. [22963]
Fisher Auto Parts Professionals [2623]
Fitch Industrial Welding Supply Inc. [16865]
Fleming Co.; T.J. [16866]
The Fletcher-Terry Company [13709]
Flickinger Co. [16867]
Flo-Pac Pacific Div. [15500]
Flo-Products Co. [16868]
Florida Bearings Inc. [16869]
Florig Equipment [8747]
Fluid-Air Components L.L.C. [16870]
Fluid Engineering Inc. [5840]
Fluid-Tech, Inc. [16023]
Forge Industries Inc. [16871]

Forged Vessel Connections Inc. [16872]
Foss Co.; W.J. [16874]
Foundry Service Supply Inc. [16876]
Fournier Rubber and Supply Co. [16877]
Frank Winne and Son Inc. [26039]
Fredericseal, Inc. [16878]
Freeman Manufacturing and Supply [16879]
Freund Can Co. [25916]
Friedman Electric Supply [8762]
FSC Educational Inc. [3768]
Fugitt Rubber & Supply Company, Inc. [16881]
Fulton, Mehring & Hauser Company, Inc. [16882]
Fulton Supply Co. [16883]
Furniture Makers Supply Co. [16884]
Gage Co. [16885]
Gage Co. Central Div. [16886]
Galco Industrial Electronics [8772]
Gardena Industrial Supply and Hardware
  Co. [16887]
Gardner and Meredith Inc. [16047]
Gary's Machinery Inc. [16888]
Gates InterAmerica [16890]
Gear Motions Inc. [16891]
Geib Industries Inc. [16892]
Gelber Industries [16051]
Genalco Inc. [7382]
General Pipe and Supply Company Inc. [23187]
General Steel Fabricators [19997]
General Tool and Supply Co. [13722]
General Tool & Supply Co. [16893]
Genesis Safety Systems Inc. [24555]
Georgino and Sons Inc.; Patsy [16894]
Gerhardt's International, Inc. [16060]
Gierston Tool Company Inc. [16063]
GKM Enterprises Inc. [22856]
GL&V/Celleco Inc. [16066]
Glass Co., Inc.; The John M. [16895]
Global Expediting and Marketing Co. [16896]
Global Fastener Inc. [13724]
Globe Machinery and Supply Co. [16897]
Glosser and Sons Inc.; M. [20010]
Goddard Industries Inc. [16898]
Goodall Rubber Co. [16899]
Gooding Rubber Co. (La Grange, Illinois) [16900]
Gooding and Shields Rubber Co. [24277]
Goodyear Tire Rubber Co. [16901]
Gopher Bearing [2692]
Gordon Rubber and Packing Company
  Inc. [24278]
Goss Supply Co. [16902]
Graphic Sciences Inc. [16903]
Grattan & Sons Inc.; Dave [13728]
Graves Fire Protection [24557]
Grayco Products [16904]
Green and Co.; Carl [16907]
Greene Rubber Company Inc. [24279]
Greensboro Pipe Company Inc. [16908]
Greno Industries Inc. [16909]
Grier and Sons Co.; R.D. [16910]
Grinnell Supply Sales Co [16911]
Grinnell Supply Sales Co. [23199]
Groth Corp. [16912]
GRS Industrial Supply Co. [16913]
GT Sales and Manufacturing Inc. [16914]
GTH Holdings, Inc. [7421]
Guilfoil and Associates Inc.; T.V. [25919]
Gusmer Enterprises Inc. [16915]
GWS Supply, Inc. [16917]
Haasco Inc. [16918]
Hadlock Paint Co. [21454]
Hagerty Brothers Co. [16919]
Haggard and Stocking Associates Inc. [16920]
Haldeman-Homme Inc. [16921]
Halsey Company Inc.; W.L. [11367]
Handy Care [19349]
Hannan Supply Co. [8826]
Hardesty Welding Supply Div. [16922]
Hardware and Supply Company of Chester
  Inc. [16923]
Hardware Supply Company Inc. [13741]
Harley Industries Inc. [16924]
Harris Pump and Supply Co. [16090]
Harris Supply Company Inc. [16925]
Haskel International, Inc. [16091]
Hasson-Bryan Hardware Co. [13744]
Hatfield and Company Inc. [16926]

Hawaii Hardware Company Ltd. [13745]
Hayden Company Inc.; C.W. [16927]
Hazlett Company Inc.; T.R. [7462]
Heartland Paper Co. [21758]
Helicoflex Co. [16929]
Hendrix Technologies Inc. [21029]
Herco Products Corp.; Ryan [22980]
Highway Equipment and Supply Co. [16100]
Hitachi America Ltd. [25233]
Hitachi Maxco Ltd. [16930]
Ho Imports, Inc. [26515]
Hoke Controls [16931]
Holloway Brothers Tools Inc. [16109]
Holo-Krome Co. [13755]
Honeywell H.P.G. [99]
Hope Group [16112]
Hopper Specialty West, Inc. [16932]
Horizon Distribution Inc. [13757]
Horn Co.; E.T. [4418]
Horsepower Control System [2761]
Hosokawa Micron International Inc. [16115]
Hotsy Cleaning Systems [25681]
H.S. Industrial Equipment [16933]
Hub/Industrial Mill Supply Co. [16934]
Hubbard Industrial Supply Co. [16119]
Hudgins Inc.; T.F. [16935]
Hughes Company Inc.; R.S. [24568]
Hunt Cleaners Inc. [4638]
Hydraquip Corp. [16128]
Hyster MidEast [16134]
IBT Inc. [16136]
IBT Inc. [16137]
ICE Export Sales Corp. [7503]
Ideal Machinery and Supply Co. [16139]
IDG [16937]
Ilapak Inc. [16141]
IMA Tool Distributors [13763]
Impex International [16940]
Independent Foundry Supply Co. [16941]
Indiana Supply Corp. [16943]
Indianapolis Belting & Supply [16148]
Indresco, Inc. [16945]
Industrial Distribution Group, Inc. [16946]
Industrial Pipe & Steel [16152]
Industrial Rubber Products Co. [24282]
Industrial Safety Supply Co. [16948]
Industrial Safety Supply Co. Interex Div. [24571]
Industrial Steel and Wire Co. [16949]
Industrial Supplies Co. [16950]
Industrial Supply Co. [16951]
Industrial Supply Co. [16952]
Industrial Supply Co. [16953]
Industrial Supply Co. [16954]
Industrial Supply Co. [16154]
Industrial Supply Co. [16955]
Industrial Supply Company Inc. (Salt Lake City,
  Utah) [16956]
Industrial Supply Corp. [16957]
Industrial Supply Corp. [16958]
Industrial Supply Solutions, Inc. [2775]
Industrial Supply Solutions, Inc. [16155]
Industrial Tool Products Inc. [16156]
Industrial Tools and Abrasives Inc. [16959]
Intech Corp. [16960]
Intermarket Imports Inc. [16163]
International Tape Products Co. [21065]
Interstate Bearing Co. [2794]
Interstate Co. [16962]
Interstate Welding Sales Corp. [16168]
Interstate Welding Sales Corp. [16963]
Iowa Machinery and Supply Company Inc. [16173]
Irby Co.; Stuart C. [16964]
Island Spring & Drive Shaft Co. [16965]
J and L Strong Tool Co. [16180]
Jabo Supply Corp. [23223]
JacksonLea [16966]
Jacob and Sons; M. [25921]
Jacobs Supply Co.; Mylon C. [2808]
Jacon Fasteners and Electronics Inc. [13768]
James and Company Inc.; E. [16968]
Jarvis Supply Co. [16183]
Jasper Engineering and Equipment Co. [16970]
Jealco International, Inc. [16185]
Jed Co.; Leonard [13770]
Jennison Industrial Supply [13771]
JLK Direct Distribution Inc. [16188]

Johnston Industrial Supply Co. [16190]
Joint and Clutch Service Inc. [2830]
Joint Production Technology Inc. [16191]
Jolley Industrial Supply Company Inc. [16971]
Jonesboro Winnelson Co. [16972]
Juno Industries Inc. [16973]
Justis Supply Company Inc. [16974]
Kalamazoo Mill Supply Co. [16975]
Kalamazoo Mill Supply Co. [20083]
Kaman Corp. [16197]
Kaman Industrial [16976]
Kaman Industrial Technologies [16977]
Kaman Industrial Technologies Inc. [111]
Kansas City Rubber and Belting Co. [24283]
Kansas City Rubber and Belting Co. [16978]
Kar Products [13781]
Kar Products, Inc. [16980]
Kelly Supply Company of Iowa [16983]
Kendall Industrial Supplies Inc. [16984]
Kennametal [16985]
Kennedy Manufacturing Co. [16986]
Kenrick Company Inc.; R. G. [16987]
Kentucky Bearings Service [16988]
Kentucky Mine Supply Co. [16989]
Kentucky Welding Supply [16990]
Kett Tool Co. [13785]
Kibar Bearings [16991]
Kiemle-Hankins Co. [8943]
King Bearing Div. [2857]
Kleen Supply Co. [4651]
Knight Corp. [16992]
Kohl Building Products [7568]
Kolda Corp. [16213]
Kornfeld-Thorp Electric Co. [8957]
La Grand Industrial Supply Co. [24582]
Lab Safety Supply Inc. [18880]
Lamons Beaumont Bolt & Gasket [16993]
Langford Tool & Drill [13792]
Laredo Hardware Co. [13793]
Laube Technology Inc. [16994]
Lawson Products Inc. [16995]
Leica Industries Inc. [20121]
Lempco Industries Inc. [16996]
Leon's Molds [16997]
Lewis-Goetz and Company Inc. [24284]
Lewis Supply Company Inc. [16998]
Lindquist Industrial Supply Co. [17000]
Linear Industries Ltd [17001]
Lipe-Rollway Corp. International Div. [17002]
Logan and Whaley Company Inc. [17003]
Lord & Hodge, Inc. [13803]
Los Angeles Rubber Co. [24285]
Losey and Company Inc. [17004]
Lotz Paper and Fixture Co.; F.W. [21814]
Louisiana Mill Supply [17005]
Louisiana Mill Supply [17006]
Lowe Supply Co.; Bert [17007]
Lumberton Industries Inc. [17008]
M & G Industries [9013]
M & G Industries Inc. [9014]
M & M Sales & Equipment [17009]
Machine Service Inc. [2903]
Machine and Welding Supply Co. [16255]
Mackay Industrial Sales Inc. [17010]
Magnum Corp. [17011]
Mahoning Valley Supply Co. [17012]
Malco Products Inc. [13809]
The Manderscheid Co. [17013]
Manson Tool and Supply Co. [17014]
Manufactured Rubber Products Inc. [17015]
Maraj International [6461]
Mars Co.; W.P. and R.S. [16266]
Marshall Co.; R.J. [4453]
Marshall Co.; R.J. [17016]
Martensen Enterprises Inc. [7651]
Martensen Enterprises Inc. [17017]
Marus and Weimer, Inc. [23252]
The Massey Company Inc. [17018]
Matthews International Corp., Marking Systems
  Div. [16274]
MBL USA Corp. [24286]
McAdams Pipe and Supply Co. [22461]
McCormick Co.; J.S. [20553]
McCoy and Son Inc.; J.B. [21828]
McGill Hose and Coupling Inc. [17021]
McGraw Group Inc. [17022]

McGraw Inc.; James [17023]
McGraw Inc.; James [16278]
McGuire Bearing [2933]
McGuire Bearing [2934]
McGuire Bearing [17024]
McGuire Bearing [17025]
McGuire-Nicholas Co., Inc. [17026]
McJunkin Corp. [9058]
McJunkin Corp. [17027]
McLean International Marketing Inc. [24589]
McLean International Marketing Inc. [17028]
MDC Industries Inc. [17029]
Mechanical Drives Co. [2936]
Mechanical Drives Inc. [16283]
Meriden Cooper Corp. [17030]
Merrill Co. [2944]
Metric & Multistandard Components Corp. [17031]
Meyer Co.; O.E. [17032]
MGA Research Corp. [16291]
Michigan Airgas [17033]
Michigan Industrial Piping Supply Company
    Inc. [23262]
Mid-America Power Drives [17035]
Mid-America Power Drives [16295]
Mid-South Oxygen Company Inc. [17036]
Mid-South Supply Corp. [21501]
Mid-State Distributing [9077]
Mid-States Industrial Div. [23266]
Mid-States Supply Company Inc. [23267]
Mid-Valley Supply Co. [17037]
Midamar Corp. [11882]
Midvale Industries Inc. [16297]
Midway Trading, Inc. [2958]
Milchap Products [7710]
Mill Supplies Corp. [17038]
Mill Supplies Inc. [17039]
Miller Bearings Inc. [17040]
Miller Bearings Inc. [2964]
Miller Bearings Inc. [2965]
Miller Bearings Inc. [2966]
Miller Bearings Inc. [2967]
Miller Bearings Inc. [17041]
Milligan-Spika Co. [17042]
Mills and Lupton Supply Co. [9087]
Mine and Mill Supply Co. [20197]
Mine Supply Co. [17043]
Minnesota Mining & Manufacturing Co. Do-It-
    Yourself Div. [17044]
MLT International Inc. [17045]
Modern Material Handling Co. [17046]
Modern Supply Company Inc. [23271]
Mohawk Rubber Sales of N.E. Inc. [24287]
Monumental Supply Company Inc. [23274]
Moody Co.; J.A. [18572]
Moonachie Co. [17048]
Moore Brothers Div. [17050]
Moore Drums Inc. [22496]
Moore Drums Inc. [17051]
Morris Co.; S.G. [16326]
Morse Co.; M.K. [13838]
Morse Distribution Inc. [17053]
Mosier Fluid Power of Ohio Inc. [17054]
Motion Ind. [2989]
Motion Industries [2990]
Motion Industries [17055]
Motion Industries [2991]
Motion Industries, Atlantic Tracy Div. [17056]
Motion Industries, Inc. [2992]
Motion Industries Inc. [17057]
Motor Parts & Bearing Co. [2994]
MSC Industrial Supply Co. [13840]
Muehlstein and Company Inc.; H. [23001]
Mueller Sales Inc. [23283]
Multicraft [25746]
Multifacet Industrial Supply Company Inc. [17061]
Mundy Enterprises, Inc.; K.C. [3003]
Munnell & Sherrill Inc. [17062]
Murdock Industrial Inc. [17064]
Murken Products Inc.; Frank [24288]
Mutual Manufacturing and Supply Co. [14615]
Mutual Sales Corp. [16334]
Myles Inc.; J.E. [17065]
National Mine Service Co. Mining Safety and
    Supply Div. [7767]
National Welders Supply Company Inc. [17067]
National Welding Supply of Algona [17068]

Nautical & Industrial Supply Inc. [18575]
Naz-Dar Cincinnati [25752]
Neff Engineering Co. [17069]
Neill-LaVielle Supply Co. [13843]
Neill-LaVielle Supply Co. [17070]
Nekoosa Corp. [17071]
Nelson-Dunn Inc. [17072]
Nelson-Jameson Inc. [16347]
Nelson-Roanoke Div. [13845]
Newmans Inc. [17074]
Norfolk Bearing & Supply Co. [17075]
Normad Fastener Company Inc. [13849]
Norris Co.; Walter [17077]
North Texas Bolt, Nut & Screw, Inc. [13851]
Northeast Airgas Inc. [17078]
Northeast Steel and Machine Products [17080]
Northern Indiana Supply Company Inc. [17081]
Northern Industrial Supply Inc. [17082]
Northwestern Equipment Supply [16354]
Novelty Machine and Supply Company
    Inc. [17083]
Nudo Products Inc. [17084]
O-Rings Inc. [17085]
Ocean Products Research, Inc. [18576]
Ohio Brake & Clutch [17086]
Ohio Overseas Corp. [16359]
Ohio Pipe Valves and Fittings Inc. [17087]
Oklahoma Rig and Supply Company Inc. [17088]
Omega Optical, Inc. [17089]
Omni Services Inc. [17090]
One Source Distributors [9156]
Oren Van Aman Company Inc. [17091]
OSG Tap and Die Inc. [17092]
Ost and Ost Inc. [3065]
Owensboro Electric Supply [9165]
Owensboro Supply Company Inc. [17093]
Pac States Electric Wholesalers [9167]
Pacific Abrasive Supply Co. [17094]
Pacific Coast Air Tool and Supply Inc. [135]
Pacific Fibre and Rope Company Inc. [17095]
Pacific Handy Cutter Inc. [17096]
Pacific Industrial Supply Company Inc. [17097]
Packaging Concepts and Design [21857]
Packers Engineering and Equipment Company
    Inc. [17098]
Packing Seals and Engineering Company
    Inc. [23305]
Pagel Safety Inc. [24611]
Parker Hannifin Corp. Fluidpower Sales
    Div. [17099]
Parnell-Martin Co. [23309]
Pathon Co. [16383]
Patron Transmission [17100]
Peacock Co./Southwestern Cordage Co.;
    R.E. [17102]
Peerless Paper Mills Inc. [4684]
Penco Corp. [22560]
Penstan Supply [23312]
Perrigo Inc. [23313]
Perry Supply Inc. [7851]
Petter Supply Co.; Henry A. [17103]
Piedmont National Corp. [21882]
Pikotek [17104]
Pioneer Equipment Inc. [5849]
Pioneer Industrial Corp. [17105]
Pipe Valve and Fitting Co. [17106]
Piping Supply Company Inc. [17107]
Plant Service Co. [17108]
Plumbers Supply Co. [23320]
Plumbers Supply Co. [23321]
PMC Specialties Group [17109]
PMI Sales and Marketing Services Inc. [23324]
PNB Trading, Inc. [16405]
Pollack Enterprises Inc.; Morton [15275]
Potomac Rubber Company Inc. [24289]
Power Drives and Bearings Div. [16413]
Power Lift Corp. [16414]
Power & Pumps Inc. [3111]
Power Torque [3112]
Prassel Lumber Company Inc. [7884]
Praxair Gas Tech [17110]
Precision Bearing [17111]
Precision Bearing Co. [17112]
Precision Bearing Co. [17113]
Precision Industrial Distributors Inc. [17114]
Precision Industries [16422]

Precision Industries Inc. [3116]
Precision Speed Instruments Inc. [17115]
Price Engineering Company, Inc. [17116]
Primark Tool Group [13875]
PrimeSource Corp. [25791]
Probst Supply Co. [23331]
Processors Equipment & Hardware [17118]
Production Tool Supply [17119]
Production Tool Supply of Jackson [17120]
Professional Aviation Associates Inc. [139]
Pump Engineering Co. [17121]
Purvis Bearings [17123]
Quality Mill Supply Company Inc. [17125]
Quimby Corp. [17126]
R and R Plumbing Supply Corp. [23333]
R and W Supply Inc. [17127]
Ram Threading Inc. [13881]
Ramclif Supply Co. [17128]
Raniville Company Inc.; F. [17130]
Rapid Controls Inc. [17131]
Rasmussen Equipment Co. [7901]
Raufeisen Enterprises [17132]
RB Royal Industries Inc. [23336]
R.C.A. America [7904]
Reade Advanced Materials [4491]
Reed Manufacturing Co. [17133]
Refco IDG. [17134]
Reichman, Crosby, Hays Inc. [17135]
Reid Tool Supply Co. [17136]
Rexel-Summers [9288]
RG Group Inc. [17137]
Riggsbee Hardware & Industrial Supply [13887]
Ritter Engineering Co. [23344]
Robco International Corporation/Advanced
    Technology International [17140]
Robert-James Sales Inc. [20323]
Roberts and Brune Co. [17141]
Roberts International, Inc. [7942]
Robnet Inc. [13889]
Rockford Industrial Welding Supply Inc. [17142]
Rod Co. Inc.; A.J. [17143]
Rodriguez Inc.; R.A. [17144]
Rogers Co.; B.W. [17145]
Roll-Rite Corp. [16459]
Root Brothers Manufacturing and Supply
    Co. [17146]
Root, Neal and Company Inc. [9318]
Rowland Co. [17147]
Royal Brass and Hose [13896]
Royal Supply Inc. [16461]
Rubber and Accessories Inc. [17148]
Rubber Plus Inc. [24292]
Ruffridge Johnson Equipment Company Inc. [7965]
Russell Associates Inc. [25806]
S & W Supply Company Inc. [1225]
Sack Company Inc.; J. R. [17151]
Saddle Brook Controls [17152]
Safety West [17154]
Sager Spuck Statewide Supply Company
    Inc. [17155]
St. Louis Coke and Foundry [17156]
St. Louis Screw and Bolt Co. [23356]
Sakash Company Inc.; John [17158]
Salina Supply Co. [23357]
Sarco Inc. [17159]
Sawyer and Company Inc.; J.E. [13904]
Saxonburg Ceramics Inc. [17160]
Schermerhorn Brothers Co. [25935]
Schrader-Bridgeport International [3196]
Seaman Mill Supplies Co. [17162]
Seattle Box Co. [25937]
Sebastian Equipment Company Inc. [16478]
Sees & Faber-Berlin Inc. [16479]
Sekisui TA Industries Inc. [17164]
Semmelmeyer-Corby Co. [17165]
Senior Flexonics Inc. Dearborn Industrial Products
    Div. [17166]
Sepco Bearing and P.T. Group [17167]
Serson Supply Inc. [17168]
Servsteel Inc. [17169]
Sewell Hardware Company Inc. [13914]
Shaheen Paint and Decorating Company,
    Inc. [21566]
Sharp Products International, Inc. [17170]
Shearer Industrial Supply Co. [16485]
Sheats Supply Services, Inc. [16486]

Shelley Company Inc.; John G. [14]
Shima American Corp. [17171]
Shop Tools Inc. [13918]
Shorewood Packaging of California Inc. [21939]
Shorewood Packaging Company of Illinois Inc. [21940]
Shuster Corp. [17174]
Sid Tool Company Inc. [16488]
Silliter/Klebes Industrial Supplies Inc. [17175]
Silver State Welding Supply Inc. [16492]
Skyline Supply Company Inc. [21272]
Slip-Not Belting Corp. [17176]
Smith Abrasives, Inc. [13922]
Smith Co.; Harold E. [16497]
Smith-Thompson Co. [17177]
Smith-Thompson Inc. [17178]
Smyth-Despard Company Inc. [16500]
Snap-on Tools Corp. [13925]
Snyder Paper Corp. [21942]
Solares Florida Corp. [16501]
Soltis & Co., Inc.; A.R. [16502]
Soule Steam Feed Works [16505]
South Bend Supply Company Inc. [17181]
Southern Belting & Transmissions [17182]
Southern California Airgas Inc. [17183]
Southern Cross and O'Fallon Building Products Co. [13929]
Southern Filters Inc. [17184]
Southern Fluid Power [17185]
Southern Hardware and Supply Company Ltd. [17186]
Southern Rubber Company Inc. [17187]
Southwire Co. [17189]
Spartan Tool Supply [13931]
Specialties Co. [24295]
Specialty Products Inc. [17190]
Spencer Chain Gear Co. [3250]
Spencer Industries [17191]
Spencer Industries Inc. [17192]
Spencer Industries Inc. (Seattle, Washington) [150]
Springfield Paper Specialties, Inc. [21948]
Squibb-Taylor Inc. [22696]
Standard Supply and Hardware Company Inc. [17194]
Stangel Co.; J.J. [17195]
State Seal Co. [17197]
Steam Supply Co. [17198]
Sterco New York Inc. [18433]
Sterling Rubber and Plastics [24296]
Stewart Fastener Corp. [13937]
Strickland Auto; Jewell [17199]
Strong Tool Co. [13941]
Stutz Co. [17200]
Summit Company [4522]
Sumter Machinery Company Inc. [17201]
Sunbelt Supply Co. [17202]
Sunkyong America Inc. [15323]
Sunset Industrial Parts [17203]
SunSource [17204]
SuperGrind Co. [17205]
Superior Insulated Wire Corp. [9444]
Supply Station Inc. [13945]
Surpless, Dunn & Co. [13947]
Sutton-Garten Co. [17207]
Svetlana Electron Devices, Inc. [17208]
Swing Machinery and Equipment Company Inc. [17209]
Sygnet [16543]
T and A Industrial Distributors [17211]
Tab Electric Supply Inc. [9454]
Tampa Rubber & Gasket Co., Inc. [24298]
Tapco USA, Inc. [17212]
Tate & Lyle Enterprises, Inc. [16548]
Taylor-Parker Co. [17213]
Tech-Aerofoam Products Inc. [8103]
Techmark Corporation [24442]
Tek-Matic, Inc. [17215]
Tempo Glove Manufacturing Inc. [25839]
Tennessee Mat Company Inc. [17216]
Tepco Corp. [17217]
Tewes Company Inc.; George B. [17218]
Texas Mill Inc. [17219]
Texas Mill Inc. [17220]
Texas Mill Inc. [17221]
Texas Mill Inc. [17222]

Texas Mill Supply and Manufacturing Company Inc. [17223]
Texas Rubber Supply Inc. [24301]
Texas Rubber Supply Inc. [17224]
Thew Supply Company Inc.; W.E. [17225]
Thomas Industrial Products Company Inc. [24876]
Thompson and Cooke Inc. [17226]
Thomson Company Inc.; Geo. S. [17227]
Thorpe Co.; B.K. [23410]
Thorpe Insulation Co. [17228]
Thrall Distribution Inc. [17229]
Threaded Fasteners Inc. [13954]
T.L.K. Industries Inc. [17230]
TML Associates Inc. [8138]
Torque-A-Matic [17231]
Torrington Supply Company Inc. [23412]
Toyo USA Inc. [22745]
The TRACOM Corporation [4225]
Trade Development Corporation of Chicago [17232]
TradeCom International Inc. [13961]
Tradex International Corp. [20436]
Trans-Cal Industries Inc. [25847]
Transmission Engineering Co. [3326]
Transmission Products, Inc. [17234]
Transply Inc. [3328]
Trelltex Inc. [24303]
Tri-Power MPT [17235]
Tri-State Bearing Co. [3337]
Troy Belting Supply Co. [17236]
Tru-Form Tool and Manufacturing Industries Inc. [16584]
Tryon Trading, Inc. [17237]
Tubular Products of Texas Inc. [17238]
Turtle and Hughes Inc. [9517]
TW Graphics Group [25850]
Ultra Hydraulics Inc. [17239]
Unibri International [17240]
Union Bearing & Transmission [3361]
Union Carbide Corp., IPX Services [16587]
Union Supply Co. [23421]
Unisorce Paper Co. [21961]
Unisource [21963]
Unisource [21965]
Unistrut Fall Arrest Systems Inc. [24649]
United Pipe and Supply Company Inc. [23422]
United Plumbing and Heating Supply Co. [23423]
United Receptacle, Inc. [25855]
United World Supply Co. [17244]
Universal Management Consultants Inc. [14749]
Uvex Safety [24653]
Valiac Inc. [17247]
Valley Welders Supply Inc. [17249]
Van Horn Company Inc.; Oliver H. [16600]
Van Leeuwen Pipe and Tube Corp. [23431]
Van Sant Equipment Corp. [17251]
Vanguard Distributors Inc. [24656]
Vantage Industries Inc. [10274]
Vellano Brothers Inc. [25865]
Victor Machinery Exchange Inc. [17252]
Victory Packaging [21985]
Victory White Metal Co. [17253]
Viking Distributing Company Inc. [17254]
Viking Formed Products [17255]
Vinson Supply Co. [23433]
Virginia Materials [16603]
Virginia Welding Supply Company Inc. [17256]
Vlcek Corp.; Jerry K. [16604]
Vogel Tool & Die Corp. [16606]
Vogel Tool and Die Corp. [17257]
Voorhies Supply Company Inc. [16608]
Voto Manufacturing Sales Company Inc. [17258]
Walke Co.; Henry [17260]
Walker Co.; James [17261]
Walker and Son Inc.; P.G. [17262]
Wallace Company Inc. [23435]
Wallace Supply Co. [23437]
Washington Belt & Drive [17263]
Washington Belt & Drive [17264]
Washington Belt & Drive [17265]
Washington Belt & Drive [17266]
Washington Chain and Supply Inc. [18634]
Water and Waste Water Equipment Co. [23439]
Water Works and Industrial Supply Co., Inc. [17267]
Waymire Drum Company Inc. [25517]

Wayne Fasteners Inc. [13986]
Webb Co.; F.W. [23446]
Wedin International Inc., Ball Screw Manufacturing and Repair, Inc. [13989]
Weiss Company Inc.; Max [16618]
Welders Supply Inc. [17269]
Welding Industrial Supply Inc. [17270]
Weldstar Co. [17271]
Welsco Inc. [17272]
Wesche Co. [13993]
WESCO Distribution Inc. [9569]
West Coast Ship Chandlers Inc. [17273]
West Penn Laco Inc. [17275]
Western Fluid Power [16628]
Western MacArthur Co. [8208]
Western Rubber and Supply Inc. [17276]
Westmoreland Industrial Supply Co. [17277]
Wheelabrator Air Pollution Control [25879]
Wheeler Consolidated Inc. [8217]
White Water Manufacturing [17279]
Wilkins Supply Co.; M.P. [23459]
Williams Equipment and Supply Company Inc. [8227]
Williams Inc.; Ralph C. [17280]
Williamson & Co. [17281]
Wilton Corp. [17282]
Winograd's Steel and Supply [20495]
Wisconsin Bearing [17283]
Wisconsin Bearing [3442]
Wisconsin Bearing [17284]
Wisconsin Bearing [17285]
Wood Brothers and Halstead Lumber [25948]
Wood Supply Co.; Walter A. [17286]
Woodlawn Hardware [17287]
World Trade Network, Ltd. [18644]
Wright Co.; F.B. [17288]
Yale/Chase Materials Handling, Inc. [16654]
Yaun Company Inc. [23468]
Yecies Inc.; Herman W. [17291]
Young Cos.; A.B. [16657]
Young Cos.; A.B. [17292]
Young and Vann Supply Co. [17293]
Zagar Inc. [16658]
Zatkoff Seals and Packings Co. [17294]
Zed Group Inc. [16659]
Ziegler's Bolt & Nut House [14005]
Zuckerman-Honickman Inc. [25950]

SIC 5087 — Service Establishment Equipment

3-D Supply Inc. [4562]
78ic Beauty Supply & Salons [14006]
A-1 Chemical Inc. [4563]
A and B Wiper Supply Inc. [26723]
A & D Maintenance [4564]
Aberdeen Vault Inc.; Wilbert [25541]
Ace Advance Paper Co. [21614]
Acme Paper and Supply Company Inc. [21615]
Acorn Distributors Inc. [21616]
Adams-Burch Inc. [24056]
ADEMCO/ADI [24468]
Advanced Maintenance Products Co. [4566]
Aerial Company Inc. [14009]
Airgas [15746]
Alaska Paper Co. Inc. [21617]
Aldelano Corp. [4567]
Aleutian Pribilof Island Association [18670]
Alkota of Western Montana [4568]
All City Barber & Beauty Supply [14013]
Almeda Beauty Shop [14017]
Altimus Distributing [4569]
Amedem Enterprises, Inc. [4570]
American Industrial Supply [16694]
American Paper Towel Co. [21630]
American Paper and Twine Co. [21631]
American Wiping Rag [4572]
AMJ Inc. [4573]
AMJ Inc. [24064]
Ammar Beauty Supply Co. [14020]
Angus Fire Armour Corp. [25553]
Apco Inc. [15014]
Apollo Sales Group Inc. [25554]

Arbuckle Coffee Roasters Inc. [24067]
Arensberg Sons Inc. [25558]
Aries Paper & Chemical Co. Inc. [4574]
Arizona Coin & Commercial Laundry
  Equipment [15032]
Arrow Sales Inc. [20812]
Artesia Fire Equipment Inc. [24509]
ATS Money Systems Inc. [25567]
Automotive Distributors Inc. [2286]
AVK II Inc. [24073]
B & A Distributing Inc. [14032]
B & G Beauty Supply Inc. [14033]
B-J Pac-A-Part [4575]
B-J Pac-A-Part [24074]
Banner Systems Inc. [4577]
Barry Pumps Inc.; R.E. [25568]
Baumann Paper Company Inc. [21647]
Bay Paper Co. Inc. [20837]
Bean and Sons Co.; D.D. [24512]
Bean's Beauty Supply [14035]
Beauty Aid Distributors [14036]
Beisler Weidmann Company Inc. [21650]
Belco Athletic Laundry Equipment Co. [15047]
Ben-Mar Paper Co. Inc. [21652]
Berint Trading, Ltd. [13593]
Bermil Industries Corp. [15050]
Best Beauty Supply Co. [14039]
Best-Klean Products [4578]
Best Way Carpet Care Inc. [4579]
Big Horn Wholesale [4580]
Big W Supplies Inc. [4581]
Black & Decker US Inc. [4582]
Black Hills Chemical Co. Inc. [4583]
Blais Enterprises; M.C. [24516]
Blue Cold Distributors [24078]
Blue Lustre, LLC [4584]
Blue Ribbon Linen Supply Inc. [4585]
Bockstanz Brothers Co. [4586]
Boelter Co. [24080]
Boyd Distributing Co. Inc. [15056]
Bozeman Distributors [2376]
BR Chemical Co. Inc. [4587]
Brady Industries Inc. [4588]
Brissman-Kennedy Inc. [4589]
Bristol Retail Solutions Inc. [20855]
C & C Distributors [15067]
C & S Specialty Inc. [24522]
C & W Distributing Inc. [4591]
Cache Beauty Supply Inc. [14054]
California Professional Manufacturing Inc. [25593]
Callahan Brothers Supply Inc. [25594]
Cameo Paper & Janitor Supply Co. [4592]
Capitol Chemical & Supply [4593]
Capitol Distributors [9756]
Capps Beauty & Barber Inc. [14055]
Carolina FireMasters Inc. [24525]
Carolina Salon Services [14058]
Casey Inc.; John R. [4594]
Central Paper Products Co. Inc. [21676]
Centre Beauty Supply [14061]
Chantal Cookware Corp. [15441]
Chapmans Shoe Repair [24710]
Clark's Store Fixtures Inc. [4599]
Classic Beauty Supply and Service Center [14065]
Classic Beauty Supply and Service Center [24095]
Columbus Paper Company Inc. [4601]
Commercial Laundry Sales [4602]
Connecticut Appliance & Fireplace Distributors,
  LLC [15094]
Conrad Memorial Cemetary; C.E. [25609]
Consolidated International Corp. [4603]
Convenience Equipment and Supplies Enterprises
  Inc. [25611]
Courtesy Sanitary Supply [4604]
Cox; Charles E. [4606]
Cunningham Distributing Inc. [25615]
Cunningham Distributing Inc. [25616]
D & H Beauty Supply [14076]
D & M Distributors Inc. [25620]
D and M Distributors Inc. [24099]
D & S Enterprises [4607]
Dakota Industrial Supply [4608]
Damon Industries, Inc. [4609]
Davison Co.; R.E. [24532]
Decker's Inc. [4611]
Defreeze Corp. [14413]

Deuster Co. [24104]
Diamond Chemical/Supply Co. [4372]
Diamond Supply Company Inc. [4612]
Dibs Chemical & Supply Co. Inc. [21708]
Dillard Paper Co. Chattanooga Div. [21710]
DPI Southwest Distributing Inc. [10990]
Dreyfus & Assoc. [2562]
E & B Beauty & Barber Supply [14088]
E and B Beauty and Barber Supply [24106]
Easterday Janitorial Supply Co. [4613]
Ecolab Inc. Textile Care Div. [4616]
Edmer Sanitary Supply Co. Inc. [4617]
Elite Supply Co. [14093]
Empire Corporation [4618]
Empire Paper Co. [21723]
Engberg Janitorial Supply & Service [4619]
Essence Beauty Supply [14097]
Exsaco Corp. [23658]
EXSL/Ultra Labs Inc. [4385]
F & S Supply Company Inc. [8728]
Faulcon Industries [14100]
Fegely Inc.; J. [16859]
Fire Boss of Louisiana Inc. [24542]
Fire Equipment Inc. [24544]
Fire Fighters Equipment Co. [24545]
Fire Fighters Equipment Co. [24119]
Fire Spec Inc. [24546]
Fire Systems Unlimited Inc. [24547]
Fire-Tec Inc. [24548]
Fire Tech & Safety of Neng [24549]
Fireman's Supply Inc. [24551]
Fisher; Karen [4620]
Fisher Paper [21727]
Fitch Dustdown Co. [4621]
Fitch Dustdown Co. [24120]
Fite; Ted G. [25652]
Flo-Pac Corp. [4623]
Follum Supply [4624]
Foresight Inc. [4625]
Forman Inc. [4626]
Fredriksen and Sons Fire Equipment Company
  Inc. [24553]
General Supply of Yakima Inc. [4627]
Ghia Corp. [25660]
Giancola Exports, Inc.; D.J. [4628]
Golden Products Co. [4629]
Goorland & Mann, Inc. [4630]
Graves Fire Protection [24557]
Great Lakes Air Systems Inc. [4631]
Great Scott Services Ltd. [21751]
Green Mountain Foam Products [25671]
Group One Capital Inc. [14117]
Guss Cleaning & Supply [4632]
Hair Depot Beauty Consultants [14120]
Hallsmith-Sysco Food Services [11366]
Hampshire Furniture Co. [25673]
Hampshire Furniture Co. [24134]
Harf Inc. [25674]
Hartsook Equipment & Pump Services [22340]
Hathaway Paper Co. [21756]
Hearn Paper Company Inc. [21757]
Hercules Vacu-Maid [4633]
Herman; Jeffrey [25677]
Hess Hair Milk Laboratories Inc. [25678]
Hettinger-Mobridge Candy & Tobacco [26306]
HGS Power House, Inc. [818]
Hickel Investment Co. [25679]
Hiller Investments Inc. [24563]
Hintz Fire Equipment Inc. [24564]
Hispania Trading Corporation [25680]
HK Laundry Equipment Inc. [4634]
Holstein Paper & Janitorial Supply [21765]
Horizon [837]
Hotsy Cleaning Systems [25681]
House of Clean Inc. [4636]
HP Products [4637]
Hunt Cleaners Inc. [4638]
Huntsville/Redstone Paper Co. [21772]
Idaho Barber & Beauty Supply Inc. [14128]
Indiana Concession Supply Inc. [11504]
Industrial Safety Supply Co. [16948]
Industrial Soap Co. [4639]
Industrial Wiper & Paper [21775]
Interstate Distributors Inc. [24145]
Interworld [4640]
J & J Cleaning Service [4641]

Jacks Fragrances [25691]
Jackson Supply Co. [4643]
Jackson Supply Co. [24147]
Jani-Serv [4644]
Janitor Supply Co. [4645]
Janitor Supply Co. [24149]
Janvey and Sons Inc.; I. [4646]
Jim's Beauty Supply [14137]
JLJ Inc. [24577]
Johnson & Associates; Steve [14138]
Johnson Company Inc.; George T. [4647]
JS Enterprises Inc. [24151]
JVLNET By Electrolarm [6413]
JVLNET By Electrolarm [24153]
Katcef Sales Inc. [25696]
Kazuhiro Ltd. [25697]
Kellermeyer Co. [4649]
Kenway Distributors Inc. [4650]
Keyston Brothers [26109]
Kirby Company of Wichita [25701]
Knapp Supply & Equipment Co. [24160]
Knight Marketing Corp. [4652]
Knoll Motel [4653]
Kranz Inc. [4654]
Kwik Stop Car Wash Supply [4655]
La Grand Industrial Supply Co. [24582]
Lab Safety Supply Inc. [18880]
LaFrance Equipment Corp. [24583]
Lake Tahoe Supplies [4656]
Landsberg Co.; Kent H. [21796]
Lane Fire Service; Donald [24584]
Lane and McClain Distributors Inc. [24162]
Laun-Dry Supply Company Inc. [4657]
Lawsons Locksmithing [25710]
Leading Products Co. [4658]
Leavenworth Paper Supply Co. [21798]
Leedal Inc. [22873]
Leland Paper Company Inc. [21105]
Leonard Paper Company Inc. [21799]
Levin and Sons Co.; J. [4659]
Lit Refrigeration Co. [25718]
M & P Sales Inc. [4662]
Macon Beauty Supply Co. [14157]
Magnolia Casket Co. [24174]
Mahowald; John G. [25723]
Main Street and Main Inc. [24175]
Mansfield Paper Company Inc. [21821]
Mark VII Equipment Inc. [24177]
Marshall Co.; A.J. [4663]
Marstan Industries Inc. [24178]
Massena Paper Company Inc. [21824]
Master Cleaners Home Service [4664]
Mattson Distributing Co.; Art [25727]
MCF Systems Atlanta Inc. [4665]
Medek Inc.; George M. [4667]
Memphis Chemical Janitorial Supply Inc. [4668]
MH Associates Ltd. [23824]
Mid City Hardware [4669]
Midwest Chemical and Supply Inc. [4670]
Midwest Cleaning Systems Inc. [4671]
Mikara Corp. [24185]
Miller Funeral Home Inc. [25741]
Mission Janitorial Supplies [4672]
Monahan Paper Co. [21841]
Monsour's Inc. [11926]
Montana Leather Co. Inc. [25743]
Monumental Paper Co. [21842]
Moore, Inc.; A.E. [4673]
More; Ruth [14167]
Moreland Wholesale Co., Inc. [11935]
Morse Wholesale Paper Company Inc. [21844]
Mt. Ellis Paper Company Inc. [21845]
MSC Industrial Supply Co. [13840]
Mutual Trading Co. Inc. [11962]
Mutual Wholesale Co. [11963]
Mutual Wholesale Co. [11964]
Nannicola Wholesale Co., Inc. [25747]
Nar Inc. [4674]
Nardini Fire Equipment Company of North
  Dakota [24598]
Nation Wide Paper Co. [21847]
National Sanitary Supply Co. Portland Div. [4675]
Nelson Company Inc.; Walter E. [4676]
New Man Barber & Beauty Supply [14177]
New Mexico Beauty & Barber Supply [14178]
NJCT Corp. [24194]

North American Parts Inc. [23849]
Northern Chemical/Janitor Sply [24195]
Northwest Arkansas Paper Co. [4677]
NUCO Industries Inc. [4678]
Nugget Distributors Inc. [12044]
Okie Dokie Services [4679]
Oliver Supply Co. [4680]
Oliver Supply Co. [24198]
On Spot Janitor Supplies & Repair [4681]
Oreck Floorcare Center [25776]
OUR Designs Inc. [25778]
PAMSCO Inc. [4682]
Paper Mart [21862]
Paper Service Company Inc. [21865]
Paper Supply Co. [4683]
Peerless Paper Mills Inc. [4684]
Perfection Distributing Co. [25781]
Petter Supply Co.; Henry A. [17103]
Phenix Supply Co. [4685]
Phillips Distribution Inc. [4686]
Pifer, Inc. [23881]
Plant Maintenance Equipment [4687]
Plastic Safety Systems, Inc. [24613]
Portsmouth Paper Co. [4688]
Pressure Service Inc. [4689]
Professional Education & Products Inc. [14196]
Professional Salon Services [14198]
Professional Salon Services [24206]
Providence Casket Co. [25792]
Pryor & Associates; Roger [25793]
Rainbow Paper Company, Inc. [21896]
Rapid City Beauty & Barber Supply [14205]
Raylon Corp. [14206]
Raylon Corp. [14208]
Redco Lighting & Maintenance [9270]
Redy Inc. [14211]
Reed Distributors [4692]
Reliable Fire Equipment Co. [24618]
Renken Distributing; M. [25801]
Rex Chemical Corp. [4694]
Richard-Ewing Equipment Co. Inc. [4696]
Rite Way Barber & Beauty Supplies [14221]
Ro-Vic Inc. [4697]
Rochester Midland Corp. [4698]
Rocky Mountain Salon Consolidated [14223]
Rose Products and Services Inc. [4699]
Royal Beauty & Barber [14225]
Rykoff & Co.; S.E. [21916]
S & D Industrial Supply Inc. [4700]
SA-SO [24620]
Sadd Laundry and Dry Cleaning Supplies [4701]
St. Paul Bar/Restaurant Equipment [24213]
Sally Beauty Company Inc. [14227]
Salon Associates [14228]
San Joaquin Supply Company Inc. [4702]
Sanderson Safety Supply Co. [24624]
Sani-Clean Distributors Inc. [4703]
Schilling Paper Co. [21923]
Schnaible Service and Supply Company Inc. [4704]
Schutte and Koerting Div. [15305]
Schuylkill Haven Casket Co. [25809]
Scissors and Shears [14231]
Scott Foam & Fabrics, Inc. [26200]
Seatronics Inc. [24627]
Select Wines & Spirits Co. [2017]
Servall Products Inc. [21934]
Seybold Co. [4706]
Ships Wheel Brand Corp. [4708]
Sierra Craft Inc. [23374]
Signature Services Corp. [25816]
Simplex Chemical Corp. [4709]
Singer Equipment Company Inc. [24220]
Smith and Co.; R.W. [25820]
Solomon M. Casket Company of Rhode Island [25823]
Solutions and Cleaning Products [4710]
Solutions and Cleaning Products [24224]
Sondras Beauty Supply [14243]
South King Kirby [25824]
Southwest Paper Company Inc. [21944]
State Beauty Supply [14246]
State Beauty Supply [14247]
State Janitorial Supply Co. [4713]
State Service Systems Inc. [14248]
Statewide Floor Waxing Distributors [4714]

Steam Way International Inc. [24227]
Stockton Service Corp. [22708]
Strickland Beauty & Barber Supply Inc. [14249]
Sullivan Candy & Supply [26354]
Sullivan Co. Inc.; C.B. [14250]
Sun Appliance Service Inc. [25833]
Sweeper Corp. [25836]
Tech Fire and Safety Co. [24642]
Tech Fire and Safety Co. [24243]
Teeters Products Inc. [25838]
Texas Mill Supply and Manufacturing Company Inc. [17223]
Thayer Inc. [4716]
Thayer Inc. [24245]
Thompsons Inc. [25842]
Thompson's State Beauty Supply [14258]
Todd; Robyn [14260]
Total Safety Inc. [25846]
TRI-Alaska [14262]
Tri M Specialties [24645]
TRI-New England [14263]
Tri State Beauty Supply Inc. [14264]
Tri-State Police Fire Equipment Inc. [24647]
TRI-Utah [14265]
Trompeter Co.; John F. [26361]
Tsuki's Hair Design [14266]
Turtle Plastics Co. [4718]
TW Systems Ltd. [4719]
Twyman Templeton Company Inc. [24648]
Unijax Div. [21959]
Unisorce Paper Co. [21961]
Unisource Midwest Inc. [21967]
Unisource Worldwide Inc. [21970]
United Beauty Equipment Co. [14269]
United Beauty Equipment Co. [24253]
United Fire Equipment Co. [24650]
United Fire Equipment Co. [24255]
U.S. Foodservice - RRS Div. [12802]
Urban Wholesale [4721]
Valley Coin Laundry Equipment Co. [4722]
Van Dyke Supply Co. [25862]
Veterans Supply & Distributing Co. [4723]
Virginia Industrial Cleaners and Equipment Co. [4724]
Vlcek Corp.; Jerry K. [16604]
Wabash Independent Oil Co. [4725]
Wahler Brothers [13983]
Wallace Inc.; Gary L. [25870]
Wards Cleaning & Supply [4726]
Warrenterprises Inc. [4727]
Western Cascade Equipment Co. [15370]
Western Facilities Supply, Inc. [4730]
Western Facilities Supply Inc. [24261]
White River Paper Company Inc. [21991]
Wholesale Supply Company Inc. [26372]
Wilbert Vault of Aroostook [25880]
Wilcox Paper Co. [21993]
Willets O'Neil Co.; A. [4732]
Wilson Paper Co. [21994]
Wink Davis Equipment Company Inc. [4733]
With Enterprises Inc. [4734]
xpedx West Region [22008]
Yankton Janitorial Supply [4735]

SIC 5088 — Transportation Equipment & Supplies

A and K Railroad Materials Inc. [23471]
AAA Interair Inc. [20]
AAA Manufacturing Inc. [20575]
AAR Corp. [21]
AAR Corp. [22]
ABSCOA Industries Inc. [23]
Adams Industries Inc. [13531]
A.E.R. Supply, Inc. [18448]
Aero Services International Inc. [24]
Aero Systems Aviation Inc. [25]
Aero Systems Inc. [26]
Aerodynamics Inc. [27]
Aeronca Inc. [28]
Aerospace Products International Inc. [29]
Aerotech World Trade Corp. [30]
Agusta Aerospace Corp. [31]

Aim Enterprises, Inc. [32]
Air Combat Exchange Ltd. [20579]
Air Comm Corp. [33]
Airbus Industry of North America Inc. [34]
Aircraft and Component Equipment Suppliers Inc. [35]
Aircraft Spruce and Specialty Co. [36]
Airmotive Inc. [37]
Alamo Aircraft, Ltd. [38]
Alco Equipment Inc. [2200]
Allied Screw Products [39]
Almerica Overseas Inc. [40]
American General Supplies Inc. [41]
American Industrial Exports Ltd. [18449]
Argo International Corp. [18450]
Arizona Electrical Prdts Inc. [8375]
ASC Industries [42]
ASC International Inc. [20592]
Associated Aircraft Supply Inc. [43]
ASW Aviation Services Inc. [44]
ATC International [2262]
Atlantic Aviation Corp. [45]
Atlantic Track and Turnout Co. [23472]
Atlas Railroad Construction Co. [23473]
Austin Aircraft (HIE); D. [46]
Auxiliary Power International Corp. [47]
AvAlaska, Inc. [48]
Avatar Alliance L.P. [49]
Aviatech Corporation [50]
Aviation Distributors Inc. [51]
Aviation Sales Co. (Miami, Florida) [52]
AWS Companies Inc. [53]
Azcon Corp. [7006]
Azimuth Corp. (Orlando, Florida) [54]
Aztech Controls Corp. [16717]
BAI Inc. [55]
Banner Aerospace Inc. [56]
Barbour Marine Supply [18451]
Barclay Marine Distributors Corp. [18452]
Barclay Marine Distributors Corp. [18453]
Barclay Marine Distributors Corp. [18454]
Barclay Marine Distributors Corp. [18455]
Barfield Inc. [57]
Barstad and Donicht Inc. [2323]
Bayjet Inc. [58]
Beacon Supply Co. [18456]
Bell Industries [18458]
Bell Industries [18459]
Benrock Inc. [18460]
Benrock of Oklahoma [18461]
Biewer; John A. [18462]
Big Island Marine [18463]
Birmingham Rail Locomotive Company Inc. [23474]
Bisho Company, Inc.; J.R. [2365]
Bizjet International Sales and Support Inc. [59]
Blue Water Ship Store [18464]
Boat America Corp. [18465]
Boater's World [18467]
Braden's Flying Service Inc. [61]
Brewer Associates Inc. [62]
Brewer, Inc.; R.G. [18469]
Brewers Chandlery East [18470]
Bridge Stone Aircraft Tire (USA), Inc. [63]
Bridon Elm Inc. [64]
British Aerospace Holdings Inc. [65]
British Aerospace North America Inc. [66]
Brown Marine Service Inc. [18471]
Brown Ship Chandlery Inc. [18472]
Bruce Industries Inc. [67]
Burningtons, Inc. [23475]
Byfield Marine Supply LLC [18473]
Certified Parts Corp. [18477]
Chapman Marine Supply [18478]
Charlotte Aerospace Co. Inc. [69]
Click Bond Inc. [70]
CMA International [15894]
Coast Air Inc. [71]
Coast Distribution [18480]
Coast Distribution [18481]
Coast Distribution [18482]
Coast Marine [18483]
Coast Marine Distribution [18484]
Coastal Distributors, Inc. [18485]
Comet Industries Inc. [15901]
Commerce Overseas Corp. [72]

Commercial Aviation Support Inc. [73]
Composite Technology Inc. [74]
Consolidated Asset Management Company
  Inc. [23476]
Continental Information Systems Corp. [6154]
Cooper Power Tools Division-Apex [75]
Corporate Rotable and Supply Inc. [76]
CPS Marketing Corporation [18757]
Crescent Airways Inc. [77]
CYN [18488]
D. Austin Aircraft [78]
DAC International Inc. [25621]
Dallas Aerospace Inc. [79]
Dealers Truck Equipment Company Inc. [2534]
Defender Industries [18489]
Defender Marine Supply NY [18490]
Derco Industries Inc. [80]
DIFCO Inc. [23477]
Diversified Marine Products [18492]
Doc Freeman's [18493]
Donovan Marine [18494]
Donovan Marine [18495]
Donovan Marine Inc. [18496]
Dunlop Aviation North America [81]
Easton Wholesale Co. [18497]
Eaton Corp. [82]
Edwards & Co.; C.G. [18498]
Electric Car Distributors [23648]
Elliott Aviation Inc. [83]
Englund Marine Supply [18499]
Ewig Inc.; Carl F. [25914]
Export Consultants Corp. [84]
Eyak Aircraft [85]
Fall City Boat Works [18500]
Far East Trading Company Inc. [86]
Federal Express Aviation Services Inc. [87]
Fisheries Supply Co. Industrial Div. [18503]
Fisherman's Marine Supply [18504]
Flight Products International [88]
Fortune Industries Inc. [89]
Freeport Marine Supply [18505]
Fremont Electric Company Inc. [2648]
Fulton Supply Co. [16883]
Fuses Unlimimted [90]
Future Metals Inc. [91]
G-N Aircraft Inc. [92]
GATX Corp. [23478]
General Handling Systems Inc. [16055]
Gillette Air Inc. [93]
Glenn-Mar Marine Supply, Inc. [18507]
Gold Coast Marine Distribution [18508]
Great Lakes Power Products [18509]
Great Lakes Power Products [18510]
Greene Equipment Co. [2706]
Greenwich Trading Co. [18511]
Gregg Company Ltd. [23479]
Gross and Janes Co. [23480]
Gulf Coast Marine Supply Inc. [18512]
Gulf King Marine [18513]
Gunderland Marine Supply, Inc. [18514]
H and L Marine Woodworking Inc. [18515]
Hamilton Marine [18516]
Hannays [18517]
Hardin Marine Inc. [18518]
Hardware & Marine Co. of Alabama [18519]
Hawker Pacific Inc. [94]
Hayden Company Inc.; C.W. [16927]
Hedrick Beechcraft Inc. [95]
Hermetic Aircraft International Corp. [96]
Hern Marine [18520]
Hibbard Aviation [20648]
Hoder-Rogers Inc. [97]
Hoffmann Aircraft Inc. [98]
Hopkins-Carter Company Inc. [18521]
HSS Group [18522]
Illinois Auto Electric Co. [16142]
Indmar Products Industrial Div. [18524]
Indusco, Ltd. [8875]
Industrial Liaison Inc. [18525]
Industry-Railway Suppliers Inc. [23481]
Intermountain Piper Inc. [100]
International Air Leases Inc. [101]
International Airline Support Group Inc. [102]
International Engine Parts Inc. [103]
International Hi-Tech Trading Corp. [2793]
International Lease Finance Corp. [104]

Irwin International Inc. [106]
Israel Aircraft Industries International [107]
ITG, Inc. [23482]
Jack & Co.; K.L. [18526]
Jacobi Hardware Co., Inc. [18527]
Jamestown Distributors Inc. [18528]
Jet Equipment and Tools [108]
Johnson Supply Co. [18529]
Jonas Aircraft and Arms Company Inc. [109]
Jonas Aircraft and Arms Company Inc. [24578]
K-Tech Aviation, Inc. [110]
Kansas City Aviation Center Inc. [112]
Keller Marine Service Inc. [18531]
Kellogg Marine Supply Inc. [18532]
Ken Dor Corp. [18533]
King & Son Inc.; T.A. [18534]
Kirkhill Aircraft Parts Co. [113]
Kirkland Marine Co. [18535]
Knutson Distributors [18536]
Kremer Marine [18538]
L.A. Marine Hardware [18539]
Labinal, Inc. [22987]
Ladd, Inc.; Bob [927]
Lake Aircraft Inc. [114]
Lambs Yacht Center [18540]
Land-N-Sea Distribution East [18541]
Land-N-Sea Distribution West [18542]
Land-N-Sea—Norfolk [18543]
Landis Rail Fastening Systems Inc. [23483]
Leader Creek Marina [18544]
Lektro Inc. [115]
Leo J. Distributors [18545]
Lewis Marine Supply [18546]
LFS Inc. [18547]
Lincoln Trading Co. [116]
Lindquist Investment Co. [117]
Linear Industries Ltd [17001]
Llewellyn Supply [18549]
Londavia Inc. [118]
Loock & Company Inc.; R.J. [2892]
Lorenz & Jones Marine Distributors, Inc. [18550]
Luden & Co., Inc.; J.J.W. [18552]
Lynton Group Inc. [119]
M & E Marine Supply, Inc. [18553]
M & M Vehicle Co. [23794]
Magee Marine Supply [18555]
Manset Marine Supply Co. [18556]
Marathon Boat Yard [18557]
Marco Marine Seattle, IMFS Div. [18558]
Marine Equipment & Supply [18559]
Marine & Industrial Supply [18560]
Marine Rescue Products Inc. [18561]
Marinovich Trawl Co. [18562]
Martec International [25930]
Maschmedt and Associates [18563]
Matrix Aviation Inc. [120]
McCaughey Brothers [18564]
McGill Distributors [18565]
McIntosh and Associates Inc.; Ron [121]
Melvin Village Marina Inc. [18566]
Memphis Group Inc. [122]
Meridian Aerospace Group Ltd. [123]
Merritt Marine Supply [18567]
Metro Crown International [124]
Metro-Jasim, Inc. [125]
Miami Aviation Corp. [126]
Michelle International, Ltd. [127]
Mid Continent Aircraft Corp. [128]
Mid-South Engine Systems Inc. [18568]
Midland Reclamation Co. [23484]
Midnight Sun Boat Company, Inc. [18569]
MidWest Air Motive Corp. [129]
Midwest Marine Supply Co. [18570]
Mitsubishi International Corp. [26151]
Moes Marine Service [18571]
Molly Corp. [23485]
Morgan Recreational Supply [18573]
National Airmotive Corp. [131]
Nautical & Industrial Supply Inc. [18575]
Ness Company Inc. [3025]
Northwest Parts & Equipment [132]
Ocean Products Research, Inc. [18576]
Ocean State Yacht Brokerage and Marine
  Services [18577]
Oceana Ltd. [18578]
O'Connor Company, Inc. [14627]

O'Day Equipment Inc. [22534]
Ontario Air Parts Inc. [133]
Overtons Sports Center, Inc. [18579]
Pac Aero [134]
Pacific O.E.M. Supply [18580]
Padre Island Supply [18581]
Parr Golf Car Company, Inc. [23873]
PAS Div. [136]
Paxton Company Inc. [18582]
Pietsch Aircraft Restoration & Repair [137]
PLM Transportation Equipment Corp. [16402]
Pohle NV Center Inc. [23888]
Poly Processing Co. [25933]
Port Electric Supply Corp. [9219]
Port Supply [18584]
Post Marine [18586]
Post Yacht Supplies [18587]
Precision Propeller Service Inc. [138]
Professional Aviation Associates Inc. [139]
Proper Tighe Marine [18588]
PullRite/Pulliam Enterprise Inc. [3123]
Rails Co. [23486]
Railway Services International [23487]
Raytheon Aircraft Services [140]
Reeve Aleutian Airways Inc. [141]
Reilly-Benton Company Inc. [18591]
Revels Tractor Company Inc. [1183]
Rice Aircraft Inc. [142]
Rockland Boat, Inc. [18592]
Rockland Marine Corp. [18593]
Roloff Manufacturing Corp. [18595]
R.S.B.I. Aerospace Inc. [143]
Rude Corp.; R.T. [15297]
Ryder Aviall Inc. [144]
Saab Aircraft of America Inc. [145]
Sacramento Sky Ranch Inc. [146]
The Sailor's Supply [18598]
Salks Hardware & Marine Inc. [18599]
Salomon Co.; Paul R. [18600]
San Diego Marine Exchange [18601]
Schrader-Bridgeport International [3196]
SCS Cases Inc. [25936]
Sea Coast Distributors, Inc. [18602]
Sea Containers America Inc. [18603]
Seaboard Manufacturing Co. [18604]
Seaboard Marine [18605]
Sealand Power Industries, Inc. [18606]
Seaside Supply Stores [18607]
Seattle Ship Supply [18609]
Securaplane Technologies L.L.C. [24628]
Shields Harper and Co. [22667]
Shores Marine [18610]
Smith Electronics; Larry [18612]
Smiths Industries [147]
Solair Inc. [148]
Spacecraft Components Corp. [149]
Spartan Lobster Traps Inc. [18613]
Spencer Industries Inc. (Seattle, Washington) [150]
SSR Pump Co. [3257]
Standard Marine Supply Co. [18614]
Standard Marine Supply Co. [18615]
Standard Marine Supply Corp. [18616]
Stein Seal Company Inc. [151]
Sterling & Son; Clarence [18617]
Stewart and Stevenson Services Inc. [3270]
Stover Greenlight Auto & Marine [18618]
Stull Enterprises Inc. [1301]
Summit Aviation Inc. [152]
Sun Aviation Inc. [153]
Sun Valley Aviation Inc. [154]
Sutliff & Son; Norman [18619]
Svendsen's Boat Works [18620]
Svendsen's Marine Distribution [18621]
Syban International Inc. [155]
Tacoma Fiberglass [18622]
Techrepco Inc. [157]
Texas Turbo Jet Inc. [158]
Thego Corporation/Acme Marine Hoist,
  inc. [18624]
Thermion Technologies Inc. [159]
Tiger Enterprises [18625]
TLD America [160]
Tower Aviation Services [161]
Toyota Aviation U.S.A. Inc. [162]
Transco Products Inc. [23488]
Triangle Inc. [3340]

Tronair Inc. [163]
Turf and Industrial Equipment Co. [1363]
Unirex Inc. [164]
United Marine Inc. [18627]
U.S. Aircraft Industries International Inc. [165]
Universal Marine [18628]
US Airways Group Inc. [166]
Venada Aviation Inc. [167]
Venture Vehicles Inc. [24029]
Venturian Corp. [3390]
Versatile Vehicles Inc. [24031]
Vida Paint & Supply Co. [18629]
Vida Paint & Supply Co. [18630]
Vita-Plate Battery, Inc. [18631]
Warren Marine Supply Inc. [18632]
Washington Avionics Inc. [168]
Washington Chain and Supply [18633]
Washington Marina Co. [18635]
Way-Point Avionics Inc. [170]
Weems & Plath, Inc. [171]
Weil Service Products Corp. [22790]
Wesmac Enterprises [18636]
West Coast Ship Chandlers Inc. [17273]
West Marine Corp. [18637]
Western Aircraft Inc. [172]
Wholesale Marine Supply Co. of Alaska,
  Inc. [18638]
Wiggins Airways Inc. Parts East [173]
Wiggins Airways Inc. Parts East; E.W. [174]
Wilcox Marine Supply Inc. [18639]
Williams and Wells Corp. [18641]
Wilson Corp.; W.S. [175]
Wolf Warehouse Distributors [18643]
World Buying Service Inc. [9605]
World Trade Network, Ltd. [18644]
WRG Corp. [177]
YAO Industries [12991]
Yingling Aircraft Inc. [178]
Zephyr Manufacturing Co., Inc. [179]
Zidell Marine Corp. [18646]
Zimco Marine [18647]
Zodiac of North America [18649]

SIC 5091 — Sporting & Recreational
Goods

3 GI Athletics Inc. [23489]
ABA Enterprise Inc. [23490]
A.B.A.C.O. Group [4740]
Access Bicycle Components Inc. [23491]
Accu-Care Supply, Inc. [23492]
Action Sports of Edmond [23493]
AcuSport Corp. [23494]
Adams & Durvin Marine Inc. [23495]
Agee's Sporting Goods [23496]
Agri Volt & Cabinet Co. [23497]
Ajay Leisure Products Inc. [23498]
Albany Bowling Supply Inc. [23499]
Albuquerque Balloon Center [23500]
Alexander & Townsend [23501]
Algoma Net Co. [23502]
All American Pool N Patio [23503]
All Quality Builders [23504]
All Star Sports Inc. [23505]
Allied Cycle Distributors Inc. [23506]
Alpine Slide of Jackson Hole [23507]
American Camper [23508]
American Exercise & Fitness Equipment
  Co. [23509]
American Fitness Products Inc. [23510]
American Outdoor Sports [23511]
American Pool Supply Inc. [23512]
American Recreation Products Inc. [23513]
American Tennis Courts Inc. [23514]
Amics International Inc. [24311]
Anazeh Sands [23515]
Anderson Bait Distributors [23517]
Anderson Recreational Design, Inc. [23518]
Anson & Co.; R.E. [23519]
Aqua Dream Pools Inc. [23520]
Aquajogger [23521]
Arcadia Merchandising Corp. [23522]
Argos Enterprises [14024]

Argus Buying Group [4781]
Arkansas Import & Distributing Co. [23523]
Artomate Co. [23524]
Arts & Craft Distributors Inc. [26400]
Asian World of Martial Arts Inc. [23525]
Atlantic Fitness Products Co. [23526]
Atlantic Skates Inc. [23528]
AutoBike Inc. [23529]
Avis Enterprises Inc. [23530]
Avon North America Inc. [23531]
AWD International Inc. [13028]
Babco International Inc. [23532]
Bacharach-Rasin Co. [23533]
Bacon Creek Gun Shop [23534]
Badger Shooters Supply Inc. [23535]
Baja Products Ltd. [23536]
Baker Hydro Inc. [23537]
Barker & Co. [23538]
Bauer Cycle Supply Inc. [23539]
Beacon Sporting Goods Inc. [23540]
Beauty Pools Inc. [23541]
Beijing Trade Exchange Inc. [24688]
Bel-Aqua Pool Supply Inc. [23542]
Benson Pool Systems [23543]
Benson Pool Systems [23544]
Benson Pump Co. [23545]
Benson Pump Co. [23546]
Benson Pump Co. [23547]
Benson Pump Co. [23548]
Benson Pump Co. [23549]
Benson Pump Co. [23550]
Benson Pump Co. [23551]
Bestex Company Inc. [24515]
Bicknell Distributors Inc. [23552]
Bicknell Distributors, Inc. [23553]
Bicknell Huston Distributors [23554]
Bicknell Huston Distributors, Inc. [23555]
Bicknell Huston Distributors, Inc. [23556]
Bicknell-Tidewater Inc. [23557]
Big Rock Sports Inc. [23558]
Bio-Tech Maintenance Products [23559]
Blankenstein Co. Inc.; F.R. [18717]
Blue Mount Quarry [23560]
Blue Ridge Sporting Supplies [23561]
The Boat Locker [18466]
Bob's Business Inc. [23562]
Bob's Machine Shop [18468]
Bocock-Stroud Co. [23563]
Bonitz Brothers Inc. [23564]
Boss Hawaii Inc. [23565]
Boswell Golf Cars, Inc. [23566]
Boyd Distributing Co. Inc. [15056]
Boyt Harness Co./Bob Allen Sportswear [4839]
Brine Inc. [23567]
Brookfield Athletic Company [23568]
Brown Bear Sporting [23569]
Brown Co.; E. Arthur [23570]
Brownells Inc. [13477]
Browning [13478]
BSE Engineering Corp. [23571]
Buck & Bass Shop [23572]
Buck Rub Archery Inc. [23573]
Buck's War Surplus [23574]
Bumble Bee Wholesale [13479]
Bumble Bee Wholesale [23575]
Burgess; Philip [23576]
Burnham; William H. [26431]
Burts Sports Specialty Inc. [23577]
C & J Bait Co. [23579]
Callaway Golf Co [23580]
Camfour Inc. [23581]
Cape Water Sports [18474]
Cariddi Sales Co. [23582]
Carolina Fisherman Supply Inc. [23583]
Carolina Pools & Patios [23584]
Casale Engineering Inc. [2432]
Cascade Pacific Lumber Co. [7150]
Cascade Yachts, Inc. [18476]
Cash Indiana [22840]
Cassemco Sporting Goods [23585]
Central Garden and Pet Co. [391]
Century Sports Inc. [23586]
Certified Parts Corp. [18477]
Champion Athletic Supply Inc. [23587]
Chattanooga Shooting Supplies [23588]
Cheerleader Supply Co. [23589]

Chesal Industries [23590]
Chesapeake Gun Works [23591]
Churchich & Associates; Ely [23592]
Churchich Recreation [23593]
Churchill Brothers [18479]
Cinderella Inc. [23594]
Cissna's Sporting Goods Inc. [23595]
Clark's Gun Shop [13481]
CMA Incorporated [10779]
CMT Sporting Goods Co. [23596]
Coach's Connection Inc. [23597]
Coastal Net Marine Co. [23598]
Cogdells Westview Inc. [13482]
Colie Sailmakers [18486]
Collins Landing [23599]
Competition Karting Inc. [23600]
Complete Golf Services Co. [23601]
Compool Corp. [23602]
Composite Engineering Inc. [18487]
Connecticut Valley Arms Inc. [13483]
Consumer Direct Inc. [23603]
Continental Sports Supply Inc. [23604]
Coosa Co. Inc. [23605]
Cormans Sporting Goods [23606]
Cortland Line Company Inc. [23607]
Counter Assault [23608]
Coyote Engineering, Inc. [23609]
CR Specialty Co. [13484]
Cressi-Sub USA Inc. [23610]
Crosman Corporation [13485]
CSI Sports, LLC [23611]
Custom Design Play Structures Inc. [23612]
Daiwa Corp. [23613]
Dalco Athletic [25624]
Darton Archery [23614]
Dave's Sport Shop [23615]
Davidson's [13486]
Day Corp.; Alan G. [18766]
Dayman USA Inc. [23616]
Deans Firearms, Ltd. [13488]
Deep See Products Inc. [23617]
Del Mar Distributing Company Inc. [23618]
Denzak & Associates, Inc.; Joan [23619]
Derby Cycle [23620]
Developed Technology Resource Inc. [23621]
Dia-Compe Inc. [23622]
Dibs Chemical & Supply Co. Inc. [21708]
Dimmer-Warren Enterprises [23623]
Dinghy Shop International [18491]
Discount Fishing Tackle [23624]
Diversified Investments Inc. [23625]
Dixon Muzzleloading Shop [13489]
Dixons Bicycling Center Inc. [23626]
Do-It Corp. [23627]
Dolphin Pools Inc. [23628]
Down River Equipment Co. [23629]
Drayton Swimming Pool Supply [23630]
Drybranch Inc. [23631]
Duck Commander Company, Inc. [23632]
Dugans Inc. [23633]
Dunns Sporting Goods Co. Inc. [23634]
Durham Boat Co. Inc. [23635]
Dyna Group International Inc. [13349]
Dyna Group International Inc. [23636]
Dynacraft Golf Products, Inc. [23637]
Dynamic Classics Ltd. [23638]
Eagle Claw Fishing Tackle [23639]
Eagle River Corp. [23640]
East Providence Cycle Co. Inc. [23641]
East Side Sporting Goods Co. [23642]
East West Trading Co. [23643]
Eaton Corp. Golf Grip Div. [23644]
Eaton; Daniel A. [26026]
Ebisuzaki Fishing Supply [23645]
Edwards & Associates; John [23646]
Efinger Sporting Goods Inc. [23647]
Electric Car Distributors [23648]
Ellett Brothers Inc. [13490]
EMSCO [23650]
EMSCO [23651]
Engan-Tooley-Doyle & Associates Inc. [23652]
Eppinger Manufacturing Co. [23653]
Ericksons Super-Pros, Inc.; Vic [23654]
Esneault Inc. [23655]
Everett Square Sporting Goods [23656]
Ewing Aquatech Pools Inc. [23657]

Extex Co. [23659]	Hornung's Pro Golf Sales Inc. [23731]	Longnecker Inc. [23793]
Exxersource [23660]	Horton Distributing Co.; Lew [23732]	Loria & Sons Westchester Corp.; V. [25720]
F & E Sportswear Inc. [23661]	House For Sports Inc. [23733]	LSI (Legacy Sports International LLC) [13500]
Faber Brothers Inc. [23662]	Huet & Associates; Pat [23734]	LU International [16250]
Fain & Associates; Gary [23663]	Hughes Golf Inc.; Art [23735]	M-Bin International Imports [18410]
Famous Mart Inc. [4945]	Hughes Supply Inc. [23216]	M & M Vehicle Co. [23794]
Fawcett Boat Supplies Inc. [18501]	Huston Distributors Inc. [23736]	Maats Enterprises [19421]
F.B.F. Inc. [13491]	Hutchinson & Associates, Inc.; Roger J. [23737]	MacGregor Sports and Fitness Inc. [23795]
FEMCO Corp. [23664]	Hutson Enterprises, Inc.; D.H. [23738]	Mackinaw Sales Inc. [18554]
Filut & Associates Inc.; R.J. [23665]	Hyperox Technologies [23739]	Magic Distributing [23796]
First Service, Div. of Straightline Enterprises, Inc. [23666]	Imperial Pools Inc. [23740]	Maine Battery Distributors [23797]
Fish Net Co. [23667]	Imperial Wax and Chemical Company Inc. [23741]	Maltby's Golfworks; Ralph [23798]
Fisher Enterprises Inc. [23668]	Imtra Corp. [18523]	Marco Marine Seattle, IMFS Div. [18558]
Fishermans Factory Outlet [23669]	Incentive Associates Inc. [15539]	Marine Electric Co. [23799]
Fitness Corporation of America [23670]	Indian Industries Inc. [23742]	Marine Equipment & Supply [18559]
Fitness Expo Inc. [23671]	Indiana Recreation Equipment & Design, Inc. [23743]	Mark-It of Colorado LLC [23800]
Fitness Shop [23672]	Industrial Liaison Inc. [18525]	Marker USA [23801]
Fitness Systems Inc. [23673]	Institutional Equipment Inc. [23744]	Marks Pro Shop; Mike [23802]
Fitness Systems Inc. [23674]	Intermountain Resources [23745]	Marksman Products Inc. [13501]
Fleet Wholesale [11144]	International Marine Industries [23746]	Markwort Sporting Goods Co. [23803]
Folsom Corp. [23675]	Island Cycle Supply Co. [23748]	Marquis Corp. [23804]
Franklin Sports Industries Inc. [23676]	Island Style [23749]	Masek Sports Inc. [23805]
French's Athletics Inc. [23677]	Izuo Brothers Ltd. [23750]	Master Cartridge Corp. [23806]
FTG Manufacturing [23678]	J and B Foam Fabricators Inc. [23751]	Master Industries Inc. [23807]
Fuji America Inc. [23679]	J & B Importers Inc. [23752]	Maumee Co. [23808]
Funco Inc. [23680]	J & B Tackle Company Inc. [23753]	Maurice Pincoffs Company Inc. [20158]
Future Pro Inc. [23681]	J & E Fishing Supplies Inc. [23754]	Maurice Sporting Goods [23809]
Gander Mountain Inc. [23682]	Jack's Tack International Distributors [5073]	Mayfield & Co. Inc. [23810]
Gared Sports Inc. [23683]	Jaytow International Inc. [5843]	Mayfield Pool Supply L.L.C. [23811]
Garrett & Co., Inc. [23684]	JBM Associates Inc. [23755]	Mc-U Sports [23812]
Garrett III & Co. Inc.; J.W. [23685]	Jenkins Metal Corp. Hunting Classics Limited Div. [15545]	McArthur Towels, Inc. [15581]
Gateway Seed Co. [729]	Jerry's Sport Center Inc. [23756]	McBroom Pool Products Inc. [23813]
Gazaway & Associates; Jerry [23686]	Jewel Box Inc. [23757]	McCabe Bait Company Inc. [23814]
Gazelle Athletics [23687]	Joannou Cycle Company Inc.; G. [23758]	McCorkle Cricket Farm Inc. [23815]
Gemini Manufacturing Inc. [23688]	Jog-A-Lite Inc. [23759]	McGuire Sun and Fitness Inc. [23816]
Getaway Sailing [18506]	Johannsens Inc. [24780]	M.E. O'Brien and Sons Inc. [23817]
Gleeson Inc. [23689]	Johnny's Crab Traps Inc. [23760]	Mel Pinto Imports Inc. [23818]
Globemaster Inc. [13725]	Johnsen Co.; Hans [23761]	Melges; Gregory N. [23819]
Gnieweks Trophies Inc.; Hank [23690]	Johnson Camping Inc. [23762]	Memphis Import Company Inc. [23820]
Go/Sportsmen's Supply Inc. [23691]	Jolly & Sons, Inc.; Jack [23763]	Memphis Pool Supply Co. Inc. [23821]
Golf Training Systems Inc. [23692]	Jonas Aircraft and Arms Company Inc. [109]	Mercantile Sales Company Inc. [23822]
Golf Ventures [23693]	Joseph's Clothing & Sporting Goods [23764]	Merrymeeting Corp. [23823]
Gould Athletic Supply [23694]	Jovino Company, Inc.; John [13496]	Mickeys Sales Co. [23825]
Grace Inc.; V.F. [14115]	Joy Enterprises [13776]	Mid-Atlantic Park & Playground Concepts [23826]
Grafalloy Corp. [23695]	Joy Optical Co. [19388]	Mid-Atlantic Spa Distributors [23827]
Great Northwest Bicycle Supply [23697]	JP International Imports & Exports [23765]	Middleground Golf Inc. [23828]
Green Associates; Dale [23698]	K & P Manufacturing [23766]	Midwest Action Cycle [20681]
Green Top Sporting Goods Inc. [23699]	K-Swiss Inc. [23767]	Midwest Pool Distributors Inc. [23829]
Gregco Inc. [23700]	K2 Corp. [23768]	Miracle Playground Sales [23830]
GSI, Inc. [13492]	Karhu USA Inc. [23769]	Miracle Recreation of Minnesota Inc. [23831]
GTH Holdings, Inc. [7421]	Kaufman Co. Inc.; Hal [22868]	Mitchell Manufacturing, Hagens Division [23832]
Gulbenkian Swim Inc. [23701]	Kawasaki Motors Corporation U.S.A. [20659]	Moates Sport Shop Inc.; Bob [13502]
Gulbranson Equipment Inc. [777]	Keller Supply Co. [23770]	Mobile Cycle Center [23833]
Gulf Pool Equipment Co. [23702]	Kerman, Inc.; A.C. [23771]	Montana Scale Co. Inc. [24402]
Gun Traders Inc. [23703]	Keys Fitness Products Inc. [23772]	Monticello Sports Inc. [23834]
Guns Of Yesteryear [13493]	Keystone Cue & Cushion Inc. [23773]	Moore-Sigler Sports World Inc. [23835]
Guptons Sporting Goods Inc. [23704]	Kilpatrick Table Tennis Co.; Martin [23774]	Morris Rothenberg and Son Inc. [23836]
Guterman International Inc. [23705]	Kiri Trading Co. Ltd. [5111]	Morrow Snowboards Inc. [23837]
Gym Source [23706]	Klein's Allsports Distributors [23776]	Mountain Shades Distributing Co. [23838]
H & W Sport Monticello Inc. [23707]	Kmart Corp. [15553]	Mountain State Muzzleloading Supplies, Inc. [13503]
H2O [23708]	Kona Marine Supply [18537]	Mountain States Sporting Goods [23839]
Hachik Distributors Inc. [23709]	Kryptonics Inc. [23777]	Multisports Inc. [23840]
Hadfield Sport Shops Inc. [23710]	K's Merchandise Mart Inc. [17494]	Mustad and Son Inc.; O. [23841]
Halbro America [23711]	Kwik Ski Products [23778]	N Pool Patio Ltd. [23842]
Hansen & Co. [23712]	Labieniec & Associates; Paul [23779]	Nabo Industries [18574]
Har-Tru Corp. [23713]	Lanahan Sales [24789]	Nashville Sporting Goods Co. [23843]
Hard Hat Inc. [23714]	Langlois Stores Inc. [15559]	Natcom International [19475]
Harman Appliance Sales [15161]	Las Vegas Discount Golf and Tennis Inc. [23780]	Nebraska Golf Discount Inc. [23844]
Harper & Associates [23715]	Lavro Inc. [23781]	Nefouse Brothers Distributing Co. [23845]
Hasley Recreation and Design Inc. [23716]	LBK Distributors [23782]	NFZ Products Inc. [13846]
Hauff Sporting Goods Co. Inc. [23717]	Ledford's Trading Post [13497]	Noland & Associates, Inc.; Tim J. [23846]
Hawaii Martial Art Supply [23718]	Lee Tennis, LLC [23783]	Nordica USA Inc. [23847]
Health and Leisure Mart Inc. [23719]	Leisurelife USA Inc. [23784]	Normark Corp. [23848]
Heckler and Koch Inc. [13494]	Leland Limited Inc. [23785]	North American Parts Inc. [23849]
Helmet House Inc. [23721]	Lenz Sports; Jerry [23786]	North Auburn Cash Market [23850]
Henbest & Associates, Inc.; Jen [23722]	Life-Link International [23787]	North Country Marketing Ltd. [23851]
Henry's Tackle L.L.C. [23723]	Lightnin Fiberglass Co. [23788]	Northland Sports Inc. [23852]
Here's Fred Golf Co. [23724]	Lipsey's Inc. [13498]	Northwest Coast Trading Company [23853]
Heritage Manufacturing Inc. [13495]	Lisk Lures [23789]	Norvel Hasley and Associates [23854]
HG International Corporation [23725]	Little River Marine Co. [18548]	Norwood Products Co. [23855]
Hicks Inc. [23726]	Lob-Ster Inc. [23790]	Numrich Gunparts Corp. [13504]
Hike A Bike [23727]	Log Cabin Sport Shop [13499]	O'Brien & Sons Inc.; M.E. [23856]
Hiltons Tent City Inc. [23728]	Lolo Sporting Goods Inc. [23791]	Ohio Pool Equipment Supply Co. [23857]
Hopkins Sporting Goods Inc. [23729]	London Bridge Trading Company Ltd. [23792]	Olhausen Billiard Manufacturing, Inc. [23858]
Horner Equipment of Florida Inc. [23730]		Olympia Sports [23859]

Orbex Inc. [23860]
Orcal Inc. [23861]
Orlando Yamaha [20701]
Oshman's Sporting Goods Inc. [23862]
Outdoor Research Inc. [23863]
Outdoor Sports Headquarters Inc. [23864]
P & B Enterprises Inc. [23865]
P & K Athletics Inc. [23866]
Pacific International Marketing Co. [23867]
Paddock Swimming Pool Co. [23868]
Palm Pool Products Inc. [23869]
Pana Bait Co. [23870]
Pape's Archery Inc. [23871]
Pappy's Customs Inc. [5268]
Park Place Recreation Designs Inc. [23872]
Parr Golf Car Company, Inc. [23873]
Paul Company Inc. [23875]
Pearl's Sports Center; Jack [23876]
Pedersen's Ski and Sport [23877]
Performance Catamarans Inc. [18583]
Pettit and Sons [23878]
Phillips Energy Inc. [23879]
Phoenix Wholesale Sporting Supplies Inc. [23880]
Pinch a Penny Pool Patio [23882]
Pinto Imports Inc.; Mel [23883]
Piper Sport Racks Inc. [23884]
Playfield Industries Inc. [23885]
Playsafe Playground Systems of N.Y. [23886]
Pocket Pool & Patio [23887]
Pohle NV Center Inc. [23888]
Point Sporting Goods Inc. [23889]
Pool Doctor [23890]
Pool Fact, Inc. [23891]
Pool Water Products [23892]
Pool Water Products [23893]
Pool Water Products [23894]
Porta-Bote International [18585]
Poseidon Adventure Inc. [23896]
Precision Sports Surfaces Inc. [23897]
PRO Sports Products [23898]
Putt-Putt Golf & Games [23899]
Queens City Distributing Co. [23900]
R & T Enterprises Inc. [23901]
Rainbow Sports [23903]
Raleigh Cycle of America [23904]
Rand International Leisure Products Ltd. [23905]
Rax Works Inc. [23906]
RC Sports Inc. [23907]
Recreation Supply Co. [23908]
Reda Sports Express [23909]
Regent Sports Corp. [23910]
Renner & Associates; E.J. [7916]
R.E.S. Associates [7918]
Resilite Sports Products Inc. [23911]
Reverse & Company [5307]
Rex International [23912]
Rex Playground Equipment Inc. [23913]
Reynolds & Sons Inc. [23914]
Rice Lake Products Inc. [25803]
Richardson Sports Inc. [23915]
Robco Corp. [23916]
Robern Skiwear Inc. [5313]
Robinson Wholesale Inc. [23917]
Robison & Associates; Jerry [23918]
Rockys II Inc. [23919]
Rogers Pool Supply, Inc. [23920]
Roller Derby Skate Corp. [23921]
Roloff Manufacturing Corp. [18595]
Romac Export Management Corp. [15639]
Rouzee Green Company Inc.; The John [23922]
Royal Golf, Inc. [23923]
Royal Golf Inc. [23924]
Royal Textile Mills Inc. [5323]
RSR Group Florida, Inc. [13505]
RSR Group Texas, Inc. [13506]
RSR Wholesale Guns Inc. [13507]
RSR Wholesale Guns Inc. [13508]
RSR Wholesale Guns Midwest, Inc. [13509]
RSR Wholesale Guns Midwest Inc. [23925]
RSR Wholesale Guns West, Inc. [13510]
Rubin Inc. [23926]
S & F Associates Inc. [23927]
S & S Firearms [13512]
Safesport Manufacturing Co. [23928]
Sailing Inc. [18597]
Salomon Co.; Paul R. [18600]

Salomon North America Inc. [23929]
Sartorius Sports Ltd. [24849]
Saunier-Wilhelm Co. [23930]
SB Developments Inc. [23360]
Schram & Associates; Mike [23931]
Schwinn Cycling and Fitness [23932]
Scientific Anglers [23933]
Seattle Marine Industrial Division [18608]
Seaway Distributors [12454]
Second Chance Golf Ball Recyclers Inc. [23934]
Sheldons', Inc. [23935]
Shimano American Corp. [23936]
Shimano American Corp. Fishing Tackle
 Div. [23937]
Sierra Pacific [23938]
Sile Distributors Inc. [13513]
Simione and Associates, Inc.; Bill [23939]
Simmons Gun Specialty Inc. [13514]
Simmons Sporting Goods Company Inc. [23940]
Sinclair Imports Inc. [23941]
Sinclair & Rush, Inc. [23942]
Site Concepts [23943]
Skane Ltd. [5361]
Skipper Bills Inc. [23944]
Skipper Shop [18611]
Skis Dynastar Inc. [23945]
Slusser Wholesale Inc. [26652]
Smith Distributing Co. [23946]
Smith Enterprises Inc.; P. [23947]
Smith Inc.; Kenneth [23948]
Smith Sporting Goods Inc.; L.L. [23949]
Soccer House Inc. [23950]
Soccer Plus Inc. [23951]
Sorcerer Lures [23953]
South Central Pool Supply, Inc. [23954]
South Central Pool Supply, Inc. [23955]
South Central Pool Supply, Inc. [23956]
South Central Pool Supply, Inc. [23957]
South Central Pool Supply, Inc. [23958]
South Central Pool Supply, Inc. [23959]
South Central Pool Supply, Inc. [23960]
South Central Pool Supply, Inc. [23961]
South Central Pool Supply, Inc. [23962]
South Central Pool Supply, Inc. [23963]
South Central Pool Supply, Inc. [23964]
South Central Pool Supply, Inc. [23965]
South Central Pool Supply, Inc. [23966]
South Central Pool Supply, Inc. [23967]
South Central Pool Supply, Inc. [23968]
South Central Pool Supply, Inc. [23969]
South Central Pool Supply, Inc. [23970]
Southeastern Skate Supply of Virginia Inc. [23971]
Southwest Sporting Goods Co. [23972]
Spalding Holdings Corp. [5376]
Spartan Sporting Goods Inc. [23973]
Spas Unlimited [23974]
Sport Shop Inc. [23976]
The Sporting House [23977]
Sportmaster Inc. [23978]
Sports Cellar [23979]
Sports Specialist Inc. [23980]
Sports Specialties Corp. [5387]
Sportsmans Inc. [23981]
Sportsware West [23982]
Stano Components [23983]
Star Sales Company of Knoxville [26668]
Starks Sport Shop [23984]
Starlight Archery Inc. [23985]
Starmac Group [5393]
Stateline Sports [23986]
Steamboat International LLC [25831]
Steamboat International LLC [23987]
Steele's Sports Co. [23988]
Stream & Lake Tackle [23989]
Striplings Tackle Co. [23990]
Sues Young and Brown Inc. [23991]
Sun America Corp. [23992]
Sun Shader International, Inc. [5405]
Sunny's Great Outdoors Inc. [23993]
Sunshine Golf, Inc. [23994]
Superb Cooking Products Co./Empire Comfort
 Systems, Inc. [23995]
Superior Pool Products Inc. [23996]
Superior Turf Equipment [23997]
Surfco Hawaii Inc. [23998]
Surplus City USA Inc. [23999]

Sussman Co.; Frank [5411]
Swimming Pool Supply Co. [24000]
T & D Sporting Goods [24001]
Tackle Craft [24002]
Tackle Service Center [24003]
Tamiami Range and Gun Distributors Inc. [13515]
Taylor Company Inc.; Nelson A. [18623]
Taylor Sports & Recreation Inc. [24004]
Team Distributors Inc. [24005]
Team Sporting Goods Inc. [24006]
Tennis Factory [24007]
Texas Recreation Corp. [24008]
Three Epsilon Inc. [24009]
Three M Leisure Time [24010]
Tiger Enterprises [18625]
Titleist Golf [24011]
Toner Sales Inc. [24012]
Trans-Global Sports Co. [24013]
Tri-Color International [24014]
Trojan Pools [24015]
Trophy Products Inc. [13966]
T.T.S. Distributors [24016]
Tulsa Bowling Supply Co. [24017]
Tulsa Firearms Training Academy [24018]
Turbo Link International Inc. [24019]
Tuscarora Corp. [24020]
Ullman Sails [18626]
United Industries Inc. [24021]
U.S. Line Co. [24022]
U.S. Marketing Services [5451]
Universal Athletic Services of Utah [24882]
Universal Bowling and Golf Co. [24023]
Utikem Products [24024]
Valley Gun of Baltimore [13516]
Vans Pro Shop [24025]
Vantage Pools Inc. [24026]
Varsity Sports Center Inc. [24027]
Vectra Fitness Inc. [24028]
Venture Vehicles Inc. [24029]
Venus Knitting Mills Inc. [24030]
Versatile Vehicles Inc. [24031]
Victor Sports [24032]
Viking Cue Manufacturing, Inc. [24033]
Viking Traders, Inc. [19102]
Vint & Associates; Keith [24034]
VMC Inc. [24035]
Volunteer Janitorial Supply Co. [24036]
Waco Sales Inc. [24037]
Wallace & Associates [24038]
Walmsley Marine Inc. [24039]
Washington Tysons Golf Center [24040]
Waters Edge Distributors Inc. [24041]
Weider Health and Fitness Inc. [14278]
Wenger N.A. [24042]
West Virginia Archery Supply [24043]
Westar Inc. [24044]
Western Export Services, Inc. [12913]
Western Golf Inc. [24045]
Western Power Sports, Inc. [3411]
White Water Manufacturing [17279]
Wildwasser Sport U.S.A. Inc. [18640]
Williams Sales & Service; Jim [24046]
Wilson Wholesale Sporting Goods; John [24047]
Wind Line Sails [18642]
Winn Inc. [24048]
Wittek Golf Supply Co., Inc. [24049]
Woodshill Pool [24050]
World Wen, Inc. [6882]
Wright; Ronald J. [18362]
Wright and Wilhelmy Co. [15381]
Wuu Jau Company Inc. [24051]
Yamaha Motor Corporation USA [20755]
Ye Old Black Powder Shop [13517]
Yeck Antique Firearms [13518]
Yellow River Systems [19113]
Zimmerman; Jerry [18648]
Zodiac of North America [18649]

SIC 5092 — Toys & Hobby Goods & Supplies

AAA-Four Aces [26378]
ABC International Traders Inc. [26379]

Acclaim Entertainment Inc. [26380]
Action Products International Inc. [26381]
Adams Co.; S.S. [26382]
Adams News Co. Inc. [3470]
AIS Construction Equipment Corp. [6927]
Aladdin Distributors Inc. [26383]
Alamex Crafts Inc. [26384]
Alan Co.; B.J. [9630]
Aluma Flight Co. [26385]
Amceco International Corp. [26386]
American Educational Products Inc. [26387]
American Importers of South Carolina [26388]
American Promotional Events, Inc. [26389]
American Visual Aids [26390]
American West Marketing Inc. [9631]
America's Hobby Center Inc. [26391]
Ammar's Inc. [26392]
Anco Management Services Inc. [3509]
Angel Associates Inc.; Mike [26393]
Applause Enterprises Inc. [26394]
Applause, Inc. [26395]
Arkin Distributing Co. [26396]
Arrow Wholesale Co. Inc. [26397]
Arrowcopter Inc. [26398]
Arrowhead Fireworks Co. [26399]
Arts & Craft Distributors Inc. [26400]
Aubford Enterprises [26401]
Aungst Wholesale; Dan [26402]
Avon Products Inc. [14029]
Ayers Art Co. [26403]
Baer Co.; Ralph A. [26404]
Bailes Inc.; Buck [26405]
Ballard Enterprises Inc. [26406]
Balloon Express [26407]
Balloon House [26408]
Balloonery Inc. [26409]
Balloons, Logos & T-Shirts [26410]
Balloons & Things [26411]
Ballpark Inc. [26412]
Banian Trading Co. [4801]
Battery Warehouse [8422]
Bayer Wood Products [26413]
Becksmith Co. [26414]
Berkley Game Distributors [26415]
Best Toy Manufacturing Ltd. [26416]
Betty's Doll House [26417]
The Bingo Company Inc. [26418]
Bingo Depot [26419]
Bingo Sales Inc.; J.D. [26420]
B.J. Toy Manufacturing Co. [26421]
Blackhawk Distributors [26422]
Blick Co.; Dick [25576]
Bloom Brothers Co. [4827]
Boutique Trim [20851]
Bowser Manufacturing [26423]
Bradley Import Co. [26424]
Brechner and Co. Inc.; Dan [26425]
Brewer Sewing Supplies [25988]
BRIO Corp. [26426]
Brohman Distributing Co. [26427]
Brown South; J.L. [26428]
Bud Plant Comic Art [3599]
Bud's Hobbies [26429]
Burda Brothers [26430]
Burnham; William H. [26431]
C & P Sales Co. [26432]
California Gift Center Inc. [26433]
California Hobby Distributors [26434]
Calus & CEI Distributors Inc. [26435]
Cappel Distributing Co. [21412]
Cardinal Inc. [26437]
Cariddi Sales Co. [23582]
Casper Pay-Less Drug Co. [26438]
Cee-J Wholesale [26439]
Celebrations Fireworks & Supply Co. Inc. [9633]
Central Arizona Distributing Co. [3620]
Central Valley Oriental Imports [26440]
Ceramics By Bob and Hazel [26441]
Checkmate International [26442]
Chernin Co.; Eugene [26003]
Chulani International [26443]
Cleveland Hobby Supply [26444]
CM School Supply [26445]
CMA Incorporated [10779]
Coins, Cards & Collectibles [26446]
Combined Sales Co. [26447]

Comics Hawaii Distributors [26448]
Comics Unlimited [26449]
Country Decor [26450]
Cousin Corporation of America [26451]
Craft Corner [26452]
Craft Enterprises [26453]
Craft Wholesalers [20936]
Cromers Inc. [24098]
CTT Distributing [26454]
Curtis Associates Inc. [26455]
CX Blaster Co. Inc. [26456]
D & D Distributing [26457]
Daigger and Company Inc. ETA/Cuisenaire;
   A. [26458]
Dakin Inc. [26459]
Dakin Inc. [26460]
Daylight Distributors [26461]
Dearing Wholesale Inc. [26462]
Dee's Delights, Inc. [26463]
Delaware Dry Goods [26017]
Delta Technical Coatings Inc. [26464]
Dentt Inc. [26465]
Dentt, Inc. [26466]
Designers Ltd. [26467]
Diamond Comic Distributors Inc. [26468]
Different Drummer [26469]
Direct Connect International Inc. [26470]
Discovery Toys Inc. [26471]
Do-My Ceramics [26472]
Dolls By Jerri [26473]
Douglas Model Distributors [26474]
Drybranch Inc. [23631]
Eaglecrafts Inc. [26475]
Emery Distributors [26477]
Esco Imports of Texas Inc. [26478]
E.T.S. Distributing [26479]
Eugene Trading Inc. [14098]
Evers Toy Store Inc. [26480]
F & S Co. Inc. [26481]
Flash Fireworks [26482]
Fleur de Paris [26036]
Flexible Flyer Co. [26483]
Florida Craft Wholesale [26484]
Flower Factory [21005]
Flying Phoenix Corp. [9634]
Flying Phoenix Corp. [26485]
Franco-American Novelty Company Inc. [13359]
Franco Distributing Co. Inc. [26486]
Franklin Stores Inc.; Ben [26487]
FVB Enterprises, Inc. [26488]
Galan Enterprises, Inc. [26489]
Gamblers General Store Inc. [26490]
Games of Tennessee [26491]
Games Unlimited [26492]
Gametree Inc. [26493]
Gann Company Inc.; E.C. [26494]
Garden State Fireworks Inc. [9635]
Gayla Industries Inc. [26495]
General Sales Co. [26496]
General Toys of Los Angeles [26497]
Geo-Hex [26498]
Georgies Ceramic & Clay Co. [26499]
Go Fly A Kite Inc. [26501]
Goldberg Models Inc.; Carl [26502]
Golden State Models [26503]
Gonsalves Inc.; Arthur J. [26504]
Great Lakes Area Distributing [26505]
Great Planes Model Distributors Co. [26506]
Gregory Inc.; E.Z. [14116]
H and H Sales Inc. [26507]
Hall Balloon Co. [26508]
Hall Enterprises; Robert J. [26509]
Hallmark Models, Inc. [26510]
Hankes Crafts [26511]
Harris & Co.; William H. [24759]
Hauler & Wade Associates Inc. [26512]
Havice Inc.; James F. [14121]
Hays Distributing Corp. [26513]
Herr's and Bernat Inc. [26514]
Herr's Inc. [26063]
Ho Imports, Inc. [26515]
Hobbies of Huntsville [26516]
Hobby Book Distributors [3830]
Hobby Crafts [26517]
Hobby House Inc. [26518]
Hobby Lobby International Inc. [26519]

Hobby Stores Distributing Inc. [26520]
HobbyGame Distributors Inc. [26521]
Hobbyquest Marketing [26522]
Hobbytyme Distributors [26523]
Hollandia Gift and Toy Co. [26524]
Hoven Inc. [26526]
H.O.W. Train Distribution [26527]
Howell Co.; R.B. [26528]
Hungates Inc. [26529]
Hunt Co. [26530]
Imperial Display Co. [26531]
Imperial Toy Corp. [26532]
Import Export Management Service Inc. [21054]
Import Warehouse Inc. [13374]
Impulse Merchandisers Inc. [2772]
Innoland Inc. [26533]
Institute for Childhood Resources [26534]
International Playthings Inc. [26535]
Interstate Bingo Supplies Inc. [26536]
Intromark Inc. [26537]
J & J Distributors Inc. [25690]
J & M Wholesale Distributors [26538]
Jagoe; Philip [26539]
James Industries Inc. [26540]
Jansco Marketing Inc. [26541]
Jarnagin; C & D [26542]
Jay Mar Sales Inc. [26543]
J.C. Sales Company Inc. [26544]
Jersey Model Distributors [26545]
Joissu Products Inc. [26546]
K & L Marketing Inc. [26547]
Kalweit Sales Company Inc. [26548]
Karshner Ceramics Inc. [26549]
Kasch Co.; M.W. [26550]
K.B. Brothers Inc. [26551]
KD Sales Inc. [26552]
Keen Jewelers [14141]
Ken's Craft Supply [21087]
Kipp Brothers Inc. [26553]
Klam International [7561]
KMS Inc. [26554]
Koch Resources Inc. [26555]
Kraft Korner Inc. [26556]
Kramer; L.C. [26114]
L H Ranch Bunk & Bisket & Hansens
   Hobby [26557]
L & L Lace [26558]
La Francis Associates; Mal [13383]
Lachman & Son Inc.; S. [26559]
Lacy Ltd.; Alice [26560]
Lake Instruments & Wholesale Corp. [26561]
LamRite West Inc. [13385]
Lankhorst Distributors Inc. [26562]
Last Gasp of San Francisco [3897]
The Last Straw Inc. [26563]
Lean Year Distributing Inc. [26564]
Learning Materials Workshop [26565]
The Learning Plant [3902]
Legends of Racing Inc. [26566]
Leisure Learning Products [26567]
Liberty Hobby [26568]
Linden Tree Children's Records & Books [3915]
Lion Notions Inc. [26125]
Marlin Distributors Inc. [26569]
Maxim Inc.; Mary [26570]
MC Sales [26571]
McCall Fireworks Inc. [26572]
Mellon Patch [26573]
Meyer Corp.; Mary [26574]
MGA Entertainment [26575]
Micro-Trains Line Co. [26576]
Mid-West Crafts Inc. [26577]
Midwest Sports Cards [26578]
Minnesota Clay Co. USA [26579]
Mizen International, Inc. [16313]
Model Rectifier Corp. [26580]
Morris Novelty Inc. [26581]
Morse Wholesale Inc.; J.D. [26582]
Mountain Lakes Distributors [26583]
Mountain Service Corp. [26584]
Mucci; Patrick J. [26585]
Mutual Sales Inc. [26586]
Myer Co.; Milton D. [26587]
Nadel and Sons Toy Corp. [26588]
Nana Development Corp. [22504]
Nasco-Catalog [26589]

National Art Supply [25748]
Neal's Gauging Trains [26590]
Nesson Sales [26591]
New Mexico Fire Works Inc. [26592]
New York Notions/Craft Supply Corp. [26593]
Nikko America Inc. [26594]
Nor-Del Productions Ltd. [4006]
Northern League Sportscards [26595]
Novel-Tees Wholesale [26596]
Old Sutler John [26597]
Original Appalachian Artworks Inc. [26598]
P & D Hobby Distributors [26600]
Pacific Group International [13417]
Pacific Model Distributing Inc. [26601]
Pacific Trading [26602]
Pal Productions Inc. [26603]
Pan American International [26604]
Paramount Sales Co. [14188]
Parkville Imports Inc. [17542]
Parris Manufacturing Co. [26605]
Patriotic Fireworks Inc. [13418]
Pat's Ceramics Tile Design Center [26606]
Paul-Son Gaming Supplies, Inc. [26607]
Peacock Alley Needlepoint [26608]
Peatfield Industries [26609]
Peck-Polymers [26610]
Peterson Co.; Dale [26611]
PFM Industries Inc. [26612]
Phase II [26613]
Phase II Distributors Inc. [26614]
Pierce Enterprises of Eagle Lake, Inc. [26615]
Plakie Inc. [26616]
Playmates Toys Inc. [26617]
Pleasant Co. [26618]
Pope Distributing Co. [5283]
Portland Merchandise Corp. [5284]
Portman Hobby Distributors [26619]
Preferred Distributors Inc. [26620]
The Premier Group [26621]
Processed Plastic Co. [26622]
Provo Craft Inc. [26181]
Punch It Distributing Inc. [26623]
Q-Snap Corp. [26624]
Quiltworks [26182]
R/C Henry Company Inc. [26625]
Rack Service Company Inc. [14203]
Rainbow Balloons Inc. [26627]
Ramer & Associates, Inc.; H. [4106]
Ramson's Imports [13433]
Random House Inc. [26628]
Rasmark Display Fireworks Inc. [26630]
Ray's Hobby [26631]
Reco International Corp. [4109]
Reichenbach Fireworks [26632]
Reno Game Sales Inc. [26633]
Representative Sales Co. [26184]
Reverse & Company [5307]
Rich Brothers Co. [26634]
Rieger's Ceramics Arts & Crafts [26635]
Rita Selections Ltd. [26636]
Rochester Imports Inc. [26637]
Royal Arts & Crafts [26638]
Royal Products Corp. [26639]
Royal Sales [26640]
Royal Toy Distributors Inc. [26641]
RPV Distributors [26642]
Rubenstein & Ziff Inc. [26194]
Rust Wholesale Company Inc. [12371]
S and G Trading Co. [26643]
S & P Whistle Stop [26644]
S and S Worldwide Inc. [26645]
Samson's Novelty Company Inc. [26646]
Sanrio Inc. [13442]
Sbar's, Inc. [26647]
Scenery Unlimited [26648]
Schwartz & Co.; Arthur [4145]
Sega of America Inc. [26649]
Sentai Distributors International [26650]
Shepher Distributors and Sales Corp. [26651]
Slusser Wholesale Inc. [26652]
Small World Toys [26653]
Smith Ceramics [26654]
Smith; Nicholas [26655]
SMP Enterprises Inc. [26656]
Sorceror Distributors [26657]
South Atlantic Distributing Co. [26658]

South Carolina Distributors Inc. [26659]
Southern Distributors Inc. [15662]
Southern Wholesale Co. [19629]
Southwest Bingo Supply [26660]
Sparks Game & Toy Co. [26661]
Special Promotion Co. [26662]
Spellbinders Inc. [26663]
Stack; Al [26665]
Staff [26666]
Stanislaus Imports Inc. [26667]
Star Sales Company of Knoxville [26668]
Starr Display Fireworks Inc. [26669]
Steven Smith/Stuffed Animals Inc. [26670]
Storck & Co.; M.A. [26671]
Strombecker Corp. [26672]
Sun Inc.; Bob [26673]
Sunset Models, Inc. [26674]
Syndee's Crafts Inc. [26675]
T & E Wholesale Outlet [13460]
Tari-Tan Ceramic Supply Inc. [26676]
Tee Pee Advertising Co. [26677]
Testor Corp. [26678]
Texas Hobby Distributors [26679]
Thomas Sales Company Inc. [26680]
TJ Wholesale Distributor [26681]
Today's Kids Inc. [26682]
Totsy Manufacturing Co., Inc. [26683]
Tower Publishing Co. [4224]
Toy Farmer Ltd. [26684]
Toy Wonders Inc. [26685]
The Toy Works, Inc. [26686]
Trags Distributors [26687]
Train Center Distributors [26688]
Tri-State Hobbycraft [26689]
Trims II Inc. [26690]
Trost Modelcraft Hobbies [26691]
Tucson Hobby Shop [26692]
Tujay's Artist Dolls [26693]
Tulsa Automatic Music Co. [26694]
Tuttle Enterprises Inc. [26695]
Twinson Co. [26696]
Unicover Corp. [26697]
Unique Crafters Co. [13465]
Unique Industries Inc. (Philadelphia, PA) [13466]
Unique Sales, Inc. [26698]
United Model Distributors Inc. [26699]
United Notions [26235]
United Notions [26236]
United Notions & Fabrics [26237]
U.S. Games Systems Inc. [26700]
Universal Card & Coin Center Inc. [26701]
Unnex Industrial Corp. [5455]
Upper Mississippi Valley Mercantile Co. [26702]
Vallery Co.; William G. [26703]
Variety Distributors Inc. [21336]
Victorian Pearl [26704]
Wal-Mart Stores Inc. [15700]
Walthers Inc.; Wm. K. [26705]
Wang's International Inc. [26706]
Wargames West [26707]
Well Made Toy Manufacturing Co. [26708]
Western Depot [26709]
Western Star Distributors [26710]
Western Toy and Hobby Inc. [26711]
Western Trading Post Inc. [26712]
Wills Co. [13474]
Winchester Sutler [26713]
Wisconsin Toy Company Inc. [26714]
Wood-N-Stuf [26715]
The Wright One Enterprises Inc. [26716]
The Yarn Center [26717]
Yesco Ltd. [26718]
ZDI Gaming Inc. [26719]
Zeiger International Inc. [26720]
Zims Inc. [26721]
Zocchi Distributors [26722]

SIC 5093 — Scrap & Waste Materials

A-1 Battery Distributors [2149]
Aaron Scrap Metals [26724]
Abbey Metal Corp. [26725]
ACC Recycling Corp. [26726]
Accurate Iron and Metal Co. [26727]

Adams International Metals Corp. [26728]
Addington Holdings Inc. [26730]
Addlestone International Corp. [26731]
Advanced Environmental Recycling Technologies
  Inc. [26732]
Advanced Petroleum Recycling Inc. [22024]
Aerospace Metals Inc. [26733]
Alcan Recycling [26734]
Allan Co. [26735]
Allan Industries Inc.; A. [26736]
Alliance Steel Service Co. [26737]
Allied Scrap Processors Inc. [26739]
Allied Vista Inc. Vista Fibers [26740]
Allwaste Inc. [26741]
Allwaste Inc. Allwaste Recycling Div. [26742]
Alma Iron and Metal Company Inc. [26743]
Alter Norfolk Corp. [26745]
Alter Scrap Processing [26746]
Alter Trading Corp. [26747]
Alter Trading Corp. [26748]
Ambit Pacific Recycling Inc. [26749]
AMCEP Inc. [26750]
American Byproducts Inc. [25957]
American Century Pallet Co. [27278]
American Commodities Inc. [22923]
American Compressed Steel Corp. [25549]
American Iron and Supply Co. [26751]
American Renaissance Paper Corp. [21632]
Annaco Inc. [26752]
Appliance Recycling Centers of America
  Inc. [15030]
Arizona Recycling Corp. [26753]
Arizona Scrap Iron and Metals Inc. [26754]
Atlantis Plastics, Inc. [22930]
Atlas Inc. [19789]
Atlas Metal and Iron Corp. [19790]
Atlas Steel Inc. [26755]
Auto Shred Recycling L.L.C. [26756]
Azcon Corp. [7006]
Baker Rubber Inc. [24268]
Baltimore Scrap Corp. [19801]
Bamberger Molding Compounds Inc.; C. [26757]
Barer and Sons; B. [26758]
Barry Metals Company Inc. [26759]
Basic Fibres Inc. [26760]
Batliner Paper Stock Co. [21646]
Bedford Recycling Inc. [26762]
Behr Iron and Steel Inc. [26763]
Behr and Sons Inc.; Joseph [26764]
Belwool Corp. [25980]
Benjamin Metals Co. [19811]
Best Disposal Inc. [26765]
BFI/Allied Recyclery Mpls [26766]
BFI Recyclery [19821]
BFI Waste Systems of North America Inc. [26767]
Bloch Metals Inc. [26768]
Bonded Insulation Company Inc. [26769]
Bradley Landfill and Recycling Center [26770]
Bristol Metal Co. Inc. [26771]
Browning-Ferris Industries of Michigan Inc. [26772]
BTM Recycling [26773]
Butech Inc. [26774]
Calbag Metals Co. [26775]
Can Land Recycling Center Inc. [26776]
Charles Bluestone Co. [19873]
Chemical Waste Management Inc. [26778]
City Metal Company Inc. [26779]
CMA Incorporated [10779]
CMC Secondary Metals Processing Div. [26780]
Columbia National Group Inc. [19883]
Columbia Ventures Corp. [19884]
Commercial Metals Co. Commercial Levin
  Div. [26781]
Commercial Waste Paper Company Inc. [26782]
Connell L.P. Luria Brothers Div. [26783]
Consolidated Scrap Processing [26784]
Consolidated Scrap Resources, Inc. [26785]
Container Recycling Alliance [26786]
Continental Paper Grading Co. [26787]
Continental Recycling Inc. [26788]
Conversion Resources Inc. [26789]
Cozzi Iron and Metal Inc. [26790]
Curcio Scrap Metal Inc. [26791]
Curtis TradeGroup Inc. [24274]
Custom-Pak Inc. [26792]
Damille Metal Supply Inc. [26793]

DC Metals Inc. [19919]
Delta Poly Plastic Inc. [26795]
Dempster Equipment [26796]
Denbo Iron and Metal Company Inc. [19925]
Denton Plastics Inc. [26797]
Discas Inc. [22955]
Dobrow Industries [26798]
Du-Wald Steel Corp. [19936]
DuBarry International Inc. [26799]
Earth Care Paper Inc. [26800]
Earth Waste Systems Inc. [26801]
Easton Iron and Metal Co. Inc. [26802]
EKCO International Metals Inc. [26803]
Elg Metals, Inc. [26804]
ELG Metals Southern, Inc. [26805]
Elgin Salvage and Supply Company Inc. [26806]
Empire Recycling Inc. [26807]
Encycle/Texas Inc. [26808]
Energy Answers Corp. [26809]
Engle and Co.; Jack [19955]
Environmental Control Inc. [26810]
EPI Technologies, Inc. [26811]
Fairway Salvage Inc. [26812]
Fibres International Inc. [26813]
Fisher Steel and Supply Co. [26814]
Five Star Trading Company [13708]
Frankfort Scrap Metal Company Inc. [26815]
Franklin Iron and Metal Corp. [26816]
Franklin Town Metals and Cores [19984]
Freedman Company Inc.; Joseph [26817]
Freedman and Son Inc.; R. [26818]
G and L Recycling Inc. [26819]
Gamtex Industries Inc. [26820]
Garbose Metal Co. [26821]
Gardena Recycling Center Inc. [26822]
GCF Inc. [19995]
General Iron Industries Inc. [26823]
General Metals of Tacoma Inc. [26824]
General Waste Products Inc. [26825]
Gershow Recycling [26827]
G.I. Industries [26828]
Glant Pacific Co. [26829]
Glant Pacific Iron and Metal Co. [26830]
Global Marketing Concepts [7399]
Global Titanium Inc. [26831]
Goldin Industries Inc. [20012]
Goodman Inc.; Harry [21744]
Gordon Waste Company Inc. [26832]
Great Western Recycling Industries Inc. [26833]
Green Team of San Jose [26834]
Grossman Iron and Steel Co. [20023]
Gulf Reduction Div. [20543]
Hans Metals, Inc. [26835]
Harding Metals Inc. [26836]
Harding Metals Inc. [26837]
Harley Metals Recycling Co. [26838]
Hartley Manufacturing Inc. [26839]
Heckett Multiserv Div. [26840]
Heckman Metals Co. [26841]
Herndon Company Inc.; J.E. [26842]
Hirschfield Sons Co.; H. [26843]
Horsehead Resource Development Company
  Inc. [20547]
Houston Wiper and Mill Supply Co. [26844]
Hugo Neu-Proler Co. [20046]
Hugo-Neu-Schnitzen East [26845]
Hummelstein Iron and Metal Inc. [26846]
Huron Valley Steel Corp. [20050]
Image Industries Inc. [26847]
IMCO Recycling Inc. [26848]
Indianapolis Materials Recycling Facility [26849]
Industrial Disposal Co. [26850]
Industrial Metal Processing Inc. [20056]
International Cellulose Inc. [26851]
International Mill Service Inc. [26852]
International Petroleum Corp. [26853]
Ireland Alloys Inc. [26854]
Iron and Metals Inc. [26855]
Jackson Iron and Metal Co. [20074]
Jacobs Iron and Metal Co. [26856]
Joseph Co.; David J. [26857]
Joseph Co., Ferrous Div.; David J. [26858]
Joseph Co. International Div.; David J. [26859]
Joseph Co. Municipal Recycling Div.; David
  J. [26860]
Joseph Co. Nonferrous Div.; David J. [26861]

K and F Industries Inc. (Indianapolis,
  Indiana) [20081]
K and K Recycling Inc. [26862]
Kelman Inc.; Nathan H. [26863]
Kendallville Iron and Metal Inc. [26864]
Keystone Resources Inc. [26865]
Keywell Corp. [26866]
Klempner Bros. Inc. [26867]
Kramer Metals [26869]
Kramer Scrap Inc. [26870]
Krentzman and Son Inc.; Joe [26871]
Krentzman Supply Co. [26872]
Kruger Recycling Inc. [26873]
Lakeside Nonferrous Metals Co. [26874]
Landfill Alternatives Inc. [26875]
Lans Sons Co.; William [26876]
Lavetan and Sons Inc.; L. [26877]
Lefton Enterprises Inc. [26879]
Lefton Iron and Metal Co. [26880]
Lenox Junk Co. [20122]
Levand Steel and Supply Corp. [20124]
Levin and Company of Tonawanda, Inc.;
  Louis [26881]
Liberty Iron and Metal Company Inc. [26883]
Lipsitz and Company Inc.; M. [26884]
Loef Company Inc. [26885]
Loef Company Inc. [26886]
Lorman Iron and Metal Co. [26887]
Los Angeles Paper Box and Board Mills. Paper
  Stock Div. [26888]
Luntz Corp. [26889]
M and M Metals International Inc. [26890]
MacLeod Group [26891]
Macon Iron and Paper Stock Company
  Inc. [26892]
Magnum Steel and Trading Inc. [20144]
Maine Scrap Metal LLC [26893]
Mallin Brothers Company Inc. [26894]
Mankato Iron and Metal Co. [26895]
Manufacturing Sciences Corp. [26896]
Marion Iron Co. [26897]
Marion Steel Co. Scrap Div. [26898]
Markovits and Fox [20153]
Matlow Company Inc. [26899]
Max Scrap Metals Inc. [26900]
McChesney Co.; C.E. [18078]
Mercury Waste Solutions Inc. [26901]
Mervis Industries Inc. [20168]
Metal Alloy Corp. [26902]
Metal Management Aerospace, Inc. [26903]
Metal Management Inc. [20169]
Metalsco Inc. [26905]
Metech International Inc. [26906]
Metro Group Inc. [26907]
Metro Metals Northwest [26908]
Metro Recycling Co. [21833]
Metro Recycling Co. Imagination Store
  Co. [26909]
Metropolitan Mining Co. [26910]
Michigan Paper Recyling Corp. [26911]
Mid-Ark Salvage Pool Inc. [2949]
Mid-City Iron and Metal Corp. [20181]
Mid-South Metals Co. [26912]
Midland Iron and Steel Co. [26913]
Midwest Metallics L.P. [20190]
Mill Waste Recovery Inc. [26914]
Millitrade International Inc. [20195]
Mindis Acquisition Corp. [26915]
Minkin Chandler Corp. [26916]
Mobile Data Shred Inc. [21840]
Morris Scrap Metal Inc. [26917]
Moskowitz Brothers [26918]
MP-Tech Inc. [20209]
MRC Polymers Inc. [26919]
M.R.D. Products Inc. [26920]
National Material L.P. [20219]
New England CR Inc. [26922]
New England Recycling Company Inc. [26923]
New Options on Waste Inc. [15593]
Newell Recycling Company Inc. [26924]
Non-Ferrous Processing Corp. [20230]
North Shore Recycled Fibers [26925]
North Star Recycling Co. [20234]
Northwest Ribbon Recycling and Supplies [26926]
Oil Recycling Inc. [26928]
OmniSource Corp. [26929]

OmniSource Lima Div. [26930]
O'Neill Div. [26162]
Otter Recycling [20257]
P & W Industries, Inc. [26931]
Pacific Hide and Fur Depot Inc. [20260]
Pacific Steel Inc. [26932]
Padnos Iron and Metal Co.; Louis [26933]
Paper Recovery Inc. [26934]
Parkans International L.L.C. [26935]
Parts Inc. [26936]
Peck Recycling Co. [26937]
Peltz Group Inc. [26938]
Phillip Metals Inc. [20275]
Phillips and Son Inc.; Max [26939]
Pielet Brothers Scrap, Iron and Metal L.P. [20277]
Plastic Recycling of Iowa Falls, Inc. [26940]
Plyler Paper Stock Co. [26941]
Plymouth Paper Company Inc. [21885]
Pollock Corp. [26942]
Pollock Steel Corp.; Mayer [26943]
Potential Industries Inc. [26944]
Powmet Inc. [26945]
Prins/Basic Waste Systems Inc. [26946]
Proler International Corp. [26947]
Prolerized Schiabo-Neu Co. [26948]
R and R Salvage Inc. [26949]
Rag Man Inc. [26950]
Rapid Disposal Services Inc. [26951]
Recycle America Northern California [26952]
Recycle Metals Corp. [26953]
Recycling Industries Inc. [26954]
Red Giant Oil Co. [22612]
Reisner Corp.; William [26955]
Republic Alloys Inc. [26956]
Research Environmental Industries [26957]
Reserve Iron and Metal L.P. [20316]
Richman Sons Inc.; S.D. [26959]
Riverside Recycling Inc. [26961]
Riverside Scrap Iron [26962]
Robinson Iron and Metal Company Inc. [26963]
Rocky Mountain Recycling [26964]
Rogers Iron and Metal Corp. [26965]
Rose Industries Inc. (Houston, Texas) [20330]
Rose Metal Processing [26967]
Rosebar Tire Shredding Inc. [24291]
RRT Empire Returns Corp. [26968]
Rubin Brothers Company Inc. [17149]
Rubino Brothers Inc. [26969]
Ruby Metal Traders Inc. [26970]
Sabel Industries Inc. [26971]
Sabel Steel Service [20349]
Sack Company Inc.; Stanley [26972]
Saco Steel Company Inc. [26973]
Sadoff and Rudoy Industries [26974]
Safety House [26975]
Safety-Kleen, Southwest [26976]
Samuels Recycling Co. [26977]
Samuels Recycling Co. Green Bay Div. [20352]
Samuels Recycling Co. Janesville Div. [26978]
Scepter Industries Inc. [26979]
Schiavone and Sons Inc.; Michael [26980]
Schlafer Iron and Steel Co. [26981]
Schnitzer Steel Products [26982]
Schwartzman Co. [26983]
Scrap Corporation of America [26984]
Seattle Iron and Metals Corp. [26985]
Segel and Son Inc. [26986]
SerVaas Inc. [24294]
Sessler Inc. [26987]
Shredded Products Corp. [26988]
Shulman and Son Co.; I. [26989]
Simon Resources Inc. [26990]
Simon & Sons; Joseph [26991]
Sims Brothers Inc. [26992]
Sims Metal America - Structural Steel Div. [26993]
Simsmetal USA Corp. [26994]
Simsmetal USA Corp. C and C Metals
  Div. [20367]
Smithey Recycling Co. [26995]
Soave Enterprises L.L.C. [26996]
Sol-Pro Inc. [26997]
Soloman Metals Corp. [26998]
Solotken and Company Inc.; J. [26999]
South Coast Recycling Inc. [27000]
Southern Holdings Inc. [27002]
Southern Metals Company Inc. [27003]

Southern Scrap Material Company Ltd. [27004]
Southern Scrap Material Company Ltd. [27005]
Southside Recycling Inc. [27006]
Spartan Iron Metal Company Inc. [27007]
SPC Corp. [27008]
State Salvage Company Inc. [27009]
Strauss Inc.; Herman [27010]
Sturgis Iron and Metal Company Inc. [27012]
Sugar Creek Scrap, Inc. [27013]
Suisman and Blumenthal Inc. [27014]
Sun Valley Paper Stock Inc. [27015]
Superior Div. [27016]
Swenson Metal Salvage Inc. [27017]
TALCO Recycling Inc. [27018]
Temple Iron and Metal Company Inc. [27019]
Tenenbaum Company Inc.; A. [27020]
Terra Haute Recycling [27021]
Tewksbury Industries Inc. [27022]
Texpack USA Inc. [27023]
Thalheimer Brothers Inc. [27024]
Titan Technologies Inc. (Albuquerque, New
    Mexico) [3312]
T.L.K. Industries Inc. [17230]
T.L.K. Industries Inc. [27025]
TRC Industries Inc. [24302]
Tri-State Iron and Metal Co. [27026]
Tribune Div. [4231]
Tube City Inc. [27027]
Tung Tai Trading Corp. [27028]
United Iron and Metal Co. [27029]
United Recycling Industries Inc. [27030]
U.S. Tire Recycling [27031]
Universal Metal and Ore Company Inc. [27032]
Universal Scrap Metals Co. [27033]
Washington Compressed Steel Corp. [27035]
Waste Management Recycle America [27036]
Waste Recovery-Illinois [27037]
Waste Recovery Inc. [22784]
Waste Reduction Systems Inc. [27038]
Weiner Steel Corp. [20483]
Weinreich Co.; Charles [27039]
Wellman Inc. [27040]
West Bay Resources Inc. [27041]
Western Gold Thermoplastics Inc. [27042]
Western Pacific Pulp and Paper [27043]
Western Scrap Processing Co. [27044]
Westreet Industries [27045]
Weyerhaeuser Co. Recycling Business
    Div. [27046]
Wichita Recycling [27047]
Wilkoff and Sons Co.; S. [27048]
Winston Brothers Iron and Metal Inc. [27049]
Wire and Metal Separation Inc. [27050]
wTe Corp. [27051]
WTE Recycling Corp. [27052]
Yaffe Iron and Metal Company Inc. [20501]
Zanker Road Resource Management Co. [27053]

SIC 5094 — Jewelry & Precious
Stones

14 Carats Ltd. [17297]
A La Carte Jewelry [17298]
A-Mark Financial Corp. [19720]
A-Mark Precious Metals Inc. [17299]
A & Z Pearls Inc. [17300]
Abco International [17301]
Accessories Palace [13288]
Accessory Resource Gallery Inc. [4745]
Accessory Wholesale [17302]
Adirondack Silver [17303]
Airmo Div. [13012]
Alaska Trophy Manufacturing [17304]
Allan Distributors [17305]
Almanzan [17306]
Amadom Corp. [17307]
American Jewelry Sales [17308]
Amerind Inc. [17309]
Anka Co. Inc. [17310]
Annie C.P. Productions Inc. [24672]
Antwerp Diamond Distributing Inc. [17311]
Apex Technologies [17312]
Arizona Mail Order Co. [4782]

Arlington Coin Co. [17313]
Art Cathedral Metal Inc. [17314]
Art's Theatrical Supply [17315]
Ashley & Company Inc.; E.H. [17316]
ASO Enterprises [17317]
Atlas Diamond Co. [17318]
Aurafin Corp. [17319]
Aurea Italia Inc. [17320]
Aurora Arts & Krafts [17321]
Ayre & Ayre Silversmiths [17322]
B & V Inc. [17323]
Baba International Inc. [17324]
Baker's Fine Jewelry and Gifts [17325]
Balfour Co.; L.G. [17326]
Ballanda Corp. [17327]
Bartky Mineralogical Enterprises Inc. [17328]
Baume and Mercier [17329]
Bazar Inc. Sales Co. [17330]
Bel Trade USA Corp. [22830]
Bellini Jewelry Co. [17332]
Belmar Inc. [17333]
Bennett Brothers Inc. [17334]
Benoit; Samuel [17335]
Benold's Jewelers [17336]
Benras Watch Co. [17337]
Bijoux Terner L.P. [17338]
Birzon Inc.; Sid [17339]
Black Hills Gold Colema [17340]
Blake Brothers [17341]
Blank Inc.; Joseph [17342]
Blue Canyon Jewelry [17343]
Blue Ribbon Awards [17345]
Bobtron International Inc. [4830]
Bock Jewelry Co. Inc. [17346]
Boone-Davis Inc. [15425]
Borel Jules & Co. [17347]
Bortman Trading Co. [17348]
Boutique Trim [20851]
Breton & Co. Inc.; Bruce [17349]
Broadway Style Showroom No. 1 [17350]
Brown Jewelry Inc.; Harold [17351]
Bruce and Co.; Donald [17352]
Brunos Turquoise Trading Post [17353]
BTE Import-Export [19204]
Bulova Corp. [17354]
Buy-Lines Co. [17355]
California Time Inc. [17356]
Capri Jewelry Inc. [17357]
Carat Diamond Corp. [17358]
Carr Inc.; Jim [17359]
Cartier Inc. [17360]
Cas Ker Co. [17361]
Cash Indiana [22840]
Casio, Inc. [17362]
Cates Associates [17363]
Cathedral Art Metal Inc. [17364]
Cellino Inc. [17365]
Chatham Created Gems Inc. [17366]
Chiefs Discount Jewelers Inc. [17367]
Chipita Accessories [17368]
Citizen Watch Company of America Inc. [17369]
Citra Trading Corp. [17370]
CJC Holdings Inc. [17371]
Clamor Impex Inc. [17372]
Clark Sales Co. [17373]
Colette Malouf Inc. [14067]
Colossal Jewelry and Accessories Inc. [17374]
Colossal Jewelry and Accessories Inc. [17375]
Connoisseurs Products Corp. [17376]
Connor and Associates Inc. [13333]
Connor & Son [17377]
Cook Brothers Inc. [15096]
Cooke Co.; David [17378]
Cousin Corporation of America [26451]
Coyne Galleries; Elaine [17379]
Craftown Inc. [17380]
Creative Imports Inc. [17381]
Cres Jewelry Factory Inc. [17382]
Crosby's Americana Arts I; Judy [17383]
Crumrine Manufacturing Jewelers [17384]
Crystaline North America Inc. [17385]
Cuba Buckles [17386]
D & D Distributing [26457]
Dallas Gold and Silver Exchange Inc. [17387]
Davenport Organisation [17388]
Dave's Jewelry & Giftware [17389]

Denison Co. Inc.; A.J. [17390]
Denver Merchandise Mart [17391]
Desert Indian Traders [17392]
Desert Star Jewelry Manufacturing [17393]
Design Accessories Inc. [17394]
DeYoung Inc.; J. and S.S. [17395]
Direct Diamonds Distributors [17396]
Divinci Ltd. [17397]
Don-Lin Jewelry Co. Inc. [17398]
Downey Designs International Inc. [17399]
Dugans Inc. [23633]
Duraffourg Gem Company Inc.; Max [17400]
Dynamic Concepts Inc. [17401]
E Big Inc. [17402]
Eagle Trophy [17403]
East Continental Gems Inc. [17404]
Eastrade Inc. [17405]
Educational Coin Co. [26476]
Elkins Inc.; Jerry [17406]
Ellis Tanner Trading Co. [17407]
Elvee/Rosenberg Inc. [17408]
Equity Industries Corp. [15490]
Evvan Importers Inc. [17409]
Excelsior International Corp. [17410]
Export USA [17411]
Fantasy Diamond Corp. [17412]
Fashion Victim [4946]
Feibelman & Krack [17413]
Field and Associates Inc. [17414]
Fine-Line Products Inc. [4953]
Fire Mountain Gems [17415]
Florida Clock & Supplies Inc. [15501]
Foreign Exchange Ltd. [20541]
Forschner Group Inc. [15505]
Fragments Inc. [17416]
Fremont Coin Co. Inc. [17417]
Friedman and Co. [17418]
Frontier [17419]
G & S Jewelry Manufacturing [17420]
Gamzon Brothers Inc. [17421]
Gattas Company Inc.; Fred P. [15512]
Gee; Donald & Rema [17422]
Gem East Corp. [17423]
Gem Enterprises, Inc. [17424]
Gem-La Jewelry Inc. [17425]
Gem Platinum Manufacturing Co. [17426]
Gemcarve [17427]
GemTek Enterprises Inc. [17428]
Genal Strap Inc. [17429]
Gerson Company Inc. [17430]
Giordano International; Michael [17431]
Global Importing Inc. [17432]
Glucksman & Associates; Barry [17433]
Gold Father's Jewelry, Inc. [17434]
Gold Findings Company Inc. [17435]
Gold & Silver Exchange [17436]
Goldman Co.; H.R. [17437]
Gordon Brothers Corp. [17438]
Gordon & Co.; Alan [17439]
Graham Co.; Mike [17440]
The Green Company, Inc. [17441]
Hahn Watch & Jewelry Co. [17442]
Hallock Coin Jewelry [17443]
Hansful Trading Company Inc. [8828]
Hard Hat Inc. [23714]
Hardy Turquoise Co. [17444]
Harold Jewelry Inc. [17445]
Harris & Co.; William H. [24759]
Heartline [17446]
Heaton Co.; G.A. [17447]
Heuer Time and Electronics Corp. [17448]
Honolulu Wholesale Jewelry Exchange [17449]
Horn EB Replacement Service [15534]
Horn EB Replacement Service [17450]
Hubb; William [17451]
Idaho Coin Galleries [17452]
Import Ltd. [17453]
Import Wholesale Co. [17454]
Indian Den Traders [17455]
Indian Mission Jewelry [17456]
Indian Trade Center Inc. [17457]
Insonic Technology, Inc. [17458]
Inter-American Trading [25689]
International Bullion and Metal Brokers
    Inc. [17459]
International Cultured Pearl & Jewelry Co. [17460]

International Importers Inc. [17461]
Interstate Wholesale Inc. [17462]
IPX [17463]
Jack LLC; Judith [17464]
Jamco [17465]
Jay's Indian Arts Inc. [17466]
JDS Industries Inc. [17467]
Jenkins Sons Company Inc.; J. [17468]
The Jewelers of Las Vegas [17469]
Jewelmasters Inc. [17470]
Jewelry By Dyan & Eduardo [17471]
Jewelry Exchange Inc. [17472]
Jewelry Trend Inc. [17473]
JGL Inc. [17474]
JJ Gold International Inc. [17475]
Johnson Safari Museum; Martin and Osa [17476]
J.R.N. Inc. [17477]
Judee K Creations Inc. [17478]
K & J Jewelry Manufacturing [17479]
K & M Associates [17480]
Kabana Inc. [17481]
Kappel Wholesale Co.; William J. [17482]
Kardas/Jelinek Gemstones [17483]
Karmily Gem Corp. [17484]
Kaye Inc.; Richard W. [17485]
Kaye Pearl Co. [17486]
Keen Jewelers [14141]
Kenilworth Creations Inc. [17487]
Kennedy; Rob E. [17488]
Key Imports [17489]
Khalsa Trading Co. Inc. [17490]
Kim International Mfg., L.P. [17491]
Kitsinian Jewelers [17492]
Koplewitz; Jane [17493]
K's Merchandise Mart Inc. [17494]
Kurman & Co.; S.J. [17495]
La Farge; Patricia Arscott [26118]
L.A. Silver [17496]
Lapis Lazuli Jewelry Distributors [17497]
LaRose, Inc.; S. [17498]
Lasting Impressions Inc. [17499]
Lata Export and Import [17500]
Lavdas Jewelry Ltd. [17501]
Levy Inc.; Victor H. [17502]
Loews Corp. [17503]
Longhill Partners Inc. [17504]
Lory's West Inc. [17505]
LW Bristol Collection [5147]
Lyles-DeGrazier Co. [17506]
Magic Novelty Company Inc. [17507]
Maine Entrepreneurs Group [17508]
Maisel Inc.; Skip [17509]
Majesti Watch Company Inc. [17510]
Marcel Watch Corp. [17511]
Marie Sales; Gina [17512]
Marketing Group Inc. (Harvey, Illinois) [17513]
Martek Ltd. [13397]
Maryland Import/Export, Inc. [17514]
Mask-Off Corp. [17515]
Mastoloni and Sons Inc.; Frank [17516]
Mathews Enterprises [17517]
Mayers Jewelry Company Inc. [17518]
McCrone Associates [17519]
Merchants Overseas Inc. [17520]
Merchants Overseas Inc. [17521]
Merrimack Jewelers Inc. [17522]
Meyer Diamond Company Inc.; Henry [17523]
MGD Enterprises [17524]
Missoula Gold & Silver Exchange [17525]
Morton Company Inc.; J.P. [17526]
Murdock Inc.; H.E. [17527]
Nacol Jewelry; C.S. [17528]
Nakai Trading Co. [17529]
Narragansett Trading Co. Ltd. [17530]
Navajo Manufacturing Co. [17531]
Nevitt; Stephen L. [17532]
Nice Time & Electronics Inc. [17533]
North American Investment Services [17534]
North American Treasures Inc. [17535]
North American Watch Corp. [17536]
Now Products [13416]
Odyssey Jewelry Inc. [17537]
Olympia Gold Inc. [17538]
Oogenesis Inc. [5254]
Orient Express [17539]
Original Designs Inc. [17540]

OroAmerica Inc. [17541]
Parkville Imports Inc. [17542]
Party Kits Unlimited Inc. [23874]
Pearson Inc.; Ronald Hayes [17543]
Peck & Co.; S.A. [17544]
Pereira Inc.; Ed [17545]
Perm Inc. [17546]
Persin and Robbin Jewelers [17547]
Platzer Company Inc.; Samuel [17548]
Polishers & Jewelers Supply Inc. [17549]
Pollack L.L.C.; J.O. [17550]
Polson's Rock Shop [17551]
Pow Wow Indian Jewelry [17552]
Pullen Inc.; Norman W. [17553]
Pyramid Studios [17554]
Quintel/Consort Watch Co. [17555]
Ramson's Imports [13433]
Rare Coins [17556]
Raymond Jewelers [17557]
Reed Inc.; Schweichert [17558]
Regency Collection Inc. [17559]
Regency Collection Inc. [17560]
Remar; Irving [17561]
Republic Jewelry & Coin Co. [17562]
Rhode Island Wholesale Jewelry [17563]
Richey Design Ltd.; William [17564]
Ridco Inc. [17565]
RMP Enterprises Inc. [17566]
Roberts Inc.; M.L. [17567]
Roeden Inc. [17569]
Roldan Products Corp. [15293]
Rolyn Inc. [17570]
Roma Chain Manufacturing [17571]
Romanoff International Supply Corp. [17572]
Ronald Hayes Pearson Inc. [17573]
Rose Goldsmith; H.M. [17574]
Rothenberg and Schloss Inc. [14224]
Royal Chain Inc. [17575]
Royal Stones Corp. [17576]
RTC Manufacturing [17577]
Ru-Mart Metal Specialties [17578]
Ru-Mart Metal Specialties [17579]
Rubins Stone House [17580]
Ryan Jewelry; Susan [17581]
S & T Jewelers [17582]
Saettele Jewelers Inc. [17583]
Sago Imports Inc. [17584]
Salvors Inc. [17585]
Samuels Jewelers [17586]
Sanchez Fine Jewelers [17587]
Sandaga [17588]
Sassounian Inc. [17589]
Sausalito Craftworks [17590]
Schachter and Company Inc.; Leo [17591]
Schneider Sales Inc.; Arthur [24852]
Schreiber Inc.; E. [17592]
Sea Level Products International [17593]
Security Silver and Gold Exchange [17594]
Seiko Corporation of America [17595]
Seiko Time West [17596]
Seville Watch Corp. [17597]
Shil La Art Gems, Inc. [17598]
Shiprock Trading Post [17599]
Shirts Unlimited [17600]
Shube Manufacturing Inc. [17601]
Silver City [17602]
Silver Dust Trading Inc. [17603]
A Silver Lining Inc. [17604]
Silver Ray [17605]
Silver Sun Wholesale Inc. [17606]
SilverSource [17607]
SKL Company Inc. [17608]
SMH (US) Inc. [17609]
SMP Enterprises Inc. [26656]
Snow & Stars Corp. [17610]
Somersault Ltd. [17611]
South Pacific Wholesale [17612]
Southern Watch Inc. [17613]
Southwestern Gold Inc. [17614]
Southwestern Jewelry & Gifts [17615]
Spaman Jewellers; W.M. [17616]
Spil Co.; Samuel [17617]
Stange Co. [17618]
Stanley-Lawrence Co. [17619]
Stanley Roberts Inc. [15667]
Star Jewelry Enterprises Inc. [17620]

Stern Watch Agency Inc.; Henri [17621]
Steven Inc.; David G. [17622]
Strygler Company Inc.; H.S. [17623]
Style Asia Inc. [13454]
Suave Noble Creations Inc. [5401]
The Sultan Co. [17624]
Sun Fashion Designs Inc. [17625]
Sun Sales [17626]
Sunwest Silver Co. [17627]
Swedes Sales [17628]
Swift Ltd.; S.A. [17629]
Swiss Army Brands Inc. [15676]
Tacoa Inc. [17630]
Tanner Trading Co.; Ellis [17631]
Taramax U.S.A., Inc. [17632]
Taxor Inc. [17633]
Teneff Jewelry Inc. [17634]
Terryberry Co. [17635]
Texas Sales Co. [15336]
Thunderbird Silver Co. [17636]
Timco Jewelers Corp. [17637]
Time Service Inc. [17638]
Tin-Nee-Ann Trading Co. [17639]
Tobe Turpen's Indian Trading Co. [13464]
Todisco Jewelry Inc. [17640]
Tool Craft Inc. [17641]
Touch Adjust Clip Co. Inc. [17642]
Trade Corporation [8140]
Troica Enterprise Inc. [17643]
Tryon Mercantile Inc. [17644]
Turquoise World [17645]
Unique Sales, Inc. [26698]
Universal Jewelers & Trading Co. [17646]
Vitriesse Glass Studio [17647]
Waldeck Jewelers [17648]
Waliga Imports and Sales Inc. [17649]
Walton's Gold Diamond Co.; George [17650]
Watches [17651]
Webster Watch Company Associates LLC [17652]
Wedlo Inc. [17653]
Weil Inc.; Cliff [21352]
Wel-Met Corp. [17654]
Wenger N.A. [24042]
Wheatland Rock Shop [17655]
Wildflower Jewelry [17656]
Wildlife Lithographs, Inc. [13472]
Wilkerson Jewelers [17657]
Winkler Group, Ltd. [17658]
Winston Inc.; Harry [17659]
Wittnauer International [17660]
Wolf and Sons Inc.; Charles [17661]
World Traders (USA) Inc. [9607]
World Wide Imports of Orlando Inc. [17662]
Wuite Traders International [17663]
Yeh Dah Ltd. [17664]
Yong's Watch & Clock Repair [17665]
York Novelty Import Inc. [17666]
Zack Trading [17667]
Zak Designs Inc. [15716]

SIC 5099 — Durable Goods Nec

AAA Fire & Safety Inc. [24466]
AB Wholesale Co. [13521]
ABKCO Music and Records Inc. [25056]
Advanced Affiliates Inc. [13536]
Adventures Unlimited Press [3474]
AIMS Multimedia [25058]
Aircraft and Component Equipment Suppliers Inc. [35]
Airway Industries Inc. [18367]
Al-WaLi Inc. [3481]
Alaska Fire & Safety Equipment [24501]
Alfreda's Film Works c/o Continnuus [3489]
Allied International Marketing Corp. [17692]
Allied-Vaughn Inc. [25063]
Almerica Overseas Inc. [40]
AmeriBag Inc. [18368]
American Accessories International Inc. [18369]
American Audio Prose Library [3497]
American Global Co. [13558]
American Media Inc. [25070]
American Mill and Manufacturing Inc. [27279]
American Wholesale Book Co. [3504]

Ancient Future Music [3508]
Andalusia Wood Products Inc. [27280]
Andersen Inc.; Earl F. [23516]
Anderson Associates Inc.; Earl F. [24066]
Appalachian Distributors [3521]
A.R. Musical Enterprises Inc. [25081]
Arctic Fire Equipment [24507]
Arista Records Inc. [25082]
Arizona Sportsman, Inc. [13476]
Army & Navy Supplies [4785]
Arnessen Corp. [25559]
Arrowhead Timber Co. [27281]
Art Essentials [20813]
ArtSource Inc. [13308]
Audio Supply Co. [25087]
Aungst Wholesale; Dan [26402]
Backstage Pass Productions and Distributing
   Inc. [25095]
Baker and Taylor Inc. [3541]
Barco Municipal Products Inc. [24511]
Barry Pumps Inc.; R.E. [25568]
Bassin Inc.; Jerry [25097]
Bennett Brothers Inc. [17334]
Bergquists Imports Inc. [15419]
Berman Leather Company Inc. [18376]
Beyda & Associates, Inc. [3553]
Beyda & Associates, Inc. [3554]
Big State Record Distribution Corp. [25103]
Blacast Entertainment [3558]
Blevins Inc. [8445]
BMG Distribution Co. [25106]
BMI Educational Services [3562]
Bobs Fire Extinguisher [24517]
Book Warehouse Inc. [3572]
Boyd Coffee Co. [10603]
Brady Distributing Co. [25579]
Brain Teaser Money Machines [25580]
Breezy Ridge Instruments [25108]
Broward Fire Equipment and Service Inc. [24519]
Bruno & Son Inc.; C. [25110]
Buckeye Fire Equipment Co. Sales Div. [24520]
Buck's War Surplus [23574]
Buttross Wholesale Co.; A. [23578]
Buy-Lines Co. [17355]
Cabin Crafters [27291]
Calato USA Div. [25116]
California Wallet Co. Inc. [18379]
Calolympic Glove and Safety Co. Inc. [24523]
Canaan Records [25117]
Canterbury Enterprises [27294]
Capcom Entertainment Inc. [26436]
Carina International Inc. [18380]
Carmichael and Carmichael Inc. [25123]
Carolina Western Inc. [7145]
Cascade Pacific Lumber Co. [7150]
Castiglione Accordion [25127]
Caye's Luggage [18381]
CD One Stop [25130]
Central South Music Inc. [25132]
Chartier Double Reed Co. [25133]
Chesbro Music Co. [25134]
Cheviot Corp. [25135]
Chicago Case International [18382]
Chidvilas, Inc. [3628]
Children's Media Center, Inc. [3629]
The Christian Broadcasting Network, Inc. [3635]
Church Doctor Resource Center [3638]
City One Stop [25138]
Clark's Gun Shop [13481]
Claymore Sieck Co. [13635]
Clipper Products [18383]
CMS Communications Inc. [5563]
Coast Wholesale Music [25141]
Coast Wholesale Music Co. [25142]
Color Brite Fabrics and Displays Inc. [25605]
Common Ground Distributors Inc. [3648]
Contemporary Arts Press Distribution [3655]
Contico International Inc. [13643]
Coolant Management Services Co. [4365]
Cooper and Associates [13335]
CR Specialty Co. [13484]
Creative Healthcare Resources [3668]
Creative Joys Inc. [3670]
Creative Source [3671]
Creative Specialties Inc. [15463]
Curtis and Sons; L.N. [24529]

Custom Music Co. [25152]
D and H Distributing Co. [15103]
Dauphin Co. [25156]
Davitt & Hansen West [25158]
Davitt and Hanser Music Co. [25159]
Day Star Productions [25161]
DayMark Corp. [13487]
Deans Firearms, Ltd. [13488]
Decorative Crafts Inc. [13086]
Deering Banjo Co. [25164]
Denver Merchandise Mart [17391]
Desert Mesquite of Arizona [10950]
DeVorss & Co. [3691]
Discipleship Resources [3694]
Display Technologies [25631]
Doughten Films, Inc.; Russ [25168]
Durkin Hayes Publishing [3704]
Dusty Strings Co. [25169]
Dynamic Classics Ltd. [23638]
E & R Sales Inc. [13350]
Eagle Creek [18390]
Eastern Enterprises [25640]
Edu-Tech Corp. [3719]
Educational Activities Inc. [25171]
Educational Record Sales, Inc. [25173]
Educational Record & Tape Distributors of
   America [25174]
Educational Technology Inc. [6236]
Eldon Rubbermaid Office Products [20987]
Elliott Sales Corp. [23649]
EME Corp. [25181]
Encyclopaedia Britannica Educational Corp. [3731]
Engineering Equipment Co. [24537]
Entertainment Music Marketing Corp. [25183]
Espana General Importers [13353]
Essex Entertainment Inc. [25185]
European Crafts/USA [25186]
Evergreen Publishing & Stationery [3738]
Everpure Inc. [25645]
Eyemark Video Services [25188]
F and B Marketing Inc. [8726]
F.B.F. Inc. [13491]
Field and Associates Inc. [17414]
Fire Appliance & Safety Co. [24541]
Fire Command Company Inc. [24543]
Fire Equipment Inc. [24544]
Fireman's Supply Inc. [24551]
Fireside Distributors [14448]
Flannery Co. [3752]
Flower Films & Video [25192]
FMC Resource Management Corp. [21006]
Folkcraft Instruments [25193]
Forgy Process Instruments Inc. [23172]
Fox, Inc.; T.E. [25197]
Fredrico Percussion [25198]
Fredriksen and Sons Fire Equipment Company
   Inc. [24553]
Full Perspective Videos Services Inc. [25201]
Fulton Corp. [13718]
Fyr Fyter Inc. [24554]
G. Leblanc Corp. [25204]
G & S Products Inc. [25205]
Garick Corp. [27308]
Gate Group USA, Inc. [22855]
General Music Corp. [25209]
George Washington University Press [3777]
Getzen Co. [25210]
Glenray Communications [25212]
Global Access Entertainment Inc. [25213]
Global Forestry Management Group [27309]
Glove Wagon Enterprises, Inc. [4991]
GMS Corp. [18395]
Golden-Lee Book Distributors Inc. [3784]
Good Karma Publishing Inc. [3786]
Good News Productions, International [25214]
Gotham Distributing Corp. [25215]
Graves Fire Protection [24557]
GSI, Inc. [13492]
Gulbransen Inc. Crystal Products [25221]
Gulf South Forest Products, Inc. [27313]
Handleman Co. [25225]
Hanford's Inc. [13365]
Harmonia Mundi U.S.A. Inc. [25226]
Harris-Teller, Inc. [3814]
Harvest Productions (E.B.M.) [25228]
Havice Inc.; James F. [14121]

HBG Export Corp. [22979]
HealthTech International Inc. [23720]
Heckler and Koch Inc. [13494]
Heritage Manufacturing [13495]
Higgins Productions, Inc.; Alfred [25231]
Highsmith Inc. [13132]
Hiller Corp.; Herbert S. [24562]
Hillmer's Luggage & Leather [18397]
Hofert Co.; J. [13369]
Hohner, Inc./HSS [25234]
Holmes Timber Company Inc. [27319]
Hondo Guitar Co. [25237]
Hoshino U.S.A. Inc. [25238]
Hotho & Co. [3835]
House of Guitars Corp. [25239]
House of Lloyd Inc. [13372]
HP Products [4637]
Hughes Company Inc.; R.S. [24568]
Hunter Co., Inc. [18398]
I.J.K. Sales Corp. [18399]
Industrial Safety Supply Co. Interex Div. [24571]
Ingram Book Co. [25243]
Ingram Entertainment [25244]
Ingram Entertainment [25245]
Ingram Entertainment Inc. [25248]
Ingram International Films [25249]
Ingram Video [25250]
International Cultural Enterprises Inc. [25252]
Intertrade, Inc. [13147]
Interwest Safety Supply Inc. [24573]
Jan-Mar Industries [25258]
Jay Mart Wholesale [25259]
Jonas Aircraft and Arms Company Inc. [109]
Jonas Aircraft and Arms Company Inc. [24578]
Jovino Company, Inc.; John [13496]
JTG of Nashville [25262]
Juergens Produce and Feed Co. [893]
Julius Kraft Company Inc. [24579]
Jupiter Band Instruments Inc. [25263]
K-Swiss Inc. [23767]
K-Tel International Inc. [25264]
K-Tel International (USA) Inc. [15547]
Kaman Music Corp. [25265]
Kaman Music Corp. Los Angeles [25266]
Kay Guitar Co. [25267]
Kemper Enterprises Inc. [25698]
Kentuckyiana Music Supply Inc. [25269]
Keyboard Decals [25271]
Kidde Safety [24580]
Kimbo Educational [25272]
Kingdom Co. [25273]
Kirby Forest Products; J. [7559]
Knape and Vogt Manufacturing Co. [7564]
Koch International [25274]
Koncor Forest Products Co. [27332]
Koplik and Sons Inc.; Perry H. [26868]
Korg U.S.A. Inc. [25275]
Koval Marketing Inc. [15556]
Kravet Fabrics Inc. [26115]
Kultur, White Star, Duke International Films Ltd.,
   Inc. [25276]
La Grand Industrial Supply Co. [24582]
LaFrance Equipment Corp. [24583]
Lakey Mouthpieces; Claude [25277]
Lang Percussion [25278]
Lata Export and Import [17500]
Latin Percussion, Inc. [25279]
Latin Trading Corp. [3898]
Lazy-Man, Inc. [15201]
The Learning Plant [3902]
Leather Connection [18405]
Leather Loft Stores [18406]
Ledford's Trading Post [13497]
Legal Star Communications [25281]
Levy Home Entertainment [3908]
Lib-Com Ltd. [13390]
Liberty Leather Products Company Inc. [18407]
Library Video Co. [25283]
Life Unlimited [3913]
Lifestyle International Inc. [18408]
Ligonier Ministries, Inc. [25285]
Linden Tree Children's Records & Books [3915]
Link Lumber Co.; C.J. [27335]
Lipsey's Inc. [13498]
LIVE Entertainment Inc. [25286]
Loveall Music Co. [25289]

LP Music Group [25291]
LPD Music International [25292]
L.P.S. Records, Inc. [25293]
LSI (Legacy Sports International LLC) [13500]
Luggage America Inc. [18409]
Luthier's Mercantile Int. Inc. [25294]
MacDonald Manufacturing; Stewart [25295]
Magnamusic Distributors Inc. [25298]
Maiden Music [25299]
Majega Records [25300]
Malletech/Marimba Productions Inc. [25301]
Mangelsen and Sons Inc.; Harold [13394]
Maranatha Music [25303]
Marketing Group Inc. (Harvey, Illinois) [17513]
Markley Strings, Inc.; Dean [25304]
Marshall and Johnson [24587]
Martinson-Nicholls [26135]
Mayfield Timber Co. [27341]
Mazel Stores Inc. [25728]
MBT International Inc. [25307]
McAlister Camera Co.; Don [22876]
McPherson & Co. Publishers [3945]
Meisel Stringed Instruments Inc. [25311]
Memtek Products/Memorex Audio, Video, CDR's, &
    Computer Peripherals [25313]
Meridian International Co. [24590]
Metamorphous Advances Product Services [3949]
Michigan Church Supply Company Inc. [3951]
Mid-Continent Fire & Safety, Inc. [24591]
Mid-East Manufacturing Inc. [25317]
MIDCO International [25319]
MIDCO International [25320]
Midco International Inc. (Effingham, Illinois) [25737]
Mill City Music Record Distribution, Inc. [25325]
Minnesota Conway [24593]
Mississippi Tool Supply Co. [24595]
Mix Bookshelf [3964]
MMB Music Inc. [25330]
Monahan Co.; Thomas [27348]
Monarch Luggage Company Inc. [18413]
Montoya/MAS International Inc. [25744]
Moody Institute of Science [25335]
Moonbeam Publications, Inc. [3967]
Mountain State Muzzleloading Supplies,
    Inc. [13503]
Murphy Co. [22881]
Music City Record Distributors Inc. [25344]
Music Distributors Inc. [25345]
Music Emporium Record Co. [25346]
Music Industries Inc. [25347]
Music People Inc. [9110]
Music Sales Corp. [3976]
Music Sales International [25349]
Nalpak Video Sales, Inc. [16336]
National Audio Company Inc. [25353]
National Book Network Inc. [3984]
National Potteries Corp. [13408]
National Safety Apparel Inc. [24600]
National Stock Sign Co. [25750]
National Wholesale [25355]
New Concepts Books & Tapes Distributors [3993]
New Cooperative Company Inc. [12000]
NewSound, LLC [25357]
N.H.F. Musical Merchandise Corp. [25358]
NMC Corp. [15251]
Northwest Wholesale [25365]
Numrich Gunparts Corp. [13504]
NYC Liquidators Inc. [25366]
O'Connor Distributing Company Inc. [25367]
Olin Corp. [4473]
Omega Publications, Inc. [4020]
Omnichron [25774]
Opportunities for Learning, Inc. [4023]
Orr Safety Corp. [24608]
Orscheln Farm and Home Supply Inc. [1109]
Oswald Supply Company Inc.; H.C. [23304]
Pacific Coast One-Stop [25373]
Paragon Music Center Inc. [25375]
Path Press Inc. [4043]
Paulist Productions [22888]
Paxton Timber Co. [27356]
Peakwon International Inc. [18979]
Pearl Corp. [25376]
Penton Overseas Inc. [25377]
Petersburg Box and Lumber Inc. [27358]
Peterson Co.; Robert H. [15618]

Petillo Masterpiece Guitars [25380]
Philadelphia Sign Company Inc. [25783]
Photocomm Inc. [25785]
Pictorial Histories Publishing Co. [4064]
Pioneer Laser Optical Products Div. [25382]
P.K. Safety Supply [24612]
Plano International [13870]
Plastic Recycling of Iowa Falls, Inc. [26940]
Plastic Safety Systems, Inc. [24613]
Platinum Entertainment Inc. [25385]
Player International; J.B. [25386]
Player Piano Company Inc. [25387]
Poolmaster Inc. [23895]
Potter-Roemer [24614]
Premiere AVD Corp. [25388]
Preston Leather Products [18421]
Price and Pierce International Inc. [21890]
Price Stern Sloan Inc. [4083]
Princeton Book Company Publishers [4084]
Pro/Am Music Resources, Inc. [4086]
Pro-Mark Corp. [25389]
Projexions Video Supply [25391]
Protech Safety Equipment [24615]
Provident Music Group [4090]
Pruitt; Richard [13213]
Pryor Novelty Co., Inc. [13430]
QCA Inc. [25395]
Quality Books Inc. [4099]
Racing Champions Corp. [26626]
Rag Man Inc. [26950]
Ramer & Associates, Inc.; H. [4106]
Rashid Sales Co. [25405]
Real Sales; Paul A. [25410]
Record Technology Inc. [25411]
RED Distribution [25413]
Reedy International Corp. [4693]
Regal Shearing [18423]
Reid Enterprises; Desmond A. [4113]
Reis Environmental Inc. [24617]
Reliable Fire Equipment Co. [24618]
RHO-Chem Div. [4695]
Robert Manufacturing Company Inc. [18425]
Roland Corporation U.S. [25420]
Romac Export Management Corp. [15639]
Rothenbuhler Engineering [5747]
Royal Publications, Inc. [4126]
RPL Supplies Inc. [22899]
R.S. Hughes Company Inc. [12]
RSR Wholesale South Inc. [13511]
S & S Firearms [13512]
S and S Worldwide Inc. [26645]
SA-SO [24620]
SAF-T-GARD International, Inc. [17153]
Safety Flare Inc. [24622]
Safety Flare Inc. [24623]
Safety Industries Inc. [3179]
St. Louis Music Supply Co. [25425]
San Francisco Center for Visual Studies [4136]
Sanderson Safety Supply Co. [24624]
Sandusco Inc. [25427]
Sandusky Distributing Co. [25428]
Schadler and Sons Inc.; John [25431]
Schoenhof's Foreign Books Inc. [4140]
Scientific Anglers [23933]
Scorpio Music Inc. [25434]
Sealaska Corp. [27372]
Sealaska Timber Corp. [27373]
Select-O-Hits Inc. [25437]
Senco of Florida Inc. [13910]
Serendipity Communications, Inc. [25438]
Seven Star Productions [25439]
Showstopper Exhibits Inc. [25814]
Signs of All Kinds [25817]
Sigo Press/Coventure [4162]
Sile Distributors Inc. [13513]
Silver Blue Associated Ltd. [18427]
Simmons Gun Specialty Inc. [13514]
Skyway Luggage Co. [18430]
Sound Words Communications, Inc. [25453]
Sounds Write Productions, Inc. [25454]
Source Books [4171]
Southeastern Skate Supply of Virginia Inc. [23971]
Southern Highland Accordions & Dulcimers
    Ltd. [25456]
Southern Territory Associates [4174]
Sparrow-Star [4179]

Spectrum Lighting/Sound & Beyond [25828]
Square Deal Recordings and Supplies [25462]
Squires Timber Co. [27379]
Stage Inc. [15665]
Steiner Inc.; S.S. [18253]
Stelling Banjo Works Ltd. [25465]
Strategic Distribution Inc. [16530]
Struve Distributing Company Inc. [25832]
Studio Film & Tape Inc. [22908]
Sugar Records [25468]
Suncook Tanning Corp. [18269]
Superlearning [4199]
SUPERVALU Champaign Distribution
    Center [12643]
Systematix Co. [4524]
Talon Associates International, Inc. [19069]
Tamiami Range and Gun Distributors Inc. [13515]
Tech Fire and Safety Co. [24642]
Telemusica Co. [25476]
TENBA Quality Cases, Ltd. [18435]
TENBA Quality Cases Ltd. [18436]
Texas A & M University Press [4210]
Thomas-Walker-Lacey Inc. [12716]
Thomson Productions [25478]
Tilton & Sons, Inc.; Ben [18281]
Time Emergency Equipment [25844]
Time Life Inc. [4219]
Titleist Golf [24011]
Trax Distributors [25483]
Tri-S Co. [24646]
Tropical Music and Pro Audio [25485]
Tulsa Automatic Music Co. [26694]
TWT Moulding Company Inc. [15690]
Tyndale House Publishers [25488]
Uni Distribution Co. [25489]
Unique Crafters Co. [13465]
United Fire Equipment Co. [24650]
Universal Percussion [25492]
USA Test, Inc. [25494]
Valdez [25495]
Valley Hardwood Inc. [8168]
Valley Media Inc. [25496]
VCI Home Video [25498]
Vestal Press Ltd. [4259]
Victor's House of Music [25502]
Victory International Productions [25503]
Video Action [25504]
Vision Video [25509]
Vitali Import Company Inc. [25510]
Volcano Press, Inc. [4262]
Vorpahl, Inc.; W.A. [24659]
Vuitton North America Inc.; Louis [18439]
Wagners [13468]
Waikiki Trader Corp. [5470]
Warner-Elektra-Atlantic Corp. [25512]
Warner Music Group [25513]
Washington Chain and Supply [18633]
Waxworks Inc. [25515]
WaxWorks/VideoWorks Inc. [25516]
Weber Piano Co. [25519]
Werleins for Music [25520]
West L.A. Music [25521]
Weston Woods Studio Inc. [25522]
Westvaco Worldwide [21990]
White Star Video [25523]
White Water Manufacturing [17279]
Wolf Imports [25527]
Word Entertainment [25530]
World Wide Pictures, Inc. [25532]
WRG Corp. [177]
WRI Education [25533]
Yamaha Corporation of America [25535]
Yamaha Corporation of America Band and
    Orchestral Division [25536]
Yorkville Sound Inc. [25538]
Zeager Brothers Inc. [27399]
Zink Safety of Arkansas Inc. [24662]
Zink Safety Equipment [24663]
The Zondervan Corp. [4307]

SIC 5111 — Printing & Writing Paper

Acorn Distributors Inc. [21616]
Alaska Paper Co. Inc. [21617]

Albert Paper Co. [21618]
Alco Standard Corp. [21620]
Alling and Cory Co. [20786]
Alpina International Inc. [21626]
Anchor Paper Co. [21633]
Andrews Paper and Chemical Co. [4323]
Andrews Paper House of York Inc. [21634]
A.T. Clayton and Company Inc. [21637]
Atlantic Corp. [21639]
Autron Inc. [21641]
Autron Inc. Precision Rolls Division [21642]
Baldwin Paper Co. [21645]
Barnaby Inc. [20831]
BCT International Inc. [21648]
Bell Paper Products Co. [21651]
Berry Company Inc.; H.T. [21653]
Blue Pearl [17344]
Borden & Riley Paper Co. [21654]
Bradner Central Co. [21656]
Business Cards Tomorrow Inc. [21660]
Butler-Dearden Paper Service Inc. [21661]
Butler Paper Co. [21662]
Capital Paper Company Div. [21666]
Capstone Paper Co. [21667]
Carolina Pad and Paper Co. [21669]
Carpenter Paper Co. [21671]
Carter Paper Co. [21672]
Case Paper Co. [21674]
Chess Business Forms Co. [21677]
Chris Cam Corp. [21678]
Cincinnati Cordage and Paper Co. [21679]
Cincinnati Cordage and Paper Co. Cordage Papers
    Cleveland Div. [21680]
Citifax Corp. [20900]
Clampitt Paper Co. [21681]
Cole Papers Inc. [21685]
Coronet Paper Corp. [21692]
Coronet Paper Products [21693]
Cox Paper & Printing Co. [21695]
Crescent Paper Co. [21696]
Danforth International Trade Associates,
    Inc. [21700]
Darling Corp.; J.L. [21701]
Dennis Paper Co. Inc. [21706]
Diamond Paper Corp. [21707]
Dillard Paper Co. Birmingham Div. [21709]
Dillard Paper Co. Chattanooga Div. [21710]
Direct Way Distributors Inc. [21713]
Eagle of Cody Printing [21717]
EcoCycle Inc. [21718]
Economy Paper Company Inc. [21719]
Elish Paper Company Inc.; Harry [21722]
Executive Converting Corp. [20995]
Farmers Cooperative Co. (Milligan,
    Nebraska) [17856]
Fidelity Paper Supply Inc. [21725]
First State Paper, Inc. [21726]
Fulton Paper Co. [21732]
Goes Lithographing Co. [21742]
Gould Paper Corp. [21745]
Grant & Associates, LLC; R.B. [21746]
Graphic Controls [21747]
Graphic Papers Inc. [21748]
Heartland Paper Co. [21758]
Heritage Paper Company Inc. [21759]
The Hillcraft Group [21761]
Hillsdale Paper Co. [21763]
Holstein Paper & Janitorial Supply [21765]
Hudson Valley Paper Co. [21770]
Industrial Paper Corp. [21773]
Industrial Wiper & Paper [21775]
Infinity Paper Inc. [21776]
Ingram Paper Co. [21777]
Inter-City Paper Co. [21778]
Jackson Paper Company Inc. [21781]
Kayboys Empire Paper Company Inc. [21789]
Kelly Paper Co. [21790]
Kenzacki Specialty Papers Inc. [21791]
Kirk Paper Co. [21792]
LaSalle Paper and Packaging Inc. [21797]
Leavenworth Paper Supply Co. [21798]
Leonard Paper Company Inc. [21799]
Leslie Paper Co. Chicago Div. [21800]
Lindenmeyer Munroe [21802]
Lindenmeyr Munroe [21808]
Lord Brothers & Higgins [21811]

Mac Papers Inc. [21816]
MacKinnon Paper Company Inc. [21818]
Macy Associates Inc. [21819]
Marquardt and Company Inc. [21823]
Matz Paper Company, Inc. [21825]
McComb Wholesale Paper Co. [21827]
McMurray Printing Co. [25733]
Mead Corp. Zellerbach Paper Co. [21830]
The Millcraft Group [21837]
Millcraft Paper Co. [21838]
Mitsui & Co. (USA), Inc. Seattle Branch [16312]
Monumental Paper Co. [21842]
Mooney General Paper Co. [21843]
New Hampshire Tobacco Corp. [26331]
Newell Paper Co. [21851]
Pacific Terminals Ltd. [4034]
Pan American Papers Inc. [21858]
Paper Center Inc. [21859]
Paper Corp. [21860]
Paper Corporation of the United States [21861]
Paper Sales Corp. [21864]
Paper Stock of Iowa [21866]
Papercraft Inc. [21204]
Parsons Paper Co.; Frank [21868]
Peek Inc.; Walter D. [21871]
Pelican Paper Products Div. [21872]
Perez Trading Company Inc. [21877]
Perkins-Goodwin Company Inc. [21878]
Peterson Paper Co. [21880]
Pierce Box & Paper Corp. [21884]
Plymouth Paper Company Inc. [21885]
Price and Pierce International Inc. [21890]
Quaker City Paper & Chemical [21891]
Quaker City Paper and Chemical [21892]
Quimby-Walstrom Paper Co. [21895]
Rainbow Paper Company, Inc. [21896]
Range Paper Corp. [21897]
Reliable Paper & Supply Company Inc. [21899]
Resource Net International [21902]
ResourceNet International (Shawnee Mission,
    Kansas) [21904]
Ris Paper Company Inc. [21906]
Riverside Paper Company Inc. [21907]
Roa Distributors [21908]
Roosevelt Paper Co. [21911]
Roto-Litho Inc. [21912]
Royal Paper Corp. [21914]
Sabin Robbins Paper Co. [21918]
Safeguard Abacus [21920]
Saxon Paper Co. [21922]
School Stationers Corp. [21925]
Scott Paper, Inc. [21928]
Seaman Paper Co.; Patrick [21930]
Seaman-Patrick Paper Co. [21931]
Select Robinson Paper Co. [21932]
Seneca Paper [21933]
Servall Products Inc. [21934]
Skyline Supply Company Inc. [21272]
Snyder Paper Corp. [21942]
Spicers Paper Inc. [21946]
Springfield Paper Specialties, Inc. [21948]
Stanford Paper Co. [21949]
Tayloe Paper Co. [21952]
Three Sixty Services Inc. [25843]
Unisorce Paper Co. [21961]
Unisource [21962]
Unisource [21963]
Unisource [21964]
Unisource [21965]
Unisource-Central Region Div. [21966]
Unisource Midwest Inc. [21967]
Unisource Worldwide Inc. [21969]
Unisource Worldwide Inc. [21970]
Unisource Worldwide Inc. Denver Div. [21971]
Unisource Worldwide Inc. West [21973]
U.S. Printing Supply Co. [25857]
United Systems Software Inc. [21978]
Universal Blueprint Paper [21979]
Universal Paper and Packaging [21982]
Ward's [25871]
Websource [21351]
West Coast Paper Co. [21988]
Westvaco Worldwide [21990]
White Rose Paper Co. [21992]
Wilcox Paper Co. [21993]
Wilson Paper Co. [21994]

Wisconsin Paper and Products Co. [21995]
WWF Paper Corp. [21998]
WWF Paper Corp. [21999]
Xpedx [22000]
xpedx [22002]
XPEDX [22003]
Xpedx/Carpenter Group [22005]
Xpedx-Carpenter Group [22006]
Xpedx/Carpenter Group [22007]
Yellowstone Paper Co. [22010]

SIC 5112 — Stationery & Office Supplies

Able Steel Equipment Co. Inc. [20765]
A.C. Supply [20767]
Acorn Distributors Inc. [21616]
Adams Printing and Stationery Co.; S.G. [20772]
Adkins Printing Company Inc. [20774]
Alabama Art Supply [20779]
Alaska Education & Recreational Products [20781]
Albert Paper Co. [21618]
Alders Wholesale; Henry [20782]
All About Offices Inc. [20783]
Allied Boise Cascade [21623]
Allied School and Office Products [20785]
Alling and Cory Co. [20786]
Allstate Office Products Inc. [20787]
Alsdorf International Ltd. [13554]
Amcraft, Inc. [20788]
American Business International Inc. [20790]
American Loose Leaf Business Products
    Inc. [20793]
American Mail-Well Co. [21628]
American Office Machines Inc. [20795]
American Paper and Twine Co. [21631]
American Renaissance Paper Corp. [21632]
Ames Supply Co. [20802]
Anchorage Reprographics Center [20804]
L'Anse Sentinel Co. [20807]
Arnold Pen Co. Inc. [20810]
Arrow Business Products Inc. [20811]
Artist Brush & Color Dist. [20814]
Atlantic Corp. [21639]
Audria's Crafts [20821]
Automated Office Products Inc. [20823]
Autron Inc. [21641]
Autron Inc. Precision Rolls Division [21642]
B & B Office Supply Inc. [20827]
B & G Export Management Associates [21644]
Balfour Printing Company Inc. [20828]
Banking Forms Supply Company Inc. [20830]
Barnaby Inc. [20831]
Barry's Office Service Inc. [20832]
Bates Manufacturing Inc. [20833]
Batliner Paper Stock Co. [21646]
Beckley-Cardy, Inc. [20838]
Bel Trade USA Corp. [22830]
Bell Paper Products Co. [21651]
Best Label Company Inc./IMS Div. [15821]
B.G. Office Products [13037]
Block and Company Inc. [20845]
Boise Cascade [20847]
Boise Cascade Corp. [27287]
Boise Cascade Office Products Corp. [20848]
Borden & Riley Paper Co. [21654]
Bottman Design Inc. [20850]
Boutique Trim [20851]
Bowlus School Supply Inc. [13042]
Bowlus School Supply Inc. [20852]
Brittain Merchandising [19201]
Brown Arts & Crafts; Stan [20860]
BSC Litho Inc. [3598]
BT Office Products USA [20862]
BT Summit Office Products Inc. [20863]
Burcham and McCune Inc. [13049]
Burgess, Anderson and Tate Inc. [13050]
Burkett's Office Supply Inc. [13051]
Buschart Office Products Inc. [20865]
Business Express of Boulder Inc. [20867]
Business Office Supply Co. [20868]
Business With Pleasure [20870]
Butler-Dearden Paper Service Inc. [21661]

Butler Paper Co. [21662]
C & P Sales Co. [26432]
Cabin-Craft Southwest [20872]
Capital Stationery Corp. [20876]
Capri Arts & Crafts [20878]
Capstone Paper Co. [21667]
Cardinal Office Systems [20880]
Carolina Office Equipment Co. [20881]
Carpenter Paper Co. [21671]
Carter Paper Co. [21672]
Carter Paper and Packaging Inc. [21673]
Cathay International [8508]
Central Office Supply Co. [20892]
Central States/Multiplex Business Forms [3623]
Champion America [25600]
Champion Industries Inc. (Huntington, West
    Virginia) [20895]
Clamyer International Corp. [21413]
Clarke and Bro. Inc.; E.H. [20902]
C.M. Paula Co. [21682]
Colonial Office Supplies Inc. [20905]
Columbia Jobbing Co. Inc. [21687]
Commercial Office Supply Inc. [20907]
Concord Technologies Inc. [6147]
Connecticut Valley Paper & Envelope Co.
    Inc. [20909]
Contemporary Office Products Inc. [20910]
Continental Craft Distributors [20911]
Continental Office Furniture and Supply
    Corp. [13080]
Cook Communications Ministries [3658]
Cook's Inc. [20913]
Copy Center Inc. [20914]
Cornelius Printed Products [21691]
Cornelius Systems Inc. [20921]
Corporate Data Products [20923]
Corporate Express [20925]
Corporate Express [20926]
Corporate Express [20927]
Corporate Express of the East Inc. [20928]
Corporate Express Inc. [20929]
Corporate Express of Northern California
    Inc. [20931]
Cosons Inc. [20933]
Cox Paper & Printing Co. [21695]
Craft & Hobby Supplies [20934]
Craft King [20935]
Craft Wholesalers [20936]
Crawfords Office Furniture & Supplies [20937]
Creative Craft Distributors [20939]
Crescent Paper Co. [21696]
Cross Co.; A.T. [20940]
Cuna Strategic Services, Inc. [20942]
C.W. Mills [20943]
Daisytek Inc. [6176]
Dale Office Plus [20944]
Darling Corp.; J.L. [21701]
Data Forms Inc. [21702]
Data Management Corp. [20950]
Data Papers Inc. [21703]
Data Print Inc. [21704]
Dealer's Discount Crafts [20952]
Decorator & Craft Corp. [20953]
Desert Stationers [20956]
Diamond Paper Corp. [21707]
Diane Ribbon Wholesale [20960]
Disc Distributing Corp. [6212]
Dittos [20968]
Dixie Art Supplies Inc. [20970]
Dixie Craft & Floral Wholesale [20971]
Doubleday Brothers and Co. [20974]
Douron Inc. [21714]
Duradex Inc. [21716]
Earthworm Inc. [20976]
Eastern Data Paper [20977]
Eaton Office Supply Company Inc. [20978]
EcoCycle Inc. [21718]
Economy Paper Company Inc. [21719]
EcoTech Recycled Products [20981]
EDM Business Interiors Inc. [20983]
Educators Resource, Inc. [20984]
EGP Inc. [20986]
Empire Paper Co. [21723]
Executive Converting Corp. [20995]
Expressive Art & Craft [20997]
F-D-C Corp. [20998]

Farner Bocken Co. [26292]
File TEC [6269]
Fineline Products, Inc. [21004]
Fisher Paper [21727]
Flower Factory [21005]
FMC Resource Management Corp. [21006]
Forms and Supplies Inc. [21007]
Fotofolio Inc. [21729]
GBS Corp. [21736]
General Business Machines Inc. [21010]
General Office Products Co. [21011]
Give Something Back Inc. [21014]
Glendale Envelope Co. [21741]
Graphic Controls [21747]
Graphic Papers Inc. [21748]
Graphic Systems Inc. (Memphis,
    Tennessee) [21019]
Hadley Office Products Inc. [21022]
Hammett Co.; J.L. [21024]
Hampton-Haddon Marketing Corp. [21025]
Harbor Packaging Inc. [21026]
Harpel's Inc. [21027]
Hathaway Paper Co. [21756]
Hearn Paper Company Inc. [21757]
Hesters/McGlaun Office Supply Co. [21031]
H.H. West Co. [21032]
Hickson's Office Supplies Co. [21033]
Highsmith Inc. [25232]
Hoeckel Co.; C.F. [21035]
Holcomb's Education Resource [21036]
Holcomb's Education Resource [21037]
Holstein Paper & Janitorial Supply [21765]
Howard Invitations and Cards [21767]
Hudson Valley Paper Co. [21770]
Humac Engineering and Equipment Inc. [7497]
Imperial Display Co. [26531]
Import Export Management Service Inc. [21054]
Industrial Paper Corp. [21773]
Industrial Wiper & Paper [21775]
Infinity Paper Inc. [21776]
Insonic Technology, Inc. [17458]
International Computer and Office Products
    Inc. [6389]
Iowa Office Supplies Inc. [21069]
Iowa Office Supply Inc. [21070]
ITM [6399]
Ives Business Forms Inc. [21073]
J-Snell & Co., Inc. [21074]
Jenkins Trading Inc. [3863]
Jewel Paula-Ronn Records [21077]
Jordan Graphics [21785]
Joyce International Inc. [21081]
K & S Tole & Craft Supply [21083]
Kalbus Office Supply [21084]
Kaneka Far West, Inc. [21085]
Kayboys Empire Paper Company Inc. [21789]
Ken's Craft Supply [21087]
Kenzacki Specialty Papers Inc. [21791]
Kern & Sons; Jacob [11604]
Keystone Office Supply Co. Inc. [21088]
Kielty and Dayton Co. [21090]
Koval Marketing Inc. [15556]
LaBelle Time Inc. [13384]
Lake County Office Equipment Inc. [21097]
Lamb's Office Products [21098]
Layton Marketing Group Inc. [21488]
Leavenworth Paper Supply Co. [21798]
Leland Paper Company Inc. [21105]
Leonard Paper Company Inc. [21799]
Leslie Paper Co. Chicago Div. [21800]
Lessco Products Inc. [21106]
Lindenmeyer Munroe [21803]
Lindenmeyer Munroe [21805]
Lindenmeyer Munroe [21806]
Lindenmeyr Munroe [21809]
Loftin Web Graphics [21810]
Los Alamos Stationers [21113]
Louisiana Office Products [21114]
Lucas Brothers Inc. [21115]
Luther's Creative Craft Studios [21116]
MacKinnon Paper Company Inc. [21818]
Majestic Penn State Inc. [21120]
The Manderscheid Co. [17013]
Mankato Business Products [21121]
Mark-Pack Inc. [21822]
Mark-Rite Distributing Corp. [21125]

Marks Paper Co. [21126]
Marks Paper Co., Inc. [21127]
Marni International [21128]
Marshall and Bruce Co. [25725]
Martin Stationers [21130]
Marysville Office Center [21133]
Matz Paper Company, Inc. [21825]
McComb Wholesale Paper Co. [21827]
McLane Western, Inc. [11835]
MDR Corp. [21136]
Media Recovery Inc. [6479]
Melo Envelope Company Inc. [21832]
Meyer Inc.; Frances [13403]
Micropoint Inc. [21141]
Midland Grocery Co. [11885]
Midwest Greeting Card Distributor [21836]
Midwest Office Furniture and Supply Company
    Inc. [21143]
Minnesota Mining & Manufacturing Co. [21147]
Modern Business Machines Inc. [21149]
Monumental Paper Co. [21842]
Mooney General Paper Co. [21843]
Nadel and Sons Toy Corp. [26588]
Nasco West [18955]
Nashua Corp. [21155]
Nebraska Book Company Inc. [3991]
Newell Office Products [21163]
Newell P.R. Ltd. [15594]
Nice Computer Inc. [6553]
Northway Acres Craft Supply [21165]
Northway Acres Craft Supply [21166]
Northwest Blueprint and Supply [13413]
O Henry Inc. [21168]
O'Connor and Raque Office Products Co. [21170]
Office America Inc. [21171]
Office Depot Inc. [21173]
Office Depot Inc. Business Services Div. [21174]
Office Equipment Sales [21177]
Office Express [21180]
Office Machine & Furniture Inc. [21183]
Office Stop Inc. [21188]
Office Systems Co. [21190]
OffiSource [21194]
Okhai-Moyer Inc. [21198]
Opler Sales Company Inc.; Jack [21854]
Pacific Interface [6580]
Pan American Papers Inc. [21858]
Paper Corp. [21860]
Paper Mart [21862]
Paper Sales Corp. [21864]
Papercraft Inc. [21204]
Paperwork Products Co. [21205]
Paramount Sales Co. [14188]
Parsons Paper Co.; Frank [21868]
Patrick and Co. [21869]
Pence International, Inc. [5273]
Perkins Stationery [21209]
Peters Office Equipment [21210]
Petersen-Arne [21211]
Peterson Business Systems Inc. [21212]
Peterson Paper Co. [21880]
Petter Supply Co.; Henry A. [17103]
Pierce Box & Paper Corp. [21884]
Pilot Corporation of America [21215]
Pioneer Photo Albums Inc. [13421]
Plus Corporation of America [21217]
Plymouth Paper Company Inc. [21885]
PMC of Indiana [21218]
Precept Business Products Inc. [21221]
Precise Industries, Inc. [21222]
Price Modern Inc. [13212]
Pro Form and File [21223]
Publix Office Supplies, Inc. [21225]
Purchasing Support Services [21226]
Quality Art [21227]
Quality Business Forms Inc. [21228]
Quality First Greetings Corp. [21894]
Rainbow Paper Company, Inc. [21896]
Range Paper Corp. [21897]
Rangel Distributing Co. [5733]
R.E.I. Glitter [21236]
Reliable Paper & Supply Company Inc. [21899]
Reliance Group of Michigan [21900]
Renick and Company Inc. [6687]
Rheas Crafts [21238]
Richards Co.; S.P. [21241]

Richards Co.; S.P. [21242]
Richmond Office Supply [21243]
Rieger's Ceramics Arts & Crafts [26635]
Riverside Paper Company Inc. [21907]
Roatan International Corporation [21244]
Robinson's Woods [21245]
Roto-Litho Inc. [21912]
Royce, Inc. [21250]
S and G Trading Co. [26643]
Safeguard International, Inc. [24621]
Safina Office Products [21255]
St. Louis Business Forms Inc. [21256]
Sanrio Inc. [13442]
Savage Universal Corp. [22902]
School Specialties Inc. [13233]
School Stationers Inc. [21925]
Schwarz Paper Co. [21260]
Seaman Paper Co.; Patrick [21930]
Second City Systems Inc. [21263]
Servall Products Inc. [21934]
Servco Pacific Inc. [3205]
Service Office Supply Corp. [21265]
Service Packaging Corp. [21935]
Shachihata Incorporated USA [21266]
Sherman Business Forms, Inc. [21937]
Sherman Business Forms Inc. [21267]
Shipman Printing Industries Inc. [21938]
Silvers Inc. [13242]
Singing Poppe's, Inc. [21270]
Source Management Inc. [21274]
Southern Business Systems Inc. [21276]
Southern Distributors Inc. [15662]
Splash Technology Inc. [21283]
The Standard Register Co [21285]
Stanford Paper Co. [21949]
Staples Business Advantage [21287]
Staples Business Advantage [21288]
Staples Business Advantage [21289]
Staples Office Products Inc. [21290]
Staples, The Office Superstore Inc. [21291]
Star Beacon Products Co. [25830]
Stationers' Corporation of Hawaii Ltd. [21294]
Stationers Inc. (Huntington, West Virginia) [21295]
Stationers Inc. (Indianapolis, Indiana) [21296]
Steinhardt & Hanson, Inc. [21298]
Stewart Co.; Douglas [6761]
Story Wright Printing [21299]
Style Asia Inc. [13454]
Sufrin Inc.; Adolph [21302]
Summervilles Inc. [21304]
SupplySource Inc. [21306]
Swanson, Inc. [21308]
SWM Inc. [21951]
Tab of Northern New England [21314]
TAB Products Co. [13254]
Target Distributing Co. [25471]
Thomas Nelson Inc. [13463]
Thompson Office Equipment Company Inc. [21318]
Time Out For Sports [5430]
Total Office Interiors [21954]
Trails West Publishing [21956]
Tri-Quality Business Forms Inc. [21322]
Trick and Murray Inc. [21323]
Unisource [21962]
Unisource [21963]
Unisource [21965]
United Envelope Co. [21975]
U.S. Office Products Co. [21329]
U.S. Printing Supply Co. [25857]
U.S. Ring Binder Corp. [21330]
United Stationers Inc. [21977]
Universal Forms, Labels, and Systems, Inc. [21980]
Universal Paper Goods Co. [21981]
University Products, Inc. [25493]
Unnex Industrial Corp. [5455]
US Office Products, Midwest District Inc. [21331]
Variety Distributors Inc. [21336]
Viking Office Products Inc. [21339]
Wang's International, Inc. [21345]
Wang's International, Inc. [21346]
Ward Thompson Paper Inc. [21347]
Weil Inc.; Cliff [21352]
Weil and Sons, Inc.; Joseph [21986]
Wescosa Inc. [21353]

Western Printing Co. [21989]
Wills Co. [13474]
Wilson Paper Co. [21994]
Wolcotts Forms Inc. [21996]
Woodmansee Inc. [21361]
World Traders (USA) Inc. [9607]
Wyoming Stationery Company of Casper [21364]
Xpedx/Carpenter Group [22005]
xpedx West Region [22008]
Yankton Office Equipment [21366]
Yarn Tree Designs [26253]
Yasutomo and Company Inc. [22009]
Yorktown Industries Inc. [21367]
Yost Office Systems, Inc. [21368]
Young Journal Inc.; Richard [6888]
Zakion; Robert [21369]
Zebra Pen Corp. [21370]

SIC 5113 — Industrial & Personal Service Paper

ABC Coffee Co. [10319]
Ace Advance Paper Co. [21614]
Acme Paper and Supply Company Inc. [21615]
Acorn Distributors Inc. [21616]
Acorn Paper Products Co [16670]
Aetna Felt Corp. Mechanical Felt and Textile Div. [25954]
Alabama Institutional Foods Inc. [10352]
Albert Paper Co. [21618]
Albright Paper & Box Corp. [21619]
Aldelano Corp. [4567]
Aldine Technologies Industries, Inc. [21621]
Alles Corp. [21622]
Allied Box Co. [21624]
Allied Box Co. [16686]
Allied Container Corp. [21625]
Alling and Cory Co. [20786]
American Excelsior Co. [14316]
American Fibre Supplies, Inc. [21627]
American Paper Products Co. [21629]
American Paper Towel Co. [21630]
American Paper and Twine Co. [21631]
Anchor Paper Co. [21633]
Andrews Paper and Chemical Co. [4323]
Andrews Paper House of York Inc. [21634]
Anle Paper Company Inc. [16699]
Archer Company Inc.; A.W. [21635]
Aries Paper & Chemical Co. Inc. [4574]
Asbury Syrup and Paper Company Inc. [21636]
Associated Packaging Inc. [16714]
Atlanta Broom Company Inc. [21638]
Atlanta Broom Company Inc. [16715]
Atlantic Corp. [21639]
Atlantic Corp. [16716]
Atlantic Paper & Twine Co. Inc. [21640]
Autron Inc. [21641]
Autron Inc. Precision Rolls Division [21642]
Avico Distributing Inc. [10475]
B and B Paper Converters Inc. [21643]
B & G Export Management Associates [21644]
Bacon Material Handling; Davis [25889]
Badalament Inc. [10484]
Batliner Paper Stock Co. [21646]
Baumann Paper Company Inc. [21647]
Bay Area Data Supply Inc. [20835]
Bay Paper Co. Inc. [20837]
Beaverhead Bar Supply Inc. [1512]
Beck Packaging Corp. [21649]
Beck Packaging Corp. [16744]
Beisler Weidmann Company Inc. [21650]
Bell Paper Products Co. [21651]
Ben-Mar Paper Co. Inc. [21652]
Berg Bag Co. [25891]
Berg Bag Co. [16750]
Berlin Packaging Inc. [25893]
Berry Company Inc.; H.T. [21653]
Best-Klean Products [4578]
Big Horn Wholesale [4580]
Bockstanz Brothers Co. [4586]
Boise Cascade Office Products Corp. [20848]
Bonita Pioneer Packaging Prods [16755]
Borden & Riley Paper Co. [21654]

The Box Maker [21655]
Boyd-Bluford Co. Inc. [10602]
Bro Tex Company Inc., Wiping Cloth Div. [21657]
Bro Tex Company Inc., Wiping Cloth Div. [16767]
Bunn Capitol Co. [10643]
Bunzl Distribution Inc. [21658]
Bunzl New Jersey Inc. [21659]
Butler-Dearden Paper Service Inc. [21661]
Butler Paper Co. [21662]
C-N Corrugated and Sheeting Inc. [21663]
Cady Industries Inc. [21664]
Callahan Grocery Co. Inc. [10679]
Calpine Containers Inc. [25897]
Camden Bag and Paper Company, Inc. [21665]
Cameo Paper & Janitor Supply Co. [4592]
Canusa Corp. [26777]
Cariba International Corp. [10700]
Carlson Systems Corp. [13620]
Carolina Retail Packaging Inc. [21670]
Carter Paper Co. [21672]
Carter Paper and Packaging Inc. [21673]
Casey's General Stores Inc. [10709]
Cash Wholesale Candy Co. [10712]
Central National-Gottesman Inc. [21675]
Central Paper Products Co. Inc. [21676]
Centre Jobbing Co. [26275]
Century Papers Inc. [4596]
CGF Cash & Carry [10731]
Chemed Corp. [4597]
Chemicraft Corp. [20897]
Chris Cam Corp. [21678]
Cincinnati Cordage and Paper Co. [21679]
Clamyer International Corp. [21413]
Clark Food Service Inc. South Bend Div. [24094]
Clean Green Packing Company of Minnesota [25903]
Coast Paper Box Co. [21683]
Cocoa Brevard Paper Co. [21684]
Coeur d'Alene Cash & Carry [10785]
Colony Papers Inc. [21686]
Commerce Packaging Corp. [21688]
ComSource Independent Foodservice Companies Inc. [10803]
Concord Sales Co. [26278]
Conley Company Inc.; M. [21689]
Convermat Corp. [21690]
Cottingham Paper Co. [21694]
Cougle Commission Co. [10853]
Cox Paper & Printing Co. [21695]
Crescent Paper Co. [21696]
Crest Paper Products Inc. [21697]
Crisci Food Equipment Co. [24097]
Crown Products Co. [21698]
Cullen Distributors Inc. [26284]
C.W. Mills [10943]
Dacotah Paper Co. [21699]
Dacotah Paper Co. [16819]
Damon Industries, Inc. [4609]
Danforth International Trade Associates, Inc. [21700]
Darter Inc. [4610]
DeHater [21705]
Des Moines Marketing Associates [10947]
Design Impressions Inc. [21427]
Diamond Chemical/Supply Co. [4372]
Dibs Chemical & Supply Co. Inc. [21708]
Dillard Paper Co. Birmingham Div. [21709]
Dillard Paper Co. Chattanooga Div. [21710]
Dillard Paper Co. Knoxville Div. [21711]
Dillard Paper Co. Macon Div. [21712]
Don and Co.; Edward [15478]
Doughtie's Foods Inc. [10984]
The Dowd Co. [21715]
Earth Care Paper Inc. [26800]
Eberle Sons Co.; C. [11019]
EcoCycle Inc. [21718]
Economy Foods [11023]
Economy Paper Company Inc. [21719]
Economy Paper Company Inc. [16845]
Edmer Sanitary Supply Co. Inc. [4617]
Eisenberg Brothers Inc. [21720]
Elgin Paper Co. [21721]
Empire Paper Co. [21723]
Ernest Paper Products [21724]
Executive Converting Corp. [20995]
F & A Food Sales Inc. [11067]

Fargo-Moorhead Jobbing Co. [11082]
Fidelity Paper Supply Inc. [21725]
Fisher Paper [21727]
Fleetwood Paper Co. [21728]
Food Services of America [11178]
Forman Inc. [4626]
Forman Inc. [16873]
Franklin Cigar and Tobacco Company Inc. [26296]
Freedman and Sons Inc.; S. [21730]
Freund Can Co. [25916]
Friedman Bag Company Inc. [16880]
Fuller Paper Company Inc. [21731]
Fulton Paper Co. [21732]
Fulton Paper Co. [21733]
Fulton Paper Company Inc. [21734]
G & O Paper & Supplies [21735]
Gem State Paper and Supply Co. [21737]
General Supply and Paper Co. [21738]
George Co., Inc.; William [11254]
Georgia-Pacific Corp. Distribution Div. [7394]
Gibbons Inc.; J.T. [11262]
Gibson Co.; C.R. [13360]
Gibson Group Inc. [21739]
GKR Industries, Inc. [21740]
Glover Wholesale Inc. [11277]
Golden State Containers Inc. [25918]
Goldman Paper Co.; G.B. [21743]
Graphic Controls [21747]
Graphic Papers Inc. [21748]
Gray's Wholesale Inc. [26300]
Great Bay Paper Co. [21749]
Great Falls Paper Co. [21750]
Great Falls Paper Co. [16905]
Great Scott Services Ltd. [21751]
Great Southern Industries Inc. [21752]
Griffin Container and Supply Co. [21753]
H & M Distributing Inc. [26301]
Hadley Braithwait Co. [11357]
Halsey Company Inc.; W.L. [11367]
Harder Paper and Packaging Inc. [21755]
Hardlines Marketing Inc. [13735]
Harris Corp.; Dub [21028]
Harvin Foods Inc. [11389]
Hathaway Paper Co. [21756]
Hawaiian Distributor Ltd. [11393]
Hearn Paper Company Inc. [21757]
Heritage Paper Company Inc. [21759]
Hettinger-Mobridge Candy & Tobacco [26306]
Hill City Wholesale Company Inc. [21760]
Holiday Wholesale Inc. [26308]
Hollinger Corp. [21764]
Holstein Paper & Janitorial Supply [21765]
Holt Distributors, Inc. [21766]
Howard Sales Inc. [21768]
Hudson Paper Co. [21769]
Hudson Valley Paper Co. [21770]
Huff Paper Co. [21771]
Huntsville/Redstone Paper Co. [21772]
Huntsville/Redstone Paper Co. [16936]
Indiana Concession Supply Inc. [11504]
Industrial Paper Corp. [21773]
Industrial Paper & Plastic Products Company
    Inc. [21774]
Industrial Wiper & Paper [21775]
Ingram Paper Co. [21777]
International Forest Products Corp. [21779]
International Tape Products Co. [21065]
Jackson Paper Company Inc. [21781]
Jacob and Sons; M. [25921]
Jacobi-Lewis Co. [24148]
James River Corporation of Connecticut [21782]
JC Paper [21783]
Jerome Distribution Inc. [1781]
Joiner Foodservice, Inc. [21784]
Joseph Orchard Siding Inc.; George F. [21786]
Judd Paper Co. [21787]
Kaiser Wholesale Inc. [26315]
Katz Paper, Foil & Cordage Corp. [21788]
Kayboys Empire Paper Company Inc. [21789]
Kenzacki Specialty Papers Inc. [21791]
Key Sales Inc. [24157]
Kings Food Service Professionals Inc.; J. [11618]
Koplik and Sons Inc.; Perry H. [26868]
Korol Co.; Leon [21793]
Kozak Distributors [21794]
Kruger Recycling Inc. [26873]

L and L Concession Co. [11658]
La Boiteaux Co. [21795]
Landsberg Co.; Kent H. [21796]
LaSalle Paper and Packaging Inc. [21797]
Leavenworth Paper Supply Co. [21798]
Ledyard Company Inc. [24164]
Leland Paper Company Inc. [21105]
Leon Supply Company, Inc. [11699]
Leonard Paper Company Inc. [21799]
Leone Food Service Corp. [11702]
Levis Paper Company Inc.; J.J. [21801]
Lindenmeyer Munroe [21804]
Lindenmeyer Munroe [21807]
Lindenmeyr Munroe [21808]
Lindenmeyr Munroe [21809]
Logan Inc. [11722]
Lorel Co. [21812]
Los Angeles Carton Co. [21813]
Lotz Paper and Fixture Co.; F.W. [21814]
M & M Chemical Supply Inc. [4661]
M and R International Inc. [21815]
Mack-Chicago Corp. [21817]
Malone Products Inc. [11768]
Mansfield Bag & Paper Company Inc. [21820]
Mansfield Paper Company Inc. [21821]
Mark-Pack Inc. [21822]
Marshall Co.; A.J. [4663]
Martin Bros. Distributing Co., Inc. [11793]
Martin-Brower Co. [11794]
Massena Paper Company Inc. [21824]
Matz Paper Company, Inc. [21825]
Mayer Myers Paper Co. [21826]
McComb Wholesale Paper Co. [21827]
McComb Wholesale Paper Co. [17020]
McConnell and Sons Inc.; F. [11820]
McMahon Paper Company Inc. [21829]
Mead Corp. Zellerbach Paper Co. [21830]
Mead Pulp Sales Inc. [21831]
Michigan Retail Packaging [21834]
Mid City Hardware [4669]
Mid States Paper/Notion Co. [14161]
Mid-West Paper Products Co. [21835]
Midland Iron and Steel Co. [26913]
Milhem & Brothers; Attea [26329]
Miller Sales Co.; Simon [21839]
Monahan Paper Co. [21841]
Monahan Paper Co. [17047]
Monsour's Inc. [11926]
Monumental Paper Co. [21842]
Mooney General Paper Co. [21843]
Mooney General Paper Co. [17049]
Moore, Inc.; A.E. [4673]
Morse Wholesale Paper Company Inc. [21844]
Mound City Industries Inc. [11940]
Mt. Ellis Paper Company Inc. [21845]
Mt. Ellis Paper Company Inc. [17058]
Mutual Distributors Inc. [11961]
Mutual Wholesale Co. [11963]
Mutual Wholesale Co. [11964]
Nagel Paper & Box Co. [21846]
Nation Wide Paper Co. [21847]
Nationwide Papers Div. [21848]
Neece Paper Company Inc. [21849]
Nelson Company Inc.; Walter E. [4676]
New England Industrial Supply Company
    Inc. [21850]
Newell Paper Co. [21851]
Newells Bar & Restaurant Supply, Inc. [24192]
NM Bakery Service Co. [12010]
Norris Co.; Garland C. [21852]
Norris Co.; Garland C. [17076]
Northwest Arkansas Paper Co. [4677]
Notini and Sons Inc.; Albert H. [26335]
NSC International [21167]
Oak Paper Products Company Inc. [21853]
Orange Distributors Inc. [21855]
Pacific Packaging Products Inc. [21856]
PAMSCO Inc. [4682]
Paper Mart [21862]
Paper Products Company Inc. [21863]
Paper Sales Corp. [21864]
Paper Service Company Inc. [21865]
Paper Supply Co. [4683]
Paragon Packaging Products Inc. [21867]
Parkway Food Service Inc. [12117]
Patterson Sales Associates [21870]

Patterson Sales Associates [17101]
Penachio Company Inc.; Nick [12135]
Peninsular Paper Company Inc. [21873]
Penmar Industries Inc. [21874]
Penn-Jersey Paper Co. [21875]
Pennsylvania Paper & Supply Co. [21876]
Perkins-Goodwin Company Inc. [21878]
Permalin Products Co. [21879]
Peterson Paper Co. [21880]
Peyton's [21881]
Piedmont National Corp. [21882]
Piedmont Paper Company Inc. [21883]
Pierce Box & Paper Corp. [21884]
Pizza Needs of Memphis Inc. [12179]
Pollock Paper Distributors [21886]
Pomerantz Diversified Services Inc. [21887]
Poritzky's Wholesale Meats and Food
    Services [12195]
Posner Sons Inc.; S. [21888]
Powell Company Inc.; W.J. [12200]
Prairie Farms Dairy Supply Inc. [24205]
Presto Paper Company Inc. [21889]
Products Corp. of North America, Inc. [12226]
Professional Marketers Inc. [12228]
Quaker City Paper Co. [21893]
Quaker City Paper Co. [17124]
Quality Foods Inc. [12250]
Rainbow Paper Company, Inc. [21896]
Range Paper Corp. [21897]
Reed Distributors [4692]
Regal Supply & Chemical Co. [21898]
Reliable Paper & Supply Company Inc. [21899]
Reliance Paper Co. [21901]
Resource Net International [21903]
ResourceNet International (Shawnee Mission,
    Kansas) [21904]
Retailers Supply Co. [21905]
Riverside Paper Company Inc. [21907]
Roberts Paper Co. [21909]
Rome Paper Co. [21910]
Rose Products and Services Inc. [4699]
Roselli's Wholesale Foods Inc. [12353]
Royal Industries [21913]
Runge Paper Co., Inc. [21915]
Rykoff & Co.; S.E. [12374]
Rykoff & Co.; S.E. [21916]
S and S Inc. [21917]
Sacks International Inc.; M. [24293]
St. Louis Paper and Box Co. [21921]
St. Louis Paper and Box Co. [17157]
San Joaquin Supply Company Inc. [4702]
Sangamon Co. [13440]
Saxon Paper Co. [21922]
Schilling Paper Co. [21923]
Schinner Co.; A.D. [21924]
Schnaible Service and Supply Company
    Inc. [4704]
Schorin Company Inc. [21926]
Schrafel Paper Corp.; A.J. [21927]
Schwarz Paper Co. [21260]
Scott Paper, Inc. [21928]
Scrivner of North Carolina Inc. [12439]
Sealed Air Corp. [21929]
Seaman Paper Co.; Patrick [21930]
Select Robinson Paper Co. [21932]
Seneca Paper [21933]
Servall Products Inc. [21934]
Seventh Generation, Inc. [21936]
Seybold Co. [4706]
Shaheen Brothers Inc. [12468]
Shipman Printing Industries Inc. [21938]
Shippers Supply Corp. [4707]
Shorr Paper Products Inc. [21941]
Smart & Final Foodservice [12505]
Smith & Sons Co.; Dale T. [12516]
Snyder Wholesale Inc. [12524]
Sofco-Mead Inc. [12525]
Southeastern Paper Group [21943]
Southwest Paper Company Inc. [21944]
Specialty Box and Packaging Co. [21945]
Springfield Paper Co. [21947]
Springfield Paper Specialties, Inc. [21948]
Stanford Paper Co. [21949]
Stanz Cheese Company Inc. [12568]
StarchTech Inc. [25940]
Stark Co. [21950]

Stark Co. [17196]
Staunton Food Inc. [12579]
Stomel and Sons; Joseph H. [12589]
Stretch and Sew Inc. [26216]
Sullivan Candy & Supply [26354]
Sunfire Corporation [12610]
Sunflower Restaurant Supply [12611]
Superior Linen Company Inc. [15673]
SWD Corp. [26355]
SYSCO Food Service, Inc. [12670]
SYSCO Food Services [12673]
Tapesolutions [25943]
Tayloe Paper Co. [21952]
Taylor Rental Corp. [1316]
Thayer Inc. [4716]
Todd-Zenner Packaging [21953]
Trade Supplies [21955]
Tucker Company Inc.; M. [24250]
Tyco Adhesives [21957]
Unger Co. [21958]
Unijax Div. [21959]
Union Paper Company Div. [21960]
Union Paper Company Inc. [17241]
Unisource [21962]
Unisource [21964]
Unisource [21965]
Unisource [4720]
Unisource-Central Region Div. [21966]
Unisource International [21325]
Unisource Worldwide [21968]
Unisource Worldwide Inc. [21970]
Unisource Worldwide Inc. Denver Div. [21971]
Unisource Worldwide Inc. (Southborough,
    Massachusetts) [21972]
United Container Corp. [21974]
United Packaging Corp. [23045]
United Paper Company Inc. [21976]
United Paper Company Inc. [17242]
Universal Paper Goods Co. [21981]
Universal Paper and Packaging [21982]
Valley Wholesalers Inc. [21983]
Van Paper Co. [21984]
Victory Packaging [21985]
Volunteer Janitorial Supply Co. [24036]
Watson Inc.; Fannie [13470]
Weil and Co.; J. [12897]
Weil and Sons, Inc.; Joseph [21986]
Werts Novelty Co. [21987]
West Coast Paper Co. [21988]
Western Facilities Supply, Inc. [4730]
White River Paper Company Inc. [21991]
White River Paper Company Inc. [17278]
White Swan, Inc. [12930]
Wholesale Supply Company Inc. [26372]
Wilcox Paper Co. [21993]
Wills Co. [13474]
Wilson Paper Co. [21994]
Wisconsin Paper and Products Co. [21995]
Wurzburg Inc. [21997]
Xpedx [22000]
Xpedx [22001]
XPEDX [22003]
xpedx [22004]
Xpedx [17290]
Yamada Distributors Ltd.; K. [25949]
York Tape and Label Co. [22011]
Zellerbach Co. [22012]
Ziff Co. [17296]

SIC 5122 — Drugs, Proprietaries & Sundries

78ic Beauty Supply & Salons [14006]
Aanns Trading Co. [4309]
Abana Pharmaceuticals Inc. [19118]
Abbaco Inc. [10317]
Abbey Medical Inc. [19120]
Accurate Chemical and Scientific Corp. [4312]
Acme Agri Supply Inc. [27056]
AcryMed Inc. [19123]
Action Laboratories Inc. [14008]
Action Laboratories Inc. [19124]
Aerobic Life Industries Inc. [14010]

Affiliated Foods Inc. [10336]
Agora Cosmetics Inc. [14011]
Airgas Intermountain [16680]
Akin Medical Equipment International [19128]
Akorn Inc. [19130]
Albers Inc. [19132]
Alberto-Culver International Inc. [14012]
Alcide Corp. [19133]
All City Barber & Beauty Supply [14013]
Allen's Supply Co. [223]
Allou Distributors Inc. [14014]
Allou Health and Beauty Care Inc. [14015]
Alma's Glow Products International [14016]
ALR Wholesale [27062]
Amber Grout Sales [27063]
AMCON Distributing Co. [10392]
American Comb Corp. [14018]
American Ex-Im Corp. [14019]
American Health Supplies [19140]
American Medical Industries [19141]
American Medserve Corp. [19143]
American Paper Towel Co. [21630]
AmeriNet/SupportHealth [19146]
AmeriSource Corp. [19147]
AmeriSource Corp. Orlando Div. [19148]
AmeriSource Corp. (Paducah, Kentucky) [19149]
AmeriSource Health Corp. [19150]
AmeriSource-Lynchburg Div. [19151]
Ammar Beauty Supply Co. [14020]
Amrion Inc. [14021]
Anda Generics Inc. [19152]
Anderson Wholesale Co. [14022]
Animal Medic Inc. [27067]
Apotheca Inc. [19155]
Applied Genetics Inc. [14023]
Aquajogger [23521]
Arco Pharmaceuticals Inc. [19158]
Argos Enterprises [14024]
Ark Manufacturing Inc. [27074]
Armstrong McCall [14025]
Arnold's Inc. [14026]
Associated Grocers of Florida Inc. [10449]
Aungst Wholesale; Dan [26402]
Auromere Inc. [14027]
Austin House Inc. [14028]
Avatex Corp. [19170]
Avon Products Inc. Newark Regional Area [14030]
Avon Products Inc. Northeast Regional
    Area [19172]
Award Pet Supply [27077]
Awareness and Health Unlimited [14031]
B Sharp Co. [27078]
Baddour International [14034]
Baker Agri Sales Inc. [17718]
Barnes Wholesale Drug Company Inc. [19174]
Baxter International Inc. (Deerfield, Illinois) [19177]
Beauty & Beauty Enterprises, Inc. [14037]
Beauty and Beauty Enterprises Inc. [19179]
Beehive Botanicals Inc. [19181]
Belcam Inc. [14038]
Bennett's Pet Center [27080]
Bergen Brunswig Corp. [19183]
Bergen Brunswig Corp. [19184]
Best Beauty Supply Co. [14039]
Billings Horn [14040]
Bindley Western [14041]
Bindley Western Drug Co. [14042]
Bindley Western Drug Co. [14043]
Bindley Western Drug Co. Dallas Div. [14044]
Bindley Western Drug Co. Mid-South Div. [14045]
Bindley Western Drug Co. Southeastern
    Div. [14046]
Bindley Western Industries Inc. [14047]
Bindley Western Industries Inc. [19187]
Bindley Western Industries Inc. Bindley Western
    Drug Div. [14048]
Bindley Western Industries Inc. Kendall
    Div. [19188]
Biopractic Group II Inc. [14049]
Blankinship Distributors Inc. [14050]
Blankinship Distributors Inc. [19193]
Blistex Inc. [14051]
Bloodline Agency [27085]
Blooming Prairie Natural Foods [10571]
Bock Pharmaceutical, Inc.; James A. [19196]
Bottenfield's Inc. [14052]

Bradley Pharmaceuticals Inc. [19197]
Breeders Edge [27092]
Brittain Merchandising [19201]
Brudnick Company Inc.; James [19203]
Brulin and Co. Inc. [4590]
BTE Import-Export [19204]
Burkmann Feed [27093]
Burkmann Feeds—Glasgow [27094]
Burkmann Feeds—London [27095]
Burkmann Mills [27096]
Butler Co.; W.A. [19206]
Buttrey Food & Drug [19207]
Buy_Low Beauty Supply [14053]
Cache Beauty Supply Inc. [14054]
Cajun Sales [27098]
Caltag Lab [19209]
Capps Beauty & Barber Inc. [14055]
Capstone Pharmacy Services [19211]
Caravan Trading Corporation [4342]
Cardinal Health-Behrens Inc. [14056]
Cardinal Health Inc. [19212]
Carewell Industries, Inc. [14057]
Cariba International Corp. [10700]
Carnrick Laboratories Inc. [19218]
Carolina Vet Supply [27102]
Casey's General Stores Inc. [10709]
Celestial Mercantile Corporation [14059]
Celestial Mercantile Corporation [19222]
Cellulite Products Inc. [14060]
Charter Pet Supplies [27108]
Chemapol USA Inc. [4350]
Chemins Company Inc. [19228]
Children's Art Corp. [14062]
Children's Art Corp. [19229]
Cinema Secrets Inc. [14063]
Clarins USA Inc. [14064]
Classic Fragrances Ltd. [14066]
Clear Eye [10767]
Clintec Nutrition Co. [19236]
Color Me Beautiful Inc. [14068]
Colorado Serum Co. [19240]
Colorcon [20906]
Colossal Jewelry and Accessories Inc. [17374]
Columbia Beauty Supply Co. [14069]
Columbus Serum Co. [27110]
Compar Inc. [14070]
Compass Foods Eight O'Clock Coffee [10802]
Congress Leather Co. [27111]
Conney Safety Products Co. [24527]
Consolidated Midland Corp. [14071]
The Consulting Scientists [19245]
Core-Mark International Inc. [10840]
Cornucopia Natural Foods Inc. [14072]
Corr-Williams Wholesale Company Inc. [26282]
Corso Inc.; Frank P. [26283]
Cosmetic Marketing Group [14073]
Cosmopolitan Trading Co. [14074]
Cost-U-Less [10847]
Costco Companies, Inc. [10850]
Cramer Products, Inc. [19255]
D & K Healthcare Resources, Inc. [19269]
D & K Wholesale Drug, Inc. [19270]
Daiichi Fine Chemicals Inc. [14077]
Dakota Drug Inc. [14078]
Daniels Co.; C.P. [27114]
Davidson & Associates; Art [14079]
Davis and Sons Inc.; F.A. [26286]
Davis Wholesale Co. Inc.; Al [14080]
Debra Inc. [14081]
Deodorant Stones of America [14082]
Derma Sciences Inc. [19277]
Diamond Products Co. [14084]
The Dipper [14085]
Dodge Company Inc. [25634]
Dohmen Co./Anoka; The F. [19287]
Dohmen Co.; F. [14086]
Dolphin Acquisition Corp. [14087]
Donico & Associates; J.P. [18778]
Drogueria Betances [19290]
Drogueria J.M. Blanco [19291]
Drug Center, Inc. [19292]
Drug Guild Distributors Inc. [15116]
DuCoa [20536]
Durr-Fillauer Medical Inc. [18781]
E-Y Laboratories Inc. [19299]
Eastern Atlantic Company Inc. [14089]

Eastern Pharmaceuticals [14090]
Eberly Inc.; John A. [13674]
Eby-Brown Company L.P. [26289]
Economy Cash and Carry Inc. [11022]
Edcat Enterprises [19303]
Edco Manufacturing Co. [27123]
Edlis Inc. [14091]
Edom Laboratories Inc. [14092]
Ed's Leather Co. [27124]
Efland Distributing Co. [27126]
Elchar Dog Bows [27127]
Elite Supply Co. [14093]
Elk River Trading Co. [14094]
Empire Equities Inc. [19304]
En Garde Health Products Inc. [14095]
Eon Labs Manufacturing, Inc. [19306]
Escada Beaute Ltd. [14096]
Eugene Trading Inc. [14098]
Experimental Applied Sciences [19312]
Express International Corp. [19313]
F and M Distributors Inc. [19319]
Famous Mart Inc. [4945]
Far-Vet Supply Co. [19322]
Farn Ltd.; Gary [14099]
Fine-Line Products Inc. [4953]
Five Continent Enterprise Inc., PMB 4022 [14101]
Fmali Inc. [11165]
Food For Health [14102]
Food Marketing Corp. [11174]
Foreign Trade Marketing [11187]
Fortune Personnel Consultants of Springfield
    Inc. [19327]
FoxMeyer Drug Co. [19328]
FoxMeyer Drug Co. Carol Stream Div. [19329]
FoxMeyer Drug Co. Slidell Div. [14103]
Fragrance International Inc. [14104]
Freeda Vitamins Inc. [14105]
French Transit Ltd. [14106]
Frontier Co-op Herbs [11220]
Fuller Supply Co. [27136]
Fuller Supply Co., Inc. [27137]
Fuller Supply Company Inc. [27138]
Gallard-Schlesinger Industries Inc. [4396]
Garber Brothers Inc. [11232]
Garner Wholesale Merchandisers Inc. [14108]
Gateway Foods Inc. [11242]
Gemini Cosmetics [14109]
Gemini Cosmetics [19335]
Gemmex Intertrade America Inc. [11247]
General Drug Co. [19336]
General Merchandise Services Inc. [14110]
General Trading Company Inc. [11252]
Generic Distributors L.P. [19338]
Geriatric Medical & Surgical [18811]
Geviderm Inc. [14111]
Gibbons Inc.; J.T. [11262]
Ginseng Co. [14112]
Girindus Corp. [4399]
GMR Division MNH [14113]
Golden Crown Corp. [27139]
Golden Neo-Life Diamite International [14114]
Golden Pride International [11286]
Golden State Medical Supply Inc. [19341]
Grace Inc.; V.F. [14115]
Graeffs Eastside Drugs; Mike [18814]
Great Western Pet Supply [27141]
Greeff Company Inc.; R.W. [19342]
Greene Rubber Company Inc. [24279]
Greenville Health Corp. [18816]
Greenwich Trading Co. [18511]
Gregory Inc.; E.Z. [14116]
GSK Products Inc. [14118]
Guarnieri Co.; Albert [21754]
Gulf Marine and Industrial Supplies [11346]
H & H Beauty & Barber Supply [14119]
Happy Acres Pet Supply [27144]
Harf Inc. [25674]
Harmony Enterprises America [18825]
Harrison Wholesale Products Inc. [27145]
Havice Inc.; James F. [14121]
Hawaiian Housewares, Ltd. [15521]
HCI Great Lakes Region [4413]
Health Food Distributors [14122]
Health Services Corporation of America [19354]
HealthComm International Inc. [14123]
HealthStyles, Inc. [19355]

Helen of Troy Ltd. [14124]
Helen of Troy Texas Corp. [14125]
HemaCare Corp. [19357]
Hess Hair Milk Laboratories Inc. [25678]
Hi-Fashion Cosmetics Inc. [14126]
Horizons Marketing Group Inc. [4635]
HPF L.L.C. [14127]
Hsu's Ginseng Enterprises Inc. [11469]
Humco Holding Group Inc. [4422]
IDE-Interstate Inc. [14129]
Imperial Distributors Inc. [14130]
Imperial Pet Products [27156]
Independent Drug Co. [19368]
Independent Pet Co-op [27157]
Indiana Botanic Gardens [11503]
Infolab Inc. [19371]
Inmed Corp. [18852]
Inter-American Trading [25689]
Interdonati, Inc.; H. [19375]
Interior Design Nutritionals [14131]
Intermountain Scientific Corp. [24374]
International Diagnostic Systems Corp. [18856]
International Organic Products Inc. [14132]
Iowa Veterinary Supply Co. [27158]
IQ Holdings Inc. [14133]
IQ Products Co. [2798]
Island Style [23749]
ITG Laboratories Inc. [19381]
I.V. Therapy Associates [19382]
Japco Exports [27159]
Jaydon Inc. [14134]
Jay's Perfume Bar [14135]
J.D. Products [14136]
Jeffers Vet Supply [27161]
Jeffers Vet Supply [27162]
JM Smith Corp. [19386]
Johnson & Associates; Steve [14138]
Joissu Products Inc. [26546]
Jonel Inc. [14139]
K & I Transeau Co. [27166]
K & K Pet Talk [27167]
K & K Vet Supply [27168]
K & R Distributors [27169]
Kamaaina Distribution [11578]
Karemor Independent Distributor [14140]
Keen Jewelers [14141]
Kelley-Clarke [11594]
Kentucky Buying Cooperative Int. [907]
Keystone Chemical Supply Inc. [4435]
Kimbet Leather [27173]
Kinray, Inc. [14142]
Kinray Inc. [19396]
Kiwi Brands [14143]
Klabin Marketing [14144]
Klabin Marketing [19397]
Kluge, Finkelstein & Co. [11627]
Knight Distributing Company Inc. [14145]
Kraft Chemical Co. [21477]
Kramer Laboratories Inc. [19401]
Krantor Corp. [11646]
Krelitz Industries Inc. [19402]
Kryolan [25708]
KS Group International [14146]
L & B Pet Supplies [27176]
L & L Pet Center [27177]
La Parfumerie Inc. [14147]
Lab Safety Supply Inc. [18880]
Lady Iris Cosmetic Company Inc. [14148]
Lafayette Drug Company Inc. [14149]
Lazartigue Inc.; J.F. [14150]
Lazartigue Inc.; J.F. [19406]
LBM Sales Inc. [11690]
Lee Brothers Corp. [14151]
Leich Div.; Charles [19407]
Leish; Bob [25711]
LEK USA Inc. [4440]
Leone's Animal Supply [27180]
Liberty Natural Products [14152]
Liberty Natural Products [19414]
Lilly and Co. Pharmaceutical Div.; Eli [19416]
Linsey's Products Inc. [14153]
Lorel Co. [21812]
Lotus Light Inc. [19417]
M and H Sales and Marketing Inc. [14156]
Malone & Hyde [14158]
Marmac Distributors Inc. [19423]

Marni International [21128]
Marshall Co.; A.W. [11789]
Mason Distributors [19425]
Maxcare International Inc. [19426]
M.C. International [19429]
McKesson Drug [19432]
McKesson Drug Co. [19433]
McKesson Drug Co. [19434]
McKesson HBOC Inc. [19435]
McKesson Health Systems [19436]
McKesson Pharmaceutical Inc. [19437]
McLane Group Interntional L.P. [11833]
McQueary Brothers Drug Co. [18906]
MD Foods Ingredients Inc. [24181]
Medica International Ltd. [1009]
Medical Advisory Systems Inc. [19442]
Meijer Inc. [11845]
Merck-Medco Managed Care Inc. [19449]
Mercury Beauty Company Inc. [14159]
Meridian Veterinary Products [27187]
Metagenics Inc. [14160]
Meyers; Tom [27188]
Miami-Luken Inc. [19453]
Mid States Paper/Notion Co. [14161]
Midwest Veterinary Supply Inc. [27189]
Mikara Corp. [14162]
Mikara Corp. [24185]
Millbrook Distribution Services [14163]
Millbrook Distributors Inc. [14164]
Minnesota Mining & Manufacturing Co. [21147]
Mize Farm & Garden Supply [27190]
MK Health Food Distributors [14165]
Modern Overseas, Inc. [14166]
Monson Chemicals Inc. [4460]
Montgomery Seed [27191]
Moore Medical Corp. [19467]
Morgan and Sampson Pacific [14168]
Morse Wholesale Inc.; J.D. [26582]
Mound City Industries Inc. [11940]
Mundy Enterprises, Inc.; K.C. [3003]
Mustela USA [14169]
Mustela USA [19472]
Nassifs Professional Pharmacy [18956]
National Specialty Services Inc. [19479]
Natrol, Inc. [14170]
Naturade Inc. [14171]
Nature's Best [11987]
Nature's Gate Herbal Cosmetics [14172]
Nature's Herbs [14173]
Network Marketing L.C. [14174]
Neuman Distributors, Inc. [14175]
Neuman Distributors Inc. [19485]
Neuman Health Services Inc. [19486]
New England Serum Co. [27194]
New England Wholesale Drug Co. [14176]
New Hampshire Tobacco Corp. [26331]
NLS Animal Health [27195]
Norstar Consumer Products Company Inc. [14179]
North Carolina Mutual Wholesale Drug
    Co. [19499]
Northeast Cooperatives [12031]
Northpoint Trading Co. Inc. [27197]
Northwest Arkansas Paper Co. [4677]
Northwestern Supply Co. [1090]
Notini and Sons Inc.; Albert H. [26335]
Novo Nordisk North America Inc. [19501]
Novo Nordisk Pharmaceuticals Inc. [19502]
Nu-Dimension Beauty Supply Inc. [14180]
Nu Skin Enterprises Inc. [19503]
Nu Skin International Inc. [14181]
NutriCology Inc. [12048]
Nutrition For Life International Inc. [14182]
Nutrition International Co. [14183]
Nutrition Medical Inc. [14184]
Ohio Valley-Clarksburg Inc. [19505]
Omnitrition [12071]
Optibal Co. [14185]
Oral Logic Inc. [14186]
Outdoor Research Inc. [23863]
Owens and Minor Inc. [18972]
PanVera Corp. [19522]
Parallel Traders Inc. [14187]
Paramount Sales Co. [14188]
Paramount Sales Co. [19524]
Parfums de Coeur Ltd. [14189]
ParMed Pharmaceuticals Inc. [19525]

Parnell Pharmaceuticals Inc. [19526]
Paulk Grocery; H.B. [12122]
Pence International, Inc. [5273]
Perfumania, Inc. [14190]
Perfumania Inc. [19532]
Perz Feed & Delivery [27204]
Pet Supply Warehouse [27211]
Pet World [27212]
Peterson's Rental [19535]
Peyton's [21881]
Pfizer Inc. Distribution Center [19536]
Pharmacy Corporation of America [19537]
PharMerica Inc./PMSI [19538]
PMI-Eisenhart Wisconsin Div. [12185]
Pola U.S.A. Inc. [14191]
Polep Distribution Services Inc.; J. [26342]
Poultry Health [27215]
Pound International Corp. [14192]
Premier Inc. (Greenwich, Connecticut) [14193]
Priddy's General Store [27216]
Prime Natural Health Laboratories Inc. [14194]
Princeton Lipids [4485]
Priority Healthcare Corp. [19551]
PRN Pharmaceutical Services Inc. [19553]
Pro-Line Corp. [14195]
Professional Education & Products Inc. [14196]
Professional Medical Services Inc. [19555]
Professional Salon Concepts Inc. [14197]
Professional Salon Services [14198]
Progressive Distributors [14199]
Prometex International Corp. [14200]
Provico Inc. [27218]
Proxycare Inc. [19560]
PTC International [19000]
Q Perfumes [14201]
Q.E.D. Exports [12244]
Quaglino Tobacco and Candy Company
    Inc. [26344]
Qualis Inc. [19562]
Quality Care Pharmaceuticals Inc. [19563]
Quality King Distributors Inc. [14202]
Quigley Corp. [19564]
Rack Service Company Inc. [14203]
Rack Service Company Inc. [19565]
Rainbow Distributing, Inc. [14204]
Rainbow Trading Company Inc. [13215]
Raylon Corp. [14206]
Raylon Corp. [14207]
Raylon Corp. [14208]
Raylon Corp. [14209]
RC International [14210]
Reese Chemical Co. [14212]
Reese Chemical Co. [19572]
Reese Pharmaceutical Co. [19573]
Reisman Corp.; H. [4492]
Reliv' International Inc. [14213]
Reliv' World Corp. [12300]
Rexall Co. [14214]
Rexall Co. [19579]
Rexall Managed Care [14215]
Rexall Sundown Inc. [14216]
RIA International [14217]
Richard Beauty Supply [14218]
Richards Products Inc. [14219]
Rio Grande Trading Co. [14220]
Rite Way Barber & Beauty Supplies [14221]
Rival/Pollenex [14222]
Rivard International Corp. [7939]
Rochester Drug Cooperative Inc. [19584]
Rochester Midland Corp. [4698]
Rorer West Inc. [19586]
Rosemont Pharmaceutical Corp. [19587]
Rothenberg and Schloss Inc. [14224]
Royal Essence Ltd. [14226]
Rx Medical Services Corp. [19590]
Ryan's Wholesale Food Distributors [12373]
Sanofi Beaute Inc. [14229]
Schein Pharmaceutical Inc. [19594]
Scherer Laboratories Inc. [19595]
Schilling Paper Co. [21923]
Scotland Yard [27229]
Scott Drug Co. [19600]
Sebastian Inc.; Paul [14232]
Segura Products Co. [19602]
Sel-Leb Marketing, Inc. [14233]
Seow Company Inc.; Anthony [19603]

Service Brokerage Inc. [12461]
Sewon America Inc. [4509]
SF Services Inc. [27231]
Shaklee Corp. [14234]
Shaklee Distributor [12469]
Shakour Inc.; R.G. [14235]
Sigma-Tau Pharmaceuticals Inc. [19611]
Silver Sage [14236]
Sime Health Ltd. [14237]
Simple Wisdom Inc. [14238]
Slusser Wholesale Inc. [26652]
Smith Drug Co. [19616]
Smith Drug Co.; C.D. [14239]
S.O.E. Ltd. [14240]
Solgar Vitamin and Herb Co. [14241]
Somerset Pharmaceuticals Inc. [19620]
Southern Distributors Inc. [15662]
Southern Wholesale Co. [19629]
SST Corp. [19634]
Standard Drug Co. [19635]
Star Sales Company of Knoxville [26213]
Steinberg Brothers Inc. [19638]
Stockman Supply Inc. [27239]
Stomel & Sons; Joseph H. [12588]
Stow Mills [12592]
Strickland Beauty & Barber Supply Inc. [14249]
Sullivan Co. Inc.; C.B. [14250]
Sunhopper Inc. [14251]
Super-Nutrition Distributors Inc. [14252]
Super Valu Inc. - Midwest Region [12628]
Superior Pharmaceutical Co. [19644]
SUPERVALU Inc. Food Marketing Div. [12647]
Swanson Health Products [14253]
T & T Distributors [14254]
Tamco Distributors Company Inc. [14255]
Tec Laboratories Inc. [14256]
Technical Marketing, Inc. [14257]
Technical Marketing Inc. [19650]
Tennessee Wholesale Drug Co. [19651]
Tetra Sales U.S.A. [19652]
Teva Pharmaceutical USA [19653]
Texas Health Distributors [12709]
Threshold Enterprises Ltd. [14259]
Top Dog Ltd. [27248]
Topicz [26360]
Transcon Trading Company, Inc. [27250]
Tree of Life Inc. Midwest [12748]
Tree of Life Inc. Northwest [12750]
Tree of Life Inc. Southeast [14261]
Tri-Blue Kennel [27251]
Tri-State Vet & Pet Supply [27253]
Tsumura International Inc. [14267]
UDL Laboratories, Inc. [19668]
UETA Inc. [26362]
Ultimate Salon Services Inc. [14268]
Unichem Industries Inc. [19671]
Union Standard Equipment Co. [19672]
United Natural Foods, Inc. [12799]
United Research Laboratories Inc. [19678]
U.S. Export & Trading Company, Inc. [14270]
United States Pharmaceutical Corp. [19681]
Universal Products Enterprises [19685]
The Validation Group Inc. [19687]
Vermillion Wholesale Drug Company Inc. [19689]
Virginia Wholesale Co. [12849]
Vita Plus Industries Inc. [14271]
Vitality Distributiors Inc. [14272]
The Vitamin Shoppe [14273]
Vitamin Specialties Corp. [14274]
Walco International Inc. [27267]
Walco International Inc. Cody Div. [1404]
Walgreen Co. [14275]
Walsh Healthcare Solutions [14276]
Walton & Post [12873]
WeCare Distributors Inc. [14277]
Weider Health and Fitness Inc. [14278]
Weinberg Supply Company Inc.; E. [4729]
Wells International [12900]
Welltep International Inc. [4551]
Wesco Merchandising [14279]
West Coast Beauty Supply [14280]
West Wholesale [27270]
Westbrook Pharmaceutical and Surgical Supply
    Co. [19698]
Western Stockmen's Inc. [19700]
Whitby Pharmaceuticals Inc. [19702]

White Cross Corporation, Inc. [19703]
Whole Herb Co. [12934]
Wild Craft Herb [12940]
The Willing Group [14282]
Willis Distribution Beauty Supply [14283]
W.L.C. Ltd. [27271]
X-S Beauty Supplies [14284]
YAO Industries [12991]
York Hannover Health Care Inc. [19716]
Young Inc.; W.F. [19717]
Yves Saint Laurent Parfums Corp. [14285]
Zenter Enterprises Ltd. [27273]
Zucca Inc.; L.J. [26377]

SIC 5131 — Piece Goods & Notions

3A Products [25951]
Acme Linen Co. [25953]
ADO Corp. [15389]
Advanced Graphics [4753]
Albuquerque Balloon Center [23500]
Allen Brown Industries Inc. [25955]
Allen; Robert [25956]
Allied Trading Companies [15758]
American Cord and Webbing Inc. [25958]
American Fast Print [25959]
American Textile and Trim Company Inc. [25961]
Amfib Fibers Ltd. [25962]
Amicale Mongolia Inc. [25963]
Anchor Specialties Co. [25964]
Anichini Inc. [25965]
ARC Mills Corp. [25967]
Arkansas Sock & Wiping Rag Co. [25968]
Around the Corner [13306]
ASAP [4786]
Associated Fabrics Corp. [25969]
Astrup Co. [25970]
ATD-American Co. [25971]
Atlas Textile Company Inc. [15410]
Baily and Company Inc.; Joshua L. [25972]
Ballantyne Cashmere USA Inc. [4799]
Barb's Knitting Machines & Supplies [25973]
Barrow Industries Inc. [25974]
Barrow Industries Inc. [25975]
Barrow Industries Inc. Merrimac Textile [25976]
Beckenstein Men's Fabrics Inc. [25978]
Bella & Co.; Frank [25979]
Belwool Corp. [25980]
Berger Co.; B. [25981]
Best Brands Home Products, Inc. [15420]
Billie's Fashion Hats [4824]
Bishops Inc. [25982]
Blumenthal-Lansing Co. [25983]
Bogatin, Inc.; Philip F. [25984]
Bond Supply Co. [25985]
Bonded Fibers and Quilting [25986]
Boutross Imports Inc. [15427]
Bowles Sales; Gay [25987]
Brewer Sewing Supplies [25988]
Brewster Wallcovering Co. [15429]
Brittany Fabrics Inc. [25989]
Bro Tex Company Inc., Wiping Cloth Div. [21657]
Brookwood Companies Inc. [25990]
Brunschwig and Fils Inc. [15430]
Burlington Industries Equity Inc. Knitted Fabrics
    Div. [25992]
Burrows Co. [19205]
C and F Enterprises [25993]
Carhartt Inc. [25995]
Carlyle Industries Inc. [25996]
Carolyn Fabrics Inc. [25997]
Cattsa Inc.; S.D. [4870]
Cavalier Fabrics, Ltd./Redrum [25998]
Celebrity, Inc. [14838]
Celestial Mercantile Corporation [14059]
Central Textile Co. [25999]
Cetex Trading Corp. [26000]
Charter Fabrics Inc. [26001]
Checker Distributors [26002]
Chernin Co.; Eugene [26003]
Chinatex America Inc. [26004]
Chori America Inc. [26005]
Churchwell Co.; J.H. [4882]
Claesson Co. [26006]

Cohen and Company Inc.; Herman [26007]
Colette Malouf Inc. [14067]
Colossal Jewelry and Accessories Inc. [17374]
Consolidated Textiles, Inc. [26008]
Corpus Christi Wholesale Mart [4896]
Culp Inc. [26009]
Cup Graphics and Screen Printing [4905]
Custom Laminations Inc. [26010]
Dakota Flags and Banner [26012]
David-Martin Co. Inc. [26013]
De Poortere of America Inc.; Louis [26014]
DeBois Textiles Inc. [26015]
Decorator & Upholstery Supply, Inc. [26016]
Delaware Dry Goods [26017]
Derby Fabrics, Inc. [26018]
DJ Associates, Inc. [13668]
Doral Fabrics Inc. [26019]
Dorell Fabrics Co. [26020]
Dorr Fabrics Inc. [26021]
Down East Wholesalers Inc. [26022]
DuBois Fabrics [26023]
Duke Sports [26024]
Duplex Novelty Corp. [26025]
Eaton; Daniel A. [26026]
Edgars Fabrics Inc. [26027]
Elna Inc. [26028]
Emerson Company Inc.; W. S. [26029]
Emser International [15489]
Euro-Knit Corp. [26030]
Fabricut Inc. [26031]
Ferman Fabrics Centers [26033]
Fisher Bag Company Inc. [26034]
Fisher, Inc.; Marc J. [26035]
Fleur de Paris [26036]
Forbex Corporation [9904]
Forte Dupee Sawyer Co. [26037]
Frank and Sons Inc.; A. [26038]
Frankel Associates Inc. [26040]
General Fabrics Co. [26041]
Geo-Synthetics Inc. [26042]
Georgia Fabrics Inc. [26043]
Goodman and Co. Inc.; C. [26044]
Greeff Fabrics Inc. [26045]
Greenburg & Hammer [26046]
Greenwood Mills Marketing Co. [26047]
Guilford of Maine Textile Resources [26049]
Guttmann Corp.; Victor [26050]
Haber Fabrics Corp. [26051]
Haik's Inc. [26052]
Hallwood Group Inc. [26053]
Hancock Fabrics Inc. [26054]
Hanes Converting Co. [26055]
Hanes Fabrics Co. [26056]
Harris & Stearns [26057]
Harwell Fabrics, Inc. [26058]
Hata Company Ltd.; S. [26059]
Hedlund Fabrics and Supply Co. [26061]
Helen of Troy Ltd. [14124]
Helen of Troy Texas Corp. [14125]
Hemisphere International [26062]
Heritage Lace Inc. [15527]
Herr's Inc. [26063]
HG International Corporation [23725]
Hoch & Selby Company, Inc. [26064]
Hoffman Company Inc.; Rube P. [26065]
Hoffman Distributing Co. [26066]
Houles USA Inc. [26067]
Humphries Decorative Fabrics; Gabe [26068]
Hunter and Company Inc. [26069]
Idaho Outdoor Equipment [26070]
IKO Notions [26071]
Institutional Linen Supply [26072]
Interiors By Loette [26073]
Irvin-Alan Fabrics [26075]
Irvin-Alan Fabrics [26076]
Irwin Sales [26077]
Jacobson Capital Services Inc. [26078]
Jaftex Corp. [26079]
JBM Sales [26080]
JHB International Inc. [26081]
Josin Fabrics [26082]
Kabat Textile Corp. [26083]
Kagedo Inc. [26084]
Kaldor Fabricmaker USA Ltd.; John [26085]
Kaplan-Simon Co. [26087]
Karystal International Inc. [26088]

KasLen Textiles [26089]
Kast Fabrics Inc. [26090]
Kaufman Inc.; P. [26091]
Keyston Brothers [26093]
Keyston Brothers [26094]
Keyston Brothers [26095]
Keyston Brothers [26096]
Keyston Brothers [26097]
Keyston Brothers [26098]
Keyston Brothers [26099]
Keyston Brothers [26100]
Keyston Brothers [26101]
Keyston Brothers [26102]
Keyston Brothers [26103]
Keyston Brothers [26104]
Keyston Brothers [26105]
Keyston Brothers [26106]
Keyston Brothers [26107]
Keyston Brothers [26108]
Kirk Artclothes; Jennifer Sly [5112]
Kirsch Fabric Corp. [26110]
Kirsch Fabrics Corp. [26111]
Klam International [7561]
Klemer and Wiseman [26112]
Kmart Trading Services, Inc. [26113]
Kramer; L.C. [26114]
Kreinik Manufacturing Company Inc. [26116]
Kwik Sew Pattern Company Inc. [26117]
La Farge; Patricia Arscott [26118]
Lamport and Brother; Alexander [26119]
Larson Fabrics, Inc. [26121]
Laundry Textile Co. [26122]
Leish; Bob [25711]
Lenzip Manufacturing Corp. [26123]
Level Export Corp. [26124]
Lewiston Rubber & Supply Inc. [25715]
Lion Notions Inc. [26125]
Lion Ribbon Company Inc. [26126]
Logantex Inc. [26127]
Logo Apparel [5139]
Logo Designs [5140]
Loomcraft Textiles Inc. [15571]
Lucerne Textiles Inc. [26128]
M & R Sales & Service Inc. [26129]
Maco Vinyl Products Corp. [26130]
Maharam Fabric Corp. [26131]
Majilite Corp. [26132]
Mannix World Imports Inc. [26133]
Marion Fabrics Inc. [26134]
Marlin Custom Embroidery [5169]
Marubeni America Corp. [26136]
Masco Fabrics Inc. [26137]
Matthews Hinsman Co. [26138]
Mayar Silk Inc. [26139]
Memphis Furniture Manufacturing Co. [26140]
Merrimac Boyce Fabrics [26141]
Meskin and Davis Inc. [26142]
Mexican Art Imports [13402]
MH World Trade Corp. [26143]
Michigan Retail Packaging [21834]
Microfibres Inc. [26145]
Mid Mountain Wholesale [26146]
Miltan Export Corp. [26147]
Miltex International Inc. [26148]
Minnetonka Mills Inc. [26149]
Miroglio Textiles U.S.A. Inc. [26150]
Mitsubishi International Corp. [26151]
Moore; Florence [26152]
Mosehart-Schleeter Company, Inc. [26153]
Motif Designs, Inc. [21507]
Muller and Company Inc.; L.P. [26154]
Name Place [5212]
Neo Fabrics, Inc. [26155]
Neo Fabrics, Inc. [26156]
Nomura America Corp. [26157]
Nordic Needle, Inc. [26158]
Notions Marketing Corp. [26159]
Ocean Originals [5246]
Oklahoma Upholstery Supply Co. [26160]
Oklahoma Upholstery Supply Co. [26161]
Orchard Yarn and Thread Company Inc./Lion Brand
    Yarn Co. [26163]
Orient Express [17539]
Original Design Silk Screen Co. [26164]
Oved Corp. [26599]
Oved Corp. [26165]

Pacific Trade Wind Inc. [5263]
Padre Island Screen Printing [5264]
Paragon Fabrics Company Inc. [26166]
Patchis Yarn Shop; Peter [26167]
Patrick Dry Goods Company Inc. [26168]
The Pawley Co. [26169]
Peachtree Fabrics Inc. [26170]
Peachtree Fabrics Inc. [26171]
Peachtree Fabrics Inc. [26172]
Peiger Co.; J.J. [26173]
Personally Yours [26174]
Phillips Industries Inc. [26175]
Pike County Cooperative [1130]
Pinetex [26177]
PL Preferred Products [26178]
Plezall Wipers Inc. [26179]
Promotional Sales Co. [26180]
Quiltworks [26182]
Raytex Fabrics Inc. [26183]
Representative Sales Co. [26184]
Revere Mills Inc. [15634]
Richard The Thread [26185]
Rivertex Company, Inc. [26186]
Robert Allen Fabrics Inc. [26187]
Rockland Industries Inc. [26188]
Rockville Fabrics Corp. [26189]
Rogers Decorative Fabrics; Miles [26190]
Rose Brand-Theatrical Fabrics Fabrications and
    Supplies [26191]
Rosenstein and Co. [26193]
R.S. Hughes Company Inc. [12]
Rubenstein & Ziff Inc. [26194]
Rushin Upholstery Supply, Inc. [26195]
St. Louis Trimming [26197]
Sanderson and Sons North America Ltd.;
    Arthur [15649]
Schenck Co.; E.E. [26198]
Schoeller Textil USA Inc. [26199]
Scott Foam & Fabrics, Inc. [26200]
Service Unlimited [3208]
Shepherd Products Co. [23033]
Sherri-Li Textile Inc. [26203]
The Showroom [26204]
Singer Textiles Inc. [26205]
SKF Textile Products Inc. [26206]
The Slosman Corp. [26207]
Soltex International Inc. [26208]
Spiral Binding Company Inc. [21282]
Springs Industries Inc. Chesterfield Div. [26211]
Staflex/Harotex Co. [26212]
Standard Textile Company Inc. [15666]
Star Sales Company of Knoxville [26213]
Stern Corp.; Paul N. [26214]
Stinson, Inc.; C.F. [26215]
Stroheim & Romann Inc. [26217]
Sun Coast Imports [26218]
Symphony Fabrics Corp. [26219]
T-Shirt Gallery and Sports [5418]
Talladega Machinery and Supply Co. [26220]
Tapetex Inc. [26221]
Tech Aerofoam Products, Inc. [26222]
Tedco Indus Inc. [26223]
TETKO Inc. [26224]
Texstyles Group Inc. [26225]
Textile Import Corp. [26226]
Thompson Silk Co.; Jim [26227]
Threadtex Inc. [26228]
Tillinghast-Stiles Co. [26229]
Tingue Brown and Company Inc. [26230]
Toggitt Ltd.; Joan [26231]
Toray Industries (America) Inc. [4531]
Toray Industries Inc. [26232]
Trade Am International Inc. [10256]
Trim-Pak Inc. [26233]
Trophy Craft Source [5441]
TW Systems Ltd. [4719]
United Fabrics, Inc. [26234]
United Notions [26235]
United Notions [26236]
United Notions & Fabrics [26237]
United Thread Mills Corp. [26238]
Unitex Inc. [26239]
The Upholstery Supply Co. [26240]
Uranus Impex Co. [5456]
Viking Sewing Machines Inc. [26241]
Viking Technology Inc. [5463]

Warren of Stafford Corp. Fabric Merchandising Div. [26243]
Wasser Morton Co. [26244]
WB Stores Inc. [13471]
Webbing Mills Co.; Elizabeth [26245]
West Coast Liquidators Inc. [5480]
Westgate Fabrics Inc. [26246]
Whittenburg, Inc.; N.A. [26247]
Wichelt Imports [26248]
Windsor Rhodes Co. [26249]
Wynn and Graff Inc. [26251]
Wynn and Graff Inc. [26252]
Yarn Tree Designs [26253]
Zabin Industries Inc. [26254]

SIC 5136 — Men's/Boys' Clothing

2BU-Wear [4736]
A and M Sales and Manufacturing Inc. [4737]
Aardvark Swim & Sports Inc. [4738]
Abbott Import-Export Co. [4741]
Abboud Apparel Corp.; Joseph [4742]
ABC School Uniforms Inc. [4743]
Abnormal Trees [4744]
Action Line/UniVogue, Inc. [4746]
Action Sales Promotions [4747]
Action Sport & Apparel [4748]
Ad-Shir-Tizing Inc. [4749]
Adele Fashion Knit Corp. [4750]
Adler Glove Co.; Marcus [4752]
Alba-Waldensian Inc. [4755]
Albain Shirt Co. [4756]
All Dressed Up [4757]
All Pro Championships Inc. [4759]
Alpena Screen Arts [4763]
Alpena Screen Arts [4764]
Amerex (USA) Inc. [4766]
American Argo Corp. Sales and Distribution [4767]
American Athletic Sales Inc. [4768]
American Industrial Exports Ltd. [18449]
American International Trading Co. [4769]
American Military Supply Inc. [4770]
Amity Hosiery Company Inc. [4771]
Anderson News Service Center [3517]
Anna Marie Designs Inc. [4773]
Antler Uniform, Division of M. Rubin & Sons, Inc. [4776]
Apparel Exprex Inc. [4777]
Apple Graphics Ltd. [4778]
Aramsco, Inc. [16707]
Argus Buying Group [4781]
Arizona Sport Shirts Inc. [4783]
Armani Fashion Corp.; Giorgio [4784]
Army & Navy Supplies [4785]
Atlanta Tees Inc. [4789]
Australian Outback Collection [4790]
Authentic Sports Inc. [4791]
AVH Inc. [4792]
Axon Import Export Corporation [4793]
B & L Leather Co. [4794]
Bacon & Co. Inc. [4798]
Ballantyne Cashmere USA Inc. [4799]
Barborie Fashions [4803]
Barbour Inc. [4804]
Bargain City [4805]
Barons Wholesale Clothiers [4806]
Bata Shoe Co. Inc. [24683]
Bay Rag [4808]
BCI Inc. [4809]
BCVG Inc. [4810]
Bee Hat Co. [4812]
Beijing Trade Exchange Inc. [24688]
Belmont Wholesale Co. Inc. [10534]
Belt Corp.; P.M. [4814]
Belts By Nadim, Inc. [4815]
Benel Manufacturing Inc. [4818]
Berger L.L.C.; Ben [4819]
Bergner and Co.; P.A. [4820]
Bernards Formal Wear Inc. [4821]
Best-Klean Products [4578]
Best Style Formal Wear Inc. [4822]
Birkenstock Footprint Sandals Inc. [24691]
Black & Black Inc. [4825]
Blackbird Ltd. [4826]

Blau; Emery [24692]
Bloomingdale's Inc. [4828]
Blue Ridge Graphics Inc. [4829]
Bluestem Farm and Ranch Supply Inc. [324]
Bobtron International Inc. [4830]
Bogner of America Inc. [4832]
Bombay Industries Inc. [4833]
Borneo Group Inc. [4834]
Boroff and Associates; Cy [4835]
Boss Manufacturing Co. [4837]
Boston Trading Ltd. Inc. [4838]
Boyt Harness Co./Bob Allen Sportswear [4839]
Branco Enterprises Inc. [4841]
Bright Lights Sportswear Inc. [4844]
Brittania Sportswear [4847]
Broder Bros., Inc. [4848]
Broner Glove Co. [4849]
Brooks Manufacturing Co. [4850]
Buffalo Inc. [4851]
Burnham Glove Co.; Frederic H. [4854]
Burtons Inc. [4855]
California Manufacturing Co. [4857]
Calolympic Glove and Safety Co. Inc. [24523]
Calvert Dry Goods Inc. [4858]
Camo Distributors [4859]
Cappel Distributing Co. [21412]
Captain TS [4860]
Carolina Made Inc. [4863]
Carousel Fashions [4865]
Castleberry Knits Ltd. [4867]
Castleberry; Tom [4868]
Casual Apparel Inc. [4869]
Cattsa Inc.; S.D. [4870]
Celebration Imports Inc. [4871]
Cellucap-Melco Manufacturing [4872]
Central Work Clothes [4873]
Centre Manufacturing Co. Inc. [4874]
Changing Colors [4876]
Cherokee Hosiery Mills [4878]
Cherry Sticks Inc. [4879]
Chock Inc.; Louis [4880]
Churchwell Co.; J.H. [4882]
CMS Casuals Inc. [4884]
CMT Sporting Goods Co. [23596]
Coach's Connection Inc. [23597]
Cofish International Inc. [24715]
College Bowl Inc. [4888]
Columbia Sportswear Co. [4889]
Command Uniforms [4890]
The Company Logo Inc. [4891]
Cooper Sportswear Manufacturing Company Inc. [4892]
Cop Shop [4893]
Corral West Ranchwear Inc. [4897]
Costa Inc.; Victor [4898]
The Cotton Exchange [4900]
CR Specialty Co. [13484]
Cromer Co. [4903]
Custom Creations Sportswear [4906]
D and T Services Inc. [13654]
Daccord Inc. [4908]
Daewoo International (America) [26011]
Damascus Worldwide, Inc. [4909]
Davis Supply Co. Inc. [16821]
Dawg Luvers & Co. [13344]
Dayman USA Inc. [23616]
Deckers Outdoor Corp. [24725]
Del-Mar Industries Inc. [4911]
Dell Rapids Co-op Grain [505]
Denton Hosiery Mill [4912]
Dentt Inc. [26465]
Denver Merchandise Mart [17391]
Diadora America [4915]
Diamond Comic Distributors Inc. [26468]
Dinorah's Sportswear [4917]
Dolgencorp [10978]
Domsey Fiber Corp. [4919]
Dorfman-Pacific Company Inc. [4921]
Dumans Custom Tailor Inc. [4924]
Dyl-Chem Inc. [4925]
Eagle Pointe Inc. [4926]
East Coast Embroidery Inc. [4927]
Eastland Screen Prints Inc. [4928]
EBSCO Industries Inc. Western Region [4929]
Eisenberg International Corp. [4931]
Eisner Bros. [4932]

Elder Hosiery Mills Inc. [4933]
Elem Corp. [4934]
Elson Import Export; Walter [4935]
Ely & Walker [4936]
Embroidery Services Inc. [4937]
The Empire Co. [4938]
Eudora Garment Corp. [4940]
Evans Inc. [4941]
F & R Sales Inc. [4942]
Fabric Art Inc. [4943]
Fairfield Line Inc. [4944]
Famous Mart Inc. [4945]
Fashion Victim [4946]
Fashions Inc. Jackson [4947]
Fidelity Sportswear Co. [4950]
Fiji Wear Inc. [4951]
Finchers Findings Inc. [4952]
Fine-Line Products Inc. [4953]
Fire-Dex Inc. [25651]
Fire-Dex Inc. [4955]
Fit-All Sportswear Inc. [4956]
Fleet Wholesale [11144]
Flirt Corp/Belldini [4959]
Fontana & Fontana Inc. [4960]
Foremost Athletic Apparel [4961]
Fortune Dogs Inc. [4962]
Forty Acres and A Mule Film Works [4963]
Fox Point Sportswear Inc. [4965]
Fox River Mills, Inc. [4966]
Fratzke Sales, Inc. [4967]
Full Line Distributors [4970]
FW Sales [4971]
G-III Apparel Group Ltd. [4972]
Gachassin Inc. [4973]
Gallagher Industrial Laundry [4974]
Garan, Inc. [4976]
Garment District Inc. [4977]
Garmirian Company Inc.; H.K. [4979]
Genny USA Inc. [4981]
Gilbert Company Inc.; S.L. [4984]
Givenchy Corp. [4985]
Glamour Glove Corp. [4986]
Glenco Hosiery Mills Inc. [4988]
Globe Industrial Supply Inc. [13123]
Glove Wagon Enterprises, Inc. [4991]
Golden Goose [4993]
Golden Needles Knitting and Glove Co. Monte Glove Div. [4994]
Goldman Brothers Inc. [4995]
Good Sports Inc. [4996]
Goodman Knitting Company Inc. [4997]
Goulds Sports Textiles Inc. [4998]
Graham Sporting Goods Burlington [4999]
Gramex Corp. [5000]
Grandoe Corp. [23696]
Great American Wearhouse [5001]
Great Graphic Originals [5002]
Greenwood Mills Inc. [5003]
Gruner & Company, Inc. [5004]
The Guild [5006]
Gulbenkian Swim Inc. [23701]
Gulf Coast Sportswear Inc. [5007]
HA-LO [5009]
Ha-Lo Marketing [5010]
Haas Outdoors Inc. [5011]
Habitat Softwear [5012]
Hagale Industries Inc. [5013]
Hampton-Haddon Marketing Corp. [21025]
Hana Hou Corp. [5015]
Hanley Sales Inc.; Pat [5016]
Happy Valley Clothing Co. [5019]
Hardy and Company Inc.; James G. [15519]
Harris & Co.; William H. [24759]
Hawaii ID Apparel [5021]
Hawaii Martial Art Supply [23718]
Hawkins Fabrics [5022]
Heikkinen Productions Inc. [5024]
Hellam Hosiery Company Inc. [5025]
Helmet House Inc. [23721]
Henco Inc. [24762]
Henry Doneger Associates Inc. [5028]
Here's Fred Golf Co. [23724]
Herman's Inc. [5029]
Highland Laundry Co. [5030]
Hilfiger USA Inc.; Tommy [5032]
Holoubek Inc. [5033]

Hoosier Screen Printer Inc. [5036]
Horizon Impex [5037]
Hosiery Sales Inc. [5038]
Host Apparel Inc. [5039]
IDA Inc. [7504]
Imex Corp. [5045]
Imports Wholesale [5047]
Incentive Associates Inc. [15539]
Indiana Tees [5049]
Industrial Uniform Company Inc. [5050]
InSport International Inc. [5052]
Institutional Linen Supply [26072]
Intercontinental Importers Inc. [5053]
Intercontinental Industries [5054]
International Components Corp. [11520]
International Imports Inc. [5057]
International Industries Inc. [5058]
International Male [5059]
International Marketing Association Ltd. [5060]
International Waters [5061]
Island Import and Export Co. [24772]
Island Snow Hawaii Inc. [5063]
Island Tee Shirt Sales Inc. [5064]
Ital Fashion Inc. [5065]
ITI Interamericana Trade Inc. [5067]
Ivars Sportswear Inc. [5068]
Izod Lacoste [5069]
J & B Wholesale Co. [5070]
J & E Feed Distributors Inc. [872]
J & M Sportswear Inc. [5071]
J.A. Apparel Corp. [5072]
Jackster Inc. [5074]
Jansport Inc. [5075]
JCG Corp. [5077]
JCS Enterprises, Inc. [5078]
JDK Enterprises Inc. [5079]
Jefferies Socks [5080]
Jelina International Ltd. [5081]
Jen-Mar Ltd. [5082]
Jennison Industrial Supply [13771]
Jewel and Co. [5083]
Jim's Formal Wear Co. [5084]
JK Miami Corp. [5085]
JK Sports [5086]
JM/Ontario Tees [5087]
JMR Inc. [5088]
Johnson and Company Wilderness Products Inc. [5090]
Johnson Garment Corp. [5091]
Jones Sportswear Company Inc. [5092]
Jones; Susan Brese [5093]
Jordan Inc.; Leslie [5095]
Jo's Designs [5096]
Joyce-Munden Co. [5097]
JT Racing Inc. [5100]
Julius Kraft Company Inc. [24579]
Kabat Textile Corp. [26083]
Karumit Associates Ltd. [5101]
Kauai Screen Print [5102]
Kaufenberg Enterprises [5103]
Kays Enterprises Inc. [5104]
KBC Bargain Center Inc. [5105]
KD Sales Associates [5106]
Keddie Kreations of California [5107]
King Louie International Inc. [5110]
Kiri Trading Co. Ltd. [5111]
Klear-Knit Sales Inc. [5113]
Kmart Corp. [15553]
Kolon America Inc. [5114]
Kombi Ltd. [5115]
L & L Shirt Shop [5117]
La Crosse Footwear, Inc. [24788]
L.A. T Sportswear Inc. [5119]
Lamport and Brother; Alexander [26119]
Last Gasp of San Francisco [3897]
Lavitt Mills Inc.; Paul [5125]
The Leather Shop [5126]
Legal Sportswear [5127]
Les Appel for Rex Lester Inc. [5128]
Leslie Company Inc.; Richard A. [5129]
Letters N Logos Inc. [5130]
Level Export Corp. [26124]
Lewis Manufacturing Co. [5134]
Livingston Apparel Inc. [5135]
Locoli Inc. [5138]
Logo-Wear Inc. [5141]

Longwear Hosiery Mill [5142]
Loveline Industries Inc. [5143]
Loving; L.A. [5144]
Lozars Total Screen Design [5145]
LW Bristol Collection [5147]
LWR Inc. [5148]
M & M Wholesale [5149]
Madaris Hosiery Mill [5151]
Mahan Western Industries, Inc. [5152]
Maier Sporting Goods Inc.; Ray [5153]
Majestic Glove Inc. [5154]
Manchester Manufacturing Inc. [5157]
Manhattan-Miami Corp. [5158]
Manhattan Shirt Company-Winnsboro Distribution Center [5159]
Manifatture Associate Cashmere USA Inc. [5160]
Mannix World Imports Inc. [26133]
Marco Polo Import & Export [5162]
Marian Group Corp. [5164]
Marketing Success [5165]
Markos Wholesale Clothing Distributors [5166]
Marks Pro Shop; Mike [23802]
Massachusetts Export Corp. [5172]
Massive Graphic Screen Printing [5173]
Maui and Sons Corp. [5174]
Mauney Hosiery Mills Inc. [5175]
McNutt Hosiery; Danny [5181]
Meade Hosiery; Elizabeth [5182]
Meca Sportswear Inc. [5183]
Merit Marketing Inc. [5185]
Metro Export and Import Co. [5187]
Meystel Inc. [5189]
MH World Trade Corp. [26143]
Miami Robes International [5190]
Michigan Glove Company Inc. [5191]
Mid-West Golf Inc. [5193]
Midland Co-Op Inc. [1030]
Midwest Athlete [5194]
Mimbres Valley Farmers Association Inc. [1042]
Modern Material Handling Co. [17046]
Mole Hole [5199]
Monarch Hosiery Mills Inc. [5200]
Montgomery Hosiery Mill Inc. [5202]
Moore Brothers Inc. [5203]
Moreland Hosiery [5204]
Morris Environmental T-Shirts; Jim [5206]
Morrow Snowboards Inc. [23837]
Mr. Logo Inc. [5208]
Multi-Line Industries Inc. [5209]
Music Emporium Record Co. [25346]
Naggar; Albert [5210]
Name Game [5211]
Nantucket Inc. [5214]
National Dry Goods [5215]
National Safety Apparel Inc. [24600]
Nautica Enterprises Inc. [5217]
Nautica International Inc. [5218]
Navasky & Company Inc.; Charles [5219]
Neff Athletic Lettering Co. [5220]
Neiman Marcus Co. [5221]
Nelsons [5222]
New American T-Shirt [5223]
New Era Cap Company Inc. [5224]
New Era Factory Outlet [5225]
New Hosiery [5227]
Newcomb Sportswear Inc.; Tony [5229]
Newsouth Athletic Co. [5230]
Ni-Co. Sales Company Inc. [5231]
Niver Western Wear Inc. [5233]
Nolan Glove Company Inc. [5235]
Nordstrom Inc. [5237]
North Star Glove Co. [5239]
North Warehouse Inc. [5241]
Northwest Designs Ink Inc. [5242]
Nu-Look Fashions Inc. [5243]
NY Apparel [5244]
Oakbrook Custom Embroidery [5245]
Ocean Pacific Apparel Corp. [5247]
Ocean Pacific Sunwear Ltd. [5248]
Officers Equipment Co. [5249]
Olson Inc.; Kenneth P. [5250]
Only Once Inc. [5253]
Orchid Uniform Retail Sales [5256]
Orsen-Porter-Rockwell International [18415]
Osborne Distributing Company Inc. [1111]
Outdoor Research Inc. [23863]

Overcast and Associates; Don [5257]
Owenby Co. [5258]
Oxford Industries Inc. Renny Div. [5260]
Oztex Inc. [5261]
Pacific Trade Wind Inc. [5263]
Paisano Publications [5265]
Palisades Beach Club [5266]
Panorama Casual [5267]
Pappy's Customs Inc. [5268]
Paradies and Co. [4039]
Paramount Manufacturing Co. [5269]
Paramount Uniform Rental Inc. [5270]
Park Manufacturing Co. [5272]
Pemalot Inc. [24830]
Pence International, Inc. [5273]
Penn Printed Shirts Corp. [5274]
Pincus Brothers Inc. [5275]
Pine State Knitwear Co. [5276]
Pioneer Industries Inc. [5277]
Piramide Imports [5278]
Pivot Rules Inc. [5279]
Polo Ralph Lauren Corp. [5282]
Pond International Inc. [18174]
Pope Distributing Co. [5283]
Portland Merchandise Corp. [5284]
Portolano Products Inc. [5285]
Predot Company Inc. [5288]
Prentiss Manufacturing Company Inc. [5289]
Pubco Corp. [5292]
Queens City Distributing Co. [23900]
Quisenberrys Inc. [5296]
Rah Rah Sales Inc. [5299]
Rainforest Inc. [5300]
Raj India Trading Corp. Inc. [5301]
Rally Products Inc. [5302]
Ram Graphics Inc. [5303]
Red Steer Glove Co. [5305]
Reebok International Ltd. [24840]
Reebok International Ltd. Reebok Metaphors [24841]
Reno; Mary Ann [5306]
Reverse & Company [5307]
Reynolds Manufacturing Co. [5308]
Ridgeview Inc. [5310]
Robela Knit Shop Ltd. [5311]
Robern Golfwear Inc. [5312]
Robern Skiwear Inc. [5313]
Robinson Co.; Frank L. [5314]
Robinson Manufacturing Company Inc. [5315]
Rockingham Cooperative Farm Bureau [1205]
Rockmount Ranch Wear Manufacturing Co. [5318]
Romac Export Management Corp. [15639]
Rooster Products International Inc./McGuire-Nicholas [13893]
Rose's Stores Inc. [5320]
Rosing; William [5321]
Royal Hawaiian Creations [5322]
Royal Textile Mills Inc. [5323]
Running Strong Inc. [5325]
Russell Corp. Knit Apparel Div. [5326]
S & S Firearms [13512]
S & W Investments [5328]
SAF-T-GARD International, Inc. [17153]
Safesport Manufacturing Co. [23928]
Safetywear [5329]
Sander Supply Co.; Joseph [5331]
Sanford Shirt Co. [5332]
Saxony Sportswear Co. [5333]
Scope Imports Inc. [5337]
Scottish Connection [5339]
Segue Ltd. [5341]
Self; William [5343]
Service Unlimited [3208]
Shawnee Garment Manufacturing Co. [5346]
Shelton Clothing Inc. [5347]
Sidneys Department Store & Uniforms, Inc. [5352]
Siegels Inc. [5353]
Signature Apparel [5354]
Simmons Hosiery Mill Inc. [5357]
Singer Hosiery Mills Inc. [5359]
Sipes Co.; Howe K. [5360]
Skane Ltd. [5361]
Skillers Workwear USA, Inc. [5362]
Slane Hosiery Mills Inc. [5363]
Small Apparel Co.; Horace [5364]
Soffe; M.J. [23952]

Soft-As-A-Grape Inc. [5366]
South Carolina Tees Inc. [5368]
Southern Apparel Corp. [5370]
Southern Apparel Corp. [5371]
Southern California Tees [5372]
Southwestern Wholesale Co. Inc. [5374]
Soyad Brothers Textile Corp. [5375]
Sparlon Hosiery Mills Inc. [5377]
Spectacular Modes Inc. [5379]
Spiewalk & Sons, Inc.; I. [5380]
Sport Obermeyer Ltd. [23975]
Sport Palace Wholesale [5382]
Sport Spectrum [5383]
Sportcap Inc. [5384]
Sportif USA Inc. [5385]
The Sporting House [23977]
Sporting Image Inc. [5386]
Sports Cellar [23979]
Sports Specialties Corp. [5387]
Sportsarama Inc. [5388]
Sportsprint Inc. [5389]
Spyder Active Sports Inc. [5390]
SST Sales Company Inc. [5391]
Starmac Group [5393]
Stephens Manufacturing Company Inc.; W.
    E. [5394]
Steven Hosiery Inc. [5395]
Stock Ltd.; Robert [5396]
Stone Island; C.P. [5398]
Stonehill Group Inc. [5399]
Striker Products [5400]
Suave Noble Creations Inc. [5401]
Suk Fashions [5402]
Summit Hats [5403]
Sun & Fun Specialties Inc. [13457]
Sun Shader International, Inc. [5405]
Sundog Productions [5406]
Sunfire Corporation [12610]
Sunny's Great Outdoors Inc. [23993]
Sunset Supply [13459]
Sunshine Cap Co. [5407]
Superba Inc. [5408]
Surratt Hosiery Mill Inc. [5409]
Sussex Company Inc. [5410]
Sussman Co.; Frank [5411]
Swany America Corp. [5412]
Sylvias Swimwear-Swim Shop [5413]
T-J Knit Enterprises Inc. [5415]
T-Shirt City Inc. [5416]
T-Shirt Factory & Odd Shop [5417]
Tacchini Apparel; Sergio [5419]
Talbert Trading Corp. [5421]
Tazewell Farm Bureau Inc. [1318]
TBI [5423]
Tees Dyes [5424]
Tempo Glove Manufacturing Inc. [25839]
Terramar Sports Worldwide Ltd. [5425]
Texas Tees [5428]
Thomas Company Inc.; Frank R. [5429]
Thomas Industrial Products Company Inc. [24876]
Tinley Performancewear [5431]
Todd Uniform Inc. [5432]
Tom Thumb Glove Co. [5433]
Top Comfo Athletic Sox Inc. [5434]
Torres Hat Company [5436]
Track 'N Trail [5439]
Traffic Control Service Inc. [24644]
Tri-Parish Cooperative Inc. [1354]
TSF Sportswear [5443]
Tuf-Nut Company Inc. [5444]
Turban Plus [5445]
Tuxedo Junction Inc. [5446]
Twin City Manufacturing Co. [5447]
Twyman Templeton Company Inc. [24648]
Tzetzo Brothers Inc. [12781]
Uniform Center of Lansing Inc. [5448]
Uniform House Inc. [5449]
United Sports Apparel Inc. [5450]
U.S. Products Inc. [5452]
United Uniforms Inc. [5453]
Universal International Inc. [5454]
Unnex Industrial Corp. [5455]
Uranus Impex Co. [5456]
Vanguard Distributors Inc. [24656]
Variety Sales, Inc. [5458]
Vass U.S.A.; Joan [5459]

Vibrint Corp. [5461]
Vickers International [5462]
Viking Technology Inc. [5463]
VIP Formal Wear Inc. [5465]
Virginia West Uniforms Inc. [5466]
Wagman and Co.; N. [5467]
Wagner Enterprises Inc. [5468]
Wagners Formal Wear of Washington [5469]
Waikiki Trader Corp. [5470]
Wam Inc. [5472]
Wearhouse [24889]
Wells Lamont Corp. [5477]
Wells Lamont Corp. [5478]
West Coast Liquidators Inc. [5480]
Westchester Marketing [5482]
Whole Pie Company Ltd. [5483]
Wholesale T-Shirt Supply [5484]
Wild West Company Inc. [5486]
Winchester Hat Corp. [5488]
Windjammer Inc. [5489]
Wise El Santo Company Inc. [5490]
Wise & Son; Frank C. [5491]
Woolworth Corp. [15379]
Work Duds [24899]
Worldwide Distributors Inc. [5492]
Wright; Ronald J. [18362]
Wuite Traders International [17663]
XNEX Inc. [5493]
Zanella Ltd. [5494]
Zimmerman Dry Goods [5495]

SIC 5137 — Women's/Children's Clothing

A & S Suppliers [15384]
AB Collections [4739]
Abbott Import-Export Co. [4741]
ABC School Uniforms Inc. [4743]
Accesories That Matter [18366]
Accessory Resource Gallery Inc. [4745]
Action Sales Promotions [4747]
Action Sport & Apparel [4748]
Adele Fashion Knit Corp. [4750]
Adler Glove Co.; Marcus [4752]
Aiken Designs Inc.; Patsy [4754]
A.L. Investors Inc. [13297]
Albain Shirt Co. [4756]
All Dressed Up [4757]
All-In-One Monogramming [4758]
All That Jazz [4760]
Allimex International [4762]
Alpena Screen Arts [4763]
Amerex (USA) Inc. [4766]
American International Trading Co. [4769]
Amics International Inc. [24311]
Amity Hosiery Company Inc. [4771]
Anderson News Service Center [3517]
Andrew Sports Club Inc. [4772]
Anna Marie Designs Inc. [4773]
Annawear [4774]
Annie C.P. Productions Inc. [24672]
Anns Uniform Center Inc. [4775]
Anthony International Inc.; Paul [24673]
Antler Uniform, Division of M. Rubin & Sons,
    Inc. [4776]
Apparel Exprex Inc. [4777]
Apple Graphics Ltd. [4778]
Aquilla Fashions Inc. [4779]
Archie's Sporting Goods of Gainesville [4780]
Argus Buying Group [4781]
Arizona Mail Order Co. [4782]
Arizona Sport Shirts Inc. [4783]
Armani Fashion Corp.; Giorgio [4784]
Arrow Wholesale Co. Inc. [26397]
Ashleys on Main [4787]
Athlon II Enterprises Inc. [4788]
Atlanta Tees Inc. [4789]
Australian Outback Collection [4790]
Authentic Sports Inc. [4791]
AVH Inc. [4792]
Axon Import Export Corporation [4793]
B J's Wholesale Club Inc. [13029]
B & L Leather Co. [4794]

B & W Hosiery, Inc. [4795]
Baby Bliss Inc. [4796]
Baby Needs Inc. [4797]
Bacon & Co. Inc. [4798]
Bag Bazaar Ltd. [18374]
Ballantyne Cashmere USA Inc. [4799]
Banash and Son Inc.; David [4800]
Banian Trading Co. [4801]
Barboglio; Jan [4802]
Barborie Fashions [4803]
Barbour Inc. [4804]
Bargain City [4805]
Bata Shoe Co. Inc. [24683]
Baxter Knitting Co. [4807]
Bay Rag [4808]
Baynes Co. Inc.; John [24687]
BCI Inc. [4809]
BCVG Inc. [4810]
Beco Helman Inc. [4811]
Bee Hat Co. [4812]
Beeba's Creations Inc. [4813]
Beijing Trade Exchange Inc. [24688]
Belmont Wholesale Co. Inc. [10534]
Belts By Nadim, Inc. [4815]
Benben Sportswear [4816]
Benedict International Inc. [4817]
Benel Manufacturing Inc. [4818]
Berger L.L.C.; Ben [4819]
Bergner and Co.; P.A. [4820]
Best-Klean Products [4578]
Best Style Formal Wear Inc. [4822]
Biflex International Inc. [4823]
Birkenstock Footprint Sandals Inc. [24691]
Black & Black Inc. [4825]
Blackbird Ltd. [4826]
Blau; Emery [24692]
Bloom Brothers Co. [4827]
Bloomingdale's Inc. [4828]
Bobtron International Inc. [4830]
Body Drama Inc. [4831]
Bogner of America Inc. [4832]
Borneo Group Inc. [4834]
Boston Trading Ltd. Inc. [4838]
Boyt Harness Co./Bob Allen Sportswear [4839]
Brach Knitting Mills Inc. [4840]
Branco Enterprises Inc. [4841]
Brazabra Corp. [4842]
Bridges Accessories; Ronna [4843]
Bright Lights Sportswear Inc. [4844]
Brindar Design Inc. [4845]
Bristol Lettering of Hartford [4846]
Brittania Sportswear [4847]
Broder Bros., Co. [4848]
Brooks Manufacturing Co. [4850]
Buckler's Inc. [13324]
Buffalo Inc. [4851]
Burke Hosiery Mills Inc. [4853]
Burnham Glove Co.; Frederic H. [4854]
Cabot Hosiery Mills Inc. [4856]
Calolympic Glove and Safety Co. Inc. [24523]
Cappel Distributing Co. [21412]
Caring Concepts Inc. [4861]
Carolina Hosiery Connection [4862]
Carolina Maid Products Inc. [4864]
Carousel Fashions Inc. [4865]
Carter Girls Fashions Inc. [4866]
Castleberry Knits Ltd. [4867]
Castleberry; Tom [4868]
Cattsa Inc.; S.D. [4870]
Celebration Imports Inc. [4871]
Cellucap-Melco Manufacturing [4872]
Centre Manufacturing Co. Inc. [4874]
Chandras [4875]
Chattanooga Manufacturing Inc. [4877]
Cherokee Hosiery Mills [4878]
Cherry Sticks Inc. [4879]
Chock Inc.; Louis [4880]
Christie Brothers Fur Corp. [4881]
Churchwell Co.; J.H. [4882]
Clark Ltd.; Vivian [4883]
CMS Casuals Inc. [4884]
CMT Sporting Goods Co. [23596]
Coach's Connection Inc. [23597]
Cofish International Inc. [24715]
Cohan Berta Showroom [4886]
Cohen Ltd.; Paula [4887]

Cole Productions Inc.; Kenneth [24716]	Givenchy Corp. [4985]	Jewel and Co. [5083]
Columbia Sportswear Co. [4889]	Glamour Glove Corp. [4986]	JK Miami Corp. [5085]
The Company Logo Inc. [4891]	Glaser and Son Inc.; H. [4987]	JM/Ontario Tees [5087]
Cop Shop [4893]	Glenco Hosiery Mills Inc. [4988]	JNT Corporation [5089]
Copy Cats Industries Inc. [4894]	Glencraft Lingerie Inc. [4989]	Johnson and Company Wilderness Products
Cornell Trading Inc. [4895]	Glentex Corp. [4990]	Inc. [5090]
Corral West Ranchwear Inc. [4897]	Glove Wagon Enterprises, Inc. [4991]	Johnson Garment Corp. [5091]
Costa Inc.; Victor [4898]	Gold Bug [4992]	Jolie Handbags/Uptown Ltd. [18402]
Cotton Caboodle Company Co. [4899]	Golden Goose [4993]	Jones; Susan Brese [5093]
The Cotton Exchange [4900]	Goldman Brothers Inc. [4995]	Jordan Fashions Corp. [5094]
Country Miss Carrollton [4901]	Good Sports Inc. [4996]	Jordan Inc.; Leslie [5095]
Coyne Galleries; Elaine [17379]	Goodman Knitting Company Inc. [4997]	Jo's Designs [5096]
CR Specialty Co. [13484]	Goulds Sports Textiles Inc. [4998]	Joyce-Munden Co. [5097]
CRH International Inc. [4902]	Gramex Corp. [5000]	Joyce Sportswear Co. [5098]
Cromer Co. [4903]	Grandoe Corp. [23696]	JP Associates [5099]
Cullens Playland Inc. [4904]	Great American Wearhouse [5001]	JT Racing Inc. [5100]
Custom Creations Sportswear [4906]	Great Graphic Originals [5002]	Kabat Textile Corp. [26083]
Daewoo International (America) [26011]	Greenwood Mills Inc. [5003]	Karumit Associates Ltd. [5101]
Davis Enterprises Inc.; Dan L. [4910]	Gruner & Company, Inc. [5004]	Kauai Screen Print [5102]
Davis Supply Co. Inc. [16821]	GSL Enterprises Inc. [5005]	Kaufenberg Enterprises [5103]
Dayman USA Inc. [23616]	The Guild [5006]	Kays Enterprises Inc. [5104]
Deckers Outdoor Corp. [24725]	Gulbenkian Swim Inc. [23701]	KBC Bargain Center Inc. [5105]
Denton Hosiery Mill [4912]	Gulf Coast Sportswear Inc. [5007]	KD Sales Associates [5106]
Dentt Inc. [26465]	Gussoff-Reslow & Associates [5008]	Keddie Kreations of California [5107]
Denver Waste Materials Inc. [4913]	HA-LO [5009]	Kentucky Derby Hosiery [5108]
Design Tees Hawaii Inc. [4914]	Hagale Industries Inc. [5013]	Kenwil Sales [5109]
Diadora America [4915]	Hamilton Inc.; David [5014]	King Louie International Inc. [5110]
Diamony International, Inc. [4916]	Hampton-Haddon Marketing Corp. [21025]	Kiri Trading Co. Ltd. [5111]
Dinorah's Sportswear [4917]	Hana Hou Corp. [5015]	Klear-Knit Sales Inc. [5113]
Direct Sales Inc. [4918]	Happy Shirts Inc. [5018]	Kmart Corp. [15553]
Dolgencorp [10978]	Happy Valley Clothing Co. [5019]	Kolon America Inc. [5114]
Domsey Fiber Corp. [4919]	Hardin Clothing Co. Inc.; J.M. [5020]	Kombi Ltd. [5115]
Don Overcast and Associates [4920]	Hardy and Company Inc.; James G. [15519]	Kory Mercantile Company [5116]
Dorfman-Pacific Company Inc. [4921]	Harris & Co.; William H. [24759]	La Crosse Footwear, Inc. [24788]
Dover Handbag Co. [18389]	Hawaii ID Apparel [5021]	L.A. Glo [5118]
Dreyer & Associates Inc. [4922]	Hawaii Martial Art Supply [23718]	L.A. T Sportswear Inc. [5119]
Dyl-Chem Inc. [4925]	Hawkins Fabrics [5022]	Lamport and Brother; Alexander [26119]
East Coast Embroidery Inc. [4927]	Hecht Manufacturing Co. [5023]	Lanz Inc. [5121]
Eaton; Daniel A. [26026]	Hellam Hosiery Company Inc. [5025]	LAT Sportswear, Inc. [5122]
EBSCO Industries Inc. Western Region [4929]	Helman Corporation [5026]	Lauren Hosiery Div.; Ralph [5123]
Ed-Burt Corp. [4930]	Henco Inc. [24762]	LaVayne Distributors [5124]
Eisner Bros. [4932]	Henig Furs Inc. [5027]	Lavitt Mills Inc.; Paul [5125]
Elder Hosiery Mills Inc. [4933]	Henry Doneger Associates Inc. [5028]	The Leather Shop [5126]
Elem Corp. [4934]	Here's Fred Golf Co. [23724]	Les Appel for Rex Lester Inc. [5128]
Elson Import Export; Walter [4935]	Herman's Inc. [5029]	Leslie Company Inc.; Richard A. [5129]
Ely & Walker [4936]	Highland Mills Inc. [5031]	Level Export Corp. [26124]
Embroidery Services Inc. [4937]	Honey Bee Fashions [5034]	Levi's Womenswear [5131]
The Empire Co. [4938]	Honey Fashions Ltd. [5035]	Levoy's [5132]
Esprit International [4939]	Hosiery Sales Inc. [5038]	Levy Inc.; Frank [5133]
Eudora Garment Corp. [4940]	House of Bianchi Inc. [5040]	Lewis Manufacturing Co. [5134]
Evans Inc. [4941]	I Play [5041]	Livingston Apparel Inc. [5135]
Fabric Art Inc. [4943]	IIRI International Inc. [5042]	Liz and Co. [5136]
Famous Mart Inc. [4945]	Imar Industries Inc. [5044]	Loco Boutique [5137]
Fashion Victim [4946]	Imex Corp. [5045]	Longwear Hosiery Mill [5142]
Fashions Inc. Jackson [4947]	Import Wholesale Co. [17454]	Loveline Industries Inc. [5143]
Felicia Grace and Co. [4948]	Incentive Associates Inc. [15539]	Loving; L.A. [5144]
Felina Lingerie [4949]	India Hand Arts [5048]	Lozars Total Screen Design [5145]
Fidelity Sportswear Co. [4950]	Indiana Tees [5049]	Lucia Inc. [5146]
Fiji Wear Inc. [4951]	Industrial Uniform Company Inc. [5050]	Lurie Associates; Fred [24797]
Finchers Findings Inc. [4952]	Infant To Teen Headwear [5051]	LW Bristol Collection [5147]
Fine-Line Products Inc. [4953]	InSport International Inc. [5052]	M & M Wholesale [5149]
Fink Brothers Inc. [4954]	Institutional Linen Supply [26072]	Mad Bomber Co. [5150]
Fire-Dex Inc. [25651]	Inter-Pacific Corp. [24769]	Madaris Hosiery Mill [5151]
Fit-All Sportswear Inc. [4956]	Intercontinental Industries [5054]	Maier Sporting Goods Inc.; Ray [5153]
Fleet Wholesale [11144]	Interknit Inc. [5055]	Malco Modes Inc. [5155]
Fleurette California [4957]	International Components Corp. [11520]	Manchester Manufacturing Acquisitions Inc. [5156]
Flirt Corp/Belldini [4959]	International Imports Inc. [5057]	Manhattan Shirt Company-Winnsboro Distribution
Foremost Athletic Apparel [4961]	International Marketing Association Ltd. [5060]	Center [5159]
Fortune Dogs Inc. [4962]	International Waters [5061]	Manifatture Associate Cashmere USA Inc. [5160]
Forty Acres and A Mule Film Works [4963]	Intimate Fashions Inc. [5062]	Manz, Jr.; Edward H. [5161]
Foster Associates Inc.; M. [4964]	Island Import and Export Co. [24772]	Marco Polo Import & Export [5162]
Fox Point Sportswear Inc. [4965]	Island Snow Hawaii Inc. [5063]	Marco and Sons; R.B. [5163]
Fox River Mills, Inc. [4966]	Island Tee Shirt Sales Inc. [5064]	Marcus Brothers [15577]
Fratzke Sales, Inc. [4967]	Ital Fashion Inc. [5065]	Marlenes Inc. [5168]
French Toast [4968]	Items Galore Inc. [5066]	Marlo Bags [18411]
Fritzi of Utah [4969]	Ivars Sportswear Inc. [5068]	Marni International [21128]
Full Line Distributors [4970]	J & B Wholesale Co. [5070]	Mary Fashion Manufacturing Company Inc. [5170]
FW Sales [4971]	J.A. Apparel Corp. [5072]	Mauney Hosiery Mills Inc. [5175]
G-III Apparel Group Ltd. [4972]	Jack's Tack International Distributors [5073]	Max Nitzberg Inc. [5176]
Gamco Manufacturing Co. [4975]	Jansport Inc. [5075]	McCubbin Hosiery Inc. [5177]
Garment Inc.; Susan [4978]	Jantzen Inc. [5076]	McCubbin Hosiery Inc. [5178]
Garmirian Company Inc.; H.K. [4979]	JCG Corp. [5077]	McFadden Inc.; Mary [5180]
Garpac Corp. [4980]	JCS Enterprises, Inc. [5078]	McNutt Hosiery; Danny [5181]
Genny USA Inc. [4981]	JDK Enterprises Inc. [5079]	Meca Sportswear Inc. [5183]
Genuine Rose Inc. [4982]	Jelina International Ltd. [5081]	Melody Gloves Inc. [5184]
GFT USA Corp. [4983]	Jen-Mar Ltd. [5082]	Merit Marketing Inc. [5185]

Meshekow Brothers Inc. [5186]
Metro Export and Import Co. [5187]
Metro Marketing Co. [5188]
Meystel Inc. [5189]
Miami Robes International [5190]
Michigan Glove Company Inc. [5191]
Mid Atlantic Accessories [5192]
Mid-West Golf Inc. [5193]
Milrank Knitwear Inc. [5196]
Miss Elliette Inc. [5197]
Mister Remo of California Inc. [5198]
Mole Hole [5199]
Monarch Hosiery Mills Inc. [5200]
Monarch Knit and Sportswear Inc. [5201]
Montgomery Hosiery Mill Inc. [5202]
Moore Brothers Inc. [5203]
Moreland Hosiery [5204]
Morelle Products Ltd., Philippe ADEC and
    Equipment [5205]
Morris Environmental T-Shirts; Jim [5206]
Morrow Snowboards Inc. [23837]
Movie Star Inc. [5207]
Music Emporium Record Co. [25346]
Naggar; Albert [5210]
Name Game [5211]
Nannette [5213]
Nantucket Inc. [5214]
Neff Athletic Lettering Co. [5220]
Neiman Marcus Co. [5221]
New American T-Shirt [5223]
New Era Cap Company Inc. [5224]
New Era Factory Outlet [5225]
New Fashion Inc. [5226]
New Hosiery [5227]
New York Enterprises [5228]
Ni-Co. Sales Company Inc. [5231]
Nitches Inc. [5232]
Niver Western Wear Inc. [5233]
Noe-Equal Hosiery Corporation [5234]
Nolan Glove Company Inc. [5235]
Nordic Wholesale Distributors Inc. [5236]
Nordstrom Inc. [5237]
North American Fur Producers New York
    Inc. [18135]
North Shore Sportswear Company Inc. [5238]
North State Garment Company Inc. [5240]
Northwest Designs Ink Inc. [5242]
NY Apparel [5244]
Oakbrook Custom Embroidery [5245]
Ocean Pacific Apparel Corp. [5247]
Ocean Pacific Sunwear Ltd. [5248]
Officers Equipment Co. [5249]
On the Beach, Inc. [5251]
Only Hearts Ltd. [5252]
Only Once Inc. [5253]
Oogenesis Inc. [5254]
Orbit Industries Inc. Clarkesville Garment
    Div. [5255]
Orchid Uniform Retail Sales [5256]
Orscheln Farm and Home Supply Inc. [1109]
Orsen-Porter-Rockwell International [18415]
Osborne Distributing Company Inc. [1111]
Outdoor Research Inc. [23863]
Overcast and Associates; Don [5257]
Oxford of Burgaw Co. [5259]
Oxford Industries Inc. Renny Div. [5260]
Oztex Inc. [5261]
Pacasa [5262]
Paisano Publications [5265]
Palisades Beach Club [5266]
Panorama Casual [5267]
Pantera International Corp. [18418]
Pappy's Customs Inc. [5268]
Paradies and Co. [4039]
Paramount Manufacturing Co. [5269]
Paramount Uniform Rental Inc. [5270]
Paris Vienna [5271]
Pemalot Inc. [24830]
Pence International, Inc. [5273]
Phillippe of California Inc. [18420]
Pincus Brothers Inc. [5275]
Pine State Knitwear Co. [5276]
Pioneer Industries Inc. [5277]
Piramide Imports [5278]
Plus Woman [5280]
Podell Industries Inc. [5281]

Polo Ralph Lauren Corp. [5282]
Pope Distributing Co. [5283]
Portland Merchandise Corp. [5284]
Portolano Products Inc. [5285]
Prairie Belle Clothing Exports [5286]
Pratt Medical Inc. [5287]
Price Direct Sales; Don [5290]
Psoul Company Inc. [5291]
Pubco Corp. [5292]
Q-T Foundations Company Inc. [5293]
Q-T Foundations Company Inc. [5294]
Quality Mill Supply Company Inc. [17125]
Queen Shebra Co. [5295]
Queens City Distributing Co. [23900]
R & J Apparel Distributors [5297]
Racewear Designs Inc. [5298]
Raj India Trading Corp. Inc. [5301]
Rally Products Inc. [5302]
Ram Graphics Inc. [5303]
Rashti and Company Inc.; Harry J. [5304]
Red Steer Glove Co. [5305]
Reebok International Ltd. [24840]
Reebok International Ltd. Reebok
    Metaphors [24841]
Regal Bag Corp. [18422]
Reynolds Manufacturing Co. [5308]
Rialto Inc. [5309]
Ridgeview Inc. [5310]
Robela Knit Shop Ltd. [5311]
Robern Golfwear Inc. [5312]
Robern Skiwear Inc. [5313]
Robinson Co.; Frank L. [5314]
Rock Candy Inc. [5316]
Rockmount of Arkansas [5317]
Ronlee Apparel Co. [5319]
Rose's Stores Inc. [5320]
Rosing; William [5321]
Royal Hawaiian Creations [5322]
Royal Textile Mills Inc. [5323]
Roye; Gene [5324]
Russell Corp. Knit Apparel Div. [5326]
Rust Wholesale Company Inc. [12371]
S & L Monograms and Embroidery [5327]
S & W Investments [5328]
SAF-T-GARD International, Inc. [17153]
Safesport Manufacturing Co. [23928]
Safetywear [5329]
Sago Imports Inc. [17584]
Samara Brothers, Inc. [5330]
Sander Supply Co.; Joseph [5331]
Schleifer and Son Inc.; H. [5334]
Schneider Sales Inc.; Arthur [24852]
Scott Associates; L.S. [5338]
Scottish Connection [5339]
Scripts For All Reasons [5340]
Segue Ltd. [5341]
Seibel & Stern Corp. [5342]
Senor's Q Inc. [5344]
Service Unlimited [3208]
Shankles Hosiery Inc. [5345]
Shaws-Healthtick [19606]
Shelton Clothing Inc. [5347]
Showroom Seven [5349]
Showroom Seven [5350]
Sidney Furs Inc.; Robert [5351]
Siegels Inc. [5353]
Signature Apparel [5354]
Silber Knitwear Corp. [5355]
Silky's Sportswear [5356]
Simons Millinery Mart [5358]
Singer Hosiery Mills Inc. [5359]
Sipes Co.; Howe K. [5360]
Sirco International Corp. [18429]
Skane Ltd. [5361]
Skillers Workwear USA, Inc. [5362]
SKL Company Inc. [17608]
Slane Hosiery Mills Inc. [5363]
Small Apparel Co.; Horace [5364]
Sockyard Company Inc. [5365]
Soffe; M.J. [23952]
Soft-As-A-Grape Inc. [5366]
Softouch Company Inc. [5367]
South Carolina Tees Inc. [5368]
South Wool [5369]
Southern Apparel Corp. [5370]
Southern Apparel Corp. [5371]

Southern California Tees [5372]
Soyad Brothers Textile Corp. [5375]
Sparlon Hosiery Mills Inc. [5377]
Specialty House Inc. [5378]
Spectacular Modes Inc. [5379]
Spiewalk & Sons, Inc.; I. [5380]
Spoiled Rotten USA Inc. [5381]
Sport Obermeyer Ltd. [23975]
Sport Palace Wholesale [5382]
Sport Spectrum [5383]
Sportcap Inc. [5384]
Sportif USA Inc. [5385]
The Sporting House [23977]
Sporting Image Inc. [5386]
Sports Cellar [23979]
Sports Specialties Corp. [5387]
Sportsprint Inc. [5389]
Spyder Active Sports Inc. [5390]
SST Sales Company Inc. [5391]
Star of India Fashions [5392]
Stephens Manufacturing Company Inc.; W.
    E. [5394]
Stevens Ltd.; Michael [18434]
Stock Ltd.; Robert [5396]
Stone Enterprises [5397]
Stonehill Group Inc. [5399]
Striker Products [5400]
Suave Noble Creations Inc. [5401]
Suk Fashions [5402]
Summit Hats [5403]
Summit Hats [5404]
Sun & Fun Specialties Inc. [13457]
Sun Shader International, Inc. [5405]
Sundog Productions [5406]
Sunny's Great Outdoors Inc. [23993]
Sunset Supply [13459]
Sunshine Cap Co. [5407]
Super Shoe Stores Inc. [24871]
Surratt Hosiery Mill Inc. [5409]
Sussex Company Inc. [5410]
Sussman Co.; Frank [5411]
Swany America Corp. [5412]
Sylvias Swimwear-Swim Shop [5413]
Symphony Designs Inc. [5414]
T-J Knit Enterprises Inc. [5415]
T-Shirt City Inc. [5416]
T-Shirt Factory & Odd Shop [5417]
Tacchini Apparel; Sergio [5419]
Taj Inc. [5420]
Talbert Trading Corp. [5421]
Tamara Imports [5422]
TBI [5423]
Tees Dyes [5424]
Terramar Sports Worldwide Ltd. [5425]
Terry Products Inc. [5426]
TET Incorporated [5427]
Texas Tees [5428]
Thomas Company Inc.; Frank R. [5429]
Thomas Industrial Products Company Inc. [24876]
Time Out For Sports [5430]
Tinley Performancewear [5431]
Todd Uniform Inc. [5432]
Tom Thumb Glove Co. [5433]
Top Comfo Athletic Sox Inc. [5434]
Topsville Inc. [5435]
Torres Hat Company [5436]
Tots Wear Company Inc. [5437]
Town Talk Cap Manufacturing Co. [5438]
Track 'N Trail [5439]
Trade Routes Ltd. [5440]
Traffic Control Service Inc. [24644]
True Blue Inc. [5442]
TSF Sportswear [5443]
Turban Plus [5445]
Twin City Manufacturing Co. [5447]
Tzetzo Brothers Inc. [12781]
Uniform Center of Lansing Inc. [5448]
United Sports Apparel Inc. [5450]
U.S. Marketing Services [5451]
U.S. Products Inc. [5452]
United Uniforms Inc. [5453]
Universal International Inc. [5454]
Unnex Industrial Corp. [5455]
Uranus Impex Co. [5456]
Vanguard Distributors Inc. [24656]
Variety Hosiery Mills [5457]

Variety Sales, Inc. [5458]
Vass U.S.A.; Joan [5459]
Venture Trading [5460]
Vibrint Corp. [5461]
Vickers International [5462]
Vine Associates Inc.; George [5464]
Viva Handbags Inc. [18438]
Vuitton North America Inc.; Louis [18439]
Wagman and Co.; N. [5467]
Wallace Sportswear [5471]
Wam Inc. [5472]
Warehouse Outlet Stores Inc. [18442]
Warnaco Inc. [5473]
Wearhouse [24889]
Weekend Exercise Co., Inc. [5475]
Weiss Inc.; Harry [18443]
Wells Designs Inc.; Victoria [5476]
Wells Lamont Corp. [5477]
Wells Lamont Corp. [5478]
The Wermers Co. [5479]
West Coast Liquidators Inc. [5480]
Westchester Marketing [5482]
Whole Pie Company Ltd. [5483]
Wholesale T-Shirt Supply [5484]
Wild West Company Inc. [5486]
Wilton Manufacturing Company Inc. [5487]
Winchester Hat Corp. [5488]
Windjammer Inc. [5489]
Woolworth Corp. [15379]
Work Duds [24899]
Worldwide Distributors Inc. [5492]
Wright; Ronald J. [18362]
XNEX Inc. [5493]
Zanella Ltd. [5494]
Zimmerman Dry Goods [5495]

SIC 5139 — Footwear

A.B.A.C.O. Group [4740]
Acfer International Inc. [22822]
Adidas America Inc./Intl Div [4751]
Aerogroup International Inc. [24664]
African Export Ltd. [24665]
Alec Corp. [24666]
Allen Trading Co. Inc. [24667]
Allen Trading Company Inc. [4761]
Alpina Sports Corp. [24668]
AmAsia International Ltd. [24669]
AmAsia International Ltd. [4765]
American Footwear Corp. [24670]
Angel-Etts Inc. [24671]
Annie C.P. Productions Inc. [24672]
Anns Uniform Center Inc. [4775]
Anthony International Inc.; Paul [24673]
Arky House Inc. [24675]
Athletic Supply Inc. [24676]
Atlas Safety Equipment Co. Inc. [24677]
Atsco Footwear Inc. [24678]
Baker Inc.; J. [24679]
Baklayan Garbis [24680]
Bally Retail Inc. [24681]
Barry Manufacturing Company, Inc. [24682]
Bata Shoe Co. Inc. [24683]
Battlefield Police Supply Inc. [24684]
Bay Corp. [24685]
Bay Merchandising Inc. [24686]
Baynes Co. Inc.; John [24687]
Beijing Trade Exchange Inc. [24688]
Benge & Co.; Jim [24689]
Bennett Importing Inc. [24690]
Berube Municipal Supply; Tom [13594]
Birkenstock Footprint Sandals Inc. [24691]
Blau; Emery [24692]
Bobbett & Associates Inc. [24693]
Boley Co.; Mel [24694]
Boot & Shoe Village [24695]
Bosler Leather Co. Inc.; George [4836]
Bostonian Shoe Co. [24696]
Brenner Companies Inc. [24697]
Brocato; Charles [24698]
Brown Group Inc. [24699]
Brown Shoe Co. [24700]
BTF Inc. [24701]
Buckhead Shoes Corp. II [24702]

Burchs Fine Footwear Inc. [24703]
Burchs Fine Footwear Inc. [4852]
Cadillac Shoe Products Inc. [24704]
Candie's Inc. [24705]
Caporicci Footwear Ltd. [24706]
Carl's Clogging Supplies [24707]
Cascade Clothing [24708]
Cels Enterprises Inc. [24709]
Chapmans Shoe Repair [24710]
Chesapeake Shoe Co. of California [24711]
Chilis Footwear Inc. [24712]
CK Footwear Inc. [24713]
Classic Sales Inc. [24714]
Coast Shoes Inc. [4885]
Cofish International Inc. [24715]
Cole Productions Inc.; Kenneth [24716]
Colonial Shoe Co. [24717]
Comfort Shoe Corp. [24718]
Consolidated Shoe Company Inc. [24719]
Continental Sports Supply Inc. [23604]
Contour Lynnsoles Inc. [24720]
Corral West Ranchwear Inc. [4897]
Corrective Shoe Repair [24721]
D and D Shoe Co. [4907]
D & D Shoe Company, LLC [24722]
Daewoo International (America) [26011]
David Shoe Co. [24723]
Davis County Cooperative Society [24724]
Dayman USA Inc. [23616]
Deckers Outdoor Corp. [24725]
Dell Rapids Co-op Grain [505]
Dentex Shoe Corp. [24726]
Diadora America [4915]
Driscoll Leather Co. Inc. [24727]
Driscoll Leather Company Inc. [4923]
Dynamic Foam Products Inc. [24728]
East Coast Connection Inc. [24729]
Easy Shoe Distributors Inc. [24730]
Eidai International, Inc. [24731]
Elan-Polo Inc. [24732]
Elliott Shoe Co. [24733]
Emerson Company Inc.; W. S. [26029]
Emit International Corp. [24734]
Ener-Gee Sales Inc. [24735]
Euroimport Co. Inc. [24736]
Eurostar Inc. [24737]
Fabiano Shoe Company Inc. [24738]
Fair Inc. [24739]
Family Shoe Center [24740]
Fancy Feet Inc. [24741]
Fashion Slippers Import USA [24742]
FE. MA. Inc. [24743]
First Native American Corp. [24744]
Flexible Feat Sandals [24745]
Flexible Feat Sandals [4958]
Fontana & Fontana Inc. [4960]
Foot Loose Inc. [24746]
Foremost Athletic Apparel [4961]
Free Shoe Shop [24747]
French Dressing Inc. [24748]
Gardners Shoes Inc. [24749]
Garpac Corp. [4980]
Gemmex Intertrade America Inc. [11247]
Gilbert & Son Shoe Company [24750]
Gilvins Boots & Shoes [24751]
Gita Sporting Goods, Ltd. [24752]
Good Sports Inc. [4996]
Goodwear Shoe Co. Inc. [24753]
Granton Shoe Imports [24754]
Graves Import Co. [24755]
Green Market Services Co. [24756]
Haney Shoe Store Inc. [24757]
Happy Feet Plus [24758]
Happy Feet Plus [5017]
Hardy and Company Inc.; James G. [15519]
Harris & Co.; William H. [24759]
Hawaii; Scott [24760]
Helpern Inc.; Joan & David [24761]
Henco Inc. [24762]
Hi-Tec Sports USA Inc. [24763]
Himex International Inc. [24764]
Hondo Boots [24765]
Hush Puppies Co. [24766]
Ilani Shoes Ltd. [24767]
Ilani Shoes Ltd. [5043]
Impo International Inc. [5046]

Imports Wholesale [5047]
IMR Corp. [24768]
Inter-Pacific Corp. [24769]
Intermountain Lea Findings Co. [24770]
Intermountain Lea Findings Co. [5056]
Iron Age Corp. [24771]
Island Import and Export Co. [24772]
Items International Airwalk Inc. [24773]
Izenco Inc. [24774]
J & B Import Ltd. Inc. [24775]
J & J Shoe Co. [24776]
Jasmine Ltd. [24777]
Jeffress Business Services [24778]
Jimlar Corp. [24779]
Johannsens Inc. [24780]
K-Swiss Inc. [23767]
Kambach & Kettman Inc. [24781]
Kearns Associates [24782]
Kilpatrick; Eddie [24783]
Kims Family Shoes Inc. [24784]
Kipling Shoe Company Inc. [24785]
Klitzner and Son Inc.; B. [24786]
Kmart Trading Services, Inc. [26113]
Knapp Shoes of Tucson Inc. [24787]
Kolon America Inc. [5114]
La Crosse Footwear, Inc. [24788]
Lanahan Sales [24789]
Lanahan Sales [5120]
Landwerlen Leather Co. Inc. [24790]
Lauren Footwear Inc.; Ralph [24791]
Left Foot Ltd. [24792]
Lehigh Safety Shoe Co. [24793]
Leisurelife USA Inc. [23784]
Linwood; Mitchell [24794]
LJO Inc. [24795]
Loeffler's Safety Shoes Inc. [24796]
London Bridge Trading Company Ltd. [23792]
Lurie Associates; Fred [24797]
Lynch Enterprises Inc.; C.O. [24798]
Mahan Western Industries, Inc. [5152]
Maier Sporting Goods Inc.; Ray [5153]
Markon Footwear Inc. [24799]
Markos Wholesale Clothing Distributors [5166]
Marlboro Footworks Ltd. [24800]
Marlboro Footworks Ltd. [5167]
Marshal Glove & Safety Supply [24801]
Maryland Industrial Inc. [24802]
Maryland Industrial Inc. [5171]
Maxwell Shoe Company Inc. [24803]
Maye Hosiery Sales [24804]
Maytown Shoe Manufacturing Company
   Inc. [24805]
McClendons Boot Store [24806]
McCullar Enterprises Inc. [24807]
McCullar Enterprises Inc. [5179]
Mercury International Trading Corp. [24808]
Mia Shoes Inc. [24809]
Michigan Industrial Shoe Co. [24810]
Mid-America Footwear Co. [24811]
Miller Safety Products [24812]
Miller Safety Products [5195]
Moccasin Tipi [24813]
Money Saver [24814]
Morse Enterprises Inc. [24815]
Munro and Co. [24816]
Myers and Sons Inc.; D. [24817]
National Rubber Footwear Inc. [24818]
National Rubber Footwear Inc. [5216]
Naturalizer [24819]
New City Shoes Inc. [24820]
Nickels Supply [24821]
Nine West Group [24822]
Norden Inc. [24823]
Nordstrom Inc. [5237]
North American Shoe Co. Inc. [24824]
North West Quality Innovations [24825]
Olathe Boot Co. [24826]
Oomphies Inc. [24827]
Pagoda Trading Co. [24828]
Parnell; Wayne [24829]
Pemalot Inc. [24830]
Peterman & Company, Inc.; D.S. [24831]
Phillips Shoe Co. Inc.; Austin [24832]
Phillips Shoes [24833]
Pierce Inc.; Jack A. [24834]
Pierre Shoes Inc. [24835]

Portland Merchandise Corp. [5284]
Propet USA, Inc. [24836]
Prosper Shevenell and Son Inc. [24837]
R & S Sales Co. Inc. [24838]
Recife Importing & Exporting Inc. [14648]
Red Wing Shoe Store [24839]
Reebok International Ltd. [24840]
Reebok International Ltd. Reebok
    Metaphors [24841]
Richards International; Lyle [24842]
Right Stuff Inc. [24843]
Robern Golfwear Inc. [5312]
Robern Skiwear Inc. [5313]
Rossignol Ski Co. [24844]
Royal Alaskan Sales [24845]
Royce International Inc. [24846]
S & L International [24847]
Salomon North America Inc. [23929]
Sand Mountain Shoe Co. [24848]
Sara Lee Corp. [12412]
Sartorius Sports Ltd. [24849]
SBC/Sporto Corp. [24850]
Schapero Co. Inc.; Eric [24851]
Schneider Sales Inc.; Arthur [24852]
Schwartz and Benjamin Inc. [24853]
Schwartz and Benjamin Inc. [5335]
Schwartz Shoes Inc.; Jack [5336]
Shane's Shoe [24854]
Shoe Barn [24855]
Shoe Corporation of Birmingham Inc. [24856]
Shoe Corp. of Birmingham Inc. [5348]
Shoe Flair [24857]
Shoe Shack Inc. [24858]
Shoes To Boot Inc. [24859]
Shore Imports Inc. [24860]
Shtofman Company Inc. [24861]
Skechers U.S.A. Inc. [24862]
Slippers International Inc. [24863]
Smith-Claypool; Shirley [24864]
South China Import Inc. [24865]
Southern Leather Co. [24866]
Southern Leather Co. [5373]
Spalding Holdings Corp. [5376]
Speen & Company Inc. [24867]
Street Cars Inc. [24868]
Sullco Inc. [24869]
Sun Pacific Trading Co. Inc. [24870]
Super Shoe Stores Inc. [24871]
Superfeet In-Shoe Systems Inc. [24872]
Sween ID Products Inc. [24873]
Swenson Imports [24874]
Tecnica USA [24875]
Thomas Industrial Products Company Inc. [24876]
Tober Industries Inc. [24877]
Topline Corp. [24878]
Track 'N Trail [5439]
Two Left Feet [24879]
Twyman Templeton Company Inc. [24648]
Uman Corp. [24880]
United Shoe Ornament Company Inc. [24881]
United Uniforms Inc. [5453]
Universal Athletic Services of Utah [24882]
Valencia Imports Co. [24883]
Valley Athletic Supply Co. Inc. [24884]
Vanguard Distributors Inc. [24656]
Vincent Jobbing Co. [24885]
Virgs Inc. [24886]
Walk Corp.; Benjamin [24887]
Warrington Group Ltd. [24888]
Washington Shoe Company [5474]
Wearhouse [24889]
Weintrob Brothers [24890]
West Coast Shoe Co. [24891]
West Coast Shoe Co. [5481]
Wesvic's Clothing and Shoe Brokers, Inc. [24892]
Whites Shoe Shop Inc. [24893]
Wigwam Inc. [24894]
Wigwam Inc. [5485]
Willard Safety Shoe Co. [24895]
Winter Port Boot Shop [24896]
Wolff Shoe Co. [24897]
Wolfpax Inc. [24898]
Work Duds [24899]
Wright and Co.; E.T. [24900]
Yearwoods Inc. [24901]

SIC 5140 — Groceries & Related Products

Frieda's Inc. [11214]
NM Bakery Service Co. [12010]

SIC 5141 — Groceries—General Line

A-1 International Foods [10315]
Abbaco Inc. [10317]
Abbott Foods Inc. [24053]
Acosta-PMI St. Louis Div. [10321]
Acosta Sales Co. [10322]
Adderton Brokerage Co. [10325]
Admiral Exchange Company Inc. [10327]
Advantage Crown [10330]
Advantage Food Marketing Corp. [10331]
Advantage Sales and Marketing [10332]
Affiliated Food Stores Inc. [10333]
Affiliated Food Stores Inc. (Tulsa,
    Oklahoma) [10334]
Affiliated Foods Cooperative Inc. [10335]
Affiliated Foods Inc. [10336]
Affiliated Foods Inc. [10337]
Affiliated Foods Midwest [10338]
Affiliated Foods Southwest Inc. [10339]
AFI Food Service Distributors Inc. [10341]
AJC International Inc. [19127]
Ajinomoto U.S.A. Inc. [10350]
Alabama Food Group Inc. [10351]
Albert Poultry Co. Inc. [10357]
Alex City Provision Inc. [10361]
Alex Lee Inc. [10362]
Alexander Koetting Poole and Buehrle Inc. [10363]
All Kitchens Inc. [10365]
Allegiance Brokerage Co. [10368]
Alliance Foods Inc. [10371]
Alliant Foodservice Inc. [10373]
Alliant Foodservice Indianapolis [10375]
Allied Grocers Cooperative Inc. [10376]
Allied International Marketing Corp. [17692]
Almena Cooperative Association [22032]
Alpena Wholesale Grocery Co. [10377]
Alper Inc.; Morris [10378]
Alpha Distributors Ltd. [10379]
Altitude Wholesale Co. Inc. [10387]
Altitude Wholesale Company Inc. [10388]
AMCON Distributing Co. [10392]
AME Food Service Inc. [10393]
American Foods [10397]
American FoodService [10398]
American Seaway Foods Inc. [10404]
AmeriServe [24063]
AmeriServe Food Distribution Inc. [10407]
Ancona/Midwest Inc. [10411]
Anderson-DuBose Co. [10412]
Antognoli and Co.; Joseph [10422]
Apple Food Sales Company Inc. [10424]
Applewood Farms Inc. [10425]
Arctic Ice Co. [10432]
Arkansas Valley Wholesale Grocers Co. [10433]
Arranaga and Co.; Robert [10436]
Arrow-Sysco Food Services Inc. [10438]
Arrowhead Mills Inc. [10439]
Associated Brokers Inc. [10443]
Associated Buyers [10444]
Associated Food Stores Inc. [10445]
Associated Food Stores Inc. [10446]
Associated Food Stores Inc. [10447]
Associated Food Stores Inc. (Salt Lake City,
    Utah) [10448]
Associated Grocers of Florida Inc. [10449]
Associated Grocers, Inc. [10450]
Associated Grocers of Maine Inc. [10451]
Associated Grocers of New England Inc. [10452]
Associated Wholesale Grocers Inc. [10457]
Astor Inc. [10460]
Atalanta Corp. [10461]
Atlas Marketing Co. Inc. [10466]
Auburn Merchandise Distributors Inc. [10468]
Avalon Distributing Inc. [10474]
Avico Distributing Inc. [10475]

B J's Wholesale Club Inc. [13029]
Badger Popcorn Co. [10487]
Balfour Maclaine Corp. [10494]
Banner Wholesale Grocers Inc. [10497]
Banner Wholesale Grocers Inc. [10498]
Banta Foods Inc. [10499]
Baraboo-Sysco Food Services Inc. [10502]
Barkett Fruit Co. Inc. [10507]
Baye & Rhodes [10517]
Beaver Street Fisheries, Inc. [10521]
Big Horn Wholesale [4580]
BiRite Foodservice [10558]
Bishop-Epicure Foods Company Inc. [10560]
Bivins Barbecue Sauce [10562]
Blackburn-Russell Company Inc. [10564]
Blackwell Stevenson Co. [10566]
Bloemer Food Service Co. [10569]
Blooming Prairie Cooperative Warehouse [10570]
Borton Brokerage Co. [10595]
Bounty Trading Co. [10599]
Boyd & Associates, Inc.; E. [10601]
Bozzuto's Inc. [10605]
BPC Foodservice Inc. [10606]
Bratt-Foster Inc. [10609]
Brenham Wholesale Grocery Company
    Inc. [10613]
Briggs Inc. [26267]
Bromar Inc. [10615]
Bromar Inc. Bromar Hawaii [10616]
Bromar Montana/Wyoming [10617]
Bromar Utah [10618]
Brown and Co.; Lewis A. [10623]
Brown and Co.; Lewis A. [10624]
Brown Food Service [10625]
Brown Moore and Flint Inc. [10627]
Bruno's Inc. [10632]
BTE Import-Export [19204]
Buchy Food Products [10636]
Budd Mayer Co. [24083]
Bunn Capitol Co. [10643]
Bur-Bee Co. Inc. [10644]
Burklund Distributors Inc. [10645]
Burlington Drug Co. [26268]
Butler National Corp. [10649]
Butler Wholesale Products [24085]
Butterfield and Company Inc. [10651]
Buttrey Food & Drug [19207]
C & R Distributors [10656]
C and S Wholesale Grocers Inc. [10657]
C and W Food Service Inc. [10658]
Cal-Growers Corp. [10667]
Cal-West Foodservice Inc. [10668]
Calhoun Enterprises [10671]
Camellia Food Stores Inc. [10683]
Campbell Supply Company Inc. [10685]
Canale Food Services Inc.; D. [24087]
Caro Foods Inc. [10701]
Caro Produce and Institutional Foods Inc. [10702]
Casa Italia [10705]
Casey's General Stores Inc. [10709]
Cash and Carry Stores Inc. [10710]
Cash Way Distributors [10711]
Catanzaro Sons and Daughters Inc.;
    Frank [10714]
Central Carolina Grocers Inc. [10718]
Central Farmers Cooperative [390]
Central Grocers Co-op Inc. [10721]
Centre Jobbing Co. [26275]
Certified Grocers Midwest Inc. [10729]
CGF Cash & Carry [10731]
Chem-Real Investment Corp. [409]
Chilay Corp. [10748]
Church Point Wholesale Groceries Inc. [10757]
Cirelli Foods Inc. [24092]
City Market Inc. [10761]
Clark Food Service Inc. [10764]
Clark Food Service Inc. South Bend Div. [24094]
Clem Wholesale Grocer Co. Inc. [10770]
Cochran Brothers Cash & Carry [10783]
Coeur d'Alene Cash & Carry [10785]
Cole Brothers and Fox Co. [26277]
Compass Foods Eight O'Clock Coffee [10802]
ComSource Independent Foodservice Companies
    Inc. [10803]
Comstock Distributing [10804]
Conco Food Service [10808]

Conco Food Service Inc. [10809]
Conrad Sales Company, Inc. [10814]
Consolidated Companies Inc. [10815]
Consolidated Foodservice Companies L.P. [10817]
Contadina Foods [10824]
Continental Foods Inc. [10829]
Convenience Store Distributing Company L.L.C. [10830]
Copps Corp. [10838]
Copps Distributing Co. [10839]
Core-Mark International Inc. [10840]
Core-Mark International Inc. Core-Mark International Incorporated Div. [10841]
Cosgrove Distributors Inc. [10845]
Cost-U-Less [10847]
Costa Fruit and Produce Co. [10848]
Costco Companies, Inc. [10850]
Costco Wholesale [10851]
Cross and Company Inc. [10869]
Cross Mark Southern California [10870]
Crown Inc. (Cerritos, California) [10874]
Crystal Farms Refrigerated Distribution Co. [10877]
Cub Foods [10880]
Daffin Mercantile Company Inc. [24101]
Dairy Maid Foods Inc. [10898]
Dallas Market Center Company Ltd. [10904]
Davenport and Sons Inc.; J.T. [10913]
Davenport-Webb Inc. [10914]
Davis & Sons; William E. [10918]
Daymon Associates Inc. [10919]
Daystar-Robinson Inc. [10920]
Daytona Beach Cold Storage Inc. [10921]
DBB Marketing Co. [10923]
Deaktor/Sysco Food Services Co. [10926]
Dearborn Wholesale Grocers L.P. [10930]
Dependable Food Corp. [10945]
Dettor, Edwards & Morris [1647]
Diaz Wholesale and Manufacturing Company Inc. [10963]
Doerle Food Services Inc. [10973]
Dolgencorp [10978]
Dot Foods Inc. [10982]
Douglas Northeast Inc. [10986]
DPI-Epicurean Fine Foods [10988]
DPI Food Products Co. [10989]
DPI Southwest Distributing Inc. [10990]
DPI-Taylor Brothers [10992]
Durst Brokerage Inc. [11001]
Dyer and Co.; B.W. [11005]
Dykstra Food Service [11006]
Eagle Food Centers Inc. [11009]
Eagle Wholesale L.P. [11011]
Eaton; Daniel A. [26026]
Eby-Brown Company L.P. [26289]
Economy Cash and Carry Inc. [11022]
Economy Foods [11023]
Economy Wholesalers [11024]
Edmiston Brothers Inc. [11028]
Edsung Foodservice Co. [11029]
Egerstrom Inc. [11033]
El Charro Mexican Foods [11035]
Elmira Distributing [1674]
Elson Import Export; Walter [4935]
Epco-JKD Food Brokers Inc. [11051]
Epicure Foods Inc. [11052]
Epicurean International Inc. [24109]
Etna Oil Company Inc. [22240]
EVCO Wholesale Foods Co. [11061]
Fadler Company Inc. [11069]
Fairco, Inc. [11071]
Fairway Foods Inc. [11074]
Fairway Foods of Michigan Inc. [11075]
Fareway Wholesale [11081]
Fargo-Moorhead Jobbing Co. [11082]
Farm Boy Meats Inc. [11083]
Federated Foods Inc. [11114]
Federated Foodservice [24115]
Federated Group, Inc. [11115]
Ferrera and Sons Inc.; James [11121]
Fiesta Foods [11124]
Fine Distributing Inc. [11126]
Fines Distributing Inc. [11127]
First Choice Ingredients [11131]
Fisher Central Coast [11133]
Fite Co.; Clifford D. [11137]
Fleet Wholesale [11144]

Fleming [11145]
Fleming Companies, Inc. [11146]
Fleming Companies, Inc. [11147]
Fleming Companies Inc. [11148]
Fleming Companies Inc. Garland Div. [11149]
Fleming Companies Inc. Heartland Div. [11150]
Fleming Companies Inc. Oklahoma City Div. [11151]
Fleming Companies Inc. Philadelphia Div. [11152]
Fleming Foods [11153]
Fleming Foods of Alabama Inc. [11154]
Fleming Foods of Ohio Inc. [11155]
Fleming Foods of Tennessee Inc. [11156]
Fleming/Gateway [11158]
Flemming and Associates Inc.; Tom [11159]
Florimex Inc. [11162]
Folloder Co. [11169]
Food Country USA [11170]
Food Marketing Corp. [11174]
Food Service Action Inc. [11177]
Food Services of America [11178]
Food Services of America [11179]
Food Services of America Inc. [11180]
Foodsales Inc. [11181]
FoodSalesWest Inc. [11182]
Foreign Trade Marketing [11187]
Foresight Partners, LLC [11188]
Forman Inc. [4626]
Fornaca Inc. [11190]
Fresh Freeze Supply Inc. [11210]
Frohman & Sons Inc.; L.H. [11219]
Fruit Distributors Inc. [11221]
Gaetano Food Distributor [11227]
Gage Food Products Co. [11228]
Gann Company Inc.; E.C. [26494]
Garber Brothers Inc. [11232]
Gardenview Eggs [11236]
Gardners Good Foods Inc. [11237]
Gateway Distributing Co. [11241]
Gateway Foods Inc. [11242]
Gateway Foods of Pennsylvania Inc. [11243]
Gaylord Cash & Carry [11246]
General Trading Company Inc. [11252]
George H. International Corp. [734]
GFG Foodservice Inc. [11259]
Ginsbergs Institutional Food Service Supplies Inc. [11266]
Glencourt Inc. [11270]
Glover Wholesale Inc. [11277]
Golden Capital Distributors [11283]
Golden State Foods Corp. [11287]
Gordon Food Service Inc. [11293]
Gourmet Award Foods [11296]
Gourmet Specialties [11299]
Gragnon Wholesale [11303]
Great Lakes Marketing Inc. [11312]
Great Southwest Sales [11314]
Great Western Meats Inc. [11316]
Green and Company Inc.; A.A. [11319]
Griffin Manufacturing [11327]
Grocers Specialty Co. [11329]
Grocers Supply Company Inc. [11331]
Grocers Wholesale Co. [11332]
Grocery Supply Co. [11333]
Grocery Supply Co., Inc. [11334]
Grocery Supply Company - Southeast [11335]
GSC Enterprises Inc. [11341]
GSC Enterprises Inc. [11342]
Guarnieri Co.; Albert [21754]
Gulf Marine and Industrial Supplies [11346]
H & H Foodservice [11349]
H & M Distributing Inc. [26301]
H n' M Associates Inc. [11352]
Hackney Co.; H.T. [11355]
Hale Brothers Inc. [11362]
Hale-Halsell Co. [11363]
Hallsmith-Sysco Food Services [11366]
Halsey Company Inc.; W.L. [11367]
Hardin's-Sysco Food Services Inc. [11377]
Harrison Company Inc. [11381]
Hartford Provision Co. [11383]
Hartford Provision Co. [11384]
Hartnett Co.; The C.D. [11385]
Hartnett Co. Food Service Div.; C.D. [11386]
Harvin Foods Inc. [11389]
Hattiesburg Grocery Co. [11391]

Hawaiian Distributor Ltd. [11393]
Hawaiian Grocery Stores Ltd. [11394]
H.E. Butt Grocery Co. San Antonio Distribution/Manufacturing Center [11400]
HealthComm International Inc. [14123]
Heddinger Brokerage Inc. [11405]
Helena Wholesale Inc. [11407]
Henderson and Co.; J.L. [15525]
Heritage Marketing Inc. [11418]
Hester Industries Inc. Pierce Foods Div. [11422]
HFM Foodservice [11423]
HI-Pac Ltd. [11425]
Hill City Wholesale Company Inc. [21760]
Hillcrest Food Service Co. [21762]
Hillcrest Foods Inc. [11433]
Hilton, Gibson, and Miller Inc. [11437]
Hipp Wholesale Foods Inc. [11440]
Holiday Cos. [11446]
Holiday Stores Inc. [11447]
HomeBase Inc. [15532]
Hopewell Valley Specialties [11459]
Hub City Foods Inc. [11470]
Hundley Brokerage Company Inc. [11477]
Husky Food Products of Anchorage [11482]
Hutchings Brokerage Co. [11483]
I.D. Foods, Inc. [11488]
IGA Inc. [11491]
IJ Co. [11492]
IJ Co. Tri-Cities Div. [11493]
I.J. Cos. [11494]
Illinois Fruit and Produce Corp. [11496]
Indiana Concession Supply Inc. [11504]
Inman Associates Inc.; Paul [11509]
Institution Food House Inc. [11510]
Institution Food House Inc. [11511]
Institutional Distributors Inc. [11512]
Institutional Distributors, Inc. [11513]
Institutional Sales Associates [11514]
Institutional Wholesale Co. [11515]
Interstate Distributors Inc. [24145]
Intexco Inc. [11528]
ITBR, Inc. [5651]
ITOCHU International Inc. [11532]
Jackson Wholesale Co. [11544]
Jackson Wholesale Company Inc.; Paul [11545]
Jacob's Store Inc. [877]
Jetro Cash and Carry Enterprises Inc. [11553]
Joiner Foodservice, Inc. [21784]
Jones Co.; J.M. [11560]
Jordanos Inc. [11565]
Jordan's Foods [11566]
Jordan's Meats Inc. [11567]
Joyce Brothers Inc. [11568]
JP Foodservice Inc. [11569]
JP Foodservice Inc. [11570]
Kaw Valley Company Inc. [11584]
Keefe Supply Co. [24154]
Kehe Food Distributors Inc. [11589]
Keith Co.; Ben E. [11590]
Keith Foods; Ben E. [11591]
Kelley-Clarke Inc. [11595]
Kellner Co., Inc.; M.J. [11596]
Ken-Son Inc. [11599]
Kennesaw Fruit Juice Co. [11602]
Kerr Pacific Corp. [11605]
Kesterson Food Company Inc. [24156]
Key Food Stores Cooperative Inc. [11607]
Kings Foodservice [11619]
Kleen Supply Co. [4651]
KLF, Inc. [11624]
Kluge, Finkelstein & Co. [11627]
Knott's Wholesale Foods Inc. [11630]
Koa Trading Co. [11631]
Kohl Grocer Company Inc.; N. [11633]
Kraft Chemical Co. [21477]
Kraft Foods Inc. Distribution, Sales, Service Div. [11641]
Kraft General Foods Group. Kraft Food Service [11643]
Kraft-Holleb [11644]
Krantor Corp. [11646]
Krasdale Foods Inc. [11647]
Krasdale Foods Inc. [11648]
Kroger Co. [11650]
Kuehn Company Inc.; Otto L. [11654]
Kwik-Way Corp. [11657]

Labatt Food Service [11663]	Mutual Trading Co. Inc. [11962]	Red Trolley Co. [12288]
Labatt Institutional Supply Company Inc. [11664]	Mutual Wholesale Co. [11963]	Reinhart Food Service Inc. [12297]
Lakeland Wholesale Grocery [11668]	Mutual Wholesale Co. [11964]	Reinhart Institutional Foods Inc. Milwaukee
Lankford-Sysco Food Services Inc. [11677]	Napoli Foodservices Inc. [11966]	Div. [12298]
Laurel Grocery Company Inc. [11684]	Nash Finch Co. [11969]	Renzi Brothers Inc. [12301]
Lee Cash & Carry [11691]	Nash Finch Co. [11970]	Reser's Fine Foods Inc. [12303]
Lee Co.; Henry [11692]	Nash Finch Co. [11971]	Rhodes Corp.; P.J. [12306]
Lee and Sons Inc.; W.S. [11693]	Nash Finch Co. [11972]	Richfood Holdings Inc. [12315]
Lehman Co.; Charles [11696]	Nash Finch Co. [11973]	Richfood Inc. [12316]
Leon Supply Company, Inc. [11699]	National Supermarkets [11979]	Ritchie Grocer Co. [12320]
Leon Supply Company Inc. [11700]	Nestle Carnation Food Service Co. [11997]	Ritter Sysco Food Services Inc. [12321]
Lewis Grocer Co. [11707]	New Age Distributing Co. [24992]	Robins Brokerage Co. [12331]
Liberty Gold Fruit Co. [11708]	New Hampshire Tobacco Corp. [26331]	Robin's Food Distribution Inc. [12332]
Lil Brave Distributors Inc./Division of Plee-Zing	Nicholas and Co. [12005]	Rocky Mountain Marketing Services Inc. [12339]
Inc. [11711]	Nichols Foodservice Inc. [12007]	Rodon Foods [12342]
Lincoln Poultry and Egg Co. [11713]	Nissho Iwai American Corp. [20226]	Rohtstein Corp. [12345]
Logan Inc. [11722]	Nonesuch Foods [12013]	Romeo & Sons [12349]
Lone Star Institutional Grocers [11728]	Normans Inc. [12020]	Roselli's Wholesale Foods Inc. [12353]
Long Wholesale Distributors Inc. [11730]	NorthCenter Foodservice Corp. [12030]	Ross and Company International; Mark [12354]
Long Wholesale Inc. [11731]	Northland Hub Inc. [12034]	Roundy's Foods [12356]
Luzo Food Service Inc. [24171]	Noyes and Son Inc.; J.C. [12042]	Roundy's, Inc. [12357]
M & B Distributors, Inc. [11749]	Nugget Distributors Inc. [12044]	Roundy's Inc. [12358]
Madison Grocery Company Inc. [11757]	Ohio Steak and Barbecue Co. [12056]	Roundy's Inc. Eldorado Div. [12359]
Maine Entrepreneurs Group [17508]	Oil Marketing Company Inc. [22538]	Roundy's Inc. Lima Div. [12360]
Maines Paper and Food Service Inc. [11761]	Olean Wholesale Grocery Cooperative Inc. [12065]	Roundy's Westville Div. [12361]
Major-Sysco Food Services Inc. [11763]	Oppenheimer Corp. Golbon [12073]	Royal Foods Distributors Inc. [12364]
Malone and Hyde Inc. [11766]	Original Chili Bowl Inc. [12076]	Rust Wholesale Company Inc. [12371]
Malone and Hyde Inc. Lafayette Div. [11767]	Orion Food Systems [12077]	Rykoff & Co.; S.E. [12374]
Maloney, Cunningham & Devic [11769]	Orr-Sysco Food Services Co.; Robert [24199]	Rykoff-Sexton Distribution Div. [12375]
Manchester Wholesale Distributors [11772]	Orrell's Food Service Inc. [12078]	Rykoff-Sexton Inc. [12376]
Mancini & Groesbeck, Inc. [11773]	O'San Products Inc. [12080]	Rykoff-Sexton Manufacturing L.L.C. [12377]
Market Specialties [11782]	Osborn Brothers Inc. [12081]	S and D Coffee Inc. [12379]
Marketing Performance Inc. [11783]	Pacific Commerce Company Inc. [12089]	S and M Food Service Inc. [12380]
Marketing Specialist Corp. [11784]	Pamida Inc. [12101]	Sales Corporation of Alaska [12393]
Marketing Specialista [11785]	Pancho's Mexican Foods Inc. [12103]	Sales Force Companies Inc. [12394]
Marmelstein and Associates Inc. [11788]	Paragon/Monteverde Food Service [12106]	Sales Force of Omaha [12395]
Marshall Co.; A.J. [4663]	Park Orchards Inc. [12111]	Sales Mark Alpha One Inc. [12396]
Marshall Co.; A.W. [11789]	Parker-Tilton Inc. [12114]	Sales Results [12397]
Martin Bros. Distributing Co., Inc. [11793]	Parks Company Inc.; Charles C. [12115]	San Jacinto Foods [12401]
Martin-Brower Co. [11794]	Pastorelli Food Products Inc. [12120]	Sandler Foods [24214]
Mascari & Associations; Charles [11800]	Paulk Grocery; H.B. [12122]	Sanford and Associates Inc.; Gene [12408]
Matthes and Associates [11806]	Paulk Grocery Inc.; H.B. [12123]	Santucci-Trigg Sales Co. [12411]
Mayer Co.; Budd [11813]	Pay Cash Grocery Co. [12124]	Sargento Foods Inc. [12414]
Mayer Myers Paper Co. [21826]	Peachey and Sons Inc.; A.J. [12125]	Saunders & Associates; Keifer [12420]
McCabe's Quality Foods Inc. [11817]	Pegler-Sysco Food Services Co. [12132]	Saval Foods [12421]
McCarty-Holman Company Inc. [11818]	Pence Company Inc.; W.J. [12136]	Scheidelman Inc. [12424]
McConnell and Sons Inc.; F. [11820]	Penn Traffic Co. [12139]	Schenck Foods Company Inc. [12426]
McDermott Food Brokers Inc. [11822]	Penn Traffic Co. Riverside Div. [12140]	Schnieber Fine Food Inc. [12430]
McFarling Foods Inc. [11826]	Performance Food Group Co. [12150]	Schultz Sav-O Stores Inc. [12431]
McGill & Co.; P. [11828]	Performance Northwest Inc. [12151]	Scrivner Inc. [12436]
McLane Company Inc. [11831]	Pezrow Food Brokers Inc. [12160]	Scrivner Inc. Buffalo Div. [12437]
McLane Company Inc. High Plains [11832]	PFG Lester [12161]	Scrivner of North Carolina Inc. [12439]
McLane Group Interntional L.P. [11833]	PFG Milton's [12162]	Scrivner of Pennsylvania Inc. [12440]
McLane Southwest, Inc. [11834]	Pick'n Save Warehouse Foods Inc. [12165]	Sealts Co.; J.M. [12450]
McLane Western, Inc. [11835]	Piedmont Distribution Centers [15620]	Seashore Food Distributors [12451]
McLemore Wholesale and Retail Inc. [11836]	Piggly Wiggly Alabama Distributing Company	Self Service Grocery [12459]
McMahon Foodservice Outlet [11838]	Inc. [12168]	Service Supply [12462]
MDG Inc. [24182]	Pizza Commissary Inc. [12178]	Services Group of America Inc. [12463]
Meijer Inc. [11845]	Plee-Zing Inc. [12181]	SGA Sales and Marketing Inc. [12467]
Mendez & Co. Inc. [1865]	Plus Distributors Inc. [12182]	Shaheen Brothers Inc. [12468]
Merchants Co. [11853]	PMI-Eisenhart [12183]	Shamrock Farms Creamery [12471]
Merchants Distributors Inc. [11854]	PMI-Eisenhart, St. Louis Div. [12184]	Shanks Co.; L.P. [12473]
Merchants Grocery Co. [11855]	PMI-Eisenhart Wisconsin Div. [12185]	Shenandoah Foods, Inc. [12477]
Merit Marketing Inc. [5185]	Pocahontas Foods USA Inc. [12186]	Shimaya Shoten Ltd. [12479]
Merkert Enterprises Inc. [11857]	Pola Foods Inc. [12187]	Shojin Natural Foods [12481]
Merrill Distributing, Inc. [11858]	Poritzky's Wholesale Meats and Food	ShopKo Stores Inc. [12482]
Metro Foods Inc. [11859]	Services [12195]	Shurfine International Inc. [12484]
Metropolitan Marketing Inc. [11860]	Powers Candy Company Inc. [12201]	Shurfine International Inc. [12485]
Micro Chef Inc. [11873]	Prairie Farms Dairy Supply Inc. [24205]	S.K.H. Management Co. [12500]
Mid-Central/Sysco Food Services Inc. [11878]	Preferred Brokerage Co. [12208]	Skidmore Sales & Distributing Company,
Mid-Mountain Foods Inc. [11879]	Preferred Products Inc. [12211]	Inc. [12501]
Midland Groceries Michigan Inc. [11884]	Premier Food Marketing Inc. [12213]	Sky Brothers Inc. [12503]
Midland Grocery Co. [11885]	President Global Corp. [12216]	Smart & Final Foodservice [12505]
Miller and Hartman Inc. [11898]	Pro-Fac Cooperative Inc. [12222]	Smith and Sons Foods Inc. [12517]
Miller and Hartman South Inc. [11899]	Professional Marketers Inc. [12228]	Sommer Advantage Food Brokers [12526]
Milton's Institutional Foods [11902]	Progressive Marketing [12230]	Sorem and Associates; L.S. [12529]
Minyard Food Stores Inc. [11909]	PYA/Monarch Chain Distribution [12240]	Southern Foods Inc. [12539]
Minyard Food Stores Inc. Carnival Food	PYA/Monarch Inc. [12241]	Spartan Stores Inc. [12547]
Stores [11910]	Quality Bakery Co. [12246]	Spartan Stores Inc. [12548]
Mitsubishi International Corp. [26151]	Quality Bakery Products Inc. [12247]	Specialty Distribution [12550]
Monroe and Associates Inc. [11924]	Quality Foods Inc. [12251]	Springfield Grocer Company Inc. [12558]
Monroe Foods [11925]	Quigley Corp. [19564]	Springfield Sugar and Products Co. [12559]
Monsour's Inc. [11926]	Ragland Co.; C.B. [12263]	Squeri FoodService [12560]
Mountain People's Warehouse Inc. [11947]	Rainbow Inc. (Pearl City, Hawaii) [12268]	Stan's Frozen Foods [12566]
Mountain Service Distributors [26330]	RAMM Global [12272]	Stanz Cheese Company Inc. [12568]
MSM Solutions [11952]	RAMM Metals Inc. [12273]	Stark & Company Inc. [12573]

Stark and Company Inc. [12574]
Stomel & Sons; Joseph H. [12588]
Stomel and Sons; Joseph H. [12589]
Suarez and Co.; V. [12597]
Suarez Food Distribution Co.; C.G. [12598]
Sunbelt Food Sales [12608]
Sunshine Market Inc. [12621]
Super Food Services Inc. [12623]
Super Rite Foods Inc. [12624]
Super Stores Industries [12626]
Super Stores Industries [12627]
Super Valu Inc. - Midwest Region [12628]
Super Valu Stores Inc. [12629]
Super Valu Stores Inc. [12630]
Super Valu Stores Inc. [12631]
Super Valu Stores Inc. [12632]
Super Valu Stores Inc. [12633]
Super Valu Stores Inc. [12634]
Super Valu Stores Inc. [12635]
Super Valu Stores Inc. Ohio Valley [12637]
Superior Foods [12639]
SUPERVALU [12642]
SUPERVALU Champaign Distribution
   Center [12643]
SuperValu Inc. [12644]
SUPERVALU Inc. [12645]
SUPERVALU Inc. Charley Brothers Div. [12646]
SUPERVALU Inc. Food Marketing Div. [12647]
SuperValu International [12648]
Supervalu - Milton Div. [12649]
SuperValu Quincy Div. [12651]
Sweet Life Foods Inc. [12654]
Switzers Inc. [12661]
Sygma Network [12662]
SYGMA Network of Ohio Inc. [12663]
SYGMA Network of Pennsylvania Inc. [12664]
SYSCO/Alamo Food Services, Inc. [12667]
Sysco Food Service of Cincinnati Inc. [12669]
SYSCO Food Service, Inc. [12670]
Sysco Food Service of Jamestown [12671]
Sysco Food Service of Seattle Inc. [12672]
SYSCO Food Services [12673]
Sysco Food Services of Atlanta Inc. [12674]
SYSCO Food Services of Atlantic City
   Inc. [12675]
Sysco Food Services of Austin Inc. [12676]
Sysco Food Services of Beaumont Inc. [12677]
Sysco Food Services-Chicago Inc. [12678]
SYSCO Food Services of Grand Rapids [12680]
Sysco Food Services of Houston Inc. [12681]
SYSCO Food Services of Indianapolis Inc. [12682]
SYSCO Food Services Los Angeles Inc. [12683]
SYSCO Food Services of Minnesota Inc. [12684]
Sysco Food Services of Philadelphia Inc. [12685]
SYSCO Food Services of Portland [12686]
Sysco Food Services of San Francisco,
   Inc. [12687]
SYSCO Food Services of South Florida [12688]
Sysco Food Services of South Florida Inc. [12689]
Sysco Intermountain Food Services Inc. [12690]
SYSCO of Louisville [12691]
Tanner Grocery Company Inc.; C.M. [12697]
Taylor and Sledd Inc. [12701]
T.B.I. Corp. [12703]
Thomas and Howard Company Inc. [12714]
Thomas-Walker-Lacey Inc. [12716]
Thompson-Clark-Gerritsen Co. [12717]
Thoms-Proestler Co. [24246]
TLC Beatrice International Holdings Inc. [12724]
Tomen America Inc. [20430]
Tom's Foods Inc. [12729]
Topco Associates Inc. [12734]
Topicz [26360]
Torn and Glasser Inc. [12735]
Transmedia Restaurant Company Inc. [24248]
Tree of Life Inc. [12747]
Tree of Life Inc. Midwest [12748]
Tri River Foods Inc. [12753]
Tri-State Wholesale Associated Grocers
   Inc. [12754]
Trinidad/Benham [12756]
Tripifoods Inc. [12757]
Triton Marketing Inc. [12758]
Tung Pec Inc. [12769]
Tusco Grocers Inc. [12777]
Twin County Grocers Inc. [12778]

Tzetzo Brothers Inc. [12781]
Uni-Marts Inc. [12784]
Union Grocery Company Inc. [12786]
UNIPRO Foodservice, Inc. [12788]
United-A.G. Cooperative Inc. [12789]
United Food Service Inc. [12793]
United Grocers, Inc. [12796]
U.S. Food Service [12801]
U.S. Foodservice Inc. [24257]
U.S. Foodservice - RRS Div. [12802]
U.R.M. Cash & Carry [12805]
U.R.M. Stores Inc. [12806]
US Food Service-Pittston Division [12807]
US FoodService Inc. Carolina Div. [12808]
Uster Imports, Inc.; Albert [12809]
Vallet Food Service Inc. [12815]
Valley Packing Service [12820]
Van Eerden Distribution Co. [12823]
VEC Inc. [12833]
Viles and Associates Inc. [12844]
Virginia Food Service Group [12848]
Virginia Wholesale Co. [12849]
Volunteer Sales Co. [12856]
Vowles Farm Fresh Foods [12857]
Wagner Candy Co. [12862]
Wakefern Food Corp. [12866]
Walker Company, Inc.; J.F. [12867]
Walton & Post [12873]
Waukesha Wholesale Foods Inc. [12884]
W.D. Trading Company Inc. [12888]
We Market Success Inc. [12889]
Weaver Co.; James A. [12890]
Webb Foods Inc.; Joseph [12891]
Weiland Associates [12898]
Westco Food Service Co. [12908]
Western Family Foods Inc. [12914]
Western North Carolina Apple Growers [12915]
Wetterau Inc. [12920]
Wetterau Inc. Northeast [12921]
White Company Inc.; John R. [12927]
White Feather Farms Inc. [12929]
White Fountain Supply Co.; Bob [24262]
White Swan, Inc. [12930]
White Swan, Inc. [12931]
White Swan, Inc. [12932]
Wilke International Inc. [12944]
Williams Inc.; M.R. [12947]
The Willing Group [14282]
Willow Run Foods Inc. [12952]
Winkler Inc. [12958]
Winters; Adam [12963]
Wise & Sons; A.B. [12968]
Witmer Foods Inc. [12969]
Witt Co.; The Eli [12970]
Wood-Fruitticher Grocery [12976]
Woodhaven Foods Inc. [12978]
Wright Brokerage Inc. [12987]
XNEX Inc. [5493]
Yankee Marketers Inc. [12990]
YAO Industries [12991]
Zanios Foods [13001]
Zatarain's [13003]

SIC 5142 — Packaged Frozen Foods

Acosta Sales Co. [10322]
Advantage Food Marketing Corp. [10331]
Advantage Sales and Marketing [10332]
Alabama Food Group Inc. [10351]
Alaskan Glacier Seafoods [10354]
Alaskan Gold Seafood Inc. [10355]
Alex City Provision Inc. [10361]
Allegiance Brokerage Co. [10368]
Alpha Star International Inc. [10380]
Alphin Brothers Inc. [10381]
Alpine Distribution Services [10382]
AME Food Service Inc. [10393]
American FoodService [10398]
Ancona Midwest Foodservices [10410]
Ancona/Midwest Inc. [10411]
Associated Brokers Inc. [10443]
Atalanta Corp. [10461]
Avalon Distributing Inc. [10474]
B & M Provision Co. [10483]

Bama Companies Inc. [10495]
Beaver Street Fisheries, Inc. [10521]
Belli-Childs Wholesale Produce [10532]
Berelson Export Corp. [10539]
Berelson Export Corp. [10540]
Blackburn-Russell Company Inc. [10564]
Blackmore Master Distributor [10565]
Blanke Sales Inc.; Bob [10568]
Bloemer Food Service Co. [10569]
Bluefin Seafoods Corp. [10582]
Bohrer Inc.; A. [10586]
Bratt-Foster Inc. [10609]
Bromar Inc. Bromar Hawaii [10616]
Brown Moore and Flint Inc. [10627]
Brown Packing Co. Inc. [10628]
Brown's Ice Cream Co. [10631]
Burris Foods Inc. [10646]
C-Corp. [10655]
Cal-West Foodservice Inc. [10668]
California Shellfish Company Inc. [10676]
Canale Food Services Inc.; D. [24087]
Catanzaro Sons and Daughters Inc.;
   Frank [10714]
Central Seaway Co. [10723]
Certified Grocers of California Ltd. [10728]
Certified Grocers Midwest Inc. [10729]
Cervena Co. [10730]
Chesapeake Fish Company Inc. [10740]
Chihade International Inc. [10746]
Chilli-O Frozen Foods Inc. [10749]
Church Point Wholesale Groceries Inc. [10757]
City Meat & Provisions Company, Inc. [10762]
Cloverhill Pastry-Vending Inc. [10776]
CMA Incorporated [10779]
Cole Brothers and Fox Co. [26277]
Consolidated Poultry and Egg Co. [10819]
Convenience Store Distributing Company
   L.L.C. [10830]
Craig & Hamilton Meat Co. [10863]
Crystal Products Corp. [10879]
Cutie Pie Corp. [10887]
Dadco Food Products Inc. [10891]
Dan Valley Foods, Inc. [10906]
Davenport-Webb Inc. [10914]
DBB Marketing Co. [10923]
Dennis Sales Ltd. [10944]
Dependable Food Corp. [10945]
Des Moines Marketing Associates [10947]
Diamond Foods Inc. [10957]
Dierks Foods Inc. [10964]
Dot Foods Inc. [10982]
Douglas Brothers Produce Co. [10985]
Downs Foods Co.; Tony [10987]
DPI Southwest Distributing Inc. [10990]
DPI Southwest Distributing Inc. [10991]
Duso Food Distributors [11002]
Eastern Shore Seafood [11017]
Economy Foods [11023]
El Encanto Inc. [11036]
Empire Fish Co. [11045]
EVCO Wholesale Foods Co. [11061]
F & A Food Sales Inc. [11067]
F and E Wholesale Food Service Inc. [11068]
Fairway Foods Inc. [11073]
Feesers Inc. [11117]
First Choice Food Distributors Inc. [11130]
Flowers Industries Inc. [11163]
Foehrkolb Inc.; Louis [11166]
Folloder Co. [11169]
FoodSalesWest Inc. [11182]
FoodSource, Inc. [11184]
Fox River Foods Inc. [11197]
French Gourmet Inc. [11204]
Fresh Fish Company Inc. [11208]
Fruit a Freeze [11222]
Garner Meats Inc.; John [11238]
Gateway Foods of Pennsylvania Inc. [11243]
Gaucho Foods Inc. [11245]
Goldberg and Solovy Food Inc. [11281]
Great Western Meats [11315]
Grocers Specialty Co. [11329]
Grocers Supply Co. [11330]
Grocers Wholesale Co. [11332]
H n' M Associates Inc. [11352]
Hanover Sales Co. [11372]
Hanover Warehousing [11373]

Harker's Distribution Inc. [11379]
Harrison Poultry Inc. [11382]
Hartford Provision Co. [11383]
Hawaiian Grocery Stores Ltd. [11394]
Hearn Kirkwood [11402]
Hoban Foods Inc. [11443]
Holberg Industries Inc. [11445]
Houk Co. Inc.; Clarence H. [11464]
ICEE-USA Corp. [24972]
Icicle Seafoods Inc. Port Chatham Div. [11487]
IGA Inc. [11491]
IJ Co. [11492]
Imperial Frozen Foods Company Inc. [11501]
Institutional Sales Associates [11514]
International Food and Beverage Inc. [11521]
Jordan Meat and Livestock Company Inc. [11564]
Jordan's Foods [11566]
Jordan's Meats Inc. [11567]
Juno Chefs Inc. [11572]
Kaelbel Wholesale Inc. [11576]
Kido Brothers Exports, Inc. [11608]
King Food Service [11613]
King Provision Corp. [11616]
Kings Food Service Professionals Inc.; J. [11618]
King's Foodservice Inc. [11620]
Kitchens of the Oceans Inc. [11623]
Knaubs Bakery [11628]
Koerner and Company Inc.; John E. [11632]
Ledyard Company Inc. [24164]
Lee and Sons Inc.; W.S. [11693]
Leone Food Service Corp. [11702]
Lil Brave Distributors Inc./Division of Plee-Zing
    Inc. [11711]
Logan International Ltd. [11723]
Lone Star Food Service Co. [11727]
Luanka Seafood Co. [11740]
M & F Foods [11750]
M and H Sales and Marketing Inc. [14156]
M & L Trading Company, Inc. [11751]
M & V Provision Company Inc. [11752]
Mallor Brokerage Co. [11765]
Malone and Hyde Inc. Lafayette Div. [11767]
Malone Products Inc. [11768]
Manassas Ice and Fuel Company Inc. [11771]
Maryland Hotel Supply Co. [11798]
Mattingly Foods Inc. [11807]
M.B.M. Corp. [11816]
M.E. Carter of Jonesboro Inc. [11840]
Meat Processors Inc. [11843]
Merchants Co. [11853]
Merchants Grocery Co. [11855]
Metropolitan Marketing Inc. [11860]
Mile Hi Frozen Food Co. [11895]
Miss Kings Kitchen Inc, The Original Yahoo!
    Baking Co. [11911]
Moore Food Distributors Inc. [11930]
Mor-Rad Foodservice [11934]
Mosey's Inc. [11937]
Murry's Inc. [11959]
Nash Finch/Bluefield [11968]
Nationwide Beef Inc. [11980]
Ne-Mo's Bakery Inc. [11989]
New Cooperative Company Inc. [12000]
New England Frozen Foods Inc. [12001]
Niagara Foods Inc. [12004]
Norpac Fisheries, Inc. [12021]
Norpac Food Sales Inc. [12023]
Olson-Kessler Meat Company Inc. [12067]
Orange Bakery Inc. [12074]
Overhill Farms [12084]
Packers Distributing Co. [12096]
Palermo's Frozen Pizza [12099]
Pan American Frozen Food Inc. [12102]
Paris Food Corp. [12109]
Parker-Tilton Inc. [12114]
Paulk Grocery; H.B. [12122]
Peco Foods Inc. [12129]
Penachio Company Inc.; Nick [12135]
Peyton Meats Inc. [12158]
Plee-Zing Inc. [12181]
Poritzky's Wholesale Meats and Food
    Services [12195]
Powell Company Inc.; W.J. [12200]
Prawn Seafoods Inc. [12207]
PrePeeled Potato Co. [12214]
Pro-Fac Cooperative Inc. [12222]

Proficient Food Co. [24207]
Pruden Packing Company Inc. [12233]
Purcell & Associates [12235]
Pyramid Agri-Products International [18184]
Quality Meat Company Inc. [12252]
R and R Provision Co. [12258]
Rainbow Inc. (Pearl City, Hawaii) [12268]
Rainsweet [12270]
Randy's Frozen Meats [12277]
REDI-FROZ [12291]
Resource Net International [21903]
Rich Products Corp. Food Service Div. [12312]
Ritter Sysco Food Services Inc. [12321]
Rocky Mountain Food Factory Inc. [12338]
Rodgers International Trading Inc. [12341]
Rogers Brothers Wholesale Inc. [12344]
Roundy's Inc. Lima Div. [12360]
Royal Cup Inc. [12363]
Ryan Company Inc.; W.E. [12372]
Rykoff-Sexton Manufacturing L.L.C. [12377]
St. John's Food Service, Inc. [12389]
San Jacinto Foods [12401]
Sanford and Associates Inc.; Gene [12408]
Santucci-Trigg Sales Co. [12411]
Schlachter Co. Inc.; Edward J. [12427]
Seafood Wholesalers Inc. [12449]
Sealts Co.; J.M. [12450]
Seaway Foods Co. [12455]
Select Foods Inc. [12458]
Self Service Grocery [12459]
Service Brokerage Inc. [12461]
Shelmar Food [12476]
Sioux Preme Packing Co. [12498]
Skinner Baking Co.; James [12502]
Sky Brothers Inc. [12503]
Smith Brothers Food Service Inc. [12508]
Snyder Wholesale Inc. [12524]
Sommer Inc.; John [12527]
Southeast Frozen Food Co. [12536]
Southern Industrial Corp. [24225]
Southern Seafood Co. [12541]
Specialty Grain Products Co. [12552]
Staunton Food Inc. [12579]
Stouffer Foods Corp. [12591]
Summit Import Corp. [12602]
Sun Glo of Idaho Inc. [12604]
Super Stores Industries [12626]
Super Valu Stores Inc. [12633]
Super Valu Stores Inc. [12636]
Superior Foods [12639]
SuperValu Inc. [12644]
SuperValu International [12648]
SuperValu—New England [12650]
SuperValu Quincy Div. [12651]
Sysco Food Service of Seattle Inc. [12672]
Sysco Food Services-Chicago Inc. [12678]
SYSCO Food Services of Detroit, LLC [12679]
SYSCO Food Services of Portland [12686]
SYSCO Food Services of South Florida [12688]
Tamarkin Company Inc. [12694]
Taylor and Sledd Inc. [12701]
Tenneva Food and Supplies Inc. [12707]
Thompson Company Inc. [12718]
Transmudo Company Inc. [12744]
Tung Pec Inc. [12769]
Turner Shellfish New Zealand Inc. [12774]
Tusco Grocers Inc. [12777]
Twin County Grocers Inc. [12778]
Tyson Seafood Group [12780]
United Foods Inc. [12794]
Valley Packing Service [12820]
VIP Sales Company Inc. [12847]
Volunteer Sales Co. [12856]
Watson Foodservice Inc. [12883]
Waxler Co. [12886]
Weems Brothers Seafood Co. [12896]
Weil and Co.; J. [12897]
Werner & Son; Max [12903]
Westco-BakeMark Las Vegas [12907]
Westco Food Service Co. [12908]
Wetterau Inc. [12919]
Wetterau Inc. [12920]
Wetterau Inc. Northeast [12921]
White and Company Inc.; L.N. [12928]
Wilcox Frozen Foods Inc. [12939]
Will Poultry Co. [12946]

Wilson Foods Company L.L.C. [12953]
Witmer Foods Inc. [12969]
Wolfstein International, Inc. [12973]
Wood Inc.; J.R. [12977]
World Food Tech Services [12982]
Wright Brokerage Inc. [12987]
Zacky Foods Co. [12999]

SIC 5143 — Dairy Products Except Dried or Canned

A. Camacho Inc. [10316]
Abbott's Premium Ice Cream Inc. [10318]
Adohr Farms Inc. [10328]
Aimonetto and Sons, Inc. [10348]
Allen Foods Inc. [10370]
Alliant Foodservice, Inc. [10372]
Alliant Foodservice Inc. [10374]
Alpine Distribution Services [10382]
Alta Dena Certified Dairy [10386]
Ambriola Co. Inc. [10391]
American Cheeseman Inc. [10395]
Anderson Erickson Dairy Co. [10413]
Angel Food Ice Cream [10418]
Applewood Farms Inc. [10425]
Ardrosson Farms [17704]
Associated Milk Producers Inc. North Central
    Region [10453]
Associated Milk Producers Inc. Southern
    Region [10454]
Associated Milk Producers Inc. Sulphur Springs
    Div. [10455]
Atalanta Corp. [10461]
Atlanta Ice Inc. [10463]
Atwater Creamery Co. [260]
Axelrod Foods Inc. [10477]
Bakalars Brothers Sausage Co. [10489]
Bar-S Foods Co. [10501]
Barkett Fruit Co. Inc. [10507]
Barnett Brothers Brokerage Co. Inc. [10509]
Baskin-Robbins USA Co. [10513]
Bassett Dairy Products Inc. [10514]
Bensinger's [10537]
Benz and Sons Inc.; George [17730]
Beyer Farms Inc. [10549]
Big Boy Ice Cream [10555]
Black Hills Milk Producers [10563]
Bloemer Food Service Co. [10569]
Borden Inc. [10590]
Borden Inc. [10591]
Borden Inc. [10592]
Borden Milk Products LLP [10593]
Boston Brands [10597]
BPC Foodservice Inc. [10606]
Branch Cheese Co. [10607]
Bratt-Foster Inc. [10609]
Broughton Foods LLC [10622]
Brown and Co.; Lewis A. [10623]
Brown Swiss/Gillette Quality Checkered
    Dairy [10629]
Brown's Ice Cream Co. [10631]
Buckman Farmers Cooperative Creamery [350]
Burris Foods Inc. [10646]
Butte Produce Co. [10650]
California Milk Producers [10672]
Cape Dairy Products Inc. [10690]
Cara Donna Provision Co. [10696]
Cardinal Frozen Distributors Co. [10697]
Cardinal Ice Cream Corp. [10698]
Central Minnesota Cooperative [397]
Chappells Cheese Co. [10735]
Cheese Importers Warehouse [10737]
China First Merchandising Co. [10750]
Chipwich Inc. [10752]
Chocolate Shoppe Ice Cream [10754]
Churny Company Inc. [10758]
Clay Cass Creamery [10766]
Clofine Dairy and Food Products Inc. [10772]
Clover Leaf Ice Cream [10774]
Co-Sales Co. [10781]
Cold Spring Cooperative Creamery [434]
Cole Brothers and Fox Co. [26277]
Coleman's Ice Cream [10789]

Colombo, Inc. [10791]
ComSource Independent Foodservice Companies Inc. [10803]
Connell Co. [10811]
Coors Brothers Co. [10837]
Country Classic Dairies Inc. [10854]
Country Fresh Inc. [10856]
Cream O' Weber [10864]
Crestar Food Products Inc. [10867]
Crown Distributing Inc. [10872]
Crystal Farms Refrigerated Distribution Co. [10877]
Crystal Food Import Corp. [10878]
Culver Dairy Inc. [10882]
Cutrufellos Creamery Inc. [10888]
Dairy Export Co. Inc. [10893]
Dairy Fresh Corp. [10894]
Dairy Fresh Products Co. [10895]
Dairy Gold Foods Co. [10896]
Dairy Maid Dairy Inc. [10897]
Dairy-Mix Inc. [10899]
Dairy-Mix Inc. [10900]
Dairy Valley [10901]
Dairylea Cooperative Inc. [10902]
Darigold [10908]
Darisil, Inc. [10909]
Dassel Cooperative Dairy Association [495]
Davis Company Inc.; H.C. [10916]
Dealers Food Products Co. [10927]
Dealers Food Products Co. [10928]
Dean Foods Co. [10929]
DeConna Ice Cream Inc. [10933]
Deli USA [10940]
Desert Delights Wholesale Ice [10949]
Detroit City Dairy Inc. [10952]
DMV USA Inc. [10970]
Doerle Food Services Inc. [10973]
Doneli Foods, Inc. [10981]
Dublin Yogurt Co. [10997]
E & M Ice Cream Distributors [11007]
Eberle Sons Co.; C. [11019]
Echo Spring Dairy Inc. [11020]
Edgerton Cooperative Farm Service Center [11027]
Equity Supply Co. [554]
EVCO Wholesale Foods Co. [11061]
F & A Dairy California [11066]
Fairview Dairy Inc. & Valley Dairy [11072]
Fairway Foods Inc. [11073]
Falcone and Italia Foods [11077]
Farm Fresh Inc. [11086]
Farmers Cooperative Co. (Dike, Iowa) [17854]
Farmers Cooperative Dairy Inc. [11097]
Farr & Sons Co.; Asael [11109]
Ference Cheese Inc. [11118]
Ferro Foods Corp. [11122]
Fieldbrook Farms Inc. [11123]
First Choice Food Distributors Inc. [11130]
Flav-O-Rich Inc. [11141]
Flav-O-Rich Inc. [11143]
Fleming [11145]
Fleming Companies Inc. [11148]
Flying J Travel Plaza [22285]
Food Lion Inc. [11173]
Forsythe Ice Cream [11191]
Foster's Good Service Dairy [11193]
Franks Inc.; M.E. [11201]
Gardenview Eggs [11236]
Gateway Foods of Pennsylvania Inc. [11243]
Gerber Cheese Company Inc. [11256]
Getchell Brothers Inc. [11258]
Gold Star Dairy [11280]
Golden State Foods Corp. [24961]
Gordon Food Company Inc. [11292]
Graf Creamery Co. [11302]
Grand River Meat Center [11305]
Granger Farmers Cooperative Creamery Association [11308]
Grassland Dairy Products Inc. [11310]
Green and Company Inc.; A.A. [11319]
Greenebaum Inc.; M.H. [11320]
Guernsey Farms Dairy [11343]
Harvin Foods Inc. [11389]
Hautly Cheese Company Inc. [11392]
Hawaiian Distributor Ltd. [11393]
Hawaiian Grocery Stores Ltd. [11394]
Hay-A-Bar Dry Ice Wholesaler [11396]

Henry's Homemade Ice Cream [11416]
Hickory Farms Inc. [11427]
Hillside Dairy Inc. [11435]
Hilmar Cheese Company Inc. [11436]
Hoban Foods Inc. [11443]
Holberg Industries Inc. [11445]
Hope Cooperative Creamery [11458]
Houston Harvest Gift Products LLC [11466]
Hudson Distributing Inc.; Mike [11474]
Hunter Farms [11479]
Hunter, Walton and Company Inc. [11480]
Ideal American Dairy [11490]
IGA Inc. [11491]
Imlers Poultry [11498]
Imperia Foods Inc. [11499]
Jack and Jill Ice Cream [11540]
Jetfreeze Distributing [11552]
Johnson Dairy Co. [11558]
Jones Dairy Farm Distributors [11561]
JR Distributors [11571]
Kemps Dairy Products Distributors [11598]
Kings Food Service Professionals Inc.; J. [11618]
Kolb-Lena Cheese Co. [11634]
Koolies Ice Cream [11636]
Kraft Food Ingredients [11640]
Kraft Foodservice Inc. [11642]
Kraft General Foods Group. Kraft Food Service [11643]
Land O Lakes Inc. [11672]
Land O Lakes Inc. [11673]
Latina Niagara Importing Co. [11680]
Lemke Cheese and Packaging Company Inc. [11698]
Level Valley Creamery, Inc. [11703]
Lifeline Food Company Inc. [11710]
London's Farm Dairy, Inc. [11725]
Lone Elm Sales Inc. [11726]
Lov-It Creamery Inc. [11737]
Luberski Inc. [11741]
Luxor California Export Corp. [11747]
M & V Provision Company Inc. [11752]
Madison Dairy Produce Company Inc. [11756]
Marmelstein and Associates Inc. [11788]
Martindale Feed Mill [990]
Maryland Hotel Supply Co. [11798]
Maryland Import/Export, Inc. [17514]
Maryland and Virginia Milk Producers Cooperative Association Inc. [11799]
Master Purveyors [11801]
Matanuska Maid Dairy [11802]
McCabe's Quality Foods Inc. [11817]
McIntosh Cooperative Creamery [11830]
Meadow Gold Dairies [11841]
Meadow Gold Dairy [11842]
Mellobuttercup Ice Cream Co. [11847]
Melody Farms Inc. [11848]
Michael Foods Inc. [11867]
Michael Foods Refrigerated Distribution Cos. [11868]
Mid-America Dairymen Inc. Brown Swiss [11874]
Mid-America Dairymen Inc. Southern Div. [11875]
Milk Marketing Inc. [11896]
Milk Products Holdings Inc. [11897]
Miller Machinery and Supply Company of Tampa [4457]
Minster Farmers Cooperative Exchange Inc. [18105]
Mohawk Dairy [11917]
Mohawk Farms Inc. [11918]
Montana International Lvstk [18111]
Mulligan Sales Inc. [11956]
Multifoods Specialty Distribution [11957]
Nelson-Ricks Creamery Co. [11994]
Neuman Distributors [11998]
New Cooperative Company Inc. [12000]
New England Frozen Foods Inc. [12001]
Nicholas and Co. [12005]
Niser Ice Cream [12008]
Nor-Joe Cheese Importing [12017]
Norseland Inc. [12024]
Northland Hub Inc. [12034]
Old Dominion Export-Import Co. Inc. [12060]
Old Home Foods Inc. [12063]
Pacific Fruit Processors Inc. [12090]
Parmalat USA [12118]
Performance Food Group Co. [12150]

PFS [12163]
Pierre's French Ice Cream Distributing Company of Akron [12167]
Pint Size Corp. [12170]
Pioneer Dairy Inc. [12171]
Plains Dairy Products [12180]
Polly-O Dairy [12189]
Prairie Farms Dairy Inc. Fort Wayne Div. [12204]
Prairie Farms Dairy Inc. Ice Cream Specialties Div. [12205]
Prasek's Hillje Smokehouse [12206]
Priscilla Gold Seal Corp. [12221]
Pure Sealed Dairy [12236]
Purity Dairies, Inc. [12237]
Radways Dairy [12262]
Reilly Dairy and Food Co. [12296]
Reinhart Institutional Foods Inc. Milwaukee Div. [12298]
Reiter Dairy [12299]
Richman's Ice Cream Div. [12317]
Rimfire Imports, Inc. [12318]
Riverside Homemade Ice Cream [12323]
Roberts Dairy Co. [12328]
Roberts Dairy Co. [12329]
Robin's Food Distribution Inc. [12332]
Rock Island North [12335]
Rock River Provision Company Inc. [12336]
Rockview Farms Inc. [12337]
Roselli's Wholesale Foods Inc. [12353]
Rous Inc.; R.J. [12362]
Russells Ice Cream [12369]
Ryan Company Inc.; W.E. [12372]
Rykoff-Sexton Distribution Div. [12375]
Sam's Ice Cream Inc. [12400]
Sargento Foods Inc. [12415]
Sartori Food Corp. [12417]
Schlachter Co. Inc.; Edward J. [12427]
Schneider Dairy [12428]
Schnieber Fine Food Inc. [12430]
Scrivner Inc. [12436]
Sculli Brothers Inc. [12441]
Shamrock Foods Co. [12472]
Simco Sales Service of Pennsylvania [12494]
Sinton Dairy Foods Co. Inc. [12496]
Smith Brothers Farms Inc. [12507]
Southeast Dairy Products [12535]
A Southern Season [12542]
Stacyville Cooperative Creamery Association [12561]
Sun-Ni Cheese Co. [12605]
Sunbelt Distributors Inc. [12607]
Sunset Ice Cream Offices and Sales [12618]
Sunshine Dairy Foods Inc. [12619]
Sunshine Dairy Foods Inc. [12620]
Super Store Industries/Fairfield Dairy Division [12625]
Super Valu Stores Inc. [12636]
SuperValu International [12648]
SuperValu—New England [12650]
SuperValu Quincy Div. [12651]
Swensen's Inc. [12659]
SYSCO Food Services of Portland [12686]
Takitani Enterprises Inc.; K. [25043]
Tamarkin Company Inc. [12694]
Thayer Food Products Inc. [12710]
Thibodeau's Farms [12711]
Thiel Cheese Inc. [12712]
Thompson Company Inc. [12718]
Tony's Fine Foods [12731]
Tree of Life/Gourmet Award Foods [12746]
Turner Dairy [12773]
Tuscan Dairy Farms Inc. [12775]
Tuscan/Lehigh Dairies L.P. [12776]
Tusco Grocers Inc. [12777]
Twin County Grocers Inc. [12778]
Umpqua Dairy Products Co. [12782]
United Dairymen of Arizona [12791]
Valley Farm Dairy Co. [12816]
Van Dam Brothers Co. [12822]
Vaughn Meat Packing Company Inc. [12832]
Velda Farms [12834]
Vermont Whey Co. [12838]
Waco Meat Service Inc. [12858]
Waddington Dairy [12859]
Waddington/Richman Inc. [12860]
Wades Dairy Inc. [12861]

Wallach's Poultry Farms [12871]
Wapsie Valley Creamery Inc. [12875]
Warren Cheese Plants [12880]
Weeks Div. [12894]
Weeks Div. [12895]
Wesley Ice Cream [12905]
Westby Cooperative Creamery [12906]
Westco-BakeMark Las Vegas [12907]
Western Dairy Products Inc. [12911]
Western Dairymen Cooperative Inc. [12912]
Wetterau Inc. [12919]
Wetterau Inc. [12920]
Wetterau Inc. Northeast [12921]
White Fountain Supply Co.; Bob [24262]
Wisco Farm Cooperative [12965]
Wormell; L.C. [18360]
Yarnell Ice Cream Company Inc. [12992]
Zanders Creamery Inc. [13000]
Zanios Foods Inc. [13002]

SIC 5144 — Poultry & Poultry Products

Agar Supply Company Inc. [10343]
Albert Poultry Co. Inc. [10357]
American FoodService [10398]
American Poultry International Ltd. [10401]
Barber's Poultry Inc. [10505]
Cagle's Inc. [10661]
Calvada Sales Co. [10681]
Case Farms of North Carolina Inc. [10708]
Central Connecticut Cooperative Farmers
  Association [17771]
Century Acres Eggs Inc. [10725]
Comer Packing Company Inc. [10797]
ConAgra Poultry Co. (Duluth, Georgia) [10806]
Consolidated Poultry and Egg Co. [10819]
Costas Provisions Corp. [10849]
Couch's Inc. [10852]
Craelius and Company Inc.; L. [10862]
Crown Foods Inc. [10873]
Crystal Farms Refrigerated Distribution Co. [10877]
CWT International Inc. [10889]
Daytona Beach Cold Storage Inc. [10921]
Decoster Egg Farms [10934]
Deen Wholesale Meat Co. [10936]
Dependable Food Corp. [10945]
Dewar & Company Inc.; John [10953]
Draper Valley Farms Inc. [10994]
Dutt and Wagner of Virginia Inc. [11004]
Entree Corp. [11050]
Extech Ltd. [18794]
Farm Boy Meats Inc. [11083]
Feather Crest Farms Inc. [11112]
Fleming Foodservice [11157]
Food Match, Inc. [11176]
Fox River Foods Inc. [11197]
FPC Foodservices [11198]
Gachot & Gachot, Inc. [11226]
Gant Food Distributors Inc. [11231]
Gardenview Eggs [11236]
Garner Meats Inc.; John [11238]
Goldberg and Solovy Food Inc. [11281]
Golden Poultry Company Inc. [11285]
Green Acre Farms Inc. [11318]
H and F Food Products Inc. [11348]
H and H Meat Products Company Inc. [11350]
Harker's Distribution Inc. [11379]
HCI Corp./International Marketing Services [18831]
Hemmelgran and Sons Inc. [11411]
Hillandale Farms Inc. of Pennsylvania [11432]
Holberg Industries Inc. [11445]
House of Raeford Farms [11465]
Imlers Poultry [11498]
International Trade & Telex Corp. [19378]
Jawd Associates Inc. [11550]
Jordan Meat and Livestock Company Inc. [11564]
Kings Food Service Professionals Inc.; J. [11618]
Kinnealey & Co.; T.F. [11621]
Lambright's Inc. [932]
Loda Poultry Company Inc. [11721]
Louis Rich Co. [11736]
Luberski [11741]

Maats Enterprises [19421]
Master Purveyors [11801]
McInerney-Miller Brothers Inc. [11829]
Metropolitan Poultry and Seafood Co. [11861]
Mims Meat Company Inc. [11904]
Murry's Inc. [11959]
Nash Finch/Bluefield [11968]
Neithart Meats Inc. [11993]
Neuman Distributors [11998]
Nichols Companies of South Carolina [12006]
Noerenberg's Wholesale Meats Inc. [12012]
Norbest Inc. [12018]
Nulaid Foods Inc. [12045]
O'San Products Inc. [12080]
Pacheco; James A. [12087]
Papetti's Hygrade Egg Products Inc. [12104]
Park Farms Inc. [12110]
Pennfield Corp. Pennfield Farms-Poultry Meat
  Div. [12142]
Petaluma Poultry Processors Inc. [12155]
PFS [12163]
Poultry Specialties Inc. [12199]
Prime Poultry Corp. [12218]
Pringle Meats Inc. [12220]
Protein Foods Inc. [12232]
Pyramid Agri-Products International [18184]
Quality Meats and Seafood Inc. [12253]
Race Street Foods Inc. [12260]
Randall Foods Inc. [12274]
Red River Barbeque and Grille [12286]
Rodgers International Trading Inc. [12341]
Rose Hill Distribution Inc. [12352]
Ryan Company Inc.; W.E. [12372]
Schlachter Co. Inc.; Edward J. [12427]
Sherwood Food Distributors [12478]
Supervalu - Milton Div. [12649]
SuperValu—New England [12650]
Sutherland Foodservice Inc. [12652]
Sweet Sue Kitchens [12657]
Thayer Food Products Inc. [12710]
Trenk and Sons; Joseph [18289]
Twin Valley Farmers Exchange Inc. [12779]
United Meat Company Inc. [12798]
Valley Farm Dairy Co. [12816]
Vaughn Meat Packing Company Inc. [12832]
Wallach's Poultry Farms [12871]
Ward Egg Ranch Corp. [12876]
Weil and Co.; J. [12897]
Werner & Son; Max [12903]
Western Beef Inc. [12909]
Wholey and Company Inc.; Robert [12936]
Will Poultry Co. [12946]
Willmar Poultry Company Inc. [12950]
Wisco Farm Cooperative [12965]
Wolfstein International, Inc. [12973]
Zacky Foods Co. [12999]
Zanios Foods Inc. [13002]
Zephyr Egg Co. [13005]

SIC 5145 — Confectionery

Aanns Trading Co. [4309]
Abraham and Sons Inc.; S. [26257]
Affy Tapple Inc. [10340]
Agricultural Survey Development
  Associates [10346]
Albert's Organics Inc. [10359]
All Season's Kitchen L.L.C. [10367]
Amcon Distributing Co. [26259]
Anderson Wholesale Co. [14022]
Andersons Candy Company [10414]
Annabelle Candy Company Inc. [10419]
Ann's House of Nuts, Inc. [10420]
Arrowhead Mills Inc. [10439]
Atlas Merchandising Co. [24072]
Auburn Merchandise Distributors Inc. [10468]
Axton Candy and Tobacco Co. [26262]
Badeaux Co.; Edward [26263]
Baker Candy Co. Inc. [10490]
Barentsen Candy Co. [26264]
Barentsen Candy Co. [10506]
Barnett Brothers Brokerage Co. Inc. [10509]
Barringer Distributing Company Inc.; R.H. [1501]
Beaverhead Bar Supply Inc. [1512]

Becksmith Co. [26414]
Beecher Candies; Katharine [10526]
Beer World [1517]
Benham and Company Inc. [10535]
Bergeron Pecan Shelling Plant, Inc.; H.J. [10541]
Blankinship Distributors Inc. [19193]
Bloemer Food Service Co. [10569]
Bob's Candies Inc. [10584]
Bon Ton Foods Inc. [10589]
Bond Wholesale, Inc. [26266]
Boyd-Bluford Co. Inc. [10602]
Bradley Distributing [24917]
Brans Nut Co. Inc. [10608]
Briggs Inc. [26267]
Bronson Syrup Company Inc. [10619]
Brost International Trading Co. [24271]
Brown & Haley [10626]
Brudnick Company Inc.; James [19203]
Bucks County Distributors [10638]
Bucky Bairdo's Inc. [10639]
Bur-Bee Co. Inc. [10644]
Burklund Distributors Inc. [10645]
Byrnes and Kiefer Company Inc. [10654]
California Naturals [10673]
Candy by Bletas [10688]
Capital Wholesale Distribution Co. [26271]
Capitol Distributing [26272]
Carolyn Candies, Inc. [10703]
Casani Candy Co. [10706]
Cash Wholesale Candy Co. [10712]
Chikara Products Inc. [10747]
Chocolate Specialty Corp. [10755]
Coclin Tobacco Corp. [26276]
Coffee Bean International Inc. [10786]
Columbia Bean & Produce Co., Inc. [10795]
Concord Sales Co. [26278]
Consolidated Wholesale Co. [26279]
Convenience Store Distributing Company
  L.L.C. [10830]
Core-Mark International Inc. [10840]
Core-Mark International Inc. Core-Mark International
  Incorporated Div. [10841]
Corr-Williams Co. [26281]
Corr-Williams Wholesale Company Inc. [26282]
Corso Inc.; Frank P. [26283]
Country Club Foods Inc. [10855]
Cowan Brothers Inc. [4605]
Cox Distributing; Dale [10861]
Crispy's Inc. [10868]
Crown Products Inc. [10875]
Cullen Distributors Inc. [26284]
D E B Industries, Inc. [10890]
Dakota Drug Inc. [14078]
Darlington Farms [10910]
Davenport and Sons Inc.; J.T. [10913]
Davis & Butler, Inc. [26285]
Davis and Sons Inc.; F.A. [26286]
De Vries Imports & Distributors [10925]
Dealers Food Products Co. [10927]
DeFranco and Sons Inc.; D. [10938]
DeSantis Distributors [10948]
Diamond Bakery Co. Ltd. [10956]
Dole Nut Co. Inc. [10977]
Dolly Madison Cake Co. [10980]
Douglas Northeast Inc. [10986]
Duffco [10998]
Eagle Wholesale L.P. [11011]
Eby-Brown Company L.P. [26289]
Edmiston Brothers Inc. [11028]
Elmira Distributing [1674]
Enstrom Candies Inc. [11049]
Equity Cooperative Association [22238]
Ethel M. Chocolates, Inc. [11055]
Euro American Trading-Merchants Inc. [11058]
Everson Distributing Company, Inc. [11062]
Falcon Trading Co. [11076]
Family Sweets Candy Co. Inc. [11078]
Fargo-Moorhead Jobbing Co. [11082]
Farner Bocken Co. [26292]
Farner Bocken Co. [11107]
Farner & Co. [11108]
Ferrara Food and Confections Inc. [11119]
Ferrara Pan Candy Co. [11120]
Five H Island Foods Inc. [11139]
Flanigan Farms [11140]
Flying J Travel Plaza [22285]

Food Match, Inc. [11176]
Foreign Candy Company Inc. [11186]
Frank, Inc.; Sam [26295]
Franklin Cigar and Tobacco Company Inc. [26296]
Frito-Lay Co. [11215]
Frito-Lay Inc. [11216]
Fritz Company Inc. [11218]
Garber Brothers Inc. [11232]
Garden Spot Distributors [11235]
Gary's Everfresh Products Inc. [11239]
Gate Petroleum Co. [11240]
Gatzke Farms Inc. [11244]
Glasgow Distributors Inc. [1718]
GNS Foods Inc. [11278]
Golden Peanut Co. De Leon Div. [11284]
Good Health Natural Foods Inc. [11290]
Gourmet Specialties [11299]
Graeffs Eastside Drugs; Mike [18814]
Gragnon Wholesale [11303]
Gray's Wholesale Inc. [26300]
Great Western Products Inc. [11317]
Grist Mill Co. [11328]
Grocers Specialty Co. [11329]
Grocery Supply Co. [11333]
Guarnieri Co.; Albert [21754]
H & M Distributing Inc. [26301]
Habys Sales Candy Co. [11354]
Hadley Braithwait Co. [11357]
Hammond Candy Co [11368]
Hammons Products Co. [11369]
Hartford Distributors Inc. [1746]
Hattiesburg Grocery Co. [11391]
Hayes and Sons; John [11398]
Heartland Distributors, Inc. [26305]
Helms Candy Company Inc. [11410]
Hennessy Ingredients; Ron [11412]
Henry's Foods Inc. [11414]
Hershey Foods Corp. [11421]
Hettinger-Mobridge Candy & Tobacco [26306]
HI Line Wholesale Co. [26307]
Hill City Wholesale Company Inc. [21760]
Hines Nut Co. [11439]
Homa Co. [11455]
Honor Snack Inc. [11456]
Hoopers Candies [11457]
Houston Harvest Gift Products LLC [11466]
Howe Company Inc.; George J. [11467]
HRD International [11468]
Hubbard Peanut Company Inc. [11471]
Humpty Dumpty Potato Chip Co. [11476]
Huser-Paul Company Inc. [26309]
Husky Food Products of Anchorage [11482]
Imperial Trading Co. [26310]
Inter-County Bakers [11516]
International Industries Corporation [11522]
J & V Vending Wholesale [26311]
JaCiva's Chocolate and Pastries [11539]
Jack's Bean Co. [11541]
Jacksonville Candy Company Inc. [11546]
Jans Distributing Inc. [26313]
Jogue Corp. [11557]
Jones-McIntosh Tobacco Company Inc. [26314]
K & L Associates, Inc. [11574]
Kaiser Wholesale Inc. [26315]
Kamaaina Distribution Co. [26316]
Keilson-Dayton Co. [26317]
Kennedy Wholesale Inc. [11601]
Kenyon, Inc.; Harry [26318]
Kern & Sons; Jacob [11604]
Key Sales Inc. [24157]
Klee Wholesale Company, Inc. [26319]
Klosterman Company Inc.; John C. [26320]
Kona Farmers Coop [11635]
K.R. International [11639]
Krema Nut Co. [11649]
KT Distributors [11652]
Kubota Inc. [1806]
L and L Jiroch Distributing Co. [26321]
Lavin Candy Company Inc. [11685]
Laymon Candy Company Inc. [11687]
LBM Sales Inc. [11689]
LBM Sales Inc. [11690]
Lee Cash & Carry [11691]
L.E.G. Inc. [11695]
Levinson Associates Inc.; Harold [26323]
Logan Inc. [11722]

Lord Brothers & Higgins [21811]
Los Angeles Nut House [11735]
Luce Candy Co. [11742]
Lutheran Distributors Inc.; A.M. [1832]
Mac Nuts of Hawaii [11753]
Marshall Co.; A.W. [11789]
MarshmallowCone Co. [11792]
Martinelli Inc.; John [11795]
Maui Potato Chip Factory [11809]
McClesky Mills Inc. [11819]
McDonald Candy Company Inc. [11823]
McDonough Brothers [11825]
McGill & Co.; P. [11828]
Melhado Co.; George [26328]
Melster Candies Inc. [11849]
Merrill Distributing, Inc. [11858]
Michaud Distributors [11869]
Michaud Distributors [11870]
Michelle's Family Bakery [11871]
Mid-Atlantic Snacks Inc. [11877]
Mid States Concession Supply [11881]
Mike-Sell's Inc. [11891]
Mike Sell's Indiana Inc. [11892]
Mike-Sell's Potato Chip Co. [11893]
Milhem & Brothers; Attea [26329]
Minter-Weisman Co. [11908]
Mitchell Products; Allen [11913]
Monel Distributors [11920]
Moore, Inc.; A.E. [4673]
Moore's Quality Snack Foods Div. [11932]
Moreland Wholesale Co., Inc. [11935]
Morse Wholesale Inc.; J.D. [26582]
Mound City Industries Inc. [11940]
Mountain Service Distributors [26330]
Mutual Distributors Inc. [11961]
Nabisco Foods. Phoenix Confections Div. [11965]
National Candy [11975]
Nebraska Popcorn, Inc. [11990]
New England Variety Distributors [24993]
New England Variety Distributors [12002]
New Hampshire Tobacco Corp. [26331]
New Hampshire Tobacco Corp. [26332]
NM Bakery Service Co. [12010]
Nor-Joe Cheese Importing [12017]
North Idaho Distributing Inc. [26333]
Northwest Tobacco and Candy Inc. [26334]
Notari Sales Co.; John [12040]
Notini and Sons Inc.; Albert H. [26335]
Noyes and Son Inc.; J.C. [12042]
Old Dutch Foods Inc. [12062]
Palmer Candy Co. [12100]
Paradies and Co. [4039]
Parkside Candy Co. [12116]
Paskesz Candies & Confectionery [12119]
Peak Distributing Co. [12126]
Peanut Processors Inc. [12127]
Penna Dutch Co. [12141]
Perugina Brands of America [12153]
Pez Candy Inc. [12159]
Piedmont Candy Co. [12166]
Pine Lesser and Sons Inc. [26340]
Pine State Tobacco and Candy Co. [26341]
Pollock; Ralph [12188]
Pond Brothers Peanut Company Inc. [12191]
Poore Brothers Distributing Inc. [12192]
Poore Brothers Inc. [12193]
Powers Candy Company Inc. [12201]
Powers Candy & Nut Co. [12202]
Preferred Products Inc. [12211]
Preferred Products Inc. [12212]
Prince of Peace Enterprises Inc. [12219]
Q.E.D. Exports [12244]
Quaglino Tobacco and Candy Company Inc. [26344]
Queen City Wholesale Inc. [12255]
Queen City Wholesale Inc. [12256]
Raketty Co.; A.E. [26345]
Red Mill Farms Inc. [12285]
Reeves Peanut Company Inc. [12294]
Rhodes Corp.; P.J. [12306]
Richardson Brands Co. [12314]
Robins Brokerage Co. [12331]
Rolet Food Products Co. [12347]
Rosario Candy Inc. [26348]
Russell Stover Candies [12367]
Russell Stover Candies [12368]

S & H Co. [26349]
Safa Enterprises Co., Inc. [12386]
Safier's Inc. [12387]
St. Louis Beverage Co. [2005]
San Saba Pecan, Inc. [12403]
Sanfilippo Co.; John B. [12407]
Sathers Inc. [12418]
Scheppers Distributing; N.H. [2011]
Sconza Candy Co. [12434]
Setton's International Foods Inc. [12465]
Shari Candies Inc. [12474]
Shoemakers Candies Inc. [12480]
SK Food International, Inc. [12499]
Slusser Wholesale Inc. [26652]
SNACC Distributing Co. [12521]
Snak King Corp. [12522]
Snyder Wholesale Inc. [12524]
Sosnick and Son; J. [12530]
A Southern Season [12542]
Stark Candy Co., Division of New England Confectionery Co. [12572]
State Line Potato Chip Co. [12578]
Sterzing Food Co. [12584]
Stomel & Sons; Joseph H. [12588]
Struve Distributing Company Inc. [25832]
Stutz Candy Co., Inc. [12596]
Sullivan Candy & Supply [26354]
Sunnyland Farms, Inc. [12617]
Superior Confections [12638]
Superior Nut Company Inc. [12640]
SuperValu International [12648]
SWD Corp. [26355]
Tastee Apple Inc. [12699]
Tayters Inc. [12702]
T.E.I./Texaco Bulk Services [12704]
Tetra Sales U.S.A. [19652]
Thompson Company Inc. [12718]
Thrift Products Company Inc. [12719]
Tidewater Wholesalers Inc. [4717]
Timber Crest Farms [12722]
Tobacco Sales Company Inc. [26357]
Tomfoolery Serious Chocolate, Inc. [12728]
Tom's Toasted Peanuts [12730]
Torn and Glasser Inc. [12735]
Totem Food Products Co. [12736]
TownTalk/Hostess [12738]
T.R. Distributing [12739]
Trophy Nut Company [12759]
Tropical Nut and Fruit [12761]
Tuong; Dam [12770]
Tzetzo Brothers Inc. [12781]
United Candy and Tobacco Co. [26363]
United Export Import, Inc. [20740]
Valley Convenience Products [26367]
Van's Candy & Tobacco Service [12830]
Vassilaros and Sons Inc.; J.A. [12831]
Vendor Supply of America Inc. [12836]
Vitner Company Inc.; C.J. [12852]
Wagner Candy Co. [12862]
Walker Distributors Inc. [12868]
Walker Distributors Inc.; Joe [12869]
Wallace's Old Fashion Skins Inc. [12870]
Warner Candy Company Inc. [12878]
Warrell Corp. [12879]
Waymouth Farms Inc. [12887]
Weaver Co.; James A. [12890]
Weeke Wholesale Company Inc. [26371]
Wertz Candies; Allen [12904]
Whaley Pecan Company Inc. [12923]
Wholesale Supply Company Inc. [26372]
Wilbur Chocolate Company Inc. [12938]
Wilkersons Pecans [12945]
Wilson Marketing & Sales [12954]
Winters; Adam [12963]
Wise Snacks Bryden Distributors [12967]
Wolfgang Candy Co. Inc.; D.E. [12972]
World Candies Inc. [12980]
World Food Tech Services [12982]
Wricley Nut Products Co. Edwards-Freeman Div. [12986]
Yorkshire Food Sales Corp. [12996]
Zenobia Co. [13004]
Zucca Inc.; L.J. [26377]

SIC 5146 — Fish & Seafoods

Agar Supply Company Inc. [10343]
Alabama Institutional Foods Inc. [10352]
Alaskan Gold Seafood Inc. [10355]
All Seas Wholesale Inc. [10366]
Alliant Foodservice, Inc. [10372]
Alphin Brothers Inc. [10381]
Amende and Schultz [10394]
American Poultry International Ltd. [10401]
Amory and Company Inc.; L.D. [10408]
Amsing International Inc. [10409]
Appert Foods [10423]
Aqua Gourmet Foods, Inc. [10427]
Aqua Star Inc. [10428]
Artemia of Utah Inc. [10440]
Atalanta Corp. [10461]
Axelrod Distributors [10476]
B and B Fisheries Inc. [10479]
B-G Lobster and Shrimp Corp. [10482]
Bakalars Brothers Sausage Co. [10489]
Bar Harbor Lobster Co. [10500]
Barnacle Seafood [10508]
Bay State Lobster Company Inc. [10515]
Bayou Caddy Fisheries Inc. [10518]
Bayou Land Seafood [10519]
Beaver Street Fisheries, Inc. [10521]
Bell Fish Company, Inc.; A.P. [10530]
Blount Seafood Corp. [10572]
Blue Ribbon Foods [10577]
Bluefin Seafoods Corp. [10582]
Bon Secour Fisheries Inc. [10588]
Borstein Seafood Inc. [10594]
Boston Sea Foods Inc. [10598]
Boyajian Inc. [10600]
Bratt-Foster Inc. [10609]
Bumble Bee Seafoods Inc. [10641]
Buy for Less Inc. [10653]
C-Corp. [10655]
California Shellfish Co. [10675]
California Shellfish Company Inc. [10676]
Calvada Sales Co. [10681]
Cape Oceanic Corp. [10691]
Central Seaway Co. [10723]
Chesapeake Fish Company Inc. [10740]
Chicago Fish House Inc. [10742]
Chin's Import Export Co. Inc. [10751]
City Provisioners Inc. [10763]
Clark Seafood Company Inc. [10765]
Clear Springs Foods Inc. [10768]
Clegg Seafood International [10769]
Clipper Quality Seafood, Inc. [10771]
Connolly Seafood; Steve [10812]
Connors Brothers Inc. [10813]
Consolidated Factors, Inc. [10816]
Cosmos Import Export Inc. [10846]
Couch's Inc. [10852]
Craig & Hamilton Meat Co. [10863]
Crystal Products Corp. [10879]
Daytona Beach Cold Storage Inc. [10921]
D.B. Brown Inc. [10922]
Deen Wholesale Meat Co. [10936]
Demerico Corp. [10943]
Depoe Bay Fish Co. [10946]
Dole and Bailey Inc. [10974]
Empire Fish Co. [11045]
Empire Seafood [11046]
Empress International Ltd. [11047]
Entree Corp. [11050]
Epicure Foods Inc. [11052]
Eureka Fisheries [11057]
Farm Fresh Catfish Co. [11084]
Fishery Products International [11135]
Fishery Products International USA [11136]
Fleming Foodservice [11157]
Floribbean Wholesale Inc. [11161]
Flower's Shellfish Distributors [11164]
Foehrkolb Inc.; Louis [11166]
Foley Company Inc.; M.F. [11168]
Fournier & Sons Seafoods; R. [11194]
Fresh Fish Company Inc. [11208]
Fresh Fish Inc. [11209]
Gant Food Distributors Inc. [11231]
Garbo Lobster Company Inc. [11233]
Gilbert Foods Inc. [11263]

Glacier Seafoods [11268]
Goldberg and Solovy Food Inc. [11281]
Gorton & Co., Inc.; Slade [11294]
Gorton and Company Inc.; Slade [11295]
Great Northern Products Ltd. [11313]
Gulf Central Seafoods Inc. [11344]
H and H Meat Products Company Inc. [11350]
H and N Fish Co. [11351]
Haley and Company Inc.; Caleb [11364]
Handy Company Inc.; John T. [11370]
Hanks Seafood Company Inc. [11371]
Hayes Associates; Marvin [11397]
Hearn Kirkwood [11402]
Herb's Seafood [11417]
Holberg Industries Inc. [11445]
Holly Sea Food Inc. [11451]
Horton's Smoked Seafoods [11463]
Hubert Co. [11472]
Ingardia Brothers Inc. [11506]
Inland Seafood Corp. [11508]
Italian Sausage Inc. [11531]
Jimmy's Seaside Co. [11555]
Josephson's Smokehouse and Dock [24150]
Kaelbel Wholesale Inc. [11576]
King Fish Inc. [11612]
King Lobster Connection [11614]
King Salmon Inc. [11617]
Kitchens of the Oceans Inc. [11623]
Kohl Grocer Company Inc.; N. [11633]
Komerex Industries, Inc. [16215]
Lascco Fish Products [11679]
Lawson Seafood Company Inc. [11686]
Lee and Sons Inc.; W.S. [11693]
Lone Star Food Service Co. [11727]
Look Company Inc.; O.W. and B.S. [11732]
Luanka Seafood Co. [11740]
Malik International Enterprises Ltd. [15574]
Marvin Hayes Fish Co. [11796]
Maxim's Import Corp. [11811]
Mayco Fish Company Ltd. [11812]
Mazzetta Co. [11815]
McCabe Bait Company Inc. [23814]
McInerney-Miller Brothers Inc. [11829]
Meier Inc.; Walter [11844]
Mendocino Sea Vegetable Co. [11851]
Meredith and Meredith Inc. [11856]
Metropolitan Poultry and Seafood Co. [11861]
Mid Atlantic Foods Inc. [11876]
Mitsubishi Intl Corp./Foods Div [11914]
Mor-Rad Foodservice [11934]
Morley Sales Company Inc. [11936]
Motivatit Seafoods Inc. [11938]
Mount Pleasant Seafood Co. [11942]
Murry's Inc. [11959]
Nash Finch/Bluefield [11968]
Natural Sales Network, Inc. [11986]
Neithart Meats Inc. [11993]
Nobel/Sysco Food Services Co. [12011]
Noerenberg's Wholesale Meats Inc. [12012]
Nomura America Corp. [26157]
Noon Hour Food Products Inc. [12014]
Nordic Delights Foods Inc. [12019]
Norpac Fisheries, Inc. [12021]
Norpac Fisheries Inc. [12022]
North Coast Sea Foods Inc. [12027]
Northern Wind, Inc. [12032]
Northwest Foods [12037]
Nunez Seafood [12046]
Ocean Crest Seafoods Inc. [12050]
Ocean Floor Abalone [12051]
Off the Dock Seafood Inc. [12054]
Olson-Kessler Meat Company Inc. [12067]
Ore-Cal Corp. [12075]
O'San Products Inc. [12080]
Pace Fish Company Inc. [12086]
Pacific Salmon Company Inc. [12093]
Pacific Sea Food Company Inc. [12094]
Packers Distributing Co. [12096]
Palacios Processors [12097]
PFS [12163]
Prawn Seafoods Inc. [12207]
Progressive Companies Inc. [12229]
Q.E.D. Exports [12244]
Quality Meats and Seafood Inc. [12253]
Race Street Foods Inc. [12260]
Rangen Inc. [18191]

Rappahannock Seafood Company Inc. [12280]
R.E.S. Associates [7918]
Resaca Inc. [12302]
Resource Trading Co. [12304]
Rimfire Imports, Inc. [12318]
Riverside Foods [12322]
Rock River Provision Company Inc. [12336]
Ross and Company International; Mark [12354]
Royal Seafoods Inc. [12365]
Rymer Foods Inc. [12378]
St. John's Food Service, Inc. [12389]
Salasnek Fisheries Inc. [12391]
Sales Force of Omaha [12395]
San Jacinto Foods [12401]
Schnieber Fine Food Inc. [12429]
Scrivner of North Carolina Inc. [12439]
Sea Harvest Packing Co. [12442]
Sea K. Fish Company Inc. [12443]
Sea View Fillet Company Inc. [12444]
Seafood Express [12446]
Seafood Marketing [12447]
Seafood Producers Cooperative [12448]
Seafood Wholesalers Inc. [12449]
Seattle Fish Co. [12453]
Seaway Distributors [12454]
Seaway Foods Co. [12455]
Shelmar Food [12476]
Shibamoto America, Inc. [16487]
Sierra Seafood Co. [12488]
Sigma International Inc. [12490]
Slavin and Sons Ltd.; M. [12504]
Smith Bros. Food Service Inc. [12506]
Smith Brothers Food Service Inc. [12508]
Smith & Son Fish; Luther [12515]
South Pier Fish Co. [12533]
Southern Seafood Co. [12541]
Southtowns Seafood & Meats [12544]
Starboard Inc. [12569]
State Fish Company Inc. [12577]
Stavis Seafoods Inc. [12580]
Steuart Investment Co. [12585]
Summers Sales Company Inc.; Barney [12600]
SuperValu—New England [12650]
SYSCO Food Services of South Florida [12688]
Tamashiro Market Inc. [12695]
Tennessee Shell Company, Inc. [12706]
Tenneva Food and Supplies Inc. [12707]
Terry Bros. Inc. [12708]
Tichon Seafood Corp. [12721]
Tri Marine International [12752]
True World Foods, Inc. of Alabama [12764]
Turner Shellfish New Zealand Inc. [12774]
U.S. World Trade Corp. [18305]
Vaughn Meat Packing Company Inc. [12832]
Victory Seafood Processors Inc. [12843]
Waco Meat Service Inc. [12858]
Walter's Meat Co. [12872]
Wards Cove Packing Co. [12877]
Weems Brothers Seafood Co. [12896]
Weinstein International Seafood Inc. [12899]
White and Company Inc.; L.N. [12928]
Wholey and Company Inc.; Robert [12936]
Will Poultry Co. [12946]
Willow Run Foods Inc. [12952]
Winter Harbor Fisheries [12961]
Wolfstein International, Inc. [12973]
World Food Tech Services [12982]
York River Seafood Company Inc. [12995]
Zanios Foods Inc. [13002]

SIC 5147 — Meats & Meat Products

Affiliated Foods Cooperative Inc. [10335]
Agar Supply Company Inc. [10343]
Alabama Institutional Foods Inc. [10352]
Albert Poultry Co. Inc. [10357]
Alderfer, Inc. [10360]
Allen Foods Inc. [10370]
Alpine Packing Co. [10383]
Amato International Inc. [10389]
AME Food Service Inc. [10393]
American Management Group [10400]
American Provisions Co. [10403]
Appert Foods [10423]

Applewood Farms Inc. [10425]
Arcadia Livestock, Inc. [17703]
Associated Wholesalers Inc. [10458]
Atalanta Corp. [10461]
Atlantic Premium Brands Ltd. [10464]
Auction Livestock, Inc. [17711]
Aurora Packing Company Inc. [10471]
B & M Provision Co. [10483]
Bailey's Slaughter House [17717]
Bakalars Brothers Sausage Co. [10489]
Becker Food Company Inc. [10523]
Belle Island International Inc. [10531]
Bensinger's [10537]
Benson-Quinn Co. [17729]
Best Sausage Inc. [10548]
Beyer Livestock; Allen [10550]
Bison Products Co. Inc. [10561]
Blanke Sales Inc.; Bob [10568]
Blue Grass Quality Meats [10574]
Blue Ribbon Foods [10577]
Blue Ribbon Meat Co. [10578]
Blue Ribbon Meat Company Inc. [10579]
Blue Ridge Beef Plant Inc. [10580]
Boyle Meat Co. [10604]
BPC Foodservice Inc. [10606]
Brown and Co.; Lewis A. [10623]
Brown Packing Co. Inc. [10628]
Bunker Hill Foods [10642]
Butler Beef Inc. [10648]
Calihan Pork Processors [10677]
Calihan Pork Processors [10678]
Calvada Sales Co. [10681]
Calvetti Meats Inc.; James [10682]
Capricorn Foods [10695]
Cara Donna Provision Co. [10696]
Casing Associates Inc. [10713]
Cattleman's Inc. [10715]
Cattleman's Meat Co. [10716]
Central Meat Packing [10722]
Certified Grocers Midwest Inc. [10729]
Chandler Foods Inc. [10733]
Chermak Sausage Co. [10738]
Chihade International Inc. [10746]
Chilay Corp. [10748]
Chilli-O Frozen Foods Inc. [10749]
Choe Meat Co. [10756]
City Market Inc. [10761]
City Provisioners Inc. [10763]
Clougherty Packing Co. [10773]
Cloverdale Foods Company Inc. [10775]
Coleman Natural Products Inc. [10788]
Colonial Beef Co. [10793]
Columbia Packing Co. Inc. [10796]
Comer Packing Company Inc. [10797]
ComSource Independent Foodservice Companies
   Inc. [10803]
Consolidated Poultry and Egg Co. [10819]
Continental Grain Co. [17792]
Costas Provisions Corp. [10849]
Couch's Inc. [10852]
Cougle Commission Co. [10853]
Country Smoked Meats Inc. [10858]
Craig & Hamilton Meat Co. [10863]
Crossmark Sales and Marketing [10871]
Crown Distributing Inc. [10872]
Crown Foods Inc. [10873]
Curtis Packing Co. Inc. [10883]
Curtis Packing Co. Inc. [10884]
Cusack Wholesale Meat Co. [10886]
Dallas City Packing Inc. [10903]
D'Artagnan Inc. [10912]
Davis Company Inc.; H.C. [10916]
Daytona Beach Cold Storage Inc. [10921]
D.B. Brown Inc. [10922]
DeBragga and Spitler Inc. [10931]
Deen Meat Co., Inc. [10935]
Deen Wholesale Meat Co. [10936]
Delaware Foods Inc. [10939]
Demakes Enterprises and Co. Inc. [10941]
Detroit City Dairy Inc. [10952]
Dewar & Company Inc.; John [10953]
Dewied International Inc. [10954]
Doerle Food Services Inc. [10973]
Dole and Bailey Inc. [10974]
Double A Provisions Inc. [10983]
Doughtie's Foods Inc. [10984]

DPM of Arkansas [10993]
Durham Meat Co. [11000]
Earp Meat Company Inc. [11012]
Ehmer Inc.; Karl [11034]
Elm Hill Meats Inc. [11042]
Empire Beef Company Inc. [11044]
Entree Corp. [11050]
Epicure Foods Inc. [11052]
European Kosher Provision [11060]
EVCO Wholesale Foods Co. [11061]
Excel Corp. [11063]
Excel Corp. DPM Foods Div. [11064]
F & A Food Sales Inc. [11067]
Fairbank Reconstruction Corp. [11070]
Fairway Foods Inc. [11073]
Farm Boy Meats Inc. [11083]
Farmer Johns Packing Co. [11087]
Farmland Foods [11106]
FDL Marketing Inc. [11110]
Federated Foods Inc. [11114]
Fiorucci Foods USA Inc. [11129]
First Choice Food Distributors Inc. [11130]
Fleming Companies Inc. [11148]
Foell Packing Co. [11167]
FoodSource, Inc. [11184]
Ford Brothers Wholesale Meats Inc. [11185]
Fort Pitt Brand Meat Co. [11192]
Fox River Foods Inc. [11197]
Freirich Food; Julian [11203]
Gachot & Gachot, Inc. [11226]
Gamble Co.; L.H. [11230]
Gant Food Distributors Inc. [11231]
Gardenview Eggs [11236]
Garner Meats Inc.; John [11238]
Gaucho Foods Inc. [11245]
Gerber Agri-Export Inc. [11255]
Gerlach Beef Inc. [11257]
GFI America Inc. [11260]
Gilbert Foods Inc. [11263]
Gilco Meats Inc. [11264]
Glen Rose Meat Services Inc. [11269]
Gliers Meats Inc. [11271]
Gordon Food Company Inc. [11292]
Grand River Meat Center [11305]
Great Western Meats [11315]
Great Western Meats Inc. [11316]
Greenebaum Inc.; M.H. [11320]
Groff Meats Inc. [11336]
Habbersett Sausage Inc. [11353]
Hahn Bros. Inc. [11359]
Hahns of Westminster [11360]
Hartford Provision Co. [11383]
Hartford Provision Co. [11384]
Harvin Choice Meats Inc. [11388]
Harvin Foods Inc. [11389]
Hatfield Quality Meats Inc. [11390]
Hazle Park Packing Co. [11399]
Hearn Kirkwood [11402]
Helmbold Inc.; Fritz [11409]
Henry J. Easy Pak Meats [11413]
Henry's Hickory House Inc. [11415]
Herring & Co.; T.L. [11420]
Hi Grade Meats Inc. [11424]
Hickory Farms Inc. [11427]
Holberg Industries Inc. [11445]
Holmes Smokehouse Inc.; S and D [11452]
Holten Meat Inc. [11453]
Hormel Foods International Corp. [11462]
Hudson Distributing Inc.; Mike [11474]
Hygrade Food Products [11485]
Imlers Poultry [11498]
Italian Sausage Inc. [11531]
J and B Meats Corp. [11534]
J and B Meats Corp. [11535]
J and B Wholesale Distribution [11536]
J & V Vending Wholesale [26311]
Jordan Meat and Livestock Company Inc. [11564]
Karn Meats Inc. [11582]
Kaye Brothers Inc. [11586]
King Cotton Foods [11611]
Kinnealey & Co.; T.F. [11621]
Knauss and Son Inc.; E.W. [11629]
Kohl Grocer Company Inc.; N. [11633]
Kowalski Sausage Company Inc. [11638]
Kroger Co. Dairy-Bakery Div. [11651]
Kunzler and Company Inc. [11656]

Lays Fine Foods [11688]
Lee and Sons Inc.; W.S. [11693]
Leidy's Inc. [11697]
Leonard and Harral Packing Company Inc. [11701]
Levonian Brothers Inc. [11705]
Lincoln Packing Co. [11712]
Lindsay Foods Inc. [11716]
Lionel Lavallee Company Inc. [11717]
Loda Poultry Company Inc. [11721]
Lone Star Food Service Co. [11727]
Lords Sausage [11733]
Lowell Packing Co. [11738]
Lumen Foods [11744]
Luter Packing Company Inc. [11746]
Lykes Bros. Inc. [11748]
M & V Provision Company Inc. [11752]
Malone and Hyde Inc. Lafayette Div. [11767]
Manassas Ice and Fuel Company Inc. [11771]
Manhattan Wholesale Meat Company Inc. [11775]
Mark's Quality Meats [11787]
Maryland Hotel Supply Co. [11798]
Master Purveyors [11801]
Mathews and Sons Inc.; G.D. [11804]
Mattingly Foods Inc. [11807]
Mattingly Foods Inc. [11808]
Maverick Ranch Lite Beef Inc. [11810]
Maxim's Import Corp. [11811]
McCabe's Quality Foods Inc. [11817]
McGee's Packing Co. [11827]
Meat Processors Inc. [11843]
Metro Foods Inc. [11859]
Metropolitan Poultry and Seafood Co. [11861]
Midamar Corp. [11882]
Midtown Packing Company Inc. [11887]
Mims Meat Company Inc. [11904]
Miniat Inc.; Ed [11905]
Monfort Inc. [11921]
Monfort International Sales Corp. [11922]
Monfort-Swift Support Centers [11923]
Montage Foods Inc. [11927]
Moore Food Distributors Inc. [11930]
Mor-Rad Foodservice [11934]
Mosey's Inc. [11937]
Mott Meat Company, Inc. [11939]
Murry's Inc. [11959]
Nash Finch/Bluefield [11968]
Natco Food Service Merchants [11974]
National Foods [11977]
National Heritage Sales Corp. [11978]
Nationwide Beef Inc. [11980]
Natural Meat Specialties [11983]
Neithart Meats Inc. [11993]
Nesson Meat Sales [11996]
Neuman Distributors [11998]
Nevada Food Service [11999]
New Cooperative Company Inc. [12000]
New Horizons Meats and Dist., L.L.C. [12003]
Nicholas and Co. [12005]
Noerenberg's Wholesale Meats Inc. [12012]
Nor-Joe Cheese Importing [12017]
Northwest Meats Inc. [12038]
Northwood Meats Inc. [12039]
Nueske Hillcrest Farm Meats [12043]
O'Brien and Co. [12049]
Olson-Kessler Meat Company Inc. [12067]
Omaha Steaks Foodservice [12068]
Omaha Steaks International [12069]
Oscars Wholesale Meats Company Inc. [12082]
Packers Distributing Co. [12096]
Parkway Food Service Inc. [12117]
Patterson Brothers Meat Co. [12121]
Peachey and Sons Inc.; A.J. [12125]
Performance Food Group Co. [12150]
Perishable Distributors of Iowa Ltd. [12152]
Peyton Meats Inc. [12158]
PFS [12163]
Pioneer Snacks Inc. [12174]
Pioneer Wholesale Meat [12175]
Pittsburgh Oakland Enterprises Inc. [12177]
Poritzky's Wholesale Meats and Food
   Services [12195]
Pork Packers International [12196]
Prasek's Hillje Smokehouse [12206]
Preferred Meats Inc. [12210]
Pringle Meats Inc. [12220]
Pruden Packing Company Inc. [12233]

Quality Meat Company Inc. [12252]
Quality Meats and Seafood Inc. [12253]
Quarex Industries Inc. [12254]
R and R Provision Co. [12258]
Race Street Foods Inc. [12260]
Randall Foods Inc. [12274]
Randy's Frozen Meats [12277]
Ray's Wholesale Meat [12281]
Red Apple Supermarkets [12283]
Reinhart Institutional Foods Inc. Milwaukee
   Div. [12298]
Rich Planned Foods [12311]
Richard's American Food Service [12313]
Rimfire Imports, Inc. [12318]
Robins Brokerage Co. [12331]
Robzens Inc. [12334]
Rock River Provision Company Inc. [12336]
Rocky Mountain Natural Meats Inc. [12340]
Rogers Brothers Wholesale Inc. [12344]
Rolet Food Products Co. [12347]
Roma Food Enterprises Inc. [12348]
Roselli's Wholesale Foods Inc. [12353]
Rykoff-Sexton Distribution Div. [12375]
Rymer Foods Inc. [12378]
S & N Sales [12382]
S and S Meat Company Inc. [12383]
Saag's Products Inc. [12384]
St. John's Food Service, Inc. [12389]
Saint Louis Restaurant Steaks Inc. [12390]
San Jacinto Foods [12401]
Santucci-Trigg Sales Co. [12411]
Saval Foods [12421]
Scariano Brothers Inc. [12422]
Schaefer's Cold Storage [12423]
Schlachter Co. Inc.; Edward J. [12427]
Schnieber Fine Food Inc. [12430]
Schumacher Wholesale Meats Inc. [12432]
Scrivner Inc. [12436]
Scrivner of North Carolina Inc. [12439]
Sculli Brothers Inc. [12441]
Shelmar Food [12476]
Sherwood Food Distributors [12478]
Shopper's Food Warehouse Corp. [12483]
Shurfine International Inc. [12484]
Sierra Meat Company Inc. [12487]
Silver Springs Farm Inc. [12493]
Sioux Preme Packing Co. [12498]
Smith Packing Company Inc. [12511]
Smith Provision Company Inc. [12514]
Smith & Sons Co.; Dale T. [12516]
Smithfield Companies Inc. [12518]
Smithfield Ham Products Co. Inc. [12519]
Sosnick and Son; J. [12530]
Standard Meat Co. [12564]
Stan's Smokehouse Inc. [12567]
Stone Commodities Corp. [12590]
Stratton's Salads; Mrs. [12593]
Super Valu Stores Inc. [12636]
SUPERVALU Inc. Food Marketing Div. [12647]
Supervalu - Milton Div. [12649]
SuperValu—New England [12650]
SuperValu Quincy Div. [12651]
Swanton Packing, Inc. [12653]
SYSCO Food Services of Minnesota Inc. [12684]
Tennessee Dressed Beef Company Inc. [12705]
Tenneva Food and Supplies Inc. [12707]
Thomas Brothers Ham Co. [12713]
Thomas and Howard Company Inc. [12714]
Thomas Meat Co. [12715]
Tomahawk Farms Inc. [12727]
Tony's Fine Foods [12731]
Totem Food Products Co. [12736]
Transmudo Company Inc. [12744]
Trax Farms Inc. [12745]
Troyer Foods Inc. [12763]
Tusco Grocers Inc. [12777]
United Heritage Corp. [12797]
United Meat Company Inc. [12798]
Uvalde Meat Processing [12811]
U.W. Provision Co. [12812]
Vaughn Meat Packing Company Inc. [12832]
Vina & Son Meat Distributors [12846]
Vowles Farm Fresh Foods [12857]
Waco Meat Service Inc. [12858]
Walter's Meat Co. [12872]
Wamplers Farm Sausage [12874]

Weil and Co.; J. [12897]
Wenzel Farm Sausage [12902]
Western Beef Inc. [12909]
Wetterau Inc. [12920]
Wexler Meat Co. [12922]
Wholey and Company Inc.; Robert [12936]
Wild Game Inc. [12941]
Will Poultry Co. [12946]
Williams Inc.; T.O. [12948]
Willow Run Foods Inc. [12952]
Wisconsin Packing Company Inc. [12966]
Wolfstein International, Inc. [12973]
Wolverine Packing Co. [12974]
Yoders Inc. [12994]
Zanios Foods Inc. [13002]

SIC 5148 — Fresh Fruits & Vegetables

Adams Brothers Produce Company Inc. [10323]
Adams Brothers Produce Company of Tuscaloosa
   Inc. [10324]
Advanced Specialties [10329]
Affiliated Foods Cooperative Inc. [10335]
Affy Tapple Inc. [10340]
Agri-Empire [10345]
Agricultural Survey Development
   Associates [10346]
Agrimor [10347]
Alabama Food Group Inc. [10351]
Alabama Institutional Foods Inc. [10352]
Albert's Organics Inc. [10359]
Alex City Provision Inc. [10361]
Allen Foods Inc. [10370]
Alsum Produce Inc. [10385]
AME Food Service Inc. [10393]
American Food Export Co. [10396]
American FoodService [10398]
Andrew and Williamson Sales Co. [10416]
Andrews Produce Inc. [10417]
Anthony Farms Inc. [10421]
Appert Foods [10423]
Armstrong Produce Ltd. [10435]
Associated Food Stores Inc. (Salt Lake City,
   Utah) [10448]
Associated Potato Growers Inc. [10456]
Associated Wholesalers Inc. [10458]
Atlas Vegetable Exchange [10467]
Aunt Mid Produce Co. [10470]
The Auster Co. Inc. [10472]
B and B Produce Inc. [10480]
Badalament Inc. [10484]
Badalament Inc. [10485]
Banana Supply Company Inc. [10496]
Barkett Fruit Co. Inc. [10507]
Bay View Food Products Co. [10516]
Beckman Produce Inc. [10524]
Bell-Carter Foods Inc. [10529]
Belli-Childs Wholesale Produce [10532]
Bell's Produce, Inc. [10533]
Bensinger's [10537]
Bertuca Co.; Teddy [10545]
Bianchi and Sons Packing Co. [10552]
Big Banana Fruit Market [10554]
Bland Farms Inc. [10567]
Blanke Sales Inc.; Bob [10568]
Blue Anchor Inc. [10573]
Blue Mountain Growers Inc. [10576]
Blue Star Growers Inc. [10581]
Bob's Fruit Market & Deli [10585]
Bohrer Inc.; A. [10586]
Brock Corp.; J.C. [10614]
Brooks and Co.; H. [10621]
Brown and Co.; Lewis A. [10623]
Buikema Produce Co. [10640]
Burrows Inc.; John H. [10647]
Buurma Farms Inc. [10652]
Caito Foods Service, Inc. [10664]
Cal Fruit [10666]
Calco of Minneapolis Inc. [10669]
California Pacific Fruit Co. [10674]
Callif Co. [10680]
Campbell's Fresh Inc. [10686]

Campbell's Fresh Inc. [10687]
Capitol City Produce [10692]
Caro Produce and Institutional Foods Inc. [10702]
Cascadian Fruit Shippers Inc. [10707]
Cavalier, Gulling, and Wilson Inc. [10717]
Central City Produce Inc. [10719]
C.H. Robinson Company Inc. [10732]
Chazy Orchards Inc. [10736]
Cherry Central, Inc. [10739]
Chestnut Hill Farms Inc. [10741]
Chico Produce, Inc. [10743]
Chief Tonasket Growers [10744]
Chief Wenatchee [10745]
Circle Produce Co. [10760]
City Market Inc. [10761]
City Provisioners Inc. [10763]
Club Chef [10778]
Coastal Berry Company [10782]
Colorado Potato Growers Exchange [10794]
Community Suffolk Inc. [10801]
Congdon Orchards Inc. [10810]
Consolidated Factors, Inc. [10816]
Consumers Produce Co. [10821]
Corids & Son Inc.; Alex D. [10842]
Cornille and Sons Inc.; George J. [10843]
Cosentino Company Inc.; J. [10844]
Costa Fruit and Produce Co. [10848]
Country Wide Transport Services Inc. [10860]
CPS Marketing Corporation [18757]
Crest Fruit Co. Inc. [10866]
Damore's Wholesale Produce [10905]
Dan Valley Foods, Inc. [10906]
D'Arrigo Brothers of Massachusetts Inc. [10911]
Davis Produce, Inc.; John [10917]
De Bruyn Produce Company Inc. [10924]
DeFranco and Sons Inc.; D. [10938]
Delta International [17817]
Demase and Manna Co. [10942]
Diamond Fruit Growers [10958]
Diamond Fruit Growers [10959]
Diamond Nut Company of California [10960]
Diamond Tager Co. [10961]
Dierks Foods Inc. [10964]
DiMare Brothers Inc. [10965]
DiMare Homestead Inc. [10966]
Dixie Produce and Packaging Inc. [10968]
Dixon Tom-A-Toe Cos. [10969]
DNE World Fruit Sales Inc. [10971]
Doerle Food Services Inc. [10973]
Dole Bakersfield Inc. [10975]
Dole Fresh Vegetables Co. [10976]
Douglas Brothers Produce Co. [10985]
DPI Food Products Co. [10989]
Dundee Citrus Growers Association [10999]
Earth Brothers Ltd. [11013]
Ebel Company Inc.; Fred C. [11018]
E.D. Packing Co. [11025]
Eden Valley Growers Inc. [11026]
Edwards Fruit Co. [11030]
Edwards Produce Co.; M and B [11031]
Egan and Co.; Bernard [11032]
Elmore & Stahl Inc. [11043]
Etheridge Produce [11056]
EVCO Wholesale Foods Co. [11061]
F & A Food Sales Inc. [11067]
F and E Wholesale Food Service Inc. [11068]
Fantastic Foods Inc. [11080]
Farm Fresh Foods Inc. [11085]
Federal Fruit and Produce Co. [11113]
Fishery Products International [11135]
Fitzgerald Ltd. [690]
Food Match, Inc. [11176]
Food Services of America Inc. [11180]
Forlizzi Brothers [11189]
FPC Foodservices [11198]
Francisco Distributing [11199]
Frankferd Farms [11200]
Fresh Advantage [11205]
Fresh America Corp. [11206]
Fresh Express [11207]
Fresh Start Produce Sales, Inc. [11211]
FreshPoint Inc. [11212]
FreshWorld Farms Inc. [11213]
Funderburk Company Inc.; G.A. [11224]
G and G Produce Company Inc. [11225]
Gateway Foods of Pennsylvania Inc. [11243]

Gatzke Farms Inc. [11244]
General Potato and Onion Inc. [11250]
General Produce Company Ltd. [11251]
George Co., Inc.; William [11254]
Gerber Agri-Export Inc. [11255]
Ghiselli Brothers [11261]
Gilbert Foods Inc. [11263]
Giumarra Brothers Fruit Company, Inc. [11267]
Global Tropical [11273]
Gloucester County Packing Co. [11276]
Glover Wholesale Inc. [11277]
GNS Foods Inc. [11278]
Goodson Farms Inc. [11291]
GPOD of Idaho [11300]
Gracewood Fruit Co. [11301]
Greenleaf Produce [11321]
Greg Orchards & Produce Inc. [11322]
Griffin and Brand Produce Sales Agency Inc. [11324]
Griffin & Brand Sales Agency, Inc. [11325]
Griffin-Holder Co. [11326]
Grocers Wholesale Co. [11332]
Grower Shipper Potato Co. [11337]
Growers Marketing Service Inc. [11338]
Growers Precooler Inc. [11339]
Grower's Produce Corp. [11340]
Harrington Produce [11380]
Hartford Provision Co. [11383]
Harvin Foods Inc. [11389]
Hauser Company; M.L. [16092]
Hearn Kirkwood [11402]
Hearne Produce Co.; William P. [11403]
Heeren Brothers, Inc. [11406]
Hellman Produce Inc.; J. [11408]
Heritage Wafers Ltd. [11419]
Hickenbottom and Sons Inc. [11426]
Highland Exchange Service Co-op [11431]
Hollandale Marketing Association [11448]
Hollar and Greene Produce [11449]
Hollar and Greene Produce Co., Inc. [11450]
Holthouse Brothers [11454]
Idaho Supreme Potatoes Inc. [11489]
Imlers Poultry [11498]
Indianapolis Fruit Company, Inc. [11505]
Ingardia Brothers Inc. [11506]
Inland Fruit and Produce Company Inc. [11507]
Iseri Produce Co.; Thomas [11530]
Italian Sausage Inc. [11531]
Jackson Produce Co. [11543]
Javi Farm Inc. [11549]
JC Produce Inc. [11551]
Jones Potatoes Inc.; Rolland [11562]
Kamaaina Distribution [11578]
Kansas City Salad Company Inc. [11581]
Kennesaw Fruit Juice Co. [11602]
Kenyon Packing Co.; Lowell C. [11603]
Kido Brothers Exports, Inc. [11608]
Kopke Jr. Inc.; William H. [11637]
Kroger Co. Dairy-Bakery Div. [11651]
Kuehl's Distributors [11653]
Lake Region Pack Association [11667]
Lamanuzzi and Pantaleo [11670]
Landsman International Inc. [11675]
Lange Co.; Tom [11676]
Latina Niagara Importing Co. [11680]
Laurel Farms [11683]
Lee Tomato Co. [11694]
Leone Food Service Corp. [11702]
Levin and Company Inc.; M. [11704]
Liberty Richter Inc. [11709]
Lindemann Produce Inc. [11714]
Lindemann Produce Inc. [11715]
Livacich Produce Inc.; John [11718]
Lomar Foods [11724]
Lone Star Produce Inc. [11729]
Lucky Fruit and Produce Company Inc. [11743]
Lun Fat Produce Inc. [11745]
M and H Sales and Marketing Inc. [14156]
M & L Trading Company, Inc. [11751]
Made in Nature Inc. [11754]
Magi Inc. [11758]
Main Street Produce Inc. [11759]
Maine Potato Growers Inc. [11760]
Majji Produce, Inc. [11762]
Malin Potato Cooperative Inc. [11764]
Matarazzo Brothers Company Inc. [11803]

Mathews and Sons Inc.; G.D. [11804]
Mathias and Company Inc. [11805]
M.B.M. Corp. [11816]
McCabe's Quality Foods Inc. [11817]
McDonald Farms, Inc. [11824]
McNabb Grain Co. [11839]
M.E. Carter of Jonesboro Inc. [11840]
Melchs Food Products Inc. [11846]
Mendocino Coast Produce, Inc. [11850]
Merchants Grocery Co. [11855]
Meyer Tomatoes [11865]
Meyer Vegetables [11866]
Mid-State Potato Distributors Inc. [11880]
Miedema Produce, Inc. [11890]
Minnesota Produce Inc. [11907]
Mission Produce Inc. [11912]
Mixon Fruit Farms Inc. [11916]
Moody Creek Produce Inc. [11929]
Moore Food Distributors Inc. [11930]
Mor-Rad Foodservice [11934]
Mountain Food Products [11945]
Movsovitz and Sons of Florida Inc. [11949]
Mr. Dell Foods, Inc. [11950]
Muir-Roberts Company Inc. [11955]
Musco Olive Products Inc. [11960]
Nash Finch/Bluefield [11968]
Nat's Garden Produce, Inc. [11981]
Natural Energy Unlimited Inc. [11982]
Naturipe Berry Growers [11988]
Nobel/Sysco Food Services Co. [12011]
Nor-Cal Produce Inc. [12016]
Normans Inc. [12020]
North Castle Produce Inc. [12025]
Northland Cranberries Inc. [12033]
Northland Hub Inc. [12034]
Northwest Foods [12037]
Ocean Mist Farms [12052]
Offutt Co.; R.D. [1098]
Ohio Farmers Inc. [12055]
Omega Produce Company Inc. [12070]
Oneonta Trading Corp. [12072]
Ozark Co-op Warehouse [12085]
Pacific Coast Fruit Co. [12088]
Pacific Fruit Processors Inc. [12090]
Pacific PreCut Produce Inc. [12092]
Packaging Concepts Corp. [12095]
Paradise Products Corp. [12105]
Paragon/Monteverde Food Service [12106]
Paramount Export Co. [12107]
Parker Banana Company Inc. [12112]
Parker Co.; Mitt [12113]
Peirone Produce Co. [12133]
Penachio Company Inc.; Nick [12135]
Perez Farms Inc. [12148]
Performance Food Group Co. [12150]
Phillips Mushroom Farms [12164]
Pirrone Produce, Inc.; Mike [12176]
Powell Company Inc.; W.J. [12200]
PPI Del Monte Tropical Fruit Co. [12203]
Prawn Seafoods Inc. [12207]
PrePeeled Potato Co. [12214]
PROACT [12223]
Produce Distributors Co. [12224]
Progressive Produce Co. [12231]
Pueblo Fruits Inc. [12234]
Quality Banana Inc. [12248]
Randazzo's Fruit Market #2 [12275]
Rapasadi Sons; Isadore A. [12279]
Red Apple Food Marts Inc. [12282]
Red Apple Supermarkets [12283]
Red's/Fisher Inc. [12292]
Red's Market Inc. [12293]
Regal Fruit Co. [12295]
Reinhart Institutional Foods Inc. Milwaukee Div. [12298]
Rinella and Company Inc.; A.J. [12319]
Riverside Potatoes Inc. [12324]
Riviana Foods Inc. [12325]
RLB Food Distributors L.P. [12326]
RMC Foods, Inc. [12327]
Roberts Foods Inc. [12330]
Robin's Food Distribution Inc. [12332]
Rodgers International Trading Inc. [12341]
Rogers Brothers Wholesale Inc. [12344]
Ron's Produce Company Inc. [12350]
Roots & Fruits Cooperative Produce [12351]

Rotelle Inc. [12355]
Royal Seeds Inc. [1217]
Russo Farms Inc. [12370]
S and M Food Service Inc. [12380]
S & M Produce [12381]
St. John's Food Service, Inc. [12389]
Sam Farm Inc.; A. [12398]
Sandridge Foods Corp. [12405]
Sandridge Gourmet Salads [12406]
Sanson Co. [12409]
Santanna Banana Co. [12410]
Saroff & Company Inc.; Sam [12416]
Saval Foods [12421]
Schnieber Fine Food Inc. [12430]
Scrivner of New York [12438]
Shopper's Food Warehouse Corp. [12483]
Shurfine International Inc. [12484]
Sierra [12486]
Smith Family Corp.; The Miles [12509]
Smith Packing Corp.; H. [12512]
Smith Potato Inc. [12513]
Smith's Sons Inc.; Leroy E. [12520]
Snokist Growers [12523]
Sommer Inc.; John [12527]
South Bay Growers Inc. [12531]
South Lake Apopka Citrus Growers Association [12532]
South Shore Produce Co. [12534]
Southern Produce Inc. [12540]
SPADA Enterprises Ltd. [12546]
Spencer Fruit Co. [12554]
Standard Fruit and Vegetable Company Inc. [12563]
Stanley Brothers Inc. [12565]
Stokes-Shaheen Produce Inc. [12587]
Stow Mills [12592]
Strohmeyer and Arpe Co. [12595]
Summertime Potato Co. [12601]
Sun-Diamond Growers of California. Mixed Nut Div. [12603]
Sun Glo of Idaho Inc. [12604]
Sunfresh Inc. [12613]
Sunkist Growers Inc. [12614]
Sunkist Growers Inc. [12615]
Super Valu Stores Inc. [12636]
SuperValu International [12648]
Sweet of Madison, Inc.; A.J. [12655]
Syracuse Banana Co. [12665]
Sysco Food Service of Seattle Inc. [12672]
SYSCO Food Services of Grand Rapids [12680]
SYSCO Food Services of Minnesota [12684]
SYSCO Food Services of Portland [12686]
Taiyo Inc. [12692]
Tam Produce Inc. [12693]
Tamarkin Company Inc. [12694]
Tamashiro Market Inc. [12695]
Tarantino Company Inc.; Lee Ray [12698]
Thomas and Howard Company Inc. [12714]
Thruway Produce Inc. [12720]
Too Goo Doo Farms Inc. [12732]
Trans World Company of Miami Inc. [12743]
Trax Farms Inc. [12745]
Tree of Life Inc. Northeast [12749]
Tripifoods Inc. [12757]
Tropical Hawaiian Products [12760]
Trout-Blue Chelan, Inc. [12762]
Tufts Ranch Packing Shed [12767]
Tumbleweed Distributors [12768]
Turbana Corp. [12772]
Twin County Grocers Inc. [12778]
UniMark Group Inc. [12785]
United Foods Inc. [12794]
United Fruit and Produce Company Inc. [12795]
U.S. World Trade Corp. [18305]
Valenti Company Inc.; J.C. [12814]
Valley Farm Dairy Co. [12816]
Valley Fruit [12818]
Valley Isle Produce Inc. [12819]
Van Solkema Produce Inc. [12825]
Vandenberg Inc.; Jac [12827]
Vanguard Trading Services Inc. [12829]
Vena Inc.; John [12835]
Vernon Produce Co.; W.R. [12840]
Vilrore Foods Company Inc. [12845]
Vitrano Co.; Tony [12853]
Volunteer Produce Co. [12855]

Wallach's Poultry Farms [12871]
Walton & Post [12873]
Washington Natural Foods and Co. [12881]
Watson Company Inc.; J.C. [12882]
Watson Foodservice Inc. [12883]
Waverly Growers Cooperative [12885]
Wells International [12900]
Wenatchee-Okanogan Cooperative Federation [12901]
Werner & Son; Max [12903]
Western Cold Storage [12910]
Western North Carolina Apple Growers [12915]
Wetterau Inc. Northeast [12921]
White Swan, Inc. [12930]
Whitenight; Delavan E. [12933]
Wholesale Produce Supply Company Inc. [12935]
Wiers Farm Inc. [12937]
Wilcox Drug Company Inc. [14281]
Williams Produce; Ron [12949]
Wilson Marketing & Sales [12954]
Winter Haven Citrus Grower Association [12962]
Woodwyk Inc.; Casey [12979]
World Variety Produce Inc. [12983]
Wright Co.; William S. [12988]
Yell-O-Glow Corp. [12993]

SIC 5149 — Groceries & Related Products Nec

3 Springs Water Co. [24902]
3 Springs Water Co. [10314]
A. Camacho Inc. [10316]
A & L Coors Inc. [1473]
Abbey Ice Co. [24903]
ABC Coffee Co. [10319]
Abita Water Company Inc. [24904]
Absolute Bottled Water Co. [24905]
Absopure Water Co. [24906]
Acadiana Culligan [24907]
Acme Food Sales Inc. [10320]
Advanced Specialties [10329]
Advantage Crown [10330]
Affiliated Foods Midwest [10338]
Affy Tapple Inc. [10340]
Agri Feed & Supply [27057]
Agrigold Juice Products [24908]
Agrimor [10347]
AIPC [10349]
Alakef Coffee Roasters Inc. [10353]
Albaco Foods Inc. [10356]
Albert W. Sisk and Son Inc. [10358]
Albert's Organics Inc. [10359]
Ale-8-One Bottling Co. Inc. [24909]
Alex City Provision Inc. [10361]
Alimenta (USA) Inc. [10364]
All Season's Kitchen L.L.C. [10367]
Allegro Coffee Co. [10369]
Alliant Foodservice, Inc. [10372]
Alliant FoodService Inc. [24059]
Allied Distributing [1480]
Allou Health and Beauty Care Inc. [14015]
Allstate Beverage Co. [1481]
Alpha Distributors Ltd. [10379]
Alpina International Inc. [21626]
Alshefski Enterprise [10384]
Amato International Inc. [10389]
Amberstar International Inc. [10390]
Ambex Inc. [15006]
AMCON Distributing Co. [10392]
AME Food Service Inc. [10393]
American Cheeseman Inc. [10395]
American FoodService [10398]
American Key Food Products Inc. [10399]
American Management Group [10400]
American Products Company Inc. [10402]
American Sweeteners Inc. [10405]
AmeriQual Foods Inc. [10406]
AmeriServe [24063]
Amway Corp. [8350]
Anapet [27065]
Ancona Midwest Foodservices [10410]
Andrews Produce Inc. [10417]
Anjo Distributors [27068]

Ann's House of Nuts, Inc. [10420]
Apple Food Sales Company Inc. [10424]
Applewood Farms Inc. [10425]
ARA-Cory Refreshment Services [24910]
ARA Services, Inc. [24911]
Araban Coffee Co. Inc. [10429]
Arbuckle Coffee Roasters Inc. [24067]
Archway Cookie Co. [10430]
Arco Coffee Co. [10431]
Armour Food Ingredients Co. [10434]
Armstrong Produce Ltd. [10435]
Arnold-Sunbelt Beverage Company L.P.; Ben [1487]
Arrow-SYSCO [10437]
Arrowhead Mills Inc. [10439]
Artesia Water Co. [10441]
Artusos Pastry Shop [10442]
Associated Food Stores Inc. [10445]
Atlantic Premium Brands Ltd. [10464]
Atlantic Promotions [25565]
Atlas Distributing, Inc. [24912]
Atlas Distributing Inc. [10465]
Auddino's Italian Bakery Inc. [10469]
Auromere Inc. [14027]
Austin Quality Foods, Inc. [10473]
Avalon Distributing Inc. [10474]
Axelrod Distributors [10476]
Azure Standard [10478]
B & B Specialty Foods [10481]
Bagatelle [10488]
Bakers Chocolate and Coconut [10491]
Bakers Choice [10492]
Bakery Management Corp. [10493]
Bama Companies Inc. [10495]
Banko Enterprises Inc. [1499]
Barbara's Bakery Inc. [10503]
Barbero Bakery Inc. [10504]
Barnie's Coffee and Tea Company Inc. [10510]
Baronet Coffee Inc. [10511]
Barr Enterprises Inc. [27079]
Base Inc. [10512]
Bassett Dairy Products Inc. [10514]
Bauer & Foss, Inc. [1505]
Bays Corp. [10520]
Beauchamp Distributing Co. [24913]
Beaverton Foods Inc. [10522]
Bedford Food Products Inc. [10525]
Beer City [1515]
Beer World [1517]
Bel Canto Fancy Foods Ltd. [10527]
Bel-Pak Foods Inc. [10528]
Belmont Wholesale Co. Inc. [10534]
Beloit Beverage Company Inc. [1519]
Benham and Company Inc. [10535]
Bennett Distributing Co. Inc. [1520]
Bennett Vending [10536]
Bensons Backery [10538]
Berelson Export Corp. [10539]
Bernick Inc.; Charles A. [24914]
Bernstein Company Inc.; William [10542]
Bertolli U.S.A. Inc. [10544]
Best Brands Inc. [10546]
Best Foods [10547]
Best Way Distributing Co. [1523]
Better Brands of Atlanta Inc. [1524]
Better Brands of Milwaukee Inc. [1525]
Bev-Tech, Inc. [14345]
B.G.B. Pet Supply Inc. [27082]
Bi Rite Foodservice Distributors [10551]
Bickford Flavors Inc. [10553]
Big Sandy Wholesale Co. [10556]
Big Shot Beverage Inc. [24915]
Bishop Baking Co. [10559]
Black Hills Distributing Co. Inc. [1533]
Black Mountain Spring Water Inc. [24916]
Blackman Industries [27084]
Bloemer Food Service Co. [10569]
Blooming Prairie Natural Foods [10571]
Blue Line Distributing [10575]
Blue Ribbon Meat Company Inc. [10579]
Blue Rock Beverage Co. [1537]
Bob's Fruit Market & Deli [10585]
Bomadi Inc. [10587]
Bosco Products Inc. [10596]
Boyajian Inc. [10600]
Boyd-Bluford Co. Inc. [10602]

Boyd Coffee Co. [10603]
Bradley Distributing [24917]
Bratt-Foster Inc. [10609]
Braun and Sons; J.F. [10610]
Brehm Inc.; Otto [10611]
Bremner Biscuit Co. [10612]
Brookfield's Great Water Inc. [24918]
Brooklyn Bagels Inc. [10620]
Brother's Gourmet Coffees Inc. (Boca Raton, Florida) [24919]
Brownlow Corp. [3595]
Browns Bakery Inc. [10630]
Bruss Co. [10633]
Bubbles Baking Co. [10634]
Buckeye Countrymark Corp. [348]
Budd Mayer Co. [24083]
Buffalo Don's Artesian Wells Ltd. [24920]
Buffalo Rock Co. Gadsden Div. [24921]
Bumble Bee Seafoods Inc. [10641]
Bunker Hill Foods [10642]
Burnham; William H. [26431]
Butler Wholesale Products [24085]
Butte Produce Co. [10650]
Buy for Less Inc. [10653]
BYE Inc. [1562]
C & K Distributors Inc. [27097]
Cade Grayson Co. [10659]
Caffe Latte [10660]
Cahokia Flour Co. [10662]
Cains Foods, L.P. [10663]
Cal Compack Foods Inc. [10665]
California Naturals [10673]
California Shellfish Company Inc. [10676]
Callahan Grocery Co. Inc. [10679]
Calvada Sales Co. [10681]
Camerican International [10684]
Canada Dry of Delaware Valley [24922]
Canfield Co.; A.J. [24923]
Canine Commissary [27099]
Cannizzaro's Distributors [10689]
Capitol Foods Inc. [10693]
Capricorn Coffees Inc. [10694]
Cardinal Distributing [1573]
Cariba International Corp. [10700]
Carolyn Candies, Inc. [10703]
Carter Distributing Co. [1578]
Castleton Beverage Corp. [1581]
Catanzaro Sons and Daughters Inc.; Frank [10714]
Centennial Beverage Corp. [1583]
Central Distributing Co. [24924]
Central Garden and Pet Supply Inc. [392]
Central Snacks [10724]
Central States Coca-Cola Bottling Co. [24925]
Cereal Byproducts Co. [404]
Cereal Food Processors, Inc. [10726]
Cerenzia Foods Inc. [10727]
Certified Grocers of California Ltd. [10728]
Chandler Foods Inc. [10733]
Chapin's Supreme Foods [10734]
Chatham Imports Inc. [1591]
Cherry Central, Inc. [10739]
Chihade International Inc. [10746]
Chikara Products Inc. [10747]
Chilli-O Frozen Foods Inc. [10749]
China First Merchandising Co. [10750]
Chin's Import Export Co. Inc. [10751]
Chock Full o'Nuts [10753]
Circle Food Products Inc. [10759]
City Beverage Co. [1596]
City Bottling Company Inc. [24926]
CJW Inc. [24927]
Clark Inc.; C.C. [3641]
Clear Eye [10767]
Clermont Inc. [24928]
Cloverleaf Farms Distributors Inc. [10777]
Co-Sales Co. [10781]
Coca-Cola Aberdeen [24929]
Coca-Cola Bottlers of Detroit Inc. [24930]
Coca-Cola Bottling Co. [24931]
Coca-Cola Bottling Co. of California [24932]
Coca-Cola Bottling Co.; Coast [24933]
Coca-Cola Bottling Co. Consolidated [24934]
Coca-Cola Bottling Co. of Lincoln [24935]
Coca-Cola Bottling Co. of Manchester [24936]
Coca-Cola Bottling Co.; Meridian [24937]

Coca-Cola Bottling Company of Mobile Inc. [24938]
Coca-Cola Bottling Company of New York Inc. [24939]
Coca-Cola Bottling Company of Shreveport [24940]
Coca-Cola Bottling Company of Virginia [24941]
Coca-Cola Bottling; Dixie [24942]
Coca-Cola Bottling Works Inc.; Valdosta [24943]
Coca-Cola Bottling Works; Lexington [24944]
Coca-Cola Co. [24945]
Coca-Cola; Johnston [24946]
Coca-Cola of Northern Arizona [24947]
Coca-Cola; Pacific [24948]
Coca-Cola; Pacific [24949]
Coca-Cola Pocatello [24950]
Coca-Cola Twin Falls Bottling Co. [3645]
Cocoa Barry U.S. [10784]
Coffee Bean International Inc. [10786]
Colombo Baking Co. [10790]
Colonial Baking Co. [10792]
Columbia Bean & Produce Co., Inc. [10795]
Columbia Distributing Co./Henry Hirsdale/Admiralty Beverage Co. [1607]
Common Health Warehouse Cooperative Association [10798]
Community Coffee Company Inc. [10799]
Community Coffee Company LLC [10800]
Compass Foods Eight O'Clock Coffee [10802]
Con-Tech International, Inc. [16805]
Concord Sales Co. [26278]
Connell Co. [10811]
Conrad Sales Company, Inc. [10814]
Consolidated Pet Foods Inc. [10818]
Consolidated Poultry and Egg Co. [10819]
Consumers Choice Coffee Inc. [10820]
Consumers Vinegar and Spice Co. [10823]
Contadina Foods [10824]
Continental Baking Co. [10825]
Continental Baking Co. [10826]
Continental Commodities L.P. [10827]
Continental Foods Corp. [10828]
Continental Foods Inc. [10829]
Conway Import Co. Inc. [10831]
Cook Chocolate Co. [10832]
Cook's Gourmet [10833]
Coors Brewing Co. [10836]
Coors Brothers Co. [10837]
Coors West [1618]
Copley Distributors Inc. [1619]
Cornucopia Natural Foods Inc. [14072]
Costa Fruit and Produce Co. [10848]
Cougle Commission Co. [10853]
Country Club Foods Inc. [10855]
Country Oven Bakery [10857]
Courtesy Distributors Inc. [24951]
Cox Distributing; Dale [10861]
Creme Curls Bakery Inc. [10865]
Crest Beverage Co. [1623]
Crestar Food Products Inc. [10867]
Crispy's Inc. [10868]
Crossmark Sales and Marketing [10871]
Crown Beverages Inc. [1625]
Crown Distributing Co. [1627]
Crown Inc. Beverage Div. [1628]
Crown Products Inc. [10875]
Crystal Bottling Company Inc. [24952]
Crystal City Bakers [10876]
Crystal Farms Refrigerated Distribution Co. [10877]
Crystal Products Corp. [10879]
Cuetara America Co. [10881]
Cullen Distributors Inc. [26284]
Culver Dairy Inc. [10882]
Cunningham Wholesale Company Inc. [1629]
Curtiss Bakery; Penny [10885]
Daily Bread Company Inc. [10892]
Dairy Fresh Products Co. [10895]
Dan Valley Foods, Inc. [10906]
Darigold [10908]
Darisil, Inc. [10909]
Darlington Farms [10910]
D'Artagnan Inc. [10912]
Davis Bakery Inc. [10915]
Davis Company Inc.; H.C. [10916]
De Vries Imports & Distributors [10925]
Dealers Food Products Co. [10927]

Decatur Bottling Co. [24953]
Decatur Coca-Cola Bottling Co. [10932]
Deerwood Rice Grain Produce [10937]
Deli Universal Inc. [26287]
Dennert Distributing Corp.; H. [1641]
Dennis Sales Ltd. [10944]
Dependable Food Corp. [10945]
Des Moines Marketing Associates [10947]
Desert Mesquite of Arizona [10950]
Detail Fresh Sandwich Co. [10951]
Dewar & Company Inc.; John [10953]
Dewied International Inc. [10954]
Di Paolo Baking Company, Inc. [10955]
Dial Corp. [14083]
Diamond Bakery Co. Ltd. [10956]
Diamond Distributors [1649]
Diamond Foods Inc. [10957]
Diaz Foods Inc. [10962]
Dierks Foods Inc. [10964]
Dimitri Wine & Spirits [1651]
Discount Drugs Wisconsin Inc. [19281]
Distribution Plus Inc. [10967]
Dr. Pepper/Seven Up, Inc. [10972]
Doerle Food Services Inc. [10973]
Dole and Bailey Inc. [10974]
Dole Fresh Vegetables Co. [10976]
Dolly Madison Bakery [10979]
Dolly Madison Cake Co. [10980]
Donico & Associates; J.P. [18778]
Dot Foods Inc. [10982]
Double A Provisions Inc. [10983]
Downs Foods Co.; Tony [10987]
DPI Food Products Co. [10989]
Drake America Div. [2559]
Drescher Company Inc.; P. [10995]
Drinks Galore Inc. [1658]
Dutch Gold Honey Inc. [11003]
Dyer and Co.; B.W. [11005]
Dynamic International Company Inc. [7295]
E-Z Mart Stores Inc. [11008]
Eagle Beverage Co. [1663]
Eagle Distributors Inc. [1666]
Eagle Family Foods [24954]
Eagle Foods Co. [11010]
Earth Grains Company of Sacramento [11014]
Earthgrains/Waldensian Bakerie [11015]
Echter Ornaments Inc. [11021]
Economy Distributors [27122]
Edsung Foodservice Co. [11029]
El Encanto Inc. [11036]
El Galindo Inc. [11037]
El Indio Shop [11038]
El Ray Distributing Company Inc. [1672]
Eldorado Artesian Springs Inc. [24955]
Eldorado Artesian Springs Inc. [11039]
Elki Corp. [11041]
Elmer's Distributing Co. [1673]
Elmira Distributing [1674]
Empire Distributing [1676]
Enrico Food Products Co. Inc. [11048]
Erwin Distributing Co. [1679]
Essex Grain Products Inc. [11053]
Estrella Tortilla Factory & Deli Store [11054]
EuroAmerican Brands LLC [11059]
Evans Distributing Company Inc. [1680]
F & A Food Sales Inc. [11067]
F and E Wholesale Food Service Inc. [11068]
Fabiano Brothers Inc. [1682]
Fairway Foods Inc. [11073]
Faithway Feed Company Inc. [27130]
Falcon Trading Co. [11076]
Falcone and Italia Foods [11077]
Fancy Fare Distributors [11079]
Fantastic Foods Inc. [11080]
Farm Fresh Foods Inc. [11085]
Farmers Cooperative Association [17845]
Farmers Cooperative Dairy Inc. [11097]
Farner Bocken Co. [11107]
Farrell Distributing [1685]
Feaster Foods Co. [11111]
Federation of Ohio River Co-ops [11116]
Feesers Inc. [11117]
Ferrara Food and Confections Inc. [11119]
Ferro Foods Corp. [11122]
Figueroa International Inc. [11125]
Fink Baking Corp. [11128]

Fisher Mills Inc. [11134]
Fitness Plus II [11138]
Flanigan Farms [11140]
Flavtek Inc. [11142]
F.L.D. Distributors Inc. [1692]
Fleming [11145]
Fleming Companies Inc. Philadelphia Div. [11152]
Flite Service [11160]
Food For Life Baking Co. [11171]
Food Gems Ltd. [11172]
Food Lion Inc. [11173]
Food Marketing Corp. [11174]
Food Masters Inc. [11175]
Food Match, Inc. [11176]
Food Services of America [11179]
Food and Spirits Distributing Company Inc. [1693]
FoodScience Corp. [11183]
FoodSource, Inc. [11184]
Foster's Good Service Dairy [11193]
Fowler Brothers [11195]
Fox River Foods Inc. [11197]
Frankferd Farms [11200]
Friendly Distributors [1698]
Frito-Lay Co. [11215]
Frito-Lay Inc. [11217]
Frontier Co-op Herbs [11220]
Fuji Natural Food Co. [11223]
Full Service Beverage Co. [24956]
Gai's Northwest Bakeries Inc. [11229]
Gamble Co.; L.H. [11230]
Garden Foods Products [11234]
Garden Spot Distributors [11235]
Gate Petroleum Co. [11240]
Gateway Foods of Pennsylvania Inc. [11243]
Gaylord Cash & Carry [11246]
General Brokerage Co. [11248]
General Merchandise Services Inc. [14110]
General Mills Operations [11249]
Genesee Natural Foods [11253]
George Co., Inc.; William [11254]
Georgia Crown Distributing Co. [1712]
Georgia Mountain Water Inc. [24957]
Gerber Cheese Company Inc. [11256]
Gibbons Inc.; J.T. [11262]
Gillies Coffee Co. [11265]
Ginseng Co. [14112]
Ginseng Up Corp. [24958]
Glasgow Distributors Inc. [1718]
Glazer's of Iowa [1719]
Global Bakeries, Inc. [11272]
Global Beverage Co. [24959]
Globe Trends Inc. [11274]
Globil Inc. [1721]
Glorybee Foods Inc. [11275]
GNS Foods Inc. [11278]
Gold Coast Beverage Distributors [1722]
Gold Medal Bakery Inc. [11279]
Goldberg and Solovy Food Inc. [11281]
Golden Boy Pies Inc. [11282]
Golden Gem Growers Inc. [24960]
Golombeck Inc.; Morris J. [11288]
Good Food Inc. [11289]
Good Health Natural Foods Inc. [11290]
Good-O-Beverage Co. [24962]
Gourmet Award Foods Tree of Life Inc. [11297]
Gourmet Regency Coffee Inc. [11298]
GOYA Foods Inc. [24963]
Gramex Corp. [5000]
Grand River Meat Center [11305]
Grandma Brown's Beans Inc. [11306]
Grandma's Bake Shoppe [11307]
Grapevine [11309]
Great Bear Spring Co. [24964]
Great Brands of Europe Inc. [24965]
Great Health [11311]
Great Southwest Sales [11314]
Great Western Meats [11315]
Great Western Products Inc. [11317]
Greg's Cookies Inc. [11323]
Grist Mill Co. [11328]
Grocers Supply Co. [11330]
Grocers Wholesale Co. [11332]
Grosslein Beverages Inc. [1734]
Guiffre Distributing Co.; Tony [1735]
Gulf Go-Fers Inc. [11345]
Gulf Marine and Industrial Supplies [11346]

Gusto Brands Inc. [1738]
H and H Meat Products Company Inc. [11350]
H & H Products Co. [24966]
H & M Distributing [24967]
Habys Sales Candy Co. [11354]
Haddon House Food Products Inc. [11356]
Hadley Braithwait Co. [11357]
Hadley Corp.; Raymond [11358]
Hahn and Phillips Grease Company Inc. [17968]
Haitai America Inc. [11361]
Hanover Sales Co. [11372]
Hanover Warehousing [11373]
Hansen Caviar Co. [11374]
Happy Refrigerated Services [11375]
Hara and Company Ltd.; T. [11376]
Hart Beverage Co. [24968]
Hartog Foods Inc. [11387]
Hartzler's Inc. Exporters [18828]
Hattiesburg Grocery Co. [11391]
Hawaiian Distributor Ltd. [11393]
Hawaiian Isles Distributors [26302]
Hawaiian Isles Distributors [26303]
Hawaiian Natural Water Company Inc. [24969]
Hawk Flour Mills Inc. [11395]
Hawkeye Seed Company Inc. [802]
HealthComm Inc. [24970]
HealthComm Inc. [11401]
HealthComm International Inc. [14123]
Heidema Brothers Inc. [20647]
Hennessy Ingredients; Ron [11412]
Henry's Foods Inc. [11414]
Heritage Wafers Ltd. [11419]
Hershey Foods Corp. [11421]
HG International Corporation [23725]
HIE Holdings, Inc. [11428]
Higdon Grocery Company Inc.; Ira [11429]
High Grade Beverage [1754]
High Grade Beverage [11430]
Hill's Pet Nutrition Inc. [27149]
Hillside Coffee of California Holding Co. [11434]
Hinckley and Schmitt Bottled Water Group [11438]
Hirt Jr., Co.; R. [11441]
HMA/International Business Development Ltd. [11442]
Hoban Foods Inc. [11443]
Homa Co. [11455]
HomeBase Inc. [15532]
Hopkinsville Milling Company Inc. [11461]
Hormel Foods International Corp. [11462]
House of Schwan Inc. [1763]
Houston Harvest Gift Products LLC [11466]
Howe Company Inc.; George J. [11467]
Hsu's Ginseng Enterprises Inc. [11469]
Hubbard Milling Co. [27152]
Huesing Corp.; A.D. [24971]
Hundley Brokerage Company Inc. [11477]
Hunt Wesson Inc. [11478]
Hunter, Walton and Company Inc. [11480]
Hybco USA [11484]
I. Wanna Distribution Company Inc. [11486]
The Iams Co. [27154]
ICEE-USA Corp. [24972]
I.D. Foods, Inc. [11488]
IJ Co. [11492]
ILHWA [11495]
Illycaffe Espresso USA Inc. [11497]
Imperia Foods Inc. [11499]
Imperial Commodities Corp. [11500]
Import Warehouse Inc. [13374]
Independent Bakers' Cooperative [11502]
Independent Distributors of America Inc. [24141]
Indiana Botanic Gardens [11503]
Indianapolis Coca-Cola Bottling Company Inc. [24973]
Indianapolis Coca-Cola Bottling Company Inc./Richmond Div. [24974]
Inter-County Bakers [11516]
Interior Design Nutritionals [14131]
Intermountain Trading Company Ltd. [11517]
International Agricultural Associates, Inc. [862]
International Baking Co. [11518]
International Baking Co. [11519]
International Food and Beverage Inc. [11521]
International Industries Corporation [11522]
International Pizza Co. [11523]
International Trading Co. [11524]

Interstate Brands Corp. [11525]
Interstate Brands Corp. Cotton Brothers Baking Co. [11526]
Interstate Brands Corp. Dolly Madison Cakes Div. [11527]
Ireland Coffee and Tea Inc. [11529]
Italian Sausage Inc. [11531]
It's Coffee Lovers Time, Inc. [11533]
J and J Food Service Inc. [11537]
J and R Bottling and Distribution Co. [24975]
J and R Bottling and Distribution Co. [11538]
JaCiva's Chocolate and Pastries [11539]
Jacks Original Pizza [11542]
Jackson Coca-Cola Bottling Co. [24976]
Jarritos Distributors [24977]
Java City Inc. [11547]
Java Dave's Executive Coffee Service [11548]
Jaytow International Inc. [5843]
Jeff Bottling Company Inc. [24978]
JFC International Inc. [11554]
J.O. Spice Company Inc. [11556]
Johnston Coca-Cola [3867]
Joiner Foodservice Inc. [11559]
Jones-McIntosh Tobacco Company Inc. [26314]
Jonesboro Coca-Cola [24979]
Jonesboro Grocer Co. [11563]
Jordanos Inc. [11565]
Just Desserts Inc. [11573]
K & L Associates, Inc. [11574]
K and N Meats [11575]
Kahn's Bakery Inc. [11577]
Kamaaina Distribution [11578]
Kane International Corp. [11579]
Kangaroo Brand Inc. [11580]
Karn Meats Inc. [11582]
Karp's BakeMark [11583]
Kay Distributing Co. [11585]
Keebler Co. [11587]
Kehe Food Distributors Inc. [11588]
Kehe Food Distributors Inc. [11589]
Kelley and Abide Company Inc. [11592]
Kelley Bean Co., Inc. [11593]
Kelley-Clarke [11594]
Kellogg Co. [11597]
Kem Distributing Inc. [1795]
Kenan Oil Co. [11600]
Kenlin Pet Supply Inc. [27171]
Kent [1796]
Kern & Sons; Jacob [11604]
Kesterson Food Company Inc. [24156]
Kettle Foods [11606]
Keystone-Ozone Pure Water Co. [24980]
Kido Brothers Exports, Inc. [11608]
Kim's Processing Plant [11609]
King Arthur Flour Co. [11610]
King Milling Co. [11615]
King Provision Corp. [11616]
King's Foodservice Inc. [11620]
Kirchhoff Distributing Co. [11622]
Klee Wholesale Company, Inc. [26319]
KLF, Inc. [11624]
Klosterman Bakery Outlet [11625]
Klosterman Baking Co. Inc. [11626]
Kobrand Corp. [1802]
Koerner and Company Inc.; John E. [11632]
Kona Farmers Coop [11635]
K.R. International [11639]
Kraft Food Ingredients [11640]
Kraft Foodservice Inc. [11642]
Kraft-Holleb [11644]
Kraft USA [11645]
Kroger Co. Dairy-Bakery Div. [11651]
Kuehl's Distributors [11653]
Kum Kee (USA) Inc.; Lee [11655]
Kunda and Sons Inc.; Watson [1807]
L and L Concession Co. [11658]
L and L Jiroch Distributing Co. [26321]
La Madeleine Inc. [11659]
La Piccolina and Co. Inc. [11660]
La Reina Inc. [11661]
La Vencedora Products [11662]
LaCROIX Beverages Inc. [24982]
Lady Baltimore Foods Inc. [11665]
Lagomarsino's Inc. [1810]
Lakeside Mills Inc. [11669]
Lambert's Coffee Services [11671]

Lambright's Inc. [932]
Land O Lakes Inc. [11673]
Landman Co. Inc.; Carl [11674]
Lantev [11678]
Larrabee Brothers Distributing Company Inc. [1813]
Latina Niagara Importing Co. [11680]
Latina Trading Corp. [11681]
Latona's Food Importing Corp. [11682]
Laurel Vending Inc. [24983]
LBM Sales Inc. [11689]
Lee Cash & Carry [11691]
Lee and Sons Inc.; W.S. [11693]
Leone Food Service Corp. [11702]
Lewis Brothers Bakeries Inc. [11706]
Liberty Richter Inc. [11709]
The Lion Brewery, Inc. [1821]
Lo-An Foods Inc. [11719]
Loda Poultry Company Inc. [11721]
Logan Inc. [11722]
Lomar Foods [11724]
Lone Star Food Service Co. [11727]
Lookout Beverages [1828]
Los Amigos Tortilla Manufacturing Inc. [11734]
Love Bottling Co. [24984]
Lovotti Brothers [1829]
L.T. Plant, Inc. [11739]
Lumen Foods [11744]
Lutheran Distributors Inc.; A.M. [1832]
M and H Sales and Marketing Inc. [14156]
MacBean Inc.; Scottie [24173]
Made-Rite Co. [24985]
Made Rite Potato Chip Company Inc. [11755]
Magnolia Marketing Co. [1839]
Main Street and Main Inc. [24175]
Major Brands [1843]
Major Brands [1844]
Malolo Beverages & Supplies, Ltd. [24986]
Malone & Hyde [14158]
Malone Products Inc. [11768]
Maloney, Cunningham & Devic [11769]
Mama Rosa's Slice of Italy [11770]
Mandala Corp. [27184]
Manhattan Coffee Co. [11774]
Manildra Milling Corp. [11776]
Maranatha [11778]
Mariani Packing Company Inc. [11779]
Marie's Quality Foods [11780]
Mark V Distributors Inc. [1850]
Market Share International Inc. [11781]
Marketing Specialists - Southern California Div. [11786]
Markstein Beverage Company of Sacramento [1852]
Marquette Bottling Works Inc. [3936]
Marshall Distributing Co. [11790]
Marshmallow Products Inc. [11791]
MarshmallowCone Co. [11792]
Martin Brothers International [26327]
Mary Ann's Baking Co. [11797]
Mathews and Sons Inc.; G.D. [11804]
Mauston Farmers Cooperative [993]
Mautino Distributing Company Inc. [1855]
McConnell and Sons Inc.; F. [11820]
McCullagh Inc.; S.J. [11821]
McDonough Brothers [11825]
McFarling Foods Inc. [11826]
McGill & Co.; P. [11828]
McLendon Co. [11837]
Meadowbrook Distributing Corp. [24987]
Melody Farms Inc. [11848]
Mer-Roc F.S. Inc. [27186]
Merchants Coffee Co. [11852]
Merkert Enterprises Inc. [11857]
Merrill Distributing, Inc. [11858]
Metz Baking Co. [11862]
Metz Baking Co. [11863]
Metz Baking Co. [11864]
Metz Beverage Company Inc. [1870]
Michael Foods Inc. [11867]
Michelle's Family Bakery [11871]
Michigan Sugar Co. [11872]
Mid-Atlantic Snacks [11877]
Mid-South Malts/Memphis Brews Inc. [1872]
Midamar Corp. [11882]
Midstate Mills Inc. [11886]

Midwest Coca-Cola Bottling Co.
  Rhinelander [24988]
Millbrook Distributors Inc. [14164]
Mille Lacs Agriculture Services Inc. [1039]
Miller's Bakery Inc. [11900]
Millitrade International Inc. [20195]
Mills Farmers Elevator [1041]
Millstone Service Div. [11901]
Milwaukee Biscuit [11903]
Mimbres Valley Farmers Association Inc. [1042]
Miniat Inc.; Ed [11905]
Minnesota Cultivated Wild Rice Council [11906]
Miss Kings Kitchen Inc, The Original Yahoo!
  Baking Co. [11911]
Mitchell Products; Allen [11913]
Mitsui and Company (U.S.A.) Inc. [20199]
Mitsui Foods, Inc. [11915]
Mom's Food Co. [11919]
Monarch Beverage Inc. [1888]
Monel Distributors [11920]
Monsour's Inc. [11926]
Montana Naturals Int'l. Inc. [11928]
Moore Food Distributors Inc. [11930]
Moore's Quality Snack Foods Div. [11932]
Moorhead and Company Inc. [11933]
Mor-Rad Foodservice [11934]
Mountain Ark Trading Co. [11944]
Mountain People's Warehouse [11946]
Mountain Service Distributors [26330]
Mountain Sun Organic Juices [11948]
Mounthood Beverage Co. [1895]
Mrs. Leeper's Pasta, Inc. [11951]
Muffin Town Inc. [11954]
Mulligan Sales Inc. [11956]
Multifoods Specialty Distribution [11957]
Murray Biscuit Co., LLC (Division of Keebler
  Co.) [11958]
Musco Olive Products Inc. [11960]
Nackard Wholesale Beverage Co.; Fred [1899]
Nardone Bakery Pizza Co. [11967]
Natchez Coca-Cola Bottling Co. [24989]
National Beverage Corp. [24990]
National Distributors Inc. [24991]
National Enzyme Co. [11976]
National Foods [11977]
National Safety Associates Inc. [23286]
National Wine and Spirits Corp. [3017]
Natural Energy Unlimited Inc. [11982]
Natural Ovens of Manitowoc Inc. [11984]
Natural Resources [11985]
Nature's Best [11987]
Nebraska Wine & Spirits Inc. [1911]
Neiman Brothers Company Inc. [11992]
Neshaminy Valley Natural Foods Distributor,
  Ltd. [11995]
Nevada Beverage Co. [1912]
New Age Distributing Co. [24992]
New Cooperative Company Inc. [12000]
New England Variety Distributors [24993]
Niagara Drinking Waters Inc. [24994]
Nichols and Company Inc.; Austin [1917]
Nissen Baking Co.; John J. [12009]
Nittany Beverage Co. [1918]
NM Bakery Service Co. [12010]
Noel Corp. [24995]
Nor-Cal Beverage Company Inc. [12015]
Nor-Joe Cheese Importing [12017]
Norpac Food Sales Inc. [12023]
North Farm Cooperative [12028]
North Star Distributors [24996]
North Star Distributors [12029]
Northeast Cooperatives [12031]
Northern California Beverage Company
  Inc. [24998]
Northern Distributing Co. [1921]
Northern Eagle Beverages Inc. [1922]
Northland Cranberries Inc. [12033]
Northland Hub Inc. [12034]
Northwest Bottling Co. [24999]
Northwest Distribution Services Inc. [24196]
Northwest Farm Food Cooperative [27198]
Northwest Farm Food Cooperative [12036]
Novartis Nutrition Corp. [12041]
Nulaid Foods Inc. [12045]
NutraSource Inc. [12047]
Nutri-Fruit Inc. [25000]

NutriCology Inc. [12048]
Oasis Drinking Waters Inc. [25001]
Odom Corp. [1927]
Oilseeds International Ltd. [12057]
Olbro Wholesalers [12059]
Old Dominion Export-Import Co. Inc. [12060]
Old Dutch Bakery Inc. [12061]
Old World Bakery [12064]
Olender and Company Inc.; P. [12066]
Omnitrition [12071]
Orange Bakery Inc. [12074]
Original Chili Bowl Inc. [12076]
O'San Products Inc. [12080]
Ottenbergs Bakery [12083]
Ozark Co-op Warehouse [12085]
Pacific Beverage Company Inc. [25002]
Pacific Coca-Cola Tacoma [4031]
Pacific Grain Products, Inc. [12091]
Pacific Wine Co. [1938]
Palagonia Italian Bread [12098]
Paradise Products Corp. [12105]
Paramount Export Co. [12107]
Parco Foods LLC [12108]
Parkway Food Service Inc. [12117]
Party Kits Unlimited Inc. [23874]
Peak Distributing Co. [12126]
Peanut Processors Inc. [12127]
The Pearl Coffee Co. [12128]
Pearlstine Distributors Inc. [1945]
Peerless Coffee Co. [12130]
Peets Coffee and Tea Inc. [12131]
Pellman Foods Inc. [12134]
Peninsula Bottling Company Inc. [25003]
Peninsula Bottling Company Inc. [12138]
Penny Curtiss Bakery [12143]
Pepper Products [12144]
Pepsi; Buffalo Rock [25004]
Pepsi-Cola Batavia Bottling Corp. [25005]
Pepsi-Cola Bottling Co. of Daytona Beach [25006]
Pepsi-Cola Bottling Company of Denver [25007]
Pepsi-Cola Bottling Company of La Crosse [4054]
Pepsi-Cola Bottling Company of Luverne
  Inc. [25008]
Pepsi-Cola Bottling Company of Marysville
  Inc. [25009]
Pepsi-Cola Bottling Company of New Bern
  Inc. [25010]
Pepsi-Cola Bottling Company of Rochester [25011]
Pepsi-Cola Bottling Company of Rockford [25012]
Pepsi-Cola Bottling Company of Salisbury [25013]
Pepsi-Cola Bottling Company of
  Shreveport [25014]
Pepsi-Cola Company of Jonesboro [25015]
Pepsi-Cola Company South [25016]
Pepsi-Cola General Bottlers of South
  Bend [25017]
Pepsi-Cola General Bottlers of South
  Bend [12145]
Pepsi-Cola Northwest [12146]
Pepsi-Cola Ogdensburg Inc. [25018]
Pepsi-Cola Pittsfield [25019]
Pepsi-Cola Pittsfield [12147]
Pepsi-Cola of Salem [25020]
Pepsi-Cola of Washington, D.C. L.P. [4055]
Perfection Bakeries Inc. [12149]
Perishable Distributors of Iowa Ltd. [12152]
Perrier Group of America Inc. [25021]
Perugina Brands of America [12153]
Pet Food Wholesale, Inc. [27206]
Pet Food Wholesale Inc. [12154]
Pet Life Foods Inc. [27207]
The Pet Pharmacy Inc. [27209]
Peter Pan of Hollywood Inc. [12156]
Petri Baking Products [12157]
Pinahs Company Inc. [12169]
Pioneer Dairy Inc. [12171]
Pioneer French Baking Company Inc. [12172]
Pistoresi Distributing Inc. [1960]
Pittman International [27214]
Pizza Commissary Inc. [12178]
Pizza Needs of Memphis Inc. [12179]
Plains Dairy Products [12180]
PM AG Products Inc. [1135]
Pompeian Inc. [12190]
Poppers Supply Co. [12194]
Port Cargo Service Inc. [12197]

Portland Bottling Co. [12198]
Potomac Adventist Book Center [4075]
Powell Company Inc.; W.J. [12200]
Powers Candy Company Inc. [12201]
Prairie Farms Dairy Supply Inc. [24205]
Preferred Brokerage Co. [12209]
Premier Distributors [1969]
Premium Beverage Company Inc. [1970]
President Baking Co., Inc. [12215]
Pricing Dynamics [12217]
Prince of Peace Enterprises Inc. [12219]
Pro-Fac Cooperative Inc. [12222]
Pro-Visions Pet Specialty Enterprises Div. [27217]
Producers Rice Mill Inc. [12225]
Proferas Pizza Bakery Inc. [12227]
Progressive Distributors [14199]
ProSource Inc. [24208]
Purcell & Associates [12235]
Pure Beverage Inc. [4097]
Purity Minonk Baking Co. [12238]
Purity Products Inc. [1973]
Purity Products Inc. (Baltimore, Maryland) [25022]
Purity Wholesale Grocers Inc. [12239]
Puro Corporation of America [25023]
Pyrenees French Bakery Inc. [12242]
Q.A. Products Inc. [12243]
QCU Inc. [13431]
Q.E.D. Exports [12244]
Quaker City Hide Co. [18186]
Quaker Oats Co. International Foods Div. [12245]
Quality Bakery Products Inc. [12247]
Quality Croutons Inc. [12249]
Quality Foods Inc. [12250]
Quality Foods Inc. [12251]
Quality King Distributors Inc. [14202]
Quality Meat Company Inc. [12252]
Quinn Coffee Co. [12257]
R and R Provision Co. [12258]
R.A.B. Holdings Inc. [12259]
Ragu Foods Co. [12264]
Rainbo Baking Co. [12265]
Rainbo Baking Co. [12266]
Rainbo Baking Co. [12267]
Rainbow Natural Foods [12269]
Ralston Purina/Pet Products [12271]
Randolph Slaughter Co. [12276]
Randy's Frozen Meats [12277]
Red Apple Supermarkets [12283]
Red Diamond Inc. [12284]
Red Mill Farms Inc. [12285]
Red River Barbeque and Grille [12286]
Red Star Yeast and Products, A Division of
  Universal Foods Corp. [12287]
Reddi-Made Foods Inc. [12289]
Reddy Ice Company Inc. [12290]
Reilly Dairy and Food Co. [12296]
Reliv' International Inc. [14213]
Reliv' World Corp. [12300]
Reuben's Wines & Spirits [1985]
Reynolds and Sons Inc.; A.T. [25024]
Rhee Bros. Inc. [12305]
Rhodes Corp.; P.J. [12306]
Ribbons Pasta Co. [12307]
Rice Growers Association of California [12308]
Riceland Foods Inc. [12309]
RiceTec Inc. [12310]
Rio Grande Trading Co. [14220]
Ritter Sysco Food Services Inc. [12321]
River Springs Cooperative Association [27222]
Riviana Foods Inc. [12325]
Roanoke Distributing Company Inc. [1995]
Robbinsdale Farm and Garden Pet Supply
  Inc. [27224]
Roberts Dairy Co. [12329]
Robins Brokerage Co. [12331]
Robinson Barbecue Sauce Company Inc. [12333]
Rock Hill Coca-Cola Bottling Co. [25025]
Rock Springs Casper Coca-Cola Bottling
  Co. [25026]
Rocky Mountain Food Factory Inc. [12338]
Rodriguez Festive Foods Inc. [12343]
Rogers Brothers Wholesale Inc. [12344]
Roland Foods [12346]
Rolet Food Products Co. [12347]
Roma Food Enterprises Inc. [12348]
Romeo & Sons [12349]

Royal Crown Beverage Co. [25027]
Royal Crown Bottling Company Inc. [25028]
Royal Essence Ltd. [14226]
Royal Foods Distributors Inc. [12364]
Royal Wine Co. [2001]
Rudis Bakery [12366]
Ryan Co.; Johnnie [25029]
Ryan's Wholesale Food Distributors [12373]
Rykoff-Sexton Distribution Div. [12375]
Rykoff-Sexton Manufacturing L.L.C. [12377]
S and D Coffee Inc. [12379]
S & H Co. [26349]
S & S [27226]
S & S Variety Beverages Inc. [25030]
Sabrett Food Products [12385]
Saccani Distributing Co. [25031]
Saelens Beverages Inc. [2004]
Safa Enterprises Co., Inc. [12386]
St. Charles County Cooperative Co. [27227]
Saleff & Son New York Pastry; Richard [12392]
Salem Coca-Cola Bottling Co. [25032]
Sales Force of Omaha [12395]
Sales Results [12397]
Sam's Gourmet [12399]
San Diego Beverage and Cup Inc. [25033]
San Jacinto Foods [12401]
San Luis Sourdough [12402]
Sanfilippo Co.; John B. [12407]
Sara Lee Corp. [12412]
Saratoga Specialties [12413]
Sathers Inc. [12418]
Satori Herbal-Business Development Labs [12419]
Scheidt Inc.; Bruno [12425]
Schlachter Co. Inc.; Edward J. [12427]
Schneider Dairy [12428]
Schnieber Fine Food Inc. [12430]
Schwan Wholesale Co. [12433]
Scotty's Foods Inc. [12435]
Scrivner Inc. [12436]
Scrivner of New York [12438]
Seasia [12452]
Seawind International [12456]
Sergeant's Pet Products Inc. [27230]
Seven-Up Baltimore Inc. [25034]
Seven-Up Dayton Div. [25035]
Seven-Up Royal Crown [25036]
Seven-Up Salem [25037]
Shaklee Corp. [14234]
Shaklee Distributor [12469]
Shaklee Distributor [12470]
Shamrock Farms Creamery [12471]
Shear Associates Inc.; Ted [12475]
Shimaya Shoten Ltd. [12479]
Shopper's Food Warehouse Corp. [12483]
Sierra [12486]
Sigel Liquor Stores Inc. [2024]
Sigma Food Distributing [12489]
Silver Foods Corp. [12491]
Silver Lake Cookie Co. [12492]
Sinbad Sweets Inc. [12495]
Sioux Honey Association [12497]
SK Food International, Inc. [12499]
Skidmore Sales & Distributing Company, Inc. [12501]
Skokie Valley Beverage Co. [2028]
Sky Brothers Inc. [12503]
Smith Brothers Food Service Inc. [12508]
Smith Inc.; Del Cher [12510]
Smith and Sons Foods Inc. [12517]
Snak King Corp. [12522]
Sommer Inc.; John [12527]
Sona & Hollen Foods Inc. [12528]
Sosnick and Son; J. [12530]
Southern Beverage Company Inc. [25038]
A Southern Season [12542]
Southern Tea Co. [12543]
Southern Wine & Spirits [2035]
Southern Wine & Spirits [2038]
Southern Wine & Spirits [2039]
Southern Wine and Spirits of California Inc. [2041]
Southwest Specialties [12545]
SPAP Company LLC [4517]
Spaz Beverage Co. [25039]
Specialized Marketing [12549]
Specialty Food Distributors, Inc. [12551]
Specialty World Foods Inc. [12553]

Spindler Co. [12555]
Spring Tree Corp. [12557]
Springfield Pepsi-Cola Bottling Co. [25040]
Springfield Sugar and Products Co. [12559]
Stahl's Bakery [12562]
Standard Distributing Company Inc. (Waterloo, Iowa) [2047]
Starbucks Corp. [12571]
StarKist Seafood/Heinz Pet Prd [12575]
Stash Distributing Inc. [2049]
Stash Tea Co. [12576]
Staton Distributing Co.; Jim [2050]
Staunton Food Inc. [12579]
Staz Food Services [12581]
Steel City Milling Inc. [12582]
Stella D'Oro Biscuit Company Inc. [12583]
Stokes Canning Co. [12586]
Storm Pet Supply Inc. [27240]
Stow Mills [12592]
Stratton's Salads; Mrs. [12593]
Straub and Co.; W.F. [12594]
Streva Distributing Co. [2059]
Struve Distributing Company Inc. [25832]
Stutz Candy Co., Inc. [12596]
Suarez and Co.; V. [12597]
Suarez Food Distribution Co.; C.G. [12598]
Sugar Foods Corp. [12599]
Summit Import Corp. [12602]
Sun Office Service [12606]
Sun States Beverage Co. [25041]
Sunbelt Food Sales [12608]
Sunburst Foods Inc. [12609]
Sundrop Inc. [25042]
Sunfire Corporation [12610]
Sunflower Restaurant Supply [12611]
Sunflower Restaurant Supply Inc. [12612]
Sunlight Foods Inc. [12616]
Sunsweet Growers Inc. [12622]
Super-Nutrition Distributors Inc. [14252]
Superior Confections [12638]
Superior Trading Co. [12641]
SuperValu Inc. [12644]
Sweet Street Desserts [12656]
Sweet Things Bakery [12658]
Swire Coca-Cola USA [12660]
Switzers Inc. [12661]
Syrex, Inc. [1311]
Sysco Corp. [12668]
Sysco Food Service of Jamestown [12671]
Sysco Food Service of Seattle Inc. [12672]
SYSCO Food Services [12673]
SYSCO Food Services of Detroit, LLC [12679]
SYSCO Food Services of Minnesota Inc. [12684]
SYSCO Food Services of Portland [12686]
T & M Inc. [2067]
Taiyo Inc. [12692]
Takitani Enterprises Inc.; K. [25043]
Talladega Beverage Co. [2068]
Tanner Enterprises, Inc. [12696]
Tastee Apple Inc. [12699]
Tasty Foods/VCA [27244]
Tasty Mix Quality Foods Inc. [12700]
Taylor Corp.; Jim [2070]
Taylor Feed & Pet Supply [27245]
Taylor and Sledd Inc. [12701]
TENGASCO Inc. [22723]
Tenneva Food and Supplies Inc. [12707]
Texas Health Distributors [12709]
Thomas and Howard Company Inc. [12714]
Timber Crest Farms [12722]
Tims Cascade Style Chips [12723]
Tipp Distributors Inc. [25044]
To Market Two Markets Inc. [12725]
Tom Cat Bakery [12726]
Tom's Foods Inc. [12729]
Tony's Fine Foods [12731]
Top Taste Bakery Inc. [12733]
Torn and Glasser Inc. [12735]
Totem Food Products Co. [12736]
Toudouze Inc. [12737]
TownTalk/Hostess [12738]
T.R. Distributing [12739]
Trader Vic's Food Products [12740]
Traditional Quality Corp. [12741]
Trailblazer Foods [12742]
Trax Farms Inc. [12745]

Tree of Life/Gourmet Award Foods [12746]
Tree of Life Inc. Midwest [12748]
Tree of Life Inc. Northeast [12749]
Tree of Life Inc. Northwest [12750]
Tree of Life Inc. Southwest [12751]
Triarc Companies Inc. [12755]
Trinidad-Benham Corp. [18293]
Triumph Pet Industries, Inc. [27254]
Tropical Nut and Fruit [12761]
Troyer Foods Inc. [12763]
Trundle and Company Inc. [25045]
Trundle and Company Inc. [12765]
Tucson Co-op Wholesale [12766]
Tumbleweed Distributors [12768]
Tupman Thurlow Company Inc. [12771]
Uncle Bens Inc. [12783]
Union Incorporated [12787]
United Beverage Inc. [12790]
United Liquors Ltd. [2092]
United Natural Foods, Inc. [12799]
United Noodles Inc. [12800]
U.S. Beverage Corp. [25046]
U.S. Food Service [12801]
U.S. Import Export Corp. [12803]
U.S. Pure Water Corp. [25858]
U.S. Sugar Company Inc. [12804]
Universal Corp. [26365]
UPCO Pet Vet Supply [27258]
V-Labs Inc. [12813]
Valley Distributors Inc. [2095]
Valley Farm Dairy Co. [12816]
Valley Foods [12817]
Val's Homemade Bagels Inc. [12821]
Van Den Bosch Co.; John A. [27261]
Van Roy Coffee Co. [12824]
Vancol Industries Inc. [12826]
Vanee Foods Co. [12828]
Vassilaros and Sons Inc.; J.A. [12831]
Veri-Best Bakers [12837]
Vermont Pet Food & Supply [27263]
Vermont Pure Holdings Ltd. [25047]
Vermont Whey Co. [12839]
Veronica Foods Co. [12841]
Very Fine Resources Inc. [12842]
Viles and Associates Inc. [12844]
Villafane Inc.; Rene Ortiz [8183]
Virginia Beach Beverages [25048]
Virginia Imports [2106]
Vista Bakery, Inc. [12850]
Vitality Foodservice Inc. [25049]
Vitex Foods Inc. [12851]
Vogue Cuisine Inc. [12854]
Wades Dairy Inc. [12861]
Wagner and Sons Inc.; John [12864]
Wakefern Food Corp. [12865]
Walker Distributors Inc. [12868]
Walker Distributors Inc.; Joe [12869]
Wallace's Old Fashion Skins Inc. [12870]
Wallach's Poultry Farms [12871]
Water Warehouse, Etc. [25050]
Watson Foodservice Inc. [12883]
Waukesha Wholesale Foods Inc. [12884]
Waymouth Farms Inc. [12887]
Weaver Co.; James A. [12890]
Wechsler Coffee Corp. [12892]
Wedemeyers Bakery [12893]
Weil and Co.; J. [12897]
Wells International [12900]
Werner & Son; Max [12903]
Westco-BakeMark Las Vegas [12907]
Westco Food Service Co. [12908]
Western Export Services [12913]
Western Farm Center [1429]
Western Wyoming Beverage Inc. [25051]
Westside Distributors [12916]
Westway Trading Corp. [12917]
Westway Trading Corp. [12918]
Wetterau Inc. [12919]
White Coffee Corp. [12925]
White Cross Corporation, Inc. [19703]
Whole Herb Co. [12934]
Wildwood Natural Foods [12942]
Wilhelm Warehouse Company Inc.; Rudie [12943]
Wilsbach Distributors Inc. [2122]
Wilson Products Company Inc. [12955]
Wilton Industries Inc. [12956]

Winchell's Donut Houses Operating Company L.P. [12957]
Wine Distributors Inc. [2124]
Winrock Bakery Inc. [12959]
Winter Gardens Quality Foods [12960]
Winward Trading Company. [12964]
Wisconsin Distributors Inc. [2134]
Wolfstein International, Inc. [12973]
Wonder Bread Thrift Store Inc. [12975]
Woolson Spice Co. [4294]
World Finer Foods Inc. [12981]
World Food Tech Services [12982]
Worldwide Wonders [12984]
Wricley Nut Products Co. [12985]
Wricley Nut Products Co. Edwards-Freeman Div. [12986]
Wright Brokerage Inc. [12987]
Wright Wisner Distributing Corp. [2140]
Xcell International Corp. [12989]
Xcell International Corp. [15382]
Xport Port Authority Trading Co. [4559]
Yorkshire Food Sales Corp. [12996]
Yum Yum Donut Shops, Inc. [12998]
Zekes Distributing Co. [2145]
Ziegler's Bakers Supply and Equipment Corp. [13006]
Zucca Inc.; L.J. [26377]

SIC 5153 — Grain & Field Beans

A & K Feed and Grain Company Inc. [17670]
Ada Farmers Exchange Co. [17672]
Adams County Co-operative Association Inc. [183]
Adams Group Inc. [17675]
ADM-Growmark Inc. [17677]
ADM-Growmark Inc. [10326]
Adrian Wheat Growers Inc. [189]
Ag Partners Co. Cannon Falls Div. [17679]
Ag Partners Co. Cannon Falls Div. [10342]
AG Partners L.L.C. [197]
Agaland CO-OP Inc. [202]
Agate Cooperative [203]
Agco Inc. [204]
Agco Inc. [10344]
Agiand Co-op [17680]
Agland Coop [17681]
Agland Cooperative [207]
Agland Cooperative [208]
AGP Grain Co. [17682]
Agrex Inc. [17683]
Agri Grain Marketing [17684]
AGRI Sales [17685]
Agri Sales Inc. [17686]
Agriland F.S. Inc. [215]
AgriPride F.S. [216]
Alabama Farmers Cooperative Inc. [17689]
Albert City Elevator Inc. [220]
Allen County Cooperative Association [222]
Alliance Grain Co. [17691]
Allied International Marketing Corp. [17692]
Alma Farmers Cooperative Association [229]
American Rice Growers Cooperative Association [235]
Amherst Cooperative Elevator Inc. [17697]
Andale Farmers Cooperative Company Inc. [17699]
Andersons Inc. [242]
Andres and Wilton Farmers Grain and Supply Co. [17701]
Anthony Farmers Cooperative and Elevator Co. [17702]
Archer Cooperative Grain Co. [248]
Arizona Grain Inc. [17705]
Arthur Companies Inc. [257]
Ashland Farmers Elevator Co. [17706]
Ashmore Grain Co. Inc. [17707]
Assumption Cooperative Grain Co. [17708]
Assumption Cooperative Grain Co. [10459]
Atchison County Farmers Union Cooperative Association [17709]
Atherton Grain Co. [17710]
Atherton Grain Co. [10462]
Auglaize Farmers Cooperative [261]
Augusta Cooperative Farm Bureau [262]

Augusta Farmers Cooperative Co. [17712]
Austinville Elevator [17713]
B and W Farm Center Inc. [266]
Badger Farmers Cooperative [268]
Badger Farmers Cooperative [10486]
Badgerland Farm Center [269]
Balfour Maclaine Corp. [10494]
Barron Farmers Union Cooperative Services Inc. [279]
Barry Grain and Feed Inc. [280]
Bartlett and Co. (Headquarters) [17725]
Bartlett Cooperative Association Inc. [281]
Battle Creek Farmers Cooperative [283]
Beardsley Farmers Elevator Co. [287]
Beattie Farmers Union Cooperative Association [17726]
Bee County Cooperative Association Inc. [292]
Beltrami Farmers Elevator [297]
Bement Grain Company Inc. [17728]
Benham and Company Inc. [10535]
Benson Farmers Cooperative [299]
Benson-Quinn Co. [17729]
Berlin Farmers Elevator [302]
Berthold Farmers Elevator Co. [10543]
Bethany Grain Company Inc. [17732]
Bickley Inc.; A.M. [17733]
Big Tex Feed Co. Inc. [312]
Big Tex Grain Company Inc. [313]
Binford Farmers Union Grain [316]
Blackwell Cooperative Elevator Association [17736]
Blanchard Valley Farmers Cooperative [17737]
Bliss Cooperative Grain Co. [17738]
Bluff Springs Farmers Elevator Co. [17740]
Bobb Brothers Inc. [17741]
Bode Cooperative [325]
Bomadi Inc. [10587]
Bond County Services Co. [328]
Bondurant Grain Company Inc.; D.E. [17743]
Booker Equity Union Exchange Inc. [330]
Booneville Cooperative Elevator Co. [331]
Bottineau Farmers Elevator Inc. [17744]
Bradfordton Cooperative Association Inc. [17745]
Brewmaster [1549]
Bricelyn Elevator Association [17746]
Brocke and Sons Inc.; George F. [337]
Brooks Farmers Cooperative Association [17748]
Broussard Rice Mill Inc. [17749]
Brown County Co-op [339]
Bryant and Son Inc.; Otis [347]
BTR Farmers Co-op [17750]
Buchanan Farmers Elevator Co. [17751]
Buchanan Farmers Elevator Co. [10635]
Buckeye Cooperative Elevator Co. [17752]
Buckeye Cooperative Elevator Co. [10637]
Buckeye Countrymark Corp. [348]
Buckingham Cooperative Co. [17753]
Buckman Farmers Cooperative Creamery [350]
Bunge Corp. [17754]
Burgess Brothers Grain Inc. [17755]
Bushland Grain Cooperative [17757]
Caledonia Farmers Elevator Co., Lake Odessa Branch [362]
Calumet Industries Inc. [17760]
Canadian Equity Cooperative [368]
Cariba International Corp. [10700]
Carrollton Farmers Elevator Co. [17765]
Carrollton Farmers Elevator Co. [10704]
Carwell Elevator Company Inc. [17766]
Cass County Service Co. [378]
Castlewood Farmers Elevator [17767]
Cedar Valley FS Inc. [381]
Cenex Harvest States [382]
Cenex Harvest States Cooperatives [17768]
Centennial Commodities Inc. [17769]
Centra Sota Cooperative [385]
Central Commodities Ltd. [17770]
Central Connecticut Cooperative Farmers Association [17771]
Central Counties Cooperative [388]
Central Farmers Cooperative [390]
Central Farmers Cooperative [10720]
Central Iowa Cooperative [396]
Cereal Byproducts Co. [404]
CGB Enterprises Inc. [17773]
Chapin Farmers Elevator Co. [17775]
Cheney Cooperative Elevator Association [411]

Chester Inc. [414]
Chokio Equity Exchange Inc. [17778]
Cisco Cooperative Grain Inc. [17779]
Clarence Cooperative Company Inc. [419]
Clarenie Cooperative Elevator Co. [420]
Clarion Farmers Elevator Cooperative [421]
Clark Landmark Inc. [423]
Clearwater Grain Co. [424]
Clifton Grain Inc. [17782]
Clinton Landmark Inc. [17783]
Co-HG [429]
Co-op Country Farmers Elevator [17785]
Co-op Country Farmers Elevator [10780]
Coast Grain Company Inc. [430]
Collingwood Grain Inc. [435]
Colusa Elevator Company Inc. [17786]
Colwell Cooperative [17787]
Commerce Consultants Inc. [22154]
ConAgra Grain Co. [17789]
ConAgra Grain Co. [10805]
ConAgra Trading Cos. [10807]
Concordia Farmers Cooperative Co. [437]
Connell Grain Growers Inc. [17790]
Conrad Cooperative [438]
Consolidated Cooperative Inc. [17791]
Consolidated Cooperatives Inc. [440]
Consumers Supply Cooperative Co. [10822]
Continental Grain Co. [17792]
Cooksville Grain Co. [17793]
Coop Country Partners [445]
Coop Services Inc. [446]
Cooperative Agricultural Services Inc. [448]
Cooperative Elevator Co. [450]
Cooperative Elevator Co. [451]
Cooperative Elevator Co. [17794]
Cooperative Elevator Co. [10834]
Cooperative Elevator, Sebewaing [17795]
Cooperative Elevator Supply Co. [452]
Cooperative Exchange [453]
Cooperative Feed Dealer Inc. [454]
Cooperative Grain and Product Co. [455]
Cooperative Grain and Supply [17796]
Cooperative Grain and Supply [17797]
Cooperative Grain and Supply [10835]
Cooperative Oil Co. [458]
Cooperative Sampo Corp. [17798]
Cooperative Union Mercantile Co. Inc. [461]
Coshocton Grain Co. [17799]
Cottage Grove Cooperative [465]
Coulter Elevator [17801]
Country Springs Farmers [10859]
Country Star Coop [17802]
Countrymark Cooperative Inc. [466]
County Line Co-op [469]
Crescent Cooperative Association [472]
Crestland Cooperative [473]
Crookston Farmers Cooperative [477]
Crowley Grain Drier Inc. [17804]
Crystal Cooperative Inc. [479]
Cullman Seed and Feed Co. [481]
Culver-Fancy Prairie Cooperative Co. [17805]
Custer Grain Co. [485]
Cyclone Grain Co. [17806]
Cylinder Cooperative Elevator [17807]
Dakota Pride Coop [487]
Dalhart Consumers Fuel and Grain Association Inc. [17808]
Danforth-Gilman Grain Co. [17810]
Danvers Farmers Elevator Co. [493]
Danvers Farmers Elevator Co. [10907]
Davenport Union Warehouse Co. [17812]
Davis Grain Corp. [17813]
DeBruce Grain Inc. [17814]
Dell Rapids Co-op Grain [505]
DeLong Company Inc. [506]
Delphos Co-Op Association Inc. [17816]
Del's Farm Supply [508]
Demeter Inc. [17818]
Dewar Elevator Co. [517]
Donovan Farmers Cooperative Elevator Inc. [17819]
Dorchester Farmers Cooperative [17820]
Dreyfus Corp.; Louis [17822]
Driscoll Grain Cooperative Inc. [17823]
Driscoll Grain Cooperative Inc. [10996]
Drummond Cooperative Elevator Inc. [526]

Dubois County Farm Bureau Cooperative [527]
Dyer Lauderdale Co-op [532]
Earlville Farmers Cooperative [17825]
East Central Iowa Cooperative [11016]
Eastern Europe, Inc. [536]
Eastern Farmers Coop [537]
Edison Non-Stock Cooperative [542]
Edmonson Wheat Growers Inc. [17826]
Edon Farmers Cooperative Association Inc. [543]
Effingham Equity [17827]
Elbow Lake Cooperative Grain [545]
Elburn Cooperative Co. [17829]
Eldridge Cooperative Co. [17830]
Elkhart Cooperative Equity Exchange [11040]
Ellsworth-William Cooperative Co. [17831]
Elwood Line Grain and Fertilizer Co. [17832]
Emma Cooperative Elevator Co. [27129]
EMP Co-op Inc. [17833]
Equity Cooperative Elevator Co. [17834]
Equity Elevator and Trading Co. [17835]
Equity Grain and General Merchant
   Exchange [17836]
Equity Supply Co. [554]
Ezell-Key Grain Company Inc. [11065]
Fairdale Farmers Cooperative Elevator Co. [560]
Farm Service Company Inc. [564]
Farm Service Cooperative Inc. [565]
Farm Service Elevator Co. [17839]
Farmers Coop Association of Jackson, Sherburn,
   Spring Lake & Trimont [568]
Farmers Cooperative [569]
Farmers Cooperative Association [571]
Farmers Cooperative Association [572]
Farmers Cooperative Association [573]
Farmers Cooperative Association [17841]
Farmers Cooperative Association [576]
Farmers Cooperative Association [578]
Farmers Cooperative Association [579]
Farmers Cooperative Association [580]
Farmers Cooperative Association [17842]
Farmers Cooperative Association [581]
Farmers Cooperative Association [17843]
Farmers Cooperative Association [582]
Farmers Cooperative Association [22254]
Farmers Cooperative Association [585]
Farmers Cooperative Association [17844]
Farmers Cooperative Association [17845]
Farmers Cooperative Association [17846]
Farmers Cooperative Association [11088]
Farmers Cooperative Association [11089]
Farmers Cooperative Association (Brule,
   Nebraska) [11090]
Farmers Cooperative Association (York,
   Nebraska) [17847]
Farmers Cooperative Business Association [586]
Farmers Cooperative (Carmen, Oklahoma) [17848]
Farmers Cooperative Co. [588]
Farmers Cooperative Co. [589]
Farmers Cooperative Co. [590]
Farmers Cooperative Co. [591]
Farmers Cooperative Co. [592]
Farmers Cooperative Co. [593]
Farmers Cooperative Co. [594]
Farmers Cooperative Co. [595]
Farmers Cooperative Co. [17849]
Farmers Cooperative Co. [17850]
Farmers Cooperative Co. [597]
Farmers Cooperative Co. [598]
Farmers Cooperative Co. [599]
Farmers Cooperative Co. [17851]
Farmers Cooperative Co. [600]
Farmers Cooperative Co. [601]
Farmers Cooperative Co. [17852]
Farmers Cooperative Co. [602]
Farmers Cooperative Co. [603]
Farmers Cooperative Co. [17853]
Farmers Cooperative Co. [11091]
Farmers Cooperative Co. [11092]
Farmers Cooperative Co. [11093]
Farmers Cooperative Co. [11094]
Farmers Cooperative Co. [11095]
Farmers Cooperative Co. (Britt, Iowa) [11096]
Farmers Cooperative Co. (Dike, Iowa) [17854]
Farmers Cooperative Co. (Hinton, Iowa) [17855]
Farmers Cooperative Company Inc. [604]

Farmers Cooperative Co. (Milligan,
   Nebraska) [17856]
Farmers Cooperative Co. (Readlyn, Iowa) [17857]
Farmers Cooperative Co. (Woolstock,
   Iowa) [17858]
Farmers Cooperative of El Campo [17860]
Farmers Cooperative Elevator [605]
Farmers Cooperative Elevator [606]
Farmers Cooperative Elevator [607]
Farmers Cooperative Elevator [608]
Farmers Cooperative Elevator [17861]
Farmers Cooperative Elevator [609]
Farmers Cooperative Elevator [17862]
Farmers Cooperative Elevator Association [17863]
Farmers Cooperative Elevator Association [610]
Farmers Cooperative Elevator Association [611]
Farmers Cooperative Elevator Association [11098]
Farmers Cooperative Elevator Co. [612]
Farmers Cooperative Elevator Co. [613]
Farmers Cooperative Elevator Co. [17864]
Farmers Cooperative Elevator Co. [614]
Farmers Cooperative Elevator Co. [615]
Farmers Cooperative Elevator Co. [616]
Farmers Cooperative Elevator Co. [17865]
Farmers Cooperative Elevator Co. [617]
Farmers Cooperative Elevator Co. [618]
Farmers Cooperative Elevator Co. [17866]
Farmers Cooperative Elevator Co. [620]
Farmers Cooperative Elevator Co. [17867]
Farmers Cooperative Elevator Co. [621]
Farmers Cooperative Elevator Co. [17868]
Farmers Cooperative Elevator Co. (Buffalo Lake,
   Minnesota) [11099]
Farmers Cooperative Elevator Co. (Everly,
   Iowa) [17869]
Farmers Cooperative Elevator Co. Lake Lillian
   Div. [622]
Farmers Cooperative Elevator (Martelle,
   Iowa) [17870]
Farmers Cooperative Elevator and Supply [17871]
Farmers Cooperative Exchange [623]
Farmers Cooperative Exchange [625]
Farmers Cooperative Exchange [626]
Farmers Cooperative Exchange [11100]
Farmers Cooperative Exchange (Elgin,
   Nebraska) [11101]
Farmers Cooperative Grain Association [628]
Farmers Cooperative Grain Association [629]
Farmers Cooperative Grain Co. [17872]
Farmers Cooperative Grain and Seed [17873]
Farmers Cooperative Grain and Seed Co. [630]
Farmers Cooperative Grain and Supply [17874]
Farmers Cooperative Grain and Supply Co. [631]
Farmers Cooperative Grain and Supply Co. [632]
Farmers Cooperative Grain and Supply
   Co. [11102]
Farmers Cooperative Mill Elevator [17875]
Farmers Cooperative (Odebolt, Iowa) [17876]
Farmers Cooperative of Pilger [17877]
Farmers Cooperative Society [637]
Farmers Cooperative Society (Sioux Center,
   Iowa) [17878]
Farmers Cooperative Trading Co. [639]
Farmers Cooperative Union [640]
Farmer's Elevator Co-op [17879]
Farmers Elevator Co. [17880]
Farmers Elevator Co. [641]
Farmers Elevator Co. [642]
Farmers Elevator Co. [17881]
Farmers Elevator Co. [643]
Farmers Elevator Co. [17882]
Farmers Elevator Co. [17883]
Farmers Elevator Co. [11103]
Farmers Elevator Company of Avoca [644]
Farmers Elevator Company of Manteno [17884]
Farmers Elevator Co. Richey Div. [17885]
Farmers Elevator Cooperative [645]
Farmers Elevator and Exchange Inc. [17886]
Farmers Elevator of Fergus Falls [17887]
Farmers Elevator Grain and Supply [646]
Farmers Elevator Inc. [17888]
Farmers Elevator and Supply Co. [17889]
Farmers Elevator Supply Co. [647]
Farmers Exchange Cooperative [649]
Farmers Gin Company Inc. [17891]
Farmers Grain Co. [651]

Farmers Grain Company of Chestnut [17892]
Farmers Grain Company of Dorans [17893]
Farmers Grain Company Inc. [653]
Farmers Grain Company Inc. [17894]
Farmers Grain Company of Julesburg [17895]
Farmers Grain Cooperative [17896]
Farmers Grain Cooperative [654]
Farmers Grain Cooperative [655]
Farmers Grain Dealers Inc. [17897]
Farmers Grain and Seed [17898]
Farmers Grain and Supply Company Inc. [17899]
Farmers Grain and Supply Company Inc. [657]
Farmers Grain Terminal [17900]
Farmers Shipping and Supply [17902]
Farmers Soybean Corp. [17903]
Farmers Supply Cooperative-AAL [658]
Farmers Union Co-op [17904]
Farmers Union Co-op [11104]
Farmers Union Cooperative Association [17905]
Farmers Union Cooperative Association (Mead,
   Nebraska) [17906]
Farmers Union Cooperative Co. [17907]
Farmers Union Cooperative Elevator Co. [17908]
Farmers Union Cooperative (Harvard,
   Nebraska) [11105]
Farmers Union Elevator [663]
Farmers Union Elevator Co. [17909]
Farmers Union Grain Cooperative [17910]
Farmers Union Oil Co. [664]
Farmland Grain Div. [17912]
Farmland Industries Inc. Union Equity Exchange
   Div. [17913]
Farmland Service Cooperative [17914]
Fayette County Cooperative Inc. [674]
Ferrin Cooperative Equity Exchange [680]
Fessenden Cooperative Association [17917]
First Cooperative Association [11132]
First Farmers Cooperative Elevator [685]
Fisher Farmers Grain and Coal Co. [17919]
Fitzgerald Ltd. [690]
Fort Recovery Equity Exchange Co. [27133]
Four Circle Cooperative [17920]
Four Seasons F.S. Inc. [17921]
Fowler Elevator Inc. [17922]
Fowler Equity Exchange Inc. [17923]
Fowler Equity Exchange Inc. [11196]
Fox Co.; C.B. [17924]
Foxley Grain [17925]
Franklin County Grain Grower Inc. [701]
Franklin Farmers Cooperative [702]
Fredericksburg Farmers Cooperative [705]
Fredonia Cooperative Association [17926]
Fredonia Cooperative Association [11202]
Fremont Cooperative Produce Co. [706]
Frick's Services Inc. [17929]
Frontier Cooperative Co. [17930]
Frontier Trading Inc. [714]
Funderburk Company Inc.; G.A. [11224]
Funks Grove Grain Co. [17931]
Galesberg Cooperative Elevator Co. [720]
Garwood Implement and Supply Co. [17934]
Gateway Co-Op [17936]
Gaylord Cash & Carry [11246]
Genesee Union Warehouse Company Inc. [17938]
Geneva Elevator Co. [733]
Ging and Co. [17941]
Glasgow Cooperative Association [742]
Gold-Eagle Cooperative [744]
Golden Belt Cooperative Association Inc. [17946]
Good Seed and Grain Company Inc. [17947]
Goodhue Elevator Association Cooperative [17948]
Gooding Seed Co. [750]
Goodland Cooperative Equity Exchange
   Inc. [17950]
Graham Grain Co. [17951]
Grain Growers Cooperative (Cimarron,
   Kansas) [17952]
Grain Land Co-op [17953]
Grain Land Cooperative [17954]
Grainland [11304]
Grainland Cooperative [17955]
Grainland Cooperative [17956]
Grand Prairie Cooperative [17957]
Graymont Cooperative Association Inc. [761]
Great Bend Cooperative Association [17960]
Great Plains Co-op [17961]

Greeley Elevator Co. [17962]
Growers Cooperative Inc. [772]
GROWMARK Inc. [17965]
Gulf Pacific Rice Company Inc. [11347]
Gully Tri-Coop Association [778]
Hadley Corp.; Raymond [11358]
Hahnaman-Albrecht Inc. [17969]
Hale Center Wheat Growers Inc. [781]
Hallock Cooperative Elevator Co. [17971]
Hallock Cooperative Elevator Co. [11365]
Halstad Elevator Co. [17972]
Hamilton County Farm Bureau [784]
Hamilton Elevator Company Inc. [17973]
Hansmeier and Son Inc. [788]
Harco Distributing Co. [17974]
Hardeman Fayette Farmers Cooperative [790]
Hardy Cooperative Elevator Co. [17975]
Hardy Cooperative Elevator Co. [11378]
Harmony Agri Services [791]
Hartsburg Grain Co. [17979]
Hartz Seed Company Inc.; Jacob [17980]
Harvest States Cooperatives. Canton Div. [798]
Harvest States Cooperatives Line Elevator
    Div. [17981]
Harvest States Soybean Processing [17982]
Hayward Cooperative [804]
Heart of Iowa Coop. [11404]
Heart of Iowa Cooperative [805]
Heartland Co-op [807]
Heartland Co-op (Trumbull, Nebraska) [17986]
Heartland Cooperative Inc. [808]
Hector Farmers Elevator [17987]
Hereford Grain Corp. [17992]
Hettinger Cooperative Equity Exchange [17995]
Hiawatha Grain Co. [17996]
High Plains Cooperative [17997]
High Plains Cooperative Association [821]
Hill Grain Co. Inc.; C.F. [17999]
Hills Beaver Creek Coop Farm Service [824]
Hillsdale Cooperative Elevator [18000]
Hoegemeyer Hybrids Inc. [18001]
Hoegemeyer Hybrids Inc. [11444]
Hoffman and Reed Inc. [830]
Holmquist Grain and Lumber Co. [18002]
Holyrood Cooperative Grain and Supply
    Co. [18003]
Hoople Farmers Grain Co. [18004]
Hopkinsville Elevator Co. [11460]
Hub Grain Company Inc. [18006]
Hull Cooperative Association [11475]
Humphreys Coop Tipton Location [18007]
Hunter Grain Co. [845]
Huskers Coop. [11481]
Hutchinson Coop Elevator [18009]
Interstate Commodities Inc. [18012]
Iowa Soybean Association [18013]
Italgrani Elevator Co. [18014]
Iuka Cooperative Inc. [18015]
Jack's Bean Co. [11541]
Jackson-Jennings Farm Bureau
    Cooperative [22381]
JaGee Corp. [18019]
James Agriculture Center Inc. [878]
Jarvis-Paris-Murphy Company Inc. [18021]
Jasper County Farm Bureau Cooperative [18022]
Jefferson County Farmco Coop. [881]
Johnson Cooperative Grain Co. [888]
Johnston Elevator Co. [18025]
Kanorado Cooperative Association [18027]
Kathryn Farmers Mutual Elevators Inc. [18028]
Kaufman Grain Co. [18029]
Keller Grain and Feed Inc. [18030]
Kemp Grain Company Inc. [18032]
Kensington Cooperative Association [906]
King Grain Company Inc. [18034]
Klein Brothers Ltd. [18036]
Klemme Cooperative Grain Co. [914]
Knightstown Elevator Co. [18038]
Knowles Produce and Trading Co. [916]
Kokomo Grain Company Inc. [18039]
K.R. International [11639]
Kragnes Farmers Elevator [18040]
Krob and Co.; F.J. [920]
La Porte County Cooperative [18041]
La Salle Farmers Grain Co. [926]
Lake Andes Farmers Cooperative Co. [929]

Lake Andes Farmers Cooperative Co. [11666]
Lake Benton Farmers Elevator Inc. [930]
Lake Region Cooperative Oil Association [22416]
Lamont Grain Growers Inc. [18043]
Lapeer County Cooperative Inc. [18044]
Lasley and Sons Inc.; Walter [940]
Latah County Grain Growers Inc. [18045]
Latham Seed Co. [18046]
Laughery Valley AG Co-Op Inc. [942]
Lawn Hill Cooperative [945]
Lawrence County Exchange [18047]
Layne and Myers Grain Co. [18048]
Le Roy Cooperative Association Inc. [18049]
Lewiston Grain Growers [18055]
Lockney Cooperative Gin [11720]
Logsdon Service Inc. [18063]
Lowe's Pellets and Grain Co. [18065]
Lucky Farmers Inc. [975]
Ludlow Cooperative Elevator Company
    Inc. [18066]
Madison Farmers Elevator Co. [18070]
Madison Landmark Inc. [18071]
Madison Service Co. [982]
Mahaska Farm Service Co. [18073]
Maple Valley Cooperative [11777]
Mapleton Grain Co. [18074]
Martinsburg Farmers Elevator Co. [18075]
Master Feed and Grain Inc. [991]
Maynard Cooperative Inc. [18076]
Maywood Cooperative Association [995]
Mazon Farmers Elevator [996]
Mazon Farmers Elevator [11814]
McBee Grain and Trucking Inc. [18077]
McChesney Co.; C.E. [18078]
McCune Farmers Union Cooperative
    Association [1001]
McGeary Grain Inc. [18083]
Meis Seed and Feed Co. [1013]
Mendota Farm Cooperative Supply Inc. [18086]
Metamora Elevator Co. [1018]
Michigan Agricultural Commodities [18088]
Mid Columbia Producers Inc. [18091]
Mid-Iowa Cooperative (Beaman, Iowa) [18092]
Mid-Kansas Cooperative Association [1027]
Mid-South Malts/Memphis Brews Inc. [1872]
Mid-States Wool Growers Cooperative [1029]
Mid-Wood Inc. [18093]
Midland Bean Co. [18094]
Midland Cooperative Inc. [1031]
Midland Cooperative Inc. [11883]
Midland Cooperative Inc. Wilcox Div. [18095]
Midland Marketing Cooperative, Inc. [18096]
Midwest Consolidated Cooperative [1034]
Midwest Coop. [11888]
Midwest Cooperatives [18097]
Midwest Farmers Cooperative [1037]
Midwest Farmers Cooperative [11889]
Milan Farmers Elevator [18098]
Milan Farmers Elevator [11894]
Mills Farmers Elevator [1041]
Minier Cooperative Grain Co. [18102]
Minneola Cooperative Inc. [18104]
Minster Farmers Cooperative Exchange
    Inc. [18105]
Mitchellville Cooperative [1043]
Monica Elevator Co. [18109]
Monroe Lawrence Farm Bureau
    Cooperative [1047]
Monroeville Co-op Grain [18110]
Montezuma Cooperative Exchange [18112]
Monticello Grain Company Inc. [18113]
Morrisonville Farmers Cooperative [18117]
Morrow County Grain Growers Inc. [18118]
Moultrie Grain Association [18119]
Mt. Horeb Farmers Coop. [11941]
Mount Pulaski Farmers Grain [18120]
Mt. Union Cooperative Elevator [18121]
Mt. Union Cooperative Elevator [11943]
Mountain View Coop. [1055]
Moweaqua Farmers Cooperative Grain Co. [18122]
Mueller Bean Co. [11953]
Mueller Feed Mill Inc. [1057]
Nathan Segal and Company Inc. [18125]
NC Plus Hybrids Coop. [18126]
Nehawka Farmers Coop. [11991]
Nehawka Farmers Cooperative [18127]

NEW Cooperative Inc. [18130]
New Horizons Ag Services [1071]
Newark Farmers Grain Co. [18131]
Nokomis Equity Elevator Co. [18132]
Nomura and Company Inc. [18133]
North Caddo Cooperative Inc. [1078]
North Central Commodities, Inc. [18136]
North Central Cooperative Association [22524]
North Central Cooperative Elevator [18137]
North Central Cooperative Inc. [1079]
North Central Farm Service Inc. [18138]
North Central Grain Coop. [12026]
North Central Grain Cooperative [1080]
North Iowa Cooperative Elevator [1081]
Northampton County Seed [1082]
Northeast Cooperative [18140]
Northern Seed Service [1085]
Northland Marketing, Inc. [12035]
Northwest Grain [18143]
Northwest Grain Growers, Inc. [18144]
Northwest Iowa Cooperative [18145]
Northwest Iowa Cooperative [1088]
Northwood Cooperative Elevator [18146]
Northwood Equity Elevators [18147]
Ocheyedan Cooperative Elevator
    Association [18148]
Odessa Trading Company Inc. [18149]
Odessa Trading Company Inc. [12053]
Odessa Union Warehouse Co-op [18150]
Ohigro Inc. [1101]
O.K. Grain Co. [18153]
Old Dominion Grain Corp. [18154]
Olton Grain Cooperative Inc. [18155]
Osage Cooperative Elevator [1110]
Osage Cooperative Elevator [12079]
Ottawa Cooperative Association Inc. [18157]
Ottawa Cooperative Association Inc. [1112]
Pacific Southwest Seed and Grain Inc. [18158]
Paoli Farmers Cooperative Elevator Co. [18159]
Paramount Feed and Supply Inc. [1118]
Parshall Farmers Union Co-op Inc. [18160]
Pendleton Grain Growers Inc. [18161]
Perdue Farms Grain Div. [18162]
Perryton Equity Exchange [18164]
Perstorp Analytical Inc. [24417]
Pettisville Grain Company Inc. [1127]
Pickrell Cooperative Elevator Association [18165]
Pied Piper Mills Inc. [27213]
Pine Island Farmers Elevator Co. [18167]
Piqua Farmers Cooperative Association [18168]
Plains Equity Exchange [18171]
Pomeroy Grain Growers Inc. [18173]
Posey County Farm Bureau Cooperative
    Association Inc. [1141]
Prairie Land Cooperative [1144]
Prins Grain Co. [18178]
Prinz Grain and Feed Inc. [18179]
Producers Cooperative Association of
    Girard [18180]
Prosper Farmers Cooperative Elevator [1159]
Protection Co-op Supply [18182]
Pulaski Chase Cooperative [1161]
Pulaski County Farm Bureau Cooperative [1162]
Pyramid Agri-Products International [18184]
Quad County Cooperative [18185]
R and L Supply Co-op [1166]
Radium Cooperative Co. [18188]
Radium Cooperative Co. [12261]
Randall Farmers Cooperative Union [18189]
Rangen Inc. [18191]
Rangen Inc. [12278]
Ray-Carroll County Grain Growers Inc. [1169]
Reading Feed and Grain Inc. [1173]
Redwood Valley Co-op Elevator [18193]
Reeds Seeds Inc. [1178]
Reese Farmers Inc. [18194]
Revere Elevator Company Inc. [18195]
Rhoads Mills Inc. [1185]
Rickett Grain Co. [18197]
Rio Farmers Union Cooperative [18198]
Rivard's Quality Seeds Inc. [18199]
River Spring Cooperative [18200]
Roberts Brothers Inc. [18202]
Rock River Lumber and Grain Co. [1203]
Rockbridge Farmers Cooperative [1204]
Rockwell and Son; H. [1206]

Rolla Cooperative Equity Exchange [18203]
Rolla Cooperative Grain Co. [18204]
Rosamond Cooperative [18205]
Rosholt Farmers Cooperative Elevator Co. [18206]
Route 16 Grain Cooperative [18209]
Rugby Farmers Union Elevator Co. [18211]
Rumbold and Kuhn Inc. [18212]
Rural Serv Inc. [18213]
Rush County Farm Bureau Cooperative [1219]
Ruth Farmers Elevator Inc. [18215]
Sabina Farmers Exchange Inc. [1226]
St. Angsar Mills Inc. [18218]
St. Angsar Mills Inc. [12388]
St. Francis Mercantile Equity Exchange [1228]
St. John Grain Growers Inc. [18219]
Sanborn Cooperative Grain Co. [1233]
Sanborn Farmers Elevator [18221]
Sanborn Farmers Elevator [12404]
Satanta Cooperative Grain [18222]
S.C. Farm Bureau Marketing Association [18223]
Schultz Seed Co.; J.M. [18225]
Schuyler-Brown FS Inc. [1239]
Scott Cooperative Association [1240]
The Scoular Co. [18227]
Seaboard Corp. [12445]
Seaman Grain Inc. [1248]
Secor Elevator Company Inc. [12457]
Seibert Equity Cooperative Association [1256]
Seifert Farm Supply [1257]
Senex Harvest States [12460]
Senrenella Enterprises Inc. [18229]
Shelby Grain and Feed Co. [1264]
Shipman Elevator Co. [18232]
Simplot AgriSource [18234]
South Central Co-op [1274]
South Central Cooperative [18239]
South Dakota Wheat Growers Association [18241]
Southeast Cooperative Service Co. [18243]
Southeastern Colorado Coop. [12537]
Southeastern Mills Inc. [12538]
Southern States Cooperative Inc. [1283]
Southern States Frederick Cooperative Inc. [1284]
Southwest Grain Farm Marketing and Supply Div. [22686]
Spokane Seed Co. [18249]
Spokane Seed Co. [12556]
Stacyville Cooperative Co. [1291]
Stafford County Flour Mills Co. [4521]
Stanford Grain Co. [18250]
Starbuck Creamery Co. [12570]
Steuben County Farm Bureau Association Inc. [27238]
Stewart Co.; Jesse C. [18255]
Stonington Cooperative Grain Co. [18259]
Stotler Grain Co. [18260]
Stratford Grain and Supply Cooperative [18262]
Sublette Cooperative, Inc. [18265]
Sublette Farmers Elevator Co. [18266]
Sullivan Inc. [18267]
Sully Cooperative Exchange Inc. [18268]
Sunray Cooperative [1304]
Sunrise Cooperative Inc. [1305]
Superior Cooperative Elevator Co. [18270]
Sutherland Farmers Cooperative [1307]
Syracuse Cooperative Exchange [18272]
Syracuse Cooperative Exchange [12666]
Tabor Grain Co. [18273]
Taintor Cooperative Co. [18274]
Tama-Benton Cooperative Co. [18275]
Tampico Farmers Elevator Co. [1313]
Texas-West Indies Co. [18278]
Texhoma Wheat Growers Inc. [1325]
Tiffin Farmers Cooperative, Inc. [1335]
Tindall Inc.; E.H. [18284]
Tomen America Inc. [20430]
Top AG Inc. [1341]
Top of Iowa Coop [18285]
Torn and Glasser Inc. [12735]
Town and Country Coop. [1345]
Tradigrain Inc. [18287]
Trainor Grain and Supply Co. [18288]
Tri Central Co-op [18290]
Tri-Line Farmers Cooperative [18291]
Tri Valley Cooperative [1356]
Trinidad Bean and Elevator Co. [18292]
Trinidad-Benham Corp. [18293]

Tropical Nut and Fruit [12761]
Troy Elevator Inc. [18295]
Truman Farmers Elevator Co. [1361]
Ulysses Cooperative Supply Co. [18297]
Union Elevator and Warehouse Co. [18299]
Union Oil Mill Inc. [1372]
United Co-op [18301]
United Co-op Inc. (Hampton, Nebraska) [1374]
United Cooperative Farmers Inc. [1375]
United Farmers Co-op [1376]
United Farmers Cooperative [1377]
United Farmers Cooperative [12792]
United Farmers Elevator Co. [18302]
United Farmers Mercantile Cooperative [18303]
U.S. World Trade Corp. [18305]
Unity Grain and Supply Co. [18306]
Universal Cooperative Inc. [1385]
Ursa Farmers Cooperative [18308]
Utica Cooperative Grain Company Inc. [18310]
Utica Cooperative Grain Company Inc. [12810]
Valley Feed Mill Inc. [1393]
Valley Seed Co. [18314]
Van Horn Hybrids Inc. [18315]
V.H. Associates Inc. [18317]
Vista Trading Corp. [18319]
W-P Milling Company Inc. [1401]
Wagner Mills Inc. [18323]
Wagner Mills Inc. [12863]
Wallace County Cooperative Equity Exchange [1407]
Walters Cooperative Elevators Association [1411]
Warren Farmers Cooperative [1413]
Watertown Cooperative Elevator Association [1414]
Watonwan Farm Services Co. [18327]
Watonwan Farm Services Co. Ormsby Div. [18328]
Webb Inc.; Fred [18329]
Wendell Farmers Elevator Co. [18333]
West Bend Elevator Co. [18335]
West Central Cooperative [18336]
West Lyon Cooperative Inc. [18337]
West Nesbitt Inc. [18338]
Western Iowa Cooperative [18340]
Wheaton Dumont Cooperative Elevator Inc. [18342]
Wheeler Brothers [18343]
Wheeler Brothers [12924]
Wheeler Brothers Grain Company Inc. [18344]
Whitaker Farmers Cooperative Grain Co. [18345]
White Cloud Grain Co. [1438]
White Commercial Corp. [12926]
Whiteside F.S. Inc. [22800]
Whitman County Growers Inc. [18346]
Wilbur-Ellis Co. [18348]
Williamsville Farmers Cooperative Grain Co. [18351]
Willow Hill Grain Inc. [18352]
Willow Hill Grain Inc. [12951]
Wilmont Farmers Elevator Co. [18353]
Windom Cooperative Association [1455]
Wolcott and Lincoln Inc. [18357]
Wolcott and Lincoln Inc. [12971]
Wolverton Farmers Elevator [18358]
Wright Lorenz Grain Company Inc. [18361]
Wyndmere Farmers Elevator Co. [1466]
Yale Farmers Cooperative [18363]
Ypsilanti Equity Elevator Company Inc. [18364]

SIC 5154 — Livestock

3K Livestock [17668]
4 Seasons Livestock [17669]
Adams-Dougherty Livestock Brokerage [17674]
Addison County Commodity Sales [17676]
Allied Order Buyers, Inc. [17693]
Allied Order Buyers, Inc. [17694]
Amber NFO Reload Corp. [17695]
Andelain Farm [17700]
Arcadia Livestock, Inc. [17703]
Ardrosson Farms [17704]
Auction Livestock, Inc. [17711]
B & B Buyers Inc. [17714]
B & B Cattle Co. [17715]
B & J Cattle Co. [17716]

Bailey's Slaughter House [17717]
Bales Continental Commission Co. [17719]
Balthauser & Moyer [17720]
Bar Lazy K Bar Ranch Inc. [17721]
Belle Fourche Livestock Exchange [17727]
Bessman Price Auctioneers [17731]
Beyer Livestock; Allen [10550]
Billingsley Ranch Outfitters Equipment [17734]
Blackfoot Livestock Commission Company Inc. [17735]
Bloxham; Jack S. [17739]
Boedeker; Robert L. [17742]
Britton Livestock Sales Inc. [17747]
Camenzind Dairy Cattle; Art [17761]
Candee; Robert G. [17762]
Central Livestock Association [17772]
Chamberlain Livestock Auction [17774]
Cherry & Son; A.W. [17776]
CJ Cattle Co. Inc. [17780]
Clark; Clayton H. [17781]
Clovis Livestock Auction [17784]
Cottonwood Sales Yard [17800]
Daniel Piroutek [17811]
El Toro Land and Cattle Co. [17828]
Erickson's Sheep Co. [17837]
Farmers Livestock Marketing Association [17901]
Ferguson Cattle Co. Inc. [17916]
Finger Lakes Livestock Exchange Inc. [17918]
Fitzgerald Ltd. [690]
Frick Hog Buying & Trucking [17928]
Gallagher's Inc. [17932]
Garrard County Stockyard [17933]
Genetic Leaders International [17939]
Gilmou Inc.; Doug [17940]
Gligorea Livestock [17943]
Gooding Livestock Community Co. [17949]
Gregory Livestock [17964]
Growmark [775]
Growmark [776]
Hackler Livestock; G.A. [17967]
Haider; Raymond [17970]
Harrison Livestock Co.; B.H. [17977]
Hauck; Donald [17983]
Hay Land and Livestock Inc. [17985]
Heinold Hog Market Inc. [17988]
Heraa Inc. [17991]
Herreid Livestock Market [17994]
Highmore Auction [17998]
Horpestad Ranch Inc. [18005]
Hunsdon; Vernon [18008]
Idaho Livestock Auction Co. [18010]
J & L Livestock [18016]
J & R Mercantile Ltd. [18017]
Jacobson Cattle Co. [18018]
Jamestown Livestock Sales [18020]
Kalispell Livestock Auction [18026]
Kelly; Dennis [18031]
Kendall; Dale B. [18033]
Kist Livestock Auction Co. [18035]
Klinker; Norman [18037]
Lea County Livestock Marketing [18050]
Lemmon Livestock Inc. [18051]
Lewis-Simpson Ranch [18053]
Lewis-Simpson Ranch [18054]
Lewiston Livestock Market Inc. [18056]
Lewistown Livestock Auction [18057]
Line & Co.; R.Q. [18059]
Linton Livestock Market Inc. [18061]
Lloyds Buying Service [18062]
Long & Hansen Commission Co. [18064]
M & R Trading Inc. [18068]
Magness Huron Livestock Exchange [18072]
Maynard Cooperative Co. [18076]
McCoy Cattle Co.; M.W. [18080]
McCraken Livestock Inc. [18081]
McDonald Livestock Inc. [18082]
McLaughlin Livestock Auction [18084]
Michigan Agricultural Commodities [18088]
Michigan Livestock Exchange [18089]
Miller Corp.; C.C. [18099]
Miller Livestock Sales Co. [18100]
Miller Stockyards; A.E. [18101]
Missouri Swine Export Federation [18106]
Montana International Lvstk [18111]
Mooney Cattle Co. Inc. [18114]
Morazan [18115]

Munsell Livestock [18123]
Napoleon Livestock Auction [18124]
Nelson; Todd [18128]
North East Kingdom Sales, Inc. [18139]
Orleans Commissions Sales [18156]
Perry; Lynn [18163]
Piroutek; Daniel [18169]
Pohlman Farms; Henry G. [18172]
Pontiac Livestock Sales [18175]
Prairie Livestock L.L.C. [18176]
Prewitt Cattle Co. [18177]
Producers Livestock Marketing Association [18181]
Public Auction Yards [18183]
Pyramid Agri-Products International [18184]
Randall Inc.; H.G. [18190]
Rangen Inc. [18191]
Redfield Livestock Auction Inc. [18192]
Robbins Livestock Auction [18201]
Roswell Livestock Auction Co. [18207]
Russell; Herbert A. [18214]
St. Albans Commission Sales [18217]
Salado Cattle Co. [18220]
Schmalenberge; Jacob [18224]
Seymour Livestock Trucking [18231]
Shoshone Sales Yard Inc. [18233]
Snipes Webb Trailer & Livestock Co. [18238]
South Dakota Livestock Sale [18240]
Speartex Grain Co. [18248]
Steele-Siman & Co. [18252]
Steinke Ranches Inc.; E.J. [18254]
Stockmen's Livestock Exchange [18256]
Stockmen's Livestock Market [18257]
Stone Commodities Corp. [12590]
Sturgis Livestock Exchange [18263]
Sutton Ranches [18271]
Thomas & Jones Sales Management [18279]
Thorpe Livestock Inc. [18280]
Tilton & Sons, Inc.; Ben [18281]
Tilton; Sumner H. [18282]
Timberline Feed Lot Inc. [18283]
Unger Cattle Marketing; Randy J. [18298]
United Producers, Inc. [18304]
Vintage Sales Stables Inc. [18318]
Wagner Livestock Auction [18322]
Walker River Pute Tribal Council [18324]
Watertown Livestock Auction, Inc. [18326]
Wegnar Livestock Inc.; Keith E. [18330]
Weiser Livestock Commission [18332]
West Nesbitt Inc. [18338]
West; Reginald [18339]
Western Livestock Inc. [18341]
Williams; Lyle L. [18350]
Windom Sales Company Inc. [18355]
Wishek Livestock Market Inc. [18356]
Worland Livestock Auction Inc. [18359]
Wormell; L.C. [18360]
Wright; Ronald J. [18362]
Zenchiku Land and Cattle Co. [18365]

SIC 5159 — Farm-Product Raw Materials Nec

ABJ Enterprises Inc. [17671]
Agricultural Survey Development
  Associates [10346]
Agrimor [10347]
Agway Inc. [17688]
American Legend Cooperative [17696]
Amex Hides Ltd. [18370]
Amsko Fur Corp. [17698]
Andersen Turf Supply [240]
Anderson's Peanuts [10415]
Barham and Co.; J.T. [17722]
Barretts Equine Sales Ltd. [17723]
Barta International Sales Corp. [17724]
Bickley; A.M. [17733]
Birdsong Corp. [10557]
Brocke and Sons Inc.; George F. [337]
Brown County Cooperative Association [340]
Calcot Ltd. [17758]
Cargill Peanut Products [10699]
Carolina Cotton Growers Association Inc. [17764]
Casa Export Ltd. [26273]

Chapin Farmers Elevator Co. [17775]
Chickasha Cotton Oil Co. [17777]
Commodity Specialists Co. [17788]
Cooperative Grain and Supply [17796]
Damascus Peanut Co. [17809]
Deli Universal Inc. [26287]
Delta International [17817]
Dover Handbag Corp. [18389]
Dreyfus Corp. Allenberg Cotton Company Div.;
  Louis [17821]
Dreyfus Corp.; Louis [17822]
Dunavant Enterprises Inc. [17824]
Elkhart Farmers Cooperative Association Inc. [546]
Farmers Cooperative Compress [17859]
Farmers Cooperative of El Campo [17860]
Farmer's Fur House [17890]
Felder & Co.; W.D. [17915]
Fitz Chem Corp. [4389]
Gass Horse Supply [17935]
General Genetics Inc. [17937]
Glen's Peanuts and Grains Inc. [17942]
Goedecke Inc.; Otto [17944]
Goldberg & Co., Inc.; H. E. [17945]
Goldmar Sales Corp. [747]
Grandview Hatchery & Locker Plant [17958]
Gray Storage and Dryer Company Inc. [17959]
Grimes Oil Company Inc. [22323]
Gruen Export Co. [17966]
Gusmer Co.; A. [16081]
Hartman Hide and Fur Company Inc. [17978]
Heitmann; Chester [17989]
Hog Inc. [831]
Humphreys Coop Tipton Location [18007]
International Service Group [18011]
Jimbo's Jumbos Inc. [18024]
Juergens Produce and Feed Co. [893]
Klemme Cooperative Grain Co. [914]
K.R. International [11639]
Lexington Trotters and Breeders
  Association [18058]
Liberal Hull Co. [22430]
Linn; John [18060]
McClesky Mills Inc. [18079]
Moffatt Hay Co. [18108]
Monahan Co.; Thomas [27348]
Nored Cotton Co.; W.H. [18134]
North Central Commodities, Inc. [18136]
Northeast Hide & Fur Corp. [18141]
Ohsman and Sons Co. [18151]
Oils of Aloha [18152]
Okleelanta Corp. [12058]
Pacific Fibers, Inc. [16372]
Pioneer Growers Co-Op [12173]
Plains Cotton Cooperative Association [18170]
Pond International Inc. [18174]
Quaker City Hide Co. [18186]
Quaker City Hide Co. [18187]
Rhode Island Tack Shop Inc. [18196]
Roswell Wool LLC [18208]
Rueb Associates Inc.; John [18210]
Sessions Company Inc. [12464]
Severn Peanut Company Inc. [12466]
Shamash and Sons; S. [26201]
Smith and Sons Inc.; Jess [18236]
Southwest Hide Co. [18246]
Southwestern Irrigated Cotton Growers
  Association [18247]
Standard Commercial Corp. [26353]
Staple Cotton Cooperative Association [18251]
Steiner Inc.; S.S. [18253]
Stone Commodities Corp. [12590]
Struthers Industries Inc. [22712]
Sutton Ranches [18271]
Taylor Co.; Jesse R. [18276]
Thorpe and Ricks Inc. [26356]
Tobacco Supply Company Inc. [26359]
Tourbillon Farm [18286]
Tropical Nut and Fruit [12761]
TruAl Inc. [1360]
Universal Corp. [26365]
Universal Semen Sales Inc. [18307]
Utah Wool Marketing Association [18309]
V and M Cotton Co. [18311]
Valley Forge Leather Co. [18313]
Weil Brothers Cotton Inc. [18331]
Wensman Seed Co. [18334]

Wonalancet Co. [26250]
Wricley Nut Products Co. [12985]
Young Pecan Shelling Company Inc. [12997]
Ziegler's Bakers Supply and Equipment
  Corp. [13006]

SIC 5162 — Plastics Materials & Basic Shapes

A-Top Polymers Inc. [22917]
Abell Corp. [181]
Advanced Plastics Inc. [22918]
Aetna Plastics Corp. [22919]
AIA Plastics Inc. [22920]
A.I.D. Inc. [4316]
AIN Plastics Inc. [22921]
AIN Plastics of Michigan Inc. [22922]
Akrochem Corp. [24266]
Allpak Co. [25887]
Aluma Panel, Inc. [21384]
American Commodities Inc. [22923]
American Laubscher Corp. [16695]
American Renolit Corp. [22924]
American Trade Co. [22925]
Anaheim Custom Extruders, Inc. [22926]
Angus-Campbell Inc. [22927]
Apex Plastic Industries Inc. [22928]
Artform Industries Inc. [22929]
Atlanta Broom Company Inc. [21638]
Atlantis Plastics, Inc. [22930]
Auburn Plastics and Rubber Inc. [22931]
Aztec Supply Co. [22932]
Bags Direct, Inc. [22933]
Bay Polymer Corp. [26761]
Beard and Associates Inc.; Robert A. [22934]
B.E.B. Ltd. [22935]
Beck Packaging Corp. [16744]
Belwool Corp. [25980]
Bevco Inc. [22936]
Bogatin, Inc.; Philip F. [25984]
Bronze and Plastic Specialties Inc. [19837]
Business Development International [22938]
Cadillac Plastic and Chemical Div. [22939]
Cadillac Plastic Group Inc. [22940]
Capital Design Inc. [22941]
Carolina Plastics Supply Inc. [23106]
Carson Industries LLC [22942]
Caye and Company Inc.; W.C. [7154]
Central Distributors Inc. [9783]
Charlotte Hardwood Center [7168]
Chemung Supply Corp. [16795]
Cincinnati Container Co. [25901]
Clark-Schwebel Distribution Corp. [22943]
Cloutier Supply Co. [22944]
Coleman; Dr. Ernest A. [22945]
Commercial Plastics and Supply Corp. [22946]
Commercial Plastics and Supply Inc. [22947]
Con-Tech International, Inc. [16805]
Conprotec Inc. [22948]
CORR TECH, Inc. [23128]
Corr Tech Inc. [22949]
Crown Glass Corp. [25909]
Curbell Inc. [22950]
Currie Industries Inc. [22951]
Depco Inc. [22953]
Dielectric Corp. [22954]
Diversified Foam Products Inc. [22956]
Dupont de Nemours and Co.; E.I. [4376]
Eager Plastics Inc. [22957]
Engineered Plastics Inc. [22958]
Fabricated Plastics Inc. [22959]
Federal Plastics Corp. [22960]
Federal Wholesale Company Inc. [15495]
Feldman Glass Co. [25915]
FFR Inc. [25649]
Fiberglass Hawaii, Inc. [22961]
FIC International Corp. [22962]
First Phillips Marketing Company Inc. [22963]
Forbex Corporation [9904]
Freund Can Co. [25916]
Galaxy Liner Company Inc. [22966]
Gar-Ron Plastics Corp. [22967]
Garci Plastics Industries [15511]

General Polymers Div. [22968]
GeoCHEM Inc. [22969]
GLS Corp. [7400]
GLS Thermoplastic Elastomers Div. [22970]
Goldmark Plastic Co. [22971]
Gordon Co.; Len [22972]
Grafix Plastic [22973]
Graphic Arts Systems Inc. [22974]
Greenstreak Inc. [22975]
Greenstreak Plastic Products [22976]
Hanna Resin Distribution Inc.; M.A. [22977]
Harbor Sales Company [7441]
Harrington Industrial Plastics Inc. [22978]
Hawaii Plastics Corp. [26060]
HBG Export Corp. [22979]
HCl Corp./International Marketing Services [18831]
Herco Products Corp.; Ryan [22980]
Holland Co.; M. [22981]
Horn Plastics Inc. [22982]
Industrial Plastics Inc. [22983]
Industrial Safety Supply Co. Interex Div. [24571]
Intersystems of Delaware [22984]
Intertech Services [26074]
JATCO Inc. [22985]
Jordan Brookes Company Inc.; E. [20078]
Kellco & Associates [15185]
Kemlite Company, Inc. [7545]
Kerr Group Inc. [22986]
Kranson Industries [25923]
Lainiere De Picardie Inc. [22988]
Laird Plastics Inc. [22989]
Lake Crescent Inc. [22990]
Laminates Unlimited Inc. [22991]
Lavanture Plastic Extrusion Technologies [22992]
Leathertone Inc. [22993]
Leed Plastics Corp. [22994]
Lusk Metals and Plastics [20139]
Marubeni America Corp. [26136]
Marval Industries Inc. [22995]
Matthews and Associates Inc. [22996]
Meyer Plastics Inc. [22997]
Midwest Plastics Supply Inc. [22998]
Milvan Packaging Company Inc. [22999]
Mooney General Paper Co. [17049]
MRC Polymers Inc. [26919]
MS Rubber Co. [17059]
MTH Corp. [23000]
Muehlstein and Company Inc.; H. [23001]
Multi-Craft Plastics, Inc. [23002]
Neita Product Management [16346]
Norris Inc.; Garland C. [21852]
Northeast Industrial Components Co. [17079]
Northern Laminate Sales Inc. [23003]
Nott-Atwater Co [16355]
Ohio Valley Supply Co. [7807]
Olympic Industries Inc. [23004]
Paper Products Company Inc. [21863]
P.A.T. Products Inc. [4479]
Percura Inc. [23005]
Plascom Trading Company [23006]
Plastic Distributing Corp. [23007]
Plastic Dress-Up Co. [13423]
Plastic Fabricators Inc. [23008]
The Plastic Man Inc. [23009]
Plastic Piping Systems Inc. [23010]
Plastic Sales Southern Inc. [23011]
Plastic Supply Inc. [23012]
Plastic Supply Inc. [23013]
Plastruct Inc. [25787]
Polymer Plastics Corp. [23014]
Port Plastics Inc. [23015]
Power Plastics Inc. [23016]
Prestige Packaging Inc. [23017]
Prime Alliance Inc. [23018]
Pro Plastics Inc. [23019]
Quality Paper & Plastic Corp. [23020]
Rapid Industrial Plastics Co. [23021]
Regal Plastic Supply Co. [23022]
Regal Plastic Supply Co. Kansas City Div. [23023]
Regal Plastic Supply Inc. [23024]
Regional Supply Inc. [23025]
Resyn Corp. [23026]
Retailers Supply Co. [21905]
Ridout Plastics Inc. [23027]
Riley and Geehr Inc. [23028]
River City Enterprises [23029]

Roberts Colonial House Inc. [23030]
Rue Plastics Inc. [23031]
Ryerson and Son Inc., Ryerson Plastics Div.;
    Joseph T. [23032]
San Esters Corp. [4500]
Signcaster Corp. [23034]
Southeastern Adhesive Co. [23035]
Southeastern Industries Inc. [27001]
Star Cutter Co. [16519]
State Seal Co. [17197]
Steel City Corp. [20392]
Sterling Rubber and Plastics [24296]
Sumitomo Plastics America Inc. [23037]
Sun Pacific Industries [25942]
Suntuf USA [23038]
Targun Plastics Co. [23039]
Tavdi Company, Inc. [16549]
Tay/Chem L.L.C. [23040]
TCB Inc. [25944]
Tekra Corp. [23041]
Texatek International [23042]
Texberry Container Corp. [23043]
Thyssen Incorporated N.A. [20423]
Tomchuck Insulators [23044]
Trade Supplies [21955]
Tricon Industries Inc. Electromechanical Div. [3341]
Tricor Braun - Div. of Kranson [25945]
Turtle Plastics Co. [4718]
Unichem Industries Inc. [19671]
Veb Plastics Inc. [23046]
Viking Formed Products [17255]
Wood & Plastics Industries [8240]

SIC 5169 — Chemicals & Allied Products Nec

3-D Supply Inc. [4562]
A & D Maintenance [4564]
A and S Corp. [4308]
Aanns Trading Co. [4309]
ABA-tron Industries Inc. [4310]
Abbaco Inc. [10317]
Abbott Foods Inc. [24053]
Able Trading Corp. [4565]
Ace Hardware Corp. [13525]
Aceto Corp. [4313]
Advanced Maintenance Products Co. [4566]
Advanced Plastics Inc. [22918]
Aeropres Corp. [4314]
Aetna Chemical Corp. [4315]
Aetna Felt Corp. Mechanical Felt and Textile
    Div. [25954]
AG Cooperative Service Inc. [17678]
AGL Welding Supply Company Inc. [16675]
A.I.D. Inc. [4316]
Aim Enterprises, Inc. [32]
Airco Gas and Gear [16678]
Airgas Inc. [16679]
Airgas West [15747]
Akin Medical Equipment International [19128]
Alco Tool Supply Inc. [13545]
Alden Autoparts Warehouse Inc. [2202]
Alkota of Western Montana [4568]
Allen Foods Inc. [10370]
Alliance Steel Corp. [19750]
Allied Container Corp. [21625]
Alma's Glow Products International [14016]
Alta Paint & Coatings [21383]
Amalgamet Inc. [4317]
Amedem Enterprises, Inc. [4570]
American Chemet Corp. [4318]
American Chemical Company Inc. [4319]
American Chemical Works Co. [4320]
American Chemicals Co. Inc. [4321]
American Homeware Inc. [4571]
American Packing and Gasket Company [1]
American Paper and Twine Co. [21631]
AMJ Inc. [4573]
Amrochem Inc. [4322]
Anatech Ltd. [21388]
Anchor Commerce Trading Corp. [6973]
Andrews Paper and Chemical Co. [4323]

Anthony Farmers Cooperative and Elevator
    Co. [17702]
Apache Nitrogen Products Inc. [4324]
Applied Biochemists, Inc. [4325]
Architects Hardware & Specialty Company
    Inc. [13563]
Arctic Industrial Supply [16708]
Aries Paper & Chemical Co. Inc. [4574]
Aronson-Campbell Industrial Supply Inc. [15780]
Arthur Companies Inc. [257]
Ashby Equity Association [258]
Ashland Chemical Co. [4326]
Ashland Chemical Co. Industrial Chemicals and
    Solvents Div. [4327]
Associated Allied Industries Inc. [2]
Asuka Inc. [19166]
A.T. Supply [21391]
Atlantis International, Inc. [22049]
Atlas Chemical Inc. [4329]
Atlas Supply Inc. [4330]
Atomergic Chemetals Corp. [4331]
Aurora Cooperative Elevator Co. [263]
Automotive International Inc. [4332]
Avico Distributing Inc. [10475]
Axchem Solutions Inc. [4333]
Axon Import Export Corporation [4793]
Axton-Cross Company Inc. [4334]
B-J Pac-A-Part [4575]
Baddour International [14034]
Balloonery Inc. [26409]
Banner Systems Inc. [4577]
Bardahl Manufacturing Corp. [22058]
Barnett Brothers Brokerage Co. Inc. [10509]
Barton Solvents Inc. [4335]
Bay Paper Co. Inc. [20837]
Beeson Hardware Industrial Sales Co. [13590]
Bell Additives Inc. [22064]
Bender Wholesale Distributors [3]
Benson Farmers Cooperative [299]
Best Way Carpet Care Inc. [4579]
Big W Supplies Inc. [4581]
Bill's Battery Co. Inc. [2362]
Bimex Incorporated [15824]
Bison Corp. [4336]
Black Hills Chemical Co. Inc. [4583]
Blue Ribbon Linen Supply Inc. [4585]
Bock Pharmaceutical, Inc.; James A. [19196]
Bodman Chemicals, Inc. [4337]
Bower Ammonia and Chemical [4338]
Boyd Distributing Co. Inc. [15056]
Brady Industries Inc. [4588]
Brenntag Inc. [4339]
Brewer Environmental Industries Inc. [335]
Brewer Environmental Industries Inc. [4340]
Brulin and Co. Inc. [4590]
Brunt Tile & Marble [9742]
Builders Hardware and Supply Co. Inc. [13612]
Burt Explosives Inc. [9632]
Butler-Dearden Paper Service Inc. [21661]
C R Laurence Company Inc. [2406]
C & W Distributing Inc. [4591]
Calsol Inc. [4341]
Camalloy Inc. [19848]
Capitol Chemical & Supply [4593]
Caravan Trading Corporation [4342]
Cargill Inc. [4343]
Carol Service Co. [4344]
Cash Supply Co. [13623]
Catawba Color and Chemical Company
    Inc. [4345]
Cedar Rapids Welding Supply Inc. [16785]
Cee Kay Supply Co. [16786]
Central Scientific Co. [4346]
Central States Airgas Inc. [16788]
Century Labs Inc. [4347]
Century Papers Inc. [4596]
Chase Trade, Inc. [407]
Chem-Central [4348]
Chem-Real Investment Corp. [409]
Chem-Serv Inc. [4349]
Chemapol USA Inc. [4350]
CHEMCENTRAL Corp. [4351]
ChemDesign Corp. [4352]
Chemical Associates of Illinois, Inc. [4353]
Chemical Export Company, Inc. [4354]
Chemical Sales Company Inc. [4355]

Chemicals Inc. [4356]
Chemisolv Inc. [4357]
Chemply Div. [4358]
Cherokee Chemical Company Inc. [4598]
Chevron Corp. [4359]
Chori America Inc. [26005]
Cirelli Foods Inc. [24092]
Citizen's Distributors [4360]
Coastal Engineering Equipment Sales LLC [22144]
Coastal States Trading [22148]
Colgate-Palmolive Co. Institutional Products Div. [4600]
Cometals Inc. [4361]
Commerce Consultants Inc. [22154]
ComSource Independent Foodservice Companies Inc. [10803]
Con-Tech International, Inc. [16805]
Connell Brothers Company Ltd. [4362]
Consolidated Coatings Corp. [21417]
Consolidated Tile and Carpet Co. [9822]
Control Solutions Inc. [4363]
Cook Composites and Polymers Co. [4364]
Coolant Management Services Co. [4365]
Coop Country Partners [445]
Cornbelt Chemical Co. [4366]
Cottonwood Cooperative Oil Co. [22175]
Counter Assault [23608]
CourterCo [4]
Courtesy Sanitary Supply [4604]
Cowan Brothers Inc. [4605]
Crisci Food Equipment Co. [24097]
Crompton and Knowles Colors Inc. [4367]
Cron Chemical Corp. [4368]
Crouch Supply Company Inc. [24343]
Curbell Inc. [22950]
D-Chem Corp. [4369]
D & S Enterprises [4607]
Dacotah Paper Co. [21699]
Dakota Industrial Supply [4608]
Damon Industries, Inc. [4609]
De Lille Oxygen Co. [16822]
Decker's Inc. [4611]
Degussa Huls [4370]
Delta Distributors Inc. [4371]
Detroit Gas Products Co. [16830]
Deuel County Farmers Union Oil Co. [22199]
Dewar Elevator Co. [517]
Diamond Chemical/Supply Co. [4372]
Diamond Supply Company Inc. [4612]
Diamond W Supply Co. Inc. [9864]
Dibs Chemical & Supply Co. Inc. [21708]
Dixie Chemical Co. Inc. [4373]
D.J. Enterprises, Inc. [20533]
Dodge Company Inc. [25634]
Douglas Products and Packaging Co. [4374]
Doussan Inc. [16838]
Dover Sales Co. Inc. [4375]
The Dowd Co. [21715]
Du Pont Co. [21435]
Dupont de Nemours and Co.; E.I. [4376]
Eager Plastics Inc. [22957]
Eagle Chemical Co. [4377]
ECCA America Inc. [4378]
Ecolab Inc. Food and Beverage Div. [4614]
Ecolab Inc. Institutional Div. [4615]
Ecolab Inc. Professional Products Div. [4379]
Ecolab Inc. Textile Care Div. [4616]
Ecological Laboratories [4380]
Economy Foods [11023]
Elan Chemical Co. [4381]
Ellis and Everard Inc. [4382]
Empire Airgas [16848]
Empire Airgas [4383]
Empire Corporation [4618]
Engberg Janitorial Supply & Service [4619]
Environmental Chemical Group Inc. [4384]
Everitt & Ray Inc. [5]
Ewing Aquatech Pools Inc. [23657]
Execu-Flow Systems, Inc. [19311]
Explosive Supply Company Inc. [7327]
EXSL/Ultra Labs Inc. [4385]
Exxon Company USA [22245]
F & S Supply Company Inc. [8728]
Farmers Cooperative Co. [596]
Farmers Cooperative Elevator Co. [17865]
Farmers Cooperative Elevator and Supply [17871]

Farmers Cooperative Exchange [627]
Farmers Cooperative Oil Co. [22255]
Farmers Elevator Co. [643]
Farmers Elevator Cooperative [645]
Farmers Grain Cooperative [655]
Farmers Union Oil Co. (Great Falls, Montana) [4387]
Farmers Union Oil Company of Kenmare [669]
Farmers Union Oil Co. (Napoleon, North Dakota) [22269]
Farwest Corrosion Control Co. [4388]
Feesers Inc. [11117]
First International Trading Company [16863]
Fisher; Karen [4620]
Fisher Scientific Co. [24360]
Fitch Dustdown Co. [4621]
Fitch Industrial Welding Supply Inc. [16865]
Fitz Chem Corp. [4389]
Flack International, Inc.; Henry [4622]
Flame Spray Inc. [4390]
Flask Chemical Corp. [4391]
Flexstik Adheso Graphics [6]
Follum Supply [4624]
Food Ingredients and Additives Group [4393]
Food Marketing Corp. [11174]
FoodSource, Inc. [11184]
Forbex Corporation [9904]
Foresight Inc. [4625]
Francis Drilling Fluids Ltd. [4394]
Fremont Chemical Company Inc. [4395]
Fullwell Products Inc. [2656]
Furniture Makers Supply Co. [16884]
Futura Adhesives & Chemicals [7]
Gallard-Schlesinger Industries Inc. [4396]
Gannon Company Inc.; G.M. [4397]
Gas Technics of Ohio [16889]
GATX Terminals Corp. [22304]
General Air Service and Supply Company Inc. [16052]
General Supply of Yakima Inc. [4627]
GEO Drilling Fluids Inc. [4398]
George H. International Corp. [734]
Georgia Steel and Chemical Co. [18810]
Getz Bros. & Company Inc. [16062]
Gibbons Inc.; J.T. [11262]
Girindus Corp. [4399]
G.J. Chemical Company Inc. [4400]
GLS Thermoplastic Elastomers Div. [22970]
GNI Group Inc. [4401]
Golden Capital Distributors [11283]
Golden Neo-Life Diamite International [14114]
Grace and Co. Grace Dearborn Div.; W.R. [25664]
Grange Supply Company Inc. [757]
Graves Fire Protection [24557]
Great Western Airgas Inc. [16906]
Grimstad, Inc.; J.M. [4402]
Grimstad, Inc.; J.M. [4403]
Grimstad, Inc.; J.M. [4404]
Growers Cooperative Inc. [772]
Guss Cleaning & Supply [4632]
Hall Div.; Howard [19346]
Hamler Industries [4405]
Harder Paper and Packaging Inc. [21755]
Hardesty Welding Supply Div. [16922]
Hardy Cooperative Elevator Co. [17975]
Harmony Enterprises America [18825]
Harris Chemical Group Inc. [4407]
Hart Seed Co.; Charles C. [796]
Hartford Provision Co. [11383]
Harwell & Associates Inc. Chemical Div. [4408]
Harwick Standard Distribution Corporation [4409]
Haviland Agricultural Inc. [4410]
Haviland Products Co. [4411]
Hayden Company Inc.; C.W. [16927]
HBG Export Corp. [22979]
hci Coastal Chemical Co., LLC [4412]
HCI Corp./International Marketing Services [18831]
HCI Great Lakes Region [4413]
Heart of Iowa Cooperative [805]
Heigl Adhesive Sales [8]
Hendrix Technologies Inc. [21029]
Henkel Corp. Chemicals Group [4414]
Heritage Industries [13752]
Hess and Company Inc.; John R. [4415]
Hill Brothers Chemical Co. [4416]

Hills Beaver Creek Coop Farm Service [824]
Hisco [8844]
Hitachi Maxco Ltd. [16930]
HM Water Technologies Inc. [4417]
Holiday Wholesale Inc. [26308]
Holston Gases Inc. [22356]
Holt Distributors, Inc. [21766]
Horizons Marketing Group Inc. [4635]
Horn Co.; E.T. [4418]
Houghton Chemical Corp. [4419]
House of Clean Inc. [4636]
Howard County Equity Cooperative Inc. [841]
Howard Sales Inc. [21768]
Howell Petroleum Products Inc. [22367]
Hubbard-Hall Inc. [4420]
Huff Paper Co. [21771]
Hughes Company Inc.; R.S. [24568]
Humco Holding Group Inc. [4422]
Hunter Trading Corporation [27322]
Husch and Husch Inc. [847]
HVC Inc. [4423]
Hydrite Chemical Co. [4424]
ICI Fluoropolymers [4425]
Ideal Chemical and Supply Co. [4426]
Import Warehouse Inc. [13374]
Indiana Oxygen Co. [16942]
Indianapolis Welding Supply Inc. [16944]
Industrial Adhesives Inc. [4427]
Industrial Environmental Products Inc. [4428]
Industrial Fumigant Co. [856]
Industrial Soap Co. [4639]
Industrial Solvents Corp. [4429]
Inland Leidy Inc. [4430]
Institutional Wholesale Co. [11515]
Interconsal Associates Inc. [4431]
Interdonati, Inc.; H. [19375]
Interstate Chemical Co. [4432]
Interstate Supply [9969]
Interworld [4640]
J & J Cleaning Service [4641]
J & K Distributors [4642]
Jackson Supply Co. [4643]
JacksonLea [16966]
Jani-Serv [4644]
Janitor Supply Co. [4645]
Janvey and Sons Inc.; I. [4646]
Jaytow International Inc. [5843]
Jefferson Farmers Cooperative [882]
Jirdon Agri Chemicals Inc. [14897]
Jonas Aircraft and Arms Company Inc. [109]
JTS Enterprises Inc. [4433]
Juno Industries Inc. [16973]
Kanematsu U.S.A. Inc. [26086]
Kay Chemical Co. [4648]
Keen Compressed Gas Co. [16981]
Keltner Enterprises Inc. [2846]
Kennametal [16985]
Keystone Aniline Corp. [4434]
Keystone Automotive Operations Inc. [2852]
Keystone Chemical Supply Inc. [4435]
Kindt Collins Co. [25700]
King Co. Inc.; E.F. [23775]
Kings Food Service Professionals Inc.; J. [11618]
Kitrick Management Company, Ltd. [24383]
KMG Chemicals Inc. [4436]
Knight Marketing Corp. [4652]
Komp Equipment Company Inc. [4437]
Kona Marine Supply [18537]
Kova Fertilizer Inc. [919]
Kraft Chemical Co. [21477]
Kwik Stop Car Wash Supply [4655]
Ladshaw Explosives Inc. [9636]
Lady Baltimore Foods Inc. [11665]
Larsen International, Inc. [4438]
Laun-Dry Supply Company Inc. [4657]
Laurence Company Inc.; C.R. [16228]
Layton Marketing Group Inc. [21488]
LCI Ltd. [4439]
Le Roy Cooperative Association Inc. [18049]
Leading Products Co. [4658]
Lenover & Son Inc.; J.E. [9]
Lester Company Inc.; Kenneth O. [24165]
Lexington Cooperative Oil Co. [22429]
Lilyblad Petroleum Inc. [22433]
Lincoln County Farmers Cooperative [960]
Lincoln Poultry and Egg Co. [11713]

Logsdon Service Inc. [18063]
Loock & Company Inc.; R.J. [2892]
Loos and Dilworth Inc. [4441]
Los Angeles Chemical Co. [4442]
Lotepro Corp. [22438]
Lotus Group [16246]
Louisiana Chemical Equipment Co. [16247]
Loveland Industries [972]
Lyk-Nu Inc. [4660]
Lynde Co. [4443]
M & M Chemical Supply Inc. [4661]
M and M Chemical Supply Inc. [4444]
M & P Sales Inc. [4662]
MacAlaster Bicknell Company of New Jersey
    Inc. [4445]
Machine and Welding Supply Co. [16255]
Madison Farmers Elevator Co. [18070]
Magic American Corp. [4446]
Magnolia Chemical and Solvents Inc. [4447]
Maintenance Engineering Corp. [4448]
Maltby Company Inc. [4449]
Management Supply Co. [23248]
Mann and Company, Inc.; George [4450]
Mansfield Paper Company Inc. [21821]
Market Actives, LLC [4451]
Marsh Inc.; Paul [4452]
Marshall Co.; R.J. [4453]
Martrex Alpha Corp. [6466]
Martrex Inc. [4454]
Marubeni America Corp. [26136]
Marval Industries Inc. [22995]
Marvin Corp. [7657]
Mascon Inc. [16269]
Massena Paper Company Inc. [21824]
Mayer Myers Paper Co. [21826]
Mayfield Pool Supply L.L.C. [23811]
Mays Chemical Co. [19427]
Mazon Farmers Elevator [996]
M.C. International [19429]
McBax Ltd. [22462]
McFadden Wholesale Company Inc.; F.B. [4666]
MEBCO Contractors Supplies [13823]
Medek Inc.; George M. [4667]
Mees Tile and Marble Inc. [10024]
Mega Systems Chemicals Inc [4455]
Mega Systems Chemicals Inc. [4456]
Merriam-Graves Corp. [18932]
Methanex Methanol Co. [22477]
Meyer Co.; O.E. [17032]
Michigan Airgas [17033]
Mid-America Airgas Inc. [17034]
Mid-South Oxygen Company Inc. [17036]
Mid-South Supply Corp. [21501]
Midway Trading, Inc. [2958]
Midwest Chemical and Supply Inc. [4670]
Midwest Cleaning Systems Inc. [4671]
Midwest Environmental Safety Supply [25738]
Midwest Farmers Cooperative [1037]
Miller Machinery and Supply Company of
    Tampa [4457]
Millers Wholesale, Inc. [25742]
Mine and Mill Supply Co. [20197]
Minnesota Chemical Co. [4458]
Minnesota Mining & Manufacturing Co. [21147]
Missouri Petroleum Products [22488]
Mitsui and Company (U.S.A.) Inc. [20199]
Mon-Dak Chemical Inc. [4459]
Monahan Paper Co. [21841]
Monarch Ceramic Tile [10048]
Monogram Sanitation Co. [23273]
Monson Chemicals Inc. [4460]
Monsour's Inc. [11926]
Monterey Chemical Co. Inc. [4461]
Montgomery Div. [22494]
Moore Brothers Div. [17050]
Moorhead and Company Inc. [4462]
Moreland Wholesale Co., Inc. [11935]
Moss Dynamics [2988]
Mozel Inc. [4463]
Mr. Hardwoods, Inc. [10068]
Murphy Co. [22881]
N Pool Patio Ltd. [23842]
Nalco Chemical Co. [4464]
NanoMaterials, Inc. [4465]
Nar Inc. [4674]
National Compressed Gases Inc. [17066]

National Sanitary Supply Co. Portland Div. [4675]
National Welders Supply Company Inc. [17067]
National Welding Supply of Algona [17068]
Naturo Co. [25751]
Neely Industries [10]
Neita Product Management [16346]
Neutron Industries Inc. [4466]
Neville Chemical Co. [4467]
Newell Paper Co. [21851]
Nippon Steel Chemical Corporation of
    America [4468]
Norco Inc. [4469]
Norman, Fox & Co. [4470]
Norris Co.; Garland C. [21852]
Northeast Airgas Inc. [17078]
NUCO Industries Inc. [4678]
Odeen International, Inc. [4471]
Ogle Service Co. [1100]
Okie Dokie Services [4679]
Old World Industries, Inc. [4472]
Olin Corp. [4473]
Olympian Oil Co. [22540]
Omega Refrigerant Reclamation Corp. [25773]
Organic Dyestuffs Corp. [4474]
Original Mink Oil Inc. [4475]
Orkin Lawn Care [14933]
Osakagodo America Inc. [4476]
OSCA Inc. [4477]
Overseas Capital Corp. [4478]
Pac Aero [134]
Parts Associates Inc. [13864]
P.A.T. Products Inc. [4479]
Patterson Brothers Oil and Gas Inc. [22552]
Patterson Oil Co. [22553]
P.B. and S. Chemical Inc. [4480]
Peninsular Paper Company Inc. [21873]
Peterson Spacecrafters [21213]
Phenix Supply Co. [4685]
Pinch a Penny Pool Patio [23882]
Pioneer Manufacturing Co. [21540]
Plant Maintenance Equipment [4687]
PMC Specialties Group [17109]
Pocahontas Welding Supply Co. [16408]
Polycoat Systems Inc. [7878]
Polysciences Inc. [4481]
Pool Doctor [23890]
Poritzky's Wholesale Meats and Food
    Services [12195]
Potash Import and Chemical Corp. [4482]
Power Chemical Company Inc. [4483]
Prairie Land Cooperative Co. [1146]
Praxah Gas Tech Inc. [22592]
Praxair Distribution/W. Div. [16421]
Praxair Gas Tech [17110]
PRC-DeSoto International Inc. Semco Application
    Systems [4484]
Pressure Service Inc. [4689]
Primrose Oil Company Inc. [22594]
Prinsburg Farmers Cooperative [1152]
Pro Cooperative [1155]
Products Corp. of North America, Inc. [12226]
Progas Service Inc. [22595]
Pueblo Chemical and Supply Co. [4486]
Puratex Inc. [4487]
Purity Cylinder Gases Inc. [16434]
PYA/Monarch Inc. Schloss and Kahn [4690]
Quaker City Paper & Chemical [21891]
Quickshine of America Inc. [4488]
Quimby Corp. [17126]
R and D Products [4691]
RAE Products and Chemical Inc. [4489]
Rausch Naval Stores Company Inc. [4490]
Reade Advanced Materials [4491]
Red Devil Inc. [13884]
Reed Distributors [4692]
Regal Supply & Chemical Co. [21898]
Reisman Corp.; H. [4492]
Research Biochemicals Inc. [4493]
Resin Management Corp. [4494]
RHO-Chem Div. [4695]
Ribelin Sales Inc. [4495]
Rice Welding Supply Co. [17138]
Richard-Ewing Equipment Co. Inc. [4696]
Riley Sales Inc. [11]
River Springs Cooperative Association [27222]
Riverside Chemical Company Inc. [4496]

Rochester Midland Corp. [4698]
Rock River Provision Company Inc. [12336]
Rock Valley Oil and Chemical Company
    Inc. [22637]
Rockford Industrial Welding Supply Inc. [17142]
Roebic Laboratories Inc. [4497]
Rogers Pool Supply, Inc. [23920]
Rolla Cooperative Equity Exchange [18203]
Romic Chemical Corp. [26966]
Rosen's Diversified Inc. [4498]
R.S. Hughes Company Inc. [12]
RSB Tile, Inc. [10132]
Rude Corp.; R.T. [15297]
Ryan's Wholesale Food Distributors [12373]
S & D Industrial Supply Inc. [4700]
Safe Stride Non-Slip USA Inc. [4499]
Safeguard International, Inc. [24621]
Safety-Kleen, Southwest [26976]
Sailor Corporation of America [13]
San Esters Corp. [4500]
San Joaquin Sulphur Company Inc. [4501]
San Joaquin Supply Company Inc. [4702]
Saratoga Specialties [12413]
Sargent-Welch Scientific Co. [24425]
Sattex Corp. [4502]
Saval Foods [12421]
Savol Bleach Co. [4503]
Schilling Paper Co. [21923]
Schultz and Sons; H. [4705]
Scientific Equipment Co. [24429]
Seaforth Mineral and Ore Company Inc. [4504]
Seegott Inc. [4505]
Seeler Industries Inc. [4506]
Semi-Gas Systems Inc. [4507]
Sessions Specialty Co. [4508]
Seventh Generation, Inc. [21936]
Seybold Co. [4706]
Seymour of Sycamore Inc. [21565]
Shaheen Brothers Inc. [12468]
Shelley Company Inc.; John G. [14]
Shin-Etsu Silicones of America Inc. [4510]
Ships Wheel Brand Corp. [4708]
Showa Denko America Inc. [20364]
Sierra Airgas Inc. [22672]
Simplex Chemical Corp. [4709]
Skidmore Sales & Distributing Company,
    Inc. [12501]
Slack Chemical Company, Inc. [4512]
Slay Industries Inc. [18235]
Snyder Wholesale Inc. [12524]
SOCO-Lynch Corp. [4513]
SOGEM-Afrimet Inc. [20372]
Soil Shield International [15659]
Soil Stabilization Products Company Inc. [4514]
Solutions and Cleaning Products [4710]
Sooner Airgas Inc. [17180]
SOS Gases Inc. [4515]
Southchem Inc. [4516]
Southeastern Adhesive Co. [23035]
Southeastern Paper Group [21943]
Southwestern Camera [22906]
SPAP Company LLC [4517]
Specialty Chemical Company, Inc. [4518]
Spectrum Labs Inc. [4519]
Speed Brite Inc. [4711]
Sprayway Inc. [4520]
SST Corp. [19634]
Stangel Co.; J.J. [17195]
Star Brite [4712]
Statewide Floor Waxing Distributors [4714]
Staunton Food Inc. [12579]
Steam Way International Inc. [24227]
Stein's Inc. [4715]
Steven Industries, Inc. [21589]
Stinnes Corp. [22706]
Stomel and Sons; Joseph H. [12589]
Stratcor Technical Sales Inc. [20570]
Stratford Grain and Supply Cooperative [18262]
Summit Company [4522]
Summitville Fairfax [10190]
Superior Epoxies & Coatings, Inc. [15]
Superior FomeBords Corp. [16]
Superior Pool Products Inc. [23996]
Sutton-Garten Co. [17207]
Sybron Chemicals Inc. [4523]
Sygnet [16543]

Syrex, Inc. [1311]
SYSCO Food Service, Inc. [12670]
SYSCO Food Services [12673]
SYSCO Food Services of South Florida [12688]
Systematix Co. [4524]
Tampa Armature Works Inc. [16546]
Tanner Industries, Inc. [4525]
Tavdi Company, Inc. [16549]
Taylor Simkins Inc. [17214]
Tetra Technologies Inc. [4526]
Texaco Additive Co. [4528]
Texo Corp. [4529]
Textile Chemical Company Inc. [4530]
Thomas Scientific [24446]
THP United Enterprises Inc. [8127]
Tidewater Wholesalers Inc. [4717]
Tile Distributor Company Inc. [10231]
Tite Co. [17]
Tomen America Inc. [20430]
Toray Industries (America) Inc. [4531]
Toyota Tsusho America Inc. [20434]
TradeCom International Inc. [13961]
Transtech Industries Inc. [4532]
Triangle Chemical Co. [4533]
Triple Crown America Inc. [4534]
Troy BioSciences Inc. [1358]
Truesdale Company Inc. [4535]
Twinco Automotive Warehouse Inc. [4536]
Ulrich Chemical Inc. [4537]
UMPQUA Technology Co. [4538]
Unelko Corp. [4539]
Unicen Wastewater Treatment Co. [25852]
Unichem Industries Inc. [19671]
United Paper Company Inc. [21976]
United Refrigeration Inc. [14748]
United Scale and Engineering Co. [25856]
U.S. Printing Supply Co. [25857]
Universal Cooperative Inc. [1385]
US Chemical Corporation [4541]
Valley Coin Laundry Equipment Co. [4722]
Valley National Gases Inc. [22766]
Valley Welding Supply Co. [16599]
Valley Wholesalers Inc. [21983]
Van Sant Equipment Corp. [17251]
Van Waters and Rogers [4542]
Van Waters & Rogers [4543]
Van Waters and Rogers Inc. [4544]
Van Waters and Rogers Inc. [22768]
Van Waters and Rogers Inc. Omaha [4545]
Van's Candy & Tobacco Service [12830]
Vermillion Elevator Co. [18316]
Versatile Industrial Products [18]
Vic Supply Co. [4547]
Vie Americas Inc. [4548]
VWR Scientific Products Corp. [24454]
Wacker Chemicals (USA) Inc. [4549]
Waco Inc. [20477]
Wagner Hardware Co. [13982]
Wards Cleaning & Supply [4726]
Warrenterprises Inc. [4727]
Water Source USA [4550]
Waxie Sanitary Supply [4728]
Web Seal Inc. [19]
Weinberg Supply Company Inc.; E. [4729]
Weingartner Company Inc.; Henry [20484]
Welco Gases Corp. [17268]
Welltep International Inc. [4551]
Welsco Inc. [17272]
West Agro Inc. [4552]
West Minerals Inc. [22793]
West Penn Laco Inc. [17275]
Westar Inc. [24044]
Western Gold Thermoplastics Inc. [27042]
Western Pioneer Inc. [22795]
Westvaco Worldwide [21990]
White Cross Corporation, Inc. [19703]
White River Cooperative [1440]
Whittaker, Clark and Daniels [4553]
Wilbur-Ellis Co. [4554]
Wilbur-Ellis Co. [4555]
Wilcox Paper Co. [21993]
WILFARM L.L.C. [4556]
Willets O'Neil Co.; A. [4732]
William/Reid Ltd. [25882]
Wilmar Industries Inc. [23461]
Wilson Paper Co. [21994]

With Enterprises Inc. [4734]
Woodburn Fertilizer Inc. [1462]
World Wide Chemnet Inc. [4557]
Xpedx [17290]
Xpedx-Birmingham [4558]
Xport Port Authority Trading Co. [4559]
Yankton Janitorial Supply [4735]
YAO Industries [12991]
Zep Manufacturing Co., Springfield [4560]
Ziff Co. [17296]
Zorbite Corp. [4561]

SIC 5171 — Petroleum Bulk Stations & Terminals

Acorn Petroleum Inc. [22020]
Agri Cooperative Inc. [210]
Alpena Oil Company Inc. [22034]
Amerada Hess Corp. [22035]
AmeriGas Propane Inc. [22036]
Ampride [22038]
ARB Inc. (Franklinton, Louisiana) [22042]
Arkla Chemical Corp. [22045]
Automotive Service Inc. [22051]
Ayers Oil Company Inc. [22054]
Badgerland Farm Center [269]
Bailey Distributing Co.; E.M. [22057]
Bayside Fuel Oil Depot Corp. [22059]
Beck Suppliers Inc. [22062]
Bell Gas Inc. [22065]
Berry-Hinkley Terminal Inc. [22070]
Black Oil Company Inc. [22076]
Blalock Oil Company Inc. [22078]
Blarney Castle Oil Co. [22080]
Boncosky Oil Co. [22084]
Bowen-Hall Petroleum Inc. [22087]
Bowen Petroleum [22088]
C and S Inc. [22102]
C and W Enterprises Inc. [22103]
Celeron Trading and Transportation Co. [22117]
Cenex-Harvest States Cooperative [22120]
Central Cooperative Oil Association [22123]
Cheatwood Oil Co. [25900]
Childs Oil Company Inc. [22137]
Circleville Oil Co. [22140]
Clinton Gas Marketing Inc. [6076]
Coastal Gas Services Co. [22146]
Coleman Oil Co. Inc. [22151]
Colonial Oil Industries Inc. [22152]
Commonwealth Oil Co. Inc. [22155]
Community Oil Company Inc. [22157]
Consumer Oil Company of Meridian [22162]
Consumers Cooperative Oil Co. [22163]
Consumers Supply Cooperative Co. [10822]
Cooperative Gas and Oil Company Inc. [22167]
Cooperative Oil Association [22168]
Cooperative Oil Co. [22169]
Coors Energy Co. [20532]
Cosbel Petroleum Corp. [22173]
Cottage Grove Cooperative [465]
Cowboy Oil Co. [22176]
Crystal Flash Petroleum Corp. [22181]
Curry Oil Company Inc. [22183]
Dalhart Consumers Fuel and Grain Association Inc. [17808]
Davies Service Co.; Jo [498]
Dean Oil Co. [22191]
Delta Oil Company Inc. [22194]
Dilmar Oil Company Inc. [22201]
Distributors Oil Co. Inc. [22203]
District Petroleum Products Inc. [22204]
East Jordan Cooperative Co. [22218]
Eastern Petroleum Corp. [22221]
Ellsworth Farmers Union Cooperative Oil Co. [549]
Empire Petroleum Inc. [22228]
Englefield Oil Co. [22232]
Enron Liquid Fuels Co. [22233]
Enron Power Services [22234]
EOTT Energy Partners L.P. [22237]
Erie Petroleum Inc. [22239]
Etna Oil Company Inc. [22240]
Evans Oil Co. [22241]
Fair City Oil [22249]

Far-Mor Cooperative [22252]
Farmers Cooperative Co. [599]
Farmers Cooperative Elevator (Martelle, Iowa) [17870]
Farmers Cooperative Oil of Balaton [635]
Farmers Exchange [648]
Farmers Exchange Cooperative [649]
Farmers Union Cooperative [22258]
Farmers Union Cooperative Oil Co. [662]
Farmers Union Oil Co. [22262]
Farmers Union Oil Co. [22266]
Farmers Union Oil Co. [22267]
Farmers Union Oil Co. [22268]
Farmers Union Oil Co. (Great Falls, Montana) [4387]
Farmers Union Oil Company of Kenmare [669]
Farmers Union Oil Co. (Napoleon, North Dakota) [22269]
Federation Cooperative [675]
Fleischli Oil Company Inc. [22279]
FOF Inc. [22287]
Fortmeyer's Inc. [22290]
Frank Carroll Oil Co. [22292]
G and B Oil Company Inc. [22298]
G and M Oil Company Inc. [22299]
Gant Oil Co. [22301]
GATX Terminals Corp. [22304]
Gerlach Oil Company Inc. [22308]
Getty Realty Corp. [22310]
Gibble Oil Company Inc. [22312]
Glover Oil Company Inc. [22315]
Grimsley Oil Company Inc. [22324]
Growmark [775]
Growmark [776]
GROWMARK Inc. [17965]
Habhegger Company Inc.; E.O. [22331]
Hicks Oil and Hicks Gas Inc. [22350]
High Point Oil Co. [22351]
Hightower Oil and Petroleum Company Inc. [22352]
Hillger Oil Company Inc. [22353]
Home Oil Co. [22358]
Hopkins-Gowen Oil Company Inc. [22364]
Howell Corp. [22366]
Illini F.S. Inc. [22371]
Jacobus Energy [22382]
James Oil Co. [22383]
Jardine Petroleum Co. [22385]
Jefferson City Oil Company Inc. [22386]
Jefferson County Farmco Coop. [881]
Johnson Oil Company of Gaylord [22389]
Kent Distribution Inc. [22401]
Knievel's Inc. [915]
Kohler Oil and Propane Co. [22410]
Lake Andes Farmers Cooperative Co. [929]
Lakeside Oil Company Inc. [22417]
Lee F.S. Inc. [949]
Leffler Inc.; Carlos R. [22424]
Lehigh Oil Co. [22426]
Lemmen Oil Co. [22427]
Lewis Oil Co.; H.C. [22428]
Local Oil Company of Anoka Inc. [22435]
Lone Star Company Inc. [22436]
Loyd LP Gas Co.; Bob [22439]
Lyon County Cooperative Oil Co. [22443]
Manley Oil Co. [22448]
McBax Ltd. [22462]
McLeieer Oil Inc. [22468]
Medford Co-operative Inc. [18085]
Meenan Oil Company L.P. [22473]
Meyer Oil Co. [22478]
Mid West Oil Ltd. [22480]
Midland 66 Oil Company Inc. [22481]
Midway Oil Co. [22482]
Midwest Oil Co. [22483]
Monroe Oil Company Inc. [22493]
Morris Cooperative Association [1053]
Morris Oil Inc. [22499]
Nana Development Corp. [22504]
National Oil and Gas Inc. [22505]
Newell Oil Company Inc. [22514]
Nittany Oil Co. [22520]
Northern Coop Services (Lake Mills, Iowa) [22526]
Northern Lakes Co-op Inc. [1084]
Ogle Service Co. [1100]
Oil Marketing Company Inc. [22538]

Olympian Oil Co. [22540]
Oxbow Corp. [22545]
Patterson Brothers Oil and Gas Inc. [22552]
Perkins Inc.; Julian W. [22564]
Petroleum World Inc. [22573]
Petron Oil Corp. [22574]
Phibro Inc. [22576]
Phillips 66 Propane Co. [22577]
Phoenix Fuel Company Inc. [22582]
Piasa Motor Fuels Inc. [22583]
Pipeline Oil Sales Inc. [22586]
Plains Equity Exchange [18171]
Polk County Farmers Cooperative [1138]
Porter Oil Company Inc. [22589]
Powell Distributing Company Inc. [22590]
Progressive Farmers Cooperative [1158]
Rad Oil Company Inc. [22607]
Raymond Oil Co. [22608]
Rebel Oil Company Inc. [22611]
Reece Oil Co. [22616]
Reeder Distributors Inc. [22617]
Rice Lake Farmers Union Cooperative [1188]
River Country Cooperative [1197]
River Valley Cooperative [1198]
Riverview FS Inc. [1199]
Rosetta Oil Inc. [22640]
Rosetta Oil Inc. [22641]
Rosetta Oil Inc. Duck Island Terminal [22642]
St. Martin Oil and Gas Inc. [22648]
Saybeck Inc. [22654]
Schaeperkoetter Store Inc. [6711]
Scott Farm Service Inc. [1242]
Service Oil Inc. [22663]
Siegel Oil Co. [22671]
South Dakota Wheat Growers Association [18241]
Southwest Grain Farm Marketing and Supply
    Div. [22686]
Spartan Petroleum Company Inc. [22688]
S.T. and H. Oil Company Inc. [22697]
Standish Oil Co. [22700]
Star Oil Company Inc. [22701]
Stone County Oil Company Inc. [22709]
Superior Cooperative Elevator Co. [18270]
Taconite Oil Company Inc. [22720]
Thaler Oil Company Inc. [22732]
Thompson Oil Co. [22734]
Time Oil Co. [22736]
Tippins Oil and Gas Company Inc. [22737]
Toms Sierra Company Inc. [22738]
Truman Arnold Co. [22752]
Turner Marine Bulk Inc. [22754]
United Pride Inc. [22762]
U.S. Oil Company Inc. [3371]
Veach Oil Co. [22771]
V.T. Petroleum [22775]
Wabash Power Equipment Co. [22777]
Wareco Service Inc. [22781]
Webb's Oil Corp. [22788]
Wilkerson Fuel Company Inc. [22803]
Williams Oil Co. [22804]
Williams Oil Co.; A.T. [22805]
Williams Oil Company Inc.; J.H. [22806]
Wooten Oil Co. [22815]
Yoder Oil Company Inc. [22818]
Zuni Investment Co. [22821]

SIC 5172 — Petroleum Products Nec

1st Call McCall Heating and Clng [15718]
3-D Energy Inc. [22013]
A-Doc Oil Co. [22015]
A and W Oil Company Inc. [22016]
Abel's Quik Shops [22018]
AC and T Company Inc. [22019]
Adams Tractor Co.; Carroll [185]
Addington Oil Co. [22021]
Adrian Wheat Growers Inc. [189]
Advance Petroleum Distributing Company
    Inc. [22022]
Advance Petroleum Inc. [22023]
AG Cooperative Service Inc. [17678]
Ag-Land FS Inc. [194]
AG ONE CO-OP Inc. [196]
AGA Welding [15741]

Agaland CO-OP Inc. [202]
AgBest Cooperative Inc. [22025]
Agland Coop [17681]
Agland Coop [205]
Agland Cooperative [206]
Agland Cooperative [207]
Agland Cooperative [208]
Agland Cooperative [22026]
Agland Inc. [209]
Agriland F.S. Inc. [22027]
Agway Energy Products [22028]
Agway Inc. [17688]
Allen Petroleum Corp. [22029]
Allied Oil and Supply Inc. [22031]
Alma Farmers Union Cooperative [230]
Almena Cooperative Association [22032]
Almena Cooperative Association [22033]
Alpena Oil Company Inc. [22034]
Amherst Cooperative Elevator Inc. [17697]
Amoco Energy Trading Corp. [22037]
Anthony Farmers Cooperative and Elevator
    Co. [17702]
Apex Oil Co. [22039]
Apollo Oil LLC [22040]
Aranosian Oil Co. Inc. [22041]
Ard Oil Co. Inc. [22043]
Arkansas Valley Companies [22044]
Arkla Chemical Corp. [22045]
Ashby Equity Association [258]
Assumption Cooperative Grain Co. [17708]
ASW Aviation Services Inc. [44]
A.T. Supply [21391]
Atlanta Fuel Company Inc. [22046]
Atlantic Aviation Service Inc. [22047]
Atlantis International, Inc. [22049]
Atlas Fuel Oil Co. [22050]
Auglaize Farmers Cooperative [261]
Aurora Cooperative Elevator Co. [263]
Avfuel Corp. [22052]
Awalt Wholesale Inc. [2301]
AWC Propane Co. [22053]
Ayers Oil Company Inc. [22054]
B & J Oil Co. [22055]
Bailey Distributing Co.; E.M. [22057]
Bales & Truitt Company Inc. [14336]
Balfour Maclaine Corp. [10494]
Ball Tire and Gas Inc. [2312]
Bardahl Manufacturing Corp. [22058]
Bayside Fuel Oil Depot Corp. [22059]
Beard Oil Pipeline Supply Inc. [22061]
Bearing Enterprises Inc. [16733]
Beck Suppliers Inc. [22062]
Bedford Valley Petroleum Corp. [22063]
Bell Additives Inc. [22064]
Bell Gas Inc. [22065]
Belle Plaine Cooperative [295]
Bemidji Cooperative Association [22066]
Benton County Cooperative [300]
Benton Oil Co. [22067]
Benz Oil Inc. [22068]
Berreth Oil Company Inc. [22069]
Besche Oil Co. Inc. [22071]
Big Horn Cooperative Market Association
    Inc. [309]
Big/Little Stores Inc. [22072]
Big Saver Inc. [22073]
Big Stone County Cooperative [310]
Biltmore Oil Co. Inc. [22074]
Bison Oil [22075]
Blackburn Oil Co. Inc. [22077]
Blalock Oil Company Inc. [22078]
Blanchardville Cooperative Oil Association [22079]
Blarney Castle Oil Co. [22080]
Blue Flame Div. [22081]
Boeing Petroleum Services Inc. [22082]
Boente Sons Inc.; Joseph F. [22083]
Boncosky Oil Co. [22084]
Bond County Services Co. [328]
Bonfield Brothers, Inc. [22085]
Boone County Farm Bureau Cooperative
    Inc. [22086]
Booneville Cooperative Elevator Co. [331]
BP America Inc. [60]
BP Oil Co. [22089]
Brentari Oil Co. [22091]
Breon and Sons Inc.; R.E. [22092]

Brewer Oil Co. [22093]
Brewer Oil Co.; Don [22094]
Broad Street Oil & Gas Co. [22095]
Brown Evans Distributing Co. [22096]
Bryant and Blount Oil Co. [22097]
Buckeye Cooperative Elevator Co. [17752]
Buckeye Cooperative Elevator Co. [10637]
Bud's Service Inc. [22098]
Buy-Rite Petroleum Ltd. [22099]
C-D Farm Service Company Inc. [354]
C and J Service Co. [22100]
C and P Oil Inc. [22101]
C and W Enterprises Inc. [22103]
Campbell Oil Co. [22105]
Cannon Valley Cooperative [370]
CAP Propane Plus Inc. [22106]
Capital City Companies Inc. [22107]
Cargill Inc. Northeast Petroleum Div. [22108]
Carleton Oil Company Inc. [21668]
Carr Oil Inc. [22109]
Carse Oil Company Inc. [22110]
Carson Co. Tri-County Oil Div. [22111]
Carson Oil Company Inc. [22112]
Carter Inc.; Jerry C. [22113]
Carver's Oil Co. [22114]
Cass County Service Co. [378]
Castle Oil Corp. [22115]
Castrol North America Holdings Inc. [22116]
Cen-Tex AG Supply [22118]
CENCO Refining Co. [22119]
Cenex-Harvest States Cooperative [22120]
Cenex Harvest States Cooperative [383]
Center Oil Co. [22121]
Center Valley Cooperative Association [22122]
Central Cooperative Oil Association [22123]
Central Illinois Enterprises Ltd. [22124]
Central Motive Power Inc. [22125]
Central Oil Company Inc. [22126]
Central Oil of Virginia Corp. [22127]
Centre Oil and Gas Co. Inc. [22128]
Chapin Co. [22129]
Chapman Inc. [22130]
Chase Oil Co. Inc. [22131]
Chemoil Corp. [22132]
Cheney Cooperative Elevator Association [411]
Chesapeake Utilities Corp. [22133]
Chevron Corp. [4359]
Chevron Industries [22134]
Childress Oil Co.; W.R. [22136]
Christensen Oil Co. [22138]
Christian County Farmers Supply Co. [416]
Chronister Oil Co. [22139]
Circleville Oil Co. [22140]
Citrus Trading Inc. [22141]
City Coal of New London Inc. [22142]
Clarks Petroleum Service Inc. [22143]
Coastal Fuels Marketing Inc. [22145]
Coastal Oil New York Inc. [22147]
Coastal States Trading [22148]
Coen Oil Co. Inc. [22149]
Cold Spring Cooperative Creamery [434]
Coleman Oil Co. Inc. [22151]
Colonial Oil Industries Inc. [22152]
Colvard Oil Company Inc. [22153]
Commerce Consultants Inc. [22154]
Community Cooperative Oil Association [22156]
Condon Oil Company Inc. [22158]
Conrad Cooperative [438]
Consolidated Cooperative Inc. [17791]
Consolidated Fuel Oil Co. Inc. [22160]
Consumer Cooperative Oil Co. [22161]
Consumer Oil Company of Meridian [22162]
Consumer Oil and Supply Co. [442]
Consumers Petroleum Co. [22164]
Continental Ozark Corp. [22165]
Cooperative Agricultural Center [447]
Cooperative Elevator, Sebewaing [17795]
Cooperative Exchange [453]
Cooperative Gas and Oil Co. (Geneseo,
    Illinois) [22166]
Cooperative Grain and Supply [17796]
Cooperative Oil Co. [458]
Cooperative Oil Co. [22169]
Cooperative Service Oil Co. [459]
Copeland Oil Co. [22170]
Cornerstone Propane G.P. Inc. [22171]

Cornerstone Propane Partners L.P. [22172]
Cosbel Petroleum Corp. [22173]
Cota and Cota Inc. [22174]
Cottonwood Cooperative Oil Co. [22175]
Craft Oil Corp. [22177]
Creameries Blending Inc. [471]
Crest Distributing Co. [22178]
Cronin Asphalt Corp. [22179]
Crus Oil Inc. [22180]
Crystal Flash Petroleum Corp. [22181]
Cumberland Oil Co. Inc. [22182]
Curry Oil Company Inc. [22183]
Curt's Oil Co. [22184]
Cuyahoga Landmark Inc. [22185]
CY Hart Distributig Co. [22186]
Dakota Pride Coop [487]
Dakota Pride Cooperative [22187]
Danco Prairie FS Cooperative [492]
Danville Gasoline and Oil Company Inc. [22188]
Dassel Cooperative Dairy Association [495]
Daubert Oil & Gas Co. [22189]
Dead River Co. [22190]
Delaware Storage Co. [22192]
Delgasco Inc. [22193]
Delta Oil Company Inc. [22194]
Delta Purchasing Federation [511]
Delta Resources Inc. [22195]
Denatec Distributors [22196]
Denton Petroleum Co. [22197]
Detlefsen Oil Inc. [22198]
Deuel County Farmers Union Oil Co. [22199]
Devine Brothers Inc. [7259]
Dickey Oil Corp. [22200]
Dilmar Oil Company Inc. [22201]
Dion and Sons Inc.; M.O. [22202]
Distributors Oil Co. Inc. [22203]
District Petroleum Products Inc. [22204]
Dixie Oil Co. Inc. [22205]
D.O. Inc. [22206]
Dooley Oil Company, Inc. [22207]
Dooley Oil Company, Inc. [22208]
Dorsey Oil Co.; B.A. [22209]
Dover Company Inc.; Bill L. [22210]
Drake Petroleum Company Inc. [22211]
Dreyfus Corp.; Louis [17822]
Drummond Cooperative Elevator Inc. [526]
Duke Energy Field Services Inc. [22212]
Dumas Oil Co. [22213]
Dunlap Oil Company Inc. [22214]
Dyna-Lube [22215]
DynAir Fueling Inc. [22216]
E-Z Serve Petroleum Marketing Co. [22217]
East Jordan Cooperative Co. [2571]
East Texas Gas Co. [22219]
Eastern Fuels Inc. [22220]
Eastern Petroleum Corp. [22221]
Eden Oil Company Inc. [22223]
Edgewood Oil Inc. [22224]
Edison Non-Stock Cooperative [542]
Effingham Equity [17827]
Elkhart County Farm Cooperative [22225]
Ellenbecker Oil Co. [22226]
Elliott Aviation Inc. [83]
Elser Oil Co. [22227]
Emery Air Charter Inc. [15984]
Empire Petroleum Inc. [22228]
Empiregas Trucking Corp. [22229]
Energy Buyers Service Corp. [22230]
EnergyNorth Propane Inc. [22231]
Enron Liquid Fuels Co. [22233]
Enron Power Services [22234]
Enterprise Oil Co. [22235]
EOTT Energy Operating L.P. [22236]
Equity Cooperative Association [22238]
Erie Petroleum Inc. [22239]
Evangeline Farmers Cooperative [17838]
Evans Oil Co. [22241]
Evans Systems Inc. [22242]
Ever-Ready Oil Co. [22243]
Exxon Company USA [22245]
Exxon Company U.S.A. Santa Ynez Unit [22246]
F and R Oil Company Inc. [22248]
Fairclough and Sons Inc.; N.B. [22250]
Fannon Petroleum Services Inc. [22251]
Far East Trading Company Inc. [86]
Farm-Oyl Company Inc. [563]

Farm Service Cooperative Inc. [565]
Farmers Cooperative Association [572]
Farmers Cooperative Association [22253]
Farmers Cooperative Association [575]
Farmers Cooperative Co. [593]
Farmers Cooperative Co. [594]
Farmers Cooperative Co. [17849]
Farmers Cooperative Co. [596]
Farmers Cooperative Co. [602]
Farmers Cooperative Company Inc. [604]
Farmers Cooperative Elevator [607]
Farmers Cooperative Elevator [608]
Farmers Cooperative Elevator [17862]
Farmers Cooperative Elevator Association [610]
Farmers Cooperative Elevator Co. [613]
Farmers Cooperative Elevator Co. [616]
Farmers Cooperative Elevator Co. [619]
Farmers Cooperative Elevator Co. [621]
Farmers Cooperative Exchange [623]
Farmers Cooperative Exchange [626]
Farmers Cooperative Exchange [627]
Farmers Cooperative Mill Elevator [17875]
Farmers Cooperative Oil Co. [22255]
Farmers Cooperative Oil Company of Clara City [22256]
Farmers Cooperative Trading Co. [639]
Farmers Cooperative Union [640]
Farmers Petroleum Cooperative Inc. [22257]
Farmers Union Cooperative Association of Alcester and Beresford South Dakota [22259]
Farmers Union Oil Co. [22260]
Farmers Union Oil Co. [664]
Farmers Union Oil Co. [22261]
Farmers Union Oil Co. [22262]
Farmers Union Oil Co. [666]
Farmers Union Oil Co. [22263]
Farmers Union Oil Co. [22264]
Farmers Union Oil Co. [22265]
Farmers Union Oil Co. [22266]
Farmers Union Oil Co. (Crookston, Minnesota) [668]
Farmers Union Oil Company of Kenmare [669]
Farmers Union Oil Co. (Napoleon, North Dakota) [22269]
Farmers Union Oil Co. (Rolla, North Dakota) [22270]
Farmers Union Oil Co. (Starbuck, Minnesota) [670]
Farmers Union Oil Cooperative [22271]
Federal Heating and Engineering Company Inc. [22272]
Fegley Oil Company Inc. [22273]
Ferrellgas Partners L.P. [22274]
FFP Operating Partners L.P. [22275]
FFP Partners L.P. [22276]
Field Oil Inc. [22277]
First International Trading Company [16863]
First State Petroleum Services [22278]
Fisher Auto Parts Professionals [2623]
Five County Farmers Association [691]
Fleischli Oil Company Inc. [22279]
Fleischli Oil Company Inc. [22280]
Fleischli Oil Company Inc. [22281]
Flintex Marketing, Inc. [22282]
Flitz International Ltd. [22283]
Flying J Inc. [22284]
Flying J Travel Plaza [22285]
FMI Hydrocarbon Co. [22286]
Ford Distributing Co.; Leid [22288]
Fort Worth Jet Center [22289]
Fortmeyer's Inc. [22290]
Four Corners Welding & Gas [19982]
Fowler Inc.; M.M. [22291]
Franklin Feed and Supply Co. [703]
Fredericksen Tank Lines [22293]
Freeborn County Cooperative Oil Co. [22294]
Frontier Texaco [22295]
Fruita Consumers Cooperative [716]
Fuel South Company Inc. [22296]
Fuller Oil Company Inc. [22297]
G and M Oil Company Inc. [22299]
Galesberg Cooperative Elevator Co. [720]
Galvin Flying Service Inc. [22300]
Gardner Inc. [725]
Gassmon Coal and Oil Company Inc. [20542]
Gate City Equipment Company Inc. [22303]
Gayle Oil Company Inc. [22305]

Geer Tank Trucks Inc. [22306]
General Air Service and Supply Company Inc. [16052]
Gerlach Oil Company Inc. [22308]
Getty Petroleum Marketing Inc. [22309]
Getty Realty Corp. [22310]
Giant Refining Co. [22311]
Gibbons and LeFort Inc. [22313]
Gillespie Oil Company Inc. [2681]
Global Petroleum Corp. [22314]
Glover Oil Company Inc. [22315]
Godwin Oil Company Inc. [22316]
Goetz Energy Corp. [22317]
Gold Eagle Co. [2688]
Gothic Energy Corp. [22319]
Grain Land Co-op [17953]
Graves Oil & Butane Co. [20016]
Grays Petroleum Inc. [22320]
Gresham Petroleum Co. [22321]
Griggs Inc.; Jack [22322]
Grimes Oil Company Inc. [22323]
Grimsley Oil Company Inc. [22324]
GTA Aviation Inc. [22325]
Guard All Chemical Company Inc. [22326]
Gulf Oil L.P. [22327]
Gull Industries Inc. [22328]
Gunderson Oil Co. [22329]
Guttman Oil Co. [22330]
Halron Oil Company Inc. [22332]
Harbor Enterprises Inc. [22334]
Harbor Fuel Company Inc. [22335]
Hardeman Fayette Farmers Cooperative [790]
Harmony Co-op [17976]
Harmony Country Cooperatives [792]
Harper Distributing Company Inc. [22336]
Harris County Oil Company Inc. [22337]
Harris Oil Co.; Bob [22338]
Harrison Oil Co. [22339]
Heating Oil Partners [22341]
Heetco Inc. [22342]
Heetco Inc. Kansas Div. [22343]
Heffner Brothers Co. [22344]
Henry Farmers Cooperative Inc. [814]
Henry Service Co. [22345]
Heritage FS Inc. [815]
Heritage F.S. Inc. [22346]
Heritage Propane Partners, L.P. [22347]
Hermes Consolidated Inc. [22348]
Hewitt Brothers Inc. [817]
Hickman & Willey, Inc. [22349]
Hicks Oil and Hicks Gas Inc. [22350]
High Plains Cooperative Association [821]
High Point Oil Co. [22351]
Hightower Oil and Petroleum Company Inc. [22352]
Highway Agricultural Services Inc. [822]
Hillger Oil Company Inc. [22353]
Hines Inc.; Angus I. [22354]
Hoffman Cooperative Oil Association [829]
Holiday Cos. [11446]
Holiday Stores Inc. [11447]
Hollar Company Inc. [22355]
Homax Oil [22357]
Home Oil Company of Sikeston Inc. [22359]
Home Oil and Gas Company Inc. [22360]
Home Service Oil Company Inc. [22361]
Hone Oil Co. [22362]
Hoople Farmers Grain Co. [18004]
Hoosier Oil Inc. [22363]
Houston Texaco Oil Co.; Harry [22365]
Howell Petroleum Products Inc. [22367]
Humboldt Petroleum Inc. [22368]
Hunt and Sons Inc. [22369]
Huntington County Farm Cooperative [846]
IGI Div. [22370]
Illinois Oil Products Inc. [22372]
Imlay City Total Oil Inc. [22373]
Industrial Fuel Co. [22374]
Interior Fuels Co. [22375]
International Marine Fuels Inc. [22376]
Interstate Petroleum Products Inc. [22377]
Intraco Corp. [2796]
Iowa Oil Co. [22378]
Iowa River Farm Service Inc. [868]
J and H Oil Co. [22379]

Jackson-Jennings Farm Bureau Cooperative [22381]
Jacobus Energy [22382]
James Oil Co. [22383]
Jardine Petroleum [22384]
Jasper Engineering and Equipment Co. [16970]
Jefferson City Oil Company Inc. [22386]
Jenkel Oil Company Inc. [22387]
Jenkins Gas and Oil Company Inc. [22388]
Johnson Cooperative Grain Co. [888]
Jones Oil Company Inc.; John E. [22391]
Jones Oil Company Inc.; N.E. [22392]
JV Inc. [22393]
Kanabec Cooperative Association [22394]
Kanematsu U.S.A. Inc. [22395]
Kansas Propane [22396]
Keller Oil Inc. [22397]
Kellerstrass Oil Co. [22398]
Kelley Inc.; Jack B. [22399]
Keltner Enterprises Inc. [2846]
Kenan Oil Co. [11600]
Kennedy Oil Company Inc. [22400]
Keystops Inc. [22402]
Kiel Brothers Oil Company Inc. [22403]
Kilburn and Company Inc.; J.C. [22404]
Kimber Petroleum Corp. [22405]
Kingman Aero Services Inc. [22406]
Kingston Oil Supply Corp. [22407]
Kirby Oil Co. [22408]
Koenig Fuel & Supply Co. [22409]
Kohler Oil and Propane Co. [22410]
Kona Marine Supply [18537]
Kunz Oil Company Inc. [22411]
L & L Gas & Oil Inc. [22413]
L & L Oil and Gas Service LLC [22414]
La Porte County Cooperative [18041]
Lake Welding Supply Co. [16226]
Lakeside Oil Company Inc. [22417]
Larsen Cooperative Company Inc. [939]
Laurel Valley Oil Co. [22418]
Laurel Valley Oil Co. [22419]
Lawes Coal Company Inc. [943]
Lawson and Son; E.T. [22420]
Leahy's Fuels Inc. [22421]
Leemon Oil Company Inc. [22422]
Leemon Shores Oil [22423]
Leffler Inc.; Carlos R. [22424]
Lehigh Gas and Oil Co. [22425]
Lehigh Oil Co. [22426]
Lexington Cooperative Oil Co. [22429]
Liberty Oil Company Inc. [22431]
Lightening Oil Co. [22432]
Lilyblad Petroleum Inc. [22433]
Lincoln County Farmers Cooperative [960]
Linn Cooperative Oil Co. [22434]
Lone Star Company Inc. [22436]
Loos and Dilworth Inc. [4441]
Lord Equipment Co. [22437]
Loyd LP Gas Co.; Bob [22439]
Lubrichem Environmental Inc. [22441]
Lyden Co. [22442]
Lyford Gin Association [18067]
M & R Trading Inc. [18068]
Machine and Welding Supply Co. [16255]
Macon Ridge Farmers Association [18069]
Maine Propane Distributors Inc. [22445]
Major Oil Inc. [22446]
Mallard Oil Co. [22447]
Manassas Ice and Fuel Company Inc. [11771]
Mansfield Oil Company of Gainesville Inc. [22449]
Marathon Ashland Petroleum L.L.C. [22450]
Marcley Oil Inc. [22451]
Mark Oil Company Inc. [22452]
Marshall County Cooperative Association [22453]
Martin Oil Co. [22454]
Martrex Alpha Corp. [6466]
Massey Wood and West Inc. [22455]
Matthews Brothers Wholesale Inc. [22456]
Maugansville Elevator and Lumber Company Inc. [22457]
Mayes County Petroleum Products [22459]
Maytag Aircraft Corp. [22460]
Maywood Cooperative Association [995]
Mazon Farmers Elevator [996]
McBax Ltd. [22462]
McBride Distributing Inc.; J.B. [22463]

McCall Oil and Chemical Co. [22464]
McGuirk Oil Company Inc. [22465]
McLain Oil Company Inc. [22467]
McLean County Service Co. [1004]
McLeieer Oil Inc. [22468]
McLeod Merchantile Inc. [22469]
McLeod Merchantile Inc. Conoco [22470]
McMillan-Shuller Oil Company Inc. [22471]
McPhails Inc. [15225]
Medina Landmark Inc. [1011]
Meeder Equipment Co. [22472]
Mega Company [2939]
Menomonie Farmers Union Cooperative [1015]
Mercury Air Center [22474]
Mercury Air Group Inc. [22475]
Merrimac Petroleum Inc. [22476]
Meyer Oil Co. [22478]
M.F.A. Oil Co. [22479]
MH World Trade Corp. [26143]
Mid-South Supply Corp. [21501]
Mid West Oil Ltd. [22480]
Midland 66 Oil Company Inc. [22481]
Midland Cooperative Inc. [1031]
Midway Oil Co. [22482]
Midway Trading, Inc. [2958]
Midwest Coop. [11888]
Miller Distributing [22484]
Miller Inc.; Luther P. [22485]
Miller Oil Co. [22486]
Misco Industries Inc. [22487]
Missouri Petroleum Products [22488]
Mitchell Supreme Fuel Co. [22489]
Mitchellville Cooperative [1043]
Moffitt Oil Company Inc. [22490]
Molo Oil Co. [22491]
Mon Valley Petroleum Inc. [22492]
Monroe Oil Company Inc. [22493]
Montour Oil Service Co. [22495]
Moore Oil Company Inc. [22497]
Moore Oil Company Inc.; Lee [22498]
Morpol Industrial Corporation Ltd. [16322]
Morris Oil Inc. [22499]
Morrison Petroleum Company Inc. [22500]
Moss Dynamics [2988]
Mt. Union Cooperative Elevator [18121]
Mulgrew Oil Co. [22501]
Mullis Petroleum Co. [22502]
Mustang Fuel Corp. [22503]
Nana Development Corp. [22504]
National Oil and Gas Inc. [22505]
National Propane Corp. [22506]
National Propane SGP Inc. [22507]
Nebraska Iowa Supply Co. [22508]
Nehawka Farmers Union [18127]
Neowa F.S. Inc. [18129]
New Horizon FS Inc. [22509]
New Horizons FS Inc. [22510]
New Richmond Farmers Union Cooperative Oil Co. [22511]
Newcomer Oil Corp. [22513]
Newell Oil Company Inc. [22514]
Newsom Oil Company Inc. [22515]
Nezperce Rochdale Company Inc. [22516]
NHC Inc. [22517]
Nielsen Oil and Propane Inc. [22518]
Nisbet Oil Co. [22519]
Nittany Oil Co. [22520]
Nobles County Cooperative Oil Co. [22521]
NOCO Energy Corp. [22522]
Norrick Petroleum [22523]
North Central Cooperative Association [22524]
North Central Cooperative Inc. [1079]
Northampton Farm Bureau Cooperative [1083]
Northeast Petroleum [22525]
Northern Coop Services (Lake Mills, Iowa) [22526]
Northville Industries Corp. [22527]
Northwest Oil Company Inc. [22528]
Norton Petroleum Corp. [22529]
Novakovich Enterprises [22531]
Nyssa Cooperative Supply Inc. [1095]
Oakes Oil Co. [22532]
O'Day Equipment Inc. [22534]
Ogden Aviation Services [24197]
Ogden Services Corp. [22535]
Oil Marketing Company Inc. [22538]
Onyx Petroleum Inc. [22541]

Orca Oil Company, Inc. [22542]
Osage Cooperative Elevator [12079]
Owens Inc.; Arnold [22543]
Owensboro Supply Company Inc. [17093]
Ownbey Enterprises Inc. [22544]
Pace Oil Company Inc. [22546]
Pacific Northern [22547]
Pam Oil Inc. [22548]
Panhandle Trading Co. [22549]
Paraco Gas Corp. [22550]
Parker Oil Company Inc. [22551]
Parts Inc. [3083]
Patterson Brothers Oil and Gas Inc. [22552]
Patterson Oil Co. [22553]
Paynesville Farmers Union Cooperative Oil Co. [22554]
PDQ Air Service Inc. [22555]
Peck's Petroleum Inc. [22556]
Pedroni Fuel Co. [22557]
Peerless Distributing Co. [22558]
Pen-Fern Oil Co. [22559]
Pendleton Grain Growers Inc. [18161]
Penfield Petroleum Products [22561]
Peoples Communitive Oil Cooperative [22562]
Peoples Gas and Oil Company Inc. [22563]
Peoria County Service Co. [1122]
Perryton Equity Exchange [18164]
Peterson Oil Co. [22565]
Petrofina Delaware Inc. [22566]
Petrolec Inc. [22567]
Petroleum Marketers Inc. [22568]
Petroleum Products Corp. [22569]
Petroleum Products Corporation North [22570]
Petroleum Sales and Service Inc. [22571]
Petroleum Service Company Inc. [22572]
Petroleum World Inc. [22573]
Phibro Inc. [22576]
Phillips Company Inc.; Tom M. [22578]
Phillips Hardware Co. [22579]
Phillips Inc.; Ira [22580]
Phillipsburg Cooperative Association [22581]
Phoenix Fuel Company Inc. [22582]
Piedmont Propane Co. [22584]
Pine City Cooperative Association [18166]
Pioneer Manufacturing Co. [21540]
Planters Cooperative Association [1133]
Ploch Co.; A.J. [22587]
Pollard-Swain Inc. [22588]
Postville Farmers Cooperative [1142]
Powell Distributing Company Inc. [22590]
Prairie Land Cooperative Co. [1146]
Precision Bearing Co. [17113]
Premier Cooperative [1147]
Premium Oil Co. [22593]
Primrose Oil Company Inc. [22594]
Pro AG Farmers Co-op [1154]
Pro Cooperative [1155]
Propane Equipment Corp. [22596]
Propane/One Inc. [22597]
P.S. Energy Group Inc. [22598]
PSNC Propane Corp. [22599]
Quad County Cooperative [18185]
Quality Oil Company L.P. [22600]
Quality Oil Company L.P. [22601]
Quality Petroleum Corp. [22602]
Queen Oil & Gas [22603]
Quogue Sinclair Fuel Inc. [22604]
R and L Supply Co-op [1166]
Racetrac Petroleum Inc. [22605]
Racine Elevator Co. [22606]
Ray-Carroll County Grain Growers Inc. [1169]
Red Giant Oil Co. [22612]
Red-Kap Sales Inc. [22613]
Red Rock Distributing Co. [22614]
Redlake County Co-op [22615]
Reece Oil Co. [22616]
Reeled Tubing Inc. [22618]
Region Oil Div. [22619]
Reif Oil Co. [22620]
Reinauer Petroleum Co. [22621]
Reiner & Company, Inc.; John [16446]
Retif Oil and Fuel Inc. [22623]
Rex Oil Company Inc. [22624]
Reynolds Industries Inc. (Watertown, Massachusetts) [22625]
Rhodes Oil Co. [22626]

Rib River Valley Cooperative [1187]
Rice Oil Company Inc. [22627]
Richter Fertilizer Co. [1190]
Riggins Oil Co.; L.S. [22628]
Riley and Son Inc.; W.H. [22629]
Risser Oil Corp. [22630]
Rite Way Oil and Gas Company Inc. [22631]
River City Petroleum Inc. [22632]
River Petroleum Inc.; James [22633]
RKA Petroleum Companies, L.L.C. [22634]
Robert Distributors Inc.; Roland J. [22635]
Roberts and Company Inc.; F.L. [22636]
Rock Valley Oil and Chemical Company
    Inc. [22637]
Romanelli and Son Inc. [22638]
Rosebud Farmers Union Cooperative Associates
    Inc. [22639]
Rosetta Oil Inc. Duck Island Terminal [22642]
Royal Fuel Corp. [22643]
Ruffridge Johnson Equipment Company Inc. [7965]
Rupp Oil Company Inc. [22644]
Russell Petroleum Corp. [22645]
Sadowsky and Son Inc.; G.A. [22646]
Sage Creek Refining Co. [22647]
St. Francis Mercantile Equity Exchange [1228]
Sampson-Bladen Oil Co. [22649]
Santa Fuel Inc. [22651]
Sapp Brothers Petroleum Inc. [22652]
Satanta Cooperative Grain [18222]
Sawyer Gas Co. [22653]
SBM Drilling Fluids [22655]
Scana Propane Supply Inc. [22656]
Schildwachter and Sons Inc.; Fred M. [22657]
Schmuckal Oil Co. [22658]
Scott Cooperative Association [1240]
Scranton Equity Exchange Inc. [7995]
Scullin Oil Co. [22659]
Sellers Oil Co. [22660]
Service Oil Company Inc. [22662]
Sharp Oil Company Inc. [22664]
Shelby Industries Inc. [22665]
Shell Lake Cooperative [22666]
Shipley Oil Co. [22668]
Shipley-Phillips Inc. [22669]
Sibco Enterprises Incorporated [3217]
Sico Co. [22670]
Siegel Oil Co. [22671]
Sinclair Oil Corp. [22673]
Sinclair Oil Corp. Eastern Region [22674]
Sioux Valley Cooperative [22675]
Slay Industries Inc. [18235]
Slick 50 Corp. [22676]
Smith Brothers of Dudley Inc. [22677]
Smith Oil Co.; Glenn [22678]
Smith Oil Company Inc. [22679]
SMO Inc. [22680]
South Central Co-op [1274]
South Central Co-op [1275]
Southeast Cooperative Service Co. [1277]
Southern LNG Inc. [22683]
Southern Valley Co-op [22684]
Southwest Energy Distributors Inc. [22685]
Spartan Oil Co. [22687]
Spartan Petroleum Company Inc. [22688]
Speaks Oil Company Inc. [22689]
Spear Oil Co. [22690]
Spencer Companies Inc. (Huntsville,
    Alabama) [22691]
Spencer County Cooperative Associates
    Inc. [1289]
Spiegel and Sons Oil Corp.; M. [22692]
Sprague Energy Corp. [22693]
Sprague Energy Corp. [22694]
Spruill Oil Company Inc. [22695]
Stahl Oil Company Inc. [22698]
Standard Cycle and Auto Supply Co. [22699]
Standish Oil Co. [22700]
Star Oil Company Inc. [22701]
State Gas and Oil Co. [22702]
Stein Distributing [22703]
Stem Brothers Inc. [22704]
Steuart Petroleum Co. [22705]
Stockton Oil Co. [22707]
Stone County Oil Company Inc. [22709]
Streett and Company Inc.; J.D. [22710]
Streicher Mobile Fueling Inc. [22711]

Stuarts' Petroleum Co. [22713]
Sun Company Inc. [22714]
Supreme Oil Company Inc. [22715]
Surner Heating Company Inc. [22716]
Sutey Oil CO. [22717]
Sutherland Farmers Cooperative [1307]
Swifty Oil Company Inc. [22718]
Switzer Petroleum Products [22719]
Tama-Benton Cooperative Co. [18275]
Tauber Oil Co. [22721]
Tenneco Energy Resources Corp. [22724]
Tenneco Gas Marketing Co. [22725]
Tesoro Petroleum Corp. [22726]
Tesoro Petroleum Distributing Co. [22727]
Tesoro Petroleum Distributing Co. [22728]
Texaco International Trader, Inc. [22729]
Texaco Oil Co. [22730]
Texaco Trading and Transportation Inc. [22731]
Thibaut Oil Company Inc. [22733]
Thompson Oil Co. [22734]
Thornhill Oil Company Inc. [22735]
Three Rivers FS Co. [1332]
Tippins Oil and Gas Company Inc. [22737]
Toney Petroleum Inc. [22739]
Toney Petroleum Inc. [22740]
TOSCO Marketing Co. [22741]
Tower Oil and Technology Co. [22742]
Town and Country Coop. [1345]
Town Pump Inc. [22743]
Townsend-Strong Inc. [22744]
Trans-Tec Services Inc. [22746]
Transammonia Inc. [1349]
TransMontaigne Product Services Inc. [22747]
Trease Distributing Co.; Dan [22748]
Tri Lakes Petroleum [22749]
Triton Marketing Inc. [22750]
Troutman Brothers [22751]
Tulco Oils Inc. [22753]
Tulia Wheat Growers Inc. [1362]
Twin County Service Co. [1368]
UCG Energy Corp. [22755]
Ultramar Diamond Shamrock Corp. [22756]
Uni-Marts Inc. [12784]
Union Carbide Corp., IPX Services [16587]
Union Distributing Co. [22757]
Union Oil Company of Maine [22758]
UniSource Energy Inc. [22759]
United Co-op Inc. (Hampton, Nebraska) [1374]
United Distributing Co. [22760]
United Farmers Co-op [1376]
United Farmers Cooperative [1377]
United Oil of the Carolinas, Inc. [22761]
United Pride Inc. [22762]
United States Exploration Inc. [22763]
Universal Companies Inc. (Wichita,
    Kansas) [22764]
Universal Lubricants Inc. [22765]
Urwiler Oil and Fertilizer Inc. [1387]
Valley Farmers Cooperative (Natchitoches,
    Louisiana) [1392]
Valley Oil Co. [22767]
Van Zeeland Oil Company Inc. [22769]
Vanguard Petroleum Corp. [22770]
Veach Oil Co. [22771]
Vesco Oil Corp. [22772]
Vintage Petroleum Inc. [22773]
Vista Oil Co. [22774]
V.T. Petroleum [22775]
Wabash Valley Service Co. [1402]
Wainoco Oil Corp. [22778]
Wakefield Oil Co. [22779]
Walla Walla Farmers Co-op Inc. [1406]
Wallace County Cooperative Equity
    Exchange [1407]
Wallace Oil Co. [22780]
Warren Co. Inc.; E.R. [22782]
Warren Corp.; George E. [22783]
Warren Farmers Cooperative [1413]
Waterloo Service Company Inc. [22785]
Waukon Equity Cooperative [1418]
WD-40 Co. [22786]
Webber Oil Co. [22787]
Webb's Oil Corp. [22788]
Wehman Inc. [22789]
Weil Service Products Corp. [22790]
Wesson, Inc. [22791]

West Liberty Oil Co. [22792]
West Minerals Inc. [22793]
Western Petroleum Co. [22794]
Western States Oil Company Inc. [22796]
Western States Petroleum Inc. [22797]
Western Stations Co. [22798]
Whitaker Oil Co. [22799]
Whiteside F.S. Inc. [22800]
Whiteville Oil Company Inc. [22801]
Wilbanks Oil Company Inc. [22802]
Wilkerson Fuel Company Inc. [22803]
Williams Inc.; Ralph C. [17280]
Williams Oil Co. [22804]
Williams Oil Co.; A.T. [22805]
Williams Oil Company Inc.; J.H. [22806]
Winnco Inc. [22810]
Winters Oil Co. [22811]
Wixson Brothers Equipment Co. [22812]
Wogaman Oil Co.; R.W. [22813]
Wolf River Country Cooperative [1458]
Wolfriver Country Cooperative [22814]
World Fuel Services Corp. [22816]
World Fuel Services Inc. [176]
World Wen, Inc. [6882]
Worsley Oil Company of Wallace Inc. [22817]
Yingling Aircraft Inc. [178]
Young Oil CO. [22819]
Youngblood Oil Company Inc. [22820]
Ziegler Tire and Supply Co. [3455]

SIC 5181 — Beer & Ale

A & B Distributors [1471]
A-B Sales Inc. [1472]
A & L Coors Inc. [1473]
Airport Beer Distributors [1475]
Alabama Crown [1476]
Alko Distributors Inc. [1477]
Allentown Beverage Company Inc. [1478]
Allied Distributing [1480]
Allstate Beverage Co. [1481]
Alpena Beverage Co. Inc. [1482]
Amoskeag Beverages Inc. [1483]
Anderson Distributing Co. [1484]
Anheuser-Busch Inc. [1485]
Arizona Beverage Distributing Co. LLC [1486]
Arnold-Sunbelt Beverage Company L.P.;
    Ben [1487]
Aroostook Beverage Co. [1488]
Atlanta Beverage Co. [1490]
Atlas Distributing, Inc. [24912]
B & B Beer Distributing [1492]
B and J Sales Inc. [1495]
Baker Distributing [1497]
Banko Enterprises Inc. [1499]
Barringer Distributing Company Inc.; R.H. [1501]
Barton Inc. [1503]
Bauer & Foss, Inc. [1505]
Baum Wine Imports Inc. [1506]
Baumgarten Distributing Company, Inc. [1507]
Bavaria House Corp. [1508]
Bayside Distributing Inc. [1509]
Beck's North America [1513]
Beechwood Distributors Inc. [1514]
Beer City [1515]
Beer Import Company [1516]
Beer World [1517]
Beloit Beverage Company Inc. [1519]
Bennett Distributing Co. Inc. [1520]
Bertolina Wholesale Co. [1521]
Best Way Distributing Co. [1523]
Better Brands of Atlanta Inc. [1524]
Better Brands of South Georgia [1526]
Beverage Distributors Co. [1527]
Beverage Wholesalers Inc. [1528]
Biersch Brewing Co.; Gordon [1529]
Bissman Company Inc. [1530]
Blach Distributing Co. [1531]
Black Forest Distributors Ltd. [1532]
Black Hills Distributing Co. Inc. [1533]
Blue Rock Beverage Co. [1537]
Bob & Joe's Wholesale [1538]
Boisset U.S.A. [1539]
Bonanza Beverage Co. [1543]

Bonded Spirits Corp. [1544]
Branded Liquors Inc. [1547]
Brewery Products Co. [1548]
Brewmaster [1549]
Briggs, Inc. [1550]
Brown Distributing [1553]
Bryson Inc. [1555]
Buck Distributing Company Inc. [1556]
BudCo Incorporated of San Antonio [1557]
Budco of San Antonio Inc. [1558]
Burke Beverage of California Inc. [1560]
Burke Beverage Inc. [1561]
C & G Distributing Co. Inc. [1563]
Cabo Distributing Co., Inc. [1564]
Caffey, Inc.; I.H. [1565]
Calumet Breweries Inc. [1566]
Canale Beverages Inc.; D. [1568]
Capital Beverage Corp. [1569]
Capital Beverages Inc. [1570]
Capital Coors Co. [1571]
Capitol Distributors Inc. [1572]
Cardinal Distributing [1573]
Carenbauer Wholesale Corp. [1574]
Carolina Beer Company Inc. [1575]
Carter Distributing Co. [1578]
Cash Distributing Co. [1580]
Cellars Beverage Inc. [1582]
Centennial Beverage Corp. [1583]
Central Distributors Inc. [1586]
Central Liquor Co. [1587]
Chatham Imports Inc. [1591]
Chicago Beer Distributing [1592]
Choice Brands, Inc. [1593]
City Beverage Co. [1595]
City Beverage Co. [1596]
City Beverage Inc. [1597]
City Beverages [1598]
Clarke Distributors Inc. [1599]
Classic City Beverages Inc. [1600]
Clausen Distributing [1602]
Clement and Muller Inc. [1603]
Coast Distributing Co. [1604]
Coastal Beverage Company Inc. [1605]
Colonial Distributors Inc. [1606]
Columbia Distributing Co./Henry Hirsdale/Admiralty Beverage Co. [1607]
Columbus Distributing Co. [1608]
Commercial Distributing Co. [1609]
Conkling Distributing Co.; John A. [1610]
Conkling Distributing Co.; John A. [1611]
Considine Sales Co. Inc. [1612]
Consolidated Beverages Inc. [1613]
Consumers of La Salle [1615]
Coors Distributing Co. [1617]
Coors West [1618]
Costello Beverage Co.; J.W. [1620]
Cox & Son Inc.; H. [1621]
Crawford Sales Co. [1622]
Crest Beverage Co. [1623]
Crown Beer Distributors Inc. [1624]
Crown Beverages Inc. [1625]
Crown Bottling Co. [1626]
Crown Distributing Co. [1627]
Crown Inc. Beverage Div. [1628]
Cunningham Wholesale Company Inc. [1629]
D & D Distributing [1630]
Dady Distributing Inc.; J.A. [1631]
Dakota Beverage Co. [1632]
Dakota Sales Co. Inc. [1633]
Dana Distributors Inc. [1635]
De Luca Liquor and Wine Ltd. [1636]
Dearing Beverage Company Inc. [1637]
DeBauge Brothers Inc. [1638]
Delaney Management Corp. [1639]
Delaware Importers Inc. [1640]
Dennert Distributing Corp.; H. [1641]
Desert Beverage Co. Inc. [1643]
Desert Eagle Distributing Co. [1644]
DET Distributing Co. [1645]
DET Distributing Co. [1646]
DeWitt Beverage [1648]
Diamond Distributors [1649]
Diamond State Distributors [1650]
Dimitri Wine & Spirits [1651]
Divine Brothers Distributing Inc. [1653]
Dixie Beverage Co. [1654]

D.M. Distributing Company Inc. [1655]
Drinks Galore Inc. [1658]
Dutchess Beer Distributors [1660]
Dwan and Company Inc. [1661]
E-Corp, Inc. [1662]
Eagle Beverage Co. [1663]
Eagle Distributing Co. [1664]
Eagle Distributing Co. Inc. [1665]
Eagle Distributors Inc. [1666]
Eagle River Distributing [1667]
East Side Beverage Co. [1668]
El Ray Distributing Company Inc. [1672]
Elmer's Distributing Co. [1673]
Elmwood Beer Distributor [1675]
Empire Distributing [1676]
Empire Distributors of NC Inc. [1677]
Erie Beer Co. [1678]
Erwin Distributing Co. [1679]
Evans Distributing Company Inc. [1680]
Evanston Wholesale Inc. [1681]
Fabiano Brothers Inc. [1682]
Farmer and Co.; Leon [1684]
Farrell Distributing [1685]
Federal Wine and Liquor Co. [1686]
Finger Lakes Bottling Co. [1690]
F.L.D. Distributors Inc. [1692]
Forester Beverage Inc. [1694]
Forman Distributing Co. [1695]
Fox Sales Co.; Henry A. [1696]
Frank Distributing [1697]
Franklin Cigar and Tobacco Company Inc. [26296]
Friendly Distributors [1698]
Fuhrer Holdings Inc.; Frank [1699]
Fuhrer Wholesale Co.; Frank B. [1700]
G and G Enterprises Inc. [1701]
Gambrinus Co. [1703]
Gate City Beverage Distributors [1705]
General Beer Distributors [1706]
General Beverage Sales Co. [1707]
General Distributing Co. [1708]
General Wholesale Co. [1709]
General Wine Co. [1710]
Georgia Crown Distributing Co. [1712]
Gidden Distributing [1714]
Gideon Distributing Inc. [1715]
Girardi Distributors Corp. [1717]
Glasgow Distributors Inc. [1718]
Glazer's of Iowa [1719]
Glazer's Wholesale Drug Co. Inc. [1720]
Globil Inc. [1721]
Gold Coast Beverage Distributors [1722]
Gold Coast Distributors Inc. [1723]
Golden Eagle of Arkansas Inc. [1724]
Golden Eagle Distributors [1725]
Goodman; C.R. [1726]
Goody-Goody Liquor Store Inc. [1727]
Grantham Distributing Company Inc. [1730]
Greene Beverage Company Inc. [1731]
Green's/Pine Avenue Beer Distributing [1732]
Grey Eagle Distributors Inc. [1733]
Grosslein Beverages Inc. [1734]
Guiffre Distributing Co.; Tony [1735]
Guinness America Inc. [1736]
Guinness Import Co. [1737]
Gusto Brands Inc. [1738]
H-H of Savannah, Inc. [1739]
Hall Inc.; Bob [1740]
Halliday-Smith Inc. [1741]
Halo Distributing Co. [1742]
Hamburg [1743]
Harbor Distributing Co. [1744]
Harbor Distributing Co. [1745]
Hartford Distributors Inc. [1746]
Haubrich Enterprises Inc. [1747]
Havre Distributors Inc. [1748]
Heidelberg Distributing Co. [1749]
Heineken USA Inc. [1750]
Hensley and Co. [1751]
High Country Sales Inc. [1753]
High Grade Beverage [1754]
High Grade Beverage [11430]
High Life Sales Co. [1755]
Highland Distributing Co. [1756]
Hillman International Brands, Ltd. [1757]
Hilltop Beer Distributing [1758]
Hirst Imports [1759]

Hitchcock Distributing Inc. [1760]
Holsten Import Corp. [1761]
Holston Distributing Co. [1762]
House of Schwan Inc. [1763]
House of Wines Inc. [1764]
Housen and Co. Inc.; G. [1765]
Hub City Distributors Inc. [1766]
Huber Brewing Co., Inc.; Joseph [1767]
Hubert Distributors Inc. [1768]
Huntsville Beverage Co. [1769]
Imperial Beverage Co. [1771]
Intermountain Beverage Company [1773]
Intermountain Distributing Co. [1774]
International Brands West [1775]
Iron City Distributing Company Inc. [1776]
Jackson Hole Distributing [1777]
Jerabek Wholesalers, Inc.; Paul [1780]
Jerome Distribution Inc. [1781]
Jerome Wholesales Inc. [1782]
JMD Beverages [1784]
Jones Distributors Inc.; Bill [1789]
JRB Corp of Lynchburg [1790]
JT Beverage Inc. [1791]
Junction City Distributing Company Inc. [1792]
Katcef Brothers Inc. [1794]
Keith Co.; Ben E. [11590]
Kem Distributing Inc. [1795]
Kenan Oil Co. [11600]
Kent [1796]
KMC Corp. [1799]
Knobel & Son Inc.; John [1800]
Kramer Beverage Company Inc. [1804]
Kunda and Sons Inc.; Watson [1807]
L & L Wine & Liquor Corp. [1808]
Labatt USA Inc. [1809]
Lagomarsino's Inc. [1810]
Lake Beverage Corp. [1811]
Lake Erie Distributors [1812]
Larrabee Brothers Distributing Company Inc. [1813]
Latah Distributors Inc. [1814]
Latrobe Brewing Company Inc. [1815]
Ledo-Dionysus [1816]
Lehrkinds Inc. [1817]
Lenore & Co.; John [1819]
The Lion Brewery, Inc. [1821]
Liquid Town [1822]
Litter Distributing Co. [1823]
Litter Industries Inc. [1824]
Little Rock Distributing Co. [1825]
Luce and Son Inc. [1831]
Lutheran Distributors Inc.; A.M. [1832]
M and M Distributors Inc. [1833]
Madison Bottling Co. [1835]
Magic City Beverage Co. [1836]
Magnolia Distributing Co. [1837]
Magnolia Liquor Lafayette Inc. [1838]
Maine Distributing Co. [1840]
Major Brands [1842]
Major Brands [1844]
Maloof & Co.; Joe G. [1846]
Maple City Ice Co. [1848]
Maris Distributing Co. [1849]
Mark V Distributors Inc. [1850]
Markstein Beverage Co. [1851]
Markstein Beverage Company of Sacramento [1852]
Mason Distributing Company [1854]
Mautino Distributing Company Inc. [1855]
Mayflower Wines & Spirits [1856]
McBride Distributing Co. [1857]
McCormick Beverage Co. [1859]
McGinley Inc.; Wilson [1861]
McLaughlin and Moran Inc. [1862]
McQuade Distributing Company, Inc. [1863]
McQuade Distributing Company Inc. [1864]
Mendez & Co. Inc. [1865]
Merchant du Vin Corp. [1866]
Merrimack Valley Distributing Company Inc. [1867]
Metz Beverage Company Inc. [1869]
Metz Beverage Company Inc. [1870]
Mid-South Malts/Memphis Brews Inc. [1872]
Mid State Distributors Inc. [1873]
Midland Bottling Co. [1874]
Midstate Beverage Inc. [1875]
Midwest Beverage Company Inc. [1876]

Miller Brands [1877]
Miller-Brands-Milwaukee L.L.C.   [1878]
Miller of Dallas Inc. [1879]
Miller Distributing Ft. Worth [1880]
Mirabile Beverage Company Inc. [1881]
Mobile Beer & Wine Co. [1885]
Moffett Co.; Preston I. [1886]
Monarch Beverage Inc. [1888]
Montgomery Beverage Co. [1891]
Moon Distributors Inc. [1892]
Morrey Distributing Co. [1894]
Mounthood Beverage Co. [1895]
Mutual Distributing Co. [1897]
Nackard Wholesale Beverage Co.; Fred [1899]
Nackard Wholesale Beverage Co.; Fred [1900]
National Beverage Company Inc. [1901]
National Distributing Co. [1902]
National Distributing Company, Inc. [1906]
National Distributing Company Inc. [1907]
National Distributing Company Inc. [1909]
National Distributing Inc. [1910]
Nevada Beverage Co. [1912]
New Belgium Brewing Co [1913]
New Hampshire Distributor Inc. [1915]
New World Wines [1916]
Nittany Beverage Co. [1918]
N.K.S. Distributors Inc. [1919]
Nor-Cal Beverage Company Inc. [12015]
Northern Beverage [1920]
Northern Distributing Co. [1921]
Northern Eagle Beverages Inc. [1922]
Northern Virginia Beverage Co. [1923]
Northstar Distributors [1924]
Oak Distributing Company Inc. [1925]
Odell Brewing Co. [1926]
Odom Corp. [1927]
Odom Northwest Beverages [1928]
Old South Distributors Company Inc. [1929]
Oley Distributing Co. [1930]
Olinde and Sons Company Inc.; B. [1931]
Origlio Inc.; Antonio [1934]
O'Sullivan Distributor Inc.; John P. [1935]
Ourrison Inc. [1936]
P & F Distributors Inc. [1937]
Pacific Beverage Company Inc. [25002]
Pacific Wine Co. [1938]
Pacini Wines [1939]
Paw Paw Wine Distributors [1943]
Pearce Co. [1944]
Pearlstine Distributors Inc. [1945]
Pehler Brothers, Inc. [1947]
Penn Distributors Inc. [1948]
Pepin Distributing Co. [1949]
Peraldo Co. Inc.; L.W. [1950]
Peter Pan of Hollywood Inc. [12156]
Peterson Distributing Co. [1951]
Phillips Beverage Co. [1952]
Phoenix Imports Ltd. [1957]
Pike Distributors Inc. [1958]
Pinnacle Distributing Co. [1959]
Pistoresi Distributing Inc. [1960]
Plattsburgh Distributing [1961]
Porter Distributing Co. [1962]
Portland Distributing Co. [1963]
Powers Distributing Company Inc. [1965]
Premier Beverage [1967]
Premier Beverage [1968]
Premier Distributors [1969]
Premium Beverage Company Inc. [1970]
Premium Distributors Incorporated of Washington,
    D.C. L.L.C. [1971]
Quality Beverage Limited Partnership [1974]
Rave Associates [1978]
Redwood Vintners [1980]
Reliance Wine & Spirits [1982]
Richard Distributing Co. [1989]
Riffel & Sons Inc.; C. [1990]
Rinella Beverage Co. [1991]
Ritchie and Page Distributing Company Inc. [1992]
Roach and Smith Distributors, Inc. [1994]
Roanoke Distributing Company Inc. [1995]
Robertson Distributing [1996]
Rose Inc.; Clare [1999]
Royal Hill Co. [2000]
Rudisill Enterprises Inc. [2002]
Saccani Distributing Co. [25031]

Saelens Beverages Inc. [2004]
St. Louis Beverage Co. [2005]
San Joaquin Beverage Co. [2006]
Santoni and Co.; V. [2007]
Sapporo U.S.A. Inc. [2008]
Savannah Distributing Company Inc. [2009]
Scheppers Distributing; N.H. [2011]
Schott Distributing Co. [2013]
Seago Distributing Co. [2015]
Seneca Beverage Corp. [2018]
Service Distributing [2019]
Servidio Beverage Distributing Co. [2020]
Shestokas Distributing Inc. [2022]
Shore Point Distributing Co. [2023]
Sigel Liquor Stores Inc. [2024]
Sinclair Produce Distributing [2026]
Skokie Valley Beverage Co. [2028]
Smoky Mountain Distributors [2030]
Sodak Distributing Co. [2031]
Solman Distributors Inc. [2032]
Southern Illinois Wholesale Company Inc. [2033]
Southern Wine & Spirits [2038]
Southern Wine & Spirits [2039]
Southern Wine and Spirits of California Inc. [2041]
SPADA Enterprises Ltd. [12546]
Spaz Beverage Co. [25039]
Spirit Distributing Co. [2043]
Standard Crown Distributing Co. [2045]
Standard Distributing Company Inc. [2046]
Standard Distributing Company Inc. (Waterloo,
    Iowa) [2047]
Stash Distributing Inc. [2049]
Staton Distributing Co.; Jim [2050]
Stein Distributing Co. [2052]
Stoudt Distributing Co. [2055]
Strathman Sales Company Inc. [2056]
Straub Brewery Company Inc. [2057]
Streva Distributing Co. [2059]
Sun Imports Inc. [2060]
Superior Distributing Co. [2062]
Superior Wines and Liquors Inc. [2063]
Supreme Beverage Co. Inc. [2064]
Sweetwater Distributors Inc. [2065]
Sweetwood Distributing Inc. [2066]
Talladega Beverage Co. [2068]
Taylor Corp.; Jim [2070]
Taylor Distributing Co.; J.J. [2071]
Taylor Distributing Miami Key-West; J.J. [2072]
Terk Distributing [2073]
Terk Distributing [2074]
Thames America Trading Company Ltd. [2076]
Thies and Sons Inc.; William [2077]
Thompson Distributing [2078]
Thompson Distributing Inc. [2079]
Thorpe Distributing Co. [2081]
Three Lakes Distributing Co. [2082]
Tippecanoe Beverages Inc. [2083]
Tri County Coors [2085]
Tryon Distributors [2086]
United Beverage, Inc. [2087]
United Distillers Group Inc. [2088]
United Distillers North America [2089]
United Liquors Corp. [2091]
United Liquors Ltd. [2092]
Valley Distributors [2093]
Valley Distributors Inc. [2094]
Valley Distributors Inc. [2095]
Valley Distributors Inc. [2096]
Valley Sales Company Inc. [2097]
Vehrs Wine Inc. [2100]
Venture South Distributors [2101]
Virginia Imports [2106]
Wallbaum Distributing; Dan [2109]
Wayne Densch Inc. [2110]
Wayne Distributing Co. [2111]
Weatherhead Distributing Co. [2112]
Western Beverage Company Inc. [2113]
Western Distributing Co. [2114]
Western Distributing Company Inc. [2115]
Western Maryland Distributing [2116]
Western Wyoming Beverage Inc. [25051]
Whitehall Company Ltd. [2117]
Whitley Central Distributing Co. [2118]
Williams Distributing Corp. [2120]
Willow Distributors Inc. [2121]
Wilsbach Distributors Inc. [2122]

The Wine Co. [2123]
Wine Distributors Inc. [2124]
Wine Warehouse [2127]
Winneva Distributing Co. Inc. [2131]
Wirtz Corp. [2132]
Wis WetGoods Co. [2133]
Wisconsin Distributors Inc. [2134]
Wisconsin Wholesale Beer Distributor [2135]
Wolfe Distributing Co. [2136]
W.O.W. Distributing Company Inc. [2139]
Wright Wisner Distributing Corp. [2140]
Zeb Pearce Cos. [2144]
Zekes Distributing Co. [2145]

SIC 5182 — Wines & Distilled Beverages

800 Spirits Inc. [1470]
A-B Sales Inc. [1472]
Admiral Wine and Liquor Co. [1474]
Alabama Crown [1476]
Alko Distributors Inc. [1477]
Allied Beverage Group, LLC [1479]
Allied Distributing [1480]
Alpena Beverage Co. Inc. [1482]
Anderson Distributing Co. [1484]
Arizona Beverage Distributing Co. LLC [1486]
Arnold-Sunbelt Beverage Company L.P.;
    Ben [1487]
Athens Distributing Co. [1489]
Atlanta Wholesale Wine Co. [1491]
Atlas Distributing, Inc. [24912]
B & B Imports [1493]
B & G Wholesalers Inc. [1494]
Badger Liquor Company Inc. [1496]
Baker Distributing [1497]
Banfi Products Corp. [1498]
Barcardi-Martini U.S.A., Inc. [1500]
Barton Brands California Inc. [1502]
Barton Inc. [1503]
Baton Rouge Wholesale [1504]
Bauer & Foss, Inc. [1505]
Baum Wine Imports Inc. [1506]
Baumgarten Distributing Company, Inc. [1507]
Beacon Distributing Co. [1510]
Beacon Liquor and Wine [1511]
Beaverhead Bar Supply Inc. [1512]
Beer Import Company [1516]
Beitzell and Company Inc. [1518]
Bennett Distributing Co. Inc. [1520]
Best Brands [1522]
Best Regards Inc. [13316]
Better Brands of Atlanta Inc. [1524]
Better Brands of Milwaukee Inc. [1525]
Beverage Distributors Co. [1527]
Blach Distributing Co. [1531]
Black Forest Distributors Ltd. [1532]
Black Hills Distributing Co. Inc. [1533]
Block Distributing Co. Inc. [1534]
Block Distributing Co. Inc. [1535]
Block Distributing Co. Inc. [1536]
Boisset U.S.A. [1539]
Bologna Brothers [1540]
Bologna Brothers [1541]
Bologna Brothers [1542]
Bonded Spirits Corp. [1544]
Boone Distributing [1545]
Bossi Sales Co. Inc. [1546]
Branded Liquors Inc. [1547]
Brewmaster [1549]
Briggs, Inc. [1550]
Brotherhood America's Oldest Winery Ltd. [1551]
Broudy-Kantor Co. Inc. [1552]
Brown-Forman Beverage Div. [1554]
Buena Vista Winery Inc. [1559]
BYE Inc. [1562]
Cabo Distributing Co., Inc. [1564]
Campari USA Inc. [1567]
Canale Beverages Inc.; D. [1568]
Capital Coors Co. [1571]
Cardinal Distributing [1573]
Carolina Wine Co. [1576]
Carriage House Imports Ltd. [1577]

Carter Distributing Co. [1578]
Casa Italia [10705]
Casa Nuestra Winery [1579]
Castleton Beverage Corp. [1581]
Cellars Beverage Inc. [1582]
Central Beverage Corporation [1584]
Central Distribution Co. [1585]
Central Distributors Inc. [1586]
Central Liquor Co. [1587]
Chaddsford Winery [1588]
Charmer Industries Inc. [1589]
Chateaux-Vineyards [1590]
Chatham Imports Inc. [1591]
Church Point Wholesale Groceries Inc. [10757]
Churchill Distributors [1594]
City Beverage Co. [1595]
City Beverage Co. [1596]
Classic Wine Imports Inc. [1601]
Clausen Distributing [1602]
Colonial Distributors Inc. [1606]
Columbia Distributing Co./Henry Hirsdale/Admiralty
    Beverage Co. [1607]
Considine Sales Co. Inc. [1612]
Constantine Wine [1614]
Consumers of La Salle [1615]
Continental Distributing Company Inc. [1616]
Copley Distributors Inc. [1619]
Cost-U-Less [10847]
Costco Companies, Inc. [10850]
Costello Beverage Co.; J.W. [1620]
Crown Beer Distributors Inc. [1624]
Crown Beverages Inc. [1625]
Crown Inc. Beverage Div. [1628]
Damour; William L. [1634]
De Luca Liquor and Wine Ltd. [1636]
Delaware Importers Inc. [1640]
Denton and Company Ltd.; Robert [1642]
Dettor, Edwards & Morris [1647]
Diamond Distributors [1649]
Diamond State Distributors [1650]
Dimitri Wine & Spirits [1651]
Diversified Imports [1652]
Dixie Beverage Co. [1654]
Domecq Importers Inc. [1656]
Dops, Inc. [1657]
Duplin Wine Cellars [1659]
E-Corp, Inc. [1662]
Eagle Distributors Inc. [1666]
Eber Brothers Wine and Liquor Corp. [1669]
Edison Liquor Corp. [1670]
Edison West Liquor [1671]
Elmira Distributing [1674]
Empire Distributing [1676]
Erwin Distributing Co. [1679]
Evans Distributing Company Inc. [1680]
Fabiano Brothers Inc. [1682]
Famous Brands Distributors Inc. [1683]
Farrell Distributing [1685]
Federal Wine and Liquor Co. [1686]
Fedway Associates Inc. [1687]
Fetzer Vineyards [1688]
Fine Wine Brokers Inc. [1689]
Finnish National Distillers Inc. [1691]
F.L.D. Distributors Inc. [1692]
Fleming [11145]
Food and Spirits Distributing Company Inc. [1693]
Forman Distributing Co. [1695]
Fox Sales Co.; Henry A. [1696]
Friendly Distributors [1698]
Gallup Sales Co. Inc. [1702]
Garco Wine [1704]
General Beverage Sales Co. [1707]
General Distributing Co. [1708]
General Wholesale Co. [1709]
General Wine Co. [1710]
Georgia Crown Distributing [1711]
Georgia Crown Distributing Co. [1712]
Gibson Wine Company Inc. [1713]
Giglio Distributing Company Inc. [1716]
Glazer's of Iowa [1719]
Glazer's Wholesale Drug Co. Inc. [1720]
Globil Inc. [1721]
Goody-Goody Liquor Store Inc. [1727]
Gourmet Wine & Spirits [1728]
Grant and Sons Inc.; William [1729]
Grantham Distributing Company Inc. [1730]

Guinness Import Co. [1737]
Halo Distributing Co. [1742]
Hamburg [1743]
Haubrich Enterprises Inc. [1747]
Heritage House Wines [1752]
Highland Distributing Co. [1756]
Hirst Imports [1759]
House of Wines Inc. [1764]
HSS Group [18522]
Ideal Wine & Spirits Co., Inc. [1770]
Imperial Beverage Co. [1771]
Independent Distribution Services Inc. [15175]
Inlet Distributors [1772]
Iron City Distributing Company Inc. [1776]
Jarboe Sales Co. [1778]
Jaydor Corp. [1779]
Jerabek Wholesalers, Inc.; Paul [1780]
Jet Wine and Spirits Inc. [1783]
JMD Beverages [1784]
Johnson Brothers Co. (St. Paul, Minnesota) [1785]
Johnson Brothers Liquor Co. [1786]
Johnson Brothers Wholesale Liquor [1787]
Johnson Brothers Wholesale Liquor Co. [1788]
JRB Corp of Lynchburg [1790]
Kacher Selections; Robert [1793]
Kent [1796]
Kings Liquor Inc. [1797]
Kiva Direct Distribution Inc. [1798]
KMC Corp. [1799]
Knoxville Beverage Co. [1801]
Kobrand Corp. [1802]
Korbel and Bros. Inc.; F. [1803]
Kronheim and Co.; Milton S. [1805]
Kubota Inc. [1806]
L & L Wine & Liquor Corp. [1808]
Ledo-Dionysus [1816]
Lemma Wine Co. [1818]
Lenore & Co.; John [1819]
Lichtman and Company Inc.; M. [1820]
Liquid Town [1822]
Little Rock Distributing Co. [1825]
Lohr Winery; J. [1826]
Longhorn Liquors, Ltd. [1827]
Lookout Beverages [1828]
Lovotti Brothers [1829]
Luce and Son Inc. [1830]
Luce and Son Inc. [1831]
Maddalena Vineyard/San Antonio Winery [1834]
Madison Bottling Co. [1835]
Magnolia Liquor Lafayette Inc. [1838]
Magnolia Marketing Co. [1839]
Maisons Marques and Domaines USA Inc. [1841]
Major Brands [1842]
Major Brands [1843]
Major Brands [1844]
Major Brands-Cape Girardeau [1845]
Manhattan Distributing Co. [1847]
Martini and Prati Wines Inc. [1853]
Mayflower Wines & Spirits [1856]
McClaskeys Wine Spirits & Cigars
    Distributor [1858]
McCormick Distilling Company Inc. [1860]
Mendez & Co. Inc. [1865]
Merrimack Valley Distributing Company Inc. [1867]
Metabran [1868]
Mid-America Wine Co. [1871]
Midwest Beverage Company Inc. [1876]
Miramar Trading International Inc. [1882]
Mirassou Sales Co. [1883]
Missouri Conrad Liquors [1884]
Mobile Beer & Wine Co. [1885]
Mohawk Distilled Products L.P. [1887]
Monarch Beverage Inc. [1888]
Monarch Wine Company of Georgia [1889]
Monsieur Touton Selections, LTD [1890]
Montgomery Beverage Co. [1891]
Moon Distributors Inc. [1892]
Moroney, Inc.; James [1893]
Mounthood Beverage Co. [1895]
MRR Traders, Ltd. [1896]
Mutual Distributing Co. [1897]
Myerson Candy Co.; Ben [1898]
Nackard Wholesale Beverage Co.; Fred [1899]
National Distributing Co. [1902]
National Distributing Co. [1903]
National Distributing Co. [1904]

National Distributing Co. [1905]
National Distributing Company, Inc. [1906]
National Distributing Company Inc. [1907]
National Distributing Co. Inc. [1908]
National Distributing Company Inc. [1909]
National Distributing Inc. [1910]
National Wine and Spirits Corp. [3017]
Nebraska Wine & Spirits Inc. [1911]
New England Wine & Spirits [1914]
New World Wines [1916]
Nichols and Company Inc.; Austin [1917]
N.K.S. Distributors Inc. [1919]
Northern Beverage [1920]
Odom Corp. [1927]
Olinger Distributing Co. [1932]
Olinger Distributing Co. [1933]
Pacific Wine Co. [1938]
Pacini Wines [1939]
Paddington Corp. [1940]
Paramount Brands, Inc. [1941]
Paramount Liquor Co. [1942]
Paw Paw Wine Distributors [1943]
Pearlstine Distributors Inc. [1945]
Peerless Importers Inc. [1946]
Pepin Distributing Co. [1949]
Phillips Beverage Co. [1952]
Phillips Distributing Corp. [1953]
Phillips and Sons (Eau Claire, Wisconsin);
    Ed [1954]
Phillips and Sons; Ed [1955]
Phillips & Sons of N.D.; Ed [1956]
Pinnacle Distributing Co. [1959]
Pistoresi Distributing Inc. [1960]
Post Familie Vineyards and Winery [1964]
Premier Beverage [1966]
Premier Beverage [1967]
Premier Beverage [1968]
Premium Beverage Company Inc. [1970]
Preston Premium Wines [1972]
Purity Products Inc. [1973]
Quality Brands Inc. [1975]
Racine Vineyard Products [1976]
Raden and Sons Inc.; G. [1977]
Rave Associates [1978]
Rays Beverage Co. [1979]
Redwood Vintners [1980]
Reitman Industries [1981]
Reliance Wine & Spirits [1982]
Remy Amerique Inc. [1983]
Republic Beverage Co. [1984]
Reuben's Wines & Spirits [1985]
Rheinpfalz Imports Ltd. [1986]
Rhoades Wine Group, Inc. [1987]
Rhode Island Distributing Co. [1988]
Richard Distributing Co. [1989]
Riffel & Sons Inc.; C. [1990]
Riverside Liquors & Wine [1993]
Roach and Smith Distributors, Inc. [1994]
Roanoke Distributing Company Inc. [1995]
Rochester Liquor Corp. [1997]
Romano Brothers Beverage Co. [1998]
Royal Wine Co. [2001]
S & C Importing [2003]
Saelens Beverages Inc. [2004]
Santoni and Co.; V. [2007]
Savannah Distributing Company Inc. [2009]
Sazerac Company Inc. [2010]
Schieffelin and Somerset Co. [2012]
Seagram Classics Wine Co. [2016]
Select Wines & Spirits Co. [2017]
Service Distributing [2019]
Shaw-Ross International Inc. [2021]
Shore Point Distributing Co. [2023]
Sigel Liquor Stores Inc. [2024]
Silverstate Co. [2025]
SJL Beverage Co. [2027]
Slocum & Sons Co. [2029]
Sodak Distributing Co. [2031]
Southern Illinois Wholesale Company Inc. [2033]
A Southern Season [12542]
Southern Wine Co. [2034]
Southern Wine & Spirits [2035]
Southern Wine & Spirits [2036]
Southern Wine & Spirits [2037]
Southern Wine & Spirits [2038]
Southern Wine & Spirits [2039]

Southern Wine and Spirits of America [2040]
Southern Wine and Spirits of California Inc. [2041]
SPADA Enterprises Ltd. [12546]
Spadafore Distributing Co. [2042]
Standard Beverage Corp. [2044]
Standard Crown Distributing Co. [2045]
Standard Distributing Company Inc. (Waterloo, Iowa) [2047]
Star Distributors [2048]
Staton Distributing Co.; Jim [2050]
Stefanelli Distributing [2051]
Sterling Distributing Co. [2053]
Stimson Lane Wine and Spirits Ltd. [2054]
Strauss Distributing [2058]
Sun Imports Inc. [2060]
Sunbelt Beverage Company L.L.C. [2061]
Superior Wines and Liquors Inc. [2063]
Sweetwater Distributors Inc. [2065]
T & M Inc. [2067]
Talladega Beverage Co. [2068]
Tarrant Distributors Inc. [2069]
Terk Distributing [2073]
Terk Distributing [2074]
Terk Distributing [2075]
Thames America Trading Company Ltd. [2076]
Thornton Wine Imports; J.W. [2080]
Todhunter Imports Ltd. [2084]
Tryon Distributors [2086]
Tung Pec Inc. [12769]
United Beverage Inc. [12790]
United Beverage, Inc. [2087]
United Distillers Group Inc. [2088]
United Distillers North America [2089]
United Distributors, Inc. [2090]
United Liquors Corp. [2091]
United Liquors Ltd. [2092]
Valley Distributors Inc. [2094]
Valley View Vineyard [2098]
Valley Vintners Inc. [2099]
Vehrs Wine Inc. [2100]
Vertner Smith Co. [2102]
Vintage House Merchants [2103]
Vintage House Merchants, Inc. [2104]
Vintwood International Ltd. [2105]
Virginia Imports [2106]
Viva Vino Import Corp. [2107]
Walker Inc.; M.S. [2108]
Western Distributing Co. [2114]
Whitehall Company Ltd. [2117]
Wildman and Sons Ltd.; Frederick [2119]
The Wine Co. [2123]
Wine Distributors Inc. [2124]
The Wine Merchant [2125]
Wine Trends, Inc. [2126]
Wine Warehouse [2127]
Winebow, Inc. [2128]
Wines and Spirits International [2129]
Winesellers Ltd. [2130]
Wirtz Corp. [2132]
World Wide Wine and Spirit Importers Inc. [2137]
Worldwide Wines, Inc. [2138]
Wyoming Liquor Division [2141]
Young's Market Co. [2142]
Young's Market Co. [2143]
Zekes Distributing Co. [2145]
Zumot and Son [2146]

SIC 5191 — Farm Supplies

A & K Feed and Grain Company Inc. [17670]
Abell Inc. [181]
Ada Farmers Exchange Co. [17672]
Ada Feed and Seed Inc. [182]
Adair Feed and Grain Co. [17673]
Adams County Co-operative Association Inc. [183]
Adams Tractor Co.; Carroll [185]
Adikes Inc.; J. & L. [187]
Adler Seeds Inc. [188]
Adrian Wheat Growers Inc. [189]
Aeon International Corp. [190]
AFI [191]
AG Cooperative Service Inc. [17678]
AG Distributors, Inc. [192]
Ag-Land FS Inc. [194]

AG ONE CO-OP Inc. [196]
Ag Partners Co. Cannon Falls Div. [17679]
AG Partners L.L.C. [197]
Ag Services of America Inc. [199]
AG Systems Inc. [200]
Ag Valley Cooperative [201]
Agaland CO-OP Inc. [202]
AgBest Cooperative Inc. [22025]
Agco Inc. [204]
Agco Inc. [10344]
Agland Coop [17681]
Agland Coop [205]
Agland Cooperative [206]
Agland Cooperative [207]
Agland Cooperative [208]
Agland Cooperative [22026]
Agland Inc. [209]
Agri-Sales Associates Inc. [211]
Agri-Tech F.S. Inc. [212]
AgriBioTech Inc. [213]
Agriland F.S. Inc. [215]
AgriPride F.S. [216]
AgriPro Seeds Inc. [17687]
Agriturf Inc. [217]
Agsco Inc. [218]
Albert City Elevator Inc. [220]
Alexander's Nursery [14799]
Allen Brothers Feed Inc. [17690]
Allen County Cooperative Association [222]
Alliance Agronomics Inc. [225]
Allied International Marketing Corp. [17692]
Allied International Marketing Corp. [226]
Allied Seed Co-Op, Inc. [227]
Alltech Inc. [228]
Alma Farmers Cooperative Association [229]
Alma Farmers Union Cooperative [230]
American Farm & Feed [232]
American Feed and Farm Supply Inc. [233]
American Pride Coop [234]
American Rice Growers Cooperative Association [235]
American Rice Growers Cooperative Association [236]
Ames Co. [237]
Ampac Seed Co. [238]
Amvac Chemical Corp. [239]
Andale Farmers Cooperative Company Inc. [17699]
Andersons Inc. [242]
Androw Fertilizer [243]
Andres and Wilton Farmers Grain and Supply Co. [17701]
Anfinson's Inc. [244]
Anthony Farmers Cooperative and Elevator Co. [17702]
Apache Farmers Cooperative [245]
Arbordale Home and Garden Showplace [247]
Archer Cooperative Grain Co. [248]
Argent Chemical Laboratories Inc. [251]
Arizona Bag Co. LLC [252]
Arizona Grain Inc. [17705]
Arkansas Valley Seed Co. [254]
Arkfeld Manufacturing & Distributing Company Inc. [255]
Arthur Companies Inc. [257]
Ashby Equity Association [258]
Ashland Farmers Elevator Co. [17706]
Associated Farmers Cooperative [259]
Assumption Cooperative Grain Co. [10459]
Atherton Grain Co. [10462]
Atlantic F.E.C. Inc. [4328]
Auglaize Farmers Cooperative [261]
Augusta Cooperative Farm Bureau [262]
Aurora Cooperative Elevator Co. [263]
Austinville Elevator [17713]
AVM Products, Inc. [27076]
B and W Farm Center Inc. [266]
Bacon Products Co. Inc. [267]
Badger Farmers Cooperative [268]
Badgerland Farm Center [269]
Bailey Seed Company, Inc. [270]
Baker Agri Sales Inc. [17718]
Baker and Brother Inc.; H.J. [271]
Bakersfield AG Co. Inc. [274]
Barenbrug U.S.A. [277]
Barham and Co.; J.T. [17722]

Barry Grain and Feed Inc. [280]
Bartlett Cooperative Association Inc. [281]
Bascom Elevator Supply Association [282]
Battle Creek Farmers Cooperative [283]
Beachley Hardy Seed Co. [286]
Beardsley Farmers Elevator Co. [287]
Beattie Farmers Union Cooperative Association [288]
Bedford Farm Bureau Cooperative [290]
Bedford Farmers Cooperative [291]
Bee County Cooperative Association Inc. [292]
Belle Plaine Cooperative [295]
Belstra Milling Co. Inc. [296]
Benton County Cooperative [300]
Berlin Farmers Elevator [302]
Berthold Farmers Elevator Co. [304]
Bertrand Cooperative [305]
Bethea Distributing Inc. [306]
Big Corn Cooperative Marketing Association Inc. [308]
Big Horn Cooperative Market Association Inc. [309]
Big Stone County Cooperative [310]
Big Valley AG Services Inc. [314]
Binford Farmers Union Grain [316]
Bion Environmental Technologies Inc. [23087]
Bixby Feed Mill Inc. [319]
Blanchard Valley Farmers Cooperative [17737]
Bleyhl Farm Service [322]
Blount Farmers Cooperative [323]
Bluestem Farm and Ranch Supply Inc. [324]
Bluff Springs Farmers Elevator Co. [17740]
Bode Cooperative [325]
Boettcher Enterprises Inc. [326]
Bolivar Farmers Exchange [327]
Bond County Services Co. [328]
Bondurant Grain Company Inc.; D.E. [17743]
Bonus Crop Fertilizer Inc. [329]
Booker Equity Union Exchange Inc. [330]
Boone County Farm Bureau Cooperative Inc. [22086]
Booneville Cooperative Elevator Co. [331]
Botkin Grain Co. Inc. [27089]
Bradfordton Cooperative Association Inc. [17745]
Brandt Consolidated Inc. [333]
Brewer Environmental Industries Inc. [335]
Bricelyn Elevator Association [17746]
Brooks Farmers Cooperative Association [17748]
Brotherton Seed Company Inc. [338]
Brown County Co-op [339]
Brown County Cooperative Association [340]
Browning Equipment Inc. [343]
Browning Seed Inc. [344]
Brownton Cooperative Agriculture Center [345]
Bryant and Son Inc.; Otis [347]
Buckeye Cooperative Elevator Co. [17752]
Buckeye Cooperative Elevator Co. [10637]
Buckeye Countrymark Corp. [348]
Buckman Farmers Cooperative Creamery [350]
Buhrman and Son Inc. [351]
Burchinal Cooperative Society [352]
Burlingham and Sons; E.F. [353]
Burnett Dairy Cooperative [17756]
C-D Farm Service Company Inc. [354]
C and J Service Co. [22100]
CADCO Div. [355]
Cairo Cooperative Equity Exchange [356]
Cal-West Seeds Inc. [358]
Calarco Inc. [359]
Caldwell Milling Company Inc. [10670]
Caldwell Supply Company Inc. [17759]
Caledonia Farmers Elevator Co., Lake Odessa Branch [362]
Calhoun County Cooperative [363]
California Ammonia Co. [364]
Calumet Industries Inc. [17760]
Calumet Industries Inc. [365]
Canadian Equity Cooperative [368]
Cannon Valley Cooperative [370]
Canton Mills Inc. [371]
Carco International Inc. [372]
Cariba International Corp. [10700]
Carroll Farmers Cooperative [374]
Carrollton Farmers Elevator Co. [10704]
Carter Service Center [375]
Cascade Seed Co. [376]

Cass County Service Co. [378]
Castle of Stockton; A.L. [379]
Castlewood Farmers Elevator [17767]
Cedar Valley FS Inc. [381]
Cenex Harvest States [382]
Cenex Harvest States Cooperative [383]
Cenex/Land O'Lakes AG Services [384]
Center Valley Cooperative Association [22122]
Centra Sota Cooperative [385]
Central Alabama Cooperative Farms Inc. [386]
Central Connecticut Cooperative Farmers
    Association [17771]
Central Cooperatives Inc. [387]
Central Counties Cooperative [388]
Central Farm Supply Inc. [389]
Central Farmers Cooperative [390]
Central Garden and Pet Co. [391]
Central Garden and Pet Supply Inc. [392]
Central Garden and Pet Supply Inc. [393]
Central Garden & Pet Supply Inc. [27107]
Central Garden Supplies [394]
Central Iowa Cooperative [396]
Central Minnesota Cooperative [397]
Central Rivers Cooperative [399]
Central Wisconsin Cooperative [401]
Cereal Byproducts Co. [404]
Cereal Byproducts Co. [405]
Chase Trade, Inc. [407]
Chem Gro of Houghton Inc. [408]
Chemi-Trol Chemical Co. [410]
Cheney Cooperative Elevator Association [411]
Cherry Farms Inc. [412]
Chester Inc. [414]
Christian County Farmers Supply Co. [416]
Claiborne Farmers Cooperative [418]
Clarence Cooperative Company Inc. [419]
Clarenie Cooperative Elevator Co. [420]
Clarion Farmers Elevator Cooperative [421]
Clark Landmark Inc. [423]
Clearwater Grain Co. [424]
Clinton AG Service Inc. [427]
Clinton Landmark Inc. [17783]
Clyde Cooperative Association [428]
Co-HG [429]
Co-op Country Farmers Elevator [17785]
Co-op Country Farmers Elevator [10780]
Coastal Plains Farmers Co-op Inc. [431]
Cocke Farmers Cooperative Inc. [432]
Coffey and Sons Inc.; Bill [433]
Cold Spring Cooperative Creamery [434]
Collingwood Grain Inc. [435]
Colwell Cooperative [17787]
Concordia Farmers Cooperative Co. [437]
Conrad Cooperative [438]
Conrad Implement Co. [439]
Consolidated Cooperative Inc. [17791]
Consolidated Cooperatives Inc. [440]
Consumer Cooperative of Walworth County [441]
Consumer Oil and Supply Co. [442]
Consumers Cooperative [443]
Consumers Cooperative Exchange [444]
Coop Country Partners [445]
Coop Services Inc. [446]
Cooperative Agricultural Center [447]
Cooperative Agricultural Services Inc. [448]
Cooperative Association No. 1 Inc. [449]
Cooperative Elevator Co. [451]
Cooperative Elevator, Sebewaing [17795]
Cooperative Elevator Supply Co. [452]
Cooperative Exchange [453]
Cooperative Feed Dealer Inc. [454]
Cooperative Grain and Product Co. [455]
Cooperative Grain and Supply [456]
Cooperative Grain and Supply [17796]
Cooperative Grain and Supply [17797]
Cooperative Grain and Supply [457]
Cooperative Oil Association [22168]
Cooperative Oil Co. [458]
Cooperative Service Oil Co. [459]
Cooperative Services of Clark County [460]
Cooperative Union Mercantile Co. Inc. [461]
Coos Grange Supply Co. [462]
Cornbelt Chemical Co. [4366]
Cory Orchard and Turf Div. [464]
Cottage Grove Cooperative [465]
Cottonwood Cooperative Oil Co. [22175]

Coulter Elevator [17801]
Country Springs Farmers [10859]
Country Star Coop [17802]
Countrymark Cooperative Inc. [466]
County General [468]
County Line Co-op [469]
Craighead Farmers Cooperative [17803]
Creameries Blending Inc. [471]
Crescent Cooperative Association [472]
Crestland Cooperative [473]
Creston Feed and Grain Co. [474]
Crites-Moscow Growers Inc. [475]
Crockett Farmers Cooperative Co. [476]
Crookston Farmers Cooperative [477]
Crystal Cooperative Inc. [479]
CT Wholesale [480]
Cullman Seed and Feed Co. [481]
Cumberland Farmers Union Cooperative [482]
Cumberland Valley Cooperative Association [483]
Curtis & Curtis, Inc. [484]
Custer Grain Co. [485]
Dairyland Seed Company Inc. [486]
Dakota Pride Coop [487]
Dakota Pride Cooperative [22187]
Dalhart Consumers Fuel and Grain Association
    Inc. [17808]
Dallas County Farmers Exchange [488]
Dalton Cooperative Creamery Association [491]
Danco Prairie FS Cooperative [492]
Danvers Farmers Elevator Co. [493]
Danvers Farmers Elevator Co. [10907]
Danville Cooperative Association [494]
Dassel Cooperative Dairy Association [495]
Davidson Farmers Cooperative [497]
Davies Service Co.; Jo [498]
Deerwood Rice Grain Produce [10937]
DeKalb-Pfizer Genetics, Crawfordsville Div. [17815]
Dell Rapids Co-op Grain [505]
DeLong Company Inc. [506]
Del's Farm Supply [508]
Delta Purchasing Federation [511]
Desoto County Cooperative [516]
Deuel County Farmers Union Oil Co. [22199]
Dewar Elevator Co. [517]
Dickson Farmers Cooperative [519]
Dodge City Cooperative Exchange Inc. [2554]
Dollar Farm Products Co. [522]
Donley Seed Co. [523]
Donovan Farmers Cooperative Elevator
    Inc. [17819]
Door County Cooperative Inc. [525]
Dorchester Farmers Cooperative [17820]
Douglas Products and Packaging Co. [4374]
Drummond Cooperative Elevator Inc. [526]
Dubois County Farm Bureau Cooperative [527]
DuBois Elevator Co. [528]
Dye Seed Ranch [531]
Dyer Lauderdale Co-op [532]
East Central Cooperative Inc. [534]
East Central Iowa Cooperative [11016]
East Jordan Cooperative Co. [22218]
East West Connect Inc. [535]
Eastern Europe, Inc. [536]
Eastern Farmers Coop [537]
Ebbert's Field Seed Inc. [540]
Eckroat Seed Co. [541]
Edison Non-Stock Cooperative [542]
Edmonson Wheat Growers Inc. [17826]
Edon Farmers Cooperative Association Inc. [543]
Elberta Farmers Cooperative [544]
Elbow Lake Cooperative Grain [545]
Elburn Cooperative Co. [17829]
Eldridge Cooperative Co. [17830]
Elkhart Cooperative Equity Exchange [11040]
Elkhart Farmers Cooperative Association Inc. [546]
Ellsworth Farmers Union Cooperative Oil Co. [549]
Ellsworth-William Cooperative Co. [17831]
Elmore County Farms Exchange [27128]
Elwood Line Grain and Fertilizer Co. [17832]
Emma Cooperative Elevator Co. [27129]
Emma Cooperative Elevator Co. [551]
EMP Co-op Inc. [17833]
Empire N.A. Inc. [552]
Equity Cooperative of Amery Inc. [553]
Equity Elevator and Trading Co. [17835]
Equity Supply Co. [554]

Erie Crawford Cooperative [555]
Evangeline Farmers Cooperative [17838]
Evergreen Mills Inc. [556]
Ezell-Key Grain Company Inc. [557]
Fairdale Farmers Cooperative Elevator Co. [560]
Faithway Feed Company Inc. [27130]
Far-Mor Cooperative [22252]
Farm Service Company Inc. [564]
Farm Service Cooperative Inc. [565]
Farm Service Inc. [566]
Farm Services Inc. [567]
Farmers Co-op Elevator and Mercantile
    Association [17840]
Farmers Coop Association of Jackson, Sherburn,
    Spring Lake & Trimont [568]
Farmers Cooperative [569]
Farmers Cooperative [570]
Farmers Cooperative Association [572]
Farmers Cooperative Association [573]
Farmers Cooperative Association [574]
Farmers Cooperative Association [575]
Farmers Cooperative Association [576]
Farmers Cooperative Association [577]
Farmers Cooperative Association [578]
Farmers Cooperative Association [579]
Farmers Cooperative Association [580]
Farmers Cooperative Association [17842]
Farmers Cooperative Association [581]
Farmers Cooperative Association [17843]
Farmers Cooperative Association [582]
Farmers Cooperative Association [583]
Farmers Cooperative Association [584]
Farmers Cooperative Association [585]
Farmers Cooperative Association [17844]
Farmers Cooperative Association [17845]
Farmers Cooperative Association [17846]
Farmers Cooperative Association (Okarche,
    Oklahoma) [4386]
Farmers Cooperative Association (York,
    Nebraska) [17847]
Farmers Cooperative Business Association [586]
Farmers Cooperative Co. [587]
Farmers Cooperative Co. [588]
Farmers Cooperative Co. [589]
Farmers Cooperative Co. [590]
Farmers Cooperative Co. [591]
Farmers Cooperative Co. [592]
Farmers Cooperative Co. [593]
Farmers Cooperative Co. [594]
Farmers Cooperative Co. [595]
Farmers Cooperative Co. [17849]
Farmers Cooperative Co. [596]
Farmers Cooperative Co. [597]
Farmers Cooperative Co. [598]
Farmers Cooperative Co. [599]
Farmers Cooperative Co. [17851]
Farmers Cooperative Co. [600]
Farmers Cooperative Co. [601]
Farmers Cooperative Co. [17852]
Farmers Cooperative Co. [602]
Farmers Cooperative Co. [603]
Farmers Cooperative Co. [17853]
Farmers Cooperative Co. (Britt, Iowa) [11096]
Farmers Cooperative Co. (Dike, Iowa) [17854]
Farmers Cooperative Co. (Hinton, Iowa) [17855]
Farmers Cooperative Company Inc. [604]
Farmers Cooperative Co. (Readlyn, Iowa) [17857]
Farmers Cooperative Co. (Woolstock,
    Iowa) [17858]
Farmers Cooperative of El Campo [17860]
Farmers Cooperative Elevator [605]
Farmers Cooperative Elevator [606]
Farmers Cooperative Elevator [607]
Farmers Cooperative Elevator [608]
Farmers Cooperative Elevator [17861]
Farmers Cooperative Elevator [609]
Farmers Cooperative Elevator Association [17863]
Farmers Cooperative Elevator Association [610]
Farmers Cooperative Elevator Association [611]
Farmers Cooperative Elevator Co. [612]
Farmers Cooperative Elevator Co. [613]
Farmers Cooperative Elevator Co. [614]
Farmers Cooperative Elevator Co. [615]
Farmers Cooperative Elevator Co. [616]
Farmers Cooperative Elevator Co. [617]
Farmers Cooperative Elevator Co. [618]

Farmers Cooperative Elevator Co. [17866]
Farmers Cooperative Elevator Co. [619]
Farmers Cooperative Elevator Co. [620]
Farmers Cooperative Elevator Co. [17867]
Farmers Cooperative Elevator Co. [621]
Farmers Cooperative Elevator Co. [17868]
Farmers Cooperative Elevator Co. Lake Lillian
    Div. [622]
Farmers Cooperative Elevator (Martelle,
    Iowa) [17870]
Farmers Cooperative Elevator and Supply [17871]
Farmers Cooperative Exchange [623]
Farmers Cooperative Exchange [624]
Farmers Cooperative Exchange [625]
Farmers Cooperative Exchange [626]
Farmers Cooperative Exchange [627]
Farmers Cooperative Exchange (Elgin,
    Nebraska) [11101]
Farmers Cooperative Grain Association [628]
Farmers Cooperative Grain Association [629]
Farmers Cooperative Grain and Seed [17873]
Farmers Cooperative Grain and Seed Co. [630]
Farmers Cooperative Grain and Supply Co. [631]
Farmers Cooperative Grain and Supply Co. [632]
Farmers Cooperative Inc. [633]
Farmers Cooperative Market [634]
Farmers Cooperative (Odebolt, Iowa) [17876]
Farmers Cooperative Oil Co. [636]
Farmers Cooperative of Pilger [17877]
Farmers Cooperative Society [637]
Farmers Cooperative Society (Sioux Center,
    Iowa) [17878]
Farmers Cooperative Supply and Shipping
    Association [638]
Farmers Cooperative Trading Co. [639]
Farmers Cooperative Union [640]
Farmers Elevator Co. [641]
Farmers Elevator Co. [642]
Farmers Elevator Co. [643]
Farmers Elevator Co. [17882]
Farmers Elevator Company of Avoca [644]
Farmers Elevator Cooperative [645]
Farmers Elevator of Fergus Falls [17887]
Farmers Elevator Grain and Supply [646]
Farmers Elevator and Supply Co. [17889]
Farmers Elevator Supply Co. [647]
Farmers Exchange [648]
Farmers Exchange Cooperative [649]
Farmers Gin Company Inc. [17891]
Farmers Grain Co. [651]
Farmers Grain Company of Charlotte [652]
Farmers Grain Company of Dorans [17893]
Farmers Grain Company Inc. [653]
Farmers Grain Cooperative [654]
Farmers Grain Cooperative [655]
Farmers Grain Exchange [656]
Farmers Grain and Supply Company Inc. [17899]
Farmers Grain and Supply Company Inc. [657]
Farmers Soybean Corp. [17903]
Farmers Supply Cooperative-AAL [658]
Farmers Union Cooperative [22258]
Farmers Union Cooperative Association [660]
Farmers Union Cooperative Association of Howard
    County [661]
Farmers Union Cooperative (Harvard,
    Nebraska) [11105]
Farmers Union Elevator [663]
Farmers Union Grain Cooperative [17910]
Farmers Union Oil Co. [664]
Farmers Union Oil Co. [22261]
Farmers Union Oil Co. [665]
Farmers Union Oil Co. [666]
Farmers Union Oil Co. [22266]
Farmers Union Oil Co. [667]
Farmers Union Oil Co. (Crookston,
    Minnesota) [668]
Farmers Union Oil Co. (Ellendale, North
    Dakota) [17911]
Farmers Union Oil Co. (Great Falls,
    Montana) [4387]
Farmers Union Oil Co. (Starbuck, Minnesota) [670]
Farmers Union Oil Co. (Willmar, Minnesota) [671]
Farmland Service Cooperative [17914]
Farmway Cooperative Inc. [672]
Fayette County Cooperative Inc. [674]
Federation Cooperative [675]

Feed Products Inc. [676]
Feed Seed and Farm Supplies Inc. [677]
Ferrin Cooperative Equity Exchange [680]
Fessenden Cooperative Association [17917]
Fey Inc. [681]
Fiebiger and Son Inc.; Jim [682]
Fieldcrest Fertilizer Inc. [683]
First Cooperative Association [11132]
First Farmers Cooperative Elevator [685]
FirstMiss Fertilizer Inc. [686]
Fisher Farmers Grain and Coal Co. [17919]
Fisher & Son Co. Inc. [689]
Fitzgerald Ltd. [690]
Five County Farmers Association [691]
Florida Seed Company Inc. [693]
Flusche Supply Inc. [695]
Fly Guard Systems Inc. [4392]
Forbes Implement Supply Inc.; Keith [697]
Forbes Seed & Grain [698]
Ford and Sons Inc.; C.D. [699]
Fort Recovery Equity Exchange Co. [27133]
Foxhome Elevator Co. [700]
Franklin County Grain Grower Inc. [701]
Franklin Farmers Cooperative [702]
Franklin Feed and Supply Co. [703]
Fredericksburg Farmers Cooperative [705]
Fremont Cooperative Produce Co. [706]
Frenchman Valley Farmer's Cooperative [17927]
Frenchman Valley Farmer's Cooperative [708]
Frick's Services Inc. [17929]
Frontier Cooperative Co. [17930]
Frontier Hybrids [709]
Frontier Trading Inc. [714]
Fruit Growers Supply Co. [715]
Fruita Consumers Cooperative [716]
F.S. Adams Inc. [717]
FS Cooperative Inc. [718]
Full Circle, Inc. [719]
Galesberg Cooperative Elevator Co. [720]
Garden Exchange Limited [13720]
Garden Grove Nursery Inc. [721]
Garden Grow Co [722]
Garden Valley Coop. [723]
Garroutte Products [726]
Gateway Co-Op [17936]
Geddie; Thomas E. [730]
Gehman Feed Mill Inc. [731]
Genesee Union Warehouse Company Inc. [17938]
Geneva Elevator Co. [733]
Gibson Farmers Cooperative [738]
Gilbert Co.; A.L. [739]
Giles Farmers Cooperative Inc. [740]
Ging and Co. [17941]
Glasgow Cooperative Association [742]
Globe Seed and Feed Company Inc. [743]
Gold-Eagle Cooperative [744]
Golden Sun Feeds Inc. Danville Div. [746]
Gooding Seed Co. [750]
Graco Fertilizer Co. [751]
Grain Growers Cooperative (Cimarron,
    Kansas) [17952]
Grain Land Co-op [17953]
Grain Land Cooperative [17954]
Grain Processing Corp. [753]
Grain Storage Corp. [754]
Grainland Cooperative [17956]
Grand River Cooperative Inc. [756]
Grange Supply Company Inc. [757]
Granite Seed [758]
Grassland West [760]
Graymont Cooperative Association Inc. [761]
Great Bend Cooperative Association [17960]
Great Plains Co-op [17961]
Greeley Elevator Co. [17962]
Green Seed Co. [764]
Green Seed Co. [17963]
Green Valley Seed [765]
Green Velvet Sod Farms [766]
Greene Farmers Cooperative [767]
Gries Seed Farms Inc. [768]
Grosz; Leland [770]
Grove City Farmers Exchange Co. [771]
Growers Cooperative Inc. [772]
Growers Fertilizer Corp. [773]
Growmark [775]
Growmark [776]

GROWMARK Inc. [17965]
Gully Tri-Coop Association [778]
HAACO Inc. [779]
Hahn and Phillips Grease Company Inc. [17968]
Hale Center Wheat Growers Inc. [781]
Halsey Seed Co. [783]
Halstad Elevator Co. [17972]
Hamilton County Farm Bureau [784]
Hansen and Peterson Inc. [787]
Hansmeier and Son Inc. [788]
Harco Distributing Co. [17974]
Hardeman Fayette Farmers Cooperative [790]
Hardy Cooperative Elevator Co. [17975]
Hardy Cooperative Elevator Co. [11378]
Harmony Agri Services [791]
Harmony Co-op [17976]
Harmony Country Cooperatives [792]
Hart Seed Co.; Charles C. [796]
Harvest Land Cooperative Inc. [797]
Harvest States Cooperatives. Canton Div. [798]
Haverhill Cooperative [17984]
Haviland Agricultural Inc. [4410]
Hawkeye Seed Company Inc. [27147]
Hawkeye Seed Company Inc. [802]
Hayward Cooperative [804]
Heart of Iowa Coop. [11404]
Heart Seed [806]
Heartland Co-op [807]
Heartland Co-op (Trumbull, Nebraska) [17986]
Heartland Cooperative Inc. [808]
Hector Farmers Elevator [17987]
Hector Turf [810]
Helena Chemical Company Hughes [811]
Helena Wholesale Inc. [11407]
Hempstead County Farmers Association [813]
Hennepin Cooperative Seed Exchange
    Inc. [17990]
Henry Farmers Cooperative Inc. [814]
Henry Service Co. [22345]
Hereford Grain Corp. [17992]
Heritage FS Inc. [815]
Heritage F.S. Inc. [22346]
Herkimer Cooperative Business
    Association [17993]
Hewitt Brothers Inc. [817]
Hi-Line Fertilizer Inc. [819]
High Plains Cooperative Association [821]
Highway Agricultural Services Inc. [822]
Hill and Co., Inc.; Geo. W. [823]
Hill Grain Co. Inc.; C.F. [17999]
Hills Beaver Creek Coop Farm Service [824]
Hills Beaver Creek Cooperative Farm
    Service [825]
Hilo Farmer's Exchange [14887]
Hoffman Cooperative Oil Association [829]
Hoffman and Reed Inc. [830]
Holden's Foundation Seeds L.L.C. [832]
Holdrege Seed and Farm Supply Inc. [833]
Holmquist Grain and Lumber Co. [18002]
Home Oil Co. [22358]
Hopkinsville Elevator Co. [11460]
Horizon [837]
Horn Seed Company Inc. [838]
Houston Moneycreek Cooperative [840]
Howard County Equity Cooperative Inc. [841]
Hull Cooperative Association [11475]
Humphreys Coop Tipton Location [18007]
Hunter Grain Co. [845]
Huntington County Farm Cooperative [846]
Husch and Husch Inc. [847]
Huskers Coop. [11481]
Hutchinson Coop Elevator [18009]
Hydro Agri North America Inc. [849]
Illini F.S. Inc. [22371]
Illinois Agricultural Association [851]
Independent Rental, Inc. [853]
Indiana Seed Co. [855]
Industrial Fumigant Co. [856]
Ingredient Resource Corp. [858]
Integrated World Enterprises [859]
Intermountain Farmers Association [861]
International Agricultural Associates, Inc. [862]
International Seeds, Inc. [865]
Interstate Payco Seed Co. [866]
Iowa River Farm Service Inc. [868]
Iowa Veterinary Supply Co. [869]

IQ Holdings Inc. [14133]
IQ Products Co. [2798]
Iuka Cooperative Inc. [18015]
J & E Feed Distributors Inc. [872]
J & R Mercantile Ltd. [18017]
Jacklin Seed Co. [873]
Jacklin Seed Co. [874]
Jacklin Seed Simplot Turf & Horticulture [875]
Jackson-Jennings Farm Bureau
  Cooperative [22381]
Jacob's Store Inc. [877]
James Agriculture Center Inc. [878]
Jasper County Farm Bureau Cooperative [18022]
Jasper Farmers Exchange Inc. [880]
Jefferson County Farmco Coop. [881]
Jefferson Farmers Cooperative [882]
Jeffrey's Seed Company Inc. [883]
Jersey County Farm Supply Co. [886]
Johnson Cooperative Grain Co. [888]
Johnston County Feed & Farm Supply [890]
Johnston Elevator Co. [18025]
Justin Seed Company Inc. [894]
K and L Feed Mill Corp. [895]
Kanabec Cooperative Association [22394]
Kaufman Seeds Inc. [898]
Keller Grain and Feed Inc. [18030]
Keller & Sons [900]
Kendall-Grundy FS Inc. [901]
Kennett Liquid Fertilizer Co. [903]
Kenosha-Racine FS Cooperative [905]
Kensington Cooperative Association [906]
Kentucky Buying Cooperative Int. [907]
Kerber Milling Co. [908]
Kettle-Lakes Cooperative [909]
Keystone Mills [910]
Kinder Seed Co. [911]
Knievel's Inc. [915]
Knowles Produce and Trading Co. [916]
Knox County Farm Bureau Cooperative
  Association [917]
Kova Fertilizer Inc. [919]
Kragnes Farmers Elevator [18040]
Krob and Co.; F.J. [920]
La Salle County Farm Supply Co. [925]
La Salle Farmers Grain Co. [926]
Lake Andes Farmers Cooperative Co. [929]
Lake Benton Farmers Elevator Inc. [930]
Lake County Farm Bureau Cooperative Association
  Inc. [22415]
Lake Preston Cooperative Association [18042]
Lake Region Cooperative Oil Association [22416]
Lakeland FS, Inc. [931]
Landiseed International, Ltd. [934]
Landmark Co-Op Inc. [935]
Landmark Supply Company Inc. [936]
Lapeer County Cooperative Inc. [18044]
Larsen Cooperative Company Inc. [939]
Laughery Valley AG Co-Op Inc. [942]
Lawes Coal Company Inc. [943]
Lawn and Golf Supply Company Inc. [944]
Lawn Hill Cooperative [945]
Lawrence County Exchange [18047]
Layne and Myers Grain Co. [18048]
Le Roy Cooperative Association Inc. [18049]
Le Roy Farmers Cooperative Creamery
  Association [946]
Lee F.S. Inc. [949]
Lewis Seed and Feed Co. [954]
Lewiston AG Inc. [955]
Lexington Cooperative Oil Co. [22429]
Lextron Inc. [27181]
Lilly Co.; Chas. H. [958]
Limestone Farmers Cooperative Inc. [959]
Lincoln County Farmers Cooperative [960]
Linn Cooperative Oil Co. [22434]
Livingston Service Co. [962]
Lobel Chemical Corp. [963]
Lockbourne Farmers Exchange Co. [964]
Lockwood Farmers Exchange Inc. [965]
Loft's Seed Inc. [966]
Logsdon Service Inc. [18063]
Lorraine Grain Fuel and Stock Co. [970]
Lostant Hatchery and Milling Company Inc. [971]
Loveland Industries [972]
Lowville Farmers Cooperative Inc. [973]
Lucky Farmers Inc. [975]

Lyssy and Eckel Inc. [976]
M-G Inc. [977]
M and M Chemical Products Inc. [979]
M & R Trading Inc. [18068]
Macon Ridge Farmers Association [18069]
Madison County Cooperative [980]
Madison County Cooperative Inc. [981]
Madison Farmers Elevator Co. [18070]
Madison Landmark Inc. [18071]
Madison Service Co. [982]
Mahaska Farm Service Co. [18073]
Manna Pro Corp. Denver Div. [984]
Manning Grain Co. [985]
Maple Valley Cooperative [11777]
Mark Seed Co. [986]
Marks Co.; D.F. [987]
Maroa Farmers Cooperative Elevator Co. [988]
Marshall Farmers Cooperative [989]
Martindale Feed Mill [990]
Master Feed and Grain Inc. [991]
Maurice Pincoffs Company Inc. [20158]
Maury Farmers Cooperative [992]
Mauston Farmers Cooperative [993]
Mayo Seed Co.; D.R. [994]
Maywood Cooperative Association [995]
Mazon Farmers Elevator [996]
McBee Grain and Trucking Inc. [18077]
McCune Farmers Union Cooperative
  Association [1001]
McFarlane Manufacturing Company Inc. [1002]
McIntosh Cooperative Creamery [11830]
McLean County Service Co. [1004]
McMann Loudan Farmers Cooperative [1005]
McNeil Marketing Co. [1006]
Medalist America Turfgrass Seed Co. [1008]
Medford Co-operative Inc. [18085]
Medica International Ltd. [1009]
Medina Farmers Exchange Co. [1010]
Medina Landmark Inc. [1011]
Meherrin Agricultural and Chemical Co. [1012]
Meis Seed and Feed Co. [1013]
Menomonie Farmers Union Cooperative [1015]
Mer-Roc F.S. Inc. [27186]
Merchant's Grain Inc. [18087]
Merschman Inc. [1016]
Metamora Elevator Co. [1018]
Meyer Seed Co. [1020]
MFA Agriservice [1023]
MFA Inc. [1024]
Michigan Glass Lined Storage Inc. [1025]
Michigan State Seed Co. [1026]
Mid-Iowa Cooperative (Beaman, Iowa) [18092]
Mid-Kansas Cooperative Association [1027]
Midland Co-Op Inc. [1030]
Midland Cooperative Inc. [1031]
Midland Cooperative Inc. Wilcox Div. [18095]
Midland Marketing Cooperative, Inc. [18096]
Midor Inc. [1033]
Midstate Mills Inc. [11886]
Midwest Consolidated Cooperative [1034]
Midwest Coop. [11888]
Midwest Cooperative [1035]
Midwest Cooperatives [18097]
Midwest Farmers Cooperative [1037]
Milan Farmers Elevator [18098]
Miles Farm Supply Inc. [1038]
Mille Lacs Agriculture Services Inc. [1039]
Mimbres Valley Farmers Association Inc. [1042]
Minn-Kota AG Products Inc. [18103]
Minneola Cooperative Inc. [18104]
Mitchellville Cooperative [1043]
Moews Seed Company Inc. [18107]
Mondovi Cooperative Equity Association
  Inc. [1045]
Monroe City Feed Mill Inc. [1046]
Monroe Lawrence Farm Bureau
  Cooperative [1047]
Monroeville Co-op Grain [18110]
Monte Vista Cooperative Inc. [1048]
Monterey Chemical Co. Inc. [4461]
Montezuma Cooperative Exchange [18112]
Montgomery Farmers Cooperative [1049]
Morgan Grain and Feed Co. [18116]
Morgan Wholesale Feed; Fred [1052]
Morris Cooperative Association [1053]
Morris Grain Company Inc. [1054]

Morrow County Grain Growers Inc. [18118]
Mt. Horeb Farmers Coop. [11941]
Mt. Union Cooperative Elevator [18121]
Mountain View Coop. [1055]
Moyer and Son Inc. [1056]
Mycogen Plant Sciences. Southern Div. [1059]
Mycogen Seeds [1060]
Mycogen Seeds [1061]
Myers Inc. [1063]
Nasco-Catalog [26589]
National Seed Co. [1065]
NC Plus Hybrids Coop. [18126]
Necessary Organics Inc. [1066]
Nehawka Farmers Coop. [11991]
Nemaha County Cooperative Association [1069]
Neowa F.S. Inc. [18129]
New AG Center Inc. [1070]
New Horizons Ag Services [1071]
New Horizons FS Inc. [22510]
New Horizons Supply Cooperative [1072]
New Richmond Farmers Union Cooperative Oil
  Co. [22511]
Newark Farmers Grain Co. [18131]
Newsom Seeds [1073]
Nichol's Farm Supply Inc. [1074]
Nielsen Oil and Propane Inc. [22518]
NK Lawn & Garden Co. [1076]
North Caddo Cooperative Inc. [1078]
North Central Cooperative Association [22524]
North Central Cooperative Inc. [1079]
North East Kingdom Sales, Inc. [18139]
North Iowa Cooperative Elevator [1081]
North Pacific Group, Inc. [7794]
Northampton County Seed [1082]
Northampton Farm Bureau Cooperative [1083]
Northeast Cooperative [18140]
Northeast Texas Farmers Cooperative Inc. [18142]
Northern Lakes Co-op Inc. [1084]
Northern Seed Service [1085]
Northrup King Co. [1086]
Northwest Grain [18143]
Northwest Iowa Co-op [1087]
Northwest Iowa Cooperative [18145]
Northwest Iowa Cooperative [1088]
Northwest Wholesale Inc. [1089]
Northwestern Supply Co. [1090]
Northwood Cooperative Elevator [18146]
Novartis Seeds Inc. [1092]
Novartis Seeds Inc. (Golden Valley,
  Minnesota) [1093]
Nyssa Cooperative Supply Inc. [1095]
Oakville Feed and Grain Inc. [1096]
Ocheyedan Cooperative Elevator
  Association [18148]
Ogle Service Co. [1100]
Ohigro Inc. [1101]
Ohio Agriculture and Turf Systems Inc. [1102]
Ohio Seed Company Inc. [1103]
Olds Seed Co.; L.L. [1104]
Oliger Seed Co. [1105]
Olsen-Fennell Seeds, Inc. [1106]
Olton Grain Cooperative Inc. [18155]
Orscheln Farm and Home Supply Inc. [1109]
Osage Cooperative Elevator [1110]
Osage Cooperative Elevator [12079]
Osborne Distributing Company Inc. [1111]
Ottawa Cooperative Association Inc. [1112]
Ouachita Fertilizer Div. [1113]
Outdoor Equipment Co. [1114]
Pacific Southwest Seed and Grain Inc. [18158]
Page Seed Co. [1116]
Papillon Agricultural Products Inc. [1117]
Paramount Feed and Supply Inc. [1118]
Paynesville Farmers Union Cooperative Oil
  Co. [22554]
Pearl's Garden Center [14939]
Peine Inc. [1120]
Pendleton Grain Growers Inc. [18161]
Pennington Seed Inc. [1121]
Peoples Communitive Oil Cooperative [22562]
Peoria County Service Co. [1122]
Perennial Gardens [14941]
Perryton Equity Exchange [18164]
Pestcon Systems Inc. [1124]
Pestorious Inc. [1125]
Peterson's North Branch Inc. [1126]

Pettisville Grain Company Inc. [1127]
Pickrell Cooperative Elevator Association [18165]
Pickseed West, Inc. [1128]
Pied Piper Mills Inc. [27213]
Pike County Cooperative [1130]
Pine City Cooperative Association [18166]
Pine Valley Supply [1131]
Plains Equity Exchange [18171]
Planters Cooperative Association [1133]
PM AG Products Inc. [1135]
Poag Grain Inc. [1136]
Polk County Farmers Cooperative [1138]
Polk County Fertilizer Co. [1139]
Posey County Farm Bureau Cooperative
   Association Inc. [1141]
Postville Farmers Cooperative [1142]
Potash Import and Chemical Corp. [4482]
Prairie Land Cooperative [1144]
Prairie Land Cooperative [1145]
Prairie Land Cooperative Co. [1146]
Premier Cooperative [1147]
Price Milling Co. [1149]
Prins Grain Co. [18178]
Prinsburg Farmers Cooperative [1152]
Prinz Grain and Feed Inc. [18179]
Pro-Ag Chem Inc. [1153]
Pro AG Farmers Co-op [1154]
Pro Cooperative [1155]
Producers Cooperative Association [1156]
Products Corp. of North America, Inc. [12226]
Progressive Farmers Cooperative [1158]
Prosper Farmers Cooperative Elevator [1159]
PTC International [19000]
Pueblo Chemical and Supply Co. [4486]
Pulaski Chase Cooperative [1161]
Pulaski County Farm Bureau Cooperative [1162]
Pure Line Seeds Inc. [1164]
Quad County Cooperative [18185]
Quitman County Farmers Association [1165]
R and L Supply Co-op [1166]
Ramsey Seed, Inc. [1167]
Ramy Seed Co. [1168]
Ray-Carroll County Grain Growers Inc. [1169]
RCH Distributors Inc. [1170]
Reading Feed and Grain Inc. [1173]
Real Veal Inc. [1174]
Recycled Wood Products [1175]
Redlake County Co-op [22615]
Redwood Valley Co-op Elevator [18193]
Reeds Seeds Inc. [1178]
Reedsville Cooperative Association [1179]
Reese Farmers Inc. [18194]
Regan Co.; Steve [1180]
Research Seeds Inc. [1182]
Rhoads Mills Inc. [1185]
Rib River Valley Cooperative [1187]
Rice Lake Farmers Union Cooperative [1188]
Rice Lake Products Inc. [25803]
Richardson Seeds Inc. [1189]
Richter Fertilizer Co. [1190]
Rickreall Farms Supply Inc. [1192]
Ridgeland Chetek Cooperative [1193]
Rio Farmers Union Cooperative [18198]
Rippey Farmers Cooperative [1195]
River Country Cooperative [1197]
River Springs Cooperative Association [27222]
River Valley Cooperative [1198]
Riverview FS Inc. [1199]
RMC Inc. [23346]
Roberts Seed Co. [1200]
Robertson Supply Inc. [23349]
Robin Seed Co.; Clyde [1201]
Rock River Lumber and Grain Co. [1203]
Rockbridge Farmers Cooperative [1204]
Rockingham Cooperative Farm Bureau [1205]
Rockwell and Son; H. [1206]
Rockwood Chemical Co. [1207]
Rolla Cooperative Equity Exchange [18203]
Rosebud Farmers Union Cooperative Associates
   Inc. [1211]
Rosebud Farmers Union Cooperative Associates
   Inc. [22639]
Rosen's Diversified Inc. [4498]
Rosen's Inc. [1213]
Rosholt Farmers Cooperative Elevator Inc. [18206]
Round Butte Seed Growers Inc. [1215]

Route 16 Grain Cooperative [18209]
Royal Seeds Inc. [1217]
Rugby Farmers Union Elevator Co. [18211]
Rural Serv Inc. [18213]
Rush County Farm Bureau Cooperative [1219]
Rutherford Farmers Cooperative [1220]
Ryan Cooperative Inc. [1221]
S & W Supply Company Inc. [1225]
Sabina Farmers Exchange Inc. [1226]
St. Clair Service Co. [1227]
St. Francis Mercantile Equity Exchange [1228]
St. Paul Feed and Supply Inc. [1229]
Sakata Seed America, Inc. [1230]
San Joaquin Sulphur Company Inc. [4501]
San Joaquin Valley Hay Growers
   Association [1232]
Sanborn Cooperative Grain Co. [1233]
Sanborn Farmers Elevator [18221]
Sand Seed Service Inc. [1235]
Satanta Cooperative Grain [18222]
Schuyler-Brown FS Inc. [1239]
Scott Cooperative Association [1240]
Scott County Cooperative [1241]
Scott Farm Service Inc. [1242]
Scott and Muscatine's Service Co. [18226]
Scott Seed Co. [1244]
Scott and Sons Co.; O.M. [1245]
The Scoular Co. [18227]
Scranton Equity Exchange Inc. [7995]
Seaboard Seed Co. [1247]
Seaman Grain Inc. [1248]
Seed Corp. of America [1250]
Seed Research of Oregon [1251]
Seed Resource Inc. [18228]
Seedex Distributors, Inc. [1252]
Seeds, Inc. [1253]
Seedway [1254]
Seedway, Inc. [1255]
Seibert Equity Cooperative Association [1256]
Seifert Farm Supply [1257]
Selma Oil Mill Inc. [1259]
Senesac Inc. [1260]
Senex Harvest States [12460]
Sexauer Company Inc. [18230]
Sharp Brothers Seed Co. [1261]
Shawano Equity Cooperative Inc. [1262]
Shawneetown Feed and Seed [1263]
Shelby Grain and Feed Co. [1264]
Shell Lake Cooperative [22666]
Shields Soil Service Inc. [1265]
Shipman Elevator Co. [18232]
Shumway Seedsman; R.H. [1266]
SIGCO Sun Products Inc. [1267]
Skinner Nursery Inc. [14951]
Slay Industries Inc. [18235]
Smith Southside Feed and Grain Inc. [18237]
Sommer Brothers Seed Co. [1273]
South Central Co-op [1274]
South Central Co-op [1275]
South Central Cooperative [18239]
South Dakota Wheat Growers Association [18241]
South Omaha Supply [18242]
Southeast Cooperative Service Co. [18243]
Southeast Cooperative Service Co. [1277]
Southeastern Colorado Coop. [12537]
Southeastern Colorado Cooperative [1278]
Southern Agriculture Insecticides Inc. [1279]
Southern Farm and Home Center [1280]
Southern Livestock Supply Co. Inc. [1281]
Southern States Cooperative Inc. [1282]
Southern States Cooperative Inc. [1283]
Southern States Frederick Cooperative Inc. [1284]
Southern States Madisonville Cooperative [18244]
Southwest Cooperative Wholesale [18245]
Sovana, Inc. [1286]
SPADA Enterprises Ltd. [12546]
Spalding Cooperative Elevator Co. [1287]
Speartex Grain Co. [18248]
Spencer County Cooperative Associates
   Inc. [1289]
Sphar & Co. [1290]
Stacyville Cooperative Co. [1291]
Stafford County Flour Mills Co. [4521]
Stanislaus Farm Supply Co. [1293]
Starbuck Creamery Co. [12570]
Statz and Sons Inc.; Carl F. [1294]

Steuben County Farm Bureau Association
   Inc. [27238]
Stewart Co.; Jesse C. [18255]
Stockton Feed and Milling Inc. [1295]
Stone and Son Inc.; E.B. [1296]
Stones Inc. [18258]
Stover Seed Company Inc. [1297]
Stratford Farmers Cooperative [18261]
Stratford Grain and Supply Cooperative [18262]
Stratton Equity Cooperative [1298]
Stratton Seed Co. [1299]
Sublette Cooperative, Inc. [18265]
Sublette Farmers Elevator Co. [18266]
Sullivan Inc. [18267]
Sully Cooperative Exchange Inc. [18268]
Sunbelt Seeds Inc. [1302]
Sunray Cooperative [1304]
Sunrise Cooperative Inc. [1305]
Superior Cooperative Elevator Co. [18270]
Superior-Deshler Inc. [1306]
Sutherland Farmers Cooperative [1307]
Sweeney Seed Co. [1309]
Swift Co-op Oil Co. [1310]
Tabor Grain Co. [18273]
Taintor Cooperative Co. [18274]
Tama-Benton Cooperative Co. [18275]
Tampico Farmers Elevator Co. [1313]
Taser International Inc. [1314]
Taylor Feed & Pet Supply [27245]
Taylor Fertilizers Co.; John [1315]
Tazewell Farm Bureau Inc. [1318]
Terra Industries Inc. [1320]
Terra International Inc. [1321]
Terral-Norris Seed Company Inc. [1322]
Terral Seed, Inc. [18277]
Terral Seed Inc. [1323]
Terre Company of New Jersey Inc. [1324]
Tex-Ag Co. [4527]
Texhoma Wheat Growers Inc. [1325]
Theisen Farm and Home Stores [1326]
Thompson Farmers Cooperative Elevator
   Co. [1328]
Thompson Sales; Larry [1331]
Thompson's Veterinary Supplies [27246]
Three Rivers FS Co. [1332]
Thurmont Cooperative Inc. [1333]
Tiffin Farmers Cooperative, Inc. [1335]
Tindle Mills Inc. [1337]
Titgemeiers Feed, Inc. [1338]
Toma International [1340]
Top of Iowa Coop [18285]
Topeka Seed and Stove Inc. [1342]
Toshin Trading Inc. [1344]
Town and Country Coop. [1345]
Tracy-Garvin Cooperative [1348]
Tradex International Corp. [19083]
Trainor Grain and Supply Co. [18288]
Transammonia Inc. [1349]
Traylor Chemical and Supply Co. [1350]
Treasure State Seed, Inc. [1351]
Tri Central Co-op [18290]
Tri-County Co-op [1352]
Tri-County Farmers Association [1353]
Tri-Parish Cooperative Inc. [1354]
Tri Star Seed Co. [1355]
Tri-State Breeders Cooperative [27252]
Tri Valley Cooperative [1356]
Triangle Chemical Co. [4533]
Triple S Ranch Supply [18294]
Troy BioSciences Inc. [1358]
Tulia Wheat Growers Inc. [1362]
Turf Merchants [1364]
Turf-Seed, Inc. [1366]
Twin County Service Co. [1368]
Twomey Co. [18296]
UAP Northwest [1370]
Union Fertilizer Co. [1371]
Union Produce Cooperative [1373]
Union Seed Company Inc. [18300]
United Co-op [18301]
United Co-op Inc. (Hampton, Nebraska) [1374]
United Farmers Cooperative [1377]
United Farmers Cooperative Inc. [1378]
United Producers Consumers Cooperative [1379]
United Services Association [1381]
U.S. Home and Garden Inc. [1383]

U.S. World Trade Corp. [18305]
United Suppliers Inc. [1384]
Ursa Farmers Cooperative [18308]
Urwiler Oil and Fertilizer Inc. [1387]
U.S.A. Marketing Alliance Inc. [1388]
Utica Cooperative Grain Company Inc. [18310]
Utica Cooperative Grain Company Inc. [12810]
Valders Cooperative [18312]
Valley Farmers Cooperative (Natchitoches, Louisiana) [1392]
Valley Feed Mill Inc. [1393]
Valley Fertilizer and Chemical Company Inc. [1394]
Van Zyverden, Inc. [14970]
VanderHave USA [1395]
Vermillion Elevator Co. [18316]
Veterinary Companies of America Inc. [1398]
V.H. Associates Inc. [18317]
Villafane Inc.; Rene Ortiz [8183]
Vita Plus Corp. [1400]
W-L Research Inc. [18320]
Wabash Elevator Co. [18321]
Wabash Valley Service Co. [1402]
Walco International Inc. [27267]
Walco International Inc. Cody Div. [1404]
Walla Walla Farmers Co-op Inc. [1406]
Wallace County Cooperative Equity Exchange [1407]
Wallace Grain Company Inc. [1408]
Wallace Hardware Co. [1409]
Walters Cooperative Elevators Association [1411]
Ward and Van Scoy Inc. [18325]
Warner Fertilizer Company Inc. [1412]
Warren Farmers Cooperative [1413]
Watertown Cooperative Elevator Association [1414]
Wathena and Bendena Grain Company Inc. [1415]
Watonwan Farm Services [1416]
Watonwan Farm Services Co. Ormsby Div. [18328]
Watseka Farmers Grain Company Cooperative [1417]
Waukon Equity Cooperative [1418]
Wedgworth's Inc. [1420]
West Agro Inc. [4552]
West Bend Elevator Inc. [1422]
West Central Cooperative [18336]
West Lyon Cooperative Inc. [18337]
West Nesbitt Inc. [18338]
West Valley Farmers Inc. [1426]
Westby Farmers Union Cooperative [1428]
Western Farm Center [1429]
Western Farm Service/Cascade [1430]
Western Farm Service Inc. [1431]
Western Seeds [1433]
Westland Seed, Inc. [1434]
Wheeler Brothers [18343]
Whitaker Farmers Cooperative Grain Co. [18345]
White Cloud Grain Co. [1438]
White County Farmers Cooperative [1439]
White River Cooperative [1440]
White Swan Ltd. [1441]
Whiteside F.S. Inc. [22800]
Whittemore Cooperative Elevator [18347]
Whittington Wholesale Company Inc. [1443]
Wilbro Inc. [1445]
Wilbur-Ellis Co. [4554]
Wilbur-Ellis Co. [4555]
Wilbur-Ellis Co. [18348]
Wilbur-Ellis Co. Southern Div. [1446]
Wilco Farmers Inc. [1447]
Wildhawk Inc. [1448]
WILFARM L.L.C. [4556]
Will-Du Page Service Co. [18349]
Willamette Seed Co. [1449]
Willette Seed Farm Inc. [1450]
Williams Fertilizer Co.; Archie [1451]
Williams Lawn Seed, Inc. [1452]
Williamsville Farmers Cooperative Grain Co. [18351]
Willmar Poultry Company Inc. [12950]
Wilmont Farmers Elevator Co. [18353]
Wilson Seeds Inc. [18354]
Windom Cooperative Association [1455]
Winona River and Rail Inc. [1456]
Wolf River Country Cooperative [1458]
Wolverton Farmers Elevator [18358]

Wood County Farm Supply [1460]
Woodard and Company Inc.; P.L. [1461]
Woodburn Fertilizer Inc. [1462]
Wright Lorenz Grain Company Inc. [18361]
Wyndmere Farmers Elevator Co. [1466]
Ypsilanti Equity Elevator Company Inc. [18364]
Zajac's Performance Seed [1467]
Zamzow's Inc. [1469]

SIC 5192 — Books, Periodicals & Newspapers

A-C Book Service [3457]
Abingdon Press [3458]
Abranovic Associates Inc. [3459]
Academi-Text Medical Wholesalers [3460]
Academic Enterprises Ltd. [3461]
Academic Therapy Publications [3462]
Academy Chicago Publishers Ltd. [3463]
Accent Books [3464]
Accents Publications Service, Inc. [3465]
Access Publishers Network [3466]
Accura Music, Inc. [3467]
ACS Publications [3468]
Action Products International Inc. [26381]
Adams Book Company, Inc. [3469]
Adams News Co. Inc. [3470]
Addor Associates, Inc. [3471]
Adler's Foreign Books Inc. [3472]
Advanced Marketing Services Inc. [3473]
Adventures Unlimited Press [3474]
Advocate Publishing Co. [20778]
Aerial Photography Services Inc. [3475]
African & Caribbean Imprint Library Services [3476]
AIDS Impact Inc. [3477]
AIMS International Books, Inc. [3478]
Akiba Press [3479]
AKJ Educational Services, Inc. [3480]
Al-WaLi Inc. [3481]
Alabama Book Store [3482]
Alamo Square Distributors [3483]
Alamo Square Distributors [3484]
Alamo Square Distributors [3485]
Alaska News Agency Inc. [3486]
Alaska Pacific University Press [3487]
Alfred Publishing Company Inc. [3488]
Alfreda's Film Works c/o Continnuus [3489]
All America Distributors Corp. [3490]
Allenson, Inc.; Alec R. [3491]
Allentown News Agency Inc. [3492]
Ally Press [3493]
Altman Map, Inc.; Bryant [3494]
Ambassador Book Service, Inc. [3495]
America West Distributors [3496]
American Book Center [3498]
American Cooking Guild [3499]
American Educational Services [3500]
American Mathematical Society [3501]
American Overseas Book Company Inc. [3502]
American Printing House for the Blind, Inc. [3503]
American Wholesale Book Co. [3504]
Americans for the Arts [3505]
AMG Publications [3506]
AMREP Corp. [3507]
Ancient Future Music [3508]
Anco Management Services Inc. [3509]
Anderson Austin News [3510]
Anderson-Gemco [3511]
Anderson News [3512]
Anderson News Co. [3513]
Anderson News Company [3514]
Anderson News Co. [3515]
Anderson News Co. Southwest [3516]
Anderson News Service Center [3517]
Anderson News of Yuma [3518]
Apollo Book [3520]
Appalachian Distributors [3521]
Applied Geographics Inc. [3522]
Aramark Magazines and Books [3523]
Arch Hunter Books and Canyon Country Distribution Services [3524]
Arrow Map Inc. [3525]

Ashgate Publishing Co. [3526]
Asian World of Martial Arts Inc. [23525]
Aspen West Publishing Co. Inc. [3527]
Assorted Book Co. [3528]
Astran Inc. [3529]
Astran Inc. [3530]
Astronomical Society of the Pacific [3531]
Audubon Prints & Books [3532]
Augsburg Fortress Publishers [3533]
Auto-Bound, Inc. [3534]
Avery Book Stores, Inc. [3535]
Avonlea Books [3536]
Awareness and Health Unlimited [14031]
Back Bay News Distributors [3537]
Bacon Pamphlet Service, Inc. [3538]
Baker Book House Co. [3539]
Baker and Taylor [3540]
Banner of Truth [3542]
Baptist Spanish Publishing House [3543]
Barclay Press [3544]
Barrett & Co. Publishers [3545]
Beekman Publishers, Inc. [3546]
Beeman Jorgensen Inc. [3547]
Before Columbus Foundation [3548]
Beijing Book Co. Inc. [3549]
Benjamin News Group [3550]
Bergano Book Co., Inc. [3551]
Bernan [3552]
Beyda & Associates, Inc. [3553]
Beyda & Associates, Inc. [3554]
Big Horn Booksellers Inc. [3555]
Bilingual Educational Services, Inc. [3556]
Bilingual Publications Co. [3557]
Blacast Entertainment [3558]
Black Gold Comics & Graphics [3559]
Blackwell North America Inc. [3560]
Blackwell's Delaware Inc. [3561]
BMI Educational Services [3562]
Bonneville News Co. Inc. [3563]
Bonus Books Inc. [3564]
Book Box, Inc. [3565]
Book Centers Inc. [3566]
Book Distribution Center [3567]
Book Distribution Center, Inc. [3568]
Book Dynamics, Inc. [3569]
Book Home, Inc. [3570]
The Book House Inc. [3571]
Book Warehouse Inc. [3572]
Book Wholesalers, Inc. [3573]
Bookazine Co., Inc. [3574]
Bookcraft Inc. [3575]
Booklegger [3576]
BookLink Distributors [3577]
Bookmark, Inc. [3578]
Bookmen, Inc. [3579]
Bookpeople [3580]
Books Nippan [3581]
Booksmith Promotional Co. [3582]
The Booksource [3583]
BookWorld Services Inc. [3584]
The Bookworm [3585]
Bouregy, Thomas & Co. Inc. [3586]
Bradford Publishing Co. [3587]
Brady News and Recycling [3588]
Branden Publishing Co. [3589]
Brethren Press [3590]
Bridge-Logos Publishers [3591]
Bridge Publications Inc. [3592]
Brodart Co. [3593]
Brotherhood of Life, Inc. [3594]
Brownells Inc. [13477]
Brownlow Corp. [3595]
Brumley & Sons; Albert E. [3596]
Brunner News Agency [3597]
BSC Litho Inc. [3598]
Bud Plant Comic Art [3599]
BUDGEText Corporation [3600]
Butterworth Co. of Cape Cod [3601]
C and W Zabel Co. [3602]
Cambridge Educational [3603]
Cambridge Law Study Aids, Inc. [3604]
Cambridge University Press [3605]
Capeway News [3606]
Capital City Distribution Inc. [3607]
Capital City Distribution Inc. [3608]
Capital City Distribution Inc. [3609]

Capitol News Distributors [3610]
Capra Press Inc. [3611]
Carolina Biological Supply Co. [3612]
Carolina News Co. [3613]
Castellon Inc.; E. [3614]
Catholic Reading Society [3615]
Caxton Printers Ltd. [3616]
CCS Printing [3617]
Celestial Arts Publishing Co. [3618]
Cellar Book Shop [3619]
Central Arizona Distributing Co. [3620]
Central Kentucky News Distributing Co. [3621]
Central News Co. [3622]
Chalice Press [3624]
Chaney, Jr. Books; Bev [3625]
Chatsworth Press [3626]
Cheng & Tsui Company [3627]
Cheviot Corp. [25135]
Chidvilas, Inc. [3628]
Children's Media Center, Inc. [3629]
Children's Small Press Collection [3630]
Chilton Co. [3631]
C.H.I.P.S. [3632]
Choice Books [3633]
Christ for the World, Inc. [3634]
The Christian Broadcasting Network, Inc. [3635]
Christian Destiny Inc. [3636]
Christian Publications Inc. [3637]
Church Doctor Resource Center [3638]
City and Suburban Delivery Systems East [3639]
Claitor's Publishing Division [3640]
Classroom Reading Service [3642]
Claymont Communications [3643]
CLEARVUE [3644]
Cogan Books [3646]
Columbia News Agency Inc. [3647]
Common Ground Distributors Inc. [3648]
Como Sales Co., Inc. [3649]
Compassion Book Service [3650]
Concordia Publishing House [3651]
Conkey's Bookstore [3652]
Connors Associates, Inc. [3653]
Consortium Book Sales and Distribution
    Inc. [3654]
Contemporary Arts Press Distribution [3655]
Continental Book Co. [3656]
Continnuus [3657]
Cook Communications Ministries [3658]
Cook Publishing Co.; David C. [3659]
Cookbook Collection, Inc. [3660]
Cook's Mart Ltd. [15454]
Coronet Books, Inc. [3661]
Coutts Library Services Inc. [3662]
Cover To Cover [3663]
Cox Subscriptions, Inc.; W.T. [3664]
CPP-Belwin Inc. [3665]
Crandall Associates [3666]
Creative Arts Book Co. [3667]
Creative Healthcare Resources [3668]
Creative Homeowner Press [3669]
Creative Joys Inc. [3670]
Creative Source [3671]
Crescent Imports & Publications [3672]
Cromland, Inc. [3673]
Crossing Press [3674]
C.S.S. Publishing Co. [3675]
Cuerno Largo Publications [3676]
Cultural Hispana/Ameriketakoa [3677]
Cypress Book (USA) Co., Inc. [3678]
Daedalus Books [3679]
The Daily Astorian [3680]
Damien Educational Services; M. [3681]
Day Star Productions [25161]
Dearborn Trade [3682]
Delmar News Agency Inc. [3683]
Delta Systems Company, Inc. [3684]
Deltiologists of America [3685]
Denver Business Journal Inc. [3686]
Derstine Book Co.; Roy [3687]
DeRu's Fine Art Books [3688]
Detroit Free Press Agency [3689]
Devin-Adair Publishers, Inc. [3690]
DeVorss & Co. [3691]
Dialogue Systems Inc. [3692]
Diamond Comic Distributors Inc. [26468]
Diamond Comic Distributors Inc. [3693]

Discipleship Resources [3694]
Discovery Toys Inc. [26471]
Distribution Services Inc. [3695]
Distribution Systems of America [3696]
Distribution Systems of America [3697]
Dixie News Co. [3698]
Document Center [3699]
Dosik International [3700]
Doussard & Associates, Inc.; Ron [3701]
DsgnHaus, Inc. [6223]
Dufour Editions, Inc. [3702]
Duke University Press [3703]
Durkin Hayes Publishing [3704]
E-Heart Press, Inc. [3705]
Eaglecrafts Inc. [26475]
East Distributors Ltd.; Ryan [3706]
East Kentucky News Inc. [3707]
East Texas Distributing Inc. [3708]
East-West Center [3709]
Eastern Book Co. [3710]
Eastview Editions [3711]
Eble Music Co. [3712]
E.C.A. Associates Press [3713]
Economical Wholesale Co. [3714]
ECS Publishing Corporation [3715]
Edelweiss Publishing Co. [3716]
Ediciones del Norte [3717]
Ediciones Universal [3718]
Edu-Tech Corp. [3719]
Education Guide Inc. [3720]
Education People, Inc. [3721]
Educational Book Distributors [3722]
Educational Geodesics Inc. [3723]
Eerdmans Publishing Co.; William B. [3724]
Eisenbrauns [3725]
Elder's Bookstore [3726]
Emery Pratt Co. [3727]
Empire Comicsl [3728]
Empire Publishing Inc. [3729]
Empire State News Corp. [3730]
Encyclopaedia Britannica Educational Corp. [3731]
Enrica Fish Books Inc. [3732]
Enslow Publishers, Inc. [3733]
ETD KroMar [3734]
European American Music Distributors
    Corp. [3735]
European Book Company Inc. [3736]
Evangel Publishing House [3737]
Evergreen Publishing & Stationery [3738]
EZ Nature Books [3739]
Fairfield Book Co., Inc. [3740]
Fairfield Book Service Co. [3741]
Fall River News Company, Inc. [3742]
Family Life Productions [3743]
Family Reading Service [3744]
Faxon Company Inc. [3745]
Feldheim, Inc.; Philipp [3746]
F.E.P. Inc. [3747]
Fiesta Book Co. [3748]
Fine Associates [3749]
Fischer Inc.; Carl [3750]
Fishing Hot Spots/FHS Maps [3751]
Flannery Co. [3752]
Florida Classics Library [3753]
Florida Craft Wholesale [26484]
The Florida News Group, Ltd. [3754]
Flynt Distribution Company Inc. [3755]
Follett Campus Resources [3756]
Follett Corp. [3757]
Follett Library Book Co. [3758]
Follett Library Resources [3759]
Ford & Bailie [3760]
Fortress Press [3761]
Franciscan Press [3762]
Franklin Book Company, Inc. [3763]
Frederick Fell Publishers, Inc. [3764]
Friendly Frank's Distribution Inc. [3765]
Friendship Press [3766]
Front Musical Literature; Theodore [3767]
Fujii Associates, Inc. [3769]
Gardner's Book Service, Inc. [3770]
Garrett Educational Corp. [3771]
Gavilanes Books from Indoamerica [3772]
Geiger Bros. [3773]
Gem Guides Book Co. [3774]
Genealogical Sources Unlimited [3775]

General Medical Publishers [3776]
George Washington University Press [3777]
Gessler Publishing Company, Inc. [3778]
Gibson Dot Publications [3779]
Gingery Publishing; David J. [3780]
Global Directions Inc. [3781]
Gnomon Inc. [3782]
Gnomon Press [3783]
Golden-Lee Book Distributors, Inc. [3784]
Good Apple [3785]
Good Karma Publishing Inc. [3786]
Good News Communications, Inc. [3787]
Gopher News Co. [3788]
Gospel Light Publications [3789]
Gospel Light Publications [3790]
Gospel Publishing House [3791]
Graham Services Inc. [3792]
Grail Foundation of America [3793]
Granary Books, Inc. [3794]
Graphic Arts Center Publishing Co. [3795]
Great Northern Distributors, Inc. [3796]
Great Outdoors Publishing Co. [3797]
Greeley Publishing Co. [3798]
Green Gate Books [3799]
Green Leaf Press [3800]
Group Publishing, Inc. [3801]
Gryphon House, Inc. [3802]
Guardian Book Co. [3803]
Guidelines Inc. [3804]
Hacker Art Books Inc. [3805]
Hamakor Judaica Inc. [3807]
Hamel Spanish Book Corp.; Bernard H. [3808]
Hamon Inc.; Gerard [3809]
Hancock House Publishers [3810]
Handleman Co. [25225]
Handleman Co. [3811]
Harcourt Brace Professional Publishing [3812]
Harper San Francisco [3813]
Harris-Teller, Inc. [3814]
Harrowood Books [3815]
Harvest House Publishers, Inc. [3816]
Harvest Publications [3817]
The Haworth Press Inc. [3818]
Haynes Manuals Inc. [2733]
HCIA Inc. [3819]
Healthcare Press [3820]
Hein and Co., Inc.; William S. [3821]
Heirloom Bible Publications [3822]
Herald House/Independence Press [3823]
Herald Press [3824]
Hermitage Publishing Co. [3825]
Heroes World Distribution, Inc. [3826]
Himber's Books [3827]
Hinrichs; E. Louis [3828]
Hispanic Books Distributors, Inc. [3829]
Hobby Book Distributors [3830]
Holmgangers Press [3831]
Homestead Book Co. [3832]
Horizon Publishers & Distributors, Inc. [3833]
Horizons Publishers and Dstbrs [3834]
Hotho & Co. [3835]
Hudson News Co. [3836]
Ideal Foreign Books, Inc. [3837]
Ideal Foreign Books Inc. [3838]
Impact Christian Books Inc. [3839]
Imperial Delivery Service Inc. [3840]
Imported Books [3841]
Independent Publishers Group Inc. [3842]
Ingham Publishing, Inc. [3843]
Ingram Book Co. [25243]
Ingram Book Group Inc. [3844]
Ingram Industries Inc. [6372]
International Book Centre [3845]
International Book Distributors Ltd. [3846]
International Business & Management
    Institute [3847]
International Marine Publishing Co. [3848]
International Periodical Distributors [3849]
International Playthings Inc. [26535]
International Service Co. [3850]
International Specialized Book Services [3851]
International Wealth Success Inc. [3852]
Interstate Distributors Inc. [3853]
Interstate Periodical Distributors Inc. [3854]
Irish Books & Media, Inc. [3855]
ISHK Book Services [3856]

SIC Index

J & L Book Co. [3857]
Jain Publishing Co. [3858]
Jalmar Press/Innerchoice Publishing [3859]
Jeanie's Classics [3860]
Jean's Dulcimer Shop and Crying Creek
    Publishers [3861]
Jellyroll Productions [3862]
Jenkins Trading Inc. [3863]
Jethro Publications [3864]
JO-D Books [3865]
Johnson Books [3866]
Jones & Bartlett Publishers Inc. [3868]
Joyce Media Inc. [3869]
Judson Press [3870]
Jung Foundation; C.G. [3871]
K & S Militaria Books [3872]
Kable News Company Inc. [3873]
Kansas City Periodical Distributing Co. [3874]
Karr & Company, Inc.; Jean [3875]
Kazi Publications [3876]
Keith Distributors Inc. [3877]
Key Curriculum Press Inc. [3878]
Kinokuniya Publications Service of New
    York [3879]
Kirkbride Bible Co.; B.B. [3880]
Kissen News Agency Inc. [3881]
Kitrick Management Company, Ltd. [24383]
Klein News Co.; George R. [3882]
Klein's Booklein [3883]
Koen Book Distributors, Inc. [3884]
Kornish Distributors Co. [3885]
Kregel Publications & Bookstores [3886]
Krieger Publishing Co. [3887]
Kurian Reference Books; George [3888]
Kurtzman Book Sales, Inc. [3889]
Kuykendall's Press [3890]
La Cite [3891]
Lake Martin Living [3892]
Landrum News Agency—Cincinnati Div. [3893]
Landrum News Agency Inc. [3894]
Langley Press, Inc. [3895]
Larry's News [3896]
Last Gasp of San Francisco [3897]
Latin Trading Corp. [3898]
Law Distributors [3899]
LEA Book Distributors [3900]
Leader Newspapers [3901]
The Learning Plant [3902]
Lectorum Publications Inc. [3903]
Legal Books Distributing [3904]
Leisure Arts, Inc. [3905]
Levine Books & Judaica; J. [3906]
Levy Co.; Charles [3907]
Levy Home Entertainment [3908]
Liberation Distributors [3909]
Liberty Publishing Co. Inc. [3910]
Library Book Selection Service, Inc. [3911]
Library Research Associates Inc. [3912]
Life Unlimited [3913]
Lincoln Industries Inc. [3914]
Linden Tree Children's Records & Books [3915]
Ling's International Books [3916]
Listening Library Inc. [3917]
Literal Books [3918]
Llewellyn Publications [3919]
Login Brothers Book Co. [3920]
Longhill Partners Inc. [17504]
Longman Publishing Group [3921]
LPC [3922]
Lutz News Co. [3923]
M & M News Agency [3924]
Mabon Business Equipment [3925]
MacAlester Park Publishing Co. [3926]
MacRae's Indian Book Distributors [3927]
Magazines Inc. [3928]
Main Court Book Fair [3929]
Main Line Book Company Inc. [3930]
Maine Writers & Publishers Alliance [3931]
Majors Scientific Books Inc. [3932]
Manson News Distributors [3933]
Many Feathers Books and Maps [3934]
Map Link Inc. [3935]
Maryland Historical Press [3937]
Maryland News Distributing Co. [3938]
Marysville Newspaper Distributor [3939]
Matthews Book Co. [3940]

MBS Textbook Exchange Inc. [3941]
McClain Printing Co. [3942]
McDonald & Woodward Publishing [3943]
McKnight Sales Company Inc. [3944]
McPherson & Co. Publishers [3945]
Melman-Moster Associates, Inc. [3946]
Melton Book Company Inc. [3947]
Meriwether Publishing, Ltd. [3948]
Metamorphous Advances Product Services [3949]
Michiana News Service, Inc. [3950]
Michigan Church Supply Company Inc. [3951]
Michigan State University Press [3952]
Mickler's Floridiana, Inc. [3953]
Mid-Penn Magazine Distributors [3954]
Mid-State Distributors [3955]
Mid-State Periodicals Inc. [3956]
Midmarch Arts Press [3957]
Midwest Distributors [3958]
Midwest Library Service [3959]
Milligan News Co., Inc. [3960]
MILTCO Corp. [3961]
Mississippi Safety Services Inc. [24594]
Missouri Archaeological Society Inc. [3962]
Missouri Archaeological Society Inc. [3963]
Mix Bookshelf [3964]
MMB Music Inc. [25330]
Montfort Publications [3965]
Mook & Blanchard Wholesale Library
    Books [3966]
Moonbeam Publications, Inc. [3967]
The Morehouse Group, Inc. [3968]
Mosby Brothers Inc. [3969]
Motorbooks International [3970]
Mott Media L.L.C. [3971]
Mountain West Printing and Publishing Ltd. [3972]
Moznaim Publishing Corp. [3973]
Mr. Paperback Publisher News [3974]
Music for Percussion, Inc. [3975]
Music Sales Corp. [3976]
Mustang Publishing Co. [3977]
NACSCORP [3978]
Najarian Music Company Inc. [3979]
Nanny Goat Productions [3980]
Napsac Reproductions [3981]
Nataraj Books [3982]
National Association of College Stores Inc. [3983]
National Book Network Inc. [3984]
National Braille Press Inc. [3985]
National Learning Corp. [3986]
Naturegraph Publishers Inc. [3987]
NavPress [3988]
Nazarene Publishing House [3989]
NEA Professional Library [3990]
Nebraska Book Company Inc. [3991]
Ner Tamid Book Distributors [3992]
New Concepts Books & Tapes Distributors [3993]
New Jersey Book Agency [3994]
New Leaf Distributing Co. [3995]
New Leaf Distributors Inc. [3996]
New Testament Christian Press [3997]
Newark Newsdealers Supply Company Inc. [3998]
Newborn Enterprises Inc. [3999]
The News Group, III [4000]
The News Group - Rocky Mount [4001]
NEWSouth Distributors [4002]
Niagara County News Company Inc. [4003]
Nippan Shuppan Hanbai [4004]
Nolo Press/Folklaw Inc. [4005]
Nor-Del Productions Ltd. [4006]
Nordic Needle, Inc. [26158]
North American Book Dealers Exchange [4007]
North Central Book Distributors [4008]
Northland Publishing [4009]
Northland Publishing Company [4010]
NTC/Contemporary Publishing Group [4012]
Oberlin College Press-Field Magazine-Field
    Translation Series-Field Poetry Series-Field
    Editions [4014]
Ocean Springs Distributors Inc. [4015]
Oceana Publications Inc. [4016]
Old Saltbox Publishing House Inc. [4017]
Oliver Worldclass Labs [4018]
Omega Publications [4019]
Omega Publications, Inc. [4020]
Omnibooks [4021]
Omnigraphics Inc. [4022]

Opportunities for Learning, Inc. [4023]
Organ Literature Foundation [4024]
Orient Book Distributors [4025]
O.S.S. Publishing Co. [4026]
Other Publishers [4027]
Overland West Press [4028]
Ozer; Jerome S. [4029]
Pacific Books [4030]
Pacific Mountain Book Associates [4032]
Pacific Northwest Books Co. [4033]
Pacific Trade Group [4035]
Paladin Press [4036]
Palmer News Inc. [4037]
Paperbacks for Educators [4038]
Paradies and Co. [4039]
Paramount International [6588]
Parks & History Association, Inc. [4040]
Partners Book Distributing Inc. [4041]
Party Kits Unlimited Inc. [23874]
Passeggiata Press, Inc. [4042]
Path Press Inc. [4043]
Pathfinder Press [4044]
Pathway Book Service [4045]
Paulsen Company Inc.; G. [4046]
P.B.D. Worldwide Fulfillment Services [4047]
P.D. Music Headquarters Inc. [4048]
Pelican Publishing Company Inc. [4049]
Penfield Press [4050]
Pennsylvania State University Press [4051]
PennWell Publishing Co. [4052]
Pentecostal Publishing House [4053]
Perin Press [4056]
Periodical Services [4057]
Perma-Bound Books [4058]
Persona Press [4059]
PFM Industries Inc. [26612]
Phiebig Inc., Services to Libraries; Albert J. [4060]
Philosophical Research Society, Inc. [4061]
Phoenix Mapping Service [4062]
Pickering Publications [4063]
Pictorial Histories Publishing Co. [4064]
Pilgrim Way Press [4065]
Plains Distribution Service, Inc. [4066]
Playboy Entertainment Group Inc. [4067]
Pleasant Co. [26618]
Plough Publishing House [4068]
PMG International Inc. [4069]
Pocahontas Press Inc. [4070]
Polycrystal Book Service [4071]
Pomona Valley News Agency Inc. [4072]
Portland News Co. [4073]
Portland State University, School of Extended
    Studies, Continuing Education Press [4074]
Potomac Adventist Book Center [4075]
Potomac Adventist Book Center [4076]
Power Sewing [4077]
Practical Cookbooks [4078]
Pratt Co.; Emery [4079]
Presbyterian & Reformed Publishing Co. [4080]
Presidio Press Inc. [4081]
Presser Co.; Theodore [4082]
Price Stern Sloan Inc. [4083]
Princeton Book Company Publishers [4084]
Printed Matter Inc. [4085]
Pro/Am Music Resources, Inc. [4086]
Professional Book Distributors, Inc. [4087]
Professional Book Service [4088]
Professional's Library [4089]
Publishers Associates [4091]
Publishers Distributing Co. [4092]
Publishers Group West Inc. [4093]
Publishers Group West Inc. [4094]
The Publishers Mark [4095]
Publishing Center for Cultural Resources [4096]
Quail Ridge Press Inc. [4098]
Quality Books Inc. [4099]
Quality Resources [4100]
The Quilt Digest Press — A division of
    NTC/Contemporary Publishing Group [4101]
Quite Specific Media Group Ltd. [4102]
R & R Technical Bookfinders Inc. [4103]
R & W Distribution Inc. [4104]
Rainbow Publishers [4105]
Ramer & Associates, Inc.; H. [4106]
Ransom Distributing Co. [4107]
Readmore Inc. [4108]

Reco International Corp. [4109]
Redwing Book Company, Inc. [4110]
Reed Publications, Inc.; Thomas [4111]
Regent Book Co. [4112]
Reid Enterprises; Desmond A. [4113]
Research Books, Inc. [4114]
Resource Publications Inc. [4115]
Rhode Island Publications Society [4116]
Richardson's Educators Inc. [4117]
Rittenhouse Book Distributors, Inc. [4118]
Riverside Book and Bible House [4119]
Riverside Distributors [4120]
Rizzoli International Inc. [4121]
Roberts Co. Inc. [4122]
Rogers Heritage Trust; Will [4123]
Rosenblum's World of Judaica, Inc. [4124]
Ross-Erikson [4125]
Royal Publications, Inc. [4126]
Rushwin Publishing [4127]
Russica Book & Art Shop Inc. [4128]
Rutgers Book Center [4129]
Rutland News Co. [4130]
Ryen, Re Associates [4131]
S & L Sales Co., Inc. [4132]
S & W Distributors Inc. [4133]
Safari Press Inc. [4134]
Saint Aepan's Press & Book Distributors, Inc. [4135]
San Francisco Center for Visual Studies [4136]
Saphrograph Corp. [4137]
S.A.V.E. Half Price Books for Libraries [4138]
S.C.B. Distributors [4139]
Schoenhof's Foreign Books Inc. [4140]
Scholarly Publications [4141]
Scholium International, Inc. [4142]
School Book Service [4143]
Schroeder's Book Haven [4144]
Schwartz & Co.; Arthur [4145]
Science and Spirit Resources, Inc. [4146]
Scientific & Medical Publications of France Inc. [4147]
Selective Books Inc. [4148]
Seneca News Agency Inc. [4149]
Sentai Distributors International [26650]
Sepher-Hermon Press [4150]
Serconia Press [4151]
Serendipity Couriers, Inc. [4152]
Serendipity Couriers Inc. [4153]
Servant Publications [4154]
Seven Hills Book Distributors Inc. [4155]
Sharpe Inc.; M.E. [4156]
Shaw Publishers; Harold [4157]
Shen's Books and Supplies [4158]
Sher Distributing Co. [4159]
Sheriar Books [4160]
Signature Books Inc. [4161]
Sigo Press/Coventure [4162]
Silver Bow News Distributing Company Inc. [4163]
Sirak & Sirak Associates [4164]
Ski America Enterprises Inc. [4165]
Slawson Communications, Inc. [4166]
Small Changes Inc. [4167]
Small Press Distribution Inc. [4168]
Society of Petroleum Engineers [4169]
SOM Publishing [4170]
Sound Words Communications, Inc. [25453]
Source Books [4171]
South Asia Books [4172]
Southern Publishers Group, Inc. [4173]
Southern Territory Associates [4174]
Southern Wisconsin News [4175]
Southwest Book Co. [4176]
Southwest Cookbook Distributors, Inc. [4177]
Spanish & European Bookstore Inc. [4178]
Sparrow-Star [4179]
Specialty Promotions Co., Inc. [4180]
The Speech Bin, Inc. [4181]
Speedimpex USA, Inc. [4182]
Spofford's Newspapers [4183]
Spring Arbor Distribution Company Inc. [4184]
Spring Publishing [4185]
Sri Aurobindo Association [4186]
Stackpole Books [4187]
Standard Publishing Co. [4188]
State Mutual Book & Periodical Service Ltd. [4189]

Sterling Publishing Co., Inc. [4190]
Stoelting Co. [4191]
Straight Talk Distributing [4192]
Strawberry Hill Press [4193]
Subterranean Co. [4194]
Sunbelt Publications [4195]
Sundance Publishing [4196]
Sunday School Publishing Board [4197]
Sunfire Corporation [12610]
Sunflower University Press [4198]
Superlearning [4199]
Swift Fulfillment Services [4200]
Swift Lizard Distributors [4201]
Syracuse University Press [4202]
Taylor & Francis, Inc. [4203]
Taylor Publishing Co. [4204]
Team Up [4205]
Team Up Services [4206]
Ten Speed Press [4207]
Terra Nova Press [4208]
Tesla Book Co. [4209]
Texas A & M University Press [4210]
Texas Book Co. [4211]
Texas State Directory Press [4212]
Thatcher Distributing Group [4213]
the distributors [4214]
Thieme New York [4215]
Thinker's Press [4216]
Thomson Corp. [4217]
Time Distribution Services Inc. [4218]
Time Life Inc. [4219]
Time Warner and Sony Direct Entertainment [4220]
Torah Umesorah Publications [4221]
Total Information [4222]
Tout de Suite a la Microwave Inc. [4223]
Tower Publishing Co. [4224]
The TRACOM Corporation [4225]
Trafalgar Square [4226]
Transamerican & Export News Co. [4227]
Treasure Chest Books, LLC [4228]
Tree Frog Trucking Co. [4229]
Tri-State Periodicals, Inc. [4230]
Triple D Publishing Inc. [4232]
Troll Associates of Memphis [4233]
Tuttle Co. Inc.; Charles E. [4234]
Ubiquity Distributors [4235]
Ultra Books, Inc. [4236]
Unicorn Books and Crafts [4237]
Unipub [4238]
United Learning Inc. [25490]
United Magazine Company [4239]
United Magazine Company [4240]
United Magazine Co. Southern Michigan Division [4241]
United Methodist Publishing House [4242]
Univelt Inc. [4243]
University of Alaska Press [4244]
University Book Service [4245]
University Marketing Group [4246]
University of Missouri Press [4247]
University Press of Colorado [4248]
University Press of Kansas [4249]
University Press of Virginia [4250]
University of Texas Press [4251]
University of Washington Press [4252]
Upper Access Books [4253]
Upper Access Inc. [4254]
Upper Room [4255]
Upstart Publishing Company Inc. [4256]
Vantage Sales & Marketing, Inc. [4257]
Vegetarian Resource Group [4258]
Vestal Press Ltd. [4259]
Vistabooks Publishing [4260]
VMS Inc. [4261]
Volcano Press, Inc. [4262]
Volcano Press Inc. [4263]
Voyageur Press, Inc. [4264]
Waffle Book Co.; O.G. [4265]
Walk Thru the Bible Ministries Inc. [4266]
Walker and Co. [4267]
Ward's [25871]
Ward's Natural Science Establishment Inc. [4268]
Warner Book Distributors; W. [4269]
Warner Press Inc. [4270]
Weider Health and Fitness Inc. [14278]

Weidner & Sons Publishing [4271]
Weiser Inc.; Samuel [4272]
WellSpring Books [4273]
Wesleyan Publishing House [4274]
West Texas News Co. [4275]
Western Book Distributors [4276]
Western Library Books [4277]
Western Merchandisers Inc. [4278]
Westview Press [4279]
Whitaker House [4280]
White Dove International [4281]
Wilcher Associates [4282]
Wildlife Publications, Inc. [4283]
Wilkie; Robert [4284]
Williamson; Darcy [4285]
Williamson Publishing Co. [4286]
Willis Music Co. [4287]
Wilshire Book Co. [4288]
Wilson & Sons [4289]
Wimmer Cookbook Distribution [4290]
Winston-Derek Publishers Group Inc. [4291]
Wishing Well Video Distributing Co. [25526]
Wolverine Distributing [4292]
Woodcrafters Lumber Sales, Inc. [4293]
Words Distributing Company [4295]
Wordware Publishing Inc. [4296]
Worldwide Books [4297]
Worldwide Media Service Inc. [4298]
Writers & Books [4299]
Wyoming Periodical Distributors [4300]
Yankee Book Peddler Inc. [4301]
Yankee Paperback & Textbook Co. [4302]
Yarn Tree Designs [26253]
Ye Olde Genealogie Shoppe [4303]
Yudkin & Associates; Samuel [4304]
Zabel Co.; C & W [4305]
Zephyr Press, Inc. [4306]
The Zondervan Corp. [4307]

SIC 5193 — Flowers & Florists' Supplies

20th Century Nursery Landscape [14790]
A & A Plants [14791]
Aarons Creek Farms [14792]
Accawmacke Ornamentals [14793]
Accent Nursery [14794]
Air Conditioned Roses, Inc. [14795]
Airport Greenhouse [14796]
Ajo Way Garden & Nursery [14797]
Alan's Tropical Plants [14798]
Alexander's Nursery [14799]
Alma, Inc. [14800]
Alpha Fern Co. [14801]
Alvin Tree Farm, Inc. [14802]
American Nursery Products [14803]
Andy's Discount Nursery & Landscape [14805]
Angle Acres Greenhouse [14806]
Anthuriums of Hawaii [14807]
Apopka Trees & Shrubs [14808]
Arbordale Home and Garden Showplace [247]
Ardinger and Son Co.; H.T. [14809]
Avalon Ornamentals [14810]
Avant Gardens Silk Plants [14811]
Avon-Lakewood Nursery Inc. [264]
Babikow Greenhouses [14812]
Bailey Nurseries Inc. [14813]
Baker's Nursery [14814]
Ball Horticultural Co. [14815]
Ball Seed Co. [14816]
Banner Place Nursery [14817]
Barrow's Greenhouses [14818]
Barton's Greenhouse & Nursery [14819]
Bartsch Greenhouses [14820]
Bath Beach Nurseries, Inc. [14821]
Baton Rouge Landscape Co. [14822]
Baucoms Nursery Farm [14823]
Bay Grove Nurseries, Inc. [14824]
Bay Houston Towing Co. [284]
Bay State Florist Supply, Inc. [14825]
Beach Growers [14826]
Beaty's Nursery [14827]
Beautiful Plants by Charlie [14828]

Biddle Service; Dorothy [14829]
Blue Mount Quarry [23560]
Boutique Trim [20851]
Brooks Nursery Inc. [14830]
Buckeye Sales Inc. [14831]
Bush Landscaping & Nursery [14832]
Capitol Wholesale Florists Inc. [14833]
Carbone Co.; R.J. [14834]
Carbone Floral Distributors [14835]
Cascade Seed Co. [376]
CCC Associates Co. [14836]
Cedars Wholesale Floral Imports [14837]
Celebrity, Inc. [14838]
Celebrity Inc. (Tyler, Texas) [14839]
CFX, Inc. [14840]
Claprood Co.; Roman J. [14841]
Cleveland Plant and Flower Co. [14842]
Color Spot Nurseries Inc. [14843]
Communications Products and Services Inc. [8552]
Conard-Pyle Co. [14844]
Concord Nurseries Inc. [14845]
Creative Distributors [14846]
Creighton & Son [14847]
Cuthbert Greenhouse Inc. [14848]
Cuthbert Greenhouse Inc. [14849]
Cuthbert Greenhouse Inc. [14850]
CWF Inc. [14851]
D'Anna B'Nana [14852]
Davids and Royston Bulb Company Inc. [14853]
Decorative Designs [14854]
Decorative Plant Service Inc. [504]
Denver Wholesale Florists [14855]
Design Craft [14856]
DIMON Inc. [14857]
Dixie Craft & Floral Wholesale [20971]
Doran Co.; Bill [14858]
Eskew, Smith & Cannon [9886]
Evelyn's Floral [14859]
Evergreen Nurseries [14860]
First American Artificial Flowers Inc. [14861]
First Coast Designs Inc. [14862]
Flora-Dec Saes, Inc. [14863]
Floral Acres Inc. [14864]
Florence Turfgrass; Paul [14866]
Florexotica Hawaii [14867]
Florimex Worldwide Inc. [14868]
Flower Factory [21005]
Flower Warehouse [14869]
Forrest-Keeling Nursery [14870]
Frinks Greenhouses Inc. [14871]
Frontier Hybrids [709]
Gardener's Supply Co. [14872]
Goble's Flower Farm [14873]
Golden Products Co. [4629]
Good Earth Farm, Inc. [14874]
Good Floral Distributors [14875]
Granite Seed [758]
Green Connection Co. [14876]
Green Mountain Florist Supply [14877]
The Greenhouse [14878]
Greenleaf Wholesale Florist [14879]
Greenleaf Wholesale Florists [14880]
Growmark [775]
Growmark [776]
Halifax Floral Co., Inc. [14881]
Hanford's Inc. [13365]
Harlow International [2725]
Hashimoto Nursery [14882]
Hawaii Protea Corp. [14883]
Hawaiian Greenhouse, Inc. [14884]
Hay Greenhouses, Inc.; Alexander [14885]
Hill Floral Products [14886]
Hilo Farmer's Exchange [14887]
Hoffman; A.H. [14888]
Home & Garden Innovations [835]
Ho'Owaiwia Farms [14889]
Houff Co.; Roy [14890]
House of Rock Inc. [839]
I.E.F. Corp. [14891]
Indianapolis Fruit Company, Inc. [11505]
Inouye Lei Flowers, Inc. [14892]
Interior Plant Designs, Ltd. [14893]
Interior Tropicals, Inc. [14894]
International Decoratives Company Inc. [14895]
Jiffy Foam, Inc. [14896]
Jirdon Agri Chemicals Inc. [14897]

JML Sales Corp. [14898]
Johnston Florist Inc. [14899]
K and D Exports Imports Corp. [14900]
Kamuela Roses, Inc. [14901]
Karthauser and Sons Inc. [14902]
K.D. Farms, Inc. [14903]
Ken's Craft Supply [21087]
Kervar Inc. [14904]
Kim Originals Inc. [14905]
Knutson Farms Inc. [14906]
Koba Nurseries & Landscaping [14907]
Kobayashi Farm & Nursery [14908]
Kubota Inc. [1806]
Kula Farm [14909]
L and L Nursery Supply Inc. [924]
Lawn and Golf Supply Company Inc. [944]
LBK Marketing Corp. [13388]
Lee Flowers and Company Inc.; W. [14910]
Lee Wholesale Floral Inc. [14911]
Lloyd's Carnation [14912]
Lorelei's Exotic Leis & Flower [14913]
LU International [16250]
Mahealani Farms Inc. [14914]
Mahoney's Garden Center [14915]
Marks Co.; D.F. [987]
Marshall Pottery Inc. [14916]
Maui Blooms [14917]
Maui Tropicals & Foliage [14918]
McGinnis Farms Inc. [1003]
McKay Nursery Company Inc. [14920]
Metrolina Greenhouses Inc. [14921]
Michigan Peat Div. [18090]
Mid American Growers [14922]
Mt. Eden Floral Co. [14923]
Mueller Co.; Charles H. [14924]
Multi-Grow Investments Inc. [14925]
Musser Forests Inc. [14926]
NAPCO & LBK Marketing Corp. [14927]
New England Pottery Co. [13410]
Nordlie Inc. [14928]
Nortex Wholesale Nursery Inc. [14929]
Novartis Seeds Inc. [1092]
Of Distinction, Inc. - The Silk Plant Co. [14930]
Orchid Plantation, Inc. [14931]
Oregon Floral Distributors [14932]
Orkin Lawn Care [14933]
Outer Bay Trading Co. [14934]
Pacific Floral Exchange, Inc. [14935]
Pallian & Co. [14936]
Paradise Flower Farms Inc. [14937]
Pasqua Florist & Greenhouse [14938]
Pearl's Garden Center [14939]
Pennock Co. [14940]
Perennial Gardens [14941]
Pikes Peak Greenhouses, Inc. [14942]
QCU Inc. [13431]
Quintal Farms [14943]
Rapers of Spencer Inc. [26629]
Reising and Co.; G. [14944]
Roak's Seven-Acre Greenhouses [14945]
Rott-Keller Supply Co. [3175]
Rowland Nursery Inc. [1216]
Sally's Flower Shop [14946]
Schluckbier Inc.; Jerry [14947]
Sequoia Floral International [14948]
Sharion's Silk Flower Outlet [14949]
Silk and Morgan Inc. [14950]
Skinner Nursery Inc. [14951]
Skyline Distributing Co. [15656]
South Cedar Greenhouses [14952]
Southern Floral Co. [14953]
Southern Importers Inc. [14954]
Spokane Flower Growers [14955]
Stein Garden and Gifts [14956]
Stevens Inc.; Gerald [14957]
Super American Import [14958]
Synnestvedt Co. [14959]
Tennessee Florist Supply Inc. [14960]
Terre Company of New Jersey Inc. [1324]
Teters Floral Products Inc. [14961]
Toma International [1340]
Tonkadale Greenhouses [14962]
Tropical Gardens of Maui [14963]
U.A.F. L.P. [14964]
Ulery Greenhouse Co. [14965]
United Floral Supply Inc. [14966]

U.S.A. Floral Products [14967]
Valley Crest Tree Co. [1390]
Van Ness Water Gardens Inc. [14968]
Van Wingerden International Inc. [14969]
Vermont Flower Exchange [14971]
Volcano Flowers & Greenery [14972]
Watanabe Floral, Inc. [14973]
Watanabe Floral, Inc. [14974]
Wetsel Inc. [14975]
Wight Nurseries Inc. [14976]
Wilderness Nursery [14977]
Wilson Nursery; Dave [14978]
Yamashiro, Inc.; A. [14979]
Yoder Brothers Inc. [14980]
Zamzow's Inc. [1469]
Zeigler's Market [14981]
Zieger and Sons Inc. [14982]
Zorbite Corp. [4561]

SIC 5194 — Tobacco & Tobacco Products

4th Street Tobacco Warehouse [26255]
800 JR Cigar Inc. [26256]
Abraham and Sons Inc.; S. [26257]
Alpena Wholesale Grocery Co. [10377]
Alternative Cigarettes Inc. [26258]
Amcon Distributing Co. [26259]
AMCON Distributing Co. [10392]
Aquafilter Corp. [26260]
Auburn Merchandise Distributors Inc. [10468]
Automatic Vendors Inc. [26261]
Axton Candy and Tobacco Co. [26262]
Badeaux Co.; Edward [26263]
Barentsen Candy Co. [26264]
Big Horn Wholesale [4580]
Birmingham Tobacco Co. [26265]
Bond Wholesale, Inc. [26266]
Briggs Inc. [26267]
Brudnick Company Inc.; James [19203]
Bur-Bee Co. Inc. [10644]
Burklund Distributors Inc. [10645]
Burlington Drug Co. [26268]
Buyers Paper & Specialty Inc. [26269]
Callahan Grocery Co. Inc. [10679]
Campbell Tobacco Rehandling Company
    Inc. [26270]
Capital Wholesale Distribution Co. [26271]
Capitol Distributing [26272]
Caravan Trading Corporation [4342]
Cash Wholesale Candy Co. [10712]
Central District Inc. [26274]
Centre Jobbing Co. [26275]
Coclin Tobacco Corp. [26276]
Cole Brothers and Fox Co. [26277]
Concord Sales Co. [26278]
Consolidated Wholesale Co. [26279]
Core-Mark International Inc. [10840]
Core-Mark International Inc. [26280]
Core-Mark International Inc. Core-Mark International
    Incorporated Div. [10841]
Corr-Williams Co. [26281]
Corr-Williams Wholesale Company Inc. [26282]
Corso Inc.; Frank P. [26283]
Cowan Brothers Inc. [4605]
Cullen Distributors Inc. [26284]
Dakota Drug Inc. [14078]
Davenport and Sons Inc.; J.T. [10913]
Davis & Butler, Inc. [26285]
Davis and Sons Inc.; F.A. [26286]
Digrazia Wholesale Distributing; Joseph E. [26288]
Douglas Northeast Inc. [10986]
Eagle Wholesale L.P. [11011]
Eby-Brown Company L.P. [26289]
Edmiston Brothers Inc. [11028]
El Grande Distributors Inc. [26290]
Elmira Distributing [1674]
Equity Cooperative Association [22238]
Famous Smoke Shop Inc. [26291]
Fargo-Moorhead Jobbing Co. [11082]
Farner Bocken Co. [26292]
Farner Bocken Co. [11107]
Farner & Co. [11108]

Fleming [11145]
Flue-Cured Tobacco Cooperative Stabilization
    Corp. [26293]
Frank and Company Inc.; S.M. [26294]
Frank, Inc.; Sam [26295]
Franklin Cigar and Tobacco Company Inc. [26296]
Freeman Tobacco Warehouse [26297]
Fritz Company Inc. [11218]
Garber Brothers Inc. [11232]
Gem State Distributors Inc. [26298]
General Trading Company Inc. [11252]
Gragnon Wholesale [11303]
Grave and Son Inc.; F.D. [26299]
Gray's Wholesale Inc. [26300]
Grocers Specialty Co. [11329]
Grocery Supply Co. [11333]
GSC Enterprises Inc. [11342]
Guarnieri Co.; Albert [21754]
H & M Distributing Inc. [26301]
Habys Sales Candy Co. [11354]
Hadley Braithwait Co. [11357]
Hattiesburg Grocery Co. [11391]
Hawaiian Isles Distributors [26302]
Hawaiian Isles Distributors [26303]
Hayward Distribution Center [26304]
Heartland Distributors, Inc. [26305]
Henry's Foods Inc. [11414]
Hettinger-Mobridge Candy & Tobacco [26306]
HI Line Wholesale Co. [26307]
HIE Holdings, Inc. [11428]
Hill City Wholesale Company Inc. [21760]
Holiday Wholesale Inc. [26308]
Huser-Paul Company Inc. [26309]
Imperial Trading Co. [26310]
J & V Vending Wholesale [26311]
J and V Vending Wholesale [26312]
Jans Distributing Inc. [26313]
Jones-McIntosh Tobacco Company Inc. [26314]
Kaiser Wholesale Inc. [26315]
Kamaaina Distribution [11578]
Kamaaina Distribution Co. [26316]
Keilson-Dayton Co. [26317]
Kenan Oil Co. [11600]
Kennedy Wholesale Inc. [11601]
Kenyon, Inc.; Harry [26318]
Kern & Sons; Jacob [11604]
Klee Wholesale Company, Inc. [26319]
Klosterman Company Inc.; John C. [26320]
L and L Jiroch Distributing Co. [26321]
Lane Ltd. [26322]
Lavin Candy Company Inc. [11685]
Lee Cash & Carry [11691]
Levinson Associates Inc.; Harold [26323]
Linco Distributors [26324]
Longo Distributors Inc. [26325]
Lord Brothers & Higgins [21811]
Luckett Tobaccos Inc. [26326]
Martin Brothers International [26327]
Melhado Co.; George [26328]
Milhem & Brothers; Attea [26329]
Miller and Hartman South Inc. [11899]
Minter-Weisman Co. [11908]
Moore, Inc.; A.E. [4673]
Moreland Wholesale Co., Inc. [11935]
Mound City Industries Inc. [11940]
Mountain Service Distributors [26330]
National Distributing Co. [1902]
New England Variety Distributors [24993]
New England Variety Distributors [12002]
New Hampshire Tobacco Corp. [26331]
New Hampshire Tobacco Corp. [26332]
North Idaho Distributing Inc. [26333]
Northwest Tobacco and Candy Inc. [26334]
Notini and Sons Inc.; Albert H. [26335]
Noyes and Son Inc.; J.C. [12042]
O.K. Distributing Company Inc. [26336]
Pablo Don Cigar Co. [26337]
Parker Tobacco Company [26338]
Philip Morris Products Inc. [26339]
Pine Lesser and Sons Inc. [26340]
Pine State Tobacco and Candy Co. [26341]
Polep Distribution Services Inc.; J. [26342]
Powers Candy Company Inc. [12201]
Premium Cigars International Ltd. [26343]
Quaglino Tobacco and Candy Company
    Inc. [26344]

Queen City Wholesale Inc. [12255]
Queen City Wholesale Inc. [12256]
Raketty Co.; A.E. [26345]
Republic Tobacco L.P. [26346]
Republic Tobacco L.P. [26347]
Reuben's Wines & Spirits [1985]
Roach and Smith Distributors, Inc. [1994]
Rosario Candy Inc. [26348]
S & H Co. [26349]
Safier's Inc. [12387]
Smiths Sons Co.; F.X. [26350]
Snyder Wholesale Inc. [12524]
Southwestern Tobacco Co. [26351]
Stalling Inc. [26352]
Stomel & Sons; Joseph H. [12588]
Stomel and Sons; Joseph H. [12589]
Sullivan Candy & Supply [26354]
Sunfire Corporation [12610]
SWD Corp. [26355]
T.B.I. Corp. [12703]
Thompson Company Inc. [12718]
Tidewater Wholesalers Inc. [4717]
Tobacco Sales Company Inc. [26357]
Tobacco Shop at Hyatt [26358]
Topicz [26360]
Tri-State Wholesale Associated Grocers
    Inc. [12754]
Trompeter Co.; John F. [26361]
UETA Inc. [26362]
United Candy and Tobacco Co. [26363]
United States Tobacco Sales and Marketing
    Co. [26364]
Universal Leaf Tobacco Company Inc. [26366]
Valley Convenience Products [26367]
Valley Vending Service Inc. [26368]
Van's Candy & Tobacco Service [12830]
Vega Enterprises Inc. [26369]
Veterans Supply & Distributing Co. [4723]
Virginia Wholesale Co. [12849]
Wagner Candy Co. [12862]
W.C. Distributors Corp. [26370]
Weeke Wholesale Company Inc. [26371]
Western Stations Co. [22798]
White and White Pharmacy Inc. [19704]
Wholesale Supply Company Inc. [26372]
Wholesale Supply Company Inc. [26373]
Wiemuth and Son Company Inc. [26374]
Windsor Shade Tobacco Co. [26375]
Winters; Adam [12963]
Witt Co.; Eli [26376]
Zucca Inc.; L.J. [26377]

SIC 5198 — Paints, Varnishes & Supplies

ABC Auto Paint Supply [21373]
Advanced Color Coatings Inc. [21374]
Ag-Land FS Inc. [194]
Akers & Chrysler Inc. [21375]
Akzo Coatings [21376]
Alaska Housewares Inc. [14996]
Alaskan Paint Manufacturing Company
    Inc. [21377]
All Paint Supply Co. [21378]
Allpro Corp. [21379]
Allpro Corp. [21380]
Allpro Corp. [21381]
Almar, Ltd. [21382]
Alta Paint & Coatings [21383]
Aluma Panel, Inc. [21384]
Ameritone Devoe Paints [21385]
Ameritone Paint Corp. [21386]
Amsterdam Brush Corp. [21387]
Anatech Ltd. [21388]
Apollo Colors Inc. [21389]
Approved Color Corp. [21390]
Architectural Surfaces, Inc. [15406]
Armitage Industrial Supply, Inc. [16710]
Asel Art Supply [25562]
A.T. Supply [21391]
Aucutt's General Store [21392]
Auto Body Paint and Supply [21393]
Auto Body Supply of Orem [21394]

Auto Wholesale and Hartsville Paint Store [21395]
B & A Paint Co. [21396]
Baldridge Lumber Co.; J.C. [7016]
Barry Sales Inc. [21397]
Bearing Distributors [16729]
Bennetts East Side Paint & Gloss [21399]
Berg Fargo Motor Supply Inc. [2350]
Berint Trading, Ltd. [13593]
Big Sky Paint Co., Heating & Air
    Conditioning [21400]
Blaine's Paint Store, Inc. [21401]
Blast-Spray Equipment Co. [25575]
Blick Co.; Dick [25576]
Boise Paint & Glass Inc. [21402]
Bond Paint Co. [21403]
Bond Paint Co. [21404]
Bradley Supply Company Inc.; R.W. [7075]
Brewster Wallcovering Co. [15429]
Bridges Smith & Co. [21405]
Broadway Industries Corp. [21406]
Brod-Dugan Co./Sherwin Williams Co. [21407]
Bruder and Sons Inc.; M.A. [21408]
Brunschwig and Fils Inc. [15430]
Budeke's Paint [21409]
Builders Hardware and Supply Co. Inc. [13612]
Builders Warehouse [7102]
Cabin Craft Southwest, Inc. [25588]
CADCO Div. [355]
Capital Carousel Inc. [21410]
Capital Paint & Glass Inc. [21411]
Cappel Distributing Co. [21412]
Carpet Mart & Wallpaper [9770]
Carpet Mart & Wallpaper Outlet [15435]
Cedar Valley FS Inc. [381]
Central Distribution Services, LLC [13626]
Century-Federman Wallcoverings Inc. [15440]
Chapman Marine Supply [18478]
Clamyer International Corp. [21413]
Clarence House Imports Ltd. [21414]
Columbia Paint & Coatings [21415]
Columbia Paint Co. [21416]
Columbus Wallcovering Co. [15451]
Consolidated Coatings Corp. [21417]
Contract Decor Inc. [15453]
Cook and Dunn Paint Corp. Adelphi
    Coating [21418]
Courtaulds Coatings Inc. Southeast Div. [21419]
Cover and Son Wholesale Lumber Inc.;
    H.A. [7225]
Coyle Inc. [15459]
Creative Paint & Glass Inc. [21420]
Crittenden Paint and Glass [21421]
Curtis & Campbell Inc. [21422]
Curtis Paint [21423]
D & A Distributing [2519]
D & D Specialties Millwork [7241]
Dale's Auto Paints & Supplies [21424]
Daret Inc. [21425]
Davis Paint Co. [21426]
Dean Supply Inc.; Bob [15934]
Deaton's Carpet One [9851]
Decorative Engineering and Supply Inc. [15938]
Decorative Products Group [9852]
Design Finishes Inc. [13087]
Design Impressions Inc. [21427]
Design Marketing Associates [13088]
Devoe Paint [21428]
Dial Battery Paint & Auto Supply [21429]
Diamond Art & Craft [25628]
Diamond Vogel Inc. [21430]
Diamond Vogel Paint Center [21431]
Diamond Vogel Paint Center [21432]
Diamond Vogel Paint Center [21433]
DJ's Alaska Rentals, Inc. [15954]
Dremont-Levy Co. [21434]
Du Pont Co. [21435]
Dupont de Nemours and Co.; E.I. [4376]
Eco Design Co. [21436]
Ellis Paint Co. [21437]
Elmwood Paint Center [21438]
Emery Waterhouse Co. [13681]
Erickson's Decorating Products, Inc. [21439]
Esty and Sons Inc.; Ralph A. [7323]
Fairview True Value Hardware [13693]
Fargo Glass and Paint Co. [21440]
FinishMaster Inc. [2617]

First Automotive Inc. [2618]
Fisher's Incorporated Painting Co. [21441]
Flamemaster Corp. [21442]
Flexi-Wall Systems [15499]
Florida Protective Coatings Consultants Inc. [21443]
Forbo America Inc. [15503]
Forbo Wallcoverings Inc. [15504]
Forbo Wallcoverings Inc. [21444]
Fortman's Paint & Glass [21445]
Fuller Color Center Inc. [21446]
Fuller-O'Brien Paint Stores [21447]
Fuller-O'Brien Paint Stores [21448]
GCM Corp. [21449]
Gehlhausen Paint Wholesalers [21450]
Genuine Parts Company of West Virginia Inc. [2679]
Glidden Paint & Wallcovering [21451]
Golden State Flooring [9923]
Greenwich Trading Co. [18511]
Griggs Paint Co. [21452]
Gross-Yowell and Company Inc. [7420]
H & R General Painting [21453]
Hadlock Paint Co. [21454]
Hamilton Equipment Inc. [785]
Hammer-Johnson Supply Inc. [7435]
Hansen-Kinney Company Inc. [21455]
Hardlines Marketing Inc. [13735]
Hardware Distributors Inc. [13737]
Hardwood Flooring & Finishes [9937]
Hawaii Hardware Company Ltd. [13745]
Hirshfield's, Inc. [21456]
Holladay Color Center [21457]
House of Glass Inc. [21458]
HPM Building Supply [27320]
Hubbard Paint and Wallpaper [21459]
Hunter and Company of North Carolina [15536]
ICI Dulux Paint Centers [21460]
ICI Dulux Paints [21461]
ICI Dulux Paints [21462]
ICI Paints [21463]
Indurall Coatings Inc. [21464]
Intermountain Specialty Coatings [21465]
Iowa Paint Manufacturing Company Inc. [21466]
J & R Industries Inc. [21468]
Jarvis Supply Co. [16183]
Jennison Industrial Supply [13771]
Jensen Distribution Services [13773]
Jetmore Distributing [15182]
Jones Blair Co. [21469]
Kauai Paint & Jalousie [21470]
Keith-Sinclair Company Inc. [21471]
Kentucky Mine Supply Co. [16989]
Key-Duncan Wallcoverings [15548]
Klenosky Co.; S. [21472]
Klinger Paint Co., Inc. [21473]
Komac Paint Center [21474]
Komac Paint Center [21475]
Komer and Co. [21476]
Kona Marine Supply [18537]
Kraft Korner Inc. [26556]
KR's Paint Shop [21478]
The Kruse Company [13789]
Kwal-Hanley Paint Co. [21479]
Kwal-Howells Inc. [21480]
Kwal-Howells Paint & Wallcovering [21481]
Kwal-Howells Paint & Wallcovering [21482]
Kwal-Howells Paint & Wallcovering [21483]
Laagco Sales [21484]
Landers-Segal Color Co. [21485]
Lannans Paint & Decorating Ctr. [21486]
Lapierre; Bill [21487]
LBI Wallcovering [21489]
Leach Company Inc.; W.W. [21490]
Leese Flooring Supply [9994]
Lehman Paint Co. Inc. [21491]
Licht Company Inc.; J.C. [21492]
Lipscomb and Co.; H.G. [13797]
Llewellyn Supply [18549]
Lloyd Ltd.; Reston [21493]
Loock & Company Inc.; R.J. [2892]
Loomis Paint & Wallpaper Ctr [21494]
Lynne Company Inc.; J.M. [15572]
Maharam Fabric Corp. [26131]
Management Supply Co. [23248]
Mantrose-Haeuser Company Inc. [21495]

Masterchem Industries Inc. [21496]
Matthews Paint Co. [21497]
Mattos Inc. [21498]
Mautz Paint Co. [21499]
Maxco Inc. [20159]
Mercantile Buyer's Service Inc. [21500]
Meyer Company Inc.; William F. [23261]
Mid-South Supply Corp. [21501]
Midwest Floors [10033]
Midwest Industrial Coatings Inc. [21502]
Mine and Mill Supply Co. [20197]
Minnesota Mining & Manufacturing Co. Do-It-Yourself Div. [17044]
Mission Paint & Glass [21503]
Mobile Paint Distributors [21504]
Modern Paint & Wallpaper Inc. [21505]
Mohawk Finishing Products Inc. [21506]
Motif Designs, Inc. [21507]
Mount Pleasant Hardware Inc. [21508]
Mountain West Paint Distributor [21509]
Muralo Company Inc. [21510]
Mutual Services of Highland Park [13841]
MVR Auto Refinishing Supplies [21511]
Nakagawa Painting, Inc.; James [21512]
Nashua Wallpaper & Paint Co. [21513]
Nason Automotive [21514]
National Paint Distributors [21515]
National Paint Distributors [21516]
National Patent Development Corp. [21517]
New United Distributors [21518]
Niles Color Center [21519]
Norwood Auto Parts Co. [3048]
Ocean Products Research, Inc. [18576]
Otto's Paint & Supply Co. [21520]
Pacific Coast Chemical Co. [21521]
Pacific Flooring Supply [10092]
Pacific Home Furnishings [15608]
Pacific Paint Center, Inc. [21522]
Padco Inc. [21523]
The Paint Bucket [21524]
Paint Dept. [21525]
Paint & Equipment Supply [21526]
Paint & Glass Supply Company Inc. [21527]
The Paint Store [21528]
Paint Supply Co. [21529]
Paint West Decor Center [21530]
Painter's Choice [21531]
Parks Corp. [21532]
Parts Associates Inc. [13864]
Parts Inc. [3083]
Passonno Paints [21533]
Pearl Paint Co., Inc. [21534]
Penn Color Inc. [21535]
Penobscot Paint Products Co. [21536]
Perschon Paint & Wallcovering [21537]
Perspectives [21538]
Phelans [15619]
Pioneer Coatings Inc. [21539]
Pioneer Manufacturing Co. [21540]
Plaza Paint Co. [21541]
Polar Supply Company Inc. [21542]
Ponderosa Paint Stores [21543]
PPG Industries, Inc. [21544]
Preservative Paint Company Inc. [21545]
Prime Coatings [21546]
Professional Paint Supply [21548]
Queens Decorative Wallcoverings Inc. [15627]
Quill, Hair & Ferrule [21549]
Ray's Workshop [21550]
Re-Neva Inc. [21551]
Red Spot Paint Varnish Co. [21552]
Redlands Auto Parts [3141]
Reece Supply Company of Dallas [25800]
Relco Engineers [21553]
Reno Brake Inc. [21554]
Ren's Clearfield Paint & Glass [21555]
Reston Lloyd Ltd. [21556]
RKB Enterprises Inc. [23345]
Roberts and Sons Inc.; Frank [7943]
Rodda Paint Co. [21557]
Romanoff Corp.; Maya [15640]
Ruidoso Paint Center Inc. [21558]
Sanborn's Paint Spot Inc. [21559]
Saria International Inc. [13903]
Schulte Paint [21560]
Scotty's Inc. [7993]

Seabrook Wallcoverings Inc. [15650]
Sentry/Liberty Hardware Distributors Inc. [13911]
Sequence (USA) Co. Ltd. [21561]
Sequoia Paint [21562]
Service Central, Inc. [21563]
Seven Paint and Wallpaper Co.; John [21564]
Seymour of Sycamore Inc. [21565]
Shaheen Paint and Decorating Company, Inc. [21566]
Sharp Products International, Inc. [17170]
Sherwin Williams Paint Co. [21567]
Sherwin Williams Paint Co. [21568]
Sherwin Williams Paint Co. [21569]
Sherwin Williams Paint Co. [21570]
Sherwin Williams Paint Co. [21571]
Sherwin Williams Paint Co. [21572]
Sherwin Williams Paint Co. [21573]
Sherwin Williams Paint Co. [21574]
Sherwin Williams Paint Co. [21575]
Sherwin Williams Paint Co. [21576]
Shur-Line Inc. [21577]
Siperstein Freehold Paint [21578]
Siperstein, Inc.; N. [21579]
Siperstein, Inc.; N. [21580]
Siperstein, Inc.; N. [21581]
Siperstein, Inc.; N. [21582]
Siperstein MK Paint [21583]
Siperstein West End [21584]
Siperstein's Middletown [21585]
Skips Ameritone Paint Center [21586]
Smith; Merle B. [10155]
SmithChem Div. [21587]
Sorrell Interiors [15661]
South Central Company Inc. [23391]
Specialty Distribution [10175]
Spokane Hardware Supply Inc. [13934]
Stein Paint Co. [21588]
Steven Industries, Inc. [21589]
Strafco Inc. [3272]
Street Art Supply Dallas [21591]
Tasso Wallcovering [15682]
Thompson Lacquer Company Inc. [21592]
Thomson Company Inc.; Geo. S. [17227]
Thybony Wallcoverings Co. [21593]
Tilers—Pergo Shop; J.R. [10247]
Tower Paint Manufacturing [21594]
Tri-County Distributors [25848]
Triangle Coatings, Inc. [21595]
Tsigonia Paint Sales [21596]
Valdes Paint & Glass [21597]
Valley Paint [21598]
Viking Woodcrafts, Inc. [21599]
Wallcoverings, Ltd. [21600]
Wallpaper Hawaii, Ltd. [21601]
Warner Manufacturing Co. [21602]
Warwick Auto Parts Inc. [21603]
Weissman & Sons Inc.; Carl [21604]
Wellborn Paint Manufacturing Co. [21605]
West Carpenter Paint & Flooring [21606]
West Penn Laco Inc. [17275]
Western Pacific Interior [10293]
Westgate Fabrics Inc. [21607]
Whisler Bearing Co. [21608]
White Inc.; H. Lynn [15707]
Wholesale Paint Center, Inc. [21609]
Williams Paint & Coatings [21610]
Wilmar Industries Inc. [23461]
Wilson and Sons Inc.; W.A. [15708]
Wiltech Corp. [21611]
Young's: The Paint Place [21612]
Zeeland Lumber and Supply Inc. [8253]
Zinsser & Co., Inc.; William [21613]

SIC 5199 — Nondurable Goods Nec

3A Products [25951]
A-Pet, Inc. [27054]
Aaraya Beauty Accents [14007]
Abba Products Corp. [27055]
Abbey Ice Co. [24903]
ABC Display and Supply Inc. [25540]
Abel Carbonic Products Inc. [4311]
Aberdeen Vault Inc.; Wilbert [25541]
Accesories That Matter [18366]

Accessories Palace [13288]
Accura Music, Inc. [3467]
Ace Bag and Burlap Co. Inc. [25952]
Achievement Products Inc. [13289]
Acme Agri Supply Inc. [27056]
Acme Machell Company Inc. [24264]
Action Products International Inc. [26381]
Ad House Inc. [13290]
Ada Feed and Seed Inc. [182]
Adams Apple Distributing L.P. [13291]
Adams Foam Rubber Co. [24265]
Adler Inc.; Kurt S. [13292]
Advertising Gifts Inc. [13293]
Advertising Products Company Inc. [13294]
A/E Supplies [13295]
Aetna Felt Corp. Mechanical Felt and Textile
   Div. [25954]
Agri Feed & Supply [27057]
Agri Supplies [27058]
Airtex Consumer Products [15392]
A.K. International [13296]
Akrochem Corp. [24266]
A.L. Investors Inc. [13297]
Alamex Crafts Inc. [26384]
Alaska Garden and Pet Supply [27059]
Alimenta (USA) Inc. [10364]
All Pet Distributors [27060]
All Star Pet Supply [27061]
Allen's Supply Co. [223]
Allstar Enterprises Inc. [13298]
Almar Industries [13299]
Alpena Screen Arts [4763]
Alpine Evergreen Company Inc. [27277]
ALR Wholesale [27062]
Alvin and Co. Inc. [25548]
Alvin and Company Inc. [24310]
A.M. Associates Inc. [13300]
Amber Grout Sales [27063]
American Accessories International Inc. [18369]
American Comb Corp. [14018]
American Cord and Webbing Inc. [25958]
American Gift Corp. [13301]
American Pet Pro [27064]
American Sandpainting [13302]
American Textile Export Co. [25960]
AMG Corp. [13303]
Anapet [27065]
Angel Gifts and Noah's Art [13304]
Animal Medic Inc. [27067]
Anjo Distributors [27068]
Another Dancing Bear Productions [13305]
Antara Music Group [3519]
Apex Plastic Industries Inc. [22928]
Apollo Pet Supply [27069]
Appalachian Distributors [3521]
Aqualife [27070]
Aquaperfect [27071]
Aquarium Pet Book Distributors [27072]
Ark Grooming [27073]
Ark Manufacturing Inc. [27074]
Army & Navy Supplies [4785]
Around the Corner [13306]
Arrow Wholesale Co. Inc. [26397]
Art Barn Enterprises [25560]
Art Craft Wallets Inc. [18371]
Art Glass House, Inc. [25561]
Artistic Stone of America [13307]
Artmark Chicago Ltd. [15407]
Asel Art Supply [25562]
Assorted Book Co. [3528]
Astra International [13309]
Atchison Leather Products [18372]
Atkins Inc.; Frederick [25563]
Atlantic Promotions [25565]
Atwood Leather Cutting [18373]
Aungst Wholesale; Dan [26402]
Aurora Cooperative Elevator Co. [263]
Avant Gardens Silk Plants [14811]
Avian Kingdom Supply Inc. [27075]
Award Pet Supply [27077]
B and F System Inc. [15411]
B-J Pac-A-Part [4575]
B Sharp Co. [27078]
Baba International Inc. [17324]
Baker's Fine Jewelry and Gifts [17325]
Ballard and Co.; W.P. [4576]

Balloon House [26408]
Banian Trading Co. [4801]
Barbuscak and Associates; John [13310]
Barrett Company Inc.; L.W. [13311]
Barry's Office Service Inc. [20832]
Basketville Inc. [13312]
Bata Shoe Co. Inc. [24683]
Beachcombers International Inc. [13313]
Beaulieu of America Inc. [25977]
Beggs and Cobb Corp. [18375]
Beistle Co. [13314]
Bell Industries Graphic [25571]
Belwool Corp. [25980]
Ben Wa Novelty Corp. [13315]
Bennett's Pet Center [27080]
Berman Leather Company Inc. [18376]
Best Pet Distributing [27081]
Big Apple Enterprises [13317]
Big Valley Plastics Inc. [22937]
Bird Toy Man [27083]
Blackman Associates, Inc.; Mel [13318]
Blaine's Art & Graphic Supply [13319]
Blick Co.; Dick [25576]
Bloodline Agency [27085]
Blue Pearl [17344]
Blue Ridge Fish Wholesale [27086]
Blue Ridge Mountain Woodcrafts Inc. [13320]
Blue Ridge Wholesale [27087]
Blumenthal-Lansing Co. [25983]
Blyth Industries Inc. [15422]
Border Leather Corp. [18377]
Boston Pet Supply, Inc. [27088]
Botkin Grain Co. Inc. [27089]
Bounty Trading Co. [10599]
Bouquet Enterprises Inc. [13321]
Bowline Family Products Inc. [25895]
Boyd & Associates; Robert W. [13322]
Brady Co.; Joseph M. [27091]
Brechner and Co. Inc.; Dan [26425]
Breeders Edge [27092]
Brighter Image Publishing [13323]
Brown & Bros. Inc.; Arthur [25583]
Brown County Co-op [339]
Buckler's Inc. [13324]
Buck's War Surplus [23574]
Bugatti Inc. [18378]
Burkmann Feed [27093]
Burkmann Feeds—Glasgow [27094]
Burkmann Feeds—London [27095]
Burkmann Mills [27096]
C-Mor Co. [15433]
C & S Distributors [25586]
Cabin Craft Southwest, Inc. [25588]
CableLink Inc. [6035]
Cady Industries Inc. [21664]
Cajun Sales [27098]
Calcom Graphic Supply, Inc. [25589]
Calcom Graphic Supply, Inc. [25590]
Calcom Graphic Supply, Inc. [25591]
Calcom Inc. [15863]
Caliendo-Savio Enterprises Inc. [13325]
California Gift Center Inc. [26433]
Camel Outdoor Products Inc. [13480]
Canine Commissary [27099]
Canson Talens, Inc. [25596]
Canvas Specialty [25994]
Capital Pet Supply [27100]
Cardona Inc. [13326]
Care-A-Lot [27101]
Carlson Dolls Co. [13327]
Carolina Vet Supply [27102]
Cascade Seed Co. [376]
Casey Inc.; John R. [4594]
Cashway Pet Supply [27103]
Catalina Cottage [25597]
Cathay International [8508]
Cathedral Art Metal Inc. [17364]
CCL Creative Ltd [13328]
Cee-J Wholesale [26439]
Celebrity, Inc. [14838]
Central Garden and Pet Co. [391]
Central Garden and Pet Co. Pet Supplies
   Div. [27104]
Central Garden and Pet Supply Inc. [392]
Central Garden and Pet Supply Inc. [27105]
Central Garden & Pet Supply Inc. [27106]

Central Garden and Pet Supply Inc. [393]
Central Garden & Pet Supply Inc. [27107]
Ceramics By Bob and Hazel [26441]
Chapin Co.; Noel R. [13329]
Charles Products Inc. [13330]
Charles River BRF Inc. [406]
Charter Pet Supplies [27108]
Cherrybrook [27109]
Chicago Import Inc. [13331]
Claymore Sieck Co. [13635]
C.M. Paula Co. [21682]
Coastal Supply Co., Inc. [25604]
Cocke Farmers Cooperative Inc. [432]
Coffee Mill Roastery [10787]
Columbia Impex Corp. [18384]
Comer Packing Company Inc. [13332]
Commercial Art Supply [25606]
Congress Leather Co. [27111]
Conkey's Bookstore [3652]
Consolidated International [13334]
Consumer Products Co. [25906]
Coop Country Partners [445]
Cork Supply International Inc. [15456]
Cornilsen's Backyard Bird [27112]
Country Originals Inc. [13336]
Cousin Corporation of America [26451]
Cowan Costume, Inc. [13337]
Coyote Pet Products Inc. [27113]
CPP-Belwin Inc. [3665]
Craft Corner [26452]
Craft Enterprises [26453]
Craft-Tex/Phase IV Inc. [13338]
Crafts Etc. Ltd. [25613]
Creative Merchandising Inc. [13339]
Cresc Corp. [13340]
Cromwell Leather Group [18385]
Crown Imports [13341]
CSL and Associates Inc. [15921]
Custom Leathercraft Manufacturing [18386]
Customline of North America, Inc. [13342]
D & J Manufacturing Inc. [13343]
D & L Stained Glass Supply, Inc. [25619]
Daniels Co.; C.P. [27114]
Dave's Jewelry & Giftware [17389]
Dawg Luvers & Co. [13344]
Debra Inc. [14081]
The Depot Ltd. [13345]
Design Craft [14856]
Design Impressions Inc. [21427]
Desmond Process Supply Co. [25627]
Dessau Brass Inc. [13346]
Diamond Art & Craft [25628]
Diamond Leather Inc. [18387]
Diamond Supply, Inc. [25629]
Dimensional Graphics Corp. Risto Division [18388]
Diversified Foam Products Inc. [22956]
DL Pet Supply [27116]
D.M.R. Distributors [25632]
DMR International [25633]
Dodge & Son Inc.; Herman [15113]
Dog Outfitters [27117]
Dogloo Inc. [27118]
Dogroom Products [27119]
Don and Co.; Edward [15478]
Dove Wholesale [27120]
Drulane/ Palmer Smith [15481]
Drybranch Inc. [23631]
Duchess Royale Inc. [15482]
Duchin Inc.; Gloria [13347]
East Distributors Ltd.; Ryan [3706]
Ebeling & Reuss Co. [13351]
Ebinger Brothers Leather Co. [18391]
Eble Music Co. [3712]
Economy Distributors [27122]
Economy Foods [11023]
ECS Publishing Corporation [3715]
Edcat Enterprises [19303]
Edco Manufacturing Co. [27123]
Ed's Leather Co. [27124]
Educational Coin Co. [26476]
Edward's Pet Supplies Co. [27125]
Efland Distributing Co. [27126]
Eide Industries Inc. [15486]
El Paso Onyx Co. Inc. [13352]
Elchar Dog Bows [27127]

Elco Manufacturing Company Inc. [18392]
Emma Cooperative Elevator Co. [27129]
The Empire Co. [4938]
Ergonomic Design Inc. [20994]
Espana General Importers [13353]
Excel Tanning Corp. [18393]
Exotic Rubber and Plastics Corp. [16852]
Export Consultant Service [24358]
Falcon Industries Inc. [26032]
Fallah Enterprises [13354]
Far Corners Importers Ltd. [13355]
Farrell Imports Inc.; Patrick [18394]
Fashion Victim [4946]
Fashions Inc. Jackson [4947]
Feldstein and Associates Inc. [13356]
FFR Inc. [25649]
Field and Associates Inc. [17414]
Fine-Line Products Inc. [4953]
Fire-Dex Inc. [25651]
Firey Pet Supplies [27131]
First Coast Pet Supply [27132]
Fischer Inc.; Carl [3750]
Flash Fireworks [26482]
Flexible Flyer Co. [26483]
Flo-Pac Pacific Div. [15500]
Floralife Inc. [14865]
Florexotica Hawaii [14867]
Florida Craft Wholesale [26484]
Flury & Co. Ltd. [13358]
Foam Factory and Upholstery Inc. [22964]
Foam Products of San Antonio Inc. [22965]
Foreign Trade Marketing [11187]
Forschner Group Inc. [15505]
Fotofolio Inc. [21729]
Franco-American Novelty Company Inc. [13359]
Franklin Stores Inc.; Ben [26487]
Friedman Bag Company Inc. [16880]
Fritz Pet Products [27134]
Fritz Pet Supply [27135]
Front Musical Literature; Theodore [3767]
FSC Educational Inc. [3768]
Fuller Supply Co. [27136]
Fuller Supply Co., Inc. [27137]
Fuller Supply Company Inc. [27138]
Gabor International Ltd.; Eva [14107]
Galan Enterprises, Inc. [26489]
Gardner Distributing Co. [724]
Garston, Inc. [25657]
Garston Sign Supplies, Inc. [25658]
Gaylord Cash & Carry [11246]
Gem State Distributors Inc. [26298]
Gemmex Intertrade America Inc. [11247]
General Sales Co. [26496]
Georgies Ceramic & Clay Co. [26499]
Gerlach Oil Company Inc. [22308]
Gibson Co.; C.R. [13360]
Glass Crafters Stain Glass Supply [13361]
Glaze Inc. [13362]
Global Products [26500]
Glucksman & Associates; Barry [17433]
GMS Corp. [18395]
Golden Crown Corp. [27139]
Golden State Foods Corp. [24961]
Golden State Trading Co. [13363]
Goldman Associates Inc. [13364]
Goldman Co.; H.R. [17437]
Gordon Rubber and Packing Company Inc. [24278]
Graeffs Eastside Drugs; Mike [18814]
Grand Stage Co., Inc. [25666]
Graphic Media [25668]
Graphic Systems Inc. [25669]
Great Eastern Pet Supply [27140]
Great Lakes Area Distributing [26505]
Great Western Pet Supply [27141]
Green Leaf Distributors, Inc. [27142]
Grover Industries Inc. [26048]
Gruen Export Co. [17966]
Gully Tri-Coop Association [778]
H & H Distributing [27143]
H & J Leather Finishing [18396]
Habitat Softwear [5012]
Hadley Cos. [3806]
Hahn and Phillips Grease Company Inc. [17968]
Hamakor Judaica Inc. [3807]
Hankes Crafts [26511]

Hanna Rubber Co. [24280]
Happy Acres Pet Supply [27144]
Harrison Wholesale Products Inc. [27145]
Hartz Group Inc. [27146]
Hawkeye Seed Company Inc. [27147]
Hemisphere International [26062]
HHS USA Inc. [13366]
Hibel Studio; Edna [13367]
High Mountain Distributing [27148]
Hillmer's Luggage & Leather [18397]
Hirten Company Inc.; William J. [13368]
Hispania Trading Corporation [25680]
Hobby Crafts [26517]
Hofert Co.; J. [13369]
Hollandia Gift and Toy Co. [26524]
Honolulu Aquarium & Pet Supplies [27150]
Horn EB Replacement Service [15534]
Horns Inc. [13370]
House of Ceramics Inc. [13371]
House of Pets Supplies [27151]
Hoven Inc. [26526]
Huckleberry People Inc. [11473]
Humboldt Industries, Inc. [27153]
Hunt Co. [26530]
Hunter Co., Inc. [18398]
Hyatt's Graphic Supply Company, Inc. [25684]
Idaho Outdoor Equipment [26070]
Idaho Souvenir [13373]
Ideal Pet Supplies [27155]
Imperial Commodities Corp. [11500]
Imperial Display Co. [26531]
Imperial Pet Products [27156]
Import Export Management Service Inc. [21054]
Import Leather Inc. [18400]
Import Warehouse Inc. [13374]
Importmex [13375]
Impulse Merchandisers Inc. [2772]
Incentive Associates Inc. [15539]
Independent Pet Co-op [27157]
Industrial Trade and Development Co. [13376]
Infocase Inc. [18401]
Inter-American Trading [25689]
International Advertising Gifts [13377]
Ives Business Forms Inc. [21073]
Jacobs Trading Co. [15543]
JanWay Co. [13378]
Japco Exports [27159]
Jay's Indian Arts Inc. [17466]
J.B. Wholesale [27160]
Jeffers Vet Supply [27161]
Jeffers Vet Supply [27162]
Jerry's Artarama Inc. [25694]
JFK Enterprises [27163]
Jimson Novelties Inc. [13379]
Julius Kraft Company Inc. [24579]
K-9 Specialists [27165]
K & I Transeau Co. [27166]
K & K Pet Talk [27167]
K & K Vet Supply [27168]
K & R Distributors [27169]
Karla's Kreations Inc. [13380]
Keeton Sales Agency Inc. [26092]
Kenlin Pet Supply [27170]
Kenlin Pet Supply Inc. [27171]
Kennel-Aire Inc. [27172]
Kentucky Buying Cooperative Int. [907]
Keyston Brothers [26109]
Kimbet Leather [27173]
King's Cage [27174]
Kmart Corp. [15553]
Knobler International Ltd. [13381]
Koldkist-Beverage Ice Company Inc. [24981]
KoolaBrew Inc. [13382]
Koval Marketing Inc. [15556]
Kraftbilt Products [25705]
Krause & Sons; M.P. [27175]
Krieger Associates; J. [25707]
Kryolan Corp. [25708]
K's Merchandise Mart Inc. [17494]
L & B Pet Supplies [27176]
L & L Lace [26558]
L & L Pet Center [27177]
L & S Trading Co. [18403]
La Francis Associates; Mal [13383]
LaBelle Time Inc. [13384]
Lad Enterprises, Ltd. [21095]

Lads Pet Supplies [27178]
Landew Sawdust Inc. [27333]
Lankhorst Distributors Inc. [26562]
Lansing Company Inc. [26120]
Larriva Corp. [13386]
Larsen and Associates Inc.; Bill [13387]
Las Cruces Leather Co. [18404]
LBK Marketing Corp. [13388]
Leather Loft Stores [18406]
The Leather Shop [5126]
Lee-Mar Aquarium and Pet Supplies, Inc. [27179]
Leeber Ltd. USA [13389]
Leisure Crafts [25712]
Leisure Time Products Inc. [25713]
Leone's Animal Supply [27180]
Lesco Corp. (Lansing, Michigan) [25714]
Levor and Company Inc.; G. [18052]
Liberty Industries Inc. [25716]
Little Brass Shack Imports [13391]
Logo-Wear Inc. [5141]
Longhorn Pet Supply [27182]
Lorel Co. [21812]
Loria & Sons Westchester Corp.; V. [25720]
Loui Michel Cie. [13392]
Lugo Hair Center Ltd. [14155]
Lynnwood Co. [13393]
M-Bin International Imports [18410]
MacPherson's-Artcraft [25721]
Mahalick Corp. [25722]
Mallory Pet Supplies [27183]
Manneco, Inc. [13395]
Marsh Inc.; Paul [4452]
Marshall Pottery Inc. [14916]
Martek Ltd. [13397]
Martexport Inc. [15579]
Martha Weems Ltd. [13398]
Maruri USA Corp. [13399]
Maryland Leather Inc. [18412]
Maxim Inc.; Mary [26570]
McCall Fireworks Inc. [26572]
McElheney, Inc.; R.H. [27185]
McLogan Supply [25730]
McLogan Supply [25731]
McLogan Supply [25732]
MDI Production [25734]
Medica International Ltd. [1009]
Mello Smello [13400]
Meredith Stained Glass Center, Inc. [25735]
Meridian Veterinary Products [27187]
Merz and Company Inc.; F.O. [13401]
Metro Export and Import Co. [5187]
Mexican Art Imports [13402]
Meyer Inc.; Frances [13403]
Meyers; Tom [27188]
Michelle Textile Corp. [26144]
Michigan Church Supply Company Inc. [3951]
Mikan Theatricals [25739]
Miller Funeral Home Inc. [25741]
Miller Safety Products [24812]
Millers Wholesale, Inc. [25742]
Minnesota Clay Co. USA [26579]
Mitchell Mogal Inc. [13406]
Mize Farm & Garden Supply [27190]
Mole Hole [5199]
Monahan Co.; Thomas [27348]
Montgomery Seed [27191]
Morris Rothenberg and Son Inc. [23836]
Moshy Brothers Inc. [3969]
MS Rubber Co. [17059]
Multicraft Inc. [25745]
Multicraft Inc. [25746]
N Squared Inc. [24407]
Nadel and Sons Toy Corp. [26588]
Najarian Music Company Inc. [3979]
Nasco-Catalog [26589]
Nashville Pet Products Center [27192]
National Art Supply [25748]
National Capital Flag Co. Inc. [13407]
National Impressions Corp. [25749]
National Potteries Corp. [13408]
Nationwide Advertising Specialty Inc. [13409]
Naz-Dar Cincinnati [25752]
Nelson-Jameson Inc. [16347]
New England Pet Supply [27193]
New England Pottery Co. [13410]
New England Serum Co. [27194]

New Jersey Art Drafting [25757]
Newton Manufacturing Co. [13411]
NLS Animal Health [27195]
Nolt's Ponds Inc. [27196]
Norcostco Inc. [25761]
Nordic Wholesale Distributors Inc. [5236]
Northeast Mississippi Coca-Cola Bottling
 Co. [24997]
Northern Sun [13412]
Northpoint Trading Co. Inc. [27197]
Northwest Blueprint and Supply [13413]
Northwest Graphic Supply Co. [25764]
Novelty Advertising Co. [4011]
Novelty Poster Co. [13414]
Novelty Poster Co. [13415]
Now Pet Products [27200]
Now Products [13416]
Nystrom Co. [4013]
Oil-Dri Corp. [22536]
Okhai-Moyer Inc. [21198]
Oklahoma Leather Products Inc. [18414]
Omaha Vaccine [27201]
Orchard Yarn and Thread Company Inc./Lion Brand
 Yarn Co. [26163]
Ordway Sign Supply [25775]
Organ Literature Foundation [4024]
ORRCO, Inc. [27202]
Orrefors Inc. [15602]
Orsen-Porter-Rockwell International [18415]
Ossoff Leather [18416]
Pacific Beverage Company Inc. [25002]
Pacific Group International [13417]
Pacific Hide & Leather Company, Inc. [18417]
Pan Am Sign Products, Inc. [25780]
Pana Bait Co. [23870]
Paradies and Co. [4039]
Party Kits Unlimited Inc. [23874]
Patnaude's Aquarium & Pet [27203]
Patriotic Fireworks Inc. [13418]
Peenware International [13419]
Penobscot Paint Products Co. [21536]
People's Coal Co. [20559]
Pepline/Wincraft [13420]
Perz Feed & Delivery [27204]
Pet Care Wholesale [27205]
Pet Food Wholesale, Inc. [27206]
Pet Lift [27208]
The Pet Pharmacy Inc. [27209]
Pet Products Associates, Inc. [27210]
Pet Supply Warehouse [27211]
Pet World [27212]
Philadelphia Hide Brokerage [18419]
Phillips Ice Service Inc. [14635]
Phillips and Jacobs Inc. [25784]
Pitman Co.; Harold M. [25786]
Pittman International [27214]
PK Imports Inc. [13422]
Podgor Co. Inc.; Joseph E. [16410]
Posters Please Inc. [13424]
Poultry Health [27215]
Preston Fuels; John [15279]
Preston Leather Products [18421]
Price Inc.; Albert E. [13426]
Priddy's General Store [27216]
Prime Resources Corp. [13427]
Primesource [25790]
PrimeSource Corp. [25791]
Print Gallery Inc. [13428]
Pro/Am Music Resources, Inc. [4086]
Progressive Distributors [14199]
Promotions Plus [13429]
Provo Craft Inc. [26181]
Pryor Novelty Co., Inc. [13430]
Punch It Distributing Inc. [26623]
QCU Inc. [13431]
Quaker City Hide Co. [18186]
Quaker City Paper & Chemical [21891]
Quaker City Paper Co. [21893]
Quality Pets, Inc. [27219]
R & R Distributors [27220]
Rack Service Company Inc. [14203]
Rainbow Sales Distributing [13432]
Raj India Trading Corp. Inc. [5301]
Ralston Purina Co., Golden Products Div. [27221]
Ramson's Imports [13433]
Ray's Beaver Bag [13434]

RCF Inc. [13435]
Recognition Systems Inc. [25799]
Recycled Wood Products [1175]
Regal Shearing [18423]
Representative Sales Co. [26184]
Reynolds Metals Co. Construction Products
 Div. [7925]
Reynolds Polymer Technology [7926]
Ri-Mat Enterprises Inc. [13436]
Rice Oil Company Inc. [22627]
Rico Industries Inc. [18424]
Riedel Crystal of America Inc. [15636]
Rieger's Ceramics Arts & Crafts [26635]
Rivard International Corp. [7939]
RNM Specialty Co. [13437]
Road Runner Pet Supplies [27223]
Robbinsdale Farm and Garden Pet Supply
 Inc. [27224]
Robert Manufacturing Company Inc. [18425]
Rock Mirrors Inc. [13438]
Rocket Jewelry Box Inc. [17568]
Rodwell Sales [15637]
Roman Inc. [13439]
Rose City Awning Co. [26192]
Rose Metal Products Inc. [20331]
Royal Arts & Crafts [26638]
Rust Wholesale Company Inc. [12371]
Ryan's Pet Supplies [27225]
Rykoff-Sexton Manufacturing L.L.C. [12377]
S & O Industries Inc. [26196]
S & S [27226]
S and S Worldwide Inc. [25807]
S-T Leather Co. [18216]
Sacks International Inc.; M. [24293]
Sacramento Bag Manufacturing Co. [21919]
Sangray Corporation [13441]
Santa Fe Pet and Vet Supply [27228]
Sara Lee Corp. [12412]
Sarah's Attic Inc. [13443]
Sbar's, Inc. [26647]
Schecter and Sons, Inc.; Nathan [13444]
Schillers Photo Graphics [22903]
Scotland Yard [27229]
Sentry/Liberty Hardware Distributors Inc. [13911]
Sequence (USA) Co. Ltd. [21561]
Sergeant's Pet Products Inc. [27230]
Service Unlimited [3208]
SF Services Inc. [27231]
Shafmaster Company Inc. [18426]
Shell's Bags Hats [13445]
Shepherd Products Co. [23033]
Sher and Mishkin Inc. [26202]
Sherwood Promotions Inc. [25813]
Shiau's Trading Co. [13446]
Sierra Chemical Co [4511]
Silver Blue Associated Ltd. [18427]
Silver Blue Associated Ltd. [18428]
Silvestri Corporation Inc.; Fitz and Floyd [15654]
Sirco International Corp. [18429]
SLC Technologies Inc. [24637]
SLS Arts, Inc. [25819]
Small Talk Inc. [27232]
Smith Inc.; Kenneth [23948]
Snow Filtration Co. [17179]
S.N.S. International Trading [13447]
South Bay Leather Corp. [18431]
Southeast Pet [27234]
Southeastern Colorado Cooperative [1278]
Southern California Trophy Co. [13448]
Southern Wholesale Co. [19629]
Southwest Hide Co. [18246]
Southwest Import Co. [13449]
Soviet American Woolens [26209]
Spartan Pet Supply [27235]
Specially Yours Inc. [13450]
Specialty Catalog Corp. [14244]
Specialty Merchandise Corp. [13451]
Speiser Pet Supplies [27236]
The Spiral Collection, Inc. [15664]
Spola Fibres International Inc. [26210]
Sporting Dog Specialties Inc. [27237]
Sports Impressions Corp. [13452]
Sportscards & Comics Center [26664]
Spradling International Inc. [18432]
Spring Arbor Distribution Company Inc. [4184]
SST Sales Company Inc. [5391]

Stanislaus Imports Inc. [26667]
Stanley Home Products [14245]
Stanz Cheese Company Inc. [12568]
Star Beacon Products Co. [25830]
Star Creation Inc. [13453]
Star Sales Company of Knoxville [26668]
Starmac Group [5393]
Sterco New York Inc. [18433]
Stockman Supply Inc. [27239]
Stomel and Sons; Joseph H. [12589]
Storm Pet Supply Inc. [27240]
Style Asia Inc. [13454]
Sullivan's [13455]
Summit Pet Products [27241]
Summit Pet Products [27242]
Sun Coast Imports [26218]
Sun/Day Distributor Corp. [13456]
Sun & Fun Specialties Inc. [13457]
Sun Hing Trading Company Inc. [13458]
Sun International [24440]
Sun Sales [17626]
Sunset Supply [13459]
Super American Import [14958]
Super Valu Stores Inc. [12634]
Super Valu Stores Inc. [12635]
Swanson, Inc. [21308]
T & E Enterprises & Development [27243]
T & E Wholesale Outlet [13460]
Taylor Company Inc.; Nelson A. [18623]
Taylor Feed & Pet Supply [27245]
Taylor Rental Corp. [1316]
TCC Industries Inc. [13461]
Teknor Apex Co. [24300]
TEM Inc. [13462]
Texas Art Supply Co. [25840]
Texas Leather Trim Inc. [18437]
Texas Recreation Corp. [24008]
Texas Screen Process Supply Co. [25841]
Thomas Sales Company Inc. [26680]
Thomas-Walker-Lacey Inc. [12716]
Thompson Sales; Larry [1331]
Thompson's Veterinary Supplies [27246]
Thunder Mountain Dog Supplies [27247]
Tilton & Sons, Inc.; Ben [18281]
Tobacco Shop at Hyatt [26358]
Top Dog Ltd. [27248]
Town & Country Pet Supply Inc. [27249]
Treasure Chest Books, LLC [4228]
Tree of Life Inc. Midwest [12748]
Tri-Blue Kennel [27251]
Tri-County Distributors [25848]
Tri-Parish Cooperative Inc. [1354]
Tri-State Vet & Pet Supply [27253]
Trims II Inc. [26690]
Trinidad-Benham Corp. [18293]
Tropical Fisheries [27255]
Tubelite Company, Inc. [9515]
Tubelite Company, Inc. [25849]
TW Graphics Group [25850]
Unique Crafters Co. [13465]
United Art Distributors [25853]
United Cooperative Farmers Inc. [1375]
United Pacific Pet L.L.C. [27256]
United Pharmacal Co. [27257]
United Receptacle, Inc. [25855]
United States Check Book Co. [21328]
Universal Corp. [26365]
UPCO Pet Vet Supply [27258]
US Reflector [3378]
Valdez [25495]
Valley Feed Mill Inc. [1393]
Valley Pet Supply [27259]
Valley Vet Supply [27260]
Valley View Vineyard [2098]
Van Den Bosch Co.; John A. [27261]
Vann Sales Co.; Hugh [27262]
Variety Distributors Inc. [15695]
Varon and Associates Inc. [25864]
Vermont Pet Food & Supply [27263]
Vickers International [5462]
Vicki Lane Design [13467]
Viva Handbags Inc. [18438]
Wagner Hardware Co. [13982]
Waikiki Trader Corp. [5470]
Walach Leather Splitting [18440]
Wang's International, Inc. [15701]

Wang's International Inc. [26706]
Warden Leathers Inc. [18441]
Warrior Inc. [13469]
Watson Inc.; Fannie [13470]
Weatherford Enterprise of Flagstaff [27268]
Weisheimer Pet Supply [27269]
Wesco Merchandising [14279]
West Ridge Designs [18444]
West Wholesale [27270]
Western Depot [26709]

Western Trading Post Inc. [26712]
Westport Corp. [18445]
Wilbert Vault of Aroostook [25880]
Wildlife Lithographs, Inc. [13472]
William's Umbrella Co. [13473]
Wills Co. [13474]
Winston-Derek Publishers Group Inc. [4291]
Wise El Santo Company Inc. [5490]
W.L.C. Ltd. [27271]
Wolverton Pet Supply [27272]

Wood-N-Stuf [26715]
World Network Trading Corp. [18446]
Worldwide Distributors Inc. [5492]
Worldwide Dreams LLC [18447]
The Yarn Center [26717]
Zeiger International Inc. [26720]
Zenter Enterprises Ltd. [27273]
Zims Inc. [26721]
The Zondervan Corp. [4307]
Zukerman and Sons Inc.; Sam [13475]

Geographic Index

Entries in this section are arranged alphabetically by state and city, then alphabetically by company name within each city. When the company name is a personal name, the company name is alphabetized by the surname unless the first name or initial(s) are part of a trade name. See the User's Guide at the front of this directory for additional information.

Alabama

Alabaster
Barton's Greenhouse & Nursery (Horticultural Supplies) [14819]
Godbee Medical Distributors (Medical, Dental, and Optical Equipment) [18813]

Albertville
Albertville Electric Motor (Electrical and Electronic Equipment and Supplies) [8288]
Genesis Manufacturing, Inc. (Household Items) [15513]
Wilks Tire and Battery Service (Automotive) [3431]

Alexander City
Alabama Food Group Inc. (Food) [10351]
Alex City Provision Inc. (Food) [10361]
Lake Martin Living (Books and Other Printed Materials) [3892]
Russell Corp. Knit Apparel Div. (Clothing) [5326]

Aliceville
Lewis Brothers Lumber Company Inc. (Construction Materials and Machinery) [7598]

Andalusia
Carquest Distribution Co. Cleaner and Equipment Div. (Automotive) [2430]

Anniston
Adco Inc. (Medical, Dental, and Optical Equipment) [18657]
McCormick Refrigeration (Heating and Cooling Equipment and Supplies) [14535]
Miller's Supply (Plumbing Materials and Fixtures) [23268]
Rite Way Barber & Beauty Supplies (Health and Beauty Aids) [14221]
Smith Distributing Co. (Recreational and Sporting Goods) [23946]
Super Valu Stores Inc. (Food) [12629]

Arab
L & L Lace (Toys and Hobby Goods) [26558]

Ashford
Art Barn Enterprises (Specialty Equipment and Products) [25560]

Athens
Kuykendall's Press (Books and Other Printed Materials) [3890]
Limestone Farmers Cooperative Inc. (Agricultural Equipment and Supplies) [959]
Sweet Sue Kitchens (Food) [12657]

Bayou la Batre
True World Foods, Inc. of Alabama (Food) [12764]

Bessemer
Piggly Wiggly Alabama Distributing Company Inc. (Food) [12168]
Simmons Sporting Goods Company Inc. (Recreational and Sporting Goods) [23940]
Southern Store Fixtures Inc. (Construction Materials and Machinery) [8054]

Birmingham
Adams Brothers Produce Company Inc. (Food) [10323]
AFGD (Household Items) [15390]
Alabama Art Supply (Office Equipment and Supplies) [20779]
Alabama Coal Cooperative (Minerals and Ores) [20508]
Alabama Crankshaft and Engine Warehouse Inc. (Automotive) [2196]
Alabama Crown (Alcoholic Beverages) [1476]
AmeriNet/SupportHealth (Medical, Dental, and Optical Supplies) [19146]
Atlas Safety Equipment Co. Inc. (Shoes) [24677]
Automatic Ice & Beverage Inc. (Heating and Cooling Equipment and Supplies) [14332]
Ballard and Co.; W.P. (Cleaning and Janitorial Supplies) [4576]
Berry Bearing Co. (Industrial Supplies) [16751]
Birmingham Electric Battery Co. (Automotive) [2364]
Birmingham Rail Locomotive Company Inc. (Railroad Equipment and Supplies) [23474]
Birmingham Tobacco Co. (Tobacco Products) [26265]
Bodine Inc. (Furniture and Fixtures) [13040]
Brungart Equipment Company Inc. (Industrial Machinery) [15851]
Bruno's Inc. (Food) [10632]
Consolidated Pipe and Supply Company Inc. (Plumbing Materials and Fixtures) [23123]
Cowin Equipment Company Inc. (Construction Materials and Machinery) [7226]
Cummins Alabama Inc. (Automotive) [2502]
Custom Supply Inc. (Electrical and Electronic Equipment and Supplies) [8601]
David Tire Co. Inc. (Automotive) [2531]
Dillard Paper Co. Birmingham Div. (Paper and Paper Products) [21709]
Dixie Store Fixtures and Sales Company Inc. (Household Items) [15476]
DMACS International Corp. (Computers and Software) [6215]
DMI Tile & Marble (Floorcovering Equipment and Supplies) [9867]
Doctor Computerized Systems (Computers and Software) [6217]
Empire Seafood (Food) [11046]
Floors, Inc. (Floorcovering Equipment and Supplies) [9898]
Fontaine Fifth Wheel Co. (Automotive) [2635]
Fontaine Industries Inc. (Construction Materials and Machinery) [7353]

Forbes Distributing Co. (Electrical and Electronic Equipment and Supplies) [8748]
Fravert Services Inc. (Electrical and Electronic Equipment and Supplies) [8759]
Fresh Fish Inc. (Food) [11209]
Fuller Supply Company Inc. (Veterinary Products) [27138]
General Machinery Company Inc. (Compressors) [5842]
Greg's Cookies Inc. (Food) [11323]
Hart-Greer Ltd. (Household Appliances) [15164]
Henry Tile Co.; Robert F. (Floorcovering Equipment and Supplies) [9941]
Hill City Wholesale Company Inc. (Paper and Paper Products) [21760]
Hinkle Metals and Supply Company Inc. (Metals) [20041]
Hoffman Distributing Co. (Textiles and Notions) [26066]
HVL Technical Services Inc. (Computers and Software) [6347]
Indurall Coatings Inc. (Paints and Varnishes) [21464]
Integrated Medical Systems (Medical, Dental, and Optical Equipment) [18853]
James International Trading Company (Specialty Equipment and Products) [25692]
Jemison Investment Company Inc. (Construction Materials and Machinery) [7533]
Jones Sportswear Company Inc. (Clothing) [5092]
LeJoy Uniforms Inc. (Medical, Dental, and Optical Equipment) [18889]
Long Lewis Inc. (Hardware) [13801]
Long Lewis Inc. (Hardware) [13802]
Marketing Performance Inc. (Food) [11783]
Masco Fabrics Inc. (Textiles and Notions) [26137]
Matthews Electric Supply Company Inc. (Electrical and Electronic Equipment and Supplies) [9046]
Mayer Electric Supply Co. (Electrical and Electronic Equipment and Supplies) [9050]
Mayer Electric Supply Co. (Electrical and Electronic Equipment and Supplies) [9051]
Mayer Electric Supply Company Inc. (Electrical and Electronic Equipment and Supplies) [9052]
Molay Supply Inc. (Household Appliances) [15239]
Money Machinery Co.; Joe (Industrial Machinery) [16320]
Motion Industries Inc. (Industrial Supplies) [17057]
O'Neal Steel Inc. (Metals) [20251]
Perry Supply Inc. (Construction Materials and Machinery) [7851]
Perry Supply Inc. (Construction Materials and Machinery) [7852]
Progressive Tire (Automotive) [3121]
Ram Tool and Supply Co. (Hardware) [13882]
Red Diamond Inc. (Food) [12284]
Reynolds Aluminum Supply (Metals) [20317]
Roberts International, Inc. (Construction Materials and Machinery) [7942]
Royal Cup Inc. (Food) [12363]
S & S Appliance Service Co. (Household Appliances) [15299]

Sema Inc. (Medical, Dental, and Optical
  Equipment) [19035]
Shaklee Distributor (Food) [12469]
Shoe Corporation of Birmingham
  Inc. (Shoes) [24856]
Shoe Corp. of Birmingham Inc. (Clothing) [5348]
Shook and Fletcher Insulation Co. (Industrial
  Supplies) [17173]
Shook and Fletcher Supply of Alabama
  Inc. (Construction Materials and
  Machinery) [8013]
South Central Pool Supply, Inc. (Recreational and
  Sporting Goods) [23955]
Southern Filters Inc. (Industrial Supplies) [17184]
Southern LNG Inc. (Petroleum, Fuels, and Related
  Equipment) [22683]
Southern Publishers Group, Inc. (Books and Other
  Printed Materials) [4173]
Spar Medical Inc. (Medical, Dental, and Optical
  Equipment) [19047]
Stratton's Salads; Mrs. (Food) [12593]
Stringfellow Lumber Co. (Construction Materials and
  Machinery) [8081]
Sunbelt Food Sales (Food) [12608]
Supreme Beverage Co. Inc. (Alcoholic
  Beverages) [2064]
Thompson Tractor Company Inc. (Construction
  Materials and Machinery) [8123]
Thypin Stainless Steel (Metals) [20421]
United Plywood and Lumber Inc. (Construction
  Materials and Machinery) [8159]
Washer and Refrigeration Supply Company
  Inc. (Household Appliances) [15365]
Wedlo Inc. (Jewelry) [17653]
Wheelock Company Inc.; George F. (Heating and
  Cooling Equipment and Supplies) [14763]
White Company Inc.; John R. (Food) [12927]
Wittichen Supply Company Inc. (Heating and
  Cooling Equipment and Supplies) [14771]
Wood-Fruitticher Grocery (Food) [12976]
Xpedx-Birmingham (Chemicals) [4558]
Young and Vann Supply Co. (Industrial
  Supplies) [17293]

Boaz

Peck's Petroleum Inc. (Petroleum, Fuels, and
  Related Equipment) [22556]

Bon Secour

Bon Secour Fisheries Inc. (Food) [10588]

Brewton

Davis Supply Co. Inc. (Industrial Supplies) [16821]

Bridgeport

Williams Oil Co. (Petroleum, Fuels, and Related
  Equipment) [22804]

Brundidge

Wallace Pump and Supply Company Inc. (Plumbing
  Materials and Fixtures) [23436]

Carrollton

Country Miss Carrollton (Clothing) [4901]

Centre

Camo Distributors (Clothing) [4859]
Centre Manufacturing Co. Inc. (Clothing) [4874]

Chickasaw

ST and T Communications Inc. (Communications
  Systems and Equipment) [5768]

Childersburg

Butler & Sons Refrigeration (Heating and Cooling
  Equipment and Supplies) [14365]

Citronelle

North American Cylinders Inc. (Automotive) [3041]

Cullman

Buettner Brothers Lumber Co. (Construction
  Materials and Machinery) [7095]
Buettner Brothers Lumber Co. (Wood and Wood
  Products) [27289]

Cullman Seed and Feed Co. (Agricultural
  Equipment and Supplies) [481]
Dean Oil Co. (Petroleum, Fuels, and Related
  Equipment) [22191]

Daphne

IPE Trade Inc. (Agricultural Equipment and
  Supplies) [870]

Decatur

Alabama Farmers Cooperative Inc. (Livestock and
  Farm Products) [17689]
Assembly Components Systems
  Inc. (Hardware) [13568]
Decatur Coca-Cola Bottling Co. (Food) [10932]
Denbo Iron and Metal Company
  Inc. (Metals) [19925]
Feralloy Corp. Birmingham Div. (Metals) [19970]
McAbee Medical Inc. (Medical, Dental, and Optical
  Equipment) [18904]
Williams Auto Parts (Automotive) [3432]
Wonderful World of Imports (Household
  Appliances) [15377]

Demopolis

Collins Communications Inc. (Electrical and
  Electronic Equipment and Supplies) [8543]

Dothan

Allied Sales Co. (Furniture and Fixtures) [13014]
Bell Supply Company Inc. (Plumbing Materials and
  Fixtures) [23081]
Danzey Oil and Tire Co. Inc. (Automotive) [2527]
Dothan Auto Auction Inc. (Motorized
  Vehicles) [20625]
Fuller Supply Co., Inc. (Veterinary
  Products) [27137]
Jeffers Vet Supply (Veterinary Products) [27162]
Jeffers Vet Supply (Medical, Dental, and Optical
  Supplies) [19384]
South Alabama Brick (Floorcovering Equipment and
  Supplies) [10158]
Tiles Plus (Floorcovering Equipment and
  Supplies) [10250]
Truck Equipment Sales Inc. (Automotive) [3348]

Elberta

Elberta Farmers Cooperative (Agricultural Equipment
  and Supplies) [544]

Enterprise

Big/Little Stores Inc. (Petroleum, Fuels, and Related
  Equipment) [22072]
Sessions Company Inc. (Food) [12464]

Eufaula

Reeves Peanut Company Inc. (Food) [12294]

Fairfield

Specialty Products Inc. (Industrial
  Supplies) [17190]

Florence

American Promotional Events, Inc. (Toys and
  Hobby Goods) [26389]
American Wholesale Book Co. (Books and Other
  Printed Materials) [3504]
Anco Management Services Inc. (Books and Other
  Printed Materials) [3509]
Blanke Sales Inc.; Bob (Food) [10568]
Martin Industries Inc. (Household
  Appliances) [15215]
Star Com Computers (Computers and
  Software) [6758]
Tile Distributors, Inc. (Floorcovering Equipment and
  Supplies) [10233]

Foley

Sports Specialist Inc. (Recreational and Sporting
  Goods) [23980]

Ft. Payne

Cherokee Hosiery Mills (Clothing) [4878]
Hi-Jac Corporation (Household Items) [15528]
Lowe Inc.; Devan (Motorized Vehicles) [20674]

McNutt Hosiery; Danny (Clothing) [5181]
Shankles Hosiery Inc. (Clothing) [5345]

Frisco City

Farmers Cooperative Market (Agricultural Equipment
  and Supplies) [634]

Gadsden

Buffalo Rock Co. Gadsden Div. (Soft
  Drinks) [24921]
Hollar Company Inc. (Petroleum, Fuels, and
  Related Equipment) [22355]
Osborn Brothers Inc. (Food) [12081]
Phillips Inc.; Ira (Petroleum, Fuels, and Related
  Equipment) [22580]
Stowers Manufacturing Inc. (Construction Materials
  and Machinery) [8078]

Geneva

Fleming Foods (Food) [11153]
Fleming Foods of Alabama Inc. (Food) [11154]

Georgiana

Ni-Co. Sales Company Inc. (Clothing) [5231]

Greensboro

Dairy Fresh Corp. (Food) [10894]

Guntersville

Faithway Feed Company Inc. (Veterinary
  Products) [27130]

Haleyville

Haleyville Drapery Manufacturing (Household
  Items) [15517]

Hollywood

Great Western Products Inc. (Food) [11317]

Huntsville

Baron Services, Inc. (Computers and
  Software) [6001]
Flooring Distributors Inc. (Floorcovering Equipment
  and Supplies) [9896]
Halsey Company Inc.; W.L. (Food) [11367]
Hobbies of Huntsville (Toys and Hobby
  Goods) [26516]
Hughes Supply Inc. (Plumbing Materials and
  Fixtures) [23215]
Huntsville Beverage Co. (Alcoholic
  Beverages) [1769]
Huntsville/Redstone Paper Co. (Paper and Paper
  Products) [21772]
Huntsville/Redstone Paper Co. (Industrial
  Supplies) [16936]
Madison County Cooperative Inc. (Agricultural
  Equipment and Supplies) [981]
Monroe Distributing Co. (Sound and Entertainment
  Equipment and Supplies) [25334]
Newcomb Company Inc. Newcomb
  Associates (Scientific and Measurement
  Devices) [24408]
Shannon Brothers Tile (Floorcovering Equipment
  and Supplies) [10146]
Sharp Communication (Communications Systems
  and Equipment) [5754]
Sirsi Corp. (Computers and Software) [6732]
Spencer Companies Inc. (Huntsville,
  Alabama) (Petroleum, Fuels, and Related
  Equipment) [22691]
Svetlana Electron Devices, Inc. (Industrial
  Supplies) [17208]
Tee Tile Distributors, Inc. (Floorcovering Equipment
  and Supplies) [10211]
Valley Hardwood Inc. (Construction Materials and
  Machinery) [8168]

Jemison

Godbee Medical Distributors (Medical, Dental, and
  Optical Equipment) [18812]

Laceys Spring

Oakes Oil Co. (Petroleum, Fuels, and Related
  Equipment) [22532]

Lafayette
East Alabama Lumber Co. (Construction Materials and Machinery) [7298]

Lanett
Skinner Corp. (Furniture and Fixtures) [13245]

Lapine
Spear Oil Co. (Petroleum, Fuels, and Related Equipment) [22690]

Livingston
Coleman Lumber Inc. (Construction Materials and Machinery) [7195]
Livingston Apparel Inc. (Clothing) [5135]

Luverne
Hicks Inc. (Recreational and Sporting Goods) [23726]
Pepsi-Cola Bottling Company of Luverne Inc. (Soft Drinks) [25008]

Madison
SEA Wire & Cable Inc. (Electrical and Electronic Equipment and Supplies) [9348]
Sundrop Inc. (Soft Drinks) [25042]

Marion
Griffin Wood Company Inc. (Wood and Wood Products) [27312]

Mobile
Alabama Crankshaft and Engine (Automotive) [2195]
Allied Electronics (Electrical and Electronic Equipment and Supplies) [8314]
American Foods (Food) [10397]
American Tennis Courts Inc. (Recreational and Sporting Goods) [23514]
Appliance Parts & Supply Co. (Household Appliances) [15028]
B & B Appliance Parts of Mobile (Household Appliances) [15044]
Bay Paper Co. Inc. (Office Equipment and Supplies) [20837]
Bedsole Medical Companies Inc. (Medical, Dental, and Optical Equipment) [18705]
Bodden Lumber Company Inc.; R.K. (Construction Materials and Machinery) [7065]
Carlisle Medical Inc. (Medical, Dental, and Optical Equipment) [18727]
Coca-Cola Bottling Company of Mobile Inc. (Soft Drinks) [24938]
Craftsmen Supply, Inc. (Floorcovering Equipment and Supplies) [9830]
Equipment Sales Corp. (Heating and Cooling Equipment and Supplies) [14435]
Floors, Inc. (Floorcovering Equipment and Supplies) [9899]
Gulf Coast Marine Supply Inc. (Marine) [18512]
Hardware & Marine Co. of Alabama (Marine) [18519]
Hiller Investments Inc. (Security and Safety Equipment) [24563]
Hutchings Brokerage Co. (Food) [11483]
Jeffrey's Steel Company Inc. (Metals) [20075]
MacKinnon Paper Company Inc. (Paper and Paper Products) [21818]
Marine Specialty Company Inc. (Plumbing Materials and Fixtures) [23251]
Micro Comm Inc. (Communications Systems and Equipment) [5674]
Mobile Beer & Wine Co. (Alcoholic Beverages) [1885]
Mobile Cycle Center (Recreational and Sporting Goods) [23833]
Nelson Wholesale Corp. (Restaurant and Commercial Foodservice Equipment and Supplies) [24191]
OPICO (Agricultural Equipment and Supplies) [1108]
Peakwon International Inc. (Medical, Dental, and Optical Equipment) [18979]
Riley-Stuart Supply Co. (Construction Materials and Machinery) [7935]

Southern Contracts (Computers and Software) [6748]
Southern Flooring Distributors (Floorcovering Equipment and Supplies) [10163]
Threaded Fasteners Inc. (Hardware) [13954]
Tricorp, Inc. (Agricultural Equipment and Supplies) [1357]
Underwood Builders Supply Co. (Construction Materials and Machinery) [8155]
Wade Distributors, Inc. (Floorcovering Equipment and Supplies) [10283]

Montgomery
Allstate Beverage Co. (Alcoholic Beverages) [1481]
Ben-Mar Paper Co. Inc. (Paper and Paper Products) [21652]
Calhoun Enterprises (Food) [10671]
Capital Pet Supply (Veterinary Products) [27100]
Capitol Chevrolet Inc. (Motorized Vehicles) [20609]
CCC Associates Co. (Horticultural Supplies) [14836]
Coates Optical Lab Inc. (Medical, Dental, and Optical Supplies) [19237]
Durr-Fillauer Medical Inc. (Medical, Dental, and Optical Equipment) [18781]
F & E Sportswear Inc. (Recreational and Sporting Goods) [23661]
Franco Distributing Co. Inc. (Toys and Hobby Goods) [26486]
Fuller Supply Co. (Veterinary Products) [27136]
Henig Furs Inc. (Clothing) [5027]
Henry Tile Co.; Robert F. (Floorcovering Equipment and Supplies) [9942]
Major Oil Inc. (Petroleum, Fuels, and Related Equipment) [22446]
Montgomery Beverage Co. (Alcoholic Beverages) [1891]
Montgomery Building Materials (Floorcovering Equipment and Supplies) [10056]
Montgomery Seed (Veterinary Products) [27191]
PYA/Monarch Inc. Schloss and Kahn (Cleaning and Janitorial Supplies) [4690]
Russell Petroleum Corp. (Petroleum, Fuels, and Related Equipment) [22645]
Sabel Industries Inc. (Used, Scrap, and Recycled Materials) [26971]
Sabel Steel Service (Metals) [20349]
Sadco Inc. (Household Appliances) [15301]
Sanford Tile Co. (Floorcovering Equipment and Supplies) [10137]
WDI United Warehouse Inc. (Automotive) [3406]
Weil Brothers Cotton Inc. (Livestock and Farm Products) [18331]

Moody
ADESA Auctions of Birmingham (Motorized Vehicles) [20577]

Moulton
Lawrence County Exchange (Livestock and Farm Products) [18047]
Shelton Clothing Inc. (Clothing) [5347]

Muscle Shoals
Opler Sales Company Inc.; Jack (Paper and Paper Products) [21854]

New Market
B & L Leather Co. (Clothing) [4794]

Northport
Huet & Associates; Pat (Recreational and Sporting Goods) [23734]

Oneonta
Alabama Truck Body & Equipment, Inc. (Automotive) [2197]

Opelika
Blackburn Oil Co. Inc. (Petroleum, Fuels, and Related Equipment) [22077]
Premium Beverage Company Inc. (Alcoholic Beverages) [1970]
Talladega Beverage Co. (Alcoholic Beverages) [2068]

Taylor Co.; Jesse R. (Livestock and Farm Products) [18276]

Opp
Anderson's Peanuts (Food) [10415]
Paulk Grocery; H.B. (Food) [12122]
Paulk Grocery Inc.; H.B. (Food) [12123]
Smith-Claypool; Shirley (Shoes) [24864]

Pelham
Lafayette Auto Electric (Electrical and Electronic Equipment and Supplies) [8964]
Moore-Handley Inc. (Food) [11931]
Southern Power Inc. (Automotive) [3243]
Spradling International Inc. (Luggage and Leather Goods) [18432]

Phenix City
Randall Tile Company, Inc. (Floorcovering Equipment and Supplies) [10114]

River Falls
Andalusia Wood Products Inc. (Wood and Wood Products) [27280]

Selma
Central Alabama Cooperative Farms Inc. (Agricultural Equipment and Supplies) [386]
Miller and Company Inc. (Construction Materials and Machinery) [7714]
Selma Oil Mill Inc. (Agricultural Equipment and Supplies) [1259]

Semmes
Educators Resource, Inc. (Office Equipment and Supplies) [20984]

Sheffield
Miller Refrigeration Supply Co. (Heating and Cooling Equipment and Supplies) [14604]
Southern Sash Sales and Supply Co. (Construction Materials and Machinery) [8051]

Summerdale
Ard Oil Co. Inc. (Petroleum, Fuels, and Related Equipment) [22043]

Sylacauga
ECCA America Inc. (Chemicals) [4378]

Talladega
Michael Supply Company Inc. (Household Appliances) [15228]
Talladega Machinery and Supply Co. (Textiles and Notions) [26220]
Talladega Machinery and Supply Company Inc. (Industrial Machinery) [16545]

Theodore
Barnett Millworks Inc. (Construction Materials and Machinery) [7024]
Mobile Paint Distributors (Paints and Varnishes) [21504]
Pauls Tops & Knobs (Construction Materials and Machinery) [7842]

Toxey
Mayfield Timber Co. (Wood and Wood Products) [27341]

Troy
Harris Tire Co. (Automotive) [2727]
Whaley Pecan Company Inc. (Food) [12923]

Trussville
Coastal Equipment Inc. (Construction Materials and Machinery) [7187]
GSI, Inc. (Guns and Weapons) [13492]
Spas Unlimited (Recreational and Sporting Goods) [23974]
Spradling Originals (Automotive) [3254]

Tuscaloosa

Adams Brothers Produce Company of Tuscaloosa Inc. (Food) [10324]
Alabama Book Store (Books and Other Printed Materials) [3482]
Alabama Institutional Foods Inc. (Food) [10352]
Almerica Overseas Inc. (Aeronautical Equipment and Supplies) [40]
Almerica Overseas Inc. (Plumbing Materials and Fixtures) [23059]
Appliance Parts Inc. (Household Appliances) [15025]
Cain Steel and Supply Co. (Metals) [19846]
Greene Beverage Company Inc. (Alcoholic Beverages) [1731]
Peco Foods Inc. (Food) [12129]
Phifer Wire Products Inc. (Furniture and Fixtures) [13208]
Southern Wine Co. (Alcoholic Beverages) [2034]
Tuscaloosa Electrical Supply Inc. (Electrical and Electronic Equipment and Supplies) [9518]
Tuscaloosa Optical Dispensary (Medical, Dental, and Optical Supplies) [19666]
Warrior Asphalt Refining Corp. (Construction Materials and Machinery) [8196]

Tuscumbia

Muscle Shoals Mack Sales Inc. (Motorized Vehicles) [20688]
Muscle Shoals Mack Sales Inc. (Industrial Machinery) [16332]

Wetumpka

Elmore County Farms Exchange (Veterinary Products) [27128]
Wam Inc. (Clothing) [5472]

Whistler

Baird Steel Inc. (Metals) [19798]

Alaska

Anchorage

Advance Scaffold of Alaska (Construction Materials and Machinery) [6916]
A/E Supplies (Gifts and Novelties) [13295]
Alaska Education & Recreational Products (Office Equipment and Supplies) [20781]
Alaska Garden and Pet Supply (Veterinary Products) [27059]
Alaska General Alarm Inc. (Security and Safety Equipment) [24502]
Alaska General Alarm Inc. (Electrical and Electronic Equipment and Supplies) [8286]
Alaska Housewares Inc. (Household Appliances) [14996]
Alaska Industrial Hardware, Inc. (Industrial Machinery) [15750]
Alaska Instrument Company Inc. (Scientific and Measurement Devices) [24308]
Alaska Insulation Supply, Inc. (Construction Materials and Machinery) [6928]
Alaska Micro Systems Inc. (Computers and Software) [5899]
Alaska News Agency Inc. (Books and Other Printed Materials) [3486]
Alaska Nut & Bolt (Hardware) [13541]
Alaska Pacific University Press (Books and Other Printed Materials) [3487]
Alaska Paper Co. Inc. (Paper and Paper Products) [21617]
Alaska Quality Control Services (Electrical and Electronic Equipment and Supplies) [8287]
Alaska Trophy Manufacturing (Jewelry) [17304]
Alaskan Paint Manufacturing Company Inc. (Paints and Varnishes) [21377]
Aleutian Pribilof Island Association (Medical, Dental, and Optical Equipment) [18670]
Allied Building Products Corp. (Construction Materials and Machinery) [6941]
Anchorage Restaurant Supply (Restaurant and Commercial Foodservice Equipment and Supplies) [24065]

Arctic Industrial Supply (Industrial Supplies) [16708]
Artistic Tile Co. Inc. (Floorcovering Equipment and Supplies) [9688]
Aurora Arts & Krafts (Jewelry) [17321]
AvAlaska, Inc. (Aeronautical Equipment and Supplies) [48]
AWS Companies Inc. (Aeronautical Equipment and Supplies) [53]
B and C Auto Supply (Automotive) [2305]
Bagoy and Associates Inc.; John P. (Electrical and Electronic Equipment and Supplies) [8410]
Blaine's Art & Graphic Supply (Gifts and Novelties) [13319]
Blaine's Paint Store, Inc. (Paints and Varnishes) [21401]
Bush Landscaping & Nursery (Horticultural Supplies) [14832]
Cash Register Sales & Service (Office Equipment and Supplies) [20885]
Cedars Wholesale Floral Imports (Horticultural Supplies) [14837]
Comware Business Systems Inc. (Computers and Software) [6145]
Curtis & Campbell Inc. (Paints and Varnishes) [21422]
Debenham Electric Supply Co. (Electrical and Electronic Equipment and Supplies) [8619]
Denali Industrial Supply Inc. (Industrial Supplies) [16826]
Diomede Enterprises, Inc. (Construction Materials and Machinery) [7266]
DJ's Alaska Rentals, Inc. (Industrial Machinery) [15954]
DW Enterprises (Scientific and Measurement Devices) [24350]
Eagle River Corp. (Recreational and Sporting Goods) [23640]
Evelyn's Floral (Horticultural Supplies) [14859]
Frigid North Co. (Electrical and Electronic Equipment and Supplies) [8763]
Fuller-O'Brien Paint Stores (Paints and Varnishes) [21447]
Gensco, Inc. (Heating and Cooling Equipment and Supplies) [14461]
Glacier Seafoods (Food) [11268]
Grace Inc.; V.F. (Health and Beauty Aids) [14115]
Green Connection Inc. (Horticultural Supplies) [14876]
Gun Traders Inc. (Recreational and Sporting Goods) [23703]
H & H Equipment Inc. (Computers and Software) [6320]
H & R General Painting (Paints and Varnishes) [21453]
Hickel Investment Co. (Specialty Equipment and Products) [25679]
Husky Food Products of Anchorage (Food) [11482]
Inlet Distributors (Alcoholic Beverages) [1772]
Interior Plant Designs, Ltd. (Horticultural Supplies) [14893]
Jans Distributing Inc. (Tobacco Products) [26313]
Koncor Forest Products Co. (Wood and Wood Products) [27332]
Leader Creek Marina (Marine) [18544]
M & M Distributors (Restaurant and Commercial Foodservice Equipment and Supplies) [24172]
Marsch Enterprises (Sound and Entertainment Equipment and Supplies) [25305]
Matanuska Maid Dairy (Food) [11802]
Midnight Sun Boat Company, Inc. (Marine) [18569]
Nana Development Corp. (Petroleum, Fuels, and Related Equipment) [22504]
Nethercott's Optical (Medical, Dental, and Optical Supplies) [19484]
North Star Sales Co. (Household Appliances) [15253]
Novakovich Enterprises (Petroleum, Fuels, and Related Equipment) [22531]
Pacific Rim Telecommunications Inc. (Communications Systems and Equipment) [5698]
Plaschem Supply & Consulting (Construction Materials and Machinery) [7869]

Plaschem Supply & Consulting Inc. (Construction Materials and Machinery) [7870]
Polar Refrigeration & Restaurant Equipment (Heating and Cooling Equipment and Supplies) [14639]
Polar Supply Company Inc. (Paints and Varnishes) [21542]
R & R Scaffold Erectors, Inc. (Construction Materials and Machinery) [7895]
Ray's Workshop (Paints and Varnishes) [21550]
Reeve Aleutian Airways Inc. (Aeronautical Equipment and Supplies) [141]
Roofing Supply Inc. (Construction Materials and Machinery) [7958]
Royal Alaskan Sales (Shoes) [24845]
Rude Corp.; R.T. (Household Appliances) [15297]
Sabus Group (Computers and Software) [6698]
Sales Corporation of Alaska (Food) [12393]
Stusser Electric Company (Electrical and Electronic Equipment and Supplies) [9438]
Surgitec (Medical, Dental, and Optical Equipment) [19065]
T & E Enterprises & Development (Veterinary Products) [27243]
Techlink Alaska (Computers and Software) [6797]
Trailer Craft (Automotive) [3325]
TRI-Alaska (Health and Beauty Aids) [14262]
Truckwell of Alaska (Automotive) [3352]
Urethane Contractors Supply (Construction Materials and Machinery) [8163]
Vision Plastics USA, Inc. (Medical, Dental, and Optical Supplies) [19690]
Walton's Gold Diamond Co.; George (Jewelry) [17650]
Wholesale Distributors of Alaska (Plumbing Materials and Fixtures) [23455]
Wholesale Distributors of Alaska (Plumbing Materials and Fixtures) [23456]
Wholesale Marine Supply Co. of Alaska, Inc. (Marine) [18638]
Yukon Equipment (Construction Materials and Machinery) [8252]

Cordova

Orca Oil Company, Inc. (Petroleum, Fuels, and Related Equipment) [22542]

Eagle River

Perennial Gardens (Horticultural Supplies) [14941]

Fairbanks

Appliance Service Center Inc. (Sound and Entertainment Equipment and Supplies) [25079]
Arctic Fire Equipment (Security and Safety Equipment) [24507]
Arctic Technical Services (Heating and Cooling Equipment and Supplies) [14326]
Brown & Sons NAPA Auto Parts (Automotive) [2398]
Coal Bunkers (Minerals and Ores) [20529]
Donnybrook Building Supply Inc. (Construction Materials and Machinery) [7279]
Independent Rental, Inc. (Agricultural Equipment and Supplies) [853]
Interior Fuels Co. (Petroleum, Fuels, and Related Equipment) [22375]
K and K Recycling Inc. (Used, Scrap, and Recycled Materials) [26862]
McCauley's Reprographics, Inc. (Scientific and Measurement Devices) [24396]
Northland Hub Inc. (Food) [12034]
The Performance Shop Inc. (Automotive) [3092]
Samson Hardware & Fairbanks (Hardware) [13901]
University of Alaska Press (Books and Other Printed Materials) [4244]

Juneau

Sealaska Corp. (Wood and Wood Products) [27372]

Ketchikan

Sealaska Timber Corp. (Wood and Wood Products) [27373]

Kodiak
Sutliff & Son; Norman (Marine)　[18619]

Palmer
Wilderness Nursery (Horticultural Supplies)　[14977]

Petersburg
Alaskan Glacier Seafoods (Food)　[10354]

Seward
Harbor Enterprises Inc. (Petroleum, Fuels, and Related Equipment)　[22334]
Suneel Alaska Corp. (Minerals and Ores)　[20572]

Soldotna
Alaskan Gold Seafood Inc. (Food)　[10355]

Thorne Bay
Alaska Fire & Safety Equipment (Security and Safety Equipment)　[24501]

Wasilla
Power Solutions (Electrical and Electronic Equipment and Supplies)　[9225]

Willow
Eyak Aircraft (Aeronautical Equipment and Supplies)　[85]

Arizona

Apache Junction
Hardy Turquoise Co. (Jewelry)　[17444]

Benson
Apache Nitrogen Products Inc. (Chemicals)　[4324]

Camp Verde
Medical Imaging Inc. (Medical, Dental, and Optical Equipment)　[18916]

Casa Grande
Arizona Grain Inc. (Livestock and Farm Products)　[17705]
Bingham Equipment Co. (Agricultural Equipment and Supplies)　[317]
Eagle Milling Co. (Veterinary Products)　[27121]
Valley Seed Co. (Livestock and Farm Products)　[18314]

Chandler
AlliedSignal Hardware Product Group (Industrial Supplies)　[16689]
Amkor Technology (Electrical and Electronic Equipment and Supplies)　[8348]
Arizona Machinery Co., Inc. (Agricultural Equipment and Supplies)　[253]
Arizona Sealing Devices Inc. (Industrial Supplies)　[16709]
Aztech Controls Corp. (Industrial Supplies)　[16717]
Chickasha Cotton Oil Co. (Livestock and Farm Products)　[17777]
DataCal Corp. (Computers and Software)　[6187]
Fas-Co Coders Inc.orporated (Office Equipment and Supplies)　[21001]
Inter-Tel Integrated Systs Inc. (Electrical and Electronic Equipment and Supplies)　[8889]
Mega Systems Chemicals Inc (Chemicals)　[4455]
Mega Systems Chemicals Inc. (Chemicals)　[4456]
Metalink Corp. (Electrical and Electronic Equipment and Supplies)　[9068]
Microchip Technology Inc. (Electrical and Electronic Equipment and Supplies)　[9074]
Pac Aero (Aeronautical Equipment and Supplies)　[134]
Pimalco Inc. (Metals)　[20279]
Savage Universal Corp. (Photographic Equipment and Supplies)　[22902]
SunSource (Industrial Supplies)　[17204]

Cortaro
Coca-Cola Co. (Soft Drinks)　[24945]

Cottonwood
Hooleon Corp. (Computers and Software)　[6339]

Flagstaff
Anderson News Co. (Books and Other Printed Materials)　[3513]
Coca-Cola of Northern Arizona (Soft Drinks)　[24947]
Jay's Indian Arts Inc. (Jewelry)　[17466]
Mountain Imaging Inc. (Medical, Dental, and Optical Equipment)　[18950]
Nackard Wholesale Beverage Co.; Fred (Alcoholic Beverages)　[1899]
Nackard Wholesale Beverage Co.; Fred (Alcoholic Beverages)　[1900]
Northland Publishing (Books and Other Printed Materials)　[4009]
Northland Publishing Company (Books and Other Printed Materials)　[4010]
Weatherford Enterprise of Flagstaff (Veterinary Products)　[27268]

Fountain Hills
Robison & Associates; Jerry (Recreational and Sporting Goods)　[23918]

Gilbert
Cerprobe Corp. (Electrical and Electronic Equipment and Supplies)　[8520]
Coast Distribution (Marine)　[18480]
World Wide Laser Service Corp. (Industrial Machinery)　[16650]

Glendale
CAD Store Inc. (Computers and Software)　[6037]
Central Arizona Distributing Co. (Books and Other Printed Materials)　[3620]
Conair Corp.oration (Household Appliances)　[15093]
Northern Chemical/Janitor Sply (Restaurant and Commercial Foodservice Equipment and Supplies)　[24195]
Valtronics Engineering and Mfg (Electrical and Electronic Equipment and Supplies)　[9534]

Goodyear
Poore Brothers Distributing Inc. (Food)　[12192]
Poore Brothers Inc. (Food)　[12193]
Simpson Norton Corp. (Agricultural Equipment and Supplies)　[1269]

Green Valley
Park Corporation (Electrical and Electronic Equipment and Supplies)　[9179]

Kingman
Great West Truck and Auto Inc. (Automotive)　[2701]
Kingman Aero Services Inc. (Petroleum, Fuels, and Related Equipment)　[22406]

Lake Havasu City
Bingo Depot (Toys and Hobby Goods)　[26419]

Laveen
Arnold Machinery Co. (Construction Materials and Machinery)　[6990]

Mesa
ADTRON. Corp (Computers and Software)　[5881]
Arizona Sash and Door Co. (Hardware)　[13565]
Berge Ford Inc. (Motorized Vehicles)　[20599]
Big-2 Oldsmobile Inc. (Motorized Vehicles)　[20600]
Brown Evans Distributing Co. (Petroleum, Fuels, and Related Equipment)　[22096]
DPI-Epicurean Fine Foods (Food)　[10988]
DPI-Taylor Brothers (Food)　[10992]
Falcon Plumbing Inc. (Plumbing Materials and Fixtures)　[23156]
HealthTech International Inc. (Recreational and Sporting Goods)　[23720]
Mesa Sprinkler Inc. (Agricultural Equipment and Supplies)　[1017]
Optek Inc. (Medical, Dental, and Optical Supplies)　[19510]

Pearce Co. (Alcoholic Beverages)　[1944]
PRI Automation Inc. (Electrical and Electronic Equipment and Supplies)　[9236]
Running Strong Inc. (Clothing)　[5325]
Spectrum Labs Inc. (Medical, Dental, and Optical Supplies)　[19632]
United Systems Software Inc. (Paper and Paper Products)　[21978]
Zeb Pearce Cos. (Alcoholic Beverages)　[2144]

Nogales
Delta Products Corp. (Nogales, Arizona) (Computers and Software)　[6197]
Hanessian Mercantile Co. (Household Appliances)　[15160]
Kims Family Shoes Inc. (Shoes)　[24784]
Kory Mercantile Company (Clothing)　[5116]
Larriva Corp. (Gifts and Novelties)　[13386]
Meyer Vegetables (Food)　[11866]
Omega Produce Company Inc. (Food)　[12070]
Wright Co.; William S. (Food)　[12988]

Phoenix
A Pickle House/Judy Blair's Rustic Collectibles (Furniture and Fixtures)　[13008]
Access Bicycle Components Inc. (Recreational and Sporting Goods)　[23491]
Access Solutions Inc. (Computers and Software)　[5868]
Accutron Inc. (Medical, Dental, and Optical Equipment)　[18656]
ACM Equipment Rental and Sales Co. (Industrial Machinery)　[15732]
ADEMCO/ADI (Security and Safety Equipment)　[24474]
Aerobic Life Industries Inc. (Health and Beauty Aids)　[14010]
Aerospace Southwest (Electrical and Electronic Equipment and Supplies)　[8281]
Air Comm Corp. (Communications Systems and Equipment)　[5504]
Allstate/GES Appliance Inc. (Household Appliances)　[15003]
American Ambulance (Medical, Dental, and Optical Equipment)　[18674]
American Excelsior Co. (Heating and Cooling Equipment and Supplies)　[14316]
Apotheca Inc. (Medical, Dental, and Optical Supplies)　[19155]
Appliance Parts Co. (Household Appliances)　[15019]
Ariz Coin & Commercial Lndry Eq. (Electrical and Electronic Equipment and Supplies)　[8373]
Arizona Bag Co. LLC (Agricultural Equipment and Supplies)　[252]
Arizona Beverage Distributing Co. LLC (Alcoholic Beverages)　[1486]
Arizona Coin & Commercial Laundry Equipment (Household Appliances)　[15032]
Arizona Commercial Lighting Co. (Electrical and Electronic Equipment and Supplies)　[8374]
Arizona Recycling Corp. (Used, Scrap, and Recycled Materials)　[26753]
Arizona Scrap Iron and Metals Inc. (Used, Scrap, and Recycled Materials)　[26754]
Arizona Therapy Source (Medical, Dental, and Optical Equipment)　[18690]
Arizona Welding Equipment Co. (Industrial Machinery)　[15777]
Arizona Wholesale Supply Co. (Household Appliances)　[15033]
Arnold Machinery Co. (Construction Materials and Machinery)　[6988]
Arraid Inc. (Computers and Software)　[5963]
Aspen Furniture Inc. (Furniture and Fixtures)　[13025]
Associated Sales (Household Appliances)　[15037]
Auto Safety House Inc. (Automotive)　[2277]
Automotive Sales Co. (Automotive)　[2295]
Bar-S Foods Co. (Food)　[10501]
Barry Metals Company Inc. (Used, Scrap, and Recycled Materials)　[26759]
BDD Inc. (Household Items)　[15417]
Bearing Belt and Chain Inc. (Industrial Supplies)　[16728]

Bedrosians Tile & Marble (Floorcovering Equipment and Supplies) [9714]

Best Disposal Inc. (Used, Scrap, and Recycled Materials) [26765]

Call Dynamics Inc. (Communications Systems and Equipment) [5542]

Capital City Distribution Inc. (Books and Other Printed Materials) [3607]

Capitol Metals Company Inc. (Metals) [19852]

Chrismann Computer Services Inc. (Computers and Software) [6065]

Chrismann Computer Services Inc. (Computers and Software) [6066]

Cimarron Materials Inc. (Construction Materials and Machinery) [7173]

City Meat & Provisions Company, Inc. (Food) [10762]

Co-Sales Co. (Food) [10781]

Complete Golf Services Co. (Recreational and Sporting Goods) [23601]

Cookson Co. (Wood and Wood Products) [27300]

Cooley Forest Products (Construction Materials and Machinery) [7215]

Cooley Industries Inc. (Construction Materials and Machinery) [7216]

Cornforths (Heating and Cooling Equipment and Supplies) [14406]

Corporate Express (Office Equipment and Supplies) [20927]

Cummins Southwest Inc. (Automotive) [2516]

Dairy Maid Foods Inc. (Food) [10898]

Dalis Electronic Supply Inc. (Electrical and Electronic Equipment and Supplies) [8607]

Davis Salvage Co. (Metals) [19918]

Decot Hy-Wyd Sport Glasses, Inc. (Medical, Dental, and Optical Supplies) [19274]

DeMar Inc.; M & T (Heating and Cooling Equipment and Supplies) [14414]

Desert Mesquite of Arizona (Food) [10950]

Diamond W Supply Co. Inc. (Floorcovering Equipment and Supplies) [9863]

Diane Ribbon Wholesale (Office Equipment and Supplies) [20960]

Empire Power Systems Inc. (Automotive) [2589]

Empire Southwest L.L.C. (Construction Materials and Machinery) [7312]

Estrella Tortilla Factory & Deli Store (Food) [11054]

Farmer Johns Packing Co. (Food) [11087]

Filtemp Sales, Inc. (Industrial Supplies) [16860]

Fine Wire Coil Company (Electrical and Electronic Equipment and Supplies) [8742]

First Native American Corp. (Shoes) [24744]

Florie Corporation Turf Irrigation and Water Works Supply (Agricultural Equipment and Supplies) [694]

Food For Health (Health and Beauty Aids) [14102]

Fuji Natural Food Co. (Food) [11223]

G & N Appliance Parts (Household Appliances) [15139]

Galan Enterprises, Inc. (Toys and Hobby Goods) [26489]

Garden Grove Nursery Inc. (Agricultural Equipment and Supplies) [721]

Gardner's Book Service, Inc. (Books and Other Printed Materials) [3770]

Great Western Pet Supply (Veterinary Products) [27141]

Griggs Paint Co. (Paints and Varnishes) [21452]

GSK Products Inc. (Health and Beauty Aids) [14118]

GTA Aviation Inc. (Petroleum, Fuels, and Related Equipment) [22325]

Handling Systems Inc. (Industrial Machinery) [16086]

Harwell Fabrics, Inc. (Textiles and Notions) [26058]

Hedlund Fabrics and Supply Co. (Textiles and Notions) [26061]

Hensley and Co. (Alcoholic Beverages) [1751]

Hopper and Son Inc.; Ora B. (Construction Materials and Machinery) [7486]

Horizon (Agricultural Equipment and Supplies) [837]

Hughes-Calihan Corp. (Office Equipment and Supplies) [21043]

Inter-Tel Technologies Inc. (Electrical and Electronic Equipment and Supplies) [8890]

International Surgical Systems (Medical, Dental, and Optical Equipment) [18859]

Jensen Tools Inc. (Electrical and Electronic Equipment and Supplies) [8912]

Jensen Tools Inc. (Industrial Machinery) [16187]

Jewel Box Inc. (Recreational and Sporting Goods) [23757]

Jones Inc.; Charlie C. (Automotive) [2834]

Kaman Industrial Technologies (Industrial Supplies) [16977]

Keyston Brothers (Textiles and Notions) [26098]

Koch-Bailey and Associates (Household Items) [15555]

KS. Electronics L.L.C. (Electrical and Electronic Equipment and Supplies) [8959]

LaSalle Paper and Packaging Inc. (Paper and Paper Products) [21797]

Lights Etc. Inc. (Electrical and Electronic Equipment and Supplies) [8990]

Main Street and Main Inc. (Restaurant and Commercial Foodservice Equipment and Supplies) [24175]

Mallco Lumber and Building Materials Inc. (Construction Materials and Machinery) [7635]

Many Feathers Books and Maps (Books and Other Printed Materials) [3934]

Martensen Enterprises Inc. (Construction Materials and Machinery) [7651]

Martensen Enterprises Inc. (Industrial Supplies) [17017]

McKesson Pharmaceutical Inc. (Medical, Dental, and Optical Supplies) [19437]

Medical Electronics Sales and Service (Medical, Dental, and Optical Supplies) [19444]

Mexican Art Imports (Gifts and Novelties) [13402]

Micro Symplex Corp. (Computers and Software) [6496]

Miller Inc.; Herman (Furniture and Fixtures) [13181]

Millitrade International Inc. (Metals) [20195]

Monarch Cermaic Tile, Inc. (Floorcovering Equipment and Supplies) [10050]

Morgan Agency; J.R. (Electrical and Electronic Equipment and Supplies) [9095]

Multicraft Inc. (Specialty Equipment and Products) [25745]

National Impressions Corp. (Specialty Equipment and Products) [25749]

Nelson Holland Inc. (Security and Safety Equipment) [24601]

Neutron Industries Inc. (Chemicals) [4466]

N.I.E. International Inc. (Computers and Software) [6556]

NIENEX Inc. (Computers and Software) [6557]

Noble Distributors Inc. (Sound and Entertainment Equipment and Supplies) [25360]

Ocotillo Lumber Sales Inc. (Construction Materials and Machinery) [7803]

Ocotillo Lumber Sales Inc. (Wood and Wood Products) [27352]

Pacific Fibers, Inc. (Industrial Machinery) [16372]

Perry Supply Company Inc.; Roy L. (Medical, Dental, and Optical Equipment) [18983]

PFT Of America Inc. (Construction Materials and Machinery) [7855]

Phase II (Toys and Hobby Goods) [26613]

Phoenix Fuel Company Inc. (Petroleum, Fuels, and Related Equipment) [22582]

Phoenix Mapping Service (Books and Other Printed Materials) [4062]

Phoenix Wholesale Sporting Supplies Inc. (Recreational and Sporting Goods) [23880]

Pioneer Equipment Inc. (Compressors) [5849]

Pioneer Equipment Inc. (Industrial Machinery) [16400]

POS Systems Company Inc. (Computers and Software) [6628]

Praxair Distribution, Inc. (Industrial Machinery) [16420]

Precision Speed Instruments Inc. (Industrial Supplies) [17115]

Premier Manufactured Systems (Specialty Equipment and Products) [25789]

Premier Manufactured Systems (Plumbing Materials and Fixtures) [23327]

Pure Water Centers, Inc. (Household Appliances) [15284]

RACER Computer Corp. (Computers and Software) [6677]

Redburn Tire (Automotive) [3140]

RLP Inc. (Medical, Dental, and Optical Equipment) [19023]

Road Machinery Co. (Specialty Equipment and Products) [25805]

The Roane Co. (Floorcovering Equipment and Supplies) [10125]

Roofing Wholesale Company Inc. (Construction Materials and Machinery) [7959]

Ryan's Pet Supplies (Veterinary Products) [27225]

Rykoff & Co.; S.E. (Food) [12374]

Safety-Kleen, Southwest (Used, Scrap, and Recycled Materials) [26976]

Sahuaro Petroleum-Asphalt Company Inc. (Construction Materials and Machinery) [7972]

Sanford and Associates Inc.; Gene (Food) [12408]

Shamrock Farms Creamery (Food) [12471]

Shamrock Foods Co. (Food) [12472]

Singing Poppe's, Inc. (Office Equipment and Supplies) [21270]

Smith Pipe and Steel Co. (Metals) [20371]

Smith Sporting Goods Inc.; L.L. (Recreational and Sporting Goods) [23949]

Smithey Recycling Co. (Used, Scrap, and Recycled Materials) [26995]

Southwest Cooperative Wholesale (Livestock and Farm Products) [18245]

Southwire Co. (Industrial Supplies) [17189]

Spellman Hardwoods Inc. (Construction Materials and Machinery) [8061]

State Seal Co. (Industrial Supplies) [17197]

Storm Products Co. (Electrical and Electronic Equipment and Supplies) [9423]

Systems Solutions Inc. (Computers and Software) [6785]

Tekvisions Inc. (Computers and Software) [6807]

Test Systems Inc. (Electrical and Electronic Equipment and Supplies) [9483]

Thompson's Veterinary Supplies (Veterinary Products) [27246]

Thorpe Insulation Co. (Industrial Supplies) [17228]

Trims II Inc. (Toys and Hobby Goods) [26690]

Troxell Communications Inc. (Sound and Entertainment Equipment and Supplies) [25486]

Troy BioSciences Inc. (Agricultural Equipment and Supplies) [1358]

Tubelite Company, Inc. (Electrical and Electronic Equipment and Supplies) [9515]

United Producers Consumers Cooperative (Agricultural Equipment and Supplies) [1379]

Utility Trailer Sales Company of Arizona (Automotive) [3380]

Virginia Hardwood Co. (Floorcovering Equipment and Supplies) [10277]

Vista Laboratories Inc. (Medical, Dental, and Optical Supplies) [19691]

Walsh Bros. (Office Equipment and Supplies) [21344]

Western States Petroleum Inc. (Petroleum, Fuels, and Related Equipment) [22797]

Western Truck Equipment Company Inc. (Automotive) [3413]

Wood Brothers and Halstead Lumber (Storage Equipment and Containers) [25948]

Yankee Photo Products Inc. (Photographic Equipment and Supplies) [22916]

Prescott

Davidson's (Guns and Weapons) [13486]

Sun Fashion Designs Inc. (Jewelry) [17625]

Wrangler Power Products Inc. (Automotive) [3447]

Queen Creek

TRW. Inc (Automotive) [3353]

St. Johns

Algol Consultants Technology (Computers and Software) [5900]

Scottsdale

AME Food Service Inc. (Food) [10393]
Associated Medical Supply Inc. (Medical, Dental, and Optical Equipment) [18694]
Barker & Co. (Recreational and Sporting Goods) [23538]
Carlton Optical Distributors (Medical, Dental, and Optical Supplies) [19217]
Deodorant Stones of America (Health and Beauty Aids) [14082]
Dial Corp. (Health and Beauty Aids) [14083]
DP Equipment Marketing Inc. (Computers and Software) [6221]
The Great Organization Inc. (Construction Materials and Machinery) [7414]
Hot Products, Inc.com (Toys and Hobby Goods) [26525]
Illycaffe Espresso USA Inc. (Food) [11497]
Marta Cooperative of America (Household Appliances) [15214]
Monarch Tile (Floorcovering Equipment and Supplies) [10051]
Nalco Chemical Co. (Chemicals) [4464]
Nova Science Inc. (Electrical and Electronic Equipment and Supplies) [9145]
Numatics Inc./Microsmith Div (Industrial Machinery) [16356]
Olsen Audio Group Inc. (Household Appliances) [15259]
Photocomm Inc. (Specialty Equipment and Products) [25785]
Premium Cigars International Ltd. (Tobacco Products) [26343]
Reinalt-Thomas Corp. (Automotive) [3142]
Semi Systems Inc. (Scientific and Measurement Devices) [24431]
Unelko Corp. (Chemicals) [4539]
U.S. Marketing Services (Clothing) [5451]
Vodavi Technology Inc. (Electrical and Electronic Equipment and Supplies) [9546]
VoiceWorld Inc. (Communications Systems and Equipment) [5807]

Sedona

Chidvilas, Inc. (Books and Other Printed Materials) [3628]

Sun City

Pohle NV Center Inc. (Recreational and Sporting Goods) [23888]
Vans Pro Shop (Recreational and Sporting Goods) [24025]

Tempe

Allied Electronics (Electrical and Electronic Equipment and Supplies) [8318]
Apple Graphics Ltd. (Clothing) [4778]
Arizona Electrical Prdts Inc. (Electrical and Electronic Equipment and Supplies) [8375]
Arizona Water Works Supply Inc. (Plumbing Materials and Fixtures) [23072]
Avant Gardens Silk Plants (Horticultural Supplies) [14811]
Avnet Computer Inc. (Computers and Software) [5995]
Blackbird Ltd. (Clothing) [4826]
Brock Supply Co. (Automotive) [2389]
C S & S Computer Systems Inc. (Computers and Software) [6034]
California Micro Devices Inc. (Electrical and Electronic Equipment and Supplies) [8486]
Canyon State Opthalmaic Lab, Inc. (Medical, Dental, and Optical Supplies) [19210]
Copeland Optical Inc. (Medical, Dental, and Optical Supplies) [19252]
Crossmark Sales and Marketing (Food) [10871]
Eclyptic Inc. (Medical, Dental, and Optical Supplies) [19302]
Electroglas Inc. (Electrical and Electronic Equipment and Supplies) [8687]
Infincom Inc. (Office Equipment and Supplies) [21057]
Insight Direct (Computers and Software) [6376]
Inter-Act Inc. (Sound and Entertainment Equipment and Supplies) [25251]

J & L Medical Supply Corp. (Medical, Dental, and Optical Equipment) [18866]
JR Electronics and Assembly Inc. (Electrical and Electronic Equipment and Supplies) [8922]
Longust Distributing Inc. (Floorcovering Equipment and Supplies) [9997]
Medi-Globe Corp. (Medical, Dental, and Optical Equipment) [18911]
MicroAge Inc. (Computers and Software) [6499]
Motorola MIMS. VLSI Tech Center (Electrical and Electronic Equipment and Supplies) [9101]
Myers Associates; Vic (Computers and Software) [6539]
Omnifax Danka Co. (Office Equipment and Supplies) [21201]
Parkville Imports Inc. (Jewelry) [17542]
Southwest Hallowell Inc. (Industrial Machinery) [16515]
Spectrum Lighting/Sound & Beyond (Specialty Equipment and Products) [25828]
Star of India Fashions (Clothing) [5392]
Stretch and Sew Inc. (Textiles and Notions) [26216]
Sutmyn America (Computers and Software) [6779]
TOSCO Marketing Co. (Petroleum, Fuels, and Related Equipment) [22741]
United Dairymen of Arizona (Food) [12791]
Unizone Inc. (Computers and Software) [6844]
Val Dere Co.; W.R. (Heating and Cooling Equipment and Supplies) [14752]
Venus Manufacturing Co. (Construction Materials and Machinery) [8178]
Viles and Associates Inc. (Food) [12844]
Ward Technologies Inc. (Industrial Machinery) [16614]

Tucson

A and H Building Materials Co. (Construction Materials and Machinery) [6895]
Action Communications Inc. (Electrical and Electronic Equipment and Supplies) [8270]
Advanced Ceramics Research Inc. (Construction Materials and Machinery) [6917]
AGM Electronics Inc. (Electrical and Electronic Equipment and Supplies) [8282]
Ajo Way Garden & Nursery (Horticultural Supplies) [14797]
AMCEP Inc. (Used, Scrap, and Recycled Materials) [26750]
American Steel Builders International, Corp. & Copper Valley Concrete (Metals) [19771]
American Tile Co. of Tucson (Floorcovering Equipment and Supplies) [9672]
Apex Data Systems Inc. (Computers and Software) [5943]
Appliance Dealer Supply Co. (Household Appliances) [15016]
Arbuckle Coffee Roasters Inc. (Restaurant and Commercial Foodservice Equipment and Supplies) [24067]
Arizona Appliance Parts (Household Appliances) [15031]
Arizona Mail Order Co. (Clothing) [4782]
Arizona Sportsman, Inc. (Guns and Weapons) [13476]
Babco International Inc. (Recreational and Sporting Goods) [23532]
Bedrosians Tile & Marble (Floorcovering Equipment and Supplies) [9715]
Bedrosians Tile and Marble (Construction Materials and Machinery) [7042]
Chapman-Dyer Steel Manufacturing (Metals) [19872]
Computer Trading Co. (Computers and Software) [6131]
Crispy's Inc. (Food) [10868]
Drilex Corporation (Industrial Machinery) [15963]
Engelhart Co.; H.C. (Computers and Software) [6250]
Envirosystems Equipment Company Inc. (Industrial Machinery) [15994]
Fluid Engineering Inc. (Compressors) [5840]
G & N Appliance Parts (Household Appliances) [15138]
Golden Eagle Distributors (Alcoholic Beverages) [1725]

Hispanic Books Distributors, Inc. (Books and Other Printed Materials) [3829]
K & K Pet Talk (Veterinary Products) [27167]
K and K Pet Talk (Medical, Dental, and Optical Supplies) [19389]
K-Tech Aviation, Inc. (Aeronautical Equipment and Supplies) [110]
Knapp Shoes of Tucson Inc. (Shoes) [24787]
Lumber Yards Inc. (Wood and Wood Products) [27337]
Magtrol Inc. (Tucson, Arizona) (Electrical and Electronic Equipment and Supplies) [9020]
Maxi Switch Inc (Computers and Software) [6471]
Mining Construction Supply (Hardware) [13830]
Modular Mining Systems Inc. (Computers and Software) [6527]
Naughton Plumbing Sales, Inc. (Plumbing Materials and Fixtures) [23287]
Naughton Plumbing Sales Inc. (Plumbing Materials and Fixtures) [23288]
Omnimedical Inc. (Medical, Dental, and Optical Equipment) [18967]
Ron's Produce Company Inc. (Food) [12350]
Securaplane Technologies L.L.C. (Security and Safety Equipment) [24628]
Treasure Chest Books, LLC (Books and Other Printed Materials) [4228]
Tucson Co-op Wholesale (Food) [12766]
Tucson Computer Products (Computers and Software) [6835]
Tucson Hobby Shop (Toys and Hobby Goods) [26692]
Union Distributing Co. (Petroleum, Fuels, and Related Equipment) [22757]
United Fire Equipment Co. (Security and Safety Equipment) [24650]
United Fire Equipment Co. (Restaurant and Commercial Foodservice Equipment and Supplies) [24255]
Veeco Process Metrology (Industrial Machinery) [16601]
Via West Interface Inc. (Computers and Software) [6850]
World Computer Inc. (Computers and Software) [6878]
Yankee Paperback & Textbook Co. (Books and Other Printed Materials) [4302]
Zephyr Press, Inc. (Books and Other Printed Materials) [4306]

Wickenburg

Bear Cat Manufacturing Inc. (Construction Materials and Machinery) [7035]

Willcox

Dunlap Oil Company Inc. (Petroleum, Fuels, and Related Equipment) [22214]

Williams

Hilites; K.C. (Electrical and Electronic Equipment and Supplies) [8842]

Yuma

Anderson News of Yuma (Books and Other Printed Materials) [3518]
Bose Corp. (Household Appliances) [15055]
Britain's Steel and Supplies (Industrial Supplies) [16766]
Consolidated Electrical Distributors° (Electrical and Electronic Equipment and Supplies) [8567]
Desert Delights Wholesale Ice (Food) [10949]
Miller Distributing (Petroleum, Fuels, and Related Equipment) [22484]
Pacific Southwest Seed and Grain Inc. (Livestock and Farm Products) [18158]
Yuma Winnelson Co. (Plumbing Materials and Fixtures) [23470]

Arkansas

Alexander

Fiser Tractor and Equipment Co. (Agricultural Equipment and Supplies) [687]

Midark Optical (Medical, Dental, and Optical
Supplies) [19455]

Altus
Post Familie Vineyards and Winery (Alcoholic
Beverages) [1964]

Arkadelphia
Southwest Sporting Goods Co. (Recreational and
Sporting Goods) [23972]

Ashdown
Kaufman Seeds Inc. (Agricultural Equipment and
Supplies) [898]

Batesville
French's Athletics Inc. (Recreational and Sporting
Goods) [23677]
Ind-Co Cable TV Inc. (Electrical and Electronic
Equipment and Supplies) [8873]
Professional Dental Technologies Inc. (Medical,
Dental, and Optical Supplies) [19554]

Benton
H & H Beauty & Barber Supply (Health and
Beauty Aids) [14119]

Bentonville
Arkansas Import & Distributing Co. (Recreational
and Sporting Goods) [23523]
Wal-Mart Stores Inc. (Household Items) [15700]

Blytheville
Farmers Soybean Corp. (Livestock and Farm
Products) [17903]
Snyder Wholesale Inc. (Food) [12524]

Bono
Craighead Farmers Cooperative (Livestock and
Farm Products) [17803]

Booneville
DPM of Arkansas (Food) [10993]
Simmons Lumber Company Inc. (Construction
Materials and Machinery) [8022]
Today's Kids Inc. (Toys and Hobby
Goods) [26682]

Brinkley
J & J Shoe Co. (Shoes) [24776]
Producers Tractor Co. (Agricultural Equipment and
Supplies) [1157]
Tri-County Farmers Association (Agricultural
Equipment and Supplies) [1353]

Bryant
Data Tech Services Inc. (Computers and
Software) [6185]

Cherry Valley
Carwell Elevator Company Inc. (Livestock and
Farm Products) [17766]

Clarksville
Clarksville Pharmacy Inc. (Medical, Dental, and
Optical Equipment) [18744]

Conway
Associated Farmers Cooperative (Agricultural
Equipment and Supplies) [259]
Mid-Ark Salvage Pool Inc. (Automotive) [2949]
Otto Dental Supply Company Inc. (Medical, Dental,
and Optical Equipment) [18971]

Corning
Harold Implement Company
Inc. (Chemicals) [4406]

De Queen
Grays Petroleum Inc. (Petroleum, Fuels, and
Related Equipment) [22320]

De Witt
Ag-Pro Inc. (Agricultural Equipment and
Supplies) [198]

Des Arc
Des Arc Implement Co. (Agricultural Equipment and
Supplies) [514]

El Dorado
Anthony Forest Products Co. (Construction
Materials and Machinery) [6979]
E and B Electric Supply Co. (Electrical and
Electronic Equipment and Supplies) [8641]
Ritchie Grocer Co. (Food) [12320]

England
Dean-Henderson Equipment Co. Inc. (Agricultural
Equipment and Supplies) [501]

Eudora
Eudora Garment Corp. (Clothing) [4940]

Fayetteville
BUDGEText Corporation (Books and Other Printed
Materials) [3600]
Continental Ozark Corp. (Petroleum, Fuels, and
Related Equipment) [22165]
Data Forms Inc. (Paper and Paper
Products) [21702]
McBride Distributing Co. (Alcoholic
Beverages) [1857]
Mountain Ark Trading Co. (Food) [11944]
Northwest Oil Company Inc. (Petroleum, Fuels, and
Related Equipment) [22528]
Northwest Tobacco and Candy Inc. (Tobacco
Products) [26334]
Ozark Co-op Warehouse (Food) [12085]
Smith Two-Way Radio Inc. (Communications
Systems and Equipment) [5760]
TransMontaigne Product Services Inc. (Petroleum,
Fuels, and Related Equipment) [22747]

Fisher
Wixson Brothers Equipment Co. (Petroleum, Fuels,
and Related Equipment) [22812]

Ft. Smith
A and W Oil Company Inc. (Petroleum, Fuels, and
Related Equipment) [22016]
Brown's Heating & Air Conditioning; Bob (Heating
and Cooling Equipment and Supplies) [14361]
Bruce-Rogers Company Inc. (Plumbing Materials
and Fixtures) [23099]
Carco International Inc. (Agricultural Equipment and
Supplies) [372]
Ceramic Tile Distributors (Floorcovering Equipment
and Supplies) [9795]
Dixie Bearings, Inc. (Automotive) [2549]
DJ Associates, Inc. (Hardware) [13668]
Eads Brothers Wholesale Furniture Co. (Furniture
and Fixtures) [13095]
Farmers Cooperative (Agricultural Equipment and
Supplies) [570]
Fort Smith Winnelson Co. (Plumbing Materials and
Fixtures) [23175]
J and B Supply Inc. (Heating and Cooling
Equipment and Supplies) [14496]
McKee-Pitts Industrials Inc. (Industrial
Machinery) [16279]
Pharmacies In Medisav Homecare (Medical, Dental,
and Optical Equipment) [18985]
Plunkett Optical Inc. (Medical, Dental, and Optical
Supplies) [19544]
Pomeco Corp. (Heating and Cooling Equipment
and Supplies) [14640]
Rockmount of Arkansas (Clothing) [5317]
Smith Hardwood Floors (Floorcovering Equipment
and Supplies) [10154]
Wise Wholesale Electronics (Electrical and
Electronic Equipment and Supplies) [9602]

Greenwood
Ark Grooming (Veterinary Products) [27073]

Gurdon
Malletech/Marimba Productions Inc. (Sound and
Entertainment Equipment and Supplies) [25301]

Harrison
Millbrook Distribution Services (Health and Beauty
Aids) [14163]
Miller Hardware Co. (Hardware) [13829]

Heber Springs
B & J Enterprises Inc. (Medical, Dental, and
Optical Equipment) [18702]

Helena
Helena Wholesale Inc. (Food) [11407]

Hope
Hempstead County Farmers
Association (Agricultural Equipment and
Supplies) [813]

Hot Springs
Arky House Inc. (Shoes) [24675]
Falk Supply Co. (Plumbing Materials and
Fixtures) [23157]
Munro and Co. (Shoes) [24816]
NSC International (Office Equipment and
Supplies) [21167]
Smith Abrasives, Inc. (Hardware) [13922]
Three Lakes Distributing Co. (Alcoholic
Beverages) [2082]

Hot Springs National Park
Bean Lumber Co.; Buddy (Construction Materials
and Machinery) [7034]
R & E Supply Inc. (Heating and Cooling
Equipment and Supplies) [14647]

Hoxie
Farm Service Inc. (Agricultural Equipment and
Supplies) [566]

Hughes
Arkansas Sock & Wiping Rag Co. (Textiles and
Notions) [25968]
Helena Chemical Company Hughes (Agricultural
Equipment and Supplies) [811]

Jacksonville
Lomanco Inc. (Heating and Cooling Equipment and
Supplies) [14527]

Jonesboro
Barton and Co.; E.C. (Construction Materials and
Machinery) [7027]
Cache Beauty Supply Inc. (Health and Beauty
Aids) [14054]
D.S.A. Materials Inc. (Electrical and Electronic
Equipment and Supplies) [8635]
Hummelstein Iron and Metal Inc. (Used, Scrap, and
Recycled Materials) [26846]
Jonesboro Coca-Cola (Soft Drinks) [24979]
Jonesboro Grocer Co. (Food) [11563]
Jonesboro Winnelson Co. (Industrial
Supplies) [16972]
Lone Star Company Inc. (Petroleum, Fuels, and
Related Equipment) [22436]
M.E. Carter of Jonesboro Inc. (Food) [11840]
Pepsi-Cola Company of Jonesboro (Soft
Drinks) [25015]

Little Rock
AFCO Metals Inc. (Metals) [19734]
Affiliated Foods Southwest Inc. (Food) [10339]
Allied Supply Inc. (Plumbing Materials and
Fixtures) [23057]
ALLTEL Corp. (Communications Systems and
Equipment) [5507]
Arnold's Inc. (Health and Beauty Aids) [14026]
Balfour Printing Company Inc. (Office Equipment
and Supplies) [20828]
Blackmon Auctions Inc.; Tom (Agricultural
Equipment and Supplies) [321]
BPI (Floorcovering Equipment and Supplies) [9735]
Brown Packing Co. Inc. (Food) [10628]

Burns Co.; Troy (Industrial Machinery) [15860]
Capital Ford New Holland Inc. (Livestock and Farm Products) [17763]
Capitol Chemical & Supply (Cleaning and Janitorial Supplies) [4593]
Carlton-Bates Co. (Electrical and Electronic Equipment and Supplies) [8504]
Central Distribution Co. (Alcoholic Beverages) [1585]
City Business Machines Inc. (Office Equipment and Supplies) [20901]
Crain Automotive Inc. (Automotive) [2491]
Croy & Associates Inc.; Ralph (Electrical and Electronic Equipment and Supplies) [8595]
Fire Appliance & Safety Co. (Security and Safety Equipment) [24541]
Gold Star Dairy (Food) [11280]
Golden Eagle of Arkansas Inc. (Alcoholic Beverages) [1724]
Graham Blue Print Co. (Specialty Equipment and Products) [25665]
Harbor Distributing Co. (Alcoholic Beverages) [1744]
Harris Enterprises Inc. (Medical, Dental, and Optical Equipment) [18827]
Heral Enterprises Inc. (Household Appliances) [15166]
Jungkind Photo-Graphic Inc. (Specialty Equipment and Products) [25695]
Leisure Arts, Inc. (Books and Other Printed Materials) [3905]
Little Rock Distributing Co. (Alcoholic Beverages) [1825]
Little Rock Drapery Co. (Household Items) [15570]
Little Rock Tool Service, Inc. (Hardware) [13798]
Mechanical Refrigeration & AC (Heating and Cooling Equipment and Supplies) [14539]
Mid-South Appliance Parts Inc. (Household Appliances) [15229]
Mole Hole (Clothing) [5199]
Moon Distributors Inc. (Alcoholic Beverages) [1892]
MP Productions Co. (Sound and Entertainment Equipment and Supplies) [25342]
Nation Wide Paper Co. (Paper and Paper Products) [21847]
New Age Distributing Co. (Soft Drinks) [24992]
Parts Warehouse Inc. (Automotive) [3085]
Quality Foods Inc. (Food) [12250]
Quality Foods Inc. (Food) [12251]
Refrigeration and Electric Supply Co. (Household Appliances) [15288]
Rushin Upholstery Supply, Inc. (Textiles and Notions) [26195]
Scanning Technologies Inc. (Computers and Software) [6709]
Strauss Distributing (Alcoholic Beverages) [2058]
SYSCO Food Services of Arkansas, Inc. (Restaurant and Commercial Foodservice Equipment and Supplies) [24237]
Tenenbaum Company Inc.; A. (Used, Scrap, and Recycled Materials) [27020]
Tennessee Valley Electric Supply Co. (Electrical and Electronic Equipment and Supplies) [9478]
Treadway Electric Co. (Electrical and Electronic Equipment and Supplies) [9502]
Win Nelson Inc. (Plumbing Materials and Fixtures) [23462]
Winburn Tile (Floorcovering Equipment and Supplies) [10302]
Zink Safety of Arkansas Inc. (Security and Safety Equipment) [24662]

Malvern

Clem Wholesale Grocer Co. Inc. (Food) [10770]
STIHL Southwest Inc. (Industrial Machinery) [16527]

Marked Tree

Ritter Equipment Co.; E. (Agricultural Equipment and Supplies) [1196]

Marmaduke

Delta Cotton Cooperative Inc. (Agricultural Equipment and Supplies) [509]

Mena

Intermountain Resources (Recreational and Sporting Goods) [23745]

Monticello

Akin Industries, Inc. (Medical, Dental, and Optical Equipment) [18666]

Morrilton

Arkansas Valley Wholesale Grocers Co. (Food) [10433]

Mountain Home

Mountain Muffler (Automotive) [3001]

Mountain View

McClung Equipment Co. (Agricultural Equipment and Supplies) [998]
Mellon Patch (Toys and Hobby Goods) [26573]

North Little Rock

Acme Agri Supply Inc. (Veterinary Products) [27056]
Arkansas Optical Co. (Medical, Dental, and Optical Supplies) [19160]
Burton Building Products Inc. (Construction Materials and Machinery) [7114]
Capitol Wholesale Florists Inc. (Horticultural Supplies) [14833]
Davies Electric Supply Co. (Electrical and Electronic Equipment and Supplies) [8612]
Jones of Little Rock Inc.; Grady W. (Industrial Machinery) [16193]
Keathley-Patterson Electric Co. (Electrical and Electronic Equipment and Supplies) [8933]
LaserTone Inc. (Computers and Software) [6431]
One Source Home and Building Centers (Construction Materials and Machinery) [7812]
President Baking Co., Inc. (Food) [12215]
Pulaski Equipment Co., Inc. (Agricultural Equipment and Supplies) [1163]
SF Services Inc. (Veterinary Products) [27231]
South Central Pool Supply, Inc. (Recreational and Sporting Goods) [23957]
Welsco Inc. (Industrial Supplies) [17272]

Osceola

Home Oil Co. (Petroleum, Fuels, and Related Equipment) [22358]

Paragould

Turner Dairy (Food) [12773]

Parkin

Farmers Cooperative Oil Co. (Petroleum, Fuels, and Related Equipment) [22255]

Piggott

Piggott Tractor and Equipment Company Inc. (Agricultural Equipment and Supplies) [1129]

Pine Bluff

Hall Balloon Co. (Toys and Hobby Goods) [26508]

Plumerville

Hightower Oil and Petroleum Company Inc. (Petroleum, Fuels, and Related Equipment) [22352]

Rogers

Computer Service and Support (Computers and Software) [6125]
Rogers Iron and Metal Corp. (Used, Scrap, and Recycled Materials) [26965]

Rose Bud

Caldwell Milling Company Inc. (Food) [10670]

Russellville

Poultry Specialties Inc. (Food) [12199]
Price Milling Co. (Agricultural Equipment and Supplies) [1149]

Searcy

McKenney Supply Inc. (Heating and Cooling Equipment and Supplies) [14538]
Ridout Lumber Cos. (Wood and Wood Products) [27363]
Yarnell Ice Cream Company Inc. (Food) [12992]

Sherwood

Centro, Inc. (Scientific and Measurement Devices) [24336]

Siloam Springs

Farmers Cooperative Association (Agricultural Equipment and Supplies) [575]

Springdale

Advanced Environmental Recycling Technologies Inc. (Used, Scrap, and Recycled Materials) [26732]
Danaher Tool Group (Hardware) [13655]
K & K Vet Supply (Veterinary Products) [27168]
K and K Vet Supply (Medical, Dental, and Optical Supplies) [19390]
Northwest Arkansas Paper Co. (Cleaning and Janitorial Supplies) [4677]
Townzen Tile & Laminates (Floorcovering Equipment and Supplies) [10255]

Stuttgart

Delta Poly Plastic Inc. (Used, Scrap, and Recycled Materials) [26795]
Harco Distributing Co. (Livestock and Farm Products) [17974]
Hartz Seed Company Inc.; Jacob (Livestock and Farm Products) [17980]
Kinder-Harris Inc. (Electrical and Electronic Equipment and Supplies) [8945]
Orbit Fluid Power Co. (Industrial Machinery) [16362]
Producers Rice Mill Inc. (Food) [12225]
Riceland Foods Inc. (Food) [12309]
Stratton Seed Co. (Agricultural Equipment and Supplies) [1299]
Stuttgart Industrial Service Inc. (Livestock and Farm Products) [18264]
Wilkerson Jewelers (Jewelry) [17657]

Texarkana

A.P. Supply Co. (Plumbing Materials and Fixtures) [23066]
Buhrman-Pharr Hardware Co. (Hardware) [13609]
Douglas Northeast Inc. (Food) [10986]
Tri-State Iron and Metal Co. (Used, Scrap, and Recycled Materials) [27026]
Twin City Marble (Floorcovering Equipment and Supplies) [10260]

Van Buren

Dales Mechanical Sales & Service (Heating and Cooling Equipment and Supplies) [14411]
Garner Meats Inc.; John (Food) [11238]
Law Office Information Systems Inc. (Sound and Entertainment Equipment and Supplies) [25280]
Yeager Hardware (Floorcovering Equipment and Supplies) [10309]

Walnut Ridge

Douglas/Quikut (Household Appliances) [15114]
Gemini Manufacturing Inc. (Recreational and Sporting Goods) [23688]

Weiner

Norseworthy and Wofford Inc. (Agricultural Equipment and Supplies) [1077]

West Helena

Southern Hardware Company Inc. (Hardware) [13930]

West Memphis

Peacock Radio & Wilds Computer Services (Communications Systems and Equipment) [5705]

California

Agoura Hills
Paisano Publications (Clothing) [5265]

Alameda
Auto-Bound, Inc. (Books and Other Printed Materials) [3534]
Cognex Corp. (Industrial Machinery) [15896]
Esprit International (Clothing) [4939]
Svendsen's Boat Works (Marine) [18620]
Svendsen's Marine Distribution (Marine) [18621]
United Beverage Inc. (Food) [12790]

Alamo
Green Associates; Dale (Recreational and Sporting Goods) [23698]

Alhambra
California Hobby Distributors (Toys and Hobby Goods) [26434]
Green Leaf Press (Books and Other Printed Materials) [3800]
Kum Kee (USA) Inc.; Lee (Food) [11655]
Lasonic Electronics Corp. (Household Appliances) [15199]
Meeder Equipment Co. (Petroleum, Fuels, and Related Equipment) [22472]
Tewes Company Inc.; George B. (Industrial Supplies) [17218]
U.S. International (Industrial Machinery) [16593]

Aliso Viejo
Bearing Engineers Inc. (Industrial Supplies) [16732]
Flex-Foot Inc. (Medical, Dental, and Optical Equipment) [18799]

Alpine
Hallmarkets International Ltd. (Office Equipment and Supplies) [21023]

American Canyon
Ramallah Inc. (Household Items) [15629]

Anaheim
Action Laboratories Inc. (Health and Beauty Aids) [14008]
Action Laboratories Inc. (Medical, Dental, and Optical Supplies) [19124]
Adams International Metals Corp. (Used, Scrap, and Recycled Materials) [26728]
ALM Surgical Equipment Inc. (Medical, Dental, and Optical Equipment) [18673]
Anaheim Custom Extruders, Inc. (Plastics) [22926]
Anaheim Extrusion Co. Inc. (Metals) [19780]
Anaheim Manufacturing Co. (Household Appliances) [15011]
Anaheim Marketing International (Household Appliances) [15012]
Ashbrook & Associates (Household Items) [15408]
Bedrosian Tile Supply (Floorcovering Equipment and Supplies) [9709]
Boone-Davis Inc. (Household Items) [15425]
Brothers' Optical Lab, Inc. (Medical, Dental, and Optical Supplies) [19202]
Burnett Engraving Co. Inc. (Industrial Machinery) [15859]
California Fasteners Inc. (Hardware) [13615]
CBS Fasteners Inc. (Hardware) [13624]
CM School Supply (Toys and Hobby Goods) [26445]
Compex Inc. (Anaheim, California) (Computers and Software) [6091]
Esojon International, Inc. (Floorcovering Equipment and Supplies) [9887]
Filter Supply Co. (Automotive) [2615]
Fujitsu Business Communication Systems Inc. (Electrical and Electronic Equipment and Supplies) [8766]
Ganahl Lumber Co. (Construction Materials and Machinery) [7375]
Hallock Coin Jewelry (Jewelry) [17443]
Hardin Marine Inc. (Marine) [18518]

HEPA Corp. (Heating and Cooling Equipment and Supplies) [14484]
Keyston Brothers (Textiles and Notions) [26094]
McLogan Supply (Specialty Equipment and Products) [25730]
Nanbren-Compsol Ltd. (Computers and Software) [6541]
Pacific Group International (Gifts and Novelties) [13417]
Pacific Supply Co. (Automotive) [3075]
Panasonic Copier Co. (Office Equipment and Supplies) [21202]
Pittman International (Veterinary Products) [27214]
Pittman International (Medical, Dental, and Optical Supplies) [19542]
Scope Office Services Inc. (Office Equipment and Supplies) [21261]
Superior Pool Products Inc. (Recreational and Sporting Goods) [23996]
Taylor-Dunn Manufacturing Co. (Industrial Machinery) [16550]
Tile Club (Floorcovering Equipment and Supplies) [10224]
Traffic Control Service Inc. (Security and Safety Equipment) [24644]
Westburne Supply Inc. (Plumbing Materials and Fixtures) [23451]
Yang Machine Tool Co. (Industrial Machinery) [16656]

Antioch
Fiberglass Representatives Inc. (Plumbing Materials and Fixtures) [23166]
Reliance Sheet and Strip Co. (Metals) [20312]

Aptos
Hike A Bike (Recreational and Sporting Goods) [23727]
Marcom (Communications Systems and Equipment) [5667]
Omnibooks (Books and Other Printed Materials) [4021]

Arcadia
Aero-K.A.P. Inc. (Electrical and Electronic Equipment and Supplies) [8278]
Hartzler's Inc. Exporters (Medical, Dental, and Optical Equipment) [18828]
Raco Manufacturing Inc. (Recreational and Sporting Goods) [23902]
Shen's Books and Supplies (Books and Other Printed Materials) [4158]

Arleta
Absolute Aqua Systems (Specialty Equipment and Products) [25542]
Expressive Art & Craft (Office Equipment and Supplies) [20997]

Arroyo Grande
BookLink Distributors (Books and Other Printed Materials) [3577]

Artesia
California Milk Producers (Food) [10672]
Daiwa Corp. (Recreational and Sporting Goods) [23613]

Atascadero
X-Ray Products Corp. (Medical, Dental, and Optical Equipment) [19112]

Atherton
China First Merchandising Co. (Food) [10750]

Atwater
Wood Inc.; J.R. (Food) [12977]

Auburn
Bedrosian Building Supply (Floorcovering Equipment and Supplies) [9698]
Mountain People's Warehouse (Food) [11946]
Mountain People's Warehouse Inc. (Food) [11947]

Azusa
Catalina Cottage (Specialty Equipment and Products) [25597]
K & P Manufacturing (Recreational and Sporting Goods) [23766]
Taxor Inc. (Jewelry) [17633]
Totten Tubes Inc. (Metals) [20433]
Virginia Hardwood Co. (Floorcovering Equipment and Supplies) [10280]

Bakersfield
Abbott Import-Export Co. (Clothing) [4741]
Auto Parts Wholesale (Automotive) [2276]
B and B Surplus Inc. (Metals) [19797]
Bakersfield AG Co. Inc. (Agricultural Equipment and Supplies) [274]
Bakersfield Sandstone Brick Co. Inc. (Construction Materials and Machinery) [7015]
Bakersfield Sandstone Brick Company Inc. (Wood and Wood Products) [27285]
Bedrosian Tile Supply (Floorcovering Equipment and Supplies) [9708]
Berchtold Equipment Company Inc. (Agricultural Equipment and Supplies) [301]
Burcham and McCune Inc. (Furniture and Fixtures) [13049]
Calcot Ltd. (Livestock and Farm Products) [17758]
Calmini Products Inc. (Automotive) [2413]
Celeron Trading and Transportation Co. (Petroleum, Fuels, and Related Equipment) [22117]
Dole Bakersfield Inc. (Food) [10975]
GEO Drilling Fluids Inc. (Chemicals) [4398]
GWS Automotive and Truck Equipment Sales Inc. (Automotive) [2712]
Jim's Supply Company Inc. (Metals) [20076]
Mazzei Injector Corp. (Industrial Machinery) [16276]
McCarthy Steel Inc. (Metals) [20161]
Pioneer Mercantile Co. (Automotive) [3098]
Pyrenees French Bakery Inc. (Food) [12242]
Sequoia Paint (Paints and Varnishes) [21562]
Smith and Sons Inc.; Jess (Livestock and Farm Products) [18236]
Stockdale Ceramic Tile Center, Inc. (Floorcovering Equipment and Supplies) [10183]
Stuarts' Petroleum Co. (Petroleum, Fuels, and Related Equipment) [22713]
Valley Auto and Truck Wrecking Inc. (Automotive) [3383]

Baldwin Park
Allan Co. (Used, Scrap, and Recycled Materials) [26735]
American Kal Enterprises Inc. (Hardware) [13559]
Gem Guides Book Co. (Books and Other Printed Materials) [3774]
Microstar Computer Technology Inc. (Computers and Software) [6509]
Sues Young and Brown Inc. (Recreational and Sporting Goods) [23991]
Unitex Inc. (Textiles and Notions) [26239]

Barstow
Barstow Truck Parts and Equipment Co. (Automotive) [2324]
Desert Stationers (Office Equipment and Supplies) [20956]

Bell Gardens
Farm Fresh Foods Inc. (Food) [11085]

Belmont
Document Center (Books and Other Printed Materials) [3699]
Erickson Wood Products (Wood and Wood Products) [27304]
Global Metrics Inc. (Automotive) [2684]
GRE America Inc. (Communications Systems and Equipment) [5626]
Howard Tire Service Inc. (Automotive) [2764]
Jacobi and Sons Inc.; Walter (Furniture and Fixtures) [13149]
Jacobi and Sons Inc.; Walter (Furniture and Fixtures) [13150]
Jameco Electronics Inc. (Electrical and Electronic Equipment and Supplies) [8905]

MicroTech Conversion Systems (Computers and Software) [6510]

Benicia

BSW Inc. (Heating and Cooling Equipment and Supplies) [14362]
Cork Supply International Inc. (Household Items) [15456]
Flickinger Co. (Industrial Supplies) [16867]
Intertile Distributors, Inc. (Floorcovering Equipment and Supplies) [9972]
Schneider Company Inc.; J.R. (Specialty Equipment and Products) [25808]
West Coast Beauty Supply (Health and Beauty Aids) [14280]

Berkeley

Berkley Game Distributors (Toys and Hobby Goods) [26415]
Celestial Arts Publishing Co. (Books and Other Printed Materials) [3618]
Creative Arts Book Co. (Books and Other Printed Materials) [3667]
Dover Sales Co. Inc. (Chemicals) [4375]
Fosburg & McLaughlin Inc. (Industrial Machinery) [16035]
Import Tile Co. (Floorcovering Equipment and Supplies) [9961]
Inlite Corp. (Electrical and Electronic Equipment and Supplies) [8880]
Intermountain Trading Company Ltd. (Food) [11517]
Key Curriculum Press Inc. (Books and Other Printed Materials) [3878]
Minnesota Western Inc. (Sound and Entertainment Equipment and Supplies) [25326]
Nolo Press/Folklaw Inc. (Books and Other Printed Materials) [4005]
Northwestern Equipment Supply (Industrial Machinery) [16354]
Omnichron (Specialty Equipment and Products) [25774]
Pacific Coast Chemical Co. (Paints and Varnishes) [21521]
Peets Coffee and Tea Inc. (Food) [12131]
Publishers Group West Inc. (Books and Other Printed Materials) [4094]
Qualitas Trading Co. (Computers and Software) [6669]
Small Press Distribution Inc. (Books and Other Printed Materials) [4168]
Sri Aurobindo Association (Books and Other Printed Materials) [4186]
Ten Speed Press (Books and Other Printed Materials) [4207]
T.W.P. Inc. (Metals) [20450]
Western Book Distributors (Books and Other Printed Materials) [4276]
Winners Circle Systems (Computers and Software) [6872]

Beverly Hills

14 Carats Ltd. (Jewelry) [17297]
ABA-tron Industries Inc. (Chemicals) [4310]
Flynt Distribution Company Inc. (Books and Other Printed Materials) [3755]
Hilton Equipment Corp. (Furniture and Fixtures) [13134]
Langer Inc.; David (Computers and Software) [6426]
Lory's West Inc. (Jewelry) [17505]
Playboy Entertainment Group Inc. (Books and Other Printed Materials) [4067]

Blythe

Toshin Trading Inc. (Agricultural Equipment and Supplies) [1344]

Bodega Bay

McCaughey Brothers (Marine) [18564]

Brawley

Rockwood Chemical Co. (Agricultural Equipment and Supplies) [1207]

Brea

American Suzuki Motor Corp. (Motorized Vehicles) [20591]
American Suzuki Motor Corp. (Automotive) [2234]
G.D.E., Inc. (Electrical and Electronic Equipment and Supplies) [8778]
Great Health (Food) [11311]
Jorgensen Co.; Earle M. (Metals) [20079]
Kirkhill Aircraft Parts Co. (Aeronautical Equipment and Supplies) [113]
Nature's Best (Food) [11987]
Pet Food Wholesale, Inc. (Veterinary Products) [27206]
Pet Food Wholesale Inc. (Food) [12154]
Progressive Marketing (Electrical and Electronic Equipment and Supplies) [9241]
RPV Distributors (Toys and Hobby Goods) [26642]

Brisbane

Hitachi America Ltd. (Electrical and Electronic Equipment and Supplies) [8846]
Persona Technologies Inc. (Electrical and Electronic Equipment and Supplies) [9191]
Sierra (Food) [12486]
Skyline Supply Company Inc. (Office Equipment and Supplies) [21272]
VWR Scientific Products (Scientific and Measurement Devices) [24453]

Buena Park

ACS Digital Solutions (Office Equipment and Supplies) [20770]
Fibertron Corp. (Communications Systems and Equipment) [5613]
Noritsu America Corp. (Photographic Equipment and Supplies) [22885]
Pacific Abrasive Supply Co. (Industrial Supplies) [17094]
President Global Corp. (Food) [12216]
The Standard Register Co (Office Equipment and Supplies) [21285]
Tung Pec Inc. (Food) [12769]
U.S. Amada Ltd. (Industrial Machinery) [16590]
Yamaha Corporation of America (Sound and Entertainment Equipment and Supplies) [25535]
Yamaha Electronics Corporation USA (Sound and Entertainment Equipment and Supplies) [25537]
Yamaha Systems Technology (Electrical and Electronic Equipment and Supplies) [9616]

Burbank

Airmotive Inc. (Aeronautical Equipment and Supplies) [37]
Aramark Magazines and Books (Books and Other Printed Materials) [3523]
Bawamba Software Inc. (Computers and Software) [6002]
California Tile Distributors (Floorcovering Equipment and Supplies) [9751]
Cinema Secrets Inc. (Health and Beauty Aids) [14063]
Cinemills Corp. (Electrical and Electronic Equipment and Supplies) [8525]
Clark Productions Inc.; Dick (Electrical and Electronic Equipment and Supplies) [8530]
Elmo Semiconductor Corp. (Electrical and Electronic Equipment and Supplies) [8700]
Geviderm Inc. (Health and Beauty Aids) [14111]
Haskel International, Inc. (Industrial Machinery) [16091]
Herco Products Corp.; Ryan (Plastics) [22980]
International Hi-Tech Trading Corp. (Automotive) [2793]
Jax International (Office Equipment and Supplies) [21075]
Kaman Industrial (Industrial Supplies) [16976]
Keyston Brothers (Textiles and Notions) [26099]
King Fish Inc. (Food) [11612]
Laagco Sales (Paints and Varnishes) [21484]
Marion Fabrics Inc. (Textiles and Notions) [26134]
OroAmerica Inc. (Jewelry) [17541]
Pool Doctor (Recreational and Sporting Goods) [23890]
Swaner Hardwood Company Inc. (Construction Materials and Machinery) [8092]

Touch Flo Manufacturing (Plumbing Materials and Fixtures) [23413]
Warner-Elektra-Atlantic Corp. (Sound and Entertainment Equipment and Supplies) [25512]

Burlingame

Caltag Lab (Medical, Dental, and Optical Supplies) [19209]
Corkey Control Systems Inc. (Security and Safety Equipment) [24528]
DTC Tool Corp. (Industrial Machinery) [15966]
French Transit Ltd. (Health and Beauty Aids) [14106]
Nomura and Company Inc. (Livestock and Farm Products) [18133]
QSound Ltd. (Sound and Entertainment Equipment and Supplies) [25397]
Signalcom Systems Inc. (Communications Systems and Equipment) [5756]
Smith Associates; Jay (Hardware) [13923]
Tung Tai Trading Corp. (Used, Scrap, and Recycled Materials) [27028]

Calabasas

Valley Crest Tree Co. (Agricultural Equipment and Supplies) [1390]

Calabasas Hills

Helmet House Inc. (Recreational and Sporting Goods) [23721]

Calexico

Circle Produce Co. (Food) [10760]

Camarillo

Howard Enterprises Inc. (Communications Systems and Equipment) [5640]
Laube Technology Inc. (Industrial Supplies) [16994]
Record Technology Inc. (Sound and Entertainment Equipment and Supplies) [25411]
Signature Housewares Inc. (Household Items) [15653]
Supra Alloys Inc. (Metals) [20414]

Campbell

Capri Arts & Crafts (Office Equipment and Supplies) [20878]
KNB Computer Werx Inc. (Computers and Software) [6422]
Mercury Computer Systems (Computers and Software) [6483]
Motor Sound Corp. (Communications Systems and Equipment) [5682]
Pana Pacific Corp. (Communications Systems and Equipment) [5702]
Savoir Technology Group Inc. (Electrical and Electronic Equipment and Supplies) [9339]
Sierra Pacific (Recreational and Sporting Goods) [23938]
Sunset Models, Inc. (Toys and Hobby Goods) [26674]

Canoga Park

Apollo Tire Co. Inc. (Automotive) [2245]
R.E.I. Glitter (Office Equipment and Supplies) [21236]

Carlsbad

Callaway Golf Co (Recreational and Sporting Goods) [23580]
Carlsbad Volvo (Motorized Vehicles) [20610]
Dyna Corp. (Medical, Dental, and Optical Supplies) [19297]
Glacier Water Services Inc. (Restaurant and Commercial Foodservice Equipment and Supplies) [24128]
Hartwell Medical Corp. (Medical, Dental, and Optical Supplies) [19350]
Liberty Woods International, Inc. (Construction Materials and Machinery) [7603]
Micro Star (Computers and Software) [6495]
Myron L Co. (Scientific and Measurement Devices) [24406]

Penton Overseas Inc. (Sound and Entertainment Equipment and Supplies) [25377]
Seawind International (Food) [12456]
Titleist Golf (Recreational and Sporting Goods) [24011]

Carmel
Hillside Coffee of California Holding Co. (Food) [11434]

Carmel Valley
Edwards & Associates; John (Recreational and Sporting Goods) [23646]

Carpinteria
CUI Corp. (Medical, Dental, and Optical Equipment) [18761]
Dako Corp. (Medical, Dental, and Optical Supplies) [19271]
Southern California Tees (Clothing) [5372]

Carson
Ad Art Electronic Sign Corp. (Restaurant and Commercial Foodservice Equipment and Supplies) [24055]
Barton Brands California Inc. (Alcoholic Beverages) [1502]
Books Nippan (Books and Other Printed Materials) [3581]
Crest Steel Corp. (Metals) [19904]
Easterday Janitorial Supply Co. (Cleaning and Janitorial Supplies) [4613]
Jalmar Press/Innerchoice Publishing (Books and Other Printed Materials) [3859]
Mark-Costello Co. (Industrial Machinery) [16264]
MQ Power Corp. (Construction Materials and Machinery) [7754]
Nippan Shuppan Hanbai (Books and Other Printed Materials) [4004]
Penberthy Lumber Co. (Construction Materials and Machinery) [7845]
Pola U.S.A. Inc. (Health and Beauty Aids) [14191]
Porteous Fastener Co. (Hardware) [13873]
Prime Natural Health Laboratories Inc. (Health and Beauty Aids) [14194]
Ragu Foods Co. (Food) [12264]
Sales International (Industrial Machinery) [16469]

Castroville
Ocean Mist Farms (Food) [12052]

Century City
AGFA Corp. (Photographic Equipment and Supplies) [22823]

Ceres
Advanced Tech Distributors (Computers and Software) [5889]
Gaylord Manufacturing Co. (Electrical and Electronic Equipment and Supplies) [8776]

Cerritas
American Isuzu Motors Inc. (Motorized Vehicles) [20589]

Cerritos
Billings Horn (Health and Beauty Aids) [14040]
California Panel and Veneer Co. (Construction Materials and Machinery) [7127]
Capital City Distribution Inc. (Books and Other Printed Materials) [3608]
Chilay Corp. (Food) [10748]
Crown Inc. (Cerritos, California) (Food) [10874]
Eide Industries Inc. (Household Items) [15486]
Fastener Controls Inc. (FASCON) (Hardware) [13697]
Isuzu Motors America Inc. (Motorized Vehicles) [20655]
Leisure Components/SF Technology (Automotive) [2878]
Marcone Appliance Parts (Household Appliances) [15210]
Proton Corp. (Sound and Entertainment Equipment and Supplies) [25392]

The Roane Co. (Floorcovering Equipment and Supplies) [10123]
The Roane Co. (Wood and Wood Products) [27364]
S and J Chevrolet Inc. (Electrical and Electronic Equipment and Supplies) [9328]
Simmons Mattress Factory Inc.; W. (Furniture and Fixtures) [13243]
Sirco International Corp. (Luggage and Leather Goods) [18429]
Southern Wine and Spirits of California Inc. (Alcoholic Beverages) [2041]
Sunset Industrial Parts (Industrial Supplies) [17203]
Yaesu U.S.A. Inc. (Sound and Entertainment Equipment and Supplies) [25534]

Chatsworth
AIMS Multimedia (Sound and Entertainment Equipment and Supplies) [25058]
AIMS Multimedia (Household Appliances) [14995]
Air Electro Inc. (Electrical and Electronic Equipment and Supplies) [8283]
Alatec Products (Hardware) [13542]
Automoco Corp. (Automotive) [2284]
Best Data Products Inc. (Computers and Software) [6014]
Chatsworth Press (Books and Other Printed Materials) [3626]
DocuSource Inc. (Office Equipment and Supplies) [20973]
Dot Line (Photographic Equipment and Supplies) [22851]
Fuses Unlimimted (Aeronautical Equipment and Supplies) [90]
Interamerican Motor Corp. (Automotive) [2790]
International Engine Parts Inc. (Aeronautical Equipment and Supplies) [103]
International Television Corp. (Electrical and Electronic Equipment and Supplies) [8895]
Jacon Fasteners and Electronics Inc. (Hardware) [13768]
Light Wave Systems (Electrical and Electronic Equipment and Supplies) [8987]
Maruri USA Corp. (Gifts and Novelties) [13399]
Max Scrap Metals Inc. (Used, Scrap, and Recycled Materials) [26900]
McBain Instruments (Scientific and Measurement Devices) [24395]
Mercury Beauty Company Inc. (Health and Beauty Aids) [14159]
Micro Metrology Inc. (Industrial Machinery) [16293]
Mil-Spec Supply Inc. (Electrical and Electronic Equipment and Supplies) [9081]
Miller Industrial Tools Inc. (Industrial Machinery) [16301]
Natrol, Inc. (Health and Beauty Aids) [14170]
Nature's Gate Herbal Cosmetics (Health and Beauty Aids) [14172]
Nor-Mar Sales Company Inc. (Hardware) [13848]
ORA Electronics (Communications Systems and Equipment) [5696]
Pioneer Photo Albums Inc. (Gifts and Novelties) [13421]
Professional Education & Products Inc. (Health and Beauty Aids) [14196]
RadServ Inc. (Medical, Dental, and Optical Equipment) [19010]
Specialty Merchandise Corp. (Gifts and Novelties) [13451]
Syncor International Corp. (Medical, Dental, and Optical Equipment) [19066]
Western Component Sales Div. (Electrical and Electronic Equipment and Supplies) [9574]

Chico
A-1 Plumbers Supply (Plumbing Materials and Fixtures) [23048]
Norfield Industries (Construction Materials and Machinery) [7790]
Pacific STIHL, Inc. (Industrial Machinery) [16376]
Stash Distributing Inc. (Alcoholic Beverages) [2049]
Tile City (Floorcovering Equipment and Supplies) [10219]

Chino
All Coast Forest Products Inc. (Construction Materials and Machinery) [6933]
American Filtration Systems Inc. (Heating and Cooling Equipment and Supplies) [14317]
Dearborn West L.P. (Electrical and Electronic Equipment and Supplies) [8618]
Harrington Industrial Plastics Inc. (Plastics) [22978]
Kemper Enterprises Inc. (Specialty Equipment and Products) [25698]
L and L Nursery Supply Inc. (Agricultural Equipment and Supplies) [924]
Lite Source Inc. (Furniture and Fixtures) [13165]
OREPAC Millwork Products (Construction Materials and Machinery) [7814]
Pacific Coast Air Tool and Supply Inc. (Aeronautical Equipment and Supplies) [135]
Parr Lumber Co. (Construction Materials and Machinery) [7835]
Uspar Enterprises Inc. (Electrical and Electronic Equipment and Supplies) [9528]
Webber Cable and Electronics (Electrical and Electronic Equipment and Supplies) [9564]
Wertz Candies; Allen (Food) [12904]

Chula Vista
American Mill and Manufacturing Inc. (Wood and Wood Products) [27279]
Banian Trading Co. (Clothing) [4801]
Border Leather Corp. (Luggage and Leather Goods) [18377]

ChuLa Vista
Coyote Pet Products Inc. (Veterinary Products) [27113]

Chula Vista
Farrell Imports Inc.; Patrick (Luggage and Leather Goods) [18394]

ChuLa Vista
IDM Satellite Division Inc. (Communications Systems and Equipment) [5643]

Chula Vista
JT Racing Inc. (Clothing) [5100]
Latin Trading Corp. (Books and Other Printed Materials) [3898]
Tesla Book Co. (Books and Other Printed Materials) [4209]
Tile Club (Floorcovering Equipment and Supplies) [10222]

Citrus Heights
Harris Industrial Gases Inc. (Industrial Machinery) [16089]

City of Commerce
A-1 International Foods (Food) [10315]
California Naturals (Food) [10673]
E and E Steel Company Inc. (Metals) [19943]
G and G Produce Company Inc. (Food) [11225]
Harris Corp.; Dub (Office Equipment and Supplies) [21028]
Ideal Sales and Distributing Company Inc. (Automotive) [2770]
Q Perfumes (Health and Beauty Aids) [14201]
Western Office Interiors (Furniture and Fixtures) [13278]
Wine Warehouse (Alcoholic Beverages) [2127]

City of Industry
All Computer Warehouse (Computers and Software) [5902]
Alta Dena Certified Dairy (Food) [10386]
Arnel Compressor Co. (Compressors) [5829]
Deuteronomy Inc. (Computers and Software) [6202]
Ingram Paper Co. (Paper and Paper Products) [21777]
Microlink Enterprises Inc. (Computers and Software) [6504]
Mulligan Sales Inc. (Food) [11956]
PC Club Inc. (Computers and Software) [6596]

Peterson Co.; Robert H. (Household
Items) [15618]
Sager Midern Computer Inc. (Computers and
Software) [6700]
Sierra Craft Inc. (Plumbing Materials and
Fixtures) [23374]
Snak King Corp. (Food) [12522]
Sun Hing Trading Company Inc. (Gifts and
Novelties) [13458]
Sun Pacific Industries (Storage Equipment and
Containers) [25942]
TIC Industries Co. (Sound and Entertainment
Equipment and Supplies) [25479]
TIC Industries Co. (Household Appliances) [15338]
United Packaging Corp. (Plastics) [23045]
Valley Detroit Diesel Allison
Inc. (Automotive) [3384]
Yum Yum Donut Shops, Inc. (Food) [12998]

Claremont
Majega Records (Sound and Entertainment
Equipment and Supplies) [25300]

Cloverdale
All Coast Lumber Products Inc. (Construction
Materials and Machinery) [6934]

Clovis
Lamanuzzi and Pantaleo (Food) [11670]

Colfax
Toms Sierra Company Inc. (Petroleum, Fuels, and
Related Equipment) [22738]

Colton
Brithinee Electric (Automotive) [2386]
Colton Piano and Organ (Furniture and
Fixtures) [13072]

Commerce
Atlas Textile Company Inc. (Household
Items) [15410]
Grocers Specialty Co. (Food) [11329]
ICI Dulux Paints (Paints and Varnishes) [21462]
Paper Mart (Paper and Paper Products) [21862]
TW Graphics Group (Specialty Equipment and
Products) [25850]

Compton
Accurate Air Engineering
Inc. (Compressors) [5823]
Accurate Air Engineering Inc. (Industrial
Machinery) [15730]
Algert Company, Inc. (Household
Appliances) [14998]
Alma's Glow Products International (Health and
Beauty Aids) [14016]
BAL RV Products Group (Industrial
Machinery) [15799]
Beauchamp Distributing Co. (Soft Drinks) [24913]
Coast Wholesale Music (Sound and Entertainment
Equipment and Supplies) [25141]
Kaman Music Corp. Los Angeles (Sound and
Entertainment Equipment and Supplies) [25266]
Kaman Music Corp. Los Angeles (Household
Appliances) [15183]
Kraco Enterprises Inc. (Automotive) [2862]
L and M Shape Burning Inc. (Metals) [20112]
Luggage America Inc. (Luggage and Leather
Goods) [18409]
Monogram Sanitation Co. (Plumbing Materials and
Fixtures) [23273]
Nankang USA Inc. (Automotive) [3014]
Pos-A-Traction Inc. (Automotive) [3104]
Rubin, Jack and Sons Inc. (Metals) [20335]
Skeels and Co.; Robert (Hardware) [13921]
Tacchini Apparel; Sergio (Clothing) [5419]
West Coast Liquidators Inc. (Clothing) [5480]

Concord
Bedrosian Tile Supply (Floorcovering Equipment
and Supplies) [9702]
Diablo Cellular Phone Stores Inc. (Communications
Systems and Equipment) [5593]

Higgins Lumber Co.; J.E. (Wood and Wood
Products) [27317]
Nordic Computers (Computers and
Software) [6560]
Office Club Inc. (Office Equipment and
Supplies) [21172]
Pacific Flooring Supply (Floorcovering Equipment
and Supplies) [10091]
Paramount Technology (Computers and
Software) [6589]
Stone Enterprises (Clothing) [5397]
Western Tile Design Center (Floorcovering
Equipment and Supplies) [10294]

Corcoran
Calarco Inc. (Agricultural Equipment and
Supplies) [359]

Corona
A-1 Metal Services Corp. (Metals) [19719]
Agrigold Juice Products (Soft Drinks) [24908]
Aircraft Spruce and Specialty Co. (Aeronautical
Equipment and Supplies) [36]
Calhoun Inc.; Nancy (Household Items) [15434]
Engineered Equipment Co. (Specialty Equipment
and Products) [25643]
Engineered Equipment Co. (Construction Materials
and Machinery) [7313]
Farris Enterprises (Specialty Equipment and
Products) [25647]
Food For Life Baking Co. (Food) [11171]
Irwin International Inc. (Aeronautical Equipment and
Supplies) [106]
Konex Corp. (Electrical and Electronic Equipment
and Supplies) [8955]
Liston Brick Company of Corona
Inc. (Metals) [20132]
Robertshaw Uni-Line North America (Heating and
Cooling Equipment and Supplies) [14664]
Sprite Industries (Plumbing Materials and
Fixtures) [23394]
TALCO Recycling Inc. (Used, Scrap, and Recycled
Materials) [27018]
Transfer Print Foils (Metals) [20437]

Costa Mesa
Alligator Technologies (Computers and
Software) [5906]
American International Trading
Co. (Clothing) [4769]
Battery Specialties Inc. (Electrical and Electronic
Equipment and Supplies) [8421]
Eaton Corp. (Aeronautical Equipment and
Supplies) [82]
Emulex Corp. (Computers and Software) [6248]
Flower Warehouse (Horticultural Supplies) [14869]
FoodSalesWest Inc. (Food) [11182]
Ingardia Brothers Inc. (Food) [11506]
McGuire-Nicholas Co., Inc. (Industrial
Supplies) [17026]
O'Connor Engineering Laboratories (Photographic
Equipment and Supplies) [22886]
Pacific Handy Cutter Inc. (Industrial
Supplies) [17096]
Phoneby (Communications Systems and
Equipment) [5709]
Playmates Toys Inc. (Toys and Hobby
Goods) [26617]
Stacoswitch Inc. (Electrical and Electronic
Equipment and Supplies) [9400]
Teaching Aids Inc. (Computers and
Software) [6791]

Cotati
Reliance Trailer Manufacturing Inc. (Motorized
Vehicles) [20711]

Crescent City
Eureka Fisheries (Food) [11057]

Crows Landing
Perez Farms Inc. (Food) [12148]

Cudahy
Coast Paper Box Co. (Paper and Paper
Products) [21683]

Culver City
Alan Desk Business Interiors (Office Equipment and
Supplies) [20780]
Body Drama Inc. (Clothing) [4831]
Daylight Distributors (Toys and Hobby
Goods) [26461]
Flanigan Farms (Food) [11140]
Fleur de Paris (Textiles and Notions) [26036]
Golden Products Co. (Cleaning and Janitorial
Supplies) [4629]
Kelley-Clarke Inc. (Food) [11595]
L. Powell Co./Generations for the 21st
Century (Furniture and Fixtures) [13159]
Labomed, Inc. (Medical, Dental, and Optical
Equipment) [18881]
Lanz Inc. (Clothing) [5121]
Orbital Trading Co. (Industrial Machinery) [16363]
Powell Co./Generations for the 21st Century;
L. (Furniture and Fixtures) [13211]
Powell Co.; L. (Household Items) [15623]
Professional Electronics Inc. (Computers and
Software) [6650]
Showscan Entertainment Inc. (Sound and
Entertainment Equipment and Supplies) [25442]
Small World Toys (Toys and Hobby
Goods) [26653]
Stanley-Lawrence Co. (Jewelry) [17619]
STRO-WARE Inc. (Computers and
Software) [6768]
Surfas Inc. (Restaurant and Commercial
Foodservice Equipment and Supplies) [24236]
TechQuest Inc. (Computers and Software) [6803]
Wagner Hydraulic Equipment Co. (Industrial
Machinery) [16611]

Cupertino
Apple Pacific Div. (Computers and
Software) [5946]
Benton Electronics Inc. (Computers and
Software) [6012]
Elite Computers and Software Inc. (Computers and
Software) [6247]

Cypress
EIZO Nanao Technologies Inc. (Computers and
Software) [6238]
KTS Services Inc. (Communications Systems and
Equipment) [5659]
Minolta Corp. (Photographic Equipment and
Supplies) [22879]
Mitsubishi Electronics America Inc. (Sound and
Entertainment Equipment and Supplies) [25329]
Mitsubishi Motor Sales of America Inc. (Motorized
Vehicles) [20684]
Nitto Tires (Automotive) [3035]
Yamaha Motor Corporation USA (Motorized
Vehicles) [20755]

Daly City
Sigma America (Medical, Dental, and Optical
Supplies) [19610]

Danville
Baye & Rhodes (Food) [10517]
Compact Performance Inc. (Automotive) [2469]
Proper Tighe Marine (Marine) [18588]

Davis
Terra Nova Press (Books and Other Printed
Materials) [4208]

Del Mar
Rax Works Inc. (Recreational and Sporting
Goods) [23906]

Delano
Whitten Pumps Inc. (Industrial Machinery) [16630]

Desert Hot Springs
Ross-Erikson (Books and Other Printed
Materials) [4125]

Diamond Bar

Aldelano Corp. (Cleaning and Janitorial Supplies) [4567]

Diamond Springs

Western Water Products, Inc. (Specialty Equipment and Products) [25878]

Dos Palos

Nylander and Sorenson Inc. (Agricultural Equipment and Supplies) [1094]

Downey

American United Global Inc. (Automotive) [2236]
Golden West Pipe & Supply Co. (Plumbing Materials and Fixtures) [23194]
Hobart Arc Welding Systems (Industrial Machinery) [16104]
Kirk Paper Co. (Paper and Paper Products) [21792]
Montero International, Inc. (Computers and Software) [6528]
Rockview Farms Inc. (Food) [12337]
Simpson Buick Co. (Motorized Vehicles) [20721]
Western Pacific Pulp and Paper (Used, Scrap, and Recycled Materials) [27043]

Duarte

Assembly Automation Industries (Industrial Machinery) [15781]
Mister Remo of California Inc. (Clothing) [5198]
Sunny Group Inc. (Computers and Software) [6773]
Zack Electronics (Communications Systems and Equipment) [5821]

Dublin

Advantage Crown (Food) [10330]
Agorra Building Supply Inc. (Construction Materials and Machinery) [6925]
Soft Solutions (Computers and Software) [6735]
Western Tile Design Center (Dublin) (Floorcovering Equipment and Supplies) [10295]

Durham

Chico Produce, Inc. (Food) [10743]
Tink Inc. (Construction Materials and Machinery) [8136]

East Palo Alto

Romic Chemical Corp. (Used, Scrap, and Recycled Materials) [26966]

East Rancho Dominguez

H and L Marine Woodworking Inc. (Marine) [18515]
Metro Marketing Inc. (Household Items) [15586]

El Cajon

Ababa - QA (Hardware) [13522]
Advanced Color Coatings Inc. (Paints and Varnishes) [21374]
Buck Knives Inc. (Household Items) [15431]
Cameo Paper & Janitor Supply Co. (Cleaning and Janitorial Supplies) [4592]
Equality Screw Co. Inc. (Hardware) [13687]
Grafalloy Corp. (Recreational and Sporting Goods) [23695]
Kerman, Inc.; A.C. (Recreational and Sporting Goods) [23771]
Nalpak Video Sales, Inc. (Industrial Machinery) [16336]
Racewear Designs Inc. (Clothing) [5298]
Sunbelt Publications (Books and Other Printed Materials) [4195]
Vowles Farm Fresh Foods (Food) [12857]

El Cerrito

Flower Films & Video (Sound and Entertainment Equipment and Supplies) [25192]
Flower Films and Video (Household Appliances) [15129]
Perfect Solution Multimedia Inc. (Computers and Software) [6608]

El Dorado Hills

Hayes Medical Inc. (Medical, Dental, and Optical Supplies) [19352]
Track 'N Trail (Clothing) [5439]

El Monte

Burke Engineering Company Inc. (Heating and Cooling Equipment and Supplies) [14363]
California Wallet Co. Inc. (Luggage and Leather Goods) [18379]
Commercial Waste Paper Company Inc. (Used, Scrap, and Recycled Materials) [26782]
Howland Electric Wholesale Co. (Electrical and Electronic Equipment and Supplies) [8862]
Quickshot Technology Inc. (Computers and Software) [6670]
Valley-Western Distributors, Inc. (Floorcovering Equipment and Supplies) [10270]

El Segundo

Burbank Aircraft Supply Inc. (Aeronautical Equipment and Supplies) [68]
Disc Distributing Corp. (Computers and Software) [6212]
En Pointe Technologies Inc. (Computers and Software) [6249]
Force Electronics Inc. (Electrical and Electronic Equipment and Supplies) [8749]
Force Electronics Inc. (Electrical and Electronic Equipment and Supplies) [8750]
Harco (Hardware) [13734]
Mac America (Computers and Software) [6449]
Merisel Inc. (Computers and Software) [6484]
Seiko Time West (Jewelry) [17596]

El Toro

Creative Source (Books and Other Printed Materials) [3671]

Elk Grove

Matheson Trucking Inc.; R.B. (Automotive) [2924]

Emeryville

Bearing Engineering (Automotive) [2338]
Bon Motif Co. (Household Items) [15424]
Coulter Steel and Forge Co. (Metals) [19901]
Diamond Supply Company Inc. (Cleaning and Janitorial Supplies) [4612]
FreshWorld Farms Inc. (Food) [11213]
Hydraulic Controls Inc. (Industrial Machinery) [16130]
Knopp Inc. (Electrical and Electronic Equipment and Supplies) [8953]
MacPherson's-Artcraft (Specialty Equipment and Products) [25721]
Maz Auto (Automotive) [2927]
Mix Bookshelf (Books and Other Printed Materials) [3964]
Pacific Flooring Supply (Floorcovering Equipment and Supplies) [10092]
Plant Insulation Co. (Construction Materials and Machinery) [7868]
Publishers Group West Inc. (Books and Other Printed Materials) [4093]
Trader Vic's Food Products (Food) [12740]
Tumbleweed Distributors (Food) [12768]

Encino

Empress Linen Import Co. (Household Items) [15488]

Escondido

Caltemp Instrument Inc. (Electrical and Electronic Equipment and Supplies) [8489]
Cange & Associates International (Household Appliances) [15073]
Escondido Lumber & True Value (Construction Materials and Machinery) [7319]
Golden State Models (Toys and Hobby Goods) [26503]
Laforza Automobiles Inc. (Automotive) [2869]
Ne-Mo's Bakery Inc. (Food) [11989]
Pine Tree Lumber Co. (Construction Materials and Machinery) [7865]

R.O. Systems International (Specialty Equipment and Products) [25804]
Sloan Electric Co (Electrical and Electronic Equipment and Supplies) [9376]
Tile Club (Floorcovering Equipment and Supplies) [10223]
Tile Club (Construction Materials and Machinery) [8133]
Tool Mart (Hardware) [13958]
U.S. Export & Trading Company, Inc. (Health and Beauty Aids) [14270]
Ward Egg Ranch Corp. (Food) [12876]

Eureka

Fresh Freeze Supply Inc. (Food) [11210]
Humboldt Petroleum Inc. (Petroleum, Fuels, and Related Equipment) [22368]

Exeter

Blue Anchor Inc. (Food) [10573]
Griggs Inc.; Jack (Petroleum, Fuels, and Related Equipment) [22322]

Fairfax

Wildwood Natural Foods (Food) [12942]

Fairfield

S & S (Veterinary Products) [27226]
Super Store Industries/Fairfield Dairy Division (Food) [12625]

Fallbrook

Family Life Productions (Books and Other Printed Materials) [3743]
Jawz Inc. (Specialty Equipment and Products) [25693]

Fontana

Flo-Pac Pacific Div. (Household Items) [15500]
Kumho U.S.A. Inc. (Automotive) [2864]
Ontario Air Parts Inc. (Aeronautical Equipment and Supplies) [133]
United Pacific Pet L.L.C. (Veterinary Products) [27256]
Utility Trailer Sales Co. (Automotive) [3379]

Foothill Ranch

ICL Inc. (Computers and Software) [6351]
Sports Specialties Corp. (Clothing) [5387]

Ft. Bragg

Mendocino Coast Produce, Inc. (Food) [11850]
Natural Sales Network, Inc. (Food) [11986]

Foster City

Diab Data Inc. (Computers and Software) [6206]
Edmund's Dummy Company Inc. (Specialty Equipment and Products) [25641]
Pure Water Centers (Household Appliances) [15283]

Fountain Valley

Abbey Medical Inc. (Medical, Dental, and Optical Supplies) [19120]
Hyundai Motor America (Motorized Vehicles) [20651]
Lynde-Ordway Company Inc. (Office Equipment and Supplies) [21117]
Prepress Supply (Photographic Equipment and Supplies) [22892]
Staples, The Office Superstore Inc. (Office Equipment and Supplies) [21291]
Telecomputer Inc. (Computers and Software) [6810]
Tri-Color International (Recreational and Sporting Goods) [24014]

Fremont

A and A Technology Inc. (Computers and Software) [5856]
ACMA Computers Inc. (Computers and Software) [5870]
AlTech International Corp. (Computers and Software) [5897]
Atlantis Software (Computers and Software) [5981]

Bay Polymer Corp. (Used, Scrap, and Recycled Materials) [26761]
Cardona Inc. (Gifts and Novelties) [13326]
EIS Com-Kyl (Industrial Supplies) [16847]
Fortron/Source Corp. (Industrial Machinery) [16034]
Golden Neo-Life Diamite International (Health and Beauty Aids) [14114]
Interworld (Cleaning and Janitorial Supplies) [4640]
Jain Publishing Co. (Books and Other Printed Materials) [3858]
KEA Electronics (Electrical and Electronic Equipment and Supplies) [8932]
LCD Systems Corp. (Electrical and Electronic Equipment and Supplies) [8976]
New DEST Corp. (Electrical and Electronic Equipment and Supplies) [9126]
NewSoft America Inc. (Computers and Software) [6552]
Oliver Worldclass Labs (Books and Other Printed Materials) [4018]
OST Inc. (Fremont, California) (Security and Safety Equipment) [24609]
Peripheral Land Inc. (Computers and Software) [6610]
Phylon Communications Inc. (Electrical and Electronic Equipment and Supplies) [9198]
Semix Inc. (Automotive) [3204]
Shuttle Computer International (Computers and Software) [6725]
Soil Shield International (Household Items) [15659]
Songtech International Inc. (Computers and Software) [6746]
Sysco Food Services of San Francisco, Inc. (Food) [12687]
T & T Distributors (Health and Beauty Aids) [14254]
Tele Path Corp. (Communications Systems and Equipment) [5780]
TriGem Corp. (Computers and Software) [6831]
UMAX Computer Corp. (Computers and Software) [6839]
Western Shower Door Inc. (Construction Materials and Machinery) [8213]
Westex Automotive Corp. (Automotive) [3414]
World-Net Microsystems Inc. (Computers and Software) [6881]
Znyx Corp. (Electrical and Electronic Equipment and Supplies) [9628]

French Camp

California Ammonia Co. (Agricultural Equipment and Supplies) [364]

Fresno

American Carrier Equipment Inc. (Motorized Vehicles) [20585]
American Carrier Systems, Inc. (Automotive) [2228]
Bedrosians (Floorcovering Equipment and Supplies) [9713]
Bedrosians (Construction Materials and Machinery) [7041]
Billings Distributing Corp. (Heating and Cooling Equipment and Supplies) [14346]
California Industrial Rubber Company Inc. (Industrial Supplies) [16775]
California School Furnishing Company Inc. (Furniture and Fixtures) [13059]
Central California Electronics Inc. (Electrical and Electronic Equipment and Supplies) [8516]
Central Valley Oriental Imports (Toys and Hobby Goods) [26440]
Cumulous Communications Co. (Communications Systems and Equipment) [5582]
Dean's Materials Inc. (Construction Materials and Machinery) [7257]
Elliott Manufacturing Company Inc. (Restaurant and Commercial Foodservice Equipment and Supplies) [24108]
Fresno Distributing Co. (Electrical and Electronic Equipment and Supplies) [8760]
Fresno Truck Center (Motorized Vehicles) [20636]
Higgins Lumber Co.; J.E. (Construction Materials and Machinery) [7471]
Intertile Distributors, Inc. (Floorcovering Equipment and Supplies) [9973]

Johnson & Associates; Steve (Health and Beauty Aids) [14138]
Kearney's Metals Inc. (Metals) [20091]
Keyston Brothers (Textiles and Notions) [26100]
King Co.; R.M. (Agricultural Equipment and Supplies) [912]
McMurray Co.; Charles (Hardware) [13822]
Monterey Chemical Co. Inc. (Chemicals) [4461]
San Joaquin Supply Company Inc. (Cleaning and Janitorial Supplies) [4702]
Sinbad Sweets Inc. (Food) [12495]
Stefanelli Distributing (Alcoholic Beverages) [2051]
Ulbrich of California Inc. (Metals) [20453]
Western Farm Service Inc. (Agricultural Equipment and Supplies) [1431]
Yosemite Technologies (Computers and Software) [6887]

Fullerton

Braymar Precision Inc. (Industrial Machinery) [15842]
DNB Engineering Inc. (Industrial Machinery) [15955]
Grinnell Supply Sales Co (Industrial Supplies) [16911]
Luberski Inc. (Food) [11741]
Riccar America Co. (Household Appliances) [15291]
Salman (Furniture and Fixtures) [13229]
Sherwood Corp. (La Mirada, California) (Sound and Entertainment Equipment and Supplies) [25440]
Syslink Computer Corp. (Computers and Software) [6782]
Systematix Co. (Chemicals) [4524]
Tam Produce Inc. (Food) [12693]
Uni Filter Inc. (Automotive) [3360]

Galt

Building Materials Distributors Inc. (Construction Materials and Machinery) [7104]
Uniquity (Medical, Dental, and Optical Supplies) [19673]

Garden Grove

Airfan Engineered Products Inc. (Heating and Cooling Equipment and Supplies) [14309]
Cannon Equipment West (Industrial Supplies) [16778]
Graphic Resources Corp. (Computers and Software) [6308]
Milrank Knitwear Inc. (Clothing) [5196]
MK Health Food Distributors (Health and Beauty Aids) [14165]
Revco Products, Inc. (Automotive) [3151]
Richey Electronics Inc. (Electrical and Electronic Equipment and Supplies) [9295]
Sekisui TA Industries Inc. (Industrial Supplies) [17164]
Swiss Precision Instruments (Industrial Machinery) [16541]
Turban Plus (Clothing) [5445]
Victory International Productions (Sound and Entertainment Equipment and Supplies) [25503]

Gardena

Active Carb Ltd. (Plumbing Materials and Fixtures) [23051]
Ambit Pacific Recycling Inc. (Used, Scrap, and Recycled Materials) [26749]
American Hardwood Co. (Construction Materials and Machinery) [6966]
Astro Business Solutions Inc. (Office Equipment and Supplies) [20816]
Astro Office Products Inc. (Office Equipment and Supplies) [20817]
Clarion Corporation of America (Communications Systems and Equipment) [5562]
Clarion Sales Corp. (Automotive) [2450]
Coast Wire and Plastic Tech Inc. (Electrical and Electronic Equipment and Supplies) [8536]
Davids and Royston Bulb Company Inc. (Horticultural Supplies) [14853]
De Best Manufacturing Company Inc. (Plumbing Materials and Fixtures) [23135]
Decorative Engineering and Supply Inc. (Industrial Machinery) [15938]

Elixir Industries (Heating and Cooling Equipment and Supplies) [14431]
Farwest Corrosion Control Co. (Chemicals) [4388]
Gardena Industrial Supply and Hardware Co. (Industrial Supplies) [16887]
Gardena Recycling Center Inc. (Used, Scrap, and Recycled Materials) [26822]
Handy Care (Medical, Dental, and Optical Supplies) [19349]
Inca Corp. (Electrical and Electronic Equipment and Supplies) [8872]
L.A. Liquid Handling Systems (Industrial Machinery) [16225]
Law Distributors (Books and Other Printed Materials) [3899]
Leonard Inc.; Charles (Metals) [20123]
Loui Michel Cie. (Gifts and Novelties) [13392]
Nissan Motor Corporation U.S.A. (Motorized Vehicles) [20695]
Nissan Motor Corporation U.S.A. Infiniti Div. (Motorized Vehicles) [20696]
Pacific Dualies, Inc. (Automotive) [3074]
Pottery Manufacturing and Distributing Inc. (Gifts and Novelties) [13425]
Pottery Manufacturing and Distributing Inc. (Household Items) [15622]
Professional Media Service Corp. (Sound and Entertainment Equipment and Supplies) [25390]
S.C.B. Distributors (Books and Other Printed Materials) [4139]
Sea-Pac Inc. (Industrial Machinery) [16476]
Sea Recovery (Plumbing Materials and Fixtures) [23365]
Superior Water Systems (Specialty Equipment and Products) [25835]
TCI Aluminum (Metals) [20417]
Transworld Alloys Inc. (Metals) [20439]
Viking Office Products Inc. (Office Equipment and Supplies) [21339]

Geyserville

Lampson Tractor and Equipment Company Inc. (Agricultural Equipment and Supplies) [933]

Gilroy

Agricultural Survey Development Associates (Food) [10346]
Silicon Valley Electronics International (Computers and Software) [6728]

Glendale

Alis-USA (Computers and Software) [5901]
Biederman Inc.; A. (Scientific and Measurement Devices) [24323]
Contadina Foods (Food) [10824]
Eritech International (Computers and Software) [6253]
Glendale Envelope Co. (Paper and Paper Products) [21741]
Granton Shoe Imports (Shoes) [24754]
Kennedy Wholesale Inc. (Food) [11601]
Leader Newspapers (Books and Other Printed Materials) [3901]
Marshall and Johnson (Security and Safety Equipment) [24587]
McGill & Co.; P. (Food) [11828]
Nestle Carnation Food Service Co. (Food) [11997]
Paging Plus Co. (Communications Systems and Equipment) [5699]
Paging Wholesalers (Communications Systems and Equipment) [5701]
Peak Computer Solutions (Computers and Software) [6606]
PRC-DeSoto International Inc. Semco Application Systems (Chemicals) [4484]
Rex International (Recreational and Sporting Goods) [23912]
R.S. Hughes Company Inc. (Adhesives) [12]
Southwest DoAll Industrial Supply (Industrial Machinery) [16514]
Total Concepts Inc. (Computers and Software) [6824]
Western Pioneer Sales Co. (Specialty Equipment and Products) [25877]

Glendora

Caltrol Inc. (Industrial Machinery) [15867]
Carson Industries LLC (Plastics) [22942]

Goleta

Deckers Outdoor Corp. (Shoes) [24725]
Santa Barbara Instrument Group
Corp. (Photographic Equipment and
Supplies) [22901]

Granite Bay

Lucky Fruit and Produce Company
Inc. (Food) [11743]

Grass Valley

Booklegger (Books and Other Printed
Materials) [3576]
Bud Plant Comic Art (Books and Other Printed
Materials) [3599]
Maier Manufacturing (Automotive) [2910]
Vector Engineering Inc. (Scientific and
Measurement Devices) [24451]

Greenbrae

U.S. Pure Water Corp. (Specialty Equipment and
Products) [25858]

Gridley

Big Valley AG Services Inc. (Agricultural Equipment
and Supplies) [314]

Guerneville

Ghia Corp. (Specialty Equipment and
Products) [25660]
Korbel and Bros. Inc.; F. (Alcoholic
Beverages) [1803]

Happy Camp

Naturegraph Publishers Inc. (Books and Other
Printed Materials) [3987]

Hawthorne

BGW Systems Inc. (Sound and Entertainment
Equipment and Supplies) [25102]
Cherokee Chemical Company Inc. (Cleaning and
Janitorial Supplies) [4598]
Graphic Media (Specialty Equipment and
Products) [25668]
Spacecraft Components Corp. (Aeronautical
Equipment and Supplies) [149]
Superior Pump Exchange Co. (Automotive) [3286]

Hayward

ACF Components and Fasteners, Inc. (Electrical
and Electronic Equipment and Supplies) [8263]
American Pet Pro (Veterinary Products) [27064]
Anderson News Service Center (Books and Other
Printed Materials) [3517]
Annabelle Candy Company Inc. (Food) [10419]
Argraph West (Electrical and Electronic Equipment
and Supplies) [8371]
Beco/Boyd Equipment Co. (Construction Materials
and Machinery) [7040]
Bedrosian Tile Supply (Floorcovering Equipment
and Supplies) [9703]
B.E.E. Industrial Supply Inc. (Industrial
Machinery) [15814]
Burke Beverage of California Inc. (Alcoholic
Beverages) [1560]
California Tire Co. (Automotive) [2410]
Davitt & Hansen West (Sound and Entertainment
Equipment and Supplies) [25158]
EDCO Electronics Inc. (Electrical and Electronic
Equipment and Supplies) [8653]
EXSL/Ultra Labs Inc. (Chemicals) [4385]
Filtrex Inc. (Specialty Equipment and
Products) [25650]
Gene Schick Co. (Household Appliances) [15145]
Gourmet Specialties (Food) [11299]
Hayward Distribution Center (Tobacco
Products) [26304]
Ingram Entertainment (Sound and Entertainment
Equipment and Supplies) [25244]
Keebler Co. (Food) [11587]

Kielty and Dayton Co. (Office Equipment and
Supplies) [21090]
Lloyd F. McKinney Associates Inc. (Sound and
Entertainment Equipment and Supplies) [25287]
Miller Brands (Alcoholic Beverages) [1877]
Milvan Packaging Company Inc. (Plastics) [22999]
Mizutani USA (Hardware) [13832]
NutriCology Inc. (Food) [12048]
Prince of Peace Enterprises Inc. (Food) [12219]
Process Equipment Inc. (Industrial
Machinery) [16429]
Richmond Optical Co. (Medical, Dental, and Optical
Supplies) [19581]
Robin Seed Co.; Clyde (Agricultural Equipment and
Supplies) [1201]
Roll-Rite Corp. (Industrial Machinery) [16459]
Select Foods Inc. (Food) [12458]
Sierra Pacific Steel Inc. (Metals) [20366]
Sigma Food Distributing (Food) [12489]
Talley Electronics (Communications Systems and
Equipment) [5774]
Tech Distributing/Supply (Automotive) [3294]
Valley Pet Supply (Veterinary Products) [27259]
Weigh-Tronix Inc. (Restaurant and Commercial
Foodservice Equipment and Supplies) [24260]
Western Rubber and Supply Inc. (Industrial
Supplies) [17276]
Wood Flooring Distributors (Floorcovering
Equipment and Supplies) [10307]
Young's Market Co. (Alcoholic Beverages) [2143]

Healdsburg

Cooling Tower Resources, Inc. (Construction
Materials and Machinery) [7217]
Luthier's Mercantile Int. Inc. (Sound and
Entertainment Equipment and Supplies) [25294]
Timber Crest Farms (Food) [12722]

Heber

El Toro Land and Cattle Co. (Livestock and Farm
Products) [17828]
Torrences Farm Implement (Agricultural Equipment
and Supplies) [1343]

Hermosa Beach

Develcon Electronics Inc. (Computers and
Software) [6203]

Hesperia

A & A Ceramic Tile, Inc. (Floorcovering Equipment
and Supplies) [9637]
Aerospace Tube & Pipe (Metals) [19733]
Noleen Racing Inc. (Automotive) [3037]

Hickman

Saunco Air Technologies (Heating and Cooling
Equipment and Supplies) [14673]
Wilson Nursery; Dave (Horticultural
Supplies) [14978]

Hilmar

Hilmar Cheese Company Inc. (Food) [11436]

Hollister

All-Right (Construction Materials and
Machinery) [6935]
Applied Chemical Solutions Inc. (Scientific and
Measurement Devices) [24315]

Hollywood

American Electronics Supply, Inc. (Sound and
Entertainment Equipment and Supplies) [25069]
Ametron (Electrical and Electronic Equipment and
Supplies) [8345]
Birns & Sawyer Inc. (Photographic Equipment and
Supplies) [22831]
European Crafts/USA (Sound and Entertainment
Equipment and Supplies) [25186]
European Crafts/USA (Household
Appliances) [15122]
Mole-Richardson Co. (Sound and Entertainment
Equipment and Supplies) [25333]
Moviola/J & R Film Company, Inc. (Photographic
Equipment and Supplies) [22880]

Pacific Radio Exchange Inc. (Electrical and
Electronic Equipment and Supplies) [9171]
Studio Film & Tape Inc. (Sound and Entertainment
Equipment and Supplies) [25467]

Huntington Beach

Andersen Turf Supply (Agricultural Equipment and
Supplies) [240]
Archway Systems Inc. (Computers and
Software) [5958]
Baron (Automotive) [2320]
Beach Supply Co. (Petroleum, Fuels, and Related
Equipment) [22060]
Children's Art Corp. (Health and Beauty
Aids) [14062]
Children's Art Corp. (Medical, Dental, and Optical
Supplies) [19229]
Digital Business Automation (Office Equipment and
Supplies) [20963]
Equality Trading (Industrial Machinery) [15995]
Gaggenau USA Corp. (Household
Appliances) [15141]
House Of Batteries (Electrical and Electronic
Equipment and Supplies) [8858]
Marksman Products Inc. (Guns and
Weapons) [13501]
Optical Laser Inc. (Computers and
Software) [6574]
Precision Industrial Distributors Inc. (Industrial
Supplies) [17114]
Pump Systems Inc. (Industrial Supplies) [17122]
Safari Press Inc. (Books and Other Printed
Materials) [4134]
SPAP Company LLC (Chemicals) [4517]
Specialty Vehicles, Inc. (Motorized
Vehicles) [20728]
Specialty Vehicles Inc. (Automotive) [3248]
STATCO Engineering and Fabricators
Inc. (Metals) [20389]
Tesserax Information Systems (Computers and
Software) [6814]
Tomfoolery Serious Chocolate, Inc. (Food) [12728]
Unisource Worldwide Inc. West (Paper and Paper
Products) [21973]
Vint & Associates; Keith (Recreational and Sporting
Goods) [24034]
Winn Inc. (Recreational and Sporting
Goods) [24048]

Huntington Park

Damille Metal Supply Inc. (Used, Scrap, and
Recycled Materials) [26793]
Maran-Wurzell Glass and Mirror Co. (Household
Items) [15575]
Marvin Corp. (Construction Materials and
Machinery) [7657]
Precision Aluminum and Sawing Service
Inc. (Metals) [20291]
Randall Foods Inc. (Food) [12274]
S and R Metals Inc. (Metals) [20348]

Ignacio

Rock Island North (Food) [12335]

Igo

Westech (Computers and Software) [6864]

Inglewood

Barnes Wholesale Drug Company Inc. (Medical,
Dental, and Optical Supplies) [19174]
IBA Protection Services (Security and Safety
Equipment) [24569]
Overhill Farms (Food) [12084]
RHO-Chem Div. (Cleaning and Janitorial
Supplies) [4695]
Storm Products Company Inc. (Electrical and
Electronic Equipment and Supplies) [9424]
Technovance Corp. (Automotive) [3297]
Zephyr Manufacturing Co., Inc. (Aeronautical
Equipment and Supplies) [179]

Irvine

A.B.A.C.O. Group (Clothing) [4740]
Advantage Sales and Marketing (Food) [10332]
Allied Electronics (Electrical and Electronic
Equipment and Supplies) [8317]

Anabolic Laboratories Inc. (Medical, Dental, and Optical Equipment) [18681]
Aquatec Water Systems Inc. (Plumbing Materials and Fixtures) [23071]
Bale Ready-Mix Concrete; Gary (Construction Materials and Machinery) [7017]
Canterbury Enterprises (Wood and Wood Products) [27294]
Commercial and Industrial Design Co. Inc. (Computers and Software) [6087]
Computer Products Center Inc. (Computers and Software) [6120]
East West Trading Co. (Recreational and Sporting Goods) [23643]
FORMation mg Inc. (Computers and Software) [6275]
General Automation Inc. (Computers and Software) [6297]
Gensia Sicor Inc. (Medical, Dental, and Optical Equipment) [18809]
Golden State Foods Corp. (Soft Drinks) [24961]
HomeBase Inc. (Household Items) [15532]
Industrial Liaison Inc. (Marine) [18525]
Just Phones (Communications Systems and Equipment) [5655]
Kentec Medical Inc. (Medical, Dental, and Optical Equipment) [18873]
Kia Motors America Inc. (Motorized Vehicles) [20662]
Master Industries Inc. (Recreational and Sporting Goods) [23807]
Mazda Motor of America Inc. (Motorized Vehicles) [20675]
Mazda North American Operations (Motorized Vehicles) [20676]
Naturade Inc. (Health and Beauty Aids) [14171]
Niagara Drinking Waters Inc. (Soft Drinks) [24994]
Nihon Kohden America Inc. (Medical, Dental, and Optical Equipment) [18961]
Nutrition International Co. (Health and Beauty Aids) [14183]
Ocean Pacific Apparel Corp. (Clothing) [5247]
Ocean Pacific Sunwear Ltd. (Clothing) [5248]
Orange Bakery Inc. (Food) [12074]
Pacific Coast Micro Inc. (Computers and Software) [6579]
Paramount International (Computers and Software) [6588]
Pick Systems (Computers and Software) [6618]
Pool Water Products (Recreational and Sporting Goods) [23893]
PrimeSource Inc. (Construction Materials and Machinery) [7886]
PSDI (Computers and Software) [6656]
Renkus-Heinz Inc. (Sound and Entertainment Equipment and Supplies) [25416]
Roland Digital Group (Computers and Software) [6692]
Royalty Carpet Mills Inc. (Floorcovering Equipment and Supplies) [10131]
Shimano American Corp. (Recreational and Sporting Goods) [23936]
Shimano American Corp. Fishing Tackle Div. (Recreational and Sporting Goods) [23937]
Shur-Lok Corp. (Hardware) [13919]
Tech 101 Inc. (Computers and Software) [6792]
Teeco Products Inc. (Petroleum, Fuels, and Related Equipment) [22722]
Toshiba America Electronic Components Inc. Storage Device Div. (Computers and Software) [6822]
Toshiba America Information Systems Inc. Network Products Div. (Computers and Software) [6823]
Union Incorporated (Food) [12787]
Western Graphtec Inc. (Computers and Software) [6866]
Wyle Electronics (Electrical and Electronic Equipment and Supplies) [9611]
Wyle Systems (Computers and Software) [6884]
Zee Service Inc. (Medical, Dental, and Optical Supplies) [19718]

Irwindale

Blue Diamond Materials Co. (Construction Materials and Machinery) [7062]
Grattan & Sons Inc.; Dave (Hardware) [13728]

RTM Inc. (Computers and Software) [6697]
Select Copy Systems of Southern California Inc. (Office Equipment and Supplies) [21264]
Sierra Alloys Company Inc. (Metals) [20365]

Joshua Tree

Wilkie; Robert (Books and Other Printed Materials) [4284]

Kentfield

Ancient Future Music (Books and Other Printed Materials) [3508]

King City

Meyer Tomatoes (Food) [11865]
V.T. Petroleum (Petroleum, Fuels, and Related Equipment) [22775]

La Canada

Horizon West Draperies (Household Items) [15533]

La Habra

Marnal Corp. (Automotive) [2918]

La Jolla

Western Pacific Data Systems Inc. (Computers and Software) [6868]
Windows Memory Corp. (Computers and Software) [6871]

La Mesa

Aztec Business Machines Inc. (Office Equipment and Supplies) [20826]

La Mirada

Bralco Metals Div. (Metals) [19833]
Cal Fruit (Food) [10666]
Cogan Books (Books and Other Printed Materials) [3646]
Daewoo International (America) (Textiles and Notions) [26011]
Forest Plywood Sales (Construction Materials and Machinery) [7361]
Horn Co.; E.T. (Chemicals) [4418]
Kittrich Corp. (Household Items) [15552]
Makita U.S.A. Inc. (Hardware) [13807]

La Palma

Arcadia Chair Co. (Furniture and Fixtures) [13022]

La Puente

ATC Computer and Business Machines Inc. (Office Equipment and Supplies) [20818]
Atlas Energy Systems Inc. (Electrical and Electronic Equipment and Supplies) [8392]
Casale Engineering Inc. (Automotive) [2432]
CompuTrend Systems Inc. (Computers and Software) [6138]
DTK Computer Inc. (Computers and Software) [6225]
Everitt & Ray Inc. (Adhesives) [5]
Flask Chemical Corp. (Chemicals) [4391]
JML Sales Corp. (Horticultural Supplies) [14898]
Mook & Blanchard Wholesale Library Books (Books and Other Printed Materials) [3966]
Plastruct Inc. (Specialty Equipment and Products) [25787]
Port Plastics Inc. (Plastics) [23015]
Safety West (Industrial Supplies) [17154]
Southern California Air-Conditioning Distributors (Heating and Cooling Equipment and Supplies) [14691]
W C L Co. (Hardware) [13981]
Yale/Chase Materials Handling, Inc. (Industrial Machinery) [16654]

La Verne

Mitsuba Corp. (Computers and Software) [6523]

Lafayette

Bell-Carter Foods Inc. (Food) [10529]
Central Garden and Pet Co. (Agricultural Equipment and Supplies) [391]
Central Garden and Pet Co. Pet Supplies Div. (Veterinary Products) [27104]

Laguna Beach

Communications World of Costa Mesa (Communications Systems and Equipment) [5574]
DeRu's Fine Art Books (Books and Other Printed Materials) [3688]
Nanny Goat Productions (Books and Other Printed Materials) [3980]

Laguna Hills

Advanced Technology Center Inc. (Computers and Software) [5890]
Cutting Edge Technology Inc. (Computers and Software) [6173]
Intec Video Systems Inc. (Security and Safety Equipment) [24572]
Maranatha Music (Sound and Entertainment Equipment and Supplies) [25303]
Western Automation Inc. (Heating and Cooling Equipment and Supplies) [14761]

Laguna Niguel

Guidelines Inc. (Books and Other Printed Materials) [3804]
Ramer & Associates, Inc.; H. (Books and Other Printed Materials) [4106]

Lake Elsinore

Elsinore Ready-Mix Co. (Construction Materials and Machinery) [7308]
Pacific Clay Brick Products Inc. (Construction Materials and Machinery) [7821]

Lake Forest

Aviation Distributors Inc. (Aeronautical Equipment and Supplies) [51]
Bellsonics (Communications Systems and Equipment) [5529]
Electric Motor Engineering Inc. (Industrial Machinery) [15979]
Insulectro Corp. (Electrical and Electronic Equipment and Supplies) [8884]
Perfection Products Inc. (Household Items) [15617]
Signal Vision, Inc. (Electrical and Electronic Equipment and Supplies) [9372]
Single Point of Contact Inc. (Communications Systems and Equipment) [5758]
Sony Precision Technology (Scientific and Measurement Devices) [24434]
Sony Precision Technology America, Inc. (Sound and Entertainment Equipment and Supplies) [25449]

Lake View Terrace

Pico Products, Inc. (Electrical and Electronic Equipment and Supplies) [9201]

Lakewood

Cel Tech Communications Inc. (Communications Systems and Equipment) [5554]
Southern California Airgas Inc. (Industrial Supplies) [17183]

Lancaster

California Tile Supply (Floorcovering Equipment and Supplies) [9752]
Van Dam Brothers Co. (Food) [12822]

Larkspur

Parnell Pharmaceuticals Inc. (Medical, Dental, and Optical Supplies) [19526]

Lathrop

Alpine Distribution Services (Food) [10382]
Libbey Owens Ford Co. (Construction Materials and Machinery) [7602]
Super Stores Industries (Food) [12626]
Super Stores Industries (Food) [12627]

Lawndale

Carbro Corp. (Industrial Machinery) [15872]
Puro Filter Co. (Specialty Equipment and Products) [25796]

Lemon Grove

Deering Banjo Co. (Sound and Entertainment Equipment and Supplies) [25164]
Deering Banjo Co. (Household Appliances) [15107]
R.C.P. Block and Brick Inc. (Construction Materials and Machinery) [7905]

Livermore

Casey-Johnston Sales Inc. (Computers and Software) [6047]
CCI Triad (Computers and Software) [6048]
Coast Wholesale Music Co. (Sound and Entertainment Equipment and Supplies) [25142]
Crown Inc. Beverage Div. (Alcoholic Beverages) [1628]
Discovery Toys Inc. (Toys and Hobby Goods) [26471]
Higgins Lumber Co.; J.E. (Construction Materials and Machinery) [7470]
Ideal Computer Services Inc. (Computers and Software) [6352]
WAFAB International (Industrial Machinery) [16610]
Warren Associates (Electrical and Electronic Equipment and Supplies) [9555]

Livingston

Francisco Distributing (Food) [11199]

Lodi

Ag-Industrial Manufacturing (Agricultural Equipment and Supplies) [193]
San Joaquin Sulphur Company Inc. (Chemicals) [4501]

Lompoc

Hinrichs; E. Louis (Books and Other Printed Materials) [3828]
Western Star Distributors (Toys and Hobby Goods) [26710]

Long Beach

Acom Computer Inc. (Computers and Software) [5871]
American Commercial Inc. (Household Items) [15396]
Belli-Childs Wholesale Produce (Food) [10532]
The Berns Co. (Industrial Machinery) [15820]
BHP Trading Inc. (Metals) [19822]
Bristol Retail Solutions Inc. (Office Equipment and Supplies) [20855]
Ceramic Tile Center Inc. (Floorcovering Equipment and Supplies) [9792]
Compass Concepts (Floorcovering Equipment and Supplies) [9821]
Control Switches International Inc. (Electrical and Electronic Equipment and Supplies) [8576]
Dion and Sons Inc.; M.O. (Petroleum, Fuels, and Related Equipment) [22202]
Douglas Brothers Produce Co. (Food) [10985]
Electrical Power and Controls Inc. (Electrical and Electronic Equipment and Supplies) [8681]
Gaines Electric Supply Co. (Electrical and Electronic Equipment and Supplies) [8771]
Harbor Distributing Co. (Alcoholic Beverages) [1745]
Heard Optical Co. (Medical, Dental, and Optical Supplies) [19356]
Industrial Trade and Development Co. (Gifts and Novelties) [13376]
International Trade & Telex Corp. (Medical, Dental, and Optical Supplies) [19378]
Kenwood USA Corp. (Sound and Entertainment Equipment and Supplies) [25270]
Merrimac Petroleum Inc. (Petroleum, Fuels, and Related Equipment) [22476]
Nippondenso of Los Angeles Inc. (Automotive) [3034]
Pioneer Electronics USA Inc. (Electrical and Electronic Equipment and Supplies) [9207]
Pioneer Electronics (USA) Inc. (Household Appliances) [15273]
Pioneer Entertainment (USA) L.P. (Computers and Software) [6622]
Pioneer North America Inc. (Sound and Entertainment Equipment and Supplies) [25383]
Power Pumps Inc. (Industrial Machinery) [16416]

Seven Star Productions (Sound and Entertainment Equipment and Supplies) [25439]
State Salvage Company Inc. (Used, Scrap, and Recycled Materials) [27009]
Tatung Company of America Inc. (Computers and Software) [6789]
Thorpe Co.; B.K. (Plumbing Materials and Fixtures) [23410]
Tires, Wheels, Etc. Wholesale Inc. (Automotive) [3309]
Toyota Aviation U.S.A. Inc. (Aeronautical Equipment and Supplies) [162]
Walters Wholesale Electric Co. (Electrical and Electronic Equipment and Supplies) [9554]

Loomis

SJS Products/Jamcor Corp. (Electrical and Electronic Equipment and Supplies) [9374]

Los Alamitos

American Netronic Inc. (Computers and Software) [5931]
Coolant Management Services Co. (Chemicals) [4365]
Frieda's Inc. (Food) [11214]
Morgan and Sampson Pacific (Health and Beauty Aids) [14168]
Patten Corp. (Industrial Machinery) [16384]
Sona & Hollen Foods Inc. (Food) [12528]

Los Altos

Landis Rail Fastening Systems Inc. (Railroad Equipment and Supplies) [23483]
Linden Tree Children's Records & Books (Books and Other Printed Materials) [3915]
Los Altos PC Inc. (Computers and Software) [6445]

Los Altos Hills

Edwards Wood Products Inc. (Portola Valley, California) (Storage Equipment and Containers) [25910]

Los Angeles

3A Products (Textiles and Notions) [25951]
A & Z Pearls Inc. (Jewelry) [17300]
AAA Glass Corp. (Household Items) [15385]
Acme Linen Co. (Textiles and Notions) [25953]
Acorn Paper Products Co (Industrial Supplies) [16670]
Airport Metals (Metals) [19738]
All America Distributors Corp. (Books and Other Printed Materials) [3490]
All Makes Office Machine Company Inc. (Office Equipment and Supplies) [20784]
All That Jazz (Clothing) [4760]
Alpert and Alpert Iron and Metal Inc. (Used, Scrap, and Recycled Materials) [26744]
American Plasma Services L.P (Medical, Dental, and Optical Supplies) [19144]
Amvac Chemical Corp. (Agricultural Equipment and Supplies) [239]
Angel-Etts Inc. (Shoes) [24671]
Army & Navy Supplies (Clothing) [4785]
Around the Corner (Gifts and Novelties) [13306]
Arranaga and Co.; Robert (Food) [10436]
Associated of Los Angeles (Electrical and Electronic Equipment and Supplies) [8386]
Atlantic Pacific Industries (Hardware) [13572]
Atlas Carpet Mills Inc. (Floorcovering Equipment and Supplies) [9693]
Atlas Vegetable Exchange (Food) [10467]
Avon-Glendale Home Medical Equipment and Supplies Inc. (Medical, Dental, and Optical Supplies) [19171]
Bacon Material Handling; Davis (Storage Equipment and Containers) [25889]
Basic Fibres Inc. (Used, Scrap, and Recycled Materials) [26760]
Baszile Metals Service Inc. (Metals) [19806]
Bell Industries Graphic (Specialty Equipment and Products) [25571]
Belts By Nadim, Inc. (Clothing) [4815]
Ben Wa Novelty Corp. (Gifts and Novelties) [13315]
Benjamin Metals Co. (Metals) [19811]

Bestex Company Inc. (Security and Safety Equipment) [24515]
Bilingual Educational Services, Inc. (Books and Other Printed Materials) [3556]
Bobco Metal Co. (Metals) [19829]
Bonded Motors, Inc. (Automotive) [2371]
Book Box, Inc. (Books and Other Printed Materials) [3565]
Bradley Co.; E.B. (Hardware) [13605]
Bradley Import Co. (Toys and Hobby Goods) [26424]
Brake Sales Co. Inc. (Automotive) [2378]
Bridge Publications Inc. (Books and Other Printed Materials) [3592]
Brunner and Lay Inc. (Construction Materials and Machinery) [7089]
Bruwiler Precise Sales Company, Inc. (Scientific and Measurement Devices) [24329]
BTM Recycling (Used, Scrap, and Recycled Materials) [26773]
Builders Brass Works Corp. (Hardware) [13610]
Buy-Lines Co. (Jewelry) [17355]
C R Laurence Company Inc. (Automotive) [2406]
Caffe Latte (Food) [10660]
California Gift Center Inc. (Toys and Hobby Goods) [26433]
California Time Inc. (Jewelry) [17356]
Calrad Electronics (Electrical and Electronic Equipment and Supplies) [8488]
Canvas Specialty (Textiles and Notions) [25994]
Carpenter Technology/Steel Div (Metals) [19860]
Cels Enterprises Inc. (Shoes) [24709]
Central Textile Co. (Textiles and Notions) [25999]
Certified Grocers of California Ltd. (Food) [10728]
Cheviot Corp. (Sound and Entertainment Equipment and Supplies) [25135]
Choe Meat Co. (Food) [10756]
City One Stop (Sound and Entertainment Equipment and Supplies) [25138]
Clougherty Packing Co. (Food) [10773]
Compotite Corp. (Construction Materials and Machinery) [7200]
Copper and Brass Sales Inc. (Metals) [19898]
Coyote Network Systems, Inc. (Electrical and Electronic Equipment and Supplies) [8584]
Custom Leathercraft Manufacturing (Luggage and Leather Goods) [18386]
D & M Distributing (Automotive) [2521]
DeFranco and Sons Inc.; D. (Food) [10938]
Diamond W Supply Co. Inc. (Floorcovering Equipment and Supplies) [9864]
Diversified Marine Products (Marine) [18492]
Dorell Fabrics Co. (Textiles and Notions) [26020]
EKCO International Metals Inc. (Used, Scrap, and Recycled Materials) [26803]
Ellis Paint Co. (Paints and Varnishes) [21437]
Emser International (Household Items) [15489]
Engle and Co.; Jack (Metals) [19955]
Eugene Trading Inc. (Health and Beauty Aids) [14098]
Eurostar Inc. (Shoes) [24737]
Evergreen Scientific Inc. (Scientific and Measurement Devices) [24357]
Fisher Central Coast (Food) [11133]
Flavtek Inc. (Food) [11142]
Fleurette California (Clothing) [4957]
Flirt Corp/Belldini (Clothing) [4959]
Forcean Inc. (Medical, Dental, and Optical Equipment) [18800]
Friedman Bag Company Inc. (Industrial Supplies) [16880]
Gehr Industries (Industrial Machinery) [16050]
General Brokerage Co. (Food) [11248]
General Toys of Los Angeles (Toys and Hobby Goods) [26497]
Genuine Rose Inc. (Clothing) [4982]
Gibson Overseas Inc. (Household Items) [15514]
Giumarra Brothers Fruit Company, Inc. (Food) [11267]
Golden State Containers Inc. (Storage Equipment and Containers) [25918]
Hamel Spanish Book Corp.; Bernard H. (Books and Other Printed Materials) [3808]
Harley Metals Recycling Co. (Used, Scrap, and Recycled Materials) [26838]

Harmonia Mundi U.S.A. Inc. (Sound and Entertainment Equipment and Supplies) [25226]
Harrington Tools Inc. (Hardware) [13743]
Hellman Produce Inc.; J. (Food) [11408]
Henry Radio Inc. (Sound and Entertainment Equipment and Supplies) [25230]
Henry Radio Inc. (Electrical and Electronic Equipment and Supplies) [8838]
Higgins Productions, Inc.; Alfred (Sound and Entertainment Equipment and Supplies) [25231]
Highland Auto and Truck Inc. (Automotive) [2751]
Highland Auto and Truck Inc. (Automotive) [2752]
Holly Sea Food Inc. (Food) [11451]
Holtzman Office Furniture Co. (Office Equipment and Supplies) [21039]
Honey Bee Fashions (Clothing) [5034]
Houles USA Inc. (Textiles and Notions) [26067]
Hybco USA (Food) [11484]
Hydro-Abrasive Machining Inc. (Industrial Machinery) [16131]
Imperial Toy Corp. (Toys and Hobby Goods) [26532]
Independent Foundry Supply Co. (Industrial Supplies) [16941]
Insonic Technology, Inc. (Jewelry) [17458]
Inter-Pacific Corp. (Shoes) [24769]
International Lease Finance Corp. (Aeronautical Equipment and Supplies) [104]
International Restaurant Equipment Company Inc. (Restaurant and Commercial Foodservice Equipment and Supplies) [24144]
International Tile and Supply Corp. (Household Items) [15541]
Ital Fashion Inc. (Clothing) [5065]
ITC Electronics (Electrical and Electronic Equipment and Supplies) [8901]
Jaunty Co., Inc. (Household Items) [15544]
JGL Inc. (Jewelry) [17474]
Jordan Brookes Company Inc.; E. (Metals) [20078]
Kelly Paper Co. (Paper and Paper Products) [21790]
King Food Service (Food) [11613]
Klemer and Wiseman (Textiles and Notions) [26112]
KPK Truck Body Manufacturing and Equipment Distributing Company Inc. (Automotive) [2861]
Kramer Metals (Used, Scrap, and Recycled Materials) [26869]
La Cite (Books and Other Printed Materials) [3891]
L.A. Glo (Clothing) [5118]
La Reina Inc. (Food) [11661]
L.A. Silver (Jewelry) [17496]
La Vencedora Products (Food) [11662]
Lascco Fish Products (Food) [11679]
Lata Export and Import (Jewelry) [17500]
Laurence Company Inc.; C.R. (Industrial Machinery) [16228]
Leed Plastics Corp. (Plastics) [22994]
Legal Books Distributing (Books and Other Printed Materials) [3904]
Legal Star Communications (Sound and Entertainment Equipment and Supplies) [25281]
Les Appel for Rex Lester Inc. (Clothing) [5128]
Levand Steel and Supply Corp. (Metals) [20124]
Levy Inc.; Victor H. (Jewelry) [17502]
Lighting Parts Inc. (Electrical and Electronic Equipment and Supplies) [8988]
LoJack of California Corp. (Automotive) [2887]
Los Angeles Nut House (Food) [11735]
Los Angeles Paper Box and Board Mills. Paper Stock Div. (Used, Scrap, and Recycled Materials) [26888]
Los Angeles Rubber Co. (Rubber) [24285]
LU International (Industrial Machinery) [16250]
Lynwood Battery Manufacturing Co. (Automotive) [2899]
Machinery Sales Co. (Industrial Machinery) [16256]
Maddalena Vineyard/San Antonio Winery (Alcoholic Beverages) [1834]
Main Electric Supply Co. (Electrical and Electronic Equipment and Supplies) [9021]
Manley Oil Co. (Petroleum, Fuels, and Related Equipment) [22448]
Mar Vista Lumber Co. (Construction Materials and Machinery) [7639]

Marvin Land Systems, Inc. (Automotive) [2919]
Master International Corp. (Electrical and Electronic Equipment and Supplies) [9045]
McLogan Supply (Specialty Equipment and Products) [25731]
McMaster-Carr Supply Co. California (Hardware) [13821]
Mechanical Drives Co. (Automotive) [2936]
Mercury Air Group Inc. (Petroleum, Fuels, and Related Equipment) [22475]
Meshekow Brothers Inc. (Clothing) [5186]
MetalCenter Inc. (Metals) [20172]
Mid-City Iron and Metal Corp. (Metals) [20181]
Mitsubishi Intl Corp./Foods Div (Food) [11914]
Monarch Knit and Sportswear Inc. (Clothing) [5201]
Monico Alloys Inc. (Metals) [20203]
Morton Company Inc.; J.P. (Jewelry) [17526]
Moss Co.; Roscoe (Construction Materials and Machinery) [7752]
MPBS Industries (Industrial Machinery) [16329]
Mutual Trading Co. Inc. (Food) [11962]
Myerson Candy Co.; Ben (Alcoholic Beverages) [1898]
National Titanium Corp. (Metals) [20221]
Naturo Co. (Specialty Equipment and Products) [25751]
NGE Inc. (Heating and Cooling Equipment and Supplies) [14619]
O-Rings Inc. (Industrial Supplies) [17085]
Oak Paper Products Company Inc. (Paper and Paper Products) [21853]
Offenhauser Sales Corp. (Automotive) [3056]
Old Masters Products Inc. (Floorcovering Equipment and Supplies) [10085]
Oliver Peoples Inc. (Medical, Dental, and Optical Supplies) [19506]
On the Beach, Inc. (Clothing) [5251]
Ore-Cal Corp. (Food) [12075]
Osterbauer Compressor Services (Compressors) [5846]
Pac States Electric Wholesalers (Electrical and Electronic Equipment and Supplies) [9167]
Pacific Combustion Engineering Inc. (Scientific and Measurement Devices) [24413]
Pacific Hide & Leather Company, Inc. (Luggage and Leather Goods) [18417]
Pacific International Marketing Co. (Recreational and Sporting Goods) [23867]
Palisades Beach Club (Clothing) [5266]
Paradise Manufacturing Company Inc. (Household Items) [15611]
Paris Vienna (Clothing) [5271]
Perfection Distributing Co. (Specialty Equipment and Products) [25781]
Peripheral Resources Inc. (Computers and Software) [6611]
Philosophical Research Society, Inc. (Books and Other Printed Materials) [4061]
Pioneer Aluminum Inc. (Metals) [20280]
Plastic Sales Southern Inc. (Plastics) [23011]
Podell Industries Inc. (Clothing) [5281]
Pollack Enterprises Inc.; Morton (Household Appliances) [15275]
Progressive Produce Co. (Food) [12231]
Promotional Sales Co. (Textiles and Notions) [26180]
Publishers Distributing Co. (Books and Other Printed Materials) [4092]
Rahn Industries, Inc. (Automotive) [3132]
Rebel and Associates Inc.; Albert (Industrial Machinery) [16444]
Reliance Steel and Aluminum Co. (Metals) [20313]
Reliance Steel Inc. (Metals) [20314]
Rialto Inc. (Clothing) [5309]
Robinson Co.; Frank L. (Clothing) [5314]
Rock Candy Inc. (Clothing) [5316]
Roland Corporation U.S. (Sound and Entertainment Equipment and Supplies) [25420]
Rolled Steel Products Corp. (Metals) [20328]
Romac Export Management Corp. (Household Items) [15639]
Roto-Litho Inc. (Paper and Paper Products) [21912]
Roye; Gene (Clothing) [5324]
Rykoff-Sexton Manufacturing L.L.C. (Food) [12377]

S & T Jewelers (Jewelry) [17582]
Sassounian Inc. (Jewelry) [17589]
Sheffield Furniture Corp. (Furniture and Fixtures) [13241]
Shepherd Machinery Co. (Construction Materials and Machinery) [8010]
Shorewood Packaging of California Inc. (Paper and Paper Products) [21939]
Sigma Electronics Inc. (Communications Systems and Equipment) [5755]
Silver City (Jewelry) [17602]
South Coast Recycling Inc. (Used, Scrap, and Recycled Materials) [27000]
Southern California Trophy Co. (Gifts and Novelties) [13448]
Spanish & European Bookstore Inc. (Books and Other Printed Materials) [4178]
Spatron Inc. (Electrical and Electronic Equipment and Supplies) [9391]
Sportcap Inc. (Clothing) [5384]
Stover Seed Company Inc. (Agricultural Equipment and Supplies) [1297]
Sun Sales (Jewelry) [17626]
Supertek (Electrical and Electronic Equipment and Supplies) [9446]
TBI (Clothing) [5423]
TD Materials Inc. (Aeronautical Equipment and Supplies) [156]
Technical Business Specialists Inc. (Computers and Software) [6799]
Telemusica Co. (Sound and Entertainment Equipment and Supplies) [25476]
Thompson Lacquer Company Inc. (Paints and Varnishes) [21592]
Thorpe Insulation Co. (Construction Materials and Machinery) [8125]
Tomco Auto Products Inc. (Automotive) [3318]
Torn and Glasser Inc. (Food) [12735]
Toyo Trading Co. (Household Items) [15686]
Trade Development Corporation of Chicago (Industrial Supplies) [17232]
Trans-Global Sports Co. (Recreational and Sporting Goods) [24013]
Triangle Brass Manufacturing Co. (Hardware) [13965]
Ultraseal International Inc. (Automotive) [3359]
United Alloys Inc. (Metals) [20463]
U.S. Equipment Company Inc. (Compressors) [5855]
Universal Paper Goods Co. (Paper and Paper Products) [21981]
Valdez (Sound and Entertainment Equipment and Supplies) [25495]
Valdez (Household Appliances) [15353]
Video Action (Sound and Entertainment Equipment and Supplies) [25504]
Vitex Foods Inc. (Food) [12851]
Viva Handbags Inc. (Luggage and Leather Goods) [18438]
Vogue Bedding Co. (Furniture and Fixtures) [13270]
Vogue Cuisine Inc. (Food) [12854]
Watches (Jewelry) [17651]
Weinreich Co.; Charles (Used, Scrap, and Recycled Materials) [27039]
Wesco Merchandising (Health and Beauty Aids) [14279]
Western Library Books (Books and Other Printed Materials) [4277]
Wholesale and Home Supply Company Inc. (Furniture and Fixtures) [13280]
Wolfstein International, Inc. (Food) [12973]
World Variety Produce Inc. (Food) [12983]
Zabin Industries Inc. (Textiles and Notions) [26254]
Ziegler Steel Service Corp. (Construction Materials and Machinery) [8254]

Los Banos

Lindemann Produce Inc. (Food) [11714]

Los Gatos

Array Microsystems Inc. (Electrical and Electronic Equipment and Supplies) [8376]
Greystone Peripherals Inc. (Computers and Software) [6313]

Geographic Index

Marathon Codestar (Computers and
Software) [6462]

Los Osos
Really Right Stuff Co. (Photographic Equipment
and Supplies) [22897]

Lynwood
Allied Distribution Systems (Construction Materials
and Machinery) [6944]
Allied Distribution Systems (Wood and Wood
Products) [27276]
Allied Plywood Corp. (Construction Materials and
Machinery) [6946]
Southwest Plywood and Lumber
Corp. (Construction Materials and
Machinery) [8056]

Madera
Norby Lumber Company Inc. (Wood and Wood
Products) [27350]
Westgate Building Materials (Construction Materials
and Machinery) [8215]

Manhattan Beach
Skechers U.S.A. Inc. (Shoes) [24862]

Manteca
Ramsey Seed, Inc. (Agricultural Equipment and
Supplies) [1167]
Valley Electric Company Inc. (Electrical and
Electronic Equipment and Supplies) [9532]

Marina Del Rey
Transparent Technology Inc. (Computers and
Software) [6828]

Marina del Rey
DeVorss & Co. (Books and Other Printed
Materials) [3691]

Mariposa
Heaton Co.; G.A. (Jewelry) [17447]

Marshall
Specialized Marketing (Food) [12549]

Martinez
Pohang Steel America Corp. (Metals) [20287]

Marysville
Excel Corp. DPM Foods Div. (Food) [11064]

Maywood
Arrow Precision Products Inc. (Plumbing Materials
and Fixtures) [23073]

Mendocino
Mendocino Sea Vegetable Co. (Food) [11851]

Menlo Park
FWB Inc. (Computers and Software) [6285]
Landman Co. Inc.; Carl (Food) [11674]
Sola International Inc. (Medical, Dental, and Optical
Supplies) [19619]
Telogy Inc. (Scientific and Measurement
Devices) [24443]

Merced
Bianchi and Sons Packing Co. (Food) [10552]
Soil Stabilization Products Company
Inc. (Chemicals) [4514]

Millbrae
Reising and Co.; G. (Horticultural
Supplies) [14944]

Milpitas
ACBEL Technologies Inc. (Computers and
Software) [5864]
ADS Inc. (Computers and Software) [5879]
APPIC Inc. (Computers and Software) [5944]
A.R.T. Multimedia Systems, Inc. (Computers and
Software) [5966]

AVerMedia Technologies Inc. (Computers and
Software) [5994]
CONTEC Microelectronics USA (Computers and
Software) [6152]
Lindsay-Ferrari (Furniture and Fixtures) [13164]
Lite-On Inc. (Computers and Software) [6440]
One Workplace L. Ferrari LLC (Furniture and
Fixtures) [13195]
Pacific Magtron Inc. (Electrical and Electronic
Equipment and Supplies) [9170]
Tatung Science and Technology Inc. (Office
Equipment and Supplies) [21315]

Mission Hills
Coast Air Inc. (Aeronautical Equipment and
Supplies) [71]

Mission Viejo
Hoffman Company Inc.; Rube P. (Textiles and
Notions) [26065]
Parasoft Corp. (Computers and Software) [6590]

Modesto
American Distributing Co. (Construction Materials
and Machinery) [6962]
Anderson News Company (Books and Other
Printed Materials) [3514]
Bedrosian Tile Supply (Floorcovering Equipment
and Supplies) [9711]
California Professional Manufacturing Inc. (Specialty
Equipment and Products) [25593]
Call Associates Inc. (Industrial Machinery) [15865]
Dow-Hammond Trucks Co. (Automotive) [2558]
Hi-Tec Sports USA Inc. (Shoes) [24763]
J.M. Equipment Co. (Industrial Machinery) [16189]
Major-Sysco Food Services Inc. (Food) [11763]
Market Specialties (Food) [11782]
Nasco West (Medical, Dental, and Optical
Equipment) [18955]
Pacific Flooring Supply (Floorcovering Equipment
and Supplies) [10093]
Processors Equipment & Hardware (Industrial
Supplies) [17118]
Stanislaus Farm Supply Co. (Agricultural Equipment
and Supplies) [1293]
Sweetwater Distributors Inc. (Alcoholic
Beverages) [2065]
Tile Expressions (Floorcovering Equipment and
Supplies) [10234]
Waltman's Inc. (Industrial Machinery) [16613]
Wille Electric Supply Co. (Electrical and Electronic
Equipment and Supplies) [9596]

Monrovia
Linear Industries Ltd (Industrial Supplies) [17001]
S.A.K. Industries (Furniture and Fixtures) [13228]
Virginia Hardwood Co. (Construction Materials and
Machinery) [8186]

Montclair
AA Equipment (Agricultural Equipment and
Supplies) [180]

Montebello
Acoustical Material Services (Sound and
Entertainment Equipment and Supplies) [25057]
Benz Engineering Inc. (Compressors) [5830]
Century Wheel & Rim Corp. (Automotive) [2440]
Haitai America Inc. (Food) [11361]
J and R Bottling and Distribution Co. (Soft
Drinks) [24975]
J and R Bottling and Distribution
Co. (Food) [11538]
Landsberg Co.; Kent H. (Paper and Paper
Products) [21796]
Nelson-Dunn Inc. (Industrial Supplies) [17072]
Recycled Wood Products (Agricultural Equipment
and Supplies) [1175]
TEAC America Inc. (Electrical and Electronic
Equipment and Supplies) [9463]
TEAC America Inc. Data Storage Products
Div. (Household Appliances) [15335]
Vanadium Pacific Steel Co. (Metals) [20471]

Monterey
Consolidated Factors, Inc. (Food) [10816]
Miramar Trading International Inc. (Alcoholic
Beverages) [1882]
PCI Tech (Computers and Software) [6603]
PROACT (Food) [12223]
Royal Seafoods Inc. (Food) [12365]
Worldwide Exporters Inc. (Electrical and Electronic
Equipment and Supplies) [9608]

Monterey Park
Bobtron International Inc. (Clothing) [4830]
Evergreen Publishing & Stationery (Books and
Other Printed Materials) [3738]
Marcone Appliance Parts Center (Household
Appliances) [15212]
Trend Pacific Inc. (Household Items) [15688]

Montrose
Shelmar Food (Food) [12476]

Moorpark
Honeywell H.P.G. (Aeronautical Equipment and
Supplies) [99]

Morgan Hill
Coast Distribution (Marine) [18481]
Global Motorsport Group Inc. (Automotive) [2685]
Redlake Imaging Corp. (Photographic Equipment
and Supplies) [22898]
Redwood Empire Inc. (Construction Materials and
Machinery) [7907]
Sakata Seed America, Inc. (Agricultural Equipment
and Supplies) [1230]
Target Electronics Inc. (Electrical and Electronic
Equipment and Supplies) [9460]

Mountain View
Compool Corp. (Recreational and Sporting
Goods) [23602]
Eakins Associates Inc. (Computers and
Software) [6232]
Educational Industrial Systems Inc. (Sound and
Entertainment Equipment and Supplies) [25172]
Franciscan Glass Co. (Construction Materials and
Machinery) [7366]
LaserCard Systems Corp. (Computers and
Software) [6430]
Medical Manager Sales and Marketing
Inc. (Computers and Software) [6480]
Micropoint Inc. (Office Equipment and
Supplies) [21141]
Minton's Lumber and Supply Co. (Construction
Materials and Machinery) [7725]
Mt. Eden Floral Co. (Horticultural
Supplies) [14923]
Polymer Plastics Corp. (Plastics) [23014]
Porta-Bote International (Marine) [18585]
Techfarm Inc. (Computers and Software) [6796]
Technical Sales Inc. (Automotive) [3296]
Victs Computers Inc. (Computers and
Software) [6852]

Napa
Capital Business Systems Inc. (Computers and
Software) [6045]
El Ray Distributing Company Inc. (Alcoholic
Beverages) [1672]
Foge Jensen Imports (Household Items) [15502]
Marinco-AFI (Electrical and Electronic Equipment
and Supplies) [9030]
Napa Pipe Corp. (Metals) [20215]
Power Industries (Automotive) [3110]

National City
Appliance Parts Center Inc. (Household
Appliances) [15018]
Appliance Parts Center Inc. (Electrical and
Electronic Equipment and Supplies) [8364]
Baker Hardwood Lumber Co. (Construction
Materials and Machinery) [7014]
Baker Hardwood Lumber Co. (Wood and Wood
Products) [27284]
Fornaca Inc. (Food) [11190]

Hyperbaric Oxygen Therapy Systems Inc. (Medical, Dental, and Optical Equipment) [18848]
Pacific Steel Inc. (Used, Scrap, and Recycled Materials) [26932]
Ranger Communications Inc. (Communications Systems and Equipment) [5734]

Newark

Advance Computer Systems (Computers and Software) [5882]
Electronic Lighting Inc. (Electrical and Electronic Equipment and Supplies) [8692]
Ultima International Corp. (Computers and Software) [6838]

Newbury Park

Haynes Manuals Inc. (Automotive) [2733]
Rx Rocker Corp. (Medical, Dental, and Optical Equipment) [19027]
Vivitar Corp. (Photographic Equipment and Supplies) [22914]

Newman

F & A Dairy California (Food) [11066]

Newport Beach

B/T Western Corp. (Automotive) [2307]
Cabo Distributing Co., Inc. (Alcoholic Beverages) [1564]
Five Continent Enterprise Inc., PMB 4022 (Health and Beauty Aids) [14101]
IEEI (Computers and Software) [6353]
Leader Technologies Inc. (Computers and Software) [6433]
Luce Candy Co. (Food) [11742]
Marquart-Wolfe Lumber Company Inc. (Construction Materials and Machinery) [7644]
Style Eyes Inc. (Medical, Dental, and Optical Supplies) [19641]
Tradex International Corp. (Medical, Dental, and Optical Equipment) [19083]
Turner Shellfish New Zealand Inc. (Food) [12774]

Nipomo

Baggs Co.; L R (Electrical and Electronic Equipment and Supplies) [8409]

North Hills

ABC International Traders Inc. (Toys and Hobby Goods) [26379]
De Vries Imports & Distributors (Food) [10925]
MGA Entertainment (Toys and Hobby Goods) [26575]

North Hollywood

ADEMCO/ADI (Security and Safety Equipment) [24473]
American Export Trading Company (Industrial Machinery) [15766]
Arrow Thompson Metals Inc. (Metals) [19783]
Associated Industries (Communications Systems and Equipment) [5518]
Associated Industries (Electrical and Electronic Equipment and Supplies) [8385]
Bedrosian Building Supply (Floorcovering Equipment and Supplies) [9699]
Bumble Bee Wholesale (Guns and Weapons) [13479]
Bumble Bee Wholesale (Recreational and Sporting Goods) [23575]
Castec Window Shading Inc. (Household Items) [15439]
Coast Shoes Inc. (Clothing) [4885]
Electronic Hardware Ltd (Electrical and Electronic Equipment and Supplies) [8690]
General Industrial Tool and Supply Inc. (Industrial Machinery) [16056]
GKM Enterprises Inc. (Photographic Equipment and Supplies) [22856]
Interactive Medical Technologies Ltd. (Medical, Dental, and Optical Equipment) [18854]
J.S. Screw Manufacturing Co. (Hardware) [13777]
Judee K Creations Inc. (Jewelry) [17478]
Peter Pan of Hollywood Inc. (Food) [12156]

Semler Inc.; Arnold A. (Communications Systems and Equipment) [5752]
Wilshire Book Co. (Books and Other Printed Materials) [4288]

Northridge

B.G. Industries Inc. (Medical, Dental, and Optical Supplies) [19186]
California Affiliated Representative Inc. (Automotive) [2409]
HB Distributors (Communications Systems and Equipment) [5633]
HB Distributors (Electrical and Electronic Equipment and Supplies) [8836]
Independent Telephone Network Inc. (Communications Systems and Equipment) [5644]
JBL Professional (Sound and Entertainment Equipment and Supplies) [25261]
Northridge Lumber Company Inc. (Construction Materials and Machinery) [7799]
Sentai Distributors International (Toys and Hobby Goods) [26650]

Norwalk

Fruit a Freeze (Food) [11222]
Lehman Co.; Charles (Food) [11696]

Novato

Academic Therapy Publications (Books and Other Printed Materials) [3462]
BCS*A (Computers and Software) [6005]
Birkenstock Footprint Sandals Inc. (Shoes) [24691]
Educational Book Distributors (Books and Other Printed Materials) [3722]
Presidio Press Inc. (Books and Other Printed Materials) [4081]
Redwood Vintners (Alcoholic Beverages) [1980]
Rhodes Corp.; P.J. (Food) [12306]
SoftKey International (Computers and Software) [6737]
Sommer Inc.; John (Food) [12527]
Tate-Reynolds Company Inc. (Motorized Vehicles) [20736]

Oakdale

Gilbert Co.; A.L. (Agricultural Equipment and Supplies) [739]

Oakhurst

Sierra Seafood Co. (Food) [12488]

Oakland

Akiba Press (Books and Other Printed Materials) [3479]
Almanzan (Jewelry) [17306]
Attorney's Briefcase (Computers and Software) [5983]
Bay Rubber Co. (Rubber) [24269]
Bay Rubber Co. (Industrial Supplies) [16726]
Bookpeople (Books and Other Printed Materials) [3580]
California Glass Co. (Construction Materials and Machinery) [7126]
Carbide Tooling & Design (Industrial Supplies) [16780]
Carrier Corp./Bldg Sys and Svc Di (Heating and Cooling Equipment and Supplies) [14367]
Coca-Cola Bottling Co. of California (Soft Drinks) [24932]
Curtis and Sons; L.N. (Security and Safety Equipment) [24529]
Epicurean International Inc. (Restaurant and Commercial Foodservice Equipment and Supplies) [24109]
Give Something Back Inc. (Office Equipment and Supplies) [21014]
Grocers Wholesale Co. (Food) [11332]
Grower's Produce Corp. (Food) [11340]
Henderson and Co.; J.L. (Household Items) [15525]
Hoopers Candies (Food) [11457]
Hunt Co.; C.P. (Automotive) [2766]
Hunt Co.; C.P. (Automotive) [2767]
Intertile Distributors, Inc. (Floorcovering Equipment and Supplies) [9974]

Lakeside Nonferrous Metals Co. (Used, Scrap, and Recycled Materials) [26874]
Lusk Metals and Plastics (Metals) [20139]
Maisons Marques and Domaines USA Inc. (Alcoholic Beverages) [1841]
Milligan-Spika Co. (Industrial Supplies) [17042]
Monahan Paper Co. (Paper and Paper Products) [21841]
Monahan Paper Co. (Industrial Supplies) [17047]
National Airmotive Corp. (Aeronautical Equipment and Supplies) [131]
Paramount Export Co. (Food) [12107]
PC Professional Inc. (Computers and Software) [6598]
Peerless Coffee Co. (Food) [12130]
P.K. Safety Supply (Security and Safety Equipment) [24612]
Pringle Meats Inc. (Food) [12220]
Recycle America Northern California (Used, Scrap, and Recycled Materials) [26952]
Rubenstein Supply Co. (Plumbing Materials and Fixtures) [23353]
Schaefer's Cold Storage (Food) [12423]
Sconza Candy Co. (Food) [12434]
Shields Harper and Co. (Petroleum, Fuels, and Related Equipment) [22667]
Thayer Food Products Inc. (Food) [12710]
Tower Aviation Services (Aeronautical Equipment and Supplies) [161]
Veronica Foods Co. (Food) [12841]
West Coast Ship Chandlers Inc. (Industrial Supplies) [17273]
Western Door and Sash Co. (Construction Materials and Machinery) [8206]
Western MacArthur Co. (Construction Materials and Machinery) [8208]
White Company Inc.; William D. (Electrical and Electronic Equipment and Supplies) [9582]
Wilco Supply (Hardware) [13997]
Words Distributing Company (Books and Other Printed Materials) [4295]
Wurzbach Company Inc.; William (Heating and Cooling Equipment and Supplies) [14773]

Ontario

American Building Supply, Inc. (Construction Materials and Machinery) [6960]
Brown Metals Co. (Metals) [19839]
California Hardware Co. (Hardware) [13616]
Coast Grain Company Inc. (Agricultural Equipment and Supplies) [430]
Dairy Fresh Products Co. (Food) [10895]
Graves Automotive Supply (Automotive) [2697]
ICEE-USA Corp. (Soft Drinks) [24972]
JM/Ontario Tees (Clothing) [5087]
Kendell Co (Medical, Dental, and Optical Supplies) [19394]
Los Angeles Freightliner (Motorized Vehicles) [20673]
Pacific Coast Cement Corp. (Construction Materials and Machinery) [7823]
Parkway Automotive Warehouse (Automotive) [3081]
Pathtrace Systems Inc. (Computers and Software) [6595]
Pomona Valley News Agency Inc. (Books and Other Printed Materials) [4072]
Porter Cable (Hardware) [13874]
Rickard Metals Inc. (Metals) [20322]
TVM Professional Monitor Corp. (Computers and Software) [6837]

Orange

Accessorie Air Compressor Systems Inc. (Compressors) [5822]
Accessorie Air Compressor Systems Inc. (Industrial Machinery) [15729]
Anapet (Veterinary Products) [27065]
Aztec Supply Co. (Storage Equipment and Containers) [25888]
Aztec Supply Co. (Plastics) [22932]
Bergen Brunswig Corp. (Medical, Dental, and Optical Supplies) [19184]
Bisco Industries Inc. (Electrical and Electronic Equipment and Supplies) [8442]

Bromar Inc. (Food) [10615]
Gary's Machinery Inc. (Industrial Supplies) [16888]
Geary Pacific Corp. (Heating and Cooling
  Equipment and Supplies) [14457]
Hill Brothers Chemical Co. (Chemicals) [4416]
Irv Seaver Motorcycles (Automotive) [2800]
Marketing Specialists - Southern California
  Div. (Food) [11786]
Orcal Inc. (Recreational and Sporting
  Goods) [23861]
Pollard-Swain Inc. (Petroleum, Fuels, and Related
  Equipment) [22588]
Wynn's International Inc. (Hardware) [14001]
Young's Market Co. (Alcoholic Beverages) [2142]

Orinda

AHM Security Inc. (Security and Safety
  Equipment) [24497]

Orland

Dole Nut Co. Inc. (Food) [10977]

Oxnard

APS Systems (Electrical and Electronic Equipment
  and Supplies) [8366]
CalMark Custom Covers (Automotive) [2412]
Dudek & Company, Inc.; R.C. (Electrical and
  Electronic Equipment and Supplies) [8636]
The Helman Group Ltd. (Household Items) [15524]
Mission Produce Inc. (Food) [11912]
Mitchell Products; Allen (Food) [11913]
Power Machinery Center (Industrial
  Machinery) [16415]
Seaboard Marine (Marine) [18605]
Virginia Hardwood Co. (Floorcovering Equipment
  and Supplies) [10278]

Pacific Palisades

Maui and Sons Corp. (Clothing) [5174]
Paulist Productions (Photographic Equipment and
  Supplies) [22888]

Pacoima

Global Bakeries, Inc. (Food) [11272]
Higgins Lumber Co.; J.E. (Construction Materials
  and Machinery) [7472]

Palm Springs

Contract Decor Inc. (Household Items) [15453]
Riverside Communications (Communications
  Systems and Equipment) [5744]

Palo Alto

Diamond Systems Corp. (Computers and
  Software) [6208]
Duke Scientific Corp. (Scientific and Measurement
  Devices) [24349]
Electrical Materials Inc. (Electrical and Electronic
  Equipment and Supplies) [8680]
Heckman Metals Co. (Used, Scrap, and Recycled
  Materials) [26841]
Hewlett-Packard Co. International (Computers and
  Software) [6331]
Ico Rally Corp. (Electrical and Electronic Equipment
  and Supplies) [8869]
Meddev Corp. (Medical, Dental, and Optical
  Equipment) [18910]
Pearson Electronics Inc. (Electrical and Electronic
  Equipment and Supplies) [9184]
Priz Co. (Scientific and Measurement
  Devices) [24420]
Shop Tools Inc. (Hardware) [13918]
TAB Products Co. (Furniture and Fixtures) [13254]

Palos Verdes Estates

Fountain Lumber Co.; Ed (Construction Materials
  and Machinery) [7362]

Palos Verdes Peninsula

MarketForce, Ltd. (Industrial Machinery) [16265]

Panorama City

Nickerson Lumber and Plywood Inc. (Construction
  Materials and Machinery) [7777]

Paramount

Blackmore Master Distributor (Food) [10565]
Kemp Hardware and Supply
  Co. (Hardware) [13783]
Pacific Model Distributing Inc. (Toys and Hobby
  Goods) [26601]
Rayvern Lighting Supply Company Inc. (Electrical
  and Electronic Equipment and Supplies) [9267]
Sona Enterprises (Hardware) [13926]
Wolcotts Forms Inc. (Paper and Paper
  Products) [21996]

Pasadena

Aircraft and Component Equipment Suppliers
  Inc. (Aeronautical Equipment and Supplies) [35]
Blue Chip Stamps (Specialty Equipment and
  Products) [25577]
Extend-A-Life Inc. (Medical, Dental, and Optical
  Supplies) [19315]
Glenray Communications (Sound and Entertainment
  Equipment and Supplies) [25212]
Hutchins Manufacturing Co. (Industrial
  Machinery) [16121]
Wesco Financial Corp. (Metals) [20487]

Paso Robles

Acme Vial and Glass Co. Inc. (Scientific and
  Measurement Devices) [24306]

Pearblossom

Wells International (Food) [12900]

Perris

Dogloo Inc. (Veterinary Products) [27118]

Petaluma

Applied Hydroponics Inc. (Agricultural Equipment
  and Supplies) [246]
Barbara's Bakery Inc. (Food) [10503]
Cox Distributing; Dale (Food) [10861]
Fantastic Foods Inc. (Food) [11080]
Firebird International, Inc. (Construction Materials
  and Machinery) [7344]
First Service, Div. of Straightline Enterprises,
  Inc. (Recreational and Sporting Goods) [23666]
Hudson Distributing Inc.; Mike (Food) [11474]
Petaluma Poultry Processors Inc. (Food) [12155]
Schoonmaker Service Parts Co. (Industrial
  Machinery) [16472]
Scott Laboratories Inc. (Alcoholic
  Beverages) [2014]
Unicorn Books and Crafts (Books and Other
  Printed Materials) [4237]
Van Bebber Brothers Inc. (Metals) [20470]

Pico Rivera

ADCO Equipment Inc. (Industrial
  Machinery) [15735]
Canfield Co.; M.E. (Industrial Machinery) [15870]
Engs Motor Truck Co. (Motorized
  Vehicles) [20633]
McLaughlin Industrial Distributors
  Inc. (Hardware) [13819]
Power Lift Corp. (Industrial Machinery) [16414]
Weiner Steel Corp. (Metals) [20483]

Pittsburg

Merit USA (Metals) [20166]

Placentia

Aerospace Materials Corp. (Electrical and Electronic
  Equipment and Supplies) [8280]
Carlberg Warren & Associates (Electrical and
  Electronic Equipment and Supplies) [8502]
Computer Lab International Inc. (Computers and
  Software) [6114]
LeadingSpect Corp. (Computers and
  Software) [6435]
Walton Manufacturing Co. (Furniture and
  Fixtures) [13272]
Walton Manufacturing Co. (Furniture and
  Fixtures) [13273]

Placerville

Columbine International (Industrial
  Machinery) [15899]

Pleasant Hill

Color Spot Nurseries Inc. (Horticultural
  Supplies) [14843]
R-Computer (Computers and Software) [6672]

Pleasanton

Ascom Timeplex Inc. (Electrical and Electronic
  Equipment and Supplies) [8382]
Simpson Strong-Tie Company Inc. (Construction
  Materials and Machinery) [8023]

Plymouth

Central House Technologies (Computers and
  Software) [6057]

Pomona

Armline (Floorcovering Equipment and
  Supplies) [9687]
Auromere Inc. (Health and Beauty Aids) [14027]
Barretts Equine Sales Ltd. (Livestock and Farm
  Products) [17723]
Calsol Inc. (Chemicals) [4341]
Familian Corp. (Household Appliances) [15125]
Keystone Automotive Industries
  Inc. (Automotive) [2851]
PCC Group Inc. (Computers and Software) [6602]
Stanline Inc. (Floorcovering Equipment and
  Supplies) [10176]
Western Gold Thermoplastics Inc. (Used, Scrap,
  and Recycled Materials) [27042]

Potter Valley

Keene Div. (Storage Equipment and
  Containers) [25922]
Keene Div. (Wood and Wood Products) [27327]

Poway

Anacomp Inc. (Specialty Equipment and
  Products) [25552]
Computer and Networking Services Inc. (Computers
  and Software) [6117]
Harbor Packaging Inc. (Office Equipment and
  Supplies) [21026]
Mrs. Leeper's Pasta, Inc. (Food) [11951]
Olhausen Billiard Manufacturing, Inc. (Recreational
  and Sporting Goods) [23858]

Rancho Cordova

Automotive Importing Manufacturing
  Inc. (Automotive) [2290]
Bedrosian Tile Supply (Floorcovering Equipment
  and Supplies) [9712]
Bio-Dental Technologies Corp. (Medical, Dental,
  and Optical Supplies) [19190]
Jamesville Office Furnishing (Furniture and
  Fixtures) [13151]
Keddie Kreations of California (Clothing) [5107]
Office Planning Group Inc. (Furniture and
  Fixtures) [13193]
Sign of the Crab Ltd. (Plumbing Materials and
  Fixtures) [23376]
Simsmetal USA Corp. C and C Metals
  Div. (Metals) [20367]
Techline Studio Inc. (Furniture and
  Fixtures) [13258]

Rancho Cucamonga

Airgas West (Industrial Machinery) [15747]
Bradshaw International Inc. (Furniture and
  Fixtures) [13044]
Cerenzia Foods Inc. (Food) [10727]
De'Vons Optics Inc. (Medical, Dental, and Optical
  Supplies) [19279]
Falken Tire Corp. (Automotive) [2607]
Leisure Crafts (Specialty Equipment and
  Products) [25712]
Proficient Food Co. (Restaurant and Commercial
  Foodservice Equipment and Supplies) [24207]
Rebco West/Vistawall (Metals) [20309]
Superior Tire Inc. (Rubber) [24297]

Rancho Dominguez

CCC Steel Inc. (Metals) [19866]
Cosmi Corp. (Computers and Software) [6164]
Engine and Equipment Co. Inc. (Industrial Machinery) [15989]
Evans Hydro (Industrial Machinery) [15999]
Mirage Rug Imports (Floorcovering Equipment and Supplies) [10041]
Standard Wire & Cable Co. (Electrical and Electronic Equipment and Supplies) [9405]

Rancho Mirage

Electric Car Distributors (Recreational and Sporting Goods) [23648]

Rancho Palos Verdes

Cherney & Associates, Inc. (Medical, Dental, and Optical Equipment) [18739]
Melan International Trading (Electrical and Electronic Equipment and Supplies) [9064]

Redding

C.D.C. Optical Lab Inc. (Medical, Dental, and Optical Supplies) [19221]
Cook Concrete Products Inc. (Construction Materials and Machinery) [7213]
Newells Bar & Restaurant Supply, Inc. (Restaurant and Commercial Foodservice Equipment and Supplies) [24192]
North Valley Distributing (Electrical and Electronic Equipment and Supplies) [9135]
Pacific Flooring Supply (Floorcovering Equipment and Supplies) [10094]
Pacific Supply (Construction Materials and Machinery) [7828]
Tile City (Floorcovering Equipment and Supplies) [10221]

Redlands

Redlands Auto Parts (Automotive) [3141]
Young Minds Inc. (Computers and Software) [6889]

Redondo Beach

Tiernay Metals Inc. (Metals) [20424]
Zorbite Corp. (Chemicals) [4561]

Redwood City

Coors West (Alcoholic Beverages) [1618]
Harris Corporation (Communications Systems and Equipment) [5631]
ITG Laboratories Inc. (Medical, Dental, and Optical Supplies) [19381]
M and M Chemical Products Inc. (Agricultural Equipment and Supplies) [979]
Oracle Corp. USA Div. (Computers and Software) [6575]
Power-Sonic Corp. (Electrical and Electronic Equipment and Supplies) [9226]
Roberts and Brune Co. (Industrial Supplies) [17141]

Reedley

Spencer Fruit Co. (Food) [12554]

Reseda

Tile Club (Floorcovering Equipment and Supplies) [10226]

Rialto

Inland Empire Equipment Inc. (Industrial Machinery) [16157]

Richmond

Color Group (Computers and Software) [6079]
Simsmetal USA Corp. (Used, Scrap, and Recycled Materials) [26994]
State Electric Supply (Electrical and Electronic Equipment and Supplies) [9412]
Urban Ore Inc. (Construction Materials and Machinery) [8162]

Rio Linda

Taylor Fertilizers Co.; John (Agricultural Equipment and Supplies) [1315]

Ripon

Nulaid Foods Inc. (Food) [12045]

Riverside

Barstow Company Inc.; A.G. (Paints and Varnishes) [21398]
Calolympic Glove and Safety Co. Inc. (Security and Safety Equipment) [24523]
Calolympic Glove and Safety Company Inc. (Industrial Supplies) [16776]
Camomile Enterprises, Inc. (Specialty Equipment and Products) [25595]
Cook's Gourmet (Food) [10833]
Livacich Produce Inc.; John (Food) [11718]
Parsons Air Gas Inc. (Riverside, California) (Industrial Machinery) [16382]
RDO Equipment Co. (Agricultural Equipment and Supplies) [1172]
Reddy Ice Company Inc. (Food) [12290]
Riverside Scrap Iron (Used, Scrap, and Recycled Materials) [26962]
SMA Equipment Inc. (Construction Materials and Machinery) [8033]
Stull Industries Inc. (Automotive) [3277]
West Coast Wire and Steel (Metals) [20489]

Rocklin

Allied Electronics (Electrical and Electronic Equipment and Supplies) [8322]
Morrow Snowboards Inc. (Recreational and Sporting Goods) [23837]
Northern Video Systems Inc. (Sound and Entertainment Equipment and Supplies) [25364]

Rohnert Park

Lemo USA, Inc. (Electrical and Electronic Equipment and Supplies) [8983]
McPhails Inc. (Household Appliances) [15225]

Rolling Hills Estates

Analytic Associates (Computers and Software) [5941]

Rosamond

Joyce Media Inc. (Books and Other Printed Materials) [3869]

Rosemead

Global Products Company (Industrial Machinery) [16068]
Mourad & Associated International Trade (Medical, Dental, and Optical Equipment) [18952]

Roseville

Comlink Inc. (Computers and Software) [6083]
Comlink Inc. (Roseville, California) (Electrical and Electronic Equipment and Supplies) [8550]
Cornilsen's Backyard Bird (Veterinary Products) [27112]
Corporate Design Group (Furniture and Fixtures) [13083]

Sacramento

All Phase Electric Supply (Electrical and Electronic Equipment and Supplies) [8294]
American Building Supply, Inc. (Construction Materials and Machinery) [6961]
Bedrosian Tile Supply (Floorcovering Equipment and Supplies) [9710]
B.G. Office Products (Furniture and Fixtures) [13037]
Brix Co.; H.G. (Communications Systems and Equipment) [5534]
Burkett's Office Supply Inc. (Furniture and Fixtures) [13051]
Burnett and Sons Mill and Lumber Co. (Construction Materials and Machinery) [7111]
Butler-Johnson Corp. (Floorcovering Equipment and Supplies) [9747]
California Shellfish Co. (Food) [10675]
California Surveying and Drafting Supply Inc. (Scientific and Measurement Devices) [24333]

Capital Telephone Co. (Communications Systems and Equipment) [5546]
Capitol Plywood Inc. (Construction Materials and Machinery) [7137]
Central Garden and Pet Supply Inc. (Veterinary Products) [27105]
Chair Place (Furniture and Fixtures) [13068]
Colombo Baking Co. (Food) [10790]
Contracted Associates Office Interiors Inc. (Furniture and Fixtures) [13082]
Crystal Bottling Company Inc. (Soft Drinks) [24952]
Del Paso Pipe and Steel Inc. (Metals) [19922]
Diamond Flower Electric Instruments Company (USA) Inc. (Computers and Software) [6207]
Eagle Communications Technology (Communications Systems and Equipment) [5599]
Earth Grains Company of Sacramento (Food) [11014]
Filco Inc. (Household Appliances) [15128]
Firey Pet Supplies (Veterinary Products) [27131]
Floor Service Supply (Floorcovering Equipment and Supplies) [9892]
General Produce Company Ltd. (Food) [11251]
Golden State Flooring Sacramento (Floorcovering Equipment and Supplies) [9924]
H and H Computers (Computers and Software) [6319]
Hunt and Sons Inc. (Petroleum, Fuels, and Related Equipment) [22369]
Jampro Antennas, Inc. (Electrical and Electronic Equipment and Supplies) [8906]
Java City Inc. (Food) [11547]
J.J.R. Enterprises Inc. (Office Equipment and Supplies) [21078]
Jones-Campbell Co. (Furniture and Fixtures) [13153]
Jurins Distributing Co. (Restaurant and Commercial Foodservice Equipment and Supplies) [24152]
Keller Group (Furniture and Fixtures) [13155]
Keyston Brothers (Textiles and Notions) [26095]
Lovotti Brothers (Alcoholic Beverages) [1829]
Lynnwood Co. (Gifts and Novelties) [13393]
Markstein Beverage Company of Sacramento (Alcoholic Beverages) [1852]
Mary Ann's Baking Co. (Food) [11797]
Moore Brothers Div. (Industrial Supplies) [17050]
Pacific Coast Building Products Inc. (Construction Materials and Machinery) [7822]
Pacific Flooring Supply (Floorcovering Equipment and Supplies) [10095]
Pocket Pool & Patio (Recreational and Sporting Goods) [23887]
Poolmaster Inc. (Recreational and Sporting Goods) [23895]
RMT Engineering, Inc. (Electrical and Electronic Equipment and Supplies) [9300]
Ruland's Used Office Furnishings (Furniture and Fixtures) [13226]
Saccani Distributing Co. (Soft Drinks) [25031]
Sacramento Bag Manufacturing Co. (Paper and Paper Products) [21919]
Sacramento Sky Ranch Inc. (Aeronautical Equipment and Supplies) [146]
Sierra Airgas Inc. (Petroleum, Fuels, and Related Equipment) [22672]
Slakey Brothers Inc. (Construction Materials and Machinery) [8030]
Smith Family Corp.; The Miles (Food) [12509]
Sun/Day Distributor Corp. (Gifts and Novelties) [13456]
Sunshine Steel Enterprises Corp. (Metals) [20413]
Supply Station Inc. (Hardware) [13945]
Telelink Communications Co. (Communications Systems and Equipment) [5785]
Throwbot Inc. (Automotive) [3303]
Unarco Commercial Products (Restaurant and Commercial Foodservice Equipment and Supplies) [24252]
United Corporate Furnishings Inc. (Furniture and Fixtures) [13265]
Von Housen Motors Inc. (Motorized Vehicles) [20746]
Western Design Tile (Floorcovering Equipment and Supplies) [10292]

St. Helena

Casa Nuestra Winery (Alcoholic Beverages) [1579]
Central Valley Builders Supply (Construction Materials and Machinery) [7161]

Salinas

Brock Corp.; J.C. (Food) [10614]
Dole Fresh Vegetables Co. (Food) [10976]
Griffin Container and Supply Co. (Paper and Paper Products) [21753]
Salinas Tile Sales Co. (Floorcovering Equipment and Supplies) [10134]
Satori Herbal-Business Development Labs (Food) [12419]

San Bernardino

California Steel Services Inc. (Metals) [19847]
Gate City Beverage Distributors (Alcoholic Beverages) [1705]
Graybar Electric Company Inc. (Electrical and Electronic Equipment and Supplies) [8812]
Keyston Brothers (Textiles and Notions) [26101]
Laymon Candy Company Inc. (Food) [11687]
New Age Water Technology (Specialty Equipment and Products) [25756]
Strickland Beauty & Barber Supply Inc. (Health and Beauty Aids) [14249]
Valley-Western, Inc. (Floorcovering Equipment and Supplies) [10272]

San Carlos

API Appliance Parts Inc. (Household Appliances) [15015]
Belmont Systems Inc. (Computers and Software) [6009]
Black Mountain Spring Water Inc. (Soft Drinks) [24916]
Controltech (Industrial Machinery) [15913]
Delta Star Inc. (Electrical and Electronic Equipment and Supplies) [8622]
Inside Source (Furniture and Fixtures) [13141]
IPS of California (Industrial Machinery) [16174]
Lodan West Inc. (Electrical and Electronic Equipment and Supplies) [8999]
Peninsula Laboratories Inc. (Medical, Dental, and Optical Supplies) [19530]
Piper Sport Racks Inc. (Recreational and Sporting Goods) [23884]
Praxair Distribution/W. Div. (Industrial Machinery) [16421]
Saria International Inc. (Hardware) [13903]

San Clemente

Cook Brothers Manufacturing and Supply Co. (Plumbing Materials and Fixtures) [23126]
Metagenics Inc. (Health and Beauty Aids) [14160]
Southwest Specialties (Food) [12545]

San Diego

Abacus Data Systems Inc. (Computers and Software) [5861]
ACS Publications (Books and Other Printed Materials) [3468]
Admiral Exchange Company Inc. (Food) [10327]
Advanced Marketing Services Inc. (Books and Other Printed Materials) [3473]
Advanced Test Equipmnt Rentals (Industrial Machinery) [15738]
ALARIS Medical Systems Inc. (Medical, Dental, and Optical Equipment) [18669]
Anacomp Inc. International Div. (Office Equipment and Supplies) [20803]
Andrew and Williamson Sales Co. (Food) [10416]
Aquanetics Systems (Plumbing Materials and Fixtures) [23070]
Atlas Chemical Inc. (Chemicals) [4329]
Auto Parts Club Inc. (Automotive) [2274]
Auxiliary Power International Corp. (Aeronautical Equipment and Supplies) [47]
Bedrosian Tile Supply (Floorcovering Equipment and Supplies) [9704]
Beeba's Creations Inc. (Clothing) [4813]
Best Regards Inc. (Gifts and Novelties) [13316]
Bext, Inc. (Electrical and Electronic Equipment and Supplies) [8436]
Bittle American Inc.; J. (Automotive) [2366]

Bumble Bee Seafoods Inc. (Food) [10641]
California Pacific Fruit Co. (Food) [10674]
Camper's Trade Emporium (Hardware) [13618]
Carlson and Beauloye (Compressors) [5833]
Centaurus Systems Inc. (Computers and Software) [6051]
Chesapeake Fish Company Inc. (Food) [10740]
Circle Food Products Inc. (Food) [10759]
Coast Distributing Co. (Alcoholic Beverages) [1604]
Copyline Corp. (Office Equipment and Supplies) [20919]
Crest Beverage Co. (Alcoholic Beverages) [1623]
Diamond W Supply Co. Inc. (Floorcovering Equipment and Supplies) [9865]
Diversified Copier Products Inc. (Office Equipment and Supplies) [20969]
Dixieline Lumber Co. (Construction Materials and Machinery) [7273]
El Indio Shop (Food) [11038]
ESD Co. (Electrical and Electronic Equipment and Supplies) [8714]
Expo Industries Inc. (Construction Materials and Machinery) [7328]
Flame Spray Inc. (Chemicals) [4390]
Frost Hardwood Lumber Co. (Construction Materials and Machinery) [7371]
Frost Hardwood Lumber Co. (Wood and Wood Products) [27307]
Gulbransen Inc. Crystal Products (Sound and Entertainment Equipment and Supplies) [25221]
Harcourt Brace Professional Publishing (Books and Other Printed Materials) [3812]
Hawthorne Machinery Inc. (Automotive) [2732]
Hawthorne Machinery Inc. Hawthorne Power Systems Div. (Agricultural Equipment and Supplies) [803]
Heating and Cooling Supply Inc. (Heating and Cooling Equipment and Supplies) [14482]
Higgins Lumber Co.; J.E. (Construction Materials and Machinery) [7473]
Hydro-Scape Products, Inc. (Agricultural Equipment and Supplies) [850]
Hyperox Technologies (Recreational and Sporting Goods) [23739]
Insight Electronics Inc. (Electrical and Electronic Equipment and Supplies) [8883]
Instrument Engineers (Scientific and Measurement Devices) [24372]
Integrated Orbital Implants Inc. (Medical, Dental, and Optical Supplies) [19374]
Interatech (Computers and Software) [6385]
International Male (Clothing) [5059]
ITM (Computers and Software) [6399]
Jaco Co. (Medical, Dental, and Optical Equipment) [18867]
JBA Headers (Automotive) [2814]
K Rep Sales (Computers and Software) [6415]
Keyston Brothers (Textiles and Notions) [26096]
King Lobster Connection (Food) [11614]
Knox Computer Systems Inc. (Computers and Software) [6423]
KS Group International (Health and Beauty Aids) [14146]
KSC Industries Inc. (Household Appliances) [15193]
Laboratory & Biomedical Supplies Inc. (Medical, Dental, and Optical Supplies) [19403]
Lenore & Co.; John (Alcoholic Beverages) [1819]
Ling's International Books (Books and Other Printed Materials) [3916]
Loftin Web Graphics (Paper and Paper Products) [21810]
Luxor California Export Corp. (Food) [11747]
Maintenance Warehouse/America Corp. (Hardware) [13806]
MC Sales (Toys and Hobby Goods) [26571]
McLogan Supply (Specialty Equipment and Products) [25732]
Mesa Microwave Inc. (Electrical and Electronic Equipment and Supplies) [9067]
Mission Janitorial Supplies (Cleaning and Janitorial Supplies) [4672]
Moonlight Products Inc. (Scientific and Measurement Devices) [24403]
Mycogen Seeds (Agricultural Equipment and Supplies) [1060]

Neostyle Eyewear Corp. (Medical, Dental, and Optical Supplies) [19482]
Networks 2000 (Computers and Software) [6550]
Nicolet Imaging Systems (Security and Safety Equipment) [24602]
Nimax Inc. (Computers and Software) [6558]
Nitches Inc. (Clothing) [5232]
Ocean Floor Abalone (Food) [12051]
One Source Distributors (Electrical and Electronic Equipment and Supplies) [9156]
Pacific Drapery Co. (Household Items) [15607]
Paper Recovery Inc. (Used, Scrap, and Recycled Materials) [26934]
Perfusion Services of Baxter Healthcare Corp. (Medical, Dental, and Optical Supplies) [19533]
PetrolSoft Corp. (Computers and Software) [6615]
PMH Associates (Industrial Machinery) [16404]
Rainbow Publishers (Books and Other Printed Materials) [4105]
Reverse & Company (Clothing) [5307]
Ridout Plastics Inc. (Plastics) [23027]
Rising Sun Import Parts Inc. (Automotive) [3162]
The Roane Co. (Floorcovering Equipment and Supplies) [10124]
Saber Enterprises Inc. (Scientific and Measurement Devices) [24424]
SalePoint Inc. (Computers and Software) [6701]
San Diego Beverage and Cup Inc. (Soft Drinks) [25033]
San Diego Marine Exchange (Marine) [18601]
SDA Security Systems, Inc. (Security and Safety Equipment) [24626]
Sierra Optical (Medical, Dental, and Optical Supplies) [19608]
Smith and Co.; R.W. (Specialty Equipment and Products) [25820]
Sounds Write Productions, Inc. (Sound and Entertainment Equipment and Supplies) [25454]
South Bay Leather Corp. (Luggage and Leather Goods) [18431]
Southern Motorcycle Supply (Automotive) [3240]
Sport Palace Wholesale (Clothing) [5382]
StarTech International (Computers and Software) [6760]
Tile Club (Floorcovering Equipment and Supplies) [10225]
Tinley Performancewear (Clothing) [5431]
Trags Distributors (Toys and Hobby Goods) [26687]
Transamerican & Export News Co. (Books and Other Printed Materials) [4227]
Univelt Inc. (Books and Other Printed Materials) [4243]
USAP (Computers and Software) [6845]
Valhalla Scientific Inc. (Electrical and Electronic Equipment and Supplies) [9531]
Valley-Western, Inc. (Floorcovering Equipment and Supplies) [10273]
Virginia Hardwood Co. (Floorcovering Equipment and Supplies) [10279]
Waxie Sanitary Supply (Cleaning and Janitorial Supplies) [4728]
WD-40 Co. (Petroleum, Fuels, and Related Equipment) [22786]
Weekend Exercise Co., Inc. (Clothing) [5475]
Western Fastener Co. (Hardware) [13995]
Western Radio Electronics Inc. (Electrical and Electronic Equipment and Supplies) [9576]
Wood Floor Wholesalers (Floorcovering Equipment and Supplies) [10305]
WRI Education (Sound and Entertainment Equipment and Supplies) [25533]
Zzyzx Peripherals Inc. (Computers and Software) [6893]

San Dimas

Bindley Western Drug Co. (Health and Beauty Aids) [14042]
Cathay International (Electrical and Electronic Equipment and Supplies) [8508]
Pacific Exports (Scientific and Measurement Devices) [24414]
PerTronix Inc. (Electrical and Electronic Equipment and Supplies) [9192]

Worldwide Environmental Products Inc. (Automotive) [3446]

San Fernando

Aleph International (Electrical and Electronic Equipment and Supplies) [8289]

Canare (Electrical and Electronic Equipment and Supplies) [8494]

Dodge & Son Inc.; Herman (Household Appliances) [15113]

Eisenberg International Corp. (Clothing) [4931]

San Francisco

2BU-Wear (Clothing) [4736]

Airmo Div. (Furniture and Fixtures) [13012]

Alamo Square Distributors (Books and Other Printed Materials) [3483]

Alamo Square Distributors (Books and Other Printed Materials) [3484]

Alamo Square Distributors (Books and Other Printed Materials) [3485]

All Seas Wholesale Inc. (Food) [10366]

American Ex-Im Corp. (Health and Beauty Aids) [14019]

American Industrial Supply (Industrial Supplies) [16694]

AMP King Battery Company Inc. (Electrical and Electronic Equipment and Supplies) [8349]

Another Dancing Bear Productions (Gifts and Novelties) [13305]

Astronomical Society of the Pacific (Books and Other Printed Materials) [3531]

Atlas Diamond Co. (Jewelry) [17318]

Barta International Sales Corp. (Livestock and Farm Products) [17724]

Berelson Export Corp. (Food) [10539]

Berelson Export Corp. (Food) [10540]

Bi Rite Foodservice Distributors (Food) [10551]

BiRite Foodservice (Food) [10558]

Bisho Company, Inc.; J.R. (Automotive) [2365]

Boisset U.S.A. (Alcoholic Beverages) [1539]

Boyd Lighting Fixture Co (Electrical and Electronic Equipment and Supplies) [8459]

California Shellfish Company Inc. (Food) [10676]

Capricorn Coffees Inc. (Food) [10694]

Casella Lighting Co. (Electrical and Electronic Equipment and Supplies) [8506]

Casella Lighting Co. (Household Items) [15438]

CGF Cash & Carry (Food) [10731]

Chatham Created Gems Inc. (Jewelry) [17366]

Chemoil Corp. (Petroleum, Fuels, and Related Equipment) [22132]

Chevron Corp. (Chemicals) [4359]

Chevron Industries (Petroleum, Fuels, and Related Equipment) [22134]

Cleasby Manufacturing Company Inc. (Construction Materials and Machinery) [7179]

Connell Brothers Company Ltd. (Chemicals) [4362]

Contemporary Arts Press Distribution (Books and Other Printed Materials) [3655]

Contemporary Computer Wear (Computers and Software) [6153]

Continental Baking Co. (Food) [10826]

Cutting Edge Audio Group L.L.C. (Sound and Entertainment Equipment and Supplies) [25154]

Cypress Book (USA) Co., Inc. (Books and Other Printed Materials) [3678]

DBB Marketing Co. (Food) [10923]

Decorative Plant Service Inc. (Agricultural Equipment and Supplies) [504]

Dolphin Acquisition Corp. (Health and Beauty Aids) [14087]

Electrical Appliance Service Co. (Household Appliances) [15120]

European Book Company Inc. (Books and Other Printed Materials) [3736]

FIC International Corp. (Plastics) [22962]

Forderer Cornice Works Co. (Construction Materials and Machinery) [7356]

Foreign Exchange Ltd. (Minerals and Ores) [20541]

Funsten and Co.; B.R. (Household Items) [15510]

Getz Bros. & Company Inc. (Industrial Machinery) [16062]

Global Directions Inc. (Books and Other Printed Materials) [3781]

Golden State Trading Co. (Gifts and Novelties) [13363]

Greenleaf Produce (Food) [11321]

H and N Fish Co. (Food) [11351]

Harper San Francisco (Books and Other Printed Materials) [3813]

Hermann Associates Inc. (Security and Safety Equipment) [24561]

Hermann Associates Inc. (Office Equipment and Supplies) [21030]

Higgins Purchasing Group (Furniture and Fixtures) [13131]

Hinshaw Supply Company of California (Heating and Cooling Equipment and Supplies) [14486]

Holzmueller Corp. (Electrical and Electronic Equipment and Supplies) [8855]

Institute for Childhood Resources (Toys and Hobby Goods) [26534]

Interknit Inc. (Clothing) [5055]

International Marine Fuels Inc. (Petroleum, Fuels, and Related Equipment) [22376]

IPC Information Systems Inc. (Electrical and Electronic Equipment and Supplies) [8899]

J-Snell & Co., Inc. (Office Equipment and Supplies) [21074]

Just Desserts Inc. (Food) [11573]

Kaye Inc.; Richard W. (Jewelry) [17485]

Keizer Associates (Industrial Machinery) [16200]

Keyston Brothers (Textiles and Notions) [26102]

Kryolan Corp. (Specialty Equipment and Products) [25708]

Last Gasp of San Francisco (Books and Other Printed Materials) [3897]

Malco Modes Inc. (Clothing) [5155]

Maltby Electric Supply Company Inc. (Electrical and Electronic Equipment and Supplies) [9024]

Mathews Enterprises (Jewelry) [17517]

M.C. International (Medical, Dental, and Optical Supplies) [19429]

McGuire Furniture Co. (Furniture and Fixtures) [13176]

McKesson Drug Co. (Medical, Dental, and Optical Supplies) [19433]

McKesson Drug Co. (Medical, Dental, and Optical Supplies) [19434]

McKesson HBOC Inc. (Medical, Dental, and Optical Supplies) [19435]

McKesson Health Systems (Medical, Dental, and Optical Supplies) [19436]

McLane Group Interntional L.P. (Food) [11833]

M.G. West (Furniture and Fixtures) [13179]

Modern Overseas, Inc. (Health and Beauty Aids) [14166]

Morgan Graphic Supply (Industrial Machinery) [16321]

New World Wines (Alcoholic Beverages) [1916]

Oilseeds International Ltd. (Food) [12057]

Orsen-Porter-Rockwell International (Luggage and Leather Goods) [18415]

Pacific Flooring Supply (Floorcovering Equipment and Supplies) [10096]

Patrick and Co. (Paper and Paper Products) [21869]

Peer Light Inc. (Electrical and Electronic Equipment and Supplies) [9185]

Persona Press (Books and Other Printed Materials) [4059]

PLM Transportation Equipment Corp. (Industrial Machinery) [16402]

Power Sewing (Books and Other Printed Materials) [4077]

R & H Wholesale Supply, Inc. (Security and Safety Equipment) [24616]

Ross and Company International; Mark (Food) [12354]

Rotometals Inc. (Marine) [18596]

San Francisco Center for Visual Studies (Books and Other Printed Materials) [4136]

San Francisco Mart (Furniture and Fixtures) [13231]

Scatena York Company (Heating and Cooling Equipment and Supplies) [14675]

Sega of America Inc. (Toys and Hobby Goods) [26649]

Shaklee Corp. (Health and Beauty Aids) [14234]

Sierra Point Lumber and Plywood Co. (Construction Materials and Machinery) [8018]

Sierra Point Lumber and Plywood Co. (Wood and Wood Products) [27377]

Sloan Miyasato (Furniture and Fixtures) [13247]

Squirrel Companies Inc. (Computers and Software) [6756]

Stan Corporation of America (Computers and Software) [6757]

Stanislaus Imports Inc. (Toys and Hobby Goods) [26667]

Summation Legal Technologies Inc. (Computers and Software) [6769]

Superior Trading Co. (Food) [12641]

Takahashi Trading Corp. (Household Items) [15681]

Thinkware (Computers and Software) [6816]

Tilia, Inc. (Industrial Machinery) [16564]

United Exporters (Medical, Dental, and Optical Supplies) [19674]

United Meat Company Inc. (Food) [12798]

U.S. Home and Garden Inc. (Agricultural Equipment and Supplies) [1383]

U.S. Import Export Corp. (Food) [12803]

Van Arsdale-Harris Lumber (Construction Materials and Machinery) [8169]

Van Arsdale-Harris Lumber (Wood and Wood Products) [27392]

Viking Distributing Company Inc. (Industrial Supplies) [17254]

West Bay Resources Inc. (Used, Scrap, and Recycled Materials) [27041]

West Coast Industries Inc. (Furniture and Fixtures) [13277]

Wilbur-Ellis Co. (Chemicals) [4554]

Wilcox Frozen Foods Inc. (Food) [12939]

San Gabriel

Ri-Mat Enterprises Inc. (Gifts and Novelties) [13436]

Valley Tile & Marble (Floorcovering Equipment and Supplies) [10269]

San Gregorio

Cybernetic Micro Systems Inc. (Electrical and Electronic Equipment and Supplies) [8604]

San Jacinto

Agri-Empire (Food) [10345]

San Jose

ACL Inc. (Electrical and Electronic Equipment and Supplies) [8266]

ADI Systems Inc. (Computers and Software) [5876]

AdvanTel Inc. (Communications Systems and Equipment) [5503]

Allied Container Corp. (Paper and Paper Products) [21625]

Alps Electric (USA) Inc. (Computers and Software) [5915]

ARM Computer Inc. (Computers and Software) [5962]

Arrowcopter Inc. (Toys and Hobby Goods) [26398]

Bacon Company Inc.; Edward R. (Construction Materials and Machinery) [7009]

Bedrosian Tile Supply (Floorcovering Equipment and Supplies) [9705]

Bell Microproducts Inc. (Electrical and Electronic Equipment and Supplies) [8429]

Biersch Brewing Co.; Gordon (Alcoholic Beverages) [1529]

Buckles-Smith Electric (Electrical and Electronic Equipment and Supplies) [8474]

Business Resource Group (Furniture and Fixtures) [13058]

Butler-Johnson Corp. (Floorcovering Equipment and Supplies) [9748]

Butler-Johnson Corp. (Construction Materials and Machinery) [7116]

Cal-Growers Corp. (Food) [10667]

Coast Counties Truck and Equipment Co. (Automotive) [2459]

Coast Distribution System (Automotive) [2460]

Competition Parts Warehouse Inc. (Automotive) [2470]

Complete Office Solutions Inc. (Furniture and Fixtures) [13077]

Connor and Associates Inc. (Gifts and Novelties) [13333]

Corporate Express of Northern California Inc. (Office Equipment and Supplies) [20931]

DistribuPro Inc. (Computers and Software) [6213]

Dudek & Company, Inc.; R.C. (Electrical and Electronic Equipment and Supplies) [8637]

Durham Meat Co. (Food) [11000]

Floor Service Supply (Floorcovering Equipment and Supplies) [9893]

Flytech Technology (USA) Inc. (Computers and Software) [6273]

Fujitsu Computer Products of America Inc. (Computers and Software) [6282]

Fujitsu Network Switching of America Inc. (Computers and Software) [6283]

Green Team of San Jose (Used, Scrap, and Recycled Materials) [26834]

Harris Semiconductor (Electrical and Electronic Equipment and Supplies) [8831]

Integrated Process Equipment Corp. (Industrial Machinery) [16161]

Integrated Sensor Solutions (Automotive) [2789]

ITC International (Electrical and Electronic Equipment and Supplies) [8902]

JC Paper (Paper and Paper Products) [21783]

JDR Microdevices Inc. (Computers and Software) [6408]

KBM Workspace (Furniture and Fixtures) [13154]

Keywest Wire Div. (Construction Materials and Machinery) [7554]

Laser Logic Inc. (Office Equipment and Supplies) [21101]

Law Cypress Distributing (Computers and Software) [6432]

Lehmann Co. Inc.; Chester C. (Electrical and Electronic Equipment and Supplies) [8981]

Lehmann Company Inc.; Chester C. (Electrical and Electronic Equipment and Supplies) [8982]

Lohr Winery; J. (Alcoholic Beverages) [1826]

MA Laboratories Inc. (Computers and Software) [6448]

Mariani Packing Company Inc. (Food) [11779]

Markovits and Fox (Metals) [20153]

Merisel Inc. Macamerica Div. (Computers and Software) [6485]

Milligan News Co., Inc. (Books and Other Printed Materials) [3960]

Miracle Computers Inc. (Computers and Software) [6522]

Mirassou Sales Co. (Alcoholic Beverages) [1883]

Mission Valley Ford Trucks Sales Inc. (Automotive) [2974]

Mr. Hub Cap (Automotive) [3002]

MSIS Semiconductor Inc. (Electrical and Electronic Equipment and Supplies) [9105]

NEC America Inc. Data and Video Communications Systems Div. (Computers and Software) [6548]

Novellus Systems Inc. (Electrical and Electronic Equipment and Supplies) [9146]

Orion Group (USA), Ltd. (Metals) [20254]

Pacific PreCut Produce Inc. (Food) [12092]

PDP Systems (Computers and Software) [6605]

Penstock (Electrical and Electronic Equipment and Supplies) [9190]

Philips Key Modules (Electrical and Electronic Equipment and Supplies) [9196]

Pivot Interiors (Furniture and Fixtures) [13209]

Pixel U.S.A. (Computers and Software) [6624]

Quement Electronics (Electrical and Electronic Equipment and Supplies) [9250]

Qumax Corp. (Computers and Software) [6671]

Race Street Foods Inc. (Food) [12260]

Raster Graphics Inc. (Office Equipment and Supplies) [21233]

Resource Publications Inc. (Books and Other Printed Materials) [4115]

RT Computers Inc. (Computers and Software) [6696]

San Jose Surgical Supply Inc. (Medical, Dental, and Optical Equipment) [19032]

Savoye Packaging Corp. (Metals) [20353]

Semi-Gas Systems Inc. (Chemicals) [4507]

Silicon Valley Technology Inc. (Computers and Software) [6729]

Sun Moon Star (Communications Systems and Equipment) [5771]

Telecom Solutions Div. (Computers and Software) [6809]

True Comp America Inc. (Computers and Software) [6834]

Vantage Pools Inc. (Recreational and Sporting Goods) [24026]

Videomedia Inc. (Sound and Entertainment Equipment and Supplies) [25506]

Western States Oil Company Inc. (Petroleum, Fuels, and Related Equipment) [22796]

Xilinx Inc. (Electrical and Electronic Equipment and Supplies) [9614]

Zack Electronics Inc. (Electrical and Electronic Equipment and Supplies) [9620]

Zanker Road Resource Management Co. (Used, Scrap, and Recycled Materials) [27053]

San Juan Capistrano

Hirsch Pipe & Supply Co. (Plumbing Materials and Fixtures) [23209]

San Leandro

Alco Iron and Metal Co. (Metals) [19743]

Barstad and Donicht Inc. (Automotive) [2323]

Brewmaster (Alcoholic Beverages) [1549]

Clydes Corner Electronics (Sound and Entertainment Equipment and Supplies) [25140]

Cummins West Inc. (Automotive) [2517]

Duhig and Co. (Plumbing Materials and Fixtures) [23139]

Duhig and Co. (Metals) [19940]

Hoffmeyer Co. (Automotive) [2759]

Keyston Brothers (Textiles and Notions) [26097]

Medallion Carpets (Floorcovering Equipment and Supplies) [10018]

Pacific Electrical Supply (Electrical and Electronic Equipment and Supplies) [9169]

Pacific Steel and Supply Corp. (Construction Materials and Machinery) [7827]

Peterson Tractor Co. (Construction Materials and Machinery) [7853]

Saag's Products Inc. (Food) [12384]

Sierra Detroit Diesel Allison Inc. (Automotive) [3220]

Triangle Coatings, Inc. (Paints and Varnishes) [21595]

Unistrut Northern California (Metals) [20462]

San Luis Obispo

Dega Technologies (Automotive) [2536]

EZ Nature Books (Books and Other Printed Materials) [3739]

San Luis Sourdough (Food) [12402]

Square Deal Recordings and Supplies (Sound and Entertainment Equipment and Supplies) [25462]

Tile Collection (Floorcovering Equipment and Supplies) [10227]

San Marcos

Applied Membranes Inc. (Specialty Equipment and Products) [25555]

Challenger Water International Inc. (Specialty Equipment and Products) [25599]

Markstein Beverage Co. (Alcoholic Beverages) [1851]

Nimbus Water Systems, Inc. (Specialty Equipment and Products) [25759]

Slawson Communications, Inc. (Books and Other Printed Materials) [4166]

Southwestern Ceramic, Tile & Marble Co. (Floorcovering Equipment and Supplies) [10171]

Southwestern Ceramic, Tile & Marble Co. (Floorcovering Equipment and Supplies) [10172]

San Mateo

Baxter Co.; J.H. (Construction Materials and Machinery) [7032]

E-Y Laboratories Inc. (Medical, Dental, and Optical Supplies) [19299]

Electronic Arts Inc. (Computers and Software) [6242]

Seagram Classics Wine Co. (Alcoholic Beverages) [2016]

San Pedro

Amsing International Inc. (Food) [10409]

First International Trading Company (Industrial Supplies) [16863]

HSS Group (Marine) [18522]

L.A. Marine Hardware (Marine) [18539]

MLH and Associates (Computers and Software) [6526]

Seaside Supply Stores (Marine) [18607]

StarKist Seafood/Heinz Pet Prd (Food) [12575]

State Fish Company Inc. (Food) [12577]

Tri Marine International (Food) [12752]

San Rafael

ComputersAmerica Inc. (Computers and Software) [6136]

Fetzer Vineyards (Alcoholic Beverages) [1688]

Fowler Brothers (Food) [11195]

Ghiselli Brothers (Food) [11261]

Rubenstein Supply Co. (Plumbing Materials and Fixtures) [23354]

Serendipity Couriers, Inc. (Books and Other Printed Materials) [4152]

Serendipity Couriers, Inc. (Books and Other Printed Materials) [4153]

Sonnen Mill Valley BMW (Motorized Vehicles) [20722]

Thames America Trading Company Ltd. (Alcoholic Beverages) [2076]

Winward Trading Company. (Food) [12964]

San Ramon

Clare Computer Solutions Inc. (Computers and Software) [6072]

Purcell & Associates (Food) [12235]

U.S. AudioTex L.L.C. (Computers and Software) [6841]

White Swan Ltd. (Agricultural Equipment and Supplies) [1441]

San Ysidro

Cattsa Inc.; S.D. (Clothing) [4870]

International Advertising Gifts (Gifts and Novelties) [13377]

Sand City

Lifeline Food Company Inc. (Food) [11710]

Salinas Tile Sales, Inc. (Floorcovering Equipment and Supplies) [10135]

Sanger

Gibson Wine Company Inc. (Alcoholic Beverages) [1713]

Senor's Q Inc. (Clothing) [5344]

Santa Ana

Adohr Farms Inc. (Food) [10328]

Advanced Enterprise Solutions (Computers and Software) [5887]

All City Barber & Beauty Supply (Health and Beauty Aids) [14013]

American Computer Hardware (Computers and Software) [5923]

American West Marketing Inc. (Explosives) [9631]

Amidon Associates Inc. (Electrical and Electronic Equipment and Supplies) [8347]

AR Industries Inc. (Computers and Software) [5956]

Cal Compack Foods Inc. (Food) [10665]

Collins & Associates; Paul (Electrical and Electronic Equipment and Supplies) [8542]

CTI Abrasives and Tools (Industrial Supplies) [16815]

Dollar Computer Corp. (Computers and Software) [6218]

Economy Distributors (Veterinary Products) [27122]

FM Systems, Inc. (Communications Systems and Equipment) [5614]

Frost Engineering Service Co. (Industrial Machinery) [16042]

Hall Research Technologies (Computers and Software) [6324]
ICC Instrument Company Inc. (Industrial Machinery) [16138]
Ingram Micro Inc. (Computers and Software) [6373]
Kawasaki Motors Corporation U.S.A. (Motorized Vehicles) [20659]
Knox Industrial Supplies Inc. (Hardware) [13788]
MAG Innovision Inc. (Computers and Software) [6453]
Mania-Testerion (Electrical and Electronic Equipment and Supplies) [9025]
Marlin Manufacturing & Distribution Inc.; R. (Gifts and Novelties) [13396]
MicroCAD Technologies Inc. (Computers and Software) [6500]
Oasis Drinking Waters Inc. (Soft Drinks) [25001]
Pacific O.E.M. Supply (Marine) [18580]
Performance Catamarans Inc. (Marine) [18583]
Potter-Roemer (Security and Safety Equipment) [24614]
Powertron Battery Co. (Automotive) [3113]
Quality Care Pharmaceuticals Inc. (Medical, Dental, and Optical Supplies) [19563]
SG Wholesale Roofing Supply Inc. (Construction Materials and Machinery) [8005]
Shurflo (Storage Equipment and Containers) [25939]
Siemens Energy and Automation Inc. (Electrical and Electronic Equipment and Supplies) [9368]
Southwest CTI Inc. (Computers and Software) [6750]
Superior Manufacturing Co. (Santa Ana, California) (Electrical and Electronic Equipment and Supplies) [9445]
U.S. Rigging Supply Corp. (Industrial Supplies) [17243]
Universal Forms, Labels, and Systems, Inc. (Paper and Paper Products) [21980]
Winchell's Donut Houses Operating Company L.P. (Food) [12957]
Wood Floor Wholesalers (Floorcovering Equipment and Supplies) [10306]

Santa Barbara

Capra Press Inc. (Books and Other Printed Materials) [3611]
Chase Com Corp. (Communications Systems and Equipment) [5559]
Fortune Dogs Inc. (Clothing) [4962]
Jordanos Inc. (Food) [11565]
Map Link Inc. (Books and Other Printed Materials) [3935]
Pacific Beverage Company Inc. (Soft Drinks) [25002]
Pacific Books (Books and Other Printed Materials) [4030]
Sportsware West (Recreational and Sporting Goods) [23982]
The Tile Collection, Inc. (Floorcovering Equipment and Supplies) [10228]
Valley Foods (Food) [12817]

Santa Clara

ARA-Cory Refreshment Services (Soft Drinks) [24910]
Calcom Inc. (Industrial Machinery) [15863]
California Eastern Laboratories Inc. (Electrical and Electronic Equipment and Supplies) [8484]
Central Computer Systems Inc. (Computers and Software) [6056]
Cumming-Henderson Inc. (Automotive) [2501]
Cutter Precision Metals Inc. (Metals) [19912]
Deanco Inc. (Electrical and Electronic Equipment and Supplies) [8617]
Greenleaf Distribution Inc. (Computers and Software) [6310]
Halted Specialties Co. (Computers and Software) [6326]
Hitachi Data Systems Corp. (Computers and Software) [6333]
Hitachi Data Systems Corp. (Computers and Software) [6334]
Hitron Systems Inc. (Computers and Software) [6336]

Intel Corp. (Computers and Software) [6379]
Keyston Brothers (Textiles and Notions) [26103]
Marketex Computer Corp. (Computers and Software) [6464]
Markley Strings, Inc.; Dean (Sound and Entertainment Equipment and Supplies) [25304]
Micro Integrated Communications Corp. (Computers and Software) [6492]
Mini-Micro Supply Company Inc. (Computers and Software) [6521]
Prima International (Computers and Software) [6635]
Probe Technology Corp. (Industrial Machinery) [16428]
Santa Clara Tile Supply (Floorcovering Equipment and Supplies) [10138]
Sejin America Inc. (Computers and Software) [6720]
Sentex Corp. (Electrical and Electronic Equipment and Supplies) [9354]
Siliconix Inc. (Automotive) [3222]
Sumitomo Plastics America Inc. (Plastics) [23037]
Superscape Inc. (Computers and Software) [6776]
Turf and Industrial Equipment Co. (Agricultural Equipment and Supplies) [1363]

Santa Clarita

Taitron Components Inc. (Electrical and Electronic Equipment and Supplies) [9456]

Santa Cruz

Continental Sales Co. of America (Medical, Dental, and Optical Supplies) [19250]
Crossing Press (Books and Other Printed Materials) [3674]
EBSCO Industries Inc. Western Region (Clothing) [4929]
Falcon Trading Co. (Food) [11076]
Fmali Inc. (Food) [11165]
Ledyard Company Inc. (Restaurant and Commercial Foodservice Equipment and Supplies) [24164]
National Stock Sign Co. (Specialty Equipment and Products) [25750]
Straight Talk Distributing (Books and Other Printed Materials) [4192]
Toma International (Agricultural Equipment and Supplies) [1340]
Wild Craft Herb (Food) [12940]
Worth Data (Electrical and Electronic Equipment and Supplies) [9609]

Santa Fe Springs

Aberdeen L.L.C. (Computers and Software) [5863]
ABSCOA Industries Inc. (Aeronautical Equipment and Supplies) [23]
ACI Distribution (Construction Materials and Machinery) [6905]
Air Mobile Systems (Communications Systems and Equipment) [5505]
Alloy Tool Steel Inc. (Metals) [19753]
Ballanda Corp. (Jewelry) [17327]
Cal-West Foodservice Inc. (Food) [10668]
CENCO Refining Co. (Petroleum, Fuels, and Related Equipment) [22119]
Century Fasteners, Inc. (Hardware) [13628]
Clark-Schwebel Distribution Corp. (Plastics) [22943]
Classroom Reading Service (Books and Other Printed Materials) [3642]
Coaster Company of America (Furniture and Fixtures) [13071]
Cross Mark Southern California (Food) [10870]
Dresco Reproduction Inc. (Specialty Equipment and Products) [25636]
Dresco Reproduction Inc. (Scientific and Measurement Devices) [24348]
E.K. Fasteners Inc. (Hardware) [13677]
Kelly Pipe Co. (Industrial Supplies) [16982]
L & D Appliance Corp. (Household Appliances) [15195]
The Lincoln Electric Co (Industrial Machinery) [16236]
Lombard Management Inc. (Automotive) [2889]
Luxury Liners (Medical, Dental, and Optical Equipment) [18893]
Luxury Liners (Medical, Dental, and Optical Supplies) [19419]

Memtek Products/Memorex Audio, Video, CDR's, & Computer Peripherals (Sound and Entertainment Equipment and Supplies) [25313]
Pro-Chem Corp. (Metals) [20296]
Pump Engineering Co. (Industrial Supplies) [17121]
Pusan Pipe America Inc. (Metals) [20303]
Relco Engineers (Paints and Varnishes) [21553]
Shoemakers Candies Inc. (Food) [12480]
Sierra Concepts Corp. (Industrial Machinery) [16489]
SMW Systems Inc. (Industrial Machinery) [16499]
SOCO-Lynch Corp. (Chemicals) [4513]
Southern California Pipe and Steel Co. (Construction Materials and Machinery) [8048]
Speed-O-Motive (Automotive) [3249]
Spicers Paper Inc. (Paper and Paper Products) [21946]
State Pipe and Supply Inc. (Metals) [20391]
Talley Communications (Communications Systems and Equipment) [5773]
Tru-Form Tool and Manufacturing Industries Inc. (Industrial Machinery) [16584]
Tube Service Co. (Metals) [20444]
Uddeholm Steel Corp. (Metals) [20452]
Unistrut Los Angeles (Metals) [20461]
Universal Aqua (Specialty Equipment and Products) [25859]
Vallen Safety Supply Co. (Medical, Dental, and Optical Supplies) [19688]
Viam Manufacturing Inc. (Automotive) [3392]
Zonne Industrial Tool Co. (Industrial Machinery) [16663]

Santa Maria

Boston Pet Supply, Inc. (Veterinary Products) [27088]
Cal-Coast Machinery (Agricultural Equipment and Supplies) [357]
Chilis Footwear Inc. (Shoes) [24712]
Higgins Lumber Co.; J.E. (Construction Materials and Machinery) [7474]
Impo International Inc. (Clothing) [5046]
Larrabee Brothers Distributing Company Inc. (Alcoholic Beverages) [1813]
Main Street Produce Inc. (Food) [11759]
Santa Maria Tire Inc. (Automotive) [3188]

Santa Monica

A-Mark Financial Corp. (Metals) [19720]
A-Mark Precious Metals Inc. (Jewelry) [17299]
Bomaine Corp. (Household Items) [15423]
Citizen America Corp. (Computers and Software) [6071]
Consolidated Pet Foods Inc. (Food) [10818]
Harvey Titanium Ltd. (Metals) [20029]
HealthStyles, Inc. (Medical, Dental, and Optical Supplies) [19355]
McIntosh and Associates Inc.; Ron (Aeronautical Equipment and Supplies) [121]
Red Trolley Co. (Food) [12288]
SilverSource (Jewelry) [17607]
Symantec Corp. Peter Norton Products Div. (Computers and Software) [6780]
Warren Distributing Inc. (Automotive) [3401]
Westgate Enterprises Inc. (Electrical and Electronic Equipment and Supplies) [9578]

Santa Rosa

Bedrosians Tile & Marble (Floorcovering Equipment and Supplies) [9716]
Cal-North Auto Brokers Inc. (Automotive) [2408]
Grapevine (Food) [11309]
Martini and Prati Wines Inc. (Alcoholic Beverages) [1853]
Milk Products Holdings Inc. (Food) [11897]
Santa Rosa Bearing (Automotive) [3189]
Sequoia Floral International (Horticultural Supplies) [14948]
Western Dairy Products Inc. (Food) [12911]
Western Farm Center (Agricultural Equipment and Supplies) [1429]
Western Tile Santa Rosa, Inc. (Floorcovering Equipment and Supplies) [10296]

Santee

Coastal Supply Co., Inc. (Specialty Equipment and Products) [25604]
Peck-Polymers (Toys and Hobby Goods) [26610]
South Bay Foundry, Inc. (Metals) [20373]

Saratoga

Mitsui Comtek Corp. (Computers and Software) [6524]
See First Technology Inc. (Computers and Software) [6718]

Sausalito

Nokia Display Products Inc. (Communications Systems and Equipment) [5690]
Omnirax (Furniture and Fixtures) [13194]
Sausalito Craftworks (Jewelry) [17590]

Scotts Valley

JSB Software Technologies PLC (Computers and Software) [6412]
Threshold Enterprises Ltd. (Health and Beauty Aids) [14259]
Wescosa Inc. (Office Equipment and Supplies) [21353]

Sebastopol

International Medcom (Industrial Machinery) [16166]
Made in Nature Inc. (Food) [11754]
Natural Resources (Food) [11985]

Shafter

Biloff Manufacturing Co. Inc. (Heating and Cooling Equipment and Supplies) [14347]
Rush Company Inc.; J D (Metals) [20338]

Sherman Oaks

Fruit Growers Supply Co. (Agricultural Equipment and Supplies) [715]
HemaCare Corp. (Medical, Dental, and Optical Supplies) [19357]
Micronetics Inc. Information Management Systems (Computers and Software) [6505]
Sunkist Growers Inc. (Food) [12614]
Wilcher Associates (Books and Other Printed Materials) [4282]

Signal Hill

Office Depot Inc. Business Services Div. (Office Equipment and Supplies) [21174]
PBI Market Equipment Inc. (Industrial Machinery) [16385]
Sea Level Products International (Jewelry) [17593]

Simi Valley

G.I. Industries (Used, Scrap, and Recycled Materials) [26828]
Ginseng Co. (Health and Beauty Aids) [14112]
Pacific Coast One-Stop (Sound and Entertainment Equipment and Supplies) [25373]
SJA Industries Inc. (Household Appliances) [15314]

Solana Beach

International Periodical Distributors (Books and Other Printed Materials) [3849]

Sonoma

Buena Vista Winery Inc. (Alcoholic Beverages) [1559]
Westberg Manufacturing Inc. (Scientific and Measurement Devices) [24456]
Whole Herb Co. (Food) [12934]
World Products Inc. (Electrical and Electronic Equipment and Supplies) [9606]

Sonora

MRL Industries (Electrical and Electronic Equipment and Supplies) [9104]

Soulsbyville

Sierra Building Supply, Inc. (Construction Materials and Machinery) [8017]

South El Monte

Frejoth International Corp. (Metals) [19988]
Miss Elliette Inc. (Clothing) [5197]
Mom's Food Co. (Food) [11919]
Plastic Dress-Up Co. (Gifts and Novelties) [13423]

South Gate

City Sound (Sound and Entertainment Equipment and Supplies) [25139]
Fairway Salvage Inc. (Used, Scrap, and Recycled Materials) [26812]
Kustom Fit (Automotive) [2866]
Los Angeles Chemical Co. (Chemicals) [4442]
MacLeod Group (Used, Scrap, and Recycled Materials) [26891]
Pacific Fruit Processors Inc. (Food) [12090]
Royal Floor Mats (Floorcovering Equipment and Supplies) [10130]
Waymire Drum Company Inc. (Sound and Entertainment Equipment and Supplies) [25517]
Westside Distributors (Food) [12916]

South Lake Tahoe

Scotty's Hardware Inc. (Hardware) [13907]

South el Monte

Bearings and Drives Inc. (Industrial Supplies) [16734]
Coast Appliance Parts Co. (Household Appliances) [15087]
Industrial Pipe & Steel (Industrial Machinery) [16152]
Nissen and Company Inc. (Construction Materials and Machinery) [7781]
Normad Fastener Company Inc. (Hardware) [13849]
Valley Cities Supply Co. (Plumbing Materials and Fixtures) [23428]
Zacky Foods Co. (Food) [12999]

South Pasadena

Amende and Schultz (Food) [10394]
Real Sales; Paul A. (Sound and Entertainment Equipment and Supplies) [25410]
Surel International, Inc. (Electrical and Electronic Equipment and Supplies) [9447]

South San Francisco

Abel Carbonic Products Inc. (Chemicals) [4311]
Allied Electronics (Electrical and Electronic Equipment and Supplies) [8323]
BAI Inc. (Aeronautical Equipment and Supplies) [55]
Bedrosian Building Supply (Floorcovering Equipment and Supplies) [9700]
Brennan-Hamilton Co. (Industrial Machinery) [15844]
Chesapeake Shoe Co. of California (Shoes) [24711]
Claricom Inc. (Electrical and Electronic Equipment and Supplies) [8529]
Comet Micro Systems Inc. (Computers and Software) [6082]
Core-Mark International Inc. (Food) [10840]
Core-Mark International Inc. (Tobacco Products) [26280]
Corids & Son Inc.; Alex D. (Food) [10842]
Far East Restaurant Equipment Mfg. Co. (Restaurant and Commercial Foodservice Equipment and Supplies) [24114]
Fastlink Network Products (Computers and Software) [6265]
Golden State Flooring (Floorcovering Equipment and Supplies) [9923]
High Performance Distributors (Automotive) [2750]
JFC International Inc. (Food) [11554]
Lessco Products Inc. (Office Equipment and Supplies) [21106]
Liberty Gold Fruit Co. (Food) [11708]
Lion Notions Inc. (Textiles and Notions) [26125]
MPS Multimedia Inc. (Computers and Software) [6533]
Muzak (Sound and Entertainment Equipment and Supplies) [25350]
Olympian Oil Co. (Petroleum, Fuels, and Related Equipment) [22540]

Otagiri Mercantile Company Inc. (Household Items) [15604]
Peters-De Laet Inc. (Electrical and Electronic Equipment and Supplies) [9193]
Sanrio Inc. (Gifts and Novelties) [13442]
Saybeck Inc. (Petroleum, Fuels, and Related Equipment) [22654]
Sosnick and Son; J. (Food) [12530]
SSF Imported Auto Parts Inc. (Automotive) [3256]
Tarantino Company Inc.; Lee Ray (Food) [12698]
TOA Electronics, Inc. (Electrical and Electronic Equipment and Supplies) [9491]
Treadways Corp. (Automotive) [3332]
Wedemeyers Bakery (Food) [12893]
Yasutomo and Company Inc. (Paper and Paper Products) [22009]

Stanton

Fallah Enterprises (Gifts and Novelties) [13354]

Stockton

Albert Paper Co. (Paper and Paper Products) [21618]
Alpine Packing Co. (Food) [10383]
Bedrosian Tile Supply (Floorcovering Equipment and Supplies) [9706]
Brannon Tire Corp. (Automotive) [2382]
Castle of Stockton; A.L. (Agricultural Equipment and Supplies) [379]
Connell Motor Truck Company Inc. (Industrial Machinery) [15908]
Craig & Hamilton Meat Co. (Food) [10863]
CT Wholesale (Agricultural Equipment and Supplies) [480]
Dorfman-Pacific Company Inc. (Clothing) [4921]
Feralloy Corp./Western Div (Metals) [19972]
Frey, Inc. (Floorcovering Equipment and Supplies) [9907]
General Communications (Communications Systems and Equipment) [5618]
General Potato and Onion Inc. (Food) [11250]
Klein Brothers Ltd. (Livestock and Farm Products) [18036]
Meyer West (Agricultural Equipment and Supplies) [1022]
Nugget Distributors Inc. (Food) [12044]
Pacific Flooring Supply (Floorcovering Equipment and Supplies) [10097]
PDM Steel Service Centers Div. (Metals) [20267]
PrePeeled Potato Co. (Food) [12214]
Rays Beverage Co. (Alcoholic Beverages) [1979]
Reed Equipment Co. (Agricultural Equipment and Supplies) [1177]
Regal Steel Supply Inc. (Metals) [20311]
San Joaquin Beverage Co. (Alcoholic Beverages) [2006]
San Joaquin Lumber Co. (Construction Materials and Machinery) [7976]
Smart & Final Foodservice (Food) [12505]
Stockton Service Corp. (Petroleum, Fuels, and Related Equipment) [22708]
United Pharmaceutical & Medical Supply Co. (Medical, Dental, and Optical Equipment) [19092]
W.B.R. Inc. (Construction Materials and Machinery) [8199]

Studio City

Laurel Farms (Food) [11683]

Suisun City

NPA West Inc. (Computers and Software) [6563]
Servidio Beverage Distributing Co. (Alcoholic Beverages) [2020]
Stone and Son Inc.; E.B. (Agricultural Equipment and Supplies) [1296]

Sun City

Alumax Building Products (Metals) [19763]

Sun Valley

Bradley Landfill and Recycling Center (Used, Scrap, and Recycled Materials) [26770]
Flamemaster Corp. (Paints and Varnishes) [21442]
Hawker Pacific Inc. (Aeronautical Equipment and Supplies) [94]

Industrial Battery Engineering Inc. (Electrical and Electronic Equipment and Supplies) [8876]
Kitcor Corp. (Restaurant and Commercial Foodservice Equipment and Supplies) [24158]
KLH Research and Development Corp. (Household Appliances) [15191]
Maltby Company Inc. (Chemicals) [4449]
Sun Valley Paper Stock Inc. (Used, Scrap, and Recycled Materials) [27015]

Sunnyvale

Bay Area Data Supply Inc. (Office Equipment and Supplies) [20835]
Bay Microfilm Inc. (Sound and Entertainment Equipment and Supplies) [25098]
Bay Microfilm Inc. Library Microfilms (Office Equipment and Supplies) [20836]
Capcom Entertainment Inc. (Toys and Hobby Goods) [26436]
Chronomix Corp. (Scientific and Measurement Devices) [24339]
ECW Enterprises Inc. (Computers and Software) [6235]
ForeSight Electronics Inc. (Electrical and Electronic Equipment and Supplies) [8752]
Hardware Knowledge Group Inc. (Computers and Software) [6328]
Hughes Company Inc.; R.S. (Security and Safety Equipment) [24568]
Idec (Electrical and Electronic Equipment and Supplies) [8870]
Interconsal Associates Inc. (Chemicals) [4431]
Legend Computer Inc. (Computers and Software) [6437]
Marubeni Solutions USA, Corp. (Computers and Software) [6467]
Micro-Comp Industries Inc. (Electrical and Electronic Equipment and Supplies) [9073]
MindWorks Corp. (Computers and Software) [6520]
OKI Semiconductor (Electrical and Electronic Equipment and Supplies) [9153]
Peninsula Engineering Group Inc. (Communications Systems and Equipment) [5706]
Perisol Technology Inc. (Computers and Software) [6612]
Pine Cone Lumber Company Inc. (Construction Materials and Machinery) [7864]
PLX Technology Inc. (Electrical and Electronic Equipment and Supplies) [9214]
Purdy Electronics Corp. (Electrical and Electronic Equipment and Supplies) [9247]
Server Technology Inc. (Electrical and Electronic Equipment and Supplies) [9356]
Splash Technology Inc. (Office Equipment and Supplies) [21283]
Sunnyvale Lumber Inc. (Construction Materials and Machinery) [8088]
Technoland Inc. (Computers and Software) [6801]
Telesensory Corp. (Electrical and Electronic Equipment and Supplies) [9476]
Twinson Co. (Toys and Hobby Goods) [26696]
Wuite Traders International (Jewelry) [17663]
Zytronix Inc. (Computers and Software) [6892]

Sylmar

Allied Wholesale Inc. (Hardware) [13552]
Best Way Distributing Co. (Alcoholic Beverages) [1523]
JZ Allied International Holdings Inc. (Hardware) [13778]
Neithart Meats Inc. (Food) [11993]
OPTEX Morse, Inc. (Security and Safety Equipment) [24606]

Tehachapi

Electric Switches Inc. (Electrical and Electronic Equipment and Supplies) [8672]

Temecula

Miracle Playground Sales (Recreational and Sporting Goods) [23830]
Specialty Metals Industries (Metals) [20381]

Terminal Island

Hugo Neu-Proler Co. (Metals) [20046]

Thousand Oaks

FLEET Specialties Co. (Electrical and Electronic Equipment and Supplies) [8746]
Fleet Specialties Div. (Automotive) [2630]

Thousand Palms

Western Golf Inc. (Recreational and Sporting Goods) [24045]

Tiburon

Sweet Things Bakery (Food) [12658]

Torrance

Adams Supply Co. (Hardware) [13532]
Aisin World Corporation of America (Automotive) [2193]
Allied Electronics (Electrical and Electronic Equipment and Supplies) [8311]
Alpine Electronics of America Inc. (Sound and Entertainment Equipment and Supplies) [25065]
American Honda Motor Company Inc. (Motorized Vehicles) [20587]
American Honda Motor Co. Inc. Acura Div. (Motorized Vehicles) [20588]
Brentwood Medical Products Inc. (Medical, Dental, and Optical Supplies) [19198]
Celestron International (Photographic Equipment and Supplies) [22842]
Ceramic Tile Center Inc. (Floorcovering Equipment and Supplies) [9793]
Classic Components Corp. (Computers and Software) [6074]
Ferro Union Inc. (Metals) [19978]
Incorporated Business Interiors Inc. (Furniture and Fixtures) [13140]
Input Automation Inc. (Office Equipment and Supplies) [21060]
Kubota Tractor Corp. (Agricultural Equipment and Supplies) [921]
L.A. TRADE (Computers and Software) [6425]
Lexus Div. (Automotive) [2880]
Lyncole XIT Grounding (Electrical and Electronic Equipment and Supplies) [9011]
Main Line Equipment, Inc. (Electrical and Electronic Equipment and Supplies) [9022]
Nakamichi America Corp. (Sound and Entertainment Equipment and Supplies) [25352]
NovaQuest InfoSystems (Computers and Software) [6562]
Optex USA Inc. (Security and Safety Equipment) [24607]
Seika Machinery, Inc. (Industrial Machinery) [16481]
Shachihata Incorporated USA (Office Equipment and Supplies) [21266]
Sumitok America Inc. (Automotive) [3281]
Toyota Motor Sales U.S.A. Inc. (Motorized Vehicles) [20737]

Trabuco Canyon

Source Books (Books and Other Printed Materials) [4171]

Tracy

Atlantic-Pacific Technologies (Electrical and Electronic Equipment and Supplies) [8390]
Musco Olive Products Inc. (Food) [11960]
San Joaquin Valley Hay Growers Association (Agricultural Equipment and Supplies) [1232]

Tulare

Linder Equipment Co. (Agricultural Equipment and Supplies) [961]
Tulare Pipe and Electric Supply Co. (Electrical and Electronic Equipment and Supplies) [9516]

Tulelake

Kenyon Packing Co.; Lowell C. (Food) [11603]

Turlock

Garton Ford Tractor Inc. (Agricultural Equipment and Supplies) [727]
Service Supply (Food) [12462]

Tustin

Argus Buying Group (Clothing) [4781]
Brownell & Associates, Inc. (Hardware) [13607]
Compusol Inc. (Computers and Software) [6097]
Dennis and Schwab Inc. (Computers and Software) [6198]
International Business & Management Institute (Books and Other Printed Materials) [3847]
JOS Projection Systems Inc. (Office Equipment and Supplies) [21080]
PairGain Technologies Inc. (Electrical and Electronic Equipment and Supplies) [9175]
Toshiba America Medical Systems Inc. (Medical, Dental, and Optical Equipment) [19081]
Toshiba America Medical Systems Inc. (Medical, Dental, and Optical Supplies) [19658]

Ukiah

Pacini Wines (Alcoholic Beverages) [1939]

Union City

Amalco Metals Inc. (Metals) [19766]
Best Label Company Inc./IMS Div. (Industrial Machinery) [15821]
ICG (Computers and Software) [6350]
JATCO Inc. (Plastics) [22985]
Peachtree Fabrics Inc. (Textiles and Notions) [26171]

Universal City

Uni Distribution Co. (Sound and Entertainment Equipment and Supplies) [25489]
Uni Distribution Co. (Household Appliances) [15347]

Upland

Sam's Gourmet (Food) [12399]
Sashco Inc. (Construction Materials and Machinery) [7980]
Van Ness Water Gardens Inc. (Horticultural Supplies) [14968]

Valencia

AA Computech Inc. (Computers and Software) [5860]
Golden State Medical Supply Inc. (Medical, Dental, and Optical Supplies) [19341]
Kustom Tool Works Inc. (Industrial Machinery) [16224]
McClintock and Bustad Inc. (Heating and Cooling Equipment and Supplies) [14534]
Whitmor/Wirenetics (Electrical and Electronic Equipment and Supplies) [9586]
Whitmor/Wirenetics (Electrical and Electronic Equipment and Supplies) [9587]

Valley Center

International Decoratives Company Inc. (Horticultural Supplies) [14895]

Van Nuys

Alfred Publishing Company Inc. (Books and Other Printed Materials) [3488]
American Lock and Supply Company Inc. (Security and Safety Equipment) [24506]
ARS Electronics (Sound and Entertainment Equipment and Supplies) [25083]
Backstage Pass Productions and Distributing Inc. (Sound and Entertainment Equipment and Supplies) [25095]
Beyda & Associates, Inc. (Books and Other Printed Materials) [3553]
Blake Wire and Cable Corp. (Electrical and Electronic Equipment and Supplies) [8444]
Bubbles Baking Co. (Food) [10634]
Cellulite Products Inc. (Health and Beauty Aids) [14060]
Economy Office Furniture (Office Equipment and Supplies) [20980]
Electro Rent Corp. Data Rentals/Sales Div. (Electrical and Electronic Equipment and Supplies) [8686]
En Garde Health Products Inc. (Health and Beauty Aids) [14095]

Exxersource (Recreational and Sporting Goods) [23660]
Familian Pipe and Supply (Plumbing Materials and Fixtures) [23159]
Front Musical Literature; Theodore (Books and Other Printed Materials) [3767]
Holga Inc. (Office Equipment and Supplies) [21038]
Kitsinian Jewelers (Jewelry) [17492]
LIVE Entertainment Inc. (Sound and Entertainment Equipment and Supplies) [25286]
Matz Paper Company, Inc. (Paper and Paper Products) [21825]
Moorhead and Company Inc. (Food) [11933]
Moorhead and Company Inc. (Chemicals) [4462]
National Electro Sales Corp. (Electrical and Electronic Equipment and Supplies) [9115]
Nikzak (Automotive) [3033]
Old Masters Products Inc. (Floorcovering Equipment and Supplies) [10086]
Ordway Sign Supply (Specialty Equipment and Products) [25775]
Performance Products (Automotive) [3091]
ProMark (Electrical and Electronic Equipment and Supplies) [9242]
Siroflex of America Inc. (Plumbing Materials and Fixtures) [23378]
Sunkist Growers Inc. (Food) [12615]
Trans-Cal Industries Inc. (Specialty Equipment and Products) [25847]
Trax Distributors (Sound and Entertainment Equipment and Supplies) [25483]
Warnaco Inc. (Clothing) [5473]

Venice
General Medical Publishers (Books and Other Printed Materials) [3776]
Pioneer French Baking Company Inc. (Food) [12172]

Ventura
Allied Distributing (Alcoholic Beverages) [1480]
Biopool International Inc. (Medical, Dental, and Optical Equipment) [18714]
Buena Tile Supply, Inc. (Floorcovering Equipment and Supplies) [9745]
California Electric Supply (Electrical and Electronic Equipment and Supplies) [8485]
Consolidated Electrical Distributors Inc. (Electrical and Electronic Equipment and Supplies) [8570]
Gospel Light Publications (Books and Other Printed Materials) [3789]
Gospel Light Publications (Books and Other Printed Materials) [3790]
Lagomarsino's Inc. (Alcoholic Beverages) [1810]

Vernon
Albert's Organics Inc. (Food) [10359]
Angus-Campbell Inc. (Plastics) [22927]
BCVG Inc. (Clothing) [4810]
Continental Commodities L.P. (Food) [10827]
Ernest Paper Products (Paper and Paper Products) [21724]
Glen Rose Meat Services Inc. (Food) [11269]
Goldberg and Solovy Food Inc. (Food) [11281]
International Baking Co. (Food) [11519]
KasLen Textiles (Textiles and Notions) [26089]
Los Angeles Carton Co. (Paper and Paper Products) [21813]
Maas-Hansen Steel Corp. (Metals) [20140]
Norman, Fox & Co. (Chemicals) [4470]
Pacific Southwest Sales Company Inc. (Electrical and Electronic Equipment and Supplies) [9172]
Trade Supplies (Paper and Paper Products) [21955]

Victorville
Flannery Co. (Books and Other Printed Materials) [3752]
H. and E. Brothers Inc. (Hardware) [13730]

VilLa Park
Multi-Grow Investments Inc. (Horticultural Supplies) [14925]
Percura Inc. (Plastics) [23005]

Vinton
Fabel Inc.; Robert A. (Agricultural Equipment and Supplies) [559]

Visalia
Bedrosian Tile Supply (Floorcovering Equipment and Supplies) [9707]
Life Unlimited (Books and Other Printed Materials) [3913]

Vista
Bio Medical Life Systems Inc. (Medical, Dental, and Optical Equipment) [18710]
Brain Teaser Money Machines (Specialty Equipment and Products) [25580]
Cade Grayson Co. (Food) [10659]
Eagle Creek (Luggage and Leather Goods) [18390]
Kiss International (Specialty Equipment and Products) [25702]
Lee-Mar Aquarium and Pet Supplies, Inc. (Veterinary Products) [27179]
Webb Foods Inc.; Joseph (Food) [12891]

Volcano
Volcano Press, Inc. (Books and Other Printed Materials) [4262]
Volcano Press Inc. (Books and Other Printed Materials) [4263]

Walnut
CWC Group Inc. (Computers and Software) [6174]
Ocean Interface Company Inc. (Computers and Software) [6567]
SunRace Technology (USA) Corp. (Computers and Software) [6775]
SYSCO Food Services Los Angeles Inc. (Food) [12683]
Titus and Sons Inc.; F.D. (Medical, Dental, and Optical Supplies) [19655]
Trinet Industries Inc. (Industrial Machinery) [16582]

Walnut Creek
Alpha Fine Computer Furniture (Furniture and Fixtures) [13015]
Calpine Containers Inc. (Storage Equipment and Containers) [25897]
Extex Co. (Recreational and Sporting Goods) [23659]
Glencourt Inc. (Food) [11270]
Imperial Wax and Chemical Company Inc. (Recreational and Sporting Goods) [23741]
Integral Systems Inc. (Computers and Software) [6378]
Keyston Brothers (Textiles and Notions) [26104]
Keyston Brothers (Textiles and Notions) [26109]
Taylor-Made Office Systems Inc. (Office Equipment and Supplies) [21316]

Watsonville
Bassi Distributing Co.; George (Storage Equipment and Containers) [25890]
Coastal Berry Company (Food) [10782]
Cornerstone Propane G.P. Inc. (Petroleum, Fuels, and Related Equipment) [22171]
Cornerstone Propane Partners L.P. (Petroleum, Fuels, and Related Equipment) [22172]
Granite Rock Co. (Construction Materials and Machinery) [7412]
Lease Wholesale Plumbing Supply; A.L. (Plumbing Materials and Fixtures) [23243]
Naturipe Berry Growers (Food) [11988]
Port Supply (Marine) [18584]
Superior Foods (Food) [12639]
Valley Packing Service (Food) [12820]

Weaverville
Florida Craft Wholesale (Toys and Hobby Goods) [26484]

West Covina
Chubbuck Sales Inc. (Hardware) [13633]
Hanson Aggregates West, Inc. (Construction Materials and Machinery) [7440]
Wesco Auto Parts (Automotive) [3408]

West Hollywood
Pacific Design Center (Furniture and Fixtures) [13199]
Richard The Thread (Textiles and Notions) [26185]
Two Left Feet (Shoes) [24879]

West Los Angeles
West L.A. Music (Sound and Entertainment Equipment and Supplies) [25521]

West Sacramento
American Metals Corp. (Metals) [19770]
Capital Coors Co. (Alcoholic Beverages) [1571]
Cen-Cal Wallboard Supply Co. (Construction Materials and Machinery) [7157]
Fredericksen Tank Lines (Petroleum, Fuels, and Related Equipment) [22293]
JC Produce Inc. (Food) [11551]
McWong International Inc.; M.W. (Electrical and Electronic Equipment and Supplies) [9061]
Medallion Carpets (Floorcovering Equipment and Supplies) [10019]
Miles Treaster and Associates (Furniture and Fixtures) [13180]
Nor-Cal Beverage Company Inc. (Food) [12015]
Nor-Cal Produce Inc. (Food) [12016]
Northern California Beverage Company Inc. (Soft Drinks) [24998]
Pacific Fluids Systems Inc. (Industrial Machinery) [16374]
River City Petroleum Inc. (Petroleum, Fuels, and Related Equipment) [22632]
Tony's Fine Foods (Food) [12731]

Westlake Village
Ball Pipe & Supply; Leif (Plumbing Materials and Fixtures) [23076]
Cadillac Motor Car (Automotive) [2407]
Consolidated Electrical Distributors Inc. (Electrical and Electronic Equipment and Supplies) [8571]
Diodes Inc. (Electrical and Electronic Equipment and Supplies) [8627]
Exxon Company U.S.A. Santa Ynez Unit (Petroleum, Fuels, and Related Equipment) [22246]
FTC Corp. (Automotive) [2654]
K-Swiss Inc. (Recreational and Sporting Goods) [23767]
Pacific Intertrade Corporation (Household Appliances) [15262]

Westminster
Blue White Industries Limited Inc. (Scientific and Measurement Devices) [24324]
Turbex Heat Transfer Corp. (Heating and Cooling Equipment and Supplies) [14740]

Whitethorn
Holmgangers Press (Books and Other Printed Materials) [3831]

Whittier
American Business Service and Computer Technologies Inc. (Computers and Software) [5921]
Bassett Co.; Russ (Furniture and Fixtures) [13033]
Delta Technical Coatings Inc. (Toys and Hobby Goods) [26464]
Metalmart Inc. (Metals) [20174]
Omega Refrigerant Reclamation Corp. (Specialty Equipment and Products) [25773]
Peck Road Ford Truck Sales Inc. (Motorized Vehicles) [20703]
Rutland Tool and Supply Company Inc. (Industrial Machinery) [16465]
United Fastener and Supply Co. (Hardware) [13972]
Vitali Import Company Inc. (Sound and Entertainment Equipment and Supplies) [25510]

Willits
Microphor (Plumbing Materials and Fixtures) [23264]

Wilmington

Coordinated Equipment Co. (Industrial Machinery) [15915]
Llewellyn Supply (Marine) [18549]
Pacific Fibre and Rope Company Inc. (Industrial Supplies) [17095]
Pasha Group Co. (Automotive) [3086]
Potential Industries Inc. (Used, Scrap, and Recycled Materials) [26944]

Winters

Tufts Ranch Packing Shed (Food) [12767]

Wofford Heights

Mitchell-Hughes Co. (Industrial Machinery) [16309]

Woodland

Adams Group Inc. (Livestock and Farm Products) [17675]
Cal-West Seeds Inc. (Agricultural Equipment and Supplies) [358]
Cranston International Inc. (Agricultural Equipment and Supplies) [470]
Hoover Tractor and Engine Co. (Agricultural Equipment and Supplies) [836]
Marie's Quality Foods (Food) [11780]
McCormick Beverage Co. (Alcoholic Beverages) [1859]
Pacific Grain Products, Inc. (Food) [12091]
Rice Growers Association of California (Food) [12308]
Santoni and Co.; V. (Alcoholic Beverages) [2007]
Valley Media Inc. (Sound and Entertainment Equipment and Supplies) [25496]

Woodland Hills

Applause Enterprises Inc. (Toys and Hobby Goods) [26394]
Applause, Inc. (Toys and Hobby Goods) [26395]
Creative Specialties Inc. (Household Items) [15463]
Dakin Inc. (Toys and Hobby Goods) [26460]
El Camino Resources International Inc. (Computers and Software) [6240]
Weider Health and Fitness Inc. (Health and Beauty Aids) [14278]
Western Purifier Water Purifier Co. (Plumbing Materials and Fixtures) [23453]

Yorba Linda

Stouffer Foods Corp. (Food) [12591]
Vlcek Corp.; Jerry K. (Industrial Machinery) [16604]
White Brothers Inc. (Automotive) [3424]

Yreka

Ozotech, Inc. (Specialty Equipment and Products) [25779]

Yuba City

California Industrial Rubber Co. (Rubber) [24272]
LRP Enterprises (Health and Beauty Aids) [14154]
LRP Enterprises (Restaurant and Commercial Foodservice Equipment and Supplies) [24169]
Sunsweet Growers Inc. (Food) [12622]
Western Depot (Toys and Hobby Goods) [26709]

Colorado

Amherst

Amherst Cooperative Elevator Inc. (Livestock and Farm Products) [17697]

Arvada

Barber-Nichols Inc. (Electrical and Electronic Equipment and Supplies) [8415]
Barone Inc. (Industrial Machinery) [15801]
C.B. Electronic Marketing (Electrical and Electronic Equipment and Supplies) [8511]
Computer Equipment Warehouse Inc. (Computers and Software) [6111]
Easter-Owens Electric Co (Electrical and Electronic Equipment and Supplies) [8645]

Electro Media of Colorado (Electrical and Electronic Equipment and Supplies) [8685]
Electronics Discount World (Computers and Software) [6244]
Farm Fresh Inc. (Food) [11086]
Hi Country Wire and Telephone Ltd. (Communications Systems and Equipment) [5635]
Mark VII Equipment Inc. (Restaurant and Commercial Foodservice Equipment and Supplies) [24177]
Sundstrand Fluid Handling Corp. (Industrial Machinery) [16538]

Aspen

Sport Obermeyer Ltd. (Recreational and Sporting Goods) [23975]

Aurora

Advertising Products Company Inc. (Gifts and Novelties) [13294]
Beverage Distributors Co. (Alcoholic Beverages) [1527]
Bibliographical Center for Research Inc. (Computers and Software) [6015]
Bowline Family Products Inc. (Storage Equipment and Containers) [25895]
Core-Mark International Inc. Core-Mark International Incorporated Div. (Food) [10841]
Flite Service (Food) [11160]
Goodyear Tire Rubber Co. (Industrial Supplies) [16901]
Hallogram Publishing (Computers and Software) [6325]
K & S Tole & Craft Supply (Office Equipment and Supplies) [21083]
Maximum Performance (Computers and Software) [6472]
Micro K Systems Inc. (Computers and Software) [6493]
Mid-America Export Inc. (Household Items) [15588]
Midwest Beverage Company Inc. (Alcoholic Beverages) [1876]
Oreck Floorcare Center (Specialty Equipment and Products) [25776]
Performance-Plus Distributing (Sound and Entertainment Equipment and Supplies) [25378]
Pinnacle Distributing Co. (Alcoholic Beverages) [1959]
Rainbow Natural Foods (Food) [12269]
Roth Distributing Co. (Household Appliances) [15295]
Super Valu Stores Inc. (Food) [12631]
Taskforce Batteries (Photographic Equipment and Supplies) [22910]
Tile For Less (Floorcovering Equipment and Supplies) [10235]
Wireless Telecom Inc. (Computers and Software) [6873]

Berthoud

Dawdys Inc. (Sound and Entertainment Equipment and Supplies) [25160]

Boulder

Access Graphics (Computers and Software) [5865]
Access Graphics Technology Inc. (Computers and Software) [5866]
Advanced Research Instruments Corp. (Scientific and Measurement Devices) [24307]
Air Comm Corp. (Aeronautical Equipment and Supplies) [33]
Allegro Coffee Co. (Food) [10369]
American Educational Products Inc. (Toys and Hobby Goods) [26387]
American Environmental Systems Inc. (Plumbing Materials and Fixtures) [23062]
Amrion Inc. (Health and Beauty Aids) [14021]
Anatel Corp. (Industrial Machinery) [15772]
Ayre Acoustics Inc. (Household Appliances) [15043]
Business Express of Boulder Inc. (Office Equipment and Supplies) [20867]
Chimera Co (Photographic Equipment and Supplies) [22845]

Churchich Recreation (Recreational and Sporting Goods) [23593]
D & L Stained Glass Supply, Inc. (Specialty Equipment and Products) [25619]
EcoCycle Inc. (Paper and Paper Products) [21718]
Hirsh Precision Products Inc. (Automotive) [2755]
Imge Guided Technologies, Inc. (Computers and Software) [6357]
Inovonics Co (Electrical and Electronic Equipment and Supplies) [8882]
Johnson Books (Books and Other Printed Materials) [3866]
McBax Ltd. (Petroleum, Fuels, and Related Equipment) [22462]
Morris Environmental T-Shirts; Jim (Clothing) [5206]
Paladin Press (Books and Other Printed Materials) [4036]
Particle Measuring Systems Inc. (Scientific and Measurement Devices) [24415]
Restaurant Design & Development (Heating and Cooling Equipment and Supplies) [14662]
Rudis Bakery (Food) [12366]
Satellite Information Systems Co. (Computers and Software) [6705]
Spyder Active Sports Inc. (Clothing) [5390]
Tactilitics Inc. (Medical, Dental, and Optical Supplies) [19647]
Taft Development Group (Computers and Software) [6787]
Tek-Gear LLC (Computers and Software) [6804]
Timberline Instruments Inc. (Scientific and Measurement Devices) [24447]
Turtle Island Herbs Inc. (Plumbing Materials and Fixtures) [23419]
Westview Press (Books and Other Printed Materials) [4279]
Wildwasser Sport U.S.A. Inc. (Marine) [18640]

Brighton

American Pride Coop (Agricultural Equipment and Supplies) [234]
Greenleaf Wholesale Florists (Horticultural Supplies) [14880]
Maxwell Microsystems Inc. (Computers and Software) [6473]

Broomfield

Ballpark Inc. (Toys and Hobby Goods) [26412]
Barber's Poultry Inc. (Food) [10505]
Bestop Inc. (Automotive) [2355]
Bio-Medical Resources Inc. (Medical, Dental, and Optical Equipment) [18711]
Call Management Products Inc. (Electrical and Electronic Equipment and Supplies) [8487]
Corporate Express Inc. (Office Equipment and Supplies) [20929]
Custom Design and Manufacturing (Electrical and Electronic Equipment and Supplies) [8600]
Knudson Manufacturing Inc. (Industrial Machinery) [16211]
McDATA Corp. (Computers and Software) [6476]

Colorado Springs

Alphatronics Engineering Corp. (Industrial Machinery) [15761]
Altura PC Systems Inc. (Computers and Software) [5918]
American Convenience Inc. (Security and Safety Equipment) [24505]
Book Home, Inc. (Books and Other Printed Materials) [3570]
Brookharts Inc. (Construction Materials and Machinery) [7084]
Chemins Company Inc. (Medical, Dental, and Optical Supplies) [19228]
Cook Communications Ministries (Books and Other Printed Materials) [3658]
Envirotechnology Inc. (Specialty Equipment and Products) [25644]
Fitness Systems Inc. (Recreational and Sporting Goods) [23674]
High Country Sales Inc. (Alcoholic Beverages) [1753]
Johnstone Supply (Heating and Cooling Equipment and Supplies) [14503]

Laser Magnetic Storage International Co. (Office Equipment and Supplies) [21102]

Maytag Aircraft Corp. (Petroleum, Fuels, and Related Equipment) [22460]

Meadow Gold Dairy (Food) [11842]

Meriwether Publishing, Ltd. (Books and Other Printed Materials) [3948]

Moccasin Tipi (Shoes) [24813]

Motor Parts and Supply Inc. (Automotive) [2995]

Mountain Aire Medical Equipment (Medical, Dental, and Optical Equipment) [18949]

Mountain States Pipe and Supply Co. (Plumbing Materials and Fixtures) [23279]

Natural Meat Specialties (Food) [11983]

NavPress (Books and Other Printed Materials) [3988]

Pikes Peak Greenhouses, Inc. (Horticultural Supplies) [14942]

PROFITsystems Inc. (Computers and Software) [6651]

Quality Monitor Systems (Medical, Dental, and Optical Equipment) [19002]

Rosing; William (Clothing) [5321]

Shaw Publishers; Harold (Books and Other Printed Materials) [4157]

Sinton Dairy Foods Co. Inc. (Food) [12496]

Spectranetics Corp. (Medical, Dental, and Optical Supplies) [19631]

Tranex Inc. (Electrical and Electronic Equipment and Supplies) [9499]

Transit Mix Concrete Co. (Construction Materials and Machinery) [8142]

Transit Mix Concrete Co. (Metals) [20438]

Water Source USA (Chemicals) [4550]

Western Scrap Processing Co. (Used, Scrap, and Recycled Materials) [27044]

Yamato Corp. (Scientific and Measurement Devices) [24459]

Commerce City

Cummins Rocky Mountain, Inc. (Automotive) [2514]

Faris Machinery Co. (Construction Materials and Machinery) [7331]

Foothills Mill & Supply Inc. (Construction Materials and Machinery) [7354]

Frontier Truck Equipment and Parts Co. (Automotive) [2653]

Mountain Sales & Service Inc. (Heating and Cooling Equipment and Supplies) [14612]

Rocky Mountain Lasers and Instruments Inc. (Scientific and Measurement Devices) [24423]

Rocky Mountain Recycling (Used, Scrap, and Recycled Materials) [26964]

Steel Inc. (Metals) [20395]

Delta

Delta Veterinary Clinic (Veterinary Products) [27115]

Denver

AAA-Four Aces (Toys and Hobby Goods) [26378]

Accent Books (Books and Other Printed Materials) [3464]

Advance Telecommunication Inc. (Communications Systems and Equipment) [5502]

AER Inc. (Automotive) [2185]

AIA Plastics Inc. (Plastics) [22920]

A.L. Investors Inc. (Gifts and Novelties) [13297]

Alfreda's Film Works c/o Continnuus (Books and Other Printed Materials) [3489]

All Seas Exporting Inc. (Computers and Software) [5903]

Allied Building Products Corp. (Construction Materials and Machinery) [6940]

Allyn International Corp. (Household Appliances) [15004]

Applied Information Solutions Inc. (Computers and Software) [5951]

Aquafilter Corp. (Tobacco Products) [26260]

Arkansas Valley Seed Co. (Agricultural Equipment and Supplies) [254]

Atlas Metal and Iron Corp. (Metals) [19790]

Auto-trol Technology Corp. (Computers and Software) [5985]

Barrett Company Inc.; L.W. (Gifts and Novelties) [13311]

Baum Wine Imports Inc. (Alcoholic Beverages) [1506]

Beam of Denver Inc. (Household Appliances) [15046]

Bear Valley Communications Inc. (Communications Systems and Equipment) [5526]

Bedrosians Tile & Marble (Floorcovering Equipment and Supplies) [9717]

Benson Pump Co. (Recreational and Sporting Goods) [23545]

The Bingo Company Inc. (Toys and Hobby Goods) [26418]

Bio-Tech Maintenance Products (Recreational and Sporting Goods) [23559]

Bion Environmental Technologies Inc. (Plumbing Materials and Fixtures) [23087]

Boyd Distributing Co. Inc. (Household Appliances) [15056]

Bradford Publishing Co. (Books and Other Printed Materials) [3587]

Bremner Biscuit Co. (Food) [10612]

Business Interiors Inc. (Denver, Colorado) (Furniture and Fixtures) [13056]

Butler Paper Co. (Paper and Paper Products) [21662]

Can Land Recycling Center Inc. (Used, Scrap, and Recycled Materials) [26776]

Car-Go Battery Co. (Automotive) [2421]

Cashway Electrical Supply Co. (Electrical and Electronic Equipment and Supplies) [8507]

Cashway Pet Supply (Veterinary Products) [27103]

Centennial Bolt Inc. (Hardware) [13625]

Central Motive Power Inc. (Petroleum, Fuels, and Related Equipment) [22125]

Chapin's Supreme Foods (Food) [10734]

Checkmate International (Toys and Hobby Goods) [26442]

Chem-Real Investment Corp. (Agricultural Equipment and Supplies) [409]

Chemical Sales Company Inc. (Chemicals) [4355]

Coleman Natural Products Inc. (Food) [10788]

Colorado Clarklift Inc. (Industrial Machinery) [15898]

Colorado Kenworth Inc. (Motorized Vehicles) [20613]

Colorado Potato Growers Exchange (Food) [10794]

Colorado Serum Co. (Medical, Dental, and Optical Supplies) [19240]

Colorado Wire and Cable Company Inc. (Electrical and Electronic Equipment and Supplies) [8547]

Conserve-A-Watt Lighting Inc. (Electrical and Electronic Equipment and Supplies) [8561]

Contact Optical Center Inc. (Medical, Dental, and Optical Supplies) [19247]

Continental Sales Co. (Medical, Dental, and Optical Supplies) [19249]

Continnuus (Books and Other Printed Materials) [3657]

Contractors Heating and Supply Co. (Hardware) [13645]

Cook's Mart Ltd. (Household Items) [15454]

Copy Sales Inc. (Office Equipment and Supplies) [20918]

CPS Distributors Inc. (Industrial Machinery) [15916]

Curtis Fluid Controls, Inc. (Industrial Supplies) [16817]

Dana Kepner Co. (Plumbing Materials and Fixtures) [23132]

Darant Distribution (Plastics) [22952]

Dencor Energy Cost Controls Inc. (Electrical and Electronic Equipment and Supplies) [8623]

Dental Enterprises Inc. (Medical, Dental, and Optical Equipment) [18770]

Denver Air Machinery Co. (Industrial Machinery) [15940]

Denver Business Journal Inc. (Books and Other Printed Materials) [3686]

Denver Hardware Co. (Hardware) [13662]

Denver Hardware Co. (Hardware) [13663]

Denver Hardwood Co. (Floorcovering Equipment and Supplies) [9855]

Denver Merchandise Mart (Jewelry) [17391]

Denver Waste Materials Inc. (Clothing) [4913]

Denver Wholesale Florists (Horticultural Supplies) [14855]

Desks Inc. (Denver, Colorado) (Furniture and Fixtures) [13090]

Diamond Vogel Inc. (Paints and Varnishes) [21430]

Drive Train Industries Inc. (Automotive) [2563]

Du-Wald Steel Corp. (Metals) [19936]

Duffens Optical (Medical, Dental, and Optical Supplies) [19294]

Duke Energy Field Services Inc. (Petroleum, Fuels, and Related Equipment) [22212]

Dumans Custom Tailor Inc. (Clothing) [4924]

Eagle Claw Fishing Tackle (Recreational and Sporting Goods) [23639]

Empire Staple Co. (Hardware) [13684]

Engine & Performance Warehouse Inc. (Automotive) [2590]

Federal Fruit and Produce Co. (Food) [11113]

Feed Products Inc. (Agricultural Equipment and Supplies) [676]

Financial Commercial Security (Security and Safety Equipment) [24539]

FMH Material Handling Solutions, Inc. (Industrial Machinery) [16025]

Fones West (Communications Systems and Equipment) [5615]

Fowler and Peth Inc. (Construction Materials and Machinery) [7365]

General Air Service and Supply Company Inc. (Industrial Machinery) [16052]

Gold Bug (Clothing) [4992]

Hammond Candy Co (Food) [11368]

Hatch Grinding Co. (Automotive) [2730]

Hercules Industries (Metals) [20034]

Hermes Consolidated Inc. (Petroleum, Fuels, and Related Equipment) [22348]

HIA Inc. (Agricultural Equipment and Supplies) [820]

Hoeckel Co.; C.F. (Office Equipment and Supplies) [21035]

IKO Notions (Textiles and Notions) [26071]

Ingram Entertainment Inc. (Sound and Entertainment Equipment and Supplies) [25248]

Installation Telephone Services Inc. (Communications Systems and Equipment) [5646]

Intermountain Wholesale Hardware Inc. (Motorized Vehicles) [20653]

Iron and Metals Inc. (Used, Scrap, and Recycled Materials) [26855]

JHB International Inc. (Textiles and Notions) [26081]

Kamen Supply Company Inc. (Plumbing Materials and Fixtures) [23226]

Kelley-Clarke (Food) [11594]

Keyston Brothers (Textiles and Notions) [26105]

Kwal-Howells Inc. (Paints and Varnishes) [21480]

Larson Distributing Company Inc. (Floorcovering Equipment and Supplies) [9991]

Ledo-Dionysus (Alcoholic Beverages) [1816]

Levy Inc.; Frank (Clothing) [5133]

Lewan and Associates Inc. (Office Equipment and Supplies) [21107]

Manna Pro Corp. Denver Div. (Agricultural Equipment and Supplies) [984]

Marco Polo Import & Export (Clothing) [5162]

Mark-It of Colorado LLC (Recreational and Sporting Goods) [23800]

Masbeirn Corp. (Medical, Dental, and Optical Supplies) [19424]

Maverick Ranch Lite Beef Inc. (Food) [11810]

McMillan Sales Corp. (Plumbing Materials and Fixtures) [23258]

MDG Inc. (Restaurant and Commercial Foodservice Equipment and Supplies) [24182]

Medical Specialists Company Inc. (Medical, Dental, and Optical Equipment) [18923]

Medical Specialists Company Inc. (Medical, Dental, and Optical Supplies) [19446]

Microtech-Tel Inc. (Communications Systems and Equipment) [5675]

Midwest Chemical and Supply Inc. (Cleaning and Janitorial Supplies) [4670]

Mile Hi Frozen Food Co. (Food) [11895]

Mile High Equipment Co. (Restaurant and Commercial Foodservice Equipment and Supplies) [24186]
Modec Inc. (Industrial Machinery) [16316]
Mountain West Printing and Publishing Ltd. (Books and Other Printed Materials) [3972]
Multifoods Specialty Distribution (Food) [11957]
Navajo Manufacturing Co. (Jewelry) [17531]
Nobel/Sysco Food Services Co. (Food) [12011]
O'Donnell Co. Inc.; Roy J. (Household Appliances) [15257]
OfficeScapes & Scott Rice (Office Equipment and Supplies) [21193]
On-Gard Systems Inc. (Medical, Dental, and Optical Equipment) [18968]
Pacific Mountain Book Associates (Books and Other Printed Materials) [4032]
Paris Tire City of Montbello Inc.; Jim (Automotive) [3079]
Pasch Optical Lab (Medical, Dental, and Optical Supplies) [19528]
The Pawley Co. (Textiles and Notions) [26169]
Pepsi-Cola Bottling Company of Denver (Soft Drinks) [25007]
Pioneer Steel and Tube Distributors (Metals) [20282]
Pipe Valve and Fitting Co. (Industrial Supplies) [17106]
PlastiCom Industries Inc. (Electrical and Electronic Equipment and Supplies) [9211]
Porta-Lung Inc. (Heating and Cooling Equipment and Supplies) [14641]
Power Motive Corp. (Motorized Vehicles) [20708]
R and S Steel Co. (Metals) [20306]
Ralston Purina/Pet Products (Food) [12271]
Raycomm Telecommunications Inc. (Communications Systems and Equipment) [5735]
Rehab Technology of Colorado (Medical, Dental, and Optical Supplies) [19577]
Renner & Associates; E.J. (Construction Materials and Machinery) [7916]
Republic Automotive (Automotive) [3149]
Rio Grande Co. (Construction Materials and Machinery) [7936]
Rio Grande Trading Co. (Health and Beauty Aids) [14220]
RKR Corp. (Industrial Supplies) [17139]
Robinson Brick Co. (Construction Materials and Machinery) [7944]
Rockmount Ranch Wear Manufacturing Co. (Clothing) [5318]
Rocky Mountain Conveyor and Equipment (Industrial Machinery) [16457]
Rocky Mountain Marketing Services Inc. (Food) [12339]
Rocky Mountain Natural Meats Inc. (Food) [12340]
Rosemont Pharmaceutical Corp. (Medical, Dental, and Optical Supplies) [19587]
Royal Products Corp. (Toys and Hobby Goods) [26639]
Royal Publications, Inc. (Books and Other Printed Materials) [4126]
Ryall Electric Supply Co. (Electrical and Electronic Equipment and Supplies) [9327]
Safesport Manufacturing Co. (Recreational and Sporting Goods) [23928]
Seattle Fish Co. (Food) [12453]
Siegel Oil Co. (Petroleum, Fuels, and Related Equipment) [22671]
Sound Marketing Concepts (Electrical and Electronic Equipment and Supplies) [9383]
Source Management Inc. (Office Equipment and Supplies) [21274]
Spitzer Electrical Co. (Automotive) [3252]
Steam Way International Inc. (Restaurant and Commercial Foodservice Equipment and Supplies) [24227]
Stokes Canning Co. (Food) [12586]
Tele-Vue Service Company Inc. (Computers and Software) [6808]
Texaco Trading and Transportation Inc. (Petroleum, Fuels, and Related Equipment) [22731]
Train Center Distributors (Toys and Hobby Goods) [26688]
TransLogic Corp. (Industrial Machinery) [16575]

Trinidad-Benham Corp. (Livestock and Farm Products) [18293]
Union Bearing & Transmission (Automotive) [3361]
Unisource Worldwide Inc. Denver Div. (Paper and Paper Products) [21971]
United Notions (Textiles and Notions) [26235]
United States Exploration Inc. (Petroleum, Fuels, and Related Equipment) [22763]
Vancol Industries Inc. (Food) [12826]
Vendor Supply of America Inc. (Food) [12836]
Walker Component Group (Electrical and Electronic Equipment and Supplies) [9552]
Watson Company, Inc.; O.J. (Automotive) [3403]
The Wermers Co. (Clothing) [5479]
Wesco Fabrics Inc. (Household Items) [15705]
Western Distributing Co. (Alcoholic Beverages) [2114]
Western Export Services, Inc. (Food) [12913]
Western Trading Post Inc. (Toys and Hobby Goods) [26712]
Western United Electric Supply Corp. (Electrical and Electronic Equipment and Supplies) [9577]
Wildflower Jewelry (Jewelry) [17656]
Wilfley and Sons Inc.; A.R. (Industrial Machinery) [16633]
xpedx West Region (Paper and Paper Products) [22008]
Zuni Investment Co. (Petroleum, Fuels, and Related Equipment) [22821]

Dolores

Mountain Sun Organic Juices (Food) [11948]

Dove Creek

Midland Bean Co. (Livestock and Farm Products) [18094]

Durango

A & L Coors Inc. (Alcoholic Beverages) [1473]
Burnett Construction Co. (Construction Materials and Machinery) [7110]
Fiji Wear Inc. (Clothing) [4951]
Flexible Feat Sandals (Shoes) [24745]
Flexible Feat Sandals (Clothing) [4958]
Throttle Up Corp. (Electrical and Electronic Equipment and Supplies) [9488]

Eagle

Genesis Technologies Inc. (Household Appliances) [15147]

Eaton

Agland Inc. (Agricultural Equipment and Supplies) [209]

Eldorado Springs

Eldorado Artesian Springs Inc. (Soft Drinks) [24955]
Eldorado Artesian Springs Inc. (Food) [11039]

Englewood

A C Systems (Computers and Software) [5857]
Altitude Wholesale Co. Inc. (Food) [10387]
Altitude Wholesale Company Inc. (Food) [10388]
Balco Metals Inc. Recycling World (Metals) [19799]
CBLX Holdings Inc. (Sound and Entertainment Equipment and Supplies) [25129]
Communications Products and Services Inc. (Electrical and Electronic Equipment and Supplies) [8552]
Continental Sports Supply Inc. (Recreational and Sporting Goods) [23604]
CREOS. Technologies LLC (Electrical and Electronic Equipment and Supplies) [8586]
Fireplace Industries Inc. (Heating and Cooling Equipment and Supplies) [14447]
Hotsy Corp. (Plumbing Materials and Fixtures) [23213]
HP Marketing Co. (Sound and Entertainment Equipment and Supplies) [25240]
InaCom Information Systems (Computers and Software) [6361]
Integrated Medical Inc. (Medical, Dental, and Optical Supplies) [19373]

Katy Industries Inc. (Electrical and Electronic Equipment and Supplies) [8931]
KCG Communications Inc. (Communications Systems and Equipment) [5658]
Medical Dynamics Inc. (Medical, Dental, and Optical Supplies) [19443]
Mega Hertz (Sound and Entertainment Equipment and Supplies) [25310]
Mueller Telecommunications Inc. (Communications Systems and Equipment) [5685]
Nova-Net Communications Inc. (Electrical and Electronic Equipment and Supplies) [9144]
OCE-Bruning Inc. (Specialty Equipment and Products) [25771]
Omni-X Inc. (Industrial Machinery) [16361]
Oxford Recycling Inc. (Construction Materials and Machinery) [7818]
Pentax Corp. (Photographic Equipment and Supplies) [22889]
Pinpoint Systems Inc. (Electrical and Electronic Equipment and Supplies) [9204]
Recycling Industries Inc. (Used, Scrap, and Recycled Materials) [26954]
Rocky Mountain Food Factory Inc. (Food) [12338]
Telewire Supply (Communications Systems and Equipment) [5788]
Trak-Air/Rair (Restaurant and Commercial Foodservice Equipment and Supplies) [24247]
Vangard Technology, Inc. (Computers and Software) [6849]
Windsor Industries Inc. (Englewood, Colorado) (Industrial Machinery) [16641]

Evergreen

Australian Outback Collection (Clothing) [4790]
Comprehensive Systems Inc. (Computers and Software) [6093]

Ft. Collins

Airgas Intermountain (Industrial Supplies) [16680]
Anderson News (Books and Other Printed Materials) [3512]
Applied Computer Technology Inc. (Computers and Software) [5949]
Big Horn Booksellers Inc. (Books and Other Printed Materials) [3555]
CBW Automation Inc. (Industrial Machinery) [15882]
Directed Energy Inc. (Electrical and Electronic Equipment and Supplies) [8628]
Fort Collins Winnelson Co. (Plumbing Materials and Fixtures) [23174]
Glove Wagon Enterprises, Inc. (Clothing) [4991]
Hixon Manufacturing and Supply (Industrial Machinery) [16103]
Ion Tech Inc. (Industrial Machinery) [16171]
New Belgium Brewing Co (Alcoholic Beverages) [1913]
Odell Brewing Co. (Alcoholic Beverages) [1926]
Rand-Scot Inc. (Medical, Dental, and Optical Supplies) [19567]
Sigo Press/Coventure (Books and Other Printed Materials) [4162]
Vetline Inc. (Veterinary Products) [27265]
Voice It Worldwide Inc. (Computers and Software) [6856]
WebAccess (Computers and Software) [6861]

Franktown

Golden Bear Services Inc. (Computers and Software) [6304]

Fruita

Fruita Consumers Cooperative (Agricultural Equipment and Supplies) [716]

Glenwood Springs

Modern Kitchen Center Inc. (Construction Materials and Machinery) [7734]

Golden

ACT Teleconferencing Inc. (Communications Systems and Equipment) [5500]
Coors Brewing Co. (Food) [10836]
Coors Distributing Co. (Alcoholic Beverages) [1617]

Coors Energy Co. (Minerals and Ores) [20532]
Copy Supply Concepts Inc. (Electrical and
  Electronic Equipment and Supplies) [8579]
D.I. Engineering Corp. of America (Industrial
  Machinery) [15948]
Experimental Applied Sciences (Medical, Dental,
  and Optical Supplies) [19312]
Mountain Cable Industries Inc. (Electrical and
  Electronic Equipment and Supplies) [9102]

Grand Junction
City Market Inc. (Food) [10761]
Enstrom Candies Inc. (Food) [11049]
Gay Johnson's Inc. (Automotive) [2664]
Great Western Airgas Inc. (Industrial
  Supplies) [16906]
Mesa Optical (Medical, Dental, and Optical
  Supplies) [19451]
Quality Meat Company Inc. (Food) [12252]
Reynolds Polymer Technology (Construction
  Materials and Machinery) [7926]
Valley Controls & Supply Co. (Heating and Cooling
  Equipment and Supplies) [14753]
Valley Controls and Supply Co. (Heating and
  Cooling Equipment and Supplies) [14754]
Western Implement Co. (Agricultural Equipment and
  Supplies) [1432]

Greeley
Action Page Inc. (Communications Systems and
  Equipment) [5501]
Ellis and Capp Equipment Co. (Agricultural
  Equipment and Supplies) [547]
Greeley Elevator Co. (Livestock and Farm
  Products) [17962]
Greeley Publishing Co. (Books and Other Printed
  Materials) [3798]
Kenwood Data Systems Inc. (Computers and
  Software) [6420]
Lextron Inc. (Veterinary Products) [27181]
Loveland Industries (Agricultural Equipment and
  Supplies) [972]
Monfort Inc. (Food) [11921]
Monfort International Sales Corp. (Food) [11922]
Monfort-Swift Support Centers (Food) [11923]
Noffsinger Manufacturing Co (Metals) [20228]
Trinidad Bean and Elevator Co. (Livestock and
  Farm Products) [18292]
Winograd's Steel and Supply (Metals) [20495]

Greenwood Village
Internet Communication Corp. (Computers and
  Software) [6392]

Henderson
DPI Food Products Co. (Food) [10989]

Highlands Ranch
The TRACOM Corporation (Books and Other
  Printed Materials) [4225]

Holly
Southeastern Colorado Coop. (Food) [12537]
Southeastern Colorado Cooperative (Agricultural
  Equipment and Supplies) [1278]

Holyoke
Jack's Bean Co. (Food) [11541]
Scholl Oil & Transport Co. (Sound and
  Entertainment Equipment and Supplies) [25433]
Scholl Oil and Transport Co. (Household
  Appliances) [15304]

Julesburg
Farmers Grain Company of Julesburg (Livestock
  and Farm Products) [17895]

Lafayette
Larcan TTC (Communications Systems and
  Equipment) [5661]
Rocky Mountain Instrument Co (Medical, Dental,
  and Optical Supplies) [19585]

Lakewood
CARQUEST Corp. (Automotive) [2428]

Deans Firearms, Ltd. (Guns and
  Weapons) [13488]
High Country Kitchens (Household
  Appliances) [15168]
Pikotek (Industrial Supplies) [17104]

Lamar
Carder Inc. (Construction Materials and
  Machinery) [7139]
WHO Manufacturing Co (Agricultural Equipment and
  Supplies) [1444]

Littleton
Business Concepts Inc. (Furniture and
  Fixtures) [13053]
Colorado Commercial Refrigeration (Heating and
  Cooling Equipment and Supplies) [14392]
E-Corp, Inc. (Alcoholic Beverages) [1662]
Myers Associates; Vic (Computers and
  Software) [6538]
R & R Technical Bookfinders Inc. (Books and
  Other Printed Materials) [4103]

Longmont
Centennial Beverage Corp. (Alcoholic
  Beverages) [1583]
Cheese Importers Warehouse (Food) [10737]
Displaytech Inc. (Scientific and Measurement
  Devices) [24346]
McLane Western, Inc. (Food) [11835]
Operator Interface Technology (Computers and
  Software) [6572]
Pharmacy Corporation of America (Medical, Dental,
  and Optical Supplies) [19537]
Summertree Medisales (Medical, Dental, and
  Optical Equipment) [19060]
TechniStar Corp. (Industrial Machinery) [16554]

Louisville
Kryptonics Inc. (Recreational and Sporting
  Goods) [23777]
Pulmonary Data Service (Medical, Dental, and
  Optical Supplies) [19561]
Storage Technology Corp. (Computers and
  Software) [6763]

Loveland
Group Publishing, Inc. (Books and Other Printed
  Materials) [3801]
Hach Co. (Specialty Equipment and
  Products) [25672]
Jorgensen Laboratories Inc. (Veterinary
  Products) [27164]

Manitou Springs
Piramide Imports (Clothing) [5278]

Monte Vista
Grower Shipper Potato Co. (Food) [11337]
Monte Vista Cooperative Inc. (Agricultural
  Equipment and Supplies) [1048]

Montrose
Franklin Medical Products (Medical, Dental, and
  Optical Supplies) [19330]
Habitat Softwear (Clothing) [5012]

Monument
Mabon Business Equipment (Books and Other
  Printed Materials) [3925]
Prescotts Inc. (Medical, Dental, and Optical
  Equipment) [18994]
Think and Tinker Ltd. (Industrial
  Machinery) [16561]

Morrison
Computer Talk Inc. (Computers and
  Software) [6130]

Niwot
University Press of Colorado (Books and Other
  Printed Materials) [4248]

Northglenn
Ergonomic Design Inc. (Office Equipment and
  Supplies) [20994]

Olathe
Pratt Medical Inc. (Clothing) [5287]

Paoli
Paoli Farmers Cooperative Elevator Co. (Livestock
  and Farm Products) [18159]

Parker
Centennial Commodities Inc. (Livestock and Farm
  Products) [17769]
Davis Associates Inc. (Computers and
  Software) [6190]

Pueblo
Andrews Produce Inc. (Food) [10417]
Gyles; Janis (Security and Safety
  Equipment) [24558]
Hillside Dairy Inc. (Food) [11435]
JETT Supply Company Inc. (Construction Materials
  and Machinery) [7534]
Passeggiata Press, Inc. (Books and Other Printed
  Materials) [4042]
Rainbo Baking Co. (Food) [12267]
Sangray Corporation (Gifts and Novelties) [13441]
Summit Brick and Tile Co. (Construction Materials
  and Machinery) [8085]

Rocky Ford
Griffin-Holder Co. (Food) [11326]

Seibert
Seibert Equity Cooperative Association (Agricultural
  Equipment and Supplies) [1256]

Silverthorne
Vistabooks Publishing (Books and Other Printed
  Materials) [4260]

Steamboat Springs
Dynamic Foam Products Inc. (Shoes) [24728]
Mountain High Technology Inc. (Computers and
  Software) [6530]

Stratton
Stratton Equity Cooperative (Agricultural Equipment
  and Supplies) [1298]

Vail
Mountain Shades Distributing Co. (Recreational and
  Sporting Goods) [23838]

Walsenburg
Acorn Petroleum Inc. (Petroleum, Fuels, and
  Related Equipment) [22020]
Chipita Accessories (Jewelry) [17368]

Westminster
Hunter Co., Inc. (Luggage and Leather
  Goods) [18398]
Melco Embroidery Systems (Industrial
  Machinery) [16287]
Respironics Colorado Inc. (Medical, Dental, and
  Optical Supplies) [19578]

Wheat Ridge
Antennas America Inc. (Electrical and Electronic
  Equipment and Supplies) [8360]
AVED Rocky Mountain Inc. (Electrical and
  Electronic Equipment and Supplies) [8402]
Colorado Electronic Hardware Inc. (Electrical and
  Electronic Equipment and Supplies) [8546]
Down River Equipment Co. (Recreational and
  Sporting Goods) [23629]
Sanders Company Inc.; George T. (Plumbing
  Materials and Fixtures) [23358]

Worthington
Industrial Management Systems Corp. (Construction
  Materials and Machinery) [7508]

Wray

Farmers Union Cooperative Elevator Co. (Livestock and Farm Products) [17908]

Yuma

L & L Implement Company Inc. (Agricultural Equipment and Supplies) [923]

Connecticut

Avon

Avon Appliance & Electric Co. Inc. (Household Appliances) [15042]
Sartorius Sports Ltd. (Shoes) [24849]
Tupman Thurlow Company Inc. (Food) [12771]

Berlin

Hadfield Sport Shops Inc. (Recreational and Sporting Goods) [23710]

Bethel

CD One Stop (Sound and Entertainment Equipment and Supplies) [25130]

Bloomfield

Dapra Corp. (Industrial Machinery) [15930]
Kaman Corp. (Industrial Machinery) [16197]
Kaman Industrial Technologies Inc. (Aeronautical Equipment and Supplies) [111]
Kaman Music Corp. (Sound and Entertainment Equipment and Supplies) [25265]
Mosey's Inc. (Food) [11937]
Sack Company Inc.; Stanley (Used, Scrap, and Recycled Materials) [26972]

Branford

Champion America (Specialty Equipment and Products) [25600]
Rose Hill Distribution Inc. (Food) [12352]
University Marketing Group (Books and Other Printed Materials) [4246]

Bridgeport

Chapin and Bangs Co. Inc. (Metals) [19871]
Gesswein and Co.; Paul H. (Industrial Machinery) [16061]
Hawley Industrial Supplies Inc. (Hardware) [13746]
Prime Resources Corp. (Gifts and Novelties) [13427]
Santa Fuel Inc. (Petroleum, Fuels, and Related Equipment) [22651]
Vitramon Inc. (Electrical and Electronic Equipment and Supplies) [9544]
Wades Dairy Inc. (Food) [12861]

Bristol

Gavlick Machinery Corporation (Industrial Machinery) [16048]
Tradequest International USA (Computers and Software) [6825]
Vivax Medical Corp. (Medical, Dental, and Optical Equipment) [19103]
Yarde Metals Inc. (Metals) [20502]

Brookfield

Accurate Office Machines Inc. (Office Equipment and Supplies) [20769]
Tile America (Floorcovering Equipment and Supplies) [10216]
Tornos Technologies U.S. Corp. (Industrial Machinery) [16568]

Brookfield Center

Fairfield Book Co., Inc. (Books and Other Printed Materials) [3740]

Cheshire

Bozzuto's Inc. (Food) [10605]
Techmark Corporation (Scientific and Measurement Devices) [24442]
Worldwide Wines, Inc. (Alcoholic Beverages) [2138]

Colchester

Eastern Refrigeration Co. (Heating and Cooling Equipment and Supplies) [14426]
S and S Worldwide Inc. (Specialty Equipment and Products) [25807]
S and S Worldwide Inc. (Toys and Hobby Goods) [26645]

Cromwell

Muzak (Sound and Entertainment Equipment and Supplies) [25351]

Danbury

American Tile Supply Company, Inc. (Floorcovering Equipment and Supplies) [9678]
F & M Electric Supply Co. (Electrical and Electronic Equipment and Supplies) [8727]
Harmony Enterprises America (Medical, Dental, and Optical Equipment) [18825]
Leahy's Fuels Inc. (Petroleum, Fuels, and Related Equipment) [22421]
Peatfield Industries (Toys and Hobby Goods) [26609]

Darien

Labatt USA Inc. (Alcoholic Beverages) [1809]
Parfums de Coeur Ltd. (Health and Beauty Aids) [14189]

Dayville

United Natural Foods, Inc. (Food) [12799]

Derby

Gordon Rubber and Packing Company Inc. (Rubber) [24278]

East Berlin

Liberty Industries Inc. (Specialty Equipment and Products) [25716]

East Granby

Peachtree Fabrics Inc. (Textiles and Notions) [26172]
REM Sales Inc. (Industrial Machinery) [16447]

East Haddam

Betty's Doll House (Toys and Hobby Goods) [26417]
Cofish International Inc. (Shoes) [24715]
Go Fly A Kite Inc. (Toys and Hobby Goods) [26501]

East Hartford

American Communications Co. (Electrical and Electronic Equipment and Supplies) [8337]
Checkpoint International (Medical, Dental, and Optical Equipment) [18736]
Duo-Fast Northeast (Hardware) [13672]
Farmstead Telephone Group Inc. (Communications Systems and Equipment) [5610]
Hobby Stores Distributing Inc. (Toys and Hobby Goods) [26520]
Hobbytyme Distributors (Toys and Hobby Goods) [26523]
Precision Optical Co. (Medical, Dental, and Optical Supplies) [19549]
Savol Bleach Co. (Chemicals) [4503]

East Haven

Associated X-Ray Corp. (Medical, Dental, and Optical Equipment) [18695]

East Windsor

Marmac Distributors Inc. (Medical, Dental, and Optical Supplies) [19423]
Motion Ind. (Automotive) [2989]
Shoe Shack Inc. (Shoes) [24858]

Enfield

Enfield Overseas Trade Co. (Industrial Machinery) [15986]
Turf Products Corp. (Agricultural Equipment and Supplies) [1365]

Essex

Brewers Chandlery East (Marine) [18470]

Fairfield

Bergano Book Co., Inc. (Books and Other Printed Materials) [3551]
Delta International (Livestock and Farm Products) [17817]
DsgnHaus, Inc. (Computers and Software) [6223]
Edu-Tech Corp. (Books and Other Printed Materials) [3719]
Elan Technical Corp. (Scientific and Measurement Devices) [24353]
Executive Business Machines, Inc. (Computers and Software) [6258]
Phoenix Computer Associates Inc. (Computers and Software) [6616]
ReproCAD Inc. (Computers and Software) [6688]
Willco Sales and Services Inc. (Specialty Equipment and Products) [25881]

Farmington

Connecticut Micro Corp. (Computers and Software) [6149]
ebm Industries, Inc. (Industrial Machinery) [15975]
Morris Co.; The Robert E. (Industrial Machinery) [16323]

Forestville

Northeast Steel and Machine Products (Industrial Supplies) [17080]

Franklin

Consolidated Utility & Equipment Service (Automotive) [2477]

Glastonbury

A-Copy Inc. (Office Equipment and Supplies) [20761]
American Ladders & Scaffolds, Inc. (Automotive) [2230]
Vie Americas Inc. (Chemicals) [4548]

Greenwich

A.T. Clayton and Company Inc. (Paper and Paper Products) [21637]
Blyth Industries Inc. (Household Items) [15422]
Decorative Crafts Inc. (Furniture and Fixtures) [13086]
Frankel & Company Inc.; Lou (Electrical and Electronic Equipment and Supplies) [8756]
Great Bear Spring Co. (Soft Drinks) [24964]
Greeff Company Inc.; R.W. (Medical, Dental, and Optical Supplies) [19342]
Hall Div.; Howard (Medical, Dental, and Optical Supplies) [19346]
Holberg Industries Inc. (Food) [11445]
Intersystems of Delaware (Plastics) [22984]
Leisure Learning Products (Toys and Hobby Goods) [26567]
M and R International Inc. (Paper and Paper Products) [21815]
North Atlantic Services Inc. (Medical, Dental, and Optical Supplies) [19498]
PanAm Sat Corp. (Communications Systems and Equipment) [5703]
Pechiney Corp. (Metals) [20268]
Pechiney World Trade (USA) Inc. (Metals) [20269]
Perrier Group of America Inc. (Soft Drinks) [25021]
Premier Inc. (Greenwich, Connecticut) (Health and Beauty Aids) [14193]
Royce International Inc. (Shoes) [24846]
Strategic Distribution Inc. (Industrial Machinery) [16530]
United States Tobacco Sales and Marketing Co. (Tobacco Products) [26364]
Welding Equipment & Supply/All State Medical Gases (Medical, Dental, and Optical Equipment) [19106]

Groton

Command Technology Inc. (Computers and Software) [6086]

Guilford

Chester Technical Services Inc. (Computers and Software) [6062]

Hamden

American Appliance Parts Co. Inc. (Household Appliances) [15008]

Lindquist Industrial Supply Co. (Industrial Supplies) [17000]

Milroy and Company Inc.; W.H. (Construction Materials and Machinery) [7718]

Plastic Fabricators Inc. (Plastics) [23008]

Recife Importing & Exporting Inc. (Heating and Cooling Equipment and Supplies) [14648]

Silliter/Klebes Industrial Supplies Inc. (Industrial Supplies) [17175]

Hampton

Export Division of Gordon E. Hansen Agency Inc. (Automotive) [2600]

Hartford

Aerospace Metals Inc. (Used, Scrap, and Recycled Materials) [26733]

Auto Parts Depot Inc. (Automotive) [2275]

Baronet Coffee Inc. (Food) [10511]

Bishop Ladder Co. Inc. (Industrial Machinery) [15826]

Bristol Lettering of Hartford (Clothing) [4846]

Capitol Light and Supply Co. (Electrical and Electronic Equipment and Supplies) [8498]

Champlin Co. (Storage Equipment and Containers) [25899]

CLS (Electrical and Electronic Equipment and Supplies) [8534]

CLS (Electrical and Electronic Equipment and Supplies) [8535]

Cummins Connecticut Inc. (Automotive) [2503]

Eckart and Finard Inc. (Hardware) [13675]

Linvar Inc. (Restaurant and Commercial Foodservice Equipment and Supplies) [24167]

Linvar LLC (Storage Equipment and Containers) [25929]

Metal Management Aerospace, Inc. (Used, Scrap, and Recycled Materials) [26903]

Small Appliance Repair Inc. (Household Appliances) [15315]

Standard Metals Inc. (Metals) [20386]

Suisman and Blumenthal Inc. (Used, Scrap, and Recycled Materials) [27014]

Windsor Shade Tobacco Co. (Tobacco Products) [26375]

Hawleyville

Desherbinin Products Inc.; W.N. (Household Items) [15470]

Killingworth

Miller Machinery Corp. (Industrial Machinery) [16302]

Lebanon

Van Woerkom; Jan (Computers and Software) [6848]

Madison

Pacon Machines Corp. (Industrial Machinery) [16378]

Research Books, Inc. (Books and Other Printed Materials) [4114]

USI Inc. (Office Equipment and Supplies) [21333]

Manchester

American Sewing Machine Distributors (Household Appliances) [15010]

Central Connecticut Cooperative Farmers Association (Livestock and Farm Products) [17771]

Garston Sign Supplies, Inc. (Specialty Equipment and Products) [25658]

Good Sports Inc. (Clothing) [4996]

Hartford Distributors Inc. (Alcoholic Beverages) [1746]

Leese Flooring Supply (Floorcovering Equipment and Supplies) [9994]

Manchester Medical Supply Inc. (Medical, Dental, and Optical Equipment) [18900]

Ro-Vic Inc. (Cleaning and Janitorial Supplies) [4697]

Uranus Impex Co. (Clothing) [5456]

Meriden

AJ Coal Co. (Minerals and Ores) [20507]

Mechanical Finishing Co. (Industrial Machinery) [16285]

Meriden Cooper Corp. (Industrial Supplies) [17030]

Middlefield

Premier Food Marketing Inc. (Food) [12213]

Middletown

Lord & Hodge, Inc. (Hardware) [13803]

Madrigal Audio Laboratories Inc. (Sound and Entertainment Equipment and Supplies) [25297]

McAuliffe Inc.; Howard (Sound and Entertainment Equipment and Supplies) [25308]

Primary Steel Inc. (Metals) [20295]

Sunshine Dairy Foods Inc. (Food) [12619]

Milford

Banner Systems Inc. (Cleaning and Janitorial Supplies) [4577]

BKM Total Office (Office Equipment and Supplies) [20844]

Bridgeport Steel Co. (Metals) [19835]

Coclin Tobacco Corp. (Tobacco Products) [26276]

Connecticut Driveshaft Inc. (Automotive) [2472]

Farn Ltd.; Gary (Health and Beauty Aids) [14099]

McMillan Conroy Machinery (Industrial Machinery) [16282]

Olympic Steel Inc. Eastern Steel and Metal Div. (Metals) [20248]

Milldale

Superior Block and Supply Co. (Construction Materials and Machinery) [8090]

Monroe

Metals Engineering Co. (Metals) [20175]

Morris

Litchfield Packaging Machinery Corp. (Industrial Machinery) [16238]

Mystic

Wilcox Marine Supply Inc. (Marine) [18639]

Naugatuck

Kombi Ltd. (Clothing) [5115]

Portmeirion USA (Household Items) [15621]

Skinner Company Inc.; S.P. (Household Items) [15655]

New Britain

Ace Advance Paper Co. (Paper and Paper Products) [21614]

Acmat Corp. (Construction Materials and Machinery) [6906]

Adkins Printing Company Inc. (Office Equipment and Supplies) [20774]

Kern Special Tools Company Inc. (Electrical and Electronic Equipment and Supplies) [8939]

Moore Medical Corp. (Medical, Dental, and Optical Supplies) [19467]

Spring and Buckley Inc. (Electrical and Electronic Equipment and Supplies) [9396]

Taylor Rental Corp. (Agricultural Equipment and Supplies) [1316]

Wayne Steel Co., Ray H. Morris Div. (Metals) [20482]

New Haven

The Amerling Co. (Sound and Entertainment Equipment and Supplies) [25073]

Feldman Glass Co. (Storage Equipment and Containers) [25915]

Grand Light and Supply Co. (Electrical and Electronic Equipment and Supplies) [8805]

Grave and Son Inc.; F.D. (Tobacco Products) [26299]

MacAlaster Bicknell Company Inc. (Scientific and Measurement Devices) [24391]

MPC Educational Systems Inc. (Sound and Entertainment Equipment and Supplies) [25343]

Perrigo Inc. (Plumbing Materials and Fixtures) [23313]

Phillips Shoe Co. Inc.; Austin (Shoes) [24832]

Systems Inc. (Office Equipment and Supplies) [21311]

Tri Lift (Industrial Machinery) [16578]

United Uniforms Inc. (Clothing) [5453]

New London

City Coal of New London Inc. (Petroleum, Fuels, and Related Equipment) [22142]

Hobby Crafts (Toys and Hobby Goods) [26517]

Radways Dairy (Food) [12262]

New Milford

Electronic World Sales & Service (Sound and Entertainment Equipment and Supplies) [25179]

Newington

Hudson Home Health Care Inc. (Medical, Dental, and Optical Equipment) [18845]

Mohawk Farms Inc. (Food) [11918]

Newtown

Fuller Associates Inc.; Arthur (Sound and Entertainment Equipment and Supplies) [25202]

Sonics and Materials Inc. (Industrial Machinery) [16504]

Niantic

J & B Tackle Company Inc. (Recreational and Sporting Goods) [23753]

New England Variety Distributors (Soft Drinks) [24993]

New England Variety Distributors (Food) [12002]

North Branford

New England Wine & Spirits (Alcoholic Beverages) [1914]

Tilcon Tomasso Inc. (Construction Materials and Machinery) [8132]

North Franklin

K and L Feed Mill Corp. (Agricultural Equipment and Supplies) [895]

North Haven

Gilbert and Richards Inc. (Industrial Machinery) [16064]

M/M Electronic Products Ltd. (Electrical and Electronic Equipment and Supplies) [9015]

National Compressed Gases Inc. (Industrial Supplies) [17066]

New Haven Body, Inc. (Automotive) [3027]

Schiavone and Sons Inc.; Michael (Used, Scrap, and Recycled Materials) [26980]

Summit Handling Systems Inc. (Industrial Machinery) [16536]

Norwalk

ABB Pressure Systems Inc. (Electrical and Electronic Equipment and Supplies) [8260]

Auto Suture Company U.S.A. (Medical, Dental, and Optical Supplies) [19169]

Belle Head International Inc. (Food) [10531]

Blau; Emery (Shoes) [24692]

Connecticut Physicians & Surgeons (Medical, Dental, and Optical Equipment) [18752]

Devine Brothers Inc. (Construction Materials and Machinery) [7259]

Gibson Co.; C.R. (Gifts and Novelties) [13360]

Greenwich Trading Co. (Marine) [18511]

Guard All Chemical Company Inc. (Petroleum, Fuels, and Related Equipment) [22326]

James River Corporation of Connecticut (Paper and Paper Products) [21782]

Muehlstein and Company Inc.; H. (Plastics) [23001]

Olin Corp. (Chemicals) [4473]

Ouzunoff & Associates (Electrical and Electronic Equipment and Supplies) [9163]

Paper Sales Corp. (Paper and Paper Products) [21864]
Paperwork Products Co. (Office Equipment and Supplies) [21205]
Penmar Industries Inc. (Paper and Paper Products) [21874]
Smiths Industries (Aeronautical Equipment and Supplies) [147]

Norwich

Heating Oil Partners (Petroleum, Fuels, and Related Equipment) [22341]
Lehigh Oil Co. (Petroleum, Fuels, and Related Equipment) [22426]
Lightolier Inc. Norwich Div. (Electrical and Electronic Equipment and Supplies) [8989]
Rogers Kitchens Inc. (Furniture and Fixtures) [13224]

Old Greenwich

Devin-Adair Publishers, Inc. (Books and Other Printed Materials) [3690]
Jack Spratt Woodwind Shop (Household Appliances) [15178]
Listening Library Inc. (Books and Other Printed Materials) [3917]

Old Saybrook

Currie Industries Inc. (Plastics) [22951]
Kellogg Marine Supply Inc. (Marine) [18532]
Primax Inc. (Computers and Software) [6637]

Orange

Avatar Alliance L.P. (Aeronautical Equipment and Supplies) [49]
F & W Welding Service Inc. (Construction Materials and Machinery) [7329]
Pez Candy Inc. (Food) [12159]
Roebic Laboratories Inc. (Chemicals) [4497]
SecurityLink Corp. (Security and Safety Equipment) [24631]
U.S. Products Inc. (Clothing) [5452]

Plainville

Ideal Machinery and Supply Co. (Industrial Machinery) [16139]

Plantsville

Fluid-O-Tech International, Inc. (Plumbing Materials and Fixtures) [23171]

Portland

Axelrods Tire Inc. (Automotive) [2302]

Rockville

Signs of All Kinds (Specialty Equipment and Products) [25817]

Rocky Hill

A & A Office Systems Inc. (Communications Systems and Equipment) [5498]
MRS Industries Inc. (Medical, Dental, and Optical Equipment) [18953]
Organization Systems Inc. (Computers and Software) [6577]

Seymour

Ally Industries Inc. (Security and Safety Equipment) [24504]

Sharon

Magnamusic Distributors Inc. (Sound and Entertainment Equipment and Supplies) [25298]
Magnamusic Distributors Inc. (Household Appliances) [15208]

Shelton

Forschner Group Inc. (Household Items) [15505]
GE Supply (Electrical and Electronic Equipment and Supplies) [8779]
Philips Medical Systems North America Co. (Medical, Dental, and Optical Supplies) [19539]
Shelton Winair Co. (Heating and Cooling Equipment and Supplies) [14679]

Swiss Army Brands Inc. (Household Items) [15676]

South Norwalk

RF Technology, Inc. (Communications Systems and Equipment) [5742]

South Windsor

Aerodyne Ulbrich Alloys (Metals) [19732]
Lawrence Eyewear (Medical, Dental, and Optical Supplies) [19405]

Southbury

Southford Garage Truck Equippers (Automotive) [3244]

Southington

Baumer Electric Ltd. (Industrial Machinery) [15809]
Connecticut Appliance & Fireplace Distributors, LLC (Household Appliances) [15094]
Gibbs Wire and Steel Co. (Metals) [20005]

Southport

Connectronics Corp. (Electrical and Electronic Equipment and Supplies) [8560]
Hansen & Co. (Recreational and Sporting Goods) [23712]
Ryan and Co.; Connor F. (Sound and Entertainment Equipment and Supplies) [25424]

Stamford

Alec Corp. (Shoes) [24666]
Baker and Brother Inc.; H.J. (Agricultural Equipment and Supplies) [271]
Beck's North America (Alcoholic Beverages) [1513]
Caemi International Inc. (Minerals and Ores) [20526]
Coleman; Dr. Ernest A. (Plastics) [22945]
Commerce Packaging Corp. (Paper and Paper Products) [21688]
Corporacion del Cobre U.S.A. Inc. (Metals) [19900]
Coutinho Caro and Company Inc. (Metals) [19902]
Crane Co. (Construction Materials and Machinery) [7230]
Daymon Associates Inc. (Food) [10919]
DCE Corp. (Computers and Software) [6191]
Ecology Detergents Inc. (Heating and Cooling Equipment and Supplies) [14427]
Fashion Slippers Import USA (Shoes) [24742]
Fuji Medical Systems USA Inc. (Medical, Dental, and Optical Equipment) [18801]
Fuji Medical Systems USA Inc. (Photographic Equipment and Supplies) [22854]
Gestetner Corp. (Office Equipment and Supplies) [21012]
Great Brands of Europe Inc. (Soft Drinks) [24965]
Guinness America Inc. (Alcoholic Beverages) [1736]
Guinness Import Co. (Alcoholic Beverages) [1737]
Hartford Provision Co. (Food) [11383]
Hartford Provision Co. (Food) [11384]
JO-D Books (Books and Other Printed Materials) [3865]
MKM Inc. (Medical, Dental, and Optical Equipment) [18945]
Nationwide Papers Div. (Paper and Paper Products) [21848]
New England Recycling Company Inc. (Used, Scrap, and Recycled Materials) [26923]
Norseland Inc. (Food) [12024]
Pasminco Inc. (Metals) [20266]
Perkins-Goodwin Company Inc. (Paper and Paper Products) [21878]
Polyconcept USA, Inc. (Electrical and Electronic Equipment and Supplies) [9217]
Price and Pierce International Inc. (Paper and Paper Products) [21890]
Royal Toy Distributors Inc. (Toys and Hobby Goods) [26641]
Rubino Brothers Inc. (Used, Scrap, and Recycled Materials) [26969]
Savin Corp. (Office Equipment and Supplies) [21258]
Sibco Enterprises Incorporated (Automotive) [3217]

United Distillers Group Inc. (Alcoholic Beverages) [2088]
United Distillers North America (Alcoholic Beverages) [2089]
U.S. Games Systems Inc. (Toys and Hobby Goods) [26700]

Stonington

Garbo Lobster Company Inc. (Food) [11233]

Storrs Mansfield

AV Associates Inc. (Electrical and Electronic Equipment and Supplies) [8399]

Stratford

Anderson Machinery Co. (Scientific and Measurement Devices) [24312]
Beck-Lee Inc. (Medical, Dental, and Optical Equipment) [18704]
Beck-Lee Inc. (Medical, Dental, and Optical Supplies) [19180]
Corporate Express of the East Inc. (Office Equipment and Supplies) [20928]
Cosmotec Inc. (Electrical and Electronic Equipment and Supplies) [8583]
Cutrufellos Creamery Inc. (Food) [10888]
Ellsworth Supply Company Inc. (Hardware) [13680]
Fairfield Book Service Co. (Books and Other Printed Materials) [3741]
Hudson Paper Co. (Paper and Paper Products) [21769]
Jackster Inc. (Clothing) [5074]
Lindquist Steels Inc. (Metals) [20130]

Torrington

Dwan and Company Inc. (Alcoholic Beverages) [1661]
Patterson Oil Co. (Petroleum, Fuels, and Related Equipment) [22553]

Trumbull

Cameca Instruments Inc. (Scientific and Measurement Devices) [24334]
Pilot Corporation of America (Office Equipment and Supplies) [21215]

Unionville

McCallum Motor Supply Co. (Automotive) [2928]

Vernon

ITS/Intertrade Scientific, Inc. (Industrial Machinery) [16177]

Wallingford

D'ELIA Associates of Connecticut Inc. (Household Appliances) [15108]
Sharp Products International, Inc. (Industrial Supplies) [17170]
Transmission Equipment International Inc. (Industrial Machinery) [16576]

Waterbury

Connecticut Optical (Medical, Dental, and Optical Supplies) [19244]
Daly and Sons Inc.; M.J. (Plumbing Materials and Fixtures) [23131]
Discas Inc. (Plastics) [22955]
Hubbard-Hall Inc. (Chemicals) [4420]
Industrial Paper & Plastic Products Company Inc. (Paper and Paper Products) [21774]
JacksonLea (Industrial Supplies) [16966]
Jay Mar Sales Inc. (Toys and Hobby Goods) [26543]
MTS Wireless Components (Restaurant and Commercial Foodservice Equipment and Supplies) [24190]
Radio Research Instrument (Electrical and Electronic Equipment and Supplies) [9257]
Starbuck Sprague Co. (Electrical and Electronic Equipment and Supplies) [9410]
Stolls Medical Rentals Inc. (Medical, Dental, and Optical Equipment) [19057]
Torrington Supply Company Inc. (Plumbing Materials and Fixtures) [23412]

Wesson, Inc. (Petroleum, Fuels, and Related Equipment) [22791]

Waterford

ABCO Welding and Industrial Supply (Industrial Supplies) [16667]
Defender Industries (Marine) [18489]

Watertown

Sun Design Ltd. (Medical, Dental, and Optical Supplies) [19643]

West Hartford

Acme Auto Inc. (Automotive) [2173]
Faxon Engineering Company Inc. (Industrial Supplies) [16858]
Guaranteed Business Services Inc. (Computers and Software) [6317]
Holo-Krome Co. (Hardware) [13755]
Industrial Safety Supply Co. (Industrial Supplies) [16948]
Industrial Safety Supply Co. Interex Div. (Security and Safety Equipment) [24571]
Lavery Appliance Co.; S.K. (Household Appliances) [15200]
Music People Inc. (Sound and Entertainment Equipment and Supplies) [25348]
Music People Inc. (Electrical and Electronic Equipment and Supplies) [9110]
Signal Electronic Supply (Electrical and Electronic Equipment and Supplies) [9370]

West Haven

H A Foodservice-HAFSCO (Restaurant and Commercial Foodservice Equipment and Supplies) [24131]
Slocum & Sons Co. (Alcoholic Beverages) [2029]
Sullivan Tile Distributors (Floorcovering Equipment and Supplies) [10185]
Torello and Son Machine Co.; F. (Automotive) [3320]

Westport

Addor Associates, Inc. (Books and Other Printed Materials) [3471]
The Boat Locker (Marine) [18466]
Domecq Importers Inc. (Alcoholic Beverages) [1656]
Hunter Trading Corporation (Wood and Wood Products) [27322]
Klear-Knit Sales Inc. (Clothing) [5113]
Mantrose-Haeuser Company Inc. (Paints and Varnishes) [21495]
Phibro Inc. (Petroleum, Fuels, and Related Equipment) [22576]
R & S Sales Co. Inc. (Shoes) [24838]
Space Page Inc. (Communications Systems and Equipment) [5764]
Weston Woods Studio Inc. (Sound and Entertainment Equipment and Supplies) [25522]

Wethersfield

Hart Seed Co.; Charles C. (Agricultural Equipment and Supplies) [796]
Soccer Plus Inc. (Recreational and Sporting Goods) [23951]

Willimantic

Brand-Rex Co. (Electrical and Electronic Equipment and Supplies) [8463]
Para-Pharm Inc. (Medical, Dental, and Optical Equipment) [18977]
Software and Electrical Engineering (Computers and Software) [6740]

Wilton

Dreyfus Corp.; Louis (Livestock and Farm Products) [17822]

Windsor

Allied Grocers Cooperative Inc. (Food) [10376]
Alvin and Co. Inc. (Specialty Equipment and Products) [25548]
Alvin and Company Inc. (Scientific and Measurement Devices) [24310]

Bicknell Huston Distributors, Inc. (Recreational and Sporting Goods) [23555]
Konica Business Technologies, Inc. (Office Equipment and Supplies) [21094]
TLD America (Aeronautical Equipment and Supplies) [160]

Windsor Locks

Adams Industries Inc. (Hardware) [13531]
Springfield Sugar and Products Co. (Food) [12559]
Sweet Life Foods Inc. (Food) [12654]

Winsted

Folkcraft Instruments (Sound and Entertainment Equipment and Supplies) [25193]
Folkcraft Instruments (Household Appliances) [15130]
Standard Cycle and Auto Supply Co. (Petroleum, Fuels, and Related Equipment) [22699]

Wolcott

Alden Corp. (Industrial Machinery) [15752]
Hayes and Sons; John (Food) [11398]

Woodbridge

Krieg Consulting and Trading Inc.; A. (Industrial Machinery) [16220]

Woodstock

Spring Publishing (Books and Other Printed Materials) [4185]

Delaware

Bridgeville

Davis Company Inc.; H.C. (Food) [10916]
Diesel Equipment Specialists (Automotive) [2544]

Dover

Battery Warehouse (Electrical and Electronic Equipment and Supplies) [8422]
Carewell Industries, Inc. (Health and Beauty Aids) [14057]
Chesapeake Utilities Corp. (Petroleum, Fuels, and Related Equipment) [22133]
Davis & Butler, Inc. (Tobacco Products) [26285]
Delaware Storage Co. (Petroleum, Fuels, and Related Equipment) [22192]
Dover Electric Supply Company Inc. (Electrical and Electronic Equipment and Supplies) [8632]
Fleet Parts Distributor (Automotive) [2628]
Great Graphic Originals (Clothing) [5002]
Holt Distributors, Inc. (Paper and Paper Products) [21766]
Murray; Thomas W. (Automotive) [3004]
Scott Paper, Inc. (Paper and Paper Products) [21928]
State Janitorial Supply Co. (Cleaning and Janitorial Supplies) [4713]

Georgetown

Arrow Safety Device Co. (Automotive) [2254]
Kruger Trailer Inc. (Industrial Machinery) [16221]
Manlove Auto Parts (Automotive) [2914]

Harrington

Callis-Thompson, Inc. (Industrial Machinery) [15866]
First State Petroleum Services (Petroleum, Fuels, and Related Equipment) [22278]

Middletown

American Fitness Products Inc. (Recreational and Sporting Goods) [23510]
Calotex Delaware, Inc. (Construction Materials and Machinery) [7128]
Calotex Inc.; D.E. (Hardware) [13617]
Quaker City Motor Parts Co. (Automotive) [3128]
Summit Aviation Inc. (Aeronautical Equipment and Supplies) [152]

Milford

Blue Hen Spring Works, Inc. (Automotive) [2369]

Burris Foods Inc. (Food) [10646]
Caulk Co.; L.D. (Medical, Dental, and Optical Equipment) [18731]
Sussex Company Inc. (Clothing) [5410]
Wharton and Barnard Inc. (Automotive) [3419]

Millsboro

Moore, Inc.; A.E. (Cleaning and Janitorial Supplies) [4673]

New Castle

Bennington Co.; J.C. (Automotive) [2348]
Delaware Importers Inc. (Alcoholic Beverages) [1640]
Delaware Plumbing Supply Co. (Plumbing Materials and Fixtures) [23136]
Delaware Valley Hydraulics (Industrial Supplies) [16825]
First State Paper, Inc. (Paper and Paper Products) [21726]
Hardy & Son; Joseph T. (Construction Materials and Machinery) [7449]
Material Supply Inc. (Construction Materials and Machinery) [7666]
Morgan's Auto Parts (Automotive) [2985]
N.K.S. Distributors Inc. (Alcoholic Beverages) [1919]
North Penn Equipment (Automotive) [3042]
Tecot Electrical Supply Company Inc. (Electrical and Electronic Equipment and Supplies) [9470]
Vail Enterprises Inc. (Plumbing Materials and Fixtures) [23427]

Newark

Avon Products Inc. Newark Regional Area (Health and Beauty Aids) [14030]
Avon Products Inc. Northeast Regional Area (Medical, Dental, and Optical Supplies) [19172]
Bells Supply Co. (Plumbing Materials and Fixtures) [23082]
Engineered Systems & Designs, Inc. (Scientific and Measurement Devices) [24354]
Fulton Paper Co. (Paper and Paper Products) [21732]
Happy Harry's Healthcare Inc. (Medical, Dental, and Optical Equipment) [18824]
Kraft Foods Inc. Distribution, Sales, Service Div. (Food) [11641]
Leeber Ltd. USA (Gifts and Novelties) [13389]
Lilly Fasteners Inc.; Gary Kenneth (Hardware) [13796]
Macintosh Inc.; Dr. (Computers and Software) [6450]
Mia Shoes Inc. (Shoes) [24809]
Norton Petroleum Corp. (Petroleum, Fuels, and Related Equipment) [22529]
Staz Food Services (Food) [12581]

Ocean View

Quaker City Paper & Chemical (Paper and Paper Products) [21891]
Quaker City Paper and Chemical (Paper and Paper Products) [21892]

Seaford

Allen Petroleum Corp. (Petroleum, Fuels, and Related Equipment) [22029]
Fisher Auto Parts Inc. Manlove Div. (Automotive) [2622]
Lord Brothers & Higgins (Paper and Paper Products) [21811]
Penco Corp. (Petroleum, Fuels, and Related Equipment) [22560]
Penco Corp. (Plumbing Materials and Fixtures) [23311]
R & F Auto Sales (Motorized Vehicles) [20709]

Selbyville

Hickman & Willey, Inc. (Petroleum, Fuels, and Related Equipment) [22349]

Smyrna

Warner Fruehauf Trailer Co. (Automotive) [3400]

Townsend

Drake's Salvage; Fred (Automotive) [2560]

Wilmington

Abnormal Trees (Clothing) [4744]
All American Truck Brokers (Industrial
Machinery) [15754]
Atlantic Aviation Corp. (Aeronautical Equipment and
Supplies) [45]
Bath/Kitchen & Tile Supply Co. (Household
Items) [15415]
C/D/R/ Inc. (Household Appliances) [15068]
Ceramic Tile Supply Co. (Floorcovering Equipment
and Supplies) [9800]
Commercial Equipment & Design, Inc. (Heating and
Cooling Equipment and Supplies) [14398]
CRW Parts, Inc. (Automotive) [2498]
Delaware Brick Co. (Construction Materials and
Machinery) [7258]
Delaware Dry Goods (Textiles and
Notions) [26017]
Diamond Chemical/Supply Co. (Chemicals) [4372]
Diamond State Distributors (Alcoholic
Beverages) [1650]
Dupont de Nemours and Co.;
E.I. (Chemicals) [4376]
Forbo America Inc. (Household Items) [15503]
Fulton Paper Co. (Paper and Paper
Products) [21733]
Goorland & Mann, Inc. (Cleaning and Janitorial
Supplies) [4630]
Harvin Foods Inc. (Food) [11389]
Holloway Brothers Tools Inc. (Industrial
Machinery) [16109]
Holloway Brothers Tools Inc. (Industrial
Machinery) [16110]
ICI Fluoropolymers (Chemicals) [4425]
Info Systems Inc. (Computers and
Software) [6366]
J & M Industries, Inc. (Construction Materials and
Machinery) [7528]
Keen Compressed Gas Co. (Industrial
Supplies) [16981]
Kenyon, Inc.; Harry (Tobacco Products) [26318]
Nason Automotive (Paints and Varnishes) [21514]
Poseidon Adventure Inc. (Recreational and Sporting
Goods) [23896]
United Electric Supply Inc. (Electrical and Electronic
Equipment and Supplies) [9524]
Young Co.; William M. (Construction Materials and
Machinery) [8250]

District of Columbia

Washington

Addison Auto Parts Co. (Automotive) [2180]
Atlantic Plumbing Supply Co. Inc. (Plumbing
Materials and Fixtures) [23074]
Banner Aerospace Inc. (Aeronautical Equipment
and Supplies) [56]
Beijing Trade Exchange Inc. (Shoes) [24688]
Beitzell and Company Inc. (Alcoholic
Beverages) [1518]
Corrective Shoe Repair (Shoes) [24721]
Fine Associates (Books and Other Printed
Materials) [3749]
Future Med, Inc. (Medical, Dental, and Optical
Supplies) [19332]
George Washington University Press (Books and
Other Printed Materials) [3777]
The Guild (Clothing) [5006]
Horizon Trading Company (Furniture and
Fixtures) [13136]
House of Wines Inc. (Alcoholic Beverages) [1764]
Jenks & Son; W.S. (Electrical and Electronic
Equipment and Supplies) [8911]
Kacher Selections; Robert (Alcoholic
Beverages) [1793]
Karr & Company, Inc.; Jean (Books and Other
Printed Materials) [3875]
Kronheim and Co.; Milton S. (Alcoholic
Beverages) [1805]
L and L Products (Computers and
Software) [6424]

Literal Books (Books and Other Printed
Materials) [3918]
Mayflower Wines & Spirits (Alcoholic
Beverages) [1856]
Mega Company (Automotive) [2939]
National Distributing Company, Inc. (Alcoholic
Beverages) [1906]
National Electronic Service Co. (Sound and
Entertainment Equipment and Supplies) [25354]
Nova International Inc. (Furniture and
Fixtures) [13190]
Ottenbergs Bakery (Food) [12083]
Paige International (Computers and
Software) [6584]
Parks & History Association, Inc. (Books and Other
Printed Materials) [4040]
Premium Distributors Incorporated of Washington,
D.C. L.L.C. (Alcoholic Beverages) [1971]
Refrigeration Supply Co. (Heating and Cooling
Equipment and Supplies) [14660]
Somerville Co.; Thomas (Plumbing Materials and
Fixtures) [23380]
Steuart Investment Co. (Food) [12585]
Steuart Petroleum Co. (Petroleum, Fuels, and
Related Equipment) [22705]
Trade Routes Ltd. (Clothing) [5440]
U.S. Office Products Co. (Office Equipment and
Supplies) [21329]
U.S.A. Floral Products (Horticultural
Supplies) [14967]
Washington Marina Co. (Marine) [18635]
Yudkin & Associates; Samuel (Books and Other
Printed Materials) [4304]

Florida

Alachua
Tamrock USA (Industrial Machinery) [16547]

Altamonte Springs
Decision Support Systems Inc. (Computers and
Software) [6193]
Filbert Refrigeration (Restaurant and Commercial
Foodservice Equipment and Supplies) [24118]

Apopka
Apopka Trees & Shrubs (Horticultural
Supplies) [14808]
Growers Precooler Inc. (Food) [11339]
Tubelite Company, Inc. (Specialty Equipment and
Products) [25849]
World Wide Imports of Orlando
Inc. (Jewelry) [17662]

Arcadia
Childs Oil Company Inc. (Petroleum, Fuels, and
Related Equipment) [22137]

Avon Park
Grimsley Oil Company Inc. (Petroleum, Fuels, and
Related Equipment) [22324]

Balm
Goodson Farms Inc. (Food) [11291]

Belle Glade
Glade and Grove Supply Inc. (Agricultural
Equipment and Supplies) [741]
Pioneer Growers Co-Op (Food) [12173]
Wedgworth's Inc. (Agricultural Equipment and
Supplies) [1420]

Belleview
Florida Clock & Supplies Inc. (Household
Items) [15501]

Boca Raton
ADT Ltd. (Security and Safety Equipment) [24486]
Alliant Foodservice, Inc. (Food) [10372]
Alliant Foodservice Inc. (Food) [10374]
Alro Metals Service Center (Metals) [19758]
Bitor America Corp. (Minerals and Ores) [20521]

Brother's Gourmet Coffees Inc. (Boca Raton,
Florida) (Soft Drinks) [24919]
Carr Co. (Plumbing Materials and
Fixtures) [23107]
Champion Computer Corp. (Computers and
Software) [6060]
Commercial Plastics and Supply
Corp. (Plastics) [22946]
Leisegang Medical Inc. (Medical, Dental, and
Optical Equipment) [18887]
Network Marketing L.C. (Health and Beauty
Aids) [14174]
Purity Wholesale Grocers Inc. (Food) [12239]
Q.E.P. Co. Inc. (Wood and Wood
Products) [27361]
Quest Electronic Hardware Inc. (Electrical and
Electronic Equipment and Supplies) [9251]
Rexall Co. (Health and Beauty Aids) [14214]
Rexall Co. (Medical, Dental, and Optical
Supplies) [19579]
Rexall Managed Care (Health and Beauty
Aids) [14215]
Teledata Concepts Inc. (Electrical and Electronic
Equipment and Supplies) [9475]
Young Steel Products Co. (Metals) [20504]

Bonifay
Arnold Lumber Company Inc. (Construction
Materials and Machinery) [6987]

Boynton Beach
American Cooking Guild (Books and Other Printed
Materials) [3499]
Paging Products Group (Communications Systems
and Equipment) [5700]

Bradenton
The Bradenton Financial Ctr. (Minerals and
Ores) [20524]
Carbon Resources of Florida (Minerals and
Ores) [20528]
Gulf Coast Auto Auction Inc. (Motorized
Vehicles) [20645]
Mixon Fruit Farms Inc. (Food) [11916]

Casselberry
Air O Quip Corp. (Heating and Cooling Equipment
and Supplies) [14304]

Clearwater
Action Fabrication & Truck Equipment,
Inc. (Automotive) [2179]
ADI (Security and Safety Equipment) [24484]
Alpha Tile Distributors, Inc. (Floorcovering
Equipment and Supplies) [9665]
Ambex Inc. (Household Appliances) [15006]
Automotive Industries Inc. (Automotive) [2291]
Communico Inc. (Communications Systems and
Equipment) [5575]
Communico Inc. Communico Supply
Div. (Communications Systems and
Equipment) [5576]
Design Data Systems Corp. (Computers and
Software) [6200]
EcoTech Recycled Products (Office Equipment and
Supplies) [20981]
ForeFront Direct Inc. (Computers and
Software) [6274]
Happy Feet Plus (Shoes) [24758]
Happy Feet Plus (Clothing) [5017]
Hauser Company; M.L. (Industrial
Machinery) [16092]
Moreland Hosiery (Clothing) [5204]
Morgan Tire and Auto Inc. (Automotive) [2984]
Risser Oil Corp. (Petroleum, Fuels, and Related
Equipment) [22630]
Russell Associates Inc. (Specialty Equipment and
Products) [25806]
St. Pete Auto Auction Inc. (Motorized
Vehicles) [20717]
Tampa Tile Center (Floorcovering Equipment and
Supplies) [10209]
Tech Data Corp. (Computers and Software) [6794]
Turbo Link International Inc. (Recreational and
Sporting Goods) [24019]

Zachary Software Inc. (Computers and Software) [6890]

Clewiston
South Bay Growers Inc. (Food) [12531]

Cocoa
Art Glass House, Inc. (Specialty Equipment and Products) [25561]
Cocoa Brevard Paper Co. (Paper and Paper Products) [21684]
D.M.R. Distributors (Specialty Equipment and Products) [25632]

Coconut Creek
It's Coffee Lovers Time, Inc. (Food) [11533]

Coral Gables
Almaly Trading Corp. (Computers and Software) [5910]
Camilo Office Furniture, Inc. (Office Equipment and Supplies) [20873]
Camilo Office Furniture Inc. (Furniture and Fixtures) [13061]
Iberia Tile (Floorcovering Equipment and Supplies) [9956]
IMT Corp. (Industrial Machinery) [16145]
PPI Del Monte Tropical Fruit Co. (Food) [12203]
Rexel Inc. (Electrical and Electronic Equipment and Supplies) [9286]
Rexel Inc. (Coral Gables, Florida) (Electrical and Electronic Equipment and Supplies) [9287]
Tate & Lyle Enterprises, Inc. (Industrial Machinery) [16548]
Turbana Corp. (Food) [12772]

Coral Springs
Bassin Inc.; Jerry (Sound and Entertainment Equipment and Supplies) [25097]
Olympia Gold Inc. (Jewelry) [17538]
Renaissance Stoneworks (Construction Materials and Machinery) [7915]
School Book Service (Books and Other Printed Materials) [4143]

Cortez
Bell Fish Company, Inc.; A.P. (Food) [10530]

Dania
Action Tool Company Inc. (Hardware) [13529]
Alan Inc.; Charles (Floorcovering Equipment and Supplies) [9649]
Windows of the World (Household Items) [15709]

Dania Beach
Design Center of the Americas (Household Items) [15471]

Davie
Speiser Pet Supplies (Veterinary Products) [27236]

Daytona Beach
B and B Fisheries Inc. (Food) [10479]
City Provisioners Inc. (Food) [10763]
Daytona Beach Cold Storage Inc. (Food) [10921]
Edcat Enterprises (Medical, Dental, and Optical Supplies) [19303]
Lore L. Ltd. (Construction Materials and Machinery) [7611]
Pepsi-Cola Bottling Co. of Daytona Beach (Soft Drinks) [25006]

Deerfield Beach
Designed Flooring Distributors (Floorcovering Equipment and Supplies) [9860]
Gemaire Distributors Inc. (Heating and Cooling Equipment and Supplies) [14458]
Hector Turf (Agricultural Equipment and Supplies) [810]
JM Family Enterprises Inc. (Motorized Vehicles) [20656]
Kitchens of the Oceans Inc. (Food) [11623]
Lens Express Inc. (Medical, Dental, and Optical Supplies) [19412]

Liberty Publishing Co. Inc. (Books and Other Printed Materials) [3910]
Micros of South Florida Inc. (Office Equipment and Supplies) [21142]
Milano Brothers International Corp. (Electrical and Electronic Equipment and Supplies) [9082]
National Distributing Co. Inc. (Alcoholic Beverages) [1908]
Southeast Toyota Distributors Inc. (Motorized Vehicles) [20724]
Tasso Wallcovering (Household Items) [15682]
Young Journal Inc.; Richard (Computers and Software) [6888]

Delray Beach
Beach Growers (Horticultural Supplies) [14826]
Brill Hygenic Products Inc. (Plumbing Materials and Fixtures) [23096]
D & B Tile (Floorcovering Equipment and Supplies) [9840]
Field and Associates Inc. (Jewelry) [17414]
Fresh Start Produce Sales, Inc. (Food) [11211]
Office Depot Inc. (Office Equipment and Supplies) [21173]

Destin
CSL and Associates Inc. (Industrial Machinery) [15921]

Dundee
Dundee Citrus Growers Association (Food) [10999]
Winter Haven Citrus Grower Association (Food) [12962]

Dunedin
RSL Trading Company, Inc. (Industrial Machinery) [16462]

Dunnellon
Flowmatic Systems (Industrial Machinery) [16017]

Eaton Park
Rubber and Accessories Inc. (Industrial Supplies) [17148]

Edgewater
Houseware Warehouse Inc. (Household Items) [15535]
Zeigler's Market (Horticultural Supplies) [14981]

Fernandina Beach
Standard Marine Supply Co. (Marine) [18615]

Ft. Lauderdale
Agrimor (Food) [10347]
Anda Generics Inc. (Medical, Dental, and Optical Supplies) [19152]
Astro-Pure Water Purifiers (Household Appliances) [15038]
Barnacle Seafood (Food) [10508]
BCT International Inc. (Paper and Paper Products) [21648]
Broward Fire Equipment and Service Inc. (Security and Safety Equipment) [24519]
Business Cards Tomorrow Inc. (Paper and Paper Products) [21660]
Butler National Services Inc. (Scientific and Measurement Devices) [24332]
Causeway Lumber Co. (Construction Materials and Machinery) [7153]
Commercial Telephone Systems Inc. (Communications Systems and Equipment) [5568]
Corporate Rotable and Supply Inc. (Aeronautical Equipment and Supplies) [76]
Drapery Hardware of Florida (Hardware) [13670]
Duffy and Lee Co. (Floorcovering Equipment and Supplies) [9873]
Duncan-Edward Co. (Industrial Supplies) [16841]
East Hampton Industries Inc. (Household Items) [15484]
Fine Distributing Inc. (Food) [11126]
Future Metals Inc. (Aeronautical Equipment and Supplies) [91]
Gold Coast Marine Distribution (Marine) [18508]

Grabber Southeast (Construction Materials and Machinery) [7405]
Gulf South Forest Products, Inc. (Wood and Wood Products) [27313]
Home Diagnostics Inc. (Medical, Dental, and Optical Equipment) [18838]
Horner Equipment of Florida Inc. (Recreational and Sporting Goods) [23730]
International Airline Support Group Inc. (Aeronautical Equipment and Supplies) [102]
Kaelbel Wholesale Inc. (Food) [11576]
Land-N-Sea Distribution East (Marine) [18541]
Lewis Marine Supply (Marine) [18546]
Metrix South Inc. (Automotive) [2947]
Modernfold of Florida, Inc. (Construction Materials and Machinery) [7737]
Modernfold of Florida Inc. (Wood and Wood Products) [27347]
Music for Percussion, Inc. (Books and Other Printed Materials) [3975]
Pelican Paper Products Div. (Paper and Paper Products) [21872]
Port Everglades Steel Corp. (Metals) [20289]
Power & Pumps Inc. (Automotive) [3111]
Proxycare Inc. (Medical, Dental, and Optical Supplies) [19560]
Quality Bakery Products Inc. (Food) [12247]
Rexall Sundown Inc. (Health and Beauty Aids) [14216]
Richards Products Inc. (Health and Beauty Aids) [14219]
Rx Medical Services Corp. (Medical, Dental, and Optical Supplies) [19590]
Solair Inc. (Aeronautical Equipment and Supplies) [148]
Star Brite (Cleaning and Janitorial Supplies) [4712]
Stevens Inc.; Gerald (Horticultural Supplies) [14957]
Streicher Mobile Fueling Inc. (Petroleum, Fuels, and Related Equipment) [22711]
Telectron Inc. (Electrical and Electronic Equipment and Supplies) [9474]
Thies and Sons Inc.; William (Alcoholic Beverages) [2077]
Thompson Office Equipment Company Inc. (Office Equipment and Supplies) [21318]
Ultra Lens (Medical, Dental, and Optical Supplies) [19669]
Unique Communications Inc. (Communications Systems and Equipment) [5800]
Vitality Distributiors Inc. (Health and Beauty Aids) [14272]
West Wholesale (Veterinary Products) [27270]

Ft. Myers
Alpha Tile Distributors, Inc. (Floorcovering Equipment and Supplies) [9661]
Beachcombers International Inc. (Gifts and Novelties) [13313]
CPS Marketing Corporation (Medical, Dental, and Optical Equipment) [18757]
Dean Supply Inc.; Bob (Industrial Machinery) [15934]
Frank Carroll Oil Co. (Petroleum, Fuels, and Related Equipment) [22292]
Fyr Fyter Inc. (Security and Safety Equipment) [24554]
Key Imports (Jewelry) [17489]
Land-N-Sea Distribution West (Marine) [18542]
Mark V Distributiors Inc. (Alcoholic Beverages) [1850]
Office Furniture & Design Center Inc. (Office Equipment and Supplies) [21181]
QCU Inc. (Gifts and Novelties) [13431]
Southwest Florida Auction Inc. (Motorized Vehicles) [20726]
Sun Coast Tile Distributors Inc. (Floorcovering Equipment and Supplies) [10194]
Water Products International, Inc. (Specialty Equipment and Products) [25873]
WINMED Products Co. (Medical, Dental, and Optical Equipment) [19109]

Ft. Pierce
DNE World Fruit Sales Inc. (Food) [10971]

Egan and Co.; Bernard (Food) [11032]
Zeroll Co. (Household Items) [15717]

Ft. Walton Beach

Cooling & Heating Inc. (Heating and Cooling Equipment and Supplies) [14404]
Ivanco Inc. (Communications Systems and Equipment) [5652]

Gainesville

Bearings and Drives, Inc. (Industrial Supplies) [16737]
Blue Pearl (Jewelry) [17344]
Bridge-Logos Publishers (Books and Other Printed Materials) [3591]
Little River Marine Co. (Marine) [18548]
Maris Distributing Co. (Alcoholic Beverages) [1849]
Market Share International Inc. (Food) [11781]
Purple Frog Software (Computers and Software) [6665]
Walker Distributors Inc.; Joe (Food) [12869]
Wildlife Publications, Inc. (Books and Other Printed Materials) [4283]

Gulfport

Surface Technology Corp. (Household Items) [15674]

Haines City

Polk County Fertilizer Co. (Agricultural Equipment and Supplies) [1139]

Hallandale

D.J.H. Inc. (Household Items) [15477]
Global Access Entertainment Inc. (Sound and Entertainment Equipment and Supplies) [25213]
Global Access Entertainment Inc. (Household Appliances) [15149]
Infra Metals (Metals) [20064]
Rheuban Associates (Automotive) [3155]
Zack Trading (Jewelry) [17667]

Hialeah

A & S Suppliers (Household Items) [15384]
ABC Cellular Corp. (Communications Systems and Equipment) [5499]
ABC School Uniforms Inc. (Clothing) [4743]
AC Sales Company Ltd. (Industrial Machinery) [15728]
Barborie Fashions (Clothing) [4803]
Bass Woodworking Machinery (Industrial Machinery) [15804]
Bass Woodworking Machinery, Inc. (Industrial Machinery) [15805]
Book Warehouse Inc. (Books and Other Printed Materials) [3572]
Brooke Distributors Inc. (Sound and Entertainment Equipment and Supplies) [25109]
CPP-Belwin Inc. (Books and Other Printed Materials) [3665]
Garci Plastics Industries (Household Items) [15511]
Manhattan-Miami Corp. (Clothing) [5158]
Mason Distributors (Medical, Dental, and Optical Supplies) [19425]
Replacement Hardware Manufacturing Inc. (Construction Materials and Machinery) [7917]
Robert Manufacturing Company Inc. (Luggage and Leather Goods) [18425]
Shelley Tractor and Equipment Co. (Construction Materials and Machinery) [8009]
Tile Mart, Inc. (Floorcovering Equipment and Supplies) [10241]
Tower Paint Manufacturing (Paints and Varnishes) [21594]

Hialeah Gardens

Plezall Wipers Inc. (Textiles and Notions) [26179]

Holiday

M.R.D. Products Inc. (Used, Scrap, and Recycled Materials) [26920]

Holly Hill

American Ceramic Tile (Floorcovering Equipment and Supplies) [9667]

Hollywood

Broadway Style Showroom No. 1 (Jewelry) [17350]
Crescent Airways Inc. (Aeronautical Equipment and Supplies) [77]
Frederick Fell Publishers, Inc. (Books and Other Printed Materials) [3764]
Gates InterAmerica (Industrial Supplies) [16890]
International Importers Inc. (Jewelry) [17461]
Magnivision (Medical, Dental, and Optical Equipment) [18897]
Mayers Jewelry Company Inc. (Jewelry) [17518]
NCD (Computers and Software) [6545]
Pool Fact, Inc. (Recreational and Sporting Goods) [23891]
Walpeco (Agricultural Equipment and Supplies) [1410]

Homestead

Atlantic F.E.C. Inc. (Chemicals) [4328]
DiMare Homestead Inc. (Food) [10966]
K and A Lumber Company Inc. (Wood and Wood Products) [27326]

Howey in the Hills

Alan's Tropical Plants (Horticultural Supplies) [14798]

Hudson

Cass Inc.; Veronica (Photographic Equipment and Supplies) [22841]

Indialantic

Action Sales Promotions (Clothing) [4747]
International Service Co. (Books and Other Printed Materials) [3850]

Inverness

EGP Inc. (Office Equipment and Supplies) [20986]
Grabarczyk Associates (Household Items) [15515]

Jacksonville

Ace Electric Supply Co. (Electrical and Electronic Equipment and Supplies) [8262]
Acosta Sales Co. (Food) [10322]
ADI Jacksonville (Household Appliances) [14993]
AFGD (Construction Materials and Machinery) [6920]
Baker Distributing Co. (Heating and Cooling Equipment and Supplies) [14333]
Barnett Brass and Copper Inc. (Plumbing Materials and Fixtures) [23077]
Barnett Inc. (Plumbing Materials and Fixtures) [23078]
Beaver Street Fisheries, Inc. (Food) [10521]
Bodyline Comfort Systems (Medical, Dental, and Optical Equipment) [18718]
Boise Cascade Office Products Corp. (Office Equipment and Supplies) [20848]
Brandons Camera (Photographic Equipment and Supplies) [22835]
Cain & Bultman, Inc. (Floorcovering Equipment and Supplies) [9750]
Cain and Bultman Inc. (Household Appliances) [15070]
Castleton Beverage Corp. (Alcoholic Beverages) [1581]
Churchwell Co.; J.H. (Clothing) [4882]
Coastal Industries Inc. (Plumbing Materials and Fixtures) [23117]
Connie's Enterprise (Petroleum, Fuels, and Related Equipment) [22159]
Connie's Enterprise (Industrial Machinery) [15909]
Copytronics Inc. (Office Equipment and Supplies) [20920]
Diamond Hill Plywood Co. (Construction Materials and Machinery) [7262]
Equipment and Technology, Inc. (Industrial Machinery) [15997]
Export Contract Corp. (Restaurant and Commercial Foodservice Equipment and Supplies) [24113]

Fire Fighters Equipment Co. (Security and Safety Equipment) [24545]
Fire Fighters Equipment Co. (Restaurant and Commercial Foodservice Equipment and Supplies) [24119]
First Coast Designs Inc. (Horticultural Supplies) [14862]
First Coast Pet Supply (Veterinary Products) [27132]
Florida Detroit Diesel-Allison North Inc. (Automotive) [2632]
Florida Hardware Co. (Hardware) [13712]
Fowler and Associates Inc.; R.W. (Construction Materials and Machinery) [7364]
Gate Petroleum Co. (Food) [11240]
Granger Lumber-Hardware, Inc. (Construction Materials and Machinery) [7409]
Henry's Hickory House Inc. (Food) [11415]
Here's Fred Golf Co. (Recreational and Sporting Goods) [23724]
Heritage Paper Company Inc. (Paper and Paper Products) [21759]
Industrial Tractor Co. (Agricultural Equipment and Supplies) [857]
ITEC Enterprises Inc. (Computers and Software) [6398]
Jacksonville Sound and Communications Inc. (Sound and Entertainment Equipment and Supplies) [25256]
Joyserv Company Ltd. (Motorized Vehicles) [20657]
Kights' Printing and Office Products (Office Equipment and Supplies) [21091]
King Provision Corp. (Food) [11616]
Kwik-Affix Products (Household Items) [15558]
Lambs Yacht Center (Marine) [18540]
LBK Marketing Corp. (Gifts and Novelties) [13388]
Mac Papers Inc. (Paper and Paper Products) [21816]
Magnolia Casket Co. (Restaurant and Commercial Foodservice Equipment and Supplies) [24174]
Martin Brothers International (Tobacco Products) [26327]
Miller Bearings Inc. (Automotive) [2965]
Miller Machinery and Supply Company of Tampa (Chemicals) [4457]
Monarch Tile (Floorcovering Equipment and Supplies) [10052]
Moody and Sons Inc.; M.D. (Construction Materials and Machinery) [7742]
Movsovitz and Sons of Florida Inc. (Food) [11949]
NAPCO & LBK Marketing Corp. (Horticultural Supplies) [14927]
National Distributing Co. (Alcoholic Beverages) [1905]
National Potteries Corp. (Gifts and Novelties) [13408]
NEWSouth Distributors (Books and Other Printed Materials) [4002]
Perdue Inc. (Office Equipment and Supplies) [21208]
Physician Sales and Service Inc. (Medical, Dental, and Optical Equipment) [18988]
Poultry Health (Veterinary Products) [27215]
R & R Distributors (Veterinary Products) [27220]
Rivers Body Co., Inc. (Automotive) [3163]
Riverside Group Inc. (Construction Materials and Machinery) [7940]
Sawyer Gas Co. (Petroleum, Fuels, and Related Equipment) [22653]
Security Data Group (Security and Safety Equipment) [24629]
Southern Industrial Corp. (Restaurant and Commercial Foodservice Equipment and Supplies) [24225]
Swindal-Powell Co. (Furniture and Fixtures) [13253]
Tech Aerofoam Products, Inc. (Textiles and Notions) [26222]
Uni-Flange Corp. (Plumbing Materials and Fixtures) [23420]
Unijax Div. (Paper and Paper Products) [21959]

Jacksonville Beach

Island Style (Recreational and Sporting Goods) [23749]

LCI Ltd. (Chemicals) [4439]

Jupiter

Ceramic Concept of Martin County (Floorcovering Equipment and Supplies) [9791]
Mr. Hardwoods (Household Items) [15591]
Mr. Hardwoods, Inc. (Floorcovering Equipment and Supplies) [10068]
Pifer, Inc. (Recreational and Sporting Goods) [23881]

Kendall

D & B Tile (Floorcovering Equipment and Supplies) [9841]

Key Biscayne

Fiesta Book Co. (Books and Other Printed Materials) [3748]

Key West

Langley Press, Inc. (Books and Other Printed Materials) [3895]
Salvors Inc. (Jewelry) [17585]
Standard Marine Supply Co. (Marine) [18614]

Kissimmee

Nordic Wholesale Distributors Inc. (Clothing) [5236]

Lake Alfred

Growers Fertilizer Corp. (Agricultural Equipment and Supplies) [773]

Lake City

The Leather Shop (Clothing) [5126]

Lake Mary

Florida Protective Coatings Consultants Inc. (Paints and Varnishes) [21443]
Ligonier Ministries, Inc. (Sound and Entertainment Equipment and Supplies) [25285]
Priority Healthcare Corp. (Medical, Dental, and Optical Supplies) [19551]

Lake Park

World Class Software Inc. (Computers and Software) [6876]

Lake Worth

Accessories Palace (Gifts and Novelties) [13288]
Adaptive Living (Computers and Software) [5874]
Floral Acres Inc. (Horticultural Supplies) [14864]
Sun Shader International, Inc. (Clothing) [5405]

Lakeland

AA Electric S.E. Inc. (Industrial Machinery) [15721]
Allied Scrap Processors Inc. (Used, Scrap, and Recycled Materials) [26739]
American and International Telephone Inc. (Communications Systems and Equipment) [5512]
Barneys Pumps Inc. (Plumbing Materials and Fixtures) [23079]
Bunn Co.; B.H. (Industrial Machinery) [15856]
Craft King (Office Equipment and Supplies) [20935]
Edwards Fruit Co. (Food) [11030]
Florida Seed Company Inc. (Agricultural Equipment and Supplies) [693]
Golf Ventures (Recreational and Sporting Goods) [23693]
Growers Marketing Service Inc. (Food) [11338]
Juno Industries Inc. (Industrial Supplies) [16973]
Lakeland Auto Auction Inc. (Motorized Vehicles) [20669]
Liberty Hobby (Toys and Hobby Goods) [26568]
Magna Graphics (Automotive) [2907]
Mine and Mill Supply Co. (Metals) [20197]
Mutual Distributors Inc. (Food) [11961]
Mutual Wholesale Co. (Food) [11964]
Quality Petroleum Corp. (Petroleum, Fuels, and Related Equipment) [22602]
Sunshine Cap Co. (Clothing) [5407]

Largo

Cousin Corporation of America (Toys and Hobby Goods) [26451]
Glenn-Mar Marine Supply, Inc. (Marine) [18507]
Southern Apparel Corp. (Clothing) [5371]

Lauderhill

Branches Medical Inc. (Medical, Dental, and Optical Equipment) [18719]

Lee

Cherry Farms Inc. (Agricultural Equipment and Supplies) [412]

Leesburg

Besco Electic Supply Company of Florida Inc. (Electrical and Electronic Equipment and Supplies) [8433]
Ditch Witch Trencher Incorporated of Florida (Construction Materials and Machinery) [7271]

Longwood

21st Century Holdings Inc. (Medical, Dental, and Optical Equipment) [18650]
Bell Additives Inc. (Petroleum, Fuels, and Related Equipment) [22064]
Merit Fasteners Corp. (Hardware) [13825]
Suarez Food Distribution Co.; C.G. (Food) [12598]
Supplyline Inc. (Computers and Software) [6777]

Maitland

Ruff and Co. Business Furniture Div.; Thomas W. (Furniture and Fixtures) [13225]
Taylor Corp.; Jim (Alcoholic Beverages) [2070]

Marathon

Clipper Quality Seafood, Inc. (Food) [10771]
Marathon Boat Yard (Marine) [18557]
Ornamental Tile and Design Center (Floorcovering Equipment and Supplies) [10090]

Margate

Floribbean Wholesale Inc. (Food) [11161]
Intercoastal Tile (Floorcovering Equipment and Supplies) [9965]

Marianna

Daffin Mercantile Company Inc. (Restaurant and Commercial Foodservice Equipment and Supplies) [24101]

Medley

Max Nitzberg Inc. (Clothing) [5176]
Topsville Inc. (Clothing) [5435]

Melbourne

ComoTec (Medical, Dental, and Optical Supplies) [19241]
Datalink Ready Inc. (Electrical and Electronic Equipment and Supplies) [8609]
East Coast Tile/Terrazzo (Floorcovering Equipment and Supplies) [9876]
Expert Tile, Inc. (Floorcovering Equipment and Supplies) [9888]
Glover Oil Company Inc. (Petroleum, Fuels, and Related Equipment) [22315]
Impression Technology Inc. (Computers and Software) [6358]
Krieger Publishing Co. (Books and Other Printed Materials) [3887]
Mid-East Manufacturing Inc. (Sound and Entertainment Equipment and Supplies) [25317]
Southern Electric Supply Company Inc. (Electrical and Electronic Equipment and Supplies) [9386]

Miami

AAA Interair Inc. (Aeronautical Equipment and Supplies) [20]
AAAA World Import Export Inc. (Sound and Entertainment Equipment and Supplies) [25054]
ADEMCO/ADI (Security and Safety Equipment) [24471]
Aero Systems Aviation Inc. (Aeronautical Equipment and Supplies) [25]

Aero Systems Inc. (Aeronautical Equipment and Supplies) [26]
Air Systems Distributors Inc. (Heating and Cooling Equipment and Supplies) [14307]
All American Semiconductor Inc. (Electrical and Electronic Equipment and Supplies) [8291]
American Gift Corp. (Gifts and Novelties) [13301]
Americas Trade & Supply Co. (Automotive) [2237]
Ampco Products Inc. (Construction Materials and Machinery) [6971]
Arabel Inc. (Household Items) [15404]
Artmark Associates Inc. (Electrical and Electronic Equipment and Supplies) [8380]
Associated Grocers of Florida Inc. (Food) [10449]
Astran Inc. (Books and Other Printed Materials) [3529]
Astran Inc. (Books and Other Printed Materials) [3530]
Atlantic Pump and Equipment Co. (Recreational and Sporting Goods) [23527]
Aviation Sales Co. (Miami, Florida) (Aeronautical Equipment and Supplies) [52]
Bakery Management Corp. (Food) [10493]
Banana Supply Company Inc. (Food) [10496]
Barcardi-Martini U.S.A., Inc. (Alcoholic Beverages) [1500]
Barfield Inc. (Aeronautical Equipment and Supplies) [57]
Bay Rag (Clothing) [4808]
BEK International Inc. (Computers and Software) [6008]
Bencruz Enterprises Corporation (Industrial Machinery) [15817]
BFI Waste Systems of North America Inc. (Used, Scrap, and Recycled Materials) [26767]
Bijoux Terner L.P. (Jewelry) [17338]
Biscayne Electric and Hardware Distributors Inc. (Electrical and Electronic Equipment and Supplies) [8441]
Bridge Stone Aircraft Tire (USA), Inc. (Aeronautical Equipment and Supplies) [63]
Century Plumbing Wholesale (Plumbing Materials and Fixtures) [23112]
CFX, Inc. (Horticultural Supplies) [14840]
Chestnut Hill Farms Inc. (Food) [10741]
CHS Electronics Inc. (Computers and Software) [6067]
Clamor Impex Inc. (Jewelry) [17372]
Coastal Fuels Marketing Inc. (Petroleum, Fuels, and Related Equipment) [22145]
Cobb Optical Lab Inc. (Medical, Dental, and Optical Supplies) [19238]
Columbia Impex Corp. (Luggage and Leather Goods) [18384]
Commercial Aviation Support Inc. (Aeronautical Equipment and Supplies) [73]
Comtech Systems Brokers (Computers and Software) [6142]
Coronet Paper Products (Paper and Paper Products) [21693]
Cromer Co. (Clothing) [4903]
Custom Creations Sportswear (Clothing) [4906]
Custom Wholesale Flooring (Floorcovering Equipment and Supplies) [9837]
Daccord Inc. (Clothing) [4908]
Dana World Trade Div. (Automotive) [2526]
Desk Concepts (Office Equipment and Supplies) [20957]
Dinorah's Sportswear (Clothing) [4917]
DMR International (Specialty Equipment and Products) [25633]
Dynamic Distributors (Construction Materials and Machinery) [7294]
Easy Shoe Distributors Inc. (Shoes) [24730]
E.C.F. Supply (Floorcovering Equipment and Supplies) [9882]
Ediciones Universal (Books and Other Printed Materials) [3718]
El Dorado Furniture Co. (Furniture and Fixtures) [13103]
Electronic Equipment Company Inc. (Electrical and Electronic Equipment and Supplies) [8689]
Espana General Importers (Gifts and Novelties) [13353]
Euro Classic Distributors Inc. (Household Items) [15491]

Evans Environmental Corp. (Sound and Entertainment Equipment and Supplies) [25187]

Ezcony Interamerica Inc. (Electrical and Electronic Equipment and Supplies) [8725]

Fairwind Sunglasses Trading Company Inc. (Medical, Dental, and Optical Supplies) [19320]

Falcone and Italia Foods (Food) [11077]

Florida Bearings Inc. (Industrial Supplies) [16869]

Future Tech International Inc. (Computers and Software) [6284]

Gold Coast Beverage Distributors (Alcoholic Beverages) [1722]

GOYA Foods Inc. (Soft Drinks) [24963]

Green and Company Inc.; A.A. (Food) [11319]

Growers Ford Tractor Co. (Agricultural Equipment and Supplies) [774]

Halpin Equipment Corp.; Tim (Automotive) [2720]

Hardware Imagination (Hardware) [13738]

Hopkins-Carter Company Inc. (Marine) [18521]

Iberia Tiles Inc. (Floorcovering Equipment and Supplies) [9958]

Inaqua International (Specialty Equipment and Products) [25687]

Intcomex (Computers and Software) [6377]

Integrated World Enterprises (Agricultural Equipment and Supplies) [859]

Intermetra Corp. (Electrical and Electronic Equipment and Supplies) [8891]

International Air Leases Inc. (Aeronautical Equipment and Supplies) [101]

Intexco Inc. (Food) [11528]

ITI Interamericana Trade Inc. (Clothing) [5067]

J & B Importers Inc. (Recreational and Sporting Goods) [23752]

Jademar Corp. (Electrical and Electronic Equipment and Supplies) [8904]

JK Miami Corp. (Clothing) [5085]

Just Drop, Inc. (Electrical and Electronic Equipment and Supplies) [8923]

Kelly Tractor Co. (Industrial Machinery) [16202]

Kramer Laboratories Inc. (Medical, Dental, and Optical Supplies) [19401]

Land, Air & Sea Tool Corp. (Hardware) [13791]

Lee Co.; Henry (Food) [11692]

LeMare Medical Inc. (Medical, Dental, and Optical Equipment) [18890]

Lindeco International Corp. (Automotive) [2884]

Lurie Associates; Fred (Shoes) [24797]

Major Appliances Inc. (Restaurant and Commercial Foodservice Equipment and Supplies) [24176]

Marco and Sons; R.B. (Clothing) [5163]

Marvitec Export Corporation (Industrial Machinery) [16268]

Maxim's Import Corp. (Food) [11811]

Med-Lab Supply Company Inc. (Medical, Dental, and Optical Equipment) [18908]

Merisel Inc. Merisel World Class Distribution (Computers and Software) [6486]

Mestre Equipment Co.; F.W. (Construction Materials and Machinery) [7699]

Miami Robes International (Clothing) [5190]

Miller Bearings Inc. (Automotive) [2966]

Miller Machinery and Supply Co. (Restaurant and Commercial Foodservice Equipment and Supplies) [24187]

Mills, Inc.; Aladin (Floorcovering Equipment and Supplies) [10040]

Monel Distributors (Food) [11920]

Nailite International Inc. (Construction Materials and Machinery) [7760]

National Candy (Food) [11975]

Opperman Co., Inc.; Matthew (Hardware) [13854]

Oved Corp. (Toys and Hobby Goods) [26599]

Oved Corp. (Textiles and Notions) [26165]

Palmetto Ford Truck Sales Inc. (Automotive) [3077]

Pan Am Sign Products, Inc. (Specialty Equipment and Products) [25780]

Pan American Frozen Food Inc. (Food) [12102]

Pan American International (Toys and Hobby Goods) [26604]

Pan American Papers Inc. (Paper and Paper Products) [21858]

Pantropic Power Products Inc. (Industrial Machinery) [16379]

Parallel Traders Inc. (Health and Beauty Aids) [14187]

Perez Trading Company Inc. (Paper and Paper Products) [21877]

Perfumania, Inc. (Health and Beauty Aids) [14190]

Perfumania Inc. (Medical, Dental, and Optical Supplies) [19532]

Perm Inc. (Jewelry) [17546]

Pound International Corp. (Health and Beauty Aids) [14192]

Prawn Seafoods Inc. (Food) [12207]

ProSource Inc. (Restaurant and Commercial Foodservice Equipment and Supplies) [24208]

Ram Turbos Inc. (Automotive) [3134]

Rex Chemical Corp. (Cleaning and Janitorial Supplies) [4694]

Richard Electric Supply Company Inc. (Electrical and Electronic Equipment and Supplies) [9292]

Richardson Brands Co. (Food) [12314]

Riverside Paper Company Inc. (Paper and Paper Products) [21907]

Rocamar Services Inc. (Plumbing Materials and Fixtures) [23350]

Roma Chain Manufacturing (Jewelry) [17571]

Rowland Equipment, Inc. (Automotive) [3176]

Rubins Stone House (Jewelry) [17580]

Santucci-Trigg Sales Co. (Food) [12411]

Shaw-Ross International Inc. (Alcoholic Beverages) [2021]

Softouch Company Inc. (Clothing) [5367]

Solares Florida Corp. (Industrial Machinery) [16501]

Southeast Frozen Food Co. (Food) [12536]

Southern Wine & Spirits (Alcoholic Beverages) [2035]

Southern Wine and Spirits of America (Alcoholic Beverages) [2040]

Spectacular Modes Inc. (Clothing) [5379]

Stein Paint Co. (Paints and Varnishes) [21588]

Sunlight Foods Inc. (Food) [12616]

Sunny International Inc. (Hardware) [13943]

Sunshine Golf, Inc. (Recreational and Sporting Goods) [23994]

Super American Import (Horticultural Supplies) [14958]

SYSCO Food Services of South Florida (Food) [12688]

Sysco Food Services of South Florida Inc. (Food) [12689]

Tamiami Range and Gun Distributors Inc. (Guns and Weapons) [13515]

Taylor Distributing Miami Key-West; J.J. (Alcoholic Beverages) [2072]

Tech-Aerofoam Products Inc. (Construction Materials and Machinery) [8103]

Telecom Engineering Consultants Inc. (Communications Systems and Equipment) [5782]

Texpack USA Inc. (Used, Scrap, and Recycled Materials) [27023]

Textiles South Inc. (Industrial Machinery) [16560]

T.R. Distributing (Food) [12739]

Trans World Company of Miami Inc. (Food) [12743]

Transmudo Company Inc. (Food) [12744]

Tropical Music and Pro Audio (Sound and Entertainment Equipment and Supplies) [25485]

United Marine Inc. (Marine) [18627]

Vina & Son Meat Distributors (Food) [12846]

Vitech America Inc. (Computers and Software) [6855]

Walton & Post (Food) [12873]

Walton Wholesale Corp. (Floorcovering Equipment and Supplies) [10284]

Whittenburg, Inc.; N.A. (Textiles and Notions) [26247]

Willets O'Neil Co.; A. (Cleaning and Janitorial Supplies) [4732]

Window Components Manufacturing (Construction Materials and Machinery) [8232]

World Network Trading Corp. (Luggage and Leather Goods) [18446]

Worldwide Manufacturing Inc. (Household Items) [15715]

Wren Electronics, Inc. (Electrical and Electronic Equipment and Supplies) [9610]

Miami Beach

Garment Inc.; Susan (Clothing) [4978]

Miami Lakes

Cuetara America Co. (Food) [10881]

Graveline Electronics Inc. (Communications Systems and Equipment) [5625]

Miami Springs

Advance Petroleum Inc. (Petroleum, Fuels, and Related Equipment) [22023]

Edwards Produce Co.; M and B (Food) [11031]

World Fuel Services Corp. (Petroleum, Fuels, and Related Equipment) [22816]

World Fuel Services Inc. (Aeronautical Equipment and Supplies) [176]

Miramar

G.A.R. International Corp. (Construction Materials and Machinery) [7376]

Jewelmasters Inc. (Jewelry) [17470]

Phillips and Jacobs Inc. (Specialty Equipment and Products) [25784]

Ruff and Company of Florida Inc.; Thomas W. (Office Equipment and Supplies) [21252]

Naples

Allen Systems Group Inc. (Computers and Software) [5905]

D & B Tile (Floorcovering Equipment and Supplies) [9842]

Graybar Electric Company Inc. (Electrical and Electronic Equipment and Supplies) [8809]

Gulf Go-Fers Inc. (Food) [11345]

Metro Tile & Marble, Inc. (Floorcovering Equipment and Supplies) [10027]

Naples Rent-All and Sales Company Inc. (Construction Materials and Machinery) [7762]

New Port Richey

PAS Div. (Aeronautical Equipment and Supplies) [136]

Welbilt Corp. (Household Appliances) [15369]

North Lauderdale

Galaxy Liner Company Inc. (Plastics) [22966]

North Miami

Air Flow Shutters Shade (Household Items) [15391]

LaBelle Time Inc. (Gifts and Novelties) [13384]

Locks Co. (Security and Safety Equipment) [24585]

Locks Co. (Hardware) [13799]

Mohawk Distilled Products L.P. (Alcoholic Beverages) [1887]

North Miami Beach

JJ Gold International Inc. (Jewelry) [17475]

Kaye Brothers Inc. (Food) [11586]

Landsman International Inc. (Food) [11675]

North Palm Beach

Zero 88 Inc. (Electrical and Electronic Equipment and Supplies) [9623]

Oakland

South Lake Apopka Citrus Growers Association (Food) [12532]

Oakland Park

Coastline Distributing (Heating and Cooling Equipment and Supplies) [14389]

Pure Water International Inc. (Specialty Equipment and Products) [25795]

TSF Sportswear (Clothing) [5443]

Ocala

All American Recycling Div. (Metals) [19744]

BAI Distributors Inc. (Electrical and Electronic Equipment and Supplies) [8411]

Broadcasters General Store Inc. (Communications Systems and Equipment) [5536]

Miller Bearings Inc. (Industrial Supplies) [17040]

Witt Co.; The Eli (Food) [12970]

Oldsmar

Datex Inc. (Electrical and Electronic Equipment and Supplies) [8610]
Selective Books Inc. (Books and Other Printed Materials) [4148]

Opa Locka

Heritage Manufacturing Inc. (Guns and Weapons) [13495]
Miami Aviation Corp. (Aeronautical Equipment and Supplies) [126]

Orange City

Lesco Distributing (Electrical and Electronic Equipment and Supplies) [8984]

Orange Lake

DeConna Ice Cream Inc. (Food) [10933]

Orlando

Aaron Scrap Metals (Used, Scrap, and Recycled Materials) [26724]
Aaron Scrap Metals, Div. of Commercial Metals Co. (Metals) [19722]
Abco International (Jewelry) [17301]
Action Products International Inc. (Toys and Hobby Goods) [26381]
Advantor Corp. (Security and Safety Equipment) [24494]
Alfa Romeo Distributors of North America (Motorized Vehicles) [20581]
All American Pool N Patio (Recreational and Sporting Goods) [23503]
Alpha Tile Distributors, Inc. (Floorcovering Equipment and Supplies) [9662]
Amateur Electronics Supply (Communications Systems and Equipment) [5510]
AmeriSource Corp. Orlando Div. (Medical, Dental, and Optical Supplies) [19148]
Azimuth Corp. (Orlando, Florida) (Aeronautical Equipment and Supplies) [54]
Bar Harbor Lobster Co. (Food) [10500]
Barnie's Coffee and Tea Company Inc. (Food) [10510]
Beyda & Associates, Inc. (Books and Other Printed Materials) [3554]
Bindley Western Drug Co. Southeastern Div. (Health and Beauty Aids) [14046]
Blackton Inc. (Floorcovering Equipment and Supplies) [9730]
Capricorn Foods (Food) [10695]
Carse Oil Company Inc. (Petroleum, Fuels, and Related Equipment) [22110]
Chip Supply Inc. (Computers and Software) [6063]
Christ for the World, Inc. (Books and Other Printed Materials) [3634]
City Beverages (Alcoholic Beverages) [1598]
C.L. Industries Inc. (Construction Materials and Machinery) [7175]
Colonial Medical Supplies (Medical, Dental, and Optical Equipment) [18746]
D & B Tile (Floorcovering Equipment and Supplies) [9843]
Desk-Mate Products Inc. (Office Equipment and Supplies) [20958]
Electronic Maintenance Supply Co. (Electrical and Electronic Equipment and Supplies) [8693]
Gear & Wheel Corp. (Automotive) [2668]
Grantham Distributing Company Inc. (Alcoholic Beverages) [1730]
Great Western Meats (Food) [11315]
Great Western Meats Inc. (Food) [11316]
H & H Products Co. (Soft Drinks) [24966]
Hammond Electronics Inc. (Electrical and Electronic Equipment and Supplies) [8825]
Hardware Imagination (Construction Materials and Machinery) [7446]
Highway Equipment and Supply Co. (Industrial Machinery) [16100]
Hughes Supply Inc. (Plumbing Materials and Fixtures) [23216]
I. Wanna Distribution Company Inc. (Food) [11486]

Joissu Products Inc. (Toys and Hobby Goods) [26546]
K & R Instruments Inc. (Scientific and Measurement Devices) [24381]
King Fleet Group (Motorized Vehicles) [20663]
Kobrin Builders Supply Inc. (Construction Materials and Machinery) [7567]
Lasting Impressions Inc. (Jewelry) [17499]
Mechanical Services of Orlando Inc. (Heating and Cooling Equipment and Supplies) [14540]
Meyer Laminates Inc. (Wood and Wood Products) [27345]
Miller Bearings Inc. (Automotive) [2964]
Miller Bearings Inc. (Industrial Supplies) [17041]
Miller Workplace Resources; Herman (Office Equipment and Supplies) [21145]
National Distributing Co. (Alcoholic Beverages) [1903]
Orange Distributors Inc. (Paper and Paper Products) [21855]
Orlando Yamaha (Motorized Vehicles) [20701]
PhotoVision Inc. (Medical, Dental, and Optical Equipment) [18987]
Power & Pumps, Inc. (Industrial Machinery) [16417]
Premier Beverage (Alcoholic Beverages) [1966]
Primary Image Inc. (Computers and Software) [6636]
Red's/Fisher Inc. (Food) [12292]
Red's Market Inc. (Food) [12293]
Senco of Florida Inc. (Hardware) [13910]
Southern Flooring Distributors (Floorcovering Equipment and Supplies) [10161]
Southern Wine & Spirits (Alcoholic Beverages) [2036]
STIHL Southeast, Inc. (Industrial Machinery) [16526]
Summitville Orlando (Floorcovering Equipment and Supplies) [10191]
Taylor Distributors (Floorcovering Equipment and Supplies) [10210]
Tempaco Inc. (Heating and Cooling Equipment and Supplies) [14715]
Transtat Equipment, Inc. (Automotive) [3331]
Traylor Chemical and Supply Co. (Agricultural Equipment and Supplies) [1350]
Truex Associates (Electrical and Electronic Equipment and Supplies) [9513]
Webb Bolt and Nut Co. (Hardware) [13988]
Willcox and Gibbs Inc. Consolidated Electric Supply (Electrical and Electronic Equipment and Supplies) [9595]
Wind-Dorf (USA) Inc. (Construction Materials and Machinery) [8231]

Oviedo

Mickler's Floridiana, Inc. (Books and Other Printed Materials) [3953]

Palm Bay

Military Industrial Supply Co. (Aeronautical Equipment and Supplies) [130]

Palm Beach

HPG Industries Inc. (Construction Materials and Machinery) [7492]

Palm Beach Gardens

Top Source Technologies Inc. (Automotive) [3319]

Palm Coast

Welltep International Inc. (Chemicals) [4551]

Palm Harbor

Girindus Corp. (Chemicals) [4399]
Pinch a Penny Pool Patio (Recreational and Sporting Goods) [23882]

Palmetto

Southern Agriculture Insecticides Inc. (Agricultural Equipment and Supplies) [1279]

Panama City

Clerf Equipment Inc. (Agricultural Equipment and Supplies) [426]

Richardson & Sons Distributors (Construction Materials and Machinery) [7930]
The Sailor's Supply (Marine) [18598]

Paxton

Paxton Timber Co. (Wood and Wood Products) [27356]

Pembroke Pines

Aquaperfect (Veterinary Products) [27071]
Asbury Worldwide Inc. (Restaurant and Commercial Foodservice Equipment and Supplies) [24068]
Baba International Inc. (Jewelry) [17324]
Sparlon Hosiery Mills Inc. (Clothing) [5377]

Pensacola

Auto Shred Recycling L.L.C. (Used, Scrap, and Recycled Materials) [26756]
Brown Marine Service Inc. (Marine) [18471]
Byfield Marine Supply LLC (Marine) [18473]
Craftsmen Supply, Inc. (Floorcovering Equipment and Supplies) [9831]
Grocery Supply Company - Southeast (Food) [11335]
Hub/Industrial Mill Supply Co. (Industrial Supplies) [16934]
Johnson Supply Co. (Marine) [18529]
National Distributing Co. (Alcoholic Beverages) [1904]
Pensacola Mill Supply Company Inc. (Hardware) [13865]
Premier Beverage (Alcoholic Beverages) [1967]
SFK Steel Inc. (Metals) [20362]
Smith Inc.; Del Cher (Food) [12510]
Southern Scrap Material Company Ltd. (Used, Scrap, and Recycled Materials) [27004]

Perry

Bassett Dairy Products Inc. (Food) [10514]

Pierson

Alpha Fern Co. (Horticultural Supplies) [14801]

Pinellas Park

A and M Supply Inc. (Construction Materials and Machinery) [6896]
Ace Tool Co. (Hardware) [13527]
Nestor Sales Co. (Industrial Machinery) [16348]
Tri Citi Auto Warehouse (Automotive) [3333]
Vector Industries Inc. (Construction Materials and Machinery) [8177]

Plant City

A. Camacho Inc. (Food) [10316]
International Petroleum Corp. (Used, Scrap, and Recycled Materials) [26853]
Mid-State Potato Distributors Inc. (Food) [11880]
Prosperity Tool Corp. (Hardware) [13877]
Specialty Food Distributors, Inc. (Food) [12551]

Plantation

National Beverage Corp. (Soft Drinks) [24990]
Technical Marketing, Inc. (Health and Beauty Aids) [14257]
Technical Marketing Inc. (Medical, Dental, and Optical Supplies) [19650]

Pompano Beach

American Sandpainting (Gifts and Novelties) [13302]
Ameritrend Corp. (Office Equipment and Supplies) [20800]
D & B Tile (Floorcovering Equipment and Supplies) [9844]
Iberia Tile (Floorcovering Equipment and Supplies) [9957]
Island Classic Automotive Inc. (Motorized Vehicles) [20654]
Kennesaw Fruit Juice Co. (Food) [11602]
Merritt Marine Supply (Marine) [18567]
Mutual Wholesale Co. (Food) [11963]
Southland Floors, Inc. (Floorcovering Equipment and Supplies) [10170]
Sultan and Sons Inc. (Household Items) [15671]

Summitville Pompano (Floorcovering Equipment and Supplies) [10192]
White Office Furniture and Interiors; J.C. (Office Equipment and Supplies) [21355]

Port St. Joe
St. Joe Communications Inc. (Communications Systems and Equipment) [5748]

Port St. Lucie
Japco Exports (Veterinary Products) [27159]

Port Salerno
Florida Classics Library (Books and Other Printed Materials) [3753]

Quail Heights
Graybar Electric Company Inc. (Electrical and Electronic Equipment and Supplies) [8813]

Quincy
SuperValu Quincy Div. (Food) [12651]

Riverview
Premier Beverage (Alcoholic Beverages) [1968]

Riviera Beach
Consulier Engineering Inc. (Automotive) [2479]
Florida Bolt and Nut Co. (Hardware) [13710]
Florida Bolt and Nut Co. (Hardware) [13711]
Hibel Studio; Edna (Gifts and Novelties) [13367]
Ner Tamid Book Distributors (Books and Other Printed Materials) [3992]
Smith Electronics; Larry (Marine) [18612]

Ruskin
Bob's Machine Shop (Marine) [18468]

Safety Harbor
Aqua Magnetics International (Specialty Equipment and Products) [25556]
Aqua Magnetics International (Plumbing Materials and Fixtures) [23068]
Cariba International Corp. (Food) [10700]

St. Augustine
Ammar Beauty Supply Co. (Health and Beauty Aids) [14020]
Ideal Division (Hardware) [13762]
St. John's Food Service, Inc. (Food) [12389]
Tree of Life Inc. (Food) [12747]
Tree of Life Inc. Southeast (Health and Beauty Aids) [14261]

St. Petersburg
ACC Recycling Corp. (Used, Scrap, and Recycled Materials) [26726]
Alpha Tile Distributors, Inc. (Floorcovering Equipment and Supplies) [9664]
America II Electronics (Electrical and Electronic Equipment and Supplies) [8336]
Best Labs (Medical, Dental, and Optical Equipment) [18706]
Best Labs (Electrical and Electronic Equipment and Supplies) [8434]
Dairy-Mix Inc. (Food) [10899]
Dairy-Mix Inc. (Food) [10900]
Danka Business Systems PLC (Office Equipment and Supplies) [20946]
Danka Industries Inc. (Office Equipment and Supplies) [20947]
Electric Fuels Corp. (Minerals and Ores) [20537]
Film Technologies International, Inc. (Photographic Equipment and Supplies) [22853]
Foreign Car Parts Inc. (Automotive) [2638]
Great Outdoors Publishing Co. (Books and Other Printed Materials) [3797]
Ingham Publishing, Inc. (Books and Other Printed Materials) [3843]
Lapure Water Coolers (Household Appliances) [15198]
Media Concepts Inc. (Sound and Entertainment Equipment and Supplies) [25309]
Office Pavillion (Furniture and Fixtures) [13192]

Si-Tex Marine Electronics Inc. (Electrical and Electronic Equipment and Supplies) [9366]
Sigma International Inc. (Food) [12490]
Solar Graphic Inc. (Household Items) [15660]

Sanford
Aero Products Corp. (Medical, Dental, and Optical Equipment) [18663]
Coastline Distribution Inc. (Heating and Cooling Equipment and Supplies) [14390]
Comfortmaker Distribution (Heating and Cooling Equipment and Supplies) [14397]
Florida Extruders International Inc. (Metals) [19980]
Wayne Densch Inc. (Alcoholic Beverages) [2110]

Sarasota
Alpha Tile Distributors, Inc. (Floorcovering Equipment and Supplies) [9666]
American Business International Inc. (Office Equipment and Supplies) [20790]
BookWorld Services Inc. (Books and Other Printed Materials) [3584]
Casa Italia (Food) [10705]
Contour Lynnsoles Inc. (Shoes) [24720]
Curtis TradeGroup Inc. (Rubber) [24274]
Eagle International, Inc. (Industrial Machinery) [15973]
Elcotel Inc. (Communications Systems and Equipment) [5601]
Foreign Trade Marketing (Food) [11187]
Glass Crafters Stain Glass Supply (Gifts and Novelties) [13361]
Imagination & Co. (Construction Materials and Machinery) [7506]
Jordan Research Corp. (Automotive) [2836]
Kinetronics Corp. (Photographic Equipment and Supplies) [22869]
Medical Equipment Repair Services Inc. (Medical, Dental, and Optical Equipment) [18914]
Stottlemyer and Shoemaker Lumber Co. (Construction Materials and Machinery) [8076]
Ullman Sails (Marine) [18626]
Wesco Turf Inc. (Agricultural Equipment and Supplies) [1421]

Seffner
Diamond Products Co. (Health and Beauty Aids) [14084]

South Bay
Okleelanta Corp. (Food) [12058]

Spring Hill
CX Blaster Co. Inc. (Toys and Hobby Goods) [26456]

Stuart
Chapman Marine Supply (Marine) [18478]
EME Corp. (Sound and Entertainment Equipment and Supplies) [25181]
Nautical & Industrial Supply Inc. (Marine) [18575]
Second Chance Golf Ball Recyclers Inc. (Recreational and Sporting Goods) [23934]
White Commercial Corp. (Food) [12926]

Sunrise
Aurafin Corp. (Jewelry) [17319]
D & B Tile Distributors (Floorcovering Equipment and Supplies) [9846]
D and B Tile Distributors (Construction Materials and Machinery) [7240]
Delta Industrial Systems Co. (Hardware) [13660]
Pavarini Business Communications Inc. (Communications Systems and Equipment) [5704]

Tallahassee
C and W Food Service Inc. (Food) [10658]
Dowling Inc.; J.H. (Construction Materials and Machinery) [7286]
Seatile Distributors (Floorcovering Equipment and Supplies) [10141]
SoftKlone Distributing Corp. (Computers and Software) [6738]

Tamarac
Graphline, Inc. (Specialty Equipment and Products) [25670]

Tampa
ADEMCO/ADI (Security and Safety Equipment) [24481]
Agri Supplies (Veterinary Products) [27058]
Allstate Office Products Inc. (Office Equipment and Supplies) [20787]
Alpha Tile Distributors, Inc. (Floorcovering Equipment and Supplies) [9663]
Anderson Home Health Supply (Medical, Dental, and Optical Equipment) [18682]
Aqua Systems International, Inc. (Plumbing Materials and Fixtures) [23069]
Ashe Industries Inc. (Construction Materials and Machinery) [6997]
Baker's Nursery (Horticultural Supplies) [14814]
Best Brands Inc. (Food) [10546]
Booker and Company Inc. (Construction Materials and Machinery) [7070]
Budd Mayer Co. (Restaurant and Commercial Foodservice Equipment and Supplies) [24083]
Cady Industries Inc. (Paper and Paper Products) [21664]
Carroll Air Systems Inc. (Heating and Cooling Equipment and Supplies) [14369]
Casey Co.; A.A. (Industrial Supplies) [16784]
Central Oil Company Inc. (Petroleum, Fuels, and Related Equipment) [22126]
Central Power Systems (Agricultural Equipment and Supplies) [398]
Coast Marine Distribution (Marine) [18484]
Columbia Jobbing Co. Inc. (Paper and Paper Products) [21687]
ComTel Industries Inc. (Communications Systems and Equipment) [5578]
Custom Cable Industries Inc. (Electrical and Electronic Equipment and Supplies) [8599]
Custom Wholesale Flooring (Floorcovering Equipment and Supplies) [9838]
Diamond Tager Co. (Food) [10961]
Dixie Building Supplies Co. (Construction Materials and Machinery) [7272]
Dow Electronics Inc. (Electrical and Electronic Equipment and Supplies) [8633]
Dynabit USA Inc. (Computers and Software) [6230]
Eagle Supply Inc. (Construction Materials and Machinery) [7296]
Encore Broadcast Equipment Sales Inc. (Communications Systems and Equipment) [5604]
F.E.P. Inc. (Books and Other Printed Materials) [3747]
Florida Hardwood Floor Supply (Floorcovering Equipment and Supplies) [9901]
Florimex Inc. (Food) [11162]
Gulf Central Corp. (Household Appliances) [15154]
Hardware Imagination (Construction Materials and Machinery) [7445]
Harris & Stearns (Textiles and Notions) [26057]
Heavy Parts International (Automotive) [2736]
Hoven Inc. (Toys and Hobby Goods) [26526]
Hydro Agri North America Inc. (Agricultural Equipment and Supplies) [849]
Infra Metals (Metals) [20063]
Johnson Brothers Liquor Co. (Alcoholic Beverages) [1786]
Lincoln Trading Co. (Aeronautical Equipment and Supplies) [116]
Lo-An Foods Inc. (Food) [11719]
Lowe Supply Co.; Bert (Industrial Supplies) [17007]
Lykes Bros. Inc. (Food) [11748]
Marcone Appliance Parts Center (Household Appliances) [15211]
Master Purveyors (Food) [11801]
McNichols Co. (Metals) [20162]
Meadow Steel Products Div. (Construction Materials and Machinery) [7687]
National Distributing Co. (Alcoholic Beverages) [1902]
Paragon Music Center Inc. (Sound and Entertainment Equipment and Supplies) [25375]

Parker Banana Company Inc. (Food) [12112]
Peninsular Paper Company Inc. (Paper and Paper Products) [21873]
Pepin Distributing Co. (Alcoholic Beverages) [1949]
PharMerica Inc./PMSI (Medical, Dental, and Optical Supplies) [19538]
Professional Medical Services Inc. (Medical, Dental, and Optical Supplies) [19555]
Raybro Electric Supplies, Inc., Utility Div. (Electrical and Electronic Equipment and Supplies) [9266]
Reddi-Made Foods Inc. (Food) [12289]
Reeves Southeastern Corp. (Construction Materials and Machinery) [7908]
Reilly Dairy and Food Co. (Food) [12296]
Reptron Electronics Inc. (Electrical and Electronic Equipment and Supplies) [9277]
Resin Management Corp. (Chemicals) [4494]
Ringhaver Equipment Co. (Industrial Machinery) [16454]
SAFLINK Corp. (Computers and Software) [6699]
Security Engineers Systems Inc. (Security and Safety Equipment) [24630]
Somerset Pharmaceuticals Inc. (Medical, Dental, and Optical Supplies) [19620]
Southeast Dairy Products (Food) [12535]
Southeastern Access Control (Construction Materials and Machinery) [8043]
Southern Wine & Spirits (Alcoholic Beverages) [2037]
Southwestern Suppliers Inc. (Metals) [20380]
Standard Marine Supply Corp. (Marine) [18616]
Tampa Appliance Parts Corp. (Household Appliances) [15330]
Tampa Armature Works Inc. (Industrial Machinery) [16546]
Tampa Rubber & Gasket Co., Inc. (Rubber) [24298]
Tech Products, Inc. (Construction Materials and Machinery) [8104]
TRCA Electronic Division (Communications Systems and Equipment) [5796]
U.A.F. L.P. (Horticultural Supplies) [14964]
Valenti Company Inc.; J.C. (Food) [12814]
Velda Farms (Food) [12834]
VersaTec (Furniture and Fixtures) [13268]
Vitality Foodservice Inc. (Soft Drinks) [25049]
Westshore Glass Corp. (Construction Materials and Machinery) [8216]
Williams Oil Company Inc.; J.H. (Petroleum, Fuels, and Related Equipment) [22806]

Tavares
Lake Region Pack Association (Food) [11667]

Tequesta
Broedell Plumbing Supply Inc. (Plumbing Materials and Fixtures) [23098]

Thonotosassa
Beautiful Plants by Charlie (Horticultural Supplies) [14828]
Fire Alarm Service Corp. (Security and Safety Equipment) [24540]

Treasure Island
Metrotek Industries Inc. (Electrical and Electronic Equipment and Supplies) [9070]

Umatilla
Golden Gem Growers Inc. (Soft Drinks) [24960]

Venice
J.R.N. Inc. (Jewelry) [17477]
Venice Convalescent Aids Medical Supply (Medical, Dental, and Optical Equipment) [19100]

Vero Beach
East Coast Tile/Terrazzo (Floorcovering Equipment and Supplies) [9877]
East Coast Tile/Terrazzo (Construction Materials and Machinery) [7300]
Gracewood Fruit Co. (Food) [11301]
Smith's Sons Inc.; Leroy E. (Food) [12520]
The Speech Bin, Inc. (Books and Other Printed Materials) [4181]

Warren Corp.; George E. (Petroleum, Fuels, and Related Equipment) [22783]

Waverly
Highland Exchange Service Co-op (Food) [11431]
Waverly Growers Cooperative (Food) [12885]

West Palm Beach
Atlantic Filter Corp. (Specialty Equipment and Products) [25564]
Brown Distributing (Alcoholic Beverages) [1553]
D & B Tile (Floorcovering Equipment and Supplies) [9845]
Distribution Services Inc. (Books and Other Printed Materials) [3695]
Eastern Electric (Household Appliances) [15118]
The Florida News Group, Ltd. (Books and Other Printed Materials) [3754]
Golden Pride International (Food) [11286]
Graybar Electric Company Inc. (Electrical and Electronic Equipment and Supplies) [8808]
Joy Enterprises (Hardware) [13776]
Joy Enterprises (Medical, Dental, and Optical Supplies) [19387]
Joy Optical Co. (Medical, Dental, and Optical Supplies) [19388]
Laird Plastics Inc. (Plastics) [22989]
The Learning Plant (Books and Other Printed Materials) [3902]
Miller Bearings Inc. (Automotive) [2967]
Montoya/MAS International Inc. (Specialty Equipment and Products) [25744]
Oxbow Carbon International Inc. (Minerals and Ores) [20556]
Oxbow Corp. (Petroleum, Fuels, and Related Equipment) [22545]
Peninsular Electric Distributors Inc. (Electrical and Electronic Equipment and Supplies) [9188]
Peninsular Electronic Distributors (Electrical and Electronic Equipment and Supplies) [9189]
Rayside Truck & Trailer (Automotive) [3136]
Sewell Hardware Company Inc. (Hardware) [13914]
Todhunter Imports Ltd. (Alcoholic Beverages) [2084]

Westville
Allenson, Inc.; Alec R. (Books and Other Printed Materials) [3491]

Winter Garden
Avalon Ornamentals (Horticultural Supplies) [14810]
Pounds Motor Company Inc. (Agricultural Equipment and Supplies) [1143]

Winter Haven
Carolyn Candies, Inc. (Food) [10703]
Fields Equipment Company Inc. (Agricultural Equipment and Supplies) [684]
Hartmann of Florida (Electrical and Electronic Equipment and Supplies) [8833]
Laundry Textile Co. (Textiles and Notions) [26122]
Myco Plastics (Automotive) [3009]
Scotty's Inc. (Construction Materials and Machinery) [7993]

Winter Park
ADEMCO/ADI (Security and Safety Equipment) [24477]
InfoSource Inc. (Computers and Software) [6370]
Members Service Corp. (Communications Systems and Equipment) [5668]
RSR Group Florida, Inc. (Guns and Weapons) [13505]
RSR Wholesale Guns Inc. (Guns and Weapons) [13508]
RSR Wholesale South Inc. (Guns and Weapons) [13511]
T & T Tile Distribution Inc. (Floorcovering Equipment and Supplies) [10208]

Zephyrhills
Zephyr Egg Co. (Food) [13005]

Georgia

Acworth
Regency Collection Inc. (Jewelry) [17559]

Albany
Alarm Services Inc. (Security and Safety Equipment) [24500]
Albany Bowling Supply Inc. (Recreational and Sporting Goods) [23499]
Anderson and Associates Inc. (Electrical and Electronic Equipment and Supplies) [8351]
Bearings & Drives, Inc. (Automotive) [2339]
Bob's Candies Inc. (Food) [10584]
Engineering and Equipment Co. (Plumbing Materials and Fixtures) [23149]
Family Reading Service (Books and Other Printed Materials) [3744]
Medley Hotel and Restaurant Supply Co. (Restaurant and Commercial Foodservice Equipment and Supplies) [24183]
Sellers Tile Distributors (Floorcovering Equipment and Supplies) [10144]
Sunnyland Farms, Inc. (Food) [12617]

Alma
Albaco Foods Inc. (Food) [10356]

Alpharetta
Addison Corp. (Construction Materials and Machinery) [6915]
Alimenta (USA) Inc. (Food) [10364]
Big River Industries Inc. (Construction Materials and Machinery) [7057]
Certified Ribbon Supply Inc. (Computers and Software) [6059]
Industrial Environmental Products Inc. (Chemicals) [4428]
MacMillan Bloedel Building Materials (Construction Materials and Machinery) [7633]
McGinnis Farms Inc. (Agricultural Equipment and Supplies) [1003]
P.B.D. Worldwide Fulfillment Services (Books and Other Printed Materials) [4047]
Professional Book Distributors, Inc. (Books and Other Printed Materials) [4087]
Regency Collection Inc. (Jewelry) [17560]
Rugby Building Products (Construction Materials and Machinery) [7966]
Seagull Software Systems Inc. (Computers and Software) [6714]
Southern Data Systems Inc. (Computers and Software) [6749]
Southern Prosthetic Supply (Medical, Dental, and Optical Equipment) [19046]
Southern Prosthetic Supply Co. (Medical, Dental, and Optical Supplies) [19628]

Americus
Design Finishes Inc. (Furniture and Fixtures) [13087]

Armuchee
Image Industries Inc. (Used, Scrap, and Recycled Materials) [26847]

Athens
Armstrong and Dobbs Inc. (Construction Materials and Machinery) [6986]
Athens Hardware Co. (Hardware) [13570]
Athens Material Handling Inc. (Industrial Machinery) [15787]
Bearings and Drives, Inc. (Industrial Supplies) [16735]
Classic City Beverages Inc. (Alcoholic Beverages) [1600]
COSMIC (Computers and Software) [6165]
Dixons Bicycling Center Inc. (Recreational and Sporting Goods) [23626]
Exploration Resources Inc. (Computers and Software) [6261]
Farmer and Co.; Leon (Alcoholic Beverages) [1684]

Green Seed Co. (Livestock and Farm
Products) [17963]
Loef Company Inc. (Used, Scrap, and Recycled
Materials) [26885]
Loef Company Inc. (Used, Scrap, and Recycled
Materials) [26886]
Southern Copy Machines (Office Equipment and
Supplies) [21277]
Trademark Dental Ceramics Inc. (Medical, Dental,
and Optical Equipment) [19082]

Atlanta

Ack Electronics (Electrical and Electronic Equipment
and Supplies) [8264]
Adelman Sales Corp. (Hardware) [13534]
ADEMCO/ADI (Security and Safety
Equipment) [24468]
Advanced Computer Distributors Inc. (Computers
and Software) [5885]
AJC International Inc. (Medical, Dental, and Optical
Supplies) [19127]
Alpha Star International Inc. (Food) [10380]
American Associated Roofing
Distributor (Construction Materials and
Machinery) [6958]
American Performance (Automotive) [2233]
American Scientific Technology, L.L.C. (Medical,
Dental, and Optical Equipment) [18679]
APD Transmission Parts (Automotive) [2244]
Apex Supply Company Inc. (Heating and Cooling
Equipment and Supplies) [14323]
Armstrong's Lock & Supply, Inc. (Security and
Safety Equipment) [24508]
Artlite Office Supply and Furniture Co. (Furniture
and Fixtures) [13024]
Atlanta Beverage Co. (Alcoholic Beverages) [1490]
Atlanta Broom Company Inc. (Paper and Paper
Products) [21638]
Atlanta Broom Company Inc. (Industrial
Supplies) [16715]
Atlanta Commercial Tire Inc. (Automotive) [2263]
Atlanta Fixture and Sails Co. (Restaurant and
Commercial Foodservice Equipment and
Supplies) [24070]
Atlanta Fuel Company Inc. (Petroleum, Fuels, and
Related Equipment) [22046]
Atlanta Wheels & Accessories,
Inc. (Automotive) [2264]
Atlanta Wholesale Wine Co. (Alcoholic
Beverages) [1491]
Atlantic Promotions (Specialty Equipment and
Products) [25565]
Auto Service and Tire Supermarts
Inc. (Automotive) [2278]
Bags Direct, Inc. (Plastics) [22933]
Ball Stalker Co. (Office Equipment and
Supplies) [20829]
B.E.B. Ltd. (Plastics) [22935]
Better Brands of Atlanta Inc. (Alcoholic
Beverages) [1524]
Bimex Incorporated (Industrial Machinery) [15824]
Bishop-Epicure Foods Company
Inc. (Food) [10560]
Brown Distributing Co. Inc. (Furniture and
Fixtures) [13046]
Brown South; J.L. (Toys and Hobby
Goods) [26428]
Buckhead Shoes Corp. II (Shoes) [24702]
Cagle's Inc. (Food) [10661]
Cain and Bultman Co. (Electrical and Electronic
Equipment and Supplies) [8482]
Capel Rugs Inc. (Floorcovering Equipment and
Supplies) [9754]
Carithers-Wallace-Courtenay Inc. (Furniture and
Fixtures) [13063]
Castleberry Office Interiors Inc. (Furniture and
Fixtures) [13066]
Caye and Company Inc.; W.C. (Construction
Materials and Machinery) [7154]
Chihade International Inc. (Food) [10746]
Colonial Shoe Co. (Shoes) [24717]
ComSource Independent Foodservice Companies
Inc. (Food) [10803]
Cornucopia Natural Foods Inc. (Health and Beauty
Aids) [14072]

Corporate Environments of Georgia Inc. (Office
Equipment and Supplies) [20924]
Cowan Supply Co. (Plumbing Materials and
Fixtures) [23129]
Cox Enterprises Inc. (Automotive) [2490]
Coyne Galleries; Elaine (Jewelry) [17379]
Dakin Inc. (Toys and Hobby Goods) [26459]
Depco Inc. (Sound and Entertainment Equipment
and Supplies) [25166]
Designer's Den Inc. (Household Items) [15473]
Diaz Foods Inc. (Food) [10962]
Diaz Wholesale and Manufacturing Company
Inc. (Food) [10963]
Digitel Corp. (Communications Systems and
Equipment) [5596]
Dixon Medical Inc. (Medical, Dental, and Optical
Equipment) [18776]
Don Overcast and Associates (Clothing) [4920]
Dreyer & Associates Inc. (Clothing) [4922]
East West Connect Inc. (Agricultural Equipment
and Supplies) [535]
EIS, Inc. (Electrical and Electronic Equipment and
Supplies) [8658]
Electronic Tele-Communications
Inc. (Communications Systems and
Equipment) [5602]
Ellis and Everard Inc. (Chemicals) [4382]
Empire Distributing (Alcoholic Beverages) [1676]
Epicure Foods Inc. (Food) [11052]
Fast Track Communications Inc. (Communications
Systems and Equipment) [5611]
Fleet Distribution, Inc. (Computers and
Software) [6272]
Fox Appliance Parts of Atlanta Inc. (Household
Appliances) [15131]
Framers On Peachtree (Household Items) [15506]
Fulton Paper Company Inc. (Paper and Paper
Products) [21734]
Fulton Supply Co. (Industrial Supplies) [16883]
General Wholesale Co. (Alcoholic
Beverages) [1709]
Genuine Parts Co. (Automotive) [2678]
Georgia Crown Distributing (Alcoholic
Beverages) [1711]
Georgia Flush Door Sales Inc. (Construction
Materials and Machinery) [7392]
Georgia Impression Products Inc. (Furniture and
Fixtures) [13121]
Georgia Lighting Supply Co. (Electrical and
Electronic Equipment and Supplies) [8786]
Georgia-Pacific Corp. Distribution Div. (Construction
Materials and Machinery) [7394]
Golden Poultry Company Inc. (Food) [11285]
Good News Communications Inc. (Books and
Other Printed Materials) [3787]
Greater Mobile Auto Auction
Div. (Automotive) [2702]
Green Seed Co. (Agricultural Equipment and
Supplies) [764]
Gunter Jr. & Associates; Guy T. (Household
Appliances) [15155]
Gussoff-Reslow & Associates (Clothing) [5008]
Hamilton Inc.; David (Clothing) [5014]
Helman Corporation (Clothing) [5026]
Hinely Aluminum Inc. (Metals) [20040]
Horizon Impex (Clothing) [5037]
Hunter and Company Inc. (Textiles and
Notions) [26069]
Ideal Optics Inc. (Medical, Dental, and Optical
Supplies) [19365]
Industrial Paper Corp. (Paper and Paper
Products) [21773]
Inland Seafood Corp. (Food) [11508]
International Business Machines Corp.
EduQuest (Computers and Software) [6388]
International Trading & Investment (Furniture and
Fixtures) [13146]
Kaufman Supply (Household Appliances) [15184]
Klockner Namasco Corp. (Metals) [20105]
Lanier Worldwide Inc. (Office Equipment and
Supplies) [21100]
Lincoln-Kaltek (Construction Materials and
Machinery) [7607]
Linsey's Products Inc. (Health and Beauty
Aids) [14153]
LOR Inc. (Industrial Machinery) [16245]

Los Amigos Tortilla Manufacturing
Inc. (Food) [11734]
Mellen Parts Company Inc. (Automotive) [2940]
Mindis Acquisition Corp. (Used, Scrap, and
Recycled Materials) [26915]
Modemsplus Inc. (Communications Systems and
Equipment) [5681]
Monarch Wine Company of Georgia (Alcoholic
Beverages) [1889]
Nalley Cos. (Automotive) [3013]
Namasco Corp. (Metals) [20213]
National Distributing Company Inc. (Alcoholic
Beverages) [1907]
Neon Co. (Specialty Equipment and
Products) [25753]
New Era Media Supply (Photographic Equipment
and Supplies) [22882]
North Brothers Co. (Construction Materials and
Machinery) [7792]
Orbilt Compressors, Inc. (Heating and Cooling
Equipment and Supplies) [14629]
Orbit Industries Inc. Clarkesville Garment
Div. (Clothing) [5255]
Orkin Lawn Care (Horticultural Supplies) [14933]
Orton Industries Inc. (Electrical and Electronic
Equipment and Supplies) [9161]
Overcast and Associates; Don (Clothing) [5257]
Paradies and Co. (Books and Other Printed
Materials) [4039]
Peachtree Fabrics Inc. (Textiles and
Notions) [26170]
Phenix Supply Co. (Cleaning and Janitorial
Supplies) [4685]
Piedmont National Corp. (Paper and Paper
Products) [21882]
Printers Xchange Inc. (Industrial
Machinery) [16427]
Production Services Atlanta Inc. (Photographic
Equipment and Supplies) [22894]
Professional Aviation Associates Inc. (Aeronautical
Equipment and Supplies) [139]
Projexions Video Supply (Sound and Entertainment
Equipment and Supplies) [25391]
P.S. Energy Group Inc. (Petroleum, Fuels, and
Related Equipment) [22598]
Randall Brothers Inc. (Construction Materials and
Machinery) [7899]
Rank America Inc. (Industrial Machinery) [16438]
RCF Inc. (Gifts and Novelties) [13435]
RealCom Office Communications
Inc. (Communications Systems and
Equipment) [5736]
Rogers Decorative Fabrics; Miles (Textiles and
Notions) [26190]
Royal Arts & Crafts (Toys and Hobby
Goods) [26638]
Rubin Brothers Company Inc. (Floorcovering
Equipment and Supplies) [10133]
Schneider Sales Inc.; Arthur (Shoes) [24852]
Servidyne System (Heating and Cooling Equipment
and Supplies) [14677]
Smarter Security Systems, Inc. (Security and Safety
Equipment) [24638]
Smarter Security Systems Inc. (Electrical and
Electronic Equipment and Supplies) [9377]
Southeastern Communications (Electrical and
Electronic Equipment and Supplies) [9384]
Southern Belting & Transmission (Industrial
Machinery) [16508]
Spectrum Data Systems Inc. (Computers and
Software) [6755]
Stag/Parkway Inc. (Motorized Vehicles) [20730]
Summitville Atlanta (Floorcovering Equipment and
Supplies) [10186]
Sunbrand Co. (Agricultural Equipment and
Supplies) [1303]
Sunlow Inc. (Restaurant and Commercial
Foodservice Equipment and Supplies) [24233]
Super Valu Stores Inc. (Food) [12630]
Symco Group Inc. (Computers and
Software) [6781]
TEC America Inc. (Specialty Equipment and
Products) [25837]
TEC America Inc. (Restaurant and Commercial
Foodservice Equipment and Supplies) [24242]

Thompson Silk Co.; Jim (Textiles and Notions) [26227]
TimeSaving Services Inc. (Computers and Software) [6818]
Transoceanic Trade, Inc. (Photographic Equipment and Supplies) [22911]
Trax Inc. (Construction Materials and Machinery) [8143]
Triton Marketing Inc. (Food) [12758]
Triton Marketing Inc. (Petroleum, Fuels, and Related Equipment) [22750]
Underwood HVAC, Inc. (Heating and Cooling Equipment and Supplies) [14743]
UNIPRO Foodservice, Inc. (Food) [12788]
Unisource (Paper and Paper Products) [21965]
U.S. Medical Supply Co. (Medical, Dental, and Optical Equipment) [19096]
Universal Blueprint Paper (Paper and Paper Products) [21979]
Vantage Industries Inc. (Floorcovering Equipment and Supplies) [10274]
Vihon Associates (Household Appliances) [15358]
Walk Thru the Bible Ministries Inc. (Books and Other Printed Materials) [4266]
Whitaker Oil Co. (Petroleum, Fuels, and Related Equipment) [22799]
Williams Detroit Diesel Allison (Automotive) [3433]
Wink Davis Equipment Company Inc. (Cleaning and Janitorial Supplies) [4733]
Wonalancet Co. (Textiles and Notions) [26250]
World Access Inc. (Communications Systems and Equipment) [5818]
Zumpano Enterprises, Inc. (Floorcovering Equipment and Supplies) [10310]

Auburn
Steri-Systems Corp. (Medical, Dental, and Optical Equipment) [19056]

Augusta
A Plus Medical, Inc. (Medical, Dental, and Optical Supplies) [19117]
Baker Hydro Inc. (Recreational and Sporting Goods) [23537]
Custom Sound of Augusta Inc. (Sound and Entertainment Equipment and Supplies) [25153]
Fox Appliance Parts of Augusta Inc. (Household Appliances) [15132]
Hennessy Ingredients; Ron (Food) [11412]
Johannsens Inc. (Shoes) [24780]
Macuch Steel Products Inc. (Metals) [20142]
Pratt & Dudley Building Materials (Construction Materials and Machinery) [7885]
Rex Auto Parts (Automotive) [3152]
Sidneys Department Store & Uniforms, Inc. (Clothing) [5352]
Sig Cox Inc. (Plumbing Materials and Fixtures) [23375]
Southern Distributing (Sound and Entertainment Equipment and Supplies) [25455]
Thomas; Johnny (Computers and Software) [6817]
The Tile Center, Inc. (Floorcovering Equipment and Supplies) [10218]

Austell
Bindley Western Drug Co. Mid-South Div. (Health and Beauty Aids) [14045]
Midsouth Electric Corp. (Sound and Entertainment Equipment and Supplies) [25321]
Seghers Better Technology (Industrial Machinery) [16480]
Southeast Pet (Veterinary Products) [27234]

Avondale Estates
Global Expediting and Marketing Co. (Industrial Supplies) [16896]
La Piccolina and Co. Inc. (Food) [11660]

Bainbridge
Callahan Grocery Co. Inc. (Food) [10679]
Dollar Farm Products Co. (Agricultural Equipment and Supplies) [522]
Harrison Livestock Co.; B.H. (Livestock and Farm Products) [17977]
Sellers Oil Co. (Petroleum, Fuels, and Related Equipment) [22660]

Stones Inc. (Livestock and Farm Products) [18258]

Ball Ground
LAT Sportswear, Inc. (Clothing) [5122]

Bethlehem
Harrison Poultry Inc. (Food) [11382]

Blairsville
Owenby Co. (Clothing) [5258]

Blakely
Early Tractor Co. Inc. (Agricultural Equipment and Supplies) [533]

Bogart
Athens Building Supply (Construction Materials and Machinery) [7000]
Bensons Backery (Food) [10538]
Custom Audio Distributors Inc. (Sound and Entertainment Equipment and Supplies) [25151]
Main Line International Inc. (Medical, Dental, and Optical Equipment) [18898]
Zumpano Enterprises, Inc. (Floorcovering Equipment and Supplies) [10311]

Bowdon
Multi-Line Industries Inc. (Clothing) [5209]

Brunswick
Modern Builders Supply (Floorcovering Equipment and Supplies) [10043]
Sea Harvest Packing Co. (Food) [12442]
Tidewater Companies Inc. (Wood and Wood Products) [27387]
Tidewater Companies Inc. (Agricultural Equipment and Supplies) [1334]

Buford
Brighter Image Publishing (Gifts and Novelties) [13323]
Sisco Products Inc. (Heating and Cooling Equipment and Supplies) [14685]

Cairo
Graco Fertilizer Co. (Agricultural Equipment and Supplies) [751]
Higdon Grocery Company Inc.; Ira (Food) [11429]
Wight Nurseries Inc. (Horticultural Supplies) [14976]

Calhoun
Bretlin Inc. (Floorcovering Equipment and Supplies) [9739]
De Poortere of America Inc.; Louis (Textiles and Notions) [26014]
LaVayne Distributors (Clothing) [5124]
Sharion's Silk Flower Outlet (Horticultural Supplies) [14949]

Camilla
O'San Products Inc. (Food) [12080]

Canton
L.A. T Sportswear Inc. (Clothing) [5119]
Meadows Company Inc.; Ben (Agricultural Equipment and Supplies) [1007]

Carrollton
Tanner Grocery Company Inc.; C.M. (Food) [12697]

Cartersville
Admiralty Mills Inc. (Floorcovering Equipment and Supplies) [9647]
Enterprise Oil Co. (Petroleum, Fuels, and Related Equipment) [22235]
Prince Street Technologies Ltd. (Floorcovering Equipment and Supplies) [10110]
Taylor Feed & Pet Supply (Veterinary Products) [27245]

Cedartown
Fite Co.; Clifford D. (Food) [11137]

Chamblee
Cresc Corp. (Gifts and Novelties) [13340]

Chatsworth
Focus Carpet Corp. (Floorcovering Equipment and Supplies) [9903]
Playfield Industries Inc. (Recreational and Sporting Goods) [23885]
The Yarn Center (Toys and Hobby Goods) [26717]

Clarkston
Custom Wholesale Flooring (Floorcovering Equipment and Supplies) [9839]
North American Security (Security and Safety Equipment) [24604]

Cleveland
Original Appalachian Artworks Inc. (Toys and Hobby Goods) [26598]

College Park
Kauffman Tire Service Inc. (Automotive) [2840]
Sysco Food Services of Atlanta Inc. (Food) [12674]

Columbus
Albert Poultry Co. Inc. (Food) [10357]
Columbus Paper Company Inc. (Cleaning and Janitorial Supplies) [4601]
Columbus Tractor Machinery Co. (Agricultural Equipment and Supplies) [436]
Fox Appliance Parts of Columbus Inc. (Household Appliances) [15133]
Georgia Crown Distributing Co. (Alcoholic Beverages) [1712]
Glover Wholesale Inc. (Food) [11277]
Pepsi; Buffalo Rock (Soft Drinks) [25004]
Southern Belting & Transmissions (Industrial Supplies) [17182]
Specialty Building Products, Inc. (Floorcovering Equipment and Supplies) [10174]
Specialty Building Products Inc. (Construction Materials and Machinery) [8060]
Valley Fir and Redwood Co. (Construction Materials and Machinery) [8167]
Williams Industrial Products, Inc.; J.H. (Hardware) [13998]

Conyers
Dickson CC Co. (Heating and Cooling Equipment and Supplies) [14420]
Metro Refrigeration Supply, Inc. (Heating and Cooling Equipment and Supplies) [14541]
Sealy Mattress Georgia (Furniture and Fixtures) [13235]

Cordele
B and W Farm Center Inc. (Agricultural Equipment and Supplies) [266]
Service Supply Systems Inc. (Plumbing Materials and Fixtures) [23369]

Cornelia
Fleming Foodservice (Food) [11157]

Cumming
Air Parts Inc. (Heating and Cooling Equipment and Supplies) [14305]
Aluma Panel, Inc. (Paints and Varnishes) [21384]
Automotive Dryers Inc. (Automotive) [2287]
Sawnee Refrigeration & Welding Supply, Inc. (Heating and Cooling Equipment and Supplies) [14674]
Vibrint Corp. (Clothing) [5461]

Dalton
Beaulieu of America Inc. (Textiles and Notions) [25977]
Buchanan Industries (Floorcovering Equipment and Supplies) [9743]
Clarklift of Dalton Inc. (Industrial Machinery) [15890]
Dalton Computer Services Inc. (Computers and Software) [6178]

Dalton Supply Co. Inc. (Heating and Cooling Equipment and Supplies) [14412]

F & R Sales Inc. (Clothing) [4942]

Glaze Supply Company Inc. (Electrical and Electronic Equipment and Supplies) [8788]

Merit Industries (Floorcovering Equipment and Supplies) [10026]

Ownbey Enterprises Inc. (Petroleum, Fuels, and Related Equipment) [22544]

Preferred Carpets (Floorcovering Equipment and Supplies) [10106]

Southern Wholesalers Inc. (Plumbing Materials and Fixtures) [23393]

Star International Ltd. (Floorcovering Equipment and Supplies) [10177]

World Carpets Inc. (Floorcovering Equipment and Supplies) [10308]

Damascus

Damascus Peanut Co. (Livestock and Farm Products) [17809]

Dawson

Cargill Peanut Products (Food) [10699]

Decatur

American Hermetics, Inc. (Heating and Cooling Equipment and Supplies) [14318]

Colonial Baking Co. (Food) [10792]

Complete Medical Products Inc. (Medical, Dental, and Optical Equipment) [18749]

Complete Medical Products Inc. (Medical, Dental, and Optical Supplies) [19242]

International Computer and Office Products Inc. (Computers and Software) [6389]

MCF Systems Atlanta Inc. (Cleaning and Janitorial Supplies) [4665]

Superior Epoxies & Coatings, Inc. (Adhesives) [15]

Technical Products Inc. (Medical, Dental, and Optical Equipment) [19072]

Dexter

Lords Sausage (Food) [11733]

Doraville

Fashion Victim (Clothing) [4946]

Full Line Distributors (Clothing) [4970]

Shibamoto America, Inc. (Industrial Machinery) [16487]

Sun States Beverage Co. (Soft Drinks) [25041]

Van Ran Communications Services Inc. (Communications Systems and Equipment) [5803]

Douglas

Lott Builders Supply Co. (Construction Materials and Machinery) [7612]

Lott Builders Supply Co. (Wood and Wood Products) [27336]

Douglasville

Accent Nursery (Horticultural Supplies) [14794]

Dublin

Cochran Brothers Cash & Carry (Food) [10783]

Farmers Furniture Company Inc. (Furniture and Fixtures) [13110]

Warehouse Home Furnishing Distributors Inc. (Furniture and Fixtures) [13274]

Duluth

Anderson Bait Distributors (Recreational and Sporting Goods) [23517]

Computer Banking Inc. (Computers and Software) [6101]

ConAgra Poultry Co. (Duluth, Georgia) (Food) [10806]

Golf Training Systems Inc. (Recreational and Sporting Goods) [23692]

Inmed Corp. (Medical, Dental, and Optical Equipment) [18852]

Knight Distributing Company Inc. (Health and Beauty Aids) [14145]

Lombardini USA Inc. (Industrial Machinery) [16242]

Wegener Communications Inc. (Communications Systems and Equipment) [5809]

East Point

Atlanta Ice Inc. (Food) [10463]

Ellijay

Blue Ridge Mountain Woodcrafts Inc. (Gifts and Novelties) [13320]

Fairburn

CCA Electronics (Communications Systems and Equipment) [5553]

Fayetteville

AIS Computers (Computers and Software) [5896]

Andy's Discount Nursery & Landscape (Horticultural Supplies) [14805]

D & J Cabinet Co. Inc. (Furniture and Fixtures) [13084]

Sailor Corporation of America (Adhesives) [13]

Fitzgerald

Lowell Packing Co. (Food) [11738]

Folkston

Hopkins-Gowen Oil Company Inc. (Petroleum, Fuels, and Related Equipment) [22364]

Forest Park

Davis Produce, Inc.; John (Food) [10917]

Dunlop Aviation North America (Aeronautical Equipment and Supplies) [81]

Parker Co.; Mitt (Food) [12113]

Sutherland Foodservice Inc. (Food) [12652]

Thermo King Atlanta Inc. (Household Appliances) [15337]

Total Supply (Heating and Cooling Equipment and Supplies) [14730]

Total Supply Inc. (Heating and Cooling Equipment and Supplies) [14732]

Tubesales (Metals) [20445]

Ft. Oglethorpe

R and D Products (Cleaning and Janitorial Supplies) [4691]

Ft. Valley

Valley Athletic Supply Co. Inc. (Shoes) [24884]

Gainesville

Archie's Sporting Goods of Gainesville (Clothing) [4780]

Carter Inc.; Jerry C. (Petroleum, Fuels, and Related Equipment) [22113]

City Plumbing & Electrical Supply (Electrical and Electronic Equipment and Supplies) [8528]

CWT International Inc. (Food) [10889]

Gainesville Industrial Supply (Automotive) [2658]

Goforth Electric Supply Inc. (Electrical and Electronic Equipment and Supplies) [8793]

Mansfield Oil Company of Gainesville Inc. (Petroleum, Fuels, and Related Equipment) [22449]

Onyx Petroleum Inc. (Petroleum, Fuels, and Related Equipment) [22541]

Protein Foods Inc. (Food) [12232]

Surfa-Shield Corp. (Hardware) [13946]

Vacuum Pump Systems Inc. (Industrial Machinery) [16596]

Glennville

Bland Farms Inc. (Food) [10567]

Rotary Corp. (Agricultural Equipment and Supplies) [1214]

Grayson

Comse Sales/John Weeks Enterprises (Sound and Entertainment Equipment and Supplies) [25147]

Greensboro

Hasley Recreation and Design Inc. (Recreational and Sporting Goods) [23716]

Norvel Hasley and Associates (Recreational and Sporting Goods) [23854]

Griffin

Atlanta Tees Inc. (Clothing) [4789]

Food Masters Inc. (Food) [11175]

Varsity Sports Center Inc. (Recreational and Sporting Goods) [24027]

Grovetown

Owens and Minor Inc. Augusta Div. (Medical, Dental, and Optical Supplies) [19521]

Hawkinsville

McCranie Motor and Tractor Inc. McCranie Implement Co. (Agricultural Equipment and Supplies) [1000]

Hazlehurst

Fuel South Company Inc. (Petroleum, Fuels, and Related Equipment) [22296]

Helen

Jewelry Trend Inc. (Jewelry) [17473]

Jasper

Phillips Company Inc.; Tom M. (Petroleum, Fuels, and Related Equipment) [22578]

Jesup

Dawg Luvers & Co. (Gifts and Novelties) [13344]

Jonesboro

Blalock Oil Company Inc. (Petroleum, Fuels, and Related Equipment) [22078]

Zumpano Enterprises, Inc. (Floorcovering Equipment and Supplies) [10312]

Kennesaw

Georgia Marble Co. (Construction Materials and Machinery) [7393]

Hitachi Maxco Ltd. (Industrial Supplies) [16930]

Pacesetter Steel Service Inc. (Metals) [20259]

Lagrange

Gusto Brands Inc. (Alcoholic Beverages) [1738]

LaGrange

User Friendly Software Hardware (Computers and Software) [6846]

Lake City

Witt Co.; Eli (Tobacco Products) [26376]

Lawrenceville

Air & Hydraulic Engineering (Industrial Machinery) [15743]

Alfa Laval Celleco Inc. (Industrial Machinery) [15753]

Associated Computers Services (Computers and Software) [5977]

Cel Air Corp. (Electrical and Electronic Equipment and Supplies) [8515]

Floor Supply Co. (Floorcovering Equipment and Supplies) [9894]

Georgia Business Solutions (Computers and Software) [6300]

GL&V/Celleco Inc. (Industrial Machinery) [16066]

Lotus Cars USA Inc. (Automotive) [2893]

Mobile Communications of Gwinnett (Communications Systems and Equipment) [5680]

Plumbing Distributors Inc. (Plumbing Materials and Fixtures) [23323]

Pureflow Ultraviolet, Inc. (Plumbing Materials and Fixtures) [23332]

Target Premiums Inc. (Household Appliances) [15333]

Lithia Springs

Al-WaLi Inc. (Books and Other Printed Materials) [3481]

Metro Refrigeration Supply, Inc. (Heating and Cooling Equipment and Supplies) [14542]

New Leaf Distributing Co. (Books and Other Printed Materials) [3995]

New Leaf Distributors Inc. (Books and Other Printed Materials) [3996]

Macon

American Military Supply Inc. (Clothing) [4770]
Bearing and Drivers Inc. (Automotive) [2337]
Bearings & Drives, Inc. (Automotive) [2340]
Bullington Lift Trucks (Industrial Machinery) [15855]
Custom Labs (Medical, Dental, and Optical Supplies) [19265]
Dillard Paper Co. Macon Div. (Paper and Paper Products) [21712]
Fox Appliance Parts of Macon Inc. (Household Appliances) [15134]
Holox Ltd. (Industrial Machinery) [16111]
Macon Beauty Supply Co. (Health and Beauty Aids) [14157]
Macon Iron and Paper Stock Company Inc. (Used, Scrap, and Recycled Materials) [26892]
McGehee & Associates; Thomas (Computers and Software) [6477]
Smith and Sons Foods Inc. (Food) [12517]
Standard Crown Distributing Co. (Alcoholic Beverages) [2045]
Stokes-Shaheen Produce Inc. (Food) [12587]
Triangle Chemical Co. (Chemicals) [4533]
Wilson Electric Supply Co. (Electrical and Electronic Equipment and Supplies) [9599]

Madison

Pennington Seed Inc. (Agricultural Equipment and Supplies) [1121]

Marietta

Adtek Computer Systems Inc. (Computers and Software) [5880]
AFGD (Construction Materials and Machinery) [6919]
Arch-I-Tech Doors Inc. (Construction Materials and Machinery) [6982]
Avant Computer Associates Inc. (Computers and Software) [5991]
Century Air Conditioning and Maintenance Supply, Inc. (Heating and Cooling Equipment and Supplies) [14379]
Communications Marketing S.E. Inc. (Communications Systems and Equipment) [5571]
Compcom Enterprises Inc. (Computers and Software) [6089]
Connections USA (Computers and Software) [6150]
Crain M-M Sales Inc. (Automotive) [2492]
DE International Inc. (Medical, Dental, and Optical Equipment) [18767]
Dickson CC Co. (Heating and Cooling Equipment and Supplies) [14421]
Dixon Tom-A-Toe Cos. (Food) [10969]
Georgia Mountain Water Inc. (Soft Drinks) [24957]
Gerber Agri-Export Inc. (Food) [11255]
Hopson Broker Inc.; Thomas R. (Construction Materials and Machinery) [7487]
Johnstone Supply (Heating and Cooling Equipment and Supplies) [14504]
Lamp Glow Industries Inc. (Electrical and Electronic Equipment and Supplies) [8969]
LTD Dozier Inc. (Restaurant and Commercial Foodservice Equipment and Supplies) [24170]
Master Works International (Medical, Dental, and Optical Equipment) [18901]
McGee Eye Fashions Inc. (Medical, Dental, and Optical Supplies) [19431]
Metro Refrigeration Supply, Inc. (Heating and Cooling Equipment and Supplies) [14543]
Office Furniture Warehouse Inc. (Furniture and Fixtures) [13191]
Southern Micro Instruments (Medical, Dental, and Optical Supplies) [19624]
Southern Tea Co. (Food) [12543]
Southern Tile Distributors Inc. (Floorcovering Equipment and Supplies) [10165]
Tatung Company of America Inc. Marietta Div. (Sound and Entertainment Equipment and Supplies) [25473]
Tite Co. (Adhesives) [17]
Toner Sales Inc. (Recreational and Sporting Goods) [24012]
V-Tek Associates (Computers and Software) [6847]

Marshallville

Bickley Inc.; A.M. (Livestock and Farm Products) [17733]

McDonough

Gainor Medical U.S.A. Inc. (Medical, Dental, and Optical Equipment) [18803]

Metter

McCorkle Cricket Farm Inc. (Recreational and Sporting Goods) [23815]

Morrow

Southern Tile Distributors Inc. (Floorcovering Equipment and Supplies) [10166]

Nashville

Dorsey Oil Co.; B.A. (Petroleum, Fuels, and Related Equipment) [22209]

Newnan

Wallace & Associates (Recreational and Sporting Goods) [24038]

Newton

Newton Appliance Sales & Service (Household Appliances) [15249]

Norcross

AARP Inc. (Electrical and Electronic Equipment and Supplies) [8258]
Akzo Coatings (Paints and Varnishes) [21376]
Allied Electronics (Electrical and Electronic Equipment and Supplies) [8301]
ALLTEL Supply Inc. (Communications Systems and Equipment) [5508]
Atlanta Tile Supply, Inc. (Floorcovering Equipment and Supplies) [9691]
Audio-Tech Inc. (Sound and Entertainment Equipment and Supplies) [25088]
BET Plant Services USA Inc. (Industrial Machinery) [15822]
BET Rentokil Plant Services (Construction Materials and Machinery) [7054]
Brighton-Best Socket Screw Manufacturing Inc. (Hardware) [13606]
Camel Outdoor Products Inc. (Guns and Weapons) [13480]
Chateaux-Vineyards (Alcoholic Beverages) [1590]
Connecticut Valley Arms Inc. (Guns and Weapons) [13483]
Durkopp Adler America Inc. (Industrial Machinery) [15968]
Ernest Telecom Inc. (Communications Systems and Equipment) [5605]
Great American Wearhouse (Clothing) [5001]
Hitachi America Ltd. Electron Tube Div. (Electrical and Electronic Equipment and Supplies) [8847]
Hitachi Home Electronics (America) Inc. Visual Technologies Div. (Household Appliances) [15169]
Hitachi Power Tools USA Ltd. (Hardware) [13754]
Infinite Solutions Inc. (Computers and Software) [6363]
Intelligent Systems Corp. (Computers and Software) [6383]
International Service Group (Livestock and Farm Products) [18011]
Interstate Distributors Inc. (Restaurant and Commercial Foodservice Equipment and Supplies) [24145]
ITM, Inc. (Automotive) [2804]
Johnstone Supply (Heating and Cooling Equipment and Supplies) [14505]
Liuski International Inc. (Electrical and Electronic Equipment and Supplies) [8996]
Mighty Distributing System of America Inc. (Automotive) [2962]
Milner Document Products Inc. (Office Equipment and Supplies) [21146]
Mingledorffs Inc. (Heating and Cooling Equipment and Supplies) [14607]
Minton-Jones Co. (Furniture and Fixtures) [13182]
North Riverside Venture Inc. (Automotive) [3044]

Office Pavillion/National Systems Inc. (Office Equipment and Supplies) [21185]
Pameco Corp. (Heating and Cooling Equipment and Supplies) [14631]
PD60 Distributors Inc. (Household Items) [15615]
Peach State Truck Centers (Automotive) [3088]
Prestige Packaging Inc. (Plastics) [23017]
RedMax Komatsu Zenoah America Inc. (Agricultural Equipment and Supplies) [1176]
Saab Cars USA Inc. (Motorized Vehicles) [20716]
Sampo Corporation of America (Computers and Software) [6702]
Scientific and Business Minicomputers Inc. (Computers and Software) [6712]
Socoloff Health Supply Inc. (Medical, Dental, and Optical Supplies) [19617]
Southern Business Communications Inc. (Computers and Software) [6747]
Southern Flooring Distributors (Floorcovering Equipment and Supplies) [10162]
Sun Data Inc. (Computers and Software) [6770]
Sunbelt Seeds Inc. (Agricultural Equipment and Supplies) [1302]
Three Epsilon Inc. (Recreational and Sporting Goods) [24009]
Total Supply (Heating and Cooling Equipment and Supplies) [14729]
Trade Am International Inc. (Floorcovering Equipment and Supplies) [10256]
Tull Metals Company Inc.; J.M. (Metals) [20447]
Wang's International, Inc. (Office Equipment and Supplies) [21346]
Waste Management Recycle America (Used, Scrap, and Recycled Materials) [27036]
Zumpano Enterprises, Inc. (Floorcovering Equipment and Supplies) [10313]
Zumpano Enterprises Inc. (Construction Materials and Machinery) [8255]

Oakwood

Milton's Institutional Foods (Food) [11902]
PFG Milton's (Food) [12162]

Ochlocknee

Oil-Dri Corp. (Petroleum, Fuels, and Related Equipment) [22536]

Ocilla

Gray Storage and Dryer Company Inc. (Livestock and Farm Products) [17959]

Peachtree City

Engineered Components Inc. (Electrical and Electronic Equipment and Supplies) [8707]
Hella Inc. (Automotive) [2740]
MET International (Computers and Software) [6487]
Triumph Motorcycles America Ltd. (Automotive) [3342]

Pembroke

Wesvic's Clothing and Shoe Brokers, Inc. (Shoes) [24892]

Quitman

Coastal Plains Farmers Co-op Inc. (Agricultural Equipment and Supplies) [431]
Southern Carbide Specialists Inc. (Hardware) [13928]

Resaca

Shaheen Carpet Mills (Floorcovering Equipment and Supplies) [10145]
Shaheen Carpet Mills (Household Items) [15651]

Riverdale

Custom Labs (Medical, Dental, and Optical Supplies) [19266]
Multifocal Rx Lens Lab (Medical, Dental, and Optical Supplies) [19471]

Rome

Battey Machinery Co. (Industrial Machinery) [15807]

Coosa Co. Inc. (Recreational and Sporting Goods) [23605]
Fairbanks Co. (Hardware) [13691]
Manis Lumber Company Inc. (Wood and Wood Products) [27339]
Roga International Div. Export-Import Marketing (Household Items) [15638]
Rome Paper Co. (Paper and Paper Products) [21910]
Southeastern Mills Inc. (Food) [12538]
Southern Wholesale Co. (Medical, Dental, and Optical Supplies) [19629]
Suhner Manufacturing, Inc. (Industrial Machinery) [16534]

Roswell

Accu Tech Cable Inc. (Electrical and Electronic Equipment and Supplies) [8261]
Dickens Data Systems Inc. (Computers and Software) [6209]
Durastill Inc. (Specialty Equipment and Products) [25639]
Gate City Equipment Company Inc. (Petroleum, Fuels, and Related Equipment) [22303]
Jealco International, Inc. (Industrial Machinery) [16185]
Majure Data Inc. (Computers and Software) [6455]
Physimetrics Inc. (Electrical and Electronic Equipment and Supplies) [9199]
Precept Business Products Inc. (Office Equipment and Supplies) [21221]

Royston

Tri-State Distributors Inc. (Heating and Cooling Equipment and Supplies) [14738]

Sandersville

Smith-Sheppard Concrete Company Inc. (Construction Materials and Machinery) [8035]
Washington Electric Membership Cooperative (Household Appliances) [15366]

Savannah

Alko Distributors Inc. (Alcoholic Beverages) [1477]
Chatham Steel Corp. (Metals) [19874]
Coastal Supply Company Inc. (Heating and Cooling Equipment and Supplies) [14388]
Colonial Oil Industries Inc. (Petroleum, Fuels, and Related Equipment) [22152]
Davis Supply Co. (Plumbing Materials and Fixtures) [23134]
Electric Sales & Service of Savannah (Sound and Entertainment Equipment and Supplies) [25176]
Electronics 21 Inc. (Sound and Entertainment Equipment and Supplies) [25180]
Friedman and Co. (Jewelry) [17418]
H-H of Savannah, Inc. (Alcoholic Beverages) [1739]
Italian Sausage Inc. (Food) [11531]
Kem Distributing Inc. (Alcoholic Beverages) [1795]
Meyer Inc.; Frances (Gifts and Novelties) [13403]
Modern Builders Supply (Floorcovering Equipment and Supplies) [10044]
Patterson Sales Associates (Paper and Paper Products) [21870]
Patterson Sales Associates (Industrial Supplies) [17101]
Savannah Communications (Communications Systems and Equipment) [5750]
Savannah Communications (Electrical and Electronic Equipment and Supplies) [9338]
Savannah Distributing Company Inc. (Alcoholic Beverages) [2009]
South Atlantic Forest Products Inc. (Wood and Wood Products) [27378]
Tradewinds International Inc. (Construction Materials and Machinery) [8141]
Vanguard Distributors Inc. (Security and Safety Equipment) [24656]

Scottdale

Futura Adhesives & Chemicals (Adhesives) [7]

Smithville

McClesky Mills Inc. (Food) [11819]

McClesky Mills Inc. (Livestock and Farm Products) [18079]

Smyrna

Astor Foods Inc. (Food) [10460]
Buckeye Vacuum Cleaner Supply Co. Inc. (Household Appliances) [15063]
Fabricated Systems of Atlanta (Heating and Cooling Equipment and Supplies) [14438]
Fines Distributing Inc. (Food) [11127]
Johnson Controls, Inc. (Heating and Cooling Equipment and Supplies) [14498]
Racetrac Petroleum Inc. (Petroleum, Fuels, and Related Equipment) [22605]
Richards Co.; S.P. (Office Equipment and Supplies) [21242]
Smyrna Truck Body & Equipment, Inc. (Automotive) [3234]
Total Supply (Heating and Cooling Equipment and Supplies) [14731]
United Distributors, Inc. (Alcoholic Beverages) [2090]
Wallace Oil Co. (Petroleum, Fuels, and Related Equipment) [22780]

Snellville

Kentec Inc. (Hardware) [13784]

Statesboro

Self; William (Clothing) [5343]

Stone Mountain

Ashford International Inc. (Computers and Software) [5971]
Benrock Inc. (Marine) [18460]
Food Service Action Inc. (Food) [11177]
Implement Sales LLC (Agricultural Equipment and Supplies) [852]
Ingraham Corp.; George (Electrical and Electronic Equipment and Supplies) [8879]
SunSource Technology Services (Industrial Machinery) [16539]

Suwanee

Barrow Industries Inc. (Textiles and Notions) [25975]
Drillot Corporation (Household Appliances) [15115]
Gas Equipment Supply Co. (Petroleum, Fuels, and Related Equipment) [22302]
Hadco Inc. (Household Appliances) [15156]
Pfaff Pegasus of USA Inc. (Industrial Machinery) [16395]

Sylvania

Feed Seed and Farm Supplies Inc. (Agricultural Equipment and Supplies) [677]

Sylvester

Wilkersons Pecans (Food) [12945]

Thomaston

Jones; Susan Brese (Clothing) [5093]

Thomasville

Archbold Health Services Inc. (Medical, Dental, and Optical Equipment) [18688]
Flowers Industries Inc. (Food) [11163]
Powell Company Inc.; W.J. (Food) [12200]
Shoe Flair (Shoes) [24857]
Thermal Equipment Company Inc. (Heating and Cooling Equipment and Supplies) [14721]

Tifton

Bearings & Drives, Inc. (Automotive) [2341]
Curtis Packing Co. Inc. (Food) [10884]
Dixie Oil Co. Inc. (Petroleum, Fuels, and Related Equipment) [22205]
Thigpen Distributing Inc. (Agricultural Equipment and Supplies) [1327]

Toccoa

Dempster Equipment (Used, Scrap, and Recycled Materials) [26796]

Tucker

Best Locking Systems of Georgia Inc. (Security and Safety Equipment) [24513]
Boring and Smith Industries Div. (Industrial Supplies) [16757]
Cofer Brothers Inc. (Construction Materials and Machinery) [7190]
Controls-Instruments-Devices (Electrical and Electronic Equipment and Supplies) [8577]
Courtaulds Coatings Inc. Southeast Div. (Paints and Varnishes) [21419]
Energy and Process Corp. (Metals) [19954]
Industrial Distribution Group, Inc. (Industrial Supplies) [16946]
Lane Ltd. (Tobacco Products) [26322]
SED International, Inc. (Computers and Software) [6717]
Whitebox Inc. (Computers and Software) [6869]

Tunnel Hill

Guns Of Yesteryear (Guns and Weapons) [13493]

Unadilla

McCranie Motor and Tractor Inc. (Agricultural Equipment and Supplies) [999]

Valdosta

Bearings & Drives, Inc. (Automotive) [2342]
Better Brands of South Georgia (Alcoholic Beverages) [1526]
Coca-Cola Bottling Works Inc.; Valdosta (Soft Drinks) [24943]
Davis Enterprises Inc.; Dan L. (Clothing) [4910]

Vidalia

Vidalia Naval Stores Co. (Construction Materials and Machinery) [8181]

VilLa Rica

Master Cartridge Corp. (Recreational and Sporting Goods) [23806]
O'Neill Div. (Textiles and Notions) [26162]

Waycross

Gibson Dot Publications (Books and Other Printed Materials) [3779]
Leon's Molds (Industrial Supplies) [16997]
S & L Sales Co., Inc. (Books and Other Printed Materials) [4132]
Striplings Tackle Co. (Recreational and Sporting Goods) [23990]

Waynesboro

Daniels Co.; C.P. (Veterinary Products) [27114]

Woodstock

Intelligent Computer Networks (Computers and Software) [6380]

Hawaii

Aiea

Chikara Products Inc. (Food) [10747]
Hawaiian Housewares, Ltd. (Household Items) [15521]
JCS Enterprises, Inc. (Clothing) [5078]
JMD Beverages (Alcoholic Beverages) [1784]
Kamaaina Distribution (Food) [11578]
Optical Suppliers Inc. (Medical, Dental, and Optical Supplies) [19517]
Pacific Interface (Computers and Software) [6580]
Paradise Optical Co. (Medical, Dental, and Optical Supplies) [19523]
Pint Size Corp. (Food) [12170]
SMP Enterprises Inc. (Toys and Hobby Goods) [26656]
Symd Inc. (Medical, Dental, and Optical Supplies) [19646]
TW Systems Ltd. (Cleaning and Janitorial Supplies) [4719]
Waikiki Trader Corp. (Clothing) [5470]
Yeh Dah Ltd. (Jewelry) [17664]

Captain Cook

Kobayashi Farm & Nursery (Horticultural Supplies) [14908]
Kona Farmers Coop (Food) [11635]
Pearl's Garden Center (Horticultural Supplies) [14939]

Ewa Beach

Honsador Inc. (Construction Materials and Machinery) [7484]

Haiku

Maui Tropicals & Foliage (Horticultural Supplies) [14918]

Haleiwa

Oogenesis Inc. (Clothing) [5254]

Hana

Mahealani Farms Inc. (Horticultural Supplies) [14914]

Hanapepe

Nakagawa Painting, Inc.; James (Paints and Varnishes) [21512]

Hilo

Ameritone Devoe Paints (Paints and Varnishes) [21385]
Anthuriums of Hawaii (Horticultural Supplies) [14807]
Carpet Isle Design Center (Floorcovering Equipment and Supplies) [9769]
Ebisuzaki Fishing Supply (Recreational and Sporting Goods) [23645]
Garden Exchange Limited (Hardware) [13720]
Hara and Company Ltd.; T. (Food) [11376]
Hawaii Hardware Company Ltd. (Hardware) [13745]
Hawaiian Isles Distributors (Tobacco Products) [26302]
Hilo Farmer's Exchange (Horticultural Supplies) [14887]
HPM Building Supply (Hardware) [13759]
HPM Building Supply (Wood and Wood Products) [27320]
HT & T Co. (Motorized Vehicles) [20650]
HT and T Company (Automotive) [2765]
Kamaaina Distribution Co. (Tobacco Products) [26316]
Pacific Machinery Inc. (Construction Materials and Machinery) [7824]
Stationers' Corporation of Hawaii Ltd. (Office Equipment and Supplies) [21294]

Honolulu

Acutron Co. (Construction Materials and Machinery) [6912]
Air Engineering Co. Inc. (Metals) [19737]
Almar, Ltd. (Paints and Varnishes) [21382]
Aloha Tap & Die Inc. (Industrial Supplies) [16690]
American Food Export Co. (Food) [10396]
Ameritone Paint Corp. (Paints and Varnishes) [21386]
Apollo Sales Group Inc. (Specialty Equipment and Products) [25554]
Architectural Surfaces, Inc. (Household Items) [15406]
Armstrong Produce Ltd. (Food) [10435]
Atecs Corp. (Medical, Dental, and Optical Equipment) [18696]
Atecs Corp. (Medical, Dental, and Optical Supplies) [19167]
AUDISSEY (Electrical and Electronic Equipment and Supplies) [8396]
Balloons & Things (Toys and Hobby Goods) [26411]
Black & Black Inc. (Clothing) [4825]
Boss Hawaii Inc. (Recreational and Sporting Goods) [23565]
Brewer Environmental Industries Inc. (Agricultural Equipment and Supplies) [335]
Brewer Environmental Industries Inc. (Chemicals) [4340]
Bromar Inc. Bromar Hawaii (Food) [10616]

Chandras (Clothing) [4875]
Changing Colors (Clothing) [4876]
Chip & Wafer Office Automation (Office Equipment and Supplies) [20898]
Classic Sales Inc. (Shoes) [24714]
CMA Incorporated (Food) [10779]
Comics Hawaii Distributors (Toys and Hobby Goods) [26448]
Commercial Motors (Automotive) [2467]
Commercial Shelving (Storage Equipment and Containers) [25905]
Cosco Inc. (Heating and Cooling Equipment and Supplies) [14407]
Davies and Company Ltd.; Theo. H. (Industrial Machinery) [15932]
Design Tees Hawaii Inc. (Clothing) [4914]
Diamond Bakery Co. Ltd. (Food) [10956]
Discount Store (Sound and Entertainment Equipment and Supplies) [25167]
Du Pont Co. (Paints and Varnishes) [21435]
East-West Center (Books and Other Printed Materials) [3709]
Edsung Foodservice Co. (Food) [11029]
Eidai International, Inc. (Shoes) [24731]
Ener-Gee Sales Inc. (Shoes) [24735]
Evergreen Nurseries (Horticultural Supplies) [14860]
Eyeglass Shoppe (Medical, Dental, and Optical Supplies) [19318]
Fiberglass Hawaii, Inc. (Plastics) [22961]
Five H Island Foods Inc. (Food) [11139]
Flora-Dec Saes, Inc. (Horticultural Supplies) [14863]
Florexotica Hawaii (Horticultural Supplies) [14867]
French Gourmet Inc. (Food) [11204]
Gamble Co.; L.H. (Food) [11230]
Gaspro (Medical, Dental, and Optical Equipment) [18804]
Goldman Brothers Inc. (Clothing) [4995]
GSL Enterprises Inc. (Clothing) [5005]
Hana Hou Corp. (Clothing) [5015]
Happy Shirts Inc. (Clothing) [5018]
Hata Company Ltd.; S. (Textiles and Notions) [26059]
Hawaii ID Apparel (Clothing) [5021]
Hawaii Instrumentation, Inc. (Security and Safety Equipment) [24560]
Hawaii Martial Art Supply (Recreational and Sporting Goods) [23718]
Hawaii Plastics Corp. (Textiles and Notions) [26060]
Hawaii; Scott (Shoes) [24760]
Hawaiian Fluid Power (Industrial Machinery) [16093]
Hawaiian Grocery Stores Ltd. (Food) [11394]
Hawaiian Sunglass Co. (Medical, Dental, and Optical Supplies) [19351]
HFM Foodservice (Food) [11423]
HI-Pac Ltd. (Food) [11425]
HIE Holdings, Inc. (Food) [11428]
Honolulu Optical (Medical, Dental, and Optical Supplies) [19361]
Honolulu Wholesale Jewelry Exchange (Jewelry) [17449]
Hunters Inc. (Office Equipment and Supplies) [21045]
Inouye Lei Flowers, Inc. (Horticultural Supplies) [14892]
Intercontinental Industries (Clothing) [5054]
Island Pacific Distributors, Inc. (Security and Safety Equipment) [24575]
Izuo Brothers Ltd. (Recreational and Sporting Goods) [23750]
J & E Fishing Supplies Inc. (Recreational and Sporting Goods) [23754]
JCG Corp. (Clothing) [5077]
Kamaaina Vision Center Inc. (Medical, Dental, and Optical Supplies) [19392]
Kamuela Roses, Inc. (Horticultural Supplies) [14901]
Keyston Brothers (Textiles and Notions) [26106]
Kilgo Co. Inc.; A.L. (Hardware) [13786]
Lees Refrigeration, Div. of Hussmann Corp. (Heating and Cooling Equipment and Supplies) [14520]

Lens Co. (Medical, Dental, and Optical Supplies) [19411]
Linwood; Mitchell (Shoes) [24794]
Loco Boutique (Clothing) [5137]
Malolo Beverages & Supplies, Ltd. (Soft Drinks) [24986]
Martin and MacArthur (Construction Materials and Machinery) [7654]
MDI Production (Specialty Equipment and Products) [25734]
Medeiros Optical Service (Medical, Dental, and Optical Supplies) [19440]
Mid Pac Lumber (Plumbing Materials and Fixtures) [23265]
Midpac Lumber Company Ltd. (Construction Materials and Machinery) [7707]
Moreira Tile (Floorcovering Equipment and Supplies) [10057]
Multimedia Pacific Inc. (Communications Systems and Equipment) [5686]
Nelson Hawaiian, Ltd. (Medical, Dental, and Optical Supplies) [19481]
New American T-Shirt (Clothing) [5223]
Norpac Fisheries, Inc. (Food) [12021]
Norpac Fisheries Inc. (Food) [12022]
Obrig Hawaii Contact Lens Lab (Medical, Dental, and Optical Supplies) [19504]
Oki Trading, Ltd.; T. (Construction Materials and Machinery) [7809]
Optique Paris Miki (Medical, Dental, and Optical Supplies) [19519]
Otake Instrument Inc. (Medical, Dental, and Optical Equipment) [18970]
Pacific Dataport Inc. (Communications Systems and Equipment) [5697]
Pacific Paint Center, Inc. (Paints and Varnishes) [21522]
Paradise Optical Co. (Medical, Dental, and Optical Equipment) [18978]
Pioneer Electric Inc. (Electrical and Electronic Equipment and Supplies) [9206]
Royal Hawaiian Creations (Clothing) [5322]
Royal Metals Company Inc. (Metals) [20332]
Rugby Building Products, Inc. (Construction Materials and Machinery) [7968]
S & L International (Shoes) [24847]
Sadd Laundry and Dry Cleaning Supplies (Cleaning and Janitorial Supplies) [4701]
Servco Pacific Inc. (Automotive) [3205]
Service Central, Inc. (Paints and Varnishes) [21563]
Shimaya Shoten Ltd. (Food) [12479]
State Optical Company, Inc. (Medical, Dental, and Optical Supplies) [19637]
The Sultan Co. (Jewelry) [17624]
Sun Inc.; Bob (Toys and Hobby Goods) [26673]
Sun Pacific Trading Co. Inc. (Shoes) [24870]
Taiyo Inc. (Food) [12692]
Taj Inc. (Clothing) [5420]
Tamashiro Market Inc. (Food) [12695]
Tobacco Shop at Hyatt (Tobacco Products) [26358]
Tsuki's Hair Design (Health and Beauty Aids) [14266]
Tuong; Dam (Food) [12770]
Uniq Distributing Group (Floorcovering Equipment and Supplies) [10263]
Vets International Inc. (Veterinary Products) [27266]
Wallcoverings, Ltd. (Paints and Varnishes) [21600]
Wallpaper Hawaii, Ltd. (Paints and Varnishes) [21601]
Watanabe Floral, Inc. (Horticultural Supplies) [14973]
W.C. Distributors Corp. (Tobacco Products) [26370]
Woolson Spice Co. (Books and Other Printed Materials) [4294]
Yamada Distributors Ltd.; K. (Storage Equipment and Containers) [25949]
Yamashiro, Inc.; A. (Horticultural Supplies) [14979]

Kahului

Eagle Distributors Inc. (Alcoholic Beverages) [1666]
Maui Potato Chip Factory (Food) [11809]

Mor-Rad Foodservice (Food) [11934]
Sturdvant Refrigeration/Air-Conditioning (Heating and Cooling Equipment and Supplies) [14700]
Valley Isle Produce Inc. (Food) [12819]

Kailua
Island Snow Hawaii Inc. (Clothing) [5063]
Rae Mel Sales Inc. (Sound and Entertainment Equipment and Supplies) [25404]

Kailua Kona
Big Island Marine (Marine) [18463]
The Greenhouse (Horticultural Supplies) [14878]
ICI Dulux Paint Centers (Paints and Varnishes) [21460]
Kona Marine Supply (Marine) [18537]
Neptune Polarized Sunglasses (Medical, Dental, and Optical Supplies) [19483]
Tile Warehouse (Floorcovering Equipment and Supplies) [10245]
Western Pacific Interior (Floorcovering Equipment and Supplies) [10293]

Kamuela
Watanabe Floral, Inc. (Horticultural Supplies) [14974]

Kaneohe
All Quality Builders (Recreational and Sporting Goods) [23504]
Island Instruments, Inc. (Sound and Entertainment Equipment and Supplies) [25255]

Kapaa
Alexander's Nursery (Horticultural Supplies) [14799]
Kubota Inc. (Alcoholic Beverages) [1806]

Kapolei
Bonded Materials Co. (Construction Materials and Machinery) [7068]
Fleming (Food) [11145]
Hawaii Modular Space Inc. (Construction Materials and Machinery) [7457]
Marlin Distributors Inc. (Toys and Hobby Goods) [26569]
Pacific Criticare Inc. (Medical, Dental, and Optical Equipment) [18974]

Kaunakakai
K.D. Farms, Inc. (Horticultural Supplies) [14903]
KR's Paint Shop (Paints and Varnishes) [21478]

Keaau
Discount Building Materials (Construction Materials and Machinery) [7268]
Pacific Floral Exchange, Inc. (Horticultural Supplies) [14935]
Tropical Hawaiian Products (Food) [12760]

Kealakekua
Mac Nuts of Hawaii (Food) [11753]
Shojin Natural Foods (Food) [12481]

Kihei
Maui Blooms (Horticultural Supplies) [14917]

Kilauea
Lightnin Fiberglass Co. (Recreational and Sporting Goods) [23788]

Kula
Goble's Flower Farm (Horticultural Supplies) [14873]
Hawaii Protea Corp. (Horticultural Supplies) [14883]
Kula Farm (Horticultural Supplies) [14909]
Lloyd's Carnation (Horticultural Supplies) [14912]
Paradise Flower Farms Inc. (Horticultural Supplies) [14937]

Kurtistown
Quintal Farms (Horticultural Supplies) [14943]

Lahaina
Shell's Bags Hats (Gifts and Novelties) [13445]

Lihue
Del's Farm Supply (Agricultural Equipment and Supplies) [508]
Garden Island Motors Ltd. (Motorized Vehicles) [20641]
Kauai Paint & Jalousie (Paints and Varnishes) [21470]
Kauai Screen Print (Clothing) [5102]
Koa Trading Co. (Food) [11631]
Nezbeda Tile, Inc. (Floorcovering Equipment and Supplies) [10078]
Nezbeda Tile Inc. (Construction Materials and Machinery) [7776]
Pacific Machinery Inc. (Industrial Machinery) [16375]
Rasco Supply Company Ltd. (Electrical and Electronic Equipment and Supplies) [9265]

Makawao
Lorelei's Exotic Leis & Flower (Horticultural Supplies) [14913]

Pahoa
D'Anna B'Nana (Horticultural Supplies) [14852]
Hashimoto Nursery (Horticultural Supplies) [14882]
Hawaiian Greenhouse, Inc. (Horticultural Supplies) [14884]
Orchid Plantation, Inc. (Horticultural Supplies) [14931]

Papaikou
Ho'Owaiwia Farms (Horticultural Supplies) [14889]

Pearl City
Hawaiian Distributor Ltd. (Food) [11393]
Hawaiian Natural Water Company Inc. (Soft Drinks) [24969]
Newtown Appliance Sales & Services (Household Appliances) [15250]
Pacific Home Furnishings (Household Items) [15608]
Rainbow Inc. (Pearl City, Hawaii) (Food) [12268]
Surfco Hawaii Inc. (Recreational and Sporting Goods) [23998]

Volcano
Volcano Flowers & Greenery (Horticultural Supplies) [14972]

Waialua
Oils of Aloha (Livestock and Farm Products) [18152]

Wailuku
Hawaiian Ceramic Tile (Floorcovering Equipment and Supplies) [9939]
Hawaiian Isles Distributors (Tobacco Products) [26303]
MVR Auto Refinishing Supplies (Paints and Varnishes) [21511]
MVR Auto Refinishing Supplies (Automotive) [3008]
Rimfire Imports, Inc. (Food) [12318]
Takitani Enterprises Inc.; K. (Soft Drinks) [25043]
Tropical Gardens of Maui (Horticultural Supplies) [14963]

Waimanalo
Koba Nurseries & Landscaping (Horticultural Supplies) [14907]

Waimea
Fiber Glass West (Marine) [18502]

Waipahu
A To Z Rental Center (Construction Materials and Machinery) [6898]
Appliance Parts Co. Inc. (Household Appliances) [15021]
Coyne Mattress Co. Ltd. (Household Items) [15460]
Davidson & Associates; Art (Health and Beauty Aids) [14079]
Hans Metals, Inc. (Used, Scrap, and Recycled Materials) [26835]

Honolulu Aquarium & Pet Supplies (Veterinary Products) [27150]
Metabran (Alcoholic Beverages) [1868]
Pacific Machinery Inc. (Agricultural Equipment and Supplies) [1115]
Pacific Trade Group (Books and Other Printed Materials) [4035]

Idaho

Blackfoot
Agriculture Services Inc. (Agricultural Equipment and Supplies) [214]
Barb's Knitting Machines & Supplies (Textiles and Notions) [25973]
Blackfoot Livestock Commission Company Inc. (Livestock and Farm Products) [17735]

Boise
A-1 Lock & Safe Co. (Office Equipment and Supplies) [20758]
Ada Copy Supplies Inc. (Office Equipment and Supplies) [20771]
All About Offices Inc. (Office Equipment and Supplies) [20783]
All Kitchens Inc. (Food) [10365]
Boise Cascade Corp. (Wood and Wood Products) [27287]
Boise Cascade Corp. Building Materials Distribution Div. (Wood and Wood Products) [27288]
Boise Paint & Glass Inc. (Paints and Varnishes) [21402]
Boise Refrigeration Service Co. (Heating and Cooling Equipment and Supplies) [14352]
Capital Paint & Glass Inc. (Paints and Varnishes) [21411]
Connolly & Associates; Barrie (Furniture and Fixtures) [13078]
Empire Wholesale Supply (Floorcovering Equipment and Supplies) [9884]
File TEC (Computers and Software) [6269]
Finch-Brown Company Inc. (Office Equipment and Supplies) [21003]
FOF Inc. (Petroleum, Fuels, and Related Equipment) [22287]
Foresight Partners, LLC (Food) [11188]
Freeman Corp. (Heating and Cooling Equipment and Supplies) [14452]
Gametree Inc. (Toys and Hobby Goods) [26493]
H & H Distributing Inc. (Construction Materials and Machinery) [7427]
Hale Industries Inc. (Restaurant and Commercial Foodservice Equipment and Supplies) [24133]
Idaho Barber & Beauty Supply Inc. (Health and Beauty Aids) [14128]
Idaho Outdoor Equipment (Textiles and Notions) [26070]
Idaho Souvenir (Gifts and Novelties) [13373]
Ifeco Inc. (Restaurant and Commercial Foodservice Equipment and Supplies) [24140]
Information Processing Center (Office Equipment and Supplies) [21058]
Interiors By Loette (Textiles and Notions) [26073]
Kaman Industrial Technology (Industrial Machinery) [16198]
Kauphusman Inc.; F.W. (Heating and Cooling Equipment and Supplies) [14507]
L & L Shirt Shop (Clothing) [5117]
L.B. Industries Inc. (Automotive) [2875]
Main Auction (Furniture and Fixtures) [13168]
The Masonry Center (Construction Materials and Machinery) [7660]
Mattson Distributing Co.; Art (Specialty Equipment and Products) [25727]
Mc-U Sports (Recreational and Sporting Goods) [23812]
Medek Inc.; George M. (Cleaning and Janitorial Supplies) [4667]
Mooney Cattle Co. Inc. (Livestock and Farm Products) [18114]
Mountain States Microfilm Inc. (Office Equipment and Supplies) [21152]
Norco Inc. (Chemicals) [4469]

Novartis Seeds Inc. (Agricultural Equipment and Supplies) [1092]
Off Road Specialty (Automotive) [3055]
Oppenheimer Corp. Golbon (Food) [12073]
Pioneer Coatings Inc. (Paints and Varnishes) [21539]
Power Tool & Machinery (Industrial Machinery) [16418]
Precision Propeller Service Inc. (Aeronautical Equipment and Supplies) [138]
Quality Art (Office Equipment and Supplies) [21227]
R & R Hardwood Floors (Floorcovering Equipment and Supplies) [10112]
Rueb Associates Inc.; John (Livestock and Farm Products) [18210]
Security Silver and Gold Exchange (Jewelry) [17594]
Simplot AgriSource (Livestock and Farm Products) [18234]
Southwest Hide Co. (Livestock and Farm Products) [18246]
Spirit Distributing Co. (Alcoholic Beverages) [2043]
Stein Distributing Co. (Alcoholic Beverages) [2052]
Sysco Food Services of Idaho Inc. (Restaurant and Commercial Foodservice Equipment and Supplies) [24238]
Tempco Contracting & Supply (Construction Materials and Machinery) [8107]
Thompsons Inc. (Specialty Equipment and Products) [25842]
TNT Insured Towing Auto Salvage (Automotive) [3313]
Treasure Valley X-Ray Inc. (Medical, Dental, and Optical Equipment) [19084]
Tri State Beauty Supply Inc. (Health and Beauty Aids) [14264]
Utility Truck Equipment Sales (Automotive) [3381]
Water and Waste Water Equipment Co. (Plumbing Materials and Fixtures) [23439]
Weil and Co.; J. (Food) [12897]
West Company; William H. (Construction Materials and Machinery) [8203]
Western Aircraft Inc. (Aeronautical Equipment and Supplies) [172]
Western Fluid Power (Industrial Machinery) [16626]
Western Power Sports, Inc. (Automotive) [3411]
Whiteman Industries (Construction Materials and Machinery) [8220]

Buhl
Buhl Animal Clinic (Medical, Dental, and Optical Equipment) [18721]
Clear Springs Foods Inc. (Food) [10768]
Rangen Inc. (Livestock and Farm Products) [18191]
Rangen Inc. (Food) [12278]

Burley
Wards Cleaning & Supply (Cleaning and Janitorial Supplies) [4726]
Western Seeds (Agricultural Equipment and Supplies) [1433]

Caldwell
All Parts Brokers (Automotive) [2206]
Caxton Printers Ltd. (Books and Other Printed Materials) [3616]
Commercial Refrigeration Inc. (Heating and Cooling Equipment and Supplies) [14399]
Craft Corner (Toys and Hobby Goods) [26452]
Darigold (Food) [10908]
Western Stockmen's Inc. (Medical, Dental, and Optical Supplies) [19700]

Coeur D Alene
Centre Beauty Supply (Health and Beauty Aids) [14061]
Coeur d'Alene Cash & Carry (Food) [10785]
Golden Crown Corp. (Veterinary Products) [27139]
Northern Beverage (Alcoholic Beverages) [1920]
Sports Cellar (Recreational and Sporting Goods) [23979]
T & R Beverage Control (Restaurant and Commercial Foodservice Equipment and Supplies) [24239]

Williams Paint & Coatings (Paints and Varnishes) [21610]

Cottonwood
Cottonwood Sales Yard (Livestock and Farm Products) [17800]

Council
Nelson; Todd (Livestock and Farm Products) [18128]

Dalton Gardens
Action Auto Parts (Automotive) [2178]

Donnelly
Williamson; Darcy (Books and Other Printed Materials) [4285]

Driggs
Comex International (Furniture and Fixtures) [13073]

Eagle
Northwest Parts & Equipment (Aeronautical Equipment and Supplies) [132]

Emmett
Northwest Distribution Services Inc. (Restaurant and Commercial Foodservice Equipment and Supplies) [24196]
T.J.T. Inc. (Construction Materials and Machinery) [8137]

Firth
Idaho Supreme Potatoes Inc. (Food) [11489]

Fruitland
B C Sales Co., Inc. (Medical, Dental, and Optical Equipment) [18701]

Genesee
Genesee Union Warehouse Company Inc. (Livestock and Farm Products) [17938]

Gooding
Gooding Seed Co. (Agricultural Equipment and Supplies) [750]

Grangeville
Brown Motors Inc. (Agricultural Equipment and Supplies) [341]
Jim Sales & Service (Scientific and Measurement Devices) [24379]

Hailey
Fisher; Karen (Cleaning and Janitorial Supplies) [4620]
Sun Valley Aviation Inc. (Aeronautical Equipment and Supplies) [154]

Hayden
North Idaho Distributing Inc. (Tobacco Products) [26333]

Heyburn
McBride Insulation Co. (Construction Materials and Machinery) [7673]

Idaho Falls
Automotive Electric and Supply Co. (Automotive) [2288]
Bennetts East Side Paint & Gloss (Paints and Varnishes) [21399]
Building Materials Wholesale (Construction Materials and Machinery) [7105]
Chesbro Music Co. (Sound and Entertainment Equipment and Supplies) [25134]
De Mott Tractor Company Inc. (Agricultural Equipment and Supplies) [500]
Decker's Inc. (Cleaning and Janitorial Supplies) [4611]
Electrical Wholesale Supply Company Inc. (Electrical and Electronic Equipment and Supplies) [8682]

Ericksons Super-Pros, Inc.; Vic (Recreational and Sporting Goods) [23654]
Globil Inc. (Alcoholic Beverages) [1721]
Hercules Vacu-Maid (Cleaning and Janitorial Supplies) [4633]
Idaho Livestock Auction Co. (Livestock and Farm Products) [18010]
Johnson Brothers (Hardware) [13774]
Lucero Computer Products (Computers and Software) [6447]
Marshall's Tile Co. (Floorcovering Equipment and Supplies) [10010]
Martin Stationers (Office Equipment and Supplies) [21130]
Norman Supply (Plumbing Materials and Fixtures) [23295]
One Stop Distributing (Heating and Cooling Equipment and Supplies) [14628]
Owen Distributors Inc. (Furniture and Fixtures) [13197]
Polson's Rock Shop (Jewelry) [17551]
R & L Data Systems Inc. (Computers and Software) [6675]
Recreational Sports and Imports Inc. (Sound and Entertainment Equipment and Supplies) [25412]
Slusser Wholesale Inc. (Toys and Hobby Goods) [26652]
Steinke Ranches Inc.; E.J. (Livestock and Farm Products) [18254]
Wheel City Inc. (Automotive) [3420]
Yost Office Systems, Inc. (Office Equipment and Supplies) [21368]

Kendrick
Brocke and Sons Inc.; George F. (Agricultural Equipment and Supplies) [337]

Ketchum
Marketing Success (Clothing) [5165]
Okie Dokie Services (Cleaning and Janitorial Supplies) [4679]
Thornton Wine Imports; J.W. (Alcoholic Beverages) [2080]
Valley Vintners Inc. (Alcoholic Beverages) [2099]

Lewiston
Bi-State Distributing Co. (Construction Materials and Machinery) [7056]
Blue Ribbon Linen Supply Inc. (Cleaning and Janitorial Supplies) [4585]
Erb Hardware Co. Ltd. (Hardware) [13688]
Freeburg Sign & Lighting (Specialty Equipment and Products) [25654]
Hahn Supply Inc. (Plumbing Materials and Fixtures) [23200]
Inland NW Services Inc. (Office Equipment and Supplies) [21059]
Lewiston Grain Growers (Livestock and Farm Products) [18055]
Lewiston Livestock Market Inc. (Livestock and Farm Products) [18056]
Lolo Sporting Goods Inc. (Recreational and Sporting Goods) [23791]
Long Machinery Inc. Lewiston (Agricultural Equipment and Supplies) [969]
Odom Northwest Beverages (Alcoholic Beverages) [1928]
P & F Distributors Inc. (Alcoholic Beverages) [1937]

Marsing
Scott's Market Equipment Inc. (Heating and Cooling Equipment and Supplies) [14676]

Mc Call
McCall Woodworks Inc. (Furniture and Fixtures) [13175]

Meridian
Automated Business Systems (Office Equipment and Supplies) [20822]
Canfor U.S.A. Corp. (Wood and Wood Products) [27293]
Capitol Distributing (Tobacco Products) [26272]
E Big Inc. (Jewelry) [17402]

Hackler Livestock; G.A. (Livestock and Farm Products) [17967]

Western States Equipment (Construction Materials and Machinery) [8214]

Middleton
CTR Used Parts & Equipment (Automotive) [2500]

Moscow
American Pennant Corp. (Computers and Software) [5932]

Bobs Fire Extinguisher (Security and Safety Equipment) [24517]

Crites-Moscow Growers Inc. (Agricultural Equipment and Supplies) [475]

Latah County Grain Growers Inc. (Livestock and Farm Products) [18045]

Latah Distributors Inc. (Alcoholic Beverages) [1814]

Pure Line Seeds Inc. (Agricultural Equipment and Supplies) [1164]

Mountain Home
Hiway 30 Auto Salvage (Automotive) [2756]

Nampa
All Foreign Used Auto Parts (Automotive) [2204]

All Hours Auto Salvage (Automotive) [2205]

Allied Seed Co-Op, Inc. (Agricultural Equipment and Supplies) [227]

Campbell Tractors and Implements Inc. (Agricultural Equipment and Supplies) [367]

Fireman's Supply Inc. (Security and Safety Equipment) [24551]

Gering; David (Restaurant and Commercial Foodservice Equipment and Supplies) [24127]

Kalbus Office Supply (Office Equipment and Supplies) [21084]

Kido Brothers Exports, Inc. (Food) [11608]

McNeil Marketing Co. (Agricultural Equipment and Supplies) [1006]

R & R Wood Products (Furniture and Fixtures) [13214]

Robertson Supply Inc. (Plumbing Materials and Fixtures) [23349]

Tri E Distributors (Furniture and Fixtures) [13262]

Union Seed Company Inc. (Livestock and Farm Products) [18300]

Woodworks (Furniture and Fixtures) [13283]

Zamzow's Inc. (Agricultural Equipment and Supplies) [1469]

Nezperce
Dokken Implement Co. Inc. (Agricultural Equipment and Supplies) [521]

Jacklin Seed Co. (Agricultural Equipment and Supplies) [873]

Nezperce Rochdale Company Inc. (Petroleum, Fuels, and Related Equipment) [22516]

Osburn
Gold Rush Wrecking (Automotive) [2689]

Parma
Watson Company Inc.; J.C. (Food) [12882]

Payette
Sioux Veneer Panel Co. (Construction Materials and Machinery) [8026]

Pocatello
Associated Food Stores Inc. (Food) [10445]

Beauty Aid Distributors (Health and Beauty Aids) [14036]

Bowen-Hall Petroleum Inc. (Petroleum, Fuels, and Related Equipment) [22087]

Bowen Petroleum (Petroleum, Fuels, and Related Equipment) [22088]

Coca-Cola Pocatello (Soft Drinks) [24950]

Cowboy Oil Co. (Petroleum, Fuels, and Related Equipment) [22176]

Gem State Distributors Inc. (Tobacco Products) [26298]

H & M Distributing (Soft Drinks) [24967]

Intermountain Beverage Company (Alcoholic Beverages) [1773]

Mountain Tile (Floorcovering Equipment and Supplies) [10067]

Paint & Equipment Supply (Paints and Varnishes) [21526]

Pickens Electronics (Office Equipment and Supplies) [21214]

Powers Candy Company Inc. (Food) [12201]

Read Optical Inc. (Medical, Dental, and Optical Supplies) [19569]

Shaw Auto Parts Inc. (Automotive) [3214]

Tee Pee Advertising Co. (Toys and Hobby Goods) [26677]

Thompson Distributing (Alcoholic Beverages) [2078]

Post Falls
Bild Industries Inc. (Hardware) [13599]

Jacklin Seed Simplot Turf & Horticulture (Agricultural Equipment and Supplies) [875]

Preston
Franklin County Grain Grower Inc. (Agricultural Equipment and Supplies) [701]

Rexburg
Sun Glo of Idaho Inc. (Food) [12604]

Rigby
Spectrum Corp. (Specialty Equipment and Products) [25827]

Rupert
Jones Potatoes Inc.; Rolland (Food) [11562]

Salmon
J & V Vending Wholesale (Tobacco Products) [26311]

J and V Vending Wholesale (Tobacco Products) [26312]

Sandpoint
Jones Distributors Inc.; Bill (Alcoholic Beverages) [1789]

Shelley
GPOD of Idaho (Food) [11300]

Shoshone
Shoshone Sales Yard Inc. (Livestock and Farm Products) [18233]

Soda Springs
Mason Distributing Company (Alcoholic Beverages) [1854]

Sterling
Hebes Motor Co. (Automotive) [2737]

Sugar City
Moody Creek Produce Inc. (Food) [11929]

Sun Valley
S & C Importing (Alcoholic Beverages) [2003]

Twin Falls
A & B Electronic Systems Inc. (Office Equipment and Supplies) [20760]

Auto Body Paint and Supply (Paints and Varnishes) [21393]

Coca-Cola Twin Falls Bottling Co. (Books and Other Printed Materials) [3645]

Creative Business Concepts (Office Equipment and Supplies) [20938]

Dunken Distributing Inc. (Floorcovering Equipment and Supplies) [9874]

Gem Equipment Inc. (Agricultural Equipment and Supplies) [732]

Gem State Paper and Supply Co. (Paper and Paper Products) [21737]

Globe Seed and Feed Company Inc. (Agricultural Equipment and Supplies) [743]

H & M Distributing Inc. (Tobacco Products) [26301]

Idaho Coin Galleries (Jewelry) [17452]

JLJ Inc. (Security and Safety Equipment) [24577]

Pedersen's Ski and Sport (Recreational and Sporting Goods) [23877]

Sound Limited Inc. (Electrical and Electronic Equipment and Supplies) [9382]

Todd; Robyn (Health and Beauty Aids) [14260]

Twin Falls Tractor and Implement Inc. (Agricultural Equipment and Supplies) [1369]

Venture South Distributors (Alcoholic Beverages) [2101]

Weiser
Merritts Auto Salvage (Automotive) [2945]

Weiser Livestock Commission (Livestock and Farm Products) [18332]

Wendell
Desert Sky Wrecking (Automotive) [2540]

Illinois

Addison
A-1 Air Compressor Corp. (Industrial Machinery) [15719]

American Printing Equipment Inc. (Industrial Machinery) [15769]

Bearings & Industrial Supply Co., Inc. (Industrial Supplies) [16741]

Chicago Electric Co. (Electrical and Electronic Equipment and Supplies) [8523]

Duo-Fast Corp. North Central Sales Div. (Hardware) [13671]

Fleetwood Paper Co. (Paper and Paper Products) [21728]

Fleming Sales Company Inc. (Agricultural Equipment and Supplies) [692]

Industrial Steel Service Center (Metals) [20059]

Kehe Food Distributors Inc. (Food) [11588]

KYB Corporation of America (Automotive) [2867]

Leslie Paper Co. Chicago Div. (Paper and Paper Products) [21800]

McCann Industries, Inc. (Construction Materials and Machinery) [7674]

MP-Tech Inc. (Metals) [20209]

Pampered Chef (Household Items) [15609]

Sprayway Inc. (Chemicals) [4520]

Thomas Tile & Carpet Supply Co. Inc. (Floorcovering Equipment and Supplies) [10212]

Yorktown Industries Inc. (Office Equipment and Supplies) [21367]

Aledo
Mer-Roc F.S. Inc. (Veterinary Products) [27186]

Algonquin
Tri-County Truck Tops, Inc. (Automotive) [3334]

Unibri International (Industrial Supplies) [17240]

Allerton
Allerton Implement Co. (Agricultural Equipment and Supplies) [224]

Alsip
Admiral Steel (Metals) [19730]

BBC Fasteners Inc. (Hardware) [13588]

Carpet Cushion Supply (Floorcovering Equipment and Supplies) [9764]

Distinctive Business Products Inc. (Office Equipment and Supplies) [20967]

George Co.; Edward (Construction Materials and Machinery) [7389]

George Co.; Edward (Construction Materials and Machinery) [7390]

Hurley Chicago Company Inc. (Specialty Equipment and Products) [25683]

McAllister Equipment Co. (Construction Materials and Machinery) [7672]

Mid-America Tile L.P. (Floorcovering Equipment and Supplies) [10032]

Nichols Motorcycle Supply, Inc. (Motorized Vehicles) [20694]

RAE Products and Chemical Inc. (Chemicals) [4489]

Reliable Fire Equipment Co. (Security and Safety Equipment) [24618]

Tilers—Pergo Shop; J.R. (Floorcovering Equipment and Supplies) [10247]

Ulbrich of Illinois Inc. (Metals) [20454]

Alton

Piasa Motor Fuels Inc. (Petroleum, Fuels, and Related Equipment) [22583]

Amboy

Lee F.S. Inc. (Agricultural Equipment and Supplies) [949]

Leffelman and Sons Inc.; W.G. (Agricultural Equipment and Supplies) [951]

Ogle Service Co. (Agricultural Equipment and Supplies) [1100]

Arcola

Mid-State Industries LLC (Metals) [20183]

Monahan Co.; Thomas (Wood and Wood Products) [27348]

Arlington Heights

Architectural Floor Systems, Inc. (Floorcovering Equipment and Supplies) [9684]

Art Metal Products (Furniture and Fixtures) [13023]

Design Toscano Inc. (Furniture and Fixtures) [13089]

Durst Brokerage Inc. (Food) [11001]

Federated Foods Inc. (Food) [11114]

Federated Foodservice (Restaurant and Commercial Foodservice Equipment and Supplies) [24115]

Federated Group, Inc. (Food) [11115]

GLS Corp. (Construction Materials and Machinery) [7400]

Harlow International (Automotive) [2725]

Harvest Publications (Books and Other Printed Materials) [3817]

Persin and Robbin Jewelers (Jewelry) [17547]

Arthur

Moultrie Grain Association (Livestock and Farm Products) [18119]

Okaw Buildings Inc. (Construction Materials and Machinery) [7808]

Ashkum

Tri Central Co-op (Livestock and Farm Products) [18290]

Ashland

Ashland Farmers Elevator Co. (Livestock and Farm Products) [17706]

Ashmore

Ashmore Grain Co. Inc. (Livestock and Farm Products) [17707]

Coffey and Sons Inc.; Bill (Agricultural Equipment and Supplies) [433]

Assumption

Assumption Cooperative Grain Co. (Livestock and Farm Products) [17708]

Assumption Cooperative Grain Co. (Food) [10459]

Sloan Implement Company Inc. (Agricultural Equipment and Supplies) [1270]

Athens

Culver-Fancy Prairie Cooperative Co. (Livestock and Farm Products) [17805]

Auburn

Beatty Implement Co. (Agricultural Equipment and Supplies) [289]

Augusta

Augusta Farmers Cooperative Co. (Livestock and Farm Products) [17712]

Aurora

Bernina of America Inc. (Household Appliances) [15051]

Illco Inc. (Heating and Cooling Equipment and Supplies) [14494]

Marcley Oil Inc. (Petroleum, Fuels, and Related Equipment) [22451]

Meyer Company Inc.; William F. (Plumbing Materials and Fixtures) [23261]

Mitutoyo/MTI Corp. (Scientific and Measurement Devices) [24400]

MTI Corp. (Scientific and Measurement Devices) [24405]

Shorr Paper Products Inc. (Paper and Paper Products) [21941]

Spong Trade Co. (Motorized Vehicles) [20729]

Superscope Technologies, Inc./Marantz Professional (Sound and Entertainment Equipment and Supplies) [25469]

Weldstar Co. (Industrial Supplies) [17271]

Avon

Neff Co. (Agricultural Equipment and Supplies) [1067]

Barrington

CAI Div. (Photographic Equipment and Supplies) [22836]

Dentec Corp. (Medical, Dental, and Optical Equipment) [18771]

ERW International, Inc. (Medical, Dental, and Optical Supplies) [19307]

Matt-Son Inc. (Plumbing Materials and Fixtures) [23255]

Maverick.com Inc. (Computers and Software) [6469]

Royal Fuel Corp. (Petroleum, Fuels, and Related Equipment) [22643]

Bartlett

Setko Fasteners Inc. (Hardware) [13913]

Batavia

All Dressed Up (Clothing) [4757]

Becker Company Inc.; Larson (Specialty Equipment and Products) [25569]

Flinn Scientific, Inc. (Scientific and Measurement Devices) [24361]

Rosario Candy Inc. (Tobacco Products) [26348]

Bedford Park

Action Threaded Products Inc. (Hardware) [13528]

CHEMCENTRAL Corp. (Chemicals) [4351]

Fail-Safe Lighting Systems Inc. (Electrical and Electronic Equipment and Supplies) [8729]

Hoist Liftruck Manufacturing (Industrial Machinery) [16108]

Lexington Steel Corp. (Metals) [20127]

Belleville

St. Clair Service Co. (Agricultural Equipment and Supplies) [1227]

Stein Distributing (Petroleum, Fuels, and Related Equipment) [22703]

Superb Cooking Products Co./Empire Comfort Systems, Inc. (Recreational and Sporting Goods) [23995]

Bellwood

Combined Metals of Chicago L.P. (Metals) [19886]

Dura Metals Inc. (Metals) [19941]

Belvidere

Central Commodities Ltd. (Livestock and Farm Products) [17770]

Bement

Bement Grain Company Inc. (Livestock and Farm Products) [17728]

Bensenville

A-Pet, Inc. (Veterinary Products) [27054]

Aaron Equipment Co. (Industrial Machinery) [15722]

Advance Refrigeration Co. (Household Appliances) [14994]

Auto Truck Inc. (Automotive) [2280]

Bearing Distributors Inc. (Automotive) [2331]

Capital City Distribution Inc. (Books and Other Printed Materials) [3609]

Fredriksen and Sons Fire Equipment Company Inc. (Security and Safety Equipment) [24553]

General Music Corp. (Sound and Entertainment Equipment and Supplies) [25209]

Industry-Railway Suppliers Inc. (Railroad Equipment and Supplies) [23481]

Kraft Foodservice Inc. (Food) [11642]

Kraft-Holleb (Food) [11644]

North States Steel Corp. (Metals) [20236]

QSN Manufacturing Inc. (Hardware) [13879]

Benson

Benson Farmers Cooperative (Agricultural Equipment and Supplies) [299]

Berkeley

Vanee Foods Co. (Food) [12828]

Berwyn

BB & W Electronics (Electrical and Electronic Equipment and Supplies) [8424]

Bethany

Bethany Grain Company Inc. (Livestock and Farm Products) [17732]

Bloomingdale

Comark Inc. (Computers and Software) [6080]

Outokumpu Metals (USA) Inc. (Metals) [20258]

PC Wholesale Inc. (Computers and Software) [6601]

Weil Service Products Corp. (Petroleum, Fuels, and Related Equipment) [22790]

Bloomington

B and J Sales Inc. (Alcoholic Beverages) [1495]

BPC Foodservice Inc. (Food) [10606]

Glass Specialty Inc. (Automotive) [2683]

Growmark (Agricultural Equipment and Supplies) [775]

Growmark (Agricultural Equipment and Supplies) [776]

GROWMARK Inc. (Livestock and Farm Products) [17965]

Hundman Lumber Do-it Center Inc. (Construction Materials and Machinery) [7499]

Illinois Agricultural Association (Agricultural Equipment and Supplies) [851]

Library Book Selection Service, Inc. (Books and Other Printed Materials) [3911]

McLean County Service Co. (Agricultural Equipment and Supplies) [1004]

McLean County Truck Company Inc. (Motorized Vehicles) [20677]

Owens Inc.; Arnold (Petroleum, Fuels, and Related Equipment) [22543]

Blue Island

Chase Supply Co. (Heating and Cooling Equipment and Supplies) [14382]

Parco Foods LLC (Food) [12108]

Sawing and Shearing Services Inc. (Metals) [20354]

Bluff Springs

Bluff Springs Farmers Elevator Co. (Livestock and Farm Products) [17740]

Bolingbrook

A & D Enterprises, Import-Export (Automotive) [2156]

Century Tile and Supply (Floorcovering Equipment and Supplies) [9788]

Sammons Preston (Medical, Dental, and Optical Equipment) [19031]

Schwinn Cycling and Fitness (Recreational and Sporting Goods) [23932]

Bourbonnais

Global Steel Trading Inc. (Metals) [20008]

Braceville

Fisher Auto Parts (Automotive) [2619]

Bradley

Fleet Pride (Automotive) [2629]
Moore Industries Inc. (Medical, Dental, and Optical Supplies) [19466]

Bridgeview

Great Central Steel Co. (Metals) [20018]
Norman Equipment Company Inc. (Industrial Machinery) [16349]
Tool Steel Service Inc. (Metals) [20432]

Bristol

Seaboard Seed Co. (Agricultural Equipment and Supplies) [1247]

Broadview

Aluminum Distributors Inc. (Metals) [19764]
Dyna Group International Inc. (Recreational and Sporting Goods) [23636]
Intech EDM Electrotools (Electrical and Electronic Equipment and Supplies) [8885]
Midwest Environmental Safety Supply (Specialty Equipment and Products) [25738]
Perlow Steel Corp. (Metals) [20272]

Brookfield

Aaraya Beauty Accents (Health and Beauty Aids) [14007]

Brookport

States Distributing (Floorcovering Equipment and Supplies) [10180]

Buffalo Grove

Akorn Inc. (Medical, Dental, and Optical Supplies) [19130]
ASAP Software Express Inc. (Computers and Software) [5969]
Cambridge Communication Inc. (Niles, Illinois) (Communications Systems and Equipment) [5543]
Sargent-Welch Scientific Co. (Scientific and Measurement Devices) [24425]

Burr Ridge

Applied Industrial Technologies (Communications Systems and Equipment) [5516]
Assembly Component Systems (Hardware) [13566]
Floralife Inc. (Horticultural Supplies) [14865]
Smith; Merle B. (Floorcovering Equipment and Supplies) [10155]

Cairo

Halliday-Smith Inc. (Alcoholic Beverages) [1741]

Calumet Park

Fabsco Corp. (Hardware) [13690]
SG Supply Co. (Plumbing Materials and Fixtures) [23371]

Cambridge

Empire N.A. Inc. (Agricultural Equipment and Supplies) [552]
Henry Service Co. (Petroleum, Fuels, and Related Equipment) [22345]
Whiteside F.S. Inc. (Petroleum, Fuels, and Related Equipment) [22800]

Campus

Hamilton Elevator Company Inc. (Livestock and Farm Products) [17973]

Carbondale

Williams Fertilizer Co.; Archie (Agricultural Equipment and Supplies) [1451]

Carlinville

Boente Sons Inc.; Joseph F. (Petroleum, Fuels, and Related Equipment) [22083]

Carlyle

Ferrin Cooperative Equity Exchange (Agricultural Equipment and Supplies) [680]

Carol Stream

Associated Material Handling Industries Inc. (Industrial Supplies) [16713]
Banner Service Corp. (Metals) [19803]
Ditch Witch of Illinois Inc. (Construction Materials and Machinery) [7269]
Fiatallis North America Inc. (Construction Materials and Machinery) [7338]
FoxMeyer Drug Co. Carol Stream Div. (Medical, Dental, and Optical Supplies) [19329]
Grayline Housewares (Metals) [20017]
Inland Detroit Diesel/Allison (Automotive) [2778]
Material Handling Services Inc. (Industrial Machinery) [16272]
Pella Windows and Doors Inc. (Construction Materials and Machinery) [7844]
WaterPro Supplies Inc. (Plumbing Materials and Fixtures) [23440]

Carrollton

Carrollton Farmers Elevator Co. (Livestock and Farm Products) [17765]
Carrollton Farmers Elevator Co. (Food) [10704]

Carterville

Southern Illinois Wholesale Company Inc. (Alcoholic Beverages) [2033]

Casey

Casey Implement Company Inc. (Agricultural Equipment and Supplies) [377]

Cerro Gordo

Van Horn Hybrids Inc. (Livestock and Farm Products) [18315]
V.H. Associates Inc. (Livestock and Farm Products) [18317]

Champaign

Great Planes Model Distributors Co. (Toys and Hobby Goods) [26506]
Hamburg (Alcoholic Beverages) [1743]
Humphries Decorative Fabrics; Gabe (Textiles and Notions) [26068]
Micro-Pace Computers Inc. (Computers and Software) [6494]
Stotler Grain Co. (Livestock and Farm Products) [18260]
SUPERVALU Champaign Distribution Center (Food) [12643]
Tepper Electrical Supply Inc. (Electrical and Electronic Equipment and Supplies) [9479]

Chapin

Chapin Farmers Elevator Co. (Livestock and Farm Products) [17775]

Chatsworth

Diller Tile Company Inc. (Plumbing Materials and Fixtures) [23138]
Farmers Grain Company of Charlotte (Agricultural Equipment and Supplies) [652]

Chebanse

Clifton Grain Inc. (Livestock and Farm Products) [17782]

Chestnut

Farmers Grain Company of Chestnut (Livestock and Farm Products) [17892]

Chicago

21st Century Telecom Group (Electrical and Electronic Equipment and Supplies) [8256]
Able Distributors (Heating and Cooling Equipment and Supplies) [14290]
Academy Chicago Publishers Ltd. (Books and Other Printed Materials) [3463]
Action Electric Sales Co. (Electrical and Electronic Equipment and Supplies) [8271]
Active Electrical Supply Co. (Electrical and Electronic Equipment and Supplies) [8272]
Adams Apple Distributing L.P. (Gifts and Novelties) [13291]
Adams Foam Rubber Co. (Rubber) [24265]

Advance Electrical Supply Co. (Electrical and Electronic Equipment and Supplies) [8274]
Affy Tapple Inc. (Food) [10340]
Airtex Corp. (Construction Materials and Machinery) [6926]
Albany Steel & Brass Corp. (Hardware) [13543]
All-Power Inc. (Automotive) [2207]
All Products Automotive Inc. (Automotive) [2208]
Alsdorf International Ltd. (Hardware) [13554]
American Hydrotech Inc. (Construction Materials and Machinery) [6967]
Antognoli and Co.; Joseph (Food) [10422]
Armitage Industrial Supply, Inc. (Industrial Supplies) [16710]
Armstrong Bros. Tool Co. (Industrial Machinery) [15778]
The Auster Co. Inc. (Food) [10472]
Azcon Corp. (Construction Materials and Machinery) [7006]
Banner Wholesale Grocers Inc. (Food) [10497]
Banner Wholesale Grocers Inc. (Food) [10498]
Barclay Marine Distributors Corp. (Marine) [18452]
Barton Inc. (Alcoholic Beverages) [1503]
Basic Wire & Cable Co. (Electrical and Electronic Equipment and Supplies) [8418]
Bays Corp. (Food) [10520]
Bel-Pak Foods Inc. (Food) [10528]
Bennett Brothers Inc. (Jewelry) [17334]
Benras Watch Co. (Jewelry) [17337]
Berlin Packaging Inc. (Storage Equipment and Containers) [25893]
Best Foods (Food) [10547]
Bird-X, Inc. (Agricultural Equipment and Supplies) [318]
Bird-X Inc. (Electrical and Electronic Equipment and Supplies) [8440]
Bomadi Inc. (Food) [10587]
Bonus Books Inc. (Books and Other Printed Materials) [3564]
Boroff and Associates; Cy (Clothing) [4835]
Bradley Supply Co. (Plumbing Materials and Fixtures) [23094]
Bradner Central Co. (Paper and Paper Products) [21656]
Brake and Wheel Parts Industries (Automotive) [2379]
Brewer Sewing Supplies (Textiles and Notions) [25988]
Brost International Trading Co. (Rubber) [24271]
Bruce and Co.; Donald (Jewelry) [17352]
Bruss Co. (Food) [10633]
Calvetti Meats Inc.; James (Food) [10682]
Cambridge Law Study Aids, Inc. (Books and Other Printed Materials) [3604]
Carina International Inc. (Luggage and Leather Goods) [18380]
Carpet Cushion Supply (Floorcovering Equipment and Supplies) [9767]
Carroll Seating Company Inc. (Furniture and Fixtures) [13064]
Centel Information Systems Inc. (Computers and Software) [6052]
Central Steel and Wire Co (Metals) [19868]
Century Tile & Carpet (Floorcovering Equipment and Supplies) [9786]
Century Tile and Carpet (Construction Materials and Machinery) [7163]
Certified Automotive Warehouse Inc. (Automotive) [2442]
Chicago Fish House Inc. (Food) [10742]
Chicago Import Inc. (Gifts and Novelties) [13331]
Chicago Tube and Iron Co. (Metals) [19876]
Clark Ltd.; Vivian (Clothing) [4883]
CLEARVUE (Books and Other Printed Materials) [3644]
Cloverhill Pastry-Vending Inc. (Food) [10776]
Cobra Electronics Corp. (Communications Systems and Equipment) [5565]
Cobra Electronics Corp. (Electrical and Electronic Equipment and Supplies) [8537]
Cold Headers Inc. (Hardware) [13638]
Columbia Pipe and Supply (Heating and Cooling Equipment and Supplies) [14393]
Consumers Vinegar and Spice Co. (Food) [10823]
Container Recycling Alliance (Used, Scrap, and Recycled Materials) [26786]

Continental Glass and Plastic Inc. (Storage Equipment and Containers) [25908]

Continental Paper Grading Co. (Used, Scrap, and Recycled Materials) [26787]

Cook Brothers Inc. (Household Appliances) [15096]

Cook Chocolate Co. (Food) [10832]

Cooper and Associates (Gifts and Novelties) [13335]

Corey Steel Co. (Metals) [19899]

Cornille and Sons Inc.; George J. (Food) [10843]

Cosentino Company Inc.; J. (Food) [10844]

Cotter and Co. (Hardware) [13648]

Cougle Commission Co. (Food) [10853]

Cozzi Iron and Metal Inc. (Used, Scrap, and Recycled Materials) [26790]

Craelius and Company Inc.; L. (Food) [10862]

Cragin Metals L.L.C. (Metals) [19903]

Crown Glass Corp. (Storage Equipment and Containers) [25909]

Crown Steel Sales Inc. (Metals) [19906]

CS Battery Inc. (Automotive) [2499]

Cushing and Company Inc. (Specialty Equipment and Products) [25617]

CYN (Marine) [18488]

D E B Industries, Inc. (Food) [10890]

Darco Enterprises Inc. (Metals) [19916]

Davies Supply Co. (Industrial Supplies) [16820]

Dearborn Trade (Books and Other Printed Materials) [3682]

Dearborn Wholesale Grocers L.P. (Food) [10930]

Desks Inc. (Chicago, Illinois) (Office Equipment and Supplies) [20959]

Duchess Royale Inc. (Household Items) [15482]

Durable Packaging Corp. (Industrial Machinery) [15967]

Eager Plastics Inc. (Plastics) [22957]

Edmunds and Company Inc.; Frank A. (Construction Materials and Machinery) [7303]

Edmunds and Company Inc.; Frank A. (Wood and Wood Products) [27303]

EESCO, A Division of WESCO Distribution, Inc. (Electrical and Electronic Equipment and Supplies) [8655]

Electro Brand Inc. (Sound and Entertainment Equipment and Supplies) [25178]

Encyclopaedia Britannica Educational Corp. (Books and Other Printed Materials) [3731]

Erickson's Decorating Products, Inc. (Paints and Varnishes) [21439]

Evans (Clothing) [4941]

Excel Corp. (Food) [11063]

Excel Electric Service Co. (Electrical and Electronic Equipment and Supplies) [8722]

Excel Specialty Corp. (Electrical and Electronic Equipment and Supplies) [8723]

Faber Brothers Inc. (Recreational and Sporting Goods) [23662]

Fantasy Diamond Corp. (Jewelry) [17412]

Fashion Bed Group (Furniture and Fixtures) [13111]

Federal Screw Products Inc. (Hardware) [13704]

Feralloy Corp. (Metals) [19969]

Feralloy Corp. Midwest Div. (Metals) [19971]

Field Tool Supply Co. (Industrial Machinery) [16008]

Fine Wine Brokers Inc. (Alcoholic Beverages) [1689]

Fixture Hardware Co. (Furniture and Fixtures) [13113]

Foell Packing Co. (Food) [11167]

Franklin Stores Inc.; Ben (Toys and Hobby Goods) [26487]

Freedman Seating Co. (Automotive) [2647]

Freund Can Co. (Storage Equipment and Containers) [25916]

GATX Corp. (Railroad Equipment and Supplies) [23478]

GATX Terminals Corp. (Petroleum, Fuels, and Related Equipment) [22304]

General Iron Industries Inc. (Used, Scrap, and Recycled Materials) [26823]

General Truck Parts and Equipment Co. (Automotive) [2676]

Gerber Inc.; Max (Plumbing Materials and Fixtures) [23189]

GF Office Furniture Ltd. (Office Equipment and Supplies) [21013]

Goes Lithographing Co. (Paper and Paper Products) [21742]

Gold Eagle Co. (Automotive) [2688]

Goldberg Models Inc.; Carl (Toys and Hobby Goods) [26502]

Grand Stage Co., Inc. (Specialty Equipment and Products) [25666]

Great Western Steel Co. (Metals) [20021]

Handelsman Co.; Hanco M. (Household Items) [15518]

Hardy Corp. (Construction Materials and Machinery) [7448]

Harris Marcus Group (Furniture and Fixtures) [13127]

Harris-Teller, Inc. (Books and Other Printed Materials) [3814]

HCI Great Lakes Region (Chemicals) [4413]

Helix Ltd. (Photographic Equipment and Supplies) [22864]

Henry J. Easy Pak Meats (Food) [11413]

Hickman, Williams and Co., Black Products Div. (Metals) [20037]

Hinckley and Schmitt Bottled Water Group (Food) [11438]

HobbyGame Distributors Inc. (Toys and Hobby Goods) [26521]

Hoffman Co.; H. (Security and Safety Equipment) [24565]

Houff Co.; Roy (Horticultural Supplies) [14890]

Howard Corp.; H.H. (Metals) [20045]

I.F. Optical Co. Inc. (Medical, Dental, and Optical Supplies) [19366]

IGA Inc. (Food) [11491]

In Products Inc. (Household Items) [15538]

Independent Bakers' Cooperative (Food) [11502]

Independent Publishers Group Inc. (Books and Other Printed Materials) [3842]

Indus-Tool (Electrical and Electronic Equipment and Supplies) [8874]

Indus-Tool Inc. (Automotive) [2773]

Industrial Steel and Wire Co. (Industrial Supplies) [16949]

Inland Steel Industries Inc. (Metals) [20065]

Interior Enterprises Inc. (Office Equipment and Supplies) [21061]

International Cellulose Inc. (Used, Scrap, and Recycled Materials) [26851]

International Components Corp. (Electrical and Electronic Equipment and Supplies) [8893]

International Healthcare Products (Medical, Dental, and Optical Equipment) [18858]

International Historic Films Inc. (Sound and Entertainment Equipment and Supplies) [25253]

International Importers Inc. (Electrical and Electronic Equipment and Supplies) [8894]

International Machine Tool Ltd. (Industrial Machinery) [16164]

International Typewriter Exchange (Office Equipment and Supplies) [21066]

ITE Distributing (Office Equipment and Supplies) [21071]

James and Company Inc.; E. (Industrial Supplies) [16968]

JC Whitney & Co. (Automotive) [2815]

Jiffy Metal Products Co. (Automotive) [2821]

Johnson and Associates Business Interiors Inc. (Furniture and Fixtures) [13152]

Johnson Pipe and Supply Co. (Plumbing Materials and Fixtures) [23225]

Jonel Inc. (Health and Beauty Aids) [14139]

Kazi Publications (Books and Other Printed Materials) [3876]

Kemeny Overseas Products Corporation (Metals) [20094]

Keystone Aniline Corp. (Chemicals) [4434]

Keystone Tube Co. (Metals) [20100]

King Salmon Inc. (Food) [11617]

Krause & Sons; M.P. (Veterinary Products) [27175]

L and W Supply Corp. (Construction Materials and Machinery) [7574]

LaCROIX Beverages Inc. (Soft Drinks) [24982]

Lance Construction Supplies Inc. (Construction Materials and Machinery) [7584]

Lapham-Hickey Steel Corp. (Metals) [20117]

Lee Lumber and Building Materials Corp. (Construction Materials and Machinery) [7591]

Leedal Inc. (Photographic Equipment and Supplies) [22873]

Lefton Co.; Geo Zolton (Household Items) [15564]

Lenzip Manufacturing Corp. (Textiles and Notions) [26123]

Levy Co.; Charles (Books and Other Printed Materials) [3907]

Liberation Distributors (Books and Other Printed Materials) [3909]

LKS International Inc. (Restaurant and Commercial Foodservice Equipment and Supplies) [24168]

LKS International Inc. (Heating and Cooling Equipment and Supplies) [14525]

Login Brothers Book Co. (Books and Other Printed Materials) [3920]

LPC (Books and Other Printed Materials) [3922]

Mack-Chicago Corp. (Paper and Paper Products) [21817]

Malik International Enterprises Ltd. (Household Items) [15574]

Maloney, Cunningham & Devic (Food) [11769]

The Manderscheid Co. (Industrial Supplies) [17013]

Marketing Group Inc. (Harvey, Illinois) (Jewelry) [17513]

Marvel Group Inc. (Office Equipment and Supplies) [21132]

Material Service Corp. (Construction Materials and Machinery) [7665]

Medica International Ltd. (Agricultural Equipment and Supplies) [1009]

Metal Management Inc. (Metals) [20169]

Metron Steel Corp. (Metals) [20178]

Meystel Inc. (Clothing) [5189]

Mid-America Wine Co. (Alcoholic Beverages) [1871]

Mid-City Automotive Warehouse Inc. (Automotive) [2950]

Mid-Lakes Distributing Inc. (Heating and Cooling Equipment and Supplies) [14602]

Mid-South Supply Corp. (Paints and Varnishes) [21501]

Midwest Coil Processing (Metals) [20189]

Midwest Labs (Medical, Dental, and Optical Supplies) [19458]

Midwest Metallics L.P. (Metals) [20190]

Midwest Truck and Auto Parts Inc. (Automotive) [2960]

Midwest Visual Equipment Co. (Sound and Entertainment Equipment and Supplies) [25324]

Miller Bros. Lumber Company Inc. (Construction Materials and Machinery) [7713]

Miniat Inc.; Ed (Food) [11905]

Monarch Steel Co. (Metals) [20201]

Moody Institute of Science (Sound and Entertainment Equipment and Supplies) [25335]

Moore Supply Co. (Heating and Cooling Equipment and Supplies) [14610]

Morley Sales Company Inc. (Food) [11936]

Motloid Co. (Medical, Dental, and Optical Supplies) [19469]

Motloid Company (Electrical and Electronic Equipment and Supplies) [9100]

MRC Polymers Inc. (Used, Scrap, and Recycled Materials) [26919]

Mutual Sales Corp. (Industrial Machinery) [16334]

Mutual Truck Parts Co. (Automotive) [3006]

National Hardware and Supplies (Electrical and Electronic Equipment and Supplies) [9116]

National Systems Corp. (Computers and Software) [6543]

Nationwide Beef Inc. (Food) [11980]

Nat's Garden Produce, Inc. (Food) [11981]

Neiman Brothers Company Inc. (Food) [11992]

New York Notions/Craft Supply Corp. (Toys and Hobby Goods) [26593]

Noon Hour Food Products Inc. (Food) [12014]

North Branch Flooring (Floorcovering Equipment and Supplies) [10080]

Nystrom Co. (Books and Other Printed Materials) [4013]

OCE-USA Inc. (Office Equipment and Supplies) [21169]
Pacific Wine Co. (Alcoholic Beverages) [1938]
Packing Seals and Engineering Company Inc. (Plumbing Materials and Fixtures) [23305]
Pastorelli Food Products Inc. (Food) [12120]
Path Press Inc. (Books and Other Printed Materials) [4043]
Peck & Co.; S.A. (Jewelry) [17544]
Pielet Brothers Scrap, Iron and Metal L.P. (Metals) [20277]
Pioneer Wholesale Meat (Food) [12175]
Pola Foods Inc. (Food) [12187]
Pollack L.L.C.; J.O. (Jewelry) [17550]
Quaker Oats Co. International Foods Div. (Food) [12245]
Quality Croutons Inc. (Food) [12249]
Quick-Rotan Inc. (Household Appliances) [15286]
Rainbow Distributing, Inc. (Health and Beauty Aids) [14204]
Rembrandt Lamps (Household Items) [15632]
Representative Sales Co. (Textiles and Notions) [26184]
Republic Tobacco L.P. (Tobacco Products) [26347]
Revere Electric Supply Co. (Electrical and Electronic Equipment and Supplies) [9283]
Rico Industries Inc. (Luggage and Leather Goods) [18424]
Robin's Food Distribution Inc. (Food) [12332]
Romano Brothers Beverage Co. (Alcoholic Beverages) [1998]
Romanoff Corp.; Maya (Household Items) [15640]
Root Brothers Manufacturing and Supply Co. (Industrial Supplies) [17146]
Rosenblum's World of Judaica, Inc. (Books and Other Printed Materials) [4124]
Rous Inc.; R.J. (Food) [12362]
Royal Crown Bottling Company Inc. (Soft Drinks) [25028]
Royal Industries (Paper and Paper Products) [21913]
Ryerson and Son Inc.; Joseph T. (Metals) [20342]
Ryerson and Son Inc., Ryerson Plastics Div.; Joseph T. (Plastics) [23032]
Ryerson Tull Inc. (Metals) [20344]
Rymer Foods Inc. (Food) [12378]
S & M Produce (Food) [12381]
Salon Associates (Health and Beauty Aids) [14228]
Sara Lee Corp. (Food) [12412]
Scrap Corporation of America (Used, Scrap, and Recycled Materials) [26984]
Serson Supply Inc. (Industrial Supplies) [17168]
Shorewood Packaging Company of Illinois Inc. (Paper and Paper Products) [21940]
SK Hand Tool Corp. (Hardware) [13920]
Solinger and Associates (Household Appliances) [15318]
Southside Ford Truck Sales Inc. (Motorized Vehicles) [20725]
Specialty Promotions Co., Inc. (Books and Other Printed Materials) [4180]
The Spiral Collection, Inc. (Household Items) [15664]
Standard Steel and Wire Corp. (Metals) [20387]
Star Tubular Products Co. (Plumbing Materials and Fixtures) [23397]
Steel Co. (Metals) [20393]
Stone Commodities Corp. (Food) [12590]
Straub and Co.; W.F. (Food) [12594]
Strombecker Corp. (Toys and Hobby Goods) [26672]
Stuck and Associates; Paul (Used, Scrap, and Recycled Materials) [27011]
Stutz Co. (Industrial Supplies) [17200]
Sunnyside Auto Finance (Automotive) [3283]
Superior FomeBords Corp. (Adhesives) [16]
Surpless, Dunn & Co. (Hardware) [13947]
Talk-A-Phone Co. (Communications Systems and Equipment) [5772]
Thybony Wallcoverings Co. (Paints and Varnishes) [21593]
Tower Oil and Technology Co. (Petroleum, Fuels, and Related Equipment) [22742]
Transco Products Inc. (Railroad Equipment and Supplies) [23488]

Tri-State Surgical Corp. (Medical, Dental, and Optical Equipment) [19087]
Tribune Co. (Books and Other Printed Materials) [4231]
Trost Modelcraft Hobbies (Toys and Hobby Goods) [26691]
TruServ Corp. (Hardware) [13968]
United Container Corp. (Paper and Paper Products) [21974]
Unity Manufacturing Co. (Automotive) [3373]
Universal Bowling and Golf Co. (Recreational and Sporting Goods) [24023]
Universal Scrap Metals Co. (Used, Scrap, and Recycled Materials) [27033]
Upstart Publishing Company Inc. (Books and Other Printed Materials) [4256]
UV Process Supply Inc. (Electrical and Electronic Equipment and Supplies) [9529]
Viking Supply Company Inc. (Electrical and Electronic Equipment and Supplies) [9539]
Vitner Company Inc.; C.J. (Food) [12852]
Wahler Brothers (Hardware) [13983]
Welding Industrial Supply Inc. (Industrial Supplies) [17270]
Wexler Meat Co. (Food) [12922]
Wild Game Inc. (Food) [12941]
Wilkens-Anderson Co. (Scientific and Measurement Devices) [24457]
Wilton Corp. (Industrial Supplies) [17282]
Wipeco Corp. (Household Items) [15711]
Wirtz Corp. (Alcoholic Beverages) [2132]
Wittek Golf Supply Co., Inc. (Recreational and Sporting Goods) [24049]
World Wide Distributors Inc. (Specialty Equipment and Products) [25883]
World Wide Distributors Inc. (Restaurant and Commercial Foodservice Equipment and Supplies) [24263]
XNEX Inc. (Clothing) [5493]
Yates & Bird (Medical, Dental, and Optical Supplies) [19715]
Yates and Bird (Electrical and Electronic Equipment and Supplies) [9618]

Chicago Heights
Century Steel Corp. (Metals) [19870]
Helsel-Jepperson Electric Inc. (Electrical and Electronic Equipment and Supplies) [8837]

Cicero
Auto Clutch/All Brake Inc. (Automotive) [2269]
Office Equipment Sales (Office Equipment and Supplies) [21177]
Sommer and Maca Industries Inc. (Industrial Machinery) [16503]

Cisco
Cisco Cooperative Grain Inc. (Livestock and Farm Products) [17779]

Cissna Park
Kaufman Grain Co. (Livestock and Farm Products) [18029]

Coal Valley
J and B Meats Corp. (Food) [11534]
J and B Meats Corp. (Food) [11535]

Collinsville
Austin, D L Steel Supply Corp. (Metals) [19792]

Colusa
Colusa Elevator Company Inc. (Livestock and Farm Products) [17786]

Cooksville
Cooksville Grain Co. (Livestock and Farm Products) [17793]

Countryside
Chicago Chain & Transmission (Automotive) [2448]

Crestwood
Cloverleaf Farms Distributors Inc. (Food) [10777]
Dodge Chicago/IBT (Industrial Machinery) [15957]

Evergreen Oak Electric Supply & Sales Co. Crest Lighting Studios Div. (Electrical and Electronic Equipment and Supplies) [8718]
Evergreen Oak Electric Supply and Sales Co. Evergreen Oak Div. (Electrical and Electronic Equipment and Supplies) [8719]
GKR Industries, Inc. (Paper and Paper Products) [21740]
Northern Industries Inc. (Metals) [20237]

Crystal Lake
Curran Contracting Co. (Construction Materials and Machinery) [7237]
Triumph Twist Drill Co. (Industrial Machinery) [16583]

Dalton City
Farmers Cooperative Grain Co. (Livestock and Farm Products) [17872]

Danforth
Danforth-Gilman Grain Co. (Livestock and Farm Products) [17810]

Danvers
Danvers Farmers Elevator Co. (Agricultural Equipment and Supplies) [493]
Danvers Farmers Elevator Co. (Food) [10907]

Danville
Bearings & Transmission (Automotive) [2343]
Bud Electronic Supply Co. (Electrical and Electronic Equipment and Supplies) [8475]
Danville Gasoline and Oil Company Inc. (Petroleum, Fuels, and Related Equipment) [22188]
Danville Gasoline & Oil Co. Inc. Leverenz Automotive & Truck Parts (Industrial Machinery) [15929]
Great Scott Services Ltd. (Paper and Paper Products) [21751]
Herr's and Bernat Inc. (Toys and Hobby Goods) [26514]
Herr's Inc. (Textiles and Notions) [26063]
Industrial Supply Co. (Industrial Supplies) [16955]
Mervis Industries Inc. (Metals) [20168]

Darien
Canfield Co.; A.J. (Soft Drinks) [24923]
Leeco Steel Products Inc. (Metals) [20120]

De Land
Hall Group Inc. (Computers and Software) [6322]

Decatur
ADM-Growmark Inc. (Livestock and Farm Products) [17677]
ADM-Growmark Inc. (Food) [10326]
Black and Co. (Industrial Supplies) [16753]
Bodine Electric of Decatur (Electrical and Electronic Equipment and Supplies) [8449]
Boland Electric Supply Inc. (Electrical and Electronic Equipment and Supplies) [8452]
Decatur Bottling Co. (Soft Drinks) [24953]
Decatur Custom Tool Inc. (Industrial Machinery) [15936]
K's Merchandise Mart Inc. (Jewelry) [17494]
Tabor Grain Co. (Livestock and Farm Products) [18273]
ZEXEL USA Corp. (Automotive) [3454]

Deerfield
Alliant FoodService Inc. (Restaurant and Commercial Foodservice Equipment and Supplies) [24059]
Baxter International Inc. (Deerfield, Illinois) (Medical, Dental, and Optical Supplies) [19177]
BT Office Products USA (Office Equipment and Supplies) [20862]
Clintec Nutrition Co. (Medical, Dental, and Optical Supplies) [19236]
International Cultural Enterprises Inc. (Sound and Entertainment Equipment and Supplies) [25252]
K & L Associates, Inc. (Food) [11574]

Kraft General Foods Group. Kraft Food
Service (Food) [11643]
Leica Inc. (Scientific and Measurement
Devices) [24387]
Rugby USA Inc. (Wood and Wood
Products) [27367]
Walgreen Co. (Health and Beauty Aids) [14275]

Des Plaines

Advent Electronics Inc. (Electrical and Electronic
Equipment and Supplies) [8275]
Alliance Steel Corp. (Metals) [19750]
dB Sound L.P. (Sound and Entertainment
Equipment and Supplies) [25162]
Do All Foreign Sales Corp. (Industrial
Machinery) [15956]
DoAll Co. (Industrial Supplies) [16836]
Filtran Div. (Automotive) [2616]
Interstate Steel Co. (Metals) [20067]
Kar Products (Hardware) [13781]
Lawson Products Inc. (Industrial Supplies) [16995]
Littelfuse Inc. (Electrical and Electronic Equipment
and Supplies) [8995]
Maine Scrap Metal LLC (Used, Scrap, and
Recycled Materials) [26893]
Microunited (Computers and Software) [6512]
Raco Industrial Corp. (Industrial
Machinery) [16436]
Roberts Industries Inc.; J.H. (Metals) [20324]
Sentry/Liberty Hardware Distributors
Inc. (Hardware) [13911]
Sysco Food Services-Chicago Inc. (Food) [12678]
United Stationers Inc. (Paper and Paper
Products) [21977]
Universal Coach Parts Inc. (Automotive) [3374]

Dewey

Fisher Farmers Grain and Coal Co. (Livestock and
Farm Products) [17919]
Shields Soil Service Inc. (Agricultural Equipment
and Supplies) [1265]

Dieterich

Schultz Seed Co.; J.M. (Livestock and Farm
Products) [18225]

Dixon

Wildlife Lithographs, Inc. (Gifts and
Novelties) [13472]

Donovan

Donovan Farmers Cooperative Elevator
Inc. (Livestock and Farm Products) [17819]

Dow

Midland Reclamation Co. (Railroad Equipment and
Supplies) [23484]

Downers Grove

Ames Industries Inc. (Office Equipment and
Supplies) [20801]
Ames Industries Inc. (Industrial Supplies) [16697]
Ames Supply Co. (Office Equipment and
Supplies) [20802]
Anderson Co.; S.W. (Electrical and Electronic
Equipment and Supplies) [8352]
Engineering Equipment Co. (Industrial
Machinery) [15992]
Engineering Equipment Co. (Security and Safety
Equipment) [24537]
National Seed Co. (Agricultural Equipment and
Supplies) [1065]
Platinum Entertainment Inc. (Sound and
Entertainment Equipment and Supplies) [25385]

Earlville

Earlville Farmers Cooperative (Livestock and Farm
Products) [17825]

East Alton

Fairfax Trailer Sales Inc. (Heating and Cooling
Equipment and Supplies) [14440]

East Dubuque

Crescent Electric Supply Co. (Electrical and
Electronic Equipment and Supplies) [8589]
Crescent Electric Supply Co. (Electrical and
Electronic Equipment and Supplies) [8592]

East Moline

Arrow-Master Inc. (Construction Materials and
Machinery) [6992]
Barjan Products, L.P. (Automotive) [2316]

East Peoria

Burklund Distributors Inc. (Food) [10645]
DeHater (Paper and Paper Products) [21705]
PAFCO Truck Bodies Inc. (Automotive) [3076]

East St. Louis

Holten Meat Inc. (Food) [11453]
Lefton Enterprises Inc. (Used, Scrap, and Recycled
Materials) [26879]
Lefton Iron and Metal Co. (Used, Scrap, and
Recycled Materials) [26880]
Switzers Inc. (Food) [12661]

Edwards

Peoria County Service Co. (Agricultural Equipment
and Supplies) [1122]

Edwardsville

Madison Service Co. (Agricultural Equipment and
Supplies) [982]

Effingham

Central Illinois Enterprises Ltd. (Petroleum, Fuels,
and Related Equipment) [22124]
Effingham Equity (Livestock and Farm
Products) [17827]
MIDCO International (Sound and Entertainment
Equipment and Supplies) [25319]
Midco International Inc. (Effingham,
Illinois) (Specialty Equipment and
Products) [25737]
Wabash Independent Oil Co. (Cleaning and
Janitorial Supplies) [4725]

Elburn

Elburn Cooperative Co. (Livestock and Farm
Products) [17829]
F & W Rallye Engineering (Automotive) [2602]
Landfill Alternatives Inc. (Used, Scrap, and
Recycled Materials) [26875]
Regal Shearing (Luggage and Leather
Goods) [18423]

Eldorado

Roundy's Inc. Eldorado Div. (Food) [12359]

Elgin

Boncosky Oil Co. (Petroleum, Fuels, and Related
Equipment) [22084]
Brethren Press (Books and Other Printed
Materials) [3590]
Cook Publishing Co.; David C. (Books and Other
Printed Materials) [3659]
Elgin Paper Co. (Paper and Paper
Products) [21721]
Elgin Salvage and Supply Company Inc. (Used,
Scrap, and Recycled Materials) [26806]
Paragon Supply Co. (Plumbing Materials and
Fixtures) [23307]
Refractory Products Co. (Heating and Cooling
Equipment and Supplies) [14652]
Seegott Inc. (Chemicals) [4505]

Elizabeth

Davies Service Co.; Jo (Agricultural Equipment and
Supplies) [498]

Elk Grove Village

Active Screw and Fastener (Hardware) [13530]
All Tile (Floorcovering Equipment and
Supplies) [9653]
Associates in Software International (Computers
and Software) [5979]

Astral Precision Equipment Co. (Industrial
Machinery) [15785]
B & K Industries Inc. (Plumbing Materials and
Fixtures) [23075]
Bell Paper Products Co. (Paper and Paper
Products) [21651]
Caravelle Distributing (Floorcovering Equipment and
Supplies) [9758]
Carpet Cushion Supply (Floorcovering Equipment
and Supplies) [9763]
Chicago Machine Tool Co. (Industrial
Machinery) [15886]
Clark Food Service Inc. (Food) [10764]
Consolidated Service Corp. (Automotive) [2475]
F-D-C Corp. (Office Equipment and
Supplies) [20998]
Gateway Supply Co. (Plumbing Materials and
Fixtures) [23184]
Gelber Industries (Industrial Machinery) [16051]
GMS Corp. (Luggage and Leather Goods) [18395]
Hawkinson (Floorcovering Equipment and
Supplies) [9940]
Korol Co.; Leon (Paper and Paper
Products) [21793]
M & G Industries (Electrical and Electronic
Equipment and Supplies) [9013]
Mapes and Sprowl Steel Ltd. (Metals) [20151]
Mid-America Tile (Floorcovering Equipment and
Supplies) [10029]
National Material L.P. (Metals) [20219]
Oakton Distributors Inc. (Household
Appliances) [15256]
Petersen Aluminum Corp. (Metals) [20273]
Q.A. Products Inc. (Food) [12243]
Rainsoft Water Conditioning Co. (Specialty
Equipment and Products) [25797]
Reliable Tire Co. (Automotive) [3146]
Rolled Steel Co. (Metals) [20327]
Runge Paper Co., Inc. (Paper and Paper
Products) [21915]
Sakata U.S.A. Corp. (Electrical and Electronic
Equipment and Supplies) [9332]
Steiner Electric Co. (Electrical and Electronic
Equipment and Supplies) [9415]
Summitville, USA (Floorcovering Equipment and
Supplies) [10193]
Tang Industries Inc. (Metals) [20416]
Warehouse Equipment Inc. (Industrial
Machinery) [16615]
WWF Paper Corp. (Paper and Paper
Products) [21999]
Zip Dee Inc. (Furniture and Fixtures) [13287]

Elmhurst

Baumbach Manufacturing Co.; E.A. (Industrial
Supplies) [16724]
Chamberlain Group Inc. (Hardware) [13630]
Chicago Communications Service
Inc. (Communications Systems and
Equipment) [5560]
Chicago Industrial Rubber (Rubber) [24273]
Fay Electric Wire Corp. (Electrical and Electronic
Equipment and Supplies) [8732]
Fitz Chem Corp. (Chemicals) [4389]
Fluid-Dynamic Midwest Inc. (Industrial
Machinery) [16018]
Illinois Auto Electric Co. (Industrial
Machinery) [16142]
Lesman Instrument Co. (Scientific and
Measurement Devices) [24388]
Patten Industries Inc. (Construction Materials and
Machinery) [7841]
S and S Automotive Inc. (Hardware) [13898]
Sakash Company Inc.; John (Industrial
Supplies) [17158]
Saratoga Specialties (Food) [12413]
Shima American Corp. (Industrial Supplies) [17171]
Vic Supply Co. (Chemicals) [4547]

Eureka

Central Illinois Harvestore Inc. (Agricultural
Equipment and Supplies) [395]
Grainland (Food) [11304]
Grainland Cooperative (Livestock and Farm
Products) [17955]

Grainland Cooperative (Livestock and Farm
Products) [17956]

Evanston

Adler's Foreign Books Inc. (Books and Other
Printed Materials) [3472]
Belmont Steel Corp. (Metals) [19808]
Goldsmith Chemical and Metal Corp.;
D.F. (Metals) [20013]
J & F Steel Corporation (Metals) [20071]
Riley and Geehr Inc. (Plastics) [23028]
Sawtooth Technologies Inc. (Computers and
Software) [6707]
Tri-County Distributors (Specialty Equipment and
Products) [25848]
Vena Tech Corp. (Specialty Equipment and
Products) [25866]

Fairfield

Associated Lumber Industries Inc. (Construction
Materials and Machinery) [6999]
Southern Illinois Lumber Co. (Construction Materials
and Machinery) [8050]

Fairview Heights

Weeke Wholesale Company Inc. (Tobacco
Products) [26371]

Farina

Ging and Co. (Livestock and Farm
Products) [17941]
Green/Line Equipment Inc. (Agricultural Equipment
and Supplies) [762]

Forest City

Rickett Grain Co. (Livestock and Farm
Products) [18197]

Forest Park

Ferrara Pan Candy Co. (Food) [11120]
Scenery Unlimited (Toys and Hobby
Goods) [26648]

Forrest

Trainor Grain and Supply Co. (Livestock and Farm
Products) [18288]

Franklin Park

Ajax Tool Works Inc. (Hardware) [13540]
Berry Tire Company Inc. (Automotive) [2351]
Binks Manufacturing Co. (Industrial
Machinery) [15825]
BWD Automotive Corp. (Automotive) [2405]
Castle and Co.; A.M. (Metals) [19862]
Central Grocers Co-op Inc. (Food) [10721]
Central Scientific Co. (Chemicals) [4346]
Consolidated Tool Manufacturers Inc. (Industrial
Machinery) [15910]
Dean Foods Co. (Food) [10929]
Geib Industries Inc. (Industrial Supplies) [16892]
Houston Harvest Gift Products LLC (Food) [11466]
Kinast Distributors Inc.; E. (Construction Materials
and Machinery) [7556]
Precision Steel Warehouse Inc. (Metals) [20293]
Semler Industries Inc. (Specialty Equipment and
Products) [25812]
Unimast Inc. (Metals) [20458]

Freeport

Honeywell Sensing and Control (Electrical and
Electronic Equipment and Supplies) [8856]
Knobel & Son Inc.; John (Alcoholic
Beverages) [1800]

Fulton

Fulton Corp. (Hardware) [13718]

Galesburg

Blick Co.; Dick (Specialty Equipment and
Products) [25576]
Rogers Brothers Wholesale Inc. (Food) [12344]
Saelens Beverages Inc. (Alcoholic
Beverages) [2004]
Westbay Equipment Co. (Agricultural Equipment
and Supplies) [1427]

Willis Steel Corp. (Metals) [20494]
Wilson Paper Co. (Paper and Paper
Products) [21994]

Galva

Gateway Co-Op (Livestock and Farm
Products) [17936]

Geneseo

Cooperative Gas and Oil Co. (Geneseo,
Illinois) (Petroleum, Fuels, and Related
Equipment) [22166]
Ford and Sons Inc.; C.D. (Agricultural Equipment
and Supplies) [699]

Geneva

Schram & Associates; Mike (Recreational and
Sporting Goods) [23931]

Gibson City

Alliance Grain Co. (Livestock and Farm
Products) [17691]
Arends and Sons Inc. (Agricultural Equipment and
Supplies) [250]

Gillespie

Aladdin Steel Inc. (Metals) [19739]

Gilman

Heritage FS Inc. (Agricultural Equipment and
Supplies) [815]
Heritage F.S. Inc. (Petroleum, Fuels, and Related
Equipment) [22346]

Gladstone

McChesney Co.; C.E. (Livestock and Farm
Products) [18078]

Glen Ellyn

CW Magnet Wire Co. (Electrical and Electronic
Equipment and Supplies) [8602]
Dreisilker Electric Motors Inc. (Electrical and
Electronic Equipment and Supplies) [8634]
M & R Sales & Service Inc. (Textiles and
Notions) [26129]
Racing Champions Corp. (Toys and Hobby
Goods) [26626]

Glendale Heights

Alps Wire Rope Corp. (Metals) [19756]
Alps Wire Rope Corp. (Metals) [19757]
C. Design International Inc. (Industrial
Machinery) [15861]
Licht Company Inc.; J.C. (Paints and
Varnishes) [21492]
Maxtec International Corp. (Electrical and Electronic
Equipment and Supplies) [9049]
OSG Tap and Die Inc. (Industrial
Supplies) [17092]

Glenview

Courtesy Distributors Inc. (Soft Drinks) [24951]
Lil Brave Distributors Inc./Division of Plee-Zing
Inc. (Food) [11711]
Plee-Zing Inc. (Food) [12181]
Plywood Discount Center (Construction Materials
and Machinery) [7874]
Republic Tobacco L.P. (Tobacco Products) [26346]
RJM Sales, Associates, Inc. (Hardware) [13888]
Young Supply North; Frank (Heating and Cooling
Equipment and Supplies) [14788]

Granite City

Affiliated Metals Co. (Metals) [19736]
Coyle Mechanical Supply (Industrial
Supplies) [16813]
Prairie Farms Dairy Supply Inc. (Restaurant and
Commercial Foodservice Equipment and
Supplies) [24205]

Grant Park

Whitaker Farmers Cooperative Grain Co. (Livestock
and Farm Products) [18345]

Granville

Mid American Growers (Horticultural
Supplies) [14922]
Moews Seed Company Inc. (Livestock and Farm
Products) [18107]

Graymont

Graymont Cooperative Association Inc. (Agricultural
Equipment and Supplies) [761]

Grayville

Wabash Valley Service Co. (Agricultural Equipment
and Supplies) [1402]

Greenfield

Hog Inc. (Agricultural Equipment and
Supplies) [831]

Greenville

Bond County Services Co. (Agricultural Equipment
and Supplies) [328]
Farmers Livestock Marketing Association (Livestock
and Farm Products) [17901]

Gurnee

Carpet Basics (Floorcovering Equipment and
Supplies) [9762]

Hammond

Unity Grain and Supply Co. (Livestock and Farm
Products) [18306]

Hartsburg

Hartsburg Grain Co. (Livestock and Farm
Products) [17979]

Harvard

AT Products Inc. (Communications Systems and
Equipment) [5519]

Harvey

Cleco Industrial Fasteners, Inc. (Hardware) [13636]
Voss Equipment Inc. (Industrial Machinery) [16609]

Hebron

Shutters Inc. (Construction Materials and
Machinery) [8016]
Vaughan and Bushnell
Manufacturing (Hardware) [13978]

Highland

DuCoa (Minerals and Ores) [20536]

Highland Park

Columbia Audio-Video Inc. (Electrical and Electronic
Equipment and Supplies) [8548]
Craftwood Lumber Co. (Construction Materials and
Machinery) [7229]
Mazzetta Co. (Food) [11815]
Menoni and Mocogni Inc. (Construction Materials
and Machinery) [7693]
Mutual Services of Highland
Park (Hardware) [13841]
Wind Line Sails (Marine) [18642]

Hillsdale

Hillsdale Cooperative Elevator (Livestock and Farm
Products) [18000]

Hillside

Garden Foods Products (Food) [11234]
Levy Home Entertainment (Books and Other
Printed Materials) [3908]
Merchants Cash Register Co. (Office Equipment
and Supplies) [21137]
Praxah Gas Tech Inc. (Petroleum, Fuels, and
Related Equipment) [22592]
Praxair Gas Tech (Industrial Supplies) [17110]

Hinsdale

Storm Products Co. (Electrical and Electronic
Equipment and Supplies) [9422]
Victor Sports (Recreational and Sporting
Goods) [24032]

Hodgkins
Certified Grocers Midwest Inc. (Food) [10729]

Hoffman Estates
Convenience Equipment and Supplies Enterprises Inc. (Specialty Equipment and Products) [25611]

Homewood
PM AG Products Inc. (Agricultural Equipment and Supplies) [1135]
Ruklic Screw Company Inc.; J.P. (Hardware) [13897]

Itasca
Boise Cascade (Office Equipment and Supplies) [20847]
Century Tile and Supply Co. (Floorcovering Equipment and Supplies) [9789]
Excelsior Manufacturing and Supply (Heating and Cooling Equipment and Supplies) [14437]
Geotronics of North America Inc. (Scientific and Measurement Devices) [24364]
MNP Fastener Distribution Group (Hardware) [13833]
NEC Technologies Inc. (Computers and Software) [6549]
Nippon Electric Glass America Inc. (Construction Materials and Machinery) [7780]
Sanyo Sales and Supply (USA) Corp. (Sound and Entertainment Equipment and Supplies) [25430]
Sports Impressions Corp. (Gifts and Novelties) [13452]
Toshiba Tungaloy America Inc. (Industrial Machinery) [16569]

Jacksonville
Baptist Electronics Supply Company Inc. (Electrical and Electronic Equipment and Supplies) [8413]
Perma-Bound Books (Books and Other Printed Materials) [4058]
Wareco Service Inc. (Petroleum, Fuels, and Related Equipment) [22781]

Jerseyville
Jersey County Farm Supply Co. (Agricultural Equipment and Supplies) [886]
Sunderland Motor Company Inc. (Motorized Vehicles) [20732]

Joliet
Amstek Metal (Metals) [19778]
Barrett Hardware and Industrial Supply Co. (Hardware) [13585]
CMC America Corp. (Specialty Equipment and Products) [25603]
CMC America Corp. (Restaurant and Commercial Foodservice Equipment and Supplies) [24096]
Crescent Electric Supply Co. (Electrical and Electronic Equipment and Supplies) [8590]
Darter Inc. (Cleaning and Janitorial Supplies) [4610]
Joliet Equipment Corp. (Automotive) [2832]
Kemlite Company, Inc. (Construction Materials and Machinery) [7545]
Primus Electronics Corp. (Communications Systems and Equipment) [5720]
Professional Salon Concepts Inc. (Health and Beauty Aids) [14197]
Promatek Medical Systems Inc. (Medical, Dental, and Optical Equipment) [18999]
Seeler Industries Inc. (Chemicals) [4506]
Will-Du Page Service Co. (Livestock and Farm Products) [18349]

Kankakee
La Beau Brothers Inc. (Motorized Vehicles) [20667]

Kempton
Adventures Unlimited Press (Books and Other Printed Materials) [3474]

Kewanee
Boss Manufacturing Co. (Clothing) [4837]

La Grange
Burk Electronics (Communications Systems and Equipment) [5537]
Burke Beverage Inc. (Alcoholic Beverages) [1561]
Fujii Associates, Inc. (Books and Other Printed Materials) [3769]
Gooding Rubber Co. (La Grange, Illinois) (Industrial Supplies) [16900]

La Grange Park
Weil and Sons, Inc.; Joseph (Paper and Paper Products) [21986]

La Salle
M & M News Agency (Books and Other Printed Materials) [3924]

Lafox
Richardson Electronics, Ltd. (Electrical and Electronic Equipment and Supplies) [9293]
Richardson Electronics, Ltd. (Electrical and Electronic Equipment and Supplies) [9294]

Lake Forest
Channer Corp. (Electrical and Electronic Equipment and Supplies) [8522]
Citifax Corp. (Office Equipment and Supplies) [20900]
Grainger Inc.; W.W. (Electrical and Electronic Equipment and Supplies) [8802]
Mabis Healthcare Inc. (Medical, Dental, and Optical Equipment) [18896]
Second City Systems Inc. (Office Equipment and Supplies) [21263]

Lake in the Hills
Doussard & Associates, Inc.; Ron (Books and Other Printed Materials) [3701]

Lake In The Hills
Joshua Distributing Co. (Computers and Software) [6410]

Lake Zurich
Colonial Hospital Supply Co. Inc. (Medical, Dental, and Optical Supplies) [19239]

Lanark
Carol Service Co. (Chemicals) [4344]

Lansing
Applewood Farms Inc. (Food) [10425]
Buikema Produce Co. (Food) [10640]
Temperature Equipment Corp. (Heating and Cooling Equipment and Supplies) [14717]

Lawrenceville
Allimex International (Clothing) [4762]

Lemont
Accurate Iron and Metal Co. (Used, Scrap, and Recycled Materials) [26727]
Alpha Distributors Ltd. (Food) [10379]
Diamond Nut Company of California (Food) [10960]
Hanna Resin Distribution Inc.; M.A. (Plastics) [22977]
Independent Distributors of America Inc. (Restaurant and Commercial Foodservice Equipment and Supplies) [24141]
Shestokas Distributing Inc. (Alcoholic Beverages) [2022]
Sun-Diamond Growers of California. Mixed Nut Div. (Food) [12603]

Lena
Kolb-Lena Cheese Co. (Food) [11634]

Lewistown
Lewiston AG Inc. (Agricultural Equipment and Supplies) [955]

Lexington
Kemp Grain Company Inc. (Livestock and Farm Products) [18032]
Myers Inc. (Agricultural Equipment and Supplies) [1063]

Libertyville
Allied Electronics (Electrical and Electronic Equipment and Supplies) [8303]
Meridian International Co. (Security and Safety Equipment) [24590]
Piher International Corporation (Electrical and Electronic Equipment and Supplies) [9202]

Lincolnshire
Armstrong Medical Industries Inc. (Medical, Dental, and Optical Equipment) [18691]
Daiichi Fine Chemicals Inc. (Health and Beauty Aids) [14077]
Quill Corp. (Office Equipment and Supplies) [21229]
Volkswagen of America Inc. Industrial Engine Div. (Motorized Vehicles) [20744]

Lincolnwood
Boelter Co. (Restaurant and Commercial Foodservice Equipment and Supplies) [24080]
Byczek Enterprises (Restaurant and Commercial Foodservice Equipment and Supplies) [24086]
Diamond Industrial Tools Inc. (Industrial Machinery) [15949]
Gerber Plumbing Fixtures Corp. (Plumbing Materials and Fixtures) [23190]
Hardwood Flooring & Finishes (Floorcovering Equipment and Supplies) [9937]
London Litho Aluminum Company Inc. (Computers and Software) [6444]
London Litho Aluminum Company Inc. (Industrial Machinery) [16243]
NTC/Contemporary Publishing Group (Books and Other Printed Materials) [4012]
The Quilt Digest Press — A division of NTC/Contemporary Publishing Group (Books and Other Printed Materials) [4101]
United Sports Apparel Inc. (Clothing) [5450]

Lisle
Chicago Furnace Supply Inc. (Heating and Cooling Equipment and Supplies) [14383]
Postalia Inc. (Office Equipment and Supplies) [21220]
Tricon Industries Inc. Electromechanical Div. (Automotive) [3341]

Litchfield
O.K. Grain Co. (Livestock and Farm Products) [18153]
Roller Derby Skate Corp. (Recreational and Sporting Goods) [23921]

Loda
Loda Poultry Company Inc. (Food) [11721]

Lombard
Anle Paper Company Inc. (Industrial Supplies) [16699]
Century Tile and Carpet (Floorcovering Equipment and Supplies) [9784]
Century Tile and Carpet (Floorcovering Equipment and Supplies) [9787]
Chemical Waste Management Inc. (Used, Scrap, and Recycled Materials) [26778]
Ergonomic Specialties Ltd. (Furniture and Fixtures) [13107]
Labinal, Inc. (Plastics) [22987]
Martin-Brower Co. (Food) [11794]
PMI-Eisenhart (Food) [12183]
Professional Marketers Inc. (Food) [12228]
Schermerhorn Brothers Co. (Storage Equipment and Containers) [25935]
Terco Computer Systems (Computers and Software) [6813]

Lostant

Lostant Hatchery and Milling Company Inc. (Agricultural Equipment and Supplies) [971]

Loves Park

Rock Valley Oil and Chemical Company Inc. (Petroleum, Fuels, and Related Equipment) [22637]
Tapco USA, Inc. (Industrial Supplies) [17212]
Tek-Matic, Inc. (Industrial Supplies) [17215]
Thrall Distribution Inc. (Industrial Supplies) [17229]
UDL Laboratories, Inc. (Medical, Dental, and Optical Supplies) [19668]
United Flooring Distributors Inc. (Floorcovering Equipment and Supplies) [10265]

Ludlow

Ludlow Cooperative Elevator Company Inc. (Livestock and Farm Products) [18066]

Lyons

Accurate Partitions Corp. (Furniture and Fixtures) [13010]
Accurate Partitions Corp. (Restaurant and Commercial Foodservice Equipment and Supplies) [24054]

Manteno

Farmers Elevator Company of Manteno (Livestock and Farm Products) [17884]

Marion

Blankenship and Company Inc.; E. (Automotive) [2368]
Twin County Service Co. (Agricultural Equipment and Supplies) [1368]
United Manufacturers Service (Automotive) [3368]

Markham

Chicago Beer Distributing (Alcoholic Beverages) [1592]
ImpoGlaztile (Floorcovering Equipment and Supplies) [9960]

Maroa

Maroa Farmers Cooperative Elevator Co. (Agricultural Equipment and Supplies) [988]

Marseilles

Waste Recovery-Illinois (Used, Scrap, and Recycled Materials) [27037]

Mascoutah

Heberer Equipment Company Inc. (Agricultural Equipment and Supplies) [809]

Mattoon

Farmers Grain Company of Dorans (Livestock and Farm Products) [17893]
Schilling Brothers Inc. (Agricultural Equipment and Supplies) [1237]

Mazon

Mazon Farmers Elevator (Agricultural Equipment and Supplies) [996]
Mazon Farmers Elevator (Food) [11814]

Mc Gaw Park

Allegiance Corp. (Medical, Dental, and Optical Supplies) [19134]
Allegiance Healthcare Corporation Hospital Supply/Scientific Products (Medical, Dental, and Optical Equipment) [18672]
Baxter Healthcare Corp. Converters/Custom Sterile Div. (Medical, Dental, and Optical Equipment) [18703]
Baxter Scientific Products (Scientific and Measurement Devices) [24322]

McHenry

Delta Systems Company, Inc. (Books and Other Printed Materials) [3684]
Follett Library Book Co. (Books and Other Printed Materials) [3758]

McLean

Follett Library Resources (Books and Other Printed Materials) [3759]
GLS Thermoplastic Elastomers Div. (Plastics) [22970]
Mid-America Information Systems Inc. (Computers and Software) [6514]

McLean

Funks Grove Grain Co. (Livestock and Farm Products) [17931]

McNabb

McNabb Grain Co. (Food) [11839]

Melrose Park

Alberto-Culver International Inc. (Health and Beauty Aids) [14012]
Auto Components Inc. (Automotive) [2271]
Gage Food Products Co. (Food) [11228]
Gerrard Steel of Illinois (Metals) [20004]
Kraft Chemical Co. (Paints and Varnishes) [21477]
Kreher Steel Company Inc. (Metals) [20110]

Melvin

Arends Brothers Inc. (Agricultural Equipment and Supplies) [249]

Mendota

Mendota Farm Cooperative Supply Inc. (Livestock and Farm Products) [18086]

Milan

Eagle Food Centers Inc. (Food) [11009]

Minier

Minier Cooperative Grain Co. (Livestock and Farm Products) [18102]
Peine Inc. (Agricultural Equipment and Supplies) [1120]

Minonk

Purity Minonk Baking Co. (Food) [12238]
Sauder and Rippel Inc. (Agricultural Equipment and Supplies) [1236]

Minooka

Minooka Grain Lumber and Supply Co. (Construction Materials and Machinery) [7723]

Moline

Consumers of La Salle (Alcoholic Beverages) [1615]
Dimock, Gould and Co. (Floorcovering Equipment and Supplies) [9866]
Dimock, Gould and Co. (Household Items) [15475]
Elliott Aviation Inc. (Aeronautical Equipment and Supplies) [83]
Great Plains (Construction Materials and Machinery) [7415]
Midland Iron and Steel Co. (Used, Scrap, and Recycled Materials) [26913]
Mutual Wheel Co. (Automotive) [3007]

Momence

Elwood Line Grain and Fertilizer Co. (Livestock and Farm Products) [17832]

Monee

New AG Center Inc. (Agricultural Equipment and Supplies) [1070]

Montgomery

Fox River Foods Inc. (Food) [11197]
Processed Plastic Co. (Toys and Hobby Goods) [26622]

Monticello

Monticello Grain Company Inc. (Livestock and Farm Products) [18113]

Morris

Kendall-Grundy FS Inc. (Agricultural Equipment and Supplies) [901]

Morrison

Farmers Elevator and Supply Co. (Livestock and Farm Products) [17889]

Morrisonville

Morrisonville Farmers Cooperative (Livestock and Farm Products) [18117]

Morton

Unisource Worldwide (Paper and Paper Products) [21968]

Mt. Prospect

Century Tile & Supply Co. (Floorcovering Equipment and Supplies) [9790]
Multigraphics Inc. (Office Equipment and Supplies) [21153]
Northwest Electrical Supply (Electrical and Electronic Equipment and Supplies) [9141]
Salton/Maxium Housewares Inc. (Household Items) [15648]
Sayers Computer Source (Computers and Software) [6708]
TDK Corporation of America (Electrical and Electronic Equipment and Supplies) [9461]

Mt. Pulaski

Mount Pulaski Farmers Grain (Livestock and Farm Products) [18120]

Mt. Sterling

Dot Foods Inc. (Food) [10982]
Prospect Energy Inc. (Minerals and Ores) [20560]

Mt. Vernon

Alexander Wholesale Inc.; W.C. (Construction Materials and Machinery) [6932]

Moweaqua

Moweaqua Farmers Cooperative Grain Co. (Livestock and Farm Products) [18122]

Mt Zion

Hagerman and Company Inc. (Computers and Software) [6321]

Mundelein

Handi-Ramp Inc. (Industrial Machinery) [16085]
Mid-America Tile, Inc. (Floorcovering Equipment and Supplies) [10031]
Rinella Beverage Co. (Alcoholic Beverages) [1991]

Naperville

Abbey Pharmaceutical Services Inc. (Medical, Dental, and Optical Equipment) [18655]
All Line Inc. (Industrial Supplies) [16683]
American Medserve Corp. (Medical, Dental, and Optical Supplies) [19143]
Dartek Corp. (Computers and Software) [6180]
Eby-Brown Company L.P. (Tobacco Products) [26289]
Joyce Sportswear Co. (Clothing) [5098]
Mercy National Purchasing Inc. (Medical, Dental, and Optical Equipment) [18928]
Mercy National Purchasing Inc. (Medical, Dental, and Optical Supplies) [19450]
Mercy Resource Management, Inc. (Medical, Dental, and Optical Equipment) [18929]
Moser Lumber Inc. (Construction Materials and Machinery) [7750]
Paoku International Company Ltd. (Computers and Software) [6585]
PSDI (Computers and Software) [6654]
West Side Tractor Sales Inc. (Agricultural Equipment and Supplies) [1424]

Nashville

AgriPride F.S. (Agricultural Equipment and Supplies) [216]

Newark

Newark Farmers Grain Co. (Livestock and Farm Products) [18131]

Niles

ADI Medical (Medical, Dental, and Optical Supplies) [19125]
Allied Safety Inc. (Medical, Dental, and Optical Supplies) [19138]
Bossert Industrial Supply Inc. (Industrial Supplies) [16758]
Dann Dee Display Fixtures Inc. (Specialty Equipment and Products) [25625]
Design/Craft Fabric Corp. (Household Items) [15472]
Dick Co.; A.B. (Office Equipment and Supplies) [20961]
Four Star Incentives Inc. (Sound and Entertainment Equipment and Supplies) [25196]
Hamakor Judaica Inc. (Books and Other Printed Materials) [3807]
Midland Computers (Computers and Software) [6516]
Niles Color Center (Paints and Varnishes) [21519]
Revere Mills Inc. (Household Items) [15634]
Scott Stainless Steel (Metals) [20358]
United Learning Inc. (Sound and Entertainment Equipment and Supplies) [25490]
Wells Lamont Corp. (Clothing) [5478]

Nokomis

Nokomis Equity Elevator Co. (Livestock and Farm Products) [18132]
Route 16 Grain Cooperative (Livestock and Farm Products) [18209]

North Aurora

Aurora Packing Company Inc. (Food) [10471]
Mar and Sons Inc.; J (Industrial Machinery) [16263]

North Chicago

King Wire Inc. (Electrical and Electronic Equipment and Supplies) [8948]

North Riverside

Don and Co.; Edward (Household Items) [15478]

Northbrook

Amcam International Inc. (Photographic Equipment and Supplies) [22825]
American Hotel Register Co. (Household Items) [15398]
Apollo Colors Inc. (Paints and Varnishes) [21389]
Atlantic Premium Brands Ltd. (Food) [10464]
Cavexsa USA Inc. (Metals) [19865]
Chilli-O Frozen Foods Inc. (Food) [10749]
Churny Company Inc. (Food) [10758]
Classic Components Supply Inc. (Electrical and Electronic Equipment and Supplies) [8531]
Columbus Wallcovering Co. (Household Items) [15451]
Fullerton Metals Co. (Metals) [19991]
Heads & Threads Co. (Hardware) [13747]
Heads and Threads Div. (Hardware) [13748]
Holland Co.; M. (Plastics) [22981]
Maurice Sporting Goods (Recreational and Sporting Goods) [23809]
Old World Industries, Inc. (Chemicals) [4472]
SAF-T-GARD International, Inc. (Industrial Supplies) [17153]
Solis America Inc. (Health and Beauty Aids) [14242]
SPRI Medical Products Corp. Ballert International Div. (Medical, Dental, and Optical Supplies) [19633]
Targun Plastics Co. (Plastics) [23039]
TriTech Graphics Inc. (Computers and Software) [6832]

Northfield

Central Seaway Co. (Food) [10723]
Christy Metals Company Inc. (Metals) [19878]

Northlake

Shurfine International Inc. (Food) [12484]
Shurfine International Inc. (Food) [12485]

Oak Brook

Ace Hardware Corp. (Hardware) [13526]
Autoline Industries Inc. (Automotive) [2283]
Blistex Inc. (Health and Beauty Aids) [14051]
IPX (Jewelry) [17463]
Lansa USA Inc. (Computers and Software) [6427]

Oak Lawn

DuBois Fabrics (Textiles and Notions) [26023]

Oak Park

Allpak Co. (Storage Equipment and Containers) [25887]
Robco International Corporation/Advanced Technology International (Industrial Supplies) [17140]
Robinson Barbecue Sauce Company Inc. (Food) [12333]

Oregon

Quality Books Inc. (Books and Other Printed Materials) [4099]

Orland Park

American Import Tile (Floorcovering Equipment and Supplies) [9670]
Consolidated Tile and Carpet Co. (Floorcovering Equipment and Supplies) [9822]
Consolidated Tile and Carpet Co. (Household Items) [15452]
Global Tile (Floorcovering Equipment and Supplies) [9922]

Ottawa

Etna Oil Company Inc. (Petroleum, Fuels, and Related Equipment) [22240]
La Salle County Farm Supply Co. (Agricultural Equipment and Supplies) [925]
MBL USA Corp. (Rubber) [24286]
Myer Brothers Implements Inc. (Agricultural Equipment and Supplies) [1062]
St. Louis Beverage Co. (Alcoholic Beverages) [2005]

Palatine

Carpet Cushion Supply (Floorcovering Equipment and Supplies) [9766]
Central Audio Visual Equipment Inc. (Photographic Equipment and Supplies) [22843]
Chicago Hardwood Flooring (Floorcovering Equipment and Supplies) [9804]
PNR International Ltd. (Industrial Machinery) [16407]
Resource Electronics, Inc. (Electrical and Electronic Equipment and Supplies) [9281]
Tactical Business Services (Computers and Software) [6786]
Tapesolutions (Storage Equipment and Containers) [25943]
Wilton Corp. (Industrial Machinery) [16638]

Palmer

Farmers Grain Co. (Agricultural Equipment and Supplies) [651]

Paloma

F.S. Adams Inc. (Agricultural Equipment and Supplies) [717]

Pana

Air Conditioned Roses, Inc. (Horticultural Supplies) [14795]
Pana Bait Co. (Recreational and Sporting Goods) [23870]

Paris

Midwest Truck Equipment Inc. (Motorized Vehicles) [20682]

Park Ridge

Frohman & Sons Inc.; L.H. (Food) [11219]

Pekin

Ag-Land FS Inc. (Agricultural Equipment and Supplies) [194]

D & W Distributing Co. Inc. (Automotive) [2523]
Sommer Brothers Seed Co. (Agricultural Equipment and Supplies) [1273]

Peoria

ATS Machinery and Equipment Co. (Industrial Machinery) [15792]
Baker-Hauser Co. (Heating and Cooling Equipment and Supplies) [14335]
Baumgarten Distributing Company, Inc. (Alcoholic Beverages) [1507]
Browning Metal Products Co. (Heating and Cooling Equipment and Supplies) [14360]
Calihan Pork Processors (Food) [10677]
Calihan Pork Processors (Food) [10678]
Carter Paper and Packaging Inc. (Paper and Paper Products) [21673]
Champion Furnace Pipe Co. (Plumbing Materials and Fixtures) [23113]
CILCORP Energy Services Inc. (Scientific and Measurement Devices) [24340]
Common Equipment Co. (Industrial Machinery) [15903]
Connor Co. (Plumbing Materials and Fixtures) [23122]
Hagerty Brothers Co. (Industrial Supplies) [16919]
ICI Dulux Paints (Paints and Varnishes) [21461]
Illinois Blueprint Corp. (Specialty Equipment and Products) [25686]
Klaus Companies (Household Appliances) [15190]
Lincoln Office Supply Company Inc. (Storage Equipment and Containers) [25928]
M.H. Equipment Corp. (Industrial Machinery) [16292]
Mississippi Valley STIHL, Inc. (Industrial Machinery) [16307]
The News Group, Ill (Books and Other Printed Materials) [4000]
O'Brien Steel Service (Metals) [20242]
River City Enterprises (Plastics) [23029]
RLI Corp. (Medical, Dental, and Optical Supplies) [19582]
SVI Systems Inc. (Sound and Entertainment Equipment and Supplies) [25470]
Yeomans Distributing Co. (Heating and Cooling Equipment and Supplies) [14774]

Peotone

Andres and Wilton Farmers Grain and Supply Co. (Livestock and Farm Products) [17701]

Peru

Home Reverse Osmosis Systems (Plumbing Materials and Fixtures) [23212]

Plano

Plano International (Hardware) [13870]

Pleasant Hill

Richter Fertilizer Co. (Agricultural Equipment and Supplies) [1190]

Pleasant Plains

Brandt Consolidated Inc. (Agricultural Equipment and Supplies) [333]

Pontiac

Livingston Service Co. (Agricultural Equipment and Supplies) [962]
Pontiac Livestock Sales (Livestock and Farm Products) [18175]

Posen

Vitco Steel Supply Corp. (Metals) [20474]

Princeton

Bearing Distributors Inc. (Industrial Machinery) [15811]

Princeville

German Implement Co.; L.E. (Agricultural Equipment and Supplies) [735]
German's Outdoor Power Equipment (Agricultural Equipment and Supplies) [736]

Monica Elevator Co. (Livestock and Farm
Products) [18109]
Rumbold and Kuhn Inc. (Livestock and Farm
Products) [18212]

Prophetstown
Rock River Lumber and Grain Co. (Agricultural
Equipment and Supplies) [1203]

Prospect Heights
Gray Machinery Co. (Industrial Machinery) [16074]
Lewis International (Agricultural Equipment and
Supplies) [953]

Quincy
Ehrhart Co.; T.F. (Heating and Cooling Equipment
and Supplies) [14430]
Franciscan Press (Books and Other Printed
Materials) [3762]
Haubrich Enterprises Inc. (Alcoholic
Beverages) [1747]
Keller & Sons (Agricultural Equipment and
Supplies) [900]
Kohl Grocer Company Inc.; N. (Food) [11633]
Mid-State Periodicals Inc. (Books and Other Printed
Materials) [3956]

Ransom
Farmers Elevator Co. (Livestock and Farm
Products) [17882]
Farmers Elevator Co. (Food) [11103]

Red Bud
Red Bud Industries Inc. (Metals) [20310]

River Grove
Follett Campus Resources (Books and Other
Printed Materials) [3756]
Follett Corp. (Books and Other Printed
Materials) [3757]
Leisure Time Products Inc. (Specialty Equipment
and Products) [25713]
Tile Helper Inc. (Floorcovering Equipment and
Supplies) [10238]

Roberts
Hicks Oil and Hicks Gas Inc. (Petroleum, Fuels,
and Related Equipment) [22350]
Rocket Supply Corp. (Motorized Vehicles) [20714]

Robinson
Bradford Supply Co. (Petroleum, Fuels, and
Related Equipment) [22090]

Rock Falls
Rock River Provision Company
Inc. (Food) [12336]

Rock Island
American Provisions Co. (Food) [10403]
Dimitri Wine & Spirits (Alcoholic Beverages) [1651]
Herman's Inc. (Clothing) [5029]
Huesing Corp.; A.D. (Soft Drinks) [24971]
Illinois Oil Products Inc. (Petroleum, Fuels, and
Related Equipment) [22372]
Jaydon Inc. (Health and Beauty Aids) [14134]
Midway Oil Co. (Petroleum, Fuels, and Related
Equipment) [22482]
Raufeisen Enterprises (Industrial Supplies) [17132]
Thoms-Proestler Co. (Restaurant and Commercial
Foodservice Equipment and Supplies) [24246]

Rockford
Aggregate Equipment and Supply (Industrial
Supplies) [16673]
Aggregate Equipment and Supply (Industrial
Supplies) [16674]
Behr Iron and Steel Inc. (Used, Scrap, and
Recycled Materials) [26763]
Behr Machinery and Equipment Corp. (Industrial
Machinery) [15815]
Behr and Sons Inc.; Joseph (Used, Scrap, and
Recycled Materials) [26764]
Benson Pump Co. (Recreational and Sporting
Goods) [23547]

Cardinal Glass Co. (Construction Materials and
Machinery) [7140]
Carlson Distributors Inc. (Construction Materials and
Machinery) [7141]
DeVlieg-Bullard Services Group (Industrial
Machinery) [15947]
Dierks Foods Inc. (Food) [10964]
Doran Co.; Bill (Horticultural Supplies) [14858]
Econo Trading Company (Hardware) [13676]
Emery Air Charter Inc. (Industrial
Machinery) [15984]
Forest City Electric Supply (Electrical and Electronic
Equipment and Supplies) [8753]
GC Thorsen Inc. (Electrical and Electronic
Equipment and Supplies) [8777]
Geraghty Industrial Equipment Inc. (Industrial
Machinery) [16059]
Grimstad, Inc.; J.M. (Chemicals) [4404]
Hahnaman-Albrecht Inc. (Livestock and Farm
Products) [17969]
Jeanie's Classics (Books and Other Printed
Materials) [3860]
Liebovich Brothers Inc. (Metals) [20128]
LKG Industries Inc. (Electrical and Electronic
Equipment and Supplies) [8998]
Mid-States Industrial Div. (Plumbing Materials and
Fixtures) [23266]
Mizen International, Inc. (Industrial
Machinery) [16313]
Muntz Electrical Supply Co.; Jack H. (Electrical and
Electronic Equipment and Supplies) [9107]
Osmonics, Aquamatic (Plumbing Materials and
Fixtures) [23303]
Pepsi-Cola Bottling Company of Rockford (Soft
Drinks) [25012]
Pierce Box & Paper Corp. (Paper and Paper
Products) [21884]
Powmet Inc. (Used, Scrap, and Recycled
Materials) [26945]
Rapid Air Corp. (Industrial Machinery) [16439]
Revere Electrical Supply Co. (Electrical and
Electronic Equipment and Supplies) [9284]
Riverview FS Inc. (Agricultural Equipment and
Supplies) [1199]
Rockford Bolt & Steel Co. (Hardware) [13890]
Rockford Industrial Welding Supply Inc. (Industrial
Supplies) [17142]
Rockford Industrial Welding Supply Inc. (Industrial
Machinery) [16456]
Rocknel Fastener Inc. (Hardware) [13891]
Rubin and Co.; J. (Metals) [20334]
Testor Corp. (Toys and Hobby Goods) [26678]

Rockton
Blackhawk Distributors (Toys and Hobby
Goods) [26422]

Rolling Meadows
Coil Sales and Manufacturing Co. (Communications
Systems and Equipment) [5566]
DS America Inc. (Industrial Machinery) [15965]
Komori America Corp. (Industrial
Machinery) [16216]
Screen (USA) (Specialty Equipment and
Products) [25810]
Steel Supply Co. (Rolling Meadows,
Illinois) (Metals) [20402]
Uddeholm Corp. (Metals) [20451]
Valiac Inc. (Industrial Supplies) [17247]

Romeoville
Kehe Food Distributors Inc. (Food) [11589]
Mid-America Tile (Floorcovering Equipment and
Supplies) [10030]

Rosamond
Rosamond Cooperative (Livestock and Farm
Products) [18205]

Roselle
Roman Inc. (Gifts and Novelties) [13439]
Service Keystone Supply (Construction Materials
and Machinery) [8001]

Rosemont
Anicom Inc. (Electrical and Electronic Equipment
and Supplies) [8356]
Comdisco Inc. (Computers and Software) [6081]
Continental Distributing Company Inc. (Alcoholic
Beverages) [1616]
Hoffman Brothers (Industrial Machinery) [16107]
Norris Co.; Walter (Industrial Supplies) [17077]
United Chemi-Con Inc. (Electrical and Electronic
Equipment and Supplies) [9521]

Round Lake
Synnestvedt Co. (Horticultural Supplies) [14959]

Ruma
Schwarz Service Co. (Household
Appliances) [15306]

Rushville
Schuyler-Brown FS Inc. (Agricultural Equipment and
Supplies) [1239]

Russell
Auto Dealers Exchange of Illinois (Motorized
Vehicles) [20595]

Sadorus
Grand Prairie Cooperative (Livestock and Farm
Products) [17957]

St. Charles
Prime Label Div. (Industrial Machinery) [16425]

Savoy
Mycogen Seeds (Agricultural Equipment and
Supplies) [1061]

Schaumburg
Avesta Sheffield—North American Division,
Inc. (Metals) [19795]
Jorgensen Steel Co. (Metals) [20080]
Machinery Systems Inc. (Industrial
Machinery) [16257]
NHK Intex Corp. (Motorized Vehicles) [20693]
Olympic Steel Inc. Chicago Div. (Metals) [20247]
Renishaw Inc. (Medical, Dental, and Optical
Equipment) [19018]
Tocos America Inc. (Electrical and Electronic
Equipment and Supplies) [9492]

Schiller Park
Artmark Chicago Ltd. (Household Items) [15407]
Atlas Lift Truck Rentals (Industrial
Machinery) [15790]
Industrial and Wholesale Lumber Inc. (Construction
Materials and Machinery) [7511]
Warner Candy Company Inc. (Food) [12878]

Secor
Secor Elevator Company Inc. (Food) [12457]

Shelbyville
Lakeland FS, Inc. (Agricultural Equipment and
Supplies) [931]

Shipman
Shipman Elevator Co. (Livestock and Farm
Products) [18232]

Skokie
Allegheny Rodney Strip Svc Ctr (Metals) [19746]
Anixter International Inc. (Electrical and Electronic
Equipment and Supplies) [8359]
Block Steel Corp. (Metals) [19826]
Cellular Wholesales (Communications Systems and
Equipment) [5557]
Chicago Case International (Luggage and Leather
Goods) [18382]
Forsythe Technology Inc. (Computers and
Software) [6277]
Jani-Serv (Cleaning and Janitorial Supplies) [4644]
PanaVise Products
International (Hardware) [13861]
Topco Associates Inc. (Food) [12734]
Winesellers Ltd. (Alcoholic Beverages) [2130]

Smithshire
Twomey Co. (Livestock and Farm Products) [18296]

South Beloit
Lans Sons Co.; William (Used, Scrap, and Recycled Materials) [26876]
New York Twist Drill Inc. (Industrial Supplies) [17073]

South Chicago Heights
Muench Woodwork Company Inc. (Wood and Wood Products) [27349]

South Elgin
Casco Industries Inc. (Construction Materials and Machinery) [7151]
Hawera Inc. (Industrial Machinery) [16094]

South Holland
Izenco Inc. (Shoes) [24774]
Mac Supply Co. (Construction Materials and Machinery) [7628]
McElheney, Inc.; R.H. (Veterinary Products) [27185]
Roberts Colonial House Inc. (Plastics) [23030]
Universal Metal Services Corp. (Metals) [20467]
Wilson Co.; H. (Electrical and Electronic Equipment and Supplies) [9598]

Spring Grove
Century Wheels Research (Electrical and Electronic Equipment and Supplies) [8518]

Spring Valley
Cosgrove Distributors Inc. (Food) [10845]
Mautino Distributing Company Inc. (Alcoholic Beverages) [1855]

Springfield
American Metals Supply Co. Inc. (Heating and Cooling Equipment and Supplies) [14319]
Bradfordton Cooperative Association Inc. (Livestock and Farm Products) [17745]
Bradley Supply Company Inc.; R.W. (Construction Materials and Machinery) [7075]
Bunn Capitol Co. (Food) [10643]
Capitol Plumbing and Heating Supply Co. (Plumbing Materials and Fixtures) [23104]
Central States Coca-Cola Bottling Co. (Soft Drinks) [24925]
Chronister Oil Co. (Petroleum, Fuels, and Related Equipment) [22139]
Dauphin Co. (Sound and Entertainment Equipment and Supplies) [25156]
Kellner Co., Inc.; M.J. (Food) [11596]
Menco Corp. (Automotive) [2941]
Nudo Products Inc. (Industrial Supplies) [17084]
Roberts Foods Inc. (Food) [12330]
Roland Machinery Co. (Construction Materials and Machinery) [7955]
Springfield Electric Supply Co. (Electrical and Electronic Equipment and Supplies) [9397]
Springfield Pepsi-Cola Bottling Co. (Soft Drinks) [25040]
Staab Battery Manufacturing Company Inc. (Electrical and Electronic Equipment and Supplies) [9399]
United States Electric Co. (Electrical and Electronic Equipment and Supplies) [9526]

Stanford
Stanford Grain Co. (Livestock and Farm Products) [18250]

Stone Park
Vogel Tool & Die Corp. (Industrial Machinery) [16606]
Vogel Tool and Die Corp. (Industrial Supplies) [17257]

Stonington
Stonington Cooperative Grain Co. (Livestock and Farm Products) [18259]

Streator
Cullen Distributors Inc. (Tobacco Products) [26284]
Illinois Fruit and Produce Corp. (Food) [11496]

Sublette
Sublette Farmers Elevator Co. (Livestock and Farm Products) [18266]

Sullivan
The Depot Ltd. (Gifts and Novelties) [13345]

Sycamore
Barnaby Inc. (Office Equipment and Supplies) [20831]
Seymour of Sycamore Inc. (Paints and Varnishes) [21565]

Tampico
Tampico Farmers Elevator Co. (Agricultural Equipment and Supplies) [1313]

Taylorville
Christian County Farmers Supply Co. (Agricultural Equipment and Supplies) [416]
Sangamon Co. (Gifts and Novelties) [13440]

Thornton
VMS Inc. (Books and Other Printed Materials) [4261]

Trenton
Jim's Formal Wear Co. (Clothing) [5084]
Lite Brite Distributors (Electrical and Electronic Equipment and Supplies) [8994]

University Park
Amtex Steel Inc. (Metals) [19779]
Benson Pool Systems (Recreational and Sporting Goods) [23543]
Federal Signal Corp. (Electrical and Electronic Equipment and Supplies) [8734]
Miller Metal Service Corp. (Metals) [20194]
National Tube Supply Co (Metals) [20222]

Urbana
American Software & Hardware Distributors, Inc. (Computers and Software) [5933]
East Side Lumberyard Supply (Floorcovering Equipment and Supplies) [9878]
Illini F.S. Inc. (Petroleum, Fuels, and Related Equipment) [22371]
Jones Co.; J.M. (Food) [11560]

Ursa
Ursa Farmers Cooperative (Livestock and Farm Products) [18308]

Vernon Hills
American Tool Companies Inc. (Hardware) [13562]
Baer Supply Co. (Hardware) [13581]
Cole-Parmer Instrument Co. (Scientific and Measurement Devices) [24341]
Daigger and Co. Inc.; A. (Scientific and Measurement Devices) [24344]
Daigger and Company Inc. ETA/Cuisenaire; A. (Toys and Hobby Goods) [26458]
Faucet-Queens Inc. (Hardware) [13703]
Loomcraft Textiles Inc. (Household Items) [15571]
Waxler Co. (Food) [12886]

Vienna
Veach Oil Co. (Petroleum, Fuels, and Related Equipment) [22771]

Virginia
Cass County Service Co. (Agricultural Equipment and Supplies) [378]

Walnut
Atherton Grain Co. (Livestock and Farm Products) [17710]
Atherton Grain Co. (Food) [10462]

Warren
Warren Cheese Plants (Food) [12880]

Warrenville
Pressotechnik Ltd. (Industrial Machinery) [16424]

Watseka
Watseka Farmers Grain Company Cooperative (Agricultural Equipment and Supplies) [1417]

Wauconda
Brans Nut Co. Inc. (Food) [10608]
Current Works Inc. (Computers and Software) [6172]
Premiere AVD Corp. (Sound and Entertainment Equipment and Supplies) [25388]

Waukegan
Allegiance Healthcare Corporation Hospital Supply/Scientific Products (Medical, Dental, and Optical Supplies) [19135]
American Fluorescent Corp. (Electrical and Electronic Equipment and Supplies) [8344]
Burgess, Anderson and Tate Inc. (Furniture and Fixtures) [13050]
Illinois Carbide Tool Co. (Industrial Machinery) [16143]
Lake County Office Equipment Inc. (Office Equipment and Supplies) [21097]
Stauber Wholesale Hardware; E. (Hardware) [13936]
United Conveyor Corp. (Industrial Machinery) [16588]
Waukegan Steel Sales Inc. (Metals) [20479]
Waukegan Steel Sales Inc. (Metals) [20480]

Waverly
Farmers Elevator Co. (Agricultural Equipment and Supplies) [643]

West Chicago
Ball Horticultural Co. (Horticultural Supplies) [14815]
Ball Seed Co. (Horticultural Supplies) [14816]
Coach House Products (Automotive) [2458]
Gorence Mobile Marketing Distribution (Automotive) [2694]
Napco Steel Inc. (Metals) [20216]
S.E.S. Inc. (Construction Materials and Machinery) [8003]
UniSource Energy Inc. (Petroleum, Fuels, and Related Equipment) [22759]
United Pacific Corp. (Scientific and Measurement Devices) [24449]
United Recycling Industries Inc. (Used, Scrap, and Recycled Materials) [27030]

West Frankfort
Special Mine Services Inc. (Electrical and Electronic Equipment and Supplies) [9392]

Westmont
Everpure Inc. (Specialty Equipment and Products) [25645]
Gaucho Foods Inc. (Food) [11245]
Senior Flexonics Inc. Dearborn Industrial Products Div. (Industrial Supplies) [17166]
Xcell International Corp. (Food) [12989]
Xcell International Corp. (Household Appliances) [15382]

Wheaton
Tyndale House Publishers (Sound and Entertainment Equipment and Supplies) [25488]

Wheeling
Block and Company Inc. (Office Equipment and Supplies) [20845]
Burrows Co. (Medical, Dental, and Optical Supplies) [19205]
Day Star Productions (Sound and Entertainment Equipment and Supplies) [25161]
Faucet-Queens Inc. (Hardware) [13702]

Hawk Electronics Inc. (Electrical and Electronic Equipment and Supplies) [8834]

Indeck Power Equipment Co. (Industrial Machinery) [16147]

Marlo Bags (Luggage and Leather Goods) [18411]

Numeridex Inc. (Computers and Software) [6564]

Quintel/Consort Watch Co. (Jewelry) [17555]

Shapco Inc. (Household Items) [15652]

Skokie Valley Beverage Co. (Alcoholic Beverages) [2028]

Tool King Inc. (Metals) [20431]

United Model Distributors Inc. (Toys and Hobby Goods) [26699]

Wabash Power Equipment Co. (Petroleum, Fuels, and Related Equipment) [22777]

Wabash Power Equipment Co. (Electrical and Electronic Equipment and Supplies) [9547]

Williamsville

Patterson Brothers Oil and Gas Inc. (Petroleum, Fuels, and Related Equipment) [22552]

Williamsville Farmers Cooperative Grain Co. (Livestock and Farm Products) [18351]

Willow Hill

Willow Hill Grain Inc. (Livestock and Farm Products) [18352]

Willow Hill Grain Inc. (Food) [12951]

Wilmette

Distribution Plus Inc. (Food) [10967]

Winchester

Scott Farm Service Inc. (Agricultural Equipment and Supplies) [1242]

Wood Dale

AAR Corp. (Aeronautical Equipment and Supplies) [22]

Industrial Tool Products Inc. (Industrial Machinery) [16156]

Komatsu America Industries Corp. (Industrial Machinery) [16214]

Renaissance Drywall and Construction Supplies Inc. (Construction Materials and Machinery) [7914]

Ryan Equipment Co., Inc. (Metals) [20340]

Sales Force Companies Inc. (Food) [12394]

Southland Carpet Supplies (Floorcovering Equipment and Supplies) [10167]

Southland Flooring Supplies Inc. (Floorcovering Equipment and Supplies) [10168]

Stoelting Co. (Books and Other Printed Materials) [4191]

Zentao Corp. (Electrical and Electronic Equipment and Supplies) [9622]

Woodridge

Publix Office Supplies, Inc. (Office Equipment and Supplies) [21225]

Wilton Industries Inc. (Food) [12956]

Woodstock

Atlantic India Rubber Co. (Rubber) [24267]

Century Tile & Carpet (Floorcovering Equipment and Supplies) [9785]

Worth

Westcott Worldwide (Floorcovering Equipment and Supplies) [10291]

Indiana

Alexandria

Ram Graphics Inc. (Clothing) [5303]

Anderson

AG ONE CO-OP Inc. (Agricultural Equipment and Supplies) [196]

Barnes Co.; A.O. (Industrial Machinery) [15800]

J.C. Sales Company Inc. (Toys and Hobby Goods) [26544]

Warner Press Inc. (Books and Other Printed Materials) [4270]

Angola

Steuben County Farm Bureau Association Inc. (Veterinary Products) [27238]

Bedford

Bedford Recycling Inc. (Used, Scrap, and Recycled Materials) [26762]

Mullis Petroleum Co. (Petroleum, Fuels, and Related Equipment) [22502]

Beech Grove

Control Sales Inc. (Industrial Machinery) [15912]

Wire Supplies Inc. (Electrical and Electronic Equipment and Supplies) [9601]

Bicknell

Scepter Industries Inc. (Used, Scrap, and Recycled Materials) [26979]

Bloomington

Johnson Dairy Co. (Food) [11558]

Monroe Lawrence Farm Bureau Cooperative (Agricultural Equipment and Supplies) [1047]

Thompson's State Beauty Supply (Health and Beauty Aids) [14258]

Tree of Life Inc. Midwest (Food) [12748]

Bluffton

National Oil and Gas Inc. (Petroleum, Fuels, and Related Equipment) [22505]

Brazil

Agri-Logic Solution Systems (Computers and Software) [5895]

Brownstown

Brownstown Electric Supply Inc. (Electrical and Electronic Equipment and Supplies) [8471]

Burns Harbor

Cash Indiana (Photographic Equipment and Supplies) [22840]

Butler

Rods Indiana Inc. (Hardware) [13892]

Carmel

Moffett Co. Inc.; J.W. (Heating and Cooling Equipment and Supplies) [14609]

Storage Solutions Inc. (Restaurant and Commercial Foodservice Equipment and Supplies) [24230]

Chrisney

Spencer County Cooperative Associates Inc. (Agricultural Equipment and Supplies) [1289]

Churubusco

Churubusco Distribution Service Center (Industrial Supplies) [16797]

Clarksville

ScanSteel Service Center Inc. (Metals) [20355]

Columbia City

Computer Management Systems (Computers and Software) [6116]

Columbus

Acme Electric Supply Inc. (Electrical and Electronic Equipment and Supplies) [8267]

Arvin Industries Inc. (Automotive) [2257]

Arvin Industries Inc. North American Automotive Div. (Automotive) [2258]

Brands Inc. (Construction Materials and Machinery) [7076]

Cummins Electronics Company Inc. (Computers and Software) [6170]

Kiel Brothers Oil Company Inc. (Petroleum, Fuels, and Related Equipment) [22403]

Quality Mill Supply Company Inc. (Industrial Supplies) [17125]

South Central Company Inc. (Plumbing Materials and Fixtures) [23391]

Connersville

Fayette County Cooperative Inc. (Agricultural Equipment and Supplies) [674]

Stant Corp. (Automotive) [3262]

Stant Manufacturing Inc. (Heating and Cooling Equipment and Supplies) [14697]

Corunna

Church Doctor Resource Center (Books and Other Printed Materials) [3638]

Corydon

Eckart Supply Company Inc. (Electrical and Electronic Equipment and Supplies) [8650]

Crawfordsville

DeKalb-Pfizer Genetics, Crawfordsville Div. (Livestock and Farm Products) [17815]

Heartland Cooperative Inc. (Agricultural Equipment and Supplies) [808]

Toney Petroleum Inc. (Petroleum, Fuels, and Related Equipment) [22739]

Toney Petroleum Inc. (Petroleum, Fuels, and Related Equipment) [22740]

Crown Point

Lake County Farm Bureau Cooperative Association Inc. (Petroleum, Fuels, and Related Equipment) [22415]

Culver

Culver Products Co. Inc. (Medical, Dental, and Optical Equipment) [18762]

Dale

Winkler Inc. (Food) [12958]

Danville

Midland Co-Op Inc. (Agricultural Equipment and Supplies) [1030]

Decatur

The Parker Company (Hardware) [13862]

Delphi

Delphi Products Co. (Agricultural Equipment and Supplies) [507]

Demotte

Belstra Milling Co. Inc. (Agricultural Equipment and Supplies) [296]

Dubois

DuBois Elevator Co. (Agricultural Equipment and Supplies) [528]

Dyer

Dyer Auto Auction Inc. (Motorized Vehicles) [20629]

East Chicago

Acro Electronics Corp. (Industrial Supplies) [16671]

Acro Electronics Corp. (Electrical and Electronic Equipment and Supplies) [8268]

Bearing Distributors (Industrial Supplies) [16730]

LB Steel Plate Co. (Used, Scrap, and Recycled Materials) [26878]

Robinson Steel Company Inc. (Metals) [20325]

Elberfeld

JH Service Company Inc. (Electrical and Electronic Equipment and Supplies) [8914]

Elkhart

AL-KO KOBER Corp. (Automotive) [2194]

Alco Tool Supply Inc. (Hardware) [13545]

ASA Audiovox Specialized Applications (Communications Systems and Equipment) [5517]

ASA Audiovox Specialized Applications (Electrical and Electronic Equipment and Supplies) [8381]
Atlantis Plastics, Inc. (Plastics) [22930]
Audiovox Specialized Applications LLC (Electrical and Electronic Equipment and Supplies) [8395]
Babsco Supply (Electrical and Electronic Equipment and Supplies) [8408]
Banks Lumber Company Inc. (Construction Materials and Machinery) [7019]
Banks Lumber Company Inc. (Wood and Wood Products) [27286]
Bender Wholesale Distributors (Adhesives) [3]
Burnstine's Distributing Corp. (Automotive) [2400]
Cast Products Corp. (Plumbing Materials and Fixtures) [23108]
C.O. Tools Inc. (Automotive) [2457]
Coachmen Industries Inc. Coachmen Vans Div. (Motorized Vehicles) [20612]
Conversion Components Inc. (Automotive) [2482]
Double-T Manufacturing Corp. (Construction Materials and Machinery) [7283]
E.W.C. Supply Inc. (Plumbing Materials and Fixtures) [23153]
Fabwel Inc. (Metals) [19962]
Fasnap Corp. (Hardware) [13694]
Fastec Industrial (Hardware) [13695]
GM International Inc. (Hardware) [13726]
Hull Lift Truck Inc. (Industrial Machinery) [16120]
Lavanture Plastic Extrusion Technologies (Plastics) [22992]
LaVanture Products Co. (Automotive) [2874]
MITO Corp. (Sound and Entertainment Equipment and Supplies) [25328]
MITO Corp. (Household Appliances) [15235]
Onan Indiana (Electrical and Electronic Equipment and Supplies) [9155]
Patrick Industries Inc. (Construction Materials and Machinery) [7839]
Pro Air Inc. (Heating and Cooling Equipment and Supplies) [14643]
Quality Window & Door (Construction Materials and Machinery) [7892]
River Park, Inc. (Sound and Entertainment Equipment and Supplies) [25419]
Sprunger Corp. (Industrial Supplies) [17193]
ST Laminating Corp. (Specialty Equipment and Products) [25829]
Steel Suppliers Inc. (Metals) [20400]
Temple Products of Indiana Inc. (Automotive) [3299]
Thunander Corp. (Construction Materials and Machinery) [8129]
Toolman Co. (Hardware) [13960]
Viking Formed Products (Industrial Supplies) [17255]
Vista Manufacturing (Electrical and Electronic Equipment and Supplies) [9543]
Yoder Oil Company Inc. (Petroleum, Fuels, and Related Equipment) [22818]

Elwood

Small Talk Inc. (Veterinary Products) [27232]

Evansville

American Resources Inc. (Minerals and Ores) [20513]
AmeriQual Foods Inc. (Food) [10406]
Black Beauty Coal Co. (Minerals and Ores) [20522]
Black Equipment Co. Inc. (Industrial Machinery) [15827]
BSH of Evansville (Construction Materials and Machinery) [7090]
CED/Superior Electrical Supply Co. (Electrical and Electronic Equipment and Supplies) [8514]
Diamond Foods Inc. (Food) [10957]
Evansville Appliance Parts (Household Appliances) [15123]
Evansville Auto Parts Inc. (Industrial Machinery) [16000]
Farm Boy Meats Inc. (Food) [11083]
Gehlhausen Paint Wholesalers (Paints and Varnishes) [21450]
General Waste Products Inc. (Used, Scrap, and Recycled Materials) [26825]
Great Lakes Power Products (Marine) [18509]

Hardesty Welding Supply Div. (Industrial Supplies) [16922]
Hutch & Son Inc. (Electrical and Electronic Equipment and Supplies) [8867]
Ideal American Dairy (Food) [11490]
Indian Industries Inc. (Recreational and Sporting Goods) [23742]
Indiana Wholesalers Inc. (Household Items) [15540]
Leich Div.; Charles (Medical, Dental, and Optical Supplies) [19407]
Lensing Wholesale, Inc. (Construction Materials and Machinery) [7595]
Lewis Brothers Bakeries Inc. (Food) [11706]
Louisville Tile Distributors, Inc. (Floorcovering Equipment and Supplies) [10001]
Louisville Tile Distributors Inc. (Construction Materials and Machinery) [7615]
Marshal Glove & Safety Supply (Shoes) [24801]
Ohio Valley Sound Inc. (Electrical and Electronic Equipment and Supplies) [9151]
Olinger Distributing Co. (Alcoholic Beverages) [1932]
O'Neal Steel Inc. Evansville (Metals) [20252]
Red Spot Paint Varnish Co. (Paints and Varnishes) [21552]
Roundy's Foods (Food) [12356]
Siegels Inc. (Clothing) [5353]
Singer Optical Co. Inc. (Medical, Dental, and Optical Supplies) [19614]
Swanson-Nunn Electric Co. (Electrical and Electronic Equipment and Supplies) [9450]
Tri-State Lighting and Supply Company Inc. (Electrical and Electronic Equipment and Supplies) [9507]
Tri-State Periodicals, Inc. (Books and Other Printed Materials) [4230]
Tri-State Vet & Pet Supply (Veterinary Products) [27253]
Truck Pro (Automotive) [3350]
Unisource (Paper and Paper Products) [21962]

Fishers

Alliant Foodservice Indianapolis (Food) [10375]
A.R. Musical Enterprises Inc. (Sound and Entertainment Equipment and Supplies) [25081]
Central Indiana Hardware Co. (Construction Materials and Machinery) [7159]

Ft. Wayne

Airport Greenhouse (Horticultural Supplies) [14796]
Belmont Wholesale Co. Inc. (Food) [10534]
Car Tape Distributors Inc. (Sound and Entertainment Equipment and Supplies) [25121]
Central Supply Co. (Plumbing Materials and Fixtures) [23110]
Clark and Mitchell Inc. (Floorcovering Equipment and Supplies) [9808]
Continental International (Industrial Supplies) [16807]
Custom Radio Corp. (Household Appliances) [15102]
Data Professionals (Computers and Software) [6183]
Do It Best Corp. (Construction Materials and Machinery) [7275]
Empire Refactory Sales Inc. (Industrial Supplies) [16849]
Executone of Fort Wayne Inc. (Communications Systems and Equipment) [5606]
Fastner House (Hardware) [13701]
Fisher Electric Motor Service (Automotive) [2624]
Fisher Paper (Paper and Paper Products) [21727]
Food Marketing Corp. (Food) [11174]
Fortmeyer's Inc. (Petroleum, Fuels, and Related Equipment) [22290]
Huser-Paul Company Inc. (Tobacco Products) [26309]
Indiana Auto Auction Inc. (Motorized Vehicles) [20652]
Ingram Video (Sound and Entertainment Equipment and Supplies) [25250]
Kaough Distributing Company, Inc. (Floorcovering Equipment and Supplies) [9984]
Kelmar Corp. (Heating and Cooling Equipment and Supplies) [14508]

Korte Brothers Inc. (Construction Materials and Machinery) [7570]
Leo Distributors Inc. (Construction Materials and Machinery) [7596]
Materials Handling Equipment Corp. (Industrial Machinery) [16273]
McMahon Paper Company Inc. (Paper and Paper Products) [21829]
Mill Supplies Inc. (Industrial Supplies) [17039]
Miller Supply Inc.; Bud (Heating and Cooling Equipment and Supplies) [14605]
Neff Engineering Co. (Industrial Supplies) [17069]
OmniSource Corp. (Used, Scrap, and Recycled Materials) [26929]
Oren Van Aman Company Inc. (Industrial Supplies) [17091]
Panoramic Corp. (Medical, Dental, and Optical Equipment) [18976]
Perfection Bakeries Inc. (Food) [12149]
Prairie Farms Dairy Inc. Fort Wayne Div. (Food) [12204]
Pure Sealed Dairy (Food) [12236]
Ridge Auto Parts Company Inc. (Automotive) [3158]
Roethele Building Materials Inc. (Construction Materials and Machinery) [7952]
Safetywear (Clothing) [5329]
Soccer House Inc. (Recreational and Sporting Goods) [23950]
Superior Div. (Used, Scrap, and Recycled Materials) [27016]
SUPERVALU Inc. Food Marketing Div. (Food) [12647]
Taylor Distributors of Indiana (Heating and Cooling Equipment and Supplies) [14712]
Thornhill Oil Company Inc. (Petroleum, Fuels, and Related Equipment) [22735]
Transmission and Fluid Equipment Inc. (Electrical and Electronic Equipment and Supplies) [9501]
Wagner-Electric of Fort Wayne Inc. (Electrical and Electronic Equipment and Supplies) [9550]
Wayne Fasteners Inc. (Hardware) [13986]
Wayne Pipe and Supply Inc. (Plumbing Materials and Fixtures) [23444]
Wayne Pipe and Supply Inc. (Plumbing Materials and Fixtures) [23445]
Xpedx-Carpenter Group (Paper and Paper Products) [22006]

Fortville

Abrasive Products Inc. (Industrial Supplies) [16668]

Fowler

Demeter Inc. (Livestock and Farm Products) [17818]
Senesac Inc. (Agricultural Equipment and Supplies) [1260]

Francesville

Cooperative Elevator Co. (Agricultural Equipment and Supplies) [451]

Frankfort

Cyclone Grain Co. (Livestock and Farm Products) [17806]

Fremont

Best-Klean Products (Cleaning and Janitorial Supplies) [4578]
LaGrange Products Inc. (Storage Equipment and Containers) [25925]

Garrett

Custer Grain Co. (Agricultural Equipment and Supplies) [485]

Gary

Berkheimer Company Inc.; G.W. (Heating and Cooling Equipment and Supplies) [14343]
Friendly Frank's Distribution Inc. (Books and Other Printed Materials) [3765]

Goshen

ACME Automotive Accessories Group (Automotive) [2174]

Arctic Clear Products Inc. (Specialty Equipment and Products) [25557]
Elkhart County Farm Cooperative (Petroleum, Fuels, and Related Equipment) [22225]
Goshen Sash and Door Co. (Wood and Wood Products) [27310]
Nagy Sales Corp.; Tom (Security and Safety Equipment) [24597]
Paragon Interiors Inc. (Household Items) [15612]
Troyer Foods Inc. (Food) [12763]

Grabill
Eastes Distributing (Computers and Software) [6234]

Granger
LESCO Distributing (Communications Systems and Equipment) [5662]

Greencastle
Skelton and Skinner Lumber Inc. (Construction Materials and Machinery) [8027]

Greenfield
Irving Materials Inc. (Construction Materials and Machinery) [7527]

Greensburg
Kova Fertilizer Inc. (Agricultural Equipment and Supplies) [919]
Lowe's Pellets and Grain Co. (Livestock and Farm Products) [18065]
Rust Wholesale Company Inc. (Food) [12371]

Greentown
Kokomo Grain Company Inc. (Livestock and Farm Products) [18039]

Greenwood
Bobbett & Associates Inc. (Shoes) [24693]
Hoosier Screen Printer Inc. (Clothing) [5036]

Griffith
Carpet Cushion Supply (Floorcovering Equipment and Supplies) [9765]
G-N Aircraft Inc. (Aeronautical Equipment and Supplies) [92]

Hamilton
CTN Data Service Inc. (Computers and Software) [6169]

Hammond
Alpha Steel Corp. (Metals) [19755]
Applied Industrial Technologies, Inc. (Industrial Supplies) [16705]
Berlin Enterprises Inc. (Metals) [19815]
Berlin Metals Inc. (Metals) [19816]
Calumet Auto Recycling and Sales Inc. (Automotive) [2414]
Calumet Breweries Inc. (Alcoholic Beverages) [1566]
Castle and Co. Hy-Alloy Steels Div.; A.M. (Metals) [19863]
Roll and Hold Warehousing and Distribution (Metals) [20326]
Time Saver Tool Corp. (Hardware) [13956]

Highland
Bell Parts Supply Inc. (Household Appliances) [15048]

Hobart
Indiana Botanic Gardens (Food) [11503]

Huntertown
H & H Sales Company, Inc. (Automotive) [2715]

Huntingburg
Dubois County Farm Bureau Cooperative (Agricultural Equipment and Supplies) [527]

Huntington
City Beverage Inc. (Alcoholic Beverages) [1597]
Coach's Connection Inc. (Recreational and Sporting Goods) [23597]
Erie Stone Company Inc. (Construction Materials and Machinery) [7318]
Homier Distributing Inc. (Hardware) [13756]
Huntington County Farm Cooperative (Agricultural Equipment and Supplies) [846]

Indianapolis
Ace Battery Inc. (Automotive) [2170]
Acorn Distributors Inc. (Paper and Paper Products) [21616]
ADESA Corp. (Automotive) [2181]
Airco Gas and Gear (Industrial Supplies) [16678]
Allied Box Co. (Paper and Paper Products) [21624]
Allied Box Co. (Industrial Supplies) [16686]
Allied Truck Equipment Corp. (Automotive) [2215]
Aluma Systems USA Inc. (Construction Materials and Machinery) [6949]
American Equipment Company Inc. (Construction Materials and Machinery) [6963]
American Equipment Marble & Tile, Inc. (Floorcovering Equipment and Supplies) [9668]
Arizona Sport Shirts Inc. (Clothing) [4783]
Associated Material Handling Industries Inc. (Industrial Machinery) [15784]
Athmann Industrial Medical Supply (Medical, Dental, and Optical Equipment) [18697]
Auburn Plastics and Rubber Inc. (Plastics) [22931]
Audio Supply Co. (Sound and Entertainment Equipment and Supplies) [25087]
Barber Cabinet Co. Inc. (Furniture and Fixtures) [13031]
Beeman Jorgensen Inc. (Books and Other Printed Materials) [3547]
Benson Pump Co. (Recreational and Sporting Goods) [23548]
Bindley Western Industries Inc. (Health and Beauty Aids) [14047]
Bindley Western Industries Inc. (Medical, Dental, and Optical Supplies) [19187]
Bindley Western Industries Inc. Bindley Western Drug Div. (Health and Beauty Aids) [14048]
Biosound Esaote Inc. (Medical, Dental, and Optical Equipment) [18715]
Bowes Industries Inc. (Automotive) [2375]
Brehob Corp. (Industrial Machinery) [15843]
Brightpoint, Inc. (Communications Systems and Equipment) [5533]
Brightpoint Inc. (Electrical and Electronic Equipment and Supplies) [8467]
Brulin and Co. Inc. (Cleaning and Janitorial Supplies) [4590]
Bryant Corp.; P.R. (Industrial Machinery) [15853]
Bud's Service Inc. (Petroleum, Fuels, and Related Equipment) [22098]
Buyers Paper & Specialty Inc. (Tobacco Products) [26269]
C and T Design and Equipment Company Inc. (Specialty Equipment and Products) [25587]
Caito Foods Service, Inc. (Food) [10664]
Carter-Lee Lumber Company Inc. (Construction Materials and Machinery) [7147]
Catheter Research Inc. (Medical, Dental, and Optical Equipment) [18730]
Celebrations Fireworks & Supply Co. Inc. (Explosives) [9633]
City Optical Company Inc./Division of The Tavel Optical Group (Medical, Dental, and Optical Supplies) [19230]
Clarklift Corporation of Indiana (Industrial Machinery) [15889]
Clay Tile Products; Allen (Floorcovering Equipment and Supplies) [9812]
Communications Products Inc. (Communications Systems and Equipment) [5572]
Container Industries Inc. (Storage Equipment and Containers) [25907]
Corinthian Healthcare Systems (Medical, Dental, and Optical Equipment) [18756]
Cornelius Printed Products (Paper and Paper Products) [21691]

Cory Orchard and Turf Div. (Agricultural Equipment and Supplies) [464]
Countrymark Cooperative Inc. (Agricultural Equipment and Supplies) [466]
CourterCo (Adhesives) [4]
Crescent Paper Co. (Paper and Paper Products) [21696]
Crystal Flash Petroleum Corp. (Petroleum, Fuels, and Related Equipment) [22181]
Cummins Midstates Power Inc. (Automotive) [2510]
Custom Phones Inc. (Communications Systems and Equipment) [5583]
Devoe Co.; Leslie M. (Electrical and Electronic Equipment and Supplies) [8624]
Downey Designs International Inc. (Jewelry) [17399]
Drey and Co. Inc.; S.E. (Industrial Supplies) [16839]
DSI Distributing, Inc. (Household Appliances) [15117]
Duncan Supply Co. Inc. (Heating and Cooling Equipment and Supplies) [14424]
EESCO Inc. Farrell-Argast Div. (Electrical and Electronic Equipment and Supplies) [8656]
Ertel Products Inc. (Automotive) [2596]
Gage Co. Central Div. (Industrial Supplies) [16886]
Gene Labs Inc. (Computers and Software) [6296]
Gilvins Boots & Shoes (Shoes) [24751]
Globe Industrial Supply Inc. (Furniture and Fixtures) [13123]
Godby Products Inc. (Heating and Cooling Equipment and Supplies) [14471]
Godwin Company, Inc. (Industrial Machinery) [16070]
Grocers Supply Co. (Food) [11330]
Haggard and Stocking Associates Inc. (Industrial Supplies) [16920]
Haggard and Stocking Associates Inc. (Industrial Machinery) [16083]
Hahn Systems (Construction Materials and Machinery) [7430]
Hausman Corp. (Construction Materials and Machinery) [7456]
Heating-Cooling Distributors Inc. (Heating and Cooling Equipment and Supplies) [14481]
High Point Oil Co. (Petroleum, Fuels, and Related Equipment) [22351]
Hoosier Company Inc. (Construction Materials and Machinery) [7485]
Horner Electric Inc. (Industrial Machinery) [16113]
Howard Sales Inc. (Paper and Paper Products) [21768]
HP Products (Cleaning and Janitorial Supplies) [4637]
HPS, Inc. (Photographic Equipment and Supplies) [22866]
HPS Inc. (Office Equipment and Supplies) [21040]
HPS Office Systems (Office Equipment and Supplies) [21041]
HPS Printing Products (Office Equipment and Supplies) [21042]
IEI Investments Inc. (Industrial Supplies) [16938]
IGC Energy Inc. (Industrial Supplies) [16939]
Indiana Carbon Company Inc. (Office Equipment and Supplies) [21056]
Indiana Concession Supply Inc. (Food) [11504]
Indiana Oxygen Co. (Industrial Supplies) [16942]
Indiana Soft Water Service Inc. (Household Appliances) [15176]
Indiana Supply Corp. (Heating and Cooling Equipment and Supplies) [14495]
Indiana Supply Corp. (Industrial Supplies) [16943]
Indiana Tees (Clothing) [5049]
Indianapolis Belting & Supply (Industrial Machinery) [16148]
Indianapolis Fruit Company, Inc. (Food) [11505]
Indianapolis Materials Recycling Facility (Used, Scrap, and Recycled Materials) [26849]
Indianapolis Welding Supply Inc. (Industrial Supplies) [16944]
J & J Distributors Inc. (Specialty Equipment and Products) [25690]
Jack's Tack International Distributors (Clothing) [5073]
Joint and Clutch Service Inc. (Automotive) [2830]

K and F Industries Inc. (Indianapolis, Indiana) (Metals) [20081]
Kahn & Son, Inc.; Irvin (Floorcovering Equipment and Supplies) [9982]
Kay Guitar Co. (Sound and Entertainment Equipment and Supplies) [25267]
Kenney Machinery Corp. (Agricultural Equipment and Supplies) [904]
Kesler-Schaefer Auto Auction Inc. (Motorized Vehicles) [20661]
Kiefaber Co.; W.H. (Plumbing Materials and Fixtures) [23235]
King Electronics Distributing (Electrical and Electronic Equipment and Supplies) [8946]
Kipp Brothers Inc. (Toys and Hobby Goods) [26553]
Kirkbride Bible Co.; B.B. (Books and Other Printed Materials) [3880]
Kulwin Electric Supply (Electrical and Electronic Equipment and Supplies) [8960]
Landwerlen Leather Co. Inc. (Shoes) [24790]
LDI, Ltd. (Motorized Vehicles) [20671]
Lee Supply Corp. (Plumbing Materials and Fixtures) [23245]
Lilly and Co. Pharmaceutical Div.; Eli (Medical, Dental, and Optical Supplies) [19416]
MacAllister Machinery Company Inc. (Construction Materials and Machinery) [7629]
Management Computer Systems Inc. (Computers and Software) [6456]
Manu Reps Inc. (Sound and Entertainment Equipment and Supplies) [25302]
Mark-Rite Distributing Corp. (Office Equipment and Supplies) [21125]
Marshall Building Specialties Company Inc. (Construction Materials and Machinery) [7648]
Mays Chemical Co. (Medical, Dental, and Optical Supplies) [19427]
McFarling Foods Inc. (Food) [11826]
McMahon Foodservice Outlet (Food) [11838]
Metal Service and Supply Inc. (Metals) [20170]
Meunier Electronics Supply Inc. (Electrical and Electronic Equipment and Supplies) [9071]
Meyer Plastics Inc. (Plastics) [22997]
Mike Sell's Indiana Inc. (Food) [11892]
Mill Contractor and Industrial Supplies, Inc. (Construction Materials and Machinery) [7711]
Monfort Electronic Marketing (Electrical and Electronic Equipment and Supplies) [9093]
Morgan-Wightman Supply Inc. Indiana (Construction Materials and Machinery) [7748]
Morse Wholesale Inc.; J.D. (Toys and Hobby Goods) [26582]
Mosier Fluid Power of Indiana Inc. (Scientific and Measurement Devices) [24404]
Mutual Pipe and Supply Inc. (Plumbing Materials and Fixtures) [23285]
National Wine and Spirits Corp. (Automotive) [3017]
Nylen Products Inc. (Automotive) [3051]
Oil Equipment Supply Corp. (Petroleum, Fuels, and Related Equipment) [22537]
Olinger Distributing Co. (Alcoholic Beverages) [1933]
Pallet Recycling Center Inc. (Storage Equipment and Containers) [25931]
Patriotic Fireworks Inc. (Gifts and Novelties) [13418]
Peerless Electric Supply Co. (Electrical and Electronic Equipment and Supplies) [9186]
Pierce Inc.; Jack A. (Shoes) [24834]
Plumbers Supply Co. (Plumbing Materials and Fixtures) [23320]
PMC of Indiana (Office Equipment and Supplies) [21218]
Printers Supply of Indiana Inc. (Industrial Machinery) [16426]
PRN Pharmaceutical Services Inc. (Medical, Dental, and Optical Supplies) [19553]
Pure Beverage Inc. (Books and Other Printed Materials) [4097]
Raub Radio and Television Co. (Sound and Entertainment Equipment and Supplies) [25406]

Raytheon Aircraft Services (Aeronautical Equipment and Supplies) [140]
RELM Communications Inc. (Communications Systems and Equipment) [5739]
SerVaas Inc. (Rubber) [24294]
Sheats Supply Services, Inc. (Industrial Machinery) [16486]
Solotken and Company Inc.; J. (Used, Scrap, and Recycled Materials) [26999]
Southeastern Supply Company Inc. (Construction Materials and Machinery) [8046]
Southland Flooring Supply (Floorcovering Equipment and Supplies) [10169]
Stationers Inc. (Indianapolis, Indiana) (Office Equipment and Supplies) [21296]
Stromberg Sales Company Inc. (Electrical and Electronic Equipment and Supplies) [9427]
Support Net Inc. (Computers and Software) [6778]
Sutton-Garten Co. (Industrial Supplies) [17207]
SYSCO Food Services of Indianapolis Inc. (Food) [12682]
Tileworks (Floorcovering Equipment and Supplies) [10251]
Trident Medical International (Medical, Dental, and Optical Supplies) [19663]
Turner Appliance (Household Appliances) [15344]
Tynan Equipment Co. (Industrial Machinery) [16585]
Ulrich Chemical Inc. (Chemicals) [4537]
Uniform House Inc. (Clothing) [5449]
Universal Sales Engineering Inc. (Industrial Supplies) [17245]
Van Ausdall and Farrar Inc. (Office Equipment and Supplies) [21335]
Wayne Distributing Inc. (Electrical and Electronic Equipment and Supplies) [9562]
Wesleyan Publishing House (Books and Other Printed Materials) [4274]
Wholesale T-Shirt Supply (Clothing) [5484]
Word Systems Inc. (Office Equipment and Supplies) [21362]
Ye Olde Genealogie Shoppe (Books and Other Printed Materials) [4303]
Young Company Inc.; A.R. (Automotive) [3451]
Young Cos.; A.B. (Industrial Machinery) [16657]
Young Cos.; A.B. (Industrial Supplies) [17292]

Indiannapolis
Butterfield and Company Inc. (Food) [10651]

Jasper
Hoosier Oil Inc. (Petroleum, Fuels, and Related Equipment) [22363]
Ruxer Ford, Lincoln, Mercury Inc. (Motorized Vehicles) [20715]

Jeffersonville
Dynafluid Products, Inc. (Industrial Machinery) [15970]

Kendallville
Kendallville Iron and Metal Inc. (Used, Scrap, and Recycled Materials) [26864]

Knightstown
Knightstown Elevator Inc. (Livestock and Farm Products) [18038]

Kokomo
Englewood Electric (Electrical and Electronic Equipment and Supplies) [8708]
Harvest Productions (E.B.M.) (Sound and Entertainment Equipment and Supplies) [25228]
Northern Indiana Supply Company Inc. (Industrial Supplies) [17081]
Schillinger Associates Inc. (Electrical and Electronic Equipment and Supplies) [9342]
Vickers International (Clothing) [5462]

Kouts
Heinold Hog Market Inc. (Livestock and Farm Products) [17988]

La Porte
La Porte County Cooperative (Livestock and Farm Products) [18041]
Light House Electrical Suppliers Inc. (Electrical and Electronic Equipment and Supplies) [8986]
Perz Feed & Delivery (Veterinary Products) [27204]
Veri-Best Bakers (Food) [12837]

Lafayette
Biggs Pump and Supply Inc. (Plumbing Materials and Fixtures) [23086]
Kirby Risk Electrical Supply (Electrical and Electronic Equipment and Supplies) [8949]
Lafayette Electronics Supply Inc. (Electrical and Electronic Equipment and Supplies) [8965]
Lafayette Electronics Supply Inc. (Household Appliances) [15197]
Leming Supply Inc. (Heating and Cooling Equipment and Supplies) [14522]
Schnaible Service and Supply Company Inc. (Cleaning and Janitorial Supplies) [4704]
Vierk Industrial Products (Plumbing Materials and Fixtures) [23432]

Lagrange
Goulds Sports Textiles Inc. (Clothing) [4998]
Lambright's Inc. (Agricultural Equipment and Supplies) [932]

Lawrence
Glass Co., Inc.; The John M. (Industrial Supplies) [16895]

Lebanon
Boone County Farm Bureau Cooperative Inc. (Petroleum, Fuels, and Related Equipment) [22086]
United Industrial Tire Inc. (Automotive) [3367]

Ligonier
G & S Products Inc. (Sound and Entertainment Equipment and Supplies) [25205]

Linden
Midwest Distributing Inc. (Agricultural Equipment and Supplies) [1036]

Logansport
ABC Metals Inc. (Metals) [19723]
Buck-Hilkert Inc. (Industrial Supplies) [16770]
Cole Hardwood Inc. (Construction Materials and Machinery) [7193]
Edlo Sales and Engineering Inc. (Industrial Machinery) [15978]
LDI MFG Co., Inc. (Heating and Cooling Equipment and Supplies) [14518]

Lowell
Harding's Inc. (Construction Materials and Machinery) [7444]
Sportscards & Comics Center (Toys and Hobby Goods) [26664]

Madison
Steinhardt & Hanson, Inc. (Office Equipment and Supplies) [21298]

Marion
Aluminum Products Co. (Construction Materials and Machinery) [6951]
Hundley Brokerage Company Inc. (Food) [11477]
Ross Supply Company Inc. (Plumbing Materials and Fixtures) [23352]

Martinsville
Affiliated Medical Research (Medical, Dental, and Optical Equipment) [18664]

McCordsville
XYZ Electronics Inc. (Computers and Software) [6886]

Merrillville

Tri-State Hospital Supply Corp. (Medical, Dental, and Optical Equipment) [19085]

Michigan City

Burnham Glove Co.; Frederic H. (Clothing) [4854]
Sprague Devices Inc. (Automotive) [3255]
Tri State Electrical Supply Inc. (Electrical and Electronic Equipment and Supplies) [9506]

Millersburg

C and P Oil Inc. (Petroleum, Fuels, and Related Equipment) [22101]

Mishawaka

Allied Screw Products (Aeronautical Equipment and Supplies) [39]
Auto Radio Specialists (Sound and Entertainment Equipment and Supplies) [25091]
Berreth Oil Company Inc. (Petroleum, Fuels, and Related Equipment) [22069]
Dewald Fluid Power Company Inc. (Industrial Supplies) [16831]
General Drug Co. (Medical, Dental, and Optical Supplies) [19336]
Kelley Manufacturing Corp. (Construction Materials and Machinery) [7544]
PullRite/Pulliam Enterprise Inc. (Automotive) [3123]
Rosenstein and Co. (Textiles and Notions) [26193]
Style Master (Metals) [20410]
Welded Products Inc. (Metals) [20485]

Monroe

Adams County Co-operative Association Inc. (Agricultural Equipment and Supplies) [183]

Monroe City

Monroe City Feed Mill Inc. (Agricultural Equipment and Supplies) [1046]

Monticello

Indiana Recreation Equipment & Design, Inc. (Recreational and Sporting Goods) [23743]
McCord Auto Supply Inc. (Automotive) [2930]

Mooresville

Tackle Service Center (Recreational and Sporting Goods) [24003]

Mt. Vernon

Posey County Farm Bureau Cooperative Association Inc. (Agricultural Equipment and Supplies) [1141]

Muncie

AgBest Cooperative Inc. (Petroleum, Fuels, and Related Equipment) [22025]
Alro Steel Corp. (Metals) [19761]
Consumer Products Co. (Storage Equipment and Containers) [25906]
Delaware Foods Inc. (Food) [10939]
Dobrow Industries (Used, Scrap, and Recycled Materials) [26798]
Grainger Industrial Supply (Electrical and Electronic Equipment and Supplies) [8803]
J & K Distributors (Storage Equipment and Containers) [25920]
KBC Bargain Center Inc. (Clothing) [5105]
Knapp Supply Company Inc. (Plumbing Materials and Fixtures) [23237]
Mid States Concession Supply (Food) [11881]
Miller Tire Co. Inc. (Automotive) [2969]
Miller Tire Distributors (Automotive) [2970]
Norrick Petroleum (Petroleum, Fuels, and Related Equipment) [22523]
Werts Novelty Co. (Paper and Paper Products) [21987]
White Feather Farms Inc. (Food) [12929]
Willco Wholesale Distributors (Heating and Cooling Equipment and Supplies) [14768]

Munster

Carpetland U.S.A. Inc. (Floorcovering Equipment and Supplies) [9772]

Nappanee

Borkholder and Company Inc.; F.D. (Construction Materials and Machinery) [7071]
Evangel Publishing House (Books and Other Printed Materials) [3737]

New Albany

Kaiser Wholesale Inc. (Tobacco Products) [26315]
Scott Seed Co. (Agricultural Equipment and Supplies) [1244]
Sphar & Co. (Agricultural Equipment and Supplies) [1290]
Supreme Oil Company Inc. (Petroleum, Fuels, and Related Equipment) [22715]
Wolf Warehouse Distributors (Marine) [18643]

New Haven

Allen County Cooperative Association (Agricultural Equipment and Supplies) [222]
McConnell and Sons Inc.; F. (Food) [11820]

New Market

Layne and Myers Grain Co. (Livestock and Farm Products) [18048]

New Palestine

Institutional Equipment Inc. (Recreational and Sporting Goods) [23744]

New Salisbury

C & D Hardwoods (Construction Materials and Machinery) [7120]

Newburgh

General Imaging Corp. (Medical, Dental, and Optical Equipment) [18806]

Noblesville

Haffner X-Ray Company Inc. (Medical, Dental, and Optical Equipment) [18820]
Hamilton County Farm Bureau (Agricultural Equipment and Supplies) [784]
Indiana Seed Co. (Agricultural Equipment and Supplies) [855]

Oakland City

Propane/One Inc. (Petroleum, Fuels, and Related Equipment) [22597]

Osceola

Stripco Sales Inc. (Metals) [20408]

Osgood

Laughery Valley AG Co-Op Inc. (Agricultural Equipment and Supplies) [942]

Palmyra

Jacobi Sales Inc. (Agricultural Equipment and Supplies) [876]

Plainfield

ADESA Indianapolis Inc. (Motorized Vehicles) [20578]
PSI Resources Inc. (Electrical and Electronic Equipment and Supplies) [9243]
Rhoades Wine Group, Inc. (Alcoholic Beverages) [1987]

Plymouth

Electric Specialties Inc. (Automotive) [2580]
Koontz Equipment Co.; Don (Construction Materials and Machinery) [7569]

Portage

Feralloy Processing Co (Metals) [19973]
Great Lakes Peterbilt Inc. (Motorized Vehicles) [20643]

Portland

Pennville Custom Cabinetry for the Home (Construction Materials and Machinery) [7849]
Pennville Custom Cabinetry for the Home (Wood and Wood Products) [27357]

Rensselaer

Castongia's Inc. (Agricultural Equipment and Supplies) [380]
Jasper County Farm Bureau Cooperative (Livestock and Farm Products) [18022]

Richmond

Allied Telecommunications Inc. (Household Appliances) [15002]
Axxis Inc. (Sound and Entertainment Equipment and Supplies) [25094]
Convenience Store Distributing Company L.L.C. (Food) [10830]
Franklin Iron and Metal Corp. (Used, Scrap, and Recycled Materials) [26816]
Harvest Land Cooperative Inc. (Agricultural Equipment and Supplies) [797]
Hill Floral Products (Horticultural Supplies) [14886]
Indianapolis Coca-Cola Bottling Company Inc./Richmond Div. (Soft Drinks) [24974]
Richmond Electric Supply Co. (Electrical and Electronic Equipment and Supplies) [9296]
Rodefeld Company Inc. (Automotive) [3171]
Warehouse Service Co. (Automotive) [3399]

Roanoke

Fort Wayne Fleet Equipment (Automotive) [2642]

Rockville

BJ Distributing (Sound and Entertainment Equipment and Supplies) [25104]

Rushville

Rush County Farm Bureau Cooperative (Agricultural Equipment and Supplies) [1219]

Russiaville

Indiana Farm Systems Inc. (Agricultural Equipment and Supplies) [854]

St. John

Locoli Inc. (Clothing) [5138]

Schererville

AAA Supply Corp. (Hardware) [13520]
Koremen Ltd. (Plumbing Materials and Fixtures) [23238]

Sellersburg

Adtek Co. (Medical, Dental, and Optical Equipment) [18659]
Adtek Co. (Medical, Dental, and Optical Supplies) [19126]

Seymour

First Class Business Systems Inc. (Computers and Software) [6271]
Jackson-Jennings Farm Bureau Cooperative (Petroleum, Fuels, and Related Equipment) [22381]
Swifty Oil Company Inc. (Petroleum, Fuels, and Related Equipment) [22718]

Sharpsville

Adler Seeds Inc. (Agricultural Equipment and Supplies) [188]

Shelbyville

Lumberman of Indiana (Construction Materials and Machinery) [7618]

Sheridan

Wallace Grain Company Inc. (Agricultural Equipment and Supplies) [1408]

Shipshewana

Mastercraft Inc. (Furniture and Fixtures) [13174]

South Bend

Acra Custom Wheel (Automotive) [2176]
Aqualife (Veterinary Products) [27070]
Baker Rubber Inc. (Rubber) [24268]

Berkheimer Company Inc. South Bend;
   G.W. (Heating and Cooling Equipment and
   Supplies) [14344]
Bernell Corp. (Medical, Dental, and Optical
   Supplies) [19185]
Clark Food Service Inc. South Bend
   Div. (Restaurant and Commercial Foodservice
   Equipment and Supplies) [24094]
Clean Seal (Industrial Supplies) [16800]
Cloud Brothers Inc. (Household
   Appliances) [15086]
Englewood Electrical Supply (Electrical and
   Electronic Equipment and Supplies) [8709]
Glass Depot (Construction Materials and
   Machinery) [7398]
Koontz-Wagner Electric Company Inc. (Electrical
   and Electronic Equipment and Supplies) [8956]
Michiana Micro Inc. (Computers and
   Software) [6489]
Midwest Sales and Service Inc. (Sound and
   Entertainment Equipment and Supplies) [25323]
Midwest Sales and Service Inc. (Household
   Appliances) [15232]
Pepsi-Cola General Bottlers of South Bend (Soft
   Drinks) [25017]
Pepsi-Cola General Bottlers of South
   Bend (Food) [12145]
Powell Tool Supply Inc. (Industrial
   Machinery) [16412]
Ridge Co. (Automotive) [3159]
Shoemaker of Indiana, Inc. (Heating and Cooling
   Equipment and Supplies) [14681]
South Bend Supply Company Inc. (Industrial
   Supplies) [17181]
Stanz Cheese Company Inc. (Food) [12568]
Steel Warehouse Company Inc. (Metals) [20403]
Sweeper Corp. (Specialty Equipment and
   Products) [25836]
the distributors (Books and Other Printed
   Materials) [4214]
Time Systems Inc. (Electrical and Electronic
   Equipment and Supplies) [9489]
The Tire Rack Wholesale (Automotive) [3306]
Vanderheyden Distributing Inc. (Household
   Appliances) [15356]

Speedway
Indianapolis Coca-Cola Bottling Company Inc. (Soft
   Drinks) [24973]

Spencer
Cable Converter Services Corp. (Electrical and
   Electronic Equipment and Supplies) [8481]

Star City
Farmers Grain and Supply Company
   Inc. (Agricultural Equipment and Supplies) [657]

Terre Haute
Graham Grain Co. (Livestock and Farm
   Products) [17951]
Growers Cooperative Inc. (Agricultural Equipment
   and Supplies) [772]
Hardware Supply Company
   Inc. (Hardware) [13741]
Hydro-Power Inc. (Industrial Machinery) [16133]
Industrial Supply Co. (Industrial Supplies) [16951]
Kleptz Aluminum Building Supply Co. (Construction
   Materials and Machinery) [7562]
Lee Company Inc. (Furniture and Fixtures) [13163]
Morgan Wholesale Feed; Fred (Agricultural
   Equipment and Supplies) [1052]
Reece Oil Co. (Petroleum, Fuels, and Related
   Equipment) [22616]
Terra Haute Recycling (Used, Scrap, and Recycled
   Materials) [27021]
Wearhouse (Shoes) [24889]
Wiemuth and Son Company Inc. (Tobacco
   Products) [26374]
Wolfe's Terre Haute Auto Auction Inc. (Motorized
   Vehicles) [20751]

Tipton
Top AG Inc. (Agricultural Equipment and
   Supplies) [1341]

Topeka
Topeka Seed and Stove Inc. (Agricultural
   Equipment and Supplies) [1342]

Valparaiso
Chester Inc. (Agricultural Equipment and
   Supplies) [414]

Vincennes
Bolk Industrial Supply Corp. (Industrial
   Supplies) [16754]
Knox County Farm Bureau Cooperative
   Association (Agricultural Equipment and
   Supplies) [917]
Niehaus Lumber Co. (Construction Materials and
   Machinery) [7778]
Valley Electric Supply Corp. (Electrical and
   Electronic Equipment and Supplies) [9533]

Wabash
LBK Distributors (Recreational and Sporting
   Goods) [23782]
North Central Cooperative Inc. (Agricultural
   Equipment and Supplies) [1079]

Warsaw
DaLite Screen Co. (Sound and Entertainment
   Equipment and Supplies) [25155]
North Central Cooperative Association (Petroleum,
   Fuels, and Related Equipment) [22524]
Penguin Point Systems Inc. (Food) [12137]
Warsaw Chemical Company Inc. (Specialty
   Equipment and Products) [25872]

Washington
White River Cooperative (Agricultural Equipment
   and Supplies) [1440]

Wawaka
Frick's Services Inc. (Livestock and Farm
   Products) [17929]

West Terre Haute
Sugar Creek Scrap, Inc. (Used, Scrap, and
   Recycled Materials) [27013]

Westfield
Altex-Mar Electronics Inc. (Electrical and Electronic
   Equipment and Supplies) [8333]
Mar Electronics Inc. (Electrical and Electronic
   Equipment and Supplies) [9027]
Mid-West Golf Inc. (Clothing) [5193]
Westfield Decorator Fashions (Household
   Items) [15706]

Westville
Midland Grocery Co. (Food) [11885]
REDI-FROZ (Food) [12291]
Roundy's Westville Div. (Food) [12361]

Whiting
Michigan Industrial Hardwood Co. (Construction
   Materials and Machinery) [7701]

Winamac
Pulaski County Farm Bureau
   Cooperative (Agricultural Equipment and
   Supplies) [1162]
Tippecanoe Beverages Inc. (Alcoholic
   Beverages) [2083]

Winchester
Professional Computer Systems (Computers and
   Software) [6649]

Winona Lake
Eisenbrauns (Books and Other Printed
   Materials) [3725]

Wolcott
Farmers Cooperative Co. (Livestock and Farm
   Products) [17850]

Woodburn
EMP Co-op Inc. (Livestock and Farm
   Products) [17833]

Iowa

Adair
Adair Feed and Grain Co. (Livestock and Farm
   Products) [17673]

Akron
Farmers Cooperative Co. (Agricultural Equipment
   and Supplies) [587]

Albert City
AG Partners L.L.C. (Agricultural Equipment and
   Supplies) [197]
Albert City Elevator Inc. (Agricultural Equipment and
   Supplies) [220]

Alexander
Latham Seed Co. (Livestock and Farm
   Products) [18046]

Algona
Electronic Specialties Inc. (Electrical and Electronic
   Equipment and Supplies) [8694]
National Welding Supply of Algona (Industrial
   Supplies) [17068]
Williams Ltd.; Ernie (Agricultural Equipment and
   Supplies) [1453]

Alta
Agland Cooperative (Agricultural Equipment and
   Supplies) [207]

Alton
Farmers Cooperative Co. (Agricultural Equipment
   and Supplies) [602]
Farmers Cooperative Co. (Food) [11095]

Ames
Yarn Tree Designs (Textiles and Notions) [26253]

Anamosa
Amber NFO Reload Corp. (Livestock and Farm
   Products) [17695]
New Horizon FS Inc. (Petroleum, Fuels, and
   Related Equipment) [22509]

Ankeny
Casey's General Stores Inc. (Food) [10709]
L & L Insulation and Supply Co. (Construction
   Materials and Machinery) [7573]
Lorenz & Jones Marine Distributors,
   Inc. (Marine) [18550]
Perishable Distributors of Iowa Ltd. (Food) [12152]

Arcadia
Farmers Cooperative Elevator Co. (Agricultural
   Equipment and Supplies) [620]

Archer
Archer Cooperative Grain Co. (Agricultural
   Equipment and Supplies) [248]

Ashton
Northwest Iowa Cooperative (Livestock and Farm
   Products) [18145]

Atlantic
Cappel Distributing Co. (Paints and
   Varnishes) [21412]

Austinville
Austinville Elevator (Livestock and Farm
   Products) [17713]

Beaman
Mid-Iowa Cooperative (Beaman, Iowa) (Livestock
   and Farm Products) [18092]

Belmond

Helland and Long Implement Co. (Agricultural Equipment and Supplies) [812]

Bettendorf

Adel Wholesalers Inc. (Plumbing Materials and Fixtures) [23053]
Alter Trading Corp. (Used, Scrap, and Recycled Materials) [26747]

Blairsburg

Farmers Cooperative Elevator Co. (Livestock and Farm Products) [17865]

Bloomfield

Troy Elevator Inc. (Livestock and Farm Products) [18295]

Bode

Bode Cooperative (Agricultural Equipment and Supplies) [325]

Boone

Archway Cookie Co. (Food) [10430]
Fareway Wholesale (Food) [11081]

Booneville

Booneville Cooperative Elevator Co. (Agricultural Equipment and Supplies) [331]

Boyden

Farmers Cooperative Association (Petroleum, Fuels, and Related Equipment) [22254]

Britt

Farmers Cooperative Co. (Britt, Iowa) (Food) [11096]

Buckeye

Buckeye Cooperative Elevator Co. (Livestock and Farm Products) [17752]
Buckeye Cooperative Elevator Co. (Food) [10637]

Buckingham

Buckingham Cooperative Co. (Livestock and Farm Products) [17753]

Buffalo Center

Farmers Cooperative Elevator (Agricultural Equipment and Supplies) [606]

Burlington

Bangert's Computer Systems (Computers and Software) [6000]
Reif Oil Co. (Petroleum, Fuels, and Related Equipment) [22620]
Sterzing Food Co. (Food) [12584]
Vista Bakery, Inc. (Food) [12850]

Carlisle

James Oil Co. (Petroleum, Fuels, and Related Equipment) [22383]

Carroll

Agri Volt & Cabinet Co. (Recreational and Sporting Goods) [23497]
Farner Bocken Co. (Tobacco Products) [26292]
Juergens Produce and Feed Co. (Agricultural Equipment and Supplies) [893]

Cedar Falls

Ag Services of America Inc. (Agricultural Equipment and Supplies) [199]
Frinks Greenhouses Inc. (Horticultural Supplies) [14871]
Grimstad, Inc.; J.M. (Industrial Machinery) [16078]
Harnack Co. (Agricultural Equipment and Supplies) [793]
Martin Bros. Distributing Co., Inc. (Food) [11793]

Cedar Rapids

Apache Hose and Belting Inc. (Industrial Supplies) [16700]
Barron Motor Inc. (Automotive) [2321]

Bell Company Inc.; James W. (Construction Materials and Machinery) [7045]
Cedar Rapids Welding Supply Inc. (Industrial Supplies) [16785]
Hawkeye Seed Company Inc. (Veterinary Products) [27147]
Hawkeye Seed Company Inc. (Agricultural Equipment and Supplies) [802]
Intertrade Ltd. (Aeronautical Equipment and Supplies) [105]
Jerabek Wholesalers, Inc.; Paul (Alcoholic Beverages) [1780]
Klinger Paint Co., Inc. (Paints and Varnishes) [21473]
Midamar Corp. (Food) [11882]
O'Connell Wholesale Lumber Co.; John J. (Construction Materials and Machinery) [7802]
Ohsman and Sons Co. (Livestock and Farm Products) [18151]
Phelans (Household Items) [15619]
PMX Industries Inc. (Metals) [20286]
Pratt Audio Visual and Video (Electrical and Electronic Equipment and Supplies) [9233]
Precision Bearing (Industrial Supplies) [17111]
Radio Communications Co. (Communications Systems and Equipment) [5730]
Rosebar Tire Shredding Inc. (Rubber) [24291]
Spreitzer Inc. (Construction Materials and Machinery) [8064]
Terry-Durin Company Inc. (Electrical and Electronic Equipment and Supplies) [9481]
Wagner Enterprises Inc. (Clothing) [5468]

Charles City

Colwell Cooperative (Livestock and Farm Products) [17787]

CharLes City

Diversified Fastening (Hardware) [13667]

Cherokee

First Cooperative Association (Food) [11132]

Clarence

Clarence Cooperative Company Inc. (Agricultural Equipment and Supplies) [419]

Clarion

Clarion Farmers Elevator Cooperative (Agricultural Equipment and Supplies) [421]
North Central Cooperative Elevator (Livestock and Farm Products) [18137]

Clear Lake

American Cheeseman Inc. (Food) [10395]
Farmers Cooperative Co. (Agricultural Equipment and Supplies) [590]
Farmers Cooperative Co. (Food) [11091]
Foxley Grain (Livestock and Farm Products) [17925]

Cleghorn

First Farmers Cooperative Elevator (Agricultural Equipment and Supplies) [685]

Clinton

Custom-Pak Inc. (Used, Scrap, and Recycled Materials) [26792]
Kirchhoff Distributing Co. (Food) [11622]

Colo

Farmers Grain Cooperative (Agricultural Equipment and Supplies) [654]

Conrad

Conrad Cooperative (Agricultural Equipment and Supplies) [438]

Coralville

McCabe Equipment Inc. (Agricultural Equipment and Supplies) [997]

Coulter

Coulter Elevator (Livestock and Farm Products) [17801]

Council Bluffs

Ballenger Automotive Service (Automotive) [2313]
Bud's Hobbies (Toys and Hobby Goods) [26429]
Farm Service Company Inc. (Agricultural Equipment and Supplies) [564]
Griffith Inc.; R.C. (Construction Materials and Machinery) [7417]
Red Giant Oil Co. (Petroleum, Fuels, and Related Equipment) [22612]

Creston

Crestland Cooperative (Agricultural Equipment and Supplies) [473]
Creston Feed and Grain Co. (Agricultural Equipment and Supplies) [474]

Cylinder

Cylinder Cooperative Elevator (Livestock and Farm Products) [17807]

Davenport

Carroll Distribution Company, Inc. (Floorcovering Equipment and Supplies) [9773]
Central States Electronics (Communications Systems and Equipment) [5558]
Crystal Refrigeration Inc. (Heating and Cooling Equipment and Supplies) [14408]
Deco Tool Supply Co. (Industrial Machinery) [15937]
Kambach & Kettman Inc. (Shoes) [24781]
Midwest Metals Inc. (Metals) [20191]
Peterson Paper Co. (Paper and Paper Products) [21880]
The Republic Companies (Electrical and Electronic Equipment and Supplies) [9278]
Rich Metals Co. (Used, Scrap, and Recycled Materials) [26958]
Samuels Jewelers (Jewelry) [17586]
TEC Industrial (Industrial Machinery) [16553]
Thinker's Press (Books and Other Printed Materials) [4216]
Upper Mississippi Valley Mercantile Co. (Toys and Hobby Goods) [26702]

Dayton

Farmers Cooperative (Agricultural Equipment and Supplies) [569]

De Witt

C and J Service Co. (Petroleum, Fuels, and Related Equipment) [22100]

Denver

Do-It Corp. (Recreational and Sporting Goods) [23627]

Des Moines

Adventure Lighting Supply Ltd. (Electrical and Electronic Equipment and Supplies) [8276]
Agri Grain Marketing (Livestock and Farm Products) [17684]
Aluminum Distributors Inc. (Construction Materials and Machinery) [6950]
Anderson Erickson Dairy Co. (Food) [10413]
Anderson News Co. (Books and Other Printed Materials) [3515]
Barton Solvents Inc. (Chemicals) [4335]
Beckman Brothers Inc. (Plumbing Materials and Fixtures) [23080]
Bolton and Hay Inc. (Restaurant and Commercial Foodservice Equipment and Supplies) [24081]
Briggs Corp. (Medical, Dental, and Optical Supplies) [19199]
Brown Co.; Herman M. (Construction Materials and Machinery) [7085]
Central Distributors Inc. (Floorcovering Equipment and Supplies) [9783]
Central States/Multiplex Business Forms (Books and Other Printed Materials) [3623]
Central Tractor Farm & Country, Inc. (Agricultural Equipment and Supplies) [400]

Component Technology (Industrial
  Machinery) [15904]
Computer Support Systems Inc. (Electrical and
  Electronic Equipment and Supplies) [8557]
CVK Corp. (Medical, Dental, and Optical
  Supplies) [19268]
Des Moines Marketing Associates (Food) [10947]
Doughten Films, Inc.; Russ (Sound and
  Entertainment Equipment and Supplies) [25168]
Electrical Engineering and Equipment Co. (Electrical
  and Electronic Equipment and Supplies) [8677]
Farmers Grain Dealers Inc. (Livestock and Farm
  Products) [17897]
Ford and Garland Inc. (Sound and Entertainment
  Equipment and Supplies) [25195]
Gifford-Brown Inc. (Sound and Entertainment
  Equipment and Supplies) [25211]
Globe Machinery and Supply Co. (Industrial
  Supplies) [16897]
Globe Machinery and Supply Co. (Industrial
  Machinery) [16069]
Herregan Distributors Inc. (Floorcovering Equipment
  and Supplies) [9943]
Hockenberg Equipment Co. (Restaurant and
  Commercial Foodservice Equipment and
  Supplies) [24138]
Hopkins Sporting Goods Inc. (Recreational and
  Sporting Goods) [23729]
Imaging Technologies (Office Equipment and
  Supplies) [21053]
Ingram International Films (Sound and
  Entertainment Equipment and Supplies) [25249]
Inland Truck Parts (Automotive) [2780]
Iowa Export Import Trading Co. (Agricultural
  Equipment and Supplies) [867]
Iowa Machinery and Supply Company
  Inc. (Industrial Machinery) [16173]
Iowa Paint Manufacturing Company Inc. (Paints
  and Varnishes) [21466]
Lehman's Commercial Service (Heating and Cooling
  Equipment and Supplies) [14521]
Lomar Foods (Food) [11724]
Maxcare International Inc. (Medical, Dental, and
  Optical Supplies) [19426]
Mid-State Distributing (Electrical and Electronic
  Equipment and Supplies) [9077]
Midwest Tile (Floorcovering Equipment and
  Supplies) [10035]
Miller Mechanical Specialties (Scientific and
  Measurement Devices) [24397]
Paper Corp. (Paper and Paper Products) [21860]
Paper Stock of Iowa (Paper and Paper
  Products) [21866]
Plumb Supply Co. (Plumbing Materials and
  Fixtures) [23319]
Pomerantz Diversified Services Inc. (Paper and
  Paper Products) [21887]
Power & Telephone Supply Company
  Inc. (Communications Systems and
  Equipment) [5714]
Precision Bearing Co. (Automotive) [3114]
Prime Alliance Inc. (Plastics) [23018]
Qualis Inc. (Medical, Dental, and Optical
  Supplies) [19562]
Roberts and Dybdahl Inc. (Construction Materials
  and Machinery) [7941]
Russ Doughten Films Inc. (Household
  Appliances) [15298]
Sandler Medical Services (Medical, Dental, and
  Optical Equipment) [19033]
Shelter Super Store Corp. (Wood and Wood
  Products) [27376]
Summertime Potato Co. (Food) [12601]
Super Valu Stores Inc. (Food) [12632]
Tesdell Refrigeration Supply Inc. (Heating and
  Cooling Equipment and Supplies) [14720]
United Services Association (Agricultural Equipment
  and Supplies) [1381]
Wahl and Wahl of Iowa Inc. (Office Equipment and
  Supplies) [21342]

Dewar
Dewar Elevator Co. (Agricultural Equipment and
  Supplies) [517]

Dike
Farmers Cooperative Co. (Dike, Iowa) (Livestock
  and Farm Products) [17854]

Dixon
Clarenie Cooperative Elevator Co. (Agricultural
  Equipment and Supplies) [420]

Donnellson
Donnellson Implement Inc. (Agricultural Equipment
  and Supplies) [524]

Dows
Farmers Cooperative Co. (Livestock and Farm
  Products) [17852]
Farmers Cooperative Co. (Food) [11094]

Dubuque
Ambraco Inc. (Industrial Supplies) [16693]
FDL Marketing Inc. (Food) [11110]
Iowa Oil Co. (Petroleum, Fuels, and Related
  Equipment) [22378]
McDonald Supply Company Inc.; A.Y. (Plumbing
  Materials and Fixtures) [23257]
Molo Oil Co. (Petroleum, Fuels, and Related
  Equipment) [22491]
Mulgrew Oil Co. (Petroleum, Fuels, and Related
  Equipment) [22501]
Roeder Implement Inc. (Agricultural Equipment and
  Supplies) [1209]
Spahn and Rose Lumber Co. (Construction
  Materials and Machinery) [8057]
Theisen Farm and Home Stores (Agricultural
  Equipment and Supplies) [1326]
Vallet Food Service Inc. (Food) [12815]

Dunkerton
Hauptly Construction and Equipment Company
  Inc. (Construction Materials and
  Machinery) [7455]

Dyersville
Evers Toy Store Inc. (Toys and Hobby
  Goods) [26480]
New Energy Distributing (Heating and Cooling
  Equipment and Supplies) [14618]
New Energy Distributors (Plumbing Materials and
  Fixtures) [23289]

Dysart
Tama-Benton Cooperative Co. (Livestock and Farm
  Products) [18275]

Earlville
Three Rivers FS Co. (Agricultural Equipment and
  Supplies) [1332]

Edgewood
Edgewood Oil Inc. (Petroleum, Fuels, and Related
  Equipment) [22224]

Eldora
United Suppliers Inc. (Agricultural Equipment and
  Supplies) [1384]

Eldridge
Eldridge Cooperative Co. (Livestock and Farm
  Products) [17830]

Ellsworth
Ellsworth-William Cooperative Co. (Livestock and
  Farm Products) [17831]

Elma
Howard County Equity Cooperative Inc. (Agricultural
  Equipment and Supplies) [841]

Ely
Krob and Co.; F.J. (Agricultural Equipment and
  Supplies) [920]

Emmetsburg
Kerber Milling Co. (Agricultural Equipment and
  Supplies) [908]

Everly
Farmers Cooperative Elevator Co. (Everly,
  Iowa) (Livestock and Farm Products) [17869]

Fairfield
Angel Gifts and Noah's Art (Gifts and
  Novelties) [13304]
Central States Airgas Inc. (Industrial
  Supplies) [16788]
Fairfield Line Inc. (Clothing) [4944]
Softcell Inc. (Computers and Software) [6736]

Farnhamville
Farmers Cooperative Co. (Agricultural Equipment
  and Supplies) [603]

Forest City
Farmers Cooperative Association (Agricultural
  Equipment and Supplies) [581]

Ft. Dodge
Electrical Materials Co. (Plumbing Materials and
  Fixtures) [23146]
Fort Dodge Machine Supply Company
  Inc. (Industrial Machinery) [16031]
Mid-America Power Drives (Industrial
  Supplies) [17035]
NEW Cooperative Inc. (Livestock and Farm
  Products) [18130]
Pederson-Sells Equipment (Industrial
  Machinery) [16389]

Ft. Madison
Progas Service Inc. (Petroleum, Fuels, and Related
  Equipment) [22595]

Garner
Farmers Cooperative Society (Agricultural
  Equipment and Supplies) [637]

Geneva
Geneva Elevator Co. (Agricultural Equipment and
  Supplies) [733]

George
Northwest Iowa Co-op (Agricultural Equipment and
  Supplies) [1087]
Northwest Iowa Cooperative (Agricultural Equipment
  and Supplies) [1088]

Gilmore City
Pro Cooperative (Agricultural Equipment and
  Supplies) [1155]

Glidden
Farmers Cooperative Co. (Agricultural Equipment
  and Supplies) [592]

Goldfield
Gold-Eagle Cooperative (Agricultural Equipment and
  Supplies) [744]

Gowrie
Consolidated Cooperative Inc. (Livestock and Farm
  Products) [17791]

Greenfield
Farmers Cooperative Co. (Livestock and Farm
  Products) [17853]

Grimes
Swimming Pool Supply Co. (Recreational and
  Sporting Goods) [24000]

Grundy Center
Farmers Cooperative Elevator Co. (Agricultural
  Equipment and Supplies) [617]

Hamburg
Good Seed and Grain Company Inc. (Livestock
  and Farm Products) [17947]

Hampton

North Central Farm Service Inc. (Livestock and Farm Products) [18138]

Harcourt

Harcourt Equipment (Agricultural Equipment and Supplies) [789]

Hardy

Hardy Cooperative Elevator Co. (Livestock and Farm Products) [17975]
Hardy Cooperative Elevator Co. (Food) [11378]

Harlan

Agriland F.S. Inc. (Agricultural Equipment and Supplies) [215]
Agriland F.S. Inc. (Petroleum, Fuels, and Related Equipment) [22027]
Farm Service Cooperative Inc. (Agricultural Equipment and Supplies) [565]
Variety Distributors Inc. (Household Items) [15695]
Variety Distributors Inc. (Office Equipment and Supplies) [21336]
Wilson Seeds Inc. (Livestock and Farm Products) [18354]

Haverhill

Haverhill Cooperative (Livestock and Farm Products) [17984]

Hiawatha

Moss Enterprises Inc. (Computers and Software) [6529]

Hinton

Farmers Cooperative Co. (Hinton, Iowa) (Livestock and Farm Products) [17855]

Hornick

Western Iowa Cooperative (Livestock and Farm Products) [18340]

Hospers

Midwest Farmers Cooperative (Agricultural Equipment and Supplies) [1037]
Midwest Farmers Cooperative (Food) [11889]

Houghton

Chem Gro of Houghton Inc. (Agricultural Equipment and Supplies) [408]

Hubbard

Hubbard Implement Inc. (Chemicals) [4421]
Prairie Land Cooperative Co. (Agricultural Equipment and Supplies) [1146]

Hudson

East Central Iowa Cooperative (Food) [11016]

Hull

Foreign Candy Company Inc. (Food) [11186]
Hull Cooperative Association (Food) [11475]

Ida Grove

Hi-Way Products Inc. (Metals) [20035]
Hultgren Implement Inc. (Agricultural Equipment and Supplies) [844]

Independence

Wapsie Valley Creamery Inc. (Food) [12875]

Indianola

Midwest Labs, Inc. (Medical, Dental, and Optical Supplies) [19459]
Sermel Inc. (Medical, Dental, and Optical Supplies) [19604]

Inwood

West Lyon Cooperative Inc. (Livestock and Farm Products) [18337]

Iowa City

Balloon House (Toys and Hobby Goods) [26408]
Blooming Prairie Cooperative Warehouse (Food) [10570]
Eble Music Co. (Books and Other Printed Materials) [3712]
Forbes Implement Supply Inc.; Keith (Agricultural Equipment and Supplies) [697]
Penfield Press (Books and Other Printed Materials) [4050]
Wilson Wholesale Sporting Goods; John (Recreational and Sporting Goods) [24047]

Iowa Falls

Campbell Supply Co. (Industrial Supplies) [16777]
Iowa Veterinary Supply Co. (Veterinary Products) [27158]
Iowa Veterinary Supply Co. (Agricultural Equipment and Supplies) [869]
Plastic Recycling of Iowa Falls, Inc. (Used, Scrap, and Recycled Materials) [26940]
Riverside Book and Bible House (Books and Other Printed Materials) [4119]
Riverside Distributors (Books and Other Printed Materials) [4120]

Ireton

Farmers Cooperative Elevator Co. (Buffalo Lake, Minnesota) (Food) [11099]

Jewell

Central Iowa Cooperative (Agricultural Equipment and Supplies) [396]

Johnston

Johnston Distributing Co. (Automotive) [2827]

Joice

Top of Iowa Coop (Livestock and Farm Products) [18285]

Kalona

Farmers Supply Sales Inc. (Agricultural Equipment and Supplies) [659]

Kellogg

Central Counties Cooperative (Agricultural Equipment and Supplies) [388]

Kingsley

Farmers Elevator Co. (Agricultural Equipment and Supplies) [642]

Klemme

Klemme Cooperative Grain Co. (Agricultural Equipment and Supplies) [914]

La Motte

Huss Implement Co. (Agricultural Equipment and Supplies) [848]

Lacona

South Central Co-op (Agricultural Equipment and Supplies) [1275]

Lake City

Bowie Manufacturing Inc. (Veterinary Products) [27090]

Lake Mills

Northern Coop Services (Lake Mills, Iowa) (Petroleum, Fuels, and Related Equipment) [22526]

Lake Park

Farmers Exchange Cooperative (Agricultural Equipment and Supplies) [649]

Lamoni

Farmers Cooperative Grain and Seed Co. (Agricultural Equipment and Supplies) [630]

Lansing

Allamakee Implement Co. (Agricultural Equipment and Supplies) [221]
Lansing Company Inc. (Textiles and Notions) [26120]

Laurens

Farmers Cooperative Association (Agricultural Equipment and Supplies) [585]

Lawton

Allied Order Buyers, Inc. (Livestock and Farm Products) [17693]

Le Mars

Harker's Distribution Inc. (Food) [11379]
Meis Seed and Feed Co. (Agricultural Equipment and Supplies) [1013]

Lime Springs

A & K Feed and Grain Company Inc. (Livestock and Farm Products) [17670]

Long Grove

Pro-Chem Ltd. Inc. (Medical, Dental, and Optical Equipment) [18997]

Lost Nation

Farmers Cooperative Co. (Agricultural Equipment and Supplies) [598]
Tri-County Co-op (Agricultural Equipment and Supplies) [1352]

Manly

Farmers Cooperative Co. (Agricultural Equipment and Supplies) [589]

Manning

Puck Implement Co. (Agricultural Equipment and Supplies) [1160]

Manson

Farmers Cooperative Co. (Livestock and Farm Products) [17849]

Mapleton

Mapleton Grain Co. (Livestock and Farm Products) [18074]

Marble Rock

Farmers Cooperative Elevator Co. (Agricultural Equipment and Supplies) [618]

Marcus

Sand Seed Service Inc. (Agricultural Equipment and Supplies) [1235]

Marion

Aeon International Corp. (Agricultural Equipment and Supplies) [190]
Linn Cooperative Oil Co. (Petroleum, Fuels, and Related Equipment) [22434]
Marion Iron Co. (Used, Scrap, and Recycled Materials) [26897]
Waffle Book Co.; O.G. (Books and Other Printed Materials) [4265]

Marshalltown

Gazaway & Associates; Jerry (Recreational and Sporting Goods) [23686]
Marshalltown Trowel Co. (Construction Materials and Machinery) [7650]

Martelle

Farmers Cooperative Elevator (Martelle, Iowa) (Livestock and Farm Products) [17870]

Mason City

Allied Purchasing (Industrial Supplies) [16687]
Dimensional Graphics Corp. Risto Division (Luggage and Leather Goods) [18388]
Key Wholesale Building Products Inc. (Construction Materials and Machinery) [7550]
North Iowa Cooperative Elevator (Agricultural Equipment and Supplies) [1081]
Schukei Chevrolet Inc. (Automotive) [3197]

Maynard
Maynard Cooperative Co. (Livestock and Farm Products) [18076]
Neowa F.S. Inc. (Livestock and Farm Products) [18129]

Mitchellville
Mitchellville Cooperative (Agricultural Equipment and Supplies) [1043]

Mondamin
Farmers Cooperative Co. (Agricultural Equipment and Supplies) [599]
Farmers Cooperative Co. (Food) [11093]

Montezuma
Brownells Inc. (Guns and Weapons) [13477]

Monticello
Monticello Sports Inc. (Recreational and Sporting Goods) [23834]

MoscoW
West Liberty Oil Co. (Petroleum, Fuels, and Related Equipment) [22792]

Mt. Pleasant
Hassenfritz Equipment Co.; Tom (Agricultural Equipment and Supplies) [799]
Hassenfritz Equipment Co.; Tom (Agricultural Equipment and Supplies) [800]
Heatilator Inc. (Construction Materials and Machinery) [7466]

Mt. Union
Mt. Union Cooperative Elevator (Livestock and Farm Products) [18121]
Mt. Union Cooperative Elevator (Food) [11943]

Muscatine
Grain Processing Corp. (Agricultural Equipment and Supplies) [753]

Nevada
Cabin Crafters (Wood and Wood Products) [27291]

New Hampton
Ag-Land Inc. (Agricultural Equipment and Supplies) [195]
Cedar Valley FS Inc. (Agricultural Equipment and Supplies) [381]
Farmers Cooperative Association (Agricultural Equipment and Supplies) [576]
Pacasa (Clothing) [5262]

New Providence
Lawn Hill Cooperative (Agricultural Equipment and Supplies) [945]

New Sharon
Taintor Cooperative Co. (Livestock and Farm Products) [18274]

Newton
Maytag Corp. (Household Appliances) [15221]
The Newton Group, Inc. (Medical, Dental, and Optical Supplies) [19493]
The Newton Group, Inc. - Newton Lab (Medical, Dental, and Optical Supplies) [19494]
Newton Manufacturing Co. (Gifts and Novelties) [13411]

North Liberty
New Horizons FS Inc. (Petroleum, Fuels, and Related Equipment) [22510]
Prybil Enterprises (Heating and Cooling Equipment and Supplies) [14645]

Northwood
Northwood Cooperative Elevator (Livestock and Farm Products) [18146]
Northwood Equipment Inc. (Agricultural Equipment and Supplies) [1091]

Northwood Meats Inc. (Food) [12039]

Norway
Frontier Co-op Herbs (Food) [11220]

Oakville
Oakville Feed and Grain Inc. (Agricultural Equipment and Supplies) [1096]

Ocheyedan
Ocheyedan Cooperative Elevator Association (Livestock and Farm Products) [18148]

Odebolt
Farmers Cooperative (Odebolt, Iowa) (Livestock and Farm Products) [17876]

Osage
Cooperative Oil Co. (Petroleum, Fuels, and Related Equipment) [22169]
Fox River Mills, Inc. (Clothing) [4966]
Osage Cooperative Elevator (Agricultural Equipment and Supplies) [1110]
Osage Cooperative Elevator (Food) [12079]

Osceola
Boyt Harness Co./Bob Allen Sportswear (Clothing) [4839]

Oskaloosa
Mahaska Farm Service Co. (Livestock and Farm Products) [18073]

Ossian
Union Produce Cooperative (Agricultural Equipment and Supplies) [1373]

Otley
Farmers Cooperative Exchange (Agricultural Equipment and Supplies) [625]

Ottumwa
Midwest Athlete (Clothing) [5194]

Packwood
Dickey Oil Corp. (Petroleum, Fuels, and Related Equipment) [22200]

Panora
Panorama Casual (Clothing) [5267]

Paullina
Farmers Cooperative Co. (Agricultural Equipment and Supplies) [595]

Pella
Farmers Cooperative Exchange (Agricultural Equipment and Supplies) [623]
Farmers Cooperative Exchange (Food) [11100]
Heritage Lace Inc. (Household Items) [15527]

Perry
Mark Seed Co. (Agricultural Equipment and Supplies) [986]

Pilot Grove
Nichting Company Inc.; J.J. (Agricultural Equipment and Supplies) [1075]

Pocahontas
Farmers Cooperative Co. (Livestock and Farm Products) [17851]

Postville
Postville Farmers Cooperative (Agricultural Equipment and Supplies) [1142]

Preston
Kunau Implement Co. (Agricultural Equipment and Supplies) [922]

Radcliffe
Farmers Cooperative Elevator Co. (Agricultural Equipment and Supplies) [615]

Rake
Farmers Cooperative Elevator Co. (Agricultural Equipment and Supplies) [619]

Ralston
West Central Cooperative (Livestock and Farm Products) [18336]

Readlyn
Farmers Cooperative Co. (Agricultural Equipment and Supplies) [601]
Farmers Cooperative Co. (Readlyn, Iowa) (Livestock and Farm Products) [17857]

Red Oak
United Farmers Mercantile Cooperative (Livestock and Farm Products) [18303]

Remsen
Farmers Cooperative Co. (Agricultural Equipment and Supplies) [600]

Ringsted
Cooperative Grain and Product Co. (Agricultural Equipment and Supplies) [455]

Rippey
Rippey Farmers Cooperative (Agricultural Equipment and Supplies) [1195]

Rock Rapids
Sturdevant Auto Supply (Automotive) [3278]

Rock Valley
Farmers Elevator Co. (Livestock and Farm Products) [17881]

Rockford
Farmers Cooperative Exchange (Agricultural Equipment and Supplies) [627]

Rockwell
Burchinal Cooperative Society (Agricultural Equipment and Supplies) [352]

Roland
Heart of Iowa Coop. (Food) [11404]
Heart of Iowa Cooperative (Agricultural Equipment and Supplies) [805]

Rudd
Farmers Cooperative Co. (Agricultural Equipment and Supplies) [596]

Ruthven
Farmers Cooperative Elevator Co. (Agricultural Equipment and Supplies) [614]

Ryan
Ryan Cooperative Inc. (Agricultural Equipment and Supplies) [1221]

St. Ansgar
St. Angsar Mills Inc. (Livestock and Farm Products) [18218]
St. Angsar Mills Inc. (Food) [12388]

Sanborn
Sanborn Cooperative Grain Co. (Agricultural Equipment and Supplies) [1233]

Scranton
Farmers Elevator Cooperative (Agricultural Equipment and Supplies) [645]

Searsboro
Golden Sun Feeds Inc. Danville Div. (Agricultural Equipment and Supplies) [746]

Sheldon

Farmers Cooperative Elevator Association (Agricultural Equipment and Supplies) [611]
Farmers Cooperative Elevator Association (Food) [11098]
Siouxland Ophthalmics Lab Inc. (Medical, Dental, and Optical Supplies) [19615]

Sioux Center

Cooperative Gas and Oil Company Inc. (Petroleum, Fuels, and Related Equipment) [22167]
Farmers Cooperative Society (Sioux Center, Iowa) (Livestock and Farm Products) [17878]
Sioux Preme Packing Co. (Food) [12498]

Sioux City

Allied Order Buyers, Inc. (Livestock and Farm Products) [17694]
AVH Inc. (Clothing) [4792]
Bennett Vending (Food) [10536]
Crescent Electric Supply Co. (Electrical and Electronic Equipment and Supplies) [8588]
Dennis Supply Co. (Heating and Cooling Equipment and Supplies) [14416]
Farner Bocken Co. (Food) [11107]
Hawkeye Building Supply Co. (Construction Materials and Machinery) [7458]
Metz Baking Co. (Food) [11864]
Midwest Electric Inc. (Household Appliances) [15231]
Novelty Machine and Supply Company Inc. (Industrial Supplies) [17083]
Office Systems Co. (Office Equipment and Supplies) [21190]
Palmer Candy Co. (Food) [12100]
Perkins Stationery (Office Equipment and Supplies) [21209]
Rogers Electric Supply Co. (Electrical and Electronic Equipment and Supplies) [9311]
Sioux Honey Association (Food) [12497]
Sportsmans Inc. (Recreational and Sporting Goods) [23981]
Terra Industries Inc. (Agricultural Equipment and Supplies) [1320]
Terra International Inc. (Agricultural Equipment and Supplies) [1321]
Western States Manufacturing Company, Inc. (Automotive) [3412]

Spencer

Arnold Motor Supply Co. (Automotive) [2252]
C-D Farm Service Company Inc. (Agricultural Equipment and Supplies) [354]
Merrill Co. (Automotive) [2944]

Spirit Lake

Progressive Companies Inc. (Food) [12229]
TET Incorporated (Clothing) [5427]

Stacyville

Stacyville Cooperative Co. (Agricultural Equipment and Supplies) [1291]
Stacyville Cooperative Creamery Association (Food) [12561]

Stanton

United Farmers Cooperative Inc. (Agricultural Equipment and Supplies) [1378]

Stockton

Farmers Cooperative Elevator (Agricultural Equipment and Supplies) [607]

Storm Lake

Iowa Office Supplies Inc. (Office Equipment and Supplies) [21069]
Iowa Office Supply Inc. (Office Equipment and Supplies) [21070]

Stratford

Stratford Grain and Supply Cooperative (Livestock and Farm Products) [18262]

Sully

Sully Cooperative Exchange Inc. (Livestock and Farm Products) [18268]

Superior

Superior Cooperative Elevator Co. (Livestock and Farm Products) [18270]

Sutherland

Sutherland Farmers Cooperative (Agricultural Equipment and Supplies) [1307]

Thompson

Farmers Cooperative Elevator (Agricultural Equipment and Supplies) [609]

Toledo

Iowa River Farm Service Inc. (Agricultural Equipment and Supplies) [868]

Urbandale

Glazer's of Iowa (Alcoholic Beverages) [1719]
Iowa Soybean Association (Livestock and Farm Products) [18013]
Super Valu Stores Inc. (Food) [12636]

Ventura

Farmers Cooperative Company Inc. (Agricultural Equipment and Supplies) [604]

Vinton

Farm Services Inc. (Agricultural Equipment and Supplies) [567]

Walcott

Scott and Muscatine's Service Co. (Livestock and Farm Products) [18226]

Wapello

Farmers Elevator and Exchange Inc. (Livestock and Farm Products) [17886]

Washington

Sitler's Electric Supply Inc. (Electrical and Electronic Equipment and Supplies) [9373]

Waterloo

Airgas-North Central (Industrial Supplies) [16681]
Industrial Steel and Machine Sales (Metals) [20058]
O'Neal Steel Inc. (Waterloo, Iowa) (Metals) [20253]
R & R CB Distributors Inc. (Sound and Entertainment Equipment and Supplies) [25400]
Standard Battery and Electric Co. (Automotive) [3259]
Standard Distributing Company Inc. (Waterloo, Iowa) (Alcoholic Beverages) [2047]
Waterloo Service Company Inc. (Petroleum, Fuels, and Related Equipment) [22785]
Winterbottom Supply Co. (Heating and Cooling Equipment and Supplies) [14769]

Waukee

Farmers Cooperative Elevator Co. (Agricultural Equipment and Supplies) [616]
Syrvet, Inc. (Medical, Dental, and Optical Equipment) [19067]

Waukon

Waukon Equity Cooperative (Agricultural Equipment and Supplies) [1418]

Waverly

Dorfman Auto Supply Inc. (Automotive) [2556]
Fredericksburg Farmers Cooperative (Agricultural Equipment and Supplies) [705]
Rada Manufacturing Co. (Household Items) [15628]

West Bend

West Bend Elevator Co. (Livestock and Farm Products) [18335]

West Burlington

Alter Scrap Processing (Used, Scrap, and Recycled Materials) [26746]
Precision Industries (Industrial Machinery) [16422]
Wilbur-Ellis Co. (Chemicals) [4555]
WILFARM L.L.C. (Chemicals) [4556]

West Des Moines

American Media Inc. (Sound and Entertainment Equipment and Supplies) [25070]
Bonded Fibers and Quilting (Textiles and Notions) [25986]
Heartland Co-op (Agricultural Equipment and Supplies) [807]
Heddinger Brokerage Inc. (Food) [11405]
Wheeler Consolidated Inc. (Construction Materials and Machinery) [8217]

West Point

Merschman Inc. (Agricultural Equipment and Supplies) [1016]

West Union

H & H Foodservice (Food) [11349]

Whittemore

Whittemore Cooperative Elevator (Livestock and Farm Products) [18347]

Williamsburg

Holden's Foundation Seeds L.L.C. (Agricultural Equipment and Supplies) [832]

Winterset

Farmers Cooperative Elevator Co. (Agricultural Equipment and Supplies) [613]
Global Products (Toys and Hobby Goods) [26500]

Woolstock

Farmers Cooperative Co. (Agricultural Equipment and Supplies) [594]
Farmers Cooperative Co. (Woolstock, Iowa) (Livestock and Farm Products) [17858]

Kansas

Andale

Andale Farmers Cooperative Company Inc. (Livestock and Farm Products) [17699]

Andover

United Biomedical Inc. (Medical, Dental, and Optical Equipment) [19091]

Anthony

Anthony Farmers Cooperative and Elevator Co. (Livestock and Farm Products) [17702]

Argonia

Botkin Grain Co. Inc. (Veterinary Products) [27089]

Arlington

Cooperative Exchange (Agricultural Equipment and Supplies) [453]

Atchison

Atchison County Farmers Union Cooperative Association (Livestock and Farm Products) [17709]
Atchison Leather Products (Luggage and Leather Goods) [18372]
Blish-Mize Co. (Hardware) [13601]

Bartlett

Bartlett Cooperative Association Inc. (Agricultural Equipment and Supplies) [281]

Bazine

Cooperative Grain and Supply (Livestock and Farm Products) [17796]
Cooperative Grain and Supply (Food) [10835]

Beattie
Beattie Farmers Union Cooperative Association (Livestock and Farm Products) [17726]
Beattie Farmers Union Cooperative Association (Agricultural Equipment and Supplies) [288]

Beloit
Boettcher Enterprises Inc. (Agricultural Equipment and Supplies) [326]
Boettcher Supply Inc. (Electrical and Electronic Equipment and Supplies) [8450]
Farmway Cooperative Inc. (Agricultural Equipment and Supplies) [672]

Bird City
Four Circle Cooperative (Livestock and Farm Products) [17920]

Bonner Springs
Coleman Equipment Inc. (Construction Materials and Machinery) [7194]

Bremen
Herkimer Cooperative Business Association (Livestock and Farm Products) [17993]

Brewster
Farmers Cooperative Association (Livestock and Farm Products) [17841]

Bucklin
Bucklin Tractor and Implement (Agricultural Equipment and Supplies) [349]

Burdett
Farmers Cooperative Grain and Supply (Livestock and Farm Products) [17874]

Burlington
Caldwell Implement Co. Inc. (Agricultural Equipment and Supplies) [360]

Chanute
Hi Lo Table Manufacturing Inc. (Furniture and Fixtures) [13130]
Johnson Safari Museum; Martin and Osa (Jewelry) [17476]
Pioneer Music Company Inc. (Electrical and Electronic Equipment and Supplies) [9208]

Cheney
Cheney Cooperative Elevator Association (Agricultural Equipment and Supplies) [411]

Cimarron
Grain Growers Cooperative (Cimarron, Kansas) (Livestock and Farm Products) [17952]

Clearwater
Clearwater Grain Co. (Agricultural Equipment and Supplies) [424]

Colby
Co-HG (Agricultural Equipment and Supplies) [429]
High Plains Cooperative Association (Agricultural Equipment and Supplies) [821]
Service Oil Company Inc. (Petroleum, Fuels, and Related Equipment) [22662]

Columbus
Farmers Cooperative Association (Agricultural Equipment and Supplies) [583]

Concordia
F & A Food Sales Inc. (Food) [11067]

Conway Springs
Farmers Cooperative Grain Association (Agricultural Equipment and Supplies) [628]

Copeland
Sublette Cooperative, Inc. (Livestock and Farm Products) [18265]

Danville
Danville Cooperative Association (Agricultural Equipment and Supplies) [494]

Delphos
Delphos Co-Op Association Inc. (Livestock and Farm Products) [17816]

Derby
Rota Systems Inc. (Medical, Dental, and Optical Supplies) [19588]

Dighton
Farmers Co-op Elevator and Mercantile Association (Livestock and Farm Products) [17840]

Dodge City
Dodge City Cooperative Exchange Inc. (Automotive) [2554]
Dodge City Implement Inc. (Agricultural Equipment and Supplies) [520]

Downs
Pork Packers International (Food) [12196]

El Dorado
Triple S Ranch Supply (Livestock and Farm Products) [18294]

Elkhart
Elkhart Cooperative Equity Exchange (Food) [11040]

Ellis
Golden Belt Cooperative Association Inc. (Livestock and Farm Products) [17946]

Emporia
Bluestem Farm and Ranch Supply Inc. (Agricultural Equipment and Supplies) [324]
DeBauge Brothers Inc. (Alcoholic Beverages) [1638]
EVCO Wholesale Foods Co. (Food) [11061]

Ft. Scott
Extrusions Inc. (Metals) [19960]

Fowler
Fowler Equity Exchange Inc. (Livestock and Farm Products) [17923]
Fowler Equity Exchange Inc. (Food) [11196]

Fredonia
Fredonia Cooperative Association (Livestock and Farm Products) [17926]
Fredonia Cooperative Association (Food) [11202]

Garden City
Pueblo Chemical and Supply Co. (Chemicals) [4486]
Williams Investigation & SEC (Communications Systems and Equipment) [5815]

Garden Plain
Farmers Cooperative Elevator Co. (Livestock and Farm Products) [17868]

Gardner
Cramer Products, Inc. (Medical, Dental, and Optical Supplies) [19255]

Girard
Producers Cooperative Association of Girard (Livestock and Farm Products) [18180]

Goodland
Goodland Cooperative Equity Exchange Inc. (Livestock and Farm Products) [17950]

Great Bend
Doonan Truck and Equipment Inc. (Motorized Vehicles) [20624]
Great Bend Cooperative Association (Livestock and Farm Products) [17960]
Stanley Home Products (Health and Beauty Aids) [14245]

Greenleaf
Farmers Cooperative Elevator Association (Agricultural Equipment and Supplies) [610]

Grinnell
Cooperative Union Mercantile Co. Inc. (Agricultural Equipment and Supplies) [461]

Hays
Kansas Electric Supply Company Inc. (Electrical and Electronic Equipment and Supplies) [8928]
Midland Marketing Cooperative, Inc. (Livestock and Farm Products) [18096]
S & W Supply Company Inc. (Agricultural Equipment and Supplies) [1225]

Healy
Sharp Brothers Seed Co. (Agricultural Equipment and Supplies) [1261]

Hiawatha
Brown County Cooperative Association (Agricultural Equipment and Supplies) [340]
RHS Inc. (Agricultural Equipment and Supplies) [1186]
White Cloud Grain Co. (Agricultural Equipment and Supplies) [1438]

Hillsboro
Christian Destiny Inc. (Books and Other Printed Materials) [3636]
Cooperative Grain and Supply (Agricultural Equipment and Supplies) [456]
Cooperative Grain and Supply (Agricultural Equipment and Supplies) [457]

Hoisington
Kansas Brick and Tile Company Inc. (Construction Materials and Machinery) [7540]
Kansas Brick and Tile Company Inc. (Construction Materials and Machinery) [7541]

Holton
B-M-B Company Inc. (Agricultural Equipment and Supplies) [265]

Holyrood
Holyrood Cooperative Grain and Supply Co. (Livestock and Farm Products) [18003]

Hoxie
Hoxie Implement Company Inc. (Agricultural Equipment and Supplies) [842]

Hudson
Stafford County Flour Mills Co. (Chemicals) [4521]

Hutchinson
Colladay Hardware Co. (Plumbing Materials and Fixtures) [23119]
Collingwood Grain Inc. (Agricultural Equipment and Supplies) [435]
Electrex Inc. (Electrical and Electronic Equipment and Supplies) [8659]
Hutchinson Health Care Services (Medical, Dental, and Optical Equipment) [18847]
Jarvis Supply Co. (Automotive) [2812]
Kansas Oxygen Inc. (Industrial Supplies) [16979]
Shears Construction L.P. (Construction Materials and Machinery) [8007]

Inman
Future Pro Inc. (Recreational and Sporting Goods) [23681]

Iola

F & S Supply Company Inc. (Electrical and Electronic Equipment and Supplies) [8728]

Iuka

Iuka Cooperative Inc. (Livestock and Farm Products) [18015]

Johnson

Johnson Cooperative Grain Co. (Agricultural Equipment and Supplies) [888]

Junction City

Junction City Distributing Company Inc. (Alcoholic Beverages) [1792]

Kanorado

Kanorado Cooperative Association (Livestock and Farm Products) [18027]

Kansas City

All Systems Inc. (Electrical and Electronic Equipment and Supplies) [8297]
Amtron Corp. (Computers and Software) [5939]
Arrow-Cold Control Appliance Parts Co. (Household Appliances) [15035]
Arrow Speed Warehouse (Automotive) [2255]
Ashland Chemical Co. Industrial Chemicals and Solvents Div. (Chemicals) [4327]
Associated Wholesale Grocers Inc. (Food) [10457]
Blackman Industries (Veterinary Products) [27084]
Burke Inc. (Medical, Dental, and Optical Equipment) [18722]
Century Labs Inc. (Chemicals) [4347]
D & H Tire Service (Automotive) [2520]
Dugan Equipment & Supply Co. (Heating and Cooling Equipment and Supplies) [14423]
Earp Meat Company Inc. (Food) [11012]
Fleming Co.; T.J. (Industrial Supplies) [16866]
Fresh Advantage (Food) [11205]
House of Rock Inc. (Agricultural Equipment and Supplies) [839]
Kansas City Salad Company Inc. (Food) [11581]
Kansas City Winnelson Co. (Plumbing Materials and Fixtures) [23227]
Kaw River Shredding Inc. (Metals) [20090]
Kornfeld-Thorp Electric Co. (Electrical and Electronic Equipment and Supplies) [8957]
Lady Baltimore Foods Inc. (Food) [11665]
Lawrence Photo-Graphic Inc. (Photographic Equipment and Supplies) [22872]
Leisure-Lift, Inc. (Medical, Dental, and Optical Equipment) [18888]
Leisure-Lift Inc. (Medical, Dental, and Optical Supplies) [19408]
Mickeys Sales Co. (Recreational and Sporting Goods) [23825]
Midwest Distributors (Books and Other Printed Materials) [3958]
Miller Safety Products (Shoes) [24812]
Miller Safety Products (Clothing) [5195]
National Compressed Steel Corp. (Metals) [20218]
Rew Material Inc. (Construction Materials and Machinery) [7923]
Rieke Equipment Co. Inc.; Ernie (Construction Materials and Machinery) [7932]
Sinclair Oil Corp. Eastern Region (Petroleum, Fuels, and Related Equipment) [22674]
Strasser Hardware Co.; A.L. (Hardware) [13940]
Van Keppel Co.; G.W. (Construction Materials and Machinery) [8171]

Kensington

Kensington Cooperative Association (Agricultural Equipment and Supplies) [906]

Larned

Pyramid Agri-Products International (Livestock and Farm Products) [18184]

Lawrence

Advanced Specialties (Food) [10329]
Heetco Inc. Kansas Div. (Petroleum, Fuels, and Related Equipment) [22343]
Hillcrest Foods Inc. (Food) [11433]

University Press of Kansas (Books and Other Printed Materials) [4249]

Le Roy

Le Roy Cooperative Association Inc. (Livestock and Farm Products) [18049]

Leavenworth

Chem-Tronics Inc. (Medical, Dental, and Optical Equipment) [18738]
Leavenworth Paper Supply Co. (Paper and Paper Products) [21798]

Lenexa

American Camper (Recreational and Sporting Goods) [23508]
Bookmark, Inc. (Books and Other Printed Materials) [3578]
Brooks Manufacturing Co. (Clothing) [4850]
Dash Inc. (Computers and Software) [6181]
First Rep Associates (Sound and Entertainment Equipment and Supplies) [25191]
The Green Company, Inc. (Jewelry) [17441]
International Marketing Association Ltd. (Clothing) [5060]
Kansas Communications Inc. (Communications Systems and Equipment) [5656]
Kansas Communications Inc. (Electrical and Electronic Equipment and Supplies) [8927]
Langley Optical Company Inc. (Medical, Dental, and Optical Supplies) [19404]
Marshall Co.; John A. (Office Equipment and Supplies) [21129]
Midwest Lens (Medical, Dental, and Optical Supplies) [19460]
Motorola Inc. Communications and Electronics Div. (Communications Systems and Equipment) [5684]
Pioneer Industries Inc. (Clothing) [5277]
RC Sports Inc. (Recreational and Sporting Goods) [23907]
Reeves-Wiedeman Co. (Plumbing Materials and Fixtures) [23337]
Santa Fe Communications (Sound and Entertainment Equipment and Supplies) [25429]
SOR Inc. (Electrical and Electronic Equipment and Supplies) [9381]
South Central Pool Supply, Inc. (Recreational and Sporting Goods) [23958]
Superior Supply Co. (Heating and Cooling Equipment and Supplies) [14703]
Unimark Inc. (Electrical and Electronic Equipment and Supplies) [9520]
U.S. Safety Corp. (Medical, Dental, and Optical Supplies) [19682]
White Inc.; H. Lynn (Household Items) [15707]
Wilke International Inc. (Food) [12944]
Zeuschel Equipment Co. (Scientific and Measurement Devices) [24463]
Zink Safety Equipment (Security and Safety Equipment) [24663]

Liberal

Liberal Hull Co. (Petroleum, Fuels, and Related Equipment) [22430]
Nash Finch Co. (Food) [11972]

Lindsborg

Farmers Union Elevator Co. (Livestock and Farm Products) [17909]

Lorraine

Lorraine Grain Fuel and Stock Co. (Agricultural Equipment and Supplies) [970]

Manhattan

Farmers Cooperative Association (Agricultural Equipment and Supplies) [578]
Harrold Engineering Group (Agricultural Equipment and Supplies) [795]
Manhattan Wholesale Meat Company Inc. (Food) [11775]
Saroff & Company Inc.; Sam (Food) [12416]
Steel and Pipe Supply Co. (Metals) [20398]

Sunflower University Press (Books and Other Printed Materials) [4198]

Marysville

Pepsi-Cola Bottling Company of Marysville Inc. (Soft Drinks) [25009]
Valley Vet Supply (Veterinary Products) [27260]

McCune

McCune Farmers Union Cooperative Association (Agricultural Equipment and Supplies) [1001]

Meade

Cooperative Elevator Supply Co. (Agricultural Equipment and Supplies) [452]

Medicine Lodge

Finchers Findings Inc. (Clothing) [4952]

Minneola

Minneola Cooperative Inc. (Livestock and Farm Products) [18104]

Mission

American Industrial Tool Co. (Industrial Machinery) [15767]
Prairie Belle Clothing Exports (Clothing) [5286]
Rothenberg and Schloss Inc. (Health and Beauty Aids) [14224]

Montezuma

Montezuma Cooperative Exchange (Livestock and Farm Products) [18112]

Moundridge

Mid-Kansas Cooperative Association (Agricultural Equipment and Supplies) [1027]

Mullinville

Equity Grain and General Merchant Exchange (Livestock and Farm Products) [17836]

Ness City

Bondurant Grain Company Inc.; D.E. (Livestock and Farm Products) [17743]

New Century

Sprint North Supply (Communications Systems and Equipment) [5767]

Oakley

Cooperative Agricultural Services Inc. (Agricultural Equipment and Supplies) [448]

Olathe

Acme Brick Co. (Floorcovering Equipment and Supplies) [9644]
Adventure Group, Inc. (Floorcovering Equipment and Supplies) [9648]
Alexander & Townsend (Recreational and Sporting Goods) [23501]
All Star Pet Supply (Veterinary Products) [27061]
Boulevard Truck Sales and Service Inc. (Automotive) [2374]
Broadway Collection (Plumbing Materials and Fixtures) [23097]
Butler National Corp. (Food) [10649]
Continental Foods Corp. (Food) [10828]
Crawford Sales Co. (Alcoholic Beverages) [1622]
Industrial Fumigant Co. (Agricultural Equipment and Supplies) [856]
Inland Associates Inc. (Computers and Software) [6375]
Kansas City Aviation Center Inc. (Aeronautical Equipment and Supplies) [112]
Lister-Petter Inc. (Automotive) [2886]
Mid-Central/Sysco Food Services Inc. (Food) [11878]
Mission Lumber Co. (Construction Materials and Machinery) [7727]
Olathe Boot Co. (Shoes) [24826]
Williams Equipment Co. (Industrial Machinery) [16636]

Osborne
Kaser Implement Inc. (Agricultural Equipment and Supplies) [897]

Otis
Ochs Inc. (Agricultural Equipment and Supplies) [1097]

Ottawa
Ottawa Cooperative Association Inc. (Livestock and Farm Products) [18157]
Ottawa Cooperative Association Inc. (Agricultural Equipment and Supplies) [1112]

Overland Park
Agrex Inc. (Livestock and Farm Products) [17683]
Brookfield's Great Water Inc. (Soft Drinks) [24918]
Case Supply, Inc. (Floorcovering Equipment and Supplies) [9777]
Childers & Associates (Household Items) [15443]
Chocolate Specialty Corp. (Food) [10755]
Creative Merchandising Inc. (Gifts and Novelties) [13339]
Golden Boy Pies Inc. (Food) [11282]
Interstate Supply (Floorcovering Equipment and Supplies) [9969]
McCray Lumber Co. (Construction Materials and Machinery) [7677]
Relco Corp. (Automotive) [3143]
Reliable Automotive of Kansas Inc. (Automotive) [3144]
S & L Monograms and Embroidery (Clothing) [5327]
Sokkia Corp. (Construction Materials and Machinery) [8039]
TIE Systems Inc. (Communications Systems and Equipment) [5794]

Penalosa
Cairo Cooperative Equity Exchange (Agricultural Equipment and Supplies) [356]

Phillipsburg
Phillipsburg Cooperative Association (Petroleum, Fuels, and Related Equipment) [22581]

Piqua
Piqua Farmers Cooperative Association (Livestock and Farm Products) [18168]

Pittsburg
American Electric Co. (Electrical and Electronic Equipment and Supplies) [8339]
Assi Computers Inc. (Computers and Software) [5976]
Bottenfield's Inc. (Health and Beauty Aids) [14052]
Bowlus School Supply Inc. (Furniture and Fixtures) [13042]
Bowlus School Supply Inc. (Office Equipment and Supplies) [20852]
Monsour's Inc. (Food) [11926]
Striker Products (Clothing) [5400]

Plains
Plains Equity Exchange (Livestock and Farm Products) [18171]

Plainville
Farm Implement and Supply Company Inc. (Agricultural Equipment and Supplies) [562]

Pratt
Stanion Wholesale Electric Company Inc. (Electrical and Electronic Equipment and Supplies) [9407]

Protection
Protection Co-op Supply (Livestock and Farm Products) [18182]

Quinter
Midwest Coop. (Food) [11888]
Midwest Cooperative (Agricultural Equipment and Supplies) [1035]

Radium
Radium Cooperative Co. (Livestock and Farm Products) [18188]
Radium Cooperative Co. (Food) [12261]

Randall
Randall Farmers Cooperative Union (Livestock and Farm Products) [18189]

Robinson
Brown County Co-op (Agricultural Equipment and Supplies) [339]

Rolla
Rolla Cooperative Equity Exchange (Livestock and Farm Products) [18203]

Russell
Agco Inc. (Agricultural Equipment and Supplies) [204]
Agco Inc. (Food) [10344]

Sabetha
Wenger Manufacturing Inc. (Industrial Machinery) [16621]

St. Francis
Flash Fireworks (Toys and Hobby Goods) [26482]
St. Francis Mercantile Equity Exchange (Agricultural Equipment and Supplies) [1228]

Salina
Mid-America Appliance Center (Sound and Entertainment Equipment and Supplies) [25315]
Salina Supply Co. (Plumbing Materials and Fixtures) [23357]
Sellers Tractor Company Inc. (Agricultural Equipment and Supplies) [1258]
Sunflower Restaurant Supply (Food) [12611]
Sunflower Restaurant Supply Inc. (Food) [12612]
Wright Lorenz Grain Company Inc. (Livestock and Farm Products) [18361]

Satanta
Satanta Cooperative Grain (Livestock and Farm Products) [18222]

Scott City
Scott Cooperative Association (Agricultural Equipment and Supplies) [1240]

Seneca
Nemaha County Cooperative Association (Agricultural Equipment and Supplies) [1069]
Todd Tractor Company Inc. (Agricultural Equipment and Supplies) [1339]

Sharon Springs
Wallace County Cooperative Equity Exchange (Agricultural Equipment and Supplies) [1407]

Shawnee
Big A Auto Parts (Automotive) [2357]
General Parts, Inc. (Automotive) [2672]
K.R. International (Food) [11639]
Smith Inc.; Kenneth (Recreational and Sporting Goods) [23948]

Shawnee Mission
AgriPro Seeds Inc. (Livestock and Farm Products) [17687]
Balno Incorporated (Computers and Software) [5998]
Benben Sportswear (Clothing) [4816]
Consolidated Fuel Oil Co. Inc. (Petroleum, Fuels, and Related Equipment) [22160]
Dennis Refrigeration & Electric (Heating and Cooling Equipment and Supplies) [14415]
Gerson Company Inc. (Jewelry) [17430]
Heart of America Bolt (Hardware) [13750]
IBT Inc. (Industrial Machinery) [16136]
Incentive Associates Inc. (Household Items) [15539]

Inland Industries Inc. (Industrial Machinery) [16158]
Inland Newspaper Machinery Corp. (Industrial Machinery) [16159]
J & M Industries Inc. (Computers and Software) [6403]
J & M Sportswear Inc. (Clothing) [5071]
J & R Industries Inc. (Paints and Varnishes) [21468]
JWS Corp. (Computers and Software) [6414]
Kansas City Periodical Distributing Co. (Books and Other Printed Materials) [3874]
Long Motor Corp. (Automotive) [2890]
Manildra Milling Corp. (Food) [11776]
Maxima Electrical Sales Company Inc. (Electrical and Electronic Equipment and Supplies) [9048]
Peterson Machine Tool Co. (Industrial Machinery) [16393]
Rangel Distributing Co. (Communications Systems and Equipment) [5733]
Resource Net International (Paper and Paper Products) [21902]
SKC Communication Products Inc. (Electrical and Electronic Equipment and Supplies) [9375]
Special-T-Metals Company Inc. (Hardware) [13932]
Tech Inc. (Automotive) [3295]
Tonnies Company Inc.; David F. (Sound and Entertainment Equipment and Supplies) [25481]
Wood Products Inc.; Stanley (Sound and Entertainment Equipment and Supplies) [25528]

South Hutchinson
Kansas Propane (Petroleum, Fuels, and Related Equipment) [22396]

Spring Hill
Simmons Gun Specialty Inc. (Guns and Weapons) [13514]
Tri Star Seed Co. (Agricultural Equipment and Supplies) [1355]

Sterling
Farmers Cooperative Union (Agricultural Equipment and Supplies) [640]
United Industries Inc. (Recreational and Sporting Goods) [24021]

Stockton
Jones Oil Company Inc.; John E. (Petroleum, Fuels, and Related Equipment) [22391]

Syracuse
Syracuse Cooperative Exchange (Livestock and Farm Products) [18272]
Syracuse Cooperative Exchange (Food) [12666]

Topeka
Allied Floors, Inc. (Floorcovering Equipment and Supplies) [9660]
American Educational Services (Books and Other Printed Materials) [3500]
Associated Bearings (Industrial Machinery) [15782]
Builders Wholesale Supply Company, Inc. (Furniture and Fixtures) [13048]
Builders Wholesale Supply Company Inc. (Wood and Wood Products) [27290]
Capitol Concrete Products Co. (Construction Materials and Machinery) [7136]
Carroll Electronics Inc. (Electrical and Electronic Equipment and Supplies) [8505]
Conger Dental Supply Co. (Medical, Dental, and Optical Equipment) [18751]
Davis Co.; Kriz (Electrical and Electronic Equipment and Supplies) [8613]
Famous Brands Distributors Inc. (Alcoholic Beverages) [1683]
Hillmer's Luggage & Leather (Luggage and Leather Goods) [18397]
Hill's Pet Nutrition Inc. (Veterinary Products) [27149]
Katch and Company Inc.; M. (Metals) [20089]
Kaw Valley Company Inc. (Food) [11584]
Martin Tractor Company Inc. (Construction Materials and Machinery) [7656]
Palmer News Inc. (Books and Other Printed Materials) [4037]

Skinner Nursery Inc. (Horticultural Supplies) [14951]
Strathman Sales Company Inc. (Alcoholic Beverages) [2056]
Superior Supply Co. (Heating and Cooling Equipment and Supplies) [14704]
Team Sporting Goods Inc. (Recreational and Sporting Goods) [24006]
Veterinary Companies of America Inc. (Agricultural Equipment and Supplies) [1398]

Ulysses
Sullivan Inc. (Livestock and Farm Products) [18267]
Ulysses Cooperative Supply Co. (Livestock and Farm Products) [18297]

Walton
Farmers Grain Cooperative (Agricultural Equipment and Supplies) [655]

Waterville
Farmers Cooperative Grain Association (Agricultural Equipment and Supplies) [629]

Wathena
Wathena and Bendena Grain Company Inc. (Agricultural Equipment and Supplies) [1415]

Wellsville
Paul Company Inc. (Recreational and Sporting Goods) [23875]

Wichita
A-B Sales Inc. (Alcoholic Beverages) [1472]
Advanced Imaging Technologies Inc. (Medical, Dental, and Optical Equipment) [18660]
Airtechnics Inc. (Electrical and Electronic Equipment and Supplies) [8284]
Airtechnics Inc. (Electrical and Electronic Equipment and Supplies) [8285]
Allpro Corp. (Paints and Varnishes) [21379]
Associated Systems Inc. (Computers and Software) [5978]
Bagatelle (Food) [10488]
Berry Companies Inc. (Construction Materials and Machinery) [7051]
Berry Tractor and Equipment Co. (Agricultural Equipment and Supplies) [303]
Bevan-Rabell Inc. (Electrical and Electronic Equipment and Supplies) [8435]
Case Supply, Inc. (Floorcovering Equipment and Supplies) [9778]
Comfort Supply Inc. (Heating and Cooling Equipment and Supplies) [14395]
Cramer Co. Inc. (Household Appliances) [15097]
Decorator & Craft Corp. (Office Equipment and Supplies) [20953]
F and E Wholesale Food Service Inc. (Food) [11068]
Finn Distributing Co. Inc. (Household Items) [15497]
Foley Equipment Co. (Agricultural Equipment and Supplies) [696]
Foley Equipment Company Inc. (Construction Materials and Machinery) [7352]
Foley Holding Co. (Industrial Machinery) [16026]
Full Service Beverage Co. (Soft Drinks) [24956]
General Distributors Inc. (Floorcovering Equipment and Supplies) [9914]
Goldsmiths Inc. (Office Equipment and Supplies) [21016]
Goldsmiths Inc. (Furniture and Fixtures) [13125]
GT Sales and Manufacturing Inc. (Industrial Supplies) [16914]
Heirloom Bible Publications (Books and Other Printed Materials) [3822]
House of Schwan Inc. (Alcoholic Beverages) [1763]
Hub Tool and Supply Inc. (Industrial Machinery) [16118]
Industrial Uniform Company Inc. (Clothing) [5050]
Information Management Inc. (Computers and Software) [6369]
Inland Truck Parts (Automotive) [2781]

Investrade Import & Export (Industrial Machinery) [16170]
Kirby Company of Wichita (Specialty Equipment and Products) [25701]
Kleeko Enterprises (Heating and Cooling Equipment and Supplies) [14510]
KMS Inc. (Toys and Hobby Goods) [26554]
Latshaw Enterprises Inc. (Agricultural Equipment and Supplies) [941]
Liberty Distributors Inc. (Household Appliances) [15205]
Matrix Aviation Inc. (Aeronautical Equipment and Supplies) [120]
Mid-Continent Fire & Safety, Inc. (Security and Safety Equipment) [24591]
Midwest Plastics Supply Inc. (Plastics) [22998]
Misco Industries Inc. (Petroleum, Fuels, and Related Equipment) [22487]
Murdock Companies Inc. (Electrical and Electronic Equipment and Supplies) [9109]
Murdock Electric and Supply Co. (Industrial Supplies) [17063]
Norandex, Inc. (Construction Materials and Machinery) [7785]
O'Connor Company, Inc. (Heating and Cooling Equipment and Supplies) [14626]
Player Piano Company Inc. (Sound and Entertainment Equipment and Supplies) [25387]
Power Drive, Inc. (Automotive) [3107]
Price Brothers Equipment Co. (Agricultural Equipment and Supplies) [1148]
Raymond Oil Company Inc. (Petroleum, Fuels, and Related Equipment) [22609]
Rieger Medical Supply Co. (Medical, Dental, and Optical Equipment) [19022]
RSC Electronics Inc. (Electrical and Electronic Equipment and Supplies) [9322]
Schmid Motor Inc.; Don (Motorized Vehicles) [20720]
Self's, Inc. (Floorcovering Equipment and Supplies) [10142]
Sisco Equipment Rental and Sales Inc. (Industrial Machinery) [16495]
Southwest Paper Company Inc. (Paper and Paper Products) [21944]
Standard Beverage Corp. (Alcoholic Beverages) [2044]
Superior Supply Company Inc. (Heating and Cooling Equipment and Supplies) [14709]
Truck Parts and Equipment Inc. (Automotive) [3349]
Unirex Inc. (Aeronautical Equipment and Supplies) [164]
Unisource (Paper and Paper Products) [21964]
United Distributors Inc. (Specialty Equipment and Products) [25854]
U.S. Machinery, Inc. (Industrial Machinery) [16594]
Universal Companies Inc. (Wichita, Kansas) (Petroleum, Fuels, and Related Equipment) [22764]
Universal Lubricants Inc. (Petroleum, Fuels, and Related Equipment) [22765]
White Star Machinery and Supply Company Inc. (Construction Materials and Machinery) [8219]
Wichita Sheet Metal Supply Co. (Heating and Cooling Equipment and Supplies) [14766]
Yingling Aircraft Inc. (Aeronautical Equipment and Supplies) [178]

Winfield
Jarvis Supply Co. (Industrial Machinery) [16183]

Kentucky

Almo
Tate Jr.'s Murray Auto Auction Inc.; Jim (Motorized Vehicles) [20735]

Ashland
Addington Holdings Inc. (Used, Scrap, and Recycled Materials) [26730]
Ashland Electric Company Inc. (Electrical and Electronic Equipment and Supplies) [8383]

Ashland Electric Company Inc. (Electrical and Electronic Equipment and Supplies) [8384]

Barbourville
Advocate Publishing Co. (Office Equipment and Supplies) [20778]
G and M Oil Company Inc. (Petroleum, Fuels, and Related Equipment) [22299]

Bardstown
Design Craft (Horticultural Supplies) [14856]
Jideco of Bardstown Inc. (Automotive) [2820]
Nally & Haydon Inc. (Construction Materials and Machinery) [7761]

Bowling Green
Bowling Green Winlectric (Electrical and Electronic Equipment and Supplies) [8458]
Carpenter-Dent-Sublett No. 1 (Medical, Dental, and Optical Equipment) [18729]
Cherry & Son; A.W. (Livestock and Farm Products) [17776]
Contractors Floor Covering (Floorcovering Equipment and Supplies) [9826]
Country Oven Bakery (Food) [10857]
DESA International Inc. (Heating and Cooling Equipment and Supplies) [14417]
McGuirk Oil Company Inc. (Petroleum, Fuels, and Related Equipment) [22465]
Mid-America Airgas Inc. (Industrial Supplies) [17034]
Phillips Ice Service Inc. (Heating and Cooling Equipment and Supplies) [14635]
Powr-Lite Electric Supplies (Electrical and Electronic Equipment and Supplies) [9232]
Rainbow Sports (Recreational and Sporting Goods) [23903]
Smith Southside Feed and Grain Inc. (Livestock and Farm Products) [18237]
Southern Foods Inc. (Food) [12539]
Wholesale Electric Supply Company Inc. (Bowling Green, Kentucky) (Electrical and Electronic Equipment and Supplies) [9590]

Buckner
Creative Engineering and Manufacturing Corp. (Industrial Machinery) [15919]

Campbellsville
Flav-O-Rich Inc. (Food) [11141]
Wholesale Hardwood Interiors Inc. (Construction Materials and Machinery) [8223]

Caneyville
Bryant and Son Inc.; Otis (Agricultural Equipment and Supplies) [347]

Cecilia
Shoe Barn (Shoes) [24855]

Central City
Central City Produce Inc. (Food) [10719]

Clinton
Burgess Brothers Grain Inc. (Livestock and Farm Products) [17755]
Farmers Gin Company Inc. (Livestock and Farm Products) [17891]

Corbin
Bacon Creek Gun Shop (Recreational and Sporting Goods) [23534]

Covington
Corken Steel Products Co. (Heating and Cooling Equipment and Supplies) [14405]
Current Software (Computers and Software) [6171]
Gliers Meats Inc. (Food) [11271]
La Boiteaux Co. (Paper and Paper Products) [21795]
Mead Corp. Zellerbach Paper Co. (Paper and Paper Products) [21830]
Noyes and Son Inc.; J.C. (Food) [12042]
OUR Designs Inc. (Specialty Equipment and Products) [25778]

ResourceNet International (Shawnee Mission, Kansas) (Paper and Paper Products) [21904]
Sportmaster Inc. (Recreational and Sporting Goods) [23978]
Westside Development Inc. (Heating and Cooling Equipment and Supplies) [14762]

Crescent Springs

Blue Grass Quality Meats (Food) [10574]

Danville

Burkmann Feed (Veterinary Products) [27093]
Burkmann Mills (Veterinary Products) [27096]

East Bernstadt

Institutional Distributors Inc. (Food) [11512]

Elizabethtown

Action Sport & Apparel (Clothing) [4748]
Elizabethtown Distributing Co. Inc. (Automotive) [2581]
Kentucky Home Care Services, Inc. (Medical, Dental, and Optical Equipment) [18875]
Lubrichem Environmental Inc. (Petroleum, Fuels, and Related Equipment) [22441]
Sunhopper Inc. (Health and Beauty Aids) [14251]

Erlanger

Embroidery Services Inc. (Clothing) [4937]
Gary's Everfresh Products Inc. (Food) [11239]
Tate Builders Supply L.L.C. (Construction Materials and Machinery) [8099]
Xpedx (Paper and Paper Products) [22001]

Falmouth

Klee Wholesale Company, Inc. (Tobacco Products) [26319]

Florence

EDM Business Interiors Inc. (Office Equipment and Supplies) [20983]
Emerald International Corp. (Minerals and Ores) [20538]
Harper Distributing Company Inc. (Petroleum, Fuels, and Related Equipment) [22336]
Hill and Co., Inc.; Geo. W. (Agricultural Equipment and Supplies) [823]
Krauss-Maffei Corp. (Specialty Equipment and Products) [25706]
Ris Paper Company Inc. (Paper and Paper Products) [21906]
Thomson Corp. (Books and Other Printed Materials) [4217]
Willis Music Co. (Books and Other Printed Materials) [4287]
ZF Group NAO (Marine) [18645]

Frankfort

Frankfort Scrap Metal Company Inc. (Used, Scrap, and Recycled Materials) [26815]
Gnomon Press (Books and Other Printed Materials) [3783]

Franklin

Keystops Inc. (Petroleum, Fuels, and Related Equipment) [22402]

Glasgow

Burkmann Feeds—Glasgow (Veterinary Products) [27094]

Greenville

Wetterau Inc. (Food) [12919]

Harlan

Croushorn Equipment Company Inc. (Agricultural Equipment and Supplies) [478]
Kentucky Mine Supply Co. (Industrial Supplies) [16989]

Harold

Big Sandy Wholesale Co. (Food) [10556]

Harrodsburg

Freeman Tobacco Warehouse (Tobacco Products) [26297]

Hazard

Black Gold Sales Inc. (Minerals and Ores) [20523]
Home Lumber Company Inc. (Construction Materials and Machinery) [7481]

Henderson

Haasco Inc. (Industrial Supplies) [16918]
Home Oil and Gas Company Inc. (Petroleum, Fuels, and Related Equipment) [22360]
P.B. and S. Chemical Inc. (Chemicals) [4480]

Hopkinsville

Cayce Mill Supply Co. (Electrical and Electronic Equipment and Supplies) [8509]
Hopkinsville Elevator Co. (Food) [11460]
Hopkinsville Milling Company Inc. (Food) [11461]
Roeder Implement Company Inc. (Agricultural Equipment and Supplies) [1208]

Horse Cave

Farmers Investment Company Inc. (Minerals and Ores) [20540]

Independence

ALR Wholesale (Veterinary Products) [27062]

Jackson

Jackson Wholesale Co. (Food) [11544]
Saturn Satellite System, Inc. (Electrical and Electronic Equipment and Supplies) [9337]

Jeffersontown

Brandeis Machinery and Supply Corp. (Specialty Equipment and Products) [25582]

La Grange

Northland Corp. (Construction Materials and Machinery) [7798]

Lancaster

Garrard County Stockyard (Livestock and Farm Products) [17933]
Shoes To Boot Inc. (Shoes) [24859]

Leitchfield

Middleground Golf Inc. (Recreational and Sporting Goods) [23828]
Miller and Hartman South Inc. (Food) [11899]

Lexington

4th Street Tobacco Warehouse (Tobacco Products) [26255]
Addington Environmental Inc. (Used, Scrap, and Recycled Materials) [26729]
Air Technologies (Compressors) [5828]
Airgas (Industrial Machinery) [15746]
Baumann Paper Company Inc. (Paper and Paper Products) [21647]
Blue Grass Optical Co. (Medical, Dental, and Optical Supplies) [19194]
Book Wholesalers, Inc. (Books and Other Printed Materials) [3573]
Brock-McVey Co. (Heating and Cooling Equipment and Supplies) [14359]
C/C Chemical and Coal Co. (Minerals and Ores) [20525]
Central District Inc. (Tobacco Products) [26274]
Central Kentucky News Distributing Co. (Books and Other Printed Materials) [3621]
Chapmans Shoe Repair (Shoes) [24710]
City Electric Motor Co. (Electrical and Electronic Equipment and Supplies) [8527]
CK Associates (Household Items) [15445]
Clay Ingels Company Inc. (Construction Materials and Machinery) [7178]
D & K Wholesale Drug, Inc. (Medical, Dental, and Optical Supplies) [19270]
Dura Med Inc. (Medical, Dental, and Optical Equipment) [18780]
Dynamic Technology (Industrial Machinery) [15971]
Graybar Electric Company Inc. (Electrical and Electronic Equipment and Supplies) [8810]
Grogan's Healthcare Supply Inc. (Medical, Dental, and Optical Equipment) [18817]
Grogan's, Inc. (Medical, Dental, and Optical Supplies) [19343]
Hurst Office Suppliers Inc. (Office Equipment and Supplies) [21046]
Kentucky Bearings Service (Industrial Supplies) [16988]
Kentucky Buying Cooperative Int. (Agricultural Equipment and Supplies) [907]
Kentucky Buying Cooperative Int. (Medical, Dental, and Optical Supplies) [19395]
Kentucky Dental Supply Co. Inc. (Medical, Dental, and Optical Equipment) [18874]
King's Foodservice Inc. (Food) [11620]
Lexington Trotters and Breeders Association (Livestock and Farm Products) [18058]
Louisville Tile Distributors, Inc. (Floorcovering Equipment and Supplies) [9999]
Mees Distributors (Floorcovering Equipment and Supplies) [10020]
Perspectives (Paints and Varnishes) [21538]
Southwestern Tobacco Co. (Tobacco Products) [26351]
Utter Company Inc. (Heating and Cooling Equipment and Supplies) [14750]

Liberty

Watson Lumber Co. (Construction Materials and Machinery) [8197]

London

Burkmann Feeds—London (Veterinary Products) [27095]
Curry Oil Company Inc. (Petroleum, Fuels, and Related Equipment) [22183]
Laurel Grocery Company Inc. (Food) [11684]

Louisa

Brown Food Service (Food) [10625]

Louisville

A and A Mechanical Inc. (Industrial Machinery) [15720]
Air Systems Inc. (Compressors) [5827]
All Pro Championships Inc. (Clothing) [4759]
Allen Brown Industries Inc. (Textiles and Notions) [25955]
Allied Tools Inc. (Industrial Supplies) [16688]
American Printing House for the Blind, Inc. (Books and Other Printed Materials) [3503]
Animal Emergency Center (Veterinary Products) [27066]
Atlas Machine and Supply Inc. (Industrial Machinery) [15791]
Axton Candy and Tobacco Co. (Tobacco Products) [26262]
Balloon Express (Toys and Hobby Goods) [26407]
Bearings Incorporated of Kentucky (Industrial Supplies) [16740]
Bloemer Food Service Co. (Food) [10569]
Bluefin Seafoods Corp. (Food) [10582]
Booker-Price Co. (Furniture and Fixtures) [13041]
Booth Co.; George E. (Scientific and Measurement Devices) [24325]
Bosler Leather Co. Inc.; George (Clothing) [4836]
Bramco Inc. (Specialty Equipment and Products) [25581]
Bridges Smith & Co. (Paints and Varnishes) [21405]
Brown-Forman Beverage Div. (Alcoholic Beverages) [1554]
Business Office Supply Co. (Office Equipment and Supplies) [20868]
C-N Corrugated and Sheeting Inc. (Paper and Paper Products) [21663]
Calvert & Hoffman (Construction Materials and Machinery) [7129]
Cardinal Carryor Inc. (Industrial Machinery) [15873]
Cardinal Carryor Inc. (Industrial Machinery) [15874]
Cardinal Frozen Distributors Co. (Food) [10697]
Cardinal Ice Cream Corp. (Food) [10698]

Carrington Distributing Company Inc. (Automotive) [2431]

Central Office Supply Co. (Office Equipment and Supplies) [20892]

Choice Medical Distribution Inc. (Computers and Software) [6064]

Cissna's Sporting Goods Inc. (Recreational and Sporting Goods) [23595]

Computer Brokers of Kentucky (Computers and Software) [6102]

Consumers Choice Coffee Inc. (Food) [10820]

Copper Electronics (Computers and Software) [6159]

Crutcher Dental Inc. (Medical, Dental, and Optical Supplies) [19260]

Cummins Cumberland Inc. (Automotive) [2504]

Derby Fabrics, Inc. (Textiles and Notions) [26018]

Derby Industries Inc. (Household Appliances) [15110]

Dispensers Optical Service Corp. (Medical, Dental, and Optical Supplies) [19282]

Dynamic Technology (Industrial Machinery) [15972]

Elchar Dog Bows (Veterinary Products) [27127]

Electro-Med Co. Inc. (Medical, Dental, and Optical Equipment) [18787]

Fall City Boat Works (Marine) [18500]

Fetzer Company-Restaurateurs (Restaurant and Commercial Foodservice Equipment and Supplies) [24117]

First Aid Plus Inc. (Medical, Dental, and Optical Equipment) [18798]

Fold-A-Way Corporation (Construction Materials and Machinery) [7351]

GE Machine Tool Services (Industrial Machinery) [16049]

Gleeson Inc. (Recreational and Sporting Goods) [23689]

Hesco Parts Corp. (Automotive) [2745]

Industrial Belting & Transmission, Inc. (Industrial Machinery) [16149]

Industrial Disposal Co. (Used, Scrap, and Recycled Materials) [26850]

Industrial Services of America Inc. (Specialty Equipment and Products) [25688]

Ingredient Resource Corp. (Agricultural Equipment and Supplies) [858]

Inter-Tel Technologies, Inc. (Communications Systems and Equipment) [5649]

Kahn & Son, Inc.; Irvin (Floorcovering Equipment and Supplies) [9983]

Kentucky Bearings Service (Automotive) [2849]

Kentucky Indiana Lumber Company Inc. (Construction Materials and Machinery) [7546]

Kentuckyiana Music Supply Inc. (Sound and Entertainment Equipment and Supplies) [25269]

Kenway Distributors Inc. (Cleaning and Janitorial Supplies) [4650]

Key-Duncan Wallcoverings (Household Items) [15548]

Klempner Bros. Inc. (Used, Scrap, and Recycled Materials) [26867]

Koch Filter Corp. (Specialty Equipment and Products) [25703]

Laboratory Supply Company (Medical, Dental, and Optical Equipment) [18882]

Lanham Hardwood Flooring Co. (Floorcovering Equipment and Supplies) [9990]

Louisville Plate Glass Company Inc. (Construction Materials and Machinery) [7613]

Louisville Tile Distributors Inc. (Floorcovering Equipment and Supplies) [10000]

Louisville Tile Distributors Inc. (Construction Materials and Machinery) [7614]

Luckett Tobaccos Inc. (Tobacco Products) [26326]

Manning Equipment Inc. (Automotive) [2915]

Masters Supply Inc. (Plumbing Materials and Fixtures) [23254]

Medical Devices Inc. (Medical, Dental, and Optical Equipment) [18913]

Mees Tile and Marble Inc. (Floorcovering Equipment and Supplies) [10024]

Mid-America Auto Auction (Motorized Vehicles) [20680]

Mid-West Paper Products Co. (Paper and Paper Products) [21835]

Mobile Data Shred Inc. (Paper and Paper Products) [21840]

Moog Louisville Wholesale (Automotive) [2982]

Murphy Elevator Company Inc. (Industrial Machinery) [16331]

Neill-LaVielle Supply Co. (Hardware) [13843]

Neill-LaVielle Supply Co. (Industrial Supplies) [17070]

O'Connor and Raque Office Products Co. (Office Equipment and Supplies) [21170]

Office Resources Inc. (Office Equipment and Supplies) [21187]

Orr Safety Corp. (Security and Safety Equipment) [24608]

Pape's Archery Inc. (Recreational and Sporting Goods) [23871]

Party Kits Unlimited Inc. (Recreational and Sporting Goods) [23874]

Pet Care Wholesale (Veterinary Products) [27205]

Peyton's (Paper and Paper Products) [21881]

Plumber's Supply Company Inc. (Plumbing Materials and Fixtures) [23322]

Primark Tool Group (Hardware) [13875]

R/C Henry Company Inc. (Toys and Hobby Goods) [26625]

Ransdell Surgical Inc. (Medical, Dental, and Optical Equipment) [19012]

Ransdell Surgical Inc. (Medical, Dental, and Optical Supplies) [19568]

Raymond Equipment Company Inc. (Construction Materials and Machinery) [7902]

Rev-A-Shelf, Inc. (Household Items) [15633]

Riverside Recycling Inc. (Used, Scrap, and Recycled Materials) [26961]

Rogers Group Inc. Louisville (Construction Materials and Machinery) [7953]

Roppel Industries Inc. (Automotive) [3174]

Rudd Equipment Co. (Construction Materials and Machinery) [7964]

Rueff Lighting Co. (Electrical and Electronic Equipment and Supplies) [9324]

Shippers Supply Corp. (Cleaning and Janitorial Supplies) [4707]

Silver Foods Corp. (Food) [12491]

Summit Company (Chemicals) [4522]

SYSCO of Louisville (Food) [12691]

Thomas Meat Co. (Food) [12715]

Tile Distributor Company Inc. (Floorcovering Equipment and Supplies) [10231]

Tile Distributor Company Inc. (Construction Materials and Machinery) [8134]

Topworx (Electrical and Electronic Equipment and Supplies) [9494]

Town Talk Cap Manufacturing Co. (Clothing) [5438]

Trompeter Co.; John F. (Tobacco Products) [26361]

Unisorce Paper Co. (Paper and Paper Products) [21961]

Universal Management Consultants Inc. (Heating and Cooling Equipment and Supplies) [14749]

VC Glass Carpet Co. (Floorcovering Equipment and Supplies) [10275]

Vertner Smith Co. (Alcoholic Beverages) [2102]

Wesley Electric and Supply Inc. (Heating and Cooling Equipment and Supplies) [14760]

Whayne Supply Co. (Agricultural Equipment and Supplies) [1436]

Wilson's Appliance Co.; Charlie (Household Appliances) [15374]

Wimsatt Brothers Inc. (Construction Materials and Machinery) [8229]

World Buying Service Inc. (Electrical and Electronic Equipment and Supplies) [9605]

Zoeller Co. (Industrial Machinery) [16662]

Madisonville

Hart Equipment Company Inc. (Security and Safety Equipment) [24559]

Madisonville Tire and Retreading Inc. (Automotive) [2905]

Southern States Madisonville Cooperative (Livestock and Farm Products) [18244]

Mayfield

Campbell Tobacco Rehandling Company Inc. (Tobacco Products) [26270]

D and D Shoe Co. (Clothing) [4907]

D & D Shoe Company, LLC (Shoes) [24722]

Dairyman's Supply Co. (Construction Materials and Machinery) [7246]

K & T Lamp & Shade Company Inc. (Household Items) [15546]

Rhodes Supply Company Inc. (Construction Materials and Machinery) [7927]

Maysville

Parker Tobacco Company (Tobacco Products) [26338]

Monticello

H & W Sport Monticello Inc. (Recreational and Sporting Goods) [23707]

Morganfield

Bickett Equipment Company Inc. (Agricultural Equipment and Supplies) [307]

Morgantown

Morgantown Tire Wholesalers (Automotive) [2986]

Mt. Sterling

Bonfield Brothers, Inc. (Petroleum, Fuels, and Related Equipment) [22085]

Nancy

Challenger Ltd. (Construction Materials and Machinery) [7167]

Newport

Clover Leaf Ice Cream (Food) [10774]

Niser Ice Cream (Food) [12008]

Scotland Yard (Veterinary Products) [27229]

Scotland Yard (Medical, Dental, and Optical Supplies) [19599]

Nicholasville

Alltech Inc. (Agricultural Equipment and Supplies) [228]

Cardinal Office Systems (Office Equipment and Supplies) [20880]

Cardinal Office Systems (Furniture and Fixtures) [13062]

Craftown Inc. (Jewelry) [17380]

Owensboro

Addwest Mining, Inc. (Minerals and Ores) [20506]

Applied Industrial Technologies (Automotive) [2246]

Big River Rubber & Gasket (Rubber) [24270]

Cox Paper & Printing Co. (Paper and Paper Products) [21695]

Gant Food Distributors Inc. (Food) [11231]

Hard Hat Inc. (Recreational and Sporting Goods) [23714]

MidAmerican Metals Company Inc. (Automotive) [2954]

Miles Farm Supply Inc. (Agricultural Equipment and Supplies) [1038]

Modern Methods Inc. (Construction Materials and Machinery) [7735]

Owensboro Electric Supply (Electrical and Electronic Equipment and Supplies) [9165]

Owensboro Supply Company Inc. (Industrial Supplies) [17093]

Storm Pet Supply Inc. (Veterinary Products) [27240]

Waxworks Inc. (Sound and Entertainment Equipment and Supplies) [25515]

WaxWorks/VideoWorks Inc. (Sound and Entertainment Equipment and Supplies) [25516]

Paducah

AmeriSource Corp. (Paducah, Kentucky) (Medical, Dental, and Optical Supplies) [19149]

Bailey Distributing Co.; E.M. (Petroleum, Fuels, and Related Equipment) [22057]

Computer Source Inc. (Computers and Software) [6126]

Distributors Warehouse Inc. (Automotive) [2548]

Hannan Supply Co. (Electrical and Electronic Equipment and Supplies) [8826]
Kitchens Inc. of Paducah (Household Items) [15551]
Petter Supply Co.; Henry A. (Industrial Supplies) [17103]
Wagner Candy Co. (Food) [12862]

Paintsville
East Kentucky News Inc. (Books and Other Printed Materials) [3707]
Van Hoose and Company Inc.; F.S. (Construction Materials and Machinery) [8170]

Pikeville
Coleman Oil Co. Inc. (Petroleum, Fuels, and Related Equipment) [22151]
Sparks Game & Toy Co. (Toys and Hobby Goods) [26661]
T & D Sporting Goods (Recreational and Sporting Goods) [24001]

Prestonsburg
Cooley Medical Equipment Inc. (Medical, Dental, and Optical Equipment) [18754]
Kentucky Welding Supply (Industrial Supplies) [16990]
World Wide Equipment Inc. (Motorized Vehicles) [20754]

Richmond
Madison Grocery Company Inc. (Food) [11757]

Scottsville
Dolgencorp (Food) [10978]

Shelbyville
Ichikoh Manufacturing Inc. (Household Items) [15537]
Shelby Industries Inc. (Automotive) [3215]

Somerset
South Kentucky Trucks Inc. (Automotive) [3238]
Warner Fertilizer Company Inc. (Agricultural Equipment and Supplies) [1412]

Springfield
Armour Food Ingredients Co. (Food) [10434]

Stanford
Cormans Sporting Goods (Recreational and Sporting Goods) [23606]

Sturgis
Grain Storage Corp. (Agricultural Equipment and Supplies) [754]

Tompkinsville
Hagan & Stone Wholesale (Agricultural Equipment and Supplies) [780]

Uniontown
Wabash Elevator Co. (Livestock and Farm Products) [18321]

Warsaw
Dorman Products Div. (Automotive) [2557]

Waverly
Union Fertilizer Co. (Agricultural Equipment and Supplies) [1371]

Whitley City
Mid-West Crafts Inc. (Toys and Hobby Goods) [26577]

Williamsburg
2-Way Radio Communications Engineering (Communications Systems and Equipment) [5496]

Winchester
Ale-8-One Bottling Co. Inc. (Soft Drinks) [24909]

Allen Company Inc. (Construction Materials and Machinery) [6937]
Apollo Oil LLC (Petroleum, Fuels, and Related Equipment) [22040]
Bloodline Agency (Veterinary Products) [27085]
Bluegrass Bandag, Inc. (Automotive) [2370]
Delgasco Inc. (Petroleum, Fuels, and Related Equipment) [22193]
Delta Resources Inc. (Petroleum, Fuels, and Related Equipment) [22195]
Hudson Company (Construction Materials and Machinery) [7493]
Old South Distributors Company Inc. (Alcoholic Beverages) [1929]

Louisiana

Abbeville
Aqua Gourmet Foods, Inc. (Food) [10427]
hci Coastal Chemical Co., LLC (Chemicals) [4412]
Victory Seafood Processors Inc. (Food) [12843]

Alexandria
Appliance Parts Inc. (Household Appliances) [15026]
Crest Industries Inc. (Alexandria, Louisiana) (Electrical and Electronic Equipment and Supplies) [8594]
Interstate Brands Corp. Cotton Brothers Baking Co. (Food) [11526]
Kazette Enterprises Inc. (Computers and Software) [6417]
Notari Sales Co.; John (Food) [12040]

Baton Rouge
Ace Appliances Inc. (Household Appliances) [14992]
Acme Brick Co. (Floorcovering Equipment and Supplies) [9641]
Acme Refrigeration (Heating and Cooling Equipment and Supplies) [14295]
Acme Refrigeration of Baton Rouge Inc. (Heating and Cooling Equipment and Supplies) [14296]
AFGD (Construction Materials and Machinery) [6924]
Analytcal Automation Specialists Inc. (Computers and Software) [5940]
Area Wholesale Tire Co., Inc. (Automotive) [2250]
AWC, Inc. (Scientific and Measurement Devices) [24319]
Baton Rouge Landscape Co. (Horticultural Supplies) [14822]
Baton Rouge Lumber Company LLC (Construction Materials and Machinery) [7031]
Baton Rouge Wholesale (Alcoholic Beverages) [1504]
Builders Center Inc. (Construction Materials and Machinery) [7099]
Capitol City Produce (Food) [10692]
Capitol Steel Inc. (Metals) [19853]
Chambers Supply Inc.; Carter (Industrial Supplies) [16791]
Claitor's Publishing Division (Books and Other Printed Materials) [3640]
Community Coffee Company Inc. (Food) [10799]
Community Coffee Company LLC (Food) [10800]
Corporate Computer Systems Inc. (Computers and Software) [6162]
Cullens Playland Inc. (Clothing) [4904]
Desselle-Maggard Corp. (Industrial Supplies) [16828]
Distributors Oil Co. Inc. (Petroleum, Fuels, and Related Equipment) [22203]
Ewing Aquatech Pools Inc. (Recreational and Sporting Goods) [23657]
Fantec Inc. (Household Appliances) [15126]
Fraenkel Wholesale Furniture Company Inc. (Furniture and Fixtures) [13115]
Head and Engguist Equipment L.L.C. (Construction Materials and Machinery) [7464]
Impulse Merchandisers Inc. (Automotive) [2772]
Interstate Companies of Louisiana (Office Equipment and Supplies) [21067]

LCR Corp. (Plumbing Materials and Fixtures) [23242]
Lipsey's Inc. (Guns and Weapons) [13498]
Louisiana Chemical Equipment Co. (Industrial Machinery) [16247]
Louisiana Welding Supply Company Inc. (Industrial Machinery) [16248]
Menard Electronics Inc. (Electrical and Electronic Equipment and Supplies) [9065]
Micro Computer Centre (Computers and Software) [6491]
Olinde and Sons Company Inc.; B. (Alcoholic Beverages) [1931]
Petro-Chem Equipment Co. (Industrial Machinery) [16394]
Riley's Electrical Supply (Electrical and Electronic Equipment and Supplies) [9297]
Southern Livestock Supply Co. Inc. (Agricultural Equipment and Supplies) [1281]
Specialty Metals and Minerals Inc. (Metals) [20382]
Sport Shop Inc. (Recreational and Sporting Goods) [23976]
Tri-Parish Communications Inc. (Communications Systems and Equipment) [5797]

Belle Chasse
Reeled Tubing Inc. (Petroleum, Fuels, and Related Equipment) [22618]

Bossier City
Harrison Company (Food) [11381]
ICEE Distributors Inc. (Heating and Cooling Equipment and Supplies) [14493]

Breaux Bridge
Bayou Land Seafood (Food) [10519]

Broussard
Butcher Air Conditioning Co. (Heating and Cooling Equipment and Supplies) [14364]
C and B Sales and Service Inc. (Compressors) [5832]
Maxam Corp. (Petroleum, Fuels, and Related Equipment) [22458]

Burnside
Robert Distributors Inc.; Roland J. (Petroleum, Fuels, and Related Equipment) [22635]

Carencro
Stemmans Inc. (Medical, Dental, and Optical Equipment) [19054]

Chalmette
Advanced Scientific Inc. (Medical, Dental, and Optical Equipment) [18662]
Nowak Dental Supplies Inc. (Medical, Dental, and Optical Equipment) [18962]

Church Point
Church Point Wholesale Groceries Inc. (Food) [10757]

Coushatta
Almond Brothers Lumber and Supply Inc. (Construction Materials and Machinery) [6947]

Covington
Information Sales and Marketing Company Inc. (Medical, Dental, and Optical Supplies) [19372]
V-Labs Inc. (Food) [12813]

Crowley
Crowley Grain Drier Inc. (Livestock and Farm Products) [17804]
Francis Drilling Fluids Ltd. (Chemicals) [4394]

Donaldsonville
Thibaut Oil Company Inc. (Petroleum, Fuels, and Related Equipment) [22733]

Ferriday

Ferriday Farm Equipment Company Inc. (Agricultural Equipment and Supplies) [679]
United Hardwood, L.L.C. (Construction Materials and Machinery) [8157]

Franklin

A Plus Sales & Service Inc. (Computers and Software) [5859]
Franklin Cigar and Tobacco Company Inc. (Tobacco Products) [26296]

Franklinton

ARB Inc. (Franklinton, Louisiana) (Petroleum, Fuels, and Related Equipment) [22042]
Fair City Oil (Petroleum, Fuels, and Related Equipment) [22249]

Gonzales

Louisiana Mill Supply (Industrial Supplies) [17006]
Tempco Supplies Inc. (Heating and Cooling Equipment and Supplies) [14716]

Gretna

Advanced Industrial Products, Inc. (Industrial Machinery) [15737]
EPR Automotive Warehouse (Automotive) [2593]
Pelican Publishing Company Inc. (Books and Other Printed Materials) [4049]
Richards Machine and Cutting Tools Inc. (Industrial Machinery) [16451]
Zatarain's (Food) [13003]

Gueydan

Gayle Oil Company Inc. (Petroleum, Fuels, and Related Equipment) [22305]

Hammond

American Homepatient, Inc. (Medical, Dental, and Optical Equipment) [18676]

Harahan

Accessory Wholesale (Jewelry) [17302]
Arrow-SYSCO (Food) [10437]
Big Shot Beverage Inc. (Soft Drinks) [24915]
Bologna Brothers (Alcoholic Beverages) [1541]
Hiller Corp.; Herbert S. (Security and Safety Equipment) [24562]
Pelican Plumbing Supply Inc. (Household Appliances) [15269]
Rodan Inc. (Computers and Software) [6691]
Shollmier Distribution Inc. (Heating and Cooling Equipment and Supplies) [14682]
Veazey Suppliers Inc. (Sound and Entertainment Equipment and Supplies) [25499]

Harvey

Bearings Service & Supply, Inc. (Industrial Supplies) [16743]
IMR Corp. (Shoes) [24768]
Intrepid Enterprises Inc. (Construction Materials and Machinery) [7525]
Mayer-Hammant Equipment Inc. (Electrical and Electronic Equipment and Supplies) [9053]
Mid-South Engine Systems Inc. (Marine) [18568]

Houma

Caro Foods Inc. (Food) [10701]
Caro Produce and Institutional Foods Inc. (Food) [10702]
EMT Electronics Inc. (Electrical and Electronic Equipment and Supplies) [8705]
Exploration Supplies of Houma Inc. (Industrial Supplies) [16854]
Falgouts Refrigeration & Appliance Service (Heating and Cooling Equipment and Supplies) [14441]
M and L Industries Inc. (Agricultural Equipment and Supplies) [978]
Marine Systems Inc. (Automotive) [2917]
Motivatit Seafoods Inc. (Food) [11938]
Vida Paint & Supply Co. (Marine) [18630]

Jefferson

Heritage House Wines (Alcoholic Beverages) [1752]

Medical Imaging Services Inc. (Medical, Dental, and Optical Equipment) [18917]
TC Computers Inc. (Computers and Software) [6790]

Jonesville

Fish Net Co. (Recreational and Sporting Goods) [23667]

Kenner

Alfreds Processor Sales & Service (Medical, Dental, and Optical Equipment) [18671]
Bayou Import-Export Corp. (Industrial Machinery) [15810]
Beacon Supply Co. (Marine) [18456]
Computer Source Inc. (Computers and Software) [6127]
Continental Screen Printing Supply (Industrial Machinery) [15911]
Dynamic International Company Inc. (Construction Materials and Machinery) [7295]
Eagle Distributors Inc. (Sound and Entertainment Equipment and Supplies) [25170]
General Biomedical Service Inc. (Medical, Dental, and Optical Equipment) [18805]
JFK Enterprises (Veterinary Products) [27163]
Lee Tractor Company Inc. (Construction Materials and Machinery) [7592]
Lehleitner and Company Inc.; Geo H. (Household Items) [15565]

Kentwood

Allen Brothers Feed Inc. (Livestock and Farm Products) [17690]
Richlund Enterprises (Household Appliances) [15292]

Lafayette

Acadiana Culligan (Soft Drinks) [24907]
Aluminum and Stainless Inc. (Metals) [19765]
Auto Comm Engineering Corp. (Communications Systems and Equipment) [5524]
Bologna Brothers (Alcoholic Beverages) [1540]
Carroll Building Specialties (Hardware) [13621]
George Inc.; Al (Industrial Machinery) [16058]
Lafayette Drug Company Inc. (Health and Beauty Aids) [14149]
Magnolia Liquor Lafayette Inc. (Alcoholic Beverages) [1838]
Malone and Hyde Inc. Lafayette Div. (Food) [11767]
Marian Group Corp. (Clothing) [5164]
OSCA Inc. (Chemicals) [4477]
Performance Medical Group, Inc. (Medical, Dental, and Optical Equipment) [18980]
Teche Electric Supply Inc. (Electrical and Electronic Equipment and Supplies) [9467]
Tout de Suite a la Microwave Inc. (Books and Other Printed Materials) [4223]
United Tile of LaFayette, LLC (Floorcovering Equipment and Supplies) [10267]

Lafitte

Nunez Seafood (Food) [12046]

Lake Charles

Appliance Parts of Lake Charles (Household Appliances) [15027]
Aries Paper & Chemical Co. Inc. (Cleaning and Janitorial Supplies) [4574]
Borden Inc. (Food) [10590]
Davidson Louisiana Inc. (Construction Materials and Machinery) [7251]
House For Sports Inc. (Recreational and Sporting Goods) [23733]
Lumen Foods (Food) [11744]
Safety House (Used, Scrap, and Recycled Materials) [26975]

Lake Providence

Terral-Norris Seed Company Inc. (Agricultural Equipment and Supplies) [1322]
Terral Seed, Inc. (Livestock and Farm Products) [18277]

Terral Seed Inc. (Agricultural Equipment and Supplies) [1323]

Lecompte

Champion Distributors Inc. (Heating and Cooling Equipment and Supplies) [14381]

Leesville

S and M Food Service Inc. (Food) [12380]

Livingston

Henderson Auctions Inc. (Restaurant and Commercial Foodservice Equipment and Supplies) [24137]
J.A.H. Enterprises, Inc. (Construction Materials and Machinery) [7530]

Loranger

L & B Pet Supplies (Veterinary Products) [27176]

Luling

Cajun Sales (Veterinary Products) [27098]

Mandeville

CGB Enterprises Inc. (Livestock and Farm Products) [17773]
P & W Industries, Inc. (Used, Scrap, and Recycled Materials) [26931]
Toland Enterprises Inc. (Floorcovering Equipment and Supplies) [10252]

Marrero

Preventive Electrical Maintenance Co. (Electrical and Electronic Equipment and Supplies) [9235]
Tomba Communications and Electronics Inc. (Computers and Software) [6821]

Mermentau

Broussard Rice Mill Inc. (Livestock and Farm Products) [17749]

Metairie

ABC Tile Distributors (Floorcovering Equipment and Supplies) [9638]
ABC Tile Distributors (Construction Materials and Machinery) [6900]
Abita Water Company Inc. (Soft Drinks) [24904]
American Office Machines Inc. (Office Equipment and Supplies) [20795]
Atlantis International, Inc. (Petroleum, Fuels, and Related Equipment) [22049]
Brown and Co.; Lewis A. (Food) [10623]
Brown and Co.; Lewis A. (Food) [10624]
Computer Discounters (Computers and Software) [6109]
Consolidated Companies Inc. (Food) [10815]
Continental Equipment Co. (Heating and Cooling Equipment and Supplies) [14401]
Crown Products Inc. (Food) [10875]
Delta Materials Inc. (Electrical and Electronic Equipment and Supplies) [8621]
Ebel Company Inc.; Fred C. (Food) [11018]
Esneault Inc. (Recreational and Sporting Goods) [23655]
Figueroa International Inc. (Food) [11125]
Fitness Expo Inc. (Recreational and Sporting Goods) [23671]
Gibbons Inc.; J.T. (Food) [11262]
Ideal Appliance Parts Inc. (Household Appliances) [15174]
Infinity Data Systems (Computers and Software) [6364]
Koen Co.; U. (Specialty Equipment and Products) [25704]
L & L Oil and Gas Service LLC (Petroleum, Fuels, and Related Equipment) [22414]
Marchand Contractors Specialties Inc.; R.J. (Construction Materials and Machinery) [7640]
Marks Paper Co. (Office Equipment and Supplies) [21126]
Marks Paper Co., Inc. (Office Equipment and Supplies) [21127]
Mayer Co.; Budd (Food) [11813]
Nor-Joe Cheese Importing (Food) [12017]

Reily Electrical Supply Inc. (Electrical and Electronic Equipment and Supplies) [9271]
Richards Co.; S.P. (Office Equipment and Supplies) [21241]
South Central Pool Supply, Inc. (Recreational and Sporting Goods) [23954]
Southeast Wholesale Equipment Distributors Inc. (Heating and Cooling Equipment and Supplies) [14690]
Sunseri's Inc. (Household Appliances) [15325]
Werleins for Music (Sound and Entertainment Equipment and Supplies) [25520]
Wilbur Chocolate Company Inc. (Food) [12938]
WJS Enterprises Inc. (Office Equipment and Supplies) [21359]
Wong's Advanced Technologies Inc. (Computers and Software) [6875]

Monroe

Abell Corp. (Agricultural Equipment and Supplies) [181]
Allied Building Stores Inc. (Wood and Wood Products) [27275]
Brunt Tile & Marble (Floorcovering Equipment and Supplies) [9742]
Buffington Corp. (Construction Materials and Machinery) [7096]
Choice Brands, Inc. (Alcoholic Beverages) [1593]
Consolidated Truck Parts Inc. (Automotive) [2476]
Generic Distributors L.P. (Medical, Dental, and Optical Supplies) [19338]
Luffeys Medical & Surgical Supplies (Medical, Dental, and Optical Supplies) [19418]
Malone & Hyde (Health and Beauty Aids) [14158]
National Optical Co. Inc. (Medical, Dental, and Optical Supplies) [19478]
Northeast Louisiana Heating & Air Distributing (Heating and Cooling Equipment and Supplies) [14624]
Ouachita Fertilizer Div. (Agricultural Equipment and Supplies) [1113]
Poly Processing Co. (Storage Equipment and Containers) [25933]
Rack Service Company Inc. (Health and Beauty Aids) [14203]
Rack Service Company Inc. (Medical, Dental, and Optical Supplies) [19565]
Scott Truck and Tractor Company Inc. (Agricultural Equipment and Supplies) [1246]
Southern Hardware and Supply Company Ltd. (Industrial Supplies) [17186]

Morgan City

Power Products Service (Petroleum, Fuels, and Related Equipment) [22591]
Rice Electronics LP (Communications Systems and Equipment) [5743]
Vida Paint & Supply Co. (Marine) [18629]

Natchitoches

Valley Farmers Cooperative (Natchitoches, Louisiana) (Agricultural Equipment and Supplies) [1392]

New Iberia

Doerle Food Services Inc. (Food) [10973]
Fire Boss of Louisiana Inc. (Security and Safety Equipment) [24542]
Gachassin Inc. (Clothing) [4973]
Gragnon Wholesale (Food) [11303]
Rainbow Paper Company, Inc. (Paper and Paper Products) [21896]
Streva Distributing Co. (Alcoholic Beverages) [2059]
Voorhies Supply Company Inc. (Industrial Machinery) [16608]

New Orleans

Accardos Appliance Parts & Services (Household Appliances) [14991]
Ace Hardware Corp. (Hardware) [13525]
ADT Security Systems (Security and Safety Equipment) [24489]
Allen Supply Company, Inc.; William B. (Security and Safety Equipment) [24503]

American Textile and Trim Company Inc. (Textiles and Notions) [25961]
Arrow-Sysco Food Services Inc. (Food) [10438]
Bana Parts Inc. (Sound and Entertainment Equipment and Supplies) [25096]
Boeing Petroleum Services Inc. (Petroleum, Fuels, and Related Equipment) [22082]
Branton Industries Inc. (Construction Materials and Machinery) [7077]
Bridon Elm Inc. (Aeronautical Equipment and Supplies) [64]
Cannizzaro's Distributors (Food) [10689]
Certex Gulf Coast (Electrical and Electronic Equipment and Supplies) [8521]
Church Business Machines (Office Equipment and Supplies) [20899]
Coastal Engineering Equipment Sales LLC (Petroleum, Fuels, and Related Equipment) [22144]
Con-Tech International, Inc. (Industrial Supplies) [16805]
Conco Food Service (Food) [10808]
Crescent City Pharmaceutical (Medical, Dental, and Optical Equipment) [18758]
Dixie Art Supplies Inc. (Office Equipment and Supplies) [20970]
Dixie Mill Inc. (Industrial Machinery) [15952]
Dixie Produce and Packaging Inc. (Food) [10968]
Domus Corp. (Floorcovering Equipment and Supplies) [9871]
Donovan Marine Inc. (Marine) [18496]
Doussan Inc. (Industrial Supplies) [16838]
Fairco, Inc. (Food) [11071]
FMI Hydrocarbon Co. (Petroleum, Fuels, and Related Equipment) [22286]
Fox Co.; C.B. (Livestock and Farm Products) [17924]
Gavilanes Books from Indoamerica (Books and Other Printed Materials) [3772]
General Mill Supplies Inc. (Plumbing Materials and Fixtures) [23186]
Gerhardt's Inc. (Automotive) [2680]
Glindmeyer Distributors Co. (Household Appliances) [15148]
Graphic Papers Inc. (Paper and Paper Products) [21748]
Gulf Enterprises (Floorcovering Equipment and Supplies) [9928]
Gulf Marine and Industrial Supplies (Food) [11346]
Gulf States Optical Labs Inc. (Medical, Dental, and Optical Supplies) [19344]
Herzogs Auto Parts Inc. (Automotive) [2744]
I.D. Foods, Inc. (Food) [11488]
IDN-ACME, Inc. (Security and Safety Equipment) [24570]
Imperial Trading Co. (Tobacco Products) [26310]
Industrial Metals of the South Inc. (Metals) [20057]
Ives Business Forms Inc. (Office Equipment and Supplies) [21073]
Johnny's Crab Traps Inc. (Recreational and Sporting Goods) [23760]
Kelley and Abide Company Inc. (Food) [11592]
Koerner and Company Inc.; John E. (Food) [11632]
Lee Engineering Supply Company, Inc. (Industrial Machinery) [16232]
Louisiana Office Products (Office Equipment and Supplies) [21114]
Magnolia Chemical and Solvents Inc. (Chemicals) [4447]
Magnolia Marketing Co. (Alcoholic Beverages) [1839]
Magnum Equipment Inc. (Heating and Cooling Equipment and Supplies) [14529]
Mama Rosa's Slice of Italy (Food) [11770]
Masonry Product Sales Inc. (Construction Materials and Machinery) [7661]
Merchants Coffee Co. (Food) [11852]
Natco Food Service Merchants (Food) [11974]
National Supermarkets (Food) [11979]
Natural Energy Unlimited Inc. (Food) [11982]
Neo Fabrics, Inc. (Textiles and Notions) [26155]
Orleans Materials and Equipment Company Inc. (Metals) [20255]
Port Cargo Service Inc. (Food) [12197]

Predot Company Inc. (Clothing) [5288]
Production Supply Co. (Metals) [20299]
Production Supply Co. (Metals) [20300]
Quaglino Tobacco and Candy Company Inc. (Tobacco Products) [26344]
Rausch Naval Stores Company Inc. (Chemicals) [4490]
Reco Crane Inc. (Construction Materials and Machinery) [7906]
Reilly-Benton Company Inc. (Marine) [18591]
Retif Oil and Fuel Inc. (Petroleum, Fuels, and Related Equipment) [22623]
Robinson Lumber Company Inc. (Construction Materials and Machinery) [7945]
Robinson Lumber Company Inc. (Wood and Wood Products) [27365]
Sazerac Company Inc. (Alcoholic Beverages) [2010]
Scariano Brothers Inc. (Food) [12422]
SLS Arts, Inc. (Specialty Equipment and Products) [25819]
Southern Electronics Supply, Inc. (Electrical and Electronic Equipment and Supplies) [9388]
Southern Flooring Distributors (Floorcovering Equipment and Supplies) [10164]
Southern Holdings Inc. (Used, Scrap, and Recycled Materials) [27002]
Southern Scrap Material Company Ltd. (Used, Scrap, and Recycled Materials) [27005]
Standard Supply and Hardware Company Inc. (Industrial Supplies) [17194]
Sunseri's Inc. (Household Appliances) [15324]
Tesoro Petroleum Distributing Co. (Petroleum, Fuels, and Related Equipment) [22727]
Tesoro Petroleum Distributing Co. (Petroleum, Fuels, and Related Equipment) [22728]
Turner Marine Bulk Inc. (Petroleum, Fuels, and Related Equipment) [22754]
Van Horn Company Inc.; Oliver H. (Industrial Machinery) [16600]
Westway Trading Corp. (Food) [12918]
Wynne Company Inc.; A.D. (Furniture and Fixtures) [13285]

New Roads

Bergeron Pecan Shelling Plant, Inc.; H.J. (Food) [10541]

Opelousas

Vermillion Wholesale Drug Company Inc. (Medical, Dental, and Optical Supplies) [19689]

Plaquemine

Cane Equipment Cooperative Inc. (Agricultural Equipment and Supplies) [369]

Rayville

Delta Ridge Implement (Agricultural Equipment and Supplies) [512]

St. Martinville

St. Martin Oil and Gas Inc. (Petroleum, Fuels, and Related Equipment) [22648]

St. Rose

ETD KroMar (Books and Other Printed Materials) [3734]
Graham Services Inc. (Books and Other Printed Materials) [3792]

Shreveport

Aeropres Corp. (Chemicals) [4314]
Allen Appliance Distributors (Household Appliances) [15001]
Allen Millwork Inc. (Construction Materials and Machinery) [6938]
Alloy Piping Products Inc. (Plumbing Materials and Fixtures) [23058]
Appliance Parts Inc. (Sound and Entertainment Equipment and Supplies) [25078]
Arkla Chemical Corp. (Petroleum, Fuels, and Related Equipment) [22045]
Bearings Service & Supply (Industrial Supplies) [16742]
Bologna Brothers (Alcoholic Beverages) [1542]

Coca-Cola Bottling Company of Shreveport (Soft Drinks) [24940]

Conco Food Service Inc. (Food) [10809]

Creger Auto Company Inc. (Automotive) [2493]

Custom Bilt Cabinet and Supply Inc. (Construction Materials and Machinery) [7238]

Dealers Truck Equipment Company Inc. (Automotive) [2534]

Eye Care Inc. (Medical, Dental, and Optical Supplies) [19316]

Gilbert Pipe and Supply Co.; A.A. (Plumbing Materials and Fixtures) [23191]

Hardware Distribution Warehouses Inc. (Hardware) [13736]

Industrial Electronic Supply Inc. (Electrical and Electronic Equipment and Supplies) [8878]

Jewel Paula-Ronn Records (Office Equipment and Supplies) [21077]

Louisiana Lift & Equipment, Inc. (Automotive) [2894]

Maxey System Inc. (Computers and Software) [6470]

Moore-Sigler Sports World Inc. (Recreational and Sporting Goods) [23835]

Neo Fabrics, Inc. (Textiles and Notions) [26156]

Noland & Associates, Inc.; Tim J. (Recreational and Sporting Goods) [23846]

Pepsi-Cola Bottling Company of Shreveport (Soft Drinks) [25014]

Red Ball Medical Supply Inc. (Medical, Dental, and Optical Equipment) [19013]

Service Brokerage Inc. (Food) [12461]

South Gateway Tire Co. (Automotive) [3237]

Southwestern Wholesale Co. Inc. (Clothing) [5374]

T & L Distributors Company Inc. (Floorcovering Equipment and Supplies) [10203]

Thornton Industries, Inc. (Hardware) [13953]

Tri-State Optical Co. Inc. (Medical, Dental, and Optical Supplies) [19661]

United Engines Inc. (Automotive) [3365]

United Tile Company, Inc. (Floorcovering Equipment and Supplies) [10266]

Williams Physicians and Surgeons Supplies (Medical, Dental, and Optical Supplies) [19706]

Yearwoods Inc. (Shoes) [24901]

Sicily Island

Macon Ridge Farmers Association (Livestock and Farm Products) [18069]

Slaughter

Tri-Parish Cooperative Inc. (Agricultural Equipment and Supplies) [1354]

Slidell

FoxMeyer Drug Co. Slidell Div. (Health and Beauty Aids) [14103]

Sulphur

Louisiana Mill Supply (Industrial Supplies) [17005]

Tallulah

Farmers Grain Terminal (Livestock and Farm Products) [17900]

Thibodaux

Badeaux Co.; Edward (Tobacco Products) [26263]

Gibbons and LeFort Inc. (Petroleum, Fuels, and Related Equipment) [22313]

National Beverage Company Inc. (Alcoholic Beverages) [1901]

Popes Parts Inc. (Automotive) [3103]

Ville Platte

Evangeline Farmers Cooperative (Livestock and Farm Products) [17838]

West Monroe

Duck Commander Company, Inc. (Recreational and Sporting Goods) [23632]

Mission Service Supply (Sound and Entertainment Equipment and Supplies) [25327]

Rexel-Summers (Electrical and Electronic Equipment and Supplies) [9288]

Rexel-Summers (Electrical and Electronic Equipment and Supplies) [9289]

Twin City ICEE Inc. (Heating and Cooling Equipment and Supplies) [14741]

Westlake

Acme-Dixie Inc. (Industrial Machinery) [15733]

Maine

Addison

Tiger Enterprises (Marine) [18625]

Alfred

Morin Steel (Metals) [20204]

Auburn

Akers & Chrysler Inc. (Paints and Varnishes) [21375]

Damon Insulation Co. (Construction Materials and Machinery) [7249]

Hayden Company Inc.; C.W. (Industrial Supplies) [16927]

North Auburn Cash Market (Recreational and Sporting Goods) [23850]

Republic Jewelry & Coin Co. (Jewelry) [17562]

Samson's Novelty Company Inc. (Toys and Hobby Goods) [26646]

Augusta

Central Maine Business Machines (Office Equipment and Supplies) [20891]

Mathews; Manfred (Construction Materials and Machinery) [7668]

N.A. Marketing Inc. (Medical, Dental, and Optical Supplies) [19473]

N.A. Marketing Inc. (Medical, Dental, and Optical Supplies) [19474]

NorthCenter Foodservice Corp. (Food) [12030]

N.R.F. Distributors, Inc. (Floorcovering Equipment and Supplies) [10081]

PID, Inc. (Industrial Machinery) [16397]

Pine State Tobacco and Candy Co. (Tobacco Products) [26341]

Bangor

ADCO Surgical Supply Inc. (Medical, Dental, and Optical Equipment) [18658]

Atlantic Communications Inc. (Sound and Entertainment Equipment and Supplies) [25085]

Atlantic Communications Inc. (Household Appliances) [15039]

Automotive Distributors Inc. (Automotive) [2286]

Bangor Steel (Metals) [19802]

Bragg and Sons; N.H. (Industrial Supplies) [16762]

Briggs, Inc. (Alcoholic Beverages) [1550]

Comtech Inc. (Office Equipment and Supplies) [20908]

Darlings (Motorized Vehicles) [20621]

Dead River Co. (Petroleum, Fuels, and Related Equipment) [22190]

Eastern Maine Healthcare (Medical, Dental, and Optical Equipment) [18782]

Fancy Fare Distributors (Food) [11079]

Flagg Co.; R.M. (Restaurant and Commercial Foodservice Equipment and Supplies) [24122]

Holmes Distributors Inc. (Electrical and Electronic Equipment and Supplies) [8852]

Home Edco Home Care (Medical, Dental, and Optical Equipment) [18839]

Johnson and Company Wilderness Products Inc. (Clothing) [5090]

Magazines Inc. (Books and Other Printed Materials) [3928]

Maine Distributing Co. (Alcoholic Beverages) [1840]

Maine Equipment Company, Inc. (Automotive) [2911]

Maine Propane Distributors Inc. (Petroleum, Fuels, and Related Equipment) [22445]

Marlenes Inc. (Clothing) [5168]

McGary Optical Co.; F.H. (Medical, Dental, and Optical Supplies) [19430]

Michaud Distributors (Food) [11869]

Northeast Tire of Maine (Automotive) [3045]

Nyle International Corp. (Medical, Dental, and Optical Equipment) [18964]

P.A.T. Products Inc. (Chemicals) [4479]

Penobscot Paint Products Co. (Paints and Varnishes) [21536]

Reliance Electric Co. (Electrical and Electronic Equipment and Supplies) [9274]

SKR Distributors (Construction Materials and Machinery) [8028]

Smith Ceramics (Toys and Hobby Goods) [26654]

Statewide Floor Waxing Distributors (Cleaning and Janitorial Supplies) [4714]

Unisource (Cleaning and Janitorial Supplies) [4720]

Webber Oil Co. (Petroleum, Fuels, and Related Equipment) [22787]

Bar Harbor

Golden Goose (Clothing) [4993]

Bath

Lacy Ltd.; Alice (Toys and Hobby Goods) [26560]

Benton

KT Distributors (Food) [11652]

Biddeford

AMJ Inc. (Cleaning and Janitorial Supplies) [4573]

AMJ Inc. (Restaurant and Commercial Foodservice Equipment and Supplies) [24064]

Centercore New England Inc. (Office Equipment and Supplies) [20888]

Maine Office Supply Co. Inc. (Office Equipment and Supplies) [21119]

Ron's Steel Sales (Metals) [20329]

Summit of New England (Automotive) [3282]

Blaine

Smith Packing Corp.; H. (Food) [12512]

Boothbay Harbor

A Silver Lining Inc. (Jewelry) [17604]

Brewer

Direct Way Distributors Inc. (Paper and Paper Products) [21713]

Emerson Company Inc.; W. S. (Textiles and Notions) [26029]

Getchell Brothers Inc. (Food) [11258]

Green Point Inc. (Automotive) [2705]

Lawsons Locksmithing (Specialty Equipment and Products) [25710]

Nyle Home Health Supplies Inc. (Specialty Equipment and Products) [25768]

Twin City Tile (Floorcovering Equipment and Supplies) [10261]

Winter Port Boot Shop (Shoes) [24896]

Brunswick

Coastal Net Marine Co. (Recreational and Sporting Goods) [23598]

General Business Machines Inc. (Office Equipment and Supplies) [21010]

Maine Writers & Publishers Alliance (Books and Other Printed Materials) [3931]

Bucksport

Pro Form and File (Office Equipment and Supplies) [21223]

Buxton

3-D Energy Inc. (Petroleum, Fuels, and Related Equipment) [22013]

Imperial Pools Inc. (Recreational and Sporting Goods) [23740]

Calais

Connors Brothers Inc. (Food) [10813]

Camden

Richey Design Ltd.; William (Jewelry) [17564]

Geographic Index

Caribou

County Optical Inc. (Medical, Dental, and Optical Supplies) [19254]
Solman Distributors Inc. (Alcoholic Beverages) [2032]

Casco

Hancock Lumber Inc. (Wood and Wood Products) [27315]

Damariscotta

Down East Wholesalers Inc. (Textiles and Notions) [26022]

Deer Isle

Pearson Inc.; Ronald Hayes (Jewelry) [17543]
Ronald Hayes Pearson Inc. (Jewelry) [17573]

East Corinth

Tilton & Sons, Inc.; Ben (Livestock and Farm Products) [18281]

East Vassalboro

Cates Associates (Jewelry) [17363]

Ellsworth

Ellsworth Builders Supply Inc. (Construction Materials and Machinery) [7307]
Pyramid Studios (Jewelry) [17554]

Fairfield

Joseph's Clothing & Sporting Goods (Recreational and Sporting Goods) [23764]

Falmouth

Med Dent Service Corp. (Medical, Dental, and Optical Equipment) [18907]

Farmington

Skane Ltd. (Clothing) [5361]

Ft. Kent Mills

Martin Sons Inc.; Frank (Industrial Machinery) [16267]

Freeport

Good Earth Farm, Inc. (Horticultural Supplies) [14874]

Fryeburg

Bear Paw Lumber Corp. (Construction Materials and Machinery) [7036]

Gardiner

Associated Grocers of Maine Inc. (Food) [10451]
Dick Company Inc.; T.W. (Metals) [19929]
Elliott Office Products Inc. (Office Equipment and Supplies) [20990]
Prescott Inc.; Everett J. (Plumbing Materials and Fixtures) [23328]
Tisdale Used Auto Parts (Automotive) [3311]

Gorham

Barrow's Greenhouses (Horticultural Supplies) [14818]

Gray

Maine Ladder & Staging Co., Inc. (Automotive) [2912]

Hallowell

Wise & Son; Frank C. (Clothing) [5491]

Hancock

Kimsco Supply Co. (Office Equipment and Supplies) [21093]

Houlton

Good Floral Distributors (Horticultural Supplies) [14875]
Wilbert Vault of Aroostook (Specialty Equipment and Products) [25880]

Jonesport

King & Son Inc.; T.A. (Marine) [18534]
Look Company Inc.; O.W. and B.S. (Food) [11732]

Kennebunk

Cressy & Sons Inc.; W. C. (Medical, Dental, and Optical Equipment) [18759]
Spofford's Newspapers (Books and Other Printed Materials) [4183]
Warren Co. Inc.; E.R. (Petroleum, Fuels, and Related Equipment) [22782]

Kennebunkport

McCabe Bait Company Inc. (Recreational and Sporting Goods) [23814]
Sundin Rand; Gloria (Furniture and Fixtures) [13252]

Kittery

Greenpages Inc. (Computers and Software) [6311]

Lewiston

Aubford Enterprises (Toys and Hobby Goods) [26401]
Callahan Brothers Supply Inc. (Specialty Equipment and Products) [25594]
Camera Service Center of Maine (Photographic Equipment and Supplies) [22838]
Central Distributors Inc. (Alcoholic Beverages) [1586]
Geiger Bros. (Books and Other Printed Materials) [3773]
Industrial Distributors (Construction Materials and Machinery) [7507]
Lewiston Rubber & Supply Inc. (Specialty Equipment and Products) [25715]
Lewiston Rubber and Supply Inc. (Scientific and Measurement Devices) [24389]
Radio City Automotive (Sound and Entertainment Equipment and Supplies) [25401]
Radio City Inc. (Sound and Entertainment Equipment and Supplies) [25402]
Reed Distributors (Cleaning and Janitorial Supplies) [4692]
Stover Broom (Household Items) [15669]
Universal Card & Coin Center Inc. (Toys and Hobby Goods) [26701]
V.I.P. Discount Auto Center (Automotive) [3393]

Lubec

Nordic Delights Foods Inc. (Food) [12019]

Manchester

Apgar Office Systems Inc. (Office Equipment and Supplies) [20808]

Monmouth

Barrows Used Auto Parts (Automotive) [2322]

New Gloucester

Oliver Stores Inc. (Construction Materials and Machinery) [7810]

Nobleboro

Venture Trading (Clothing) [5460]

Norway

French Refrigeration Co. (Heating and Cooling Equipment and Supplies) [14453]

Oakland

Valley Distributors Inc. (Alcoholic Beverages) [2095]

Ogunquit

Leon Supply Company, Inc. (Food) [11699]
Molly Corp. (Railroad Equipment and Supplies) [23485]

Orono

Gass Horse Supply (Livestock and Farm Products) [17935]

Peru

Lane Fire Service; Donald (Security and Safety Equipment) [24584]

Porter

Soviet American Woolens (Textiles and Notions) [26209]

Portland

Alma, Inc. (Horticultural Supplies) [14800]
Applicator Sales & Service (Construction Materials and Machinery) [6981]
Bicknell Huston Distributors, Inc. (Recreational and Sporting Goods) [23556]
Brookline Machine Co. Williams Brothers Div. (Automotive) [2395]
Brown Ship Chandlery Inc. (Marine) [18472]
Creighton & Son (Horticultural Supplies) [14847]
D & M Distributors Inc. (Specialty Equipment and Products) [25620]
D and M Distributors Inc. (Restaurant and Commercial Foodservice Equipment and Supplies) [24099]
Deveault; Ed (Scientific and Measurement Devices) [24345]
Eastern Book Co. (Books and Other Printed Materials) [3710]
Emery Waterhouse Co. (Hardware) [13681]
Gage Co. Redlon and Johnson Plumbing Supply Div. (Plumbing Materials and Fixtures) [23181]
Humpty Dumpty Potato Chip Co. (Food) [11476]
Jack & Co.; K.L. (Marine) [18526]
Jordan's Foods (Food) [11566]
Jordan's Meats Inc. (Food) [11567]
Konica Quality Photo East (Photographic Equipment and Supplies) [22870]
Lindenmeyer Munroe (Paper and Paper Products) [21805]
Lindenmeyer Munroe (Paper and Paper Products) [21807]
Maine Entrepreneurs Group (Jewelry) [17508]
Modern Paint & Wallpaper Inc. (Paints and Varnishes) [21505]
Motion Industries, Atlantic Tracy Div. (Industrial Supplies) [17056]
Nar Inc. (Cleaning and Janitorial Supplies) [4674]
Paper Center Inc. (Paper and Paper Products) [21859]
Pullen Inc.; Norman W. (Jewelry) [17553]
Remar; Irving (Jewelry) [17561]
Resource Trading Co. (Food) [12304]
Retail Service Company Inc. (Furniture and Fixtures) [13220]
Richardson Dana Div. (Construction Materials and Machinery) [7929]
RKB Enterprises Inc. (Plumbing Materials and Fixtures) [23345]
Roak's Seven-Acre Greenhouses (Horticultural Supplies) [14945]
Sani-Clean Distributors Inc. (Cleaning and Janitorial Supplies) [4703]
Select Robinson Paper Co. (Paper and Paper Products) [21932]
Storck & Co.; M.A. (Toys and Hobby Goods) [26671]
Stultz Fluid Power (Industrial Machinery) [16532]
Tomra Maine (Specialty Equipment and Products) [25845]
Westco./DoAll Industrial Distribution (Industrial Machinery) [16624]
Wetterau Inc. Northeast (Food) [12921]

Presque Isle

Academy Optical Inc. (Medical, Dental, and Optical Supplies) [19121]
Aroostook Beverage Co. (Alcoholic Beverages) [1488]
Maine Potato Growers Inc. (Food) [11760]
Netherland Typewriter (Office Equipment and Supplies) [21157]

Rockland

Manset Marine Supply Co. (Marine) [18556]
Rockland Boat, Inc. (Marine) [18592]
Rockland Marine Corp. (Marine) [18593]

Saco

Atlantis Restaurant Equipment (Restaurant and Commercial Foodservice Equipment and Supplies) [24071]
Earth Waste Systems Inc. (Used, Scrap, and Recycled Materials) [26801]
Saco Steel Company Inc. (Used, Scrap, and Recycled Materials) [26973]
Thibodeau's Farms (Food) [12711]

Sanford

Hercules Tire & Rubber Products (Automotive) [2743]
Rainbow Rug Inc. (Floorcovering Equipment and Supplies) [10113]

Scarborough

Blue Cold Distributors (Restaurant and Commercial Foodservice Equipment and Supplies) [24078]
Castle Distributors Inc. (Household Appliances) [15080]
Florig Equipment of Portland, Inc. (Industrial Machinery) [16016]
Maine Battery Distributors (Recreational and Sporting Goods) [23797]
Michaud Distributors (Food) [11870]
Nonesuch Foods (Food) [12013]
Parker-Tilton Inc. (Food) [12114]
Pelreco Inc. (Heating and Cooling Equipment and Supplies) [14634]
Portland News Co. (Books and Other Printed Materials) [4073]
Scarborough Auto Parts Inc. (Automotive) [3192]

Searsport

Hamilton Marine (Marine) [18516]

Skowhegan

Clark; Clayton H. (Livestock and Farm Products) [17781]

Solon

Different Drummer (Toys and Hobby Goods) [26469]

South Berwick

Emery; Stuart (Automotive) [2588]

South Portland

Broadway Industries Corp. (Paints and Varnishes) [21406]
Hews Company Inc. (Construction Materials and Machinery) [7468]
National Distributing Inc. (Alcoholic Beverages) [1910]
National Distributors Inc. (Soft Drinks) [24991]
Union Oil Company of Maine (Petroleum, Fuels, and Related Equipment) [22758]

Southwest Harbor

Village Electronics (Sound and Entertainment Equipment and Supplies) [25508]

Standish

Tower Publishing Co. (Books and Other Printed Materials) [4224]

Turner

Decoster Egg Farms (Food) [10934]

Union

Wesmac Enterprises (Marine) [18636]

Warren

Seaboard Manufacturing Co. (Marine) [18604]

Waterboro

Horton's Smoked Seafoods (Food) [11463]
Northeast Hide & Fur Corp. (Livestock and Farm Products) [18141]

Waterville

Colonial Distributors Inc. (Alcoholic Beverages) [1606]

Medical Supplies Inc. (Medical, Dental, and Optical Equipment) [18924]
Murdock Inc.; H.E. (Jewelry) [17527]
Swift Ltd.; S.A. (Jewelry) [17629]

Wells

Home Fasions Distributor (Household Items) [15530]
Pallian & Co. (Horticultural Supplies) [14936]
Seacoast Gallery (Specialty Equipment and Products) [25811]

Westbrook

C & R Tile (Floorcovering Equipment and Supplies) [9749]
Chadwick-BaRoss Inc. (Construction Materials and Machinery) [7166]
Environetics (Scientific and Measurement Devices) [24355]
New England Pet Supply (Veterinary Products) [27193]
Wormell; L.C. (Livestock and Farm Products) [18360]

Windham

Ricci; Robert (Restaurant and Commercial Foodservice Equipment and Supplies) [24210]

Winthrop

Bounty Trading Co. (Food) [10599]
Fire Tech & Safety of Neng (Security and Safety Equipment) [24549]
Progressive Distributors (Health and Beauty Aids) [14199]

Woolwich

Merrymeeting Corp. (Recreational and Sporting Goods) [23823]

Yarmouth

Maine Cottage Furniture Inc. (Furniture and Fixtures) [13169]
Ring's Coal Co. (Minerals and Ores) [20562]

York

Bev-Tech, Inc. (Heating and Cooling Equipment and Supplies) [14345]

York Beach

Burnham; William H. (Toys and Hobby Goods) [26431]
Weiser Inc.; Samuel (Books and Other Printed Materials) [4272]

Maryland

Aberdeen

Folcomer Equipment Corporation (Construction Materials and Machinery) [7350]
Harco Electronics Inc. (Electrical and Electronic Equipment and Supplies) [8829]

Abingdon

Somerville, Co.; Thomas (Plumbing Materials and Fixtures) [23383]

Annapolis

American Bus Sales (Automotive) [2227]
Bay Merchandising Inc. (Shoes) [24686]
Fawcett Boat Supplies Inc. (Marine) [18501]
Gardner Inc.; E.L. (Construction Materials and Machinery) [7379]
Gomoljak Block (Construction Materials and Machinery) [7403]
H-A Distributors Inc. (Sound and Entertainment Equipment and Supplies) [25222]
J & K Distributors (Cleaning and Janitorial Supplies) [4642]
Katcef Brothers Inc. (Alcoholic Beverages) [1794]
Katcef Sales Inc. (Specialty Equipment and Products) [25696]
Michel Company Inc.; R.E. (Heating and Cooling Equipment and Supplies) [14545]

Oceana Ltd. (Marine) [18578]
Somerville Co.; Thomas (Plumbing Materials and Fixtures) [23384]
Specialized Marketing (Office Equipment and Supplies) [21280]
Specialized Marketing (Furniture and Fixtures) [13249]
Team Distributors Inc. (Recreational and Sporting Goods) [24005]
Technology Specialists Inc. (Computers and Software) [6802]
Weems & Plath, Inc. (Aeronautical Equipment and Supplies) [171]

Annapolis Junction

Cummins-Wagner Company Inc. (Compressors) [5837]
Georgia Steel and Chemical Co. (Medical, Dental, and Optical Equipment) [18810]
Michel Company Inc.; R.E. (Heating and Cooling Equipment and Supplies) [14546]
NEA Professional Library (Books and Other Printed Materials) [3990]
United Strategies Inc. (Computers and Software) [6843]

Arbutus

Seed Corp. of America (Agricultural Equipment and Supplies) [1250]

Baltimore

African Export Ltd. (Shoes) [24665]
Alban Tractor Company Inc. (Industrial Machinery) [15751]
Ansam Metals Corp. (Metals) [19782]
Artform Industries Inc. (Plastics) [22929]
Atlantic Solar Products Inc. (Electrical and Electronic Equipment and Supplies) [8391]
Atlantic Tire Wholesaler (Automotive) [2267]
Babikow Greenhouses (Horticultural Supplies) [14812]
Baklayan Garbis (Shoes) [24680]
Balloonery Inc. (Toys and Hobby Goods) [26409]
Baltimore Hydraulics Inc. (Industrial Supplies) [16719]
Baltimore Scrap Corp. (Metals) [19801]
Bee Jay Refrigeration Inc. (Heating and Cooling Equipment and Supplies) [14341]
Belair Road Supply Company Inc. (Construction Materials and Machinery) [7044]
Benson Company Inc.; L.A. (Industrial Supplies) [16749]
Best Battery Company Inc. (Automotive) [2352]
Better Buildings, Inc. (Construction Materials and Machinery) [7055]
Bond Co.; T. Talbott (Office Equipment and Supplies) [20849]
Bronze and Plastic Specialties Inc. (Metals) [19837]
Budeke's Paint (Paints and Varnishes) [21409]
Calvert Dry Goods Inc. (Clothing) [4858]
Canusa Corp. (Used, Scrap, and Recycled Materials) [26777]
Capital Lighting & Supply - Baltimore/Lee Electric Div. (Electrical and Electronic Equipment and Supplies) [8496]
Carey Machinery & Supply Co. (Security and Safety Equipment) [24524]
Chesapeake Rim & Wheel Distributors Inc. (Automotive) [2447]
Choice Medical Inc. (Medical, Dental, and Optical Equipment) [18743]
Churchill Distributors (Alcoholic Beverages) [1594]
Claymore Sieck Co. (Hardware) [13635]
CoalARBED International Trading Co. (Minerals and Ores) [20531]
College Bowl Inc. (Clothing) [4888]
Conklin and Company Inc.; Lyon (Heating and Cooling Equipment and Supplies) [14400]
Continental Foods Inc. (Food) [10829]
Corporate Express of the MidAtlantic Inc. (Office Equipment and Supplies) [20930]
Crown Optical Ltd. (Medical, Dental, and Optical Supplies) [19259]
Dashew Inc.; J. (Industrial Machinery) [15931]

Davis and Sons Inc.; F.A. (Tobacco Products) [26286]

DeBois Textiles Inc. (Textiles and Notions) [26015]

DEI Inc. (Security and Safety Equipment) [24533]

Durrett-Sheppard Steel Co. (Metals) [19942]

East Distributors Ltd.; Ryan (Books and Other Printed Materials) [3706]

Electric Motor Repair Co. (Restaurant and Commercial Foodservice Equipment and Supplies) [24107]

Emanuel Tire Co. (Automotive) [2586]

European Kosher Provision (Food) [11060]

Fitch Dustdown Co. (Cleaning and Janitorial Supplies) [4621]

Fitch Dustdown Co. (Restaurant and Commercial Foodservice Equipment and Supplies) [24120]

Forman Inc. (Cleaning and Janitorial Supplies) [4626]

Forman Inc. (Industrial Supplies) [16873]

Foundry Service Supply Inc. (Industrial Supplies) [16876]

Fox Auctioneers Inc.; Michael (Industrial Machinery) [16037]

Fox International Inc.; Michael (Industrial Machinery) [16038]

Frank and Sons Inc.; A. (Textiles and Notions) [26038]

Franklin Town Metals and Cores (Metals) [19984]

G and L Recycling Inc. (Used, Scrap, and Recycled Materials) [26819]

Gar-Ron Plastics Corp. (Plastics) [22967]

General Plumbing Supply Company of Maryland Inc. (Plumbing Materials and Fixtures) [23188]

Getaway Sailing (Marine) [18506]

Gilco Meats Inc. (Food) [11264]

Golden Capital Distributors (Food) [11283]

Goldmar Sales Corp. (Agricultural Equipment and Supplies) [747]

Gonzalez International Inc. (Industrial Machinery) [16071]

Grasmick Lumber Company Inc.; Louis J. (Construction Materials and Machinery) [7413]

Gunther and Co.; Albert (Construction Materials and Machinery) [7424]

HCIA Inc. (Books and Other Printed Materials) [3819]

Home Safety Products (Sound and Entertainment Equipment and Supplies) [25236]

Importmex (Gifts and Novelties) [13375]

Independent Distribution Services Inc. (Household Appliances) [15175]

Inland Leidy Inc. (Chemicals) [4430]

International Eyewear Inc. (Medical, Dental, and Optical Supplies) [19376]

Jarvis Steel and Lumber Company Inc. (Construction Materials and Machinery) [7531]

Jed Co.; Leonard (Hardware) [13770]

Jenkins Sons Company Inc.; J. (Jewelry) [17468]

J.O. Spice Company Inc. (Food) [11556]

Kayboys Empire Paper Company Inc. (Paper and Paper Products) [21789]

Kimmel Automotive Inc. (Automotive) [2855]

Kreinik Manufacturing Company Inc. (Textiles and Notions) [26116]

Leonard Paper Company Inc. (Paper and Paper Products) [21799]

Loock & Company Inc.; R.J. (Automotive) [2892]

Lucas Brothers Inc. (Office Equipment and Supplies) [21115]

M & E Sales - A Honeywell Business (Scientific and Measurement Devices) [24390]

Marlen Trading Company Inc. (Metals) [20154]

Maryland Hotel Supply Co. (Food) [11798]

Maryland Industrial Inc. (Shoes) [24802]

Maryland Industrial Inc. (Clothing) [5171]

Maryland Leather Inc. (Luggage and Leather Goods) [18412]

Maryland News Distributing Co. (Books and Other Printed Materials) [3938]

Maryland Tile Distributors (Floorcovering Equipment and Supplies) [10011]

Medical Procedures Inc. (Medical, Dental, and Optical Equipment) [18921]

Meyer Seed Co. (Agricultural Equipment and Supplies) [1020]

Microcomputer Company of Maryland Inc. (Computers and Software) [6501]

Mitchell Inc.; E. Stewart (Construction Materials and Machinery) [7730]

Modern Equipment Sales and Rental Co. (Construction Materials and Machinery) [7733]

Monumental Supply Company Inc. (Plumbing Materials and Fixtures) [23274]

Myers and Sons Inc.; D. (Shoes) [24817]

National Rubber Footwear Inc. (Shoes) [24818]

National Rubber Footwear Inc. (Clothing) [5216]

National Wholesale (Sound and Entertainment Equipment and Supplies) [25355]

New City Optical Company Inc. (Medical, Dental, and Optical Supplies) [19489]

NFZ Products Inc. (Hardware) [13846]

Noe-Equal Hosiery Corporation (Clothing) [5234]

Old World Bakery (Food) [12064]

Pikesville Lumber Co. (Construction Materials and Machinery) [7863]

Piraeus International (Sound and Entertainment Equipment and Supplies) [25384]

Pompeian Inc. (Food) [12190]

Price Modern Inc. (Furniture and Fixtures) [13212]

Production Machinery Inc. (Industrial Machinery) [16432]

PTC International (Medical, Dental, and Optical Equipment) [19000]

Purity Products Inc. (Alcoholic Beverages) [1973]

Purity Products Inc. (Baltimore, Maryland) (Soft Drinks) [25022]

Radio Resources and Services Corp. (Communications Systems and Equipment) [5732]

Radio Resources and Services Corp. (Electrical and Electronic Equipment and Supplies) [9258]

Robins L.L.C.; A.K. (Restaurant and Commercial Foodservice Equipment and Supplies) [24211]

Robnet Inc. (Hardware) [13889]

Rockland Industries Inc. (Textiles and Notions) [26188]

Sanders Co. (Construction Materials and Machinery) [7978]

Sanford Shirt Co. (Clothing) [5332]

Schelle Cellular Group Inc. (Communications Systems and Equipment) [5751]

Shane's Shoe (Shoes) [24854]

Shepherd Electric Company Inc. (Electrical and Electronic Equipment and Supplies) [9362]

Smith Associates; Bernie (Sound and Entertainment Equipment and Supplies) [25445]

Standard Equipment Co. (Agricultural Equipment and Supplies) [1292]

Standard Plumbing Supply Company Inc. (Plumbing Materials and Fixtures) [23396]

Standard Textile Company Inc. (Household Items) [15666]

Stone Steel Corp. (Metals) [20407]

Summers Fuel Inc. (Minerals and Ores) [20571]

Sunbelt Beverage Company L.L.C. (Alcoholic Beverages) [2061]

Superior Products, Inc. (Floorcovering Equipment and Supplies) [10195]

Szco Supplier Inc. (Household Items) [15678]

Target Appliances (Household Appliances) [15331]

Tate Engineering Systems, Inc. (Compressors) [5853]

Tedco Indus Inc. (Textiles and Notions) [26223]

Time Out For Sports (Clothing) [5430]

Total Office Interiors (Paper and Paper Products) [21954]

Tots Wear Company Inc. (Clothing) [5437]

Town & Country Pet Supply Inc. (Veterinary Products) [27249]

United Iron and Metal Co. (Used, Scrap, and Recycled Materials) [27029]

United Steel Associates Inc. (Metals) [20465]

Universal Marble and Granite Inc. (Construction Materials and Machinery) [8161]

Valley Gun of Baltimore (Guns and Weapons) [13516]

Vegetarian Resource Group (Books and Other Printed Materials) [4258]

Walker Co.; James (Industrial Supplies) [17261]

Wareheim Air Brakes (Automotive) [3398]

Watson Co.; Ray V. (Automotive) [3404]

Westreet Industries (Used, Scrap, and Recycled Materials) [27045]

White Rose Paper Co. (Paper and Paper Products) [21992]

Zamoiski Company Inc. (Household Appliances) [15383]

Bel Air

Kiddie Academy International Inc. (Office Equipment and Supplies) [21089]

Kunkel Services Co. (Automotive) [2865]

Belcamp

Bata Shoe Co. Inc. (Shoes) [24683]

Beltsville

Boater's World (Marine) [18467]

Bray and Scarff Inc. (Sound and Entertainment Equipment and Supplies) [25107]

Capitol Copy Products Inc. (Office Equipment and Supplies) [20877]

Closet Centers America (Household Items) [15447]

Contract Kitchen Distributors (Household Appliances) [15095]

Gryphon House, Inc. (Books and Other Printed Materials) [3802]

Hazlett Company Inc.; T.R. (Construction Materials and Machinery) [7462]

Maryland Clay Products (Construction Materials and Machinery) [7658]

Maryland Clay Products (Construction Materials and Machinery) [7659]

Mid-South Building Supply of Maryland Inc. (Construction Materials and Machinery) [7705]

Triangle Pacific Corp. Beltsville Div. (Construction Materials and Machinery) [8148]

Veb Plastics Inc. (Plastics) [23046]

Berlin

Somerville Co.; Thomas (Plumbing Materials and Fixtures) [23385]

Bethesda

ASCII Group Inc. (Computers and Software) [5970]

Bartley Tile Concepts Inc. (Construction Materials and Machinery) [7026]

Capitol Entertainment & Home (Photographic Equipment and Supplies) [22839]

Enright Co.; J.R. (Sound and Entertainment Equipment and Supplies) [25182]

H n' M Associates Inc. (Food) [11352]

International Telecom Systems Inc. (Communications Systems and Equipment) [5650]

U.S.-China Industrial Exchange Inc. (Medical, Dental, and Optical Equipment) [19094]

Bladensburg

Joy Company Inc.; B. Frank (Electrical and Electronic Equipment and Supplies) [8921]

Maier Inc.; Ernest (Construction Materials and Machinery) [7634]

Thompson and Cooke Inc. (Industrial Supplies) [17226]

Braddock Heights

AAA Distributors Inc. (Office Equipment and Supplies) [20763]

AAA Distributors Inc. (Household Appliances) [14988]

Brandywine

Brandywine Auto Parts Inc. (Automotive) [2381]

Brentwood

Michelle's Family Bakery (Food) [11871]

Cambridge

Chesapeake Medical Systems (Medical, Dental, and Optical Equipment) [18740]

Phillips Hardware Co. (Petroleum, Fuels, and Related Equipment) [22579]

Camp Springs

Mattos Inc. (Paints and Varnishes) [21498]

Capitol Heights

Advanced Equipment Company Inc. (Industrial Machinery) [15736]
Capital Carousel Inc. (Paints and Varnishes) [21410]
Hockstein Inc.; David (Floorcovering Equipment and Supplies) [9951]
Potomac Industrial Trucks Inc. (Industrial Machinery) [16411]
Potomac Rubber Company Inc. (Rubber) [24289]
Sita Tile Distributors, Inc. (Floorcovering Equipment and Supplies) [10150]
U.S. Recording Co. (Sound and Entertainment Equipment and Supplies) [25491]

Cheverly

Michel Company Inc.; R.E. (Heating and Cooling Equipment and Supplies) [14547]
Roland Foods (Food) [12346]
Washington Natural Foods and Co. (Food) [12881]

Clinton

J.A. Optronics (Medical, Dental, and Optical Supplies) [19383]

Cockeysville

Advance Business Systems and Supply Co. (Office Equipment and Supplies) [20775]
Artomate Co. (Recreational and Sporting Goods) [23524]
Glover Equipment Inc. (Furniture and Fixtures) [13124]

College Park

Full Bore - Cycle Lines USA (Motorized Vehicles) [20638]
Full Bore - Cycle Lines USA (Automotive) [2655]

Columbia

Allied Electronics (Electrical and Electronic Equipment and Supplies) [8302]
Biocoustics Instruments Inc. (Medical, Dental, and Optical Equipment) [18712]
JP Foodservice Inc. (Food) [11569]
JP Foodservice Inc. (Food) [11570]
Kluge, Finkelstein & Co. (Food) [11627]
Peak Technologies Inc. (Columbia, Maryland) (Office Equipment and Supplies) [21207]
Rhee Bros. Inc. (Food) [12305]
Rykoff-Sexton Distribution Div. (Food) [12375]
Rykoff-Sexton Inc. (Food) [12376]
S and G Trading Co. (Toys and Hobby Goods) [26643]
Sales and Marketing Services Inc. (Medical, Dental, and Optical Equipment) [19030]
Standard Medical Imaging Inc. (Medical, Dental, and Optical Equipment) [19052]
U.S. Foodservice Inc. (Restaurant and Commercial Foodservice Equipment and Supplies) [24257]
Vair Corp. (Heating and Cooling Equipment and Supplies) [14751]

Crisfield

Carvel Hall Inc. (Household Items) [15436]
Handy Company Inc.; John T. (Food) [11370]
Sterling & Son; Clarence (Marine) [18617]

Crofton

Kane X-Ray Company Inc. (Medical, Dental, and Optical Equipment) [18872]

Cumberland

Burtons Inc. (Clothing) [4855]
Lee/Star Tire Co. (Automotive) [2877]
Super Shoe Stores Inc. (Shoes) [24871]
Western Maryland Distributing (Alcoholic Beverages) [2116]

Easton

Ames Sciences Inc. (Computers and Software) [5936]
Charter Distributing Inc. (Household Appliances) [15083]
Easton Steel Service Inc. (Metals) [19947]
Easton Wholesale Co. (Marine) [18497]
Elliott Equipment Company Inc. (Motorized Vehicles) [20632]
Hanks Seafood Company Inc. (Food) [11371]
Papillon Agricultural Products Inc. (Agricultural Equipment and Supplies) [1117]
Whalen Co. (Cleaning and Janitorial Supplies) [4731]

Elkridge

Alban Engine Power Systems (Automotive) [2198]
Development Through Self-Reliance Inc. (Computers and Software) [6204]
Saval Foods (Food) [12421]
Sunny's Great Outdoors Inc. (Recreational and Sporting Goods) [23993]

Elkton

Summit Instruments Corp. (Medical, Dental, and Optical Equipment) [19061]

Ellicott City

Calus & CEI Distributors Inc. (Toys and Hobby Goods) [26435]
Himex International Inc. (Shoes) [24764]
Phoenix Imports Ltd. (Alcoholic Beverages) [1957]

Forestville

Pepsi-Cola of Washington, D.C. L.P. (Books and Other Printed Materials) [4055]
Remco Business Systems Inc. (Office Equipment and Supplies) [21237]

Ft. Washington

Dops, Inc. (Alcoholic Beverages) [1657]
Tuxedo Junction Inc. (Clothing) [5446]

Frederick

Dairy Maid Dairy Inc. (Food) [10897]
Duvall Inc.; H.B. (Agricultural Equipment and Supplies) [530]
Erwin Distributing Co. (Alcoholic Beverages) [1679]
FPC Foodservices (Food) [11198]
Frederick Trading Co. (Hardware) [13715]
Nelson Roanoke Corp. (Hardware) [13844]
Nelson-Roanoke Div. (Hardware) [13845]
Phoenix Inc. (Construction Materials and Machinery) [7862]
Rice Tire Co.; Donald B. (Automotive) [3156]
Southern States Frederick Cooperative Inc. (Agricultural Equipment and Supplies) [1284]
Werres Corp. (Industrial Machinery) [16622]

Gaithersburg

American General Supplies Inc. (Aeronautical Equipment and Supplies) [41]
Arbee Associates (Office Equipment and Supplies) [20809]
Axis Electronics Inc. (Electrical and Electronic Equipment and Supplies) [8405]
Biomedical Research & Development Laboratories, Inc. (Medical, Dental, and Optical Equipment) [18713]
Commercial Washer Dryer Sales Co. (Household Appliances) [15092]
Computer Graphics Distributing Co. (Computers and Software) [6112]
GE Capital Information Technology Solutions (Computers and Software) [6295]
GTS Scientific Inc. (Medical, Dental, and Optical Equipment) [18818]
Keep It Simple Technology Inc. (Computers and Software) [6418]
Key Distribution, Inc. (Electrical and Electronic Equipment and Supplies) [8940]
Morris Tile Distributors (Floorcovering Equipment and Supplies) [10058]

Pioneer-Standard Electronics Inc. (Computers and Software) [6623]
Sigma-Tau Pharmaceuticals Inc. (Medical, Dental, and Optical Supplies) [19611]
Standard Supplies Inc. (Construction Materials and Machinery) [8069]
Total Orthopedic Div. (Medical, Dental, and Optical Supplies) [19659]
Uster Imports, Inc.; Albert (Food) [12809]
Visual Aids Electronics (Communications Systems and Equipment) [5806]

Gambrills

Clark; Frank (Computers and Software) [6073]

Glen Arm

Happy Valley Clothing Co. (Clothing) [5019]

Glen Burnie

Central Atlantic Toyota Distributors Inc. (Automotive) [2437]
Haines & Company, Inc.; J.J. (Floorcovering Equipment and Supplies) [9931]
Michel Company Inc.; R.E. (Heating and Cooling Equipment and Supplies) [14601]
Quality Brands Inc. (Alcoholic Beverages) [1975]

Grantsville

Yoders Inc. (Food) [12994]

Greenbelt

NYMA Inc. (Computers and Software) [6565]

Hagerstown

AC and T Company Inc. (Petroleum, Fuels, and Related Equipment) [22019]
Blaine Window Hardware Inc. (Hardware) [13600]
Foltz Manufacturing and Supply Co. (Hardware) [13714]
The Gage Co. (Plumbing Materials and Fixtures) [23180]
Har-Tru Corp. (Recreational and Sporting Goods) [23713]
Keyboard Decals (Sound and Entertainment Equipment and Supplies) [25271]
Packaging Concepts Corp. (Food) [12095]
Paramount Feed and Supply Inc. (Agricultural Equipment and Supplies) [1118]
Sokol Electronics Inc. (Computers and Software) [6744]
Tristate Electrical & Electronics Supply Company Inc./Uagemeyer N.V. (Electrical and Electronic Equipment and Supplies) [9511]
Tristate Electrical Supply Company Inc. (Electrical and Electronic Equipment and Supplies) [9512]

Hampstead

Black and Decker Corp. Products Service Div. (Household Appliances) [15053]

Hancock

Sky Knob Technologies LLC (Computers and Software) [6734]

Hanover

Almo Distributing (Computers and Software) [5913]
Capstone Pharmacy Services (Medical, Dental, and Optical Supplies) [19211]
Gilbert Foods Inc. (Food) [11263]
Hearn Kirkwood (Food) [11402]
Thermo King of Baltimore Inc. (Heating and Cooling Equipment and Supplies) [14723]

Hunt Valley

Coaxis Inc. Insight Distribution Systems (Computers and Software) [6078]
ITC Inc. (Paper and Paper Products) [21780]
Tessco Technologies Inc. (Communications Systems and Equipment) [5791]
TESSCO Technologies Inc. (Communications Systems and Equipment) [5792]

Hyattsville

Adams-Burch Inc. (Restaurant and Commercial Foodservice Equipment and Supplies) [24056]

Daedalus Books (Books and Other Printed Materials) [3679]

D.C. Materials Inc. (Used, Scrap, and Recycled Materials) [26794]

Morris Tile Distributors Inc. (Floorcovering Equipment and Supplies) [10060]

Noland Co. (Plumbing Materials and Fixtures) [23291]

The Premier Group (Toys and Hobby Goods) [26621]

Shankle Co. Inc.; Earle (Automotive) [3212]

Ijamsville

Comus Computer Corp. (Computers and Software) [6144]

Jarrettsville

Aquarium Pet Book Distributors (Veterinary Products) [27072]

Jessup

Ann's House of Nuts, Inc. (Food) [10420]

Auto Collision Inc. (Automotive) [2270]

Foehrkolb Inc.; Louis (Food) [11166]

Leasure & Associates Inc.; Ralph (Medical, Dental, and Optical Equipment) [18885]

Monumental Paper Co. (Paper and Paper Products) [21842]

Smellkinson Sysco Food Services Inc. (Restaurant and Commercial Foodservice Equipment and Supplies) [24223]

Southern Seafood Co. (Food) [12541]

Vitrano Co.; Tony (Food) [12853]

Joppa

Brocato; Charles (Shoes) [24698]

La Plata

SMO Inc. (Petroleum, Fuels, and Related Equipment) [22680]

Landover

A.W. Industries (Furniture and Fixtures) [13027]

CERBCO Inc. (Office Equipment and Supplies) [20894]

Dynamic Computer Concepts (Computers and Software) [6231]

Freedman and Sons Inc.; S. (Paper and Paper Products) [21730]

Metropolitan Poultry and Seafood Co. (Food) [11861]

Night Owl Security Inc. (Security and Safety Equipment) [24603]

Parsons Paper Co.; Frank (Paper and Paper Products) [21868]

Sel-Tronics, Inc. (Electrical and Electronic Equipment and Supplies) [9351]

Stanford Paper Co. (Paper and Paper Products) [21949]

Wilson Capital Truck L.L.C.; Elliot (Motorized Vehicles) [20750]

Lanham

Accents Publications Service, Inc. (Books and Other Printed Materials) [3465]

Bernan (Books and Other Printed Materials) [3552]

Integral Marketing Inc. (Electrical and Electronic Equipment and Supplies) [8886]

Maryland Historical Press (Books and Other Printed Materials) [3937]

National Book Network Inc. (Books and Other Printed Materials) [3984]

Pulsar Data Systems Inc. (Computers and Software) [6664]

Shopper's Food Warehouse Corp. (Food) [12483]

Unipub (Books and Other Printed Materials) [4238]

Vestal Press Ltd. (Books and Other Printed Materials) [4259]

Lanham Seabrook

Automated Office Products Inc. (Office Equipment and Supplies) [20823]

Land Rover North America Inc. (Automotive) [2872]

Rohde and Schwarz Inc. (Electrical and Electronic Equipment and Supplies) [9312]

Largo

Jewel and Co. (Clothing) [5083]

Laurel

International Organic Products Inc. (Health and Beauty Aids) [14132]

System Solutions Technology Inc. (Computers and Software) [6783]

Lavale

Witmer Foods Inc. (Food) [12969]

Leonardtown

Up-Rad Inc. (Medical, Dental, and Optical Equipment) [19097]

Lexington Park

Colonial Office Supplies Inc. (Office Equipment and Supplies) [20905]

Linthicum Heights

Atlantic Fitness Products Co. (Recreational and Sporting Goods) [23526]

Fitness Corporation of America (Recreational and Sporting Goods) [23670]

Lutherville Timonium

Day Corp.; Alan G. (Medical, Dental, and Optical Equipment) [18766]

Maugansville

Maugansville Elevator and Lumber Company Inc. (Petroleum, Fuels, and Related Equipment) [22457]

Mechanicsville

Noland Co. (Plumbing Materials and Fixtures) [23292]

Monkton

Great Bay Paper Co. (Paper and Paper Products) [21749]

Mt. Airy

Baltimore & Washington Truck Equipment, Inc. (Automotive) [2314]

Mt. Rainier

Coleman Interior Service Co. (Household Items) [15450]

New Carrollton

CMA International (Industrial Machinery) [15894]

Ocean City

Atlantic Skates Inc. (Recreational and Sporting Goods) [23528]

Spectrum Computer & Business Supplies (Computers and Software) [6754]

Odenton

Lachman & Son Inc.; S. (Toys and Hobby Goods) [26559]

Techmart Computer Products (Office Equipment and Supplies) [21317]

Olney

Maryland Import/Export, Inc. (Jewelry) [17514]

Owings

Carl Beatty and Associates (Medical, Dental, and Optical Supplies) [19216]

Medical Advisory Systems Inc. (Medical, Dental, and Optical Supplies) [19442]

Owings Mills

Cameo Electronics Company Inc. (Electrical and Electronic Equipment and Supplies) [8492]

Douron Inc. (Paper and Paper Products) [21714]

Douron Incorporated Corporate Furniture (Furniture and Fixtures) [13094]

Fluid Power Inc. (Industrial Machinery) [16020]

Gaylon Distributing Inc. (Electrical and Electronic Equipment and Supplies) [8775]

Holstein Paper & Janitorial Supply (Paper and Paper Products) [21765]

Master Building Supply and Lumber Co. (Construction Materials and Machinery) [7664]

NLS Animal Health (Veterinary Products) [27195]

Somerville Co.; Thomas (Plumbing Materials and Fixtures) [23381]

Thomas Industrial Products Company Inc. (Shoes) [24876]

Tradeways Inc. (Furniture and Fixtures) [13260]

Universal Security Instruments Inc. (Security and Safety Equipment) [24652]

Wilf Corp.; Elias (Floorcovering Equipment and Supplies) [10300]

Oxon Hill

Tribles of Maryland Inc. (Household Appliances) [15343]

Pasadena

D.M. Distributing Company Inc. (Alcoholic Beverages) [1655]

Perryville

Bay Grove Nurseries, Inc. (Horticultural Supplies) [14824]

Pocomoke City

Lankford-Sysco Food Services Inc. (Food) [11677]

Mid Atlantic Foods Inc. (Food) [11876]

Preston

Albert W. Sisk and Son Inc. (Food) [10358]

Princess Anne

Hollandia Gift and Toy Co. (Toys and Hobby Goods) [26524]

Quantico

Dave's Sport Shop (Recreational and Sporting Goods) [23615]

Reisterstown

International Purchasers, Inc. (Construction Materials and Machinery) [7521]

The Test Connection Inc. (Scientific and Measurement Devices) [24444]

Rockville

AKJ Educational Services, Inc. (Books and Other Printed Materials) [3480]

Ando Corp. Measuring Instruments Div. (Scientific and Measurement Devices) [24313]

Charles Products Inc. (Gifts and Novelties) [13330]

Computer Data Systems, Inc. (Computers and Software) [6108]

Cosons Inc. (Office Equipment and Supplies) [20933]

Devlin Lumber and Supply Corp. (Construction Materials and Machinery) [7260]

Discount Drugs Wisconsin Inc. (Medical, Dental, and Optical Supplies) [19281]

Empire Recycling Inc. (Used, Scrap, and Recycled Materials) [26807]

FIC Corp. (Electrical and Electronic Equipment and Supplies) [8739]

IDEAL Scanners & Systems, Inc. (Office Equipment and Supplies) [21048]

Intercontinental Trade Development (Medical, Dental, and Optical Equipment) [18855]

M & A Sales (Electrical and Electronic Equipment and Supplies) [9012]

Manugistics Group Inc. (Computers and Software) [6460]

Mid-Atlantic Marketing Inc. (Sound and Entertainment Equipment and Supplies) [25316]

Newsom Seeds (Agricultural Equipment and Supplies) [1073]

Noland Co. (Plumbing Materials and Fixtures) [23293]

Paddock Swimming Pool Co. (Recreational and Sporting Goods) [23868]
RCI Custom Products (Sound and Entertainment Equipment and Supplies) [25408]
R.J. Marketing, Ltd. (Electrical and Electronic Equipment and Supplies) [9298]
Roberts Oxygen Company Inc. (Medical, Dental, and Optical Equipment) [19025]
Rockville Fuel and Feed Company Inc. (Construction Materials and Machinery) [7948]
Somerville Co.; Thomas (Plumbing Materials and Fixtures) [23382]
Target Distributing Co. (Sound and Entertainment Equipment and Supplies) [25471]
Target Distributing Co. (Household Appliances) [15332]

Salisbury

Coastline Parts Co. (Household Appliances) [15088]
Dennis Sales Ltd. (Food) [10944]
Grier and Sons Co.; R.D. (Industrial Supplies) [16910]
Hearne Produce Co.; William P. (Food) [11403]
Pepsi-Cola Bottling Company of Salisbury (Soft Drinks) [25013]
Perdue Farms Grain Div. (Livestock and Farm Products) [18162]
Shore Distributors Inc. (Heating and Cooling Equipment and Supplies) [14683]

Savage

Acme Paper and Supply Company Inc. (Paper and Paper Products) [21615]
Carapace Corp. (Hardware) [13619]

Silver Spring

American International Exports (Household Appliances) [15009]
Antronnix Antenna Co. Inc. (Electrical and Electronic Equipment and Supplies) [8362]
Concrete Supply Corp. (Construction Materials and Machinery) [7205]
Cultural Hispana/Ameriketakoa (Books and Other Printed Materials) [3677]
Dosik International (Books and Other Printed Materials) [3700]
Export of International Appliances (Household Appliances) [15124]
Formtronix Inc. (Computers and Software) [6276]
IMS Systems, Inc. (Sound and Entertainment Equipment and Supplies) [25241]
Meredith Stained Glass Center, Inc. (Specialty Equipment and Products) [25735]
Noland Co. (Plumbing Materials and Fixtures) [23294]
Perstorp Analytical Inc. (Scientific and Measurement Devices) [24417]
Potomac Adventist Book Center (Books and Other Printed Materials) [4075]
Scantek Inc. (Scientific and Measurement Devices) [24426]
Scripts For All Reasons (Clothing) [5340]
Sorceror Distributors (Toys and Hobby Goods) [26657]
Summit Pet Products (Veterinary Products) [27241]

Sparks

Arundel Corp. (Construction Materials and Machinery) [6995]

Stevensville

Casele Associates Inc. (Sound and Entertainment Equipment and Supplies) [25125]
Office Manager, Inc. (Computers and Software) [6568]
Zodiac of North America (Marine) [18649]

Sudlersville

Harbor Sales Company (Construction Materials and Machinery) [7441]
Harbor Sales Co. (Wood and Wood Products) [27316]

Sykesville

Constantine Wine (Alcoholic Beverages) [1614]

Takoma Park

Appliance Distributors Unlimited (Household Appliances) [15017]
Potomac Adventist Book Center (Books and Other Printed Materials) [4076]

Thurmont

Andelain Farm (Livestock and Farm Products) [17700]
Thurmont Cooperative Inc. (Agricultural Equipment and Supplies) [1333]

Timonium

Communications Electronics Inc. (Communications Systems and Equipment) [5569]
Diamond Comic Distributors Inc. (Toys and Hobby Goods) [26468]
Kitchen Distributors Maryland (Household Appliances) [15189]
Omni Group Inc. (Security and Safety Equipment) [24605]
Schumacher and Seiler Inc. (Plumbing Materials and Fixtures) [23361]
Summitville Baltimore (Floorcovering Equipment and Supplies) [10187]

Toddville

Meredith and Meredith Inc. (Food) [11856]

Towson

Bacharach-Rasin Co. (Recreational and Sporting Goods) [23533]
Nolan Scott Chatard L.L.C. (Construction Materials and Machinery) [7784]

Tuxedo

Morris Tile Distributors (Floorcovering Equipment and Supplies) [10059]

Upper Marlboro

Branch Electric Supply Co. (Electrical and Electronic Equipment and Supplies) [8462]
Buck Distributing Company Inc. (Alcoholic Beverages) [1556]
Electronic Security Services (Security and Safety Equipment) [24536]
Europa Consulting (Computers and Software) [6257]
Hall Inc.; Bob (Alcoholic Beverages) [1740]
Murry's Inc. (Food) [11959]
Walston Co.; William H. (Construction Materials and Machinery) [8194]

Waldorf

Bailey Lumber Co. (Construction Materials and Machinery) [7011]
Besche Oil Co. Inc. (Petroleum, Fuels, and Related Equipment) [22071]
Cenna International Corp. (Medical, Dental, and Optical Supplies) [19223]
Yeatman Architectural Hardware Inc. (Hardware) [14004]

Westminster

Hahn Bros. Inc. (Food) [11359]
Hahns of Westminster (Food) [11360]
Michel Company Inc.; R.E. (Heating and Cooling Equipment and Supplies) [14548]
Mills Communication Inc. (Electrical and Electronic Equipment and Supplies) [9086]

Wheaton

Classic Beauty Supply and Service Center (Health and Beauty Aids) [14065]
Classic Beauty Supply and Service Center (Restaurant and Commercial Foodservice Equipment and Supplies) [24095]

White Hall

Blue Mount Quarry (Recreational and Sporting Goods) [23560]

White Marsh

Gibson McIlvain Co.; J. (Construction Materials and Machinery) [7396]

Massachusetts

Acton

First Phillips Marketing Company Inc. (Plastics) [22963]
Leading Edge Products Inc. (Computers and Software) [6434]
Rex Lumber Co. (Acton, Massachusetts) (Construction Materials and Machinery) [7924]

Adams

Berkshire Valley (Metals) [19814]
Butler Wholesale Products (Restaurant and Commercial Foodservice Equipment and Supplies) [24085]

Agawam

Alco Equipment Inc. (Automotive) [2200]

Allston

Cambridge Street Metal Company Inc. (Metals) [19849]
Houghton Chemical Corp. (Chemicals) [4419]

Amesbury

Shaheen Brothers Inc. (Food) [12468]
Zakion; Robert (Office Equipment and Supplies) [21369]

Amherst

AMS Imports Inc. (Household Items) [15401]
Surner Heating Company Inc. (Petroleum, Fuels, and Related Equipment) [22716]

Andover

ABC Systems and Development Inc. (Computers and Software) [5862]
Brockway-Smith Co. (Construction Materials and Machinery) [7082]
Intelliphone Inc. (Communications Systems and Equipment) [5647]
RW Electronics Inc. (Electrical and Electronic Equipment and Supplies) [9325]
Standard Duplicating Machines Corp. (Office Equipment and Supplies) [21284]
Swensen's Inc. (Food) [12659]

Arlington

Boston Metal Door Company Inc. (Construction Materials and Machinery) [7072]
Hall Electric Supply Co., Inc. (HESCO) (Household Appliances) [15157]

Ashburnham

Lombard Co.; F.W. (Furniture and Fixtures) [13166]

Athol

Girardi Distributors Corp. (Alcoholic Beverages) [1717]

Attleboro

Universal/Univis Inc. (Medical, Dental, and Optical Supplies) [19686]

Attleboro Falls

Antex Incorporated (Electrical and Electronic Equipment and Supplies) [8361]

Auburn

Aimtek Inc. Welding Supply Div. (Industrial Supplies) [16676]
Aronson Tire Co. Inc. (Automotive) [2253]
Atlas Distributing, Inc. (Soft Drinks) [24912]
Atlas Distributing Inc. (Food) [10465]
Consolidated Beverages Inc. (Alcoholic Beverages) [1613]

Imperial Distributors Inc. (Health and Beauty Aids) [14130]
Mastermans (Medical, Dental, and Optical Equipment) [18902]

Avon
Atsco Footwear Inc. (Shoes) [24678]
Datel Communications Corp. (Communications Systems and Equipment) [5589]
Dutton Co.; Andrew (Household Items) [15483]
Sheehy Inc.; Charles D. (Plumbing Materials and Fixtures) [23372]
Southeastern Construction Inc. (Construction Materials and Machinery) [8044]
Tetra Laval Convenience Food Inc. (Restaurant and Commercial Foodservice Equipment and Supplies) [24244]
Tetra Laval Convenience Food Inc. (Industrial Machinery) [16559]

Ayer
Cains Foods, L.P. (Food) [10663]
Plastic Distributing Corp. (Plastics) [23007]
Ryerson-Thypin - Div. of Ryerson Tull (Metals) [20343]

Barre
Berube Municipal Supply; Tom (Hardware) [13594]

Bedford
Continental Resources Inc. (Bedford, Massachusetts) (Computers and Software) [6155]
La Francis Associates; Mal (Gifts and Novelties) [13383]
PSDI (Computers and Software) [6657]
wTe Corp. (Used, Scrap, and Recycled Materials) [27051]
WTE Recycling Corp. (Used, Scrap, and Recycled Materials) [27052]

Belmont
Cooperative Reserve Supply Inc. (Construction Materials and Machinery) [7218]
Ford & Bailie (Books and Other Printed Materials) [3760]

Beverly
C-Corp. (Food) [10655]
Cargill Inc. Northeast Petroleum Div. (Petroleum, Fuels, and Related Equipment) [22108]
Eliza Corporation (Communications Systems and Equipment) [5603]
Moynihan Lumber (Construction Materials and Machinery) [7753]

Billerica
Boshco Inc. (Industrial Machinery) [15835]
Boshco Inc. (Industrial Machinery) [15836]
Interface Data Inc. (Computers and Software) [6386]
Lehigh-Armstrong Inc. (Hardware) [13795]
Peroni Business Systems Inc. (Computers and Software) [6613]

Bolton
Future Electronics Corporation (Electrical and Electronic Equipment and Supplies) [8769]

Boston
Agar Supply Company Inc. (Food) [10343]
Alretta Truck Parts Inc. (Automotive) [2222]
American Wiping Rag (Cleaning and Janitorial Supplies) [4572]
Applied Geographics Inc. (Books and Other Printed Materials) [3522]
Asmara Inc. (Household Items) [15409]
Asmara Oriental Rugs (Floorcovering Equipment and Supplies) [9689]
Back Bay News Distributors (Books and Other Printed Materials) [3537]
Bay State Computer Group Inc. (Computers and Software) [6003]
Bearing Enterprises Inc. (Industrial Supplies) [16733]

Bentley Mills Inc. (Floorcovering Equipment and Supplies) [9722]
Berman Leather Company Inc. (Luggage and Leather Goods) [18376]
Boston Brands (Food) [10597]
Boston Productions Inc. (Photographic Equipment and Supplies) [22834]
Brookline Machine Co. (Automotive) [2391]
Capitol News Distributors (Books and Other Printed Materials) [3610]
Cara Donna Provision Co. (Food) [10696]
Carbone Floral Distributors (Horticultural Supplies) [14835]
Chemical Export Company, Inc. (Chemicals) [4354]
Cheng & Tsui Company (Books and Other Printed Materials) [3627]
Classic Wine Imports Inc. (Alcoholic Beverages) [1601]
Commonwealth Films Inc. (Sound and Entertainment Equipment and Supplies) [25143]
Computer Sports Systems Inc. (Electrical and Electronic Equipment and Supplies) [8556]
Connors Associates, Inc. (Books and Other Printed Materials) [3653]
Costas Provisions Corp. (Food) [10849]
Creative Distributors (Horticultural Supplies) [14846]
Crystal Food Import Corp. (Food) [10878]
Davison Inc. (Furniture and Fixtures) [13085]
Dewar & Company Inc.; John (Food) [10953]
DeYoung Inc.; J. and S.S. (Jewelry) [17395]
Direct Diamonds Distributors (Jewelry) [17396]
Dremont-Levy Co. (Paints and Varnishes) [21434]
ECS Publishing Corporation (Books and Other Printed Materials) [3715]
Edwards & Co.; C.G. (Marine) [18498]
Ellis Inc. (Automotive) [2584]
Eyelet Enterprises Inc. (Industrial Machinery) [16002]
Fabiano Shoe Company Inc. (Shoes) [24738]
Gordon Brothers Corp. (Jewelry) [17438]
Gorton & Co., Inc.; Slade (Food) [11294]
Gorton and Company Inc.; Slade (Food) [11295]
Grimes Oil Company Inc. (Petroleum, Fuels, and Related Equipment) [22323]
Hiltons Tent City Inc. (Recreational and Sporting Goods) [23728]
Horn EB Replacement Service (Household Items) [15534]
Horn EB Replacement Service (Jewelry) [17450]
International Forest Products Corp. (Paper and Paper Products) [21779]
Jimmy's Seaside Co. (Food) [11555]
Kinnealey & Co.; T.F. (Food) [11621]
Lee Jay Bed and Bath (Household Items) [15563]
Lincoln Packing Co. (Food) [11712]
Lun Fat Produce Inc. (Food) [11745]
Marr Scaffolding Company Inc. (Construction Materials and Machinery) [7646]
Masco Corp. Beacon Hill Showroom (Furniture and Fixtures) [13173]
Massachusetts Gas and Electric Lighting Supply Co. (Electrical and Electronic Equipment and Supplies) [9044]
Mathews and Sons Inc.; G.D. (Food) [11804]
National Braille Press Inc. (Books and Other Printed Materials) [3985]
North Coast Sea Foods Inc. (Food) [12027]
Peabody Office Furniture Corp. (Office Equipment and Supplies) [21206]
Pill Electric Supply Co.; Ralph (Electrical and Electronic Equipment and Supplies) [9203]
Prime Poultry Corp. (Food) [12218]
R & R Sales Inc. (Construction Materials and Machinery) [7894]
SBC/Sporto Corp. (Shoes) [24850]
Schapero Co. Inc.; Eric (Shoes) [24851]
Schawbel Corp. (Health and Beauty Aids) [14230]
Shared Technologies Cellular Inc. (Communications Systems and Equipment) [5753]
Stavis Seafoods Inc. (Food) [12580]
Swift Instruments, Inc. (Medical, Dental, and Optical Supplies) [19645]
Tuttle Co. Inc.; Charles E. (Books and Other Printed Materials) [4234]
US TeleCenters (Communications Systems and Equipment) [5801]

Waldo Brothers Co. (Construction Materials and Machinery) [8193]
WB Stores Inc. (Gifts and Novelties) [13471]

Boylston
Butler-Dearden Paper Service Inc. (Paper and Paper Products) [21661]
Refco IDG. (Industrial Supplies) [17134]

Bradford
Custom Industries Inc. (Wood and Wood Products) [27301]

Braintree
Diamond Optical Corp. (Medical, Dental, and Optical Supplies) [19280]
Hammett Co.; J.L. (Office Equipment and Supplies) [21024]
Kaplan-Simon Co. (Textiles and Notions) [26087]
Millard Metal Service Center (Metals) [20193]
Organ Literature Foundation (Books and Other Printed Materials) [4024]

Brewster
Creative Joys Inc. (Books and Other Printed Materials) [3670]

Bridgewater
Arrow Map Inc. (Books and Other Printed Materials) [3525]
HIM Mechanical Systems Inc. (Heating and Cooling Equipment and Supplies) [14485]

Brighton
Automotive Parts Wholesaler (Automotive) [2294]
Truck Equipment Boston, Inc. (Automotive) [3344]
Truesdale Company Inc. (Chemicals) [4535]

Brockton
Cirelli Foods Inc. (Restaurant and Commercial Foodservice Equipment and Supplies) [24092]
Goodman Knitting Company Inc. (Clothing) [4997]
Green Market Services Co. (Shoes) [24756]
Hickey and Associates (Computers and Software) [6332]
New England Wholesale Drug Co. (Health and Beauty Aids) [14176]
Signature Apparel (Clothing) [5354]

Brookline
Allen Trading Co. Inc. (Shoes) [24667]
Allen Trading Company Inc. (Clothing) [4761]
Boston Electronics Corporation (Photographic Equipment and Supplies) [22833]
Redwing Book Company, Inc. (Books and Other Printed Materials) [4110]

Burlington
AmAsia International Ltd. (Shoes) [24669]
AmAsia International Ltd. (Clothing) [4765]
Bardon Trimount Inc. (Construction Materials and Machinery) [7021]
Callback Software (Computers and Software) [6042]
Compass Technology of Burlington Massachusetts (Electrical and Electronic Equipment and Supplies) [8553]
Genesis Associates Inc. (Electrical and Electronic Equipment and Supplies) [8785]
Johnson Company Inc.; George T. (Cleaning and Janitorial Supplies) [4647]
Primeon (Computers and Software) [6639]
Right Stuff Inc. (Shoes) [24843]
Techexport, Inc. (Computers and Software) [6795]
United Distributors, Inc. (Floorcovering Equipment and Supplies) [10264]
Webb Co.; F.W. (Plumbing Materials and Fixtures) [23446]

Cambridge
Access International Software (Computers and Software) [5867]
Boston Pipe and Fittings Company Inc. (Plumbing Materials and Fixtures) [23093]

Centerline Software Inc. (Computers and Software) [6054]
Dodge Company Inc. (Specialty Equipment and Products) [25634]
Garment District Inc. (Clothing) [4977]
Harvard Associates Inc. (Computers and Software) [6329]
ISHK Book Services (Books and Other Printed Materials) [3856]
Massachusetts Lumber Co. (Construction Materials and Machinery) [7662]
Programart Corp. (Computers and Software) [6652]
Protech Safety Equipment (Security and Safety Equipment) [24615]
PSDI (Computers and Software) [6661]
Schoenhof's Foreign Books Inc. (Books and Other Printed Materials) [4140]
SEC International (Computers and Software) [6716]
Superior Nut Company Inc. (Food) [12640]

Canton

Baker Inc.; J. (Shoes) [24679]
Barrow Industries Inc. (Textiles and Notions) [25974]
Berry Company Inc.; H.T. (Paper and Paper Products) [21653]
Blackman Associates, Inc.; Mel (Gifts and Novelties) [13318]
Carousel Fashions Inc. (Clothing) [4865]
CRH International Inc. (Clothing) [4902]
Ferrera and Sons Inc.; James (Food) [11121]
Home Entertainment Distributors (Sound and Entertainment Equipment and Supplies) [25235]
Hub Material Co. (Electrical and Electronic Equipment and Supplies) [8863]
Merkert Enterprises Inc. (Food) [11857]
Morris Co.; Walter F. (Plumbing Materials and Fixtures) [23277]
New England Door Corp. (Construction Materials and Machinery) [7773]
Pierce Aluminum Company Inc. (Metals) [20278]
Reiser and Co.; Robert (Household Appliances) [15289]
Stream International Inc. (Computers and Software) [6766]

Carlisle

ESI Computing (Computers and Software) [6255]

Charlestown

Costa Fruit and Produce Co. (Food) [10848]
Cunningham Co.; C.A. (Hardware) [13651]
East Coast Mill Sales Co. (Construction Materials and Machinery) [7299]
Prins/Basic Waste Systems Inc. (Used, Scrap, and Recycled Materials) [26946]
United International Inc. (Construction Materials and Machinery) [8158]

Chelmsford

American Business Systems Inc. (Computers and Software) [5922]
Thompson & Son Inc.; Edwin L. (Communications Systems and Equipment) [5793]

Chelsea

Chelsea Clock Co. Inc. (Medical, Dental, and Optical Equipment) [18737]
D'Arrigo Brothers of Massachusetts Inc. (Food) [10911]
DiMare Brothers Inc. (Food) [10965]
Forlizzi Brothers (Food) [11189]
Gulf Oil L.P. (Petroleum, Fuels, and Related Equipment) [22327]
Industrial Wiper & Paper (Paper and Paper Products) [21775]
Jenkins Trading Inc. (Books and Other Printed Materials) [3863]
Matarazzo Brothers Company Inc. (Food) [11803]
Reliable Fabrics Inc. (Household Items) [15631]
Slippers International Inc. (Shoes) [24863]
Yell-O-Glow Corp. (Food) [12993]
Zed Group Inc. (Industrial Machinery) [16659]

Chestnut Hill

Curtis Associates Inc. (Toys and Hobby Goods) [26455]
Seaboard Corp. (Food) [12445]

Chicopee

Chicopee Medical Supplies (Medical, Dental, and Optical Equipment) [18741]
Everson Distributing Company, Inc. (Food) [11062]
Polep Distribution Services Inc.; J. (Tobacco Products) [26342]
Spalding Holdings Corp. (Clothing) [5376]

Clinton

Reisner Corp.; William (Used, Scrap, and Recycled Materials) [26955]

Cohasset

Massa Associates; Ronald A. (Electrical and Electronic Equipment and Supplies) [9043]
Target Industries Inc. (Medical, Dental, and Optical Supplies) [19648]

Concord

Bradford Publishing Co.; William K. (Computers and Software) [6021]
Composite Engineering Inc. (Marine) [18487]

Dalton

Perferx Optical Co. Inc. (Medical, Dental, and Optical Supplies) [19531]

Danvers

Behrens Machinery Co.; C. (Industrial Machinery) [15816]
Fishery Products International (Food) [11135]
Fishery Products International USA (Food) [11136]
Merrimack Valley Distributing Company Inc. (Alcoholic Beverages) [1867]
TurningPoint Systems Inc. (Computers and Software) [6836]

Dedham

Prudential Building Materials (Construction Materials and Machinery) [7887]
Prudential Metal Supply Corp. (Construction Materials and Machinery) [7888]
West Marine Corp. (Marine) [18637]

Dorchester

Lenox Junk Co. (Metals) [20122]
Yale Electric Supply Company Inc. (Electrical and Electronic Equipment and Supplies) [9615]

Dracut

Majilite Corp. (Textiles and Notions) [26132]

East Boston

Bellesteel Industries Inc. (Metals) [19807]
Bugatti Inc. (Luggage and Leather Goods) [18378]
Towle Manufacturing Co. (Household Items) [15685]
Wigglesworth Machine Co. (Industrial Machinery) [16632]

East Falmouth

Falmouth Supply Co. Inc. (Sound and Entertainment Equipment and Supplies) [25190]

East Longmeadow

American Saw & Manufacturing Co. (Hardware) [13561]
Fortune Personnel Consultants of Springfield Inc. (Medical, Dental, and Optical Supplies) [19327]
McGill Hose and Coupling Inc. (Industrial Supplies) [17021]
Tyler Equipment Corp. (Construction Materials and Machinery) [8154]

East Walpole

Pilgrim Instrument & Controls (Industrial Machinery) [16399]

Everett

CK Footwear Inc. (Shoes) [24713]
Community Suffolk Inc. (Food) [10801]
Everett Square Sporting Goods (Recreational and Sporting Goods) [23656]
Fidelity Sportswear Co. (Clothing) [4950]
Geriatric Medical & Surgical (Medical, Dental, and Optical Equipment) [18811]
Helpern Inc.; Joan & David (Shoes) [24761]
Metropolitan AC & Refrigeration (Heating and Cooling Equipment and Supplies) [14544]
New England Industrial Supply Company Inc. (Paper and Paper Products) [21850]
Rainbow Balloons Inc. (Toys and Hobby Goods) [26627]
W.D. Trading Company Inc. (Food) [12888]

Fall River

AFGD (Construction Materials and Machinery) [6921]
BSE Engineering Corp. (Recreational and Sporting Goods) [23571]
Cosmos Import Export Inc. (Food) [10846]
Fall River News Company, Inc. (Books and Other Printed Materials) [3742]
Gold Medal Bakery Inc. (Food) [11279]
Haddad Electronic Supply Inc. (Communications Systems and Equipment) [5629]
J & B Import Ltd. Inc. (Shoes) [24775]
JDM Data Systems Inc. (Computers and Software) [6407]
Leach Company Inc.; W.W. (Paints and Varnishes) [21490]
Parks Corp. (Paints and Varnishes) [21532]

Falmouth

Burts Sports Specialty Inc. (Recreational and Sporting Goods) [23577]
Stat Surgical Center Inc. (Medical, Dental, and Optical Equipment) [19053]

Fitchburg

American Footwear Corp. (Shoes) [24670]
Cano Corp. (Office Equipment and Supplies) [20874]
ChemDesign Corp. (Chemicals) [4352]
The Dowd Co. (Paper and Paper Products) [21715]
United Cooperative Farmers Inc. (Agricultural Equipment and Supplies) [1375]

Foxboro

BTR Inc. (Electrical and Electronic Equipment and Supplies) [8473]
JBM Associates Inc. (Recreational and Sporting Goods) [23755]
New England Pottery Co. (Gifts and Novelties) [13410]

Framingham

Allan Distributors (Jewelry) [17305]
Ameriglobe Irrigation Distributors (Horticultural Supplies) [14804]
Atlantic International Corp. (Motorized Vehicles) [20593]
Clay Classics Inc. (Construction Materials and Machinery) [7177]
Colonial Floors Inc. (Floorcovering Equipment and Supplies) [9818]
Hansen Electrical Supply (Electrical and Electronic Equipment and Supplies) [8827]
Jomar Distributors Inc. (Heating and Cooling Equipment and Supplies) [14506]
Lapis Lazuli Jewelry Distributors (Jewelry) [17497]
New England Sand and Gravel Co. (Construction Materials and Machinery) [7774]
Roberts Co. Inc. (Books and Other Printed Materials) [4122]
Staples Office Products Inc. (Office Equipment and Supplies) [21290]
Stimpson Productions; John (Photographic Equipment and Supplies) [22907]
Trillennium (Electrical and Electronic Equipment and Supplies) [9509]
Wells Designs Inc.; Victoria (Clothing) [5476]

Franklin
Key Boston Inc. (Household Appliances) [15187]
Thomson National Press Co. (Industrial Machinery) [16563]

Gardner
Money Saver (Shoes) [24814]

Georgetown
Radiology Services Inc. (Medical, Dental, and Optical Equipment) [19009]

Gloucester
Nelsons (Clothing) [5222]
Ocean Crest Seafoods Inc. (Food) [12050]

Greenfield
Couzon USA (Household Items) [15458]
Kramer Scrap Inc. (Used, Scrap, and Recycled Materials) [26870]
Rice Oil Company Inc. (Petroleum, Fuels, and Related Equipment) [22627]
Rugg Manufacturing Company Inc. (Agricultural Equipment and Supplies) [1218]

Groveland
Esty and Sons Inc.; Ralph A. (Construction Materials and Machinery) [7323]

Hanover
BL Associates, Inc. (Computers and Software) [6017]

Harwich Port
Cape Water Sports (Marine) [18474]

Hatfield
Agriturf Inc. (Agricultural Equipment and Supplies) [217]

Haverhill
Cedar Group US Inc. (Computers and Software) [6050]
Comfort Shoe Corp. (Shoes) [24718]
Garston, Inc. (Specialty Equipment and Products) [25657]
Harvey Lumber Company Inc. (Construction Materials and Machinery) [7452]
Lionel Lavallee Company Inc. (Food) [11717]
Morgan Scientific, Inc. (Medical, Dental, and Optical Equipment) [18947]

Hingham
Araban Coffee Co. Inc. (Food) [10429]
Mohawk Rubber Sales of N.E. Inc. (Rubber) [24287]
Sager Electronics Inc. (Electrical and Electronic Equipment and Supplies) [9331]
Sontek Industries Inc. (Medical, Dental, and Optical Equipment) [19044]

Holliston
Axton-Cross Company Inc. (Chemicals) [4334]
Glaser and Son Inc.; H. (Clothing) [4987]
Harvard Apparatus, Inc. (Medical, Dental, and Optical Equipment) [18829]
St. Louis Ostomy Distributors Inc. (Medical, Dental, and Optical Equipment) [19029]
Suburban Ostomy Supply Company Inc. (Medical, Dental, and Optical Supplies) [19642]

Holyoke
Autron Inc. (Paper and Paper Products) [21641]
B & G Export Management Associates (Paper and Paper Products) [21644]
Highland Laundry Co. (Clothing) [5030]
Judd Paper Co. (Paper and Paper Products) [21787]
Plymouth Paper Company Inc. (Paper and Paper Products) [21885]
Totsy Manufacturing Co., Inc. (Toys and Hobby Goods) [26683]
University Products, Inc. (Sound and Entertainment Equipment and Supplies) [25493]

Hopkinton
Bicknell Distributors Inc. (Recreational and Sporting Goods) [23552]
Rudel Machinery Company Inc. (Industrial Machinery) [16463]
South Central Pool Supply, Inc. (Recreational and Sporting Goods) [23970]

Huntington
Gateway Auto Parts (Automotive) [2662]

Hyannis
AGR Warehouse Distributors (Automotive) [2188]
Cape Dairy Products Inc. (Food) [10690]
Cape & Island Steel Co. (Metals) [19851]
Cape Oceanic Corp. (Food) [10691]
Capeway News (Books and Other Printed Materials) [3606]
Cloutier Supply Co. (Plastics) [22944]
Hubbard Paint and Wallpaper (Paints and Varnishes) [21459]
Vehicle Vibres Inc. (Sound and Entertainment Equipment and Supplies) [25500]

HyDe Park
Howden Fan Co. (Industrial Machinery) [16117]

Ipswich
Ebinger Brothers Leather Co. (Luggage and Leather Goods) [18391]
Preston Leather Products (Luggage and Leather Goods) [18421]

Lakeville
Atlantic Building Products (Construction Materials and Machinery) [7001]

Lawrence
Brodie Inc. (Industrial Machinery) [15846]
House of Bianchi Inc. (Clothing) [5040]
Lawrence Plate Glass Co. (Construction Materials and Machinery) [7588]
Levis Paper Company Inc.; J.J. (Paper and Paper Products) [21801]
Oomphies Inc. (Shoes) [24827]
Simpson's Inc. (Construction Materials and Machinery) [8024]
Standard Automotive Parts Corp. (Automotive) [3258]

Lee
Brazabra Corp. (Clothing) [4842]

Leicester
Millbrook Distributors Inc. (Health and Beauty Aids) [14164]

Leominster
Fitchburg Hardware Company Inc. (Hardware) [13707]
Monson Chemicals Inc. (Chemicals) [4460]
Point of Sale System Services Inc. (Computers and Software) [6626]
Regional Home Care Inc. (Medical, Dental, and Optical Equipment) [19015]

Littleton
HNSX Supercomputers Inc. (Computers and Software) [6338]
Sundance Publishing (Books and Other Printed Materials) [4196]

Lowell
Electrical Distributors Inc. (Electrical and Electronic Equipment and Supplies) [8676]
Etchomatic Inc. (Electrical and Electronic Equipment and Supplies) [8716]
Genes Appliance Parts Inc. (Household Appliances) [15146]
Notini and Sons Inc.; Albert H. (Tobacco Products) [26335]

Ludlow
East Coast Tile Imports—East (Floorcovering Equipment and Supplies) [9875]

Lunenburg
Graves Fire Protection (Security and Safety Equipment) [24557]

Lynn
Barry Manufacturing Company, Inc. (Shoes) [24682]
Bay State Lobster Company Inc. (Food) [10515]
Boston Trading Ltd. Inc. (Clothing) [4838]
Demakes Enterprises and Co. Inc. (Food) [10941]
Essex Electrical Supply Company Inc. (Electrical and Electronic Equipment and Supplies) [8715]
Malco Industries (Hardware) [13808]
Patten Inc.; H.I. (Restaurant and Commercial Foodservice Equipment and Supplies) [24203]
Schwartz and Benjamin Inc. (Shoes) [24853]
Schwartz and Benjamin Inc. (Clothing) [5335]
Soloman Metals Corp. (Used, Scrap, and Recycled Materials) [26998]

Malden
Brudnick Company Inc.; James (Medical, Dental, and Optical Supplies) [19203]
Eastern Auto Parts Company Inc. (Automotive) [2572]
Gans Tire Company Inc. (Automotive) [2661]
Smethurst & Sons; William (Floorcovering Equipment and Supplies) [10151]
World Food Tech Services (Food) [12982]

Manchester
Sullco Inc. (Shoes) [24869]

Mansfield
Allen; Robert (Textiles and Notions) [25956]
The Belknap White Group (Floorcovering Equipment and Supplies) [9719]
Lindenmeyer Munroe (Paper and Paper Products) [21802]
Robert Allen Fabrics Inc. (Textiles and Notions) [26187]
Toyota Motor Distributors Inc. (Automotive) [3322]

Marlborough
Alper Inc.; Morris (Food) [10378]
Business Systems (Computers and Software) [6032]
Comlink Inc. (Marlborough, Massachusetts) (Communications Systems and Equipment) [5567]
Concord Technologies Inc. (Computers and Software) [6147]
Cunningham Sales Corp. (Medical, Dental, and Optical Supplies) [19263]
Fleming Associates Inc.; J.S. (Heating and Cooling Equipment and Supplies) [14450]
Maconomy NE Inc. (Computers and Software) [6451]
PCs Compleat Inc. (Computers and Software) [6604]
Standard Tube Sales Corp. (Metals) [20388]

Marshfield
Century-Federman Wallcoverings Inc. (Household Items) [15440]
Jansco Marketing Inc. (Toys and Hobby Goods) [26541]

Mashpee
Durr and Partners (Computers and Software) [6227]
Tees Dyes (Clothing) [5424]

Medfield
Hosey and Port Sales Corp. (Household Appliances) [15172]
M.E. O'Brien and Sons Inc. (Recreational and Sporting Goods) [23817]
O'Brien & Sons Inc.; M.E. (Recreational and Sporting Goods) [23856]

Medford
Fire Equipment Inc. (Security and Safety Equipment) [24544]

Ideal Wine & Spirits Co., Inc. (Alcoholic
Beverages) [1770]
Rowenta Inc. (Household Appliances) [15296]

Melrose
Bowman Associates Inc.; A.D. (Storage Equipment
and Containers) [25896]
Melrose Appliance Inc. (Sound and Entertainment
Equipment and Supplies) [25312]

Methuen
Bracken Company Inc. (Industrial
Machinery) [15839]
Pricing Dynamics (Food) [12217]
Radiology Resources Inc. (Medical, Dental, and
Optical Equipment) [19008]

Middleton
Yankee Marketers Inc. (Food) [12990]

Milford
Academic Enterprises Ltd. (Books and Other
Printed Materials) [3461]
Brine Inc. (Recreational and Sporting
Goods) [23567]
Electronic Hook-up (Electrical and Electronic
Equipment and Supplies) [8691]
PAGG Corp. (Computers and Software) [6583]
Southworth-Milton Inc. (Agricultural Equipment and
Supplies) [1285]

Millis
Pearse Pearson Co. (Industrial Machinery) [16388]

Monson
Diversified Metals Inc. (Metals) [19933]

Natick
B J's Wholesale Club Inc. (Furniture and
Fixtures) [13029]
Fertility Technologies Inc. (Medical, Dental, and
Optical Equipment) [18796]
Forte Dupee Sawyer Co. (Textiles and
Notions) [26037]
Research Biochemicals Inc. (Chemicals) [4493]
Sanford Process Corp. (Industrial
Machinery) [16470]
Simsim Inc. (Computers and Software) [6731]

Needham
Brady Co.; Joseph M. (Veterinary
Products) [27091]
Northeast Group Inc. (Household
Appliances) [15254]
Piper Associates (Electrical and Electronic
Equipment and Supplies) [9210]

Needham Heights
Genalco Inc. (Construction Materials and
Machinery) [7382]

New Bedford
Atlas Screw and Specialty Co.;
L.P. (Hardware) [13575]
Babbitt Steam Specialty Co. (Industrial
Supplies) [16718]
Beckman Co.; C.C. (Marine) [18457]
Dyl-Chem Inc. (Clothing) [4925]
Enos Home Oxygen Therapy Inc. (Medical, Dental,
and Optical Equipment) [18792]
Enos Home Oxygen Therapy Inc. (Medical, Dental,
and Optical Supplies) [19305]
Fiber Optic Center Inc. (Communications Systems
and Equipment) [5612]
Foley Company Inc.; M.F. (Food) [11168]
Imtra Corp. (Marine) [18523]
Luzo Food Service Inc. (Restaurant and
Commercial Foodservice Equipment and
Supplies) [24171]
Northern Wind, Inc. (Food) [12032]
Optical Laboratory of New Bedford (Medical,
Dental, and Optical Supplies) [19513]
Patnaude's Aquarium & Pet (Veterinary
Products) [27203]
Sea View Fillet Company Inc. (Food) [12444]

Shuster Corp. (Industrial Supplies) [17174]
Tichon Seafood Corp. (Food) [12721]

Newburyport
Computalabel International Ltd. (Computers and
Software) [6100]
Dean Associates Inc.; Richard (Sound and
Entertainment Equipment and Supplies) [25163]
McCarty & Son; H.J. (Household Items) [15584]
Rochester Electronics Inc. (Electrical and Electronic
Equipment and Supplies) [9305]

Newton
Accent Lamp and Shade Co. Inc. (Household
Items) [15387]
Alles Corp. (Paper and Paper Products) [21622]
Atlas Water Systems Inc. (Specialty Equipment and
Products) [25566]
Bennett Importing Inc. (Shoes) [24690]
Fowler Company Inc.; Fred V. (Scientific and
Measurement Devices) [24362]
Marlboro Footworks Ltd. (Shoes) [24800]
Marlboro Footworks Ltd. (Clothing) [5167]
North Atlantic Engineering Co. (Electrical and
Electronic Equipment and Supplies) [9132]

Newton Upper Falls
Gerrity Company Inc. (Construction Materials and
Machinery) [7395]

Norfolk
CableLAN Express Inc. (Communications Systems
and Equipment) [5541]
Diagnostic Equipment Service Corp. (Medical,
Dental, and Optical Equipment) [18774]

North Adams
Cariddi Sales Co. (Recreational and Sporting
Goods) [23582]
Nassifs Professional Pharmacy (Medical, Dental,
and Optical Equipment) [18956]

North Andover
Brookline Machine Co. (Industrial
Machinery) [15847]
L-com Inc. (Electrical and Electronic Equipment and
Supplies) [8961]
Mutual Sales Inc. (Toys and Hobby
Goods) [26586]
Pervone (Computers and Software) [6614]
Watts Regulator Co. (Plumbing Materials and
Fixtures) [23441]
Watts/Taras Valve Corp. (Plumbing Materials and
Fixtures) [23442]

North Attleboro
Mercury International Trading
Corp. (Shoes) [24808]
Riley and Son Inc.; W.H. (Petroleum, Fuels, and
Related Equipment) [22629]
Teknis Corp. (Electrical and Electronic Equipment
and Supplies) [9471]

North Billerica
For-Tek (Construction Materials and
Machinery) [7355]
McQuesten Company Inc.; Geo. (Wood and Wood
Products) [27343]
Mobile Automotive Diagnostic (Automotive) [2978]
MuTech Corp. (Computers and Software) [6536]

North Chatham
N Pool Patio Ltd. (Recreational and Sporting
Goods) [23842]

North Chelmsford
McKittrick Company Inc.; Frank G.W. (Industrial
Machinery) [16281]

North Dartmouth
Taylor Distributing Co.; J.J. (Alcoholic
Beverages) [2071]

North Dighton
Kimbet Leather (Veterinary Products) [27173]

North Quincy
Interstate Distributors Inc. (Books and Other Printed
Materials) [3853]

North Reading
Alpha-Omega Sales Corp. (Electrical and Electronic
Equipment and Supplies) [8330]
Gonsalves Inc.; Arthur J. (Toys and Hobby
Goods) [26504]
Lindenmeyr Munroe (Paper and Paper
Products) [21808]

Northborough
Emuge Corp. (Industrial Supplies) [16850]
Hope Group (Industrial Machinery) [16112]

Norton
Hallsmith-Sysco Food Services (Food) [11366]

Norwell
BrainTree Technology Inc. (Computers and
Software) [6023]
New Resource Inc. (Sound and Entertainment
Equipment and Supplies) [25356]
New Resource Inc. (Household
Appliances) [15247]
Reed Export, Inc.; Charles H. (Floorcovering
Equipment and Supplies) [10117]

Norwood
ACT Services Inc. (Electrical and Electronic
Equipment and Supplies) [8269]
Altman Map, Inc.; Bryant (Books and Other Printed
Materials) [3494]
Barrow Industries Inc. Merrimac Textile (Textiles
and Notions) [25976]
Boston Warehouse Trading Corp. (Household
Items) [15426]
Boyajian Inc. (Food) [10600]
Branded Liquors Inc. (Alcoholic Beverages) [1547]
Emtel Electronics Inc. (Electrical and Electronic
Equipment and Supplies) [8706]
Gerber Radio Supply Co. (Electrical and Electronic
Equipment and Supplies) [8787]
King Co. Inc.; E.F. (Recreational and Sporting
Goods) [23775]
SilverPlatter Information Inc. (Computers and
Software) [6730]
Tyco Adhesives (Paper and Paper
Products) [21957]
Whitehall Company Ltd. (Alcoholic
Beverages) [2117]
Wiggins Airways Inc. Parts East (Aeronautical
Equipment and Supplies) [173]
Wiggins Airways Inc. Parts East; E.W. (Aeronautical
Equipment and Supplies) [174]

Nutting Lake
Boise Cascade (Construction Materials and
Machinery) [7067]

Paxton
Guterman International Inc. (Recreational and
Sporting Goods) [23705]

Peabody
Beggs and Cobb Corp. (Luggage and Leather
Goods) [18375]
Boyle Machine and Supply Co. (Industrial
Supplies) [16761]
Brookfield Athletic Company (Recreational and
Sporting Goods) [23568]
Daly Inc.; James W. (Medical, Dental, and Optical
Equipment) [18764]
JEOL U.S.A. Inc. (Scientific and Measurement
Devices) [24378]
NECX Inc. (Electrical and Electronic Equipment and
Supplies) [9119]
Ossoff Leather (Luggage and Leather
Goods) [18416]
Suncook Tanning Corp. (Livestock and Farm
Products) [18269]
Valenti Inc.; F.M. (Security and Safety
Equipment) [24654]

Walach Leather Splitting (Luggage and Leather Goods) [18440]

Pembroke
IVI Corp. (Industrial Machinery) [16178]

Pittsfield
Schilling TV Inc. (Sound and Entertainment Equipment and Supplies) [25432]
Ski America Enterprises Inc. (Books and Other Printed Materials) [4165]
York Hannover Health Care Inc. (Medical, Dental, and Optical Supplies) [19716]

Plymouth
Automated Office Systems of New England (Computers and Software) [5987]
Ellis Inc.; A.L. (Household Items) [15487]
Plymouth Rock Associates (Computers and Software) [6625]

Quincy
Beacon Sporting Goods Inc. (Recreational and Sporting Goods) [23540]
Granite City Electric Supply Co. (Electrical and Electronic Equipment and Supplies) [8807]
World Source Trading Inc. (Sound and Entertainment Equipment and Supplies) [25531]

Randolph
Brewster Wallcovering Co. (Household Items) [15429]
Burgess; Philip (Recreational and Sporting Goods) [23576]
Education Guide Inc. (Books and Other Printed Materials) [3720]
Emerson-Swan Inc. (Plumbing Materials and Fixtures) [23148]
Fetco International Corp. (Gifts and Novelties) [13357]
Garber Brothers Inc. (Food) [11232]
Medi Inc. (Medical, Dental, and Optical Supplies) [19441]
Medi Inc. - School Health Div. (Medical, Dental, and Optical Equipment) [18912]

Raynham
Fire Spec Inc. (Security and Safety Equipment) [24546]
Pacheco; James A. (Food) [12087]

Reading
Boston Stove Co. (Heating and Cooling Equipment and Supplies) [14353]
Graham Radio Inc. (Sound and Entertainment Equipment and Supplies) [25219]
Griffin Refrigeration Inc. (Heating and Cooling Equipment and Supplies) [14474]

Readville
Maxwell Shoe Company Inc. (Shoes) [24803]

Rehoboth
Dyer Co.; H.G. (Plumbing Materials and Fixtures) [23143]

Revere
Beach Sales Inc. (Sound and Entertainment Equipment and Supplies) [25099]

Rockland
TRI-New England (Health and Beauty Aids) [14263]

Roxbury
Connolly Seafood; Steve (Food) [10812]

Salem
Brake & Clutch, Inc. (Automotive) [2377]
North Shore Recycled Fibers (Used, Scrap, and Recycled Materials) [26925]
Old Saltbox Publishing House Inc. (Books and Other Printed Materials) [4017]
Rolls Battery Engineering Inc. (Marine) [18594]

Saugus
Brenner Companies Inc. (Shoes) [24697]

Seekonk
Choquette and Company Inc. (Household Appliances) [15084]
Copier Supply Inc. (Communications Systems and Equipment) [5579]

Sharon
Melhado Co.; George (Tobacco Products) [26328]
Simplex Chemical Corp. (Cleaning and Janitorial Supplies) [4709]

Shelburne Falls
Mayhew Steel Products (Hardware) [13817]

Shrewsbury
Boston Tile Distributors of Shrewsbury (Floorcovering Equipment and Supplies) [9733]
International Industries Inc. (Clothing) [5058]
Rayco Car Electronics Inc. (Sound and Entertainment Equipment and Supplies) [25407]

Somerset
Alden Autoparts Warehouse Inc. (Automotive) [2202]
Fran-TEC Computer (Computers and Software) [6280]

Somerville
Bornstein and Company Inc.; L. (Floorcovering Equipment and Supplies) [9731]
Boston Computer Exchange Corp. (Computers and Software) [6019]
Central Steel Supply Company Inc. (Metals) [19867]
Earthworm Inc. (Office Equipment and Supplies) [20976]
Gray Sales Co. Inc. (Computers and Software) [6309]
MRR Traders, Ltd. (Alcoholic Beverages) [1896]
Spaulding Brick Company Inc. (Construction Materials and Machinery) [8058]
Walker Inc.; M.S. (Alcoholic Beverages) [2108]

South Attleboro
Continental Craft Distributors (Office Equipment and Supplies) [20911]

South Boston
Coastal Distributors, Inc. (Marine) [18485]
Reed Publications, Inc.; Thomas (Books and Other Printed Materials) [4111]

South Easton
A.M. Associates Inc. (Gifts and Novelties) [13300]
AutoBike Inc. (Recreational and Sporting Goods) [23529]
Marine Optical Inc. (Medical, Dental, and Optical Supplies) [19422]
Medical Specialties Company Inc. (Medical, Dental, and Optical Supplies) [19447]
Specialty Catalog Corp. (Health and Beauty Aids) [14244]

South Hadley
Canson Talens, Inc. (Specialty Equipment and Products) [25596]

South Weymouth
Certified Data Processing Inc. (Computers and Software) [6058]

South Yarmouth
Cape Electronics (Communications Systems and Equipment) [5544]

Southborough
Defreeze Corp. (Heating and Cooling Equipment and Supplies) [14413]
New England Frozen Foods Inc. (Food) [12001]

Unisource Worldwide Inc. (Southborough, Massachusetts) (Paper and Paper Products) [21972]

Southwick
Pioneer Dairy Inc. (Food) [12171]

Springfield
Allied Distributors Inc. (Floorcovering Equipment and Supplies) [9655]
Bay State Florist Supply, Inc. (Horticultural Supplies) [14825]
Boston Sea Foods Inc. (Food) [10598]
Boston Tile (Floorcovering Equipment and Supplies) [9732]
Command Computer Maintenance (Computers and Software) [6084]
Cushing Inc.; T.F. (Electrical and Electronic Equipment and Supplies) [8598]
Farmland Foods (Food) [11106]
Freedman Company Inc.; Joseph (Used, Scrap, and Recycled Materials) [26817]
Goodman Inc.; Harry (Paper and Paper Products) [21744]
Heatbath Corp. (Industrial Supplies) [16928]
Kenzacki Specialty Papers Inc. (Paper and Paper Products) [21791]
Kittredge Equipment Co. (Restaurant and Commercial Foodservice Equipment and Supplies) [24159]
Martin Millwork Inc. (Construction Materials and Machinery) [7655]
Martinelli Inc.; John (Food) [11795]
Roberts and Company Inc.; F.L. (Petroleum, Fuels, and Related Equipment) [22636]
Toolkraft Distributing (Industrial Machinery) [16566]
Williams Distributing Corp. (Alcoholic Beverages) [2120]
Young Inc.; W.F. (Medical, Dental, and Optical Supplies) [19717]

Sterling
Eastern States Components Inc. (Electrical and Electronic Equipment and Supplies) [8648]

Still River
The Wakanta Group (Computers and Software) [6858]

Stockbridge
South Wool (Clothing) [5369]

Stoughton
American Data Systems Marketing (Computers and Software) [5925]
Franklin Sports Industries Inc. (Recreational and Sporting Goods) [23676]
Hoboken Wood Floors (Floorcovering Equipment and Supplies) [9950]
JBM Sales (Textiles and Notions) [26080]
Left Foot Ltd. (Shoes) [24792]
Ophthalmic Instrument Co. Inc. (Medical, Dental, and Optical Supplies) [19508]
Reebok International Ltd. (Shoes) [24840]
Richards International; Lyle (Shoes) [24842]
Spaulding Company Inc. (Sound and Entertainment Equipment and Supplies) [25458]

Sturbridge
Fabricating and Production Machinery Inc. (Industrial Machinery) [16003]

Sudbury
House of Representatives Inc. (Computers and Software) [6343]
Jones & Bartlett Publishers Inc. (Books and Other Printed Materials) [3868]
Laser Resale Inc. (Scientific and Measurement Devices) [24386]

Sunderland
Deerfield Data Systems Inc. (Computers and Software) [6194]

Swansea

Pilottes Transport Refrigeration (Heating and Cooling Equipment and Supplies) [14637]

Taunton

Decatur Hopkins (Hardware) [13657]
Princess House Inc. (Household Items) [15625]
Quality Beverage Limited Partnership (Alcoholic Beverages) [1974]

Tewksbury

Datex-Ohmeda, Inc. (Medical, Dental, and Optical Equipment) [18765]
Datex-Ohmeda Inc. (Medical, Dental, and Optical Supplies) [19272]
Holt and Bugbee Co. (Floorcovering Equipment and Supplies) [9952]
Preferred Distributors Inc. (Toys and Hobby Goods) [26620]
Tewksbury Industries Inc. (Used, Scrap, and Recycled Materials) [27022]
Yankee Custom, Inc. (Automotive) [3450]

Topsfield

New England Serum Co. (Veterinary Products) [27194]
New England Serum Co. (Medical, Dental, and Optical Supplies) [19491]

Wakefield

Apem Components, Inc. (Electrical and Electronic Equipment and Supplies) [8363]
ERM Recycling Inc./Crazy Bob's (Computers and Software) [6254]

Walpole

Banash and Son Inc.; David (Clothing) [4800]

Waltham

Adjustable Clamp Co. (Hardware) [13535]
Allied Cycle Distributors Inc. (Recreational and Sporting Goods) [23506]
Authentica Security Technology (Computers and Software) [5984]
Burton-Rogers Co. Inc. (Scientific and Measurement Devices) [24331]
Burton-Rogers Company Inc. (Automotive) [2403]
Cambridge Development Laboratory (Computers and Software) [6043]
Clauss Cutlery Co. (Household Items) [15446]
Danka E.B.S. (Computers and Software) [6179]
Deuer Manufacturing Co. (Industrial Machinery) [15945]
Dispenser Services Inc. (Specialty Equipment and Products) [25630]
Eastern Bearings Inc. (Automotive) [2573]
Eastern Bearings Inc. (Electrical and Electronic Equipment and Supplies) [8646]
Electronic Fasteners Inc. (Hardware) [13679]
Fasteners & Metal Products Corp. (Hardware) [13700]
The Fletcher-Terry Company (Hardware) [13709]
Global Petroleum Corp. (Petroleum, Fuels, and Related Equipment) [22314]
Hampton-Haddon Marketing Corp. (Office Equipment and Supplies) [21025]
Harvey Industries Inc. (Construction Materials and Machinery) [7451]
Hyster New England, Inc. (Industrial Machinery) [16135]
Mass Hardware and Supply Inc. (Hardware) [13814]
McEllin Company, Inc. (Floorcovering Equipment and Supplies) [10015]
McKim Group (Hardware) [13818]
MIRA Inc. (Medical, Dental, and Optical Equipment) [18940]
Najarian Music Company Inc. (Books and Other Printed Materials) [3979]
Tayters Inc. (Food) [12702]
Tile International (Floorcovering Equipment and Supplies) [10240]
Vaughan & Bushnell Manufacturing Co. (Hardware) [13979]

Ward Hill

Masda Corp. New England (Household Appliances) [15217]

Ware

Wilton Manufacturing Company Inc. (Clothing) [5487]

Wareham

Soft-As-A-Grape Inc. (Clothing) [5366]

Washington

Insular Lumber Sales Corp. (Construction Materials and Machinery) [7513]

Watertown

Elite Consumer Products (Plumbing Materials and Fixtures) [23147]
Reynolds Industries Inc. (Watertown, Massachusetts) (Petroleum, Fuels, and Related Equipment) [22625]

Wellesley

Branden Publishing Co. (Books and Other Printed Materials) [3589]
Spivack's Antiques (Furniture and Fixtures) [13250]

Wellesley Hills

Shelley Company Inc.; John G. (Adhesives) [14]

Wenham

Atlantic Software (Computers and Software) [5980]

West Boylston

Ziff Co. (Industrial Supplies) [17296]

West Bridgewater

Optech Inc. (Medical, Dental, and Optical Supplies) [19509]
United Liquors Ltd. (Alcoholic Beverages) [2092]

West Concord

Atlantic Pre-Hung Doors Inc. (Construction Materials and Machinery) [7004]

West Falmouth

African & Caribbean Imprint Library Services (Books and Other Printed Materials) [3476]

West Harwich

Thistle Co.; R.F. (Sound and Entertainment Equipment and Supplies) [25477]

West Lynn

Lynn Ladder and Scaffolding Company Inc. (Construction Materials and Machinery) [7625]

West Roxbury

Carolina Wine Co. (Alcoholic Beverages) [1576]

West Springfield

Carter Paper Co. (Paper and Paper Products) [21672]
Connecticut Driveshaft Inc. (Automotive) [2473]
Foss Co.; W.J. (Industrial Supplies) [16874]
J.S. Woodhouse Co. (Agricultural Equipment and Supplies) [892]
Long Inc.; E.W. (Sound and Entertainment Equipment and Supplies) [25288]
Mansfield Paper Company Inc. (Paper and Paper Products) [21821]
Merriam-Graves Corp. (Medical, Dental, and Optical Equipment) [18931]
Valley Sales Company Inc. (Sound and Entertainment Equipment and Supplies) [25497]
Valley Sales Company Inc. (Household Appliances) [15355]
Woodhouse Co.; J.S. (Agricultural Equipment and Supplies) [1463]

Westborough

BTF Inc. (Shoes) [24701]

Horton Distributing Co.; Lew (Recreational and Sporting Goods) [23732]
Shakour Inc.; R.G. (Health and Beauty Aids) [14235]

Westfield

A.C.T. Vehicle Equipment, Inc. (Automotive) [2177]
Air Compressor Engineering Company Inc. (Compressors) [5824]
Camfour Inc. (Recreational and Sporting Goods) [23581]
Commercial Distributing Co. (Alcoholic Beverages) [1609]
U.S. Line Co. (Recreational and Sporting Goods) [24022]
Wilson Marketing & Sales (Food) [12954]

Westminster

Aubuchon Company Inc.; W.E. (Hardware) [13576]

Weston

Eastern Enterprises (Specialty Equipment and Products) [25640]
Shore Imports Inc. (Shoes) [24860]

Westwood

Faxon Company Inc. (Books and Other Printed Materials) [3745]
Harbor Tool Supply Inc. (Industrial Machinery) [16088]
The Northeast Group, Inc. (Sound and Entertainment Equipment and Supplies) [25362]
Scales Company Inc.; R.H. (Automotive) [3191]

Whitinsville

Auburn Merchandise Distributors Inc. (Food) [10468]
Longo Distributors Inc. (Tobacco Products) [26325]

Whitman

All Stainless Inc. (Hardware) [13548]

Wilbraham

State Line Potato Chip Co. (Food) [12578]

Wilmington

Northland Industrial Truck Company Inc. (Motorized Vehicles) [20699]
Northland Industrial Truck Company Inc. (Industrial Machinery) [16353]
Pacific Packaging Products Inc. (Paper and Paper Products) [21856]
Redington USA Inc. (Computers and Software) [6686]
Roberts Co.; D.B. (Electrical and Electronic Equipment and Supplies) [9301]
Xpedx (Industrial Supplies) [17290]

Winchester

Federal Heating and Engineering Company Inc. (Petroleum, Fuels, and Related Equipment) [22272]
Mahoney's Garden Center (Horticultural Supplies) [14915]

Winthrop

J & B Wholesale Co. (Clothing) [5070]
Muffin Town Inc. (Food) [11954]

Woburn

Abel and Company Inc.; Robert (Industrial Machinery) [15724]
Admiral Metals Inc. (Metals) [19729]
Amchem Inc. (Industrial Machinery) [15763]
Andover Communications Inc. (Office Equipment and Supplies) [20806]
Axis Communications Inc. (Office Equipment and Supplies) [20825]
Connoisseurs Products Corp. (Jewelry) [17376]
Dole and Bailey Inc. (Food) [10974]
Fitzgerald Inc.; Albert F. (Floorcovering Equipment and Supplies) [9890]
Florig Equipment (Industrial Machinery) [16011]
Greene Rubber Company Inc. (Rubber) [24279]

Image Processing Solutions (Computers and
  Software) [6355]
International Procurement Services,
  Inc. (Construction Materials and
  Machinery) [7520]
Mannix World Imports Inc. (Textiles and
  Notions) [26133]
Markuse Corp. (Household Items) [15578]
Mascon Inc. (Industrial Machinery) [16269]
Mascon Inc. (Industrial Machinery) [16270]
Metro Marketing Co. (Clothing) [5188]
Pierre Shoes Inc. (Shoes) [24835]
Rohtstein Corp. (Food) [12345]
Speen & Company Inc. (Shoes) [24867]
Star Sales and Distributing Co. (Construction
  Materials and Machinery) [8073]
Watkins & Associates; Steen (Computers and
  Software) [6860]
WellSpring Books (Books and Other Printed
  Materials) [4273]

Worcester

ADT Security Systems (Security and Safety
  Equipment) [24487]
Arrow Wholesale Co. Inc. (Toys and Hobby
  Goods) [26397]
Central Electric Supply Co. (Electrical and
  Electronic Equipment and Supplies) [8517]
Central Supply Co. (Plumbing Materials and
  Fixtures) [23111]
CNEAD Division (Automotive) [2456]
Economical Wholesale Co. (Books and Other
  Printed Materials) [3714]
Garbose Metal Co. (Used, Scrap, and Recycled
  Materials) [26821]
Goddard Industries Inc. (Industrial
  Supplies) [16898]
Jones Inc.; Ken (Automotive) [2835]
Kesseli Morse Company Inc. (Construction Materials
  and Machinery) [7548]
Leon Supply Company Inc. (Food) [11700]
Lowell Corp. (Hardware) [13804]
Manoog Inc.; Charles (Plumbing Materials and
  Fixtures) [23250]
Massachusetts Export Corp. (Clothing) [5172]
McCoy and Company Inc.; Lawrence
  R. (Construction Materials and
  Machinery) [7676]
McCoy and Company Inc.; Lawrence R. (Wood
  and Wood Products) [27342]
Nissen Baking Co.; John J. (Food) [12009]
Omni Services Inc. (Industrial Supplies) [17090]
Parker Metal Goods Corp. (Hardware) [13863]
Quinsig Automotive Warehouse
  Inc. (Automotive) [3130]
R and R Plumbing Supply Corp. (Plumbing
  Materials and Fixtures) [23333]
Talbert Trading Corp. (Clothing) [5421]
Tri-State Ladder & Scaffolding Company,
  Inc. (Automotive) [3338]
US Reflector (Automotive) [3378]
Washburn-Garfield Corp. (Plumbing Materials and
  Fixtures) [23438]
Webstone Company Inc. (Plumbing Materials and
  Fixtures) [23447]
Wire and Metal Separation Inc. (Used, Scrap, and
  Recycled Materials) [27050]
Worad Inc. (Communications Systems and
  Equipment) [5817]

Yarmouth Port

Butterworth Co. of Cape Cod (Books and Other
  Printed Materials) [3601]

Michigan

Ada

Amway Corp. (Electrical and Electronic Equipment
  and Supplies) [8350]
Amway Global Inc. (Sound and Entertainment
  Equipment and Supplies) [25074]
Baker Book House Co. (Books and Other Printed
  Materials) [3539]

Northern Equipment Company Inc. (Construction
  Materials and Machinery) [7795]

Adrian

Maumee Co. (Recreational and Sporting
  Goods) [23808]
Wacker Chemicals (USA) Inc. (Chemicals) [4549]

Allen Park

Tokico (USA) Inc. (Automotive) [3316]

Alma

Alma Iron and Metal Company Inc. (Used, Scrap,
  and Recycled Materials) [26743]
Medler Electric Co. (Electrical and Electronic
  Equipment and Supplies) [9062]

Alpena

Alpena Beverage Co. Inc. (Alcoholic
  Beverages) [1482]
Alpena Oil Company Inc. (Petroleum, Fuels, and
  Related Equipment) [22034]
Alpena Screen Arts (Clothing) [4763]
Alpena Screen Arts (Clothing) [4764]
Alpena Wholesale Grocery Co. (Food) [10377]
Ball Tire and Gas Inc. (Automotive) [2312]

Ann Arbor

Allied Inc. (Automotive) [2213]
Avfuel Corp. (Petroleum, Fuels, and Related
  Equipment) [22052]
Avis Enterprises Inc. (Recreational and Sporting
  Goods) [23530]
Children's Small Press Collection (Books and Other
  Printed Materials) [3630]
Communications Electronics Inc. (Communications
  Systems and Equipment) [5570]
Crescent Imports & Publications (Books and Other
  Printed Materials) [3672]
Diversified Data Products Inc. (Computers and
  Software) [6214]
Fingerle Lumber Co. (Construction Materials and
  Machinery) [7341]
H & H Distributing (Veterinary Products) [27143]
Interface Systems Inc. (Computers and
  Software) [6387]
J.D. Products (Health and Beauty Aids) [14136]
Olympia Sports (Recreational and Sporting
  Goods) [23859]
Rave Associates (Alcoholic Beverages) [1978]
ReCellular Inc. (Communications Systems and
  Equipment) [5737]
Servant Publications (Books and Other Printed
  Materials) [4154]
Thalner Electronic Labs Inc. (Electrical and
  Electronic Equipment and Supplies) [9484]
UMI (Photographic Equipment and
  Supplies) [22912]
Unistrut Fall Arrest Systems Inc. (Security and
  Safety Equipment) [24649]
Wedemeyer Electronic Supply Co. (Electrical and
  Electronic Equipment and Supplies) [9566]
Young Co.; Behler (Heating and Cooling Equipment
  and Supplies) [14783]

L' Anse

L'Anse Sentinel Co. (Office Equipment and
  Supplies) [20807]

Athens

House of Raeford Farms (Food) [11465]

Attica

Dimmer-Warren Enterprises (Recreational and
  Sporting Goods) [23623]

Auburn

Ye Old Black Powder Shop (Guns and
  Weapons) [13517]

Auburn Hills

Alaron Inc. (Sound and Entertainment Equipment
  and Supplies) [25060]
Audi of America Inc. (Motorized Vehicles) [20594]
Broner Glove Co. (Clothing) [4849]

Coca-Cola Bottlers of Detroit Inc. (Soft
  Drinks) [24930]
Denton and Company Ltd.; Robert (Alcoholic
  Beverages) [1642]
Impex International (Industrial Supplies) [16940]
North Electric Supply Inc. (Electrical and Electronic
  Equipment and Supplies) [9134]
Scherer Truck Equipment, Inc. (Automotive) [3194]
Shelving Inc. (Storage Equipment and
  Containers) [25938]
Shelving Inc. (Restaurant and Commercial
  Foodservice Equipment and Supplies) [24218]
Siemens Automotive Corp. (Automotive) [3219]
Trevarrow Inc. (Household Appliances) [15342]
Volkswagen of America Inc. (Motorized
  Vehicles) [20743]
World Computer Corp. (Computers and
  Software) [6877]

Bad Axe

S.T. and H. Oil Company Inc. (Petroleum, Fuels,
  and Related Equipment) [22697]

Battle Creek

Ackerman Electrical Supply Co. (Electrical and
  Electronic Equipment and Supplies) [8265]
Anatech Ltd. (Paints and Varnishes) [21388]
Gallagher Industrial Laundry (Clothing) [4974]
Galloup Co.; J.O. (Plumbing Materials and
  Fixtures) [23182]
Great Lakes Electronics Supply Div. (Electrical and
  Electronic Equipment and Supplies) [8816]
Kendall Electric Inc. (Electrical and Electronic
  Equipment and Supplies) [8935]
Kendall Industrial Supplies Inc. (Industrial
  Supplies) [16984]
Millers Wholesale, Inc. (Specialty Equipment and
  Products) [25742]
Normans Inc. (Food) [12020]
Pearl's Sports Center; Jack (Recreational and
  Sporting Goods) [23876]

Bay City

Bingo Sales Inc.; J.D. (Toys and Hobby
  Goods) [26420]
Cellars Beverage Inc. (Alcoholic Beverages) [1582]
Duro Supply Co. (Plumbing Materials and
  Fixtures) [23141]
First Automotive Inc. (Automotive) [2618]
Great Lakes Area Distributing (Toys and Hobby
  Goods) [26505]
Hirschfield Sons Co.; H. (Used, Scrap, and
  Recycled Materials) [26843]
Jennison Industrial Supply (Hardware) [13771]
Made Rite Potato Chip Company
  Inc. (Food) [11755]
Michigan Airgas (Industrial Supplies) [17033]
Rupp Oil Company Inc. (Petroleum, Fuels, and
  Related Equipment) [22644]
Standish Oil Co. (Petroleum, Fuels, and Related
  Equipment) [22700]

Bear Lake

Blarney Castle Oil Co. (Petroleum, Fuels, and
  Related Equipment) [22080]

Belleville

Happy Acres Pet Supply (Veterinary
  Products) [27144]
Huron Valley Steel Corp. (Metals) [20050]
Splane Electric Supply (Electrical and Electronic
  Equipment and Supplies) [9395]

Benton Harbor

All Phase Electric Supply Co. (Electrical and
  Electronic Equipment and Supplies) [8295]
Applied Industrial Technologies (Industrial
  Supplies) [16704]
Barentsen Candy Co. (Tobacco Products) [26264]
Barentsen Candy Co. (Food) [10506]
Brammall Supply Co. (Industrial Supplies) [16764]
Greg Orchards & Produce Inc. (Food) [11322]
Lakeland Wholesale Grocery (Food) [11668]
Thayer Inc. (Cleaning and Janitorial
  Supplies) [4716]

Thayer Inc. (Restaurant and Commercial Foodservice Equipment and Supplies) [24245]

Berkley

Barbuscak and Associates; John (Gifts and Novelties) [13310]
Cornelius Systems Inc. (Office Equipment and Supplies) [20921]
Discount Office Equipment Inc. (Office Equipment and Supplies) [20966]
Discount Office Equipment Inc. (Furniture and Fixtures) [13092]

Berrien Springs

Brohman Distributing Co. (Toys and Hobby Goods) [26427]

Beverly Hills

Varon and Associates Inc. (Specialty Equipment and Products) [25864]

Bingham Farms

Magnum Corp. (Industrial Supplies) [17011]

Birmingham

Byrne Plywood Co. (Construction Materials and Machinery) [7119]
La Belle Provence Ltd. (Furniture and Fixtures) [13160]
Silk and Morgan Inc. (Horticultural Supplies) [14950]

Blissfield

Michigan Agricultural Commodities (Livestock and Farm Products) [18088]

Bloomfield

Young Co.; Behler (Heating and Cooling Equipment and Supplies) [14784]

Bloomfield Hills

B & B Specialty Foods (Food) [10481]
Brown-Campbell Co (Metals) [19838]
Kurtzman Book Sales, Inc. (Books and Other Printed Materials) [3889]
Lynn Medical Instrument Co. (Medical, Dental, and Optical Equipment) [18894]
Molls Inc. (Hardware) [13834]
United Export Import, Inc. (Motorized Vehicles) [20740]
Vine Associates Inc.; George (Clothing) [5464]

Bridgeport

Amigo Mobility International Inc. (Medical, Dental, and Optical Equipment) [18680]
Selectware Technologies, Inc. (Computers and Software) [6723]

Bridgman

Bosch Corp. Packaging Machinery Div.; Robert (Industrial Machinery) [15833]

Brighton

FOX Systems Inc. (Computers and Software) [6279]
K.M.H. Equipment Co. (Construction Materials and Machinery) [7563]
Lowry Computer Products Inc. (Computers and Software) [6446]

Brooklyn

Penn Printed Shirts Corp. (Clothing) [5274]

Brown City

Kohler Oil and Propane Co. (Petroleum, Fuels, and Related Equipment) [22410]

Burton

B.G.B. Pet Supply Inc. (Veterinary Products) [27082]
Genesee Ceramic Tile Distributors (Floorcovering Equipment and Supplies) [9917]
Vacuum Center Central Michigan (Household Appliances) [15352]

Byron Center

Absopure Water Co. (Soft Drinks) [24906]
Van Solkema Produce Inc. (Food) [12825]

Cadillac

Avon North America Inc. (Recreational and Sporting Goods) [23531]
Fiamm Technologies (Automotive) [2614]
Pells Radio Center (Household Appliances) [15270]
Wedin International Inc., Ball Screw Manufacturing and Repair, Inc. (Hardware) [13989]

Canton

Burda Brothers (Toys and Hobby Goods) [26430]
Competitive Edge (Computers and Software) [6090]
Packaged Software Solutions Inc. (Computers and Software) [6581]
ProCoil Corp. (Metals) [20297]
Staples Business Advantage (Office Equipment and Supplies) [21288]
West Side Distributors Ltd. (Automotive) [3409]

Cassopolis

Best Plastics Inc. (Automotive) [2354]

Cedar Springs

Ho Imports, Inc. (Toys and Hobby Goods) [26515]

Center Line

Binson's Hospital Supplies Inc. (Medical, Dental, and Optical Equipment) [18708]
Commodity Steel and Processing Inc. (Metals) [19889]
Dealer's Discount Crafts (Office Equipment and Supplies) [20952]
Servall Co. (Household Appliances) [15308]

Chassell

Anderson & Jarvi Lumber (Construction Materials and Machinery) [6975]

Chesaning

Sarah's Attic Inc. (Gifts and Novelties) [13443]

Chesterfield

AM-DYN-IC Fluid Power (Industrial Supplies) [16692]
Brown Bear Sporting (Recreational and Sporting Goods) [23569]

Clare

Johnston Elevator Co. (Livestock and Farm Products) [18025]

Clarkston

Cordial/Riley Marketing (Electrical and Electronic Equipment and Supplies) [8581]

Clawson

House of Plastic Inc. (Medical, Dental, and Optical Supplies) [19362]
Sun Medical Equipment and Supply Co. (Medical, Dental, and Optical Equipment) [19063]

Clinton Township

Avanti 4 International Corp. (Computers and Software) [5992]
Barclay Marine Distributors Corp. (Marine) [18453]
Haig Lighting & Electric (Electrical and Electronic Equipment and Supplies) [8822]
Pharm-Med Inc. (Medical, Dental, and Optical Equipment) [18984]

Clio

Industrial Communications Co. (Communications Systems and Equipment) [5645]

Coldwater

Alliance Foods Inc. (Food) [10371]

Comstock Park

Dykstra Food Service (Food) [11006]

Coopersville

Lemmen Oil Co. (Petroleum, Fuels, and Related Equipment) [22427]
Mark-Pack Inc. (Paper and Paper Products) [21822]

Davison

TNT Optical Supply, Inc. (Medical, Dental, and Optical Supplies) [19657]

Dearborn

Arun Technology Inc. (Scientific and Measurement Devices) [24317]
Carhartt Inc. (Textiles and Notions) [25995]
Energy International Corp. (Heating and Cooling Equipment and Supplies) [14432]
Eppinger Manufacturing Co. (Recreational and Sporting Goods) [23653]
Freedland Industries Corp. (Automotive) [2646]
Gnieweks Trophies Inc.; Hank (Recreational and Sporting Goods) [23690]
Kenwal Steel Corp. (Metals) [20097]
Metropolitan X-Ray Sales Inc. (Medical, Dental, and Optical Equipment) [18934]
Rogers Electric Supply; Chas. (Electrical and Electronic Equipment and Supplies) [9310]
S & N Sales (Food) [12382]
Standard Building Products (Construction Materials and Machinery) [8067]
Weldtube Inc. (Metals) [20486]
Wright Co.; F.B. (Industrial Supplies) [17288]

Dearborn Heights

Parkway Drapery Co. (Household Items) [15613]
Televan Sales Inc. (Industrial Machinery) [16556]
XWW Alloys, Inc. (Industrial Machinery) [16653]

Detroit

Acme Group (Automotive) [2175]
Advance Steel Co. (Metals) [19731]
Allied Metals Corp. (Used, Scrap, and Recycled Materials) [26738]
Ambassador Steel Company Inc. (Metals) [19767]
Andrew Co.; W.T. (Plumbing Materials and Fixtures) [23065]
Arrow Trucks and Parts Co. (Automotive) [2256]
Aunt Mid Produce Co. (Food) [10470]
Auto Trends Inc. (Automotive) [2279]
Badalament Inc. (Food) [10484]
Badalament Inc. (Food) [10485]
Boyer Steel Inc. (Industrial Supplies) [16760]
Canton China and Equipment Co. (Restaurant and Commercial Foodservice Equipment and Supplies) [24088]
Cattleman's Inc. (Food) [10715]
Cattleman's Meat Co. (Food) [10716]
Cellar Book Shop (Books and Other Printed Materials) [3619]
Century Saw and Tool Co. Inc. (Hardware) [13629]
Circle Glass Co. (Construction Materials and Machinery) [7174]
Colonial Brick Co. (Construction Materials and Machinery) [7197]
Consumers Petroleum Co. (Petroleum, Fuels, and Related Equipment) [22164]
Continental Wood Preservers Inc. (Construction Materials and Machinery) [7210]
Continental Wood Preservers Inc. (Wood and Wood Products) [27299]
Crystal Home Health Care Inc. (Medical, Dental, and Optical Equipment) [18760]
Crystal Home Health Care Inc. (Medical, Dental, and Optical Supplies) [19261]
Davidson Lumber Co.; Howard A. (Construction Materials and Machinery) [7252]
Dearborn Fabricating and Engineering Corp. (Industrial Machinery) [15935]
Detroit Ball Bearing Company Executive Offices (Industrial Supplies) [16829]
Detroit Diesel Overseas Corp. (Automotive) [2541]
Detroit Pump and Manufacturing Co. (Plumbing Materials and Fixtures) [23137]
Dopar Support Systems Inc. (Computers and Software) [6219]

Eastside Wholesale Supply Co. (Floorcovering Equipment and Supplies) [9880]
Economy Wholesalers (Food) [11024]
Factory Steel and Metal Supply Co., LLC (Metals) [19963]
Federal Pipe and Supply Co. (Construction Materials and Machinery) [7332]
Federal Pipe and Supply Co. (Construction Materials and Machinery) [7333]
Fleischman Carpet Co. (Floorcovering Equipment and Supplies) [9891]
Gell and Co.; Jack (Medical, Dental, and Optical Supplies) [19334]
George H. International Corp. (Agricultural Equipment and Supplies) [734]
Global Titanium Inc. (Used, Scrap, and Recycled Materials) [26831]
Grand River Meat Center (Food) [11305]
HD Communications Inc. (Communications Systems and Equipment) [5634]
Hirt Jr., Co.; R. (Food) [11441]
Hoban Foods Inc. (Food) [11443]
Howard Electric Co. (Electrical and Electronic Equipment and Supplies) [8861]
Huron Steel Company Inc. (Metals) [20049]
Jogue Corp. (Food) [11557]
Johnston Company Inc.; George L. (Heating and Cooling Equipment and Supplies) [14502]
Joint Clutch and Gear Service Inc. (Automotive) [2829]
Jonner Steel Industries (Metals) [20077]
Kasle Steel Corp. (Metals) [20087]
Keywell Corp. (Used, Scrap, and Recycled Materials) [26866]
Koenig Fuel & Supply Co. (Petroleum, Fuels, and Related Equipment) [22409]
Kuhlman and Co.; A. (Medical, Dental, and Optical Equipment) [18878]
Kurtz Steel; James H. (Metals) [20111]
Lafayette Steel Co. (Metals) [20114]
Leemon Oil Company Inc. (Petroleum, Fuels, and Related Equipment) [22422]
Leemon Shores Oil (Petroleum, Fuels, and Related Equipment) [22423]
Leonard Refrigeration & Heating Sales & Service (Heating and Cooling Equipment and Supplies) [14523]
Letts Equipment Div. (Automotive) [2879]
Levin and Sons Co.; J. (Cleaning and Janitorial Supplies) [4659]
Lutz News Co. (Books and Other Printed Materials) [3923]
Majji Produce, Inc. (Food) [11762]
Maldaver Company Inc. (Automotive) [2913]
Mark's Quality Meats (Food) [11787]
Martin Universal Design Inc. (Furniture and Fixtures) [13172]
McInerney-Miller Brothers Inc. (Food) [11829]
Meskin and Davis Inc. (Textiles and Notions) [26142]
Metropolitan Diesel Supply Co. (Automotive) [2948]
Michigan Industrial Shoe Co. (Shoes) [24810]
Minkin Chandler Corp. (Used, Scrap, and Recycled Materials) [26916]
Montgomery Div. (Petroleum, Fuels, and Related Equipment) [22494]
National Dry Goods (Clothing) [5215]
National Metal Processing Inc. (Metals) [20220]
National Paint Distributors (Paints and Varnishes) [21515]
Nordlie Inc. (Horticultural Supplies) [14928]
Omnigraphics Inc. (Books and Other Printed Materials) [4022]
Pioneer Steel Corp. (Metals) [20281]
Pollard Co.; C.E. (Motorized Vehicles) [20706]
Pollard Co.; C.E. (Automotive) [3101]
Reliable Architectural Metals Co. (Construction Materials and Machinery) [7911]
Reliable Glass Co. (Construction Materials and Machinery) [7912]
Rose Caster Co. (Hardware) [13894]
Salasnek Fisheries Inc. (Food) [12391]
Salomon Co.; Paul R. (Marine) [18600]
Samuel-Whittar Inc. (Minerals and Ores) [20567]
Schlafer Iron and Steel Co. (Used, Scrap, and Recycled Materials) [26981]

Seaman Paper Co.; Patrick (Paper and Paper Products) [21930]
Seaman-Patrick Paper Co. (Paper and Paper Products) [21931]
Service Tire Co. (Automotive) [3207]
Silvers Inc. (Furniture and Fixtures) [13242]
Soave Enterprises L.L.C. (Used, Scrap, and Recycled Materials) [26996]
Steel Industries Inc. (Metals) [20396]
Stella Products Co.; F.D. (Restaurant and Commercial Foodservice Equipment and Supplies) [24228]
Sun Appliance Service Inc. (Specialty Equipment and Products) [25833]
SYSCO Food Services of Detroit, LLC (Food) [12679]
Taylor Optical Supplies Inc. (Medical, Dental, and Optical Supplies) [19649]
Taylor Supply Co. (Plumbing Materials and Fixtures) [23406]
Thyssen Incorporated N.A. (Metals) [20423]
U.S. Equipment Co. (Industrial Machinery) [16591]
Watson Inc.; Fannie (Gifts and Novelties) [13470]
Wetherbee and Co.; George C. (Automotive) [3416]
Winston Brothers Iron and Metal Inc. (Used, Scrap, and Recycled Materials) [27049]
Wolverine Packing Co. (Food) [12974]
Wolverine Tractor and Equipment (Agricultural Equipment and Supplies) [1459]
Young Supply Co. (Heating and Cooling Equipment and Supplies) [14787]

Dexter

Mager Scientific Inc. (Scientific and Measurement Devices) [24393]
Packtronics Inc. (Sound and Entertainment Equipment and Supplies) [25374]

Dimondale

Greater Lansing Auto Auction Inc. (Motorized Vehicles) [20644]

Dollar Bay

Horner Flooring Company Inc. (Floorcovering Equipment and Supplies) [9953]

Dundee

Yeck Antique Firearms (Guns and Weapons) [13518]

Durand

Durand Equipment and Manufacturing Co. (Construction Materials and Machinery) [7291]

East Jordan

East Jordan Cooperative Co. (Automotive) [2571]
East Jordan Cooperative Co. (Petroleum, Fuels, and Related Equipment) [22218]

East Lansing

Cruse Communication Co. (Household Appliances) [15100]
Mackinaw Sales Inc. (Marine) [18554]
Michigan State University Press (Books and Other Printed Materials) [3952]

Eastpointe

All State Fastener Corp. (Hardware) [13549]
Copper and Brass Sales Inc. (Metals) [19896]
Copper and Brass Sales Inc. (Metals) [19897]

Ecorse

Ecorse Sales and Machinery Inc. (Industrial Machinery) [15976]

Elkton

Cooperative Elevator Co. (Livestock and Farm Products) [17794]

Escanaba

Northern Plumbing & Heating Supply (Plumbing Materials and Fixtures) [23298]

Fairgrove

Laethem Farm Service Co. (Agricultural Equipment and Supplies) [928]

Farmington

Exotic Rubber and Plastics Corp. (Industrial Supplies) [16852]
Hackett Co.; J. Lee (Industrial Machinery) [16082]
Jay-Cee Sales and Rivet Inc. (Hardware) [13769]
Star Cutter Co. (Industrial Machinery) [16519]
Zatkoff Seals and Packings Co. (Industrial Supplies) [17294]

Farmington Hills

American Exercise & Fitness Equipment Co. (Recreational and Sporting Goods) [23509]
Atlas Copco Tools Inc. (Hardware) [13574]
Bamal Fastener Corp. (Hardware) [13582]
Barons Wholesale Clothiers (Clothing) [4806]
Blue Line Distributing (Food) [10575]
Corrosion Fluid Products Corp. (Industrial Supplies) [16811]
Electro-Matic Products Inc. (Electrical and Electronic Equipment and Supplies) [8684]
Electro-Matic Products Inc. (Industrial Machinery) [15980]
Genesee Ceramic Tile Distributors (Floorcovering Equipment and Supplies) [9920]
Implant Dynamic (Medical, Dental, and Optical Equipment) [18850]
Inman Associates Inc.; Paul (Food) [11509]
Jacob and Sons; M. (Storage Equipment and Containers) [25921]
Management Supply Co. (Plumbing Materials and Fixtures) [23248]
Mascari & Associations; Charles (Food) [11800]
Methods and Equipment Associates (Industrial Machinery) [16290]
Pioneer Snacks Inc. (Food) [12174]
Reliance Group of Michigan (Paper and Paper Products) [21900]
RP Sales, Inc. (Electrical and Electronic Equipment and Supplies) [9321]
Stark & Company Inc. (Food) [12573]
Stark and Company Inc. (Food) [12574]
Virginia Tile Co. (Floorcovering Equipment and Supplies) [10281]

Fennville

Campbell's Fresh Inc. (Food) [10686]

Fenton

Bently Sand & Gravel (Construction Materials and Machinery) [7046]
Mott Media L.L.C. (Books and Other Printed Materials) [3971]

Ferndale

Custom Music Co. (Sound and Entertainment Equipment and Supplies) [25152]
Detroit Air Compressor and Pump Co. (Industrial Machinery) [15944]
Detroit Gas Products Co. (Industrial Supplies) [16830]
Engine Center Inc. (Industrial Machinery) [15987]
Erickson's Flooring & Supply (Floorcovering Equipment and Supplies) [9885]
Optical Center Laboratory Inc. (Medical, Dental, and Optical Supplies) [19512]

Flint

Advance Glove & Safety Co. (Security and Safety Equipment) [24492]
American Commodities Inc. (Plastics) [22923]
Apco Inc. (Household Appliances) [15013]
Auto-Blankers (Metals) [19794]
Bel Air Distributors (Sound and Entertainment Equipment and Supplies) [25100]
Bell's Produce, Inc. (Food) [10533]
Bivins Barbecue Sauce (Food) [10562]
Brannon; Thomas (Heating and Cooling Equipment and Supplies) [14357]
Brown and Sons Co. Inc. (Automotive) [2397]
Charter Distributing (Floorcovering Equipment and Supplies) [9803]

Clark's Store Fixtures Inc. (Cleaning and Janitorial Supplies) [4599]

Denatec Distributors (Petroleum, Fuels, and Related Equipment) [22196]

Dukes Car Stereo Inc. (Communications Systems and Equipment) [5598]

Genesis Medical Equipment (Medical, Dental, and Optical Equipment) [18808]

GM Service Parts Operations (Automotive) [2687]

Gruener Sales Inc. (Automotive) [2709]

Hay-A-Bar Dry Ice Wholesaler (Food) [11396]

Hicks Equipment (Electrical and Electronic Equipment and Supplies) [8841]

Hill Steel & Builders Supplies (Metals) [20039]

Hougen Manufacturing Inc. (Industrial Machinery) [16116]

Hubbard Industrial Supply Co. (Industrial Machinery) [16119]

Iron Mike's Welding & Fab (Metals) [20070]

Keith Distributors Inc. (Books and Other Printed Materials) [3877]

Kenrick Company Inc.; R. G. (Industrial Supplies) [16987]

Koolies Ice Cream (Food) [11636]

Lorbec Metals USA Ltd. (Metals) [20134]

M & R Distributors Inc. (Automotive) [2901]

McNaughton-McKay Electric Company (Electrical and Electronic Equipment and Supplies) [9059]

Michigan Lumber Co. (Construction Materials and Machinery) [7702]

North Warehouse Inc. (Clothing) [5241]

O'Sullivan Distributor Inc.; John P. (Alcoholic Beverages) [1935]

Royalite Co. (Electrical and Electronic Equipment and Supplies) [9319]

White Fountain Supply Co.; Bob (Restaurant and Commercial Foodservice Equipment and Supplies) [24262]

Young Co.; Behler (Heating and Cooling Equipment and Supplies) [14777]

Flushing

S & M Lumber Co. (Construction Materials and Machinery) [7970]

S and M Lumber Co. (Wood and Wood Products) [27368]

Fowlerville

Klein's Booklein (Books and Other Printed Materials) [3883]

Fraser

Artistic Stone of America (Gifts and Novelties) [13307]

Dale Office Plus (Office Equipment and Supplies) [20944]

Hogan and Associates Inc.; T.J. (Automotive) [2760]

Mucci; Patrick J. (Toys and Hobby Goods) [26585]

P & D Hobby Distributors (Toys and Hobby Goods) [26600]

Roselli's Wholesale Foods Inc. (Food) [12353]

Fremont

Fremont Cooperative Produce Co. (Agricultural Equipment and Supplies) [706]

Gaylord

Gaylord Cash & Carry (Food) [11246]

Johnson Oil Company of Gaylord (Petroleum, Fuels, and Related Equipment) [22389]

Scientific Brake and Equipment Co. (Automotive) [3199]

Gladstone

Besse Forest Products Group (Construction Materials and Machinery) [7052]

Grand Blanc

AC-Delco/GM Service Parts Operation (Automotive) [2166]

Grand Blanc Cement Products (Construction Materials and Machinery) [7407]

Grand Haven

Artist Brush & Color Dist. (Office Equipment and Supplies) [20814]

Dawson Industries Inc. (Specialty Equipment and Products) [25626]

Grand Haven Steel Products (Metals) [20015]

Grand Transformers Inc. (Electrical and Electronic Equipment and Supplies) [8806]

Heyboer Transformers Inc. (Electrical and Electronic Equipment and Supplies) [8839]

Lakeside Spring Products (Hardware) [13790]

Ottawa Electric Inc. (Electrical and Electronic Equipment and Supplies) [9162]

Grand Ledge

Michigan State Seed Co. (Agricultural Equipment and Supplies) [1026]

Grand Rapids

Abraham and Sons Inc.; S. (Tobacco Products) [26257]

AIS Construction Equipment Corp. (Construction Materials and Machinery) [6927]

Allied Electronics (Electrical and Electronic Equipment and Supplies) [8310]

AM-DYN-IC Fluid Power (Industrial Machinery) [15762]

American Seating Co. (Furniture and Fixtures) [13018]

Anazeh Sands (Recreational and Sporting Goods) [23515]

Auto Wares Inc. (Automotive) [2281]

B & B Beer Distributing (Alcoholic Beverages) [1492]

Bar Beverage Control Inc. (Heating and Cooling Equipment and Supplies) [14337]

Behler-Young Co. (Heating and Cooling Equipment and Supplies) [14342]

Bertsch Co. (Industrial Supplies) [16752]

Bishop Distributing Co. (Floorcovering Equipment and Supplies) [9728]

Budres Lumber Co. (Construction Materials and Machinery) [7094]

Bursma Electronic Distributing Inc. (Sound and Entertainment Equipment and Supplies) [25113]

Bursma Electronic Distributing Inc. (Electrical and Electronic Equipment and Supplies) [8478]

C & J Tool & Gage Co. (Industrial Machinery) [15862]

Carpenter Paper Co. (Paper and Paper Products) [21671]

Cascade Optical Inc. (Medical, Dental, and Optical Supplies) [19220]

Central Distribution Services, LLC (Hardware) [13626]

Country Fresh Inc. (Food) [10856]

Dennen Steel Corp. (Metals) [19927]

Eerdmans Publishing Co.; William B. (Books and Other Printed Materials) [3724]

Eikenhout and Sons Inc. (Construction Materials and Machinery) [7304]

Ferguson Supply Co. (Plumbing Materials and Fixtures) [23165]

Flaherty Company Inc.; L.H. (Automotive) [2627]

Fox Sales Co.; Henry A. (Alcoholic Beverages) [1696]

Fuller Supply Co. (Plumbing Materials and Fixtures) [23179]

Genesee Ceramic Tile Distributors (Floorcovering Equipment and Supplies) [9921]

Gordon Food Service Inc. (Food) [11293]

Grand Rapids Sash and Door (Construction Materials and Machinery) [7408]

Great Lakes Sales, Inc. (Floorcovering Equipment and Supplies) [9925]

Green and Co.; Carl (Industrial Supplies) [16907]

GRS Industrial Supply Co. (Industrial Supplies) [16913]

Guilford of Maine Textile Resources (Textiles and Notions) [26049]

Hager Lumber Company Inc.; T.W. (Construction Materials and Machinery) [7428]

Hager Lumber Company Inc.; T.W. (Wood and Wood Products) [27314]

Harmony International Corporation (Household Appliances) [15162]

Haviland Products Co. (Chemicals) [4411]

Heeren Brothers, Inc. (Food) [11406]

Hemisphere International (Textiles and Notions) [26062]

HJV Inc. (Computers and Software) [6337]

Hoekstra Truck Equipment Company, Inc. (Automotive) [2758]

Irvin-Alan Fabrics (Textiles and Notions) [26075]

Kawasaki Motors Corporation U.S.A. Engine Div. (Automotive) [2841]

Knape and Vogt Manufacturing Co. (Construction Materials and Machinery) [7564]

Kregel Publications & Bookstores (Books and Other Printed Materials) [3886]

L and L Jiroch Distributing Co. (Tobacco Products) [26321]

Land & Sea Products (Storage Equipment and Containers) [25926]

Lumbermen's Inc. (Construction Materials and Machinery) [7619]

Mackay Industrial Sales Inc. (Industrial Supplies) [17010]

Marks Pro Shop; Mike (Recreational and Sporting Goods) [23802]

Marquette Lumbermen's Warehouse Inc. (Construction Materials and Machinery) [7645]

Meijer Inc. (Food) [11845]

Mill Steel Co. (Metals) [20192]

Morrison Industrial Equipment Co. (Industrial Machinery) [16327]

Morrison Industries Inc. (Industrial Supplies) [17052]

North Central Optical Co. (Medical, Dental, and Optical Supplies) [19500]

Notions Marketing Corp. (Textiles and Notions) [26159]

Optical Supply (Medical, Dental, and Optical Supplies) [19518]

Oshtemo Hill Inc. (Construction Materials and Machinery) [7815]

Peacock Alley Needlepoint (Toys and Hobby Goods) [26608]

Pfeiffer Hijet (Automotive) [3096]

Potter Distributing Inc. (Heating and Cooling Equipment and Supplies) [14642]

Potter Distributing Inc. (Household Appliances) [15277]

Purity Cylinder Gases Inc. (Industrial Machinery) [16434]

Quimby-Walstrom Paper Co. (Paper and Paper Products) [21895]

Raniville Company Inc.; F. (Industrial Supplies) [17130]

Reynolds & Sons Inc. (Recreational and Sporting Goods) [23914]

Richards Manufacturing Company Inc. (Plumbing Materials and Fixtures) [23341]

Richards Quality Bedding (Furniture and Fixtures) [13222]

Sack Company Inc.; J. R. (Industrial Supplies) [17151]

Seven Paint and Wallpaper Co.; John (Paints and Varnishes) [21564]

Skytron (Medical, Dental, and Optical Equipment) [19041]

Spartan Stores Inc. (Food) [12547]

Spartan Stores Inc. (Food) [12548]

Stiles Machinery Inc. (Industrial Machinery) [16528]

Stream & Lake Tackle (Recreational and Sporting Goods) [23989]

Superior Appliance Service Co. (Household Appliances) [15326]

SYSCO Food Services of Grand Rapids (Food) [12680]

Tari-Tan Ceramic Supply Inc. (Toys and Hobby Goods) [26676]

Terryberry Co. (Jewelry) [17635]

Thrift Products Company Inc. (Food) [12719]

Transnational Motors Inc. (Motorized Vehicles) [20738]

United Art Distributors (Specialty Equipment and Products) [25853]

Universal Forest Products, Inc. (Wood and Wood Products) [27391]

Van Eerden Distribution Co. (Food) [12823]

VEC Inc. (Food) [12833]
We Market Success Inc. (Food) [12889]
White and White Pharmacy Inc. (Medical, Dental, and Optical Supplies) [19704]
Williams Distributing Co. (Household Appliances) [15373]
Xpedx/Carpenter Group (Paper and Paper Products) [22005]
Xpedx/Carpenter Group (Paper and Paper Products) [22007]
Yamaha Corporation of America Band and Orchestral Division (Sound and Entertainment Equipment and Supplies) [25536]
The Zondervan Corp. (Books and Other Printed Materials) [4307]

Grandville

C.W. Mills (Office Equipment and Supplies) [20943]
Hascall Steel Company Inc. (Metals) [20030]
Postema Sales Co. Inc. (Household Appliances) [15276]

Grawn

Access Publishers Network (Books and Other Printed Materials) [3466]

Grayling

Stephan Wood Products Inc. (Wood and Wood Products) [27382]

Grosse Pointe

Gallagher Steel Co. (Metals) [19993]
Maiale Metal Products (Metals) [20145]
Marmon Group (Hardware) [13813]

Grosse Pointe Woods

Drucker Associates, Inc. (Automotive) [2566]
Michigan Paper Recyling Corp. (Used, Scrap, and Recycled Materials) [26911]

Hale

Darton Archery (Recreational and Sporting Goods) [23614]

Hamilton

Pet Life Foods Inc. (Veterinary Products) [27207]

Hamtramck

Kowalski Sausage Company Inc. (Food) [11638]
Veterans Supply & Distributing Co. (Cleaning and Janitorial Supplies) [4723]

Harrison Township

Econ Equipment & Supplies Inc. (Medical, Dental, and Optical Equipment) [18783]
International Imports Inc. (Clothing) [5057]

Hartford

Neil's Automotive Service, Inc. (Automotive) [3023]

Hazel Park

Meier Metal Servicenters Inc. (Metals) [20163]
Sibley Industrial Tool Co. (Electrical and Electronic Equipment and Supplies) [9367]

Highland Park

Detroit City Dairy Inc. (Food) [10952]
General Wine Co. (Alcoholic Beverages) [1710]

Holland

Genzink Steel (Metals) [20000]
Genzink Steel (Metals) [20001]
Hansen Machine Co. (Metals) [20027]
Heidema Brothers Inc. (Motorized Vehicles) [20647]
Padnos Iron and Metal Co.; Louis (Used, Scrap, and Recycled Materials) [26933]
Worden Co. (Furniture and Fixtures) [13284]

Holt

Partners Book Distributing Inc. (Books and Other Printed Materials) [4041]

Houghton Lake

Halliday Sand and Gravel Co. (Construction Materials and Machinery) [7432]

Howell

Coil Center Corp. (Metals) [19880]
ESCO Industries (Automotive) [2597]

Hudsonville

Creme Curls Bakery Inc. (Food) [10865]
Miedema Produce, Inc. (Food) [11890]
Woodwyk Inc.; Casey (Food) [12979]

Inkster

Unirak Storage Systems (Storage Equipment and Containers) [25946]

Ionia

Kay Distributing Co. (Food) [11585]

Iron Mountain

Thompson Company Inc.; W.B. (Automotive) [3302]
Wittock Supply Co. (Plumbing Materials and Fixtures) [23465]

Ishpeming

Virgs Inc. (Shoes) [24886]

Jackson

Alro Steel Corp. (Metals) [19759]
Anderson Distributing Co. (Alcoholic Beverages) [1484]
Cruse Communication Co. (Sound and Entertainment Equipment and Supplies) [25149]
Fulton Radio Supply Co. (Electrical and Electronic Equipment and Supplies) [8767]
General Materials Inc. (Construction Materials and Machinery) [7385]
Jackson Iron and Metal Co. (Metals) [20074]
McGowan Electric Supply Inc. (Electrical and Electronic Equipment and Supplies) [9057]
New World Acquisition Inc. (Petroleum, Fuels, and Related Equipment) [22512]
Nova Vista Industries Inc. (Petroleum, Fuels, and Related Equipment) [22530]
Pipeline Oil Sales Inc. (Petroleum, Fuels, and Related Equipment) [22586]
Preston Corp.; J.A. (Medical, Dental, and Optical Equipment) [18995]
Production Tool Supply of Jackson (Industrial Supplies) [17120]
Refrigeration Sales Inc. (Heating and Cooling Equipment and Supplies) [14658]
United Magazine Co. Southern Michigan Division (Books and Other Printed Materials) [4241]
Young Co.; Behler (Heating and Cooling Equipment and Supplies) [14779]

Jonesville

The Book House Inc. (Books and Other Printed Materials) [3571]

Kalamazoo

Aero-Motive Co. (Electrical and Electronic Equipment and Supplies) [8279]
Automotive Diagnostics (Automotive) [2285]
Clausing Industrial Inc. (Industrial Machinery) [15893]
Doubleday Brothers and Co. (Office Equipment and Supplies) [20974]
Douglas and Sons, Inc. (Industrial Supplies) [16837]
Great Lakes Technologies Corp. (Photographic Equipment and Supplies) [22859]
Hearing Aid Centers of America (Medical, Dental, and Optical Equipment) [18833]
Imperial Beverage Co. (Alcoholic Beverages) [1771]
Kalamazoo Dental Supply (Medical, Dental, and Optical Equipment) [18871]
Kalamazoo Mill Supply Co. (Industrial Supplies) [16975]
Kalamazoo Mill Supply Co. (Metals) [20083]

Kalamazoo Steel Processing Inc. (Metals) [20084]
KD Sales Inc. (Toys and Hobby Goods) [26552]
Klosterman Company Inc.; John C. (Tobacco Products) [26320]
McLeieer Oil Inc. (Petroleum, Fuels, and Related Equipment) [22468]
Neil's Automotive Service, Inc. (Automotive) [3022]
Newhouse Printers Supply Inc. (Specialty Equipment and Products) [25758]
Roe-Comm Inc. (Electrical and Electronic Equipment and Supplies) [9309]
Spaman Jewellers; W.M. (Jewelry) [17616]
Wesley Ice Cream (Food) [12905]
Young Co.; Behler (Heating and Cooling Equipment and Supplies) [14778]

Kentwood

FinishMaster Inc. (Automotive) [2617]

Lake Odessa

Caledonia Farmers Elevator Co., Lake Odessa Branch (Agricultural Equipment and Supplies) [362]
Michigan Glass Lined Storage Inc. (Agricultural Equipment and Supplies) [1025]

Lake Orion

Kay Automotive Graphics (Automotive) [2842]
Midwest Telephone Inc. (Communications Systems and Equipment) [5677]
Powers Distributing Company Inc. (Alcoholic Beverages) [1965]

Lansing

Advance Glove & Safety Co. (Security and Safety Equipment) [24491]
Allied Building Products (Construction Materials and Machinery) [6939]
Alro Steel Corp. (Metals) [19760]
Apco Inc. (Household Appliances) [15014]
Capital Wholesale Distribution Co. (Tobacco Products) [26271]
Decker and Company Inc. (Agricultural Equipment and Supplies) [503]
Farmers Petroleum Cooperative Inc. (Petroleum, Fuels, and Related Equipment) [22257]
Imlay City Total Oil Inc. (Petroleum, Fuels, and Related Equipment) [22373]
International Consulting & Contracting Services (Construction Materials and Machinery) [7517]
Kent Electronics Inc. (Sound and Entertainment Equipment and Supplies) [25268]
Lesco Corp. (Lansing, Michigan) (Specialty Equipment and Products) [25714]
M and M Distributors Inc. (Alcoholic Beverages) [1833]
Maxco Inc. (Metals) [20159]
McDaniels Sales Co. (Household Appliances) [15224]
Michigan Supply Co. (Plumbing Materials and Fixtures) [23263]
Microform Systems Inc. (Office Equipment and Supplies) [21140]
Mill Supplies Corp. (Industrial Supplies) [17038]
Oldsmobile Div. (Automotive) [3062]
Schultz Snyder Steele Lumber Co. (Construction Materials and Machinery) [7989]
Schultz Snyder Steele Lumber Co. (Wood and Wood Products) [27369]
Servall Co. (Household Appliances) [15307]
Soffe; M.J. (Recreational and Sporting Goods) [23952]
Spadafore Distributing Co. (Alcoholic Beverages) [2042]
Uniform Center of Lansing Inc. (Clothing) [5448]
Wallace Opticians Inc. (Medical, Dental, and Optical Supplies) [19693]
Wolverton Pet Supply (Veterinary Products) [27272]
Young Co.; Behler (Heating and Cooling Equipment and Supplies) [14782]

Lapeer

Basic Service Corp. (Scientific and Measurement Devices) [24321]

Lapeer County Cooperative Inc. (Livestock and Farm Products) [18044]
Pro Systems, Inc. (Computers and Software) [6641]

Lincoln Park

ABC Appliance Inc. White Automotive Association Div. (Heating and Cooling Equipment and Supplies) [14288]
Central Work Clothes (Clothing) [4873]

Livonia

All City Refrigeration Co. Inc. (Heating and Cooling Equipment and Supplies) [14311]
Allen Electric Supply Co. (Electrical and Electronic Equipment and Supplies) [8299]
Allied Electronics (Electrical and Electronic Equipment and Supplies) [8308]
Allied Electronics (Electrical and Electronic Equipment and Supplies) [8326]
Allied-Vaughn Inc. (Sound and Entertainment Equipment and Supplies) [25063]
Benson Pump Co. (Recreational and Sporting Goods) [23549]
Blackburn and Co.; Don (Electrical and Electronic Equipment and Supplies) [8443]
Bockstanz Brothers Co. (Cleaning and Janitorial Supplies) [4586]
Contractors Steel Co. (Metals) [19894]
Custom Design Security & Sound (Security and Safety Equipment) [24530]
General Fasteners Company Inc. (Hardware) [13721]
Great Lakes Sales, Inc. (Floorcovering Equipment and Supplies) [9926]
Harrison Piping Supply Co. (Plumbing Materials and Fixtures) [23205]
Hickman, Williams and Co. (Metals) [20036]
Ingram Co.; G.A. (Medical, Dental, and Optical Equipment) [18851]
Larson Fabrics, Inc. (Textiles and Notions) [26121]
Lenover & Son Inc.; J.E. (Adhesives) [9]
Leone Food Service Corp. (Food) [11702]
Melody Farms Inc. (Food) [11848]
Multi Communication Systems (Electrical and Electronic Equipment and Supplies) [9106]
National Sales Engineering (Industrial Machinery) [16343]
National Temperature Control Centers Inc. (Heating and Cooling Equipment and Supplies) [14617]
Northwest Blueprint and Supply (Gifts and Novelties) [13413]
Purchased Parts Group (Hardware) [13878]
Soltis & Co., Inc.; A.R. (Industrial Machinery) [16502]
Sound Engineering (Communications Systems and Equipment) [5761]
Talays Inc. (Electrical and Electronic Equipment and Supplies) [9457]
Talcup, Inc. (Electrical and Electronic Equipment and Supplies) [9458]
Three Sixty Services Inc. (Specialty Equipment and Products) [25843]

Lowell

King Milling Co. (Food) [11615]

Ludington

J and B Foam Fabricators Inc. (Recreational and Sporting Goods) [23751]

Macomb

Joint Production Technology Inc. (Industrial Machinery) [16191]
Pirrone Produce, Inc.; Mike (Food) [12176]
Randazzo's Fruit Market #2 (Food) [12275]

Madison Heights

Century Rain Aid (Agricultural Equipment and Supplies) [403]
Cochrane Supply and Engineering, Inc. (Heating and Cooling Equipment and Supplies) [14391]
Fauver Co. (Industrial Supplies) [16857]
Galco Industrial Electronics (Electrical and Electronic Equipment and Supplies) [8772]

Great Lakes Air Systems Inc. (Cleaning and Janitorial Supplies) [4631]
Jahm Inc. (Automotive) [2810]
LPD Music International (Sound and Entertainment Equipment and Supplies) [25292]
Magna Communications Inc. (Communications Systems and Equipment) [5664]
McNaughton-McKay Electric Company Inc. (Electrical and Electronic Equipment and Supplies) [9060]
Med-Tech Inc. (Medical, Dental, and Optical Equipment) [18909]
Ollesheimer & Son Inc.; Louis T. (Construction Materials and Machinery) [7811]
Optical Measurements Inc. (Medical, Dental, and Optical Supplies) [19514]
Packaging Concepts and Design (Paper and Paper Products) [21857]
Sennett Steel Corp. (Metals) [20359]
T & E Timers Inc. (Household Appliances) [15327]

Manistee

Axchem Solutions Inc. (Chemicals) [4333]

Manton

Central Door & Hardware (Construction Materials and Machinery) [7158]

Marquette

Generic Computer Products Inc. (Computers and Software) [6299]
Marquette Bottling Works Inc. (Books and Other Printed Materials) [3936]
TR Systems (Household Appliances) [15340]

Marysville

Banking Forms Supply Company Inc. (Office Equipment and Supplies) [20830]
Biewer; John A. (Marine) [18462]
JP International Imports & Exports (Recreational and Sporting Goods) [23765]

Mason

C & R Distributors (Food) [10656]

Mendon

Service Unlimited (Automotive) [3208]

Menominee

Fairway Foods of Michigan Inc. (Food) [11075]

Middleville

Baby Bliss Inc. (Clothing) [4796]

Midland

Brady News and Recycling (Books and Other Printed Materials) [3588]
Detail Fresh Sandwich Co. (Food) [10951]
Fisher Sand and Gravel Co. (Construction Materials and Machinery) [7347]
Ken's Craft Supply (Office Equipment and Supplies) [21087]
Mid-Michigan Regional Health Systems (Medical, Dental, and Optical Equipment) [18937]
Midland Steel (Metals) [20187]
Misaba Steel Products Inc. (Metals) [20198]
Mohr Vinyl & Carpet Supplier (Floorcovering Equipment and Supplies) [10045]
Smith Distributors; Laurence (Household Items) [15657]
Three M Leisure Time (Recreational and Sporting Goods) [24010]

Milan

SB Developments Inc. (Plumbing Materials and Fixtures) [23360]

Milford

EASI (Electronic Applications Specialists Inc.) (Electrical and Electronic Equipment and Supplies) [8644]
Kirk Artclothes; Jennifer Sly (Clothing) [5112]
Surface Sealing Inc. (Construction Materials and Machinery) [8091]

Monroe

Fedor Steel Co. (Metals) [19968]
Heartland Distributors, Inc. (Tobacco Products) [26305]
Monroe Foods (Food) [11925]
Shaklee Distributor (Food) [12470]
Sygma Network (Food) [12662]

Mt. Clemens

Grinnell Door Inc. (GS & D) (Construction Materials and Machinery) [7418]

Mt. Morris

Michigan Church Supply Company Inc. (Books and Other Printed Materials) [3951]

Mt. Pleasant

Beard Oil Pipeline Supply Inc. (Petroleum, Fuels, and Related Equipment) [22061]
Fabiano Brothers Inc. (Alcoholic Beverages) [1682]
Michigan Retail Packaging (Paper and Paper Products) [21834]

Muskegon

Fisher Steel and Supply Co. (Used, Scrap, and Recycled Materials) [26814]
Fitzpatrick Electric Supply Co. (Electrical and Electronic Equipment and Supplies) [8743]
Hardware Distributors Inc. (Hardware) [13737]
Lake Welding Supply Co. (Industrial Machinery) [16226]
Langlois Stores Inc. (Household Items) [15559]
Midland Groceries Michigan Inc. (Food) [11884]
Northern Machine Tool Co. (Industrial Machinery) [16351]
Reid Tool Supply Co. (Industrial Supplies) [17136]
Skipper Heating, Air Conditioning & Fireplace Showroom (Heating and Cooling Equipment and Supplies) [14686]
Structural Concepts Corp. (Restaurant and Commercial Foodservice Equipment and Supplies) [24231]
Watkins Pharmaceutical & Surgical Supply (Medical, Dental, and Optical Equipment) [19105]

Muskegon Heights

Cee-J Wholesale (Toys and Hobby Goods) [26439]

New Baltimore

Stahl's Bakery (Food) [12562]

New Hudson

Lee Wholesale Supply Company Inc. (Construction Materials and Machinery) [7593]
Sky-Reach Inc. (Construction Materials and Machinery) [8029]

Newberry

Pike Distributors Inc. (Alcoholic Beverages) [1958]

Niles

A-1 Telecom Inc. (Household Appliances) [14985]
Derda Inc. (Industrial Machinery) [15942]
Michiana News Service, Inc. (Books and Other Printed Materials) [3950]
Mr. Paperback Publisher News (Books and Other Printed Materials) [3974]

Northville

Climate Technologies (Heating and Cooling Equipment and Supplies) [14385]
Guernsey Farms Dairy (Food) [11343]
Paramount Manufacturing Co. (Clothing) [5269]
Willard Safety Shoe Co. (Shoes) [24895]

Novi

American Isuzu Motors Inc. (Automotive) [2229]
Arkin Distributing Co. (Toys and Hobby Goods) [26396]
Cummins Michigan Inc. (Automotive) [2509]
Fife Electric Co. (Electrical and Electronic Equipment and Supplies) [8741]
Ichikoh America Inc. (Automotive) [2769]

Medical Equipment Resale, Inc. (Medical, Dental, and Optical Equipment) [18915]
Medical Equipment Resale Inc. (Medical, Dental, and Optical Supplies) [19445]
Michigan Tractor and Machinery Co. (Construction Materials and Machinery) [7703]

Oak Park

Allied-National Inc. (Electrical and Electronic Equipment and Supplies) [8329]
Brann Associates Inc.; Don (Office Equipment and Supplies) [20854]
Cloverdale Equipment Co. (Construction Materials and Machinery) [7185]
Contractors Machinery Co. (Construction Materials and Machinery) [7211]
Eaton Steel Corp. (Metals) [19948]
Fancy Feet Inc. (Shoes) [24741]
Herald Wholesalers Inc. (Hardware) [13751]
Kerr Pump and Supply Inc. (Industrial Machinery) [16205]
Mel Farr Automotive Group Inc. (Motorized Vehicles) [20678]
Michigan Glove Company Inc. (Clothing) [5191]
Mid-East Materials Co. (Metals) [20182]
Progress Electrical Supply Co. (Electrical and Electronic Equipment and Supplies) [9240]
Wickman Corp. (Industrial Machinery) [16631]

Okemos

Engan-Tooley-Doyle & Associates Inc. (Recreational and Sporting Goods) [23652]

Orion

Dawn Co. (Communications Systems and Equipment) [5591]

Oscoda

Norwood Products Co. (Recreational and Sporting Goods) [23855]

Ottawa Lake

Guardian Book Co. (Books and Other Printed Materials) [3803]

Owosso

Emery Pratt Co. (Books and Other Printed Materials) [3727]
Pratt Co.; Emery (Books and Other Printed Materials) [4079]
Systems Medical Co. Inc. (Medical, Dental, and Optical Equipment) [19068]

Paw Paw

Paw Paw Wine Distributors (Alcoholic Beverages) [1943]
Sporting Image Inc. (Clothing) [5386]

Pigeon

Cooperative Elevator Co. (Agricultural Equipment and Supplies) [450]
Cooperative Elevator Co. (Food) [10834]
Gettel and Co. (Agricultural Equipment and Supplies) [737]

Pinconning

Bay View Food Products Co. (Food) [10516]

Plymouth

Broder Bros., Co. (Clothing) [4848]
Buffalo Don's Artesian Wells Ltd. (Soft Drinks) [24920]
Creative Health Products (Medical, Dental, and Optical Supplies) [19256]
Koyo Corporation of USA (Industrial Machinery) [16219]
PMC Machinery, Inc. (Industrial Machinery) [16403]
Simpson Industries Inc. (Industrial Machinery) [16493]
U.S. Industrial Tool Supply (Hardware) [13976]
Victory Packaging (Paper and Paper Products) [21985]

Pontiac

Allen and Son Inc.; Sam (Metals) [19747]

Altron International (Sound and Entertainment Equipment and Supplies) [25066]
Altron International (Household Appliances) [15005]
American Medical Services (Medical, Dental, and Optical Supplies) [19142]
Ceramics By Bob and Hazel (Toys and Hobby Goods) [26441]
Hubert Distributors Inc. (Alcoholic Beverages) [1768]
Inland Plywood Co. (Construction Materials and Machinery) [7512]
Magic Distributing (Recreational and Sporting Goods) [23796]
Midway Motor Supply Core Supplier (Automotive) [2956]
Oliver Supply Co. (Cleaning and Janitorial Supplies) [4680]
Oliver Supply Co. (Restaurant and Commercial Foodservice Equipment and Supplies) [24198]
Southern Automotive Inc. (Automotive) [3239]
Wholesale Heating Supply Co. (Heating and Cooling Equipment and Supplies) [14765]

Port Huron

Detroit Free Press Agency (Books and Other Printed Materials) [3689]
Ferguson Steel Co. (Metals) [19976]
London's Farm Dairy, Inc. (Food) [11725]
Mapal Aaro, Inc. (Industrial Machinery) [16262]
Marysville Newspaper Distributor (Books and Other Printed Materials) [3939]
Maxim Inc.; Mary (Toys and Hobby Goods) [26570]
Port Huron Electric Motor (Electrical and Electronic Equipment and Supplies) [9220]
Star Oil Company Inc. (Petroleum, Fuels, and Related Equipment) [22701]
Textron Automotive (Automotive) [3301]
U.S. Manufacturing Corp. (Automotive) [3370]
Wallbank Springs Inc.; P.J. (Hardware) [13984]

Portage

Shepherd Products Co. (Plastics) [23033]

Potterville

Mid Michigan Trailer & Truck Equipment, Inc. (Automotive) [2951]

Quincy

Crotty Corp. (Automotive) [2497]

Reading

Reading Feed and Grain Inc. (Agricultural Equipment and Supplies) [1173]

Redford

C & J Fasteners (Hardware) [13614]
Instrument Sales-East (Scientific and Measurement Devices) [24373]
Material Sales Company Inc. (Industrial Supplies) [17019]
Milart Ceramics Inc. (Specialty Equipment and Products) [25740]
Steel Industries Inc. (Industrial Machinery) [16521]
Young Co.; Behler (Heating and Cooling Equipment and Supplies) [14786]

Reese

Reese Farmers Inc. (Livestock and Farm Products) [18194]

Richland

Keltech, Inc. (Plumbing Materials and Fixtures) [23231]
Keltech Inc. (Plumbing Materials and Fixtures) [23232]

River Rouge

Baxter and Co. Inc.; A.J. (Industrial Supplies) [16725]
Metal Alloy Corp. (Used, Scrap, and Recycled Materials) [26902]

Riverview

Down River Home Health Supply (Medical, Dental, and Optical Equipment) [18779]
Kasperek Optical Inc. (Medical, Dental, and Optical Supplies) [19393]

Rochester

Rittner Products Inc. (Construction Materials and Machinery) [7938]

Rochester Hills

Kearns Associates (Shoes) [24782]
Macro Computer Products Inc. (Computers and Software) [6452]
Stinson, Inc.; C.F. (Textiles and Notions) [26215]
Time Emergency Equipment (Specialty Equipment and Products) [25844]
Unisource (Paper and Paper Products) [21963]

Rockford

Burch Body Works Inc. (Industrial Machinery) [15857]
Hush Puppies Co. (Shoes) [24766]

Rockwood

Mirror Lite Co. (Gifts and Novelties) [13405]

Romeo

Action Water Treatment Service (Specialty Equipment and Products) [25545]

Romulus

Cartell Inc. (Communications Systems and Equipment) [5549]
GMA Industries Inc. (Metals) [20011]
RKA Petroleum Companies, L.L.C. (Petroleum, Fuels, and Related Equipment) [22634]
Service Electric Supply Inc. (Electrical and Electronic Equipment and Supplies) [9357]

Roseville

Fraza Equipment Inc. (Industrial Machinery) [16040]
JC Industrial Motor Service Inc. (Industrial Machinery) [16184]
McCausey Lumber Co. (Construction Materials and Machinery) [7675]
NBC Truck Equipment Inc. (Automotive) [3018]

Royal Oak

Berg Steel Corp. (Metals) [19813]
Interior Systems Contract Group Inc. (Furniture and Fixtures) [13144]
Nefouse Brothers Distributing Co. (Recreational and Sporting Goods) [23845]
Quigley Sales and Marketing and Associates (Construction Materials and Machinery) [7893]
Richard Beauty Supply (Health and Beauty Aids) [14218]
Royal Radio Sales & Service (Sound and Entertainment Equipment and Supplies) [25422]
US Farathane Inc. (Automotive) [3377]

Ruth

Ruth Farmers Elevator Inc. (Livestock and Farm Products) [18215]

Saginaw

Agri Sales Inc. (Livestock and Farm Products) [17686]
Beckley Equipment Co. (Industrial Supplies) [16745]
Cinderella Inc. (Recreational and Sporting Goods) [23594]
Damore's Wholesale Produce (Food) [10905]
Delphi Saginaw Steering Systems (Automotive) [2537]
HI-Tech Optical Inc. (Medical, Dental, and Optical Supplies) [19358]
Mahar Tool Supply Inc. (Hardware) [13805]
Michigan Sugar Co. (Food) [11872]
Nagel Paper & Box Co. (Paper and Paper Products) [21846]

Northern Industrial Supply Inc. (Industrial
Supplies) [17082]
Pabco Fluid Power Co. (Industrial
Machinery) [16367]
Riffel & Sons Inc.; C. (Alcoholic Beverages) [1990]
Scientific Brake and Equipment
Co. (Automotive) [3200]
Standard Electric Co. (Electrical and Electronic
Equipment and Supplies) [9401]
Wolohan Lumber Co. (Construction Materials and
Machinery) [8238]
Wolpert Refrigeration Inc. (Heating and Cooling
Equipment and Supplies) [14772]
Young Co.; Behler (Heating and Cooling Equipment
and Supplies) [14781]

St. Clair Shores
Midwest Marine Supply Co. (Marine) [18570]
Shores Marine (Marine) [18610]

St. Johns
Mason Co.; F.C. (Industrial Machinery) [16271]

St. Joseph
International Diagnostic Systems Corp. (Medical,
Dental, and Optical Equipment) [18856]
Punch It Distributing Inc. (Toys and Hobby
Goods) [26623]

Sand Lake
General Genetics Inc. (Livestock and Farm
Products) [17937]

Sandusky
Jensen Bridge and Supply Co. (Plumbing Materials
and Fixtures) [23224]

Scotts
Independent Pet Co-op (Veterinary
Products) [27157]

Sebewaing
Cooperative Elevator, Sebewaing (Livestock and
Farm Products) [17795]

Shelby Township
Clark Brothers Instrument Co. (Automotive) [2451]

South Haven
Kalamazoo International, Inc. (Industrial
Machinery) [16196]
Lake Instruments & Wholesale Corp. (Toys and
Hobby Goods) [26561]

South Lyon
Boutique Trim (Office Equipment and
Supplies) [20851]

Southfield
ABC Coffee Co. (Food) [10319]
ABC Supply Co., Inc. (Construction Materials and
Machinery) [6899]
AIN Plastics of Michigan Inc. (Plastics) [22922]
Bakers Choice (Food) [10492]
Classic Optical Inc. (Medical, Dental, and Optical
Supplies) [19233]
Comtel Corp. (Computers and Software) [6143]
Genesee Ceramic Tile Distributors (Floorcovering
Equipment and Supplies) [9918]
Industrial Development & Procurement (Industrial
Machinery) [16150]
Intercontinental Importers Inc. (Clothing) [5053]
Intertrade, Inc. (Furniture and Fixtures) [13147]
Marshall Co.; R.J. (Chemicals) [4453]
Marshall Co.; R.J. (Industrial Supplies) [17016]
MMI Inc. (Medical, Dental, and Optical
Equipment) [18946]
Peerless Distributing Co. (Petroleum, Fuels, and
Related Equipment) [22558]
Print Gallery Inc. (Gifts and Novelties) [13428]
The Reynolds and Reynolds Co. (Computers and
Software) [6689]
Segal, Alpert, McPherson & Associates (Sound and
Entertainment Equipment and Supplies) [25436]

Triangle Industrial Sales, Inc. (Industrial
Machinery) [16581]
Vesco Oil Corp. (Petroleum, Fuels, and Related
Equipment) [22772]
Wolverine X-Ray Sales and Service (Medical,
Dental, and Optical Equipment) [19110]

Southgate
Bob's Fruit Market & Deli (Food) [10585]
Palco Electronics (Electrical and Electronic
Equipment and Supplies) [9176]

Sparta
Haviland Agricultural Inc. (Chemicals) [4410]
Spartan Distributors Inc. (Agricultural Equipment
and Supplies) [1288]

Sterling Heights
Aargus Truck & Auto (Automotive) [2162]
Borg Warner Automotive Friction
Products (Automotive) [2372]
Burke Equipment Co. (Construction Materials and
Machinery) [7108]
Courtesy Sanitary Supply (Cleaning and Janitorial
Supplies) [4604]
Ex-Cell-O North American Sales and Service
Inc. (Industrial Machinery) [16001]
Foam Factory and Upholstery
Inc. (Plastics) [22964]
Frito-Lay Inc. (Food) [11216]
General Automation Manufacturing Inc. (Industrial
Machinery) [16053]
Genesee Ceramic Tile Distributors (Floorcovering
Equipment and Supplies) [9919]
Integrity Steel Co (Metals) [20066]
Marshall Co.; A.J. (Cleaning and Janitorial
Supplies) [4663]
Rave Computer Association Inc. (Computers and
Software) [6685]
Unisteel Inc. (Metals) [20459]
Virginia Tile Co. (Floorcovering Equipment and
Supplies) [10282]

Sturgis
First Choice Tool Co. (Hardware) [13706]
Sportsarama Inc. (Clothing) [5388]
Sturgis Iron and Metal Company Inc. (Used, Scrap,
and Recycled Materials) [27012]

Sunfield
AGRI Sales (Livestock and Farm
Products) [17685]
Mueller Bean Co. (Food) [11953]

Taylor
Detroit Auto Auction (Motorized Vehicles) [20622]
Microcomputer Cable Company Inc. (Electrical and
Electronic Equipment and Supplies) [9075]
Olender and Company Inc.; P. (Food) [12066]
Z-Weigh Inc. (Scientific and Measurement
Devices) [24460]

Tecumseh
Standard Electric Time Corp. (Security and Safety
Equipment) [24640]

Three Oaks
Seifert Farm Supply (Agricultural Equipment and
Supplies) [1257]

Three Rivers
Armstrong International Inc. Three Rivers
Div. (Household Appliances) [15034]

Traverse City
Actron Steel (Metals) [19725]
Beaver Distributors (Construction Materials and
Machinery) [7038]
Cherry Central, Inc. (Food) [10739]
Cox & Son Inc.; H. (Alcoholic Beverages) [1621]
Direct Distributors (Construction Materials and
Machinery) [7267]
Gold Coast Distributors Inc. (Alcoholic
Beverages) [1723]
Great Lakes Forge, Inc. (Metals) [20019]

GTR Truck Equipment (Automotive) [2710]
Jacklin Steel Supply Co. (Metals) [20073]
Moonbeam Publications, Inc. (Books and Other
Printed Materials) [3967]
Phillips Energy Inc. (Recreational and Sporting
Goods) [23879]
Schmuckal Oil Co. (Petroleum, Fuels, and Related
Equipment) [22658]
Young Co.; Behler (Heating and Cooling Equipment
and Supplies) [14780]

Trenton
Mercer's Dix Equipment (Construction Materials and
Machinery) [7696]

Troy
Blue Birds International Corp. (Sound and
Entertainment Equipment and Supplies) [25105]
Cadillac Plastic and Chemical
Div. (Plastics) [22939]
Cadillac Plastic Group Inc. (Plastics) [22940]
Cannon Engineering and Equipment Co.
LLC (Industrial Machinery) [15871]
City Animation Co. (Sound and Entertainment
Equipment and Supplies) [25137]
Clarklift of Detroit Inc. (Industrial
Machinery) [15891]
Desmond Process Supply Co. (Specialty Equipment
and Products) [25627]
Foremost Athletic Apparel (Clothing) [4961]
General Electric Supply (Electrical and Electronic
Equipment and Supplies) [8783]
Genesee Ceramic Tile Distribution (Floorcovering
Equipment and Supplies) [9916]
Handleman Co. (Sound and Entertainment
Equipment and Supplies) [25225]
Handleman Co. (Books and Other Printed
Materials) [3811]
Health Food Distributors (Health and Beauty
Aids) [14122]
International Book Centre (Books and Other Printed
Materials) [3845]
Intraco Corp. (Automotive) [2796]
Kmart Corp. (Household Items) [15553]
Kmart Trading Services, Inc. (Textiles and
Notions) [26113]
L and L Concession Co. (Food) [11658]
L & L Wine & Liquor Corp. (Alcoholic
Beverages) [1808]
Lucas Industries Inc. Aftermarket Operations
Div. (Automotive) [2895]
Mascotech Forming Technologies (Metals) [20156]
Myles Inc.; J.E. (Industrial Machinery) [16335]
Myles Inc.; J.E. (Industrial Supplies) [17065]
O/E Automation Inc. (Computers and
Software) [6566]
Parker Hannifin Corp. Fluidpower Sales
Div. (Industrial Supplies) [17099]
Peters Associates; George R. (Sound and
Entertainment Equipment and Supplies) [25379]
Producers Tape Service-All Media (Electrical and
Electronic Equipment and Supplies) [9238]
Ram Meter Inc. (Electrical and Electronic
Equipment and Supplies) [9261]
Salinger Electric Co. (Electrical and Electronic
Equipment and Supplies) [9333]
Schluckbier Inc.; Jerry (Horticultural
Supplies) [14947]
SMARTEYE Corp. (Electrical and Electronic
Equipment and Supplies) [9378]
Synergy Steel Inc. (Metals) [20415]
Teal Electric Company Inc. (Electrical and
Electronic Equipment and Supplies) [9465]
Test Equipment Distributors (Scientific and
Measurement Devices) [24445]
Troy Biologicals Inc. (Medical, Dental, and Optical
Supplies) [19665]
Wright Tool Co. (Automotive) [3449]
X-Ray Industries Inc. (Electrical and Electronic
Equipment and Supplies) [9612]

Utica
Nu-Way Supply Company Inc. (Plumbing Materials
and Fixtures) [23301]

Vandalia

North American Aqua Inc. (Specialty Equipment and Products) [25762]

Walled Lake

ASA Builders Supply Inc. (Construction Materials and Machinery) [6996]

Far Corners Importers Ltd. (Gifts and Novelties) [13355]

Haggerty Lumber (Construction Materials and Machinery) [7429]

QMI Inc. (Sound and Entertainment Equipment and Supplies) [25396]

Romar Industries Inc. (Electrical and Electronic Equipment and Supplies) [9313]

Varilease Corp. (Communications Systems and Equipment) [5804]

Warren

A-Air Conditioning Contractor (Household Appliances) [14986]

Baker's Kneads (Restaurant and Commercial Foodservice Equipment and Supplies) [24075]

Behling Building Products; Gil (Construction Materials and Machinery) [7043]

BT Office Products International Inc. Detroit Div. (Office Equipment and Supplies) [20861]

Cadillac Glass Co. (Construction Materials and Machinery) [7123]

Carlson Dimond and Wright (Industrial Machinery) [15877]

Castiglione Accordion (Sound and Entertainment Equipment and Supplies) [25127]

Central Air Compressor Co. (Compressors) [5835]

Claeys and Co.; H.L. (Plumbing Materials and Fixtures) [23116]

Darling Bolt Co. (Hardware) [13656]

East Side Sporting Goods Co. (Recreational and Sporting Goods) [23642]

F and M Distributors Inc. (Medical, Dental, and Optical Supplies) [19319]

General Polymers Div. (Plastics) [22968]

Great Lakes Power Products (Automotive) [2699]

Grinders Clearing House Inc. (Industrial Machinery) [16080]

Items Galore Inc. (Clothing) [5066]

K-9 Specialists (Veterinary Products) [27165]

K & R Distributors (Veterinary Products) [27169]

Keo Cutters Inc. (Industrial Machinery) [16204]

Lavdas Jewelry Ltd. (Jewelry) [17501]

Link Lumber Co.; C.J. (Wood and Wood Products) [27335]

Madison Electric Co. (Sound and Entertainment Equipment and Supplies) [25296]

Madison Electric Co. (Household Appliances) [15207]

Menlo Tool Company Inc. (Medical, Dental, and Optical Equipment) [18927]

National Lumber Co. (Construction Materials and Machinery) [7765]

Omicron Electronics (Computers and Software) [6570]

Palm Pool Products Inc. (Recreational and Sporting Goods) [23869]

Plywood-Detroit Inc. (Construction Materials and Machinery) [7873]

Production Carbide and Steel (Metals) [20298]

Production Tool Supply (Industrial Supplies) [17119]

Reif Carbide Tool Company, Inc. (Industrial Machinery) [16445]

Royal Carpet Distribution, Inc. (Floorcovering Equipment and Supplies) [10129]

Satterlund Supply Co. (Plumbing Materials and Fixtures) [23359]

Scion Steel Co. (Metals) [20357]

Soyad Brothers Textile Corp. (Clothing) [5375]

Star Steel Supply Co. (Heating and Cooling Equipment and Supplies) [14699]

Starlight Archery Inc. (Recreational and Sporting Goods) [23985]

United Automotive Supply Co. (Automotive) [3363]

Wolverine Metal Company Inc. (Metals) [20498]

Young Co.; Behler (Heating and Cooling Equipment and Supplies) [14785]

Waterford

Aerodynamics Inc. (Aeronautical Equipment and Supplies) [27]

Drayton Swimming Pool Supply (Recreational and Sporting Goods) [23630]

Oak Distributing Company Inc. (Alcoholic Beverages) [1925]

Wayland

Waco Sales Inc. (Recreational and Sporting Goods) [24037]

Wayne

Browning-Ferris Industries of Michigan Inc. (Used, Scrap, and Recycled Materials) [26772]

Complex Steel Wire Corp. (Metals) [19891]

Handicapped Driving Aids of Michigan Inc. (Medical, Dental, and Optical Equipment) [18823]

Keystone Chemical Supply Inc. (Chemicals) [4435]

Unistrut Detroit Service Co. (Metals) [20460]

West Bloomfield

Lamport and Brother; Alexander (Textiles and Notions) [26119]

Morpol Industrial Corporation Ltd. (Industrial Machinery) [16322]

O2 Emergency Medical Care Service Corp. (Medical, Dental, and Optical Equipment) [18965]

Safe Stride Non-Slip USA Inc. (Chemicals) [4499]

Sorrell Interiors (Household Items) [15661]

Stuart's Federal Fireplace, Inc. (Household Items) [15670]

Westland

Fruehauf Trailer Services, Inc. (Motorized Vehicles) [20637]

RHM Fluid Power Inc. (Industrial Machinery) [16450]

White Pigeon

Centurion Vehicles Inc. (Automotive) [2439]

Williamston

Michigan Livestock Exchange (Livestock and Farm Products) [18089]

Wisconsin Dells

Progressive Tire Group (Automotive) [3122]

Wixom

Almetals Co. (Metals) [19754]

American Terminal Supply Company, Inc. (Sound and Entertainment Equipment and Supplies) [25071]

Automatic Controls Co. (Electrical and Electronic Equipment and Supplies) [8397]

Cadillac Shoe Products Inc. (Shoes) [24704]

Key Electronics Inc. (Electrical and Electronic Equipment and Supplies) [8941]

Michigan Hardwood Distributors (Floorcovering Equipment and Supplies) [10028]

Mueller Sales Inc. (Plumbing Materials and Fixtures) [23283]

Triangle Computer Corp. (Computers and Software) [6830]

Wholesale Builder Supply Inc. (Household Appliances) [15372]

Wyandotte

D.A. Distributors Inc. (Construction Materials and Machinery) [7244]

Michigan Industrial Piping Supply Company Inc. (Plumbing Materials and Fixtures) [23262]

Wyoming

Berendsen Fluid Power, Inc. (Industrial Machinery) [15818]

Chem-Central (Chemicals) [4348]

Frito-Lay Inc. (Food) [11217]

J and H Oil Co. (Petroleum, Fuels, and Related Equipment) [22379]

Kent (Alcoholic Beverages) [1796]

Millbrook Sales & Service Co. (Communications Systems and Equipment) [5678]

Walker Company, Inc.; J.F. (Food) [12867]

Ypsilanti

Heikkinen Productions Inc. (Clothing) [5024]

Mitchell Home Medical (Medical, Dental, and Optical Equipment) [18943]

Zeeland

De Bruyn Produce Company Inc. (Food) [10924]

The Empire Company, Inc. (Construction Materials and Machinery) [7310]

Internal Sound Communications (Electrical and Electronic Equipment and Supplies) [8892]

Van Den Bosch Co.; John A. (Veterinary Products) [27261]

Zeeland Lumber and Supply Inc. (Construction Materials and Machinery) [8253]

Minnesota

Ada

Ada Feed and Seed Inc. (Agricultural Equipment and Supplies) [182]

Aitkin

Lake States Lumber Inc. (Construction Materials and Machinery) [7581]

Albert Lea

Freeborn County Cooperative Oil Co. (Petroleum, Fuels, and Related Equipment) [22294]

Pestorious Inc. (Agricultural Equipment and Supplies) [1125]

Albertville

Fraser Steel Co. (Metals) [19985]

Alexandria

Brown Co.; E. Arthur (Recreational and Sporting Goods) [23570]

Henry's Foods Inc. (Food) [11414]

Amboy

Watonwan Farm Services (Agricultural Equipment and Supplies) [1416]

Annandale

Malco Products Inc. (Hardware) [13809]

Anoka

Dohmen Co./Anoka; The F. (Medical, Dental, and Optical Supplies) [19287]

Grosslein Beverages Inc. (Alcoholic Beverages) [1734]

Local Oil Company of Anoka Inc. (Petroleum, Fuels, and Related Equipment) [22435]

Schwartzman Co. (Used, Scrap, and Recycled Materials) [26983]

Apple Valley

Enderes Tool Co. Inc. (Hardware) [13685]

Arden Hills

East Side Beverage Co. (Alcoholic Beverages) [1668]

Argyle

Rivard's Quality Seeds Inc. (Livestock and Farm Products) [18199]

Ashby

Ashby Equity Association (Agricultural Equipment and Supplies) [258]

Atwater

Atwater Creamery Co. (Agricultural Equipment and Supplies) [260]

Austin

Hormel Foods International Corp. (Food) [11462]

Balaton
Farmers Cooperative Oil of Balaton (Agricultural Equipment and Supplies) [635]

Beardsley
Beardsley Farmers Elevator Co. (Agricultural Equipment and Supplies) [287]

Beaver Creek
Hills Beaver Creek Coop Farm Service (Agricultural Equipment and Supplies) [824]

Belle Plaine
Belle Plaine Cooperative (Agricultural Equipment and Supplies) [295]

Beltrami
Beltrami Farmers Elevator (Agricultural Equipment and Supplies) [297]

Bemidji
Bemidji Cooperative Association (Petroleum, Fuels, and Related Equipment) [22066]
Walters Inc.; Dave (Motorized Vehicles) [20748]

Benson
Swift Co-op Oil Co. (Agricultural Equipment and Supplies) [1310]

Bigelow
United Co-op (Livestock and Farm Products) [18301]

Blaine
Kolstad Company Inc. (Motorized Vehicles) [20665]

Blooming Prairie
Bixby Feed Mill Inc. (Agricultural Equipment and Supplies) [319]

Bloomington
Advanced Communication Design Inc. (Computers and Software) [5884]
Andersen Inc.; Earl F. (Recreational and Sporting Goods) [23516]
Anderson Associates Inc.; Earl F. (Restaurant and Commercial Foodservice Equipment and Supplies) [24066]
Banana Educational Software Distributors (Computers and Software) [5999]
Bosch Power Tools; Robert (Industrial Machinery) [15834]
Clarklift of Minnesota Inc. (Industrial Machinery) [15892]
Decorative Designs (Horticultural Supplies) [14854]
Hadley Cos. (Books and Other Printed Materials) [3806]
Holiday Stores Inc. (Food) [11447]
Interstate Bearing Co. (Automotive) [2794]
Loving; L.A. (Clothing) [5144]
Mars Co.; W.P. and R.S. (Industrial Machinery) [16266]
Midwest Industrial Coatings Inc. (Paints and Varnishes) [21502]
Monarch Industries Incorporated U.S.A. (Industrial Machinery) [16319]
Of Distinction, Inc. - The Silk Plant Co. (Horticultural Supplies) [14930]
Pro-Med Supplies Inc. (Medical, Dental, and Optical Equipment) [18998]
Quiltworks (Textiles and Notions) [26182]
Seelye Plastics Inc. (Industrial Supplies) [17163]
Select Sales (Computers and Software) [6721]
Select Sales Inc. (Computers and Software) [6722]
Shurail Supply Inc. (Heating and Cooling Equipment and Supplies) [14684]
Sorem and Associates; L.S. (Food) [12529]
Vendor's Supply and Service Inc. (Specialty Equipment and Products) [25867]
WirthCo Engineering Inc. (Automotive) [3441]

Blue Earth
Grain Land Cooperative (Livestock and Farm Products) [17954]
Hankes Crafts (Toys and Hobby Goods) [26511]

Brainerd
Electric Garage Supply Co. (Automotive) [2579]
Fleet Wholesale (Food) [11144]
Service Drug of Brainerd Inc. (Medical, Dental, and Optical Equipment) [19036]

Breckenridge
Minn-Kota AG Products Inc. (Livestock and Farm Products) [18103]
SIGCO Sun Products Inc. (Agricultural Equipment and Supplies) [1267]

Bricelyn
Bricelyn Elevator Association (Livestock and Farm Products) [17746]

Brooklyn Center
River Trading Co. (Minerals and Ores) [20563]

Brooklyn Park
Coyne's Inc. (Household Items) [15461]
Cutting Tools Inc. (Hardware) [13653]
SCS Cases Inc. (Storage Equipment and Containers) [25936]

Brooks
Brooks Farmers Cooperative Association (Livestock and Farm Products) [17748]
Redlake County Co-op (Petroleum, Fuels, and Related Equipment) [22615]

Brownsdale
Ashleys on Main (Clothing) [4787]

Brownton
Brownton Cooperative Agriculture Center (Agricultural Equipment and Supplies) [345]

Buckman
Buckman Farmers Cooperative Creamery (Agricultural Equipment and Supplies) [350]

Buffalo
Centra Sota Cooperative (Agricultural Equipment and Supplies) [385]

Burnsville
Aladdin Distributors Inc. (Toys and Hobby Goods) [26383]
Apothecary Products Inc. (Medical, Dental, and Optical Supplies) [19156]
FORCE America Inc. (Industrial Machinery) [16027]
Kuehn Company Inc.; J.W. (Industrial Machinery) [16223]
Martin Instrument Co. (Burnsville, Minnesota) (Scientific and Measurement Devices) [24394]
Midwest Machinery (Industrial Machinery) [16298]
Midwest Veterinary Supply Inc. (Veterinary Products) [27189]
RDO Equipment Co. (Industrial Machinery) [16441]

Canby
Farmers Cooperative Association (Petroleum, Fuels, and Related Equipment) [22253]

Cannon Falls
Ag Partners Co. Cannon Falls Div. (Livestock and Farm Products) [17679]
Ag Partners Co. Cannon Falls Div. (Food) [10342]

Chanhassen
Consan Inc. (Computers and Software) [6151]
Waytek Inc. (Electrical and Electronic Equipment and Supplies) [9563]

Chatfield
Chatfield Lumber Company Inc. (Construction Materials and Machinery) [7169]

Chokio
Chokio Equity Exchange Inc. (Livestock and Farm Products) [17778]

Circle Pines
Orbex Inc. (Recreational and Sporting Goods) [23860]

Clara City
Farmers Cooperative Oil Company of Clara City (Petroleum, Fuels, and Related Equipment) [22256]

Clarkfield
Tri-Line Farmers Cooperative (Livestock and Farm Products) [18291]

Climax
Farmers Union Oil Co. (Petroleum, Fuels, and Related Equipment) [22266]

Clinton
Big Stone County Cooperative (Agricultural Equipment and Supplies) [310]
Clinton AG Service Inc. (Agricultural Equipment and Supplies) [427]

Cloquet
Bergquists Imports Inc. (Household Items) [15419]

Cokato
Airtex Consumer Products (Household Items) [15392]

Cold Spring
Cold Spring Cooperative Creamery (Agricultural Equipment and Supplies) [434]

Columbia Heights
Hiawatha Grain Co. (Livestock and Farm Products) [17996]

Cottonwood
Cottonwood Cooperative Oil Co. (Petroleum, Fuels, and Related Equipment) [22175]

Crookston
Crookston Farmers Cooperative (Agricultural Equipment and Supplies) [477]
Farmers Union Oil Co. (Petroleum, Fuels, and Related Equipment) [22260]
Farmers Union Oil Co. (Crookston, Minnesota) (Agricultural Equipment and Supplies) [668]

Cyrus
Midwest Consolidated Cooperative (Agricultural Equipment and Supplies) [1034]

Dalton
Dalton Cooperative Creamery Association (Agricultural Equipment and Supplies) [491]

Dassel
Dassel Cooperative Dairy Association (Agricultural Equipment and Supplies) [495]

Dawson
Farmers Cooperative Elevator Co. (Livestock and Farm Products) [17866]

Deer River
Rajala Lumber Co. (Construction Materials and Machinery) [7898]

Deerwood
Deerwood Rice Grain Produce (Food) [10937]

Delavan
Willette Seed Farm Inc. (Agricultural Equipment and Supplies) [1450]

Dent

Collins Landing (Recreational and Sporting
Goods) [23599]

Detroit Lakes

Hartman Hide and Fur Company Inc. (Livestock
and Farm Products) [17978]
Hedahl's Automotive Center (Automotive) [2739]

Dodge Center

Southern Minnesota Machinery Sales Inc. (Industrial
Machinery) [16511]

Duluth

Alakef Coffee Roasters Inc. (Food) [10353]
Arrowhead Supply Inc. (Household
Appliances) [15036]
Chromaline Corp. (Photographic Equipment and
Supplies) [22846]
Congdon Orchards Inc. (Food) [10810]
Duluth Plumbing Supply Co. (Plumbing Materials
and Fixtures) [23140]
Energy Plus (Heating and Cooling Equipment and
Supplies) [14433]
Equipment Rental (Automotive) [2595]
Gartner Refrigeration Inc. (Heating and Cooling
Equipment and Supplies) [14455]
Kelly Furniture Co.; F.S. (Furniture and
Fixtures) [13156]
Leo J. Distributors (Marine) [18545]
O.K. Auto Parts (Automotive) [3060]
Owens Forest Products (Wood and Wood
Products) [27353]
Sorcerer Lures (Recreational and Sporting
Goods) [23953]

Eagan

Continental Safety Equipment Inc. (Medical, Dental,
and Optical Supplies) [19248]
Hanco Corp. (Automotive) [2721]
Herregan Distributors, Inc. (Floorcovering Equipment
and Supplies) [9944]
Universal Cooperative Inc. (Agricultural Equipment
and Supplies) [1385]

Eagle Lake

Pierce Enterprises of Eagle Lake, Inc. (Toys and
Hobby Goods) [26615]

Echo

Farmers Cooperative Elevator Co. (Livestock and
Farm Products) [17867]

Eden Prairie

Associated Business Products Inc. Scanning
Systems (Office Equipment and
Supplies) [20815]
Broich Enterprises Inc. (Household
Appliances) [15060]
C Companies, Inc. (Computers and
Software) [6033]
C-Tech Systems Div. (Industrial Supplies) [16774]
C.H. Robinson Company Inc. (Food) [10732]
Command Electronics Inc. (Computers and
Software) [6085]
Computer Commodities Inc. (Computers and
Software) [6104]
Elna Inc. (Textiles and Notions) [26028]
Excellence Marketing (Electrical and Electronic
Equipment and Supplies) [8724]
GBC Technologies Inc. (Computers and
Software) [6294]
Great Lakes Orthopedics Inc. (Medical, Dental, and
Optical Equipment) [18815]
GTI (Computers and Software) [6316]
Heigl Adhesive Sales (Adhesives) [8]
Inland Truck Parts (Automotive) [2782]
Minnesota Supply Co. (Industrial
Machinery) [16306]
Musolf Distributing Inc.; Lon (Floorcovering
Equipment and Supplies) [10071]
Nova Technology Inc. (Computers and
Software) [6561]
Osgood SM Company Inc. (Heating and Cooling
Equipment and Supplies) [14630]

Phillips and Temro Industries (Automotive) [3097]
Preferred Products Inc. (Food) [12212]
Rorke Data Inc. (Computers and Software) [6693]
Speaker Company, Inc.; Guy (Scientific and
Measurement Devices) [24435]
Timm Medical Systems (Medical, Dental, and
Optical Equipment) [19079]
Western Petroleum Co. (Petroleum, Fuels, and
Related Equipment) [22794]

Edgerton

Air-Ax Suspension Systems (Automotive) [2191]
Edgerton Cooperative Farm Service
Center (Food) [11027]

Edina

Bergquist Co. Inc. (Electrical and Electronic
Equipment and Supplies) [8432]
Developed Technology Resource Inc. (Recreational
and Sporting Goods) [23621]
JDL Technologies Inc. (Computers and
Software) [6406]
Minnesota Conway (Security and Safety
Equipment) [24593]
North Star Recycling Co. (Metals) [20234]

Eitzen

Capacitor Associates (Electrical and Electronic
Equipment and Supplies) [8495]

Elbow Lake

Cosmos Enterprises, Inc. (Automotive) [2487]
Elbow Lake Cooperative Grain (Agricultural
Equipment and Supplies) [545]

Essig

Community Cooperative Oil Association (Petroleum,
Fuels, and Related Equipment) [22156]

Excelsior

Lyman Lumber Co. (Construction Materials and
Machinery) [7623]

Fairfax

South Central Co-op (Agricultural Equipment and
Supplies) [1274]

Fairmont

Fairmont Tamper (Hardware) [13692]
Rosen's Diversified Inc. (Chemicals) [4498]
Rosen's Inc. (Agricultural Equipment and
Supplies) [1213]

Faribault

Randy's Frozen Meats (Food) [12277]

Farmington

South Cedar Greenhouses (Horticultural
Supplies) [14952]

Fergus Falls

Farmers Elevator of Fergus Falls (Livestock and
Farm Products) [17887]
Hanley Sales Inc.; Pat (Clothing) [5016]
JK Sports (Clothing) [5086]

Foxhome

Foxhome Elevator Co. (Agricultural Equipment and
Supplies) [700]

Gaylord

Agland Cooperative (Petroleum, Fuels, and Related
Equipment) [22026]

Golden Valley

Clean Green Packing Company of
Minnesota (Storage Equipment and
Containers) [25903]
Hennepin Cooperative Seed Exchange
Inc. (Livestock and Farm Products) [17990]
Northrup King Co. (Agricultural Equipment and
Supplies) [1086]
Novartis Seeds Inc. (Golden Valley,
Minnesota) (Agricultural Equipment and
Supplies) [1093]

Redline Healthcare Corp. (Medical, Dental, and
Optical Equipment) [19014]
Redline Healthcare Corp. (Medical, Dental, and
Optical Supplies) [19570]
Roberts-Hamilton Co., Div. of Hajoca
Corp. (Plumbing Materials and Fixtures) [23347]
Schumacher Wholesale Meats Inc. (Food) [12432]
StarchTech Inc. (Storage Equipment and
Containers) [25940]

Goodhue

Goodhue Elevator Association
Cooperative (Livestock and Farm
Products) [17948]

Grand Rapids

Computer Enterprises of Grand Rapids (Computers
and Software) [6110]
North Country Equipment Inc. (Industrial
Machinery) [16350]

Granger

Granger Farmers Cooperative Creamery
Association (Food) [11308]

Gully

Gully Tri-Coop Association (Agricultural Equipment
and Supplies) [778]

Hallock

Hallock Cooperative Elevator Co. (Livestock and
Farm Products) [17971]
Hallock Cooperative Elevator Co. (Food) [11365]

Halstad

Halstad Elevator Co. (Livestock and Farm
Products) [17972]

Hamel

Air & Water Purification Inc. (Specialty Equipment
and Products) [25547]
Twinco Automotive Warehouse
Inc. (Chemicals) [4536]
Twinco Romax Inc. (Automotive) [3356]

Harmony

Harmony Agri Services (Agricultural Equipment and
Supplies) [791]

Hastings

Miracle Recreation of Minnesota Inc. (Recreational
and Sporting Goods) [23831]

Hayward

Hayward Cooperative (Agricultural Equipment and
Supplies) [804]

Hector

Hector Farmers Elevator (Livestock and Farm
Products) [17987]

Herman

New Horizons Ag Services (Agricultural Equipment
and Supplies) [1071]

Hibbing

Continental Sales and Equipment Co. (Specialty
Equipment and Products) [25610]
Dom-Ex Inc. (Construction Materials and
Machinery) [7278]
Jasper Engineering and Equipment Co. (Industrial
Supplies) [16970]
Mesabi Radial Tire Co. (Automotive) [2946]
Sullivan Candy & Supply (Tobacco
Products) [26354]
T-Shirt Factory & Odd Shop (Clothing) [5417]

Hills

Hills Beaver Creek Cooperative Farm
Service (Agricultural Equipment and
Supplies) [825]

Hoffman
Hoffman Cooperative Oil Association (Agricultural Equipment and Supplies) [829]

Holland
Prins Grain Co. (Livestock and Farm Products) [18178]

Hollandale
Hollandale Marketing Association (Food) [11448]

Hope
Hope Cooperative Creamery (Food) [11458]

Hopkins
Kunz Oil Company Inc. (Petroleum, Fuels, and Related Equipment) [22411]
Lankhorst Distributors Inc. (Toys and Hobby Goods) [26562]
Minnetonka Mills Inc. (Textiles and Notions) [26149]
Super Valu Stores Inc. (Food) [12633]
Venturian Corp. (Automotive) [3390]

Houston
Houston Moneycreek Cooperative (Agricultural Equipment and Supplies) [840]

Hugo
North Country Marketing Ltd. (Recreational and Sporting Goods) [23851]
United Service Dental Chair (Medical, Dental, and Optical Equipment) [19093]

Hutchinson
AG Systems Inc. (Agricultural Equipment and Supplies) [200]
Hutchinson Coop Elevator (Livestock and Farm Products) [18009]

Jackson
Farmers Coop Association of Jackson, Sherburn, Spring Lake & Trimont (Agricultural Equipment and Supplies) [568]
Farmers Cooperative Association (Livestock and Farm Products) [17846]

Jasper
Eastern Farmers Coop (Agricultural Equipment and Supplies) [537]

Jeffers
Prairie Land Cooperative (Agricultural Equipment and Supplies) [1145]

Kellogg
Bouquet Enterprises Inc. (Gifts and Novelties) [13321]

Kettle River
CAP Propane Plus Inc. (Petroleum, Fuels, and Related Equipment) [22106]

La Salle
La Salle Farmers Grain Co. (Agricultural Equipment and Supplies) [926]

Lafayette
United Farmers Cooperative (Agricultural Equipment and Supplies) [1377]
United Farmers Cooperative (Food) [12792]

Lake Benton
Lake Benton Farmers Elevator Inc. (Agricultural Equipment and Supplies) [930]

Lake Bronson
Farmers Union Oil Co. (Petroleum, Fuels, and Related Equipment) [22261]
Farmers Union Oil Co. (Agricultural Equipment and Supplies) [667]

Lake Crystal
Crystal Cooperative Inc. (Agricultural Equipment and Supplies) [479]

Lake George
Wigwam Inc. (Shoes) [24894]
Wigwam Inc. (Clothing) [5485]

Lake Lillian
Farmers Cooperative Elevator Co. Lake Lillian Div. (Agricultural Equipment and Supplies) [622]

Lakefield
Cooperative Agricultural Center (Agricultural Equipment and Supplies) [447]

Lakeville
Grist Mill Co. (Food) [11328]
Rosemount Office Systems, Inc. (Office Equipment and Supplies) [21248]
Viking Acoustical Corp. (Office Equipment and Supplies) [21338]

Le Center
Highway Agricultural Services Inc. (Agricultural Equipment and Supplies) [822]

Le Roy
Hanson Tire Service Inc. (Automotive) [2724]
Le Roy Farmers Cooperative Creamery Association (Agricultural Equipment and Supplies) [946]
Le Roy Farmers Cooperative Grain and Stock Co. (Agricultural Equipment and Supplies) [947]

Lewisville
TruAl Inc. (Agricultural Equipment and Supplies) [1360]

Little Falls
Creameries Blending Inc. (Agricultural Equipment and Supplies) [471]

Luverne
Farmers Union Cooperative Oil Co. (Agricultural Equipment and Supplies) [662]
Frakco Inc. (Plumbing Materials and Fixtures) [23176]
Land O Lakes Inc. (Food) [11673]
Sturdevant Auto Supply (Automotive) [3279]

Madison
Fieldcrest Fertilizer Inc. (Agricultural Equipment and Supplies) [683]
Madison Bottling Co. (Alcoholic Beverages) [1835]

Mankato
Crown Bottling Co. (Alcoholic Beverages) [1626]
Harvest States Soybean Processing (Livestock and Farm Products) [17982]
Hubbard Milling Co. (Veterinary Products) [27152]
Kato Radiator Diesel Systems (Automotive) [2839]
Katolight Corp. (Electrical and Electronic Equipment and Supplies) [8930]
Mankato Iron and Metal Co. (Used, Scrap, and Recycled Materials) [26895]
Mankato-Kasota Stone (Construction Materials and Machinery) [7636]
Mercury Waste Solutions Inc. (Used, Scrap, and Recycled Materials) [26901]
Paper Service Company Inc. (Paper and Paper Products) [21865]
Ramy Seed Co. (Agricultural Equipment and Supplies) [1168]
Shari Candies Inc. (Food) [12474]
Southern Valley Co-op (Petroleum, Fuels, and Related Equipment) [22684]
Sween ID Products Inc. (Shoes) [24873]

Maple Grove
Wiurth Adams Nut and Bolt (Hardware) [13999]

Maple Lake
Carlson Dolls Co. (Gifts and Novelties) [13327]

Lake Region Cooperative Oil
Association (Petroleum, Fuels, and Related Equipment) [22416]

Maple Plain
Herc-U-Lift Inc. (Industrial Machinery) [16098]

Marshall
Lyon County Cooperative Oil Co. (Petroleum, Fuels, and Related Equipment) [22443]

McIntosh
McIntosh Cooperative Creamery (Food) [11830]

Medina
Thorpe Distributing Co. (Alcoholic Beverages) [2081]

Menahga
Cooperative Sampo Corp. (Livestock and Farm Products) [17798]

Mendota Heights
Industrial Supply Co. (Industrial Supplies) [16953]

Milan
Milan Farmers Elevator (Livestock and Farm Products) [18098]
Milan Farmers Elevator (Food) [11894]

Milroy
Farmers Cooperative Association (Livestock and Farm Products) [17845]

Miltona
Pro AG Farmers Co-op (Agricultural Equipment and Supplies) [1154]

Minneapolis
Abrasive Specialists Inc. (Industrial Machinery) [15726]
ADP Hollander Inc. (Computers and Software) [5878]
AEI Electronic Parts (Electrical and Electronic Equipment and Supplies) [8277]
AeroSpace Computer Supplies, Inc. (Computers and Software) [5892]
Air Power Equipment Corp. (Compressors) [5825]
All Star Sports Inc. (Recreational and Sporting Goods) [23505]
Allanson Business Products (Computers and Software) [5904]
Alliance Steel Service Co. (Used, Scrap, and Recycled Materials) [26737]
American Iron and Supply Co. (Used, Scrap, and Recycled Materials) [26751]
American Telephone Systems (Communications Systems and Equipment) [5513]
AmeriData Inc. (Computers and Software) [5934]
Amex Inc. (Computers and Software) [5937]
Appliance Recycling Centers of America Inc. (Household Appliances) [15030]
Arrowhead Fireworks Co. (Toys and Hobby Goods) [26399]
Augsburg Fortress Publishers (Books and Other Printed Materials) [3533]
Bauer Cycle Supply Inc. (Recreational and Sporting Goods) [23539]
Beco Helman Inc. (Clothing) [4811]
Benson Pump Co. (Recreational and Sporting Goods) [23550]
Benson-Quinn Co. (Livestock and Farm Products) [17729]
Berg Bag Co. (Storage Equipment and Containers) [25891]
Berg Bag Co. (Industrial Supplies) [16750]
Best Buy Co. Inc. (Sound and Entertainment Equipment and Supplies) [25101]
BFI/Allied Recyclery Mpls (Used, Scrap, and Recycled Materials) [26766]
Blooming Prairie Natural Foods (Food) [10571]
Bookmen, Inc. (Books and Other Printed Materials) [3579]
Borneo Group Inc. (Clothing) [4834]

Boustead Electric and Manufacturing Co. (Electrical and Electronic Equipment and Supplies) [8457]

Brin-Northwestern Glass Co. (Construction Materials and Machinery) [7079]

Brooks and Co.; H. (Food) [10621]

Brown's Ice Cream Co. (Food) [10631]

Calco of Minneapolis Inc. (Food) [10669]

Cannon Technologies Inc. (Computers and Software) [6044]

Cargill Inc. (Chemicals) [4343]

Caribiner International (Sound and Entertainment Equipment and Supplies) [25122]

Caribiner International (Household Appliances) [15075]

Cash Register Sales Inc. (Office Equipment and Supplies) [20884]

Central Medical Inc. (Medical, Dental, and Optical Supplies) [19224]

Chem-Serv Inc. (Chemicals) [4349]

Colombo, Inc. (Food) [10791]

Commodity Specialists Co. (Livestock and Farm Products) [17788]

ConAgra Grain Co. (Food) [10805]

ConAgra Trading Cos. (Food) [10807]

Cosmopolitan Trading Co. (Health and Beauty Aids) [14074]

Creative Healthcare Resources (Books and Other Printed Materials) [3668]

Crystal Farms Refrigerated Distribution Co. (Food) [10877]

Datalink Corp. (Computers and Software) [6188]

Datron Corp. (Agricultural Equipment and Supplies) [496]

Duncan Co. (Industrial Supplies) [16840]

Ed-Burt Corp. (Clothing) [4930]

Elias Sales & Service, Inc.; T.J. (Industrial Machinery) [15982]

Emit International Corp. (Shoes) [24734]

Enrica Fish Books Inc. (Books and Other Printed Materials) [3732]

Fairway Foods Inc. (Food) [11073]

Fairway Foods Inc. (Food) [11074]

Feed-Rite Controls Inc. (Specialty Equipment and Products) [25648]

Filut & Associates Inc.; R.J. (Recreational and Sporting Goods) [23665]

Fleming/Gateway (Food) [11158]

Flo-Pac Corp. (Cleaning and Janitorial Supplies) [4623]

Floors Northwest Inc. (Floorcovering Equipment and Supplies) [9900]

Fortress Press (Books and Other Printed Materials) [3761]

G-Riffco (Industrial Machinery) [16044]

Gander Mountain Inc. (Recreational and Sporting Goods) [23682]

Gardner Hardware Co. (Construction Materials and Machinery) [7378]

GFI America Inc. (Food) [11260]

Gibb Co.; Clark R. (Computers and Software) [6301]

Goodin Co. (Plumbing Materials and Fixtures) [23196]

Gopher News Co. (Books and Other Printed Materials) [3788]

Gourmet Award Foods Tree of Life Inc. (Food) [11297]

Grimstad, Inc.; J.M. (Chemicals) [4403]

GT Interactive Software Corp. Value Products Div. (Computers and Software) [6315]

H Enterprises International Inc. (Medical, Dental, and Optical Supplies) [19345]

Haldeman-Homme Inc. (Industrial Supplies) [16921]

Hannays (Marine) [18517]

Hawkins Chemical Inc. (Industrial Machinery) [16095]

Hayden-Murphy Equipment Co. (Construction Materials and Machinery) [7460]

Hirshfield's, Inc. (Paints and Varnishes) [21456]

Holiday Cos. (Food) [11446]

Humac Engineering and Equipment Inc. (Construction Materials and Machinery) [7497]

Hydra-Power, Inc. (Industrial Machinery) [16122]

Inter-City Paper Co. (Paper and Paper Products) [21778]

Interior Tropicals, Inc. (Horticultural Supplies) [14894]

International Dairy Queen Inc. (Restaurant and Commercial Foodservice Equipment and Supplies) [24143]

International Office Systems Inc. (Office Equipment and Supplies) [21064]

Interstate Co. (Industrial Supplies) [16962]

Interstate Detroit Diesel Inc. (Industrial Machinery) [16167]

Irish Books & Media, Inc. (Books and Other Printed Materials) [3855]

Island Cycle Supply Co. (Recreational and Sporting Goods) [23748]

J-Mark (Automotive) [2806]

Jacobs Trading Co. (Household Items) [15543]

K-Tel International Inc. (Sound and Entertainment Equipment and Supplies) [25264]

K-Tel International (USA) Inc. (Household Items) [15547]

Kalweit Sales Company Inc. (Toys and Hobby Goods) [26548]

Keelor Steel Inc. (Metals) [20092]

Kirsch Fabric Corp. (Textiles and Notions) [26110]

Kirsch Fabrics Corp. (Textiles and Notions) [26111]

Krelitz Industries Inc. (Medical, Dental, and Optical Supplies) [19402]

Kwik Sew Pattern Company Inc. (Textiles and Notions) [26117]

Lakeland Engineer Equipment Co. (Electrical and Electronic Equipment and Supplies) [8966]

Landvest Development Corp. (Construction Materials and Machinery) [7585]

Langford Tool & Drill (Hardware) [13792]

Larson Co.; J.H. (Electrical and Electronic Equipment and Supplies) [8973]

Loffler Business Systems Inc. (Electrical and Electronic Equipment and Supplies) [9001]

Lynde Co. (Chemicals) [4443]

MacAlester Park Publishing Co. (Books and Other Printed Materials) [3926]

Magnum Tire Corp. (Automotive) [2909]

Marine Electric Co. (Recreational and Sporting Goods) [23799]

Mello Smello (Gifts and Novelties) [13400]

Michael Foods Inc. (Food) [11867]

Michael Foods Refrigerated Distribution Cos. (Food) [11868]

Micro Ear Technology Inc. (Medical, Dental, and Optical Equipment) [18936]

Mid America Ribbon & Supply Co. (Computers and Software) [6515]

Mid-West Steel Supply Co. (Metals) [20185]

Midwest Sports Cards (Toys and Hobby Goods) [26578]

Mikara Corp. (Health and Beauty Aids) [14162]

Mikara Corp. (Restaurant and Commercial Foodservice Equipment and Supplies) [24185]

Mill City Music Record Distribution, Inc. (Sound and Entertainment Equipment and Supplies) [25325]

Minneapolis Equipment Co. (Construction Materials and Machinery) [7720]

Minnesota Clay Co. USA (Toys and Hobby Goods) [26579]

Minnesota Produce Inc. (Food) [11907]

Motivaction Inc. (Sound and Entertainment Equipment and Supplies) [25340]

Nada Concepts Inc. (Medical, Dental, and Optical Equipment) [18954]

Nash Finch Co. (Food) [11973]

Newark Electronics Corp. (Electrical and Electronic Equipment and Supplies) [9129]

Norcostco Inc. (Specialty Equipment and Products) [25761]

Northern Sun (Gifts and Novelties) [13412]

Northland Electric Supply Co. (Electrical and Electronic Equipment and Supplies) [9140]

Northwest Graphic Supply Co. (Specialty Equipment and Products) [25764]

Novartis Nutrition Corp. (Food) [12041]

Nutrition Medical Inc. (Health and Beauty Aids) [14184]

Olympic Steel Inc. Juster Steel Div. (Metals) [20249]

Optical Advantage (Computers and Software) [6573]

Original Marketing Concepts Ltd. (Sound and Entertainment Equipment and Supplies) [25371]

Padco Inc. (Paints and Varnishes) [21523]

Page Inc.; T.H. (Medical, Dental, and Optical Equipment) [18975]

Palay Display Industries Inc. (Furniture and Fixtures) [13203]

Palm Brothers Inc. (Restaurant and Commercial Foodservice Equipment and Supplies) [24201]

Partners 4 Design Inc. (Household Appliances) [15266]

PC Drilling Control Co. (Electrical and Electronic Equipment and Supplies) [9181]

Perfection Type Inc. (Industrial Machinery) [16391]

Phillips Beverage Co. (Alcoholic Beverages) [1952]

Photo Control Corp. (Photographic Equipment and Supplies) [22891]

Plant and Flanged Equipment (Plumbing Materials and Fixtures) [23317]

Plant and Flanged Equipment (Metals) [20285]

Powertronics Inc. (Electrical and Electronic Equipment and Supplies) [9231]

Practical Cookbooks (Books and Other Printed Materials) [4078]

Preferred Products Inc. (Food) [12211]

Quality Business Forms Inc. (Office Equipment and Supplies) [21228]

Quantum Labs Inc. (Medical, Dental, and Optical Equipment) [19003]

Re-Mark Co. (Sound and Entertainment Equipment and Supplies) [25409]

Robbinsdale Farm and Garden Pet Supply Inc. (Veterinary Products) [27224]

Robco Corp. (Recreational and Sporting Goods) [23916]

Roots & Fruits Cooperative Produce (Food) [12351]

Rovac Inc. (Computers and Software) [6695]

Rubenstein & Ziff Inc. (Textiles and Notions) [26194]

Ruffridge Johnson Equipment Company Inc. (Construction Materials and Machinery) [7965]

Ryerson Coil Processing Co. (Metals) [20341]

St. Paul Appliance Center Inc. (Household Appliances) [15302]

Signcaster Corp. (Plastics) [23034]

Specially Yours Inc. (Gifts and Novelties) [13450]

SPS Company Inc. (Plumbing Materials and Fixtures) [23395]

Stark Electronics Inc. (Electrical and Electronic Equipment and Supplies) [9411]

Stewart Lumber Co. (Construction Materials and Machinery) [8075]

SUPERVALU Inc. (Food) [12645]

Surgical Instrument Associates (Medical, Dental, and Optical Equipment) [19064]

Sygnet (Industrial Machinery) [16543]

TCB Inc. (Storage Equipment and Containers) [25944]

Tradewinds International Inc. (Computers and Software) [6826]

Tri-State Bearing Co. (Automotive) [3337]

Twin City Optical Inc. (Medical, Dental, and Optical Supplies) [19667]

United Noodles Inc. (Food) [12800]

Viking Materials Inc. (Metals) [20472]

Vincent Metal Goods (Metals) [20473]

Waldor Pump and Equipment (Specialty Equipment and Products) [25869]

Waldor Pump and Equipment (Plumbing Materials and Fixtures) [23434]

Walman Optical Co. (Medical, Dental, and Optical Supplies) [19694]

Warner Manufacturing Co. (Paints and Varnishes) [21602]

Weinberg Supply Company Inc.; E. (Cleaning and Janitorial Supplies) [4729]

Weinstein International Seafood Inc. (Food) [12899]

Westway Trading Corp. (Food) [12917]

Wholesale Produce Supply Company Inc. (Food) [12935]

The Wine Co. (Alcoholic Beverages) [2123]

World Trade Network, Ltd. (Marine) [18644]
World Wide Pictures, Inc. (Sound and Entertainment Equipment and Supplies) [25532]
World Wide Pictures Inc. (Household Appliances) [15380]

Minnesota City
Canton Mills Inc. (Agricultural Equipment and Supplies) [371]

Minnesota Lake
Grain Land Co-op (Livestock and Farm Products) [17953]

Minnetonka
Abbey Home Healthcare (Medical, Dental, and Optical Supplies) [19119]
Allied Electronics (Electrical and Electronic Equipment and Supplies) [8313]
Anodyne Inc. (Medical, Dental, and Optical Supplies) [19154]
Compar, Inc. (Computers and Software) [6088]
Cutlery (Hardware) [13652]
Flemming and Associates Inc.; Tom (Food) [11159]
Imar Industries Inc. (Clothing) [5044]
Keomed Inc. (Medical, Dental, and Optical Equipment) [18876]
Martrex Alpha Corp. (Computers and Software) [6466]
Martrex Inc. (Chemicals) [4454]
Minneapolis Rusco Inc. (Construction Materials and Machinery) [7722]
NCS Assessments (Computers and Software) [6546]
Normark Corp. (Recreational and Sporting Goods) [23848]
Norstan Inc. (Communications Systems and Equipment) [5692]
Osmonics, Inc. (Specialty Equipment and Products) [25777]
Roth Distributing Co. (Household Appliances) [15294]
Tonkadale Greenhouses (Horticultural Supplies) [14962]
World Data Products Inc. (Computers and Software) [6879]
World Data Products Inc. (Computers and Software) [6880]

Montevideo
Harvest States Cooperatives Line Elevator Div. (Livestock and Farm Products) [17981]

Moorhead
Kragnes Farmers Elevator (Livestock and Farm Products) [18040]
Stein's Inc. (Cleaning and Janitorial Supplies) [4715]

Moose Lake
Sun Coast Imports (Textiles and Notions) [26218]

Mora
Kanabec Cooperative Association (Petroleum, Fuels, and Related Equipment) [22394]

Morgan
Morgan Grain and Feed Co. (Livestock and Farm Products) [18116]

Morris
Elmer's Distributing Co. (Alcoholic Beverages) [1673]
Morris Cooperative Association (Agricultural Equipment and Supplies) [1053]
Morris Grain Company Inc. (Agricultural Equipment and Supplies) [1054]

Mounds View
SYSCO Food Services of Minnesota Inc. (Food) [12684]

Mountain Lake
Cooperative Oil Association (Petroleum, Fuels, and Related Equipment) [22168]

Murdock
United Farmers Elevator Co. (Livestock and Farm Products) [18302]

New Brighton
General Office Products Co. (Office Equipment and Supplies) [21011]
Spectrum Labs Inc. (Chemicals) [4519]

New Hope
Navarre Corp. (Computers and Software) [6544]
Universal International Inc. (Clothing) [5454]
Waymouth Farms Inc. (Food) [12887]

New London
Melges; Gregory N. (Recreational and Sporting Goods) [23819]

New Ulm
Associated Milk Producers Inc. North Central Region (Food) [10453]

New York Mills
Mills Farmers Elevator (Agricultural Equipment and Supplies) [1041]

Newport
Fritz Company Inc. (Food) [11218]

North Branch
Peterson's North Branch Inc. (Agricultural Equipment and Supplies) [1126]

North Mankato
Kaye Corp. (Agricultural Equipment and Supplies) [899]
Mankato Business Products (Office Equipment and Supplies) [21121]
Neubert Millwork Co. (Construction Materials and Machinery) [7772]

Northfield
Cannon Valley Cooperative (Agricultural Equipment and Supplies) [370]

Oakdale
Flexo-Printing Equipment Corp. (Specialty Equipment and Products) [25653]
Flexo-Printing Equipment Corp. (Industrial Machinery) [16010]

Ormsby
Watonwan Farm Services Co. Ormsby Div. (Livestock and Farm Products) [18328]

Oslo
Farmers Cooperative Elevator (Livestock and Farm Products) [17861]
Farmers Union Oil Co. (Agricultural Equipment and Supplies) [666]

Osseo
Jane Co. (Computers and Software) [6405]

Owatonna
Central Cooperative Oil Association (Petroleum, Fuels, and Related Equipment) [22123]

Park Rapids
Gulbranson Equipment Inc. (Agricultural Equipment and Supplies) [777]

Paynesville
Paynesville Farmers Union Cooperative Oil Co. (Petroleum, Fuels, and Related Equipment) [22554]

Pease
Mille Lacs Agriculture Services Inc. (Agricultural Equipment and Supplies) [1039]

Perham
Auction Livestock, Inc. (Livestock and Farm Products) [17711]
Pabco Inc. (Electrical and Electronic Equipment and Supplies) [9166]

Pine City
Pine City Cooperative Association (Livestock and Farm Products) [18166]

Pine Island
Pine Island Farmers Elevator Co. (Livestock and Farm Products) [18167]

Plymouth
Appliance Parts Inc. (Household Appliances) [15024]
Applied Microcomputer Solutions (Computers and Software) [5952]
Bloom Brothers Co. (Clothing) [4827]
Computer Parts and Services Inc. (Computers and Software) [6118]
ELA Medical Inc. (Medical, Dental, and Optical Equipment) [18785]
Graybow-Daniels Co. (Plumbing Materials and Fixtures) [23198]
Hartzell Acquisition Corp. (Furniture and Fixtures) [13129]
Industrial Supply Co. (Industrial Supplies) [16952]
Kate-Lo Div. (Floorcovering Equipment and Supplies) [9985]
Kennel-Aire Inc. (Veterinary Products) [27172]
Minneapolis Glass Co. (Construction Materials and Machinery) [7721]
Minter-Weisman Co. (Food) [11908]
RBC Tile & Stone (Floorcovering Equipment and Supplies) [10115]
RBC Tile and Stone (Construction Materials and Machinery) [7903]
United Hardware Distributing Co. (Hardware) [13973]

Princeton
Central Rivers Cooperative (Agricultural Equipment and Supplies) [399]

Prinsburg
Prinsburg Farmers Cooperative (Agricultural Equipment and Supplies) [1152]

Prior Lake
Gourmet Regency Coffee Inc. (Food) [11298]

Racine
Racine Elevator Co. (Petroleum, Fuels, and Related Equipment) [22606]

Ramsey
Alexon Trend Inc. (Scientific and Measurement Devices) [24309]

Red Wing
Behrens Supply Co. (Automotive) [2346]
Bob's Business Inc. (Recreational and Sporting Goods) [23562]

Redwood Falls
Redwood Valley Co-op Elevator (Livestock and Farm Products) [18193]

Renville
Co-op Country Farmers Elevator (Livestock and Farm Products) [17785]
Co-op Country Farmers Elevator (Food) [10780]

Revere
Revere Elevator Company Inc. (Livestock and Farm Products) [18195]

Richfield
Fadson International Company (Heating and Cooling Equipment and Supplies) [14439]

Geographic Index

Rochester

Anderson's Wheelchair Therapeutic Supply (Medical, Dental, and Optical Equipment) [18684]
Fisher Auto Parts Professionals (Automotive) [2623]
Pace Electronics Inc. (Electrical and Electronic Equipment and Supplies) [9168]
Pepsi-Cola Bottling Company of Rochester (Soft Drinks) [25011]
Schilling Paper Co. (Paper and Paper Products) [21923]

Rosemount

Oil Recycling Inc. (Used, Scrap, and Recycled Materials) [26928]

Roseville

Bradley Distributing (Soft Drinks) [24917]
Fair Inc. (Shoes) [24739]
Hickory Tech-Enterprise Solutions (Communications Systems and Equipment) [5636]
L-Z Truck Equipment Co., Inc. (Automotive) [2868]
Lynch Enterprises Inc.; C.O. (Shoes) [24798]
Old Dutch Foods Inc. (Food) [12062]

Round Lake

Sathers Inc. (Food) [12418]

Rushford

Farmers Cooperative Elevator Co. (Agricultural Equipment and Supplies) [612]

Rushmore

United Farmers Co-op (Agricultural Equipment and Supplies) [1376]

St. Cloud

Appert Foods (Food) [10423]
Automotive Parts Headquarters Inc. (Automotive) [2293]
Bernick Inc.; Charles A. (Soft Drinks) [24914]
Electric Motor Service (Electrical and Electronic Equipment and Supplies) [8663]
Eye Kraft Optical Inc. (Medical, Dental, and Optical Supplies) [19317]
Granite City Ready Mix Inc. (Construction Materials and Machinery) [7410]
Granite City Ready Mix Inc. (Construction Materials and Machinery) [7411]
Index 53 Optical (Medical, Dental, and Optical Supplies) [19369]
Marco Business Products Inc. (Computers and Software) [6463]
Midwest Vision Distributors Inc. (Medical, Dental, and Optical Equipment) [18939]
Nash Finch Co. (Food) [11970]
National Bushing and Parts Company Inc. (Automotive) [3015]
Northwest Diesel & Refrigeration Services (Heating and Cooling Equipment and Supplies) [14625]
Northwestern Supply Co. (Agricultural Equipment and Supplies) [1090]
Schmidt Laboratories (Medical, Dental, and Optical Supplies) [19596]

St. Hilaire

Northwest Grain (Livestock and Farm Products) [18143]

St. James

Downs Foods Co.; Tony (Food) [10987]

St. Joseph

DBL Labs (Medical, Dental, and Optical Supplies) [19273]

St. Louis Park

Globe Inc. (Plumbing Materials and Fixtures) [23193]
Olson Inc.; Kenneth P. (Clothing) [5250]

St. Louis Pk.

Pink Business Interiors Inc. (Floorcovering Equipment and Supplies) [10105]

St. Michael

J and B Wholesale Distribution (Food) [11536]

St. Paul

Ally Press (Books and Other Printed Materials) [3493]
Anchor Paper Co. (Paper and Paper Products) [21633]
A.P.I. Inc. (Construction Materials and Machinery) [6980]
Automotive Trades Div. (Automotive) [2298]
AVAC Corp. (Household Appliances) [15041]
Bailey Nurseries Inc. (Horticultural Supplies) [14813]
Battery and Tire Warehouse Inc. (Automotive) [2327]
Beckman Produce Inc. (Food) [10524]
Benz and Sons Inc.; George (Livestock and Farm Products) [17730]
Bio Instruments Inc. (Medical, Dental, and Optical Supplies) [19191]
Birnberg & Sons Inc. (Household Appliances) [15052]
Brissman-Kennedy Inc. (Cleaning and Janitorial Supplies) [4589]
Bro Tex Company Inc., Wiping Cloth Div. (Paper and Paper Products) [21657]
Bro Tex Company Inc., Wiping Cloth Div. (Industrial Supplies) [16767]
Capitol Electronics Inc. (Communications Systems and Equipment) [5547]
Capitol Sales Company Inc. (Sound and Entertainment Equipment and Supplies) [25120]
Capitol Sales Company Inc. (Household Appliances) [15074]
Cenex Harvest States Cooperatives (Livestock and Farm Products) [17768]
Cenex/Land O'Lakes AG Services (Agricultural Equipment and Supplies) [384]
Champion Auto Stores Inc. (Automotive) [2443]
Clayhill (Compressors) [5836]
Consortium Book Sales and Distribution Inc. (Books and Other Printed Materials) [3654]
Corning-Donohue Inc. (Construction Materials and Machinery) [7222]
Countryman Co.; D.F. (Communications Systems and Equipment) [5580]
Cummins Diesel Sales Inc. (Industrial Machinery) [15922]
Cummins North Central Inc. (Automotive) [2511]
Dahlco Music & Vending (Specialty Equipment and Products) [25622]
Ecolab Inc. Food and Beverage Div. (Cleaning and Janitorial Supplies) [4614]
Ecolab Inc. Institutional Div. (Cleaning and Janitorial Supplies) [4615]
Ecolab Inc. Professional Products Div. (Chemicals) [4379]
Ecolab Inc. Textile Care Div. (Cleaning and Janitorial Supplies) [4616]
Electronics and Information Systems (Computers and Software) [6245]
Elliott Auto Supply Company Inc. (Automotive) [2583]
Executone Systems of St. Paul Inc. (Communications Systems and Equipment) [5607]
Far-Vet Supply Co. (Medical, Dental, and Optical Supplies) [19322]
Farm-Oyl Company Inc. (Agricultural Equipment and Supplies) [563]
Gopher Bearing (Automotive) [2692]
Gopher Electronics Co. (Electrical and Electronic Equipment and Supplies) [8797]
Great Western Recycling Industries Inc. (Used, Scrap, and Recycled Materials) [26833]
Hess Hair Milk Laboratories Inc. (Specialty Equipment and Products) [25678]
Horizon Medical Inc. (Medical, Dental, and Optical Equipment) [18842]
Island Import and Export Co. (Shoes) [24772]
Johnson Brothers Co. (St. Paul, Minnesota) (Alcoholic Beverages) [1785]
Johnson Brothers Wholesale Liquor (Alcoholic Beverages) [1787]

Johnson Brothers Wholesale Liquor Co. (Alcoholic Beverages) [1788]
Johnson RDO Communications Co. (Electrical and Electronic Equipment and Supplies) [8917]
Kelly Computer Supplies (Computers and Software) [6419]
Lahr Co.; W.E. (Automotive) [2870]
Lampert Yards Inc. (Construction Materials and Machinery) [7583]
Layton Marketing Group Inc. (Paints and Varnishes) [21488]
Lean Year Distributing Inc. (Toys and Hobby Goods) [26564]
Lintex Corp. (Medical, Dental, and Optical Equipment) [18891]
Llewellyn Publications (Books and Other Printed Materials) [3919]
Loeffler's Safety Shoes Inc. (Shoes) [24796]
MacArthur Co. (Construction Materials and Machinery) [7630]
MacQueen Equipment Inc. (Industrial Machinery) [16258]
McKee Enterprises Inc. (Floorcovering Equipment and Supplies) [10017]
Midwest Auto Parts Distributors Inc. (Automotive) [2959]
Minnesota Chemical Co. (Chemicals) [4458]
Minnesota Cultivated Wild Rice Council (Food) [11906]
Minnesota Mining & Manufacturing Co. (Office Equipment and Supplies) [21147]
Minnesota Mining & Manufacturing Co. Do-It-Yourself Div. (Industrial Supplies) [17044]
Musolf Distributing Inc.; Lon (Floorcovering Equipment and Supplies) [10070]
Nasco Inc. (Industrial Machinery) [16338]
Norden Inc. (Shoes) [24823]
Office to Office Inc. (Office Equipment and Supplies) [21184]
Old Home Foods Inc. (Food) [12063]
Patterson Dental Co. (Medical, Dental, and Optical Supplies) [19529]
Power/mation Inc. (Electrical and Electronic Equipment and Supplies) [9224]
Rihm Motor Co. (Motorized Vehicles) [20712]
Road Rescue Inc. (Automotive) [3165]
Royal Crown Beverage Co. (Soft Drinks) [25027]
Rue Plastics Inc. (Plastics) [23031]
R.W. Sales, Inc. (Electrical and Electronic Equipment and Supplies) [9326]
St. Jude Medical Inc. (Medical, Dental, and Optical Equipment) [19028]
St. Paul Bar/Restaurant Equipment (Restaurant and Commercial Foodservice Equipment and Supplies) [24213]
Scientific Anglers (Recreational and Sporting Goods) [23933]
Shaw Lumber Co. (Construction Materials and Machinery) [8006]
Soderburg Optical Services (Medical, Dental, and Optical Supplies) [19618]
State Supply Co. (Plumbing Materials and Fixtures) [23398]
Superior Products (Restaurant and Commercial Foodservice Equipment and Supplies) [24234]
Superior Products Manufacturing Co. (Restaurant and Commercial Foodservice Equipment and Supplies) [24235]
Ternes Register System (Industrial Machinery) [16557]
Tru-Part Manufacturing Corp. (Agricultural Equipment and Supplies) [1359]
Twin City Hardware Company Inc. (Hardware) [13969]
Van Paper Co. (Paper and Paper Products) [21984]
VMC Inc. (Recreational and Sporting Goods) [24035]
White Co.; Brock (Construction Materials and Machinery) [8218]
Zimmerman Dry Goods (Clothing) [5495]

Sanborn

Sanborn Farmers Elevator (Livestock and Farm Products) [18221]
Sanborn Farmers Elevator (Food) [12404]

Sauk Centre

Central Minnesota Cooperative (Agricultural Equipment and Supplies) [397]
Centre Jobbing Co. (Tobacco Products) [26275]

Sauk Rapids

CSI Sports, LLC (Recreational and Sporting Goods) [23611]

Savage

Heat-N-Glo Fireplaces (Heating and Cooling Equipment and Supplies) [14480]
Versatile Vehicles Inc. (Recreational and Sporting Goods) [24031]

Shakopee

Lano Equipment Inc. (Agricultural Equipment and Supplies) [937]
Minneapolis Northstar Auto Auction Inc. (Motorized Vehicles) [20683]

Sleepy Eye

Miller Sellner Implement Inc. (Agricultural Equipment and Supplies) [1040]

South St. Paul

Allstate Sales and Leasing Corp. (Motorized Vehicles) [20583]
Allstate Sales and Leasing Corp. (Automotive) [2219]
Bell Industries (Marine) [18458]
Central Livestock Association (Livestock and Farm Products) [17772]

Starbuck

Farmers Union Oil Co. (Starbuck, Minnesota) (Agricultural Equipment and Supplies) [670]
Starbuck Creamery Co. (Food) [12570]

Stillwater

Cub Foods (Food) [10880]
U.S.A. Marketing Alliance Inc. (Agricultural Equipment and Supplies) [1388]
Voyageur Press, Inc. (Books and Other Printed Materials) [4264]

Taconite

Troumbly Brothers Inc. (Construction Materials and Machinery) [8150]

Thief River Falls

Farmers Cooperative Grain and Seed (Livestock and Farm Products) [17873]
H and H Sales Inc. (Toys and Hobby Goods) [26507]
Wilson Brothers Co. (Automotive) [3439]

Tracy

Tracy-Garvin Cooperative (Agricultural Equipment and Supplies) [1348]

Truman

Truman Farmers Elevator Co. (Agricultural Equipment and Supplies) [1361]
Watonwan Farm Services Co. (Livestock and Farm Products) [18327]

Tyler

Cenex-Harvest States Cooperative (Petroleum, Fuels, and Related Equipment) [22120]

Vadnais Heights

Dey Appliance Parts (Electrical and Electronic Equipment and Supplies) [8625]

Vermillion

Vermillion Elevator Co. (Livestock and Farm Products) [18316]

Virginia

Anderson & Spring Firestone (Automotive) [2240]
Coca-Cola Bottling Company of Virginia (Soft Drinks) [24941]

Langer Equipment Company Inc. (Motorized Vehicles) [20670]
Range Paper Corp. (Paper and Paper Products) [21897]
Taconite Oil Company Inc. (Petroleum, Fuels, and Related Equipment) [22720]

Wabasha

Uni-Patch (Medical, Dental, and Optical Supplies) [19670]

Wadena

Wensman Seed Co. (Livestock and Farm Products) [18334]

Wanamingo

Hermann Implement Inc. (Agricultural Equipment and Supplies) [816]

Warren

Marshall County Cooperative Association (Petroleum, Fuels, and Related Equipment) [22453]

Waseca

Viking Woodcrafts, Inc. (Paints and Varnishes) [21599]
Wills Co. (Gifts and Novelties) [13474]

Wendell

Wendell Farmers Elevator Co. (Livestock and Farm Products) [18333]

Westbrook

Farmers Elevator Company of Avoca (Agricultural Equipment and Supplies) [644]

Wheaton

Sturdevant Auto Supply (Automotive) [3280]
Wheaton Dumont Cooperative Elevator Inc. (Livestock and Farm Products) [18342]

White Bear Lake

Barclay Marine Distributors Corp. (Marine) [18454]

Willmar

Computers of Willmar Inc. (Computers and Software) [6135]
Farm Service Elevator Co. (Livestock and Farm Products) [17839]
Farmers Union Oil Co. (Willmar, Minnesota) (Agricultural Equipment and Supplies) [671]
Minnesota Electrical Supply Co. (Electrical and Electronic Equipment and Supplies) [9088]
Nelson Leasing Inc. (Automotive) [3024]
West Central Steel Inc. (Metals) [20488]
Willmar Poultry Company Inc. (Food) [12950]

Wilmont

Wilmont Farmers Elevator Co. (Livestock and Farm Products) [18353]

Windom

Prairie Land Cooperative (Agricultural Equipment and Supplies) [1144]
Windom Cooperative Association (Agricultural Equipment and Supplies) [1455]
Windom Sales Company Inc. (Livestock and Farm Products) [18355]

Winona

Fastenal Co. (Hardware) [13696]
Fratzke Sales, Inc. (Clothing) [4967]
Pepline/Wincraft (Gifts and Novelties) [13420]
Schott Distributing Co. (Alcoholic Beverages) [2013]
Valley Wholesalers Inc. (Paper and Paper Products) [21983]
Winona River and Rail Inc. (Agricultural Equipment and Supplies) [1456]

Wolverton

Wolverton Farmers Elevator (Livestock and Farm Products) [18358]

Wood Lake

Equity Elevator and Trading Co. (Livestock and Farm Products) [17835]

Woodbury

North Star Water Conditioning (Specialty Equipment and Products) [25763]
North Star Water Conditioning (Plumbing Materials and Fixtures) [23297]

Worthington

Consolidated Cooperatives Inc. (Agricultural Equipment and Supplies) [440]
Nobles County Cooperative Oil Co. (Petroleum, Fuels, and Related Equipment) [22521]

Zumbrota

Jerrine Company Inc. (Agricultural Equipment and Supplies) [885]

Mississippi

Aberdeen

Comer Packing Company Inc. (Gifts and Novelties) [13332]
Comer Packing Company Inc. (Food) [10797]

Ashland

Benton County Cooperative (Agricultural Equipment and Supplies) [300]

Batesville

Dunlap and Kyle Company Inc. (Motorized Vehicles) [20628]

Bay St. Louis

Dixie Craft & Floral Wholesale (Office Equipment and Supplies) [20971]

Belzoni

Belzoni Tractor Co. Inc. (Agricultural Equipment and Supplies) [298]

Biloxi

Corso Inc.; Frank P. (Tobacco Products) [26283]
Fournier & Sons Seafoods; R. (Food) [11194]
Gulf Central Seafoods Inc. (Food) [11344]
Kennedy Engine Co. (Automotive) [2848]
Marinovich Trawl Co. (Marine) [18562]
Weems Brothers Seafood Co. (Food) [12896]

Blue Mountain

BenchCraft (Furniture and Fixtures) [13035]

Booneville

Prentiss Manufacturing Company Inc. (Clothing) [5289]

Brandon

Quail Ridge Press Inc. (Books and Other Printed Materials) [4098]

Brookhaven

Phillips Brothers Lumber Company Inc. (Wood and Wood Products) [27359]

Calhoun City

Calhoun County Cooperative (Agricultural Equipment and Supplies) [363]
Hardin Clothing Co. Inc.; J.M. (Clothing) [5020]
Hawkins Auto Parts (Automotive) [2731]

Canton

Cole Brothers and Fox Co. (Tobacco Products) [26277]
Madison County Cooperative (Agricultural Equipment and Supplies) [980]
Thomas-Walker-Lacey Inc. (Food) [12716]

Carthage

Central Snacks (Food) [10724]

Clarksdale
Delta Wholesale Hardware Co. (Hardware) [13661]
Five County Farmers Association (Agricultural Equipment and Supplies) [691]
Infolab Inc. (Medical, Dental, and Optical Supplies) [19371]
Kim's Processing Plant (Food) [11609]

Cleveland
West Implement Company Inc. (Agricultural Equipment and Supplies) [1423]

Clinton
KLH Industries Inc. (Electrical and Electronic Equipment and Supplies) [8951]
Mississippi Safety Services Inc. (Security and Safety Equipment) [24594]

Columbia
Morris Oil Inc. (Petroleum, Fuels, and Related Equipment) [22499]

Columbus
Cash Distributing Co. (Alcoholic Beverages) [1580]
Columbus Metals Supply Inc. (Metals) [19885]
Lawrin Lighting, Inc. (Household Items) [15561]
Waters Truck and Tractor Company Inc. (Automotive) [3402]

Corinth
Briggs Inc. (Tobacco Products) [26267]
Jarnagin; C & D (Toys and Hobby Goods) [26542]
Long Wholesale Distributors Inc. (Food) [11730]
M.L. Sandy Lumber Sales Company Inc. (Wood and Wood Products) [27346]
Sandy Lumber Sales Company Inc.; M.L. (Construction Materials and Machinery) [7979]

Drew
Lewis Seed and Feed Co. (Agricultural Equipment and Supplies) [954]

Flowood
Putt-Putt Golf & Games (Recreational and Sporting Goods) [23899]
Specialty Supply Co. (Electrical and Electronic Equipment and Supplies) [9394]

Forest
Scott County Cooperative (Agricultural Equipment and Supplies) [1241]

Golden
Mississippi Tool Supply Co. (Security and Safety Equipment) [24595]
Mississippi Tool Supply Co. (Scientific and Measurement Devices) [24398]

Greenville
Friedman Steel Company Inc. (Metals) [19990]
Joe's Firestone Inc. (Automotive) [2823]

Greenwood
Delta Purchasing Federation (Agricultural Equipment and Supplies) [511]
Farmers Supply Cooperative-AAL (Agricultural Equipment and Supplies) [658]
Henderson and Baird Hardware Company Inc. (Household Appliances) [15165]
Nored Cotton Co.; W.H. (Livestock and Farm Products) [18134]
Staple Cotton Cooperative Association (Livestock and Farm Products) [18251]
Union Oil Mill Inc. (Agricultural Equipment and Supplies) [1372]

Grenada
Dixie Auto Auction Inc. (Motorized Vehicles) [20623]
Hankins Lumber Company, Inc. (Construction Materials and Machinery) [7439]

Gulfport
A-1 Battery Distributors (Automotive) [2149]
Anderson-Gemco (Books and Other Printed Materials) [3511]
C & C Distributors (Household Appliances) [15067]
Coastal Energy Co. (Automotive) [2461]
Coca-Cola Bottling Co.; Coast (Soft Drinks) [24933]
Deas Tire Co. (Automotive) [2535]
Dibs Chemical & Supply Co. Inc. (Paper and Paper Products) [21708]
Goldin Industries Inc. (Metals) [20012]
Gulf Coast Software & Systems (Computers and Software) [6318]
Jetfreeze Distributing (Food) [11552]
Kremer Marine (Marine) [18538]
Newman Lumber Co. (Construction Materials and Machinery) [7775]
Ocean Springs Distributors Inc. (Books and Other Printed Materials) [4015]
Periodical Services (Books and Other Printed Materials) [4057]
United Tire Distributors Inc. (Automotive) [3372]
Viking Distributors Inc. (Floorcovering Equipment and Supplies) [10276]
Wade Distributors Inc. (Construction Materials and Machinery) [8190]

Hattiesburg
Caremed (Medical, Dental, and Optical Supplies) [19214]
Grover Brothers Equipment Inc. (Heating and Cooling Equipment and Supplies) [14475]
Hattiesburg Grocery Co. (Food) [11391]
J & J Computer Resources (Computers and Software) [6402]
Komp Equipment Company Inc. (Industrial Machinery) [16217]
Komp Equipment Company Inc. (Chemicals) [4437]
Merchants Co. (Food) [11853]
Sherron Broom & Associates (Computers and Software) [6724]
Southern Farm and Home Center (Agricultural Equipment and Supplies) [1280]

Hazlehurst
Harrell Co.; Hollis (Hardware) [13742]

Hernando
Desoto County Cooperative (Agricultural Equipment and Supplies) [516]

Hollandale
Farm Fresh Catfish Co. (Food) [11084]

Holly Springs
Zocchi Distributors (Toys and Hobby Goods) [26722]

Indianola
Gresham Petroleum Co. (Petroleum, Fuels, and Related Equipment) [22321]
Lewis Grocer Co. (Food) [11707]

Inverness
V and M Cotton Co. (Livestock and Farm Products) [18311]

Jackson
Addkison Hardware Co. Inc. (Hardware) [13533]
American Poultry International Ltd. (Food) [10401]
Benton Ballard Co. (Computers and Software) [6011]
B.J.'s Ceramic Tile Distributing Company, Inc. (Floorcovering Equipment and Supplies) [9729]
Bozeman Distributors (Automotive) [2376]
BPI Inc. (Floorcovering Equipment and Supplies) [9737]
Capitol Corp. (Industrial Supplies) [16779]
Corr-Williams Co. (Tobacco Products) [26281]
Country Originals Inc. (Gifts and Novelties) [13336]
Delta Steel Inc. (Metals) [19924]
Divesco Inc. (Industrial Supplies) [16833]
Equipment Inc. (Industrial Machinery) [15996]
Fashions Inc. Jackson (Clothing) [4947]
FirstMiss Fertilizer Inc. (Agricultural Equipment and Supplies) [686]
Great Southern Industries Inc. (Paper and Paper Products) [21752]
Harris Tire Co. (Automotive) [2728]
Hesselbein Tire Company Inc. (Automotive) [2747]
Irby Co.; Stuart C. (Industrial Supplies) [16964]
Jackson Coca-Cola Bottling Co. (Soft Drinks) [24976]
Jackson Paper Company Inc. (Paper and Paper Products) [21781]
JTM Tile Distributing, Inc. (Floorcovering Equipment and Supplies) [9981]
Lee Tomato Co. (Food) [11694]
May & Company Inc. (Household Appliances) [15218]
McCarty-Holman Company Inc. (Food) [11818]
McLemore Wholesale and Retail Inc. (Food) [11836]
Missco Corporation of Jackson (Furniture and Fixtures) [13183]
Mississippi School Supply Co./MISSCO Corp. (Office Equipment and Supplies) [21148]
Mississippi Serum Distributors (Medical, Dental, and Optical Equipment) [18941]
MS Rubber Co. (Industrial Supplies) [17059]
Natchez Electric Supply (Electrical and Electronic Equipment and Supplies) [9112]
Nitek Metal Service Inc. (Metals) [20227]
Noel's Automotive Warehouse (Automotive) [3036]
OffiSource (Office Equipment and Supplies) [21194]
Prassel Lumber Company Inc. (Construction Materials and Machinery) [7884]
Produce Distributors Co. (Food) [12224]
Puckett Machinery Co. (Construction Materials and Machinery) [7889]
Saunders & Associates; Keifer (Food) [12420]
South Central Pool Supply, Inc. (Recreational and Sporting Goods) [23961]
Southern Beverage Company Inc. (Soft Drinks) [25038]
Southern Ice Equipment Distributor (Industrial Machinery) [16509]
Stribling Equipment Inc. (Agricultural Equipment and Supplies) [1300]
Surplus City USA Inc. (Recreational and Sporting Goods) [23999]
Thomas Company Inc.; Frank R. (Clothing) [5429]
Tri-State Brick and Tile Co. (Construction Materials and Machinery) [8144]
Unitech Inc. (Office Equipment and Supplies) [21326]
United Builders Supply of Jackson Inc. (Construction Materials and Machinery) [8156]
Westland International Corp. (Electrical and Electronic Equipment and Supplies) [9580]
Worldwide Medical (Medical, Dental, and Optical Equipment) [19111]

Lakeshore
Bayou Caddy Fisheries Inc. (Food) [10518]

Laurel
Laurel Center (Construction Materials and Machinery) [7587]
Scruggs & Associates Inc. (Computers and Software) [6713]
Stover Smith Electric Supplies Inc. (Electrical and Electronic Equipment and Supplies) [9425]

Learned
Barrett & Co. Publishers (Books and Other Printed Materials) [3545]

Louisville
D and T Services Inc. (Hardware) [13654]

Madison
Angel Food Ice Cream (Food) [10418]
E & L Steel Co. Inc. (Metals) [19944]
Nsa Independent Distributor (Specialty Equipment and Products) [25767]

Magee

Pace Oil Company Inc. (Petroleum, Fuels, and Related Equipment) [22546]

Marks

Quitman County Farmers Association (Agricultural Equipment and Supplies) [1165]

McComb

Custom Audio (Sound and Entertainment Equipment and Supplies) [25150]
McComb Wholesale Paper Co. (Paper and Paper Products) [21827]
McComb Wholesale Paper Co. (Industrial Supplies) [17020]
Pike County Cooperative (Agricultural Equipment and Supplies) [1130]

Meridian

Carter Girls Fashions Inc. (Clothing) [4866]
Coca-Cola Bottling Co.; Meridian (Soft Drinks) [24937]
Consumer Oil Company of Meridian (Petroleum, Fuels, and Related Equipment) [22162]
Corr-Williams Wholesale Company Inc. (Tobacco Products) [26282]
Henderson Steel Corp. (Metals) [20033]
Hooper Electronics Supply (Electrical and Electronic Equipment and Supplies) [8857]
Kimbrell Ruffer Lumber (Construction Materials and Machinery) [7555]
Long Wholesale Inc. (Food) [11731]
McGinnis Lumber Company Inc. (Construction Materials and Machinery) [7681]
Meridian Mattress Factory Inc. (Furniture and Fixtures) [13178]
Music Emporium Record Co. (Sound and Entertainment Equipment and Supplies) [25346]
Newell Paper Co. (Paper and Paper Products) [21851]
Soule Steam Feed Works (Industrial Machinery) [16505]
Soule Steam Feed Works (Industrial Machinery) [16506]
Southern Electric Supply Company Inc. (Electrical and Electronic Equipment and Supplies) [9387]
Van Zyverden, Inc. (Horticultural Supplies) [14970]

Moss Point

Phase II Distributors Inc. (Toys and Hobby Goods) [26614]

Natchez

Blankenstein Co. Inc.; F.R. (Medical, Dental, and Optical Equipment) [18717]
Buttross Wholesale Co.; A. (Recreational and Sporting Goods) [23578]
Kiri Trading Co. Ltd. (Clothing) [5111]
Natchez Coca-Cola Bottling Co. (Soft Drinks) [24989]
Natchez Equipment Company Inc. (Motorized Vehicles) [20690]
Tanner Forest Products Inc. (Construction Materials and Machinery) [8097]

New Albany

Carr Oil Inc. (Petroleum, Fuels, and Related Equipment) [22109]
Union Grocery Company Inc. (Food) [12786]

Olive Branch

Metro Foods Inc. (Food) [11859]
Unicorn International Inc. (Furniture and Fixtures) [13264]

Pascagoula

Clark Seafood Company Inc. (Food) [10765]
Concrete Products and Supply Co. Inc. (Construction Materials and Machinery) [7203]

Philadelphia

Wells Lamont Corp. (Clothing) [5477]

Picayune

Park Supply Co. Inc. (Household Appliances) [15265]

Port Gibson

Farmers Cooperative Association (Agricultural Equipment and Supplies) [574]

Potts Camp

Ash Woodyard Inc.; J.M. (Wood and Wood Products) [27282]

Ridgeland

Camsco Wholesalers Inc. (Household Appliances) [15072]
Gulf South Medical Supply Inc. (Medical, Dental, and Optical Equipment) [18819]
Specialty Metals Supply Inc. (Metals) [20383]

Rolling Fork

Delta Implement Co. (Agricultural Equipment and Supplies) [510]

Rosedale

Ampco/Rosedale Fabricators (Furniture and Fixtures) [13019]
Rosedale Fabricators/Ampco (Office Equipment and Supplies) [21247]

Sebastopol

Green Acre Farms Inc. (Food) [11318]

Sherman

Morris Scrap Metal Inc. (Used, Scrap, and Recycled Materials) [26917]

Starkville

Clark Inc.; C.C. (Books and Other Printed Materials) [3641]
Northeast Mississippi Coca-Cola Bottling Co. (Soft Drinks) [24997]

Tunica

Whittington Wholesale Company Inc. (Agricultural Equipment and Supplies) [1443]

Tupelo

Hancock Fabrics Inc. (Textiles and Notions) [26054]
Jeter Store Equipment, Inc.; Ken (Heating and Cooling Equipment and Supplies) [14497]
M.W. Manufacturers Inc. (Construction Materials and Machinery) [7756]
Nesco Electrical Distributors Inc. (Electrical and Electronic Equipment and Supplies) [9123]
Tom's Toasted Peanuts (Food) [12730]

Union

Carleton Oil Company Inc. (Paper and Paper Products) [21668]

Vicksburg

Irby Co.; Stuart C. (Electrical and Electronic Equipment and Supplies) [8900]

Waynesboro

Buck & Bass Shop (Recreational and Sporting Goods) [23572]

West Point

Flexible Flyer Co. (Toys and Hobby Goods) [26483]
Haas Outdoors Inc. (Clothing) [5011]
Prairie Livestock L.L.C. (Livestock and Farm Products) [18176]

Woodville

Netterville Lumber; Fred (Construction Materials and Machinery) [7771]

Yazoo City

Kermit Nolan Lumber Sales (Construction Materials and Machinery) [7547]

Missouri

Advance

Mirly Truck Center Inc. (Automotive) [2973]
Southeast Cooperative Service Co. (Livestock and Farm Products) [18243]
Southeast Cooperative Service Co. (Agricultural Equipment and Supplies) [1277]

Alma

Alma Farmers Cooperative Association (Agricultural Equipment and Supplies) [229]

Arnold

Medart Inc. (Automotive) [2938]

Ballwin

HRD International (Food) [11468]
Napoli Foodservices Inc. (Food) [11966]
Roldan Products Corp. (Household Appliances) [15293]
Sinclair & Rush, Inc. (Recreational and Sporting Goods) [23942]

Barnhart

Home Service Oil Company Inc. (Petroleum, Fuels, and Related Equipment) [22361]
Masterchem Industries Inc. (Paints and Varnishes) [21496]

Belton

Cookbook Collection, Inc. (Books and Other Printed Materials) [3660]

Bernie

The IXL Group (Hardware) [13767]

Bolivar

Bolivar Farmers Exchange (Agricultural Equipment and Supplies) [327]
Teters Floral Products Inc. (Horticultural Supplies) [14961]

Bourbon

Reynolds Manufacturing Co. (Clothing) [5308]

Branson

AMS Enterprises (Floorcovering Equipment and Supplies) [9680]
Loyd's Electric Supply Co. (Electrical and Electronic Equipment and Supplies) [9005]
Tri Lakes Petroleum (Petroleum, Fuels, and Related Equipment) [22749]
United School Bus Seat Services (Automotive) [3369]

Braymer

Consumer Oil and Supply Co. (Agricultural Equipment and Supplies) [442]

Bridgeton

Crown Distributing Inc. (Food) [10872]
Gramex Corp. (Clothing) [5000]
Jackson Produce Co. (Food) [11543]
Jaeckle Distributors (Floorcovering Equipment and Supplies) [9977]
Midwest Library Service (Books and Other Printed Materials) [3959]
Midwest Medical Supply Company Inc. (Medical, Dental, and Optical Supplies) [19461]

Buffalo

Dallas County Farmers Exchange (Agricultural Equipment and Supplies) [488]

California

California Manufacturing Co. (Clothing) [4857]

Canton

Ayers Oil Company Inc. (Petroleum, Fuels, and Related Equipment) [22054]

Cape Girardeau

Health Services Corporation of America (Medical, Dental, and Optical Supplies) [19354]
Major Brands-Cape Girardeau (Alcoholic Beverages) [1845]
Motorcycle Stuff Inc. (Automotive) [2997]
Ralston Purina Co., Golden Products Div. (Veterinary Products) [27221]
Rhodes Oil Co. (Petroleum, Fuels, and Related Equipment) [22626]
United Distributing Co. (Petroleum, Fuels, and Related Equipment) [22760]
Wilson Co.; Jim (Automotive) [3440]

Carrollton

Carroll County Equipment Co. (Agricultural Equipment and Supplies) [373]

Carthage

Empiregas Trucking Corp. (Petroleum, Fuels, and Related Equipment) [22229]

Charleston

French Implement Company Inc. (Agricultural Equipment and Supplies) [707]

Chesterfield

Alexander Koetting Poole and Buehrle Inc. (Food) [10363]
CMS Communications Inc. (Communications Systems and Equipment) [5563]
Outdoor Equipment Co. (Agricultural Equipment and Supplies) [1114]
Price Turf Equipment Inc.; Howard (Agricultural Equipment and Supplies) [1150]
Reliv' International Inc. (Health and Beauty Aids) [14213]
Reliv' World Corp. (Food) [12300]
UMPQUA Technology Co. (Chemicals) [4538]

Chillicothe

Cooke Sales and Service Company Inc. (Construction Materials and Machinery) [7214]
Reeds Seeds Inc. (Agricultural Equipment and Supplies) [1178]

Chula

Chula Farmers Cooperative (Agricultural Equipment and Supplies) [417]

Clinton

Farmers Elevator Supply Co. (Agricultural Equipment and Supplies) [647]

Cole Camp

Dowler Enterprises Inc. (Specialty Equipment and Products) [25635]

Columbia

American Audio Prose Library (Books and Other Printed Materials) [3497]
Award Pet Supply (Veterinary Products) [27077]
Boone Distributing (Alcoholic Beverages) [1545]
Major Brands (Alcoholic Beverages) [1843]
MBS Textbook Exchange Inc. (Books and Other Printed Materials) [3941]
MFA Inc. (Agricultural Equipment and Supplies) [1024]
Missouri Archaeological Society Inc. (Books and Other Printed Materials) [3962]
Missouri Archaeological Society Inc. (Books and Other Printed Materials) [3963]
Missouri Power Transmission (Automotive) [2975]
Missouri Swine Export Federation (Livestock and Farm Products) [18106]
Paramount Liquor Co. (Alcoholic Beverages) [1942]
Philips and Co. (Electrical and Electronic Equipment and Supplies) [9195]
Riback Supply Company Inc. (Plumbing Materials and Fixtures) [23340]
South Asia Books (Books and Other Printed Materials) [4172]

Superior Supply Co. (Heating and Cooling Equipment and Supplies) [14706]
University of Missouri Press (Books and Other Printed Materials) [4247]

Concordia

Concordia Farmers Cooperative Co. (Agricultural Equipment and Supplies) [437]

Crane

Stone County Oil Company Inc. (Petroleum, Fuels, and Related Equipment) [22709]

Crestwood

Tallman Company Inc. (Plumbing Materials and Fixtures) [23405]

Curryville

Jennings Implement Company Inc. (Agricultural Equipment and Supplies) [884]

De Soto

Nation Wide Die Steel and Machinery Co. (Industrial Machinery) [16339]

Dexter

Dexter Implement Co. (Agricultural Equipment and Supplies) [518]

Earth City

Beltservice Corp. (Industrial Supplies) [16748]
Everest and Jennings International Ltd. (Medical, Dental, and Optical Supplies) [19310]
Manufacturers Supplies Co. (Industrial Machinery) [16261]
Phoenix Textile Corp. (Textiles and Notions) [26176]
Three States (Heating and Cooling Equipment and Supplies) [14727]

Elsberry

Forrest-Keeling Nursery (Horticultural Supplies) [14870]

Excelsior Springs

AIPC (Food) [10349]

Fenton

Blue Lustre, LLC (Cleaning and Janitorial Supplies) [4584]
Convenience Products (Construction Materials and Machinery) [7212]
Erb Equipment Company Inc. (Construction Materials and Machinery) [7315]
Fabick Tractor Co.; John (Construction Materials and Machinery) [7330]
Gross and Janes Co. (Railroad Equipment and Supplies) [23480]
Lee-Rowan Co. (Storage Equipment and Containers) [25927]
Machine Maintenance Inc. (Construction Materials and Machinery) [7632]
Peterson Business Systems Inc. (Office Equipment and Supplies) [21212]
Peterson Spacecrafters (Office Equipment and Supplies) [21213]
Power Torque (Automotive) [3112]
St. Louis Business Forms Inc. (Office Equipment and Supplies) [21256]
Tacony Corp. (Household Appliances) [15328]
Wolff Shoe Co. (Shoes) [24897]

Florissant

Schulte Paint (Paints and Varnishes) [21560]
Sugar Records (Sound and Entertainment Equipment and Supplies) [25468]

Fordland

Gingery Publishing; David J. (Books and Other Printed Materials) [3780]

Forsyth

National Enzyme Co. (Food) [11976]

Glasgow

Glasgow Cooperative Association (Agricultural Equipment and Supplies) [742]

Grain Valley

Consolidated Asset Management Company Inc. (Railroad Equipment and Supplies) [23476]

Grandview

Citywide Floor Service (Floorcovering Equipment and Supplies) [9807]
House of Lloyd Inc. (Gifts and Novelties) [13372]
King Louie International Inc. (Clothing) [5110]

Hannibal

Duffens Optical (Medical, Dental, and Optical Supplies) [19293]

Hayti

Mid Continent Aircraft Corp. (Aeronautical Equipment and Supplies) [128]

Hazelwood

Pentecostal Publishing House (Books and Other Printed Materials) [4053]

Independence

Custom Car Center (Motorized Vehicles) [20618]
Herald House/Independence Press (Books and Other Printed Materials) [3823]
Manneco, Inc. (Gifts and Novelties) [13395]

Jackson

Shawneetown Feed and Seed (Agricultural Equipment and Supplies) [1263]

Jasper

Jasper Farmers Exchange Inc. (Agricultural Equipment and Supplies) [880]

Jefferson City

Jefferson City Oil Company Inc. (Petroleum, Fuels, and Related Equipment) [22386]
Scheppers Distributing; N.H. (Alcoholic Beverages) [2011]

Joplin

Acme Brick, Tile and More (Construction Materials and Machinery) [6908]
Belden Electric Co.; Russell (Office Equipment and Supplies) [20839]
General Steel Fabricators (Metals) [19997]
Good News Productions, International (Sound and Entertainment Equipment and Supplies) [25214]
McDonald Supply Co.; A.Y. (Heating and Cooling Equipment and Supplies) [14537]
Sebastian Equipment Company Inc. (Industrial Machinery) [16478]
Superior Supply Co. (Heating and Cooling Equipment and Supplies) [14708]

Kansas City

AFI (Agricultural Equipment and Supplies) [191]
Akin Medical Equipment International (Medical, Dental, and Optical Supplies) [19128]
American Farm & Feed (Agricultural Equipment and Supplies) [232]
Arrow Truck Sales Inc. (Agricultural Equipment and Supplies) [256]
Associated Bearings (Industrial Machinery) [15783]
Barclay Marine Distributors Corp. (Marine) [18455]
Bartlett and Co. (Headquarters) (Livestock and Farm Products) [17725]
Batliner Paper Stock Co. (Paper and Paper Products) [21646]
Blankinship Distributors Inc. (Health and Beauty Aids) [14050]
Blankinship Distributors Inc. (Medical, Dental, and Optical Supplies) [19193]
Borel Jules & Co. (Jewelry) [17347]
Boyle Meat Co. (Food) [10604]
Carpet Factory Outlet (Floorcovering Equipment and Supplies) [9768]
Carter-Waters Corp. (Construction Materials and Machinery) [7149]

Case Supply, Inc. (Floorcovering Equipment and Supplies) [9776]

Cimarron Lumber and Supply Co. (Construction Materials and Machinery) [7172]

Cimarron Lumber and Supply Co. (Wood and Wood Products) [27297]

Comet Industries Inc. (Industrial Machinery) [15901]

CR Specialty Co. (Guns and Weapons) [13484]

Dean Machinery Co. (Agricultural Equipment and Supplies) [502]

DeBruce Grain Inc. (Livestock and Farm Products) [17814]

DIT-MCO International Corp. (Electrical and Electronic Equipment and Supplies) [8629]

Egerstrom Inc. (Food) [11033]

Electronics Supply Co. (Electrical and Electronic Equipment and Supplies) [8696]

Epstein Co.; Harry J. (Hardware) [13686]

Farmland Grain Div. (Livestock and Farm Products) [17912]

Fineline Products, Inc. (Office Equipment and Supplies) [21004]

Fleming Companies Inc. Heartland Div. (Food) [11150]

Foley-Belsaw Co. (Hardware) [13713]

Force America Inc. (Industrial Machinery) [16028]

Frederick Manufacturing Corp. (Agricultural Equipment and Supplies) [704]

Function Junction Inc. (Household Items) [15509]

Gabor International Ltd.; Eva (Health and Beauty Aids) [14107]

Gooch Brake and Equipment Co. (Automotive) [2690]

Hanna Rubber Co. (Rubber) [24280]

High Life Sales Co. (Alcoholic Beverages) [1755]

Horsepower Control System (Automotive) [2761]

Industrial Parts Distributors Inc. (Automotive) [2774]

Inland Truck Parts (Automotive) [2783]

Interstate Brands Corp. Dolly Madison Cakes Div. (Food) [11527]

Kansas City Auto Auction Inc. (Motorized Vehicles) [20658]

Kansas City Auto Auction Inc. (Automotive) [2838]

Kansas City Bolt, Nut and Screw Co. (Hardware) [13780]

Kansas City Rubber and Belting Co. (Rubber) [24283]

Kansas City Rubber and Belting Co. (Industrial Supplies) [16978]

Knit-Rite Inc. (Medical, Dental, and Optical Equipment) [18877]

Lift Truck Sales and Service Inc. (Industrial Machinery) [16233]

Major Brands (Alcoholic Beverages) [1844]

Mallin Brothers Company Inc. (Used, Scrap, and Recycled Materials) [26894]

Metro Crown International (Aeronautical Equipment and Supplies) [124]

Mid-America Industrial Equipment Co. (Industrial Machinery) [16294]

Mid-States Supply Company Inc. (Plumbing Materials and Fixtures) [23267]

Midwest Sales Company of Iowa Inc. (Construction Materials and Machinery) [7708]

Missouri Conrad Liquors (Alcoholic Beverages) [1884]

Missouri Valley Electric Co. (Electrical and Electronic Equipment and Supplies) [9089]

Modern Distributing Co. (Agricultural Equipment and Supplies) [1044]

National Art Supply (Specialty Equipment and Products) [25748]

National Equipment Co. (Furniture and Fixtures) [13186]

Nazarene Publishing House (Books and Other Printed Materials) [3989]

Nielsen Co. Inc.; E.A. (Construction Materials and Machinery) [7779]

Pacific Mutual Door Co. (Construction Materials and Machinery) [7825]

Paxton Co.; Frank (Wood and Wood Products) [27355]

Phillips Co.; Victor L. (Construction Materials and Machinery) [7860]

Precision Built Parts (Automotive) [3115]

Regal Plastic Supply Co. Kansas City Div. (Plastics) [23023]

Reliance Paper Co. (Paper and Paper Products) [21901]

Rexel Glasco (Electrical and Electronic Equipment and Supplies) [9285]

Rice of Kansas City Inc.; Scott (Office Equipment and Supplies) [21240]

Richards and Conover Steel Co. (Metals) [20320]

Rival/Pollenex (Health and Beauty Aids) [14222]

Roberts Dairy Co. (Food) [12329]

Russell Stover Candies (Food) [12367]

Russell Stover Candies (Food) [12368]

S and S Meat Company Inc. (Food) [12383]

Scherer Truck Equipment, Inc. (Automotive) [3193]

Schutte Lumber Company Inc. (Construction Materials and Machinery) [7990]

Schutte Lumber Company Inc. (Wood and Wood Products) [27370]

Steel Manufacturing and Warehouse Co. (Metals) [20397]

Summers Sales Company Inc.; Barney (Food) [12600]

Sun Imports Inc. (Alcoholic Beverages) [2060]

Superior Wines and Liquors Inc. (Alcoholic Beverages) [2063]

VID COM Distributing (Electrical and Electronic Equipment and Supplies) [9536]

VID COM Distributing (Electrical and Electronic Equipment and Supplies) [9537]

VLP Holding Co. (Construction Materials and Machinery) [8188]

Waechtersbach U.S.A. (Household Items) [15699]

West Agro Inc. (Chemicals) [4552]

Western Extralite Co. (Electrical and Electronic Equipment and Supplies) [9575]

Wolcott and Lincoln Inc. (Livestock and Farm Products) [18357]

Wolcott and Lincoln Inc. (Food) [12971]

Xebec Corp. (Electrical and Electronic Equipment and Supplies) [9613]

Kearney

Mr. Dell Foods, Inc. (Food) [11950]

Variform Inc. (Construction Materials and Machinery) [8173]

Kennett

Baker Implement Co. (Agricultural Equipment and Supplies) [272]

Baker Implement Co. (Agricultural Equipment and Supplies) [273]

Kennett Liquid Fertilizer Co. (Agricultural Equipment and Supplies) [903]

Riggs Supply Co. (Hardware) [13886]

Kirkwood

Impact Christian Books Inc. (Books and Other Printed Materials) [3839]

Lake Winnebago

Custom Design Play Structures Inc. (Recreational and Sporting Goods) [23612]

Lebanon

D & A Distributing (Automotive) [2519]

MFA Agriservice (Agricultural Equipment and Supplies) [1023]

Lees Summit

FTG Manufacturing (Recreational and Sporting Goods) [23678]

M.F.A. Oil Co. (Petroleum, Fuels, and Related Equipment) [22479]

R.S.B.I. Aerospace Inc. (Aeronautical Equipment and Supplies) [143]

Lewistown

Heetco Inc. (Petroleum, Fuels, and Related Equipment) [22342]

Liberty

Douglas Products and Packaging Co. (Chemicals) [4374]

Ferrellgas Partners L.P. (Petroleum, Fuels, and Related Equipment) [22274]

Linn Creek

Superior Supply Co. (Heating and Cooling Equipment and Supplies) [14707]

Lockwood

Lockwood Farmers Exchange Inc. (Agricultural Equipment and Supplies) [965]

Louisiana

Abel's Quik Shops (Petroleum, Fuels, and Related Equipment) [22018]

Allparts Inc. (Automotive) [2218]

Midwest Veneer Company (Construction Materials and Machinery) [7709]

Marble Hill

Crader Distributing Co. (Industrial Machinery) [15917]

Napsac Reproductions (Books and Other Printed Materials) [3981]

Marshall

Hahn and Phillips Grease Company Inc. (Livestock and Farm Products) [17968]

Martinsburg

Martinsburg Farmers Elevator Co. (Livestock and Farm Products) [18075]

Maryland Heights

Acme Brick Co. (Construction Materials and Machinery) [6907]

Acosta-PMI St. Louis Div. (Food) [10321]

Adderton Brokerage Co. (Food) [10325]

Benson Pump Co. (Recreational and Sporting Goods) [23546]

Engineered Sales Inc. (Industrial Machinery) [15991]

Flo-Products Co. (Industrial Supplies) [16868]

Ford Steel Co (Metals) [19981]

Grey Eagle Distributors Inc. (Alcoholic Beverages) [1733]

Manhattan Distributing Co. (Alcoholic Beverages) [1847]

Matthes and Associates (Food) [11806]

Matthews Book Co. (Books and Other Printed Materials) [3940]

Misco Shawnee Inc. (Floorcovering Equipment and Supplies) [10042]

Misco Shawnee Inc. (Household Items) [15589]

Monarch Tile (Floorcovering Equipment and Supplies) [10053]

Progressive Wholesale Supply Co. (Heating and Cooling Equipment and Supplies) [14644]

Streett and Company Inc.; J.D. (Petroleum, Fuels, and Related Equipment) [22710]

Maryville

Williams Lawn Seed, Inc. (Agricultural Equipment and Supplies) [1452]

Mexico

M & M Vehicle Co. (Recreational and Sporting Goods) [23794]

McGee's Packing Co. (Food) [11827]

Moberly

Mid-AM Building Supply Inc. (Construction Materials and Machinery) [7704]

Orscheln Farm and Home Supply Inc. (Agricultural Equipment and Supplies) [1109]

Monett

Friend Tire Co. (Automotive) [2650]

Monroe City

White Electric Supply Co. (Monroe City, Missouri) (Electrical and Electronic Equipment and Supplies) [9584]

Mt. Sterling

Schaeperkoetter Store Inc. (Computers and Software) [6711]

Neelyville

James Agriculture Center Inc. (Agricultural Equipment and Supplies) [878]

Nevada

Tuf-Nut Company Inc. (Clothing) [5444]

New Haven

New Haven Filter Co. (Automotive) [3028]

Newtown

Fowler Elevator Inc. (Livestock and Farm Products) [17922]

North Kansas City

Chapman Co.; J.T. (Automotive) [2444]
Cook Composites and Polymers Co. (Chemicals) [4364]
Davis Paint Co. (Paints and Varnishes) [21426]
Ebling Distribution, Inc. (Floorcovering Equipment and Supplies) [9881]
General Heating and Cooling Co. (Heating and Cooling Equipment and Supplies) [14459]
Grinnell Supply Sales Co. (Plumbing Materials and Fixtures) [23199]
Herregan Distributors Inc. (Floorcovering Equipment and Supplies) [9945]
Merchandise International (Electrical and Electronic Equipment and Supplies) [9066]
Midwest Bolt and Supply Inc. (Hardware) [13828]
National Manufacturing, Inc. (Construction Materials and Machinery) [7766]
O'Connor Company, Inc. (Heating and Cooling Equipment and Supplies) [14627]
Refrigeration Equipment Co. (Heating and Cooling Equipment and Supplies) [14655]
Regal Plastic Supply Co. (Plastics) [23022]
Siggins Co. (Industrial Machinery) [16490]

O Fallon

Southern Cross and O'Fallon Building Products Co. (Hardware) [13929]
Southern Cross and O'Fallon Building Products Co. (Construction Materials and Machinery) [8049]

Ozark

Hagale Industries Inc. (Clothing) [5013]

Pevely

Dunns Sporting Goods Co. Inc. (Recreational and Sporting Goods) [23634]

Pleasant Hill

Central Cooperatives Inc. (Agricultural Equipment and Supplies) [387]

Poplar Bluff

Duckett Truck Center Inc. (Motorized Vehicles) [20627]
Riggs Wholesale Supply (Construction Materials and Machinery) [7934]

Portage Des Sioux

Universal Marine (Marine) [18628]

Powell

Brumley & Sons; Albert E. (Books and Other Printed Materials) [3596]

Raytown

Sun Aviation Inc. (Aeronautical Equipment and Supplies) [153]

Richmond

Ray-Carroll County Grain Growers Inc. (Agricultural Equipment and Supplies) [1169]
Tippins Oil and Gas Company Inc. (Petroleum, Fuels, and Related Equipment) [22737]

Rockville

Mott Meat Company, Inc. (Food) [11939]

St. Charles

St. Charles County Cooperative Co. (Veterinary Products) [27227]

St. Clair

Par-Way/Tryson Co. (Restaurant and Commercial Foodservice Equipment and Supplies) [24202]

St. Joseph

American Electric Co. (Electrical and Electronic Equipment and Supplies) [8340]
American Electric Co. (Electrical and Electronic Equipment and Supplies) [8342]
Midland Bottling Co. (Alcoholic Beverages) [1874]
Research Seeds Inc. (Agricultural Equipment and Supplies) [1182]
Ross-Frazer Supply Co. (Hardware) [13895]
Royal Seeds Inc. (Agricultural Equipment and Supplies) [1217]
Smith Drug Co.; C.D. (Health and Beauty Aids) [14239]
Superior Supply Co. (Heating and Cooling Equipment and Supplies) [14705]
United Pharmacal Co. (Veterinary Products) [27257]

St. Louis

A.A. Importing Co. Inc. (Furniture and Fixtures) [13009]
Abana Pharmaceuticals Inc. (Medical, Dental, and Optical Supplies) [19118]
Adams Printing and Stationery Co.; S.G. (Office Equipment and Supplies) [20772]
Affinitec Corp. (Computers and Software) [5893]
Ahrens and McCarron Inc. (Plumbing Materials and Fixtures) [23054]
Alcan Aluminum Corp. Metal Goods Service Center Div. (Metals) [19742]
Allen Foods Inc. (Food) [10370]
Allied Construction Equipment Co. (Construction Materials and Machinery) [6943]
Allied Industrial Equipment Corp. (Industrial Machinery) [15757]
Alter Trading Corp. (Used, Scrap, and Recycled Materials) [26748]
AMC Tile Supply (Construction Materials and Machinery) [6954]
American Foundry and Manufacturing Co. (Plumbing Materials and Fixtures) [23063]
American Loose Leaf Business Products Inc. (Office Equipment and Supplies) [20793]
American Recreation Products Inc. (Recreational and Sporting Goods) [23513]
Anheuser-Busch Inc. (Alcoholic Beverages) [1485]
Apex Oil Co. (Petroleum, Fuels, and Related Equipment) [22039]
Arch Coal Sales Company Inc. (Minerals and Ores) [20519]
Arnold Inc.; S.M. (Automotive) [2251]
Autco (Security and Safety Equipment) [24510]
Authorized Motor Parts (Automotive) [2268]
Authorized Refrigeration Parts Co. (Heating and Cooling Equipment and Supplies) [14329]
Bee Hat Co. (Clothing) [4812]
Bensinger's (Food) [10537]
The Booksource (Books and Other Printed Materials) [3583]
Borton Brokerage Co. (Food) [10595]
Brauer Supply Co. (Heating and Cooling Equipment and Supplies) [14358]
Brauner Export Co. (Electrical and Electronic Equipment and Supplies) [8466]
Breckenridge Material (Construction Materials and Machinery) [7078]
The Brightman Co. (Household Appliances) [15059]
Broadway Office Interiors (Office Equipment and Supplies) [20856]
Brod-Dugan Co./Sherwin Williams Co. (Paints and Varnishes) [21407]
Brown Group Inc. (Shoes) [24699]
Brown Shoe Co. (Shoes) [24700]

Bunge Corp. (Livestock and Farm Products) [17754]
Bunzl Distribution Inc. (Paper and Paper Products) [21658]
Buschart Office Products Inc. (Office Equipment and Supplies) [20865]
Buy-Rite Petroleum Ltd. (Petroleum, Fuels, and Related Equipment) [22099]
Cahokia Flour Co. (Food) [10662]
Capital GBS Communications Corp. (Communications Systems and Equipment) [5545]
Cee Kay Supply Co. (Industrial Supplies) [16786]
Center Oil Co. (Petroleum, Fuels, and Related Equipment) [22121]
Cereal Byproducts Co. (Agricultural Equipment and Supplies) [404]
Cereal Byproducts Co. (Agricultural Equipment and Supplies) [405]
Chalice Press (Books and Other Printed Materials) [3624]
Christy Refractories Co. L.L.C. (Construction Materials and Machinery) [7171]
Community Tire Co. Inc. (Automotive) [2468]
Component Technology (Industrial Machinery) [15905]
Computer Sales International Inc. (Computers and Software) [6124]
Concordia Publishing House (Books and Other Printed Materials) [3651]
Contico International Inc. (Hardware) [13643]
Conveyor & Drive Equipment (Industrial Machinery) [15914]
Crown Foods Inc. (Food) [10873]
Cummings, McGowan and West Inc. (Construction Materials and Machinery) [7236]
Cummins Gateway Inc. (Automotive) [2505]
Curtis Toledo Inc. (Compressors) [5838]
D-Chem Corp. (Chemicals) [4369]
D & K Healthcare Resources, Inc. (Medical, Dental, and Optical Supplies) [19269]
Dealer Chemical Corp. (Automotive) [2533]
Elan-Polo Inc. (Shoes) [24732]
Electrorep Energy Products Inc. (Electrical and Electronic Equipment and Supplies) [8697]
Energy Group P.L.C. (Minerals and Ores) [20539]
Ermco Inc. (Plumbing Materials and Fixtures) [23151]
Falcon Products Inc. (Furniture and Fixtures) [13109]
Forgy Process Instruments Inc. (Plumbing Materials and Fixtures) [23172]
Foster Company of St. Louis Inc.; John Henry (Industrial Machinery) [16036]
Fresh Fish Company Inc. (Food) [11208]
Garco Wine (Alcoholic Beverages) [1704]
Gared Sports Inc. (Recreational and Sporting Goods) [23683]
Gateway Seed Co. (Agricultural Equipment and Supplies) [729]
Goedecke Company Inc.; Vernon L. (Construction Materials and Machinery) [7401]
Goldman Associates Inc. (Gifts and Novelties) [13364]
GPX Inc. (Electrical and Electronic Equipment and Supplies) [8798]
GPX Inc. (Household Appliances) [15151]
GPX Inc. (St. Louis, Missouri) (Sound and Entertainment Equipment and Supplies) [25218]
Graybar Electric Company Inc. (Electrical and Electronic Equipment and Supplies) [8814]
Greenstreak Inc. (Plastics) [22975]
Greenstreak Plastic Products (Plastics) [22976]
Grossman Iron and Steel Co. (Metals) [20023]
Group One Capital Inc. (Health and Beauty Aids) [14117]
Hager Companies (Hardware) [13732]
Hall Inc.; Melville B. (Electrical and Electronic Equipment and Supplies) [8823]
Hammond Sheet Metal Company Inc. (Heating and Cooling Equipment and Supplies) [14477]
Hautly Cheese Company Inc. (Food) [11392]
Heap Lumber Sales Company Inc. (Construction Materials and Machinery) [7465]
Hispania Trading Corporation (Specialty Equipment and Products) [25680]

Illmo Rx Service Inc. (Medical, Dental, and Optical Supplies) [19367]

Industrial Soap Co. (Cleaning and Janitorial Supplies) [4639]

Industrial Vision Corp. (Medical, Dental, and Optical Supplies) [19370]

Interstate Brands Corp. (Food) [11525]

Interstate Supply Co. (Floorcovering Equipment and Supplies) [9971]

Intoximeters Inc. (Scientific and Measurement Devices) [24376]

Italgrani Elevator Co. (Livestock and Farm Products) [18014]

Johnson Heater Corp. (Heating and Cooling Equipment and Supplies) [14499]

Kataman Metals Inc. (Metals) [20088]

Keefe Supply Co. (Restaurant and Commercial Foodservice Equipment and Supplies) [24154]

Kranson Industries (Storage Equipment and Containers) [25923]

Kranz Automotive Supply (Automotive) [2863]

La Barge Pipe and Steel (Metals) [20113]

Lapham-Hickey Steel Corp. (Metals) [20116]

Lay International Consulting Services (Heating and Cooling Equipment and Supplies) [14517]

Lee Brothers Corp. (Health and Beauty Aids) [14151]

Lowy Group Inc. (Floorcovering Equipment and Supplies) [10002]

Lumberyard Supply Co. (Construction Materials and Machinery) [7622]

Mahne Company Inc.; William P. (Household Items) [15573]

Major Brands (Alcoholic Beverages) [1842]

Management Techniques Inc. (Computers and Software) [6457]

Manhattan Coffee Co. (Food) [11774]

Manufacturers Steel Supply Company Inc. (Metals) [20149]

Marco Sales Inc. (Heating and Cooling Equipment and Supplies) [14531]

Marcone Appliance Parts Center Inc. (Household Appliances) [15213]

Markwort Sporting Goods Co. (Recreational and Sporting Goods) [23803]

Matthews Hinsman Co. (Textiles and Notions) [26138]

Mercantile Sales Company Inc. (Recreational and Sporting Goods) [23822]

Metal Commodities Inc. (Computers and Software) [6488]

Metal Recovery Systems Inc. (Used, Scrap, and Recycled Materials) [26904]

Metalsco Inc. (Used, Scrap, and Recycled Materials) [26905]

Midvale Industries Inc. (Industrial Machinery) [16297]

Midwest Floors (Floorcovering Equipment and Supplies) [10033]

Millman Lumber Co. (Construction Materials and Machinery) [7717]

Mississippi Valley Equipment Co. (Construction Materials and Machinery) [7728]

Missouri Petroleum Products (Petroleum, Fuels, and Related Equipment) [22488]

Missouri Pipe Fittings Co. (Plumbing Materials and Fixtures) [23269]

Missouri Power Transmission (Automotive) [2976]

Mitek Industries Inc. (Industrial Machinery) [16311]

MMB Music Inc. (Sound and Entertainment Equipment and Supplies) [25330]

Mobile Power and Hydraulics (Industrial Machinery) [16315]

Moore Food Distributors Inc. (Food) [11930]

Morgan-Wightman Supply Company (Construction Materials and Machinery) [7747]

Mound City Industries Inc. (Food) [11940]

Mozel Inc. (Chemicals) [4463]

Ness Trading Co. (Automotive) [3026]

Nu-Way Concrete Forms Inc. (Construction Materials and Machinery) [7801]

Oilfield Pipe and Supply Inc. (Metals) [20244]

Pagoda Trading Co. (Shoes) [24828]

Paint Supply Co. (Paints and Varnishes) [21529]

Peabody COALSALES Co. (Minerals and Ores) [20557]

Peabody Group (Minerals and Ores) [20558]

Pioneer Industrial Corp. (Industrial Supplies) [17105]

Plaza Fleet Parts (Automotive) [3099]

PMI-Eisenhart, St. Louis Div. (Food) [12184]

Power Drive & Equipment (Automotive) [3106]

PowerSolutions for Business (Computers and Software) [6631]

Prairie Farms Dairy Inc. Ice Cream Specialties Div. (Food) [12205]

Pro-Visions Pet Specialty Enterprises Div. (Veterinary Products) [27217]

PRODUCT4 (Computers and Software) [6648]

Rancilio Associates (Electrical and Electronic Equipment and Supplies) [9262]

Refrigeration Supply Inc. (Furniture and Fixtures) [13217]

Reis Environmental Inc. (Security and Safety Equipment) [24617]

Road Tested Recycled Auto Parts Inc. (Automotive) [3167]

Royal Prestige of Missouri Inc. (Household Items) [15643]

Saettele Jewelers Inc. (Jewelry) [17583]

St. Louis Coke and Foundry (Industrial Supplies) [17156]

St. Louis Music Supply Co. (Sound and Entertainment Equipment and Supplies) [25425]

St. Louis Paper and Box Co. (Paper and Paper Products) [21921]

St. Louis Paper and Box Co. (Industrial Supplies) [17157]

Saint Louis Restaurant Steaks Inc. (Food) [12390]

St. Louis Screw and Bolt Co. (Plumbing Materials and Fixtures) [23356]

St. Louis Trimming (Textiles and Notions) [26197]

Schillers Photo Graphics (Photographic Equipment and Supplies) [22903]

Schuco Inc. (Medical, Dental, and Optical Equipment) [19034]

Semmelmeyer-Corby Co. (Industrial Supplies) [17165]

Senrenella Enterprises Inc. (Livestock and Farm Products) [18229]

Shehan-Cary Lumber Co. (Construction Materials and Machinery) [8008]

Shehan-Cary Lumber Co. (Wood and Wood Products) [27375]

Showcase Kitchens and Baths Inc. (Plumbing Materials and Fixtures) [23373]

Siboney Learning Group (Computers and Software) [6726]

Sidener Supply Co. (Specialty Equipment and Products) [25815]

Slay Industries Inc. (Livestock and Farm Products) [18235]

Southside Recycling Inc. (Used, Scrap, and Recycled Materials) [27006]

Southwest Steel Supply Co. (Metals) [20378]

Sportsprint Inc. (Clothing) [5389]

Stange Co. (Jewelry) [17618]

State Electric Company Inc. (Automotive) [3263]

SWM Inc. (Paper and Paper Products) [21951]

Thau-Nolde Inc. (Medical, Dental, and Optical Supplies) [19654]

Thomas and Proetz Lumber Co. (Construction Materials and Machinery) [8122]

Tober Industries Inc. (Shoes) [24877]

Todd Uniform Inc. (Clothing) [5432]

Tri-Star Industrial Supply Inc. (Industrial Machinery) [16580]

Tricor Braun - Div. of Kranson (Storage Equipment and Containers) [25945]

Truck Equipment Co. (Automotive) [3345]

Tubular Steel Inc. (Metals) [20446]

Unique Crafters Co. (Gifts and Novelties) [13465]

Unisource-Central Region Div. (Paper and Paper Products) [21966]

United Electric Supply Co. (Electrical and Electronic Equipment and Supplies) [9522]

United Fruit and Produce Company Inc. (Food) [12795]

U.S. Ring Binder Corp. (Office Equipment and Supplies) [21330]

Universal Sewing Supply Inc. (Household Appliances) [15350]

US Office Products, Midwest District Inc. (Office Equipment and Supplies) [21331]

Valley Farm Dairy Co. (Food) [12816]

ValuNet Div. (Medical, Dental, and Optical Equipment) [19099]

Villa Lighting Supply Company Inc. (Electrical and Electronic Equipment and Supplies) [9540]

Waggener Lumber Co. (Construction Materials and Machinery) [8191]

Wallace Inc.; Gary L. (Specialty Equipment and Products) [25870]

Weber Industries Inc. (Industrial Machinery) [16617]

Wise El Santo Company Inc. (Clothing) [5490]

Wolf Imports (Sound and Entertainment Equipment and Supplies) [25527]

Word Technology Systems Inc. (Office Equipment and Supplies) [21363]

World Communications Inc. (Communications Systems and Equipment) [5819]

Young Sales Corp. (Construction Materials and Machinery) [8251]

Zeller Electric Inc. (Automotive) [3453]

Zeuschel Equipment Co. (Scientific and Measurement Devices) [24462]

Zeuschel Equipment Co. (Scientific and Measurement Devices) [24464]

St. Peters

G and S Motors Inc. (Motorized Vehicles) [20640]

Kaplan Lumber Company Inc. (Construction Materials and Machinery) [7542]

Scott City

Wetterau Inc. (Food) [12920]

Sedalia

AG Cooperative Service Inc. (Livestock and Farm Products) [17678]

Baker Agri Sales Inc. (Livestock and Farm Products) [17718]

Kim Originals Inc. (Horticultural Supplies) [14905]

Sedalia Implement Company Inc. (Agricultural Equipment and Supplies) [1249]

Sikeston

Home Oil Company of Sikeston Inc. (Petroleum, Fuels, and Related Equipment) [22359]

J.R.M. Inc. (Office Equipment and Supplies) [21082]

Slater

Cooperative Association No. 1 Inc. (Agricultural Equipment and Supplies) [449]

Smithville

Halferty and Sons Inc.; H.H. (Agricultural Equipment and Supplies) [782]

Springfield

Acme Brick Co. (Floorcovering Equipment and Supplies) [9642]

Audio Acoustics (Sound and Entertainment Equipment and Supplies) [25086]

Banta Foods Inc. (Food) [10499]

Best Bilt Parts (Automotive) [2353]

Bossi Sales Co. Inc. (Alcoholic Beverages) [1546]

Bryant and Blount Oil Co. (Petroleum, Fuels, and Related Equipment) [22097]

Chock Full o'Nuts (Food) [10753]

Gospel Publishing House (Books and Other Printed Materials) [3791]

Haik's Inc. (Textiles and Notions) [26052]

Hoag Enterprises, Inc. (Photographic Equipment and Supplies) [22865]

Hubbell Mechanical Supply Co. (Heating and Cooling Equipment and Supplies) [14490]

Huntco Steel Inc. (Metals) [20047]

Interior Specialties of the Ozarks (Floorcovering Equipment and Supplies) [9966]

International Division, Inc. (Agricultural Equipment and Supplies) [863]

Johnston Industrial Supply Co. (Industrial Machinery) [16190]

Keltner Enterprises Inc. (Automotive) [2846]

Martin Co.; E.A. (Construction Materials and Machinery) [7652]

Martin Co.; E.A. (Construction Materials and Machinery) [7653]

McQueary Brothers Drug Co. (Medical, Dental, and Optical Equipment) [18906]

Mid-America Dairymen Inc. Southern Div. (Food) [11875]

Missouri Export Trading Company (Industrial Machinery) [16308]

Montgomery GMC Trucks Inc. (Motorized Vehicles) [20686]

National Audio Company Inc. (Sound and Entertainment Equipment and Supplies) [25353]

Nattinger Materials Co. (Construction Materials and Machinery) [7769]

O'Reilly Automotive Inc. (Automotive) [3064]

Ozark Automotive Distributors Inc. (Automotive) [3066]

Packers Distributing Co. (Food) [12096]

Quinn Coffee Co. (Food) [12257]

Reliable Chevrolet Inc. (Motorized Vehicles) [20710]

Rose Metal Products Inc. (Metals) [20331]

Self's, Inc. (Floorcovering Equipment and Supplies) [10143]

SJL Beverage Co. (Alcoholic Beverages) [2027]

Springfield Grocer Company Inc. (Food) [12558]

Springfield Paper Co. (Paper and Paper Products) [21947]

Tindle Mills Inc. (Agricultural Equipment and Supplies) [1337]

Walker and Son Inc.; P.G. (Industrial Supplies) [17262]

Stockton
Hammons Products Co. (Food) [11369]

Stover
Stover Greenlight Auto & Marine (Marine) [18618]

Sullivan
Ditch Witch Sales Inc. (Construction Materials and Machinery) [7270]

Sweet Springs
Emma Cooperative Elevator Co. (Veterinary Products) [27129]

Emma Cooperative Elevator Co. (Agricultural Equipment and Supplies) [551]

Thayer
Cover and Son Wholesale Lumber Inc.; H.A. (Construction Materials and Machinery) [7225]

Trenton
Bond Wholesale, Inc. (Tobacco Products) [26266]

Hoffman and Reed Inc. (Agricultural Equipment and Supplies) [830]

Troy
Hutchinson & Associates, Inc.; Roger J. (Recreational and Sporting Goods) [23737]

Lincoln County Farmers Cooperative (Agricultural Equipment and Supplies) [960]

Tuscumbia
Pryor Novelty Co., Inc. (Gifts and Novelties) [13430]

Warrensburg
Team Up (Books and Other Printed Materials) [4205]

Washington
Paperbacks for Educators (Books and Other Printed Materials) [4038]

Wayland
Logsdon Service Inc. (Livestock and Farm Products) [18063]

West Plains
Jeffers Vet Supply (Veterinary Products) [27161]

Weston
McCormick Distilling Company Inc. (Alcoholic Beverages) [1860]

Windyville
SOM Publishing (Books and Other Printed Materials) [4170]

Woodson Terrace
IBT Inc. (Industrial Machinery) [16137]

Montana

Alder
McLeod Merchantile Inc. (Petroleum, Fuels, and Related Equipment) [22469]

Arlee
Montana Naturals Int'l. Inc. (Food) [11928]

Baker
Jacobson Cattle Co. (Livestock and Farm Products) [18018]

Belgrade
AF & T Salvage (Automotive) [2186]

Kamp Implement Co. (Agricultural Equipment and Supplies) [896]

Bigfork
Valley Coin Laundry Equipment Co. (Cleaning and Janitorial Supplies) [4722]

Billings
A 1 Accredited Batteries (Automotive) [2148]

A & H Turf & Specialties Inc. (Hardware) [13519]

Altimus Distributing (Cleaning and Janitorial Supplies) [4569]

Automated Office Systems Inc. (Office Equipment and Supplies) [20824]

B & J Cattle Co. (Livestock and Farm Products) [17716]

B & L Scales (Scientific and Measurement Devices) [24320]

Bevco Inc. (Plastics) [22936]

Big Sky Auto Auction Inc. (Motorized Vehicles) [20601]

Big Sky Auto Auction Inc. (Automotive) [2360]

Big Sky Office Products Inc. (Office Equipment and Supplies) [20843]

Billings Truck Center (Motorized Vehicles) [20602]

Bromar Montana/Wyoming (Food) [10617]

Business Data Systems Inc. (Office Equipment and Supplies) [20866]

BYE Inc. (Alcoholic Beverages) [1562]

Carquest Distribution Co. (Automotive) [2429]

Catey Controls (Industrial Machinery) [15880]

Computers Unlimited Inc. (Computers and Software) [6134]

Countryside Marketing (Agricultural Equipment and Supplies) [467]

D & D Transport Refrigeration Services (Heating and Cooling Equipment and Supplies) [14409]

Elite Denture Center (Medical, Dental, and Optical Equipment) [18789]

Empire Sand and Gravel Company Inc. (Construction Materials and Machinery) [7311]

Erickson's Sheep Co. (Livestock and Farm Products) [17837]

Food Services of America (Food) [11179]

Gardner Distributing Co. (Agricultural Equipment and Supplies) [724]

Gemcarve (Jewelry) [17427]

Go/Sportsmen's Supply Inc. (Recreational and Sporting Goods) [23691]

Hanser Automotive Co. (Automotive) [2722]

Hanser's Pick A Part Inc. (Automotive) [2723]

Harken Inc. (Heating and Cooling Equipment and Supplies) [14478]

Horns Inc. (Gifts and Novelties) [13370]

Inland Northwest Distributors Inc. (Floorcovering Equipment and Supplies) [9962]

Inland Truck Parts (Automotive) [2784]

Intermountain Distributing Co. (Alcoholic Beverages) [1774]

McCoy Cattle Co.; M.W. (Livestock and Farm Products) [18080]

Midland Implement Co. (Agricultural Equipment and Supplies) [1032]

Montana Leather Co. Inc. (Specialty Equipment and Products) [25743]

Moore; Florence (Textiles and Notions) [26152]

Mountain View Supply Inc. (Restaurant and Commercial Foodservice Equipment and Supplies) [24189]

Northwest Pipe Fittings Inc. (Plumbing Materials and Fixtures) [23299]

Northwest Truck and Trailer Sales Inc. (Motorized Vehicles) [20700]

Paint Dept. (Paints and Varnishes) [21525]

Photo-Cine Labs (Photographic Equipment and Supplies) [22890]

Public Auction Yards (Livestock and Farm Products) [18183]

Reichenbach Fireworks (Toys and Hobby Goods) [26632]

Ryan's Wholesale Food Distributors (Food) [12373]

Sherwin Williams Paint Co. (Paints and Varnishes) [21571]

Star Office Machines (Office Equipment and Supplies) [21292]

Stockton Oil Co. (Petroleum, Fuels, and Related Equipment) [22707]

Thermax Insulation Inc. (Construction Materials and Machinery) [8119]

Tractor and Equipment Co. (Agricultural Equipment and Supplies) [1346]

Tri-State Truck and Equipment Inc. (Construction Materials and Machinery) [8146]

Valley Welders Supply Inc. (Industrial Supplies) [17249]

Western Office Equipment (Office Equipment and Supplies) [21354]

Western Plains Machinery Co. (Construction Materials and Machinery) [8210]

Wyo-Ben Inc. (Industrial Supplies) [17289]

Yellowstone Paper Co. (Paper and Paper Products) [22010]

Black Eagle
Bloxham; Jack S. (Livestock and Farm Products) [17739]

Bozeman
America West Distributors (Books and Other Printed Materials) [3496]

Bozeman Safe & Lock (Security and Safety Equipment) [24518]

Cardinal Distributing (Alcoholic Beverages) [1573]

Commercial Laundry Sales (Cleaning and Janitorial Supplies) [4602]

Country Classic Dairies Inc. (Food) [10854]

Ferguson Cattle Co. Inc. (Livestock and Farm Products) [17916]

Fitness Plus II (Food) [11138]

House of Clean Inc. (Cleaning and Janitorial Supplies) [4636]

Lehrkinds Inc. (Alcoholic Beverages) [1817]

Rasmark Display Fireworks Inc. (Toys and Hobby Goods) [26630]

Rocky Mountain Salon Consolidated (Health and Beauty Aids) [14223]

Universal Athletic Services of Utah (Shoes) [24882]

Wild West Company Inc. (Clothing) [5486]

Browning
Glacier Studio (Photographic Equipment and Supplies) [22857]

Butte
Alcoa Authorized Distributing (Construction Materials and Machinery) [6931]

Benjamin News Group (Books and Other Printed Materials) [3550]

Bob & Joe's Wholesale (Alcoholic Beverages) [1538]

Butte Produce Co. (Food) [10650]

CJ Cattle Co. Inc. (Livestock and Farm
Products) [17780]
Harrington Co. (Restaurant and Commercial
Foodservice Equipment and Supplies) [24136]
I-90 Auto Salvage & Sales (Automotive) [2768]
Lees Office Equipment & Supplies (Office
Equipment and Supplies) [21104]
Lisac's Inc. (Automotive) [2885]
McBride Distributing Inc.; J.B. (Petroleum, Fuels,
and Related Equipment) [22463]
Office Stop Inc. (Office Equipment and
Supplies) [21188]
Pacific Steel and Recycling (Metals) [20263]
Roach and Smith Distributors, Inc. (Alcoholic
Beverages) [1994]
Seymour Livestock Trucking (Livestock and Farm
Products) [18231]
Sherwin Williams Paint Co. (Paints and
Varnishes) [21572]
Silver Bow News Distributing Company Inc. (Books
and Other Printed Materials) [4163]
Sutey Oil CO. (Petroleum, Fuels, and Related
Equipment) [22717]
Thompson Distributing Inc. (Alcoholic
Beverages) [2079]
Town Pump Inc. (Petroleum, Fuels, and Related
Equipment) [22743]
Ward Thompson Paper Inc. (Office Equipment and
Supplies) [21347]
Whalen Tire (Automotive) [3418]

Chinook
B & B Buyers Inc. (Livestock and Farm
Products) [17714]

Choteau
4 Seasons Livestock (Livestock and Farm
Products) [17669]

Circle
Farmers Elevator Co. (Livestock and Farm
Products) [17883]

Columbus
Davey Motor Co. (Automotive) [2530]

Conrad
Conrad Implement Co. (Agricultural Equipment and
Supplies) [439]
Northern Seed Service (Agricultural Equipment and
Supplies) [1085]

Corvallis
Tri M Specialties (Security and Safety
Equipment) [24645]

Cut Bank
Heitmann; Chester (Livestock and Farm
Products) [17989]
P & K Athletics Inc. (Recreational and Sporting
Goods) [23866]

Dillon
Beaverhead Bar Supply Inc. (Alcoholic
Beverages) [1512]
Intermountain Irrigation (Plumbing Materials and
Fixtures) [23221]
Zenchiku Land and Cattle Co. (Livestock and Farm
Products) [18365]

Dutton
Mountain View Coop. (Agricultural Equipment and
Supplies) [1055]

East Helena
American Chemet Corp. (Chemicals) [4318]

Fairfield
Klinker; Norman (Livestock and Farm
Products) [18037]
Treasure State Seed, Inc. (Agricultural Equipment
and Supplies) [1351]

Fromberg
Gateway Software Corp. (Computers and
Software) [6293]

Glasgow
Billingsley Ranch Outfitters Equipment (Livestock
and Farm Products) [17734]
Glasgow Distributors Inc. (Alcoholic
Beverages) [1718]
Sinclair Produce Distributing (Alcoholic
Beverages) [2026]

Glendive
Con-Mat Supply (Construction Materials and
Machinery) [7202]

Gold Creek
L H Ranch Bunk & Bisket & Hansens
Hobby (Toys and Hobby Goods) [26557]

Great Falls
B-J Pac-A-Part (Cleaning and Janitorial
Supplies) [4575]
B-J Pac-A-Part (Restaurant and Commercial
Foodservice Equipment and Supplies) [24074]
Divine Brothers Distributing Inc. (Alcoholic
Beverages) [1653]
Farmers Union Oil Co. (Great Falls,
Montana) (Chemicals) [4387]
Gagnons Reprographics Co. (Computers and
Software) [6286]
Great Falls Paper Co. (Paper and Paper
Products) [21750]
Great Falls Paper Co. (Industrial Supplies) [16905]
Hansen-Kinney Company Inc. (Paints and
Varnishes) [21455]
House of Hubcaps (Automotive) [2762]
JB Junk & Salvage Inc. (Automotive) [2813]
Johnson Distributing, Inc. (Automotive) [2824]
Kardas/Jelinek Gemstones (Jewelry) [17483]
Limestone Detailers (Specialty Equipment and
Products) [25717]
Malisani, Inc. (Floorcovering Equipment and
Supplies) [10005]
Moderne Cabinet Shop (Construction Materials and
Machinery) [7736]
Northwestern Systems (Specialty Equipment and
Products) [25765]
Pacific Hide and Fur Depot Inc. (Metals) [20260]
Peterson's Rental (Medical, Dental, and Optical
Supplies) [19535]
Skyline Distributing Co. (Household Items) [15656]
Trails West Publishing (Paper and Paper
Products) [21956]
Universal Semen Sales Inc. (Livestock and Farm
Products) [18307]
Warrenterprises Inc. (Cleaning and Janitorial
Supplies) [4727]
Weissman & Sons Inc.; Carl (Paints and
Varnishes) [21604]
Weissman and Sons Inc.; Carl (Hardware) [13991]
White Inc. (Heating and Cooling Equipment and
Supplies) [14764]
Williamson; Gary (Office Equipment and
Supplies) [21356]

Hamilton
Guss Cleaning & Supply (Cleaning and Janitorial
Supplies) [4632]
Reds Office Supply (Office Equipment and
Supplies) [21235]

Havre
Evans Optical (Medical, Dental, and Optical
Supplies) [19309]
Farmers Grain Exchange (Agricultural Equipment
and Supplies) [656]
Havre Distributors Inc. (Alcoholic
Beverages) [1748]
Office Equipment Co. (Office Equipment and
Supplies) [21176]
Valley Motor Supply Inc. (Automotive) [3386]

Helena
Aluma Flight Co. (Toys and Hobby
Goods) [26385]
Clausen Distributing (Alcoholic Beverages) [1602]
Empire Office Machines Inc. (Office Equipment and
Supplies) [20992]
Green Meadow Auto Salvage,
Inc. (Automotive) [2704]
Lee's Refrigeration (Heating and Cooling Equipment
and Supplies) [14519]
Master Cleaners Home Service (Cleaning and
Janitorial Supplies) [4664]
Mid Mountain Wholesale (Textiles and
Notions) [26146]
Montana International Lvstk (Livestock and Farm
Products) [18111]
North American Treasures Inc. (Jewelry) [17535]
Sherwin Williams Paint Co. (Paints and
Varnishes) [21573]
Zekes Distributing Co. (Alcoholic
Beverages) [2145]

Hingham
Hi-Line Fertilizer Inc. (Agricultural Equipment and
Supplies) [819]

Hungry Horse
Fire Systems Unlimited Inc. (Security and Safety
Equipment) [24547]

Kalispell
Conrad Memorial Cemetary; C.E. (Specialty
Equipment and Products) [25609]
Counter Assault (Recreational and Sporting
Goods) [23608]
Dittos (Office Equipment and Supplies) [20968]
Equity Supply Co. (Agricultural Equipment and
Supplies) [554]
Flight Products International (Aeronautical
Equipment and Supplies) [88]
Kalispell Livestock Auction (Livestock and Farm
Products) [18026]
Sherwin Williams Paint Co. (Paints and
Varnishes) [21574]
Thermal Tech, Inc. (Construction Materials and
Machinery) [8118]

Laurel
Heights Pump & Supply (Scientific and
Measurement Devices) [24370]

Lavina
Horpestad Ranch Inc. (Livestock and Farm
Products) [18005]

Lewistown
Big Sky Fire Equipment (Medical, Dental, and
Optical Equipment) [18707]
Eastman Sign Co. (Furniture and Fixtures) [13100]
Lewistown Livestock Auction (Livestock and Farm
Products) [18057]

Livingston
J & J Cleaning Service (Cleaning and Janitorial
Supplies) [4641]

Malta
Equity Cooperative Association (Petroleum, Fuels,
and Related Equipment) [22238]

MiLes City
Custer Supply & Fixtures (Specialty Equipment and
Products) [25618]
JS Enterprises Inc. (Restaurant and Commercial
Foodservice Equipment and Supplies) [24151]
Munsell Livestock (Livestock and Farm
Products) [18123]
Sherwin Williams Paint Co. (Paints and
Varnishes) [21575]

Milltown
Montana Truck Parts (Automotive) [2981]

Missoula

4 BS Wholesale Supply Inc. (Restaurant and Commercial Foodservice Equipment and Supplies) [24052]
A C Auto Recycling (Automotive) [2153]
Ace Auto Salvage (Automotive) [2169]
Alkota of Western Montana (Cleaning and Janitorial Supplies) [4568]
Anders Office Equipment Co. (Office Equipment and Supplies) [20805]
Bleecker Furniture Inc. (Furniture and Fixtures) [13039]
Catey Controls (Industrial Machinery) [15881]
Creative Paint & Glass Inc. (Paints and Varnishes) [21420]
High Mountain Distributing (Veterinary Products) [27148]
Hotsy Cleaning Systems (Specialty Equipment and Products) [25681]
Huckleberry People Inc. (Food) [11473]
Inland Truck Parts (Automotive) [2785]
Long Machinery (Agricultural Equipment and Supplies) [968]
Long Machinery Inc. (Construction Materials and Machinery) [7610]
Meadow Gold Dairies (Food) [11841]
Mission Paint & Glass (Paints and Varnishes) [21503]
Missoula Gold & Silver Exchange (Jewelry) [17525]
Missoula Hearing (Medical, Dental, and Optical Equipment) [18942]
Mountain Supply Co. (Plumbing Materials and Fixtures) [23281]
Pictorial Histories Publishing Co. (Books and Other Printed Materials) [4064]
Robbins Livestock Auction (Livestock and Farm Products) [18201]
Sherwin Williams Paint Co. (Paints and Varnishes) [21576]
Stratton Electronics Inc. (Electrical and Electronic Equipment and Supplies) [9426]
Vehrs Wine Inc. (Alcoholic Beverages) [2100]

Norris

McLeod Merchantile Inc. Conoco (Petroleum, Fuels, and Related Equipment) [22470]

Nye

Russell; Herbert A. (Livestock and Farm Products) [18214]

Philipsburg

Lightening Oil Co. (Petroleum, Fuels, and Related Equipment) [22432]

Polson

Lozars Total Screen Design (Clothing) [5145]
Montana Scale Co. Inc. (Scientific and Measurement Devices) [24402]
Montana Scale Company Inc. (Restaurant and Commercial Foodservice Equipment and Supplies) [24188]

Raynesford

Swedes Sales (Jewelry) [17628]

Richey

Candee; Robert G. (Livestock and Farm Products) [17762]
Farmers Elevator Co. Richey Div. (Livestock and Farm Products) [17885]

Ronan

Big Sky Paint Co., Heating & Air Conditioning (Paints and Varnishes) [21400]
Tomchuck Insulators (Plastics) [23044]
Westland Seed, Inc. (Agricultural Equipment and Supplies) [1434]
Woody's Big Sky Supply, Inc. (Construction Materials and Machinery) [8241]

Shelby

Perry; Lynn (Livestock and Farm Products) [18163]

Sheridan

Elser Oil Co. (Petroleum, Fuels, and Related Equipment) [22227]

Sidney

Blue Rock Beverage Co. (Alcoholic Beverages) [1537]
Prewitt Cattle Co. (Livestock and Farm Products) [18177]
Sidney Auto Wrecking Inc. (Automotive) [3218]

Stevensville

Farmers Exchange (Agricultural Equipment and Supplies) [648]

Vaughn

Morazan (Livestock and Farm Products) [18115]

Wolf Point

HI Line Wholesale Co. (Tobacco Products) [26307]

Nebraska

Allen

Farmers Cooperative Association (Agricultural Equipment and Supplies) [580]

Alliance

Burningtons, Inc. (Railroad Equipment and Supplies) [23475]

Alma

Cooperative Oil Co. (Agricultural Equipment and Supplies) [458]

Arapahoe

Ag Valley Cooperative (Agricultural Equipment and Supplies) [201]

Aurora

Aurora Cooperative Elevator Co. (Agricultural Equipment and Supplies) [263]

Axtell

Midland Cooperative Inc. (Agricultural Equipment and Supplies) [1031]
Midland Cooperative Inc. (Food) [11883]

Bassett

Miller Livestock Sales Co. (Livestock and Farm Products) [18100]

Battle Creek

Battle Creek Farmers Cooperative (Agricultural Equipment and Supplies) [283]

Beatrice

Grandma's Bake Shoppe (Food) [11307]

Bellevue

O'Brien and Co. (Food) [12049]

Benedict

Great Plains Co-op (Livestock and Farm Products) [17961]

Benkelman

Valley Farm Inc. (Agricultural Equipment and Supplies) [1391]

Bertrand

Bertrand Cooperative (Agricultural Equipment and Supplies) [305]

Blair

Nebraska Iowa Supply Co. (Petroleum, Fuels, and Related Equipment) [22508]

Blue Springs

Farmers Union Co-op (Livestock and Farm Products) [17904]
Farmers Union Co-op (Food) [11104]

Bridgeport

Bridgeport Equipment Co. Inc. (Agricultural Equipment and Supplies) [336]

Brule

Farmers Cooperative Association (Livestock and Farm Products) [17844]
Farmers Cooperative Association (Brule, Nebraska) (Food) [11090]

Chappell

Farmers Elevator Co. (Livestock and Farm Products) [17880]

Clearwater

Nebraska Popcorn, Inc. (Food) [11990]

Cody

Walco International Inc. Cody Div. (Agricultural Equipment and Supplies) [1404]

Columbus

Hadley Braithwait Co. (Food) [11357]
Huskers Coop. (Food) [11481]
Sand Livestock Systems Inc. (Agricultural Equipment and Supplies) [1234]

Cornlea

Cornlea Auction Co. (Agricultural Equipment and Supplies) [463]

Cozad

Hunt Cleaners Inc. (Cleaning and Janitorial Supplies) [4638]

Davenport

Superior-Deshler Inc. (Agricultural Equipment and Supplies) [1306]

David City

Frontier Cooperative Co. (Livestock and Farm Products) [17930]

Dodge

Cooperative Supply Inc. (Construction Materials and Machinery) [7219]

Dorchester

Dorchester Farmers Cooperative (Livestock and Farm Products) [17820]

Edison

Edison Non-Stock Cooperative (Agricultural Equipment and Supplies) [542]

Elgin

Farmers Cooperative Exchange (Elgin, Nebraska) (Food) [11101]

Elkhorn

Milliken & Co. (Floorcovering Equipment and Supplies) [10039]

Elwood

Bellamy's Inc. (Agricultural Equipment and Supplies) [294]

Ewing

Knievel's Inc. (Agricultural Equipment and Supplies) [915]

Exeter

Quad County Cooperative (Livestock and Farm Products) [18185]

Fairbury

Delta Enterprises Inc. (Medical, Dental, and Optical Supplies) [19275]

Fairbury Winnelson Co. (Plumbing Materials and Fixtures) [23155]

Fairmont
Manning Grain Co. (Agricultural Equipment and Supplies) [985]

Fremont
Doneli Foods, Inc. (Food) [10981]
Nebraska Medical Mart II (Medical, Dental, and Optical Equipment) [18959]
Standard Distributing Company Inc. (Alcoholic Beverages) [2046]

Friend
Farmers Union Cooperative Co. (Livestock and Farm Products) [17907]

Gering
Masek Distributing Inc. (Automotive) [2921]

Glenvil
AGP Grain Co. (Livestock and Farm Products) [17682]

Gothenburg
Farmland Service Cooperative (Livestock and Farm Products) [17914]

Grand Island
Builders Warehouse (Construction Materials and Machinery) [7102]
Kelly Supply Company of Iowa (Industrial Supplies) [16983]
Quality Sew & Vac (Household Items) [15626]
Quality Sew and Vac (Household Appliances) [15285]
Thompson Company Inc. (Food) [12718]

Hampton
United Co-op Inc. (Hampton, Nebraska) (Agricultural Equipment and Supplies) [1374]

Harvard
Farmers Union Cooperative (Harvard, Nebraska) (Food) [11105]

Hastings
Friend Truck Equipment, Inc.; Matt (Automotive) [2651]
Matt Friend Truck Equipment Inc. (Automotive) [2926]

Holdrege
Agri Cooperative Inc. (Agricultural Equipment and Supplies) [210]
Holdrege Seed and Farm Supply Inc. (Agricultural Equipment and Supplies) [833]
South Central Cooperative (Livestock and Farm Products) [18239]

Hooper
Agland Coop (Livestock and Farm Products) [17681]
Hoegemeyer Hybrids Inc. (Livestock and Farm Products) [18001]
Hoegemeyer Hybrids Inc. (Food) [11444]
Mid States Classic Cars (Automotive) [2953]

Imperial
Frenchman Valley Farmer's Cooperative (Livestock and Farm Products) [17927]
Frenchman Valley Farmer's Cooperative (Agricultural Equipment and Supplies) [708]

Kearney
Ayers Art Co. (Toys and Hobby Goods) [26403]
Cash Way Distributors (Food) [10711]
Central Nebraska Home Care (Medical, Dental, and Optical Equipment) [18732]
Coleman Powermate Inc. (Electrical and Electronic Equipment and Supplies) [8540]
Holmes Plumbing and Heating Supply Inc. (Plumbing Materials and Fixtures) [23211]

L and W Enterprises Inc. (Household Appliances) [15196]

Kimball
Central Vac International (Cleaning and Janitorial Supplies) [4595]
High Plains Cooperative (Livestock and Farm Products) [17997]

Laurel
Urwiler Oil and Fertilizer Inc. (Agricultural Equipment and Supplies) [1387]

Leigh
Maple Valley Cooperative (Food) [11777]

Lexington
Lexington Cooperative Oil Co. (Petroleum, Fuels, and Related Equipment) [22429]
Veetronix Inc. (Communications Systems and Equipment) [5805]

Lincoln
A-1 Refrigeration Inc. (Heating and Cooling Equipment and Supplies) [14286]
Best Style Formal Wear Inc. (Clothing) [4822]
Beynon Farm Products Corp. (Storage Equipment and Containers) [25894]
Business Media Inc. (Computers and Software) [6031]
Central Lumber Sales Inc. (Construction Materials and Machinery) [7160]
Central Lumber Sales Inc. (Wood and Wood Products) [27296]
Clover Auto Supply Inc. (Automotive) [2455]
Coca-Cola Bottling Co. of Lincoln (Soft Drinks) [24935]
Colin Electric Motor Services (Electrical and Electronic Equipment and Supplies) [8541]
Consolidated Electrical Distributors (Electrical and Electronic Equipment and Supplies) [8568]
Cornhusker International (Motorized Vehicles) [20616]
Cubs Distributing Inc. (Floorcovering Equipment and Supplies) [9836]
D & D Distributing (Alcoholic Beverages) [1630]
Data Source Media Inc. (Computers and Software) [6184]
Donley Medical Supply Co. (Medical, Dental, and Optical Supplies) [19288]
EH Engineering Ltd. (Electrical and Electronic Equipment and Supplies) [8657]
Electronic Contracting Co. (Electrical and Electronic Equipment and Supplies) [8688]
Funk Machine and Supply (Hardware) [13719]
Kuehl's Distributors (Food) [11653]
Lincoln Clutch and Brake Supply (Automotive) [2883]
Lincoln Industries Inc. (Books and Other Printed Materials) [3914]
Lincoln Machine (Metals) [20129]
Lincoln Office Equipment Co. (Office Equipment and Supplies) [21109]
Lincoln Part Supply Inc. (Electrical and Electronic Equipment and Supplies) [8992]
Lincoln Poultry and Egg Co. (Food) [11713]
Midland Medical Supply Co. (Medical, Dental, and Optical Supplies) [19457]
Midland Suppliers Inc. (Electrical and Electronic Equipment and Supplies) [9078]
Midwest Tile (Floorcovering Equipment and Supplies) [10034]
NC Plus Hybrids Coop. (Livestock and Farm Products) [18126]
Nebraska Book Company Inc. (Books and Other Printed Materials) [3991]
Pegler-Sysco Food Services Co. (Food) [12132]
Precision Bearing Co. (Industrial Supplies) [17112]
Schnieber Fine Food Inc. (Food) [12430]
Schwarz Paper Co. (Office Equipment and Supplies) [21260]
Scott Electronics (Electrical and Electronic Equipment and Supplies) [9346]
Software Technology Inc. (Computers and Software) [6742]

Sound Words Communications, Inc. (Sound and Entertainment Equipment and Supplies) [25453]
Standard Meat Co. (Food) [12564]
T.O. Haas Holding Co. (Automotive) [3314]
T.O. Haas Tire Company Inc. (Automotive) [3315]
Tool House Inc. (Hardware) [13957]
University Publishing Co. (Furniture and Fixtures) [13266]
Westar Inc. (Recreational and Sporting Goods) [24044]
White Electric Supply Co. (Electrical and Electronic Equipment and Supplies) [9583]

Lindsay
Farmers Cooperative Association (Livestock and Farm Products) [17842]
Farmers Cooperative Association (Food) [11089]

Maywood
Maywood Cooperative Association (Agricultural Equipment and Supplies) [995]

McCook
Cornbelt Chemical Co. (Chemicals) [4366]

Mead
Farmers Union Cooperative Association (Mead, Nebraska) (Livestock and Farm Products) [17906]

Milligan
Farmers Cooperative Co. (Milligan, Nebraska) (Livestock and Farm Products) [17856]

Minden
Farmers Cooperative Grain and Supply Co. (Agricultural Equipment and Supplies) [631]
Farmers Cooperative Grain and Supply Co. (Food) [11102]

Morrill
Jirdon Agri Chemicals Inc. (Horticultural Supplies) [14897]

Nehawka
Nehawka Farmers Coop. (Food) [11991]
Nehawka Farmers Cooperative (Livestock and Farm Products) [18127]

Newman Grove
Farmers Cooperative Oil Co. (Agricultural Equipment and Supplies) [636]

Nora
Farmers Union Cooperative Association (Livestock and Farm Products) [17905]

Norfolk
Affiliated Foods Cooperative Inc. (Food) [10335]
Affiliated Foods Midwest (Food) [10338]
Alter Norfolk Corp. (Used, Scrap, and Recycled Materials) [26745]
Arkfeld Manufacturing & Distributing Company Inc. (Agricultural Equipment and Supplies) [255]
Business Management Software (Computers and Software) [6030]
Cover To Cover (Books and Other Printed Materials) [3663]
Farner & Co. (Food) [11108]
Norfolk Iron and Metal Co. (Metals) [20231]
Precision Bearing Co. (Industrial Supplies) [17113]
Robertson Distributing (Alcoholic Beverages) [1996]
Telebeep Wireless Inc. (Electrical and Electronic Equipment and Supplies) [9472]

North Platte
Detlefsen Oil Inc. (Petroleum, Fuels, and Related Equipment) [22198]
Hipp Wholesale Foods Inc. (Food) [11440]
Inland Truck Parts (Automotive) [2786]

O' Neill
Central Farmers Cooperative (Food) [10720]

Oakland

Agiand Co-op (Livestock and Farm Products) [17680]

Agland Cooperative (Agricultural Equipment and Supplies) [208]

Holmquist Grain and Lumber Co. (Livestock and Farm Products) [18002]

Omaha

Able Trading Corp. (Cleaning and Janitorial Supplies) [4565]

Affiliated Holdings Inc. (Heating and Cooling Equipment and Supplies) [14303]

Allied Electronics (Electrical and Electronic Equipment and Supplies) [8316]

Allied Oil and Supply Inc. (Petroleum, Fuels, and Related Equipment) [22031]

Amcon Distributing Co. (Tobacco Products) [26259]

AMCON Distributing Co. (Food) [10392]

Amcraft, Inc. (Office Equipment and Supplies) [20788]

American Business Network and Associates Inc. (Computers and Software) [5920]

American Feed and Farm Supply Inc. (Agricultural Equipment and Supplies) [233]

Ancona Midwest Foodservices (Food) [10410]

Ancona/Midwest Inc. (Food) [10411]

Badger Body and Truck Equipment Co. (Automotive) [2308]

Barco Municipal Products Inc. (Security and Safety Equipment) [24511]

Baum Iron Co. (Industrial Machinery) [15808]

Benson Pool Systems (Recreational and Sporting Goods) [23544]

Briggs Incorporated of Omaha (Plumbing Materials and Fixtures) [23095]

Browns Medical Imaging (Medical, Dental, and Optical Equipment) [18720]

Camenzind Dairy Cattle; Art (Livestock and Farm Products) [17761]

Carlson Systems Corp. (Hardware) [13620]

Central Distributing Co. (Specialty Equipment and Products) [25598]

Central Plains Distributing Inc. (Heating and Cooling Equipment and Supplies) [14377]

Churchich & Associates; Ely (Recreational and Sporting Goods) [23592]

Coins, Cards & Collectibles (Toys and Hobby Goods) [26446]

Computer Systems Inc. (Computers and Software) [6128]

ConAgra Grain Co. (Livestock and Farm Products) [17789]

Cummins Great Plains Diesel Inc. (Automotive) [2507]

Cummins Great Plains Diesel Inc. (Industrial Machinery) [15923]

Day Co.; John (Industrial Machinery) [15933]

Day Co.; John (Agricultural Equipment and Supplies) [499]

Diesel Power Equipment Co. (Automotive) [2545]

Driscoll Leather Co. Inc. (Shoes) [24727]

Driscoll Leather Company Inc. (Clothing) [4923]

Electric Fixture and Supply Co. (Electrical and Electronic Equipment and Supplies) [8660]

Factory Motor Parts (Automotive) [2604]

Feaster Foods Co. (Food) [11111]

Ferer and Sons Co.; Aaron (Metals) [19974]

Fuchs Machinery Inc. (Industrial Machinery) [16043]

Funco Inc. (Recreational and Sporting Goods) [23680]

Furniture on Consignment Inc. (Furniture and Fixtures) [13116]

Haney Shoe Store Inc. (Shoes) [24757]

Harman Appliance Sales (Household Appliances) [15161]

Hauff Sporting Goods Co. Inc. (Recreational and Sporting Goods) [23717]

Herregan Distributors, Inc. (Floorcovering Equipment and Supplies) [9946]

InaCom Corp. (Computers and Software) [6360]

Inland Truck Parts (Automotive) [2787]

Johnson Hardware Company Inc. (Construction Materials and Machinery) [7537]

Josin Fabrics (Textiles and Notions) [26082]

Karla's Kreations Inc. (Gifts and Novelties) [13380]

Kiewit Mining Group, Inc. (Minerals and Ores) [20549]

Koley's Medical Supply Company Inc. (Medical, Dental, and Optical Supplies) [19399]

Kopecky & Co.; J. M. (Heating and Cooling Equipment and Supplies) [14514]

Lyman-Richey Corp. (Construction Materials and Machinery) [7624]

Mangelsen and Sons Inc.; Harold (Gifts and Novelties) [13394]

Micro-Tron Inc. (Computers and Software) [6497]

Midwest Refrigeration Supply Inc. (Compressors) [5844]

Midwest Refrigeration Supply Inc. (Industrial Machinery) [16299]

Midwest Tile Supply Co. (Floorcovering Equipment and Supplies) [10036]

Miller Electric Co. (Omaha, Nebraska) (Electrical and Electronic Equipment and Supplies) [9084]

MSM Solutions (Food) [11952]

Nebraska Golf Discount Inc. (Recreational and Sporting Goods) [23844]

Nebraska Machinery Co. (Construction Materials and Machinery) [7770]

Nebraska Wine & Spirits Inc. (Alcoholic Beverages) [1911]

Omaha Steaks Foodservice (Food) [12068]

Omaha Steaks International (Food) [12069]

Omaha Vaccine (Veterinary Products) [27201]

Packers Engineering and Equipment Company Inc. (Industrial Supplies) [17098]

Pamida Inc. (Food) [12101]

Physicians Optical Supply Inc. (Medical, Dental, and Optical Supplies) [19540]

Power Drives and Bearings Div. (Industrial Machinery) [16413]

Precision Industries Inc. (Automotive) [3116]

Probe Technology Inc. (Computers and Software) [6644]

QA Technologies Inc. (Computers and Software) [6667]

RC International (Health and Beauty Aids) [14210]

Riekes Equipment Co. (Industrial Machinery) [16453]

Rite Way Oil and Gas Company Inc. (Petroleum, Fuels, and Related Equipment) [22631]

Roberts Dairy Co. (Food) [12328]

Sales Force of Omaha (Food) [12395]

Sapp Brothers Petroleum Inc. (Petroleum, Fuels, and Related Equipment) [22652]

Schnieber Fine Food Inc. (Food) [12429]

The Scoular Co. (Livestock and Farm Products) [18227]

Seaway Importing Co. (Sound and Entertainment Equipment and Supplies) [25435]

Sergeant's Pet Products Inc. (Veterinary Products) [27230]

Shared Service Systems Inc. (Medical, Dental, and Optical Supplies) [19605]

Skinner Baking Co.; James (Food) [12502]

South Omaha Supply (Livestock and Farm Products) [18242]

Specialty Grain Products Co. (Food) [12552]

Sterling Distributing Co. (Alcoholic Beverages) [2053]

Strategic Products and Services Inc. (Computers and Software) [6765]

Telesystems Inc. (Communications Systems and Equipment) [5787]

Tires Inc. (Automotive) [3308]

United-A.G. Cooperative Inc. (Food) [12789]

United States Check Book Co. (Office Equipment and Supplies) [21328]

Van Waters and Rogers Inc. (Petroleum, Fuels, and Related Equipment) [22768]

Van Waters and Rogers Inc. Omaha (Chemicals) [4545]

Wright and Wilhelmy Co. (Household Appliances) [15381]

ONeill

Central Farmers Cooperative (Agricultural Equipment and Supplies) [390]

Ord

Farmers Cooperative Elevator (Agricultural Equipment and Supplies) [605]

Pickrell

Pickrell Cooperative Elevator Association (Livestock and Farm Products) [18165]

Pilger

Farmers Cooperative of Pilger (Livestock and Farm Products) [17877]

Plymouth

Farmers Cooperative Elevator Co. (Agricultural Equipment and Supplies) [621]

Roseland

Cooperative Grain and Supply (Livestock and Farm Products) [17797]

St. Edward

Tri Valley Cooperative (Agricultural Equipment and Supplies) [1356]

St. Paul

Farmers Union Cooperative Association of Howard County (Agricultural Equipment and Supplies) [661]

Schuyler

Wagner Mills Inc. (Livestock and Farm Products) [18323]

Wagner Mills Inc. (Food) [12863]

Scottsbluff

Kelley Bean Co., Inc. (Food) [11593]

Scribner

Agland Coop (Agricultural Equipment and Supplies) [205]

Shelby

Farmers Cooperative Business Association (Agricultural Equipment and Supplies) [586]

Sidney

Far-Mor Cooperative (Petroleum, Fuels, and Related Equipment) [22252]

South Sioux City

Fishermans Factory Outlet (Recreational and Sporting Goods) [23669]

Hart Beverage Co. (Soft Drinks) [24968]

Spalding

Spalding Cooperative Elevator Co. (Agricultural Equipment and Supplies) [1287]

Swanton

Farmer's Elevator Co-op (Livestock and Farm Products) [17879]

Trumbull

Heartland Co-op (Trumbull, Nebraska) (Livestock and Farm Products) [17986]

Utica

Utica Cooperative Grain Company Inc. (Livestock and Farm Products) [18310]

Utica Cooperative Grain Company Inc. (Food) [12810]

Waverly

Farmers Cooperative Co. (Agricultural Equipment and Supplies) [593]

West Point

Farmers Cooperative Co. (Agricultural Equipment and Supplies) [597]

Nielsen Oil and Propane Inc. (Petroleum, Fuels, and Related Equipment) [22518]

Northeast Cooperative (Livestock and Farm Products) [18140]

Prinz Grain and Feed Inc. (Livestock and Farm Products) [18179]

Wilcox

Midland Cooperative Inc. Wilcox Div. (Livestock and Farm Products) [18095]

Wisner

Northeast Cooperative (Petroleum, Fuels, and Related Equipment) [22525]

York

Farmers Cooperative Association (York, Nebraska) (Livestock and Farm Products) [17847]
Scott-Hourigan Co. (Agricultural Equipment and Supplies) [1243]

Nevada

Boulder City

Brunos Turquoise Trading Post (Jewelry) [17353]

Carson City

AAA Manufacturing Inc. (Motorized Vehicles) [20575]
Accupart International (Automotive) [2168]
Air Combat Exchange Ltd. (Motorized Vehicles) [20579]
Allied Tire and Auto Services (Automotive) [2214]
Blue Mountain Steel (Metals) [19827]
Capital Beverages Inc. (Alcoholic Beverages) [1570]
Carson Masonry and Steel Supply (Metals) [19861]
Cavallero Heating and Air Conditioning Inc. (Heating and Cooling Equipment and Supplies) [14371]
Ceramic Tile Center (Construction Materials and Machinery) [7164]
Click Bond Inc. (Aeronautical Equipment and Supplies) [70]
Click Bond Inc. (Hardware) [13637]
Comstock Distributing (Food) [10804]
Consolidated Electrical Distributing (Electrical and Electronic Equipment and Supplies) [8564]
Cox; Charles E. (Cleaning and Janitorial Supplies) [4606]
General Tire Inc. (Automotive) [2674]
Gnomon Inc. (Books and Other Printed Materials) [3782]
Hibbard Aviation (Motorized Vehicles) [20648]
Im-Pruv-All (Automotive) [2771]
Mallory Inc. (Electrical and Electronic Equipment and Supplies) [9023]
Moustrak Inc. (Computers and Software) [6532]
Stano Components (Recreational and Sporting Goods) [23983]
Virginia City Furniture Inc. (Furniture and Fixtures) [13269]

Crystal Bay

Koch Resources Inc. (Toys and Hobby Goods) [26555]

Dayton

Bruce Industries Inc. (Aeronautical Equipment and Supplies) [67]

Elko

Blach Distributing Co. (Alcoholic Beverages) [1531]
Paoletti and Urriola Inc. (Office Equipment and Supplies) [21203]

Ely

Ely Auto Dismantlers (Automotive) [2585]

Fallon

Light Creations (Photographic Equipment and Supplies) [22874]
McKenzie; C.D. (Construction Materials and Machinery) [7685]

Valley Distributors Inc. (Alcoholic Beverages) [2096]

Fernley

Enco Manufacturing Co. (Industrial Machinery) [15985]

Gardnerville

Silver State Roofing Materials (Construction Materials and Machinery) [8021]

Henderson

AgriBioTech Inc. (Agricultural Equipment and Supplies) [213]
Any & All Auto Parts Inc. (Automotive) [2242]
DuBarry International Inc. (Used, Scrap, and Recycled Materials) [26799]
Ethel M. Chocolates, Inc. (Food) [11055]
Gooding Livestock Community Co. (Livestock and Farm Products) [17949]
Key Products Co. (Computers and Software) [6421]
OK Hafens Tire Store Inc. (Automotive) [3061]
Roeden Inc. (Jewelry) [17569]
Skips Ameritone Paint Center (Paints and Varnishes) [21586]
Spinal Analysis Machine (Medical, Dental, and Optical Equipment) [19051]
Wood-N-Stuf (Toys and Hobby Goods) [26715]

Incline Village

Connor & Son (Jewelry) [17377]
Hubb; William (Jewelry) [17451]
Lake Tahoe Supplies (Cleaning and Janitorial Supplies) [4656]
The Publishers Mark (Books and Other Printed Materials) [4095]

Las Vegas

3-D Supply Inc. (Cleaning and Janitorial Supplies) [4562]
Access International Marketing Inc. (Hardware) [13524]
Alumacast Inc. (Furniture and Fixtures) [13016]
American Pool Supply Inc. (Recreational and Sporting Goods) [23512]
Anicom Multimedia Wiring Systems (Electrical and Electronic Equipment and Supplies) [8357]
Anthony International Inc.; Paul (Shoes) [24673]
Appliance Parts Center Inc. (Sound and Entertainment Equipment and Supplies) [25077]
Appliance Parts Co. (Household Appliances) [15020]
Bat Rentals (Construction Materials and Machinery) [7030]
Beal's Royal Glass and Mirror Inc. (Construction Materials and Machinery) [7033]
Bearing Belt Chain Co. (Industrial Supplies) [16727]
Bedrosians Tile & Marble (Floorcovering Equipment and Supplies) [9718]
Bellini Co. (Floorcovering Equipment and Supplies) [9721]
Best Glass Co. (Construction Materials and Machinery) [7053]
Bonanza Beverage Co. (Alcoholic Beverages) [1543]
Brady Industries Inc. (Cleaning and Janitorial Supplies) [4588]
Brennans Ltd. (Furniture and Fixtures) [13045]
Buck's War Surplus (Recreational and Sporting Goods) [23574]
Charleston Auto Parts Company Inc. (Automotive) [2445]
Clark County Bar & Restaurant Supply (Restaurant and Commercial Foodservice Equipment and Supplies) [24093]
Clark County Wholesale Inc. (Automotive) [2452]
Costello Beverage Co.; J.W. (Alcoholic Beverages) [1620]
De Luca Liquor and Wine Ltd. (Alcoholic Beverages) [1636]
Desert Design Inc. (Agricultural Equipment and Supplies) [515]
Diamond Prairie Ranch Company Inc. (Automotive) [2542]

Divinci Ltd. (Jewelry) [17397]
ECR Sales & Service Inc. (Office Equipment and Supplies) [20982]
Fremont Coin Co. Inc. (Jewelry) [17417]
Frontier Radio Inc. (Communications Systems and Equipment) [5616]
Frontier Radio Inc. (Electrical and Electronic Equipment and Supplies) [8765]
Gamblers General Store Inc. (Toys and Hobby Goods) [26490]
Gateswood Software Inc. (Computers and Software) [6292]
Gee; Donald & Rema (Jewelry) [17422]
Gold Father's Jewelry, Inc. (Jewelry) [17434]
Goldman Co.; H.R. (Jewelry) [17437]
Gordon Co.; Len (Plastics) [22972]
Imports Wholesale (Clothing) [5047]
International Food and Beverage Inc. (Food) [11521]
Jacks Fragrances (Specialty Equipment and Products) [25691]
Jenik Automotive Distributors Inc. (Automotive) [2817]
The Jewelers of Las Vegas (Jewelry) [17469]
Jewelry Exchange Inc. (Jewelry) [17472]
Jones Office Equipment; Al (Office Equipment and Supplies) [21079]
Kaufenberg Enterprises (Clothing) [5103]
Kelly's Pipe and Supply Co. (Plumbing Materials and Fixtures) [23230]
Kennedy; Rob E. (Jewelry) [17488]
KG Engineering Inc. (Specialty Equipment and Products) [25699]
Kiesub Corp. (Electrical and Electronic Equipment and Supplies) [8944]
Las Vegas Discount Golf and Tennis Inc. (Recreational and Sporting Goods) [23780]
Leish; Bob (Specialty Equipment and Products) [25711]
Lloyd's Refrigeration Inc. (Heating and Cooling Equipment and Supplies) [14526]
M & P Sales Inc. (Cleaning and Janitorial Supplies) [4662]
Marshall Building Supply (Construction Materials and Machinery) [7649]
MBI Inc. (Medical, Dental, and Optical Equipment) [18903]
MBI Inc. (Medical, Dental, and Optical Supplies) [19428]
MELIBRAD (Medical, Dental, and Optical Supplies) [19448]
Monarch Beverage Inc. (Alcoholic Beverages) [1888]
Monarch Tile (Floorcovering Equipment and Supplies) [10054]
More; Ruth (Health and Beauty Aids) [14167]
N & L Inc. (Construction Materials and Machinery) [7759]
NEDCO Supply (Electrical and Electronic Equipment and Supplies) [9120]
Nevada Beverage Co. (Alcoholic Beverages) [1912]
Nevada Business Systems Inc. (Office Equipment and Supplies) [21158]
Nevada Cash Register Inc. (Office Equipment and Supplies) [21159]
Nevada Food Service (Food) [11999]
Nevada Illumination Inc. (Electrical and Electronic Equipment and Supplies) [9124]
Northern Telecom Inc. (Electrical and Electronic Equipment and Supplies) [9139]
Office Planning Group Inc. (Office Equipment and Supplies) [21186]
Oriental Furniture Warehouse (Furniture and Fixtures) [13196]
Pablo Don Cigar Co. (Tobacco Products) [26337]
Pat's Ceramics Tile Design Center (Toys and Hobby Goods) [26606]
Paul-Son Gaming Supplies, Inc. (Toys and Hobby Goods) [26607]
The Plastic Man Inc. (Plastics) [23009]
Precision Instruments Inc. (Medical, Dental, and Optical Equipment) [18991]
The Premium Connection (Household Items) [15624]
Pruitt; Richard (Furniture and Fixtures) [13213]

QED (Electrical and Electronic Equipment and Supplies) [9249]

Ray's Beaver Bag (Gifts and Novelties) [13434]

Rebel Oil Company Inc. (Petroleum, Fuels, and Related Equipment) [22611]

Redy Inc. (Health and Beauty Aids) [14211]

Refrigeration & Air-Conditioning Maintenance Co. (Heating and Cooling Equipment and Supplies) [14653]

Rita Selections Ltd. (Toys and Hobby Goods) [26636]

The Roane Co. (Floorcovering Equipment and Supplies) [10126]

Sherwin Williams Paint Co. (Paints and Varnishes) [21567]

Shetakis Distributing Co.; Jim L. (Restaurant and Commercial Foodservice Equipment and Supplies) [24219]

Sloan International, Inc. (Specialty Equipment and Products) [25818]

Soukup Brothers Mechanical Inc. (Heating and Cooling Equipment and Supplies) [14689]

Southern Nevada T.B.A. Supply Inc. (Automotive) [3242]

Southern Wine & Spirits (Alcoholic Beverages) [2038]

State Restaurant Equipment Inc. (Restaurant and Commercial Foodservice Equipment and Supplies) [24226]

Steamboat International LLC (Specialty Equipment and Products) [25831]

Steamboat International LLC (Recreational and Sporting Goods) [23987]

Steel Engineers Inc. (Metals) [20394]

Stromberg; J. Edward (Office Equipment and Supplies) [21301]

Superior Tire Inc. (Automotive) [3287]

Syndee's Crafts Inc. (Toys and Hobby Goods) [26675]

Technical Advisory Service (Electrical and Electronic Equipment and Supplies) [9468]

Tires Wholesale Inc. (Automotive) [3310]

TJ Wholesale Distributor (Toys and Hobby Goods) [26681]

Universal Service and Supply (Household Appliances) [15349]

Valley-Western Distributors, Inc. (Floorcovering Equipment and Supplies) [10271]

Vega Enterprises Inc. (Tobacco Products) [26369]

Venada Aviation (Aeronautical Equipment and Supplies) [167]

Vita Plus Industries Inc. (Health and Beauty Aids) [14271]

Yong's Watch & Clock Repair (Jewelry) [17665]

Laughlin

L & M Food Service (Restaurant and Commercial Foodservice Equipment and Supplies) [24161]

Mc Gill

Safety Industries Inc. (Automotive) [3179]

Minden

Bing Construction Company of Nevada (Construction Materials and Machinery) [7058]

North Las Vegas

A & A Midwest Distributing Inc. (Automotive) [2152]

A-City Auto Glass (Automotive) [2154]

Advanced Equipment Inc. (Construction Materials and Machinery) [6918]

Fiesta Foods (Food) [11124]

Silver State Welding Supply Inc. (Industrial Machinery) [16492]

Simpson Norton Corp. (Agricultural Equipment and Supplies) [1268]

Southern Nevada Auto Parts Inc. (Automotive) [3241]

Westco-BakeMark Las Vegas (Food) [12907]

Westco Food Service Co. (Food) [12908]

Reno

B & G Beauty Supply Inc. (Health and Beauty Aids) [14033]

BEST Cash Registers (Office Equipment and Supplies) [20842]

Boyd & Associates; Robert W. (Gifts and Novelties) [13322]

Bulbman Inc. (Electrical and Electronic Equipment and Supplies) [8476]

Compusolve (Computers and Software) [6098]

Crumrine Manufacturing Jewelers (Jewelry) [17384]

D & P Enterprises Inc. (Restaurant and Commercial Foodservice Equipment and Supplies) [24100]

Electronic Bus Systems of Nevada (Office Equipment and Supplies) [20988]

Falk Corp. (Industrial Machinery) [16004]

Fuller Color Center Inc. (Paints and Varnishes) [21446]

Hamilton Medical Inc. (Medical, Dental, and Optical Equipment) [18822]

Hamilton Medical Inc. (Medical, Dental, and Optical Supplies) [19347]

Horizon USA Data Supplies Inc. (Computers and Software) [6342]

iGo (Electrical and Electronic Equipment and Supplies) [8871]

Imports International (Furniture and Fixtures) [13139]

Kar Products, Inc. (Industrial Supplies) [16980]

Keystone Cue & Cushion Inc. (Recreational and Sporting Goods) [23773]

Kold Temp Refigeration Inc. (Heating and Cooling Equipment and Supplies) [14513]

Lindemann Produce Inc. (Food) [11715]

Luce and Son Inc. (Alcoholic Beverages) [1830]

Luce and Son Inc. (Alcoholic Beverages) [1831]

MCM Enterprise (Automotive) [2935]

Mercury Air Center (Petroleum, Fuels, and Related Equipment) [22474]

Nevada Office Machines Inc. (Office Equipment and Supplies) [21160]

Rare Coins (Jewelry) [17556]

Reno Auto Wrecking Inc. (Automotive) [3148]

Reno Brake Inc. (Paints and Varnishes) [21554]

Reno Game Sales Inc. (Toys and Hobby Goods) [26633]

RSR Wholesale Guns West, Inc. (Guns and Weapons) [13510]

Safeguard Abacus (Paper and Paper Products) [21920]

Shamrock Auto Parts Inc. (Automotive) [3210]

Sierra Meat Company Inc. (Food) [12487]

Sierra Roofing Corp. (Construction Materials and Machinery) [8019]

Sierra Scales (Scientific and Measurement Devices) [24432]

Siri Office Equipment Inc. (Office Equipment and Supplies) [21271]

Tarrant Service Agency, Inc. (Heating and Cooling Equipment and Supplies) [14710]

Vaughn Materials Company Inc. (Construction Materials and Machinery) [8176]

Wedco Inc. (Electrical and Electronic Equipment and Supplies) [9565]

Wheel Masters Inc. (Automotive) [3421]

Schurz

Walker River Pute Tribal Council (Livestock and Farm Products) [18324]

Sparks

A-1 Chemical Inc. (Cleaning and Janitorial Supplies) [4563]

A & D Maintenance (Cleaning and Janitorial Supplies) [4564]

Adams Hard-Facing Company of California (Agricultural Equipment and Supplies) [184]

Beacon Distributing Co. (Alcoholic Beverages) [1510]

Beacon Liquor and Wine (Alcoholic Beverages) [1511]

Bedrosian Tile & Marble Supply (Floorcovering Equipment and Supplies) [9701]

Berry-Hinkley Terminal Inc. (Petroleum, Fuels, and Related Equipment) [22070]

Blue Ribbon Meat Co. (Food) [10578]

BMG Distribution Co. (Sound and Entertainment Equipment and Supplies) [25106]

Bonanza Nut and Bolt Inc. (Hardware) [13603]

Burrows Inc.; John H. (Food) [10647]

Calvada Sales Co. (Food) [10681]

Ceramic Tile Center, Inc. (Floorcovering Equipment and Supplies) [9794]

Choquettes' Used Trucks & Equipment (Industrial Machinery) [15887]

Crown Beverages Inc. (Alcoholic Beverages) [1625]

Discount Desk Etc., Inc. (Office Equipment and Supplies) [20965]

Discount Desk Etc. Inc. (Furniture and Fixtures) [13091]

Ecco Corp. (Office Equipment and Supplies) [20979]

Engs Motor Truck Co. (Automotive) [2592]

Gemini Cosmetics (Health and Beauty Aids) [14109]

Gemini Cosmetics (Medical, Dental, and Optical Supplies) [19335]

Hofert Co.; J. (Gifts and Novelties) [13369]

Key Sales Inc. (Restaurant and Commercial Foodservice Equipment and Supplies) [24157]

Morrey Distributing Co. (Alcoholic Beverages) [1894]

Personally Yours (Textiles and Notions) [26174]

Ransom Distributing Co. (Books and Other Printed Materials) [4107]

Re-Neva Inc. (Paints and Varnishes) [21551]

Renken Distributing; M. (Specialty Equipment and Products) [25801]

Retailers Supply Co. (Paper and Paper Products) [21905]

Rorer West Inc. (Medical, Dental, and Optical Supplies) [19586]

Shirts Unlimited (Jewelry) [17600]

Sierra Chemical Co (Chemicals) [4511]

Silverstate Co. (Alcoholic Beverages) [2025]

Smith Detroit Diesel (Automotive) [3231]

Southern Wine & Spirits (Alcoholic Beverages) [2039]

Sportif USA Inc. (Clothing) [5385]

Water Safety Corporation of America (Specialty Equipment and Products) [25874]

Western Nevada Supply Co. (Plumbing Materials and Fixtures) [23452]

Stateline

Duke Sports (Textiles and Notions) [26024]

Verdi

Sinclair Imports Inc. (Recreational and Sporting Goods) [23941]

Wells

Digrazia Wholesale Distributing; Joseph E. (Tobacco Products) [26288]

Winnemucca

Peraldo Co. Inc.; L.W. (Alcoholic Beverages) [1950]

Winneva Distributing Co. Inc. (Alcoholic Beverages) [2131]

Zephyr Cove

Jo's Designs (Clothing) [5096]

New Hampshire

Amherst

Blake Brothers (Jewelry) [17341]

Consolidated Utility Equipment Service, Inc. (Automotive) [2478]

International Data Acquisition and Control Inc. (Computers and Software) [6390]

MTH Corp. (Plastics) [23000]

Atkinson

Northern Laminate Sales Inc. (Plastics) [23003]

Auburn

Northeast Scale Company Inc. (Scientific and Measurement Devices) [24410]

Barrington

Associated Buyers (Food) [10444]
Londavia Inc. (Aeronautical Equipment and Supplies) [118]
Walk Corp.; Benjamin (Shoes) [24887]

Bedford

Franki Sales Co. (Electrical and Electronic Equipment and Supplies) [8757]
Granite State Office Supplies, Inc. (Office Equipment and Supplies) [21018]
Zytronics Inc. (Electrical and Electronic Equipment and Supplies) [9629]

Belmont

Major Medical Supply Co. Inc. (Medical, Dental, and Optical Equipment) [18899]

Brentwood

Shorts Wholesale Supply Co. (Construction Materials and Machinery) [8014]

Canaan

Vine Trading Company (Computers and Software) [6853]

Candia

Action Equipment Company Inc. (Construction Materials and Machinery) [6911]

Center Ossipee

Mitee-Bite Products Inc. (Industrial Machinery) [16310]

Center Sandwich

Bortman Trading Co. (Jewelry) [17348]

Charlestown

Merriam-Graves Corp. (Medical, Dental, and Optical Equipment) [18932]
Saxonville USA (Construction Materials and Machinery) [7984]
Waters Edge Distributors Inc. (Recreational and Sporting Goods) [24041]

Chesterfield

Stow Mills (Food) [12592]

Claremont

General Auto Sales Company Inc. (Automotive) [2670]
Reliable Paper & Supply Company Inc. (Paper and Paper Products) [21899]

Colebrook

Manchester Manufacturing Acquisitions Inc. (Clothing) [5156]
Manchester Manufacturing Inc. (Clothing) [5157]
Sambito; William B. (Office Equipment and Supplies) [21257]

Concord

Aranosian Oil Co. Inc. (Petroleum, Fuels, and Related Equipment) [22041]
Automotive Supply Associates (Automotive) [2296]
Ballard Enterprises Inc. (Toys and Hobby Goods) [26406]
Capitol Distributors Inc. (Alcoholic Beverages) [1572]
Capitol Plumbing and Heating Supply Company Inc. (Plumbing Materials and Fixtures) [23105]
Corriveau-Routhier, Inc. (Floorcovering Equipment and Supplies) [9827]
Data Information Service (Office Equipment and Supplies) [20949]
EnergyNorth Propane Inc. (Petroleum, Fuels, and Related Equipment) [22231]
Facit Div. (Computers and Software) [6263]
Great Northern Video (Sound and Entertainment Equipment and Supplies) [25220]

Little & Son; Michael (Office Equipment and Supplies) [21110]
New Hampshire Distributor Inc. (Alcoholic Beverages) [1915]
New Hampshire Optical Co. (Medical, Dental, and Optical Supplies) [19492]
Sanel Auto Parts Inc. (Automotive) [3187]
Science and Spirit Resources, Inc. (Books and Other Printed Materials) [4146]
Tilton; Sumner H. (Livestock and Farm Products) [18282]
Tujay's Artist Dolls (Toys and Hobby Goods) [26693]
United Beverage, Inc. (Alcoholic Beverages) [2087]
Weeks Div. (Food) [12894]
Weeks Div. (Food) [12895]
West Carpenter Paint & Flooring (Paints and Varnishes) [21606]

Contoocook

Depco Inc. (Plastics) [22953]
Venture Vehicles Inc. (Recreational and Sporting Goods) [24029]
Yankee Book Peddler Inc. (Books and Other Printed Materials) [4301]

Conway

Abbott's Premium Ice Cream Inc. (Food) [10318]
Duffco (Food) [10998]
Enfield Industries Inc. (Furniture and Fixtures) [13105]

Deerfield

Computer Craft Co. (Computers and Software) [6107]

Derry

Gem Enterprises, Inc. (Jewelry) [17424]
Merrimack Valley Wood Products Inc. (Construction Materials and Machinery) [7698]

Dover

Corriveau-Routhier, Inc. (Construction Materials and Machinery) [7223]
Fibredyne Inc. (Plumbing Materials and Fixtures) [23167]
Prosper Shevenell and Son Inc. (Shoes) [24837]
Quimby Co. Inc.; Edward H. (Office Equipment and Supplies) [21230]
Robbins Auto Parts Inc. (Automotive) [3168]
Tab of Northern New England (Office Equipment and Supplies) [21314]

Durham

Durham Boat Co. Inc. (Recreational and Sporting Goods) [23635]

Epping

Bayside Distributing Inc. (Alcoholic Beverages) [1509]

Exeter

Import Leather Inc. (Luggage and Leather Goods) [18400]
Leather Loft Stores (Luggage and Leather Goods) [18406]
Shafmaster Company Inc. (Luggage and Leather Goods) [18426]

Gilsum

Pathway Book Service (Books and Other Printed Materials) [4045]

Goffstown

Choice Metals (Metals) [19877]
Gold Key Electronics Inc. (Electrical and Electronic Equipment and Supplies) [8794]
Hampshire Furniture Co. (Specialty Equipment and Products) [25673]
Hampshire Furniture Co. (Restaurant and Commercial Foodservice Equipment and Supplies) [24134]
Village Products (Heating and Cooling Equipment and Supplies) [14755]

Grafton

McDow & Sons Salvage; V.H. (Automotive) [2932]

Greenville

Approved Color Corp. (Paints and Varnishes) [21390]

Guild

Dorr Fabrics Inc. (Textiles and Notions) [26021]

Hampton

Davenport Organisation (Jewelry) [17388]
Fisher Scientific International Inc. (Security and Safety Equipment) [24552]
Hampton Vision Center (Medical, Dental, and Optical Supplies) [19348]
Inventory Conversion Inc. (Computers and Software) [6394]
Mikan Theatricals (Specialty Equipment and Products) [25739]
Neal's Gauging Trains (Toys and Hobby Goods) [26590]
New England CR Inc. (Used, Scrap, and Recycled Materials) [26922]
Transco South Inc. (Office Equipment and Supplies) [21321]

Hanover

Alpina Sports Corp. (Shoes) [24668]
Bridge Technology Inc. (Computers and Software) [6024]
Ediciones del Norte (Books and Other Printed Materials) [3717]

Henniker

Damour; William L. (Alcoholic Beverages) [1634]

Hooksett

Gorton Communications Inc. (Communications Systems and Equipment) [5622]
Sullivan Co. Inc.; C.B. (Health and Beauty Aids) [14250]
Syban International Inc. (Aeronautical Equipment and Supplies) [155]

Hudson

Computer Optics Inc. (Photographic Equipment and Supplies) [22848]
Heat Inc. (Heating and Cooling Equipment and Supplies) [14479]
Howtek Inc. (Computers and Software) [6344]
RST Reclaiming Co. Inc. (Office Equipment and Supplies) [21251]
Sitek Inc. (Computers and Software) [6733]

Jaffrey

Bean and Sons Co.; D.D. (Security and Safety Equipment) [24512]
Macy Associates Inc. (Paper and Paper Products) [21819]

Keene

Clarke Distributors Inc. (Alcoholic Beverages) [1599]
Housen and Co. Inc.; G. (Alcoholic Beverages) [1765]
Lex Computing and Management Corp. (Computers and Software) [6438]
Schleicher and Schuell Inc. (Scientific and Measurement Devices) [24428]

Laconia

Brewer Associates Inc. (Aeronautical Equipment and Supplies) [62]
Lake Aircraft Inc. (Aeronautical Equipment and Supplies) [114]

Lancaster

Timberland Machines (Agricultural Equipment and Supplies) [1336]

Lebanon

Barker Steel Co. Inc. Lebanon Div. (Construction Materials and Machinery) [7023]

Lincoln
Scottish Connection (Clothing) [5339]

Londonderry
Cadec Corporation (Computers and Software) [6040]
Rally Products, Inc. (Medical, Dental, and Optical Supplies) [19566]
Sharpe; Cliff (Furniture and Fixtures) [13239]
SIS Human Factor Technologies Inc. (Furniture and Fixtures) [13244]
WTI (Computers and Software) [6883]

Manchester
Advanced Maintenance Products Co. (Cleaning and Janitorial Supplies) [4566]
Amoskeag Beverages Inc. (Alcoholic Beverages) [1483]
Applied Educational Systems Inc. (Computers and Software) [5950]
Associated Grocers of New England Inc. (Food) [10452]
Central Paper Products Co. Inc. (Paper and Paper Products) [21676]
Coca-Cola Bottling Co. of Manchester (Soft Drinks) [24936]
Corriveau-Routhier Inc. (Floorcovering Equipment and Supplies) [9828]
Corriveau-Routhier Inc. (Construction Materials and Machinery) [7224]
D-J, Inc. (Construction Materials and Machinery) [7242]
Electronic Surplus Services (Electrical and Electronic Equipment and Supplies) [8695]
Frederickseal, Inc. (Industrial Supplies) [16878]
G & C Restaurant Equipment (Restaurant and Commercial Foodservice Equipment and Supplies) [24125]
Gills Automotive Inc. (Heating and Cooling Equipment and Supplies) [14470]
Goulet Supply Company Inc. (Plumbing Materials and Fixtures) [23197]
Institutional Contract Sales (Furniture and Fixtures) [13142]
Interstate Restaurant Equipment Corp. (Restaurant and Commercial Foodservice Equipment and Supplies) [24146]
Jet Wine and Spirits Inc. (Alcoholic Beverages) [1783]
Lindenmeyer Munroe (Paper and Paper Products) [21803]
Manchester Wholesale Distributors (Food) [11772]
Northern Electronics Automation (Electrical and Electronic Equipment and Supplies) [9136]
Northern Electronics Automation (Electrical and Electronic Equipment and Supplies) [9137]
Northstar Steel and Aluminum Inc. (Metals) [20239]
Plastic Supply Inc. (Plastics) [23012]
Seamans Supply Company Inc. (Electrical and Electronic Equipment and Supplies) [9349]
Shohet Frederick of New Hampshire Inc. (Hardware) [13916]
Sound Warehouse Inc. (Automotive) [3236]
State Scale Co., Inc. (Scientific and Measurement Devices) [24438]
Stonehill Group Inc. (Clothing) [5399]
Surplus Office Equipment Inc. (Office Equipment and Supplies) [21307]
T.B.I. Corp. (Food) [12703]
Tri-State (Restaurant and Commercial Foodservice Equipment and Supplies) [24249]
Tucker Library Interiors LLC (Furniture and Fixtures) [13263]
Viking (Construction Materials and Machinery) [8182]
Wolfpax Inc. (Shoes) [24898]
Yankee Electronics Inc. (Electrical and Electronic Equipment and Supplies) [9617]

Mason
Compol Inc. (Sound and Entertainment Equipment and Supplies) [25145]

Melvin Village
Melvin Village Marina Inc. (Marine) [18566]

Meredith
Designers Ltd. (Toys and Hobby Goods) [26467]

Merrimack
American Copy Inc. (Office Equipment and Supplies) [20792]
KD Sales Associates (Clothing) [5106]
Merrimack Jewelers Inc. (Jewelry) [17522]
Transupport Inc. (Industrial Machinery) [16577]

Milford
Barbour Inc. (Clothing) [4804]

Nashua
Breton & Co. Inc.; Bruce (Jewelry) [17349]
Charron Medical Equipment Inc. (Medical, Dental, and Optical Equipment) [18735]
Chess Business Forms Co. (Paper and Paper Products) [21677]
Cirrus Technology Inc. (Computers and Software) [6069]
Complete Computer Solutions of New England (Computers and Software) [6092]
Corriveau-Routhier, Inc. (Floorcovering Equipment and Supplies) [9829]
Edgcomb Metals Co. New England Div. (Metals) [19950]
Faulcon Industries (Health and Beauty Aids) [14100]
Ferman Fabrics Centers (Textiles and Notions) [26033]
Heating Specialties of New Hampshire (Heating and Cooling Equipment and Supplies) [14483]
Horizon Business Systems (Computers and Software) [6340]
Marion Office Products Inc. (Office Equipment and Supplies) [21124]
Nashua Corp. (Office Equipment and Supplies) [21155]
Nashua Wallpaper & Paint Co. (Paints and Varnishes) [21513]
New Hampshire Tobacco Corp. (Tobacco Products) [26331]
New Hampshire Tobacco Corp. (Tobacco Products) [26332]
Oasis Imaging Products (Specialty Equipment and Products) [25770]

New London
Sigma Data Inc. (Computers and Software) [6727]

Newington
Rockingham Electrical Supplies Inc. (Electrical and Electronic Equipment and Supplies) [9307]

Newport
Skyline Designs (Furniture and Fixtures) [13246]
Skyline Designs (Restaurant and Commercial Foodservice Equipment and Supplies) [24222]

North Conway
Porter Office Machine Corp. (Office Equipment and Supplies) [21219]

North Hampton
Officeland of the N.H. Seacoast (Office Equipment and Supplies) [21192]

North Sutton
Labsphere (Electrical and Electronic Equipment and Supplies) [8962]

North Woodstock
Attraction Services Corp. (Photographic Equipment and Supplies) [22828]
Original Design Silk Screen Co. (Textiles and Notions) [26164]

Northwood
Harding Metals Inc. (Used, Scrap, and Recycled Materials) [26836]
Harding Metals Inc. (Used, Scrap, and Recycled Materials) [26837]

Ossipee
PL Preferred Products (Textiles and Notions) [26178]
Preston Fuels; John (Household Appliances) [15279]

Pelham
Carr Inc.; Jim (Jewelry) [17359]
Dave's Jewelry & Giftware (Jewelry) [17389]
RGA Tire Shop (Automotive) [3154]

Pembroke
New Hampshire Tile Distributors (Floorcovering Equipment and Supplies) [10076]
Paulsen Company Inc.; G. (Books and Other Printed Materials) [4046]

Peterborough
Appropriate Solutions (Computers and Software) [5955]

Plaistow
Aqua Dream Pools Inc. (Recreational and Sporting Goods) [23520]
Gani International Inc.; J. (Specialty Equipment and Products) [25656]
United Business Machines Inc. (Office Equipment and Supplies) [21327]

Portsmouth
Amedem Enterprises, Inc. (Cleaning and Janitorial Supplies) [4570]
Anns Uniform Center Inc. (Clothing) [4775]
Burgon Tool Steel Company Inc. (Metals) [19844]
Daily Bread Company Inc. (Food) [10892]
Gigatec (U.S.A.) Inc. (Computers and Software) [6302]
Portsmouth Paper Co. (Cleaning and Janitorial Supplies) [4688]
Sprague Energy Corp. (Petroleum, Fuels, and Related Equipment) [22693]
Sprague Energy Corp. (Petroleum, Fuels, and Related Equipment) [22694]
Warrington Group Ltd. (Shoes) [24888]

Salem
Andover Corp. (Medical, Dental, and Optical Supplies) [19153]
Buderus Hydronic Systems Inc. (Plumbing Materials and Fixtures) [23100]
Conprotec Inc. (Plastics) [22948]
Eagle Trophy (Jewelry) [17403]
Mifax-New Hampshire (Office Equipment and Supplies) [21144]
Northeast Airgas Inc. (Industrial Supplies) [17078]
Publishers Supply Inc. (Specialty Equipment and Products) [25794]
Salem Coca-Cola Bottling Co. (Soft Drinks) [25032]
Wescorp International Ltd. (Computers and Software) [6862]

Silver Lake
Jog-A-Lite Inc. (Recreational and Sporting Goods) [23759]

Stoddard
Eaton; Daniel A. (Textiles and Notions) [26026]

Stratham
Stratham Hardware & Lumber Co. (Paints and Varnishes) [21590]
Stratham Tire Inc. (Automotive) [3273]

Walpole
Johnson Inc.; R.N. (Agricultural Equipment and Supplies) [889]

West Lebanon
Stateline Sports (Recreational and Sporting Goods) [23986]
Tecnica USA (Shoes) [24875]

Westmoreland
Castor; Stanley (Heating and Cooling Equipment and Supplies) [14370]

Whitefield
Austin Aircraft (HIE); D. (Aeronautical Equipment and Supplies) [46]
D. Austin Aircraft (Aeronautical Equipment and Supplies) [78]

Wilmot
Brain Corp. (Office Equipment and Supplies) [20853]

Wilton
Draper Energy Co. Inc. (Minerals and Ores) [20535]

Winchester
Wallock; John M. (Automotive) [3397]

Windham
A-Top Polymers Inc. (Plastics) [22917]
Nationwide Ladder & Equipment Company Inc. (Construction Materials and Machinery) [7768]
Nationwide Ladder and Equipment Company Inc. (Industrial Machinery) [16344]
United Beauty Equipment Co. (Health and Beauty Aids) [14269]
United Beauty Equipment Co. (Restaurant and Commercial Foodservice Equipment and Supplies) [24253]

Wolfeboro Falls
Zee Medical Service Co. (Medical, Dental, and Optical Equipment) [19114]

New Jersey

Adelphia
Shore Point Distributing Co. (Alcoholic Beverages) [2023]
Weber and Sons Inc. (Office Equipment and Supplies) [21350]

Allendale
Control Associates Inc. (Automotive) [2481]
Plus Corporation of America (Office Equipment and Supplies) [21217]

Alloway
Waddington Dairy (Food) [12859]

Asbury Park
Asbury Syrup and Paper Company Inc. (Paper and Paper Products) [21636]

Atlantic City
Franklin Electric Company Inc. (Atlantic City, New Jersey) (Electrical and Electronic Equipment and Supplies) [8758]

Avenel
Rea International Corp. (Electrical and Electronic Equipment and Supplies) [9268]
R.S.R. Electronics Inc. (Electrical and Electronic Equipment and Supplies) [9323]

Barnegat
HM Water Technologies Inc. (Chemicals) [4417]

Barrington
Edmund Scientific Co., Industrial Optics Div. (Scientific and Measurement Devices) [24352]

Basking Ridge
Axon Import Export Corporation (Clothing) [4793]

Bayonne
Bookazine Co., Inc. (Books and Other Printed Materials) [3574]
Muralo Company Inc. (Paints and Varnishes) [21510]
Steven Industries, Inc. (Paints and Varnishes) [21589]

Bedminster
Leland Limited Inc. (Recreational and Sporting Goods) [23785]

Belleville
Beisler Weidmann Company Inc. (Paper and Paper Products) [21650]
ILHWA (Food) [11495]

Bellmawr
Price Inc.; Albert E. (Gifts and Novelties) [13426]

Belvidere
Lazy-Man, Inc. (Household Appliances) [15201]

Bergenfield
Cornell Surgical Co. (Medical, Dental, and Optical Supplies) [19253]
Hansen Caviar Co. (Food) [11374]
Lady Iris Cosmetic Company Inc. (Health and Beauty Aids) [14148]
Palermo Supply Company Inc. (Plumbing Materials and Fixtures) [23306]
Roofers Supplies Inc. (Construction Materials and Machinery) [7956]
Siperstein, Inc.; N. (Paints and Varnishes) [21579]

Berkeley Heights
Enslow Publishers, Inc. (Books and Other Printed Materials) [3733]
ESSROC Corp. (Construction Materials and Machinery) [7321]

Berlin
Garden State Tile Design Center (Floorcovering Equipment and Supplies) [9908]
Orrefors Inc. (Household Items) [15602]

Bernardsville
Dyer and Co.; B.W. (Food) [11005]
Eastview Editions (Books and Other Printed Materials) [3711]
Samuel Specialty Metals Inc. (Metals) [20351]

Birmingham
Sybron Chemicals Inc. (Chemicals) [4523]

Blackwood
Associated Building Specialties (Furniture and Fixtures) [13026]
Associated Building Specialties (Restaurant and Commercial Foodservice Equipment and Supplies) [24069]
I See Optical Co. (Medical, Dental, and Optical Supplies) [19364]
Seaboard Automotive Inc. (Automotive) [3202]

Blairstown
Operations Technology Inc. (Electrical and Electronic Equipment and Supplies) [9158]

Bloomfield
Atlantic Track and Turnout Co. (Railroad Equipment and Supplies) [23472]
NTE Electronics Inc. (Electrical and Electronic Equipment and Supplies) [9147]
World Finer Foods Inc. (Food) [12981]

Boonton
Allure Home Creation Company Inc. (Household Items) [15395]
Carbone of America (Communications Systems and Equipment) [5548]

Bordentown
Nordica USA Inc. (Recreational and Sporting Goods) [23847]

Bound Brook
Bicknell Huston Distributors (Recreational and Sporting Goods) [23554]
Efinger Sporting Goods Inc. (Recreational and Sporting Goods) [23647]
Michel Company Inc.; R.E. (Heating and Cooling Equipment and Supplies) [14556]

Branchburg
Office Interiors Inc. (Office Equipment and Supplies) [21182]

Brick
Indusco, Ltd. (Electrical and Electronic Equipment and Supplies) [8875]
The Tile Place (Floorcovering Equipment and Supplies) [10244]

Bridgeport
Anchor Sales Associates Inc. (Industrial Supplies) [16698]
Forbo Wallcoverings Inc. (Household Items) [15504]
Forbo Wallcoverings Inc. (Paints and Varnishes) [21444]

Bridgewater
Baker & Taylor (Computers and Software) [5997]
Brother International Corp. (Office Equipment and Supplies) [20858]
Hamamatsu Photonic Systems (Photographic Equipment and Supplies) [22862]
Olivetti Office USA Inc. (Office Equipment and Supplies) [21199]
Photonics Management Corp. (Electrical and Electronic Equipment and Supplies) [9197]

Broadway
Cherrybrook (Veterinary Products) [27109]

Brooklawn
Tile Gallery Inc. (Floorcovering Equipment and Supplies) [10236]

Burlington
Dupli-Fax Inc. (Office Equipment and Supplies) [20975]
Multifacet Industrial Supply Company Inc. (Industrial Supplies) [17061]
Wallace Sportswear (Clothing) [5471]

Caldwell
Anderson and Vreeland Inc. (Industrial Machinery) [15773]

Camden
Camden Iron and Metal Co. (Metals) [19850]
Eisenberg Brothers Inc. (Paper and Paper Products) [21720]
Engine Distributors Inc. (Industrial Machinery) [15988]
NJ Rivet Co. (Hardware) [13847]
Paris Food Corp. (Food) [12109]
Reliable Tire Distributors Inc. (Automotive) [3147]
Reliable Tire Distributors Inc. (Rubber) [24290]

Carlstadt
Aldine Technologies Industries, Inc. (Paper and Paper Products) [21621]
Argraph Central (Electrical and Electronic Equipment and Supplies) [8369]
Argraph Corp. (Electrical and Electronic Equipment and Supplies) [8370]
Bamberger Molding Compounds Inc.; C. (Used, Scrap, and Recycled Materials) [26757]
Beauty & Beauty Enterprises, Inc. (Health and Beauty Aids) [14037]
Beauty and Beauty Enterprises Inc. (Medical, Dental, and Optical Supplies) [19179]
Beta Screen Corp. (Specialty Equipment and Products) [25572]

Betti Industries Inc.; H. (Specialty Equipment and Products) [25573]
Blumenthal-Lansing Co. (Textiles and Notions) [25983]
Carlyle Industries Inc. (Textiles and Notions) [25996]
Cook and Dunn Paint Corp. Adelphi Coating (Paints and Varnishes) [21418]
Coronet Paper Corp. (Paper and Paper Products) [21692]
Dixon Co.; William (Industrial Machinery) [15953]
Dreyco Inc. (Automotive) [2561]
General Trading Company Inc. (Food) [11252]
Halebian; Michael (Floorcovering Equipment and Supplies) [9934]
Reiner & Company, Inc.; John (Industrial Machinery) [16446]
Style Asia Inc. (Gifts and Novelties) [13454]
Teaneck Graphics Inc. (Furniture and Fixtures) [13257]

Carteret

D.B. Brown Inc. (Food) [10922]
Gemini Sound Products Corp. (Sound and Entertainment Equipment and Supplies) [25208]
Plaza Paint Co. (Paints and Varnishes) [21541]

Cedar Grove

Pro-Flo Products (Plumbing Materials and Fixtures) [23330]

Cedar Knolls

AlphaNet Solutions Inc. (Computers and Software) [5914]
Carnrick Laboratories Inc. (Medical, Dental, and Optical Supplies) [19218]
Consolidated Bearing Co. (Automotive) [2474]

Chatham

Globe Trends Inc. (Food) [11274]
Modern Mass Media Inc. (Sound and Entertainment Equipment and Supplies) [25331]
Modern Mass Media Inc. (Household Appliances) [15237]

Cherry Hill

The Bookworm (Books and Other Printed Materials) [3585]
Fewkes and Co.; Joseph T. (Electrical and Electronic Equipment and Supplies) [8738]
Harrison Wholesale Products Inc. (Veterinary Products) [27145]
Infinity Paper Inc. (Paper and Paper Products) [21776]
inTEST Corp. (Scientific and Measurement Devices) [24375]
National Keystone Mizzy Tridynamics (Medical, Dental, and Optical Supplies) [19476]
New Jersey Art Drafting (Specialty Equipment and Products) [25757]
Optibal Co. (Health and Beauty Aids) [14185]
Subaru of America Inc. (Motorized Vehicles) [20731]
Trinkle Sales Inc. (Electrical and Electronic Equipment and Supplies) [9510]

Chester

Lion Ribbon Company Inc. (Textiles and Notions) [26126]
Toggitt Ltd.; Joan (Textiles and Notions) [26231]

Clark

Knitting Machine and Supply Company Inc. (Industrial Machinery) [16210]

CliffsiDe Park

Marburn Stores Inc. (Household Items) [15576]

Cliffwood

Federated Purchaser Inc. (Electrical and Electronic Equipment and Supplies) [8735]

Clifton

AGL Welding Supply Company Inc. (Industrial Supplies) [16675]

Cantel Medical Corp. (Medical, Dental, and Optical Equipment) [18725]
Chulani International (Toys and Hobby Goods) [26443]
Denman and Davis (Metals) [19926]
Duradex Inc. (Paper and Paper Products) [21716]
Fine Organics Corp. (Industrial Supplies) [16862]
Glen Mills Inc. (Scientific and Measurement Devices) [24366]
Hopewell Valley Specialties (Food) [11459]
Mills Inc.; Glen (Industrial Machinery) [16304]
Passaic Metal & Building Supplies Co. (Construction Materials and Machinery) [7838]
Pfizer Inc. Distribution Center (Medical, Dental, and Optical Supplies) [19536]
Pine Lesser and Sons Inc. (Tobacco Products) [26340]
Schadler and Sons Inc.; John (Sound and Entertainment Equipment and Supplies) [25431]
SST Corp. (Medical, Dental, and Optical Supplies) [19634]
Systems House Inc. (Computers and Software) [6784]
Tele-Measurements Inc. (Sound and Entertainment Equipment and Supplies) [25475]
Terre Company of New Jersey Inc. (Agricultural Equipment and Supplies) [1324]
X-Ray Industrial Distributor Corp. (Scientific and Measurement Devices) [24458]

Closter

American Key Food Products Inc. (Food) [10399]
Cressi-Sub USA Inc. (Recreational and Sporting Goods) [23610]
Hi-Fashion Cosmetics Inc. (Health and Beauty Aids) [14126]
Intech Corp. (Industrial Supplies) [16960]
Moulinex Appliances Inc. (Household Appliances) [15242]

Collingswood

Diener Brick Co. (Construction Materials and Machinery) [7264]
M & E Marine Supply, Inc. (Marine) [18553]
Raymond Jewelers (Jewelry) [17557]

Cranbury

FRP Supplies Inc. (Construction Materials and Machinery) [7372]

Cranford

Federal Plastics Corp. (Plastics) [22960]
Gusmer Co.; A. (Industrial Machinery) [16081]
Gusmer Enterprises Inc. (Industrial Supplies) [16915]

Dayton

BMI Educational Services (Books and Other Printed Materials) [3562]
Bunzl New Jersey Inc. (Paper and Paper Products) [21659]
Garden State Tile Distributors (Floorcovering Equipment and Supplies) [9910]

Delanco

Huston Distributors Inc. (Recreational and Sporting Goods) [23736]
Prosteel Service Centers Inc. (Metals) [20301]

Delran

East Coast Connection Inc. (Shoes) [24729]
South Jersey X-Ray Supply Co. (Medical, Dental, and Optical Equipment) [19045]

Denville

Elmco Distributors Inc. (Agricultural Equipment and Supplies) [550]
FGH Systems Inc. (Industrial Machinery) [16007]

Dover

Casio, Inc. (Jewelry) [17362]
Kahant Electrical Supply Co. (Electrical and Electronic Equipment and Supplies) [8925]

Region Oil Div. (Petroleum, Fuels, and Related Equipment) [22619]
Spartan Oil Co. (Petroleum, Fuels, and Related Equipment) [22687]

East Brunswick

Book Dynamics, Inc. (Books and Other Printed Materials) [3569]

East Hanover

Achievement Products Inc. (Gifts and Novelties) [13289]
Fidelity Paper Supply Inc. (Paper and Paper Products) [21725]
International Tape Products Co. (Office Equipment and Supplies) [21065]

East Newark

Harrison Supply Co. (Construction Materials and Machinery) [7450]

East Orange

M & F Foods (Food) [11750]
Pierson Co.; J.W. (Petroleum, Fuels, and Related Equipment) [22585]

East Rutherford

Allied Building Products Corp. (Construction Materials and Machinery) [6942]
Commtron Corporation (Sound and Entertainment Equipment and Supplies) [25144]
Hoke Controls (Industrial Supplies) [16931]
Lello Appliances Corp. (Household Appliances) [15204]
Worldwide Media Service Inc. (Books and Other Printed Materials) [4298]

Eatontown

Cooper Electric Supply Co. (Electrical and Electronic Equipment and Supplies) [8578]
Huntleigh Technology Inc. (Medical, Dental, and Optical Equipment) [18846]
PCE Inc. (Electrical and Electronic Equipment and Supplies) [9182]

Edison

Aerogroup International Inc. (Shoes) [24664]
Allied Electronics (Electrical and Electronic Equipment and Supplies) [8315]
Bay State Computer of New Jersey Inc. (Computers and Software) [6004]
Contech Instrumentation (Electrical and Electronic Equipment and Supplies) [8574]
Execu-Flow Systems, Inc. (Medical, Dental, and Optical Supplies) [19311]
Glaze Inc. (Gifts and Novelties) [13362]
Golden-Lee Book Distributors, Inc. (Books and Other Printed Materials) [3784]
Grant and Sons Inc.; William (Alcoholic Beverages) [1729]
Gross and Hecht Trucking Corp. (Automotive) [2708]
International Piecework Controls Co. (Household Appliances) [15177]
Metro/North (Electrical and Electronic Equipment and Supplies) [9069]
Model Rectifier Corp. (Toys and Hobby Goods) [26580]
Permark, Inc. (Medical, Dental, and Optical Equipment) [18982]
Raritan Supply Co. (Plumbing Materials and Fixtures) [23335]
Samara Brothers, Inc. (Clothing) [5330]
Sinar-Bron Inc. (Photographic Equipment and Supplies) [22905]
Singer Sewing Co. (Household Appliances) [15313]
Star Micronics America Inc. (Computers and Software) [6759]
Twin County Grocers Inc. (Food) [12778]
York International Corp. (Heating and Cooling Equipment and Supplies) [14775]
Zebra Pen Corp. (Office Equipment and Supplies) [21370]

Elizabeth

Abba Products Corp. (Veterinary Products) [27055]
AFI Food Service Distributors Inc. (Food) [10341]
Alpha Wire Co. (Electrical and Electronic Equipment and Supplies) [8332]
Atalanta Corp. (Food) [10461]
BFI/Specmark (Furniture and Fixtures) [13036]
Classic Tile, Inc. (Floorcovering Equipment and Supplies) [9811]
Jacobson & Company Inc. (Construction Materials and Machinery) [7529]
Papetti's Hygrade Egg Products Inc. (Food) [12104]
Port Electric Supply Corp. (Electrical and Electronic Equipment and Supplies) [9219]
Ritter Sysco Food Services Inc. (Food) [12321]
Stulz-Sickles Steel Co. (Metals) [20409]
Wakefern Food Corp. (Food) [12865]
Wakefern Food Corp. (Food) [12866]
Wayne Steel Co. (Metals) [20481]

Elmwood Park

Aetna Chemical Corp. (Chemicals) [4315]
JVC Professional Products Co. (Electrical and Electronic Equipment and Supplies) [8924]
Northern Jersey Reserve Supply Co. (Construction Materials and Machinery) [7796]

Englewood

ATS Money Systems Inc. (Specialty Equipment and Products) [25567]
ATS Money Systems Inc. (Computers and Software) [5982]
Coffin Turbo Pump Inc. (Industrial Machinery) [15895]
Fisher Brothers Steel Corp. (Metals) [19979]
Ozer; Jerome S. (Books and Other Printed Materials) [4029]
Rapac Network International (Automotive) [3135]
Royal Sovereign Corp. (Heating and Cooling Equipment and Supplies) [14669]
Sanderson and Sons North America Ltd.; Arthur (Household Items) [15649]
Techmedia Computer Systems Corp. (Computers and Software) [6798]

Englewood Cliffs

Chemapol USA Inc. (Chemicals) [4350]
Chick Master International Inc. (Agricultural Equipment and Supplies) [415]
Commonwealth Metal Corp. (Metals) [19890]
Ferrari North America Inc. (Automotive) [2613]
Irrideco International Corp. (Agricultural Equipment and Supplies) [871]
Konica U.S.A. Inc. (Photographic Equipment and Supplies) [22871]
LEK USA Inc. (Chemicals) [4440]

Englishtown

Bargain City (Clothing) [4805]
Siperstein Freehold Paint (Paints and Varnishes) [21578]
Washington Forge Inc. (Household Items) [15702]

Fair Lawn

Lake Crescent Inc. (Plastics) [22990]
Maxell Corporation of America (Sound and Entertainment Equipment and Supplies) [25306]
Rock Lumber and Supply Co.; Glen (Construction Materials and Machinery) [7947]

Fairfield

Bradley Pharmaceuticals Inc. (Medical, Dental, and Optical Supplies) [19197]
Clinical Homecare Corp. Haemotronic Ltd. (Medical, Dental, and Optical Supplies) [19235]
Electronic Office Systems (Office Equipment and Supplies) [20989]
Hermes Machine Tool Company Inc. (Industrial Machinery) [16099]
Marshall Industries (Electrical and Electronic Equipment and Supplies) [9033]
Monarch Electric Company Inc. (Electrical and Electronic Equipment and Supplies) [9092]

Olflex Wire and Cable Inc. (Electrical and Electronic Equipment and Supplies) [9154]
Palmieri Associates (Electrical and Electronic Equipment and Supplies) [9177]
Palmieri Associates (Household Appliances) [15263]
PHONEXPRESS Inc. (Communications Systems and Equipment) [5710]
Quickshine of America Inc. (Chemicals) [4488]

Farmingdale

Copy Center Inc. (Office Equipment and Supplies) [20914]
Copy Center Inc. (Office Equipment and Supplies) [20915]
Garden State Tile Distributors (Floorcovering Equipment and Supplies) [9911]
Loft's Seed Inc. (Agricultural Equipment and Supplies) [966]
RABCO Equipment Corp. (Office Equipment and Supplies) [21232]
Schroth Inc.; Emil A. (Metals) [20356]

Flemington

Flemington Block and Supply Inc. (Construction Materials and Machinery) [7349]

Florham Park

Aftec Inc. (Computers and Software) [5894]
RIA International (Health and Beauty Aids) [14217]
Schein Pharmaceutical Inc. (Medical, Dental, and Optical Supplies) [19594]

Fords

Datamatics Management Services, Inc. (Computers and Software) [6189]
Siperstein, Inc.; N. (Paints and Varnishes) [21580]

Ft. Lee

Okaya U.S.A. Inc. (Metals) [20245]
Paddington Corp. (Alcoholic Beverages) [1940]
Torosian Brothers (Floorcovering Equipment and Supplies) [10254]

Franklin Lakes

Fagan Inc.; Ed (Metals) [19964]
Teleparts, Inc. (Automotive) [3298]

Garfield

C-Mor Co. (Household Items) [15433]
Latin Percussion Inc. (Sound and Entertainment Equipment and Supplies) [25279]
LP Music Group (Sound and Entertainment Equipment and Supplies) [25291]

Glen Rock

Direct Connect International Inc. (Toys and Hobby Goods) [26470]

Gloucester City

Ply-Gem Manufacturing Co. (Storage Equipment and Containers) [25932]

Green Brook

Tile Country Inc. (Floorcovering Equipment and Supplies) [10229]

Hackensack

800 Spirits Inc. (Alcoholic Beverages) [1470]
American Paper Towel Co. (Paper and Paper Products) [21630]
Conserve Electric (Electrical and Electronic Equipment and Supplies) [8562]
Gregg Company Ltd. (Railroad Equipment and Supplies) [23479]
Jacoby Appliance Parts (Household Appliances) [15179]
Patron Transmission (Automotive) [3087]
Reinauer Petroleum Co. (Petroleum, Fuels, and Related Equipment) [22621]
Sewon America Inc. (Chemicals) [4509]
Superior Linen Company Inc. (Household Items) [15673]

Hackettstown

Alacrity Systems Inc. (Computers and Software) [5898]
Bates Manufacturing Co. (Office Equipment and Supplies) [20833]

Haddonfield

Read-Ferry Company Ltd. (Industrial Machinery) [16442]

Hainesport

Cho-Pat Inc. (Medical, Dental, and Optical Equipment) [18742]
Perry Videx, LLC (Industrial Machinery) [16392]

Hamburg

Wayne Tile Co. (Floorcovering Equipment and Supplies) [10287]

Hamilton

Pericom Inc. (Computers and Software) [6609]

Harrington Park

Capresso Inc. (Restaurant and Commercial Foodservice Equipment and Supplies) [24090]

Harrison

Fedco Steel Corp. (Metals) [19967]
Newark Newsdealers Supply Company Inc. (Books and Other Printed Materials) [3998]
Tucker Company Inc.; M. (Restaurant and Commercial Foodservice Equipment and Supplies) [24250]
Tucker Company Inc.; M. (Restaurant and Commercial Foodservice Equipment and Supplies) [24251]

Hasbrouck Heights

Coastal Oil New York Inc. (Petroleum, Fuels, and Related Equipment) [22147]
Logon Inc. (Computers and Software) [6443]

Hawthorne

Frezzolini Electronics Inc. (Electrical and Electronic Equipment and Supplies) [8761]
J.B. Wholesale (Veterinary Products) [27160]
Kirsch Energy System (Heating and Cooling Equipment and Supplies) [14509]

Hazlet

Interstate Electronics, Inc. (Sound and Entertainment Equipment and Supplies) [25254]
Vantage Sales & Marketing, Inc. (Books and Other Printed Materials) [4257]

Highland Park

Rutgers Book Center (Books and Other Printed Materials) [4129]

Hightstown

Princeton Book Company Publishers (Books and Other Printed Materials) [4084]

Hillsdale

Jan-Mar Industries (Sound and Entertainment Equipment and Supplies) [25258]
Saint Aepan's Press & Book Distributors, Inc. (Books and Other Printed Materials) [4135]

Hillside

Brookline Machine Company, Inc. (Automotive) [2394]
Gerber Metal Supply Co. (Used, Scrap, and Recycled Materials) [26826]
Mooney General Paper Co. (Paper and Paper Products) [21843]
Mooney General Paper Co. (Industrial Supplies) [17049]

Ho Ho Kus

Winebow, Inc. (Alcoholic Beverages) [2128]

Hoboken

Baily and Company Inc.; Joshua L. (Textiles and Notions) [25972]

Holmdel

Globus Industries (Electrical and Electronic Equipment and Supplies) [8791]

Hurffville

Mitchell Hardware Co. (Plumbing Materials and Fixtures) [23270]

Irvington

Admiral Wine and Liquor Co. (Alcoholic Beverages) [1474]
Manufacturers Reserve Supply Inc. (Construction Materials and Machinery) [7637]
Tesco Distributors Inc. (Heating and Cooling Equipment and Supplies) [14719]

Jackson

Marmelstein and Associates Inc. (Food) [11788]
Mundy Enterprises, Inc.; K.C. (Automotive) [3003]
Sebastian Inc.; Paul (Health and Beauty Aids) [14232]

Jamesburg

Canon U.S.A. Inc., Office Products Div. (Office Equipment and Supplies) [20875]

Jersey City

A To Z Vending Service Corp. (Specialty Equipment and Products) [25539]
Ambriola Co. Inc. (Food) [10391]
American Mail-Well Co. (Paper and Paper Products) [21628]
Baldwin Steel Co. (Metals) [19800]
Bass Inc.; Rudolf (Industrial Machinery) [15803]
Booksmith Promotional Co. (Books and Other Printed Materials) [3582]
Decorative Aides Co. Inc. (Household Items) [15468]
Hugo-Neu-Schnitzen East (Used, Scrap, and Recycled Materials) [26845]
Ideal Supply Co. (Plumbing Materials and Fixtures) [23218]
North American Plywood Corp. (Construction Materials and Machinery) [7791]
North East Auto-Marine Terminal Inc. (Motorized Vehicles) [20697]
Prolerized Schiabo-Neu Co. (Used, Scrap, and Recycled Materials) [26948]
R & W Distribution Inc. (Books and Other Printed Materials) [4104]
Rapid Industrial Plastics Co. (Plastics) [23021]
Sabrett Food Products (Food) [12385]
Siperstein, Inc.; N. (Paints and Varnishes) [21582]

Kearny

Federal Wine and Liquor Co. (Alcoholic Beverages) [1686]
Fedway Associates Inc. (Alcoholic Beverages) [1687]
SOS Gases Inc. (Chemicals) [4515]

Kenilworth

Belting Industry Company Inc. (Industrial Supplies) [16747]

Keyport

R.C.A. America (Construction Materials and Machinery) [7904]
Reedy International Corp. (Cleaning and Janitorial Supplies) [4693]
Semcor Equipment & Manufacturing Corp. (Hardware) [13909]

Kinnelon

Derstine Book Co.; Roy (Books and Other Printed Materials) [3687]

Lakewood

Century Sports Inc. (Recreational and Sporting Goods) [23586]

Harold Import Company Inc. (Household Items) [15520]
Intruder Alert Security (Security and Safety Equipment) [24574]
Van Sant Equipment Corp. (Industrial Supplies) [17251]

Laurence Harbor

Duferco Trading Corp. (Metals) [19939]

Lawrenceville

Tindall Inc.; E.H. (Livestock and Farm Products) [18284]

Lebanon

Construction Specialties Inc. (Construction Materials and Machinery) [7209]
The Tile Barn (Floorcovering Equipment and Supplies) [10217]
Weiland Associates (Food) [12898]

Leonia

Apple Food Sales Company Inc. (Food) [10424]
C and W Zabel Co. (Books and Other Printed Materials) [3602]
Zabel Co.; C & W (Books and Other Printed Materials) [4305]

Liberty Corner

Kimber Petroleum Corp. (Petroleum, Fuels, and Related Equipment) [22405]

Linden

Beijing Book Co. Inc. (Books and Other Printed Materials) [3549]
Birdsall and Company Inc.; W.A. (Plumbing Materials and Fixtures) [23088]
Pro Plastics Inc. (Plastics) [23019]
Resyn Corp. (Plastics) [23026]
Sealand Power Industries, Inc. (Marine) [18606]
Thor Electronics Corp. (Electrical and Electronic Equipment and Supplies) [9487]
Transco Inc. (Sound and Entertainment Equipment and Supplies) [25482]
Turtle and Hughes Inc. (Electrical and Electronic Equipment and Supplies) [9517]

Linwood

Clofine Dairy and Food Products Inc. (Food) [10772]

Little Falls

Eastern Data Paper (Office Equipment and Supplies) [20977]
Peugeot Citroen Engines (Automotive) [3095]

Little Ferry

Conesco Industries Ltd. (Construction Materials and Machinery) [7207]

Little Silver

Builders General Supply Co. (Construction Materials and Machinery) [7100]

Livingston

Bartky Mineralogical Enterprises Inc. (Jewelry) [17328]
Briel America Inc. (Household Appliances) [15058]
Hammill and Gillespie Inc. (Minerals and Ores) [20544]
Orient Book Distributors (Books and Other Printed Materials) [4025]

Lodi

Atlantic Detroit Diesel-Allison Inc. (Automotive) [2265]
Siperstein, Inc.; N. (Paints and Varnishes) [21581]
Stanley Roberts Inc. (Household Items) [15667]

Long Branch

Kimbo Educational (Sound and Entertainment Equipment and Supplies) [25272]
Norwood Auto Parts Co. (Automotive) [3048]
Servall Products Inc. (Paper and Paper Products) [21934]

Siperstein West End (Paints and Varnishes) [21584]

Lyndhurst

Benedict-Miller Inc. (Metals) [19810]
Citizen Watch Company of America Inc. (Jewelry) [17369]
Knapp Company Inc.; R.S. (Scientific and Measurement Devices) [24384]
North American Fur Producers New York Inc. (Livestock and Farm Products) [18135]
North American Watch Corp. (Jewelry) [17536]
Ronlee Apparel Co. (Clothing) [5319]

Madison

AMG Corp. (Gifts and Novelties) [13303]
Heller Co.; E.P. (Industrial Machinery) [16097]

Magnolia

FVB Enterprises, Inc. (Toys and Hobby Goods) [26488]

Mahwah

Aiwa America Inc. (Sound and Entertainment Equipment and Supplies) [25059]
Baker Linen Co.; H.W. (Household Items) [15413]
Castellon Inc.; E. (Books and Other Printed Materials) [3614]
Catholic Reading Society (Books and Other Printed Materials) [3615]
Folsom Corp. (Recreational and Sporting Goods) [23675]
Jaguar Cars (Automotive) [2809]
Kenlin Pet Supply Inc. (Veterinary Products) [27171]
Philips Electronic Instruments Co. (Scientific and Measurement Devices) [24418]
Ridgewood Corp. (Plumbing Materials and Fixtures) [23343]
Scriptex Enterprises Ltd. (Office Equipment and Supplies) [21262]
Seiko Corporation of America (Jewelry) [17595]
Thermion Technologies Inc. (Aeronautical Equipment and Supplies) [159]

Manalapan

Global Exports, Inc. (Plumbing Materials and Fixtures) [23192]
Huntleigh Technology Inc. (Medical, Dental, and Optical Supplies) [19363]

Manasquan

Post Yacht Supplies (Marine) [18587]

Maple Shade

Eastern Lift Truck Co. (Industrial Machinery) [15974]
Philadelphia Hide Brokerage (Luggage and Leather Goods) [18419]

Maplewood

Lehrhoff and Company Inc.; I. (Household Appliances) [15203]
Rails Co. (Railroad Equipment and Supplies) [23486]

Marlboro

Jay's Perfume Bar (Health and Beauty Aids) [14135]

Marlton

Bell Atlantic Meridian Systems Inc. (Communications Systems and Equipment) [5527]
Celestial Mercantile Corporation (Health and Beauty Aids) [14059]
Celestial Mercantile Corporation (Medical, Dental, and Optical Supplies) [19222]

Matawan

Manzo Contracting Co. (Construction Materials and Machinery) [7638]
Water Warehouse, Etc. (Soft Drinks) [25050]

Maywood

Colossal Jewelry and Accessories Inc. (Jewelry) [17374]

Medford

DuBell Lumber Co. (Construction Materials and Machinery) [7288]
Haddon House Food Products Inc. (Food) [11356]

Mendham

Viking Traders, Inc. (Medical, Dental, and Optical Equipment) [19102]

Middlesex

Export Consultants Corp. (Aeronautical Equipment and Supplies) [84]
Segura Products Co. (Medical, Dental, and Optical Supplies) [19602]

Midland Park

Selsi Company Inc. (Scientific and Measurement Devices) [24430]

Milford

Stem Brothers Inc. (Petroleum, Fuels, and Related Equipment) [22704]

Millburn

Arcadia Merchandising Corp. (Recreational and Sporting Goods) [23522]
Jaydor Corp. (Alcoholic Beverages) [1779]

Millington

Garden State Fireworks Inc. (Explosives) [9635]

Milltown

New Process Development (Computers and Software) [6551]

Millville

Durand International (Gifts and Novelties) [13348]
Kane Steel Co. (Metals) [20086]
MacAlaster Bicknell Company of New Jersey Inc. (Chemicals) [4445]
Macalaster Bicknell Company of NJ, Inc. (Scientific and Measurement Devices) [24392]

Monmouth Junction

Allstar Enterprises Inc. (Gifts and Novelties) [13298]
Guest Supply Inc. (Restaurant and Commercial Foodservice Equipment and Supplies) [24130]

Montclair

Full Perspective Videos Services Inc. (Sound and Entertainment Equipment and Supplies) [25201]

Montvale

Compass Foods Eight O'Clock Coffee (Food) [10802]
Hansco Technologies, Inc. (Industrial Machinery) [16087]
Landers-Segal Color Co. (Paints and Varnishes) [21485]
Mercedes-Benz of North America Inc. (Motorized Vehicles) [20679]
Merck-Medco Managed Care Inc. (Medical, Dental, and Optical Supplies) [19449]

Montville

L.T. Plant, Inc. (Food) [11739]
Sirak & Sirak Associates (Books and Other Printed Materials) [4164]
Vernitron Corp. AST Bearings Div. (Automotive) [3391]

Moonachie

Abbey Metal Corp. (Used, Scrap, and Recycled Materials) [26725]
Bohrer Inc.; A. (Food) [10586]
Crystal Products Corp. (Food) [10879]
Dessau Brass Inc. (Gifts and Novelties) [13346]
Moonachie Co. (Industrial Supplies) [17048]

Neuman Distributors, Inc. (Health and Beauty Aids) [14175]
Toy Wonders Inc. (Toys and Hobby Goods) [26685]
Wechsler Coffee Corp. (Food) [12892]
Williams and Wells Corp. (Marine) [18641]

Moorestown

Government Electronic Systems Div. (Communications Systems and Equipment) [5623]
Graphic Systems Inc. (Specialty Equipment and Products) [25669]
Jolly & Sons, Inc.; Jack (Recreational and Sporting Goods) [23763]
Koen Book Distributors, Inc. (Books and Other Printed Materials) [3884]
Sbar's, Inc. (Toys and Hobby Goods) [26647]
Shingle & Gibb Co. (Industrial Supplies) [17172]
Wilmar Industries Inc. (Plumbing Materials and Fixtures) [23461]

Morganville

Valencia Imports Co. (Shoes) [24883]

Morris Plains

Charmant Incorporated USA (Medical, Dental, and Optical Equipment) [18734]
New Jersey Book Agency (Books and Other Printed Materials) [3994]
Tetra Sales U.S.A. (Medical, Dental, and Optical Supplies) [19652]

Morristown

Colgate-Palmolive Co. Institutional Products Div. (Cleaning and Janitorial Supplies) [4600]
Fabricated Plastics Inc. (Plastics) [22959]
Lynton Group Inc. (Aeronautical Equipment and Supplies) [119]
Miller Wholesale Electric Supply Co., Inc.—Morristown Division (Electrical and Electronic Equipment and Supplies) [9085]
RF Management Corp. (Medical, Dental, and Optical Equipment) [19020]

Mt. Ephraim

All Brand Appliance Parts Inc. (Household Appliances) [14999]

Mt. Holly

Amherst Electrical Supply (Electrical and Electronic Equipment and Supplies) [8346]
Herb's Seafood (Food) [11417]

Mt. Laurel

Camden Bag and Paper Company, Inc. (Paper and Paper Products) [21665]
Ideal Tile Co. (Floorcovering Equipment and Supplies) [9959]
Johnson and Towers Inc. (Automotive) [2826]
Marshall Industries (Electrical and Electronic Equipment and Supplies) [9032]
Roosevelt Paper Co. (Paper and Paper Products) [21911]

Mountain Lakes

Mountain Lakes Distributors (Toys and Hobby Goods) [26583]

Mountainside

Biglow Industrial Company Inc. (Automotive) [2361]
DRG International Inc. (Medical, Dental, and Optical Supplies) [19289]
Durst Corp. (Plumbing Materials and Fixtures) [23142]
Klingelhofer Corp. (Industrial Machinery) [16208]
Richton International Corp. (Agricultural Equipment and Supplies) [1191]
Wisner Manufacturing Inc. (Industrial Machinery) [16644]

Murray Hill

The Consulting Scientists (Medical, Dental, and Optical Supplies) [19245]

Venus Knitting Mills Inc. (Recreational and Sporting Goods) [24030]

Neptune

Adams Co.; S.S. (Toys and Hobby Goods) [26382]
Standard Supply Company Inc. (Construction Materials and Machinery) [8070]

New Brunswick

Thatcher Distributing Group (Books and Other Printed Materials) [4213]

New Providence

Wood Co.; W.B. (Office Equipment and Supplies) [21360]

Newark

Cooper Sportswear Manufacturing Company Inc. (Clothing) [4892]
D'Artagnan Inc. (Food) [10912]
Elan Chemical Co. (Chemicals) [4381]
Ferranti Steel and Aluminum Inc. (Metals) [19977]
G.J. Chemical Company Inc. (Chemicals) [4400]
Landew Sawdust Inc. (Wood and Wood Products) [27333]
Mathewson Co.; George A. (Automotive) [2925]
Naporano Iron and Metal Co. (Used, Scrap, and Recycled Materials) [26921]
Newark Wire Cloth Co. (Metals) [20225]
Trenk and Sons; Joseph (Livestock and Farm Products) [18289]
Welco Gases Corp. (Industrial Supplies) [17268]
Windsor Distributors Co. (Electrical and Electronic Equipment and Supplies) [9600]

North Bergen

Asuka Corp. (Medical, Dental, and Optical Supplies) [19166]
De Sisti Lighting Corp. (Electrical and Electronic Equipment and Supplies) [8615]
Hudson News Co. (Books and Other Printed Materials) [3836]
Lewisohn Sales Company Inc. (Construction Materials and Machinery) [7600]
Production Arts Lighting Inc. (Electrical and Electronic Equipment and Supplies) [9239]
Reuther Material Co. (Construction Materials and Machinery) [7921]
Rockwell (Construction Materials and Machinery) [7949]
Tree of Life Inc. Northeast (Food) [12749]
United Candy and Tobacco Co. (Tobacco Products) [26363]
The Vitamin Shoppe (Health and Beauty Aids) [14273]

North Brunswick

High Grade Beverage (Alcoholic Beverages) [1754]
High Grade Beverage (Food) [11430]
KG Specialty Steel Inc. (Metals) [20101]

North Haledon

Hay Greenhouses, Inc.; Alexander (Horticultural Supplies) [14885]
Zajac's Performance Seed (Agricultural Equipment and Supplies) [1467]

North Plainfield

Siperstein MK Paint (Paints and Varnishes) [21583]

Northvale

Joannou Cycle Company Inc.; G. (Recreational and Sporting Goods) [23758]
Norstar Consumer Products Company Inc. (Health and Beauty Aids) [14179]
Silhouette Optical Ltd. (Medical, Dental, and Optical Supplies) [19612]

Norwood

American Overseas Book Company Inc. (Books and Other Printed Materials) [3502]
Mitsui Foods, Inc. (Food) [11915]

Precision Technology Inc. (Norwood, New Jersey) (Medical, Dental, and Optical Equipment) [18992]
Q-T Foundations Company Inc. (Clothing) [5293]
Q-T Foundations Company Inc. (Clothing) [5294]
World Wide Wine and Spirit Importers Inc. (Alcoholic Beverages) [2137]

Oakhurst
The Tile Place (Floorcovering Equipment and Supplies) [10242]

Oakland
Fuji America Inc. (Recreational and Sporting Goods) [23679]
Relay Specialties Inc. (Electrical and Electronic Equipment and Supplies) [9272]
Ultra Books, Inc. (Books and Other Printed Materials) [4236]

Oaklyn
Rock Mirrors Inc. (Gifts and Novelties) [13438]

Ocean
Petillo Masterpiece Guitars (Sound and Entertainment Equipment and Supplies) [25380]

Ocean City
Seashore Supply Company Inc. (Plumbing Materials and Fixtures) [23366]

Old Bridge
Micro Central Inc. (Computers and Software) [6490]
The Tile Place (Floorcovering Equipment and Supplies) [10243]

Oradell
Ryen, Re Associates (Books and Other Printed Materials) [4131]
Sylvan Ginsbury Ltd. (Electrical and Electronic Equipment and Supplies) [9452]

Orange
CIMID Corp. (Industrial Supplies) [16798]
Mitchell Supreme Fuel Co. (Petroleum, Fuels, and Related Equipment) [22489]
Reisman Corp.; H. (Chemicals) [4492]

Oxford
OxTech Industries Inc. (Hardware) [13857]

Palmyra
Philadelphia Sign Company Inc. (Specialty Equipment and Products) [25783]

Paramus
Ajinomoto U.S.A. Inc. (Food) [10350]
Camerican International (Food) [10684]
Elish Paper Company Inc.; Harry (Paper and Paper Products) [21722]
EuroAmerican Brands LLC (Food) [11059]
HAAKE (Scientific and Measurement Devices) [24367]
HB Instruments Inc. (Scientific and Measurement Devices) [24369]
LoJack of New Jersey Corp. (Security and Safety Equipment) [24586]
LoJack of New Jersey Corp. (Automotive) [2888]
New York Fastener Corp. (Electrical and Electronic Equipment and Supplies) [9128]
Regional Communications Inc. (Communications Systems and Equipment) [5738]
Victor's House of Music (Sound and Entertainment Equipment and Supplies) [25502]

Park Ridge
Sony Corp. Business and Professional Products Group (Sound and Entertainment Equipment and Supplies) [25448]

Parsippany
A and S Corp. (Chemicals) [4308]
Emerson Radio Corp. (Electrical and Electronic Equipment and Supplies) [8701]

Greenebaum Inc.; M.H. (Food) [11320]
Heroes World Distribution, Inc. (Books and Other Printed Materials) [3826]
Homa Co. (Food) [11455]
International Playthings Inc. (Toys and Hobby Goods) [26535]

Passaic
Sharut Furniture Co. (Furniture and Fixtures) [13240]
SmithChem Div. (Paints and Varnishes) [21587]
Spola Fibres International Inc. (Textiles and Notions) [26210]
Stern Corp.; Paul N. (Textiles and Notions) [26214]
Utikem Products (Recreational and Sporting Goods) [24024]
Yecies Inc.; Herman W. (Industrial Supplies) [17291]

Paterson
American Comb Corp. (Health and Beauty Aids) [14018]
Axelrod Foods Inc. (Food) [10477]
Chew International Bascom Div. (Industrial Machinery) [15885]
Connecticut Valley Paper & Envelope Co. Inc. (Office Equipment and Supplies) [20909]
Custom Laminations Inc. (Textiles and Notions) [26010]
Fairclough and Sons Inc.; N.B. (Petroleum, Fuels, and Related Equipment) [22250]
Goodman and Co. Inc.; C. (Textiles and Notions) [26044]
Kessler Industries Inc. (Plumbing Materials and Fixtures) [23233]
Safety Truck Equipment Inc. (Automotive) [3181]
Sel-Leb Marketing, Inc. (Health and Beauty Aids) [14233]
Steelfab (Automotive) [3265]
Thermwell Products Co. Inc. (Construction Materials and Machinery) [8120]
Warehouse Outlet Stores Inc. (Luggage and Leather Goods) [18442]

Pennsauken
Allied Beverage Group, LLC (Alcoholic Beverages) [1479]
Canada Dry of Delaware Valley (Soft Drinks) [24922]
CEO/United Electric Supply Co. (Electrical and Electronic Equipment and Supplies) [8519]
Cocoa Barry U.S. (Food) [10784]
Diversified Foam Products Inc. (Plastics) [22956]
Fessenden Hall Inc. (Construction Materials and Machinery) [7337]
Jasmine Ltd. (Shoes) [24777]
N.H.F. Musical Merchandise Corp. (Sound and Entertainment Equipment and Supplies) [25358]
Patco Inc. (Heating and Cooling Equipment and Supplies) [14633]
Podgor Co. Inc.; Joseph E. (Industrial Machinery) [16410]
PrimeSource Corp. (Specialty Equipment and Products) [25791]
Puratex Co. (Chemicals) [4487]
Ultra Hardware Products LLC (Hardware) [13970]
United Fabrics, Inc. (Textiles and Notions) [26234]

Pennsville
A.I.D. Inc. (Chemicals) [4316]

Perth Amboy
Central Jersey Supply Co. (Industrial Supplies) [16787]
O.K. Electric Supply Co. (Electrical and Electronic Equipment and Supplies) [9152]

Phillipsburg
AccuPro Inc. (Specialty Equipment and Products) [25543]
Presbyterian & Reformed Publishing Co. (Books and Other Printed Materials) [4080]

Pine Brook
Cony Computers Systems Inc. (Computers and Software) [6157]
Indresco, Inc. (Industrial Supplies) [16945]
T-Fal Corp. (Household Items) [15680]
Westport Corp. (Luggage and Leather Goods) [18445]

Piscataway
Hoffman International Inc. (Construction Materials and Machinery) [7476]
JWS Technologies Inc. (Industrial Machinery) [16195]
Roma Food Enterprises Inc. (Food) [12348]
Transtech Industries Inc. (Chemicals) [4532]
Unichem Industries Inc. (Medical, Dental, and Optical Supplies) [19671]

Pitman
Sheridan Optical Co. (Medical, Dental, and Optical Supplies) [19607]

Plainfield
Lob-Ster Inc. (Recreational and Sporting Goods) [23790]

Pleasantville
Ireland Coffee and Tea Inc. (Food) [11529]
Kramer Beverage Company Inc. (Alcoholic Beverages) [1804]
Sovereign Distributors, Inc. (Floorcovering Equipment and Supplies) [10173]
SYSCO Food Services of Atlantic City Inc. (Food) [12675]
Wheelchair Pit-Stop (Medical, Dental, and Optical Supplies) [19701]

Point Pleasant
Colie Sailmakers (Marine) [18486]
Danforth International Trade Associates, Inc. (Paper and Paper Products) [21700]

Pompton Lakes
Valley Appliance Parts Co. (Household Appliances) [15354]

Princeton
American ELTEC Inc. (Computers and Software) [5929]
Derma Sciences Inc. (Medical, Dental, and Optical Supplies) [19277]
Novo Nordisk Pharmaceuticals Inc. (Medical, Dental, and Optical Supplies) [19502]
Princeton Lipids (Chemicals) [4485]
R5 Trading International Inc. (Medical, Dental, and Optical Equipment) [19005]
Urken Supply Company Inc. (Household Items) [15693]
Villeroy and Boch Tableware Ltd. (Household Items) [15696]

Rahway
Cardinal Inc. (Toys and Hobby Goods) [26437]
Gaffney-Kroese Electrical Supply Corp. (Electrical and Electronic Equipment and Supplies) [8770]
SDI Technologies Inc. (Electrical and Electronic Equipment and Supplies) [9347]

Ramsey
Aero Tec Laboratories Inc. (Industrial Supplies) [16672]
American Industrial Exports Ltd. (Marine) [18449]
Bogen Photo Corp. (Photographic Equipment and Supplies) [22832]
Jersey Model Distributors (Toys and Hobby Goods) [26545]
Minolta Corp. (Photographic Equipment and Supplies) [22878]
Onkyo USA Corp. (Sound and Entertainment Equipment and Supplies) [25369]
Pezrow Food Brokers Inc. (Food) [12160]
Werner and Pfleiderer Corp. (Plastics) [23047]

Randolph

Mas-Tech International Inc. (Computers and Software) [6468]
Seikosha America Inc. (Computers and Software) [6719]

Red Bank

Hobbyquest Marketing (Toys and Hobby Goods) [26522]
Siperstein's Middletown (Paints and Varnishes) [21585]

Ridgefield

Neuman Distributors Inc. (Medical, Dental, and Optical Supplies) [19485]
Neuman Health Services Inc. (Medical, Dental, and Optical Supplies) [19486]

Ridgefield Park

Crystal Clear Industries Inc. (Household Items) [15464]
Degussa Huls (Chemicals) [4370]
Horizon High Reach, Inc. (Construction Materials and Machinery) [7488]
Horizon High Reach Inc. (Construction Materials and Machinery) [7489]
Samsung Electronics America Inc. (Sound and Entertainment Equipment and Supplies) [25426]

Ridgewood

Pharis Organization Inc. (Construction Materials and Machinery) [7857]

Ringwood

Daret Inc. (Paints and Varnishes) [21425]

Rio Grande

Seashore Food Distributors (Food) [12451]

Riverdale

CustomCraft (Construction Materials and Machinery) [7239]

Riverton

Weidner & Sons Publishing (Books and Other Printed Materials) [4271]

Robbinsville

Universal Process Equipment Inc. (Industrial Machinery) [16595]

Rochelle Park

PSDI (Computers and Software) [6658]

Rockaway

CPS Technologies Inc. (Computers and Software) [6166]
Erika-Record Inc. (Restaurant and Commercial Foodservice Equipment and Supplies) [24110]
Jaytow International Inc. (Compressors) [5843]
Wayne Tile Co. (Floorcovering Equipment and Supplies) [10288]

Rockleigh

Volvo Cars of North America Inc. (Motorized Vehicles) [20745]

Roosevelt

Universal Process Equipment Inc. (Chemicals) [4540]

Roseland

Amano Partners USA Inc. (Electrical and Electronic Equipment and Supplies) [8334]

Roselle

Arnessen Corp. (Specialty Equipment and Products) [25559]

Roselle Park

Garden State Tile Distributors, Inc. (Floorcovering Equipment and Supplies) [9912]

Rutherford

BSTC Group Inc. (Construction Materials and Machinery) [7091]
Lindenmeyer Munroe (Paper and Paper Products) [21804]

Saddle Brook

Azco Steel Co. (Metals) [19796]
Colossal Jewelry and Accessories Inc. (Jewelry) [17375]
Curcio Scrap Metal Inc. (Used, Scrap, and Recycled Materials) [26791]
Dana-Lu Imports Inc. (Restaurant and Commercial Foodservice Equipment and Supplies) [24103]
DeLonghi America Inc. (Household Appliances) [15109]
IMA Tool Distributors (Hardware) [13763]
JPA Electronics Supply Inc. (Marine) [18530]
Liberty Richter Inc. (Food) [11709]
Noury and Sons Ltd. (Household Items) [15599]
Perugina Brands of America (Food) [12153]
Regent Book Co. (Books and Other Printed Materials) [4112]
RPL Supplies Inc. (Photographic Equipment and Supplies) [22899]
Saddle Brook Controls (Industrial Supplies) [17152]
Scheinert & Son Inc.; Sidney (Hardware) [13905]
Sealed Air Corp. (Paper and Paper Products) [21929]
SKL Company Inc. (Jewelry) [17608]
Tingue Brown and Company Inc. (Textiles and Notions) [26230]

Saddle River

McKee Brothers Inc. (Construction Materials and Machinery) [7684]

Sayreville

Heads and Threads International, LLC (Hardware) [13749]

Secaucus

Bertolli U.S.A. Inc. (Food) [10544]
Drug Guild Distributors Inc. (Household Appliances) [15116]
Hoogovens Aluminium Corp. (Metals) [20044]
Lifestyle International Inc. (Luggage and Leather Goods) [18408]
Marcel Watch Corp. (Jewelry) [17511]
Noonoo Rug Company Inc. (Household Items) [15596]
Noritake Company Inc. (Household Items) [15598]
Panasonic Broadcast and Television Systems Co. (Household Appliances) [15264]
Panasonic Industrial Co. (Electrical and Electronic Equipment and Supplies) [9178]
Samsung Opto-Electronics America Inc. (Photographic Equipment and Supplies) [22900]
Tsumura International Inc. (Health and Beauty Aids) [14267]
Weber Piano Co. (Sound and Entertainment Equipment and Supplies) [25519]

Short Hills

Strohmeyer and Arpe Co. (Food) [12595]

Shrewsbury

Lawes Coal Company Inc. (Agricultural Equipment and Supplies) [943]
Wellman Inc. (Used, Scrap, and Recycled Materials) [27040]

Somerdale

Raylon Corp. (Health and Beauty Aids) [14207]

Somerset

Hubbard Printing Equipment (Specialty Equipment and Products) [25682]
Rapid Disposal Services Inc. (Used, Scrap, and Recycled Materials) [26951]
Raritan Computer Inc. (Computers and Software) [6683]
Raritan Computer Inc. (Computers and Software) [6684]

Royal Doulton USA Inc. (Household

Royal Doulton USA Inc. (Household Items) [15642]
Slingman Industries (Automotive) [3229]
Technical Telephone Systems Inc. (Communications Systems and Equipment) [5777]
World Wide Metric, Inc. (Plumbing Materials and Fixtures) [23467]
Zinsser & Co., Inc.; William (Paints and Varnishes) [21613]

Somerville

TransNet Corp. (Computers and Software) [6827]

South Hackensack

AC & R Specialty Supply (Heating and Cooling Equipment and Supplies) [14292]
Apex Foot Health Industries (Shoes) [24674]
AVAS VIP (Sound and Entertainment Equipment and Supplies) [25092]
Comprehensive Video Group (Photographic Equipment and Supplies) [22847]
Standard Telecommunications Systems Inc. (Communications Systems and Equipment) [5769]

South Kearny

American Chemical Company Inc. (Chemicals) [4319]
American Chemicals Co. Inc. (Chemicals) [4321]

South Orange

Jarett Industries Inc. (Industrial Supplies) [16969]

South Plainfield

All American Food Group Inc. (Restaurant and Commercial Foodservice Equipment and Supplies) [24058]
Ewig Inc.; Carl F. (Storage Equipment and Containers) [25914]
Hunter, Walton and Company Inc. (Food) [11480]
Imperia Foods Inc. (Food) [11499]
J & H Berge, Inc. (Scientific and Measurement Devices) [24377]
Martec International (Storage Equipment and Containers) [25930]
Whittaker, Clark and Daniels (Chemicals) [4553]

Spring Lake

Medical International Inc. (Medical, Dental, and Optical Equipment) [18918]

Spring Lake Heights

Taramax U.S.A., Inc. (Jewelry) [17632]

Springfield

Carriage House Imports Ltd. (Alcoholic Beverages) [1577]
Gotham Sales Co. (Sound and Entertainment Equipment and Supplies) [25216]
Heuer Time and Electronics Corp. (Jewelry) [17448]
Meisel Stringed Instruments Inc. (Sound and Entertainment Equipment and Supplies) [25311]
New Jersey Semiconductor Products Inc. (Electrical and Electronic Equipment and Supplies) [9127]
Zep Manufacturing Co., Springfield (Chemicals) [4560]

Succasunna

Almar Industries (Gifts and Novelties) [13299]
Bird Toy Man (Veterinary Products) [27083]
Exmart International, Inc. (Restaurant and Commercial Foodservice Equipment and Supplies) [24112]

Swedesboro

Thomas Scientific (Scientific and Measurement Devices) [24446]

Teaneck

American Medical Export Inc. (Medical, Dental, and Optical Equipment) [18677]
PC L.P. (Computers and Software) [6597]
System Brunner USA Inc. (Industrial Supplies) [17210]

Trans-Tec Services Inc. (Petroleum, Fuels, and Related Equipment) [22746]

Tenafly
Hermitage Publishing Co. (Books and Other Printed Materials) [3825]
Med-X International, Inc. (Medical, Dental, and Optical Supplies) [19439]

Teterboro
Data Net Inc. (Communications Systems and Equipment) [5587]
Funai Corp. (Sound and Entertainment Equipment and Supplies) [25203]
Sunnytech Inc. (Computers and Software) [6774]
WMT Machine Tool Company Inc. (Industrial Machinery) [16645]

Thorofare
Aramsco, Inc. (Industrial Supplies) [16707]
Marine Equipment & Supply (Marine) [18559]

Tinton Falls
Propane Equipment Corp. (Petroleum, Fuels, and Related Equipment) [22596]
Standard Roofings Inc. (Construction Materials and Machinery) [8068]

Toms River
Wallach's Poultry Farms (Food) [12871]

Totowa
Holzberg Communications, Inc. (Communications Systems and Equipment) [5638]
Pitman Co.; Harold M. (Specialty Equipment and Products) [25786]
Sher Distributing Co. (Books and Other Printed Materials) [4159]
Spiral Binding Company Inc. (Office Equipment and Supplies) [21282]
Star Stainless Screw Co. (Hardware) [13935]

Towaco
Bosco Products Inc. (Food) [10596]

Trenton
Barbero Bakery Inc. (Food) [10504]
Crest Paper Products Inc. (Paper and Paper Products) [21697]
Hub City Distributors Inc. (Alcoholic Beverages) [1766]
Michel Company Inc.; R.E. (Heating and Cooling Equipment and Supplies) [14557]
New American Electric Distributors, Inc. (Electrical and Electronic Equipment and Supplies) [9125]
Plascom Trading Company (Plastics) [23006]
Ritchie and Page Distributing Company Inc. (Alcoholic Beverages) [1992]
Rosetta Oil Inc. (Petroleum, Fuels, and Related Equipment) [22641]
Rosetta Oil Inc. Duck Island Terminal (Petroleum, Fuels, and Related Equipment) [22642]
Royal Inc.; H.M. (Minerals and Ores) [20566]
Scorpio Music Inc. (Sound and Entertainment Equipment and Supplies) [25434]
Trenton Iron and Metal Corp. (Metals) [20441]
Yardville Supply Co. (Construction Materials and Machinery) [8245]
Zeiger International Inc. (Toys and Hobby Goods) [26720]

Union
ACuPowder International, LLC (Metals) [19726]
Beer Import Company (Alcoholic Beverages) [1516]
Berk Co.; O. (Storage Equipment and Containers) [25892]
Force Machinery Company Inc. (Industrial Machinery) [16029]
Foreign Tire Sales Inc. (Automotive) [2640]
General Office Interiors (Furniture and Fixtures) [13120]
HALCO (Restaurant and Commercial Foodservice Equipment and Supplies) [24132]

Jasco Tile Company, Inc. (Floorcovering Equipment and Supplies) [9979]
KII, Inc. (Plumbing Materials and Fixtures) [23236]
MD Foods Ingredients Inc. (Restaurant and Commercial Foodservice Equipment and Supplies) [24181]
Paige Electric Company L.P. (Electrical and Electronic Equipment and Supplies) [9173]
Red Devil Inc. (Hardware) [13884]
Reisen Lumber and Millwork Co. (Construction Materials and Machinery) [7910]
Schultz and Sons; H. (Cleaning and Janitorial Supplies) [4705]
Tuscan Dairy Farms Inc. (Food) [12775]
Tuscan/Lehigh Dairies L.P. (Food) [12776]

Union City
Royal Essence Ltd. (Health and Beauty Aids) [14226]
Swift Electric Supply Co. (Electrical and Electronic Equipment and Supplies) [9451]

Upper Saddle River
Creative Homeowner Press (Books and Other Printed Materials) [3669]
Pioneer Laser Optical Products Div. (Sound and Entertainment Equipment and Supplies) [25382]
Rodico Inc. (Storage Equipment and Containers) [25934]

Vineland
Ace Plumbing and Electrical Supply, Inc. (Plumbing Materials and Fixtures) [23050]
Joffe Lumber and Supply Company Inc. (Construction Materials and Machinery) [7535]
Michel Company Inc.; R.E. (Heating and Cooling Equipment and Supplies) [14558]
Pedroni Fuel Co. (Petroleum, Fuels, and Related Equipment) [22557]
Riggins Oil Co.; L.S. (Petroleum, Fuels, and Related Equipment) [22628]
Russo Farms Inc. (Food) [12370]
Vineland Electric CED/Supply, Inc. (Electrical and Electronic Equipment and Supplies) [9542]
Wallace Supply Co. (Plumbing Materials and Fixtures) [23437]
Zucca Inc.; L.J. (Tobacco Products) [26377]

Voorhees
RF Power Products Inc. (Electrical and Electronic Equipment and Supplies) [9291]
Sarco Inc. (Industrial Supplies) [17159]

Wall
Crown Beer Distributors Inc. (Alcoholic Beverages) [1624]
Jersey Truck Equipment Co. (Automotive) [2818]
Wedgwood U.S.A. Inc. (Household Items) [15704]

Wallington
Parmalat USA (Food) [12118]

Wayne
Atlas Copco North America Inc. (Hardware) [13573]
Castrol North America Holdings Inc. (Petroleum, Fuels, and Related Equipment) [22116]
Genesis Safety Systems Inc. (Security and Safety Equipment) [24555]
Hoboken Wood Flooring Corp. (Household Items) [15529]
Hoboken Wood Floors (Floorcovering Equipment and Supplies) [9949]
LJO Inc. (Shoes) [24795]
Toshiba America Consumer Products Inc. (Electrical and Electronic Equipment and Supplies) [9495]
Wayne Tile Co. (Floorcovering Equipment and Supplies) [10289]

Wenonah
Starmac Group (Clothing) [5393]

West Berlin
Garden State Tile Distributors (Floorcovering Equipment and Supplies) [9909]
Garden State Tile Distributors (Construction Materials and Machinery) [7377]
Stomel & Sons; Joseph H. (Food) [12588]

West Caldwell
Eastern Tool Warehouse Corp. (Automotive) [2574]
NJCT Corp. (Restaurant and Commercial Foodservice Equipment and Supplies) [24194]
Reitman Industries (Alcoholic Beverages) [1981]
RLB Food Distributors L.P. (Food) [12326]

West Long Branch
Kultur, White Star, Duke International Films Ltd., Inc. (Sound and Entertainment Equipment and Supplies) [25276]
Kultur, White Star, Duke International Films Ltd. Inc. (Household Appliances) [15194]
White Star Video (Sound and Entertainment Equipment and Supplies) [25523]

West New York
Cres Jewelry Factory Inc. (Jewelry) [17382]

West Orange
Hockman Lewis Ltd. (Industrial Machinery) [16106]

West Paterson
Tri-Lite Optical (Medical, Dental, and Optical Supplies) [19660]

Westfield
Connell Co. (Food) [10811]

Westville
Berkowitz L.P.; J.E. (Construction Materials and Machinery) [7049]

Westwood
BMW of North America Inc. (Motorized Vehicles) [20603]

Wharton
Whittier-Ruhle Millwork (Construction Materials and Machinery) [8221]

Whippany
800 JR Cigar Inc. (Tobacco Products) [26256]
American Renolit Corp. (Plastics) [22924]
Corporate Express (Office Equipment and Supplies) [20926]
Masda Corp. (Household Appliances) [15216]

Williamstown
Mechanic's Auto Parts, Inc. (Automotive) [2937]
Shamrock Custom Truck Caps, Inc. (Automotive) [3211]

Wood Ridge
Latona's Food Importing Corp. (Food) [11682]

Woodbridge
Amalgamet Inc. (Chemicals) [4317]
Royal Foods Distributors Inc. (Food) [12364]

Woodbury
Gloucester County Packing Co. (Food) [11276]
Henry Corp.; E.P. (Construction Materials and Machinery) [7467]

Woodbury Heights
S.M.S. Distributors (Heating and Cooling Equipment and Supplies) [14687]

Woodstown
Richman's Ice Cream Div. (Food) [12317]
Waddington/Richman Inc. (Food) [12860]

Wyckoff
Melman-Moster Associates, Inc. (Books and Other Printed Materials) [3946]

New Mexico

Alamogordo

AA Water Service (Household Appliances) [14987]
Alfredos Restaurant Equipment (Restaurant and Commercial Foodservice Equipment and Supplies) [24057]
Basin Pipe & Metal (Metals) [19805]
Mickey's Mobile Metal Mending (Metals) [20180]
North 54 Salvage Yard (Automotive) [3040]
The Pet Pharmacy Inc. (Veterinary Products) [27209]
Roy's Welding & Wrought Iron (Metals) [20333]
Southwestern Jewelry & Gifts (Jewelry) [17615]
Vision Broadcasting Network (Photographic Equipment and Supplies) [22913]

Albuquerque

1st Source Parts Center (Household Appliances) [14983]
A Timely Tech Services (Office Equipment and Supplies) [20762]
A to Z Tire & Battery Inc. (Automotive) [2159]
Albuquerque Balloon Center (Recreational and Sporting Goods) [23500]
Albuquerque Bolt & Fastener (Hardware) [13544]
Albuquerque Foreign Auto Parts (Automotive) [2199]
Albuquerque Winnelson Co. (Plumbing Materials and Fixtures) [23056]
Allied School and Office Products (Office Equipment and Supplies) [20785]
Almeda Beauty Shop (Health and Beauty Aids) [14017]
American Mailing Systems Inc. (Office Equipment and Supplies) [20794]
Architectural Surfaces, Inc. (Floorcovering Equipment and Supplies) [9685]
B & V Inc. (Jewelry) [17323]
Baldridge Lumber Co.; J.C. (Construction Materials and Machinery) [7016]
The Bell Group (Jewelry) [17331]
Best Way Carpet Care Inc. (Cleaning and Janitorial Supplies) [4579]
Blue Canyon Jewelry (Jewelry) [17343]
Bond Paint Co. (Paints and Varnishes) [21404]
Brotherhood of Life, Inc. (Books and Other Printed Materials) [3594]
Business Environments Inc. (Furniture and Fixtures) [13054]
Capos Auto Parts Inc. (Automotive) [2419]
Cash & Carry Electronics Inc. (Sound and Entertainment Equipment and Supplies) [25126]
Cash Register Systems Inc. (Office Equipment and Supplies) [20886]
Chartier Double Reed Co. (Sound and Entertainment Equipment and Supplies) [25133]
Commercial Body Corp. (Automotive) [2462]
Complete Auto & Truck Parts (Automotive) [2471]
Computer Corner Inc. (Computers and Software) [6106]
Condeck Corp. (Construction Materials and Machinery) [7206]
Contract Associates Inc. (Office Equipment and Supplies) [20912]
Coronado Auto Recyclers Inc. (Automotive) [2484]
Crosby's Americana Arts I; Judy (Jewelry) [17383]
Cunningham Distributing Inc. (Specialty Equipment and Products) [25616]
D & D Specialties Millwork (Construction Materials and Machinery) [7241]
Dakota Flags and Banner (Textiles and Notions) [26012]
Desert Star Jewelry Manufacturing (Jewelry) [17393]
Dick Products of Albuquerque; A.B. (Office Equipment and Supplies) [20962]
DPI Southwest Distributing Inc. (Food) [10990]
DPI Southwest Distributing Inc. (Food) [10991]
EDS Refrigeration Inc. (Heating and Cooling Equipment and Supplies) [14429]
El Encanto Inc. (Food) [11036]
El Mexicano Auto Salvage (Automotive) [2578]
El Rey Stucco Co. (Construction Materials and Machinery) [7305]

Essence Beauty Supply (Health and Beauty Aids) [14097]
Ever-Ready Oil Co. (Petroleum, Fuels, and Related Equipment) [22243]
F & S Co. Inc. (Toys and Hobby Goods) [26481]
Five Foreign Auto Salvage (Automotive) [2625]
Five JS Auto Parts Inc. (Automotive) [2626]
Frank's Supply Company Inc. (Construction Materials and Machinery) [7368]
G & S Jewelry Manufacturing (Jewelry) [17420]
Glidden Paint & Wallcovering (Paints and Varnishes) [21451]
Gold & Silver Exchange (Jewelry) [17436]
Goodmans Design Interior (Office Equipment and Supplies) [21017]
Graham Co.; Mike (Jewelry) [17440]
Graves Oil & Butane Co. (Metals) [20016]
Greenleaf Wholesale Florist (Horticultural Supplies) [14879]
Hopper Specialty West, Inc. (Industrial Supplies) [16932]
Interstate Glass Distributors (Construction Materials and Machinery) [7523]
Jamco (Jewelry) [17465]
Kabana Inc. (Jewelry) [17481]
Keith Foods; Ben E. (Food) [11591]
Khalsa Trading Co. Inc. (Jewelry) [17490]
Korber and Co.; J. (Automotive) [2859]
La Plante Gallery Inc. (Furniture and Fixtures) [13161]
Lumber Inc. (Construction Materials and Machinery) [7617]
Maisel Inc.; Skip (Jewelry) [17509]
Mallory Pet Supplies (Veterinary Products) [27183]
Maloof & Co.; Joe G. (Alcoholic Beverages) [1846]
Man-I-Can Store Fixtures, Inc. (Furniture and Fixtures) [13170]
Maneto Wholesale Flooring, Inc. (Floorcovering Equipment and Supplies) [10007]
McBride and Associates Inc. (Computers and Software) [6475]
McComas Sales Co. Inc. (Restaurant and Commercial Foodservice Equipment and Supplies) [24180]
Medical Scientific Service (Medical, Dental, and Optical Equipment) [18922]
Merit Insulation Inc. (Construction Materials and Machinery) [7697]
Monarch Ceramic Tile (Floorcovering Equipment and Supplies) [10047]
Mountain States Sporting Goods (Recreational and Sporting Goods) [23839]
Myers Associates Inc.; Vic (Computers and Software) [6537]
Nakai Trading Co. (Jewelry) [17529]
National Distributing Company Inc. (Alcoholic Beverages) [1909]
National Electric Supply Co. (Household Appliances) [15245]
New Man Barber & Beauty Supply (Health and Beauty Aids) [14177]
New Mexico Fire Works Inc. (Toys and Hobby Goods) [26592]
New Mexico International Trade & Development (Office Equipment and Supplies) [21161]
New Mexico Mattress Co. Inc. (Furniture and Fixtures) [13187]
New Mexico Orthopedic Supplies (Medical, Dental, and Optical Equipment) [18960]
New Mexico Salvage Pool (Automotive) [3029]
New Mexico School Products Co. (Office Equipment and Supplies) [21162]
NM Bakery Service Co. (Food) [12010]
North American Investment Services (Jewelry) [17534]
On Spot Janitor Supplies & Repair (Cleaning and Janitorial Supplies) [4681]
Patio Production Inc. (Furniture and Fixtures) [13206]
Plains Auto Refrigeration (Heating and Cooling Equipment and Supplies) [14638]
Plastic Supply Inc. (Plastics) [23013]
Preferred Brokerage Co. (Food) [12209]

Professional Paint Supply (Paints and Varnishes) [21548]
Pueblo Fruits Inc. (Food) [12234]
Quality Paper & Plastic Corp. (Plastics) [23020]
R & B Service Co. (Heating and Cooling Equipment and Supplies) [14646]
Reed Optical Co. Inc.; Fred (Medical, Dental, and Optical Supplies) [19571]
Reserve Industries Corp. (Construction Materials and Machinery) [7919]
Richard Distributing Co. (Alcoholic Beverages) [1989]
Rowland Nursery Inc. (Agricultural Equipment and Supplies) [1216]
Ryan Jewelry; Susan (Jewelry) [17581]
Safety Flare Inc. (Security and Safety Equipment) [24622]
Safety Flare Inc. (Security and Safety Equipment) [24623]
Sagebrush Sales Inc. (Construction Materials and Machinery) [7971]
Sam's Ice Cream Inc. (Food) [12400]
Shube Manufacturing Inc. (Jewelry) [17601]
Silver Ray (Jewelry) [17605]
Silver Sun Wholesale Inc. (Jewelry) [17606]
Snipes Webb Trailer & Livestock Co. (Livestock and Farm Products) [18238]
South Central Pool Supply, Inc. (Recreational and Sporting Goods) [23965]
Southwest Bingo Supply (Toys and Hobby Goods) [26660]
Southwestern Gold Inc. (Jewelry) [17614]
Stan's Frozen Foods (Food) [12566]
Stewart & Stevenson (Automotive) [3267]
Summit Electric Supply Inc. (Electrical and Electronic Equipment and Supplies) [9439]
Sunrise Glass Distributors (Construction Materials and Machinery) [8089]
Sunwest Silver Co. (Jewelry) [17627]
Tab Business Systems Inc. (Office Equipment and Supplies) [21313]
Table Supply Co. (Restaurant and Commercial Foodservice Equipment and Supplies) [24240]
Taylor Restaurant Equipment (Restaurant and Commercial Foodservice Equipment and Supplies) [24241]
Techrepco Inc. (Aeronautical Equipment and Supplies) [157]
Thunderbird Steel Div. (Construction Materials and Machinery) [8130]
Tire Welder Inc. (Automotive) [3307]
Titan Technologies Inc. (Albuquerque, New Mexico) (Automotive) [3312]
Turquoise World (Jewelry) [17645]
U-Joints, Inc. (Automotive) [3357]
Universal Jewelers & Trading Co. (Jewelry) [17646]
UPCO Pet Vet Supply (Veterinary Products) [27258]
Val-Comm Inc. (Electrical and Electronic Equipment and Supplies) [9530]
Waldeck Jewelers (Jewelry) [17648]
Wargames West (Toys and Hobby Goods) [26707]
WD Industries Inc. (Construction Materials and Machinery) [8200]
Wellborn Paint Manufacturing Co. (Paints and Varnishes) [21605]
Winrock Bakery Inc. (Food) [12959]
With Enterprises Inc. (Cleaning and Janitorial Supplies) [4734]
Zanios Foods (Food) [13001]
Zanios Foods Inc. (Food) [13002]

Angel Fire

MIMICS Inc. (Computers and Software) [6519]

Anthony

Sharp Oil Company Inc. (Petroleum, Fuels, and Related Equipment) [22664]

Artesia

Artesia Fire Equipment Inc. (Security and Safety Equipment) [24509]
Baker-Stephens Tire Co. (Automotive) [2310]
Brewer Oil Co. (Petroleum, Fuels, and Related Equipment) [22093]

Belen

Castillo Ready-Mix Concrete (Construction Materials and Machinery) [7152]

Carlsbad

Edcor Electronics (Electrical and Electronic Equipment and Supplies) [8654]
El Grande Distributors Inc. (Tobacco Products) [26290]
Lehman Paint Co. Inc. (Paints and Varnishes) [21491]
Mine Supply Co. (Industrial Supplies) [17043]
Moffatt Hay Co. (Livestock and Farm Products) [18108]

Clovis

American Auto Salvage (Automotive) [2226]
Aucutt's General Store (Paints and Varnishes) [21392]
Clovis Livestock Auction (Livestock and Farm Products) [17784]
Curtis & Curtis, Inc. (Agricultural Equipment and Supplies) [484]
Dent and Co. (Agricultural Equipment and Supplies) [513]

Cuba

Cuba Buckles (Jewelry) [17386]
Gunderson Oil Co. (Petroleum, Fuels, and Related Equipment) [22329]

Deming

Mimbres Valley Farmers Association Inc. (Agricultural Equipment and Supplies) [1042]
Teague Refrigeration Service (Heating and Cooling Equipment and Supplies) [14714]
Vogann Business Machines (Office Equipment and Supplies) [21341]

Dexter

Daubert Oil & Gas Co. (Petroleum, Fuels, and Related Equipment) [22189]

Espanola

Road Runner Pet Supplies (Veterinary Products) [27223]

Farmington

All Paint Supply Co. (Paints and Varnishes) [21378]
Antenna Farms Inc. (Sound and Entertainment Equipment and Supplies) [25075]
Bond Paint Co. (Paints and Varnishes) [21403]
D & S Enterprises (Cleaning and Janitorial Supplies) [4607]
Diamond Vogel Paint Center (Paints and Varnishes) [21433]
Discount Engine Exchange Inc. (Automotive) [2547]
Four States Industrial Distributors (Construction Materials and Machinery) [7363]
Justis Supply Company Inc. (Industrial Supplies) [16974]
Komac Paint Center (Paints and Varnishes) [21475]
Stewart & Stevenson (Automotive) [3268]
Thunderbird Silver Co. (Jewelry) [17636]

Gallup

Abeita Glass Co. (Construction Materials and Machinery) [6901]
Amadom Corp. (Jewelry) [17307]
Arctic Ice Co. (Food) [10432]
Brentari Oil Co. (Petroleum, Fuels, and Related Equipment) [22091]
Desert Indian Traders (Jewelry) [17392]
Elkins Inc.; Jerry (Jewelry) [17406]
Ellis Tanner Trading Co. (Jewelry) [17407]
Four Corners Welding & Gas (Metals) [19982]
Gallup Sales Co. Inc. (Alcoholic Beverages) [1702]
Gallup Welding Co. (Metals) [19994]
Indian Den Traders (Jewelry) [17455]
Indian Trade Center Inc. (Jewelry) [17457]

J & R Mercantile Ltd. (Livestock and Farm Products) [18017]
M & R Trading Inc. (Livestock and Farm Products) [18068]
Pow Wow Indian Jewelry (Jewelry) [17552]
Silver Dust Trading Inc. (Jewelry) [17603]
Tanner Trading Co.; Ellis (Jewelry) [17631]
Tobe Turpen's Indian Trading Co. (Gifts and Novelties) [13464]

Hobbs

Brown Jewelry Inc.; Harold (Jewelry) [17351]
Dale's Auto Paints & Supplies (Paints and Varnishes) [21424]
Olympic Industries Inc. (Plastics) [23004]
Watson Truck and Supply Inc. (Automotive) [3405]

Jamestown

Giant Refining Co. (Petroleum, Fuels, and Related Equipment) [22311]

Las Cruces

Bayjet Inc. (Aeronautical Equipment and Supplies) [58]
Big Boy Ice Cream (Food) [10555]
Craft Enterprises (Toys and Hobby Goods) [26453]
Dove Wholesale (Veterinary Products) [27120]
Foreign Car Parts Inc. (Automotive) [2639]
Hillger Oil Company Inc. (Petroleum, Fuels, and Related Equipment) [22353]
Jewelry By Dyan & Eduardo (Jewelry) [17471]
Kwal-Hanley Paint Co. (Paints and Varnishes) [21479]
Las Cruces Leather Co. (Luggage and Leather Goods) [18404]
Porter Oil Company Inc. (Petroleum, Fuels, and Related Equipment) [22589]
Sewing Machines Distributors (Industrial Machinery) [16484]
South West New Mexico Communications, Inc. (Communications Systems and Equipment) [5763]
Southwest Steel (Metals) [20377]
Sun & Fun Specialties Inc. (Gifts and Novelties) [13457]

Los Alamos

Los Alamos Stationers (Office Equipment and Supplies) [21113]

Lovington

Lea County Livestock Marketing (Livestock and Farm Products) [18050]

Mayhill

Queen Oil & Gas (Petroleum, Fuels, and Related Equipment) [22603]

MesilLa Park

Casa Mexicana (Floorcovering Equipment and Supplies) [9775]

Mesilla Park

Southern New Mexico Office Machines (Office Equipment and Supplies) [21278]

Milan

A-X Propane Co. (Petroleum, Fuels, and Related Equipment) [22017]
Carver's Oil Co. (Petroleum, Fuels, and Related Equipment) [22114]

Moriarty

Ayre & Ayre Silversmiths (Jewelry) [17322]

Peralta

Tayo's Tile Co. (Construction Materials and Machinery) [8101]

Portales

C and S Inc. (Petroleum, Fuels, and Related Equipment) [22102]
Glen's Peanuts and Grains Inc. (Livestock and Farm Products) [17942]

Prewitt

Indian Mission Jewelry (Jewelry) [17456]

Raton

Kenco (Automotive) [2847]

Rio Rancho

Byrne Co. (Construction Materials and Machinery) [7118]
Leading Products Co. (Cleaning and Janitorial Supplies) [4658]

Roswell

A-Doc Oil Co. (Petroleum, Fuels, and Related Equipment) [22015]
All Seasons Engines Inc. (Heating and Cooling Equipment and Supplies) [14312]
Allison Inc. (Motorized Vehicles) [20582]
AWC Propane Co. (Petroleum, Fuels, and Related Equipment) [22053]
Bell Gas Inc. (Petroleum, Fuels, and Related Equipment) [22065]
Brewer Oil Co.; Don (Petroleum, Fuels, and Related Equipment) [22094]
Dodson Wholesale Lumber Company Inc. (Construction Materials and Machinery) [7277]
El Charro Mexican Foods (Food) [11035]
Goode's Welding Inc. (Metals) [20014]
Martinez; Gus (Office Equipment and Supplies) [21131]
New Mexico Beauty & Barber Supply (Health and Beauty Aids) [14178]
Rons Office Equipment Inc. (Office Equipment and Supplies) [21246]
Roswell Livestock Auction Co. (Livestock and Farm Products) [18207]
Roswell Winnelson Co. (Heating and Cooling Equipment and Supplies) [14668]
Roswell Wool LLC (Livestock and Farm Products) [18208]
South Main Metal Building (Metals) [20374]
Wakefield Oil Co. (Petroleum, Fuels, and Related Equipment) [22779]
Young's: The Paint Place (Paints and Varnishes) [21612]

Ruidoso

Ruidoso Paint Center Inc. (Paints and Varnishes) [21558]

Santa Fe

Artesanos Imports Company Inc. (Construction Materials and Machinery) [6993]
C & W Distributing Inc. (Cleaning and Janitorial Supplies) [4591]
Clear Optics Inc. (Medical, Dental, and Optical Supplies) [19234]
Dahl (Plumbing Materials and Fixtures) [23130]
Eco Design Co. (Paints and Varnishes) [21436]
Environmental Control Inc. (Used, Scrap, and Recycled Materials) [26810]
Heartline (Jewelry) [17446]
Kiva Direct Distribution Inc. (Alcoholic Beverages) [1798]
La Farge; Patricia Arscott (Textiles and Notions) [26118]
Quintana Sales (Photographic Equipment and Supplies) [22895]
RMP Enterprises Inc. (Jewelry) [17566]
Santa Fe Pet and Vet Supply (Veterinary Products) [27228]
Seret & Sons Inc. (Furniture and Fixtures) [13237]
State Beauty Supply (Health and Beauty Aids) [14247]
Tin-Nee-Ann Trading Co. (Jewelry) [17639]
Valdes Paint & Glass (Paints and Varnishes) [21597]

Shiprock

Shiprock Trading Post (Jewelry) [17599]

Silver City

Interstate Copy Shop (Office Equipment and Supplies) [21068]

Socorro

L & L Gas & Oil Inc. (Petroleum, Fuels, and Related Equipment) [22413]

Swift Lizard Distributors (Books and Other Printed Materials) [4201]

TBT Industries Inc. (Furniture and Fixtures) [13256]

Taos

El Rancho Laundry Equipment (Household Appliances) [15119]

Randall's Lumber (Construction Materials and Machinery) [7900]

Saltillo Tile Co. (Construction Materials and Machinery) [7973]

White Dove International (Books and Other Printed Materials) [4281]

Texico

Hoffmann Aircraft Inc. (Aeronautical Equipment and Supplies) [98]

Truth or Consequences

Swanson Sales and Service (Office Equipment and Supplies) [21309]

Truth Or Consequences

Sunland Steel Inc. (Metals) [20412]

Tucumcari

Shipley-Phillips Inc. (Petroleum, Fuels, and Related Equipment) [22669]

Veguita

Heraa Inc. (Livestock and Farm Products) [17991]

New York

Akron

Burgmaster (Industrial Machinery) [15858]

MGA Research Corp. (Industrial Machinery) [16291]

Albany

Adirondack Electronics Inc. (Electrical and Electronic Equipment and Supplies) [8273]

Adirondack Silver (Jewelry) [17303]

Albany Ladder Company Inc. (Construction Materials and Machinery) [6929]

Albany Tile Supply (Floorcovering Equipment and Supplies) [9650]

Architects Hardware & Specialty Company Inc. (Hardware) [13563]

Audio-Video Corp. (Sound and Entertainment Equipment and Supplies) [25090]

Bicknell Distributors, Inc. (Recreational and Sporting Goods) [23553]

BRS Software Products (Computers and Software) [6026]

CMP Industries Inc. (Medical, Dental, and Optical Equipment) [18745]

Dorsey Millwork Inc. (Industrial Machinery) [15958]

Energy Answers Corp. (Used, Scrap, and Recycled Materials) [26809]

Four Wheeler Communications (Computers and Software) [6278]

Frank Brothers Flooring Distributors (Floorcovering Equipment and Supplies) [9906]

Gourmet Award Foods (Food) [11296]

Grainger, Inc. (Industrial Machinery) [16073]

H.L. Gage Sales Inc. (Automotive) [2757]

Hoboken Wood Flooring Corp. (Floorcovering Equipment and Supplies) [9948]

Hudson Valley Paper Co. (Paper and Paper Products) [21770]

Hudson Valley Tile Co. (Floorcovering Equipment and Supplies) [9955]

Klein's Allsports Distributors (Recreational and Sporting Goods) [23776]

Kruger Recycling Inc. (Used, Scrap, and Recycled Materials) [26873]

Larry's News (Books and Other Printed Materials) [3896]

McDermott Food Brokers Inc. (Food) [11822]

Moore's Wholesale Tire Sales (Automotive) [2983]

New Options on Waste Inc. (Household Items) [15593]

Orange Motor Company Inc. (Automotive) [3063]

Rinella and Company Inc.; A.J. (Food) [12319]

Sager Spuck Statewide Supply Company Inc. (Industrial Supplies) [17155]

Sommer Advantage Food Brokers (Food) [12526]

Specialty Box and Packaging Co. (Paper and Paper Products) [21945]

Specialty World Foods Inc. (Food) [12553]

Trojan Pools (Recreational and Sporting Goods) [24015]

United Food Service Inc. (Food) [12793]

White Bear Equipment, Inc. (Automotive) [3423]

Wolberg Electrical Supply Company Inc. (Electrical and Electronic Equipment and Supplies) [9603]

Yaun Company Inc. (Plumbing Materials and Fixtures) [23468]

Albertson

Forbex Corporation (Floorcovering Equipment and Supplies) [9904]

Alexandra Bay

Seaway Distributors (Food) [12454]

Amherst

Andromeda Software Inc. (Computers and Software) [5942]

Arbordale Home and Garden Showplace (Agricultural Equipment and Supplies) [247]

A.T. Supply (Paints and Varnishes) [21391]

Buffalo Hotel Supply Company Inc. (Specialty Equipment and Products) [25585]

Eaton Office Supply Company Inc. (Office Equipment and Supplies) [20978]

Florig Equipment of Buffalo, Inc. (Industrial Machinery) [16015]

Lang and Washburn Electric Inc. (Electrical and Electronic Equipment and Supplies) [8970]

Standard Electronics (Electrical and Electronic Equipment and Supplies) [9403]

Amityville

Components Specialties Inc. (Sound and Entertainment Equipment and Supplies) [25146]

Dinghy Shop International (Marine) [18491]

IDE-Interstate Inc. (Health and Beauty Aids) [14129]

International Screw & Bolt (Hardware) [13766]

Meadowbrook Distributing Corp. (Soft Drinks) [24987]

Mega Cabinets Inc. (Construction Materials and Machinery) [7689]

Romanoff International Supply Corp. (Jewelry) [17572]

Schwartz Co.; Louis J. (Furniture and Fixtures) [13234]

Amsterdam

Amsterdam Brush Corp. (Paints and Varnishes) [21387]

Mohawk Dairy (Food) [11917]

Mohawk Finishing Products Inc. (Paints and Varnishes) [21506]

Steinberg Brothers Inc. (Medical, Dental, and Optical Supplies) [19638]

Angola

Lads Pet Supplies (Veterinary Products) [27178]

Arcade

Koike America Inc. (Industrial Machinery) [16212]

Roberts Auto Parts; Fred (Automotive) [3169]

Ardsley

Earthworm Inc. (Construction Materials and Machinery) [7297]

Armonk

HK Laundry Equipment Inc. (Cleaning and Janitorial Supplies) [4634]

Sharpe Inc.; M.E. (Books and Other Printed Materials) [4156]

Ashville

Fairbank Reconstruction Corp. (Food) [11070]

Astoria

Charmer Industries Inc. (Alcoholic Beverages) [1589]

Parma Tile Mosaic & Marble (Floorcovering Equipment and Supplies) [10101]

Tsigonia Paint Sales (Paints and Varnishes) [21596]

Auburn

Consolidated Scrap Processing (Used, Scrap, and Recycled Materials) [26784]

Finger Lakes Bottling Co. (Alcoholic Beverages) [1690]

Julius Kraft Company Inc. (Security and Safety Equipment) [24579]

Mustad and Son Inc.; O. (Recreational and Sporting Goods) [23841]

Rood Utilities (Heating and Cooling Equipment and Supplies) [14666]

Baldwin

Ecological Laboratories (Chemicals) [4380]

Educational Activities Inc. (Sound and Entertainment Equipment and Supplies) [25171]

Baldwin Place

Kurian Reference Books; George (Books and Other Printed Materials) [3888]

Baldwinsville

JRE Computing (Computers and Software) [6411]

Barrytown

Other Publishers (Books and Other Printed Materials) [4027]

Batavia

Pepsi-Cola Batavia Bottling Corp. (Soft Drinks) [25005]

Summit Wholesale (Heating and Cooling Equipment and Supplies) [14702]

Summit Wholesale (Plumbing Materials and Fixtures) [23399]

Bay Shore

Montfort Publications (Books and Other Printed Materials) [3965]

Wholesale Tire Company Auto Centers (Automotive) [3428]

Bayport

Stimpson Company Inc. (Hardware) [13939]

Thego Corporation/Acme Marine Hoist, inc. (Marine) [18624]

Bayside

Lundahl Inc.; Warner T. (Automotive) [2898]

Bayville

Flower's Shellfish Distributors (Food) [11164]

Bedford

Duraffourg Gem Company Inc.; Max (Jewelry) [17400]

Bedford Hills

Burquip Truck Bodies & Equipment (Automotive) [2401]

Bethpage

Kravet Fabrics Inc. (Textiles and Notions) [26115]

RNM Specialty Co. (Gifts and Novelties) [13437]

Binghamton

Binghamton Truck Body & Equipment Corp. (Automotive) [2363]

Grail Foundation of America (Books and Other Printed Materials) [3793]

The Haworth Press Inc. (Books and Other Printed Materials) [3818]
Johnson Camping Inc. (Recreational and Sporting Goods) [23762]
Mainline Supply Corp. (Floorcovering Equipment and Supplies) [10004]
Old Sutler John (Toys and Hobby Goods) [26597]
West Nesbitt Inc. (Livestock and Farm Products) [18338]
Willow Run Foods Inc. (Food) [12952]

Blasdell
Eaton Equipment Corp. (Agricultural Equipment and Supplies) [539]
Southtowns Seafood & Meats (Food) [12544]

Blauvelt
Arriflex Corp. (Photographic Equipment and Supplies) [22827]
First American Artificial Flowers Inc. (Horticultural Supplies) [14861]

Bohemia
Arco Pharmaceuticals Inc. (Medical, Dental, and Optical Supplies) [19158]
ARvee Systems Inc. (Computers and Software) [5968]
Bronson Syrup Company Inc. (Food) [10619]
Omega Products Corporation (Hardware) [13853]
Riedel Crystal of America Inc. (Household Items) [15636]
Touch Adjust Clip Co. Inc. (Jewelry) [17642]
Versatile Industrial Products (Adhesives) [18]

Brentwood
All Pet Distributors (Veterinary Products) [27060]
Allou Distributors Inc. (Health and Beauty Aids) [14014]
Allou Health and Beauty Care Inc. (Health and Beauty Aids) [14015]
Distribution Systems of America (Books and Other Printed Materials) [3697]
U.S. Lock Corp. (Security and Safety Equipment) [24651]
Wizard Equipment Corp. (Construction Materials and Machinery) [8236]

Brewerton
Magee Marine Supply (Marine) [18555]
Northway Acres Craft Supply (Office Equipment and Supplies) [21165]
Northway Acres Craft Supply (Office Equipment and Supplies) [21166]

Brewster
Consolidated Midland Corp. (Health and Beauty Aids) [14071]
Interstate Petroleum Products Inc. (Petroleum, Fuels, and Related Equipment) [22377]
Sonin Inc. (Hardware) [13927]

Briarcliff Manor
TETKO Inc. (Textiles and Notions) [26224]

Brockport
Sporting Dog Specialties Inc. (Veterinary Products) [27237]

Bronx
Artusos Pastry Shop (Food) [10442]
Atlas Fuel Oil Co. (Petroleum, Fuels, and Related Equipment) [22050]
Byrne Compressed Air Equipment Company, Inc. (Compressors) [5831]
Capital Beverage Corp. (Alcoholic Beverages) [1569]
Casing Associates Inc. (Food) [10713]
Continental Recycling Inc. (Used, Scrap, and Recycled Materials) [26788]
Drinks Galore Inc. (Alcoholic Beverages) [1658]
Gassmon Coal and Oil Company Inc. (Minerals and Ores) [20542]
Good-O-Beverage Co. (Soft Drinks) [24962]
Kass Industrial Supply Corp. (Hardware) [13782]
Keystone Steel Sales Inc. (Metals) [20099]

Loveline Industries Inc. (Clothing) [5143]
Metropolis Metal Spinning and Stamping Inc. (Hardware) [13826]
Midland Steel Warehouse Co. (Metals) [20188]
National Equipment Corp. (Industrial Machinery) [16340]
National Foods (Food) [11977]
National Medical Excess (Medical, Dental, and Optical Equipment) [18957]
Paradise Products Corp. (Food) [12105]
Penachio Company Inc.; Nick (Food) [12135]
Power Chemical Company Inc. (Chemicals) [4483]
Quality Tile Corp. (Floorcovering Equipment and Supplies) [10111]
Rocket Jewelry Box Inc. (Jewelry) [17568]
Royce Industries Inc. (Electrical and Electronic Equipment and Supplies) [9320]
Schildwachter and Sons Inc.; Fred M. (Petroleum, Fuels, and Related Equipment) [22657]
Selby Furniture Hardware Company Inc. (Hardware) [13908]
Spoiled Rotten USA Inc. (Clothing) [5381]
Stella D'Oro Biscuit Company Inc. (Food) [12583]
Tulnoy Lumber Inc. (Construction Materials and Machinery) [8152]
Union Standard Equipment Co. (Medical, Dental, and Optical Supplies) [19672]
Weingart & Sons (Hardware) [13990]
Woodlawn Hardware (Industrial Supplies) [17287]
Zenobia Co. (Food) [13004]

Brooklyn
A & A Brake Service Co. Inc. (Automotive) [2151]
A-C Book Service (Books and Other Printed Materials) [3457]
Able Welding Co. (Automotive) [2165]
Ace Bag and Burlap Co. Inc. (Textiles and Notions) [25952]
Adams Book Company, Inc. (Books and Other Printed Materials) [3469]
Alicia Comforts (Household Items) [15393]
American Book Center (Books and Other Printed Materials) [3498]
American Visual Aids (Toys and Hobby Goods) [26390]
Avery Book Stores, Inc. (Books and Other Printed Materials) [3535]
Bath Beach Nurseries, Inc. (Horticultural Supplies) [14821]
Bayside Fuel Oil Depot Corp. (Petroleum, Fuels, and Related Equipment) [22059]
Bedford Food Products Inc. (Food) [10525]
Belmont Automotive Co. (Automotive) [2347]
Belt Corp.; P.M. (Clothing) [4814]
Berger and Company Inc.; Howard (Hardware) [13592]
Best Toy Manufacturing Ltd. (Toys and Hobby Goods) [26416]
Beyer Farms Inc. (Food) [10549]
Bicor Processing Corp. (Household Items) [15421]
Boutross Imports Inc. (Household Items) [15427]
Brainum Junior Inc.; Harry (Metals) [19832]
Burt Millwork Corp. (Construction Materials and Machinery) [7113]
Concord Sales Co. (Tobacco Products) [26278]
Continental Flooring Inc. (Floorcovering Equipment and Supplies) [9825]
Coronet Parts Manufacturing Co. Inc. (Automotive) [2485]
Creative Technologies Corp. (Household Appliances) [15098]
Dandee Creations Ltd. (Household Items) [15466]
Davidson Pipe Supply Company Inc. (Plumbing Materials and Fixtures) [23133]
Dealers Electric Motor (Electrical and Electronic Equipment and Supplies) [8616]
Dependable Food Corp. (Food) [10945]
Domsey Fiber Corp. (Clothing) [4919]
Duromotive Industries (Automotive) [2568]
Elson Import Export; Walter (Clothing) [4935]
Euro-Knit Corp. (Textiles and Notions) [26030]
Ferro Foods Corp. (Food) [11122]
Forty Acres and A Mule Film Works (Clothing) [4963]
Frontier (Jewelry) [17419]
Ganin Tire Company Inc. (Automotive) [2659]

Ganin Tire Inc. (Automotive) [2660]
Gillies Coffee Co. (Food) [11265]
Global Tropical (Food) [11273]
Gold & Reiss Corp. (Construction Materials and Machinery) [7402]
Golombeck Inc.; Morris J. (Food) [11288]
Granada Electronics Corp. (Electrical and Electronic Equipment and Supplies) [8804]
Haywin Textile Products Inc. (Household Items) [15522]
Hirten Company Inc.; William J. (Gifts and Novelties) [13368]
Howell Petroleum Products Inc. (Petroleum, Fuels, and Related Equipment) [22367]
Juno Chefs Inc. (Food) [11572]
K.B. Brothers Inc. (Toys and Hobby Goods) [26551]
Key Food Stores Cooperative Inc. (Food) [11607]
Klenosky Co.; S. (Paints and Varnishes) [21472]
Lang Percussion (Sound and Entertainment Equipment and Supplies) [25278]
Lantev (Food) [11678]
L.B. Electric Supply Company Inc. (Electrical and Electronic Equipment and Supplies) [8975]
Leather Connection (Luggage and Leather Goods) [18405]
Liberty Leather Products Company Inc. (Luggage and Leather Goods) [18407]
Lugo Hair Center Ltd. (Health and Beauty Aids) [14155]
Lumber Exchange Terminal Inc. (Construction Materials and Machinery) [7616]
M & V Provision Company Inc. (Food) [11752]
Marcus Brothers (Household Items) [15577]
Marino Marble & Tile (Floorcovering Equipment and Supplies) [10009]
Mendon Leasing Corp. (Automotive) [2942]
Milford Enterprises, Inc. (Floorcovering Equipment and Supplies) [10037]
Monarch Luggage Company Inc. (Luggage and Leather Goods) [18413]
Moznaim Publishing Corp. (Books and Other Printed Materials) [3973]
Nabisco Foods. Phoenix Confections Div. (Food) [11965]
Non-Ferrous Processing Corp. (Metals) [20230]
Nova Clutch Inc. (Automotive) [3049]
Novelty Cord and Tassel Company Inc. (Household Items) [15600]
Palagonia Italian Bread (Food) [12098]
Parkset Supply Ltd. (Plumbing Materials and Fixtures) [23308]
Paskesz Candies & Confectionery (Food) [12119]
Peerless Importers Inc. (Alcoholic Beverages) [1946]
Penthouse Industries Inc. (Household Items) [15616]
Pet Lift (Veterinary Products) [27208]
Playsafe Playground Systems of N.Y. (Recreational and Sporting Goods) [23886]
Polly-O Dairy (Food) [12189]
Psoul Company Inc. (Clothing) [5291]
Queen Shebra Co. (Clothing) [5295]
Rashid Sales Co. (Sound and Entertainment Equipment and Supplies) [25405]
Red Mill Farms Inc. (Food) [12285]
Reid Enterprises; Desmond A. (Books and Other Printed Materials) [4113]
Reynolds Tire and Rubber Div. (Automotive) [3153]
Rolet Food Products Co. (Food) [12347]
Royal Sales (Toys and Hobby Goods) [26640]
Royal Wine Co. (Alcoholic Beverages) [2001]
S. and S. Machinery Co. (Industrial Machinery) [16466]
Sander Supply Co.; Joseph (Clothing) [5331]
Saphrograph Corp. (Books and Other Printed Materials) [4137]
Sepher-Hermon Press (Books and Other Printed Materials) [4150]
Serconia Press (Books and Other Printed Materials) [4151]
Shepher Distributors and Sales Corp. (Toys and Hobby Goods) [26651]
Silber Knitwear Corp. (Clothing) [5355]

Silent Hoist and Crane Co. (Industrial Machinery) [16491]

Slavin and Sons Ltd.; M. (Food) [12504]

Sound Around Inc. (Sound and Entertainment Equipment and Supplies) [25451]

Sound Around Inc. (Household Appliances) [15319]

Steven Smith/Stuffed Animals Inc. (Toys and Hobby Goods) [26670]

Sticht Company Inc.; Herman H. (Scientific and Measurement Devices) [24439]

Super Glass Corp. (Household Items) [15672]

Tasty Mix Quality Foods Inc. (Food) [12700]

TENBA Quality Cases, Ltd. (Luggage and Leather Goods) [18435]

Torah Umesorah Publications (Books and Other Printed Materials) [4221]

Ubiquity Distributors (Books and Other Printed Materials) [4235]

Universal Marine Medical Supply Co. (Medical, Dental, and Optical Supplies) [19684]

Vasso Systems, Inc. (Automotive) [3388]

Very Fine Resources Inc. (Food) [12842]

Window Headquarters Inc. (Construction Materials and Machinery) [8233]

World Candies Inc. (Food) [12980]

Buffalo

ADI (Security and Safety Equipment) [24483]

AirSep Corporation (Industrial Machinery) [15748]

Alternative Cigarettes Inc. (Tobacco Products) [26258]

Appliance Parts Distributors Inc. (Household Appliances) [15022]

Austin House Inc. (Health and Beauty Aids) [14028]

Automatic Firing Inc. (Heating and Cooling Equipment and Supplies) [14331]

Automatic Firing Inc. (Electrical and Electronic Equipment and Supplies) [8398]

Birzon Inc.; Sid (Jewelry) [17339]

Bison Products Co. Inc. (Food) [10561]

Brookline Machine Co. (Automotive) [2392]

Buffalo Office Interiors Inc. (Office Equipment and Supplies) [20864]

Buffalo Scale and Supply Co. Inc. (Scientific and Measurement Devices) [24330]

Buffalo White GMC Inc. (Motorized Vehicles) [20607]

Crest Audio/Video/Electronics (Electrical and Electronic Equipment and Supplies) [8593]

D & M Plywood, Inc. (Construction Materials and Machinery) [7243]

Davenport-Webb Inc. (Food) [10914]

Day Manufacturing Co.; S.A. (Automotive) [2532]

Denzak & Associates, Inc.; Joan (Recreational and Sporting Goods) [23619]

Dunlop Tire Corp. (Automotive) [2567]

EEV, Inc. (Communications Systems and Equipment) [5600]

Empire/EMCO Inc. (Storage Equipment and Containers) [25911]

ESI-Technologies Inc. (Computers and Software) [6256]

Ferguson Electric Construction Company Inc. (Electrical and Electronic Equipment and Supplies) [8737]

Frey the Wheelman Inc. (Automotive) [2649]

Frontier Lumber Co. (Construction Materials and Machinery) [7369]

Frontier Water and Steam Supply Co. (Plumbing Materials and Fixtures) [23178]

GCF Inc. (Metals) [19995]

Gibraltar Steel Corp. (Metals) [20006]

Gibraltar Steel Products (Metals) [20007]

GMR Division MNH (Health and Beauty Aids) [14113]

Goetz Energy Corp. (Petroleum, Fuels, and Related Equipment) [22317]

Gor-den Industries Inc. (Automotive) [2693]

Graphic Controls (Paper and Paper Products) [21747]

H and F Food Products Inc. (Food) [11348]

Hein and Co., Inc.; William S. (Books and Other Printed Materials) [3821]

Hurwitz Brothers Iron and Metal Company Inc. (Metals) [20051]

Hyatt's Graphic Supply Company, Inc. (Specialty Equipment and Products) [25684]

Langley Company Inc.; Frank P. (Plumbing Materials and Fixtures) [23240]

LBM Sales Inc. (Food) [11690]

Levin and Company of Tonawanda, Inc.; Louis (Used, Scrap, and Recycled Materials) [26881]

Luther's Creative Craft Studios (Office Equipment and Supplies) [21116]

McCullagh Inc.; S.J. (Food) [11821]

Milhem & Brothers; Attea (Tobacco Products) [26329]

Parkside Candy Co. (Food) [12116]

Petroleum Sales and Service Inc. (Petroleum, Fuels, and Related Equipment) [22571]

R and R Salvage Inc. (Used, Scrap, and Recycled Materials) [26949]

Rich Products Corp. Food Service Div. (Food) [12312]

Robert-James Sales Inc. (Metals) [20323]

Root, Neal and Company Inc. (Electrical and Electronic Equipment and Supplies) [9318]

Seneca Plumbing and Heating Supply Company Inc. (Plumbing Materials and Fixtures) [23368]

T-W Truck Equippers, Inc. (Automotive) [3291]

Traditional Quality Corp. (Food) [12741]

Tripifoods Inc. (Food) [12757]

Tzetzo Brothers Inc. (Food) [12781]

UMBRA U.S.A. Inc. (Household Items) [15692]

U.S. Sugar Company Inc. (Food) [12804]

Volland Electric Equipment Corp. (Industrial Machinery) [16607]

Wehle Electric Div. (Electrical and Electronic Equipment and Supplies) [9567]

Will Poultry Co. (Food) [12946]

Woolley Inc.; L.A. (Electrical and Electronic Equipment and Supplies) [9604]

Zappia Enterprises Inc. (Motorized Vehicles) [20757]

Cairo

Black Forest Distributors Ltd. (Alcoholic Beverages) [1532]

Calverton

W.L.C. Ltd. (Veterinary Products) [27271]

Cambria Heights

Blacast Entertainment (Books and Other Printed Materials) [3558]

Camillus

Crucible Service Centers (Metals) [19908]

Campbell Hall

Alders Wholesale; Henry (Office Equipment and Supplies) [20782]

Canandaigua

Finger Lakes Livestock Exchange Inc. (Livestock and Farm Products) [17918]

S & P Whistle Stop (Toys and Hobby Goods) [26644]

Canastota

Clarks Petroleum Service Inc. (Petroleum, Fuels, and Related Equipment) [22143]

Rapasadi Sons; Isadore A. (Food) [12279]

Carle Place

Nuclear Associates (Medical, Dental, and Optical Equipment) [18963]

Scales Air Compressor Corp. (Compressors) [5851]

Carthage

Slack Chemical Company, Inc. (Chemicals) [4512]

Center Moriches

Triconic Labs Inc. (Medical, Dental, and Optical Supplies) [19662]

Central Islip

CBS WhitCom Technologies Corp. (Communications Systems and Equipment) [5552]

Duraline (Electrical and Electronic Equipment and Supplies) [8639]

Flexbar Machine Corp. (Industrial Machinery) [16009]

Lib-Com Ltd. (Gifts and Novelties) [13390]

Chappaqua

Education People, Inc. (Books and Other Printed Materials) [3721]

Chazy

Chazy Orchards Inc. (Food) [10736]

Cheektowaga

Davis Electrical Supply Company Inc. (Electrical and Electronic Equipment and Supplies) [8614]

Dobkin Company, Inc.; W.W. (Floorcovering Equipment and Supplies) [9868]

Empire State News Corp. (Books and Other Printed Materials) [3730]

Scrivner Inc. Buffalo Div. (Food) [12437]

Scrivner of New York (Food) [12438]

Sorce, Inc. (Floorcovering Equipment and Supplies) [10156]

Chenango Bridge

Cooperative Feed Dealer Inc. (Agricultural Equipment and Supplies) [454]

Cicero

A & P Auto Parts Inc. (Automotive) [2158]

ACI Controls (Industrial Machinery) [15731]

Clarence

Mitscher Company Inc.; R.W. (Electrical and Electronic Equipment and Supplies) [9090]

North American Parts Inc. (Recreational and Sporting Goods) [23849]

Clayton

Gray's Wholesale Inc. (Tobacco Products) [26300]

Clifton Park

Northeast Interior Systems Inc. (Furniture and Fixtures) [13188]

Cohoes

Kelman Inc.; Nathan H. (Used, Scrap, and Recycled Materials) [26863]

Ontario Supply Corp. (Electrical and Electronic Equipment and Supplies) [9157]

Cold Spring Harbor

Interdonati, Inc.; H. (Medical, Dental, and Optical Supplies) [19375]

College Point

Display Technologies (Specialty Equipment and Products) [25631]

Jetro Cash and Carry Enterprises Inc. (Food) [11553]

Knese, Inc.; Henry (Industrial Machinery) [16209]

Commack

A & M Trading Company Inc. (Automotive) [2157]

All Appliance Parts Inc. (Electrical and Electronic Equipment and Supplies) [8292]

Heritage Marketing Inc. (Food) [11418]

Precision Type Inc. (Computers and Software) [6634]

Setton's International Foods Inc. (Food) [12465]

Spartan Pet Supply (Veterinary Products) [27235]

Zetex Inc. (Electrical and Electronic Equipment and Supplies) [9625]

Conklin

Maines Paper and Food Service Inc. (Food) [11761]

Maines Paper and Food Service Inc. Equipment and Supply Div. (Heating and Cooling Equipment and Supplies) [14530]

Copiague
Acme Heat & Power (Heating and Cooling
Equipment and Supplies) [14293]
Sea Coast Distributors, Inc. (Marine) [18602]

Corning
Corning Inc. (Household Items) [15457]
Crystal City Bakers (Food) [10876]

Cornwall
Applied Systems Technology and
Resources (Computers and Software) [5953]

Corona
U.S. Industrial Products Corp. (Hardware) [13975]

Cortland
Cortland Line Company Inc. (Recreational and
Sporting Goods) [23607]

Deer Park
Alarm Controls Corp. (Security and Safety
Equipment) [24498]
Best Way Tools (Hardware) [13596]
Edom Laboratories Inc. (Health and Beauty
Aids) [14092]
Entertainment Music Marketing Corp. (Sound and
Entertainment Equipment and Supplies) [25183]
High Frequency Technology Company
Inc. (Communications Systems and
Equipment) [5637]
Krantor Corp. (Food) [11646]
Schenck Trebel Corp. (Scientific and Measurement
Devices) [24427]
Surge Components Inc. (Electrical and Electronic
Equipment and Supplies) [9448]

Delmar
DayMark Corp. (Guns and Weapons) [13487]

Derby
Hazard and Sons Inc.; L.A. (Plumbing Materials
and Fixtures) [23206]
New Era Cap Company Inc. (Clothing) [5224]

DeWitt
Agway, Inc. (Agricultural Equipment and
Supplies) [219]

Dobbs Ferry
Oceana Publications Inc. (Books and Other Printed
Materials) [4016]

Dunkirk
AA & A Enterprises Inc. (Metals) [19721]
Fieldbrook Farms Inc. (Food) [11123]
Sam Farm Inc.; A. (Food) [12398]

East Bloomfield
Crosman Corporation (Guns and
Weapons) [13485]

East Chatham
Bacon Pamphlet Service, Inc. (Books and Other
Printed Materials) [3538]

East Farmingdale
Doral Fabrics Inc. (Textiles and Notions) [26019]
Imperial Delivery Service Inc. (Books and Other
Printed Materials) [3840]

East Jewett
Winter Harbor Fisheries (Food) [12961]

East Meadow
Edmer Sanitary Supply Co. Inc. (Cleaning and
Janitorial Supplies) [4617]
Mausner Equipment Company Inc. (Industrial
Machinery) [16275]
Pearl Paint Co., Inc. (Paints and
Varnishes) [21534]
Super-Nutrition Distributors Inc. (Health and Beauty
Aids) [14252]

East Rochester
Country Wide Transport Services
Inc. (Food) [10860]
Monroe Insulation & Gutter Company
Inc. (Construction Materials and
Machinery) [7739]

East Syracuse
CIS Corp. (Computers and Software) [6070]
Green Leaf Distributors, Inc. (Veterinary
Products) [27142]
Liftech Handling Inc. (Industrial Machinery) [16234]
Liland Trade & Radiator Service
Inc. (Automotive) [2882]
NEC Business Communication Systems East
Inc. (Communications Systems and
Equipment) [5688]
STS Truck Equipment and Trailer
Sales (Automotive) [3276]
Thompson and Johnson Equipment Company
Inc. (Industrial Machinery) [16562]
Ziegler's Bakers Supply and Equipment
Corp. (Food) [13006]

East Worcester
Herzog Supply Inc.; C. (Plumbing Materials and
Fixtures) [23208]

Eastchester
Westcon Inc. (Communications Systems and
Equipment) [5811]

Eden
Eden Valley Growers Inc. (Food) [11026]

Ellenville
Duso Food Distributors (Food) [11002]

Ellicottville
Fitzpatrick and Weller Inc. (Construction Materials
and Machinery) [7348]

Elmhurst
Acarex Inc. (Automotive) [2167]
Century Fasteners Corp. (Hardware) [13627]

Elmira
Booth Inc.; I.D. (Plumbing Materials and
Fixtures) [23092]
Chemung Supply Corp. (Industrial
Supplies) [16795]
Chemung Supply Corp. (Metals) [19875]
Elmira Distributing (Alcoholic Beverages) [1674]
Empire Airgas (Industrial Supplies) [16848]
Empire Airgas (Chemicals) [4383]
Gierston Tool Company Inc. (Industrial
Machinery) [16063]
LaFrance Equipment Corp. (Security and Safety
Equipment) [24583]
Purolator Products (Automotive) [3124]
Seneca Beverage Corp. (Alcoholic
Beverages) [2018]
Shulman and Son Co.; I. (Used, Scrap, and
Recycled Materials) [26989]
Winchester Optical Company Inc. (Medical, Dental,
and Optical Supplies) [19711]

Elmont
Fiorano Design Center (Floorcovering Equipment
and Supplies) [9889]
Warner Book Distributors; W. (Books and Other
Printed Materials) [4269]

Elmsford
Conway Import Co. Inc. (Food) [10831]
EEV, Inc. (Medical, Dental, and Optical
Equipment) [18784]
Gerber Cheese Company Inc. (Food) [11256]
Holsten Import Corp. (Alcoholic Beverages) [1761]
Mamiya America Corp. (Photographic Equipment
and Supplies) [22875]
Varta Batteries Inc. (Electrical and Electronic
Equipment and Supplies) [9535]

Endicott
Lehigh Safety Shoe Co. (Shoes) [24793]
Marshall Industries (Electrical and Electronic
Equipment and Supplies) [9034]
MDR Corp. (Office Equipment and
Supplies) [21136]

Esperance
Cable Technologies International of New York
Inc. (Sound and Entertainment Equipment and
Supplies) [25115]

Fairport
Gilman Industrial Exports, Inc. (Scientific and
Measurement Devices) [24365]
Happy Refrigerated Services (Food) [11375]
OCE-USA Inc. (Specialty Equipment and
Products) [25772]

Falconer
Clark Supply Co. (Hardware) [13634]

Farmingdale
Allied Transmission, Inc. (Industrial
Machinery) [15759]
American Laubscher Corp. (Industrial
Supplies) [16695]
American Laubscher Corp. (Industrial
Machinery) [15768]
American Outdoor Sports (Recreational and
Sporting Goods) [23511]
Atomergic Chemetals Corp. (Chemicals) [4331]
Beyerdynamic (Communications Systems and
Equipment) [5532]
Bulbtronics (Electrical and Electronic Equipment and
Supplies) [8477]
Colorado Prime Foods (Household
Appliances) [15090]
GEM Electronics (Electrical and Electronic
Equipment and Supplies) [8781]
GMI Photographic Inc. (Photographic Equipment
and Supplies) [22858]
Group One Ltd. (Communications Systems and
Equipment) [5627]
King's Cage (Veterinary Products) [27174]
Lindenmeyr Munroe (Paper and Paper
Products) [21809]
Long Island Transmission Corp. (Industrial
Machinery) [16244]
M & N Supply Corp. (Construction Materials and
Machinery) [7627]
NUCO Industries Inc. (Cleaning and Janitorial
Supplies) [4678]
Patron Transmission (Industrial Supplies) [17100]
Perigon Medical Dist. Corp. (Medical, Dental, and
Optical Supplies) [19534]
Rand International Leisure Products
Ltd. (Recreational and Sporting Goods) [23905]
Semispecialists of America Inc. (Electrical and
Electronic Equipment and Supplies) [9352]
Semispecialists of America Inc. (Electrical and
Electronic Equipment and Supplies) [9353]
Tapeswitch Corp. (Electrical and Electronic
Equipment and Supplies) [9459]
TW Communication Corp. (Communications
Systems and Equipment) [5798]
Waldner Company Inc.; D. (Office Equipment and
Supplies) [21343]
WMF of America (Household Items) [15712]
WMF Hutschenreuther USA (Household
Items) [15713]

Farmington
Seneca Paper (Paper and Paper
Products) [21933]

Farmingville
Cancos Tile Corp. (Floorcovering Equipment and
Supplies) [9753]
Cancos Tile Corp. (Construction Materials and
Machinery) [7133]

Fayetteville
LBM Sales Inc. (Food) [11689]

Floral Park

Music Industries Inc. (Sound and Entertainment Equipment and Supplies) [25347]
Music Industries Inc. (Household Appliances) [15244]
Schrafel Paper Corp.; A.J. (Paper and Paper Products) [21927]
Silver Loom Associates (Floorcovering Equipment and Supplies) [10148]

Florida

Brach Knitting Mills Inc. (Clothing) [4840]

Flushing

Advanced Affiliates Inc. (Hardware) [13536]
Amex Hides Ltd. (Luggage and Leather Goods) [18370]
Campari USA Inc. (Alcoholic Beverages) [1567]
Express International Corp. (Medical, Dental, and Optical Supplies) [19313]
H & D Transmission (Automotive) [2713]
Liconix Industries Inc. (Industrial Supplies) [16999]
McDermott Corp.; Julian A. (Security and Safety Equipment) [24588]
Prime Care Medical Supplies Inc. (Medical, Dental, and Optical Equipment) [18996]
Scott Associates; L.S. (Clothing) [5338]
Shiau's Trading Co. (Gifts and Novelties) [13446]
Thermax Wire Corp. (Electrical and Electronic Equipment and Supplies) [9485]
Travers Tool Co. (Hardware) [13963]
Travers Tool Co., Inc. (Hardware) [13964]
Vassilaros and Sons Inc.; J.A. (Food) [12831]

Forest Hills

Electronic Security Integration, Inc. (Security and Safety Equipment) [24535]
Hahn Watch & Jewelry Co. (Jewelry) [17442]
Hall & Reis, Inc. (Construction Materials and Machinery) [7431]

Freeport

ABC Display and Supply Inc. (Specialty Equipment and Products) [25540]
Applied Genetics Inc. (Health and Beauty Aids) [14023]
B & N Industries (Hardware) [13578]
CCL Creative Ltd (Gifts and Novelties) [13328]
Educational Record & Tape Distributors of America (Sound and Entertainment Equipment and Supplies) [25174]
Freeport Marine Supply (Marine) [18505]
Monarch Toilet Partition (Furniture and Fixtures) [13184]
North American Vision Services (Medical, Dental, and Optical Supplies) [19497]
Prestige Marble & Tile Co. (Floorcovering Equipment and Supplies) [10107]

Fresh Meadows

Silton USA Corp. (Medical, Dental, and Optical Supplies) [19613]

Gansevoort

Railway Services International (Railroad Equipment and Supplies) [23487]

Garden City

Export Oil Field Supply Company Inc. (Petroleum, Fuels, and Related Equipment) [22244]
Gallard-Schlesinger Industries Inc. (Chemicals) [4396]
W.A.C. Lighting (Electrical and Electronic Equipment and Supplies) [9548]

Garden City Park

Amity Hosiery Company Inc. (Clothing) [4771]

Gasport

Perry and Son Inc.; C.J. (Agricultural Equipment and Supplies) [1123]

Geneva

Seneca News Agency Inc. (Books and Other Printed Materials) [4149]

Winchester Optical (Medical, Dental, and Optical Supplies) [19709]

Getzville

Service Office Supply Corp. (Office Equipment and Supplies) [21265]
Watmet Inc. (Electrical and Electronic Equipment and Supplies) [9559]

Glen Cove

Acclaim Entertainment Inc. (Toys and Hobby Goods) [26380]
North Shore Sportswear Company Inc. (Clothing) [5238]
Royal Golf, Inc. (Recreational and Sporting Goods) [23923]
Royal Golf Inc. (Recreational and Sporting Goods) [23924]

Glen Head

Banfi Products Corp. (Alcoholic Beverages) [1498]

Glendale

C & K Distributors Inc. (Veterinary Products) [27097]
Continental Book Co. (Books and Other Printed Materials) [3656]
Franco-American Novelty Company Inc. (Gifts and Novelties) [13359]
LI Tinsmith Supply Corp. (Construction Materials and Machinery) [7601]
Mechanics Building Materials Inc. (Construction Materials and Machinery) [7688]
S & S Firearms (Guns and Weapons) [13512]
Sharp Wholesale Corp. (Household Appliances) [15311]

Glens Falls

Leland Paper Company Inc. (Office Equipment and Supplies) [21105]
Northern Distributing Co. (Alcoholic Beverages) [1921]
Sawyer and Company Inc.; J.E. (Hardware) [13904]

Gloversville

Grandoe Corp. (Recreational and Sporting Goods) [23696]
Hawkins Fabrics (Clothing) [5022]
Levor and Company Inc.; G. (Livestock and Farm Products) [18052]
Swany America Corp. (Clothing) [5412]
Taylor Company Inc.; Nelson A. (Marine) [18623]
Warden Leathers Inc. (Luggage and Leather Goods) [18441]

Goshen

LAM Electrical Supply Company, Inc. (Electrical and Electronic Equipment and Supplies) [8967]

Great Neck

Avent Inc. (Computers and Software) [5993]
Clamyer International Corp. (Paints and Varnishes) [21413]
Convermat Corp. (Paper and Paper Products) [21690]
Imperial Frozen Foods Company Inc. (Food) [11501]
Imrex Company Inc. (Computers and Software) [6359]
Jimlar Corp. (Shoes) [24779]
Sherman Business Forms, Inc. (Paper and Paper Products) [21937]
Sherman Business Forms Inc. (Office Equipment and Supplies) [21267]
Tradex International Corp. (Metals) [20436]

Green Island

Freedman and Son Inc.; R. (Used, Scrap, and Recycled Materials) [26818]

Greene

Page Seed Co. (Agricultural Equipment and Supplies) [1116]

Raymond Sales Corp. (Industrial Machinery) [16440]

Guilderland Center

Intermarket Imports Inc. (Industrial Machinery) [16163]

Hagaman

Bonded Insulation Company Inc. (Used, Scrap, and Recycled Materials) [26769]

Hall

Seedway (Agricultural Equipment and Supplies) [1254]
Seedway, Inc. (Agricultural Equipment and Supplies) [1255]

Hamburg

Baillie Lumber Co. (Construction Materials and Machinery) [7012]
Globe-Hamburg, Import/Export (Electrical and Electronic Equipment and Supplies) [8790]
Superior Auto Sales Inc. (Motorized Vehicles) [20733]
Superior Auto Sales Inc. (Automotive) [3285]

Hampton Bays

Quogue Sinclair Fuel Inc. (Petroleum, Fuels, and Related Equipment) [22604]

Harrison

Castle Oil Corp. (Petroleum, Fuels, and Related Equipment) [22115]
Rail Europe Group (Computers and Software) [6679]
Rail Europe Holding (Computers and Software) [6680]

Hartsdale

Singer Products Export Company Inc. (Industrial Machinery) [16494]
Singer Products Export Company Inc. (Automotive) [3224]
Stern & Company, Inc.; Henry (Electrical and Electronic Equipment and Supplies) [9417]

Hauppauge

American Marketing International (Automotive) [2231]
Apex Plastic Industries Inc. (Plastics) [22928]
Arista Enterprises Inc. (Computers and Software) [5960]
Atlantic Fluid Power (Industrial Machinery) [15788]
Audiovox Corp. (Communications Systems and Equipment) [5523]
Avon Electrical Supplies, Inc. (Electrical and Electronic Equipment and Supplies) [8404]
Busby Metals Inc. (Metals) [19845]
Dan Communications Inc.; Lee (Communications Systems and Equipment) [5586]
Electrograph Systems Inc. (Computers and Software) [6241]
Essex Entertainment Inc. (Sound and Entertainment Equipment and Supplies) [25185]
International Components Corp. (Food) [11520]
Jaco Electronics Inc. (Electrical and Electronic Equipment and Supplies) [8903]
Knogo North America Inc. (Household Appliances) [15192]
Leader Instruments Corp. (Electrical and Electronic Equipment and Supplies) [8977]
Maharam Fabric Corp. (Textiles and Notions) [26131]
Manchester Equipment Company Inc. (Computers and Software) [6458]
Milgray Electronics Inc. (Electrical and Electronic Equipment and Supplies) [9083]
PSDI (Computers and Software) [6659]
Regent Sports Corp. (Recreational and Sporting Goods) [23910]
Rice Aircraft Inc. (Aeronautical Equipment and Supplies) [142]
Schneider Optics Inc. (Medical, Dental, and Optical Supplies) [19597]

Sentry Technology Corp. (Security and Safety Equipment) [24635]

Sherburn Electronics Corp. (Electrical and Electronic Equipment and Supplies) [9364]

Stok Software Inc. (Computers and Software) [6762]

Stomel and Sons; Joseph H. (Food) [12589]

Vanguard Imaging Corp. (Chemicals) [4546]

Video Sentry Corp. (Security and Safety Equipment) [24658]

Hawthorne

AAR Corp. (Aeronautical Equipment and Supplies) [21]

Commerce Overseas Corp. (Aeronautical Equipment and Supplies) [72]

Corstar Business Computing Inc. (Computers and Software) [6163]

Metric & Multistandard Components Corp. (Industrial Supplies) [17031]

Hempstead

Ambassador Book Service, Inc. (Books and Other Printed Materials) [3495]

Barry Optical Co., Inc. (Medical, Dental, and Optical Supplies) [19175]

Dogroom Products (Veterinary Products) [27119]

Janvey and Sons Inc.; I. (Cleaning and Janitorial Supplies) [4646]

Henrietta

Matthews and Fields Lumber of Henrietta (Construction Materials and Machinery) [7670]

Monroe Tractor and Implement Company Inc. (Motorized Vehicles) [20685]

Tri-Line Corp. (Compressors) [5854]

Tri-Line Corp. (Industrial Machinery) [16579]

Hewlett

American Cut Crystal (Household Items) [15397]

Hicksville

Anchor Commerce Trading Corp. (Construction Materials and Machinery) [6973]

Bella & Co.; Frank (Textiles and Notions) [25979]

Distribution Systems of America (Books and Other Printed Materials) [3696]

ERS Distributors, Inc. (Sound and Entertainment Equipment and Supplies) [25184]

Firestone Plywood (Construction Materials and Machinery) [7345]

Levinson Associates Inc.; Harold (Tobacco Products) [26323]

Malvese Equipment Company Inc. (Agricultural Equipment and Supplies) [983]

Nemo Tile Company, Inc. (Floorcovering Equipment and Supplies) [10074]

Priscilla Gold Seal Corp. (Food) [12221]

Hilton

PM Marketing (Electrical and Electronic Equipment and Supplies) [9215]

Hollis

Borden & Riley Paper Co. (Paper and Paper Products) [21654]

Well Made Toy Manufacturing Co. (Toys and Hobby Goods) [26708]

Holtsville

Hermetic Aircraft International Corp. (Aeronautical Equipment and Supplies) [96]

Kings Food Service Professionals Inc.; J. (Food) [11618]

L.J. Technical Systems Inc. (Computers and Software) [6441]

National Electrical Supply Corp. (Electrical and Electronic Equipment and Supplies) [9114]

Picone Building Products (Heating and Cooling Equipment and Supplies) [14636]

Tower Fasteners Company, Inc. (Electrical and Electronic Equipment and Supplies) [9497]

Hopewell Junction

Granada Systems Design Inc. (Communications Systems and Equipment) [5624]

Howard Beach

Atlantic Ceramic Tile (Floorcovering Equipment and Supplies) [9692]

Hudson

Clermont Inc. (Soft Drinks) [24928]

Columbia News Agency Inc. (Books and Other Printed Materials) [3647]

Ginsbergs Institutional Food Service Supplies Inc. (Food) [11266]

HAVE Inc. (Sound and Entertainment Equipment and Supplies) [25229]

Hudson Falls

Polycoat Systems Inc. (Construction Materials and Machinery) [7878]

Huntington

Knutson Distributors (Marine) [18536]

Vintwood International Ltd. (Alcoholic Beverages) [2105]

Huntington Station

Big Blue Products Inc. (Computers and Software) [6016]

HGS Power House, Inc. (Agricultural Equipment and Supplies) [818]

Protein Databases Inc. (Scientific and Measurement Devices) [24421]

Rees Ceramic Tile; Cynthia (Floorcovering Equipment and Supplies) [10118]

Inwood

Bermil Industries Corp. (Household Appliances) [15050]

The Last Straw Inc. (Toys and Hobby Goods) [26563]

Islandia

CBS WhitCom Technologies Corp. (Electrical and Electronic Equipment and Supplies) [8512]

Islip

Silver Lake Cookie Co. (Food) [12492]

Ithaca

Sawtooth Builders (Floorcovering Equipment and Supplies) [10139]

Seneca Supply and Equipment Co. (Construction Materials and Machinery) [7999]

Worldwide Books (Books and Other Printed Materials) [4297]

Jamaica

Adikes Inc.; J. & L. (Agricultural Equipment and Supplies) [187]

Associated Food Stores Inc. (Food) [10446]

King Wire and Cable Corp. (Electrical and Electronic Equipment and Supplies) [8947]

LEA Book Distributors (Books and Other Printed Materials) [3900]

Loroman Co. (Electrical and Electronic Equipment and Supplies) [9003]

Mallor Brokerage Co. (Food) [11765]

Nemo Tile Company, Inc. (Floorcovering Equipment and Supplies) [10073]

Queens Decorative Wallcoverings Inc. (Household Items) [15627]

Verby Company Inc.; H. (Construction Materials and Machinery) [8179]

Jamestown

American Locker Security Systems Inc. (Furniture and Fixtures) [13017]

Sysco Food Service of Jamestown (Food) [12671]

WEB Machinery Co. (Industrial Machinery) [16616]

Westburgh Electric Inc. (Electrical and Electronic Equipment and Supplies) [9572]

Jericho

Getty Petroleum Marketing Inc. (Petroleum, Fuels, and Related Equipment) [22309]

Getty Realty Corp. (Petroleum, Fuels, and Related Equipment) [22310]

Winter Wolff Inc. (Metals) [20496]

Johnstown

H & J Leather Finishing (Luggage and Leather Goods) [18396]

Knight Marketing Corp. (Cleaning and Janitorial Supplies) [4652]

Kew Gardens

Kelaty International Inc. (Floorcovering Equipment and Supplies) [9986]

Kiamesha Lake

Reynolds and Sons Inc.; A.T. (Soft Drinks) [25024]

Kinderhook

International Book Distributors Ltd. (Books and Other Printed Materials) [3846]

Kingston

AmeriBag Inc. (Luggage and Leather Goods) [18368]

Educational Coin Co. (Toys and Hobby Goods) [26476]

Entronic Industries Inc. (Electrical and Electronic Equipment and Supplies) [8711]

Greylock Electronics Distributors (Electrical and Electronic Equipment and Supplies) [8819]

McPherson & Co. Publishers (Books and Other Printed Materials) [3945]

Wonderly Company Inc. (Household Items) [15714]

Lackawanna

Lake Erie Distributors (Alcoholic Beverages) [1812]

Lafayette

Archer Associates; C.F. (Household Items) [15405]

Lake Success

Daystar-Robinson Inc. (Food) [10920]

Lancaster

Allied-Eastern Distributors (Floorcovering Equipment and Supplies) [9656]

Hoffman Inc.; A.H. (Horticultural Supplies) [14888]

Osgood Machinery Inc. (Industrial Machinery) [16365]

Shur-Line Inc. (Paints and Varnishes) [21577]

Larchmont

Felicia Grace and Co. (Clothing) [4948]

SBM Industries Inc. (Electrical and Electronic Equipment and Supplies) [9340]

Shear Associates Inc.; Ted (Food) [12475]

Techcom Systems Inc. (Communications Systems and Equipment) [5776]

Latham

Grassland Equipment (Agricultural Equipment and Supplies) [759]

Pepsi-Cola Pittsfield (Soft Drinks) [25019]

Pepsi-Cola Pittsfield (Food) [12147]

Vellano Brothers Inc. (Specialty Equipment and Products) [25865]

Laurelton

Eon Labs Manufacturing, Inc. (Medical, Dental, and Optical Supplies) [19306]

Leicester

CPAC Inc. (Photographic Equipment and Supplies) [22849]

Lewiston

Coutts Library Services Inc. (Books and Other Printed Materials) [3662]

Lindenhurst
Inter-County Bakers (Food) [11516]
Romanelli and Son Inc. (Petroleum, Fuels, and Related Equipment) [22638]

Little Valley
Lyons Equipment Co. (Construction Materials and Machinery) [7626]
Lyons Sawmill and Logging Equipment Co. (Wood and Wood Products) [27338]

Liverpool
American Granby Inc. (Specialty Equipment and Products) [25550]
Drescher Company Inc.; P. (Food) [10995]
Lichtman and Company Inc.; M. (Alcoholic Beverages) [1820]
Lipe-Rollway Corp. International Div. (Industrial Supplies) [17002]
RRT Empire Returns Corp. (Used, Scrap, and Recycled Materials) [26968]

Locke
Hewitt Brothers Inc. (Agricultural Equipment and Supplies) [817]

Lockport
General Motors Corporation - Harrison Div. (Heating and Cooling Equipment and Supplies) [14460]
Kern & Sons; Jacob (Food) [11604]
Kohl Sales; Walter A. (Motorized Vehicles) [20664]
Niagara County News Company Inc. (Books and Other Printed Materials) [4003]

Locust Valley
Dalton, Cooper Gates Corp. (Agricultural Equipment and Supplies) [490]

Long Beach
Fire Command Company Inc. (Security and Safety Equipment) [24543]

Long Island City
ABCO Refrigeration Supply Corp. (Heating and Cooling Equipment and Supplies) [14289]
Able Steel Equipment Co. Inc. (Office Equipment and Supplies) [20765]
Adirondack Chair Company Inc. (Office Equipment and Supplies) [20773]
Adirondack Chair Company Inc. (Furniture and Fixtures) [13011]
American Global Co. (Hardware) [13558]
Antler Uniform, Division of M. Rubin & Sons, Inc. (Clothing) [4776]
Apon Record Company, Inc. (Sound and Entertainment Equipment and Supplies) [25076]
B and B Motor and Control Inc. (Automotive) [2303]
Beardslee Transmission Equipment Company Inc. (Automotive) [2330]
Case Paper Co. (Paper and Paper Products) [21674]
City and Suburban Delivery Systems East (Books and Other Printed Materials) [3639]
Con Serve Electric Supply (Electrical and Electronic Equipment and Supplies) [8558]
Dalis, Inc.; H.L. (Communications Systems and Equipment) [5585]
Fink Baking Corp. (Food) [11128]
Freirich Food; Julian (Food) [11203]
Genal Strap Inc. (Jewelry) [17429]
Glamour Glove Corp. (Clothing) [4986]
Globe Electric Supply Company, Inc. (Electrical and Electronic Equipment and Supplies) [8789]
Hal-Hen Company Inc. (Medical, Dental, and Optical Equipment) [18821]
Hardware Specialty Company Inc. (Hardware) [13740]
Long Inc.; Duncan (Office Equipment and Supplies) [21112]
Original Designs Inc. (Jewelry) [17540]
Plaza Stationery & Printing Inc. (Office Equipment and Supplies) [21216]

Qualiton Imports Ltd. (Sound and Entertainment Equipment and Supplies) [25398]
Rainbow Trading Company Inc. (Furniture and Fixtures) [13215]
Refron Inc. (Heating and Cooling Equipment and Supplies) [14661]
Rozin Optical Export Corp. (Medical, Dental, and Optical Supplies) [19589]
Saxon Paper Co. (Paper and Paper Products) [21922]
Speedimpex USA, Inc. (Books and Other Printed Materials) [4182]
Standard Motor Products Inc. (Electrical and Electronic Equipment and Supplies) [9404]
Stepic Corp. (Medical, Dental, and Optical Equipment) [19055]
Stroheim & Romann Inc. (Textiles and Notions) [26217]
Thypin Steel Co. (Metals) [20422]
Todisco Jewelry Inc. (Jewelry) [17640]
Tom Cat Bakery (Food) [12726]
Ward's (Specialty Equipment and Products) [25871]
White Coffee Corp. (Food) [12925]

Lowville
Lowville Farmers Cooperative Inc. (Agricultural Equipment and Supplies) [973]

Lynbrook
Baisley Lumber Corp. (Construction Materials and Machinery) [7013]
Solgar Vitamin and Herb Co. (Health and Beauty Aids) [14241]
Swift Fulfillment Services (Books and Other Printed Materials) [4200]

Lyndonville
Thruway Produce Inc. (Food) [12720]

Mamaroneck
Brewer, Inc.; R.G. (Marine) [18469]
Cromwell Leather Group (Luggage and Leather Goods) [18385]
Excel Tanning Corp. (Luggage and Leather Goods) [18393]
Hamon Inc.; Gerard (Books and Other Printed Materials) [3809]
Lensland (Medical, Dental, and Optical Supplies) [19413]
Marval Industries Inc. (Plastics) [22995]
MKM Electronic Components Inc. (Electrical and Electronic Equipment and Supplies) [9091]

Manhasset
ICE Export Sales Corp. (Construction Materials and Machinery) [7503]
Northeast Engineering Inc. (Scientific and Measurement Devices) [24409]

Maspeth
Babco, Inc. (Electrical and Electronic Equipment and Supplies) [8407]
Bel Canto Fancy Foods Ltd. (Food) [10527]
Manhattan Brass and Copper Company Inc. (Metals) [20147]
Marc Sales Corp.; Ken (Electrical and Electronic Equipment and Supplies) [9029]
Metropolitan Mining Co. (Used, Scrap, and Recycled Materials) [26910]
Puro Corporation of America (Soft Drinks) [25023]

Massapequa
South Shore Produce Co. (Food) [12534]

Massapequa Park
Crown Tile & Marble (Floorcovering Equipment and Supplies) [9835]

Massena
Massena Paper Company Inc. (Paper and Paper Products) [21824]

Mechanicville
Troy Top Soil Company Inc. (Construction Materials and Machinery) [8151]

Medford
Blackman Medford Corp. (Plumbing Materials and Fixtures) [23089]
Gershow Recycling (Used, Scrap, and Recycled Materials) [26827]
Neil Parts Distribution Corp. (Automotive) [3021]
Penfield Petroleum Products (Petroleum, Fuels, and Related Equipment) [22561]

Medina
Standfix Air Distribution Products - ACME (Heating and Cooling Equipment and Supplies) [14696]

Melville
Arrow Electronics Inc. (Computers and Software) [5964]
Arrow Electronics Inc. (Electrical and Electronic Equipment and Supplies) [8377]
Arrow-Kierulff Electronics Group (Electrical and Electronic Equipment and Supplies) [8378]
Henry Schein Inc. Dental Div. (Medical, Dental, and Optical Equipment) [18834]
Korg U.S.A. Inc. (Sound and Entertainment Equipment and Supplies) [25275]
MSC Industrial Direct Inc. (Industrial Supplies) [17060]
Nikon Inc. (Photographic Equipment and Supplies) [22883]
Northville Industries Corp. (Petroleum, Fuels, and Related Equipment) [22527]
Nu Horizons Electronics Corp. (Electrical and Electronic Equipment and Supplies) [9148]
Olympus America Inc. (Photographic Equipment and Supplies) [22887]
THC Systems Inc. (Household Items) [15683]

Merrick
Educational Technology Inc. (Computers and Software) [6236]

Mexico
Grandma Brown's Beans Inc. (Food) [11306]

Middle Falls
The Toy Works, Inc. (Toys and Hobby Goods) [26686]

Middle Village
Renault Telephone Supplies (Communications Systems and Equipment) [5740]

Middleport
Niagara Foods Inc. (Food) [12004]

Middletown
Dana Distributors Inc. (Alcoholic Beverages) [1635]
Kissen News Agency Inc. (Books and Other Printed Materials) [3881]
Kornish Distributors Co. (Books and Other Printed Materials) [3885]
RAL Corp. (Plumbing Materials and Fixtures) [23334]

Millwood
American Pecco Corp. (Construction Materials and Machinery) [6970]

Mineola
Allen Avionics, Inc. (Electrical and Electronic Equipment and Supplies) [8298]
Capital Stationery Corp. (Office Equipment and Supplies) [20876]
Van Son Holland Corporation of America (Specialty Equipment and Products) [25863]

Monroe
Library Research Associates Inc. (Books and Other Printed Materials) [3912]
RSB Tile, Inc. (Floorcovering Equipment and Supplies) [10132]

RSB Tile Inc. (Construction Materials and
Machinery) [7963]

Monsey
Rockland Tire and Service
Co. (Automotive) [3170]

Montgomery
Big Saver Inc. (Petroleum, Fuels, and Related
Equipment) [22073]

Monticello
Catskill Electronics (Sound and Entertainment
Equipment and Supplies) [25128]

Mt. Kisco
ABM International Corp. (Metals) [19724]
Mt. Kisco Truck & Auto Parts (Automotive) [2998]
Mt. Kisco Truck and Fleet
Supply (Automotive) [2999]

Mt. Morris
Riverside Liquors & Wine (Alcoholic
Beverages) [1993]

Mt. Vernon
AIN Plastics Inc. (Plastics) [22921]
Globe Motorist Supply Company
Inc. (Automotive) [2686]
Janesway Electronic Corp. (Electrical and Electronic
Equipment and Supplies) [8907]
Main Court Book Fair (Books and Other Printed
Materials) [3929]
National Medical Excess (Medical, Dental, and
Optical Supplies) [19477]
Stone Medical Supply Corp. (Medical, Dental, and
Optical Supplies) [19639]
Universal Metal and Ore Company Inc. (Used,
Scrap, and Recycled Materials) [27032]
Walker and Zanger Inc. (Furniture and
Fixtures) [13271]

Nanuet
Feldheim, Inc.; Philipp (Books and Other Printed
Materials) [3746]

Neponsit
Echter Ornaments Inc. (Food) [11021]

New City
Mailers Equipment Co. (Computers and
Software) [6454]

New Hartford
Cabinet & Cupboard Inc. (Construction Materials
and Machinery) [7121]
Jay-K Independent Lumber Corp. (Construction
Materials and Machinery) [7532]

New HyDe Park
Aceto Corp. (Chemicals) [4313]

New Hyde Park
Goldmark Plastic Co. (Plastics) [22971]
Kopke Jr. Inc.; William H. (Food) [11637]
Metro-Jasim, Inc. (Aeronautical Equipment and
Supplies) [125]
Pollard Company Inc.; Joseph G. (Metals) [20288]
S & O Industries Inc. (Textiles and
Notions) [26196]
Superior Auto Electric (Automotive) [3284]
Yorkshire Food Sales Corp. (Food) [12996]

New Lebanon
Omega Publications, Inc. (Books and Other Printed
Materials) [4020]

New Paltz
Ulster Scientific Inc. (Medical, Dental, and Optical
Equipment) [19090]

New Rochelle
Bally Retail Inc. (Shoes) [24681]

Bel-Aqua Pool Supply Inc. (Recreational and
Sporting Goods) [23542]
Defender Marine Supply NY (Marine) [18490]
Dunn Sales; Skip (Specialty Equipment and
Products) [25638]
Garmirian Company Inc.; H.K. (Clothing) [4979]
Monarch Brass and Copper
Corp. (Hardware) [13835]
Motif Designs, Inc. (Paints and Varnishes) [21507]
Plunkett Webster Inc. (Construction Materials and
Machinery) [7871]
Post Marine (Marine) [18586]
Sadek Import Company Inc.; Charles (Household
Items) [15645]
Skip Dunn Sales (Restaurant and Commercial
Foodservice Equipment and Supplies) [24221]
Wittnauer International (Jewelry) [17660]

New Windsor
Mt. Ellis Paper Company Inc. (Paper and Paper
Products) [21845]
Mt. Ellis Paper Company Inc. (Industrial
Supplies) [17058]

New York
AB Collections (Clothing) [4739]
Abbaco Inc. (Food) [10317]
Abboud Apparel Corp.; Joseph (Clothing) [4742]
ABKCO Music and Records Inc. (Sound and
Entertainment Equipment and Supplies) [25056]
Accesories That Matter (Luggage and Leather
Goods) [18366]
Accessory Resource Gallery Inc. (Clothing) [4745]
Acme-Danneman Company Inc. (Industrial
Supplies) [16669]
Actrade International Corp. (Heating and Cooling
Equipment and Supplies) [14299]
Adele Fashion Knit Corp. (Clothing) [4750]
Adler Glove Co.; Marcus (Clothing) [4752]
Adler Inc.; Kurt S. (Gifts and Novelties) [13292]
Advertising Gifts Inc. (Gifts and Novelties) [13293]
Agora Cosmetics Inc. (Health and Beauty
Aids) [14011]
AI Automotive Corp. (Automotive) [2189]
AI International Corp. (Automotive) [2190]
Alpina International Inc. (Paper and Paper
Products) [21626]
Alpine Corp. (Construction Materials and
Machinery) [6948]
Amato International Inc. (Food) [10389]
Amerada Hess Corp. (Petroleum, Fuels, and
Related Equipment) [22035]
Amerex (USA) Inc. (Clothing) [4766]
American Argo Sales and
Distribution (Clothing) [4767]
American Contex Corp. (Electrical and Electronic
Equipment and Supplies) [8338]
American Liquidators (Computers and
Software) [5930]
American Pacific Enterprises Inc. (Household
Items) [15399]
Americans for the Arts (Books and Other Printed
Materials) [3505]
America's Hobby Center Inc. (Toys and Hobby
Goods) [26391]
Amerind Inc. (Jewelry) [17309]
Amicale Mongolia Inc. (Textiles and
Notions) [25963]
AMREP Corp. (Books and Other Printed
Materials) [3507]
Amsko Fur Corp. (Livestock and Farm
Products) [17698]
Andrea by Sadek (Household Items) [15403]
Andrew Sports Club Inc. (Clothing) [4772]
Antwerp Diamond Distributing
Inc. (Jewelry) [17311]
Apex Technologies (Jewelry) [17312]
Applied Computer Solutions Inc. (New York, New
York) (Computers and Software) [5948]
ARC Mills Corp. (Textiles and Notions) [25967]
AremisSoft Corp. (Computers and Software) [5959]
Argo International Corp. (Marine) [18450]
Arista Records Inc. (Sound and Entertainment
Equipment and Supplies) [25082]
Armani Fashion Corp.; Giorgio (Clothing) [4784]

Art Craft Wallets Inc. (Luggage and Leather
Goods) [18371]
Asia Pacific Trading Co. (Medical, Dental, and
Optical Supplies) [19163]
Associated Fabrics Corp. (Textiles and
Notions) [25969]
Assorted Book Co. (Books and Other Printed
Materials) [3528]
Astra International (Gifts and Novelties) [13309]
Atkins Inc.; Frederick (Specialty Equipment and
Products) [25563]
Atlantic Hardware and Supply
Corp. (Hardware) [13571]
Atlantic Trading Company Ltd. (Petroleum, Fuels,
and Related Equipment) [22048]
Atlantic Trading Company Ltd. (Industrial
Machinery) [15789]
Authentic Sports Inc. (Clothing) [4791]
Avon Products Inc. (Health and Beauty
Aids) [14029]
B-G Lobster and Shrimp Corp. (Food) [10482]
Bag Bazaar Ltd. (Luggage and Leather
Goods) [18374]
Baldwin Paper Co. (Paper and Paper
Products) [21645]
Balfour Maclaine Corp. (Food) [10494]
Ballantyne Cashmere USA Inc. (Clothing) [4799]
Baume and Mercier (Jewelry) [17329]
Beckenstein Men's Fabrics Inc. (Textiles and
Notions) [25978]
Bel Trade USA Corp. (Photographic Equipment and
Supplies) [22830]
The Bella Tile Company, Inc. (Floorcovering
Equipment and Supplies) [9720]
Belwool Corp. (Textiles and Notions) [25980]
Berger L.L.C.; Ben (Clothing) [4819]
Bernstein Company Inc.; William (Food) [10542]
Best Brands Home Products, Inc. (Household
Items) [15420]
Biflex International Inc. (Clothing) [4823]
Big Apple Enterprises (Gifts and Novelties) [13317]
Bilingual Publications Co. (Books and Other Printed
Materials) [3557]
Blank Inc.; Joseph (Jewelry) [17342]
Bloomingdale's Inc. (Clothing) [4828]
BMT Commodity Corp. (Food) [10583]
Bombay Industries Inc. (Clothing) [4833]
Bond Supply Co. (Textiles and Notions) [25985]
Bondy Export Corp. (Electrical and Electronic
Equipment and Supplies) [8454]
Bouregy, Thomas & Co. Inc. (Books and Other
Printed Materials) [3586]
Bright Lights Sportswear Inc. (Clothing) [4844]
Brittania Sportswear (Clothing) [4847]
Brittany Fabrics Inc. (Textiles and Notions) [25989]
Brookwood Companies Inc. (Textiles and
Notions) [25990]
Brown & Bros. Inc.; Arthur (Specialty Equipment
and Products) [25583]
Browne Dreyfus International Ltd. (Industrial
Machinery) [15849]
Brownstone Gallery Ltd. (Textiles and
Notions) [25991]
BT Summit Office Products Inc. (Office Equipment
and Supplies) [20863]
Buckler's Inc. (Gifts and Novelties) [13324]
Burlington Industries Equity Inc. Knitted Fabrics
Div. (Textiles and Notions) [25992]
Business Development
International (Plastics) [22938]
Cables & Chips Inc. (Computers and
Software) [6036]
Cambridge University Press (Books and Other
Printed Materials) [3605]
Capital Paper Company Div. (Paper and Paper
Products) [21666]
Capitol Motion Picture Corp. (Sound and
Entertainment Equipment and Supplies) [25119]
Capri Jewelry Inc. (Jewelry) [17357]
Captre Electrical Supply (Electrical and Electronic
Equipment and Supplies) [8500]
Carat Diamond Corp. (Jewelry) [17358]
Caravan Trading Corporation (Chemicals) [4342]
Caring Concepts Inc. (Clothing) [4861]
Cartier Inc. (Jewelry) [17360]
Castleberry Knits Ltd. (Clothing) [4867]

Celebration Imports Inc. (Clothing) [4871]
Cellino Inc. (Jewelry) [17365]
Centrex Inc. (Medical, Dental, and Optical Supplies) [19226]
Centrotrade Minerals and Metals Inc. (Metals) [19869]
Cervena Co. (Food) [10730]
Cetex Trading Corp. (Textiles and Notions) [26000]
Charter Fabrics Inc. (Textiles and Notions) [26001]
Chase Trade, Inc. (Agricultural Equipment and Supplies) [407]
Chatham Imports Inc. (Alcoholic Beverages) [1591]
Chattanooga Manufacturing Inc. (Clothing) [4877]
Chemicraft Corp. (Office Equipment and Supplies) [20897]
Cherry Sticks Inc. (Clothing) [4879]
Chinatex America Inc. (Textiles and Notions) [26004]
Chock Inc.; Louis (Clothing) [4880]
Chori America Inc. (Textiles and Notions) [26005]
Christie Brothers Fur Corp. (Clothing) [4881]
Cine 60 Inc. (Sound and Entertainment Equipment and Supplies) [25136]
Citra Trading Corp. (Jewelry) [17370]
Clarence House Imports Ltd. (Paints and Varnishes) [21414]
Clarins USA Inc. (Health and Beauty Aids) [14064]
Classic Fragrances Ltd. (Health and Beauty Aids) [14066]
Cohan Berta Showroom (Clothing) [4886]
Cohen and Company Inc.; Herman (Textiles and Notions) [26007]
Cohen Ltd.; Paula (Clothing) [4887]
Cole Productions Inc.; Kenneth (Shoes) [24716]
Colette Malouf Inc. (Health and Beauty Aids) [14067]
Colonial Hardware Corp. (Hardware) [13640]
Colonial Hardware Corp. (Industrial Supplies) [16803]
Cometals Inc. (Chemicals) [4361]
Como Sales Co., Inc. (Books and Other Printed Materials) [3649]
Compar Inc. (Health and Beauty Aids) [14070]
CompuLink Electronic Inc. (Electrical and Electronic Equipment and Supplies) [8555]
Continental Grain Co. (Livestock and Farm Products) [17792]
Continental Information Systems Corp. (Computers and Software) [6154]
Copy Cats Industries Inc. (Clothing) [4894]
Customline of North America, Inc. (Gifts and Novelties) [13342]
Dale Electronics Corp. (Electrical and Electronic Equipment and Supplies) [8606]
Dancker, Sellew and Douglas Inc. (Office Equipment and Supplies) [20945]
David-Martin Co. Inc. (Textiles and Notions) [26013]
Debra Inc. (Health and Beauty Aids) [14081]
DeBragga and Spitler Inc. (Food) [10931]
Dialogue Systems Inc. (Books and Other Printed Materials) [3692]
Dover Handbag Corp. (Luggage and Leather Goods) [18389]
Dreyfus & Assoc. (Automotive) [2562]
Duplex Novelty Corp. (Textiles and Notions) [26025]
Dynamic Classics Ltd. (Recreational and Sporting Goods) [23638]
East Continental Gems Inc. (Jewelry) [17404]
Eastern Europe, Inc. (Agricultural Equipment and Supplies) [536]
Eastrade Inc. (Jewelry) [17405]
Edgars Fabrics Inc. (Textiles and Notions) [26027]
Educational Record Sales, Inc. (Sound and Entertainment Equipment and Supplies) [25173]
Eisner Bros. (Clothing) [4932]
Elco Manufacturing Company Inc. (Luggage and Leather Goods) [18392]
E.L.F. Software Co. (Computers and Software) [6246]
Elvee/Rosenberg Inc. (Jewelry) [17408]

Empire State Marble Manufacturing Corp. (Floorcovering Equipment and Supplies) [9883]
Epic Inc. (Scientific and Measurement Devices) [24356]
Equipment and Parts Export Inc. (Automotive) [2594]
Escada Beaute Ltd. (Health and Beauty Aids) [14096]
Evvan Importers Inc. (Jewelry) [17409]
F and S Alloys and Minerals Corp. (Metals) [19961]
Famous Smoke Shop Inc. (Tobacco Products) [26291]
FE. MA. Inc. (Shoes) [24743]
Felina Lingerie (Clothing) [4949]
Ferrara Food and Confections Inc. (Food) [11119]
Ferrex International, Inc. (Construction Materials and Machinery) [7336]
Fink Brothers Inc. (Clothing) [4954]
Finnish National Distillers Inc. (Alcoholic Beverages) [1691]
First National Trading Company Inc. (Household Items) [15498]
Fischer Inc.; Carl (Books and Other Printed Materials) [3750]
Fisher, Inc.; Marc J. (Textiles and Notions) [26035]
Flash Clinic Inc. (Electrical and Electronic Equipment and Supplies) [8744]
Food Match, Inc. (Food) [11176]
Fotofolio Inc. (Paper and Paper Products) [21729]
Fragments Inc. (Jewelry) [17416]
Francosteel Corp. (Metals) [19983]
Freeda Vitamins Inc. (Health and Beauty Aids) [14105]
French Toast (Clothing) [4968]
Freund, Freund and Company Inc. (Household Items) [15507]
Friendship Press (Books and Other Printed Materials) [3766]
Furniture Consultants Inc. (Office Equipment and Supplies) [21009]
G-III Apparel Group Ltd. (Clothing) [4972]
Gachot & Gachot, Inc. (Food) [11226]
Gamzon Brothers Inc. (Jewelry) [17421]
Garpac Corp. (Clothing) [4980]
Gate Group USA, Inc. (Photographic Equipment and Supplies) [22855]
Gem Platinum Manufacturing Co. (Jewelry) [17426]
Genny USA Inc. (Clothing) [4981]
Georgia Fabrics Inc. (Textiles and Notions) [26043]
Gerber and Company Inc.; J. (Metals) [20003]
Gerlach Beef Inc. (Food) [11257]
GFT USA Corp. (Clothing) [4983]
Gilbert Company Inc.; S.L. (Clothing) [4984]
Ginseng Up Corp. (Soft Drinks) [24958]
Giordano International; Michael (Jewelry) [17431]
Givenchy Corp. (Clothing) [4985]
Glencraft Lingerie Inc. (Clothing) [4989]
Glentex Corp. (Clothing) [4990]
Gold Findings Company Inc. (Jewelry) [17435]
Goodwear Shoe Co. Inc. (Shoes) [24753]
Gould Paper Corp. (Paper and Paper Products) [21745]
GPrime Ltd. (Sound and Entertainment Equipment and Supplies) [25217]
Granary Books, Inc. (Books and Other Printed Materials) [3794]
Greeff Fabrics Inc. (Textiles and Notions) [26045]
Greenburg & Hammer (Textiles and Notions) [26046]
Greenwood Mills Marketing Co. (Textiles and Notions) [26047]
Gruner & Company, Inc. (Clothing) [5004]
GT Interactive Software Corp. (Computers and Software) [6314]
Guttmann Corp.; Victor (Textiles and Notions) [26050]
Gym Source (Recreational and Sporting Goods) [23706]
Hacker Art Books Inc. (Books and Other Printed Materials) [3805]
Haley and Company Inc.; Caleb (Food) [11364]

Hansful Trading Company Inc. (Electrical and Electronic Equipment and Supplies) [8828]
Hardy and Company Inc.; James G. (Household Items) [15519]
Harold Jewelry Inc. (Jewelry) [17445]
Harris Chemical Group Inc. (Chemicals) [4407]
Hartog Foods Inc. (Food) [11387]
Hartz Group Inc. (Veterinary Products) [27146]
Hebard and Associates Inc.; R.W. (Metals) [20031]
Henry Doneger Associates Inc. (Clothing) [5028]
Hilfiger USA Inc.; Tommy (Clothing) [5032]
Honey Fashions Ltd. (Clothing) [5035]
Horsehead Resource Development Company Inc. (Minerals and Ores) [20547]
Hosiery Sales Inc. (Clothing) [5038]
Hosokawa Micron International Inc. (Industrial Machinery) [16115]
Host Apparel Inc. (Clothing) [5039]
ICF Gropu Showroom (Furniture and Fixtures) [13138]
Ilani Shoes Ltd. (Shoes) [24767]
Ilani Shoes Ltd. (Clothing) [5043]
Imperial Commodities Corp. (Food) [11500]
Infant To Teen Headwear (Clothing) [5051]
Inter-Ocean Industries Inc. (Communications Systems and Equipment) [5648]
International Bullion and Metal Brokers Inc. (Jewelry) [17459]
International Cultured Pearl & Jewelry Co. (Jewelry) [17460]
International Waters (Clothing) [5061]
Interroyal Hospital Supply Corp. (Medical, Dental, and Optical Equipment) [18861]
Intertech Services (Textiles and Notions) [26074]
IOA Data Corp. (Computers and Software) [6395]
Israel Aircraft Industries International (Aeronautical Equipment and Supplies) [107]
ITOCHU International Inc. (Food) [11532]
Izod Lacoste (Clothing) [5069]
J.A. Apparel Corp. (Clothing) [5072]
Jack LLC; Judith (Jewelry) [17464]
Jaftex Corp. (Textiles and Notions) [26079]
Jahn and Son Inc.; Henry R. (Industrial Machinery) [16182]
Jawd Associates Inc. (Food) [11550]
Jelina International Ltd. (Clothing) [5081]
Jen-Mar Ltd. (Clothing) [5082]
Jimson Novelties Inc. (Gifts and Novelties) [13379]
Jolie Handbags/Uptown Ltd. (Luggage and Leather Goods) [18402]
Jonas Aircraft and Arms Company Inc. (Aeronautical Equipment and Supplies) [109]
Jonas Aircraft and Arms Company Inc. (Security and Safety Equipment) [24578]
Jordan Fashions Corp. (Clothing) [5094]
Jovino Company, Inc.; John (Guns and Weapons) [13496]
Joyce International Inc. (Office Equipment and Supplies) [21081]
JP Associates (Clothing) [5099]
Jung Foundation; C.G. (Books and Other Printed Materials) [3871]
K and D Exports Imports Corp. (Horticultural Supplies) [14900]
Kabat Textile Corp. (Textiles and Notions) [26083]
Kable News Company Inc. (Books and Other Printed Materials) [3873]
Kaldor Fabricmaker USA Ltd.; John (Textiles and Notions) [26085]
Kanematsu U.S.A. Inc. (Petroleum, Fuels, and Related Equipment) [22395]
Kanematsu U.S.A. Inc. (Textiles and Notions) [26086]
Karmily Gem Corp. (Jewelry) [17484]
Kaufman Inc.; P. (Textiles and Notions) [26091]
Kervar Inc. (Horticultural Supplies) [14904]
Kinokuniya Publications Service of New York (Books and Other Printed Materials) [3879]
Klabin Marketing (Health and Beauty Aids) [14144]
Klabin Marketing (Medical, Dental, and Optical Supplies) [19397]
Klam International (Construction Materials and Machinery) [7561]

Kluyskens Company Inc.; Gerard (Medical, Dental, and Optical Supplies) [19398]
Knobler International Ltd. (Gifts and Novelties) [13381]
Kobrand Corp. (Alcoholic Beverages) [1802]
Kolon America Inc. (Clothing) [5114]
Koplik and Sons Inc.; Perry H. (Used, Scrap, and Recycled Materials) [26868]
Kraft Hardware Inc. (Household Items) [15557]
Kurman & Co.; S.J. (Jewelry) [17495]
L-3 Communications Corp. (Communications Systems and Equipment) [5660]
La Parfumerie Inc. (Health and Beauty Aids) [14147]
Lane Office Furniture Inc. (Office Equipment and Supplies) [21099]
Lauren Footwear Inc.; Ralph (Shoes) [24791]
Lauren Hosiery Div.; Ralph (Clothing) [5123]
Lazartigue Inc.; J.F. (Health and Beauty Aids) [14150]
Lazartigue Inc.; J.F. (Medical, Dental, and Optical Supplies) [19406]
Lectorum Publications Inc. (Books and Other Printed Materials) [3903]
Legal Sportswear (Clothing) [5127]
Leico Industries Inc. (Metals) [20121]
Leifheit Sales Inc. (Household Items) [15566]
Level Export Corp. (Textiles and Notions) [26124]
Levine Books & Judaica; J. (Books and Other Printed Materials) [3906]
Levi's Womenswear (Clothing) [5131]
Levy, Inc.; Harris (Household Items) [15567]
Lipper International Inc. (Household Items) [15569]
Liz and Co. (Clothing) [5136]
Lobel Chemical Corp. (Agricultural Equipment and Supplies) [963]
Loews Corp. (Jewelry) [17503]
Logantex Inc. (Textiles and Notions) [26127]
Lucerne Textiles Inc. (Textiles and Notions) [26128]
Lucoral Company Inc. (Electrical and Electronic Equipment and Supplies) [9010]
Magic Novelty Company Inc. (Jewelry) [17507]
Majesti Watch Company Inc. (Jewelry) [17510]
Manhattan Office Products Inc. (Computers and Software) [6459]
Manifatture Associate Cashmere USA Inc. (Clothing) [5160]
Mannesmann Corp. (Industrial Machinery) [16260]
Manson News Distributors (Books and Other Printed Materials) [3933]
Markon Footwear Inc. (Shoes) [24799]
Marquardt and Company Inc. (Paper and Paper Products) [21823]
Marsh Inc.; Paul (Chemicals) [4452]
Martexport Inc. (Household Items) [15579]
Marubeni America Corp. (Textiles and Notions) [26136]
Mastoloni and Sons Inc.; Frank (Jewelry) [17516]
Mayar Silk Inc. (Textiles and Notions) [26139]
McFadden Inc.; Mary (Clothing) [5180]
Melo Envelope Company Inc. (Paper and Paper Products) [21832]
Melody Gloves Inc. (Clothing) [5184]
Mer Communications Systems Inc. (Communications Systems and Equipment) [5670]
Messina and Zucker Inc. (Household Items) [15585]
Metallurg International Resources (Metals) [20173]
Metro Export and Import Co. (Clothing) [5187]
Meyer Diamond Company Inc.; Henry (Jewelry) [17523]
MH World Trade Corp. (Textiles and Notions) [26143]
Mid City Hardware (Cleaning and Janitorial Supplies) [4669]
Midmarch Arts Press (Books and Other Printed Materials) [3957]
Midtown Electric Supply (Electrical and Electronic Equipment and Supplies) [9079]
Midtown Packing Company Inc. (Food) [11887]
Miltan Export Corp. (Textiles and Notions) [26147]
Miroglio Textiles U.S.A. Inc. (Textiles and Notions) [26150]

Mitsubishi International Corp. (Textiles and Notions) [26151]
Mitsui and Company (U.S.A.) Inc. (Metals) [20199]
Momeni Inc. (Floorcovering Equipment and Supplies) [10046]
Monsieur Touton Selections, LTD (Alcoholic Beverages) [1890]
Morelle Products Ltd., Philippe ADEC and Equipment (Clothing) [5205]
Moshy Brothers Inc. (Books and Other Printed Materials) [3969]
Mottahedeh and Co. (Household Items) [15590]
Movie Star Inc. (Clothing) [5207]
Music Sales Corp. (Books and Other Printed Materials) [3976]
Nabo Industries (Marine) [18574]
Nadel and Sons Toy Corp. (Toys and Hobby Goods) [26588]
Naggar; Albert (Clothing) [5210]
Nannette (Clothing) [5213]
National Patent Development Corp. (Paints and Varnishes) [21517]
Nautica Enterprises Inc. (Clothing) [5217]
Nautica International Inc. (Clothing) [5218]
Nelco Sewing Machine Sales Corp. (Household Appliances) [15246]
Nemo Tile Company, Inc. (Floorcovering Equipment and Supplies) [10075]
Neuwirth Co. (Household Items) [15592]
New City Shoes Inc. (Shoes) [24820]
New Era Factory Outlet (Clothing) [5225]
New World Research Corp. (Automotive) [3030]
New York Enterprises (Clothing) [5228]
Nice Time & Electronics Inc. (Jewelry) [17533]
Nichols and Company Inc.; Austin (Alcoholic Beverages) [1917]
Nikiforov, Inc.; George (Heating and Cooling Equipment and Supplies) [14620]
Nippon Steel Chemical Corporation of America (Chemicals) [4468]
Nissho Iwai American Corp. (Metals) [20226]
NKK Electronics America Inc. (Sound and Entertainment Equipment and Supplies) [25359]
NMC Corp. (Household Appliances) [15251]
Nolan Glove Company Inc. (Clothing) [5235]
Nomura America Corp. (Textiles and Notions) [26157]
Novo Nordisk North America Inc. (Medical, Dental, and Optical Supplies) [19501]
NY Apparel (Clothing) [5244]
NYC Liquidators Inc. (Sound and Entertainment Equipment and Supplies) [25366]
Ogden Services Corp. (Petroleum, Fuels, and Related Equipment) [22535]
Only Hearts Ltd. (Clothing) [5252]
Orchard Yarn and Thread Company Inc./Lion Brand Yarn Co. (Textiles and Notions) [26163]
Oremco Inc. (Minerals and Ores) [20555]
Osakagodo America Inc. (Chemicals) [4476]
Oswald Supply Company Inc.; H.C. (Plumbing Materials and Fixtures) [23304]
Oxford Industries Inc. Renny Div. (Clothing) [5260]
Pande Cameron/Fritz and La Rue (Household Items) [15610]
Pantera International Corp. (Luggage and Leather Goods) [18418]
Paper Corporation of the United States (Paper and Paper Products) [21861]
Paragon Fabrics Company Inc. (Textiles and Notions) [26166]
Pathfinder Press (Books and Other Printed Materials) [4044]
P.D. Music Headquarters Inc. (Books and Other Printed Materials) [4048]
Permalin Products Co. (Paper and Paper Products) [21879]
Phillippe of California Inc. (Luggage and Leather Goods) [18420]
Pinetex (Textiles and Notions) [26177]
Pivot Rules Inc. (Clothing) [5279]
PK Imports Inc. (Gifts and Novelties) [13422]
Platzer Company Inc.; Samuel (Jewelry) [17548]
Polo Ralph Lauren Corp. (Clothing) [5282]
Portland Merchandise Corp. (Clothing) [5284]
Portolano Products Inc. (Clothing) [5285]

Posner Sons Inc.; S. (Paper and Paper Products) [21888]
Posters Please Inc. (Gifts and Novelties) [13424]
Potash Import and Chemical Corp. (Chemicals) [4482]
Presto Paper Company Inc. (Paper and Paper Products) [21889]
Price Stern Sloan Inc. (Books and Other Printed Materials) [4083]
Printed Matter Inc. (Books and Other Printed Materials) [4085]
Private Eyes Sunglasses Shop (Medical, Dental, and Optical Supplies) [19552]
Publishing Center for Cultural Resources (Books and Other Printed Materials) [4096]
Quite Specific Media Group Ltd. (Books and Other Printed Materials) [4102]
R.A.B. Holdings Inc. (Food) [12259]
Rainforest Inc. (Clothing) [5300]
Random House Inc. (Toys and Hobby Goods) [26628]
Rashti and Company Inc.; Harry J. (Clothing) [5304]
Raytex Fabrics Inc. (Textiles and Notions) [26183]
Readmore Inc. (Books and Other Printed Materials) [4108]
Red Apple Supermarkets (Food) [12283]
RED Distribution (Sound and Entertainment Equipment and Supplies) [25413]
Reebok International Ltd. Reebok Metaphors (Shoes) [24841]
Reeves Audio Visual Systems Inc. (Sound and Entertainment Equipment and Supplies) [25415]
Remy Amerique Inc. (Alcoholic Beverages) [1983]
Renco Corp. (Metals) [20315]
Rhapsody Film Inc. (Sound and Entertainment Equipment and Supplies) [25417]
Richard-Ginori 1735, Inc. (Household Items) [15635]
Rivertex Company, Inc. (Textiles and Notions) [26186]
Rizzoli International Inc. (Books and Other Printed Materials) [4121]
Roatan International Corporation (Office Equipment and Supplies) [21244]
Robern Skiwear Inc. (Clothing) [5313]
Rocket World Trade Enterprise (Compressors) [5850]
Rockville Fabrics Corp. (Textiles and Notions) [26189]
Rose Brand-Theatrical Fabrics Fabrications and Supplies (Textiles and Notions) [26191]
Royal Chain Inc. (Jewelry) [17575]
Royal Paper Corp. (Paper and Paper Products) [21914]
Royal Stones Corp. (Jewelry) [17576]
Russica Book & Art Shop Inc. (Books and Other Printed Materials) [4128]
Sago Imports Inc. (Jewelry) [17584]
San Esters Corp. (Chemicals) [4500]
Sandaga (Jewelry) [17588]
Sanofi Beaute Inc. (Health and Beauty Aids) [14229]
Sapporo U.S.A. Inc. (Alcoholic Beverages) [2008]
Schachter and Company Inc.; Leo (Jewelry) [17591]
Scheidt Inc.; Bruno (Food) [12425]
Schieffelin and Somerset Co. (Alcoholic Beverages) [2012]
Schiffer Wholesale Hardware; Leslie (Security and Safety Equipment) [24625]
Schleifer and Son Inc.; H. (Clothing) [5334]
Schreiber Inc.; E. (Jewelry) [17592]
Schwartz Shoes Inc.; Jack (Clothing) [5336]
Scientific & Medical Publications of France Inc. (Books and Other Printed Materials) [4147]
Sea Containers America Inc. (Marine) [18603]
Segue Ltd. (Clothing) [5341]
Seibel & Stern Corp. (Clothing) [5342]
Seville Watch Corp. (Jewelry) [17597]
Shamash and Sons; S. (Textiles and Notions) [26201]
Sheldon and Company Inc.; H.D. (Restaurant and Commercial Foodservice Equipment and Supplies) [24217]
Shil La Art Gems, Inc. (Jewelry) [17598]

Showa Denko America Inc. (Metals) [20364]
Showroom Seven (Clothing) [5349]
Showroom Seven (Clothing) [5350]
Sidney Furs Inc.; Robert (Clothing) [5351]
Siemens Audio Inc. (Sound and Entertainment Equipment and Supplies) [25443]
Sile Distributors Inc. (Guns and Weapons) [13513]
Silo International Inc. (Construction Materials and Machinery) [8020]
Silver Blue Associated Ltd. (Luggage and Leather Goods) [18427]
Silver Blue Associated Ltd. (Luggage and Leather Goods) [18428]
Singer Sewing Inc. (Sound and Entertainment Equipment and Supplies) [25444]
Singer Textiles Inc. (Textiles and Notions) [26205]
SMH (US) Inc. (Jewelry) [17609]
Sockyard Company Inc. (Clothing) [5365]
SOGEM-Afrimet Inc. (Metals) [20372]
Somersault Ltd. (Jewelry) [17611]
South China Import Inc. (Shoes) [24865]
Southern Watch Inc. (Jewelry) [17613]
Specialty House Inc. (Clothing) [5378]
Spiewalk & Sons, Inc.; I. (Clothing) [5380]
Stark Carpet Corp. (Floorcovering Equipment and Supplies) [10178]
Stark Carpet Corp. (Household Items) [15668]
State Mutual Book & Periodical Service Ltd. (Books and Other Printed Materials) [4189]
Steel Partners L.P. (Office Equipment and Supplies) [21297]
Steiner Inc.; S.S. (Livestock and Farm Products) [18253]
Sterling Publishing Co., Inc. (Books and Other Printed Materials) [4190]
Stern Watch Agency Inc.; Henri (Jewelry) [17621]
Steven Inc.; David G. (Jewelry) [17622]
Stevens Ltd.; Michael (Luggage and Leather Goods) [18434]
Stinnes Intercoal Inc. (Minerals and Ores) [20569]
Stock Ltd.; Robert (Clothing) [5396]
Stone Island; C.P. (Clothing) [5398]
Strygler Company Inc.; H.S. (Jewelry) [17623]
Studio Film & Tape Inc. (Photographic Equipment and Supplies) [22908]
Suave Noble Creations Inc. (Clothing) [5401]
Sugar Foods Corp. (Food) [12599]
Sumitomo Corporation of America (Metals) [20411]
Summit Import Corp. (Food) [12602]
Sunkyong America Inc. (Household Appliances) [15323]
Superba Inc. (Clothing) [5408]
Superlearning (Books and Other Printed Materials) [4199]
Symphony Fabrics Corp. (Textiles and Notions) [26219]
T-J Knit Enterprises Inc. (Clothing) [5415]
Tacoa Inc. (Jewelry) [17630]
Tadiran Electronic Industries Inc. (Household Appliances) [15329]
Talon Associates International, Inc. (Medical, Dental, and Optical Equipment) [19069]
TDA Industries Inc. (Construction Materials and Machinery) [8102]
Telmar Group Inc. (Computers and Software) [6811]
TENBA Quality Cases Ltd. (Luggage and Leather Goods) [18436]
Terralink International (Communications Systems and Equipment) [5790]
Terrile Export & Import Corp. (Electrical and Electronic Equipment and Supplies) [9480]
TES (USA) Corp. (Industrial Machinery) [16558]
Texstyles Group Inc. (Textiles and Notions) [26225]
Textile Import Corp. (Textiles and Notions) [26226]
Thackeray Corp. (Hardware) [13951]
Thieme New York (Books and Other Printed Materials) [4215]
Threadtex Inc. (Textiles and Notions) [26228]
Time Distribution Services Inc. (Books and Other Printed Materials) [4218]
Time Warner and Sony Direct Entertainment (Books and Other Printed Materials) [4220]
Titan Industrial Corp. (Metals) [20425]

TLC Beatrice International Holdings Inc. (Food) [12724]
Tomen America Inc. (Metals) [20430]
Toray Industries (America) Inc. (Chemicals) [4531]
Toray Industries Inc. (Textiles and Notions) [26232]
Toyota Tsusho America Inc. (Metals) [20434]
Traco Industrial Corp. (Heating and Cooling Equipment and Supplies) [14733]
Tradearbed Inc. (Metals) [20435]
Transammonia Inc. (Agricultural Equipment and Supplies) [1349]
Transmedia Restaurant Company Inc. (Restaurant and Commercial Foodservice Equipment and Supplies) [24248]
Transocean Coal Company L.P. (Minerals and Ores) [20574]
Transworld Metal USA Ltd. (Metals) [20440]
Triarc Companies Inc. (Food) [12755]
Troica Enterprise Inc. (Jewelry) [17643]
Trundle and Company Inc. (Soft Drinks) [25045]
Trundle and Company Inc. (Food) [12765]
Tryon Mercantile Inc. (Jewelry) [17644]
Twin Panda Inc./Katha Diddel Home Collection (Household Items) [15689]
Ulster Linen Company, Inc. (Household Items) [15691]
Ultima (Heating and Cooling Equipment and Supplies) [14742]
United Envelope Co. (Paper and Paper Products) [21975]
Unnex Industrial Corp. (Clothing) [5455]
Vass U.S.A.; Joan (Clothing) [5459]
Victor Machinery Exchange Inc. (Industrial Supplies) [17252]
VideoTape Distributors Inc. (Sound and Entertainment Equipment and Supplies) [25507]
Vuitton North America Inc.; Louis (Luggage and Leather Goods) [18439]
Wagman and Co.; N. (Clothing) [5467]
Walker and Co. (Books and Other Printed Materials) [4267]
Warner Music Group (Sound and Entertainment Equipment and Supplies) [25513]
Warren of Stafford Corp. Fabric Merchandising Div. (Textiles and Notions) [26243]
Wasser Morton Co. (Textiles and Notions) [26244]
Websource (Office Equipment and Supplies) [21351]
Webster Watch Company Associates LLC (Jewelry) [17652]
Weiss Inc.; Harry (Luggage and Leather Goods) [18443]
Werner & Son; Max (Food) [12903]
Westvaco Worldwide (Paper and Paper Products) [21990]
White and Company Inc.; L.N. (Food) [12928]
Wildman and Sons Ltd.; Frederick (Alcoholic Beverages) [2119]
Winston Inc.; Harry (Jewelry) [17659]
Wisconsin Toy Company Inc. (Toys and Hobby Goods) [26714]
Wolf and Sons Inc.; Charles (Jewelry) [17661]
Woolworth Corp. (Household Appliances) [15379]
Worldwide Dreams LLC (Luggage and Leather Goods) [18447]
Xport Port Authority Trading Co. (Chemicals) [4559]
YAO Industries (Food) [12991]
Yellow River Systems (Medical, Dental, and Optical Equipment) [19113]
York Novelty Import Inc. (Jewelry) [17666]
Yves Saint Laurent Parfums Corp. (Health and Beauty Aids) [14285]
Zanella Ltd. (Clothing) [5494]

Newburgh
Hilton, Gibson, and Miller Inc. (Food) [11437]
Regal Bag Corp. (Luggage and Leather Goods) [18422]

Niagara Falls
Calato USA Div. (Sound and Entertainment Equipment and Supplies) [25116]
Durkin Hayes Publishing (Books and Other Printed Materials) [3704]

Everpower Co. (Electrical and Electronic Equipment and Supplies) [8720]
ParMed Pharmaceuticals Inc. (Medical, Dental, and Optical Supplies) [19525]
Ryan Co.; Johnnie (Soft Drinks) [25029]
Shipman Printing Industries Inc. (Paper and Paper Products) [21938]
Yorkville Sound Inc. (Sound and Entertainment Equipment and Supplies) [25538]

North Collins
Concord Nurseries Inc. (Horticultural Supplies) [14845]

North Creek
Creative Stage Lighting Company Inc. (Electrical and Electronic Equipment and Supplies) [8585]

North Merrick
Sterco New York Inc. (Luggage and Leather Goods) [18433]

North Tonawanda
Irr Supply Centers Inc. (Plumbing Materials and Fixtures) [23222]
Riverside Chemical Company Inc. (Chemicals) [4496]
Savage Inc. (Motorized Vehicles) [20718]
Thruway Fasteners Inc. (Hardware) [13955]

North White Plains
Brunschwig and Fils Inc. (Household Items) [15430]
North Castle Produce Inc. (Food) [12025]

North Woodmere
I.J.K. Sales Corp. (Luggage and Leather Goods) [18399]

Northport
Good Health Natural Foods Inc. (Food) [11290]

Oakdale
Graywell Equipment Corp. (Automotive) [2698]

Oceanside
Burlington A/V Recording Media, Inc. (Sound and Entertainment Equipment and Supplies) [25112]
Xetal Inc. (Medical, Dental, and Optical Supplies) [19714]

Ogdensburg
Pepsi-Cola Ogdensburg Inc. (Soft Drinks) [25018]

Olean
Olean Wholesale Grocery Cooperative Inc. (Food) [12065]

Oneonta
Northern Eagle Beverages Inc. (Alcoholic Beverages) [1922]

Orangeburg
Aristo Import Company Inc. (Scientific and Measurement Devices) [24316]
Leslie Company Inc.; Richard A. (Clothing) [5129]
Wenger N.A. (Recreational and Sporting Goods) [24042]

Orchard Park
Angle Acres Greenhouse (Horticultural Supplies) [14806]
Azerty Inc. (Computers and Software) [5996]
Capriotto and Sons Inc. (Automotive) [2420]
Curbell Inc. (Plastics) [22950]
Tiles International (Floorcovering Equipment and Supplies) [10249]
Zenter Enterprises Ltd. (Veterinary Products) [27273]

Ossining
Bauer Optical Co. (Medical, Dental, and Optical Supplies) [19176]

Chaney, Jr. Books; Bev (Books and Other Printed Materials) [3625]

Oswego
Northern Steel Corp. (Metals) [20238]

Owego
Ward and Van Scoy Inc. (Livestock and Farm Products) [18325]

Oyster Bay
Autoxport Inc. (Automotive) [2300]
Harbor Fuel Company Inc. (Petroleum, Fuels, and Related Equipment) [22335]

Ozone Park
Food Gems Ltd. (Food) [11172]
Ottavino Corp.; A. (Construction Materials and Machinery) [7816]

Patchogue
Rose Inc.; Clare (Alcoholic Beverages) [1999]

Peekskill
Frank and Company Inc.; S.M. (Tobacco Products) [26294]
Hudson Glass Company Inc. (Construction Materials and Machinery) [7495]
Jacobson Capital Services Inc. (Textiles and Notions) [26078]
Poritzky's Wholesale Meats and Food Services (Food) [12195]
Portman Hobby Distributors (Toys and Hobby Goods) [26619]
Shokai Far East Ltd. (Electrical and Electronic Equipment and Supplies) [9365]
Winters; Adam (Food) [12963]

Pelham
Tri-State Medical Supply Inc. (Medical, Dental, and Optical Equipment) [19086]

Pelham Manor
Micro Bio-Medics Inc. (Medical, Dental, and Optical Supplies) [19454]

Piermont
Chipwich Inc. (Food) [10752]

Pittsford
Coyote Vision USA (Health and Beauty Aids) [14075]
PNB Trading, Inc. (Industrial Machinery) [16405]
Sloan and Company Inc. (Plumbing Materials and Fixtures) [23379]

Plainview
Astrex Inc. (Electrical and Electronic Equipment and Supplies) [8387]
AVest Inc. (Electrical and Electronic Equipment and Supplies) [8403]
Capstone Paper Co. (Paper and Paper Products) [21667]
Drybranch Inc. (Recreational and Sporting Goods) [23631]
Ex-Eltronics Inc. (Electrical and Electronic Equipment and Supplies) [8721]
MSC Industrial Supply Co. (Hardware) [13840]
North Atlantic Communications Inc. (Communications Systems and Equipment) [5694]
North Atlantic Communications Inc. (Electrical and Electronic Equipment and Supplies) [9131]
Sid Tool Company Inc. (Industrial Machinery) [16488]
Specialty Hearse and Ambulance Sales Corp. (Motorized Vehicles) [20727]
Specialty Hearse and Ambulance Sales Corp. (Automotive) [3247]
Video Hi-Teck Inc. (Sound and Entertainment Equipment and Supplies) [25505]

Plattsburgh
Brushtech Inc. (Industrial Supplies) [16769]
Lavin Candy Company Inc. (Food) [11685]

Plattsburgh Distributing (Alcoholic Beverages) [1961]

Pleasant Valley
Dutchess Quarry and Supply Company Inc. (Construction Materials and Machinery) [7292]

Pleasantville
Gulbenkian Swim Inc. (Recreational and Sporting Goods) [23701]
The Wine Enthusiast Companies (Household Items) [15710]

Port Chester
ICS Intercounty Supply (Plumbing Materials and Fixtures) [23217]
Ledu Corp. (Electrical and Electronic Equipment and Supplies) [8978]
Paramount Brands, Inc. (Alcoholic Beverages) [1941]
Terramar Sports Worldwide Ltd. (Clothing) [5425]
X-S Beauty Supplies (Health and Beauty Aids) [14284]

Port Ewen
Kingston Oil Supply Corp. (Petroleum, Fuels, and Related Equipment) [22407]

Port Washington
American Rotary Tools Company Inc. (Industrial Machinery) [15770]
Andrews Paper and Chemical Co. (Chemicals) [4323]
Bruckner Machine (Hardware) [13608]
Bruckner Supply Co. Inc. (Industrial Supplies) [16768]
Empress International Ltd. (Food) [11047]
Global Computer Corp. (Computers and Software) [6303]
Industrial Fasteners Corp. (Hardware) [13764]
Koch International (Sound and Entertainment Equipment and Supplies) [25274]
Miracle Exclusives, Inc. (Household Appliances) [15234]
Reco International Corp. (Books and Other Printed Materials) [4109]
Recognition Systems Inc. (Specialty Equipment and Products) [25799]
Rodi Automotive Inc. (Automotive) [3172]
Rodriguez Inc.; R.A. (Industrial Supplies) [17144]
Scholium International, Inc. (Books and Other Printed Materials) [4142]
TDK Electronics Corp. (Sound and Entertainment Equipment and Supplies) [25474]
TDK Electronics Corp. (Electrical and Electronic Equipment and Supplies) [9462]
TDK U.S.A. Corp. (Communications Systems and Equipment) [5775]
Wilson Corp.; W.S. (Aeronautical Equipment and Supplies) [175]

Potsdam
Shelly Electric Inc. (Electrical and Electronic Equipment and Supplies) [9361]

Poughkeepsie
Allied Electronics (Electrical and Electronic Equipment and Supplies) [8320]
Apollo Book (Books and Other Printed Materials) [3520]
Dutchess Beer Distributors (Alcoholic Beverages) [1660]
Fairview True Value Hardware (Hardware) [13693]
Fargo Manufacturing Company Inc. (Electrical and Electronic Equipment and Supplies) [8731]
Labieniec & Associates; Paul (Recreational and Sporting Goods) [23779]
Penn Machinery Company Inc.; H.O. (Construction Materials and Machinery) [7847]

Purchase
Amrochem Inc. (Chemicals) [4322]
Candie's Inc. (Shoes) [24705]

Central National-Gottesman Inc. (Paper and Paper Products) [21675]
Maco Vinyl Products Corp. (Textiles and Notions) [26130]
Paraco Gas Corp. (Petroleum, Fuels, and Related Equipment) [22550]
Rad Oil Company Inc. (Petroleum, Fuels, and Related Equipment) [22607]
Wines and Spirits International (Alcoholic Beverages) [2129]

Putnam Valley
Mahalick Corp. (Specialty Equipment and Products) [25722]

Queens Village
All Standard Tile Corp. (Floorcovering Equipment and Supplies) [9652]
New York Motorcycle, Ltd. (Motorized Vehicles) [20692]

Queensbury
Britton Explosive Supply Inc. (Construction Materials and Machinery) [7080]
Double A Provisions Inc. (Food) [10983]

Rego Park
World Traders (USA) Inc. (Electrical and Electronic Equipment and Supplies) [9607]

Rensselaer
Simione and Associates, Inc.; Bill (Recreational and Sporting Goods) [23939]

Richmond Hill
Commercial Plastics and Supply Inc. (Plastics) [22947]
Ideal Foreign Books, Inc. (Books and Other Printed Materials) [3837]
Ideal Foreign Books Inc. (Books and Other Printed Materials) [3838]

Ridgewood
Ehmer Inc.; Karl (Food) [11034]
Frankel Associates Inc. (Textiles and Notions) [26040]
Great Eastern Pet Supply (Veterinary Products) [27140]
Quarex Industries Inc. (Food) [12254]
Western Beef Inc. (Food) [12909]

Rochester
ABR Wholesale, Inc. (Heating and Cooling Equipment and Supplies) [14291]
Abrasive-Tool Corp. (Hardware) [13523]
Abrasive-Tool Corp. (Industrial Machinery) [15727]
Alling and Cory Co. (Office Equipment and Supplies) [20786]
Batty & Hoyt Inc. (Office Equipment and Supplies) [20834]
Chamberlin Rubber Company Inc. (Industrial Supplies) [16790]
Computer Clearing House Inc. (Computers and Software) [6103]
Continental Baking Co. (Food) [10825]
Cook Iron Store Co. (Industrial Supplies) [16810]
Cooper Industries Inc. (Computers and Software) [6158]
Davis Wholesale Co. Inc.; Al (Health and Beauty Aids) [14080]
Di Paolo Baking Company, Inc. (Food) [10955]
Eber Brothers Wine and Liquor Corp. (Alcoholic Beverages) [1669]
Economy Paper Company Inc. (Paper and Paper Products) [21719]
Economy Paper Company Inc. (Industrial Supplies) [16845]
Eltrex Industries Inc. (Office Equipment and Supplies) [20991]
Empire Beef Company Inc. (Food) [11044]
Empire Comicsl (Books and Other Printed Materials) [3728]
Forster Co.; John M. (Automotive) [2641]
Frontier Network Systems Inc. (Sound and Entertainment Equipment and Supplies) [25200]

Genesee Reserve Supply Inc. (Construction Materials and Machinery) [7386]
Genuine Auto Parts Co. (Automotive) [2677]
Global Beverage Co. (Soft Drinks) [24959]
Hahn Automotive Warehouse Inc. (Automotive) [2717]
Houk Co. Inc.; Clarence H. (Food) [11464]
House of Guitars Corp. (Sound and Entertainment Equipment and Supplies) [25239]
H.S. Industrial Equipment (Industrial Supplies) [16933]
ICS-Executone Telecom Inc. (Communications Systems and Equipment) [5642]
Jilnance Corp. (Automotive) [2822]
Keystone Builders Supply Co. (Construction Materials and Machinery) [7551]
Keystone Builders Supply Co. (Construction Materials and Machinery) [7552]
Klein Steel Service Inc. (Metals) [20104]
Kovalsky-Carr Electric Supply Company Inc. (Electrical and Electronic Equipment and Supplies) [8958]
Kozel and Son Inc.; J. (Metals) [20108]
Larsen International, Inc. (Chemicals) [4438]
Light Impressions (Sound and Entertainment Equipment and Supplies) [25284]
Macke Business Products (Furniture and Fixtures) [13167]
Merkel Donohue Inc. (Office Equipment and Supplies) [21139]
Nor-Del Productions Ltd. (Books and Other Printed Materials) [4006]
Office Express (Office Equipment and Supplies) [21180]
Olbro Wholesalers (Food) [12059]
Pet World (Veterinary Products) [27212]
PicturePhone Direct (Communications Systems and Equipment) [5711]
Power Equipment Co. (Automotive) [3109]
Pro-Fac Cooperative Inc. (Food) [12222]
Rero Distribution Co., Inc. (Electrical and Electronic Equipment and Supplies) [9280]
Roberts Co.; D.B. (Electrical and Electronic Equipment and Supplies) [9303]
Rochester Drug Cooperative Inc. (Medical, Dental, and Optical Supplies) [19584]
Rochester Instrument Systems Inc. (Electrical and Electronic Equipment and Supplies) [9306]
Rochester Liquor Corp. (Alcoholic Beverages) [1997]
Rochester Midland Corp. (Cleaning and Janitorial Supplies) [4698]
RSR Wholesale Guns Inc. (Guns and Weapons) [13507]
Rutland News Co. (Books and Other Printed Materials) [4130]
Sentry Group (Security and Safety Equipment) [24634]
Shaheen Paint and Decorating Company, Inc. (Paints and Varnishes) [21566]
Spectronic Instruments Inc. (Scientific and Measurement Devices) [24436]
SRS International (Electrical and Electronic Equipment and Supplies) [9398]
Staples Business Advantage (Office Equipment and Supplies) [21289]
Tapetex Inc. (Textiles and Notions) [26221]
Telecommunications Bank Inc. (Communications Systems and Equipment) [5783]
Tile Wholesalers of Rochester (Floorcovering Equipment and Supplies) [10246]
Total Information (Books and Other Printed Materials) [4222]
Ward's Natural Science Establishment Inc. (Books and Other Printed Materials) [4268]
Web Seal Inc. (Adhesives) [19]
Wright Wisner Distributing Corp. (Alcoholic Beverages) [2140]
Writers & Books (Books and Other Printed Materials) [4299]

Rockville Centre

Futter Lumber Corp. (Construction Materials and Machinery) [7373]
International Wealth Success Inc. (Books and Other Printed Materials) [3852]

Nurnberg Thermometer Co. (Scientific and Measurement Devices) [24411]
United Thread Mills Corp. (Textiles and Notions) [26238]

Rome

Rome Cable Corp. (Electrical and Electronic Equipment and Supplies) [9314]

Ronkonkoma

Apollo Space Systems Inc. (Photographic Equipment and Supplies) [22826]
Compucon Distributors Inc. (Computers and Software) [6095]
Florig Equipment (Industrial Machinery) [16012]
ITTCO Sales Co., Inc. (Automotive) [2805]
Kash 'N Gold Ltd. (Communications Systems and Equipment) [5657]
M-Tron Components Inc. (Electrical and Electronic Equipment and Supplies) [9016]
Over and Back Inc. (Household Items) [15605]
Quality King Distributors Inc. (Health and Beauty Aids) [14202]
Sigma Corporation of America (Photographic Equipment and Supplies) [22904]

Roslyn

Himark Enterprises Inc. (Furniture and Fixtures) [13135]
Triangle Inc. (Automotive) [3340]

Roslyn Heights

Advantage Food Marketing Corp. (Food) [10331]
Hirschmann Corp. (Industrial Machinery) [16102]
USA Test, Inc. (Sound and Entertainment Equipment and Supplies) [25494]
Video Aided Instruction Inc. (Household Appliances) [15357]

Rouses Point

Belcam Inc. (Health and Beauty Aids) [14038]

Rye

Benson Eyecare Corp. (Electrical and Electronic Equipment and Supplies) [8431]
Burack Inc.; I. (Plumbing Materials and Fixtures) [23101]
Industrial Solvents Corp. (Chemicals) [4429]
Kane International Corp. (Food) [11579]
Peek Inc.; Walter D. (Paper and Paper Products) [21871]
White Cross Corporation, Inc. (Medical, Dental, and Optical Supplies) [19703]

Salem

Salem Farm Supply Inc. (Agricultural Equipment and Supplies) [1231]

Saugerties

Fehr Bros. Industries Inc. (Hardware) [13705]

Savannah

Clear Eye (Food) [10767]

Scarsdale

Dilmaghani and Company Inc. (Household Items) [15474]
Eastern Atlantic Company Inc. (Health and Beauty Aids) [14089]
Interchange Corp. (Agricultural Equipment and Supplies) [860]
Sexauer Inc.; J.A. (Plumbing Materials and Fixtures) [23370]
Weingartner Company Inc.; Henry (Metals) [20484]
William's Umbrella Co. (Gifts and Novelties) [13473]

Schenectady

American Electric Supply (Electrical and Electronic Equipment and Supplies) [8343]
Best Tile Distributors of Albany, Inc. (Floorcovering Equipment and Supplies) [9723]
Greno Industries Inc. (Industrial Supplies) [16909]
Mid-State Industries Ltd. (Construction Materials and Machinery) [7706]

Murken Products Inc.; Frank (Rubber) [24288]
Red-Kap Sales Inc. (Petroleum, Fuels, and Related Equipment) [22613]

Scotia

AFGD (Construction Materials and Machinery) [6922]
Sofco-Mead Inc. (Food) [12525]

Sea Cliff

Archer Company Inc.; A.W. (Paper and Paper Products) [21635]

Selden

EKD Computer Sales and Supplies Corp. (Computers and Software) [6239]

Selkirk

Security Supply Corp. (Plumbing Materials and Fixtures) [23367]

Setauket

Electronic Product Tool (Industrial Machinery) [15981]

Shirley

Shredex Inc. (Office Equipment and Supplies) [21269]

Shoreham

Stanis Trading Corp. (Medical, Dental, and Optical Supplies) [19636]

Silver Creek

Petri Baking Products (Food) [12157]

Smithtown

Coca-Cola Bottling Company of New York Inc. (Soft Drinks) [24939]
Hendrix Technologies Inc. (Office Equipment and Supplies) [21029]
Lynne Company Inc.; J.M. (Household Items) [15572]
Morris Rothenberg and Son Inc. (Recreational and Sporting Goods) [23836]
Sperry Instruments Inc.; A.W. (Scientific and Measurement Devices) [24437]

Solvay

Matlow Company Inc. (Used, Scrap, and Recycled Materials) [26899]

South Fallsburg

Mountain Service Distributors (Tobacco Products) [26330]

Southampton

Southampton Brick & Tile, Inc. (Floorcovering Equipment and Supplies) [10159]

Spencer

Hadley Corp.; Raymond (Food) [11358]

Spring Valley

Abbey Ice Co. (Soft Drinks) [24903]
Total Recall Corp. (Security and Safety Equipment) [24643]

Springfield Gardens

Brueton Industries Inc. (Furniture and Fixtures) [13047]

Staten Island

AAT Communications Systems Corp. (Sound and Entertainment Equipment and Supplies) [25055]
AAT Communications Systems Corp. (Household Appliances) [14989]
Anjo Distributors (Veterinary Products) [27068]
Colombian Development Corp. (Electrical and Electronic Equipment and Supplies) [8544]
Comics Unlimited (Toys and Hobby Goods) [26449]
Latina Trading Corp. (Food) [11681]
Superior Confections (Food) [12638]

Total Electric Distributors Inc. (Electrical and Electronic Equipment and Supplies) [9496]

Stony Point
Superior Insulated Wire Corp. (Electrical and Electronic Equipment and Supplies) [9444]

Suffern
Darisil, Inc. (Food) [10909]

Syosset
Ademco Distribution Inc. (Security and Safety Equipment) [24482]
AFA Protective Systems Inc. (Security and Safety Equipment) [24495]
Brechner and Co. Inc.; Dan (Toys and Hobby Goods) [26425]
Kojemi Corp. (Metals) [20106]
Meenan Oil Company L.P. (Petroleum, Fuels, and Related Equipment) [22473]
Morse Typewriter Company Inc. (Office Equipment and Supplies) [21151]
National Learning Corp. (Books and Other Printed Materials) [3986]
Samson Technologies Inc. (Communications Systems and Equipment) [5749]
United Manufacturers Supplies Inc. (Hardware) [13974]

Syracuse
Agway Energy Products (Petroleum, Fuels, and Related Equipment) [22028]
Agway Inc. (Livestock and Farm Products) [17688]
Allied-Eastern Distributors (Floorcovering Equipment and Supplies) [9657]
The Anderson Group (Metals) [19781]
Argos Enterprises (Health and Beauty Aids) [14024]
B & L Equipment (Construction Materials and Machinery) [7007]
Best Tile Distributors of Syracuse, Inc. (Floorcovering Equipment and Supplies) [9724]
Bratt-Foster Inc. (Food) [10609]
Burns Brothers Contractors (Plumbing Materials and Fixtures) [23102]
Burns Supply/Great Lakes Inc. (Plumbing Materials and Fixtures) [23103]
Commercial Art Supply (Specialty Equipment and Products) [25606]
Curtiss Bakery; Penny (Food) [10885]
Dairylea Cooperative Inc. (Food) [10902]
De-Tec Inc. (Medical, Dental, and Optical Equipment) [18768]
Dobkin Company, Inc.; W.W. (Floorcovering Equipment and Supplies) [9869]
Eberly Inc.; John A. (Hardware) [13674]
Enrico Food Products Co. Inc. (Food) [11048]
Gaylord Brothers (Sound and Entertainment Equipment and Supplies) [25207]
Gear Motions Inc. (Industrial Supplies) [16891]
Giancola Exports, Inc.; D.J. (Cleaning and Janitorial Supplies) [4628]
Guilfoil and Associates Inc.; T.V. (Storage Equipment and Containers) [25919]
Gypsum Wholesalers Inc. (Construction Materials and Machinery) [7426]
Inland Supply Inc. (Plumbing Materials and Fixtures) [23220]
Jones-McIntosh Tobacco Company Inc. (Tobacco Products) [26314]
Joy Co.; Edward (Electrical and Electronic Equipment and Supplies) [8920]
K.J. Electric Inc. (Electrical and Electronic Equipment and Supplies) [8950]
Michel Company Inc.; R.E. (Heating and Cooling Equipment and Supplies) [14559]
Minfelt Wholesale Company Inc. (Construction Materials and Machinery) [7719]
MKS Industries Inc. (Construction Materials and Machinery) [7731]
Penn Traffic Co. (Food) [12139]
Penny Curtiss Bakery (Food) [12143]
Reserve Supply of Central New York Inc. (Construction Materials and Machinery) [7920]

Roma Tile Co., Inc. (Floorcovering Equipment and Supplies) [10128]
Syracuse Banana Co. (Food) [12665]
Syracuse China Corp. (Household Items) [15677]
Syracuse Supply Co. (Construction Materials and Machinery) [8095]
Syracuse University Press (Books and Other Printed Materials) [4202]
Syrex, Inc. (Agricultural Equipment and Supplies) [1311]
Tech Arts (Computers and Software) [6793]
Vitto Sheet Metal Inc.; Nicholas (Metals) [20475]
Wilcox Paper Co. (Paper and Paper Products) [21993]

Tappan
Fallani and Cohn (Household Items) [15494]

Tarrytown
Hitachi America Ltd. (Sound and Entertainment Equipment and Supplies) [25233]
M and H Sales and Marketing Inc. (Health and Beauty Aids) [14156]
Motion Pictures Enterprises (Sound and Entertainment Equipment and Supplies) [25339]
SGA Sales and Marketing Inc. (Food) [12467]
Stinnes Corp. (Petroleum, Fuels, and Related Equipment) [22706]
Westcon Inc. (Computers and Software) [6863]

Thornwood
Manson Tool and Supply Co. (Industrial Supplies) [17014]
Zeiss Inc.; Carl (Scientific and Measurement Devices) [24461]

Tonawanda
Latina Niagara Importing Co. (Food) [11680]
NOCO Energy Corp. (Petroleum, Fuels, and Related Equipment) [22522]
Ready Made Sign Co. (Specialty Equipment and Products) [25798]
Ronco Communications and Electronics (Electrical and Electronic Equipment and Supplies) [9315]
Ronco Communications and Electronics Inc. (Communications Systems and Equipment) [5746]
Ronco Power Systems Inc. (Electrical and Electronic Equipment and Supplies) [9316]
Ronco Specialized Systems Inc. (Electrical and Electronic Equipment and Supplies) [9317]
U and S Services Inc. (Electrical and Electronic Equipment and Supplies) [9519]

Troy
Action Chevrolet-Subaru-Geo (Motorized Vehicles) [20576]
Comfort Mart Dist. Inc. (Heating and Cooling Equipment and Supplies) [14394]
Helmbold Inc.; Fritz (Food) [11409]
Interstate Commodities Inc. (Livestock and Farm Products) [18012]
Kibar Bearings (Industrial Supplies) [16991]
Levonian Brothers Inc. (Food) [11705]

Trumansburg
Halsey Seed Co. (Agricultural Equipment and Supplies) [783]

Tuxedo
Spiegel and Sons Oil Corp.; M. (Petroleum, Fuels, and Related Equipment) [22692]

Uniondale
Primary Industries (USA) Inc. (Metals) [20294]

Utica
Avico Distributing Inc. (Food) [10475]
Flihan Co.; Joseph (Restaurant and Commercial Foodservice Equipment and Supplies) [24123]
Scheidelman Inc. (Food) [12424]
Smith Packing Company Inc. (Food) [12511]
Smyth-Despard Company Inc. (Industrial Machinery) [16500]

Utica Plumbing Supply Co. (Plumbing Materials and Fixtures) [23426]

Valhalla
Lotepro Corp. (Petroleum, Fuels, and Related Equipment) [22438]

Valley Cottage
Complete Medical Supplies Inc. (Medical, Dental, and Optical Supplies) [19243]
Micros-to-Mainframes Inc. (Computers and Software) [6506]

Valley Stream
Cooke Co.; David (Jewelry) [17378]
Novelty Poster Co. (Gifts and Novelties) [13414]
Novelty Poster Co. (Gifts and Novelties) [13415]

Vestal
Jayark Corp. (Sound and Entertainment Equipment and Supplies) [25260]
Sun Control Window Tinting and Shades (Construction Materials and Machinery) [8087]
Sun Control Window Tinting and Shades (Wood and Wood Products) [27383]
Tri-Bro Supply Co. (Plumbing Materials and Fixtures) [23416]

Victor
Hadlock Paint Co. (Paints and Varnishes) [21454]
Morgan Recreational Supply (Marine) [18573]

Wantagh
Children's Media Center, Inc. (Books and Other Printed Materials) [3629]
Jetmore Distributing (Household Appliances) [15182]

Warwick
Triumph Pet Industries, Inc. (Veterinary Products) [27254]

Washingtonville
Brotherhood America's Oldest Winery Ltd. (Alcoholic Beverages) [1551]

Waterford
Kivort Steel Inc. (Metals) [20103]

Waterloo
Eagle Family Foods (Soft Drinks) [24954]

Watertown
Jeff Bottling Company Inc. (Soft Drinks) [24978]
Renzi Brothers Inc. (Food) [12301]

Watervliet
Passonno Paints (Paints and Varnishes) [21533]
Tech Fire and Safety Co. (Security and Safety Equipment) [24642]
Tech Fire and Safety Co. (Restaurant and Commercial Foodservice Equipment and Supplies) [24243]
Troy Belting Supply Co. (Industrial Supplies) [17236]

Watkins Glen
Professional's Library (Books and Other Printed Materials) [4089]

Webster
Culver Dairy Inc. (Food) [10882]
Lill and Son Inc.; Frank (Industrial Machinery) [16235]

Wellsville
Harris Supply Company Inc. (Industrial Supplies) [16925]
Harris Supply Company Inc. (Plumbing Materials and Fixtures) [23204]

West Amherst

Associated Healthcare Systems Inc. (Medical, Dental, and Optical Equipment) [18693]
Buffalo Structural Steel (Metals) [19841]
Purchasing Support Services (Office Equipment and Supplies) [21226]

West Babylon

Home Crafts, Inc. (Heating and Cooling Equipment and Supplies) [14487]
U.S. Aircraft Industries International Inc. (Aeronautical Equipment and Supplies) [165]

West Hempstead

Bakertowne Company, Inc. (Household Items) [15414]
Mitchell Mogal Inc. (Gifts and Novelties) [13406]

West Henrietta

Lake Beverage Corp. (Alcoholic Beverages) [1811]

West Hurley

Numrich Gunparts Corp. (Guns and Weapons) [13504]

West Islip

Industrial Municipal Equipment Inc. (Industrial Machinery) [16151]

West Seneca

ACI Controls (Scientific and Measurement Devices) [24305]
Beauty Pools Inc. (Recreational and Sporting Goods) [23541]

West Valley

Ford Brothers Wholesale Meats Inc. (Food) [11185]

Westbury

Accurate Chemical and Scientific Corp. (Chemicals) [4312]
Braun and Sons; J.F. (Food) [10610]
Brinkmann Instruments, Inc. (Scientific and Measurement Devices) [24328]
Brinkmann Instruments Inc. (Medical, Dental, and Optical Supplies) [19200]
Dynamic Medical Equipment Ltd. (Medical, Dental, and Optical Supplies) [19298]
Flexstik Adheso Graphics (Adhesives) [6]
Grayco Products (Industrial Supplies) [16904]
Kenclaire Electrical Agencies Inc. (Electrical and Electronic Equipment and Supplies) [8934]
Lifetime Hoan Corp. (Household Items) [15568]
Prior Inc.; John (Automotive) [3118]
Symphony Designs Inc. (Clothing) [5414]

White Plains

Aerotech World Trade Corp. (Aeronautical Equipment and Supplies) [30]
Asoma Corp. (Metals) [19786]
AST USA Inc. (Metals) [19788]
Avonlea Books (Books and Other Printed Materials) [3536]
Benfield Electric Supply Co.; H.H. (Electrical and Electronic Equipment and Supplies) [8430]
Berint Trading, Ltd. (Hardware) [13593]
Dorian International Inc. (Restaurant and Commercial Foodservice Equipment and Supplies) [24105]
Drake America Div. (Automotive) [2559]
Gardners Good Foods Inc. (Food) [11237]
Heineken USA Inc. (Alcoholic Beverages) [1750]
Ilva USA Inc. (Metals) [20053]
Klarman Sales Inc. (Hardware) [13787]
Krasdale Foods Inc. (Food) [11647]
Krasdale Foods Inc. (Food) [11648]
Longman Publishing Group (Books and Other Printed Materials) [3921]
Phiebig Inc., Services to Libraries; Albert J. (Books and Other Printed Materials) [4060]
Pro/Am Music Resources, Inc. (Books and Other Printed Materials) [4086]

Quality Resources (Books and Other Printed Materials) [4100]
Texaco Internatinal Trader, Inc. (Petroleum, Fuels, and Related Equipment) [22729]

Whitesboro

Corts Truck Equipment, Inc. (Automotive) [2486]

Whitestone

Kinray, Inc. (Health and Beauty Aids) [14142]
Kinray Inc. (Medical, Dental, and Optical Supplies) [19396]

Williamsville

Ingram Micro Inc. (Computers and Software) [6374]
Rand & Jones Enterprises Co., Inc. (Industrial Machinery) [16437]

Woodbury

Polar Electro Inc. (Medical, Dental, and Optical Equipment) [18990]
Polar Electro Inc. (Medical, Dental, and Optical Supplies) [19547]
Telrad Telecommunications Inc. (Communications Systems and Equipment) [5789]

Woodmere

Intimate Fashions Inc. (Clothing) [5062]
Magna Automotive Industries (Automotive) [2906]

Woodside

Area Distributors, Inc. (Automotive) [2249]
Bulova Corp. (Jewelry) [17354]
Firecom Inc. (Security and Safety Equipment) [24550]
Heitz Service Corp. (Photographic Equipment and Supplies) [22863]
Kaye Pearl Co. (Jewelry) [17486]

Woodstock

Allyn Air Seat Co. (Automotive) [2221]
Beekman Publishers, Inc. (Books and Other Printed Materials) [3546]
Schwartz & Co.; Arthur (Books and Other Printed Materials) [4145]

Yonkers

Amco-McLean Corp. (Sound and Entertainment Equipment and Supplies) [25068]
Amco-McLean Corp. (Household Appliances) [15007]
Brehm Inc.; Otto (Food) [10611]
Crown Products Co. (Paper and Paper Products) [21698]
D.N. Motors Ltd. (Automotive) [2553]
Loria & Sons Westchester Corp.; V. (Specialty Equipment and Products) [25720]
Minami International Corp. (Gifts and Novelties) [13404]
Samuels Tile (Floorcovering Equipment and Supplies) [10136]
Saw Mill Auto Wreckers (Automotive) [3190]
Vandenberg Inc.; Jac (Food) [12827]
The Willing Group (Health and Beauty Aids) [14282]

Yorktown Heights

Best Plumbing Supply Inc. (Plumbing Materials and Fixtures) [23084]

Yorkville

Meyda Tiffany (Household Items) [15587]

North Carolina

Aberdeen

Nolarec Industries, Inc. (Household Items) [15595]

Advance

Genetic Leaders International (Livestock and Farm Products) [17939]

Ahoskie

Basnight and Company Inc.; W.H. (Construction Materials and Machinery) [7029]
Eastern Fuels Inc. (Petroleum, Fuels, and Related Equipment) [22220]

Albemarle

Alpha Communications Inc. (Communications Systems and Equipment) [5509]
Bowers Implement Co. Inc. (Agricultural Equipment and Supplies) [332]
Donovan Marine (Marine) [18494]

Angier

Angus Fire Armour Corp. (Specialty Equipment and Products) [25553]
Moto America Inc. (Motorized Vehicles) [20687]

Apex

Goodwin Refrigeration Co. Inc. (Heating and Cooling Equipment and Supplies) [14473]
Norris Co.; Garland C. (Paper and Paper Products) [21852]
Norris Co.; Garland C. (Industrial Supplies) [17076]

Archdale

Hafele America Co. (Hardware) [13731]

Arden

Associated Springs (Hardware) [13569]
Clark's Wholesale Tire Co. (Automotive) [2454]
Empire Distributors of NC Inc. (Alcoholic Beverages) [1677]
Power Machine Service (Electrical and Electronic Equipment and Supplies) [9223]

Asheboro

Branco Enterprises Inc. (Clothing) [4841]
Thomas Brothers Ham Co. (Food) [12713]

Asheville

AAA Parts of Biltmore Inc. (Automotive) [2160]
Asheville Steel & Salvage Co. (Metals) [19785]
Biltmore Oil Co. Inc. (Petroleum, Fuels, and Related Equipment) [22074]
Black Forest Tile Distributors (Construction Materials and Machinery) [7061]
Blue Ridge Electric Motor Repair (Electrical and Electronic Equipment and Supplies) [8446]
Central Air Conditioning Distributor (Heating and Cooling Equipment and Supplies) [14373]
Common Ground Distributors Inc. (Books and Other Printed Materials) [3648]
Consolidated Electrical Distributor (Electrical and Electronic Equipment and Supplies) [8566]
Dave Steel Co. Inc. (Metals) [19917]
Deverger Systems Inc. (Computers and Software) [6205]
Electric Supply Co. (Asheville, North Carolina) (Electrical and Electronic Equipment and Supplies) [8667]
Farm Equipment Company of Asheville Inc. (Agricultural Equipment and Supplies) [561]
Ference Cheese Inc. (Food) [11118]
Gennett Lumber Co. (Construction Materials and Machinery) [7388]
Grainger Inc. (Electrical and Electronic Equipment and Supplies) [8801]
Hayes & Lunsford Motor Repair (Electrical and Electronic Equipment and Supplies) [8835]
I Play (Clothing) [5041]
InterACT Systems Inc. (Computers and Software) [6384]
Johnson Electric NA Inc. (Electrical and Electronic Equipment and Supplies) [8915]
Morris Associates; William (Medical, Dental, and Optical Equipment) [18948]
Mountain Food Products (Food) [11945]
Pickering Publications (Books and Other Printed Materials) [4063]
Piedmont Paper Company Inc. (Paper and Paper Products) [21883]
Professional Optical (Medical, Dental, and Optical Supplies) [19557]

Seafood Express (Food) [12446]
The Slosman Corp. (Textiles and Notions) [26207]
Smoky Mountain Distributors (Alcoholic
    Beverages) [2030]
Union Butterfield Corp. (Hardware) [13971]
Western Carolina Optical Inc. (Medical, Dental, and
    Optical Supplies) [19699]
W.N.C. Tile Distributors (Floorcovering Equipment
    and Supplies) [10304]

Atlantic

Smith & Son Fish; Luther (Food) [12515]

Beaufort

Atlantic Veneer Corp. (Wood and Wood
    Products) [27283]
Barbour Marine Supply (Marine) [18451]

Belmont

Dixie Industrial Supply Co. (Industrial
    Supplies) [16834]
Dixie Industrial Supply Div. (Industrial
    Supplies) [16835]
Transit Services Inc. (Scientific and Measurement
    Devices) [24448]

Boone

Fisher Enterprises Inc. (Recreational and Sporting
    Goods) [23668]
Hollar and Greene Produce (Food) [11449]
Hollar and Greene Produce Co.,
    Inc. (Food) [11450]
Wilcox Drug Company Inc. (Health and Beauty
    Aids) [14281]

Browns Summit

A & A Plants (Horticultural Supplies) [14791]

Burlington

Baby Needs Inc. (Clothing) [4797]
Best Pet Distributing (Veterinary Products) [27081]
Camera Corner Inc. (Photographic Equipment and
    Supplies) [22837]
Carolina Biological Supply Co. (Books and Other
    Printed Materials) [3612]
Commercial Metals Co. Commercial Levin
    Div. (Used, Scrap, and Recycled
    Materials) [26781]
Elder Hosiery Mills Inc. (Clothing) [4933]
Elem Corp. (Clothing) [4934]
Falcon Industries Inc. (Textiles and
    Notions) [26032]
Graham Sporting Goods
    Burlington (Clothing) [4999]
Ivars Sportswear Inc. (Clothing) [5068]
Jefferies Socks (Clothing) [5080]
Meade Hosiery; Elizabeth (Clothing) [5182]
Michel Company Inc.; R.E. (Heating and Cooling
    Equipment and Supplies) [14549]
Monarch Hosiery Mills Inc. (Clothing) [5200]
Protech Communications (Communications Systems
    and Equipment) [5724]

Burnsville

Compassion Book Service (Books and Other
    Printed Materials) [3650]

Calabash

KoolaBrew Inc. (Gifts and Novelties) [13382]

Camden

Watermark Association of Artisans Inc. (Household
    Items) [15703]

Candler

W.N.C. Pallet & Forest Products Company
    Inc. (Construction Materials and
    Machinery) [8237]
W.N.C. Pallet and Forest Products Company
    Inc. (Wood and Wood Products) [27395]

Carrboro

Basnight & Sons; S.H. (Hardware) [13586]

Cary

Austin Quality Foods, Inc. (Food) [10473]
DS Design (Computers and Software) [6222]
Radio Communications Co. (Sound and
    Entertainment Equipment and Supplies) [25403]
Walker Distributors Inc. (Food) [12868]

Chapel Hill

Alamex Crafts Inc. (Toys and Hobby
    Goods) [26384]
Coffee Mill Roastery (Food) [10787]
Kenan Oil Co. (Food) [11600]
Meridian Veterinary Products (Veterinary
    Products) [27187]
Sequence (USA) Co. Ltd. (Paints and
    Varnishes) [21561]
A Southern Season (Food) [12542]

Charlotte

A-1 Janitorial Supply & Equipment (Household
    Appliances) [14984]
ADEMCO/ADI (Security and Safety
    Equipment) [24469]
Aerial Photography Services Inc. (Books and Other
    Printed Materials) [3475]
Allegiance Brokerage Co. (Food) [10368]
Allison-Erwin Co. (Computers and Software) [5907]
American Barmag Corp. (Industrial
    Machinery) [15764]
AMS International Corp. (Metals) [19775]
Anderson Medical Inc. (Medical, Dental, and Optical
    Equipment) [18683]
Atlas Marketing Co. Inc. (Food) [10466]
Bailes Inc.; Buck (Toys and Hobby
    Goods) [26405]
Baker and Taylor (Books and Other Printed
    Materials) [3540]
Baker and Taylor Inc. (Books and Other Printed
    Materials) [3541]
Baucoms Nursery Farm (Horticultural
    Supplies) [14823]
Bearing Distributors Inc. (Industrial
    Supplies) [16731]
Belco Athletic Laundry Equipment Co. (Household
    Appliances) [15047]
Bindley Western Drug Co. (Health and Beauty
    Aids) [14043]
Black & Decker US Inc. (Cleaning and Janitorial
    Supplies) [4582]
Brackett Supply Inc. (Heating and Cooling
    Equipment and Supplies) [14356]
Brady Distributing Co. (Specialty Equipment and
    Products) [25579]
Caffey, Inc.; I.H. (Alcoholic Beverages) [1565]
Carolina Fluid Components (Industrial
    Supplies) [16781]
Carolina Handling Inc. (Industrial
    Machinery) [15878]
Carolina Pad and Paper Co. (Paper and Paper
    Products) [21669]
Carolina Plastics Supply Inc. (Plumbing Materials
    and Fixtures) [23106]
Carolina Rim and Wheel Co. (Marine) [18475]
Carolina Tractor/CAT (Construction Materials and
    Machinery) [7144]
Carolina's Auto Supply House,
    Inc. (Automotive) [2426]
Carrier North Carolina (Heating and Cooling
    Equipment and Supplies) [14368]
Central Air Conditioning Distributors Inc. (Heating
    and Cooling Equipment and Supplies) [14374]
Charlotte Aerospace Co. Inc. (Aeronautical
    Equipment and Supplies) [69]
Charlotte Copy Data Inc. (Office Equipment and
    Supplies) [20896]
Charlotte Hardwood Center (Construction Materials
    and Machinery) [7168]
Charlotte Tile & Stone (Floorcovering Equipment
    and Supplies) [9802]
CIC Systems Inc. (Computers and
    Software) [6068]
Clarks Distributing Co. (Heating and Cooling
    Equipment and Supplies) [14384]
Coca-Cola Bottling Co. Consolidated (Soft
    Drinks) [24934]

Columbia Beauty Supply Co. (Health and Beauty
    Aids) [14069]
Comer Inc. (Industrial Machinery) [15900]
Concrete Supply Co. (Construction Materials and
    Machinery) [7204]
Consolidated Communications Corp. (Electrical and
    Electronic Equipment and Supplies) [8563]
Consolidated Textiles, Inc. (Textiles and
    Notions) [26008]
Corporate Data Products (Office Equipment and
    Supplies) [20923]
Crompton and Knowles Colors
    Inc. (Chemicals) [4367]
Cunningham Wholesale Company Inc. (Alcoholic
    Beverages) [1629]
D & L Appliance Parts Company, Inc. (Household
    Appliances) [15104]
Diamond Supply, Inc. (Specialty Equipment and
    Products) [25629]
Dickson Co.; C.C. (Heating and Cooling Equipment
    and Supplies) [14422]
Dixie News Co. (Books and Other Printed
    Materials) [3698]
Dolls By Jerri (Toys and Hobby Goods) [26473]
Duo-Fast Carolinas Inc. (Compressors) [5839]
Emco Inc. (Industrial Machinery) [15983]
F and R Oil Company Inc. (Petroleum, Fuels, and
    Related Equipment) [22248]
Famous Mart Inc. (Clothing) [4945]
Fastener Supply Co. (Hardware) [13698]
Freeman's Car Stereo Inc. (Sound and
    Entertainment Equipment and Supplies) [25199]
Frieling USA Inc. (Household Items) [15508]
Furniture Distributors Inc. (Furniture and
    Fixtures) [13117]
Gardner and Benoit Inc. (Restaurant and
    Commercial Foodservice Equipment and
    Supplies) [24126]
Georgetown Unimetal Sales (Metals) [20002]
Gita Sporting Goods, Ltd. (Shoes) [24752]
Global Marketing Concepts (Construction Materials
    and Machinery) [7399]
Hanford's Inc. (Gifts and Novelties) [13365]
Highland Mills Inc. (Clothing) [5031]
Homelite, Inc. (Construction Materials and
    Machinery) [7482]
Hunter Farms (Food) [11479]
Hydradyene Hydraulics Inc. (Industrial
    Machinery) [16124]
Hydradyne Hydraulics (Industrial
    Machinery) [16125]
IHC Services Inc. (Construction Materials and
    Machinery) [7505]
Joint and Clutch Service Inc. (Automotive) [2831]
Jordan Graphics (Paper and Paper
    Products) [21785]
LCI Corp. (Industrial Machinery) [16229]
L.C.I. Process Division (Industrial
    Machinery) [16230]
Legends of Racing Inc. (Toys and Hobby
    Goods) [26566]
Livingston & Haven, Inc. (Industrial
    Machinery) [16239]
Logical Choice (Computers and Software) [6442]
Lotus Group (Industrial Machinery) [16246]
Mark Oil Company Inc. (Petroleum, Fuels, and
    Related Equipment) [22452]
Martek Ltd. (Gifts and Novelties) [13397]
Maye Hosiery Sales (Shoes) [24804]
McGraw Group Inc. (Industrial Supplies) [17022]
McGuire Sun and Fitness Inc. (Recreational and
    Sporting Goods) [23816]
Michel Company Inc.; R.E. (Heating and Cooling
    Equipment and Supplies) [14550]
Michelle Textile Corp. (Textiles and
    Notions) [26144]
Mid Atlantic Accessories (Clothing) [5192]
Mitchell Distributing Co. (Construction Materials and
    Machinery) [7729]
MMRF Inc. (Household Appliances) [15236]
Muller and Company Inc.; L.P. (Textiles and
    Notions) [26154]
Murata of America Inc. (Industrial
    Machinery) [16330]
Murray Biscuit Co., LLC (Division of Keebler
    Co.) (Food) [11958]

National Welders Supply Company Inc. (Industrial Supplies) [17067]
Nisbet Oil Co. (Petroleum, Fuels, and Related Equipment) [22519]
Office Environments Inc. (Office Equipment and Supplies) [21175]
Parnell-Martin Co. (Plumbing Materials and Fixtures) [23309]
Pattons Inc. (Compressors) [5847]
Piedmont Distribution Centers (Household Items) [15620]
Piedmont Propane Co. (Petroleum, Fuels, and Related Equipment) [22584]
Piedmont Technology Group Inc. (Computers and Software) [6619]
Plastic Piping Systems Inc. (Plastics) [23010]
Power Drives, Inc. (Automotive) [3108]
Primeco Inc. Southeast Div. (Hardware) [13876]
Pritchard Paint and Glass Co. (Paints and Varnishes) [21547]
Pumps, Parts and Service Inc. (Industrial Machinery) [16433]
Ragan Inc.; Brad (Automotive) [3131]
Renfrow Tile Distributing Company, Inc. (Floorcovering Equipment and Supplies) [10120]
Republic Alloys Inc. (Used, Scrap, and Recycled Materials) [26956]
Salem Sales Associates (Industrial Machinery) [16468]
Saurer Textile Systems Charlotte (Industrial Machinery) [16471]
Scott Drug Co. (Medical, Dental, and Optical Supplies) [19600]
Security Forces Inc. (Electrical and Electronic Equipment and Supplies) [9350]
Smith Group Inc.; E.J. (Agricultural Equipment and Supplies) [1271]
Smith Turf & Irrigation Co. (Agricultural Equipment and Supplies) [1272]
Source Technologies Inc. (Office Equipment and Supplies) [21275]
South Central Pool Supply, Inc. (Recreational and Sporting Goods) [23964]
Southern Electric Service Company, Inc. (Electrical and Electronic Equipment and Supplies) [9385]
Southern Flooring Distributors (Floorcovering Equipment and Supplies) [10160]
Southern Metals Company Inc. (Used, Scrap, and Recycled Materials) [27003]
Southern Pump and Tank Co. (Industrial Machinery) [16513]
Spil Co.; Samuel (Jewelry) [17617]
Starboard Inc. (Food) [12569]
Stewart Fastener Corp. (Hardware) [13937]
Summitville Charlotte (Floorcovering Equipment and Supplies) [10189]
Sun America Corp. (Recreational and Sporting Goods) [23992]
Tekmatex Inc. (Industrial Machinery) [16555]
Tens of Charlotte Inc. (Medical, Dental, and Optical Equipment) [19073]
Trim-Pak Inc. (Textiles and Notions) [26233]
Tropical Nut and Fruit (Food) [12761]
Tryon Distributors (Alcoholic Beverages) [2086]
Universal Fastener Co. (Hardware) [13977]
Upchurch Co.; Frank J. (Industrial Supplies) [17246]
WeCare Distributors Inc. (Health and Beauty Aids) [14277]
Winchester Surgical Supply Co. (Medical, Dental, and Optical Supplies) [19712]
Witherspoon Supply; Yandle (Heating and Cooling Equipment and Supplies) [14770]
Wrenn Brungart (Industrial Machinery) [16651]
Yesco Ltd. (Toys and Hobby Goods) [26718]

China Grove

Kenlin Pet Supply (Veterinary Products) [27170]

Clemmons

GSI Corp. (Office Equipment and Supplies) [21021]
King Sash and Door Inc. (Construction Materials and Machinery) [7558]

Water Works (Specialty Equipment and Products) [25875]
Young-Phillips Sales Co. (Specialty Equipment and Products) [25884]

Cliffside

Petroleum World Inc. (Petroleum, Fuels, and Related Equipment) [22573]
Spartan Petroleum Company Inc. (Petroleum, Fuels, and Related Equipment) [22688]

Clinton

A & W Medical & Oxygen Supply (Medical, Dental, and Optical Equipment) [18653]
Big Blue Store (Hardware) [13597]

Coats

Pope Distributing Co. (Clothing) [5283]

Colfax

Thomas Sales Company Inc. (Toys and Hobby Goods) [26680]

Concord

Allred Optical Laboratory (Medical, Dental, and Optical Supplies) [19139]
S and D Coffee Inc. (Food) [12379]
U.S. Tire Recycling (Used, Scrap, and Recycled Materials) [27031]

Conover

Hanes Converting Co. (Textiles and Notions) [26055]
Hanes Fabrics Co. (Textiles and Notions) [26056]

Cornelius

Baynes Co. Inc.; John (Shoes) [24687]

Dallas

Newsouth Athletic Co. (Clothing) [5230]

Denton

Denton Hosiery Mill (Clothing) [4912]
Surratt Hosiery Mill Inc. (Clothing) [5409]

Dublin

Peanut Processors Inc. (Food) [12127]

Dudley

Smith Brothers of Dudley Inc. (Petroleum, Fuels, and Related Equipment) [22677]

Dunn

ABJ Enterprises Inc. (Livestock and Farm Products) [17671]
Alphin Brothers Inc. (Food) [10381]
Benel Manufacturing Inc. (Clothing) [4818]
Machine and Welding Supply Co. (Industrial Machinery) [16255]
Tomahawk Farms Inc. (Food) [12727]

Durham

Bernards Formal Wear Inc. (Clothing) [4821]
Carolina Door Controls (Construction Materials and Machinery) [7143]
Carolina Door Controls (Wood and Wood Products) [27295]
Dealers Supply Co. (Floorcovering Equipment and Supplies) [9850]
Duke University Press (Books and Other Printed Materials) [3703]
E-Z Serve Petroleum Marketing Co. (Petroleum, Fuels, and Related Equipment) [22217]
Fowler Inc.; M.M. (Petroleum, Fuels, and Related Equipment) [22291]
HG International Corporation (Recreational and Sporting Goods) [23725]
Mid-Atlantic STIHL, Inc. (Industrial Machinery) [16296]
North Carolina Mutual Wholesale Drug Co. (Medical, Dental, and Optical Supplies) [19499]
Southchem Inc. (Chemicals) [4516]
Tecan US Inc. (Medical, Dental, and Optical Equipment) [19071]

Edenton

Hobbs Implement Company Inc. (Agricultural Equipment and Supplies) [827]
Jimbo's Jumbos Inc. (Livestock and Farm Products) [18024]

Efland

Efland Distributing Co. (Veterinary Products) [27126]

Elizabeth City

City Beverage Co. (Alcoholic Beverages) [1596]

Elizabethtown

Sampson-Bladen Oil Co. (Petroleum, Fuels, and Related Equipment) [22649]
Squires Timber Co. (Wood and Wood Products) [27379]

Elkin

Cash and Carry Stores Inc. (Food) [10710]
G and B Oil Company Inc. (Petroleum, Fuels, and Related Equipment) [22298]

Ellenboro

Carpet Barn Inc. (Floorcovering Equipment and Supplies) [9761]

Enfield

Eastern Petroleum Corp. (Petroleum, Fuels, and Related Equipment) [22221]

Fair Bluff

Meares & Son Inc.; Ellis (Household Appliances) [15226]
Scotts Inc. (Plumbing Materials and Fixtures) [23363]

Fairmont

Gaston Sealey Company Inc. (Agricultural Equipment and Supplies) [728]

Fairview

Plus Woman (Clothing) [5280]

Farmville

North State Garment Company Inc. (Clothing) [5240]

Fayetteville

American Tile Distributors (Floorcovering Equipment and Supplies) [9673]
Arts & Craft Distributors Inc. (Toys and Hobby Goods) [26400]
Brantley Electrical Supply Inc. (Electrical and Electronic Equipment and Supplies) [8465]
Carolina News Co. (Books and Other Printed Materials) [3613]
Cashwell Appliance Parts Inc. (Household Appliances) [15079]
Comtech (Construction Materials and Machinery) [7201]
Electric Supply Company of Fayetteville Inc. (Electrical and Electronic Equipment and Supplies) [8668]
Fayetteville Automotive Warehouse (Automotive) [2608]
Fuller Oil Company Inc. (Petroleum, Fuels, and Related Equipment) [22297]
Highland Distributing Co. (Alcoholic Beverages) [1756]
Hubbard Pipe and Supply Inc. (Plumbing Materials and Fixtures) [23214]
International Domestic Development Corp. (Medical, Dental, and Optical Equipment) [18857]
Intraoptics Inc. (Medical, Dental, and Optical Supplies) [19379]
Kelly Springfield Tire (Automotive) [2845]
McDonald Lumber Company Inc. (Construction Materials and Machinery) [7679]
McMillan-Shuller Oil Company Inc. (Petroleum, Fuels, and Related Equipment) [22471]
Quality Sound Enterprise Inc. (Sound and Entertainment Equipment and Supplies) [25399]

Restonic Carolina Inc. (Furniture and
Fixtures) [13219]
Systel Business Equipment Inc. (Office Equipment
and Supplies) [21310]
Tile Inc. of Fayetteville (Floorcovering Equipment
and Supplies) [10239]

Fletcher

Dia-Compe Inc. (Recreational and Sporting
Goods) [23622]
Plus Distributors Inc. (Food) [12182]
Van Wingerden International Inc. (Horticultural
Supplies) [14969]

Fuquay Varina

Revels Tractor Company Inc. (Agricultural
Equipment and Supplies) [1183]
Revels Tractor Company Inc. (Agricultural
Equipment and Supplies) [1184]

Garner

Wyatt-Quarles Seed Company Inc. (Agricultural
Equipment and Supplies) [1464]

Gastonia

American Textile Export Co. (Textiles and
Notions) [25960]
Carolina Pools & Patios (Recreational and Sporting
Goods) [23584]
Jenkins Metal Corp. Hunting Classics Limited
Div. (Household Items) [15545]
PSNC Propane Corp. (Petroleum, Fuels, and
Related Equipment) [22599]
Rudisill Enterprises Inc. (Alcoholic
Beverages) [2002]
Shiflet and Dickson Inc. (Sound and Entertainment
Equipment and Supplies) [25441]
SKF Textile Products Inc. (Textiles and
Notions) [26206]
TCI Machinery Inc. (Industrial Machinery) [16552]
United Oil of the Carolinas, Inc. (Petroleum, Fuels,
and Related Equipment) [22761]

Gibsonville

Engineered Plastics Inc. (Plastics) [22958]

Goldsboro

Automotive Wholesalers Co. (Automotive) [2299]
Cox Subscriptions, Inc.; W.T. (Books and Other
Printed Materials) [3664]
Dumas Oil Co. (Petroleum, Fuels, and Related
Equipment) [22213]
Haines & Co.; J.J. (Floorcovering Equipment and
Supplies) [9933]
Jeffrey's Seed Company Inc. (Agricultural
Equipment and Supplies) [883]
Shepherd Electric Supply Company Inc. (Electrical
and Electronic Equipment and Supplies) [9363]
Smith Hardware Company Inc. (Hardware) [13924]
Southern Optical Co. (Medical, Dental, and Optical
Supplies) [19625]
Sunburst Foods Inc. (Food) [12609]
Wooten Oil Co. (Petroleum, Fuels, and Related
Equipment) [22815]

Graham

Variety Hosiery Mills (Clothing) [5457]

Granite Quarry

Carolina Maid Products Inc. (Clothing) [4864]

Greensboro

Abacon Electronics Corp. (Electrical and Electronic
Equipment and Supplies) [8259]
ADA Computer Supplies Inc. (Computers and
Software) [5873]
Atlantic Corp. (Paper and Paper Products) [21639]
Atlantic Corp. (Industrial Supplies) [16716]
Atlantic Mobile Homes and RV Supplies
Corp. (Automotive) [2266]
Barringer Distributing Company Inc.; R.H. (Alcoholic
Beverages) [1501]
Beard Hardwood Lumber Inc.; E.N. (Construction
Materials and Machinery) [7037]
Bearing Distributors Inc. (Automotive) [2332]

Brown Lumber Corp.; Pat (Construction Materials
and Machinery) [7087]
Business Communications Inc. (Communications
Systems and Equipment) [5539]
Carolina Steel Corp. (Metals) [19859]
Carquest (Automotive) [2427]
Chandler Foods Inc. (Food) [10733]
Covington Detroit Diesel Inc. (Automotive) [2488]
Covington Diesel Inc. (Automotive) [2489]
Craft & Hobby Supplies (Office Equipment and
Supplies) [20934]
Craven Co.; E.F. (Construction Materials and
Machinery) [7231]
Cross Co. (Automotive) [2496]
Curtis Packing Co. Inc. (Food) [10883]
Disston Co. (Hardware) [13666]
DSi (Computers and Software) [6224]
Electric Supply and Equipment Company
Inc. (Electrical and Electronic Equipment and
Supplies) [8671]
Emco Inc. (Automotive) [2587]
Ford Body Company Inc. (Motorized
Vehicles) [20635]
Geneva Corp. (Construction Materials and
Machinery) [7387]
Greensboro Pipe Company Inc. (Industrial
Supplies) [16908]
HMA/International Business Development
Ltd. (Food) [11442]
Hodgin Supply Company Inc. (Construction
Materials and Machinery) [7475]
Hubbard Wholesale Lumber Corp.; A.P. (Wood and
Wood Products) [27321]
Industrial Electrics Inc. (Electrical and Electronic
Equipment and Supplies) [8877]
Industrial Transmission Inc. (Automotive) [2777]
Kay Chemical Co. (Cleaning and Janitorial
Supplies) [4648]
LaRose, Inc.; S. (Jewelry) [17498]
Lisk Lures (Recreational and Sporting
Goods) [23789]
Mac Thrift Clearance Center (Office Equipment and
Supplies) [21118]
Marsh Kitchens Greensboro Inc. (Construction
Materials and Machinery) [7647]
Michel Company Inc.; R.E. (Heating and Cooling
Equipment and Supplies) [14551]
O Henry Inc. (Office Equipment and
Supplies) [21168]
Rafferty-Brown Steel Co. (Metals) [20308]
S & W Distributors Inc. (Books and Other Printed
Materials) [4133]
Sentry Watch Inc. (Security and Safety
Equipment) [24636]
Southern Importers Inc. (Horticultural
Supplies) [14954]
Southern Office Furniture Distributors Inc. (Office
Equipment and Supplies) [21279]
Southern Optical, Inc. (Medical, Dental, and Optical
Supplies) [19627]
Southern Rubber Company Inc. (Industrial
Supplies) [17187]
Staton Distributing Co.; Jim (Alcoholic
Beverages) [2050]
Summit Pet Products (Veterinary Products) [27242]
Sunline USA Group Inc. (Hardware) [13942]
Theraquip Inc. (Medical, Dental, and Optical
Equipment) [19074]
Walke Co.; Henry (Industrial Supplies) [17260]
Wholesale Ceramic Tile (Floorcovering Equipment
and Supplies) [10298]
xpedx (Paper and Paper Products) [22002]

Greenville

Garner Wholesale Merchandisers Inc. (Health and
Beauty Aids) [14108]
Hungates Inc. (Toys and Hobby Goods) [26529]
Industrial Transmission Inc. (Automotive) [2776]
Maddux Supply Co. (Electrical and Electronic
Equipment and Supplies) [9017]
Michel Company Inc.; R.E. (Heating and Cooling
Equipment and Supplies) [14552]
Mid-South Metals Co. (Used, Scrap, and Recycled
Materials) [26912]
Overtons Sports Center, Inc. (Marine) [18579]

Pair Electronics Inc. (Electrical and Electronic
Equipment and Supplies) [9174]
Webb Inc.; Fred (Livestock and Farm
Products) [18329]

Grover

Grover Industries Inc. (Textiles and
Notions) [26048]

Henderson

Guptons Sporting Goods Inc. (Recreational and
Sporting Goods) [23704]
Rose's Stores Inc. (Clothing) [5320]
Williams Inc.; M.R. (Food) [12947]

Hendersonville

Banjo's Performancenter Inc. (Automotive) [2315]
Dal-Kawa Hijet (Motorized Vehicles) [20619]
Smith Floor Covering (Floorcovering Equipment and
Supplies) [10152]
Southland Distributors (Construction Materials and
Machinery) [8055]
Western North Carolina Apple
Growers (Food) [12915]
Youngblood Oil Company Inc. (Petroleum, Fuels,
and Related Equipment) [22820]

Hickory

Alarm-It Distributors Inc. (Security and Safety
Equipment) [24499]
Alex Lee Inc. (Food) [10362]
Atwood Leather Cutting (Luggage and Leather
Goods) [18373]
Automated Data Systems Inc. (Computers and
Software) [5986]
B & W Hosiery, Inc. (Clothing) [4795]
Baxter Knitting Co. (Clothing) [4807]
Benco Steel Inc. (Metals) [19809]
Carolina Office Equipment Co. (Office Equipment
and Supplies) [20881]
Carolina Steel Corp. (Metals) [19858]
Catawba Color and Chemical Company
Inc. (Chemicals) [4345]
Drillers Service Inc. (Specialty Equipment and
Products) [25637]
Efficient Computer System (Computers and
Software) [6237]
Flowers Auto Parts Co. (Automotive) [2634]
Forest City Tool Co. (Industrial Machinery) [16030]
Hickory Auto Parts Inc. (Automotive) [2749]
Industrial Fuel Co. (Petroleum, Fuels, and Related
Equipment) [22374]
Institution Food House Inc. (Food) [11510]
Institution Food House Inc. (Food) [11511]
ITP Business Communications (Office Equipment
and Supplies) [21072]
Lavitt Mills Inc.; Paul (Clothing) [5125]
Ledford's Trading Post (Guns and
Weapons) [13497]
Madaris Hosiery Mill (Clothing) [5151]
Merchants Distributors Inc. (Food) [11854]
Shook Builder Supply Co. (Hardware) [13917]
Simmons Hosiery Mill Inc. (Clothing) [5357]
Snyder Paper Corp. (Paper and Paper
Products) [21942]
Steven Hosiery Inc. (Clothing) [5395]

High Point

Adwood Corp. (Industrial Machinery) [15739]
Air Power Inc. (Industrial Machinery) [15745]
Amceco International Corp. (Toys and Hobby
Goods) [26386]
Beeson Hardware Industrial Sales
Co. (Hardware) [13590]
Carolyn Fabrics Inc. (Textiles and Notions) [25997]
Craft-Tex/Phase IV Inc. (Gifts and
Novelties) [13338]
Culp Inc. (Textiles and Notions) [26009]
Hunter and Company of North Carolina (Household
Items) [15536]
International Paper Co. McEwen Lumber
Co. (Construction Materials and
Machinery) [7519]
Kennedy Oil Company Inc. (Petroleum, Fuels, and
Related Equipment) [22400]

Mannington Wood Floors (Floorcovering Equipment and Supplies) [10008]

Merrimac Boyce Fabrics (Textiles and Notions) [26141]

Phillips Industries Inc. (Textiles and Notions) [26175]

Slane Hosiery Mills Inc. (Clothing) [5363]

Swaim Supply Company Inc. (Plumbing Materials and Fixtures) [23401]

Yarborough and Co. (Hardware) [14003]

Highlands

Annawear (Clothing) [4774]

Hildebran

Burke Hosiery Mills Inc. (Clothing) [4853]

Longwear Hosiery Mill (Clothing) [5142]

Hillsborough

Tarheel Communications (Sound and Entertainment Equipment and Supplies) [25472]

Huntersville

Greenwich Instruments USA (Computers and Software) [6312]

Metrolina Greenhouses Inc. (Horticultural Supplies) [14921]

Indian Trail

Carolina Made Inc. (Clothing) [4863]

Fontana & Fontana Inc. (Clothing) [4960]

Jacksonville

Del-Mar Industries Inc. (Clothing) [4911]

Jacksonville Mechanical Supply Inc. (Industrial Supplies) [16967]

Target Tire and Automotive Corp. (Automotive) [3292]

Jefferson

American Emergency Vehicles (Motorized Vehicles) [20586]

Kannapolis

Terry Products Inc. (Clothing) [5426]

Kernersville

Bales & Truitt Company Inc. (Heating and Cooling Equipment and Supplies) [14336]

Blue Ridge Fish Wholesale (Veterinary Products) [27086]

Blue Ridge Wholesale (Veterinary Products) [27087]

Central Carolina Grocers Inc. (Food) [10718]

Kings Mountain

Buckeye Fire Equipment Co. Sales Div. (Security and Safety Equipment) [24520]

Harris Welco (Metals) [20028]

Herndon Company Inc.; J.E. (Used, Scrap, and Recycled Materials) [26842]

Mauney Hosiery Mills Inc. (Clothing) [5175]

Kinston

Albain Shirt Co. (Clothing) [4756]

Mallard Oil Co. (Petroleum, Fuels, and Related Equipment) [22447]

Nantucket Inc. (Clothing) [5214]

Knightdale

Tractor Place Inc. (Agricultural Equipment and Supplies) [1347]

La Grange

Sasser Lumber Company Inc. (Construction Materials and Machinery) [7981]

Laurinburg

Eaton Corp. Golf Grip Div. (Recreational and Sporting Goods) [23644]

Electrical Equipment Co. (Electrical and Electronic Equipment and Supplies) [8678]

Luter Packing Company Inc. (Food) [11746]

Sinclair Lumber Co. (Construction Materials and Machinery) [8025]

Lawndale

Beaver's Rugs (Floorcovering Equipment and Supplies) [9697]

North State Metals Inc. (Metals) [20235]

Lenoir

Southeastern Adhesive Co. (Plastics) [23035]

Western Carolina Electrical Supply Co. (Electrical and Electronic Equipment and Supplies) [9573]

Lewisville

Sessions Specialty Co. (Chemicals) [4508]

Lexington

Furniture Makers Supply Co. (Industrial Supplies) [16884]

Piedmont Candy Co. (Food) [12166]

Power & Telephone Supply Company, Inc. (Communications Systems and Equipment) [5715]

Smith Lumber Co.; G.W. (Construction Materials and Machinery) [8034]

Lincolnton

Heafner Company Inc.; J.H. (Automotive) [2734]

Viking Technology Inc. (Clothing) [5463]

Linwood

Orrell's Food Service Inc. (Food) [12078]

Locust

Locust Lumber Company Inc. (Construction Materials and Machinery) [7608]

Lumberton

Biggs Inc.; K.M. (Agricultural Equipment and Supplies) [315]

Eagle Distributing Co. (Alcoholic Beverages) [1664]

Nash Finch Co. (Food) [11969]

Madison

Empire Publishing Inc. (Books and Other Printed Materials) [3729]

Marshville

Morgan Lumber Company Inc. (Construction Materials and Machinery) [7746]

Matthews

Carotek Inc. (Industrial Machinery) [15879]

Mechanical Equipment Company Inc. (Industrial Machinery) [16284]

Ortho-Care Southeast Inc. (Medical, Dental, and Optical Equipment) [18969]

Pro Systems Inc. (Computers and Software) [6642]

Maxton

Peoples Gas and Oil Company Inc. (Petroleum, Fuels, and Related Equipment) [22563]

Mebane

JDK Enterprises Inc. (Clothing) [5079]

Kidde Safety (Security and Safety Equipment) [24580]

Mocksville

Seaford and Sons Lumber; C.A. (Construction Materials and Machinery) [7996]

Tri-Power, Inc. (Automotive) [3335]

Monroe

Monroe Hardware Co. (Hardware) [13837]

Monroe Oil Company Inc. (Petroleum, Fuels, and Related Equipment) [22493]

Perfect Fit Industries, Inc. (Industrial Machinery) [16390]

Usco Inc. (Plumbing Materials and Fixtures) [23425]

Mooresboro

Colonial Braided Rug Co. (Floorcovering Equipment and Supplies) [9817]

Mooresville

Spectrum Financial System Inc. (Office Equipment and Supplies) [21281]

Morehead City

Big Rock Sports Inc. (Recreational and Sporting Goods) [23558]

Henry's Tackle L.L.C. (Recreational and Sporting Goods) [23723]

Morganton

Case Farms of North Carolina Inc. (Food) [10708]

Hardwoods of Morganton Inc. (Construction Materials and Machinery) [7447]

Morrisville

Golden Electronics Inc. (Electrical and Electronic Equipment and Supplies) [8795]

Mt. Airy

Kentucky Derby Hosiery (Clothing) [5108]

Merritt Machine Inc. (Metals) [20167]

Pine State Knitwear Co. (Clothing) [5276]

Water-Vac Distributors-Rainbow (Household Appliances) [15367]

Mt. Gilead

Jordan Lumber and Supply Inc. (Construction Materials and Machinery) [7538]

McRae Industries Inc. (Office Equipment and Supplies) [21135]

Mt. Holly

The Massey Company Inc. (Industrial Supplies) [17018]

P & B Enterprises Inc. (Recreational and Sporting Goods) [23865]

Robela Knit Shop Ltd. (Clothing) [5311]

New Bern

Coastal Electronics Inc. (Communications Systems and Equipment) [5564]

Pepsi-Cola Bottling Company of New Bern Inc. (Soft Drinks) [25010]

Tab Electric Supply Inc. (Electrical and Electronic Equipment and Supplies) [9454]

Tab Electric Supply Inc. (Electrical and Electronic Equipment and Supplies) [9455]

New London

Culp Lumber Co.; H.W. (Construction Materials and Machinery) [7235]

Newton

Midstate Mills Inc. (Food) [11886]

Ridgeview Inc. (Clothing) [5310]

North Wilkesboro

Forester Beverage Inc. (Alcoholic Beverages) [1694]

Lowes Home Centers Inc. (Sound and Entertainment Equipment and Supplies) [25290]

Pantego

Younce and W.T. Ralph Lumber Company Inc.; J.W. (Wood and Wood Products) [27398]

Pfafftown

Carolina First Aid Inc. (Medical, Dental, and Optical Equipment) [18728]

Pikeville

Thigpen Pharmacy Inc. (Medical, Dental, and Optical Equipment) [19076]

Pilot Mountain

Fit-All Sportswear Inc. (Clothing) [4956]

Pineville

American Photocopy Equipment Co. (Office Equipment and Supplies) [20797]

Innoland Inc. (Toys and Hobby Goods) [26533]

SCMS Inc. (Electrical and Electronic Equipment and Supplies) [9345]

Pollocksville

Jenkins Gas and Oil Company Inc. (Petroleum, Fuels, and Related Equipment) [22388]

Raleigh

Aiken Designs Inc.; Patsy (Clothing) [4754]
Allied Electronics (Electrical and Electronic Equipment and Supplies) [8321]
Associated Brokers Inc. (Food) [10443]
Batts Distributing Co.; James B. (Floorcovering Equipment and Supplies) [9695]
Boatwright Insulation Co. (Construction Materials and Machinery) [7064]
Boyd & Associates, Inc.; E. (Food) [10601]
Burroughs Communications Inc. (Communications Systems and Equipment) [5538]
Business Machines Inc. (Computers and Software) [6029]
Cameron & Barkley (Electrical and Electronic Equipment and Supplies) [8493]
Capitol Ceramic Inc. (Floorcovering Equipment and Supplies) [9755]
Carolina Cotton Growers Association Inc. (Livestock and Farm Products) [17764]
Cash; Jeff (Household Appliances) [15078]
CLG Inc. (Computers and Software) [6075]
Dillon Supply Co. (Industrial Machinery) [15951]
Electric Supply Co. (Electrical and Electronic Equipment and Supplies) [8666]
Electric Supply Co. (Raleigh, North Carolina) (Electrical and Electronic Equipment and Supplies) [8669]
Electrical Equipment Co. (Electrical and Electronic Equipment and Supplies) [8679]
Etheridge Produce (Food) [11056]
Ferguson Enterprises Inc. (Plumbing Materials and Fixtures) [23163]
Fireside Distributors (Heating and Cooling Equipment and Supplies) [14448]
Flue-Cured Tobacco Cooperative Stabilization Corp. (Tobacco Products) [26293]
General Parts Inc. (Automotive) [2673]
The Godfrey Group Inc. (Specialty Equipment and Products) [25662]
Industrial Power Sales Inc. (Hardware) [13765]
Jerry's Artarama Inc. (Specialty Equipment and Products) [25694]
McCarthy Drapery Company Inc. (Household Items) [15583]
Michel Company Inc.; R.E. (Heating and Cooling Equipment and Supplies) [14553]
Moore Equipment Co.; R.W. (Agricultural Equipment and Supplies) [1051]
Mutual Distributing Co. (Alcoholic Beverages) [1897]
North Carolina Equipment (Construction Materials and Machinery) [7793]
Parks Software Services Inc. (Computers and Software) [6592]
Piedmont Optical Co. (Medical, Dental, and Optical Supplies) [19541]
Poole Equipment Co.; Gregory (Construction Materials and Machinery) [7879]
Right of Way Equipment Co. (Agricultural Equipment and Supplies) [1194]
Service Engineering Co. (Medical, Dental, and Optical Equipment) [19037]
Siemens Energy and Automation Inc. Electrical Apparatus Div. (Electrical and Electronic Equipment and Supplies) [9369]
Stone Heavy Vehicle Specialists Inc. (Automotive) [3271]
Tay/Chem L.L.C. (Plastics) [23040]
Trade Corporation (Construction Materials and Machinery) [8140]
VIP Formal Wear Inc. (Clothing) [5465]
Warren Distributing Corp. (Household Appliances) [15364]
Wilkinson Supply Inc. (Plumbing Materials and Fixtures) [23460]

Reidsville

Eden Oil Company Inc. (Petroleum, Fuels, and Related Equipment) [22223]
Southeastern Industries Inc. (Used, Scrap, and Recycled Materials) [27001]

Twin City Manufacturing Co. (Clothing) [5447]

Research Triangle Park

ATCOM Inc. (Communications Systems and Equipment) [5521]
BroadBand Technologies Inc. (Electrical and Electronic Equipment and Supplies) [8469]
Troxler World Trade Corp. (Medical, Dental, and Optical Equipment) [19088]

Roanoke Rapids

Lors Medical Corp. (Medical, Dental, and Optical Equipment) [18892]
Newsom Oil Company Inc. (Petroleum, Fuels, and Related Equipment) [22515]
NHC Inc. (Petroleum, Fuels, and Related Equipment) [22517]

Robersonville

Southern Apparel Corp. (Clothing) [5370]

Rockingham

Seago Distributing Co. (Alcoholic Beverages) [2015]

Rocky Mount

Carolina Office Equipment Co. (Office Equipment and Supplies) [20882]
Designer Tile Co. East (Floorcovering Equipment and Supplies) [9861]
DMS Systems Corp. (Computers and Software) [6216]
Eastern Electric Supply Co. (Electrical and Electronic Equipment and Supplies) [8647]
Klitzner and Son Inc.; B. (Shoes) [24786]
M.B.M. Corp. (Food) [11816]
Michel Company Inc.; R.E. (Heating and Cooling Equipment and Supplies) [14554]
The News Group - Rocky Mount (Books and Other Printed Materials) [4001]
Thorpe and Ricks Inc. (Tobacco Products) [26356]
Tuscarora Corp. (Recreational and Sporting Goods) [24020]
Wholesale Paint Center, Inc. (Paints and Varnishes) [21609]

Rose Hill

Duplin Wine Cellars (Alcoholic Beverages) [1659]

Roseboro

DuBose Steel Incorporated of North Carolina (Metals) [19938]

Roxboro

Hercules Sales, Inc. (Household Items) [15526]

Salisbury

Baja Products Ltd. (Recreational and Sporting Goods) [23536]
Bennett Distributing Co. Inc. (Alcoholic Beverages) [1520]
Food Lion Inc. (Food) [11173]
Industrial Supply Solutions, Inc. (Automotive) [2775]
Speed Brite Inc. (Cleaning and Janitorial Supplies) [4711]

Sanford

Carolina Training Associates (Computers and Software) [6046]
CWF Inc. (Horticultural Supplies) [14851]
Davenport and Sons Inc.; J.T. (Food) [10913]
Global House (Industrial Machinery) [16067]
Moore Oil Company Inc.; Lee (Petroleum, Fuels, and Related Equipment) [22498]

Selma

Merchant's Grain Inc. (Livestock and Farm Products) [18087]

Severn

Meherrin Agricultural and Chemical Co. (Agricultural Equipment and Supplies) [1012]
Severn Peanut Company Inc. (Food) [12466]

Shawboro

Roberts Brothers Inc. (Livestock and Farm Products) [18202]

Shelby

Bindley Western Industries Inc. Kendall Div. (Medical, Dental, and Optical Supplies) [19188]
Carolina Braided Rug (Floorcovering Equipment and Supplies) [9760]
Carolina Vet Supply (Veterinary Products) [27102]
Carolina Vet Supply (Medical, Dental, and Optical Supplies) [19219]
Cleveland Electric Motors (Electrical and Electronic Equipment and Supplies) [8532]
Davis Rug Co. (Floorcovering Equipment and Supplies) [9848]
Ed's Leather Co. (Veterinary Products) [27124]
Pearson Rug Manufacturing Co.; Billy D. (Floorcovering Equipment and Supplies) [10102]
Shelby Supply Company Inc. (Electrical and Electronic Equipment and Supplies) [9360]
Simmons Yarn & Rug Co. (Floorcovering Equipment and Supplies) [10149]
Sound Advice (Sound and Entertainment Equipment and Supplies) [25450]
Stroud Braided Rug Co. (Floorcovering Equipment and Supplies) [10184]
Triple D Publishing Inc. (Books and Other Printed Materials) [4232]

Siler City

Hart Furniture Company Inc. (Siler City, North Carolina) (Furniture and Fixtures) [13128]

Skyland

South Atlantic Distributing Co. (Toys and Hobby Goods) [26658]

Smithfield

Casa Export Ltd. (Tobacco Products) [26273]

Sneads Ferry

Carolina Fisherman Supply Inc. (Recreational and Sporting Goods) [23583]

Sophia

Banner Place Nursery (Horticultural Supplies) [14817]

Southern Pines

Aro Corp. (Industrial Machinery) [15779]

Southport

Intrade, Inc. (Electrical and Electronic Equipment and Supplies) [8898]

Spencer

Rapers of Spencer Inc. (Toys and Hobby Goods) [26629]

Spindale

Lakeside Mills Inc. (Food) [11669]

Spruce Pine

Carson Co. Tri-County Oil Div. (Petroleum, Fuels, and Related Equipment) [22111]
Explosive Supply Company Inc. (Construction Materials and Machinery) [7327]

Star

Montgomery Hosiery Mill Inc. (Clothing) [5202]

Statesville

Fox, Inc.; T.E. (Sound and Entertainment Equipment and Supplies) [25197]
Interstate Equipment Co. (Construction Materials and Machinery) [7522]

Sunbury

Eastern Pharmaceuticals (Health and Beauty Aids) [14090]

Swannanoa

Owen Manufacturing Company Inc.; Charles D. (Household Items) [15606]

Tabor City

Tabor City Lumber Inc. (Construction Materials and Machinery) [8096]

Thomasville

Rex Oil Company Inc. (Petroleum, Fuels, and Related Equipment) [22624]
Singer Hosiery Mills Inc. (Clothing) [5359]

Tryon

Tryon Trading, Inc. (Industrial Supplies) [17237]

Union Grove

Somers Lumber and Manufacturing Inc. (Construction Materials and Machinery) [8040]

Valdese

Alba-Waldensian Inc. (Clothing) [4755]
Earthgrains/Waldensian Bakerie (Food) [11015]

Wadesboro

CMH Flooring Products Inc. (Floorcovering Equipment and Supplies) [9814]
CMH Flooring Products Inc. (Construction Materials and Machinery) [7186]

Walkertown

Gant Oil Co. (Petroleum, Fuels, and Related Equipment) [22301]

Wallace

Nichols Foodservice Inc. (Food) [12007]
Worsley Oil Company of Wallace Inc. (Petroleum, Fuels, and Related Equipment) [22817]

Warsaw

Scrivner of North Carolina Inc. (Food) [12439]

Washington

Frischkorn Distributors Inc. (Plumbing Materials and Fixtures) [23177]

Waxhaw

Hutson Enterprises, Inc.; D.H. (Recreational and Sporting Goods) [23738]

Waynesville

Haywood Builders Supply Inc. (Construction Materials and Machinery) [7461]
Powell Wholesale Lumber Co. (Construction Materials and Machinery) [7880]

Weaverville

Karpen Steel Custom Doors & Frames (Construction Materials and Machinery) [7543]

Welcome

Competition Karting Inc. (Recreational and Sporting Goods) [23600]
Walker and Associates Inc. (Electrical and Electronic Equipment and Supplies) [9551]
Walker and Associates Inc. (Welcome, North Carolina) (Communications Systems and Equipment) [5808]
Walker Group Inc. (Electrical and Electronic Equipment and Supplies) [9553]

Wendell

The Cotton Exchange (Clothing) [4900]
Wagners (Gifts and Novelties) [13468]

West Jefferson

Colvard Oil Company Inc. (Petroleum, Fuels, and Related Equipment) [22153]

Whiteville

Whiteville Oil Company Inc. (Petroleum, Fuels, and Related Equipment) [22801]

Wilkesboro

Golden Needles Knitting and Glove Co. Monte Glove Div. (Clothing) [4994]
Tom Thumb Glove Co. (Clothing) [5433]

Williamston

Chesson and Sons Inc.; Mark (Agricultural Equipment and Supplies) [413]

Wilmington

All Spec Static Control Inc. (Electrical and Electronic Equipment and Supplies) [8296]
Bavaria House Corp. (Alcoholic Beverages) [1508]
Becker Builders Supply Co. (Construction Materials and Machinery) [7039]
Clemmons Corp. (Industrial Supplies) [16801]
Coastal Beverage Company Inc. (Alcoholic Beverages) [1605]
Godwin Oil Company Inc. (Petroleum, Fuels, and Related Equipment) [22316]
Industrial Sales Company Inc. (Plumbing Materials and Fixtures) [23219]
Jacobi Hardware Co., Inc. (Marine) [18527]
Jacobi-Lewis Co. (Restaurant and Commercial Foodservice Equipment and Supplies) [24148]
Longley Supply Company Inc. (Plumbing Materials and Fixtures) [23247]
Owens Electric Supply Companies Inc. (Electrical and Electronic Equipment and Supplies) [9164]
Owens Electric Supply Inc. (Sound and Entertainment Equipment and Supplies) [25372]
Owens Electric Supply Inc. (Household Appliances) [15261]
Queensboro Steel Corp. (Metals) [20304]
Strickland Auto; Jewell (Industrial Supplies) [17199]
Sun International (Scientific and Measurement Devices) [24440]
Wilmington Hospital Supply (Medical, Dental, and Optical Supplies) [19707]

Wilson

Barnes Motor and Parts Co. (Automotive) [2318]
Batts Distributing Co.; James B. (Floorcovering Equipment and Supplies) [9696]
DSW Inc. (Motorized Vehicles) [20626]
Electric Supply Co. (Wilson, North Carolina) (Electrical and Electronic Equipment and Supplies) [8670]
Herring & Co.; T.L. (Food) [11420]
Itco Tire Co. (Automotive) [2802]
Kilpatrick Table Tennis Co.; Martin (Recreational and Sporting Goods) [23774]
Mellobuttercup Ice Cream Co. (Food) [11847]
Pestcon Systems Inc. (Agricultural Equipment and Supplies) [1124]
Quality Truck Bodies & Repair, Inc. (Automotive) [3129]
Sarreid Ltd. (Furniture and Fixtures) [13232]
Simpson Equipment Corp. (Automotive) [3223]
Stancil Refrigeration Services Inc.; Bruce (Heating and Cooling Equipment and Supplies) [14695]
Standard Commercial Corp. (Tobacco Products) [26353]
White's Herring Tractor and Truck Inc. (Automotive) [3427]
Woodard and Company Inc.; P.L. (Agricultural Equipment and Supplies) [1461]

Windsor

Spruill Oil Company Inc. (Petroleum, Fuels, and Related Equipment) [22695]

Winston-Salem

Bearing Distributors Inc. (Automotive) [2333]
Bio-Medical Imaging Inc. (Medical, Dental, and Optical Equipment) [18709]
Bocock-Stroud Co. (Recreational and Sporting Goods) [23563]

Winston Salem

Boot & Shoe Village (Shoes) [24695]

Winston-Salem

Brown-Rogers-Dixson Co. (Household Appliances) [15062]
Carolina C & E, Inc. (Sound and Entertainment Equipment and Supplies) [25124]
Carolina C and E Inc. (Household Appliances) [15076]
Carswell Distributing Co. (Household Appliances) [15077]
The Company Logo Inc. (Clothing) [4891]
Family Sweets Candy Co. Inc. (Food) [11078]
Hanover Warehousing (Food) [11373]
Holladay Surgical Supply Co. (Medical, Dental, and Optical Equipment) [18836]
Holladay Surgical Supply Co. (Medical, Dental, and Optical Supplies) [19360]
Joyce Brothers Inc. (Food) [11568]
Joyce-Munden Co. (Clothing) [5097]
Karumit Associates Ltd. (Clothing) [5101]
Ligon Electric Supply Co. (Electrical and Electronic Equipment and Supplies) [8991]
Lucia Inc. (Clothing) [5146]
Meridian Aerospace Group Ltd. (Aeronautical Equipment and Supplies) [123]
Michel Company Inc.; R.E. (Heating and Cooling Equipment and Supplies) [14555]
Paper Supply Co. (Cleaning and Janitorial Supplies) [4683]
Pleasants Hardware Co. (Hardware) [13871]
Quality Oil Company L.P. (Petroleum, Fuels, and Related Equipment) [22600]
Quality Oil Company L.P. (Petroleum, Fuels, and Related Equipment) [22601]
Rehab Equipment Co. (Medical, Dental, and Optical Supplies) [19574]
Salem Optical Co. Inc. (Medical, Dental, and Optical Supplies) [19592]
Salem Refrigeration Company Inc. (Heating and Cooling Equipment and Supplies) [14672]
Vernon Produce Co.; W.R. (Food) [12840]
Williams Oil Co.; A.T. (Petroleum, Fuels, and Related Equipment) [22805]

Woodland

Lewis Manufacturing Co. (Clothing) [5134]

Yanceyville

Royal Textile Mills Inc. (Clothing) [5323]

Youngsville

Variety Sales, Inc. (Clothing) [5458]

Zebulon

Veterinary Medical Supply (Veterinary Products) [27264]

North Dakota

Agate

Agate Cooperative (Agricultural Equipment and Supplies) [203]

Arthur

Arthur Companies Inc. (Agricultural Equipment and Supplies) [257]

Ashley

Fey Inc. (Agricultural Equipment and Supplies) [681]

Belfield

R-K Market (Medical, Dental, and Optical Equipment) [19007]

Berlin

Berlin Farmers Elevator (Agricultural Equipment and Supplies) [302]

Berthold

Berthold Farmers Elevator Co. (Agricultural Equipment and Supplies) [304]
Berthold Farmers Elevator Co. (Food) [10543]

Binford

Binford Farmers Union Grain (Agricultural Equipment and Supplies) [316]

Bisbee

North Central Grain Coop. (Food) [12026]
North Central Grain Cooperative (Agricultural Equipment and Supplies) [1080]

Bismarck

ABM of Bismarck Inc. (Office Equipment and Supplies) [20766]
Capital City Restaurant Supply Co. (Restaurant and Commercial Foodservice Equipment and Supplies) [24089]
Capital Scale (Scientific and Measurement Devices) [24335]
Dakota Communications Service (Communications Systems and Equipment) [5584]
Dave's Auto Inc. (Automotive) [2528]
Dependable Business Machines (Office Equipment and Supplies) [20955]
E & B Beauty & Barber Supply (Health and Beauty Aids) [14088]
E and B Beauty and Barber Supply (Restaurant and Commercial Foodservice Equipment and Supplies) [24106]
Farmers Union Oil Cooperative (Petroleum, Fuels, and Related Equipment) [22271]
Fireside Office Products Inc. (Computers and Software) [6270]
Hedahl's Auto Parts (Automotive) [2738]
McQuade Distributing Company, Inc. (Alcoholic Beverages) [1863]
McQuade Distributing Company Inc. (Alcoholic Beverages) [1864]
MidWest Air Motive Corp. (Aeronautical Equipment and Supplies) [129]
Northern League Sportscards (Toys and Hobby Goods) [26595]
Office System Inc. (Office Equipment and Supplies) [21189]
Recreation Supply Co. (Recreational and Sporting Goods) [23908]
Star Restaurant Equipment & Supplies (Heating and Cooling Equipment and Supplies) [14698]
SuperValu Inc. (Food) [12644]
Taylor Dakota Distributors (Heating and Cooling Equipment and Supplies) [14711]
Way-Point Avionics Inc. (Aeronautical Equipment and Supplies) [170]
Western Steel and Plumbing Inc. (Plumbing Materials and Fixtures) [23454]
Woodmansee Inc. (Office Equipment and Supplies) [21361]

Bottineau

Bottineau Farmers Elevator Inc. (Livestock and Farm Products) [17744]

Buchanan

Buchanan Farmers Elevator Co. (Livestock and Farm Products) [17751]
Buchanan Farmers Elevator Co. (Food) [10635]

Buxton

Farmers Union Elevator (Agricultural Equipment and Supplies) [663]

Carrington

Central Distributing Co. (Soft Drinks) [24924]
Rosenau Equipment Co. (Agricultural Equipment and Supplies) [1212]

Casselton

Offutt Co.; R.D. (Agricultural Equipment and Supplies) [1099]
Wegnar Livestock Inc.; Keith E. (Livestock and Farm Products) [18330]

Cavalier

Farmers Cooperative Elevator Co. (Livestock and Farm Products) [17864]

Cayuga

Farmer's Fur House (Livestock and Farm Products) [17890]

Crosby

Engberg Janitorial Supply & Service (Cleaning and Janitorial Supplies) [4619]

Cummings

K & L Marketing Inc. (Toys and Hobby Goods) [26547]

Devils Lake

Farmers Union Oil Co. (Petroleum, Fuels, and Related Equipment) [22264]
Jerome Wholesales Inc. (Alcoholic Beverages) [1782]
Paint & Glass Supply Company Inc. (Paints and Varnishes) [21527]
Schwan Wholesale Co. (Food) [12433]

Dickinson

Anfinson's Inc. (Agricultural Equipment and Supplies) [244]
Dickinson Supply Inc. (Automotive) [2543]
Jerome Distribution Inc. (Alcoholic Beverages) [1781]
Sadowsky and Son Inc.; G.A. (Petroleum, Fuels, and Related Equipment) [22646]
Stockmen's Livestock Exchange (Livestock and Farm Products) [18256]
Western Livestock Inc. (Livestock and Farm Products) [18341]

Dunseith

T & M Inc. (Alcoholic Beverages) [2067]

Edgeley

Anderson Brothers Inc. (Agricultural Equipment and Supplies) [241]
Farmers Union Grain Cooperative (Livestock and Farm Products) [17910]

Edmore

Farmers Shipping and Supply (Livestock and Farm Products) [17902]

Ellendale

Farmers Union Oil Co. (Petroleum, Fuels, and Related Equipment) [22262]
Farmers Union Oil Co. (Petroleum, Fuels, and Related Equipment) [22268]
Farmers Union Oil Co. (Ellendale, North Dakota) (Livestock and Farm Products) [17911]

Fairdale

Fairdale Farmers Cooperative Elevator Co. (Agricultural Equipment and Supplies) [560]

Fargo

Accent Business Products (Office Equipment and Supplies) [20768]
Berg Fargo Motor Supply Inc. (Automotive) [2350]
Beverage Wholesalers Inc. (Alcoholic Beverages) [1528]
Border States Electric Supply (Electrical and Electronic Equipment and Supplies) [8455]
Border States Industries Inc. (Electrical and Electronic Equipment and Supplies) [8456]
Business Support Services (Office Equipment and Supplies) [20869]
Clay Cass Creamery (Food) [10766]
Cole Papers Inc. (Paper and Paper Products) [21685]
Cole Wholesale Flooring (Floorcovering Equipment and Supplies) [9816]
Dacotah Paper Co. (Paper and Paper Products) [21699]
Dacotah Paper Co. (Industrial Supplies) [16819]
Dakota Electric Supply Co. (Electrical and Electronic Equipment and Supplies) [8605]
Dakota Food Equipment Inc. (Restaurant and Commercial Foodservice Equipment and Supplies) [24102]
Dakota Refrigeration Inc. (Heating and Cooling Equipment and Supplies) [14410]
Fargo Glass and Paint Co. (Paints and Varnishes) [21440]
Fargo-Moorhead Jobbing Co. (Food) [11082]

Food Services of America (Food) [11178]
General Equipment and Supplies Inc. (Construction Materials and Machinery) [7383]
Hintz Fire Equipment Inc. (Security and Safety Equipment) [24564]
Horn Plastics Inc. (Plastics) [22982]
International Marketing Systems Ltd. (Agricultural Equipment and Supplies) [864]
Liberty Business Systems Inc. (Office Equipment and Supplies) [21108]
Marketing Specialista (Food) [11785]
McKee Enterprises Inc. (Floorcovering Equipment and Supplies) [10016]
Meidlinger Inc.; H.E. (Restaurant and Commercial Foodservice Equipment and Supplies) [24184]
MH Associates Ltd. (Recreational and Sporting Goods) [23824]
Midland Hospital Supply Inc. (Medical, Dental, and Optical Equipment) [18938]
Nardini Fire Equipment Company of North Dakota (Security and Safety Equipment) [24598]
Nordic Needle, Inc. (Textiles and Notions) [26158]
Northern Plains Distributing (Sound and Entertainment Equipment and Supplies) [25363]
Northland Marketing, Inc. (Food) [12035]
O'Day Equipment Inc. (Petroleum, Fuels, and Related Equipment) [22534]
Office Machine & Furniture Inc. (Office Equipment and Supplies) [21183]
Offutt Co.; R.D. (Agricultural Equipment and Supplies) [1098]
Phillips & Sons of N.D.; Ed (Alcoholic Beverages) [1956]
Plains Distribution Service, Inc. (Books and Other Printed Materials) [4066]
Promotions Plus (Gifts and Novelties) [13429]
RDO Equipment Co. (Agricultural Equipment and Supplies) [1171]
Refrigeration Heating Inc. (Heating and Cooling Equipment and Supplies) [14656]
Rott-Keller Supply Co. (Automotive) [3175]
S & R Inc. (Office Equipment and Supplies) [21254]
S/S Electronics Inc. (Household Appliances) [15300]
Starr Display Fireworks Inc. (Toys and Hobby Goods) [26669]
Structural Materials Inc. (Construction Materials and Machinery) [8084]
SUPERVALU (Food) [12642]
Swanson Health Products (Health and Beauty Aids) [14253]
Sweeney Brothers Tractor Co. (Agricultural Equipment and Supplies) [1308]
Wallwork Inc.; W.W. (Motorized Vehicles) [20747]
Westeel Inc.; W.S. (Storage Equipment and Containers) [25947]
Western Products Inc. (Construction Materials and Machinery) [8212]

Fessenden

Fessenden Cooperative Association (Livestock and Farm Products) [17917]

Finley

Top Taste Bakery Inc. (Food) [12733]

Ft. Yates

Good Karma Publishing Inc. (Books and Other Printed Materials) [3786]

Galesburg

Galesberg Cooperative Elevator Co. (Agricultural Equipment and Supplies) [720]

Garrison

Grosz; Leland (Agricultural Equipment and Supplies) [770]

Grand Forks

Agsco Inc. (Agricultural Equipment and Supplies) [218]
Associated Potato Growers Inc. (Food) [10456]
BR Chemical Co. Inc. (Cleaning and Janitorial Supplies) [4587]

D & H Beauty Supply (Health and Beauty
Aids) [14076]
Dakota Sales Co. Inc. (Alcoholic
Beverages) [1633]
GFG Foodservice Inc. (Food) [11259]
Grand Forks Equipment Inc. (Agricultural Equipment
and Supplies) [755]
K & J Jewelry Manufacturing (Jewelry) [17479]
Mahowald; John G. (Specialty Equipment and
Products) [25723]
Modern Information Systems (Office Equipment and
Supplies) [21150]
North Central Commodities, Inc. (Livestock and
Farm Products) [18136]
Palay Display Industries Inc. (Furniture and
Fixtures) [13202]
Weekley Auto Parts Inc. (Automotive) [3407]

Harvey
Farmers Union Oil Co. (Petroleum, Fuels, and
Related Equipment) [22263]

Harwood
Prosper Farmers Cooperative Elevator (Agricultural
Equipment and Supplies) [1159]

Hebron
Schmalenberge; Jacob (Livestock and Farm
Products) [18224]

Hettinger
County General (Agricultural Equipment and
Supplies) [468]
Hettinger Cooperative Equity Exchange (Livestock
and Farm Products) [17995]
Hettinger-Mobridge Candy & Tobacco (Tobacco
Products) [26306]

Hoople
Hoople Farmers Grain Co. (Livestock and Farm
Products) [18004]

Hunter
Hunter Grain Co. (Agricultural Equipment and
Supplies) [845]

Jamestown
Central Business Systems Inc. (Office Equipment
and Supplies) [20890]
Jamestown Implement Inc. (Agricultural Equipment
and Supplies) [879]
Jamestown Livestock Sales (Livestock and Farm
Products) [18020]
JT Beverage Inc. (Alcoholic Beverages) [1791]
Kostelecky's Fiberglass (Automotive) [2860]
Microage (Computers and Software) [6498]
Valley Sales Company Inc. (Alcoholic
Beverages) [2097]

Kathryn
Kathryn Farmers Mutual Elevators Inc. (Livestock
and Farm Products) [18028]

Kenmare
Farmers Union Oil Company of
Kenmare (Agricultural Equipment and
Supplies) [669]

Lamoure
Toy Farmer Ltd. (Toys and Hobby Goods) [26684]

Leeds
BTR Farmers Co-op (Livestock and Farm
Products) [17750]

Lisbon
Meyer Equipment Inc. (Agricultural Equipment and
Supplies) [1019]

Maddock
Farmers Union Oil Co. (Agricultural Equipment and
Supplies) [664]

Mandan
Cloverdale Foods Company Inc. (Food) [10775]

Haider; Raymond (Livestock and Farm
Products) [17970]
Kist Livestock Auction Co. (Livestock and Farm
Products) [18035]
Leingang Siding and Window (Construction
Materials and Machinery) [7594]
Twin City Implement Inc. (Agricultural Equipment
and Supplies) [1367]

Mcville
Senex Harvest States (Food) [12460]

Michigan
SSR Pump Co. (Automotive) [3257]

Milnor
Peterson Co.; Dale (Toys and Hobby
Goods) [26611]

Minot
Clute Office Equipment Inc. (Office Equipment and
Supplies) [20903]
Coulter Welding Inc. (Industrial Supplies) [16812]
Dakota Drug Inc. (Health and Beauty
Aids) [14078]
Familiar Northwest (Plumbing Materials and
Fixtures) [23160]
Hair Depot Beauty Consultants (Health and Beauty
Aids) [14120]
Hauck; Donald (Livestock and Farm
Products) [17983]
Magic City Beverage Co. (Alcoholic
Beverages) [1836]
Minot Builders Supply Association (Construction
Materials and Machinery) [7724]
Nash Finch Co. (Food) [11971]
Northland Sports Inc. (Recreational and Sporting
Goods) [23852]
Oral Logic Inc. (Health and Beauty Aids) [14186]
Pietsch Aircraft Restoration & Repair (Aeronautical
Equipment and Supplies) [137]
Reeve's Refrigeration & Heating Supply (Heating
and Cooling Equipment and Supplies) [14651]
Rice Lake Products Inc. (Specialty Equipment and
Products) [25803]
Souris River Telephone Mutual Aid
Cooperative (Communications Systems and
Equipment) [5762]
Wholesale Supply Company Inc. (Tobacco
Products) [26373]

Mott
Mott Equity Exchange (Hardware) [13839]

Napoleon
Farmers Union Oil Co. (Petroleum, Fuels, and
Related Equipment) [22267]
Farmers Union Oil Co. (Napoleon, North
Dakota) (Petroleum, Fuels, and Related
Equipment) [22269]
Linton Livestock Market Inc. (Livestock and Farm
Products) [18061]
Napoleon Livestock Auction (Livestock and Farm
Products) [18124]

New Rockford
Ziegler Repair (Heating and Cooling Equipment and
Supplies) [14789]

New Town
Williams Sales & Service; Jim (Recreational and
Sporting Goods) [24046]

Northwood
Northwood Equity Elevators (Livestock and Farm
Products) [18147]

Oakes
Weatherhead Distributing Co. (Alcoholic
Beverages) [2112]

Parshall
Parshall Farmers Union Co-op Inc. (Livestock and
Farm Products) [18160]

Rolla
Farmers Union Oil Co. (Rolla, North
Dakota) (Petroleum, Fuels, and Related
Equipment) [22270]
Rolla Cooperative Grain Co. (Livestock and Farm
Products) [18204]

Rugby
Rugby Farmers Union Elevator Co. (Livestock and
Farm Products) [18211]

Scranton
Scranton Equity Exchange Inc. (Construction
Materials and Machinery) [7995]

Sharon
Farmers Cooperative Elevator (Livestock and Farm
Products) [17862]

Sheyenne
Equity Cooperative Elevator Co. (Livestock and
Farm Products) [17834]

Thompson
Thompson Farmers Cooperative Elevator
Co. (Agricultural Equipment and
Supplies) [1328]

Valley City
Dakota Industrial Supply (Cleaning and Janitorial
Supplies) [4608]
Farmers Union Oil Co. (Petroleum, Fuels, and
Related Equipment) [22265]
Sheyenne Publishing Co. (Office Equipment and
Supplies) [21268]

Velva
Mike's Refrigeration Inc. (Heating and Cooling
Equipment and Supplies) [14603]

Wahpeton
Frontier Inc. (Agricultural Equipment and
Supplies) [710]
Frontier Inc. (Agricultural Equipment and
Supplies) [712]
Lillegard Inc. (Agricultural Equipment and
Supplies) [957]
SK Food International, Inc. (Food) [12499]

Washburn
Mon-Dak Chemical Inc. (Chemicals) [4459]

West Fargo
Balthauser & Moyer (Livestock and Farm
Products) [17720]
Interstate Payco Seed Co. (Agricultural Equipment
and Supplies) [866]
McDonald Livestock Co. (Livestock and Farm
Products) [18082]
Quality Meats and Seafood Inc. (Food) [12253]
Service Oil Inc. (Petroleum, Fuels, and Related
Equipment) [22663]
Stockman Supply Inc. (Veterinary
Products) [27239]
Tri-State Auction Company
Inc. (Automotive) [3336]
VanderHave USA (Agricultural Equipment and
Supplies) [1395]

Williston
A-1 New & Used Auto Parts,
Inc. (Automotive) [2150]
Delaney Management Corp. (Alcoholic
Beverages) [1639]
O.K. Distributing Company Inc. (Tobacco
Products) [26336]
Sukut Office Equipment Co. (Office Equipment and
Supplies) [21303]
Williston Industrial Supply Corp. (Petroleum, Fuels,
and Related Equipment) [22807]

Wishek
Wishek Livestock Market Inc. (Livestock and Farm
Products) [18356]

Wyndmere

Wyndmere Farmers Elevator Co. (Agricultural Equipment and Supplies) [1466]

Ypsilanti

Ypsilanti Equity Elevator Company Inc. (Livestock and Farm Products) [18364]

Ohio

Ada

Ada Farmers Exchange Co. (Livestock and Farm Products) [17672]

Akron

Akro-Mils Inc. (Storage Equipment and Containers) [25886]
Akrochem Corp. (Rubber) [24266]
Akron Auto Auction Inc. (Motorized Vehicles) [20580]
Akron Overseas Inc. (Industrial Machinery) [15749]
Annaco Inc. (Used, Scrap, and Recycled Materials) [26752]
BFI Recyclery (Metals) [19821]
Big B Automotive Warehouse (Automotive) [2358]
Brown-Graves Co. (Construction Materials and Machinery) [7086]
Burger Iron Co. (Metals) [19843]
C & P Sales Co. (Toys and Hobby Goods) [26432]
Custom Trim of America (Automotive) [2518]
Falls Welding & Fabricating, FWF Medical Products Div. (Medical, Dental, and Optical Equipment) [18795]
Falls Welding and Fabrication, Medical Products Div. (Medical, Dental, and Optical Supplies) [19321]
Fallsway Equipment Company Inc. (Industrial Machinery) [16005]
Famous Enterprises Inc. (Heating and Cooling Equipment and Supplies) [14442]
Famous Industries (Plumbing Materials and Fixtures) [23161]
Famous Manufacturing Co. (Industrial Machinery) [16006]
Famous Telephone Supply Inc. (Communications Systems and Equipment) [5609]
Harwick Standard Distribution Corporation (Chemicals) [4409]
IM/EX Port Inc. (Industrial Machinery) [16144]
Industrial Tube and Steel Corp. (Metals) [20062]
Jeter Systems Corp. (Office Equipment and Supplies) [21076]
Milk Marketing Inc. (Food) [11896]
Miller's Adaptive Technologies (Medical, Dental, and Optical Supplies) [19464]
Murdock Industrial Inc. (Industrial Supplies) [17064]
Musson Rubber Co. (Floorcovering Equipment and Supplies) [10072]
Myers Industries Inc. (Automotive) [3011]
Myers Industries Inc. Myers Tire Supply (Automotive) [3012]
Natcom International (Medical, Dental, and Optical Supplies) [19475]
Oliger Seed Co. (Agricultural Equipment and Supplies) [1105]
Parry Corp. (Industrial Machinery) [16381]
The Pearl Coffee Co. (Food) [12128]
Pierre's French Ice Cream Distributing Company of Akron (Food) [12167]
Rogers Co.; B.W. (Industrial Supplies) [17145]
Sacks Electrical Supply Co. (Electrical and Electronic Equipment and Supplies) [9329]
Sacks International Inc.; M. (Rubber) [24293]
Shin-Etsu Silicones of America Inc. (Chemicals) [4510]
Summervilles Inc. (Office Equipment and Supplies) [21304]
Trade America (Industrial Machinery) [16573]
Tri-Power MPT (Industrial Supplies) [17235]
United Automatic Heating Supplies (Heating and Cooling Equipment and Supplies) [14745]

Alliance

Clem Lumber Distributing Company Inc. (Construction Materials and Machinery) [7180]
Damon Industries, Inc. (Cleaning and Janitorial Supplies) [4609]
Morgan Engineering Systems Inc. (Construction Materials and Machinery) [7744]
Robertson Heating Supply Co. (Plumbing Materials and Fixtures) [23348]

Alpha

Art Essentials (Office Equipment and Supplies) [20813]

Amelia

Kroger Co. Dairy-Bakery Div. (Food) [11651]

Archbold

Liechty Farm Equipment Inc. (Agricultural Equipment and Supplies) [956]

Ashland

Donley Seed Co. (Agricultural Equipment and Supplies) [523]

Ashtabula

A. Louis Supply Co. (Industrial Supplies) [16665]
Louis Steel Co.; Arthur (Metals) [20135]
Michel Company Inc.; R.E. (Heating and Cooling Equipment and Supplies) [14560]

Ashville

Brown Tractor and Implement Inc. (Agricultural Equipment and Supplies) [342]

Athens

Accura Music, Inc. (Books and Other Printed Materials) [3467]
Ace Technical Resources Inc. (Computers and Software) [5869]
MacDonald Manufacturing; Stewart (Sound and Entertainment Equipment and Supplies) [25295]

Aurora

Sherwood Promotions Inc. (Specialty Equipment and Products) [25813]

Avon

Avon-Lakewood Nursery Inc. (Agricultural Equipment and Supplies) [264]
Freeman Manufacturing and Supply (Industrial Supplies) [16879]
Jenne Distributors (Communications Systems and Equipment) [5653]

Barberton

Yoder Brothers Inc. (Horticultural Supplies) [14980]

Bascom

Bascom Elevator Supply Association (Agricultural Equipment and Supplies) [282]

Batavia

Bore Technology Inc. (Industrial Machinery) [15831]

Bath

Hazra Associates, Inc. (Medical, Dental, and Optical Equipment) [18830]

Beachwood

Buckeye Rubber and Packing Co. (Industrial Supplies) [16771]
Consolidated Coatings Corp. (Paints and Varnishes) [21417]
Design Surfaces (Floorcovering Equipment and Supplies) [9859]
Magic American Corp. (Chemicals) [4446]
Salazar International, Inc. (Automotive) [3183]

Bedford

Olympic Steel Inc. (Metals) [20246]

Bedford Heights

American Seaway Foods Inc. (Food) [10404]
Gunton Corp. (Construction Materials and Machinery) [7425]
Loveman Steel Corp. (Metals) [20138]
Majestic Steel Service Inc. (Metals) [20146]
State Ceramic Tile, Inc. (Floorcovering Equipment and Supplies) [10179]
Waxman Industries Inc. (Plumbing Materials and Fixtures) [23443]

Bellaire

J.H. Service Company Inc. (Electrical and Electronic Equipment and Supplies) [8913]

Bellbrook

Green Velvet Sod Farms (Agricultural Equipment and Supplies) [766]

Bellefontaine

AcuSport Corp. (Recreational and Sporting Goods) [23494]
General Merchandise Services Inc. (Health and Beauty Aids) [14110]
Gillespie Oil Company Inc. (Automotive) [2681]
Goff Custom Spring Inc. (Hardware) [13727]

Berea

GLF/SAE (Hardware) [13723]
Maraj International (Computers and Software) [6461]
MEBCO Contractors Supplies (Hardware) [13823]
Sound Com Corp. (Sound and Entertainment Equipment and Supplies) [25452]

Berlin

Holmes Limestone Co. (Minerals and Ores) [20546]

Blacklick

Columbus Steel Drum Co. (Storage Equipment and Containers) [25904]
International Marine Publishing Co. (Books and Other Printed Materials) [3848]
Weisheimer Pet Supply (Veterinary Products) [27269]

Bluffton

McBee Grain and Trucking Inc. (Livestock and Farm Products) [18077]

Boardman

Buckeye Ceramic Tile (Floorcovering Equipment and Supplies) [9744]
Buckeye Ceramic Tile (Construction Materials and Machinery) [7092]
Summitville Boardman (Floorcovering Equipment and Supplies) [10188]
Vector Security Systems Inc. (Security and Safety Equipment) [24657]

Botkins

Provico Inc. (Veterinary Products) [27218]

Bowersville

Seaman Grain Inc. (Agricultural Equipment and Supplies) [1248]

Bowling Green

Country Smoked Meats Inc. (Food) [10858]
Mid-Wood Inc. (Livestock and Farm Products) [18093]

Bridgeport

Scott Lumber Co. (Construction Materials and Machinery) [7992]

Broadview Heights

Anicom (Electrical and Electronic Equipment and Supplies) [8355]
Ohio Machinery Co. (Construction Materials and Machinery) [7805]
Wine Trends, Inc. (Alcoholic Beverages) [2126]

Brook Park

Calvert Wire and Cable Corp. (Electrical and Electronic Equipment and Supplies) [8490]
Steele's Sports Co. (Recreational and Sporting Goods) [23988]

Brookfield

United Steel Service Inc. (Metals) [20466]

Brooklyn Heights

All Foils Inc. (Metals) [19745]

Bucyrus

Fairfield Supply Co. (Automotive) [2606]
Now Products (Gifts and Novelties) [13416]

Cambridge

Southeastern Equipment Company Inc. (Construction Materials and Machinery) [8045]

Canal Fulton

Avalon Distributing Inc. (Food) [10474]

Canal Winchester

Mid-States Wool Growers Cooperative (Agricultural Equipment and Supplies) [1029]
Taylor and Sons Equipment Co. (Agricultural Equipment and Supplies) [1317]

Canfield

Agaland CO-OP Inc. (Agricultural Equipment and Supplies) [202]
Green Valley Seed (Agricultural Equipment and Supplies) [765]
Myers Equipment Corp. (Automotive) [3010]

Canton

AGA Welding (Industrial Machinery) [15741]
Bison Corp. (Chemicals) [4336]
Conley Company Inc.; M. (Paper and Paper Products) [21689]
Consumer Direct Inc. (Recreational and Sporting Goods) [23603]
Furbay Electric Supply Co. (Electrical and Electronic Equipment and Supplies) [8768]
Hart Co. Inc.; Edward R. (Floorcovering Equipment and Supplies) [9938]
Hillsdale Paper Co. (Paper and Paper Products) [21763]
Luntz Corp. (Used, Scrap, and Recycled Materials) [26889]
McCoy and Son Inc.; J.B. (Paper and Paper Products) [21828]
Morse Co.; M.K. (Hardware) [13838]
Park Farms Inc. (Food) [12110]
Sommer Electric Corp. (Electrical and Electronic Equipment and Supplies) [9380]
Williams Inc.; Ralph C. (Industrial Supplies) [17280]
Ziegler's Bolt & Nut House (Hardware) [14005]

Carroll

Diamond Electronics, Inc. (Security and Safety Equipment) [24534]

Centerville

Endolite North America Ltd. (Medical, Dental, and Optical Equipment) [18791]

Chagrin Falls

Marus and Weimer, Inc. (Plumbing Materials and Fixtures) [23252]
Olicom USA Inc. (Computers and Software) [6569]

Chesterland

Hobby House Inc. (Toys and Hobby Goods) [26518]

Chillicothe

Litter Distributing Co. (Alcoholic Beverages) [1823]
Litter Industries Inc. (Alcoholic Beverages) [1824]

Cincinnati

A/E MicroSystems Inc. (Computers and Software) [5858]
Adam Wholesalers Inc. (Construction Materials and Machinery) [6913]
Advanced Office Systems Inc. (Office Equipment and Supplies) [20777]
AIMS International Books, Inc. (Books and Other Printed Materials) [3478]
Alco Building Products Co. (Construction Materials and Machinery) [6930]
Allied Electronics (Electrical and Electronic Equipment and Supplies) [8304]
American Compressed Steel Corp. (Specialty Equipment and Products) [25549]
Arling Lumber Inc. (Construction Materials and Machinery) [6985]
Ashwood Computer Co. (Computers and Software) [5972]
Automotive International Inc. (Chemicals) [4332]
Becker Electric Supply (Electrical and Electronic Equipment and Supplies) [8427]
Becksmith Co. (Toys and Hobby Goods) [26414]
Belmer Co.; H. (Hardware) [13591]
Best Sausage Inc. (Food) [10548]
Better Telephones and Technology Inc. (Communications Systems and Equipment) [5531]
Bill's Battery Co. Inc. (Automotive) [2362]
Breeders Edge (Veterinary Products) [27092]
Buckeye Sales Inc. (Horticultural Supplies) [14831]
Cas Ker Co. (Jewelry) [17361]
Castle Metals Inc. (Metals) [19864]
Catanzaro Sons and Daughters Inc.; Frank (Food) [10714]
CBS Contractors Supply Co. (Construction Materials and Machinery) [7155]
CBS Technologies LLC (Communications Systems and Equipment) [5551]
CDC (Floorcovering Equipment and Supplies) [9781]
Chemed Corp. (Cleaning and Janitorial Supplies) [4597]
Cincinnati Bell Long Distance Inc. (Communications Systems and Equipment) [5561]
Cincinnati Belt & Transmission (Automotive) [2449]
Cincinnati Container Co. (Storage Equipment and Containers) [25901]
Cincinnati Cordage and Paper Co. (Paper and Paper Products) [21679]
Cincinnati Gasket Packing Manufacturing Inc. (Industrial Supplies) [16799]
Cincinnati Steel Products (Metals) [19879]
Cinti Floor Co. (Floorcovering Equipment and Supplies) [9805]
Cinti Floor Co. (Household Items) [15444]
Clarke Detroit Diesel-Allison Inc. (Automotive) [2453]
Clipper Products (Luggage and Leather Goods) [18383]
Club Chef (Food) [10778]
Color Brite Fabrics and Displays Inc. (Specialty Equipment and Products) [25605]
Command Uniforms (Clothing) [4890]
Contract Interiors (Furniture and Fixtures) [13081]
Coors Brothers Co. (Food) [10837]
Cornerstone Controls Inc. (Electrical and Electronic Equipment and Supplies) [8582]
David Shoe Co. (Shoes) [24723]
Davitt and Hanser Music Co. (Sound and Entertainment Equipment and Supplies) [25159]
Davitt and Hanser Music Co. (Household Appliances) [15105]
Dennert Distributing Corp.; H. (Alcoholic Beverages) [1641]
Diehl Steel Co (Metals) [19931]
Diversified Ophthalmics, Inc. (Medical, Dental, and Optical Supplies) [19285]
Douglass Co.; J.R. (Scientific and Measurement Devices) [24347]
Dynamic Technology (Industrial Supplies) [16844]
Eberle Sons Co.; C. (Food) [11019]
Frederick Steel Co. (Metals) [19986]
Gateway Tire Company Inc. (Automotive) [2663]
Gateway Tire Company Inc. (Rubber) [24276]

General Electric Co. Marine and Industrial Engines Div. (Industrial Machinery) [16054]
General Sales Co. (Toys and Hobby Goods) [26496]
Gibson Group Inc. (Paper and Paper Products) [21739]
Globe Business Resources Inc. (Furniture and Fixtures) [13122]
Gold Medal Products Co. (Specialty Equipment and Products) [25663]
Habegger Corp. (Heating and Cooling Equipment and Supplies) [14476]
Henkel Corp. Chemicals Group (Chemicals) [4414]
Hill and Griffith Co. (Minerals and Ores) [20545]
Hillman Fastener (Hardware) [13753]
Hughes-Peters Inc. (Electrical and Electronic Equipment and Supplies) [8864]
HVC Inc. (Chemicals) [4423]
Hyster MidEast (Industrial Machinery) [16134]
IDG (Industrial Supplies) [16937]
Infocase Inc. (Luggage and Leather Goods) [18401]
Interior Services Inc. (Office Equipment and Supplies) [21062]
Interior Services Inc. (Furniture and Fixtures) [13143]
Ion Technologies Corp. (Industrial Machinery) [16172]
Jay Instrument and Specialty Co. (Electrical and Electronic Equipment and Supplies) [8909]
Johnson-Doppler Lumber Co. (Construction Materials and Machinery) [7536]
Johnson Electric Supply Co. (Electrical and Electronic Equipment and Supplies) [8916]
Johnson Supply Controls Center (Electrical and Electronic Equipment and Supplies) [8918]
Joseph Co.; David J. (Used, Scrap, and Recycled Materials) [26857]
Joseph Co., Ferrous Div.; David J. (Used, Scrap, and Recycled Materials) [26858]
Joseph Co. International Div.; David J. (Used, Scrap, and Recycled Materials) [26859]
Joseph Co. Municipal Recycling Div.; David J. (Used, Scrap, and Recycled Materials) [26860]
Joseph Co. Nonferrous Div.; David J. (Used, Scrap, and Recycled Materials) [26861]
Kalthoff International (Computers and Software) [6416]
KD Lamp Co. (Automotive) [2843]
Keidel Supply Co. (Plumbing Materials and Fixtures) [23228]
Kett Tool Co. (Hardware) [13785]
Kindel Co.; J.A. (Furniture and Fixtures) [13157]
Kitrick Management Company, Ltd. (Scientific and Measurement Devices) [24383]
Klosterman Baking Co. Inc. (Food) [11626]
Kramig Company Inc.; R.E. (Construction Materials and Machinery) [7571]
Landrum News Agency—Cincinnati Div. (Books and Other Printed Materials) [3893]
Lawrence Electric Co.; F.D. (Electrical and Electronic Equipment and Supplies) [8974]
Levine & Co.; L (Metals) [20125]
Lovejoy Industries, Inc. (Metals) [20136]
M & B Distributors, Inc. (Food) [11749]
M and M Metals International Inc. (Used, Scrap, and Recycled Materials) [26890]
Machine Drive (Industrial Machinery) [16253]
Marshmallow Products Inc. (Food) [11791]
MarshmallowCone Co. (Food) [11792]
Mees Distributors (Floorcovering Equipment and Supplies) [10021]
Metro Recycling Co. (Paper and Paper Products) [21833]
Metro Recycling Co. Imagination Store Co. (Used, Scrap, and Recycled Materials) [26909]
Midwest Music Distributors (Sound and Entertainment Equipment and Supplies) [25322]
Mohawk Machinery Inc. (Industrial Machinery) [16318]
Moskowitz Brothers (Used, Scrap, and Recycled Materials) [26918]
Murphy Door Specialties Inc.; Don (Construction Materials and Machinery) [7755]

Mutual Manufacturing and Supply Co. (Heating and Cooling Equipment and Supplies) [14615]
New Horizons Meats and Dist., L.L.C. (Food) [12003]
Nightingale Medical Equipment Services Inc. (Medical, Dental, and Optical Supplies) [19496]
Nine West Group (Shoes) [24822]
Ohio Agriculture and Turf Systems Inc. (Agricultural Equipment and Supplies) [1102]
Ohio Tile & Marble Co. (Floorcovering Equipment and Supplies) [10083]
Ohio Tile and Marble Co. (Construction Materials and Machinery) [7806]
Ohio Truck Equipment, Inc. (Automotive) [3059]
Ohio Valley Flooring (Floorcovering Equipment and Supplies) [10084]
Ohio Valley Supply Co. (Construction Materials and Machinery) [7807]
OKI Systems Ltd. (Industrial Machinery) [16360]
Olympic Flooring Distributors Inc. (Floorcovering Equipment and Supplies) [10087]
Otis Distributors (Restaurant and Commercial Foodservice Equipment and Supplies) [24200]
P-G Products Inc. (Automotive) [3069]
Pabco Fluid Power Co. (Industrial Machinery) [16369]
Paddock Seating Co. (Furniture and Fixtures) [13200]
Pearsol's Parts Center (Household Appliances) [15268]
Phone Land Inc. (Computers and Software) [6617]
Primesource (Specialty Equipment and Products) [25790]
Primesource (Photographic Equipment and Supplies) [22893]
Professional Telecommunication Services Inc. (Communications Systems and Equipment) [5721]
Pugh & Associates, Inc.; C.L. (Electrical and Electronic Equipment and Supplies) [9246]
QCA Inc. (Sound and Entertainment Equipment and Supplies) [25395]
Queen City Home Health Care Inc. (Medical, Dental, and Optical Equipment) [19004]
Reiner Enterprises (Plumbing Materials and Fixtures) [23338]
Riemeier Lumber Company Inc. (Construction Materials and Machinery) [7933]
Rim and Wheel Service Inc. (Automotive) [3160]
Rivard International Corp. (Construction Materials and Machinery) [7939]
Roma Enterprises (Sound and Entertainment Equipment and Supplies) [25421]
Roofing Distributing Company Inc. (Construction Materials and Machinery) [7957]
Sabin Robbins Paper Co. (Paper and Paper Products) [21918]
Schlachter Co. Inc.; Edward J. (Food) [12427]
Schuster Electronics Inc. (Electrical and Electronic Equipment and Supplies) [9343]
Seven Hills Book Distributors Inc. (Books and Other Printed Materials) [4155]
Seven-Up Royal Crown (Soft Drinks) [25036]
S.G. & B. Inc. (Furniture and Fixtures) [13238]
SNACC Distributing Co. (Food) [12521]
South Central Pool Supply, Inc. (Recreational and Sporting Goods) [23959]
Squeri FoodService (Food) [12560]
Standard Publishing Co. (Books and Other Printed Materials) [4188]
Superior Pharmaceutical Co. (Medical, Dental, and Optical Equipment) [19644]
Sysco Food Service of Cincinnati Inc. (Food) [12669]
T-Shirt City Inc. (Clothing) [5416]
Tasty Foods/VCA (Veterinary Products) [27244]
Tel-Data Communications Inc. (Communications Systems and Equipment) [5779]
Texo Corp. (Chemicals) [4529]
Topicz (Tobacco Products) [26360]
United States Medical Corp. (Medical, Dental, and Optical Equipment) [19095]
United States Medical Corp. (Medical, Dental, and Optical Supplies) [19680]

Valley National Gases, Inc. (Industrial Machinery) [16598]
Western Home Center Inc. (Construction Materials and Machinery) [8207]
Western Home Center Inc. (Wood and Wood Products) [27394]
xpedx (Paper and Paper Products) [22004]

Circleville
Circleville Oil Co. (Petroleum, Fuels, and Related Equipment) [22140]

Cleveland
A and D Auto Parts Inc. (Automotive) [2155]
Advanced Federated Protection Inc. (Security and Safety Equipment) [24493]
Aetna Plastics Corp. (Plastics) [22919]
American Fastener Specialty Company (Hardware) [13557]
American Tank and Fabricating Co (Metals) [19773]
Americo Wholesale Plumbing Supply Co. (Plumbing Materials and Fixtures) [23064]
Applied Industrial Technologies Inc. (Automotive) [2247]
Applied Technology Ventures Inc. (Computers and Software) [5954]
Aspen Imaging International Inc. (Computers and Software) [5975]
Associated Steel Corp. (Metals) [19787]
Astrokam (Electrical and Electronic Equipment and Supplies) [8389]
Astrup Co. (Textiles and Notions) [25970]
Atlas Inc. (Metals) [19789]
Auto Bolt & Nut Co. (Hardware) [13577]
Avcom, Inc. (Electrical and Electronic Equipment and Supplies) [8400]
B and B Paper Converters Inc. (Paper and Paper Products) [21643]
Bearing Distributors (Industrial Supplies) [16729]
Bearings Inc. (Industrial Supplies) [16739]
Bickford Flavors Inc. (Food) [10553]
Bissett Steel Co (Metals) [19824]
Bolts & Nuts Inc. (Electrical and Electronic Equipment and Supplies) [8453]
Bowman Distribution (Industrial Supplies) [16759]
BP America Inc. (Aeronautical Equipment and Supplies) [60]
BP Oil Co. (Petroleum, Fuels, and Related Equipment) [22089]
Bruening Bearings Inc. (Industrial Machinery) [15850]
Carnegie Body Co. (Automotive) [2425]
Cavalier, Gulling, and Wilson Inc. (Food) [10717]
Chandler Products Co. (Hardware) [13631]
Chilcote Co. (Photographic Equipment and Supplies) [22844]
Cleveland Hobby Supply (Toys and Hobby Goods) [26444]
Cleveland Plant and Flower Co. (Horticultural Supplies) [14842]
Cleveland Plywood Co. (Construction Materials and Machinery) [7183]
Columbia Iron and Metal Co. (Metals) [19882]
Columbia National Group Inc. (Metals) [19883]
Commerce Consultants Inc. (Petroleum, Fuels, and Related Equipment) [22154]
Commercial Electric Products Corp. (Electrical and Electronic Equipment and Supplies) [8551]
Connell L.P. Luria Brothers Div. (Used, Scrap, and Recycled Materials) [26783]
Consumers Plumbing Heating Supply (Plumbing Materials and Fixtures) [23125]
Consumers Steel Products Co. (Metals) [19893]
Contemporary Office Products Inc. (Office Equipment and Supplies) [20910]
D and B Steel Co. (Metals) [19913]
Davis Bakery Inc. (Food) [10915]
Dealers Food Products Co. (Food) [10927]
Dealers Food Products Co. (Food) [10928]
Decker Steel and Supply Inc. (Metals) [19921]
Dixie Bearings Inc. (Automotive) [2550]
D.J. Enterprises, Inc. (Minerals and Ores) [20533]
Dougherty Hanna Resources Co. (Construction Materials and Machinery) [7284]

Dougherty Lumber Co. (Construction Materials and Machinery) [7285]
Downing Coal Co. (Minerals and Ores) [20534]
FFR Inc. (Specialty Equipment and Products) [25649]
Forest City-Babin Co. (Construction Materials and Machinery) [7357]
Forest City Enterprises Inc. (Wood and Wood Products) [27305]
Forest City-North America Lumber (Construction Materials and Machinery) [7358]
Fullwell Products Inc. (Automotive) [2656]
Gahr Machine Co. (Industrial Machinery) [16046]
Garick Corp. (Wood and Wood Products) [27308]
General Steel Corp. (Metals) [19996]
Gillmore Security Systems Inc. (Security and Safety Equipment) [24556]
Grafix Plastic (Plastics) [22973]
Graphco (Specialty Equipment and Products) [25667]
Graphic Arts Systems Inc. (Plastics) [22974]
HA-LO (Clothing) [5009]
Ha-Lo Marketing (Clothing) [5010]
Hattenbach Co. (Construction Materials and Machinery) [7454]
Heritage Industries (Hardware) [13752]
Highway Metal Services Inc. (Metals) [20038]
The Hillcraft Group (Paper and Paper Products) [21761]
Hillcrest Food Service Co. (Paper and Paper Products) [21762]
Holcomb's Education Resource (Office Equipment and Supplies) [21036]
Holcomb's Education Resource (Office Equipment and Supplies) [21037]
Honeywell Protection Services (Security and Safety Equipment) [24567]
HSB Computer Laboratories (Computers and Software) [6345]
ICI Paints (Paints and Varnishes) [21463]
J and L Strong Tool Co. (Industrial Machinery) [16180]
Jay Mart Wholesale (Sound and Entertainment Equipment and Supplies) [25259]
Ken-Mac Metals Inc. (Metals) [20095]
Kindt Collins Co. (Specialty Equipment and Products) [25700]
Kraft Korner Inc. (Toys and Hobby Goods) [26556]
Lakeside Supply Company Inc. (Plumbing Materials and Fixtures) [23239]
Leff Electric Co.; H. (Electrical and Electronic Equipment and Supplies) [8979]
Lempco Industries Inc. (Industrial Supplies) [16996]
LTV Corp. (Petroleum, Fuels, and Related Equipment) [22440]
Martindale Electric Co. (Electrical and Electronic Equipment and Supplies) [9042]
Matex Products, Inc. (Metals) [20157]
MBS/Net, Inc. (Computers and Software) [6474]
Meier Transmission Ltd. (Electrical and Electronic Equipment and Supplies) [9063]
Melin Tool Company Inc. (Industrial Machinery) [16288]
Midland Aluminum Corp. (Metals) [20186]
The Millcraft Group (Paper and Paper Products) [21837]
Millcraft Paper Co. (Paper and Paper Products) [21838]
Millers Rents & Sells (Medical, Dental, and Optical Supplies) [19465]
Miltex International Inc. (Textiles and Notions) [26148]
Monarch Steel Company Inc. (Metals) [20202]
Morris Co.; S.G. (Industrial Machinery) [16324]
Multicraft Inc. (Specialty Equipment and Products) [25746]
National Safety Apparel Inc. (Security and Safety Equipment) [24600]
New United Distributors (Paints and Varnishes) [21518]
Northcoast Business Systems Inc. (Office Equipment and Supplies) [21164]
Northern Ohio Lumber and Timber Co. (Construction Materials and Machinery) [7797]

Northern Ohio Lumber and Timber Co. (Wood and Wood Products) [27351]
Ohio Business Machines Inc. (Office Equipment and Supplies) [21195]
Ohio Calculating Inc. (Office Equipment and Supplies) [21196]
Ohio Desk Co. (Office Equipment and Supplies) [21197]
Ohio Farmers Inc. (Food) [12055]
Ohio Kitchen and Bath (Household Items) [15601]
Ohio Pipe and Supply Company Inc. (Plumbing Materials and Fixtures) [23302]
Ohio Pipe Valves and Fittings Inc. (Industrial Supplies) [17087]
Overseas Capital Corp. (Chemicals) [4478]
Parts Associates Inc. (Hardware) [13864]
Phillips, Day and Maddock Inc. (Construction Materials and Machinery) [7861]
Pickands Mather, Ltd. (Metals) [20276]
Pioneer Manufacturing Co. (Paints and Varnishes) [21540]
Pioneer-Standard Electronics Inc. (Electrical and Electronic Equipment and Supplies) [9209]
Plastic Safety Systems, Inc. (Security and Safety Equipment) [24613]
PMC Specialties Group (Industrial Supplies) [17109]
Premier Farnell Corp. (Electrical and Electronic Equipment and Supplies) [9234]
Premier Industrial Corp. (Automotive) [3117]
Premier Medical Supplies Inc. (Medical, Dental, and Optical Equipment) [18993]
Pubco (Clothing) [5292]
Pugh & Associates, Inc.; C.L. (Electrical and Electronic Equipment and Supplies) [9244]
Quality First Greetings Corp. (Paper and Paper Products) [21894]
Racom Products Inc. (Communications Systems and Equipment) [5726]
Radix Wire Co. (Electrical and Electronic Equipment and Supplies) [9260]
Randolph Distributing Corp. (Furniture and Fixtures) [13216]
Reese Chemical Co. (Health and Beauty Aids) [14212]
Reese Chemical Co. (Medical, Dental, and Optical Supplies) [19572]
Reese Pharmaceutical Co. (Medical, Dental, and Optical Supplies) [19573]
Refrigeration Sales Corp. (Heating and Cooling Equipment and Supplies) [14657]
Research Environmental Industries (Used, Scrap, and Recycled Materials) [26957]
Reserve Iron and Metal L.P. (Metals) [20316]
Revere Products (Construction Materials and Machinery) [7922]
Riverside Drives Inc. (Automotive) [3164]
S and S Inc. (Paper and Paper Products) [21917]
Safeway Tire Co. (Automotive) [3182]
Safier's Inc. (Food) [12387]
Sailing Inc. (Marine) [18597]
Samsel Supply Co. (Construction Materials and Machinery) [7974]
Sanson Co. (Food) [12409]
Seaforth Mineral and Ore Company Inc. (Chemicals) [4504]
Servall Co. (Household Appliances) [15309]
Slife and Associates; Robert M. (Industrial Machinery) [16496]
Staples Business Advantage (Office Equipment and Supplies) [21287]
Strong Tool Co. (Hardware) [13941]
Sunshine Industries Inc. (Hardware) [13944]
Sussen Inc. (Automotive) [3288]
S.W. Controls, Inc. (Scientific and Measurement Devices) [24441]
Towlift Inc. (Industrial Machinery) [16571]
Udelson Equipment Co. (Industrial Machinery) [16586]
Unger Co. (Paper and Paper Products) [21958]
United Automatic Heating Supplies (Heating and Cooling Equipment and Supplies) [14744]
Universal Steel Co. (Metals) [20468]
Valley Ford Truck Sales (Automotive) [3385]
Van Roy Coffee Co. (Food) [12824]

Victory White Metal Co. (Industrial Supplies) [17253]
VillaWare Manufacturing Co. (Household Appliances) [15360]
Vita-Mix Corp. (Household Appliances) [15361]
VWS Inc. (Sound and Entertainment Equipment and Supplies) [25511]
WACO Scaffolding and Equipment Co. (Construction Materials and Machinery) [8189]
Weber Co.; H.J. (Floorcovering Equipment and Supplies) [10290]
Weiler Wilhelm Window and Door Co. (Construction Materials and Machinery) [8201]
Weldon Tool Co. (Industrial Machinery) [16620]
Welker-McKee Supply Co. Division of Hajoca (Plumbing Materials and Fixtures) [23449]
White Sewing Machine Co. (Household Appliances) [15371]
Wilkoff and Sons Co.; S. (Used, Scrap, and Recycled Materials) [27048]
Yen Enterprises Inc. (Metals) [20503]
Zagar Inc. (Industrial Machinery) [16658]

Coldwater

Hemmelgran and Sons Inc. (Food) [11411]
Lefeld Implement Inc. (Agricultural Equipment and Supplies) [950]

Columbiana

Witmer's Inc. (Agricultural Equipment and Supplies) [1457]

Columbus

Abbott Foods Inc. (Restaurant and Commercial Foodservice Equipment and Supplies) [24053]
Apparel Exprex Inc. (Clothing) [4777]
Ashland Chemical Co. (Chemicals) [4326]
Auddino's Italian Bakery Inc. (Food) [10469]
Awareness and Health Unlimited (Health and Beauty Aids) [14031]
B & A Paint Co. (Paints and Varnishes) [21396]
Barnebey and Sutcliffe Corp. (Heating and Cooling Equipment and Supplies) [14338]
Bauer & Foss, Inc. (Alcoholic Beverages) [1505]
Berwick Steel Co (Metals) [19817]
Broad Street Oil & Gas Co. (Petroleum, Fuels, and Related Equipment) [22095]
Brothers Office Supply Inc. (Office Equipment and Supplies) [20859]
Brown Steel Div. (Metals) [19840]
Buckeye Industrial Supply Company (Industrial Machinery) [15854]
Byers Sons Inc.; Geo. (Motorized Vehicles) [20608]
Callif Co. (Food) [10680]
Cantwell Machinery Co. (Construction Materials and Machinery) [7135]
CDC (Floorcovering Equipment and Supplies) [9782]
Cisco Electrical Supply Co. (Electrical and Electronic Equipment and Supplies) [8526]
Claprood Co.; Roman J. (Horticultural Supplies) [14841]
Clinton Gas Marketing Inc. (Computers and Software) [6076]
Columbus Distributing Co. (Alcoholic Beverages) [1608]
Columbus Fair Auto Auction Inc. (Motorized Vehicles) [20614]
Columbus Hardware Supplies Inc. (Hardware) [13641]
Columbus Pipe and Equipment Co. (Plumbing Materials and Fixtures) [23120]
Columbus Serum Co. (Veterinary Products) [27110]
Consolidated International (Gifts and Novelties) [13334]
Continental Office Furniture and Supply Corp. (Furniture and Fixtures) [13080]
Cottingham Paper Co. (Paper and Paper Products) [21694]
Cranel Inc. (Computers and Software) [6167]
De Lille Oxygen Co. (Industrial Supplies) [16822]
Dixie International Co. (Automotive) [2551]

Eastern Moulding, Inc. (Furniture and Fixtures) [13099]
Electric Motor and Control Corp. (Electrical and Electronic Equipment and Supplies) [8661]
Federation of Ohio River Co-ops (Food) [11116]
Florida Tile (Floorcovering Equipment and Supplies) [9902]
Florig Equipment (Electrical and Electronic Equipment and Supplies) [8747]
Fournier Rubber and Supply Co. (Industrial Supplies) [16877]
Fyda Freightliner Inc. (Motorized Vehicles) [20639]
Gardner Inc. (Agricultural Equipment and Supplies) [725]
Good Apple (Books and Other Printed Materials) [3785]
Hamilton-Parker, Co. (Floorcovering Equipment and Supplies) [9935]
Hammond Electronics (Sound and Entertainment Equipment and Supplies) [25224]
Health and Leisure Mart Inc. (Recreational and Sporting Goods) [23719]
Hydraulic and Air Controls (Industrial Machinery) [16129]
Interior Supply Inc. (Construction Materials and Machinery) [7515]
Karn Meats Inc. (Food) [11582]
Karshner Ceramics Inc. (Toys and Hobby Goods) [26549]
Klosterman Bakery Outlet (Food) [11625]
Krema Nut Co. (Food) [11649]
Landrum News Agency Inc. (Books and Other Printed Materials) [3894]
Loeb Electric Co. (Electrical and Electronic Equipment and Supplies) [9000]
Mason Supply Co. (Heating and Cooling Equipment and Supplies) [14533]
McAlister Camera Co.; Don (Photographic Equipment and Supplies) [22876]
Mees Distributors (Floorcovering Equipment and Supplies) [10022]
Mid-State Bolt and Nut Company Inc. (Hardware) [13827]
Mooney Process Equipment Co. (Plumbing Materials and Fixtures) [23275]
Morgan Forest Products (Construction Materials and Machinery) [7745]
Murphy Co. (Photographic Equipment and Supplies) [22881]
Nu-Look Fashions Inc. (Clothing) [5243]
OASIS Corp. (Specialty Equipment and Products) [25769]
Ohio Auto Rebuilders Supply, Inc. (Automotive) [3057]
Ohio Steak and Barbecue Co. (Food) [12056]
Ohio Transmission Corp. (Compressors) [5845]
PDQ Air Service Inc. (Petroleum, Fuels, and Related Equipment) [22555]
Pugh & Associates, Inc.; C.L. (Electrical and Electronic Equipment and Supplies) [9245]
Quality Bakery Co. (Food) [12246]
Ramson's Imports (Gifts and Novelties) [13433]
Rose Products and Services Inc. (Cleaning and Janitorial Supplies) [4699]
Ross-Willoughby Co. (Industrial Machinery) [16460]
Ruff and Co.; Thomas W. (Office Equipment and Supplies) [21253]
S-T Leather Co. (Livestock and Farm Products) [18216]
Sales Results (Food) [12397]
SARCOM Inc. (Computers and Software) [6704]
Southard Supply Inc. (Plumbing Materials and Fixtures) [23392]
Spartan Tool Supply (Hardware) [13931]
Squire Supply Corp. (Heating and Cooling Equipment and Supplies) [14694]
Star Beacon Products Co. (Specialty Equipment and Products) [25830]
SYGMA Network of Ohio Inc. (Food) [12663]
Tanner Enterprises, Inc. (Food) [12696]
Tiger Machinery Co. (Construction Materials and Machinery) [8131]
Tomasco Mulciber Inc. (Automotive) [3317]
Toombs Truck and Equipment Co. (Industrial Machinery) [16567]

Twyman Templeton Company Inc. (Security and Safety Equipment) [24648]
Ultra Hydraulics Inc. (Industrial Supplies) [17239]
Unico Alloys Inc. (Metals) [20457]
United Producers, Inc. (Livestock and Farm Products) [18304]
University Book Service (Books and Other Printed Materials) [4245]
Value City Furniture Div. (Furniture and Fixtures) [13267]
Vorys Brothers Inc. (Heating and Cooling Equipment and Supplies) [14757]
Wasserstrom Co. (Office Equipment and Supplies) [21348]
Williams Co.; W.W. (Industrial Machinery) [16635]
Williams Detroit Diesel Allison (Automotive) [3434]
Worthington Industries Inc. (Metals) [20499]
Worthington Steel Co. (Metals) [20500]

Conover
Fiebiger and Son Inc.; Jim (Agricultural Equipment and Supplies) [682]

Copley
Chemical Associates of Illinois, Inc. (Chemicals) [4353]
Fromm, Inc.; R.K. (Industrial Machinery) [16041]

Coshocton
Coshocton Grain Co. (Livestock and Farm Products) [17799]
Novelty Advertising Co. (Books and Other Printed Materials) [4011]

Covington
Ebbert's Field Seed Inc. (Agricultural Equipment and Supplies) [540]

Croton
Ohio Seed Company Inc. (Agricultural Equipment and Supplies) [1103]

Cuyahoga Falls
Cenweld Corp. (Automotive) [2441]
Vital Image Technology Inc. (Computers and Software) [6854]

Danville
Patented Products Inc. (Household Items) [15614]

Dayton
Astro Industries Inc. (Electrical and Electronic Equipment and Supplies) [8388]
Becker Co.; J.A. (Electrical and Electronic Equipment and Supplies) [8426]
BMS Inc. - Barcoded Management Systems, Inc. (Computers and Software) [6018]
Consolidated Electronics Inc. (Electrical and Electronic Equipment and Supplies) [8573]
Cooper Power Tools Division-Apex (Aeronautical Equipment and Supplies) [75]
Dayton Appliance Parts Co. (Household Appliances) [15106]
Dayton Door Sales Inc. (Construction Materials and Machinery) [7253]
Dills Supply Co./Division of Dayton Supply and Tool (Industrial Supplies) [16832]
Duellman Electric Co. (Electrical and Electronic Equipment and Supplies) [8638]
Dynamic Technology (Industrial Supplies) [16843]
Electro-Line Inc. (Electrical and Electronic Equipment and Supplies) [8683]
Erb Lumber Co. Materials Distributors Div. (Construction Materials and Machinery) [7316]
Fair Company Inc.; R.E. (Automotive) [2605]
Gosiger Inc. (Industrial Machinery) [16072]
Grismer Tire Co. (Automotive) [2707]
HAZCO Services Inc. (Scientific and Measurement Devices) [24368]
The Iams Co. (Veterinary Products) [27154]
Keilson-Dayton Co. (Tobacco Products) [26317]
KK Motorcycle Supply (Automotive) [2858]
Lotz Paper and Fixture Co.; F.W. (Paper and Paper Products) [21814]

Mead Pulp Sales Inc. (Paper and Paper Products) [21831]
Mees Distributors (Floorcovering Equipment and Supplies) [10023]
Midwest Optical Laboratories, Inc. (Medical, Dental, and Optical Supplies) [19462]
Mike-Sell's Inc. (Food) [11891]
Mike-Sell's Potato Chip Co. (Food) [11893]
Outdoor Sports Headquarters Inc. (Recreational and Sporting Goods) [23864]
Palmer-Donovan Manufacturing (Construction Materials and Machinery) [7831]
Pickrel Brothers Inc. (Plumbing Materials and Fixtures) [23315]
Polycrystal Book Service (Books and Other Printed Materials) [4071]
Primus Inc. (Plumbing Materials and Fixtures) [23329]
Scott Industrial Systems Inc. (Industrial Supplies) [17161]
Seven-Up Dayton Div. (Soft Drinks) [25035]
Sterling Rubber and Plastics (Rubber) [24296]
Super Food Services Inc. (Food) [12623]
Supply One Corp. (Plumbing Materials and Fixtures) [23400]
Wagner-Smith Co. (Industrial Supplies) [17259]
Winnelson Inc. (Plumbing Materials and Fixtures) [23463]
World Wen, Inc. (Computers and Software) [6882]

Defiance
Browns Bakery Inc. (Food) [10630]
City Beverage Co. (Alcoholic Beverages) [1595]
Motor Master Products (Automotive) [2993]

Delphos
Drapery Stitch of Delphos (Household Items) [15480]
Miller Stockyards; A.E. (Livestock and Farm Products) [18101]

Dennison
Tusco Grocers Inc. (Food) [12777]

Dillonvale
New Cooperative Company Inc. (Food) [12000]
Valley Distributors Inc. (Alcoholic Beverages) [2094]

Dover
Barkett Fruit Co. Inc. (Food) [10507]
Ohio Light Truck Parts Co. (Automotive) [3058]

Dublin
Butler Co.; W.A. (Medical, Dental, and Optical Supplies) [19206]
Cardinal Health Inc. (Medical, Dental, and Optical Supplies) [19212]
Dublin Metal Corp. (Metals) [19937]
Dublin Yogurt Co. (Food) [10997]
Klein News Co.; George R. (Books and Other Printed Materials) [3882]
United Magazine Company (Books and Other Printed Materials) [4239]
United Magazine Company (Books and Other Printed Materials) [4240]

East Liverpool
Hill and Co., Inc.; O.S. (Motorized Vehicles) [20649]

Eaton
Wogaman Oil Co.; R.W. (Petroleum, Fuels, and Related Equipment) [22813]

Edgerton
Edgerton Forge Inc. (Industrial Machinery) [15977]

Edon
Edon Farmers Cooperative Association Inc. (Agricultural Equipment and Supplies) [543]

Elyria
Perkins Inc.; Julian W. (Petroleum, Fuels, and Related Equipment) [22564]

Royal Supply Inc. (Industrial Machinery) [16461]
Superior Electric Supply Co. (Elyria, Ohio) (Electrical and Electronic Equipment and Supplies) [9443]

Englewood
Northmont Sand and Gravel Co. (Minerals and Ores) [20554]

Euclid
U.S. Metal Service Inc. (Metals) [20464]

Fairfield
Blue Flame Div. (Petroleum, Fuels, and Related Equipment) [22081]
Chemicals Inc. (Chemicals) [4356]
Hern Marine (Marine) [18520]
Karp's BakeMark (Food) [11583]
The Kruse Company (Hardware) [13789]
Naz-Dar Cincinnati (Specialty Equipment and Products) [25752]

Findlay
Capitol Tire Shop (Automotive) [2417]
Cooper Tire & Rubber Co. (Automotive) [2483]
DIFCO Inc. (Railroad Equipment and Supplies) [23477]
Hercules/CEDCO (Automotive) [2742]
Hercules Tire and Rubber Co. (Rubber) [24281]
Marathon Ashland Petroleum L.L.C. (Petroleum, Fuels, and Related Equipment) [22450]
Reiter Dairy (Food) [12299]

Fletcher
Infotel (Computers and Software) [6371]
MidWest Micro (Computers and Software) [6517]
Teeters Products Inc. (Specialty Equipment and Products) [25838]

Forest Park
Irvin-Alan Fabrics (Textiles and Notions) [26076]

Ft. Loramie
Marwil Products Co. (Automotive) [2920]

Ft. Recovery
Fort Recovery Equity Exchange Co. (Veterinary Products) [27133]

Fostoria
Superior Distributing Co. (Alcoholic Beverages) [2062]

Fredericktown
Gregg Manufacturing Co. (Household Items) [15516]

Fremont
Beck Suppliers Inc. (Petroleum, Fuels, and Related Equipment) [22062]
Gries Seed Farms Inc. (Agricultural Equipment and Supplies) [768]
Rural Serv Inc. (Livestock and Farm Products) [18213]
Universal Industries Inc. (Specialty Equipment and Products) [25860]
Universal Industries Inc. (Construction Materials and Machinery) [8160]

Gahanna
Unisource Midwest Inc. (Paper and Paper Products) [21967]

Gibsonburg
CADCO Div. (Agricultural Equipment and Supplies) [355]
Chemi-Trol Chemical Co. (Agricultural Equipment and Supplies) [410]

Girard
Liberty Industries Inc. (Wood and Wood Products) [27334]
Robinson's Woods (Office Equipment and Supplies) [21245]

Stancorp Inc. (Construction Materials and
Machinery) [8066]
U.S. Extrusion Tool and Die (Industrial
Machinery) [16592]

Grafton
Town and Country Coop. (Agricultural Equipment
and Supplies) [1345]

Green Springs
Country Springs Farmers (Food) [10859]
River Springs Cooperative Association (Veterinary
Products) [27222]

Greenville
Buchy Food Products (Food) [10636]
Keller Grain and Feed Inc. (Livestock and Farm
Products) [18030]
Neff Athletic Lettering Co. (Clothing) [5220]
Treaty Co. (Plumbing Materials and
Fixtures) [23415]

Grove City
Ace Truck Body, Inc. (Automotive) [2171]
Grove City Farmers Exchange Co. (Agricultural
Equipment and Supplies) [771]

Groveport
Cuthbert Greenhouse Inc. (Horticultural
Supplies) [14848]
Cuthbert Greenhouse Inc. (Horticultural
Supplies) [14849]
Cuthbert Greenhouse Inc. (Horticultural
Supplies) [14850]
Willis Distribution Beauty Supply (Health and
Beauty Aids) [14283]

Hamilton
Ferguson Metals, Inc. (Metals) [19975]
Kornylak Corp. (Industrial Machinery) [16218]
R & L Electronics (Communications Systems and
Equipment) [5725]
Southwestern Ohio Steel Inc. (Metals) [20379]
Wise & Sons; A.B. (Food) [12968]

Harrison
Campbell Group (Industrial Machinery) [15869]
Hubert Co. (Food) [11472]

Hebron
Strait and Lamp Lumber Company
Inc. (Construction Materials and
Machinery) [8079]

Hicksville
Wholesale House (Sound and Entertainment
Equipment and Supplies) [25524]

Highland Heights
Morris Co.; S.G. (Industrial Machinery) [16326]

Hilliard
Cummins Ohio Inc. (Automotive) [2512]

Holland
International Projects Inc. (Recreational and
Sporting Goods) [23747]
Ruth Corp. (Industrial Machinery) [16464]
Tronair Inc. (Aeronautical Equipment and
Supplies) [163]

Hubbard
Federal Wholesale Company Inc. (Household
Items) [15495]

Hudson
Coyote Loader Sales Inc. (Construction Materials
and Machinery) [7228]
Design Impressions Inc. (Paints and
Varnishes) [21427]
Magnum Steel and Trading Inc. (Metals) [20144]

Independence
Allied Electronics (Electrical and Electronic
Equipment and Supplies) [8305]
MRK Technologies Ltd. (Computers and
Software) [6534]

Ironton
Mid-Valley Supply Co. (Industrial Supplies) [17037]

Jackson
Dearing Wholesale Inc. (Toys and Hobby
Goods) [26462]

Kalida
Unverferth Manufacturing Company Inc. (Agricultural
Equipment and Supplies) [1386]

Kent
Carter Lumber Co. (Construction Materials and
Machinery) [7148]
Components & Equipment International (Industrial
Machinery) [15907]
Land O Lakes Inc. (Food) [11672]
RB & W Corp. (Hardware) [13883]
Spellbinders Inc. (Toys and Hobby Goods) [26663]

Kenton
Robinson Fin Machines Inc. (Heating and Cooling
Equipment and Supplies) [14665]

Kingsville
Congress Leather Co. (Veterinary
Products) [27111]

Lakewood
Air Rite Filters Inc. (Heating and Cooling
Equipment and Supplies) [14306]

Leavittsburg
Denman Tire Corp. (Automotive) [2538]

Leesburg
Bobb Brothers Inc. (Livestock and Farm
Products) [17741]

Lemoyne
Williams Detroit Diesel Allison (Automotive) [3435]

Lewis Center
Digital Storage Inc. (Computers and
Software) [6210]

Lima
Better Brake Parts Inc. (Automotive) [2356]
Bornell Supply (Automotive) [2373]
Brunner News Agency (Books and Other Printed
Materials) [3597]
C & G Distributing Co. Inc. (Alcoholic
Beverages) [1563]
C.S.S. Publishing Co. (Books and Other Printed
Materials) [3675]
Diamond Distributors (Alcoholic Beverages) [1649]
Fruit Distributors Inc. (Food) [11221]
Green Gate Books (Books and Other Printed
Materials) [3799]
International Brake Industries
Inc. (Automotive) [2792]
OmniSource Lima Div. (Used, Scrap, and Recycled
Materials) [26930]
O.S.S. Publishing Co. (Books and Other Printed
Materials) [4026]
Rhoda Brothers-Steel & Welding (Metals) [20319]
Roundy's Inc. (Food) [12358]
Roundy's Inc. Lima Div. (Food) [12360]
Sealts Co.; J.M. (Food) [12450]
Siferd-Hossellman Co. (Automotive) [3221]
SWD Corp. (Tobacco Products) [26355]

Lisbon
Dickey and Son Inc.; D.W. (Construction Materials
and Machinery) [7263]

Lockbourne
Lockbourne Farmers Exchange Co. (Agricultural
Equipment and Supplies) [964]
Sand and Gravel Co.; J.P. (Construction Materials
and Machinery) [7977]

Lodi
Amazing Wind Machines Inc. (Agricultural
Equipment and Supplies) [231]
Log Cabin Sport Shop (Guns and
Weapons) [13499]

Logan
Elberfeld Company Inc. (Furniture and
Fixtures) [13104]

London
Madison Landmark Inc. (Livestock and Farm
Products) [18071]
Norse Motors Inc. (Automotive) [3039]

Lorain
Bostwick-Braun Lorain Div. (Industrial
Machinery) [15837]
DeSantis Distributors (Food) [10948]
Lakeland Enterprises, Inc. (Automotive) [2871]
Turtle Plastics Co. (Cleaning and Janitorial
Supplies) [4718]

Loveland
Bell; Philip M. (Furniture and Fixtures) [13034]
Bryan Equipment Sales Inc. (Industrial
Machinery) [15852]
Down Lite International (Household Items) [15479]
Seybold Co. (Cleaning and Janitorial
Supplies) [4706]
Vallery Co.; William G. (Toys and Hobby
Goods) [26703]

Macedonia
Berger Co.; B. (Textiles and Notions) [25981]
Bussert Industrial Supply Inc. (Industrial
Supplies) [16773]
Norandex Inc. (Construction Materials and
Machinery) [7787]
Norandex/Reynolds Distribution Co. (Construction
Materials and Machinery) [7788]

Malinta
Pohlman Farms; Henry G. (Livestock and Farm
Products) [18172]

Mansfield
Beckley-Cardy, Inc. (Office Equipment and
Supplies) [20838]
Beckly Cardy Group (Specialty Equipment and
Products) [25570]
Bissman Company Inc. (Alcoholic
Beverages) [1530]
Caldwell and Bloor Company Inc. (Medical, Dental,
and Optical Supplies) [19208]
Frey Scientific (Scientific and Measurement
Devices) [24363]
FSC Educational Inc. (Books and Other Printed
Materials) [3768]
Hartman-Spreng Co. (Electrical and Electronic
Equipment and Supplies) [8832]
Hoover Instrument Service Inc. (Scientific and
Measurement Devices) [24371]
Mansfield Bag & Paper Company Inc. (Paper and
Paper Products) [21820]
Mansfield Electric Supply Inc. (Electrical and
Electronic Equipment and Supplies) [9026]
Mansfield Typewriter Co. (Office Equipment and
Supplies) [21122]
Opportunities for Learning, Inc. (Books and Other
Printed Materials) [4023]
Wagner Hardware Co. (Hardware) [13982]

Maple Heights
The Metal Store (Metals) [20171]
Sherwood Food Distributors (Food) [12478]
Wine Distributors Inc. (Alcoholic Beverages) [2124]

Marietta
Broughton Foods LLC (Food) [10622]
Kardex Systems Inc. (Office Equipment and Supplies) [21086]
Marietta Ignition Inc. (Automotive) [2916]

Marion
Marion Steel Co. Scrap Div. (Used, Scrap, and Recycled Materials) [26898]
Probst Supply Co. (Plumbing Materials and Fixtures) [23331]
Riverside Homemade Ice Cream (Food) [12323]
Sims Brothers Inc. (Used, Scrap, and Recycled Materials) [26992]

Martins Ferry
Valley Vending Service Inc. (Tobacco Products) [26368]

Marysville
Florence Turfgrass; Paul (Horticultural Supplies) [14866]
Marysville Office Center (Office Equipment and Supplies) [21133]
Scott and Sons Co.; O.M. (Agricultural Equipment and Supplies) [1245]

Mason
C.M. Paula Co. (Paper and Paper Products) [21682]
Forte Industrial Equipment Systems Inc. (Industrial Machinery) [16032]
Forte Industries (Industrial Machinery) [16033]
Harris Corp. (Communications Systems and Equipment) [5630]

Massillon
ABM Distributors Inc. (Plumbing Materials and Fixtures) [23049]
Campbell Oil Co. (Petroleum, Fuels, and Related Equipment) [22105]
Fleming Foods of Ohio Inc. (Food) [11155]
Hydro Dyne Inc. (Industrial Machinery) [16132]
Ziegler Tire and Supply Co. (Automotive) [3455]

Maumee
Andersons Inc. (Agricultural Equipment and Supplies) [242]
Checker Distributors (Textiles and Notions) [26002]
Feldstein and Associates Inc. (Gifts and Novelties) [13356]
Hickory Farms Inc. (Food) [11427]

McComb
Blanchard Valley Farmers Cooperative (Livestock and Farm Products) [17737]

Medina
Anderson Recreational Design, Inc. (Recreational and Sporting Goods) [23518]
Bennett's Pet Center (Veterinary Products) [27080]
Fire-Dex Inc. (Specialty Equipment and Products) [25651]
Fire-Dex Inc. (Clothing) [4955]
Lumberton Industries Inc. (Industrial Supplies) [17008]
Medina Farmers Exchange Co. (Agricultural Equipment and Supplies) [1010]
Medina Landmark Inc. (Agricultural Equipment and Supplies) [1011]
Melchs Food Products Inc. (Food) [11846]
Pathon Co. (Industrial Machinery) [16383]
RPM Inc. (Construction Materials and Machinery) [7962]
Sandridge Foods Corp. (Food) [12405]
Sandridge Gourmet Salads (Food) [12406]
Wolff Brothers Supply Inc. (Plumbing Materials and Fixtures) [23466]

Mentor
Great Lakes Power Products (Marine) [18510]
Hauler & Wade Associates Inc. (Toys and Hobby Goods) [26512]
Mentor Lumber and Supply Company Inc. (Construction Materials and Machinery) [7694]
SuperGrind Co. (Industrial Supplies) [17205]

Metamora
Metamora Elevator Co. (Agricultural Equipment and Supplies) [1018]

Miamisburg
Mosier Fluid Power of Ohio Inc. (Industrial Supplies) [17054]
Zellerbach Co. (Paper and Paper Products) [22012]

Middleburg Heights
Music Sales International (Sound and Entertainment Equipment and Supplies) [25349]

Middlefield
Middlefield Optical Company, Inc. (Medical, Dental, and Optical Supplies) [19456]

Middletown
Aeronca Inc. (Aeronautical Equipment and Supplies) [28]
Namasco Div. (Metals) [20214]

Milford
Clermont Lumber Co. (Construction Materials and Machinery) [7181]
Zonic A and D Co. (Scientific and Measurement Devices) [24465]

Millersburg
Millersburg Tire Service Inc. (Automotive) [2972]

Millersport
Continental Midland (Hardware) [13644]

Minerva
Kepcor Inc. (Floorcovering Equipment and Supplies) [9988]

Mingo Junction
Iron City Distributing Company Inc. (Alcoholic Beverages) [1776]
KMC Corp. (Alcoholic Beverages) [1799]

Minster
Minster Farmers Cooperative Exchange Inc. (Livestock and Farm Products) [18105]

Mogadore
BICO Akron Inc. (Metals) [19823]

Monroe
Westchester Marketing (Clothing) [5482]

Monroeville
Midway Inc. (Automotive) [2955]

New Bavaria
Farmers Elevator Grain and Supply (Agricultural Equipment and Supplies) [646]

New Philadelphia
Fenton Brothers Electrical (Electrical and Electronic Equipment and Supplies) [8736]
Landmark Co-Op Inc. (Agricultural Equipment and Supplies) [935]

New Washington
Country Star Coop (Livestock and Farm Products) [17802]
White Co.; The C.E. (Automotive) [3425]

Newark
Dynacraft Golf Products, Inc. (Recreational and Sporting Goods) [23637]
Englefield Oil Co. (Petroleum, Fuels, and Related Equipment) [22232]
Maltby's Golfworks; Ralph (Recreational and Sporting Goods) [23798]

Newcomerstown
Tastee Apple Inc. (Food) [12699]

North Bend
Dee's Delights, Inc. (Toys and Hobby Goods) [26463]
Hobby Book Distributors (Books and Other Printed Materials) [3830]

North Canton
ADT Security Systems, Mid-South Inc. (Security and Safety Equipment) [24490]
ASW Aviation Services Inc. (Aeronautical Equipment and Supplies) [44]
Flower Factory (Office Equipment and Supplies) [21005]
GBS Corp. (Paper and Paper Products) [21736]
The Hoover Co. (Household Appliances) [15171]
Mathie Supply Inc. (Construction Materials and Machinery) [7669]
Muncer and Associates Inc.; J.B. (Computers and Software) [6535]
Service Packaging Corp. (Paper and Paper Products) [21935]
Spindler Co. (Food) [12555]
United Floral Supply Inc. (Horticultural Supplies) [14966]
Wilkof Morris Steel Corp. (Metals) [20491]

North Jackson
National Industrial Lumber Co. (Construction Materials and Machinery) [7764]

North Royalton
Gas Technics of Ohio (Industrial Supplies) [16889]
H and D Steel Service Inc. (Metals) [20024]
Reddish Supply; Phil (Sound and Entertainment Equipment and Supplies) [25414]

Norwalk
DL Pet Supply (Veterinary Products) [27116]
Hampton House (Furniture and Fixtures) [13126]
Maple City Ice Co. (Alcoholic Beverages) [1848]
Monroeville Co-op Grain (Livestock and Farm Products) [18110]
Sunrise Cooperative Inc. (Agricultural Equipment and Supplies) [1305]

Oberlin
NACSCORP (Books and Other Printed Materials) [3978]
National Association of College Stores Inc. (Books and Other Printed Materials) [3983]
Oberlin College Press-Field Magazine-Field Translation Series-Field Poetry Series-Field Editions (Books and Other Printed Materials) [4014]

Old Fort
River Spring Cooperative (Livestock and Farm Products) [18200]

Orrville
ORRCO, Inc. (Veterinary Products) [27202]

Painesville
Active Plumbing Supply Co. (Plumbing Materials and Fixtures) [23052]
Colony Lumber Co. (Construction Materials and Machinery) [7198]

Parma
Earnest Machine Products Co. (Hardware) [13673]

Pataskala
Allen Refractories Co. (Industrial Supplies) [16684]

Perry
Mid-West Materials Inc. (Metals) [20184]

Perrysburg
Defiance Inc. (Electrical and Electronic Equipment and Supplies) [8620]
Generic Systems Inc. (Electrical and Electronic Equipment and Supplies) [8784]

Heidelberg Distributing Co. (Alcoholic Beverages) [1749]

Morris Co.; S.G. (Industrial Machinery) [16325]

Temp Glass (Construction Materials and Machinery) [8105]

Pettisville

Pettisville Grain Company Inc. (Agricultural Equipment and Supplies) [1127]

Piqua

Berwick Steel Co. (Metals) [19818]

Bornell Supply Company Inc. (Industrial Machinery) [15832]

Forsythe Ice Cream (Food) [11191]

Miami Valley Steel Service Inc. (Metals) [20179]

Shank Spring Design Inc. (Hardware) [13915]

Plain City

Clark's Carpet Connection (Floorcovering Equipment and Supplies) [9809]

Judson Lumber Co. (Construction Materials and Machinery) [7539]

Judson Lumber Co. (Wood and Wood Products) [27325]

Poland

Conrad Sales Company, Inc. (Food) [10814]

Mahoning Valley Supply Co. (Industrial Supplies) [17012]

Port Clinton

Vita-Plate Battery, Inc. (Marine) [18631]

Reynoldsburg

Craft Wholesalers (Office Equipment and Supplies) [20936]

VMC/USA (Household Items) [15697]

Richfield

Park Orchards Inc. (Food) [12111]

Richmond

Anthony Mining, Inc. (Minerals and Ores) [20518]

Rising Sun

County Line Co-op (Agricultural Equipment and Supplies) [469]

Rocky River

LESCO Inc. (Agricultural Equipment and Supplies) [952]

Sabina

Sabina Farmers Exchange Inc. (Agricultural Equipment and Supplies) [1226]

Salem

Butech Inc. (Used, Scrap, and Recycled Materials) [26774]

Sandusky

Balloons, Logos & T-Shirts (Toys and Hobby Goods) [26410]

Brohl and Appell Inc. (Electrical and Electronic Equipment and Supplies) [8470]

District Petroleum Products Inc. (Petroleum, Fuels, and Related Equipment) [22204]

Meyer Co.; O.E. (Industrial Supplies) [17032]

Sandusky Electrical Inc. (Electrical and Electronic Equipment and Supplies) [9335]

Sandusky Industrial Supply (Automotive) [3186]

Sharon Center

Ohio Brake & Clutch (Industrial Supplies) [17086]

Shelby

Shelby Grain and Feed Co. (Agricultural Equipment and Supplies) [1264]

Sidney

Dixie Parts and Equipment Co. (Automotive) [2552]

Smithville

Gilbert Lumber/IFCO Systems (Storage Equipment and Containers) [25917]

Solon

Anderson Co.; SW (Electrical and Electronic Equipment and Supplies) [8353]

Anderson-DuBose Co. (Food) [10412]

Cincinnati Cordage and Paper Co. Cordage Papers Cleveland Div. (Paper and Paper Products) [21680]

Cone Instruments Inc. (Medical, Dental, and Optical Equipment) [18750]

Ehrke & Co.; A. (Industrial Supplies) [16846]

Marshall Industries (Electrical and Electronic Equipment and Supplies) [9035]

Mazel Stores Inc. (Specialty Equipment and Products) [25728]

North American Wire Products (Metals) [20232]

Pioneer (Electrical and Electronic Equipment and Supplies) [9205]

Stopol Inc. (Plastics) [23036]

TradeCom International Inc. (Hardware) [13961]

White Associates; Bob (Communications Systems and Equipment) [5813]

Southington

Tri-Blue Kennel (Veterinary Products) [27251]

Springboro

Darlington Farms (Food) [10910]

Miami-Luken Inc. (Medical, Dental, and Optical Supplies) [19453]

Mound Steel Corp. (Metals) [20208]

Springfield

Benjamin Steel Company Inc. (Metals) [19812]

Clark Landmark Inc. (Agricultural Equipment and Supplies) [423]

Eagle Beverage Co. (Alcoholic Beverages) [1663]

Fontaine Modification Co. (Automotive) [2636]

Pence International, Inc. (Clothing) [5273]

Ulery Greenhouse Co. (Horticultural Supplies) [14965]

Steubenville

Berkman Co.; Louis (Industrial Machinery) [15819]

Voto Manufacturing Sales Company Inc. (Industrial Supplies) [17258]

Stillwater

Laurel Valley Oil Co. (Petroleum, Fuels, and Related Equipment) [22418]

Laurel Valley Oil Co. (Petroleum, Fuels, and Related Equipment) [22419]

Stow

Audio-Technica U.S. Inc. (Electrical and Electronic Equipment and Supplies) [8394]

Audio-Technica U.S., Inc. (Sound and Entertainment Equipment and Supplies) [25089]

Matco Tools Corp. (Automotive) [2922]

TRC Industries Inc. (Rubber) [24302]

Streetsboro

Conversion Resources Inc. (Used, Scrap, and Recycled Materials) [26789]

Joseph Industries Inc. (Industrial Machinery) [16194]

Lovejoy Industries Inc. (Metals) [20137]

Mills Alloy Steel Co. (Metals) [20196]

Sandusco Inc. (Sound and Entertainment Equipment and Supplies) [25427]

Sandusco Inc. (Electrical and Electronic Equipment and Supplies) [9334]

Sandusky Distributing Co. (Sound and Entertainment Equipment and Supplies) [25428]

Singer Steel Co. (Metals) [20368]

St Lawrence Steel Corp. (Metals) [20385]

Strongsville

Aardvark Controls Equipment (Scientific and Measurement Devices) [24304]

A.C. Supply (Office Equipment and Supplies) [20767]

Cuyahoga Landmark Inc. (Petroleum, Fuels, and Related Equipment) [22185]

EMSCO (Recreational and Sporting Goods) [23650]

Fay Industries (Metals) [19966]

LamRite West Inc. (Gifts and Novelties) [13385]

Ohio Pool Equipment Supply Co. (Recreational and Sporting Goods) [23857]

Struthers

Universal Percussion (Sound and Entertainment Equipment and Supplies) [25492]

Sylvania

Angel Associates Inc.; Mike (Toys and Hobby Goods) [26393]

Jacobson Computer Inc. (Computers and Software) [6404]

Tallmadge

Independent Drug Co. (Medical, Dental, and Optical Supplies) [19368]

Leppo Inc. (Construction Materials and Machinery) [7597]

Ultrasource Inc. (Specialty Equipment and Products) [25851]

Tiffin

S & S Variety Beverages Inc. (Soft Drinks) [25030]

Tiffin Farmers Cooperative, Inc. (Agricultural Equipment and Supplies) [1335]

Titan Steel Co. (Metals) [20426]

Tipp City

Nova Steel Processing Inc. (Metals) [20241]

Trophy Nut Company (Food) [12759]

Toledo

Able Equipment Inc. (Construction Materials and Machinery) [6904]

Academi-Text Medical Wholesalers (Books and Other Printed Materials) [3460]

AP Parts Co. (Automotive) [2243]

Art Iron Inc. (Metals) [19784]

Baron Drawn Steel Corp. (Metals) [19804]

Bayer Wood Products (Toys and Hobby Goods) [26413]

Bohl Equipment Co. (Industrial Machinery) [15828]

Bostwick-Braun Co. (Hardware) [13604]

Brennan Industrial Truck Co. (Motorized Vehicles) [20605]

Capital Tire Inc. (Automotive) [2416]

Century Equipment Inc. (Agricultural Equipment and Supplies) [402]

Component Technology (Industrial Machinery) [15906]

D & J Manufacturing Inc. (Gifts and Novelties) [13343]

Derkin and Wise Inc. (Industrial Supplies) [16827]

Doral Steel Inc. (Metals) [19935]

Empire Petroleum Inc. (Petroleum, Fuels, and Related Equipment) [22228]

EPI Technologies, Inc. (Used, Scrap, and Recycled Materials) [26811]

Gross Electric Inc. (Electrical and Electronic Equipment and Supplies) [8820]

Heidtman Steel Products Inc. (Metals) [20032]

Kellermeyer Co. (Cleaning and Janitorial Supplies) [4649]

Kiemle-Hankins Co. (Electrical and Electronic Equipment and Supplies) [8943]

Kuhlman Corp. (Construction Materials and Machinery) [7572]

Meridian National Corp. (Metals) [20165]

Ohio Belt & Transmission (Industrial Machinery) [16358]

Ohio Overseas Corp. (Industrial Machinery) [16359]

Ottawa River Steel Co. (Metals) [20256]

Parker Steel Co. (Metals) [20265]

Perfect Measuring Tape Co. (Scientific and Measurement Devices) [24416]

Poll Electric Co.; H. (Electrical and Electronic Equipment and Supplies) [9216]

Reliable Belt & Transmission (Automotive) [3145]

Stump & Company Inc.; Weldon F. (Industrial
Machinery) [16533]
Tibbet Inc. (Office Equipment and
Supplies) [21319]
Time Service Inc. (Jewelry) [17638]
Titgemeiers Feed, Inc. (Agricultural Equipment and
Supplies) [1338]
Toledo Pickling and Steel Inc. (Metals) [20428]
Toledo Pickling and Steel Sales
Inc. (Metals) [20429]
Toledo Tile (Floorcovering Equipment and
Supplies) [10253]
Transport Equipment, Inc. (Automotive) [3329]
Tri-State Aluminum (Metals) [20442]
TW Metals Co. (Metals) [20449]
United Automatic Heating Supplies (Heating and
Cooling Equipment and Supplies) [14747]
West Equipment Company Inc. (Construction
Materials and Machinery) [8204]
Wilkins Supply Co.; M.P. (Plumbing Materials and
Fixtures) [23459]

Troy

Hobart Corp. (Industrial Machinery) [16105]
International Pizza Co. (Food) [11523]
Pal Productions Inc. (Toys and Hobby
Goods) [26603]

Twinsburg

Atlas Steel Products Co. (Metals) [19791]
Commercial Alloys Corp. (Metals) [19887]
Hitachi Medical Systems America Inc. (Computers
and Software) [6335]
Proctor Co.; Stanley M. (Industrial
Machinery) [16431]
RGH Enterprises Inc. (Medical, Dental, and Optical
Equipment) [19021]
RGH Enterprises Inc. (Medical, Dental, and Optical
Supplies) [19580]
Spencer Products Co. (Hardware) [13933]
Westguard Inc. (Security and Safety
Equipment) [24661]

Uniontown

American Business Machines (Office Equipment
and Supplies) [20791]
Hall Enterprises; Robert J. (Toys and Hobby
Goods) [26509]

Upper Sandusky

Schmidt Machine Co. (Agricultural Equipment and
Supplies) [1238]

Valley City

Independent Steel Co. (Metals) [20054]

Van Wert

Kennedy-Kuhn Inc. (Agricultural Equipment and
Supplies) [902]
Kennedy Manufacturing Co. (Industrial
Supplies) [16986]

Vermilion

Now Pet Products (Veterinary Products) [27200]

Vienna

Axelrod Distributors (Food) [10476]

Waldo

Ohigro Inc. (Agricultural Equipment and
Supplies) [1101]

Walton Hills

Mantua Manufacturing Co. (Furniture and
Fixtures) [13171]
Transtar Industries Inc. (Automotive) [3330]

Wapakoneta

Auglaize Farmers Cooperative (Agricultural
Equipment and Supplies) [261]

Warren

Guarnieri Co.; Albert (Paper and Paper
Products) [21754]
Kenilworth Steel Co (Metals) [20096]

Nannicola Wholesale Co., Inc. (Specialty Equipment
and Products) [25747]
REM Electronics Supply Company Inc. (Electrical
and Electronic Equipment and Supplies) [9275]
Specialty Pipe and Tube Co. (Metals) [20384]
Torque Drive (Automotive) [3321]
Trumbull Industries Inc. (Plumbing Materials and
Fixtures) [23418]
West Minerals Inc. (Petroleum, Fuels, and Related
Equipment) [22793]

Warrensville Heights

Daewoo Equipment Corp. (Industrial
Machinery) [15928]
Horrigan & Associates; E.C. (Industrial
Machinery) [16114]
North Coast Distributing, Inc. (Hardware) [13850]

Waterville

Seedex Distributors, Inc. (Agricultural Equipment
and Supplies) [1252]

West Chester

Alternative Computer Technology Inc. (Computers
and Software) [5917]
Skidmore Sales & Distributing Company,
Inc. (Food) [12501]
Snow Filtration Co. (Industrial Supplies) [17179]

Westerville

Amber Grout Sales (Veterinary Products) [27063]
Bell-Haun Systems Inc. (Communications Systems
and Equipment) [5528]
Foster's Good Service Dairy (Food) [11193]
Hunt Co. (Toys and Hobby Goods) [26530]
Industrial Tube & Steel (Metals) [20061]
Pabco Fluid Power Co. (Industrial
Machinery) [16368]

Westlake

Aluminum Line Products Co. (Automotive) [2223]
Design Surfaces (Floorcovering Equipment and
Supplies) [9858]
Hyde Marine Inc. (Specialty Equipment and
Products) [25685]
Viking Sewing Machines Inc. (Textiles and
Notions) [26241]
Western DataCom Company Inc. (Computers and
Software) [6865]

Wickliffe

Amateur Electronics Supply (Sound and
Entertainment Equipment and Supplies) [25067]
PHD, Inc. (Household Appliances) [15272]

Willard

Buurma Farms Inc. (Food) [10652]
Holthouse Brothers (Food) [11454]
Wiers Farm Inc. (Food) [12937]

Willoughby

BP Products Inc. (Heating and Cooling Equipment
and Supplies) [14355]
Lake Business Products (Office Equipment and
Supplies) [21096]
Martinson-Nicholls (Textiles and Notions) [26135]
McDonald Equipment Co. (Electrical and Electronic
Equipment and Supplies) [9056]

Willoughby Hills

Ontario Stone Corp. (Construction Materials and
Machinery) [7813]

Willowick

Applied Industrial Technologies (Industrial
Supplies) [16703]

Wilmington

Bock Pharmaceutical, Inc.; James A. (Medical,
Dental, and Optical Supplies) [19196]
Clinton Landmark Inc. (Livestock and Farm
Products) [17783]

Wintersville

Snyder Wholesale Tire Co. (Sound and
Entertainment Equipment and Supplies) [25447]

Woodlawn

Dolly Madison Bakery (Food) [10979]

Woodville

Lucky Farmers Inc. (Agricultural Equipment and
Supplies) [975]

Wooster

Central Farm Supply Inc. (Agricultural Equipment
and Supplies) [389]
COFSCO Inc. (Petroleum, Fuels, and Related
Equipment) [22150]
Prentke Romich Co. (Communications Systems and
Equipment) [5719]
Sandy Supply Co. (Petroleum, Fuels, and Related
Equipment) [22650]

Worthington

Allied Electronics (Electrical and Electronic
Equipment and Supplies) [8306]
Dal Tile Corp. (Floorcovering Equipment and
Supplies) [9847]
HomeReach Inc. (Medical, Dental, and Optical
Equipment) [18841]
MacBean Inc.; Scottie (Restaurant and Commercial
Foodservice Equipment and Supplies) [24173]

Xenia

Buckeye Countrymark Corp. (Agricultural Equipment
and Supplies) [348]
Super Valu Stores Inc. Ohio Valley (Food) [12637]

Youngstown

Acme Coal Co. (Construction Materials and
Machinery) [6909]
Alan Co.; B.J. (Explosives) [9630]
Central Optical of Youngstown Inc. (Medical,
Dental, and Optical Supplies) [19225]
Economy Electric Company Inc. (Electrical and
Electronic Equipment and Supplies) [8651]
Forge Industries Inc. (Industrial Supplies) [16871]
Fragrance International Inc. (Health and Beauty
Aids) [14104]
Hearn Paper Company Inc. (Paper and Paper
Products) [21757]
Hynes Industries Inc. (Metals) [20052]
Lyden Co. (Petroleum, Fuels, and Related
Equipment) [22442]
McCrudden Heating Supply (Heating and Cooling
Equipment and Supplies) [14536]
Michel Company Inc.; R.E. (Heating and Cooling
Equipment and Supplies) [14561]
Ohio Alloy Steels Inc. (Metals) [20243]
Optical One, Inc. (Medical, Dental, and Optical
Supplies) [19515]
Plakie Inc. (Toys and Hobby Goods) [26616]
Steel City Corp. (Metals) [20392]
Steel City Milling Inc. (Food) [12582]
Tamarkin Company Inc. (Food) [12694]
Tamco Distributors Company Inc. (Health and
Beauty Aids) [14255]
Tasco Insulations Inc. (Construction Materials and
Machinery) [8098]
United Automatic Heating Supplies (Heating and
Cooling Equipment and Supplies) [14746]
V & V Appliance Parts Inc. (Household
Appliances) [15351]
Valley Industrial Trucks Inc. (Industrial
Machinery) [16597]

Zanesville

Ace Truck Equipment Co. (Automotive) [2172]
Goss Supply Co. (Industrial Supplies) [16902]
Mattingly Foods Inc. (Food) [11807]
Mattingly Foods Inc. (Food) [11808]
Roekel Co. (Plumbing Materials and
Fixtures) [23351]

Oklahoma

Abilene
Affiliated Food Stores Inc. (Food) [10333]

Ada
Ada Iron and Metal Co. (Metals) [19727]
Evergreen Mills Inc. (Agricultural Equipment and Supplies) [556]
Garrett Educational Corp. (Books and Other Printed Materials) [3771]

Alva
Farmers Cooperative Association (Agricultural Equipment and Supplies) [582]
Wheeler Brothers (Livestock and Farm Products) [18343]
Wheeler Brothers (Food) [12924]

Apache
Apache Farmers Cooperative (Agricultural Equipment and Supplies) [245]

Ardmore
Auto Electric Sales and Service Co. (Automotive) [2272]
Fite; Ted G. (Specialty Equipment and Products) [25652]
Lumbermens Millwork and Supply Co. (Construction Materials and Machinery) [7621]

Bartlesville
ABA Enterprise Inc. (Recreational and Sporting Goods) [23490]
American Electric Co. (Electrical and Electronic Equipment and Supplies) [8341]
Phillips 66 Propane Co. (Petroleum, Fuels, and Related Equipment) [22577]

Bessie
Farmers Cooperative Exchange (Agricultural Equipment and Supplies) [626]

Blackwell
Blackwell Cooperative Elevator Association (Livestock and Farm Products) [17736]

Broken Arrow
Electronic Label Technology Inc. (Computers and Software) [6243]
Farmers Cooperative Association (Agricultural Equipment and Supplies) [573]
Jacobs Supply Co.; Mylon C. (Automotive) [2808]
Logo-Wear Inc. (Clothing) [5141]
Parnell; Wayne (Shoes) [24829]

Calumet
Calumet Industries Inc. (Livestock and Farm Products) [17760]
Calumet Industries Inc. (Agricultural Equipment and Supplies) [365]

Carmen
Farmers Cooperative (Carmen, Oklahoma) (Livestock and Farm Products) [17848]
Farmers Cooperative Co. (Agricultural Equipment and Supplies) [588]

Carnegie
Farmers Cooperative Mill Elevator (Livestock and Farm Products) [17875]

Chickasha
Poag Grain Inc. (Agricultural Equipment and Supplies) [1136]
Pro-Ag Chem Inc. (Agricultural Equipment and Supplies) [1153]

Claremore
Gaffey Inc. (Industrial Machinery) [16045]

Rogers Heritage Trust; Will (Books and Other Printed Materials) [4123]

Clinton
Elk Supply Company Inc. (Construction Materials and Machinery) [7306]
Farmers Cooperative Association (Livestock and Farm Products) [17843]
Smith Oil Company Inc. (Petroleum, Fuels, and Related Equipment) [22679]

Crescent
Crescent Cooperative Association (Agricultural Equipment and Supplies) [472]

Cushing
Gibble Oil Company Inc. (Petroleum, Fuels, and Related Equipment) [22312]

Del City
NCS Healthcare (Medical, Dental, and Optical Equipment) [18958]
NCS Healthcare (Medical, Dental, and Optical Supplies) [19480]

Drummond
Drummond Cooperative Elevator Inc. (Agricultural Equipment and Supplies) [526]

Duncan
Duncan Equipment Co. (Industrial Supplies) [16842]
M and M Supply Co. (Petroleum, Fuels, and Related Equipment) [22444]
M and M Supply Co. (Industrial Machinery) [16252]
Maier Sporting Goods Inc.; Ray (Clothing) [5153]

Durant
Hitchcock Distributing Inc. (Alcoholic Beverages) [1760]

Edmond
Action Sports of Edmond (Recreational and Sporting Goods) [23493]
Midwest Wrecking Co. (Automotive) [2961]
Pinnacle Business Systems Inc. (Computers and Software) [6620]
Wuu Jau Company Inc. (Recreational and Sporting Goods) [24051]

El Reno
Stan's Smokehouse Inc. (Food) [12567]

Eldorado
Farmers Cooperative Association (Agricultural Equipment and Supplies) [584]

Enid
Farmland Industries Inc. Union Equity Exchange Div. (Livestock and Farm Products) [17913]
Gale Force Compression Service (Compressors) [5841]
Long Equipment Co. (Agricultural Equipment and Supplies) [967]
Mid West Oil Ltd. (Petroleum, Fuels, and Related Equipment) [22480]
Northwest Vet Supply Inc. (Veterinary Products) [27199]
Singer Steel Inc. (Metals) [20369]
Uni-Steel Inc. (Metals) [20456]
Vater Implement Inc. (Agricultural Equipment and Supplies) [1397]
Walker Vacuum Supply (Household Appliances) [15363]

Ft. Gibson
Optronics Inc. (Electrical and Electronic Equipment and Supplies) [9160]

Guymon
S and H Tractor Co. (Agricultural Equipment and Supplies) [1223]

Hinton
North Caddo Cooperative Inc. (Agricultural Equipment and Supplies) [1078]

Hobart
Braun & Son Implement Inc. (Agricultural Equipment and Supplies) [334]

Idabel
Copeland Oil Co. (Petroleum, Fuels, and Related Equipment) [22170]
Houston Texaco Oil Co.; Harry (Petroleum, Fuels, and Related Equipment) [22365]
Setco Solid Tire and Rim (Automotive) [3209]
Texaco Oil Co. (Petroleum, Fuels, and Related Equipment) [22730]
Young Oil CO. (Petroleum, Fuels, and Related Equipment) [22819]

Jenks
Specialties of Surgery Inc. (Medical, Dental, and Optical Equipment) [19049]

Kellyville
Red Wing Products Inc. (Electrical and Electronic Equipment and Supplies) [9269]

Kremlin
Farmers Grain Company Inc. (Agricultural Equipment and Supplies) [653]
Zaloudek Co.; Florein W. (Agricultural Equipment and Supplies) [1468]

Langley
Hadon Security Company Inc. (Automotive) [2716]

Lawton
Brittain Merchandising (Medical, Dental, and Optical Supplies) [19201]
CED Inc. (Electrical and Electronic Equipment and Supplies) [8513]
Comanche Lumber Company Inc. (Construction Materials and Machinery) [7199]
Coop Services Inc. (Agricultural Equipment and Supplies) [446]
Dunlaw Optical Laboratories (Medical, Dental, and Optical Supplies) [19295]
Fitch Industrial Welding Supply Inc. (Industrial Supplies) [16865]
United Sewing Machine Distributing (Household Appliances) [15348]

Lone Wolf
Planters Cooperative Association (Agricultural Equipment and Supplies) [1133]

Marietta
Earth Energy Technology and Supply Inc. (Heating and Cooling Equipment and Supplies) [14425]

Marland
Bliss Cooperative Grain Co. (Livestock and Farm Products) [17738]

McAlester
McCall Fireworks Inc. (Toys and Hobby Goods) [26572]
McClendons Boot Store (Shoes) [24806]

Medford
Clyde Cooperative Association (Agricultural Equipment and Supplies) [428]

Meno
Farmers Cooperative Association (Agricultural Equipment and Supplies) [579]
Farmers Cooperative Association (Food) [11088]

Miami
Oklahoma Leather Products Inc. (Luggage and Leather Goods) [18414]

Mooreland

Farmers Cooperative Trading Co. (Agricultural Equipment and Supplies) [639]

Muskogee

A & B Distributors (Alcoholic Beverages) [1471]
Anderson Wholesale Co. (Health and Beauty Aids) [14022]
B & J Oil Co. (Petroleum, Fuels, and Related Equipment) [22055]
Curt's Oil Co. (Petroleum, Fuels, and Related Equipment) [22184]
Griffin Manufacturing (Food) [11327]
Harrison Oil Co. (Petroleum, Fuels, and Related Equipment) [22339]
J & E Feed Distributors Inc. (Agricultural Equipment and Supplies) [872]
Love Bottling Co. (Soft Drinks) [24984]
Mayes County Petroleum Products (Petroleum, Fuels, and Related Equipment) [22459]
McAdams Pipe and Supply Co. (Petroleum, Fuels, and Related Equipment) [22461]
Oklahoma Rig and Supply Company Inc. (Industrial Supplies) [17088]
Quikservice Steel Co. (Metals) [20305]
Schrader-Bridgeport International (Automotive) [3196]
Smith Oil Co.; Glenn (Petroleum, Fuels, and Related Equipment) [22678]
Uni-Steel Inc. (Metals) [20455]
W-P Milling Company Inc. (Agricultural Equipment and Supplies) [1401]
Yaffe Iron and Metal Company Inc. (Metals) [20501]

Newkirk

Farmers Cooperative Elevator and Supply (Livestock and Farm Products) [17871]

Norman

Malone Products Inc. (Food) [11768]
Massive Graphic Screen Printing (Clothing) [5173]
Ramacom Inc. (Computers and Software) [6682]
TD's Radio & TV (Heating and Cooling Equipment and Supplies) [14713]

Okarche

Farmers Cooperative Association (Agricultural Equipment and Supplies) [577]
Farmers Cooperative Association (Okarche, Oklahoma) (Chemicals) [4386]

Oklahoma City

Acme Brick Co. (Floorcovering Equipment and Supplies) [9643]
ADEMCO/ADI (Security and Safety Equipment) [24476]
AES of Oklahoma Inc. (Heating and Cooling Equipment and Supplies) [14301]
American Century Pallet Co. (Wood and Wood Products) [27278]
American Education Corp. (Computers and Software) [5928]
Associated Appliance Service (Heating and Cooling Equipment and Supplies) [14327]
Athlon II Enterprises Inc. (Clothing) [4788]
B & B Medical Service Inc. (Medical, Dental, and Optical Equipment) [18700]
Berg-Dorf Pipe & Supply Co. Inc. (Plumbing Materials and Fixtures) [23083]
Boyd Company Inc.; C.L. (Construction Materials and Machinery) [7074]
Brittain Brothers Inc. (Automotive) [2387]
Celsco Inc. (Heating and Cooling Equipment and Supplies) [14372]
Central Equipment Distributing Co. (Heating and Cooling Equipment and Supplies) [14376]
Central Liquor Co. (Alcoholic Beverages) [1587]
Consolidated Wholesale Co. (Tobacco Products) [26279]
Crafts Etc. Ltd. (Specialty Equipment and Products) [25613]
Cusack Wholesale Meat Co. (Food) [10886]
Design Systems Inc. (Computers and Software) [6201]

Eckroat Seed Co. (Agricultural Equipment and Supplies) [541]
EMSCO Electric Supply Company Inc. (Electrical and Electronic Equipment and Supplies) [8704]
F.B.F. Inc. (Guns and Weapons) [13491]
Federal Corp. (Heating and Cooling Equipment and Supplies) [14443]
Fleming Companies Inc. (Food) [11148]
Fleming Companies Inc. Oklahoma City Div. (Food) [11151]
Ford Audio-Video Systems Inc. (Sound and Entertainment Equipment and Supplies) [25194]
Gas & Electrical Equipment Co. (Sound and Entertainment Equipment and Supplies) [25206]
Gordon & Co.; Alan (Jewelry) [17439]
Grant Truck Equipment Co. (Automotive) [2696]
Harris Discount Supply (Medical, Dental, and Optical Equipment) [18826]
Hibdon Tire Center Inc. (Automotive) [2748]
Hirst Imports (Alcoholic Beverages) [1759]
Horn Seed Company Inc. (Agricultural Equipment and Supplies) [838]
Hunzicker Brothers Inc. (Electrical and Electronic Equipment and Supplies) [8866]
Interstate Supply Co. (Floorcovering Equipment and Supplies) [9970]
Laminates Unlimited Inc. (Plastics) [22991]
McCubbin Hosiery Inc. (Clothing) [5178]
Mid-America Footwear Co. (Shoes) [24811]
Miller-Jackson Co. (Communications Systems and Equipment) [5679]
Mustang Fuel Corp. (Petroleum, Fuels, and Related Equipment) [22503]
Newcomb Sportswear Inc.; Tony (Clothing) [5229]
Norman Supply Co. (Plumbing Materials and Fixtures) [23296]
OCT Equipment Inc. (Construction Materials and Machinery) [7804]
OK Distributing Company Inc. (Household Appliances) [15258]
Oklahoma Upholstery Supply Co. (Textiles and Notions) [26160]
Orchid Uniform Retail Sales (Clothing) [5256]
Pacific Trading (Toys and Hobby Goods) [26602]
Parr Golf Car Company, Inc. (Recreational and Sporting Goods) [23873]
Perfection Equipment Co. (Motorized Vehicles) [20704]
Phi Technologies Inc. (Sound and Entertainment Equipment and Supplies) [25381]
Precision Fitting & Gauge Co. (Plumbing Materials and Fixtures) [23325]
Pyramid Supply Inc. (Electrical and Electronic Equipment and Supplies) [9248]
Quality Pets, Inc. (Veterinary Products) [27219]
Rainbo Baking Co. (Food) [12265]
RECO (Heating and Cooling Equipment and Supplies) [14649]
Red Rock Distributing Co. (Petroleum, Fuels, and Related Equipment) [22614]
Reno; Mary Ann (Clothing) [5306]
Rex Playground Equipment Inc. (Recreational and Sporting Goods) [23913]
Safa Enterprises Co., Inc. (Food) [12386]
Scrivner Inc. (Food) [12436]
Sooner Airgas Inc. (Industrial Supplies) [17180]
South Central Pool Supply, Inc. (Recreational and Sporting Goods) [23962]
Southwest Modern Data Systems (Computers and Software) [6751]
Steel Supply Co. (Metals) [20401]
Sunbelt Data Systems Inc. (Computers and Software) [6771]
Swansons Tire Company Inc. (Automotive) [3289]
Thrifty Medical Supply Inc. (Medical, Dental, and Optical Equipment) [19078]
Tru-Care Health Systems Inc. (Medical, Dental, and Optical Equipment) [19089]
United Engines Inc. (Automotive) [3366]
United Engines Inc. (Industrial Machinery) [16589]
VZ Ltd. (Medical, Dental, and Optical Supplies) [19692]
Walters Optical Inc.; Wendel (Medical, Dental, and Optical Supplies) [19695]
Wilson Supply Co. (Petroleum, Fuels, and Related Equipment) [22809]

Paden

Cheatwood Oil Co. (Storage Equipment and Containers) [25900]

Ponca City

Garroutte Products (Agricultural Equipment and Supplies) [726]
Modern Supply Company Inc. (Plumbing Materials and Fixtures) [23271]

Pond Creek

Farmers Grain Company Inc. (Livestock and Farm Products) [17894]

Pryor

ViaGrafix Corp. (Computers and Software) [6851]

Purcell

C & J Bait Co. (Recreational and Sporting Goods) [23579]

Rocky

Farmers Cooperative Grain and Supply Co. (Agricultural Equipment and Supplies) [632]

Roff

Frontier Trading Inc. (Agricultural Equipment and Supplies) [714]

Sand Springs

Buy for Less Inc. (Food) [10653]
Fain & Associates; Gary (Recreational and Sporting Goods) [23663]

Shawnee

Buford White Lumber Company Inc. (Construction Materials and Machinery) [7097]
Discount Fishing Tackle (Recreational and Sporting Goods) [23624]
J & J Supply, Inc. (Medical, Dental, and Optical Equipment) [18865]
Shawnee Garment Manufacturing Co. (Clothing) [5346]
United Optical Corp. (Medical, Dental, and Optical Supplies) [19677]

Stratford

ABC Marketing (Automotive) [2163]

Tahlequah

Oil Marketing Company Inc. (Petroleum, Fuels, and Related Equipment) [22538]

Tecumseh

Bryson Inc. (Alcoholic Beverages) [1555]

Temple

Farmers Elevator Inc. (Livestock and Farm Products) [17888]

Texhoma

Texhoma Wheat Growers Inc. (Agricultural Equipment and Supplies) [1325]

Tipton

Humphreys Coop Tipton Location (Livestock and Farm Products) [18007]

Tishomingo

Johnston County Feed & Farm Supply (Agricultural Equipment and Supplies) [890]
Washita Refrigeration & Equipment Co. (Heating and Cooling Equipment and Supplies) [14758]

Tulsa

78ic Beauty Supply & Salons (Health and Beauty Aids) [14006]
Aberdeen Dynamics (Industrial Machinery) [15725]
Affiliated Food Stores Inc. (Tulsa, Oklahoma) (Food) [10334]
Allied Bearing Supply (Industrial Supplies) [16685]
AlliedSignal Automotive Catalyst Co. (Automotive) [2217]

American Nursery Products (Horticultural Supplies) [14803]

American Respiratory Inc. (Medical, Dental, and Optical Equipment) [18678]

Annie C.P. Productions Inc. (Shoes) [24672]

Arkansas Valley Companies (Petroleum, Fuels, and Related Equipment) [22044]

ASEC Manufacturing (Automotive) [2260]

Bama Companies Inc. (Food) [10495]

Base Inc. (Food) [10512]

Benrock of Oklahoma (Marine) [18461]

Bizjet International Sales and Support Inc. (Aeronautical Equipment and Supplies) [59]

Black Gold Comics & Graphics (Books and Other Printed Materials) [3559]

Borg Compressed Steel Corp. (Metals) [19831]

Budco (Sound and Entertainment Equipment and Supplies) [25111]

C & S Distributors (Specialty Equipment and Products) [25586]

Capps Beauty & Barber Inc. (Health and Beauty Aids) [14055]

Commercial/Medical Electronics (Medical, Dental, and Optical Equipment) [18748]

Computing Technology Inc. (Computers and Software) [6137]

Davis & Sons; William E. (Food) [10918]

Direct Sales Inc. (Clothing) [4918]

Dolphin Pools Inc. (Recreational and Sporting Goods) [23628]

Downs Supply Co. (Floorcovering Equipment and Supplies) [9872]

Elk River Trading Co. (Health and Beauty Aids) [14094]

Fabricut Inc. (Textiles and Notions) [26031]

Fadler Company Inc. (Food) [11069]

Fairview-AFX Inc. (Electrical and Electronic Equipment and Supplies) [8730]

Ferguson Enterprises Inc. (Heating and Cooling Equipment and Supplies) [14444]

Gothic Energy Corp. (Petroleum, Fuels, and Related Equipment) [22319]

Grant Manufacturing & Equipment Co. (Automotive) [2695]

Great Plains Stainless Inc. (Metals) [20020]

Greer Appliance Parts Inc. (Household Appliances) [15153]

Hale-Halsell Co. (Food) [11363]

Harley Industries Inc. (Industrial Supplies) [16924]

Harwell & Associates Inc. Chemical Div. (Chemicals) [4408]

Heatwave Supply Inc. (Plumbing Materials and Fixtures) [23207]

Heritage Propane Partners, L.P. (Petroleum, Fuels, and Related Equipment) [22347]

Honor Snack Inc. (Food) [11456]

Hurst Supply (Construction Materials and Machinery) [7501]

Jarboe Sales Co. (Alcoholic Beverages) [1778]

Java Dave's Executive Coffee Service (Food) [11548]

Kraftbilt Products (Specialty Equipment and Products) [25705]

Laufen International Inc. (Floorcovering Equipment and Supplies) [9992]

Lowrance Electronics Inc. (Marine) [18551]

Lyntech Corp. (Medical, Dental, and Optical Equipment) [18895]

Magic Refrigeration Co. (Heating and Cooling Equipment and Supplies) [14528]

Metro Builders Supply Inc. (Household Appliances) [15227]

Mill Creek Lumber and Supply Co. (Construction Materials and Machinery) [7712]

Nelson Electric Supply Co. (Electrical and Electronic Equipment and Supplies) [9121]

Noble and Associates (Specialty Equipment and Products) [25760]

Oklahoma Upholstery Supply Co. (Textiles and Notions) [26161]

Original Chili Bowl Inc. (Food) [12076]

Overhead Door Company Inc. (Construction Materials and Machinery) [7817]

Peacock Co./Southwestern Cordage Co.; R.E. (Industrial Supplies) [17102]

PennWell Publishing Co. (Books and Other Printed Materials) [4052]

Petrotank Equipment Inc. (Petroleum, Fuels, and Related Equipment) [22575]

Pinnacle Business Systems, Inc. (Computers and Software) [6621]

Precision Fitting & Gauge Co. (Plumbing Materials and Fixtures) [23326]

Rally Products Inc. (Clothing) [5302]

Reliance Wine & Spirits (Alcoholic Beverages) [1982]

Smith-Thompson Co. (Industrial Supplies) [17177]

Sooner Pipe Inc. (Petroleum, Fuels, and Related Equipment) [22681]

South Central Pool Supply, Inc. (Recreational and Sporting Goods) [23963]

Star Beam/Nightray Div. Gralco Corp. (Electrical and Electronic Equipment and Supplies) [9408]

Star Electric Supply Company Inc. (Electrical and Electronic Equipment and Supplies) [9409]

State Service Systems Inc. (Health and Beauty Aids) [14248]

Steves Electronics Service (Sound and Entertainment Equipment and Supplies) [25466]

Struthers Industries Inc. (Petroleum, Fuels, and Related Equipment) [22712]

SYSCO Food Service, Inc. (Food) [12670]

Tayloe Paper Co. (Paper and Paper Products) [21952]

Thermafil/Tulsa Dental Products (Medical, Dental, and Optical Equipment) [19075]

TMA Systems L.L.C. (Computers and Software) [6819]

Truck Equipment Distributors (Automotive) [3346]

Tulco Oils Inc. (Petroleum, Fuels, and Related Equipment) [22753]

Tulsa Automatic Music Co. (Toys and Hobby Goods) [26694]

Tulsa Bowling Supply Co. (Recreational and Sporting Goods) [24017]

Tulsa Firearms Training Academy (Recreational and Sporting Goods) [24018]

Tulsa Metal Processing Co. (Metals) [20448]

United Engines (Automotive) [3364]

Universal Joint Specialists Inc. (Automotive) [3375]

Utility Supply Co. (Specialty Equipment and Products) [25861]

VCI Home Video (Sound and Entertainment Equipment and Supplies) [25498]

Vinson Supply Co. (Plumbing Materials and Fixtures) [23433]

Vintage Petroleum Inc. (Petroleum, Fuels, and Related Equipment) [22773]

VIP Sales Company Inc. (Food) [12847]

Wesche Co. (Hardware) [13993]

Williams Companies Inc. (Communications Systems and Equipment) [5814]

Williams Produce; Ron (Food) [12949]

Womack Machine (Automotive) [3444]

World Wide Chemnet Inc. (Chemicals) [4557]

WorldCom Network Services Inc. (Communications Systems and Equipment) [5820]

Vici

Farmers Cooperative Association (Agricultural Equipment and Supplies) [572]

Vinita

C and L Supply Inc. (Household Appliances) [15069]

Wakita

Farmers Cooperative Elevator (Agricultural Equipment and Supplies) [608]

Walters

Walters Cooperative Elevators Association (Agricultural Equipment and Supplies) [1411]

Watonga

Wheeler Brothers Grain Company Inc. (Livestock and Farm Products) [18344]

Weatherford

Farmers Cooperative Exchange (Agricultural Equipment and Supplies) [624]

Winnco Inc. (Petroleum, Fuels, and Related Equipment) [22810]

Oregon

Albany

CB Distributing (Electrical and Electronic Equipment and Supplies) [8510]

Fisher Implement Co. (Agricultural Equipment and Supplies) [688]

Jacklin Seed Co. (Agricultural Equipment and Supplies) [874]

Medalist America Turfgrass Seed Co. (Agricultural Equipment and Supplies) [1008]

Optical Associates (Medical, Dental, and Optical Supplies) [19511]

Tec Laboratories Inc. (Health and Beauty Aids) [14256]

Ashland

Maranatha (Food) [11778]

Astoria

The Daily Astorian (Books and Other Printed Materials) [3680]

Englund Marine Supply (Marine) [18499]

Josephson's Smokehouse and Dock (Restaurant and Commercial Foodservice Equipment and Supplies) [24150]

Beavercreek

Beaver Creek Cooperative Telephone Co. (Electrical and Electronic Equipment and Supplies) [8425]

Beaverton

ADEMCO/ADI (Security and Safety Equipment) [24479]

Allied Electronics (Electrical and Electronic Equipment and Supplies) [8319]

American International Forest Products Inc. (Construction Materials and Machinery) [6968]

Aristo Computers Inc. (Computers and Software) [5961]

Beaverton Foods Inc. (Food) [10522]

Cobb Rock Div. (Construction Materials and Machinery) [7188]

Cobb Rock Inc. (Construction Materials and Machinery) [7189]

Com-Kyl (Electrical and Electronic Equipment and Supplies) [8549]

Component Resources Inc. (Electrical and Electronic Equipment and Supplies) [8554]

CUI Stack Inc. (Electrical and Electronic Equipment and Supplies) [8597]

Fitness Shop (Recreational and Sporting Goods) [23672]

InControl Solutions (Computers and Software) [6362]

InSport International Inc. (Clothing) [5052]

Letters N Logos Inc. (Clothing) [5130]

Marshall Industries (Electrical and Electronic Equipment and Supplies) [9036]

NCUBE (Computers and Software) [6547]

Northwest Ribbon Recycling and Supplies (Used, Scrap, and Recycled Materials) [26926]

Norvac Electronics Inc. (Electrical and Electronic Equipment and Supplies) [9142]

Nu-Dimension Beauty Supply Inc. (Health and Beauty Aids) [14180]

Oztex Inc. (Clothing) [5261]

Platt Electric Supply Inc. (Electrical and Electronic Equipment and Supplies) [9212]

Poorman-Douglas Corp. (Computers and Software) [6627]

Protocol Systems Inc. (Medical, Dental, and Optical Supplies) [19559]

Reser's Fine Foods Inc. (Food) [12303]

Salomon North America Inc. (Recreational and Sporting Goods) [23929]

Bend

Tektronix Inc. (Computers and Software) [6805]
Textronix Inc. Semiconductor Test Div. (Computers and Software) [6815]

Bend

Cascade Clothing (Shoes) [24708]
Deschutes Optical (Medical, Dental, and Optical Supplies) [19278]
Dubl-Click Software Corp. (Computers and Software) [6226]
Gensco, Inc. (Heating and Cooling Equipment and Supplies) [14464]

Boardman

Barenbrug U.S.A. (Agricultural Equipment and Supplies) [277]
Logan International Ltd. (Food) [11723]

Brownsville

3K Livestock (Livestock and Farm Products) [17668]

Burns

Harney County Farm Supply Co. (Agricultural Equipment and Supplies) [794]

Carver

Arrowhead Timber Co. (Wood and Wood Products) [27281]

Cave Junction

Fire Mountain Gems (Jewelry) [17415]

Clackamas

Central Garden and Pet Supply Inc. (Agricultural Equipment and Supplies) [393]
Ingram Entertainment (Sound and Entertainment Equipment and Supplies) [25245]
Marketor International Corp. (Construction Materials and Machinery) [7642]
NeuroCom International Inc. (Medical, Dental, and Optical Supplies) [19487]
North Pacific Supply Co. Inc. (Sound and Entertainment Equipment and Supplies) [25361]
Optical Plastics (Medical, Dental, and Optical Supplies) [19516]
Pacific Sea Food Company Inc. (Food) [12094]
Rag Man Inc. (Used, Scrap, and Recycled Materials) [26950]
Scotsco Inc. (Industrial Machinery) [16473]
Tree of Life/Gourmet Award Foods (Food) [12746]
Utility Trailer Sales of Oregon Inc. (Motorized Vehicles) [20742]
Val's Homemade Bagels Inc. (Food) [12821]

Coburg

Mill-Log Equipment Company Inc. (Industrial Machinery) [16300]

Coos Bay

Coos Grange Supply Co. (Agricultural Equipment and Supplies) [462]

Corvallis

Seed Research of Oregon (Agricultural Equipment and Supplies) [1251]

Cottage Grove

North American Book Dealers Exchange (Books and Other Printed Materials) [4007]
Starfire Lumber Co. (Wood and Wood Products) [27380]

Culver

Round Butte Seed Growers Inc. (Agricultural Equipment and Supplies) [1215]

The Dalles

Gazelle Athletics (Recreational and Sporting Goods) [23687]
Oregon Equipment Co. Inc. (Household Appliances) [15260]

Dufur

Azure Standard (Food) [10478]

Dundee

The Bag Connection Inc. (Industrial Machinery) [15797]

Eugene

3-D Optical Lab Inc. (Medical, Dental, and Optical Supplies) [19116]
Aquajogger (Recreational and Sporting Goods) [23521]
Burchs Fine Footwear Inc. (Shoes) [24703]
Burchs Fine Footwear Inc. (Clothing) [4852]
The Cronin Co. (Floorcovering Equipment and Supplies) [9833]
Damien Educational Services; M. (Books and Other Printed Materials) [3681]
DC Metals Inc. (Metals) [19919]
Echo Spring Dairy Inc. (Food) [11020]
Excalibur Cutlery & Gifts (Household Items) [15492]
Farwest Steel Corp. (Metals) [19965]
Gaetano Food Distributor (Food) [11227]
Galaxie Hardware Publishers Inc. (Computers and Software) [6287]
Glorybee Foods Inc. (Food) [11275]
Hammer Lumber Company Inc. (Construction Materials and Machinery) [7436]
Harvest House Publishers, Inc. (Books and Other Printed Materials) [3816]
Himber's Books (Books and Other Printed Materials) [3827]
Industrial Adhesives Inc. (Chemicals) [4427]
Industrial Source (Industrial Machinery) [16153]
Kaneka Far West, Inc. (Office Equipment and Supplies) [21085]
McDiarmid Controls Inc. (Electrical and Electronic Equipment and Supplies) [9055]
McDonald Candy Company Inc. (Food) [11823]
McGuire Bearing (Automotive) [2933]
Myrmo and Sons Inc. (Construction Materials and Machinery) [7758]
Pape Brothers Inc. (Construction Materials and Machinery) [7834]
Petersen-Arne (Office Equipment and Supplies) [21211]
Pilgrim Way Press (Books and Other Printed Materials) [4065]
Premier Distributors (Alcoholic Beverages) [1969]
Richardson Sports Inc. (Recreational and Sporting Goods) [23915]
Road-Runner Tire Service (Automotive) [3166]
Ross Corp. (Construction Materials and Machinery) [7960]
Scharpfs Twin Oaks Builders Supply Co. (Construction Materials and Machinery) [7985]
Sessler Inc. (Used, Scrap, and Recycled Materials) [26987]
Silke Communications Inc. (Communications Systems and Equipment) [5757]
Six States Distributors Inc. (Automotive) [3227]
Smeed Communication Services (Household Appliances) [15316]
Smeed Sound Service Inc. (Communications Systems and Equipment) [5759]
Tri-Quality Business Forms Inc. (Office Equipment and Supplies) [21322]
United Pipe and Supply Company Inc. (Plumbing Materials and Fixtures) [23422]
Victorian Pearl (Toys and Hobby Goods) [26704]
Vintage House Merchants (Alcoholic Beverages) [2103]
Vitus Electric Supply Co. (Electrical and Electronic Equipment and Supplies) [9545]
Wesco Cedar Inc. (Construction Materials and Machinery) [8202]
Western Fluid Power (Industrial Machinery) [16627]
Wildish Land Co. (Construction Materials and Machinery) [8224]
Wildish Sand and Gravel Co. (Construction Materials and Machinery) [8225]
Willamette Graystone Inc. (Construction Materials and Machinery) [8226]

Fairview

Trailblazer Foods (Food) [12742]

Forest Grove

Burlingham and Sons; E.F. (Agricultural Equipment and Supplies) [353]

Glendale

Superior Lumber Co. (Wood and Wood Products) [27384]

Grants Pass

Copeland Paving Inc. (Construction Materials and Machinery) [7220]
GreenTek Inc. (Industrial Machinery) [16077]
White Water Manufacturing (Industrial Supplies) [17279]

Gresham

Brindar Design Inc. (Clothing) [4845]
Cosmetic Marketing Group (Health and Beauty Aids) [14073]
Franz Optical Company Inc. (Medical, Dental, and Optical Supplies) [19331]
Refrigeration Contractors Inc. (Heating and Cooling Equipment and Supplies) [14654]

Halsey

International Seeds, Inc. (Agricultural Equipment and Supplies) [865]

Hillsboro

Cascade Wholesale Hardware, Inc. (Hardware) [13622]
Centerspan Communications Corp. (Computers and Software) [6055]
Forest Medical Products Inc. (Medical, Dental, and Optical Supplies) [19326]
Intel Corp. (Electrical and Electronic Equipment and Supplies) [8887]
La Cie. Ltd. (Storage Equipment and Containers) [25924]

Hood River

Diamond Fruit Growers (Food) [10958]
Diamond Fruit Growers (Food) [10959]

Hubbard

Turf-Seed, Inc. (Agricultural Equipment and Supplies) [1366]

Independence

Garden Grow Co (Agricultural Equipment and Supplies) [722]
Marquis Corp. (Recreational and Sporting Goods) [23804]

Jacksonville

Valley View Vineyard (Alcoholic Beverages) [2098]

Junction City

A and R Lumber Sales Inc. (Construction Materials and Machinery) [6897]
Forbes Seed & Grain (Agricultural Equipment and Supplies) [698]

Keizer

Willamette Seed Co. (Agricultural Equipment and Supplies) [1449]

Klamath Falls

Clean Water Systems International (Specialty Equipment and Products) [25602]
Specialized Sales and Service Inc. (Automotive) [3246]

Lake Oswego

Biotronik Inc. (Medical, Dental, and Optical Equipment) [18716]
Blackwell North America Inc. (Books and Other Printed Materials) [3560]
Blackwell's Delaware Inc. (Books and Other Printed Materials) [3561]
Moshofsky Enterprises (Construction Materials and Machinery) [7751]
Norpac Food Sales Inc. (Food) [12023]
North West Quality Innovations (Shoes) [24825]

SCR Inc. (Construction Materials and Machinery) [7994]
SCR Inc. (Wood and Wood Products) [27371]
Star Sales Company of Knoxville (Textiles and Notions) [26213]
Westmark Industries Inc. (Industrial Machinery) [16629]

Lexington
Morrow County Grain Growers Inc. (Livestock and Farm Products) [18118]

Madras
Full Circle, Inc. (Agricultural Equipment and Supplies) [719]

Maupin
Specialty Distribution (Floorcovering Equipment and Supplies) [10175]

McMinnville
RB Rubber Products Inc. (Household Items) [15630]
Solutions (Computers and Software) [6745]
West Valley Farmers Inc. (Agricultural Equipment and Supplies) [1426]

Medford
F.L.D. Distributors Inc. (Alcoholic Beverages) [1692]
GEC Alsthom Balteau, Inc. (Electrical and Electronic Equipment and Supplies) [8780]
Northwest Wholesale (Sound and Entertainment Equipment and Supplies) [25365]
Omega Publications (Books and Other Printed Materials) [4019]
Pacific Northwest Books Co. (Books and Other Printed Materials) [4033]
Rogue Aggregates Inc. (Construction Materials and Machinery) [7954]
SOS Alarm (Security and Safety Equipment) [24639]
Tile City (Floorcovering Equipment and Supplies) [10220]
Timber Products Co. Medford (Wood and Wood Products) [27388]
Viking Distributing Company Inc. (Household Appliances) [15359]

Merrill
Malin Potato Cooperative Inc. (Food) [11764]
Riverside Potatoes Inc. (Food) [12324]

Mill City
Northwest Wood Products Inc. (Construction Materials and Machinery) [7800]

Milton-Freewater
Blue Mountain Growers Inc. (Food) [10576]

Milwaukie
Coral Sales Co. (Electrical and Electronic Equipment and Supplies) [8580]
National Sanitary Supply Co. Portland Div. (Cleaning and Janitorial Supplies) [4675]
United Grocers, Inc. (Food) [12796]
Wilhelm Warehouse Company Inc.; Rudie (Food) [12943]

Monroe
Subterranean Co. (Books and Other Printed Materials) [4194]

Moro
Mid Columbia Producers Inc. (Livestock and Farm Products) [18091]

Mt. Angel
Wilco Farmers Inc. (Agricultural Equipment and Supplies) [1447]

Newberg
A-Dec Inc. (Furniture and Fixtures) [13007]
A-Dec International Inc. (Medical, Dental, and Optical Equipment) [18652]

Barclay Press (Books and Other Printed Materials) [3544]

Newport
Action Business Systems (Computers and Software) [5872]
Depoe Bay Fish Co. (Food) [10946]

Nyssa
Farmers Grain and Seed (Livestock and Farm Products) [17898]
Nyssa Cooperative Supply Inc. (Agricultural Equipment and Supplies) [1095]

Ontario
Hollingsworths' Inc. (Agricultural Equipment and Supplies) [834]
Iseri Produce Co.; Thomas (Food) [11530]
Stone Electronic (Electrical and Electronic Equipment and Supplies) [9419]

Oregon City
Spainhower; Vic (Computers and Software) [6752]

Pendleton
Mountain Marketing (Sound and Entertainment Equipment and Supplies) [25341]
Pendleton Grain Growers Inc. (Livestock and Farm Products) [18161]
Pioneer Implement Corp. (Agricultural Equipment and Supplies) [1132]
Woodpecker Truck and Equipment Inc. (Motorized Vehicles) [20753]

Portland
1st Call McCall Heating and Clng (Industrial Machinery) [15718]
A and L Distributing Co. (Electrical and Electronic Equipment and Supplies) [8257]
AcryMed Inc. (Medical, Dental, and Optical Supplies) [19123]
Adidas America Inc./Intl Div (Clothing) [4751]
Air Flow Systems Inc. (Automotive) [2192]
Air-Oil Products Corp. (Industrial Supplies) [16677]
American Fibre Supplies, Inc. (Paper and Paper Products) [21627]
American Industries Inc. (Metals) [19769]
American Steel L.L.C. (Metals) [19772]
Anchorage Reprographics Center (Office Equipment and Supplies) [20804]
Apollo Pet Supply (Veterinary Products) [27069]
Arndt Optical Supplies; Ray (Medical, Dental, and Optical Supplies) [19161]
Arthur Lumber Trading Co. (Construction Materials and Machinery) [6994]
ARTiSan Software Tools (Computers and Software) [5967]
Auto Wheel Service Inc. (Automotive) [2282]
Baer Co.; Ralph A. (Toys and Hobby Goods) [26404]
Balzer Pacific Equipment Co. (Construction Materials and Machinery) [7018]
Battin Power Service; John (Electrical and Electronic Equipment and Supplies) [8423]
Beall Transport Equipment Co (Automotive) [2329]
Bioject Medical Technologies Inc. (Medical, Dental, and Optical Supplies) [19192]
Blue Ribbon Business Products Co. (Office Equipment and Supplies) [20846]
Bonita Pioneer Packaging Prods (Industrial Supplies) [16755]
Book Centers Inc. (Books and Other Printed Materials) [3566]
Boyd Coffee Co. (Food) [10603]
Brake Systems Inc. (Industrial Supplies) [16763]
Branom Instrument Co. Inc. (Industrial Supplies) [16765]
Brown Arts & Crafts; Stan (Office Equipment and Supplies) [20860]
Buckeye Pacific Corp. (Construction Materials and Machinery) [7093]
Bushwacker Inc. (Security and Safety Equipment) [24521]
Calbag Metals Co. (Used, Scrap, and Recycled Materials) [26775]

Calcom Graphic Supply, Inc. (Specialty Equipment and Products) [25589]
Calcom Graphic Supply, Inc. (Specialty Equipment and Products) [25590]
Calcom Graphic Supply, Inc. (Specialty Equipment and Products) [25591]
Care Medical Equipment Inc. (Medical, Dental, and Optical Equipment) [18726]
Carson Oil Company Inc. (Petroleum, Fuels, and Related Equipment) [22112]
Cascade Pacific Lumber Co. (Construction Materials and Machinery) [7150]
Cascade Yachts, Inc. (Marine) [18476]
Caye's Luggage (Luggage and Leather Goods) [18381]
Cereal Food Processors, Inc. (Food) [10726]
Chin's Import Export Co. Inc. (Food) [10751]
Coast Cutlery Co. (Household Items) [15449]
Coffee Bean International, Inc. (Food) [10786]
Columbia Distributing Co./Henry Hirsdale/Admiralty Beverage Co. (Alcoholic Beverages) [1607]
Columbia Sportswear Co. (Clothing) [4889]
Commercial Dishwashers (Household Appliances) [15091]
Copeland Lumber Yard Inc. (Hardware) [13646]
Copeland Lumber Yard Inc. (Hardware) [13647]
The Cronin Co. (Floorcovering Equipment and Supplies) [9834]
Cyber-Tech Inc. (Electrical and Electronic Equipment and Supplies) [8603]
Data Print Inc. (Paper and Paper Products) [21704]
Dealers Supply Co. (Construction Materials and Machinery) [7254]
Dealers Supply Co. (Construction Materials and Machinery) [7255]
Denton Plastics Inc. (Used, Scrap, and Recycled Materials) [26797]
Double O Electronic Distributors (Electrical and Electronic Equipment and Supplies) [8631]
Double T Holding Co. (Construction Materials and Machinery) [7282]
Electrical Construction Co. (Electrical and Electronic Equipment and Supplies) [8674]
Electrical Distributing Inc. (Sound and Entertainment Equipment and Supplies) [25177]
Emerson Hardwood Co. (Construction Materials and Machinery) [7309]
The Empire Co. (Clothing) [4938]
Exhaust Specialties II (Automotive) [2599]
Fabric Art Inc. (Clothing) [4943]
Familian Northwest Inc. (Plumbing Materials and Fixtures) [23158]
Feenaughty Machinery Co. (Construction Materials and Machinery) [7334]
Fireside Distributors of Oregon, Inc. (Heating and Cooling Equipment and Supplies) [14449]
Fisherman's Marine Supply (Marine) [18504]
Fluid-Air Components L.L.C. (Industrial Supplies) [16870]
Forest City Trading Group Inc. (Construction Materials and Machinery) [7359]
General Tool and Supply Co. (Hardware) [13722]
Gensco, Inc. (Heating and Cooling Equipment and Supplies) [14462]
Geo-Hex (Toys and Hobby Goods) [26498]
Georgies Ceramic & Clay Co. (Toys and Hobby Goods) [26499]
Glasparts Inc. (Automotive) [2682]
Global Forestry Management Group (Wood and Wood Products) [27309]
Graphic Arts Center Publishing Co. (Books and Other Printed Materials) [3795]
Graphic Sciences Inc. (Industrial Supplies) [16903]
Great Northwest Bicycle Supply (Recreational and Sporting Goods) [23697]
Halton Co. (Construction Materials and Machinery) [7434]
Hampton Affiliates Inc. (Construction Materials and Machinery) [7437]
Hampton Lumber Sales Co. (Construction Materials and Machinery) [7438]
Hoch & Selby Company, Inc. (Textiles and Notions) [26064]
Horizon Micro Distributors (Computers and Software) [6341]

Howell Co.; R.B. (Toys and Hobby Goods) [26528]
Humke Co.; Ken R. (Hardware) [13761]
Ikon Office Solutions (Office Equipment and Supplies) [21050]
Integrated Systems Inc. (Industrial Machinery) [16162]
International Specialized Book Services (Books and Other Printed Materials) [3851]
IPD Co., Inc. (Automotive) [2797]
Isspro Inc. (Automotive) [2801]
Isspro Inc. (Industrial Machinery) [16176]
JaCiva's Chocolate and Pastries (Food) [11539]
Johnson Heating Supply (Heating and Cooling Equipment and Supplies) [14500]
Jordan Inc.; Leslie (Clothing) [5095]
Kako International Inc. (Medical, Dental, and Optical Equipment) [18870]
Kerr Pacific Corp. (Food) [11605]
Koldkist-Beverage Ice Company Inc. (Soft Drinks) [24981]
Kramer; L.C. (Textiles and Notions) [26114]
La Grand Industrial Supply Co. (Security and Safety Equipment) [24582]
Lacey-Harmer Co (Electrical and Electronic Equipment and Supplies) [8963]
Lanahan Sales (Shoes) [24789]
Lanahan Sales (Clothing) [5120]
Landiseed International, Ltd. (Agricultural Equipment and Supplies) [934]
Leatherman Tool Group Inc. (Hardware) [13794]
Lemma Wine Co. (Alcoholic Beverages) [1818]
Liberty Natural Products (Health and Beauty Aids) [14152]
Liberty Natural Products (Medical, Dental, and Optical Supplies) [19414]
Lucky Distributing (Agricultural Equipment and Supplies) [974]
Market Actives, LLC (Chemicals) [4451]
May Company Inc.; W.L. (Household Appliances) [15219]
McCabe's Quality Foods Inc. (Food) [11817]
McCall Oil and Chemical Co. (Petroleum, Fuels, and Related Equipment) [22464]
McClaskeys Wine Spirits & Cigars Distributor (Alcoholic Beverages) [1858]
McGuire Bearing (Automotive) [2934]
Metamorphous Advances Product Services (Books and Other Printed Materials) [3949]
Metaresearch Inc. (Industrial Machinery) [16289]
Metro Metals Northwest (Used, Scrap, and Recycled Materials) [26908]
Microware Inc. (Computers and Software) [6513]
Microwave Oven Company of Oregon (Sound and Entertainment Equipment and Supplies) [25314]
Moore Co. (Sound and Entertainment Equipment and Supplies) [25336]
MOORE Co. (Household Appliances) [15240]
Mounthood Beverage Co. (Alcoholic Beverages) [1895]
Multi-Craft Plastics, Inc. (Plastics) [23002]
Munnell & Sherrill Inc. (Industrial Supplies) [17062]
Nelson Company Inc.; Walter E. (Cleaning and Janitorial Supplies) [4676]
Nor-Mon Distributing Inc. (Household Appliances) [15252]
North Pacific Group, Inc. (Construction Materials and Machinery) [7794]
Northwest Futon Co. (Furniture and Fixtures) [13189]
Northwest Wholesale Distributors (Household Appliances) [15255]
Original Mink Oil Inc. (Chemicals) [4475]
Overland West Press (Books and Other Printed Materials) [4028]
Pac-West Inc. (Construction Materials and Machinery) [7819]
Pacific Airgas Inc. (Industrial Machinery) [16370]
Pacific Coast Fruit Co. (Food) [12088]
Pacific Detroit Diesel Allison Co. (Industrial Machinery) [16371]
Pacific Fluid Systems Corp. (Industrial Machinery) [16373]
Pacific Machinery and Tool Steel Co. (Metals) [20261]
Pacific Metal Co. (Metals) [20262]

Pacific Trade Wind Inc. (Clothing) [5263]
Pacific Utility Equipment Co. (Industrial Machinery) [16377]
Patrick Lumber Company Inc. (Construction Materials and Machinery) [7840]
Peake Marketing Inc. (Computers and Software) [6607]
Performance Northwest Inc. (Food) [12151]
Plywood Tropics USA Inc. (Construction Materials and Machinery) [7876]
Pollock; Ralph (Food) [12188]
Poppers Supply Co. (Food) [12194]
Portland Bottling Co. (Food) [12198]
Portland State University, School of Extended Studies, Continuing Education Press (Books and Other Printed Materials) [4074]
Potter-Webster Co. (Automotive) [3105]
Powell Distributing Company Inc. (Petroleum, Fuels, and Related Equipment) [22590]
Power & Telephone Supply Company, Inc. (Communications Systems and Equipment) [5717]
Products Corp. of North America, Inc. (Food) [12226]
Quimby Corp. (Industrial Supplies) [17126]
Quimby Corp. (Industrial Machinery) [16435]
Radar Electric (Electrical and Electronic Equipment and Supplies) [9255]
Redhawk Industries Inc. (Wood and Wood Products) [27362]
Rexel-Taylor (Electrical and Electronic Equipment and Supplies) [9290]
Roberts Motor Co. (Motorized Vehicles) [20713]
Roberts Motor Co. (Industrial Machinery) [16455]
Rodda Paint Co. (Paints and Varnishes) [21557]
Rogers Machinery Company Inc. (Industrial Machinery) [16458]
Rose City Awning Co. (Textiles and Notions) [26192]
Ross Island Sand and Gravel Co. (Construction Materials and Machinery) [7961]
Rykoff & Co.; S.E. (Paper and Paper Products) [21916]
S & F Associates Inc. (Recreational and Sporting Goods) [23927]
S & W Farm Equipment (Agricultural Equipment and Supplies) [1224]
Sanderson Safety Supply Co. (Security and Safety Equipment) [24624]
Schenck Co.; E.E. (Textiles and Notions) [26198]
Schetky Northwest Sales Inc. (Motorized Vehicles) [20719]
Schnitzer Steel Products (Used, Scrap, and Recycled Materials) [26982]
School Specialty Inc. (Office Equipment and Supplies) [21259]
Scotty's Foods Inc. (Food) [12435]
Sewing Center Supply Co. (Household Appliances) [15310]
Shaws-Healthtick (Medical, Dental, and Optical Supplies) [19606]
Shepler Refrigeration Inc. (Heating and Cooling Equipment and Supplies) [14680]
Smith Brothers Office Environments Inc. (Office Equipment and Supplies) [21273]
SPADA Enterprises Ltd. (Food) [12546]
Spar Tek Industries Inc. (Industrial Machinery) [16516]
Spectronics Inc. (Industrial Machinery) [16517]
Stash Tea Co. (Food) [12576]
Steel Yard Inc. (Metals) [20404]
StorageTek (Computers and Software) [6764]
Strawberry Hill Press (Books and Other Printed Materials) [4193]
Sunshine Dairy Foods Inc. (Food) [12620]
Thompson Tile Co., Inc. (Floorcovering Equipment and Supplies) [10215]
Tile Distributors Inc. (Floorcovering Equipment and Supplies) [10232]
Tiles For Less (Floorcovering Equipment and Supplies) [10248]
Timberwork Oregon Inc. (Wood and Wood Products) [27389]
TMX (Metals) [20427]
Transco Industries Inc. (Industrial Machinery) [16574]

Transmission Exchange Co. (Automotive) [3327]
Tree Frog Trucking Co. (Books and Other Printed Materials) [4229]
Triad Machinery Inc. (Construction Materials and Machinery) [8147]
TRM Copy Centers Corp. (Office Equipment and Supplies) [21324]
Trym-Tex, Inc. (Floorcovering Equipment and Supplies) [10259]
Tumac Lumber Company Inc. (Construction Materials and Machinery) [8153]
U.S. World Trade Corp. (Livestock and Farm Products) [18305]
VantageParts Inc. (Automotive) [3387]
Vintage House Merchants, Inc. (Alcoholic Beverages) [2104]
Wade and Co.; R.M. (Agricultural Equipment and Supplies) [1403]
Wanke Cascade (Floorcovering Equipment and Supplies) [10286]
West Coast Wire Rope and Rigging Inc. (Industrial Supplies) [17274]
West Ridge Designs (Luggage and Leather Goods) [18444]
Western Family Foods Inc. (Food) [12914]
Western Fluid Power (Industrial Machinery) [16628]
Western Photo Packaging (Photographic Equipment and Supplies) [22915]
Western Stations Co. (Petroleum, Fuels, and Related Equipment) [22798]
Willamette Electric Products Co. (Industrial Machinery) [16634]
Wood Feathers Inc. (Construction Materials and Machinery) [8239]
Woodcrafters Lumber Sales, Inc. (Books and Other Printed Materials) [4293]
Worldwide Wonders (Food) [12984]
Yancey Machine Tool Co. (Industrial Machinery) [16655]
Zidell Marine Corp. (Marine) [18646]

Prineville

Schwab Warehouse Center Inc.; Les (Automotive) [3198]

Redmond

Sat-Pak Inc. (Electrical and Electronic Equipment and Supplies) [9336]

Rickreall

Polk County Farmers Cooperative (Agricultural Equipment and Supplies) [1138]
Rickreall Farms Supply Inc. (Agricultural Equipment and Supplies) [1192]

Roseburg

Jackson Wholesale Company Inc.; Paul (Food) [11545]
Umpqua Dairy Products Co. (Food) [12782]

St. Paul

St. Paul Feed and Supply Inc. (Agricultural Equipment and Supplies) [1229]

Salem

Ark Manufacturing Inc. (Veterinary Products) [27074]
Bailey Seed Company, Inc. (Agricultural Equipment and Supplies) [270]
Capital City Companies Inc. (Petroleum, Fuels, and Related Equipment) [22107]
Eoff Electric Co. (Electrical and Electronic Equipment and Supplies) [8712]
Gensco, Inc. (Heating and Cooling Equipment and Supplies) [14463]
Kettle Foods (Food) [11606]
Mill Supply Corp. (Automotive) [2963]
Morrow Equipment Company L.L.C. (Industrial Machinery) [16328]
Olsen-Fennell Seeds, Inc. (Agricultural Equipment and Supplies) [1106]
Oregon Educational Technology Consortium (Computers and Software) [6576]
Pepsi-Cola of Salem (Soft Drinks) [25020]
Pumilite-Salem Inc. (Construction Materials and Machinery) [7891]

Rainsweet (Food) [12270]
Red Steer Glove Co. (Clothing) [5305]
Saffron Supply Co. (Hardware) [13899]
Seven-Up Salem (Soft Drinks) [25037]
Steelco Inc. (Metals) [20405]
Stusser Electric Co. (Electrical and Electronic
Equipment and Supplies) [9437]
Valley Oil Co. (Petroleum, Fuels, and Related
Equipment) [22767]
Valley Welding Supply Inc. (Industrial
Supplies) [17250]
Western Tool Supply Inc. (Hardware) [13996]

Scappoose
West Coast Shoe Co. (Shoes) [24891]
West Coast Shoe Co. (Clothing) [5481]

Sheridan
Taylor Lumber and Treating Inc. (Construction
Materials and Machinery) [8100]

Sisters
Keeter Manufacturing, Inc. (Automotive) [2844]

Springfield
International Brands West (Alcoholic
Beverages) [1775]
Mr. Logo Inc. (Clothing) [5208]
Oregon Floral Distributors (Horticultural
Supplies) [14932]
Practical Computer Inc. (Computers and
Software) [6632]
Red Wing Shoe Store (Shoes) [24839]
Timber Products Co. (Construction Materials and
Machinery) [8135]
True Value Regional
Distributor (Hardware) [13967]
Vicki Lane Design (Gifts and Novelties) [13467]
Zilkoski's Auto Electric (Electrical and Electronic
Equipment and Supplies) [9627]

Sutherlin
Orenco Systems Inc. (Industrial Machinery) [16364]

Sweet Home
Fly Guard Systems Inc. (Chemicals) [4392]

Talent
Micro-Trains Line Co. (Toys and Hobby
Goods) [26576]

Tangent
Ampac Seed Co. (Agricultural Equipment and
Supplies) [238]
NK Lawn & Garden Co. (Agricultural Equipment
and Supplies) [1076]
Pickseed West, Inc. (Agricultural Equipment and
Supplies) [1128]
Roberts Seed Co. (Agricultural Equipment and
Supplies) [1200]
Turf Merchants (Agricultural Equipment and
Supplies) [1364]
Western Farm Service/Cascade (Agricultural
Equipment and Supplies) [1430]

Tigard
Barnsley-Weis Associates Inc. (Household
Appliances) [15045]
Empire Equities Inc. (Medical, Dental, and Optical
Supplies) [19304]
MICROTECH Systems Inc. (Computers and
Software) [6511]

Tualatin
Continental Marketing (Electrical and Electronic
Equipment and Supplies) [8575]
Crystal Lite Manufacturing Co (Metals) [19909]
Delta Engineering and Manufacturing
Co. (Metals) [19923]
Dependable Foundry Equipment Co. (Industrial
Machinery) [15941]
FEI America Inc. (Computers and Software) [6268]
Monje Forest Products Co. (Construction Materials
and Machinery) [7738]

Sentrol Inc. (Electrical and Electronic Equipment
and Supplies) [9355]
SLC Technologies Inc. (Security and Safety
Equipment) [24637]
Todd-Zenner Packaging (Paper and Paper
Products) [21953]

Vale
Quisenberrys Inc. (Clothing) [5296]

Warrenton
Comstor Technology Inc. (Computers and
Software) [6141]
Lektro Inc. (Aeronautical Equipment and
Supplies) [115]

White City
Medply (Wood and Wood Products) [27344]
Sattex Corp. (Chemicals) [4502]

Wilsonville
Caffall Brothers Forest Products Inc. (Construction
Materials and Machinery) [7124]
Extech Ltd. (Medical, Dental, and Optical
Equipment) [18794]
Hillsdale Sash and Door Co (Wood and Wood
Products) [27318]
JMR Inc. (Clothing) [5088]
LPKF Laser and Electronics (Industrial
Machinery) [16249]
Pacific Commerce Company Inc. (Food) [12089]
PML Inc. (Medical, Dental, and Optical
Supplies) [19545]
PML Microbiologicals Inc. (Medical, Dental, and
Optical Supplies) [19546]
Stusser Electric Co. (Electrical and Electronic
Equipment and Supplies) [9436]
SYSCO Food Services of Portland (Food) [12686]
Tektronix Inc. Logic Analyzer Div. (Computers and
Software) [6806]

Woodburn
Woodburn Fertilizer Inc. (Agricultural Equipment and
Supplies) [1462]

Pennsylvania

Abington
Volz Truck Equipment, Inc.;
L.W. (Automotive) [3394]

Allentown
Aetna Felt Corp. Mechanical Felt and Textile
Div. (Textiles and Notions) [25954]
Allentown Beverage Company Inc. (Alcoholic
Beverages) [1478]
Allentown News Agency Inc. (Books and Other
Printed Materials) [3492]
Allentown Optical Corp. (Medical, Dental, and
Optical Supplies) [19136]
B & M Provision Co. (Food) [10483]
Banko Enterprises Inc. (Alcoholic
Beverages) [1499]
Coleman Electric Company Inc. (Electrical and
Electronic Equipment and Supplies) [8539]
Ebeling & Reuss Co. (Gifts and Novelties) [13351]
Engineered Drives (Automotive) [2591]
Hale Trailer Brake & Wheel (Automotive) [2719]
Hawk Flour Mills Inc. (Food) [11395]
Kinder Seed Co. (Agricultural Equipment and
Supplies) [911]
Luckenbach and Johnson Inc. (Electrical and
Electronic Equipment and Supplies) [9008]
Michel Company Inc.; R.E. (Heating and Cooling
Equipment and Supplies) [14562]
Suk Fashions (Clothing) [5402]
Vitra Seating Inc. (Office Equipment and
Supplies) [21340]
Wagner Appliance Parts Inc. (Household
Appliances) [15362]

Allison Park
Allegheny Inc. (Floorcovering Equipment and
Supplies) [9654]
Allegheny Inc. (Household Items) [15394]

Altoona
ADT Security Systems (Security and Safety
Equipment) [24488]
Allegheny Electronics Inc. (Sound and
Entertainment Equipment and Supplies) [25061]
Electric Motor and Supply Inc. (Electrical and
Electronic Equipment and Supplies) [8664]
Hite Co. (Electrical and Electronic Equipment and
Supplies) [8850]
Imlers Poultry (Food) [11498]
Items International Airwalk Inc. (Shoes) [24773]
Lee and Sons Inc.; W.S. (Food) [11693]
Maytown Shoe Manufacturing Company
Inc. (Shoes) [24805]
Michel Company Inc.; R.E. (Heating and Cooling
Equipment and Supplies) [14563]
Newborn Enterprises Inc. (Books and Other Printed
Materials) [3999]
Sky Brothers Inc. (Food) [12503]
To Market Two Markets Inc. (Food) [12725]

Ambridge
Central Radio and TV Inc. (Sound and
Entertainment Equipment and Supplies) [25131]
United States Export Co. (Motorized
Vehicles) [20741]

Ardara
Precise Industries, Inc. (Office Equipment and
Supplies) [21222]

Ardmore
Gotham Distributing Corp. (Sound and
Entertainment Equipment and Supplies) [25215]
Hajoca Corp. (Plumbing Materials and
Fixtures) [23201]
Kelleigh Corporation (Industrial Machinery) [16201]
Knight Corp. (Industrial Supplies) [16992]
The Wine Merchant (Alcoholic Beverages) [2125]

Arnold
City Bottling Company Inc. (Soft Drinks) [24926]

Aston
Bodman Chemicals, Inc. (Chemicals) [4337]
Goodall Rubber Co. (Industrial Supplies) [16899]
Scientific Equipment Co. (Scientific and
Measurement Devices) [24429]
Smith-Koch Inc. (Industrial Machinery) [16498]

Austin
Emporium Specialties Company Inc. (Electrical and
Electronic Equipment and Supplies) [8703]

Avoca
Craft Oil Corp. (Petroleum, Fuels, and Related
Equipment) [22177]

Baden
Andersons Candy Company (Food) [10414]

Bala Cynwyd
Aamco Transmissions Inc. (Automotive) [2161]

BaLa Cynwyd
American Renaissance Paper Corp. (Paper and
Paper Products) [21632]

Bala Cynwyd
WWF Paper Corp. (Paper and Paper
Products) [21998]

Bangor
Windjammer Inc. (Clothing) [5489]

Bath
Keystone Cement Co. (Construction Materials and
Machinery) [7553]

Mary Fashion Manufacturing Company
Inc. (Clothing) [5170]
Northampton County Seed (Agricultural Equipment
and Supplies) [1082]

Beaver Meadows
Lehigh Gas and Oil Co. (Petroleum, Fuels, and
Related Equipment) [22425]

Bedford
Bedford Farm Bureau Cooperative (Agricultural
Equipment and Supplies) [290]
Blackburn-Russell Company Inc. (Food) [10564]

Belle Vernon
Guttman Oil Co. (Petroleum, Fuels, and Related
Equipment) [22330]

Bellefonte
Centre Oil and Gas Co. Inc. (Petroleum, Fuels,
and Related Equipment) [22128]

Belleville
Peachey and Sons Inc.; A.J. (Food) [12125]

Bellwood
Martin Oil Co. (Petroleum, Fuels, and Related
Equipment) [22454]

Bensalem
Afy Security Distributros (Security and Safety
Equipment) [24496]
Airline Hydraulics Corp. (Industrial
Supplies) [16682]
Brown of Pennsylvania Corp.; D.P. (Industrial
Machinery) [15848]
Bucks County Distributors (Food) [10638]
Bundy Enterprises Inc. (Metals) [19842]
Carpet Warehouse Connection (Floorcovering
Equipment and Supplies) [9771]
CCC Heavy Duty Trucks Co. (Automotive) [2436]
Crystal Tile (Construction Materials and
Machinery) [7234]
Daltile (Construction Materials and
Machinery) [7248]
Eastern Furniture Distributors (Furniture and
Fixtures) [13098]
Edgcomb Corp. (Metals) [19949]
General Floor (Floorcovering Equipment and
Supplies) [9915]
Giles and Ransome Inc. (Industrial
Machinery) [16065]
Hoshino U.S.A. Inc. (Sound and Entertainment
Equipment and Supplies) [25238]
Jack and Jill Ice Cream (Food) [11540]
JR Distributors (Food) [11571]
K & S Distributors (Medical, Dental, and Optical
Supplies) [19391]
Macsteel Service Centers USA - Edgcomb Metals
Div. (Metals) [20141]
Pako Steel Inc. (Metals) [20264]
Pennsylvania Steel Co. (Metals) [20271]
Schutte and Koerting Div. (Household
Appliances) [15305]
Simco Sales Service of
Pennsylvania (Food) [12494]
Tile Gallery Inc. (Floorcovering Equipment and
Supplies) [10237]

Berwick
Bennies Warehouse Distribution Center (Household
Appliances) [15049]

Berwyn
Royce, Inc. (Office Equipment and
Supplies) [21250]

Bethel Park
ATI Communications (Communications Systems and
Equipment) [5522]
Blackwell Stevenson Co. (Food) [10566]
Michel Company Inc.; R.E. (Heating and Cooling
Equipment and Supplies) [14564]
Programma Incorporated (Computers and
Software) [6653]

Tri River Foods Inc. (Food) [12753]

Bethlehem
Apria Healthcare (Medical, Dental, and Optical
Supplies) [19157]
Bethlehem Steel Export Corp. (Metals) [19820]
Cromland, Inc. (Books and Other Printed
Materials) [3673]

Blakeslee
Farmers Cooperative Dairy Inc. (Food) [11097]

Blandon
Campbell's Fresh Inc. (Food) [10687]
Old Dutch Bakery Inc. (Food) [12061]

Blossburg
Ward Manufacturing Inc. (Metals) [20478]

Blue Bell
Fluid Power Inc. (Industrial Machinery) [16021]

Boothwyn
Delaware County Supply Co. (Hardware) [13658]
Huff Paper Co. (Paper and Paper
Products) [21771]

Bowmansville
Crest Truck Equipment Co.
Inc. (Automotive) [2495]

Braddock
Leff Electronics Inc. (Electrical and Electronic
Equipment and Supplies) [8980]

Bradford
KOA Speer Electronics Inc. (Electrical and
Electronic Equipment and Supplies) [8954]
State Line Supply Co. (Metals) [20390]

Bridgeville
Anderson Equipment Co. (Construction Materials
and Machinery) [6974]
Queens City Distributing Co. (Recreational and
Sporting Goods) [23900]
RAMM Global (Food) [12272]
RAMM Metals Inc. (Food) [12273]

Bristol
Cummins Power Systems Inc. (Automotive) [2513]
Loos and Dilworth Inc. (Chemicals) [4441]
Modern Group Ltd. (Industrial Machinery) [16317]
Otter Recycling (Metals) [20257]
Service Plus Distributors Inc. (Hardware) [13912]
Stephens; Stanley (Floorcovering Equipment and
Supplies) [10181]
Weed Chevrolet Company Inc. (Motorized
Vehicles) [20749]

Brookville
McMurray Printing Co. (Specialty Equipment and
Products) [25733]

Broomall
Bruder and Sons Inc.; M.A. (Paints and
Varnishes) [21408]
Main Line Book Company Inc. (Books and Other
Printed Materials) [3930]
Smith; Nicholas (Toys and Hobby Goods) [26655]

Brownsville
Express Optical Lab (Medical, Dental, and Optical
Supplies) [19314]

Bryn Mawr
Presser Co.; Theodore (Books and Other Printed
Materials) [4082]

Butler
Butler County Motor Company
Inc. (Automotive) [2404]
GTH Holdings, Inc. (Construction Materials and
Machinery) [7421]

Heckett Multiserv Div. (Used, Scrap, and Recycled
Materials) [26840]
Logan Inc. (Food) [11722]
Marmon/Keystone Corp. (Metals) [20155]
SERVISTAR Corp. (Construction Materials and
Machinery) [8002]
Skillers Workwear USA, Inc. (Clothing) [5362]

Callery
Byrnes and Kiefer Company Inc. (Food) [10654]

Camp Hill
Amalgamated Automotive Industries
Inc. (Automotive) [2224]
Beecher Candies; Katharine (Food) [10526]
Christian Publications Inc. (Books and Other Printed
Materials) [3637]
Consumers Financial Corp. (Automotive) [2480]
Fager Company Inc.; R.F. (Plumbing Materials and
Fixtures) [23154]

Canonsburg
Computer Research Inc. (Computers and
Software) [6123]

Canton
Rockwell and Son; H. (Agricultural Equipment and
Supplies) [1206]

Carlisle
Banner of Truth (Books and Other Printed
Materials) [3542]

Carnegie
Alpha Video & Electronics Co. (Sound and
Entertainment Equipment and Supplies) [25064]
BMI-France Inc. (Construction Materials and
Machinery) [7063]
E.W. Tire & Service Centers (Automotive) [2598]
Myer Co.; Milton D. (Toys and Hobby
Goods) [26587]
Petroleum Pipe and Supply Inc. (Metals) [20274]

Center Valley
Breezy Ridge Instruments (Sound and
Entertainment Equipment and Supplies) [25108]

Chadds Ford
Chaddsford Winery (Alcoholic Beverages) [1588]

Chambersburg
Brown Inc.; C. Earl (Motorized Vehicles) [20606]
Franklin Feed and Supply Co. (Agricultural
Equipment and Supplies) [703]
Gabler Inc.; H.C. (Rubber) [24275]
JCA Technology Group, A TVC
Company (Household Appliances) [15181]
Mid-State Distributors (Books and Other Printed
Materials) [3955]
Nitterhouse Concrete Product Inc. (Construction
Materials and Machinery) [7782]
Nitterhouse Masonry Products, LLC (Construction
Materials and Machinery) [7783]
Somerville Co.; Thomas (Plumbing Materials and
Fixtures) [23387]
TVC Technology Group (Sound and Entertainment
Equipment and Supplies) [25487]

Charleroi
Atlas Merchandising Co. (Restaurant and
Commercial Foodservice Equipment and
Supplies) [24072]

Cheltenham
Dittmar Inc. (Medical, Dental, and Optical
Supplies) [19283]

Chester
Hardware and Supply Company of Chester
Inc. (Industrial Supplies) [16923]
Michel Company Inc.; R.E. (Heating and Cooling
Equipment and Supplies) [14565]
Safeguard International, Inc. (Security and Safety
Equipment) [24621]

Chester Springs
AVM Products, Inc. (Veterinary Products) [27076]
Dufour Editions, Inc. (Books and Other Printed Materials) [3702]

Clarks Summit
Krieger Associates; J. (Specialty Equipment and Products) [25707]

Clearfield
JV Inc. (Petroleum, Fuels, and Related Equipment) [22393]
Petrolec Inc. (Petroleum, Fuels, and Related Equipment) [22567]
Soult Wholesale Co. (Construction Materials and Machinery) [8041]

Cleona
Meyer Oil Co. (Petroleum, Fuels, and Related Equipment) [22478]

Clifford
Walczak Lumber Inc. (Construction Materials and Machinery) [8192]

Clifton Heights
Capp Inc. (Electrical and Electronic Equipment and Supplies) [8499]
Vehicle Services/Commercial Truck & Van Equipment (Automotive) [3389]

Cogan Station
JanWay Co. (Gifts and Novelties) [13378]

Collegeville
Euro American Trading-Merchants Inc. (Food) [11058]

Collingdale
Copper and Brass Sales (Metals) [19895]

Colmar
Royal Auto Supply Inc. (Automotive) [3177]

Columbia
Gordon Waste Company Inc. (Used, Scrap, and Recycled Materials) [26832]

Concordville
Stull Enterprises Inc. (Agricultural Equipment and Supplies) [1301]
Watkins System Inc. (Aeronautical Equipment and Supplies) [169]

Conneautville
Master Feed and Grain Inc. (Agricultural Equipment and Supplies) [991]

Conshohocken
Asbury Automotive Group (Automotive) [2259]
Florig Equipment (Industrial Machinery) [16013]
Recycle Metals Corp. (Used, Scrap, and Recycled Materials) [26953]
The Validation Group Inc. (Medical, Dental, and Optical Supplies) [19687]
Wricley Nut Products Co. Edwards-Freeman Div. (Food) [12986]
Young Windows Inc. (Automotive) [3452]

Coraopolis
Equipment Corporation of America (Construction Materials and Machinery) [7314]
Export Consultant Service (Scientific and Measurement Devices) [24358]
FW Sales (Clothing) [4971]

Corry
Hillandale Farms Inc. of Pennsylvania (Food) [11432]
Xander Co. Inc.; A.L. (Industrial Machinery) [16652]

Cranberry Township
Doyle Equipment Co. (Construction Materials and Machinery) [7287]
Three Rivers Aluminum Co. (Construction Materials and Machinery) [8128]

Cranberry Twp
Penn Telecom Inc. (Communications Systems and Equipment) [5707]

Croydon
Appliance Parts Distributors Inc. (Household Appliances) [15023]
Philadelphia Reserve Supply Co. (Construction Materials and Machinery) [7859]

Dallas
Pen-Fern Oil Co. (Petroleum, Fuels, and Related Equipment) [22559]

Danville
FABTEX Inc. (Household Items) [15493]
Whitenight; Delavan E. (Food) [12933]

Denver
Gehman Feed Mill Inc. (Agricultural Equipment and Supplies) [731]

Douglassville
Kiwi Brands (Health and Beauty Aids) [14143]

Downingtown
Ivystone Group (Household Items) [15542]
Kruse Inc. (Motorized Vehicles) [20666]

Doylestown
Penn Color Inc. (Paints and Varnishes) [21535]
Quigley Corp. (Medical, Dental, and Optical Supplies) [19564]

Du Bois
E & G Auto Parts Inc. (Automotive) [2570]
Penn Traffic Co. Riverside Div. (Food) [12140]

Duquesne
Myers Group Inc.; J.B. (Heating and Cooling Equipment and Supplies) [14616]

East Berlin
Andgrow Fertilizer (Agricultural Equipment and Supplies) [243]

East Stroudsburg
Red Apple Food Marts Inc. (Food) [12282]

Easton
Braden's Flying Service Inc. (Aeronautical Equipment and Supplies) [61]
Easton Iron and Metal Co. Inc. (Used, Scrap, and Recycled Materials) [26802]
Emery Distributors (Toys and Hobby Goods) [26477]
Fuller Paper Company Inc. (Paper and Paper Products) [21731]
Losey and Company Inc. (Industrial Supplies) [17004]
Moss Dynamics (Automotive) [2988]
R and R Provision Co. (Food) [12258]
Reda Sports Express (Recreational and Sporting Goods) [23909]

Eddystone
Viva Vino Import Corp. (Alcoholic Beverages) [2107]

Effort
B Sharp Co. (Veterinary Products) [27078]

Eighty Four
84 Lumber Co. (Construction Materials and Machinery) [6894]
Atlas Railroad Construction Co. (Railroad Equipment and Supplies) [23473]

Elizabeth
Charles Bluestone Co. (Metals) [19873]

Elizabethtown
Groff Meats Inc. (Food) [11336]
Newcomer Oil Corp. (Petroleum, Fuels, and Related Equipment) [22513]

Elizabethville
Metal Industries Inc. (Construction Materials and Machinery) [7700]

Elkins Park
Bitzer Company Inc.; R.D. (Heating and Cooling Equipment and Supplies) [14348]
Franklin Book Company, Inc. (Books and Other Printed Materials) [3763]

Ellwood City
Airway Industries Inc. (Luggage and Leather Goods) [18367]

Emmaus
Software Associates Inc. (Computers and Software) [6739]

Ephrata
Hamilton Equipment Inc. (Agricultural Equipment and Supplies) [785]
Keystone Mills (Agricultural Equipment and Supplies) [910]

Erie
Airport Beer Distributors (Alcoholic Beverages) [1475]
Allied Eastern Distributors (Floorcovering Equipment and Supplies) [9658]
ASI Erie (Automotive) [2261]
Brina Steel Products Inc. (Metals) [19836]
Builders Hardware & Specialties (Hardware) [13611]
Curtze Steel Inc. (Metals) [19910]
Decker Steel & Supply Co. (Metals) [19920]
Donico & Associates; J.P. (Medical, Dental, and Optical Equipment) [18778]
Elmwood Beer Distributor (Alcoholic Beverages) [1675]
Erie Beer Co. (Alcoholic Beverages) [1678]
Erie Concrete Steel (Metals) [19956]
Erie Concrete and Steel Supply Co. (Metals) [19957]
Erie Industrial Supply Co. (Industrial Machinery) [15998]
Erie Petroleum Inc. (Petroleum, Fuels, and Related Equipment) [22239]
Erie Sand and Gravel Co. (Construction Materials and Machinery) [7317]
Erie Steel Products Inc. (Metals) [19958]
Findley Welding Supply Inc. (Industrial Supplies) [16861]
Green's/Pine Avenue Beer Distibuting (Alcoholic Beverages) [1732]
Hilltop Beer Distributing (Alcoholic Beverages) [1758]
Lake Erie Supply, Inc. (Construction Materials and Machinery) [7577]
Liberty Iron and Metal Company Inc. (Used, Scrap, and Recycled Materials) [26883]
Michel Company Inc.; R.E. (Heating and Cooling Equipment and Supplies) [14566]
Niagara Medical (Medical, Dental, and Optical Supplies) [19495]
Reed Manufacturing Co. (Industrial Supplies) [17133]
Rehab Specialties (Medical, Dental, and Optical Supplies) [19575]
Smith Provision Company Inc. (Food) [12514]
Walter's Meat Co. (Food) [12872]
West Penn Optical (Medical, Dental, and Optical Supplies) [19697]

Evans City
Fort Pitt Brand Meat Co. (Food) [11192]
Paracca & Sons; Peter (Floorcovering Equipment and Supplies) [10099]

Pittsburgh Plug and Products (Plumbing Materials and Fixtures) [23316]

Everett
Bedford Valley Petroleum Corp. (Petroleum, Fuels, and Related Equipment) [22063]

Exeter
American Office Systems (Office Equipment and Supplies) [20796]
Friedman Electric Supply (Electrical and Electronic Equipment and Supplies) [8762]
Keystone Automotive Operations Inc. (Automotive) [2852]

Exton
Chiral Technologies Inc. (Scientific and Measurement Devices) [24338]
Icon Office Solutions (Office Equipment and Supplies) [21047]
Intelligent Electronics Inc. (Computers and Software) [6381]
Intelligent Electronics Inc. Advanced Systems Div. (Computers and Software) [6382]
Pamas and Company Inc. (Construction Materials and Machinery) [7832]
Trotter and Company Inc.; Nathan (Metals) [20443]
Unisource Worldwide Inc. (Paper and Paper Products) [21970]
Wolfington Body Company Inc. (Motorized Vehicles) [20752]

Fairless Hills
Graebers Lumber Co. (Construction Materials and Machinery) [7406]

Farmington
Plough Publishing House (Books and Other Printed Materials) [4068]

Feasterville
Berger Building Products Corp. (Construction Materials and Machinery) [7048]
Epco-JKD Food Brokers Inc. (Food) [11051]
Tile Creations (Floorcovering Equipment and Supplies) [10230]

Fernwood
Arch Associates Corp. (Computers and Software) [5957]

Finleyville
Trax Farms Inc. (Food) [12745]

Fleetwood
Penn Detroit Diesel (Automotive) [3089]

Folcroft
Habbersett Sausage Inc. (Food) [11353]

Ford City
Meyers; Tom (Veterinary Products) [27188]

Forest City
Jerry's Sport Center Inc. (Recreational and Sporting Goods) [23756]

Ft. Washington
Beemer Precision Inc. (Industrial Supplies) [16746]
Kennametal (Industrial Supplies) [16985]
Springfield Paper Specialties, Inc. (Paper and Paper Products) [21948]

Franklin
Sehman Tire Service Inc. (Automotive) [3203]

Frazer
American Sweeteners Inc. (Food) [10405]
Barker Pipe Fittings Inc. (Industrial Supplies) [16720]
Decision Data Service Inc. (Computers and Software) [6192]
Essex Grain Products Co. (Food) [11053]

Fredericksburg
Pennfield Corp. Pennfield Farms-Poultry Meat Div. (Food) [12142]

Gallitzin
Seven D Wholesale (Construction Materials and Machinery) [8004]

Genesee
Genesee Natural Foods (Food) [11253]

Gettysburg
TEM Inc. (Gifts and Novelties) [13462]

Gibsonia
Bon Tool Co. (Hardware) [13602]
North Pittsburgh Systems Inc. (Communications Systems and Equipment) [5695]

Girard
Paragon Packaging Products Inc. (Paper and Paper Products) [21867]

Gladwyne
Seven-Up Baltimore Inc. (Soft Drinks) [25034]

Glasgow
Hommer Lumber Co.; J.H. (Construction Materials and Machinery) [7483]

Glassport
Tube City Inc. (Used, Scrap, and Recycled Materials) [27027]

Glenolden
LDC Corporation of America (Medical, Dental, and Optical Equipment) [18883]

Glenside
Ledgerwood-Herwig Associates Ltd. (Household Appliances) [15202]

Gratz
Kwik-Way Corp. (Food) [11657]

Greeley
Biddle Service; Dorothy (Horticultural Supplies) [14829]

Greencastle
Fresh Express (Food) [11207]

Greensburg
Allegheny High Lift Inc. (Industrial Machinery) [15756]
Laurel Vending Inc. (Soft Drinks) [24983]
Michel Company Inc.; R.E. (Heating and Cooling Equipment and Supplies) [14567]
Parkway Food Service Inc. (Food) [12117]
Pet Supply Warehouse (Veterinary Products) [27211]
Rugby Building Products Inc. (Construction Materials and Machinery) [7967]
Rugby Building Products Inc. (Wood and Wood Products) [27366]
Stuart Medical Inc. (Medical, Dental, and Optical Equipment) [19058]
Stuart's Hospital Supply Co. (Medical, Dental, and Optical Supplies) [19640]
Westmoreland Industrial Supply Co. (Industrial Supplies) [17277]

Grove City
Howe Company Inc.; George J. (Food) [11467]

Halifax
Greene Equipment Co. (Automotive) [2706]

Hanover
Best Beauty Supply Co. (Health and Beauty Aids) [14039]
Cam Industries, Inc. (Industrial Machinery) [15868]
Hanover Sales Co. (Food) [11372]

McIlvain Co.; T. Baird (Construction Materials and Machinery) [7683]
Staff (Toys and Hobby Goods) [26666]
Swam Electric Company Inc. (Electrical and Electronic Equipment and Supplies) [9449]

Harleysville
Alderfer, Inc. (Food) [10360]
Silver Springs Farm Inc. (Food) [12493]

Harmony
Deaktor/Sysco Food Services Co. (Food) [10926]

Harrisburg
Beer World (Alcoholic Beverages) [1517]
Bonitz Brothers Inc. (Recreational and Sporting Goods) [23564]
BSC Litho Inc. (Books and Other Printed Materials) [3598]
Cleveland Brothers Equipment Company Inc. (Construction Materials and Machinery) [7182]
Consolidated Scrap Resources, Inc. (Used, Scrap, and Recycled Materials) [26785]
D and H Distributing Co. (Computers and Software) [6175]
D and H Distributing Co. (Household Appliances) [15103]
Dauphin Electrical Supply Co. (Electrical and Electronic Equipment and Supplies) [8611]
Direct Office Furniture Outlet (Office Equipment and Supplies) [20964]
Environmental Interiors (Office Equipment and Supplies) [20993]
Feesers Inc. (Food) [11117]
Industrial Motor Supply Inc. (Construction Materials and Machinery) [7509]
KLF, Inc. (Food) [11624]
McCombs Supply Co. (Household Appliances) [15222]
Michel Company Inc.; R.E. (Heating and Cooling Equipment and Supplies) [14568]
MILTCO Corp. (Books and Other Printed Materials) [3961]
The Morehouse Group, Inc. (Books and Other Printed Materials) [3968]
Petroleum Products Corp. (Petroleum, Fuels, and Related Equipment) [22569]
Raylon Corp. (Health and Beauty Aids) [14209]
Resource Net International (Paper and Paper Products) [21903]
Rubin Brothers Company Inc. (Industrial Supplies) [17149]
Santanna Banana Co. (Food) [12410]
Schaedler/Yesco Distribution (Electrical and Electronic Equipment and Supplies) [9341]
Stephenson Equipment Inc. (Construction Materials and Machinery) [8074]
Super Rite Foods Inc. (Food) [12624]
Swartz Supply Company Inc. (Plumbing Materials and Fixtures) [23402]
SYGMA Network of Pennsylvania Inc. (Food) [12664]
United Restaurant Equipment (Restaurant and Commercial Foodservice Equipment and Supplies) [24256]
Wilsbach Distributors Inc. (Alcoholic Beverages) [2122]
York Electrical Supply Co. (Electrical and Electronic Equipment and Supplies) [9619]

Hartstown
Lakeland Sand and Gravel Inc. (Minerals and Ores) [20551]

Hatboro
HPF L.L.C. (Health and Beauty Aids) [14127]
Stutz Candy Co., Inc. (Food) [12596]

Hatfield
Green Bay Supply Company Inc. (Metals) [20022]
Harf Inc. (Specialty Equipment and Products) [25674]
Hatfield Quality Meats Inc. (Food) [11390]
Transmission Engineering Co. (Automotive) [3326]

Haverford

Philadelphia Fire Retardant Company Inc. (Construction Materials and Machinery) [7858]

Havertown

Kass Electronics Distributors Inc. (Electrical and Electronic Equipment and Supplies) [8929]

Lynch Machinery Co. (Industrial Machinery) [16251]

Hawthorn

Heffner Brothers Co. (Petroleum, Fuels, and Related Equipment) [22344]

Hazleton

Caldwell, Inc.; Bradley (Agricultural Equipment and Supplies) [361]

Caldwell Supply Company Inc. (Livestock and Farm Products) [17759]

Dog Outfitters (Veterinary Products) [27117]

Forbo Industries Inc. (Floorcovering Equipment and Supplies) [9905]

Howard Invitations and Cards (Paper and Paper Products) [21767]

Humboldt Industries, Inc. (Veterinary Products) [27153]

Thomas Kitchens, Inc. (Construction Materials and Machinery) [8121]

Hegins

Twin Valley Farmers Exchange Inc. (Food) [12779]

Hellam

Hellam Hosiery Company Inc. (Clothing) [5025]

Hermitage

Interstate Chemical Co. (Chemicals) [4432]

Hershey

Hershey Foods Corp. (Food) [11421]

Hillsgrove

Lewis Company Inc.; Dwight G. (Construction Materials and Machinery) [7599]

Hollidaysburg

James Industries Inc. (Toys and Hobby Goods) [26540]

Homestead

Elite Supply Co. (Health and Beauty Aids) [14093]

Keystone Plumbing Sales Co. (Plumbing Materials and Fixtures) [23234]

Honesdale

Baer Sport Center (Motorized Vehicles) [20597]

Honey Brook

Good Food Inc. (Food) [11289]

Horsham

Advanced Medical Systems Inc. (Medical, Dental, and Optical Equipment) [18661]

International Mill Service Inc. (Used, Scrap, and Recycled Materials) [26852]

Professional Book Service (Books and Other Printed Materials) [4088]

Renaissance Ceramic Tile (Floorcovering Equipment and Supplies) [10119]

Reptron Electronics Inc. (Electrical and Electronic Equipment and Supplies) [9276]

Staneco Corp. (Electrical and Electronic Equipment and Supplies) [9406]

Stokes Equipment Co. (Industrial Machinery) [16529]

Toner Cable Equipment, Inc. (Sound and Entertainment Equipment and Supplies) [25480]

Toner Cable Equipment Inc. (Household Appliances) [15339]

Houston

Pennsylvania Sewing Machine Co. (Household Appliances) [15271]

Huntingdon

Gateway Foods of Pennsylvania Inc. (Food) [11243]

Huntingdon Valley

Mid-Atlantic Spa Distributors (Recreational and Sporting Goods) [23827]

Indiana

Musser Forests Inc. (Horticultural Supplies) [14926]

National Mine Service Co. Mining Safety and Supply Div. (Construction Materials and Machinery) [7767]

National Mine Service Inc. (Security and Safety Equipment) [24599]

Irwin

Shuster's Builders Supply Co. (Construction Materials and Machinery) [8015]

Ivyland

Iiyama North America, Inc. (Computers and Software) [6354]

Keystone Wire & Cable Company Inc. (Electrical and Electronic Equipment and Supplies) [8942]

Neshaminy Valley Natural Foods Distributor, Ltd. (Food) [11995]

Wagner and Sons Inc.; John (Food) [12864]

Jeannette

National Plastics Corp. (Electrical and Electronic Equipment and Supplies) [9117]

Jenkintown

Domestic & International Technology (Automotive) [2555]

Sees & Faber-Berlin Inc. (Industrial Machinery) [16479]

Johnstown

Beerman Auto Supply Inc. (Automotive) [2345]

Glosser and Sons Inc.; M. (Metals) [20010]

Johnstown Axle Works Inc. (Automotive) [2828]

Page Foam Cushion Products Inc. (Furniture and Fixtures) [13201]

Penstan Supply (Plumbing Materials and Fixtures) [23312]

Rose Goldsmith; H.M. (Jewelry) [17574]

Kempton

Dixon Muzzleloading Shop (Guns and Weapons) [13489]

Kennett Square

Bostonian Shoe Co. (Shoes) [24696]

Phillips Mushroom Farms (Food) [12164]

King of Prussia

A and A Connections Inc. (Communications Systems and Equipment) [5497]

Colonial Electric Supply Company Inc. (Electrical and Electronic Equipment and Supplies) [8545]

Ferguson Enterprises Inc. (Heating and Cooling Equipment and Supplies) [14446]

Kunda and Sons Inc.; Watson (Alcoholic Beverages) [1807]

Nero Systems, Inc. (Specialty Equipment and Products) [25755]

Rittenhouse Book Distributors, Inc. (Books and Other Printed Materials) [4118]

Sellers Process Equipment Co. (Industrial Machinery) [16482]

Sweeney Seed Co. (Agricultural Equipment and Supplies) [1309]

Vimco Concrete Accessories Inc. (Construction Materials and Machinery) [8184]

Zuckerman-Honickman Inc. (Storage Equipment and Containers) [25950]

Kingston

Strober Building Supply Center Inc. (Construction Materials and Machinery) [8083]

Vivian Corp. (Construction Materials and Machinery) [8187]

Kittanning

Abranovic Associates Inc. (Books and Other Printed Materials) [3459]

Klingerstown

Troutman Brothers (Petroleum, Fuels, and Related Equipment) [22751]

Kulpsville

Stein Seal Company Inc. (Aeronautical Equipment and Supplies) [151]

Lancaster

Admiral Metals (Metals) [19728]

A.K. International (Gifts and Novelties) [13296]

Carpet Mart & Wallpaper (Floorcovering Equipment and Supplies) [9770]

Carpet Mart & Wallpaper Outlet (Household Items) [15435]

Coast Distribution (Marine) [18482]

Coleman's Ice Cream (Food) [10789]

Conestoga Heating and Plumbing Supply Inc. (Plumbing Materials and Fixtures) [23121]

D-M Tire Supply (Automotive) [2522]

Dutch Gold Honey Inc. (Food) [11003]

Irex Corp. (Construction Materials and Machinery) [7526]

K & W Tire Co. (Automotive) [2837]

Kerr Group Inc. (Plastics) [22986]

Kunzler and Company Inc. (Food) [11656]

Lebzelter and Son Co.; Philip (Automotive) [2876]

Lindenmeyer Munroe (Paper and Paper Products) [21806]

McCarthy Tire Service (Automotive) [2929]

McCombs Supply Company Inc. (Household Appliances) [15223]

McGeary Grain Inc. (Livestock and Farm Products) [18083]

Michel Company Inc.; R.E. (Heating and Cooling Equipment and Supplies) [14569]

Miller and Hartman Inc. (Food) [11898]

Roa Distributors (Paper and Paper Products) [21908]

Rubin Steel Co. (Metals) [20336]

Weaver Co.; James A. (Food) [12890]

Yorktowne Kitchens (Construction Materials and Machinery) [8249]

Langhorne

Computer Hardware Maintenance Company Inc. (Computers and Software) [6113]

Lainiere De Picardie Inc. (Plastics) [22988]

Lansford

Aquilla Fashions Inc. (Clothing) [4779]

Latrobe

Couch's Inc. (Food) [10852]

JLK Direct Distribution Inc. (Industrial Machinery) [16188]

Kennametal Inc. Metalworking Systems Div. (Industrial Machinery) [16203]

Latrobe Brewing Company Inc. (Alcoholic Beverages) [1815]

Lebanon

APR Supply Co. (Heating and Cooling Equipment and Supplies) [14325]

APR Supply Co. (Plumbing Materials and Fixtures) [23067]

Boyer Printing Co. (Specialty Equipment and Products) [25578]

Boyer Printing Co. (Restaurant and Commercial Foodservice Equipment and Supplies) [24082]

Harpel's Inc. (Office Equipment and Supplies) [21027]

Lebanon Building Supply Co. (Construction Materials and Machinery) [7590]

Plasterer Equipment Company Inc. (Agricultural
Equipment and Supplies) [1134]

Leesport
Ram Motors and Controls Inc. (Automotive) [3133]

Leetsdale
Mulach Steel Corp. (Metals) [20211]

Lehigh Valley
Beck Packaging Corp. (Paper and Paper
Products) [21649]
Beck Packaging Corp. (Industrial Supplies) [16744]
Biopractic Group II Inc. (Health and Beauty
Aids) [14049]

Levittown
Terry Inc.; Jesse E. (Plumbing Materials and
Fixtures) [23407]

Lewistown
Havice Inc.; James F. (Health and Beauty
Aids) [14121]
Krentzman and Son Inc.; Joe (Used, Scrap, and
Recycled Materials) [26871]
Krentzman Supply Co. (Used, Scrap, and Recycled
Materials) [26872]
Mann Edge Tool Co. Collins Axe
Div. (Hardware) [13810]

Library
Gage Co. (Industrial Supplies) [16885]

Line Lexington
Burns Industries Inc. (Construction Materials and
Machinery) [7112]
MLT International Inc. (Industrial Supplies) [17045]

Lionville
Petron Oil Corp. (Petroleum, Fuels, and Related
Equipment) [22574]

Lititz
S.K.H. Management Co. (Food) [12500]
Westlake Inc. (Automotive) [3415]

Lock Haven
E.T.S. Distributing (Toys and Hobby
Goods) [26479]

Luzerne
Wasserott's Medical Services Inc. (Medical, Dental,
and Optical Supplies) [19696]

Malvern
Applied Controls Inc. (Electrical and Electronic
Equipment and Supplies) [8365]
Dev-Air Corp. (Industrial Machinery) [15946]
Fisher & Son Co. Inc. (Agricultural Equipment and
Supplies) [689]
Foodsales Inc. (Food) [11181]
Moody Co.; J.A. (Marine) [18572]
PhoneAmerica Corp. (Communications Systems and
Equipment) [5708]
RVS Controls Co. (Industrial Supplies) [17150]

Manchester
Animal Medic Inc. (Veterinary Products) [27067]

Mansfield
Kingdom Co. (Sound and Entertainment Equipment
and Supplies) [25273]

Marcus Hook
McIlvain Co.; Alan (Construction Materials and
Machinery) [7682]

Marion
Statler Body Works (Automotive) [3264]

Mars
Keystone Resources Inc. (Used, Scrap, and
Recycled Materials) [26865]

Michel Company Inc.; R.E. (Heating and Cooling
Equipment and Supplies) [14570]

Mc Kees Rocks
Value Added Distribution Inc. (Metals) [20469]

Mc Keesport
Barno Electronics Corp. (Electrical and Electronic
Equipment and Supplies) [8417]
Elg Metals, Inc. (Used, Scrap, and Recycled
Materials) [26804]
Ireland Alloys Inc. (Used, Scrap, and Recycled
Materials) [26854]
Mon Valley Petroleum Inc. (Petroleum, Fuels, and
Related Equipment) [22492]
Sunray Electric Supply Co. (Electrical and
Electronic Equipment and Supplies) [9442]

McAdoo
More Mobility (Medical, Dental, and Optical
Supplies) [19468]

McKees Rocks
Breen International (Metals) [19834]

McMurray
H and H Distributors Inc. (Automotive) [2714]

McSherrystown
Smiths Sons Co.; F.X. (Tobacco Products) [26350]

Meadville
Channellock Inc. (Hardware) [13632]
J and J Food Service Inc. (Food) [11537]
Michel Company Inc.; R.E. (Heating and Cooling
Equipment and Supplies) [14571]

Mechanicsburg
Fredrico Percussion (Sound and Entertainment
Equipment and Supplies) [25198]
Morgan Distribution Inc. (Construction Materials and
Machinery) [7743]
Stackpole Books (Books and Other Printed
Materials) [4187]

Media
New Testament Christian Press (Books and Other
Printed Materials) [3997]

Merion Station
Valley Forge Leather Co. (Livestock and Farm
Products) [18313]

Meyersdale
Clapper's Building Materials Inc. (Furniture and
Fixtures) [13069]

Middleburg
Petroleum Products Corporation North (Petroleum,
Fuels, and Related Equipment) [22570]

Middletown
Service Motor Parts (Automotive) [3206]
Zeager Brothers Inc. (Wood and Wood
Products) [27399]

Mifflintown
Cameo Kitchens Inc. (Furniture and
Fixtures) [13060]
Keystone STIHL, Inc. (Industrial
Machinery) [16207]
Silky's Sportswear (Clothing) [5356]

Milford
Sparkomatic Corp. (Sound and Entertainment
Equipment and Supplies) [25457]

Milton
Engineered Drives (Industrial Machinery) [15990]

Minersville
Beer City (Alcoholic Beverages) [1515]

Monroeville
Document Solutions Inc. (Office Equipment and
Supplies) [20972]
Glantz & Son; N. (Specialty Equipment and
Products) [25661]
Pennsylvania Floor Coverings (Floorcovering
Equipment and Supplies) [10104]
Raylon Corp. (Health and Beauty Aids) [14208]

Montgomeryville
Closet City Ltd. (Household Items) [15448]
Jetzon Tire and Rubber Company
Inc. (Automotive) [2819]
MIL-Pack Inc. (Electrical and Electronic Equipment
and Supplies) [9080]

Montoursville
Bowser Manufacturing (Toys and Hobby
Goods) [26423]
Montour Oil Service Co. (Petroleum, Fuels, and
Related Equipment) [22495]

Morgan
Servsteel Inc. (Industrial Supplies) [17169]

Morton
FEA Industries, Inc. (Medical, Dental, and Optical
Supplies) [19323]

Mt. Holly Springs
Penna Dutch Co. (Food) [12141]

Mt. Joy
Sico Co. (Petroleum, Fuels, and Related
Equipment) [22670]

Mt. Pleasant
Smith Glass Co.; L.E. (Household Items) [15658]

Mt. Wolf
New York Wire Co. (Metals) [20224]

Muncy
Data Papers Inc. (Paper and Paper
Products) [21703]

Murrysville
Leone's Animal Supply (Veterinary
Products) [27180]

Nanticoke
Phoenix Manufacturing Incorporated (Motorized
Vehicles) [20705]

Nazareth
ESSROC Corp. (Construction Materials and
Machinery) [7322]

New Brighton
Strayer Products (Office Equipment and
Supplies) [21300]

New Britain
International Agricultural Associates,
Inc. (Agricultural Equipment and Supplies) [862]

New Castle
Bruce and Merrilee's Electric Co. (Electrical and
Electronic Equipment and Supplies) [8472]
Crisci Food Equipment Co. (Restaurant and
Commercial Foodservice Equipment and
Supplies) [24097]
Ellwood Quality Steels Co. (Metals) [19952]

New Cumberland
Guthrie-Linebaugh-Coffey, Inc. (Floorcovering
Equipment and Supplies) [9930]

New Freedom
Mann and Parker Lumber Co. (Wood and Wood
Products) [27340]

New Holland
Garden Spot Distributors (Food) [11235]

Pellman Foods Inc. (Food) [12134]

New Hope

Mueller Co.; Charles H. (Horticultural
Supplies) [14924]

New Kensington

Keibler-Thompson Corp. (Metals) [20093]
Whitaker House (Books and Other Printed
Materials) [4280]

New Oxford

Winter Gardens Quality Foods (Food) [12960]

New Stanton

SUPERVALU Inc. Charley Brothers
Div. (Food) [12646]

Newtown

Aero Services International Inc. (Aeronautical
Equipment and Supplies) [24]
Ilapak Inc. (Industrial Machinery) [16141]

Newtown Square

Harrowood Books (Books and Other Printed
Materials) [3815]
National Equipment Development Corp. (Computers
and Software) [6542]
SAP America, Inc. (Computers and
Software) [6703]

Norristown

All Brand Appliance Parts of
Pennsylvania (Household Appliances) [15000]
Laramie Tire Distributors (Automotive) [2873]
Mirabile Beverage Company Inc. (Alcoholic
Beverages) [1881]
Spectrum Communications Corp. (Communications
Systems and Equipment) [5765]

North Huntingdon

EMSCO (Recreational and Sporting
Goods) [23651]
Johnston Florist Inc. (Horticultural
Supplies) [14899]

Norwood

Deltiologists of America (Books and Other Printed
Materials) [3685]

Nuremberg

Edelweiss Publishing Co. (Books and Other Printed
Materials) [3716]

Oaks

Fleming Companies Inc. Philadelphia
Div. (Food) [11152]
Haines & Company, Inc.; J.J. (Floorcovering
Equipment and Supplies) [9932]
Peerless Paper Mills Inc. (Cleaning and Janitorial
Supplies) [4684]
Valley Forge Scientific Corp. (Medical, Dental, and
Optical Equipment) [19098]

Old Forge

Mariotti Building Products Inc. (Construction
Materials and Machinery) [7641]

Palmyra

D.A.S. Distributors, Inc. (Electrical and Electronic
Equipment and Supplies) [8608]

Paradise

Vintage Sales Stables Inc. (Livestock and Farm
Products) [18318]

Parker Ford

Koons Steel Inc. (Metals) [20107]

Pen Argyl

B.J. Toy Manufacturing Co. (Toys and Hobby
Goods) [26421]

Penfield

Georgino and Sons Inc.; Patsy (Industrial
Supplies) [16894]

Penndel

Bernstein Office Machine Co. (Office Equipment
and Supplies) [20840]

Perkasie

Triple Crown America Inc. (Chemicals) [4534]

Philadelphia

A and B Wiper Supply Inc. (Used, Scrap, and
Recycled Materials) [26723]
Acme Manufacturing Co. (Heating and Cooling
Equipment and Supplies) [14294]
Agusta Aerospace Corp. (Aeronautical Equipment
and Supplies) [31]
Airmatic Inc. (Hardware) [13539]
ALMO (Computers and Software) [5911]
Almo Corp. (Computers and Software) [5912]
American Byproducts Inc. (Textiles and
Notions) [25957]
American Paper Products Co. (Paper and Paper
Products) [21629]
Angelo Brothers Co. (Electrical and Electronic
Equipment and Supplies) [8354]
Arbill Inc. (Textiles and Notions) [25966]
Asian World of Martial Arts Inc. (Recreational and
Sporting Goods) [23525]
Associated Medical (Medical, Dental, and Optical
Supplies) [19164]
Associated Services for the Blind (Medical, Dental,
and Optical Supplies) [19165]
Atlantic Aviation Service Inc. (Petroleum, Fuels, and
Related Equipment) [22047]
B & G Optics (Medical, Dental, and Optical
Supplies) [19173]
Bartlett Bearing Co. Inc. (Industrial
Supplies) [16722]
Bean's Beauty Supply (Health and Beauty
Aids) [14035]
Billows Electric Supply Co. (Electrical and
Electronic Equipment and Supplies) [8439]
Bogatin, Inc.; Philip F. (Textiles and
Notions) [25984]
Bower Ammonia and Chemical (Chemicals) [4338]
Brooklyn Bagels Inc. (Food) [10620]
Casani Candy Co. (Food) [10706]
Cellucap-Melco Manufacturing (Clothing) [4872]
Chernin Co.; Eugene (Textiles and
Notions) [26003]
Clement and Muller Inc. (Alcoholic
Beverages) [1603]
Clisby Agency Inc. (Industrial Supplies) [16802]
Coil Plus Pennsylvania Inc. (Metals) [19881]
Colonial Beef Co. (Food) [10793]
CompuData Inc. (Computers and Software) [6096]
Continental Ceramic Tile (Floorcovering Equipment
and Supplies) [9824]
Coronet Books, Inc. (Books and Other Printed
Materials) [3661]
Cunningham Equipment Inc.; J.A. (Industrial
Supplies) [16816]
Esco Electric Supply Co. (Electrical and Electronic
Equipment and Supplies) [8713]
Frank Winne and Son Inc. (Textiles and
Notions) [26039]
Fretz Corp. (Household Appliances) [15136]
Fried Brothers Inc. (Hardware) [13716]
Goldman Paper Co.; G.B. (Paper and Paper
Products) [21743]
Goldner Company Inc.; Herman (Plumbing Materials
and Fixtures) [23195]
Hachik Distributors Inc. (Recreational and Sporting
Goods) [23709]
Hadro Aluminum & Metal Corp. (Metals) [20026]
Hamler Industries (Chemicals) [4405]
Hecht Inc.; William (Specialty Equipment and
Products) [25675]
Hill and Son Co.; Fred (Furniture and
Fixtures) [13133]
Hill and Son Co.; Fred (Industrial
Machinery) [16101]
Holloway Corp. (Plumbing Materials and
Fixtures) [23210]

Holmes Protection Inc. (Security and Safety
Equipment) [24566]
Hygrade Food Products (Food) [11485]
India Hand Arts (Clothing) [5048]
Industrial Supplies Co. (Industrial Supplies) [16950]
Interstate Steel Supply Co (Metals) [20068]
Interstate Steel Supply Co. (Metals) [20069]
Kieser and Sons; Ellwood (Automotive) [2854]
Kozak Distributors (Paper and Paper
Products) [21794]
Levin and Company Inc.; M. (Food) [11704]
Maats Enterprises (Medical, Dental, and Optical
Supplies) [19421]
Majestic Penn State Inc. (Office Equipment and
Supplies) [21120]
Manufactured Rubber Products Inc. (Industrial
Supplies) [17015]
Marstan Industries Inc. (Restaurant and Commercial
Foodservice Equipment and Supplies) [24178]
McCullough Distributing Company,
Inc. (Automotive) [2931]
MDC Industries Inc. (Industrial Supplies) [17029]
Miller Sales Co.; Simon (Paper and Paper
Products) [21839]
Moroney, Inc.; James (Alcoholic Beverages) [1893]
Morris Tile Distributors Inc. (Floorcovering
Equipment and Supplies) [10061]
Morweco Steel Co. (Metals) [20206]
National Industrial Hardware Inc. (Industrial
Machinery) [16341]
O'Connor Truck Sales Inc. (Automotive) [3053]
Ogden Aviation Services (Restaurant and
Commercial Foodservice Equipment and
Supplies) [24197]
Origlio Inc.; Antonio (Alcoholic Beverages) [1934]
Oxford Metal Products (Furniture and
Fixtures) [13198]
Pacor Inc. (Construction Materials and
Machinery) [7830]
PEI Genesis (Electrical and Electronic Equipment
and Supplies) [9187]
Penn Detroit Diesel Allison
Inc. (Automotive) [3090]
Penn Distributors Inc. (Alcoholic Beverages) [1948]
Penn-Jersey Paper Co. (Paper and Paper
Products) [21875]
Pennock Co. (Horticultural Supplies) [14940]
Pincus Brothers Inc. (Clothing) [5275]
Pine Valley Supply (Agricultural Equipment and
Supplies) [1131]
Powell Electronics Inc. (Electrical and Electronic
Equipment and Supplies) [9221]
Reliance Bedding Corp. (Furniture and
Fixtures) [13218]
Richman Sons Inc.; S.D. (Used, Scrap, and
Recycled Materials) [26959]
R.J. Marketing, Ltd. (Electrical and Electronic
Equipment and Supplies) [9299]
Rowland Co. (Industrial Supplies) [17147]
Ryan Company Inc.; W.E. (Food) [12372]
Saleff & Son New York Pastry;
Richard (Food) [12392]
Sanson and Rowland Inc. (Hardware) [13902]
Saxony Sportswear Co. (Clothing) [5333]
Schecter and Sons, Inc.; Nathan (Gifts and
Novelties) [13444]
Sculli Brothers Inc. (Food) [12441]
Seaboard Industrial Supply (Industrial
Machinery) [16477]
Simons Millinery Mart (Clothing) [5358]
Southwark Metal Manufacturing
Co. (Metals) [20375]
Spartan Iron Metal Company Inc. (Used, Scrap,
and Recycled Materials) [27007]
SPC Corp. (Used, Scrap, and Recycled
Materials) [27008]
Stark Co. (Paper and Paper Products) [21950]
Stark Co. (Industrial Supplies) [17196]
Summit Trading Co. (Medical, Dental, and Optical
Equipment) [19062]
Sun Company Inc. (Petroleum, Fuels, and Related
Equipment) [22714]
Sun Distributors L.P. (Industrial Machinery) [16537]
Sussman Co.; Frank (Clothing) [5411]
Sysco Food Services of Philadelphia
Inc. (Food) [12685]

Taylor & Francis, Inc. (Books and Other Printed Materials) [4203]
Thalheimer Brothers Inc. (Used, Scrap, and Recycled Materials) [27024]
Thompson Mahogany Co. (Wood and Wood Products) [27386]
Tianjin-Philadelphia Rug Co. (Household Items) [15684]
Trans-Atlantic Co. (Hardware) [13962]
Unique Industries Inc. (Philadelphia, PA) (Gifts and Novelties) [13466]
Unisource International (Office Equipment and Supplies) [21325]
Unisource Worldwide Inc. (Paper and Paper Products) [21969]
United Light Co. (Electrical and Electronic Equipment and Supplies) [9525]
United Refrigeration Inc. (Heating and Cooling Equipment and Supplies) [14748]
United Research Laboratories Inc. (Medical, Dental, and Optical Supplies) [19678]
Vena Inc.; John (Food) [12835]
Washington Compressed Steel Corp. (Used, Scrap, and Recycled Materials) [27035]
West Philadelphia Electric Supply Co. (Electrical and Electronic Equipment and Supplies) [9570]
Wilf Corp.; Elias (Floorcovering Equipment and Supplies) [10301]
Woodhaven Foods Inc. (Food) [12978]
Wricley Nut Products Co. (Food) [12985]
Zieger and Sons Inc. (Horticultural Supplies) [14982]

Philipsburg

Navasky & Company Inc.; Charles (Clothing) [5219]
Nittany Oil Co. (Petroleum, Fuels, and Related Equipment) [22520]

Phoenixville

Cardamation Company Inc. (Office Equipment and Supplies) [20879]
Lawn and Golf Supply Company Inc. (Agricultural Equipment and Supplies) [944]
Sher and Mishkin Inc. (Textiles and Notions) [26202]

Pipersville

Schorr Insulated Glass Inc.; Norm (Construction Materials and Machinery) [7988]

Pittsburgh

Accent On Tile (Floorcovering Equipment and Supplies) [9639]
ADEMCO/ADI (Security and Safety Equipment) [24478]
Allied Electronics Corp. (Electrical and Electronic Equipment and Supplies) [8327]
American Textile Co. (Household Items) [15400]
Anixter Inc. (Electrical and Electronic Equipment and Supplies) [8358]
Automotive Ignition Company Inc. (Automotive) [2289]
Bartsch Greenhouses (Horticultural Supplies) [14820]
Bishops Inc. (Textiles and Notions) [25982]
Cardel Sales Inc. (Metals) [19855]
Cardello Electric Supply Co. (Electrical and Electronic Equipment and Supplies) [8501]
Castriota Chevrolet Inc. (Automotive) [2433]
Charken Co. Inc. (Industrial Supplies) [16792]
Chemply Div. (Chemicals) [4358]
Coal Hill Mining Co. (Minerals and Ores) [20530]
Collins Appliance Parts Inc. (Household Appliances) [15089]
Consumers Produce Co. (Food) [10821]
Corporate Express (Office Equipment and Supplies) [20925]
Decorator & Upholstery Supply, Inc. (Textiles and Notions) [26016]
Demase and Manna Co. (Food) [10942]
Edlis Inc. (Health and Beauty Aids) [14091]
Eickoff Corp. (Specialty Equipment and Products) [25642]
Eyemark Video Services (Sound and Entertainment Equipment and Supplies) [25188]

Fisher Scientific Co. (Scientific and Measurement Devices) [24360]
Fisher Scientific Co. (Medical, Dental, and Optical Supplies) [19325]
Forest Lumber Co. (Construction Materials and Machinery) [7360]
Foster Co.; L.B. (Industrial Supplies) [16875]
F.R. Industries Inc. (Electrical and Electronic Equipment and Supplies) [8754]
Freeport Steel Co. (Metals) [19987]
Fuhrer Holdings Inc.; Frank (Alcoholic Beverages) [1699]
Fuhrer Wholesale Co.; Frank B. (Alcoholic Beverages) [1700]
Games Unlimited (Toys and Hobby Goods) [26492]
Gooding and Shields Rubber Co. (Rubber) [24277]
Great Lakes Power Products (Automotive) [2700]
Hamburg Brothers (Household Appliances) [15158]
Harris Pump and Supply Co. (Industrial Machinery) [16090]
Houston-Starr Co. (Construction Materials and Machinery) [7491]
Intromark Inc. (Toys and Hobby Goods) [26537]
Iron Age Corp. (Shoes) [24771]
Island Spring & Drive Shaft Co. (Industrial Supplies) [16965]
Jackson Welding Supply (Industrial Machinery) [16181]
Kappel Wholesale Co.; William J. (Jewelry) [17482]
Keystone Iron and Metal Company Inc. (Metals) [20098]
KOBOLD Instruments Inc. (Scientific and Measurement Devices) [24385]
Lange Co.; Tom (Food) [11676]
Levinson Steel Co. (Metals) [20126]
Lewis-Goetz and Company Inc. (Rubber) [24284]
Liberto Inc.; R.J. (Used, Scrap, and Recycled Materials) [26882]
Lockhart Co. (Metals) [20133]
Mathias Reprographics (Specialty Equipment and Products) [25726]
Matthews International Corp., Marking Systems Div. (Industrial Machinery) [16274]
Mauro Co.; A.G. (Hardware) [13815]
McCormick Co.; J.S. (Minerals and Ores) [20553]
McCullough Electric Co. (Electrical and Electronic Equipment and Supplies) [9054]
McGinley Inc.; Wilson (Alcoholic Beverages) [1861]
McKenzie Co.; P.C. (Industrial Machinery) [16280]
McKnight Sales Company Inc. (Books and Other Printed Materials) [3944]
Mosebach Electric and Supply Co. (Electrical and Electronic Equipment and Supplies) [9099]
National Paint Distributors (Paints and Varnishes) [21516]
Network Access Corp. (Pittsburgh, Pennsylvania) (Communications Systems and Equipment) [5689]
Neville Chemical Co. (Chemicals) [4467]
Noftz Sheet Metal (Metals) [20229]
Paper Products Company Inc. (Paper and Paper Products) [21863]
Paragon/Monteverde Food Service (Food) [12106]
Peiger Co.; J.J. (Textiles and Notions) [26173]
Pitt-Des Moines Inc. (Metals) [20284]
Pittsburgh Oakland Enterprises Inc. (Food) [12177]
Plant Service Co. (Industrial Supplies) [17108]
Point Spring Co. (Automotive) [3100]
The Rehab Tech Center (Medical, Dental, and Optical Supplies) [19576]
RoData Inc. (Communications Systems and Equipment) [5745]
S & H Co. (Tobacco Products) [26349]
Saunier-Wilhelm Co. (Recreational and Sporting Goods) [23930]
Schmann Auto Parts (Automotive) [3195]
Schneider Dairy (Food) [12428]
Schorin Company Inc. (Paper and Paper Products) [21926]
Smith Co.; A and B (Scientific and Measurement Devices) [24433]
Snavely Forest Products Inc. (Construction Materials and Machinery) [8037]

Stanford Lumber Company Inc. (Construction Materials and Machinery) [8071]
Stewart Co.; Jesse C. (Livestock and Farm Products) [18255]
Stratcor Technical Sales Inc. (Minerals and Ores) [20570]
Studer Industrial Tool (Industrial Machinery) [16531]
Sufrin Inc.; Adolph (Office Equipment and Supplies) [21302]
TownTalk/Hostess (Food) [12738]
Tri-State Hobbycraft (Toys and Hobby Goods) [26689]
U.S. Printing Supply Co. (Specialty Equipment and Products) [25857]
USA Plastics Inc. (Household Items) [15694]
Vincent Metal Goods (Used, Scrap, and Recycled Materials) [27034]
WCI International Co. (Household Appliances) [15368]
WESCO Distribution Inc. (Electrical and Electronic Equipment and Supplies) [9569]
West Penn Laco Inc. (Industrial Supplies) [17275]
Westbrook Pharmaceutical and Surgical Supply Co. (Medical, Dental, and Optical Supplies) [19698]
Westinghouse Electric Corp. Trading Co. (Communications Systems and Equipment) [5812]
Wheelabrator Air Pollution Control (Specialty Equipment and Products) [25879]
Wholey and Company Inc.; Robert (Food) [12936]
Wilcox Brothers Co. (Automotive) [3430]
Williams and Company Inc. (Metals) [20492]
Wood & Plastics Industries (Construction Materials and Machinery) [8240]
Zenith Supply Company Inc. (Industrial Supplies) [17295]
Zukerman and Sons Inc.; Sam (Gifts and Novelties) [13475]

Pittston

Pittston Lumber and Manufacturing Co. (Construction Materials and Machinery) [7867]
US Food Service-Pittston Division (Food) [12807]

Plains

Altec Industries Inc. Eastern Div. (Motorized Vehicles) [20584]

Plymouth Meeting

Riley Sales Inc. (Adhesives) [11]

Port Carbon

Liberty Oil Company Inc. (Petroleum, Fuels, and Related Equipment) [22431]

Port Trevorton

Keller Marine Service Inc. (Marine) [18531]

Pottstown

Albright Paper & Box Corp. (Paper and Paper Products) [21619]
Dees Corp. (Industrial Supplies) [16823]
Fegely Inc.; J. (Industrial Supplies) [16859]
Micro-Coax, Inc. (Electrical and Electronic Equipment and Supplies) [9072]
Neapco Inc. (Automotive) [3019]
Pollock Corp. (Used, Scrap, and Recycled Materials) [26942]
Pollock Steel Corp.; Mayer (Used, Scrap, and Recycled Materials) [26943]
Pottstown Truck Sales Inc. (Motorized Vehicles) [20707]

Pottsville

Ost and Ost Inc. (Automotive) [3065]
United Receptacle, Inc. (Specialty Equipment and Products) [25855]

Prospect Park

Keesler Inc.; C.C. and F.F. (Industrial Machinery) [16199]

Punxsutawney

Roberts and Sons Inc.; Frank (Construction Materials and Machinery) [7943]

Quakertown

Bastian Inc.; Owen M. (Floorcovering Equipment and Supplies) [9694]
Knauss and Son Inc.; E.W. (Food) [11629]
Penn Stainless Products Inc. (Metals) [20270]
R & J Apparel Distributors (Clothing) [5297]

Radnor

Airgas Inc. (Industrial Supplies) [16679]
Chilton Co. (Books and Other Printed Materials) [3631]
S.O.E. Ltd. (Health and Beauty Aids) [14240]
Superior Group Inc. (Industrial Supplies) [17206]

Reading

Automotive Service Inc. (Petroleum, Fuels, and Related Equipment) [22051]
Barbey Electronics Corp. (Electrical and Electronic Equipment and Supplies) [8416]
Barco Industries Inc. (Hardware) [13583]
Berks Products Corp. (Construction Materials and Machinery) [7050]
Brenntag Inc. (Chemicals) [4339]
Eagle Chemical Co. (Chemicals) [4377]
Fromm Electric Supply Corp. (Electrical and Electronic Equipment and Supplies) [8764]
Kohl Building Products (Construction Materials and Machinery) [7568]
L.E.G. Inc. (Food) [11695]
Michel Company Inc.; R.E. (Heating and Cooling Equipment and Supplies) [14572]
Parallel PCs Inc. (Computers and Software) [6587]
Raylon Corp. (Health and Beauty Aids) [14206]
Reading Crane and Engineering Co. (Industrial Machinery) [16443]
Seaman Mill Supplies Co. (Industrial Supplies) [17162]
Singer Equipment Company Inc. (Restaurant and Commercial Foodservice Equipment and Supplies) [24220]
Sweet Street Desserts (Food) [12656]
Textile Chemical Company Inc. (Chemicals) [4530]
Thomas Hardware, Parts and Fasteners Inc. (Hardware) [13952]
Wells Fargo Alarm Services Inc. (Security and Safety Equipment) [24660]

Reamstown

Power & Telephone Supply Company, Inc. (Communications Systems and Equipment) [5718]

Rebersburg

Breon and Sons Inc.; R.E. (Petroleum, Fuels, and Related Equipment) [22092]

Red Lion

Yorktowne Inc. (Construction Materials and Machinery) [8247]

Reedsville

Gardenview Eggs (Food) [11236]

Richboro

Robern Golfwear Inc. (Clothing) [5312]

Richland

Leffler Inc.; Carlos R. (Petroleum, Fuels, and Related Equipment) [22424]

Robesonia

Associated Wholesalers Inc. (Food) [10458]

Rockledge

Rosetta Oil Inc. (Petroleum, Fuels, and Related Equipment) [22640]

Rosemont

Desso USA Inc. (Floorcovering Equipment and Supplies) [9862]

Royersford

Plotts Brothers (Plumbing Materials and Fixtures) [23318]
Wetherill Associates Inc. (Automotive) [3417]

St. Marys

Keller Oil Inc. (Petroleum, Fuels, and Related Equipment) [22397]
Straub Brewery Company Inc. (Alcoholic Beverages) [2057]

Saxonburg

Saxonburg Ceramics Inc. (Industrial Supplies) [17160]

Schuylkill Haven

Schuylkill Haven Casket Co. (Specialty Equipment and Products) [25809]

Scottdale

Herald Press (Books and Other Printed Materials) [3824]

Scranton

Arley Wholesale Inc. (Floorcovering Equipment and Supplies) [9686]
Great Northern Distributors, Inc. (Books and Other Printed Materials) [3796]
Michel Company. Inc.; R.E. (Heating and Cooling Equipment and Supplies) [14573]
Mid-Penn Magazine Distributors (Books and Other Printed Materials) [3954]
Montage Foods Inc. (Food) [11927]
Pennsylvania Paper & Supply Co. (Paper and Paper Products) [21876]
Proferas Pizza Bakery Inc. (Food) [12227]
Robzens Inc. (Food) [12334]
Scranton Sales Co. (Plumbing Materials and Fixtures) [23364]
Williams Tire Co.; Jack (Automotive) [3438]

Selinsgrove

Rhoads Mills Inc. (Agricultural Equipment and Supplies) [1185]

Sellersville

Teva Pharmaceutical USA (Medical, Dental, and Optical Supplies) [19653]

Sewickley

Benthin Systems, Inc. (Household Items) [15418]
Vorberger Group Ltd. (Metals) [20476]

Shamokin

Jones Hardware Company Inc. (Hardware) [13775]

Sharon

Jolley Industrial Supply Company Inc. (Industrial Supplies) [16971]
Medal, Inc. (Hardware) [13824]
Metz Baking Co. (Food) [11862]

Shippensburg

Beistle Co. (Gifts and Novelties) [13314]
Cumberland Valley Cooperative Association (Agricultural Equipment and Supplies) [483]

Shiremanstown

Beachley Hardy Seed Co. (Agricultural Equipment and Supplies) [286]
Warrell Corp. (Food) [12879]

Silver Spring

Nolt's Ponds Inc. (Veterinary Products) [27196]

Smithfield

Friend Bit Service Inc. (Specialty Equipment and Products) [25655]

Somerset

Miller Inc.; Luther P. (Petroleum, Fuels, and Related Equipment) [22485]

Rhoads Co.; D.W. (Plumbing Materials and Fixtures) [23339]
Stahl Oil Company Inc. (Petroleum, Fuels, and Related Equipment) [22698]
Wheeler Brothers Inc. (Automotive) [3422]

Souderton

Bearings & Drives Unlimited, Inc. (Industrial Supplies) [16738]
Leidy's Inc. (Food) [11697]
Moyer and Son Inc. (Agricultural Equipment and Supplies) [1056]
Young's (Furniture and Fixtures) [13286]

Southampton

Tanner Industries, Inc. (Chemicals) [4525]

State College

Hite Co. (Electrical and Electronic Equipment and Supplies) [8849]
Michel Company Inc.; R.E. (Heating and Cooling Equipment and Supplies) [14574]
Murata Erie North America Inc. State College Div. (Electrical and Electronic Equipment and Supplies) [9108]
Nittany Beverage Co. (Alcoholic Beverages) [1918]
State Gas and Oil Co. (Petroleum, Fuels, and Related Equipment) [22702]
Uni-Marts Inc. (Food) [12784]
Whitehill Lighting and Supply Inc. (Electrical and Electronic Equipment and Supplies) [9585]

Sunbury

Resilite Sports Products Inc. (Recreational and Sporting Goods) [23911]
Scullin Oil Co. (Petroleum, Fuels, and Related Equipment) [22659]

Tamaqua

Fegley Oil Company Inc. (Petroleum, Fuels, and Related Equipment) [22273]

Tarentum

Dura Sales Inc. (Construction Materials and Machinery) [7290]

Tatamy

Northampton Farm Bureau Cooperative (Agricultural Equipment and Supplies) [1083]

Temple

Bun Patch Supply Corp. (Construction Materials and Machinery) [7107]

Terre Hill

Terre Hill Concrete Products (Construction Materials and Machinery) [8111]

Trevose

GMP (Communications Systems and Equipment) [5621]
GMP (Electrical and Electronic Equipment and Supplies) [8792]
Grace and Co. Grace Dearborn Div.; W.R. (Specialty Equipment and Products) [25664]
Jade Electronics Distributors (Sound and Entertainment Equipment and Supplies) [25257]
Trevose Electronics Inc. (Sound and Entertainment Equipment and Supplies) [25484]

Tunkhannock

Mid-Atlantic Park & Playground Concepts (Recreational and Sporting Goods) [23826]

Union City

Erie Crawford Cooperative (Agricultural Equipment and Supplies) [555]

Uniontown

Big Banana Fruit Market (Food) [10554]
COE Distributing, Inc. (Office Equipment and Supplies) [20904]

Michel Company Inc.; R.E. (Heating and Cooling Equipment and Supplies) [14575]
Romeo & Sons (Food) [12349]
Standard Machine and Equipment Co. (Industrial Machinery) [16518]
Yezbak Enterprises (Wood and Wood Products) [27397]
Yezbak Lumber Inc. (Construction Materials and Machinery) [8246]

University Park
Pennsylvania State University Press (Books and Other Printed Materials) [4051]

Upland
Intercon, Inc. (Automotive) [2791]

Upper Darby
Jones Co.; Shelby (Scientific and Measurement Devices) [24380]
Michel Company Inc.; R.E. (Heating and Cooling Equipment and Supplies) [14576]
Sun-Ni Cheese Co. (Food) [12605]

Valencia
Frankferd Farms (Food) [11200]

Valley Forge
Alco Standard Corp. (Paper and Paper Products) [21620]
AmeriGas Propane Inc. (Petroleum, Fuels, and Related Equipment) [22036]
AmeriSource Corp. (Medical, Dental, and Optical Supplies) [19147]
AmeriSource Health Corp. (Medical, Dental, and Optical Supplies) [19150]
European American Music Distributors Corp. (Books and Other Printed Materials) [3735]
IKON Office Solutions Inc. (Office Equipment and Supplies) [21051]
Judson Press (Books and Other Printed Materials) [3870]

Verona
RPC Video Inc. (Sound and Entertainment Equipment and Supplies) [25423]

Villanova
Ardrosson Farms (Livestock and Farm Products) [17704]

Walnutport
Aungst Wholesale; Dan (Toys and Hobby Goods) [26402]
Imperial Pet Products (Veterinary Products) [27156]

Warfordsburg
Mellott Estate Inc.; H.B. (Construction Materials and Machinery) [7691]

Warren
Interlectric Corp. (Industrial Supplies) [16961]
Segel and Son Inc. (Used, Scrap, and Recycled Materials) [26986]

Warrington
Merit Metal Products Corp. (Plumbing Materials and Fixtures) [23260]
Michel Company Inc.; R.E. (Heating and Cooling Equipment and Supplies) [14577]
Polysciences Inc. (Chemicals) [4481]

Washington
Alternative Computer Solutions Ltd. (Computers and Software) [5916]
American Mobile Home Products Inc. (Automotive) [2232]
Camalloy Inc. (Metals) [19848]
Chaneaco Supply Co. (Industrial Machinery) [15884]
Coen Oil Co. Inc. (Petroleum, Fuels, and Related Equipment) [22149]
Fairmont Supply Co. (Specialty Equipment and Products) [25646]

Fairmont Supply Co. (Washington, Pennsylvania) (Industrial Supplies) [16855]
Hickson's Office Supplies Co. (Office Equipment and Supplies) [21033]

Washington Crossing
Keystone-Ozone Pure Water Co. (Soft Drinks) [24980]

Wayne
Franks Inc.; M.E. (Food) [11201]
IGI Div. (Petroleum, Fuels, and Related Equipment) [22370]
Lumbermen's Merchandising Corp. (Construction Materials and Machinery) [7620]
Radnor Alloys Inc. (Metals) [20307]

Waynesboro
Thompson Oil Co. (Petroleum, Fuels, and Related Equipment) [22734]

Waynesburg
Kiwi Fence Systems Inc. (Construction Materials and Machinery) [7560]

West Chester
Alliance Metals Inc. (Metals) [19749]
Expanko Cork Co. (Industrial Supplies) [16853]
Laser Technologies and Services Inc. (Office Equipment and Supplies) [21103]
Michel Company Inc.; R.E. (Heating and Cooling Equipment and Supplies) [14578]
Pneumatic and Electric Equipment Co. (Construction Materials and Machinery) [7877]
Sklar Instrument Company Inc. (Medical, Dental, and Optical Equipment) [19039]
Spaz Beverage Co. (Soft Drinks) [25039]
VWR Scientific Products Corp. (Scientific and Measurement Devices) [24454]
VWR Scientific Products Corp. (Textiles and Notions) [26242]

West Grove
Conard-Pyle Co. (Horticultural Supplies) [14844]

West Hazleton
Alshefski Enterprise (Food) [10384]
Hazle Park Packing Co. (Food) [11399]

West Mifflin
Lutheran Distributors Inc.; A.M. (Alcoholic Beverages) [1832]

West Milton
Susquehanna Motor Company Inc. (Motorized Vehicles) [20734]

West Point
Colorcon (Office Equipment and Supplies) [20906]
Rotelle Inc. (Food) [12355]

West Reading
Edward Business Machines Inc. (Office Equipment and Supplies) [20985]

Wexford
Best Tile Distributors of Wexford, Inc. (Floorcovering Equipment and Supplies) [9725]
Red River Barbeque and Grille (Food) [12286]

Wilkes Barre
3 Springs Water Co. (Soft Drinks) [24902]
3 Springs Water Co. (Food) [10314]
Allan Industries Inc.; A. (Used, Scrap, and Recycled Materials) [26736]
Eastern Penn Supply Co. (Plumbing Materials and Fixtures) [23144]
General Supply and Paper Co. (Paper and Paper Products) [21738]
General Supply and Paper Co. (Industrial Machinery) [16057]
The Lion Brewery, Inc. (Alcoholic Beverages) [1821]

L.S.I. Lectro Science Inc. (Electrical and Electronic Equipment and Supplies) [9006]
Luzerne Optical Labs, Ltd. (Medical, Dental, and Optical Supplies) [19420]
Nardone Bakery Pizza Co. (Food) [11967]
Petroleum Service Company Inc. (Petroleum, Fuels, and Related Equipment) [22572]
Save On Software (Computers and Software) [6706]
Sunshine Market Inc. (Food) [12621]
Superior Distributors (Specialty Equipment and Products) [25834]

Williamsport
Brodart Co. (Books and Other Printed Materials) [3593]
Cable Services Co. Inc. (Sound and Entertainment Equipment and Supplies) [25114]
Eastern Wood Products Company Inc. (Floorcovering Equipment and Supplies) [9879]
Manufacturing Distributors (Household Appliances) [15209]
Neece Paper Company Inc. (Paper and Paper Products) [21849]
Simon Resources Inc. (Used, Scrap, and Recycled Materials) [26990]
Sunset Ice Cream Offices and Sales (Food) [12618]
SupplySource Inc. (Office Equipment and Supplies) [21306]
Winchester Optical (Medical, Dental, and Optical Supplies) [19710]
Wise Snacks Bryden Distributors (Food) [12967]

Willow Grove
AmeriQuest Technologies Inc. (Computers and Software) [5935]
Arbor Handling Services Inc. (Industrial Machinery) [15776]
Derr Flooring Co. (Household Items) [15469]
Weinstein Supply Corp. (Plumbing Materials and Fixtures) [23448]

Windber
Fairview Dairy Inc. & Valley Dairy (Food) [11072]

Worcester
Techni-Tool, Inc. (Hardware) [13948]
Vision Video (Sound and Entertainment Equipment and Supplies) [25509]

Wyncote
ATD-American Co. (Textiles and Notions) [25971]
Quaker City Hide Co. (Livestock and Farm Products) [18186]
Quaker City Hide Co. (Livestock and Farm Products) [18187]
Vitamin Specialties Corp. (Health and Beauty Aids) [14274]

Wynnewood
Library Video Co. (Sound and Entertainment Equipment and Supplies) [25283]

Yeadon
Habhegger Company Inc.; E.O. (Petroleum, Fuels, and Related Equipment) [22331]

York
Andrews Paper House of York Inc. (Paper and Paper Products) [21634]
Beasley Ford Inc.; Carl (Motorized Vehicles) [20598]
Bon Ton Foods Inc. (Food) [10589]
Brewery Products Co. (Alcoholic Beverages) [1548]
Colony Papers Inc. (Paper and Paper Products) [21686]
Die-A-Matic Corp. (Industrial Machinery) [15950]
FES (Restaurant and Commercial Foodservice Equipment and Supplies) [24116]
Fluid Power Inc. (Industrial Machinery) [16022]
Fulton, Mehring & Hauser Company, Inc. (Industrial Supplies) [16882]
Goodyear Tire & Rubber Co. (Automotive) [2691]

Habot Steel Company Inc. (Metals) [20025]
Klinge Corp. (Heating and Cooling Equipment and Supplies) [14512]
Knaubs Bakery (Food) [11628]
Lavetan and Sons Inc.; L. (Used, Scrap, and Recycled Materials) [26877]
Michel Company Inc.; R.E. (Heating and Cooling Equipment and Supplies) [14579]
Mid-Atlantic Snacks Inc. (Food) [11877]
Motorola Communications (Communications Systems and Equipment) [5683]
Myers and Son Inc.; John H. (Construction Materials and Machinery) [7757]
Ness Company Inc. (Automotive) [3025]
Pennsylvania Plywood & Lumber (Construction Materials and Machinery) [7848]
Peterman & Company, Inc.; D.S. (Shoes) [24831]
Quaker City Paper Co. (Paper and Paper Products) [21893]
Quaker City Paper Co. (Industrial Supplies) [17124]
Ramclif Supply Co. (Industrial Supplies) [17128]
RG Group Inc. (Industrial Supplies) [17137]
Rodwell Sales (Household Items) [15637]
RTI Technologies, Inc. (Heating and Cooling Equipment and Supplies) [14670]
Scrivner of Pennsylvania Inc. (Food) [12440]
Shearer Industrial Supply Co. (Industrial Machinery) [16485]
Shipley Oil Co. (Petroleum, Fuels, and Related Equipment) [22668]
Smith Co.; Harold E. (Industrial Machinery) [16497]
Somerville Co.; Thomas (Plumbing Materials and Fixtures) [23386]
Transply Inc. (Automotive) [3328]
Wolfgang Candy Co. Inc.; D.E. (Food) [12972]
York Corrugating Co. (Plumbing Materials and Fixtures) [23469]
York Tape and Label Co. (Paper and Paper Products) [22011]
York Truck Center Inc. (Motorized Vehicles) [20756]
Yorktowne Kitchens (Construction Materials and Machinery) [8248]

Zelienople

Keystone Detroit Diesel Allison Inc. (Automotive) [2853]
Ritter Engineering Co. (Plumbing Materials and Fixtures) [23344]

Puerto Rico

Aguada

Paradise Ceramics (Floorcovering Equipment and Supplies) [10100]

Caguas

Drogueria Betances (Medical, Dental, and Optical Supplies) [19290]

Carolina

Newell P.R. Ltd. (Household Items) [15594]

Guaynabo

Pet Products Associates, Inc. (Veterinary Products) [27210]

Naguabo

Ideal Pet Supplies (Veterinary Products) [27155]

Ponce

Commecial de Azulejos (Floorcovering Equipment and Supplies) [9819]
Naturalizer (Shoes) [24819]

Puerto Nuevo

MGM Optical Laboratory (Medical, Dental, and Optical Supplies) [19452]

Puerto Real

Skipper Shop (Marine) [18611]

Rio Piedras

Caribe Optical Lab/Lens (Medical, Dental, and Optical Supplies) [19215]

San Juan

Carabel Export & Import (Floorcovering Equipment and Supplies) [9757]
Drogueria J.M. Blanco (Medical, Dental, and Optical Supplies) [19291]
Drug Center, Inc. (Medical, Dental, and Optical Supplies) [19292]
Food and Spirits Distributing Company Inc. (Alcoholic Beverages) [1693]
Mendez & Co. Inc. (Alcoholic Beverages) [1865]
Nido, Inc.; Rafael J. (Floorcovering Equipment and Supplies) [10079]
Suarez and Co.; V. (Food) [12597]
Villafane Inc.; Rene Ortiz (Construction Materials and Machinery) [8183]

San Sebastian

Commercial Plamar (Floorcovering Equipment and Supplies) [9820]

Santurce

Casas Office Machines Inc. (Office Equipment and Supplies) [20883]

Rhode Island

Barrington

NanoMaterials, Inc. (Chemicals) [4465]
Tavdi Company, Inc. (Industrial Machinery) [16549]

Bristol

Bristol Metal Co. Inc. (Used, Scrap, and Recycled Materials) [26771]
Campagna Inc. (Medical, Dental, and Optical Equipment) [18724]
Jack's Salvage & Auto Parts Inc. (Automotive) [2807]
M & G Industries Inc. (Electrical and Electronic Equipment and Supplies) [9014]
Northeast Industrial Components Co. (Industrial Supplies) [17079]
Ships Wheel Brand Corp. (Cleaning and Janitorial Supplies) [4708]

Central Falls

Crest Distributors (Floorcovering Equipment and Supplies) [9832]
King Auto Parts Inc. (Automotive) [2856]
Patchis Yarn Shop; Peter (Textiles and Notions) [26167]

Chepachet

Herman; Jeffrey (Specialty Equipment and Products) [25677]

Coventry

Central Procurement Inc. (Restaurant and Commercial Foodservice Equipment and Supplies) [24091]
Rhode Island Distributing Co. (Alcoholic Beverages) [1988]

Cranston

Arlington Coin Co. (Jewelry) [17313]
Barry Pumps Inc.; R.E. (Specialty Equipment and Products) [25568]
Barry Sales Inc. (Paints and Varnishes) [21397]
Carbone Co.; R.J. (Horticultural Supplies) [14834]
Casey Inc.; John R. (Cleaning and Janitorial Supplies) [4594]
Considine Sales Co. Inc. (Alcoholic Beverages) [1612]
Crystaline North America Inc. (Jewelry) [17385]
Dynamic Concepts Inc. (Jewelry) [17401]
F & E Check Protector Co. Inc. (Office Equipment and Supplies) [20999]
Feibelman & Krack (Jewelry) [17413]
GemTek Enterprises Inc. (Jewelry) [17428]

Hess and Company Inc.; John R. (Chemicals) [4415]
Mandala Corp. (Veterinary Products) [27184]
May Engineering Company Inc. (Restaurant and Commercial Foodservice Equipment and Supplies) [24179]
McLaughlin and Moran Inc. (Alcoholic Beverages) [1862]
Ocean State Yacht Brokerage and Marine Services (Marine) [18577]
Pereira Inc.; Ed (Jewelry) [17545]
Professional Salon Services (Health and Beauty Aids) [14198]
Professional Salon Services (Restaurant and Commercial Foodservice Equipment and Supplies) [24206]
Rhode Island Tile/G & M Co. (Floorcovering Equipment and Supplies) [10121]
Rolyn Inc. (Jewelry) [17570]
Solomon M. Casket Company of Rhode Island (Specialty Equipment and Products) [25823]
Spaulding Brick Company Inc. (Construction Materials and Machinery) [8059]
Stiller Distributors Inc. (Floorcovering Equipment and Supplies) [10182]
SuperValu—New England (Food) [12650]
Time Products Inc. (Office Equipment and Supplies) [21320]
Wayne Distributing Co. (Alcoholic Beverages) [2111]
Wel-Met Corp. (Jewelry) [17654]

Cumberland

Dave's Used Auto Parts Inc. (Automotive) [2529]
People's Coal Co. (Minerals and Ores) [20559]

East Greenwich

Consolidated International Corp. (Cleaning and Janitorial Supplies) [4603]

East Providence

Bazar Inc. Sales Co. (Jewelry) [17330]
Benoit; Samuel (Jewelry) [17335]
Brookline Machine Co. (Automotive) [2393]
Capital Design Inc. (Plastics) [22941]
Claflin Co. (Medical, Dental, and Optical Supplies) [19231]
Crellin Handling Equipment Inc. (Industrial Machinery) [15920]
Cronin Asphalt Corp. (Petroleum, Fuels, and Related Equipment) [22179]
Dexter Sales Inc. (Metals) [19928]
Dial Battery Paint & Auto Supply (Paints and Varnishes) [21429]
East Coast Embroidery Inc. (Clothing) [4927]
East Providence Cycle Co. Inc. (Recreational and Sporting Goods) [23641]
Evans Findings Company, Inc. (Hardware) [13689]
Gregory and Sons Inc.; J.J. (Construction Materials and Machinery) [7416]
Halbro America (Recreational and Sporting Goods) [23711]
Hoder-Rogers Inc. (Aeronautical Equipment and Supplies) [97]
North American Shoe Co. Inc. (Shoes) [24824]
Organic Dyestuffs Corp. (Chemicals) [4474]
Redco Lighting & Maintenance (Electrical and Electronic Equipment and Supplies) [9270]
RI Business Equipment Co. Inc. (Office Equipment and Supplies) [21239]
Tillinghast-Stiles Co. (Textiles and Notions) [26229]
Tri-State Police Fire Equipment Inc. (Security and Safety Equipment) [24647]

Greenville

Crown Optical Co. Inc. (Medical, Dental, and Optical Supplies) [19258]

Jamestown

Jamestown Distributors Inc. (Marine) [18528]

Johnston

Accu Rx Optical (Medical, Dental, and Optical Supplies) [19122]
American Jewelry Sales (Jewelry) [17308]

Bellini Jewelry Co. (Jewelry) [17332]
Belmar Inc. (Jewelry) [17333]
Cardillo Brothers Inc. (Automotive) [2424]
Global Importing Inc. (Jewelry) [17432]
Institutional Linen Supply (Textiles and
    Notions) [26072]
Rhode Island Wholesale Jewelry (Jewelry) [17563]
RI Roof Truss Co. Inc. (Construction Materials and
    Machinery) [7928]
Roberts Inc.; M.L. (Jewelry) [17567]
Ru-Mart Metal Specialties (Jewelry) [17578]
Ru-Mart Metal Specialties (Jewelry) [17579]
Tool Craft Inc. (Jewelry) [17641]
Truck Body Manufacturing Company,
    Inc. (Automotive) [3343]
Waliga Imports and Sales Inc. (Jewelry) [17649]

Kingston
Grant & Associates, LLC; R.B. (Paper and Paper
    Products) [21746]

Lincoln
Alpine Restaurant Equipment (Restaurant and
    Commercial Foodservice Equipment and
    Supplies) [24061]
Classic Designs (Furniture and Fixtures) [13070]
Cross Co.; A.T. (Office Equipment and
    Supplies) [20940]
Providence Casket Co. (Specialty Equipment and
    Products) [25792]
Windmoeller and Hoelscher Corp. (Industrial
    Machinery) [16640]
Zero US Corp. (Office Equipment and
    Supplies) [21371]

Manville
Creative Craft Distributors (Office Equipment and
    Supplies) [20939]
Fire-Tec Inc. (Security and Safety
    Equipment) [24548]

Mapleville
Metech International Inc. (Used, Scrap, and
    Recycled Materials) [26906]

Narragansett
Spartan Lobster Traps Inc. (Marine) [18613]

Newport
International Marine Industries (Recreational and
    Sporting Goods) [23746]
Jiffy Foam, Inc. (Horticultural Supplies) [14896]
Marine Rescue Products Inc. (Marine) [18561]

North Kingstown
Castle Copiers & More Inc. (Office Equipment and
    Supplies) [20887]

North Providence
Faella Co. Inc.; Don (Sound and Entertainment
    Equipment and Supplies) [25189]
Gem-La Jewelry Inc. (Jewelry) [17425]
Marie Sales; Gina (Jewelry) [17512]

North Scituate
Atlantis Eyewear, Inc. (Medical, Dental, and Optical
    Supplies) [19168]
Rhode Island Tack Shop Inc. (Livestock and Farm
    Products) [18196]
Tourbillon Farm (Livestock and Farm
    Products) [18286]

North Smithfield
C & S Specialty Inc. (Security and Safety
    Equipment) [24522]

Pawtucket
Allstate Restaurant Equipment Inc. (Restaurant and
    Commercial Foodservice Equipment and
    Supplies) [24060]
Atlantic Paper & Twine Co. Inc. (Paper and Paper
    Products) [21640]
Broadway Tire Inc. (Automotive) [2388]
Builders Specialties Co. (Construction Materials and
    Machinery) [7101]

Hills Office Supply Co. Inc. (Office Equipment and
    Supplies) [21034]
IIRI International Inc. (Clothing) [5042]
Microfibres Inc. (Textiles and Notions) [26145]
Morris Novelty Inc. (Toys and Hobby
    Goods) [26581]
Paramount Sales Co. (Health and Beauty
    Aids) [14188]
Paramount Sales Co. (Medical, Dental, and Optical
    Supplies) [19524]
Tailor-Made Signs (Furniture and Fixtures) [13255]
Teknor Apex Co. (Rubber) [24300]
Webbing Mills Co.; Elizabeth (Textiles and
    Notions) [26245]
Windsor Rhodes Co. (Textiles and
    Notions) [26249]

Providence
Accu-Care Supply, Inc. (Recreational and Sporting
    Goods) [23492]
Allston Street Used Auto Parts (Automotive) [2220]
American Chemical Works Co. (Chemicals) [4320]
American Chemical Works Co. (Industrial
    Machinery) [15765]
American Mathematical Society (Books and Other
    Printed Materials) [3501]
American Safe and Lock Co. (Office Equipment
    and Supplies) [20798]
Art Cathedral Metal Inc. (Jewelry) [17314]
ASO Enterprises (Jewelry) [17317]
Aurea Italia Inc. (Jewelry) [17320]
Bay Colony Mills Inc. (Household Items) [15416]
Cathedral Art Metal Inc. (Jewelry) [17364]
Don-Lin Jewelry Co. Inc. (Jewelry) [17398]
Drake Petroleum Company Inc. (Petroleum, Fuels,
    and Related Equipment) [22211]
Eastern Butcher Block Corp. (Furniture and
    Fixtures) [13096]
Eastern Butcher Block Corp. (Furniture and
    Fixtures) [13097]
Eastern Wire Products (Metals) [19946]
Elmwood Paint Center (Paints and
    Varnishes) [21438]
Excelsior International Corp. (Jewelry) [17410]
Fountain Dispensers Co. Inc. (Heating and Cooling
    Equipment and Supplies) [14451]
Furnace & Duct Supply Co. (Heating and Cooling
    Equipment and Supplies) [14454]
Gem Furniture Co. Inc. (Furniture and
    Fixtures) [13119]
General Fabrics Co. (Textiles and
    Notions) [26041]
Halifax Floral Co., Inc. (Horticultural
    Supplies) [14881]
Holden, Inc.; John W.W. (Medical, Dental, and
    Optical Supplies) [19359]
Hudson Cos. (Construction Materials and
    Machinery) [7494]
Hudson Liquid Asphalts, Inc. (Construction Materials
    and Machinery) [7496]
Industrial Service Co. (Photographic Equipment and
    Supplies) [22867]
K & M Associates (Jewelry) [17480]
Kenilworth Creations Inc. (Jewelry) [17487]
Keystone Office Supply Co. Inc. (Office Equipment
    and Supplies) [21088]
Lapham-Hickey Steel Corp. Clifford Metal
    Div. (Metals) [20119]
Mann and Company, Inc.;
    George (Chemicals) [4450]
McLeod Optical Company Inc. (Medical, Dental,
    and Optical Supplies) [19438]
Merchants Overseas Inc. (Jewelry) [17520]
Merchants Overseas Inc. (Jewelry) [17521]
Mount Pleasant Hardware Inc. (Paints and
    Varnishes) [21508]
National Trading Co. Inc. (Office Equipment and
    Supplies) [21156]
North Providence Auto
    Salvation (Automotive) [3043]
Odyssey Jewelry Inc. (Jewelry) [17537]
Orient Express (Jewelry) [17539]
Packings & Insulations Corp. (Construction
    Materials and Machinery) [7829]
Polishers & Jewelers Supply Inc. (Jewelry) [17549]

RI Refrigeration Supply Co. (Heating and Cooling
    Equipment and Supplies) [14663]
Sherri-Li Textile Inc. (Textiles and Notions) [26203]
Smith-Holden Inc. (Medical, Dental, and Optical
    Equipment) [19042]
SNA Inc. (Medical, Dental, and Optical
    Equipment) [19043]
Snow & Stars Corp. (Jewelry) [17610]
Sondras Beauty Supply (Health and Beauty
    Aids) [14243]
Star Creation Inc. (Gifts and Novelties) [13453]
Star Jewelry Enterprises Inc. (Jewelry) [17620]
Sydney Supply Co. (Plumbing Materials and
    Fixtures) [23403]
Twin City Supply Company (Household
    Appliances) [15346]
Union Paper Company Div. (Paper and Paper
    Products) [21960]
Union Paper Company Inc. (Industrial
    Supplies) [17241]
United Shoe Ornament Company
    Inc. (Shoes) [24881]
VNA of Rhode Island Inc. (Medical, Dental, and
    Optical Equipment) [19104]
Winkler Group, Ltd. (Jewelry) [17658]
Winkler Store Fixtures Co. (Furniture and
    Fixtures) [13281]

Riverside
Ashley & Company Inc.; E.H. (Jewelry) [17316]
Atlantic Coast Fiberglass Co. (Construction
    Materials and Machinery) [7002]
Denison Co. Inc.; A.J. (Jewelry) [17390]
Gauntlett Agency Ltd. (Specialty Equipment and
    Products) [25659]
Q.E.D. Exports (Food) [12244]
Reade Advanced Materials (Chemicals) [4491]
Rhode Island Publications Society (Books and
    Other Printed Materials) [4116]

Rumford
AlliedSignal Automotive
    Aftermarket (Automotive) [2216]
American Coffee Co. Inc. (Restaurant and
    Commercial Foodservice Equipment and
    Supplies) [24062]
Duchin Inc.; Gloria (Gifts and Novelties) [13347]
Scissors and Shears (Health and Beauty
    Aids) [14231]

Smithfield
City Metal Company Inc. (Used, Scrap, and
    Recycled Materials) [26779]
Elan Pharmaceuticals (Medical, Dental, and Optical
    Equipment) [18786]
Magnum Diversified Industries
    Inc. (Metals) [20143]
Uvex Safety (Security and Safety
    Equipment) [24653]

Tiverton
General Auto Parts Inc. (Automotive) [2669]
Humphrey Company Inc.; P.D. (Construction
    Materials and Machinery) [7498]
Jagoe; Philip (Toys and Hobby Goods) [26539]

Wakefield
South Pier Fish Co. (Food) [12533]

Warren
Blount Seafood Corp. (Food) [10572]
Karystal International Inc. (Textiles and
    Notions) [26088]
Pasqua Florist & Greenhouse (Horticultural
    Supplies) [14938]
Walmsley Marine Inc. (Recreational and Sporting
    Goods) [24039]
Warren Marine Supply Inc. (Marine) [18632]

Warwick
ADEMCO/ADI (Security and Safety
    Equipment) [24480]
Anchor Specialties Co. (Textiles and
    Notions) [25964]
Anka Co. Inc. (Jewelry) [17310]

B & A Distributing Inc. (Health and Beauty Aids) [14032]
Boston Tile of Rhode Island (Floorcovering Equipment and Supplies) [9734]
Chernov Brothers Inc. (Household Items) [15442]
Chiefs Discount Jewelers Inc. (Jewelry) [17367]
Creative Imports Inc. (Jewelry) [17381]
Gannon Company Inc.; G.M. (Chemicals) [4397]
GCM Corp. (Paints and Varnishes) [21449]
Glucksman & Associates; Barry (Jewelry) [17433]
Great Northern Products Ltd. (Food) [11313]
McCrone Associates (Jewelry) [17519]
Motion Industries (Automotive) [2990]
Narragansett Trading Co. Ltd. (Jewelry) [17530]
Ray's Hobby (Toys and Hobby Goods) [26631]
R.E.S. Associates (Construction Materials and Machinery) [7918]
Salks Hardware & Marine Inc. (Marine) [18599]
T & L Industries Co. (Automotive) [3290]
Warwick Auto Parts Inc. (Paints and Varnishes) [21603]

West Greenwich

Central Beverage Corporation (Alcoholic Beverages) [1584]
Copley Distributors Inc. (Alcoholic Beverages) [1619]
GJ Sales Co. (Construction Materials and Machinery) [7397]
Highway Auto Parts Inc. (Automotive) [2753]

West Warwick

Amtrol International Inc. (Heating and Cooling Equipment and Supplies) [14321]
Perpall Enterprises; Michael E. (Automotive) [3093]
Valley Convenience Products (Tobacco Products) [26367]

Westerly

Jerry's At Misquamicut Inc. (Medical, Dental, and Optical Supplies) [19385]
Kenney Distributors; J.F. (Restaurant and Commercial Foodservice Equipment and Supplies) [24155]
Red Stone Inc. (Automotive) [3139]

Woonsocket

American Cord and Webbing Inc. (Textiles and Notions) [25958]
Leathertone Inc. (Plastics) [22993]
Mask-Off Corp. (Jewelry) [17515]
Privilege Auto Parts (Automotive) [3119]
Standard Drug Co. (Medical, Dental, and Optical Supplies) [19635]
United East Foodservice Supply Co. (Restaurant and Commercial Foodservice Equipment and Supplies) [24254]

South Carolina

Abbeville

The Rug Barn Inc. (Household Items) [15644]

Aiken

Sprawls Service and Sound (Sound and Entertainment Equipment and Supplies) [25461]

Anderson

Allstates Textile Machinery Inc. (Industrial Machinery) [15760]
Anderson Auto Parts Co. (Automotive) [2239]
Carolina Beer Company Inc. (Alcoholic Beverages) [1575]
Crescent Electric Supply Co. (Electrical and Electronic Equipment and Supplies) [8587]
Frank Distributing (Alcoholic Beverages) [1697]
Harris Appliance Parts Company Inc. (Household Appliances) [15163]
Jim's Beauty Supply (Health and Beauty Aids) [14137]
Orian Rugs Inc. (Floorcovering Equipment and Supplies) [10089]

Ryobi America Corp. (Agricultural Equipment and Supplies) [1222]
Wintenna Inc. (Communications Systems and Equipment) [5816]

Batesburg

M & M Wholesale (Clothing) [5149]

Belton

Blue Ridge Beef Plant Inc. (Food) [10580]

Bennettsville

Carolina FireMasters Inc. (Security and Safety Equipment) [24525]

Camden

Miller Lumber Inc.; William T. (Construction Materials and Machinery) [7715]
Speaks Oil Company Inc. (Petroleum, Fuels, and Related Equipment) [22689]

Cayce

Dealers Supply Co. (Floorcovering Equipment and Supplies) [9849]
Miller Brothers Giant Tire Service Inc. (Automotive) [2968]
S.C. Farm Bureau Marketing Association (Livestock and Farm Products) [18223]

Chapin

Ellett Brothers Inc. (Guns and Weapons) [13490]

Charleston

Addlestone International Corp. (Used, Scrap, and Recycled Materials) [26731]
Bearing Distributors, Inc. (Automotive) [2334]
Bird and Company Inc.; William M. (Floorcovering Equipment and Supplies) [9727]
Bridges Accessories; Ronna (Clothing) [4843]
Diversified Distributors (Household Appliances) [15112]
Hondo Guitar Co. (Sound and Entertainment Equipment and Supplies) [25237]
I.V. Therapy Associates (Medical, Dental, and Optical Supplies) [19382]
Luden & Co., Inc.; J.J.W. (Marine) [18552]
MBM Corp. (Charleston, South Carolina) (Industrial Machinery) [16277]
MBT International Inc. (Sound and Entertainment Equipment and Supplies) [25307]
Moore Drums Inc. (Petroleum, Fuels, and Related Equipment) [22496]
Moore Drums Inc. (Industrial Supplies) [17051]
Pearlstine Distributors Inc. (Alcoholic Beverages) [1945]
Player International; J.B. (Sound and Entertainment Equipment and Supplies) [25386]

Cheraw

Moore Brothers Inc. (Clothing) [5203]

Cherokee Falls

South Carolina Distributors Inc. (Toys and Hobby Goods) [26659]

Columbia

AKMS, Inc. (Medical, Dental, and Optical Equipment) [18667]
AKMS Inc. (Medical, Dental, and Optical Supplies) [19129]
Applied Video Systems Inc. (Sound and Entertainment Equipment and Supplies) [25080]
Associated Industrial Supply Co. (Industrial Supplies) [16712]
Bearing Distributors Inc. (Automotive) [2335]
Cate-McLaurin Company Inc. (Automotive) [2435]
Central News Co. (Books and Other Printed Materials) [3622]
Climatic Corp. (Heating and Cooling Equipment and Supplies) [14387]
Consolidated Electrical Distributors Inc. Perry-Mann Electrical (Electrical and Electronic Equipment and Supplies) [8572]
Cromers Inc. (Restaurant and Commercial Foodservice Equipment and Supplies) [24098]

Dixie Electronics (Communications Systems and Equipment) [5597]
Durr Medical Corp. (Medical, Dental, and Optical Supplies) [19296]
G & E Parts Center, Inc. (Household Appliances) [15137]
Gateway Supply Company Inc. (Plumbing Materials and Fixtures) [23185]
Helicoflex Co. (Industrial Supplies) [16929]
Hobgood Electric & Machinery Company, Inc. (Electrical and Electronic Equipment and Supplies) [8851]
Livingston & Haven, Inc. (Industrial Machinery) [16240]
Mid State Distributors Inc. (Alcoholic Beverages) [1873]
Miller Tire Service Inc. (Automotive) [2971]
Oxford of Burgaw Co. (Clothing) [5259]
Palmetto Tile Distributor (Floorcovering Equipment and Supplies) [10098]
Quill, Hair & Ferrule (Paints and Varnishes) [21549]
Resource Electronics Inc. (Electrical and Electronic Equipment and Supplies) [9282]
Robertson Optical Labs, Inc. (Medical, Dental, and Optical Supplies) [19583]
South Carolina Tees Inc. (Clothing) [5368]
Special Care Medical Inc. (Medical, Dental, and Optical Equipment) [19048]
Thomas and Howard Company Inc. (Food) [12714]
Thompson Dental Company Inc. (Medical, Dental, and Optical Equipment) [19077]

Conway

Canal Industries Inc. (Construction Materials and Machinery) [7132]

Cowpens

Glenco Hosiery Mills Inc. (Clothing) [4988]
Merz and Company Inc.; F.O. (Gifts and Novelties) [13401]

Darlington

Diamond Hill Plywood Co. (Construction Materials and Machinery) [7261]

Dillon

Bethea Distributing Inc. (Agricultural Equipment and Supplies) [306]

Easley

Harold's Tire and Auto (Automotive) [2726]

Florence

Bearing Distributors Inc. (Automotive) [2336]
Caloric Corp. (Household Appliances) [15071]
The Car Place (Construction Materials and Machinery) [7138]
Carolina Hardware & Supply, Inc. (Industrial Supplies) [16782]
Chase Oil Co. Inc. (Petroleum, Fuels, and Related Equipment) [22131]
Dilmar Oil Company Inc. (Petroleum, Fuels, and Related Equipment) [22201]
Nichols Companies of South Carolina (Food) [12006]
Sadisco of Florence (Automotive) [3178]
Trayco Inc. (Plumbing Materials and Fixtures) [23414]
W & W Body (Automotive) [3395]
Wallace's Old Fashion Skins Inc. (Food) [12870]
Young Pecan Shelling Company Inc. (Food) [12997]

Ft. Mill

Laboratory Design and Equipment (Furniture and Fixtures) [13162]
Medfax Corp. (Computers and Software) [6478]
Owsley and Sons Inc. (Industrial Machinery) [16366]
US FoodService Inc. Carolina Div. (Food) [12808]

Fountain Inn

Vermont American Tool Co. (Hardware) [13980]

Gaffney
Peeler's Rug Co. (Floorcovering Equipment and Supplies) [10103]

Graniteville
Shumway Seedsman; R.H. (Agricultural Equipment and Supplies) [1266]

Greenville
American Equipment Company Inc. (Greenville, South Carolina) (Construction Materials and Machinery) [6964]
American Health Systems Inc. (Medical, Dental, and Optical Equipment) [18675]
Amtec International Inc. (Furniture and Fixtures) [13020]
Batson Co.; Louis P. (Industrial Machinery) [15806]
Bruce Vehicle/Equipment Auction Services Inc. (Agricultural Equipment and Supplies) [346]
Builder Marts of America Inc. (Construction Materials and Machinery) [7098]
Buy_Low Beauty Supply (Health and Beauty Aids) [14053]
Caro-Tile Ltd. (Floorcovering Equipment and Supplies) [9759]
Carolina Western Inc. (Construction Materials and Machinery) [7145]
Catalyst Telecom (Communications Systems and Equipment) [5550]
Cimarron Corporation Inc. (Industrial Machinery) [15888]
Clayton Tile (Floorcovering Equipment and Supplies) [9813]
Dealers Supply and Lumber Inc. (Construction Materials and Machinery) [7256]
Enterprise Computer Systems Inc. (Computers and Software) [6251]
Frank & Thomas, Inc. (Industrial Machinery) [16039]
Gates/Arrow Distributing Inc. (Computers and Software) [6290]
Gates Arrow Distributing Inc. (Electrical and Electronic Equipment and Supplies) [8774]
Gates/FA Distributing Inc. (Computers and Software) [6291]
Greenville Health Corp. (Medical, Dental, and Optical Equipment) [18816]
Greenville Tile Distributors (Floorcovering Equipment and Supplies) [9927]
Home/Office Communications Supply (Communications Systems and Equipment) [5639]
Ikon Office Solutions (Office Equipment and Supplies) [21049]
Izumi International, Inc. (Industrial Machinery) [16179]
Long Trailer & Body Service, Inc. (Automotive) [2891]
MacGregor Sports and Fitness Inc. (Recreational and Sporting Goods) [23795]
Mann U.V. Technology, Inc. (Specialty Equipment and Products) [25724]
MJL Corp. (Industrial Machinery) [16314]
Modern Material Handling Co. (Industrial Supplies) [17046]
Orders Distributing Company Inc. (Floorcovering Equipment and Supplies) [10088]
Picanol of America Inc. (Industrial Machinery) [16396]
Piedmont Clarklift Inc. (Industrial Machinery) [16398]
Poe Corp. (Hardware) [13872]
The Print Machine Inc. (Computers and Software) [6640]
PYA/Monarch Chain Distribution (Food) [12240]
PYA/Monarch Inc. (Food) [12241]
Roane-Barker Inc. (Medical, Dental, and Optical Equipment) [19024]
ScanSource Inc. (Computers and Software) [6710]
Shealy Electrical Wholesalers Incorporated Co. (Electrical and Electronic Equipment and Supplies) [9358]
Soltex International Inc. (Textiles and Notions) [26208]

Southern Optical Co. (Medical, Dental, and Optical Supplies) [19626]
Specialty Distribution (Food) [12550]
Teleco Inc. (Communications Systems and Equipment) [5781]
Top Dog Ltd. (Veterinary Products) [27248]

Greenwood
Greenwood Mills Inc. (Clothing) [5003]
Greenwood Supply Company Inc. (Electrical and Electronic Equipment and Supplies) [8817]

Greer
Vaughn Meat Packing Company Inc. (Food) [12832]
Williams Detroit Diesel Allison (Automotive) [3436]
Williamson & Co. (Industrial Supplies) [17281]

Hartsville
Auto Wholesale and Hartsville Paint Store (Paints and Varnishes) [21395]
Plyler Paper Stock Co. (Used, Scrap, and Recycled Materials) [26941]

Hilton Head Island
Broz, Inc.; John V. (Construction Materials and Machinery) [7088]
Espy Lumber Co. (Construction Materials and Machinery) [7320]
Island Tee Shirt Sales Inc. (Clothing) [5064]

Inman
Derma-Therm Inc. (Medical, Dental, and Optical Equipment) [18772]

Irmo
Foot Loose Inc. (Shoes) [24746]
Rah Rah Sales Inc. (Clothing) [5299]
Transcon Trading Company, Inc. (Veterinary Products) [27250]

Iva
New Fashion Inc. (Clothing) [5226]

Jefferson
Funderburk Company Inc.; G.A. (Food) [11224]

Johnston
Holmes Timber Company Inc. (Wood and Wood Products) [27319]

Kingstree
McGill Distributors (Marine) [18565]

Lake City
E.D. Packing Co. (Food) [11025]
Gaskins; Carlton J. (Heating and Cooling Equipment and Supplies) [14456]
Lee Flowers and Company Inc.; W. (Horticultural Supplies) [14910]
Red Gaskins and Co.; J. (Restaurant and Commercial Foodservice Equipment and Supplies) [24209]

Lancaster
Lad Enterprises, Ltd. (Office Equipment and Supplies) [21095]
Springs Industries Inc. Chesterfield Div. (Textiles and Notions) [26211]

Landrum
Bigelow-Sanford (Floorcovering Equipment and Supplies) [9726]

Latta
Coastal Tile & Roofing Co., Inc. (Floorcovering Equipment and Supplies) [9815]

Laurens
Southern States Lumber Company Inc. (Construction Materials and Machinery) [8053]

Lexington
Carolina Retail Packaging Inc. (Paper and Paper Products) [21670]
Clarkson Co. Inc.; R.J. (Household Appliances) [15085]
Pioneer Machinery Inc. (Industrial Machinery) [16401]
Wells & Associates; Kenyon (Medical, Dental, and Optical Equipment) [19107]

Liberty
Flexi-Wall Systems (Household Items) [15499]

Lyman
Industrial Metal Processing Inc. (Metals) [20056]
S.A.C.M. Textile Inc. (Industrial Machinery) [16467]

Manning
Moore Oil Company Inc. (Petroleum, Fuels, and Related Equipment) [22497]

Mauldin
Heafner Tires & Products (Automotive) [2735]

Mt. Pleasant
Mount Pleasant Seafood Co. (Food) [11942]
sjs X-Ray Corp. (Medical, Dental, and Optical Equipment) [19038]
Zimmerman; Jerry (Marine) [18648]

Myrtle Beach
Chapin Co. (Petroleum, Fuels, and Related Equipment) [22129]

Newberry
Louis Rich Co. (Food) [11736]

Nichols
Nichol's Farm Supply Inc. (Agricultural Equipment and Supplies) [1074]

North Charleston
Allied-Crawford Steel (Metals) [19751]
Kru-Kel Co. Inc. (Heating and Cooling Equipment and Supplies) [14515]

North Myrtle Beach
Sheriar Books (Books and Other Printed Materials) [4160]

Norway
Wilbro Inc. (Agricultural Equipment and Supplies) [1445]

Okatie
Ebbtide & Associates (Household Items) [15485]

Orangeburg
Cox Industries, Inc. (Construction Materials and Machinery) [7227]

Piedmont
Parts Inc. (Used, Scrap, and Recycled Materials) [26936]

Pineland
Applied Business Computers Inc. (Computers and Software) [5947]

Ridgeway
Arnold-Sunbelt Beverage Company L.P.; Ben (Alcoholic Beverages) [1487]

Rock Hill
Amida Industries Inc. (Industrial Machinery) [15771]
Carolina Salon Services (Health and Beauty Aids) [14058]
Compusystems Inc. South Carolina (Computers and Software) [6099]
Desoutter Inc. (Industrial Machinery) [15943]
HBG Export Corp. (Plastics) [22979]
Ice Systems & Supplies Inc. (Heating and Cooling Equipment and Supplies) [14492]

Medical Mart Inc. (Medical, Dental, and Optical Equipment) [18920]
Mid-Carolina Electric Supply Company, Inc. (Electrical and Electronic Equipment and Supplies) [9076]
Ostrow Textile L.L.C. (Household Items) [15603]
Rock Hill Coca-Cola Bottling Co. (Soft Drinks) [25025]
Wilkerson Fuel Company Inc. (Petroleum, Fuels, and Related Equipment) [22803]

Rowesville
American Importers of South Carolina (Toys and Hobby Goods) [26388]

Salem
Carl's Clogging Supplies (Shoes) [24707]

Sandy Springs
Coker International Trading Inc. (Industrial Machinery) [15897]

Seneca
Jantzen Inc. (Clothing) [5076]
Rochester Imports Inc. (Toys and Hobby Goods) [26637]

Simpsonville
Builderway Inc. (Household Appliances) [15065]

Spartanburg
ADO Corp. (Household Items) [15389]
All Phase Electric Supply (Electrical and Electronic Equipment and Supplies) [8293]
American Fast Print (Textiles and Notions) [25959]
Bolliger Corp. (Industrial Machinery) [15829]
Cannon and Sons Inc.; C.L. (Construction Materials and Machinery) [7134]
Cash Supply Co. (Hardware) [13623]
Computer Trends (Computers and Software) [6132]
Gilbert & Son Shoe Company (Shoes) [24750]
International Industries Corporation (Food) [11522]
JM Smith Corp. (Medical, Dental, and Optical Supplies) [19386]
Jones Tractor Company Inc. (Agricultural Equipment and Supplies) [891]
Smith Drug Co. (Medical, Dental, and Optical Supplies) [19616]
Southeastern Paper Group (Paper and Paper Products) [21943]
Symtech Inc. (Industrial Machinery) [16544]
TML Associates Inc. (Construction Materials and Machinery) [8138]
Zima Corp. (Industrial Machinery) [16660]
Zimmer Machinery Corp. (Industrial Machinery) [16661]

Summerville
Oakbrook Custom Embroidery (Clothing) [5245]
Seago Export (Construction Materials and Machinery) [7997]

Sumter
Cities Supply Company Inc. (Plumbing Materials and Fixtures) [23115]
Harvin Choice Meats Inc. (Food) [11388]
Scana Propane Supply Inc. (Petroleum, Fuels, and Related Equipment) [22656]
Sumter Machinery Company Inc. (Industrial Supplies) [17201]
Sumter Wood Preserving Company Inc. (Construction Materials and Machinery) [8086]

SurfsiDe Beach
Builder Contract Sales Inc. (Household Appliances) [15064]
Unique Sales, Inc. (Toys and Hobby Goods) [26698]

Taylors
Staflex/Harotex Co. (Textiles and Notions) [26212]
Western Beverage Company Inc. (Alcoholic Beverages) [2113]

Union
Claesson Co. (Textiles and Notions) [26006]
Conso Products Co. (Furniture and Fixtures) [13079]
Free Shoe Shop (Shoes) [24747]

West Columbia
American Systems of the Southeast Inc. (Office Equipment and Supplies) [20799]
Magic Touch Enterprises, Inc. (Floorcovering Equipment and Supplies) [10003]
Meyers Medical Inc. (Medical, Dental, and Optical Equipment) [18935]
Smith Enterprises Inc.; P. (Recreational and Sporting Goods) [23947]
Trans World Investments, Ltd. (Household Items) [15687]
Tri-City Fuel and Heating Company Inc. (Heating and Cooling Equipment and Supplies) [14737]
Virginia Carolina Tools Inc. (Industrial Machinery) [16602]
Williams Detroit Diesel Allison (Automotive) [3437]

White Rock
Vann Sales Co.; Hugh (Veterinary Products) [27262]

Winnsboro
Manhattan Shirt Company-Winnsboro Distribution Center (Clothing) [5159]

Woodruff
Intedge Industries Inc. (Restaurant and Commercial Foodservice Equipment and Supplies) [24142]

Yemassee
Le Creuset of America Inc. (Household Items) [15562]

Yonges Island
Too Goo Doo Farms Inc. (Food) [12732]

York
Black Enterprises Inc. (Agricultural Equipment and Supplies) [320]
Rouzee Green Company Inc.; The John (Recreational and Sporting Goods) [23922]

South Dakota

Aberdeen
Aberdeen Vault Inc.; Wilbert (Specialty Equipment and Products) [25541]
Clark Implement Company Inc.; H.C. (Agricultural Equipment and Supplies) [422]
Coca-Cola Aberdeen (Soft Drinks) [24929]
House of Glass Inc. (Paints and Varnishes) [21458]
Janitor Supply Co. (Cleaning and Janitorial Supplies) [4645]
Janitor Supply Co. (Restaurant and Commercial Foodservice Equipment and Supplies) [24149]
Plainsco Inc. (Household Appliances) [15274]
South Dakota Wheat Growers Association (Livestock and Farm Products) [18241]
Thorpe Livestock Inc. (Livestock and Farm Products) [18280]
Western Printing Co. (Paper and Paper Products) [21989]

Alcester
Midwest Cleaning Systems Inc. (Cleaning and Janitorial Supplies) [4671]

Badger
Badger Farmers Cooperative (Agricultural Equipment and Supplies) [268]
Badger Farmers Cooperative (Food) [10486]

Belle Fourche
Belle Fourche Livestock Exchange (Livestock and Farm Products) [17727]
Grandview Hatchery & Locker Plant (Livestock and Farm Products) [17958]

Beresford
Farmers Union Cooperative Association of Alcester and Beresford South Dakota (Petroleum, Fuels, and Related Equipment) [22259]

Box Elder
Williams; Lyle L. (Livestock and Farm Products) [18350]

Bristol
Hansmeier and Son Inc. (Agricultural Equipment and Supplies) [788]

Britton
Britton Livestock Sales Inc. (Livestock and Farm Products) [17747]

Brookings
Central Business Supply Inc. (Office Equipment and Supplies) [20889]
Farmers Cooperative Co. (Agricultural Equipment and Supplies) [591]
Farmers Cooperative Co. (Food) [11092]
Sexauer Company Inc. (Livestock and Farm Products) [18230]

Canton
Harvest States Cooperatives. Canton Div. (Agricultural Equipment and Supplies) [798]

Castlewood
Castlewood Farmers Elevator (Livestock and Farm Products) [17767]

Chamberlain
Chamberlain Livestock Auction (Livestock and Farm Products) [17774]

Corsica
Cenex Harvest States Cooperative (Agricultural Equipment and Supplies) [383]

Dell Rapids
American Medical Industries (Medical, Dental, and Optical Supplies) [19141]
Dell Rapids Co-op Grain (Agricultural Equipment and Supplies) [505]

Elk Point
Farmers Elevator Co. (Agricultural Equipment and Supplies) [641]

Garretson
Cenex Harvest States (Agricultural Equipment and Supplies) [382]
Nordstroms (Automotive) [3038]

Gettysburg
Midway Parts Inc. (Automotive) [2957]

Gregory
Gregory Livestock (Livestock and Farm Products) [17964]
Rosebud Farmers Union Cooperative Associates Inc. (Agricultural Equipment and Supplies) [1211]
Rosebud Farmers Union Cooperative Associates Inc. (Petroleum, Fuels, and Related Equipment) [22639]

Herreid
Herreid Livestock Market (Livestock and Farm Products) [17994]

Highmore
Highmore Auction (Livestock and Farm Products) [17998]

Huron

Alexander; Steve (Electrical and Electronic Equipment and Supplies) [8290]

Ampride (Petroleum, Fuels, and Related Equipment) [22038]

Bales Continental Commission Co. (Livestock and Farm Products) [17719]

Jensen Lloyd and Willis (Livestock and Farm Products) [18023]

Magness Huron Livestock Exchange (Livestock and Farm Products) [18072]

Office Equipment Service (Office Equipment and Supplies) [21178]

Raymond Oil Co. (Petroleum, Fuels, and Related Equipment) [22608]

Lake Andes

Lake Andes Farmers Cooperative Co. (Agricultural Equipment and Supplies) [929]

Lake Andes Farmers Cooperative Co. (Food) [11666]

Lake Preston

Lake Preston Cooperative Association (Livestock and Farm Products) [18042]

Lemmon

G & O Paper & Supplies (Paper and Paper Products) [21735]

Lemmon Livestock Inc. (Livestock and Farm Products) [18051]

Southwest Grain Farm Marketing and Supply Div. (Petroleum, Fuels, and Related Equipment) [22686]

Letcher

Putnam Truck Parts (Automotive) [3127]

Madison

Bessman Price Auctioneers (Livestock and Farm Products) [17731]

Madison Farmers Elevator Co. (Livestock and Farm Products) [18070]

Murdock, Inc.; G.A. (Plumbing Materials and Fixtures) [23284]

Martin

Mueller Feed Mill Inc. (Agricultural Equipment and Supplies) [1057]

Mc Laughlin

McLaughlin Livestock Auction (Livestock and Farm Products) [18084]

Menno

Farmers Union Oil Co. (Agricultural Equipment and Supplies) [665]

Milbank

Valley Office Products Inc. (Office Equipment and Supplies) [21334]

Milesville

Daniel Piroutek (Livestock and Farm Products) [17811]

Piroutek; Daniel (Livestock and Farm Products) [18169]

Miller

Tri-State Insulation Co. (Construction Materials and Machinery) [8145]

Mitchell

Krall Optometric Professional LLC (Medical, Dental, and Optical Supplies) [19400]

Mitchell Manufacturing, Hagens Division (Recreational and Sporting Goods) [23832]

Porter Distributing Co. (Alcoholic Beverages) [1962]

United Auto Parts Inc. (Automotive) [3362]

Wholesale Electronics Inc. (Electrical and Electronic Equipment and Supplies) [9593]

Mobridge

Rieger's Ceramics Arts & Crafts (Toys and Hobby Goods) [26635]

Onida

Sutton Ranches (Livestock and Farm Products) [18271]

Parkston

Agland Cooperative (Agricultural Equipment and Supplies) [206]

Pierre

Midwest Cooperatives (Livestock and Farm Products) [18097]

Moodie Implement Co. (Agricultural Equipment and Supplies) [1050]

Presho

Bar Lazy K Bar Ranch Inc. (Livestock and Farm Products) [17721]

Rapid City

Abacus (Office Equipment and Supplies) [20764]

Black Hills Chemical Co. Inc. (Cleaning and Janitorial Supplies) [4583]

Black Hills Gold Colema (Jewelry) [17340]

Black Hills Jewelers Supply (Specialty Equipment and Products) [25574]

Black Hills Milk Producers (Food) [10563]

Brown Swiss/Gillette Quality Checkered Dairy (Food) [10629]

Country Time Ceramic Supply Inc. (Specialty Equipment and Products) [25612]

Dakota Steel and Supply Co. (Metals) [19915]

Dal CAM Oil Co. Inc. (Construction Materials and Machinery) [7247]

Follum Supply (Cleaning and Janitorial Supplies) [4624]

Hardco, Inc. (Floorcovering Equipment and Supplies) [9936]

Inland Truck Parts (Automotive) [2788]

Jalopy Jungle Inc. (Automotive) [2811]

Knecht Home Lumber Center Inc. (Construction Materials and Machinery) [7565]

Knecht Home Lumber Center Inc. (Wood and Wood Products) [27331]

Kwik Stop Car Wash Supply (Cleaning and Janitorial Supplies) [4655]

Mid-America Dairymen Inc. Brown Swiss (Food) [11874]

Northern Power Technologies (Electrical and Electronic Equipment and Supplies) [9138]

Pressure Service Inc. (Cleaning and Janitorial Supplies) [4689]

Pryor & Associates; Roger (Specialty Equipment and Products) [25793]

Rapid City Beauty & Barber Supply (Health and Beauty Aids) [14205]

Rapid Controls Inc. (Industrial Supplies) [17131]

Ridco Inc. (Jewelry) [17565]

Rushmore Health Care Products (Medical, Dental, and Optical Equipment) [19026]

Sodak Gaming Inc. (Specialty Equipment and Products) [25821]

Sunset Supply (Gifts and Novelties) [13459]

Sweetwood Distributing Inc. (Alcoholic Beverages) [2066]

Tepco Corp. (Industrial Supplies) [17217]

Time Machine (Automotive) [3304]

Urban Wholesale (Cleaning and Janitorial Supplies) [4721]

Whisler Bearing Co. (Paints and Varnishes) [21608]

Redfield

Redfield Livestock Auction Inc. (Livestock and Farm Products) [18192]

Rosholt

Consumers Cooperative Oil Co. (Petroleum, Fuels, and Related Equipment) [22163]

Rosholt Farmers Cooperative Elevator Co. (Livestock and Farm Products) [18206]

Salem

Farmers Union Cooperative Association (Agricultural Equipment and Supplies) [660]

Sioux Falls

A & B Business Equipment Inc. (Office Equipment and Supplies) [20759]

Adams-Dougherty Livestock Brokerage (Livestock and Farm Products) [17674]

Apex Medical Corp. (Medical, Dental, and Optical Equipment) [18687]

Barneys Auto Salvage Inc. (Automotive) [2319]

Bens Inc. (Automotive) [2349]

Best Business Products Inc. (Office Equipment and Supplies) [20841]

Campbell Supply Company Inc. (Food) [10685]

Chris Cam Corp. (Paper and Paper Products) [21678]

CMOV, Inc. (Computers and Software) [6077]

Commercial Interior Decor (Specialty Equipment and Products) [25607]

Dakota Beverage Co. (Alcoholic Beverages) [1632]

Dakota Chemical Inc. (Specialty Equipment and Products) [25623]

Diesel Machinery Inc. (Construction Materials and Machinery) [7265]

Egger Steel Co. (Metals) [19951]

Evans Inc.; J.D. (Construction Materials and Machinery) [7324]

Foresight Inc. (Cleaning and Janitorial Supplies) [4625]

Heartland Paper Co. (Paper and Paper Products) [21758]

Industrial Supply Co. (Industrial Supplies) [16954]

International Business Equipment (Office Equipment and Supplies) [21063]

Interstate Wholesale Inc. (Jewelry) [17462]

J & L Livestock (Livestock and Farm Products) [18016]

JDS Industries Inc. (Jewelry) [17467]

Lease Surgical Inc. (Medical, Dental, and Optical Equipment) [18884]

Line & Co.; R.Q. (Livestock and Farm Products) [18059]

Long & Hansen Commission Co. (Livestock and Farm Products) [18064]

Midwest Oil Co. (Petroleum, Fuels, and Related Equipment) [22483]

Miller Funeral Home Inc. (Specialty Equipment and Products) [25741]

Mulder Refrigeration (Heating and Cooling Equipment and Supplies) [14614]

Nelson Laboratories L.P. (Agricultural Equipment and Supplies) [1068]

Northern Truck Equip. Corp. (Motorized Vehicles) [20698]

Northern Truck Equip. Corp. (Industrial Machinery) [16352]

Orion Food Systems (Food) [12077]

Pam Oil Inc. (Petroleum, Fuels, and Related Equipment) [22548]

Pam Oil Inc. (Automotive) [3078]

Queen City Wholesale Inc. (Food) [12255]

Queen City Wholesale Inc. (Food) [12256]

Rich Brothers Co. (Toys and Hobby Goods) [26634]

Richard-Ewing Equipment Co. Inc. (Cleaning and Janitorial Supplies) [4696]

Sodak Distributing Co. (Alcoholic Beverages) [2031]

Steele-Siman & Co. (Livestock and Farm Products) [18252]

Sullivan's (Gifts and Novelties) [13455]

Sweetman Construction Co. (Construction Materials and Machinery) [8094]

Systems Unlimited Inc. (Office Equipment and Supplies) [21312]

Syverson Tile, Inc. (Floorcovering Equipment and Supplies) [10201]

Thermo King of Sioux Falls (Heating and Cooling Equipment and Supplies) [14726]

Transport Refrigeration of Sioux Falls (Heating and Cooling Equipment and Supplies) [14736]

Tri State Electric Company Inc. (Electrical and Electronic Equipment and Supplies) [9505]

Tri State Warehouse Inc. (Automotive) [3339]

United Pride Inc. (Petroleum, Fuels, and Related Equipment) [22762]
Warren Supply Co. (Electrical and Electronic Equipment and Supplies) [9558]

Sisseton

Dady Distributing Inc.; J.A. (Alcoholic Beverages) [1631]

Spearfish

National Impala Association (Automotive) [3016]
Valley Auto Parts (Automotive) [3382]

Sturgis

Automatic Vendors Inc. (Tobacco Products) [26261]
Sturgis Livestock Exchange (Livestock and Farm Products) [18263]

Tea

Lund Truck Parts Inc. (Automotive) [2897]

Toronto

Deuel County Farmers Union Oil Co. (Petroleum, Fuels, and Related Equipment) [22199]

Tripp

Hard Times Vending Inc. (Restaurant and Commercial Foodservice Equipment and Supplies) [24135]

Wagner

Wagner Livestock Auction (Livestock and Farm Products) [18322]

Watertown

Building Products Inc. (Construction Materials and Machinery) [7106]
Cook's Inc. (Office Equipment and Supplies) [20913]
Metz Baking Co. (Food) [11863]
Sioux Valley Cooperative (Petroleum, Fuels, and Related Equipment) [22675]
South Dakota Livestock Sale (Livestock and Farm Products) [18240]
Unger Cattle Marketing; Randy J. (Livestock and Farm Products) [18298]
Watertown Cooperative Elevator Association (Agricultural Equipment and Supplies) [1414]
Watertown Livestock Auction, Inc. (Livestock and Farm Products) [18326]

Webster

Webster Scale Inc. (Scientific and Measurement Devices) [24455]

Winner

B & D Auto Salvage & Repair (Automotive) [2306]
Dakota Pride Coop (Agricultural Equipment and Supplies) [487]
Dakota Pride Cooperative (Petroleum, Fuels, and Related Equipment) [22187]
Grossenburg Implement Inc. (Agricultural Equipment and Supplies) [769]
Kelly; Dennis (Livestock and Farm Products) [18031]
Whitley Central Distributing Co. (Alcoholic Beverages) [2118]

Woonsocket

Van Dyke Supply Co. (Specialty Equipment and Products) [25862]

Yale

Yale Farmers Cooperative (Livestock and Farm Products) [18363]

Yankton

A La Carte Jewelry (Jewelry) [17298]
Conkling Distributing Co.; John A. (Alcoholic Beverages) [1610]
Conkling Distributing Co.; John A. (Alcoholic Beverages) [1611]

Frick Hog Buying & Trucking (Livestock and Farm Products) [17928]
Morgen Manufacturing Co. (Construction Materials and Machinery) [7749]
Promicro Systems (Office Equipment and Supplies) [21224]
Stockmen's Livestock Market (Livestock and Farm Products) [18257]
Wallbaum Distributing; Dan (Alcoholic Beverages) [2109]
Wholesale Supply Company Inc. (Tobacco Products) [26372]
Yankton Janitorial Supply (Cleaning and Janitorial Supplies) [4735]
Yankton Office Equipment (Office Equipment and Supplies) [21366]

Tennessee

Adamsville

Garan, Inc. (Clothing) [4976]

Alamo

Crockett Farmers Cooperative Co. (Agricultural Equipment and Supplies) [476]

Antioch

Commercial Laminations (Furniture and Fixtures) [13075]

Athens

Hammer-Johnson Supply Inc. (Construction Materials and Machinery) [7435]
McMann Loudan Farmers Cooperative (Agricultural Equipment and Supplies) [1005]
Moore Discount Inc. (Household Appliances) [15241]
Safety Optical (Medical, Dental, and Optical Supplies) [19591]

Bells

Farmers Gin Co. (Agricultural Equipment and Supplies) [650]
United Foods Inc. (Food) [12794]

Blountville

Nickels Supply (Shoes) [24821]

Bolivar

Motor Parts & Bearing Co. (Automotive) [2994]

Brentwood

ADD Enterprises Inc. (Computers and Software) [5875]
Alcoa Conductors Products Co. (Automotive) [2201]
AMI Metals Inc. (Metals) [19774]
Fenders and More Inc. (Automotive) [2610]
Fitness Systems Inc. (Recreational and Sporting Goods) [23673]
Hobby Lobby International Inc. (Toys and Hobby Goods) [26519]
Mitchell Orthopedic Supply Inc. (Medical, Dental, and Optical Equipment) [18944]
Republic Automotive Parts Inc. (Automotive) [3150]
Sparrow-Star (Books and Other Printed Materials) [4179]

Bristol

Industrial Gas and Supply Co. (Industrial Supplies) [16947]
LW Bristol Collection (Clothing) [5147]
Mitchell-Powers Hardware (Hardware) [13831]

Burns

Crestar Food Products Inc. (Food) [10867]

Camden

Tennessee Shell Company, Inc. (Food) [12706]

Chattanooga

Absolute Appliance Distributors Inc. (Household Appliances) [14990]
Air & Hydraulic Equipment, Inc. (Industrial Machinery) [15744]
Allied Trading Companies (Industrial Machinery) [15758]
AMG Publications (Books and Other Printed Materials) [3506]
Appliance Parts Warehouse Inc. (Household Appliances) [15029]
Bacon Products Co. Inc. (Agricultural Equipment and Supplies) [267]
Bearings & Drives Inc. (Industrial Machinery) [15812]
Boiler and Heat Exchange Systems Inc. (Plumbing Materials and Fixtures) [23091]
Carter Distributing Co. (Alcoholic Beverages) [1578]
Ceramic Tile Supply, Inc. (Floorcovering Equipment and Supplies) [9801]
Chattanooga Shooting Supplies (Recreational and Sporting Goods) [23588]
Dillard Paper Co. Chattanooga Div. (Paper and Paper Products) [21710]
Dolly Madison Cake Co. (Food) [10980]
Elevators Etc. (Medical, Dental, and Optical Equipment) [18788]
Fillauer Inc. (Medical, Dental, and Optical Equipment) [18797]
G & N Distributors Inc. (Household Appliances) [15140]
Gardner and Meredith Inc. (Industrial Machinery) [16047]
Industrial Tools and Abrasives Inc. (Industrial Supplies) [16959]
Lookout Beverages (Alcoholic Beverages) [1828]
Manz, Jr.; Edward H. (Clothing) [5161]
Mechanical Drives Inc. (Industrial Machinery) [16283]
Mills and Lupton Supply Co. (Electrical and Electronic Equipment and Supplies) [9087]
Mitchell Industrial Tire Co. (Automotive) [2977]
New Hosiery (Clothing) [5227]
Nichols Fleet Equipment (Automotive) [3031]
O'Neal Metals Co. (Metals) [20250]
Piping Supply Company Inc. (Industrial Supplies) [17107]
RAD Graphics (Computers and Software) [6678]
Siskin Steel and Supply Company Inc. (Metals) [20370]
SM Building Supply Coompany, Inc. (Construction Materials and Machinery) [8032]
Southern Fluid Power (Industrial Supplies) [17185]
Sport Spectrum (Clothing) [5383]
Tennessee-Carolina Lumber Company Inc. (Construction Materials and Machinery) [8109]
Thermo King of Chattanooga (Heating and Cooling Equipment and Supplies) [14724]
Tri-S Co. (Security and Safety Equipment) [24646]
Volunteer Sales Co. (Food) [12856]
Whelchel Co.; Harry J. (Agricultural Equipment and Supplies) [1437]
Wood Supply Co.; Walter A. (Industrial Supplies) [17286]
Xpedx (Paper and Paper Products) [22000]

Clarksville

Averitt Lumber Company Inc. (Construction Materials and Machinery) [7005]
Lyk-Nu Inc. (Cleaning and Janitorial Supplies) [4660]
Montgomery Farmers Cooperative (Agricultural Equipment and Supplies) [1049]
Randolph, Hale & Matthews (Electrical and Electronic Equipment and Supplies) [9263]
Red River Electric & Refrigeration Supply (Heating and Cooling Equipment and Supplies) [14650]

Cleveland

Bearings and Drives, Inc. (Industrial Supplies) [16736]
Beattie Systems Inc. (Photographic Equipment and Supplies) [22829]
Bishop Baking Co. (Food) [10559]

Maycor Appliance Parts and Service
Co. (Household Appliances) [15220]
Quinn Electric Supply Co. (Electrical and Electronic
Equipment and Supplies) [9253]
Specialty Chemical Company,
Inc. (Chemicals) [4518]
Wholesale Supply Group Inc. (Plumbing Materials
and Fixtures) [23457]

Collegedale
Rehab Medical Equipment Inc. (Medical, Dental,
and Optical Equipment) [19016]

Collierville
Computer AC (Communications Systems and
Equipment) [5577]

Columbia
Maury Farmers Cooperative (Agricultural Equipment
and Supplies) [992]
Rippey Auto Parts Company
Inc. (Automotive) [3161]

Cookeville
American Custom Software (Computers and
Software) [5924]
Cassemco Sporting Goods (Recreational and
Sporting Goods) [23585]
Fixture-World, Inc. (Restaurant and Commercial
Foodservice Equipment and Supplies) [24121]
Institutional Wholesale Co. (Food) [11515]
Respiratory Homecare Inc. (Medical, Dental, and
Optical Equipment) [19019]

Cordova
Dreyfus Corp. Allenberg Cotton Company Div.;
Louis (Livestock and Farm Products) [17821]
King Cotton Foods (Food) [11611]
Mid South Marketing Inc. (Sound and Entertainment
Equipment and Supplies) [25318]
Modern Door and Hardware Inc. (Construction
Materials and Machinery) [7732]
Pizza Needs of Memphis Inc. (Food) [12179]

Cosby
Jean's Dulcimer Shop and Crying Creek
Publishers (Books and Other Printed
Materials) [3861]

Crossville
Advanced Technology Specialist (Computers and
Software) [5891]
Shanks Co.; L.P. (Food) [12473]

Dandridge
Jefferson Farmers Cooperative (Agricultural
Equipment and Supplies) [882]

Dayton
Robinson Manufacturing Company
Inc. (Clothing) [5315]
Suburban Manufacturing Co. (Heating and Cooling
Equipment and Supplies) [14701]

Decherd
Franklin Farmers Cooperative (Agricultural
Equipment and Supplies) [702]

Dickson
Dickson Farmers Cooperative (Agricultural
Equipment and Supplies) [519]

Donelson
Melton Book Company Inc. (Books and Other
Printed Materials) [3947]

Dyer
Dyer Motor Co. (Motorized Vehicles) [20630]

Dyersburg
Dyer Lauderdale Co-op (Agricultural Equipment and
Supplies) [532]
Tuckers Tire & Oil Company
Inc. (Automotive) [3355]

West Tennessee Communications (Communications
Systems and Equipment) [5810]
West Tennessee Communications (Electrical and
Electronic Equipment and Supplies) [9571]

Eagleville
Crosslin Supply Company Inc. (Construction
Materials and Machinery) [7232]

Elizabethton
Price Direct Sales; Don (Clothing) [5290]

Franklin
20th Century Nursery Landscape (Horticultural
Supplies) [14790]
Canaan Records (Sound and Entertainment
Equipment and Supplies) [25117]
McCullar Enterprises Inc. (Shoes) [24807]
McCullar Enterprises Inc. (Clothing) [5179]
Provident Music Group (Books and Other Printed
Materials) [4090]
UCG Energy Corp. (Petroleum, Fuels, and Related
Equipment) [22755]

Gallatin
Kilpatrick; Eddie (Shoes) [24783]
Parks Company Inc.; Charles C. (Food) [12115]

Gallaway
Precision Optical Laboratory (Medical, Dental, and
Optical Supplies) [19550]

Germantown
Ezon Inc. (Automotive) [2601]
Stadelman and Co.; Russell (Construction Materials
and Machinery) [8065]

Goodlettsville
Associated Packaging Inc. (Industrial
Supplies) [16714]
Fleming Foods of Tennessee Inc. (Food) [11156]
P and E Inc. (Automotive) [3068]
Remedpar Inc. (Medical, Dental, and Optical
Equipment) [19017]
Warrior Inc. (Gifts and Novelties) [13469]

Greeneville
Adams Wholesale Co. Inc. (Construction Materials
and Machinery) [6914]
Greene Farmers Cooperative (Agricultural
Equipment and Supplies) [767]

Harriman
Christmas Lumber Company Inc. (Construction
Materials and Machinery) [7170]

Henderson
A and M Sales and Manufacturing
Inc. (Clothing) [4737]

Humboldt
Lewis Electronics Co. (Electrical and Electronic
Equipment and Supplies) [8985]

Huntingdon
Carroll Farmers Cooperative (Agricultural Equipment
and Supplies) [374]

Jackson
Deaton's Carpet One (Floorcovering Equipment and
Supplies) [9851]
DET Distributing Co. (Alcoholic Beverages) [1645]
Future Optics Inc. (Medical, Dental, and Optical
Supplies) [19333]
Machine Tool and Supply Corp. (Industrial
Machinery) [16254]
Power & Telephone Supply Company,
Inc. (Electrical and Electronic Equipment and
Supplies) [9228]
Townsend Supply Co. (Electrical and Electronic
Equipment and Supplies) [9498]
Volunteer Janitorial Supply Co. (Recreational and
Sporting Goods) [24036]

Jamestown
Gamco Manufacturing Co. (Clothing) [4975]
Park Manufacturing Co. (Clothing) [5272]

Johnson City
Appalachian Distributors (Books and Other Printed
Materials) [3521]
B and B Produce Inc. (Food) [10480]
Edco Manufacturing Co. (Veterinary
Products) [27123]
Free Service Tire Company
Inc. (Automotive) [2645]
General Mills Operations (Food) [11249]
Holston Distributing Co. (Alcoholic
Beverages) [1762]
IJ Co. Tri-Cities Div. (Food) [11493]
Mayes Brothers Tool
Manufacturing (Hardware) [13816]
Mize Farm & Garden Supply (Veterinary
Products) [27190]
Summers Induserve Supply (Industrial
Machinery) [16535]

Kingsport
American Video & Audio Corp. (Sound and
Entertainment Equipment and Supplies) [25072]
Decorative Products Group (Floorcovering
Equipment and Supplies) [9852]
Delta-Southland International (Medical, Dental, and
Optical Equipment) [18769]
Holston Builders Supply Company Inc. (Construction
Materials and Machinery) [7479]
Pappy's Customs Inc. (Clothing) [5268]
Slip-Not Belting Corp. (Industrial Supplies) [17176]

Knoxville
A-Welders & Medical Supply (Medical, Dental, and
Optical Equipment) [18654]
Agri Feed & Supply (Veterinary Products) [27057]
Albers Inc. (Medical, Dental, and Optical
Supplies) [19132]
Allen's Supply Co. (Agricultural Equipment and
Supplies) [223]
Allied Flooring Supply (Floorcovering Equipment
and Supplies) [9659]
American Accessories International Inc. (Luggage
and Leather Goods) [18369]
American Limestone Company Inc. (Construction
Materials and Machinery) [6969]
Bacon & Co. Inc. (Clothing) [4798]
Braden's Wholesale Furniture Company
Inc. (Furniture and Fixtures) [13043]
Brown Appliance Parts Co. Inc. (Household
Appliances) [15061]
CISU of Dalton, Inc. (Floorcovering Equipment and
Supplies) [9806]
Clancy, Jr.; Arthur V. (Medical, Dental, and Optical
Supplies) [19232]
Coca-Cola; Johnston (Soft Drinks) [24946]
Control-Equip of Tennessee, Inc. (Heating and
Cooling Equipment and Supplies) [14402]
Corporate Interiors Inc. (Office Equipment and
Supplies) [20932]
Decorative Products Group (Floorcovering
Equipment and Supplies) [9853]
Dillard Paper Co. Knoxville Div. (Paper and Paper
Products) [21711]
Eagle Distributing Co. Inc. (Alcoholic
Beverages) [1665]
Eastern Ophthalmic Supply & Repair (Medical,
Dental, and Optical Supplies) [19301]
Elliott Shoe Co. (Shoes) [24733]
Genealogical Sources Unlimited (Books and Other
Printed Materials) [3775]
General Parts Corp. (Automotive) [2671]
Goodwin Machinery Co. (Construction Materials and
Machinery) [7404]
Hackney Co.; H.T. (Food) [11355]
Hamilton Appliance Parts Inc. (Household
Appliances) [15159]
Hill; Gary A. (Medical, Dental, and Optical
Equipment) [18835]
Holston Gases Inc. (Petroleum, Fuels, and Related
Equipment) [22356]
House-Hasson Hardware Inc. (Hardware) [13758]

HyperGlot Software Company Inc. (Computers and Software) [6348]
IJ Co. (Food) [11492]
I.J. Cos. (Food) [11494]
Jones & Lee Supply Co. (Electrical and Electronic Equipment and Supplies) [8919]
Knoxville Beverage Co. (Alcoholic Beverages) [1801]
Lays Fine Foods (Food) [11688]
Leisurelife USA Inc. (Recreational and Sporting Goods) [23784]
Linco Distributors (Tobacco Products) [26324]
Livingston & Haven, Inc. (Industrial Machinery) [16241]
Mayo Seed Co.; D.R. (Agricultural Equipment and Supplies) [994]
Mid-State Automotive (Automotive) [2952]
Modern Supply Company Inc. (Household Appliances) [15238]
Modern Supply Company Inc. (Knoxville, Tennessee) (Plumbing Materials and Fixtures) [23272]
Motor Products Company Inc. (Automotive) [2996]
Peterbilt of Knoxville Inc. (Automotive) [3094]
Power Equipment Co. (Construction Materials and Machinery) [7881]
Power & Telephone Supply Company, Inc. (Electrical and Electronic Equipment and Supplies) [9229]
Pratt & Co.; L.F. (Computers and Software) [6633]
Primavera Distributing (Floorcovering Equipment and Supplies) [10109]
Process Supplies & Accessories, Inc. (Industrial Supplies) [17117]
Rainbow Raster Graphics (Computers and Software) [6681]
RBM Company Inc. (Petroleum, Fuels, and Related Equipment) [22610]
Roden Electrical Supply Co. (Electrical and Electronic Equipment and Supplies) [9308]
Royal Beauty & Barber (Health and Beauty Aids) [14225]
Royal Brass and Hose (Hardware) [13896]
Rubber Plus Inc. (Rubber) [24292]
Skyland Hospital Supply Inc. (Medical, Dental, and Optical Equipment) [19040]
Smoky Mountain Coal Corp. (Minerals and Ores) [20568]
Stage Inc. (Household Items) [15665]
Star Sales Company of Knoxville (Toys and Hobby Goods) [26668]
Stokes Electric Co. (Electrical and Electronic Equipment and Supplies) [9418]
Stowers Machinery Corp. (Construction Materials and Machinery) [8077]
TENGASCO Inc. (Petroleum, Fuels, and Related Equipment) [22723]
Tennessee Florist Supply Inc. (Horticultural Supplies) [14960]
Tom's Foods Inc. (Food) [12729]
Trimble Company Inc.; William S. (Construction Materials and Machinery) [8149]
Vaughn Lumber Co.; Emmet (Construction Materials and Machinery) [8175]
Volunteer Produce Co. (Food) [12855]
Wynn and Graff Inc. (Textiles and Notions) [26252]

La Follette

Shelby Industries Inc. (Petroleum, Fuels, and Related Equipment) [22665]

La Vergne

Ingram Book Co. (Sound and Entertainment Equipment and Supplies) [25243]
Ingram Book Group Inc. (Books and Other Printed Materials) [3844]
Spring Arbor Distribution Company Inc. (Books and Other Printed Materials) [4184]
Tennessee Farmers Cooperative (Agricultural Equipment and Supplies) [1319]

Lebanon

Ely & Walker (Clothing) [4936]

Lester Company Inc.; Kenneth O. (Restaurant and Commercial Foodservice Equipment and Supplies) [24165]
PFG Lester (Food) [12161]

Lenoir City

Elm Hill Meats Inc. (Food) [11042]
Wamplers Farm Sausage (Food) [12874]

Lewisburg

Marshall Farmers Cooperative (Agricultural Equipment and Supplies) [989]

Lexington

Coca-Cola Bottling Works; Lexington (Soft Drinks) [24944]

Linden

Graham-Hardison Hardwood Inc. (Wood and Wood Products) [27311]

Madisonville

Kenwil Sales (Clothing) [5109]

Manchester

Manchester Wholesale Supply Inc. (Plumbing Materials and Fixtures) [23249]

Martin

Vincent Implements Inc. (Agricultural Equipment and Supplies) [1399]
Vincent Jobbing Co. (Shoes) [24885]

Maryville

Blount Farmers Cooperative (Agricultural Equipment and Supplies) [323]
Eldon Rubbermaid Office Products (Office Equipment and Supplies) [20987]
Maryville Wholesale Supply Inc. (Plumbing Materials and Fixtures) [23253]
Wholesale Supply Group, Inc. Maryville Division (Plumbing Materials and Fixtures) [23458]

Mc Minnville

Beaty's Nursery (Horticultural Supplies) [14827]
Warren Farmers Cooperative (Agricultural Equipment and Supplies) [1413]

Memphis

A & R Supply Co. Inc. (Heating and Cooling Equipment and Supplies) [14287]
Acme Brick & Tile (Floorcovering Equipment and Supplies) [9645]
Ad House Inc. (Gifts and Novelties) [13290]
ADEMCO/ADI (Security and Safety Equipment) [24470]
Admark Corp. (Computers and Software) [5877]
Aerospace Products International Inc. (Aeronautical Equipment and Supplies) [29]
Air Temperature Inc. (Heating and Cooling Equipment and Supplies) [14308]
Allied Medical, Inc. (Medical, Dental, and Optical Supplies) [19137]
Arrow Business Products Inc. (Office Equipment and Supplies) [20811]
Assembly Components Systems Co. (Hardware) [13567]
Auto Chlor System Inc. (Household Appliances) [15040]
Baddour International (Health and Beauty Aids) [14034]
Bakers Chocolate and Coconut (Food) [10491]
Ball Auto Tech Inc. (Electrical and Electronic Equipment and Supplies) [8412]
Barnett Supply Co. Inc. (Heating and Cooling Equipment and Supplies) [14339]
Barton Group Inc. (Industrial Machinery) [15802]
Barton Truck Center Inc. (Industrial Supplies) [16723]
Binswanger Glass Co. (Construction Materials and Machinery) [7059]
Bluff City Electronics (Electrical and Electronic Equipment and Supplies) [8447]

B.P.I. (Floorcovering Equipment and Supplies) [9736]
Building Plastics Inc. (Floorcovering Equipment and Supplies) [9746]
Canale Beverages Inc.; D. (Alcoholic Beverages) [1568]
Canale Food Services Inc.; D. (Restaurant and Commercial Foodservice Equipment and Supplies) [24087]
Capitol Foods Inc. (Food) [10693]
Carloss Well Supply Co. (Industrial Machinery) [15876]
Centro, Inc. (Industrial Supplies) [16789]
Clarke and Bro. Inc.; E.H. (Office Equipment and Supplies) [20902]
Colco Fine Woods and Tools Inc. (Construction Materials and Machinery) [7192]
Colco Fine Woods and Tools Inc. (Wood and Wood Products) [27298]
Concord Computing Corp. (Computers and Software) [6146]
Consolidated Poultry and Egg Co. (Food) [10819]
Cora Medical Products Inc. (Medical, Dental, and Optical Equipment) [18755]
Corporate Copy Inc. (Office Equipment and Supplies) [20922]
Cruzen Equipment Company Inc. (Industrial Supplies) [16814]
Cummins Mid-South Inc. (Industrial Machinery) [15924]
Curtis Co. (Household Appliances) [15101]
Dabney-Hoover Supply Company Inc. (Industrial Supplies) [16818]
Davis Electric Supply Company Inc.; W.B. (Communications Systems and Equipment) [5590]
Delta Materials Handling Inc. (Industrial Machinery) [15939]
Dunavant Enterprises Inc. (Livestock and Farm Products) [17824]
Eagle Sales Company Inc. (Electrical and Electronic Equipment and Supplies) [8643]
Electrical Communications (Electrical and Electronic Equipment and Supplies) [8673]
Farnsworth Armored Inc. (Motorized Vehicles) [20634]
Federal Express Aviation Services Inc. (Aeronautical Equipment and Supplies) [87]
Fischer Lime and Cement Co. (Construction Materials and Machinery) [7346]
Forms and Supplies Inc. (Office Equipment and Supplies) [21007]
Fugitt Rubber & Supply Company, Inc. (Industrial Supplies) [16881]
Gamma Inc. (Furniture and Fixtures) [13118]
Gattas Company Inc.; Fred P. (Household Items) [15512]
General Pipe and Supply Company Inc. (Plumbing Materials and Fixtures) [23187]
Gordon Food Company Inc. (Food) [11292]
Graphic Systems Inc. (Memphis, Tennessee) (Office Equipment and Supplies) [21019]
Hardin's-Sysco Food Services Inc. (Food) [11377]
Harris & Co.; William H. (Shoes) [24759]
Hawkins Machinery Inc. (Construction Materials and Machinery) [7459]
Heavy Machines Inc. (Industrial Machinery) [16096]
Home-Bound Medical Care Inc. (Medical, Dental, and Optical Equipment) [18837]
House of Ceramics Inc. (Gifts and Novelties) [13371]
Hunt Wesson Inc. (Food) [11478]
HVAC Sales and Supply Co. (Heating and Cooling Equipment and Supplies) [14491]
IDA Inc. (Construction Materials and Machinery) [7504]
Ideal Chemical and Supply Co. (Chemicals) [4426]
Info-Mation Services Co. (Computers and Software) [6365]
Jenkins Co.; H.W. (Wood and Wood Products) [27324]
Jones Company of Memphis Inc.; Grady W. (Industrial Machinery) [16192]
Kaufman Co. Inc.; Hal (Photographic Equipment and Supplies) [22868]

Kazuhiro Ltd. (Specialty Equipment and Products) [25697]

Kellogg Co. (Food) [11597]

King Kitchens Inc. (Household Appliances) [15188]

Kraft Food Ingredients (Food) [11640]

L & S Trading Co. (Luggage and Leather Goods) [18403]

Ladd, Inc.; Bob (Agricultural Equipment and Supplies) [927]

Lambert's Coffee Services (Food) [11671]

Lamination Services Inc. (Industrial Machinery) [16227]

Lewis Supply Company Inc. (Industrial Supplies) [16998]

Lit Refrigeration Co. (Specialty Equipment and Products) [25718]

Lucky Electric Supply (Electrical and Electronic Equipment and Supplies) [9009]

M-Bin International Imports (Luggage and Leather Goods) [18410]

Majestic Communications (Communications Systems and Equipment) [5666]

Malone and Hyde Inc. (Food) [11766]

Mayer Myers Paper Co. (Paper and Paper Products) [21826]

Memphis Chemical Janitorial Supply Inc. (Cleaning and Janitorial Supplies) [4668]

Memphis Communications Corporation (Communications Systems and Equipment) [5669]

Memphis Ford New Holland Inc. (Agricultural Equipment and Supplies) [1014]

Memphis Furniture Manufacturing Co. (Textiles and Notions) [26140]

Memphis Group Inc. (Aeronautical Equipment and Supplies) [122]

Memphis Import Company Inc. (Recreational and Sporting Goods) [23820]

Memphis Pool Supply Co. Inc. (Recreational and Sporting Goods) [23821]

Memphis Serum Company Inc. (Medical, Dental, and Optical Equipment) [18926]

Mid-South Malts/Memphis Brews Inc. (Alcoholic Beverages) [1872]

Mid-South Oxygen Company Inc. (Industrial Supplies) [17036]

Mills Wilson George Inc. (Industrial Machinery) [16305]

Mustang Publishing Co. (Books and Other Printed Materials) [3977]

Name Game (Clothing) [5211]

National Safety Associates Inc. (Plumbing Materials and Fixtures) [23286]

Odeen International, Inc. (Chemicals) [4471]

Odell Hardware Company Inc. (Hardware) [13852]

Off the Dock Seafood Inc. (Food) [12054]

Office Equipment Service Inc. (Office Equipment and Supplies) [21179]

Orgill Inc. (Hardware) [13855]

Pancho's Mexican Foods Inc. (Food) [12103]

Paramount Uniform Rental Inc. (Clothing) [5270]

Parts Inc. (Automotive) [3083]

Parts Industries Corp. (Agricultural Equipment and Supplies) [1119]

Parts Plus of Dearborn (Automotive) [3084]

Power and Telephone Supply Company Inc. (Communications Systems and Equipment) [5713]

Quality Control Consultants (Medical, Dental, and Optical Equipment) [19001]

RCH Distributors Inc. (Agricultural Equipment and Supplies) [1170]

Reichman, Crosby, Hays Inc. (Industrial Supplies) [17135]

Rex Mid-South Service (Furniture and Fixtures) [13221]

Rogers Pool Supply, Inc. (Recreational and Sporting Goods) [23920]

S and I Steel Supply Div. (Metals) [20347]

Scott Foam & Fabrics, Inc. (Textiles and Notions) [26200]

Scruggs Equipment Company Inc. (Automotive) [3201]

Seabrook Wallcoverings Inc. (Household Items) [15650]

Select-O-Hits Inc. (Sound and Entertainment Equipment and Supplies) [25437]

Sharon Piping and Equipment Inc. (Metals) [20363]

Shelby Electric Company Inc. (Electrical and Electronic Equipment and Supplies) [9359]

Shelby-Skipwith Inc. (Heating and Cooling Equipment and Supplies) [14678]

Siano Appliance Distributors Inc. (Household Appliances) [15312]

Simple Wisdom Inc. (Health and Beauty Aids) [14238]

Sipes Co.; Howe K. (Clothing) [5360]

South Central Pool Supply, Inc. (Recreational and Sporting Goods) [23956]

Southern Business Systems Inc. (Office Equipment and Supplies) [21276]

Southern Interiors Inc. (Household Items) [15663]

Southern Leather Co. (Shoes) [24866]

Southern Leather Co. (Clothing) [5373]

Southern Lighting and Supply Company Inc. (Electrical and Electronic Equipment and Supplies) [9389]

Southern Pump and Filter Inc. (Specialty Equipment and Products) [25826]

Southern Pump and Filter Inc. (Industrial Machinery) [16512]

Star Distributors (Alcoholic Beverages) [2048]

Steepleton Tire Co. (Automotive) [3266]

Stein World Inc. (Furniture and Fixtures) [13251]

TBC Corp. (Automotive) [3293]

TBC Corp. (Rubber) [24299]

Techno Steel Corp. (Metals) [20418]

Tennison Brothers Inc. (Construction Materials and Machinery) [8110]

Term City Furniture & Appliance (Furniture and Fixtures) [13259]

Three States Supply Co. (Heating and Cooling Equipment and Supplies) [14728]

Tradigrain Inc. (Livestock and Farm Products) [18287]

Tri-State Armature and Electrical Works Inc. (Electrical and Electronic Equipment and Supplies) [9504]

Troll Associates of Memphis (Books and Other Printed Materials) [4233]

Turner Sherwood Corp. (Household Appliances) [15345]

United Liquors Corp. (Alcoholic Beverages) [2091]

Universal Case Company Inc./Designer Optical (Medical, Dental, and Optical Supplies) [19683]

U.S.A. Woods International (Construction Materials and Machinery) [8164]

Victor Business Systems Inc. (Office Equipment and Supplies) [21337]

VVP America Inc. (Household Items) [15698]

Wang's International, Inc. (Office Equipment and Supplies) [21345]

Wang's International, Inc. (Household Items) [15701]

Wang's International Inc. (Toys and Hobby Goods) [26706]

West Union Corp. (Hardware) [13994]

Williams Equipment and Supply Company Inc. (Construction Materials and Machinery) [8227]

Wimmer Cookbook Distribution (Books and Other Printed Materials) [4290]

W.L. Roberts Inc. (Household Appliances) [15376]

Woodson & Bozeman Inc. (Sound and Entertainment Equipment and Supplies) [25529]

Woodson and Bozeman Inc. (Household Appliances) [15378]

Wurzburg Inc. (Paper and Paper Products) [21997]

Millington

Indmar Products Industrial Div. (Marine) [18524]

Monterey

Phillips Shoes (Shoes) [24833]

Morristown

Hale Brothers Inc. (Food) [11362]

Hasson-Bryan Hardware Co. (Hardware) [13744]

Morristown Electric Wholesalers Co. (Electrical and Electronic Equipment and Supplies) [9097]

Wallace Hardware Co. (Agricultural Equipment and Supplies) [1409]

Mt. Carmel

Thompson Sales; Larry (Agricultural Equipment and Supplies) [1331]

Mt. Pleasant

Industrial Products Co. (Construction Materials and Machinery) [7510]

Murfreesboro

Agee's Sporting Goods (Recreational and Sporting Goods) [23496]

Cutters Exchange Inc. (Industrial Machinery) [15926]

Procon Products (Industrial Machinery) [16430]

Rutherford Farmers Cooperative (Agricultural Equipment and Supplies) [1220]

Swanson, Inc. (Office Equipment and Supplies) [21308]

Nashville

Abc Mobile Brake (Automotive) [2164]

Abingdon Press (Books and Other Printed Materials) [3458]

ADEMCO/ADI (Security and Safety Equipment) [24472]

ADT Automotive Inc. (Automotive) [2182]

Advanced Plastics Inc. (Plastics) [22918]

AG Distributors, Inc. (Agricultural Equipment and Supplies) [192]

Agri-Sales Associates Inc. (Agricultural Equipment and Supplies) [211]

Aladdin Synergetics Inc. (Medical, Dental, and Optical Equipment) [18668]

Alley-Cassetty Coal Co. (Minerals and Ores) [20510]

Allied Bearings & Supply (Automotive) [2210]

Allied Sound Inc. (Sound and Entertainment Equipment and Supplies) [25062]

American Paper and Twine Co. (Paper and Paper Products) [21631]

Amway Distributors (Household Items) [15402]

Anderson Austin News (Books and Other Printed Materials) [3510]

Andrews Distributing Company Inc. (Heating and Cooling Equipment and Supplies) [14322]

Antara Music Group (Books and Other Printed Materials) [3519]

Applied Industrial Tech, Inc. (Industrial Supplies) [16702]

Athens Distributing Co. (Alcoholic Beverages) [1489]

Automotive Parts Distributors (Automotive) [2292]

B & C Distributors (Electrical and Electronic Equipment and Supplies) [8406]

B & G Wholesalers Inc. (Alcoholic Beverages) [1494]

Bailey Company Inc. (Industrial Machinery) [15798]

Beck-Arnley Worldparts Corp. (Automotive) [2344]

Besco Steel Supply, Inc. (Metals) [19819]

Best Brands (Alcoholic Beverages) [1522]

Blevins Inc. (Electrical and Electronic Equipment and Supplies) [8445]

BNA Optical Supply Inc. (Medical, Dental, and Optical Supplies) [19195]

Boswell Golf Cars, Inc. (Recreational and Sporting Goods) [23566]

BPI Inc. (Floorcovering and Supplies) [9738]

Braid Electric Company Inc. (Electrical and Electronic Equipment and Supplies) [8461]

Bridgestone Firestone, Inc. (Automotive) [2384]

Bridgestone/Firestone Tire Sales Co. (Automotive) [2385]

Buford Brothers Inc. (Industrial Supplies) [16772]

Cargill Steel & Wire (Metals) [19856]

Carmichael and Carmichael Inc. (Sound and Entertainment Equipment and Supplies) [25123]

Castleberry; Tom (Clothing) [4868]

Central South Music Inc. (Sound and Entertainment Equipment and Supplies) [25132]

Centro, Inc. (Scientific and Measurement Devices) [24337]

Ceramic Tile Distributors, Inc. (Floorcovering Equipment and Supplies) [9796]

Computer Maintenance Service (Computers and Software) [6115]

Consolidated Electrical Distributor (Electrical and Electronic Equipment and Supplies) [8565]

Crucible Service Center (Metals) [19907]

Cumberland Oil Co. Inc. (Petroleum, Fuels, and Related Equipment) [22182]

Cumberland Optical Company Inc. (Medical, Dental, and Optical Supplies) [19262]

CY Hart Distributig Co. (Petroleum, Fuels, and Related Equipment) [22186]

D & F Distributors (Industrial Machinery) [15927]

Davidson Farmers Cooperative (Agricultural Equipment and Supplies) [497]

Dennis Paper Co. Inc. (Paper and Paper Products) [21706]

DET Distributing Co. (Alcoholic Beverages) [1646]

Dialysis Clinic Inc. (Medical, Dental, and Optical Equipment) [18775]

Discipleship Resources (Books and Other Printed Materials) [3694]

Elder's Bookstore (Books and Other Printed Materials) [3726]

Enco Materials Inc. (Metals) [19953]

Epley Sales Co. (Security and Safety Equipment) [24538]

Florig Equipment (Industrial Machinery) [16014]

Franklin Industries Inc. (Construction Materials and Machinery) [7367]

Gas Equipment Distributors (Household Appliances) [15142]

Globe Business Furniture Inc. (Office Equipment and Supplies) [21015]

Grainger, Inc. (Electrical and Electronic Equipment and Supplies) [8800]

Graves Import Co. Inc. (Shoes) [24755]

Hermitage Electric Supply Corp. (Household Appliances) [15167]

Ingram Industries Inc. (Computers and Software) [6372]

Institutional Distributors, Inc. (Food) [11513]

JTG of Nashville (Sound and Entertainment Equipment and Supplies) [25262]

Kagiya Trading Co. Ltd. of America (Hardware) [13779]

Karemor Independent Distributor (Health and Beauty Aids) [14140]

Keith-Sinclair Company Inc. (Paints and Varnishes) [21471]

Kenco Distributors, Inc. (Floorcovering Equipment and Supplies) [9987]

Kenworth of Tennessee Inc. (Automotive) [2850]

Kgs Steel, Inc. (Metals) [20102]

Kings Foodservice (Food) [11619]

Kroger Co. (Food) [11650]

Lipscomb and Co.; H.G. (Hardware) [13797]

Louisville Tile Distributors (Floorcovering Equipment and Supplies) [9998]

MagneTek, Inc. (Electrical and Electronic Equipment and Supplies) [9018]

Marathon Electric Manufacturing Corp. (Electrical and Electronic Equipment and Supplies) [9028]

Marshall and Bruce Co. (Specialty Equipment and Products) [25725]

McDougall Company Inc.; John W. (Construction Materials and Machinery) [7680]

McQuiddy Office Designers Inc. (Office Equipment and Supplies) [21134]

Mid States Paper/Notion Co. (Health and Beauty Aids) [14161]

Milam Optical Co. Inc.; J.S. (Medical, Dental, and Optical Supplies) [19463]

Moore; Robert J. (Sound and Entertainment Equipment and Supplies) [25337]

Music City Record Distributors Inc. (Sound and Entertainment Equipment and Supplies) [25344]

Nashville Auto Auction Inc. (Motorized Vehicles) [20689]

Nashville Pet Products Center (Veterinary Products) [27192]

Nashville Sash and Door Co. (Construction Materials and Machinery) [7763]

Nashville Sporting Goods Co. (Recreational and Sporting Goods) [23843]

Nashville Steel Corp. (Metals) [20217]

National Specialty Services Inc. (Medical, Dental, and Optical Supplies) [19479]

Neely Coble Company Inc. (Motorized Vehicles) [20691]

Nixon Power Services Co. (Electrical and Electronic Equipment and Supplies) [9130]

Options International Inc. (Sound and Entertainment Equipment and Supplies) [25370]

Orr-Sysco Food Services Co.; Robert (Restaurant and Commercial Foodservice Equipment and Supplies) [24199]

Pargh Company Inc.; B.A. (Computers and Software) [6591]

Parrish-Keith-Simmons Inc. (Industrial Machinery) [16380]

Patrick Electric Supply Co. (Electrical and Electronic Equipment and Supplies) [9180]

Pearl Corp. (Sound and Entertainment Equipment and Supplies) [25376]

Pearl Equipment Co. (Industrial Machinery) [16387]

Peterson Machinery Company Inc. (Compressors) [5848]

Phillip Metals Inc. (Metals) [20275]

Power & Telephone Supply Company, Inc. (Communications Systems and Equipment) [5716]

Primavera Distributing (Floorcovering Equipment and Supplies) [10108]

ProDiesel (Automotive) [3120]

Purity Dairies, Inc. (Food) [12237]

Ragland Co.; C.B. (Food) [12263]

Randolph & Rice (Electrical and Electronic Equipment and Supplies) [9264]

Rickwood Radio Service of Tennessee (Sound and Entertainment Equipment and Supplies) [25418]

Safety Service Co. (Automotive) [3180]

Small Apparel Co.; Horace (Clothing) [5364]

South Central Pool Supply, Inc. (Recreational and Sporting Goods) [23960]

Southern Machinery Company Inc. (Industrial Machinery) [16510]

Specialty Surgical Instrumentation Inc. (Medical, Dental, and Optical Equipment) [19050]

SST Sales Company Inc. (Clothing) [5391]

Stephens Manufacturing Company Inc.; W. E. (Clothing) [5394]

Stringfellow, Inc. (Automotive) [3275]

Sunday School Publishing Board (Books and Other Printed Materials) [4197]

Tennessee Building Products Inc. (Construction Materials and Machinery) [8108]

Tennessee Dressed Beef Company Inc. (Food) [12705]

Tennessee Electric Motor Co. (Electrical and Electronic Equipment and Supplies) [9477]

Tennessee Mat Company Inc. (Industrial Supplies) [17216]

Tennessee Wholesale Drug Co. (Medical, Dental, and Optical Supplies) [19651]

Thermo King of Nashville Inc. (Heating and Cooling Equipment and Supplies) [14725]

Thomas Nelson Inc. (Gifts and Novelties) [13463]

United Methodist Publishing House (Books and Other Printed Materials) [4242]

Upper Room (Books and Other Printed Materials) [4255]

Voorhees Company Inc.; The Bill (Heating and Cooling Equipment and Supplies) [14756]

Warner's Parts Co.; Eddie (Sound and Entertainment Equipment and Supplies) [25514]

Webbs Appliance Service Ctr. (Sound and Entertainment Equipment and Supplies) [25518]

Williams Optical Laboratory Inc. (Medical, Dental, and Optical Supplies) [19705]

Wilson Audio Sales (Sound and Entertainment Equipment and Supplies) [25525]

Winston-Derek Publishers Group Inc. (Books and Other Printed Materials) [4291]

Word Entertainment (Sound and Entertainment Equipment and Supplies) [25530]

Wynn and Graff Inc. (Textiles and Notions) [26251]

Zortec International Inc. (Computers and Software) [6891]

New Tazewell

Claiborne Farmers Cooperative (Agricultural Equipment and Supplies) [418]

Newport

Cocke Farmers Cooperative Inc. (Agricultural Equipment and Supplies) [432]

Oak Ridge

Manufacturing Sciences Corp. (Used, Scrap, and Recycled Materials) [26896]

PPG Industries, Inc. (Paints and Varnishes) [21544]

Oneida

Royal Fuel Co. (Minerals and Ores) [20565]

Paris

Henry Farmers Cooperative Inc. (Agricultural Equipment and Supplies) [814]

Kesterson Food Company Inc. (Restaurant and Commercial Foodservice Equipment and Supplies) [24156]

Knott's Wholesale Foods Inc. (Food) [11630]

Southern States Industrial Sales (Household Appliances) [15320]

Parsons

Q-Snap Corp. (Toys and Hobby Goods) [26624]

Powell

DeRoyal (Medical, Dental, and Optical Equipment) [18773]

Gregco Inc. (Recreational and Sporting Goods) [23700]

Pulaski

Giles Farmers Cooperative Inc. (Agricultural Equipment and Supplies) [740]

Rockwood

Johnston Coca-Cola (Books and Other Printed Materials) [3867]

Samburg

Hayes Associates; Marvin (Food) [11397]

Marvin Hayes Fish Co. (Food) [11796]

Savannah

Parris Manufacturing Co. (Toys and Hobby Goods) [26605]

Sharon

Sand Mountain Shoe Co. (Shoes) [24848]

Shelbyville

Alcan Recycling (Used, Scrap, and Recycled Materials) [26734]

Bedford Farmers Cooperative (Agricultural Equipment and Supplies) [291]

Games of Tennessee (Toys and Hobby Goods) [26491]

Smithville

Ferodo America (Automotive) [2612]

Middle Tennessee Utility District (Household Appliances) [15230]

Smyrna

Delker Electronics Inc. (Computers and Software) [6195]

FoodSource, Inc. (Food) [11184]

Soddy-Daisy

Screen Industry Art Inc. (Industrial Machinery) [16475]

Somerville

Hardeman Fayette Farmers Cooperative (Agricultural Equipment and Supplies) [790]

Sparta

Casual Apparel Inc. (Clothing) [4869]
White County Farmers Cooperative (Agricultural Equipment and Supplies) [1439]

Springfield

Tobacco Supply Company Inc. (Tobacco Products) [26359]

Strawberry Plains

Anderson's Woodwork Inc. (Furniture and Fixtures) [13021]

Thorn Hill

Kincaid Coal Co. Inc.; Elmer (Minerals and Ores) [20550]

Trenton

Gibson Farmers Cooperative (Agricultural Equipment and Supplies) [738]

Tullahoma

Applied Industrial Tech (Industrial Supplies) [16701]

Winchester

Winchester Hat Corp. (Clothing) [5488]

Texas

Abernathy

Frontier Hybrids (Agricultural Equipment and Supplies) [709]
Thompson Implement Co.; Joe (Agricultural Equipment and Supplies) [1329]

Abilene

Abilene Lumber Inc. (Construction Materials and Machinery) [6902]
Candy by Bletas (Food) [10688]
Casey's Tile Supply Co. (Floorcovering Equipment and Supplies) [9779]
Gerlach Oil Company Inc. (Petroleum, Fuels, and Related Equipment) [22308]
Sun Supply Corp. (Electrical and Electronic Equipment and Supplies) [9440]
Terk Distributing (Alcoholic Beverages) [2073]
West Texas Wholesale Supply Co. (Plumbing Materials and Fixtures) [23450]

Addison

AmeriServe (Restaurant and Commercial Foodservice Equipment and Supplies) [24063]
Malin and Associates Inc.; N.J. (Industrial Machinery) [16259]
Wilson Co. (Industrial Machinery) [16637]

Adrian

Adrian Wheat Growers Inc. (Agricultural Equipment and Supplies) [189]

Alamo

Crest Fruit Co. Inc. (Food) [10866]

Allen

Harper & Associates (Recreational and Sporting Goods) [23715]

Alpine

K & S Militaria Books (Books and Other Printed Materials) [3872]
Newell Oil Company Inc. (Petroleum, Fuels, and Related Equipment) [22514]

Alvarado

Exsaco Corp. (Recreational and Sporting Goods) [23658]

Alvin

Alvin Equipment Company Inc. (Construction Materials and Machinery) [6952]

Alvin Tree Farm, Inc. (Horticultural Supplies) [14802]
RiceTec Inc. (Food) [12310]

Amarillo

Affiliated Foods Inc. (Food) [10336]
Affiliated Foods Inc. (Food) [10337]
Amarillo Building Products Inc. (Construction Materials and Machinery) [6953]
Amarillo Clutch & Driveshaft Co. (Automotive) [2225]
Amarillo Hardware Co. (Hardware) [13555]
Amarillo Winnelson Co. (Plumbing Materials and Fixtures) [23060]
Amcamex Electronics Corp. (Communications Systems and Equipment) [5511]
Cummins Utility Supply (Hardware) [13650]
Golden Light Equipment Co. (Restaurant and Commercial Foodservice Equipment and Supplies) [24129]
Jackson Supply Co. (Cleaning and Janitorial Supplies) [4643]
Jackson Supply Co. (Restaurant and Commercial Foodservice Equipment and Supplies) [24147]
Jones Electric Company Inc.; G.E. (Automotive) [2833]
Kelley Inc.; Jack B. (Petroleum, Fuels, and Related Equipment) [22399]
Lake Steel Inc. (Metals) [20115]
Nunn Electric Supply Corp. (Electrical and Electronic Equipment and Supplies) [9149]
Plains Dairy Products (Food) [12180]
Roberts Paper Co. (Paper and Paper Products) [21909]
S & D Industrial Supply Inc. (Cleaning and Janitorial Supplies) [4700]
San Jacinto Foods (Food) [12401]
Scottco Service Co. (Plumbing Materials and Fixtures) [23362]
Sharp Co.; William G. (Floorcovering Equipment and Supplies) [10147]
Smith-Thompson Inc. (Industrial Supplies) [17178]
Sterling Security Services Inc. (Security and Safety Equipment) [24641]
Terk Distributing (Alcoholic Beverages) [2074]
Western Merchandisers Inc. (Books and Other Printed Materials) [4278]

Aransas Pass

Commercial Motor Co. (Motorized Vehicles) [20615]
Gulf King Marine (Marine) [18513]

Argyle

UniMark Group Inc. (Food) [12785]

Arlington

All-Pro Fasteners Inc. (Hardware) [13547]
ASC Industries (Aeronautical Equipment and Supplies) [42]
ASC International Inc. (Motorized Vehicles) [20592]
Commercial Body Corp. (Automotive) [2463]
Cummins Southern Plains Inc. (Automotive) [2515]
Dallas Wheels & Accessories, Inc. (Automotive) [2525]
GNS Foods Inc. (Food) [11278]
Hydraquip Corp. (Industrial Machinery) [16126]
International Baking Co. (Food) [11518]
Longhorn Liquors, Ltd. (Alcoholic Beverages) [1827]
Mayfield Building Supply Co. (Construction Materials and Machinery) [7671]
Nationwide Advertising Specialty Inc. (Gifts and Novelties) [13409]
Neely Industries (Adhesives) [10]
Petsche Company Inc.; A.E. (Electrical and Electronic Equipment and Supplies) [9194]
Priester Supply Company Inc. (Electrical and Electronic Equipment and Supplies) [9237]
RTC Manufacturing (Jewelry) [17577]
Saladmaster Inc. (Household Items) [15646]
Sietec Inc. (Medical, Dental, and Optical Supplies) [19609]
Southern Territory Associates (Books and Other Printed Materials) [4174]
WBH Industries (Hardware) [13987]

Witch Equipment Company Inc. (Construction Materials and Machinery) [8235]

Athens

Geddie; Thomas E. (Agricultural Equipment and Supplies) [730]

Austin

American Tile Supply (Floorcovering Equipment and Supplies) [9677]
Armstrong McCall (Health and Beauty Aids) [14025]
Austin Metal and Iron Company Inc. (Metals) [19793]
Balfour Co.; L.G. (Jewelry) [17326]
Benold's Jewelers (Jewelry) [17336]
Block Distributing Co. Inc. (Alcoholic Beverages) [1536]
Calcasieu Lumber Co. (Construction Materials and Machinery) [7125]
Calcasieu Lumber Co. (Wood and Wood Products) [27292]
CJC Holdings Inc. (Jewelry) [17371]
Cuerno Largo Publications (Books and Other Printed Materials) [3676]
DAC International Inc. (Specialty Equipment and Products) [25621]
Dynamic Reprographics Inc. (Scientific and Measurement Devices) [24351]
El Galindo Inc. (Food) [11037]
Hamilton Electric Works Inc. (Electrical and Electronic Equipment and Supplies) [8824]
IOB Distributors (Computers and Software) [6396]
ITBR, Inc. (Communications Systems and Equipment) [5651]
Jupiter Band Instruments Inc. (Sound and Entertainment Equipment and Supplies) [25263]
Lamar Wholesale and Supply Inc. (Electrical and Electronic Equipment and Supplies) [8968]
Lone Star Food Service Co. (Food) [11727]
Marshall Industries (Electrical and Electronic Equipment and Supplies) [9037]
Memory Technologies Texas Inc. (Computers and Software) [6482]
Mercury Communication Services, Inc. (Communications Systems and Equipment) [5672]
Montopolis Supply Co. (Construction Materials and Machinery) [7740]
OmniFax (Office Equipment and Supplies) [21200]
PRO Sports Products (Recreational and Sporting Goods) [23898]
Rainhart Co. (Medical, Dental, and Optical Equipment) [19011]
Reuben's Wines & Spirits (Alcoholic Beverages) [1985]
South Central Pool Supply, Inc. (Recreational and Sporting Goods) [23966]
Stripling Blake Lumber Co. (Construction Materials and Machinery) [8082]
Sun Office Service (Food) [12606]
Sysco Food Services of Austin Inc. (Food) [12676]
T & L Distributors Company Inc. (Floorcovering Equipment and Supplies) [10204]
TCC Industries Inc. (Gifts and Novelties) [13461]
Tescom (Electrical and Electronic Equipment and Supplies) [9482]
Texas Health Distributors (Food) [12709]
Texas State Directory Press (Books and Other Printed Materials) [4212]
Texas Tees (Clothing) [5428]
Travis Tile Sales (Floorcovering Equipment and Supplies) [10257]
Triton Electronics (Computers and Software) [6833]
Ultimate Salon Services Inc. (Health and Beauty Aids) [14268]
University of Texas Press (Books and Other Printed Materials) [4251]
White Swan, Inc. (Food) [12931]
Whitson and Co. (Electrical and Electronic Equipment and Supplies) [9588]
XML Corp. (Computers and Software) [6885]

Avinger

Robroy Industries (Electrical and Electronic Equipment and Supplies) [9304]

Bartlett
Hill Grain Co. Inc.; C.F. (Livestock and Farm Products) [17999]

Bay City
Bonus Crop Fertilizer Inc. (Agricultural Equipment and Supplies) [329]
Dependable Motor Parts (Automotive) [2539]
Evans Oil Co. (Petroleum, Fuels, and Related Equipment) [22241]
Evans Systems Inc. (Petroleum, Fuels, and Related Equipment) [22242]

Baytown
B & B Office Supply Inc. (Office Equipment and Supplies) [20827]
Irwin Sales (Textiles and Notions) [26077]

Beaumont
Automatic Pump and Equipment Company Inc. (Industrial Machinery) [15793]
Coburn Supply Co. Inc. (Plumbing Materials and Fixtures) [23118]
Gideon Distributing Inc. (Alcoholic Beverages) [1715]
Giglio Distributing Company Inc. (Alcoholic Beverages) [1716]
Lamb's Office Products (Office Equipment and Supplies) [21098]
Lamons Beaumont Bolt & Gasket (Industrial Supplies) [16993]
Ram Threading Inc. (Hardware) [13881]
Sampson Steel Corp. (Metals) [20350]
SYSCO Food Services (Food) [12673]
Sysco Food Services of Beaumont Inc. (Food) [12677]
Warren Equipment Co. (Restaurant and Commercial Foodservice Equipment and Supplies) [24259]

Bedford
Cabin Craft Southwest, Inc. (Specialty Equipment and Products) [25588]

Beeville
B.A. Box Tank and Supply Inc. (Petroleum, Fuels, and Related Equipment) [22056]

Bellaire
TMC Orthopedic Supplies Inc. (Medical, Dental, and Optical Supplies) [19656]

Big Spring
Cain Electrical Supply Corp. (Electrical and Electronic Equipment and Supplies) [8483]

Boerne
C and L Communications Inc. (Communications Systems and Equipment) [5540]

Boling
Brooks Nursery Inc. (Horticultural Supplies) [14830]

Bonham
Southwest Cookbook Distributors, Inc. (Books and Other Printed Materials) [4177]

Booker
Booker Equity Union Exchange Inc. (Agricultural Equipment and Supplies) [330]

Bovina
T-Bone's Salvage and Equipment Inc. (Agricultural Equipment and Supplies) [1312]

Bowie
Bowie Industries Inc. (Construction Materials and Machinery) [7073]

Brady
Texas Mining Co. (Construction Materials and Machinery) [8115]

Brenham
Brenham Wholesale Grocery Company Inc. (Food) [10613]

Brownfield
BE Implemented Partners Ltd. (Agricultural Equipment and Supplies) [285]

Brownsville
Demerico Corp. (Food) [10943]
Donie Chair Co. (Furniture and Fixtures) [13093]
Eagle Foods Co. (Food) [11010]
Edelsteins Better Furniture Inc. (Furniture and Fixtures) [13101]
Hinojosa Parts Warehouse (Automotive) [2754]
Hisco (Electrical and Electronic Equipment and Supplies) [8843]
Pace Fish Company Inc. (Food) [12086]
Resaca Inc. (Food) [12302]
Riviera Tile Inc. (Floorcovering Equipment and Supplies) [10122]

Brownwood
TWT Moulding Company Inc. (Household Items) [15690]

Bryan
Baskin-Robbins USA Co. (Food) [10513]
Feather Crest Farms Inc. (Food) [11112]
Goodman; C.R. (Alcoholic Beverages) [1726]
Producers Cooperative Association (Agricultural Equipment and Supplies) [1156]

Buna
Rushwin Publishing (Books and Other Printed Materials) [4127]

Burkburnett
Moore Sales Co. (Sound and Entertainment Equipment and Supplies) [25338]

Burleson
Burly Corporation of North America (Construction Materials and Machinery) [7109]
Leonard's Stone & Fireplace (Heating and Cooling Equipment and Supplies) [14524]

Bushland
Bushland Grain Cooperative (Livestock and Farm Products) [17757]

Cameron
Sams Inc.; L.L. (Furniture and Fixtures) [13230]

Canadian
Canadian Equity Cooperative (Agricultural Equipment and Supplies) [368]

Canyon
Consumers Supply Cooperative Co. (Food) [10822]

Carmine
Jacob's Store Inc. (Agricultural Equipment and Supplies) [877]

Carrollton
Adleta Corp. (Floorcovering Equipment and Supplies) [9646]
Adleta Corp. (Household Items) [15388]
Attention Medical Co. (Medical, Dental, and Optical Equipment) [18698]
CellStar Corp. (Communications Systems and Equipment) [5555]
CellStar Ltd. (Communications Systems and Equipment) [5556]
Dallas Aerospace Inc. (Aeronautical Equipment and Supplies) [79]
Frigi-Cool/RVAC Inc. (Automotive) [2652]
Hutton Communications Inc. (Communications Systems and Equipment) [5641]
Ingram Entertainment (Sound and Entertainment Equipment and Supplies) [25246]
Neopost (Specialty Equipment and Products) [25754]

Norvell
Norvell Electronics Inc. (Electrical and Electronic Equipment and Supplies) [9143]
Omnitrition (Food) [12071]
Roberts Co.; D.B. (Electrical and Electronic Equipment and Supplies) [9302]

Castroville
Habys Sales Candy Co. (Food) [11354]

Cleburne
Cowan Costume, Inc. (Gifts and Novelties) [13337]
Four M Parts Warehouse (Automotive) [2643]
GOEX International Inc. (Petroleum, Fuels, and Related Equipment) [22318]
Harris Oil Co.; Bob (Petroleum, Fuels, and Related Equipment) [22338]
National Heritage Sales Corp. (Food) [11978]
Tree of Life Inc. Southwest (Food) [12751]
United Heritage Corp. (Food) [12797]
Wilbanks Oil Company Inc. (Petroleum, Fuels, and Related Equipment) [22802]

Clute
Warren Electric Co. (Electrical and Electronic Equipment and Supplies) [9556]

Coleman
Rhone Company Inc.; George D. (Hardware) [13885]

College Station
Texas A & M University Press (Books and Other Printed Materials) [4210]

Conroe
Moore Supply Co. (Plumbing Materials and Fixtures) [23276]
Repro Technology Inc. (Specialty Equipment and Products) [25802]
Royal Hill Co. (Alcoholic Beverages) [2000]

Coppell
Briggs-Weaver Inc. (Industrial Machinery) [15845]
Craftmade International Inc. (Household Items) [15462]
Minyard Food Stores Inc. (Food) [11909]
Minyard Food Stores Inc. Carnival Food Stores (Food) [11910]

Corpus Christi
Advanced Graphics (Clothing) [4753]
Air & Pump Co. (Compressors) [5826]
Ajax Supply Co. (Heating and Cooling Equipment and Supplies) [14310]
Anderson Machinery Company Inc. (Construction Materials and Machinery) [6977]
ASAP (Clothing) [4786]
Billie's Fashion Hats (Clothing) [4824]
Block Distributing Co. Inc. (Alcoholic Beverages) [1535]
Corpus Christi Wholesale Mart (Clothing) [4896]
Cup Graphics and Screen Printing (Clothing) [4905]
Del Mar Distributing Company Inc. (Recreational and Sporting Goods) [23618]
Encycle/Texas Inc. (Used, Scrap, and Recycled Materials) [26808]
Flato Electric Supply Co. (Electrical and Electronic Equipment and Supplies) [8745]
Gunderland Marine Supply, Inc. (Marine) [18514]
Intile Designs, Inc. (Floorcovering Equipment and Supplies) [9975]
Liquid Town (Alcoholic Beverages) [1822]
Logo Apparel (Clothing) [5139]
Logo Designs (Clothing) [5140]
Marlin Custom Embroidery (Clothing) [5169]
Name Place (Clothing) [5212]
Nueces Tile Sales (Floorcovering Equipment and Supplies) [10082]
Ocean Originals (Clothing) [5246]
Olson-Kessler Meat Company Inc. (Food) [12067]
Padre Island Screen Printing (Clothing) [5264]
Padre Island Supply (Marine) [18581]
Rosas Computer Co. (Computers and Software) [6694]

Scholl Forest Industries (Construction Materials and Machinery) [7986]
SLM Power Group Inc. (Automotive) [3230]
Standard Appliance Parts Corporation (Household Appliances) [15321]
Sterett Supply Co. (Electrical and Electronic Equipment and Supplies) [9416]
Swiff-Train Co. (Floorcovering Equipment and Supplies) [10196]
Swiff-Train Co. (Household Items) [15675]
T-Shirt Gallery and Sports (Clothing) [5418]
Texas Mill Inc. (Industrial Supplies) [17222]
Trophy Craft Source (Clothing) [5441]

Corsicana

Purvis Bearing Service (Automotive) [3125]
Winters Oil Co. (Petroleum, Fuels, and Related Equipment) [22811]

Crockett

Edmiston Brothers Inc. (Food) [11028]

Crowell

Farmers Cooperative Elevator Association (Livestock and Farm Products) [17863]

Cypress

F and R International (Petroleum, Fuels, and Related Equipment) [22247]
McGuffy Company Inc.; Lynn (Specialty Equipment and Products) [25729]

Dalhart

Dalhart Consumers Fuel and Grain Association Inc. (Livestock and Farm Products) [17808]

Dallas

A & W Bearings & Supply (Industrial Supplies) [16666]
Abatix Environmental Corp. (Security and Safety Equipment) [24467]
Action Line/UniVogue, Inc. (Clothing) [4746]
Albums Inc. (Photographic Equipment and Supplies) [22824]
Allan and Co.; G.B. (Industrial Machinery) [15755]
Allied Belting and Transmission Inc. (Automotive) [2211]
Allied Electronics (Electrical and Electronic Equipment and Supplies) [8307]
American FoodService (Food) [10398]
American Homeware Inc. (Cleaning and Janitorial Supplies) [4571]
American Management Group (Food) [10400]
American Products Company Inc. (Food) [10402]
American Tile Supply Inc. (Floorcovering Equipment and Supplies) [9679]
AMRE Inc. (Construction Materials and Machinery) [6972]
Anderson News Co. Southwest (Books and Other Printed Materials) [3516]
Applied Energy Company Inc. (Industrial Machinery) [15774]
APW/Wyott Food Service Equipment Co. (Food) [10426]
Ardinger and Son Co.; H.T. (Horticultural Supplies) [14809]
Asel Art Supply (Specialty Equipment and Products) [25562]
Ashley Aluminum Inc. (Construction Materials and Machinery) [6998]
Associated Aircraft Supply Inc. (Aeronautical Equipment and Supplies) [43]
Automation Image Inc. (Computers and Software) [5990]
Avatex Corp. (Medical, Dental, and Optical Supplies) [19170]
Avian Kingdom Supply Inc. (Veterinary Products) [27075]
B and F System Inc. (Household Items) [15411]
Barboglio; Jan (Clothing) [4802]
Baylor Biomedical Services (Medical, Dental, and Optical Supplies) [19178]
BG Electronics Inc. (Electrical and Electronic Equipment and Supplies) [8437]
BGE and C Inc. (Electrical and Electronic Equipment and Supplies) [8438]

Big D Bolt & Screw Co. (Hardware) [13598]
Big State Record Distribution Corp. (Sound and Entertainment Equipment and Supplies) [25103]
Bindley Western Drug Co. Dallas Div. (Health and Beauty Aids) [14044]
Bock Jewelry Co. Inc. (Jewelry) [17346]
Bond Equipment Company Inc. (Motorized Vehicles) [20604]
Brinkmann Corp. (Electrical and Electronic Equipment and Supplies) [8468]
Cameron Ashley Building Products Inc. (Construction Materials and Machinery) [7130]
Canine Commissary (Veterinary Products) [27099]
Cannon Inc.; W.W. (Storage Equipment and Containers) [25898]
Casa Linda Draperies (Household Items) [15437]
CCS Printing (Books and Other Printed Materials) [3617]
Central Engineering & Supply Co. (Heating and Cooling Equipment and Supplies) [14375]
Central Garden & Pet Supply Inc. (Veterinary Products) [27106]
Ceramic Tile International (Floorcovering Equipment and Supplies) [9798]
Chapin Co.; Noel R. (Gifts and Novelties) [13329]
Chase Industries Inc. (Industrial Supplies) [16793]
Clampitt Paper Co. (Paper and Paper Products) [21681]
CMC Secondary Metals Processing Div. (Used, Scrap, and Recycled Materials) [26780]
Columbia Packing Co. Inc. (Food) [10796]
Commercial Metals Co. (Metals) [19888]
Commercial Music Co. Inc. (Specialty Equipment and Products) [25608]
CompuCom Systems Inc. (Computers and Software) [6094]
Conformance Technology Inc. (Electrical and Electronic Equipment and Supplies) [8559]
Convoy Servicing Co. Inc. (Heating and Cooling Equipment and Supplies) [14403]
Copy-Co Inc. (Office Equipment and Supplies) [20916]
Costa Inc.; Victor (Clothing) [4898]
Crown Imports (Gifts and Novelties) [13341]
CTT Distributing (Toys and Hobby Goods) [26454]
Custom Manufacturing Co. (Industrial Machinery) [15925]
Custom Photo Manufacturing (Photographic Equipment and Supplies) [22850]
Custom Vision Optical (Medical, Dental, and Optical Supplies) [19267]
Dallas Auto Auction Inc. (Motorized Vehicles) [20620]
Dallas City Packing Inc. (Food) [10903]
Dallas Gold and Silver Exchange Inc. (Jewelry) [17387]
Dallas Market Center Company Ltd. (Food) [10904]
Dallas Peterbilt Inc. (Automotive) [2524]
Danka Inwood Business Systems Inc. (Office Equipment and Supplies) [20948]
Darr Equipment Company Inc. (Construction Materials and Machinery) [7250]
Davis Co.; J.W. (Sound and Entertainment Equipment and Supplies) [25157]
Diamond Art & Craft (Specialty Equipment and Products) [25628]
Dimco Steel, Inc. (Metals) [19932]
Dresser Industries Inc. (Industrial Machinery) [15962]
DVH Co. (Automotive) [2569]
DW Distribution (Construction Materials and Machinery) [7293]
E-Heart Press, Inc. (Books and Other Printed Materials) [3705]
Executive Converting Corp. (Office Equipment and Supplies) [20995]
Export Services Inc. (Computers and Software) [6262]
Ferguson Manufacturing and Equipment Co. (Construction Materials and Machinery) [7335]
Foster Associates Inc.; M. (Clothing) [4964]
FoxMeyer Drug Co. (Medical, Dental, and Optical Supplies) [19328]

Fresh America Corp. (Food) [11206]
FreshPoint Inc. (Food) [11212]
Fritz Pet Supply (Veterinary Products) [27135]
Glazer's Wholesale Drug Co. Inc. (Alcoholic Beverages) [1720]
Global Fastener Inc. (Hardware) [13724]
Goody-Goody Liquor Store Inc. (Alcoholic Beverages) [1727]
Graybar Electric Company Inc. (Electrical and Electronic Equipment and Supplies) [8811]
Halasz from Dallas (Automotive) [2718]
Hall-Mark Electronics Corp. (Computers and Software) [6323]
Hallmark Models, Inc. (Toys and Hobby Goods) [26510]
Hallwood Group Inc. (Textiles and Notions) [26053]
Harrington Produce (Food) [11380]
Hi-Line Electric Co. (Electrical and Electronic Equipment and Supplies) [8840]
Hines Nut Co. (Food) [11439]
Hisco (Electrical and Electronic Equipment and Supplies) [8844]
Home Interiors and Gifts Inc. (Household Items) [15531]
Import Export Management Service Inc. (Office Equipment and Supplies) [21054]
Import Warehouse Inc. (Gifts and Novelties) [13374]
Import Wholesale Co. (Jewelry) [17454]
Imported Books (Books and Other Printed Materials) [3841]
INOTEK Technologies Corp. (Electrical and Electronic Equipment and Supplies) [8881]
Inotek Technologies Corp. (Industrial Machinery) [16160]
Intelligence Technology Corp. (Electrical and Electronic Equipment and Supplies) [8888]
International Trade Group (Medical, Dental, and Optical Equipment) [18860]
Interstate Battery System of Dallas Inc. (Electrical and Electronic Equipment and Supplies) [8896]
Jackson Associates Inc.; Bill (Furniture and Fixtures) [13148]
Jacobs Iron and Metal Co. (Used, Scrap, and Recycled Materials) [26856]
Jarrell Distributors Inc. (Household Appliances) [15180]
Johnsen Co.; Hans (Recreational and Sporting Goods) [23761]
Jones Blair Co. (Paints and Varnishes) [21469]
Keys Fitness Products Inc. (Recreational and Sporting Goods) [23772]
Kilpatrick Equipment Co. (Office Equipment and Supplies) [21092]
Kim International Mfg., L.P. (Jewelry) [17491]
King Bearing Div. (Automotive) [2857]
Knight Electronics Inc. (Electrical and Electronic Equipment and Supplies) [8952]
Knox Tile & Marble (Floorcovering Equipment and Supplies) [9989]
La Madeleine Inc. (Food) [11659]
Lane and McClain Distributors Inc. (Restaurant and Commercial Foodservice Equipment and Supplies) [24162]
Leecom Data Systems (Computers and Software) [6436]
Lightbourn Equipment Co. (Automotive) [2881]
Loboflor Bonar Flotex (Floorcovering Equipment and Supplies) [9996]
Lofland Co. (Construction Materials and Machinery) [7609]
Lone Star Institutional Grocers (Food) [11728]
Lyles-DeGrazier Co. (Jewelry) [17506]
Majors Scientific Books Inc. (Books and Other Printed Materials) [3932]
Marine & Industrial Supply (Marine) [18560]
Marketing Specialist Corp. (Food) [11784]
Matthews and Associates Inc. (Plastics) [22996]
Maverick Electric Supply Inc. (Electrical and Electronic Equipment and Supplies) [9047]
McCubbin Hosiery Inc. (Clothing) [5177]
McLendon Co. (Food) [11837]
Mercury Communication Services, Inc. (Communications Systems and Equipment) [5671]

Methanex Methanol Co. (Petroleum, Fuels, and Related Equipment) [22477]
Metropolitan Marketing Inc. (Food) [11860]
Miller of Dallas Inc. (Alcoholic Beverages) [1879]
Momentum Metals Inc. (Metals) [20200]
MPL Industries, Inc. (Metals) [20210]
Neiman Marcus Co. (Clothing) [5221]
O'Connor Distributing Company Inc. (Sound and Entertainment Equipment and Supplies) [25367]
Omega Optical Co. (Medical, Dental, and Optical Supplies) [19507]
Patterson Brothers Meat Co. (Food) [12121]
PC Service Source Inc. (Computers and Software) [6599]
Pearsol Appliance Company (Household Appliances) [15267]
Petrofina Delaware Inc. (Petroleum, Fuels, and Related Equipment) [22566]
Peysen Inc.; David (Furniture and Fixtures) [13207]
Piper Weatherford Co. (Hardware) [13869]
Pollock Paper Distributors (Paper and Paper Products) [21886]
Polyphase Corp. (Agricultural Equipment and Supplies) [1140]
Pool Water Products (Recreational and Sporting Goods) [23892]
Preferred Meats Inc. (Food) [12210]
Primrose Oil Company Inc. (Petroleum, Fuels, and Related Equipment) [22594]
Pro-Line Corp. (Health and Beauty Aids) [14195]
Professional Optical Supply (Medical, Dental, and Optical Supplies) [19558]
ProNet Inc. (Communications Systems and Equipment) [5723]
Regal Plastic Supply Inc. (Plastics) [23024]
Republic Supply Co. (Dallas, Texas) (Petroleum, Fuels, and Related Equipment) [22622]
Ryder Aviall Inc. (Aeronautical Equipment and Supplies) [144]
Sigel Liquor Stores Inc. (Alcoholic Beverages) [2024]
Signature Services Corp. (Specialty Equipment and Products) [25816]
Slaughter Industries (Construction Materials and Machinery) [8031]
Southwest Import Co. (Gifts and Novelties) [13449]
Squibb-Taylor Inc. (Petroleum, Fuels, and Related Equipment) [22696]
Standard Fruit and Vegetable Company Inc. (Food) [12563]
Stewart & Stevenson (Automotive) [3269]
Storage Equipment Company Inc. (Storage Equipment and Containers) [25941]
Storage Equipment Company Inc. (Restaurant and Commercial Foodservice Equipment and Supplies) [24229]
Strawn Merchandise Inc. (Construction Materials and Machinery) [8080]
Street Art Supply Dallas (Paints and Varnishes) [21591]
T & L Distributors Company Inc. (Floorcovering Equipment and Supplies) [10205]
Tamara Imports (Clothing) [5422]
Taylor Publishing Co. (Books and Other Printed Materials) [4204]
Tech Electro Industries Inc. (Electrical and Electronic Equipment and Supplies) [9466]
Tex-Mastic International Inc. (Construction Materials and Machinery) [8113]
Texas Kenworth Co. (Automotive) [3300]
Texas Rubber Supply Inc. (Rubber) [24301]
Texas Rubber Supply Inc. (Industrial Supplies) [17224]
Texas Screen Process Supply Co. (Specialty Equipment and Products) [25841]
Tobacco Sales Company Inc. (Tobacco Products) [26357]
Toppan Printronics (USA) Inc. (Electrical and Electronic Equipment and Supplies) [9493]
Triangle Supply Company Inc. (Plumbing Materials and Fixtures) [23417]
TRW Replacement (Automotive) [3354]
Uniplex Software Inc. (Computers and Software) [6840]

United Notions (Textiles and Notions) [26236]
United Notions & Fabrics (Textiles and Notions) [26237]
Waste Recovery Inc. (Petroleum, Fuels, and Related Equipment) [22784]
Watson Associates Inc.; Vivian (Furniture and Fixtures) [13275]
Watson Electric Supply Co. (Electrical and Electronic Equipment and Supplies) [9561]
Welders Supply Inc. (Industrial Supplies) [17269]
Wholesale Electronic Supply Inc. (Electrical and Electronic Equipment and Supplies) [9592]
Willow Distributors Inc. (Alcoholic Beverages) [2121]
Womack Machine (Industrial Machinery) [16647]
Womack Machine Supply (Industrial Machinery) [16649]

Dayton

American Rice Growers Cooperative Association (Agricultural Equipment and Supplies) [236]

De Leon

Golden Peanut Co. De Leon Div. (Food) [11284]

Deer Park

GNI Group Inc. (Chemicals) [4401]

Denton

Murray Lighting Inc. (Household Appliances) [15243]
Sally Beauty Company Inc. (Health and Beauty Aids) [14227]
Weathertrol Supply Company Inc. (Heating and Cooling Equipment and Supplies) [14759]

Desoto

American Tile Supply (Floorcovering Equipment and Supplies) [9675]

Dickinson

Dirt Cheap Drives Inc. (Computers and Software) [6211]
MEGA HAUS Hard Drives (Computers and Software) [6481]

Dimmitt

Tulia Wheat Growers Inc. (Agricultural Equipment and Supplies) [1362]

Driscoll

Denton Petroleum Co. (Petroleum, Fuels, and Related Equipment) [22197]
Driscoll Grain Cooperative Inc. (Livestock and Farm Products) [17823]
Driscoll Grain Cooperative Inc. (Food) [10996]

Duncanville

Team Up Services (Books and Other Printed Materials) [4206]

Edinburg

Del Sol Tile Co. (Floorcovering Equipment and Supplies) [9854]
Wilbur-Ellis Co. Southern Div. (Agricultural Equipment and Supplies) [1446]

Edmonson

Edmonson Wheat Growers Inc. (Livestock and Farm Products) [17826]

El Campo

Farmers Cooperative of El Campo (Livestock and Farm Products) [17860]
Prasek's Hillje Smokehouse (Food) [12206]
Texas-West Indies Co. (Livestock and Farm Products) [18278]

El Paso

4 Wheel Center Inc. (Automotive) [2147]
Allied Electronics (Electrical and Electronic Equipment and Supplies) [8309]
Arie Incorporated (Electrical and Electronic Equipment and Supplies) [8372]

B & B Imports (Alcoholic Beverages) [1493]
Baptist Spanish Publishing House (Books and Other Printed Materials) [3543]
Brey Appliance Parts Inc. (Household Appliances) [15057]
Cantrell Auto Supply Company Inc. (Automotive) [2415]
Casa Carpet Wholesale Distributors (Floorcovering Equipment and Supplies) [9774]
Ceramic Tile International (Floorcovering Equipment and Supplies) [9799]
Cunningham Distributing Inc. (Specialty Equipment and Products) [25615]
Desert Eagle Distributing Co. (Alcoholic Beverages) [1644]
Diamond Leather Inc. (Luggage and Leather Goods) [18387]
Economy Cash and Carry Inc. (Food) [11022]
El Paso Onyx Co. Inc. (Gifts and Novelties) [13352]
El Paso Saw and Belting Supply Co. (Hardware) [13678]
EPPSCO Supply (Heating and Cooling Equipment and Supplies) [14434]
FMH Material Handling Solutions, Inc. (Industrial Machinery) [16024]
Gross-Medick-Barrows Inc. (Photographic Equipment and Supplies) [22861]
Helen of Troy Ltd. (Health and Beauty Aids) [14124]
Helen of Troy Texas Corp. (Health and Beauty Aids) [14125]
Hondo Boots (Shoes) [24765]
House of Carpets, Inc. (Floorcovering Equipment and Supplies) [9954]
Hydra-Power Systems Inc. (Industrial Machinery) [16123]
Jarritos Distributors (Soft Drinks) [24977]
Kahn's Bakery Inc. (Food) [11577]
Laun-Dry Supply Company Inc. (Cleaning and Janitorial Supplies) [4657]
Mahan Western Industries, Inc. (Clothing) [5152]
Mayfield Pool Supply L.L.C. (Recreational and Sporting Goods) [23811]
Morse Enterprises Inc. (Shoes) [24815]
Passage Supply Co. (Heating and Cooling Equipment and Supplies) [14632]
Peyton Meats Inc. (Food) [12158]
Preferred Brokerage Co. (Food) [12208]
Regal Supply & Chemical Co. (Paper and Paper Products) [21898]
Southwestern Irrigated Cotton Growers Association (Livestock and Farm Products) [18247]
Taylor Simkins Inc. (Industrial Supplies) [17214]
Texas Sales Co. (Household Appliances) [15336]
Thomson Company Inc.; Geo. S. (Industrial Supplies) [17227]
Tipp Distributors Inc. (Soft Drinks) [25044]
Tool World (Hardware) [13959]
Tri-State Wholesale Associated Grocers Inc. (Food) [12754]
Triangle Electric Supply Co. (Electrical and Electronic Equipment and Supplies) [9508]
U-Joints, Inc. (Automotive) [3358]
West Texas News Co. (Books and Other Printed Materials) [4275]
Wholesale Building Materials Co. (Construction Materials and Machinery) [8222]
Wilson Optical Company Inc. (Medical, Dental, and Optical Supplies) [19708]

Electra

Flusche Supply Inc. (Agricultural Equipment and Supplies) [695]

Elkhart

Elkhart Farmers Cooperative Association Inc. (Agricultural Equipment and Supplies) [546]

Ennis

Able Enterprises Inc. (Construction Materials and Machinery) [6903]

Euless

Cabin-Craft Southwest (Office Equipment and Supplies) [20872]
Gates Co. Inc.; B. (Plumbing Materials and Fixtures) [23183]
T-Electra/TICA of Dallas Inc. (Electrical and Electronic Equipment and Supplies) [9453]

Fairfield

Awalt Wholesale Inc. (Automotive) [2301]
Texas Mill Inc. (Industrial Supplies) [17221]

Farmers Branch

Autron Inc. Precision Rolls Division (Paper and Paper Products) [21642]
Benson Pump Co. (Recreational and Sporting Goods) [23551]
Cisco-Eagle, Inc. (Storage Equipment and Containers) [25902]
Force Electronics Inc. Texas Div. (Electrical and Electronic Equipment and Supplies) [8751]

Flower Mound

Jones Sales Group (Communications Systems and Equipment) [5654]

Follett

Farmers Grain and Supply Company Inc. (Livestock and Farm Products) [17899]

Forney

Big Reds Antiques (Furniture and Fixtures) [13038]

Ft. Stockton

Stockton Feed and Milling Inc. (Agricultural Equipment and Supplies) [1295]

Ft. Worth

A and A International Corp. (Sound and Entertainment Equipment and Supplies) [25052]
Advance Petroleum Distributing Company Inc. (Petroleum, Fuels, and Related Equipment) [22022]
Allied Electronics (Electrical and Electronic Equipment and Supplies) [8300]
Allied Electronics, Inc. (Electrical and Electronic Equipment and Supplies) [8328]
American Marazzi Tile, Inc. (Floorcovering Equipment and Supplies) [9671]
American Tile Supply (Floorcovering Equipment and Supplies) [9676]
Amsco Steel Company Inc. (Metals) [19776]
Audria's Crafts (Office Equipment and Supplies) [20821]
Bowen Supply Inc. (Household Items) [15428]
Brownlow Corp. (Books and Other Printed Materials) [3595]
Caple-Shaw Industries Inc. (Automotive) [2418]
Childress Oil Co.; W.R. (Petroleum, Fuels, and Related Equipment) [22136]
Clemons Tractor Co. (Agricultural Equipment and Supplies) [425]
Coast Marine (Marine) [18483]
Crouch Supply Company Inc. (Scientific and Measurement Devices) [24343]
Deen Meat Co., Inc. (Food) [10935]
Deen Wholesale Meat Co. (Food) [10936]
FFP Operating Partners L.P. (Petroleum, Fuels, and Related Equipment) [22275]
FFP Partners L.P. (Petroleum, Fuels, and Related Equipment) [22276]
First Choice Food Distributors Inc. (Food) [11130]
Fort Worth Jet Center (Petroleum, Fuels, and Related Equipment) [22289]
Fort Worth Lumber Co. (Wood and Wood Products) [27306]
Fortune Industries Inc. (Aeronautical Equipment and Supplies) [89]
Gamtex Industries Inc. (Used, Scrap, and Recycled Materials) [26820]
Goldthwaites of Texas Inc. (Agricultural Equipment and Supplies) [749]
Greer Industries Inc. (Electrical and Electronic Equipment and Supplies) [8818]

Hartnett Co. Food Service Div.; C.D. (Food) [11386]
Hawk Electronics (Communications Systems and Equipment) [5632]
Hotho & Co. (Books and Other Printed Materials) [3835]
House of Pets Supplies (Veterinary Products) [27151]
J & J Supply, Inc. (Paints and Varnishes) [21467]
JaGee Corp. (Livestock and Farm Products) [18019]
Keith Co.; Ben E. (Food) [11590]
Kevco Inc. (Wood and Wood Products) [27329]
Kings Liquor Inc. (Alcoholic Beverages) [1797]
Miller Distributing Ft. Worth (Alcoholic Beverages) [1880]
Morrison Supply Co. (Plumbing Materials and Fixtures) [23278]
Niver Western Wear Inc. (Clothing) [5233]
Norton Metal Products Inc. (Metals) [20240]
Oley Distributing Co. (Alcoholic Beverages) [1930]
Progressive Concepts Inc. (Communications Systems and Equipment) [5722]
Purvis Bearings (Industrial Supplies) [17123]
RadioShack Corp. (Electrical and Electronic Equipment and Supplies) [9259]
Reeder Distributors Inc. (Petroleum, Fuels, and Related Equipment) [22617]
Rodriguez Festive Foods Inc. (Food) [12343]
Sweeney Company Inc.; R.E. (Construction Materials and Machinery) [8093]
Texas Leather Trim Inc. (Luggage and Leather Goods) [18437]
Texas Turbo Jet Inc. (Aeronautical Equipment and Supplies) [158]
Tracom Inc. (Automotive) [3324]
TTI Inc. (Electrical and Electronic Equipment and Supplies) [9514]
Uniden America Corp. (Communications Systems and Equipment) [5799]
United Medical Supply Company Inc. (Medical, Dental, and Optical Supplies) [19675]

Freeport

Sepco Bearing and P.T. Group (Industrial Supplies) [17167]

Friona

Hub Grain Company Inc. (Livestock and Farm Products) [18006]

Galena Park

Texas Mill Supply and Manufacturing Company Inc. (Industrial Supplies) [17223]

Galveston

Industrial Material Corp. (Metals) [20055]
Kleen Supply Co. (Cleaning and Janitorial Supplies) [4651]
Peters Office Equipment (Office Equipment and Supplies) [21210]

Garland

Ceramic Tile International (Floorcovering Equipment and Supplies) [9797]
Cheerleader Supply Co. (Recreational and Sporting Goods) [23589]
Dalco Athletic (Specialty Equipment and Products) [25624]
Fleming Companies Inc. Garland Div. (Food) [11149]
Interceramic Inc. (Floorcovering Equipment and Supplies) [9964]
MIDCO International (Sound and Entertainment Equipment and Supplies) [25320]
Pay Cash Grocery Co. (Food) [12124]
Ribelin Sales Inc. (Chemicals) [4495]
Software Spectrum Inc. (Computers and Software) [6741]
SPH Crane and Hoist Div. (Construction Materials and Machinery) [8062]
Telephony International Inc. (Communications Systems and Equipment) [5786]
Tradex Corporation (Heating and Cooling Equipment and Supplies) [14734]

Garwood

Garwood Implement and Supply Co. (Livestock and Farm Products) [17934]

Georgetown

Georgetown Energy Inc. (Construction Materials and Machinery) [7391]

Graham

Media Recovery Inc. (Computers and Software) [6479]

Grand Prairie

Composite Technology Inc. (Aeronautical Equipment and Supplies) [74]
Freed Appliance Distributing (Household Appliances) [15135]
Keyston Brothers (Textiles and Notions) [26107]
North Texas Bolt, Nut & Screw, Inc. (Hardware) [13851]
RSR Group Texas, Inc. (Guns and Weapons) [13506]
SA-SO (Security and Safety Equipment) [24620]
Temp Glass Southern, Inc. (Construction Materials and Machinery) [8106]
Texas Plywood and Lumber Company Inc. (Construction Materials and Machinery) [8116]
Texas Plywood and Lumber Company Inc. (Wood and Wood Products) [27385]
Westgate Fabrics Inc. (Textiles and Notions) [26246]
Westgate Fabrics Inc. (Paints and Varnishes) [21607]

Grapevine

Associated Milk Producers Inc. Southern Region (Food) [10454]
Walco International Inc. (Veterinary Products) [27267]

Greenville

Texas Book Co. (Books and Other Printed Materials) [4211]

Hale Center

Hale Center Wheat Growers Inc. (Agricultural Equipment and Supplies) [781]

Hallettsville

Goedecke Inc.; Otto (Livestock and Farm Products) [17944]

Haltom City

Music Distributors Inc. (Sound and Entertainment Equipment and Supplies) [25345]
Stewart Supply Inc. (Hardware) [13938]

Hamlin

Pied Piper Mills Inc. (Veterinary Products) [27213]

Harlingen

Bush Supply Co. (Electrical and Electronic Equipment and Supplies) [8479]
Elliff Motors Inc. (Automotive) [2582]
Joiner Foodservice, Inc. (Paper and Paper Products) [21784]
Joiner Foodservice Inc. (Food) [11559]
Luanka Seafood Co. (Food) [11740]
Menchaca Brick & Tile Co. (Floorcovering Equipment and Supplies) [10025]
Seafood Marketing (Food) [12447]
Swiff-Train Co. (Floorcovering Equipment and Supplies) [10197]

Hart

Smith Potato Inc. (Food) [12513]

Hempstead

Barry Grain and Feed Inc. (Agricultural Equipment and Supplies) [280]

Hereford

Arrowhead Mills Inc. (Food) [10439]

Big T Pump Company Inc. (Agricultural Equipment and Supplies) [311]

Griffin and Brand Produce Sales Agency Inc. (Food) [11324]

Griffin & Brand Sales Agency, Inc. (Food) [11325]

Hereford Grain Corp. (Livestock and Farm Products) [17992]

Highland Village

Charter Pet Supplies (Veterinary Products) [27108]

Houston

Abrahams Oriental Rugs (Household Items) [15386]

ACR Group Inc. (Heating and Cooling Equipment and Supplies) [14297]

ACR Supply Inc. (Houston, Texas) (Heating and Cooling Equipment and Supplies) [14298]

Air-Dreco (Industrial Machinery) [15742]

Alliance Maintenance and Services Inc. (Petroleum, Fuels, and Related Equipment) [22030]

Allied Metals Inc. (Metals) [19752]

Allstar Systems Inc. (Computers and Software) [5908]

Allwaste Inc. (Used, Scrap, and Recycled Materials) [26741]

Allwaste Inc. Allwaste Recycling Div. (Used, Scrap, and Recycled Materials) [26742]

American Alloy Steel Inc. (Metals) [19768]

American Gulf Co. (Construction Materials and Machinery) [6965]

American Packing and Gasket Company (Adhesives) [1]

American Trade Co. (Plastics) [22925]

Americo International Trading, Ltd. (Medical, Dental, and Optical Supplies) [19145]

Amoco Energy Trading Corp. (Petroleum, Fuels, and Related Equipment) [22037]

Amtel Communications (Communications Systems and Equipment) [5515]

A.P.S. Inc. (Automotive) [2248]

ARA Services, Inc. (Soft Drinks) [24911]

ATC International (Automotive) [2262]

Aucoin and Miller Electric Supply Inc. (Electrical and Electronic Equipment and Supplies) [8393]

AVES Audio Visual Systems Inc. (Sound and Entertainment Equipment and Supplies) [25093]

B & B Parts Distributing (Automotive) [2304]

Bay Houston Towing Co. (Agricultural Equipment and Supplies) [284]

Beeco Motors and Controls Inc. (Electrical and Electronic Equipment and Supplies) [8428]

Beta Supply Co. (Industrial Machinery) [15823]

Big Inch Marine Systems Inc. (Plumbing Materials and Fixtures) [23085]

Bindley Western (Health and Beauty Aids) [14041]

Bison Building Materials Inc. (Construction Materials and Machinery) [7060]

Book Distribution Center (Books and Other Printed Materials) [3567]

Brance-Krachy Company Inc. (Industrial Machinery) [15840]

Brocks Auto Supply (Automotive) [2390]

Brooks Duplicator Co. (Office Equipment and Supplies) [20857]

Business Furnishings Co. (Furniture and Fixtures) [13055]

Business Integrators (Computers and Software) [6028]

Cactus Pipe and Supply Co. (Petroleum, Fuels, and Related Equipment) [22104]

CADCentre Inc. (Computers and Software) [6038]

Carbon and Alloy Metals Inc. (Metals) [19854]

Carroll's Discount Office Furniture Co. (Furniture and Fixtures) [13065]

Central Supply Division of Central Consolidated Inc. (Household Appliances) [15082]

Century Air Conditioning Supply Inc. (Heating and Cooling Equipment and Supplies) [14380]

Century Business Equipment Inc. (Office Equipment and Supplies) [20893]

Century Papers Inc. (Cleaning and Janitorial Supplies) [4596]

Ceramic Tile International (Construction Materials and Machinery) [7165]

Chair King Furniture Co. (Furniture and Fixtures) [13067]

Chantal Cookware Corp. (Household Items) [15441]

Charles River BRF Inc. (Agricultural Equipment and Supplies) [406]

Chemisolv Inc. (Chemicals) [4357]

Chickasaw Distributors Inc. (Petroleum, Fuels, and Related Equipment) [22135]

Citrus Trading Inc. (Petroleum, Fuels, and Related Equipment) [22141]

Clipper Energy Supply Co. (Construction Materials and Machinery) [7184]

Coastal Gas Services Co. (Petroleum, Fuels, and Related Equipment) [22146]

Coastal States Trading (Petroleum, Fuels, and Related Equipment) [22148]

Comfort Supply Inc. (Heating and Cooling Equipment and Supplies) [14396]

Commercial Body Corp. (Automotive) [2464]

Commercial Body Corp. (Automotive) [2466]

Commercial Furniture Services Inc. (Furniture and Fixtures) [13074]

Confederate Steel Corp. (Metals) [19892]

Contractors Parts Supply, Inc. (Industrial Supplies) [16808]

Control Specialties Inc. (Industrial Supplies) [16809]

Cornerstone Group (Construction Materials and Machinery) [7221]

CORR TECH, Inc. (Plumbing Materials and Fixtures) [23128]

Corr Tech Inc. (Plastics) [22949]

Cosbel Petroleum Corp. (Petroleum, Fuels, and Related Equipment) [22173]

Crandall Associates (Books and Other Printed Materials) [3666]

The Crispin Co. (Metals) [19905]

Cron Chemical Corp. (Chemicals) [4368]

Cross and Company Inc. (Food) [10869]

Cunill Motors Inc. (Motorized Vehicles) [20617]

Custom Drapery and Blinds Inc. (Household Items) [15465]

D/A Mid South Inc. (Security and Safety Equipment) [24531]

DATA COM (Computers and Software) [6182]

DATAVOX Inc. (Communications Systems and Equipment) [5588]

Delmar News Agency Inc. (Books and Other Printed Materials) [3683]

Delta Fastener Corp. (Hardware) [13659]

Diamony International, Inc. (Clothing) [4916]

Dictaphone Corp. (Communications Systems and Equipment) [5594]

The Dipper (Health and Beauty Aids) [14085]

Dixie Chemical Co. Inc. (Chemicals) [4373]

Dixie Pipe Sales Inc. (Metals) [19934]

Donovan Marine (Marine) [18495]

Doortown Inc. (Construction Materials and Machinery) [7281]

Drillers Supply Inc. (Industrial Machinery) [15964]

DXP Enterprises Inc. (Industrial Machinery) [15969]

Dyna Marketing (Computers and Software) [6228]

Dynamic Engineers Inc. (Electrical and Electronic Equipment and Supplies) [8640]

E. M J Co (Metals) [19945]

East Texas Distributing Inc. (Books and Other Printed Materials) [3708]

Electrical Controller Products Co. (Electrical and Electronic Equipment and Supplies) [8675]

Electrotex Inc. (Electrical and Electronic Equipment and Supplies) [8698]

ELG Metals Southern, Inc. (Used, Scrap, and Recycled Materials) [26805]

Energy Buyers Service Corp. (Petroleum, Fuels, and Related Equipment) [22230]

Enraf Inc. (Storage Equipment and Containers) [25912]

Enron Liquid Fuels Co. (Petroleum, Fuels, and Related Equipment) [22233]

Enron Power Services (Petroleum, Fuels, and Related Equipment) [22234]

Environment Ltd. (Furniture and Fixtures) [13106]

EOTT Energy Operating L.P. (Petroleum, Fuels, and Related Equipment) [22236]

EOTT Energy Partners L.P. (Petroleum, Fuels, and Related Equipment) [22237]

Equipment Valve and Supply Inc. (Plumbing Materials and Fixtures) [23150]

Everett and Co.; R.B. (Construction Materials and Machinery) [7325]

Farmer Office Products Inc. (Office Equipment and Supplies) [21000]

Fields and Co.; J.D. (Construction Materials and Machinery) [7340]

Finger Office Furniture (Furniture and Fixtures) [13112]

Fisher Healthcare (Scientific and Measurement Devices) [24359]

Fisher Healthcare (Medical, Dental, and Optical Supplies) [19324]

Flintex Marketing, Inc. (Petroleum, Fuels, and Related Equipment) [22282]

Flooring Distributors Inc. (Floorcovering Equipment and Supplies) [9897]

Folloder Co. (Food) [11169]

Food Equipment Specialists (Restaurant and Commercial Foodservice Equipment and Supplies) [24124]

Forged Vessel Connections Inc. (Industrial Supplies) [16872]

Frank's Auto Parts Co.; Johnny (Automotive) [2644]

Friedman Industries Inc. (Metals) [19989]

Frontier Fasteners Inc. (Hardware) [13717]

Gallagher Co.; R.J. (Metals) [19992]

Gayla Industries Inc. (Toys and Hobby Goods) [26495]

Gemini Enterprises Inc. (Petroleum, Fuels, and Related Equipment) [22307]

Gemini Ex-Im (Household Appliances) [15144]

Genesis Telecom Inc. (Communications Systems and Equipment) [5619]

Gerhardt's International, Inc. (Industrial Machinery) [16060]

Globemaster Inc. (Hardware) [13725]

Graham/Davis, Inc. (Electrical and Electronic Equipment and Supplies) [8799]

Grocers Supply Company Inc. (Food) [11331]

Groth Corp. (Industrial Supplies) [16912]

Gulf Coast Electric Supply Company Inc. (Electrical and Electronic Equipment and Supplies) [8821]

Gulf Pacific Rice Company Inc. (Food) [11347]

Gulf Reduction Div. (Minerals and Ores) [20543]

Gulf States Toyota Inc. (Automotive) [2711]

Handy Hardware Wholesale Inc. (Hardware) [13733]

Hanover Compression (Petroleum, Fuels, and Related Equipment) [22333]

Harris County Oil Company Inc. (Petroleum, Fuels, and Related Equipment) [22337]

Hedrick Beechcraft Inc. (Aeronautical Equipment and Supplies) [95]

Hillman International Brands, Ltd. (Alcoholic Beverages) [1757]

Hisco (Electrical and Electronic Equipment and Supplies) [8845]

Holland Southwest International Inc. (Construction Materials and Machinery) [7477]

Houston Peterbilt Inc. (Automotive) [2763]

Houston Stained Glass Supply (Construction Materials and Machinery) [7490]

Houston Trane (Heating and Cooling Equipment and Supplies) [14488]

Houston Wholesale Electronics Inc. (Electrical and Electronic Equipment and Supplies) [8859]

Houston Wiper and Mill Supply Co. (Used, Scrap, and Recycled Materials) [26844]

Houston Wire and Cable Co. (Electrical and Electronic Equipment and Supplies) [8860]

Howell Corp. (Petroleum, Fuels, and Related Equipment) [22366]

Hudgins Inc.; T.F. (Industrial Supplies) [16935]

HWC Distribution Corp. (Electrical and Electronic Equipment and Supplies) [8868]

Hydraquip Corp. (Industrial Machinery) [16127]

IKR Corporation (Industrial Machinery) [16140]

Imex Corp. (Clothing) [5045]

Infomax Inc. (Computers and Software) [6367]

Ingram Entertainment (Sound and Entertainment Equipment and Supplies) [25247]

Institutional Sales Associates (Food) [11514]
Interior Systems and Installation Inc. (Furniture and Fixtures) [13145]
International Trading Co. (Food) [11524]
Intile Designs Inc. (Construction Materials and Machinery) [7524]
Intramar Inc. (Industrial Machinery) [16169]
IQ Holdings Inc. (Health and Beauty Aids) [14133]
IQ Products Co. (Automotive) [2798]
IQ2000 (Computers and Software) [6397]
J.C. Supply (Electrical and Electronic Equipment and Supplies) [8910]
Johnson Supply and Equipment Corp. (Heating and Cooling Equipment and Supplies) [14501]
JTS Enterprises Inc. (Chemicals) [4433]
K & I Transeau Co. (Veterinary Products) [27166]
Kenkingdon & Associates (Electrical and Electronic Equipment and Supplies) [8936]
Key Oil Co. (Industrial Machinery) [16206]
Keyston Brothers (Textiles and Notions) [26108]
King Safe and Lock Company Inc. (Security and Safety Equipment) [24581]
KMG Chemicals Inc. (Chemicals) [4436]
Kobelco Welding of America Inc. (Construction Materials and Machinery) [7566]
Kolda Corp. (Industrial Machinery) [16213]
Komerex Industries, Inc. (Industrial Machinery) [16215]
L-K Industries Inc. (Petroleum, Fuels, and Related Equipment) [22412]
L & L Pet Center (Veterinary Products) [27177]
Lansdowne-Moody Company Inc. (Agricultural Equipment and Supplies) [938]
Life-Tech Inc. (Medical, Dental, and Optical Supplies) [19415]
Lone Star Produce Inc. (Food) [11729]
Longhorn Pet Supply (Veterinary Products) [27182]
Lorel Co. (Paper and Paper Products) [21812]
Magneto Diesel Injector Service Inc. (Automotive) [2908]
Maintenance Engineering Corp. (Chemicals) [4448]
Mannesmann Pipe and Steel Corp. (Metals) [20148]
Marimon Business Machines Inc. (Office Equipment and Supplies) [21123]
Markle Steel Co. (Metals) [20152]
Marshall Industries (Electrical and Electronic Equipment and Supplies) [9039]
Master Tile (Floorcovering Equipment and Supplies) [10012]
Maurice Pincoffs Company Inc. (Metals) [20158]
McKenzie Galleries and Commercial (Furniture and Fixtures) [13177]
Melton Steel Corp. (Metals) [20164]
Merfish Supply Co.; N. (Plumbing Materials and Fixtures) [23259]
Metals USA Inc. (Metals) [20176]
Michigan Peat Div. (Livestock and Farm Products) [18090]
Microsearch Inc. (Computers and Software) [6507]
Mims Meat Company Inc. (Food) [11904]
Moffitt Oil Company Inc. (Petroleum, Fuels, and Related Equipment) [22490]
Morse Wholesale Paper Company Inc. (Paper and Paper Products) [21844]
Mosehart-Schleeter Company, Inc. (Textiles and Notions) [26153]
Multisports Inc. (Recreational and Sporting Goods) [23840]
Mustang Industrial Equipment Co. (Industrial Machinery) [16333]
Mustang Power Systems (Automotive) [3005]
Mustang Tractor and Equipment Co. (Agricultural Equipment and Supplies) [1058]
Namasco (Metals) [20212]
Nappco Fastener Co. (Electrical and Electronic Equipment and Supplies) [9111]
Nathan Segal and Company Inc. (Livestock and Farm Products) [18125]
Neely TBA (Automotive) [3020]
New Concepts Books & Tapes Distributors (Books and Other Printed Materials) [3993]
New Process Steel Corp. (Metals) [20223]
Newmans Inc. (Industrial Supplies) [17074]
North Shore Supply Company Inc. (Metals) [20233]

Nutrition For Life International Inc. (Health and Beauty Aids) [14182]
Oceanex Services International, Inc. (Petroleum, Fuels, and Related Equipment) [22533]
Ochterbeck Distributing Company Inc. (Automotive) [3052]
Office Systems of Texas (Office Equipment and Supplies) [21191]
Oilworld Supply Co. (Petroleum, Fuels, and Related Equipment) [22539]
Omni USA Inc. (Agricultural Equipment and Supplies) [1107]
Oshman's Sporting Goods Inc. (Recreational and Sporting Goods) [23862]
Panhandle Trading Co. (Petroleum, Fuels, and Related Equipment) [22549]
Parkans International L.L.C. (Used, Scrap, and Recycled Materials) [26935]
Parker Brothers and Company Inc. (Automotive) [3080]
Pearce Industries Inc. (Industrial Machinery) [16386]
Peenware International (Gifts and Novelties) [13419]
Pentacon Inc. (Hardware) [13866]
PFS (Food) [12163]
Pipe Distributors Inc. (Metals) [20283]
Platt Hardin Inc. (Electrical and Electronic Equipment and Supplies) [9213]
PMI Sales and Marketing Services Inc. (Plumbing Materials and Fixtures) [23324]
Polo-Ray Sunglass, Inc. (Medical, Dental, and Optical Supplies) [19548]
Pool Water Products (Recreational and Sporting Goods) [23894]
Power Plastics Inc. (Plastics) [23016]
Power Supply, Inc. (Electrical and Electronic Equipment and Supplies) [9227]
Power & Telephone Supply Company Inc. (Communications Systems and Equipment) [5712]
Precision Tool and Supply (Industrial Machinery) [16423]
Prime Systems (Computers and Software) [6638]
Pro-Mark Corp. (Sound and Entertainment Equipment and Supplies) [25389]
Pro-Mark Corp. (Household Appliances) [15280]
Proler International Corp. (Used, Scrap, and Recycled Materials) [26947]
Prometex International Corp. (Health and Beauty Aids) [14200]
Public Software Library (Computers and Software) [6662]
Quality Banana Inc. (Food) [12248]
R and W Technical Services Ltd. (Computers and Software) [6676]
Radio Holland U.S.A. (Marine) [18590]
Rainbo Baking Co. (Food) [12266]
Rawson and Company Inc. (Scientific and Measurement Devices) [24422]
Readers Wholesale Distributors Inc. (Floorcovering Equipment and Supplies) [10116]
Renick and Company Inc. (Computers and Software) [6687]
Republic Beverage Co. (Alcoholic Beverages) [1984]
Rex Supply Co. (Industrial Machinery) [16449]
Rice Welding Supply Co. (Industrial Supplies) [17138]
Richardson's Educators Inc. (Books and Other Printed Materials) [4117]
Riggsbee Hardware & Industrial Supply (Hardware) [13887]
Riviana Foods Inc. (Food) [12325]
Robinson Iron and Metal Company Inc. (Used, Scrap, and Recycled Materials) [26963]
Rod Co. Inc.; A.J. (Industrial Supplies) [17143]
Rol-Lift Corp. (Automotive) [3173]
Rose Industries Inc. (Houston, Texas) (Metals) [20330]
Rose Metal Processing (Used, Scrap, and Recycled Materials) [26967]
Ruby Metal Traders Inc. (Used, Scrap, and Recycled Materials) [26970]
Safina Office Products (Office Equipment and Supplies) [21255]

SBM Drilling Fluids (Petroleum, Fuels, and Related Equipment) [22655]
Scholarly Publications (Books and Other Printed Materials) [4141]
Scholl Forest Products Inc. (Construction Materials and Machinery) [7987]
Scope Imports Inc. (Clothing) [5337]
Sepco-Industries Inc. (Industrial Machinery) [16483]
September Enterprises Inc. (Petroleum, Fuels, and Related Equipment) [22661]
Serendipity Communications, Inc. (Sound and Entertainment Equipment and Supplies) [25438]
SFI-Gray Steel Services Inc. (Metals) [20361]
Shepler International Inc. (Construction Materials and Machinery) [8011]
Shepler's Equipment Company Inc. (Construction Materials and Machinery) [8012]
Slick 50 Corp. (Petroleum, Fuels, and Related Equipment) [22676]
Snap Products Inc. (Automotive) [3235]
S.N.S. International Trading (Gifts and Novelties) [13447]
South Central Pool Supply, Inc. (Recreational and Sporting Goods) [23967]
Southern Architectural Systems, Inc. (Construction Materials and Machinery) [8047]
Southern Floral Co. (Horticultural Supplies) [14953]
Southern Produce Inc. (Food) [12540]
Southwest Business Furniture (Furniture and Fixtures) [13248]
Southwest Stainless Inc. (Metals) [20376]
Southwest Wire Rope Inc. (Industrial Supplies) [17188]
Southwestern Camera (Photographic Equipment and Supplies) [22906]
Specialties Co. (Rubber) [24295]
Star Middle East USA Inc. (Industrial Machinery) [16520]
Stargel Office Systems Inc. (Office Equipment and Supplies) [21293]
Stewart and Stevenson Services Inc. (Automotive) [3270]
Stewart and Stevenson Services Inc. Texas (Industrial Machinery) [16524]
Summit Hats (Clothing) [5403]
Summit Hats (Clothing) [5404]
Sunbelt Distributors Inc. (Food) [12607]
Sunbelt Supply Co. (Industrial Supplies) [17202]
Swiff-Train Co. (Floorcovering Equipment and Supplies) [10198]
Sysco Corp. (Food) [12668]
Sysco Food Services of Houston Inc. (Food) [12681]
T & L Distributors Company Inc. (Floorcovering Equipment and Supplies) [10206]
Tarrant Distributors Inc. (Alcoholic Beverages) [2069]
Taser International Inc. (Agricultural Equipment and Supplies) [1314]
Tauber Oil Co. (Petroleum, Fuels, and Related Equipment) [22721]
Technical and Scientific Application Inc. (Computers and Software) [6800]
Tenneco Energy Resources Corp. (Petroleum, Fuels, and Related Equipment) [22724]
Tenneco Gas Marketing Co. (Petroleum, Fuels, and Related Equipment) [22725]
Tex Isle Supply Inc. (Metals) [20419]
Texaco Additive Co. (Chemicals) [4528]
Texas Art Supply Co. (Specialty Equipment and Products) [25840]
Texas Pipe and Supply Company Inc. (Metals) [20420]
Texas Staple Company Inc. (Hardware) [13950]
Texatek International (Plastics) [23042]
Texberry Container Corp. (Plastics) [23043]
Thorpe Corp. (Construction Materials and Machinery) [8124]
Thorpe Products Co. (Construction Materials and Machinery) [8126]
Toole and Company Inc. (Plumbing Materials and Fixtures) [23411]
Toray Marketing and Sales (America) Inc. (Medical, Dental, and Optical Equipment) [19080]
Total Safety Inc. (Specialty Equipment and Products) [25846]

Toyo USA Inc. (Petroleum, Fuels, and Related Equipment) [22745]
Trelltex Inc. (Rubber) [24303]
Trophy Products Inc. (Hardware) [13966]
Tubular Products of Texas Inc. (Industrial Supplies) [17238]
Uncle Bens Inc. (Food) [12783]
Universal Products Enterprises (Medical, Dental, and Optical Supplies) [19685]
Vallen Corp. (Security and Safety Equipment) [24655]
Vallen Safety Supply Co. (Industrial Supplies) [17248]
Van Leeuwen Pipe and Tube Corp. (Plumbing Materials and Fixtures) [23431]
Vanguard Petroleum Corp. (Petroleum, Fuels, and Related Equipment) [22770]
Vista Trading Corp. (Livestock and Farm Products) [18319]
Wahlberg-McCreary Inc. (Automotive) [3396]
Wainoco Oil Corp. (Petroleum, Fuels, and Related Equipment) [22778]
Wallace Company Inc. (Plumbing Materials and Fixtures) [23435]
Warren Electric Group (Electrical and Electronic Equipment and Supplies) [9557]
Waste Reduction Systems Inc. (Used, Scrap, and Recycled Materials) [27038]
Wells and Kimich Inc. (Furniture and Fixtures) [13276]
White Swan, Inc. (Food) [12932]
White's Inc. (Agricultural Equipment and Supplies) [1442]
Wholesale Electric Supply Company of Houston Inc. (Electrical and Electronic Equipment and Supplies) [9589]
Wholesale Furniture Distributors (Furniture and Fixtures) [13279]
Wilson Industries Inc. (Petroleum, Fuels, and Related Equipment) [22808]
Winco Distributors Inc. (Construction Materials and Machinery) [8230]
Womack Machine (Industrial Machinery) [16648]

Humble
Lohr Structural Fasteners Inc. (Hardware) [13800]

Huntsville
Mitcham Industries Inc. (Scientific and Measurement Devices) [24399]

Hurst
Hurst Lumber Company Inc. (Construction Materials and Machinery) [7500]
Spectrum (Sound and Entertainment Equipment and Supplies) [25460]

Irving
Bollinger Healthcare (Industrial Machinery) [15830]
Brown Moore and Flint Inc. (Food) [10627]
Dallas Ford New Holland Inc. (Agricultural Equipment and Supplies) [489]
Dyna Marketing (Computers and Software) [6229]
Entrelec Inc. (Electrical and Electronic Equipment and Supplies) [8710]
Goldthwaites of Texas, Inc. (Agricultural Equipment and Supplies) [748]
GTE Supply (Communications Systems and Equipment) [5628]
Haber Fabrics Corp. (Textiles and Notions) [26051]
IMCO Recycling Inc. (Used, Scrap, and Recycled Materials) [26848]
L.E.S. Distributing (Sound and Entertainment Equipment and Supplies) [25282]
Mitsumi Electronics Corp. (Computers and Software) [6525]
Nokia Inc. (Computers and Software) [6559]
PSDI (Computers and Software) [6655]
Publishers Associates (Books and Other Printed Materials) [4091]
Reece Supply Company of Dallas (Specialty Equipment and Products) [25800]
Sovana, Inc. (Agricultural Equipment and Supplies) [1286]
Street Cars Inc. (Shoes) [24868]

Texas Contractors Supply Co. (Construction Materials and Machinery) [8114]
Texas Mill Supply Inc. (Hardware) [13949]
VHA Supply Co. (Medical, Dental, and Optical Equipment) [19101]

Italy
Carter Service Center (Agricultural Equipment and Supplies) [375]

Jacksboro
Geer Tank Trucks Inc. (Petroleum, Fuels, and Related Equipment) [22306]

Jacksonville
Jacksonville Candy Company Inc. (Food) [11546]

Jasper
Dover Company Inc.; Bill L. (Petroleum, Fuels, and Related Equipment) [22210]

Justin
Justin Seed Company Inc. (Agricultural Equipment and Supplies) [894]

Katy
Heines Custom Draperies (Household Items) [15523]

Keller
E.A.P. Co. (Computers and Software) [6233]

Kemah
Blue Water Ship Store (Marine) [18464]

Kerrville
Marni International (Office Equipment and Supplies) [21128]

Kilgore
Johnston-Lawrence Co. (Petroleum, Fuels, and Related Equipment) [22390]

Kingsville
Kleberg County Farmers Cooperative (Agricultural Equipment and Supplies) [913]

La Joya
Alfredo's Tile Distributors (Floorcovering Equipment and Supplies) [9651]

Lake Jackson
Gulf Coast Sportswear Inc. (Clothing) [5007]

Laredo
Centenario Technologies, Inc. (Computers and Software) [6053]
Dentex Shoe Corp. (Shoes) [24726]
Doctor Ike's Home Center Inc. (Construction Materials and Machinery) [7276]
Integral Kitchens (Floorcovering Equipment and Supplies) [9963]
Integral Kitchens (Construction Materials and Machinery) [7514]
Laredo Hardware Co. (Hardware) [13793]
Randolph Slaughter Co. (Food) [12276]
Torres Hat Company (Clothing) [5436]
Villarreal Electric Company Inc. (Electrical and Electronic Equipment and Supplies) [9541]
Vilrore Foods Company Inc. (Food) [12845]

League City
Schroeder's Book Haven (Books and Other Printed Materials) [4144]

Leander
Supercircuits Inc. (Photographic Equipment and Supplies) [22909]

Lewisville
Benedict Optical (Medical, Dental, and Optical Supplies) [19182]
Brinkman and Co.; LD (Floorcovering Equipment and Supplies) [9740]

National Switchgear Systems (Electrical and Electronic Equipment and Supplies) [9118]
Silvestri Corporation Inc.; Fitz and Floyd (Household Items) [15654]

Littlefield
R and W Supply Inc. (Industrial Supplies) [17127]

Llano
Buttery Hardware Company Inc. (Hardware) [13613]

Lockney
Lockney Cooperative Gin (Food) [11720]

Longview
Delta Distributors Inc. (Chemicals) [4371]
Dunaway Supply Co. (Construction Materials and Machinery) [7289]
Industrial Steel Warehouse Inc. (Metals) [20060]
Made-Rite Co. (Soft Drinks) [24985]
Stoudt Distributing Co. (Alcoholic Beverages) [2055]
Texas Mill Inc. (Industrial Supplies) [17220]
U.S. Beverage Corp. (Soft Drinks) [25046]

Lubbock
Accent Tile (Floorcovering Equipment and Supplies) [9640]
Art's Theatrical Supply (Jewelry) [17315]
Barnett Brothers Brokerage Co. Inc. (Food) [10509]
Becknell Wholesale Co. (Hardware) [13589]
Benton Oil Co. (Petroleum, Fuels, and Related Equipment) [22067]
Brandon and Clark Inc. (Electrical and Electronic Equipment and Supplies) [8464]
Cathey Wholesale Co. (Floorcovering Equipment and Supplies) [9780]
Central Garden Supplies (Agricultural Equipment and Supplies) [394]
Farmers Cooperative Compress (Livestock and Farm Products) [17859]
Felder & Co.; W.D. (Livestock and Farm Products) [17915]
Fields and Company of Lubbock Inc. (Plumbing Materials and Fixtures) [23168]
Frontier Wholesale Co. (Construction Materials and Machinery) [7370]
Gear Clutch & Joint (Automotive) [2667]
General Steel Warehouse Inc. (Metals) [19998]
Great Southwest Sales (Food) [11314]
Hesters/McGlaun Office Supply Co. (Office Equipment and Supplies) [21031]
Higginbotham-Bartlett Co. (Construction Materials and Machinery) [7469]
Lee Wholesale Floral Inc. (Horticultural Supplies) [14911]
Lubbock Electric Co. (Electrical and Electronic Equipment and Supplies) [9007]
McLain Oil Company Inc. (Petroleum, Fuels, and Related Equipment) [22467]
McLane Company Inc. High Plains (Food) [11832]
Plains Cotton Cooperative Association (Livestock and Farm Products) [18170]
R and R Electronic Supply Co. (Electrical and Electronic Equipment and Supplies) [9254]
Rheas Crafts (Office Equipment and Supplies) [21238]
Townsend-Strong Inc. (Petroleum, Fuels, and Related Equipment) [22744]
Watson Foodservice Inc. (Food) [12883]
White Swan, Inc. (Food) [12930]
Woody Tire Company Inc. (Automotive) [3445]

Lufkin
DuBose and Son Co.; W.A. (Agricultural Equipment and Supplies) [529]
George Co., Inc.; William (Food) [11254]
Story Wright Printing (Office Equipment and Supplies) [21299]
Watson Electric Supply Co. (Electrical and Electronic Equipment and Supplies) [9560]

Lyford

Lyford Gin Association (Livestock and Farm
Products) [18067]

Mansfield

Mouser Electronics (Electrical and Electronic
Equipment and Supplies) [9103]

Marshall

Logan and Whaley Company Inc. (Industrial
Supplies) [17003]
Marshall Pottery Inc. (Horticultural
Supplies) [14916]

McAllen

BCI Inc. (Clothing) [4809]
Bertuca Co.; Teddy (Food) [10545]
Carlos Franco (Electrical and Electronic Equipment
and Supplies) [8503]
Clark Chevrolet Co.; Charles (Motorized
Vehicles) [20611]
Franco; Carlos (Electrical and Electronic Equipment
and Supplies) [8755]
Tire Corral Inc. (Automotive) [3305]
Vista Oil Co. (Petroleum, Fuels, and Related
Equipment) [22774]

McGregor

Cen-Tex AG Supply (Petroleum, Fuels, and Related
Equipment) [22118]

McKinney

Teague Industries Inc. (Electrical and Electronic
Equipment and Supplies) [9464]

Mercedes

H and H Meat Products Company
Inc. (Food) [11350]

Mesquite

Fritz Pet Products (Veterinary Products) [27134]
Hatfield and Company Inc. (Industrial
Supplies) [16926]
Monarch Ceramic Tile Inc. (Floorcovering
Equipment and Supplies) [10049]
Pepsi-Cola Company South (Soft Drinks) [25016]

Midland

Anderson Tile Sales (Floorcovering Equipment and
Supplies) [9683]
Avionix Medical Devices (Medical, Dental, and
Optical Equipment) [18699]
Kent Distribution Inc. (Petroleum, Fuels, and
Related Equipment) [22401]
Leamco-Ruthco (Industrial Machinery) [16231]
Midland 66 Oil Company Inc. (Petroleum, Fuels,
and Related Equipment) [22481]
Midland Lock & Safe Service (Security and Safety
Equipment) [24592]
Palmer Pipe and Supply Inc. (Hardware) [13859]
South-Tex Treaters Inc. (Industrial
Machinery) [16507]
Union Supply Co. (Plumbing Materials and
Fixtures) [23421]
West Texas Equipment Co. (Agricultural Equipment
and Supplies) [1425]

Mineola

Benham and Company Inc. (Food) [10535]
East Texas Gas Co. (Petroleum, Fuels, and
Related Equipment) [22219]
Trinidad/Benham (Food) [12756]

Mission

Tex-Ag Co. (Chemicals) [4527]
Weaks Martin Implement Co. (Agricultural
Equipment and Supplies) [1419]

Muleshoe

King Grain Company Inc. (Livestock and Farm
Products) [18034]

Nacogdoches

Elliot Electric Supply (Electrical and Electronic
Equipment and Supplies) [8699]

Naples

Cofil Inc. (Construction Materials and
Machinery) [7191]

New Braunfels

Dyna Group International Inc. (Gifts and
Novelties) [13349]
Educational Geodesics Inc. (Books and Other
Printed Materials) [3723]
Ladshaw Explosives Inc. (Explosives) [9636]
T.R. Trading Co. (Industrial Machinery) [16572]

Odessa

Anderson Tile Sales (Floorcovering Equipment and
Supplies) [9682]
Consolidated Electrical Distributors Inc. (Electrical
and Electronic Equipment and Supplies) [8569]
Drivetrain Specialists (Automotive) [2565]
Engine Service and Supply Co. (Industrial
Supplies) [16851]
Fabco Industries, Inc. (Automotive) [2603]
J & J Steel and Supply Co. (Petroleum, Fuels, and
Related Equipment) [22380]
J and J Steel and Supply Co. (Metals) [20072]
Lindsey Completion Systems (Industrial
Machinery) [16237]
M & M Sales & Equipment (Industrial
Supplies) [17009]
Southwest Energy Distributors Inc. (Petroleum,
Fuels, and Related Equipment) [22685]
Terk Distributing (Alcoholic Beverages) [2075]
White Inc.; Billy D. (Automotive) [3426]

Olton

Olton Grain Cooperative Inc. (Livestock and Farm
Products) [18155]
Thompson Implement Inc. (Agricultural Equipment
and Supplies) [1330]

Orange

Harding and Lawler Inc. (Construction Materials
and Machinery) [7443]
Texas Mill Inc. (Industrial Supplies) [17219]

Ovilla

Texxon Enterprises Inc. (Construction Materials and
Machinery) [8117]

Ozona

South Texas Lumber Co. (Construction Materials
and Machinery) [8042]

Palacios

Palacios Processors (Food) [12097]

Palestine

B & B Cattle Co. (Livestock and Farm
Products) [17715]
Huffman Equipment Co. (Agricultural Equipment
and Supplies) [843]

Pampa

W-B Supply Co. (Petroleum, Fuels, and Related
Equipment) [22776]

Paris

Big Tex Feed Co. Inc. (Agricultural Equipment and
Supplies) [312]
Valley Feed Mill Inc. (Agricultural Equipment and
Supplies) [1393]

Pasadena

Control Solutions Inc. (Chemicals) [4363]
Kast Fabrics Inc. (Textiles and Notions) [26090]

Perryton

Perryton Equity Exchange (Livestock and Farm
Products) [18164]

Petersburg

Wylie and Son Inc. (Agricultural Equipment and
Supplies) [1465]

Pharr

Elmore & Stahl Inc. (Food) [11043]
Javi Farm Inc. (Food) [11549]

Plainview

Browning Seed Inc. (Agricultural Equipment and
Supplies) [344]
Lee Equipment Co.; Ray (Agricultural Equipment
and Supplies) [948]
Mycogen Plant Sciences. Southern Div. (Agricultural
Equipment and Supplies) [1059]

Plano

Alden Comfort Mills (Furniture and
Fixtures) [13013]
American Tile Supply (Floorcovering Equipment and
Supplies) [9674]
Daisytek Inc. (Computers and Software) [6176]
Dallas Digital Corp. (Computers and
Software) [6177]
Dr. Pepper/Seven Up, Inc. (Food) [10972]
First Choice Ingredients (Food) [11131]
Flack International, Inc.; Henry (Cleaning and
Janitorial Supplies) [4622]
Frito-Lay Co. (Food) [11215]
General Handling Systems Inc. (Industrial
Machinery) [16055]
Graico International (Agricultural Equipment and
Supplies) [752]
Henry's Homemade Ice Cream (Food) [11416]
Hitachi Inverter (Electrical and Electronic Equipment
and Supplies) [8848]
International Marketing Specialists Inc. (Industrial
Machinery) [16165]
Kreher Steel Co. (Metals) [20109]
K's Distributors (Specialty Equipment and
Products) [25709]
MediQuip International (Medical, Dental, and Optical
Equipment) [18925]
Micro Chef Inc. (Food) [11873]
Murata Business Systems Inc. (Office Equipment
and Supplies) [21154]
Nikko America Inc. (Toys and Hobby
Goods) [26594]
Sales Mark Alpha One Inc. (Food) [12396]
Scherer Laboratories Inc. (Medical, Dental, and
Optical Supplies) [19595]
Switzer Petroleum Products (Petroleum, Fuels, and
Related Equipment) [22719]
Telecom Electric Supply Co. (Electrical and
Electronic Equipment and Supplies) [9473]
U.S. Clinical Products (Medical, Dental, and Optical
Supplies) [19679]
Wordware Publishing Inc. (Books and Other Printed
Materials) [4296]

Pleasanton

Wehman Inc. (Petroleum, Fuels, and Related
Equipment) [22789]

Port Arthur

Drago Supply Co. Inc. (Hardware) [13669]
Drago Supply Company Inc. (Industrial
Machinery) [15961]
Nacol Jewelry; C.S. (Jewelry) [17528]

Port Isabel

Zimco Marine (Marine) [18647]

Port Lavaca

Clegg Seafood International (Food) [10769]

Poth

Lyssy and Eckel Inc. (Agricultural Equipment and
Supplies) [976]

Raymondville

Hocott Implement Company Inc. (Agricultural
Equipment and Supplies) [828]

Raywood

American Rice Growers Cooperative
Association (Agricultural Equipment and
Supplies) [235]

Richardson

Advanced Micro Solutions Inc. (Computers and Software) [5888]

Anritsu Co. (Scientific and Measurement Devices) [24314]

Chubb Security Systems Inc. (Security and Safety Equipment) [24526]

CONVEX Computer Corp. (Computers and Software) [6156]

Leeward Inc. (Medical, Dental, and Optical Equipment) [18886]

Marshall Industries (Electrical and Electronic Equipment and Supplies) [9038]

Nortel Federal Systems (Communications Systems and Equipment) [5693]

Richardson Trident Co (Metals) [20321]

Society of Petroleum Engineers (Books and Other Printed Materials) [4169]

USA Datafax Inc. (Office Equipment and Supplies) [21332]

Roanoke

Aviatech Corporation (Aeronautical Equipment and Supplies) [50]

Robert Lee

Lewis-Simpson Ranch (Livestock and Farm Products) [18053]

Lewis-Simpson Ranch (Livestock and Farm Products) [18054]

Robstown

Robstown Hardware Co. (Agricultural Equipment and Supplies) [1202]

Rogers

Environmental Chemical Group Inc. (Chemicals) [4384]

Rosenberg

Holmes Smokehouse Inc.; S and D (Food) [11452]

Round Rock

Carroll Touch Inc. (Construction Materials and Machinery) [7146]

Dell Computer Corp. Dell Marketing L.P. (Computers and Software) [6196]

Salado

Salado Cattle Co. (Livestock and Farm Products) [18220]

San Angelo

Anderson Tile Sales (Floorcovering Equipment and Supplies) [9681]

C and W Enterprises Inc. (Petroleum, Fuels, and Related Equipment) [22103]

Coca-Cola Bottling Co. (Soft Drinks) [24931]

Simmons-Huggins Supply Co. (Plumbing Materials and Fixtures) [23377]

San Antonio

A and A Pump Co. (Petroleum, Fuels, and Related Equipment) [22014]

Acfer International Inc. (Photographic Equipment and Supplies) [22822]

Alamo Aircraft, Ltd. (Aeronautical Equipment and Supplies) [38]

Alamo Iron Works (Metals) [19740]

Allen and Allen Company Inc. (Construction Materials and Machinery) [6936]

Alliant Foodservice Inc. (Food) [10373]

Allied Vista Inc. Vista Fibers (Used, Scrap, and Recycled Materials) [26740]

Amberstar International Inc. (Food) [10390]

AMC Industries Inc. (Plumbing Materials and Fixtures) [23061]

Anderson Machinery San Antonio Inc. (Construction Materials and Machinery) [6978]

Artesia Water Co. (Food) [10441]

ASNA Inc. (Computers and Software) [5973]

Associated Tile Sales (Floorcovering Equipment and Supplies) [9690]

Baxter International Representations Inc. (Hardware) [13587]

Big Tex Grain Company Inc. (Agricultural Equipment and Supplies) [313]

Block Distributing Co. Inc. (Alcoholic Beverages) [1534]

Bruno & Son Inc.; C. (Sound and Entertainment Equipment and Supplies) [25110]

BTE Import-Export (Medical, Dental, and Optical Supplies) [19204]

BudCo Incorporated of San Antonio (Alcoholic Beverages) [1557]

Budco of San Antonio Inc. (Alcoholic Beverages) [1558]

Callahan Inc.; S.X. (Automotive) [2411]

Central Distributing Co. (Household Appliances) [15081]

Commercial Body Corp. (Automotive) [2465]

Commercial Body Corp. (Industrial Machinery) [15902]

DEA Specialties Co. (Office Equipment and Supplies) [20951]

Dewied International Inc. (Food) [10954]

Esco Imports of Texas Inc. (Toys and Hobby Goods) [26478]

Esco Supply Company Inc. (Plumbing Materials and Fixtures) [23152]

Foam Products of San Antonio Inc. (Plastics) [22965]

Gambrinus Co. (Alcoholic Beverages) [1703]

Gourmet Wine & Spirits (Alcoholic Beverages) [1728]

Grocery Supply Co., Inc. (Food) [11334]

Guido Inc.; Gino (Construction Materials and Machinery) [7422]

Guido Lumber Company Inc. (Construction Materials and Machinery) [7423]

Gulf Pool Equipment Co. (Recreational and Sporting Goods) [23702]

Halo Distributing Co. (Alcoholic Beverages) [1742]

H.E. Butt Grocery Co. San Antonio Distribution/Manufacturing Center (Food) [11400]

Holt Company of Texas (Construction Materials and Machinery) [7480]

Huffaker's Inc. (Hardware) [13760]

Hydraquip Corp. (Industrial Machinery) [16128]

International Parts Inc. (Computers and Software) [6391]

J & J Distributors (Security and Safety Equipment) [24576]

King Koil Sleep Product (Household Items) [15549]

Labatt Food Service (Food) [11663]

Labatt Institutional Supply Company Inc. (Food) [11664]

Leonard and Harral Packing Company Inc. (Food) [11701]

Loyd Armature Works Inc. (Electrical and Electronic Equipment and Supplies) [9004]

Monarch Tile (Floorcovering Equipment and Supplies) [10055]

Monroe and Associates Inc. (Food) [11924]

Neuman Distributors (Food) [11998]

Newell Recycling Company Inc. (Used, Scrap, and Recycled Materials) [26924]

Ortho-Tex Inc. (Medical, Dental, and Optical Supplies) [19520]

Pak-Mor Manufacturing Co. (Motorized Vehicles) [20702]

Pan Am Distributing Inc. (Construction Materials and Machinery) [7833]

Park Place Recreation Designs Inc. (Recreational and Sporting Goods) [23872]

Pepper Products (Food) [12144]

Phillips Distribution Inc. (Cleaning and Janitorial Supplies) [4686]

Ploch Co.; A.J. (Petroleum, Fuels, and Related Equipment) [22587]

PMG International Inc. (Books and Other Printed Materials) [4069]

Progressive Marketing (Food) [12230]

Q.I.V. Systems Inc. (Computers and Software) [6668]

Reliable Battery Co. (Electrical and Electronic Equipment and Supplies) [9273]

River City Steel and Recycling Inc. (Used, Scrap, and Recycled Materials) [26960]

Roddis Lumber and Veneer Company Inc. (Construction Materials and Machinery) [7951]

Rooster Products International Inc./McGuire-Nicholas (Hardware) [13893]

Samuels Glass Co. (Construction Materials and Machinery) [7975]

San Antonio Brake and Clutch Service Inc. (Automotive) [3185]

Seafood Wholesalers Inc. (Food) [12449]

Smith Motor Sales (Automotive) [3233]

Snell; V.A. (Veterinary Products) [27233]

South Central Pool Supply, Inc. (Recreational and Sporting Goods) [23968]

Steelhead Inc. (Industrial Machinery) [16522]

Stewart & Stevenson (Industrial Machinery) [16523]

Strafco Inc. (Automotive) [3272]

Straus Frank Co. (Automotive) [3274]

Sunfire Corporation (Food) [12610]

Swiff-Train Co. (Floorcovering Equipment and Supplies) [10199]

Swing Machinery and Equipment Company Inc. (Industrial Supplies) [17209]

SYSCO/Alamo Food Services, Inc. (Food) [12667]

T & L Distributors Company Inc. (Floorcovering Equipment and Supplies) [10207]

Tesoro Petroleum Corp. (Petroleum, Fuels, and Related Equipment) [22726]

Texas Hobby Distributors (Toys and Hobby Goods) [26679]

Toudouze Inc. (Food) [12737]

Travis Tile Sales (Floorcovering Equipment and Supplies) [10258]

Tropical Fisheries (Veterinary Products) [27255]

UETA Inc. (Tobacco Products) [26362]

Ultramar Diamond Shamrock Corp. (Petroleum, Fuels, and Related Equipment) [22756]

U.S. Food Service (Food) [12801]

Vaughan and Sons Inc. (Construction Materials and Machinery) [8174]

Western Micro Technology Inc. (Computers and Software) [6867]

Wittigs Office Interiors (Office Equipment and Supplies) [21358]

Wittigs Office Interiors (Furniture and Fixtures) [13282]

Xerographic Copier Services Inc. (Office Equipment and Supplies) [21365]

York International Corp. Frick/Reco Div. (Heating and Cooling Equipment and Supplies) [14776]

San Marcos

Lafarge Concrete (Construction Materials and Machinery) [7575]

T.T.S. Distributors (Recreational and Sporting Goods) [24016]

San Saba

San Saba Pecan, Inc. (Food) [12403]

Schertz

Chandler Enterprises (Computers and Software) [6061]

GCR Rose Truck Tire Center (Automotive) [2665]

Schulenburg

S.A.V.E. Half Price Books for Libraries (Books and Other Printed Materials) [4138]

Seabrook

A.E.R. Supply, Inc. (Marine) [18448]

Selma

Sanfilippo Co.; John B. (Food) [12407]

Sherman

Chapman Inc. (Petroleum, Fuels, and Related Equipment) [22130]

Miss Kings Kitchen Inc, The Original Yahoo! Baking Co. (Food) [11911]

Slaton

Southern Highland Accordions & Dulcimers Ltd. (Sound and Entertainment Equipment and Supplies) [25456]

Snyder

Ezell-Key Grain Company Inc. (Agricultural Equipment and Supplies) [557]
Ezell-Key Grain Company Inc. (Food) [11065]

Spearman

Speartex Grain Co. (Livestock and Farm Products) [18248]

Stafford

Atec, Inc. (Scientific and Measurement Devices) [24318]
Atec Inc. (Industrial Machinery) [15786]
Jones Business Systems Inc. (Computers and Software) [6409]
Kays Enterprises Inc. (Clothing) [5104]
N Squared Inc. (Scientific and Measurement Devices) [24407]
Southwest Book Co. (Books and Other Printed Materials) [4176]
Southwest Electronics Inc. (Electrical and Electronic Equipment and Supplies) [9390]
Symbol Inc. (Compressors) [5852]

Stratford

Lasley and Sons Inc.; Walter (Agricultural Equipment and Supplies) [940]

Streetman

Rustic Creations (Furniture and Fixtures) [13227]

Sugar Land

Export USA (Jewelry) [17411]

Sulphur Springs

Associated Milk Producers Inc. Sulphur Springs Div. (Food) [10455]
Borden Inc. (Food) [10591]
Grocery Supply Co. (Food) [11333]
GSC Enterprises Inc. (Food) [11341]
GSC Enterprises Inc. (Food) [11342]
Northeast Texas Farmers Cooperative Inc. (Livestock and Farm Products) [18142]

Sunray

Sunray Cooperative (Agricultural Equipment and Supplies) [1304]

Taft

South Texas Implement Co. (Agricultural Equipment and Supplies) [1276]

Temple

Gidden Distributing (Alcoholic Beverages) [1714]
Ham and McCreight Inc. (Plumbing Materials and Fixtures) [23202]
McLane Company Inc. (Food) [11831]
McLane Southwest, Inc. (Food) [11834]
Sunbelt Transformer Inc. (Electrical and Electronic Equipment and Supplies) [9441]
Temple Iron and Metal Company Inc. (Used, Scrap, and Recycled Materials) [27019]

Terrell

Green Manufacturing Company Inc. (Automotive) [2703]
Tejas Resources Inc. (Minerals and Ores) [20573]
Wolfe Distributing Co. (Alcoholic Beverages) [2136]

Texarkana

E-Z Mart Stores Inc. (Food) [11008]
Humco Holding Group Inc. (Chemicals) [4422]
Jones Oil Company Inc.; N.E. (Petroleum, Fuels, and Related Equipment) [22392]
Loveall Music Co. (Sound and Entertainment Equipment and Supplies) [25289]
Truman Arnold Co. (Petroleum, Fuels, and Related Equipment) [22752]
Walsh Healthcare Solutions (Health and Beauty Aids) [14276]

Wholesale Electric Supply Company Inc. (Texarkana, Texas) (Electrical and Electronic Equipment and Supplies) [9591]

Texas City

Uman Corp. (Shoes) [24880]

Tulia

Seed Resource Inc. (Livestock and Farm Products) [18228]

Tyler

Bloch Metals Inc. (Used, Scrap, and Recycled Materials) [26768]
Borden Inc. (Food) [10592]
Celebrity, Inc. (Horticultural Supplies) [14838]
Celebrity Inc. (Tyler, Texas) (Horticultural Supplies) [14839]
Eagle Wholesale L.P. (Food) [11011]
Kirby Oil Co. (Petroleum, Fuels, and Related Equipment) [22408]
Remixer Contracting Inc. (Construction Materials and Machinery) [7913]
Shtofman Company Inc. (Shoes) [24861]
TDI Air Conditioning Appliances (Household Appliances) [15334]

Tynan

Bee County Cooperative Association Inc. (Agricultural Equipment and Supplies) [292]

Uvalde

Uvalde Meat Processing (Food) [12811]

Valley View

Martindale Feed Mill (Agricultural Equipment and Supplies) [990]

Vega

Richardson Seeds Inc. (Agricultural Equipment and Supplies) [1189]

Vernon

Osborne Distributing Company Inc. (Agricultural Equipment and Supplies) [1111]

Victoria

Accurate Water (Specialty Equipment and Products) [25544]
Gulf Bolt & Supply (Hardware) [13729]
ITG, Inc. (Railroad Equipment and Supplies) [23482]
Lenz Sports; Jerry (Recreational and Sporting Goods) [23786]
Swiff-Train Co. (Floorcovering Equipment and Supplies) [10200]
United World Supply Co. (Industrial Supplies) [17244]
Welders Equipment Company Inc. (Industrial Machinery) [16619]

Waco

Borden Milk Products LLP (Food) [10593]
Car Quest Auto Parts Co. (Automotive) [2423]
Cardinal Health-Behrens Inc. (Health and Beauty Aids) [14056]
Cogdells Westview Inc. (Guns and Weapons) [13482]
Diesel Power Supply Co. (Automotive) [2546]
Easy Gardener Inc. (Agricultural Equipment and Supplies) [538]
Gross-Yowell and Company Inc. (Construction Materials and Machinery) [7420]
Jarvis-Paris-Murphy Company Inc. (Livestock and Farm Products) [18021]
Keeton Sales Agency Inc. (Textiles and Notions) [26092]
Lipsitz and Company Inc.; M. (Used, Scrap, and Recycled Materials) [26884]
Midstate Beverage Inc. (Alcoholic Beverages) [1875]
Purvis Bearing Service (Automotive) [3126]
Waco Meat Service Inc. (Food) [12858]
Westside Tile Co. (Floorcovering Equipment and Supplies) [10297]

Weatherford

CSSI Cellular (Communications Systems and Equipment) [5581]
Hartnett Co.; The C.D. (Food) [11385]

Webster

Specialty Control Systems Inc. (Electrical and Electronic Equipment and Supplies) [9393]

Weimar

C.H.I.P.S. (Books and Other Printed Materials) [3632]
M-G Inc. (Agricultural Equipment and Supplies) [977]

Weslaco

Barbee-Neuhaus Implement Co. (Agricultural Equipment and Supplies) [276]
Burton Auto Supply Inc. (Automotive) [2402]

Wichita Falls

Amsco Steel Products Co. (Metals) [19777]
CESSCO Rental and Sales Inc. (Industrial Machinery) [15883]
Empire Paper Co. (Paper and Paper Products) [21723]
Murphy's Tile & Marble (Floorcovering Equipment and Supplies) [10069]
Texas Recreation Corp. (Recreational and Sporting Goods) [24008]
Wichita Falls Nunn Electrical Supply (Electrical and Electronic Equipment and Supplies) [9594]
Wichita Recycling (Used, Scrap, and Recycled Materials) [27047]

Winters

Loyd LP Gas Co.; Bob (Petroleum, Fuels, and Related Equipment) [22439]

The Woodlands

Tetra Technologies Inc. (Chemicals) [4526]

Wylie

AllerMed Corp. (Heating and Cooling Equipment and Supplies) [14313]
Nortex Wholesale Nursery Inc. (Horticultural Supplies) [14929]

Utah

Alpine

Anson & Co.; R.E. (Recreational and Sporting Goods) [23519]

American Fork

Nature's Herbs (Health and Beauty Aids) [14173]
Roberts Manufacturing Inc. (Furniture and Fixtures) [13223]

Bountiful

Benchmark Systems Inc. of Utah (Computers and Software) [6010]
Horizon Publishers & Distributors, Inc. (Books and Other Printed Materials) [3833]
Horizons Publishers and Dstbrs (Books and Other Printed Materials) [3834]
The TK Group, Inc. (Electrical and Electronic Equipment and Supplies) [9490]
United States Pharmaceutical Corp. (Medical, Dental, and Optical Supplies) [19681]

Brigham City

Flying J Inc. (Petroleum, Fuels, and Related Equipment) [22284]

Cedar City

Cedar Builders Supply Company Inc. (Plumbing Materials and Fixtures) [23109]

Centerville

Pro-Tect Computer Products (Computers and Software) [6643]

Clearfield
Ren's Clearfield Paint & Glass (Paints and Varnishes) [21555]

Draper
Back to Basics Products Inc. (Household Items) [15412]
Smith & Sons Co.; Dale T. (Food) [12516]

Farmington
Artemia of Utah Inc. (Food) [10440]

Heber City
Parts Inc. (Construction Materials and Machinery) [7837]

Holladay
Holladay Color Center (Paints and Varnishes) [21457]

Hooper
Trease Distributing Co.; Dan (Petroleum, Fuels, and Related Equipment) [22748]

Kaysville
Amemco (Computers and Software) [5919]
Country Club Foods Inc. (Food) [10855]
Intermountain Scientific Corp. (Scientific and Measurement Devices) [24374]
ISC/BioExpress (Medical, Dental, and Optical Equipment) [18864]
ISC/BioExpress (Medical, Dental, and Optical Supplies) [19380]

Layton
Special Promotion Co. (Toys and Hobby Goods) [26662]

Lehi
Granite Seed (Agricultural Equipment and Supplies) [758]
Hutchs TV and Appliance (Household Appliances) [15173]

Lindon
Alta Sales Inc. (Industrial Supplies) [16691]
Western Flat Rolled Steel (Metals) [20490]

Loa
Chappells Cheese Co. (Food) [10735]

Logan
Cache Valley Builders Supply (Construction Materials and Machinery) [7122]
Ellis Equipment Co. Inc. (Agricultural Equipment and Supplies) [548]

Midvale
Amco Equipment and Steel Inc. (Construction Materials and Machinery) [6955]
Butterfield Building Supply (Construction Materials and Machinery) [7117]
Dentt, Inc. (Toys and Hobby Goods) [26466]
Norbest Inc. (Food) [12018]

Moab
Burt Explosives Inc. (Explosives) [9632]

Monticello
Black Oil Company Inc. (Petroleum, Fuels, and Related Equipment) [22076]

Morgan
Browning (Guns and Weapons) [13478]

Murray
Garrett & Co., Inc. (Recreational and Sporting Goods) [23684]
Kwal-Howells Paint & Wallcovering (Paints and Varnishes) [21482]
LBI Wallcovering (Paints and Varnishes) [21489]
Regan Co.; Steve (Agricultural Equipment and Supplies) [1180]
Wonder Bread Thrift Store Inc. (Food) [12975]

North Salt Lake
Combined Sales Co. (Toys and Hobby Goods) [26447]
Producers Livestock Marketing Association (Livestock and Farm Products) [18181]

Oakley
Zimmer & Associates; Jackson (Medical, Dental, and Optical Equipment) [19115]

Ogden
Anderson Lumber Co. (Construction Materials and Machinery) [6976]
Auto Parts Association (Automotive) [2273]
Basic Convenience Foods (Automotive) [2325]
Boman and Kemp Steel and Supply Inc. (Metals) [19830]
BPC Supply Co. (Industrial Machinery) [15838]
Christensen Electric Motor Inc. (Electrical and Electronic Equipment and Supplies) [8524]
Components West (Hardware) [13642]
Crittenden Paint and Glass (Paints and Varnishes) [21421]
Dyna-Lube (Petroleum, Fuels, and Related Equipment) [22215]
Eaglecrafts Inc. (Toys and Hobby Goods) [26475]
Farmers Grain Cooperative (Livestock and Farm Products) [17896]
Farr & Sons Co.; Asael (Food) [11109]
Field Oil Inc. (Petroleum, Fuels, and Related Equipment) [22277]
Fuller-O'Brien Paint Stores (Paints and Varnishes) [21448]
Gateway Distributing Co. (Food) [11241]
Hone Oil Co. (Petroleum, Fuels, and Related Equipment) [22362]
Intermountain Specialty Coatings (Paints and Varnishes) [21465]
Jardine Petroleum (Petroleum, Fuels, and Related Equipment) [22384]
Kaman Industrial Technologies (Electrical and Electronic Equipment and Supplies) [8926]
Kellerstrass Oil Co. (Petroleum, Fuels, and Related Equipment) [22398]
Lindquist Investment Co. (Aeronautical Equipment and Supplies) [117]
Metalwest (Metals) [20177]
Mountain West Paint Distributor (Paints and Varnishes) [21509]
Oscars Wholesale Meats Company Inc. (Food) [12082]
Parson Cos.; Jack B. (Construction Materials and Machinery) [7836]
Rubin Inc. (Recreational and Sporting Goods) [23926]

Orem
Auto Body Supply of Orem (Paints and Varnishes) [21394]
Bonneville Industrial (Industrial Supplies) [16756]
Computer Recyclers Inc. (Computers and Software) [6122]
Kwal-Howells Paint & Wallcovering (Paints and Varnishes) [21481]
Mountainland Supply Co. (Plumbing Materials and Fixtures) [23282]
Seow Company Inc.; Anthony (Medical, Dental, and Optical Supplies) [19603]
Thomson Productions (Sound and Entertainment Equipment and Supplies) [25478]
Tolman Computer Supply Group (Computers and Software) [6820]
TRI-Utah (Health and Beauty Aids) [14265]
Tuttle Enterprises Inc. (Toys and Hobby Goods) [26695]

Payson
Buttrey Food & Drug (Medical, Dental, and Optical Supplies) [19207]

Price
Andalex Resources, Inc. (Minerals and Ores) [20515]
Fairmont Supply Co. Western Operations (Industrial Supplies) [16856]

Providence
Aspen Data (Computers and Software) [5974]

Provo
Ahlander Wholesale Hardware Co. (Hardware) [13537]
Cedar Co. (Computers and Software) [6049]
Christensen Oil Co. (Petroleum, Fuels, and Related Equipment) [22138]
Crest Distributing Co. (Petroleum, Fuels, and Related Equipment) [22178]
Home Medical Supply Inc. (Medical, Dental, and Optical Equipment) [18840]
Interior Design Nutritionals (Health and Beauty Aids) [14131]
Interwest Safety Supply Inc. (Security and Safety Equipment) [24573]
Lantec Inc. (Computers and Software) [6428]
Nu Skin Enterprises Inc. (Medical, Dental, and Optical Supplies) [19503]
Nu Skin International Inc. (Health and Beauty Aids) [14181]
Peterson Oil Co. (Petroleum, Fuels, and Related Equipment) [22565]
Provo Craft Inc. (Textiles and Notions) [26181]
Silver Sage (Health and Beauty Aids) [14236]

Roy
Bernoulli Collection Inc. (Computers and Software) [6013]

St. George
Painter's Choice (Paints and Varnishes) [21531]
RMC Foods, Inc. (Food) [12327]

Salt Lake City
A and K Railroad Materials Inc. (Railroad Equipment and Supplies) [23471]
ABC Auto Paint Supply (Paints and Varnishes) [21373]
Advanced Petroleum Recycling Inc. (Petroleum, Fuels, and Related Equipment) [22024]
Affiliated Metals (Metals) [19735]
AG Truck Equipment Co. (Automotive) [2187]
Allen Steel Co. (Metals) [19748]
Allred's Inc. (Heating and Cooling Equipment and Supplies) [14315]
Alpine Supply (Hardware) [13553]
Alta Industries Ltd. (Metals) [19762]
Alta Paint & Coatings (Paints and Varnishes) [21383]
American Athletic Sales Inc. (Clothing) [4768]
Architectural Building Supply (Hardware) [13564]
Arnold Machinery Co. (Construction Materials and Machinery) [6989]
Arnold Machinery Co. (Construction Materials and Machinery) [6991]
Associated Food Stores Inc. (Food) [10447]
Associated Food Stores Inc. (Salt Lake City, Utah) (Food) [10448]
Atlas Steel Inc. (Used, Scrap, and Recycled Materials) [26755]
Bergen Brunswig Corp. (Medical, Dental, and Optical Supplies) [19183]
Bintz Distributing Co. (Restaurant and Commercial Foodservice Equipment and Supplies) [24076]
Blast-Spray Equipment Co. (Specialty Equipment and Products) [25575]
Boley Co.; Mel (Shoes) [24694]
Bonneville News Co. Inc. (Books and Other Printed Materials) [3563]
Bookcraft Inc. (Books and Other Printed Materials) [3575]
Bottman Design Inc. (Office Equipment and Supplies) [20850]
CableLink Inc. (Computers and Software) [6035]
Central Garden and Pet Supply Inc. (Agricultural Equipment and Supplies) [392]
Codale Electric Supply Inc. (Electrical and Electronic Equipment and Supplies) [8538]
Contempo Ceramic Tile (Floorcovering Equipment and Supplies) [9823]
Cream O' Weber (Food) [10864]
Crus Oil Inc. (Petroleum, Fuels, and Related Equipment) [22180]
Cummins Intermountain Inc. (Automotive) [2508]

Curtis Paint (Paints and Varnishes) [21423]

Cutie Pie Corp. (Food) [10887]

Davis County Cooperative Society (Shoes) [24724]

Delta Hi-Tech Inc. (Medical, Dental, and Optical Supplies) [19276]

Dentt Inc. (Toys and Hobby Goods) [26465]

Design Marketing Associates (Furniture and Fixtures) [13088]

Distribution Holdings Inc. (Household Appliances) [15111]

Domestic Import Tile (Floorcovering Equipment and Supplies) [9870]

Douglas Model Distributors (Toys and Hobby Goods) [26474]

Economy Builders Supply Inc. (Construction Materials and Machinery) [7302]

Edwards Co.; Frank (Automotive) [2576]

Edward's Pet Supplies Co. (Veterinary Products) [27125]

Eskay Corp. (Storage Equipment and Containers) [25913]

Exodus Computers, Inc. (Computers and Software) [6260]

Felt Auto Supply (Automotive) [2609]

Franklin Quest Co. (Computers and Software) [6281]

General Distributing Co. (Alcoholic Beverages) [1708]

H2O (Recreational and Sporting Goods) [23708]

Hammond Computer Inc. (Computers and Software) [6327]

Henderson Wheel and Warehouse Supply (Automotive) [2741]

Hi Grade Meats Inc. (Food) [11424]

Howmedica Mountain States, Inc. (Medical, Dental, and Optical Equipment) [18843]

I-O Corp. (Computers and Software) [6349]

Industrial Supply Co. (Industrial Machinery) [16154]

Industrial Supply Company Inc. (Salt Lake City, Utah) (Industrial Supplies) [16956]

Intermountain Farmers Association (Agricultural Equipment and Supplies) [861]

Intermountain Lea Findings Co. (Shoes) [24770]

Intermountain Lea Findings Co. (Clothing) [5056]

Intermountain Lumber Co. (Construction Materials and Machinery) [7516]

Intermountain Piper Inc. (Aeronautical Equipment and Supplies) [100]

Intermountain Wood Products (Wood and Wood Products) [27323]

International Optical Supply Co. (Medical, Dental, and Optical Supplies) [19377]

Interwest Home Medical Inc. (Medical, Dental, and Optical Equipment) [18862]

Interwest Medical Equipment Distributors Inc. (Medical, Dental, and Optical Equipment) [18863]

Jardine Petroleum Co. (Petroleum, Fuels, and Related Equipment) [22385]

JB Tile Co. (Floorcovering Equipment and Supplies) [9980]

Jordan Meat and Livestock Company Inc. (Food) [11564]

Ken-Son Inc. (Food) [11599]

Kenworth Sales Company Inc. (Motorized Vehicles) [20660]

Keyston Brothers (Textiles and Notions) [26093]

Koch-Bailey Associates (Household Items) [15554]

Kraft USA (Food) [11645]

Kwal-Howells Paint & Wallcovering (Paints and Varnishes) [21483]

Lawson-Yates Inc. (Plumbing Materials and Fixtures) [23241]

L.B.I. Company (Floorcovering Equipment and Supplies) [9993]

L.B.I. Company (Construction Materials and Machinery) [7589]

Levoy's (Clothing) [5132]

Mancini & Groesbeck, Inc. (Food) [11773]

Manware Inc. (Hardware) [13811]

Marker USA (Recreational and Sporting Goods) [23801]

Marshall Co.; A.W. (Food) [11789]

Marshall Distributing Co. (Food) [11790]

Marshall Industries (Electrical and Electronic Equipment and Supplies) [9040]

McKesson Drug (Medical, Dental, and Optical Supplies) [19432]

Medical Marketing Inc. (Medical, Dental, and Optical Equipment) [18919]

Metro Group Inc. (Used, Scrap, and Recycled Materials) [26907]

Midwest Office Furniture and Supply Company Inc. (Office Equipment and Supplies) [21143]

Mountain States Medical Inc. (Medical, Dental, and Optical Equipment) [18951]

Mountain States Supply Inc. (Plumbing Materials and Fixtures) [23280]

Muir-Roberts Company Inc. (Food) [11955]

Myers Associates; Vic (Computers and Software) [6540]

Nelson-Ricks Creamery Co. (Food) [11994]

Nice Computer Inc. (Computers and Software) [6553]

Nicholas and Co. (Food) [12005]

Norandex Sales Co. (Construction Materials and Machinery) [7789]

Novel-Tees Wholesale (Toys and Hobby Goods) [26596]

Number One International (Automotive) [3050]

Patrick Dry Goods Company Inc. (Textiles and Notions) [26168]

Peak Distributing Co. (Food) [12126]

Physicians Supply Co. (Medical, Dental, and Optical Equipment) [18989]

Plumbers Supply Co. (Plumbing Materials and Fixtures) [23321]

Pneumatrek, Inc. (Industrial Machinery) [16406]

Premium Oil Co. (Petroleum, Fuels, and Related Equipment) [22593]

Prime Coatings (Paints and Varnishes) [21546]

Rasmussen Equipment Co. (Construction Materials and Machinery) [7901]

Regional Supply Inc. (Plastics) [23025]

Robins Brokerage Co. (Food) [12331]

Robison Distributors Co. (Floorcovering Equipment and Supplies) [10127]

Rocky Mountain Machinery Co. (Construction Materials and Machinery) [7950]

Russells Ice Cream (Food) [12369]

Sabol and Rice Inc. (Heating and Cooling Equipment and Supplies) [14671]

Salco Inc. (Household Items) [15647]

Salt Lake Optical Inc. (Medical, Dental, and Optical Supplies) [19593]

Scott Machinery Co. (Industrial Machinery) [16474]

The Showroom (Textiles and Notions) [26204]

Signature Books Inc. (Books and Other Printed Materials) [4161]

Sinclair Oil Corp. (Petroleum, Fuels, and Related Equipment) [22673]

Six States Distributors (Automotive) [3226]

Smith Crown Co. (Sound and Entertainment Equipment and Supplies) [25446]

Smith Detroit Diesel Allison Inc. (Automotive) [3232]

SR Distributing (Sound and Entertainment Equipment and Supplies) [25463]

Standard Supply Co. (Sound and Entertainment Equipment and Supplies) [25464]

Struve Distributing Company Inc. (Specialty Equipment and Products) [25832]

Struve Distributing Company Inc. (Restaurant and Commercial Foodservice Equipment and Supplies) [24232]

Sundog Technologies (Computers and Software) [6772]

Suntuf USA (Plastics) [23038]

Sysco Intermountain Food Services Inc. (Food) [12690]

Technical Devices Co. (Electrical and Electronic Equipment and Supplies) [9469]

Tenet Information Service Inc. (Computers and Software) [6812]

United Electric Supply Co. (Salt Lake City, Utah) (Electrical and Electronic Equipment and Supplies) [9523]

United Optical Co. (Medical, Dental, and Optical Supplies) [19676]

United Service and Sales (Agricultural Equipment and Supplies) [1380]

Utah Wool Marketing Association (Livestock and Farm Products) [18309]

Valley Paint (Paints and Varnishes) [21598]

Wanke Cascade (Floorcovering Equipment and Supplies) [10285]

Western Dairymen Cooperative Inc. (Food) [12912]

Western Toy and Hobby Inc. (Toys and Hobby Goods) [26711]

Wilson Foods Company L.L.C. (Food) [12953]

Wilson Products Company Inc. (Food) [12955]

Wilson Supply Inc. (Agricultural Equipment and Supplies) [1454]

Zims Inc. (Toys and Hobby Goods) [26721]

Sandy

Aspen West Publishing Co. Inc. (Books and Other Printed Materials) [3527]

Clark Sales Co. (Jewelry) [17373]

Columbia Paint & Coatings (Paints and Varnishes) [21415]

Contract Appliance Sales Inc. (Sound and Entertainment Equipment and Supplies) [25148]

Pond International Inc. (Livestock and Farm Products) [18174]

Smithfield

R & R Mill Company (Household Appliances) [15287]

South Salt Lake

Devoe Paint (Paints and Varnishes) [21428]

Perschon Paint & Wallcovering (Paints and Varnishes) [21537]

Taylor & Sons, Inc.; Robert (Industrial Machinery) [16551]

Spanish Fork

Fritzi of Utah (Clothing) [4969]

Swenson Metal Salvage Inc. (Used, Scrap, and Recycled Materials) [27017]

Thompson

Arch Hunter Books and Canyon Country Distribution Services (Books and Other Printed Materials) [3524]

Tooele

Kellco & Associates (Household Appliances) [15185]

Tremonton

Golden Spike Equipment Co. (Agricultural Equipment and Supplies) [745]

Harris Truck Equipment Co.; Jay Dee (Motorized Vehicles) [20646]

West Jordan

Rodon Foods (Food) [12342]

West Valley City

Bromar Utah (Food) [10618]

Paint West Decor Center (Paints and Varnishes) [21530]

Ponderosa Paint Stores (Paints and Varnishes) [21543]

Woods Cross

Morrison Petroleum Company Inc. (Petroleum, Fuels, and Related Equipment) [22500]

Vermont

Barnet

Gilmou Inc.; Doug (Livestock and Farm Products) [17940]

Kendall; Dale B. (Livestock and Farm Products) [18033]

Barre

Knoll Motel (Cleaning and Janitorial Supplies) [4653]

Barton
North East Kingdom Sales, Inc. (Livestock and Farm Products) [18139]

Beecher Falls
Bruces Tire Ltd. (Automotive) [2399]

Bellows Falls
Cota and Cota Inc. (Petroleum, Fuels, and Related Equipment) [22174]

Bethel
Clifford of Vermont Inc. (Electrical and Electronic Equipment and Supplies) [8533]

Bomoseen
Brown Associates Inc.; Roger G. (Automotive) [2396]

Brattleboro
Brattleboro Auto Parts (Automotive) [2383]
C and S Wholesale Grocers Inc. (Food) [10657]
DeWitt Beverage (Alcoholic Beverages) [1648]
Nevitt; Stephen L. (Jewelry) [17532]
Northeast Cooperatives (Food) [12031]
Omega Optical, Inc. (Industrial Supplies) [17089]
Recycled Auto Parts of Brattleboro Inc. (Automotive) [3138]
Spring Tree Corp. (Food) [12557]
Wright Supplier (Automotive) [3448]

Brookfield
Ashgate Publishing Co. (Books and Other Printed Materials) [3526]

Burlington
All Season's Kitchen L.L.C. (Food) [10367]
Blodgett International Sales; G.S. (Restaurant and Commercial Foodservice Equipment and Supplies) [24077]
Burlington Futon Co. Inc. (Household Items) [15432]
Cambridge Engineering Inc. (Electrical and Electronic Equipment and Supplies) [8491]
Citizen's Distributors (Chemicals) [4360]
E & M Ice Cream Distributors (Food) [11007]
Empire Corporation (Cleaning and Janitorial Supplies) [4618]
Gardener's Supply Co. (Horticultural Supplies) [14872]
Greentree Productions Inc. (Photographic Equipment and Supplies) [22860]
Home & Garden Innovations (Agricultural Equipment and Supplies) [835]
Koplewitz; Jane (Jewelry) [17493]
Learning Materials Workshop (Toys and Hobby Goods) [26565]
Living Systems Instrumentation (Electrical and Electronic Equipment and Supplies) [8997]
Napa Auto Parts (Burlington, Vermont) (Hardware) [13842]
Noodle Head Network (Photographic Equipment and Supplies) [22884]
Only Once Inc. (Clothing) [5253]
Seventh Generation, Inc. (Paper and Paper Products) [21936]
Vermont Hardware Company Inc. (Sound and Entertainment Equipment and Supplies) [25501]
Video Products Distributors (Electrical and Electronic Equipment and Supplies) [9538]

Charlotte
Vermont Optechs (Scientific and Measurement Devices) [24452]
Williamson Publishing Co. (Books and Other Printed Materials) [4286]

Chester
Hunsdon; Vernon (Livestock and Farm Products) [18008]

Colchester
American Technotherm Corp. (Heating and Cooling Equipment and Supplies) [14320]
Bay Corp. (Shoes) [24685]

Champlain Winair Co. (Plumbing Materials and Fixtures) [23114]
Outer Bay Trading Co. (Horticultural Supplies) [14934]
Skis Dynastar Inc. (Recreational and Sporting Goods) [23945]

Dorset
Adams Company Inc.; J.K. (Wood and Wood Products) [27274]

East Fairfield
Snowbelt Insulation Company Inc. (Construction Materials and Machinery) [8038]

East Montpelier
South Pacific Wholesale (Jewelry) [17612]

Essex Junction
FoodScience Corp. (Food) [11183]

Fairlee
Britton Lumber Company Inc. (Construction Materials and Machinery) [7081]

Franklin
West; Reginald (Livestock and Farm Products) [18339]

Georgia
Vermont Whey Co. (Food) [12839]

Hardwick
Bailey's Slaughter House (Livestock and Farm Products) [17717]

Hinesburg
Iroquois Manufacturing Company, Inc. (Automotive) [2799]
Upper Access Books (Books and Other Printed Materials) [4253]
Upper Access Inc. (Books and Other Printed Materials) [4254]

Jamaica
Interstate Bingo Supplies Inc. (Toys and Hobby Goods) [26536]

Ludlow
Ludlow Telephone Company Inc. (Communications Systems and Equipment) [5663]

Lyndonville
AVK II Inc. (Restaurant and Commercial Foodservice Equipment and Supplies) [24073]

Manchester Center
Business World Inc. (Office Equipment and Supplies) [20871]

Middlebury
Addison County Commodity Sales (Livestock and Farm Products) [17676]
Green Mountain Tractor Inc. (Agricultural Equipment and Supplies) [763]

Milton
Burlington Drug Co. (Tobacco Products) [26268]
Collins; James (Construction Materials and Machinery) [7196]
Vermont Whey Co. (Food) [12838]

Montpelier
Green Mountain Florist Supply (Horticultural Supplies) [14877]

Morrisville
Hess; Charles (Automotive) [2746]
Miller Corp.; C.C. (Livestock and Farm Products) [18099]

Mt. Holly
Blais Enterprises; M.C. (Security and Safety Equipment) [24516]

Newport
Bogner of America Inc. (Clothing) [4832]
Lapierre; Bill (Paints and Varnishes) [21487]
Schoeller Textil USA Inc. (Textiles and Notions) [26199]
Wright; Ronald J. (Livestock and Farm Products) [18362]

North Bennington
Big Boys Toys (Automotive) [2359]

North Clarendon
Baker Distributing (Alcoholic Beverages) [1497]

North Ferrisburg
Do-My Ceramics (Toys and Hobby Goods) [26472]

North Pomfret
Trafalgar Square (Books and Other Printed Materials) [4226]

Northfield
Cabot Hosiery Mills Inc. (Clothing) [4856]

Norwich
King Arthur Flour Co. (Food) [11610]

Orleans
Orleans Commissions Sales (Livestock and Farm Products) [18156]

Poultney
Loomis Paint & Wallpaper Ctr (Paints and Varnishes) [21494]

Proctorsville
Earth Brothers Ltd. (Food) [11013]

Putney
Basketville Inc. (Gifts and Novelties) [13312]

Randolph
Vermont Pure Holdings Ltd. (Soft Drinks) [25047]

Richmond
Linn; John (Livestock and Farm Products) [18060]

Rutland
Damascus Worldwide, Inc. (Clothing) [4909]
Frank, Inc.; Sam (Tobacco Products) [26295]
Home & Farm Center Inc. (Household Appliances) [15170]
Lenco, Inc. (Medical, Dental, and Optical Supplies) [19409]
Lenco Inc. (Medical, Dental, and Optical Supplies) [19410]
McLaughlin Distributor; J.E. (Construction Materials and Machinery) [7686]
Mintzer Brothers Inc. (Construction Materials and Machinery) [7726]
Sanborn's Paint Spot Inc. (Paints and Varnishes) [21559]
Timco Jewelers Corp. (Jewelry) [17637]
Vermont Flower Exchange (Horticultural Supplies) [14971]

St. Albans
Bonnette Supply Co. (Construction Materials and Machinery) [7069]
Gallagher's Inc. (Livestock and Farm Products) [17932]
McCraken Livestock Inc. (Livestock and Farm Products) [18081]
St. Albans Commission Sales (Livestock and Farm Products) [18217]

St. Johnsbury
JDB Merchandising (Automotive) [2816]

Shaftsbury
Dailey Inc.; William E. (Construction Materials and Machinery) [7245]

Shelburne

Artec Distributing Inc. (Sound and Entertainment Equipment and Supplies) [25084]
Computer Products of Vermont Inc. (Computers and Software) [6121]

South Burlington

Burlington House Inc. (Furniture and Fixtures) [13052]
Farrell Distributing (Alcoholic Beverages) [1685]
Karhu USA Inc. (Recreational and Sporting Goods) [23769]
Vermont Pet Food & Supply (Veterinary Products) [27263]

South Royalton

Ferro Co.; Michael (Office Equipment and Supplies) [21002]

Springfield

Wiggins Concrete Products, Inc. (Floorcovering Equipment and Supplies) [10299]

Stowe

Amfib Fibers Ltd. (Textiles and Notions) [25962]

Swanton

Swanton Packing, Inc. (Food) [12653]
Woodshill Pool (Recreational and Sporting Goods) [24050]

Townshend

Janos Technology Inc. (Medical, Dental, and Optical Equipment) [18868]
Meyer Corp.; Mary (Toys and Hobby Goods) [26574]

Tunbridge

Anichini Inc. (Textiles and Notions) [25965]

Underhill

Green Mountain Foam Products (Specialty Equipment and Products) [25671]

Underhill Center

Rheinpfalz Imports Ltd. (Alcoholic Beverages) [1986]

Vergennes

Davison Co.; R.E. (Security and Safety Equipment) [24532]

Vernon

Stan's Towing & Repair (Automotive) [3261]

Waterbury

NewSound, LLC (Sound and Entertainment Equipment and Supplies) [25357]
NewSound L.L.C. (Household Appliances) [15248]

West Rutland

Cardinal Optics, Inc. (Medical, Dental, and Optical Supplies) [19213]

Weston

Vitriesse Glass Studio (Jewelry) [17647]

White River Junction

Chadwick Optical Inc. (Medical, Dental, and Optical Supplies) [19227]
Computer Concepts Inc. (Computers and Software) [6105]
Neita Product Management (Industrial Machinery) [16346]
White River Paper Company Inc. (Paper and Paper Products) [21991]
White River Paper Company Inc. (Industrial Supplies) [17278]

Williston

Blodgett Supply Co. Inc. (Household Appliances) [15054]
Catamount North (Automotive) [2434]
Cornell Trading Inc. (Clothing) [4895]

French Dressing Inc. (Shoes) [24748]
Griswold and Company Inc.; S.T. (Construction Materials and Machinery) [7419]
Norandex, Inc. (Construction Materials and Machinery) [7786]
Rossignol Ski Co. (Shoes) [24844]
SPL Associates Inc. (Heating and Cooling Equipment and Supplies) [14693]

Winooski

Sally's Flower Shop (Horticultural Supplies) [14946]

Woodstock

Longhill Partners Inc. (Jewelry) [17504]

Virginia

Abingdon

Dutt and Wagner of Virginia Inc. (Food) [11004]
EMP International Corp. (Medical, Dental, and Optical Equipment) [18790]
Food Country USA (Food) [11170]
Mid-Mountain Foods Inc. (Food) [11879]
Mountain Systems Inc. (Computers and Software) [6531]

Afton

Stelling Banjo Works Ltd. (Sound and Entertainment Equipment and Supplies) [25465]

Alexandria

Aitcheson Inc.; J and H (Plumbing Materials and Fixtures) [23055]
Allied Plywood Corp. (Construction Materials and Machinery) [6945]
Arcade Electronics Inc. (Electrical and Electronic Equipment and Supplies) [8368]
Boat America Corp. (Marine) [18465]
CADD Microsystems, Inc. (Computers and Software) [6039]
Capital Lighting & Supply Inc. (Electrical and Electronic Equipment and Supplies) [8497]
Computer Systems Supply Corp. (Computers and Software) [6129]
Fannon Petroleum Services Inc. (Petroleum, Fuels, and Related Equipment) [22251]
Forbes & Co. (Automotive) [2637]
LSI (Legacy Sports International LLC) (Guns and Weapons) [13500]
Mount Vernon Auto Parts (Automotive) [3000]
National Capital Flag Co. Inc. (Gifts and Novelties) [13407]
Summitville Fairfax (Floorcovering Equipment and Supplies) [10190]
Thomson-CSF Inc. (Electrical and Electronic Equipment and Supplies) [9486]
Time Life Inc. (Books and Other Printed Materials) [4219]
Virginia Imports (Alcoholic Beverages) [2106]
Zeroid and Company Inc. (Office Equipment and Supplies) [21372]

Altavista

Wakely; Austin B. (Computers and Software) [6859]

Arlington

Aanns Trading Co. (Chemicals) [4309]
Dominion Electric Supply Co. (Electrical and Electronic Equipment and Supplies) [8630]
MetaSystems Design Group Inc. (Communications Systems and Equipment) [5673]
Michel Company Inc.; R.E. (Heating and Cooling Equipment and Supplies) [14580]
Republic Group (Electrical and Electronic Equipment and Supplies) [9279]
Southern Commercial Machines (Specialty Equipment and Products) [25825]
Tennis Factory (Recreational and Sporting Goods) [24007]
US Airways Group Inc. (Aeronautical Equipment and Supplies) [166]

Ashland

Industrial Video Systems Inc. (Sound and Entertainment Equipment and Supplies) [25242]
RBI Corp. (Automotive) [3137]
South Central Pool Supply, Inc. (Recreational and Sporting Goods) [23969]

Bastian

General Injectables and Vaccines Inc. (Medical, Dental, and Optical Supplies) [19337]

Bedford

Bunker Hill Foods (Food) [10642]

Blacksburg

McDonald & Woodward Publishing (Books and Other Printed Materials) [3943]
Pocahontas Press Inc. (Books and Other Printed Materials) [4070]

Bluefield

AB Wholesale Co. (Hardware) [13521]
Ammar's Inc. (Toys and Hobby Goods) [26392]
Nash Finch/Bluefield (Food) [11968]

Bristol

Coca-Cola Bottling; Dixie (Soft Drinks) [24942]
Cowan Brothers Inc. (Cleaning and Janitorial Supplies) [4605]
Electric Motor Repair & Sales (Electrical and Electronic Equipment and Supplies) [8662]
Flay-O-Rich Inc. (Food) [11143]
Gurley's Georgia Carpet (Floorcovering Equipment and Supplies) [9929]
Helms Candy Company Inc. (Food) [11410]
Holston Steel Services (Metals) [20043]
J & M Wholesale Distributors (Toys and Hobby Goods) [26538]
Line Power Manufacturing Co. (Metals) [20131]
Moore's Quality Snack Foods Div. (Food) [11932]
Mountain Service Corp. (Toys and Hobby Goods) [26584]
Tenneva Food and Supplies Inc. (Food) [12707]
Virginia Wholesale Co. (Food) [12849]

Buffalo Junction

Aarons Creek Farms (Horticultural Supplies) [14792]

Capron

Barham and Co.; J.T. (Livestock and Farm Products) [17722]

Chantilly

Aardvark Swim & Sports Inc. (Clothing) [4738]
British Aerospace Holdings Inc. (Aeronautical Equipment and Supplies) [65]
British Aerospace North America Inc. (Aeronautical Equipment and Supplies) [66]
Color Me Beautiful Inc. (Health and Beauty Aids) [14068]
Comstor (Computers and Software) [6140]
Fairchild Communications Services Co. (Communications Systems and Equipment) [5608]
Government Technology Services Inc. (Computers and Software) [6306]
Kirby Forest Products; J. (Construction Materials and Machinery) [7559]

Charlottesville

Amvest Coal Sales Inc. (Minerals and Ores) [20514]
Blue Ridge Graphics Inc. (Clothing) [4829]
Lee Tennis, LLC (Recreational and Sporting Goods) [23783]
Michel Company Inc.; R.E. (Heating and Cooling Equipment and Supplies) [14581]
Precision Sports Surfaces Inc. (Recreational and Sporting Goods) [23897]
University Press of Virginia (Books and Other Printed Materials) [4250]

Chase City

Garrett III & Co. Inc.; J.W. (Recreational and Sporting Goods) [23685]

Chesapeake

Allied Boise Cascade (Paper and Paper Products) [21623]
Burton Lumber Corp. (Construction Materials and Machinery) [7115]
Central Meat Packing (Food) [10722]
Country Decor (Toys and Hobby Goods) [26450]
Davis Grain Corp. (Livestock and Farm Products) [17813]
E.C.A. Associates Press (Books and Other Printed Materials) [3713]
Executive Productivity Systems (Computers and Software) [6259]
Hughes Golf Inc.; Art (Recreational and Sporting Goods) [23735]
International Tile & Marble, Ltd. (Floorcovering Equipment and Supplies) [9967]
Site Concepts (Recreational and Sporting Goods) [23943]
Somerville Co.; Thomas (Plumbing Materials and Fixtures) [23390]

Chester

Tri City Electrical Supply Co. (Electrical and Electronic Equipment and Supplies) [9503]

Christiansburg

Michel Company Inc.; R.E. (Heating and Cooling Equipment and Supplies) [14582]

Collinsville

Self Service Grocery (Food) [12459]

Colonial Heights

Fiorucci Foods USA Inc. (Food) [11129]
PartsPort Ltd. (Computers and Software) [6594]

Covington

T & E Wholesale Outlet (Gifts and Novelties) [13460]

Culpeper

Merchants Grocery Co. (Food) [11855]

Danville

Dan Valley Foods, Inc. (Food) [10906]
DIMON Inc. (Horticultural Supplies) [14857]
Florimex Worldwide Inc. (Horticultural Supplies) [14868]

Diggs

Ocean Products Research, Inc. (Marine) [18576]

Dillwyn

Central VA Chimney (Heating and Cooling Equipment and Supplies) [14378]

Fairfax

AEA Distributors (Automotive) [2184]
Aquatronics Inc. (Electrical and Electronic Equipment and Supplies) [8367]
Brand Co. (Automotive) [2380]
Brooks Designer Rugs; J. (Floorcovering Equipment and Supplies) [9741]
Burgess Lighting and Distributing (Household Appliances) [15066]
Capitol Distributors (Floorcovering Equipment and Supplies) [9756]
Caporicci Footwear Ltd. (Shoes) [24706]
Chesapeake Rim and Wheel Distributors (Automotive) [2446]
CSM International Corp. (Computers and Software) [6168]
Eastland Screen Prints Inc. (Clothing) [4928]
Far East Trading Company Inc. (Aeronautical Equipment and Supplies) [86]
Information Analysis Inc. (Computers and Software) [6368]
Media Communications Corp. (Photographic Equipment and Supplies) [22877]
Modi Rubber Ltd. (Automotive) [2979]

Northstar Distributors (Alcoholic Beverages) [1924]
Sci-Rep Inc. (Electrical and Electronic Equipment and Supplies) [9344]
Somerville Co.; Thomas (Plumbing Materials and Fixtures) [23388]
Sundog Productions (Clothing) [5406]
Zeta Associates Inc. (Electrical and Electronic Equipment and Supplies) [9624]

Fairfax Station

Economy Maintenance Supply Company Inc. (Electrical and Electronic Equipment and Supplies) [8652]
Health Systems Technology Corp. (Computers and Software) [6330]
Healthcare Services International (Medical, Dental, and Optical Equipment) [18832]

Falls Church

Area Access Inc. (Medical, Dental, and Optical Equipment) [18689]
Area Access Inc. (Medical, Dental, and Optical Supplies) [19159]
Davic Drapery Co. (Household Items) [15467]
Federal Computer Corp. (Computers and Software) [6266]
Federal Systems Group Inc. (Computers and Software) [6267]
Mel Pinto Imports Inc. (Recreational and Sporting Goods) [23818]
Noland Co. (Heating and Cooling Equipment and Supplies) [14621]
Pinto Imports Inc.; Mel (Recreational and Sporting Goods) [23883]
Williams Industries Inc. (Construction Materials and Machinery) [8228]

Farmville

Farmers Cooperative Inc. (Agricultural Equipment and Supplies) [633]

Fredericksburg

Columbia Diagnostics Inc. (Medical, Dental, and Optical Equipment) [18747]
Euroven Corp. (Restaurant and Commercial Foodservice Equipment and Supplies) [24111]
Hollinger Corp. (Paper and Paper Products) [21764]
Michel Company Inc.; R.E. (Heating and Cooling Equipment and Supplies) [14583]
PSDI (Computers and Software) [6660]
US Lighting & Electrical Supply (Electrical and Electronic Equipment and Supplies) [9527]

Galax

Dixon Lumber Company Inc. (Construction Materials and Machinery) [7274]

Gate City

Addington Oil Co. (Petroleum, Fuels, and Related Equipment) [22021]

Glen Allen

Goldberg Company Inc. (Household Appliances) [15150]
Green Top Sporting Goods Inc. (Recreational and Sporting Goods) [23699]
McCullough Ceramic (Floorcovering Equipment and Supplies) [10014]
Office America Inc. (Office Equipment and Supplies) [21171]
Owens and Minor Inc. (Medical, Dental, and Optical Equipment) [18972]
Radio Communications Co. (Communications Systems and Equipment) [5729]

Great Falls

Girzen, Res. (Medical, Dental, and Optical Supplies) [19339]
Great Falls Business Services (Office Equipment and Supplies) [21020]

Grimstead

Dettor, Edwards & Morris (Alcoholic Beverages) [1647]

Grundy

American Carbon Corporation (Minerals and Ores) [20512]

Hampton

Amory and Company Inc.; L.D. (Food) [10408]
Bicknell-Tidewater Inc. (Recreational and Sporting Goods) [23557]
Gately Communication Company Inc. (Communications Systems and Equipment) [5617]
Gately Communications Company Inc. (Electrical and Electronic Equipment and Supplies) [8773]
Komer and Co. (Paints and Varnishes) [21476]
Lawson Seafood Company Inc. (Food) [11686]
Lawson and Son; E.T. (Petroleum, Fuels, and Related Equipment) [22420]
Little Brass Shack Imports (Gifts and Novelties) [13391]
Refrigeration Suppliers Inc. (Heating and Cooling Equipment and Supplies) [14659]

Harrisonburg

Choice Books (Books and Other Printed Materials) [3633]
Denton Enterprises Inc. (Communications Systems and Equipment) [5592]
Michel Company Inc.; R.E. (Heating and Cooling Equipment and Supplies) [14584]
RMC Inc. (Plumbing Materials and Fixtures) [23346]
Rocco Building Supplies Inc. (Construction Materials and Machinery) [7946]
Rockingham Cooperative Farm Bureau (Agricultural Equipment and Supplies) [1205]
Special Fleet Service (Automotive) [3245]
Truck Enterprises Inc. (Motorized Vehicles) [20739]
Truck Thermo King Inc. (Heating and Cooling Equipment and Supplies) [14739]
Wetsel, Inc. (Agricultural Equipment and Supplies) [1435]
Wetsel Inc. (Horticultural Supplies) [14975]

Hayes

York River Seafood Company Inc. (Food) [12995]

Herndon

Airbus Industry of North America Inc. (Aeronautical Equipment and Supplies) [34]
Ameru Trading Co. (Industrial Supplies) [16696]
Atlantic Microsystems Inc. (Office Equipment and Supplies) [20819]
NEC America Inc. (Communications Systems and Equipment) [5687]

Huddleston

Eagle Pointe Inc. (Clothing) [4926]

Kilmarnock

Rappahannock Seafood Company Inc. (Food) [12280]

Lebanon

Mikes Computerland (Computers and Software) [6518]

Leesburg

Barber and Ross Co. (Construction Materials and Machinery) [7020]

Lexington

HCI Corp./International Marketing Services (Medical, Dental, and Optical Equipment) [18831]
Rockbridge Farmers Cooperative (Agricultural Equipment and Supplies) [1204]

Lorton

Service Distributing (Alcoholic Beverages) [2019]

Lynchburg

AmeriSource-Lynchburg Div. (Medical, Dental, and Optical Supplies) [19151]
Barker-Jennings Corp. (Automotive) [2317]
Barker-Jennings Corp. (Hardware) [13584]

Campbell-Payne Inc. (Construction Materials and Machinery) [7131]

Carolina Hosiery Connection (Clothing) [4862]

Commonwealth Oil Co. Inc. (Petroleum, Fuels, and Related Equipment) [22155]

Consolidated Shoe Company Inc. (Shoes) [24719]

Database Computer Systems Inc. (Computers and Software) [6186]

Harrington Corp. (Plumbing Materials and Fixtures) [23203]

LWR Inc. (Clothing) [5148]

Michel Company Inc.; R.E. (Heating and Cooling Equipment and Supplies) [14585]

Stalling Inc. (Tobacco Products) [26352]

Top Comfo Athletic Sox Inc. (Clothing) [5434]

Westinghouse Electical Supply (Electrical and Electronic Equipment and Supplies) [9579]

Manassas

Aim Enterprises, Inc. (Aeronautical Equipment and Supplies) [32]

Battlefield Police Supply Inc. (Shoes) [24684]

Government Micro Resources Inc. (Computers and Software) [6305]

Manassas Ice and Fuel Company Inc. (Food) [11771]

Merchants Inc. (Automotive) [2943]

Noland Co. (Heating and Cooling Equipment and Supplies) [14622]

Tinder Inc.; W.M. (Wood and Wood Products) [27390]

VSS Inc. (Computers and Software) [6857]

Manassas Park

Michel Company Inc.; R.E. (Heating and Cooling Equipment and Supplies) [14586]

Mappsville

Eastern Shore Seafood (Food) [11017]

Marion

Copenhaver Industries Inc.; Laura (Household Items) [15455]

Evans Distributing Company Inc. (Alcoholic Beverages) [1680]

Family Shoe Center (Shoes) [24740]

Marley Mouldings Inc. (Construction Materials and Machinery) [7643]

McLean

Imagex Inc. (Computers and Software) [6356]

Iverson P.C. Warehouse Inc. (Computers and Software) [6401]

Zumot and Son (Alcoholic Beverages) [2146]

Mechanicsville

Adams & Durvin Marine Inc. (Recreational and Sporting Goods) [23495]

Alliance Agronomics Inc. (Agricultural Equipment and Supplies) [225]

Specialty Marketing Inc. (Sound and Entertainment Equipment and Supplies) [25459]

Weil Inc.; Cliff (Office Equipment and Supplies) [21352]

Wright Brokerage Inc. (Food) [12987]

Merrifield

Filter Fresh of Northern Virginia Inc. (Household Items) [15496]

Midlothian

ABB Power Generation (Industrial Machinery) [15723]

Amics International Inc. (Scientific and Measurement Devices) [24311]

E & R Sales Inc. (Gifts and Novelties) [13350]

Moates Sport Shop Inc.; Bob (Guns and Weapons) [13502]

Reed Inc.; Schweichert (Jewelry) [17558]

Somerville Co.; Thomas (Plumbing Materials and Fixtures) [23389]

Mineral

Walton Lumber Company Inc. (Construction Materials and Machinery) [8195]

Montross

Miller Lumber Industries Inc. (Construction Materials and Machinery) [7716]

Montrose Hardwood Company Inc. (Construction Materials and Machinery) [7741]

Mt. Jackson

Valley Fertilizer and Chemical Company Inc. (Agricultural Equipment and Supplies) [1394]

New Castle

Necessary Organics Inc. (Agricultural Equipment and Supplies) [1066]

Newport News

C and F Enterprises (Textiles and Notions) [25993]

Ferguson Enterprises, Inc. (Heating and Cooling Equipment and Supplies) [14445]

Ferguson Enterprises Inc. (Plumbing Materials and Fixtures) [23164]

International Tile & Marble Ltd. (Floorcovering Equipment and Supplies) [9968]

JNT Corporation (Clothing) [5089]

Liebherr-America Inc. (Construction Materials and Machinery) [7604]

Liebherr Construction Equipment Co. (Construction Materials and Machinery) [7605]

Liebherr Mining Equipment Co. (Construction Materials and Machinery) [7606]

Lindox Equipment Corp. (Restaurant and Commercial Foodservice Equipment and Supplies) [24166]

Microhelp Inc. (Computers and Software) [6503]

Noland Co. (Plumbing Materials and Fixtures) [23290]

Peebles Supply Div. (Plumbing Materials and Fixtures) [23310]

Peninsula Supply Company Inc. (Construction Materials and Machinery) [7846]

Norfolk

AES of Norfolk Inc. (Heating and Cooling Equipment and Supplies) [14300]

Allpro Corp. (Paints and Varnishes) [21380]

B & S Bolts Corp. (Hardware) [13579]

Baker's Fine Jewelry and Gifts (Jewelry) [17325]

Boyd-Bluford Co. Inc. (Food) [10602]

Broudy-Kantor Co. Inc. (Alcoholic Beverages) [1552]

Camellia Food Stores Inc. (Food) [10683]

Cardinal State Fasteners (Industrial Machinery) [15875]

Carolina Building Co. (Construction Materials and Machinery) [7142]

Central Wholesale Supply Corp. (Construction Materials and Machinery) [7162]

Continental Trading Co. Inc. (Medical, Dental, and Optical Supplies) [19251]

Custom Healthcare Systems (Medical, Dental, and Optical Supplies) [19264]

Door Engineering Corp. (Construction Materials and Machinery) [7280]

Empire Machinery and Supply Co. (Hardware) [13683]

Gateway Distributors Inc. (Floorcovering Equipment and Supplies) [9913]

Globe Iron Construction Company Inc. (Metals) [20009]

Hale & Associates; Robert (Sound and Entertainment Equipment and Supplies) [25223]

Henco Inc. (Shoes) [24762]

Land-N-Sea—Norfolk (Marine) [18543]

Lee Company Inc.; George G. (Plumbing Materials and Fixtures) [23244]

Michel Company Inc.; R.E. (Heating and Cooling Equipment and Supplies) [14588]

Miller Oil Co. (Petroleum, Fuels, and Related Equipment) [22486]

Morris Tile Distributors of Norfolk, Inc. (Floorcovering Equipment and Supplies) [10062]

Nesson Meat Sales (Food) [11996]

Nesson Sales (Toys and Hobby Goods) [26591]

Norfolk Bearing & Supply Co. (Industrial Supplies) [17075]

Paxton Company Inc. (Marine) [18582]

Pottery Art Studio Inc. (Specialty Equipment and Products) [25788]

Sun Electrical Appliance Sales & Service (Household Appliances) [15322]

Taylor-Parker Co. (Industrial Supplies) [17213]

Virginia Materials (Industrial Machinery) [16603]

Watters and Martin Inc. (Hardware) [13985]

North Tazewell

Tazewell Farm Bureau Inc. (Agricultural Equipment and Supplies) [1318]

Norton

AT&T Business Markets Group Div. (Communications Systems and Equipment) [5520]

Petersburg

Arnold Pen Co. Inc. (Office Equipment and Supplies) [20810]

Delta Oil Company Inc. (Petroleum, Fuels, and Related Equipment) [22194]

Michel Company Inc.; R.E. (Heating and Cooling Equipment and Supplies) [14589]

Petersburg Box and Lumber Inc. (Wood and Wood Products) [27358]

Portsmouth

Doughtie's Foods Inc. (Food) [10984]

Michel Company Inc.; R.E. (Heating and Cooling Equipment and Supplies) [14590]

Morse Parker Motor Supply (Automotive) [2987]

Sales Systems Ltd. (Hardware) [13900]

Smithfield Companies Inc. (Food) [12518]

Western Branch Diesel Inc. (Industrial Machinery) [16625]

Williams Inc.; T.O. (Food) [12948]

Pound

Ambrose Branch Coal Co. Inc. (Minerals and Ores) [20511]

Purcellville

Browning Equipment Inc. (Agricultural Equipment and Supplies) [343]

Radford

Harvey Chevrolet Corp. (Automotive) [2729]

Reston

Apple Computer Inc. Federal Systems Group (Computers and Software) [5945]

Coroant Inc. (Computers and Software) [6160]

DynAir Fueling Inc. (Petroleum, Fuels, and Related Equipment) [22216]

Lafarge Corp. (Construction Materials and Machinery) [7576]

Lloyd Ltd.; Reston (Paints and Varnishes) [21493]

Maryland and Virginia Milk Producers Cooperative Association Inc. (Food) [11799]

Meridian Synapse Corporation (Medical, Dental, and Optical Equipment) [18930]

Midway Trading, Inc. (Automotive) [2958]

Reston Lloyd Ltd. (Paints and Varnishes) [21556]

SPOT Image Corp. (Communications Systems and Equipment) [5766]

Wheat International Communications Corp. (Electrical and Electronic Equipment and Supplies) [9581]

Richmond

Acoustical Solutions, Inc. (Construction Materials and Machinery) [6910]

AFGD (Construction Materials and Machinery) [6923]

Atlantic Construction Fabrics Inc. (Construction Materials and Machinery) [7003]

Automatic Equipment Sales of Virginia Inc. (Heating and Cooling Equipment and Supplies) [14330]

Avec Electronics Corp. (Electrical and Electronic Equipment and Supplies) [8401]

Baker Distributing Co. (Heating and Cooling Equipment and Supplies) [14334]
Blu-Ridge Sales Inc. (Heating and Cooling Equipment and Supplies) [14349]
BMG Metals Inc. (Metals) [19828]
Buhrman and Son Inc. (Agricultural Equipment and Supplies) [351]
Cavalier Fabrics, Ltd./Redrum (Textiles and Notions) [25998]
Central Diesel, Inc. (Automotive) [2438]
Central Virginia Medical Inc. (Medical, Dental, and Optical Equipment) [18733]
Crenshaw Corp. (Automotive) [2494]
Dalco International, Inc. (Medical, Dental, and Optical Equipment) [18763]
Dees Fluid Power (Industrial Supplies) [16824]
Deli Universal Inc. (Tobacco Products) [26287]
Design Carpets (Floorcovering Equipment and Supplies) [9856]
Eck Supply Co. (Electrical and Electronic Equipment and Supplies) [8649]
FEMCO Corp. (Recreational and Sporting Goods) [23664]
Fidus Instrument Corp. (Electrical and Electronic Equipment and Supplies) [8740]
Florig Equipment (Automotive) [2633]
Flowers School Equipment Company Inc. (Furniture and Fixtures) [13114]
Gardners Shoes Inc. (Shoes) [24749]
General Medical Corp. (Medical, Dental, and Optical Equipment) [18807]
Hohner, Inc./HSS (Sound and Entertainment Equipment and Supplies) [25234]
Imaging Concepts Inc. (Medical, Dental, and Optical Equipment) [18849]
Industrial Supply Corp. (Industrial Supplies) [16958]
James River Coal Sales, Inc. (Minerals and Ores) [20548]
Kitchen Specialties Inc. (Household Items) [15550]
KSB Inc. (Industrial Machinery) [16222]
Lansing Corp.; Ted (Construction Materials and Machinery) [7586]
Lewis Supply Company Inc. (Plumbing Materials and Fixtures) [23246]
Massey Builders Supply Corp. (Construction Materials and Machinery) [7663]
Massey Coal Company Inc.; A.T. (Minerals and Ores) [20552]
Massey Wood and West Inc. (Petroleum, Fuels, and Related Equipment) [22455]
McGraw Inc.; James (Industrial Supplies) [17023]
McGraw Inc.; James (Industrial Machinery) [16278]
McKesson General Medical Corp. (Medical, Dental, and Optical Equipment) [18905]
Michel Company Inc.; R.E. (Heating and Cooling Equipment and Supplies) [14591]
Morris Tile Distributors of Richmond (Floorcovering Equipment and Supplies) [10063]
Mosaic Tile (Floorcovering Equipment and Supplies) [10065]
Nance Corp. (Industrial Machinery) [16337]
National Propane Corp. (Petroleum, Fuels, and Related Equipment) [22506]
National Propane SGP Inc. (Petroleum, Fuels, and Related Equipment) [22507]
Nott Co.; Frank H. (Used, Scrap, and Recycled Materials) [26927]
Oxygen Co. Inc. (Medical, Dental, and Optical Equipment) [18973]
Peck Recycling Co. (Used, Scrap, and Recycled Materials) [26937]
Performance Food Group Co. (Food) [12150]
Philip Morris Products Inc. (Tobacco Products) [26339]
Pioneer Machinery (Wood and Wood Products) [27360]
Pioneer Machinery (Construction Materials and Machinery) [7866]
Pocahontas Foods USA Inc. (Food) [12186]
Reynolds Aluminum Supply Co. (Metals) [20318]
Reynolds Metals Co. Construction Products Div. (Construction Materials and Machinery) [7925]
Rich Planned Foods (Food) [12311]
Richfood Holdings Inc. (Food) [12315]

Richfood Inc. (Food) [12316]
Richmond Foundry Inc. (Plumbing Materials and Fixtures) [23342]
Richmond Machinery and Equipment Inc. (Construction Materials and Machinery) [7931]
Richmond Office Supply (Office Equipment and Supplies) [21243]
River Petroleum Inc.; James (Petroleum, Fuels, and Related Equipment) [22633]
S and M Equipment Company Corp. (Construction Materials and Machinery) [7969]
Saunders Oil Company Inc. (Construction Materials and Machinery) [7982]
Sealey Optical Co. (Medical, Dental, and Optical Supplies) [19601]
Showstopper Exhibits Inc. (Specialty Equipment and Products) [25814]
Sims Metal America - Structural Steel Div. (Used, Scrap, and Recycled Materials) [26993]
Southern Distributors Inc. (Household Items) [15662]
Southern Specialty Corp. (Construction Materials and Machinery) [8052]
Southern States Cooperative Inc. (Agricultural Equipment and Supplies) [1282]
Southern States Cooperative Inc. (Agricultural Equipment and Supplies) [1283]
Standard Parts Corp. (Automotive) [3260]
Steel Services Inc. (Metals) [20399]
The Supply Room Companies, Inc. (Office Equipment and Supplies) [21305]
Sydnor Hydrodynamics Inc. (Industrial Machinery) [16542]
Taylor and Sledd Inc. (Food) [12701]
Transmission Products, Inc. (Industrial Supplies) [17233]
United Paper Company Inc. (Paper and Paper Products) [21976]
United Paper Company Inc. (Industrial Supplies) [17242]
U.S. Filter/Diversified Engineering (Computers and Software) [6842]
Universal Corp. (Tobacco Products) [26365]
Universal Leaf Tobacco Company Inc. (Tobacco Products) [26366]
UTECO Inc. (Agricultural Equipment and Supplies) [1389]
Vamac Inc. (Plumbing Materials and Fixtures) [23430]
Virginia Food Service Group (Food) [12848]
Whitby Pharmaceuticals Inc. (Medical, Dental, and Optical Supplies) [19702]
Whitlock Group (Computers and Software) [6870]
Work Duds (Shoes) [24899]

Roanoke

Advance Stores Company Inc. (Automotive) [2183]
AES of Roanoke Inc. (Heating and Cooling Equipment and Supplies) [14302]
ANR Coal Company L.L.C. (Minerals and Ores) [20517]
BellSouth Communication Systems Inc. (Communications Systems and Equipment) [5530]
Classic Flooring Distributors (Floorcovering Equipment and Supplies) [9810]
CMT Sporting Goods Co. (Recreational and Sporting Goods) [23596]
Commonwealth Tool Specialty Inc. (Industrial Supplies) [16804]
Dayman USA Inc. (Recreational and Sporting Goods) [23616]
Design Accessories Inc. (Jewelry) [17394]
Design Distributing (Floorcovering Equipment and Supplies) [9857]
Fluid-Tech, Inc. (Industrial Machinery) [16023]
General Truck Body Co. (Automotive) [2675]
Gessler Publishing Company, Inc. (Books and Other Printed Materials) [3778]
Hartman & Sons Equipment; Lee (Sound and Entertainment Equipment and Supplies) [25227]
HC Supply (Construction Materials and Machinery) [7463]
Interstate Electric Supply (Electrical and Electronic Equipment and Supplies) [8897]

Marco Supply Company Inc. (Hardware) [13812]
Michel Company Inc.; R.E. (Heating and Cooling Equipment and Supplies) [14592]
Morris Tile Distributors of Roanoke, Inc. (Floorcovering Equipment and Supplies) [10064]
Optical Cable Corp. (Electrical and Electronic Equipment and Supplies) [9159]
Parts Depot Company L.P. (Automotive) [3082]
Passport Furniture (Furniture and Fixtures) [13205]
Petroleum Marketers Inc. (Petroleum, Fuels, and Related Equipment) [22568]
Pocahontas Welding Supply Co. (Industrial Machinery) [16408]
Professional Ophthalmic Labs Inc. (Medical, Dental, and Optical Supplies) [19556]
Radio Communications Company Inc. (Communications Systems and Equipment) [5731]
Roanoke Distributing Company Inc. (Alcoholic Beverages) [1995]
Schroeder Optical Company Inc. (Medical, Dental, and Optical Supplies) [19598]
Shepherd's Auto Supply Inc. (Automotive) [3216]
Southeastern Optical Corp. (Medical, Dental, and Optical Supplies) [19623]
Southeastern Skate Supply of Virginia Inc. (Recreational and Sporting Goods) [23971]
Southern Refrigeration Corp. (Heating and Cooling Equipment and Supplies) [14692]
Transmission Products, Inc. (Industrial Supplies) [17234]
Virginia Construction Supply Inc. (Construction Materials and Machinery) [8185]
Virginia Industrial Cleaners and Equipment Co. (Cleaning and Janitorial Supplies) [4724]
Webb's Oil Corp. (Petroleum, Fuels, and Related Equipment) [22788]
Williams Supply Inc. (Electrical and Electronic Equipment and Supplies) [9597]

Rocky Mount

Central Oil of Virginia Corp. (Petroleum, Fuels, and Related Equipment) [22127]
Shredded Products Corp. (Used, Scrap, and Recycled Materials) [26988]

Salem

Blue Ridge Sporting Supplies (Recreational and Sporting Goods) [23561]
U.S. Foodservice - RRS Div. (Food) [12802]
Valley Tile Distributors (Floorcovering Equipment and Supplies) [10268]

Sandston

Waco Inc. (Metals) [20477]

Sedley

Hubbard Peanut Company Inc. (Food) [11471]

Smithfield

Smithfield Ham Products Co. Inc. (Food) [12519]

South Boston

Fisher Auto Parts Inc. (Automotive) [2620]

South Hill

Parker Oil Company Inc. (Petroleum, Fuels, and Related Equipment) [22551]

Speedwell

Javatec Inc. (Electrical and Electronic Equipment and Supplies) [8908]

Springfield

A & A Reconditioned Medical (Medical, Dental, and Optical Equipment) [18651]
Allied Electronics (Electrical and Electronic Equipment and Supplies) [8324]
Forman Distributing Co. (Alcoholic Beverages) [1695]
Galliher and Brother Inc.; W.T. (Construction Materials and Machinery) [7374]
Guiffre Distributing Co.; Tony (Alcoholic Beverages) [1735]

LogEtronics Corp. (Office Equipment and
    Supplies) [21111]
Moniteq Research Labs, Inc. (Security and Safety
    Equipment) [24596]
Moniteq Research Labs Inc. (Electrical and
    Electronic Equipment and Supplies) [9094]
Mosaic Tile Co. (Floorcovering Equipment and
    Supplies) [10066]
Nataraj Books (Books and Other Printed
    Materials) [3982]
Northern Virginia Beverage Co. (Alcoholic
    Beverages) [1923]
Potomac Steel and Supply Inc. (Metals) [20290]
Reico Distributors Inc. (Construction Materials and
    Machinery) [7909]
Telecommunications Concepts Inc. (Communications
    Systems and Equipment) [5784]

Stafford
Officers Equipment Co. (Clothing) [5249]

Staunton
Augusta Cooperative Farm Bureau (Agricultural
    Equipment and Supplies) [262]
Fisher Auto Parts Inc. (Automotive) [2621]
Staunton Food Inc. (Food) [12579]

Sterling
Diamond Paper Corp. (Paper and Paper
    Products) [21707]
Heckler and Koch Inc. (Guns and
    Weapons) [13494]
Laser-Scan Inc. (Computers and Software) [6429]
Saab Aircraft of America Inc. (Aeronautical
    Equipment and Supplies) [145]

Suffolk
Birdsong Corp. (Food) [10557]
Golden State Foods Corp. (Food) [11287]
Hines Inc.; Angus I. (Petroleum, Fuels, and Related
    Equipment) [22354]
Nansemond Ford Tractor Inc. (Agricultural
    Equipment and Supplies) [1064]
Pond Brothers Peanut Company
    Inc. (Food) [12191]
Pruden Packing Company Inc. (Food) [12233]
Saunders Supply Company Inc. (Construction
    Materials and Machinery) [7983]
Tidewater Wholesalers Inc. (Cleaning and Janitorial
    Supplies) [4717]

Tasley
Accawmacke Ornamentals (Horticultural
    Supplies) [14793]
Michel Company Inc.; R.E. (Heating and Cooling
    Equipment and Supplies) [14593]

Tazewell
Candlewax Smokeless Fuel Company Inc. (Minerals
    and Ores) [20527]

Trevilians
Maiden Music (Sound and Entertainment Equipment
    and Supplies) [25299]

Vansant
Vansant Lumber (Construction Materials and
    Machinery) [8172]

Verona
JRB Corp of Lynchburg (Alcoholic
    Beverages) [1790]

Vienna
Allied International Marketing Corp. (Livestock and
    Farm Products) [17692]
Allied International Marketing Corp. (Agricultural
    Equipment and Supplies) [226]
American Business Concepts (Office Equipment
    and Supplies) [20789]
Audubon Prints & Books (Books and Other Printed
    Materials) [3532]
Comsel Corp. (Computers and Software) [6139]
Martha Weems Ltd. (Gifts and Novelties) [13398]

Michel Company Inc.; R.E. (Heating and Cooling
    Equipment and Supplies) [14587]
Old Dominion Export-Import Co.
    Inc. (Food) [12060]
Paragram Sales Co. Inc. (Computers and
    Software) [6586]

Virginia Beach
Absolute Bottled Water Co. (Soft Drinks) [24905]
Allied Electronics (Electrical and Electronic
    Equipment and Supplies) [8325]
AWD International Inc. (Furniture and
    Fixtures) [13028]
Book Distribution Center, Inc. (Books and Other
    Printed Materials) [3568]
Care-A-Lot (Veterinary Products) [27101]
Chesapeake Gun Works (Recreational and Sporting
    Goods) [23591]
The Christian Broadcasting Network, Inc. (Books
    and Other Printed Materials) [3635]
Consolidated Foodservice Companies
    L.P. (Food) [10817]
Densons Sound Systems Inc. (Sound and
    Entertainment Equipment and Supplies) [25165]
Desfosses and Associates; John J. (Computers and
    Software) [6199]
Equity Industries Corp. (Household Items) [15490]
Evans Inc. (Heating and Cooling Equipment and
    Supplies) [14436]
Holland Corp.; J. Henry (Metals) [20042]
HRS Corp. (Heating and Cooling Equipment and
    Supplies) [14489]
London Bridge Trading Company Ltd. (Recreational
    and Sporting Goods) [23792]
Merit Marketing Inc. (Clothing) [5185]
Michel Company Inc.; R.E. (Heating and Cooling
    Equipment and Supplies) [14594]
MMC Metrology Lab Inc. (Scientific and
    Measurement Devices) [24401]
Mohawk Marketing Corp. (Sound and Entertainment
    Equipment and Supplies) [25332]
New City Optical Company Inc. (Medical, Dental,
    and Optical Supplies) [19490]
Norfolk Wire and Electronics Inc. (Communications
    Systems and Equipment) [5691]
PCI Rutherford Controls Intl. Corp. (Electrical and
    Electronic Equipment and Supplies) [9183]
Penrod Co. (Construction Materials and
    Machinery) [7850]
Rutherford Controls Int'l. (Security and Safety
    Equipment) [24619]
Sandler Foods (Restaurant and Commercial
    Foodservice Equipment and Supplies) [24214]
Select Security Inc. (Security and Safety
    Equipment) [24632]
Virginia Beach Beverages (Soft Drinks) [25048]

Warrenton
BMI Equipment Dist. (Heating and Cooling
    Equipment and Supplies) [14350]
Clark's Gun Shop (Guns and Weapons) [13481]
Noland Co. (Heating and Cooling Equipment and
    Supplies) [14623]

Waynesboro
Hathaway Paper Co. (Paper and Paper
    Products) [21756]
Industrial Supply Corp. (Industrial
    Supplies) [16957]

West McLean
Gemmex Intertrade America Inc. (Food) [11247]
Washington Tysons Golf Center (Recreational and
    Sporting Goods) [24040]

West Point
Old Dominion Grain Corp. (Livestock and Farm
    Products) [18154]

Williamsburg
Michel Company Inc.; R.E. (Heating and Cooling
    Equipment and Supplies) [14595]
Southern Company Inc. (Petroleum, Fuels, and
    Related Equipment) [22682]
Wacker Chemical Corp. (Electrical and Electronic
    Equipment and Supplies) [9549]

Willis Wharf
Terry Bros. Inc. (Food) [12708]

Winchester
Dearing Beverage Company Inc. (Alcoholic
    Beverages) [1637]
Dixie Beverage Co. (Alcoholic Beverages) [1654]
Global Telecommunications (Communications
    Systems and Equipment) [5620]
Hester Industries Inc. Pierce Foods
    Div. (Food) [11422]
Mad Bomber Co. (Clothing) [5150]
McDonald Farms, Inc. (Food) [11824]
Metropolitan Medical Inc. (Medical, Dental, and
    Optical Equipment) [18933]
Moffett Co.; Preston I. (Alcoholic
    Beverages) [1886]
Schenck Foods Company Inc. (Food) [12426]
Shenandoah Foods, Inc. (Food) [12477]
Technicom Corp. (Communications Systems and
    Equipment) [5778]
Winchester Equipment Co. (Industrial
    Machinery) [16639]
Winchester Sutler (Toys and Hobby
    Goods) [26713]
Zuckerman, Charles and Son Inc. (Metals) [20505]

Woodbridge
Independent Photocopy Inc. (Office Equipment and
    Supplies) [21055]

Wytheville
Itco Tire Co. (Automotive) [2803]
Magnetic Technology (Electrical and Electronic
    Equipment and Supplies) [9019]
Power Equipment Corp. (Electrical and Electronic
    Equipment and Supplies) [9222]

Yorktown
McBroom Pool Products Inc. (Recreational and
    Sporting Goods) [23813]

Washington

Aberdeen
Grays Harbor Equipment Inc. (Industrial
    Machinery) [16075]

Airway Heights
Ad-Shir-Tizing Inc. (Clothing) [4749]

Algona
Dynacraft Co. (Motorized Vehicles) [20631]

Arlington
Clark-Schwebel Distribution Corp. (Construction
    Materials and Machinery) [7176]
Deep See Products Inc. (Recreational and Sporting
    Goods) [23617]
Trace Engineering (Automotive) [3323]

Auburn
Central Garden & Pet Supply Inc. (Veterinary
    Products) [27107]
Connect Air International Inc. (Industrial
    Supplies) [16806]
Farwest Equipment, Inc. (Agricultural Equipment
    and Supplies) [673]
Jet Equipment and Tools (Aeronautical Equipment
    and Supplies) [108]
N.R.G. Enterprises, Inc. (Specialty Equipment and
    Products) [25766]
N.R.G. Enterprises Inc. (Plumbing Materials and
    Fixtures) [23300]
NutraSource Inc. (Food) [12047]
PGL Building Products (Construction Materials and
    Machinery) [7856]
Sarco Inc. (Restaurant and Commercial
    Foodservice Equipment and Supplies) [24215]
Seatronics Inc. (Security and Safety
    Equipment) [24627]
Tims Cascade Style Chips (Food) [12723]

Westmed Specialties Inc. (Medical, Dental, and Optical Equipment) [19108]

Bainbridge Island
Five Star Trading Company (Hardware) [13708]

Bellevue
Aronson-Campbell Industrial Supply Inc. (Industrial Machinery) [15780]
Arrow Electronics Inc. Almac/Arrow Electronics Div. (Computers and Software) [5965]
Barclay Dean Interiors (Furniture and Fixtures) [13032]
BEAR Computers Inc. (Computers and Software) [6007]
Brigadoon.Com Inc. (Computers and Software) [6025]
CMS Casuals Inc. (Clothing) [4884]
Computers & Applications Inc. (Computers and Software) [6133]
Cost-U-Less (Food) [10847]
ECS Marketing Services Inc. (Heating and Cooling Equipment and Supplies) [14428]
Fibres International Inc. (Used, Scrap, and Recycled Materials) [26813]
Fumoto Engineering of America (Automotive) [2657]
General Microsystems Inc. (Bellevue, Washington) (Computers and Software) [6298]
Hunt & Associates; Robert W. (Computers and Software) [6346]
La Pointique International (Medical, Dental, and Optical Equipment) [18879]
North Coast Electric Co. (Electrical and Electronic Equipment and Supplies) [9133]
Northwest Designs Ink Inc. (Clothing) [5242]
PACCAR International (Automotive) [3071]
PACCAR Leasing Corp. (Automotive) [3072]
Pascal Company Inc. (Medical, Dental, and Optical Supplies) [19527]
PowerData Corp. (Computers and Software) [6630]
PWI Technologies (Computers and Software) [6666]
R and D Industries Inc. (Computers and Software) [6673]
Special Purpose Systems Inc. (Computers and Software) [6753]
Stusser Electric Co. (Electrical and Electronic Equipment and Supplies) [9429]
Sylvias Swimwear-Swim Shop (Clothing) [5413]
Topline Corp. (Shoes) [24878]
Unicen Wastewater Treatment Co. (Specialty Equipment and Products) [25852]
Western Cascade Equipment Co. (Household Appliances) [15370]

Bellingham
Baron Telecommunications (Communications Systems and Equipment) [5525]
Borstein Seafood Inc. (Food) [10594]
Business Computer Solutions (Computers and Software) [6027]
Gensco, Inc. (Heating and Cooling Equipment and Supplies) [14469]
IMT Inc. (Industrial Machinery) [16146]
LFS Inc. (Marine) [18547]
L.P.S. Records, Inc. (Sound and Entertainment Equipment and Supplies) [25293]
Morse Distribution Inc. (Industrial Supplies) [17053]
Northwest Foods (Food) [12037]
Radar Marine Electronics (Marine) [18589]
S & W Investments (Clothing) [5328]
Seafood Producers Cooperative (Food) [12448]
Stusser Electric Co. (Electrical and Electronic Equipment and Supplies) [9430]
Washington Loggers Corp. (Wood and Wood Products) [27393]

Black Diamond
Anesthesia Equipment Supply (Medical, Dental, and Optical Equipment) [18685]

Blaine
Bar Code Applications Inc. (Electrical and Electronic Equipment and Supplies) [8414]

Hancock House Publishers (Books and Other Printed Materials) [3810]
HHS USA Inc. (Gifts and Novelties) [13366]
Sea K. Fish Company Inc. (Food) [12443]

Bothell
ADEMCO/ADI (Security and Safety Equipment) [24475]
Commercial Office Supply Inc. (Office Equipment and Supplies) [20907]
Conductive Rubber Tech Inc. (Computers and Software) [6148]
M & L Trading Company, Inc. (Food) [11751]
Puget Sound Data Systems Inc. (Computers and Software) [6663]
Rykoff-Sexton Inc. (Restaurant and Commercial Foodservice Equipment and Supplies) [24212]

Bremerton
Fitzgerald Ltd. (Agricultural Equipment and Supplies) [690]
Stusser Electric Co. (Electrical and Electronic Equipment and Supplies) [9431]

Brewster
Magi Inc. (Food) [11758]

Browns Point
Michelle International, Ltd. (Aeronautical Equipment and Supplies) [127]

Burlington
Hansen and Peterson Inc. (Agricultural Equipment and Supplies) [787]
Northwest Farm Food Cooperative (Veterinary Products) [27198]
Northwest Farm Food Cooperative (Food) [12036]
UAP Northwest (Agricultural Equipment and Supplies) [1370]

Cashmere
Blue Star Growers Inc. (Food) [10581]

Chehalis
Pemalot Inc. (Shoes) [24830]
STIHL Northwest (Industrial Machinery) [16525]

Chelan
Trout-Blue Chelan, Inc. (Food) [12762]

Clarkston
Grassland West (Agricultural Equipment and Supplies) [760]

Colfax
Whitman County Growers Inc. (Livestock and Farm Products) [18346]

Colville
Gannsoft Publishing Co. (Computers and Software) [6288]
Vaagen Brothers Lumber Inc. (Construction Materials and Machinery) [8165]
Washington Belt & Drive (Industrial Supplies) [17264]

Connell
Connell Grain Growers Inc. (Livestock and Farm Products) [17790]

Coulee City
Jess Implements Inc.; Jim (Agricultural Equipment and Supplies) [887]

Davenport
Davenport Union Warehouse Co. (Livestock and Farm Products) [17812]

Edmonds
PFM Industries Inc. (Toys and Hobby Goods) [26612]

Enumclaw
Enumclaw Co.; Garrett (Industrial Machinery) [15993]
MacRae's Indian Book Distributors (Books and Other Printed Materials) [3927]

Everett
Acrowood Corp. (Industrial Machinery) [15734]
Churchill Brothers (Marine) [18479]
Crown Distributing Co. (Alcoholic Beverages) [1627]
Elki Corp. (Food) [11041]
Everett Anchor and Chain (Metals) [19959]
Friendly Distributors (Alcoholic Beverages) [1698]
Lee Cash & Carry (Food) [11691]
Nordic Products Inc. (Household Items) [15597]
North Star Distributors (Soft Drinks) [24996]
North Star Distributors (Food) [12029]
Panama Machinery and Equipment Co. (Hardware) [13860]
Raj India Trading Corp. Inc. (Clothing) [5301]
Strata Inc. (Communications Systems and Equipment) [5770]
Stusser Electric Co. (Electrical and Electronic Equipment and Supplies) [9432]
Western Facilities Supply, Inc. (Cleaning and Janitorial Supplies) [4730]
Western Facilities Supply Inc. (Restaurant and Commercial Foodservice Equipment and Supplies) [24261]
The Wright One Enterprises Inc. (Toys and Hobby Goods) [26716]

Fairfield
Heart Seed (Agricultural Equipment and Supplies) [806]

Ferndale
Superfeet In-Shoe Systems Inc. (Shoes) [24872]

Gig Harbor
HealthComm Inc. (Soft Drinks) [24970]
HealthComm Inc. (Food) [11401]
HealthComm International Inc. (Health and Beauty Aids) [14123]
Rep Associates Inc. (Household Appliances) [15290]

Grandview
Bleyhl Farm Service (Agricultural Equipment and Supplies) [322]

Harrah
Husch and Husch Inc. (Agricultural Equipment and Supplies) [847]

Issaquah
Bacon Building Materials Inc.; Henry (Construction Materials and Machinery) [7008]
Costco Companies, Inc. (Food) [10850]
Costco Wholesale (Food) [10851]
Jeffress Business Services (Shoes) [24778]
Loppnow & Associates (Electrical and Electronic Equipment and Supplies) [9002]
Procise Corp. (Computers and Software) [6645]
RF Ltd. Inc. (Communications Systems and Equipment) [5741]
Tower Equipment Company Inc. (Industrial Machinery) [16570]
Vanguard Trading Services Inc. (Food) [12829]
Wilson & Sons (Books and Other Printed Materials) [4289]

Kenmore
Plywood Supply Inc. (Construction Materials and Machinery) [7875]
Sepia Interior Supply (Construction Materials and Machinery) [8000]

Kennewick
Bartells Co.; E. J (Industrial Supplies) [16721]
Kennewick Industrial and Electrical Supply Inc. (Electrical and Electronic Equipment and Supplies) [8937]

Kennewick Industry & Electric Supply (Electrical
and Electronic Equipment and Supplies) [8938]
Kennewick Industry and Electric Supply (Household
Appliances) [15186]
Mayfield & Co. Inc. (Recreational and Sporting
Goods) [23810]

Kent

ADI (Security and Safety Equipment) [24485]
The Box Maker (Paper and Paper
Products) [21655]
Calhook (Specialty Equipment and
Products) [25592]
Crowe and Co.; F.T. (Construction Materials and
Machinery) [7233]
Derby Cycle (Recreational and Sporting
Goods) [23620]
Diadora America (Clothing) [4915]
Dugans Inc. (Recreational and Sporting
Goods) [23633]
Gateway Appliance Distributing Co. (Household
Appliances) [15143]
Keller Supply Co. (Recreational and Sporting
Goods) [23770]
Millstone Service Div. (Food) [11901]
Morse Industries Inc. (Metals) [20205]
Peripheral Visions Inc. (Medical, Dental, and Optical
Equipment) [18981]
Propet USA, Inc. (Shoes) [24836]
Puget Sound Pipe and Supply
Inc. (Metals) [20302]
Raleigh Cycle of America (Recreational and
Sporting Goods) [23904]
Seattle Box Co. (Storage Equipment and
Containers) [25937]
Smith Brothers Farms Inc. (Food) [12507]
Solar Pacific Inc. (Specialty Equipment and
Products) [25822]
Stusser Electric Co. (Electrical and Electronic
Equipment and Supplies) [9434]
Sysco Food Service of Seattle Inc. (Food) [12672]
Totem Food Products Co. (Food) [12736]
West Coast Paper Co. (Paper and Paper
Products) [21988]

Kirkland

ADVANCED BusinessLink Corp. (Computers and
Software) [5883]
BCSR Inc. (Computers and Software) [6006]
DeYoung Mfg Inc. (Electrical and Electronic
Equipment and Supplies) [8626]
Eagle Electric Manufacturing Co. (Electrical and
Electronic Equipment and Supplies) [8642]
Gensco, Inc. (Heating and Cooling Equipment and
Supplies) [14467]
Main Office Machine Co. (Communications Systems
and Equipment) [5665]
Ponto Associates; (Electrical and Electronic
Equipment and Supplies) [9218]
Portland Distributing Co. (Alcoholic
Beverages) [1963]
Van Waters & Rogers (Chemicals) [4543]

Lacey

Applied Power Corp. (Heating and Cooling
Equipment and Supplies) [14324]

Lakewood

Benedict International Inc. (Clothing) [4817]

Lamont

Lamont Grain Growers Inc. (Livestock and Farm
Products) [18043]

Lind

Union Elevator and Warehouse Co. (Livestock and
Farm Products) [18299]

Longview

Coleman Industrial Supply Inc. (Hardware) [13639]
PAMSCO Inc. (Cleaning and Janitorial
Supplies) [4682]
Wiltech Corp. (Paints and Varnishes) [21611]

Lynden

Korvan Industries Inc. (Agricultural Equipment and
Supplies) [918]

Lynnwood

Allview Services Inc. (Computers and
Software) [5909]
Gann Company Inc.; E.C. (Toys and Hobby
Goods) [26494]
Miller's Interiors Inc. (Floorcovering Equipment and
Supplies) [10038]
Safety Signals Systems Inc. (Electrical and
Electronic Equipment and Supplies) [9330]
South Border Imports, Inc. (Medical, Dental, and
Optical Supplies) [19622]

Marysville

Garka Mill Company Inc. (Construction Materials
and Machinery) [7380]

Mercer Island

Kwik Ski Products (Recreational and Sporting
Goods) [23778]
Pozzolanic Northwest Inc. (Construction Materials
and Machinery) [7883]

Milton

Flex-a-Lite Consolidated (Automotive) [2631]

Monroe

FMC Resource Management Corp. (Office
Equipment and Supplies) [21006]
Lavro Inc. (Recreational and Sporting
Goods) [23781]

Moses Lake

Brotherton Seed Company Inc. (Agricultural
Equipment and Supplies) [338]
Columbia Bean & Produce Co.,
Inc. (Food) [10795]
Moses Lake Steel Supply Inc. (Metals) [20207]

Mt. Vernon

Barnett Implement Co. Inc. (Agricultural Equipment
and Supplies) [278]
Dairy Valley (Food) [10901]
Draper Valley Farms Inc. (Food) [10994]
Paccar Technical Ctr. (Automotive) [3073]
Tri-Dee Distributors (Furniture and
Fixtures) [13261]

Mukilteo

Koval Marketing Inc. (Household Items) [15556]

Odessa

Odessa Trading Company Inc. (Livestock and Farm
Products) [18149]
Odessa Trading Company Inc. (Food) [12053]
Odessa Union Warehouse Co-op (Livestock and
Farm Products) [18150]

Olympia

AMOs Inc. (Computers and Software) [5938]
Capitol Communications (Sound and Entertainment
Equipment and Supplies) [25118]
Gensco, Inc. (Metals) [19999]
Longnecker Inc. (Recreational and Sporting
Goods) [23793]
Stusser Electric Co. (Electrical and Electronic
Equipment and Supplies) [9433]

Omak

Pistoresi Distributing Inc. (Alcoholic
Beverages) [1960]

Othello

Western Cold Storage (Food) [12910]

Pasco

Monarch Machine and Tool Company
Inc. (Hardware) [13836]
Preston Premium Wines (Alcoholic
Beverages) [1972]

Pomeroy

Dye Seed Ranch (Agricultural Equipment and
Supplies) [531]
Pomeroy Grain Growers Inc. (Livestock and Farm
Products) [18173]

Port Angeles

Angeles Medical Supply Inc. (Medical, Dental, and
Optical Equipment) [18686]
Captain TS (Clothing) [4860]
Peninsula Bottling Company Inc. (Soft
Drinks) [25003]
Peninsula Bottling Company Inc. (Food) [12138]

Port Orchard

Alpine Evergreen Company Inc. (Wood and Wood
Products) [27277]

Port Townsend

Jellyroll Productions (Books and Other Printed
Materials) [3862]

Poulsbo

Boxlight Corp. (Computers and Software) [6020]
Seattle Orthotics Group (Computers and
Software) [6715]

Pullman

Grange Supply Company Inc. (Agricultural
Equipment and Supplies) [757]

Redmond

Alcide Corp. (Medical, Dental, and Optical
Supplies) [19133]
Argent Chemical Laboratories Inc. (Agricultural
Equipment and Supplies) [251]
ETMA (Electrical and Electronic Equipment and
Supplies) [8717]
Fukuda Denshi USA, Inc. (Medical, Dental, and
Optical Equipment) [18802]
HSO Corp. (Medical, Dental, and Optical
Equipment) [18844]
Lakey Mouthpieces; Claude (Sound and
Entertainment Equipment and Supplies) [25277]
Larsen Co., Inc.; A. R. (Restaurant and
Commercial Foodservice Equipment and
Supplies) [24163]
Marshall Industries (Electrical and Electronic
Equipment and Supplies) [9041]
Microsoft Corp. (Computers and Software) [6508]
NIDI Northwest Inc. (Computers and
Software) [6554]
NIDI Technologies Inc. (Computers and
Software) [6555]
Perezi & Associates; K.M. (Hardware) [13867]
SpaceLabs Medical Inc. (Medical, Dental, and
Optical Supplies) [19630]
Vectra Fitness Inc. (Recreational and Sporting
Goods) [24028]

Renton

B and T Wholesale Distributors
Inc. (Hardware) [13580]
Bartells Co.; E.J. (Construction Materials and
Machinery) [7025]
Diversified Imports (Alcoholic Beverages) [1652]
GeoCHEM Inc. (Plastics) [22969]
K and N Meats (Food) [11575]
McLendon Hardware Inc. (Hardware) [13820]
PACCAR Inc. Parts Div. (Automotive) [3070]
Pop's E-Z Popcorn & Supply Co. (Restaurant and
Commercial Foodservice Equipment and
Supplies) [24204]
Raden and Sons Inc.; G. (Alcoholic
Beverages) [1977]
Sound Ford Inc. (Motorized Vehicles) [20723]
Taneum Computer Products Inc. (Computers and
Software) [6788]
Vreeken Enterprises Inc. (Restaurant and
Commercial Foodservice Equipment and
Supplies) [24258]

Richland

POSitive Software Co. (Computers and
Software) [6629]

Rollingbay

Healthcare Press (Books and Other Printed Materials) [3820]

Royal City

Sunfresh Inc. (Food) [12613]

St. John

St. John Grain Growers Inc. (Livestock and Farm Products) [18219]

Seattle

3 GI Athletics Inc. (Recreational and Sporting Goods) [23489]

A & V TapeHandlers, Inc. (Sound and Entertainment Equipment and Supplies) [25053]

AAA Fire & Safety Inc. (Security and Safety Equipment) [24466]

Ace Tank and Equipment Co. (Storage Equipment and Containers) [25885]

Acme Food Sales Inc. (Food) [10320]

Adams News Co. Inc. (Books and Other Printed Materials) [3470]

AEROGO, Inc. (Industrial Machinery) [15740]

AIDS Impact Inc. (Books and Other Printed Materials) [3477]

Aimonetto and Sons, Inc. (Food) [10348]

Aimsco Inc. (Hardware) [13538]

Alaskan Copper & Brass Co. (Metals) [19741]

Allied Body Works Inc. (Automotive) [2212]

Allied Bolt Co. (Hardware) [13551]

American Lease Co. (Motorized Vehicles) [20590]

American Legend Cooperative (Livestock and Farm Products) [17696]

American Telephone Technology (Communications Systems and Equipment) [5514]

Ample Technology (Automotive) [2238]

Aqua Star Inc. (Food) [10428]

Arensberg Sons Inc. (Specialty Equipment and Products) [25558]

Associated Grocers, Inc. (Food) [10450]

Athletic Supply Inc. (Shoes) [24676]

Atlas Supply Inc. (Chemicals) [4330]

Automated Register Systems, Inc. (Computers and Software) [5988]

B & J Industrial Supply Co. (Industrial Machinery) [15794]

Baker Candy Co. Inc. (Food) [10490]

Bank and Office Interiors (Furniture and Fixtures) [13030]

Bardahl Manufacturing Corp. (Petroleum, Fuels, and Related Equipment) [22058]

Beckwith Kuffel Industries Inc. (Industrial Machinery) [15813]

Before Columbus Foundation (Books and Other Printed Materials) [3548]

Benge & Co.; Jim (Shoes) [24689]

Bingham Enterprises Inc. (Medical, Dental, and Optical Supplies) [19189]

Blanchard Auto Electric Co. (Automotive) [2367]

Bloch Steel Industries (Metals) [19825]

Boat Electric Co. Inc. (Heating and Cooling Equipment and Supplies) [14351]

Bowman Refrigeration Inc. (Heating and Cooling Equipment and Supplies) [14354]

Branom Instrument Company Inc. (Scientific and Measurement Devices) [24326]

Branom Instrument Company Inc. (Industrial Machinery) [15841]

Budget Sales Inc. (Restaurant and Commercial Foodservice Equipment and Supplies) [24084]

Builders Hardware and Supply Co. Inc. (Hardware) [13612]

Cascade Machinery and Electric Inc. (Compressors) [5834]

Cheler Corp. (Industrial Supplies) [16794]

China House Trading Co. (Industrial Supplies) [16796]

Commercial Office Interiors Inc. (Furniture and Fixtures) [13076]

Communications Wholesale (Communications Systems and Equipment) [5573]

Corporate Computer Inc. (Computers and Software) [6161]

Cotton Caboodle Company Co. (Clothing) [4899]

Coyote Engineering, Inc. (Recreational and Sporting Goods) [23609]

Crawfords Office Furniture & Supplies (Office Equipment and Supplies) [20937]

Cutter Precision Metals Inc. (Metals) [19911]

Dairy Export Co. Inc. (Food) [10893]

Doc Freeman's (Marine) [18493]

Dockters X-Ray Inc. (Medical, Dental, and Optical Equipment) [18777]

Dockters X-Ray Inc. (Medical, Dental, and Optical Supplies) [19286]

Dusty Strings Co. (Sound and Entertainment Equipment and Supplies) [25169]

Euroimport Co. Inc. (Shoes) [24736]

Facility Resource Inc. (Seattle, Washington) (Furniture and Fixtures) [13108]

Fasteners Inc. (Hardware) [13699]

Fiberlay Inc. (Construction Materials and Machinery) [7339]

First Line Marketing, Inc. (Industrial Supplies) [16864]

Fisher Bag Company Inc. (Textiles and Notions) [26034]

Fisher Mills Inc. (Food) [11134]

Fisheries Supply Co. Industrial Div. (Marine) [18503]

Flury & Co. Ltd. (Gifts and Novelties) [13358]

Food Services of America Inc. (Food) [11180]

Fremont Electric Company Inc. (Automotive) [2648]

Gai's Northwest Bakeries Inc. (Food) [11229]

Galvin Flying Service Inc. (Petroleum, Fuels, and Related Equipment) [22300]

Gem East Corp. (Jewelry) [17423]

General Tool & Supply Co. (Industrial Supplies) [16893]

Gensco, Inc. (Heating and Cooling Equipment and Supplies) [14466]

Glant Pacific Co. (Used, Scrap, and Recycled Materials) [26829]

Glant Pacific Iron and Metal Co. (Used, Scrap, and Recycled Materials) [26830]

Goldberg & Co., Inc.; H. E. (Livestock and Farm Products) [17945]

Greaves Company Inc. (Industrial Machinery) [16076]

Gull Industries Inc. (Petroleum, Fuels, and Related Equipment) [22328]

Hallidie Machinery Company Inc. (Industrial Machinery) [16084]

Hardie Export; James (Construction Materials and Machinery) [7442]

Hardware Specialties Co. (Hardware) [13739]

Harris Electric Inc. (Electrical and Electronic Equipment and Supplies) [8830]

Hays Distributing Corp. (Toys and Hobby Goods) [26513]

Homestead Book Co. (Books and Other Printed Materials) [3832]

Icicle Seafoods Inc. Port Chatham Div. (Food) [11487]

Imagetech RICOH Corp. (Office Equipment and Supplies) [21052]

Inter-American Trading (Specialty Equipment and Products) [25689]

Kagedo Inc. (Textiles and Notions) [26084]

Katz Paper, Foil & Cordage Corp. (Paper and Paper Products) [21788]

Keller Supply Co. (Plumbing Materials and Fixtures) [23229]

Ketcham Forest Products Inc. (Wood and Wood Products) [27328]

Ketcham Lumber Company Inc. (Construction Materials and Machinery) [7549]

Kirkland Marine Co. (Marine) [18535]

Lilly Co.; Chas. H. (Agricultural Equipment and Supplies) [958]

Marco Marine Seattle, IMFS Div. (Marine) [18558]

Marketware Corp. (Computers and Software) [6465]

Maschmedt and Associates (Marine) [18563]

McDonald Industries Inc. (Construction Materials and Machinery) [7678]

McGuire Bearing (Industrial Supplies) [17024]

Mehrer Drywall Inc. (Construction Materials and Machinery) [7690]

Merchants Information Solutions Inc. (Office Equipment and Supplies) [21138]

Mitsui & Co. (USA), Inc. Seattle Branch (Industrial Machinery) [16312]

Mortemp Inc. (Heating and Cooling Equipment and Supplies) [14611]

National Barricade Co (Electrical and Electronic Equipment and Supplies) [9113]

NC Machinery Co. (Industrial Machinery) [16345]

Newell Company Inc.; C.A. (Floorcovering Equipment and Supplies) [10077]

Nordstrom Inc. (Clothing) [5237]

Northwest Bottling Co. (Soft Drinks) [24999]

Northwest Coast Trading Company (Recreational and Sporting Goods) [23853]

Odom Corp. (Alcoholic Beverages) [1927]

Office Pavilion/MBI Systems Inc. (Medical, Dental, and Optical Equipment) [18966]

Ogle & Co.; Jack (Industrial Machinery) [16357]

Outdoor Research Inc. (Recreational and Sporting Goods) [23863]

Pacific American Commercial Co. (Construction Materials and Machinery) [7820]

Pacific Industrial Supply Company Inc. (Industrial Supplies) [17097]

Pacific Lumber and Shipping Co. (Wood and Wood Products) [27354]

Pacific North Equipment Co. (Construction Materials and Machinery) [7826]

Pacific Northern (Petroleum, Fuels, and Related Equipment) [22547]

Pacific Salmon Company Inc. (Food) [12093]

Pacific Terminals Ltd. (Books and Other Printed Materials) [4034]

Pepsi-Cola Northwest (Food) [12146]

Perine Co.; John (Hardware) [13868]

Phoenix Group HI-TEC Corp. (Medical, Dental, and Optical Equipment) [18986]

Plant Maintenance Equipment (Cleaning and Janitorial Supplies) [4687]

Preservative Paint Company Inc. (Paints and Varnishes) [21545]

Prodata Computer Marketing Corp. (Computers and Software) [6646]

Prodata Systems Inc. (Computers and Software) [6647]

Puget Sound Instrument Co. Inc. (Sound and Entertainment Equipment and Supplies) [25394]

Radar, Inc. (Electrical and Electronic Equipment and Supplies) [9256]

Raketty Co.; A.E. (Tobacco Products) [26345]

Ribbons Pasta Co. (Food) [12307]

Rosanna Inc. (Household Items) [15641]

Ryerson Tull Inc. (Metals) [20345]

Sarco Inc. (Household Appliances) [15303]

Sea-Pac Sales Co. (Floorcovering Equipment and Supplies) [10140]

Seasia (Food) [12452]

Seattle Iron and Metals Corp. (Used, Scrap, and Recycled Materials) [26985]

Seattle Kitchen Design Inc. (Furniture and Fixtures) [13236]

Seattle Kitchen Design Inc. (Wood and Wood Products) [27374]

Seattle Marine Industrial Division (Marine) [18608]

Seattle Ship Supply (Marine) [18609]

Services Group of America Inc. (Food) [12463]

Signal Equipment Inc. (Electrical and Electronic Equipment and Supplies) [9371]

Sime Health Ltd. (Health and Beauty Aids) [14237]

Six Robblees Inc. (Automotive) [3225]

Skyway Luggage Co. (Luggage and Leather Goods) [18430]

Small Changes Inc. (Books and Other Printed Materials) [4167]

South King Kirby (Specialty Equipment and Products) [25824]

Spencer Chain Gear Co. (Automotive) [3250]

Spencer Industries Inc. (Industrial Supplies) [17192]

Spencer Industries Inc. Chain Gear Div. (Automotive) [3251]

Spencer Industries Inc. (Seattle, Washington) (Aeronautical Equipment and Supplies) [150]

Stack; Al (Toys and Hobby Goods) [26665]

Star Industries Inc. (Construction Materials and Machinery) [8072]

Starbucks Corp. (Food) [12571]

Steam Supply Co. (Industrial Supplies) [17198]

Steeler Inc. (Wood and Wood Products) [27381]

Stoneway Electric Supply Co. (Electrical and Electronic Equipment and Supplies) [9421]

Stusser Electric Co. (Electrical and Electronic Equipment and Supplies) [9428]

Swenson Imports (Shoes) [24874]

T & A Supply Co. (Floorcovering Equipment and Supplies) [10202]

T and A Supply Co. (Household Items) [15679]

Thermal Supply Inc. (Heating and Cooling Equipment and Supplies) [14722]

Time Oil Co. (Petroleum, Fuels, and Related Equipment) [22736]

ToteVision (Communications Systems and Equipment) [5795]

Trans West Communication Systems (Electrical and Electronic Equipment and Supplies) [9500]

Tree of Life Inc. Northwest (Food) [12750]

Trick and Murray Inc. (Office Equipment and Supplies) [21323]

True Blue Inc. (Clothing) [5442]

Tyson Seafood Group (Food) [12780]

U.S. Global Resources (Agricultural Equipment and Supplies) [1382]

University of Washington Press (Books and Other Printed Materials) [4252]

Van Waters and Rogers (Chemicals) [4542]

Van Waters and Rogers Inc. (Chemicals) [4544]

Wards Cove Packing Co. (Food) [12877]

Washington Avionics Inc. (Aeronautical Equipment and Supplies) [168]

Washington Belt & Drive (Industrial Supplies) [17265]

Washington Chain and Supply (Marine) [18633]

Washington Chain and Supply Inc. (Marine) [18634]

Washington Shoe Company (Clothing) [5474]

West Coast Machine Tools (Industrial Machinery) [16623]

Western Pioneer Inc. (Petroleum, Fuels, and Related Equipment) [22795]

Wilbur-Ellis Co. (Livestock and Farm Products) [18348]

Worldwide Distributors Inc. (Clothing) [5492]

WRG Corp. (Aeronautical Equipment and Supplies) [177]

Zapper Inc. (Electrical and Electronic Equipment and Supplies) [9621]

Sedro Woolley

Rothenbuhler Engineering (Communications Systems and Equipment) [5747]

Snohomish

Dunbar Doors and Millwork (Wood and Wood Products) [27302]

Spanaway

I.E.F. Corp. (Horticultural Supplies) [14891]

Spokane

Adams Tractor Company Inc. (Agricultural Equipment and Supplies) [186]

All-In-One Monogramming (Clothing) [4758]

Branom Instrument Company Inc. (Scientific and Measurement Devices) [24327]

Buffalo Inc. (Clothing) [4851]

Calkins Fluid Power, Inc. (Industrial Machinery) [15864]

Cascade Seed Co. (Agricultural Equipment and Supplies) [376]

Coca-Cola; Pacific (Soft Drinks) [24948]

Consolidated Supply Co. (Plumbing Materials and Fixtures) [23124]

Construction Products of Washington (Construction Materials and Machinery) [7208]

Cop Shop (Clothing) [4893]

Diversified Ophthalmics Inc. (Medical, Dental, and Optical Supplies) [19284]

Eagle Optical (Medical, Dental, and Optical Supplies) [19300]

Exchange Lumber and Manufacturing Div. (Construction Materials and Machinery) [7326]

Fiedler; John W. (Household Appliances) [15127]

Floor Supply Distributing Inc. (Floorcovering Equipment and Supplies) [9895]

Island-Northwest Distributing, Inc. (Floorcovering Equipment and Supplies) [9976]

Itron Inc. (Computers and Software) [6400]

J & L Book Co. (Books and Other Printed Materials) [3857]

Jensen-Byrd Company Inc. (Hardware) [13772]

Jensen Distribution Services (Hardware) [13773]

Market Equipment Company Inc. (Heating and Cooling Equipment and Supplies) [14532]

McGuire Bearing (Industrial Supplies) [17025]

Mobile Fleet Service of Spokane (Heating and Cooling Equipment and Supplies) [14608]

Nott-Atwater Co (Industrial Machinery) [16355]

OEM Parts Center Inc. (Automotive) [3054]

Packet Engines (Computers and Software) [6582]

Peirone Produce Co. (Food) [12133]

Plastoptics Inc. (Medical, Dental, and Optical Supplies) [19543]

Powers Candy & Nut Co. (Food) [12202]

Prudential Builders Center (Household Appliances) [15281]

Prudential Distributors Inc. (Household Appliances) [15282]

R and D Industries Inc. (Computers and Software) [6674]

Skaggs Automotive Inc. (Automotive) [3228]

Skipper Bills Inc. (Recreational and Sporting Goods) [23944]

Spokane Diesel Inc. (Automotive) [3253]

Spokane Flower Growers (Horticultural Supplies) [14955]

Spokane Hardware Supply Inc. (Hardware) [13934]

Spokane Machinery Company Inc. (Construction Materials and Machinery) [8063]

Spokane Seed Co. (Livestock and Farm Products) [18249]

Spokane Seed Co. (Food) [12556]

Stock Steel (Metals) [20406]

Stoneway Electric Supply Co. (Electrical and Electronic Equipment and Supplies) [9420]

Super Valu Stores Inc. (Food) [12634]

Superior Turf Equipment (Recreational and Sporting Goods) [23997]

Teneff Jewelry Inc. (Jewelry) [17634]

Thompson Tile Co., Inc. (Floorcovering Equipment and Supplies) [10213]

Thunder Mountain Dog Supplies (Veterinary Products) [27247]

Torque-A-Matic (Industrial Supplies) [17231]

Uniq Distributing Corp. (Floorcovering Equipment and Supplies) [10262]

U.R.M. Cash & Carry (Food) [12805]

U.R.M. Stores Inc. (Food) [12806]

Valley Best-Way Building Supply (Construction Materials and Machinery) [8166]

Wagners Formal Wear of Washington (Clothing) [5469]

Whites Shoe Shop Inc. (Shoes) [24893]

Willar Corp. (Heating and Cooling Equipment and Supplies) [14767]

Zak Designs Inc. (Household Items) [15716]

Sumner

Big Valley Plastics Inc. (Plastics) [22937]

Knutson Farms Inc. (Horticultural Supplies) [14906]

McConkey and Company Inc.; J.M. (Horticultural Supplies) [14919]

Nutri-Fruit Inc. (Soft Drinks) [25000]

Sunnyside

Hickenbottom and Sons Inc. (Food) [11426]

Tacoma

Architectural Words Inc. (Construction Materials and Machinery) [6983]

Berg Equipment and Scaffolding Company Inc. (Construction Materials and Machinery) [7047]

Broadcast Supply Worldwide (Communications Systems and Equipment) [5535]

Brookdale Lumber Inc. (Construction Materials and Machinery) [7083]

Brown & Haley (Food) [10626]

Burkhart Dental Supply (Medical, Dental, and Optical Equipment) [18723]

Business Interiors Northwest Inc. (Furniture and Fixtures) [13057]

C & G Electronics Co. (Electrical and Electronic Equipment and Supplies) [8480]

Champion Athletic Supply Inc. (Recreational and Sporting Goods) [23587]

Coca-Cola; Pacific (Soft Drinks) [24949]

D & D Distributing (Toys and Hobby Goods) [26457]

Darling Corp.; J.L. (Paper and Paper Products) [21701]

Elliott Sales Corp. (Recreational and Sporting Goods) [23649]

Fircrest Pre-Fit Door Co. (Construction Materials and Machinery) [7342]

General Metals of Tacoma Inc. (Used, Scrap, and Recycled Materials) [26824]

Gensco Inc. (Heating and Cooling Equipment and Supplies) [14465]

K and M Metals Inc. (Metals) [20082]

Larsen and Associates Inc.; Bill (Gifts and Novelties) [13387]

Lilyblad Petroleum Inc. (Petroleum, Fuels, and Related Equipment) [22433]

Mayco Fish Company Ltd. (Food) [11812]

North Star Glove Co. (Clothing) [5239]

Northpoint Trading Co. Inc. (Veterinary Products) [27197]

Northwest Meats Inc. (Food) [12038]

NWCS Inc. (Electrical and Electronic Equipment and Supplies) [9150]

Pacific Coca-Cola Tacoma (Books and Other Printed Materials) [4031]

Pacific Hardware & Specialties Inc. (Hardware) [13858]

Puget Sound Audio (Sound and Entertainment Equipment and Supplies) [25393]

Puget Sound Manufacturing Co. (Construction Materials and Machinery) [7890]

Scofield Company Inc.; George (Construction Materials and Machinery) [7991]

Service Steel Aerospace Corp. (Metals) [20360]

Shaub Ellison Co. (Automotive) [3213]

Simon & Sons; Joseph (Used, Scrap, and Recycled Materials) [26991]

Smith Tractor and Equipment Co. (Construction Materials and Machinery) [8036]

Sol-Pro Inc. (Used, Scrap, and Recycled Materials) [26997]

Sound Optical (Medical, Dental, and Optical Supplies) [19621]

Super Valu Stores Inc. (Food) [12635]

SuperValu International (Food) [12648]

Tacoma Fiberglass (Marine) [18622]

Wallace Coast Machinery Co. (Industrial Machinery) [16612]

Weyerhaeuser Co. Recycling Business Div. (Used, Scrap, and Recycled Materials) [27046]

Zinc Positive Inc. (Automotive) [3456]

Tekoa

Seeds, Inc. (Agricultural Equipment and Supplies) [1253]

Tonasket

Chief Tonasket Growers (Food) [10744]

Regal Fruit Co. (Food) [12295]

Tukwila

Carlyle Inc. (Metals) [19857]

Merchant du Vin Corp. (Alcoholic Beverages) [1866]

Sound Floor Coverings Inc. (Floorcovering Equipment and Supplies) [10157]

Thompson Tile Co., Inc. (Floorcovering Equipment and Supplies) [10214]

Tumwater

Black Hills Distributing Co. Inc. (Alcoholic Beverages) [1533]

Vancouver

Alanco Eyewear (Medical, Dental, and Optical Supplies) [19131]
Columbia Ventures Corp. (Metals) [19884]
Graeffs Eastside Drugs; Mike (Medical, Dental, and Optical Equipment) [18814]
KIC International (Wood and Wood Products) [27330]
Nicewonger Co. (Restaurant and Commercial Foodservice Equipment and Supplies) [24193]
Wacom Technology Corp. (Specialty Equipment and Products) [25868]
Western Power and Equipment Corp. (Construction Materials and Machinery) [8211]
ZDI Gaming Inc. (Toys and Hobby Goods) [26719]

Vashon

K2 Corp. (Recreational and Sporting Goods) [23768]

Vashon Island

The Sporting House (Recreational and Sporting Goods) [23977]

WalLa Walla

Adams Tractor Co.; Carroll (Agricultural Equipment and Supplies) [185]
Barer and Sons; B. (Used, Scrap, and Recycled Materials) [26758]
Bur-Bee Co. Inc. (Food) [10644]
Ford Distributing Co.; Leid (Petroleum, Fuels, and Related Equipment) [22288]

Walla Walla

Northwest Grain Growers, Inc. (Livestock and Farm Products) [18144]

WalLa Walla

Radak Electronics (Communications Systems and Equipment) [5727]

Walla Walla

Swire Coca-Cola USA (Food) [12660]

WalLa Walla

Walla Walla Farmers Co-op Inc. (Agricultural Equipment and Supplies) [1406]

Wapato

Inland Fruit and Produce Company Inc. (Food) [11507]
Joseph Orchard Siding Inc.; George F. (Paper and Paper Products) [21786]
Valley Fruit (Food) [12818]

Washougal

Industrial Plastics Inc. (Plastics) [22983]

Wenatchee

Blue Ribbon Foods (Food) [10577]
Blue Ribbon Meat Company Inc. (Food) [10579]
Cascadian Fruit Shippers Inc. (Food) [10707]
Chief Wenatchee (Food) [10745]
Northwest Wholesale Inc. (Agricultural Equipment and Supplies) [1089]
Oneonta Trading Corp. (Food) [12072]
Rockys II Inc. (Recreational and Sporting Goods) [23919]
Washington Belt & Drive (Industrial Supplies) [17263]
Washington Belt & Drive (Industrial Supplies) [17266]
Wells and Wade Hardware (Hardware) [13992]
Wenatchee-Okanogan Cooperative Federation (Food) [12901]

Woodinville

American Health Supplies (Medical, Dental, and Optical Supplies) [19140]
Aseptico, Inc. (Medical, Dental, and Optical Equipment) [18692]
Fast Multimedia U.S. Inc. (Computers and Software) [6264]

Ganson Engineering Inc. (Computers and Software) [6289]
Justlin Medical Inc. (Medical, Dental, and Optical Equipment) [18869]
Majestic Glove Inc. (Clothing) [5154]
Marks Co.; D.F. (Agricultural Equipment and Supplies) [987]
Matheus Lumber Company Inc. (Construction Materials and Machinery) [7667]
Stimson Lane Wine and Spirits Ltd. (Alcoholic Beverages) [2054]
TransPro Marketing (Computers and Software) [6829]

Yakima

AMB Tools & Equipment (Hardware) [13556]
General Supply of Yakima Inc. (Cleaning and Janitorial Supplies) [4627]
Gensco, Inc. (Heating and Cooling Equipment and Supplies) [14468]
Hauff Co.; H.F. (Agricultural Equipment and Supplies) [801]
Horizon Distribution Inc. (Hardware) [13757]
Morton Supply Inc. (Electrical and Electronic Equipment and Supplies) [9098]
Noel Corp. (Soft Drinks) [24995]
Picatti Brothers Inc. (Electrical and Electronic Equipment and Supplies) [9200]
Ray's Wholesale Meat (Food) [12281]
Snokist Growers (Food) [12523]
Spencer Industries (Industrial Supplies) [17191]
Stusser Electric Co. (Electrical and Electronic Equipment and Supplies) [9435]
Valley Communications (Communications Systems and Equipment) [5802]
Western Materials Inc. (Construction Materials and Machinery) [8209]
Yakima Hardware Co. (Hardware) [14002]

Yelm

Rodgers International Trading Inc. (Food) [12341]

West Virginia

Barboursville

SMC Electrical Products Inc. (Electrical and Electronic Equipment and Supplies) [9379]

Beckley

Lucas Tire Inc. (Automotive) [2896]
Michel Company Inc.; R.E. (Heating and Cooling Equipment and Supplies) [14596]
Raleigh Hardware Co. (Hardware) [13880]
Spartan Sporting Goods Inc. (Recreational and Sporting Goods) [23973]

Berkeley Springs

Eddie's Tire Service Inc. (Automotive) [2575]

Bluefield

Rish Equipment Co. (Construction Materials and Machinery) [7937]

Bridgeport

R & T Enterprises Inc. (Recreational and Sporting Goods) [23901]

Chapmanville

Guyan Machinery Company Inc. (Industrial Supplies) [16916]

CharLes Town

Claymont Communications (Books and Other Printed Materials) [3643]

Charles Town

Community Oil Company Inc. (Petroleum, Fuels, and Related Equipment) [22157]

Charleston

Ashmore Optical Co. Inc. (Medical, Dental, and Optical Supplies) [19162]

Cambridge Educational (Books and Other Printed Materials) [3603]
Computer Plus, Inc. (Computers and Software) [6119]
Elden Enterprises (Sound and Entertainment Equipment and Supplies) [25175]
Eskew, Smith & Cannon (Floorcovering Equipment and Supplies) [9886]
General Glass Company Inc. (Construction Materials and Machinery) [7384]
Goldfarb Electric Supply Company Inc. (Electrical and Electronic Equipment and Supplies) [8796]
Industrial Rubber Products Co. (Rubber) [24282]
Industrial Supply Solutions, Inc. (Industrial Machinery) [16155]
Kanawha Steel and Equipment Inc. (Metals) [20085]
Kyle Furniture Co.; R.H. (Furniture and Fixtures) [13158]
McJunkin Appalachian Oil Field Supply Co. (Petroleum, Fuels, and Related Equipment) [22466]
McJunkin Corp. (Industrial Supplies) [17027]
Michel Company Inc.; R.E. (Heating and Cooling Equipment and Supplies) [14597]
P-80 Systems (Computers and Software) [6578]
Pfaff and Smith Builders Supply Co. (Construction Materials and Machinery) [7854]
RCP Inc. (Office Equipment and Supplies) [21234]
Riverton Coal Co. (Minerals and Ores) [20564]
Smith Floor Covering Distributors (Floorcovering Equipment and Supplies) [10153]
Virginia Welding Supply Company Inc. (Industrial Supplies) [17256]
Virginia West Uniforms Inc. (Clothing) [5466]
Walker Machinery Co.; Cecil I. (Agricultural Equipment and Supplies) [1405]
West Virginia Archery Supply (Recreational and Sporting Goods) [24043]
West Virginia Tractor Co. (Construction Materials and Machinery) [8205]

Clarksburg

Matthews Brothers Wholesale Inc. (Petroleum, Fuels, and Related Equipment) [22456]
Osborn Machinery Company Inc. (Hardware) [13856]
Wholesale Tire Inc. (Automotive) [3429]

Davisville

Building and Industrial Wholesale Co. (Construction Materials and Machinery) [7103]

Elkins

Valley Distributors (Alcoholic Beverages) [2093]
Valley Supply Co. (Plumbing Materials and Fixtures) [23429]

Fairmont

McDonough Brothers (Food) [11825]

Farmington

Drulane/ Palmer Smith (Household Items) [15481]

Gilbert

International Industries Inc. (Construction Materials and Machinery) [7518]

Huntington

Arthurs Enterprises Inc. (Electrical and Electronic Equipment and Supplies) [8379]
Champion Industries Inc. (Huntington, West Virginia) (Office Equipment and Supplies) [20895]
Columbia Paint Co. (Paints and Varnishes) [21416]
Economy Foods (Food) [11023]
Electronic Supply (Household Appliances) [15121]
Great American Floor Care Center (Household Appliances) [15152]
Health Care Services, Inc. (Medical, Dental, and Optical Supplies) [19353]
Huntington Steel and Supply Company Inc. (Metals) [20048]

Huntington Wholesale Furniture Company Inc. (Furniture and Fixtures) [13137]
Jabo Supply Corp. (Plumbing Materials and Fixtures) [23223]
Keen Jewelers (Health and Beauty Aids) [14141]
Logan Corp. (Specialty Equipment and Products) [25719]
Michel Company Inc.; R.E. (Heating and Cooling Equipment and Supplies) [14598]
MR Supply Inc. (Heating and Cooling Equipment and Supplies) [14613]
Okhai-Moyer Inc. (Office Equipment and Supplies) [21198]
One Valley Bank of Huntington (Sound and Entertainment Equipment and Supplies) [25368]
Stanley Brothers Inc. (Food) [12565]
State Electric Supply Co. (Electrical and Electronic Equipment and Supplies) [9413]
Stationers Inc. (Huntington, West Virginia) (Office Equipment and Supplies) [21295]
Strictly Business Computer Systems Inc. (Computers and Software) [6767]
Thornburg Co. Inc.; C.I. (Plumbing Materials and Fixtures) [23409]
Water Works and Industrial Supply Co., Inc. (Industrial Supplies) [17267]

Hurricane

Baker Truck Equipment (Automotive) [2311]
Quorum Corp. (Office Equipment and Supplies) [21231]

Inwood

Library Corp. (Computers and Software) [6439]

Jane Lew

Masterpiece Crystal (Household Items) [15580]

Lanark

Tamarack Ltd. (Medical, Dental, and Optical Equipment) [19070]

Lewisburg

Allegheny Mining Corp. (Minerals and Ores) [20509]

Martinsburg

Somerville Co.; Thomas (Heating and Cooling Equipment and Supplies) [14688]
Taylor Sports & Recreation Inc. (Recreational and Sporting Goods) [24004]

Milton

Kipling Shoe Company Inc. (Shoes) [24785]
Supervalu - Milton Div. (Food) [12649]

Morgantown

Anker Energy Corp. (Minerals and Ores) [20516]
Barry's Office Service Inc. (Office Equipment and Supplies) [20832]
Michel Company Inc.; R.E. (Heating and Cooling Equipment and Supplies) [14599]
R & B Orthopedics Inc. (Medical, Dental, and Optical Equipment) [19006]
University Motors Ltd. (Automotive) [3376]
Weintrob Brothers (Shoes) [24890]

Moundsville

Sam Yanen Ford Sales Inc. (Automotive) [3184]

New Martinsville

Magnolia Distributing Co. (Alcoholic Beverages) [1837]

Newell

Laughlin China Co.; Homer (Household Items) [15560]

Nitro

American Tire Distributors (Automotive) [2235]

Oak Hill

Camco Services Inc. (Heating and Cooling Equipment and Supplies) [14366]

Parkersburg

Ames Co. (Agricultural Equipment and Supplies) [237]
Batteries Direct (Electrical and Electronic Equipment and Supplies) [8419]
Kanawha Scales and Systems (Scientific and Measurement Devices) [24382]
Matheny Motor Truck Co. (Automotive) [2923]
Universal Supply Company Inc. (Plumbing Materials and Fixtures) [23424]
Woodings-Verona Tool Works Inc. (Hardware) [14000]

Parsons

McClain Printing Co. (Books and Other Printed Materials) [3942]

Petersburg

Mathias and Company Inc. (Food) [11805]

Prichard

Persinger Supply Co. (Specialty Equipment and Products) [25782]

Princeton

Downard Hydraulics Inc. (Industrial Machinery) [15959]
McJunkin Corp. (Electrical and Electronic Equipment and Supplies) [9058]

Ravenswood

Hartley Manufacturing Inc. (Used, Scrap, and Recycled Materials) [26839]

St. Albans

Jefferds Corp. (Industrial Machinery) [16186]
Preiser Scientific (Scientific and Measurement Devices) [24419]
Smith Kitchen Specialties; W.H. (Household Appliances) [15317]

Sophia

Priddy's General Store (Veterinary Products) [27216]

South Charleston

General Truck Sales Corp. (Motorized Vehicles) [20642]
Union Carbide Corp., IPX Services (Industrial Machinery) [16587]

Summersville

Campbell Tractor and Equipment Co. (Agricultural Equipment and Supplies) [366]

Weirton

Ferguson Tire Service Inc. (Automotive) [2611]

Welch

Lewis Oil Co.; H.C. (Petroleum, Fuels, and Related Equipment) [22428]

Westover

Neville Optical Inc. (Medical, Dental, and Optical Supplies) [19488]

Wheeling

Allpro Corp. (Paints and Varnishes) [21381]
Bob's Gard Duty (Electrical and Electronic Equipment and Supplies) [8448]
Call-A-Tech Inc. (Computers and Software) [6041]
Carenbauer Wholesale Corp. (Alcoholic Beverages) [1574]
Genuine Parts Company of West Virginia Inc. (Automotive) [2679]
Imperial Display Co. (Toys and Hobby Goods) [26531]
Michel Company Inc.; R.E. (Heating and Cooling Equipment and Supplies) [14600]
Multi Vision Optical (Medical, Dental, and Optical Supplies) [19470]
Ohio Valley-Clarksburg Inc. (Medical, Dental, and Optical Supplies) [19505]
Strauss Inc.; Herman (Used, Scrap, and Recycled Materials) [27010]

T and L Supply Inc. (Plumbing Materials and Fixtures) [23404]
Valley National Gases Inc. (Petroleum, Fuels, and Related Equipment) [22766]
Valley Welding Supply Co. (Industrial Machinery) [16599]
West Virginia Ohio Motor Sales Inc. (Automotive) [3410]
Wilson and Sons Inc.; W.A. (Household Items) [15708]

Williamstown

Mountain State Muzzleloading Supplies, Inc. (Guns and Weapons) [13503]

Yolyn

Arch of West Virginia Inc. (Minerals and Ores) [20520]

Wisconsin

Adams

Farmers Union Cooperative (Petroleum, Fuels, and Related Equipment) [22258]

Algoma

Algoma Net Co. (Recreational and Sporting Goods) [23502]

Alma

Alma Farmers Union Cooperative (Agricultural Equipment and Supplies) [230]

Almena

Almena Cooperative Association (Petroleum, Fuels, and Related Equipment) [22032]
Almena Cooperative Association (Petroleum, Fuels, and Related Equipment) [22033]
Cumberland Farmers Union Cooperative (Agricultural Equipment and Supplies) [482]

Amery

Equity Cooperative of Amery Inc. (Agricultural Equipment and Supplies) [553]
Omnium Corp. (Computers and Software) [6571]

Amherst Junction

FS Cooperative Inc. (Agricultural Equipment and Supplies) [718]

Antigo

All-Car Distributors Inc. (Automotive) [2203]
Sheldons', Inc. (Recreational and Sporting Goods) [23935]

Appleton

Allied Fire Lite Fireplace (Heating and Cooling Equipment and Supplies) [14314]
American Digital Cartography Inc. (Computers and Software) [5926]
Automotive Supply Co. (Automotive) [2297]
Conkey's Bookstore (Books and Other Printed Materials) [3652]
Crescent Electric Supply (Appleton, Wisconsin) (Household Appliances) [15099]
Crescent Electric Supply Co. (Electrical and Electronic Equipment and Supplies) [8591]
Educational Distributors of America (Furniture and Fixtures) [13102]
GWS Supply, Inc. (Industrial Supplies) [16917]
Jansport Inc. (Clothing) [5075]
Langstadt Electric Supply Co. (Electrical and Electronic Equipment and Supplies) [8971]
Miller Welding Supply Company Inc. (Industrial Machinery) [16303]
Motion Industries, Inc. (Automotive) [2992]
Perin Press (Books and Other Printed Materials) [4056]
Russel Metals-Bahcall Group (Metals) [20339]
Schlafer Supply Company Inc. (Hardware) [13906]
School Specialties Inc. (Furniture and Fixtures) [13233]

Sentry Alarm, Inc. (Security and Safety
  Equipment) [24633]
Universal Paper and Packaging (Paper and Paper
  Products) [21982]

Arcadia

Arcadia Livestock, Inc. (Livestock and Farm
  Products) [17703]
Pehler Brothers, Inc. (Alcoholic Beverages) [1947]

Arpin

Wood County Farm Supply (Agricultural Equipment
  and Supplies) [1460]

Ashland

Anna Marie Designs Inc. (Clothing) [4773]

Bangor

MacDonald and Owen Lumber (Construction
  Materials and Machinery) [7631]

Baraboo

Baraboo-Sysco Food Services Inc. (Food) [10502]
McArthur Towels, Inc. (Household Items) [15581]
McArthur Towels Inc. (Household Items) [15582]
Tri-State Breeders Cooperative (Veterinary
  Products) [27252]

Barron

Barron Farmers Union Cooperative Services
  Inc. (Agricultural Equipment and Supplies) [279]

Beloit

American Builders and Contractors Supply
  Company Inc. (Construction Materials and
  Machinery) [6959]

Black River Falls

Federation Cooperative (Agricultural Equipment and
  Supplies) [675]

Blanchardville

Blanchardville Cooperative Oil
  Association (Petroleum, Fuels, and Related
  Equipment) [22079]

Brokaw

Mill Waste Recovery Inc. (Used, Scrap, and
  Recycled Materials) [26914]

Brookfield

AmeriServe Food Distribution Inc. (Food) [10407]
Artz Inc.; E.G. (Industrial Supplies) [16711]
Boehm-Madisen Lumber Company
  Inc. (Construction Materials and
  Machinery) [7066]
Edison Liquor Corp. (Alcoholic Beverages) [1670]
Entre (Computers and Software) [6252]
Geis Building Products Inc. (Construction Materials
  and Machinery) [7381]
Hydrite Chemical Co. (Chemicals) [4424]
Intrepid Systems Inc. (Computers and
  Software) [6393]
Kuehn Company Inc.; Otto L. (Food) [11654]
Meier Inc.; Walter (Food) [11844]
Milwaukee Appliance Parts Company
  Inc. (Household Appliances) [15233]
Palmer/Snyder Furniture Co. (Furniture and
  Fixtures) [13204]
P.C. Solutions Inc., Entre' (Computers and
  Software) [6600]
T and A Industrial Distributors (Industrial
  Supplies) [17211]
Theis Company Inc.; H.W. (Plumbing Materials and
  Fixtures) [23408]
The Upholstery Supply Co. (Textiles and
  Notions) [26240]
US Chemical Corporation (Chemicals) [4541]
Wisconsin Lift Truck Corp. (Industrial
  Machinery) [16643]
Ziegenbein Associates Inc. (Electrical and Electronic
  Equipment and Supplies) [9626]

Butler

Aring Equipment Company Inc. (Construction
  Materials and Machinery) [6984]
Butler Beef Inc. (Food) [10648]
Crucible Service Center (Hardware) [13649]
Data Management Corp. (Office Equipment and
  Supplies) [20950]
Inland Detroit Diesel-Allison
  Inc. (Automotive) [2779]
Richards Machinery Company Inc.; L.L. (Industrial
  Machinery) [16452]
Wisconsin Packing Company Inc. (Food) [12966]

Cambridge

Melster Candies Inc. (Food) [11849]

Cedarburg

Cedarburg Lumber Company Inc. (Construction
  Materials and Machinery) [7156]
Horizons Marketing Group Inc. (Cleaning and
  Janitorial Supplies) [4635]
Landmark Supply Company Inc. (Agricultural
  Equipment and Supplies) [936]
Mustela USA (Health and Beauty Aids) [14169]
Mustela USA (Medical, Dental, and Optical
  Supplies) [19472]

Chilton

Cooperative Service Oil Co. (Agricultural Equipment
  and Supplies) [459]

Chippewa Falls

River Country Cooperative (Agricultural Equipment
  and Supplies) [1197]
Tackle Craft (Recreational and Sporting
  Goods) [24002]
Thaler Oil Company Inc. (Petroleum, Fuels, and
  Related Equipment) [22732]
Wright and Co.; E.T. (Shoes) [24900]

Cleveland

East Central Cooperative Inc. (Agricultural
  Equipment and Supplies) [534]

Clinton

DeLong Company Inc. (Agricultural Equipment and
  Supplies) [506]

Colby

Harmony Co-op (Livestock and Farm
  Products) [17976]
Harmony Country Cooperatives (Agricultural
  Equipment and Supplies) [792]

Columbus

Hughes Company Inc. of Columbus (Restaurant
  and Commercial Foodservice Equipment and
  Supplies) [24139]
May Steel Corp. (Metals) [20160]
Mid State Power and Equipment Inc. (Agricultural
  Equipment and Supplies) [1028]

Combined Locks

Jenkel Oil Company Inc. (Petroleum, Fuels, and
  Related Equipment) [22387]
U.S. Oil Company Inc. (Automotive) [3371]

Cottage Grove

Cottage Grove Cooperative (Agricultural Equipment
  and Supplies) [465]

Cross Plains

Zanders Creamery Inc. (Food) [13000]

Darlington

Agri-Tech F.S. Inc. (Agricultural Equipment and
  Supplies) [212]
Peoples Communitive Oil Cooperative (Petroleum,
  Fuels, and Related Equipment) [22562]

De Pere

Cummins Great Lakes Inc. (Automotive) [2506]
Progressive Farmers Cooperative (Agricultural
  Equipment and Supplies) [1158]
Wisconsin Bearing (Automotive) [3442]

Delavan

Ajay Leisure Products Inc. (Recreational and
  Sporting Goods) [23498]
Flotec-Town and Country (Plumbing Materials and
  Fixtures) [23170]

Dorchester

Cooperative Services of Clark County (Agricultural
  Equipment and Supplies) [460]

Durand

Bauer Built Inc. (Automotive) [2328]

Eagle River

Eagle River Distributing (Alcoholic
  Beverages) [1667]

Eau Claire

Dadco Food Products Inc. (Food) [10891]
Eau Claire Plumbing Supply Co. (Plumbing
  Materials and Fixtures) [23145]
M & L Motor Supply Co. (Automotive) [2900]
Phillips and Son Inc.; Max (Used, Scrap, and
  Recycled Materials) [26939]
Phillips and Sons (Eau Claire, Wisconsin);
  Ed (Alcoholic Beverages) [1954]
Phillips and Sons; Ed (Alcoholic Beverages) [1955]

Edgerton

Southern Wisconsin News (Books and Other
  Printed Materials) [4175]

Elk Mound

Four Seasons F.S. Inc. (Livestock and Farm
  Products) [17921]

Elkhorn

Consumer Cooperative of Walworth
  County (Agricultural Equipment and
  Supplies) [441]
Getzen Co. (Sound and Entertainment Equipment
  and Supplies) [25210]

Ellsworth

Ellsworth Farmers Union Cooperative Oil
  Co. (Agricultural Equipment and Supplies) [549]

Elm Grove

Reinders, Inc. (Agricultural Equipment and
  Supplies) [1181]

Elroy

Midor Ltd. (Agricultural Equipment and
  Supplies) [1033]

Evansville

W-L Research Inc. (Livestock and Farm
  Products) [18320]

Fennimore

New Horizons Supply Cooperative (Agricultural
  Equipment and Supplies) [1072]

Fond du Lac

Badger Liquor Company Inc. (Alcoholic
  Beverages) [1496]
Fedco Electronics Inc. (Electrical and Electronic
  Equipment and Supplies) [8733]
Hornung's Pro Golf Sales Inc. (Recreational and
  Sporting Goods) [23731]
Interstate Bearing
  Technologies (Automotive) [2795]
RB Royal Industries Inc. (Plumbing Materials and
  Fixtures) [23336]
Sadoff and Rudoy Industries (Used, Scrap, and
  Recycled Materials) [26974]
Wisconsin Bearing (Industrial Supplies) [17283]

Forest

GCR Truck Tire Center (Automotive) [2666]

Ft. Atkinson

Highsmith Inc. (Sound and Entertainment
  Equipment and Supplies) [25232]

Highsmith Inc. (Furniture and Fixtures) [13132]
Jones Dairy Farm Distributors (Food) [11561]
Lorman Iron and Metal Co. (Used, Scrap, and Recycled Materials) [26887]
Nasco-Catalog (Toys and Hobby Goods) [26589]

Franklin
Ken Dor Corp. (Marine) [18533]

Franksville
Quick Cable Corporation (Electrical and Electronic Equipment and Supplies) [9252]
Supa Machinery Sales Inc. (Industrial Machinery) [16540]

Fredonia
Petersen Products Co. (Plumbing Materials and Fixtures) [23314]

Friesland
Alsum Produce Inc. (Food) [10385]

Gays Mills
Pettit and Sons (Recreational and Sporting Goods) [23878]

Genoa City
Robinson Wholesale Inc. (Recreational and Sporting Goods) [23917]

Germantown
Airgas Safety (Medical, Dental, and Optical Equipment) [18665]
Applied Biochemists, Inc. (Chemicals) [4325]
Bell Industries (Marine) [18459]
BRIO Corp. (Toys and Hobby Goods) [26426]
Design House Inc. (Hardware) [13664]
Dohmen Co.; F. (Health and Beauty Aids) [14086]
Forrer Supply Company Inc. (Plumbing Materials and Fixtures) [23173]
Karthauser and Sons Inc. (Horticultural Supplies) [14902]
William/Reid Ltd. (Specialty Equipment and Products) [25882]

Glendale
Allcomm of Wisconsin (Communications Systems and Equipment) [5506]

Grafton
Fine-Line Products Inc. (Clothing) [4953]

Grantsburg
Burnett Dairy Cooperative (Livestock and Farm Products) [17756]

Green Bay
Amerhart Ltd. (Construction Materials and Machinery) [6956]
American Floor Covering (Floorcovering Equipment and Supplies) [9669]
Bark River Culvert and Equipment Co. (Construction Materials and Machinery) [7022]
Dey Distributing (Heating and Cooling Equipment and Supplies) [14419]
Executive Office Furniture Outlet (Office Equipment and Supplies) [20996]
Global Optics Inc. (Medical, Dental, and Optical Supplies) [19340]
Grimstad, Inc.; J.M. (Chemicals) [4402]
Halron Oil Company Inc. (Petroleum, Fuels, and Related Equipment) [22332]
Huttig Sash & Door Co. (Construction Materials and Machinery) [7502]
Lov-It Creamery Inc. (Food) [11737]
Machine Service, Inc. (Automotive) [2902]
Meat Processors Inc. (Food) [11843]
Morley Murphy Co. (Electrical and Electronic Equipment and Supplies) [9096]
Pomps Tire Service Inc. (Automotive) [3102]
Samuels Recycling Co. Green Bay Div. (Metals) [20352]
Seaway Foods Co. (Food) [12455]
ShopKo Stores Inc. (Food) [12482]

Thew Supply Company Inc.; W.E. (Industrial Supplies) [17225]
Truck Equipment Inc. (Automotive) [3347]
United Scale and Engr. Corp. (Scientific and Measurement Devices) [24450]
Van's Supply and Equipment Inc. (Agricultural Equipment and Supplies) [1396]
VerHalen Inc. (Construction Materials and Machinery) [8180]
Vorpahl, Inc.; W.A. (Security and Safety Equipment) [24659]
WOS Inc. (Medical, Dental, and Optical Supplies) [19713]

Greendale
Dewco Milwaukee Sales (Hardware) [13665]

Greenwood
Barr Enterprises Inc. (Veterinary Products) [27079]
Grassland Dairy Products Inc. (Food) [11310]

Hartford
Automating Peripherals Inc. (Computers and Software) [5989]

Hartland
Batteries Plus L.P. (Automotive) [2326]
Battery Products Inc. (Electrical and Electronic Equipment and Supplies) [8420]
Eye Communication Systems Inc. (Photographic Equipment and Supplies) [22852]
Holt Electric Inc. (Electrical and Electronic Equipment and Supplies) [8853]

Hatley
Hatley Lumber Co. Inc. (Construction Materials and Machinery) [7453]

Hayward
Beehive Botanicals Inc. (Medical, Dental, and Optical Supplies) [19181]
Northern Lakes Co-op Inc. (Agricultural Equipment and Supplies) [1084]

Hilbert
Thiel Cheese Inc. (Food) [12712]

Hillsboro
Hillsboro Equipment Inc. (Agricultural Equipment and Supplies) [826]

Ixonia
Real Veal Inc. (Agricultural Equipment and Supplies) [1174]

Janesville
Addie Water Systems (Specialty Equipment and Products) [25546]
Bowles Sales; Gay (Textiles and Notions) [25987]
Certified Parts Corp. (Marine) [18477]
JVLNET By Electrolarm (Computers and Software) [6413]
JVLNET By Electrolarm (Restaurant and Commercial Foodservice Equipment and Supplies) [24153]
Lab Safety Supply Inc. (Medical, Dental, and Optical Equipment) [18880]
LeMans Corp. (Motorized Vehicles) [20672]
Northland Equipment Company, Inc. (Automotive) [3047]
Samuels Recycling Co. Janesville Div. (Used, Scrap, and Recycled Materials) [26978]
Schlueter Company Inc. (Restaurant and Commercial Foodservice Equipment and Supplies) [24216]
State Electrical Supply Inc. (Electrical and Electronic Equipment and Supplies) [9414]
Wis WetGoods Co. (Alcoholic Beverages) [2133]

Jefferson
Jefferson County Farmco Coop. (Agricultural Equipment and Supplies) [881]

Kansasville
Kenosha-Racine FS Cooperative (Agricultural Equipment and Supplies) [905]

Kaukauna
Roloff Manufacturing Corp. (Marine) [18595]

Kenosha
Beard and Associates Inc.; Robert A. (Plastics) [22934]
G. Leblanc Corp. (Sound and Entertainment Equipment and Supplies) [25204]
Matthews Paint Co. (Paints and Varnishes) [21497]
Snap-on Tools Corp. (Hardware) [13925]

Kimberly
Crane Engineering Sales Inc. (Industrial Machinery) [15918]
Design Air (Heating and Cooling Equipment and Supplies) [14418]

La Crosse
Badger Corrugating Co. (Construction Materials and Machinery) [7010]
Bakalars Brothers Sausage Co. (Food) [10489]
Gateway Foods Inc. (Food) [11242]
La Crosse Footwear, Inc. (Shoes) [24788]
La Crosse Truck Center Inc. (Motorized Vehicles) [20668]
Markos Wholesale Clothing Distributors (Clothing) [5166]
Pepsi-Cola Bottling Company of La Crosse (Books and Other Printed Materials) [4054]
Randall-Graw Company Inc. (Industrial Supplies) [17129]
Reinhart Food Service Inc. (Food) [12297]
Roosevelt Co.; W.A. (Heating and Cooling Equipment and Supplies) [14667]
Trane Co (Heating and Cooling Equipment and Supplies) [14735]
Wisconsin Bearing (Industrial Machinery) [16642]

Lake Geneva
Midwest Action Cycle (Motorized Vehicles) [20681]

Lake Mills
Wisco Farm Cooperative (Food) [12965]

Lancaster
Eastman-Cartwright Lumber Co. (Construction Materials and Machinery) [7301]

Larsen
Larsen Cooperative Company Inc. (Agricultural Equipment and Supplies) [939]

Lena
Branch Cheese Co. (Food) [10607]

Little Chute
Jacks Original Pizza (Food) [11542]
Van Zeeland Oil Company Inc. (Petroleum, Fuels, and Related Equipment) [22769]

Lomira
Knowles Produce and Trading Co. (Agricultural Equipment and Supplies) [916]

Madison
Badger Popcorn Co. (Food) [10487]
Chocolate Shoppe Ice Cream (Food) [10754]
Conney Safety Products Co. (Security and Safety Equipment) [24527]
Coyle Inc. (Household Items) [15459]
Cuna Strategic Services, Inc. (Office Equipment and Supplies) [20942]
Dailey Metal Group Inc. (Metals) [19914]
Danco Prairie FS Cooperative (Agricultural Equipment and Supplies) [492]
Demco Inc. (Office Equipment and Supplies) [20954]
Diamond Comic Distributors Inc. (Books and Other Printed Materials) [3693]
Dick's Superior Metal Sales (Metals) [19930]

Douglas Stewart Co. (Computers and Software) [6220]
Earth Care Paper Inc. (Used, Scrap, and Recycled Materials) [26800]
Edison West Liquor (Alcoholic Beverages) [1671]
Eggimann Motor and Equipment Sales Inc. (Automotive) [2577]
Electric Motors Unlimited Inc. (Electrical and Electronic Equipment and Supplies) [8665]
First Supply Group (Plumbing Materials and Fixtures) [23169]
General Beer Distributors (Alcoholic Beverages) [1706]
General Beverage Sales Co. (Alcoholic Beverages) [1707]
Great Lake Distributors (Electrical and Electronic Equipment and Supplies) [8815]
Gregory Inc.; E.Z. (Health and Beauty Aids) [14116]
HAACO Inc. (Agricultural Equipment and Supplies) [779]
Harder Paper and Packaging Inc. (Paper and Paper Products) [21755]
Interstate Periodical Distributors Inc. (Books and Other Printed Materials) [3854]
Jaeckle Wholesale Inc. (Floorcovering Equipment and Supplies) [9978]
Kinetics Inc. (Construction Materials and Machinery) [7557]
Machine Service Inc. (Automotive) [2903]
Madison Appliance Parts Inc. (Household Appliances) [15206]
Madison Dairy Produce Company Inc. (Food) [11756]
Mautz Paint Co. (Paints and Varnishes) [21499]
Newell Office Products (Office Equipment and Supplies) [21163]
North Farm Cooperative (Food) [12028]
Olds Seed Co.; L.L. (Agricultural Equipment and Supplies) [1104]
P & B Truck Accessories (Automotive) [3067]
PanVera Corp. (Medical, Dental, and Optical Supplies) [19522]
Parts Now! Inc. (Computers and Software) [6593]
Phillips Distributing Corp. (Alcoholic Beverages) [1953]
Rowley-Schlimgen Inc. (Office Equipment and Supplies) [21249]
Samuels Recycling Co. (Used, Scrap, and Recycled Materials) [26977]
Stewart Co.; Douglas (Computers and Software) [6761]
Sweet of Madison, Inc.; A.J. (Food) [12655]
Temperature Systems Inc. (Heating and Cooling Equipment and Supplies) [14718]
Viking Cue Manufacturing, Inc. (Recreational and Sporting Goods) [24033]
Vita Plus Corp. (Agricultural Equipment and Supplies) [1400]
Wisconsin Bearing (Industrial Supplies) [17284]
Wisconsin Brick & Block Corp. (Floorcovering Equipment and Supplies) [10303]
Wisconsin Distributors Inc. (Alcoholic Beverages) [2134]
Wisconsin Drywall Distributors (Construction Materials and Machinery) [8234]
Wisconsin Supply Corp. (Plumbing Materials and Fixtures) [23464]
Wisconsin Wholesale Beer Distributor (Alcoholic Beverages) [2135]

Manitowoc

Chermak Sausage Co. (Food) [10738]
Natural Ovens of Manitowoc Inc. (Food) [11984]
Radandt Sons Inc.; Fred (Construction Materials and Machinery) [7896]
Stangel Co.; J.J. (Industrial Supplies) [17195]

Marathon

Rib River Valley Cooperative (Agricultural Equipment and Supplies) [1187]

Marinette

Aerial Company Inc. (Health and Beauty Aids) [14009]

Interstate Welding Sales Corp. (Industrial Machinery) [16168]
Interstate Welding Sales Corp. (Industrial Supplies) [16963]

Markesan

Grand River Cooperative Inc. (Agricultural Equipment and Supplies) [756]

Marshfield

Fleming Companies, Inc. (Food) [11146]
Hub City Foods Inc. (Food) [11470]
Johnson Garment Corp. (Clothing) [5091]
Nelson-Jameson Inc. (Industrial Machinery) [16347]
Northern Auto Supply Co. (Automotive) [3046]
Prince Corp. (Agricultural Equipment and Supplies) [1151]
Wenzel Farm Sausage (Food) [12902]

Mauston

Mauston Farmers Cooperative (Agricultural Equipment and Supplies) [993]

Mayville

Deli USA (Food) [10940]
RuMar Manufacturing Corp. (Metals) [20337]

Mc Farland

Diversified Investments Inc. (Recreational and Sporting Goods) [23625]
Ferguson Enterprises (Plumbing Materials and Fixtures) [23162]
Midwest Greeting Card Distributor (Paper and Paper Products) [21836]

Medford

Medford Co-operative Inc. (Livestock and Farm Products) [18085]

Menomonee Falls

Babush Corp. (Industrial Machinery) [15796]
Cream City Scale Company Inc. (Scientific and Measurement Devices) [24342]
Deuster Co. (Restaurant and Commercial Foodservice Equipment and Supplies) [24104]
Dielectric Corp. (Plastics) [22954]
North Central Book Distributors (Books and Other Printed Materials) [4008]
Pagel Safety Inc. (Security and Safety Equipment) [24610]
Weimer Bearing & Transmission Inc. (Electrical and Electronic Equipment and Supplies) [9568]

Menomonie

Menomonie Farmers Union Cooperative (Agricultural Equipment and Supplies) [1015]

Mequon

Granite Microsystems, Inc. (Computers and Software) [6307]
Kasch Co.; M.W. (Toys and Hobby Goods) [26550]
McLean International Marketing Inc. (Security and Safety Equipment) [24589]
McLean International Marketing Inc. (Industrial Supplies) [17028]
Softworks Development Corp. (Computers and Software) [6743]

Merrill

Consumers Cooperative Exchange (Agricultural Equipment and Supplies) [444]
Merrill Distributing, Inc. (Food) [11858]

Middleton

Mid-Plains Communications Systems Inc. (Communications Systems and Equipment) [5676]
Midwest Pool Distributors Inc. (Recreational and Sporting Goods) [23829]
Pleasant Co. (Toys and Hobby Goods) [26618]
U.W. Provision Co. (Food) [12812]
Whole Pie Company Ltd. (Clothing) [5483]

Milwaukee

A-C Supply Inc. (Industrial Supplies) [16664]
Advanced Concepts Inc. (Computers and Software) [5886]
Allied Bearing (Automotive) [2209]
Alpha Source Inc. (Electrical and Electronic Equipment and Supplies) [8331]
Amateur Electronics Supply (Electrical and Electronic Equipment and Supplies) [8335]
American Millwork & Hardware, Inc. (Hardware) [13560]
Applied Industrial Technologies (Industrial Machinery) [15775]
Associated Allied Industries Inc. (Adhesives) [2]
Auer Steel & Heating Supply (Heating and Cooling Equipment and Supplies) [14328]
Babush Conveyor Corp. (Industrial Machinery) [15795]
Badger Trailer and Equipment Corp. (Automotive) [2309]
Badger Truck Center Inc. (Motorized Vehicles) [20596]
BDT Engineering Company Inc. - Industrial Products Div. (Heating and Cooling Equipment and Supplies) [14340]
Becker Food Company Inc. (Food) [10523]
Belarus Machinery Inc. (Agricultural Equipment and Supplies) [293]
Beloit Beverage Company Inc. (Alcoholic Beverages) [1519]
Benz Oil Inc. (Petroleum, Fuels, and Related Equipment) [22068]
Bergner and Co.; P.A. (Clothing) [4820]
Better Brands of Milwaukee Inc. (Alcoholic Beverages) [1525]
Boelter Companies Inc. (Restaurant and Commercial Foodservice Equipment and Supplies) [24079]
Boggis-Johnson Electric Co. (Electrical and Electronic Equipment and Supplies) [8451]
Brady Co. Xymox Div.; W.H. (Electrical and Electronic Equipment and Supplies) [8460]
Brady Corp. (Computers and Software) [6022]
Bruner Corp. (Specialty Equipment and Products) [25584]
Car Parts Inc. (Automotive) [2422]
Carpenter Brothers Inc. (Industrial Supplies) [16783]
Chesal Industries (Recreational and Sporting Goods) [23590]
Climatic Control Company Inc. (Heating and Cooling Equipment and Supplies) [14386]
Copy Plus Inc. (Office Equipment and Supplies) [20917]
Creative Store Design Inc. (Specialty Equipment and Products) [25614]
Derco Industries Inc. (Aeronautical Equipment and Supplies) [80]
Digicorp Inc. (Communications Systems and Equipment) [5595]
Dozier Equipment Co. (Industrial Machinery) [15960]
Empire Fish Co. (Food) [11045]
Entree Corp. (Food) [11050]
F and B Marketing Inc. (Electrical and Electronic Equipment and Supplies) [8726]
FABCO Equipment Inc. (Agricultural Equipment and Supplies) [558]
Fire Brick Engineers Co. (Construction Materials and Machinery) [7343]
Gould Athletic Supply (Recreational and Sporting Goods) [23694]
Grimstad Inc.; J.M. (Industrial Machinery) [16079]
Gruen Export Co. (Livestock and Farm Products) [17966]
Hallmark Building Supplies Inc. (Construction Materials and Machinery) [7433]
Hardlines Marketing Inc. (Hardware) [13735]
Herregan Distributors Inc. (Floorcovering Equipment and Supplies) [9947]
H.H. West Co. (Office Equipment and Supplies) [21032]
Holt Electric Motor Co. (Electrical and Electronic Equipment and Supplies) [8854]
Import Ltd. (Jewelry) [17453]

Jacobus Energy (Petroleum, Fuels, and Related Equipment) [22382]
Kangaroo Brand Inc. (Food) [11580]
Lakeside Oil Company Inc. (Petroleum, Fuels, and Related Equipment) [22417]
Lindsay Foods Inc. (Food) [11716]
Machine Service, Inc. (Automotive) [2904]
Manutec Inc. (Metals) [20150]
Marsh Electronics Inc. (Electrical and Electronic Equipment and Supplies) [9031]
MEE Material Handling Equipment (Industrial Machinery) [16286]
Mercantile Buyer's Service Inc. (Paints and Varnishes) [21500]
Milchap Products (Construction Materials and Machinery) [7710]
Miller's Bakery Inc. (Food) [11900]
Milwaukee Biscuit (Food) [11903]
Milwaukee Stove and Furnace Supply Company Inc. (Heating and Cooling Equipment and Supplies) [14606]
Modern Business Machines Inc. (Office Equipment and Supplies) [21149]
Monarch Ceramic Tile (Floorcovering Equipment and Supplies) [10048]
Motion Industries (Industrial Supplies) [17055]
National Business Furniture Inc. (Furniture and Fixtures) [13185]
Noerenberg's Wholesale Meats Inc. (Food) [12012]
Palermo's Frozen Pizza (Food) [12099]
Papercraft Inc. (Office Equipment and Supplies) [21204]
Peltz Group Inc. (Used, Scrap, and Recycled Materials) [26938]
Power Equipment Company (Household Appliances) [15278]
Precision Metals Inc. (Metals) [20292]
Radcom, Inc. (Communications Systems and Equipment) [5728]
Red Star Yeast and Products, A Division of Universal Foods Corp. (Food) [12287]
Ricom Electronics Ltd. (Computers and Software) [6690]
RSR Wholesale Guns Midwest, Inc. (Guns and Weapons) [13509]
RSR Wholesale Guns Midwest Inc. (Recreational and Sporting Goods) [23925]
Schinner Co.; A.D. (Paper and Paper Products) [21924]
Select Wines & Spirits Co. (Alcoholic Beverages) [2017]
Standard Electric Supply Co. (Electrical and Electronic Equipment and Supplies) [9402]
Stein Garden and Gifts (Horticultural Supplies) [14956]
Tempo Glove Manufacturing Inc. (Specialty Equipment and Products) [25839]
Tews Co. (Construction Materials and Machinery) [8112]
THP United Enterprises Inc. (Construction Materials and Machinery) [8127]
Tool Service Corp. (Industrial Machinery) [16565]
Trioptics, Inc. (Medical, Dental, and Optical Supplies) [19664]
United Plumbing and Heating Supply Co. (Plumbing Materials and Fixtures) [23423]
Walthers Inc.; Wm. K. (Toys and Hobby Goods) [26705]
Weiss Company Inc.; Max (Industrial Machinery) [16618]
Williams Steel and Supply Company Inc. (Metals) [20493]
Wisconsin Brake and Wheel Inc. (Automotive) [3443]
Wisconsin Office Systems (Office Equipment and Supplies) [21357]
Wisconsin Paper and Products Co. (Paper and Paper Products) [21995]
Wisconsin Steel and Tube Corp. (Metals) [20497]
Wolff Corp. (Industrial Machinery) [16646]

Mondovi

Mondovi Cooperative Equity Association Inc. (Agricultural Equipment and Supplies) [1045]

Monico

Ison Equipment Inc. (Industrial Machinery) [16175]

Monroe

Arrow Sales Inc. (Office Equipment and Supplies) [20812]
Huber Brewing Co., Inc.; Joseph (Alcoholic Beverages) [1767]
Monroe Truck Equipment Inc. (Automotive) [2980]

Montello

Gatzke Farms Inc. (Food) [11244]

Mt. Horeb

Mt. Horeb Farmers Coop. (Food) [11941]
Premier Cooperative (Agricultural Equipment and Supplies) [1147]

Mukwonago

Empire Level Manufacturing Corp. (Hardware) [13682]

Muskego

Richard's American Food Service (Food) [12313]

Nashotah

Best Locking Systems of Wisconsin Inc. (Security and Safety Equipment) [24514]

Neenah

Power & Telephone Supply Company, Inc. (Electrical and Electronic Equipment and Supplies) [9230]

Nekoosa

Nekoosa Corp. (Industrial Supplies) [17071]

Neopit

Menominee Tribal Enterprises (Construction Materials and Machinery) [7692]

New Berlin

ArtSource Inc. (Gifts and Novelties) [13308]
Beechwood Distributors Inc. (Alcoholic Beverages) [1514]
Caliendo-Savio Enterprises Inc. (Gifts and Novelties) [13325]
Rundle-Spence Manufacturing Co. (Plumbing Materials and Fixtures) [23355]
Tekra Corp. (Plastics) [23041]
United Scale and Engineering Co. (Specialty Equipment and Products) [25856]

New Holstein

Lakeside Harvestore Inc. (Construction Materials and Machinery) [7582]

New London

Wolf River Country Cooperative (Agricultural Equipment and Supplies) [1458]

New Richmond

Frontier Inc. (Agricultural Equipment and Supplies) [711]
Frontier Inc. (New Richmond, Wisconsin) (Agricultural Equipment and Supplies) [713]
Johnson Motor Sales Inc. (Automotive) [2825]
New Richmond Farmers Union Cooperative Oil Co. (Petroleum, Fuels, and Related Equipment) [22511]
Polfus Implement Inc. (Agricultural Equipment and Supplies) [1137]

Oak Creek

Reinhart Institutional Foods Inc. Milwaukee Div. (Food) [12298]

Oconomowoc

Bonded Spirits Corp. (Alcoholic Beverages) [1544]
Henbest & Associates, Inc.; Jen (Recreational and Sporting Goods) [23722]

Omro

H.O.W. Train Distribution (Toys and Hobby Goods) [26527]

Onalaska

DMV USA Inc. (Food) [10970]

Ontario

Meca Sportswear Inc. (Clothing) [5183]

Osceola

Motorbooks International (Books and Other Printed Materials) [3970]

Oshkosh

Lapham-Hickey Steel Corp. (Metals) [20118]
McDermott Co. Inc.; A.I. (Plumbing Materials and Fixtures) [23256]
Moes Marine Service (Marine) [18571]
Pluswood Distributors (Construction Materials and Machinery) [7872]
Plywood Oshkosh Inc. (Furniture and Fixtures) [13210]
Radford Co. (Construction Materials and Machinery) [7897]
School Stationers Corp. (Paper and Paper Products) [21925]

Owen

Badger Shooters Supply Inc. (Recreational and Sporting Goods) [23535]

Pewaukee

American Disc Corp. (Computers and Software) [5927]
Larson Co.; Gustave A. (Heating and Cooling Equipment and Supplies) [14516]
Roundy's, Inc. (Food) [12357]
Stark Candy Co., Division of New England Confectionery Co. (Food) [12572]
XPEDX (Paper and Paper Products) [22003]

Pleasant Prairie

Super Valu Inc. - Midwest Region (Food) [12628]

Plymouth

Consumer Care Products Inc. (Medical, Dental, and Optical Equipment) [18753]
Sargento Foods Inc. (Food) [12414]
Sargento Foods Inc. (Food) [12415]
Sartori Food Corp. (Food) [12417]

Port Washington

Century Acres Eggs Inc. (Food) [10725]
Smith Bros. Food Service Inc. (Food) [12506]
Smith Brothers Food Service Inc. (Food) [12508]

Portage

S I Metals (Metals) [20346]

Prairie du Chien

Prairie Tool Co. (Industrial Machinery) [16419]
Starks Sport Shop (Recreational and Sporting Goods) [23984]

Pulaski

Pulaski Chase Cooperative (Agricultural Equipment and Supplies) [1161]

Racine

All Fasteners Inc. (Hardware) [13546]
All Tool Sales Inc. (Hardware) [13550]
Best Electric Supply (Hardware) [13595]
CJW Inc. (Soft Drinks) [24927]
Creative Rehab (Medical, Dental, and Optical Supplies) [19257]
Kranz Inc. (Cleaning and Janitorial Supplies) [4654]
Nelson Electric Supply Company Inc. (Electrical and Electronic Equipment and Supplies) [9122]
Racine Vineyard Products (Alcoholic Beverages) [1976]

Random Lake

Kettle-Lakes Cooperative (Agricultural Equipment and Supplies) [909]

Reedsburg

R and L Supply Co-op (Agricultural Equipment and Supplies) [1166]

Reedsville

Reedsville Cooperative Association (Agricultural Equipment and Supplies) [1179]

Rhinelander

Fishing Hot Spots/FHS Maps (Books and Other Printed Materials) [3751]
Midwest Coca-Cola Bottling Co. Rhinelander (Soft Drinks) [24988]

Rice Lake

Rice Lake Farmers Union Cooperative (Agricultural Equipment and Supplies) [1188]

Richland Center

Consumers Cooperative (Agricultural Equipment and Supplies) [443]

Ridgeland

Ridgeland Chetek Cooperative (Agricultural Equipment and Supplies) [1193]

Rio

Rio Farmers Union Cooperative (Livestock and Farm Products) [18198]

Ripon

Condon Oil Company Inc. (Petroleum, Fuels, and Related Equipment) [22158]
Heritage Wafers Ltd. (Food) [11419]
Kemps Dairy Products Distributors (Food) [11598]

River Hills

Hecht Manufacturing Co. (Clothing) [5023]

Sauk City

Consumer Cooperative Oil Co. (Petroleum, Fuels, and Related Equipment) [22161]
Coop Country Partners (Agricultural Equipment and Supplies) [445]
McFarlane Manufacturing Company Inc. (Agricultural Equipment and Supplies) [1002]

Scandinavia

Anthony Farms Inc. (Food) [10421]

Schofield

Lake States Lumber (Construction Materials and Machinery) [7580]

Seymour

Center Valley Cooperative Association (Petroleum, Fuels, and Related Equipment) [22122]

Shawano

Shawano Equity Cooperative Inc. (Agricultural Equipment and Supplies) [1262]

Sheboygan

American Plumber (Specialty Equipment and Products) [25551]
Consumer Care Products Inc. (Medical, Dental, and Optical Supplies) [19246]
Reiss Coal Co.; C. (Minerals and Ores) [20561]
Schultz Sav-O Stores Inc. (Food) [12431]
Wisconsin Bearing (Industrial Supplies) [17285]

Sheboygan Falls

Feldmann Engineering & Manufacturing Company, Inc. (Agricultural Equipment and Supplies) [678]

Shell Lake

Shell Lake Cooperative (Petroleum, Fuels, and Related Equipment) [22666]

Silver Lake

Lotus Light Inc. (Medical, Dental, and Optical Supplies) [19417]
Wishing Well Video Distributing Co. (Sound and Entertainment Equipment and Supplies) [25526]
Wishing Well Video Distributing Co. (Household Appliances) [15375]

Sparta

Lake States Lumber (Construction Materials and Machinery) [7578]

Spring Green

Richland Ltd. (Automotive) [3157]

Stetsonville

Beyer Livestock; Allen (Food) [10550]

Stevens Point

Copps Corp. (Food) [10838]
Copps Distributing Co. (Food) [10839]
Kleenaire Corp. (Heating and Cooling Equipment and Supplies) [14511]
Point Sporting Goods Inc. (Recreational and Sporting Goods) [23889]

Stoddard

Wichelt Imports Inc. (Textiles and Notions) [26248]

Stone Lake

Bar-H-Implement Inc. (Agricultural Equipment and Supplies) [275]

Stratford

Central Wisconsin Cooperative (Agricultural Equipment and Supplies) [401]
Stratford Farmers Cooperative (Livestock and Farm Products) [18261]

Sturgeon Bay

Door County Cooperative Inc. (Agricultural Equipment and Supplies) [525]

Sturtevant

Poclain Hydraulics Inc. (Industrial Machinery) [16409]

Sullivan

Meyer and Son of Sullivan Inc.; L.W. (Agricultural Equipment and Supplies) [1021]

Sun Prairie

Hanley Company Inc. (Agricultural Equipment and Supplies) [786]
Maly (Floorcovering Equipment and Supplies) [10006]

Superior

Arco Coffee Co. (Food) [10431]
Common Health Warehouse Cooperative Association (Food) [10798]
Fleming Companies, Inc. (Food) [11147]
Lake States Lumber (Construction Materials and Machinery) [7579]
T.L.K. Industries Inc. (Industrial Supplies) [17230]
T.L.K. Industries Inc. (Used, Scrap, and Recycled Materials) [27025]

Sussex

Repete Corp. (Industrial Machinery) [16448]

Thiensville

Empire Generator Corp. (Electrical and Electronic Equipment and Supplies) [8702]
Mequon Distributors Inc. (Construction Materials and Machinery) [7695]

Tomah

Randall Inc.; H.G. (Livestock and Farm Products) [18190]

Two Rivers

Riverside Foods (Food) [12322]

Valders

Valders Cooperative (Livestock and Farm Products) [18312]

Van Dyne

Lone Elm Sales Inc. (Food) [11726]

Warrens

Wildhawk Inc. (Agricultural Equipment and Supplies) [1448]

Waterford

Flitz International Ltd. (Petroleum, Fuels, and Related Equipment) [22283]

Waterloo

McKay Nursery Company Inc. (Horticultural Supplies) [14920]
Micrographics (Computers and Software) [6502]
Trek Corp. (Household Appliances) [15341]

Watertown

River Valley Cooperative (Agricultural Equipment and Supplies) [1198]

Waukesha

Acme Machell Company Inc. (Rubber) [24264]
Buck Rub Archery Inc. (Recreational and Sporting Goods) [23573]
Etac USA Inc. (Medical, Dental, and Optical Equipment) [18793]
Etac USA Inc. (Medical, Dental, and Optical Supplies) [19308]
Food Ingredients and Additives Group (Chemicals) [4393]
Fox Point Sportswear Inc. (Clothing) [4965]
Generac Corp. (Electrical and Electronic Equipment and Supplies) [8782]
Geo-Synthetics Inc. (Textiles and Notions) [26042]
Great Lakes Marketing Inc. (Food) [11312]
Holoubek Inc. (Clothing) [5033]
Hunt Electric Supply Co. (Electrical and Electronic Equipment and Supplies) [8865]
Mermaid Water Services (Specialty Equipment and Products) [25736]
Mid-America Power Drives (Industrial Machinery) [16295]
Outdoor Outfitters of Wisconsin Inc. (Scientific and Measurement Devices) [24412]
Pagel Safety Inc. (Security and Safety Equipment) [24611]
Payne & Dolan Inc. Muskego Site (Construction Materials and Machinery) [7843]
Pence Company Inc.; W.J. (Food) [12136]
Pinahs Company Inc. (Food) [12169]
Pizza Commissary Inc. (Food) [12178]
PMI-Eisenhart Wisconsin Div. (Food) [12185]
Price Engineering Company, Inc. (Industrial Supplies) [17116]
Thompson-Clark-Gerritsen Co. (Food) [12717]
Voell Machinery Company Inc. (Industrial Machinery) [16605]
Waukesha Wholesale Foods Inc. (Food) [12884]
Wiscomp Systems Inc. (Computers and Software) [6874]
W.O.W. Distributing Company Inc. (Alcoholic Beverages) [2139]

Waumandee

Garden Valley Coop. (Agricultural Equipment and Supplies) [723]

Waunakee

Hellenbrand Water Conditioners Inc. (Specialty Equipment and Products) [25676]
Statz and Sons Inc.; Carl F. (Agricultural Equipment and Supplies) [1294]
Yahara Materials Inc. (Construction Materials and Machinery) [8244]

Wausau

Hadley Office Products Inc. (Office Equipment and Supplies) [21022]
Hsu's Ginseng Enterprises Inc. (Food) [11469]

Lemke Cheese and Packaging Company Inc. (Food) [11698]
Linder Electric Motors Inc. (Electrical and Electronic Equipment and Supplies) [8993]
Motion Industries (Automotive) [2991]
Wausau Supply Co. (Construction Materials and Machinery) [8198]

Wauwatosa

Larsen Associates Inc. (Electrical and Electronic Equipment and Supplies) [8972]
Miller-Brands-Milwaukee L.L.C. (Alcoholic Beverages) [1878]
Pick'n Save Warehouse Foods Inc. (Food) [12165]

West Allis

Allied Electronics (Electrical and Electronic Equipment and Supplies) [8312]
Fuchs Copy Systems Inc. (Office Equipment and Supplies) [21008]
Lexco Tile (Floorcovering Equipment and Supplies) [9995]
Rainbow Sales Distributing (Gifts and Novelties) [13432]
Sullivan Dental Products Inc. (Medical, Dental, and Optical Equipment) [19059]

West Bend

Albert Trading Co. (Household Appliances) [14997]
Dairyland Seed Company Inc. (Agricultural Equipment and Supplies) [486]
Level Valley Creamery, Inc. (Food) [11703]
West Bend Elevator Inc. (Agricultural Equipment and Supplies) [1422]
West Bend Water Systems (Specialty Equipment and Products) [25876]

West Salem

Farmers Cooperative Supply and Shipping Association (Agricultural Equipment and Supplies) [638]

Westby

Westby Cooperative Creamery (Food) [12906]
Westby Farmers Union Cooperative (Agricultural Equipment and Supplies) [1428]

Westfield

McCartney Carpet (Floorcovering Equipment and Supplies) [10013]

Weyauwega

Wolfriver Country Cooperative (Petroleum, Fuels, and Related Equipment) [22814]

Whitefish Bay

Bucky Bairdo's Inc. (Food) [10639]

Whitewater

Badgerland Farm Center (Agricultural Equipment and Supplies) [269]

Windsor

Clack Corp. (Specialty Equipment and Products) [25601]

Wisconsin Dells

Holiday Wholesale Inc. (Tobacco Products) [26308]

Wisconsin Rapids

Applied Industrial Technologies, Inc. (Industrial Supplies) [16706]
Northland Cranberries Inc. (Food) [12033]

Wittenberg

Nueske Hillcrest Farm Meats (Food) [12043]

Zachow

Graf Creamery Co. (Food) [11302]

Wyoming

Basin

Wolverine Distributing (Books and Other Printed Materials) [4292]

Burns

Antelope Truck Stop (Automotive) [2241]

Casper

Ameri-Tech Equipment Co. (Construction Materials and Machinery) [6957]
Atlas Reproduction Inc. (Office Equipment and Supplies) [20820]
Blue Ribbon Awards (Jewelry) [17345]
Casper Pay-Less Drug Co. (Toys and Hobby Goods) [26438]
CRS Business Products (Office Equipment and Supplies) [20941]
Crum Electrical Supply Inc. (Electrical and Electronic Equipment and Supplies) [8596]
Diamond Vogel Paint Center (Paints and Varnishes) [21432]
Drive Train Industries Inc. (Automotive) [2564]
Eaton Metal Products Co. (Petroleum, Fuels, and Related Equipment) [22222]
Fleischli Oil Company Inc. (Petroleum, Fuels, and Related Equipment) [22281]
Homax Oil (Petroleum, Fuels, and Related Equipment) [22357]
Knapp Supply & Equipment Co. (Restaurant and Commercial Foodservice Equipment and Supplies) [24160]
Lord Equipment Co. (Petroleum, Fuels, and Related Equipment) [22437]
M & M Chemical Supply Inc. (Cleaning and Janitorial Supplies) [4661]
M and M Chemical Supply Inc. (Chemicals) [4444]
National Oil Well Inc. (Industrial Machinery) [16342]
Nick's Junk Inc. (Automotive) [3032]
The Paint Store (Paints and Varnishes) [21528]
Sedmak; Louie (Construction Materials and Machinery) [7998]
Sherwin Williams Paint Co. (Paints and Varnishes) [21568]
Toolpushers Supply Co. (Construction Materials and Machinery) [8139]
Western Distributing Company Inc. (Alcoholic Beverages) [2115]
Woodworker's Supply Inc. (Wood and Wood Products) [27396]
Wyoming Machinery Co. (Construction Materials and Machinery) [8242]
Wyoming Periodical Distributors (Books and Other Printed Materials) [4300]
Wyoming Stationery Company of Casper (Office Equipment and Supplies) [21364]

Cheyenne

Advanced Financial Systems (Office Equipment and Supplies) [20776]
Big W Supplies Inc. (Cleaning and Janitorial Supplies) [4581]
Cook Co.; P.S. (Plumbing Materials and Fixtures) [23127]
Corral West Ranchwear Inc. (Clothing) [4897]
Dairy Gold Foods Co. (Food) [10896]
Diamond Vogel Paint Center (Paints and Varnishes) [21431]
Ellenbecker Oil Co. (Petroleum, Fuels, and Related Equipment) [22226]
Fisher's Incorporated Painting Co. (Paints and Varnishes) [21441]
Fleischli Oil Company Inc. (Petroleum, Fuels, and Related Equipment) [22279]
Hartsook Equipment & Pump Services (Petroleum, Fuels, and Related Equipment) [22340]
Holmes A-One Inc. (Construction Materials and Machinery) [7478]
Komac Paint Center (Paints and Varnishes) [21474]
Moreland Wholesale Co., Inc. (Food) [11935]
Otto's Paint & Supply Co. (Paints and Varnishes) [21520]

Ourrison Inc. (Alcoholic Beverages) [1936]
Powers Products Co. (Construction Materials and Machinery) [7882]
Sherwin Williams Paint Co. (Paints and Varnishes) [21569]
Stanfields Inc. (Office Equipment and Supplies) [21286]
State Beauty Supply (Health and Beauty Aids) [14246]
Thomas & Jones Sales Management (Livestock and Farm Products) [18279]
Unicover Corp. (Toys and Hobby Goods) [26697]
Wyoming Liquor Division (Alcoholic Beverages) [2141]
Wyoming Machinery Co. (Construction Materials and Machinery) [8243]

Cody

Big Horn Wholesale (Cleaning and Janitorial Supplies) [4580]
Cash Wholesale Candy Co. (Food) [10712]
Eagle of Cody Printing (Paper and Paper Products) [21717]
T.E.I./Texaco Bulk Services (Food) [12704]

Evanston

Evanston Wholesale Inc. (Alcoholic Beverages) [1681]
Flying J Travel Plaza (Petroleum, Fuels, and Related Equipment) [22285]

Evansville

Dooley Oil Company, Inc. (Petroleum, Fuels, and Related Equipment) [22207]

Gillette

D.O. Inc. (Petroleum, Fuels, and Related Equipment) [22206]
Farmers Cooperative Association (Agricultural Equipment and Supplies) [571]
Gillette Air Inc. (Aeronautical Equipment and Supplies) [93]
Goodell's Refrigeration (Heating and Cooling Equipment and Supplies) [14472]

Greybull

Big Corn Cooperative Marketing Association Inc. (Agricultural Equipment and Supplies) [308]
Big Horn Cooperative Market Association Inc. (Agricultural Equipment and Supplies) [309]
Lloyds Buying Service (Livestock and Farm Products) [18062]

Jackson

Alpine Slide of Jackson Hole (Recreational and Sporting Goods) [23507]
Frontier Texaco (Petroleum, Fuels, and Related Equipment) [22295]
Jackson Hole Distributing (Alcoholic Beverages) [1777]
Life-Link International (Recreational and Sporting Goods) [23787]
Sanchez Fine Jewelers (Jewelry) [17587]

La Barge

Exxon Company USA (Petroleum, Fuels, and Related Equipment) [22245]

Lander

Boedeker; Robert L. (Livestock and Farm Products) [17742]

Laramie

Dooley Oil Company, Inc. (Petroleum, Fuels, and Related Equipment) [22208]
Fortman's Paint & Glass (Paints and Varnishes) [21445]
G and G Enterprises Inc. (Alcoholic Beverages) [1701]
Jethro Publications (Books and Other Printed Materials) [3864]
Rainbow Photography (Photographic Equipment and Supplies) [22896]
Van's Candy & Tobacco Service (Food) [12830]

Lingle

Rose Brothers Inc. (Agricultural Equipment and Supplies) [1210]

Lovell

Sage Creek Refining Co. (Petroleum, Fuels, and Related Equipment) [22647]

Midwest

MGD Enterprises (Jewelry) [17524]

Mills

Fluid Power Equipment (Industrial Machinery) [16019]
Masek Sports Inc. (Recreational and Sporting Goods) [23805]
Truckways Inc. (Automotive) [3351]

Pine Bluffs

Bluffs Budget Plumbing (Plumbing Materials and Fixtures) [23090]

Pinedale

Hay Land and Livestock Inc. (Livestock and Farm Products) [17985]

Rawlins

Desert Beverage Co. Inc. (Alcoholic Beverages) [1643]
Kilburn and Company Inc.; J.C. (Petroleum, Fuels, and Related Equipment) [22404]

Riverton

Flying Phoenix Corp. (Explosives) [9634]
Flying Phoenix Corp. (Toys and Hobby Goods) [26485]
Fremont Chemical Company Inc. (Chemicals) [4395]
Hunter The Typewriter Man (Office Equipment and Supplies) [21044]
Peterson Distributing Co. (Alcoholic Beverages) [1951]
Weber Office Supply Inc. (Office Equipment and Supplies) [21349]

Rock Springs

Bertolina Wholesale Co. (Alcoholic Beverages) [1521]
Fleischli Oil Company Inc. (Petroleum, Fuels, and Related Equipment) [22280]
McFadden Wholesale Company Inc.; F.B. (Cleaning and Janitorial Supplies) [4666]
Rock Springs Casper Coca-Cola Bottling Co. (Soft Drinks) [25026]
Western Wyoming Beverage Inc. (Soft Drinks) [25051]

Sheridan

Bison Oil (Petroleum, Fuels, and Related Equipment) [22075]
Gligorea Livestock (Livestock and Farm Products) [17943]
Lannans Paint & Decorating Ctr. (Paints and Varnishes) [21486]

Metz Beverage Company Inc. (Alcoholic Beverages) [1869]
Metz Beverage Company Inc. (Alcoholic Beverages) [1870]
Sherwin Williams Paint Co. (Paints and Varnishes) [21570]
Solutions and Cleaning Products (Cleaning and Janitorial Supplies) [4710]
Solutions and Cleaning Products (Restaurant and Commercial Foodservice Equipment and Supplies) [24224]

Thermopolis

Business With Pleasure (Office Equipment and Supplies) [20870]

Torrington

Tri County Coors (Alcoholic Beverages) [2085]

Wheatland

Basins Inc. (Construction Materials and Machinery) [7028]
Wheatland Rock Shop (Jewelry) [17655]

Worland

Timberline Feed Lot Inc. (Livestock and Farm Products) [18283]
Worland Livestock Auction Inc. (Livestock and Farm Products) [18359]

Alphabetic Index

This index provides an alphabetical arrangement of all the companies in this directory. When the company name is a personal name, the company name is alphabetized by the surname unless the first name or initial(s) are part of a trade name. See the User's Guide at the front of this directory for additional information.

1-800-Batteries, 9393 Gateway Dr., Reno, NV 89511-8910, (775)746-6140 [8871]

1st Call McCall Heating and Clng, 1650 NE Lombard St., Portland, OR 97211, (503)231-3311 [15718]

1st Source Parts Center, 3442 Stanford NE, Albuquerque, NM 87107, (505)884-0166 [14983]

2-Way Radio Communications Engineering, 309 Main St., PO Box 209, Williamsburg, KY 40769-0209, (606)549-2250 [5496]

2BU-Wear, 188 Clayton St., San Francisco, CA 94117, (415)752-9820 [4736]

3-D Energy Inc., Pierce Rd., Buxton, ME 04093, (207)929-8804 [22013]

3-D Optical Lab Inc., 1370 S Bertolsen Rd., PO Box 2842, Eugene, OR 97402, (541)683-3898 [19116]

3-D Supply Inc., 3540 W Sahara Ave., Ste. 290, Las Vegas, NV 89102-5816, (702)877-0805 [4562]

3 GI Athletics Inc., 9037 14th Ave. NW, Seattle, WA 98117, (206)782-5860 [23489]

3 Springs Water Co., 1800 Pine Run Rd., Wilkes Barre, PA 18702-9419, (717)823-7019 [24902]

3 Springs Water Co., 1800 Pine Run Rd., Wilkes Barre, PA 18702-9419, (717)823-7019 [10314]

3A Products, 1006 S San Pedro St., Los Angeles, CA 90015, (213)747-6090 [25951]

3K Livestock, 35375 Hwy. 228, Brownsville, OR 97327, (541)466-5161 [17668]

3M, 3M Ctr., Bldg. 223-4NE-513, St. Paul, MN 55144-1000, (651)733-4751 [23933]

3M, 3M Center, St. Paul, MN 55144-1000, (612)737-6501 [21147]

4 BS Wholesale Supply Inc., PO Box 7369, Missoula, MT 59807-7369, (406)543-8265 [24052]

4 Seasons Livestock, PO Box 509, Choteau, MT 59422-0509, (406)466-2169 [17669]

4 Wheel Center Inc., 7210 Gateway Blvd. E, El Paso, TX 79915-1301, (915)593-4848 [2147]

4th Street Tobacco Warehouse, 551 W 4th St., Lexington, KY 40508, (606)744-3191 [26255]

14 Carats Ltd., 314 S Beverly Dr., Beverly Hills, CA 90212, (310)551-1212 [17297]

20th Century Nursery Landscape, 1348 Liberty Pike, Franklin, TN 37064, (615)790-2790 [14790]

21st Century Holdings Inc., 2170 W State Rd. 434, Ste. 200, Longwood, FL 32779, (407)880-7200 [18650]

21st Century Telecom Group, 350 N Orleans St., Chicago, IL 60654-1509, (312)955-2100 [8256]

78ic Beauty Supply & Salons, Woodland Hills, 7021 S Memorial, Ste. 147, Tulsa, OK 74133, (918)252-4486 [14006]

84 Lumber Co., Rte. 519, Box 8484, Eighty Four, PA 15330, (412)228-8820 [6894]

800 JR Cigar Inc., 301 Rt. 10, E, Whippany, NJ 07981, (973)884-9555 [26256]

800 Spirits Inc., 385 Prospect Ave., Ste. 3, Hackensack, NJ 07601, (201)342-6330 [1470]

100,000 Parts, 2373 S Kinnickinnic Ave., Milwaukee, WI 53207, (414)744-3210 [15278]

A 1 Accredited Batteries, 714 Central Ave., Billings, MT 59102-5817, (406)245-9839 [2148]

A-1 Air Compressor Corp., 679 W Winthrop Ave., Addison, IL 60101, (630)543-2606 [15719]

A-1 Battery Distributors, 3220 A Ave., Gulfport, MS 39507, (228)868-6482 [2149]

A-1 Chemical Inc., 1197 Greg St., Sparks, NV 89431-6004, (702)331-7627 [4563]

A-1 International Foods, 5560 E Slauson Ave., City of Commerce, CA 90040, (213)722-2100 [10315]

A-1 Janitorial Supply & Equipment, 1419 Eastway Dr., Charlotte, NC 28205-2205, (704)537-9921 [14984]

A-1 Lock & Safe Co., 8485 Overland Rd., Boise, ID 83709-1642, (208)377-4500 [20758]

A-1 Metal Services Corp., 1275 Railroad St., Ste. A, Corona, CA 91718, (714)774-2800 [19719]

A-1 New & Used Auto Parts, Inc., PO Box 1087, Williston, ND 58802-1087, (701)774-8315 [2150]

A-1 Plumbers Supply, 994 20th St., Chico, CA 95928, (530)891-6428 [23048]

A-1 Refrigeration Inc., 1134 N 21st St., Lincoln, NE 68503, (402)476-2323 [14286]

A-1 Telecom Inc., PO Box 336, Niles, MI 49120-0336, (616)683-3870 [14985]

A & A Brake Service Co. Inc., 224 3rd Ave., Brooklyn, NY 11217-3036, (718)624-4488 [2151]

A & A Ceramic Tile, Inc., 11908 Mariposa Rd., Hesperia, CA 92345-1636, (760)948-3970 [9637]

A and A Connections Inc., 530 S Henderson Rd., King of Prussia, PA 19406, (610)354-9070 [5497]

A and A International Corp., 1200 1 Tandy Ctr., Ft. Worth, TX 76102, (817)390-3011 [25052]

A & A Midwest Distributing Inc., 2580 N Commerce St., North Las Vegas, NV 89030-3876, (702)649-7776 [2152]

A & A Office Systems Inc., 16 Old Forge Rd., Rocky Hill, CT 06067-3729, (860)257-4646 [5498]

A & A Plants, 5392 E NC 150 Hwy., Browns Summit, NC 27214, (919)656-7881 [14791]

A and A Pump Co., 1119 Camden St., San Antonio, TX 78215, (210)226-1191 [22014]

A & A Reconditioned Medical, 8601 Kenilworth Dr., Springfield, VA 22151, (703)978-4510 [18651]

A and A Technology Inc., 45277 Fremont Blvd., Ste. 11, Fremont, CA 94538, (510)226-8650 [5856]

A-Air Conditioning Contractor, 27332 Van Dyke Ave., Warren, MI 48093-2850, (313)372-5500 [14986]

A & B Business Equipment Inc., 2904 W Russell St., Sioux Falls, SD 57107-0706, (605)335-8520 [20759]

A & B Distributors, 3901 Tull Ave., Muskogee, OK 74403, (918)682-6331 [1471]

A & B Electronic Systems Inc., 612 Main Ave. N, Twin Falls, ID 83301-5740, (208)734-1740 [20760]

A-B Sales Inc., 435 Eldora St., Wichita, KS 67202, (316)264-1354 [1472]

A and B Wiper Supply Inc., 116 Fountain St., Philadelphia, PA 19127, (215)482-6100 [26723]

A C Auto Recycling, 6705 Juniper Dr., Missoula, MT 59802-5751, (406)258-6141 [2153]

A-C Book Service, 60 St. Felix St., Brooklyn, NY 11217-1206, (718)855-0600 [3457]

A-C Supply Inc., 8220 W Sleske, Milwaukee, WI 53223, (414)357-7350 [16664]

A C Systems, 3990 S Lipan St., Englewood, CO 80110-4422, (303)771-5000 [5857]

A. Camacho Inc., 2502 Walden Woods Dr., Plant City, FL 33566, (813)305-4534 [10316]

A-City Auto Glass, 2220 N Commerce St., North Las Vegas, NV 89030-4147, (702)649-3905 [2154]

A-Copy Inc., 7551 Winding Brook Dr., Glastonbury, CT 06033, (860)633-6070 [20761]

A and D Auto Parts Inc., 12166 York Rd., Cleveland, OH 44133-3601, (440)237-9300 [2155]

A & D Enterprises, Import-Export, 1128 Collingwood Lane, Bolingbrook, IL 60440, (630)378-1944 [2156]

A & D Maintenance, 230 Moonbeam Dr., Sparks, NV 89436-7262, (702)359-6394 [4564]

A. Daigger and Company Inc. Educational Teaching Aids, 500 Greenview Ct., Vernon Hills, IL 60061, (847)816-5050 [26458]

A-Dec Inc., PO Box 111, Newberg, OR 97132, (503)538-9471 [13007]

A-Dec International Inc., PO Box 111, Newberg, OR 97132-0111, (503)538-9471 [18652]

A-Doc Oil Co., 1617 N Garden Ave., Roswell, NM 88201, (505)622-4210 [22015]

A/E MicroSystems Inc., 4380 Malsbary Rd., Cincinnati, OH 45242-5644, (513)772-6700 [5858]

A and H Building Materials Co., 3361 E 36th St., Tucson, AZ 85713, (520)622-4741 [6895]

A & H Turf & Specialties Inc., 468 S Moore Ln., Billings, MT 59101-4729, (406)245-8466 [13519]

A & K Feed and Grain Company Inc., PO Box 158, Lime Springs, IA 52155, (319)566-2291 [17670]

A-K Medical Software Inc., PO Box 50329, Columbia, SC 29250, (803)695-5001 [18667]

A and K Railroad Materials Inc., PO Box 30076, Salt Lake City, UT 84130, (801)974-5484 [23471]

A & L Coors Inc., PO Box 215, Durango, CO 81302, (970)247-3620 [1473]

A and L Distributing Co., 13970 SW 72nd Ave., Portland, OR 97223, (503)684-9384 [8257]

A La Carte Jewelry, 1006 Pine St., Yankton, SD 57078-3056, (605)665-4179 [17298]

A. Louis Supply Co., 5610 Main Ave., Ashtabula, OH 44004-7200, (440)997-5161 [16665]

A and M Sales and Manufacturing Inc., 3605 Hwy. 45 N, Henderson, TN 38340, (901)989-9925 [4737]

A and M Supply Inc., 6701 90th Ave. N, Pinellas Park, FL 33782, (813)541-6631 [6896]

A & M Trading Company Inc., 25 Austin Blvd., Commack, NY 11725, (631)543-4490 [2157]

A-Mark Financial Corp., 100 Wilshire Blvd., 3rd Fl., Santa Monica, CA 90401, (310)319-0200 [19720]

A-Mark Precious Metals Inc., 100 Wilshire Blvd., 3rd Fl., Santa Monica, CA 90401, (310)319-0200 [17299]

A and A Mechanical Inc., 1101 Ulrich Ave., Louisville, KY 40219, (502)968-0164 [15720]

A-P-A Auto Parts, 8572 Brewezton Rd., Cicero, NY 13039, (315)699-2728 [2158]

A & P Auto Parts Inc., 8572 Brewezton Rd., Cicero, NY 13039, (315)699-2728 [2158]

A-Pet, Inc., 299 Beeline Dr., Bensenville, IL 60106, (708)595-6808 [27054]

A Pickle House/Judy Blair's Rustic Collectibles, 1401 E Van Buren St., Phoenix, AZ 85006-3523, (602)257-1915 [13008]

A Plus Medical, Inc., 948 Walton Way, Augusta, GA 30901-2893, (404)321-9478 [19117]

A Plus Sales & Service Inc., 1114 Iberia St., Franklin, LA 70538-4720, (318)828-4470 [5859]

A and R Lumber Sales Inc., PO Box 39, Junction City, OR 97448, (541)998-3700 [6897]

A & R Supply Co. Inc., 296 S Pauline St., Memphis, TN 38104, (901)527-0338 [14287]

A and S Corp., 819 Edwards Rd., Parsippany, NJ 07054, (201)575-6330 [4308]

A & S Suppliers, 1970 W 84 St., Hialeah, FL 33014, (305)557-1688 [15384]

A Timely Tech Services, 10301 Comanche Rd. NE, Albuquerque, NM 87111-3602, (505)296-6331 [20762]

A To Z Rental Center, 94-172 Leoole St., Waipahu, HI 96797, (808)677-9181 [6898]

A To Z Vending Service Corp., 109 Port Jersey Blvd., Jersey City, NJ 07305, (201)333-4900 [25539]

A-Top Polymers Inc., 47 Rockingham Rd., Windham, NH 03087-1307, (603)893-4366 [22917]

A & V TapeHandlers, Inc., Bemis Bldg., 55 S Atlantic St., Ste. 1A, Seattle, WA 98134-1217, (206)621-9222 [25053]

A & W Bearings & Supply, PO Box 561069, Dallas, TX 75247, (214)630-7681 [16666]

A & W Medical & Oxygen Supply, 100 Sampson St., Clinton, NC 28328-4037, (910)592-3882 [18653]

A and W Oil Company Inc., PO Box 6608, Ft. Smith, AR 72906, (501)646-0595 [22016]

A-Welders & Medical Supply, PO Box 3457, Knoxville, TN 37927-3457, (865)522-8350 [18654]

A-X Propane Co., 300 Airport Rd., Milan, NM 87021, (505)287-4346 [22017]

A & Z Pearls Inc., 550 S Hill, Ste. 660, Los Angeles, CA 90013-2401, (213)627-3030 [17300]

A to Z Tire & Battery Inc., 613 Broadway Blvd. SE, Albuquerque, NM 87101, (505)247-0134 [2159]

A2M Supply, 6189 Grovedale Ct., Alexandria, VA 22310, (703)922-2805 [6945]

AA-1 Used Auto Parts Inc., PO Box 1087, Williston, ND 58802-1087, (701)774-8315 [2150]

AA & A Enterprises Inc., 23-25 Lake Shore Dr. E, PO Box 284, Dunkirk, NY 14048, (716)366-0002 [19721]

AA Computech Inc., 28170 Crocker Ave., Ste. 105, Valencia, CA 91355, (805)257-6801 [5860]

AA Electric S.E. Inc., 2011 S Combee Rd., Lakeland, FL 33801, (863)665-6941 [15721]

AA Equipment, 10611 Ramona Ave., Montclair, CA 91763, (714)626-8586 [180]

A.A. Importing Co. Inc., 7700 Hall St., St. Louis, MO 63147, (314)383-8800 [13009]

AA Water Service, 300 N White Sands Blvd., No. C, Alamogordo, NM 88310-7062, (505)434-2977 [14987]

AAA Distributors Inc., PO Box 415, Braddock Heights, MD 21714-0415, (301)428-0330 [20763]

AAA Distributors Inc., PO Box 415, Braddock Heights, MD 21714-0415, (301)428-0330 [14988]

AAA Fire & Safety Inc., 3013 3rd Ave. N, Seattle, WA 98109-1602, (206)284-1721 [24466]

AAA-Four Aces, 855 Inca St., Denver, CO 80204-4342, (303)595-0237 [26378]

AAA Glass Corp., 2800 E 12th, Los Angeles, CA 90023-3622, (213)263-2177 [15385]

AAA Interair Inc., PO Box 522230, Miami, FL 33152, (305)889-6111 [20]

AAA Manufacturing Inc., 5055 Convair Dr., Carson City, NV 89706, (775)883-6901 [20575]

AAA Parts of Biltmore Inc., 5 Brook St., Asheville, NC 28803, (828)274-3781 [2160]

AAA Supply Corp., 608 Rte. 41, Schererville, IN 46375, (219)865-8500 [13520]

AAAA World Import Export Inc., 11400 NW 32nd Ave., Miami, FL 33167, (305)688-1000 [25054]

Aamco Transmissions Inc., 1 Presidential Blvd., Bala Cynwyd, PA 19004, (610)668-2900 [2161]

Aanns Trading Co., 1805 Crystal Dr., Ste. 809, Arlington, VA 22202, (703)920-2708 [4309]

AAR Corp., 200 Saw Mill River Rd., Hawthorne, NY 10532, (914)747-0500 [21]

AAR Corp., 1100 N Wood Dale Rd., Wood Dale, IL 60191, (630)227-2000 [22]

AAR Hardware Inc., 12774 Florence Ave., Santa Fe Springs, CA 90670-3906, (562)903-7801 [23]

Aaraya Beauty Accents, 8827 W Ogden Ave., Ste. 122, Brookfield, IL 60513, (630)241-3366 [14007]

Aardvark Controls Equipment, 19571 Progress Dr., Strongsville, OH 44136, (440)572-1368 [24304]

Aardvark Swim & Sports Inc., 4212-F Technology Ct., Chantilly, VA 20151-1214, (703)631-6045 [4738]

Aargus Truck & Auto, 6145 D Wall St., Sterling Heights, MI 48312, (810)979-2114 [2162]

Aaron Equipment Co., 735 E Green St., Bensenville, IL 60106, (630)350-2200 [15722]

Aaron Scrap Metals, PO Box 607069, Orlando, FL 32860-7069, (407)293-6584 [26724]

Aaron Scrap Metals, Div. of Commercial Metals Co., PO Box 607069, Orlando, FL 32860-7069, (407)293-6584 [19722]

Aarons Creek Farms, 380 Greenhouse Dr., Buffalo Junction, VA 24529, (804)374-2174 [14792]

AARP Inc., 6019 Goshen Springs Rd., Norcross, GA 30071-3502, (404)446-0400 [8258]

AAT Communications Systems Corp., 1854 Hylan Blvd., Staten Island, NY 10305, (718)351-4782 [25055]

AAT Communications Systems Corp., 1854 Hylan Blvd., Staten Island, NY 10305, (718)351-4782 [14989]

AB Collections, 1466 Broadway, Ste. 1603, New York, NY 10036, (212)944-5950 [4739]

AB Wholesale Co., 710 S College Ave., Bluefield, VA 24605-1639, (703)322-4686 [13521]

ABA Enterprise Inc., PO Box 3424, Bartlesville, OK 74006-3424, (918)333-0941 [23490]

ABA-Tron Industries Inc., 300 Quaker Ln., Ste. 7 (PMB 151), Warwick, RI 02886-6682, (401)884-1504 [3290]

ABA-tron Industries Inc., PO Box 6341, Beverly Hills, CA 90212-1341, (213)857-8358 [4310]

Ababa - QA, 1466 Pioneer Way No. 1, El Cajon, CA 92020, (619)440-1781 [13522]

Abaco Buying Group, Skypark Business Park, PO Box 4082, Irvine, CA 92616-4082, (949)552-8494 [4740]

A.B.A.C.O. Group, Skypark Business Park, PO Box 4082, Irvine, CA 92616-4082, (949)552-8494 [4740]

Abaco Group, Skypark Business Park, PO Box 4082, Irvine, CA 92616-4082, (949)552-8494 [4740]

Abacon Electronics Corp., PO Box 4565, Greensboro, NC 27404-4565, (910)275-5655 [8259]

Abacus, PO Box 1242, Rapid City, SD 57709-1242, (605)343-3726 [20764]

Abacus Data Systems Inc., 6725 Mesa Ridge Rd., No. 204, San Diego, CA 92121, (619)452-4245 [5861]

Abana Pharmaceuticals Inc., PO Box 46903, St. Louis, MO 63146-6903, (314)390-2133 [19118]

Abatix Environmental Corp., 8311 Eastpoint Dr., Ste. 400, Dallas, TX 75227, (214)381-1146 [24467]

ABB Power Generation, 5309 Commonwealth Center Pkwy., Ste. 400, Midlothian, VA 23112, (804)763-2000 [15723]

ABB Pressure Systems Inc., 501 Merritt 7, No. 5308, Norwalk, CT 06851-7000, (203)329-8771 [8260]

Abba Products Corp., 1004 Elizabeth Ave., Elizabeth, NJ 07201, (908)353-0669 [27055]

Abbaco Inc., 230 5th Ave., Ste. 1409, New York, NY 10001, (212)679-4550 [10317]

Abbey, 2041 Ave. C, Ste. 400, Bethlehem, PA 18017, (610)266-6333 [19157]

Abbey Home Healthcare, 131 Cheshire Ln., No. 500, Minnetonka, MN 55305-1058, (612)827-8251 [19119]

Abbey Ice Co., 1 Hoffman St., Spring Valley, NY 10977, (914)356-1700 [24903]

Abbey Medical Inc., PO Box 9100, Fountain Valley, CA 92728-9100, (714)957-2000 [19120]

Abbey Metal Corp., 70 Commercial Ave., Moonachie, NJ 07074, (201)438-0330 [26725]

Abbey Pharmaceutical Services Inc., 1771 W Diehl Rd., Naperville, IL 60563, (630)305-8000 [18655]

Abbott Foods Inc., 2400 Harrison Rd., Columbus, OH 43204, (614)272-0658 [24053]

Abbott Import-Export Co., 2924 Sunset Ave., Bakersfield, CA 93304, (805)324-2833 [4741]

Abbott's Premium Ice Cream Inc., PO Box 411, Conway, NH 03818, (603)356-2344 [10318]

Abboud Apparel Corp.; Joseph, 650 5th Ave., 27th Fl., New York, NY 10019, (212)586-9140 [4742]

ABC Appliance Inc. White Automotive Association Div., 3377 Fort St., Lincoln Park, MI 48146-3634, (248)549-2300 [14288]

ABC Auto Paint Supply, 3099 South 300 West, Salt Lake City, UT 84115, (801)466-9195 [21373]

ABC Cellular Corp., 16500 NW 52nd Ave., Hialeah, FL 33014-6214, (305)621-6000 [5499]

ABC Coffee Co., 24691 Telegraph Rd., Southfield, MI 48034, (248)352-1222 [10319]

ABC Display and Supply Inc., 100 Cleveland Ave., Freeport, NY 11520, (516)867-8400 [25540]

ABC International Traders Inc., 16730 Schoenborn St., North Hills, CA 91343-6122, (818)894-2525 [26575]

ABC International Traders Inc., 16730 Schoenborn St., North Hills, CA 91343-6122, (818)894-2525 [26379]

ABC Marketing, RR 2 Box 123-A, Stratford, OK 74872-9400, (580)332-0110 [2163]

ABC Metals Inc., PO Box 7012, Logansport, IN 46947-7012, (219)753-0471 [19723]

Abc Mobile Brake, 105 Rains Ave., Nashville, TN 37203, (615)254-2223 [2164]

ABC School Uniforms Inc., 1085 E 31st St., Hialeah, FL 33013-3589, (305)836-5000 [4743]

ABC Supply Co., Inc., 21000 W 8 Mile Rd., Southfield, MI 48075-5639, (248)542-2730 [6899]

ABC Systems and Development Inc., 9 Bartlet St., Ste. 255, Andover, MA 01810, (978)463-8602 [5862]

ABC Theatricals, 602 W 22nd St., Tempe, AZ 85282, (480)968-4334 [25828]

ABC Tile Distributors, 3105 18th St., PO Box 7428, Metairie, LA 70010, (504)833-5543 [9638]

ABC Tile Distributors, 3105 18th St., Metairie, LA 70010, (504)833-5543 [6900]

Abco International, PO Box 574125, Orlando, FL 32857-4125, (407)896-6000 [17301]

ABCO Refrigeration Supply Corp., 49-70 31st St., Long Island City, NY 11101, (718)937-9000 [14289]

ABCO Welding and Industrial Supply, PO Box 296, Waterford, CT 06385, (860)442-0363 [16667]

Abeita Glass Co., 600 W Coal Ave., Gallup, NM 87301, (505)722-7676 [6901]

Abel Carbonic Products Inc., 315 Harbor Way, South San Francisco, CA 94080, (650)873-4212 [4311]

Abel and Company Inc.; Robert, 195 Merrimac St., Woburn, MA 01888, (781)935-7860 [15724]

Abell Corp., PO Box 8056, Monroe, LA 71211, (318)345-2600 [181]

Abel's Quik Shops, PO Box 532, Louisiana, MO 63353, (314)754-5595 [22018]

Aberdeen Dynamics, 17717 E Admiral Pl., PO Box 582510, Tulsa, OK 74158, (918)437-8000 [15725]

Aberdeen L.L.C., 9728 Alburtis St., Santa Fe Springs, CA 90670, (562)695-5570 [5863]

Aberdeen Vault Inc.; Wilbert, 2422 S Hwy. 281, Aberdeen, SD 57401-8747, (605)225-5255 [25541]

Abilene Lumber Inc., 2025 Industrial Blvd., Abilene, TX 79604, (915)698-4465 [6902]

Abingdon Press, PO Box 801, Nashville, TN 37202, (615)749-6451 [3458]

Abita Water Company Inc., 101 Airline Hwy., Metairie, LA 70001, (504)465-0022 [24904]

ABJ Enterprises Inc., PO Box 428, Dunn, NC 28335, (910)892-1357 [17671]

ABKCO Music and Records Inc., 1700 Broadway, New York, NY 10019, (212)399-0300 [25056]

Able Distributors, 2501 N Central Ave., Chicago, IL 60639, (773)889-5555 [14290]

Able Enterprises Inc., 2205 Park St., Ennis, TX 75119-1624, (972)875-8451 [6903]

Able Equipment Inc., 5745 Angola Rd., Toledo, OH 43615, (419)865-5539 [6904]

Able Steel Equipment Co. Inc., 50-02 23rd St., Long Island City, NY 11101, (718)361-9240 [20765]

Able Trading Corp., 2320 Keystone Dr., Omaha, NE 68134, (402)391-4161 [4565]

Able Welding Co., 1527 62nd St., Brooklyn, NY 11219, (718)259-3616 [2165]

ABM of Bismarck Inc., PO Box 2658, Bismarck, ND 58502-2658, (701)258-0210 [20766]

ABM Distributors Inc., 3316 Lincoln Way E, Massillon, OH 44646, (330)833-2661 [23049]

ABM International Corp., 275 Kisco Ave., Mt. Kisco, NY 10549, (914)241-2828 [19724]

Abnormal Trees, 4 Copper Dr., Wilmington, DE 19804-2413 [4744]

Abnormalities, 4 Copper Dr., Wilmington, DE 19804-2413 [4744]

ABR Wholesale, Inc., 510 N Goodman St., Rochester, NY 14609, (716)482-3601 [14291]

Abraham and Sons Inc.; S., PO Box 1768, Grand Rapids, MI 49501, (616)453-6358 [26257]

Abrahams Oriental Rugs, 5120 Wood Way, Houston, TX 77056, (713)622-4444 [15386]

Abrams Co. Inc.; Herbert, 1655 Imperial Way, Thorofare, NJ 08086, (609)848-5330 [16707]

Abranovic Associates Inc., 161 S McKean St., Kittanning, PA 16201, (412)543-2005 [3459]

Abrasive Products Inc., PO Box 250, Fortville, IN 46040, (317)485-7701 [16668]

Abrasive Specialists Inc., 7521 Commerce Ln., Minneapolis, MN 55432, (612)571-4111 [15726]

Abrasive-Tool Corp., 1555 Emerson St., Rochester, NY 14606, (716)254-4500 [13523]

Abrasive-Tool Corp., 1555 Emerson St., Rochester, NY 14606, (716)254-4500 [15727]

ABS, 315 Littleton Rd., Chelmsford, MA 01824, (978)250-9600 [5922]

ABS Corp., 1936 N Shiloh Dr., PO Box 1487, Fayetteville, AR 72702-1487, (501)443-9205 [3600]

ABSCOA Industries Inc., 12774 Florence Ave., Santa Fe Springs, CA 90670-3906, (562)903-7801 [23]

Absolute Appliance Distributors Inc., 4295 Cromwell Rd., Ste. 403, Chattanooga, TN 37421, (615)490-0015 [14990]

Absolute Aqua Systems, 8811 Woodman Ave., No. 3, Arleta, CA 91331, (818)891-9207 [25542]

Absolute Bottled Water Co., 849 Seahawk Circle, Virginia Beach, VA 23452, (757)468-4426 [24905]

Absopure Water Co., 96 84th St. SW, Byron Center, MI 49315, (616)385-2771 [24906]

AC-Delco/GM Service Parts Operation, PO Box 6020, Grand Blanc, MI 48439, (810)606-2000 [2166]

AC & R Specialty Supply, PO Box 1912, South Hackensack, NJ 07606, (201)652-7400 [14292]

AC Sales Company Ltd., 1080 E 29th St., Hialeah, FL 33013, (305)696-7880 [15728]

A.C. Supply, 21160 Drake Rd., Strongsville, OH 44136, (440)238-9150 [20767]

AC and T Company Inc., PO Box 4217, Hagerstown, MD 21740, (301)582-2700 [22019]

Academi-Text Medical Wholesalers, 330 N Superior, Toledo, OH 43604-1422, (419)255-9755 [3460]

Academic Enterprises Ltd., 20 Simmons Dr., Milford, MA 01757, (508)473-8034 [3461]

Academic Therapy Publications, High Noon Bks/Arena Press, 20 Commercial Blvd., Novato, CA 94949-6191, (415)883-3314 [3462]

Academy Chicago Publishers Ltd., 363 W Erie St., Chicago, IL 60610, (312)751-7300 [3463]

Academy Optical Inc., PO Box 809, Presque Isle, ME 04769-0809, (207)764-4900 [19121]

Acadiana Culligan, 708 Eraste Landry, Lafayette, LA 70506, (318)233-1645 [24907]

Acarex Inc., 91-31 Queens Blvd., Elmhurst, NY 11373, (718)424-5551 [2167]

ACBEL Technologies Inc., 472 Vista Way, Milpitas, CA 95035-5406, (408)452-7811 [5864]

ACC Recycling Corp., 1190 20th St. N, St. Petersburg, FL 33713, (813)896-9600 [26726]

Accardos Appliance Parts & Services, 8640 Oak St., New Orleans, LA 70118-1222, (504)866-1951 [14991]

Accawmacke Ornamentals, PO Box 4, Tasley, VA 23441, (757)787-8128 [14793]

Accent Books, PO Box 15337, Denver, CO 80215, (303)988-5300 [3464]

Accent Business Products, PO Box 1310, Fargo, ND 58107-1310, (701)236-6702 [20768]

Accent Lamp and Shade Co. Inc., PO Box 95128, Newton, MA 02495, (617)527-3900 [15387]

Accent Nursery, 4448 Hwy. 92, Douglasville, GA 30135, (404)949-4144 [14794]

Accent On Tile, 3700 Liberty Ave., Pittsburgh, PA 15201, (412)687-8453 [9639]

Accent Tile, 4801 Frankford Ave., Bldg. B-1, Lubbock, TX 79424, (806)796-2772 [9640]

Accents Publications Service, Inc., 4611 Assembly Dr., Ste. F, Lanham, MD 20706-4843, (301)588-5496 [3465]

Accesories That Matter, 320 5th Ave., #609, New York, NY 10001, (212)947-3012 [18366]

Access Bicycle Components Inc., 3838 N 36th Ave., Phoenix, AZ 85019-3214, (602)278-5506 [23491]

Access Graphics, 1426 Pearl St., Boulder, CO 80302, (303)938-9333 [5865]

Access Graphics Technology Inc., 1426 Pearl St., Boulder, CO 80302, (303)938-9333 [5866]

Access International Marketing Inc., 330 S Decatur, Ste. 322, Las Vegas, NV 89107, (702)870-3906 [13524]

Access International Software, 432 Columbia St., Cambridge, MA 02141-1000, (617)494-0066 [5867]

Access Publishers Network, 6893 Sullivan Rd., Grawn, MI 49637, (616)276-5196 [3466]

Access Solutions Inc., 11801 N Tatum Blvd., Ste. 108, Phoenix, AZ 85028, (602)953-7374 [5868]

Accessorie Air Compressor Systems Inc., 1858 N Case St., Orange, CA 92865-4241, (714)634-2292 [5822]

Accessorie Air Compressor Systems Inc., 1858 N Case St., Orange, CA 92865-4241, (714)634-2292 [15729]

Accessories Palace, Gaslight Business Park, 1953 10th Ave. N, Lake Worth, FL 33461, (561)582-1812 [13288]

Accessory Brainstorms, 5 W 36th St., Ste. 500, New York, NY 10018, (212)971-7300 [4745]

Accessory Resource Gallery Inc., 5 W 36th St., Ste. 500, New York, NY 10018, (212)971-7300 [4745]

Accessory Wholesale, 550 Wholesalers Pkwy. C, Harahan, LA 70123-3308, (504)736-0357 [17302]

Acclaim Entertainment Inc., 1 Acclaim Plz., Glen Cove, NY 11542, (516)624-8888 [26380]

Accu-Care Supply, Inc., 95 Hathaway Ctr., H-36, Providence, RI 02907, (401)785-9577 [23492]

Accu Rx Optical, 100 Federal Way, Johnston, RI 02919, (401)454-2920 [19122]

Accu Tech Cable Inc., 200 Hembree Park Dr., Roswell, GA 30076-3868, (404)751-9473 [8261]

Accupart International, 11 Black Rock Rd., Carson City, NV 89706, (775)246-5990 [2168]

AccuPro Inc., 1011 Hwy. 22 W, Bldg. C, Box 8, Phillipsburg, NJ 08865, (908)454-5998 [25543]

Accura Music, Inc., 13398 Mansfield Rd., PO Box 4260, Athens, OH 45701-4260 [3467]

Accurate Air Engineering Inc., PO Box 5526, Compton, CA 90224, (310)537-1350 [5823]

Accurate Air Engineering Inc., PO Box 5526, Compton, CA 90224, (310)537-1350 [15730]

Accurate Chemical and Scientific Corp., 300 Shames Dr., Westbury, NY 11590, (516)333-2221 [4312]

Accurate Iron and Metal Co., 25 Horseshoe Ln., Lemont, IL 60439-9150, (773)404-7771 [26727]

Accurate Office Machines Inc., 246 Federal Rd., Brookfield, CT 06804-2647, (203)775-9668 [20769]

Accurate Partitions Corp., PO Box 287, Lyons, IL 60534, (708)442-6800 [13010]

Accurate Partitions Corp., PO Box 287, Lyons, IL 60534, (708)442-6801 [24054]

Accurate Water, 6601 N Navarro, Victoria, TX 77904, (512)576-1501 [25544]

Accutron Inc., 2020 W Melinda Ln., Phoenix, AZ 85027, (602)780-2020 [18656]

Ace Advance Paper Co., 46 St. Claire Ave., New Britain, CT 06051, (860)224-2485 [21614]

Ace Appliances Inc., 2450 N Sherwood Forest Blvd., Baton Rouge, LA 70815, (504)275-6220 [14992]

Ace Auto Salvage, 10131 Garrymoore Ln., Missoula, MT 59802-5674, (406)543-7614 [2169]

Ace Bag and Burlap Co. Inc., 205 Water St., Brooklyn, NY 11201, (718)852-4705 [25952]

Ace Battery Inc., 2166 Bluff Rd., Indianapolis, IN 46225, (317)786-2717 [2170]

Ace Electric Supply Co., 5911 Phillips Hwy., Jacksonville, FL 32216, (904)731-5900 [8262]

Ace Hardware Corp., 8338 Oak St., New Orleans, LA 70118, (504)861-4502 [13525]

Ace Hardware Corp., 2200 Kensington Court, Oak Brook, IL 60523-2100, (630)990-6600 [13526]

Ace Plumbing and Electrical Supply, Inc., 601 S Delsea Dr., Vineland, NJ 08360-4458, (856)692-9374 [23050]

Ace Tank and Equipment Co., PO Box 9039, Seattle, WA 98109, (206)281-5000 [25885]

Ace Technical Resources Inc., 18 W State St., Ste. 42, Athens, OH 45701, (740)593-5993 [5869]

Ace Tool Co., PO Box 1650, Pinellas Park, FL 33780, (813)544-4331 [13527]

Ace Truck Body, Inc., 1600 Thrailkill Rd., PO Box 459, Grove City, OH 43123, (614)871-3100 [2171]

Ace Truck Equipment Co., PO Box 2605, Zanesville, OH 43702-2605, (740)453-0551 [2172]

Aceto Corp., 1 Hollow Ln., Ste. 201, New HyDe Park, NY 11042-1215, (516)627-6000 [4313]

ACF Components and Fasteners, Inc., 31012 Huntwood Ave., Hayward, CA 94544, (510)487-2100 [8263]

Acfer International Inc., 4218 Center Gate, San Antonio, TX 78217, (210)653-6800 [22822]

Achievement Products Inc., PO Box 388, 294 Rt. 10 W, East Hanover, NJ 07936, (973)887-5090 [13289]

ACI, 1950 N Mannheim Rd., Melrose Park, IL 60160, (708)345-8675 [2271]

ACI Controls, 5604 Business Ave., Cicero, NY 13039, (315)452-1171 [15731]

ACI Controls, 295 Main St., West Seneca, NY 14224, (716)675-9450 [24305]

ACI Distribution, 9010 S Norwalk Blvd., Santa Fe Springs, CA 90670, (562)692-0395 [6905]

Ack Electronics, 554 Deering Rd. NW, Atlanta, GA 30309-2267, (404)351-6340 [8264]

Ackerman Electrical Supply Co., 131 Grand Trunk Ave., Battle Creek, MI 49015, (616)459-8327 [8265]

ACL Inc., 2151 Bering Dr., San Jose, CA 95131, (408)432-0270 [8266]

ACM Equipment Rental and Sales Co., 4010 South 22nd St., Phoenix, AZ 85040-1437, (602)232-0600 [15732]

ACMA Computers Inc., 1505 Reliance Way, Fremont, CA 94539, (510)623-1212 [5870]

Acmat Corp., PO Box 2350, New Britain, CT 06050-2350, (860)229-9000 [6906]

Acme Agri Supply Inc., 1527 E Broadway St., North Little Rock, AR 72114-5934, (501)374-0625 [27056]

Acme Auto Inc., PO Box 330666, West Hartford, CT 06133-0666, (860)246-2540 [2173]

ACME Automotive Accessories Group, 17103 SR-4 E, Goshen, IN 46526, (219)534-1516 [2174]

Acme Brick Co., 2510 Adie Rd., Maryland Heights, MO 63043, (314)739-1810 [6907]

Acme Brick Co., 4747 Choctaw, Baton Rouge, LA 70805, (504)356-5281 [9641]

Acme Brick Co., 2325 W Battlefield, Springfield, MO 65807, (417)883-0502 [9642]

Acme Brick Co., 2500 NW 10th, Oklahoma City, OK 73107, (405)525-7421 [9643]

Acme Brick Co., 307 W Santa Fe, Olathe, KS 66061, (913)782-9500 [9644]

Acme Brick & Tile, 5690 Summer Ave., Memphis, TN 38134, (901)387-4540 [9645]

Acme Brick, Tile and More, Rte. 7, Box 337, Joplin, MO 64801, (417)781-1931 [6908]

Acme Coal Co., Harvard Blvd., Youngstown, OH 44514, (330)758-2313 [6909]

Acme-Danneman Company Inc., 480 Canal St., New York, NY 10013-1803, (212)966-4204 [16669]

Acme-Dixie Inc., PO Box 218, Westlake, LA 70669, (318)882-6467 [15733]

Acme Electric Supply Inc., 2737 Central Ave., Columbus, IN 47201, (812)372-8871 [8267]

Acme Electronics, Inc., 224 Washington Ave. N, Minneapolis, MN 55401, (612)338-4754 [8277]

Acme Food Sales Inc., 5940 1st Ave. S, Seattle, WA 98108-3248, (206)762-5150 [10320]

Acme Group, 5151 Loraine Ave., Detroit, MI 48208, (313)894-7110 [2175]

Acme Heat & Power, 21 Grand St., Copiague, NY 11726, (516)842-7077 [14293]

Acme Linen Co., 5136 E Triggs St., Los Angeles, CA 90022, (213)266-4000 [25953]

Acme Machell Company Inc., PO Box 1617, Waukesha, WI 53187, (262)521-2870 [24264]

Acme Manufacturing Co., 214 Commercial St., Medina, NY 14103, (716)798-0300 [14696]

Acme Manufacturing Co., 7500 State Rd., Philadelphia, PA 19136, (215)338-2850 [14294]

Acme Paper and Supply Company Inc., PO Box 422, Savage, MD 20763-0422, (410)792-2333 [21615]

Acme Refrigeration, 5339 Choctaw Dr., Baton Rouge, LA 70805, (504)355-2263 [14295]

Acme Refrigeration of Baton Rouge Inc., 11844 S Choctaw Dr., Baton Rouge, LA 70815-2184, (225)273-1740 [14296]

Acme Vial and Glass Co. Inc., 1601 Commerce Way, Paso Robles, CA 93446-3644, (805)239-2666 [24306]

Acom Computer Inc., 2850 East 29th St., Long Beach, CA 90806-2313, (562)424-7899 [5871]

Acorn Distributors Inc., 5820 Fortune Cir. W, Indianapolis, IN 46241-5503, (317)924-6345 [21616]

Acorn Paper Products Co, PO Box 23965, Los Angeles, CA 90023, (323)268-0507 [16670]

Acorn Petroleum Inc., PO Box 112, Walsenburg, CO 81089, (719)738-1966 [22020]

Acosta-PMI St. Louis Div., 3171 Riverport Tech. Ct. Dr., Maryland Heights, MO 63043, (314)991-3992 [10321]

Acosta Sales Co., 6850 Belfort Oaks Pl., Jacksonville, FL 32216, (904)281-9800 [10322]

AcousTech Mastering, 486 S Dawson Dr., No. 45, Camarillo, CA 93012-8049, (805)484-2747 [25411]

Acoustical Material Services, 1620 S Maple Ave., Montebello, CA 90640, (213)721-9011 [25057]

Acoustical Solutions, Inc., 3603 Mayland Ct., Richmond, VA 23233, (804)346-8350 [6910]

Acqua Group of Arizona, 2419 N Black Canyon Hwy., Ste. 10, Phoenix, AZ 85009, (602)254-6323 [15284]

ACR Group Inc., 3200 Wilcrest Dr., Ste. 440, Houston, TX 77042-6019, (713)780-8532 [14297]

ACR Supply Inc. (Houston, Texas), PO Box 630929, Houston, TX 77263, (713)787-6776 [14298]

Acra Custom Wheel, PO Box 1292, 2310 N Foundation Dr., South Bend, IN 46624, (219)233-3114 [2176]

Acro Electronics Corp., 1101 W Chicago Ave., East Chicago, IN 46312, (219)397-8681 [16671]

Acro Electronics Corp., 1101 W Chicago Ave., East Chicago, IN 46312, (219)397-8681 [8268]

Acrowood Corp., PO Box 1028, Everett, WA 98061, (425)258-3555 [15734]

AcryMed Inc., 12232 SW Garden Pl., Portland, OR 97223, (503)624-9830 [19123]

ACS Digital Solutions, PO Box 2163, Buena Park, CA 90621, (714)999-7733 [20770]

ACS Publications, PO Box 34487, San Diego, CA 92163-4487, (619)297-9203 [3468]

ACT Services Inc., 916 Pleasant St., Norwood, MA 02062, (781)255-0978 [8269]

ACT Teleconferencing Inc., 1658 Cole Blvd., Ste. 130, Golden, CO 80401, (303)233-3500 [5500]

A.C.T. Vehicle Equipment, Inc., 946 Southampton Rd., Westfield, MA 01085-1364, (413)568-6173 [2177]

Action Auto Parts, 2606 N 10th St., Dalton Gardens, ID 83815-4926, (208)664-9126 [2178]

Action Business Systems, 151 E Olive St., Newport, OR 97365-3052, (541)265-8226 [5872]

Action Chevrolet-Subaru-Geo, 795 Hoosick Rd., Troy, NY 12180, (518)279-1741 [20576]

Action Communications Inc., 2816 N Stone Ave., Tucson, AZ 85705, (520)792-0326 [8270]

Action Electric Sales Co., 3900 N Rockwell St., Chicago, IL 60618, (312)266-2600 [8271]

Action Equipment Company Inc., PO Box 736, Candia, NH 03034, (603)483-2900 [6911]

Action Fabrication & Truck Equipment, Inc., 4481 107th Cir. N, Clearwater, FL 33762-5029, (813)572-6319 [2179]

Action Laboratories Inc., Via Martens, Anaheim, CA 92806, (714)630-5941 [14008]

Action Laboratories Inc., Via Martens, Anaheim, CA 92806, (714)630-5941 [19124]

Action Line, 12091 Forestgate Dr., Dallas, TX 75243, (214)341-7300 [4746]

Action Line/UniVogue, Inc., 12091 Forestgate Dr., Dallas, TX 75243, (214)341-7300 [4746]

Action Page Inc., PO Box 5338, Greeley, CO 80634, (303)292-1204 [5501]

Action Products International Inc., 390 N Orange Ave., Orlando, FL 32801, (407)481-8007 [26381]

Action Sales Promotions, PO Box 03-4044, Indialantic, FL 32903-0944, (407)639-0290 [4747]

Action Sport & Apparel, 532 W Dixie Ave., Elizabethtown, KY 42701-2437, (502)769-3188 [4748]

Action Sports of Edmond, 1601 S Broadway St., Edmond, OK 73013-4037, (405)340-1680 [23493]

Action Threaded Products Inc., 6955 S Harlem Ave., Bedford Park, IL 60638, (708)496-0100 [13528]

Action Tool Company Inc., 1959 Tigertail Blvd., Dania, FL 33004, (954)920-2700 [13529]

Action Water Treatment Service, 110 W St. Clair St., Romeo, MI 48065, (810)752-7600 [25545]

Activation Inc., 5390 E Ponce de Leon Ave., Ste. E, Stone Mountain, GA 30083, (770)491-6900 [16539]

Active Carb Ltd., PO Box 238, Gardena, CA 90248, (310)366-7663 [23051]

Active Electrical Supply Co., 4240 W Lawrence Ave., Chicago, IL 60630, (312)282-6300 [8272]

Active Plumbing Supply Co., 216 Richmond St., Painesville, OH 44077, (440)352-4411 [23052]

Active Screw and Fastener, 1065 Chase Ave., Elk Grove Village, IL 60007-4827, (847)427-0500 [13530]

Actrade International Corp., 7 Penn Plz., Ste. 422, New York, NY 10001, (212)563-1036 [14299]

Actron Steel, 2866 Cass Rd., Traverse City, MI 49684, (616)947-3981 [19725]

ACuPowder International, LLC, 901 Lehigh Ave., Union, NJ 07083, (908)851-4500 [19726]

AcuSport Corp., One Hunter Pl., Bellefontaine, OH 43311-3001, (937)593-7010 [23494]

Acutron Co., 501 Sumner St., No. 601, Honolulu, HI 96817, (808)521-1151 [6912]

Ad Art Electronic Sign Corp., 19603 Figueroa St., Carson, CA 90745, (310)523-9500 [24055]

Ad House Inc., 1801 Shelby Oaks Dr., Memphis, TN 38104, (901)387-5555 [13290]

Ad-Shir-Tizing Inc., PO Box 1122, Airway Heights, WA 99001-1122, (509)244-3363 [4749]

ADA Computer Supplies Inc., PO Box 21704, Greensboro, NC 27420, (336)274-3441 [5873]

Ada Copy Supplies Inc., 8361 W State St., Boise, ID 83703-6071, (208)853-2026 [20771]

Ada Farmers Exchange Co., 332 W Lincoln Ave., Ada, OH 45810, (419)634-3030 [17672]

Ada Feed and Seed Inc., 12 W Thorp Ave., PO Box 231, Ada, MN 56510, (218)784-7158 [182]

Ada Iron and Metal Co., PO Box 306, Ada, OK 74820, (580)332-1165 [19727]

Adair Feed and Grain Co., PO Box 417, Adair, IA 50002, (515)742-3855 [17673]

Adam Wholesalers Inc., 3005 Kemper E Rd., Cincinnati, OH 45241, (513)772-9092 [6913]

Adams Apple Distributing L.P., 5100 N Ravenswood, Chicago, IL 60640, (312)275-7800 [13291]

Adams Book Company, Inc., 537 Sackett St., Brooklyn, NY 11211, (718)875-5464 [3469]

Adams Brothers Produce Company Inc., PO Box 2682, Birmingham, AL 35202, (205)323-2455 [10323]

Adams Brothers Produce Company of Tuscaloosa Inc., PO Box 2474, Tuscaloosa, AL 35403, (205)758-2891 [10324]

Adams-Burch Inc., 5556 Tuxedo Rd., Hyattsville, MD 20781, (301)341-1600 [24056]

Adams Company Inc.; J.K., PO Box 248, Dorset, VT 05251, (802)362-2303 [27274]

Adams Co.; S.S., PO Box 850, Neptune, NJ 07754-0850, (732)774-0570 [26382]

Adams County Co-operative Association Inc., 109 E Andrews St., Monroe, IN 46772, (219)692-6111 [183]

Adams-Dougherty Livestock Brokerage, 803 E Rice St., Sioux Falls, SD 57103-0157, (605)336-3830 [17674]

Adams & Durvin Marine Inc., 5607 Mechanicsville Pke., Mechanicsville, VA 23111-1218, (804)746-5930 [23495]

Adams Foam Rubber Co., 4737 S Christiana Ave., Chicago, IL 60632, (312)523-5252 [24265]

Adams Group Inc., 1020 East St., Woodland, CA 95776, (530)662-7351 [17675]

Adams Hard-Facing Company of California, 10 Greg St., Sparks, NV 89431-6276, (775)359-0399 [184]

Adams Industries Inc., PO Box 291, Windsor Locks, CT 06096, (860)668-1201 [13531]

Adams International Metals Corp., 3200 E Frontera Rd., Anaheim, CA 92806, (714)630-8901 [26728]

Adams News Co. Inc., 1555 W Galer St., Seattle, WA 98119-3166, (206)284-7617 [3470]

Adams Nut and Bolt Co., 10100 85th Ave. N, Maple Grove, MN 55369, (763)424-3374 [13999]

Adams Printing and Stationery Co.; S.G., 1611 Locust St., St. Louis, MO 63103, (314)621-2213 [20772]

Adams Supply Co., PO Box 2938, Torrance, CA 90501, (310)533-8088 [13532]

Adams Tractor Co.; Carroll, 902 W Rose St., WalLa Walla, WA 99362, (509)525-4550 [185]

Adams Tractor Company Inc., PO Box 3043, Spokane, WA 99202-3043, (509)535-1708 [186]

Adams Wholesale Co. Inc., PO Box 8, Greeneville, TN 37744, (423)638-4101 [6914]

Adaptive Living, 403 N L St., Lake Worth, FL 33460-3025, (561)235-7270 [5874]

Adaro Envirocoal Americas, 1401 Manatee Ave. W, Ste 520, Bradenton, FL 34205, (941)747-2630 [20524]

ADCO Equipment Inc., 3455 San Gabriel River Pkwy., Pico Rivera, CA 90660, (213)623-8514 [15735]

Adco Inc., 1320 Leighton Ave., Ste. B, Anniston, AL 36201-4614, (205)236-2593 [18657]

ADCO Surgical Supply Inc., PO Box 1328, Bangor, ME 04402-1328, (207)942-5273 [18658]

ADD Enterprises Inc., 1552 Lost Hollow Dr., Brentwood, TN 37027, (615)370-9646 [5875]

Adderton Brokerage Co., 140 Weldon Pkwy., Maryland Heights, MO 63043-3102, (314)298-7000 [10325]

Addie Water Systems, 1604 Plainfield Ave., Janesville, WI 53545, (608)755-5780 [25546]

Addington Environmental Inc., 2343 Alexandria Dr., Ste. 400, Lexington, KY 40504, (606)223-3824 [26729]

Addington Holdings Inc., 1500 N Big Run, Ashland, KY 41102, (606)928-3433 [26730]

Addington Oil Co., PO Box 125, Gate City, VA 24251, (703)386-3961 [22021]

Addison Auto Parts Co., 3908 Pennsylvania Ave., Washington, DC 20020, (202)581-2900 [2180]

Addison Corp., 2575 Westside Pkwy., No. 800, Alpharetta, GA 30004, (404)551-8900 [6915]

Addison County Commodity Sales, PO Box 214, Middlebury, VT 05753, (802)388-2639 [17676]

Addkison Hardware Co. Inc., 126 E Amite St., PO Box 102, Jackson, MS 39205-0102, (601)354-3756 [13533]

Addlestone International Corp., PO Drawer 979, Charleston, SC 29402, (803)577-9300 [26731]

Addor Associates, Inc., 115 Roseville Rd., PO Box 2128, Westport, CT 06880, (203)226-9791 [3471]

Addwest Mining, Inc., 313 Frederica St., Owensboro, KY 42301, (502)684-2490 [20506]

Adel Wholesalers Inc., PO Box B, Bettendorf, IA 52722, (319)355-4734 [23053]

Adele Accessories Corp., 1370 Broadway, New York, NY 10018-7302, (212)695-3244 [4750]

Adele Fashion Knit Corp., 1370 Broadway, New York, NY 10018-7302, (212)695-3244 [4750]

Adelman Sales Corp., 4153 Roswell Rd. NE, Atlanta, GA 30342-3715, (404)255-8096 [13534]

ADEMCO, 307 Cayuga Rd., Ste. 160, Buffalo, NY 14225, (716)631-2197 [24483]

ADEMCO/ADI, 5300 D. Fulton Industrial Blvd., Atlanta, GA 30336, (404)346-7800 [24468]

ADEMCO/ADI, 5300 Old Pineville Rd., Ste. 152, Charlotte, NC 28217, (704)525-8899 [24469]

ADEMCO/ADI, 1801 Shelby Oaks Dr. N, Ste. 16, Memphis, TN 38134, (901)377-0033 [24470]

ADEMCO/ADI, Beacon Centre, Bldg. 10, 1910 NW 84th Ave., Miami, FL 33126, (305)477-5504 [24471]

ADEMCO/ADI, 1410 Donelson Pike Ste. A3, Nashville, TN 37217, (615)361-5254 [24472]

ADEMCO/ADI, 7260 Radford Ave., North Hollywood, CA 91605, (818)764-4202 [24473]

ADEMCO/ADI, 3140 N 35th Ave., Ste. 4 & 5, Phoenix, AZ 85017, (602)484-7484 [24474]

ADEMCO/ADI, 22121 17th Ave. SE, Ste. 103, Bothell, WA 98021, (425)485-3938 [24475]

ADEMCO/ADI, 304 N Meridian Ave., Ste. 7, Oklahoma City, OK 73107, (405)946-2177 [24476]

ADEMCO/ADI, 811 S Orlando Ave., Ste A, Winter Park, FL 32789, (407)740-5622 [24477]

ADEMCO/ADI, 2833 Banksville Rd., Pittsburgh, PA 15216-2815, (412)928-0100 [24478]

ADEMCO/ADI, 2755 NW 153RD Ave., Beaverton, OR 97006-5365 [24479]

ADEMCO/ADI, 235 Elm St., Warwick, RI 02888, (401)781-2190 [24480]

ADEMCO/ADI, 3902 Corporex Park Dr., Tampa, FL 33619, (813)623-1269 [24481]

Ademco Distribution Inc., 165 Eileen Way, Syosset, NY 11791, (516)921-6700 [24482]

ADESA Auctions of Birmingham, PO Box 130, Moody, AL 35004, (205)640-1010 [20577]

ADESA Corp., 2 Parkwood Crossing, Ste. 400, 310 E 96th St., Indianapolis, IN 46240, (317)815-1100 [2181]

ADESA Indianapolis Inc., 2950 E Main St., Plainfield, IN 46168-2723, (317)298-9700 [20578]

ADI, 307 Cayuga Rd., Ste. 160, Buffalo, NY 14225, (716)631-2197 [24483]

ADI, 13190 56th Ct., Ste. 401-404, Clearwater, FL 33760, (813)573-1166 [24484]

ADI, West Valley Business Center, 7112 S 212th St., Kent, WA 98032, (253)872-7128 [24485]

ADI Jacksonville, 2757 Earnest St., Jacksonville, FL 32205, (904)384-0620 [14993]

ADI Medical, 5745 W Howard, Niles, IL 60714, (847)647-7699 [19125]

ADI Systems Inc., 2115 Ringwood Ave., San Jose, CA 95131, (408)944-0100 [5876]

Adidas America Inc./Intl Div, 541 NE 20th Ave Ste. 207, Portland, OR 97232, (503)230-2920 [4751]

Adikes Inc.; J. & L., PO Box 310600, Jamaica, NY 11431-0600, (718)739-4400 [187]

Adirondack Chair Company Inc., 31-01 Vernon Blvd., Long Island City, NY 11106, 800-221-2444 [20773]

Adirondack Chair Company Inc., 31-01 Vernon Blvd., Long Island City, NY 11106 [13011]

Adirondack Electronics Inc., PO Box 12759, Albany, NY 12212, (518)456-0203 [8273]

Adirondack Silver, PO Box 13536, Albany, NY 12212, (518)456-8110 [17303]

Adjustable Clamp Co., 225 Riverview Ave., Waltham, MA 02454, (781)647-5560 [13535]

Adkins Printing Company Inc., PO Box 2440, New Britain, CT 06050, (203)229-1673 [20774]

Adler Glove Co.; Marcus, 32 W 39th, New York, NY 10018-3810, (212)840-8652 [4752]

Adler Inc.; Kurt S., 1107 Broadway, New York, NY 10010, (212)924-0900 [13292]

Adler Seeds Inc., 6085 W 550 N, Sharpsville, IN 46068, (765)963-5397 [188]

Adler's Foreign Books Inc., 915 Foster St., Evanston, IL 60201-3199, (847)866-6329 [3472]

Adleta Corp., 1645 Diplomat Dr., Carrollton, TX 75006, (972)620-5600 [9646]

Adleta Corp., 1645 Diplomat Dr., Carrollton, TX 75006, (972)620-5600 [15388]

ADM-Growmark Inc., PO Box 1470, Decatur, IL 62525, (217)424-5900 [17677]

ADM-Growmark Inc., PO Box 1470, Decatur, IL 62525, (217)424-5900 [10326]

Admark Corp., 2502 Mt. Moriah Rd., Ste. A-140, Memphis, TN 38115-1515, (901)795-8200 [5877]

Admiral Exchange Company Inc., 1443 Union St., San Diego, CA 92101, (619)239-2165 [10327]

Admiral Metals, 1821 Oregon Pke., Lancaster, PA 17601, (717)519-1565 [19728]

Admiral Metals Inc., 11 Forbes Rd., Woburn, MA 01801, (781)933-8300 [19729]

Admiral Steel, 4152 W 123rd St., Alsip, IL 60803-1869, (708)388-9600 [19730]

Admiral Wine and Liquor Co., 603 S 21st St., Irvington, NJ 07111, (973)371-2211 [1474]

Admiralty Mills Inc., PO Box 745, 639 Peeples Valley Rd., Cartersville, GA 30120, (404)382-8244 [9647]

Admiration Hosiery Mill, PO Box 33775, Charlotte, NC 28233, (704)375-3333 [5031]

ADO Corp., 851 Simuel Rd., Spartanburg, SC 29301-8830, (864)574-2731 [15389]

Adohr Farms Inc., PO Box 1945, Santa Ana, CA 92702, (714)775-7600 [10328]

ADP Hollander Inc., PO Box 9405, Minneapolis, MN 55440, (612)553-0644 [5878]

Adrian Wheat Growers Inc., PO Box 219, Adrian, TX 79001, (806)538-6222 [189]

ADS Inc., 355 Sinclair Frontage Rd., Milpitas, CA 95035, (408)956-0800 [5879]

ADT Automotive Inc., 435 Metroplex Dr., Nashville, TN 37211, (615)333-1400 [2182]

ADT Ltd., PO Box 5035, Boca Raton, FL 33431-0835, (561)988-3600 [24486]

ADT Security Systems, 315 Hamilton St., Worcester, MA 01604, (508)791-6265 [24487]

ADT Security Systems, 2032 E Pleasant Valley Blvd., Altoona, PA 16602, (814)946-4389 [24488]

ADT Security Systems, 231 Harbor Cir., New Orleans, LA 70126-1103, (504)246-7800 [24489]

ADT Security Systems, Mid-South Inc., 5590 Lauby Rd. NW, North Canton, OH 44720, (330)497-5325 [24490]

Adtek Co., PO Box 264, Sellersburg, IN 47172-0264, (812)246-5418 [18659]

Adtek Co., PO Box 264, Sellersburg, IN 47172-0264, (812)246-5418 [19126]

Adtek Computer Systems Inc., 4026 Devonshire Dr., Marietta, GA 30066-2526, (404)565-0323 [5880]

ADTRON. Corp, 3050 S Country Club Dr Ste 24, Mesa, AZ 85210, (480)926-9324 [5881]

Advance Business Systems and Supply Co., PO Box 627, Cockeysville, MD 21030, (410)252-4800 [20775]

Advance Computer Systems, 39675 Cedar Blvd., Ste. 1004, Newark, CA 94560-5490, (408)732-6200 [5882]

Advance Electric Supply Company Inc., 1011 E 5th Ave., Flint, MI 48501, (810)238-5611 [9059]

Advance Electrical Supply Co., 263 N Oakley Blvd., Chicago, IL 60612, (312)421-2300 [8274]

Advance Glove & Safety Co., 1008 Terminal Rd., Lansing, MI 48906, (517)323-8400 [24491]

Advance Glove & Safety Co., 3638 S Saginaw, Flint, MI 48503, (810)235-3000 [24492]

Advance Machinery Company Inc., PO Box 32036, Louisville, KY 40232, (502)969-3126 [16049]

Advance Petroleum Distributing Company Inc., 2451 Great Southwest Pkwy., Ft. Worth, TX 76106, (817)626-5458 [22022]

Advance Petroleum Inc., 700 S Royal Poinciana Blvd., Ste. 800, Miami Springs, FL 33166, (305)883-8554 [22023]

Advance Refrigeration Co., 1177 Industrial Dr., Bensenville, IL 60106, (708)766-2000 [14994]

Advance Scaffold of Alaska, 2607 Barrow St., Anchorage, AK 99503, (907)277-1803 [6916]

Advance Steel Co., 9635 French Rd., Detroit, MI 48213, (313)571-6700 [19731]

Advance Stores Company Inc., PO Box 2710, Roanoke, VA 24001, (540)345-4911 [2183]

Advance Telecommunication Inc., 2120 S Grape St., Denver, CO 80222, (303)691-2220 [5502]

Advanced Affiliates Inc., 9612 43rd Ave., Flushing, NY 11368-2143, (718)335-3566 [13536]

ADVANCED BusinessLink Corp., 5808 Lake Washington Blvd. NE 100, Kirkland, WA 98033-7350, (425)602-4777 [5883]

Advanced Ceramics Research Inc., 3292 E Hemisphere Loop, Tucson, AZ 85706, (520)573-6300 [6917]

Advanced Color Coatings Inc., 806 Jackman St., El Cajon, CA 92020, (619)447-1400 [21374]

Advanced Communication Design Inc., 7901 12th Ave. S, Bloomington, MN 55425, (612)854-4000 [5884]

Advanced Computer Distributors Inc., 2395 Pleasantdale Rd., Ste. 13, Atlanta, GA 30340, (770)453-9200 [5885]

Advanced Concepts Inc., 8875 N 55th St., No. 200, Milwaukee, WI 53223-2311, (414)362-9640 [5886]

Advanced Enterprise Solutions, 1805 E Dyer Rd., Ste. 212, Santa Ana, CA 92705, (949)756-0588 [5887]

Advanced Environmental Recycling Technologies Inc., PO Box 1237, Springdale, AR 72765, (501)750-1299 [26732]

Advanced Equipment Company Inc., PO Box 3370, Capitol Heights, MD 20791, (301)336-0200 [15736]

Advanced Equipment Inc., PO Box 336720, North Las Vegas, NV 89033-0029, (702)644-4445 [6918]

Advanced Federated Protection Inc., 2108 Payne Ave., Ste. 714, Cleveland, OH 44114-4440, (216)696-8739 [24493]

Advanced Financial Systems, 6827 Valley View Pl., Cheyenne, WY 82009-2558, (307)634-7402 [20776]

Advanced Graphics, 421 Schatzel St., Corpus Christi, TX 78401, (512)879-0019 [4753]

Advanced Imaging Technologies Inc., 212 S Hydraulic St., Ste. 200, Wichita, KS 67211, (316)267-7844 [18660]

Advanced Industrial Products, Inc., 2125 Whitney Ave., Gretna, LA 70056, (504)367-1257 [15737]

Advanced Maintenance Products Co., PO Box 6547, Manchester, NH 03108-6547, (603)669-9565 [4566]

Advanced Marketing Services Inc., 5880 Oberlin Dr., Ste. 400, San Diego, CA 92121, (619)457-2500 [3473]

Advanced Medical Systems Inc., 935 Horsham Rd., Ste. M, Horsham, PA 19044, (215)443-5424 [18661]

Advanced Micro Solutions Inc., PO Box 830547, Richardson, TX 75083-0547, (972)480-8336 [5888]

Advanced Office Systems Inc., 2744 E Kemper Rd., Cincinnati, OH 45241-1818, (513)771-1200 [20777]

Advanced Petroleum Recycling Inc., PO Box 16747, Salt Lake City, UT 84116-0747, (801)364-9444 [22024]

Advanced Plastics Inc., 7360 Cockrill Bend Blvd., Nashville, TN 37209-1024, (615)350-6500 [22918]

Advanced Research Instruments Corp., 2434 30th St., Boulder, CO 80301, (303)449-2288 [24307]

Advanced Scientific Inc., PO Box 101, Chalmette, LA 70044-0101, (504)277-7562 [18662]

Advanced Specialties, 974 E 650 Rd., Lawrence, KS 66047, (785)748-9847 [10329]

Advanced Tech Distributors, 1571 Whitmore Ave., Ceres, CA 95307, (209)541-1111 [5889]

Advanced Technology Center Inc., 22982 Mill Creek Dr., Laguna Hills, CA 92653-1214, (714)583-9119 [5890]

Advanced Technology Specialist, 116 Daten Dr., Crossville, TN 38555-9809, (931)707-1662 [5891]

Advanced Test Equipmnt Rentals, PO Box 910036, San Diego, CA 92191, (858)558-6500 [15738]

Advantage Crown, 11875 Dublin Blvd., Ste. C 258, Dublin, CA 94568-2834, (510)828-0126 [10330]

Advantage Food Marketing Corp., PO Box 367, Roslyn Heights, NY 11577, (516)625-2600 [10331]

Advantage Sales and Marketing, PO Box 3650, Syracuse, NY 13220, (315)488-3840 [10609]

Advantage Sales and Marketing, 18851 Bardeen Ave., Irvine, CA 92612-1520, (949)833-1200 [10332]

Advantage Tennis Supply, 235 Arcadia St., Richmond, VA 23225-5611, (804)276-0011 [23664]

AdvanTel Inc., 2237 Paragon Dr., San Jose, CA 95131, (408)435-5436 [5503]

Advantor Corp., 6101 Lake Ellenor Dr., Orlando, FL 32809, (407)859-3350 [24494]

Advent Electronics Inc., 2400 E Devon Ave., Ste. 205, Des Plaines, IL 60018, (847)297-6200 [8275]

Adventure Group, Inc., 1351F W 56 Hwy., Olathe, KS 66061, (913)780-1195 [9648]

Adventure Lighting Supply Ltd., 90 Washington Ave., Des Moines, IA 50314, (515)288-0444 [8276]

Adventures Unlimited Press, PO Box 74, Kempton, IL 60946-0074, (815)253-6390 [3474]

Advertising Gifts Inc., 39 W 19th St., New York, NY 10011, (212)255-4300 [13293]

Advertising Products Company Inc., 10670 E Bathany Dr., Aurora, CO 80014, (303)751-4300 [13294]

Advocate Publishing Co., 214 Knox St., Barbourville, KY 40906-1428, (606)546-9225 [20778]

Adwood Corp., PO Box 1195, High Point, NC 27261, (336)884-1846 [15739]

A/E Supplies, 3695 Springer St., Anchorage, AK 99503-5810, (907)277-2506 [13295]

AEA Distributors, 2947 Prosperity Ave., Fairfax, VA 22031, (703)560-0404 [2184]

AEI Electronic Parts, 224 Washington Ave. N, Minneapolis, MN 55401, (612)338-4754 [8277]

Aeon International Corp., 459 6th Ave., Marion, IA 52302-9122, (319)377-7415 [190]

AER Inc., 7103 E 47 Ave. Dr., Denver, CO 80216, (303)399-3673 [2185]

A.E.R. Supply, Inc., 2301 Nasa Rd., No. 1, PO Box 349, Seabrook, TX 77586, (281)474-3276 [18448]

Aerial Company Inc., PO Box 197, Marinette, WI 54143, (715)735-9323 [14009]

Aerial Photography Services Inc., 2511 S Tryon St., Charlotte, NC 28203, (704)333-5143 [3475]

Aero-K.A.P. Inc., PO Box 661240, Arcadia, CA 91066, (818)574-1704 [8278]

Aero-Motive Co., PO Box 2678, Kalamazoo, MI 49003, (616)381-1242 [8279]

Aero Products Corp., 700 Aero Ln., Sanford, FL 32771-6656, (407)330-5911 [18663]

Aero Services International Inc., 660 Newtown-Yardley Rd., Newtown, PA 18940, (215)860-5600 [24]

Aero Systems Aviation Inc., PO Box 52-2221, Miami, FL 33152-2221, (305)871-1300 [25]

Aero Systems Inc., PO Box 52-2221, Miami, FL 33152-2221, (305)871-1300 [26]

Aero Tec Laboratories Inc., Spear Rd. Industrial Park, Ramsey, NJ 07446, (201)825-1400 [16672]

Aerobic Life Industries Inc., 2916 N 35th Ave., Ste. 8, Phoenix, AZ 85017-5264, (602)455-6380 [14010]

Aerodynamics Inc., PO Box 270100, Waterford, MI 48327, (810)666-3500 [27]

Aerodyne Ulbrich Alloys, 125 S Satellite Rd., South Windsor, CT 06074, (860)289-6011 [19732]

AEROGO, Inc., 1170 Andover Pk. W, Seattle, WA 98188-3909, (206)575-3344 [15740]

Aerogroup International Inc., 201 Meadow Rd., Edison, NJ 08817, (732)985-6900 [24664]

Aeronca Inc., 1712 Germantown Rd., Middletown, OH 45042, (513)422-2751 [28]

Aeropres Corp., PO Box 78588, Shreveport, LA 71137-8588, (318)221-6282 [4314]

Aerospace Alloys Inc., 3475 Symmes Rd., Hamilton, OH 45015, (513)860-6500 [19975]

Aerospace Bearing Support Inc., 11953 Challenger Ct., Moorpark, CA 93021, (805)531-0001 [99]

AeroSpace Computer Supplies, Inc., 9270 Bryant Ave. S, Minneapolis, MN 55420, (612)884-4725 [5892]

Aerospace Materials Corp., 1940 Petra Ln., No. D, Placentia, CA 92870-6750, (714)863-0811 [8280]

Aerospace Metals Inc., 500 Flatbush Ave., Hartford, CT 06106, (860)522-3123 [26903]

Aerospace Metals Inc., 500 Flatbush Ave., Hartford, CT 06106, (860)522-3123 [26733]

Aerospace Products International Inc., 3778 Distirplex Dr., N, Memphis, TN 38118, (901)365-3470 [29]

Aerospace Southwest, 21450 N 3rd Ave., Phoenix, AZ 85027, (602)582-2779 [8281]

Aerospace Tube & Pipe, 9165 Olema Ave., Hesperia, CA 92345, (760)956-8000 [19733]

Aerotech World Trade Corp., 11 New King St., White Plains, NY 10604, (914)681-3000 [30]

AES of Norfolk Inc., 3501 Progress Rd., Norfolk, VA 23510, (757)857-6061 [14300]

AES of Oklahoma Inc., PO Box 270360, Oklahoma City, OK 73137, (405)947-8700 [14301]

AES of Roanoke Inc., PO Box 4230, Roanoke, VA 24015, (540)343-8054 [14302]

Aetna Chemical Corp., PO Box 430, Elmwood Park, NJ 07407, (201)796-0230 [4315]

Aetna Felt Corp. Mechanical Felt and Textile Div., 2401 W Emaus Ave., Allentown, PA 18103, (215)791-0900 [25954]

Aetna Plastics Corp., 1702 St. Clair Ave., Cleveland, OH 44114, (216)781-4421 [22919]

AF & T Salvage, 6125 Jackrabbit Ln., Belgrade, MT 59714-9021, (406)388-4735 [2186]

AFA Protective Systems Inc., 155 Michael Dr., Syosset, NY 11791, (516)496-2322 [24495]

AFCO Metals Inc., PO Box 95010, Little Rock, AR 72295-5010, (501)490-2255 [19734]

Affiliated Food Stores Inc., PO Box 2938, Abilene, OK 79604-2938 [10333]

Affiliated Food Stores Inc. (Tulsa, Oklahoma), PO Box 629, Tulsa, OK 74101, (918)446-5531 [10334]

Affiliated Foods Cooperative Inc., PO Box 1067, Norfolk, NE 68702-1067, (402)371-0555 [10335]

Affiliated Foods Inc., PO Box 1067, Norfolk, NE 68701, (402)371-0555 [10338]

Affiliated Foods Inc., PO Box 30300, Amarillo, TX 79120, (806)372-1404 [10336]

Affiliated Foods Inc., PO Box 30300, Amarillo, TX 79120, (806)372-1404 [10337]

Affiliated Foods Midwest, PO Box 1067, Norfolk, NE 68701, (402)371-0555 [10338]

Affiliated Foods Southwest Inc., PO Box 3627, Little Rock, AR 72203, (501)455-3590 [10339]

Affiliated Holdings Inc., 6009 Center St., Omaha, NE 68106, (402)558-0988 [14303]

Affiliated Medical Research, 180 Robert Curry Dr., Martinsville, IN 46151-8076, (765)342-0578 [18664]

Affiliated Metals, 450 Billy Mitchell Rd., Salt Lake City, UT 84122-0990, (801)363-1711 [19735]

Affiliated Metals Co., PO Box 1306, Granite City, IL 62040 [19736]

Affinitec Corp., 11737 Administration, St. Louis, MO 63146, (314)569-3450 [5893]

Affy Tapple Inc., 7110 N Clark St., Chicago, IL 60626, (773)338-1100 [10340]

AFGD, 3200 Austell Rd., Marietta, GA 30060, (404)434-2041 [6919]

AFGD, 3740 Pampas Dr., Jacksonville, FL 32207, (904)398-8471 [6920]

AFGD, 3350 Ball St., Birmingham, AL 35234, (205)841-6785 [15390]

AFGD, 575 Currant Rd., Fall River, MA 02720, (508)675-9220 [6921]

AFGD, 803 Prestige Pkwy., Scotia, NY 12302, (518)374-3812 [6922]

AFGD, 6200 Gorman Rd., Richmond, VA 23231, (804)222-0120 [6923]

AFGD, 1419 Julia St., Baton Rouge, LA 70802, (504)344-9401 [6924]

AFI, PO Box 7305, Kansas City, MO 64116, (816)459-6000 [191]

AFI Food Service Distributors Inc., PO Box 6070, Elizabeth, NJ 07207-6070, (908)629-1800 [10341]

African & Caribbean Imprint Library Services, PO Box 350, West Falmouth, MA 02574, (508)540-5378 [3476]

African Export Ltd., 2401 Sinclair Ln., Baltimore, MD 21213-1331, (410)563-9118 [24665]

Aftec Inc., 222 Columbia Tpke., Florham Park, NJ 07932-1299, (908)789-3222 [5894]

Afy Security Distributros, 1548 Bristol Pke., Bensalem, PA 19020, (215)638-3880 [24496]

AG Cooperative Service Inc., 2420 Clinton Rd., Sedalia, MO 65301, (660)826-5327 [17678]

AG Distributors, Inc., 6615 Robertson Ave., Nashville, TN 37209, (615)356-9113 [192]

Ag-Industrial Manufacturing, PO Box 53, Lodi, CA 95241, (209)369-1994 [193]

Ag-Land FS Inc., 1505 Valle Vista, Pekin, IL 61554, (309)346-4145 [194]

Ag-Land Inc., 1819 McCloud Ave., New Hampton, IA 50659, (515)394-4226 [195]

AG ONE CO-OP Inc., PO Box 2009, Anderson, IN 46018, (765)643-6639 [196]

Ag Partners Co. Cannon Falls Div., PO Box 308, Cannon Falls, MN 55009, (507)263-4651 [17679]

Ag Partners Co. Cannon Falls Div., PO Box 308, Cannon Falls, MN 55009, (507)263-4651 [10342]

AG Partners L.L.C., PO Box 38, Albert City, IA 50510, (712)843-2291 [197]

Ag-Pro Inc., Hwy. 165 S, De Witt, AR 72042, (870)946-3564 [198]

Ag Services of America Inc., PO Box 668, Cedar Falls, IA 50613, (319)277-0261 [199]

AG Systems Inc., 1100 Hwy. 7 E, Hutchinson, MN 55350, (612)587-4030 [200]

AG Truck Equipment Co., 2256 West 1500 South, PO Box 359, Salt Lake City, UT 84110, (801)975-0400 [2187]

Ag Valley Cooperative, PO Box 450, Arapahoe, NE 68922-0450, (308)962-7790 [201]

AGA Welding, 905 Belden Ave., SE, Canton, OH 44711, (330)453-8414 [15741]

Agaland CO-OP Inc., PO Box 369, Canfield, OH 44406-0369, (216)533-5551 [202]

Agar Supply Company Inc., 1100 Massachusetts Ave., Boston, MA 02125, (617)442-8989 [10343]

Agate Cooperative, PO Box 10, Agate, ND 58310, (701)656-3213 [203]

AgBest Cooperative Inc., PO Box 392, Muncie, IN 47305, (317)288-5001 [22025]

Agco Inc., PO Box 668, Russell, KS 67665, (785)483-2128 [204]

Agco Inc., PO Box 668, Russell, KS 67665, (785)483-2128 [10344]

Agee's Sporting Goods, PO Box 755, Murfreesboro, TN 37133-0755, (615)896-1272 [23496]

AGFA Corp., 1801 Century Park E, Ste. 110, Century City, CA 90067-2302, (310)552-9622 [22823]

Aggregate Equipment and Supply, 1601 N Main St., Rockford, IL 61110, (309)694-6644 [16673]

Aggregate Equipment and Supply, 301 N Madison St., Rockford, IL 61110, (815)968-2418 [16674]

Agiand Co-op, PO Box 125, Oakland, NE 68045, (402)685-5613 [17680]

AGL Welding Supply Company Inc., PO Box 1707, Clifton, NJ 07015, (201)478-5000 [16675]

Agland Coop, PO Box 466, Hooper, NE 68031, (402)654-3323 [17681]

Agland Coop, PO Box 350, Scribner, NE 68057, (402)664-2256 [205]

Agland Cooperative, PO Box C, Parkston, SD 57366, (605)928-3381 [206]

Agland Cooperative, 14 N Main St., Alta, IA 51002, (712)284-2332 [207]

Agland Cooperative, PO Box 125, Oakland, NE 68045, (402)685-5613 [208]

Agland Cooperative, PO Box 777, Gaylord, MN 55334, (507)237-2210 [22026]

Agland Inc., 260 Factory Rd., Eaton, CO 80615, (303)454-3391 [209]

AGM Electronics Inc., PO Box 32227, Tucson, AZ 85751, (520)722-1000 [8282]

Agora Cosmetics Inc., 580 Broadway, Ste. 1002, New York, NY 10012, (212)941-0890 [14011]

Agorra Building Supply Inc., 5965 Dougherty Rd., Dublin, CA 94568, (925)829-2200 [6925]

AGP Grain Co., Rte. 1, Box 56, Glenvil, NE 68941, (402)726-2266 [17682]

AGR Warehouse Distributors, 135 Barnstable Rd., Hyannis, MA 02601, (508)771-0443 [2188]

Agrex Inc., 9300 W 110th St. No. 500, Overland Park, KS 66210, (913)345-5400 [17683]

Agri Cooperative Inc., 310 Logan Rd., Holdrege, NE 68949-0548, (308)995-8626 [210]

Agri-Empire, PO Box 490, San Jacinto, CA 92581, (909)654-7311 [10345]

Agri Feed & Supply, 5716 Middlebrooke Pike, Knoxville, TN 37921, (423)584-3959 [27057]

Agri Grain Marketing, PO Box 8129, Des Moines, IA 50301, (515)224-2600 [17684]

Agri-Logic Solution Systems, State Rd. 59 S, Brazil, IN 47834, (812)448-8590 [5895]

AGRI Sales, 254 Main St., Sunfield, MI 48890, (517)566-8031 [17685]

Agri-Sales Associates Inc., 209 Louise Ave., Nashville, TN 37203, (615)329-1141 [211]

Agri Sales Inc., 385 Morley Dr., Saginaw, MI 48605, (517)753-5432 [17686]

Agri Supplies, 15001 N Nebraska, Tampa, FL 33613, (813)977-8500 [27058]

Agri-Tech F.S. Inc., 16119 Hwy. 81 W, Darlington, WI 53530, (608)776-4600 [212]

Agri Volt & Cabinet Co., PO Box 767, Carroll, IA 51401-0767, (712)792-3376 [23497]

AgriBioTech Inc., 120 Corporate Park Dr., Henderson, NV 89014, (702)566-2440 [213]

Agricultural Survey Development Associates, 380 Tomkins Ct., Gilroy, CA 95020, (408)848-1090 [10346]

Agriculture Services Inc., PO Box 627, Blackfoot, ID 83221, (208)785-1717 [214]

Agrigold Juice Products, PO Box 1630, 355 N Joy St., Corona, CA 91718-1630, (714)272-2600 [24908]

Agriland F.S. Inc., PO Box 680, Harlan, IA 51537, (712)755-5141 [215]

Agriland F.S. Inc., PO Box 680, Harlan, IA 51537, (712)755-5141 [22027]

Agrimor, 5861 SW 99th Lane, Ft. Lauderdale, FL 33328, (954)434-9848 [10347]

AgriPride F.S., PO Box 329, Nashville, IL 62263, (618)327-3046 [216]

AgriPro Seeds Inc., 6700 Antioch Rd., PO Box 2962, Shawnee Mission, KS 66204, (913)384-4940 [17687]

Agriturf Inc., 59 Dwight St., Hatfield, MA 01038, (413)247-5687 [217]

Agsco Inc., PO Box 13458, Grand Forks, ND 58201, (701)775-5325 [218]

Agusta Aerospace Corp., PO Box 16002, Philadelphia, PA 19114, (215)281-1400 [31]

Agway Energy Products, PO Box 4852, Syracuse, NY 13221-4852, (315)449-7380 [22028]

Agway, Inc., 333 Butternut Dr., DeWitt, NY 13214-1803, (315)449-7061 [219]

Agway Inc., PO Box 4933, Syracuse, NY 13221, (315)449-6436 [17688]

Ahlander Wholesale Hardware Co., 490 S University Ave., Provo, UT 84601, (801)373-6463 [13537]

AHM Security Inc., 23 Orinda Way, Orinda, CA 94563-2520, (510)254-2566 [24497]

Ahrens and McCarron Inc., 4621 Beck Ave., St. Louis, MO 63116, (314)772-8400 [23054]

AI Automotive Corp., 414 E 75th St., New York, NY 10021, (212)737-3000 [2189]

AI International Corp., 414 E 75th St., New York, NY 10021, (212)245-6262 [2190]

AIA Plastics Inc., 290 E 56th Ave., Denver, CO 80216, (303)296-9696 [22920]

A.I.D. Inc., PO Box 427, Pennsville, NJ 08070, (609)678-4142 [4316]

AIDS Impact Inc., PO Box 9443, Seattle, WA 98109, (206)284-3865 [3477]

Aiken Designs Inc.; Patsy, PO Box 97457, Raleigh, NC 27624-7457, (919)872-8789 [4754]

Aim Enterprises, Inc., 10126 Residency Rd., Manassas, VA 20110-2007, (703)361-7177 [32]

Aimonetto and Sons, Inc., 5950 6th Ave. S, Ste. 204, Seattle, WA 98108-3305, (206)767-2777 [10348]

AIMS International Books, Inc., 7709 Hamilton Ave., Cincinnati, OH 45231-3103, (513)521-5590 [3478]

AIMS Multimedia, 9710 De Soto Ave., Chatsworth, CA 91311-4409, (818)773-4300 [25058]

AIMS Multimedia, 9710 De Soto Ave., Chatsworth, CA 91311-4409, (818)773-4300 [14995]

Aimsco Inc., PO Box 80304, Seattle, WA 98108-0304, (206)762-8014 [13538]

Aimtek Inc. Welding Supply Div., 201 Washington St., Auburn, MA 01501, (508)832-5035 [16676]

AIN Plastics Inc., PO Box 151, Mt. Vernon, NY 10551-0151, (914)668-6800 [22921]

AIN Plastics of Michigan Inc., PO Box 102, Southfield, MI 48037-0102, (810)356-4000 [22922]

AIPC, 1000 Italian Way, Excelsior Springs, MO 64024, (816)637-6400 [10349]

Air-Ax Suspension Systems, PO Box 64, Edgerton, MN 56128, (507)442-8201 [2191]

Air Combat Exchange Ltd., 2533 N Carson St., Carson City, NV 89706, (775)841-4015 [20579]

Air Comm Corp., 4614 E McDowell Rd., Phoenix, AZ 85008-4508, (602)275-4505 [5504]

Air Comm Corp., 3300 Airport Rd., Boulder, CO 80301, (303)440-4075 [33]

Air Compressor Engineering Company Inc., 17 Meadow St., Westfield, MA 01085, (413)568-2884 [5824]

Air Conditioned Roses, Inc., PO Box 184, Pana, IL 62557, (217)562-2421 [14795]

Air-Draulics Co., 5750 W Erie St., Chandler, AZ 85226, (602)254-8414 [17204]

Air-Dreco, 1833 Johanna, Houston, TX 77055, (281)602-5500 [15742]

Air Electro Inc., 9452 De Soto Ave., Chatsworth, CA 91311-2231, (818)407-5400 [8283]

Air Engineering Co. Inc., 2308 Pahounui Dr., Honolulu, HI 96819, (808)848-1040 [19737]

Air Flow Shutters Shade, 1825 NE 144th St., North Miami, FL 33181-1419, (305)949-7416 [15391]

Air Flow Systems Inc., 5272 SE International Way, Portland, OR 97222, (503)659-9120 [2192]

Air Gas Inc., 1118 NE Frontage Rd., Ft. Collins, CO 80524-9218, (970)490-7700 [16680]

Air & Hydraulic Engineering, 585 Old Norcross Rd., Ste. F, Lawrenceville, GA 30045-8702, (404)458-3115 [15743]

Air & Hydraulic Equipment, Inc., PO Box 3247, Chattanooga, TN 37404-0247, (423)756-2000 [15744]

Air Mobile Systems, 14120 Alondra Blvd., Ste. G, Santa Fe Springs, CA 90670-5805, (562)921-6996 [5505]

Air O Quip Corp., PO Box 108308, Casselberry, FL 32718, (407)831-3600 [14304]

Air-Oil Products Corp., 2400 E Burnside St., Portland, OR 97214, (503)234-0866 [16677]

Air Parts Inc., PO Box 170, Cumming, GA 30028, (404)781-6640 [14305]

Air Power Equipment Corp., 2400 N Washington Ave., Minneapolis, MN 55411, (612)522-7000 [5825]

Air Power Inc., PO Box 5406, High Point, NC 27262, (910)886-5081 [15745]

Air & Pump Co., 585 S Padre Island Dr., Corpus Christi, TX 78405, (512)289-7000 [5826]

Air Rite Filters Inc., 1290 W 117th St., Lakewood, OH 44107, (216)228-8200 [14306]

Air Systems Distributors Inc., 5600 NW 84th Ave., Miami, FL 33166, (305)592-3809 [14307]

Air Systems Inc., 4512 Bishop Ln., Louisville, KY 40218, (502)452-6312 [5827]

Air Technologies, 2501 Sandersville Rd., Lexington, KY 40511, (606)254-2520 [5828]

Air Temperature Inc., 802 Rozelle St., Memphis, TN 38104, (901)278-7211 [14308]

Air & Water Purification Inc., 300 Hwy. 55, Hamel, MN 55340, (612)478-6050 [25547]

Airbus Industry of North America Inc., 198 Van Buren St., No. 300, Herndon, VA 20170-5338, (703)834-3400 [34]

Airco A and R Equipment Co., 9950 4th St., Rancho Cucamonga, CA 91730, (909)987-6295 [15747]

Airco Gas and Gear, 5430 W Morris St., Indianapolis, IN 46241, (317)243-6601 [16678]

Aircraft and Component Equipment Suppliers Inc., PO Box 60968, Pasadena, CA 91116-6968, (213)564-2421 [35]

Aircraft Spruce and Specialty Co., 225 Airport Cir., Corona, CA 92880, (909)372-9555 [36]

Airfan Engineered Products Inc., 10259 Stanford Ave., Garden Grove, CA 92840-4860, (213)723-3354 [14309]

Airgas, 500 Codell Dr., Lexington, KY 40509, (606)252-0343 [15746]

Airgas Inc., PO Box 6675, Radnor, PA 19087-5240, (610)687-5253 [16679]

Airgas Intermountain, 1118 NE Frontage Rd., Ft. Collins, CO 80524-9218, (970)490-7700 [16680]

Airgas-North Central, 10 W 4th St., Waterloo, IA 50701, (319)233-3540 [16681]

Airgas Safety, PO Box 1010, W185 N11300 Whitney Dr., Germantown, WI 53022-8210, (414)255-7300 [18665]

Airgas West, 9950 4th St., Rancho Cucamonga, CA 91730, (909)987-6295 [15747]

Airline Hydraulics Corp., I-95 Business Ctr., Bensalem, PA 19020, (215)638-4700 [16682]

Airmatic Inc., 7317 State Rd., Philadelphia, PA 19136-4292, (215)333-5600 [13539]

Airmo Div., 950 Mason St., San Francisco, CA 94106, (415)772-5336 [13012]

Airmotive Inc., 3400 Winona Ave., Burbank, CA 91504, (818)845-7423 [37]

Airport Beer Distributors, 4850 W Lake Rd., Erie, PA 16505-2920, (814)833-9781 [1475]

Airport Greenhouse, 11330 Smith Rd., Ft. Wayne, IN 46809, (219)747-3356 [14796]

Airport Metals, 6099 Triangle Dr., Los Angeles, CA 90040, (323)722-2500 [19738]

AirSep Corporation, 290 Creekside Dr., Buffalo, NY 14228-2070, (716)691-0202 [15748]

Airtechnics Inc., 230 Ida, PO Box 3466, Wichita, KS 67201-3466, (316)267-2849 [8284]

Airtechnics Inc., 230 Ida, Wichita, KS 67201-3466, (316)267-2849 [8285]

Airtex Consumer Products, 150 Industrial Park Rd., Cokato, MN 55321, (320)286-2696 [15392]

Airtex Corp., 2900 N Western Ave., Chicago, IL 60618, (312)463-2500 [6926]

Airway Industries Inc., Airway Park, Ellwood City, PA 16117, (724)752-0012 [18367]

AIS Computers, 165 Carnegie Pl., Fayetteville, GA 30214, (770)461-2147 [5896]

AIS Construction Equipment Corp., 600 44th SW, Grand Rapids, MI 49548, (616)538-2400 [6927]

Aisin World Corporation of America, 24330 Garnier St., Torrance, CA 90505, (310)326-8681 [2193]

Aitcheson Inc.; J and H, 100 Dove St., Alexandria, VA 22314, (703)548-7600 [23055]

AITech International Corp., 47971 Fremont Blvd., Fremont, CA 94538-4508, (510)226-8960 [5897]

Aiwa America Inc., 800 Corporate Dr., Mahwah, NJ 07430, (201)512-3600 [25059]

AJ Coal Co., PO Box 387, Meriden, CT 06450-0387, (203)235-6358 [20507]

Ajax Supply Co., 5714 Ayers, Corpus Christi, TX 78415, (512)855-6284 [14310]

Ajax Tool Works Inc., 10801 Franklin, Franklin Park, IL 60131, (847)455-5420 [13540]

Ajay Leisure Products Inc., 1501 E Wisconsin St., Delavan, WI 53115, (414)728-5521 [23498]

AJC International Inc., 5188 Roswell Rd., Atlanta, GA 30342, (404)252-6750 [19127]

Ajinomoto U.S.A. Inc., Country Club Plz., 115 W Century Rd., Paramus, NJ 07652-1432, (201)261-1789 [10350]

Ajo Way Garden & Nursery, 3220 E Ajo Way, Tucson, AZ 85713, (520)294-9611 [14797]

A.K. International, 1116 Marshall Ave., Lancaster, PA 17601, (717)394-0202 [13296]

Akers & Chrysler Inc., PO Box 1050, Auburn, ME 04211-1050, (207)764-1511 [21375]

Akiba Press, 5949 Estates Dr., Oakland, CA 94611, (510)339-1283 [3479]

Akin Industries, Inc., 147 Commerce Dr., Monticello, AR 71655, (501)367-6263 [18666]

Akin Medical Equipment International, PO Box 412632, Kansas City, MO 64141, (816)753-3219 [19128]

AKJ Educational Services, Inc., 5609-2A Fishers Ln., Rockville, MD 20852, (301)770-4030 [3480]

AKMS, Inc., PO Box 50329, Columbia, SC 29250, (803)695-5001 [18667]

AKMS Inc., PO Box 50329, Columbia, SC 29250, (803)695-5001 [19129]

Akorn Inc., 2500 Mill Brook Dr., Buffalo Grove, IL 60089, 800-93-AKORN [19130]

Akro-Mils Inc., PO Box 989, Akron, OH 44309, (216)253-5592 [25886]

Akrochem Corp., 255 Fountain St., Akron, OH 44304, (330)535-2108 [24266]

Akron Auto Auction Inc., 2471 Ley Dr., Akron, OH 44319, (216)773-8245 [20580]

Akron Overseas Inc., PO Box 5418, Akron, OH 44334, (330)864-6411 [15749]

Akzo Coatings, 5555 Spalding Dr., Norcross, GA 30092, (404)662-8464 [21376]

A.L. Investors Inc., 5601 Logan, Denver, CO 80216, (303)295-0196 [13297]

AL-KO KOBER Corp., 25784 Borg Rd., Elkhart, IN 46514, (219)264-0631 [2194]

Al Nyman and Son, 1500 S 66th Ave., Hollywood, FL 33023, (954)986-9000 [18897]

Al-WaLi Inc., 401 Thornton Rd., Lithia Springs, GA 30122, (770)948-7845 [3481]

Alabama Art Supply, 2229 Magnolia Ave. S, Birmingham, AL 35205, (205)326-2132 [20779]

Alabama Book Store, PO Box 1279, Tuscaloosa, AL 35403-1279, (205)758-4532 [3482]

Alabama Coal Cooperative, 2870 Old Rocky Ridge Dr., Birmingham, AL 35243, (205)979-5963 [20508]

Alabama Crankshaft and Engine, 1900-B S Broad St., Unit 3, Mobile, AL 36615-1821, (205)433-3691 [2195]

Alabama Crankshaft and Engine Warehouse Inc., 1432 Mims Ave. SW, Birmingham, AL 35211, (205)925-4616 [2196]

Alabama Crown, 421 Industrial Dr., Birmingham, AL 35259, (205)941-1155 [1476]

Alabama Farmers Cooperative Inc., PO Box 2227, Decatur, AL 35609-2227, (256)353-6843 [17689]

Alabama Food Group Inc., P.O. Drawer 1207, Alexander City, AL 35011-1207, (256)234-5071 [10351]

Alabama Institutional Foods Inc., 1801 39th St., PO Box 1420, Tuscaloosa, AL 35403, (205)345-0474 [10352]

Alabama Lamp, Inc., PO Box 252, Albertville, AL 35950, (205)878-1003 [15513]

Alabama Truck Body & Equipment, Inc., 190 Industrial Park Rd., Oneonta, AL 35121, (205)274-4900 [2197]

Alacrity Systems Inc., 43 Newburg Rd., Hackettstown, NJ 07840, (908)813-2400 [5898]

Aladdin Distributors Inc., 1420 Cliff Rd. E, Burnsville, MN 55337-1414, (612)890-8700 [26383]

Aladdin Steel Inc., Rte. 16 E, Gillespie, IL 62033, (217)839-2121 [19739]

Aladdin Synergetics Inc., 555 Marriot Dr., No. 400, Nashville, TN 37214, (615)748-3830 [18668]

Alakef Coffee Roasters Inc., 1600 London Rd., Duluth, MN 55812, (218)724-6849 [10353]

Alamex Crafts Inc., 118 Old Durham Rd., No. A, Chapel Hill, NC 27514-2293, (919)479-8795 [26384]

Alamo Aircraft, Ltd., PO Box 37343, San Antonio, TX 78237, (210)434-5577 [38]

Alamo Aircraft Supply Inc., PO Box 37343, San Antonio, TX 78237, (210)434-5577 [38]

Alamo Forest Products, Inc., PO Box 17258, San Antonio, TX 78217, (210)352-1300 [8174]

Alamo Iron Works, PO Box 231, San Antonio, TX 78291-0231, (210)223-6161 [19740]

Alamo Square Distributors, 4530 19th St., PO Box 14543, San Francisco, CA 94114, (415)863-7410 [3483]

Alamo Square Distributors, 4530 18th St., San Francisco, CA 94114, (415)863-7410 [3484]

Alamo Square Distributors, 4530 18th St., San Francisco, CA 94114, (415)863-7410 [3485]

Alan Co.; B.J., 555 Martin Luther King Jr. Blvd., Youngstown, OH 44502-1102, (330)746-1064 [9630]

Alan Desk Business Interiors, 8575 Washington Blvd., Culver City, CA 90232, (323)655-6655 [20780]

Alan Inc.; Charles, 1942 Tigertail Blvd., Dania, FL 33004-2105, (954)922-9663 [9649]

Alanco Eyewear, 8117 NE 13th Ave., Vancouver, WA 98665, (360)574-0065 [19131]

Alanco Optical Inc., 8117 NE 13th Ave., Vancouver, WA 98665, (360)574-0065 [19131]

Alan's Tropical Plants, 300 E Croton Way, Howey in the Hills, FL 34737-3215, (352)934-2920 [14798]

ALARIS Medical Systems Inc., 10221 Wateridge Cir., San Diego, CA 92121, (619)458-7000 [18669]

Alarm Controls Corp., 19 Brandywine Dr., Deer Park, NY 11729-5721, (516)586-4220 [24498]

Alarm-It Distributors Inc., 1930 19th Avenue Dr. NE, Hickory, NC 28601, (828)328-2074 [24499]

Alarm Services Inc., 204 N Magnolia St., Albany, GA 31707-4223, (912)436-7000 [24500]

Alaron Inc., PO Box 215287, Auburn Hills, MI 48321-5287, (248)340-7500 [25060]

Alaska Education & Recreational Products, 3520 B Balchen, PO Box 190333, Anchorage, AK 99519-0333, (907)243-8773 [20781]

Alaska Fire & Safety Equipment, 416 Shoreline Dr., Thorne Bay, AK 99919, (907)828-3346 [24501]

Alaska Garden and Pet Supply, 114 Orca, Anchorage, AK 99510, (907)279-4519 [27059]

Alaska General Alarm Inc., 405 W 27th Ave., Anchorage, AK 99503-2612, (907)279-8511 [24502]

Alaska General Alarm Inc., 405 W 27th Ave., Anchorage, AK 99503-2612, (907)279-8511 [8286]

Alaska Housewares Inc., 501 West 58th Ave., Anchorage, AK 99518-1431, (907)561-2240 [14996]

Alaska Industrial Hardware, Inc., 2192 Viking Dr., Anchorage, AK 99501, (907)276-7201 [15750]

Alaska Instrument Company Inc., PO Box 230087, Anchorage, AK 99523-0087, (907)561-7511 [24308]

Alaska Insulation Supply, Inc., 261 E 56th Ave., Bldg. B, Anchorage, AK 99518, (907)563-4125 [6928]

Alaska Micro Systems Inc., 3211 Denali St., Anchorage, AK 99503, (907)278-3900 [5899]

Alaska Mill Feed Co., 114 Orca, Anchorage, AK 99510, (907)279-4519 [27059]

Alaska News Agency Inc., 325 W Potter Dr., Anchorage, AK 99518, (907)563-3251 [3486]

Alaska Nut & Bolt, 3041 Cottonwood, Anchorage, AK 99508-4316, (907)276-3885 [13541]

Alaska Pacific University Press, Alaska Pacific University, 4101 University Dr., Anchorage, AK 99508, (907)564-8218 [3487]

Alaska Paper Co. Inc., PO Box 101977, Anchorage, AK 99510-1977, (907)274-6681 [21617]

Alaska Quality Control Services, 184 E 53rd Ave., Anchorage, AK 99518-1222, (907)562-6439 [8287]

Alaska Trophy Manufacturing, 845 E Loop Dr., Anchorage, AK 99501-3739, (907)272-2172 [17304]

Alaskan Copper & Brass Co., 3223 6th S, PO Box 3546, Seattle, WA 98134, (206)623-5800 [19741]

Alaskan Glacier Seafoods, PO Box 209, Petersburg, AK 99833, (907)772-3333 [10354]

Alaskan Gold Seafood Inc., PO Box 806, Soldotna, AK 99669, (907)262-5797 [10355]

Alaskan Paint Manufacturing Company Inc., 2040 Spar Ave., Anchorage, AK 99501, (907)272-2942 [21377]

Alaskan Paint & Paper, 747 Gaffney Rd., Fairbanks, AK 99701, (907)479-6125 [3092]

Alatec Products, 21123 Nordoff St., Chatsworth, CA 91311, (818)727-7800 [13542]

Alba-Waldensian Inc., PO Box 100, Valdese, NC 28690, (828)874-2191 [4755]

Albaco Foods Inc., Rte. 1, Box 744, Alma, GA 31510-9801, (912)632-7213 [10356]

Albain Shirt Co., PO Box 429, Kinston, NC 28501, (919)523-2151 [4756]

Alban Engine Power Systems, PO Box 9595, Baltimore, MD 21237, (410)686-7777 [15751]

Alban Engine Power Systems, 6455 Washington Blvd., Elkridge, MD 21075-5398, (410)796-8000 [2198]

Alban Machinery and Hydraulic Services, PO Box 9595, Baltimore, MD 21237, (410)686-7777 [15751]

Alban Tractor Company Inc., PO Box 9595, Baltimore, MD 21237, (410)686-7777 [15751]

Albany Bowling Supply Inc., PO Box 3346, Albany, GA 31706-3346, (912)435-8751 [23499]

Albany Ladder Company Inc., 1586 Central Ave., Albany, NY 12205, (518)869-5335 [6929]

Albany Steel & Brass Corp., 1900 W Grand, Chicago, IL 60622-6286, (312)733-1900 [13543]

Albany Tile Supply, 452 N Pearl St., Albany, NY 12204-1511, (518)434-0155 [9650]

Albers Inc., PO Box 51030, Knoxville, TN 37950-1030, (423)524-5492 [19132]

Albert City Elevator Inc., PO Box 38, Albert City, IA 50510, (712)843-2291 [197]

Albert City Elevator Inc., PO Box 38, Albert City, IA 50510, (712)843-2291 [220]

Albert Paper Co., PO Box 8630, Stockton, CA 95208, (209)466-7931 [21618]

Albert Poultry Co. Inc., 318 10th Ave., Columbus, GA 31901-3310, (706)323-6096 [10357]

Albert Trading Co., PO Box 433, West Bend, WI 53095, (414)334-9295 [14997]

Albert W. Sisk and Son Inc., 3601 Choptawk Rd., PO Box 70, Preston, MD 21655, (410)673-7111 [10358]

Alberto-Culver International Inc., 2525 Armitage Ave., Melrose Park, IL 60160, (708)450-3000 [14012]

Albert's Organics Inc., 3268 E Vernon Ave., Vernon, CA 90058, (323)587-6367 [10359]

Albertville Electric Motor, 6621 U.S Hwy. 431, Albertville, AL 35950, (256)878-0491 [8288]

Albright Paper & Box Corp., 14 Robison St., Pottstown, PA 19464, (610)327-4990 [21619]

Albums Inc., 11422 Grissom, Dallas, TX 75229-2352, (972)247-0677 [22824]

Albuquerque Balloon Center, 523 Rankin Rd. NE, Albuquerque, NM 87107-2238, (505)344-5844 [23500]

Albuquerque Bolt & Fastener, 2926 2nd St. NW, Albuquerque, NM 87107-1416, (505)345-5869 [13544]

Albuquerque Foreign Auto Parts, 5028 Broadway Blvd. SE, Albuquerque, NM 87105-7414, (505)877-4856 [2199]

Albuquerque Winnelson Co., 3545 Princeton NE, Albuquerque, NM 87107, (505)884-1553 [23056]

Alcan Aluminum Corp, Alcan Powder and Pigments, 901 Lehigh Ave., Union, NJ 07083, (908)851-4500 [19726]

Alcan Aluminum Corp. Metal Goods Service Center Div., 8800 Page Blvd., St. Louis, MO 63114, (314)427-1234 [19742]

Alcan Recycling, PO Box 127, Shelbyville, TN 37162, (615)684-0300 [26734]

Alcide Corp., 8561 154th Ave. NE, Redmond, WA 98052, (425)882-2555 [19133]

Alco Building Products Co., 4835 Para Dr., Cincinnati, OH 45237-5008, (513)242-1100 [6930]

Alco Equipment Inc., PO Box 386, Agawam, MA 01001-0386, (413)789-0330 [2200]

Alco Health Services Corp., PO Box 10069, Lynchburg, VA 24506-0069, (804)239-6971 [19151]

Alco Iron and Metal Co., 1091 Doolittle Dr., San Leandro, CA 94577, (510)562-1107 [19743]

Alco Standard Corp., PO Box 834, Valley Forge, PA 19482-0834, (610)296-8000 [21620]

Alco Tool Supply Inc., 54847 County Rd. 17, Elkhart, IN 46516-9792, (219)295-5535 [13545]

Alcoa Authorized Distributing, 34 S Main St., Butte, MT 59701, (406)782-6536 [6931]

Alcoa Conductors Products Co., 105 Westpark Dr., Brentwood, TN 37027, (615)370-4300 [2201]

Aldelano Corp., 24021 Lodge Pole Rd., Diamond Bar, CA 91765, (909)861-3970 [4567]

Alden Autoparts Warehouse Inc., 535 Grand Army Hwy., Somerset, MA 02725, (508)673-4233 [2202]

Alden Comfort Mills, 1708 14th, Plano, TX 75074-6404, (972)423-4000 [13013]

Alden Corp., 251 Munson Rd., Wolcott, CT 06716, (203)879-4889 [15752]

Alderfer Bologna Inc., PO Box 2, 382 Main St., Harleysville, PA 19438, (215)256-8818 [10360]

Alderfer, Inc., PO Box 2, 382 Main St., Harleysville, PA 19438, (215)256-8818 [10360]

Alders Wholesale; Henry, Egbertson Rd., Campbell Hall, NY 10916, (914)496-9191 [20782]

Aldine Technologies Industries, Inc., 585 Industrial Rd., Carlstadt, NJ 07072, (201)935-1110 [21621]

Ale-8-One Bottling Co. Inc., PO Box 645, Winchester, KY 40391, (606)744-3484 [24909]

Alec Corp., PO Box 15229, Stamford, CT 06901-0229, (203)327-0922 [24666]

Aleph International, 1026 Griswold Ave., San Fernando, CA 91340, (818)365-9856 [8289]

Aleutian Pribilof Island Association, 201 E 3rd Ave., Anchorage, AK 99501-2503, (907)276-2700 [18670]

Alex City Provision Inc., PO Box 1207, Alexander City, AL 35011, (256)234-5071 [10361]

Alex Lee Inc., PO Box 800, Hickory, NC 28603, (828)323-4424 [10362]

Alexander Koetting Poole and Buehrle Inc., 737 Goddard Ave., Chesterfield, MO 63005, (314)537-5200 [10363]

Alexander; Steve, 124 2nd St. SE, Huron, SD 57350-2045, (605)352-6941 [8290]

Alexander & Townsend, 507 N Mur Len Rd., Ste. A, Olathe, KS 66062-1267, (913)829-3266 [23501]

Alexander Wholesale Inc.; W.C., PO Box 727, 2000 Forest St., Mt. Vernon, IL 62864, (618)242-6515 [6932]

Alexander's Nursery, 6566 Kuamoo Rd. No. C, Kapaa, HI 96746, (808)822-5398 [14799]

Alexon Trend Inc., 14000 Unity St. NW, Ramsey, MN 55303, (612)323-7800 [24309]

Alfa Laval Celleco Inc., 1000 Laval Blvd., Lawrenceville, GA 30043, (770)963-2100 [15753]

Alfa Romeo Distributors of North America, PO Box 598026, Orlando, FL 32859-8026, (407)856-5000 [20581]

Alfred Publishing Company Inc., PO Box 10003, Van Nuys, CA 91410-0003, (818)891-5999 [3488]

Alfreda's Film Works c/o Continnuus, PO Box 416, Denver, CO 80201-0416, (303)575-5676 [3489]

Alfredos Restaurant Equipment, 801 Delaware Ave., Alamogordo, NM 88310-7103, (505)437-1745 [24057]

Alfredo's Tile Distributors, Expy. 83, La Joya, TX 78560, (512)585-7200 [9651]

Alfreds Processor Sales & Service, 122 W Union St., Kenner, LA 70062-4822, (504)464-5914 [18671]

Algert Company, Inc., 2121 E Del Amo Blvd., Compton, CA 90220, (213)632-7777 [14998]

Algol Consultants Technology, PO Box 1762, St. Johns, AZ 85936, (520)337-3694 [5900]

Algoma Net Co., 1525 Mueller St., Algoma, WI 54201, (920)487-5577 [23502]

Alicia Comforts, 5 Cook, Brooklyn, NY 11206, (718)384-2100 [15393]

Alimenta (USA) Inc., 100 N Point Cir., No. 450, Alpharetta, GA 30022-8230, (404)255-5050 [10364]

Alis-USA, 600 W Broadway, Glendale, CA 91214 [5901]

Alko Distributors Inc., PO Box 60757, Savannah, GA 31420, (912)920-9999 [1477]

Alkota of Western Montana, PO Box 18104, Missoula, MT 59808-8104 [4568]

All About Offices Inc., PO Box 7826, Boise, ID 83707-1826, (208)336-4700 [20783]

All America Distributors Corp., 8431 Melrose Pl., Los Angeles, CA 90069, (323)651-2650 [3490]

All American Food Group Inc., 4475 S Clinton Ave., South Plainfield, NJ 07080, (908)757-3022 [24058]

All American Pool N Patio, 2021 Curry Ford Rd., Orlando, FL 32806-2419, (407)898-8722 [23503]

All American Recycling Div., PO Box 1556, Ocala, FL 34478, (904)622-0101 [19744]

All American Semiconductor Inc., 16085 NW 52nd Ave., Miami, FL 33014, (305)621-8282 [8291]

All American Truck Brokers, PO Box 12365, Wilmington, DE 19850, (302)654-6101 [15754]

All Appliance Parts Inc., 40 Austin Blvd., Commack, NY 11725, (516)543-4000 [8292]

All Brand Appliance Parts Inc., 170 N Blackhorse Pike, Mt. Ephraim, NJ 08059, (609)933-2300 [14999]

All Brand Appliance Parts of Pennsylvania, 949 E Main St., Norristown, PA 19401, (215)277-5175 [15000]

All-Car Distributors Inc., PO Box 27, Antigo, WI 54409-0027, (715)623-3791 [2203]

All City Barber & Beauty Supply, 408 S Main St., Santa Ana, CA 92701, (714)835-8727 [14013]

All City Refrigeration Co. Inc., 32425 W 8 Mile Rd., Livonia, MI 48152-1301, (248)478-8780 [14311]

All Coast Forest Products Inc., PO Box M, Chino, CA 91708, (909)627-8551 [6933]

All Coast Lumber Products Inc., PO Box 9, Cloverdale, CA 95425, (707)894-4281 [6934]

All Computer Warehouse, 224 S 5th Ave., City of Industry, CA 91746, (626)369-4181 [5902]

All Dressed Up, 150 S Water, Batavia, IL 60510, (630)879-5130 [4757]

All Fasteners Inc., 2620 4 Mile Rd., PO Box 427, Racine, WI 53401-0427, (414)639-4200 [13546]

All Foils Inc., 4597 Van Epps Rd., Brooklyn Heights, OH 44131, (216)661-0211 [19745]

All Foreign Used Auto Parts, 916 N Kings Rd., Nampa, ID 83687-3193, (208)465-3272 [2204]

All Hours Auto Salvage, 3110 Caldwell Blvd., Nampa, ID 83651-6418, (208)466-9848 [2205]

All-In-One Monogramming, 909 W Garland Ave., Spokane, WA 99205-2820, (509)325-4838 [4758]

All Kitchens Inc., 209 W Main St., Boise, ID 83702, (208)336-7003 [11188]

All Kitchens Inc., 209 W Main St., Boise, ID 83702, (208)336-7003 [10365]

All Line Inc., 31 W 310 91st St., Naperville, IL 60564, (630)820-1800 [16683]

All Makes Office Machine Company Inc., 150 W 24th St., Los Angeles, CA 90007, (213)749-7483 [20784]

All Paint Supply Co., 325 W Main St., Farmington, NM 87401-8422, (505)327-2468 [21378]

All Parts Brokers, 3515 Cleveland Blvd., Caldwell, ID 83605-6043, (208)454-0713 [2206]

All Pet Distributors, 355 Crooked Hill Rd., Brentwood, NY 11717, (516)273-6363 [27060]

All Phase Electric Supply, 539 Union St., Spartanburg, SC 29301-4469, (864)585-0103 [8293]

All Phase Electric Supply, 731 N Market Blvd., Sacramento, CA 95834-1211, (916)648-0134 [8294]

All Phase Electric Supply Co., 875 Riverview Dr., Benton Harbor, MI 49022, (616)926-6194 [8295]

All-Power Inc., 3435 S Racine Ave., Chicago, IL 60608, (773)650-7400 [2207]

All Pro Championships Inc., 2541 Holloway Rd., Louisville, KY 40299-6104, (502)267-7836 [4759]

All-Pro Fasteners, Inc., 1916 Peyco Dr. N, PO Box 151227, Arlington, TX 76015, (817)467-5700 [13547]

All Products Automotive Inc., 4701 W Courtland Ave., Chicago, IL 60639, (312)889-4500 [2208]

All Quality Builders, 47-237 Kam Hwy., Kaneohe, HI 96744, (808)247-4245 [23504]

All-Right, 1500 Shelton Dr., Hollister, CA 95023, (831)636-9566 [6935]

All Seas Exporting Inc., 11630 Garfield St., Denver, CO 80233-1618, (303)451-8313 [5903]

All Seas Wholesale Inc., 2414 San Bruno Ave., San Francisco, CA 94134-1503, (415)468-4800 [10366]

All Seasons Engines Inc., 126 S Main St., Roswell, NM 88203, (505)625-0800 [14312]

All Season's Kitchen L.L.C., PO Box 64887, Burlington, VT 05406-4887, (802)865-0412 [10367]

All Spec Static Control Inc., PO Box 1200, Wilmington, NC 28402-1200, (910)763-8111 [8296]

All Stainless Inc., 992 Temple St., Ste. 2, Whitman, MA 02382-1066, (781)749-7100 [13548]

All Standard Tile Corp., 21470 Jamaica Ave., Queens Village, NY 11428, (718)389-2520 [9652]

All Star Pet Supply, 19935 W 157th St., Olathe, KS 66062, (913)764-4232 [27061]

All Star Sports Inc., 7321 42nd Ave. N, Minneapolis, MN 55427-1317, (612)535-3312 [23505]

All State Fastener Corp., PO Box 356, Eastpointe, MI 48021, (810)773-5400 [13549]

All Systems Inc., 3241 N 7th St. Trfy., Kansas City, KS 66115-1105, (913)677-5333 [8297]

All That Jazz, 4505 Bandini Blvd., Los Angeles, CA 90040, (213)869-1832 [4760]

All Tile, 1201 Chase Ave., Elk Grove Village, IL 60007, (847)364-9191 [9653]

All Tool Sales Inc., PO Box 517, Racine, WI 53401, (414)637-7447 [13550]

Allamakee Implement Co., 1736 Lansing Harpers Rd., Lansing, IA 52151-7577, (319)568-3463 [221]

Allan Co., 14620 Joanbridge St., Baldwin Park, CA 91706, (626)962-4047 [26735]

Allan and Co.; G.B., PO Box 816146, Dallas, TX 75381-6146, (972)620-7655 [15755]

Allan Distributors, 801 Water St., No. 105, Framingham, MA 01701-3200, (508)877-8655 [17305]

Allan Industries Inc.; A., PO Box 999, Wilkes Barre, PA 18701, (717)826-0123 [26736]

Allanson Business Products, 10740 Lyndale Ave. S, Minneapolis, MN 55420-5615, (612)881-1151 [5904]

Allcar Automotive Centers, PO Box 27, Antigo, WI 54409-0027, (715)623-3791 [2203]

Allcomm of Wisconsin, 2045 W Mill Rd., Glendale, WI 53209-3444, (414)228-4000 [5506]

Allegheny Electronics Inc., PO Box 1963, Altoona, PA 16603, (814)946-0871 [25061]

Allegheny High Lift Inc., R.D. 6, Box 510, Greensburg, PA 15601, (412)836-1535 [15756]

Allegheny Inc., 3600 William Flynn Hwy., Allison Park, PA 15101, (412)486-5500 [9654]

Allegheny Inc., 3600 William Flynn Hwy., Allison Park, PA 15101, (412)486-5500 [15394]

Allegheny Mining Corp., 321 N Jefferson St., Lewisburg, WV 24901-1116, (304)693-7621 [20509]

Allegheny Rodney Strip Svc Ctr, PO Box 366, Skokie, IL 60076, (847)676-5900 [19746]

Allegiance Brokerage Co., PO Drawer 410529, Charlotte, NC 28241-0529, (704)529-1176 [10368]

Allegiance Corp., 1430 Waukegan Rd., Mc Gaw Park, IL 60085, (847)578-4240 [19134]

Allegiance Healthcare Corporation Hospital Supply/Scientific Products, 1450 Waukegan Rd., Mc Gaw Park, IL 60085, (847)689-8410 [18672]

Allegiance Healthcare Corporation Hospital Supply/Scientific Products, 1450 Waukegan Rd., Waukegan, IL 60085, (847)689-8410 [19135]

Allegro Coffee Co., 1930 Central Ave., Boulder, CO 80301, (303)444-4844 [10369]

Allen and Allen Company Inc., PO Box 5140, San Antonio, TX 78284, (210)733-9191 [6936]

Allen Appliance Distributors, 6505 St. Vincent Ave., Shreveport, LA 71136-6480, (318)868-6541 [15001]

Allen Avionics, Inc., 224 E 2nd. St., Box 350, Mineola, NY 11501, (516)248-8080 [8298]

Allen Brothers Feed Inc., 300 3rd St., Kentwood, LA 70444, (504)229-5521 [17690]

Allen Brown Industries Inc., 1720 Watterson Tr., Louisville, KY 40299-2430, (502)499-0628 [25955]

Allen Company Inc., PO Box 537, Winchester, KY 40392-0537, (606)744-3361 [6937]

Allen County Cooperative Association, PO Box 97, New Haven, IN 46774, (219)749-5130 [222]

Allen Electric Supply Co., 31750 Plymouth Rd., Livonia, MI 48151-1906, (734)421-9300 [8299]

Allen Foods Inc., 8543 Page Ave., St. Louis, MO 63114, (314)426-4100 [10370]

Allen Millwork Inc., PO Box 6480, Shreveport, LA 71136, (318)868-6541 [6938]

Allen Petroleum Corp., PO Box 210, Seaford, DE 19973, (302)629-9428 [22029]

Allen Refractories Co., 131 Shackelford Rd., Pataskala, OH 43062, (740)927-8000 [16684]

Allen; Robert, 55 Cabot Blvd., Mansfield, MA 02048, (508)333-9151 [25956]

Allen and Son Inc.; Sam, PO Box 430002, Pontiac, MI 48343, (248)335-8141 [19747]

Allen Steel Co., 1340 South 200 West, Salt Lake City, UT 84115, (801)484-8591 [19748]

Allen Supply Company, Inc.; William B., 301 N Rampart, New Orleans, LA 70112-3015, (504)525-8222 [24503]

Allen Systems Group Inc., 750 11th St., S, Naples, FL 34102, (941)435-2200 [5905]

Allen Trading Co. Inc., 275 Dean Rd., Brookline, MA 02445-4144, (617)232-7747 [24667]

Allen Trading Company Inc., 275 Dean Rd., Brookline, MA 02445-4144, (617)232-7747 [4761]

Allen's Supply Co., 7248 Ashville Hwy., Knoxville, TN 37924, (865)525-9200 [223]

Allenson, Inc.; Alec R., 1307 Highway 179A, Westville, FL 32464, (850)956-2817 [3491]

Allentown Beverage Company Inc., 1249 N Quebec St., Allentown, PA 18103, (610)432-4581 [1478]

Allentown News Agency Inc., 719-723 Liberty St., Allentown, PA 18105-0446, (610)432-4441 [3492]

Allentown Optical Corp., 525 Business Park Ln., PO Box 25003, Allentown, PA 18103, (215)433-5269 [19136]

AllerMed Corp., 31 Steel Rd., Wylie, TX 75098, (972)442-4898 [14313]

Allerton Implement Co., PO Box 80, Allerton, IL 61810, (217)834-3305 [224]

Alles Corp., 177 Wells Ave., Newton, MA 02459, (617)965-1800 [21622]

Alley-Cassetty-Building Supplies, PO Box 23305, Nashville, TN 37202, (615)244-7077 [20510]

Alley-Cassetty Coal Co., PO Box 23305, Nashville, TN 37202, (615)244-7077 [20510]

Alliance Agronomics Inc., 7104 Mechanicsville Tpk. Ste. 217, Mechanicsville, VA 23111, (804)730-2900 [225]

Alliance Foods Inc., PO Box 339, Coldwater, MI 49036, (517)278-2396 [10371]

Alliance Grain Co., PO Box 546, Gibson City, IL 60936, (217)784-4284 [17691]

Alliance Maintenance and Services Inc., 3355 W 11th St., Houston, TX 77008, (713)863-0000 [22030]

Alliance Metals Inc., 905 Fern Hill Rd., West Chester, PA 19380, (215)436-8600 [19749]

Alliance Products Company, 6189 Grovedale Ct., Alexandria, VA 22310, (703)922-2805 [6945]

Alliance Steel Corp., 275 Old Higgins Rd., Des Plaines, IL 60018, (708)297-7000 [19750]

Alliance Steel Service Co., 115 31st Ave. N, Minneapolis, MN 55411, (612)588-2721 [26737]

Alliant Foodservice, Inc., 7598 NW 6th Ave., Boca Raton, FL 33487, (561)994-8500 [10372]

Alliant Foodservice Inc., 12000 Crown Pt. Dr., Ste. 125, San Antonio, TX 78233, (210)657-6901 [10373]

Alliant FoodService Inc., One Parkway North Ctr., Deerfield, IL 60015, (847)405-8500 [24059]

Alliant Foodservice Inc., 7598 NW 6th Ave., Boca Raton, FL 33487, (561)994-8500 [10374]

Alliant Foodservice Indianapolis, 12301 Cumberland Rd., Fishers, IN 46038, (317)585-6600 [10375]

Allied Bearing, 3525 W Lincoln Ave., PO Box 340066, Milwaukee, WI 53215, (414)672-3111 [2209]

Allied Bearing Supply, 416 S Utica, PO Box 3263, Tulsa, OK 74104, (918)583-0164 [16685]

Allied Bearings & Supply, 932 8th Ave., Nashville, TN 37203, (615)255-1204 [2210]

Allied Belting and Transmission Inc., PO Box 565713, Dallas, TX 75356, (214)631-7670 [2211]

Allied Beverage Group, LLC, 7800 Browning Rd., Pennsauken, NJ 08109, (609)486-4000 [1479]

Allied Body Works Inc., 625 S 96th St., Seattle, WA 98108-4914, (206)763-7811 [2212]

Allied Boise Cascade, 1100 International Plz. S, Chesapeake, VA 23323, (757)485-1500 [21623]

Allied Bolt Co., PO Box 80604, Seattle, WA 98108, (206)763-2275 [13551]

Allied Box Co., 1931 Stout Field West Dr., Indianapolis, IN 46241-4020, (317)352-0083 [21624]

Allied Box Co., 1931 Stout Field West Dr., Indianapolis, IN 46241-4020, (317)352-0083 [16686]

Allied Building Products, 622 E Grand River Ave., Lansing, MI 48906-5338, (517)485-7121 [6939]

Allied Building Products Corp., 5252 Sherman St., Denver, CO 80216, (303)296-2222 [6940]

Allied Building Products Corp., 8207 Hartzell Rd., Anchorage, AK 99507-3109, (907)349-6668 [6941]

Allied Building Products Corp., 15 E Union Ave., East Rutherford, NJ 07073, (201)507-8400 [6942]

Allied Building Stores Inc., PO Box 8030, Monroe, LA 71211, (318)699-9100 [27275]

Allied Construction Equipment Co., 4015 Forest Park Ave., St. Louis, MO 63108, (314)371-1818 [6943]

Allied Container Corp., 435 E Hedding St., San Jose, CA 95112, (408)293-3628 [21625]

Allied-Crawford Steel, 7135 Bryhawke Cir., North Charleston, SC 29418, (803)552-6300 [19751]

Allied Cycle Distributors Inc., PO Box 430, Waltham, MA 02454-0430, (781)899-3571 [23506]

Allied Distributing, 3810 Transport St., Ventura, CA 93003, (805)644-2201 [1480]

Allied Distribution Systems, 11852 Alameda St., Lynwood, CA 90262-4019 [6944]

Allied Distribution Systems, 11852 Alameda St., Lynwood, CA 90262-4019 [27276]

Allied Distributors Inc., 555 State St., Springfield, MA 01109, (413)781-7100 [9655]

Allied-Eastern Distributors, 100 W Drullard Ave., Lancaster, NY 14086, (716)684-0234 [9656]

Allied-Eastern Distributors, 110 Baker St., Syracuse, NY 13206, (315)437-2465 [9657]

Allied Eastern Distributors, 1913 Commercial St., Erie, PA 16503, (814)453-5648 [9658]

Allied Electronics, 7410 Pebble Dr., Ft. Worth, TX 76118, (817)595-3500 [8300]

Allied Electronics, 154 Technology Pkwy., Ste. 280, Norcross, GA 30092, (770)242-0699 [8301]

Allied Electronics, 7134 Columbia Gateway Dr., Ste. 200, Columbia, MD 21046, (410)312-0810 [8302]

Allied Electronics, 1580 S Milwaukee Ave., Ste 408, Libertyville, IL 60048, (847)918-0250 [8303]

Allied Electronics, 260 Northland Blvd., Ste. 213, Cincinnati, OH 45246, (513)771-6990 [8304]

Allied Electronics, 5755 Granger Rd., Ste. 756, Independence, OH 44131-1459, (216)831-4900 [8305]

Allied Electronics, 659 Lakeview Plaza Blvd., Ste. A, Worthington, OH 43085-4775, (614)785-1270 [8306]

Allied Electronics, 9550 Forest Ln., Ste. 511, Dallas, TX 75243, (214)553-4370 [8307]

Allied Electronics, 32180 Schoolcraft Rd., Livonia, MI 48150, (734)266-0660 [8308]

Allied Electronics, 7500 Viscount, Ste. 118, El Paso, TX 79925, (915)779-6294 [8309]

Allied Electronics, 5500 Northland Dr. NE, Grand Rapids, MI 49505, (616)365-9960 [8310]

Allied Electronics, 2421 W 205 St., Ste. D-206B, Torrance, CA 90505, (310)783-0601 [8311]

Allied Electronics, 2448 S 102nd St., Ste. 150, West Allis, WI 53227, (414)543-3372 [8312]

Allied Electronics, 6110 Blue Circle Dr., Ste. 220, Minnetonka, MN 55343, (612)938-5633 [8313]

Allied Electronics, 2970 Cottage Hill Rd., Bell Air Park, Ste. 174, Mobile, AL 36606, (205)476-1875 [8314]

Allied Electronics, 860 U.S. Rte. 1, North, Edison, NJ 08817, (732)572-9600 [8315]

Allied Electronics, 10824 Old Mill Rd., Ste. 5, Omaha, NE 68154, (402)697-0038 [8316]

Allied Electronics, 140 Technology, Ste. 400, Irvine, CA 92618-2426, (949)727-3010 [8317]

Allied Electronics, 2111 E Baseball Rd., No. F3, Tempe, AZ 85283, (480)831-2002 [8318]

Allied Electronics, 9750 SW Nimbus Ave., Beaverton, OR 97005, (503)626-9921 [8319]

Allied Electronics, 22 Freedom Plains Rd., Ste. 138, Poughkeepsie, NY 12603-2670, (914)452-1470 [8320]

Allied Electronics, 5236 Greens Dairy Rd., Raleigh, NC 27604, (919)876-5845 [8321]

Allied Electronics, 580 Menlo Dr., Ste. 2, Rocklin, CA 95765, (916)632-3104 [8322]

Allied Electronics, 156 S Spruce, No. 204, South San Francisco, CA 94080, (650)952-9599 [8323]

Allied Electronics, 7406 Alban Station Ct., Ste. 211, Springfield, VA 22150, (703)644-9515 [8324]

Allied Electronics, 4525 E Honeygrove Rd., Ste. 201, Virginia Beach, VA 23455, (757)363-8662 [8325]

Allied Electronics, 32180 Schoolcraft, Livonia, MI 48150 [8326]

Allied Electronics Corp., 4530 McKnight Rd., Pittsburgh, PA 15237-3162, (412)931-2774 [8327]

Allied Electronics, Inc., 7410 Pebble Dr., Ft. Worth, TX 76118, (817)595-3500 [8328]

Allied Film Laboratory, Inc., 11923 Brookfield, Livonia, MI 48150, (734)462-5543 [25063]

Allied Fire Lite Fireplace, 310 Westhill Blvd., Appleton, WI 54914, (920)733-4911 [14314]

Allied Flooring Supply, PO Box 52005, Box 9, Knoxville, TN 37950-2005, (423)584-2386 [9659]

Allied Floors, Inc., 1815 S Kansas Ave., PO Box 2453, Topeka, KS 66612, (785)232-0381 [9660]

Allied Grocers Cooperative Inc., 1 Market Cir., Windsor, CT 06095, (860)688-8341 [10376]

Allied Inc., 260 Metty Dr., Ann Arbor, MI 48106, (734)665-4419 [2213]

Allied Industrial Equipment Corp., 9388 Dielman Industrial Dr., St. Louis, MO 63132, (314)569-2100 [15757]

Allied International Marketing Corp., 380 Maple Ave., Ste. 202, Vienna, VA 22180, (703)255-6400 [17692]

Allied International Marketing Corp., 380 Maple Ave., Ste. 202, Vienna, VA 22180, (703)255-6400 [226]

Allied Kitchen & Custom Cabinet, 6189 Grovedale Ct., Alexandria, VA 22310, (703)922-2805 [6945]

Allied Medical, Inc., 690 S Mendenhall Rd., Memphis, TN 38117, (901)683-3543 [19137]

Allied Metals Corp., 320 E Seven Mile Rd., Detroit, MI 48203, (313)368-7110 [26738]

Allied Metals Inc., 2220 Canada Dry St., Houston, TX 77023, (713)923-9491 [19752]

Allied-National Inc., 13270 Capital St., Oak Park, MI 48237-3107, (248)543-1232 [8329]

Allied Oil and Supply Inc., PO Box 3687, Omaha, NE 68103, (402)344-4343 [22031]

Allied Order Buyers, Inc., 1908 Hwy. 20, Lawton, IA 51030, (712)944-5175 [17693]

Allied Order Buyers, Inc., 333 Livestock Exchange Bldg., Sioux City, IA 51101, (712)252-3614 [17694]

Allied Plywood Corp., 6189 Grovedale Ct., Alexandria, VA 22310, (703)922-2805 [6945]

Allied Plywood Corp., 11852 Alameda St., Lynwood, CA 90262-4019, (978)371-3399 [6946]

Allied Purchasing, 1334 18th St. SW, Mason City, IA 50401, (515)423-1824 [16687]

Allied Safety Inc., 5959 W Howard St., Niles, IL 60714, (847)647-4000 [19138]

Allied Sales Co., 509 N Saint Andrews St., Dothan, AL 36303-4557, (334)792-1627 [13014]

Allied School and Office Products, PO Box 92677, Albuquerque, NM 87199-2677, (505)884-4900 [20785]

Allied Scrap Processors Inc., PO Box 1585, Lakeland, FL 33802, (941)665-7157 [26739]

Allied Screw Products, PO Box 543, Mishawaka, IN 46546-0543, (219)255-4718 [39]

Allied Seed Co-Op, Inc., 1917 E Fargo, Nampa, ID 83687, (208)466-9218 [227]

Allied Sound Inc., 230 Cumberland Bnd, Nashville, TN 37228-1807, (615)248-2800 [25062]

Allied Supply Inc., 6300 Murray St., Little Rock, AR 72209-8532, (501)562-6180 [23057]

Allied Telecommunications Inc., PO Box 2106, Richmond, IN 47375-2106, (765)935-1538 [25094]

Allied Telecommunications Inc., PO Box 2106, Richmond, IN 47375-2106, (765)935-1538 [15002]

Allied Tire and Auto Services, 4749 US Highway 50 E, Carson City, NV 89701, (775)883-3101 [2214]

Allied Tools Inc., PO Box 34367, Louisville, KY 40232, (502)966-4114 [16688]

Allied Trading Companies, PO Box 3603, Chattanooga, TN 37415, (423)877-2000 [15758]

Allied Transmission, Inc., 215 K Central Ave., Farmingdale, NY 11735, (718)335-1800 [15759]

Allied Truck Equipment Corp., 4821 Massachusetts Ave., Indianapolis, IN 46218, (317)545-1227 [2215]

Allied-Vaughn Inc., 11923 Brookfield, Livonia, MI 48150, (734)462-5543 [25063]

Allied Vista Inc. Vista Fibers, PO Box 807, San Antonio, TX 78293, (210)226-6371 [26740]

Allied Wholesale Inc., 13207 Bradley Ave., Sylmar, CA 91342, (818)364-2333 [13552]

AlliedSignal Automotive Aftermarket, 105 Pawtucket Ave., Rumford, RI 02916-2422, (401)434-7000 [2216]

AlliedSignal Automotive Catalyst Co., PO Box 580970, Tulsa, OK 74158-0970, (918)266-1400 [2217]

AlliedSignal Hardware Product Group, 120 S Webber Dr., Chandler, AZ 85226, (602)365-2611 [16689]

Alligator Technologies, 2900 Bristol St., Ste. E-101, Costa Mesa, CA 92626-7906, (714)850-9984 [5906]

Allimex International, 412 Washington St., Lawrenceville, IL 62439-3159 [4762]

Alling and Cory Co., PO Box 20403, Rochester, NY 14602-0403, (716)581-4100 [20786]

Allison-Erwin Co., 2920 N Tryon St., Charlotte, NC 28232, (704)334-8621 [5907]

Allison Inc., 114 W Bland, Roswell, NM 88201, (505)624-0151 [20582]

Allou Distributors Inc., 50 Emjay Blvd., Brentwood, NY 11717, (516)273-4000 [14014]

Allou Health and Beauty Care Inc., 50 Emjay Blvd., Brentwood, NY 11717, (516)273-4000 [14015]

Alloy Piping Products Inc., PO Box 7368, Shreveport, LA 71137, (318)226-9851 [23058]

Alloy Tool Steel Inc., 13525 E Freeway Dr., Santa Fe Springs, CA 90670, (310)921-8605 [19753]

Allpak Co., 1010 Lake St., Oak Park, IL 60301, (708)383-7200 [25887]

Allparts Inc., RR 2 Box 153-A, Louisiana, MO 63353-9802 [2218]

Allpro Corp., 2310 E Douglas, Wichita, KS 67214, (316)267-3329 [21379]

Allpro Corp., 1373 Ingleside Rd., Norfolk, VA 23502, (757)853-4371 [21380]

Allpro Corp., Sixth Industrial Park Dr., Wheeling, WV 26003, (304)232-2200 [21381]

Allred Optical Laboratory, 845 Church St. N, Concord, NC 28025-4300, (704)788-3937 [19139]

Allred's Inc., PO Box 57160, Salt Lake City, UT 84157-0160, (801)266-4413 [14315]

Allstar Enterprises Inc., 51 Stouts Ln., Ste. 1, Monmouth Junction, NJ 08852, (732)329-6095 [13298]

Allstar Systems Inc., 6401 Southwest Frwy., Houston, TX 77074, (713)795-2000 [5908]

Allstate Beverage Co., 1580 Parallel St., Montgomery, AL 36104, (334)265-0507 [1481]

Allstate/GES Appliance Inc., 2001 N 23rd Ave., Phoenix, AZ 85009-2918, (602)252-6507 [15003]

Allstate Office Products Inc., 1605 E Hillsborough Ave., Tampa, FL 33610, (813)238-9571 [20787]

Allstate Restaurant Equipment Inc., 125 Esten Ave., Pawtucket, RI 02860-4877, (401)727-0880 [24060]

Allstate Sales and Leasing Corp., 558 E Villaume Ave., South St. Paul, MN 55075, (612)455-6500 [20583]

Allstate Sales and Leasing Corp., 558 E Villaume Ave., South St. Paul, MN 55075, (612)455-6500 [2219]

Allstates Textile Machinery Inc., PO Box 266, Anderson, SC 29622, (864)226-6195 [15760]

Allston Street Used Auto Parts, 72 Allston St., Providence, RI 02908-5311, (401)273-6739 [2220]

Alltech Business Solutions Inc., PO Box 2163, Buena Park, CA 90621, (714)999-7733 [20770]

Alltech Inc., 3031 Catnip Hill Pike, Nicholasville, KY 40356, (606)885-9613 [228]

ALLTEL Corp., 1 Allied Dr., Little Rock, AR 72202, (501)661-8000 [5507]

ALLTEL Supply Inc., 6625 The Corners Pkwy., Norcross, GA 30092, (404)448-5210 [5508]

Allure Home Creation Company Inc., 85 Fulton St., Boonton, NJ 07005, (973)402-8888 [15395]

Allview Services Inc., 2215 S Castle Way, Lynnwood, WA 98036, (425)483-6103 [5909]

Allwaste Inc., 5151 San Felipe, No. 1600, Houston, TX 77056, (713)623-8777 [26741]

Allwaste Inc. Allwaste Recycling Div., 4200 Fidelity Rd., Houston, TX 77029, (713)676-1500 [26742]

Ally Industries Inc., 30-A Progress Ave., Seymour, CT 06483, (203)366-5410 [24504]

Ally Press, 524 Orleans St., St. Paul, MN 55107, (612)291-2652 [3493]

Allyn Air Seat Co., 18 Millstream Rd., Woodstock, NY 12498, (914)679-2051 [2221]

Allyn International Corp., 1075 Santa Fe Dr., Denver, CO 80204-3900, (303)825-5200 [15004]

ALM Surgical Equipment Inc., 1820 N Lemon St., Anaheim, CA 92801-1009, (714)578-1234 [18673]

Alma Farmers Cooperative Association, Clay and Collins St., Alma, MO 64001, (660)674-2291 [229]

Alma Farmers Union Cooperative, 1300 Main St. S, Alma, WI 54610, (608)685-4481 [230]

Alma, Inc., 270 Lancaster St., Portland, ME 04101, (207)773-5667 [14800]

Alma Iron and Metal Company Inc., PO Box 729, Alma, MI 48801, (517)463-2131 [26743]

Almaly Trading Corp., 325 Alhambra Cir., Coral Gables, FL 33134, (305)448-3033 [5910]

Almanzan, PO Box 10113, Oakland, CA 94610-0113, (510)532-8700 [17306]

Almàr Industries, Rte. 10 E, Bldg. 2, Succasunna, NJ 07876, (973)927-3050 [13299]

Almar, Ltd., 607 Ala Moana Blvd., Honolulu, HI 96813, (808)521-7566 [21382]

Alma's Glow Products International, 1806 E Alondra Blvd., Compton, CA 90221, (310)764-4247 [14016]

Almeda Beauty Shop, 10121 4th St. NW, Albuquerque, NM 87114-2211, (505)898-0686 [14017]

Almena Cooperative Association, PO Box 118, Almena, WI 54805, (715)357-3650 [22032]

Almena Cooperative Association, PO Box 118, Almena, WI 54805, (715)357-3650 [22033]

Almerica Overseas Inc., PO Box 2188, Tuscaloosa, AL 35403, (205)758-1311 [40]

Almerica Overseas Inc., PO Box 2188, Tuscaloosa, AL 35403, (205)758-1311 [23059]

Almetals Co., 51035 Grand River Ave., Wixom, MI 48393, (248)348-7722 [19754]

ALMO, 9815 Roosevelt Blvd., Philadelphia, PA 19114, (215)698-4000 [5911]

Almo Corp., 9815 Roosevelt Blvd., Philadelphia, PA 19114, (215)698-4080 [5912]

Almo Distributing, 1349A Charwood Rd., Hanover, MD 21076-3114, (301)459-2100 [5913]

Almond Brothers Lumber and Supply Inc., 403 Ringgold, Coushatta, LA 71019, (318)932-4041 [6947]

Aloha State Sales Company Inc., 2829 Awaawaloa St., Honolulu, HI 96819, (808)833-2731 [7968]

Aloha Tap & Die Inc., 1240 Mookaula, Honolulu, HI 96817-4621, (808)845-7252 [16690]

Alpena Beverage Co. Inc., 1313 Kline Rd., Alpena, MI 49707-8108, (517)354-4329 [1482]

Alpena Oil Company Inc., 235 Water St., Alpena, MI 49707, (517)356-1098 [22034]

Alpena Screen Arts, 2577 US Hwy. 23 S, Alpena, MI 49707-4825, (517)354-5198 [4763]

Alpena Screen Arts, 2577 US Hwy. 23 S, Alpena, MI 49707-4825, (517)354-5198 [4764]

Alpena Wholesale Grocery Co., 170 N Industrial Hwy., Alpena, MI 49707, (517)356-2281 [10377]

Alper Inc.; Morris, 130 Lizotte Dr., Marlborough, MA 01752-3080, (508)875-5600 [10378]

Alpert and Alpert Iron and Metal Inc., 1815 S Soto St., Los Angeles, CA 90023, (323)265-4040 [26744]

Alpha Communications Inc., 951 N 1st St., Albemarle, NC 28001-3353, (704)983-5252 [5509]

Alpha Distributors Ltd., 20W151 101st St., Lemont, IL 60439-8876 [10379]

Alpha Fern Co., PO Box 535, Pierson, FL 32180, (904)749-2786 [14801]

Alpha Fine Computer Furniture, 2241 N Main St., Walnut Creek, CA 94596, (925)930-0277 [13015]

Alpha-Omega Sales Corp., 325 Main St., North Reading, MA 01864-1360, (978)664-1118 [8330]

Alpha Source Inc., 12104 West Carmen Ave., Milwaukee, WI 53225, (414)760-2222 [8331]

Alpha Star International Inc., 550 Pharr Rd., Atlanta, GA 30305, (404)237-7175 [10380]

Alpha Steel Corp., 141-141st St., Hammond, IN 46327, (219)933-1000 [19755]

Alpha Tile Distributors, Inc., 10898 Metro Pkwy., Ft. Myers, FL 33912, (941)275-8288 [9661]

Alpha Tile Distributors, Inc., 2603 Ace Rd, Orlando, FL 32804-1910 [9662]

Alpha Tile Distributors, Inc., 2443 Tampa East Blvd., Tampa, FL 33619, (813)620-9000 [9663]

Alpha Tile Distributors, Inc., 4301 31st St. N, St. Petersburg, FL 33714, (813)525-1213 [9664]

Alpha Tile Distributors, Inc., 12350 Automobile Blvd. Rd., Clearwater, FL 33762-4425, (813)796-6569 [9665]

Alpha Tile Distributors, Inc., 1808 Whitfield Ave., Sarasota, FL 34243-3919, (941)351-3484 [9666]

Alpha Video & Electronics Co., 200 Keystone Dr., Carnegie, PA 15106, (412)429-2000 [25064]

Alpha Wire Co., 711 Lidgerwood Ave., Elizabeth, NJ 07207-0711, (908)925-8000 [8332]

AlphaNet Solutions Inc., 7 Ridgedale Ave., Cedar Knolls, NJ 07927, (973)267-0088 [5914]

Alphatronics Engineering Corp., 154 Talamine Ct, Colorado Springs, CO 80907, (719)520-5880 [15761]

Alphin Brothers Inc., Rte. 8, Box 40, Dunn, NC 28334, (910)892-8751 [10381]

Alpina International Inc., 102 Madison Ave., New York, NY 10016-7318, (212)683-3511 [21626]

Alpina Sports Corp., PO Box 23, Hanover, NH 03755-0023, (603)448-3101 [24668]

Alpine Corp., 250 W 57th St., New York, NY 10019, (212)697-5167 [6948]

Alpine Distribution Services, 16956 S Harlan Rd., Lathrop, CA 95330-8737, (510)795-4100 [10382]

Alpine Electronics of America Inc., PO Box 2859, Torrance, CA 90509, (310)326-8000 [25065]

Alpine Evergreen Company Inc., 7124 State Hwy. 3 SW, Port Orchard, WA 98367, (360)674-2303 [27277]

Alpine Packing Co., 9900 Lower Sacramento Rd., Stockton, CA 95210, (209)477-2691 [10383]

Alpine Restaurant Equipment, 1661 Lonsdale Ave., Lincoln, RI 02865-1707, (401)723-1300 [24061]

Alpine Slide of Jackson Hole, PO Box SKI, Jackson, WY 83001-1846, (307)733-7680 [23507]

Alpine Supply, 2841 W Parkway Blvd., Salt Lake City, UT 84119, (801)972-0477 [13553]

Alps Electric (USA) Inc., 3553 N 1st St., San Jose, CA 95134, (408)432-6000 [5915]

Alps Wire Rope Corp., 1947 Quincy Ct., Glendale Heights, IL 60139, (708)893-3888 [19756]

Alps Wire Rope Corp., 1947 Quincy Ct., Glendale Heights, IL 60139, (708)893-3888 [19757]

ALR Wholesale, 115 Sylvan Dr., Independence, KY 41051, (606)356-7220 [27062]

Alretta Truck Parts Inc., 207 A St., Boston, MA 02210, (617)268-8116 [2222]

Alro Metals Service Center, PO Box 3031, Boca Raton, FL 33431-0931, (407)997-6766 [19758]

Alro Steel Corp., PO Box 927, Jackson, MI 49204, (517)787-5500 [19759]

Alro Steel Corp., 1800 W Willow St., Lansing, MI 48915, (517)371-9600 [19760]

Alro Steel Corp., 2301 S Walnut St., Muncie, IN 47302, (765)282-5335 [19761]

Alsdorf International Ltd., 209 E Lake Shore Rd., No. 15W, Chicago, IL 60611-1307, (847)501-3335 [13554]

Alshefski Enterprise, Rte. 93, Box 330B, West Hazleton, PA 18201, (717)455-1577 [10384]

Alsum Produce Inc., N9083 Highway EF, PO Box 188, Friesland, WI 53935-0188, (920)348-5127 [10385]

Alta Dena Certified Dairy, 17637 E Valley Blvd., City of Industry, CA 91744, (626)964-6401 [10386]

Alta Industries Ltd., PO Box 510, Salt Lake City, UT 84110, (801)972-8160 [19762]

Alta Paint & Coatings, 136 West 3300 South, Salt Lake City, UT 84115, (801)466-9625 [21383]

Alta-Robbin, 110 S 1200 W, Lindon, UT 84042, (801)785-1114 [16691]

Alta Sales Inc., 110 S 1200 W, Lindon, UT 84042, (801)785-1114 [16691]

Altec Industries Inc. Eastern Div., 250 Laird St., Plains, PA 18705, (717)822-3104 [20584]

Alter Norfolk Corp., 500 Washington Ave., Norfolk, NE 68701, (402)371-2200 [26745]

Alter Scrap Processing, PO Box 220, West Burlington, IA 52655, (319)752-3643 [26746]

Alter Trading Corp., 2117 State St., Bettendorf, IA 52722, (319)344-5200 [26747]

Alter Trading Corp., 555 N New Ballas Rd., St. Louis, MO 63141, (314)872-2400 [26748]

Alternative Cigarettes Inc., PO Box 678, Buffalo, NY 14207, (716)877-2983 [26258]

Alternative Computer Solutions Ltd., 990 Washington Rd., Washington, PA 15301-9633, (412)429-5370 [5916]

Alternative Computer Technology Inc., 7908 Cin-Day Rd., West Chester, OH 45069, (513)755-1957 [5917]

Altex-Mar Electronics Inc., 17201 Westfield Park Rd., Westfield, IN 46074, (317)867-4000 [8333]

Altimus Distributing, PO Box 1724, Billings, MT 59103-1724, (406)259-9816 [4569]

Altitude Wholesale Co. Inc., 6334 S Racine Cir 200, Englewood, CO 80111-6426 [10387]

Altitude Wholesale Company Inc., 6334 S Racine Cir., No. 200, Englewood, CO 80111-6426, (303)779-1141 [10388]

Altman Map, Inc.; Bryant, Norwood Commerce Center, Bldg. 26, Endicott St., Norwood, MA 02062, (781)762-3339 [3494]

Altron International, 314 W Walton Blvd., Pontiac, MI 48340-1041, (248)334-2549 [25066]

Altron International, 314 W Walton Blvd., Pontiac, MI 48340-1041, (248)334-2519 [15005]

Altura PC Systems Inc., 2842A Janitell Rd., Colorado Springs, CO 80909, (719)538-1014 [5918]

Aluma Flight Co., PO Box 5983, Helena, MT 59604-5983, (406)442-4977 [26385]

Aluma Panel, Inc., 2410 Oak St. W, Cumming, GA 30041-6456, (404)889-3996 [21384]

Aluma Systems USA Inc., 6435 E 30th St., Indianapolis, IN 46219, (317)543-4625 [6949]

Alumacast Inc., 3112 S Highland Dr., Las Vegas, NV 89109, (702)871-7944 [13016]

Alumax Building Products, 28921 E Hwy. 74, Sun City, CA 92586, (714)928-1000 [19763]

Aluminum Distributors Inc., 706 E 2nd St., Des Moines, IA 50309, (515)283-2383 [6950]

Aluminum Distributors Inc., 2107 Gardner Rd., Broadview, IL 60153, (708)681-1900 [19764]

Aluminum Line Products Co., 24460 Sperry Circle, Westlake, OH 44145, (440)835-8880 [2223]

Aluminum Products Co., 3307 S Washington, Marion, IN 46953, (765)674-7759 [6951]

Aluminum and Stainless Inc., PO Box 3484, Lafayette, LA 70502, (337)837-4381 [19765]

Alvin and Co. Inc., PO Box 188, Windsor, CT 06095, (860)243-8991 [25548]

Alvin and Company Inc., PO Box 188, Windsor, CT 06095, (860)243-8991 [24310]

Alvin Equipment Company Inc., PO Box 1907, Alvin, TX 77512, (281)331-3177 [6952]

Alvin Tree Farm, Inc., RR 7, Box 1, Alvin, TX 77511, (281)331-0190 [14802]

A.M. Associates Inc., 21 Hampden Dr. 9, South Easton, MA 02375-1183, (508)230-2401 [13300]

AM-DYN-IC Fluid Power, 3755 Linden Ave. SE, Grand Rapids, MI 49548, (616)241-4695 [15762]

AM-DYN-IC Fluid Power, 25340 Terra Industrial Dr., Chesterfield, MI 48051, (810)949-6860 [16692]

A.M. Roehl Sales Inc., 3919 Renate Dr., Las Vegas, NV 89103-1804, (702)362-2113 [23009]

Amadom Corp., 801 E Aztec Ave., Gallup, NM 87301-5509, (505)722-5452 [17307]

Amalco Metals Inc., 33955 7th St., Union City, CA 94587-3521, (510)487-1300 [19766]

Amalgamated Automotive Industries Inc., PO Box 149, Camp Hill, PA 17001-0149, (717)939-7893 [2224]

Amalgamet Inc., 1480 US Hwy. 9 N, Ste. 207, Woodbridge, NJ 07095-1401, (732)634-6034 [4317]

Amano Partners USA Inc., 140 Harrison Ave., Roseland, NJ 07068, (973)227-8256 [8334]

Amarillo Building Products Inc., PO Box 9026, Amarillo, TX 79105, (806)373-4205 [6953]

Amarillo Clutch & Driveshaft Co., 4420 I-40 E, Amarillo, TX 79103, (806)372-3893 [2225]

Amarillo Hardware Co., PO Box 1891, Amarillo, TX 79172, (806)376-4722 [13555]

Amarillo Winnelson Co., PO Box 1306, Amarillo, TX 79105, (806)372-2259 [23060]

AmAsia International Ltd., 34 3rd Ave., Burlington, MA 01803-4414, (781)229-6611 [24669]

AmAsia International Ltd., 34 3rd Ave., Burlington, MA 01803, (781)229-6611 [4765]

Amateur Electronics Supply, 621 Commonwealth Ave., Orlando, FL 32803, (407)894-3238 [5510]

Amateur Electronics Supply, 28940 Euclid Ave., Wickliffe, OH 44092, (440)585-7388 [25067]

Amateur Electronics Supply, 5710 W Good Hope Rd., Milwaukee, WI 53223, (414)358-0333 [8335]

Amato International Inc., 11 Broadway, New York, NY 10004, (212)943-4974 [10389]

Amazing Wind Machines Inc., 7839 Greenwich Rd., Lodi, OH 44254-9709, (978)952-2889 [231]

AMB Tools & Equipment, 608 W Nob Hill Blvd., Yakima, WA 98902-5559, (509)452-7123 [13556]

Ambassador Book Service, Inc., 42 Chasner St., Hempstead, NY 11550, (516)489-4011 [3495]

Ambassador Steel Company Inc., 1469 E Atwater St., Detroit, MI 48207, (313)259-6600 [19767]

Amber Grout Sales, 6114 Bolamo Ct., Westerville, OH 43081-4151, (614)572-5033 [27063]

Amber NFO Reload Corp., RR 3, Anamosa, IA 52205, (319)462-2968 [17695]

Amberstar International Inc., 105 E Laurel, San Antonio, TX 78212, (210)227-7289 [10390]

Ambex Inc., 1917 Drew St., Clearwater, FL 33765, (727)442-2727 [15006]

Ambit Pacific Recycling Inc., 16222 S Figueroa St., Gardena, CA 90247, (310)327-2227 [26749]

Ambraco Inc., Hwy. 61-151 S, Dubuque, IA 52001, (319)583-3035 [16693]

Ambriola Co. Inc., 2 Burma Rd., Jersey City, NJ 07305, (201)434-6289 [10391]

Ambrose Branch Coal Co. Inc., PO Box 806, Pound, VA 24279, (540)796-4941 [20511]

AMC Industries Inc., PO Box 171290, San Antonio, TX 78217-8290, (210)226-8218 [23061]

AMC Tile Supply, 3905 Forest Park Blvd., St. Louis, MO 63108, (314)371-2200 [6954]

Amcam International Inc., 601 Academy Dr., Northbrook, IL 60062-1915, (847)291-1560 [22825]

Amcamex Electronics Corp., PO Box 50775, Amarillo, TX 79159, (806)354-2690 [5511]

Amceco International Corp., 1314 Long St., Ste. 110, High Point, NC 27262-2568, (910)887-8647 [26386]

AMCEP Inc., 4484 E Tennessee St., Tucson, AZ 85714, (520)748-1900 [26750]

Amchem Inc., 155 N New Boston St., Woburn, MA 01801, (781)938-0700 [15763]

Amco Equipment and Steel Inc., PO Box 125, Midvale, UT 84047, (801)255-4257 [6955]

Amco-McLean Corp., 766 McLean Ave., Yonkers, NY 10704, (914)237-4000 [25068]

Amco-McLean Corp., 766 McLean Ave., Yonkers, NY 10704, (914)237-4000 [15007]

Amcon Distributing Co., 10223 L St., Omaha, NE 68127, (402)331-3727 [26259]

AMCON Distributing Co., PO Box 241230, Omaha, NE 68124, (402)331-3727 [10392]

Amcraft, Inc., 4348 S 90th St., Omaha, NE 68127, (402)339-7950 [20788]

AME Food Service Inc., PO Box 3105, Scottsdale, AZ 85271-3105, (602)947-8021 [10393]

Amedem Enterprises, Inc., 224 State St., Ste. 2, Portsmouth, NH 03801-4035, (603)436-7489 [4570]

Amemco, 697 North 700 East, Kaysville, UT 84037-0211, (801)544-9999 [5919]

Amende and Schultz, PO Box 788, South Pasadena, CA 91030, (213)682-3806 [10394]

Amerada Hess Corp., 1185 Ave. of the Amer., New York, NY 10036, (212)997-8500 [22035]

Amerex (USA) Inc., 350 5th Ave., No. 7418, New York, NY 10118, (212)967-3330 [4766]

Amerhart Ltd., PO Box 10097, Green Bay, WI 54307-0097, (920)494-4744 [6956]

Ameri-Tech Equipment Co., PO Box 3075, Casper, WY 82602, (307)234-9921 [6957]

AmeriBag Inc., 55 Greenkill Ave., Kingston, NY 12401, (914)339-1292 [18368]

America II Electronics, 2600 118th Ave. N, St. Petersburg, FL 33716, (813)573-0900 [8336]

America West Distributors, PO Box 3300, Bozeman, MT 59772, (406)585-0700 [3496]

American Accessories International Inc., 901 E Summit Hill Dr., No. 302, Knoxville, TN 37915-1200, (423)525-9100 [18369]

American Alloy Steel Inc., PO Box 40469, Houston, TX 77240, (713)462-8081 [19768]

American Ambulance, 1401 E Washington St., Phoenix, AZ 85034, (602)255-0131 [18674]

American Appliance Parts Co. Inc., 1180 Sherman Ave., Hamden, CT 06514-1322, (203)248-4444 [15008]

American Argo Corp. Sales and Distribution, 1385 Broadway, 24th Fl., New York, NY 10018, (212)764-0700 [4767]

American Associated Roofing Distributor, PO Box 4056, Atlanta, GA 30302, (404)522-7060 [6958]

American Athletic Sales Inc., 916 S Main St., Salt Lake City, UT 84101-2923, (801)531-8032 [4768]

American Audio Prose Library, PO Box 842, Columbia, MO 65205-0842, (573)443-0361 [3497]

American Auto Salvage, PO Box 925, Clovis, NM 88102-0925, (505)763-4812 [2226]

American Barmag Corp., PO Box 7046, Charlotte, NC 28241, (704)588-0072 [15764]

American Book Center, Brooklyn Navy Yard, Bldg. 3, Brooklyn, NY 11205, (718)834-0170 [3498]

American Builders and Contractors Supply Company Inc., One ABC Pkwy., Beloit, WI 53511, (608)362-7777 [6959]

American Building Supply, Inc., 4190 E Santa Ana, Ontario, CA 91761, (909)390-1700 [6960]

American Building Supply, Inc., 8920 43rd Ave., Sacramento, CA 95828, (916)387-4100 [6961]

American Bus Sales, 195 Defense Hwy., Annapolis, MD 21401, (410)269-0251 [2227]

American Business Concepts, 2800 Gallows Rd., Ste. C, Vienna, VA 22180, (703)573-9313 [20789]

American Business International Inc., 7860 Estancia Way, Sarasota, FL 34238, (941)921-1201 [20790]

American Business Machines, 3475 Forest Lake Dr., Uniontown, OH 44685-8105, (330)699-9912 [20791]

American Business Network and Associates Inc., 2544 S 156th Cir., Omaha, NE 68130, (402)691-8248 [5920]

American Business Service and Computer Technologies Inc., 9999 Rose Hills Rd., Whittier, CA 90601-1701, (626)280-5150 [5921]

American Business Systems Inc., 315 Littleton Rd., Chelmsford, MA 01824, (978)250-9600 [5922]

American Byproducts Inc., 5601 Paschall Ave., Philadelphia, PA 19143, (215)533-4660 [25957]

American Camper, 14760 Santa Fe Tr. Dr., Lenexa, KS 66215, (913)492-3200 [23508]

American Carbon Corporation, PO Box 837, Grundy, VA 24614, (540)531-8626 [20512]

American Carrier Equipment Inc., 2285 East Date Ave., Fresno, CA 93745-2615, (559)442-1500 [20585]

American Carrier Systems, Inc., 2285 E Date Ave., Fresno, CA 93706-5477, (559)442-1500 [2228]

American Century Pallet Co., PO Box 26704, Oklahoma City, OK 73126, (405)232-9649 [27278]

American Ceramic Tile, 324 11th St., Holly Hill, FL 32117, (904)672-1285 [9667]

American Cheeseman Inc., PO Box 261, Clear Lake, IA 50428, (515)357-7176 [10395]

American Chemet Corp., PO Box 1160, East Helena, MT 59635, (406)227-5302 [4318]

American Chemical Company Inc., 49 Central Ave., South Kearny, NJ 07032, (973)344-3600 [4319]

American Chemical Works Co., PO Box 6031, Providence, RI 02940, (401)421-0828 [4320]

American Chemical Works Co., PO Box 6031, Providence, RI 02940, (401)421-0828 [15765]

American Chemicals Co. Inc., 49 Central Ave., South Kearny, NJ 07032, (973)344-3600 [4321]

American Coffee Co. Inc., PO Box 4789, Rumford, RI 02916-0789, (401)438-8666 [24062]

American Comb Corp., 22 Kentucky Ave., Paterson, NJ 07503, (973)523-6551 [14018]

American Commercial Inc., 20633 S Fordyce Ave., Long Beach, CA 90810, (310)886-3700 [15396]

American Commodities Inc., 2945 Davison Rd., Flint, MI 48506, (810)767-3800 [22923]

American Communications Co., 180 Roberts St., East Hartford, CT 06108, (860)289-3491 [8337]

American Compressed Steel Corp., PO Box 1817, Cincinnati, OH 45201, (513)948-0300 [25549]

American Computer Hardware, 2205 S Wright St., Santa Ana, CA 92705, (714)549-2688 [5923]

American Contex Corp., 964 3rd Ave., New York, NY 10155, (212)421-5430 [3183]

American Convenience Inc., 5625 N Academy Blvd., Colorado Springs, CO 80918-3658, (719)548-9500 [24505]

American Cooking Guild, 3600-K S Congress Ave., Boynton Beach, FL 33426, (561)732-8111 [3499]

American Copy Inc., PO Box 777, Merrimack, NH 03054-0777, (603)424-4771 [20792]

American Cord and Webbing Inc., 88 Century Dr., Woonsocket, RI 02895, (401)762-5500 [25958]

American Council for the Arts, 1 E 53rd St., 2nd Fl., New York, NY 10022, (212)223-2787 [3505]

American Custom Safety, 18 High St., PO Box 125, Silver Lake, NH 03875, (603)367-4741 [23759]

American Custom Software, 1210 N Willow Ave., Cookeville, TN 38501, (931)526-6100 [5924]

American Cut Crystal, 1150 Broadway, Hewlett, NY 11557-2338, (516)569-1300 [15397]

American Data Systems Marketing, 63 Independent Ave., Stoughton, MA 02072-0065, (781)341-0171 [5925]

American Digital Cartography Inc., 115 W Washington St., Appleton, WI 54911-4751, (920)733-6678 [5926]

American Disc Corp., W 231 N 2811 Round Circle E Ste. 100, Pewaukee, WI 53072, (414)970-0500 [5927]

American Dismantlers & Recycling, Inc., 1791 Bellevue, Detroit, MI 48207, (313)579-2110 [2913]

American Distributing Co., PO Box 829, Modesto, CA 95353, (209)524-7425 [6962]

American Education Corp., 7506 N Broadway, Oklahoma City, OK 73116-9016, (405)840-6031 [5928]

American Educational Products Inc., 6550 Gunpark Dr.Ste. 200, Boulder, CO 80301, (303)527-3230 [26387]

American Educational Services, 2101 NW Topeka Blvd., Topeka, KS 66608, (785)233-4252 [3500]

American Electric Co., 911 S Stilwell, Pittsburg, KS 66762-5955, (316)231-3080 [8339]

American Electric Co., 302 N 3rd St., PO Box 878, St. Joseph, MO 64502, (816)279-7405 [8340]

American Electric Co., 115 SE Cholwell Ave., Bartlesville, OK 74006-2302, (918)333-2596 [8341]

American Electric Co., PO Box 878, St. Joseph, MO 64502, (816)279-7405 [8342]

American Electric Supply, 778 Albany St., Schenectady, NY 12307-1324, (518)377-8509 [8343]

American Electronics Supply, Inc., 1546 N Argyle Ave., Hollywood, CA 90028, (323)464-1144 [25069]

American ELTEC Inc., 101 College Rd., E, Princeton, NJ 08540, (609)452-1555 [5929]

American Emergency Vehicles, 165 American Way, Jefferson, NC 28640 [20586]

American Environmental Systems Inc., 2840 Wilderness Pl Ste. C, Boulder, CO 80301, (303)449-3670 [23062]

American Equipment Company Inc., 7001 Hawthorn Park Dr., Indianapolis, IN 46220, (317)849-5400 [9668]

American Equipment Company Inc., 7001 Hawthorne Park Dr., Indianapolis, IN 46220, (317)849-5400 [6963]

American Equipment Company Inc. (Greenville, South Carolina), 2106 Anderson Dr., Greenville, SC 29602, (864)295-7800 [6964]

American Equipment Marble & Tile, Inc., 7001 Hawthorn Park Dr., Indianapolis, IN 46220, (317)849-5400 [9668]

American Ex-Im Corp., 805 Kearny, San Francisco, CA 94108, (415)362-2255 [14019]

American Excelsior Co., 200 S 49th Ave., Phoenix, AZ 85043, (602)269-3860 [14316]

American Exercise & Fitness Equipment Co., 23966 Freeway Park Dr., Farmington Hills, MI 48335-2816, (248)476-4017 [23509]

American Export Trading Company, 10919 Van Owen, North Hollywood, CA 91605, (818)985-5114 [15766]

American Farm & Feed, 1533 Knox St., Kansas City, MO 64116-3744, (816)842-1905 [232]

American Fast Print, PO Box 5765, Spartanburg, SC 29304, (803)578-2020 [25959]

American Fastener Specialty Company, 5900 Park Ave., Cleveland, OH 44105-4993, (216)883-1550 [13557]

American Feed and Farm Supply Inc., PO Box 7218, Omaha, NE 68107, (402)731-1662 [233]

American Fibre Supplies, Inc., PO Box 4345, Portland, OR 97208, (503)292-1908 [21627]

American Filtration Systems Inc., 3668 Placentia Ct., Chino, CA 91710, (909)613-1500 [14317]

American Fitness Products Inc., 623 Shallcross Lake Rd., Middletown, DE 19709-9440, (302)378-2997 [23510]

American Floor Covering, PO Box 10094, Green Bay, WI 54307, (920)337-0707 [9669]

American Fluorescent Corp., 2345 Ernie Krueger Cir., Waukegan, IL 60087, (847)249-5970 [8344]

American Food Export Co., 1290-D Maunakea St. No. 238, Honolulu, HI 96817, (808)523-3500 [10396]

American Foods, 131 New Jersey St., Mobile, AL 36603, (334)433-2528 [10397]

American FoodService, 4721 Simonton Rd., Dallas, TX 75244, (972)385-5800 [10398]

American Footwear Corp., 1 Oak Hill Rd., Fitchburg, MA 01420-3986 [24670]

American Foundry and Manufacturing Co., 920 Palm St., St. Louis, MO 63147, (314)231-6114 [23063]

American General Supplies Inc., 7840 Airpark Rd., No. 9200, Gaithersburg, MD 20879, (301)294-8900 [41]

American Gift Corp., 6600 NW 74th Ave., Miami, FL 33166, (305)884-6800 [13301]

American Global Co., 4305 35th, Long Island City, NY 11101-1205, (718)729-7500 [13558]

American Granby Inc., 7645 Henry Clay Blvd., PO Box 7000, Liverpool, NY 13088, (315)451-1100 [25550]

American Gulf Co., PO Box 721494, Houston, TX 77272, (281)561-6273 [6965]

American Hardwood Co., 15411 S Figueroa St., Gardena, CA 90248-2122, (310)527-9066 [6966]

American Health Supplies, 7610 225th St., SE, Woodinville, WA 98072, (425)486-4875 [19140]

American Health Systems Inc., PO Box 26688, Greenville, SC 29616-1688, (843)234-0496 [18675]

American Hermetics, Inc., 2935 E Ponce de Leon Ave., Decatur, GA 30030, (404)373-8782 [14318]

American Homepatient, Inc., 42014 Veterans Ave., Hammond, LA 70403, (504)542-4343 [18676]

American Homeware Inc., 4715 McEwen Rd., Dallas, TX 75244, (972)233-5541 [4571]

American Honda Motor Company Inc., 1919 Torrance Blvd., Torrance, CA 90504-2746, (310)783-2000 [20587]

American Honda Motor Co. Inc. Acura Div., 1919 Torrance Blvd., Torrance, CA 90501-2746, (310)783-2000 [20588]

American Hotel Register Co., 2775 Shermer Rd., Northbrook, IL 60062, (847)564-4000 [15398]

American Hydrotech Inc., 541 N Fairbanks St., Chicago, IL 60611, (312)337-4998 [6967]

American Import Tile, 7000 Wheeler Dr., Orland Park, IL 60462, (708)614-8100 [9670]

American Importers of South Carolina, PO Box 308, Rowesville, SC 29133-0308, (803)534-8221 [26388]

American Industrial Exports Ltd., 39 Spring St., Ramsey, NJ 07446, (201)785-1280 [18449]

American Industrial Supply, 519 Potrero Ave., San Francisco, CA 94110, (415)826-1144 [16694]

American Industrial Tool Co., 4710 Mission Rd., Mission, KS 66205, (913)432-4332 [15767]

American Industries Inc., PO Box 10086, Portland, OR 97210, (503)226-1511 [19769]

American International Exports, 8834 Monard Dr., Silver Spring, MD 20910-1815, (301)585-7448 [15009]

American International Forest Products Inc., 5560 SW 107th Ave., Beaverton, OR 97005, (503)641-1611 [6968]

American and International Telephone Inc., 3612 Ventura Dr. E, Lakeland, FL 33811, (813)647-5885 [5512]

American International Trading Co., 604 W Bay St., Costa Mesa, CA 92627, (949)645-2202 [4769]

American Iron and Supply Co., 2800 Pacific St. N, Minneapolis, MN 55411, (612)529-9221 [26751]

American Isuzu Motors Inc., 13340 183rd St., Cerritos, CA 90703, (562)229-5000 [20589]

American Isuzu Motors Inc., 41280 Bridge St., Novi, MI 48375-1301, (248)426-4200 [2229]

American Jewelry Sales, PO Box 19309, Johnston, RI 02919, (401)942-8080 [17308]

American Kal Enterprises Inc., 4265 Puenta Ave., Baldwin Park, CA 91706-3420, (626)961-9471 [13559]

American Key Food Products Inc., 1 Reuten Dr., Closter, NJ 07624-2115, (201)767-8022 [10399]

American Ladders & Scaffolds, Inc., 129 Kreiger Ln., Glastonbury, CT 06033, (860)657-9252 [2230]

American Laubscher Corp., 80 Finn Ct., Farmingdale, NY 11735, (516)694-5900 [16695]

American Laubscher Corp., 80 Finn Ct., Farmingdale, NY 11735, (516)694-5900 [15768]

American Lease Co., PO Box 27069, Seattle, WA 98125, (206)367-3300 [20590]

American Legend Cooperative, PO Box 58308, Seattle, WA 98188, (425)251-3100 [17696]

American Limestone Company Inc., PO Box 2389, Knoxville, TN 37901, (423)573-4501 [6969]

American Liquidators, 365 Canal St., New York, NY 10013, (212)219-8521 [5930]

American Lock and Supply Company Inc., PO Box 8500, Van Nuys, CA 91409-8500, (714)996-8882 [24506]

American Locker Security Systems Inc., 608 Allen St., Jamestown, NY 14701-3966, (716)664-9600 [13017]

American Loose Leaf Business Products Inc., 4015 Papin St., St. Louis, MO 63110, (314)535-1414 [21331]

American Loose Leaf Business Products Inc., 4015 Papin St., St. Louis, MO 63110, (314)535-1414 [20793]

American Mail-Well Co., 25 Linden Ave. E, Jersey City, NJ 07305, (201)434-2100 [21628]

American Mailing Systems Inc., PO Box 6808, Albuquerque, NM 87197-6808, (505)344-8704 [20794]

American Management Group, PO Box 701809, Dallas, TX 75370, (972)349-1100 [10400]

American Marazzi Tile, Inc., Sales Service Ctr., 6313-A Airport Fwy., Ft. Worth, TX 76117, (817)222-0510 [9671]

American Marketing International, 150 Engineers Rd., Hauppauge, NY 11788, (516)435-4555 [2231]

American Mathematical Society, PO Box 6248, Providence, RI 02940, (401)455-4000 [3501]

American Media Inc., 4900 University Ave., Ste. 100, West Des Moines, IA 50266-6779, (515)224-0919 [25070]

American Medical Export Inc., 316 Van Buren Ave., Teaneck, NJ 07666, (201)836-1429 [18677]

American Medical Industries, 330 1/2 E 3rd St., Dell Rapids, SD 57022, (605)428-5501 [19141]

American Medical Services, 825 W Huron, Pontiac, MI 48341, (248)338-6118 [19142]

American Medserve Corp., 184 Shuman Blvd., Ste. 200, Naperville, IL 60563, (708)717-2904 [19143]

American Metals Corp., 1499 Parkway Blvd., West Sacramento, CA 95691, (916)371-7700 [19770]

American Metals Supply Co. Inc., PO Box 1325, Springfield, IL 62705, (217)528-7553 [14319]

American Military Supply Inc., PO Box 2265, Macon, GA 31203-2265, (912)477-8206 [4770]

American Mill and Manufacturing Inc., 676 Moss St., Chula Vista, CA 91911, (619)420-7343 [27279]

American Millwork, Forbes Industrial Park, 7215 S Topeka Blvd., No. 9C, PO Box 19286, Topeka, KS 66619-1423, (913)642-4334 [13048]

American Millwork & Hardware, Inc., 4505 W Woolworth Ave., Milwaukee, WI 53218-1414, (414)353-1234 [13560]

American Mobile Home Products Inc., 817 E Maiden St., Washington, PA 15301, (412)225-7200 [2232]

American Netronic Inc., 5212 Katella Ave., Ste. 104, Los Alamitos, CA 90720, (562)795-0147 [5931]

American Nursery Products, 7010 S Yale, No. 101, Tulsa, OK 74136, (918)523-9665 [14803]

American Office Machines Inc., PO Box 9429, Metairie, LA 70055, (504)833-1964 [20795]

American Office Systems, 1089 Wyoming Ave., Exeter, PA 18643-1915, (717)655-4587 [20796]

American Outdoor Sports, 2040 Broad Hollow Rd., Farmingdale, NY 11735, (516)249-1832 [23511]

American Overseas Book Company Inc., 550 Walnut St., Norwood, NJ 07648, (201)767-7600 [3502]

American Pacific Enterprises Inc., 70 W 40th St., New York, NY 10018, (212)944-6799 [15399]

American Packing and Gasket Company, PO Box 213, Houston, TX 77001, (713)675-5271 [1]

American Paper Products Co., 2113 E Rush St., Philadelphia, PA 19134, (215)739-5718 [21629]

American Paper Towel Co., 145 Meyer St., Hackensack, NJ 07602, (201)487-2500 [21630]

American Paper and Twine Co., 7400 Cockrill Bend Blvd., Nashville, TN 37209-1047, (615)350-9000 [21631]

American Pecco Corp., PO Box 670, Millwood, NY 10546, (914)762-0550 [6970]

American Pennant Corp., PO Box 9627, Moscow, ID 83843-0178, (208)882-6323 [5932]

American Performance, 1799 Marietta Blvd., NW, Atlanta, GA 30318-3690, (404)355-8711 [2233]

American Pet Pro, 2313 American Ave., Hayward, CA 94545, (510)732-2781 [27064]

American Photocopy Equipment Co., 9349 China Grove Church Rd., Pineville, NC 28134, (704)551-8640 [20797]

American Plasma Services L.P, 1925 Century Park E #1970, Los Angeles, CA 90067-2701 [19144]

American Plumber, 502 Indiana Ave., Sheboygan, WI 53081, 800-645-5428 [25551]

American Pool Supply Inc., 4195 Pioneer Ave., Las Vegas, NV 89102-8225, (702)876-1634 [23512]

American Poultry International Ltd., PO Box 16805, Jackson, MS 39236, (601)956-1715 [10401]

American Pride Coop, 55 W Bromley Ln., Brighton, CO 80601, (303)659-1230 [234]

American Printing Equipment Inc., PO Box 678, Addison, IL 60101, (630)832-5858 [15769]

American Printing House for the Blind, Inc., PO Box 6085, Louisville, KY 40206-0085, (502)895-2405 [3503]

American Produce & Vegetable Co., 4721 Simonton Rd., Dallas, TX 75244, (972)385-5800 [10398]

American Products Company Inc., 10741 Miller Rd., Dallas, TX 75238-1303, (214)357-3961 [10402]

American Promotional Events, Inc., 4511 Helton Dr. at Rasch Rd., Florence, AL 35630, (205)764-6131 [26389]

American Provisions Co., 103 19th, Rock Island, IL 61201, (309)786-7757 [10403]

American Recreation Products Inc., 1224 Fern Ridge Park Way, St. Louis, MO 63141, (314)576-8000 [23513]

American Renaissance Paper Corp., 33 Rock Hill Rd., BaLa Cynwyd, PA 19004, (610)668-7200 [21632]

American Renolit Corp., 135 Algonquin Pkwy., Whippany, NJ 07981, (973)386-9200 [22924]

American Resources Inc., PO Box 592, Evansville, IN 47704, (812)424-9000 [20513]

American Respiratory Inc., 3220 E 21st St., Tulsa, OK 74114-1814, (918)664-9173 [18678]

American Rice Growers Cooperative Association, PO Box 188, Raywood, TX 77582, (281)456-0788 [235]

American Rice Growers Cooperative Association, PO Box 129, Dayton, TX 77535, (409)258-2681 [236]

American Rotary Tools Company Inc., 30 Beechwood Ave., PO Box 809, Port Washington, NY 11050-0232, (516)883-2887 [15770]

American Safe and Lock Co., 117 N Main St., Providence, RI 02903-1309, (401)331-3013 [20798]

American Sandpainting, 2421 NW 16th Ln., No. 3, Pompano Beach, FL 33064, (954)971-0021 [13302]

American Saw & Manufacturing Co., 301 Chestnut St., East Longmeadow, MA 01028, (413)525-3961 [13561]

American Scientific Technology, L.L.C., 2541 Welland Ave. SE, Ste. A, Atlanta, GA 30316-4135, (404)243-6166 [18679]

American Seating Co., 401 American Seating Ctr., Grand Rapids, MI 49504, (616)732-6600 [13018]

American Seaway Foods Inc., 5300 Richmond Rd., Bedford Heights, OH 44146, (216)641-2360 [10404]

American Sewing Machine Distributors, 165 Middle Tpke. W, Manchester, CT 06040-4024, (860)649-0545 [15010]

American Small Business Computers, Inc., 1 American Way, Pryor, OK 74361, (918)825-4844 [6851]

American Software & Hardware Distributors, Inc., 502 E Anthony Dr., Urbana, IL 61801, (217)384-2050 [5933]

American Steel Builders International, Corp. & Copper Valley Concrete, 7011 N Camino Martin, Tucson, AZ 85741, (520)744-6950 [19771]

American Steel L.L.C., PO Box 10086, Portland, OR 97210, (503)226-1511 [19772]

American Suzuki Motor Corp., PO Box 1100, Brea, CA 92822-1100, (714)996-7040 [20591]

American Suzuki Motor Corp., PO Box 1100, Brea, CA 92822-1100, (714)996-7040 [2234]

American Sweeteners Inc., 11 Lee Blvd., Frazer, PA 19355, (610)647-2905 [10405]

American Systems of the Southeast Inc., 999 Harbor Dr., West Columbia, SC 29169-3608, (803)796-9790 [20799]

American Tank and Fabricating Co, 12314 Elmwood Ave., Cleveland, OH 44111, (216)252-1500 [19773]

American Technotherm Corp., 1 Barnes Ave., Colchester, VT 05446, (802)655-4061 [14320]

American Telephone Systems, 5265 Edina Industrial Blvd., Minneapolis, MN 55439-2910, (612)831-0888 [5513]

American Telephone Technology, 12668 Interurban Ave. S, Seattle, WA 98168-3314, (206)622-5199 [5514]

American Tennis Courts Inc., 163 N Florida St., Mobile, AL 36607-3009, (205)476-4714 [23514]

American Terminal Supply Company, Inc., 48925 West Rd., Wixom, MI 48393-3555, (248)380-8887 [25071]

American Textile Co., PO Box 4006, Pittsburgh, PA 15201-0006, (412)681-9404 [15400]

American Textile Export Co., PO Box 66, Gastonia, NC 28053, (704)824-7803 [25960]

American Textile and Trim Company Inc., 3830 Euphrosine St., New Orleans, LA 70125-1427, (504)821-0452 [25961]

American Tile Co. of Tucson, 2300 S Friebus, Ste. 103, Tucson, AZ 85713-4248, (520)323-9822 [9672]

American Tile Distributors, 927 Bragg Blvd., PO Box 58208, Fayetteville, NC 28305, (919)433-2757 [9673]

American Tile Supply, 1701 Summit Ave., Plano, TX 75074, (972)516-4926 [9674]

American Tile Supply, 1707 Falcon Dr., Desoto, TX 75115, (972)228-0066 [9675]

American Tile Supply, 200 E Felix, Ft. Worth, TX 76115, (817)924-2231 [9676]

American Tile Supply, 2020-G Rutland Dr., Austin, TX 78758, (512)837-2843 [9677]

American Tile Supply Company, Inc., 69 Main St., Danbury, CT 06810-8011, (203)794-1191 [9678]

American Tile Supply Inc., 2839 Merrell, Dallas, TX 75229, (972)243-2377 [9679]

American Tire Distributors, 9073 Euclid Ave., Manassas, VA 20110-5306, (703)368-3171 [2943]

American Tire Distributors, PO Box 515, Nitro, WV 25143, (304)755-8473 [2235]

American Tool Companies Inc., 701 Woodlands Pky., Vernon Hills, IL 60061, 800-838-7845 [13562]

American Trade Co., 1314 Texas Ave., No. 1419, Houston, TX 77002-3515, (713)229-8602 [22925]

American United Global Inc., 11634 Patton Rd., Downey, CA 90241, (562)862-8163 [2236]

American Video & Audio Corp., 1567 N Eastman Rd., Kingsport, TN 37664-0010, (423)239-4222 [25072]

American Visual Aids, 1 Hanson Pl., Brooklyn, NY 11243, (718)636-9100 [26390]

American Volkmann Corp., 4200 Performance Rd., Charlotte, NC 28214, (704)394-8111 [16471]

American West Marketing Inc., 2002 E McFadden Ave., No. 250, Santa Ana, CA 92705-4706, (714)550-6003 [9631]

American Wholesale Book Co., Helton Dr., PO Box 219, Florence, AL 35630, (205)766-3789 [3504]

American Wiping Rag, 51 Melcher St., No. 1, Boston, MA 02210, (617)426-4130 [4572]

American Wireless, 565 Display Way, Sacramento, CA 95838, (916)646-9805 [5534]

Americans for the Arts, 1 E 53rd St., 2nd Fl., New York, NY 10022, (212)223-2787 [3505]

America's Hobby Center Inc., 146 W 22nd St., New York, NY 10011-2466, (212)675-8922 [26391]

Americas Trade & Supply Co., 7630 NW 63rd St., Miami, FL 33166, (305)594-0797 [2237]

Americo International Trading, Ltd., 13607 Belinda Court, Houston, TX 77069, (281)580-2343 [19145]

Americo Wholesale Plumbing Supply Co., 3500 Woodland Ave., Cleveland, OH 44115, (216)696-1910 [23064]

AmeriData Inc., 10200 51st Ave. N, Minneapolis, MN 55442, (612)557-2500 [5934]

AmeriGas Propane Inc., PO Box 965, Valley Forge, PA 19482, (610)337-7000 [22036]

Ameriglobe Irrigation Distributors, 19 Blandin Ave., Framingham, MA 01702-7019, (508)820-4444 [14804]

Amerind Inc., 580 5th Ave., New York, NY 10036, (212)382-0210 [17309]

AmeriNet/SupportHealth, 2204 Lakeshore Dr., Ste. 140, Birmingham, AL 35209, (205)802-1682 [19146]

AmeriQual Foods Inc., PO Box 4597, Evansville, IN 47724-0597, (812)867-1444 [10406]

AmeriQuest Technologies Inc., 2465 Maryland Rd., Willow Grove, PA, (215)658-8900 [5935]

AmeriServe, PO Box 9016, Addison, TX 75001, (972)338-7000 [24063]

AmeriServe Food Distribution Inc., 17975 W Sarah Ln., Ste. 100, Brookfield, WI 53045, (414)792-9300 [10407]

AmeriSource Corp., PO Box 959, Valley Forge, PA 19482-0959, (610)296-4480 [19147]

AmeriSource Corp. Orlando Div., 2100 Directors Row, Orlando, FL 32809-6234, (407)856-6239 [19148]

AmeriSource Corp. (Paducah, Kentucky), PO Box 330, Paducah, KY 42001-0330, (502)444-7300 [19149]

AmeriSource Health Corp., PO Box 959, Valley Forge, PA 19482-0959, (610)296-4480 [19150]

AmeriSource-Lynchburg Div., PO Box 10069, Lynchburg, VA 24506-0069, (804)239-6971 [19151]

Ameritone Devoe Paints, 18 Pohaku St., No. A, Hilo, HI 96720, (808)935-2011 [21385]

Ameritone Paint Corp., 1353 Dillingham Blvd., Honolulu, HI 96817, (808)841-3693 [21386]

Ameritrend Corp., 3710 Park Central Blvd., Pompano Beach, FL 33064, (954)970-4900 [20800]

The Amerling Co., PO Box 3028, New Haven, CT 06515-0128, (203)934-7901 [25073]

Ameru Trading Co., 1043 Sterling Rd., Ste. 201, Herndon, VA 20170, (703)709-1900 [16696]

Ames Co., PO Box 1774, 3801 Camden at Broadway, Parkersburg, WV 26101, (304)424-3000 [237]

Ames Industries Inc., 2537 Curtiss St., Downers Grove, IL 60515, (630)964-2440 [20801]

Ames Industries Inc., 2537 Curtiss St., Downers Grove, IL 60515, (630)964-2440 [16697]

Ames Sciences Inc., 501 South St., Easton, MD 21601-3845, (410)476-3200 [5936]

Ames Supply Co., 2537 Curtiss St., Downers Grove, IL 60515, (630)964-2440 [20802]

AMETEK Inc., 502 Indiana Ave., Sheboygan, WI 53081, 800-645-5428 [25551]

Ametron, 1546 N Argyle Ave., Hollywood, CA 90028, (323)466-4321 [8345]

Amex Hides Ltd., 3220 88th St., Flushing, NY 11369, (212)777-5557 [18370]

Amex Inc., 2724 Summer St. NE, Minneapolis, MN 55413, (612)331-3063 [5937]

Amfib Fibers Ltd., 740 Edson Hill Rd., Stowe, VT 05672-4175, (802)253-9732 [25962]

AMG Corp., PO Box 130, Madison, NJ 07940, (973)377-4300 [13303]

AMG Publications, 6815 Shallowford Rd., Chattanooga, TN 37421, (423)894-6060 [3506]

Amherst Cooperative Elevator Inc., PO Box 115, Amherst, CO 80721, (303)854-3141 [17697]

Amherst Electrical Supply, 1591 State Hwy. 38, Mt. Holly, NJ 08060-2751, (609)267-0900 [8346]

AMI Metals Inc., 1738 Gen. George Patton Dr., Brentwood, TN 37027, (615)377-0400 [19774]

Amicale Mongolia Inc., 1375 Broadway, New York, NY 10018, (212)398-0300 [25963]

Amics International Inc., 2430 Pagehurst Dr., PO Box 1027, Midlothian, VA 23113, (804)379-2305 [24311]

Amida Industries Inc., PO Box 3147, Rock Hill, SC 29732, (803)324-3011 [15771]

Amidon Associates Inc., PO Box 25867, Santa Ana, CA 92799, (714)850-4660 [8347]

Amigo Mobility International Inc., 6693 Dixie Hwy., Bridgeport, MI 48722, (517)777-0910 [18680]

Amity Hosiery Company Inc., 107 5th Ave., Garden City Park, NY 11040, (516)741-2606 [4771]

AMJ Inc., 25 Precourt St., Biddeford, ME 04005-4315, (207)284-5731 [4573]

AMJ Inc., 25 Precourt St., Biddeford, ME 04005-4315, (207)284-5731 [24064]

Amkor Technology, 1900 S Price Rd., Chandler, AZ 85248, (480)821-5000 [8348]

Ammar Beauty Supply Co., 223 W King St., St. Augustine, FL 32084, (904)829-6544 [14020]

Ammar's Inc., S College Ave., Bluefield, VA 24605, (540)322-4686 [26392]

Amoco Energy Trading Corp., PO Box 3092, Houston, TX 77253, (281)556-3338 [22037]

Amory and Company Inc.; L.D., 101 S King St., Hampton, VA 23669, (804)722-1915 [10408]

AMOs Inc., 2735 Harrison Ave. NW, Olympia, WA 98502-5240, (425)786-5112 [5938]

Amoskeag Beverages Inc., PO Box 6540, Manchester, NH 03108, (603)622-9033 [1483]

AMP King Battery Company Inc., 10 Loomis St., San Francisco, CA 94124, (415)648-7650 [8349]

Ampac Seed Co., PO Box 318, Tangent, OR 97389, (541)928-1651 [238]

Ampco Products Inc., 11400 NW 36 Avenue, Miami, FL 33167-2907, (305)821-5700 [6971]

Ampco/Rosedale Fabricators, PO Box 608, Rosedale, MS 38769, (601)759-3521 [13019]

Ample Technology, 2442 NW Market St., No. 43, Seattle, WA 98107, (206)789-0827 [2238]

Ampride, 2075 Dakota S, Huron, SD 57350, (605)352-6493 [22038]

AMR Combs/API, 3778 Distirplex Dr., N, Memphis, TN 38118, (901)365-3470 [29]

AMRE Inc., 3710 Rawlins St., Ste. 1220, Dallas, TX 75219-4276, (972)929-4088 [6972]

AMREP Corp., 641 Lexington Ave., New York, NY 10022, (212)541-5100 [3507]

Amrion Inc., 6565 Odell Pl., Boulder, CO 80301-3306, (303)530-2525 [14021]

Amrochem Inc., 2975 Westchester Ave., Purchase, NY 10577, (914)694-4788 [4322]

AMS Enterprises, 1940 State Highway, Branson, MO 65616, (417)337-7640 [9680]

AMS Imports Inc., 23 Ash Ln., Amherst, MA 01002, (413)253-2644 [15401]

AMS International Corp., 10718 Carmel Commons Blvd., Ste. 230, Charlotte, NC 28226, (704)543-8404 [19775]

Amsco Steel Company Inc., 3430 McCart St., Ft. Worth, TX 76110, (817)926-3355 [19776]

Amsco Steel Products Co., PO Box 97545, Wichita Falls, TX 76307-7545, (940)723-2715 [19777]

Amsing International Inc., PO Box 1467, San Pedro, CA 90733-1467, (310)834-3514 [10409]

Amsko Fur Corp., 247 W 30th St., New York, NY 10001, (212)736-9035 [17698]

Amstek Metal, PO Box 3848, Joliet, IL 60434-3848, (815)725-2520 [19778]

Amsterdam Brush Corp., PO Box 71, Amsterdam, NY 12010, (518)842-2470 [21387]

AMTEC, PO Box 66, Gastonia, NC 28053, (704)824-7803 [25960]

Amtec International Inc., 1200 Woodruff Rd., No. A-2, Greenville, SC 29607-5730, (864)288-5064 [13020]

Amtel Communications, 8503 Gulf Fwy., Houston, TX 77017-5038, (713)223-5522 [5515]

Amtex Steel Inc., 700 Central Ave., University Park, IL 60466-3138, (773)927-1080 [19779]

Amtrol International Inc., PO Box 1008, West Warwick, RI 02893-0908, (401)884-6300 [14321]

Amtron Corp., PO Box 2686, Kansas City, KS 66110-0686, (913)788-5000 [5939]

Amvac Chemical Corp., 4100 E Washington Blvd., Los Angeles, CA 90023, (213)264-3910 [239]

Amvest Coal Sales Inc., PO Box 5347, Charlottesville, VA 22905, (804)977-3350 [20514]

Amway Corp., 7575 Fulton St. E, Ada, MI 49355-0001, (616)787-6000 [8350]

Amway Distributors, 858 Todd Preis Dr., Nashville, TN 37221, (615)646-4060 [15402]

Amway Global Inc., 7575 E Fulton St., Ada, MI 49301-9117, (616)676-6000 [25074]

Anabolic Laboratories Inc., 17802 Gillette Ave., Irvine, CA 92614, (949)863-0340 [18681]

Anacomp Inc., 12365 Crosthwaite Cir., Poway, CA 92064, (619)679-9797 [25552]

Anacomp Inc. International Div., PO Box 509005, San Diego, CA 92150, (619)679-9797 [20803]

Anaheim Custom Extruders, Inc., 4640 E La Palma Ave., Anaheim, CA 92807-1910, (714)693-8508 [22926]

Anaheim Extrusion Co. Inc., PO Box 6380, Anaheim, CA 92816, (714)630-3111 [19780]

Anaheim Manufacturing Co., PO Box 4146, Anaheim, CA 92803, (714)524-7770 [15011]

Anaheim Marketing International, 4332 E La Palma Ave., Anaheim, CA 92807, (714)993-1707 [15012]

Analytcal Automation Specialists Inc., 11723 Sun Belt Ct., Baton Rouge, LA 70809-4211, (504)753-5467 [5940]

Analytic Associates, 4817 Browndeer Ln., Rolling Hills Estates, CA 90275, (310)541-0418 [5941]

Anan Grain Co., Rte. 1, Box 56, Glenvil, NE 68941, (402)726-2266 [17682]

Anapet, 1431 N Main, Orange, CA 92867, (714)532-4200 [27065]

Anatech Ltd., 1020 Harts Lake Rd., Battle Creek, MI 49015, (616)964-6450 [21388]

Anatel Corp., 2200 Central Ave., Boulder, CO 80301, (303)442-5533 [15772]

Anazeh Sands, 1339 28th St. SW, Grand Rapids, MI 49509-2703, (616)538-0810 [23515]

Anchor Commerce Trading Corp., PO Box 813, Hicksville, NY 11802, (516)822-1914 [6973]

Anchor Paper Co., 480 Broadway St., St. Paul, MN 55101, (612)298-1311 [21633]

Anchor Sales Associates Inc., 614 Heron Dr., Unit 9, Bridgeport, NJ 08014, (856)467-1133 [16698]

Anchor Specialties Co., 205 Hallene Rd., Warwick, RI 02886, (401)738-1510 [25964]

Anchorage Reprographics Center, 851 SW 6th Ave., Ste. 625, Portland, OR 97204-1343 [20804]

Anchorage Restaurant Supply, PO Box 10399, Anchorage, AK 99510, (907)276-7044 [24065]

Ancient Future Music, PO Box 264, Kentfield, CA 94914, (415)459-1892 [3508]

Anco Management Services Inc., 202 N Court St., Florence, AL 35630, (256)766-3824 [3509]

Ancona Brothers Co., PO Box 27787, 9320 J St., Omaha, NE 68127-0787, (402)331-6262 [10410]

Ancona Midwest Foodservices, PO Box 27787, 9320 J St., Omaha, NE 68127-0787, (402)331-6262 [10410]

Ancona/Midwest Inc., PO Box 27787, Omaha, NE 68127-0787, (402)331-6262 [10411]

Anda Generics Inc., 4001 SW 47th Ave., Bldg. 201, Ft. Lauderdale, FL 33314, (954)584-0300 [19152]

Andale Farmers Cooperative Company Inc., PO Box 18, Andale, KS 67001, (316)444-2141 [17699]

Andalex Resources, Inc., PO Box 902, Price, UT 84501, (435)637-5385 [20515]

Andalusia Wood Products Inc., PO Box 159, River Falls, AL 36476, (205)222-2224 [27280]

Andelain Farm, 14740 Mud College Rd., Thurmont, MD 21788, (301)271-4191 [17700]

Anders Office Equipment Co., 1525 S Russell St., Missoula, MT 59801, (406)549-4143 [20805]

Andersen Inc.; Earl F., 9808 James Cir., Bloomington, MN 55431, (612)884-7300 [23516]

Andersen Turf Supply, 5462 Oceanus, Unit C, Huntington Beach, CA 92649, (714)897-0202 [240]

Anderson and Associates Inc., 3007 N Slappey Blvd., Albany, GA 31707, (912)436-4651 [8351]

Anderson Associates Inc.; Earl F., 9808 James Cir., Bloomington, MN 55431, (612)884-7300 [24066]

Anderson Austin News, 499 Merritt Ave., Nashville, TN 37203, (615)242-7603 [3510]

Anderson Auto Parts Co., PO Box 767, Anderson, SC 29622, (803)224-0388 [2239]

Anderson Bait Distributors, 4569 Hwy. 120, Duluth, GA 30026, (404)476-2461 [23517]

Anderson Brothers Inc., PO Box 277, Edgeley, ND 58433, (701)493-2241 [241]

Anderson Co.; S.W., 2425 Wisconsin Ave., PO Box 460, Downers Grove, IL 60515, (630)964-2600 [8352]

Anderson Co.; SW, 7703 First Place, Unit E, Solon, OH 44139, (440)232-4415 [8353]

Anderson Distributing Co., 144 W Porter St., PO Box 752, Jackson, MI 49202, (517)782-8179 [1484]

Anderson-DuBose Co., 6575 Davis Industrial Pkwy., Solon, OH 44139, (440)248-8800 [10412]

Anderson Equipment Co., PO Box 339, Bridgeville, PA 15017, (412)343-2300 [6974]

Anderson Erickson Dairy Co., 2229 Hubbell, Des Moines, IA 50317-2599, (515)265-2521 [10413]

Anderson-Gemco, 1444 34th St., Gulfport, MS 39501, (228)864-1044 [3511]

The Anderson Group, 6489 Ridings Rd., Syracuse, NY 13206, (315)437-7556 [19781]

Anderson Home Health Supply, 4063 Henderson Blvd., Tampa, FL 33629, (813)289-3811 [18682]

Anderson & Jarvi Lumber, U.S 41, Chassell, MI 49916, (906)523-4265 [6975]

Anderson Lumber Co., PO Box 9459, Ogden, UT 84409, (801)479-3400 [6976]

Anderson Machinery Co., PO Box 245, Stratford, CT 06615, (203)375-4481 [24312]

Anderson Machinery Company Inc., PO Box 4806, Corpus Christi, TX 78469, (512)289-6043 [6977]

Anderson Machinery San Antonio Inc., PO Box 200380, San Antonio, TX 78220-0380, (210)661-2366 [6978]

Anderson Medical Inc., 4024 Beresford Rd., Charlotte, NC 28211-3808, (704)442-1990 [18683]

Anderson News, 106 N Link, PO Box 2105, Ft. Collins, CO 80524, (970)221-2330 [3512]

Anderson News Co., 1709 N East St., Flagstaff, AZ 86004-4910, (520)774-6171 [3513]

Anderson News Company, 1324 Coldwell Ave., Modesto, CA 95350-5702, (209)577-5551 [3514]

Anderson News Co., 5501 Park Ave., PO Box 1297, Des Moines, IA 50305, (515)244-0044 [3515]

Anderson News Co. Southwest, 11325 Gemini Ln., Dallas, TX 75229, (972)501-5500 [3516]

Anderson News Service Center, 26545 Danti Ct., Hayward, CA 94545-3917, (650)349-7023 [3517]

Anderson News of Yuma, PO Box 4427, Yuma, AZ 85366-4427, (520)782-1822 [3518]

Anderson Recreational Design, Inc., PO Box 465, Medina, OH 44258, (330)722-8804 [23518]

Anderson & Spring Firestone, 5471 17th Ave. W, Virginia, MN 55792-3368, (218)741-1646 [2240]

Anderson Tile Sales, 120 S Madison, San Angelo, TX 76903, (915)655-0646 [9681]

Anderson Tile Sales, 1801 Kermit Hwy., Odessa, TX 79761, (915)337-0081 [9682]

Anderson Tile Sales, 1703 S Midkiff, Midland, TX 79705, (915)683-5116 [9683]

Anderson and Vreeland Inc., PO Box 1246, Caldwell, NJ 07007, (973)227-2270 [15773]

Anderson Wholesale Co., PO Box 69, Muskogee, OK 74402, (918)682-5568 [14022]

Andersons Candy Company, 1010 State, Baden, PA 15005-1338, (724)869-3018 [10414]

Andersons Inc., 480 W Dussel Dr., Maumee, OH 43537, (419)893-5050 [242]

Anderson's Peanuts, PO Drawer 420, Opp, AL 36467-0420, (205)493-4591 [10415]

Anderson's Wheelchair Therapeutic Supply, 1117 2nd St. SW, Rochester, MN 55902-1936, (507)288-0113 [18684]

Anderson's Woodwork Inc., 3220 Anderson Way, Strawberry Plains, TN 37871, (423)933-8662 [13021]

Andgrow Fertilizer, 3150 Stoney Point Rd., East Berlin, PA 17316, (717)259-9573 [243]

Ando Corp. Measuring Instruments Div., 7617 Standish Pl., Rockville, MD 20855, (301)294-3365 [24313]

Andover Communications Inc., 500 W Cummings Park, Woburn, MA 01801-6503, (781)932-3400 [20806]

Andover Corp., 4 Commercial Dr., Salem, NH 03079, (603)686-0660 [19153]

Andrea by Sadek, 19 E 26th St., New York, NY 10010, (212)679-8121 [15403]

Andres and Wilton Farmers Grain and Supply Co., 28451 S Rte. 45, Peotone, IL 60468, (708)258-3268 [17701]

Andrew Co.; W.T., 15815 Hamilton Ave., Detroit, MI 48203, (313)883-2000 [23065]

Andrew Sports Club Inc., 1407 Broadway, No. 1209, New York, NY 10018, (212)764-6225 [4772]

Andrew and Williamson Sales Co., 9940 Marconi Dr., San Diego, CA 92173, (619)661-6000 [10416]

Andrews Distributing Company Inc., PO Box 17557, Nashville, TN 37217-0557, (615)399-1776 [14322]

Andrews Paper and Chemical Co., PO Box 509, 1 Channel Dr., Port Washington, NY 11050, (516)767-2800 [4323]

Andrews Paper House of York Inc., 351 East St., PO Box 1227, York, PA 17405-1227, (717)846-8816 [21634]

Andrews Produce Inc., 100 S Main, PO Box 1027, Pueblo, CO 81002, (719)543-3846 [10417]

Andromeda Software Inc., 123 Bucyrus Dr., Amherst, NY 14228-1946, (716)691-4510 [5942]

Andy's Discount Nursery & Landscape, 1807 Hwy. 85 N, Fayetteville, GA 30214, (404)461-6089 [14805]

Anesthesia Equipment Supply, 24301 Roberts Dr., Black Diamond, WA 98010-9205, (253)631-8008 [18685]

Anfinson's Inc., 1700 I94 Business Loop E, Dickinson, ND 58601-9802, (701)227-1226 [244]

Angel Associates Inc.; Mike, 3728 Hampstead Dr., Sylvania, OH 43560-5503, (419)841-1862 [26393]

Angel-Etts Inc., 5900 Rodeo Rd., Los Angeles, CA 90016, (213)870-4637 [24671]

Angel Food Ice Cream, 368 Industrial Dr. S, Madison, MS 39110, (601)898-0081 [10418]

Angel Gifts and Noah's Art, PO Box 530, Fairfield, IA 52556, (515)472-5481 [13304]

Angel Graphics and Signature Series, PO Box 530, Fairfield, IA 52556, (515)472-5481 [13304]

Angeles Medical Supply Inc., PO Box 2366, Port Angeles, WA 98362-0305, (425)452-4724 [18686]

Angelo Brothers Co., 12401 McNulty Rd., Philadelphia, PA 19154-3297, (215)671-2000 [8354]

Angle Acres Greenhouse, 2855 Angle Rd., Orchard Park, NY 14127, (716)674-8754 [14806]

Angus-Campbell Inc., 4417 S Soto St., Vernon, CA 90058, (213)587-1236 [22927]

Angus Fire Armour Corp., 1000 Junny Rd., PO Box 879, Angier, NC 27501-8974, (919)639-6151 [25553]

Anheuser-Busch Inc., 1 Busch Pl., St. Louis, MO 63118, (314)577-2000 [1485]

Anichini Inc., Rte. 110, PO Box 67, Tunbridge, VT 05077, (802)889-9430 [25965]

Anicom, 9299 Market Pl., Broadview Heights, OH 44147, (440)546-2600 [8355]

Anicom Inc., 6133 N River Rd., Ste. 410, Rosemont, IL 60018-5171, (847)518-8700 [8356]

Anicom Multimedia Wiring Systems, 5475 S Wynn Rd., Ste. 100, Las Vegas, NV 89118, (702)739-9641 [8357]

Animal Emergency Center, 4306 Bishop Ln., Louisville, KY 40218-4518, (502)456-4145 [27066]

Animal Medic Inc., PO Box 575, Manchester, PA 17345, (717)266-5611 [27067]

Anixter Inc., 10 Parkway View Dr., Bldg. O, Pittsburgh, PA 15205, (412)494-4320 [8358]

Anixter International Inc., 4711 Golf Rd., Skokie, IL 60076-1224, (847)677-2600 [8359]

Anjo Distributors, 4380 Victory Blvd., Staten Island, NY 10314, (718)698-6550 [27068]

Anka Co. Inc., 12 Greco Ln., Ste. 18, Warwick, RI 02886-1242, (401)467-6868 [17310]

Anker Energy Corp., 2708 Cranberry Sq., Morgantown, WV 26505, (304)594-1616 [20516]

Anle Paper Company Inc., 100 Progress Rd., Lombard, IL 60148, (630)629-9700 [16699]

Ann Arbor Therapy Oxygen Inc., 4811 Carpenter Rd., Ypsilanti, MI 48197, (734)572-0203 [18943]

Anna Marie Designs Inc., 811 3rd Ave. W, PO Box 777, Ashland, WI 54806-0777, (715)682-9569 [4773]

Annabelle Candy Company Inc., 27211 Industrial Blvd., Hayward, CA 94545-3347, (510)783-2900 [10419]

Annaco Inc., PO Box 1148, Akron, OH 44309, (216)376-1400 [26752]

Annawear, PO Box 2364, Highlands, NC 28741-2364, (704)526-4660 [4774]

Annie C.P. Productions Inc., PO Box 701287, Tulsa, OK 74170-1287, (918)298-0770 [24672]

Ann's House of Nuts, Inc., 8375 Patuxent Range Rd., Jessup, MD 20794, (301)317-0900 [10420]

Anns Uniform Center Inc., 2800 Lafayette Rd., Portsmouth, NH 03801-5915, (603)431-6367 [4775]

Anodyne Inc., 10912 Greenbrier Rd., Minnetonka, MN 55305-3474, (612)831-6130 [19154]

Another Dancing Bear Productions, 220 Montgomery St., No. 975, San Francisco, CA 94104, (415)291-8200 [13305]

Another Language Press, 7709 Hamilton Ave., Cincinnati, OH 45231-3103, (513)521-5590 [3478]

ANR Coal Company L.L.C., PO Box 1871, Roanoke, VA 24008-1871, (540)983-0222 [20517]

Anritsu Co., 1155 E Collins Blvd., Richardson, TX 75081, (972)644-1777 [24314]

Anritsu Wiltron Sales Co., 1155 E Collins Blvd., Richardson, TX 75081, (972)644-1777 [24314]

Ansam Metals Corp., PO Box 3408, 1026 E Patapsco Ave., Baltimore, MD 21225, (410)355-8220 [19782]

L'Anse Sentinel Co., PO Box 7, L' Anse, MI 49946, (906)524-6194 [20807]

Anson & Co.; R.E., 484 Westfield Rd., Alpine, UT 84004-1501, (801)756-5221 [23519]

Antara Music Group, 468 McNally Dr., Nashville, TN 37211-3318, (615)361-3053 [3519]

Antelope Truck Stop, 4850 I-80 Service Rd., Burns, WY 82053, (307)547-3334 [2241]

Antenna Farms Inc., 4403 Lomas St., Farmington, NM 87401-3633, (505)762-9801 [25075]

Antennas America Inc., 4860 Robb St. Ste. 101, Wheat Ridge, CO 80033, (303)421-4063 [8360]

Antex Incorporated, PO Box 2570, Attleboro Falls, MA 02763, (508)699-6911 [8361]

Anthony Farmers Cooperative and Elevator Co., PO Box 111, Anthony, KS 67003, (316)842-5181 [17702]

Anthony Farms Inc., PO Box 4, Scandinavia, WI 54977, (715)467-2212 [10421]

Anthony Forest Products Co., PO Box 1877, El Dorado, AR 71730, (870)862-3414 [6979]

Anthony International Inc.; Paul, 5165 N Riley St., Las Vegas, NV 89129-4136, (702)645-5751 [24673]

Anthony Mining, Inc., State Rt. 43, Richmond, OH 43944, (740)765-4185 [20518]

Anthuriums of Hawaii, 530 Ainaola Dr., Hilo, HI 96720, (808)959-8717 [14807]

Antler Uniform, Division of M. Rubin & Sons, Inc., 34-01 38th Ave., Long Island City, NY 11101, (718)361-2800 [4776]

Antognoli and Co.; Joseph, 1800 N Pulaski Rd., Chicago, IL 60639-4916, (312)772-1800 [10422]

Antronnix Antenna Co. Inc., 8800 Monard Dr., Silver Spring, MD 20910-1815, (301)589-8857 [8362]

Antwerp Diamond Distributing Inc., 587 5th Ave., New York, NY 10017, (212)319-3300 [17311]

Any & All Auto Parts Inc., 755 W Sunset Rd., Henderson, NV 89015-2601, (702)564-1212 [2242]

AP Parts Co., PO Box 64010, Toledo, OH 43612-0010, (419)891-8400 [2243]

A.P. Supply Co., PO Box 1927, Texarkana, AR 71854, (870)773-6586 [23066]

Apache Farmers Cooperative, PO Box 332, Apache, OK 73006, (580)588-3351 [245]

Apache Hose and Belting Inc., 4805 Bowling St. SW, PO Box 1719, Cedar Rapids, IA 52406-1719, (319)365-0471 [16700]

Apache Nitrogen Products Inc., PO Box 700, Benson, AZ 85602, (520)720-2217 [4324]

Apco Inc., 1834 Bagwell St., Flint, MI 48503-4406, (810)732-8933 [15013]

Apco Inc., 3305 S Pennsylvania, Lansing, MI 48910-4732, (517)882-5785 [15014]

APD Transmission Parts, 824 Memorial Dr. SE, Atlanta, GA 30316-1232, (404)688-1517 [2244]

Apem Components, Inc., 134 Water St., Wakefield, MA 01880, (781)246-1007 [8363]

Apex Data Systems Inc., 6464 E Grant Rd., Tucson, AZ 85715, (520)298-1991 [5943]

Apex Foot Health Industries, 170 Wesley St., South Hackensack, NJ 07606, (201)487-2739 [24674]

Apex Medical Corp., 800 S Van Eps Ave., PO Box 1235, Sioux Falls, SD 57101-1235, (605)332-6689 [18687]

Apex Oil Co., 8182 Maryland Ave., St. Louis, MO 63105, (314)889-9600 [22039]

Apex Plastic Industries Inc., 155 Marcus Blvd., Hauppauge, NY 11788, (516)231-8888 [22928]

Apex Supply Company Inc., 2500 Button Gwinnett Dr., Atlanta, GA 30340, (404)449-7000 [14323]

Apex Technologies, 392 5th Ave., New York, NY 10018, (212)268-3535 [17312]

APF Inc., 4195 Pioneer Ave., Las Vegas, NV 89102-8225, (702)876-1634 [23512]

Apgar Office Systems Inc., PO Box 2207, Manchester, ME 04351, (207)623-2674 [20808]

API Appliance Parts Inc., 1645 Old County Rd., San Carlos, CA 94070-1347, (650)591-4467 [15015]

A.P.I. Inc., 2366 Rose Pl., St. Paul, MN 55113, (612)636-4320 [6980]

Apollo Book, PO Box 3839, Poughkeepsie, NY 12603, (914)462-0040 [3520]

Apollo Colors Inc., 3000 Dundee Rd., No. 415, Northbrook, IL 60062, (847)564-9190 [21389]

Apollo Oil LLC, 1175 Early Dr., PO Box 4040, Winchester, KY 40392-4040, (606)744-5444 [22040]

Apollo Oil and Warehouse Distributors, Inc., 1175 Early Dr., PO Box 4040, Winchester, KY 40392-4040, (606)744-5444 [22040]

Apollo Pet Supply, 216 SE Washington St., Portland, OR 97214, (503)239-5768 [27069]

Apollo Sales Group Inc., 24 Sand Island Access Rd., No. 17, Honolulu, HI 96819-2221, (808)841-1679 [25554]

Apollo Space Systems Inc., 60 Trade Zone Ct., Ronkonkoma, NY 11779, (516)467-8033 [22826]

Apollo Tire Co. Inc., 21339 Saticoy, Canoga Park, CA 91304, (818)348-6142 [2245]

Apon Record Company, Inc., PO Box 3082, Steinway Sta., Long Island City, NY 11103, (718)721-5599 [25076]

Apopka Trees & Shrubs, 1616 N Schopke Rd., Apopka, FL 32712, (407)886-1060 [14808]

Apotheca Inc., 1622 N 16th St., Phoenix, AZ 85006, (602)252-5244 [19155]

Apothecary Products Inc., 11750 12th Ave. S, Burnsville, MN 55337, (612)890-1940 [19156]

Appalachian Bible Co. & Christian Books, 522 Princeton Rd., Johnson City, TN 37601, (423)282-9475 [3521]

Appalachian Distributors, 522 Princeton Rd., Johnson City, TN 37601, (423)282-9475 [3521]

Apparel Exprex Inc., 1184 Bonham Ave., Columbus, OH 43211, (614)291-5651 [4777]

Appert Foods, 809 SE Hwy. 10, St. Cloud, MN 56304-1808, (320)251-3200 [10423]

APPIC Inc., 623 S Main St., Milpitas, CA 95035, (408)719-7575 [5944]

Applause Enterprises Inc., PO Box 4183, Woodland Hills, CA 91365-4183, (818)992-6000 [26394]

Applause, Inc., 6101 Variel Ave., PO Box 4183, Woodland Hills, CA 91367, (818)595-2701 [26395]

Apple Computer Inc. Federal Systems Group, 1892 Preston White Dr., Reston, VA 20191-4359, (703)264-5155 [5945]

Apple Food Sales Company Inc., 117 Fort Lee Rd., Leonia, NJ 07605, (201)592-0277 [10424]

Apple Graphics Ltd., 1536 W Todd Dr., Ste. 105, Tempe, AZ 85283-4804, (602)731-9970 [4778]

Apple Pacific Div., 20525 Mariani Ave., Cupertino, CA 95014, (408)996-1010 [5946]

Applewood Farms Inc., PO Box 445, Lansing, IL 60438-0445 [10425]

Appliance Dealer Supply Co., 6237 E 22nd St., Tucson, AZ 85711-5230, (602)252-7506 [15016]

Appliance Distributors Unlimited, 729 Erie Ave., Takoma Park, MD 20912, (301)608-2600 [15017]

Appliance Parts Center Inc., 222 E 8th St., National City, CA 91950, (619)474-6781 [15018]

Appliance Parts Center Inc., 501 N Eastern Ave., Las Vegas, NV 89101-3422, (702)384-7759 [25077]

Appliance Parts Center Inc., 222 E 8th St., National City, CA 91950, (619)474-6781 [8364]

Appliance Parts Co., 2742 W Medowell Rd., Phoenix, AZ 85009, (602)269-6385 [15019]

Appliance Parts Co., 2001 S Western Ave., Las Vegas, NV 89102, (702)382-6532 [15020]

Appliance Parts Co. Inc., 94-472 Ukee St., Waipahu, HI 96797, (808)676-2664 [15021]

Appliance Parts Distributors Inc., 1175 William St., Buffalo, NY 14240, (716)856-5005 [15022]

Appliance Parts Distributors Inc., 400 Bristol Pke., PO Box 40, Croydon, PA 19021, (215)785-6282 [15023]

Appliance Parts Inc., 14105 13th Ave. N, Plymouth, MN 55441-4369, (612)333-0931 [15024]

Appliance Parts Inc., 228 14th St., Ste 101, Tuscaloosa, AL 35401-7408, (205)345-2828 [15025]

Appliance Parts Inc., 5520 Jewella Ave., Shreveport, LA 71109-7641, (318)631-9591 [25078]

Appliance Parts Inc., PO Box 6001, Alexandria, LA 71307-6001, (318)448-3454 [15026]

Appliance Parts of Lake Charles, 1700 Common St., Lake Charles, LA 70601-6136, (318)439-1797 [15027]

Appliance Parts & Supply Co., 805 Church St., Mobile, AL 36602-1112, (205)432-6634 [15028]

Appliance Parts Warehouse Inc., 2311 E 23rd St., PO Box 71925, Chattanooga, TN 37407, (423)698-1731 [15029]

Appliance Recycling Centers of America Inc., 7400 Excelsior Blvd., Minneapolis, MN 55426, (612)930-9000 [15030]

Appliance Service Center Inc., 700 23rd Ave., Fairbanks, AK 99701-7026, (907)452-1000 [25079]

Applicator Sales & Service, PO Box 10109, Portland, ME 04104-0109, (207)797-7950 [6981]

Applied Biochemists, Inc., 11163 Stonewood Dr., Germantown, WI 53022-6500, (262)255-4449 [4325]

Applied Business Computers Inc., R.R. Box 44A, Hwy. 321, Pineland, SC 29934, (843)726-6767 [5947]

Applied Chemical Solutions Inc., 307 Fallon Rd., Hollister, CA 95023, (408)637-0969 [24315]

Applied Computer Solutions Inc. (New York, New York), 1826 2nd Ave., Ste. 191, New York, NY 10016, (212)996-6609 [5948]

Applied Computer Technology Inc., 2573 Midpoint Dr., Ft. Collins, CO 80525-4417, (970)490-1849 [5949]

Applied Controls Inc., 47 General Warren Blvd., Malvern, PA 19355, (610)408-8000 [8365]

Applied Educational Systems Inc., 540 N Commercial St., Manchester, NH 03101-1122, (603)225-5511 [5950]

Applied Energy Company Inc., 11431 Chairman Dr., Dallas, TX 75243, (214)349-1171 [15774]

Applied Genetics Inc., 205 Buffalo Ave., Freeport, NY 11520, (516)868-9026 [14023]

Applied Geographics Inc., 100 Franklin St., Fl. 7, Boston, MA 02110, (617)292-7125 [3522]

Applied Hydroponics Inc., 755 Southpoint Blvd., Petaluma, CA 94954, (707)765-9990 [246]

Applied Industrial Tech, 205 Industrial Park Blvd., PO Box 1628, Tullahoma, TN 37388, (931)455-6990 [16701]

Applied Industrial Tech, Inc., 1240 Polk Ave., Nashville, TN 37210, (615)244-6462 [16702]

Applied Industrial Technologies, PO Box 5426, Willowick, OH 44095-0426, (216)426-4000 [16703]

Applied Industrial Technologies, 291 Frontage Rd., Burr Ridge, IL 60521, (630)325-7575 [5516]

Applied Industrial Technologies, 1948 Plaza Dr., Benton Harbor, MI 49022-2210, (616)927-4425 [16704]

Applied Industrial Technologies, 900 E 2nd St., Owensboro, KY 42303-3304, (270)684-9601 [2246]

Applied Industrial Technologies, 8475 N 87th St., PO Box 23488, Milwaukee, WI 53224, (414)355-5500 [15775]

Applied Industrial Technologies, Inc., 8021 New Jersey Ave., Hammond, IN 46323, (219)844-5090 [16705]

Applied Industrial Technologies, Inc., 2130 Industrial St., Wisconsin Rapids, WI 54495, (715)421-1730 [16706]

Applied Industrial Technologies Inc., PO Box 6925, Cleveland, OH 44101-9986, (216)881-8900 [2247]

Applied Information Solutions Inc., 1660 17th St. Ste. 400, Denver, CO 80202, (303)893-8936 [5951]

Applied Membranes Inc., 110 Bosstick Blvd., San Marcos, CA 92069, (760)727-3711 [25555]

Applied Microcomputer Solutions, PO Box 47234, Plymouth, MN 55447-0234, (612)473-8167 [5952]

Applied Power Corp., 1210 Hornann Dr. SE, Lacey, WA 98503, (360)438-2110 [14324]

Applied Systems Technology and Resources, 2570 Route 900, Cornwall, NY 12518, (914)534-7100 [5953]

Applied Technology Ventures Inc., 4577 Hinkley Industrial Pkwy, Cleveland, OH 44109-6009, (216)459-0700 [5954]

Applied Video Systems Inc., 5816 Shakespeare Rd. D, Columbia, SC 29223-7233, (803)735-1120 [25080]

Appropriate Solutions, PO Box 458, Peterborough, NH 03458, (603)924-6079 [5955]

Approved Color Corp., PO Box 413, Greenville, NH 03048-0413, (603)878-1470 [21390]

APR Supply Co., 305 N 5th St., Lebanon, PA 17046, (717)274-5999 [14325]

APR Supply Co., 305 N 5th St., Lebanon, PA 17046, (717)273-9375 [23067]

Apria Healthcare, 2041 Ave. C, Ste. 400, Bethlehem, PA 18017, (610)266-6333 [19157]

Aprons Unlimited Inc., PO Box 3639, Brockton, MA 02304-3639, (508)587-2900 [5354]

A.P.S. Inc., 3000 Pawnee St., Houston, TX 77054-3301, (713)507-1100 [2248]

APS Systems, 3535 W 5th St., Oxnard, CA 93030, (805)984-0300 [8366]

APW/Wyott Food Service Equipment Co., 729 3rd Ave., Dallas, TX 75226, (214)421-7366 [10426]

Aqua Dream Pools Inc., 7 Main St., Plaistow, NH 03865-3002, (603)382-4900 [23520]

Aqua Gourmet Foods, Inc., Hwy. 694, Abbeville, LA 70510, (318)893-9494 [10427]

Aqua Magnetics International, 915-B Harbor Lake Dr., Safety Harbor, FL 34695, (813)447-2575 [25556]

Aqua Magnetics International, 915-B Harbor Lake Dr., Safety Harbor, FL 34695, (813)447-2575 [23068]

Aqua Star Inc., 2025 1st Ave., Seattle, WA 98121, (206)448-5400 [10428]

Aqua Systems International, Inc., 4627 Bay Crest Dr., Tampa, FL 33615-4901, (813)287-8802 [23069]

Aquafilter Corp., 4880 Havana St., Denver, CO 80239-2416, (954)491-2200 [26260]

Aquajogger, PO Box 1453, Eugene, OR 97440, (541)484-2454 [23521]

Aqualife, 51800 Laurel Rd., South Bend, IN 46637, (219)272-7777 [27070]

Aquanetics Systems, 5252 Lovelock St., San Diego, CA 92110, (619)291-8444 [23070]

Aquaperfect, 7889 A Pines Blvd., Pembroke Pines, FL 33024, (954)981-5120 [27071]

Aquarium Pet Book Distributors, PO Box 298, Jarrettsville, MD 21084, (410)557-9173 [27072]

Aquatec Water Systems Inc., 17422 Pullman St., Irvine, CA 92614, (714)535-8300 [23071]

Aquatronics Inc., 10706 Orchard St., Fairfax, VA 22030, (703)273-3736 [8367]

Aquilla Fashions Inc., 863 E Patterson St., Lansford, PA 18232-1708, (717)645-7738 [4779]

AR Industries Inc., 3203 S Shannon St., Santa Ana, CA 92704-6352, (714)434-8600 [5956]

A.R. Musical Enterprises Inc., 9031 Technology Dr., Fishers, IN 46038, (317)577-6999 [25081]

ARA-Cory Refreshment Services, 750 Nuttman St., Santa Clara, CA 95054, (408)988-8211 [24910]

ARA Services, Inc., 1665 Townhurst, Houston, TX 77043, (713)932-0093 [24911]

Araban Coffee Co. Inc., 2 Keith Way, Hingham, MA 02043-4204, (617)439-3900 [10429]

Arabel Inc., 16301 NW 49th Ave., Miami, FL 33014, (305)623-8302 [15404]

Aramark Magazines and Books, 2970 N Ontario St., Burbank, CA 91504-2016, (213)857-7634 [3523]

Aramsco, Inc., 1655 Imperial Way, Thorofare, NJ 08086, (609)848-5330 [16707]

Aranosian Oil Co. Inc., 557 N State St., Concord, NH 03301, (603)224-7500 [22041]

ARB Inc. (Franklinton, Louisiana), PO Box 625, Franklinton, LA 70438, (504)839-4494 [22042]

Arbee Associates, 15890 Gaither Dr., Gaithersburg, MD 20877-1404, (301)963-3900 [20809]

Arbill Inc., 10450 Drummond Rd., Philadelphia, PA 19132, (215)228-4011 [25966]

Arbor Handling Services Inc., PO Box 91, Willow Grove, PA 19090, (215)657-2700 [15776]

Arbordale Home and Garden Showplace, 480 Dodge Rd., Amherst, NY 14068, (716)688-9125 [247]

Arbuckle Coffee Roasters Inc., 3498 S Dodge Blvd Ste 100, Tucson, AZ 85713, (520)790-5282 [24067]

ARC Mills Corp., 221 W 37th St., New York, NY 10018, (212)221-8400 [25967]

Arcade Electronics Inc., 5655 F. General Wash Dr., Alexandria, VA 22312, (703)256-4610 [8368]

Arcadia Chair Co., 5692 Fresca Dr., La Palma, CA 90623, (714)562-8200 [13022]

Arcadia Livestock, Inc., PO Box 27, Arcadia, WI 54612, (608)323-7795 [17703]

Arcadia Merchandising Corp., PO Box 140, Millburn, NJ 07041, (973)467-2856 [23522]

Arch Associates Corp., PO Box 427, Fernwood, PA 19050, (215)626-2724 [5957]

Arch Coal Sales Company Inc., City Place 1, Ste. 300, St. Louis, MO 63141, (314)994-2700 [20519]

Arch Hunter Books and Canyon Country Distribution Services, PO Box 400034, 18 Ballard Ct., Thompson, UT 84540-0034, (435)285-2210 [3524]

Arch-I-Tech Doors Inc., 799 Allgood Rd., Marietta, GA 30062, (404)426-0773 [6982]

Arch of West Virginia Inc., PO Box 156, Yolyn, WV 25654-0156, (304)792-8200 [20520]

Archbold Health Services Inc., 400 Old Albany Rd., Thomasville, GA 31792, (912)227-6800 [18688]

Archer Associates; C.F., RD 2, 2976 Persse Rd., Lafayette, NY 13084, (315)677-3263 [15405]

Archer Company Inc.; A.W., 185 Glen Cove Ave., Sea Cliff, NY 11579, (516)671-4100 [21635]

Archer Cooperative Grain Co., PO Box 147, Archer, IA 51231, (712)723-5233 [248]

Archie's Sporting Goods of Gainesville, 1500 Brownsbridge Rd., Gainesville, GA 30501, (404)532-9951 [4780]

Architects Hardware & Specialty Company Inc., Railroad & Dott Aves., Albany, NY 12205, (518)489-4478 [13563]

Architectural Building Supply, 2965 S Main St., Salt Lake City, UT 84115, (801)486-3481 [13564]

Architectural Floor Systems, Inc., 206 Campus Dr., Arlington Heights, IL 60004-1402, (847)394-3944 [9684]

Architectural Surfaces, Inc., 560 N Nimitz Hwy., No. 29-217E, Honolulu, HI 96817-5330, (808)523-7866 [15406]

Architectural Surfaces, Inc., 3535 Princeton Dr. NE, Albuquerque, NM 87107-4213, (505)889-0124 [9685]

Architectural Words Inc., 1201 Puyallup Ave., Tacoma, WA 98421, (253)383-5484 [6983]

Archway Cookie Co., 2419 Industrial Park Rd., Boone, IA 50036, (515)432-4084 [10430]

Archway Systems Inc., 2130 Main St., #145, Huntington Beach, CA 92648, (714)374-0440 [5958]

Arco Coffee Co., 2206 Winter, Superior, WI 54880-1437, (715)392-4771 [10431]

Arco Pharmaceuticals Inc., 90 Orville Dr., Bohemia, NY 11716, (516)567-9500 [19158]

Arctic Clear Products Inc., 2130 W Wilden Ave., Goshen, IN 46526, (219)533-7671 [25557]

Arctic Fire Equipment, 702 30th Ave., Fairbanks, AK 99701, (907)452-7806 [24507]

Arctic Ice Co., Industrial Park W, Gallup, NM 87301, (505)722-9470 [10432]

Arctic Industrial Supply, 6510 Arctic Spur Rd., Anchorage, AK 99518, (907)561-1520 [16708]

Arctic Technical Services, 1318 Well St., Fairbanks, AK 99701, (907)452-8368 [14326]

Ard Oil Co. Inc., PO Box 100, Summerdale, AL 36580, (205)947-2302 [22043]

Ardinger and Son Co.; H.T., PO Box 569360, Dallas, TX 75356-9360, (214)631-9830 [14809]

Ardrosson Farms, Darby-Paoli Rd., PO Box 567, Villanova, PA 19085, (215)688-2651 [17704]

Area Access Inc., 8117 Ransell Rd., Falls Church, VA 22042-1015, (703)573-2111 [18689]

Area Access Inc., 8117 Ransell Rd., Falls Church, VA 22042-1015, (703)573-2111 [19159]

Area Distributors, Inc., 61-02 31st Ave., Woodside, NY 11377, (718)726-9200 [2249]

Area Wholesale Tire Co., Inc., 5620 Airline Hwy., PO Box 2723, Baton Rouge, LA 70821-2723, (504)356-2548 [2250]

AremisSoft Corp., 200 Central Park S, New York, NY 10019, (212)765-7383 [5959]

Arends Brothers Inc., Rte. 54 N, Melvin, IL 60952, (217)388-7717 [249]

Arends and Sons Inc., 715 S Sangamon Ave., Gibson City, IL 60936, (217)784-4241 [250]

Arensberg Sons Inc., 1428 10th Ave., Seattle, WA 98122-3805, (206)323-7111 [25558]

Argent Chemical Laboratories Inc., 8702 152nd Ave. NW, Redmond, WA 98052, (425)885-3777 [251]

Argo International Corp., 140 Franklin St., New York, NY 10013, (212)431-1700 [18450]

Argos Enterprises, 101 Westfall Dr., Syracuse, NY 13219, (315)468-0297 [14024]

Argraph Central, 111 Asia Pl., Carlstadt, NJ 07072-2412 [8369]

Argraph Corp., 111 Asia Pl., Carlstadt, NJ 07072 [8370]

Argraph West, 2710 McCone Ave., Hayward, CA 94545 [8371]

Argus Buying Group, California Ctr., 1st St., PO Box 3271, Tustin, CA 92781-3271, (714)552-8494 [4781]

Arie Incorporated, 3405 Okeefe Dr., El Paso, TX 79902-2023, (915)542-1848 [8372]

Aries Paper & Chemical Co. Inc., PO Box 1864, Lake Charles, LA 70602, (337)433-8794 [4574]

Aring Equipment Company Inc., 13001 W Silver Spring Dr., Butler, WI 53007, (414)781-3770 [6984]

Arista Enterprises Inc., 125 Commerce Dr., Hauppauge, NY 11788, (516)435-0200 [5960]

Arista Records Inc., 6 W 57th St., New York, NY 10019, (212)489-7400 [25082]

Aristo Computers Inc., 6700 SW 105th Ave., Ste. 300, Beaverton, OR 97008-5484, (503)626-6333 [5961]

Aristo Import Company Inc., 15 Hunt Rd., Orangeburg, NY 10962, (914)359-0720 [24316]

Ariz Coin & Commercial Lndry Eq., 740 W Grant, Phoenix, AZ 85007, (602)258-9274 [8373]

Arizona Appliance Parts, 6237 E 22nd St., Tucson, AZ 85711, (520)748-2222 [15031]

Arizona Bag Co. LLC, PO Box 6650, Phoenix, AZ 85005-6650, (602)272-1333 [252]

Arizona Beverage Distributing Co. LLC, 1115 N 47th Ave., Phoenix, AZ 85043-1801, (602)272-3751 [1486]

Arizona Coin & Commercial Laundry Equipment, 1831 W Buckeye Rd., Phoenix, AZ 85007-3522, (602)258-9274 [15032]

Arizona Commercial Lighting Co., 4510 N 16th St., Phoenix, AZ 85016, (602)230-8770 [8374]

Arizona Electrical Prdts Inc., 1867 E 3rd St., Tempe, AZ 85281, (480)966-2167 [8375]

Arizona Grain Inc., PO Box 11188, Casa Grande, AZ 85230, (602)836-8228 [17705]

Arizona Machinery Co., Inc., 197 W Warner Rd., Chandler, AZ 85224, (602)963-4531 [253]

Arizona Mail Order Co., PO Box 27800, Tucson, AZ 85726, (520)745-4500 [4782]

Arizona Recycling Corp., 400 S 15th Ave., Phoenix, AZ 85007, (602)258-5323 [26753]

Arizona Sash and Door Co., 1265 S Pima, Mesa, AZ 85210-5347, (602)253-3151 [13565]

Arizona Scrap Iron and Metals Inc., 433 S 7th Ave., Phoenix, AZ 85007, (602)252-8423 [26754]

Arizona Sealing Devices Inc., 150 E Alamo Dr., Chandler, AZ 85225, (602)892-7325 [16709]

Arizona Sport Shirts Inc., 100 Gasoline Alley, Indianapolis, IN 46222-3965, (317)244-3905 [4783]

Arizona Sportsman, Inc., 5146 E Pima St., Tucson, AZ 85712, (520)321-3878 [13476]

Arizona Therapy Source, 338 N 16th St., Phoenix, AZ 85006-3706, (602)252-5891 [18690]

Arizona Water Works Supply Inc., PO Box 219, Tempe, AZ 85280, (602)966-5804 [23072]

Arizona Welding Equipment Co., 4030 W Lincoln St., Phoenix, AZ 85009-5398, (602)269-2151 [16420]

Arizona Welding Equipment Co., 4030 W Lincoln St., Phoenix, AZ 85009-5398, (602)269-2151 [15777]

Arizona Wholesale Supply Co., PO Box 2979, Phoenix, AZ 85062, (602)258-7901 [15033]

Ark Grooming, 3225 Eagle Dr., Greenwood, AR 72936, (501)996-0085 [27073]

Ark Manufacturing Inc., 3780 Boone Rd. SE, Salem, OR 97301, (503)581-6702 [27074]

Arkansas Import & Distributing Co., 702 SW 8th St., Bentonville, AR 72712-6299, (501)273-4173 [23523]

Arkansas Optical Co., PO Box 9004, North Little Rock, AR 72119-9004, (501)372-1923 [19160]

Arkansas Sock & Wiping Rag Co., PO Box 457, Hughes, AR 72348-0457, (870)633-0691 [25968]

Arkansas Valley Companies, 8316 E 73rd St., Tulsa, OK 74133, (918)252-0508 [22044]

Arkansas Valley Seed Co., PO Box 16025, Denver, CO 80216, (303)320-7500 [254]

Arkansas Valley Wholesale Grocers Co., PO Box 380, Morrilton, AR 72110, (501)354-3451 [10433]

Arkfeld Manufacturing & Distributing Company Inc., 1230 Monroe Ave., PO BOX 54, Norfolk, NE 68702-0054, (402)371-9430 [255]

Arkin Distributing Co., 43100 9 Mile, Novi, MI 48375-3113, (248)349-9300 [26396]

Arkla Chemical Corp., PO Box 21734, Shreveport, LA 71151, (318)429-2700 [22045]

Arky House Inc., 218 E Grand Ave., Hot Springs, AR 71901-4132, (501)624-0605 [24675]

Arley Wholesale Inc., 700 N South Rd., Scranton, PA 18504-1432, (717)451-8880 [9686]

Arling Lumber Inc., PO Box 58359, Cincinnati, OH 45258-0359, (513)451-5700 [6985]

Arlington Coin Co., 140 Gansett Ave., Cranston, RI 02910-2549, (401)942-3188 [17313]

ARM Computer Inc., 998 Rock Ave., San Jose, CA 95131-1615, (408)935-9800 [5962]

Armani Fashion Corp.; Giorgio, 11 W 42nd St., 19th Fl., New York, NY 10036-8002, (212)265-2760 [4784]

Armitage Industrial Supply, Inc., 4930 W Belmont Ave., Chicago, IL 60641-4331, (773)202-8300 [16710]

Armline, 2855 S Reservoir, Pomona, CA 91766, (714)591-0541 [9687]

Armour Food Co., 223 Progress Rd., Springfield, KY 40069, (606)336-3922 [10434]

Armour Food Ingredients Co., 223 Progress Rd., Springfield, KY 40069, (606)336-3922 [10434]

Armstrong Bros. Tool Co., 5200 W Armstrong Ave., Chicago, IL 60646, (773)763-3333 [15778]

Armstrong and Dobbs Inc., PO Box 8027, Athens, GA 30603-8027, (706)543-8271 [6986]

Armstrong International Inc. Three Rivers Div., 816 Maple St., Three Rivers, MI 49093, (616)273-1415 [15034]

Armstrong McCall, PO Box 17068, Austin, TX 78760-7068, (512)444-1757 [14025]

Armstrong Medical Industries Inc., PO Box 700, Lincolnshire, IL 60069, (847)913-0101 [18691]

Armstrong Produce Ltd., 651 Ilalo Bldg. 1, Honolulu, HI 96813-5525, (808)538-7051 [10435]

Armstrong's Lock & Supply, Inc., 1440 Dutch Valley Pl. NE, Atlanta, GA 30324-5302, (404)875-0136 [24508]

Army & Navy Supplies, 2835 E 26th St., Los Angeles, CA 90023, (213)263-8564 [4785]

Arndt Optical Supplies; Ray, 820 NW 18th Ave., Portland, OR 97209-2317, (503)223-6106 [19161]

Arnel Compressor Co., 114 N Sunset Ave., City of Industry, CA 91744, (626)968-3836 [5829]

Arnessen Corp., 1100 Walnut St., Roselle, NJ 07203, (908)241-3535 [25559]

Arnold Inc.; S.M., 7901 Michigan Ave., St. Louis, MO 63111-3594, (314)544-4103 [2251]

Arnold Lumber Company Inc., Rte. 1, Bonifay, FL 32425, (850)547-5733 [6987]

Arnold Machinery Co., PO Box 21005, Phoenix, AZ 85036, (602)237-3755 [6988]

Arnold Machinery Co., PO Box 30020, Salt Lake City, UT 84130, (801)972-4000 [6989]

Arnold Machinery Co., 6024 W Southern Ave., Laveen, AZ 85339-9652, (602)237-3755 [6990]

Arnold Machinery Co., PO Box 30020, Salt Lake City, UT 84130, (801)972-4000 [6991]

Arnold Motor Supply Co., PO Box 320, Spencer, IA 51301-0320, (712)262-4885 [2252]

Arnold Pen Co. Inc., PO Box 791, Petersburg, VA 23804, (804)733-6612 [20810]

Arnold-Sunbelt Beverage Company L.P.; Ben, PO Box 480, Ridgeway, SC 29130, (803)337-3500 [1487]

Arnold's Inc., PO Box 190260, Little Rock, AR 72219, (501)562-0675 [14026]

Arntzen Electric Company Inc., 6319 Northwest Hwy., Chicago, IL 60631-1669, (773)775-5797 [9539]

Aro Corp., 1725 US Hwy. 1 N, Southern Pines, NC 28387, (919)692-8700 [15779]

Aronson-Campbell Industrial Supply Inc., 1700 136th PL, NE, Bellevue, WA 98005-2328 [15780]

Aronson Tire Co. Inc., 510 Washington St., Auburn, MA 01501, (508)832-3244 [2253]

Aroostook Beverage Co., 52 Rice St., Presque Isle, ME 04769-2260, (207)769-2081 [1488]

Around the Corner, 618 N Doheny Dr., Los Angeles, CA 90069-5506, (310)276-8635 [13306]

AROW Components and Fasteners Inc., 31012 Huntwood Ave., Hayward, CA 94544, (510)487-2100 [8263]

Arraid Inc., PO Box 86249, Phoenix, AZ 85080, (623)582-4592 [5963]

Arranaga and Co.; Robert, 216 S Alameda St., Los Angeles, CA 90012, (213)622-7249 [10436]

Array Microsystems Inc., 987 University Ave. Ste. 6, Los Gatos, CA 95032, (408)399-1505 [8376]

Arriflex Corp., 617 Rte. 303, Blauvelt, NY 10913, (845)353-1200 [22827]

Arrow Business Products Inc., 3770 S Perkins Rd., Memphis, TN 38118, (901)362-8355 [20811]

Arrow-Cold Control Appliance Parts Co., PO Box 171275, Kansas City, KS 66117-0275, (913)371-4677 [15035]

Arrow Distributing Co., 11012 Aurora Hudson Rd., Streetsboro, OH 44241, (330)528-0410 [25427]

Arrow Electronics Inc., 25 Hub Dr., Melville, NY 11747, (516)391-1300 [5964]

Arrow Electronics Inc., 25 Hub Dr., Melville, NY 11747, (516)391-1300 [8377]

Arrow Electronics Inc. Almac/Arrow Electronics Div., 3310 146th Pl. SE, Ste. B, Bellevue, WA 98007-6471, (425)643-9992 [5965]

Arrow-Kierulff Electronics Group, 25 Hub Dr., Melville, NY 11747, (516)391-1300 [8378]

Arrow Map Inc., 50 Scotland Blvd., Bridgewater, MA 02324, (508)880-2880 [3525]

Arrow-Master Inc., 1201 7th St., East Moline, IL 61244-1465 [6992]

Arrow Precision Products Inc., 5026 E Slauson Ave., Maywood, CA 90270, (213)562-3300 [23073]

Arrow Safety Device Co., 301 S DuPont Hwy., PO Box 299, Georgetown, DE 19947-0299, (302)856-2516 [2254]

Arrow Sales Inc., 1215 17th St., Monroe, WI 53566-2403, (608)325-4260 [20812]

Arrow Speed Warehouse, 686 S Adams, Kansas City, KS 66105, (913)321-1200 [2255]

Arrow-SYSCO, 1451 River Oaks W, Harahan, LA 70123, (504)734-1015 [10437]

Arrow-Sysco Food Services Inc., PO Box 10038, New Orleans, LA 70181, (504)837-1015 [10438]

Arrow Thompson Metals Inc., 6880 Troost Ave., North Hollywood, CA 91605, (818)765-0522 [19783]

Arrow Truck Sales Inc., 3200 Manchester Traffic Way, Kansas City, MO 64129, (816)923-5000 [256]

Arrow Trucks and Parts Co., 2637 W Fort St., Detroit, MI 48216, (313)496-0900 [2256]

Arrow Wholesale Co. Inc., PO Box 108, Worcester, MA 01613-0108, (508)753-5830 [26397]

Arrowcopter Inc., Box 6480, San Jose, CA 95150, (408)978-1771 [26398]

Arrowhead Fireworks Co., 3400 Republic Ave., Minneapolis, MN 55426-4133, (612)929-8255 [26399]

Arrowhead Mills Inc., PO Box 2059, Hereford, TX 79045-2059, (806)364-0730 [10439]

Arrowhead Supply Inc., 18 N 19th Ave. W, Duluth, MN 55806-2127, (218)722-6699 [15036]

Arrowhead Timber Co., PO Box 85, Carver, OR 97015, (503)658-5151 [27281]

ARS Electronics, 7110 Decelis Pl., Van Nuys, CA 91406, (818)997-6279 [25083]

Art Barn Enterprises, 366 Paulk Rd., Ashford, AL 36312, (334)899-3503 [25560]

Art Cathedral Metal Inc., PO Box 6146, Providence, RI 02940-6146, (401)273-7200 [17314]

Art Computer Tech Inc., 56 S Abel St., Milpitas, CA 95035, (408)946-7852 [5966]

Art Craft Wallets Inc., 380 Lafayette St., New York, NY 10003, (212)674-3332 [18371]

Art Essentials, PO Box 148, Alpha, OH 45301-0148, (937)426-3503 [20813]

Art Glass House, Inc., 3445 North Hwy. 1, Cocoa, FL 32926, (407)631-4477 [25561]

Art Iron Inc., PO Box 964, Toledo, OH 43697, (419)241-1261 [19784]

Art Metal Products, 115 S Wilke Rd., Arlington Heights, IL 60006, (708)577-0330 [13023]

A.R.T. Multimedia Systems, Inc., 56 S Abel St., Milpitas, CA 95035, (408)946-7852 [5966]

Art Supply Enterprises Inc., 1351 Ocean Ave., Emeryville, CA 94608, (510)428-9011 [25721]

Artcarved Bridal, PO Box 149056, Austin, TX 78714-9056, (512)444-0571 [17371]

Artcarved Class Rings, PO Box 149056, Austin, TX 78714-9056, (512)444-0571 [17371]

Artcarved College Rings, PO Box 149056, Austin, TX 78714-9056, (512)444-0571 [17371]

Artec Distributing Inc., 1 Pine Haven Shore Rd., Shelburne, VT 05482, (802)985-9411 [25084]

Artemia of Utah Inc., PO Box 978, Farmington, UT 84025, (801)532-5426 [10440]

Artesanos Imports Company Inc., 1414 Maclovia, PO Box G, Santa Fe, NM 87505, (505)471-8020 [6993]

Artesia Fire Equipment Inc., PO Box 1367, Artesia, NM 88211-1367, (505)746-6111 [24509]

Artesia Water Co., PO Box 790210, San Antonio, TX 78279-0210, (210)654-0293 [10441]

Artform Industries Inc., 3310 Towanda Ave., Baltimore, MD 21215, (410)664-2800 [22929]

Arthur Companies Inc., PO Box 145, Arthur, ND 58006, (701)967-8312 [257]

Arthur Lumber Trading Co., 5550 SW Macadam Ave., No. 230, Portland, OR 97201-3771, (503)228-8160 [6994]

Arthurs Enterprises Inc., PO Box 5654, Huntington, WV 25703, (304)523-7491 [8379]

ARTiSan Software Tools, 2 Lincoln Center Ste. 370, Portland, OR 97223, (503)245-6200 [5967]

Artist Brush & Color Dist., Hofcraft Catalog, 1730-B Air Park Dr., Grand Haven, MI 49417, (616)847-8989 [20814]

Artistic Stone of America, 33757 Groesbeck Hwy., Fraser, MI 48026, (810)293-2120 [13307]

Artistic Tile Co. Inc., 661 E 48th Ave., Anchorage, AK 99503-2929, (907)562-2122 [9688]

Artlite Office Supply and Furniture Co., 1851 Piedmont Rd., Atlanta, GA 30324, (404)875-7271 [13024]

Artmark Associates Inc., 11315 NW 36th Ter., Miami, FL 33178, (305)715-9800 [8380]

Artmark Chicago Ltd., 4136 United Pky., Schiller Park, IL 60176-1708, (312)266-1111 [15407]

Artomate Co., PO Box 172, Cockeysville, MD 21030-0172, (410)666-9429 [23524]

Artpost, 561 Broadway, New York, NY 10012, (212)226-0923 [21729]

Arts & Craft Distributors Inc., 6304 Yadkin Rd., Fayetteville, NC 28303-2647, (910)867-1050 [26400]

Art's Theatrical Supply, 3306 83rd, Lubbock, TX 79423, (806)792-2136 [17315]

ArtSource Inc., 5515 S Westridge Dr., New Berlin, WI 53151, (414)860-4260 [13308]

Artusos Pastry Shop, 670 E 187th, Bronx, NY 10458-6802, (718)367-2515 [10442]

Artz Inc.; E.G., PO Box 97, Brookfield, WI 53008, (262)781-5700 [16711]

Arun Technology Inc., PO Box 2947, Dearborn, MI 48123-2947, (313)277-8186 [24317]

Arundel Corp., PO Box 5000, Sparks, MD 21152, (410)329-5000 [6995]

ARvee Systems Inc., 1461 Lakeland Ave., Ste. 19, Bohemia, NY 11716, (516)567-9409 [5968]

Arvin Industries Inc., PO Box 3000, Columbus, IN 47202-3000, (812)379-3000 [2257]

Arvin Industries Inc. North American Automotive Div., 1531 13th St., Columbus, IN 47201, (812)379-3000 [2258]

As Is Office Furniture, 1352 Reber St., Green Bay, WI 54301, (920)436-6820 [20996]

ASA Audiovox Specialized Applications, 23319 Cooper Dr., Elkhart, IN 46514, (219)264-3135 [5517]

ASA Audiovox Specialized Applications, 23319 Cooper Dr., Elkhart, IN 46514, (219)264-3135 [8381]

ASA Builders Supply Inc., 2040 Easy St., Walled Lake, MI 48390, (248)624-7400 [6996]

ASAP, PO Box 271393, Corpus Christi, TX 78427, (512)985-2727 [4786]

ASAP Software Express Inc., 850 Asbury Dr., Buffalo Grove, IL 60089, (847)465-3710 [5969]

Asbury Automotive Group, One Tower Bridge, Ste. 1440, Conshohocken, PA 19428, (610)260-9800 [2259]

Asbury Syrup and Paper Company Inc., 904 Sunset Ave., Asbury Park, NJ 07712, (732)774-5746 [21636]

Asbury Worldwide Inc., 10011 Pines Blvd., Ste. 101, Pembroke Pines, FL 33024-6167, (954)438-4381 [24068]

ASC Industries, PO Box 5068, Arlington, TX 76006, (817)640-1300 [42]

ASC International Inc., PO Box 5068, Arlington, TX 76006, (817)640-1300 [20592]

ASCII Group Inc., 7101 Wisconsin Ave., Ste. 1000, Bethesda, MD 20814-4805, (301)718-2600 [5970]

Ascom Timeplex Inc., 7060 Koll Center Pkwy Ste. 340, Pleasanton, CA 94566, (925)461-2300 [8382]

ASEC Manufacturing, PO Box 580970, Tulsa, OK 74158-0970, (918)266-1400 [2260]

Asel Art Supply, 2701 Cedar Springs, Dallas, TX 75201-1384, (214)871-2425 [25562]

Aseptico, Inc., PO Box 1548, Woodinville, WA 98072-1548, (425)487-3157 [18692]

Ash Woodyard Inc.; J.M., PO Box 128, Potts Camp, MS 38659, (601)252-1777 [27282]

Ashbrook & Associates, 1271 N Blue Gum St., Anaheim, CA 92806-2414, (714)765-5900 [15408]

Ashby Equity Association, 101 Main St., Ashby, MN 56309, (218)747-2219 [258]

Ashe Industries Inc., 4505 Transport Dr., Tampa, FL 33605, (813)247-2743 [6997]

Asheville Steel & Salvage Co., 314 Riverside Dr., Asheville, NC 28801, (828)252-1061 [19785]

Ashford International Inc., 2305 W Park Place Blvd ., No. N, Stone Mountain, GA 30087, (770)879-6266 [5971]

Ashgate Publishing Co., Old Post Rd., Brookfield, VT 05036, (802)276-3162 [3526]

Ashland Chemical Co., PO Box 2219, Columbus, OH 43216, (614)790-3333 [4326]

Ashland Chemical Co. Industrial Chemicals and Solvents Div., 5420 Speaker Rd., Kansas City, KS 66106, (913)621-3388 [4327]

Ashland Electric Company Inc., 2430 Carter Ave., Ashland, KY 41101-7828, (606)329-8544 [8383]

Ashland Electric Company Inc., 2430 Carter Ave., Ashland, KY 41101-7828, (606)329-8544 [8384]

Ashland Farmers Elevator Co., PO Box 199, Ashland, IL 62612, (217)476-3318 [17706]

Ashley Aluminum Inc., 11651 Plano Rd., Dallas, TX 75243, (214)860-5100 [6998]

Ashley & Company Inc.; E.H., PO Box 15067, Riverside, RI 02915-0067, (401)431-0950 [17316]

Ashleys on Main, PO Box 312, Brownsdale, MN 55918-0312, (507)433-8841 [4787]

Ashmore Grain Co. Inc., PO Box 100, Ashmore, IL 61912, (217)349-8221 [17707]

Ashmore Optical Co. Inc., PO Box 2961, Charleston, WV 25330-2961, (304)344-2366 [19162]

Ashwood Computer Co., 10671 Techwoods Cir., Cincinnati, OH 45242, (513)563-2800 [5972]

ASI Erie, 345 E 16th St., Erie, PA 16503-1902, (814)459-3000 [2261]

Asia Pacific Trading Co., 35 W 31st St., New York, NY 10001, (212)736-5220 [19163]

Asian World of Martial Arts Inc., 917-21 Arch St., Philadelphia, PA 19107-2477, (215)925-1161 [23525]

Asmara Inc., Fargo Bldg., Boston, MA 02210, (617)261-0222 [15409]

Asmara Oriental Rugs, 451 D St., Boston, MA 02210, (617)261-0222 [9689]

ASNA Inc., 14855 Blanco Rd. Ste. 300, San Antonio, TX 78216, (210)408-0212 [5973]

ASO Enterprises, 171 Elmgrove Ave., Providence, RI 02906-4222, (401)331-7051 [17317]

Asoma Corp., 105 Corporate Park Dr., White Plains, NY 10604, (914)251-5400 [19786]

Aspen Data, 345 Edgewood Dr., Providence, UT 84332-9441, (435)863-5746 [5974]

Aspen Furniture Inc., 2929 Grand Ave., Phoenix, AZ 85017-4933, (602)233-0224 [13025]

Aspen Imaging International Inc., 3830 Kelley Ave., Cleveland, OH 44114, (216)881-5300 [5975]

Aspen West Publishing Co. Inc., PO Box 1245, Sandy, UT 84091, (801)565-1370 [3527]

Assembly Automation Industries, 1858 Business Center Dr., Duarte, CA 91010, (626)303-2777 [15781]

Assembly Component Systems, 240 W 83rd St., Burr Ridge, IL 60521, (630)654-1113 [13566]

Assembly Components Systems Co., PO Box 22536, Memphis, TN 38122, (901)274-0050 [13567]

Assembly Components Systems Inc., PO Box 1608, Decatur, AL 35602, (256)353-1931 [13568]

Assi Computers Inc., 620 N Broadway, Pittsburg, KS 66762, (316)231-7833 [5976]

Associated Aircraft Supply Inc., 6020 Cedar Springs Rd., PO Box 35788, Dallas, TX 75235-5788, (214)331-4381 [43]

Associated Allied Industries Inc., 5151 N 32nd St., Milwaukee, WI 53209, (414)461-5050 [2]

Associated Appliance Service, 2318 NW 12th St., Oklahoma City, OK 73107-5606, (405)525-2003 [14327]

Associated Bearings, 115 N Jackson, Topeka, KS 66603, (785)232-5508 [15782]

Associated Bearings, 2029 Wyandotte, Kansas City, MO 64108, (816)421-0407 [15783]

Associated Brokers Inc., PO Box 26328, Raleigh, NC 27611, (919)833-2651 [10443]

Associated Building Specialties, 20 Frankford Ave., Blackwood, NJ 08012-2850, (609)227-3900 [13026]

Associated Building Specialties, 20 Frankford Ave., Blackwood, NJ 08012-2850, (609)227-3900 [24069]

Associated Business Products Inc. Scanning Systems, 11413 Valley View Rd., Eden Prairie, MN 55344, (612)941-2585 [20815]

Associated Buyers, PO Box 399, Barrington, NH 03825, (603)664-5656 [10444]

Associated Computers Services, PO Box 464057, Lawrenceville, GA 30042-4057, (404)962-7760 [5977]

Associated Fabrics Corp., 104 E 25th St., New York, NY 10010, (212)689-7186 [25969]

Associated Farmers Cooperative, 695 Exchange Ave., Conway, AR 72032, (501)329-2971 [259]

Associated Food Stores Inc., 305 W Quinn Rd., Pocatello, ID 83202-1932, (208)237-4511 [10445]

Associated Food Stores Inc., 122-20 Merrick Blvd., Jamaica, NY 11433, (718)341-2100 [10446]

Associated Food Stores Inc., PO Box 30430, Salt Lake City, UT 84130, (801)973-4400 [10447]

Associated Food Stores Inc. (Salt Lake City, Utah), PO Box 30430, Salt Lake City, UT 84130, (801)973-4400 [10448]

Associated Grocers of Florida Inc., 7000 NW 32nd Ave., Miami, FL 33147, (305)696-0080 [10449]

Associated Grocers, Inc., 3301 S Norfolk, Seattle, WA 98118, (206)762-2100 [10450]

Associated Grocers of Maine Inc., PO Box 1000, Gardiner, ME 04345, (207)582-6500 [10451]

Associated Grocers of New England Inc., PO Box 5200, Manchester, NH 03108, (603)669-3250 [10452]

Associated Healthcare Systems Inc., 85 Woodridge Dr., West Amherst, NY 14228, (716)564-4500 [18693]

Associated Industrial Supply Co., PO Box 208, Columbia, SC 29202-0208, (803)765-0990 [16712]

Associated Industries, 11347 Vanowen St., North Hollywood, CA 91605, (818)760-1000 [5518]

Associated Industries, 11347 Vanowen St., North Hollywood, CA 91605, (818)760-1000 [5752]

Associated Industries, 11347 Van Owens St., North Hollywood, CA 91605, (818)760-1000 [8385]

Associated of Los Angeles, 2585 E Olympic Blvd., Los Angeles, CA 90023, (323)268-8411 [8386]

Associated Lumber Industries Inc., 204 W Main St., Fairfield, IL 62837, (618)842-3733 [6999]

Associated Material Handling Industries Inc., 1230 Brookville Way, Indianapolis, IN 46239-1048, (317)576-0300 [15784]

Associated Material Handling Industries Inc., 550 Kenoe Blvd., Carol Stream, IL 60188-1838, (630)588-8800 [16713]

Associated Medical, 2901 S Hampton Rd., Philadelphia, PA 19154, (215)677-0589 [19164]

Associated Medical Supply Inc., 15210 N 75th St., Scottsdale, AZ 85260, (480)998-1684 [18694]

Associated Milk Producers Inc. North Central Region, PO Box 455, New Ulm, MN 56073, (507)354-8295 [10453]

Associated Milk Producers Inc. Southern Region, 3500 William D. Tate Ave., No. 100, Grapevine, TX 76051-8734, (817)461-2674 [10454]

Associated Milk Producers Inc. Sulphur Springs Div., PO Box 939, Sulphur Springs, TX 75482, (903)885-6518 [10455]

Associated Packaging Inc., 215 Connell St., Goodlettsville, TN 37072, (615)859-3737 [16714]

Associated Potato Growers Inc., 2001 North 6th Street, Grand Forks, ND 58203, (701)775-4614 [10456]

Associated R.V. Ent., Inc., 1500 Shelton Dr., Hollister, CA 95023, (831)636-9566 [6935]

Associated Sales, 4201 W Camelback Rd., Phoenix, AZ 85019-2860, (602)242-7561 [15037]

Associated Services for the Blind, 919 Walnut St., Philadelphia, PA 19107, (215)627-0600 [19165]

Associated Springs, 100 Underwood Rd., Arden, NC 28704, (828)684-7836 [13569]

Associated Steel Corp., 18200 Miles Rd., Cleveland, OH 44128-0335, (216)475-8000 [19787]

Associated Systems Inc., 1425 N Broadway, Wichita, KS 67214-1103, (316)263-1035 [5978]

Associated Tile Sales, 9203 Broadway, San Antonio, TX 78218, (210)828-5761 [9690]

Associated Wholesale Grocers, 5000 Kansas Ave., Kansas City, KS 66106, (913)321-1313 [10457]

Associated Wholesalers Inc., PO Box 67, Robesonia, PA 19551, (610)693-3161 [10458]

Associated X-Ray Corp., PO Box 120559, East Haven, CT 06512-0559, (203)466-2446 [18695]

Associates in Software International, 180 Crossen Ave., Elk Grove Village, IL 60007, (847)763-5000 [5979]

Assorted Book Co., 230 5th Ave., Ste. 1811, New York, NY 10001, (212)684-9000 [3528]

Assumption Cooperative Grain Co., 104 W North St., Assumption, IL 62510, (217)226-3213 [17708]

Assumption Cooperative Grain Co., 104 W North St., Assumption, IL 62510, (217)226-3213 [10459]

AST USA Inc., 222 Bloomingdale Rd., No. 401, White Plains, NY 10605-1511, (914)428-6010 [19788]

Astor Foods Inc., 4000 Highlands Pkwy., Smyrna, GA 30082, (770)436-0411 [10460]

Astra International, 1140 Broadway, New York, NY 10001, (212)251-0120 [13309]

Astra Trading Corp., 1140 Broadway, New York, NY 10001, (212)251-0120 [13309]

Astral Precision Equipment Co., 800 Busse Rd., Elk Grove Village, IL 60007, (847)439-1650 [15785]

Astran Inc., 591 SW 8th St., Miami, FL 33130, (305)858-4300 [3529]

Astran Inc., 591 SW 8th St., Miami, FL 33130, (305)858-4300 [3530]

Astrex Inc., 205 Express St., Plainview, NY 11803, (516)433-1700 [8387]

Astro Business Solutions Inc., 110 W Walnut St., Gardena, CA 90248, (310)217-3000 [20816]

Astro Industries Inc., 4403 Dayton-Xenia Rd., Dayton, OH 45432, (937)429-5900 [8388]

Astro Office Products Inc., 110 Walnut St., Gardena, CA 90248, (310)217-3000 [20817]

Astro-Pure Water Purifiers, 3025 SW 2nd Ave., Ft. Lauderdale, FL 33315-3309, (954)832-0630 [15038]

Astrokam, 9800 Rockside Rd., Cleveland, OH 44125, (216)447-0404 [8389]

Astronomical Society of the Pacific, 390 Ashton Ave., San Francisco, CA 94112, (415)337-1100 [3531]

Astrup Co., 2937 W 25th St., Cleveland, OH 44113, (216)696-2820 [25970]

Asuka Corp., 7800 River Rd., North Bergen, NJ 07047, (201)861-5450 [19166]

ASW Aviation Services Inc., 6060 W Airport Dr., North Canton, OH 44720, (216)494-6104 [44]

A.T. Clayton and Company Inc., 2 Pickwick Plz., Greenwich, CT 06830, (203)861-1190 [21637]

AT Products Inc., PO Box 625, Harvard, IL 60033, (815)943-3590 [5519]

A.T. Supply, PO Box 663, Amherst, NY 14228, (716)691-3331 [21391]

Atalanta Corp., 1 Atalanta Plz., Elizabeth, NJ 07206, (908)351-8000 [10461]

AT&T Business Markets Group Div., 831 Park Ave. SW, Norton, VA 24273-1927, (540)443-7000 [5520]

ATC Computer and Business Machines Inc., 15703 E Valley Blvd., La Puente, CA 91744-3932, (626)333-0193 [20818]

ATC International, 16000 Memorial Dr., Ste. 210, Houston, TX 77079-4008, (713)622-3047 [2262]

Atchison County Farmers Union Cooperative Association, PO Drawer B, Atchison, KS 66002, (913)367-0318 [17709]

Atchison Leather Products, 201 Main, Atchison, KS 66002-2838, (913)367-6431 [18372]

ATCOM Inc., PO Box 13476, Research Triangle Park, NC 27709, (919)314-1001 [5521]

ATD-American Co., 135 Greenwood Ave., Wyncote, PA 19095, (215)576-1000 [25971]

Atec, Inc., 12600 Executive Dr., Stafford, TX 77477-3064, (281)276-2700 [24318]

Atec Inc., 12600 Executive Dr., Stafford, TX 77477-3064, (281)276-2700 [15786]

Atecs Corp., 156 Mokauea St., Honolulu, HI 96819-3105, (808)845-2991 [18696]

Atecs Corp., 156 Mokauea St., Honolulu, HI 96819-3105, (808)845-2991 [19167]

Athens Building Supply, 120 Ben Burton Rd., Bogart, GA 30622, (706)546-8318 [7000]

Athens Distributing Co., 1000 Herman, Nashville, TN 37208, (615)254-0101 [1489]

Athens Hardware Co., PO Box 552, Athens, GA 30603-0552, (706)543-4391 [13570]

Athens Material Handling Inc., PO Box 6685, Athens, GA 30604, (706)543-7410 [15787]

Atherton Grain Co., PO Box 366, Walnut, IL 61376, (815)379-2177 [17710]

Atherton Grain Co., PO Box 366, Walnut, IL 61376, (815)379-2177 [10462]

Athletic Supply Inc., PO Box C19050, Seattle, WA 98109, (206)623-8972 [24676]

Athlon II Enterprises Inc., 1684 SW 86th St., Oklahoma City, OK 73159-6229, (405)685-3737 [4788]

Athmann Industrial Medical Supply, PO Box 26445, Indianapolis, IN 46226-0445, (317)898-3344 [18697]

ATI Communications, 105 Broughton Rd., Bethel Park, PA 15102-2801, (412)831-1300 [5522]

Atkins Inc.; Frederick, 1515 Broadway, New York, NY 10036, (212)840-7000 [25563]

Atlanta Beverage Co., PO Box 44008, Atlanta, GA 30336, (404)699-6700 [1490]

Atlanta Broom Company Inc., 4750 Bakers Ferry Rd. SW, Atlanta, GA 30336, (404)696-4600 [21638]

Atlanta Broom Company Inc., 4750 Bakers Ferry Rd. SW, Atlanta, GA 30336-2246, (404)696-4600 [16715]

Atlanta Commercial Tire Inc., 1495 Northside NW, Atlanta, GA 30318, (404)351-9016 [2263]

Atlanta Fixture and Sails Co., 3185 NE Expressway, Atlanta, GA 30341, (404)455-8844 [24070]

Atlanta Fuel Company Inc., PO Box 93586, Atlanta, GA 30377, (404)792-9888 [22046]

Atlanta Ice Inc., 1587 E Taylor Ave., East Point, GA 30344, (404)762-0139 [10463]

Atlanta Tees Inc., PO Box 264, Griffin, GA 30224-0264, (404)228-0940 [4789]

Atlanta Tile Supply, Inc., 5845-C Oakbrook Pkwy., Norcross, GA 30093, (770)409-8200 [9691]

Atlanta Wheels & Accessories, Inc., 777 11th St. NW, Atlanta, GA 30318-5523, (404)876-5847 [2264]

Atlanta Wholesale Wine Co., 275 Spring St. SW, Atlanta, GA 30303, (404)522-3358 [1491]

Atlantic Aviation Corp., PO Box 15000, Wilmington, DE 19850, (302)322-7000 [45]

Atlantic Aviation Service Inc., Philadelphia International Airport, H1, Philadelphia, PA 19153, (215)492-2970 [22047]

Atlantic Building Products, PO Box 1287, Lakeville, MA 02347, (508)947-5000 [7001]

Atlantic Ceramic Tile, 158-01 Crossbay Blvd., Howard Beach, NY 11414-3137, (516)586-1080 [9692]

Atlantic Coast Fiberglass Co., 510 Bullocks Point Ave., Riverside, RI 02915, (401)433-2990 [7002]

Atlantic Communications Inc., PO Box 596, Bangor, ME 04402-0596, (207)947-2575 [25085]

Atlantic Communications Inc., PO Box 596, Bangor, ME 04402-0596, (207)947-2575 [15039]

Atlantic Construction Fabrics Inc., 1801-A Willis Rd., Richmond, VA 23237, (804)271-2363 [7003]

Atlantic Corp., 8400 Triad Dr., Greensboro, NC 27409, (919)668-0081 [21639]

Atlantic Corp., 8400 Triad Dr., Greensboro, NC 27409, (919)668-0081 [16716]

Atlantic Detroit Diesel-Allison Inc., PO Box 950, Lodi, NJ 07644, (201)489-5800 [2265]

Atlantic F.E.C. Inc., PO Box 1488, Homestead, FL 33090, (305)247-8800 [4328]

Atlantic Filter Corp., 3112 45th St., West Palm Beach, FL 33407, (561)683-0101 [25564]

Atlantic Fitness Products, PO Box 300, Linthicum Heights, MD 21090-0300, (410)859-3538 [23670]

Atlantic Fitness Products Co., PO Box 300, Linthicum Heights, MD 21090-0300, (410)488-2020 [23526]

Atlantic Fluid Power, 111 Bridge Rd., Hauppauge, NY 11788, (516)234-3131 [15788]

Atlantic Hardware and Supply Corp., 601 W 26th St., New York, NY 10001, (212)924-0700 [13571]

Atlantic India Rubber Co., 1425 Lake Ave., Woodstock, IL 60098-7419, (815)334-9230 [24267]

Atlantic International Corp., PO Box 1657, Framingham, MA 01701, (508)875-6286 [20593]

Atlantic Microsystems Inc., 585 Grove St., Herndon, VA 20170, (703)478-2764 [20819]

Atlantic Mobile Homes and RV Supplies Corp., PO Box 7853, Greensboro, NC 27407, (910)299-4691 [2266]

Atlantic Pacific Industries, 4223 W Jefferson Blvd., Los Angeles, CA 90016, (213)766-9075 [13572]

Atlantic-Pacific Technologies, 450 E 10th St., Tracy, CA 95376, (209)836-4888 [8390]

Atlantic Paper & Twine Co. Inc., 85 York Ave., PO Box 443, Pawtucket, RI 02862, (401)725-0950 [21640]

Atlantic Plumbing Supply Co. Inc., 807 V St. NW, Washington, DC 20001, (202)667-6500 [23074]

Atlantic Pre-Hung Doors Inc., 143 W Concord, PO BOX 1258, West Concord, MA 01742, (978)369-5600 [7004]

Atlantic Premium Brands Ltd., 650 Dundee Rd., Ste. 370, Northbrook, IL 60062, (847)480-4000 [10464]

Atlantic Promotions, 17 Executive Park Dr. NE, Ste. 100, Atlanta, GA 30329-2222, (404)355-0515 [25565]

Atlantic Pump and Equipment Co., 3055 NW 84th Ave., Miami, FL 33122, (305)597-8300 [23527]

Atlantic Skates Inc., 12632 Sunset Ave., Ocean City, MD 21842-9662, (410)213-0680 [23528]

Atlantic Software, PO Box 299, Wenham, MA 01984, (508)922-4352 [5980]

Atlantic Solar Products Inc., 9351-J Philadelphia Rd., Baltimore, MD 21237, (410)686-2500 [8391]

Atlantic Tire Wholesaler, 7307 Pulaski Hwy., Baltimore, MD 21237, (410)866-6400 [2267]

Atlantic Track and Turnout Co., PO Box 1589, Bloomfield, NJ 07003, (973)748-5885 [23472]

Atlantic Tracy, Inc., PO Box 764, East Windsor, CT 06088-0764, (860)292-6091 [2989]

Atlantic Tracy Inc., 80 Access Rd., Warwick, RI 02886-1002, (401)736-0515 [2990]

Atlantic Trading Company Ltd., 225 W 34th St., Ste. 2015, New York, NY 10122, (212)268-4487 [22048]

Atlantic Trading Company Ltd., 225 W 34th St., Ste. 2015, New York, NY 10122, (212)268-4487 [15789]

Atlantic Veneer Corp., PO Box 660, Beaufort, NC 28516, (919)728-3169 [27283]

Atlantis Eyewear, Inc., 177 Elmdale Rd., North Scituate, RI 02857-1308, (401)353-4930 [19168]

Atlantis International, 4744 Kawanee Ave., Metairie, LA 70006, (504)455-6509 [22049]

Atlantis Plastics, Inc., PO Box 2118, Elkhart, IN 46515, (219)294-6502 [22930]

Atlantis Restaurant Equipment, 27 Industrial Park Rd., Saco, ME 04072, (207)284-7394 [24071]

Atlantis Software, 34740 Blackstone Way, Fremont, CA 94555, (510)796-2180 [5981]

Atlas Carpet Mills Inc., 2200 Saybrook Ave., Los Angeles, CA 90040-1720, (323)724-9000 [9693]

Atlas Chemical Inc., 2929 Commercial St., San Diego, CA 92113-1393, (619)232-7391 [4329]

Atlas Copco North America Inc., 1211 Hamburg Tpk., Wayne, NJ 07470, (973)439-3400 [13573]

Atlas Copco Tools Inc., 37735 Enterprise Ct. Ste.300, Farmington Hills, MI 48331-3480, (248)489-1260 [13574]

Atlas Diamond Co., 760 Market St., Ste. 765, San Francisco, CA 94102-2302, (415)433-5123 [17318]

Atlas Distributing, Inc., 44 Southbridge St., Auburn, MA 01501, (508)791-6221 [24912]

Atlas Distributing, Inc., 44 Southbridge St., Auburn, MA 01501, (508)791-6221 [10465]

Atlas Energy Systems Inc., 530 Baldwin Park Blvd., La Puente, CA 91746, (626)855-0485 [8392]

Atlas Fuel Oil Co., 1110 Bronx River Ave., Bronx, NY 10472, (718)893-4400 [22050]

Atlas Inc., 8550 Aetna Rd., Cleveland, OH 44105, (216)441-3800 [19789]

Atlas Lift Truck Rentals, 5050 River Rd., Schiller Park, IL 60176, (847)678-3450 [15790]

Atlas Machine and Supply Inc., 7000 Global Dr., Louisville, KY 40258-1976, (502)584-7262 [15791]

Atlas Marketing Co. Inc., PO Box 29100, Charlotte, NC 28229-9100, (704)847-8600 [10466]

Atlas Merchandising Co., 138-142 McKean Ave., Charleroi, PA 15022, (412)489-9561 [24072]

Atlas Metal and Iron Corp., 318 Walnut St., Denver, CO 80204, (303)825-7166 [19790]

Atlas Railroad Construction Co., PO Box 8, Eighty Four, PA 15330, (724)228-4500 [23473]

Atlas Reproduction Inc., PO Box 2901, Casper, WY 82602-2901, (307)237-9523 [20820]

Atlas Safety Equipment Co. Inc., 132 Industrial Dr., Birmingham, AL 35211-4444, (205)942-4070 [24677]

Atlas Screw and Specialty Co.; L.P., PO Box 41389, New Bedford, MA 02744-1389, (508)990-2054 [13575]

Atlas Steel Inc., 4221 W 700 S, Salt Lake City, UT 84104, (801)975-9669 [26755]

Atlas Steel Products Co., 7990 Bavaria Rd., Twinsburg, OH 44087-2252, (216)425-1600 [19791]

Atlas Supply Inc., 1736 4th Ave. S, Seattle, WA 98134, (206)623-4697 [4330]

Atlas Textile Company Inc., PO Box 911008, Commerce, CA 90091-1008, (213)888-8700 [15410]

Atlas Vegetable Exchange, PO Box 36A88, Los Angeles, CA 90036-1135, (213)749-4347 [10467]

Atlas Water Systems Inc., 86 Los Angeles St., Newton, MA 02458-1019, (617)244-8550 [25566]

Atomergic Chemetals Corp., 71 Carolyn Blvd., Farmingdale, NY 11735-1527, (516)694-9000 [4331]

ATS Machinery and Equipment Co., 515 S Maxwell Rd., Peoria, IL 61607, (309)697-5530 [15792]

ATS Money Systems Inc., 25 Rockwood Pl., Englewood, NJ 07631, (201)894-1700 [25567]

ATS Money Systems Inc., 25 Rockwood Pl., Englewood, NJ 07631, (201)894-1700 [5982]

Atsco Footwear Inc., 500 Bodwell St., Avon, MA 02322-1000, (508)583-7600 [24678]

Attention Medical Co., 1419 Dunn Dr., Carrollton, TX 75006, (972)245-0908 [18698]

Attorney's Briefcase, 519 17th St. FL. 7, Oakland, CA 94612-1527, (510)836-2743 [5983]

Attraction Services Corp., PO Box 176, North Woodstock, NH 03262-0176, (603)745-8720 [22828]

Atwater Creamery Co., PO Box 629, Atwater, MN 56209, (320)974-8820 [260]

Atwood Leather Cutting, PO Box 3882, Hickory, NC 28603-3882, (704)322-7020 [18373]

Aubford Enterprises, 9 Saratoga St., Lewiston, ME 04240-3527, (207)784-3828 [26401]

Aubuchon Company Inc.; W.E., 95 Aubuchon Dr., Westminster, MA 01473, (508)874-0521 [13576]

Auburn Merchandise Distributors Inc., 355 Main St., Whitinsville, MA 01588-1860, (508)234-9000 [10468]

Auburn Plastics and Rubber Inc., PO Box 19871, Indianapolis, IN 46219, (317)352-1565 [22931]

Aucoin and Miller Electric Supply Inc., PO Box 53122, Houston, TX 77052, (713)224-2400 [8393]

Auction Livestock, Inc., Old Highway 10 E, Perham, MN 56573, (218)346-3415 [17711]

Aucutt's General Store, 2600 Mabry Dr., Clovis, NM 88101-8372, (505)762-3333 [21392]

Aucutt's Paint Store, 2600 Mabry Dr., Clovis, NM 88101-8372, (505)762-3333 [21392]

Auddino's Italian Bakery Inc., 1490 Clara St., Columbus, OH 43211, (614)294-2577 [10469]

Audi of America Inc., 3800 Hamlin Rd., Auburn Hills, MI 48326, (313)340-5000 [20594]

Audio Acoustics, 800 N Cedarbrook Ave., Springfield, MO 65802, (417)869-0770 [25086]

Audio Supply Co., 1416 N Pennsylvania St., Indianapolis, IN 46202, (317)634-1016 [25087]

Audio-Tech Inc., 5600 Oakbrook Pky., Ste. 200, Norcross, GA 30093-1843, (404)448-3988 [25088]

Audio-Technica U.S. Inc., 1221 Commerce Dr., Stow, OH 44224, (330)686-2600 [8394]

Audio-Technica U.S., Inc., 1221 Commerce Dr., Stow, OH 44224, (330)686-2600 [25089]

Audio-Video Corp., 213 Broadway, Albany, NY 12204, (518)449-7213 [25090]

Audiovox Corp., 150 Marcus Blvd., Hauppauge, NY 11788, (516)231-7750 [5523]

Audiovox Specialized Applications LLC, 23319 Cooper Dr., Elkhart, IN 46514, (219)264-3135 [8395]

Audiovox Specialty Markets Co., 23319 Cooper Dr., Elkhart, IN 46514, (219)264-3135 [8395]

AUDISSEY, 841 Pohukaina St., Ste. B, Honolulu, HI 96813-5332, (808)591-2791 [8396]

Audria's Crafts, 6821 McCart, Ft. Worth, TX 76133, (817)346-2494 [20821]

Audubon Prints & Books, 9720 Spring Ridge Ln., Vienna, VA 22182, (703)759-5567 [3532]

Auer Steel & Heating Supply, 2935 W Silver Spring Dr., Milwaukee, WI 53209, (414)463-1234 [14328]

Auglaize Farmers Cooperative, PO Box 360, Wapakoneta, OH 45895, (419)738-2137 [261]

Augsburg Fortress Publishers, PO Box 1209, PO Box 1209, Minneapolis, MN 55440, (612)330-3300 [3533]

Augusta Cooperative Farm Bureau, 1205-B Richmond Rd., Staunton, VA 24401, (540)885-1265 [262]

Augusta Farmers Cooperative Co., 410 W Green St., Augusta, IL 62311, (217)392-2184 [17712]

Aungst Wholesale; Dan, 4570 Maple Dr., Walnutport, PA 18088-9709, (215)797-9475 [26402]

Aunt Mid Produce Co., 7939 W Lafayette, Detroit, MI 48209, (313)841-1420 [10470]

Aurafin Corp., 14001 NW 4th St., Sunrise, FL 33325, (954)846-8099 [17319]

Aurea Italia Inc., 16 Florence St., Providence, RI 02904-3527, (401)232-3303 [17320]

Auromere Inc., 1291 Weber St., Pomona, CA 91768, (909)629-0108 [14027]

Aurora Arts & Krafts, 1426 E 26th Ave., Anchorage, AK 99508-3935, (907)279-0330 [17321]

Aurora Cooperative Elevator Co., PO Box 209, Aurora, NE 68818, (402)694-2106 [263]

Aurora Packing Company Inc., PO Box 209, North Aurora, IL 60542, (630)897-0551 [10471]

The Auster Co. Inc., 51 S Water Market, Chicago, IL 60608-2209, (312)829-6550 [10472]

Austin Aircraft (HIE); D., RR 1, Box 397, Whitefield, NH 03598, (603)837-2627 [46]

Austin, D L Steel Supply Corp., PO Box 166, Collinsville, IL 62234, (618)345-7200 [19792]

Austin House Inc., PO Box 665, Buffalo, NY 14226-0665, (716)825-2650 [14028]

Austin Metal and Iron Company Inc., PO Box 2115, Austin, TX 78768, (512)472-6452 [19793]

Austin Quality Foods, Inc., 1 Quality Ln., Cary, NC 27513-2004, (919)677-3400 [10473]

Austinville Elevator, 77 Sunset St., Austinville, IA 50608, (515)847-2832 [17713]

Australian Outback Collection, PO Box 987, Evergreen, CO 80439-0987, (303)670-3933 [4790]

Autco, 10900 Midwest, St. Louis, MO 63132-1631, (314)426-6524 [24510]

Authentic Imports Inc., 372 5th Ave., Apt. 10H, New York, NY 10018-8110, (212)736-2121 [4791]

Authentic Sports Inc., 372 5th Ave., Apt. 10H, New York, NY 10018-8110, (212)736-2121 [4791]

Authentica Security Technology, 135 2nd Ave., Waltham, MA 02451, (781)290-0418 [5984]

Authorized Motor Parts, 525 S Jefferson Ave., St. Louis, MO 63103, (314)533-0243 [2268]

Authorized Refrigeration Parts Co., 301 S Vandeventer Ave., St. Louis, MO 63110, (314)371-2773 [14329]

Auto-Blankers, 1301 Alabama Ave., Flint, MI 48505, (810)767-4300 [19794]

Auto Body Paint and Supply, 339 4th Ave. W, Twin Falls, ID 83301-5816, (208)733-5731 [21393]

Auto Body Supply of Orem, 115 North 1200 West, Orem, UT 84057, (801)225-1155 [21394]

Auto Bolt & Nut Co., 4619 Perkins Ave., Cleveland, OH 44103-3595, (216)881-3913 [13577]

Auto-Bound, Inc., 909 Marina Village Pky., No. 678, Alameda, CA 94501, (510)521-8630 [3534]

Auto Chlor System Inc., 746 Poplar Ave., Memphis, TN 38105, (901)579-2300 [15040]

Auto Clutch/All Brake Inc., 5551 W Ogden Ave., Cicero, IL 60804-3507, (708)656-2100 [2269]

Auto Clutch & Parts Service Inc., 5551 W Ogden Ave., Cicero, IL 60804-3507, (708)656-2100 [2269]

Auto Collision Inc., PO Box 354, Jessup, MD 20794, (410)799-5680 [2270]

Auto Comm Engineering Corp., 3014 Cameron, Lafayette, LA 70506-1519, (318)232-9610 [5524]

Auto Components Inc., 1950 N Mannheim Rd., Melrose Park, IL 60160, (708)345-8675 [2271]

Auto Dealers Exchange of Illinois, 43363 Old Hwy. 41, Russell, IL 60075, (847)395-7570 [20595]

Auto Electric Sales and Service Co., PO Box 609, Ardmore, OK 73402, (580)223-8000 [2272]

Auto Parts Association, 1170 W Riverdale Rd., Ogden, UT 84405, (801)394-4700 [2273]

Auto Parts Club Inc., 5825 Oberlin St., No. 100, San Diego, CA 92121, (619)622-5050 [2274]

Auto Parts Depot Inc., 741 Windsor St., Hartford, CT 06120, (860)522-1104 [2275]

Auto Parts Wholesale, PO Box 3289, Bakersfield, CA 93385, (661)322-5011 [2276]

Auto Radio Specialists, 1335 Lincoln Way E, Mishawaka, IN 46544-2713, (219)255-6434 [25091]

Auto Safety House Inc., 2630 W Buckeye Rd., Phoenix, AZ 85009, (602)269-9721 [2277]

Auto Service and Tire Supermarts Inc., 5861 Roswell Rd. NE, Atlanta, GA 30328, (404)252-1603 [2278]

Auto Shred Recycling L.L.C., PO Box 17188, Pensacola, FL 32522, (904)432-0977 [26756]

Auto Suture Company U.S.A., 150 Glover Ave., Norwalk, CT 06856, (203)845-1000 [19169]

Auto Trends Inc., 9818 Grinnell, Detroit, MI 48213, (313)571-7300 [2279]

Auto-trol Technology Corp., 12500 N Washington St., Denver, CO 80241-2400, (303)452-4919 [5985]

Auto Truck Inc., 1160 N Ellis St., Bensenville, IL 60106, (708)860-5600 [2280]

Auto Wares Inc., 440 Kirtland St. SW, Grand Rapids, MI 49507, (616)243-2125 [2281]

Auto Wheel Service Inc., 1400 NW Raleigh St., Portland, OR 97209, (503)228-9346 [2282]

Auto Wholesale and Hartsville Paint Store, 1525 S 5th St., Hartsville, SC 29550, (803)332-8586 [21395]

AutoBike Inc., 108 Black Brook Rd., South Easton, MA 02375, (508)238-9651 [23529]

Autoline Industries Inc., 625 Enterprise Dr., Oak Brook, IL 60523-8813, (630)990-3200 [2283]

Automated Business Systems, 2332 N Wingate Pl., Meridian, ID 83642-7337, (208)344-8442 [20822]

Automated Data Systems Inc., PO Box 1076, Hickory, NC 28603-1076, (704)328-9365 [5986]

Automated Office Products Inc., 9700A M.L. King Jr., Lanham Seabrook, MD 20706, (301)731-4000 [20823]

Automated Office Systems, Inc., 12100 SW Garden Pl., Portland, OR 97223, (503)620-2800 [21050]

Automated Office Systems Inc., 6th Ave. N, PO Box 2404, Billings, MT 59105-0208, (406)245-3171 [20824]

Automated Office Systems of New England, 8 North St. R., Plymouth, MA 02360, (508)747-0808 [5987]

Automated Register Systems, Inc., 1437 S Jackson St., Seattle, WA 98144-2022, (206)325-8922 [5988]

Automatic Controls Co., 50222 W Pontiac Tr., Wixom, MI 48393-2023, (248)624-1990 [8397]

Automatic Equipment Sales of Virginia Inc., PO Box 27305, Richmond, VA 23261, (804)355-0651 [14330]

Automatic Firing Inc., 2100 Fillmore Ave., Buffalo, NY 14214, (716)836-0300 [14331]

Automatic Firing Inc., 2100 Fillmore Ave., Buffalo, NY 14214, (716)836-0300 [8398]

Automatic Ice & Beverage Inc., PO Box 110159, Birmingham, AL 35211-0159, (205)787-9640 [14332]

Automatic Pump and Equipment Company Inc., PO Box 26012, Beaumont, TX 77720-6012, (409)866-2314 [15793]

Automatic Vendors Inc., 2695 Hwy. 14A, Sturgis, SD 57785, (605)578-8500 [26261]

Automating Peripherals Inc., 310 N Wilson Ave., Hartford, WI 53027, (414)673-6815 [5989]

Automation Image Inc., 2650 Valley View Ln., Ste. 100, Dallas, TX 75234-6273, (972)247-8816 [5990]

Automoco Corp., 9142 Independance Ave., Chatsworth, CA 91311-5902, (818)882-6422 [2284]

Automotive Diagnostics, 8001 Angling Rd., Kalamazoo, MI 49002, (616)329-7600 [2285]

Automotive Distributors Inc., 10 Liberty Dr., Bangor, ME 04401, (207)848-2233 [2286]

Automotive Dryers Inc., PO Box 170, Cumming, GA 30028, (404)781-6653 [2287]

Automotive Electric and Supply Co., 935 Lindsay Blvd., Idaho Falls, ID 83402-1817, (208)523-1442 [2288]

Automotive Ignition Company Inc., 301 Meade St., PO Box 91039, Pittsburgh, PA 15221, (412)243-3080 [2289]

Automotive Importing Manufacturing Inc., 3920 Security Park Dr., Rancho Cordova, CA 95742, (916)985-8505 [2290]

Automotive Industries Inc., 2021 Sunnydale Blvd., Clearwater, FL 33765-1202, (904)355-7511 [2291]

Automotive International Inc., 11308 Tamarco Dr., Cincinnati, OH 45242, (513)489-7883 [4332]

Automotive Parts Distributors, 900b South St., Nashville, TN 37203, (615)259-2725 [2292]

Automotive Parts Headquarters Inc., 125 29th Ave. S, St. Cloud, MN 56301, (612)252-5411 [2293]

Automotive Parts Wholesaler, 131 Holton St., Brighton, MA 02135-1313, (617)437-8433 [2294]

Automotive Parts Wholesaler, 1870 Fillmore Ave., Buffalo, NY 14214, (716)891-5611 [2392]

Automotive Sales Co., 1801 N Black Cnyn Hwy., Phoenix, AZ 85009, (602)258-8851 [2295]

Automotive Service Inc., Box 2157, Reading, PA 19608, (215)678-3421 [22051]

Automotive Supply Associates, 129 Manchester, Concord, NH 03301, (603)225-4000 [2296]

Automotive Supply Co., PO Box 145, Appleton, WI 54912, (920)734-2651 [2297]

Automotive Trades Div., 3M Center Bldg. 223-6NW-01, St. Paul, MN 55144, (612)733-5547 [2298]

Automotive Wholesalers Co., PO Box 1676, Goldsboro, NC 27533, (919)735-3236 [2299]

Autoxport Inc., 111 Mill River Rd., Oyster Bay, NY 11771-2736, (212)349-1168 [2300]

Autron Inc., 5 Appleton St., Holyoke, MA 01040, (413)535-4200 [21641]

Autron Inc. Precision Rolls Division, 4205 McEwen Rd., Farmers Branch, TX 75234, (214)630-1210 [21642]

Autron Inc. Z Paper Div., 189 Van Rensselear St., PO Box 1271, Buffalo, NY 14240-1271, (716)853-7500 [21747]

Auxiliary Power International Corp., 4400 Ruffin Rd., PO Box 85757, San Diego, CA 92186-5757, (619)627-6501 [47]

AV Associates Inc., 1768 Storrs Rd., Storrs Mansfield, CT 06268-1207, (860)487-1330 [8399]

AV Tapehandlers, Bemis Bldg., 55 S Atlantic St., Ste. 1A, Seattle, WA 98134-1217, (206)621-9222 [25053]

AVAC Corp., 666 University Ave. W, St. Paul, MN 55104-4801, (651)222-0763 [15041]

AvAlaska, Inc., 4340 Postmark Dr., Anchorage, AK 99502, (907)248-7070 [48]

Avalon Distributing Inc., 1 Avalon Dr., PO Box 536, Canal Fulton, OH 44614-0536, (330)854-4551 [10474]

Avalon Ornamentals, 16515 E Davenport Rd., Winter Garden, FL 34787, (407)656-7687 [14810]

Avant Computer Associates Inc., 102 Powers Ferry Rd., Marietta, GA 30067-7558, (404)977-7255 [5991]

Avant Gardens Silk Plants, 6922 S Butte Ave., Tempe, AZ 85283-4151, (602)940-1903 [14811]

Avanti 4 International Corp., 42400 Garfield Rd., Ste. D, Clinton Township, MI 48038, (810)228-7090 [5992]

AVAS VIP, 55 Ruta Ct., South Hackensack, NJ 07606, (201)229-4270 [25092]

Avatar Alliance L.P., PO Box 1238, Orange, CT 06477-7238, (203)380-9377 [49]

Avatex Corp., 5910 N Central Expy., Dallas, TX 75206, (214)365-7450 [19170]

Avcom, Inc., 20827 Lorain Rd., Cleveland, OH 44126, (440)333-0111 [8400]

Avec Electronics Corp., 2002 Staples Mill Rd., Richmond, VA 23230, (804)359-6071 [8401]

AVED Rocky Mountain Inc., 4090 Youngfield St., Wheat Ridge, CO 80033-3862, (303)422-1701 [8402]

Avent Inc., 80 Cutter Mill Rd., Great Neck, NY 11021, (516)466-7000 [5993]

Averitt Lumber Company Inc., PO Box 2217, Clarksville, TN 37042-2217, (931)647-8394 [7005]

AVerMedia Technologies Inc., 1161 Cadillac Ct., Milpitas, CA 95035-3055, (510)770-9899 [5994]

Avery Book Stores, Inc., 308 Livingston St., Brooklyn, NY 11217, (718)858-3606 [3535]

AVES Audio Visual Systems Inc., PO Box 740620, Houston, TX 77274-0620, (713)783-3440 [25093]

AVest Inc., 205 Express St., Plainview, NY 11803, (516)433-1700 [8403]

Avesta Sheffield—North American Division, Inc., 425 N Martingale Rd., No. 2000, Schaumburg, IL 60173-2218, (847)517-4050 [19795]

Avfuel Corp., 47 W Ellesworth Rd., Ann Arbor, MI 48104, (734)663-6466 [22052]

AVH Inc., PO Box 1887, Sioux City, IA 51102-1887, (712)277-4223 [4792]

Avian Kingdom Supply Inc., 6350 LBJ Fwy., Ste. 151, Dallas, TX 75247, (972)631-2473 [27075]

Aviatech Corporation, 912 Airport Rd., Roanoke, TX 76262, (817)430-4784 [50]

Aviation Distributors Inc., 1 Capital Dr., Lake Forest, CA 92630, (949)586-7558 [51]

Aviation Sales Co. (Miami, Florida), 6905 NW 25th St., Miami, FL 33122-1898, (305)592-4055 [52]

Avico Distributing Inc., 729 Broad, Utica, NY 13501-1313, (315)724-8243 [10475]

Avionix Medical Devices, PO Box 9669, Midland, TX 79708, (915)686-0188 [18699]

Avis Enterprises Inc., 900 Avis Dr., Ann Arbor, MI 48108, (313)761-2800 [23530]

AVK II Inc., PO Box 310, Lyndonville, VT 05851-0310, (802)626-9274 [24073]

AVM Products, Inc., PO Box 667, Chester Springs, PA 19425, (215)827-7039 [27076]

Avnet Computer Inc., 3011 S 52nd St., Tempe, AZ 85282, (602)414-6700 [5995]

Avon Appliance & Electric Co. Inc., PO Box 407, Avon, CT 06001-0407, (860)678-1927 [15042]

Avon Electrical Supplies, Inc., 60 Hoffman Ave., Hauppauge, NY 11788, (516)582-4770 [8404]

Avon-Glendale Home Medical Equipment and Supplies Inc., PO Box 17776, Los Angeles, CA 90017, (213)487-1180 [19171]

Avon-Lakewood Nursery Inc., 39115 Detroit Rd., Avon, OH 44011, (440)934-5832 [264]

Avon North America Inc., 805 W 13th St., Cadillac, MI 49601-9281, (616)775-1345 [23531]

Avon Products Inc., 1345 Avenue of the Americas, New York, NY 10105-0302, (212)282-5000 [14029]

Avon Products Inc. Newark Regional Area, 2100 Ogletown Rd., Newark, DE 19712, (302)453-7700 [14030]

Avon Products Inc. Northeast Regional Area, 2100 Ogletown Rd., Newark, DE 19712, (302)453-7700 [19172]

Avonlea Books, PO Box 74, Main Sta., White Plains, NY 10602-0074, (914)946-5923 [3536]

AVSEEDS, PO Box 16025, Denver, CO 80216, (303)320-7500 [254]

A.W. Industries, 8415 Ardmore Rd., Landover, MD 20785, (301)322-1000 [13027]

Awalt Wholesale Inc., PO Box 907, Fairfield, TX 75840, (903)389-2159 [2301]

Award Pet Supply, 1610 B, I-70 Dr. SW, Columbia, MO 65203, (573)445-8249 [27077]

Awareness and Health Unlimited, 3509 N High St., Columbus, OH 43214, (614)262-7087 [14031]

AWC, Inc., 6655 Exchequer Dr., Baton Rouge, LA 70809, (504)752-1100 [24319]

AWC Propane Co., 813 N Virginia Ave., Roswell, NM 88201, (505)622-1130 [22053]

AWD International Inc., 410 Oakmears Cres, Ste. 202, Virginia Beach, VA 23462-4235, (757)625-0883 [13028]

AWS Companies Inc., 2113 Merrill Field Dr., Anchorage, AK 99501-4117, (907)272-4397 [53]

Axchem Inc., 317 Washington St., Manistee, MI 49660-1259, (231)723-2521 [4333]

Axchem Solutions Inc., 317 Washington St., Manistee, MI 49660-1259, (231)723-2521 [4333]

Axelrod Distributors, 4646 King Graves Rd., Vienna, OH 44473-9700, (216)721-6010 [10476]

Axelrod Foods Inc., PO Box 795, Paterson, NJ 07533, (973)684-0600 [10477]

Axelrods Tire Inc., Rte. 66, Portland, CT 06480, (860)342-0102 [2302]

Axis Communications Inc., 4 Constitution Way, No. G, Woburn, MA 01801-1042, (781)938-1188 [20825]

Axis Electronics Inc., 22 Cessna Ct., Gaithersburg, MD 20879-4145, (301)840-9640 [8405]

Axon Import Export Corporation, 36 Compton Court, Basking Ridge, NJ 07920, (908)647-2346 [4793]

Axton Candy and Tobacco Co., PO Box 32219, Louisville, KY 40232, (502)634-8000 [26262]

Axton-Cross Company Inc., PO Box 6529, Holliston, MA 01746, (508)429-6766 [4334]

Axxis Inc., PO Box 2106, Richmond, IN 47375-2106, (765)935-1538 [25094]

Ayers Art Co., 2504 Hwy. 30 E, Kearney, NE 68847-9763, (308)237-3566 [26403]

Ayers Oil Company Inc., PO Box 229, Canton, MO 63435, (314)288-4466 [22054]

Ayre Acoustics Inc., 2300 Central Ave Ste. B, Boulder, CO 80301, (303)442-7300 [15043]

Ayre & Ayre Silversmiths, PO Box 1049, Moriarty, NM 87035-1049, (505)832-4344 [17322]

Azco Steel Co., 100 Midland Ave., Saddle Brook, NJ 07663-6152, (201)791-0600 [19796]

Azcon Corp., 13733 S Ave. O, Chicago, IL 60633-1547, (312)362-0066 [7006]

Azerty Inc., 13 Centre Dr., Orchard Park, NY 14127, (716)662-0200 [5996]

Azimuth Corp. (Orlando, Florida), 3600 Rio Vista Ave., Ste. A, Orlando, FL 32805-6005, (407)849-0480 [54]

Aztec Business Machines Inc., 3663 Via Mercado, La Mesa, CA 91941, (619)660-1300 [20826]

Aztec Supply Co., 954 N Batavia St., Orange, CA 92867-5502, (714)771-6580 [25888]

Aztec Supply Co., 954 N Batavia St., Orange, CA 92867, (714)771-6580 [22932]

Aztech Controls Corp., 324 S Bracken Ln., Chandler, AZ 85224-4700, (480)782-6000 [16717]

Azure Standard, 79709 Dufur Valley Rd., Dufur, OR 97021, (541)467-2230 [10478]

B & A Distributing Inc., 1800 Post Rd., Warwick, RI 02886-1534, (401)739-9707 [14032]

B & A Paint Co., 287 Neil Ave., Columbus, OH 43215, (614)224-6161 [21396]

B. Abrams and Sons Inc., PO Box 1761, Harrisburg, PA 17105, (717)233-7927 [26785]

B & B Appliance Parts of Mobile, PO Box 6707, Mobile, AL 36660-0707, (205)478-8485 [15044]

B & B Beer Distributing, 505 Ball NE, Grand Rapids, MI 49503-2011, (616)458-1177 [1492]

B & B Buyers Inc., RR 1, Box 26, Chinook, MT 59523-9703, (406)357-3800 [17714]

B & B Cattle Co., PO Box 1850, Palestine, TX 75802, (903)729-6277 [17715]

B and B Fisheries Inc., 715 E International, Daytona Beach, FL 32118, (904)252-6542 [10479]

B and B Group Inc., 12521 Oxnard St., North Hollywood, CA 91606, (818)985-2939 [23575]

B & B Imports, 3020 N Piedras, Ste. B, El Paso, TX 79930, (915)562-0309 [1493]

B & B Medical Service Inc., 2236 NW 10th St., Bldg. 103, Oklahoma City, OK 73107-5658, (405)235-9548 [18700]

B and B Motor and Control Inc., 39-40 Cresent St., Long Island City, NY 11101, (718)784-1313 [2303]

B & B Office Supply Inc., 3923 Garth Rd., Baytown, TX 77521-3105, (281)422-8151 [20827]

B and B Paper Converters Inc., 12500 Elmwood Ave., Cleveland, OH 44111-5987, (216)941-8100 [21643]

B & B Parts Distributing, 1805 W 34th St., Houston, TX 77018-6105, (713)222-6633 [2304]

B and B Produce Inc., PO Box 415, Johnson City, TN 37605, (423)926-2191 [10480]

B & B Specialty Foods, 4050 Stoneleigh Rd., Bloomfield Hills, MI 48302, (248)645-2096 [10481]

B and B Surplus Inc., 7020 Rosedale Hwy., Bakersfield, CA 93308, (805)589-0381 [19797]

B and C Auto Supply, 5491 Minnesota Dr., Anchorage, AK 99518, (907)562-2047 [2305]

B & C Distributors, 143 Space Park S, Nashville, TN 37211, (615)831-7074 [8406]

B C Sales Co., Inc., 2395 SW 1st Ave., Fruitland, ID 83619-3745, (208)452-4707 [18701]

B & D Auto Salvage & Repair, PO Box 456, Winner, SD 57580-0456, (605)842-2877 [2306]

B and F System Inc., 3920 S Walton Walker, Dallas, TX 75236-0036, (214)333-2111 [15411]

B & G Beauty Supply Inc., 1300 E Plumb Ln., Reno, NV 89502-6915, (702)829-2704 [14033]

B & G Export Management Associates, 300 High St., PO Box 71, Holyoke, MA 01041, (413)536-4565 [21644]

B-G Lobster and Shrimp Corp., 95 South St., New York, NY 10038, (212)732-3060 [10482]

B & G Optics, 1320 Unity St., Philadelphia, PA 19124, (215)289-2480 [19173]

B & G Wholesalers Inc., 337 28th Ave., Nashville, TN 37209, (615)320-7292 [1494]

B & I Wholesale, 12 Davisville Rd., PO Box 70, Davisville, WV 26142, (304)485-6500 [7103]

B & J Cattle Co., 18th & Minnesota Ave., Billings, MT 59103, (406)252-6072 [17716]

B & J Enterprises Inc., 1001 Highway 25 N, Heber Springs, AR 72543-2010, (501)362-3727 [18702]

B & J Industrial Supply Co., PO Box 80526, Seattle, WA 98108, (206)762-4430 [15794]

B & J Oil Co., 402 S B St., Muskogee, OK 74403, (918)687-4181 [22055]

B-J Pac-A-Part, 410 25th Ave. S, Great Falls, MT 59405-7147, (406)761-4487 [4575]

B-J Pac-A-Part, 410 25th Ave. S, Great Falls, MT 59405-7147, (406)761-4487 [24074]

B and J Sales Inc., 1105 E Lafayette St., Bloomington, IL 61701, (309)662-1373 [1495]

B J's Wholesale Club Inc., PO Box 9601, Natick, MA 01760, (508)651-7400 [13029]

B & K Industries Inc., 2600 Elmhurst Rd., Elk Grove Village, IL 60007, (708)773-8585 [23075]

B & L Equipment, PO Box 2278, Syracuse, NY 13220-2278, (315)458-9500 [7007]

B & L Leather Co., 8125 Winchester Rd., New Market, AL 35761-7856, (205)379-3550 [4794]

B & L Scales, 503 Wicks Ln., Billings, MT 59105-4444, (406)248-4531 [24320]

B-M-B Company Inc., 9th & Vermont, Holton, KS 66436, (785)364-2186 [265]

B & M Provision Co., 1040 N Graham, Allentown, PA 18103, (215)434-9611 [10483]

B & N Industries, 111 Albany Ave., Freeport, NY 11520-4715, (516)623-1440 [13578]

B & S Bolts Corp., 2610 Arkansas Ave., Norfolk, VA 23513-4402, (757)855-2000 [13579]

B Sharp Co., 74 Jennifer Ln., Effort, PA 18330, (717)629-3952 [27078]

B/T Western Corp., 4 Upper Newport Plz., No. 200, Newport Beach, CA 92660, (714)476-8424 [2307]

B and T Wholesale Distributors Inc., 846 Lind SW, Renton, WA 98055, (206)235-3592 [13580]

B & V Inc., 5701 Central NE, Albuquerque, NM 87108, (505)265-8911 [17323]

B and W Farm Center Inc., PO Box 876, Cordele, GA 31015, (912)273-3398 [266]

B & W Hosiery, Inc., 332 1st Ave. SW, Hickory, NC 28602-2939, (704)327-7005 [4795]

B.A. Box Tank and Supply Inc., PO Box 547, Beeville, TX 78104, (512)358-1984 [22056]

Baba International Inc., 7177 Pembrooke Rd., Pembroke Pines, FL 33023, (954)989-1100 [17324]

Babbitt Steam Specialty Co., PO Box 51208, New Bedford, MA 02745, (508)995-9533 [16718]

Babco, Inc., 60-10 Maurice Ave., Maspeth, NY 11378 [8407]

Babco International Inc., PO Box 27187, Tucson, AZ 85726-7187, (520)628-7596 [23532]

Babikow Greenhouses, 7838 Babikow Rd., Baltimore, MD 21237, (410)391-4200 [14812]

Babsco, PO Box 1447, Elkhart, IN 46517, (219)293-0631 [8408]

Babsco Supply, PO Box 1447, Elkhart, IN 46517, (219)293-0631 [8408]

Babush Conveyor Corp., 10605 W Glenbrook Ct., Milwaukee, WI 53224, (414)362-7100 [15795]

Babush Corp., 10605 W Glenbrook Ct., Milwaukee, WI 53224, (414)362-7100 [15795]

Babush Corp., PO Box 660, Menomonee Falls, WI 53052, (414)255-5300 [15796]

Baby Bliss Inc., 227 Spring St., PO Box 9, Middleville, MI 49333, (616)795-3341 [4796]

Baby Needs Inc., 605 Cameron St., Burlington, NC 27215-5915, (919)227-6202 [4797]

Bacharach-Rasin Co., 802 Gleneagles Ct., Towson, MD 21204, (410)825-6747 [23533]

Back to Basics Products Inc., 11660 S State St., Draper, UT 84020-9455, (801)571-7349 [15412]

Back Bay News Distributors, 51 Melcher St., Boston, MA 02210, (617)350-7170 [3537]

Backstage Pass Productions and Distributing Inc., 6930 Valjean Ave., Van Nuys, CA 91406-4747, (818)786-2222 [25095]

Bacon Building Materials Inc.; Henry, PO Box 7012, Issaquah, WA 98027-7012, (206)391-8000 [7008]

Bacon & Co. Inc., PO Box 78, Knoxville, TN 37901-0078, (865)523-9181 [4798]

Bacon Company Inc.; Edward R., PO Box 21550, San Jose, CA 95151, (408)288-9500 [7009]

Bacon Creek Gun Shop, 1205 Cumberland Falls Hwy., Corbin, KY 40701-2718, (606)528-4860 [23534]

Bacon Material Handling; Davis, 5000 Valley Blvd., Los Angeles, CA 90032, (323)227-1921 [25889]

Bacon Pamphlet Service, Inc., 187 Hand Hollow Rd., East Chatham, NY 12060, (518)794-7722 [3538]

Bacon Products Co. Inc., PO Box 22187, Chattanooga, TN 37422, (423)892-0414 [267]

Badalament Inc., 515 10th St., Detroit, MI 48216, (313)963-0746 [10484]

Badalament Inc., 515 10th St., Detroit, MI 48216, (313)963-0746 [10485]

Baddour International, 4300 New Getwell Rd., Memphis, TN 38118, (901)365-1191 [14034]

Badeaux Co.; Edward, 311 Jackson, PO Box 710, Thibodaux, LA 70302, (504)447-3338 [26263]

Badger Bearing, 244-A W Pioneer Rd., Fond du Lac, WI 54936, (920)921-8816 [2795]

Badger Body and Truck Equipment Co., 6336 Grover St., Omaha, NE 68106, (402)558-5300 [2308]

Badger Corrugating Co., PO Box 1837, La Crosse, WI 54601, (608)788-0100 [7010]

Badger Farmers Cooperative, PO Box 97, Badger, SD 57214, (605)983-3241 [268]

Badger Farmers Cooperative, PO Box 97, Badger, SD 57214, (605)983-3241 [10486]

Badger Liquor Company Inc., 850 S Morris St., Fond du Lac, WI 54936, (920)922-0550 [1496]

Badger Popcorn Co., 2914 Latham Dr., Madison, WI 53701, (608)274-5058 [10487]

Badger Shooters Supply Inc., PO Box 397, Owen, WI 54460, (715)229-2101 [23535]

Badger Trailer and Equipment Corp., 415 S 3rd St., Milwaukee, WI 53204, (414)271-8273 [2309]

Badger Truck Center Inc., 2326 W St. Paul Ave., Milwaukee, WI 53201-1530, (414)344-9500 [20596]

Badgerland Farm Center, PO Box 119, Whitewater, WI 53190, (414)473-2410 [269]

Baer Co.; Ralph A., 9100 N Vancouver Ave., Portland, OR 97217-7560, (503)283-1180 [26404]

Baer Sport Center, Rte. 6 E, Honesdale, PA 18431, (570)253-2000 [20597]

Baer Supply Co., 909 Forest Edge Dr., Vernon Hills, IL 60061, (847)913-2237 [13581]

Bag Bazaar Ltd., 1 E 33rd St., New York, NY 10016, (212)689-3508 [18374]

The Bag Connection Inc., 459 SW 9th St., Dundee, OR 97115, (503)538-8180 [15797]

Bagatelle, 1425 N Pershing, Wichita, KS 67208-2211, (316)684-5662 [10488]

Baggs Co.; L R, 483 N Frontage Rd., Nipomo, CA 93444, (805)929-3544 [8409]

Bagoy & Associates, Inc.; John P., PO Box 877489, Wasilla, AK 99687, (907)229-0567 [9225]

Bagoy and Associates Inc.; John P., 3210 Rampart Dr., Anchorage, AK 99501-3133, (907)274-8531 [8410]

Bags Direct, Inc., 3482 Oakcliff Rd., Ste. B-2, Atlanta, GA 30340, (770)454-7276 [22933]

Bags R Us, Inc., 3482 Oakcliff Rd., Ste. B-2, Atlanta, GA 30340, (770)454-7276 [22933]

Bahlsen, Inc., 1 Quality Ln., Cary, NC 27513-2004, (919)677-3400 [10473]

BAI Distributors Inc., 2312 NE 29 Ave., Ocala, FL 34470, (352)732-7009 [8411]

BAI Inc., 21 Airport Blvd., South San Francisco, CA 94080, (650)872-1955 [55]

Bailes Inc.; Buck, PO Box 11172, Charlotte, NC 28220-1172, (704)342-0650 [26405]

Bailey Company Inc., PO Box 80565, Nashville, TN 37208, (615)242-0351 [15798]

Bailey Distributing Co.; E.M., 1000 S 8th St., Paducah, KY 42001, (502)442-4306 [22057]

Bailey Lumber Co., 5200 Christmas Pl., Waldorf, MD 20601, (301)274-4116 [7011]

Bailey Nurseries Inc., 1325 Bailey Rd., St. Paul, MN 55119, (612)459-9744 [14813]

Bailey Seed Company, Inc., PO Box 13517, Salem, OR 97309, (503)362-9700 [270]

Bailey's Slaughter House, PO Box 696, Hardwick, VT 05843, (802)472-5578 [17717]

Baillie Lumber Co., 4002 Legion Dr., Hamburg, NY 14075, (716)649-2850 [7012]

Baily and Company Inc.; Joshua L., PO Box 9501, Hoboken, NJ 07030-9501, (201)656-7777 [25972]

Baird Steel Inc., 2926 W Main St., Whistler, AL 36612, (205)457-9513 [19798]

Baisley Lumber Corp., 193 Horton Ave., Lynbrook, NY 11563, (516)599-8100 [7013]

Baja Products Ltd., 515 Airport Rd., Salisbury, NC 28144-8446, (704)633-0498 [23536]

Bakalars Brothers Sausage Co., 2219 South Ave., La Crosse, WI 54601, (608)784-0384 [10489]

Baker Agri Sales Inc., 3415 W Main St., Sedalia, MO 65301, (816)826-5955 [17718]

Baker Book House Co., 6030 E Fulton SE, Ada, MI 49301, (616)676-9185 [3539]

Baker and Brother Inc.; H.J., 595 Summer St., Stamford, CT 06901-1407, (203)328-9200 [271]

Baker Candy Co. Inc., 12534 Lake City Way N, Seattle, WA 98125, (206)363-5227 [10490]

Baker Distributing, North Shrewsbury Rd., North Clarendon, VT 05759, (802)773-3397 [1497]

Baker Distributing Co., 7892 Baymeadows Way, Jacksonville, FL 32256, (904)733-9633 [14333]

Baker Distributing Co., 2113 N Hamilton St., PO Box 27527, Richmond, VA 23261, (804)353-7141 [14334]

Baker Hardwood Lumber Co., 3131 Hoover Ave., National City, CA 91950-7221, (619)263-8102 [7014]

Baker Hardwood Lumber Co., PO Box 936, National City, CA 91951-0936, (619)263-8102 [27284]

Baker-Hauser Co., 1601 W Detweiller Dr., Peoria, IL 61615-1644, (309)692-5151 [14335]

Baker Hydro Inc., 1812 Tobacco Rd., Augusta, GA 30906, (706)793-7291 [23537]

Baker Implement Co., PO Box 787, Kennett, MO 63857-0787, (573)888-4646 [272]

Baker Implement Co., PO Box 787, Kennett, MO 63857, (573)888-4646 [273]

Baker Inc.; J., 555 Turnpike St., Canton, MA 02021, (781)828-9300 [24679]

Baker Linen Co.; H.W., PO Box 544, Mahwah, NJ 07430, (201)825-2000 [15413]

Baker Rubber Inc., PO Box 2438, South Bend, IN 46680, (219)237-6200 [24268]

Baker-Stephens Tire Co., 305 N 1st St., Artesia, NM 88210, (505)734-6001 [2310]

Baker & Taylor, PO Box 6885, Bridgewater, NJ 08807-0885, (908)541-7305 [5997]

Baker and Taylor, 2709 Water Ridge Pkwy., Charlotte, NC 28217, (704)357-3500 [3540]

Baker and Taylor Inc., 2709 Water Ridge Pky., Charlotte, NC 28217, (704)357-3500 [3541]

Baker Truck Equipment, State Rte. 60 at Mynes Rd., PO Box 482, Hurricane, WV 25526, (304)722-3814 [2311]

Bakers Chocolate and Coconut, PO Box 398, Memphis, TN 38101, (901)766-2100 [10491]

Bakers Choice, 21400 Telegraph Rd., Southfield, MI 48034, (248)827-7500 [10492]

Baker's Fine Jewelry and Gifts, 760 W 22nd St., Norfolk, VA 23517, (757)625-2529 [17325]

Baker's Kneads, 5598 E 10 Mile Rd., Warren, MI 48091, (734)758-4440 [24075]

Baker's Nursery, 3408 Colwell Ave., Tampa, FL 33614, (813)932-6527 [14814]

Bakersfield AG Co. Inc., 34710 7th Standard Rd., Bakersfield, CA 93312, (805)399-9191 [274]

Bakersfield Sandstone Brick Co. Inc., PO Box 866, Bakersfield, CA 93302, (805)325-5722 [7015]

Bakersfield Sandstone Brick Company Inc., PO Box 866, Bakersfield, CA 93302, (805)325-5722 [27285]

Bakertowne Company, Inc., 136 Cherry Valley Ave., West Hempstead, NY 11552, (516)489-6002 [15414]

Bakery Management Corp., 15625 NW 15th Ave., Miami, FL 33169, (305)623-3838 [10493]

Baklayan Garbis, 531 S Broadway, Baltimore, MD 21231, (410)276-2234 [24680]

BAL RV Products Group, 365 W Victoria St., Compton, CA 90220, (310)639-4000 [15799]

Balco Metals Inc. Recycling World, 9780 S Meridian Blvd., Ste. 180, Englewood, CO 80112-5926 [19799]

Baldridge Lumber Co.; J.C., PO Box 13537, Albuquerque, NM 87192, (505)298-5531 [7016]

Baldwin Paper Co., 161 Ave. of the Americas, New York, NY 10013, (212)255-1600 [21645]

Baldwin Steel Co., 500 Rte 440, Jersey City, NJ 07305, (201)333-7000 [19800]

Bale Ready-Mix Concrete; Gary, 16351 1/2 Construction Cir., Irvine, CA 92614, (949)786-9441 [7017]

Bales Continental Commission Co., PO Box 1337, Huron, SD 57350, (605)352-8682 [17719]

Bales & Truitt Company Inc., PO Box 818, Kernersville, NC 27285-0818, (910)996-3531 [14336]

Balfour Co.; L.G., 7211 Circle South Rd., Austin, TX 78745-6603, (512)222-3600 [17326]

Balfour Maclaine Corp., 61 Broadway, Ste. 2700, New York, NY 10006-2704, (212)269-0800 [10494]

Balfour Printing Company Inc., 320 W 7th, Little Rock, AR 72201-4210, (501)374-2363 [20828]

Ball Auto Tech Inc., 2298 Young Ave., Memphis, TN 38104-5755, (901)278-4922 [8412]

Ball Furniture & Appliances, 8075 Reading Rd., Ste. 408, Cincinnati, OH 45237-1417, (513)761-2600 [13238]

Ball Horticultural Co., 622 Town Rd., PO Box 2698, West Chicago, IL 60185-2698, (630)231-3600 [14815]

Ball Pipe & Supply; Leif, 31240 W Cedar Valley Dr., Westlake Village, CA 91362-4035, (805)495-8458 [23076]

Ball Seed Co., 622 Town Rd., West Chicago, IL 60185, (630)231-3500 [14816]

Ball Stalker Co., 1636 Northeast Expwy., Atlanta, GA 30318, (404)679-8999 [20829]

Ball Tire and Gas Inc., 620 Ripley Blvd., Alpena, MI 49707, (517)354-4186 [2312]

Ballanda Corp., 10020 Pioneer Blvd., Ste. 105, Santa Fe Springs, CA 90670, (562)801-6192 [17327]

Ballantyne Cashmere USA Inc., 499 7th Ave., 17th Fl., New York, NY 10018, (212)736-4228 [4799]

Ballard and Co.; W.P., PO Box 12246, Birmingham, AL 35202, (205)251-7272 [4576]

Ballard Enterprises Inc., 7 Broadway, Concord, NH 03301-2843, (603)225-5666 [26406]

Ballenger Automotive Service, 125 W Pierce, Council Bluffs, IA 51503-4396, (712)322-6636 [2313]

Balloon Express, 2906 Pailersville Rd., Louisville, KY 40205, (502)459-6337 [26407]

Balloon House, 3590 Utah Ave. NE, Iowa City, IA 52240-9283, (319)354-3471 [26408]

Balloonery Inc., 5240 Benson Ave., Baltimore, MD 21227-2512, (410)242-6380 [26409]

Balloons, Logos & T-Shirts, 220 W Perkins Ave., Sandusky, OH 44870-4707, (419)625-6968 [26410]

Balloons & Things, 993 Waimanu St., Honolulu, HI 96814, (808)538-0076 [26411]

Ballpark Inc., 10791 W 107th Cir., Broomfield, CO 80021-7331, (303)425-1480 [26412]

Bally Retail Inc., 1 Bally Pl., New Rochelle, NY 10801, (914)632-4444 [24681]

Balno Incorporated, 13506 W 72nd St., Shawnee Mission, KS 66216-3721, (913)631-9979 [5998]

Balthauser & Moyer, Exchange Bldg., West Fargo, ND 58078-1100, (701)282-4245 [17720]

Baltimore Hydraulics Inc., 708 E 25th St., Baltimore, MD 21218-5436, (410)467-8088 [16719]

Baltimore Scrap Corp., 1600 Carbon Ave., Baltimore, MD 21226, (410)355-4455 [19801]

Baltimore Stationery Co., PO Box 16010, Baltimore, MD 21218, (410)366-6000 [21954]

Baltimore & Washington Truck Equipment, Inc., 1001 E Ridgeville Blvd., PO Box 450, Mt. Airy, MD 21771, (301)831-7020 [2314]

Balzer Pacific Equipment Co., 2136 SE 8th St., Portland, OR 97214, (503)232-5141 [7018]

Bama Companies Inc., PO Box 4829, Tulsa, OK 74159, (918)592-0778 [10495]

Bama Shrimp Co., 9 8th St., Palacios, TX 77465, (512)972-3932 [12097]

Bamal Fastener Corp., 23240 Industrial Park Dr., Farmington Hills, MI 48335, (248)477-8101 [13582]

Bamberger Molding Compounds Inc.; C., PO Box 67, Carlstadt, NJ 07072, (201)933-6262 [26757]

Bana Parts Inc., PO Box 23388, New Orleans, LA 70183-0388, (504)734-0076 [25096]

Banana Educational Software Distributors, 2501 W 84th St., Bloomington, MN 55431, (612)944-0104 [5999]

Banana Supply Company Inc., 3030 NE 2nd Ave., Miami, FL 33137, (305)573-7610 [10496]

Banash and Son Inc.; David, 16 Rainbow Pond Dr., Walpole, MA 02081-3454, (617)482-5478 [4800]

Banfi Products Corp., 1111 Cedar Swamp Rd., Glen Head, NY 11545-2121, (516)626-9200 [1498]

Bangert's Computer Systems, 506 Jefferson St., Burlington, IA 52601-5426, (319)752-5484 [6000]

Bangor Steel, 123 Dowd Rd., Bangor, ME 04401, (207)947-2773 [19802]

Banian Trading Co., 2252 Main St., Ste. 9 W, Chula Vista, CA 91911, (619)423-9975 [4801]

Banjo's Performancenter Inc., 64 Cabinwood Dr., Hendersonville, NC 28792-7644, (704)684-7814 [2315]

Bank and Office Interiors, 5601 6th Ave. S, Seattle, WA 98108, (206)768-8000 [13030]

Banking Forms Supply Company Inc., PO Box 210, Marysville, MI 48040, (810)364-5000 [20830]

Banko Enterprises Inc., 2124 Hanover Ave., Allentown, PA 18103, (215)434-0147 [1499]

Banks Lumber Company Inc., PO Box 2299, Elkhart, IN 46515, (219)294-5671 [7019]

Banks Lumber Company Inc., PO Box 2299, Elkhart, IN 46515, (219)294-5671 [27286]

Banner Aerospace Inc., PO Box 20260, Washington, DC 20041, (202)478-5790 [56]

Banner Place Nursery, RR 3, Box 510, Sophia, NC 27350-9803, (919)861-1400 [14817]

Banner Service Corp., 494 E Lies Rd., Carol Stream, IL 60188, (630)653-7500 [19803]

Banner Systems Inc., PO Box 3-302, Milford, CT 06460, (203)878-6524 [4577]

Banner of Truth, 63 E Louther St., PO Box 621, Carlisle, PA 17013, (717)249-5747 [3542]

Banner Wholesale Grocers Inc., 115 S Water Market St., Chicago, IL 60608, (312)421-2650 [10497]

Banner Wholesale Grocers Inc., 115 S Water Market St., Chicago, IL 60608, (312)421-2650 [10498]

Banta Foods Inc., PO Box 8246, Springfield, MO 65801, (417)862-6644 [10499]

Baptist Electronics Supply Company Inc., 419 S Mauvaisterre St., Jacksonville, IL 62650, (217)245-6063 [8413]

Baptist Spanish Publishing House, PO Box 4255, El Paso, TX 79914, (915)566-9656 [3543]

Bar-B-Que Industries Inc., 4460 W Armitage Ave., Chicago, IL 60639, (773)227-5400 [11413]

Bar Beverage Control Inc., 4540 E Paris Ave. SE, A, Grand Rapids, MI 49512-5444, (616)698-8828 [14337]

Bar Code Applications Inc., 816 Peace Portal Way, No. 113, Blaine, WA 98231, (604)451-7878 [8414]

Bar-H-Implement Inc., Rte. 1, Stone Lake, WI 54876, (715)865-6211 [275]

Bar Harbor Lobster Co., 2000 Premier Row, Orlando, FL 32809, (407)851-4001 [10500]

Bar Lazy K Bar Ranch Inc., PO Box 337, Presho, SD 57568-0337, (605)669-2767 [17721]

Bar-S Foods Co., PO Box 29049, Phoenix, AZ 85038, (602)264-7272 [10501]

Baraboo-Sysco Food Services Inc., 910 South Blvd., Baraboo, WI 53913, (608)356-8711 [10502]

Barbara's Bakery Inc., 3900 Cypress Dr., Petaluma, CA 94954, (707)765-2273 [10503]

Barbee-Neuhaus Implement Co., 2000 W Expwy. 83, Weslaco, TX 78596, (956)968-7502 [276]

Barber Cabinet Co. Inc., 2957 Collier St., Indianapolis, IN 46241-5903, (317)247-4747 [13031]

Barber-Nichols Inc., 6325 W 55th Ave., Arvada, CO 80002, (303)421-8111 [8415]

Barber and Ross Co., PO Box 1294, Leesburg, VA 20177-1294, (703)478-1970 [7020]

Barbero Bakery Inc., 51-61 Conrad, Trenton, NJ 08611-1011, (609)394-5122 [10504]

Barber's Poultry Inc., PO Box 363, Broomfield, CO 80038, (303)466-7338 [10505]

Barbey Electronics Corp., PO Box 2, Reading, PA 19603, (610)376-7451 [8416]

Barboglio; Jan, 509 N Montclair Ave., Dallas, TX 75208-5450, (214)688-0020 [4802]

Barborie Fashions, 490 W 18th St., Hialeah, FL 33010-2622, (305)883-5089 [4803]

Barbour Inc., 55 Meadowbrook Dr., Milford, NH 03055-4613, (603)673-1313 [4804]

Barbour Marine Supply, 410 Hedrick St., PO Box 248, Beaufort, NC 28516, (252)728-2136 [18451]

Barb's Knitting Machines & Supplies, 870 West 100 South, Blackfoot, ID 83221-2016, (208)684-4391 [25973]

Barbuscak and Associates; John, 3856 W 12 Mile Rd., Berkley, MI 48072-1111, (248)544-2800 [13310]

Barcardi Imports, Inc., 2100 Biscayne Blvd., Miami, FL 33137, (305)573-8511 [1500]

Barcardi-Martini U.S.A., Inc., 2100 Biscayne Blvd., Miami, FL 33137, (305)573-8511 [1500]

Barclay Dean Interiors, 1917 120th Ave. NE, Bellevue, WA 98005, (425)451-8940 [13032]

Barclay Marine Distributors Corp., 2323 W Fulton St., Chicago, IL 60612, (312)829-0500 [18452]

Barclay Marine Distributors Corp., 24600 Maplehurst Dr., Clinton Township, MI 48036, (810)469-9910 [18453]

Barclay Marine Distributors Corp., 1755 Buerkle Rd., White Bear Lake, MN 55110, (612)770-8515 [18454]

Barclay Marine Distributors Corp., 55 Design Dr., Kansas City, MO 64116 [18455]

Barclay Press, 110 S Elliott Rd., Newberg, OR 97132-2144, (503)538-7345 [3544]

Barco Industries Inc., 1020 MacArthur Rd., Reading, PA 19605-9404 [13583]

Barco Municipal Products Inc., PO Box 45507, Omaha, NE 68145-0507, (402)334-8000 [24511]

Bardahl Manufacturing Corp., PO Box 70607, Seattle, WA 98107, (206)783-4851 [22058]

Bardon Trimount Inc., PO Box 39, Burlington, MA 01803, (617)221-8400 [7021]

Barenbrug U.S.A., PO Box 820, Boardman, OR 97818-0820, (503)481-4001 [277]

Barentsen Candy Co., PO Box 686, Benton Harbor, MI 49023-0686, (616)927-3171 [26264]

Barentsen Candy Co., PO Box 686, Benton Harbor, MI 49023-0686, (616)927-3171 [10506]

Barer and Sons; B., PO Box 1492, WalLa Walla, WA 99362, (509)529-3060 [26758]

Barfield Inc., PO Box 025367, Miami, FL 33102-5367, (305)871-3900 [57]

Bargain City, 14 Pinewood Dr., Englishtown, NJ 07726, (732)536-7626 [4805]

Barham and Co.; J.T., 22711 Main St., Capron, VA 23829, (804)658-4239 [17722]

Barjan Products, L.P., 2751 Morton Dr., East Moline, IL 61244-1802, (309)755-4546 [2316]

Bark River Culvert and Equipment Co., PO Box 10947, Green Bay, WI 54307-0947, (414)435-6676 [7022]

Barker & Co., 7745 E Redfield, Ste. 100, Scottsdale, AZ 85260, (602)483-0780 [23538]

Barker-Jennings Corp., PO Box 11289, Lynchburg, VA 24506, (804)846-8471 [2317]

Barker-Jennings Corp., PO Box 11289, Lynchburg, VA 24506, (804)846-8471 [13584]

Barker Pipe Fittings Inc., 271 Lancaster Ave., Frazer, PA 19355, (215)644-7400 [16720]

Barker Steel Co. Inc. Lebanon Div., PO Box 436, Lebanon, NH 03766, (603)448-6030 [7023]

Barkett Fruit Co. Inc., 205 Deeds Dr., Dover, OH 44622-9652, (330)364-6645 [10507]

Barnaby Inc., 1620 De Kalb Ave., Sycamore, IL 60178, (815)895-6555 [20831]

Barnacle Marine, Inc., 13 B St., South Boston, MA 02127, (617)268-5500 [4111]

Barnacle Seafood, 5301 NW 35th Ave., Ft. Lauderdale, FL 33309-6315, (954)486-8000 [10508]

Barnebey and Sutcliffe Corp., 835 N Cassady Ave., Columbus, OH 43219, (614)258-9501 [14338]

Barnes Co.; A.O., PO Box 2539, Anderson, IN 46018, (765)643-5364 [15800]

Barnes Motor and Parts Co., PO Box 1207, Wilson, NC 27893, (252)243-2161 [2318]

Barnes Wholesale Drug Company Inc., PO Box 17010, Inglewood, CA 90308, (310)641-1885 [19174]

Barnett Brass and Copper Inc., PO Box 2317, Rt. 3333 Lenox Ave., Jacksonville, FL 32203-2317, (904)384-6530 [23077]

Barnett Brothers Brokerage Co. Inc., 2509 74th St., Lubbock, TX 79423, (806)745-7575 [10509]

Barnett Implement Co. Inc., PO Box 666, Mt. Vernon, WA 98273, (206)424-7995 [278]

Barnett Inc., PO Box 2317, Jacksonville, FL 32203-2317, (904)384-6530 [23078]

Barnett Millworks Inc., PO Box 389, Theodore, AL 36590, (334)443-7710 [7024]

Barnett Supply Co. Inc., PO Box 40891, Memphis, TN 38174-0891, (901)278-0440 [14339]

Barneys Auto Salvage Inc., 2700 N Cliff Ave., Sioux Falls, SD 57104-0972, (605)338-7041 [2319]

Barneys Pumps Inc., PO Box 3529, Lakeland, FL 33802-3529, (941)665-8500 [23079]

Barnie's Coffee and Tea Company Inc., 340 N Primrose Dr., Orlando, FL 32803, (407)894-1416 [10510]

Barno Electronics Corp., 5403 W Smithfield St., PO Box 93, Mc Keesport, PA 15135-1259, (412)751-5966 [8417]

Barno Radio Company, 5403 W Smithfield St., PO Box 93, Mc Keesport, PA 15135-1259, (412)751-5966 [8417]

Barnsley-Weis Associates Inc., 10130 SW North Dakota St., Tigard, OR 97223-4236, (503)624-8758 [15045]

Baron, 15321 Transistor Ln., Huntington Beach, CA 92649-1143, (714)898-1255 [2320]

Baron Drawn Steel Corp., PO Box 3275, Toledo, OH 43607, (419)531-5525 [19804]

Baron Services, Inc., 4930 Research Dr. NW, Huntsville, AL 35805, (256)881-8811 [6001]

Baron Telecommunications, 1204 Railroad Ave., No. 101, Bellingham, WA 98225-5008, (360)734-5082 [5525]

Barone Inc., 5879 W 58th Ave., Arvada, CO 80002, (303)424-4497 [15801]

Baronet Coffee Inc., PO Box 987, Hartford, CT 06143-0987, (860)527-7253 [10511]

Baronet Gourmet Coffee Inc., PO Box 987, Hartford, CT 06143-0987, (860)527-7253 [10511]

Barons Wholesale Clothiers, 27888 Orchard Lake Rd., Farmington Hills, MI 48334-3756, (248)539-0525 [4806]

Barr Enterprises Inc., W 7276 Chickadee Rd., Greenwood, WI 54437, (715)267-6335 [27079]

Barrett Company Inc.; L.W., PO Box 19430, Denver, CO 80219, (303)934-5755 [13311]

Barrett & Co. Publishers, PO Box 2008, Learned, MS 39154, (601)885-2288 [3545]

Barrett Hardware and Industrial Supply Co., 324 Henderson Ave., Joliet, IL 60432, (815)726-4341 [13585]

Barretts Equine Sales Ltd., PO Box 2010, Pomona, CA 91769, (909)629-3099 [17723]

Barringer Distributing Company Inc.; R.H., 1620 Fairfax Rd., Greensboro, NC 27407-4139, (336)854-0555 [1501]

Barron Farmers Union Cooperative Services Inc., 505 E Grove Ave., Barron, WI 54812, (715)537-3181 [279]

Barron Motor Inc., PO Box 1327, Cedar Rapids, IA 52406, (319)393-6220 [2321]

Barrow Industries Inc., 5 Dan Rd., Canton, MA 02021, (617)828-6750 [25974]

Barrow Industries Inc., 75 Crestridge Dr., Suwanee, GA 30024-3573 [25975]

Barrow Industries Inc. Merrimac Textile, 3 Edgewater Dr., Norwood, MA 02062, (781)440-2666 [25976]

Barrow's Greenhouses, 312 Main St., Gorham, ME 04038, (207)839-3321 [14818]

Barrows Used Auto Parts, 49 Townfarm, Monmouth, ME 04259-9801, (207)268-4262 [2322]

Barry Grain and Feed Inc., PO Box 902, Hempstead, TX 77445, (409)826-6190 [280]

Barry Manufacturing Company, Inc., Bubier St., Lynn, MA 01901, (781)598-1055 [24682]

Barry Metals Company Inc., 3014 N 30th Ave., Phoenix, AZ 85017, (602)484-7186 [26759]

Barry Optical Co., Inc., 281 Clinton St., PO Box 456, Hempstead, NY 11550, (516)481-9656 [19175]

Barry Pumps Inc.; R.E., 415 Atwood Ave., Cranston, RI 02920-4358, (401)942-5300 [25568]

Barry Sales Inc., 1155 Park Ave., Cranston, RI 02910-3145, (401)943-0090 [21397]

Barry's Office Service Inc., 1370 University Ave., Morgantown, WV 26505-5518, (304)296-2594 [20832]

Barstad and Donicht Inc., 795 Aladdin Ave., San Leandro, CA 94577, (510)357-0777 [2323]

Barstow Company Inc.; A.G., 1211 Madera Way, Riverside, CA 92503, (909)372-2900 [21398]

Barstow Truck Parts and Equipment Co., 2431 W Main St., Barstow, CA 92311, (760)256-1086 [2324]

Barta International Sales Corp., 2400 Vallejo St., San Francisco, CA 94123, (415)346-6090 [17724]

Bartells Co.; E. J, PO Box 5477, Kennewick, WA 99336, (509)582-4985 [16721]

Bartells Co.; E.J., PO Box 4160, Renton, WA 98057-4160, (206)228-4111 [7025]

Bartkus Oil Co., 3501 Pearl St., Boulder, CO 80301, (303)442-6000 [22462]

Bartky Mineralogical Enterprises Inc., 375 Walnut St., Livingston, NJ 07039-5011, (973)992-9451 [17328]

Bartlett Bearing Co. Inc., 4320 H St., Philadelphia, PA 19124, (215)743-8963 [16722]

Bartlett and Co. (Headquarters), 4800 Main St., Kansas City, MO 64112, (816)753-6300 [17725]

Bartlett Cooperative Association Inc., PO Box 4675, Bartlett, KS 67332, (316)226-3322 [281]

Bartley Tile Concepts Inc., 6931 Arlington Rd., Bethesda, MD 20814, (301)913-9113 [7026]

Barton Brands California Inc., PO Box 6263, Carson, CA 90749-6263, (310)604-0017 [1502]

Barton and Co.; E.C., PO Box 4040, Jonesboro, AR 72403-4040, (501)932-6673 [7027]

Barton Group Inc., 1505 Corporate Ave., Memphis, TN 38132, (901)345-5294 [15802]

Barton Inc., 55 E Monroe St., Ste. 1700, Chicago, IL 60603, (312)346-9200 [1503]

Barton Solvents Inc., PO Box 221, Des Moines, IA 50301, (515)265-7998 [4335]

Barton Truck Center Inc., PO Box 30154, Memphis, TN 38130, (901)345-5294 [16723]

Barton's Greenhouse & Nursery, Hwy. 26, Alabaster, AL 35007, (205)664-2964 [14819]

Bartsch Greenhouses, 567 Wible Run Rd., Pittsburgh, PA 15209, (412)486-3174 [14820]

Bascom Elevator Supply Association, PO Box 305, Bascom, OH 44809, (419)937-2233 [282]

Base Inc., 5307 E Pine St., Tulsa, OK 74115-5329, (918)732-2540 [10512]

Basic Convenience Foods, 2675 Industrial Dr., No. 202, Ogden, UT 84401, (801)399-0440 [2325]

Basic Fibres Inc., 6019 S Manhattan Pl., Los Angeles, CA 90047, (213)753-3491 [26760]

Basic Service Corp., 2525 Imlay City Rd., Lapeer, MI 48446-3215, (810)667-1800 [24321]

Basic Wire & Cable Co., 3900 N Rockwell, Chicago, IL 60618-3719, (773)266-2600 [8418]

Basin Pipe & Metal, 6960 Hwy. 70 N, Alamogordo, NM 88310, (505)437-6272 [19805]

Basins Inc., PO Box 845, Wheatland, WY 82201, (307)322-2479 [7028]

Basketville Inc., PO Box 710, Putney, VT 05346, (802)387-5509 [13312]

Baskin-Robbins USA Co., 1918 S Texas Ave., Bryan, TX 77802-1831, (409)779-0091 [10513]

Basnight and Company Inc.; W.H., PO Box 1365, Ahoskie, NC 27910, (919)332-3131 [7029]

Basnight & Sons; S.H., PO Drawer 249, Carrboro, NC 27510-0249, (919)942-3158 [13586]

Bass Inc.; Rudolf, 45 Halladay St., Jersey City, NJ 07304, (201)433-3800 [15803]

Bass Woodworking Machinery, 1080 E 29th St., Hialeah, FL 33013-3518, (305)691-2277 [15804]

Bass Woodworking Machinery, Inc., PO Box 173932, Hialeah, FL 33017-3932, (305)691-2277 [15805]

Bassett Co.; Russ, 8189 Byron Rd., Whittier, CA 90606, (562)945-2445 [13033]

Bassett Dairy Products Inc., 2197 S Byron Butler Pkwy., Perry, FL 32347, (850)584-5149 [10514]

Bassi Distributing Co.; George, PO Box 1169, Watsonville, CA 95077, (408)724-1028 [25890]

Bassin Inc.; Jerry, 4250 Coral Ridge Dr., Coral Springs, FL 33065, (954)346-4024 [25097]

Bastian Inc.; Owen M., 333 W Broad St., Quakertown, PA 18951, (215)536-7939 [9694]

Baszile Metals Service Inc., 2554 E 25th St., Los Angeles, CA 90058, (213)583-6922 [19806]

Bat Rentals, 2771 S Industrial Rd., Las Vegas, NV 89109-1199, (702)731-1122 [7030]

Bata Shoe Co. Inc., U.S Hwy. 40, 4501 Pulaski Hwy., Belcamp, MD 21017, (410)272-2000 [24683]

Bates Manufacturing Co., 36 Newburgh Rd., Hackettstown, NJ 07840, (908)852-9300 [20833]

Bath Beach Nurseries, Inc., 8410 New Utrecht Ave., Brooklyn, NY 11214, (718)256-8336 [14821]

Bath/Kitchen & Tile Supply Co., 103 Greenbank Rd., Wilmington, DE 19808, (302)992-9200 [15415]

Batliner Paper Stock Co., 2501 Front St., Kansas City, MO 64120, (816)483-3343 [21646]

Baton Rouge Landscape Co., 12136 Oakwild Ave., Baton Rouge, LA 70810-7109, (504)766-1203 [14822]

Baton Rouge Lumber Company Inc., 8675 S Choctaw, Baton Rouge, LA 70895, (225)927-2400 [7031]

Baton Rouge Lumber Company LLC, 8675 S Choctaw, Baton Rouge, LA 70895, (225)927-2400 [7031]

Baton Rouge Wholesale, PO Box 3928, Baton Rouge, LA 70821, (504)343-9551 [1504]

Batson Co.; Louis P., PO Box 3978, Greenville, SC 29608, (864)242-5262 [15806]

Batteries Direct, 713 Gladstone St., Parkersburg, WV 26101-5661, (304)428-2296 [8419]

Batteries Plus L.P., 625 Walnut Ridge Dr.Ste. 106, Hartland, WI 53029, (414)369-0690 [2326]

Battery Products Inc., PO Box 589, Hartland, WI 53029-0589, (262)367-2411 [8420]

Battery Specialties Inc., 3530 Cadillac Ave., Costa Mesa, CA 92626, (714)755-0888 [8421]

Battery and Tire Warehouse Inc., 625 N Fairview Ave., St. Paul, MN 55104, (612)646-2265 [2327]

Battery Warehouse, 324 Martin St., Dover, DE 19901, (302)674-4020 [8422]

Battey Machinery Co., PO Box 33, Rome, GA 30162-0033, (706)291-4141 [15807]

Battin Power Service; John, 5004 SE Junction Creek Blvd., Portland, OR 97222, (503)777-3065 [8423]

Battle Creek Farmers Cooperative, PO Box 10, Battle Creek, NE 68715, (402)675-2375 [283]

Battlefield Police Supply Inc., 7221 Nathan Ct., Manassas, VA 20109-2436, (703)330-1902 [24684]

Batts Distributing Co.; James B., 6616 Fleetwood Dr., Raleigh, NC 27612-1837, (919)782-2982 [9695]

Batts Distributing Co.; James B., 2146 Stantonsburg Rd., Wilson, NC 27893-1000, (919)243-2134 [9696]

Batty & Hoyt Inc., 1444 Emerson St., Rochester, NY 14606-3086, (716)647-9400 [20834]

Baucoms Nursery Farm, 10020 John Russell Rd., Charlotte, NC 28213, (704)596-3220 [14823]

Bauer Built Inc., Hwy. 25 S, PO Box 248, Durand, WI 54736-0248, (715)672-4295 [2328]

Bauer Cycle Supply Inc., 404 3rd Ave. N, Minneapolis, MN 55401, (612)333-2581 [23539]

Bauer & Foss, Inc., 3940 Gantz Rd., Columbus, OH 43213-4845, (614)575-1112 [1505]

Bauer Optical Co., 23-25 Spring St., PO Box 350, Ossining, NY 10562-0350, (914)944-9016 [19176]

Baum Iron Co., 1221 Harney St., Omaha, NE 68102, (402)345-4122 [15808]

Baum Wine Imports Inc., 3870 Paris St., No. 3, Denver, CO 80239-3333, (303)322-3421 [1506]

Baumann Paper Company Inc., PO Box 13022, Lexington, KY 40512, (859)252-8891 [21647]

Baumbach Manufacturing Co.; E.A., 650 W Grand Ave., Elmhurst, IL 60126, (630)941-0505 [16724]

Baume and Mercier, 663 5th Ave., New York, NY 10022, (212)593-0444 [17329]

Baumer Electric Ltd., 122 Spring St., No. C-6, Southington, CT 06489, (860)621-2121 [15809]

Baumgarten Distributing Company, Inc., 1618 W Detweiller Dr., Peoria, IL 61615-1610, (309)691-4200 [1507]

Bavaria House Corp., 1121 S Front St., Wilmington, NC 28401, (910)251-0998 [1508]

Bawamba Software Inc., 150 E Olive Ave., Burbank, CA 91502, (818)843-1627 [6002]

Baxter and Co. Inc.; A.J., 10171 W Jefferson Ave., River Rouge, MI 48218, (313)843-1153 [16725]

Baxter Co.; J.H., PO Box 5902, San Mateo, CA 94402-0902, (650)349-0201 [7032]

Baxter Healthcare Corp. Converters/Custom Sterile Div., 1500 Waukegan Rd., Mc Gaw Park, IL 60085, (847)473-1500 [18703]

Baxter International Inc. (Deerfield, Illinois), 1 Baxter Pkwy., Deerfield, IL 60015, (847)948-2000 [19177]

Baxter International Representatives Inc., 303 W Sunset Rd., Ste. 100B, San Antonio, TX 78209, (210)829-7793 [13587]

Baxter Knitting Co., 1555 33rd St. SW, Hickory, NC 28602-4639, (704)327-0131 [4807]

Baxter Scientific Products, 1430 Waukegan Rd., Mc Gaw Park, IL 60085, (847)689-8410 [24322]

Baxter Warehouse, 7800 Browning Rd., Pennsauken, NJ 08109, (609)486-4000 [1479]

Bay Area Data Supply Inc., 1282 Hammerwood Ave., Sunnyvale, CA 94089, (408)745-6435 [20835]

Bay Colony Mills Inc., PO Box 2396, Providence, RI 02906-0396, (401)831-3505 [15416]

Bay Corp., PO Box 124, Colchester, VT 05446-0124, (802)863-2653 [24685]

Bay Grove Nurseries, Inc., PO Box 377, Perryville, MD 21903-0377, (410)397-3337 [14824]

Bay Houston Towing Co., PO Box 3006, Houston, TX 77253, (713)529-3755 [284]

Bay Merchandising Inc., 68 Old Mill Bottom Rd. N, Annapolis, MD 21401-5418, (410)757-5926 [24686]

Bay Microfilm Inc., 1115 E Arques Ave., Sunnyvale, CA 94086, (408)736-7444 [25098]

Bay Microfilm Inc. Library Microfilms, 1115 E Arques Ave., Sunnyvale, CA 94086, (408)736-7444 [20836]

Bay Paper Co. Inc., 1 Bay Paper Dr., Mobile, AL 36607, (205)476-9791 [20837]

Bay Polymer Corp., 44530 Grimmer Blvd., Fremont, CA 94538, (510)490-1791 [26761]

Bay Rag, 6250 NW 35th Ave., Miami, FL 33147, (305)691-5502 [4808]

Bay Rubber Co., 404 Pendleton Way, Oakland, CA 94621, (510)635-9151 [24269]

Bay Rubber Co., 404 Pendleton Way, Oakland, CA 94621, (510)635-9151 [16726]

Bay State Computer Group Inc., 52 Roland St., Boston, MA 02129, (617)623-3100 [6003]

Bay State Computer of New Jersey Inc., 375 Raritan Ctr. Pkwy., Edison, NJ 08837, (732)417-1122 [6004]

Bay State Florist Supply, Inc., 36 Martone Pl., Springfield, MA 01109, (413)736-7771 [14825]

Bay State Lobster Company Inc., PO Box 347, Lynn, MA 01905-0647, (617)523-4588 [10515]

Bay View Food Products Co., 2606 N Huron Rd., Pinconning, MI 48650, (517)879-3555 [10516]

Baye & Rhodes, 181 Joaquin Circle, Danville, CA 94526-3014, (510)837-9147 [10517]

Bayer Wood Products, 5122 Dorr St., Toledo, OH 43615-3849, (419)536-7416 [26413]

Bayjet Inc., 410 W Thorpe Rd., Las Cruces, NM 88005-5830, (505)526-3353 [58]

Baylor Biomedical Services, 2625 Elm St., Dallas, TX 75226, (214)820-2176 [19178]

Baynes Co. Inc.; John, 16234 Sasanoa Dr., Cornelius, NC 28031-8740, (704)527-2440 [24687]

Bayou Caddy Fisheries Inc., PO Box 44, Lakeshore, MS 39558, (228)467-4332 [10518]

Bayou Import-Export Corp., 2110 31st Ct., Kenner, LA 70065, (504)461-8797 [15810]

Bayou Land Seafood, 1008 Vincent Berard Rd., Breaux Bridge, LA 70517, (318)667-6118 [10519]

Bays Corp., PO Box 1455, Chicago, IL 60690-1455, (312)346-5757 [10520]

Bayside Distributing Inc., PO Box 710, Epping, NH 03042-0710, (603)679-2302 [1509]

Bayside Fuel Oil Depot Corp., 1776 Shore Pkwy., Brooklyn, NY 11214, (718)372-9800 [22059]

Bazar Inc. Sales Co., 793 Waterman Ave., East Providence, RI 02914-1713, (401)434-2595 [17330]

BB & W Electronics, 2137 Euclid, Berwyn, IL 60402-1800, (708)749-1710 [8424]

BBC Fasteners Inc., 4210 Shirley Ln., Alsip, IL 60803, (708)597-9100 [13588]

BBC Industrial Supply Co., 3501 Aldebaran St., Las Vegas, NV 89102, (702)876-4225 [16727]

BCI Inc., 1009 E Miracle Mile, Box 3961, McAllen, TX 78502, (956)630-2761 [4809]

BCS*A, 385 Belmarin Keyes Blvd., Novato, CA 94949, (415)883-7392 [6005]

BCSR Inc., 12015 115th Ave. NE, Ste. 130, Kirkland, WA 98034, (425)823-1188 [6006]

BCT International Inc., 3000 Northeast 30th Place, 5th Fl., Ft. Lauderdale, FL 33306, (954)563-1224 [21648]

BCVG Inc., 2761 Fruitland Ave., Vernon, CA 90058, (213)589-2224 [4810]

BDD Inc., 4318 E University Dr., Phoenix, AZ 85034-7318, (602)437-0549 [15417]

BDT Engineering Company Inc. - Industrial Products Div., 4810 N 124th St., Milwaukee, WI 53225-3601, (414)353-3112 [14340]

BE Implemented Partners Ltd., PO Box 752, Brownfield, TX 79316, (806)637-3594 [285]

Beach Growers, 9176 W Atlantic Ave., Delray Beach, FL 33446, (561)498-3030 [14826]

Beach Sales Inc., 80 VFW Pkwy., Revere, MA 02151, (781)284-0130 [25099]

Beach Supply Co., 19061 Crystal St., Huntington Beach, CA 92648, (714)847-7144 [22060]

Beachcombers International Inc., PO Box 250, Ft. Myers, FL 33902, (941)731-2111 [13313]

Beachley Hardy Seed Co., PO Box 3147, Shiremanstown, PA 17011, 800-442-7391 [286]

Beachville USA, 1936 Mateo, Los Angeles, CA 90021, (213)623-9233 [5266]

Beacon Distributing Co., 325 E Nugget Ave., Sparks, NV 89431, (702)323-3101 [1510]

Beacon Liquor and Wine, 325 E Nugget Ave., Sparks, NV 89431, (702)331-3400 [1511]

Beacon Sporting Goods Inc., 1240 Furnace Brook Pkwy., Quincy, MA 02169-4718, (617)479-8537 [23540]

Beacon Supply Co., 821 Industry Rd., Kenner, LA 70062-6868, (504)467-9200 [18456]

Beall Transport Equipment Co, PO Box 17095, Portland, OR 97217, (503)285-5959 [2329]

Beal's Royal Glass and Mirror Inc., 3350 Ali Baba Ln., Las Vegas, NV 89118, (702)736-8788 [7033]

Beam of Denver Inc., 750 E 71st Ave. B, Denver, CO 80229-6800, (303)286-7123 [15046]

Bean Lumber Co.; Buddy, 3900 Malvern Ave., Hot Springs National Park, AR 71901, (501)262-2820 [7034]

Bean and Sons Co.; D.D., PO Box 348, 207 Peterborough St., Jaffrey, NH 03452, (603)532-8311 [24512]

Bean's Beauty Supply, 4405 Main St., Philadelphia, PA 19127, (215)487-3333 [14035]

Bear Cat Manufacturing Inc., 3650 N Sabin Brown Rd., Wickenburg, AZ 85390, (520)684-7851 [7035]

BEAR Computers Inc., 12727 Northup Way., Ste. 8, Bellevue, WA 98005-1917, (425)869-5900 [6007]

Bear Paw Lumber Corp., PO Box 20, Fryeburg, ME 04037, (207)935-2951 [7036]

Bear Valley Communications Inc., PO Box 27496, Denver, CO 80227-0496, (303)987-2680 [5526]

Beard and Associates Inc.; Robert A., 4918 70th St., Kenosha, WI 53142-1626, (414)658-1778 [22934]

Beard Hardwood Lumber Inc.; E.N., PO Box 13608, Greensboro, NC 27415, (919)378-1265 [7037]

Beard Oil Pipeline Supply Inc., PO Box 485, Mt. Pleasant, MI 48804-0485, (517)773-9957 [22061]

Beardslee Transmission Equipment Company Inc., 27-22 Jackson Ave., Long Island City, NY 11101, (718)784-4100 [2330]

Beardsley Farmers Elevator Co., PO Box 297, Beardsley, MN 56211, (612)265-6933 [287]

Bearing Belt Chain Co., 3501 Aldebaran St., Las Vegas, NV 89102, (702)876-4225 [16727]

Bearing Belt and Chain Inc., 729 E Buckeye Rd., Phoenix, AZ 85034, (602)252-6541 [16728]

Bearing Distributors, 8000 Hub Pkwy., Cleveland, OH 44125, (216)642-9100 [16729]

Bearing Distributors, PO Box 3490, East Chicago, IN 46312, (219)398-3300 [16730]

Bearing Distributors Inc., 140 Eastern Ave., Bensenville, IL 60106, (708)595-9034 [2331]

Bearing Distributors Inc., 25 S 6th St., PO Box 537, Princeton, IL 61356, (815)875-3386 [15811]

Bearing Distributors Inc., 3002 Executive Dr., PO Box 16364, Greensboro, NC 27406, (919)724-8401 [2332]

Bearing Distributors Inc., 4400 Indiana Ave., Ste. B, PO Box 4453, Winston-Salem, NC 27105, (919)661-1199 [2333]

Bearing Distributors Inc., 1036 Atando Ave., PO Box 33716, Charlotte, NC 28233, (704)375-0061 [16731]

Bearing Distributors Inc., 2039 Meeting St., PO Box 7527, Charleston, SC 29405, (803)747-0473 [2334]

Bearing Distributors Inc., 930 Stadium Rd., PO Box 2347, Columbia, SC 29202, (803)799-0834 [2335]

Bearing Distributors Inc., 1814 Trade St., PO Box 4109, Florence, SC 29502, (803)665-1500 [2336]

Bearing and Drivers Inc., PO Box 4325, Macon, GA 31201, (912)743-6711 [2337]

Bearing Engineering, 5861 Christie Ave., Emeryville, CA 94608, (510)653-3913 [2338]

Bearing Engineers Inc., 27 Argonaut, Aliso Viejo, CA 92656, (949)586-7442 [16732]

Bearing Enterprises Inc., 203 Brighton Ave., Boston, MA 02134, (617)782-1400 [16733]

Bearings and Drives Inc., 9508 E Rush St., South el Monte, CA 91733, (626)575-1307 [16734]

Bearings & Drives, Inc., 2216 Toledo Dr., Albany, GA 31705, (912)432-5158 [2339]

Bearings and Drives, Inc., PO Box 1842, Athens, GA 30603-1842, (706)546-8640 [16735]

Bearings & Drives, Inc., 607 Lower Poplar St., PO Box 4325, Macon, GA 31213, (912)743-6711 [2340]

Bearings & Drives, Inc., Hwy. 41 S, PO Box 828, Tifton, GA 31793, (912)382-2125 [2341]

Bearings & Drives, Inc., 206 S Toombs St., PO Box 1225, Valdosta, GA 31601, (912)242-0214 [2342]

Bearings & Drives Inc., 3012 Freeman St., PO Box 5267, Chattanooga, TN 37406, (423)624-8333 [15812]

Bearings and Drives, Inc., 363 1st St. SW, PO Box 83, Cleveland, TN 37312, (423)472-3291 [16736]

Bearings and Drives, Inc., 2540 NW 74th Pl., Gainesville, FL 32653, (352)375-0568 [16737]

Bearings & Drives Unlimited, Inc., Bethlehem Pike & Cherry Ln., Souderton, PA 18964, (215)723-0938 [16738]

Bearings Inc., PO Box 6925, Cleveland, OH 44101-9986, (216)881-8900 [16739]

Bearings Incorporated of Kentucky, PO Box 17286, Louisville, KY 40217, (502)637-1445 [16740]

Bearings & Industrial Supply Co., Inc., 431 Irmen Dr., Addison, IL 60101, (630)628-1966 [16741]

Bearings Service & Supply, 1327 N Market, Box 7497, Shreveport, LA 71137-7497, (318)424-1447 [16742]

Bearings Service & Supply, Inc., 2129 Peters Rd., Harvey, LA 70058-1736, (504)366-4111 [16743]

Bearings & Transmission, 1301 E Voorhies, Danville, IL 61832, (217)443-2460 [2343]

Beasley Ford Inc.; Carl, PO Box 3115, York, PA 17402-3115, (717)755-2911 [20598]

Beattie Farmers Union Cooperative Association, PO Box 79, Beattie, KS 66406, (785)353-2237 [17726]

Beattie Farmers Union Cooperative Association, PO Box 79, Beattie, KS 66406, (785)353-2237 [288]

Beattie Systems Inc., 2407 Guthrie Ave. NW, Cleveland, TN 37311-3651, (423)479-8566 [22829]

Beatty Implement Co., PO Box 288, Auburn, IL 62615, (217)438-6111 [289]

Beaty's Nursery, 1933 Mike Muncey Rd., Mc Minnville, TN 37110, (931)934-2364 [14827]

Beauchamp Distributing Co., 1911 S Santa Fe Ave., Compton, CA 90221, (310)639-5320 [24913]

Beaulieu of America Inc., PO Box 4539, Dalton, GA 30721, (706)278-6666 [25977]

Beaumont Bolt & Gasket, PO Box 1710, Beaumont, TX 77704, (409)838-6304 [16993]

Beautiful Plants by Charlie, 10421 State Rd. 579, Thonotosassa, FL 33592, (813)986-4473 [14828]

Beauty Aid Distributors, PO Box 1405, Pocatello, ID 83204-1405, (208)232-5972 [14036]

Beauty & Beauty Enterprises, Inc., 30 Universal Pl., Carlstadt, NJ 07072, (201)935-8887 [14037]

Beauty and Beauty Enterprises Inc., 30 Universal Pl., Carlstadt, NJ 07072, (201)935-8887 [19179]

Beauty Pools Inc., 2700 Transit Rd., West Seneca, NY 14224-2523, (716)674-3500 [23541]

Beaver Creek Cooperative Elevator, PO Box 69, Beaver Creek, MN 56116, (507)673-2388 [824]

Beaver Creek Cooperative Telephone Co., PO Box 69, Beavercreek, OR 97004-0069, (503)632-3113 [8425]

Beaver Distributors, 1564 Northern Star Dr., Traverse City, MI 49686, (231)929-9800 [7038]

Beaver Street Fisheries, Inc., 1741 W Beaver St., Jacksonville, FL 32209, (904)354-8533 [10521]

Beaverhead Bar Supply Inc., 129 N Montana St., Dillon, MT 59725-3307 [1512]

Beaver's Rugs, 4745 Delight Rd., Lawndale, NC 28090, (704)538-3141 [9697]

Beaverton Foods Inc., 4220 SW Cedar Hills Blvd., Beaverton, OR 97005-2029, (503)646-8138 [10522]

B.E.B. Ltd., 5970 River Chase Cir., Atlanta, GA 30328, (404)850-0795 [22935]

Beck-Arnley Worldparts Corp., PO Box 110910, Nashville, TN 37222, (615)834-8080 [2344]

Beck-Lee Inc., PO Box 528, Stratford, CT 06615-0528, (203)332-7678 [18704]

Beck-Lee Inc., PO Box 425, Stratford, CT 06615-0425, (203)332-7678 [19180]

Beck Packaging Corp., PO Box 20250, Lehigh Valley, PA 18002-0250, (610)264-0551 [21649]

Beck Packaging Corp., PO Box 20250, Lehigh Valley, PA 18002-0250, (610)264-0551 [16744]

Beck Suppliers Inc., PO Box 808, Fremont, OH 43420, (419)332-5527 [22062]

Beckenstein Men's Fabrics Inc., 133 Orchard St., New York, NY 10002-3103, (212)475-6666 [25978]

Becker Builders Supply Co., PO Box 1697, Wilmington, NC 28402, (910)791-7761 [7039]

Becker Company Inc.; Larson, PO Box 340, Batavia, IL 60510, (630)879-1316 [25569]

Becker Co.; J.A., 1341 E 4th St., Dayton, OH 45401, (513)226-1341 [8426]

Becker Electric Supply, 11310 Mosteller Rd., Cincinnati, OH 45241-1828, (513)771-2550 [8427]

Becker Food Company Inc., 4160 N Port Washington Rd., Milwaukee, WI 53212, (414)964-5353 [10523]

Beckley-Cardy, Inc., 100 Paragon Pky., Mansfield, OH 44903, (419)589-1900 [20838]

Beckley Equipment Co., 2850 University Dr., Saginaw, MI 48603, (517)793-5922 [16745]

Beckly Cardy Group, 100 Paragon Pky., Mansfield, OH 44903, (419)589-2100 [25570]

Beckman Brothers Inc., 320 SE 6th St., Des Moines, IA 50309, (515)244-2233 [23080]

Beckman Co.; C.C., 11 Commercial St., New Bedford, MA 02740, (508)994-9674 [18457]

Beckman Produce Inc., 415 Grove St., St. Paul, MN 55101, (612)222-1212 [10524]

Becknell Wholesale Co., PO Box 2008, Lubbock, TX 79408, (806)747-3201 [13589]

Beck's North America, 1 Station Pl., PO Box 120 007, Stamford, CT 06912-0007, (203)388-2325 [1513]

Becksmith Co., 5005 Barrow Ave., PO Box 9068, Cincinnati, OH 45209, (513)531-4151 [26414]

Beckwith Kuffel Industries Inc., 5930 1st Ave. S, Seattle, WA 98108-3248, (206)767-6700 [15813]

Beco/Boyd Equipment Co., 1896 National Ave., Hayward, CA 94545-1708, (510)782-1500 [7040]

Beco Helman Inc., 801 Washington Ave. N, Minneapolis, MN 55401-1132, (612)338-5634 [4811]

Bedford Farm Bureau Cooperative, 102 Industrial Ave., Bedford, PA 15522, (814)623-6194 [290]

Bedford Farmers Cooperative, PO Box 64, Shelbyville, TN 37160-0064, (931)684-3506 [291]

Bedford Food Products Inc., 1320 Avenue N, Brooklyn, NY 11230-5906, (718)237-9595 [10525]

Bedford Recycling Inc., PO Box 155, Bedford, IN 47421, (812)275-6883 [26762]

Bedford Valley Petroleum Corp., PO Box 120, Everett, PA 15537, (814)623-5151 [22063]

Bedrosian Building Supply, 4055 Grass Valley Hwy. 110, Auburn, CA 95602, (530)888-1500 [9698]

Bedrosian Building Supply, 13405 Sherman Way, North Hollywood, CA 91605, (818)787-7310 [9699]

Bedrosian Building Supply, 426 Littlefield, South San Francisco, CA 94080, (650)876-0100 [9700]

Bedrosian Tile and Marble, 4285 N Golden State Blvd., Fresno, CA 93722-6397, (209)275-5000 [9713]

Bedrosian Tile & Marble Supply, 798 E Glendale, Sparks, NV 89431, (775)331-4802 [9701]

Bedrosian Tile Supply, 1001 Shary Cir., Concord, CA 94518, (510)676-4858 [9702]

Bedrosian Tile Supply, 27695 Mission Blvd., Hayward, CA 94544, (510)582-5000 [9703]

Bedrosian Tile Supply, Canyon Industrial Center, 9444 Chesapeake Dr., San Diego, CA 92122, (619)565-1215 [9704]

Bedrosian Tile Supply, 2301 Junction Ave., San Jose, CA 95131, (408)435-5544 [9705]

Bedrosian Tile Supply, 2538 N West Ln., Bldg. A, Stockton, CA 95205, (209)463-5000 [9706]

Bedrosian Tile Supply, 2045 E Main St., Visalia, CA 93291, (209)734-4035 [9707]

Bedrosian Tile Supply, 2701 Brundage Ln., Bakersfield, CA 93304, (805)324-5000 [9708]

Bedrosian Tile Supply, 1301 S State College Blvd., Ste. A, Anaheim, CA 92806, (714)778-8453 [9709]

Bedrosian Tile Supply, 7319 Roseville Rd., Sacramento, CA 95842, (916)348-4000 [9710]

Bedrosian Tile Supply, 500 N Carpenter Rd., Modesto, CA 95351, (209)579-5000 [9711]

Bedrosian Tile Supply, 11225 Trade Center Dr., Rancho Cordova, CA 95742, (916)852-1000 [9712]

Bedrosians, 4285 N Golden State Blvd., Fresno, CA 93722-6397, (209)275-5000 [9713]

Bedrosians, 4285 N Golden State Blvd., Fresno, CA 93722-6397, (209)275-5000 [7041]

Bedrosians Tile & Marble, 2946 E Broadway Rd., Phoenix, AZ 85040-0700, (602)966-7800 [9714]

Bedrosians Tile & Marble, 4651 S Butterfield Dr., Tucson, AZ 85714, (520)747-2200 [9715]

Bedrosians Tile & Marble, 3646 Standish Ave., Santa Rosa, CA 95407, (707)586-1800 [9716]

Bedrosians Tile & Marble, 756 S Jason St., Unit 8-11, Denver, CO 80223, (303)722-2200 [9717]

Bedrosians Tile & Marble, 6335 S Industrial Rd., Las Vegas, NV 89103, (702)765-7400 [9718]

Bedrosians Tile and Marble, 4651 S Butterfield Dr., Tucson, AZ 85714, (520)747-2000 [7042]

Bedsole Medical Companies Inc., 3280 Dauphin St., Ste. 115-C, Mobile, AL 36606-4050, (205)476-3635 [18705]

Bee County Cooperative Association Inc., PO Box 128, Tynan, TX 78391, (512)547-3366 [292]

Bee Hat Co., 2839 Olive St., St. Louis, MO 63103-1427, (314)231-6631 [4812]

B.E.E. Industrial Supply Inc., 25634 Nickel Pl., Hayward, CA 94545-3222, (510)293-3180 [15814]

Bee Jay Refrigeration Inc., 4216 Springwood Ave., Baltimore, MD 21206-1933, (410)483-3954 [14341]

Beeba's Creations Inc., 10280 Camino Santa Fe, San Diego, CA 92121-3105, (619)549-2922 [4813]

Beecher Candies; Katharine, PO Box 3411, Camp Hill, PA 17011-3411, (717)266-3641 [10526]

Beechwood Distributors Inc., PO Box 510946, New Berlin, WI 53151-0946, (414)821-1400 [1514]

Beeco Motors and Controls Inc., 5630 Guhn Rd., No. 116, Houston, TX 77040, (713)690-0311 [8428]

Beehive Botanicals Inc., Rte. 8, Box 8257, Hayward, WI 54843, (715)634-4274 [19181]

Beekman Publishers, Inc., 2626 Rte. 212, PO Box 888, Woodstock, NY 12498, (914)679-2300 [3546]

Beeman Jorgensen Inc., 7510 Allisonville Rd., Indianapolis, IN 46250, (317)841-7677 [3547]

Beemer Precision Inc., 230 New York Dr., Ft. Washington, PA 19034, (215)646-8440 [16746]

Beer City, Furnace Grove, Minersville, PA 17954-0126, (717)544-4701 [1515]

Beer Import Company, 2536 Springfield Ave., Union, NJ 07083, (908)686-0800 [1516]

Beer World, 520 S 29th, Harrisburg, PA 17104-2105, (717)238-2337 [1517]

Beerman Auto Supply Inc., 86 Bridge St., Johnstown, PA 15902, (814)536-3583 [2345]

Beeson Hardware Industrial Sales Co., 1114 Dorris Ave., PO Box 1390, High Point, NC 27260-1390, (336)821-2145 [13590]

Before Columbus Foundation, American Ethnic Studies, GN-80, University of Washington, Seattle, WA 98195, (206)543-4264 [3548]

Beggs and Cobb Corp., 139 Lynnfield St., Peabody, MA 01960, (978)532-3080 [18375]

Behler-Young Co., PO Box 946, Grand Rapids, MI 49509, (616)531-3400 [14342]

Behling Building Products; Gil, 7101 E 8 Mile Rd., Warren, MI 48091, (810)757-3500 [7043]

Behr Iron and Steel Inc., PO Box 740, Rockford, IL 61105, (815)987-2600 [26763]

Behr Machinery and Equipment Corp., PO Box 1318, Rockford, IL 61105, (815)987-2640 [15815]

Behr and Sons Inc.; Joseph, 1100 Seminary St., Rockford, IL 61108, (815)987-2600 [26764]

Behrens Machinery Co.; C., Danvers Indust. Park, Danvers, MA 01923, (978)774-4200 [15816]

Behrens Supply Co., 211 Main St., PO Box 61, Red Wing, MN 55066-0061, (612)388-9443 [2346]

B.E.I. Packaging, 13540 Lake City Way, Seattle, WA 98125, (206)367-3128 [19189]

Beijing Book Co. Inc., 701 E Linden Ave., Linden, NJ 07036-2495, (908)862-0909 [3549]

Beijing Trade Exchange Inc., 701 E St. SE, Washington, DC 20003-2841, (202)546-5534 [24688]

Beisler Weidmann Company Inc., 233 Cortlandt St., Belleville, NJ 07109, (973)759-5020 [21650]

Beistle Co., PO Box 10, Shippensburg, PA 17257, (717)532-2131 [13314]

Beitzell and Company Inc., 705 Edgewood St. NE, Washington, DC 20017, (202)526-1234 [1518]

BEK International Inc., 2804 NW 72nd Ave., Miami, FL 33122, (305)594-3756 [6008]

Bel Air Distributors, 2002 W Pierson Rd., Flint, MI 48504-1926, (810)785-0859 [25100]

Bel-Aqua Pool Supply Inc., 750 Main St., New Rochelle, NY 10805, (914)235-2200 [23542]

Bel Canto Fancy Foods Ltd., 57-01 49th Pl., Maspeth, NY 11378, (718)497-3888 [10527]

Bel-Pak Foods Inc., 1411 W Chicago Ave., Chicago, IL 60622, (312)421-2440 [10528]

Bel Trade USA Corp., 55 W 47th St., New York, NY 10036, (212)840-3920 [22830]

Belair Road Supply Company Inc., 7750 Pulaski Hwy., Baltimore, MD 21237, (410)687-4200 [7044]

Belarus Machinery Inc., 7075 W Parkland Ct., Milwaukee, WI 53223, (414)355-2000 [293]

Belcam Inc., 4 Montgomery St., Rouses Point, NY 12979, (518)297-6641 [14038]

Belco Athletic Laundry Equipment Co., PO Box 241655, Charlotte, NC 28224-1655, (704)525-2078 [15047]

Belco Beauty and Barber Supply Co. and Salon, 4225 E Sahara Ave., Ste. 10, Las Vegas, NV 89104-6331, (702)641-5400 [25711]

Belden Electric Co.; Russell, PO Box 167, Joplin, MO 64802, (417)624-5650 [20839]

The Belknap White Group, 111 Plymouth St., Mansfield, MA 02048, (508)337-2700 [9719]

Bell Additives Inc., 1340 Bennett Dr., Longwood, FL 32750, (407)831-5021 [22064]

Bell Atlantic Meridian Systems Inc., 5 Greentree Ctr., No. 400, Marlton, NJ 08053, (609)988-5600 [5527]

Bell-Carter Foods Inc., 3742 Mt Diablo Blvd., Lafayette, CA 94549, (925)284-5933 [10529]

Bell Company Inc.; James W., 1720 I Ave. NE, Cedar Rapids, IA 52406, (319)362-1151 [7045]

Bell Fish Company, Inc.; A.P., 4600 124th St. W, PO Box 276, Cortez, FL 34215, (941)794-1249 [10530]

Bell Gas Inc., PO Box 490, Roswell, NM 88202, (505)622-4800 [22065]

The Bell Group, 7500 Bluewater Rd. NW, Albuquerque, NM 87121-1962, (505)839-3000 [17331]

Bell-Haun Systems Inc., 935 Eastwind Dr., Westerville, OH 43081, (614)882-4040 [5528]

Bell Industries, 500 Hardman Ave., PO Box 538, South St. Paul, MN 55075, (612)450-9020 [18458]

Bell Industries, Fulton Dr., Germantown, WI 53022, (414)781-1860 [18459]

Bell Industries Graphic, 4425 Sheila, Los Angeles, CA 90023-4328, (213)268-9500 [25571]

Bell Microproducts Inc., 1941 Ringwood Ave., San Jose, CA 95131-1721, (408)451-9400 [8429]

Bell Paper Products Co., 1001 D Nicholas Blvd., Elk Grove Village, IL 60007-2581, (847)640-1310 [21651]

Bell Parts Supply Inc., 2609 45th St., Highland, IN 46322, (219)924-1200 [15048]

Bell; Philip M., 118 Northeast Dr., Loveland, OH 45140, (513)683-6300 [13034]

Bell Supply Company Inc., 262 Fortner St., Dothan, AL 36302, (205)793-4500 [23081]

Bella & Co.; Frank, 48517 S Broadway, Hicksville, NY 11801, (516)932-3838 [25979]

The Bella Tile Company, Inc., 178 1st Ave., New York, NY 10009-4508, (212)475-2909 [9720]

Bellamy's Inc., Box 106, Elwood, NE 68937, (308)785-3311 [294]

Belle Fourche Livestock Exchange, PO Box 126, Belle Fourche, SD 57717-0126, (605)892-2655 [17727]

Belle Island International Inc., 3 Mary Austin Pl., Norwalk, CT 06850, (203)840-8890 [10531]

Belle Plaine Cooperative, 820 E Main St., Belle Plaine, MN 56011, (612)873-4244 [295]

Bellesteel Industries Inc., PO Box 490, East Boston, MA 02128, (617)569-9100 [19807]

Belli-Childs Wholesale Produce, 512 W Cowles, Long Beach, CA 90813, (562)437-7441 [10532]

Bellini Co., 5550 Cameron St., Ste. A, Las Vegas, NV 89118-6221, (702)732-7275 [9721]

Bellini Jewelry Co., 1478 Atwood Ave., Johnston, RI 02919, (401)521-2233 [17332]

Bell's Produce, Inc., 3401 Michigan Ave., Flint, MI 48505, (810)235-6668 [10533]

Bells Supply Co., 718 Stanton Christiana Rd., Newark, DE 19713, (302)998-0800 [23082]

Bellsonics, PO Box 1390, Lake Forest, CA 92630, (949)581-8101 [5529]

BellSouth Communication Systems Inc., 1936 Blue Hills Dr. NE, Roanoke, VA 24012, (540)983-6000 [5530]

Belmar Inc., 554 Killingly St., Johnston, RI 02919-5227, (401)454-4430 [17333]

Belmer Co.; H., 555 Carr St., Cincinnati, OH 45203, (513)241-4341 [13591]

Belmont Automotive Co., 1918 Pitkin Ave., Brooklyn, NY 11207-3327, (718)385-4343 [2347]

Belmont Steel Corp., 2424 Oakton St., Evanston, IL 60202-2796, (847)866-2100 [19808]

Belmont Steel Corp., 2424 Oakton St., Evanston, IL 60202-2796, (847)866-2100 [20071]

Belmont Systems Inc., 1555 Industrial Rd., San Carlos, CA 94070, (650)598-9058 [6009]

Belmont Wholesale Co. Inc., 4432 Ardmore Ave., Ft. Wayne, IN 46809, (219)747-7582 [10534]

Beloit Beverage Company Inc., 4059 W Bradley Rd., Milwaukee, WI 53209-1796, (414)362-5000 [1519]

Belstra Milling Co. Inc., PO Box 460, Demotte, IN 46310, (219)987-4343 [296]

Belt Corp.; P.M., 131 32nd St., PO Box 320650, Brooklyn, NY 11232, (718)369-9800 [4814]

Belting Industry Company Inc., 20 Boright Ave., Kenilworth, NJ 07033, (908)272-8591 [16747]

Beltrami Farmers Elevator, PO Box 8, Beltrami, MN 56517, (218)926-5522 [297]

Belts By Nadim, Inc., 303 E 4th St., No. 2, Los Angeles, CA 90013-1575, (213)680-3483 [4815]

Beltservice Corp., 4143 N Rider Trail, Earth City, MO 63045-1102, (314)344-8500 [16748]

Beltwall Division of Beltservice Corp., 4143 N Rider Trail, Earth City, MO 63045-1102, (314)344-8500 [16748]

Belwool Corp., 855 Avenue of the Americas, New York, NY 10001, (212)594-7195 [25980]

Belzoni Tractor Co. Inc., PO Box 297, Belzoni, MS 39038, (601)247-3414 [298]

Bement Grain Company Inc., 400 E Bodman St., Bement, IL 61813, (217)678-2261 [17728]

Bemidji Cooperative Association, PO Box 980, Bemidji, MN 56601, (218)751-4260 [22066]

Ben Arnold-Heritage Beverage Company L.P., PO Box 480, Ridgeway, SC 29130, (803)337-3500 [1487]

Ben-Mar Paper Co. Inc., PO Box 250304, Montgomery, AL 36125, (205)263-4448 [21652]

Ben Wa Novelty Corp., 4731 W Jefferson Blvd., Los Angeles, CA 90016, (323)731-2424 [13315]

Benben Sportswear, 8119 Rosehill Rd., Shawnee Mission, KS 66215-2632, (913)541-0028 [4816]

BenchCraft, PO Box 86, Blue Mountain, MS 38610, (662)685-4711 [13035]

Benchmark Systems Inc. of Utah, PO Box 782, Bountiful, UT 84011-0782, (801)298-8200 [6010]

Benco Steel Inc., PO Box 2053, Hickory, NC 28603, (828)328-1714 [19809]

Bencruz Enterprises Corporation, 7820 SW 93rd Ave., Miami, FL 33173, (305)595-2668 [15817]

Bender Wholesale Distributors, 2911 Moose Trail, Elkhart, IN 46514, (219)264-4409 [3]

Benedict International Inc., 8640-C Onyx Dr. SW, Lakewood, WA 98498-4880 [4817]

Benedict-Miller Inc., PO Box 912, Lyndhurst, NJ 07071, (201)438-3000 [19810]

Benedict Optical, 341 Bennett Ln., Lewisville, TX 75067, (972)221-4141 [19182]

Benel Manufacturing Inc., Rfd. 1, PO Box 1301, Dunn, NC 28334-9801, (919)892-4925 [4818]

Benfield Control Systems, 25 Lafayette Ave., White Plains, NY 10603, (914)948-6660 [8430]

Benfield Electric International, Ltd., 25 Lafayette Ave., White Plains, NY 10603, (914)948-6660 [8430]

Benfield Electric Supply Co.; H.H., 25 Lafayette Ave., White Plains, NY 10603, (914)948-6660 [8430]

Benge & Co.; Jim, 927 N Northlake Way, Seattle, WA 98103-8871, (206)545-4262 [24689]

Benham and Company Inc., PO Box 29, Mineola, TX 75773, (903)569-2636 [10535]

Benjamin Metals Co., PO Box 59906, Los Angeles, CA 90059, (213)321-1700 [19811]

Benjamin News Group, 219 E Park St., Butte, MT 59701, (406)782-6995 [3550]

Benjamin Steel Company Inc., 777 Benjamin Dr., Springfield, OH 45502-8846, (513)322-8000 [19812]

Bennett Brothers Inc., 30 E Adams St., Chicago, IL 60603, (312)263-4800 [17334]

Bennett Distributing Co. Inc., 320 Circle M Dr., PO Box 142, Salisbury, NC 28145-0142, (704)636-7743 [1520]

Bennett Importing Inc., 145 Wells Ave., Newton, MA 02459, (617)332-7500 [24690]

Bennett Vending, 2032 S St. Aubin, Sioux City, IA 51106, (712)276-0173 [10536]

Bennetts East Side Paint & Gloss, PO Box 1605, Idaho Falls, ID 83403-1605, (208)522-5630 [21399]

Bennett's Pet Center, 986 Medina Rd., Medina, OH 44256, (330)239-1240 [27080]

Bennies Warehouse Distribution Center, R.D. 1, Rural Box 1997, Berwick, PA 18603, (570)759-2201 [15049]

Bennington Co.; J.C., 66 Southgate Blvd., New Castle, DE 19720, (302)322-3700 [2348]

Benoit; Samuel, 879 Waterman Ave., East Providence, RI 02914-1313, (401)431-1520 [17335]

Benold's Jewelers, 2900 W Anderson Ln., Ste. F, Austin, TX 78757, (512)452-6491 [17336]

Benras Watch Co., 1550 W Carroll, Chicago, IL 60607, (312)243-3300 [17337]

Benrock Inc., 4841 Lewis Rd., Stone Mountain, GA 30083 [18460]

Benrock of Oklahoma, 15233 E Skelly Dr., Tulsa, OK 74116, (918)437-2371 [18461]

Bens Inc., 3311 N Cliff Ave., Sioux Falls, SD 57104-0847, (605)334-6944 [2349]

Bensinger's, 8543 Page Ave., St. Louis, MO 63114, (314)426-5100 [10537]

Benson Company Inc.; L.A., PO Box 2137, Baltimore, MD 21203, (410)342-9225 [16749]

Benson Eyecare Corp., 555 Theodore Fremd Ave., Rye, NY 10580, (914)967-9400 [8431]

Benson Farmers Cooperative, PO Box 407, Benson, IL 61516, (309)394-2293 [299]

Benson Pool Systems, 800 Central Ave., University Park, IL 60466, (708)534-0505 [23543]

Benson Pool Systems, 14535 Grover St., Omaha, NE 68144, (402)330-8424 [23544]

Benson Pump Co., 5390 E 39th Ave., Denver, CO 80207, (303)322-8978 [23545]

Benson Pump Co., 150 Millwell Dr., Maryland Heights, MO 63043, (314)344-9991 [23546]

Benson Pump Co., 1936 11th St., Rockford, IL 61104, (815)964-9000 [23547]

Benson Pump Co., 6885 E 34th St., Indianapolis, IN 46226, (317)542-1091 [23548]

Benson Pump Co., 800 Central Ave., University Park, IL 60466, (708)534-0505 [23543]

Benson Pump Co., 13345 Merriman Rd., Livonia, MI 48150-1815, (517)548-1010 [23549]

Benson Pump Co., 2468 Louisiana Ave. N, Minneapolis, MN 55427, (612)545-5606 [23550]

Benson Pump Co., 4505 McEwen, Farmers Branch, TX 75244, (972)490-3367 [23551]

Benson-Quinn Co., 1075 Grain Exchange, Minneapolis, MN 55415, (612)340-5900 [17729]

Bensons Backery, PO Box 429, Bogart, GA 30622, (770)725-5711 [10538]

Benthin Systems, Inc., 79 N Industrial Pk., 510 North Ave., Sewickley, PA 15143, (412)749-5200 [15418]

Bentley Mills Inc., 451 D St., No. 919, Boston, MA 02210, (617)951-2575 [9722]

Bently Sand & Gravel, 9220 Bennett Lake Rd., Fenton, MI 48430, (810)629-6172 [7046]

Benton Ballard Co., PO Box 12375, Jackson, MS 39236-2375, (601)956-3560 [6011]

Benton County Cooperative, PO Box 278, Ashland, MS 38603, (601)224-8933 [300]

Benton Electronics Inc., 1191 Elmsford Dr., Cupertino, CA 95014-4960, (408)996-1701 [6012]

Benton Oil Co., PO Box 31, Lubbock, TX 79408, (806)763-5301 [22067]

Benz Engineering Inc., PO Box 729, Montebello, CA 90640-6325, (213)722-6603 [5830]

Benz Oil Inc., 2724 W Hampton Ave., Milwaukee, WI 53209, (414)442-2900 [22068]

Benz and Sons Inc.; George, 5th & Minnesota St., St. Paul, MN 55101, (612)224-1351 [17730]

Berchtold Equipment Company Inc., PO Box 3098, Bakersfield, CA 93385, (805)323-7818 [301]

Berelson Export Corp., 291 Geary St., Ste. 407, San Francisco, CA 94102, (415)956-6600 [10539]

Berelson Export Corp., 291 Geary St., Ste. 407, San Francisco, CA 94102, (415)956-6600 [10540]

Berendsen Fluid Power, Inc., 3528 Roger Chaffe Memorial Dr., Wyoming, MI 49548, (616)452-4560 [15818]

Berg Bag Co., 410 3rd Ave. N, Minneapolis, MN 55401, (612)332-8845 [25891]

Berg Bag Co., 410 3rd Ave. N, Minneapolis, MN 55401, (612)332-8845 [16750]

Berg-Dorf Pipe & Supply Co. Inc., 3300 South High, PO Box 95638, Oklahoma City, OK 73143, (405)672-3381 [23083]

Berg Equipment and Scaffolding Company Inc., 2130 E D St., Tacoma, WA 98421, (253)383-2035 [7047]

Berg Fargo Motor Supply Inc., 324 N Pacific Ave., Fargo, ND 58108, (701)232-8821 [2350]

Berg Steel Corp., 4306 Normandy Ct., Royal Oak, MI 48073, (248)549-6066 [19813]

Bergano Book Co., Inc., PO Box 190, Fairfield, CT 06430, (203)254-2054 [3551]

Berge Ford Inc., PO Box 4008, Mesa, AZ 85211, (602)497-1111 [20599]

Bergen Brunswig Corp., 1765 Fremont Dr., Salt Lake City, UT 84104, (801)972-4131 [19183]

Bergen Brunswig Corp., 4000 Metropolitan Dr., Orange, CA 92868-3510, (714)385-4000 [19184]

Berger Building Products Corp., 805 Pennsylvania Ave., Feasterville, PA 19053, (215)355-1200 [7048]

Berger Co.; B., PO Box 8009, Macedonia, OH 44056, (330)425-3838 [25981]

Berger and Company Inc.; Howard, 808 Georgia Ave., Brooklyn, NY 11207, (718)272-1540 [13592]

Berger L.L.C.; Ben, 15 W 37th St., 15th Fl., New York, NY 10018, (212)220-8886 [4819]

Berger and Son Inc.; Ben, 15 W 37th St., 15th Fl., New York, NY 10018, (212)220-8886 [4819]

Bergeron Pecan Shelling Plant, Inc.; H.J., 10003 False River Rd., New Roads, LA 70760, (504)638-7667 [10541]

Bergner and Co.; P.A., 331 W Wisconsin Ave., Milwaukee, WI 53203, (414)347-4141 [4820]

Bergquist Co. Inc., 5300 Edina Industrial Blvd., Edina, MN 55439, (612)835-2322 [8432]

Bergquists Imports Inc., 1412 S Hwy. 33, Cloquet, MN 55720-2627, (218)879-3343 [15419]

Berint Trading, Ltd., 12 Westchester Ave., White Plains, NY 10601, (914)948-0030 [13593]

Berk Co.; O., 3 Milltown Crt., PO Box 1690, Union, NJ 07083, (908)851-9500 [25892]

Berkheimer Company Inc.; G.W., 3460 Taft St., Gary, IN 46408, (219)887-0141 [14343]

Berkheimer Company Inc. South Bend; G.W., 612 Chapin St., South Bend, IN 46601, (219)288-4741 [14344]

Berkley Game Distributors, 2950 San Pablo Ave., Berkeley, CA 94702, (510)845-9851 [26415]

Berkman Co.; Louis, PO Box 820, Steubenville, OH 43952, (740)283-3722 [15819]

Berkowitz L.P.; J.E., PO Box 186, Westville, NJ 08093, (609)456-7800 [7049]

Berks Products Corp., PO Box 421, Reading, PA 19603, (610)374-5131 [7050]

Berkshire Valley, PO Box 150, Adams, MA 01220, (413)743-4240 [19814]

Berlin Enterprises Inc., 3200 Sheffield Ave., Hammond, IN 46320, (219)933-0233 [19815]

Berlin Farmers Elevator, PO Box 28, Berlin, ND 58415, (701)883-5347 [302]

Berlin Metals Inc., 3200 Sheffield Ave., Hammond, IN 46327, (219)933-0111 [19816]

Berlin Packaging Inc., 111 N Canal St., Chicago, IL 60606, (847)640-4790 [25893]

Berman Leather Company Inc., 229 A St., Boston, MA 02210-1309, (617)426-0870 [18376]

Bermil Industries Corp., 461 Doughty Blvd., Inwood, NY 11096, (516)371-4400 [15050]

Bernan, 4611-F Assembly Dr., Lanham, MD 20706-4391, (301)459-7666 [3552]

Bernards Formal Wear Inc., 734 9th St., Durham, NC 27705-4803, (919)286-3633 [4821]

Bernell Corp., PO Box 4637, South Bend, IN 46601, (219)234-3200 [19185]

Bernick Inc.; Charles A., PO Box 7008, St. Cloud, MN 56302, (320)252-6441 [24914]

Bernina of America Inc., 3500 Thayer Ct., Aurora, IL 60504-6182, (630)978-2500 [15051]

Bernoulli Collection Inc., 1821 West 4000 South, Roy, UT 84067, (801)524-2000 [6013]

The Berns Co., 1250 W 17th St., Long Beach, CA 90813, (562)437-0471 [15820]

Bernstein Company Inc.; William, 155 W 72nd St., New York, NY 10023, (212)799-3200 [10542]

Bernstein Office Machine Co., 389 W Lincoln Hwy., Penndel, PA 19047, (215)750-8740 [20840]

Berreth Oil Company Inc., 1301 W 6th St., Mishawaka, IN 46544, (219)255-1255 [22069]

Berry Bearing Co., 1605 Alton Rd., Birmingham, AL 35210-3770 [16751]

Berry Companies Inc., PO Box 829, Wichita, KS 67201, (316)832-0171 [7051]

Berry Company Inc.; H.T., 50 North St., Canton, MA 02021-3356, (781)828-6000 [21653]

Berry-Hinkley Terminal Inc., 147 S Stanford Way, Sparks, NV 89431, (702)359-3778 [22070]

Berry Tire Company Inc., 9229 W Grand, Franklin Park, IL 60131, (708)451-2200 [2351]

Berry Tractor and Equipment Co., PO Box 12288, Wichita, KS 67277, (316)943-4246 [303]

Berthold Farmers Elevator Co., PO Box 38, Berthold, ND 58718, (701)453-3431 [304]

Berthold Farmers Elevator Co., PO Box 38, Berthold, ND 58718, (701)453-3431 [10543]

Bertolina Wholesale Co., 520 Creek Ave., Rock Springs, WY 82901-5244, (307)362-3482 [1521]

Bertolli U.S.A. Inc., 300 Harmon Meadow Blvd., Secaucus, NJ 07094, (201)863-2088 [10544]

Bertrand Cooperative, PO Box 67, Bertrand, NE 68927, (308)472-3415 [305]

Bertsch Co., 1655 Steele Ave. SW, Grand Rapids, MI 49507, (616)452-3251 [16752]

Bertuca Co.; Teddy, PO Box 217, McAllen, TX 78502, (956)631-7123 [10545]

Berube Municipal Supply; Tom, 421 Worcester Rd., Barre, MA 01005-9006, (978)355-2366 [13594]

Berwick Steel Co, PO Box 27278, Columbus, OH 43227, (614)866-1338 [19817]

Berwick Steel Co., 100 Steelway Pl., Piqua, OH 45356, (937)778-8884 [19818]

Besche Oil Co. Inc., PO Box 277, Waldorf, MD 20604, (301)645-7061 [22071]

Besco Electic Supply Company of Florida Inc., 711 S 14th St., Leesburg, FL 34748, (352)787-4542 [8433]

Besco Steel Supply, Inc., 1801 Linder Industrial Dr., Nashville, TN 37209, (615)251-8087 [19819]

Besse Forest Products Group, 933 N 8th St., PO Box 352, Gladstone, MI 49837-0352, (906)428-3113 [7052]

Bessman Price Auctioneers, PO Box 353, Madison, SD 57042-0353, (605)256-9156 [17731]

Best American Co., 2921 S Lacienega Blvd., Culver City, CA 90232, (310)202-0814 [18881]

Best Battery Company Inc., 4015 Fleet St., Baltimore, MD 21224, (410)342-8060 [2352]

Best Beauty Supply Co., 516 Baltimore St., Hanover, PA 17331, (717)637-4232 [14039]

Best of the Best, PO Box 346, Piermont, NY 10968-0346 [10752]

Best Bilt Parts, 2527 E Kearney, Springfield, MO 65803, (417)831-4470 [2353]

Best Brands, PO Box 290155, Nashville, TN 37229-0155, (615)350-8500 [1522]

Best Brands Home Products, Inc., 325 5th Ave., Ste. 518, New York, NY 10016, (212)684-7456 [15420]

Best Brands Inc., 6307 N 53rd St., Tampa, FL 33610, (813)621-7802 [10546]

Best Business Products Inc., PO Box 749, Sioux Falls, SD 57101-0749, (605)336-1484 [20841]

Best Buy Co. Inc., PO Box 9312, Minneapolis, MN 55440-9312, (612)947-2000 [25101]

BEST Cash Registers, 418 W 5th St., Reno, NV 89503-4412, (702)322-7054 [20842]

Best Data Products Inc., 19748 Dearborn St., Chatsworth, CA 91311, (818)773-9600 [6014]

Best Disposal Inc., PO Box 6644, Phoenix, AZ 85005, (602)237-2078 [26765]

Best Electric Supply, 6201 Regency West Dr., Racine, WI 53406-4947, (414)554-0600 [13595]

Best Foods, 2816 S Kilbourn, Chicago, IL 60623-4299, (773)247-5800 [10547]

Best Glass Co., 1225 S Commerce, Las Vegas, NV 89102-2528, (702)382-7502 [7053]

Best-Klean Products, PO Box 127, 5875 N Wayne St., Fremont, IN 46737-0127, (219)495-9706 [4578]

Best Label Company Inc./IMS Div., 2943 Whipple Rd., Union City, CA 94587, (510)489-5400 [15821]

Best Labs, PO Box 20468, St. Petersburg, FL 33742, (813)525-0255 [18706]

Best Labs, PO Box 20468, St. Petersburg, FL 33742, (813)525-0255 [8434]

Best Locking Systems of Georgia Inc., 1901 Montreal Rd., Ste. 122, Tucker, GA 30084, (770)491-3101 [24513]

Best Locking Systems of Wisconsin Inc., N45 W33490 Wisconsin Ave., Nashotah, WI 53058, (414)367-8316 [24514]

Best Pet Distributing, 3580 S Church St., Burlington, NC 27215-9100, (336)366-4456 [27081]

Best Plastics Inc., 19300 Grange St., Cassopolis, MI 49031, (616)641-5811 [2354]

Best Plumbing Supply Inc., 3333-1 Crompond Rd., Yorktown Heights, NY 10598, (914)736-2468 [23084]

Best Regards Inc., 344 7th Ave., San Diego, CA 92101, (619)685-5840 [13316]

Best Rents, 945 W Wilshire, Oklahoma City, OK 73116, (405)843-8886 [19692]

Best Sausage Inc., 805 E Kemper Rd., Cincinnati, OH 45246-2515 [10548]

Best Style Formal Wear Inc., 200 S 19th St., Lincoln, NE 68510-1003, (402)474-0062 [4822]

Best Tile Distributors of Albany, Inc., 2241 Central Ave., Schenectady, NY 12304-4379, (518)869-0219 [9723]

Best Tile Distributors of Syracuse, Inc., 5891 Firestone Dr., Syracuse, NY 13206-1102, (315)437-1606 [9724]

Best Tile Distributors of Wexford, Inc., 11040 Perry Hwy., Wexford, PA 15090-8331, (412)935-6965 [9725]

Best Toy Manufacturing Ltd., 43 Hall St., Brooklyn, NY 11205-1303, (718)855-9040 [26416]

Best Way Carpet Care Inc., PO Box 3693, Albuquerque, NM 87190-3693, (505)344-6838 [4579]

Best Way Distributing Co., 13287 Ralston Ave., Sylmar, CA 91342-1296, (818)362-9333 [1523]

Best Way Tools, 171 Brook Ave., Deer Park, NY 11729, (516)586-4702 [13596]

Bestex Company Inc., 3368 San Fernando Rd., Unit 110, Los Angeles, CA 90065, (323)255-4477 [24515]

Bestmark International, 33-00 Broadway, Ste. 202, Fair Lawn, NJ 07410, (201)794-3500 [22990]

Bestop Inc., PO Box 307, Broomfield, CO 80038, (303)465-1755 [2355]

BET Plant Services USA Inc., 4067 Industrial Park Dr., #3A, Norcross, GA 30071-1638 [15822]

BET Rentokil Plant Services, 4067 Industrial Park Dr., No. 3A, Norcross, GA 30071-1638, (404)321-6067 [7054]

Beta Screen Corp., 707 Commercial Ave., Carlstadt, NJ 07072, (201)939-2400 [25572]

Beta Supply Co., PO Box 5217, Houston, TX 77262, (713)921-3600 [15823]

Bethany Grain Company Inc., PO Box 350, Bethany, IL 61914-0350, (217)665-3392 [17732]

Bethea Distributing Inc., 500 S 1st Ave., Dillon, SC 29536, (803)774-6891 [306]

Bethlehem Steel Export Corp., 701 E 3rd St., Bethlehem, PA 18016, (215)694-2424 [19820]

Better Brake Parts Inc., 915 Shawnee Rd., Lima, OH 45801, (419)227-0685 [2356]

Better Brands, 4110 High Country Rd., Colorado Springs, CO 80907-4319, (719)598-9200 [1753]

Better Brands of Atlanta Inc., 755 NW Jefferson St., Atlanta, GA 30377, (404)872-4731 [1524]

Better Brands of Milwaukee Inc., 3241 S 20th St., Milwaukee, WI 53215, (414)645-2900 [1525]

Better Brands of South Georgia, 103 Ave. B S, Valdosta, GA 31601-5153, (912)244-0447 [1526]

Better Buildings, Inc., 625 S Smallwood St., Baltimore, MD 21223, (410)945-7733 [7055]

Better Telephones and Technology Inc., PO Box 15050, Cincinnati, OH 45215-0050, (513)821-8075 [5531]

Betti Industries Inc.; H., 303 Paterson Plank Rd., Carlstadt, NJ 07072, (201)438-1300 [25573]

Betty's Doll House, Rte. 82, East Haddam, CT 06423, (860)434-2086 [26417]

Bev-Tech, Inc., PO Box 130, York, ME 03909-0130, (207)363-2707 [14345]

Bevan-Rabell Inc., 1880 Airport Rd., Wichita, KS 67209-1943, (316)946-4870 [8435]

Bevco Inc., PO Box 3494, Billings, MT 59103-3494, (406)248-2670 [22936]

Beverage Distributors Co., 14200 E Montcrieff Pl., Ste. E, Aurora, CO 80011, (303)371-3421 [1527]

Beverage Wholesalers Inc., 701 N 4th Ave., Fargo, ND 58102, (701)293-7404 [1528]

Bext, Inc., 1045 10th Ave., San Diego, CA 92101-6961, (619)239-8462 [8436]

Beyda & Associates, Inc., 6943 Valjean Ave., Van Nuys, CA 91406, (818)988-3102 [3553]

Beyda & Associates, Inc., 2150 Premier Row, Orlando, FL 32809, (407)438-6700 [3554]

Beyer Farms Inc., 265 Malta St., Brooklyn, NY 11207, (718)272-4500 [10549]

Beyer Livestock; Allen, N942 State Rd. 13, PO Box 1, Stetsonville, WI 54480, (715)678-2711 [10550]

Beyerdynamic, 56 Central Ave., Farmingdale, NY 11735, (631)293-3200 [5532]

Beynon Farm Products Corp., PO Box 82226, Lincoln, NE 68501, (402)476-2100 [25894]

BFI/Allied Recyclery Mpls, 725 44th Ave. N, Minneapolis, MN 55412, (612)522-6558 [26766]

BFI Recyclery, 964 Hazel St., Akron, OH 44305, (330)434-9183 [19821]

BFI/Specmark, 133 Rahway Ave., Elizabeth, NJ 07202, (908)355-3400 [13036]

BFI Waste Systems of North America Inc., 3840 NW 37th Ct., Miami, FL 33142, (305)638-3800 [26767]

BG Electronics Inc., PO Box 810498, Dallas, TX 75381-0498, (972)492-7877 [8437]

B.G. Industries Inc., 8550 Balboa Blvd., Ste. 214, Northridge, CA 91325, (818)894-0744 [19186]

B.G. Office Products, 3236 Auburn Blvd., Sacramento, CA 95821, (916)484-7300 [13037]

B.G.B. Pet Supply Inc., G1234 N Center Rd., Burton, MI 48509, (810)742-8760 [27082]

BGE and C Inc., PO Box 810498, Dallas, TX 75381-0498, (972)492-7877 [8438]

BGW Systems Inc., 13130 Yukon Ave., Hawthorne, CA 90250, (310)973-8090 [25102]

BHP Trading Inc., 111 W Ocean Blvd., Long Beach, CA 90802, (562)491-1441 [19822]

B.I. Chemicals, Inc., 8300 SW 71st Ave., Portland, OR 97223, (503)244-0166 [4451]

Bi Rite Foodservice Distributors, PO Box 410417, San Francisco, CA 94141-0417, (415)656-0254 [10551]

Bi-State Distributing Co., 3333 11th St., Lewiston, ID 83501, (208)746-8295 [7056]

Bianchi and Sons Packing Co., PO Box 190, Merced, CA 95341-0190, (209)722-8134 [10552]

Bibliographical Center for Research Inc., 14394 E Evans Ave., Aurora, CO 80014-1478, (303)751-6277 [6015]

Bickett Equipment Company Inc., PO Box 619, Morganfield, KY 42437, (502)389-1424 [307]

Bickford Flavors Inc., 19007 St. Clair Ave., Cleveland, OH 44117, (216)531-6006 [10553]

Bickley Inc.; A.M., PO Box 91, Marshallville, GA 31057, (912)967-2291 [17733]

Bicknell Distributors Inc., 12 Parkwood Dr., Hopkinton, MA 01748-1660, (508)435-2321 [23552]

Bicknell Distributors, Inc., 45 Industrial Park Rd., Albany, NY 12206-2021, (518)489-4401 [23553]

Bicknell Huston Distributors, 6E Easy St., PO Box 391, Bound Brook, NJ 08805, (732)271-1177 [23554]

Bicknell Huston Distributors, Inc., 436 Hayden Station Rd., Windsor, CT 06095, (860)687-1437 [23555]

Bicknell Huston Distributors, Inc., 520 Riverside Industrial Pky., Portland, ME 04103, (207)878-3888 [23556]

Bicknell-Tidewater Inc., 707 Industry Dr., Hampton, VA 23661-1002, (804)826-4001 [23557]

BICO Akron Inc., 3100 Gilchrist Rd., Mogadore, OH 44260, (330)794-1716 [19823]

Bicor Processing Corp., 362 Dewitt Ave., Brooklyn, NY 11207, (718)649-9595 [15421]

Biddeford & Saco Paper Co., 25 Precourt St., Biddeford, ME 04005-4315, (207)284-5731 [4573]

Biddle Service; Dorothy, 348 Greeley Lake Rd., Greeley, PA 18425-9799, (570)226-3239 [14829]

Biederman Inc.; A., 1425 Grand Central Ave., Glendale, CA 91201-3095, (818)246-8431 [24323]

Biersch Brewing Co.; Gordon, 33 E San Fernando St., San Jose, CA 95113, (408)294-6785 [1529]

Biewer; John A., 2555 Busha Hwy., Marysville, MI 48040, (810)364-9744 [18462]

Biflex International Inc., 183 Madison Ave., New York, NY 10016, (212)725-2800 [4823]

Big-2 Oldsmobile Inc., PO Box 4007, Mesa, AZ 85211, (602)898-6000 [20600]

Big A Auto Parts, 6523 Merle Hay Rd., PO Box 345, Johnston, IA 50131-0345, (515)276-5485 [2827]

Big A Auto Parts, 7751 Nieman Rd., Shawnee, KS 66214-1406, (316)792-3553 [2357]

Big Apple Enterprises, 230 5th Ave., New York, NY 10010, (212)685-6755 [13317]

Big B Automotive Warehouse, 489 Grant St., Akron, OH 44311-1156, (330)376-7121 [2358]

Big Banana Fruit Market, Bute Rd., Uniontown, PA 15401, (412)438-4980 [10554]

Big Blue Products Inc., 386 Oakwood Rd., Huntington Station, NY 11746-7223, (516)261-1000 [6016]

Big Blue Store, 149 South Blvd., Clinton, NC 28328-4617, (910)592-6707 [13597]

Big Boy Ice Cream, 602 E Lohman Ave., Las Cruces, NM 88001, (505)541-0413 [10555]

Big Boys Toys, Rte. 67 A, RD No. 1, Box 174A, North Bennington, VT 05257, (802)447-1721 [2359]

Big Corn Cooperative Marketing Association Inc., PO Box 591, Greybull, WY 82426, (307)765-2058 [308]

Big D Bolt & Screw Co., 11112 Grader St., Dallas, TX 75238-2403, (214)349-8162 [13598]

Big Horn Booksellers Inc., 1813 E Mulberry, Ft. Collins, CO 80524, (970)224-1579 [3555]

Big Horn Cooperative Market Association Inc., PO Box 591, Greybull, WY 82426, (307)765-2061 [309]

Big Horn Wholesale, 231 Blackburn Ave., Cody, WY 82414-8432, (307)587-4929 [4580]

Big Inch Marine Systems Inc., 12235 FM 529, Houston, TX 77041-2805, (713)896-1501 [23085]

Big Island Marine, 73-4840 Kanalani St., Kailua Kona, HI 96740, (808)329-3719 [18463]

Big/Little Stores Inc., PO Box 1236, Enterprise, AL 36331, (334)347-9546 [22072]

Big Reds Antiques, PO Box 160, Forney, TX 75126, (214)552-2949 [13038]

Big River Industries Inc., 3700 Mansell Rd., No. 250, Alpharetta, GA 30022-8246, (678)461-2830 [7057]

Big River Rubber & Gasket, 214 W 10th St., Owensboro, KY 42303, (270)926-0241 [24270]

Big Rock Sports Inc., Hwy. 24 W Hankinson Dr., PO Drawer 1107, Morehead City, NC 28557, (252)726-6186 [23558]

Big Sandy Wholesale Co., PO Box 249, Harold, KY 41635, (606)478-9591 [10556]

Big Saver Inc., PO Box 198, Montgomery, NY 12549, (914)457-9622 [22073]

Big Shot Beverage Inc., 272 Plauche St., Harahan, LA 70123, (504)733-4343 [24915]

Big Sky Auto Auction Inc., 1236 Cordova St., Billings, MT 59101, (406)259-5999 [20601]

Big Sky Auto Auction Inc., 1236 Cordova St., Billings, MT 59101, (406)259-5999 [2360]

Big Sky Fire Equipment, 207 W Janeaux, Lewistown, MT 59457-3036, (406)538-9303 [18707]

Big Sky Office Products Inc., 501 N 23rd St., Billings, MT 59101, (406)252-9210 [20843]

Big Sky Paint Co., Heating & Air Conditioning, 505 Main St. SW, Ronan, MT 59864, (406)676-0700 [21400]

Big Sky Trading Co., 19994 U.S Highway 93 N, Arlee, MT 59821, (406)726-3214 [11928]

Big State Record Distribution Corp., 4830 Lakawana, Ste. 121, Dallas, TX 75247, (214)631-1100 [25103]

Big Stone County Cooperative, PO Box 362, Clinton, MN 56225, (612)325-5466 [310]

Big T Pump Company Inc., PO Drawer 2278, Hereford, TX 79045, (806)364-0353 [311]

Big Tex Feed Co. Inc., 3720 Lamar Ave., Paris, TX 75460, (903)785-1681 [312]

Big Tex Grain Company Inc., 401 Blue Star St., San Antonio, TX 78204, (210)227-3462 [313]

Big Valley AG Services Inc., PO Box 926, Gridley, CA 95948, (530)846-5612 [314]

Big Valley Plastics Inc., PO Box 1690, Sumner, WA 98390, (253)863-8111 [22937]

Big W Supplies Inc., 650 W 18th St., Cheyenne, WY 82001-4305, (307)634-5502 [4581]

Bigelow-Sanford, 300 Landrum Mill Rd., Landrum, SC 29356, (864)457-3391 [9726]

Biggs Inc.; K.M., PO Box 967, Lumberton, NC 28359, (919)738-5206 [315]

Biggs Pump and Supply Inc., PO Box 7208, Lafayette, IN 47903, (765)447-1141 [23086]

Biglow Industrial Company Inc., PO Box 1251, Mountainside, NJ 07092-0251, (908)233-6500 [2361]

Bijoux Terner L.P., 7200 NW 7th St., Miami, FL 33126, (305)266-9000 [17338]

Bild Industries Inc., 800 Clear Water Loop, Post Falls, ID 83854, (208)773-0630 [13599]

Bilingual Educational Services, Inc., 2514 S Grand Ave., Los Angeles, CA 90007-2688, (213)749-6213 [3556]

Bilingual Publications Co., 270 Lafayette St., New York, NY 10012, (212)431-3500 [3557]

Bill Veazey's Rehab & Home Care Equipment, 945 W Wilshire, Oklahoma City, OK 73116, (405)843-8886 [19692]

Billie's Fashion Hats, 2521 Wainwright St., Corpus Christi, TX 78405, (512)887-6261 [4824]

Billings Distributing Corp., 260 Fulton St., Fresno, CA 93721, (209)268-6314 [14346]

Billings Horn, 12881 166th St., Cerritos, CA 90703-2103, (714)220-2313 [14040]

Billings Truck Center, PO Box 30236, Billings, MT 59107, (406)252-5121 [20602]

Billingsley Ranch Outfitters Equipment, PO Box 768, Glasgow, MT 59230-0768, (406)367-5577 [17734]

Billows Electric Supply Co., 9100 State Rd., Philadelphia, PA 19136, (267)332-9700 [8439]

Bill's Battery Co. Inc., 5221 Crookshank Rd., Cincinnati, OH 45238, (513)922-0100 [2362]

Biloff Manufacturing Co. Inc., PO Box 726, Shafter, CA 93263, (661)746-3976 [14347]

Biltmore Oil Co. Inc., 191 Amboy Rd., Asheville, NC 28806, (828)253-4591 [22074]

Bimex Incorporated, 3617 Shallford Rd., Atlanta, GA 30340, (404)451-2525 [15824]

Bindley Western, 9727 Tanner Rd., Houston, TX 77041-7620, (713)460-8588 [14041]

Bindley Western Drug Co., 542 Covina Blvd., San Dimas, CA 91773, (909)394-0067 [14042]

Bindley Western Drug Co., Carolina Division, Charlotte, NC 28203, (704)333-9393 [14043]

Bindley Western Drug Co. Dallas Div., 4217 Mint Way, Dallas, TX 75237, (214)339-3744 [14044]

Bindley Western Drug Co. Mid-South Div., 8055 Troon Circle, Ste. F, Austell, GA 30168-7849, (404)739-5030 [14045]

Bindley Western Drug Co. Southeastern Div., 2600 Pitan Row, Orlando, FL 32809, (407)438-0500 [14046]

Bindley Western Industries Inc., 8909 Purdue Rd., Indianapolis, IN 46268, (317)704-4000 [14047]

Bindley Western Industries Inc., 8909 Purdue Rd., Indianapolis, IN 46268-3135, (317)704-4000 [19187]

Bindley Western Industries Inc. Bindley Western Drug Div., 4212 W 71st St., Indianapolis, IN 46268, (317)298-9900 [14048]

Bindley Western Industries Inc. Kendall Div., PO Box 1060, Shelby, NC 28150, (704)482-2481 [19188]

Binford Farmers Union Grain, PO Box 165, Binford, ND 58416, (701)676-2481 [316]

Bing Construction Company of Nevada, PO Box 487, Minden, NV 89423, (702)265-3641 [7058]

Bingham Enterprises Inc., 13540 Lake City Way, Seattle, WA 98125, (206)367-3128 [19189]

Bingham Equipment Co., 815 Gila Bend Hwy., Casa Grande, AZ 85222, (602)836-8700 [317]

Binghamton Truck Body & Equipment Corp., 25 Alice St., PO Box 27, Binghamton, NY 13904, (607)723-8993 [2363]

The Bingo Company Inc., 700 W Mississippi Ave., Unit 2, Bldg. A, Denver, CO 80223-3172, (303)744-3332 [26418]

Bingo Depot, PO Box 903, Lake Havasu City, AZ 86405-0903, (907)561-7115 [26419]

Bingo Sales Inc.; J.D., 1500 Kosciuszko Ave., Bay City, MI 48708-8028, (517)894-4004 [26420]

Binks Manufacturing Co., 9201 W Belmont Ave., Franklin Park, IL 60131-2887, (847)671-3000 [15825]

Binson's Hospital Supplies Inc., 26834 Lawrence Ave., Center Line, MI 48015, (810)755-2300 [18708]

Binswanger Glass Co., PO Box 171173, Memphis, TN 38187, (901)767-7111 [7059]

Bintz Distributing Co., 1855 S 300 W, Salt Lake City, UT 84115, (801)463-1515 [24076]

Bio-Dental Technologies Corp., 11291 Sunrise Park Dr., Rancho Cordova, CA 95742, (916)638-8147 [19190]

Bio Instruments Inc., 271 Silver Lake Rd., St. Paul, MN 55112, (612)631-3380 [19191]

Bio-Medical Imaging Inc., PO Box 5364, Winston-Salem, NC 27113-5364, (336)768-9506 [18709]

Bio Medical Life Systems Inc., PO Box 1360, Vista, CA 92085-1360, (619)727-5600 [18710]

Bio-Medical Resources Inc., 2150 W 6th Ave., Broomfield, CO 80020, (303)469-1746 [18711]

Bio-Tech Maintenance Products, 2635 S Santa Fe Dr., Unit 2A, Denver, CO 80223, (970)774-8285 [23559]

Biocoustics Instruments Inc., 6925 Oakland Mills Rd., Ste. H, Columbia, MD 21045-4714, (410)995-6131 [18712]

Bioject Medical Technologies Inc., 7620 SW Bridgeport Rd., Portland, OR 97224, (503)639-7221 [19192]

Biomedical Research & Development Laboratories, Inc., 8561 Atlas Dr., Gaithersburg, MD 20877-4135, (301)948-6506 [18713]

Bion Environmental Technologies Inc., 555 17th St., Denver, CO 80202, (303)294-0750 [23087]

Biopool International Inc., 6025 Nicolle St., Ventura, CA 93003, (805)654-0643 [18714]

Biopractic Group II Inc., PO Box 22164, Lehigh Valley, PA 18002-2164 [14049]

Biosound Esaote Inc., 8000 Castleway Dr., Indianapolis, IN 46250-1943, (317)849-1793 [18715]

Biotronik Inc., 6024 Jean Rd., Lake Oswego, OR 97035-5369, (503)635-3594 [18716]

Bird and Company Inc.; William M., PO Box 20040, Charleston, SC 29413, (803)722-5930 [9727]

Bird Toy Man, 197 S Hillside Ave., Succasunna, NJ 07876, (973)584-0756 [27083]

Bird-X, Inc., 300 N Elizabeth St., 2N, Chicago, IL 60607, (312)226-2473 [318]

Bird-X Inc., 300 N Elizabeth St., Chicago, IL 60607, (312)226-2473 [8440]

Birdie Jackets, 7 Corporate Dr., Orangeburg, NY 10962-2615, (914)359-5200 [5129]

Birds Eye Veneer Co., 933 N 8th St., PO Box 352, Gladstone, MI 49837-0352, (906)428-3113 [7052]

Birdsall and Company Inc.; W.A., 1819 W Elizabeth Ave., Linden, NJ 07036, (908)862-4455 [23088]

Birdsong Corp., 612 Madison Ave., Suffolk, VA 23434, (804)539-3456 [10557]

BiRite Foodservice, 201 Alabama St., San Francisco, CA 94103, (415)621-6909 [10558]

Birkenstock Footprint Sandals Inc., PO Box 6140, Novato, CA 94948, (415)892-4200 [24691]

Birmingham Electric Battery Co., 2230 2nd Ave., Birmingham, AL 35233, (205)251-3211 [2364]

Birmingham Rail Locomotive Company Inc., PO Box 530157, Birmingham, AL 35253, (205)424-7245 [23474]

Birmingham Tobacco Co., PO Box 11021, Birmingham, AL 35202, (205)324-2581 [26265]

Birnberg & Sons Inc., 516 N Prior Ave., St. Paul, MN 55104, (612)645-4521 [15052]

Birns & Sawyer Inc., 1026 N Highland Ave., Hollywood, CA 90038-2407, (213)466-8211 [22831]

Birzon Inc.; Sid, 686 Main St., Buffalo, NY 14202, (716)856-8255 [17339]

Biscayne Electric and Hardware Distributors Inc., 1140 NW 159th Dr., Miami, FL 33169, (305)625-8526 [8441]

Bisco Industries Inc., 704 W Southern Ave., Orange, CA 92865, (714)283-7140 [8442]

Bisho Company, Inc.; J.R., 564 Market St., San Francisco, CA 94104, (415)397-0767 [2365]

Bishop Baking Co., PO Box 3720, Cleveland, TN 37320, (423)472-1561 [10559]

Bishop Distributing Co., 5200 36th SE, Grand Rapids, MI 49508, (616)942-9734 [9728]

Bishop-Epicure Foods Company Inc., PO Box 48426, Atlanta, GA 30362-1428, (404)441-2227 [10560]

Bishop Ladder Co. Inc., 1400 Park St., Hartford, CT 06106, (860)951-3246 [15826]

Bishops Inc., 112 Lincoln Ave., Pittsburgh, PA 15209-2620, (412)821-3333 [25982]

Bison Building Materials Inc., PO Box 19849, Houston, TX 77224, (713)467-6700 [7060]

Bison Corp., 1935 SE Allen Ave., Canton, OH 44707, (330)455-0282 [4336]

Bison Oil, PO Box 807, Sheridan, WY 82801, (307)672-2363 [22075]

Bison Products Co. Inc., 81 Dingens St., Buffalo, NY 14206, (716)826-2700 [10561]

Bissett Steel Co, 9005 Bank St., Cleveland, OH 44125, (216)447-4000 [19824]

Bissman Company Inc., 30 W 5th St., Mansfield, OH 44901, (419)524-2337 [1530]

Bitor America Corp., 5200 Town Center Cir., Ste. 301, Boca Raton, FL 33486, (561)392-0026 [20521]

Bittle American Inc.; J., 7149 Mission Gorge Rd., San Diego, CA 92120-1130, (619)560-2030 [2366]

Bittle American Inc.; J., 7149 Mission Gorge Rd., San Diego, CA 92120-1130, (619)229-7797 [2814]

Bitzer Company Inc.; R.D., 1330 Willow Ave., Elkins Park, PA 19027, (215)224-2112 [14348]

Bivins Barbecue Sauce, 6129 N Dort Hwy., Flint, MI 48505, (810)789-5444 [10562]

Bixby Feed Mill Inc., Rte. 2, Blooming Prairie, MN 55917, (507)583-7231 [319]

Bizjet International Sales and Support Inc., 3515 N Sheridan Rd., Tulsa, OK 74115, (918)832-7733 [59]

BJ Distributing, R.R. 1, Box 432, Rockville, IN 47872, (765)344-1046 [25104]

B.J. Toy Manufacturing Co., Applegate Ave., Pen Argyl, PA 18072-1403, (215)863-9191 [26421]

B.J.'s Ceramic Tile Distributing Company, Inc., 512 Dexter Dr., Jackson, MS 39208, (601)939-0111 [9729]

BKM Total Office, 340 Woodmont Rd., Milford, CT 06460, (203)324-3138 [20844]

BL Associates, Inc., 145 Webster St., Hanover, MA 02339, (781)982-9664 [6017]

Blacast Entertainment, PO Box 175, Cambria Heights, NY 11411, (718)712-2300 [3558]

Blach Distributing Co., PO Box 2690, Elko, NV 89803-2690, (702)738-5147 [1531]

Black Beauty Coal Co., PO Box 312, Evansville, IN 47702, (812)424-9000 [20522]

Black & Black Inc., 3081 La Pietra Circle, Honolulu, HI 96815, (808)926-2626 [4825]

Black and Co., 1717 E Garfield Ave., Decatur, IL 62525, (217)428-4424 [16753]

Black and Decker Corp. Products Service Div., 626 Hanover Pike, Hampstead, MD 21074, (410)239-5000 [15053]

Black & Decker US Inc., 3007 E Independence Blvd., Charlotte, NC 28205-7036, (704)374-1779 [4582]

Black Enterprises Inc., 1807 Black Hwy., York, SC 29745, (803)684-4971 [320]

Black Equipment Co. Inc., PO Box 5286, Evansville, IN 47716, (812)477-6481 [15827]

Black Forest Distributors Ltd., Co. Rte. 84, PO Box 607, Cairo, NY 12413, (518)622-9888 [1532]

Black Forest Tile Distributors, 1900 Hendersonville Rd., Asheville, NC 28803, (828)681-9597 [7061]

Black Gold Comics & Graphics, 2130 S Sheridan Rd., Tulsa, OK 74129-1002 [3559]

Black Gold Sales Inc., PO Box 1097, Hazard, KY 41701, (606)439-4559 [20523]

Black Hills Chemical Co. Inc., PO Box 2082, Rapid City, SD 57709-2082, (605)342-0788 [4583]

Black Hills Distributing Co. Inc., 6080 SW Linderson Way, Tumwater, WA 98501-5229, (425)357-5579 [1533]

Black Hills Gold Colema, PO Box 6400, Rapid City, SD 57701-4670, (605)394-3700 [17340]

Black Hills Jewelers Supply, 713 Main St., Rapid City, SD 57701-2737, (605)343-5678 [25574]

Black Hills Milk Producers, PO Box 2084, Rapid City, SD 57709, (605)342-3780 [10563]

Black Mountain Spring Water Inc., PO Box 3010, San Carlos, CA 94070-3010, (650)595-3800 [24916]

Black Oil Company Inc., PO Box 159, Monticello, UT 84535-0159, (435)587-2215 [22076]

Blackbird Ltd., 1143 E Broadmor, Tempe, AZ 85282, (602)966-7384 [4826]

Blackburn and Co.; Don, 13335 Farmington Rd., Livonia, MI 48150, (734)261-9100 [8443]

Blackburn Oil Co. Inc., PO Box 430, Opelika, AL 36803-0430, (334)745-2951 [22077]

Blackburn-Russell Company Inc., PO Box 157, Bedford, PA 15522-0157, (814)623-5181 [10564]

Blackfoot Livestock Commission Company Inc., PO Box 830, Blackfoot, ID 83221, (208)785-0500 [17735]

Blackhawk Distributors, 14225 Hansberry Rd., Rockton, IL 61072, (815)624-7227 [26422]

Blackman Associates, Inc.; Mel, PO Box 284, Canton, MA 02021, (781)828-9020 [13318]

Blackman Industries, 1401 Minnesota Ave., Kansas City, KS 66102-4309, (913)342-5010 [27084]

Blackman Medford Corp., 2700 Rte. 112, Medford, NY 11763-2553, (516)475-3170 [23089]

Blackmon Auctions Inc.; Tom, PO Box 7464, Little Rock, AR 72217, (501)664-4526 [321]

Blackmore Master Distributor, 7100 Jackson St., Paramount, CA 90723, (562)634-5600 [10565]

Blackton Inc., PO Bxo 536155, Orlando, FL 32853, (407)898-2661 [9730]

Blackwell Cooperative Elevator Association, 410 N Main St., Blackwell, OK 74631, (580)363-1461 [17736]

Blackwell North America Inc., 6024 SW Jean Rd., Lake Oswego, OR 97035, (503)684-1140 [3560]

Blackwell Stevenson Co., 3270 Sunnyside Rd., Bethel Park, PA 15102-1247, (412)257-1470 [10566]

Blackwell's Delaware Inc., 6024 SW Jean Rd., Lake Oswego, OR 97035, (503)684-1140 [3561]

Blaine Window Hardware Inc., 17319 Blaine Dr., Hagerstown, MD 21740, (301)797-6500 [13600]

Blaine's Art & Graphic Supply, 2803 Spenard Rd., Anchorage, AK 99503, (907)561-5344 [13319]

Blaine's Paint Store, Inc., 360 E International Airport Rd., Anchorage, AK 99518, (907)563-3412 [21401]

Blais Enterprises; M.C., RR 1 Box 19, Mt. Holly, VT 05758-9703, (802)259-2213 [24516]

Blake Brothers, 13 Columbia Dr. Unit 3, Amherst, NH 03031-2319, (603)377-8058 [17341]

Blake Wire and Cable Corp., 16134 Runnymede St., Van Nuys, CA 91406, (818)781-8300 [8444]

Blalock Oil Company Inc., PO Box 775, Jonesboro, GA 30236, (770)478-8888 [22078]

Blanchard Auto Electric Co., PO Box 24626, Seattle, WA 98124, (206)682-2981 [2367]

Blanchard Valley Farmers Cooperative, PO Box 607, McComb, OH 45858, (419)293-2311 [22079]

Blanchardville Cooperative Oil Association, 401 S Main St., Box 88, Blanchardville, WI 53516, (608)523-4294 [22079]

Bland Farms Inc., PO Box 506, Glennville, GA 30427, (912)654-1426 [10567]

Blank Inc.; Joseph, 15 W 47th St., New York, NY 10036, (212)575-9050 [17342]

Blanke Sales Inc.; Bob, 1549 Helton Dr., Florence, AL 35631, (205)764-5983 [10568]

Blankenship and Company Inc.; E., 704 W Main St., Marion, IL 62959, (618)993-2643 [2368]

Blankenstein Co. Inc.; F.R., PO Box 986, Natchez, MS 39121-0986, (601)445-5618 [18717]

Blankinship Distributors Inc., 1927 Vine St., Kansas City, MO 64108, (816)842-6825 [14050]

Blankinship Distributors Inc., 1927 Vine St., Kansas City, MO 64108, (816)842-6825 [19193]

Blarney Castle Oil Co., PO Box 246, Bear Lake, MI 49614, (616)864-3111 [22080]

Blast-Spray Equipment Co., 1810 Fortune Rd., Ste. G, Salt Lake City, UT 84104-3808, (801)486-0803 [25575]

Blau; Emery, 20 Pumpkin Ln., Norwalk, CT 06851-1421, (203)846-9606 [24692]

Bleecker Furniture Inc., PO Box 5084, Missoula, MT 59806-5084, (406)543-8593 [13039]

Blevins Inc., 421 Hart Ln., Nashville, TN 37216, (615)227-7772 [8445]

Bleyhl Farm Service, 119 E Main, Grandview, WA 98930, (509)882-1225 [322]

Blick Co.; Dick, PO Box 1267, Galesburg, IL 61401, (309)343-6181 [25576]

Blickman Supply, 280 Midland Ave., Bldg. M-1, Saddle Brook, NJ 07663, (201)791-2244 [24103]

Blish-Mize Co., 223 S 5th St., Atchison, KS 66002, (913)367-1250 [13601]

Bliss Cooperative Grain Co., PO Box 549, Marland, OK 74644, (580)268-3316 [17738]

Blistex Inc., 1800 Swift Dr., Oak Brook, IL 60523, (630)571-2870 [14051]

Bloch Metals Inc., PO Box 306, Tyler, TX 75710, (903)597-4552 [26768]

Bloch Steel Industries, PO Box 24063, Seattle, WA 98124, (206)763-0200 [19825]

Block and Company Inc., 1111 S Wheeling Rd., Wheeling, IL 60090, (847)537-7200 [20845]

Block Distributing Co. Inc., PO Box 8157, San Antonio, TX 78208, (210)224-7531 [1534]

Block Distributing Co. Inc., PO Box 9429, Corpus Christi, TX 78469, (512)882-4273 [1535]

Block Distributing Co. Inc., 2112 Rutland Dr., Ste. 140, Austin, TX 78758, (512)834-9742 [1536]

Block Steel Corp., 6101 W Oakton, Skokie, IL 60077, (847)966-3000 [19826]

Blodgett International Sales; G.S., PO Box 586, Burlington, VT 05402-0586, (802)658-6600 [24077]

Blodgett Supply Co. Inc., PO Box 759, Williston, VT 05495-0759, (802)864-9831 [15054]

Bloemer Food Service Co., 925 S 7th St., Louisville, KY 40203, (502)584-8338 [10569]

Blonders of Hartford, 741 Windsor St., Hartford, CT 06120, (860)522-1104 [2275]

Bloodline Agency, Attn: Terry Boyarsky, 101 Hud Rd., Winchester, KY 40391, (606)745-6601 [27085]

Bloom Brothers Co., 15350 25th Ave. N, No. 114, Plymouth, MN 55447-2081, (612)832-3250 [4827]

Blooming Prairie, 2340 Heinz Rd., Iowa City, IA 52240, (319)337-6448 [10570]

Blooming Prairie Cooperative Warehouse, 2340 Heinz Rd., Iowa City, IA 52240, (319)337-6448 [10570]

Blooming Prairie Natural Foods, 510 Kasota Ave. SE, Minneapolis, MN 55414, (612)378-9774 [10571]

Bloomingdale's Inc., 1000 3rd Ave., New York, NY 10022, (212)705-2000 [4828]

Blossoms, 33866 Woodward Ave., Birmingham, MI 48009-0914, (248)644-4411 [14950]

Blount Farmers Cooperative, 1514 W Broadway Ave., Maryville, TN 37801, (615)982-2761 [323]

Blount Seafood Corp., PO Box 327, Warren, RI 02885, (401)245-8800 [10572]

Bloxham; Jack S., 348 Bootlegger Tr., Black Eagle, MT 59414-0328, (406)761-4492 [17739]

Blu-Ridge Sales Inc., 11613 Busy St., Richmond, VA 23236-4059, (804)379-2774 [14349]

Blue Anchor Inc., 301 North G St., Exeter, CA 93221-1123, (916)929-3050 [10573]

Blue Birds International Corp., 6110 Ledwin Dr., Troy, MI 48098, (248)828-7972 [25105]

Blue Canyon Jewelry, 10918 Cochiti Rd. SE, Albuquerque, NM 87123-3350, (505)298-3096 [17343]

Blue Chip Stamps, PO Box 831, Pasadena, CA 91102, (626)585-6714 [25577]

Blue Cold Distributors, 323 Pine Point Rd., Scarborough, ME 04074, (207)885-0107 [24078]

Blue Diamond Materials Co., 1245 Arrow Hwy., Irwindale, CA 91706-6601, (626)303-2623 [7062]

Blue Flame Div., 6502 Dixie Hwy., Ste. 240, Fairfield, OH 45014, (513)247-0660 [22081]

Blue Grass Optical Co., 140 S Forbes Rd., Lexington, KY 40511, (606)255-0743 [19194]

Blue Grass Quality Meats, PO Box 17658, Crescent Springs, KY 41017, (606)331-7100 [10574]

Blue Hen Spring Works, Inc., 112 N Rehoboth Blvd., Milford, DE 19963, (302)422-6600 [2369]

Blue Line Distributing, 24120 Haggerty Rd., Farmington Hills, MI 48335, (248)478-6200 [10575]

Blue Lustre, LLC, 997 Horan Dr., Fenton, MO 63026-2401, (314)343-5106 [4584]

Blue Mount Quarry, 17701 Big Falls Rd., White Hall, MD 21161-9208, (410)343-0500 [23560]

Blue Mountain Growers Inc., PO Box 156, Milton-Freewater, OR 97862, (541)938-3391 [10576]

Blue Mountain Steel, 10097 US Highway 50 E, Carson City, NV 89701, (775)246-7770 [19827]

Blue Pearl, PO Box 5127, Gainesville, FL 32602 [17344]

Blue Ribbon Awards, 1935 S Lennox Ave., Casper, WY 82601-4944, (307)266-6401 [17345]

Blue Ribbon Business Products Co., 930 SE Sherman St., Portland, OR 97214-4655, (503)233-7288 [20846]

Blue Ribbon Foods, PO Box 1805, Wenatchee, WA 98801, (509)662-2181 [10577]

Blue Ribbon Linen Supply Inc., PO Box 798, Lewiston, ID 83501-0798, (208)743-5521 [4585]

Blue Ribbon Meat Co., PO Box 633, Sparks, NV 89431, (702)358-8116 [10578]

Blue Ribbon Meat Company Inc., PO Box 1805, Wenatchee, WA 98801, (509)662-2181 [10579]

Blue Ridge Beef Plant Inc., PO Box 397, Belton, SC 29627, (803)338-5544 [10580]

Blue Ridge Electric Motor Repair, 629 Emma Rd., Asheville, NC 28806, (828)258-0800 [8446]

Blue Ridge Fish Wholesale, 330 Berry Garden Rd., Kernersville, NC 27284, (910)996-3200 [27086]

Blue Ridge Graphics Inc., 550 Meade Ave., Charlottesville, VA 22902-5461, (804)296-9746 [4829]

Blue Ridge Mountain Woodcrafts Inc., PO Box 566, Ellijay, GA 30540, (706)276-2222 [13320]

Blue Ridge Sporting Supplies, PO Box 1537, Salem, VA 24153-0019, (540)389-1368 [23561]

Blue Ridge Wholesale, 299 Berry Garden Rd., Kernersville, NC 27284, (910)996-3200 [27087]

Blue Rock Beverage Co., PO Box 1705, Sidney, MT 59270, (406)228-8249 [1537]

Blue Star Growers Inc., PO Box I, Cashmere, WA 98815, (509)782-2922 [10581]

Blue Water Ship Store, 2030 FM 2094, PO Box 989, Kemah, TX 77565, (281)334-7583 [18464]

Blue White Industries Limited Inc., 14931 Chestnut St., Westminster, CA 92683, (714)893-8529 [24324]

Bluefin Seafoods Corp., 141 N Spring St., Louisville, KY 40206, (502)587-1505 [10582]

Bluegrass Bandag, Inc., 1101 Enterprise Dr., PO Box 756, Winchester, KY 40392-0756, (606)745-2850 [2370]

Bluestem Farm and Ranch Supply Inc., 2611 W 50 Hwy., Emporia, KS 66801, (316)342-5502 [324]

Bluff City Electronics, 3339 Fontaine Rd., Memphis, TN 38116, (901)345-9500 [8447]

Bluff Springs Farmers Elevator Co., PO Box 50, Bluff Springs, IL 62622, (217)323-2815 [17740]

Bluffs Budget Plumbing, PO Box 255, Pine Bluffs, WY 82082-0255, (307)245-9224 [23090]

Blumenthal-Lansing Co., 1 Palmer Ter., Carlstadt, NJ 07072, (201)935-6220 [25983]

Blyth Industries Inc., 100 Field Point Rd., Greenwich, CT 06830-6442, (203)661-1926 [15422]

BMG Distribution Co., 974 United Cir., Sparks, NV 89431, (702)331-6600 [25106]

BMG Metals Inc., PO Box 7536, Richmond, VA 23231, (804)226-1024 [19828]

BMI Educational Services, 26 Hay Press Rd., PO Box 800, Dayton, NJ 08810-0800, (732)329-6991 [3562]

BMI Equipment Dist., 5431 Old Alexandria Tpke., Warrenton, VA 20187, (540)341-4330 [14350]

BMI-France Inc., 27 Noblestown Rd., Carnegie, PA 15106, (412)923-2525 [7063]

BMS Inc. - Barcoded Management Systems, Inc., PO Box 49310, Dayton, OH 45449-0310, (937)643-2006 [6018]

BMT Commodity Corp., 750 Lexington Ave., New York, NY 10022, (212)759-4505 [10583]

BMW of North America Inc., PO Box 1227, Westwood, NJ 07675-1227, (201)307-4000 [20603]

BNA Optical Supply Inc., 2819 Columbine Pl., Nashville, TN 37204-3103, (615)383-7036 [19195]

Boat America Corp., 880 S Pickett St., Alexandria, VA 22304, (703)370-4202 [18465]

Boat Electric Co. Inc., 2520 Westlake Ave. N, Seattle, WA 98109-2234, (206)281-7570 [14351]

The Boat Locker, 1543 Post Rd. E, Westport, CT 06880, (203)259-7808 [18466]

Boater's World, 6711 Ritz Way, Beltsville, MD 20705, (301)953-9611 [18467]

Boatwright Insulation Co., PO Box 25516, Raleigh, NC 27611, (919)828-7102 [7064]

Bob Allen Sportswear, 220 S Main St., Osceola, IA 50213, (515)342-6773 [4839]

Bob & Joe's Wholesale, 1011 E 2nd St., Butte, MT 59701-2984, (406)723-5455 [1538]

Bobb Brothers Inc., PO Box 306, Leesburg, OH 45135, (513)780-2241 [17741]

Bobbett & Associates Inc., 263 N Madison Ave., Greenwood, IN 46142-3633, (317)882-6051 [24693]

Bobco Metal Co., 2000 S Alameda St., Los Angeles, CA 90058, (213)748-5171 [19829]

Bob's Business Inc., PO Box 35, Red Wing, MN 55066-0035, (612)388-4742 [23562]

Bob's Candies Inc., PO Box 3170, Albany, GA 31707, (912)430-8300 [10584]

Bobs Fire Extinguisher, 1033 N Polk Ext., Moscow, ID 83843-9271, (208)882-3693 [24517]

Bob's Fruit Market & Deli, 12418 Dix-Toledo, Southgate, MI 48195, (810)282-1057 [10585]

Bob's Gard Duty, 901 Market St., Wheeling, WV 26003-2909, (304)234-7667 [8448]

Bob's Machine Shop, 1501 33rd St. SE, Ruskin, FL 33570, (813)645-3966 [18468]

Bobtron International Inc., 1101 Monterey Pass Rd., Monterey Park, CA 91754, (213)748-9466 [4830]

Bock Jewelry Co. Inc., 6019 Berkshire Lane, Dallas, TX 75225-5706, (214)692-9000 [17346]

Bock Pharmaceutical, Inc.; James A., PO Box 785, Wilmington, OH 45177, (937)382-4545 [19196]

Bockstanz Brothers Co., 32553 Schoolcraft, Livonia, MI 48150-4307, (734)458-2006 [4586]

Bocock-Stroud Co., PO Box 25746, Winston-Salem, NC 27114, (919)724-2421 [23563]

Bodden Lumber Company Inc.; R.K., PO Box 203, Mobile, AL 36601, (334)433-2736 [7065]

Bode Cooperative, PO Box 155, Bode, IA 50519, (515)379-1754 [325]

Bode-Finn Co., 3480 Spring Grove Ave., Cincinnati, OH 45223, (513)541-0401 [16134]

Bodine Electric of Decatur, 1845 N 22nd St., Decatur, IL 62526, (217)423-2593 [8449]

Bodine Inc., 2141 14th Ave. S, Birmingham, AL 35205, (205)933-9100 [13040]

Bodman Chemicals, Inc., PO Box 2421, Aston, PA 19014, (610)459-5600 [4337]

Body Drama Inc., 5840 Uplander Way, No. 202, Culver City, CA 90230-6620, (310)410-5090 [4831]

Bodyline Comfort Systems, 3730 Kori Rd., Jacksonville, FL 32257, (904)262-4068 [18718]

Boedeker; Robert L., PO Box 482, Lander, WY 82520-0482, (307)332-3703 [17742]

Boehm-Madisen Lumber Company Inc., PO Box 906, Brookfield, WI 53008-0906, (262)544-4660 [7066]

Boeing Petroleum Services Inc., 850 S Clearview Pkwy., New Orleans, LA 70123, (504)734-4200 [22082]

Boelter Companies Inc., 11100 W Silver Spr Rd, Milwaukee, WI 53225, (414)461-3400 [24079]

Boelter Co., 7370 N Lincoln Ave., Lincolnwood, IL 60646, (773)267-0505 [24080]

Boente Sons Inc.; Joseph F., 543 W Main St., Carlinville, IL 62626-0288, (217)854-3164 [22083]

Boettcher Enterprises Inc., 118 W Court St., Beloit, KS 67420, (785)738-5761 [326]

Boettcher Supply Inc., PO Box 486, Beloit, KS 67420, (785)738-5781 [8450]

Bogatin, Inc.; Philip F., 2011 Walnut St., Philadelphia, PA 19103, (215)568-1464 [25984]

Bogen Photo Corp., 565 E Crescent Ave., PO Box 506, Ramsey, NJ 07446-0506, (201)818-9500 [22832]

Boggis-Johnson Electric Co., 2900 N 112th St., Milwaukee, WI 53222, (414)475-6900 [8451]

Bogner of America Inc., PO Box 644, Newport, VT 05855, (802)334-6507 [4832]

Bohl Equipment Co., 534 Laskey Rd., Toledo, OH 43612, (419)476-7525 [15828]

Bohrer Inc.; A., 50 Knickerbocker Rd., Moonachie, NJ 07074, (201)935-1600 [10586]

Boiler and Heat Exchange Systems Inc., PO Box 23566, Chattanooga, TN 37422, (423)899-6600 [23091]

Boise Cascade, PO Box 130, Nutting Lake, MA 01865, (978)670-3800 [7067]

Boise Cascade, 800 W Bryn Mawr Ave., Itasca, IL 60143, (708)773-5000 [20847]

Boise Cascade Corp., PO Box 50, Boise, ID 83728, (208)384-6161 [27287]

Boise Cascade Corp. Building Materials Distribution Div., 1111 W Jefferson St., Boise, ID 83702, (208)384-6354 [27288]

Boise Cascade Office Products Corp., 3025 Powers Ave., Jacksonville, FL 32207-8011, (904)773-5000 [20848]

Boise Paint & Glass Inc., 410 N Orchard St., Boise, ID 83706-1977, (208)343-4811 [21402]

Boise Refrigeration Service Co., 202 W 39th St., Boise, ID 83714-6404, (208)344-0709 [14352]

Boisset U.S.A., 650 5th St., Ste. 403, San Francisco, CA 94107, (415)979-0630 [1539]

Boland Electric Supply Inc., PO Box 3430, Decatur, IL 62524-3430, (217)423-3495 [8452]

Boley Co.; Mel, 1484 S State St., Salt Lake City, UT 84115-5424, (801)484-5372 [24694]

Boliden Metech Inc., 120 Mapleville Main St., Mapleville, RI 02839, (401)568-0711 [26906]

Bolivar Farmers Exchange, PO Box 27, Bolivar, MO 65613, (417)326-5231 [327]

Bolk Industrial Supply Corp., PO Box 279, Vincennes, IN 47591, (812)882-4090 [16754]

Bolliger Corp., P.O. Box 2949, Spartanburg, SC 29304, (864)582-1900 [15829]

Bollinger Healthcare, 222 W Airport Fwy., Irving, TX 75062-6322 [15830]

Bologna Brothers, PO Box 90737, Lafayette, LA 70509-0737, (318)235-8555 [1540]

Bologna Brothers, 6321 Humphreys St., Harahan, LA 70123, (504)733-4361 [1541]

Bologna Brothers, PO Box 8727, Shreveport, LA 71148, (318)869-2053 [1542]

Bolton and Hay Inc., PO Box 3247, Des Moines, IA 50316, (515)265-2554 [24081]

Bolts & Nuts Inc., 17407 Lorain Ave., Cleveland, OH 44111-4022, (216)671-6670 [8453]

Bomadi Inc., 28 E Jackson Blvd., Ste. 1109, Chicago, IL 60604, (312)663-3880 [10587]

Bomaine Corp., 2716 Ocean Park Blvd., Ste. 1065, Santa Monica, CA 90405, (310)450-2303 [15423]

Boman and Kemp Steel and Supply Inc., PO Box 9725, Ogden, UT 84409, (801)731-0615 [19830]

Bombay Industries Inc.; 989 6th Ave., 15th Fl., New York, NY 10018, (212)564-3099 [4833]

Bon Motif Co., 4045 Horton St., Emeryville, CA 94608, (510)655-2000 [15424]

Bon Secour Fisheries Inc., PO Box 60, Bon Secour, AL 36511, (334)949-7411 [10588]

Bon Ton Foods Inc., 1120 Zinns Quarry Rd., York, PA 17404, (717)843-0738 [10589]

Bon Tool Co., 4430 Gibsonia Rd., Gibsonia, PA 15044, (724)443-7080 [13602]

Bonanza Beverage Co., 6333 S Ensworth St., Las Vegas, NV 89119, (702)361-4166 [1543]

Bonanza Nut and Bolt Inc., 1890 Purina Way, Sparks, NV 89431, (702)358-2638 [13603]

Boncosky Oil Co., 739 N State St., Elgin, IL 60123, (847)741-2577 [22084]

Bond Co.; T. Talbott, 7138 Windsor Blvd., Baltimore, MD 21244, (410)265-8600 [20849]

Bond County Services Co., 822 S 2nd St., Greenville, IL 62246, (618)664-2030 [328]

Bond Equipment Company Inc., 2946 Irving Blvd., Dallas, TX 75247, (214)637-0760 [20604]

Bond Paint Co., 1802 San Juan Blvd., Farmington, NM 87401, (505)326-3368 [21403]

Bond Paint Co., 2512 Graceland Dr. NE, Albuquerque, NM 87110-3802, (505)888-3737 [21404]

Bond Supply Co., 147 W 35th St., New York, NY 10001, (212)695-2672 [25985]

Bond Wholesale, Inc., 3025 Mable, Trenton, MO 64683, (660)359-3710 [26266]

Bonded Fibers and Quilting, 1720 Fuller Rd., West Des Moines, IA 50265, (515)223-5668 [25986]

Bonded Insulation Company Inc., PO Box 337, Hagaman, NY 12086, (518)842-1470 [26769]

Bonded Materials Co., 91-400 Komohana St., Kapolei, HI 96707-1785, (808)832-1155 [7068]

Bonded Motors, Inc., 7522 S Maie Ave., Los Angeles, CA 90001, (323)583-8631 [2371]

Bonded Spirits Corp., PO Box 265, Oconomowoc, WI 53066, (414)786-7770 [1544]

Bondurant Grain Company Inc.; D.E., PO Box 280, Ness City, KS 67560, (913)798-3322 [17743]

Bondy Export Corp., 40 Canal St., New York, NY 10002, (212)925-7785 [8454]

Bonfield Brothers, Inc., Calk Ave., Box 450, Mt. Sterling, KY 40353, (606)498-1993 [22085]

Bonita Pioneer Packaging Prods, 7333 SW Bonita Rd., Portland, OR 97224, (503)684-6542 [16755]

Bonitz Brothers Inc., 931 Dana Dr., Harrisburg, PA 17109-5937, (717)545-3754 [23564]

Bonnette Supply Inc., PO Box 709, St. Albans, VT 05478-0709, (802)524-3806 [7069]

Bonneville Industrial, 45 South 1500 West, Orem, UT 84058, (801)225-7770 [16756]

Bonneville News Co. Inc., 965 Beardsley Pl., Salt Lake City, UT 84119, (801)972-5454 [3563]

Bonus Books Inc., 160 E Illinois St., Chicago, IL 60611, (312)467-0580 [3564]

Bonus Crop Fertilizer Inc., PO Box 1725, Bay City, TX 77404-1725, (409)245-4825 [329]

Book Box, Inc., 3126 Purdue Ave., Los Angeles, CA 90066, (310)391-2313 [3565]

Book Centers Inc., 5600 NE Hassalo St., Portland, OR 97213, (503)287-6657 [3566]

Book Distribution Center, PO Box 31669, Houston, TX 77235, (713)721-1980 [3567]

Book Distribution Center, Inc., 4617 N Witchduck Rd., Virginia Beach, VA 23455, (757)456-0005 [3568]

Book Dynamics, Inc., 26 Kennedy Blvd., East Brunswick, NJ 08816, (732)545-5151 [3569]

Book Home, Inc., 119 E Dale St., PO Box 825, Colorado Springs, CO 80901, (719)634-5885 [3570]

The Book House Inc., 208 W Chicago St., Jonesville, MI 49250-0125, (517)849-2117 [3571]

Book Warehouse Inc., 5154 NW 165th St., Palmetto Lakes Industrial Pk., Hialeah, FL 33014-6335, (305)624-4545 [3572]

Book Wholesalers, Inc., 1847 Mercer Rd., Lexington, KY 40511, (606)231-9789 [3573]

Bookazine Co., Inc., 75 Hook Rd., Bayonne, NJ 07002, (201)339-7777 [3574]

Bookcraft Inc., 40 E South Temple, Salt Lake City, UT 84111-1003, (801)908-3400 [3575]

Booker and Company Inc., 4720 Oak Fair Blvd., Tampa, FL 33610, (813)229-0931 [7070]

Booker Equity Union Exchange Inc., PO Box 230, Booker, TX 79005-0230, (806)658-4541 [330]

Booker-Price Co., 1318 McHenry St., Louisville, KY 40217, (502)637-2531 [13041]

Booklegger, PO Box 2626, Grass Valley, CA 95945, (530)272-1556 [3576]

BookLink Distributors, PO Box 840, Arroyo Grande, CA 93421-0840, (805)473-1947 [3577]

Bookmark, Inc., 14643 W 95th St., Lenexa, KS 66215, (913)894-1288 [3578]

Bookmen, Inc., 525 N 3rd St., Minneapolis, MN 55401, (612)359-5757 [3579]

Bookpeople, 7900 Edgewater Dr., Oakland, CA 94621, (510)632-4700 [3580]

Books Nippan, 1123 Dominguez St., Ste. K, Carson, CA 90746, (310)604-9701 [4004]

Books Nippan, 1123K Dominguez St., Carson, CA 90746, (310)604-9701 [3581]

Booksmith Promotional Co., 100 Paterson Plank Rd., Jersey City, NJ 07307, (201)659-2768 [3582]

The Booksource, 1230 Macklind Ave., St. Louis, MO 63110, (314)647-0600 [3583]

BookWorld Services Inc., 1933 Whitfield Park Loop, Sarasota, FL 34243, (941)758-8094 [3584]

The Bookworm, 417 Monmouth Dr., Cherry Hill, NJ 08002, (609)667-5884 [3585]

Boone County Farm Bureau Cooperative Inc., PO Box 626, Lebanon, IN 46052, (765)482-5600 [22086]

Boone-Davis Inc., 1346 N Knollwood Cir., Anaheim, CA 92801, (714)229-9900 [15425]

Boone Distributing, 4300 Chateau Rd., Columbia, MO 65202-6725, (573)474-6153 [1545]

Booneville Cooperative Elevator Co., PO Box 34, Booneville, IA 50038, (515)987-4533 [331]

Boot & Shoe Village, 5704 Vickie Dr., Winston Salem, NC 27106-9655, (910)969-6408 [24695]

Booth Co.; George E., 800 Cawthon St., Ste. 100, Louisville, KY 40203, (502)589-1056 [24325]

Booth Inc.; I.D., PO Box 579, Elmira, NY 14902, (607)733-9121 [23092]

Borden Inc., 103 W 11th, Lake Charles, LA 70601-6034, (318)494-3830 [10590]

Borden Inc., 500 N Jackson, Sulphur Springs, TX 75482-2846, (903)885-7573 [10591]

Borden Inc., 805 W Front, Tyler, TX 75702-7953, (903)595-4461 [10592]

Borden Inc., PO Box 7651, Waco, TX 76714-7651, (254)420-3374 [10593]

Borden Milk Products LLP, PO Box 7651, Waco, TX 76714-7651, (254)420-3374 [10593]

Borden & Riley Paper Co., 184-10 Jamaica Ave., Hollis, NY 11423, (718)454-0791 [21654]

Border Leather Corp., 261 Broadway, Chula Vista, CA 91910-2319, (619)691-1657 [18377]

Border Sales Inc., 255 S Regent St., Port Chester, NY 10573, (914)939-4350 [23217]

Border States Electric Supply, 105 25th St., N, Fargo, ND 58102-4030, (701)293-5834 [8455]

Border States Industries Inc., PO Box 2767, Fargo, ND 58108-2767, (701)293-5834 [8456]

Bore Technology Inc., 5977 Hutchinson Rd., Batavia, OH 45103, (513)625-8374 [15831]

Borel Jules & Co., 1110 Grand, Kansas City, MO 64106-2306, (816)421-6110 [17347]

Borg Compressed Steel Corp., 1032 N Lewis Ave., Tulsa, OK 74110, (918)587-2437 [19831]

Borg Warner Automotive Friction Products, 6700 18 1/2 Mile Rd., PO Box 8023, Sterling Heights, MI 48311-8023, (810)726-4470 [2372]

Boring and Smith Industries Div., 2500 Royal Pl., Tucker, GA 30084, (404)934-6341 [16757]

Borkholder and Company Inc.; F.D., PO Box 32, Nappanee, IN 46550, (219)773-3144 [7071]

Bornell Supply, 180 Eastom Cir., Lima, OH 45804, (419)221-2080 [2373]

Bornell Supply Company Inc., 8550 North 25A, PO Box 1138, Piqua, OH 45356, (937)773-5323 [15832]

Borneo Group Inc., 2317 E 34th St., Minneapolis, MN 55406-2414, (612)331-6136 [4834]

Bornstein and Company Inc.; L., PO Box 172, Somerville, MA 02143, (617)776-3555 [9731]

Boroff and Associates; Cy, 804 Apparel Ctr., Chicago, IL 60654, (312)644-7020 [4835]

Borstein Seafood Inc., PO Box 188, Bellingham, WA 98227, (360)734-7990 [10594]

Bortman Trading Co., PO Box 134, Center Sandwich, NH 03227-0134, (603)284-7068 [17348]

Borton Brokerage Co., PO Box 410167, St. Louis, MO 63141, (314)991-3355 [10595]

Bosch Corp. Packaging Machinery Div.; Robert, PO Box 579, Bridgman, MI 49106-0579, (616)466-4149 [15833]

Bosch Power Tools; Robert, 9401 James Ave. S, Bloomington, MN 55431-2500, (612)881-6979 [15834]

Bosco Products Inc., 441 Main Rd., Towaco, NJ 07082, (973)334-7777 [10596]

Bosco Trading Corp., 1605 NW 82nd Ave., Miami, FL 33122, (305)591-5888 [9610]

Bose Corp., 3550 E 40th St., Yuma, AZ 85365, (520)726-1820 [15055]

Boshco Inc., 42 Manning Rd., Billerica, MA 01821, (978)667-1911 [15835]

Boshco Inc., 42 Manning Rd., Billerica, MA 01821, (978)667-1911 [15836]

Bosler Leather Co. Inc.; George, 3106 Sunny Ln., Louisville, KY 40205-2825, (502)454-0416 [4836]

Boss Hawaii Inc., 3210 F. Koapaka St., Honolulu, HI 96819, (808)839-1057 [23565]

Boss Manufacturing Co., 221 W 1st St., Kewanee, IL 61443, (309)852-2131 [4837]

Bossert Industrial Supply Inc., 5959 W Howard St., Niles, IL 60714, (708)647-0515 [16758]

Bossi Sales Co. Inc., PO Box 3375, Springfield, MO 65802, (417)862-9351 [1546]

Boston Brands, 8 Faneuil Hall Market Pl., Boston, MA 02109, (617)973-9100 [10597]

Boston Clock, 284 Everett Ave., Chelsea, MA 02150, (617)884-0250 [18737]

Boston Computer Exchange Corp., 100 Charlestown St., Somerville, MA 02143, (617)625-7722 [6019]

Boston Electronics Corporation, 91 Boylston St., Brookline, MA 02445-7602, (617)566-3821 [22833]

Boston Metal Door Company Inc., 60 Lowell St., Arlington, MA 02474, (781)648-6890 [7072]

Boston Pet Supply, Inc., 1341 W McCoy Ln., Santa Maria, CA 93454, (805)922-2175 [27088]

Boston Pipe and Fittings Company Inc., 171 Sidney St., Cambridge, MA 02139, (617)876-7800 [23093]

Boston Productions Inc., 648 Beacon St., No. 2, Boston, MA 02215, (617)236-1180 [22834]

Boston Sea Foods Inc., 982 Main, Springfield, MA 01103-2120, (413)732-3663 [10598]

Boston Stove Co., 155 John St., Reading, MA 01867, (617)944-1045 [14353]

Boston Tile, 632 White St., Springfield, MA 01108-3221, (413)732-4191 [9732]

Boston Tile Distributors of Shrewsbury, Rte. 9, 512 Turnpike Rd., Shrewsbury, MA 01545-5970, (508)842-0178 [9733]

Boston Tile of Rhode Island, 1112 Jefferson Blvd., Warwick, RI 02886-2203, (401)738-2450 [9734]

Boston Trading Ltd. Inc., 315 Washington St., Lynn, MA 01902-4727, (781)592-4603 [4838]

Boston Warehouse Trading Corp., 59 Davis Ave., Norwood, MA 02062, (617)769-8550 [15426]

Bostonian Shoe Co., 520 S Broad St., Kennett Square, PA 19348, (215)444-6550 [24696]

Bostwick-Braun Co., PO Box 912, Toledo, OH 43697, (419)259-3600 [13604]

Bostwick-Braun Lorain Div., 5000 Grove Ave., Lorain, OH 44055-3612, (440)277-8288 [15837]

Boswell Golf Cars, Inc., 401 Fesslers Ln., Nashville, TN 37210, (615)256-0737 [23566]

Botkin Grain Co. Inc., PO Box 145, Argonia, KS 67004, (316)435-6510 [27089]

Bottenfield's Inc., PO Box 769, Pittsburg, KS 66762, (316)231-3900 [14052]

Bottineau Farmers Elevator Inc., PO Box 7, Bottineau, ND 58318, (701)228-2294 [17744]

Bottman Design Inc., 340 Whitney Ave., Salt Lake City, UT 84115-5120, (801)973-5410 [20850]

Boulevard Truck Sales and Service Inc., PMB 109, 119 N Parker St., Olathe, KS 66061-3139 [2374]

Bounty Food Co., PO Box 5, Winthrop, ME 04364, (207)377-6900 [10599]

Bounty Trading Co., PO Box 5, Winthrop, ME 04364, (207)377-6900 [10599]

Bouquet Enterprises Inc., 233 Glasgow Ave., Kellogg, MN 55945, (507)767-4994 [13321]

Bouregy, Thomas & Co. Inc., 160 Madison Ave., 5th Fl., New York, NY 10016-5412, (212)598-0222 [3586]

Boustead Electric and Manufacturing Co., 7135 Madison Ave. W, Minneapolis, MN 55427, (763)544-9131 [8457]

Boutique Trim, 21200 Pontiac Trl., South Lyon, MI 48178, (248)437-2017 [20851]

Boutross Imports Inc., 209 25th St., Brooklyn, NY 11232, (718)965-0070 [15427]

Bowen-Hall Petroleum Inc., PO Box 2012, Pocatello, ID 83201, (208)233-2794 [22087]

Bowen Petroleum, PO Box 2012, Pocatello, ID 83206, (208)233-2794 [22088]

Bowen Supply Inc., PO Box 947015, Ft. Worth, TX 76147-9015, (912)924-9076 [15428]

Bower Ammonia and Chemical, 5811 Tacony St., Philadelphia, PA 19135, (215)535-7530 [4338]

Bowers Implement Co. Inc., 338 Hwy. 24-27Bypass E, Albemarle, NC 28001, (704)983-2161 [332]

Bowes Industries Inc., PO Box 18802, Indianapolis, IN 46218-0802, (317)547-5245 [2375]

Bowie Industries Inc., PO Box 931, Bowie, TX 76230, (940)872-1106 [7073]

Bowie Manufacturing Inc., 313 S Hancock St., Lake City, IA 51449, (712)464-3191 [27090]

Bowles Sales; Gay, 3930 Enterprise Dr., PO Box 1060, Janesville, WI 53547, (608)754-9466 [25987]

Bowline Family Products Inc., 1564 Elmira St., Aurora, CO 80010, (303)340-4500 [25895]

Bowling Green Winlectric, 1001A Shive Ln., Bowling Green, KY 42101, (502)842-6153 [8458]

Bowlus School Supply Inc., PO Box 1349, Pittsburg, KS 66762, (316)231-3450 [13042]

Bowlus School Supply Inc., PO Box 1349, Pittsburg, KS 66762, (316)231-3450 [20852]

Bowman Associates Inc.; A.D., PO Box 770, Melrose, MA 02176, (781)662-7411 [25896]

Bowman Distribution, PO Box 6908, Cleveland, OH 44101-9990, (216)416-7200 [16759]

Bowman Refrigeration Inc., 1135 NW 46th St., Seattle, WA 98107-4633, (206)706-3033 [14354]

Bowmar Productions Inc., PO Box 157, Wilson, NC 27894-0157, (919)291-8202 [23774]

Bowser Manufacturing, 21 Howard St., Montoursville, PA 17754, (717)368-2516 [26423]

The Box Maker, 6412 S 190th St., Kent, WA 98032, (425)251-9892 [21655]

Boxlight Corp., 19332 Powder Hill Pl., Poulsbo, WA 98370, (360)779-7901 [6020]

Boyajian Inc., 349 Lenox St., Norwood, MA 02062-3417, (617)965-5800 [10600]

Boyd & Associates, Inc.; E., 7009 Harps Mill Rd., PO Box 99189, Raleigh, NC 27624-9189, (919)846-8000 [10601]

Boyd & Associates; Robert W., PO Box 7442, Reno, NV 89510-7442, (702)847-9399 [13322]

Boyd-Bluford Co. Inc., PO Box 12240, Norfolk, VA 23541-0240, (757)855-6036 [10602]

Boyd Coffee Co., PO Box 20547, Portland, OR 97294, (503)666-4545 [10603]

Boyd Company Inc.; C.L., PO Box 26427, Oklahoma City, OK 73126, (405)942-8000 [7074]

Boyd Distributing Co. Inc., 1400 W 3rd Ave., Denver, CO 80223, (303)534-7706 [15056]

Boyd Lighting Fixture Co, 944 Folsom St., San Francisco, CA 94107, (415)778-4300 [8459]

Boyer Printing Co., PO Box 509, Lebanon, PA 17042-0509, (717)272-5691 [25578]

Boyer Printing Co., PO Box 509, Lebanon, PA 17042-0509, (717)272-5691 [24082]

Boyer Steel Inc., 19640 Charleston Ave., Detroit, MI 48203, (313)368-8760 [16760]

Boyle Machine and Supply Co., PO Box 352, Peabody, MA 01960-6852, (978)531-1920 [16761]

Boyle Meat Co., 1638 St. Louis Ave., Kansas City, MO 64101, (816)842-5852 [10604]

Boyt Harness Co./Bob Allen Sportswear, 220 S Main St., Osceola, IA 50213, (515)342-6773 [4839]

Bozeman Distributors, 5341 I 55 N, Jackson, MS 39206, (601)368-9274 [2376]

Bozeman Safe & Lock, 2304F N 7th Ave., Bozeman, MT 59715, (406)587-8911 [24518]

Bozzuto's Inc., 275 Schoolhouse Rd., Cheshire, CT 06410-0340, (203)272-3511 [10605]

BP, 2340 Heinz Rd., Iowa City, IA 52240, (319)337-6448 [10570]

BP America Inc., 200 Public Sq., Cleveland, OH 44114, (216)586-4141 [60]

BP Oil Co., 200 Public Sq., Cleveland, OH 44114, (216)586-4141 [22089]

BP Products Inc., 4780 Beidler Rd., Willoughby, OH 44094, (440)975-4300 [14355]

BPC Foodservice Inc., PO Box 301, Bloomington, IL 61702, (309)828-6271 [10606]

BPC Supply Co., 2753 Midland Dr., Ogden, UT 84401, (801)399-5564 [15838]

BPI, 6001 Lindsey Rd., Little Rock, AR 72206, (501)490-1924 [9735]

B.P.I., 3263 Sharpe Ave., Memphis, TN 38111, (901)744-6414 [9736]

BPI Inc., 2295 Bolling St., Jackson, MS 39213, (601)981-6060 [9737]

BPI Inc., 507A Mapleleaf Dr., Nashville, TN 37210, (615)391-3901 [9738]

BR Chemical Co. Inc., 405 24th Ave. S, Grand Forks, ND 58201-7413, (701)775-5455 [4587]

Brach Knitting Mills Inc., 12 Roosevelt Ave., Florida, NY 10921-1808, (914)651-4615 [4840]

Bracken Company Inc., 109 Lindberg Ave., Methuen, MA 01844, (978)685-2200 [15839]

Brackett Supply Inc., PO Box 669046, Charlotte, NC 28208, (704)393-7827 [14356]

Braden's Flying Service Inc., 3800 Sullivan Trail, Easton, PA 18040, (610)258-1706 [61]

Braden's Wholesale Furniture Company Inc., 1335 Western Ave., Knoxville, TN 37921, (423)549-5000 [13043]

The Bradenton Financial Ctr., 1401 Manatee Ave. W, Ste 520, Bradenton, FL 34205, (941)747-2630 [20524]

Bradford Publishing Co., PO Box 448, Denver, CO 80201, (303)292-2500 [3587]

Bradford Publishing Co.; William K., 35 Forest Ridge Rd., Concord, MA 01742-3834, (978)263-6996 [6021]

Bradford Supply Co., PO Box 246, Robinson, IL 62454, (618)544-3171 [22090]

Bradfordton Cooperative Association Inc., 4440 West Jefferson St., Springfield, IL 62707, (217)546-1206 [17745]

Bradley Co.; E.B., 5080 S Alameda St., Los Angeles, CA 90058-2810, (323)585-9201 [13605]

Bradley Distributing, 1975 W County Rd., B-2, Roseville, MN 55113, (612)639-0523 [24917]

Bradley Import Co., 1400 N Spring St., Los Angeles, CA 90012, (213)221-4162 [26424]

Bradley Landfill and Recycling Center, 9081 Tujunga Ave., No. 2, Sun Valley, CA 91352-1516, (818)767-6180 [26770]

Bradley Pharmaceuticals Inc., 383 Rte. 46 W, Fairfield, NJ 07004-2402, (973)882-1505 [19197]

Bradley Supply Co., PO Box 29096, Chicago, IL 60629, (773)434-7400 [23094]

Bradley Supply Company Inc.; R.W., 403 N 4th St., Springfield, IL 62702, (217)528-8438 [7075]

Bradner Central Co., 333 S Des Plaines St., Chicago, IL 60661-5596, (312)454-1852 [21656]

Bradshaw International Inc., 9409 Buffalo Ave., Rancho Cucamonga, CA 91730-6012, (310)946-7466 [13044]

Brady Co.; Joseph M., PO Box 307, Needham, MA 02492, (781)444-0781 [27091]

Brady Co. Xymox Div.; W.H., PO Box 571, Milwaukee, WI 53223, (414)355-8300 [8460]

Brady Corp., PO Box 571, Milwaukee, WI 53202-0571, (414)358-6600 [6022]

Brady Distributing Co., PO Box 19269, Charlotte, NC 28219, (704)357-6284 [25579]

Brady Industries Inc., 4175 Arville St., Las Vegas, NV 89103-3736, (702)876-3990 [4588]

Brady News and Recycling, 3240 Schuette Rd., Midland, MI 48642, (517)496-9900 [3588]

Bradys Industrial Tool & Supplies, 3400 Hwy. 30 W, Pocatello, ID 83201-6071, (208)232-8665 [21526]

Bragg and Sons; N.H., 92 Perry Rd., Bangor, ME 04402-0927, (207)947-8611 [16762]

Braid Electric Company Inc., PO Box 23710, Nashville, TN 37202, (615)242-6511 [8461]

Brain Corp., HC 66 Box 94A, Wilmot, NH 03287-9617, (603)668-3325 [20853]

Brain Teaser Money Machines, PO Box 2065, Vista, CA 92085-2065, (760)630-5300 [25580]

BrainTree Technology Inc., 200 Cordwainer Dr., Norwell, MA 02061-1619, (617)982-0200 [6023]

Brainum Junior Inc.; Harry, 360 McGuinness Blvd., Brooklyn, NY 11222, (718)389-4080 [19832]

Brake & Clutch, Inc., 63 Bridge St., Salem, MA 01970, (978)745-2500 [2377]

Brake Sales Co. Inc., 999 N La Brea Ave., Los Angeles, CA 90038-2321, (213)874-8880 [2378]

Brake Systems Inc., 2221 NE Hoyt St., Portland, OR 97232, (503)236-2116 [16763]

Brake and Wheel Parts Industries, 2415 W 21st St., Chicago, IL 60608, (773)847-7000 [2379]

Bralco Metals Div., 15090 Northam St., La Mirada, CA 90638-5757, (714)736-4800 [19833]

Bramco Inc., PO Box 32230, Louisville, KY 40232, (502)493-4300 [25581]

Brammall Supply Co., PO Box 396, Benton Harbor, MI 49023, (616)926-2111 [16764]

Brance-Krachy Company Inc., PO Box 1724, Houston, TX 77011, (713)225-6661 [15840]

Branch Cheese Co., PO Box 198, Lena, WI 54139-0198, (920)684-0121 [10607]

Branch Electric Supply Co., 1049 Prince Georges Blvd., Upper Marlboro, MD 20774, (301)249-5005 [8462]

Branches Medical Inc., 3652 NW 16th St., Lauderhill, FL 33311, (305)321-6339 [18719]

Branco Enterprises Inc., PO Box 280, Asheboro, NC 27204-0280, (910)629-1090 [4841]

Brand Co., 10560 Main St., Fairfax, VA 22030, (703)385-2817 [2380]

Brand-Rex Co., 1600 W Main St., Willimantic, CT 06226-1128, (860)456-8000 [8463]

Branded Liquors Inc., 750 Everett St., Norwood, MA 02062, (781)769-6500 [1547]

Brandeis Machinery and Supply Corp., 1801 Watterson Trail, Jeffersontown, KY 40299, (502)491-4000 [25582]

Branden Publishing Co., PO Box 094, Wellesley, MA 02482, (781)235-3634 [3589]

Brandon Auto Supply, 605 S Gallatin, PO Box 3487, Jackson, MS 39207, (601)948-4381 [3036]

Brandon and Clark Inc., 3623 Interstate 27, Lubbock, TX 79404, (806)747-3861 [8464]

Brandons Camera, 1819 Kings Ave., Jacksonville, FL 32207-8787, (904)398-1591 [22835]

Brands Inc., PO Box 90, Columbus, IN 47202, (812)379-9566 [7076]

Brandt Consolidated Inc., Rte. 125 W, Pleasant Plains, IL 62677, (217)626-1123 [333]

Brandywine Auto Parts Inc., PO Box 68, Brandywine, MD 20613, (301)372-1000 [2381]

Brann Associates Inc.; Don, 21840 Wyoming Pl., Oak Park, MI 48237, (248)543-1950 [20854]

Brannon; Thomas, PO Box 1049, Flint, MI 48501-1049, (810)235-1322 [14357]

Brannon Tire Corp., PO Box 2496, Stockton, CA 95201, (209)943-2771 [2382]

Branom Instrument Co. Inc., 8435 N Interstate Pl., Portland, OR 97217, (503)283-2555 [16765]

Branom Instrument Company Inc., PO Box 80307, Seattle, WA 98108-0307, (206)762-6050 [24326]

Branom Instrument Company Inc., 626 N Helena, Spokane, WA 99202, (509)534-9395 [24327]

Branom Instrument Company Inc., PO Box 80307, Seattle, WA 98108, (206)762-6050 [15841]

Brans Nut Co. Inc., 581 Bonner Rd., Wauconda, IL 60084-1103, (847)526-0700 [10608]

Brantley Electrical Supply Inc., 2913 A Fort Bragg Rd., Fayetteville, NC 28303, (910)485-2100 [8465]

Branton Industries Inc., PO Box 10536, New Orleans, LA 70181-0536, (504)733-7770 [7077]

Bratt-Foster Inc., PO Box 3650, Syracuse, NY 13220, (315)488-3840 [10609]

Brattleboro Auto Parts, RR 6, Box 32, Brattleboro, VT 05301-8542, (802)254-9034 [2383]

Brauer Supply Co., 4260 Forest Park, St. Louis, MO 63108, (314)534-7150 [14358]

Braun & Son Implement Inc., 1027 S Broadway St., Hobart, OK 73651, (580)726-3337 [334]

Braun and Sons; J.F., 265 Post Ave., Westbury, NY 11590, (516)997-2200 [10610]

Brauner Export Co., 1600 N Warson Rd., St. Louis, MO 63132, (314)426-2600 [8466]

Bray and Scarff Inc., 11950 Baltimore Ave., Beltsville, MD 20705-1235, (301)470-3555 [25107]

Braymar Precision Inc., 1889 W Commonwealth Ave., Ste. P, Fullerton, CA 92833-3028, (714)870-1411 [15842]

Brazabra Corp., 8 Run Way, PO Box 698, Lee, MA 01238, (413)243-4690 [4842]

Brechner and Co. Inc.; Dan, PO Box 510, Syosset, NY 11791-0510, (516)437-8400 [26425]

Breckenridge Material, 2833 Breckenridge Rd., St. Louis, MO 63144, (314)962-1234 [7078]

Breeders Edge, PO Box 16027, Cincinnati, OH 45216-0027, (513)542-9933 [27092]

Breen International, 5458 Steubenville Pike, No. 1st Fl., McKees Rocks, PA 15136-1412, (724)695-8990 [19834]

Breezy Ridge Instruments, PO Box 295, Center Valley, PA 18034, (610)691-3302 [25108]

Brehm Inc.; Otto, 75 Tuckahoe Rd., Yonkers, NY 10710-5321, (914)968-6100 [10611]

Brehob Corp., 1334 S Meridian St., Indianapolis, IN 46225, (317)231-8080 [15843]

Bremner Biscuit Co., 4600 Joliet St., Denver, CO 80239, (303)371-8180 [10612]

Brenham Wholesale Grocery Company Inc., PO Box 584, Brenham, TX 77834, (409)836-7925 [10613]

Brennan-Hamilton Co., PO Box 2626, South San Francisco, CA 94083, (650)589-2700 [15844]

Brennan Industrial Truck Co., 3409 South Ave., Toledo, OH 43609, (419)385-4601 [20605]

Brennans Ltd., 2770 E Flamingo Rd., Las Vegas, NV 89121-5210, (702)731-2001 [13045]

Brenner Companies Inc., 27-31 Osprey Rd., Saugus, MA 01906, (781)231-0555 [24697]

Brenntag Inc., PO Box 13786, Reading, PA 19612, (610)926-6100 [4339]

Brentari Oil Co., 661 E Hwy. 66, Gallup, NM 87301, (505)863-4562 [22091]

Brentwood Medical Products Inc., 3300 Fujita St., Torrance, CA 90505, (310)530-5955 [19198]

Breon and Sons Inc.; R.E., PO Box 27, Rebersburg, PA 16872, (814)349-5681 [22092]

Brethren Press, 1451 Dundee Ave., Elgin, IL 60120, (708)742-5100 [3590]

Bretlin Inc., 185 S Industrial Blvd., Calhoun, GA 30701, (706)695-6734 [9739]

Breton & Co. Inc.; Bruce, 427 Amherst St., Nashua, NH 03063-1258, (603)882-2050 [17349]

Brett Aqualine, 7215 Bermuda Rd., Las Vegas, NV 89119-4304, (702)361-0600 [25831]

Brett Aqualine Inc., 7215 Bermuda Rd., Las Vegas, NV 89119, (702)361-0600 [23987]

Brewer Associates Inc., 68 Franklin St., Laconia, NH 03246-2322, (603)524-9225 [62]

Brewer Environmental Industries Inc., 311 Pacific St., Honolulu, HI 96817, (808)532-7400 [335]

Brewer Environmental Industries Inc., 311 Pacific St., Honolulu, HI 96817, (808)532-7400 [4340]

Brewer, Inc.; R.G., 161 E Boston Post Rd., Mamaroneck, NY 10543, (914)698-3232 [18469]

Brewer Oil Co., PO Box 1347, Artesia, NM 88210, (505)748-1248 [22093]

Brewer Oil Co.; Don, 300 E 2nd St., Roswell, NM 88201, (505)622-8560 [22094]

Brewer Sewing Supplies, 3800 W 42nd St., Chicago, IL 60632, (773)247-2121 [25988]

Brewers Chandlery East, 19 Novelty Ln., Essex, CT 06426, (860)767-8267 [18470]

Brewery Products Co., 1017 N Sherman, York, PA 17402-2130, (717)757-3515 [1548]

Brewmaster, 2315 Verna Ct., San Leandro, CA 94577-4205, (510)351-8920 [1549]

Brewster Wallcovering Co., 67 Pacella Park Dr., Randolph, MA 02368, (781)963-4800 [15429]

Brey Appliance Parts Inc., 1345 Geronimo, El Paso, TX 79925, (915)778-2739 [15057]

Bricelyn Elevator Association, PO Box 368, Bricelyn, MN 56014, (507)653-4448 [17746]

Bridge-Logos Publishers, PO Box 141630, Gainesville, FL 32614-1630, (352)472-7900 [3591]

Bridge Publications Inc., 4751 Fountain Ave., Los Angeles, CA 90029, (323)953-3320 [3592]

Bridge Stone Aircraft Tire (USA), Inc., 7775 NW 12th St., Miami, FL 33126, (305)592-3530 [63]

Bridge Technology Inc., 45 Lyme Rd., Ste. 306, Hanover, NH 03755-1224, (603)643-6355 [6024]

Bridgeport Equipment Co. Inc., PO Box 310, Bridgeport, NE 69336, (308)262-1342 [336]

Bridgeport Steel Co., 1034 Bridgeport Ave., Milford, CT 06460, (203)874-2591 [19835]

Bridges Accessories; Ronna, 1852-F Wallace School Rd., Charleston, SC 29407-4822, (803)763-7070 [4843]

Bridges Smith & Co., 118-122 E Main St., Louisville, KY 40202, (502)584-4173 [21405]

Bridgestone Firestone, Inc., 50 Century Blvd., Nashville, TN 37214, (615)872-5000 [2384]

Bridgestone/Firestone Tire Sales Co., 1 Bridgestone Park, Nashville, TN 37214, (615)391-0088 [2385]

Bridon Elm Inc., PO Box 10367, New Orleans, LA 70181-0367, (504)734-5871 [64]

Briel America Inc., 256 S Livingston Ave., Livingston, NJ 07039, (973)716-0999 [15058]

Brigadoon.Com Inc., PO Box 53168, Bellevue, WA 98015, (206)652-9365 [6025]

Briggs Corp., PO Box 1698, Des Moines, IA 50306, (515)327-6400 [19199]

Briggs Inc., 504 S Cass St., PO Box 455, Corinth, MS 38835-0455, (601)286-3312 [26267]

Briggs, Inc., PO Box 1403, Bangor, ME 04402-1403, (207)947-8671 [1550]

Briggs Incorporated of Omaha, 113 S 10th St., Omaha, NE 68102, (402)342-0778 [23095]

Briggs-Weaver Inc., 306 Airline Dr. Ste. 100A, Coppell, TX 75019, (972)304-7200 [15845]

Bright Lights Sportswear Inc., 1400 Broadway, New York, NY 10018, (212)354-0177 [4844]

Brighter Image Publishing, 2040 Amber Creek, Buford, GA 30518, (404)339-1361 [13323]

The Brightman Co., 10411 Baur Blvd., St. Louis, MO 63132, (314)993-2233 [15059]

Brighton-Best Socket Screw Manufacturing Inc., 3105 Medlock Bridge Rd., Norcross, GA 30071, (770)368-2300 [13606]

Brightpoint, Inc., 6402 Corporate Dr., Indianapolis, IN 46278, (317)297-6100 [5533]

Brightpoint, Inc., 6402 Corporate Dr., Indianapolis, IN 46278, (317)297-6100 [8467]

Brill Hygenic Products Inc., 2905 S Congress Ave., Ste. E, Delray Beach, FL 33445-7337, (561)278-5600 [23096]

Brin-Northwestern Glass Co., 2300 N 2nd St., Minneapolis, MN 55411, (612)529-9671 [7079]

Brina Steel Products Inc., 2230 E 17th St., Erie, PA 16504, (814)898-2842 [19836]

Brindar Design Inc., 370 NE 219th Ave., Gresham, OR 97030-8419, (503)661-5464 [4845]

Brine Inc., 47 Sumner St., Milford, MA 01757, (508)478-3250 [23567]

Brinkman and Co.; LD, 1655 Waters Ridge Dr., Lewisville, TX 75057, (972)353-3500 [9740]

Brinkmann Corp., 4215 McEwen Rd., Dallas, TX 75244, (972)387-4939 [8468]

Brinkmann Instruments, Inc., 1 Cantiague Rd., PO Box 1019, Westbury, NY 11590-0207, (516)334-7500 [24328]

Brinkmann Instruments Inc., 1 Cantiague Rd., Westbury, NY 11590-0207, (516)334-7500 [19200]

BRIO Corp., PO Box 1013, Germantown, WI 53022-8213, (262)250-3240 [26426]

Brissman-Kennedy Inc., 295 Pennsylvania Ave. E, St. Paul, MN 55101-2455, (651)646-7933 [4589]

Bristol Lettering of Hartford, 2034 Park St., Hartford, CT 06106-2024, (860)232-5739 [4846]

Bristol Metal Co. Inc., PO Box 596, Bristol, RI 02809, (401)253-4070 [26771]

Bristol Retail Solutions Inc., 3760 Kilroy Airport Way, Ste. 450, Long Beach, CA 90806-2484, (562)988-3660 [20855]

Britain's Steel and Supplies, 1335 S Pacific Ave., Yuma, AZ 85365, (520)782-4731 [16766]

Brithinee Electric, 620 S Rancho Ave., Colton, CA 92324, (909)825-7971 [2386]

British Aerospace Holdings Inc., 15000 Conference Center Dr., Ste. 200, Chantilly, VA 20151-3819, (703)802-0080 [66]

British Aerospace Holdings Inc., 15000 Conference Center Dr., Ste, Chantilly, VA 20151-3819, (703)227-1500 [65]

British Aerospace North America Inc., 15000 Conference Center Dr., Ste. 200, Chantilly, VA 20151-3819, (703)802-0080 [66]

Brittain Brothers Inc., 700 S Western, Oklahoma City, OK 73125, (405)235-1785 [2387]

Brittain Merchandising, PO Box 449, Lawton, OK 73502, (580)355-4430 [19201]

Brittania Sportswear, 1411 Broadway, New York, NY 10018-3403, (212)921-0060 [4847]

Brittany Fabrics Inc., 8 W 40th St., New York, NY 10018, (212)391-1250 [25989]

Britton Explosive Supply Inc., 125 Cronin Rd., Queensbury, NY 12804, (518)793-4767 [7080]

Britton Livestock Auction, Inc., S Hwy. 27, Britton, SD 57430, (605)448-5911 [17747]

Britton Livestock Sales Inc., S Hwy. 27, Britton, SD 57430, (605)448-5911 [17747]

Britton Lumber Company Inc., PO Box 38, Fairlee, VT 05045, (802)333-4388 [7081]

Brix Co.; H.G., 565 Display Way, Sacramento, CA 95838, (916)646-9805 [5534]

Brizard Wine & Spirits, USA; Marie, 11900 Biscayne Blvd., No. 600, North Miami, FL 33181-2726, (305)893-3394 [1887]

Bro Tex Company Inc., Wiping Cloth Div., 800 Hampden Ave., St. Paul, MN 55114, (651)645-5721 [21657]

Bro Tex Company Inc., Wiping Cloth Div., 800 Hampden Ave., St. Paul, MN 55114, (612)645-5721 [16767]

Broad Street Oil & Gas Co., 125 Dillmont Dr., Columbus, OH 43085, (614)786-1801 [22095]

BroadBand Technologies Inc., PO Box 13737, Research Triangle Park, NC 27709-3737, (919)544-0015 [8469]

Broadcast Supply West, 7012 27th St. W, Tacoma, WA 98466, (253)565-2301 [5535]

Broadcast Supply Worldwide, 7012 27th St. W, Tacoma, WA 98466, (253)565-2301 [5535]

Broadcasters General Store Inc., 2480 SE 52nd St., Ocala, FL 34480, (352)622-7700 [5536]

Broadway Collection, PO Box 1210, Olathe, KS 66051-1210, (913)782-6244 [23097]

Broadway Industries Corp., 2066 W Broadway, South Portland, ME 04106-3223, (207)774-7707 [21406]

Broadway Movies, 960 Old Mounta, Statesville, NC 28687, (704)528-9162 [25197]

Broadway Office Interiors, 2115 Locust St., St. Louis, MO 63103, (314)421-0753 [20856]

Broadway Style Showroom No. 1, 2850D Stirling Rd., Hollywood, FL 33020, (954)922-6336 [17350]

Broadway Tire Inc., 588 Broadway, Pawtucket, RI 02860, (401)725-3535 [2388]

Brocato; Charles, 1618 Stockton Rd., Joppa, MD 21085-1825, (410)679-6534 [24698]

Brock Corp.; J.C., River Ranch Northeast, 1156 Abbott St., Salinas, CA 93901-4503 [10614]

Brock-McVey Co., 1100 Brock McVey Dr., PO Box 55487, Lexington, KY 40555, (606)255-1412 [14359]

Brock Supply Co., 2150 E Rio Salado Pkwy., PO Box 1000, Tempe, AZ 85280-1000, (602)968-2222 [2389]

Brocke and Sons Inc.; George F., PO Box 159, Kendrick, ID 83537, (208)289-4231 [337]

Brocks Auto Supply, 221 Hamilton, Houston, TX 77002-2333, (713)222-9928 [2390]

Brockway-Smith Co., 146 Dascomb Rd., Andover, MA 01810, (508)475-7100 [7082]

Brod-Dugan Co./Sherwin Williams Co., 2145 Schuetz Rd., St. Louis, MO 63146, (314)567-1111 [21407]

Brodart Co., 500 Arch St., Williamsport, PA 17705, (570)326-2461 [3593]

Broder Bros., Co., 45555 Port St., Plymouth, MI 48170, (734)454-4800 [4848]

Brodie Inc., 10 Ballard Rd., Lawrence, MA 01843, (508)682-6300 [15846]

Broedell Plumbing Supply Inc., 19686 U.S Hwy. 1, Tequesta, FL 33469, (561)747-8000 [23098]

Brohl and Appell Inc., PO Box 1419, Sandusky, OH 44871, (419)625-6761 [8470]

Brohman Distributing Co., 333-335 Pam Dr., Berrien Springs, MI 49103, (616)471-1111 [26427]

Broich Enterprises Inc., 6440 City West Pky., Eden Prairie, MN 55344, (952)941-2270 [15060]

Broken Arrow, 104 Open Buckle Rd, Vaughn, MT 59487-9514 [18115]

Brokerage Services International, 1204 H St., Anchorage, AK 99501-4359, (907)276-6862 [6797]

Bromar Inc., 744 N Eckhoff St., Orange, CA 92868-1020, (714)640-6221 [10615]

Bromar Inc. Bromar Hawaii, 2770 Waiwai Loop, Honolulu, HI 96819, (808)836-3553 [10616]

Bromar Inc. Southern California Div., 744 N Eckhuff St., Orange, CA 92868-1020, (714)939-6275 [11786]

Bromar Montana/Wyoming, PO Box 22599, Billings, MT 59102, (406)245-5134 [10617]

Bromar Utah, 1279 W 2200 S, Ste. C, West Valley City, UT 84119, (801)973-8669 [10618]

Broner Glove Co., 1750 Harmon, Auburn Hills, MI 48326, (248)391-5006 [4849]

Bronson Syrup Company Inc., 1650 Locust Ave., Bohemia, NY 11716, (516)563-1177 [10619]

Bronze and Plastic Specialties Inc., 2025 Inverness Ave., Baltimore, MD 21230, (410)644-0440 [19837]

Brookdale Lumber Inc., 13602 Pacific Ave., Tacoma, WA 98444, (253)537-8669 [7083]

Brooke Distributors Inc., PO Box 4730, Hialeah, FL 33014, (305)624-9752 [25109]

Brookfield Athletic Company, 13 Centennial Dr., Peabody, MA 01960, (978)532-9000 [23568]

Brookfield's Great Water Inc., 9533 Nall Ave., Overland Park, KS 66207, (913)648-1234 [24918]

Brookharts Inc., 3105 N Stone Ave., Colorado Springs, CO 80907-5305, (719)471-4500 [7084]

Brookline Machine Co., 131 Holton St., Boston, MA 02135, (617)782-4018 [2391]

Brookline Machine Co., 87 Belmont St., No. 1, North Andover, MA 01845-2304, (978)689-0750 [15847]

Brookline Machine Co., 1870 Fillmore Ave., Buffalo, NY 14214, (716)891-5611 [2392]

Brookline Machine Co., 333 Waterman Ave., East Providence, RI 02914, (401)438-3650 [2393]

Brookline Machine Company, Inc., 535 Sweetland Ave., Hillside, NJ 07205, (908)688-6050 [2394]

Brookline Machine Co. Williams Brothers Div., 296 Warren Ave., Portland, ME 04103, (207)878-2994 [2395]

Brooklyn Bagels Inc., 7412 Bustleton Ave., Philadelphia, PA 19152-4312, (215)342-1661 [10620]

Brooks and Co.; H., 2521 E Hennepin Ave., Minneapolis, MN 55413, (612)331-8413 [10621]

Brooks Designer Rugs; J., 2928 Prosperity Ave., Fairfax, VA 22031, (703)698-0790 [9741]

Brooks Duplicator Co., 10402 Rockley Rd., Houston, TX 77099, (281)568-9787 [20857]

Brooks Farmers Cooperative Association, PO Box 8, Brooks, MN 56715, (218)698-4275 [17748]

Brooks Manufacturing Co., 8439 Quivira, Lenexa, KS 66215, (913)492-1455 [4850]

Brooks Nursery Inc., PO Box 263, Boling, TX 77420, (409)657-2465 [14830]

Brookwood Companies Inc., 232 Madison Ave., 10th Fl., New York, NY 10016, (212)551-0100 [25990]

Brost International Trading Co., 222 W 33rd St., Chicago, IL 60616-3700, (312)225-4900 [24271]

Brost International Trading Co., 2918 S Poplar Ave., Chicago, IL 60608, (312)225-3600 [10890]

Brother International Corp., 100 Somerset Corporate Blvd., Bridgewater, NJ 08807, (908)704-1700 [20858]

Brotherhood America's Oldest Winery Ltd., 100 Brotherhood Plaza Dr., PO Box 190, Washingtonville, NY 10992, (914)496-9101 [1551]

Brotherhood of Life, Inc., 110 Dartmouth SE, Albuquerque, NM 87106, (505)265-0888 [3594]

Brother's Gourmet Coffees Inc. (Boca Raton, Florida), 2255 Glades Rd., Boca Raton, FL 33431, (561)995-2600 [24919]

Brothers Office Supply Inc., 901 Hilliard Rome Rd., Columbus, OH 43228, (614)870-6414 [20859]

Brothers' Optical Lab, Inc., 2125 S Manchester Ave., Anaheim, CA 92802, (714)634-9303 [19202]

Brotherton Seed Company Inc., PO Box 1136, Moses Lake, WA 98837, (509)765-1816 [338]

Broudy-Kantor Co. Inc., 3501 E Princess Anne Rd., Norfolk, VA 23502, (757)855-6081 [1552]

Broughton Foods Co., PO Box 656, Marietta, OH 45750, (740)373-4121 [10622]

Broughton Foods LLC, PO Box 656, Marietta, OH 45750, (740)373-4121 [10622]

Broussard Rice Mill Inc., PO Drawer 160, Mermentau, LA 70556-0160, (318)824-2409 [17749]

Broward Fire Equipment and Service Inc., 101 SW 6th St., Ft. Lauderdale, FL 33301, (954)467-6625 [24519]

Brown Appliance Parts Co. Inc., 857 N Central Ave., PO Box 27010, Knoxville, TN 37927, (423)525-9363 [15061]

Brown Arts & Crafts; Stan, 13435 Whitaker Way, Portland, OR 97230, (503)257-0559 [20860]

Brown Associates Inc.; Roger G., PO Box 275, Bomoseen, VT 05732-0275, (802)265-4548 [2396]

Brown Bear Sporting, 46853 Gratiot Ave., Chesterfield, MI 48051, (810)949-5348 [23569]

Brown & Bros. Inc.; Arthur, 2 W 46th St., New York, NY 10036, (212)575-5555 [25583]

Brown-Campbell Co., 1383 S Woodward Ave., Ste. 200, Bloomfield Hills, MI 48302, (248)338-4980 [19838]

Brown Co.; E. Arthur, 3404 Pawnee Dr. SE, Alexandria, MN 56308-8984, (320)762-8847 [23570]

Brown Co.; Herman M., PO Box 995, Des Moines, IA 50304, (515)282-0404 [7085]

Brown and Co.; Lewis A., PO Box 9336, Metairie, LA 70055, (504)835-4201 [10623]

Brown and Co.; Lewis A., PO Box 9336, Metairie, LA 70055, (504)835-4201 [10624]

Brown County Co-op, PO Box 8, Robinson, KS 66532-0008, (785)544-6512 [339]

Brown County Cooperative Association, Rte. 5, Hiawatha, KS 66434, (913)742-2196 [340]

Brown Distributing, PO Box 056667, 1300 Allendale Rd., West Palm Beach, FL 33405, (561)655-3791 [1553]

Brown Distributing Co. Inc., 6085 Lagrange Blvd. SW, Atlanta, GA 30336-2817, (404)753-6136 [13046]

Brown Evans Distributing Co., PO Box 5840, Mesa, AZ 85211, (602)962-6111 [22096]

Brown Food Service, PO Box 690, Louisa, KY 41230, (606)638-1139 [10625]

Brown-Forman Beverage Div., PO Box 1080, Louisville, KY 40201, (502)585-1100 [1554]

Brown-Graves Co., PO Box 869, Akron, OH 44309-0869, (330)434-7111 [7086]

Brown Group Inc., PO Box 29, St. Louis, MO 63166-0029, (314)854-4000 [24699]

Brown & Haley, PO Box 1596, Tacoma, WA 98401-1596, (253)620-3000 [10626]

Brown Inc.; C. Earl, PO Box 420, Chambersburg, PA 17201, (717)264-6151 [20606]

Brown Jewelry Inc.; Harold, 316 W Bender Blvd., Hobbs, NM 88240-2269, (505)392-6046 [17351]

Brown Lumber Corp.; Pat, PO Box 19065, Greensboro, NC 27419, (336)299-7755 [7087]

Brown Marine Service Inc., PO Box 1415, Pensacola, FL 32596, (850)453-3471 [18471]

Brown Metals Co., 4225 Airport Dr., Ontario, CA 91761, (909)390-3199 [19839]

Brown Moore and Flint Inc., 1920 Westridge, Irving, TX 75038-2901, (972)518-1442 [10627]

Brown Motors Inc., PO Box 230, Grangeville, ID 83530-0230, (208)983-1730 [341]

Brown Packing Co. Inc., PO Box 2378, Little Rock, AR 72203, (501)565-2351 [10628]

Brown of Pennsylvania Corp.; D.P., 710 Street Rd., Bensalem, PA 19020, (215)245-6800 [15848]

Brown-Rogers-Dixson Co., 675 N Main St., Winston-Salem, NC 27102-2111, (910)722-1112 [15062]

Brown Ship Chandlery Inc., 36 Union Wharf, Portland, ME 04101-4607, (207)772-3796 [18472]

Brown Shoe Co., PO Box 29, St. Louis, MO 63166-0029, (314)854-4000 [24700]

Brown and Sons Co. Inc., 1720 Davison Rd., Flint, MI 48506, (810)238-3242 [2397]

Brown & Sons NAPA Auto Parts, 1001 College Rd., Fairbanks, AK 99701, (907)456-7312 [2398]

Brown South; J.L., 140 Mendel Dr., Atlanta, GA 30336, (404)691-9435 [26428]

Brown Steel Div., PO Box 16505, Columbus, OH 43216, (614)443-4881 [19840]

Brown Swiss/Gillette Quality Checkered Dairy, PO Box 2553, Rapid City, SD 57701-4177, (605)348-1500 [10629]

Brown Tractor and Implement Inc., 269 W Main St., Ashville, OH 43103, (740)983-2951 [342]

Browne Dreyfus International Ltd., 305 Madison Ave., Ste. 420, New York, NY 10165, (212)867-7700 [15849]

Brownell & Associates, Inc., 14731-E Franklin Ave., Tustin, CA 92780, (714)544-8003 [13607]

Brownells Inc., 200 S Front St., Montezuma, IA 50171, (515)623-5401 [13477]

Browning, 1 Browning Pl., Morgan, UT 84050-9326, (801)876-2711 [13478]

Browning Equipment Inc., 800 E Main St., Purcellville, VA 20132-3163, (540)338-7123 [343]

Browning-Ferris Industries of Michigan Inc., 5400 Cogswell Rd., Wayne, MI 48184, (734)729-8200 [26772]

Browning Metal Products Co., 7700 N Harker Dr., No. B, Peoria, IL 61615-1852, (309)682-1015 [14360]

Browning Seed Inc., S Interstate 27, PO Box 1836, Plainview, TX 79073, (806)293-5271 [344]

Brownlow Corp., 6309 Airport Fwy., Ft. Worth, TX 76117, (817)831-3831 [3595]

Brownlow Publishing Company, Inc., 6309 Airport Fwy., Ft. Worth, TX 76117, (817)831-3831 [3595]

Browns Bakery Inc., PO Box 1040, Defiance, OH 43512, (419)784-3330 [10630]

Brown's Heating & Air Conditioning; Bob, 2616 N C St., Ft. Smith, AR 72901-3444, (501)783-0217 [14361]

Brown's Ice Cream Co., 2929 University Ave. SE, Minneapolis, MN 55414, (612)378-1075 [10631]

Browns Medical Imaging, 14315 C Cir., Omaha, NE 68144-3349, (402)330-2168 [18720]

Brownstone Gallery Ltd., 295 5th Ave., Ste. 1618, New York, NY 10016, (212)696-4663 [25991]

Brownstown Electric Supply Inc., 690 E State Rd., No. 250, Brownstown, IN 47220, (812)358-4555 [8471]

Brownton Cooperative Agriculture Center, PO Box 189, Brownton, MN 55312, (320)328-5211 [345]

Broz, Inc.; John V., PO Box 21345, Hilton Head Island, SC 29925, (803)689-9900 [7088]

BRS Software Products, 5 Computer Dr. S, Albany, NY 12205-1608, (518)437-4000 [6026]

Bruce and Co.; Donald, 3600 N Talman Ave., Chicago, IL 60618, (312)477-8100 [17352]

Bruce Industries Inc., PO Box 1700, Dayton, NV 89403-1700, (702)246-0101 [67]

Bruce and Merrilee's Electric Co., 930 Cass St., New Castle, PA 16101, (724)652-5566 [8472]

Bruce-Rogers Company Inc., PO Box 879, Ft. Smith, AR 72902-0879, (501)782-7901 [23099]

Bruce Vehicle/Equipment Auction Services Inc., PO Box 3825, Greenville, SC 29608-3825, (864)242-3090 [346]

Bruces Tire Ltd., PO Box 276, Beecher Falls, VT 05902-0276, (802)266-7734 [2399]

Bruckner Machine, 36 Harbor Park Dr., Port Washington, NY 11050, (516)484-6070 [13608]

Bruckner Supply Co. Inc., 36 Harbor Park Dr., Port Washington, NY 11050-4602, (516)484-6070 [16768]

Bruder and Sons Inc.; M.A., PO Box 600, Broomall, PA 19008, (215)353-5100 [21408]

Brudnick Company Inc.; James, 219 Medford St., Malden, MA 02148, (781)321-6800 [19203]

Bruening Bearings Inc., 3600 Euclid Ave., Cleveland, OH 44115, (216)881-8900 [15850]

Brueton Industries Inc., 145-68 228th St., Springfield Gardens, NY 11413, (718)527-3000 [13047]

Brulin and Co. Inc., PO Box 270, Indianapolis, IN 46206, (317)923-3211 [4590]

Brumley & Sons; Albert E., 100 Albert E Brumley Pkwy., Powell, MO 65730, (417)435-2225 [3596]

Bruner Corp., 700 W Virginia St., Milwaukee, WI 53204, (414)747-3700 [25584]

Brungart Equipment Company Inc., 3930 Pinson Valley Pkwy., Birmingham, AL 35217-1856, (205)520-2000 [15851]

Brunner and Lay Inc., 2425 E 37th St., Los Angeles, CA 90058, (213)587-1233 [7089]

Brunner News Agency, 217 Flanders Ave., PO Box 598, Lima, OH 45802, (419)225-5826 [3597]

Bruno & Son Inc.; C., 3443 E Commerce St., San Antonio, TX 78294, (512)226-6353 [25110]

Bruno's Inc., PO Box 2486, Birmingham, AL 35201-2486, (205)940-9400 [10632]

Brunos Turquoise Trading Post, PO Box 60307, Boulder City, NV 89006-0307 [17353]

Brunschwig and Fils Inc., 75 Virginia Rd., North White Plains, NY 10603, (914)684-5800 [15430]

Brunt Tile & Marble, 3036 De Siard St., Monroe, LA 71211, (318)361-0100 [9742]

Brushtech Inc., PO Box 1130, Plattsburgh, NY 12901, (518)563-8420 [16769]

Bruss Co., 3548 N Kostner Ave., Chicago, IL 60641, (773)282-2900 [10633]

Bruwiler Precise Sales Company, Inc., 4308 Burns Ave., Los Angeles, CA 90029, (323)666-4551 [24329]

Bryan Equipment Sales Inc., 457 Wards Corner Rd., Loveland, OH 45140, (513)248-2000 [15852]

Bryant and Blount Oil Co., 1200 E Woodhurst Dr., Ste. G-200, Springfield, MO 65804-3776, (417)883-1611 [22097]

Bryant Corp.; P.R., 2229 Massachusetts Ave., Indianapolis, IN 46218-4341, (317)262-0695 [15853]

Bryant and Son Inc.; Otis, PO Box 148, Caneyville, KY 42721, (502)879-3221 [347]

Bryson Inc., 1301 E Highland, Tecumseh, OK 74873, (405)598-6514 [1555]

BSC Litho Inc., 3000 Canby St., Harrisburg, PA 17103, (717)238-9469 [3598]

BSE Engineering Corp., 986-998 Cherry St., Fall River, MA 02720, (508)678-4419 [23571]

BSH of Evansville, 2534 Locust Creek Dr, Evansville, IN 47720, (812)424-2901 [7090]

BSTC Group Inc., 75 Union Ave., Rutherford, NJ 07070, (201)939-1200 [7091]

BSW Inc., 4680 E 2nd St., Ste. A, Benicia, CA 94510, (707)745-8175 [14362]

BT Office Products, PO Box 9339, Pittsburgh, PA 15225, (412)741-6494 [20925]

BT Office Products International Inc. Detroit Div., 28241 Mound Rd., Warren, MI 48092, (810)573-8877 [20861]

BT Office Products USA, 6 Parkway N, Deerfield, IL 60015-2544, (708)808-3000 [20862]

BT Summit Office Products Inc., 303 W 10th St., New York, NY 10014, (914)997-9400 [20863]

BTC Corp., 1204 Railroad Ave., No. 101, Bellingham, WA 98225-5008, (360)734-5082 [5525]

BTE Import-Export, 11765 West Ave., No. 253, San Antonio, TX 78216, (210)663-0979 [19204]

BTF Inc., PO Box 408, Westborough, MA 01581-0408, (508)366-0638 [24701]

BTM Recycling, PO Box 641461, Los Angeles, CA 90047, (310)477-9636 [26773]

BTR Farmers Co-op, PO Box 244, Leeds, ND 58346, (701)466-2231 [17750]

BTR Inc., 33 Commercial St., No. B5251, Foxboro, MA 02035-2530 [8473]

Bubbles Baking Co., 15215 Keswick St., Van Nuys, CA 91405, (818)786-1700 [10634]

Buchanan Farmers Elevator Co., PO Box 100, Buchanan, ND 58420, (701)252-6622 [17751]

Buchanan Farmers Elevator Co., PO Box 100, Buchanan, ND 58420, (701)252-6622 [10635]

Buchanan Industries, 3358 Carpet Capital Dr. SW, Dalton, GA 30720-4900, (404)277-3066 [9743]

Buchy Food Products, 195 N Broadway, PO Box 899, Greenville, OH 45331-2251, (937)548-2128 [10636]

Buck & Bass Shop, 905 Azalea Dr., Waynesboro, MS 39367-2501, (601)735-4867 [23572]

Buck Distributing Company Inc., PO Box 1490, Upper Marlboro, MD 20773, (301)952-0400 [1556]

Buck-Hilkert Inc., 1001 E Broadway, Logansport, IN 46947-0510, (219)753-2555 [16770]

Buck Knives Inc., 1900 Weld Blvd., El Cajon, CA 92022, (619)449-1100 [15431]

Buck Rub Archery Inc., 157 Bank St., Waukesha, WI 53188, (414)547-0535 [23573]

Buck & Son; A.J., 11407 Cronhill Dr., Ste. D-W, Owings Mills, MD 21117, (410)581-1800 [27195]

Buck Work-Man, 1900 Weld Blvd., El Cajon, CA 92022, (619)449-1100 [15431]

Buckeye Ceramic Tile, 388 McClurg Rd., No. 5, Boardman, OH 44512, (330)758-5749 [9744]

Buckeye Ceramic Tile, 388 McClurg Rd., No. 5, Boardman, OH 44512, (330)758-5749 [7092]

Buckeye Cooperative Elevator Co., PO Box 2037, Buckeye, IA 50043, (515)855-4141 [17752]

Buckeye Cooperative Elevator Co., PO Box 2037, Buckeye, IA 50043, (515)855-4141 [10637]

Buckeye Countrymark Corp., PO Box 189, Xenia, OH 45385, (513)372-3541 [348]

Buckeye Fire Equipment Co. Sales Div., 110 Kings Rd., Kings Mountain, NC 28086, (704)739-7415 [24520]

Buckeye Industrial Supply Company, 3989 Groves Rd., PO Box 328967, Columbus, OH 43232, (614)864-8400 [15854]

Buckeye Pacific Corp., 4380 S Macadam Ave., Portland, OR 97207, (503)228-3330 [7093]

Buckeye Rubber and Packing Co., 23940 Mercantile Rd., Beachwood, OH 44122, (216)464-8900 [16771]

Buckeye Sales Inc., 1009 Race St., Cincinnati, OH 45202, (513)621-2391 [14831]

Buckeye Vacuum Cleaner Supply Co. Inc., 2870 Plant Atkinson Rd., Smyrna, GA 30080-7240, (404)351-7300 [15063]

Buckhead Shoes Corp. II, PO Box 13523, Atlanta, GA 30324, (404)233-5554 [24702]

Buckingham Cooperative Co., 1236 Dwan St., Buckingham, IA 50612, (319)478-2331 [17753]

Buckler's Inc., 225 5th Ave., New York, NY 10010, (212)684-1534 [13324]

Buckles-Smith Electric, 801 Savaker Ave., San Jose, CA 95126, (408)280-7777 [8474]

Bucklin Tractor and Implement, Hwy. 54, Bucklin, KS 67834, (316)826-3271 [349]

Buckman Farmers Cooperative Creamery, PO Box 458, Buckman, MN 56317, (612)468-6433 [350]

Bucks County Distributors, 1724 Eagen Ct., Bensalem, PA 19020, (215)638-2687 [10638]

Buck's War Surplus, 45 Lailani St., Las Vegas, NV 89110-5110, (702)452-8076 [23574]

Bucky Bairdo's Inc., 103 E Silverspring Dr., Whitefish Bay, WI 53217, (414)332-9007 [10639]

Bud Electronic Supply Co., 22 N Jackson St., Danville, IL 61832, (217)446-0925 [8475]

Bud Plant Comic Art, 13393 Grass Valley Ave., No. 7, PO Box 1689, Grass Valley, CA 95945, (530)273-2166 [3599]

Budco, PO Box 3065, Tulsa, OK 74101, (918)252-3420 [25111]

BudCo Incorporated of San Antonio, PO Box 937, San Antonio, TX 78294, (210)225-3044 [1557]

Budco of San Antonio Inc., PO Box 937, San Antonio, TX 78294, (210)225-3044 [1558]

Budd Mayer Co., 3444 Memorial Hwy., Tampa, FL 33607, (813)282-6900 [24083]

Budeke's Paint, 418 S Broadway, Baltimore, MD 21231, (410)732-4354 [21409]

Buderus Hydronic Systems Inc., PO Box 647, Salem, NH 03079, (603)898-0505 [23100]

Budget Sales Inc., 1534 1st Ave. S, Seattle, WA 98134, (206)621-9500 [24084]

BUDGEText Corporation, 1936 N Shiloh Dr., PO Box 1487, Fayetteville, AR 72702-1487, (501)443-9205 [3600]

Budres Lumber Co., 657 76th St. SW, Grand Rapids, MI 49509, (616)455-3510 [7094]

Bud's Hobbies, 2301 N Broadway, Council Bluffs, IA 51503-4333, (712)322-1378 [26429]

Bud's Service Inc., 5148 N Meridian St., Indianapolis, IN 46208-2626, (317)781-5600 [22098]

Buena Tile Supply, Inc.; 1717 Palma Dr., Ventura, CA 93003, (805)650-1252 [9745]

Buena Vista Winery Inc., PO Box 182, Sonoma, CA 95476, (707)252-7117 [1559]

Buettner Brothers Lumber Co., PO Box 1087, Cullman, AL 35056-1087, (205)734-4221 [7095]

Buettner Brothers Lumber Co., PO Box 1087, Cullman, AL 35056-1087, (205)734-4221 [27289]

Buffalo Don's Artesian Wells Ltd., PO Box 2500-C, Plymouth, MI 48170, (313)455-3600 [24920]

Buffalo Hotel Supply Company Inc., PO Box 646, Amherst, NY 14226, (716)691-8080 [25585]

Buffalo Inc., PO Box 2865, Spokane, WA 99202-0865, (509)534-1333 [4851]

Buffalo Office Interiors Inc., 1418 Niagra St., Buffalo, NY 14213, (716)883-8222 [20864]

Buffalo Rock Co. Gadsden Div., PO Box 2307, Gadsden, AL 35903, (256)492-8400 [24921]

Buffalo Scale and Supply Co. Inc., PO Box 140, Buffalo, NY 14205, (716)847-2880 [24330]

Buffalo Structural Steel, 20 John James Audobon Pkwy., West Amherst, NY 14228, (716)639-7714 [19841]

Buffalo White GMC Inc., 271 Dingens St., Buffalo, NY 14206, (716)821-9911 [20607]

Buffington Corp., PO Drawer 7420, Monroe, LA 71211, (318)387-0671 [7096]

Buford Brothers Inc., 909 Division St., Nashville, TN 37203, (615)256-4681 [16772]

Buford White Lumber Company Inc., PO Box 1029, Shawnee, OK 74802-1029, (405)275-4900 [7097]

Bugatti Inc., 100 Condor St., East Boston, MA 02128, (617)567-7600 [18378]

Buhl Animal Clinic, 201 11th Ave. S, Buhl, ID 83316-1301, (208)543-4326 [18721]

Buhrman-Pharr Hardware Co., PO Box 1818, Texarkana, AR 71854, (501)773-3122 [13609]

Buhrman and Son Inc., PO Box 5305, Richmond, VA 23220, (804)358-6776 [351]

Buikema Produce Co., 2150 Bernice Rd., Lansing, IL 60438, (708)474-5750 [10640]

Builder Contract Sales Inc., PO Box 14829, SurfsiDe Beach, SC 29587-4829, (803)651-3303 [15064]

Builder Marts of America Inc., PO Box 47, Greenville, SC 29602, (864)297-6101 [7098]

Builders Brass Works Corp., 3528 Emery St., Los Angeles, CA 90023, (213)269-8111 [13610]

Builders Center Inc., 12911 Florida Blvd., Baton Rouge, LA 70815, (504)275-4125 [7099]

Builders General Supply Co., PO Box 95, Little Silver, NJ 07739, (732)747-0808 [7100]

Builders Hardware & Specialties, 2002 W 16th St., Erie, PA 16505-4816, (814)453-4736 [13611]

Builders Hardware and Supply Co. Inc., 1516 15th Ave. W, Box C79005, Seattle, WA 98119-3185, (206)281-3700 [13612]

Builders Specialties Co., PO Box 969, Pawtucket, RI 02862, (401)722-2988 [7101]

Builders Warehouse, PO Box 1447, Grand Island, NE 68802, (308)382-9656 [7102]

Builders Wholesale Supply Company, Inc., Forbes Industrial Park, 7215 S Topeka Blvd., No. 9C, PO Box 19286, Topeka, KS 66619-1423, (913)642-4334 [13048]

Builders Wholesale Supply Company Inc., Forbes Industrial Park, Topeka, KS 66619-1423, (913)642-4334 [27290]

Builderway Inc., PO Box 429, Simpsonville, SC 29681-0429, (803)297-6266 [15065]

Building and Industrial Wholesale Co., 12 Davisville Rd., PO Box 70, Davisville, WV 26142, (304)485-6500 [7103]

Building Materials Distributors Inc., PO Box 606, Galt, CA 95632, (209)745-3001 [7104]

Building Materials Wholesale, 1571 W Sunnyside Rd., Idaho Falls, ID 83402-4349, (208)529-8162 [7105]

Building Plastics Inc., 3263 Sharpe Ave., Memphis, TN 38111, (901)744-6414 [9746]

Building Products Inc., PO Box 1390, Watertown, SD 57201, (605)886-3495 [7106]

Bulbman Inc., PO Box 12280, Reno, NV 89510-2280 [8476]

Bulbtronics, 45 Banfi Plz., Farmingdale, NY 11735, (631)249-2272 [8477]

Bullington Lift Trucks, 2790 Broadway, PO Box 763, Macon, GA 31298, (912)788-0520 [15855]

Bulova Corp., 1 Bulova Ave., Woodside, NY 11377-7874, (718)204-3300 [17354]

Bumble Bee Seafoods Inc., PO Box 85362, San Diego, CA 92186-5362, (619)550-4000 [10641]

Bumble Bee Wholesale, 12521 Oxnard St., North Hollywood, CA 91606, (818)985-2329 [13479]

Bumble Bee Wholesale, 12521 Oxnard St., North Hollywood, CA 91606, (818)985-2939 [23575]

Bumper to Bumper, 414 E 75th St., New York, NY 10021, (212)737-3000 [2189]

Bun Patch Supply Corp., 155 Tuckerton Rd., Temple, PA 19560, (215)929-3668 [7107]

Bundy Enterprises Inc., 2522 State Rd., Bensalem, PA 19020, (215)245-1099 [19842]

Bunge Corp., 11720 Borman Dr., St. Louis, MO 63146, (314)872-3030 [17754]

Bunker Hill Foods, PO Box 1048, Bedford, VA 24523-1048, (540)586-8274 [10642]

Bunn Capitol Co., PO Box 4227, Springfield, IL 62708, (217)529-5401 [10643]

Bunn Co.; B.H., 2730 Drane Field Rd., Lakeland, FL 33811-1395, (813)647-1555 [15856]

Bunzl Distribution Inc., 701 Emerson Rd., No. 500, St. Louis, MO 63141, (314)997-5959 [21658]

Bunzl Distribution USA, 701 Emerson Rd., No. 500, St. Louis, MO 63141, (314)997-5959 [21658]

Bunzl New Jersey Inc., PO Box 668, Dayton, NJ 08810-0668, (732)821-7000 [21659]

Bur-Bee Co. Inc., PO Box 797, WalLa Walla, WA 99362-0252, (509)525-5040 [10644]

Burack Inc.; I., 59 Kenilworth Rd., Rye, NY 10580-1910, (914)968-8100 [23101]

Burbank Aircraft Supply Inc., 2333 Utah Ave., El Segundo, CA 90245, (310)727-5000 [68]

Burch Body Works Inc., 22 N Monroe St., Rockford, MI 49341, (616)866-4421 [15857]

Burcham and McCune Inc., 5300 District Blvd., Bakersfield, CA 93313, (805)397-5300 [13049]

Burchinal Cooperative Society, 11745 B. 2nd St., Rockwell, IA 50469-8705, (515)822-4660 [352]

Burchs Fine Footwear Inc., 16 Oakway Ctr., Eugene, OR 97401-5612, (541)485-2070 [24703]

Burchs Fine Footwear Inc., 223 1/2 Valley River Ctr., Eugene, OR 97401-2176, (541)485-2070 [4852]

Burda Brothers, 47725 Michigan, Canton, MI 48188, (734)397-1441 [26430]

Burger Iron Co., 1324 Firestone Pkwy., Akron, OH 44301, (330)253-5121 [19843]

Burgess, Anderson and Tate Inc., 1455 S Lakeside Dr., Waukegan, IL 60085-8314, (847)872-4543 [13050]

Burgess Brothers Grain Inc., U.S Hwy. 51 S, Clinton, KY 42031, (502)653-4346 [17755]

Burgess Lighting and Distributing, 10358 Lee Hwy., Fairfax, VA 22030, (703)385-6660 [15066]

Burgess; Philip, 300 Union St., Randolph, MA 02368-4930, (781)963-1710 [23576]

Burgmaster, 12975 Clarence Center Rd., Akron, NY 14001-1321 [15858]

Burgon Tool Steel Company Inc., 20 Durham St., Portsmouth, NH 03801, (603)430-9200 [19844]

Burk Electronics, 35 N Kensington, La Grange, IL 60525, (708)482-9310 [5537]

Burke Beverage of California Inc., 31281 Wiegman Rd., Hayward, CA 94544-7809, (510)489-1919 [1560]

Burke Beverage Inc., 536 East Ave., La Grange, IL 60525, (708)579-0333 [1561]

Burke Engineering Company Inc., PO Box 3427, El Monte, CA 91733, (626)579-6763 [14363]

Burke Equipment Co., PO Box 8010, Sterling Heights, MI 48311-8010, (810)939-4400 [7108]

Burke Hosiery Mills Inc., PO Box 406, Hildebran, NC 28637-0406, (704)328-1725 [4853]

Burke Inc., 1800 Merriam Ln., Kansas City, KS 66106, (913)722-5658 [18888]

Burke Inc., 1800 Merriam Ln., Kansas City, KS 66106, (913)722-5658 [18722]

Burkett's Office Supply Inc., 8520 Younger Creek Dr., Sacramento, CA 95828, (916)387-8900 [13051]

Burkhart Dental Supply, PO Box 11265, Tacoma, WA 98411-0265, (253)474-7761 [18723]

Burklund Distributors Inc., 2500 N Main St., Ste. 3, East Peoria, IL 61611-1789, (309)694-1900 [10645]

Burkmann Feed, 1111 Perryville Rd., Danville, KY 40422-1306, (606)336-3400 [27093]

Burkmann Feeds—Glasgow, Attn: Eugene Myatt, 100 Georgetown Ln., Glasgow, KY 42141, (502)651-8000 [27094]

Burkmann Feeds—London, Attn: Gary Allen, 1115 S Laurel, London, KY 40741, (606)877-3333 [27095]

Burkmann Mills, 1111 Perryville Rd., Danville, KY 40422, (606)236-0400 [27096]

Burlingham and Sons; E.F., PO Box 217, Forest Grove, OR 97116-0217, (503)357-2141 [353]

Burlington A/V Recording Media, Inc., 106 Mott St., Oceanside, NY 11572, (516)678-4414 [25112]

Burlington Drug Co., 92 Catamount Dr., Milton, VT 05468, (802)893-5105 [26268]

Burlington Futon Co. Inc., 388 Pine St., Burlington, VT 05401-4779, (802)658-6685 [15432]

Burlington House Inc., 1250 Shelburne Rd., South Burlington, VT 05403-7707, (802)863-7902 [13052]

Burlington Industries Equity Inc. Knitted Fabrics Div., 1345 Ave. of the Americas, New York, NY 10105, (212)621-3000 [25992]

Burly Corporation of North America, 754 N Burleson Blvd., Burleson, TX 76028, (817)295-1128 [7109]

Burnett Construction Co., PO Box 2707, Durango, CO 81302, (970)247-2172 [7110]

Burnett Dairy Cooperative, 11631 State Rd. 70, Grantsburg, WI 54840-0188, (715)689-2468 [17756]

Burnett Engraving Co. Inc., 1351 N Hudley, Anaheim, CA 92806, (714)632-0870 [15859]

Burnett and Sons Mill and Lumber Co., PO Box 1646, Sacramento, CA 95812-1646, (916)442-0493 [7111]

Burnham Glove Co.; Frederic H., 1602 Tennessee St., PO Box 276, Michigan City, IN 46360, (219)874-5205 [4854]

Burnham; William H., 1 Main St., York Beach, ME 03910, (207)363-4622 [26431]

Burningtons, Inc., 824 Laramie Ave., Alliance, NE 69301-2952, (308)762-8716 [23475]

Burns Brothers Contractors, 400 Leavenworth Ave., Syracuse, NY 13204, (315)422-0261 [23102]

Burns Co.; Troy, 6723 Asher Ave., PO Box 4050, Little Rock, AR 72204, (501)562-1111 [15860]

Burns Industries Inc., PO Box 338, Line Lexington, PA 18932-0338, (215)699-5313 [7112]

Burns Supply/Great Lakes Inc., 760 W Genesee St., Syracuse, NY 13204, (315)474-7471 [23103]

Burnstine's Distributing Corp., PO Box 2367, Elkhart, IN 46515, (219)293-1571 [2400]

Burquip Truck Bodies & Equipment, 235 Adams St., PO Box 769, Bedford Hills, NY 10507, (914)241-0950 [2401]

Burris Foods Inc., PO Box 219, Milford, DE 19963, (302)422-4531 [10646]

Burroughs Communications Inc., 4701 Newbern Ave., Raleigh, NC 27610, (919)212-7700 [5538]

Burrows Co., 230 West Palatine Rd., Wheeling, IL 60090, (847)537-7300 [19205]

Burrows Inc.; John H., PO Box 604, Sparks, NV 89431, (702)358-2442 [10647]

Bursma Electronic Distributing Inc., 2851 Buchanan SW, Grand Rapids, MI 49548, (616)831-0080 [25113]

Bursma Electronic Distributing Inc., 2851 Buchanan Ave., SW, Grand Rapids, MI 49548-1025, (616)831-0080 [8478]

Burt Explosives Inc., 294 North 500 West, Moab, UT 84532, (801)259-7181 [9632]

Burt Millwork Corp., 1010 Stanley Ave., Brooklyn, NY 11208, (718)257-4601 [7113]

Burton Auto Supply Inc., PO Box 297, Weslaco, TX 78596, (210)968-3121 [2402]

Burton Building Products Inc., 9900 Maumelle Blvd., North Little Rock, AR 72113-6610 [7114]

Burton Lumber Corp., 835 Wilson Rd., Chesapeake, VA 23324, (757)545-4613 [7115]

Burton-Rogers Co. Inc., 220 Grove St., Waltham, MA 02453, (781)894-6440 [24331]

Burton-Rogers Company Inc., 220 Grove St., Waltham, MA 02453, (781)894-6440 [2403]

Burtons Inc., 800 Frederick St., Cumberland, MD 21502, (301)777-3866 [4855]

Burts Sports Specialty Inc., 850 Main St., Falmouth, MA 02540-3656, (508)540-0644 [23577]

Busby Metals Inc., 55 Davids Dr., Hauppauge, NY 11788, (631)434-3400 [19845]

Buschart Office Products Inc., 1834 Walton Rd., St. Louis, MO 63114, (314)426-7222 [20865]

Bush Landscaping & Nursery, 2848 Lore Rd., Anchorage, AK 99507, (907)344-2775 [14832]

Bush Supply Co., 1121 W Van Buren, Harlingen, TX 78550, (956)428-2425 [8479]

Bushland Grain Cooperative, PO Box 129, Bushland, TX 79012, (806)358-2411 [17757]

Bushwacker Inc., 9200 N Decatur, Portland, OR 97203-2819, (503)283-4335 [24521]

Business Cards Tomorrow Inc., 3000 NE 30th Pl., 5th Fl., Ft. Lauderdale, FL 33306, (954)563-1224 [21660]

Business Communications Inc., 7903 Thorndike Rd., Greensboro, NC 27409, (336)668-4488 [5539]

Business Computer Solutions, 1301 Fraser St., Ste. 11-A, Bellingham, WA 98226-5832, (360)671-9630 [6027]

Business Concepts Inc., PO Box 261400, Littleton, CO 80163-1400, (303)755-4988 [13053]

Business Data Systems Inc., 1 Swords Ln., Billings, MT 59105-3029, (406)256-3782 [20866]

Business Development International, 45 E End Ave., Ste. 11D, New York, NY 10028, (212)650-1689 [22938]

Business Environments Inc., 4121 Prospect Ave. NE, Albuquerque, NM 87110-3817, (505)888-4400 [13054]

Business Express of Boulder Inc., 1904 Pearl St., Boulder, CO 80302, (303)443-9300 [20867]

Business Furnishings Co., 10801 Kempwood Dr., Ste. 8, Houston, TX 77043, (713)462-5742 [13055]

Business Integrators, 1240 Blalock, Houston, TX 77055, (713)973-8811 [6028]

Business Interiors Inc. (Denver, Colorado), 4141 Colorado Blvd., Denver, CO 80216, (303)321-6671 [13056]

Business Interiors Northwest Inc., 710 Pacific Ave., Tacoma, WA 98402, (253)627-1000 [13057]

Business Machines Inc., 549 Pylon Dr., Raleigh, NC 27606-1414, (919)834-0100 [6029]

Business Management Software, PO Box 228, Norfolk, NE 68702-0228, (402)371-1992 [6030]

Business Media Inc., 300 Oak Creek Dr., Lincoln, NE 68528, (402)476-6222 [6031]

Business Office Supply Co., 816 E Broadway St., Louisville, KY 40204, (502)589-8400 [20868]

Business Resource Group, 2150 N 1st St., Ste. 101, San Jose, CA 95131, (408)325-3200 [13058]

Business Support Services, 1810 49th St. S, Apt. 206, Fargo, ND 58103-7705, (701)232-8221 [20869]

Business Systems, 734 Forest St., Marlborough, MA 01752-3002, (508)624-4600 [6032]

Business With Pleasure, PO Box 309, Thermopolis, WY 82443-0309, (307)864-2385 [20870]

Business World Inc., PO Box 624, Manchester Center, VT 05255, (802)362-3318 [20871]

Bussert Industrial Supply Inc., 8211 Bavaria Dr. E, Macedonia, OH 44056-2259, (216)441-3000 [16773]

Butcher Air Conditioning Co., 101 Boyce Rd., Broussard, LA 70518, (318)837-2000 [14364]

Butech Inc., 777 S Ellsworth Ave., Salem, OH 44460, (330)332-9913 [26774]

Butler Beef Inc., 4700 N 132nd, Butler, WI 53007-1603, (414)781-4545 [10648]

Butler Co.; W.A., 5600 Blazer Pkwy., Dublin, OH 43017, (614)761-9095 [19206]

Butler County Motor Company Inc., PO Box 1028, Butler, PA 16003, (724)287-2766 [2404]

Butler-Dearden Paper Service Inc., 80 Shrewsbury St., Boylston, MA 01505, (508)869-9000 [21661]

Butler-Johnson Corp., 5031 24th St., Sacramento, CA 95822, (916)454-3512 [9747]

Butler-Johnson Corp., PO Box 612110, San Jose, CA 95161-2110, (408)259-1800 [9748]

Butler-Johnson Corp., PO Box 612110, San Jose, CA 95161-2110, (408)259-1800 [7116]

Butler National Corp., 19920 W 161st St., Olathe, KS 66062-2700, (913)780-9595 [10649]

Butler National Services Inc., 2772 NW 31st Ave., Ft. Lauderdale, FL 33311, (954)733-7511 [24332]

Butler Paper Co., 12601 E 38th Ave., Denver, CO 80239-3408, (303)790-8343 [21662]

Butler & Sons Refrigeration, PO Box 336, Childersburg, AL 35044-0336, (205)378-3480 [14365]

Butler Wholesale Products, 37 Pleasant St., PO Box 308, Adams, MA 01220, (413)743-3885 [24085]

Butte Produce Co., 605 Utah Ave., Butte, MT 59701-2607, (406)782-2369 [10650]

Butterfield Building Supply, 375 N Main, Midvale, UT 84047-2486, (801)255-4201 [7117]

Butterfield and Company Inc., 6930 Atrium Boardwalk S, Ste. 300, Indianapolis, IN 46250, (317)841-6500 [10651]

Butterworth Co. of Cape Cod, 89 Willow St., Yarmouth Port, MA 02675-1742, (508)790-1111 [3601]

Buttery Hardware Company Inc., 201 W Main, Llano, TX 78643, (915)247-4141 [13613]

Buttrey Food & Drug, 999 W Utah Ave., Payson, UT 84651, (801)465-4831 [19207]

Buttross Wholesale Co.; A., Drawer 1206, Natchez, MS 39121-1206, (601)445-4112 [23578]

Buurma Farms Inc., 3909 Kok Rd., Willard, OH 44890, (419)935-6411 [10652]

Buy for Less Inc., 730 E Charles Page Blvd., Sand Springs, OK 74063-8507, (918)742-2456 [10653]

Buy-Lines Co., 5444 Melrose Ave., Los Angeles, CA 90038, (323)463-4855 [17355]

Buy-Rite Petroleum Ltd., 11724 Parkshire Dr., St. Louis, MO 63126, (314)421-1100 [22099]

Buyers Paper & Specialty Inc., 510 W Mill St., Indianapolis, IN 46225-1429, (317)639-2591 [26269]

Buy_Low Beauty Supply, 2738 N Pleasantburg Dr., Greenville, SC 29609, (864)232-7996 [14053]

BWD Automotive Corp., 11045 Gage Ave., Franklin Park, IL 60131, (708)455-3120 [2405]

Byczek Enterprises, 3924 W Devon Ave., Lincolnwood, IL 60659, (847)673-6050 [24086]

BYE Inc., PO Box 31093, Billings, MT 59107-1093, (406)252-5391 [1562]

Byers Sons Inc.; Geo., PO Box 16513, Columbus, OH 43216, (614)228-5111 [20608]

Byfield Marine Supply Co., 175 Olive Rd., Pensacola, FL 32514, (850)477-8011 [18473]

Byfield Marine Supply LLC, 175 Olive Rd., Pensacola, FL 32514, (850)477-8011 [18473]

Byrne Co., 200 Cabeza Negra Ct. SE, Rio Rancho, NM 87124-1344, (505)836-2600 [7118]

Byrne Compressed Air Equipment Company, Inc., 796 E 140th St., Bronx, NY 10454, (718)292-7726 [5831]

Byrne Plywood Co., 2400 Cole Ave., Birmingham, MI 48009, (248)642-8800 [7119]

Byrnes and Kiefer Company Inc., 131 Kline Ave., Callery, PA 16024, (412)321-1900 [10654]

Byron Systems International Inc., 12081-B Tech Rd., Silver Spring, MD 20904, (301)680-0006 [25241]

C and B Sales and Service Inc., 119 Nolan Rd., Broussard, LA 70518, (318)837-2701 [5832]

C/C Chemical and Coal Co., 2321 Fortune Dr., Lexington, KY 40505, (606)299-0026 [20525]

C & C Distributors, PO Box 22610, Santa Fe, NM 87502-2610, (505)982-3341 [4591]

C & C Distributors, 12463 Little Fawn Rd., Gulfport, MS 39503-7691, (228)868-1220 [15067]

C Companies, Inc., 10000 Flying Cloud Dr., Eden Prairie, MN 55347, (612)942-6630 [6033]

C-Corp., 30 Beaver Pond Rd., Beverly, MA 01915-1203, (978)281-6490 [10655]

C-D Farm Service Company Inc., PO Box 560, Spencer, IA 51301-0560, (712)262-4205 [354]

C & D Hardwoods, PO Box 14, Hwy. 64 W, New Salisbury, IN 47161, (812)347-3278 [7120]

C/D/R/ Inc., 300 Delware Ave., Ste. 1704, Wilmington, DE 19801, (302)427-5865 [15068]

C. Design International Inc., 1967 Quincy Ct., Glendale Heights, IL 60139, (708)582-2600 [15861]

C & E Carolina Inc., 651 Pilot View St., Winston-Salem, NC 27101-2717, (336)788-9191 [25124]

C and F Enterprises, 819 Blue Crab Rd., Newport News, VA 23606, (757)873-0410 [25993]

C & G Distributing Co. Inc., 3535 St. Johns Rd., Lima, OH 45804-4016, (419)221-2337 [1563]

C & G Electronics Co., PO Box 1316, Tacoma, WA 98401, (253)272-3181 [8480]

C & J Bait Co., PO Box 251, Purcell, OK 73080-0251, (405)527-2586 [23579]

C & J Fasteners, 25136 5 Mile Rd., Redford, MI 48239-3717, (313)535-8835 [13614]

C and J Service Co., PO Box 178, De Witt, IA 52742, (319)659-5145 [22100]

C & J Tool & Gage Co., 4830 S Division Ave., Grand Rapids, MI 49548, (616)534-6071 [15862]

C & K Distributors Inc., 8202 Cooper Ave., Glendale, NY 11385, (718)894-4302 [27097]

C and L Communications Inc., 26254 Interstate Hwy. 10 W, Boerne, TX 78006, (210)698-3380 [5540]

C and L Supply Inc., PO Box 578, Vinita, OK 74301, (918)256-6411 [15069]

C-Mor Co., 7 Jewell St., Garfield, NJ 07026, (201)478-3900 [15433]

C-N Corrugated and Sheeting Inc., PO Box 23570, Louisville, KY 40223, (502)244-5333 [21663]

C and P Oil Inc., PO Box 157, Millersburg, IN 46543, (219)642-3823 [22101]

C & P Sales Co., 540 S Main St., Bldg. 121, Akron, OH 44311-1023, (330)535-1141 [26432]

C & R Distributors, 1615 Tomlinson, Mason, MI 48854-9257, (517)694-7218 [10656]

C R Laurence Company Inc., PO Box 58923, Los Angeles, CA 90058, (323)588-1281 [2406]

C & R Tile, 1 Chabot St., Westbrook, ME 04092, (207)854-2077 [9749]

C & S Distributors, PO Box 471915, Tulsa, OK 74145-1915, (918)664-6400 [25586]

C and S Inc., PO Box 388, Portales, NM 88130, (505)356-4496 [22102]

C S & S Computer Systems Inc., 1515 W University Dr., Ste. 103, Tempe, AZ 85281-3279, (602)968-8585 [6034]

C & S Specialty Inc., 1181 Old Smithfield Rd., North Smithfield, RI 02896, (401)769-2260 [24522]

C and S Wholesale Grocers Inc., PO Box 821, Brattleboro, VT 05302, (802)257-4371 [10657]

C and T Design and Equipment Company Inc., 2855 Toby Dr., Indianapolis, IN 46219, (317)898-9602 [25237]

C-Tech Systems Div., 6450 Carlson Dr., Eden Prairie, MN 55346, (612)974-1700 [16774]

C & W Distributing Inc., PO Box 22610, Santa Fe, NM 87502-2610, (505)982-3341 [4591]

C and W Enterprises Inc., 317 N Farr St., San Angelo, TX 76903, (915)655-5795 [22103]

C and W Food Service Inc., PO Box 5346, Tallahassee, FL 32314-5346, (850)877-5853 [10658]

C and W Zabel Co., PO Box 41, Leonia, NJ 07605-0041, (732)254-1000 [3602]

Cabin-Craft Southwest, 1500 Westpark Way, Euless, TX 76040, (817)571-4925 [20872]

Cabin Craft Southwest, Inc., PO Box 876, Bedford, TX 76095, (817)571-3837 [25588]

Cabin Crafters, 1225 W 1st St., Nevada, IA 50201, (515)382-5406 [27291]

Cabinet & Cupboard Inc., PO Box 378, Seneca Tpke., New Hartford, NY 13413, (315)735-4665 [7121]

Cable & Computer Connection, 3404 Canton Rd., Marietta, GA 30066-2615, (770)420-8990 [6150]

Cable Converter Services Corp., 54 E Market St., Box 407, Spencer, IN 47460, (812)829-4833 [8481]

Cable Services Co. Inc., 2113 Marydale Ave., Williamsport, PA 17701, (717)323-8518 [25114]

Cable Technologies International of New York Inc., Rte. 20, Box 278, Esperance, NY 12066-6101, (518)664-7500 [25115]

CableLAN Express Inc., PO Box 196, Norfolk, MA 02056, (508)384-7811 [5541]

CableLink Inc., 255 W 2950 S, Salt Lake City, UT 84115, (801)467-4511 [6035]

Cables & Chips Inc., 121 Fulton St., 4th Fl., New York, NY 10038, (212)619-3132 [6036]

Cabo Distributing Co., Inc., PO Box 10007, Newport Beach, CA 92658-0007, (626)575-8090 [1564]

Cabot Hosiery Mills Inc., 35 N Main St., Northfield, VT 05663, (802)485-6066 [4856]

Cache Beauty Supply Inc., 2826 E Highland Dr., PO Box 8070, Jonesboro, AR 72401, (870)972-5300 [14054]

Cache Valley Builders Supply, PO Box 324, 1488 N Zoowest, Logan, UT 84341, (435)752-6200 [7122]

Cactus Pipe and Supply Co., 1 Greenway Plz., Ste. 450, Houston, TX 77046, (713)877-1948 [22104]

CAD Store Inc., 4494 W Peoria Ave., Ste. 105, Glendale, AZ 85302 [6037]

CADCentre Inc., 10700 Richmond Ave., No. 300, Houston, TX 77042, (713)977-1225 [6038]

CADCO Div., 2776 County Rd. 69, Gibsonburg, OH 43431, (419)665-2367 [355]

CADD Microsystems, Inc., 6183 Grovedale Ct., Ste. 200, Alexandria, VA 22310, (703)719-0500 [6039]

Cade Grayson Co., 2445 Cade's Way, Vista, CA 92083-7831, (760)727-1000 [10659]

Cadec Corporation, 8 E Perimeter Rd., Londonderry, NH 03053, (603)668-1010 [6040]

Cadillac Glass Co., 11801 Commerce St., Warren, MI 48089, (810)754-5277 [7123]

Cadillac Motor Car, PO Box 5018, Westlake Village, CA 91359, (805)373-9787 [2407]

Cadillac Plastic and Chemical Div., 2855 Coolidge Hwy., Ste. 300, Troy, MI 48084-3217, (810)583-1200 [22939]

Cadillac Plastic Group Inc., 2855 Coolidge Hwy., Ste. 300, Troy, MI 48084, (248)205-3100 [22940]

Cadillac Shoe Products Inc., 50761 W Pontiac Trl., Wixom, MI 48393, (248)624-5800 [24704]

Cady Industries Inc., PO Box 15085, Tampa, FL 33684, (813)876-2474 [21664]

Caemi International Inc., 100 1st Stamford Pl., Stamford, CT 06902-6732, (203)969-1442 [20526]

Caffall Brothers Forest Products Inc., PO Box 725, Wilsonville, OR 97070, (503)682-1910 [7124]

Caffe Latte, 6254 Wilshire Blvd., Los Angeles, CA 90048, (213)936-5213 [10660]

Caffey, Inc.; I.H., PO Box 410368, Charlotte, NC 28241-0368, (704)588-0930 [1565]

Cagle's Inc., 2000 Hills Ave. NW, Atlanta, GA 30318, (404)355-2820 [10661]

Cahokia Flour Co., 2701 Hereford St., St. Louis, MO 63139-1021, (314)781-1211 [10662]

CAI Div., 550 W Northwest Hwy., Barrington, IL 60010, (847)381-2400 [22836]

Cain and Bultman Co., 4825 Fulton Industrial Blvd., Atlanta, GA 30336, (404)691-0730 [8482]

Cain & Bultman, Inc., PO Box 2815, Jacksonville, FL 32203-2815, (305)625-0461 [9750]

Cain and Bultman Inc., PO Box 2815, Jacksonville, FL 32204, (904)356-4812 [15070]

Cain Electrical Supply Corp., PO Box 2158, Big Spring, TX 79720, (915)263-8421 [8483]

Cain Steel and Supply Co., PO Box 1369, Tuscaloosa, AL 35403, (205)349-2751 [19846]

Cain's Coffee Co., 1455 E Chestnut Expy., Springfield, MO 65802, (417)869-5523 [10753]

Cains Foods, Inc., E Main St., Ayer, MA 01432-1832, (978)772-0300 [10663]

Cains Foods, L.P., E Main St., Ayer, MA 01432-1832, (978)772-0300 [10663]

Cairo Cooperative Equity Exchange, 265 S Penalosa St., Penalosa, KS 67035, (316)532-5106 [356]

Caito Foods Service, Inc., 3120 N Post Rd., Indianapolis, IN 46226, (317)897-2009 [10664]

Cajun Sales, Attn: Bruce Perilloux, 412 Oak Ln., Luling, LA 70070, (504)785-1644 [27098]

Cal-Coast Machinery, 617 S Blosser Rd., Santa Maria, CA 93454, (805)925-0931 [357]

Cal Compack Foods Inc., 4906 W 1st St., Santa Ana, CA 92703, (714)775-7757 [10665]

Cal Fresh Products, 2705 5th St., Ste. 5, Sacramento, CA 95818, (916)442-1292 [12509]

Cal Fruit, 14310 Gannet, La Mirada, CA 90638-5221, (562)941-8794 [10666]

Cal-Growers Corp., 447 N 1st St., San Jose, CA 95112-4018, (408)573-1000 [10667]

Cal-North Auto Brokers Inc., PO Box 7305, Santa Rosa, CA 95407, (707)578-9245 [2408]

Cal-West Foodservice Inc., 12015 Slauson Ave., Ste. F, Santa Fe Springs, CA 90670, (562)945-1355 [10668]

Cal-West Seeds Inc., PO Box 1428, Woodland, CA 95776, (530)666-3331 [358]

Calarco Inc., PO Box 727, Corcoran, CA 93212, (209)992-3127 [359]

Calato USA Div., 4501 Hyde Park Blvd., Niagara Falls, NY 14305, (716)285-3546 [25116]

Calbag Metals Co., PO Box 10067, Portland, OR 97210, (503)226-3441 [26775]

Calcasieu Lumber Co., PO Box 17097, Austin, TX 78760, (512)444-3172 [7125]

Calcasieu Lumber Co., PO Box 17097, Austin, TX 78760, (512)444-3172 [27292]

Calco of Minneapolis Inc., 2751 Minnehaha Ave. S, Minneapolis, MN 55406, (612)724-0067 [10669]

Calcom Graphic Supply, Inc., 8215 SW Glencreek Ct., Portland, OR 97223-9330 [25589]

Calcom Graphic Supply, Inc., 8215 SW Glencreek Ct., Portland, OR 97223-9330 [25590]

Calcom Graphic Supply, Inc., 1822 NE Grand Ave., Portland, OR 97212-3912, (503)281-9698 [25591]

Calcom Inc., 3433 Edward, Santa Clara, CA 95051, (408)727-5353 [15863]

Calcot Ltd., PO Box 259, Bakersfield, CA 93302, (661)327-5961 [17758]

Caldwell and Bloor Company Inc., 80 W 3rd St., Mansfield, OH 44902, (419)522-3011 [19208]

Caldwell Implement Co. Inc., PO Box 295, Burlington, KS 66839, (316)364-5327 [360]

Caldwell, Inc.; Bradley, 200 Kiwanis Blvd., PO Box T, Hazleton, PA 18201, (717)455-7511 [361]

Caldwell Milling Company Inc., PO Box 179, Rose Bud, AR 72137-0179, (501)556-5121 [10670]

Caldwell Supply Company Inc., PO Box T, Hazleton, PA 18201, (717)455-7511 [17759]

Caledonia Farmers Elevator Co., Lake Odessa Branch, 1018 3rd Ave., Lake Odessa, MI 48849-1157, (616)374-8061 [362]

Calhook, 6205 S 231st St., Kent, WA 98032, (253)749-8822 [25592]

Calhoun County Cooperative, PO Box 900, Calhoun City, MS 38916, (601)628-6682 [363]

Calhoun Enterprises, 810 S West Blvd., Montgomery, AL 36105, (205)272-4400 [10671]

Calhoun Inc.; Nancy, PO Box 130, Corona, CA 92878-0130, (714)529-4700 [15434]

Calhoun's Shoes, 1415 1st Ave. S, Birmingham, AL 35233, (205)326-2800 [24856]

Calibron Instruments Div., 220 Grove St., Waltham, MA 02453, (781)894-6440 [24331]

Calico Trading Private Ltd. Co., PO Box 380039, Jacksonville, FL 32205-0539 [24113]

Caliendo-Savio Enterprises Inc., 16800 W Cleveland Ave., New Berlin, WI 53151, (262)786-8400 [13325]

California Affiliated Representative Inc., 9420 Reseda Blvd., No. 224, Northridge, CA 91324-2932, (213)589-6566 [2409]

California Ammonia Co., PO Box 280, French Camp, CA 95231-0280, (209)982-1000 [364]

California Artichoke and Vegetable Growers Corp., 10855 Cara Mia Pkwy., Castroville, CA 95012, (831)633-2144 [12052]

California Eastern Laboratories Inc., 4590 Patrick Henry Dr., Santa Clara, CA 95056, (408)988-3500 [8484]

California Electric Supply, 1201 Callens Rd., Ventura, CA 93003-5614, (805)642-2181 [8485]

California Fasteners Inc., PO Box 18328, Anaheim, CA 92817, (714)970-9090 [13615]

California Gift Center Inc., 1425 S Main St., Los Angeles, CA 90015, (213)747-5809 [26433]

California Glass Co., 155 98th Ave., Oakland, CA 94603, (510)635-7700 [7126]

California Hardware Co., PO Box 3640, Ontario, CA 91764, (909)390-6100 [13616]

California Hobby Distributors, 415 S Palm Ave., Alhambra, CA 91803, (626)289-8857 [26434]

California Industrial Rubber Co., Yuba City Branch, 1690 Sierra Ave., Yuba City, CA 95993, (530)674-2444 [24272]

California Industrial Rubber Company Inc., 2732 S Cherry Ave., Fresno, CA 93706, (209)485-1487 [16775]

California Manufacturing Co., Rte. 3, California, MO 65018-9416, (573)796-2133 [4857]

California Micro Devices Inc., 2000 W 14th St., Tempe, AZ 85281, (480)921-6000 [8486]

California Milk Producers, 11709 E Artesia Blvd., Artesia, CA 90701, (562)865-1291 [10672]

California Naturals, 2054 S Garfield Ave., City of Commerce, CA 90040, (213)889-6889 [10673]

California Pacific Fruit Co., 2001 Main St., San Diego, CA 92113-2216, (619)236-9100 [10674]

California Panel and Veneer Co., PO Box 3250, Cerritos, CA 90703, (562)926-5834 [7127]

California Professional Manufacturing Inc., PO Box 4832, Modesto, CA 95352, (209)527-2686 [25593]

California School Furnishing Company Inc., 4450 N Brawley St., No. 125, Fresno, CA 93722, (559)276-0561 [13059]

California Shellfish Co., 2601 5th, Sacramento, CA 95818, (916)446-0251 [10675]

California Shellfish Company Inc., 505 Beach Court, Ste. 200, San Francisco, CA 94133-1321, (415)923-7400 [10676]

California Steel Services Inc., 1212 S Mountain View, San Bernardino, CA 92408, (909)796-2222 [19847]

California Surveying and Drafting Supply Inc., 4733 Auburn Blvd., Sacramento, CA 95841, (916)344-0232 [24333]

California Tile Distributors, 1306 W Magnolia Blvd., Burbank, CA 91506, (213)849-1468 [9751]

California Tile Supply, 42704 10th St. W, Lancaster, CA 93534-7029, (661)942-2545 [9752]

California Time Inc., 1250 S Broadway, Los Angeles, CA 90015, (213)749-9949 [17356]

California Tire Co., 2295 Davis Ct., Hayward, CA 94545, (510)487-5777 [2410]

California Wallet Co. Inc., 3728 Rockwell Ave., El Monte, CA 91731, (626)443-6888 [18379]

Calihan and Co., One South St., Peoria, IL 61602, (309)674-9175 [10677]

Calihan and Co., PO Box 1155, Peoria, IL 61653, (309)674-9175 [10678]

Calihan Pork Processors, One South St., Peoria, IL 61602, (309)674-9175 [10677]

Calihan Pork Processors, PO Box 1155, Peoria, IL 61653, (309)674-9175 [10678]

Calkins Distributing, E 5417 Broadway, Spokane, WA 99212, (509)536-7642 [15864]

Calkins Fluid Power, Inc., E 5417 Broadway, Spokane, WA 99212, (509)536-7642 [15864]

Call-A-Tech Inc., 2135 Market, Wheeling, WV 26003-2840, (304)233-1771 [6041]

Call Associates Inc., 4230 Kiernan Ave., No. 210, Modesto, CA 95356-9323, (650)875-1911 [15865]

Call Dynamics Inc., 2020 N Central Ave., No. 1010, Phoenix, AZ 85016, (602)252-5800 [5542]

Call Management Products Inc., 510 Compton St. Ste. 102, Broomfield, CO 80020, (303)465-0651 [8487]

Callahan Brothers Supply Inc., PO Box 493, Lewiston, ME 04243-0493, (207)784-5897 [25594]

Callahan Grocery Co. Inc., 528 N Broad St., Bainbridge, GA 31717, (912)246-0844 [10679]

Callahan Inc.; S.X., 824 S Laredo St., San Antonio, TX 78204, (210)224-1625 [2411]

Callaway Golf Co, 2285 Rutherford Rd., Carlsbad, CA 92008-8815, (760)931-1771 [23580]

Callback Software, 265 Winn St., Burlington, MA 01803, (781)273-3044 [6042]

Callif Co., 4561 E 5th Ave., Columbus, OH 43219, (614)238-7300 [10680]

Callis-Thompson, Inc., Rte. 13 S, Harrington, DE 19952, (302)398-3068 [15866]

CalMark Custom Covers, 1617 Pacific Ave., Ste. 111, Oxnard, CA 93033, (805)486-3863 [2412]

Calmark Resources Inc., 1617 Pacific Ave., Ste. 111, Oxnard, CA 93033, (805)486-3863 [2412]

Calmini Products Inc., 6600-B McDivitt Dr., Bakersfield, CA 93313, (805)398-9500 [2413]

Calolympic Glove and Safety Co. Inc., PO Box 2323, Riverside, CA 92516-2323, (909)369-0165 [24523]

Calolympic Glove and Safety Company Inc., PO Box 2323, Riverside, CA 92516-2323, (909)369-0165 [16776]

Caloric Corp., PO Box 6255, Florence, SC 29502, (803)667-1191 [15071]

Calotex Delaware, Inc., 17 Wood St., Middletown, DE 19709, (302)378-9568 [7128]

Calotex Inc.; D.E., 24 W Main St., Middletown, DE 19709-1039, (302)378-2461 [13617]

Calpine Containers Inc., PO Box 5050, Walnut Creek, CA 94596, (510)798-3010 [25897]

Calrad Electronics, 819 N Highland Ave., Los Angeles, CA 90038, (323)465-2131 [8488]

Calsol Inc., PO Box 3983, Pomona, CA 91769, (909)623-6426 [4341]

Caltag Lab, 1849 Bayshore Hwy., Burlingame, CA 94010, (650)652-0468 [19209]

Caltemp Instrument Inc., 1871 Jeffrey Ave., Escondido, CA 92027, (619)743-2800 [8489]

Caltrol Inc., PO Box 5020, Glendora, CA 91740, (818)963-1010 [15867]

Caltronics Business Systems, 10491 Old Placerville Rd., No. 150, Sacramento, CA 95827, (916)363-2666 [21078]

Calumet Auto Recycling and Sales Inc., 6205 Indianapolis Blvd., Hammond, IN 46320, (219)844-6600 [2414]

Calumet Breweries Inc., 6535 Osborn Ave., Hammond, IN 46320, (219)845-2242 [1566]

Calumet Industries Inc., Rte. 2, Box 30, Calumet, OK 73014, (405)262-2263 [17760]

Calumet Industries Inc., Rte. 2, Box 30, Calumet, OK 73014, (405)262-2263 [365]

Calus & CEI Distributors Inc., 2625 Turf Valley Rd., Ellicott City, MD 21042, (410)465-0044 [26435]

Calvada Sales Co., 950 Southern Way, Sparks, NV 89431-6120, (702)359-4740 [10681]

Calvert Dry Goods Inc., 409 W Baltimore St., Baltimore, MD 21201-1716, (410)752-8253 [4858]

Calvert & Hoffman, PO Box 20277, Louisville, KY 40250-0277, (502)459-0936 [7129]

Calvert Wire and Cable Corp., 5091 W 164th St., Brook Park, OH 44142, (216)433-7600 [8490]

Calvetti Meats Inc.; James, 4240 S Morgan St., Chicago, IL 60609, (773)927-9242 [10682]

Cam Industries, Inc., 215 Philadelphia St., PO Box 227, Hanover, PA 17331, (717)637-5988 [15868]

Camalloy Inc., PO Box 248, Washington, PA 15301, (724)228-1880 [19848]

Cambridge Communication Inc. (Niles, Illinois), 1425 Busch Pkwy., Buffalo Grove, IL 60089-4506, (847)647-8100 [5543]

Cambridge Development Laboratory, 86 West St., Waltham, MA 02451-1110, (781)890-4640 [6043]

Cambridge Educational, PO Box 2153, Charleston, WV 25328 [3603]

Cambridge Engineering Inc., 233 Van Patten Hwy., Burlington, VT 05401, (802)860-7228 [8491]

Cambridge Law Study Aids, Inc., 4814 S Pulaski Rd., Chicago, IL 60632-4194, (773)376-1713 [3604]

Cambridge Street Metal Company Inc., 500 Lincoln St., Allston, MA 02134, (617)254-7580 [19849]

Cambridge University Press, 40 W 20th St., New York, NY 10011, (212)924-3900 [3605]

Camco Services Inc., PO Box 24, Oak Hill, WV 25901-0024, (304)469-6445 [14366]

Camden Bag and Paper Company, Inc., 114 Gaither Dr., Mt. Laurel, NJ 08054-1702, (856)727-3313 [21665]

Camden Iron and Metal Co., 1500 S 6th St., Camden, NJ 08104, (609)365-7500 [19850]

Cameca Instruments Inc., 204 Spring Hill Rd., Trumbull, CT 06611, (203)459-0623 [24334]

Camel Outdoor Products Inc., PO Box 7225, Norcross, GA 30091, (404)449-4687 [13480]

Camel Products Div., 500 S 45th St. E, Muskogee, OK 74403, (918)687-5427 [3196]

Camellia Food Stores Inc., PO Box 2320, Norfolk, VA 23501, (757)855-3371 [10683]

Camenzind Dairy Cattle; Art, 10406 State St., Omaha, NE 68122, (402)571-0522 [17761]

Cameo, 3757 S Ashland, Chicago, IL 60609-2130, (773)247-7500 [13127]

Cameo Electronics Company Inc., PO Box 724, Owings Mills, MD 21117, (410)363-6161 [8492]

Cameo Kitchens Inc., PO Box 191, Mifflintown, PA 17059-0191, (717)436-9598 [13060]

Cameo Paper & Janitor Supply Co., 433 Cypress Ln., PO Box 1692, El Cajon, CA 92022, (619)442-2526 [4592]

Camera Corner Inc., PO Box 1899, Burlington, NC 27216-1899, (919)228-0251 [22837]

Camera Service Center of Maine, 40 Lisbon St., Lewiston, ME 04240-7116, (207)784-1509 [22838]

Camerican International, 45 Eisenhower Dr., Paramus, NJ 07652, (201)587-0101 [10684]

Cameron Ashley Building Products Inc., 11651 Plano Rd., Ste. 100, Dallas, TX 75243, (214)860-5100 [7130]

Cameron & Barkley, PO Box 40519, Raleigh, NC 27629-0519, (919)834-6010 [8493]

Camfour Inc., 65 Westfield Industrial Park, Westfield, MA 01085, (413)568-3371 [23581]

Camilo Office Furniture, Inc., 4110 Laguna St., Coral Gables, FL 33146, (305)445-3505 [20873]

Camilo Office Furniture Inc., 4110 Laguna St., Coral Gables, FL 33146, (305)445-3505 [13061]

Camo Distributors, PO Box 863, Centre, AL 35960-9455, (205)475-3660 [4859]

Camomile Enterprises, Inc., 7853 Standish Ave., Riverside, CA 92509, (909)685-7540 [25595]

Campagna Inc., 173 State St., Bristol, RI 02809-2205, (401)253-8808 [18724]

Campari USA Inc., 6913 Fleet St., Flushing, NY 11351, (212)753-8220 [1567]

Campbell Group, 100 Production Dr., Harrison, OH 45030, (513)367-3152 [15869]

Campbell Oil Co., PO Box 907, Massillon, OH 44648-0907, (330)833-8555 [22105]

Campbell-Payne Inc., PO Box 11255, Lynchburg, VA 24506, (804)847-8803 [7131]

Campbell Supply Co., 710 S Oak St., Iowa Falls, IA 50126, (515)648-4621 [16777]

Campbell Supply Company Inc., 1526 N Industrial Ave., Sioux Falls, SD 57104, (605)331-5470 [10685]

Campbell Tobacco Rehandling Company Inc., PO Box 678, Mayfield, KY 42066, (502)247-0991 [26270]

Campbell Tractor and Equipment Co., PO Box 430, Summersville, WV 26651, (304)872-2611 [366]

Campbell Tractors and Implements Inc., 2014 Franklin Blvd., Nampa, ID 83687, (208)466-8414 [367]

Campbell's Fresh Inc., 1501 62nd St., Fennville, MI 49408, (616)236-5024 [10686]

Campbell's Fresh Inc., PO Box 169, Blandon, PA 19510, (610)926-4101 [10687]

Camper's Trade Emporium, PO Box 131097, San Diego, CA 92170-1097, (619)264-5578 [13618]

Camsco Wholesalers Inc., 291 Hwy. 51 C-1, Ridgeland, MS 39157-3934, (601)856-5550 [15072]

Can Land Recycling Center Inc., 6141 N Federal Blvd., Denver, CO 80221, (303)426-4141 [26776]

Canaan Records, 274 Mallory Station Rd., Franklin, TN 37067-8244, (615)327-1240 [25117]

Canada Dry of Delaware Valley, 8275 Rte. 130, Pennsauken, NJ 08110, (609)662-6767 [24922]

Canada Produce and Plants, Inc., PO Box 441, Danville, VA 24543, (804)792-4311 [10906]

Canadian Equity Cooperative, 302 S 1st St., Canadian, TX 79014, (806)323-6428 [368]

Canal Industries Inc., PO Box 260001, Conway, SC 29526-2601, (843)347-4251 [7132]

Canale Beverages Inc.; D., 45 Eh Crump Blvd. W, Memphis, TN 38106, (901)948-4543 [1568]

Canale Food Services Inc.; D., PO Box 1739, Memphis, TN 38101-1739, (901)525-6811 [24087]

Canare, 531 5th St., Unit A, San Fernando, CA 91340, (818)365-2446 [8494]

Cancos Tile Corp., 1085 Portion Rd., Farmingville, NY 11738, (516)736-0770 [9753]

Cancos Tile Corp., 1085 Portion Rd., Farmingville, NY 11738, (516)736-0770 [7133]

Candee; Robert G., Rte. 4, Box 2010, Richey, MT 59259, (406)773-5674 [17762]

Candie's Inc., 2975 Westchester Ave., Purchase, NY 10577, (914)694-8600 [24705]

Candlewax Smokeless Fuel Company Inc., PO Box 29, Tazewell, VA 24651, (540)988-2591 [20527]

Candy by Bletas, PO Box 57, Abilene, TX 79604, (915)673-2505 [10688]

Cane Equipment Cooperative Inc., PO Box 556, Plaquemine, LA 70764, (504)687-2050 [369]

Canfield Co.; A.J., 7955 S Cass Ave., No. 201, Darien, IL 60561-5009, (773)483-7000 [24923]

Canfield Co.; M.E., 8314 E Slavson Ave., Pico Rivera, CA 90660, (213)264-5050 [15870]

Canfor U.S.A. Corp., PO Box 674, Meridian, ID 83642, (208)888-2456 [27293]

Cange & Associates International, 3725 Orchid Gln., Escondido, CA 92025-7916, (619)276-7301 [15073]

Canine Commissary, 11504 Garland Rd., Dallas, TX 75218, (972)840-2181 [27099]

Cannizzaro's Distributors, 4373 Michoud Blvd., New Orleans, LA 70129, (504)254-4000 [10689]

Cannon Engineering and Equipment Co. LLC, 2011 Heide, Troy, MI 48084, (248)362-0560 [15871]

Cannon Equipment West, 12822 Monarch St., Garden Grove, CA 92841, (714)373-5800 [16778]

Cannon Inc.; W.W., 10323 Harry Hines Blvd., Dallas, TX 75220, (214)357-2846 [25898]

Cannon and Sons Inc.; C.L., PO Box 2404, Spartanburg, SC 29304, (864)503-3401 [7134]

Cannon Technologies Inc., 505 Hwy. 169 N, Ste. 600, Minneapolis, MN 55441-6448, (612)544-7756 [6044]

Cannon Valley Cooperative, PO Box 200, Northfield, MN 55057, (507)645-9556 [370]

Cano Corp., 225 Industrial Rd., Fitchburg, MA 01420-4603, (978)342-0953 [20874]

Canon U.S.A. Inc., Office Products Div., PO Box 1000, Jamesburg, NJ 08831, (732)521-7000 [20875]

Canson Talens, Inc., PO Box 220, South Hadley, MA 01075, (413)538-9250 [25596]

Cantel Industries Inc., 1135 Broad St., Ste. 203, Clifton, NJ 07013, (973)470-8700 [18725]

Cantel Medical Corp., 1135 Broad St., Ste. 203, Clifton, NJ 07013, (973)470-8700 [18725]

Canterbury Enterprises, PO Box 16369, Irvine, CA 92623-6369, (949)496-7313 [27294]

Canton China and Equipment Co., 6309 Mack Ave., Detroit, MI 48207, (313)925-3100 [24088]

Canton Mills Inc., PO Box 97, Minnesota City, MN 55959, (507)689-2131 [371]

Cantrell Auto Supply Company Inc., 2411 Alameda Ave., El Paso, TX 79942, (915)542-1575 [2415]

Cantwell Machinery Co., PO Box 44130, Columbus, OH 43204-0130, (614)276-5171 [7135]

Canusa Corp., 1616 Shakespeare St., Baltimore, MD 21231, (410)522-0110 [26777]

Canvas Specialty, PO Box 22268, Los Angeles, CA 90022, (323)723-8311 [25994]

Canyon Country Distribution, PO Box 400034, 18 Ballard Ct., Thompson, UT 84540-0034, (435)285-2210 [3524]

Canyon State Opthalmaic Lab, Inc., 2123 S Priest Rd., Ste. 203, Tempe, AZ 85282, (602)967-5834 [19210]

CAP Propane Plus Inc., PO Box 38, Kettle River, MN 55757, (218)273-4850 [22106]

Capacitor Associates, 486 Main St., Eitzen, MN 55931-0486, (507)495-3306 [8495]

Capcom Entertainment Inc., 475 Oakmead Pkwy., Sunnyvale, CA 94086-4709, (408)774-0500 [26436]

Cape Dairy Products Inc., 44 Bodick Rd., Hyannis, MA 02601, (508)771-4700 [10690]

Cape Electronics, 19 Dupont Ave., South Yarmouth, MA 02664-1203, (508)394-2405 [5544]

Cape & Island Steel Co., 200 Airport Way, Hyannis, MA 02601, (508)775-2022 [19851]

Cape Oceanic Corp., 41 Rosary Ln., Hyannis, MA 02601-2024, (508)775-8693 [10691]

Cape Water Sports, 337 Main St., Rte. 28, Harwich Port, MA 02646, (508)432-7079 [18474]

Capel Rugs Inc., 6F6 Atlanta Merchandise Mart, 240 Peachtree St., Atlanta, GA 30303, (404)577-4320 [9754]

Capeway News, 2 Hinckley Rd., Hyannis, MA 02601, (508)790-4103 [3606]

Capital 2-Way Communications, 836 Prior Ave. N, St. Paul, MN 55104-1040, (651)646-2511 [5547]

Capital Beverage Corp., 1111 E Tremont Ave., Bronx, NY 10460, (718)409-2337 [1569]

Capital Beverages Inc., 2333 Fairview Dr., Carson City, NV 89701-5858, (702)882-2122 [1570]

Capital Business Systems Inc., PO Box 2088, Napa, CA 94558, (707)252-9122 [6045]

Capital Carousel Inc., 520 Hampton Park Blvd., Capitol Heights, MD 20743, (301)350-5400 [21410]

Capital City Companies Inc., 1295 Johnson St. NE, Salem, OR 97303, (503)362-5558 [22107]

Capital City Distribution Inc., 3702 E Roeser Rd., Unit 26, Phoenix, AZ 85040, (602)437-2502 [3607]

Capital City Distribution Inc., 16643 Valley View Ave., Cerritos, CA 90701, (562)802-5222 [3608]

Capital City Distribution Inc., 107 Leland Ct., Bensenville, IL 60106, (708)595-1100 [3609]

Capital City Restaurant Supply Co., 321 S 1st St., PO Box 721, Bismarck, ND 58502-0721, (701)255-4576 [24089]

Capital Coors Co., 2424 Del Monte, West Sacramento, CA 95691-3808, (916)371-8164 [1571]

Capital Design Inc., 860 a Waterman Ave., East Providence, RI 02914, (401)431-2150 [22941]

Capital Ford New Holland Inc., PO Box 16568, Little Rock, AR 72231-6568, (501)834-9999 [17763]

Capital GBS Communications Corp., 1137 Hanley Indstl. Ct., St. Louis, MO 63144, (314)961-0557 [5545]

Capital Lighting & Supply - Baltimore/Lee Electric Div., 600 W Hamburg St., Baltimore, MD 21230, (410)752-4080 [8496]

Capital Lighting & Supply Inc., 3950 Wheeler Ave., Alexandria, VA 22304-6429, (703)823-6000 [8497]

Capital Paint & Glass Inc., PO Box 8287, Boise, ID 83707-2287, (208)342-5656 [21411]

Capital Paper Company Div., 315 Park Ave. S, 18th Fl., New York, NY 10010-3607, (212)505-1000 [21666]

Capital Pet Supply, 1200 Newell Pkwy., Montgomery, AL 36110, (205)279-0566 [27100]

Capital Petroleum Equipment Co., PO Box 11238, Jacksonville, FL 32239, (904)353-0604 [22159]

Capital Scale, PO Box 2021, Bismarck, ND 58502-2021, (701)255-1556 [24335]

Capital Stationery Corp., PO Box 230, Mineola, NY 11501-0230, (516)248-3700 [20876]

Capital Telephone Co., 6800 Willowwood Way, Sacramento, CA 95831-2131, (916)393-2700 [5546]

Capital Tire Inc., 1001 Cherry St., Toledo, OH 43608, (419)241-5111 [2416]

Capital Wholesale Distribution Co., 1149 S Pennsylvania Ave., Lansing, MI 48912, (517)485-7208 [26271]

Capitol Ceramic Inc., 4804 Thorton Rd., PO Box 61174, Raleigh, NC 27661, (919)872-8263 [9755]

Capitol Chemical & Supply, 6600 Allied Way, Little Rock, AR 72209, (501)565-5288 [4593]

Capitol Chevrolet Inc., 711 Eastern Blvd., Montgomery, AL 36117, (205)272-8700 [20609]

Capitol City Produce, 12509 S Choctaw Dr., Baton Rouge, LA 70815-2195, (504)272-8153 [10692]

Capitol Communications, 1247 85th Ave. SE, Olympia, WA 98501, (206)943-5378 [25118]

Capitol Concrete Products Co., PO Box 8159, Topeka, KS 66608, (785)233-3271 [7136]

Capitol Copy Products Inc., 12000 Old Baltimore Pike, Beltsville, MD 20705, (301)937-5030 [20877]

Capitol Corp., 233 E Rankin St., Jackson, MS 39202, (601)969-9266 [16779]

Capitol Distributing, 3500 Commercial Ct., Meridian, ID 83642-6006, (208)888-5112 [26272]

Capitol Distributors, 2801 Juniper St., Fairfax, VA 22031, (703)560-8750 [9756]

Capitol Distributors Inc., 114 Hall St., Concord, NH 03301-3425, (603)224-3348 [1572]

Capitol Electronics Inc., 836 Prior Ave. N, St. Paul, MN 55104-1040, (651)646-2511 [5547]

Capitol Entertainment & Home, 6205 Adelaide Dr., Bethesda, MD 20817, (301)564-9700 [22839]

Capitol Foods Inc., 555 Beale St., Memphis, TN 38103, (901)526-9300 [10693]

Capitol Light and Supply Co., 270 Locust St., Hartford, CT 06141-0179, (203)549-1230 [8498]

Capitol Light and Supply Inc. Co., 270 Locust St., Hartford, CT 06141-0179, (860)549-1230 [8534]

Capitol Metals Company Inc., 4131 E Washington St., Phoenix, AZ 85034, (602)275-4131 [19852]

Capitol Motion Picture Corp., 630 9th Ave., New York, NY 10036, (212)757-4510 [25119]

Capitol News Distributors, 1960 Washington St., Boston, MA 02118, (617)427-5578 [3610]

Capitol Plumbing and Heating Supply Co., 1900 S 8th St., Springfield, IL 62703, (217)753-6900 [23104]

Capitol Plumbing and Heating Supply Company Inc., 6 Storrs St., Concord, NH 03301, (603)224-1901 [23105]

Capitol Plywood Inc., 160 Commerce Cir., Sacramento, CA 95815, (916)922-8861 [7137]

Capitol Sales Company Inc., 3110 Neil Armstrong Blvd., St. Paul, MN 55121-2234, (612)688-6830 [25120]

Capitol Sales Company Inc., 3110 Neil Armstrong Blvd., St. Paul, MN 55121-2234, (612)688-6830 [15074]

Capitol Steel Inc., PO Box 66636, Baton Rouge, LA 70896, (504)356-4631 [19853]

Capitol Tire Shop, 414 W Main Cross St., Findlay, OH 45839, (419)422-4554 [2417]

Capitol Wholesale Florists Inc., 11740 Maumelle Blvd., North Little Rock, AR 72113, (501)758-0006 [14833]

Caple-Shaw Industries Inc., 1112 NE 29th St., Ft. Worth, TX 76106, (817)626-2816 [2418]

Caporicci Footwear Ltd., 11325 Lee Hwy. 103, Fairfax, VA 22030-5610, (703)591-6000 [24706]

Capos Auto Parts Inc., 5701 Broadway Blvd. SE, Albuquerque, NM 87105-7427, (505)873-0665 [2419]

Capp Inc., 201 Marple Ave., Clifton Heights, PA 19018-2414, (215)472-7700 [8499]

Cappel Distributing Co., 116 Chestnut St., Atlantic, IA 50022, (712)243-4712 [21412]

Capps Beauty & Barber Inc., 9034 E 31, Tulsa, OK 74145, (918)622-1652 [14055]

Capra Press Inc., PO Box 2068, Santa Barbara, CA 93120, (805)966-4590 [3611]

Capresso Inc., 39 Rugen Dr., Harrington Park, NJ 07640, (201)767-3999 [24090]

Capri Arts & Crafts, 06864 McGlincey Ln., Campbell, CA 95008, (408)377-3833 [20878]

Capri Jewelry Inc., 392 5th Ave., New York, NY 10018, (212)947-5280 [17357]

Capricorn Coffees Inc., 353 10th St., San Francisco, CA 94103, (415)621-8500 [10694]

Capricorn Foods, 2540 Shader Rd., Orlando, FL 32804, (407)291-9035 [10695]

Capriotto and Sons Inc., S-3100 Abbott Rd., Orchard Park, NY 14127, (716)823-5024 [2420]

Capstone Paper Co., 1464 Old Country Rd., Plainview, NY 11803, (516)752-4242 [21667]

Capstone Pharmacy Services, 7170 Standard Dr., Hanover, MD 21076-1321, (410)646-7373 [19211]

Captain Clean Inc., 208 W Brundage St., Sheridan, WY 82801, (307)672-1846 [4710]

Captain TS, PO Box 993, Port Angeles, WA 98362-0806, (425)452-6549 [4860]

Captre Electrical Supply, 2289 3rd Ave., New York, NY 10035, (212)534-3546 [8500]

Car Care Products Inc., 1 Rotary Park Dr., PO Box 3390, Clarksville, TN 37043-3390, (931)647-0139 [4660]

Car-Go Battery Co., 3860 Blake St., Denver, CO 80205, (303)296-8763 [2421]

Car Parts Inc., 613 N 36th St., Milwaukee, WI 53208, (414)342-7070 [2422]

The Car Place, PO Box 13624, Florence, SC 29504, (803)665-2880 [7138]

Car Quest Auto Parts Co., 1818 Franklin St., Waco, TX 76701, (254)752-5556 [2423]

Car Tape Distributors Inc., PO Box 5122, Ft. Wayne, IN 46895-5122, (219)484-2556 [25121]

Cara Donna Provision Co., 55 Food Mart Rd., Boston, MA 02118, (617)268-0346 [10696]

Carabel Export & Import, 948 Roosevelt Ave., San Juan, PR 00921, (787)781-2229 [9757]

Carando Inc., 20 Carando Dr., Springfield, MA 01104, (413)781-5620 [11106]

Carapace Corp., 8705 Bollman Pl., Ste. C, Savage, MD 20763-9775, (301)403-2900 [13619]

Carat Diamond Corp., 1156 Avenue of the Americas, New York, NY 10036-2702, (212)869-8666 [17358]

Caravan Trading Corporation, 45 John St., New York, NY 10038, (212)943-3257 [4342]

Caravelle Distributing, 1615 Greenleaf Ave., Elk Grove Village, IL 60007, (847)593-5240 [9758]

Caravelle Distributors, 1615 Greenleaf Ave., Elk Grove Village, IL 60007, (847)593-5240 [9758]

Carbide Tooling & Design, 1232 51st Ave., Oakland, CA 94601-5602, (510)532-7669 [16780]

Carbon and Alloy Metals Inc., PO Box 1756, Houston, TX 77251, (713)690-5518 [19854]

Carbon Resources of Florida, 1401 Manatee Ave. W, Ste 520, Bradenton, FL 34205, (941)747-2630 [20524]

Carbon Resources of Florida, 1111 Third Ave. W, Ste. 140, Bradenton, FL 34205, (941)747-2630 [20528]

Carbone of America, 400 Myrtle Ave., Boonton, NJ 07005, (973)334-0700 [5548]

Carbone Co.; R.J., 1 Goddard Dr., Cranston, RI 02920, (401)463-3333 [14834]

Carbone Floral Distributors, 540 Albany St., Boston, MA 02118, (617)728-7979 [14835]

Carbro Corp., 15724 Condon Ave., PO Box 278, Lawndale, CA 90260, (310)643-8400 [15872]

Carco International Inc., 2721 Midland Blvd., Ft. Smith, AR 72904, (501)441-3270 [372]

Cardamation Company Inc., PO Box 329, Phoenixville, PA 19460, (610)935-9700 [20879]

Cardel Sales Inc., 211 Parkwest Dr., Pittsburgh, PA 15275-1003, (412)322-5400 [19855]

Cardello Electric Supply Co., 701 Chateau St., Pittsburgh, PA 15233, (412)322-8031 [8501]

Carder Inc., PO Box 721, Lamar, CO 81052, (719)336-3479 [7139]

Cardillo Brothers Inc., 1757 Plainfield Pike, Johnston, RI 02919-5919, (401)942-0331 [2424]

Cardinal Carryor Inc., 1055 Grade Ln., Louisville, KY 40213, (502)363-6641 [15873]

Cardinal Carryor Inc., 1055 Grade Ln., Louisville, KY 40213, (502)363-6641 [15874]

Cardinal Distributing, 1750 Evergreen, Bozeman, MT 59715-1289, (406)586-0241 [1573]

Cardinal Frozen Distributors Co., 617 E Washington St., Louisville, KY 40202, (502)589-0378 [10697]

Cardinal Glass Co., PO Box 707, Rockford, IL 61105-0707, (815)394-1400 [7140]

Cardinal Health-Behrens Inc., PO Box 2520, Waco, TX 76702-2520, (254)776-7583 [14056]

Cardinal Health Inc., 5555 Glendon Ct., Dublin, OH 43016, (614)717-5000 [19212]

Cardinal Ice Cream Corp., 617 E Washington St., Louisville, KY 40202, (502)589-0378 [10698]

Cardinal Inc., 1421 Pinewood St., Rahway, NJ 07065, (732)388-6160 [26437]

Cardinal Office Systems, 101 Bradley Dr., Nicholasville, KY 40356, (606)885-6161 [20880]

Cardinal Office Systems, 101 Bradley Dr., Nicholasville, KY 40356, (606)885-6161 [13062]

Cardinal Optics, Inc., Rt. 133 Clarendon Rd., West Rutland, VT 05777, (802)438-5426 [19213]

Cardinal State Fasteners, 1130 Kingwood Ave., Norfolk, VA 23502-5603, (757)855-2041 [15875]

Cardona Inc., PO Box 81, Fremont, CA 94537, (510)786-0159 [13326]

Care-A-Lot, 1617 Diamond Springs Rd., Virginia Beach, VA 23455, (757)460-9771 [27101]

Care Medical Equipment Inc., 1877 NE 7th Ave., Portland, OR 97212-3905, (503)288-8174 [18726]

Caremed, 5702 Hwy. 49, Hattiesburg, MS 39401, (601)584-4300 [19214]

Carenbauer Wholesale Corp., 1900 Jacob St., Wheeling, WV 26003, (304)232-3000 [1574]

Carewell Industries, Inc., PO Box 7016, Dover, DE 19903, (302)995-9277 [14057]

Carey Machinery & Supply Co., 9108 Yellow Brick Rd., No. B, Baltimore, MD 21237-4701, (410)485-2323 [24524]

Cargill Inc., PO Box 9300, Minneapolis, MN 55440, (612)475-7575 [4343]

Cargill Inc. Northeast Petroleum Div., 72 Cherry Hill Dr., Beverly, MA 01915, (978)524-1500 [22108]

Cargill Peanut Products, PO Box 272, Dawson, GA 31742, (912)995-2111 [10699]

Cargill Steel & Wire, 600 Cowan St., Nashville, TN 37207, (615)782-8500 [19856]

Carhartt Inc., 3 Parklane Blvd., PO Box 600, Dearborn, MI 48121, (313)271-8460 [25995]

Cariba International Corp., 1020 Harbor Lake Dr., Safety Harbor, FL 34695, (813)725-2517 [10700]

Caribe Optical Lab/Lens, Urb Lariviera, Ave. Dediego 929, Rio Piedras, PR 00926, (787)781-4945 [19215]

Caribiner International, 525 N Washington Ave., Minneapolis, MN 55401, (612)333-1271 [25122]

Caribiner International, 525 N Washington Ave., Minneapolis, MN 55401, (612)333-1271 [15075]

Cariddi Sales Co., 508 State Rd., North Adams, MA 01247-3045, (413)663-3722 [23582]

Carina International Inc., 4657 N Pulaski St., Chicago, IL 60630, (773)509-0016 [18380]

Caring Concepts Inc., 469 7th Ave., New York, NY 10018, (212)564-3400 [4861]

Carithers-Wallace-Courtenay Inc., 4343 Northeast Expwy., Atlanta, GA 30301, (770)493-8200 [13063]

Carl Beatty and Associates, 7659 Lake Shore Dr., Owings, MD 20736, (301)855-0154 [19216]

Carl Fisher Music Distributors, 62 Cooper Sq., New York, NY 10003, (212)777-0900 [3750]

Carlberg Warren & Associates, 181 W Orangethorpe, Ste. E, Placentia, CA 92870-6931, (714)961-7300 [8502]

Carleton Oil Company Inc., PO Box 220, Union, MS 39365, (601)774-9205 [21668]

Carlisle Medical Inc., PO Box 9814, Mobile, AL 36691-0814, (205)344-7988 [18727]

Carlos Franco, 311 S Broadway, McAllen, TX 78501, (956)687-4662 [8503]

Carloss Well Supply Co., 4000 Runway Rd., Memphis, TN 38118, (901)360-8047 [15876]

Carl's Clogging Supplies, 525 Poverty Ln., Salem, SC 29676-2414, (864)944-8125 [24707]

Carlsbad Volvo, 6830 Avenida Encinas, Carlsbad, CA 92009, (760)931-7100 [20610]

Carlson and Beauloye, PO Box 13622, San Diego, CA 92170, (619)234-2256 [5833]

Carlson Dimond and Wright, 2338 Morrissey Ave., Warren, MI 48091, (734)758-6611 [15877]

Carlson Distributors Inc., 2501 Charles St., Rockford, IL 61108, (815)397-3101 [7141]

Carlson Dolls Co., 210 W 1st St., PO Box 279, Maple Lake, MN 55358, (320)963-3713 [13327]

Carlson Systems Corp., 8990 F St., Omaha, NE 68127, (402)593-5300 [13620]

Carlton-Bates Co., PO Box 192320, Little Rock, AR 72219, (501)562-9100 [8504]

Carlton Optical Distributors, 9419 E San Salvador Dr., Ste. 102, Scottsdale, AZ 85258-5510, (480)860-1801 [19217]

Carlyle Inc., PO Box 58999, Tukwila, WA 98138, (425)251-0700 [19857]

Carlyle Industries Inc., 1 Palmer Terr., Carlstadt, NJ 07072, (201)935-6220 [25996]

Carmichael and Carmichael Inc., PO Box 305151, Nashville, TN 37230-5151, (615)742-3852 [25123]

Carnegie Body Co., 9500 Brookpark Rd., Cleveland, OH 44129, (216)749-5000 [2425]

Carnrick Laboratories Inc., 65 Horsehill Rd., Cedar Knolls, NJ 07927, (973)267-2670 [19218]

Caro Foods Inc., 2324 Bayou Blue Rd., Houma, LA 70364, (504)872-1483 [10701]

Caro Produce and Institutional Foods Inc., 2324 Bayou Blue Rd., Houma, LA 70364, (504)872-1483 [10701]

Caro Produce and Institutional Foods Inc., 2324 Bayou Blue Rd., Houma, LA 70364, (504)872-1483 [10702]

Caro-Tile Ltd., 7 Task Industrial Ct., Greenville, SC 29607, (864)297-1496 [9759]

Carol Service Co., PO Box 25, Lanark, IL 61046, (815)493-2181 [4344]

Carolina Beer Company Inc., PO Box 938, Anderson, SC 29622, (803)225-1668 [1575]

Carolina Biological Supply Co., 2700 York Rd., Burlington, NC 27215, (919)584-0381 [3612]

Carolina Braided Rug, 622 Meswain Rd., Shelby, NC 28150, (704)434-6483 [9760]

Carolina Building Co., 1050 Berkley Ave. Ext., Norfolk, VA 23523-1899, (757)543-6836 [7142]

Carolina C & E, Inc., 651 Pilot View St., Winston-Salem, NC 27101-2717, (336)788-9191 [25124]

Carolina C and E Inc., 651 Pilot View St., Winston-Salem, NC 27101-2717, (336)788-9191 [15076]

Carolina Cotton Growers Association Inc., 209 Oberlin Rd., Raleigh, NC 27605, (919)833-2048 [17764]

Carolina Door Controls, PO Box 15639, Durham, NC 27704, (919)381-0094 [7143]

Carolina Door Controls, PO Box 15639, Durham, NC 27704, (919)381-0094 [27295]

Carolina FireMasters Inc., PO Box 1116, Bennettsville, SC 29512, (803)479-3871 [24525]

Carolina First Aid Inc., PO Box 147, Pfafftown, NC 27040-0147, (910)922-3916 [18728]

Carolina Fisherman Supply Inc., 2507 NC Hwy. 172, Sneads Ferry, NC 28460-6637, (910)327-2560 [23583]

Carolina Fluid Components, 9309 Stockport Pl., Charlotte, NC 28273, (704)588-6101 [16781]

Carolina Handling Inc., PO Box 7548, Charlotte, NC 28241, (704)357-6273 [15878]

Carolina Hardware & Supply, Inc., 218 W 2nd Loop Rd., PO Box 13559, Florence, SC 29504-1559, (803)662-0702 [16782]

Carolina Hosiery Connection, 525 Alleghany Ave., Lynchburg, VA 24501-2609, (804)846-5099 [4862]

Carolina Made Inc., 400 Indian Trail Rd., Indian Trail, NC 28079, (704)821-6425 [4863]

Carolina Maid Products Inc., PO Box 308, Granite Quarry, NC 28072, (704)279-7221 [4864]

Carolina News Co., 245 Tillinghast St., Fayetteville, NC 28301, (919)483-4135 [3613]

Carolina Office Equipment Co., 1030 2nd Ave. NW, PO Box 2145, Hickory, NC 28601, (704)322-6190 [20881]

Carolina Office Equipment Co., PO Box 1888, Rocky Mount, NC 27801, (919)977-1121 [20882]

Carolina Pad and Paper Co., PO Box 7525, Charlotte, NC 28241, (704)588-3190 [21669]

Carolina Plastics Supply Inc., 100 D Forsyth Hall Dr., Charlotte, NC 28273, (704)588-0541 [23106]

Carolina Pools & Patios, 1312 W 2nd Ave., Gastonia, NC 28052-3773, (704)865-9586 [23584]

Carolina Poultry Sales, PO Box 827, Florence, SC 29503, (803)667-0096 [12006]

Carolina Retail Packaging Inc., 138 Zenker Rd., Lexington, SC 29072, (803)359-0036 [21670]

Carolina Rim and Wheel Co., PO Box 30126, Charlotte, NC 28230, (704)334-7276 [18475]

Carolina Salon Services, 684 Huey Rd., Rock Hill, SC 29731-6528 [14058]

Carolina Steel Corp., 1115 Old Lenoir Rd., Hickory, NC, (828)322-9420 [19858]

Carolina Steel Corp., PO Box 20888, Greensboro, NC 27420, (336)275-9711 [19859]

Carolina Tractor/CAT, PO Box 1095, Charlotte, NC 28201-1095, (704)596-6700 [7144]

Carolina Training Associates, PO Box 816, Sanford, NC 27331-0816, (919)776-8161 [6046]

Carolina Vet Supply, PO Box 2812, Shelby, NC 28150, (704)482-7158 [27102]

Carolina Vet Supply, PO Box 2812, Shelby, NC 28150, (704)482-7158 [19219]

Carolina Western Inc., PO Box 2524, Greenville, SC 29602, (803)246-0908 [7145]

Carolina Wine Co., 99 Rivermoor St., West Roxbury, MA 02132, (617)327-1600 [1576]

Carolina's Auto Supply House, Inc., PO Box 36409, Charlotte, NC 28236, (704)334-4646 [2426]

Carolyn Candies, Inc., PO Box 7689, Winter Haven, FL 33883-7689, (352)394-8555 [10703]

Carolyn Fabrics Inc., PO Box 2758, 1948 W Green Dr., High Point, NC 27261, (919)887-3101 [25997]

Carotek Inc., PO Box 1395, Matthews, NC 28106, (704)847-4406 [15879]

Carousel Fashions Inc., 770 Dedham St., Canton, MA 02021-1404, (781)821-0821 [4865]

Carpenter Brothers Inc., 4555 W Schroeder Dr., Milwaukee, WI 53223-1400, (414)354-6555 [16783]

Carpenter-Dent-Sublett No. 1, PO Box 1747, Bowling Green, KY 42102-1747, (502)781-5310 [18729]

Carpenter Paper Co., PO Box 2709, Grand Rapids, MI 49501, (616)452-9741 [21671]

Carpenter Paper of Indiana, 401 Fernhill Ave., Ft. Wayne, IN 46805, (219)482-4686 [22006]

Carpenter Technology/Steel Div, PO Box 58880, Los Angeles, CA 90058, (323)587-9131 [19860]

Carpenter & Wither Inc., 124 Hall St., Concord, NH 03301-3442, (603)225-2832 [21606]

Carpet Barn Inc., 106 Pinehurst Rd., Ellenboro, NC 28040, (828)245-2100 [9761]

Carpet Basics, 101 Ambrogio Dr., Ste. L, Gurnee, IL 60031, (847)360-1303 [9762]

Carpet Cushion Supply, 1001 Arthur Ave., PO Box 653, Elk Grove Village, IL 60007, (847)364-6760 [9763]

Carpet Cushion Supply, 4620 W 120th St., Alsip, IL 60803-2317, (708)389-6460 [9764]

Carpet Cushion Supply, 1941 Woodlawn Ave., Griffith, IN 46319, (219)838-9664 [9765]

Carpet Cushion Supply, 543 S Vermont, Palatine, IL 60067, (847)991-4343 [9766]

Carpet Cushion Supply, 5515 N Northwest Hwy., Chicago, IL 60630, (773)631-0420 [9767]

Carpet Factory Outlet, 2501 Broadway St., Kansas City, MO 64108, (816)421-3170 [9768]

Carpet Isle Design Center, 741 Kanoelehua Ave., Hilo, HI 96720, (808)935-0047 [9769]

Carpet Mart & Wallpaper, 1271 Manheim Pike, Lancaster, PA 17601-3121, (717)299-2381 [9770]

Carpet Mart & Wallpaper Outlet, 1271 Manheim Pke., Lancaster, PA 17601, (717)299-2381 [15435]

Carpet Warehouse Connection, 1548 Ford Rd., Bensalem, PA 19020, (215)633-9444 [9771]

Carpetland U.S.A. Inc., 8201 Calumet Ave., Munster, IN 46321, (219)836-5555 [9772]

Carquest, 5307 W Market St., Greensboro, NC 27409-2809, (910)294-5632 [2427]

CARQUEST Corp., 12596 W Bayaud Ave., No. 400, Lakewood, CO 80228, (303)984-2000 [2428]

Carquest Distribution Co., PO Box 31437, Billings, MT 59107, (406)259-4577 [2429]

Carquest Distribution Co. Cleaner and Equipment Div., 208 E 3 Notch St., Andalusia, AL 36420, (205)222-6534 [2430]

Carr Co., 6000 Park of Commerce Blvd., Boca Raton, FL 33487, (407)997-0999 [23107]

Carr Inc.; Jim, 100 Bridge St., Pelham, NH 03076, (603)635-3143 [17359]

Carr Oil Inc., 1001 W Bankhead St., New Albany, MS 38652, (601)534-6314 [22109]

Carriage House Imports Ltd., 99 Morris Ave., Springfield, NJ 07081, (973)467-9646 [1577]

Carrier Corp./Bldg Sys and Svc Di, PO Box 23130, Oakland, CA 94623, (510)769-6000 [14367]

Carrier North Carolina, 4300 Golf Acres Dr., Charlotte, NC 28208, (704)394-7311 [14368]

Carrington Distributing Company Inc., 1905 Trevilian Way, Louisville, KY 40205, (502)366-2913 [2431]

Carroll Air Systems Inc., 3711 W Walnut St., Tampa, FL 33607, (813)879-5790 [14369]

Carroll Building Specialties, PO Box 61928, Lafayette, LA 70596, (318)233-6311 [13621]

Carroll County Equipment Co., PO Box 610, Carrollton, MO 64633, (660)542-2485 [373]

Carroll Distribution Company, Inc., PO Box 2647, Davenport, IA 52809, (319)391-7500 [9773]

Carroll Electronics Inc., PO Box 1513, Topeka, KS 66601-1513, (785)234-6677 [8505]

Carroll Farmers Cooperative, PO Box 546, Huntingdon, TN 38344, (901)986-8271 [374]

Carroll Seating Company Inc., 1835 W Armitage Ave., Chicago, IL 60622, (773)772-0160 [13064]

Carroll Touch Inc., 2800 Oakmont Dr., Round Rock, TX 78664, (512)244-3500 [7146]

Carroll's Discount Office Furniture Co., 5615 S Rice Ave., Houston, TX 77081, (713)667-6668 [13065]

Carrollton Farmers Elevator Co., PO Box 264, Carrollton, IL 62016, (217)942-6922 [17765]

Carrollton Farmers Elevator Co., PO Box 264, Carrollton, IL 62016, (217)942-6922 [10704]

Carse Oil Company Inc., 1700 S Bumby Ave., Orlando, FL 32806, (407)898-9494 [22110]

Carson-Brooks Plastics, Inc., 1160 Nicole Ct, Glendora, CA 91740-5386, (909)592-6272 [22942]

Carson Co. Tri-County Oil Div., 101 Summit St., Spruce Pine, NC 28777, (704)765-6171 [22111]

Carson Industries, Inc., 1160 Nicole Ct, Glendora, CA 91740-5386, (909)592-6272 [22942]

Carson Industries LLC, 1160 Nicole Ct, Glendora, CA 91740-5386, (909)592-6272 [22942]

Carson Masonry and Steel Supply, 4783 US Highway 50 E, Carson City, NV 89701, (775)882-3832 [19861]

Carson Oil Company Inc., PO Box 10948, Portland, OR 97296-0948, (503)224-8500 [22112]

Carswell Distributing Co., PO Box 4193, Winston-Salem, NC 27115-4193, (910)767-7700 [15077]

Cartell Inc., 34364 Goddard Rd., Romulus, MI 48174, (313)941-5400 [5549]

Carter Distributing Co., PO Box 388, Chattanooga, TN 37401-0349, (615)266-0056 [1578]

Carter Girls Fashions Inc., PO Box 4324, Meridian, MS 39304-4324, (601)693-1141 [4866]

Carter Inc.; Jerry C., PO Box 18, Gainesville, GA 30503, (770)534-5129 [22113]

Carter-Lee Lumber Company Inc., 1621 W Washington St., Indianapolis, IN 46222, (317)639-5431 [7147]

Carter Lumber Co., 601 Talmadge Rd., Kent, OH 44240, (330)673-6100 [7148]

Carter Paper Co., 136 Wayside Ave., PO Box 315, West Springfield, MA 01090-0315, (413)785-1961 [21672]

Carter Paper and Packaging Inc., PO Box 1349, Peoria, IL 61654-1349, (309)637-7711 [21673]

Carter Service Center, PO Box 213, Italy, TX 76651, (972)483-6027 [375]

Carter-Waters Corp., PO Box 412676, Kansas City, MO 64141, (816)471-2570 [7149]

Cartier Inc., 653 5th Ave., New York, NY 10022, (212)753-0111 [17360]

Carvel Hall Inc., PO Box 271, Crisfield, MD 21817, (410)968-0500 [15436]

Carver's Oil Co., 304 Uranium Ave., Milan, NM 87021, (505)287-4291 [22114]

Carwell Elevator Company Inc., PO Box 187, Cherry Valley, AR 72324, (501)588-3381 [17766]

Cas Ker Co., 2121 Spring Grove Ave., Cincinnati, OH 45214-1721, (513)241-7073 [17361]

Casa Carpet Wholesale Distributors, 3737 Gateway Blvd. W, El Paso, TX 79903-4555, (915)562-9521 [9774]

Casa Export Ltd., PO Box 1337, Smithfield, NC 27577, (919)934-7101 [26273]

Casa Italia, 2080 Constitution Blvd., Sarasota, FL 34231, (941)924-9293 [10705]

Casa Linda Draperies, 4111 Elva St., Dallas, TX 75227-3813, (214)388-4721 [15437]

Casa Mexicana, Main St., MesiLa Park, NM 88047, (505)523-2777 [9775]

Casa Nuestra Winery, 3451 Silverado Trl. N, St. Helena, CA 94574-9721, (707)963-5783 [1579]

Casale Engineering Inc., 161 8th Ave., La Puente, CA 91746, (626)330-6830 [2432]

Casani Candy Co., 145 N 2nd St., Philadelphia, PA 19106, (215)627-2570 [10706]

Casas Office Machines Inc., PO Box 13666, Santurce, PR 00908, (787)781-0040 [20883]

Cascade Clothing, 1707 NE Woodridge Ln., Bend, OR 97701-5847, (541)389-1454 [24708]

Cascade Machinery and Electric Inc., PO Box 3575, Seattle, WA 98124, (206)762-0500 [5834]

Cascade Optical Inc., 6740 Cascade Rd. SE, Grand Rapids, MI 49546-6850, (616)942-9886 [19220]

Cascade Pacific Lumber Co., 1975 SW 5th Ave., Portland, OR 97201, (503)223-2173 [7150]

Cascade Seed Co., PO Box 2544 T.A., Spokane, WA 99220, (509)534-9431 [376]

Cascade Wholesale Hardware, Inc., PO Box 1659, Hillsboro, OR 97123, (503)614-2600 [13622]

Cascade Yachts, Inc., 7030 NE 42nd, Portland, OR 97218, (503)287-5794 [18476]

Cascadian Fruit Shippers Inc., 2701 Euclid Ave., Wenatchee, WA 98801-5913, (509)662-8131 [10707]

Casco, 4801 E Independence Blvd., Ste. 1101, Charlotte, NC 28212, (704)536-1921 [69]

Casco Industries Inc., 540 W Division St., South Elgin, IL 60177, (847)741-9595 [7151]

Case Farms of North Carolina Inc., PO Box 308, Morganton, NC 28655, (704)438-6900 [10708]

Case Paper Co., 23-30 Borden Ave., Long Island City, NY 11101, (718)361-9000 [21674]

Case Supply, Inc., 507 N Montgall Ave., Kansas City, MO 64120-1530, (816)231-2530 [9776]

Case Supply, Inc., 14851 101st Ter., Overland Park, KS 66215, (913)492-6677 [9777]

Case Supply, Inc., 355 N Rock Island St., Wichita, KS 67202-2725, (316)265-6653 [9778]

Casele Associates Inc., 102 E Main St., Stevensville, MD 21666-4000, (410)643-8950 [25125]

Casella Lighting Co., 111 Rhode Island St., San Francisco, CA 94103, (415)626-9600 [8506]

Casella Lighting Co., 111 Rhode Island St., San Francisco, CA 94103, (415)626-9600 [15438]

Casey Co.; A.A., 5124 Nebraska Ave., Tampa, FL 33603-2364, (813)234-8831 [16784]

Casey Implement Company Inc., PO Box 246, Casey, IL 62420, (217)932-5941 [377]

Casey Inc.; John R., 300 Station St., Cranston, RI 02910-1322, (401)467-8020 [4594]

Casey-Johnston Sales Inc., 4555 Las Positas Rd., Ste. B, Livermore, CA 94550-9615, (510)371-5900 [6047]

Casey's General Stores Inc., 1 Convenience Blvd., Ankeny, IA 50021, (515)965-6280 [10709]

Casey's Tile Supply Co., 1402 S Clack, Abilene, TX 79605, (915)692-6621 [9779]

Cash & Carry Electronics Inc., 120 Wyoming Blvd. SE, Albuquerque, NM 87123-3105, (505)266-2224 [25126]

Cash and Carry Stores Inc., PO Box 308, Elkin, NC 28621, (919)835-4405 [10710]

Cash Distributing Co., 223 22nd St. N, PO Box 2687, Columbus, MS 39704, (601)328-3551 [1580]

Cash Indiana, 387 Melton Rd., Burns Harbor, IN 46304, (219)787-8311 [22840]

Cash; Jeff, 5512 Old Wake Forest Rd., Raleigh, NC 27609-5014, (919)790-1331 [15078]

Cash Register Sales Inc., 2909 Anthony Ln. NE, Minneapolis, MN 55418, (612)781-3474 [20884]

Cash Register Sales & Service, 2080 Dimond Dr., Anchorage, AK 99507-1359, (907)563-0761 [20885]

Cash Register Systems Inc., 60110 Constitution NE, Albuquerque, NM 87110, (505)265-5979 [20886]

Cash Supply Co., PO Box 2311, Spartanburg, SC 29304-2311, (864)585-9326 [13623]

Cash Way Distributors, PO Box 309, Kearney, NE 68848, (308)237-3151 [10711]

Cash Wholesale Candy Co., PO Box 53, Cody, WY 82414-0053, (307)587-6226 [10712]

Cashway Electrical Supply Co., 275 Mariposa St., Denver, CO 80223, (303)623-0151 [8507]

Cashway Pet Supply, 1325 S Cherokee, Denver, CO 80223, (303)744-6131 [27103]

Cashwell Appliance Parts Inc., 3485 Clinton Rd., Fayetteville, NC 28302, (919)323-1111 [15079]

Casing Associates Inc., 1120 Close Ave., Bronx, NY 10472, (212)842-7151 [10713]

Casio, Inc., 570 Mt. Pleasant Ave., Dover, NJ 07801, (973)361-5400 [17362]

Casper Pay-Less Drug Co., PO Box 1252, Casper, WY 82602-1252, (307)265-1914 [26438]

Cass County Service Co., 342 N Main St., Virginia, IL 62691, (217)452-7751 [378]

Cass Inc.; Veronica, PO Box 5519, Hudson, FL 34674, (727)863-2738 [22841]

Cassemco Sporting Goods, 728 E 15th St., PO Box 1495, Cookeville, TN 38503-1495, (931)528-6588 [23585]

Cast Products Corp., PO Box 1368, Elkhart, IN 46515, (219)294-2684 [23108]

Castec Window Shading Inc., 7531 Coldwater Canyon Ave., North Hollywood, CA 91605-2007, (818)503-8300 [15439]

Castellon Inc.; E., PO Box 505, Mahwah, NJ 07430-0505, (973)772-7712 [3614]

Castiglione Accordion, 13300 E 11 Mile, Ste. A, Warren, MI 48089, (810)755-6050 [25127]

Castillo Ready-Mix Concrete, 304 Rosedale Cir., Belen, NM 87002, (505)854-2492 [7152]

Castle and Co.; A.M., 3400 N Wolf Rd., Franklin Park, IL 60131, (847)455-7111 [19862]

Castle and Co. Hy-Alloy Steels Div.; A.M., 4527 Columbia Ave., Hammond, IN 46327, (773)582-3200 [19863]

Castle Copiers & More Inc., 23 Austin Rd., North Kingstown, RI 02852-1313, (401)884-1180 [20887]

Castle Distributors Inc., 137 Pleasant Hill Rd., Scarborough, ME 04074-9309, (207)883-8901 [15080]

Castle Metals Inc., 298 Crescentville Rd., Cincinnati, OH 45246, (513)772-7000 [19864]

Castle Oil Corp., 500 Mamaroneck Ave., Harrison, NY 10528, (914)381-6500 [22115]

Castle of Stockton; A.L., 5700 Cherokee Rd., Stockton, CA 95215, (209)931-0684 [379]

Castleberry Knits Ltd., 530 7th Ave., New York, NY 10018-4872, (212)221-4333 [4867]

Castleberry Office Interiors Inc., 3600 American Dr., Atlanta, GA 30341, (404)452-6600 [13066]

Castleberry; Tom, PO Box 140937, Nashville, TN 37214-0937, (615)367-9628 [4868]

Castleton Beverage Corp., PO Box 26368, Jacksonville, FL 32226, (904)757-1290 [1581]

Castlewood Farmers Elevator, PO Box 200, Castlewood, SD 57223, (605)793-2181 [17767]

Castongia's Inc., PO Box 157, Rensselaer, IN 47978, (219)866-5117 [380]

Castor; Stanley, 1017 Rte. 12, Westmoreland, NH 03467-9711, (603)399-7737 [14370]

Castriota Chevrolet Inc., 1701 W Liberty Ave., Pittsburgh, PA 15226, (412)343-2100 [2433]

Castrol North America Holdings Inc., 1500 Valley Rd., Wayne, NJ 07470, (201)633-2200 [22116]

Casual Apparel Inc., PO Box 544, Sparta, TN 38583-0544, (931)836-3004 [4869]

Catalina Cottage, 125 N Aspan, No. 5, Azusa, CA 91702, (626)969-4001 [25597]

Catalyst Telecom, 6 Logue Ct., Ste. G, Greenville, SC 29615, (864)288-2432 [5550]

Catamount North, Dorset Lane Pk., Williston, VT 05495, (802)879-7172 [2434]

Catanzaro Sons and Daughters Inc.; Frank, 535 Shepherd Ave., Cincinnati, OH 45215-3115, (513)421-9184 [10714]

Catawba Color and Chemical Company Inc., 157 21st St. NW, Hickory, NC 28601, (704)322-3203 [4345]

Cate-McLaurin Company Inc., 1001 Idlewild Blvd., Columbia, SC 29201, (803)799-1955 [2435]

Cates Associates, Route 32, East Vassalboro, ME 04935, (207)923-3101 [17363]

Catey Controls, 535 Moore Ln., Billings, MT 59101, (406)259-3703 [15880]

Catey Controls, 3102 W Broadway, PO Box 7496, Missoula, MT 59807, (406)728-7860 [15881]

Cathay International, 290 W Arrow Hwy., San Dimas, CA 91773, (909)394-7806 [8508]

Cathedral Art Metal Inc., PO Box 6146, Providence, RI 02940-6146, (401)273-7200 [17364]

Catheter Research Inc., 6131 W 80th St., Indianapolis, IN 46278, (317)872-0074 [18730]

Cathey Wholesale Co., 202 36th St., Lubbock, TX 79404-2414, (806)747-3121 [9780]

Catholic Reading Society, 997 Macarthur Blvd., Mahwah, NJ 07430, (201)825-7300 [3615]

Catskill Electronics, 4050 Rte. 42 N, No. 12, Monticello, NY 12701, (914)794-6560 [25128]

Cattleman's Inc., 1825 Scott St., Detroit, MI 48207, (313)833-2700 [10715]

Cattleman's Meat Co., 1825 Scott St., Detroit, MI 48207, (313)833-2700 [10716]

Cattsa Inc.; S.D., 320 Calle Primera, Ste. E, San Ysidro, CA 92173, (619)428-4909 [4870]

Caulk Co.; L.D., PO Box 359, Milford, DE 19963, (302)422-4511 [18731]

Causeway Lumber Co., PO Box 21088, Ft. Lauderdale, FL 33335, (305)763-1224 [7153]

Cavalier Fabrics, Ltd./Redrum, 4716 Richneil Rd., Richmond, VA 23231, (804)222-5730 [25998]

Cavalier, Gulling, and Wilson Inc., 3800 Orange Ave., Cleveland, OH 44115, (216)431-2117 [10717]

Cavallero Heating and Air Conditioning Inc., 5541 Hwy. 50 E, Carson City, NV 89706, (702)883-2066 [14371]

Cavexsa USA Inc., 3701 Commercial Ave., Ste. 12, Northbrook, IL 60062-1830, (708)730-0030 [19865]

Caxton Printers Ltd., 312 Main St., Caldwell, ID 83605, (208)459-7421 [3616]

Cayce Mill Supply Co., PO Box 689, Hopkinsville, KY 42241-0689, (502)886-3335 [8509]

Caye and Company Inc.; W.C., PO Box 4508, Atlanta, GA 30302, (404)688-2177 [7154]

Caye's Luggage, PO Box 891, Portland, OR 97207-0891, (503)227-4322 [18381]

CB Distributing, 3297 Salem Ave. SE, Albany, OR 97321, (541)926-1027 [8510]

C.B. Electronic Marketing, 6429 Iris Way, Arvada, CO 80004, (303)422-0561 [8511]

CBLX Holdings Inc., 5730 E Otero Ave., Englewood, CO 80112, (303)694-6789 [25129]

CBS Contractors Supply Co., 3650 Hauck Rd., Cincinnati, OH 45241, (513)769-6700 [7155]

CBS Fasteners Inc., 1345 N Brasher St., Anaheim, CA 92807, (714)779-6368 [13624]

CBS Technologies LLC, 6900 Steger Dr., Cincinnati, OH 45237, (513)361-9600 [5551]

CBS WhitCom Technologies Corp., 2990 Express Dr. S, Central Islip, NY 11722, (516)582-3200 [5552]

CBS WhitCom Technologies Corp., 2990 Express Dr. S, Islandia, NY 11749, (516)582-3200 [8512]

CBW Automation Inc., 3939 Automation Way, Ft. Collins, CO 80525, (970)229-9500 [15882]

CCA Electronics, 360 Bohannon Rd., Box 426, Fairburn, GA 30213, (404)964-3530 [5553]

CCC Associates Co., PO Box 3508, Montgomery, AL 36109, (334)272-2140 [14836]

CCC Heavy Duty Trucks Co., 3955 Bristol Pke., Bensalem, PA 19020, (215)638-1474 [2436]

CCC Steel Inc., 2576 E Victoria St., Rancho Dominguez, CA 90220, (310)637-0111 [19866]

CCI Triad, 3055 Triad Dr., Livermore, CA 94550, (925)449-0606 [6048]

CCL Creative Ltd, 354 N Main St., Freeport, NY 11520, (516)223-9800 [13328]

CCL Products Ent. Inc., 354 N Main St., Freeport, NY 11520, (516)223-9800 [13328]

CCS Printing, 111 Oak Lawn Ave., Dallas, TX 75207, (214)748-6622 [3617]

CD One Stop, 13 Francis J. Clarke Cir., Bethel, CT 06801, (203)798-6590 [25130]

CDC, 10511 Medallion Dr., Cincinnati, OH 45241-3193, (513)771-3100 [9781]

CDC, 5019 Trans-America Dr., Columbus, OH 43228, (614)876-4057 [9782]

C.D.C. Optical Lab Inc., 20724 Cattle Dr., Redding, CA 96003, (530)223-0152 [19221]

CED Inc., 16 SE I Ave., Lawton, OK 73501-2449, (580)355-5883 [8513]

CED/Superior Electrical Supply Co., PO Box 3156, Evansville, IN 47731, (812)423-7837 [8514]

Cedar Builders Supply Company Inc., 309 N 200 W, Cedar City, UT 84720, (801)586-9424 [23109]

Cedar Co., 1502 North 150 West, Provo, UT 84604-2526, (801)375-3393 [6049]

Cedar Group US Inc., 57 Wingate Street, Haverhill, MA 01832, (978)372-0770 [6050]

Cedar Rapids Welding Supply Inc., PO Box 453, Cedar Rapids, IA 52406, (319)365-1466 [16785]

Cedar Valley FS Inc., PO Box 409, New Hampton, IA 50659, (515)394-3031 [381]

Cedarburg Lumber Company Inc., PO Box 999, Cedarburg, WI 53012, (262)377-2345 [7156]

Cedars Wholesale Floral Imports, 6151 B St., Anchorage, AK 99518, (907)563-5566 [14837]

Cee-J Wholesale, 260 E Broadway Ave., Muskegon Heights, MI 49444-2158, (616)733-1293 [26439]

Cee Kay Supply Co., 5835 Manchester Ave., St. Louis, MO 63110, (314)644-3500 [16786]

Cel Air Corp., 1605 Lakes Pkwy., Lawrenceville, GA 30043, (770)339-1672 [8515]

Cel Tech Communications Inc., PO Box 430, Lakewood, CA 90714-0430, (562)421-2205 [5554]

Celebration Halloween, 5860 N Michigan Rd., Indianapolis, IN 46208, (317)257-9446 [9633]

Celebration Imports Inc., 350 5th Ave., New York, NY 10118, (212)239-6670 [4871]

Celebrations Creations, 5860 N Michigan Rd., Indianapolis, IN 46208, (317)257-9446 [9633]

Celebrations Fireworks & Supply Co. Inc., 5860 N Michigan Rd., Indianapolis, IN 46208, (317)257-9446 [9633]

Celebrity, Inc., 4520 Old Troup Rd., Tyler, TX 75707, (903)561-3981 [14838]

Celebrity Inc. (Tyler, Texas), PO Box 6666, Tyler, TX 75707, (903)561-3981 [14839]

Celeron Trading and Transportation Co., PO Box 40160, Bakersfield, CA 93384, (805)664-5300 [22117]

Celestial Arts Publishing Co., PO Box 7123, Berkeley, CA 94707, (510)559-1600 [3618]

Celestial Mercantile Corporation, 5 Eves Dr., Ste. 140, Marlton, NJ 08053, (856)985-8936 [14059]

Celestial Mercantile Corporation, 5 Eves Dr., Ste. 140, Marlton, NJ 08053, (609)985-8936 [19222]

Celestron International, 2835 Columbia St., Torrance, CA 90503, (310)328-9560 [22842]

Cellar Book Shop, 18090 Wyoming, Detroit, MI 48221, (313)861-1776 [3619]

Cellars Beverage Inc., PO Box 1294, Bay City, MI 48706-0294, (517)754-6550 [1582]

Celleco Hedemora Inc., 1000 Laval Blvd., Lawrenceville, GA 30043, (404)963-2100 [16066]

Cellino Inc., 31 W 47th St., No. 103, New York, NY 10036-2808, (212)382-0959 [17365]

CellStar Corp., 1730 Briercroft Ct., Carrollton, TX 75006, (972)323-0600 [5555]

CellStar Ltd., 1730 Briercroft Ct., Carrollton, TX 75006, (972)323-0600 [5556]

Cellucap-Melco Manufacturing, 4626 N 15th St., Philadelphia, PA 19019, (215)324-0213 [4872]

Cellular Wholesales, 5151 Church St., Skokie, IL 60076, (847)965-2300 [5557]

Cellulite Products Inc., 6835 Valjean Ave., Van Nuys, CA 91406, (818)989-5760 [14060]

Cels Enterprises Inc., 3485 S La Cienega, Los Angeles, CA 90016, (310)838-2103 [24709]

Celsco Bros., 5620 N Western Ave., Oklahoma City, OK 73118-4008, (405)840-6006 [14372]

Cen-Cal Wallboard Supply Co., 880 S River Rd., West Sacramento, CA 95691, (916)372-2320 [7157]

Cen-Tex AG Supply, 201 W 4th St., McGregor, TX 76657, (254)840-3288 [22118]

CENCO Refining Co., PO Box 2108, Santa Fe Springs, CA 90670-9883, (562)944-6111 [22119]

Cenex Harvest States, PO Box A, Garretson, SD 57030, (605)594-3415 [382]

Cenex-Harvest States Cooperative, PO Box 190, Tyler, MN 56178, (507)247-5586 [22120]

Cenex Harvest States Cooperative, PO Box 65, Corsica, SD 57328-0065, (605)946-5491 [383]

Cenex Harvest States Cooperatives, PO Box 64594, St. Paul, MN 55164, (651)451-5151 [17768]

Cenex/Land O'Lakes AG Services, PO Box 64089, St. Paul, MN 55164-0089, (612)451-5151 [384]

Cenna International Corp., 7 Post Office Rd., 7F, Waldorf, MD 20602-2744, (301)932-8666 [19223]

Centaurus Systems Inc., 4425 Cass St., Ste. A, San Diego, CA 92109, (858)270-4552 [6051]

Centel Information Systems Inc., 8725 Haggins Rd., Chicago, IL 60631, (773)399-2735 [6052]

Centenario Technologies, Inc., 14208 Atlanta Dr., Laredo, TX 78041, (956)724-1887 [6053]

Centennial Beverage Corp., PO Box 951, 1850 Lefthand Cir., Longmont, CO 80501-6720, (303)772-1955 [1583]

Centennial Bolt Inc., 555 Joliet St., Denver, CO 80239-2006, (303)371-1370 [13625]

Centennial Commodities Inc., 4000 N Bayou Hills Ln., Parker, CO 80134, (303)840-0644 [17769]

Center Oil Co., 600 Mason Ridge Center Dr., St. Louis, MO 63141, (314)682-3500 [22121]

Center Valley Cooperative Association, PO Box 158, Seymour, WI 54165-0156, (920)734-1409 [22122]

Centercore New England Inc., 23 Lincoln St., Biddeford, ME 04005-2019, (207)283-0147 [20888]

Centerline Software Inc., 10 Fawcett St., Cambridge, MA 02138-1110, (617)498-3000 [6054]

Centerspan Communications Corp., 7175 NW Evergreen Pkwy. Ste. 400, Hillsboro, OR 97124, (503)615-3200 [6055]

Centra Sota Cooperative, PO Box 210, Buffalo, MN 55313, (612)682-1464 [385]

Central Air Compressor Co., 28600 Lorna Ave., Warren, MI 48092-3929, (810)558-9100 [5835]

Central Air Conditioning Distributor, 121 Sweeten Creek Rd., Asheville, NC 28803 [14373]

Central Air Conditioning Distributors Inc., 100 Clanton Rd., Charlotte, NC 28217, (704)523-0306 [14374]

Central Alabama Cooperative Farms Inc., PO Box 1079, Selma, AL 36701, (205)874-9083 [386]

Central Arizona Distributing Co., 4932 W Pasadena Ave., Glendale, AZ 85301-1466, (602)939-6511 [3620]

Central Atlantic Toyota Distributors Inc., 6710 Baymeadow Dr., Glen Burnie, MD 21060, (410)760-1500 [2437]

Central Audio Visual Equipment Inc., 271 E Helen Rd., Palatine, IL 60067-6954, (847)776-9200 [22843]

Central Beer Distributing, 3030 Pine Ave., Erie, PA 16504, (814)453-2094 [1732]

Central Beverage Corporation, PO Box 1427, 123 Hopkins Hill Rd., West Greenwich, RI 02817, (401)392-3580 [1584]

Central Business Supply Inc., PO Box 807, Brookings, SD 57006-0807, (605)692-6363 [20889]

Central Business Systems Inc., 2514 Hwy. 281 S, Jamestown, ND 58401-6606, (701)252-7474 [20890]

Central California Electronics Inc., 139 E Belmont St., Fresno, CA 93701, (209)485-1254 [8516]

Central Carolina Grocers Inc., 829 Graves St., Kernersville, NC 27284, (919)996-2501 [10718]

Central City Produce Inc., E 2nd, Box 227, Central City, KY 42330-1227, (502)754-1991 [10719]

Central Commodities Ltd., 1140 W Locust St., Belvidere, IL 61008, (815)544-3455 [17770]

Central Computer Systems Inc., 3777 Stevens Creek Blvd., Santa Clara, CA 95051, (408)248-5888 [6056]

Central Connecticut Cooperative Farmers Association, PO Box 8500, Manchester, CT 06040, (203)649-4523 [17771]

Central Cooperative Oil Association, 712 N Cedar St., Owatonna, MN 55060, (507)451-1230 [22123]

Central Cooperatives Inc., PO Box 26, Pleasant Hill, MO 64080, (816)987-2196 [387]

Central Counties Cooperative, 125 High St., Kellogg, IA 50135, (515)526-8236 [388]

Central Diesel, Inc., 1422 Commerce Rd., Richmond, VA 23224, (804)233-9814 [2438]

Central Distributing Co., PO Box 1229, San Antonio, TX 78293, (210)225-1541 [15081]

Central Distributing Co., 609 N 108 St., Omaha, NE 68154, (402)493-5600 [25598]

Central Distributing Co., 695 S 6th, Carrington, ND 58421-2322, (701)652-2141 [24924]

Central Distribution Co., PO Box 165207, Little Rock, AR 72216, (501)372-3158 [1585]

Central Distribution Services, LLC, 5400 33rd St. SE, Grand Rapids, MI 49512, (616)940-3540 [13626]

Central Distributors Inc., 117 College Ave., Des Moines, IA 50314, (515)244-8103 [9783]

Central Distributors Inc., PO Box 1936, Lewiston, ME 04241, (207)784-4026 [1586]

Central District Inc., 640 S Broadway, Lexington, KY 40508, (606)255-4453 [26274]

Central Door & Hardware, 656 RW Harris, Manton, MI 49663-9775, (616)824-3041 [7158]

Central Electric Supply Co., PO Box 1025, Worcester, MA 01613, (508)755-1271 [8517]

Central Engineering & Supply Co., 2422 Butler St., Box 35907, Dallas, TX 75235, (214)951-0270 [14375]

Central Equipment Distributing Co., 1120 N Vermont Ave., Oklahoma City, OK 73107-5008, (405)947-7867 [14376]

Central Farm Supply Inc., PO Box 167, Wooster, OH 44691, (330)264-0282 [389]

Central Farmers Cooperative, Box 330, ONeill, NE 68763-0330, (402)843-2223 [390]

Central Farmers Cooperative, Box 330, O' Neill, NE 68763-0330, (402)843-2223 [10720]

Central Garden and Pet Co., 3697 Mt. Diablo Blvd., Ste. 310, Lafayette, CA 94549, (510)283-4573 [391]

Central Garden and Pet Co. Pet Supplies Div., 3697 Mt. Diablo Blvd., Ste. 310, Lafayette, CA 94549, (925)283-4573 [27104]

Central Garden and Pet Supply Inc., PO Box 27126, Salt Lake City, UT 84127, (801)973-7514 [392]

Central Garden and Pet Supply Inc., 4601 Florin Perkins Rd., No. 100, Sacramento, CA 95826-4820, (916)928-1925 [27105]

Central Garden & Pet Supply Inc., PO Box 655650, Dallas, TX 75265-5650, (972)466-0069 [27106]

Central Garden and Pet Supply Inc., 16179 SE 98th Ave., Clackamas, OR 97015, (503)650-4400 [393]

Central Garden & Pet Supply Inc., PO Box 95001, Auburn, WA 98071, (253)833-7771 [27107]

Central Garden Supplies, 925 E 66th St., Lubbock, TX 79404, (806)745-8668 [394]

Central Grocers Co-op Inc., 3701 N Centralia St., Franklin Park, IL 60131, (708)678-0660 [10721]

Central House Technologies, PO Box 1030, Plymouth, CA 95669, (209)245-5900 [6057]

Central Illinois Enterprises Ltd., 707 E Fayette Ave., Effingham, IL 62401, (217)342-9755 [22124]

Central Illinois Harvestore Inc., 208 N Rolla St., Eureka, IL 61530, (309)467-2334 [395]

Central Indiana Hardware Co., PO Box 6097, Fishers, IN 46038-6097, (317)253-6421 [7159]

Central Iowa Cooperative, PO Box 190, Jewell, IA 50130, (515)827-5431 [396]

Central Jersey Supply Co., PO Box 549, Perth Amboy, NJ 08862-0549, (732)826-7400 [16787]

Central Kentucky News Distributing Co., 808 Newtown Cir. No. B, Lexington, KY 40511-1230, (606)254-2765 [3621]

Central Liquor Co., PO Box 75447, Oklahoma City, OK 73147-0447, (405)947-8050 [1587]

Central Livestock Association, PO Box 419, South St. Paul, MN 55075, (651)451-1844 [17772]

Central Lumber Sales Inc., PO Box 22723, Lincoln, NE 68542-2723, (402)474-4441 [7160]

Central Lumber Sales Inc., PO Box 22723, Lincoln, NE 68542-2723, (402)474-4441 [27296]

Central Maine Business Machines, 84 Western Ave., Augusta, ME 04330-7225, (207)622-6100 [20891]

Central Meat Packing, 1120 Kempsville Rd., Chesapeake, VA 23320-8127, (757)547-2161 [10722]

Central Medical Inc., 3836 Minnehaha Ave., Minneapolis, MN 55406-3230, (612)724-0474 [19224]

Central Minnesota Cooperative, PO Box 192, Sauk Centre, MN 56378, (320)352-6533 [397]

Central Motive Power Inc., 6301 Broadway, Denver, CO 80216, (303)428-3611 [22125]

Central National-Gottesman Inc., 3 Manhattanville Rd., Purchase, NY 10577-2110, (914)696-9000 [21675]

Central Nebraska Home Care, PO Box 1146, Kearney, NE 68848-1146, (308)234-6094 [18732]

Central News Co., 920 Hemlock Dr., Columbia, SC 29201, (803)799-3414 [3622]

Central Office Supply Co., 1408 Bunton Rd., Louisville, KY 40213-1857, (502)456-4080 [20892]

Central Oil Company Inc., 1001 McCloskey Blvd., Tampa, FL 33605, (813)248-2105 [22126]

Central Oil of Virginia Corp., PO Box 587, Rocky Mount, VA 24151, (703)483-5342 [22127]

Central Optical of Youngstown Inc., PO Box 6210, Youngstown, OH 44501, (330)783-9660 [19225]

Central Paper Products Co. Inc., Brown Ave. Industrial Park, PO Box 4480, Manchester, NH 03108, (603)624-4064 [21676]

Central Plains Distributing Inc., 13202 I St., Omaha, NE 68137 [14377]

Central Power Systems, 1114 W Cass St., Tampa, FL 33606, (813)253-6035 [398]

Central Procurement Inc., 1 Kingfisher Dr., Coventry, RI 02816-6826, (401)823-8600 [24091]

Central Radio and TV Inc., 1910 Duss Ave., Ambridge, PA 15003, (412)266-9100 [25131]

Central Rivers Cooperative, 502 S 2nd St., Princeton, MN 55371, (612)389-2582 [399]

Central Scientific Co., 3300 Cenco Pkwy., Franklin Park, IL 60131, (847)451-0150 [4346]

Central Seaway Co., 1845 Oak St., Ste. 1, Northvale, IL 60093, (847)446-3720 [10723]

Central Snacks, 1700 N Pearl St., Carthage, MS 39051, (601)267-3023 [10724]

Central South Music Inc., 3730 Vulcan Dr., Nashville, TN 37211, (615)833-5960 [25132]

Central States Airgas Inc., 200 S 23rd St., Fairfield, IA 52556-4203, (515)472-3141 [16788]

Central States Coca-Cola Bottling Co., 3495 Sangamon Ave., Springfield, IL 62707, (217)544-4891 [24925]

Central States Electronics, 317 W 13th St., Davenport, IA 52803-4901, (319)323-0180 [5558]

Central States/Multiplex Business Forms, 4685 Merle Hay Rd., Ste. 205, Des Moines, IA 50322, (515)270-8382 [3623]

Central Steel Supply Company Inc., 99 Foley St., Somerville, MA 02145, (617)625-3232 [19867]

Central Steel and Wire Co, PO Box 5100, Chicago, IL 60680, (773)471-3800 [19868]

Central Supply Co., 701 E Wallace, Ft. Wayne, IN 46803, (219)745-4961 [23110]

Central Supply Co., PO Box 337, Worcester, MA 01613, (508)755-6121 [23111]

Central Supply Division of Central Consolidated Inc., PO Box 631009, Houston, TX 77263-1009, (713)688-6660 [15082]

Central Textile Co., 12900 W Sunset Blvd., Los Angeles, CA 90049-2644, (213)748-8782 [25999]

Central Tractor Farm & Country, Inc., PO Box 3330, Des Moines, IA 50316, (515)266-3101 [400]

Central VA Chimney, Rte. 2, Box 253, Dillwyn, VA 23936, (804)983-2988 [14378]

Central Vac International, PO Box 160, Kimball, NE 69145-0160, (308)235-4139 [4595]

Central Valley Builders Supply, 1100 Vintage Ave., St. Helena, CA 94574, (707)963-3622 [7161]

Central Valley Oriental Imports, 3209 N Marks, Fresno, CA 93722, (209)237-7115 [26440]

Central Virginia Medical Inc., 5406 B. Distributor Dr., Richmond, VA 23225-6106, (804)233-5508 [18733]

Central Wholesale Supply Corp., 1532 Ingleside Rd., Norfolk, VA 23502, (804)855-3131 [7162]

Central Wisconsin Cooperative, PO Box 14, Stratford, WI 54484, (715)687-4443 [401]

Central Work Clothes, 2017 Fort St., Lincoln Park, MI 48146-2402, (313)382-0988 [4873]

Centre Beauty Supply, 4055 N Government Way Unit 4, Coeur D Alene, ID 83815-9230, (208)765-9197 [14061]

Centre Jobbing Co., 223 S Main, Sauk Centre, MN 56378-1346, (320)352-2009 [26275]

Centre Manufacturing Co. Inc., PO Box 579, Centre, AL 35960-0579, (205)927-5541 [4874]

Centre Oil and Gas Co. Inc., 206 S Potter St., Bellefonte, PA 16823, (814)355-4749 [22128]

Centrex Inc., 38 West 32nd St., New York, NY 10001, (212)695-3320 [19226]

Centro, Inc., 7600 Hardin Dr., PO Box 6248, Sherwood, AR 72117, (501)835-2193 [24336]

Centro, Inc., 321 Hill Ave., Nashville, TN 37210-4711, (615)255-2220 [24337]

Centro, Inc., 3315 Overton Crossing, PO Box 27161, Memphis, TN 38167-0161, (901)357-1261 [16789]

Centrotrade Minerals and Metals Inc., 521 5th Ave., 30th Fl., New York, NY 10175-0003, (212)808-4900 [19869]

Centry Tile & Supply Co., 5719 Diversey, Chicago, IL 60639, (773)622-6800 [9786]

Centurion Vehicles Inc., 69651 US 131 S, PO Box 715, White Pigeon, MI 49099, (616)483-9659 [2439]

Century Acres Eggs Inc., 3420 Hwy. W, Port Washington, WI 53074, (414)284-0568 [10725]

Century Air Conditioning and Maintenance Supply, Inc., 1750 Enterprise Way, Marietta, GA 30067, (770)933-8833 [14379]

Century Air Conditioning Supply Inc., 5381 Gulfton St., Houston, TX 77081, (713)663-6661 [14380]

Century Business Equipment Inc., 1080 W Sam Houston Pkwy. N, Houston, TX 77043, (713)973-6147 [20893]

Century Equipment Inc., 5959 Angola Rd., Toledo, OH 43615, (419)865-7400 [402]

Century Fasteners Corp., 50-20 Ireland St., Elmhurst, NY 11373, (718)446-5000 [13627]

Century Fasteners, Inc., 11333 Greenstone Ave., Santa Fe Springs, CA 90670-4618, (213)583-6721 [13628]

Century-Federman Wallcoverings Inc., 18 Holly Hill Cir., Marshfield, MA 02050-1728, (781)337-9300 [15440]

Century Labs Inc., 3200 S 24th St., Kansas City, KS 66106, (913)262-0227 [4347]

Century Papers Inc., PO Box 1908, Houston, TX 77251, (713)921-7800 [4596]

Century Plumbing Wholesale, 901 SW 69th Ave., Miami, FL 33144, (305)261-4731 [23112]

Century Rain Aid, 31691 Dequindre, Madison Heights, MI 48071, (248)588-2990 [403]

Century Saw and Tool Co. Inc., 19347 Mount Elliot St., Detroit, MI 48234, (313)893-2280 [13629]

Century Sports Inc., 1995 Rutgers University Blvd., PO Box 2035, Lakewood, NJ 08701-8035, (908)905-4422 [23586]

Century Steel Corp., 300 E Joe Orr Rd., Chicago Heights, IL 60411, (708)758-0900 [19870]

Century Supply Corp., 747 E Roosevelt Rd., Lombard, IL 60148, (708)889-0800 [9787]

Century Tile and Carpet, 747 E Roosevelt Rd., Lombard, IL 60148, (630)495-2300 [9784]

Century Tile & Carpet, 200 Washington St., Woodstock, IL 60098, (815)337-0400 [9785]

Century Tile & Carpet, 5719 Diversey, Chicago, IL 60639, (773)622-6800 [9786]

Century Tile and Carpet, 747 E Roosevelt Rd., Lombard, IL 60148, (708)889-0800 [9787]

Century Tile and Carpet, 5719 Diversey, Chicago, IL 60639, (773)622-6800 [7163]

Century Tile and Supply, 374 South Rt. 53, Bolingbrook, IL 60440, (630)972-1700 [9788]

Century Tile and Supply Co., 1220 Norwood, Itasca, IL 60143, (708)250-8000 [9789]

Century Tile and Supply Co., 747 E Roosevelt Rd., Lombard, IL 60148, (630)495-2300 [9784]

Century Tile & Supply Co., 915 E Rand, Mt. Prospect, IL 60056, (847)392-4700 [9790]

Century Wheel & Rim Corp., 1550 Gage Rd., Montebello, CA 90640-6600, (323)728-3901 [2440]

Century Wheels Research, 7800 Winn Rd., Spring Grove, IL 60081-9687, (815)675-2366 [8518]

Cenweld Corp., 230 E Portage Trail, Cuyahoga Falls, OH 44221, (216)923-9717 [2441]

CEO/United Electric Supply Co., 6910 Central Hwy., Pennsauken, NJ 08109-4110 [8519]

Ceramic Concept of Martin County, 200 N Old Dixie Hwy., Jupiter, FL 33458, (561)746-2230 [9791]

Ceramic Tile Center, 4388 N Carson St., Carson City, NV 89706, (775)883-0833 [7164]

Ceramic Tile Center Inc., 3945 Vernon St., Long Beach, CA 90815-1727, (562)498-2336 [9792]

Ceramic Tile Center Inc., 525 S Van Ness Ave., Torrance, CA 90501-1424, (310)533-8231 [9793]

Ceramic Tile Center, Inc., 50 E Greg St., Ste. 114, Sparks, NV 89431-6595, (702)359-6770 [9794]

Ceramic Tile Distributors, PO Box 1107, Ft. Smith, AR 72902-1107, (501)646-7600 [9795]

Ceramic Tile Distributors, Inc., 712 Fogg St., Nashville, TN 37203, (615)255-6669 [9796]

Ceramic Tile International, 2333 S Jupiter Rd., Garland, TX 75041, (214)503-5500 [9797]

Ceramic Tile International, 2682 Forest Lane, Dallas, TX 75234, (972)243-4465 [9798]

Ceramic Tile International, 1458 Lee Trevino, El Paso, TX 79936, (915)593-7357 [9799]

Ceramic Tile International, 11525 Todd St., Houston, TX 77055-1308, (713)686-8453 [7165]

Ceramic Tile Outlet, 487 Federal Rd., Brookfield, CT 06804, (203)740-8858 [10216]

Ceramic Tile Supply Co., 103 Green Bank Rd., Wilmington, DE 19808-5963, (302)992-9212 [9800]

Ceramic Tile Supply, Inc., 1601 E 27th St., Chattanooga, TN 37404-5722, (423)698-1512 [9801]

Ceramics By Bob and Hazel, 108 N Saginaw St., Pontiac, MI 48342-2112, (248)334-8521 [26441]

CERBCO Inc., 3421 Pennsy Dr., Landover, MD 20785, (301)773-1784 [20894]

Cereal Byproducts Co., 763 New Ballas Rd. S, St. Louis, MO 63141, (314)569-2915 [404]

Cereal Byproducts Co., 763 New Ballas Rd. S, St. Louis, MO 63141, (314)569-2915 [405]

Cereal Food Processors, Inc., Foot of N Lombard, Portland, OR 97217, (503)286-1656 [10726]

Cerenzia Foods Inc., 8707 Utica, Rancho Cucamonga, CA 91730, (909)989-4000 [10727]

Cerprobe Corp., 1150 N Fiesta Blvd., Gilbert, AZ 85233-2237, (480)333-1500 [8520]

Certex Gulf Coast, PO Box 10367, New Orleans, LA 70181-0367, (504)734-5871 [8521]

Certified Automotive Warehouse Inc., 2301 S Ashland Ave., Chicago, IL 60608, (312)829-6440 [2442]

Certified Data Processing Inc., 1155 Main St., South Weymouth, MA 02190-1514, (781)337-5495 [6058]

Certified Grocers of California Ltd., PO Box 3396, Terminal Annex, Los Angeles, CA 90051, (213)726-2601 [10728]

Certified Grocers of Florida Inc., PO Box 1510, 8305 SE 58th Ave., Ocala, FL 34480, (352)245-5151 [12970]

Certified Grocers Midwest Inc., 1 Certified Dr., Hodgkins, IL 60525, (708)579-2100 [10729]

Certified Parts Corp., PO Box 8468, Janesville, WI 53547-8468, (608)752-9441 [18477]

Certified Ribbon Supply Inc., 335 Creekview Ter 100, Alpharetta, GA 30005-4697, (404)740-1600 [6059]

Cervena Co., 780 3rd. Ave., Ste. 1904, New York, NY 10017, (212)832-7964 [10730]

CESSCO Rental and Sales Inc., 703 E Scott St., Wichita Falls, TX 76307, (940)766-0238 [15883]

Cetex Trading Corp., 385 Broadway, New York, NY 10013, (212)925-6774 [26000]

CFX, Inc., 1800 NW 89th Pl., Miami, FL 33172, (305)592-4478 [14840]

CGB Enterprises Inc., PO Box 249, Mandeville, LA 70470, (504)867-3500 [17773]

CGF Cash & Carry, 455 Toland, San Francisco, CA 94124-1624, (415)285-9333 [10731]

C.H. Robinson Company Inc., 8100 Mitchell Rd., Eden Prairie, MN 55344, (612)937-8500 [10732]

Chaddsford Winery, 632 Baltimore Pike, Chadds Ford, PA 19317-9305, (610)388-6221 [1588]

Chadwick-BaRoss Inc., 160 Warren Ave., Westbrook, ME 04092, (207)854-8411 [7166]

Chadwick Optical Inc., PO Box 485, White River Junction, VT 05001-0485, (802)295-5933 [19227]

Chair King Furniture Co., 4701 Blalock Dr., Houston, TX 77041-9240, (713)690-1919 [13067]

Chair Place, 2623 J St., Sacramento, CA 95816, (916)446-1771 [13068]

Chalice Press, PO Box 179, St. Louis, MO 63166-0179, (314)231-8500 [3624]

Challenger Ltd., PO Box 185, Nancy, KY 42544-9326, (606)636-6900 [7167]

Challenger Water International Inc., 133 Newport Dr., San Marcos, CA 92069, (760)471-2282 [25599]

Chamberlain Group Inc., 845 Larch Ave., Elmhurst, IL 60126, (630)279-3600 [13630]

Chamberlain Livestock Auction, PO Box 244, Chamberlain, SD 57325-0244, (605)734-6037 [17774]

Chamberlin Rubber Company Inc., PO Box 22700, Rochester, NY 14692, (716)427-7780 [16790]

Chambers Supply Inc.; Carter, PO Box 15705, Baton Rouge, LA 70895, (504)926-2123 [16791]

Champion America, PO Box 3092, Branford, CT 06405, (203)315-1181 [25600]

Champion Athletic Supply Inc., 14806 Pacific Ave. S, Tacoma, WA 98444-4655, (253)537-4204 [23587]

Champion Auto Stores Inc., 101 5th St. E, St. Paul, MN 55101-1820, (612)391-6655 [2443]

Champion Computer Corp., 6421 Congress Ave., Boca Raton, FL 33487, (561)997-2900 [6060]

Champion Distributors Inc., PO Box 691, Lecompte, LA 71346-0691, (318)776-5011 [14381]

Champion Furnace Pipe Co., 6021 N Galena Rd., Peoria, IL 61614-3603, (309)685-1031 [23113]

Champion Industries Inc. (Huntington, West Virginia), PO Box 2968, Huntington, WV 25728, (304)528-2791 [20895]

Champion Machinery Co., 210 S Center St., Joliet, IL 60436, (815)726-4336 [25603]

Champlain Winair Co., 921 Hercules Dr., Ste. 1, Colchester, VT 05446, 800-343-1350 [23114]

Champlin Co., 236 Hamilton St., Hartford, CT 06106-2910, (860)951-9217 [25899]

Chandler Enterprises, 3925 Arroyo Seco, Schertz, TX 78154-2687 [6061]

Chandler Foods Inc., 2727 Immanuel Rd., Greensboro, NC 27407-2515, (336)299-1934 [10733]

Chandler Products Co., 1491 Chardon Rd., Cleveland, OH 44117, (216)481-4400 [13631]

Chandras, 1005 Kalahu Pl., Honolulu, HI 96825-1331, (808)521-4068 [4875]

Chaneaco Supply Co., 32 Park Ave., Washington, PA 15301, (724)222-0960 [15884]

Chanens Scrap and Steel Inc., PO Box 220, West Burlington, IA 52655, (319)752-3643 [26746]

Chaney, Jr. Books; Bev, 73 Croton Ave., Ossining, NY 10562, (914)941-1002 [3625]

Changing Colors, 1131 Bishop St., Unit 116, Honolulu, HI 96813-2822, (808)841-5607 [4876]

Channellock Inc., 1306 S Main St., PO Box 519, Meadville, PA 16335, (814)724-8700 [13632]

Channer Corp., 13720 Polo Trail Dr., Lake Forest, IL 60045, (847)816-7000 [8522]

Chantal Cookware Corp., 2030 W Sam Houston, Houston, TX 77043, (713)467-9949 [15441]

Chapin and Bangs Co. Inc., PO Box 1117, Bridgeport, CT 06601, (203)333-4183 [19871]

Chapin Co., PO Box 2568, Myrtle Beach, SC 29578-2568, (803)448-6955 [22129]

Chapin Co.; Noel R., 1201 S Ervay St., Dallas, TX 75215, (214)565-1883 [13329]

Chapin Farmers Elevator Co., PO Box 349, Chapin, IL 62628, (217)472-5771 [17775]

Chapin's Supreme Foods, 4190 Garfield, Denver, CO 80216, (303)321-1985 [10734]

Chapman Co.; J.T., 310 Armour Rd., North Kansas City, MO 64116, (816)842-4488 [2444]

Chapman-Dyer Steel Manufacturing, PO Box 27365, Tucson, AZ 85726, (520)623-6318 [19872]

Chapman Inc., PO Box 1298, Sherman, TX 75091, (903)893-8106 [22130]

Chapman Marine Supply, 2201 SE Indian St., A-5, Stuart, FL 34997, (561)283-9110 [18478]

Chapmans Shoe Repair, 110 N Mill St., Lexington, KY 40507-1207, (606)231-7463 [24710]

Chappells Cheese Co., 922 W Hwy. 24, Loa, UT 84747-0307, (435)836-2821 [10735]

Charken Co. Inc., PO Box 13052, Pittsburgh, PA 15243, (412)745-7979 [16792]

Charles Bluestone Co., PO Box 326, Elizabeth, PA 15037, (412)384-7400 [19873]

Charles Products Inc., 12118 Nebel St., Rockville, MD 20852, (301)881-1966 [13330]

Charles River BRF Inc., 305 Almeda-Genoa Rd., Houston, TX 77047, (713)433-5846 [406]

Charleston Auto Parts Company Inc., PO Box 15291, Las Vegas, NV 89114, (702)642-5557 [2445]

Charlotte Aerospace Co. Inc., 4801 E Independence Blvd., Ste. 1101, Charlotte, NC 28212, (704)536-1921 [69]

Charlotte Copy Data Inc., 4404-A Stuart Andrew Blvd., Charlotte, NC 28217, (704)523-3333 [20896]

Charlotte Hardwood Center, 4250 Golf Acres Dr., Charlotte, NC 28208, (704)394-9479 [7168]

Charlotte Salvage Co., PO Box 220268, Charlotte, NC 28222, (704)333-5157 [4945]

Charlotte Tile & Stone, 1220 Commercial Ave., Charlotte, NC 28205, (704)372-8180 [9802]

Charmant Incorporated USA, 400 American Rd., Morris Plains, NJ 07950-2400, (201)538-1511 [18734]

Charmer Industries Inc., 1950 48th St., Astoria, NY 11105, (718)726-2500 [1589]

Charron Medical Equipment Inc., 1 E Hollis St., Nashua, NH 03060-2942, (603)889-7220 [18735]

Charter Distributing, 4054 Dolan Dr., Flint, MI 48504, (810)789-5071 [9803]

Charter Distributing, 509 South St., Easton, MD 21601-3845, (410)822-2323 [15083]

Charter Fabrics Inc., 1430 Broadway, New York, NY 10018, (212)391-8110 [26001]

Charter Pet Supplies, 634 Medina, Highland Village, TX 75077-7273, (972)317-3524 [27108]

Chartier Double Reed Co., PO Box 13344, Albuquerque, NM 87192, (505)881-0843 [25133]

Chase Com Corp., 1604 State St., Santa Barbara, CA 93101, (805)963-4864 [5559]

Chase Industries Inc., 5400 Renaissance Tower 1201 Elm St., Dallas, TX 75270 [16793]

Chase Oil Co. Inc., PO Box 1599, Florence, SC 29503, (803)662-1594 [22131]

Chase Supply Co., 12431 Vincennes Rd., Blue Island, IL 60406-1640, (773)785-0500 [14382]

Chase Trade, Inc., One Chase Manhattan Plaza, New York, NY 10081, (212)552-1264 [407]

Chateaux-Vineyards, 6009 Goshen Springs Rd., Norcross, GA 30071, (404)416-1880 [1590]

Chatfield Lumber Company Inc., 25 W 3rd St., Chatfield, MN 55923, (507)867-3300 [7169]

Chatham Created Gems Inc., 111 Maiden Ln., 5th Fl., San Francisco, CA 94108, (415)397-8450 [17366]

Chatham Imports Inc., 257 Park Ave. S, New York, NY 10010, (212)473-1100 [1591]

Chatham Steel Corp., PO Box 2567, Savannah, GA 31498, (912)233-4182 [19874]

Chatsworth Press, 9135 Alabama Ave., Ste. B, Chatsworth, CA 91311, (818)341-3156 [3626]

Chattanooga Manufacturing Inc., 1407 3rd Fl., New York, NY 10018, (212)921-1755 [4877]

Chattanooga Shooting Supplies, 2600 Walker Rd., Chattanooga, TN 37421, (423)894-3007 [23588]

Chazy Orchards Inc., 9486 Rte. 9, Chazy, NY 12921, (518)846-7171 [10736]

Cheatwood Oil Co., PO Box 208, Paden, OK 74860, (405)932-4455 [25900]

Checker Distributors, 400-B W Dussel Dr., Maumee, OH 43537, (419)893-3636 [26002]

Checkmate International, 1415 E 58th Ave., Denver, CO 80216, (303)292-1000 [26442]

Checkpoint International, PO Box 280883, East Hartford, CT 06128-0883, (860)724-1811 [18736]

Cheerleader Supply Co., 2010 Merritt Dr., Garland, TX 75041, (972)840-1233 [23589]

Cheese Importers Warehouse, PO Box 1717, Longmont, CO 80501, (303)443-4444 [10737]

Cheler Corp., PO Box 1750, Seattle, WA 98111-1750, (206)624-9699 [16794]

Chelsea Clock Co. Inc., 284 Everett Ave., Chelsea, MA 02150, (617)884-0250 [18737]

Chem-Central, PO Box 9188, Wyoming, MI 49509, (616)245-9111 [4348]

Chem Gro of Houghton Inc., PO Box 76, Houghton, IA 52631, (319)469-2611 [408]

Chem-Real Investment Corp., 12015 E 46th Ave., No. 460, Denver, CO 80239, (303)375-1203 [409]

Chem-Serv Inc., 715 SE 8th St., Minneapolis, MN 55414, (612)379-4411 [4349]

Chem-Tronics Inc., PO Box 627, Leavenworth, KS 66048-1097, (913)651-3930 [18738]

Chemapol USA Inc., 560 Sylvan Ave., Englewood Cliffs, NJ 07632, (201)816-1382 [4350]

CHEMCENTRAL Corp., PO Box 730, Bedford Park, IL 60499, (708)594-7000 [4351]

ChemDesign Corp., 99 Development Rd., Fitchburg, MA 01420, (978)345-9999 [4352]

Chemed Corp., 255 E 5th St., Cincinnati, OH 45202-4726, (513)762-6900 [4597]

Chemi-Trol Chemical Co., 2776 County Rd. 69, Gibsonburg, OH 43431, (419)665-2367 [410]

Chemical Associates of Illinois, Inc., 1270 S Cleveland Massillon Rd., Copley, OH 44321, (330)666-5200 [4353]

Chemical Associates Inc., 1270 S Cleveland Massillon Rd., Copley, OH 44321, (330)666-5200 [4353]

Chemical Export Company, Inc., 77 Summer St., Boston, MA 02210, (617)292-7773 [4354]

Chemical Sales Company Inc., 4661 Monaco St., Denver, CO 80216, (303)333-8511 [4355]

Chemical Waste Management Inc., 720 E Butterfield Rd., 2nd Fl., Lombard, IL 60148-5689, (630)218-1500 [26778]

Chemicals Inc., 270 Osborne Dr., Fairfield, OH 45014-2246, (513)682-2000 [4356]

Chemicraft Corp., 351 W 35th St., New York, NY 10001, (212)563-5278 [20897]

Chemins Company Inc., PO Box 2498, Colorado Springs, CO 80901, (719)579-9650 [19228]

Chemisolv Inc., 5200 Cedar Crest Blvd., Houston, TX 77087, (713)644-3797 [4357]

Chemoil Corp., 4 Embarcadero Ctr., Ste. 1800, San Francisco, CA 94111-5951, (415)268-2700 [22132]

Chemply Div., PO Box 18049, Pittsburgh, PA 15236, (412)384-5353 [4358]

Chemung Supply Corp., PO Box 527, Elmira, NY 14902, (607)733-5506 [16795]

Chemung Supply Corp., PO Box 527, Elmira, NY 14902, (607)733-5506 [19875]

Cheney Cooperative Elevator Association, PO Box 340, Cheney, KS 67025, (316)542-3181 [411]

Cheng & Tsui Company, 25 West St., Boston, MA 02111-1213, (617)988-2401 [3627]

Chermak Sausage Co., 2915 Calumet Ave., PO Box, Manitowoc, WI 54221-1267, (920)683-5980 [10738]

Cherney & Associates, Inc., 28910 Indian Valley Rd., Rancho Palos Verdes, CA 90275-4805, (310)541-6620 [18739]

Chernin Co.; Eugene, 1401 Germantown Ave., Philadelphia, PA 19122-3799, (215)235-2700 [26003]

Chernov Brothers Inc., 219 Larchwood Dr., Warwick, RI 02886-8551, (401)751-4910 [15442]

Cherokee Chemical Company Inc., 12600 S Daphne Ave., Hawthorne, CA 90250, (213)757-8112 [4598]

Cherokee Hosiery Mills, 208 35th NE, Ft. Payne, AL 35967-3953, (205)845-0004 [4878]

Cherry Central Cooperative Inc., PO Box 988, Traverse City, MI 49685-0988, (231)946-1860 [10739]

Cherry Central, Inc., PO Box 988, Traverse City, MI 49685-0988, (231)946-1860 [10739]

Cherry Farms Inc., PO Box 128, Lee, FL 32059, (850)971-5558 [412]

Cherry & Son; A.W., PO Box 3260, Bowling Green, KY 42102, (502)782-1902 [17776]

Cherry Sticks Inc., 1407 Broadway, No. 1503, New York, NY 10018, (212)947-9400 [4879]

Cherrybrook, PO Box 15, Rte. 57, Broadway, NJ 08808, (908)689-7979 [27109]

Chesal Industries, 6702 N Lake Dr., Milwaukee, WI 53217-3620, (414)228-7920 [23590]

Chesapeake Fish Company Inc., 535 Harbor Ln., San Diego, CA 92101, (619)238-0526 [10740]

Chesapeake Gun Works, 6644 Indian River Rd., Virginia Beach, VA 23464, (757)420-1712 [23591]

Chesapeake Medical Systems, 7 Cedar St., Cambridge, MD 21613, (410)228-0221 [18740]

Chesapeake Rim and Wheel Distributors, 2730 Dorr St., Fairfax, VA 22031, (703)560-4900 [2446]

Chesapeake Rim & Wheel Distributors Inc., 7601 Pulaski Hwy., Baltimore, MD 21237-2605, (410)866-3337 [2447]

Chesapeake Shoe Co. of California, 284 Harbor Way, South San Francisco, CA 94080, (650)873-1434 [24711]

Chesapeake Utilities Corp., 909 Silver Lake Blvd., Dover, DE 19904, (302)734-6799 [22133]

Chesbro Music Co., PO Box 2009, Idaho Falls, ID 83403, (208)522-8691 [25134]

Chess Business Forms Co., 25 Burnside St., PO Box 436, Nashua, NH 03061-0436, (603)889-1786 [21677]

Chesson and Sons Inc.; Mark, 101 Chesson Dr., Williamston, NC 27892, (919)792-1566 [413]

Chester Inc., PO Box 2237, Valparaiso, IN 46384, (219)462-1131 [414]

Chester Technical Services Inc., 47 Clapboard Hill Rd., Guilford, CT 06437-2200, (203)453-6209 [6062]

Chestnut Hill Farms Inc., 1500 Port Blvd., Miami, FL 33132, (305)530-4700 [10741]

Cheviot Corp., PO Box 34485, Los Angeles, CA 90034-0485, (310)836-4678 [25135]

Chevron Corp., PO Box 7753, San Francisco, CA 94120, (415)894-7700 [4359]

Chevron Industries, PO Box 7643, San Francisco, CA 94104, (415)894-7700 [22134]

Chew International Bascom Div., 495 River St., Paterson, NJ 07524, (973)345-1802 [15885]

Chicago Beer Distributing, 2064 W 167th St., Markham, IL 60426, (708)333-4360 [1592]

Chicago Case International, PO Box 584, Skokie, IL 60076, (847)674-9888 [18382]

Chicago Chain & Transmission, 650 E Plainfield Rd., PO Box 705, Countryside, IL 60525, (312)482-9000 [2448]

Chicago Combustion Corporation, 616 Hardwick St., PO Box 327, Belvidere, NJ 07823, (908)475-5315 [15201]

Chicago Communications Service Inc., 200 Spangler Ave., Elmhurst, IL 60126-1524, (312)585-4300 [5560]

Chicago Electric Co., 901 S Route 53, No. H, Addison, IL 60101, (630)495-2900 [8523]

Chicago Fish House Inc., 1455 W Willow St., Chicago, IL 60622-1525, (773)227-7000 [10742]

Chicago Furnace Supply Inc., 4929 S Lincoln, Lisle, IL 60532, (708)971-0400 [14383]

Chicago Hardwood Flooring, 509 S Vermont, Palatine, IL 60067, (847)991-9663 [9804]

Chicago Import Inc., 3311 W Montrose Ave., Chicago, IL 60618-1205, (773)588-3399 [13331]

Chicago Industrial Rubber, 862 Industrial Blvd., Elmhurst, IL 60126, (708)834-2950 [24273]

Chicago Machine Tool Co., 2150 Touhy Ave., Elk Grove Village, IL 60007, (708)364-4700 [15886]

Chicago Tube and Iron Co., 2531 W 48th St., Chicago, IL 60632, (312)523-1441 [19876]

Chick Master International Inc., 120 Sylvan Ave., PO Box 1250, Englewood Cliffs, NJ 07632, (201)947-8810 [415]

Chickasaw Distributors Inc., 800 Bering Dr., Ste. 330, Houston, TX 77057, (713)974-2905 [22135]

Chickasha Cotton Oil Co., PO Box 2710, Chandler, AZ 85244, (602)963-5300 [17777]

Chico Produce, Inc., PO Box 1069, Durham, CA 95938, (530)893-0596 [10743]

Chicopee Medical Supplies, 920 Front St., Chicopee, MA 01020-1724, (413)594-8383 [18741]

Chidvilas, Inc., PO Box 3849, Sedona, AZ 86340 [3628]

Chief Tonasket Growers, 437 S Railroad Ave., Tonasket, WA 98855-0545, (509)486-2914 [10744]

Chief Wenatchee, PO Box 1091, Wenatchee, WA 98807-1091, (509)662-5197 [10745]

Chiefs Discount Jewelers Inc., 1724 Post Rd., Warwick, RI 02888-5941, (401)737-4331 [17367]

Chihade International Inc., PO Box 451329, Atlanta, GA 31145, (404)292-5033 [10746]

Chikara Products Inc., 99-1245 Halawa Valley St., Aiea, HI 96701-3281, (808)486-3000 [10747]

Chilay Corp., 12881 166th St., Cerritos, CA 90703-2103, (714)632-9332 [10748]

Chilcote Co., 2160 Superior Ave., Cleveland, OH 44114, (216)781-6000 [22844]

Childers & Associates, 6800 W 115th St., Ste. 110, Overland Park, KS 66211, (913)345-8844 [15443]

Children's Art Corp., 6342 Myrtle Dr., Huntington Beach, CA 92647 [14062]

Children's Art Corp., 6342 Myrtle Dr., Huntington Beach, CA 92647 [19229]

Children's Media Center, Inc., 2878 Bayview Ave., Wantagh, NY 11793, (516)826-0901 [3629]

Children's Media Productions, PO Box 40400, Pasadena, CA 91114-7400, (626)797-5462 [25212]

Children's Small Press Collection, 719 N 4th Ave., Ann Arbor, MI 48104, (734)668-8056 [3630]

Childress Farm Service Inc., Rte. 1, PO Box 39, Linden, IN 47955, (765)339-7283 [1036]

Childress Oil Co.; W.R., 2729 NE 28th St., Ft. Worth, TX 76111, (817)834-1901 [22136]

Childs Oil Company Inc., PO Box 1417, Arcadia, FL 34265, (941)494-2605 [22137]

Chilis Footwear Inc., PO Box 1658, Santa Maria, CA 93456, (805)922-7753 [24712]

Chilli-O Frozen Foods Inc., 1251 Shermer Rd., Northbrook, IL 60062, (847)562-1991 [10749]

Chilton Co., 201 King of Prussia Rd., Radnor, PA 19087, (610)964-4000 [3631]

Chimera Co., 1812 Valtec Ln., Boulder, CO 80301, (303)444-8000 [22845]

China First Merchandising Co., 101 Fair Oaks Lane, Atherton, CA 94027, (650)327-7850 [10750]

China House Trading Co., 2040 Westlake Ave. N, Seattle, WA 98109, (206)283-1301 [16796]

China Trade Development Corp., 2049 Century Park E, Ste. 480, Los Angeles, 41400, 90067, (310)556-8091 [17232]

Chinatex America Inc., 209 W 40th St. 4th Fl., New York, NY 10018, (212)719-3250 [26004]

Chin's Import Export Co. Inc., 2035 NW Overton St., Portland, OR 97209, (503)224-4082 [10751]

Chip Supply Inc., 7725 N Orange Blossom, Orlando, FL 32810, (407)298-7100 [6063]

Chip & Wafer Office Automation, PO Box 17290, Honolulu, HI 96817-0290, (808)842-5146 [20898]

Chipita Accessories, 110 E 7th St., Walsenburg, CO 81089, (719)738-3991 [17368]

C.H.I.P.S., 10777 Mazoch Rd., Weimar, TX 78962-5022, (979)263-5683 [3632]

Chipwich Inc., PO Box 346, Piermont, NY 10968-0346 [10752]

Chiral Technologies Inc., PO Box 564, Exton, PA 19341, (610)594-2100 [24338]

Cho-Pat Inc., PO Box 293, Hainesport, NJ 08036, (609)261-1336 [18742]

Chock Full o'Nuts, 1455 E Chestnut Expy., Springfield, MO 65802, (417)869-5523 [10753]

Chock Inc.; Louis, 74 Orchard, New York, NY 10002-4515, (212)473-1929 [4880]

Chocolate Shoppe Ice Cream, 2221 Daniels St., Madison, WI 53701, (608)221-8640 [10754]

Chocolate Specialty Corp., 10308 Metcalf, Ste. 215, Overland Park, KS 66202, (913)941-3088 [10755]

Choe Meat Co., 2637 E Vernon Ave., Los Angeles, CA 90058, (213)589-5271 [10756]

Choice Books, 2387 Grace Chapel Rd., Harrisonburg, VA 22801, (540)434-1827 [3633]

Choice Brands, Inc., 310 Powell Ave., Monroe, LA 71211, (318)387-0432 [1593]

Choice Medical Distribution Inc., 9960 Corporate Campus Dr., Ste. 1000, Louisville, KY 40223, (502)357-6300 [6064]

Choice Medical Inc., 6311 Clearspring Rd., Baltimore, MD 21212-2602, (410)377-3753 [18743]

Choice Metals, 36 Cote Ave., Goffstown, NH 03045, (603)626-5500 [19877]

Chokio Equity Exchange Inc., PO Box 126, Chokio, MN 56221, (612)324-2477 [17778]

Choquette and Company Inc., PO Box 88, Seekonk, MA 02771, (508)761-4300 [15084]

Choquettes' Used Trucks & Equipment, 1230 Glendale Ave., Sparks, NV 89431, (775)358-1500 [15887]

Chori America Inc., 1180 Ave. of the Americas, New York, NY 10036, (212)563-3264 [26005]

Chris Cam Corp., 808 W Cherokee St., Sioux Falls, SD 57104, (605)336-1190 [21678]

Chrismann Computer Services Inc., 2601 W Dunlap Ave., Phoenix, AZ 85021, (602)395-1500 [6065]

Chrismann Computer Services Inc., 2601 W Dunlap Ave. Ste 15, Phoenix, AZ 85021, (602)249-2385 [6066]

Christ for the World, Inc., PO Box 3428, Orlando, FL 32802, (407)423-3172 [3634]

Christensen Electric Motor Inc., 2645 Lincoln Ave., Ogden, UT 84401, (801)392-5309 [8524]

Christensen Oil Co., 200 East 600 South, Provo, UT 84606, (801)373-7970 [22138]

Christhilf and Son Inc.; S.M., 7667 Pulaski Hwy., Baltimore, MD 21237-2669, (410)918-9770 [7733]

The Christian Broadcasting Network, Inc., 700 CBN Center, Virginia Beach, VA 23463, (757)424-7777 [3635]

Christian County Farmers Supply Co., PO Box 377, Taylorville, IL 62568, (217)824-2205 [416]

Christian Destiny Inc., 902 E D St., PO Box C, Hillsboro, KS 67063, (316)947-2345 [3636]

Christian Publications Inc., 3825 Hartzdale Dr., Camp Hill, PA 17011, (717)761-7044 [3637]

Christie Brothers Fur Corp., 333 7th Ave., New York, NY 10001, (212)736-6944 [4881]

Christmas Lumber Company Inc., 101 Roane St., PO Box 3, Harriman, TN 37748, (615)882-2362 [7170]

Christy Metals Company Inc., PO Box 8206, Northfield, IL 60093, (708)729-5744 [19878]

Christy Refractories Co. L.L.C., 4641 McRee Ave., St. Louis, MO 63110, (314)773-7500 [7171]

Chromaline Corp., 4832 Grand Ave., Duluth, MN 55807, (218)628-2217 [22846]

Chronister Oil Co., 2026 Republic Ave., Springfield, IL 62702, (217)523-5050 [22139]

Chronomix Corp., 650F Vaqueros Ave., Sunnyvale, CA 94086-3580, (408)737-1920 [24339]

CHS Electronics Inc., 2000 NW 84th Ave., Miami, FL 33122, (305)908-7200 [6067]

Chubb Security Systems Inc., 903 N Bowser, No. 250, Richardson, TX 75081, (972)690-4691 [24526]

Chubbuck Sales Inc., 3536 S Whitingham Dr., West Covina, CA 91792-2947, (909)869-0069 [13633]

Chula Farmers Cooperative, PO Box 10, Chula, MO 64635, (660)639-3125 [417]

Chulani International, PO Box 2844, Clifton, NJ 07015, (973)773-8100 [26443]

Church Business Machines, 7901 Earhart Blvd., Ste. F, New Orleans, LA 70125, (504)488-8763 [20899]

Church Doctor Resource Center, 1230 U.S Hwy. 6, PO Box 145, Corunna, IN 46730-0145, (219)281-2452 [3638]

Church Point Wholesale Groceries Inc., Hwy. 35 S, Church Point, LA 70525, (318)684-5413 [10757]

Churchich & Associates; Ely, 11818 Oakair Plz., Omaha, NE 68137-3509, (402)861-8880 [23592]

Churchich Recreation, 7174 Four Rivers Rd., Boulder, CO 80301, (303)530-4414 [23593]

Churchill Brothers, 1130 W Marine View Dr., Everett, WA 98201-1500, (425)259-3500 [18479]

Churchill Distributors, 7621 Energy Pkwy., Baltimore, MD 21226-1734, (410)536-5500 [1594]

Churchwell Co.; J.H., PO Box 1019, Jacksonville, FL 32201-1019, (904)356-5721 [4882]

Churny Company Inc., 2215 Sanders Rd., No. 550, Northbrook, IL 60062, (847)480-5500 [10758]

Churubusco Distribution Service Center, PO Box 245, Churubusco, IN 46723, (219)693-2111 [16797]

CIC Systems Inc., 2425 Crown Pointe Executive Dr., Charlotte, NC 28201-0000, (704)847-7800 [6068]

CILCORP Energy Services Inc., 300 Liberty St., Peoria, IL 61602, (309)672-5271 [24340]

Cimarron Corporation Inc., PO Box 5519, Greenville, SC 29606, (864)288-5475 [15888]

Cimarron Lumber and Supply Co., 4000 Main St., Kansas City, MO 64111, (816)931-8700 [7172]

Cimarron Lumber and Supply Co., 4000 Main St., Kansas City, MO 64111, (816)756-3000 [27297]

Cimarron Materials Inc., 901 S 12th St., Phoenix, AZ 85034-4124, (602)252-2525 [7173]

CIMID Corp., 50 S Center St., Orange, NJ 07050, (973)672-5000 [16798]

Cincinnati Bell Long Distance Inc., 36 E 7th St., Cincinnati, OH 45202, (513)369-2100 [5561]

Cincinnati Bell Supply Co., 6900 Steger Dr., Cincinnati, OH 45237, (513)361-9600 [5551]

Cincinnati Belt & Transmission, 737 W 6th St., Cincinnati, OH 45203, (513)621-9050 [2449]

Cincinnati Container Co., 5060 Duff Dr., Cincinnati, OH 45246, (513)874-6874 [25901]

Cincinnati Cordage and Paper Co., PO Box 17125, 800 E Ross Ave., Cincinnati, OH 45217, (513)242-3600 [21679]

Cincinnati Cordage and Paper Co. Cordage Papers Cleveland Div., 5370 Naiman Pkwy., Solon, OH 44139-1086, (216)349-1231 [21680]

Cincinnati Gasket Packing Manufacturing Inc., 40 Illinois Ave., Cincinnati, OH 45215, (513)761-3458 [16799]

Cincinnati Steel Products, 4540 Steel Pl., Cincinnati, OH 45209, (513)871-4444 [19879]

Cinderella Inc., 1215 S Jefferson St., Saginaw, MI 48601, (517)755-7741 [23594]

Cine 60 Inc., 630 9th Ave., New York, NY 10036, (212)586-8782 [25136]

Cinema Secrets Inc., 4400 Riverside Dr., Burbank, CA 91505, (818)846-0579 [14063]

Cinemills Corp., 3500 W Magnolia Blvd., Burbank, CA 91505, (818)843-4560 [8525]

Cinti Floor Co., 5162 Broerman Ave., Cincinnati, OH 45217, (513)641-4500 [9805]

Cinti Floor Co., 5162 Broerman Ave., Cincinnati, OH 45217, (513)641-4500 [15444]

Circle Food Products Inc., 3959 Lockridge St., San Diego, CA 92102-4507, (619)263-8000 [10759]

Circle Glass Co., 8801 Fenkell, Detroit, MI 48238-1797, (313)931-5900 [7174]

Circle Produce Co., 2360 M. L. King Ave., Calexico, CA 92231-1737, (760)357-5454 [10760]

Circleville Oil Co., PO Box 189, Circleville, OH 43113, (614)474-7544 [22140]

Cirelli Foods Inc., 970 W Chestnut St., Brockton, MA 02301, (508)584-6700 [24092]

Cirrus Technology Inc., PO Box 1126, Nashua, NH 03061-1126, (603)882-2619 [6069]

CIS Corp., 6619 Joy Rd., East Syracuse, NY 13057-1107, (315)432-1642 [6070]

Cisco Cooperative Grain Inc., PO Box 69, Cisco, IL 61830, (217)669-2141 [17779]

Cisco-Eagle, Inc., 2120 Valley View Ln., Farmers Branch, TX 75234-8911, (972)406-9330 [25902]

Cisco Electrical Supply Co., 883 King Ave., Columbus, OH 43212, (614)299-6606 [8526]

Cisco Material Handling Inc., 2120 Valley View Ln., Farmers Branch, TX 75234-8911, (972)406-9330 [25902]

Cissna's Sporting Goods Inc., 1026 Clarks Ln., PO Box 17051, Louisville, KY 40217-0051, (502)636-1885 [23595]

CISU of Dalton, Inc., 5102 Middlebrook Pl., Knoxville, TN 37921-5908, (423)584-1854 [9806]

Cities Supply Company Inc., PO Box 309, Sumter, SC 29151, (803)775-7355 [23115]

Citifax Corp., 28427 N Ballard Dr., Lake Forest, IL 60045, (847)362-3300 [20900]

Citizen America Corp., PO Box 4003, Santa Monica, CA 90411-4003, (310)453-0614 [6071]

Citizen Watch Company of America Inc., 1200 Wall St. W, Lyndhurst, NJ 07071, (201)438-8150 [17369]

Citizen's Distributors, 377 Pine St., Burlington, VT 05401, (802)865-6992 [4360]

Citra Trading Corp., 590 5th Ave., New York, NY 10036, (212)354-1000 [17370]

Citrus Trading Inc., 1400 Smith St., Ste. 3902, Houston, TX 77002, (713)853-6569 [22141]

City Animation Co., 57 Park St., Troy, MI 48083-2753, (248)589-0600 [25137]

City Beverage Co., Box 432, Defiance, OH 43512-0432, (419)782-7065 [1595]

City Beverage Co., PO Box 1036, Elizabeth City, NC 27909, (919)330-5539 [1596]

City Beverage Inc., 1103 Riverside Dr., Huntington, IN 46750, (219)356-6910 [1597]

City Beverages, PO Box 620006, Orlando, FL 32862-0006, (407)851-7100 [1598]

City Bottling Company Inc., 1820 5th Ave., Arnold, PA 15068, (724)335-3350 [24926]

City Business Machines Inc., 2201 Brockwood Dr., Ste. 112, Little Rock, AR 72202, (501)663-4044 [20901]

City Coal of New London Inc., 410 Bank St., New London, CT 06320, (860)442-4321 [22142]

City Electric Motor Co., 631 Kennedy Rd., Lexington, KY 40511-1821, (859)254-5581 [8527]

City Market Inc., PO Box 729, Grand Junction, CO 81502, (970)241-0750 [10761]

City Meat & Provisions Company, Inc., 2721 W Willetta, Phoenix, AZ 85009-3501, (602)269-7717 [10762]

City Metal Company Inc., 279 Jenckes Hill Rd., Smithfield, RI 02917-1905 [26779]

City One Stop, 2551 S Alameda, Los Angeles, CA 90058-1309, (213)234-3336 [25138]

City Optical Company Inc./Division of The Tavel Optical Group, 2839 Lafayette Rd., Indianapolis, IN 46222-2147, (317)924-1300 [19230]

City Plumbing & Electrical Supply, 206 College Ave. SE, Gainesville, GA 30501-4512, (404)532-4123 [8528]

City Provisioners Inc., PO Box 2246, Daytona Beach, FL 32115, (904)673-2443 [10763]

City Sound, 4925 E Firestone Blvd., South Gate, CA 90280, (213)563-1173 [25139]

City and Suburban Delivery Systems East, 4725 34th St., Long Island City, NY 11101, (718)349-5378 [3639]

City-Wide Discount Office Supply, Inc., 2655 W Georgia Ave., Phoenix, AZ 85017-2728, (602)242-2200 [20927]

Citywide Floor Service, 4011 E 138 St., Grandview, MO 64030, (816)842-3151 [9807]

CJ Cattle Co. Inc., PO Box 3177, Butte, MT 59702-3177, (406)494-2670 [17780]

CJC Holdings Inc., PO Box 149056, Austin, TX 78714-9056, (512)444-0571 [17371]

CJW Inc., 2437 Chicory Rd., Racine, WI 53403, (414)554-4288 [24927]

CK Associates, PO Box 23127, Lexington, KY 40523, (859)266-2171 [15445]

CK Footwear Inc., 1935 Revere Beach Pky., Everett, MA 02149-5945, (781)307-5005 [24713]

C.L. Industries Inc., PO Box 593704, Orlando, FL 32854-3704, (407)851-2660 [7175]

Clack Corp., PO Box 500, Windsor, WI 53598, (608)251-3010 [25601]

Claesson Co., PO Box 326, Union, SC 29379-0326, (864)363-5059 [26006]

Claeys and Co.; H.L., 31239 Mound Rd., Warren, MI 48090, (810)264-2561 [23116]

Claflin Co., 1070 Willett Ave., East Providence, RI 02915, (401)437-1870 [19231]

Claiborne Farmers Cooperative, PO Box 160, New Tazewell, TN 37824-0160, (423)626-5251 [418]

Claitor's Publishing Division, 3165 S Acadian at Interstate 10, PO Box 261333, Baton Rouge, LA 70826-1333, (504)344-0476 [3640]

Clamor Impex Inc., 214 NE 1st St., Miami, FL 33132, (305)379-1701 [17372]

Clampitt Paper Co., 9207 Ambassador Row, Dallas, TX 75247, (214)638-3300 [21681]

Clamyer International Corp., 55 Northern Blvd., Great Neck, NY 11021, (516)504-9292 [21413]

Clancy, Jr.; Arthur V., 625 S Gay St., Knoxville, TN 37902-1608, (423)523-4161 [19232]

Clapper's Building Materials Inc., PO Box 335, Meyersdale, PA 15552, (814)634-5931 [13069]

Claprood Co.; Roman J., 242 N Grant Ave., Columbus, OH 43215, (614)221-5515 [14841]

Clare Computer Solutions Inc., 2580 San Ramon Valley Blvd., Ste. B-107, San Ramon, CA 94583, (925)277-0690 [6072]

Clarence Cooperative Company Inc., 619 Lombard St., Clarence, IA 52216, (319)452-3805 [419]

Clarence House Imports Ltd., 211 E 58th St., New York, NY 10021, (212)752-2890 [21414]

Clarenie Cooperative Elevator Co., 29434 Allen Grove Rd., Dixon, IA 52745, (319)843-2115 [420]

Claricom Inc., 850 Dubuque Ave., South San Francisco, CA 94080, (650)952-2000 [8529]

Clarins USA Inc., 110 E 59th St., New York, NY 10022-1304, (212)980-1800 [14064]

Clarion Corporation of America, 661 W Redondo Beach Blvd., Gardena, CA 90247, (310)327-9100 [5562]

Clarion Farmers Elevator Cooperative, PO Box 313, Clarion, IA 50525, (515)532-2881 [421]

Clarion Sales Corp., 661 W Redondo Beach Blvd., Gardena, CA 90247, (310)327-9100 [2450]

Clark Brothers, 1006 James Madison Hwy., Warrenton, VA 20186-7820, (703)439-8988 [13481]

Clark Brothers Instrument Co., 56680 Mound Rd., Shelby Township, MI 48316, (810)781-7000 [2451]

Clark Chevrolet Co.; Charles, PO Box 938, McAllen, TX 78502, (956)686-5441 [20611]

Clark; Clayton H., RFD 3 Box 1900, Skowhegan, ME 04976, (207)474-5825 [17781]

Clark County Bar & Restaurant Supply, 1117 S Commerce St., Las Vegas, NV 89102-2526, (702)382-6762 [24093]

Clark County Wholesale Inc., PO Box 2018, Las Vegas, NV 89125-2018, (702)382-7700 [2452]

Clark Food Service Inc., 950 Arthur Ave., Elk Grove Village, IL 60007, (708)956-1730 [10764]

Clark Food Service Inc. South Bend Div., 1901 Bendix Dr., South Bend, IN 46628, (219)234-5011 [24094]

Clark; Frank, 202 Mustang Ct, Gambrills, MD 21054-1133, (410)551-9815 [6073]

Clark Implement Company Inc.; H.C., PO Box 1158, Aberdeen, SD 57402, (605)225-8170 [422]

Clark Inc.; C.C., PO Box 966, Starkville, MS 39760, (601)323-4317 [3641]

Clark Landmark Inc., PO Box 687, Springfield, OH 45501, (937)323-7536 [423]

Clark Ltd.; Vivian, 12111 The Apparel Center, Chicago, IL 60654, (312)222-1120 [4883]

Clark and Mitchell Inc., 7820 Bluffton Rd., Ft. Wayne, IN 46809, (219)747-7431 [9808]

Clark Productions Inc.; Dick, 3003 W Olive Ave., Burbank, CA 91510-7811, (818)841-3003 [8530]

Clark Sales Co., PO Box 900398, Sandy, UT 84093, (801)942-7021 [17373]

Clark-Schwebel Distribution Corp., PO Box 25, Arlington, WA 98223, (253)435-5501 [7176]

Clark-Schwebel Distribution Corp., PO Box 3448, Santa Fe Springs, CA 90670, (562)921-9926 [22943]

Clark Seafood Company Inc., 4401 Clark St., Pascagoula, MS 39567, (601)762-4511 [10765]

Clark Supply Co., PO Box 24, Falconer, NY 14733, (716)665-4120 [13634]

Clarke and Bro. Inc.; E.H., 3272 Winbrook Dr., Memphis, TN 38116, (901)398-5700 [20902]

Clarke Detroit Diesel-Allison Inc., 3133 E Kemper Rd., Cincinnati, OH 45241, (513)771-2200 [2453]

Clarke Distributors Inc., PO Box 624, Keene, NH 03431, (603)352-0344 [1599]

Clarklift Corporation of Indiana, 6902 E 32nd St., Indianapolis, IN 46226, (317)545-6631 [15889]

Clarklift of Dalton Inc., PO Box 1045, Dalton, GA 30722-1045, (706)278-1104 [15890]

Clarklift of Detroit Inc., PO Box 487, Troy, MI 48099, (248)528-2100 [15891]

Clarklift of Minnesota Inc., 501 W 78th St., Bloomington, MN 55420, (952)887-5400 [15892]

Clark's Carpet Connection, 7450 Montgomery Rd., Plain City, OH 43064, (614)873-6108 [9809]

Clarks Distributing Co., PO Box 33294, Charlotte, NC 28233, (704)375-4456 [14384]

Clark's Gun Shop, 1006 James Madison Hwy., Warrenton, VA 20186-7820, (703)439-8988 [13481]

Clarks Petroleum Service Inc., 7846 Oxbow Rd., Canastota, NY 13032, (315)697-2278 [22143]

Clark's Store Fixtures Inc., 1830 S Dort Hwy., Flint, MI 48503, (810)239-4667 [4599]

Clark's Wholesale Tire Co., 3578 Sweeten Creek Rd., Arden, NC 28704, (828)681-8100 [2454]

Clarkson Co. Inc.; R.J., 4436 Augusta Rd., Lexington, SC 29073-7945, (803)356-4710 [15085]

Clarksville Pharmacy Inc., 602 McKennon St., Clarksville, AR 72830-3524, (501)754-8402 [18744]

Classic Beauty Supplies, Glenmont Shopping Ctr., 12335 E Georgia Ave., Wheaton, MD 20906, (301)946-2223 [14065]

Classic Beauty Supply and Service Center, Glenmont Shopping Ctr., 12335 E Georgia Ave., Wheaton, MD 20906, (301)946-2223 [14065]

Classic Beauty Supply and Service Center, Glenmont Shopping Ctr., Wheaton, MD 20906, (301)946-2223 [24095]

Classic City Beverages Inc., PO Box 549, Athens, GA 30603, (706)353-1650 [1600]

Classic Components Corp., 23605 Telo Ave., Torrance, CA 90505-4028, (310)217-8020 [6074]

Classic Components Supply Inc., 3336 Commercial Ave., Northbrook, IL 60062, (708)272-9650 [8531]

Classic Designs, 35 Angell Rd., Lincoln, RI 02865-4708, (401)725-8083 [13070]

Classic Flooring Distributors, PO Box 11706, Roanoke, VA 24022-1706, (804)329-4150 [9810]

Classic Fragrances Ltd., 132 W 36th St., New York, NY 10018, (212)929-2266 [14066]

Classic Optical Inc., 21177 Hilltop St., Southfield, MI 48034, (248)358-5895 [19233]

Classic Sales Inc., 1754 Hoe St., Honolulu, HI 96819-3124, (808)845-0122 [24714]

Classic Tile, Inc., PO Box 6680, Elizabeth, NJ 07206-1999, (908)289-8400 [9811]

Classic Wine Imports Inc., 1356 Commonwealth Ave., Boston, MA 02134, (617)731-6644 [1601]

Classroom Reading Service, 9830 Norwalk Blvd., Ste. 174, Santa Fe Springs, CA 90670, (562)906-1366 [3642]

Clausen Distributing, PO Box 238, Helena, MT 59624, (406)442-2675 [1602]

Clausing Industrial Inc., 1819 N Pitcher St., Kalamazoo, MI 49007, (616)345-7155 [15893]

Clauss Cutlery Co., 225 Riverview Ave., Waltham, MA 02454, (781)647-5560 [15446]

Clay Cass Creamery, 200 N 20th, Fargo, ND 58102, (701)293-6455 [10766]

Clay Classics Inc., 763 Waverly St., Framingham, MA 01702, (508)875-0055 [7177]

Clay Ingels Company Inc., PO Box 2120, Lexington, KY 40594-2120, (606)252-0836 [7178]

Clay Tile Products; Allen, 7301 Georgetown Rd., Ste. 213, Indianapolis, IN 46268-4128, (317)872-5980 [9812]

Clayhill, 141 S Lafayette Rd., St. Paul, MN 55107, (651)290-0000 [5836]

Claymont Communications, RR 1 Box 279, CharLes Town, WV 25414-9765, (304)725-1523 [3643]

Claymore Sieck Co., 311 E Chase St., Baltimore, MD 21202, (410)685-4660 [13635]

Clayton Tile, PO Box 6151, Greenville, SC 29607, (864)288-6290 [9813]

Clean Green Packing Company of Minnesota, 720 Florida Ave., Golden Valley, MN 55426-1704, (612)545-5400 [25903]

Clean Seal, PO Box 2919, South Bend, IN 46680-2919, (219)299-1888 [16800]

Clean Water Systems International, 2322 Marina Dr., Klamath Falls, OR 97601, (541)882-9993 [25602]

Clear Eye, 302 Route 89 S, Savannah, NY 13146, (315)365-2816 [10767]

Clear Optics Inc., 430 Alta Vista St., No. 1, Santa Fe, NM 87505-4104, (505)983-5075 [19234]

Clear Springs Foods Inc., 1500 E 4424 N, Buhl, ID 83316, (208)543-4316 [10768]

CLEARVUE, 6465 N Avondale, Chicago, IL 60631, (773)775-9433 [3644]

Clearwater Grain Co., PO Box 427, Clearwater, KS 67026, (316)584-2011 [424]

Cleasby Manufacturing Company Inc., 1414 Bancroft Ave., San Francisco, CA 94124, (415)822-6565 [7179]

Cleco Industrial Fasteners, Inc., 16701 Lathrop, Harvey, IL 60426-6029, (708)339-3600 [13636]

Clegg Seafood International, PO Drawer C, Port Lavaca, TX 77979, (512)552-3761 [10769]

Clem Lumber Distributing Company Inc., 16055 NE Waverly Ave., Alliance, OH 44601, (216)821-2130 [7180]

Clem Wholesale Grocer Co. Inc., PO Box 666, Malvern, AR 72104, (501)332-5406 [10770]

Clement and Muller Inc., 2800 Grand Ave., Philadelphia, PA 19114, (215)676-7575 [1603]

Clemmons Corp., PO Box 4697, Wilmington, NC 28406, (910)763-3131 [16801]

Clemons Tractor Co., PO Box 7707, Ft. Worth, TX 76111, (817)834-8131 [425]

Clerf Equipment Inc., 228 Beachwood Ln., Panama City, FL 32413-2791 [426]

Clermont Inc., HCO1, Box 117, Hudson, NY 12534, (518)537-6251 [24928]

Clermont Lumber Co., 105 Water St., Milford, OH 45150, (513)831-2226 [7181]

Cleveland Brothers Equipment Company Inc., PO Box 2535, Harrisburg, PA 17105, (717)564-2121 [7182]

Cleveland Electric Motors, 2536 W Dixon Blvd., Shelby, NC 28152, (704)484-0186 [8532]

Cleveland Hobby Supply, PO Box 33034, Cleveland, OH 44133, (440)237-3900 [26444]

Cleveland Plant and Flower Co., 2419 E 9th St., Cleveland, OH 44115, (216)241-3290 [14842]

Cleveland Plywood Co., 5900 Harvard Ave., Cleveland, OH 44105, (216)641-6600 [7183]

Cleveland Reclaim Industries Inc., 7450 A Industrial Pk., Lorain, OH 44053, (440)282-8008 [4718]

CLG Inc., 3001 Spring Forest Rd., Raleigh, NC 27604, (919)872-7920 [6075]

Click Bond Inc., 2151 Lockheed Way, Carson City, NV 89706, (702)885-8000 [70]

Click Bond Inc., 2151 Lockheed Way, Carson City, NV 89706, (702)885-8000 [13637]

Clifford of Vermont Inc., Rte. 107, Box 51, Bethel, VT 05032, (802)234-9921 [8533]

Clifton Grain Inc., PO Box 293, Chebanse, IL 60922-0293, (815)694-2397 [17782]

Climate Technologies, 43334 W 7 Mile Rd., Northville, MI 48167-2280, (248)380-2020 [14385]

Climatic Control Company Inc., 5061 W State St., Milwaukee, WI 53208, (414)259-9070 [14386]

Climatic Corp., PO Box 25189, Columbia, SC 29224-5189, (803)736-7770 [14387]

Clinical Homecare Corp. Haemotronic Ltd., 45 Kulick Rd., Fairfield, NJ 07004, (201)575-0614 [19235]

Clintec Nutrition Co., 3 Pkwy. N, No. 500, Deerfield, IL 60015, (847)317-2800 [19236]

Clinton AG Service Inc., PO Box 24228, Clinton, MN 56225, (320)325-5203 [427]

Clinton Gas Marketing Inc., 4770 Indianola Ave., Columbus, OH 43214, (614)888-9588 [6076]

Clinton Landmark Inc., PO Box 512, Wilmington, OH 45177, (513)382-1633 [17783]

Clipper Energy Supply Co., 2900 Weslayan, Ste. 600, Houston, TX 77027, (713)965-0006 [7184]

Clipper International Trading Co., 2900 Weslayan, Ste. 600, Houston, TX 77027, (713)965-0006 [7184]

Clipper Products, 675 Cincinnati-Batavia Pike, Cincinnati, OH 45245, (513)528-7011 [18383]

Clipper Quality Seafood, Inc., 3502 Gulfview Ave., Marathon, FL 33050-2341, (305)743-3637 [10771]

Clique, 1031 S Broadway, No. 934, Los Angeles, CA 90015-4006, (213)747-4120 [4982]

Clisby Agency Inc., 4300 H St., Philadelphia, PA 19124, (215)535-3900 [16802]

Clofine Dairy and Food Products Inc., PO Box 335, Linwood, NJ 08221, (609)653-1000 [10772]

Closet Centers America, 6700 Distribution Dr., Beltsville, MD 20705-1401, (301)595-4100 [15447]

Closet City Ltd., 619 Bethlehem Pke., PO Box 779, Montgomeryville, PA 18936-0779, (215)855-4400 [15448]

Cloud Brothers Inc., 1617 N Bendix Dr., South Bend, IN 46628-2836, (219)289-0395 [15086]

Clougherty Packing Co., PO Box 58870, Los Angeles, CA 90058, (213)583-4621 [10773]

Cloutier Supply Co., 445 W Main St., Hyannis, MA 02601, (508)775-6100 [22944]

Clover Auto Supply Inc., 412 S 9th, Lincoln, NE 68508-2217, (402)474-1741 [2455]

Clover Leaf Ice Cream, 16 E 11th, Newport, KY 41071-2110, (606)431-7550 [10774]

Cloverdale Equipment Co., 13133 Cloverdale, Oak Park, MI 48237-3272, (248)399-6600 [7185]

Cloverdale Foods Company Inc., PO Box 667, Mandan, ND 58554, (701)663-9511 [10775]

Cloverhill Pastry-Vending Inc., 2020 N Parkside Ave., Chicago, IL 60639-2991, (312)745-9800 [10776]

Cloverleaf Farms Distributors Inc., 13835 S Kostner Ave., Crestwood, IL 60445, (708)597-2200 [10777]

Clovis Livestock Auction, PO Box 187, Clovis, NM 88102-0187, (505)762-4422 [17784]

CLS, 270 Locust St., Hartford, CT 06141-0179, (860)549-1230 [8534]

CLS, 270 Locust St., Hartford, CT 06141-0179, (860)549-1230 [8535]

Club Chef, 800 Bank St., Cincinnati, OH 45214, (513)562-4200 [10778]

Clute Office Equipment Inc., PO Box 1745, Minot, ND 58702-1745, (701)838-8624 [20903]

Clyde Cooperative Association, PO Box 86, Medford, OK 73759, (580)395-3341 [428]

Clydes Corner Electronics, 15796 E 14th St., San Leandro, CA 94578, (510)276-8739 [25140]

C.M. Paula Co., 6049 HiTech Ct., Mason, OH 45040, (513)336-3100 [21682]

CM School Supply, 1025 E Orangethorpe Ave., Anaheim, CA 92801-1135, (714)680-6681 [26445]

CMA Incorporated, 904 Kohou St., Ste. 308, Honolulu, HI 96817, (808)841-8011 [10779]

CMA International, 7515 Topton St., Ste. 100, New Carrollton, MD 20784, (301)577-9340 [15894]

CMC America Corp., 210 S Center St., Joliet, IL 60436, (815)726-4336 [25603]

CMC America Corp., 210 S Center St., Joliet, IL 60436, (815)726-4336 [24096]

CMC Recycling Div., PO Box 1046, Dallas, TX 75221, (214)689-4300 [26780]

CMC Secondary Metals Processing Div., PO Box 1046, Dallas, TX 75221, (214)689-4300 [26780]

CMH Flooring Products Inc., Hwy. 74 E, Wadesboro, NC 28170, (704)694-6213 [9814]

CMH Flooring Products Inc., Hwy. 74 E, Wadesboro, NC 28170, (704)694-6213 [7186]

CMOV, Inc., 100 S Marion Rd., Sioux Falls, SD 57107, (605)338-6645 [6077]

CMP Industries Inc., PO Box 350, Albany, NY 12201, (518)434-3147 [18745]

CMS Casuals Inc., 13200 SE 30th St., Bellevue, WA 98005-4403, (425)643-5270 [4884]

CMS Communications Inc., 715 Goddard Ave., Chesterfield, MO 63005-1106, (314)530-1320 [5563]

CMT Sporting Goods Co., 3475 Brandon Ave. SW, Roanoke, VA 24018-1521, (540)343-5533 [23596]

CMV Software Specialists Inc., 100 S Marion Rd., Sioux Falls, SD 57107, (605)338-6645 [6077]

CNEAD Division, 1 Jacques St., Worcester, MA 01603-1901, (508)755-0840 [2456]

Co-HG, 116 Misner, Mingo, Colby, KS 67701, (785)462-2033 [429]

Co-op Country Farmers Elevator, PO Box 604, Renville, MN 56284, (612)329-8377 [17785]

Co-op Country Farmers Elevator, PO Box 604, Renville, MN 56284, (320)329-8377 [10780]

Co-Sales Co., PO Box 551, Phoenix, AZ 85001, (602)254-5555 [10781]

C.O. Tools Inc., 25837 Borg Rd., PO Box 988, Elkhart, IN 46515, (219)262-1527 [2457]

Coach House Products, 484 Main St., West Chicago, IL 60185-2864, (630)231-5770 [2458]

Coachmen Industries Inc. Coachmen Vans Div., PO Box 50, Elkhart, IN 46515, (219)262-3474 [20612]

Coach's Connection Inc., PO Box 1123, Huntington, IN 46750-4138, (219)356-0400 [23597]

Coal Bunkers, 270 Illinois St., Fairbanks, AK 99701, (907)456-5005 [20529]

Coal Hill Mining Co., 405 Virginia Ave., Pittsburgh, PA 15215, (412)782-1814 [20530]

CoalARBED International Trading Co., 210 E Lombard St., Baltimore, MD 21202, (410)727-4600 [20531]

Coast Air Inc., 11134 Sepulveda Blvd., Mission Hills, CA 91345, (818)898-2288 [71]

Coast Appliance Parts Co., 2606 Lee Ave., South el Monte, CA 91733, (626)579-1500 [15087]

Coast Counties Truck and Equipment Co., 1740 N 4th St., San Jose, CA 95112, (408)453-5510 [2459]

Coast Cutlery Co., PO Box 5821, Portland, OR 97228, (503)234-4545 [15449]

Coast Distributing Co., PO Box 80758, San Diego, CA 92138, (619)275-4600 [1604]

Coast Distribution, 1400 N Fiesta Blvd., Gilbert, AZ 85234, (602)497-0083 [18480]

Coast Distribution, PO Box 1449, Morgan Hill, CA 95038-1449, (18481]

Coast Distribution, 175 Greenfield Rd., Lancaster, PA 17601 [18482]

Coast Distribution System, 1982 Zanker Rd., San Jose, CA 95112, (408)436-8611 [2460]

Coast Grain Company Inc., 5355 E Airport Dr., Ontario, CA 91761-0961, (909)390-9766 [430]

Coast Marine, 7133 Burns, Ft. Worth, TX 76118, (972)247-9080 [18483]

Coast Marine Distribution, 230A Kelsey Ln., Tampa, FL 33619, (813)622-7427 [18484]

Coast Paper Box Co., 4650 Ardine St., Cudahy, CA 90201, (213)771-8772 [21683]

Coast Shoes Inc., 13401 Saticoy St., North Hollywood, CA 91605-3413, (818)786-0717 [4885]

Coast Wholesale Music, 1215 W Walnut St., PO Box 5686, Compton, CA 90224-5686, (310)537-1712 [25266]

Coast Wholesale Music, PO Box 5686, Compton, CA 90224-5686, (310)537-1712 [25141]

Coast Wholesale Music Co., 1381 Calais Ave., Livermore, CA 94550-6019, (510)796-3487 [25142]

Coast Wire and Plastic Tech Inc., 1510 W 135th St., Gardena, CA 90249, (310)327-5260 [8536]

Coastal Berry Company, 480 W Beach St., Watsonville, CA 95076-4510, (408)724-1366 [10782]

Coastal Beverage Company Inc., PO Box 10159, Wilmington, NC 28405, (910)799-3011 [1605]

Coastal Chemical Co., LLC, PO Box 820, Abbeville, LA 70511-0820, (337)898-0001 [4412]

Coastal Distributors, Inc., PO Box 358, South Boston, MA 02127-0913, (781)749-7130 [18485]

Coastal Electronics Inc., PO Box 12007, New Bern, NC 28561, (919)637-3167 [5564]

Coastal Energy Co., PO Box 1269, Gulfport, MS 39502-1269, (228)863-0041 [2461]

Coastal Engineering Corp., PO Box 23526, New Orleans, LA 70183-0526, (504)733-8511 [22144]

Coastal Engineering Equipment Sales LLC, PO Box 23526, New Orleans, LA 70183-0526, (504)733-8511 [22144]

Coastal Equipment Inc., 4871 Commerce Dr., Trussville, AL 35173-2810, (205)849-5786 [7187]

Coastal Fuels Marketing Inc., PO Box 025500, Miami, FL 33102-5500, (305)551-5200 [22145]

Coastal Gas Services Co., Nine Greenway Plz., Houston, TX 77046, (713)877-1400 [22146]

Coastal Industries Inc., 3700 St. Johns Industrial Pkwy. W, PO Box 16091, Jacksonville, FL 32245, (904)642-3970 [23117]

Coastal International Inc., 29 Water St., Newburyport, MA 01950-2763, (978)462-0993 [6100]

Coastal Net Marine Co., 23 Battle Rd., Brunswick, ME 04011, (207)725-1052 [23598]

Coastal Oil New York Inc., PO Box 818, Hasbrouck Heights, NJ 07604, (201)393-9494 [22147]

Coastal Plains Farmers Co-op Inc., PO Box 590, Quitman, GA 31643, (912)263-7564 [431]

Coastal States Trading, 9 E Greenway Plz, Houston, TX 77046, (713)877-1400 [22148]

Coastal Supply Company Inc., 407 Harmon St., Savannah, GA 31401, (912)233-9621 [14388]

Coastal Supply Co., Inc., 8650 Argent St., Santee, CA 92071, (619)562-8880 [25604]

Coastal Tile & Roofing Co., Inc., 307 S Richardson, PO Box 638, Latta, SC 29565, (803)752-5851 [9815]

Coaster Company of America, 12928 Sandoval St., Santa Fe Springs, CA 90670-4061, (562)944-7899 [13071]

Coastline Distributing, 4120 NW 10th Ave., Oakland Park, FL 33309-4601, (954)776-4811 [14389]

Coastline Distribution Inc., 601 Codisco Way, Sanford, FL 32771, (407)323-8500 [14390]

Coastline Parts Co., 818 Snow Hill Rd., Salisbury, MD 21801, (410)742-8634 [15088]

Coates Optical Lab Inc., PO Box 20200, Montgomery, AL 36125, (205)288-2021 [19237]

Coaxis Inc. Insight Distribution Systems, 222 Schilling Cir., Ste. 275, Hunt Valley, MD 21031, (410)329-1158 [6078]

Cobb Optical Lab Inc., 78 NW 37th St., Miami, FL 33127, (305)576-1700 [19238]

Cobb Rock Div., 21305 SW Koehler Rd., Beaverton, OR 97007, (503)649-5661 [7188]

Cobb Rock Inc., 21305 SW Koehler, Beaverton, OR 97007, (503)649-5661 [7189]

Cobra Electronics Corp., 6500 W Cortland St., Chicago, IL 60707, (773)889-8870 [5565]

Cobra Electronics Corp., 6500 W Cortland St., Chicago, IL 60707, (773)889-8870 [8537]

Coburn Supply Co. Inc., PO Box 2177, Beaumont, TX 77704, (409)838-6363 [23118]

Coca-Cola Aberdeen, PO Box 38, Aberdeen, SD 57402-3308, (605)225-6780 [24929]

Coca-Cola Bottlers of Detroit Inc., 880 Doris Rd., Auburn Hills, MI 48326, (248)373-2653 [24930]

Coca-Cola Bottling Co., 69 N Chadbourne St., San Angelo, TX 76903, (915)655-6991 [24931]

Coca-Cola Bottling Co. of California, 7901 Oakport St., Oakland, CA 94621, (510)638-5001 [24932]

Coca-Cola Bottling Co.; Coast, PO Drawer E, Gulfport, MS 39502, (228)864-1122 [24933]

Coca-Cola Bottling Co. Consolidated, PO Box 31487, Charlotte, NC 28231, (704)551-4400 [24934]

Coca-Cola Bottling Co. of Lincoln, 1200 King Bird Rd., Lincoln, NE 68521-3008, (402)475-3749 [24935]

Coca-Cola Bottling Co. of Manchester, 99 Eddy Rd., Manchester, NH 03102, (603)623-6033 [24936]

Coca-Cola Bottling Co.; Meridian, PO Box 5207, Meridian, MS 39302-5207, (601)483-5272 [24937]

Coca-Cola Bottling Company of Mobile Inc., PO Box 190129, Mobile, AL 36619, (205)666-2410 [24938]

Coca-Cola Bottling Company of New York Inc., 375 Wireless Blvd., Smithtown, NY 11787, (516)849-8200 [24939]

Coca-Cola Bottling Company of Shreveport, 305 Stoner Ave., Shreveport, LA 71101-4154, (318)429-0205 [24940]

Coca-Cola Bottling Company of Virginia, 832 17th St. N, Virginia, MN 55792, (218)741-7690 [24941]

Coca-Cola Bottling; Dixie, 1913 W State St., Bristol, VA 24201, (540)669-3124 [24942]

Coca-Cola Bottling Works Inc.; Valdosta, PO Box 189, Valdosta, GA 31603, (912)242-6325 [24943]

Coca-Cola Bottling Works; Lexington, 10 Front St., Lexington, TN 38351, (901)968-3636 [24944]

Coca-Cola Co., PO Box 1500, Cortaro, AZ 85652-0529, (520)744-1333 [24945]

Coca-Cola; Johnston, PO Box 50338, Knoxville, TN 37950-0338 [24946]

Coca-Cola of Northern Arizona, PO Box 2848, Flagstaff, AZ 86003-2848, (520)526-2239 [24947]

Coca-Cola; Pacific, 9705 E Montgomery, Spokane, WA 99206, (509)921-6200 [24948]

Coca-Cola; Pacific, 3333 S 38th St., Tacoma, WA 98409, (253)474-9567 [24949]

Coca-Cola Pocatello, PO Box 607, Pocatello, ID 83204, (208)232-0762 [24950]

Coca-Cola Twin Falls Bottling Co., Box 86, Twin Falls, ID 83303-0086, (208)733-3833 [3645]

Cochran Brothers Cash & Carry, PO Box 370, Dublin, GA 31040, (912)272-5144 [10783]

Cochrane Supply and Engineering, Inc., 30303 Stephenson Hwy., Madison Heights, MI 48071-1633, (248)588-9260 [14391]

Cockcroft Co., 333 Waterman Ave., East Providence, RI 02914, (401)438-3650 [2393]

Cocke Farmers Cooperative Inc., PO Box 309, Newport, TN 37821, (423)623-2331 [432]

Coclin Tobacco Corp., 290 Boston Post Rd., Milford, CT 06460, (203)877-0341 [26276]

Cocoa Barry U.S., 1500 Suckle Hwy., Pennsauken, NJ 08110-1432, (609)663-2260 [10784]

Cocoa Brevard Paper Co., 105 Forrest Ave., Cocoa, FL 32922, (407)632-8200 [21684]

Codale Electric Supply Inc., PO Box 651418, Salt Lake City, UT 84165, (801)263-3000 [8538]

COE Distributing, Inc., Franklin Commercial Park, Rte. 51 N, Uniontown, PA 15401, (724)437-8202 [20904]

Coen Oil Co. Inc., 1100 W Chestnut St., Washington, PA 15301, (412)225-1300 [22149]

Coeur d'Alene Cash & Carry, 1114 N 4th St., Coeur D Alene, ID 83814-3217, (208)765-4924 [10785]

Cofer Brothers Inc., 2300 Main St., Tucker, GA 30084, (404)938-3200 [7190]

Coffee Bean International Inc., 2181 NW Nicolai St., Portland, OR 97210, (503)227-4490 [10786]

Coffee Mill Roastery, 161 E Franklin St., Chapel Hill, NC 27514, (919)929-1727 [10787]

Coffey and Sons Inc.; Bill, Rte. 16, Ashmore, IL 61912, (217)349-8338 [433]

Coffin Turbo Pump Inc., PO Box 9833, Englewood, NJ 07631, (201)568-4700 [15895]

Cofil Inc., PO Box 657, Naples, TX 75568, (903)897-5467 [7191]

Cofish International Inc., PO Box 242, East Haddam, CT 06423, (860)873-9500 [24715]

COFSCO Inc., 291 Branstetter St., Wooster, OH 44691, (216)264-2131 [22150]

Cogan Books, 15020 Desman Rd., La Mirada, CA 90638, (562)941-5017 [3646]

Cogdells Westview Inc., 615 N Valley Mills, Waco, TX 76710, (254)772-8224 [13482]

Cognex Corp., 2060 Challenger Dr., Alameda, CA 94501-1037, (510)749-4000 [15896]

Cohan Berta Showroom, 214 W 39th St., Ste. 1003, New York, NY 10018, (212)840-0600 [4886]

Cohen and Company Inc.; Herman, 401 Broadway, Ste. 7048, New York, NY 10013, (212)925-0613 [26007]

Cohen Ltd.; Paula, 498 7th Ave., New York, NY 10018, (212)947-8252 [4887]

COI, PO Box 7, Hudson, NH 03051, (603)889-2116 [22848]

Coil Center Corp., 1415 Durant Dr., Howell, MI 48843, (517)548-0100 [19880]

Coil Plus Pennsylvania Inc., 5135 Milnor St. & Bleigh St., Philadelphia, PA 19136, (215)331-5200 [19881]

Coil Sales and Manufacturing Co., 5600 Apollo Dr., Rolling Meadows, IL 60008, (847)806-6300 [5566]

Coins, Cards & Collectibles, 8128 Girard Plz, Omaha, NE 68122-1455, (402)968-5973 [26446]

Coker International Trading Inc., PO Box 443, Sandy Springs, SC 29677, (864)287-5000 [15897]

Colco Fine Woods and Tools Inc., PO Box 820449, Memphis, TN 38182-0449, (901)452-9663 [7192]

Colco Fine Woods and Tools Inc., PO Box 820449, Memphis, TN 38182-0449, (901)452-9663 [27298]

Cold Headers Inc., 5514 N Elston Ave., Chicago, IL 60630, (773)775-7900 [13638]

Cold Spring Cooperative Creamery, 301 1st St. S, PO Box 423, Cold Spring, MN 56320, (320)685-8651 [434]

Cole Brothers and Fox Co., 252 Yandell Ave., Canton, MS 39046, (601)859-1414 [26277]

Cole Hardwood Inc., PO Box 568, Logansport, IN 46947, (219)753-3151 [7193]

Cole Papers Inc., PO Box 2967, 1300 38th St NW, Fargo, ND 58108-2967, (701)282-5311 [21685]

Cole-Parmer Instrument Co., 625 E Bunker Ct., Vernon Hills, IL 60061-1844, (847)647-7600 [24341]

Cole Productions Inc.; Kenneth, 152 W 57th St., New York, NY 10019, (212)265-1500 [24716]

Cole Wholesale Flooring, 1300 38th St. NW, PO Box 2967, Fargo, ND 58108-2967, (701)282-5311 [9816]

Coleman; Dr. Ernest A., 293 Janes Ln., Stamford, CT 06903-4822, (203)329-3693 [22945]

Coleman Electric Company Inc., 222 Hamilton St, Allentown, PA 18101, (610)434-4881 [8539]

Coleman Equipment Inc., PO Box 456, Bonner Springs, KS 66012, (913)422-3040 [7194]

Coleman Industrial Supply Inc., 1331 Industrial Way, PO Box 1516, Longview, WA 98632-1017, (206)425-3620 [13639]

Coleman Interior Service Co., 3233 Rhode Island Ave., Mt. Rainier, MD 20712, (301)699-0730 [15450]

Coleman Lumber Inc., 4144 Bellamy 21, Rte. 1, Box 23, Livingston, AL 35470, (205)652-1132 [7195]

Coleman Natural Products Inc., 5140 Race Ct. Ste. 4, Denver, CO 80216, (303)297-9393 [10788]

Coleman Oil Co. Inc., PO Box 2009, Pikeville, KY 41502, (606)432-1476 [22151]

Coleman Powermate Inc., PO Box 6001, Kearney, NE 68848-6001, (308)237-2181 [8540]

Coleman's Ice Cream, 2195 Old Philadelphia Pke., Lancaster, PA 17601, (717)394-8815 [10789]

Colette Malouf Inc., 594 Broadway, New York, NY 10012, (212)941-9588 [14067]

Colgate-Palmolive Co. Institutional Products Div., 191 E Hanover Ave., Morristown, NJ 07962-1905, (973)631-9000 [4600]

Colie Sailmakers, 1649 Bay Ave., Point Pleasant, NJ 08742, (732)892-4344 [18486]

Colin Electric Motor Services, 520 W O St., Lincoln, NE 68528, (402)476-2121 [8541]

Colladay Hardware Co., PO Box 766, Hutchinson, KS 67504, (316)663-4477 [23119]

The Collection, 2500 E 195th St., Belton, MO 64012, (816)322-2122 [3660]

College Bowl Inc., 333 W Baltimore St., Baltimore, MD 21201-2512, (410)685-0661 [4888]

Collingwood Grain Inc., PO Box 2150, Hutchinson, KS 67504-2150, (316)663-7121 [435]

Collins Appliance Parts Inc., 1533 Metropolitan St., Pittsburgh, PA 15233, (412)321-3700 [15089]

Collins & Associates; Paul, 1700 E Garry Ave., Ste. 101, Santa Ana, CA 92705-5828, (949)833-9949 [8542]

Collins Communications Inc., 1009 W Jackson St., Demopolis, AL 36732-1617, (334)289-0439 [8543]

Collins Communications Systems Co., 2920 Centre Pointe Dr., Roseville, MN 55113, (651)634-1800 [5636]

Collins; James, PO Box 478, Milton, VT 05468-0478, (802)893-4746 [7196]

Collins Landing, 10 Miles SW, Dent, MN 56528, (218)758-2697 [23599]

Colombian Development Corp., 194 Melba St., Staten Island, NY 10314-5335, (718)494-6034 [8544]

Colombo Baking Co., 1329 Fee Dr., Sacramento, CA 95815, (916)648-1011 [10790]

Colombo, Inc., PO Box 1113, Minneapolis, MN 55440-1113, (612)797-8866 [10791]

Colonial Baking Co., 3310 Panthersville, Decatur, GA 30034, (404)284-7477 [10792]

Colonial Beef Co., 3333 S 3rd St., Philadelphia, PA 19148, (215)467-0900 [10793]

Colonial Braided Rug Co., 4345 W Dixon Blvd., Mooresboro, NC 28114, (704)434-6922 [9817]

Colonial Brick Co., 12844 Greenfield, Detroit, MI 48227, (313)272-2160 [7197]

Colonial Distributors Inc., PO Box 378, Waterville, ME 04903-0378, (207)873-1143 [1606]

Colonial Electric Distributor, 417 Jeff Davis Hwy., Fredericksburg, VA 22401-3118, (703)373-8404 [9527]

Colonial Electric Supply Company Inc., 485 S Henderson Rd., King of Prussia, PA 19406, (610)312-8100 [8545]

Colonial Floors Inc., 117 Waverly St., Framingham, MA 01702-7127, (508)875-5521 [9818]

Colonial Hardware Corp., 163 Varick St., New York, NY 10013, (212)741-8989 [13640]

Colonial Hardware Corp., 163 Varick St., New York, NY 10013, (212)741-8989 [16803]

Colonial Hospital Supply Co. Inc., 555 Oakwood Rd., Lake Zurich, IL 60047, (847)438-2900 [19239]

Colonial Medical Supplies, 915 S Orange Ave., Orlando, FL 32806, (407)849-6455 [18746]

Colonial Office Supplies Inc., 21710 Great Mills Rd., PO Box 250, Lexington Park, MD 20653-0250, (301)862-2760 [20905]

Colonial Oil Industries Inc., PO Box 576, Savannah, GA 31402, (912)236-1331 [22152]

Colonial Shoe Co., PO Box 43001, Atlanta, GA 30336-0001, (404)691-4141 [24717]

Colony Lumber Co., 1083 Mentor Ave., Painesville, OH 44077, (440)352-3351 [7198]

Colony Papers Inc., 1776 Stanley Dr., York, PA 17404, (717)764-5088 [21686]

Color Brite Fabrics and Displays Inc., 212 E 8th St., Cincinnati, OH 45202, (513)721-4402 [25605]

Color Group, 6822 Del Monte Ave., Richmond, CA 94805, (510)237-5577 [6079]

Color Me Beautiful Inc., 14000 Thunderbolt Pl., Ste. E, Chantilly, VA 20151, (703)471-6400 [14068]

Color Spot Nurseries Inc., 3478 Buskirk Ave., Pleasant Hill, CA 94523, (925)934-4443 [14843]

Colorado Clarklift Inc., 4105 Globeville Rd., Denver, CO 80216, (303)292-5438 [15898]

Colorado Commercial Refrigeration, 12445 Mead Way, Littleton, CO 80125-9759, (303)791-7878 [14392]

Colorado Electronic Hardware Inc., 4975 Iris St., Wheat Ridge, CO 80033, (303)431-4334 [8546]

Colorado Kenworth Inc., 4901 York St., Denver, CO 80216, (303)292-0833 [20613]

Colorado Potato Growers Exchange, 2401 Larimer St., Denver, CO 80205, (303)292-0159 [10794]

Colorado Prime Foods, 500 BI County Blvd., Ste. 400, Farmingdale, NY 11735-3996, (516)694-1111 [15090]

Colorado Seeds, PO Box 16025, Denver, CO 80216, (303)320-7500 [254]

Colorado Serum Co., PO Box 16428, Denver, CO 80216, (303)295-7527 [19240]

Colorado Wire and Cable Company Inc., 485 Osage St., Denver, CO 80204, (303)534-0114 [8547]

Colorcon, Moyer Blvd., West Point, PA 19486, (215)699-7733 [20906]

Colossal Jewelry and Accessories Inc., 217 Hergesell Ave., Maywood, NJ 07607, (201)556-0202 [17374]

Colossal Jewelry and Accessories Inc., 406 N Midland Ave., Saddle Brook, NJ 07663, (201)794-6533 [17375]

Colton Piano and Organ, 1405 W Valley Blvd., Colton, CA 92324, (909)825-5537 [13072]

Columbia Audio-Video Inc., 1741 2nd St., Highland Park, IL 60035, (847)433-6010 [8548]

Columbia Bean & Produce Co., Inc., 2705 Rd. O, PO Box 122, Moses Lake, WA 98837, (509)765-8893 [10795]

Columbia Beauty Supply Co., PO Box 32786, Charlotte, NC 28232-2786, (704)845-2888 [14069]

Columbia Diagnostics Inc., 1127 International Pky., No. 201, Fredericksburg, VA 22406-1142, (703)569-7511 [18747]

Columbia Distributing Co., PO Box 17195, Portland, OR 97217-0195, (503)289-9600 [1607]

Columbia Distributing Co./Henry Hirsdale/Admiralty Beverage Co., PO Box 17195, Portland, OR 97217-0195, (503)289-9600 [1607]

Columbia Farms, PO Box 827, Florence, SC 29503, (803)667-0096 [12006]

Columbia Impex Corp., 16112-A NW 13th Ave., Miami, FL 33169-5748, (305)625-0511 [18384]

Columbia Iron and Metal Co., 6600 Grant Ave., Cleveland, OH 44105, (216)883-4972 [19882]

Columbia Jobbing Co. Inc., 1702 5th Ave., Tampa, FL 33605-5116, (813)248-4142 [21687]

Columbia National Group Inc., 6600 Grant Ave., Cleveland, OH 44105, (216)883-4972 [19883]

Columbia News Agency Inc., 135 Warren, Hudson, NY 12534-3118, (518)828-1017 [3647]

Columbia Packing Co. Inc., 2807 E 11th St., Dallas, TX 75203-2010, (214)946-8171 [10796]

Columbia Paint & Coatings, 9275 South 700 East, Sandy, UT 84070, (801)561-7117 [21415]

Columbia Paint Co., 641 Jackson Ave., Huntington, WV 25728, (304)529-8070 [21416]

Columbia Pipe and Supply, 1120 W Pershing Rd., Chicago, IL 60609, (312)927-6600 [14393]

Columbia Sportswear Co., 6635 N Baltimore Ave., Portland, OR 97203-5402, (573)887-3681 [4889]

Columbia Ventures Corp., 1220 Main St. Ste. 200, Vancouver, WA 98660, (360)693-1336 [19884]

Columbine International, 5441 Merchant Cir., Placerville, CA 95667, (530)622-2791 [15899]

Columbus Distributing Co., 4949 Freeway Dr. E, Columbus, OH 43229-5401, (614)846-1000 [1608]

Columbus Fair Auto Auction Inc., PO Box 32490, Columbus, OH 43232, (614)497-2000 [20614]

Columbus Hardware Supplies Inc., 944 W 5th Ave., Columbus, OH 43212, (614)294-8665 [13641]

Columbus Metals Supply Inc., 302 7th Ave. S, Columbus, MS 39701, (601)329-3889 [19885]

Columbus Paper Company Inc., PO Box 6369, Columbus, GA 31995-1699, (706)689-1361 [4601]

Columbus Pipe and Equipment Co., 773 E Markison Ave., Columbus, OH 43207, (614)444-7871 [23120]

Columbus Serum Co., 2025 S High St., Columbus, OH 43207, (614)444-1155 [27110]

Columbus Steel Drum Co., 1385 Blatt Blvd., Blacklick, OH 43004, (614)864-1900 [25904]

Columbus Tractor Machinery Co., PO Box 2407, Columbus, GA 31902, (706)687-0752 [436]

Columbus Wallcovering Co., 2301 Shermer Rd., Northbrook, IL 60062, (708)882-7474 [15451]

Colusa Elevator Company Inc., PO Box 26, Colusa, IL 62329, (217)755-4221 [17786]

Colvard Oil Company Inc., 317 S Jefferson Ave., West Jefferson, NC 28694, (919)246-4231 [22153]

Colwell Cooperative, PO Box 605, Charles City, IA 50616, (515)228-3123 [17787]

Com-Kyl, 7939 SW Cirrus Dr., Beaverton, OR 97005, (503)626-6633 [8549]

Com-Kyl, 41444 Christy St., Fremont, CA 94538, (510)979-0070 [16847]

Comanche Lumber Company Inc., 2 SW C Ave., Lawton, OK 73501, (580)357-8630 [7199]

Comark Inc., 444 Scott Dr., Bloomingdale, IL 60108, (630)351-9700 [6080]

Combined Metals of Chicago L.P., 2401 W Grant St., Bellwood, IL 60104, (708)547-8800 [19886]

Combined Sales Co., PO Box 3, North Salt Lake, UT 84054, (801)936-7302 [26447]

Comdisco Inc., 6111 N River Rd., Rosemont, IL 60018-5159, (847)698-3000 [6081]

Comer Inc., PO Box 410305, Charlotte, NC 28241, (704)588-8400 [15900]

Comer Packing Company Inc., PO Box 33, Aberdeen, MS 39730, (601)369-9325 [13332]

Comer Packing Company Inc., PO Box 33, Aberdeen, MS 39730, (601)369-9325 [10797]

Comet Industries Inc., 4800 Deramus, Kansas City, MO 64120, (816)245-9400 [15901]

Comet Micro Systems Inc., 1301 Grandview Dr., South San Francisco, CA 94080, (650)615-9123 [6082]

Cometals Inc., 1 Penn Plz., Ste. 4330, New York, NY 10119, (212)760-1200 [4361]

Comex International, PO Box 545, Driggs, ID 83422-0545, (208)354-8801 [13073]

Comfort Mart Dist. Inc., 520 Congress St., Troy, NY 12180, (518)272-2022 [14394]

Comfort Shoe Corp., PO Box 1360, Haverhill, MA 01831-1860, (978)373-0133 [24718]

Comfort Supply Inc., 3500 S Hoover Rd., Wichita, KS 67215, (316)945-8268 [14395]

Comfort Supply Inc., PO Box 262806, Houston, TX 77207, (713)845-4705 [14396]

Comfortmaker Distribution, 601 Codisco Way, Sanford, FL 32771, (407)323-8500 [14397]

Comics Hawaii Distributors, 4420 Lawehana St., Apt. 3, Honolulu, HI 96818, (808)423-0265 [26448]

Comics Unlimited, 28 Yacht Club Cv, Staten Island, NY 10308-3531, (718)948-2223 [26449]

Comlink Inc., 1052 Melody Ln., No. 280, Roseville, CA 95678, (916)783-8885 [6083]

Comlink Inc. (Marlborough, Massachusetts), 295 Donald Lynch Blvd., Marlborough, MA 01752-4702, (508)460-7800 [5567]

Comlink Inc. (Roseville, California), 1052 Melody Ln., No. 280, Roseville, CA 95678, (916)783-8885 [8550]

Command Computer Maintenance, PO Box 3051, Springfield, MA 01101-3051, (413)782-9900 [6084]

Command Electronics Inc., 10100 Crosstown Cir., Eden Prairie, MN 55344-3302, (612)943-1598 [6085]

Command Technology Inc., 404 Thames St., Groton, CT 06340-3959, (860)445-0156 [6086]

Command Uniforms, 4545 Malsbary Rd., Cincinnati, OH 45242-5624 [4890]

Commecial de Azulejos, Ave. Hostos 131, Ponce, PR 00731, (787)844-0888 [9819]

Commerce Consultants Inc., 6815 Bradley Ave., Cleveland, OH 44129, (440)845-5682 [22154]

Commerce Overseas Corp., 200 Saw Mill River Rd., Hawthorne, NY 10532, (914)773-2100 [72]

Commerce Packaging Corp., 850 Canal St., Stamford, CT 06904, (203)327-4200 [21688]

Commercial Alloys Corp., 1831 Highland Rd., Twinsburg, OH 44087-2222, (330)405-5440 [19887]

Commercial Art Supply, 935 Erie Blvd. E, Syracuse, NY 13210, (315)474-1000 [25606]

Commercial Aviation Support Inc., 8550 W Flagler St., Ste. 101, Miami, FL 33144-2037, (305)594-0084 [73]

Commercial Body Corp., 5601 Edith NE, Albuquerque, NM 87107, (505)344-8411 [2462]

Commercial Body Corp., 1005 Commercial Blvd. S, Arlington, TX 76017, (817)467-1005 [2463]

Commercial Body Corp., 10800 Northwest Fwy., Houston, TX 77092-7304, (713)688-7990 [2464]

Commercial Body Corp., PO Box 1119, San Antonio, TX 78219, (210)476-7777 [2465]

Commercial Body Corp., PO Box 1119, San Antonio, TX 78294, (210)224-1931 [15902]

Commercial Body Corp., 6010 Milwee, Houston, TX 77092, (713)688-7990 [2466]

Commercial Dishwashers, 5001 NE 82nd Ave., Portland, OR 97220-4928, (503)284-3449 [15091]

Commercial Distributing Co., PO Box 1476, Westfield, MA 01086, (413)562-9691 [1609]

Commercial Electric Products Corp., 1738 E 30th St., Cleveland, OH 44114-4408, (216)241-2886 [8551]

Commercial Equipment & Design, Inc., 904 E 16th St., Wilmington, DE 19802, (302)656-7752 [14398]

Commercial Furniture Services Inc., PO Box 24220, Houston, TX 77029-4220, (713)673-2100 [13074]

Commercial and Industrial Design Co. Inc., 1711 Langley Ave., Irvine, CA 92614-5621, (949)261-5524 [6087]

Commercial Interior Decor, 3205 W Sencore Dr., Sioux Falls, SD 57107-0728, (605)334-9288 [25607]

Commercial Laminations, 2801 Murfreesboro Rd., Antioch, TN 37013, (615)361-0000 [13075]

Commercial Laundry Sales, PO Box 391, Bozeman, MT 59771-0391, (406)587-5148 [4602]

Commercial/Medical Electronics, PO Box 690206, Tulsa, OK 74169-0206, (918)749-6151 [18748]

Commercial Metals Co., 7800 Stemmons Frwy., Dallas, TX 75247-4227, (214)689-4300 [19888]

Commercial Metals Co. Commercial Levin Div., PO Box 30, Burlington, NC 27216, (336)584-0333 [26781]

Commercial Motor Co., 160 S Commercial St., Aransas Pass, TX 78336, (512)758-5361 [20615]

Commercial Motors, 2101 Auiki St., Honolulu, HI 96819-2254, (808)845-6421 [2467]

Commercial Music Co. Inc., 1550 Edison St., Dallas, TX 75207, (214)741-6381 [25608]

Commercial Office Interiors Inc., 2601 4th Ave., Ste. 100, Seattle, WA 98121, (206)448-7333 [13076]

Commercial Office Supply Inc., 11822 N Creek Pkwy. N, Ste. 109, Bothell, WA 98011, (425)485-6900 [20907]

Commercial Plamar, 1175 Ave. Emerito Estrada, San Sebastian, PR 00685, (787)896-2735 [9820]

Commercial Plastics and Supply Corp., 543 NW 77th St., Boca Raton, FL 33487, (561)994-0076 [22946]

Commercial Plastics and Supply Inc., 9831 Jamaica Ave., Richmond Hill, NY 11418, (718)849-9000 [22947]

Commercial Refrigeration Inc., 15870 Yoder Ave., Caldwell, ID 83605-8342, (208)454-3031 [14399]

Commercial Shelving, 2835 Ualena St., Honolulu, HI 96819-1911, (808)836-3811 [25905]

Commercial Telephone Systems Inc., 3531 Griffin Rd., Ft. Lauderdale, FL 33312, (954)981-2586 [5568]

Commercial Washer Dryer Sales Co., PO Box 2858, Gaithersburg, MD 20886-2858, (301)258-9030 [15092]

Commercial Waste Paper Company Inc., PO Box 3583, El Monte, CA 91733-0583, (626)448-6649 [26782]

Commodity Specialists Co., 301 4th Ave., 780 Grain Exchange Bldg., Minneapolis, MN 55415, (612)330-9889 [17788]

Commodity Steel and Processing Inc., PO Box 3758, Center Line, MI 48015-0758, (810)758-1040 [19889]

Common Equipment Co., PO Box 988, Peoria, IL 61603, (309)672-9300 [15903]

Common Ground Distributors Inc., 115 Fairview Rd., Asheville, NC 28803, (828)274-5575 [3648]

Common Health Foods, 1505 N 8th St., Superior, WI 54880-6610, (715)392-9862 [10798]

Common Health Warehouse Cooperative Association, 1505 N 8th St., Superior, WI 54880-6610, (715)392-9862 [10798]

Commonwealth Films Inc., 223 Commonwealth Ave., Boston, MA 02116, (617)262-5634 [25143]

Commonwealth Metal Corp., 560 Sylvan Avenue, PO Box 1426, Englewood Cliffs, NJ 07632-0426, (201)569-2000 [19890]

Commonwealth Oil Co. Inc., 2328 Lakeside Dr., Lynchburg, VA 24501, (804)385-5140 [22155]

Commonwealth Tool Specialty Inc., PO Box 20039, Roanoke, VA 24018-0502, (540)989-4368 [16804]

Commtron Corporation, 11103 E 53rd Ave., Denver, CO 80239, (303)371-8372 [25248]

Commtron Corporation, 405 Murray Hill Pkwy., Ste. 2020, East Rutherford, NJ 07073, (201)933-9797 [25144]

Commtron Corp., 12600 SE Highway 212 Bldg. B, Clackamas, OR 97015-9081, (503)281-2673 [25245]

Communications Electronics Inc., 9494 Deereco Rd., Timonium, MD 21093-2102, (410)252-1222 [5569]

Communications Electronics Inc., Emergency Operations Center, PO Box 2797, Ann Arbor, MI 48106-2797, (734)996-8888 [5570]

Communications Marketing S.E. Inc., PO Box 823, Marietta, GA 30061, (404)424-9097 [5571]

Communications Products Inc., PO Box 509125, Indianapolis, IN 46250, (317)576-0332 [5572]

Communications Products and Services Inc., 1740 W Warren Ave., Englewood, CO 80110, (303)922-4519 [8552]

Communications Wholesale, 17541 15th Ave. NE, Seattle, WA 98155, (206)364-6410 [5573]

Communications World of Costa Mesa, 1278 Glenneyre St., Ste. 218, Laguna Beach, CA 92651, (714)491-1174 [5574]

Communico Inc., 1710 N Hercules Ave., Ste. 111, Clearwater, FL 33764, (727)447-8145 [5575]

Communico Inc. Communico Supply Div., 1710 N Hercules Ave., Clearwater, FL 33765-1100, (813)442-8143 [5576]

Community Coffee Company Inc., PO Box 791, Baton Rouge, LA 70821, (504)291-3900 [10799]

Community Coffee Company Inc., PO Box 791, Baton Rouge, LA 70821, (504)291-3900 [10800]

Community Coffee Company LLC, PO Box 791, Baton Rouge, LA 70821, (504)291-3900 [10800]

Community Cooperative Oil Association, PO Box 665, Essig, MN 56030, (507)354-5490 [22156]

Community Oil Company Inc., PO Box 400, Charles Town, WV 25414, (304)725-7021 [22157]

Community Suffolk Inc., 304 2nd St., Everett, MA 02149, (617)389-5200 [10801]

Community Tire Co. Inc., 1307 N 7th St., St. Louis, MO 63147, (314)241-3737 [2468]

Como Sales Co., Inc., 799 Broadway, New York, NY 10003, (212)677-1720 [3649]

ComoTec, 5130 Commercial Dr., Ste. E, Melbourne, FL 32940-7175, (407)638-4244 [19241]

Compact Performance Inc., 931 Hartz Way, Danville, CA 94526-3413, (510)831-1050 [2469]

The Company Logo Inc., PO Box 5042, Winston-Salem, NC 27113-5042, (336)722-6016 [4891]

Compar Inc., 70 E 55th St., New York, NY 10022, (212)980-9620 [14070]

Compar, Inc., 10301 Yellow Cir. Dr., Minnetonka, MN 55343-9101, (612)945-0300 [6088]

Compass Concepts, 2220 E Artesia Blvd., Long Beach, CA 90805, (562)422-6992 [9821]

Compass Foods Eight O'Clock Coffee, 2 Paragon Dr., Montvale, NJ 07645, (201)573-9700 [10802]

Compass Technology of Burlington Massachusetts, 111 S Bedford St., Burlington, MA 01803, (781)272-9990 [8553]

Compassion Book Service, 477 Hannah Branch Rd., Burnsville, NC 28714, (828)675-9670 [3650]

Compcom Enterprises Inc., 3185 Birchfield Trce, Marietta, GA 30068-3810, (404)971-6288 [6089]

Competition Karting Inc., PO Box 1777, Welcome, NC 27374-1777, (336)731-6111 [23600]

Competition Parts Warehouse Inc., 1140 Campbell Ave., San Jose, CA 95126, (408)243-3400 [2470]

Competitive Edge, 41806 Ford Rd., Canton, MI 48187-3600, (734)981-8104 [6090]

Compex Inc. (Anaheim, California), 4051 E La Palma Ave., Ste. A, Anaheim, CA 92807, (714)630-7302 [6091]

Complete Auto & Truck Parts, 4510 Broadway Blvd. SE, Albuquerque, NM 87105-7404, (505)877-5960 [2471]

Complete Computer Solutions of New England, 31 Syracuse Rd., Nashua, NH 03060-1752, (603)880-0482 [6092]

Complete Golf Services Co., 2410 W Evans Dr., Phoenix, AZ 85023, (602)863-1233 [23601]

Complete Medical Products Inc., 2052 N Decatur Rd., Decatur, GA 30033, (404)728-0010 [18749]

Complete Medical Products Inc., 2052 N Decatur Rd., Decatur, GA 30033, (404)728-0010 [19242]

Complete Medical Supplies Inc., 10 Ford Products Rd., Valley Cottage, NY 10989, (914)353-0434 [19243]

Complete Office Solutions Inc., 600 Meridian Ave., San Jose, CA 95126, (408)275-9700 [13077]

Complex Steel Wire Corp., 36254 Annapolis, Wayne, MI 48184-2044, (734)326-1600 [19891]

Compol Inc., 415 Campbell Mill Rd., Mason, NH 03048-4902, (603)878-3458 [25145]

Component Resources Inc., 14525 SW Walker Rd., Beaverton, OR 97006-5921, (503)641-8488 [8554]

Component Technology, 1225 Illinois St., Des Moines, IA 50314, (515)244-7411 [15904]

Component Technology, 3303 Washington Blvd., St. Louis, MO 63103, (314)535-7411 [15905]

Component Technology, 200 Indiana Ave., Toledo, OH 43624, (419)243-7411 [15906]

Components & Equipment International, 849 W Main St., PO Box 903, Kent, OH 44240, (330)673-8886 [15907]

Components Specialties Inc., PO Box 726, Amityville, NY 11701-0726, (516)957-8700 [25146]

Components West, 6658 Hwy. 89, Ogden, UT 84405, (801)479-1997 [13642]

Compool Corp., 599 Fairchild Dr., Mountain View, CA 94043, (650)964-2201 [23602]

Composite Engineering Inc., 277 Baker Ave., Concord, MA 01742, (978)371-3132 [18487]

Composite Technology Inc., 1001 Avenue R., Grand Prairie, TX 75050-1506, (972)556-0744 [74]

Compotite Corp., 355 Glendale Blvd., Los Angeles, CA 90026, (213)483-4444 [7200]

Comprehensive Systems Inc., PO Box 760, Evergreen, CO 80439-0760, (303)697-9798 [6093]

Comprehensive Video Group, 55 Ruta Ct., South Hackensack, NJ 07606, (201)229-4270 [25092]

Comprehensive Video Group, 55 Ruta Ct., South Hackensack, NJ 07606, (201)229-0025 [22847]

CompuCom Systems Inc., 7171 Forest Ln., Dallas, TX 75230-2306, (972)856-3600 [6094]

Compucon Distributors Inc., 701-1 Koehler Ave., Ronkonkoma, NY 11779, (516)981-8810 [6095]

CompuData Inc., 10501 Drummond Rd., Philadelphia, PA 19154, (215)824-3000 [6096]

CompuLink Electronic Inc., 875 Ave. of the Amer., No. 2411, New York, NY 10001, (212)695-5465 [8555]

Compusol Inc., 2832-C Walnut Ave., Tustin, CA 92780, (714)734-1990 [6097]

Compusolve, 1135 Terminal Way, Ste. 108, Reno, NV 89502-2145, (702)324-6995 [6098]

Compusystems Inc. South Carolina, PO Box 4739, Rock Hill, SC 29732-6739, (803)366-8904 [6099]

Computalabel International Ltd., 29 Water St., Newburyport, MA 01950-2763, (978)462-0993 [6100]

Computer AC, 721 Chaney, Collierville, TN 38017-2993, (901)854-5951 [5577]

Computer Banking Inc., 4994 Waterport Way, Duluth, GA 30096-2927, (404)448-2990 [6101]

Computer Brokers of Kentucky, 2006 High Ridge Rd., Louisville, KY 40207-1126, (502)897-1829 [6102]

Computer Clearing House Inc., 246 Commerce Dr., Rochester, NY 14623, (716)334-0550 [6103]

Computer Commodities Inc., 7161 Shady Oak Rd., Eden Prairie, MN 55344-3737, (612)942-0992 [6104]

Computer Concepts Inc., PO Box 338, White River Junction, VT 05001-0338, (802)295-3089 [6105]

Computer Corner Inc., 4700 San Mateo Blvd. NE, Albuquerque, NM 87109-2422, (505)296-8424 [6106]

Computer Craft Co., 119 North Rd., Deerfield, NH 03037-1107, (603)463-5530 [6107]

Computer Data Systems, Inc., 1 Curie Court, Rockville, MD 20850-4389, (301)921-7000 [6108]

Computer Discounters, 5416 Veterans Blvd., Metairie, LA 70003, (504)885-1635 [6109]

Computer Enterprises of Grand Rapids, 28 NW 4th St., Grand Rapids, MN 55744-2714, (218)326-1897 [6110]

Computer Equipment Warehouse Inc., 7585 W 66th Ave., Arvada, CO 80003-3909, (303)424-9710 [6111]

Computer Graphics Distributing Co., 620 E Diamond Ave., Gaithersburg, MD 20877, (301)921-0011 [6112]

Computer Hardware Maintenance Company Inc., PO Box 2025, Langhorne, PA 19047, (215)752-2221 [6113]

Computer Lab International Inc., 580 S Melrose St., Placentia, CA 92870, (714)527-8000 [6114]

Computer Maintenance Service, PO Box 17503, Nashville, TN 37217-0503, (615)831-0055 [6115]

Computer Management Systems, PO Box 407, Columbia City, IN 46725-1013, (219)248-2191 [6116]

Computer and Networking Services Inc., 14813 Morningside Dr., Poway, CA 92064, (858)486-4707 [6117]

Computer Optics Inc., PO Box 7, Hudson, NH 03051, (603)889-2116 [22848]

Computer Parts and Services Inc., 10205 51st Ave., Plymouth, MN 55442, (612)553-1514 [6118]

Computer Plus, Inc., 1101 Jefferson Rd., Charleston, WV 25309-9780, (304)744-1832 [6119]

Computer Products Center Inc., 21 Morgan St., Irvine, CA 92618, (949)588-9800 [6120]

Computer Products of Vermont Inc., 14 Tracy Dr., Shelburne, VT 05482, (802)862-1486 [6121]

Computer Recyclers Inc., 1005 N State St., Orem, UT 84057-3153, (801)226-1892 [6122]

Computer Research Inc., 400 Southpoint Blvd., Ste. 300, Canonsburg, PA 15317, (724)745-0600 [6123]

Computer Sales International Inc., 10845 Olive Blvd., Ste. 300, St. Louis, MO 63141-7760, (314)997-7010 [6124]

Computer Service and Support, PO Box 776, Rogers, AR 72757-0776, (501)631-0469 [6125]

Computer Source Inc., 211 Broadway, Paducah, KY 42001-0711, (270)442-9726 [6126]

Computer Source Inc., 3814 Williams Blvd., Kenner, LA 70065, (504)443-4100 [6127]

Computer Sports Systems Inc., 385 Western Ave., Boston, MA 02135-1005, (617)492-6500 [8556]

Computer Support Systems Inc., PO Box 7738, Des Moines, IA 50322-0958, (515)276-8826 [8557]

Computer Systems Inc., 2819 S 125th Ave., Ste. 276, Omaha, NE 68144, (402)330-3600 [6128]

Computer Systems Supply Corp., 85 S Bragg St., Alexandria, VA 22312-2731, (703)941-0336 [6129]

Computer Talk Inc., PO Box 148, Morrison, CO 80465, (303)697-5485 [6130]

Computer Trading Co., 2508 E 6th St., Tucson, AZ 85716-4404, (520)323-3539 [6131]

Computer Trends, PO Box 4757, Spartanburg, SC 29305-4757, (864)582-2021 [6132]

Computers & Applications Inc., 10623 NE 8th St., Bellevue, WA 98004, (425)451-8077 [6133]

Computers Unlimited Inc., 2407 Montana Ave., Billings, MT 59101-2336, (406)255-9500 [6134]

Computers of Willmar Inc., 1401 1st St. S, Willmar, MN 56201-4221, (320)235-6425 [6135]

ComputersAmerica Inc., PO Box 9127, San Rafael, CA 94912-9127, (415)257-1010 [6136]

Computing Technology Inc., 5314 S Yale Ave., Ste. 715, Tulsa, OK 74135-6274, (918)496-2570 [6137]

CompuTrend Systems Inc., 938 Radecki Ct., La Puente, CA 91748-1132, (818)333-5121 [6138]

Comse Sales/John Weeks Enterprises, 75 Grayson Industrial Pkwy., Grayson, GA 30017, (404)963-7870 [25147]

Comsel Corp., 8453 N Tyco Rd., Vienna, VA 22182, (703)734-3880 [6139]

ComSource Independent Foodservice Companies Inc., 2500 Cumberland Pky., Atlanta, GA 30339, (770)952-0871 [10803]

ComSource Independent Foodservice Companies Inc., 2500 Cumberland Pky., Atlanta, GA 30339, (770)952-0871 [10803]

ComSource Independent Foodservice Companies Inc., 2500 Cumberland Pkwy. , No. 600, Atlanta, GA 30339, (770)952-0871 [12788]

Comspan Inc., 201 Santa Monica Blvd., Ste. 400, Santa Monica, CA 90401, (310)451-9476 [19355]

Comstock Distributing, 1897 N Edmonds Dr., Carson City, NV 89701, (775)882-7067 [10804]

Comstor, 14116 Newbrook Dr., Chantilly, VA 20151, (703)802-0222 [6140]

Comstor Productivity Centers Inc., 3021 Hawkins Rd., Warrenton, OR 97146-9758 [6141]

Comstor Technology Inc., 3021 Hawkins Rd., Warrenton, OR 97146-9758 [6141]

Comtech, PO Box 40408, Fayetteville, NC 28309-0408, (910)864-8787 [7201]

Comtech Inc., 2001 Hammond St., Bangor, ME 04401-5725, (207)848-2801 [20908]

Comtech Systems Brokers, 7860 NW 71st St., Miami, FL 33166, (305)591-8248 [6142]

Comtel Corp., PO Box 5034, Southfield, MI 48086, (313)358-2510 [6143]

ComTel Industries Inc., 6801 N 54th St., Tampa, FL 33610, (813)623-3974 [5578]

Comtel Instruments Co., PO Box 5034, Southfield, MI 48086, (313)358-2510 [6143]

Comus Computer Corp., 2502 Urbana Pke., Ijamsville, MD 21754, (301)874-2900 [6144]

Comware Business Systems Inc., 2440 E 88th Ave., Anchorage, AK 99507-3812, (907)522-1188 [6145]

Con-Mat Supply, PO Box 1383, Glendive, MT 59330-1383, (406)365-6461 [7202]

Con Serve Electric Supply, 78 Myer St., Hackensack, NJ 07601, (201)996-6090 [8562]

Con Serve Electric Supply, 3905 Crescent St., Long Island City, NY 11101-3801, (718)937-6671 [8558]

Con-Tech International, Inc., PO Box 53313, New Orleans, LA 70153, (504)523-4785 [16805]

ConAgra Grain Co., 11 Conagra Dr., Omaha, NE 68102-5011 [17789]

ConAgra Grain Co., 730 2nd Ave. S 14th Fl., Minneapolis, MN 55402, (612)370-7500 [10805]

ConAgra Poultry Co. (Duluth, Georgia), 2475 Meadow Brook Pkwy., Duluth, GA 30096, (770)232-4200 [10806]

ConAgra Trading Cos., PO Box 2910, Minneapolis, MN 55402, (612)370-7500 [10807]

Conair Corp.oration, 7475 N Glen Harbor Blvd., Glendale, AZ 85307, (623)872-8750 [15093]

Conard-Pyle Co., 372 Rose Hill Rd., West Grove, PA 19390, (610)869-2426 [14844]

Conco Food Service, PO Box 61028, New Orleans, LA 70161, (504)733-5200 [10808]

Conco Food Service Inc., 524 W 61st, Shreveport, LA 71106, (318)869-3061 [10809]

Concord Computing Corp., 2525 Horizon Lake Dr., Memphis, TN 38133, (901)371-8000 [6146]

Concord Nurseries Inc., 10175 Mile Black Rd., North Collins, NY 14111, (716)337-2485 [14845]

Concord Sales Co., 7116 20th Ave., Brooklyn, NY 11204-5320, (718)331-0135 [26278]

Concord Technologies Inc., 600 Nickerson Rd., Marlborough, MA 01752-4661, (508)460-9795 [6147]

Concordia Farmers Cooperative Co., 708 Bismark St., Concordia, MO 64020, (816)463-2256 [437]

Concordia Publishing House, 3558 S Jefferson Ave., St. Louis, MO 63118, (314)664-7000 [3651]

Concrete Products and Supply Co. Inc., PO Box 1388, Pascagoula, MS 39568, (228)762-8911 [7203]

Concrete Supply Co., 3823 Raleigh St., Charlotte, NC 28206, (704)372-2930 [7204]

Concrete Supply Corp., 11700 Cherry Hill Rd., Silver Spring, MD 20904, (301)622-2990 [7205]

Condeck Corp., 3230 Matthew Ave. NE, Albuquerque, NM 87107-1927, (505)837-1112 [7206]

Condon Oil Company Inc., PO Box 184, Ripon, WI 54971-0184, (920)748-3186 [22158]

Conductive Rubber Tech Inc., 22125 17th Ave SE Ste. 117, Bothell, WA 98021, (425)486-8559 [6148]

Cone Instruments Inc., 5201 Naiman Pkwy., Solon, OH 44139, (216)248-1035 [18750]

Conesco Industries Ltd., 214 Gates Rd., Little Ferry, NJ 07643, (201)641-6500 [7207]

Conestoga Heating and Plumbing Supply Inc., 340 W Roseville Rd., Lancaster, PA 17601, (717)569-3246 [23121]

Confederate Steel Corp., PO Box 266386, Houston, TX 77207, (713)643-8526 [19892]

Conformance Technology Inc., PO Box 801207, Dallas, TX 75380, (972)233-0020 [8559]

Congdon Orchards Inc., 302 W Superior St., No. 510, Duluth, MN 55802, (218)722-4757 [10810]

Conger Dental Supply Co., 1917 SW Gage Blvd., Topeka, KS 66604-3390, (785)271-8073 [18751]

Congress Leather Co., Rte. 193, Kingsville, OH 44048, (440)224-2133 [27111]

Conkey's Bookstore, 226 E College Ave., Appleton, WI 54911, (920)735-6223 [3652]

Conklin and Company Inc.; Lyon, 2101 Race St., Baltimore, MD 21230, (410)752-6800 [14400]

Conkling Distributing Co.; John A., 44414 SD Hwy. S, Yankton, SD 57078-6454, (605)665-9351 [1610]

Conkling Distributing Co.; John A., 44414 SD Hwy. S, Yankton, SD 57078-6454, (605)665-9351 [1611]

Conley Company Inc.; M., 1312 4th St. SE, Canton, OH 44701, (216)456-8243 [21689]

Conn Associates, Inc.; Jerry, 130 Industrial Dr., Chambersburg, PA 17201-0444, (717)263-8258 [25487]

Connect Air International Inc., 4240 B St NW, Auburn, WA 98001, (253)813-5599 [16806]

Connecticut Appliance & Fireplace Distributors, LLC, 50 Graham Pl., Southington, CT 06489-1511, (860)621-9313 [15094]

Connecticut Driveshaft Inc., 470 Naugatuck Ave., Milford, CT 06460, (203)877-2716 [2472]

Connecticut Driveshaft Inc., 59 Kelso Ave., West Springfield, MA 01089-3701, (413)736-7207 [2473]

Connecticut Micro Corp., PO Box 1067, Farmington, CT 06034-1067, (860)677-4344 [6149]

Connecticut Optical, PO Box 572, Waterbury, CT 06720, (203)573-9107 [19244]

Connecticut Physicians & Surgeons, PO Box 429, Norwalk, CT 06852-0429, (203)838-2354 [18752]

Connecticut Valley Arms Inc., 5988 Peachtree Corners E, Norcross, GA 30071, (404)449-4687 [13483]

Connecticut Valley Paper & Envelope Co. Inc., 239 Lindbergh Place, Paterson, NJ 07503, (973)278-4004 [20909]

Connections USA, 3404 Canton Rd., Marietta, GA 30066-2615, (770)420-8990 [6150]

Connectronics Corp., PO Box 908, Southport, CT 06490-0908, (203)375-5577 [8560]

Connell Brothers Company Ltd., 345 California St., 27th Fl., San Francisco, CA 94104, (415)772-4000 [4362]

Connell Co., 45 Cardinal Dr., Westfield, NJ 07090, (908)233-0700 [10811]

Connell Grain Growers Inc., PO Box 220, Connell, WA 99326, (509)234-2641 [17790]

Connell L.P. Luria Brothers Div., 20521 Chagrin Blvd., Cleveland, OH 44122, (216)752-4000 [26783]

Connell Motor Truck Company Inc., PO Box 8467, Stockton, CA 95208, (209)948-3434 [15908]

Conney Safety Products Co., 3202 Latham Dr., Madison, WI 53713-4614 [24527]

Connie's Enterprise, PO Box 11238, Jacksonville, FL 32239, (904)353-0604 [22159]

Connie's Enterprise, PO Box 11238, Jacksonville, FL 32239, (904)353-0604 [15909]

Connoisseurs Products Corp., 17 Presidential Way, Woburn, MA 01801-1040, (781)932-3949 [17376]

Connolly & Associates; Barrie, 2188 Bluestem Ln., Boise, ID 83706-6116, (208)345-6225 [13078]

Connolly Seafood; Steve, 34 Newmarket Sq., Roxbury, MA 02118-2601, (617)427-7700 [10812]

Connor and Associates Inc., 3595 Almaden Rd., San Jose, CA 95118-1503, (408)445-0911 [13333]

Connor Co., 2800 NE Adams St., PO Box 5007, Peoria, IL 61601-5007, (309)688-1068 [23122]

Connor & Son, PO Box 6016, Incline Village, NV 89450-6016, (702)831-2741 [17377]

Connors Associates, Inc., 15 Lilac Ter., Boston, MA 02131, (617)323-7029 [3653]

Connors Brothers Inc., PO Box 308, Calais, ME 04619-0308, (207)941-6900 [10813]

Conprotec Inc., 6 Raymond Ave., Salem, NH 03079-2945, (603)893-2727 [22948]

Conrad Cooperative, PO Box 160, Conrad, IA 50621-0160, (515)366-2040 [438]

Conrad Implement Co., PO Box 1207, Conrad, MT 59425, (406)278-5531 [439]

Conrad Memorial Cemetary; C.E., 641 Conrad Dr., Kalispell, MT 59901-4629, (406)257-5303 [25609]

Conrad Sales Company, Inc., 81 McKinley Way, PO Box 5087, Poland, OH 44514-1953, (330)757-0711 [10814]

Consan Inc., 18750 Lake Dr., E, Chanhassen, MN 55317, (612)949-0053 [6151]

Conserve-A-Watt Lighting Inc., PO Box 4279, Denver, CO 80204, (303)629-0066 [8561]

Conserve Electric, 78 Myer St., Hackensack, NJ 07601, (201)996-6090 [8562]

Considine Sales Co. Inc., 45 Sharpe Dr., Cranston, RI 02920-4408, (401)463-7020 [1612]

Conso Products Co., PO Box 326, Union, SC 29379, (864)427-9004 [13079]

Consolidated Asset Management Company Inc., PO Box 600, Grain Valley, MO 64029-0600, (660)226-8985 [23476]

Consolidated Bearing Co., 10 Wing Dr., Cedar Knolls, NJ 07927, (973)539-8300 [2474]

Consolidated Beverages Co., PO Box C, Auburn, MA 01501, (508)832-5311 [1613]

Consolidated Coatings Corp., 3735 Green Rd., Beachwood, OH 44122, (216)514-7596 [21417]

Consolidated Communications Corp., 6715 Cedar Springs Rd., Charlotte, NC 28212, (704)536-8804 [8563]

Consolidated Companies Inc., PO Box 6096, Metairie, LA 70009, (504)834-4082 [10815]

Consolidated Cooperative Inc., PO Box 48, Gowrie, IA 50543, (515)352-3851 [17791]

Consolidated Cooperatives Inc., PO Box 877, Worthington, MN 56187, (507)376-4113 [440]

Consolidated Electrical Distributing, 223 Sage St., Carson City, NV 89706, (775)883-4508 [8564]

Consolidated Electrical Distributor, 330 19th Ave. N, Nashville, TN 37203, (615)340-7750 [8565]

Consolidated Electrical Distributor, 343 Hilliard Ave., Asheville, NC 28801, (828)252-5313 [8566]

Consolidated Electrical Distributors°, 649 E 18th Pl., Yuma, AZ 85365, (520)782-2586 [8567]

Consolidated Electrical Distributors, 2611 Kimco Dr., No. 1, Lincoln, NE 68521, (402)465-5151 [8568]

Consolidated Electrical Distributors Inc., 305 E University, Odessa, TX 79762-7664, (915)333-2812 [8569]

Consolidated Electrical Distributors Inc., 1807 Palma Dr., Ventura, CA 93003, (805)642-0361 [8570]

Consolidated Electrical Distributors Inc., 31356 Via Colinas, Ste. 107, Westlake Village, CA 91362, (818)991-9000 [8571]

Consolidated Electrical Distributors Inc. Perry-Mann Electrical, 431 Williams St., Columbia, SC 29201, (803)252-4373 [8572]

Consolidated Electronics Inc., PO Box 20070, Dayton, OH 45420-0070, (937)252-5662 [8573]

Consolidated Factors, Inc., 140 Olivier St., Monterey, CA 93940, (408)375-5121 [10816]

Consolidated Foodservice Companies L.P., PO Box 8790, Virginia Beach, VA 23450, (757)463-5000 [10817]

Consolidated Fuel Oil Co. Inc., PO Box 7226, Shawnee Mission, KS 66207, (913)451-3764 [22160]

Consolidated International, 300 Phillipi Rd., Columbus, OH 43228, (614)278-3700 [13334]

Consolidated International Corp., 333 Main St., East Greenwich, RI 02818-3660, (401)884-0160 [4603]

Consolidated Midland Corp., 20 Main St., Brewster, NY 10509, (914)279-6108 [14071]

Consolidated Pet Foods Inc., 1840 14th St., Santa Monica, CA 90404, (310)393-9393 [10818]

Consolidated Pipe and Supply Company Inc., PO Box 2472, Birmingham, AL 35201, (205)323-7261 [23123]

Consolidated Poultry and Egg Co., 426 St. Paul Ave., Memphis, TN 38126, (901)526-7392 [10819]

Consolidated Scrap Processing, 23 Perrine St., Auburn, NY 13021, (315)253-0373 [26784]

Consolidated Scrap Resources, Inc., PO Box 1761, Harrisburg, PA 17105, (717)233-7927 [26785]

Consolidated Service Corp., 2500 Devon Ave., Elk Grove Village, IL 60007, (708)640-2600 [2475]

Consolidated Shoe Company Inc., PO Box 10549, Lynchburg, VA 24506-0549, (804)239-0391 [24719]

Consolidated Supply Co., PO Box 3183, Spokane, WA 99220-3183, (509)535-0896 [23124]

Consolidated Textiles, Inc., PO Box 240416, Charlotte, NC 28224, (704)554-8621 [26008]

Consolidated Tile and Carpet Co., 15100 Ravinia Ave., Orland Park, IL 60462-3745, (708)403-5000 [9822]

Consolidated Tile and Carpet Co., 15100 Ravinia Ave., Orland Park, IL 60462-3745, (708)403-5000 [15452]

Consolidated Tool Manufacturers Inc., 10927 Franklin Ave., Franklin Park, IL 60131, (708)451-9050 [15910]

Consolidated Truck Parts Inc., PO Box 4844, Monroe, LA 71211, (318)325-1948 [2476]

Consolidated Utility & Equipment Service, 53 Lebanon Rd., Franklin, CT 06254, (860)886-7081 [2477]

Consolidated Utility Equipment Service, Inc., 14 Caldwell Dr., Amherst, NH 03031, (603)889-4071 [2478]

Consolidated Wholesale Co., PO Box 26903, Oklahoma City, OK 73126, (405)232-5593 [26279]

Consortium Book Sales and Distribution Inc., 1045 Westgate Dr., No. 90, St. Paul, MN 55114, (612)221-9035 [3654]

Constantine Wine, 5320 L Enterprise St., Sykesville, MD 21784, (410)549-9463 [1614]

Construction Material Supplies, PO Box 1547, Fresno, CA 93716, (209)268-9301 [7257]

Construction Products of Washington, North 3515 Haven, Spokane, WA 99207, (509)489-0830 [7208]

Construction Specialties Inc., 3 Werner Wy., Lebanon, NJ 08833, (908)236-0800 [7209]

Consulier Engineering Inc., 2391 Old Dixie Hwy., Riviera Beach, FL 33404-5456, (561)842-2492 [2479]

The Consulting Scientists, 44 Murray Hill Sq., Murray Hill, NJ 07974, (908)508-0690 [19245]

Consumer Care Products Inc., 1446 Pilgrim Rd., Plymouth, WI 53073, (920)893-4614 [18753]

Consumer Care Products Inc., PO Box 684, Sheboygan, WI 53082-0684, (920)459-8353 [19246]

Consumer Cooperative Oil Co., PO Box 668, Sauk City, WI 53583, (608)643-3301 [22161]

Consumer Cooperative of Walworth County, PO Box 377, Elkhorn, WI 53121, (414)723-3150 [441]

Consumer Direct Inc., 1375 Raff Rd. SW, Canton, OH 44750, (330)478-0755 [23603]

Consumer Oil Company of Meridian, PO Box 950, Meridian, MS 39301, (601)693-3933 [22162]

Consumer Oil and Supply Co., PO Box 38, Braymer, MO 64624, (816)645-2215 [442]

Consumer Products Co., PO Box 2729, Muncie, IN 47305-2398, (765)281-5019 [25906]

Consumers Choice Coffee Inc., 4271 Produce Rd., Louisville, KY 40218, (502)968-4151 [10820]

Consumers Cooperative, PO Box 533, Richland Center, WI 53581, (608)647-6171 [443]

Consumers Cooperative Exchange, 1400 Logan St., Merrill, WI 54452, (715)536-2491 [444]

Consumers Cooperative Oil Co., PO Box 76, Rosholt, SD 57260, (605)537-4216 [22163]

Consumers Financial Corp., PO Box 26, Camp Hill, PA 17001-0026, (717)761-4230 [2480]

Consumers of La Salle, 1701 5th Ave., Moline, IL 61265-7908, (815)223-2480 [1615]

Consumers Petroleum Co., 13507 Auburn Ave., Detroit, MI 48223, (313)272-3800 [22164]

Consumers Plumbing Heating Supply, 23233 Aurora Rd., Cleveland, OH 44146-1704, (440)232-8400 [23125]

Consumers Produce Co., 1 21st St., Pittsburgh, PA 15222, (412)281-0722 [10821]

Consumers Steel Products Co., 8510 Bessemer Ave., Cleveland, OH 44127, (216)883-7171 [19893]

Consumers Supply Cooperative Co., PO Box 868, Canyon, TX 79015, (806)655-2134 [10822]

Consumers Vinegar and Spice Co., 4723 S Washtenaw Ave., Chicago, IL 60632, (773)376-4100 [10823]

Contact Optical Center Inc., 12301 N Grant, Unit G, Denver, CO 80241, (303)457-1118 [19247]

Contadina Foods, PO Box 29059, Glendale, CA 91209, (818)549-6000 [10824]

Container Industries Inc., 4401 W 62nd St., Indianapolis, IN 46268, (317)299-5000 [25907]

Container Recycling Alliance, 8770 W Bryn Mawr Ave., No. 10R, Chicago, IL 60631, (312)399-8400 [26786]

CONTEC Microelectronics USA, 744 S Hillview Dr., Milpitas, CA 95035, (408)719-8200 [6152]

Contech Instrumentation, 7 State Route 27, Ste. 103, Edison, NJ 08820-3965, (732)560-0702 [8574]

Contempo Ceramic Tile, 3732 S 330 W, Salt Lake City, UT 84115-9314, (801)262-1717 [9823]

Contemporary Arts Press Distribution, PO Box 3123, Rincon Annex, San Francisco, CA 94119, (415)431-7524 [3655]

Contemporary Computer Wear, 201 Chester Ave., San Francisco, CA 94132, (415)587-3002 [6153]

Contemporary Office Products Inc., 3904 St. Clair Ave., Cleveland, OH 44114, (216)391-5555 [20910]

Contico International Inc., 1101 Warson Rd., St. Louis, MO 63132, (314)997-5900 [13643]

Continental Baking Co., 3645 W Henrietta Rd., Rochester, NY 14623-3529, (716)334-2340 [10825]

Continental Baking Co., 6301 N Broadway, St. Louis, MO 63147-2802, (314)385-1600 [11525]

Continental Baking Co., 1525 Bryant, San Francisco, CA 94103-4889, (415)552-0950 [10826]

Continental Book Co., 80-00 Cooper Ave., Bldg. 29, Glendale, NY 11385, (718)326-0560 [3656]

Continental Ceramic Tile, 2030 Grant Ave., Philadelphia, PA 19115, (215)676-1119 [9824]

Continental Commodities L.P., 2750 Jewel Ave., Vernon, CA 90058, (213)588-2274 [10827]

Continental Craft Distributors, PO Box 3373, South Attleboro, MA 02703-0933, (617)726-9091 [20911]

Continental Distributing Company Inc., 9800 W Balmoral Ave., Rosemont, IL 60018, (847)671-7700 [1616]

Continental Equipment Co., 2309 N Hullen St., Metairie, LA 70001-1930, (504)835-5151 [14401]

Continental Flooring Inc., 1446 39th St., Brooklyn, NY 11218, (718)854-5800 [9825]

Continental Foods Corp., 1701 E 123rd Ave., Olathe, KS 66061, (913)829-2293 [10828]

Continental Foods Inc., 2730 Wilmarco Ave., Baltimore, MD 21223-3306, (410)233-5500 [10829]

Continental Glass and Plastic Inc., 841 W Cermak Rd., Chicago, IL 60608, (312)666-2050 [25908]

Continental Grain Co., 277 Park Ave., New York, NY 10172, (212)207-5100 [17792]

Continental Information Systems Corp., 45 Broadway Atrium, Ste. 1105, New York, NY 10006-3007, (212)771-1000 [6154]

Continental International, 6723 S Hanna, Ft. Wayne, IN 46816, (219)447-7000 [16807]

Continental Marketing, 18175 SW 100th Ct., Tualatin, OR 97062-9482, (503)692-8138 [8575]

Continental Midland, PO Box 248, Millersport, OH 43046-9748, (740)467-2677 [13644]

Continental Office Furniture and Supply Corp., 2061 Silver Dr., Columbus, OH 43211, (614)262-8088 [13080]

Continental Ozark Corp., PO Box 1503, Fayetteville, AR 72702, (501)521-5565 [22165]

Continental Paper Grading Co., 1623 S Lumber St., Chicago, IL 60616, (312)226-2010 [26787]

Continental Recycling Inc., 620 Truxton St., Bronx, NY 10474, (718)842-2842 [26788]

Continental Resources Inc. (Bedford, Massachusetts), PO Box 9137, Bedford, MA 01730, (781)275-0850 [6155]

Continental Safety Equipment Inc., 899 Apollo Rd., Eagan, MN 55121, (651)454-7233 [19248]

Continental Sales Co., 4890 Ironton, Unit G1, Denver, CO 80239, (303)373-2390 [19249]

Continental Sales Co. of America, PO Box 1002, Santa Cruz, CA 95061, (408)426-7423 [19250]

Continental Sales and Equipment Co., PO Box 428, Hibbing, MN 55746, (218)263-6861 [25610]

Continental Screen Printing Supply, 2110 31st Ct., Kenner, LA 70065-4537, (504)461-8797 [15911]

Continental Sports Supply Inc., PO Box 1251, Englewood, CO 80150, (303)934-5657 [23604]

Continental Trading Co. Inc., 4807 Colley Ave., Norfolk, VA 23508-2036, (757)440-0617 [19251]

Continental Wood Preservers Inc., 7500 E Davison Ave., Detroit, MI 48212, (313)365-4200 [7210]

Continental Wood Preservers Inc., 7500 E Davison St., Detroit, MI 48212, (313)365-4200 [27299]

Continnuus, PO Box 416, Denver, CO 80201-0416, (303)575-5676 [3657]

Contour Lynnsoles Inc., PO Box 20016, Sarasota, FL 34276, (941)921-0790 [24720]

Contract Appliance Sales Inc., PO Box 1818, Sandy, UT 84091-1818, (801)569-8850 [25148]

Contract Associates Inc., 4545 McLeod Rd. NE, Ste. B, Albuquerque, NM 87109-2202, (505)888-7536 [20912]

Contract Decor Inc., 1243 N Gene Autrey Trail, Palm Springs, CA 92262, (760)320-5566 [15453]

Contract Interiors, 950 Laidlaw Ave., Cincinnati, OH 45237, (513)641-3700 [13081]

Contract Kitchen Distributors, 12002 Old Baltimore Pike, Beltsville, MD 20705-1412, (301)595-4477 [15095]

Contracted Associates Office Interiors Inc., 3111 Fite Cir., Ste. 101, Sacramento, CA 95827, (916)366-7878 [13082]

Contractors Floor Covering, 1440 Campbell Ln., PO Box 20016, Bowling Green, KY 42104, (270)843-1542 [9826]

Contractors Heating and Supply Co., 70 Santa Fe Dr., Denver, CO 80223, (303)893-1120 [13645]

Contractors Machinery Co., 13200 Northend Ave., Oak Park, MI 48237, (248)543-4770 [7211]

Contractors Parts Supply, Inc., 55 Lyerly Bldg. 313, Houston, TX 77022, (713)695-7162 [16808]

Contractors Steel Co., 36555 Amrhein Rd., Livonia, MI 48150, (313)464-4000 [19894]

Contractors Supply Corp., 920 Crooked Hill Rd., Brentwood, NY 11717, (631)231-6200 [8236]

Control Associates Inc., 20 Commerce Dr., Allendale, NJ 07401-1600, (201)568-5513 [2481]

Control-Equip of Tennessee, Inc., 2044 E Magnolia Ave., Knoxville, TN 37917-8026, (865)522-5656 [14402]

Control Sales Inc., PO Box 469, Beech Grove, IN 46107, (317)786-2272 [15912]

Control Solutions Inc., 2739 Pasadena Blvd., Pasadena, TX 77502, (713)473-4946 [4363]

Control Specialties Inc., PO Box 266724, Houston, TX 77207, (713)644-5353 [16809]

Control Switches International Inc., 2405 Mira Mar Ave., Long Beach, CA 90815, (562)498-3599 [8576]

Controls-Instruments-Devices, 1810 Auger Dr., Ste. G, Tucker, GA 30084-6603, (404)491-3143 [8577]

Controltech, PO Box 1524, San Carlos, CA 94070, (650)593-2111 [15913]

Convenience Equipment and Supplies Enterprises Inc., 2300 N Barrington, No. 400, Hoffman Estates, IL 60195-7855, (708)397-9247 [25611]

Convenience Products, 866 Horan Dr., Fenton, MO 63026-2416, (636)349-5333 [7212]

Convenience Store Distributing Company L.L.C., PO Box 1799, Richmond, IN 47374, (317)962-8521 [10830]

Convermat Corp., 45 N Station Plz, Ste. 400, Great Neck, NY 11021-5011, (516)487-7100 [21690]

Conversion Components Inc., PO Box 429, 23537 CR-106, Elkhart, IN 46515-0429, (219)264-4181 [2482]

Conversion Resources Inc., 10145 Philipp Pky., Streetsboro, OH 44241-4706, (440)786-7700 [26789]

CONVEX Computer Corp., PO Box 83351, Richardson, TX 75083-3851, (972)497-4000 [6156]

Conveyor & Drive Equipment, PO Box 191100, St. Louis, MO 63119, (314)961-1200 [15914]

Convoy Servicing Co. Inc., 3323 Jane Ln., Dallas, TX 75247, (214)638-3053 [14403]

Conway Import Co. Inc., 5 Warehouse Ln., Elmsford, NY 10523, (914)592-1310 [10831]

Cony Computers Systems Inc., PO Box 712, Pine Brook, NJ 07058-0712, (973)276-0800 [6157]

Conyngham and Company Inc., 700 Scott St., Wilkes Barre, PA 18705, (570)823-1181 [23144]

Cook Brothers Inc., 240 N Ashland, Chicago, IL 60607, (773)384-4663 [15096]

Cook Brothers Manufacturing and Supply Co., 1030 Calle Recodo, San Clemente, CA 92672, (949)361-8767 [23126]

Cook Chocolate Co., 4801 S Lawndale Ave., Chicago, IL 60632-3062, (773)847-4600 [10832]

Cook Communications Ministries, 4050 Lee Vance View, Colorado Springs, CO 80918, (719)535-2905 [3658]

Cook Co.; P.S., 400 W 15th St., Cheyenne, WY 82001, (307)634-4481 [23127]

Cook Composites and Polymers Co., 820 E 14th Ave., North Kansas City, MO 64116, (816)391-6000 [4364]

Cook Concrete Products Inc., PO Box 720280, Redding, CA 96099, (530)243-2562 [7213]

Cook Distribution Services, LLC, 5400 33rd St. SE, Grand Rapids, MI 49512, (616)940-3540 [13626]

Cook Distributors Inc.; L.G., 5400 33rd St. SE, Grand Rapids, MI 49512, (616)940-3540 [13626]

Cook and Dunn Paint Corp. Adelphi Coating, 700 Gotham Pkwy., Carlstadt, NJ 07072, (201)935-4900 [21418]

Cook Iron Store Co., PO Box 1237, Rochester, NY 14603, (716)454-5840 [16810]

Cook Publishing Co.; David C., 850 N Grove Ave., Elgin, IL 60120, (708)741-2400 [3659]

Cookbook Collection, Inc., 2500 E 195th St., Belton, MO 64012, (816)322-2122 [3660]

Cooke Co.; David, 57 E Carpenter St., Valley Stream, NY 11580-4403, (516)785-0565 [17378]

Cooke Sales and Service Company Inc., PO Box 170, Chillicothe, MO 64601, (816)646-1166 [7214]

Cook's Gourmet, 5821 Wilderness Ave., Riverside, CA 92504, (909)352-5700 [10833]

Cook's Inc., 807 S Broadway St., Watertown, SD 57201, (605)886-5892 [20913]

Cook's Mart Ltd., 3000 E 3rd. Ave., Denver, CO 80206, (303)388-5933 [15454]

Cookson Co., 2417 S 50th Ave., Phoenix, AZ 85043, (602)272-4244 [27300]

Cooksville Grain Co., PO Box 200, Cooksville, IL 61730, (309)725-3214 [17793]

Coolant Management Services Co., 11052 Via El Mercado, Los Alamitos, CA 90720, (562)795-0470 [4365]

Cooley Forest Products, PO Box 20188, Phoenix, AZ 85036-0188, (602)276-2402 [7215]

Cooley Industries, Inc., PO Box 20188, Phoenix, AZ 85036-0188, (602)276-2402 [7215]

Cooley Industries Inc., PO Box 20188, Phoenix, AZ 85036, (602)243-4288 [7216]

Cooley Medical Equipment Inc., 490 S Lake Dr., Prestonsburg, KY 41653-1359, (606)886-9267 [18754]

Cooling & Heating Inc., 70 Eglin Pkwy. NE, Ft. Walton Beach, FL 32548-4957, (850)244-6161 [14404]

Cooling Tower Resources, Inc., PO Box 159, Healdsburg, CA 95448, (707)433-3900 [7217]

Coop Country Partners, PO Box 517, Sauk City, WI 53583, (608)643-3345 [445]

Coop Services Inc., PO Box 2187, Lawton, OK 73502, (580)355-3700 [446]

Cooper and Associates, 333 West North Ave., Chicago, IL 60610, (312)988-7766 [13335]

Cooper Electric Supply Co., 70 Apple St., Eatontown, NJ 07724, (908)747-2233 [8578]

Cooper Industries Inc., 67 Willowcrest Dr., Ste. 1441, Rochester, NY 14604, (716)256-0971 [6158]

Cooper Power Tools Division-Apex, 762 W Stewart St., Dayton, OH 45408, (937)222-7871 [75]

Cooper Sportswear Manufacturing Company Inc., 720 Frelinghuysen Ave., Newark, NJ 07114, (201)824-3400 [4892]

Cooper Tire & Rubber Co., 701 Lima Ave., Findlay, OH 45839, (419)423-1321 [2483]

Cooperative Agricultural Center, PO Box 770, Lakefield, MN 56150, (507)662-5285 [447]

Cooperative Agricultural Services Inc., 411 W 2nd, Oakley, KS 67748, (785)672-3300 [448]

Cooperative Association No. 1 Inc., 201 E Front St., Slater, MO 65349, (660)529-2244 [449]

Cooperative Country Farmer's Elevator, PO Box 604, Renville, MN 56284, (612)329-8377 [17785]

Cooperative Elevator Co., 7211 E Michigan Ave., Pigeon, MI 48755, (517)453-4500 [450]

Cooperative Elevator Co., PO Box 338, Francesville, IN 47946, (219)567-9132 [451]

Cooperative Elevator Co., 4878 Mill St., Elkton, MI 48731, (517)375-2281 [17794]

Cooperative Elevator Co., 7211 E Michigan Ave., Pigeon, MI 48755, (517)453-4500 [10834]

Cooperative Elevator, Sebewaing, 969 E Pine St., Sebewaing, MI 48759, (517)883-3030 [17795]

Cooperative Elevator Supply Co., PO Box 220, Meade, KS 67864, (316)873-2161 [452]

Cooperative Exchange, PO Box 156, Arlington, KS 67514, (316)538-2331 [453]

Cooperative Feed Dealer Inc., PO Box 670, Chenango Bridge, NY 13745, (607)648-4194 [454]

Cooperative Gas and Oil Co. (Geneseo, Illinois), 324 E Exchange St., Geneseo, IL 61254, (309)944-4616 [22166]

Cooperative Gas and Oil Company Inc., PO Box 117, Sioux Center, IA 51250, (712)722-2501 [22167]

Cooperative Grain and Product Co., PO Box 128, Ringsted, IA 50578, (712)866-0581 [455]

Cooperative Grain and Supply, 107 W Grand St., Hillsboro, KS 67063, (316)947-3917 [456]

Cooperative Grain and Supply, PO Box 8, Bazine, KS 67516, (785)398-2271 [17796]

Cooperative Grain and Supply, PO Box 7, Roseland, NE 68973, (402)756-6201 [17797]

Cooperative Grain and Supply, 107 W Grand St., Hillsboro, KS 67063, (316)947-3917 [457]

Cooperative Grain and Supply, PO Box 8, Bazine, KS 67516, (785)398-2271 [10835]

Cooperative Oil Association, 1110 3rd Ave., Mountain Lake, MN 56159, (507)427-2333 [22168]

Cooperative Oil Co., PO Box 289, Alma, NE 68920, (308)928-2126 [458]

Cooperative Oil Co., PO Box 30, Osage, IA 50461, (515)732-3716 [22169]

Cooperative Reserve Supply Inc., PO Box 39, Belmont, MA 02478, (617)864-1444 [7218]

Cooperative Sampo Corp., Box 220, Menahga, MN 56464, (218)564-4534 [17798]

Cooperative Service Oil Co., 208 E Grand St., Chilton, WI 53014, (920)849-2377 [459]

Cooperative Services of Clark County, PO Box 260, Dorchester, WI 54425-0260, (715)267-6105 [460]

Cooperative Services Inc., PO Box 2187, Lawton, OK 73502, (580)355-3700 [446]

Cooperative Supply Inc., PO Box 278, Dodge, NE 68633, (402)693-2261 [7219]

Cooperative Union Mercantile Co. Inc., PO Box 274, Grinnell, KS 67738, (785)824-3201 [461]

Coordinated Equipment Co., 1707 E Anaheim St., Wilmington, CA 90744, (310)834-8535 [15915]

Coors Brewing Co., PO Box 4030, Golden, CO 80401, (303)279-6565 [10836]

Coors Brothers Co., 4354 Boomer Rd., Cincinnati, OH 45247-7947, (513)541-3271 [10837]

Coors Distributing Co., 12th & Ford Sts., Golden, CO 80401, (303)433-6541 [1617]

Coors Energy Co., PO Box 467, Golden, CO 80402, (303)277-6042 [20532]

Coors West, 2700 Middlefield Rd., Bldg. B, PO Box 5036, Redwood City, CA 94063-3404, (650)367-7070 [1618]

Coos Grange Supply Co., 1085 S 2nd St., Coos Bay, OR 97420, (541)267-7051 [462]

Coosa Co. Inc., PO Box 367, Rome, GA 30162-0367, (706)291-0199 [23605]

Cop Shop, 1306 N Howard St., Spokane, WA 99201-2412, (509)534-5068 [4893]

Copeland Fuel Inc., PO Box 608, Grants Pass, OR 97528-0261, (541)476-4441 [7220]

Copeland Lumber Yard Inc., 901 NE Glisan St., Portland, OR 97232, (503)232-7181 [13646]

Copeland Lumber Yard Inc., 901 NE Glisan St., Portland, OR 97232, (503)232-7181 [13647]

Copeland Oil Co., Hwy. 259, Idabel, OK 74745, (580)286-3272 [22170]

Copeland Optical Inc., 738 S Perry Ln., Ste. 17, Tempe, AZ 85281, (602)267-0682 [19252]

Copeland Paving Inc., PO Box 608, Grants Pass, OR 97528-0261, (541)476-4441 [7220]

Copenhaver Industries Inc.; Laura, PO Box 149 Dept. D, Marion, VA 24354, (540)783-4663 [15455]

Copier Supply Inc., 120 Amaral St., PO Box 382, Seekonk, MA 02771, (508)431-9100 [5579]

Copley Distributors Inc., PO Box 1427, 123 Hopkins Hill Rd., West Greenwich, RI 02817, (401)392-3580 [1619]

Copper and Brass Sales, 414 MacDade Blvd., Collingdale, PA 19023, (215)586-1800 [19895]

Copper and Brass Sales Inc., 17401 10 Mile Rd., Eastpointe, MI 48021, (313)775-7710 [19896]

Copper and Brass Sales Inc., 17401 E 10 Mile Rd., Eastpointe, MI 48021, (810)775-7710 [19897]

Copper and Brass Sales Inc., 2131 Garfield Ave., Los Angeles, CA 90040, (323)726-7610 [19898]

Copper Electronics, 3315 Gilmore Industrial Blvd., Louisville, KY 40213, (502)968-8500 [6159]

Copps Corp., 2828 Wayne St., Stevens Point, WI 54481, (715)344-5900 [10838]

Copps Distributing Co., 2828 Wayne St., Stevens Point, WI 54481, (715)344-5900 [10839]

Copy Cats Industries Inc., 525 7th Ave., New York, NY 10018-4999, (212)921-1595 [4894]

Copy Center Inc., PO Box 2428, Farmingdale, NJ 07727, (908)280-1333 [20914]

Copy Center Inc., PO Box 2428, Farmingdale, NJ 07727, (908)280-1333 [20915]

Copy-Co Inc., 10014 Monroe Dr., Dallas, TX 75229, (972)699-9911 [20916]

Copy Plus Inc., 7100 W Good Hope Rd., Milwaukee, WI 53223-4611, (414)353-2704 [20917]

Copy Sales Inc., 4950 E Evans Ave., Denver, CO 80222-5209, (303)758-0797 [20918]

Copy Supply Concepts Inc., 14998 W 6th Ave., Ste. E-550, Golden, CO 80401-5025, (303)271-1100 [8579]

Copyline Corp., PO Box 880367, San Diego, CA 92111, (619)220-0500 [20919]

Copytronics Inc., 2461 Rolac Rd., Jacksonville, FL 32207, (904)731-5100 [20920]

Cora Medical Products Inc., 3615 Goodlett St., Memphis, TN 38118-6213, (901)794-7174 [18755]

Coral Sales Co., PO Box 22385, Milwaukie, OR 97269-2385, (503)655-6351 [8580]

Cordial/Riley Marketing, 5104 Bronco Dr., Clarkston, MI 48346, (248)625-2420 [8581]

Core-Mark International Inc., 395 Oyster Point Blvd., No. 415, South San Francisco, CA 94080, (650)589-9445 [10840]

Core-Mark International Inc., 395 Oyster Point Blvd., No. 415, South San Francisco, CA 94080, (650)589-9445 [26280]

Core-Mark International Inc. Core-Mark International Incorporated Div., 3650 Fraser St., Aurora, CO 80011, (303)373-2300 [10841]

Corey Steel Co., PO Box 5137, Chicago, IL 60680, (708)863-8000 [19899]

Corids & Son Inc.; Alex D., 212 Shaw Rd., South San Francisco, CA 94080-6604, (650)873-1900 [10842]

Corinthian Healthcare Systems, 8227 Northwest Blvd., Indianapolis, IN 46278-1378, (317)875-9026 [18756]

Cork Supply International Inc., 537 Stone Rd., Benicia, CA 94510, (707)746-0353 [15456]

Corken Steel Products Co., PO Box 2650, Covington, KY 41012, (606)291-4664 [14405]

Corkey Control Systems Inc., 846 Mahler Rd., Burlingame, CA 94010-1604, (510)786-4241 [24528]

Cormans Sporting Goods, PO Box 144, Stanford, KY 40484-0144, (606)365-2463 [23606]

Cornbelt Chemical Co., PO Box 410, McCook, NE 69001, (308)345-5057 [4366]

Cornelius Business Forms, Inc., 2700 E 55th Pl., Indianapolis, IN 46220-3545, (317)251-8990 [21691]

Cornelius Printed Products, 2700 E 55th Pl., Indianapolis, IN 46220-3545, (317)251-8990 [21691]

Cornelius Systems Inc., 3966 11 Mile Rd., No. 1A, Berkley, MI 48072-1005, (248)545-5558 [20921]

Cornell Surgical Co., 30 New Bridge Rd., Bergenfield, NJ 07621-4304, (201)384-9000 [19253]

Cornell Trading Inc., PO Box 1710, Williston, VT 05495-1710, (802)862-1144 [4895]

Cornerstone Controls Inc., 7251 E Kemper Rd., Cincinnati, OH 45249, (513)489-2500 [8582]

Cornerstone Group, 2900 Patio Dr., Houston, TX 77017, (713)946-9000 [7221]

Cornerstone Propane G.P. Inc., 432 Westridge Dr., Watsonville, CA 95076, (408)724-1921 [22171]

Cornerstone Propane Partners L.P., 432 Westridge Dr., Watsonville, CA 95076, (831)724-1921 [22172]

Cornforths, 5625 N 7th St., Phoenix, AZ 85014-2505, (602)277-6855 [14406]

Cornhusker International, 3131 Cornhusker Hwy., Lincoln, NE 68504, (402)466-8461 [20616]

Cornille and Sons Inc.; George J., 60 S Water Mkt. W, Chicago, IL 60608, (312)226-1015 [10843]

Cornilsen's Backyard Bird, 1514 Pine Valley Cir., Roseville, CA 95661, (916)783-2243 [27112]

Corning-Donohue Inc., 1407 Marshall Ave., St. Paul, MN 55104, (612)646-8000 [7222]

Corning Inc., Houghton Park, Corning, NY 14831, (607)974-9000 [15457]

Cornlea Auction Co., R.R. 1, Cornlea, NE 68642, (402)923-0894 [463]

Cornucopia Natural Foods Inc., PO Box 999, Dayville, CT 06241, (860)779-2800 [12799]

Cornucopia Natural Foods Inc., 4200 Shirley Dr., Atlanta, GA 30336, (404)696-4667 [14072]

Coroant Inc., 11400 Commerce Park Dr., Reston, VA 20191, (703)758-7000 [6160]

Coronado Auto Recyclers Inc., 9320 San Pedro Dr. NE, Albuquerque, NM 87113-2123, (505)821-0440 [2484]

Coronet Books, Inc., 311 Bainbridge St., Philadelphia, PA 19147, (215)925-2762 [3661]

Coronet Paper Corp., 484 Washington Ave., Carlstadt, NJ 07072, (201)933-5400 [21692]

Coronet Paper Products, 3200 NW 119th St., Miami, FL 33167-2925, (305)688-6601 [21693]

Coronet Parts Manufacturing Co. Inc., 883-93 Elton St., Brooklyn, NY 11208-5315, (718)649-1750 [2485]

Corporacion del Cobre U.S.A. Inc., 177 Broad St., Stamford, CT 06901-2048, (203)425-4321 [19900]

Corporate Computer Inc., 11330 25th Ave. NE, Seattle, WA 98125, (206)365-3113 [6161]

Corporate Computer Systems Inc., 11925 Wentling Ave., Baton Rouge, LA 70816-6057, (504)296-6800 [6162]

Corporate Copy Inc., 3967 Hickory Hill, Memphis, TN 38115, (901)367-9500 [20922]

Corporate Data Products, PO Box 7148, Charlotte, NC 28241, (704)522-1234 [20923]

Corporate Design Group, 2150 Douglas Blvd., Ste. 225, Roseville, CA 95661, (916)781-6543 [13083]

Corporate Environments of Georgia Inc., PO Box 29725, Atlanta, GA 30359-0725, (404)679-8999 [20924]

Corporate Express, PO Box 9339, Pittsburgh, PA 15225, (412)741-6494 [20925]

Corporate Express, 35 Melanie Ln., Whippany, NJ 07981, (973)386-8900 [20926]

Corporate Express, 2655 W Georgia Ave., Phoenix, AZ 85017-2728, (602)242-2200 [20927]

Corporate Express of the East Inc., 160 Avon St., Stratford, CT 06615, (203)383-6300 [20928]

Corporate Express Inc., 1 Environmental Way, Broomfield, CO 80021-3416, (303)664-2000 [20929]

Corporate Express of the MidAtlantic Inc., 7700 Port Capital Dr., Baltimore, MD 21227, (410)799-7700 [20930]

Corporate Express of Northern California Inc., 2010 North 1st St., Ste. 530, San Jose, CA 95131-2040, (408)000-0000 [20931]

Corporate Interiors Inc., 318 W Depot Ave., Knoxville, TN 37917-7522, (865)637-3214 [20932]

Corporate Rotable and Supply Inc., 6701 NW 12th Ave., Ft. Lauderdale, FL 33309, (954)972-2807 [76]

Corpus Christi Wholesale Mart, 3229 Ayers St., Corpus Christi, TX 78415, (512)887-8184 [4896]

CORR TECH, Inc., 4545 Homestead Rd., Houston, TX 77028, (713)674-7887 [23128]

Corr Tech Inc., 4545 Homestead Rd., Houston, TX 77028, (713)674-7887 [22949]

Corr-Williams Co., PO Box 2570, Jackson, MS 39207, (601)353-5871 [26281]

Corr-Williams Wholesale Company Inc., 5173 Pioneer Dr., Meridian, MS 39303, (601)693-6081 [26282]

Corral West Ranchwear Inc., 4519 Frontier Mall Dr., Cheyenne, WY 82009, (307)632-0951 [4897]

Corrective Shoe Repair, 1502 21st St. NW, Washington, DC 20036-1008, (202)232-9749 [24721]

Corriveau-Routhier, Inc., 375 N State, Concord, NH 03301, (603)228-0631 [9827]

Corriveau-Routhier, Inc., 71 Broadway, Dover, NH 03820, (603)742-1901 [7223]

Corriveau-Routhier Inc., 266 Clay St., PO Box 4127, Manchester, NH 03103, (603)627-3805 [9828]

Corriveau-Routhier, Inc., 159 Temple St., Nashua, NH 03060, (603)889-2157 [9829]

Corriveau-Routhier, Inc., 266 Clay St., Manchester, NH 03103, (603)627-3805 [7224]

Corrosion Fluid Products Corp., 24450 Indoplex Ct., Farmington Hills, MI 48335, (248)478-0100 [16811]

Corsica Cooperative Association Inc., PO Box 65, Corsica, SD 57328-0065, (605)946-5491 [383]

Corso Inc.; Frank P., PO Box 488, Biloxi, MS 39533, (601)436-4697 [26283]

Corstar Business Computing Inc., 50 Saw Mill River Rd., Hawthorne, NY 10532, (914)347-2700 [6163]

Cortland Line Company Inc., 3736 Kellogg, Cortland, NY 13045, (607)756-2851 [23607]

Corts Truck Equipment, Inc., 145 Mohawk St., Whitesboro, NY 13492, (315)736-6641 [2486]

Cory Orchard and Turf Div., 6739 Guion Rd., Indianapolis, IN 46268, (317)328-1000 [464]

Cosbel Petroleum Corp., 9 Greenway Plz., Houston, TX 77046-0995, (713)877-1400 [22173]

Cosco Inc., 1369 Colburn St., Honolulu, HI 96817, (808)845-2234 [14407]

Cosco Supply, 1369 Colburn St., Honolulu, HI 96817, (808)845-2234 [14407]

Cosentino Company Inc.; J., 88 S Water Market, Chicago, IL 60608, (312)421-2000 [10844]

Cosgrove Distributors Inc., 120 S Greenwood St., Spring Valley, IL 61362, (815)664-4121 [10845]

Coshocton Grain Co., PO Box 606, Coshocton, OH 43812, (614)622-0941 [17799]

Cosmetic Marketing Group, PO Box 1138, Gresham, OR 97030-0244, (503)253-4327 [14073]

Cosmi Corp., 2600 Homestead Pl., Rancho Dominguez, CA 90220, (310)833-2000 [6164]

COSMIC, 382 E Broad St., Athens, GA 30602-4272, (706)542-3265 [6165]

Cosmopolitan Trading Co., PO Box 7024, Minneapolis, MN 55407, (612)722-5512 [14074]

Cosmos Enterprises, Inc., 15 12th Ave. SE, Elbow Lake, MN 56531-4734, (218)685-4403 [2487]

Cosmos Import Export Inc., PO Box 2797, Fall River, MA 02722, (508)674-8451 [10846]

Cosmotec Inc., 300 Long Beach Blvd., Stratford, CT 06497-7153, (203)378-8388 [8583]

Cosons Inc., 12115 Parklawn, Rockville, MD 20852, (301)816-6900 [20933]

Cost-U-Less, 12410 SE 32nd St., Bellevue, WA 98005, (425)644-4241 [10847]

Costa Fruit and Produce Co., 414 Rutherford Ave., Charlestown, MA 02129, (617)241-8007 [10848]

Costa Inc.; Victor, 5412 Vista Meadow Dr., Dallas, TX 75248-2023, (214)634-1133 [4898]

Costas Provisions Corp., 255 S Hampton St., Boston, MA 02119, (617)427-0900 [10849]

Costco Companies, Inc., 999 Lake Dr., Issaquah, WA 98027, (425)313-8100 [10850]

Costco Wholesale, 999 Lake Dr., Issaquah, WA 98027, (425)313-8100 [10851]

Costello Beverage Co.; J.W., PO Box 95007, Las Vegas, NV 89193-5007, (702)876-4000 [1620]

Cota and Cota Inc., 4 Green St., Bellows Falls, VT 05101, (802)463-4150 [22174]

Cottage Grove Cooperative, 203 W Cottage Grove Rd., Cottage Grove, WI 53527, (608)839-4511 [465]

Cotter and Co., 8600 W Bryn Mawr Ave., Chicago, IL 60631-3579, (773)975-2700 [13648]

Cottingham Paper Co., PO Box 163579, Columbus, OH 43216, (614)294-6444 [21694]

Cotton Caboodle Company Co., 203 W Thomas St., Seattle, WA 98119-4213, (206)282-0075 [4899]

The Cotton Exchange, PO Box 825, Wendell, NC 27591-0825, (919)365-5900 [4900]

Cottonwood Cooperative Oil Co., Hwy. 23 S, Cottonwood, MN 56229, (507)423-6282 [22175]

Cottonwood Sales Yard, PO Box 178, Cottonwood, ID 83522-0178, (208)962-3284 [17800]

Couch's Inc., U.S 30, Latrobe, PA 15650, (412)539-2238 [10852]

Cougle Commission Co., 345 N Aberdeen, Chicago, IL 60607, (312)666-7861 [10853]

Coulter Elevator, PO Box 177, Coulter, IA 50431, (515)866-6921 [17801]

Coulter Steel and Forge Co., PO Box 8008, Emeryville, CA 94662, (510)420-3500 [19901]

Coulter Welding Inc., 2816 S Broadway, Minot, ND 58701-7114, (701)852-4044 [16812]

Counter Assault, 120 Industry Ct., Kalispell, MT 59901, (406)257-4740 [23608]

Country Classic Dairies Inc., 1001 N 7th Ave., Bozeman, MT 59715, (406)586-5425 [10854]

Country Club Foods Inc., PO Box 228, Kaysville, UT 84037, (801)546-1201 [10855]

Country Decor, 1107 S Military Hwy. B, Chesapeake, VA 23320-2343, (757)420-8236 [26450]

Country Fresh Inc., 2555 Buchanan SW, Grand Rapids, MI 49508-1006, (616)243-0173 [10856]

Country Miss Carrollton, Rte. 1, Box 67H, Carrollton, AL 35447-9784, (205)367-8171 [4901]

Country Originals Inc., 3844 W Northside Dr., Jackson, MS 39209, (601)366-4229 [13336]

Country Oven Bakery, 2840 Pioneer Dr., Bowling Green, KY 42102, (502)782-3200 [10857]

Country Smoked Meats Inc., PO Box 46, Bowling Green, OH 43402, (419)353-0783 [10858]

Country Springs Farmers, 8419 N State Rte. 19, Green Springs, OH 44836, (419)639-2242 [10859]

Country Star Coop, PO Box 428, New Washington, OH 44854, (419)492-2548 [17802]

Country Time Ceramic Supply Inc., 3200 N Haines Ave., Rapid City, SD 57701-9562, (605)342-2505 [25612]

Country Wide Transport Services Inc., 119 Despatch Dr., East Rochester, NY 14445, (716)381-5470 [10860]

Countryman Co.; D.F., 480 N Pryor, St. Paul, MN 55104, (612)645-9153 [5580]

Countrymark Cooperative Inc., 950 N Meridian St., Indianapolis, IN 46204-3909, (317)685-3000 [466]

Countryside Marketing, PO Box 80110, Billings, MT 59108-0110, (406)245-6627 [467]

County General, RR 1, Box 500, Hettinger, ND 58639, (701)567-2412 [468]

County Line Co-op, 555 Main St., Rising Sun, OH 43457, (419)457-5711 [469]

County Optical Inc., PO Box 909, Caribou, ME 04736-0909, (207)493-3329 [19254]

Courtaulds Coatings Inc. Southeast Div., 3658 Lawrenceville Hwy., Tucker, GA 30084, (404)938-4600 [21419]

CourterCo, 5373 W 79th St., Indianapolis, IN 46268-1631, (317)875-7550 [4]

Courtesy Distributors Inc., PO Box 2217, Glenview, IL 60025-6217, (708)495-5480 [24951]

Courtesy Sanitary Supply, 33533 Mound Rd., Sterling Heights, MI 48310-6527, (810)979-8010 [4604]

Cousin Corporation of America, 12333 Enterprise Blvd., PO Box 2939, Largo, FL 33779, (813)536-3568 [26451]

Coutinho Caro and Company Inc., 300 First Stamford Pl., Stamford, CT 06902, (203)356-4840 [19902]

Coutts Library Services Inc., 736 Cayuga St., Lewiston, NY 14092, (716)754-4304 [3662]

Couzon USA, 298 Federal St., PO Box 905, Greenfield, MA 01302-0905, (413)774-3481 [15458]

Cove Distributors, 6325 Erdman Ave., Baltimore, MD 21205, (410)325-1298 [3706]

Cover and Son Wholesale Lumber Inc.; H.A., 798 Front St., Thayer, MO 65791, (417)264-7232 [7225]

Cover To Cover, 439 Norfolk Ave., Norfolk, NE 68701, (402)371-1600 [3663]

Covington Detroit Diesel Inc., PO Box 18949, Greensboro, NC 27419, (336)292-9240 [2488]

Covington Diesel Inc., PO Box 18949, Greensboro, NC 27419, (919)292-9240 [2489]

Cowan Brothers Inc., 809 State St., Bristol, VA 24201, (703)669-8342 [4605]

Cowan Costume, Inc., 108 S Caddo, Cleburne, TX 76031, (817)641-3126 [13337]

Cowan Supply Co., 485 Bishop St., Atlanta, GA 30361, (404)351-6351 [23129]

Cowboy Oil Co., PO Box L, Pocatello, ID 83201, (208)232-7814 [22176]

Cower Publishing Company Ltd., Old Post Rd., Brookfield, VT 05036, (802)276-3162 [3526]

Cowin Equipment Company Inc., PO Box 10624, Birmingham, AL 35202, (205)841-6666 [7226]

Cox; Charles E., PO Box 127, Carson City, NV 89702-0127, (702)883-9119 [4606]

Cox Distributing; Dale, 2210 Pineview, Petaluma, CA 94954, (707)778-7793 [10861]

Cox Enterprises Inc., PO Box 105357, Atlanta, GA 30348, (404)843-5000 [2490]

Cox Industries, Inc., PO Drawer 1124, Orangeburg, SC 29116, (803)534-7467 [7227]

Cox Paper & Printing Co., 1160 Carter Rd., Owensboro, KY 42301, (270)684-1436 [21695]

Cox & Son Inc.; H., 1402 Sawyer Rd., Traverse City, MI 49684, (616)943-4730 [1621]

Cox Subscriptions, Inc.; W.T., 411 Marcia Dr., Goldsboro, NC 27530, (919)735-1001 [3664]

Cox Wood Preserving Co., PO Drawer 1124, Orangeburg, SC 29116, (803)534-7467 [7227]

Coyle Inc., 250 W Beltline Hwy., Madison, WI 53713, (608)257-0291 [15459]

Coyle Mechanical Supply, PO Box 578, Granite City, IL 62040, (618)797-1760 [16813]

Coyne Galleries; Elaine, Peachtree Business Center, 3039 Amwiler Rd., Ste. 120, Atlanta, GA 30360, (404)448-8101 [17379]

Coyne Mattress Co. Ltd., 94-134 Leowwena St., Waipahu, HI 96797, (808)671-4071 [15460]

Coyne's Inc., 7400 Boone Ave., N, Brooklyn Park, MN 55428, (612)425-8666 [15461]

Coyote Engineering, Inc., 11555 27th Ave. NE, Seattle, WA 98125-5341, (206)363-5047 [23609]

Coyote Loader Sales Inc., 6721 Chittenden Rd., Hudson, OH 44236-4423, (330)650-5101 [7228]

Coyote Network Systems, Inc., 1640 S Sepulveda Blvd., Los Angeles, CA 90040, (818)735-7600 [8584]

Coyote Pet Products Inc., 750 Design Port, Ste. 108, ChuLa Vista, CA 91911, (619)421-5431 [27113]

Coyote Vision USA, PO Box 277, Pittsford, NY 14534, (716)385-7580 [14075]

Cozzi Iron and Metal Inc., 2232 S Blue Island Ave., Chicago, IL 60608, (773)254-1200 [26790]

CPA Services Inc., 525 B St., Ste. 1900, San Diego, CA 92101-4495, (619)699-6716 [3812]

CPAC Inc., 2364 Leicester Rd., Leicester, NY 14481, (716)382-3223 [22849]

CPP-Belwin Inc., 15800 NW 48th Ave., PO Box 4340, Hialeah, FL 33014, (305)620-1500 [3665]

CPS Distributors Inc., 4275 Forest St., Denver, CO 80216, (303)394-6040 [15916]

CPS Marketing Corporation, 2000 Main St., Ste. 500, Ft. Myers, FL 33901, (941)466-8343 [18757]

CPS Technologies Inc., 350 Rte. 46, Ste. 7, Rockaway, NJ 07866, (973)625-7900 [6166]

CR Specialty Co., 1701 Baltimore, Kansas City, MO 64108, (816)221-3550 [13484]

Crader Distributing Co., Rte. 3, Box 3135, Marble Hill, MO 63764, (573)238-2676 [15917]

Craelius and Company Inc.; L., 1100 W Fulton St., Chicago, IL 60607, (312)666-7100 [10862]

Craft Corner, 719 Main St., Caldwell, ID 83605-3745, (208)454-2351 [26452]

Craft Enterprises, 810 W Picacho Ave., Las Cruces, NM 88005-2236, (505)527-1470 [26453]

Craft & Hobby Supplies, 118 Edwardia Dr., Greensboro, NC 27409, (910)855-8880 [20934]

Craft King, 5675 N Tampa Hwy., PO Box 90637, Lakeland, FL 33801, (941)680-1313 [20935]

Craft Oil Corp., 837 Cherry St., Avoca, PA 18641, (717)457-5485 [22177]

Craft-Tex/Phase IV Inc., 2637 E Green Dr., High Point, NC 27260-7112, (919)861-2009 [13338]

Craft Wholesalers, 77 Cypress St. SW, Reynoldsburg, OH 43068-9673, (740)964-6210 [20936]

Craftmade International Inc., PO Box 1037, Coppell, TX 75019-1037, (972)393-3800 [15462]

Craftown Inc., 109 A McArthur Ct., Nicholasville, KY 40356-9109, (859)885-4720 [17380]

Crafts Etc. Ltd., 7717 SW 44th St., Oklahoma City, OK 73179-4808, (405)745-1200 [25613]

Craftsmen Supply, Inc., 1170-A South Beltline, PO Box 16641, Mobile, AL 36609, (205)343-3398 [9830]

Craftsmen Supply, Inc., 7457 Gunter Rd., Pensacola, FL 32526-3843, (850)455-5429 [9831]

Craftwood Lumber Co., 1590 Old Deerfield Rd., Highland Park, IL 60035, (847)831-2800 [7229]

Cragin Metals L.L.C., 2900 N Kearsarge Ave., Chicago, IL 60641, (773)283-2201 [19903]

Craig & Hamilton Meat Co., 721 N Union, Stockton, CA 95205-4150, (209)465-5838 [10863]

Craighead Farmers Cooperative, Rte. 2, Box 348, Bono, AR 72416, (870)932-3623 [17803]

Crain Automotive Inc., PO Box 15178, Little Rock, AR 72231-5178, (501)945-8383 [2491]

Crain M-M Sales Inc., 765 PickensInd'l DrExt, Marietta, GA 30062, (404)428-4421 [2492]

Cramer Co. Inc., 811 E Waterman St., Wichita, KS 67202-4729, (316)263-6145 [15097]

Cramer Products, Inc., PO Box 1001, Gardner, KS 66030, (913)856-7511 [19255]

Crandall Associates, 6107 Waltway Dr., Houston, TX 77008-6259, (713)681-4376 [3666]

Crane Co., 100 1st Stamford Pl., Stamford, CT 06902, (203)363-7300 [7230]

Crane Engineering Sales Inc., PO Box 38, Kimberly, WI 54136, (920)733-4425 [15918]

Cranel Inc., 8999 Gemini Pkwy., Columbus, OH 43240-2010, (614)431-8000 [6167]

Cranston International Inc., PO Box 820, Woodland, CA 95776, (530)662-7373 [470]

Craven Co.; E.F., PO Box 20807, Greensboro, NC 27420, (919)292-6921 [7231]

Crawford Sales Co., 1377 Hamilton Circle, Olathe, KS 66061-4526, (913)782-0801 [1622]

Crawfords Office Furniture & Supplies, 435 Westlake N, Seattle, WA 98109-5221, (206)682-1757 [20937]

Cream City Scale Company Inc., PO Box 749, Menomonee Falls, WI 53051, (414)255-5640 [24342]

Cream O' Weber, 4282 W 1730 South, Salt Lake City, UT 84104, (801)973-9922 [10864]

Creameries Blending Inc., 303 6th St. NE, Little Falls, MN 56345, (612)632-3631 [471]

Creative Arts Book Co., 833 Bancroft Way, Berkeley, CA 94710, (510)848-4777 [3667]

Creative Business Concepts, PO Box 2354, Twin Falls, ID 83303-2354, (208)734-9988 [20938]

Creative Craft Distributors, PO Box 134, Manville, RI 02838, (401)769-4010 [20939]

Creative Distributors, 96 Union Pk., Boston, MA 02118, (617)426-5525 [14846]

Creative Engineering and Manufacturing Corp., 3510 Mattingly Rd., Buckner, KY 40010-8801, (502)241-7144 [15919]

Creative Health Products, 5148 Saddle Ridge Rd., Plymouth, MI 48170, (734)996-5900 [19256]

Creative Healthcare Resources, 1701 E 79th St., Ste. 1, Minneapolis, MN 55425-1151, (612)854-9389 [3668]

Creative Homeowner Press, 24 Park Way, Upper Saddle River, NJ 07458, (201)934-7100 [3669]

Creative Imports Inc., 205 Hallene Rd. 210B, Warwick, RI 02886-2450, (401)738-8240 [17381]

Creative Joys Inc., Southern Eagle Cartway, Brewster, MA 02631, (508)255-4685 [3670]

Creative Merchandising Inc., 9917 Glenwood St., Overland Park, KS 66212, (913)642-3816 [13339]

Creative Paint & Glass Inc., 1204 Strand Ave., Missoula, MT 59801-5609, (406)543-7158 [21420]

Creative Rehab, 1817 State St., Racine, WI 53404, (414)635-0211 [19257]

Creative Source, 20702 El Toro Rd., Ste. 555, El Toro, CA 92630, (714)458-7971 [3671]

Creative Specialties Inc., 20969 Ventura Blvd., Ste. 21, Woodland Hills, CA 91364-2364, (818)367-2131 [15463]

Creative Stage Lighting Company Inc., 149 Rte. 28 N, PO Box 567, North Creek, NY 12853-0567, (518)251-3302 [8585]

Creative Store Design Inc., 3728 N Fretney St., Milwaukee, WI 53212, (414)963-1900 [25614]

Creative Technologies Corp., 170 53rd St., Brooklyn, NY 11232, (718)492-8400 [15098]

Creger Auto Company Inc., PO Box 7281, Shreveport, LA 71137-7281, (318)425-4292 [2493]

Creighton & Son, 123 Washington Ave., Portland, ME 04101, (207)774-3812 [14847]

Crellin Handling Equipment Inc., 12 Commercial Way, East Providence, RI 02914, (401)438-6400 [15920]

Creme Curls Bakery Inc., 5292 Lawndale, POB 276, Hudsonville, MI 49426, (616)669-6230 [10865]

Crenshaw Corp., 1700 Commerce Rd., PO Box 24217, Richmond, VA 23224, (804)231-6241 [2494]

CREOS. Technologies LLC, 7388 S Revere Pkwy Ste. 1003, Englewood, CO 80112, (303)790-8888 [8586]

Cres Jewelry Factory Inc., PO Box 800, West New York, NJ 07093-0800 [17382]

Cresc Corp., 3550 Broad St., Ste. H-1, Chamblee, GA 30341, (404)452-1155 [13340]

Crescent Airways Inc., 7501 Pembroke Rd., Hollywood, FL 33023-2579, (954)987-1900 [77]

Crescent City Pharmaceutical, 200 Loyola Ave., New Orleans, LA 70112-2002, (504)524-2254 [18758]

Crescent Cooperative Association, PO Box 316, Crescent, OK 73028, (405)969-3334 [472]

Crescent Electric Supply (Appleton, Wisconsin), PO Box 1157, Appleton, WI 54912, (920)734-4517 [15099]

Crescent Electric Supply Co., 516 W Market St., Anderson, SC 29624-1441, (864)225-4904 [8587]

Crescent Electric Supply Co., 2222 6th, Sioux City, IA 51101-1888, (712)277-1273 [8588]

Crescent Electric Supply Co., PO Box 500, East Dubuque, IL 61025-4420, (815)747-3145 [8589]

Crescent Electric Supply Co., 200 S Larkin Ave., Joliet, IL 60436-1248, (815)725-3020 [8590]

Crescent Electric Supply Co., PO Box 1157, Appleton, WI 54912, (920)734-4517 [8591]

Crescent Electric Supply Co., PO Box 500, East Dubuque, IL 61025-4420, (815)747-3145 [8592]

Crescent Imports & Publications, PO Box 7827, Ann Arbor, MI 48107-7827, (734)665-3492 [3672]

Crescent Paper Co., 1940 W Oliver Ave., PO Box 1983, Indianapolis, IN 46221, (317)236-6900 [21696]

Cressi-Sub USA Inc., 10 Reuten Dr., Closter, NJ 07624, (201)784-1005 [23610]

Cressy & Sons Inc.; W. C., Old Alewive Rd., Kennebunk, ME 04043, (207)985-6111 [18759]

Crest Audio/Video/Electronics, 1662 Main St., Buffalo, NY 14209, (716)885-5878 [8593]

Crest Beverage Co., PO Box 26640, San Diego, CA 92126, (619)566-1010 [1623]

Crest Distributing Co., PO Box 818, Provo, UT 84603, (801)373-7970 [22178]

Crest Distributors, 1136 Longsdale Ave., Central Falls, RI 02863, (401)723-9774 [9832]

Crest Fruit Co. Inc., 100 N Tower Rd., Alamo, TX 78516, (956)787-9971 [10866]

Crest Industries Inc. (Alexandria, Louisiana), PO Box 6115, Alexandria, LA 71307-6115, (318)448-8287 [8594]

Crest Paper Products Inc., 457 Mulberry St., Trenton, NJ 08638, (609)394-5357 [21697]

Crest Steel Corp., 1250 E 223rd St., Ste. 108, Carson, CA 90745-4214, (310)830-2651 [19904]

Crest Truck Equipment Co. Inc., Rte. 625, Bowmansville Rd., PO Box 555, Bowmansville, PA 17507, (717)445-6746 [2495]

Crestar Food Products Inc., 750 Old Hickory Blvd., Burns, TN 37029, (615)377-4400 [10867]

Crestland Cooperative, PO Box 329, Creston, IA 50801-0329, (515)782-6411 [473]

Creston Feed and Grain Co., PO Box 603, Creston, IA 50801-0603, (515)782-7202 [474]

CRH International Inc., 15 Dan Rd., Canton, MA 02021-2847, (781)821-1000 [4902]

Crisci Food Equipment Co., 1103 Croton Ave., PO Box 8327, New Castle, PA 16107, (412)654-6609 [24097]

The Crispin Co., 2929 Allen Pkwy., Ste. 2222, Houston, TX 77019, (713)224-8000 [19905]

Crispy's Inc., 544 E 24th St., Tucson, AZ 85713, (520)623-3403 [10868]

Crites-Moscow Growers Inc., PO Box 8912, Moscow, ID 83843, (208)882-5519 [475]

Crittenden Paint and Glass, 248 24th St., Ogden, UT 84401, (801)394-4643 [21421]

Crockett Farmers Cooperative Co., 359 W Main St., Alamo, TN 38001, (901)696-5528 [476]

Cromer Co., 55 NE 7th St., Miami, FL 33132, (305)373-5414 [4903]

Cromers Inc., PO Box 163, Columbia, SC 29202, (803)779-1147 [24098]

Cromland, Inc., 1995 Highland Ave., Ste. 200, Bethlehem, PA 18020, (610)997-3000 [3673]

Crompton and Knowles Colors Inc., PO Box 33188, Charlotte, NC 28233, (704)372-5890 [4367]

Cromwell Leather Group, 147 Palmer Ave., Mamaroneck, NY 10543, (914)381-0100 [18385]

Cron Chemical Corp., PO Box 14042, Houston, TX 77221, (713)644-7561 [4368]

Cronin Asphalt Corp., PO Box 4257, East Providence, RI 02914-4257, (401)434-5252 [22179]

The Cronin Co., 2601 W 5th Ave., Eugene, OR 97402, (541)485-6280 [9833]

The Cronin Co., 1205 NW Marshall, Portland, OR 97209, (503)226-3508 [9834]

Crookston Farmers Cooperative, PO Box 398, Crookston, MN 56716, (218)281-2881 [477]

Crosby's Americana Arts I; Judy, PO Box 7365, Albuquerque, NM 87194-7365, (505)266-2324 [17383]

Crosman Corporation, Rtes. 5 & 20, East Bloomfield, NY 14443, (716)657-6161 [13485]

Crosman Seed Corp., Rtes. 5 & 20, East Bloomfield, NY 14443, (716)657-6161 [13485]

Cross Co., PO Box 18508, Greensboro, NC 27419-8508, (336)856-6000 [2496]

Cross Co.; A.T., One Albion Rd., Lincoln, RI 02865, (401)333-1200 [20940]

Cross and Company Inc., PO Box 920628, Houston, TX 77058-2504, (713)673-3100 [10869]

Cross Mark Southern California, 12131 Telegraph Rd., Santa Fe Springs, CA 90670, (562)946-7333 [10870]

Cross Sales and Engineering Co., PO Box 18508, Greensboro, NC 27419-8508, (336)856-6000 [2496]

Crossing Press, 1201 Shaffer Rd. No. B, Santa Cruz, CA 95060-5729, (831)420-1110 [3674]

Crosslin Supply Company Inc., 140 N Main St., Eagleville, TN 37060, (615)274-6237 [7232]

Crossmark Sales and Marketing, 444 W 21st St., Ste. 101, Tempe, AZ 85282, (602)437-0616 [10871]

Crotty Corp., PO Box 37, Quincy, MI 49082, (517)639-8787 [2497]

Crouch Supply Company Inc., PO Box 163829, Ft. Worth, TX 76161-3829, (817)332-2118 [24343]

Croushorn Equipment Company Inc., PO Box 796, Harlan, KY 40831, (606)573-2454 [478]

Crowe and Co.; F.T., 21229 84th Ave., Kent, WA 98032, (253)872-9696 [7233]

Crowley Grain Drier Inc., PO Box 677, Crowley, LA 70526, (318)783-3284 [17804]

Crown Beer Distributors Inc., PO Box 1255, Wall, NJ 07719, (908)223-9100 [1624]

Crown Beverages Inc., 1650 Linda Way, Sparks, NV 89431-6159, (702)358-2428 [1625]

Crown Bottling Co., PO Box 1906, Mankato, MN 56002-1906, (507)345-4715 [1626]

Crown Distributing Co., 3409 McDougal Ave., Everett, WA 98201-5040, (425)252-4192 [1627]

Crown Distributing Inc., 3401 Bridgeland Dr., Bridgeton, MO 63045, (314)291-5545 [10872]

Crown Foods Inc., 5243 Manchester Rd., St. Louis, MO 63110, (314)645-5300 [10873]

Crown Glass Corp., 2345 W Hubbard St., Chicago, IL 60612, (312)666-2000 [25909]

Crown Imports, 11311 Harry Hines, No. 302, PO Box 59872, Dallas, TX 75229, (972)241-0401 [13341]

Crown Inc. Beverage Div., 2321 Bluebell Dr., Livermore, CA 94550-1007, (310)404-7452 [1628]

Crown Inc. (Cerritos, California), 12881 166th St., Cerritos, CA 90703, (562)926-3939 [10874]

Crown Optical Co. Inc., 15 Commerce St., Greenville, RI 02828, (401)949-3400 [19258]

Crown Optical Ltd., 2111 Van Deman St., Baltimore, MD 21224, (410)685-7373 [19259]

Crown Products Co., 450 Nepperhan Ave., Yonkers, NY 10701, (914)968-2222 [21698]

Crown Products Inc., 3500 North Causeway Blvd., Ste. 1548, Metairie, LA 70002, (504)837-5342 [10875]

Crown Steel Sales Inc., 3355 W 31st St., Chicago, IL 60623, (312)376-1700 [19906]

Crown Tile & Marble, 4722 Sunrise Hwy., Massapequa Park, NY 11762, (516)798-2457 [9835]

Croy & Associates Inc.; Ralph, 701 W Capitol Ave., Little Rock, AR 72201-3203, (501)378-0109 [8595]

CRS Business Products, 142 N Kimball St., Casper, WY 82601-2028, (307)235-8822 [20941]

Crucible Service Center, PO Box 445, Butler, WI 53007, (414)781-6710 [13649]

Crucible Service Center, 568 Brick Church Park Dr., Nashville, TN 37207-3200, (615)361-6699 [19907]

Crucible Service Centers, 5639 W Genesee St., Camillus, NY 13031-0991, (315)487-0800 [19908]

Crum Electrical Supply Inc., 1165 W English, Casper, WY 82601 [8596]

Crumrine Manufacturing Jewelers, 145 Catron Dr., Reno, NV 89512-1001, (702)786-3712 [17384]

Crus Oil Inc., 2260 SW Temple, Salt Lake City, UT 84115, (801)466-8783 [22180]

Cruse Communication Co., 230 N Higby St., Jackson, MI 49202-4021, (517)332-3579 [25149]

Cruse Communication Co., 4903 Dawn Ave., East Lansing, MI 48823-5689, (517)332-3579 [15100]

Crutcher Dental Inc., 849 S 3rd St., Louisville, KY 40203, (502)584-5104 [19260]

Cruzen Equipment Company Inc., 160 W Mallory Ave., Memphis, TN 38109, (901)774-3130 [16814]

CRW Parts, Inc., 3 James Ct., Wilmington, DE 19801, (302)651-9300 [2498]

Crystal Bottling Company Inc., 575 Display Way, Sacramento, CA 95838, (916)568-3300 [24952]

Crystal Cave Enterprises, PO Box 1000, Taos, NM 87571, (505)758-5400 [4281]

Crystal City Bakers, 25 Riverside Dr., Corning, NY 14830-2237, (607)937-5331 [10876]

Crystal Clear Industries Inc., 2 Bergen Tpk., Ridgefield Park, NJ 07660, (201)440-4200 [15464]

Crystal Cooperative Inc., PO Box 210, Lake Crystal, MN 56055, (507)726-6455 [479]

Crystal Farms Refrigerated Distribution Co., 6465 Wayzata Blvd., Ste. 200, Minneapolis, MN 55426, (612)544-8101 [10877]

Crystal Flash Petroleum Corp., PO Box 684, Indianapolis, IN 46206, (317)879-2849 [22181]

Crystal Food Import Corp., 245 Sumner St. E, Boston, MA 02128-2121, (617)569-7500 [10878]

Crystal Home Health Care Inc., 15819 Schoolcraft St., Detroit, MI 48227-1749, (313)493-4900 [18760]

Crystal Home Health Care Inc., 15819 Schoolcraft St., Detroit, MI 48227-1749, (313)493-4900 [19261]

Crystal Lite Manufacturing Co, 18500 SW 108th Ave., Tualatin, OR 97062, (503)692-3024 [19909]

Crystal Products Corp., 50 Knickerbocker Rd., Moonachie, NJ 07074-1613, (908)249-6602 [10879]

Crystal Refrigeration Inc., 710 E 59th St., Davenport, IA 52807-2627, (319)386-1000 [14408]

Crystal Tile, 2011 Beech Ln., Bensalem, PA 19020, (215)245-6739 [7234]

Crystaline North America Inc., 1170-B Pontiac Ave., Cranston, RI 02920-7926, (401)461-2104 [17385]

CS Battery Inc., 4555 W 59th St., Chicago, IL 60629, (773)582-3050 [2499]

CSI Sports, LLC, 360 Industrial Blvd., Sauk Rapids, MN 56379, (320)252-4193 [23611]

CSL and Associates Inc., 10 Commerce St., Ste. B, Destin, FL 32541-2359, (850)650-6602 [15921]

CSM International Corp., 3545 Chain Bridge Rd., Ste. 210, Fairfax, VA 22030-2708, (703)591-2626 [6168]

CSS Corp., 85 S Bragg St., Alexandria, VA 22312-2731, (703)941-0336 [6129]

C.S.S. Publishing Co., 517 S Main St., PO Box 4503, Lima, OH 45802-4503, (419)227-1818 [3675]

CSSI Cellular, 905 Palo Pinto St., Weatherford, TX 76086-4135, (817)341-2337 [5581]

CT Wholesale, PO Box 31510, Stockton, CA 95213, (209)983-8484 [480]

CTI Abrasives and Tools, 2650 S Grand Ave., Santa Ana, CA 92705, (714)662-0909 [16815]

CTN Data Service Inc., PO Box 250, Hamilton, IN 46742-0250, (219)488-3388 [6169]

CTR Used Parts & Equipment, 12867 Hwy. 44, Middleton, ID 83644, (208)454-8878 [2500]

CTT Distributing, 109 Medallion Ctr., Dallas, TX 75214, (214)373-9469 [26454]

Cub Foods, 421 S 3rd St., PO Box 9, Stillwater, MN 55082-0009, (612)439-7200 [10880]

Cuba Buckles, PO Box 1327, Cuba, NM 87013-1327, (505)289-3918 [17386]

Cubs Distributing Inc., 3333 N 20th St., Lincoln, NE 68521, (402)477-4411 [9836]

Cuerno Largo Publications, 6406 Old Harbor Ln., Austin, TX 78739, (512)288-3478 [3676]

Cuetara America Co., 15925 NW 52nd Ave., Miami Lakes, FL 33014, (305)625-8888 [10881]

CUI Corp., 1160 Mark Ave., Carpinteria, CA 93013, (805)684-7617 [18761]

CUI Stack Inc., PO Box 609, Beaverton, OR 97075, (503)643-4899 [8597]

Cullen Distributors Inc., 125 S Park St., Streator, IL 61364, (815)672-2975 [26284]

Cullens Playland Inc., 8424 Florida Blvd., Baton Rouge, LA 70806-4838, (504)927-9305 [4904]

Cullman Seed and Feed Co., PO Box 548, Cullman, AL 35056, (205)734-3892 [481]

Culp Inc., PO Box 2686, High Point, NC 27261-2686, (910)889-5161 [26009]

Culp Lumber Co.; H.W., PO Box 235, New London, NC 28127, (704)463-7311 [7235]

Cultural Hispana/Ameriketakoa, PO Box 7729, Silver Spring, MD 20907, (301)585-0134 [3677]

Culver Dairy Inc., 868 Bridle Ln., Webster, NY 14580-2606, (716)671-6709 [10882]

Culver-Fancy Prairie Cooperative Co., PO Box 222, Athens, IL 62613, (217)636-7171 [17805]

Culver Products Co. Inc., PO Box 230, Culver, IN 46511-0230, (219)842-3465 [18762]

Cumberland Farmers Union Cooperative, PO Box 118, Almena, WI 54805-0118 [482]

Cumberland Oil Co. Inc., 7260 Centennial Blvd., Nashville, TN 37209, (615)350-7333 [22182]

Cumberland Optical Company Inc., 806 Olympic St., Nashville, TN 37203, (615)254-5868 [19262]

Cumberland Valley Cooperative Association, PO Box 350, Shippensburg, PA 17257, (717)532-2191 [483]

Cumming-Henderson Inc., PO Box 330, Santa Clara, CA 95052, (408)727-4440 [2501]

Cummings, McGowan and West Inc., 8668 Olive Blvd., St. Louis, MO 63132, (314)993-1336 [7236]

Cummins Alabama Inc., PO Box 1147, Birmingham, AL 35201, (205)841-0421 [2502]

Cummins Connecticut Inc., 260 Murphy Rd., Hartford, CT 06114, (203)527-9156 [2503]

Cummins Cumberland Inc., 9822 Bluegrass Pkwy., Louisville, KY 40299, (502)491-6060 [2504]

Cummins Diesel Sales Inc., 2690 Cleveland Ave. N, St. Paul, MN 55113, (612)636-1000 [15922]

Cummins Electronics Company Inc., 2851 State St., Columbus, IN 47201, (812)377-8601 [6170]

Cummins Gateway Inc., 7210 Hall St., St. Louis, MO 63147, (314)389-5400 [2505]

Cummins Great Lakes Inc., PO Box 530, De Pere, WI 54115, (414)337-1991 [2506]

Cummins Great Plains Diesel Inc., PO Box 6068, Omaha, NE 68106, (402)551-7678 [2507]

Cummins Great Plains Diesel Inc., 5515 Center St., Omaha, NE 68106, (402)551-7678 [15923]

Cummins Intermountain Inc., PO Box 25428, Salt Lake City, UT 84125, (801)355-6500 [2508]

Cummins Michigan Inc., 41216 Vincenti Ct., Novi, MI 48375, (313)478-9700 [2509]

Cummins Mid-South Inc., 1784 E Brooks Rd., Memphis, TN 38116, (901)345-1784 [15924]

Cummins Midstates Power Inc., 3762 W Morris St., Indianapolis, IN 46242, (317)243-7979 [2510]

Cummins North Central Inc., 2690 Cleveland Ave. N, St. Paul, MN 55113, (651)636-1000 [2511]

Cummins Ohio Inc., 4000 Lyman Dr., Hilliard, OH 43026, (614)771-1000 [2512]

Cummins Power Inc., 5100 E 58th Ave., Commerce City, CO 80022, (303)287-0201 [2514]

Cummins Power Systems Inc., 2727 Ford Rd., Bristol, PA 19007, (215)781-2955 [2513]

Cummins Rocky Mountain, Inc., 5100 E 58th Ave., Commerce City, CO 80022, (303)287-0201 [2514]

Cummins Southern Plains Inc., 600 Watson Dr., Arlington, TX 76011, (817)640-6801 [2515]

Cummins Southwest Inc., 2239 N Black Canyon Hwy., Phoenix, AZ 85009-2706, (602)252-8021 [2516]

Cummins Utility Supply, 513 N Nelson, Amarillo, TX 79107-7904, (806)373-1808 [13650]

Cummins-Wagner Company Inc., 10901 Pump House Rd., Annapolis Junction, MD 20701, (410)792-4230 [5837]

Cummins West Inc., 14775 Wicks Blvd., San Leandro, CA 94577, (510)351-6101 [2517]

Cumulous Communications Co., 6622 N Blackstone Ave., Fresno, CA 93710, (209)431-1414 [5582]

Cuna Service Group Inc., PO Box 431, Madison, WI 53701, (608)231-4000 [20942]

Cuna Strategic Services, Inc., PO Box 431, Madison, WI 53701, (608)231-4000 [20942]

Cunill Motors Inc., PO Box 10189, Houston, TX 77206, (713)695-2981 [20617]

Cunningham Co.; C.A., 545 Medford St., PO Box 45, Charlestown, MA 02129, (617)242-5345 [13651]

Cunningham Distributing Inc., 2015 Mills St., El Paso, TX 79901, (915)533-6993 [25615]

Cunningham Distributing Inc., 615 Haines Ave. NW, Albuquerque, NM 87102-1225, (505)247-8838 [25616]

Cunningham Equipment Inc.; J.A., 2025 Trenton Ave., Philadelphia, PA 19125, (215)426-6650 [16816]

Cunningham Sales Corp., 180 Cedar Hill St., Marlborough, MA 01752-3017, (508)481-2940 [19263]

Cunningham Wholesale Company Inc., PO Box 32651, Charlotte, NC 28232, (704)392-8371 [1629]

Cup Graphics and Screen Printing, 4307 S Port Ave., No. 142, Corpus Christi, TX 78415, (512)992-5114 [4905]

Curbell Inc., 7 Cobham Dr., Orchard Park, NY 14127-4180, (716)667-3377 [22950]

Curcio Scrap Metal Inc., 416 Lanza Ave., Saddle Brook, NJ 07663-6405, (973)478-3133 [26791]

The Curlery, PO Box 1138, Gresham, OR 97030-0244, (503)253-4327 [14073]

Curran Contracting Co., 7502 S Main St., Crystal Lake, IL 60014, (815)455-5100 [7237]

Current Software, 3037 Dixie Hwy., Ste. 209, Covington, KY 41017-2364, (606)341-0702 [6171]

Current Works Inc., 1000 N Rand Rd Ste. 123, Wauconda, IL 60084, (847)526-1121 [6172]

Currie Industries Inc., PO Box 567, Old Saybrook, CT 06475, (203)388-4638 [22951]

Curry Oil Company Inc., 1450 S Main St., London, KY 40741, (606)864-5119 [22183]

Curtin Matheson Scientific Inc., 9999 Veterans Memorial Dr., Houston, TX 77038-2499, 800-640-0640 [24359]

Curtis Associates Inc., PO Box 67171, Chestnut Hill, MA 02467-0002, (781)455-9191 [26455]

Curtis & Campbell Inc., 6239 B St., No. 102, Anchorage, AK 99518-1728, (907)561-6011 [21422]

Curtis Co., 731 E Brooks Rd., Memphis, TN 38116, (901)332-1414 [15101]

Curtis & Curtis, Inc., Star Rte., Box 8-A, Clovis, NM 88101, (505)762-4759 [484]

Curtis Fluid Controls, Inc., 2170 S Lipan, Denver, CO 80223, (303)922-4564 [16817]

Curtis Packing Co. Inc., 2416 Randolph Ave., Greensboro, NC 27406, (910)275-7684 [10883]

Curtis Packing Co. Inc., 115 Sycamore St., Tifton, GA 31794-9511, (912)382-4014 [10884]

Curtis Paint, 751 S 200 W, Salt Lake City, UT 84101-2708, (801)364-1933 [21423]

Curtis and Sons; L.N., 1800 Peralta St., Oakland, CA 94607, (510)839-5111 [24529]

Curtis Toledo Inc., 1905 Kienlen Ave., St. Louis, MO 63133, (314)383-1300 [5838]

Curtis TradeGroup Inc., PO Box 17575, Sarasota, FL 34276-0575, (941)927-2333 [24274]

Curtiss Bakery; Penny, PO Box 486, Syracuse, NY 13211-0486, (315)454-3241 [10885]

Curt's Oil Co., 2220 E Shawnee Rd., Muskogee, OK 74403, (918)682-7888 [22184]

Curtze Steel Inc., 1103 Bacon St., Erie, PA 16511, (814)456-2008 [19910]

Cusack Wholesale Meat Co., PO Box 25111, Oklahoma City, OK 73125, (405)232-2115 [10886]

Cushing and Company Inc., 325 W Huron St., Chicago, IL 60610, (312)266-8228 [25617]

Cushing Inc.; T.F., PO Box 2049, Springfield, MA 01101, (413)788-7341 [8598]

Custer Grain Co., 2006 Tony Country Rd., Garrett, IN 46738, (219)357-5432 [485]

Custer Supply & Fixtures, 721 Missouri Ave., MiLes City, MT 59301-4226, (406)232-7826 [25618]

Custom Audio, 422 S Broadway St., McComb, MS 39648-4118, (601)684-2869 [25150]

Custom Audio Distributors Inc., PO Box 327, Bogart, GA 30622-0327, (706)353-1380 [25151]

Custom Bilt Cabinet and Supply Inc., PO Drawer 8969, Shreveport, LA 71148-8969, (318)865-1412 [7238]

Custom Cable Industries Inc., 3221 Cherry Palm Dr., Tampa, FL 33619, (813)623-2232 [8599]

Custom Car Center, 10541 Independence Ave., Independence, MO 64053, (816)254-1177 [20618]

Custom Creations Sportswear, 6950 NW 37th Ave., Miami, FL 33147-6514, (305)693-7873 [4906]

Custom Design and Manufacturing, 555 Alter St Ste. E, Broomfield, CO 80020, (303)465-2646 [8600]

Custom Design Play Structures Inc., 444 Winnebago Dr., Lake Winnebago, MO 64034, (816)537-7171 [23612]

Custom Design Security & Sound, 33305 W 7 Mile, Livonia, MI 48152, (248)442-2233 [24530]

Custom Drapery and Blinds Inc., 1312 Live Oak St., Houston, TX 77003, (713)225-9211 [15465]

Custom Healthcare Systems, 919 W 21st St., Norfolk, VA 23517-1515, (757)622-8334 [19264]

Custom Industries Inc., 2 S Grove St., Bradford, MA 01835-7518, (978)374-6331 [27301]

Custom Labs, 2641 2nd St., Macon, GA 31206, (912)742-2615 [19265]

Custom Labs, 6398 Hwy. 85, PO Box 488, Riverdale, GA 30274, (404)997-3344 [19266]

Custom Laminations Inc., 932 Market St., Paterson, NJ 07509, (973)279-9174 [26010]

Custom Leathercraft Manufacturing, 811 W 58th St., Los Angeles, CA 90037, (213)752-2221 [18386]

Custom Manufacturing Co., 5501 S Lamar, Dallas, TX 75215, (214)428-5173 [15925]

Custom Music Co., 1930 Hilton, Ferndale, MI 48220, (248)546-4135 [25152]

Custom-Pak Inc., PO Box 3083, Clinton, IA 52732, (319)242-1801 [26792]

Custom Phones Inc., 638 Virginia Ave., Indianapolis, IN 46203, (317)638-6385 [5583]

Custom Photo Manufacturing, 10830 Sanden Dr., Dallas, TX 75238-1337, (214)349-9779 [22850]

Custom Radio Corp., 4012 Merchant Rd., Ft. Wayne, IN 46818-1246, (219)489-2062 [15102]

Custom Sound of Augusta Inc., 2029 Gordon Hwy., Augusta, GA 30909, (706)738-8181 [25153]

Custom Supply Inc., 2509 5th Ave. S, Birmingham, AL 35233-3303, (205)252-0141 [8601]

Custom Trim of Akron, 777 E Market St., Akron, OH 44305, (330)253-6893 [2518]

Custom Trim of America, 777 E Market St., Akron, OH 44305, (330)253-6893 [2518]

Custom Truck Sales and Service, PO Box 23305, Nashville, TN 37202, (615)244-7077 [20510]

Custom Vision Optical, 2341 Charles St., PO Box 28019, Dallas, TX 75228, (214)321-4347 [19267]

Custom Wholesale Flooring, 2020 NW 23rd St., Miami, FL 33142, (305)635-6421 [9837]

Custom Wholesale Flooring, 5910 D Breckenridge Pkwy., Tampa, FL 33610, (813)626-8840 [9838]

Custom Wholesale Flooring, 735 Park North Blvd., Clarkston, GA 30021, (404)296-9663 [9839]

CustomCraft, 40 Rte. 23, Riverdale, NJ 07457, (973)839-4286 [7239]

Customline of North America, Inc., 438 W 37th St., Ste. 3B, New York, NY 10018-4095, (212)967-6266 [13342]

Cuthbert Greenhouse Inc., 4900 Hendron Rd., Groveport, OH 43125, (614)836-3866 [14848]

Cuthbert Greenhouse Inc., 4900 Hendron Rd., Groveport, OH 43125, (614)836-3866 [14849]

Cuthbert Greenhouse Inc., 4900 Hendron Rd., Groveport, OH 43125, (614)836-3866 [14850]

Cutie Pie Corp., 443 W 400 N, Salt Lake City, UT 84103, (801)533-9550 [10887]

Cutlery, 12503 A Wayzata Blvd., Ridgedale Center, Minnetonka, MN 55343, (612)545-1484 [13652]

Cutrufellos Creamery Inc., 1390 Barnum Ave., Stratford, CT 06497, (203)378-2651 [10888]

Cutter Precision Metals Inc., PO Box 88488, Seattle, WA 98138, (206)575-4120 [19911]

Cutter Precision Metals Inc., 700 Comstock St., Santa Clara, CA 95054, (408)727-0333 [19912]

Cutters Exchange Inc., PO Box 7001, Murfreesboro, TN 37133, (615)895-8070 [15926]

Cutting Edge Audio Group L.L.C., 290 Division St., Ste. 103, San Francisco, CA 94103, (415)487-2323 [25154]

Cutting Edge Technology Inc., 26071 Merit Circle, Ste. 108, Laguna Hills, CA 92653, (949)582-1946 [6173]

Cutting Tools & Abrasives, 5605 Pike Rd., Loves Park, IL 61111, (815)877-4039 [17212]

Cutting Tools Inc., 8601 73rd Ave. N, Brooklyn Park, MN 55428-1571, (612)535-7757 [13653]

Cuyahoga Landmark Inc., PO Box 361189, Strongsville, OH 44136, (440)238-6600 [22185]

CVK Corp., 3725 Ingersoll Ave., Des Moines, IA 50312-3410, (515)279-2020 [19268]

CW Magnet Wire Co., 739 Roosevelt Rd., Ste. 301, Glen Ellyn, IL 60137, (630)469-8484 [8602]

C.W. Mills, 2900 Dixie Ave., Grandville, MI 49418-1159, (616)538-4009 [20943]

CWC Group Inc., 290 Paseo Sonrisa, Walnut, CA 91789, (909)598-9366 [6174]

CWF Inc., 3015 Beechtree Dr., Sanford, NC 27330, (919)775-3631 [14851]

CWT International Inc., PO Box 1396, Gainesville, GA 30501, (404)532-3181 [10889]

CX Blaster Co. Inc., 13218 Jessica Dr., Spring Hill, FL 34609, (352)683-4862 [26456]

CY Hart Distributig Co., 433 Atlas Dr., Nashville, TN 37211, (615)834-1652 [22186]

Cyber-Tech Inc., PO Box 23801, Portland, OR 97281, (503)620-2285 [8603]

Cybernetic Micro Systems Inc., PO Box 3000, San Gregorio, CA 94074, (650)726-3000 [8604]

Cycle Lines USA - Full Bore, 9515 51st Ave., Unit 12, College Park, MD 20740, (301)474-9119 [20638]

Cyclone Grain Co., 4079 E County Rd. 400 S, Frankfort, IN 46041-8630, (765)654-4466 [17806]

Cylinder Cooperative Elevator, PO Box 67, Cylinder, IA 50528, (712)424-3335 [17807]

CYN, 1661 N Elston Ave., Chicago, IL 60622, (773)227-7627 [18488]

Cypress Book (USA) Co., Inc., 3450 3rd St., Unit 4B, San Francisco, CA 94124, (415)821-3582 [3678]

D & A Distributing, PO Box 1199, Lebanon, MO 65536-3213, (417)532-6198 [2519]

D/A Mid South Inc., 9000 Jameel, No. 100, Houston, TX 77040, (713)895-0090 [24531]

D. Austin Aircraft, RR 1, Box 397, Whitefield, NH 03598, (603)837-2627 [78]

D and B Steel Co., 5221 W 164th St., Cleveland, OH 44142, (216)267-5500 [19913]

D & B Tile, 781 S Congress Ave., Delray Beach, FL 33445, (561)272-7022 [9840]

D & B Tile, 8550 SW 129th Ter., Kendall, FL 33176, (305)238-1909 [9841]

D & B Tile, 4431 Corporate Sq., Naples, FL 34104-4796, (941)643-7099 [9842]

D & B Tile, 4241 L.B. McLeod Dr., Orlando, FL 32856, (407)849-6590 [9843]

D & B Tile, 1551 N Powerline Rd., Pompano Beach, FL 33069, (954)979-2066 [9844]

D & B Tile, 3346 45th St., West Palm Beach, FL 33407, (561)478-4242 [9845]

D & B Tile Distributors, 14200 NW 4th St., Sunrise, FL 33325, (954)846-2660 [9846]

D and B Tile Distributors, 14200 NW 4th St., Sunrise, FL 33325, (954)846-2660 [7240]

D-Chem Corp., PO Box 460462, St. Louis, MO 63146, (314)772-8700 [4369]

D & D Distributing, 14615 C St. S, Tacoma, WA 98444-4571, (253)536-2236 [26457]

D & D Distributing, 5840 N 70th St., Lincoln, NE 68507, (402)467-3573 [1630]

D and D Shoe Co., 200 S 5th St., Mayfield, KY 42066, (502)251-2055 [4907]

D & D Shoe Company, LLC, 200 S 5th St., Mayfield, KY 42066, (270)251-2055 [24722]

D & D Specialties Millwork, 3535 Princeton Dr. NE, Albuquerque, NM 87107, (505)888-4880 [7241]

D & D Transport Refrigeration Services, PO Box 30737, Billings, MT 59107-0737, (406)656-6290 [14409]

D E B Industries, Inc., 2918 S Poplar Ave., Chicago, IL 60608, (312)225-3600 [10890]

D & F Distributors, 2317 Cruzen St., Nashville, TN 37211, (615)259-9090 [15927]

D & H Beauty Supply, PO Box 14565, Grand Forks, ND 58206-1255, (701)746-5471 [14076]

D and H Distributing Co., 2525 N 7th St., PO Box 5967, Harrisburg, PA 17110, (717)236-8001 [6175]

D and H Distributing Co., 2525 N 7th St., Harrisburg, PA 17110, (717)236-8001 [15103]

D & H Tire Service, 919 Troup St., Kansas City, KS 66104, (913)621-1155 [2520]

D & J Cabinet Co. Inc., 285 Industrial Way, Fayetteville, GA 30214-6816, (404)461-1260 [13084]

D-J, Inc., PO Box 5240, Manchester, NH 03108-5240, (603)647-1301 [7242]

D & J Manufacturing Inc., 4758 Angola Rd., Toledo, OH 43615, (419)382-1327 [13343]

D & K Healthcare Resources, Inc., 8000 Maryland Ave., Ste. 920, St. Louis, MO 63105, (314)727-3485 [19269]

D & K Wholesale Drug, Inc., 2040 Creative Dr., No. 300, Lexington, KY 40505-4283, (606)254-5534 [19270]

D and K Wholesale Drug Inc., 8000 Maryland Ave., Ste. 920, St. Louis, MO 63105, (314)727-3485 [19269]

D and K Wholesale Drugs Inc., 8000 Maryland Ave., Ste. 920, St. Louis, MO 63105, (314)727-3485 [19269]

D & L Appliance Parts Company, Inc., 2100 Freedom Dr., Charlotte, NC 28208-5154, (704)374-0400 [15104]

D & L Stained Glass Supply, Inc., 4939 N Broadway, Boulder, CO 80304, (303)449-8737 [25619]

D & M Distributing, 3970 E Olympic Blvd., Los Angeles, CA 90023-3248, (213)268-9958 [2521]

D & M Distributors Inc., 273 Presumpscot St., Portland, ME 04103-5226, (207)772-4796 [25620]

D and M Distributors Inc., 273 Presumpscot St., Portland, ME 04103-5226, (207)772-4796 [24099]

D & M Plywood, Inc., 340 Seneca St., Buffalo, NY 14204, (716)856-5656 [7243]

D-M Tire Supply, 1259 Manheim Pke., Lancaster, PA 17601, (717)291-4493 [2522]

D-MAR Corp., PO Box 599, Bay City, MI 48707, (517)892-9042 [26505]

D & P Enterprises Inc., 960 S Virginia St., Reno, NV 89502-2416, (702)786-6565 [24100]

D & S Enterprises, 1901 Meadowlark, Farmington, NM 87401, (505)325-7445 [4607]

D and T Services Inc., 123 N Columbus Ave., Louisville, MS 39339, (601)773-5024 [13654]

D & W Distributing Co. Inc., 309 Mechanic St., Pekin, IL 61554, (309)347-6194 [2523]

D.A. Distributors Inc., 1128 Eureka, Wyandotte, MI 48192, (734)285-3350 [7244]

Daber Inc., PO Box 190, Woodland, NC 27897, (919)587-5221 [5134]

Dabney-Hoover Supply Company Inc., 61 W Georgia Ave., Memphis, TN 38103, (901)523-8061 [16818]

Dabro Supply Co., PO Box 148, Braceville, IL 60407, (815)237-2166 [2619]

DAC International Inc., 6702 McNeil Dr., Austin, TX 78729, (512)331-5323 [25621]

Daccord Inc., 545 NW 28th St., Miami, FL 33127-4137, (305)576-0926 [4908]

Dacotah Paper Co., 3940 15th NW, Fargo, ND 58108, (701)281-1730 [21699]

Dacotah Paper Co., 3940 15th NW, Fargo, ND 58108, (701)281-1730 [16819]

Dadco Food Products Inc., PO Box 1107, Eau Claire, WI 54702-1107, (715)834-3418 [10891]

Dady Distributing Inc.; J.A., PO Box 40, Sisseton, SD 57262-0040, (605)698-3261 [1631]

Daedalus Books, 4601 Decatur St., Hyattsville, MD 20781, (410)309-2705 [3679]

Daewoo Equipment Corp., 4350 Emery Industrial Pkwy., Warrensville Heights, OH 44128, (216)595-1212 [15928]

Daewoo International (America), 14848 Northam St., La Mirada, CA 90638, (714)228-8800 [26011]

Daffin Mercantile Company Inc., PO Box 779, Marianna, FL 32447, (850)482-4026 [24101]

Dahl, 1000 Siler Park Ln., Santa Fe, NM 87505-3116, (505)471-1968 [23130]

Dahlco Music & Vending, 296 N Pascal, St. Paul, MN 55104, (612)645-1111 [25622]

Daigger and Co. Inc.; A., 620 Lakeview Pkwy., Vernon Hills, IL 60061 [24344]

Daigger and Company Inc. ETA/Cuisenaire; A., 500 Greenview Ct., Vernon Hills, IL 60061, (847)816-5050 [26458]

Daiichi Fine Chemicals Inc., 1 Overlook Point, Ste. 250, Lincolnshire, IL 60069, (847)634-7251 [14077]

Dailey Inc.; William E., PO Box 51, Shaftsbury, VT 05262, (802)442-9923 [7245]

Dailey Metal Group Inc., 1113 N Sherman Ave., No. 3, Madison, WI 53701, (608)244-5542 [19914]

The Daily Astorian, PO Box 210, Astoria, OR 97103, (503)325-3211 [3680]

Daily Bread Company Inc., PO Box 1091, Portsmouth, NH 03802, (603)436-2722 [10892]

Dairy Export Co. Inc., 635 Elliott W, Seattle, WA 98119, (206)284-7220 [10893]

Dairy Fresh Corp., PO Box 159, Greensboro, AL 36744, (334)624-3041 [10894]

Dairy Fresh Products Co., 601 Rockefeller Ave., Ontario, CA 91761, (909)975-1019 [10895]

Dairy Gold Foods Co., 909 E 21st St., Cheyenne, WY 82001, (307)634-4433 [10896]

Dairy Maid Dairy Inc., 706 Vernon Ave., Frederick, MD 21701, (301)663-5114 [10897]

Dairy Maid Foods Inc., 2434 E Pecan St., Phoenix, AZ 85040, (602)243-3090 [10898]

Dairy-Mix Inc., 3020 46th Ave. N, St. Petersburg, FL 33714, (813)525-6101 [10899]

Dairy-Mix Inc., 3020 46th Ave. N, St. Petersburg, FL 33714, (727)525-6101 [10900]

Dairy Valley, 1201 S 1st St., Mt. Vernon, WA 98273, (360)424-7091 [10901]

Dairyland Seed Company Inc., PO Box 958, West Bend, WI 53095, (414)338-0163 [486]

Dairylea Cooperative Inc., PO Box 4844, Syracuse, NY 13221, (315)433-0100 [10902]

Dairyman's Supply Co., PO Box 528, Mayfield, KY 42066, (502)247-5642 [7246]

Daisytek Inc., 500 N Central Expwy., Plano, TX 75074, (972)881-4700 [6176]

Daiwa Corp., PO Box 6031, Artesia, CA 90702-6031, (562)802-9589 [23613]

Daiwa Golf Co., PO Box 6031, Artesia, CA 90702-6031, (562)802-9589 [23613]

Dakin Inc., 230 Spring St. NW, Ste. 1810A, Atlanta, GA 30303, (404)584-7424 [26459]

Dakin Inc., 6101 Variel Ave., Woodland Hills, CA 91365, (818)992-6000 [26460]

Dako Corp., 6392 Via Real, Carpinteria, CA 93013, (805)566-6655 [19271]

Dakota Beverage Co., PO Box 967, Sioux Falls, SD 57101, (605)339-2337 [1632]

Dakota Chemical Inc., PO Box 88111, Sioux Falls, SD 57109-1001, (605)225-6290 [25623]

Dakota Communications Service, PO Box 2341, Bismarck, ND 58502-2341, (701)223-9581 [5584]

Dakota Corp., PO Box 543, Rutland, VT 05702, (802)775-6062 [4909]

Dakota Drug Inc., PO Box 5009, Minot, ND 58702-5009, (701)852-2141 [14078]

Dakota Electric Supply Co., PO Box 2886, Fargo, ND 58108, (701)237-9440 [8605]

Dakota Flags and Banner, 308 LA Plata Rd. NW, Albuquerque, NM 87107-5429, (505)345-7882 [26012]

Dakota Food Equipment Inc., PO Box 2925, Fargo, ND 58108-2925, (701)232-4428 [24102]

Dakota Industrial Supply, 340 Main St. E, Valley City, ND 58072-3441, (701)845-2632 [4608]

Dakota Pride Coop, 648 W 2nd St., Winner, SD 57580, (605)842-2711 [487]

Dakota Pride Cooperative, 648 W 2nd St., Winner, SD 57580, (605)842-2711 [22187]

Dakota Refrigeration Inc., 515 19th St. N, Fargo, ND 58102-4133, (701)235-9698 [14410]

Dakota Sales Co. Inc., PO Box 12209, Grand Forks, ND 58208-2209, (701)746-0341 [1633]

Dakota Steel and Supply Co., PO Box 2920, Rapid City, SD 57709-2920, (605)394-7200 [19915]

Dal CAM Oil Co. Inc., PO Box 1761, Rapid City, SD 57709-1761, (605)341-5934 [7247]

Dal-Kawa Hijet, 312 Kanuga St., Hendersonville, NC 28739, (704)692-7519 [20619]

Dal Tile Corp., 730 Dearborn Park Ln., Worthington, OH 43085, (614)433-9181 [9847]

Dalco Athletic, 3719 Cavalier, Garland, TX 75042, (972)494-1455 [25624]

Dalco International, Inc., 8433 Glazebrook Ave., Richmond, VA 23228, (804)266-7702 [18763]

Dale Electronics Corp., 7 E 20th St., New York, NY 10003, (212)475-1124 [8606]

Dale Office Plus, 31938 Groesbeck, Fraser, MI 48026-3914, (810)296-2340 [20944]

Dale's Auto Paints & Supplies, 1101 W Broadway St., Hobbs, NM 88240-5501, (505)393-1541 [21424]

Dales Mechanical Sales & Service, 1701 E Main St., Van Buren, AR 72956-4736, (501)474-6844 [14411]

Dalhart Consumers Fuel and Grain Association Inc., PO Box 671, Dalhart, TX 79022, (806)249-5695 [17808]

Dalis Electronic Supply Inc., 2455 S 7th St., Bldg. 175, Phoenix, AZ 85034, (602)275-2626 [8607]

Dalis, Inc.; H.L., 35-35 24th St., Long Island City, NY 11106, (718)361-1100 [5585]

DaLite Screen Co., 3100 N Detroit St., Warsaw, IN 46580, (219)267-8101 [25155]

Dallas Aerospace Inc., 1875 N IH-35, Carrollton, TX 75006-3761, (214)539-1993 [79]

Dallas Auto Auction Inc., 5333 W Keist Blvd., Dallas, TX 75236, (214)330-1800 [20620]

Dallas City Packing Inc., 3049 Morrell St., Dallas, TX 75203, (214)948-3901 [10903]

Dallas County Farmers Exchange, PO Box 1024, Buffalo, MO 65622, (417)345-2121 [488]

Dallas Digital Corp., 624 Krona Dr., No. 160, Plano, TX 75074, (214)424-2800 [6177]

Dallas Ford New Holland Inc., 1351 S Loop 12, Irving, TX 75060, (972)579-9999 [489]

Dallas Gold and Silver Exchange Inc., 2817 Forest Ln., Dallas, TX 75234, (972)484-3662 [17387]

Dallas Market Center Company Ltd., 2100 Stemmons Fwy., Dallas, TX 75207, (214)655-6100 [10904]

Dallas Peterbilt Inc., PO Box 560228, Dallas, TX 75356, (972)445-7505 [2524]

Dallas Wheels & Accessories, Inc., 3510 Dalworth, Arlington, TX 76011, (817)640-7575 [2525]

Dallas Wholesale Builders Supply Inc., PO Box 271023, Dallas, TX 75227, (214)381-2200 [7293]

Daltile, 350 Dunksferry Rd., Bensalem, PA 19020, (215)441-4977 [7248]

Dalton Computer Services Inc., PO Box 2469, Dalton, GA 30722-2469, (706)259-3327 [6178]

Dalton, Cooper Gates Corp., 68 Forest Ave., Locust Valley, NY 11560, (516)759-2011 [490]

Dalton Cooperative Creamery Association, PO Box 248, Dalton, MN 56324, (218)589-8806 [491]

Dalton Supply Co. Inc., PO Box 1246, Dalton, GA 30722-1246, (706)278-1264 [14412]

Daly Inc.; James W., PO Box 6041, Peabody, MA 01961, (978)532-6900 [18764]

Daly and Sons Inc.; M.J., 110 Mattheuck, Waterbury, CT 06705, (203)753-5131 [23131]

Damascus Peanut Co., State Hwy. 200 W, Damascus, GA 31741, (912)725-3353 [17809]

Damascus Worldwide, Inc., PO Box 543, Rutland, VT 05702, (802)775-6062 [4909]

Damien Educational Services; M., 4810 Mahalo Dr., Eugene, OR 97405, (541)687-9055 [3681]

Damille Metal Supply Inc., PO Box 2512, Huntington Park, CA 90255, (213)587-6001 [26793]

Damon Chemical Co., Inc., PO Box 2120, Alliance, OH 44601-0120, (330)821-5310 [4609]

Damon Industries, Inc., PO Box 2120, Alliance, OH 44601-0120, (330)821-5310 [4609]

Damon Insulation Co., PO Box 1212, Auburn, ME 04211-1212, (207)783-4240 [7249]

Damore's Wholesale Produce, 2206 Delaware Blvd., Saginaw, MI 48602-5226, (517)793-1511 [10905]

Damour; William L., PO Box 426, Henniker, NH 03242-0426, (603)428-9463 [1634]

Dan Communications Inc.; Lee, 155 Adams Ave., Hauppauge, NY 11788-3699, (631)231-1414 [5586]

Dan Valley Foods, Inc., PO Box 441, Danville, VA 24543, (804)792-4311 [10906]

Dana Distributors Inc., 1750 Rte. 211 E, Middletown, NY 10940, (914)692-6766 [1635]

Dana Kepner Co., 700 Alcott, Denver, CO 80204, (303)623-6161 [23132]

Dana-Lu Imports Inc., 280 Midland Ave., Bldg. M-1, Saddle Brook, NJ 07663, (201)791-2244 [24103]

Dana World Trade Div., 10800 NW 103rd St., Ste. 11, Miami, FL 33178, (305)499-5100 [2526]

Danacolors, 1930 Fairway Dr., San Leandro, CA 94577, (510)895-8000 [21595]

Danaher Tool Group, 1609 Old Missouri Rd., Springdale, AR 72764-2699, (501)751-8500 [13655]

Dancker, Sellew and Douglas Inc., 53 Park Pl., New York, NY 10007, (212)619-7171 [20945]

Danco Prairie FS Cooperative, 5371 Farmco Dr., Madison, WI 53718-1425, (608)241-4181 [492]

Dandee Creations Ltd., 94 Thames, Brooklyn, NY 11237-1620, (718)366-5911 [15466]

Dane County Farmers Union Cooperative, 203 W Cottage Grove Rd., Cottage Grove, WI 53527, (608)839-4511 [465]

Danforth-Gilman Grain Co., PO Box 166, Danforth, IL 60930, (815)269-2390 [17810]

Danforth International Trade Associates, Inc., 3156 Route 88, Point Pleasant, NJ 08742, (732)892-4454 [21700]

Daniel Piroutek, HCR 1 Box6-A, Milesville, SD 57553, (605)544-3316 [17811]

Daniels Co.; C.P., PO Box 119, Waynesboro, GA 30830, (706)554-2446 [27114]

Daniels-McCray Lumber Co., 10741 Del Monte Ln., Overland Park, KS 66211, (913)341-6900 [7677]

Danka Business Systems PLC, 11201 Danka Cir. N, St. Petersburg, FL 33716, (813)576-6003 [20946]

Danka E.B.S., 411 Waverly Oaks Rd., Bldg. 1, Waltham, MA 02454-8414, (617)894-6283 [6179]

Danka Industries Inc., 11201 Danka Cir. N, St. Petersburg, FL 33716-3712, (813)579-2300 [20947]

Danka Inwood Business Systems Inc., 10280 Miller Rd., Dallas, TX 75238, (214)484-7720 [20948]

Dann Dee Display Fixtures Inc., 7555 N Caldwell Ave., Niles, IL 60714, (708)588-1600 [25625]

D'Anna B'Nana, 15-1293 Auina Rd., Pahoa, HI 96778, (808)965-6262 [14852]

Danvers Farmers Elevator Co., PO Box 160, Danvers, IL 61732, (309)963-4305 [493]

Danvers Farmers Elevator Co., 200 S W St., Danvers, IL 61732, (309)963-4305 [10907]

Danville Cooperative Association, PO Box 67, Danville, KS 67036, (316)962-5238 [494]

Danville Gasoline and Oil Company Inc., 201 W Main St., Danville, IL 61832-5709, (217)446-8500 [22188]

Danville Gasoline & Oil Co. Inc. Leverenz Automotive & Truck Parts, 201 W Main St., Danville, IL 61832-5709, (217)442-8500 [15929]

Danzey Oil and Tire Co. Inc., PO Box 1646, Dothan, AL 36302, (205)792-4159 [2527]

Dapra Corp., 66 Granby St., Bloomfield, CT 06002, (860)242-8539 [15930]

Darant Distribution, 1832 E 68th Ave., Denver, CO 80229, (303)289-2220 [22952]

Darco Enterprises Inc., 1600 S Laflin St., Chicago, IL 60608, (312)243-3000 [19916]

Daret Inc., 33 Daret Dr., Ringwood, NJ 07456, (973)962-6001 [21425]

Darigold, 520 E Albany, Caldwell, ID 83605-3539, (208)459-3687 [10908]

Darisil, Inc., PO Box 457, Suffern, NY 10901, (914)357-2740 [10909]

Darling Bolt Co., PO Box 2035, Warren, MI 48090, (313)757-4100 [13656]

Darling Corp.; J.L., 2614 Pacific Hwy. E, Tacoma, WA 98424-1017, (253)922-5000 [21701]

Darlings, 153 Perry Rd., Bangor, ME 04401, (207)941-1240 [20621]

Darlington Farms, PO Box 390, Springboro, OH 45066-0390 [10910]

Darr Equipment Company Inc., PO Box 540788, Dallas, TX 75354, (214)721-2000 [7250]

D'Arrigo Brothers of Massachusetts Inc., 105 New England Produce Ctr., Chelsea, MA 02150, (617)884-0316 [10911]

D'Artagnan Inc., 280 Wilson Ave., Newark, NJ 07105, (973)344-0565 [10912]

Dartek Corp., 175 Ambassador Dr., Naperville, IL 60540, (630)941-1000 [6180]

Darter Inc., 1701 Crossroads Dr., Joliet, IL 60431-9503, (708)534-7550 [4610]

Darton Archery, 3540 Darton Dr., Hale, MI 48739-9003, (517)728-4231 [23614]

D.A.S. Distributors, Inc., RR 2, Box 275K, Palmyra, PA 17078, (717)964-3642 [8608]

Dash Inc., 8226 Nieman Rd., Lenexa, KS 66214, (913)888-6555 [6181]

Dashew; J., 2709 Frederick Ave., Baltimore, MD 21223, (410)233-1660 [15931]

Dassel Cooperative Dairy Association, PO Box E, Dassel, MN 55325, (320)275-2257 [495]

DATA COM, 11205 S Main St., #109, Houston, TX 77025-5642, (713)665-5752 [6182]

Data Forms Inc., PO Box 1050, Fayetteville, AR 72701, (501)443-0099 [21702]

Data Information Service, 13 Partridge Rd., Concord, NH 03301-7886, (603)228-3549 [20949]

Data Management Corp., PO Box 70, Butler, WI 53007, (414)783-6910 [20950]

Data Net Inc., 900 Huyler St., Teterboro, NJ 07608, (201)288-9444 [5587]

Data Papers Inc., PO Box 149, Muncy, PA 17756, (717)546-2201 [21703]

Data Print Inc., 4810 N Lagoon Ave., Ste. 300, Portland, OR 97217-7665 [21704]

Data Professionals, 10716 N Westlakes Dr., Ft. Wayne, IN 46804-8601 [6183]

Data Source Media Inc., PO Box 4397, Lincoln, NE 68504, (402)466-3342 [6184]

Data Tech Services Inc., PO Box 82, Bryant, AR 72089-0082, (501)847-8998 [6185]

Database Computer Systems Inc., RR 1, Box 228, Lynchburg, VA 24502-9701, (804)385-6020 [6186]

DataCal Corp., 531 E Elliot Rd., Chandler, AZ 85225, (480)813-3100 [6187]

Datalink Corp., 7423 Washington Ave. S, Minneapolis, MN 55439-2410, (612)944-3462 [6188]

Datalink Ready Inc., PO Box 2169, Melbourne, FL 32902-2169, (321)676-0500 [8609]

Datamatics Management Services, Inc., 330 New Brunswick Ave., Fords, NJ 08863, (732)738-9600 [6189]

Datanet Services Inc., 20A Oak Branch Dr., Greensboro, NC 27407-2145, (336)294-0141 [6224]

DATAVOX Inc., 5300 Memorial, 3rd Fl., Houston, TX 77007, (713)741-6161 [5588]

Datel Communications Corp., 145 Bodwell St., Avon, MA 02322-1114, (508)580-2500 [5589]

Datex Inc., 320 Mears Blvd., Oldsmar, FL 34677, (813)891-6464 [8610]

Datex Medical Instrumentation Inc., 3 Highwood Dr., Tewksbury, MA 01876, (978)640-0460 [18765]

Datex-Ohmeda, Inc., 3 Highwood Dr., Tewksbury, MA 01876, (978)640-0460 [18765]

Datex-Ohmeda Inc., 2 Highwood Dr., Tewksbury, MA 01876, (978)640-0460 [19272]

Datron Corp., 5001 W 80th St., Minneapolis, MN 55437, (612)831-1626 [496]

Daubert Oil & Gas Co., 110 E 1st St., Dexter, NM 88230, (505)734-6001 [22189]

Dauphin Co., PO Box 5137, Springfield, IL 62705, (217)793-2424 [25156]

Dauphin Electrical Supply Co., PO Box 2206, Harrisburg, PA 17105, (717)986-9300 [8611]

Dave Steel Co. Inc., PO Box 2630, Asheville, NC 28802, (828)252-2771 [19917]

Davenport Organisation, 1 Merrill Industrial Dr., Ste. 18, Hampton, NH 03842-1981, (603)926-9266 [17388]

Davenport and Sons Inc.; J.T., PO Box 1105, Sanford, NC 27330, (919)774-9444 [10913]

Davenport Union Warehouse Co., 10th & Jefferson, Davenport, WA 99122, (509)725-7081 [17812]

Davenport-Webb Inc., 1190 Harlem Rd., Buffalo, NY 14216, (716)834-9443 [10914]

Dave's Auto Inc., PO Box 2292, Bismarck, ND 58502-0932, (701)255-1194 [2528]

Dave's Jewelry & Giftware, PO Box 740, Pelham, NH 03076, (603)635-2881 [17389]

Dave's Sport Shop, 23701 Nantocoke Rd., Quantico, MD 21856, (410)742-2454 [23615]

Dave's Used Auto Parts Inc., PO Box 7118, Cumberland, RI 02864-0892, (401)334-2900 [2529]

Davey Motor Co., PO Box 1249, Columbus, MT 59019-1249, (406)322-5346 [2530]

Davic Drapery Co., 410 S Maple Ave., Falls Church, VA 22046-4222, (703)532-6600 [15467]

David-Martin Co. Inc., 29 W 34th St., New York, NY 10001, (212)947-8452 [26013]

David Shoe Co., 1201 Edgecliff Pl., Apt. 1051, Cincinnati, OH 45206-2853 [24723]

David Tire Co. Inc., PO Box 2284, Birmingham, AL 35201, (205)251-8473 [2531]

Davids and Royston Bulb Company Inc., 550 W 135th St., Gardena, CA 90248, (310)532-2313 [14853]

Davidson & Associates; Art, PO Box 68, Waipahu, HI 96797-0068, (808)677-2422 [14079]

Davidson Farmers Cooperative, 3511 Dickerson Rd., Nashville, TN 37207-1705, (615)255-5797 [497]

Davidson Louisiana Inc., PO Box 1119, Lake Charles, LA 70602, (318)439-8393 [7251]

Davidson Lumber Co.; Howard A., PO Box 27066, Detroit, MI 48227, (313)834-6770 [7252]

Davidson Pipe Supply Company Inc., 5002 2nd Ave., Brooklyn, NY 11232, (718)439-6300 [23133]

Davidson's, 6100 Wilkinson Dr., Prescott, AZ 86301, (520)776-8055 [13486]

Davies and Company Ltd.; Theo. H., 560 N Nimitz Hwy., Ste. 207, Honolulu, HI 96817-5315, (808)531-5971 [15932]

Davies Electric Supply Co., PO Drawer 759, North Little Rock, AR 72114, (501)375-3330 [8612]

Davies Service Co.; Jo, 313 W Sycamore St., Elizabeth, IL 61028, (815)858-2238 [498]

Davies Supply Co., 6601 W Grand Ave., Chicago, IL 60707-2298, (773)637-7800 [16820]

Davis Associates Inc., PO Box 803, Parker, CO 80134-0803, (303)841-8648 [6190]

Davis Bakery Inc., 13940 Cedar Rd., Cleveland, OH 44118, (216)932-7788 [10915]

Davis & Butler, Inc., 1235 E Division St., Dover, DE 19901, (302)734-8100 [26285]

Davis Company Inc.; H.C., PO Box 346, Bridgeville, DE 19933, (302)337-7001 [10916]

Davis Co.; J.W., 3030 Canton, Dallas, TX 75226-1605, (214)651-7341 [25157]

Davis Co.; Kriz, 401 NW Norris, Topeka, KS 66608-1573, (785)354-9532 [8613]

Davis County Cooperative Society, 3500 S West Temple, Salt Lake City, UT 84115-4408, (801)467-4003 [24724]

Davis Electric Supply Company Inc.; W.B., 525 N Hollywood, Memphis, TN 38112-2544, (901)452-7363 [5590]

Davis Electrical Supply Company Inc., 24 Anderson Rd., Cheektowaga, NY 14225, (716)896-0100 [8614]

Davis Enterprises Inc.; Dan L., 402 Murray Rd., Valdosta, GA 31602-4000, (912)247-4120 [4910]

Davis Grain Corp., 5512 Bainbridge Blvd., Chesapeake, VA 23324, (804)543-2041 [17813]

Davis Paint Co., PO Box 7589, North Kansas City, MO 64116, (816)471-4447 [21426]

Davis Produce, Inc.; John, State Farmers Mkt. Bldg. C, PO Box 713, Forest Park, GA 30298, (404)366-0150 [10917]

Davis Rug Co., 3937 Barclay Rd., Shelby, NC 28152, (704)434-7231 [9848]

Davis Salvage Co., 3337 E Washington St., Phoenix, AZ 85034, (602)267-7208 [19918]

Davis and Sons Inc.; F.A., 6610 Cabot Dr., Baltimore, MD 21226-1754, (410)360-6000 [26286]

Davis & Sons; William E., 5333 G. S Mingo, Tulsa, OK 74145, (918)665-3737 [10918]

Davis Supply Co., PO Box 22189, Savannah, GA 31403-2189, (770)449-7000 [23134]

Davis Supply Co. Inc., PO Box 437, Brewton, AL 36427-0437, (205)867-6864 [16821]

Davis Wholesale Co. Inc.; Al, 767 Main St. W, Rochester, NY 14611, (716)328-6565 [14080]

Davison Co.; R.E., 170 Green St., Vergennes, VT 05491-8656, (802)877-3469 [24532]

Davison Inc., 1 Design Ctr. Pl., No. 410, Boston, MA 02210, (617)348-2870 [13085]

Davitt & Hansen West, 1859 Sabre St., Hayward, CA 94545, (510)293-0388 [25158]

Davitt and Hanser Music Co., 4940 Delhi Ave., Cincinnati, OH 45238, (513)451-5000 [25159]

Davitt and Hanser Music Co., 4940 Delhi Ave., Cincinnati, OH 45238, (513)451-5000 [15105]

Dawdys Inc., PO Box 206, Berthoud, CO 80513-0206, (970)532-3525 [25160]

Dawg Luvers & Co., 2600 Lanes Bridge Rd., Jesup, GA 31545, (912)427-6178 [13344]

Dawn Co., 3340 S Lapeer Rd., Orion, MI 48359, (248)391-9200 [5591]

Dawn Satellite Inc., 3340 S Lapeer Rd., Orion, MI 48359, (248)391-9200 [5591]

Dawson Industries Inc., 1627 Marion Ave., Grand Haven, MI 49417-2365, (313)771-5200 [25626]

Day Co.; John, PO Box 3541, Omaha, NE 68110, (402)455-8000 [15933]

Day Co.; John, PO Box 3541, Omaha, NE 68103, (402)455-8000 [499]

Day Corp.; Alan G., PO Box 5245, Lutherville Timonium, MD 21094-5245, (410)561-9995 [18766]

Day Manufacturing Co.; S.A., 1489 Niagara St., Buffalo, NY 14213, (716)881-3030 [2532]

Day Star Productions, 326 S Wille Ave., Wheeling, IL 60090, (847)541-5200 [25161]

Daylight Distributors, 4411 Sepulveda Blvd., Culver City, CA 90230, (310)313-9370 [26461]

Dayman USA Inc., 1111 Service Ave. SE, Roanoke, VA 24013-2923, (540)586-2803 [23616]

DayMark Corp., PO Box 350, Delmar, NY 12054, (518)439-9985 [13487]

Daymon Associates Inc., 700 Fairfield Ave., Stamford, CT 06902, (203)352-7500 [10919]

Daystar-Robinson Inc., 1979 Marcus Ave., #234, Lake Success, NY 11042, (516)328-3900 [10920]

Dayton Appliance Parts Co., 122 Sears St., Dayton, OH 45402, (937)224-3531 [15106]

Dayton Door Sales Inc., 1112 Springfield St., Dayton, OH 45403, (937)253-9181 [7253]

Daytona Beach Cold Storage Inc., PO Box 1752, Daytona Beach, FL 32115-1752, (904)252-3746 [10921]

D.B. Brown Inc., 400 Port Carteret Dr., Carteret, NJ 07008, (732)541-0200 [10922]

dB Sound L.P., 1219 Rand Rd., Des Plaines, IL 60016, (847)299-0357 [25162]

DBB Marketing Co., 155 Sansome St., Ste. 810, San Francisco, CA 94104, (415)956-7860 [10923]

DBL Labs, 30840 Joseph St., PO Box 280, St. Joseph, MN 56374, (320)363-7211 [19273]

D.C. Materials Inc., 3334 Kenilworth Ave., Ste. B, Hyattsville, MD 20781, (301)403-0200 [26794]

DC Metals Inc., 380 S Danebo St., Eugene, OR 97402, (503)344-3741 [19919]

DCE Corp., 5 Hillandale Ave., Stamford, CT 06902-2843, (203)358-3940 [6191]

DDS, 267 Amherst Rd., PO Box 471, Sunderland, MA 01375-0471, (413)665-3742 [6194]

De Best Manufacturing Company Inc., PO Box 2002, Gardena, CA 90247, (310)352-3030 [23135]

De Bruyn Produce Company Inc., PO Box 76, Zeeland, MI 49464, (616)772-2102 [10924]

DE International Inc., 1377 Barclay Cir., Ste. F, Marietta, GA 30060-2907, (404)422-8836 [18767]

De Lille Oxygen Co., 772 Marion Rd., Columbus, OH 43207, (614)444-1177 [16822]

De Luca Liquor and Wine Ltd., 2548 W Desert Inn Rd., Las Vegas, NV 89109, (702)735-9144 [1636]

De Mott Tractor Company Inc., 2235 E 25th St., Ste. 230, Idaho Falls, ID 83404-7538, (208)522-6372 [500]

De Poortere of America Inc.; Louis, 185 Rus Dr., Calhoun, GA 30701, (706)624-3110 [26014]

De Sisti Lighting Corp., 1109 Grand Ave., North Bergen, NJ 07047-1628, (201)319-1100 [8615]

De-Tec Inc., 1744 W Genesee St., Syracuse, NY 13204, (315)487-0909 [18768]

De Vries Imports & Distributors, 16700 Schoenborn St., North Hills, CA 91343, (818)893-6906 [10925]

DEA Specialties Co., 6874 Alamo Downs Pkwy., San Antonio, TX 78238, (210)523-1073 [20951]

Dead River Co., PO Box 1427, Bangor, ME 04401, (207)947-8641 [22190]

Deaktor/Sysco Food Services Co., PO Box 1000, Harmony, PA 16037, (724)452-2100 [10926]

Dealer Chemical Corp., PO Box 460462, St. Louis, MO 63146, (314)576-1333 [2533]

Dealers Dairy Products Co., 23800 Commerce Park Rd., Ste. D, Cleveland, OH 44122-5828, (216)292-6666 [10927]

Dealer's Discount Crafts, 8199 10 Mile Rd., Center Line, MI 48015, (810)757-2690 [20952]

Dealers Electric Motor, Brooklyn Navy Yard, Box 217, Brooklyn, NY 11205, (718)522-1110 [8616]

Dealers Food Products Co., 23800 Commerce Park Rd., Ste. D, Cleveland, OH 44122-5828, (216)292-6666 [10927]

Dealers Food Products Co., 23800 Commerce Park Rd., Ste. D, Cleveland, OH 44122-5828, (216)292-6666 [10928]

Dealers Supply Co., 110 SE Washington St., Portland, OR 97214, (503)236-1195 [7254]

Dealers Supply Co., 2100 Commerce Dr., Cayce, SC 29033, (803)796-2495 [9849]

Dealers Supply Co., PO Box 2628, Durham, NC 27715-2628, (919)383-7451 [9850]

Dealers Supply Co., 110 SE Washington St., Portland, OR 97214, (503)236-1195 [7255]

Dealers Supply and Lumber Inc., PO Box 5025, Sta. B, Greenville, SC 29606, (803)242-6571 [7256]

Dealers Truck Equipment Company Inc., PO Box 31435, Shreveport, LA 71130, (318)635-7567 [2534]

Dean Associates Inc.; Richard, 1 Harris St., Newburyport, MA 01950-2600, (978)462-1150 [25163]

Dean Foods Co., 3600 N River Rd., Franklin Park, IL 60131 [10929]

Dean-Henderson Equipment Co. Inc., Hwy. 165 S, England, AR 72046, (501)842-2521 [501]

Dean Machinery Co., 1201 W 31st St., Kansas City, MO 64108, (816)753-5300 [502]

Dean Oil Co., PO Box 9, Cullman, AL 35055, (256)734-6831 [22191]

Dean Supply Inc.; Bob, 2624 Hanson St., Ft. Myers, FL 33901-7488, (941)332-1131 [15934]

Deana Griebe, 5151 Loraine Ave., Detroit, MI 48208, (313)894-7110 [2175]

Deanco Inc., 3230 Scott Blvd., Santa Clara, CA 95054-3011, (408)654-9100 [8617]

Deans Firearms, Ltd., 7024 W Colfax, Lakewood, CO 80215, (303)234-1111 [13488]

Dean's Materials Inc., PO Box 1547, Fresno, CA 93716, (209)268-9301 [7257]

Dearborn Fabricating and Engineering Corp., 19440 Glendale Ave., Detroit, MI 48223, (313)273-2800 [15935]

Dearborn Trade, 155 N Wacker Dr., Chicago, IL 60606-1719, (312)836-4400 [3682]

Dearborn West L.P., 5236 Bell Ct., Chino, CA 91710-5701, (909)591-9393 [8618]

Dearborn Wholesale Grocers L.P., 2801 S Western Ave., Chicago, IL 60608, (773)254-4300 [10930]

Dearing Beverage Company Inc., 1520 Commerce St., Winchester, VA 22601, (540)662-0561 [1637]

Dearing Wholesale Inc., 366 Gay Pl., Jackson, OH 45640, (740)286-1046 [26462]

Deas Tire Co., PO Box 1678, Gulfport, MS 39502-1678, (228)863-5072 [2535]

Deaton's Carpet One, 1000 Hwy. 45 Bypass, Jackson, TN 38301, (901)664-5200 [9851]

DeBauge Brothers Inc., 2915 W 15th, Emporia, KS 66801, (316)342-4663 [1638]

Debenham Electric Supply Co., 5333 Fairbanks St., Anchorage, AK 99518-1258, (907)562-2800 [8619]

DeBois Textiles Inc., 1835 Washington Blvd., Baltimore, MD 21230, (410)837-8081 [26015]

Debra Inc., 125 E 87th, Ste. 3C, New York, NY 10128, (212)534-6654 [14081]

DeBragga and Spitler Inc., 826-D Washington St., New York, NY 10014, (212)924-1311 [10931]

DeBruce Grain Inc., 2702 Rock Creek Pkwy., Ste. 4, Kansas City, MO 64117-2519, (816)421-8182 [17814]

Decatur Bottling Co., PO Box 3520, Decatur, IL 62524-3250, (217)429-5415 [24953]

Decatur Coca-Cola Bottling Co., PO Box 1687, Decatur, AL 35602, (205)353-9211 [10932]

Decatur Custom Tool Inc., 410 N Jasper St., Decatur, IL 62521, (217)423-3639 [15936]

Decatur Hopkins, 800 John Quincy Adams, Taunton, MA 02780-1094, (508)824-8650 [13657]

Decision Data Service Inc., PO Box 3004, Frazer, PA 19355-0704, (215)674-3300 [6192]

Decision Support Systems Inc., 380 S State Rd., Ste. 1004-117, Altamonte Springs, FL 32714, (407)778-6447 [6193]

Decker and Company Inc., 16438 Felton Rd., Lansing, MI 48906, (517)321-7231 [503]

Decker Steel & Supply Co., 1625 Ash St., Erie, PA 16503, (814)454-2446 [19920]

Decker Steel and Supply Inc., 4500 Train Ave., Cleveland, OH 44102, (216)281-7900 [19921]

Decker's Inc., PO Box 51268, Idaho Falls, ID 83405-1268, (208)522-2551 [4611]

Deckers Outdoor Corp., 495-A S Fairview Ave., Goleta, CA 93117, (805)967-7611 [24725]

Deco Tool Supply Co., 415 W 76th St., Davenport, IA 52808, (319)386-5970 [15937]

DeConna Ice Cream Inc., PO Box 39, Orange Lake, FL 32681, (904)591-1530 [10933]

Decorative Aides Co. Inc., 317 St. Paul Ave., Jersey City, NJ 07306, (201)656-8813 [15468]

Decorative Crafts Inc., 50 Chestnut St., Greenwich, CT 06830, (203)531-1500 [13086]

Decorative Designs, 301 W 92 St., Bloomington, MN 55420-3632, (612)881-3389 [14854]

Decorative Engineering and Supply Inc., 17000 S Western Ave., PO Box 559, Gardena, CA 90248-0559, (310)532-4013 [15938]

Decorative Home Accents Inc., PO Box 1187, Abbeville, SC 29620, (864)446-2123 [15644]

Decorative Plant Service Inc., 1150 Phelps St., San Francisco, CA 94124, (415)826-8181 [504]

Decorative Products Group, 128 Regional Park Dr., Kingsport, TN 37660, (423)349-4129 [9852]

Decorative Products Group, 917 Dinwiddie, Knoxville, TN 37921, (423)525-0207 [9853]

Decorator & Craft Corp., 428 S Zelta, Wichita, KS 67207, (316)685-6265 [20953]

Decorator & Upholstery Supply, Inc., 501 McNeilly Rd., Pittsburgh, PA 15226, (412)561-3770 [26016]

Decoster Egg Farms, PO Box 216, Turner, ME 04282, (207)224-8222 [10934]

Decot Hy-Wyd Sport Glasses, Inc., PO Box 15830, Phoenix, AZ 85060-5830, (602)955-7625 [19274]

Deen Meat Co., Inc., PO Box 4155, Ft. Worth, TX 76164, (817)335-2257 [10935]

Deen Wholesale Meat Co., PO Box 4155, Ft. Worth, TX 76164, (817)335-2257 [10936]

Deep See Products Inc., 18935 59th Ave. NE, Arlington, WA 98223-8763, (253)435-6696 [23617]

Deerfield Data Systems Inc., 267 Amherst Rd., PO Box 471, Sunderland, MA 01375-0471, (413)665-3742 [6194]

Deering Banjo Co., 7936-D Lester Ave., Lemon Grove, CA 91945, (619)464-8252 [25164]

Deering Banjo Co., 7936-D Lester Ave., Lemon Grove, CA 91945, (619)464-8252 [15107]

Deerwood Rice Grain Produce, 21926 County Rd. 10, Deerwood, MN 56444, (218)534-3762 [10937]

Dees Corp., 110 Industrial Dr., No. 105, Pottstown, PA 19464-3460, (610)574-2900 [16823]

Dee's Delights, Inc., 3150 State Line Rd., North Bend, OH 45052, (513)353-3390 [26463]

Dees Fluid Power, 7611 White Pine Rd., Richmond, VA 23234, (804)275-9222 [16824]

Defender Industries, 42 Great Neck Rd., Waterford, CT 06385, (860)701-3400 [18489]

Defender Marine Supply NY, 321 Main St., New Rochelle, NY 10801, (914)632-2318 [18490]

Defiance Inc., 28271 Cedar Park Blvd., Perrysburg, OH 43551, (419)661-1333 [8620]

DeFranco and Sons Inc.; D., 1000 Lawrence St., Los Angeles, CA 90021, (213)627-8575 [10938]

Defreeze Corp., 20 Deerfoot Rd., Southborough, MA 01772, (508)485-8512 [14413]

Dega Technologies, 1530 Monterey St., San Luis Obispo, CA 93401-2928, (805)546-0444 [2536]

Degussa Huls, 65 Challenger Rd., Ridgefield Park, NJ 07660-2100, (201)641-6100 [4370]

DeHater, 3201 N Main, East Peoria, IL 61611-1718, (309)694-2083 [21705]

DEI Inc., 900 N Lehigh St., Baltimore, MD 21205, (410)522-3700 [24533]

DeKalb-Pfizer Genetics, Crawfordsville Div., PO Box 683, Crawfordsville, IN 47933-0683, (765)362-2104 [17815]

Del Mar Distributing Company Inc., PO Box 270300, Corpus Christi, TX 78427-0300, (361)992-8901 [23618]

Del-Mar Industries Inc., PO Box 496, Jacksonville, NC 28540, (919)347-1095 [4911]

Del Paso Pipe and Steel Inc., 1113 Del Paso Blvd., Sacramento, CA 95815, (916)925-1792 [19922]

Del Sol Tile Co., 920 S 5th St., Edinburg, TX 78539-4205, (956)381-4834 [9854]

Delaney Management Corp., PO Box 1185, Williston, ND 58802-1185, (701)572-1827 [1639]

Delaware Brick Co., 1114 Centerville Rd., Wilmington, DE 19804, (302)994-0949 [7258]

Delaware County Supply Co., 1000 Randall Ave., Boothwyn, PA 19061-3538, (610)485-1812 [13658]

Delaware Dry Goods, PO Box 10424, Wilmington, DE 19850, (302)731-0500 [26017]

Delaware Foods Inc., 313 E Centennial Ave., Muncie, IN 47303, (765)284-1406 [10939]

Delaware Importers Inc., PO Box 271, New Castle, DE 19720, (302)656-4487 [1640]

Delaware Plumbing Supply Co., 2309 N Dupont Hwy., New Castle, DE 19720-6300, (302)656-5437 [23136]

Delaware Storage Co., PO Box 313, Dover, DE 19903, (302)736-1774 [22192]

Delaware Valley Hydraulics, 325 Quigley Blvd., New Castle, DE 19720, (302)322-1555 [16825]

Delgasco Inc., 3617 Lexington Rd., Winchester, KY 40391, (606)744-6171 [22193]

Deli Universal Inc., PO Box 25099, Richmond, VA 23261, (804)359-9311 [26287]

Deli USA, PO Box 106, Mayville, WI 53050, (920)387-5740 [10940]

D'ELIA Associates of Connecticut Inc., 4 Laser Ln., Wallingford, CT 06492-1928, (203)234-0667 [15108]

Delker Electronics Inc., PO Box 897, Smyrna, TN 37167-0897, (615)459-2636 [6195]

Dell Computer Corp. Dell Marketing L.P., 1 Dell Way, Round Rock, TX 78682-0001, (512)338-4400 [6196]

Dell Rapids Co-op Grain, PO Box 70, Dell Rapids, SD 57022, (605)428-5494 [505]

Delmar News Agency Inc., 7120 Grand Blvd., Houston, TX 77054-3408, (713)654-9921 [3683]

DeLong Company Inc., PO Box 552, Clinton, WI 53525, (608)676-2255 [506]

DeLonghi America Inc., Park 80 W, Plaza One, Saddle Brook, NJ 07663, (201)909-4000 [15109]

Delphi Products Co., PO Box 149, Delphi, IN 46923, (765)564-3752 [507]

Delphi Saginaw Steering Systems, 3900 Hallond Rd., Saginaw, MI 48601-9494, (517)757-4005 [2537]

Delphos Co-Op Association Inc., 413 W 1st St., Delphos, KS 67436, (785)523-4213 [17816]

Del's Farm Supply, 1856 Haleukana St., Lihue, HI 96766-1459, (808)245-9200 [508]

Delta Cotton Cooperative Inc., Hwy. 34 E, Marmaduke, AR 72443, (501)597-2741 [509]

Delta Distributors Inc., 610 Fisher Rd., Longview, TX 75604, (903)759-7151 [4371]

Delta Engineering and Manufacturing Co., 19500 SW Teton Ave., Tualatin, OR 97062, (503)692-4435 [19923]

Delta Enterprises Inc., PO Box 647, Fairbury, NE 68352-0647, (402)729-3366 [19275]

Delta Fastener Corp., 7122 Old Katy Rd., Houston, TX 77024-2112, (713)868-2351 [13659]

Delta Hi-Tech Inc., 3762 S 150 E, Salt Lake City, UT 84115, (801)263-0975 [19276]

Delta Implement Co., PO Box 460, Rolling Fork, MS 39159, (662)873-2661 [510]

Delta Industrial Systems Co., 1275 Sawgrass Corporate Pkwy., Sunrise, FL 33323-2812, (305)822-9977 [13660]

Delta International, PO Box 188, Fairfield, CT 06430, (203)255-1969 [17817]

Delta Materials Handling Inc., 4676 Clarke Rd., Memphis, TN 38141, (901)795-7230 [15939]

Delta Materials Inc., 3525 N Causeway, Ste. 620, Metairie, LA 70002, (504)219-9653 [8621]

Delta Oil Company Inc., PO Box 829, Petersburg, VA 23803, (804)733-3582 [22194]

Delta Poly Plastic Inc., PO Box 799, Stuttgart, AR 72160, (870)673-7458 [26795]

Delta Products Corp. (Nogales, Arizona), 1650 W Calle Plata, Nogales, AZ 85621, (520)761-1111 [6197]

Delta Purchasing Federation, PO Box 8177, Greenwood, MS 38930, (601)453-7374 [511]

Delta Resources Inc., 3617 Lexington Rd., Winchester, KY 40391, (606)744-6171 [22195]

Delta Ridge Implement, PO Box 240, Rayville, LA 71269, (318)728-6423 [512]

Delta-Southland International, PO Box 3606, Kingsport, TN 37664-0606, (423)378-5997 [18769]

Delta Star Inc., 270 Industrial Rd., San Carlos, CA 94070-6212, (650)508-2850 [8622]

Delta Steel Inc., 111 Beasley Rd., Jackson, MS 39206, (601)956-4141 [19924]

Delta Systems Company, Inc., 1400 Miller Pkwy., McHenry, IL 60050-7030, (815)363-3582 [3684]

Delta Technical Coatings Inc., 2550 Pellissier Pl, Whittier, CA 90601, (562)695-7969 [26464]

Delta Veterinary Clinic, 1520 Bluff St., Delta, CO 81416-2141, (970)874-4486 [27115]

Delta Wholesale Hardware Co., PO Box 729, Clarksdale, MS 38614, (601)627-4141 [13661]

Deltiologists of America, PO Box 8, Norwood, PA 19074, (610)485-8572 [3685]

Demakes Enterprises and Co. Inc., 37 Waterhill St., Lynn, MA 01905, (781)595-1557 [10941]

DeMar Inc.; M & T, 4237 E University Dr., Phoenix, AZ 85034-7315, (602)437-8002 [14414]

Demase and Manna Co., 110 19th St., Pittsburgh, PA 15222, (412)281-8880 [10942]

Demco Inc., PO Box 7488, Madison, WI 53707, (608)241-1201 [20954]

Demerico Corp., 6605 E 14th St., Brownsville, TX 78521, (956)838-1290 [10943]

Demeter Inc., PO Box 465, Fowler, IN 47944, (317)884-0600 [17818]

Dempster Equipment, PO Box 1388, Toccoa, GA 30577-6388, (706)886-2327 [26796]

Dena Pedynowski Aviaries, 197 S Hillside Ave., Succasunna, NJ 07876, (973)584-0756 [27083]

Denali Industrial Supply Inc., 3933 Spenard Rd., Anchorage, AK 99517, (907)248-0090 [16826]

Denatec Distributors, 5254 S Saginaw Rd., No. 200, Flint, MI 48507, (810)694-3300 [22196]

Denbo Iron and Metal Company Inc., PO Box 1553, Decatur, AL 35602-1553, (256)353-6351 [19925]

Dencor Energy Cost Controls Inc., 1450 W Evans Ave., Denver, CO 80223, (303)922-1888 [8623]

Denison Co. Inc.; A.J., 1 East St., Riverside, RI 02915-4414, (401)433-3232 [17390]

Denman and Davis, 1 Broad St., Clifton, NJ 07011, (201)684-3900 [19926]

Denman Tire Corp., 400 Diehl South Rd., Leavittsburg, OH 44430-9741, (330)675-4242 [2538]

Dennen Steel Corp., PO Box 3200, Grand Rapids, MI 49501, (616)784-2000 [19927]

Dennert Distributing Corp.; H., 351 Wilmer Ave., Cincinnati, OH 45226-1831, (513)871-7272 [1641]

Dennis Paper Co. Inc., 1940 Elm Tree Dr., Nashville, TN 37210, (615)883-9010 [21706]

Dennis Refrigeration & Electric, 23850 W 102nd Ter., Shawnee Mission, KS 66227-4626, (913)764-6232 [14415]

Dennis Sales Ltd., PO Box 4056, Salisbury, MD 21803-4056, (410)742-1585 [10944]

Dennis and Schwab Inc., 505 E 1st St., Ste. B, Tustin, CA 92780, (714)505-1270 [6198]

Dennis Supply Co., PO Box 3376, Sioux City, IA 51102, (712)255-7637 [14416]

Densons Sound Systems Inc., 519 N Witchduck Rd., Virginia Beach, VA 23462-1914, (757)499-9005 [25165]

Dent and Co., 5800 E Mabry Dr., Clovis, NM 88101, (505)763-5517 [513]

Dental Enterprises Inc., 795 S Jason St., Denver, CO 80223-3911, (303)777-6717 [18770]

Dentec Corp., 25560 W Lake Shore Dr., Barrington, IL 60010-1461, (847)241-5966 [18771]

Dentex Shoe Corp., PO Box 1774, Laredo, TX 78041, (956)727-3591 [24726]

Denton and Company Ltd.; Robert, 2724 Auburn Rd., Auburn Hills, MI 48326, (313)299-0600 [1642]

Denton Enterprises Inc., PO Box 632, Harrisonburg, VA 22801-0632, (540)434-3193 [5592]

Denton Hosiery Mill, PO Box 476, Denton, NC 27239-0476, (336)859-2116 [4912]

Denton Petroleum Co., PO Box 360, Driscoll, TX 78351, (512)387-0592 [22197]

Denton Plastics Inc., 4427 NE 158th Ave., Portland, OR 97230, (503)257-9945 [26797]

Dentt Inc., 4171 Marquis Way, Salt Lake City, UT 84124, (801)277-7056 [26465]

Dentt, Inc., 1088 Fort Union Blvd., Midvale, UT 84047, (801)561-3821 [26466]

Denver Air Machinery Co., 1421 Blake St., Denver, CO 80202-1334, (303)893-0507 [15940]

Denver Business Journal Inc., 1700 Broadway Ste. 515, Denver, CO 80290, (303)837-3500 [3686]

Denver Hardware Co., 3200 Walnut St., Denver, CO 80205, (303)292-3550 [13662]

Denver Hardware Co., 3200 Walnut St., Denver, CO 80205, (303)292-3550 [13663]

Denver Hardwood Co., 4700B National Western Dr., Denver, CO 80216, (303)296-1168 [9855]

Denver Merchandise Mart, 451 E 58th Ave., Denver, CO 80216, (303)292-6278 [17391]

Denver Waste Materials Inc., 2363 Larimer St., Denver, CO 80205-2120, (303)295-7737 [4913]

Denver Wholesale Florists, PO Box 173354, Denver, CO 80217-3354, (303)399-0970 [14855]

Denzak & Associates, Inc.; Joan, PO Box 176, Buffalo, NY 14217, (716)876-0752 [23619]

Deodorant Stones of America, 9420 E Doubletree Ranch Rd., Ste. 101, Scottsdale, AZ 85258, (480)451-4981 [14082]

Depco Inc., 1637 Mount Vernon Rd., Atlanta, GA 30338-4205, (404)394-0643 [25166]

Depco Inc., PO Box 486, Contoocook, NH 03229-0486, (603)226-4393 [22953]

Dependable Business Machines, 2521 Railroad Ave., Bismarck, ND 58501-5072, (701)258-7676 [20955]

Dependable Food Corp., 593 McDonald Ave., Brooklyn, NY 11218, (718)435-4880 [10945]

Dependable Foundry Equipment Co., PO Box 1687, Tualatin, OR 97062, (503)692-5552 [15941]

Dependable Motor Parts, PO Box 1746, Bay City, TX 77404-1746, (409)245-5506 [2539]

Depoe Bay Fish Co., 617 SW Bay Blvd., Newport, OR 97365-4718, (541)265-8833 [10946]

The Depot Ltd., 1015 W Jackson St., Sullivan, IL 61951, (217)728-2567 [13345]

DER Duplicating Services, Inc., 212 NW 4th Ave., Hallandale, FL 33009-4015, (954)458-7505 [25213]

Derby Cycle, 22710 72nd Ave. S, Kent, WA 98032-1926 [23620]

Derby Fabrics, Inc., 630 Industry Rd., PO Box 2556, Louisville, KY 40201, (502)637-1466 [26018]

Derby Industries Inc., 4451 Robards Ln., Louisville, KY 40218-4513, (502)966-4206 [15110]

Derco Industries Inc., PO Box 25549, Milwaukee, WI 53225, (414)355-3066 [80]

Derda Inc., 1195 W Bertrand Rd., Niles, MI 49120-8772, (616)683-6666 [15942]

Derkin and Wise Inc., PO Box 1015, Toledo, OH 43697, (419)248-4411 [16827]

Derma Sciences Inc., 214 Carnegie Ctr., Ste. 100, Princeton, NJ 08540, (609)514-4744 [19277]

Derma-Therm Inc., 155 Edgewater Rd., Inman, SC 29349-6911, 800-788-1106 [18772]

DeRoyal, 200 Debusk Ln., Powell, TN 37849, (615)938-7828 [18773]

DeRoyal Industries Inc., 200 Debusk Ln., Powell, TN 37849, (615)938-7828 [18773]

Derr Flooring Co., 525 Davisville Rd., Willow Grove, PA 19090, (215)657-6300 [15469]

Derstine Book Co.; Roy, 14 Birch Rd., Kinnelon, NJ 07405, (201)838-1109 [3687]

DeRu's Fine Art Books, 1590 S Coast Hwy., Laguna Beach, CA 92651, (714)376-3785 [3688]

Des Arc Implement Co., PO Box 250, Des Arc, AR 72040, (870)256-4121 [514]

Des Moines Marketing Associates, 2231 NW 108th St., Des Moines, IA 50322-3714, (515)270-9595 [10947]

DESA International Inc., PO Box 90004, Bowling Green, KY 42102, (502)781-9600 [14417]

DeSantis Distributors, 3179 W 21st, Lorain, OH 44053-1115, (440)282-9742 [10948]

Deschutes Optical, 20332 Empire Rd., Ste. F-5, PO Box 7229, Bend, OR 97708, (503)288-8244 [19278]

Desert Beverage Co. Inc., 908 E Cedar St., Rawlins, WY 82301-5847, (307)324-5003 [1643]

Desert Delights Wholesale Ice, 2305 E Palo Verde St., Yuma, AZ 85365, (520)344-2311 [10949]

Desert Design Inc., 7460 Ranch Destino, Las Vegas, NV 89123, (702)361-4677 [515]

Desert Eagle Distributing Co., 6949 Market St., El Paso, TX 79915, (915)772-4246 [1644]

Desert Indian Traders, 1009 W Highway 66, Gallup, NM 87301-6830, (505)722-5554 [17392]

Desert Mesquite of Arizona, 3458 E Illini St., Phoenix, AZ 85040-1839, (602)437-3135 [10950]

Desert Sky Wrecking, 2742 Hwy. 46, Wendell, ID 83355, (208)536-6606 [2540]

Desert Star Jewelry Manufacturing, 10901 Acoma SE, Albuquerque, NM 87123, (505)296-6238 [17393]

Desert Stationers, 212 E Main St., Barstow, CA 92311-2324, (760)256-2161 [20956]

Desfosses and Associates; John J., 1728 Virginia Beach Blvd., Ste. 115, Virginia Beach, VA 23454-4536, (757)491-2882 [6199]

Desherbinin Products Inc.; W.N., PO Box 63, Hawleyville, CT 06440-0063, (203)791-0494 [15470]

Design Accessories Inc., 3636 Aerial Way Dr., Roanoke, VA 24018, (540)344-8958 [17394]

Design Air, PO Box 39, Kimberly, WI 54136, (920)739-7005 [14418]

Design Carpets, PO Box 15780, Richmond, VA 23227-5780, (804)550-2255 [9856]

Design Center of the Americas, 1855 Griffin Rd., Dania Beach, FL 33004, (954)920-7997 [15471]

Design Craft, 225 W John Rowan Blvd., Bardstown, KY 40004-2602, (502)348-4275 [14856]

Design/Craft Fabric Corp., 7227 Oak Park Ave., Niles, IL 60714, (847)647-2022 [15472]

Design Data Systems Corp., 13830 58th St. N, Ste. 401, Clearwater, FL 33760-3720, (727)539-1077 [6200]

Design Distributing, 1529 Seibel Dr. NE, Roanoke, VA 24012, (540)342-3471 [9857]

Design Finishes Inc., PO Box E, Americus, GA 31709, (912)924-0341 [13087]

Design House Inc., PO Box 1001, Germantown, WI 53022, (414)255-1970 [13664]

Design Impressions Inc., PO Box 2149, Hudson, OH 44236, (330)425-8011 [21427]

Design Marketing Associates, 329 East 300 South, Salt Lake City, UT 84111, (801)531-9903 [13088]

Design Surfaces, 24000 Sperry Dr., Westlake, OH 44145, (440)899-9900 [9858]

Design Surfaces, 23225 Mercantile Rd., Beachwood, OH 44122, (216)464-3430 [9859]

Design Systems Inc., PO Box 25964, Oklahoma City, OK 73125-0964, (405)341-7353 [6201]

Design Tees Hawaii Inc., PO Box 2515, Honolulu, HI 96804-2515, (808)848-4877 [4914]

Design Toscano Inc., 17 E Campbell St., Arlington Heights, IL 60004, (847)255-6799 [13089]

Designed Flooring Distributors, 3251 SW 13th Dr., Deerfield Beach, FL 33442, (954)481-1900 [9860]

Designer Tile Co. East, 145 English Rd., PO Box 7334, Rocky Mount, NC 27804-0334, (919)937-6090 [9861]

Designer Vertical Blind, 2655 Courtright, Columbus, OH 43232, (614)338-8111 [11625]

Designer Vertical Blinds, 27209 W Warren, Dearborn Heights, MI 48127-1804, (313)565-7300 [15613]

Designer's Den Inc., 1869 W Harvard Ave., Atlanta, GA 30337, (404)767-8763 [15473]

Designers Ltd., PO Box 1046, Meredith, NH 03253-1046, (603)279-8692 [26467]

Desk Concepts, 3670 NW 76th St., Miami, FL 33147, (305)696-3376 [20957]

Desk-Mate Products Inc., 7492 Chancellor Dr., Orlando, FL 32809-6242, (407)826-0600 [20958]

Desks Inc. (Chicago, Illinois), 2323 W Pershing Rd., Chicago, IL 60609, (312)664-8500 [20959]

Desks Inc. (Denver, Colorado), 1385 S Santa Fe Dr., Denver, CO 80223, (303)777-8880 [13090]

Desmond Process Supply Co., 2277 Elliott Ave., Troy, MI 48083-4502, (248)589-9100 [25627]

Desoto County Cooperative, 2425 Mount Pleasant Rd., Hernando, MS 38632, (601)429-4407 [516]

Desoutter Inc., 1800 Overview Dr., Rock Hill, SC 29730 [15943]

Dessau Brass Inc., 39 Graphic Pl., Moonachie, NJ 07074, (201)440-5150 [13346]

Desselle-Maggard Corp., PO Box 86630, Baton Rouge, LA 70879, (504)753-3290 [16828]

Desso USA Inc., 387 Strathmore Rd., Rosemont, PA 19010-1262, (215)526-9517 [9862]

DET Distributing Co., 35 Conalco Dr., Jackson, TN 38301-3665, (901)423-3344 [1645]

DET Distributing Co., 301 Great Circle Rd., Nashville, TN 37228, (615)244-4113 [1646]

Detail Fresh Sandwich Co., 414 W Isabella Rd., Midland, MI 48640, (517)631-6240 [10951]

Detlefsen Oil Inc., PO Box 728, North Platte, NE 69103-0728, (308)532-8780 [22198]

Detroit Air Compressor and Pump Co., 3205 Bermuda, Ferndale, MI 48220, (248)544-2982 [15944]

Detroit Auto Auction, 20911 Gladwin Rd., Taylor, MI 48180, (734)285-7300 [20622]

Detroit Ball Bearing Company Executive Offices, 1400 Howard St., Detroit, MI 48216, (313)963-6011 [16829]

Detroit City Dairy Inc., 15004 3rd Ave., Highland Park, MI 48203, (313)868-5511 [10952]

Detroit Diesel Overseas Corp., 13400 W Outer Dr., Detroit, MI 48239, (313)592-5000 [2541]

Detroit Free Press Agency, 1117 Bancroft St., Port Huron, MI 48060, (810)984-8767 [3689]

Detroit Gas Products Co., 1200 Farrow Ave., Ferndale, MI 48220, (248)543-4012 [16830]

Detroit Pump and Manufacturing Co., 18943 John R., Detroit, MI 48203-2090, (313)893-4242 [23137]

Dettor, Edwards & Morris, PO Box 443, Grimstead, VA 23064-0443, (804)295-7526 [1647]

Deuel County Farmers Union Oil Co., PO Box 430, Toronto, SD 57268, (605)794-4861 [22199]

Deuer Manufacturing Co., 225 Riverview Ave., Waltham, MA 02454, (781)647-5560 [15945]

Deuster Co., N57 W13636 Carman Ave., Menomonee Falls, WI 53051, (414)783-4140 [24104]

Deuteronomy Inc., 224 S 5th Ave., City of Industry, CA 91746, (626)369-4181 [6202]

Dev-Air Corp., 380 N Morehall Rd., Malvern, PA 19355, (215)647-3677 [15946]

Deveault; Ed, PO Box 932, Portland, ME 04104-0932, (207)772-3451 [24345]

Develcon Electronics Inc., 1431 Bonnie Brae St., Hermosa Beach, CA 90254-3207 [6203]

Developed Technology Resource Inc., 7300 Metro Blvd., Ste. 550, Edina, MN 55439, (612)820-0022 [23621]

Development Through Self-Reliance Inc., 6679-P Santa Barbara Rd., Elkridge, MD 21075, (410)579-4508 [6204]

Deverger Systems Inc., 7 1/2 Biltmore Ave., Asheville, NC 28801-3603, (704)253-2255 [6205]

Devin-Adair Publishers, Inc., Box A, Old Greenwich, CT 06870, (203)531-7755 [3690]

Devine Brothers Inc., PO Box 189, Norwalk, CT 06852, (203)866-4421 [7259]

DeVlieg-Bullard Services Group, 10100 Forest Hills Rd., Rockford, IL 61114, (815)544-8120 [15947]

Devlin Lumber and Supply Corp., PO Box 1306, Rockville, MD 20849, (301)881-1000 [7260]

Devoe Co.; Leslie M., 4371 E 82nd St. D, Indianapolis, IN 46250-1678, (317)842-3245 [8624]

Devoe Paint, 2179 South 300 West, No. 1, South Salt Lake, UT 84115, (801)486-2211 [21428]

De'Vons Optics Inc., 10823 Bell Ct., Rancho Cucamonga, CA 91730, (909)466-4700 [19279]

DeVorss & Co., 1046 Princeton Dr., Marina del Rey, CA 90295-0550, (310)822-8940 [3691]

Devtec Corp., 812 Bloomfield Ave., Windsor, CT 06095, (860)688-9520 [160]

Dewald Fluid Power Company Inc., 1023 W 8th St., Mishawaka, IN 46544, (219)255-4776 [16831]

Dewar & Company Inc.; John, 136 Newmarket Sq., Boston, MA 02118-2603, (617)442-4292 [10953]

Dewar Elevator Co., Box 80, Dewar, IA 50623, (319)234-1392 [517]

Dewco Milwaukee Sales, 6235 Industrial Ct., Greendale, WI 53129, (414)421-2650 [13665]

Dewied International Inc., 5010 E I-Hwy 10, San Antonio, TX 78219, (210)661-6161 [10954]

DeWitt Beverage, PO Box 596, Brattleboro, VT 05302, (802)254-6063 [1648]

Dexter Implement Co., PO Box 217, Dexter, MO 63841, (573)624-7467 [518]

Dexter Sales Inc., 860A Waterman Ave., East Providence, RI 02914, (401)431-2170 [19928]

Dey Appliance Parts, 1401 Wolters Blvd., Vadnais Heights, MN 55110, (612)490-9191 [8625]

Dey Distributing, 1418 N Irwin Ave., Green Bay, WI 54302-1614, (920)437-7022 [14419]

DeYoung Inc.; J. and S.S., 38 Newbury St., Boston, MA 02116-3210, (617)266-0100 [17395]

DeYoung Mfg Inc., 12920 NE 125th Way, Kirkland, WA 98034, (425)823-4798 [8626]

D.I. Engineering Corp. of America, 1658 Cole Blvd., Bldg. 6, Ste. 290, Golden, CO 80401, (303)231-0045 [15948]

Di Paolo Baking Company, Inc., 598 Plymouth Ave. N, Rochester, NY 14608-1629, (716)232-3510 [10955]

Di-Tech Systems, Inc., 965 Park Center Dr., Vista, CA 92083, (760)599-0200 [25702]

Dia-Compe Inc., PO Box 798, Fletcher, NC 28732, (828)684-3551 [23622]

Diab Data Inc., 323 Vintage Park Dr. Ste. C, Foster City, CA 94404, (650)571-1700 [6206]

Diablo Cellular Phone Stores Inc., 1957 Arnold Industrial Way, Concord, CA 94520-5312, (510)674-9214 [5593]

Diadora America, 6419 S 228th St., Kent, WA 98032-1874, (253)395-4644 [4915]

Diagnostic Equipment Service Corp., PO Box 303, Norfolk, MA 02056-0303, (508)520-0040 [18774]

Dial Battery Paint & Auto Supply, 414 Taunton Ave., East Providence, RI 02914-2646, (401)434-2770 [21429]

Dial Corp., 15501 N Dial Blvd., Scottsdale, AZ 85260-1619, (602)754-3425 [14083]

Dialogue Systems Inc., 33 Irving Pl., Fl. 11, New York, NY 10003-2332, (212)647-1000 [3692]

Dialysis Clinic Inc., 1600 Hayes St., Ste. 300, Nashville, TN 37203-3020, (615)327-3061 [18775]

Diamond Art & Craft, 2207 Royal Ln., Dallas, TX 75229, (972)620-9653 [25628]

Diamond Bakery Co. Ltd., PO Box 17760, Honolulu, HI 96817, (808)847-3551 [10956]

Diamond Chemical/Supply Co., 524 S Walnut St. Plaza, Wilmington, DE 19801, (302)656-7786 [4372]

Diamond Comic Distributors Inc., 1966 Greenspring Dr., Ste. 300, Timonium, MD 21093, (410)560-7100 [26468]

Diamond Comic Distributors Inc., 101 Nob Hill Rd., Madison, WI 53701, (608)274-5010 [3693]

Diamond Distributors, 1918 Bible Rd., Lima, OH 45801, (419)227-5132 [1649]

Diamond Electronics, Inc., 4445 Coonpath Rd., Carroll, OH 43112, (740)756-9222 [24534]

Diamond Flower Electric Instruments Company (USA) Inc., 135 Main Ave., Sacramento, CA 95838-2041, (916)568-1234 [6207]

Diamond Foods Inc., 4916 Ohara Dr., Evansville, IN 47711-2474, (812)425-2685 [10957]

Diamond Fruit Growers, PO Box 180, Hood River, OR 97031, (541)354-5300 [10958]

Diamond Fruit Growers, PO Box 180, Hood River, OR 97031, (541)354-5300 [10959]

Diamond Hill Plywood Co., 600 E Broad St., Darlington, SC 29532, (843)393-2803 [7261]

Diamond Hill Plywood Co., PO Box 3296, Jacksonville, FL 32206, (904)355-3592 [7262]

Diamond Industrial Tools Inc., 6712 Crawford Avenue, Lincolnwood, IL 60712, (847)676-9700 [15949]

Diamond Leather Inc., 11401 Gateway W, El Paso, TX 79936-6419, (915)598-1874 [18387]

Diamond Nut Company of California, 16500 W 103rd St., Lemont, IL 60439, (630)739-3000 [10960]

Diamond Optical Corp., 101 French Ave., Ste. A, Braintree, MA 02184-6503, (781)848-5999 [19280]

Diamond Paper Corp., PO Box 7000, Sterling, VA 20167-1049, (703)450-0000 [21707]

Diamond Prairie Ranch Company Inc., 1254 S 9th St., Las Vegas, NV 89104-1503, (702)384-6478 [2542]

Diamond Products Co., PO Box 878, Seffner, FL 33584, (813)681-4611 [14084]

Diamond State Distributors, PO Box 1223, Wilmington, DE 19899-1223, (302)888-2511 [1650]

Diamond Sun Ltd., 12410 N 28th Dr., Phoenix, AZ 85029-2433, (602)993-1130 [26613]

Diamond Supply Company Inc., 6101 Valley Jo St., Emeryville, CA 94608, (510)655-3313 [4612]

Diamond Supply, Inc., 200 Dalton Ave., PO Box 5115, Charlotte, NC 28225, (704)376-2125 [25629]

Diamond Systems Corp., 450 San Antonio Rd., Ste. 46, Palo Alto, CA 94306, (650)813-1100 [6208]

Diamond Tager Co., 28th St., PO Box 310085, Tampa, FL 33680, (813)238-3111 [10961]

Diamond Vogel Inc., 4500 E 48th Ave., Denver, CO 80216, (303)333-4499 [21430]

Diamond Vogel Paint Center, 119 Cole Shopping Ctr., Cheyenne, WY 82001, (307)635-6803 [21431]

Diamond Vogel Paint Center, 1700 W 1st, Casper, WY 82604, (307)577-0172 [21432]

Diamond Vogel Paint Center, 215 W Broadway, Farmington, NM 87401, (505)325-9851 [21433]

Diamond W Supply Co. Inc., 2017 N 23rd Ave., Phoenix, AZ 85009, (602)252-5841 [9863]

Diamond W Supply Co. Inc., PO Box 2383, Los Angeles, CA 90051, (213)685-7400 [9864]

Diamond W Supply Co. Inc., 6101 Valley Jo St., Emeryville, CA 94608, (510)655-3313 [4612]

Diamond W Supply Co. Inc., 8410 Ajong Dr., San Diego, CA 92126, (619)578-3260 [9865]

Diamony International, Inc., 7670 Woodway, Ste. 160, Houston, TX 77063, (713)266-7604 [4916]

Diana Corp., 1640 S Sepulveda Blvd., Los Angeles, CA 90040, (818)735-7600 [8584]

Diane Ribbon Wholesale, 2319 W Holly, Phoenix, AZ 85009, (602)271-9273 [20960]

Diaz Foods Inc., 5500 Bucknell Dr. SW, Atlanta, GA 30336-2531, (404)344-5421 [10962]

Diaz Wholesale and Manufacturing Company Inc., 5500 Bucknell Dr. SW, Atlanta, GA 30336-2531, (404)344-5421 [10963]

Dibs Chemical & Supply Co. Inc., 205 Courthouse Rd., Gulfport, MS 39507-1215, (228)896-7811 [21708]

Dick Co.; A.B., 5700 W Touhy Ave., Niles, IL 60714, (847)779-1900 [20961]

Dick Company Inc.; T.W., 1-25 Summer St., Gardiner, ME 04345, (207)582-5350 [19929]

Dick Products of Albuquerque; A.B., 1430 Girard Blvd. NE, Albuquerque, NM 87106-1821, (505)265-1212 [20962]

Dickens Data Systems Inc., 1175 Northmeadow Pkwy., Ste. 150, Roswell, GA 30076-4922, (404)475-8860 [6209]

Dickey Oil Corp., PO Box 809, Packwood, IA 52580, (319)695-3601 [22200]

Dickey and Son Inc.; D.W., 7896 Dickey Dr., Lisbon, OH 44432, (216)424-1441 [7263]

Dickinson Supply Inc., 37 3rd Ave. E, PO Box 1151, Dickinson, ND 58601, (701)225-8591 [2543]

Dick's Superior Metal Sales, 4298 Acker Rd., Madison, WI 53701, (608)244-9332 [19930]

Dickson CC Co., 2100 Sigman Rd. NW, Conyers, GA 30012, (770)388-7373 [14420]

Dickson CC Co., 1050 Industrial Park Dr., Marietta, GA 30062, (770)425-0121 [14421]

Dickson Co.; C.C., 927 East Blvd., Charlotte, NC 28203, (704)372-2604 [14422]

Dickson Farmers Cooperative, 705 Henslee Dr., Dickson, TN 37055, (615)446-2343 [519]

Dickson Furniture Industries, 7015 Grand Blvd., Houston, TX 77054-2205, (713)747-1167 [13279]

Dictaphone Corp., 340 N Sam Houston Pkwy. E, Ste. 180, Houston, TX 77060, (281)999-2323 [5594]

Die-A-Matic Corp., 650 N State St., York, PA 17403, (717)846-9300 [15950]

Diehl Steel Co, PO Box 17010, Cincinnati, OH 45217, (513)242-8900 [19931]

Dielectric Corp., N 83 W 13330 Leon Rd., Menomonee Falls, WI 53051, (414)255-2600 [22954]

Diener Brick Co., PO Box 130, Collingswood, NJ 08108, (856)858-2000 [7264]

Dierks Foods Inc., PO Box 2579, Rockford, IL 61103-2579, (815)877-7031 [10964]

Diesel Equipment Specialists, Rt. 13, Bridgeville, DE 19933, (302)337-8742 [2544]

Diesel Machinery Inc., 4301 N Cliff Ave., Sioux Falls, SD 57104, (605)336-0411 [7265]

Diesel Power Equipment Co., 15225 Industrial Rd., Omaha, NE 68144, (402)330-5100 [2545]

Diesel Power Supply Co., 2525 University Parks, Waco, TX 76707, (254)753-1587 [2546]

DIFCO Inc., PO Box 238, Findlay, OH 45839-0238, (419)422-0525 [23477]

Different Drummer, RR1 Box 3509, Solon, ME 04979, (207)643-2572 [26469]

Digicorp Inc., 2322 W Clybourn St., Milwaukee, WI 53233, (414)343-1080 [5595]

Digital Business Automation, 15121 Graham, Unit 101, Huntington Beach, CA 92649, (714)379-9300 [20963]

Digital Storage Inc., 7611 Green Meadows Dr., Lewis Center, OH 43035-9445, (614)548-7179 [6210]

Digitel Corp., 2600 School Dr., Atlanta, GA 30360, (770)451-1111 [5596]

Digrazia Wholesale Distributing; Joseph E., PO Box 458, Wells, NV 89835-0458, (702)752-3326 [26288]

Dillard, PO Box 21767, Greensboro, NC 27420, (336)299-1211 [22002]

Dillard Paper Co., PO Box 1567, Chattanooga, TN 37401-1567, (423)698-8111 [22000]

Dillard Paper Co. Birmingham Div., PO Box 11367, Birmingham, AL 35202, (205)798-8380 [21709]

Dillard Paper Co. Chattanooga Div., PO Box 1567, Chattanooga, TN 37401-1567, (615)698-8111 [21710]

Dillard Paper Co. Knoxville Div., PO Box 50008, Knoxville, TN 37950-0008, (615)584-5741 [21711]

Dillard Paper Co. Macon Div., 3115 Hillcrest Ave., Macon, GA 31204, (912)746-8501 [21712]

Diller Tile Company Inc., PO Box 727, Chatsworth, IL 60921, (815)635-3131 [23138]

Dillon Supply Co., PO Box 1111, Raleigh, NC 27602, (919)832-7771 [15951]

Dills Supply Co./Division of Dayton Supply and Tool, 242 Leo St., Dayton, OH 45404, (937)228-3201 [16832]

Dilmaghani and Company Inc., 540 Central Ave., Scarsdale, NY 10583, (914)472-1700 [15474]

Dilmar Oil Company Inc., PO Box 5629, Florence, SC 29502-5629, (803)752-5611 [22201]

DiMare Brothers Inc., 84 New England Produce Ctr., Chelsea, MA 02150, (617)889-3800 [10965]

DiMare Homestead Inc., PO Box 900460, Homestead, FL 33090-0460, (305)245-4211 [10966]

Dimco Steel, Inc., 3901 S Lamar St., Dallas, TX 75215, (214)428-8336 [19932]

Dimensional Graphics Corp. Risto Division, 325 N Jackson Ave., PO Box 1893, Mason City, IA 50401, (515)423-8931 [18388]

Dimitri Wine & Spirits, PO Box 5046, Rock Island, IL 61204, (309)793-0055 [1651]

Dimmer-Warren Enterprises, 1470 Mitchell Lake Rd., Attica, MI 48412-9217, (810)724-0228 [23623]

Dimock, Gould and Co., 190 22nd St., Moline, IL 61265, (309)797-0650 [9866]

Dimock, Gould and Co., 190 22nd St., Moline, IL 61265, (309)797-0650 [15475]

DIMON Inc., PO Box 681, Danville, VA 24543, (804)792-7511 [14857]

Dinghy Shop International, 334 S Bayview Ave., PO Box 431, Amityville, NY 11701, (516)264-0005 [18491]

Dinorah's Sportswear, 5101 NW 36th Ave., Miami, FL 33142, (305)633-1488 [4917]

Diodes Inc., 3050 E Hillcrest Dr., Westlake Village, CA 91362, (805)446-4800 [8627]

Diomede Enterprises, Inc., 12790 Old Seward Hwy., Ste. B, Anchorage, AK 99515, (907)345-0043 [7266]

Dion and Sons Inc.; M.O., 1543 W 16th St., Long Beach, CA 90813, (562)432-3949 [22202]

The Dipper, 12216 Hodges, Houston, TX 77085, (713)721-4227 [14085]

Direct Connect International Inc., 266 Harristown Rd., Ste. 108, Glen Rock, NJ 07452, (201)445-2101 [26470]

Direct Diamonds Distributors, 333 Washington St., Boston, MA 02108, (617)523-0444 [17396]

Direct Distributors, 1933 Northern Star Dr., Traverse City, MI 49686, (616)929-7031 [7267]

Direct Office Furniture Outlet, 2525 Paxton St., Harrisburg, PA 17111, (717)236-7200 [20964]

Direct Sales Inc., 212 S Garnett Rd., Tulsa, OK 74128-1806, (918)438-2680 [4918]

Direct Way Distributors Inc., 12 Acme Rd., No. 215, Brewer, ME 04412, (207)989-2162 [21713]

Directed Energy Inc., 2401 Research Blvd Ste. 108, Ft. Collins, CO 80526, (970)493-1901 [8628]

Dirt Cheap Drives Inc., 3716 Timber Dr., Dickinson, TX 77539, (281)534-4140 [6211]

Disc Distributing Corp., 390 N Sepulveda Blvd., Ste. 3000, El Segundo, CA 90245, (310)322-6700 [6212]

Discas Inc., 567-1 S Leonard St., Bldg. 1, Waterbury, CT 06708, (203)753-5147 [22955]

Discipleship Resources, 1908 Grand Ave., PO Box 840, Nashville, TN 37202, (615)340-7068 [3694]

Discount Building Materials, 18 Old Volcano Rd., PO Box 1539, Keaau, HI 96749, (808)966-7402 [7268]

Discount Desk Etc., Inc., 955 S McCarrah, Sparks, NV 89431-5815, (702)359-4440 [20965]

Discount Desk Etc. Inc., 955 S McCarrah, Sparks, NV 89431-5815, (702)359-4440 [13091]

Discount Drugs Wisconsin Inc., 4945 Wyconda Rd., Rockville, MD 20852, (301)230-8930 [19281]

Discount Engine Exchange Inc., 2112 W Main St., Farmington, NM 87401-3221, (505)327-0319 [2547]

Discount Fishing Tackle, 203 S Union St., Shawnee, OK 74801-7942, (405)275-8151 [23624]

Discount Office Equipment Inc., 1991 Coolidge Hwy., Berkley, MI 48072, (248)548-6900 [20966]

Discount Office Equipment Inc., 1991 Coolidge Hwy., Berkley, MI 48072, (248)548-6900 [13092]

Discount Store, 64 S Hotel St., Honolulu, HI 96813-3106, (808)531-7777 [25167]

Discovery Toys Inc., 6400 Brisa St., Livermore, CA 94550, (925)606-2600 [26471]

Dispenser Services Inc., 117 Beaver St., Waltham, MA 02454, (781)891-6595 [25630]

Dispensers Optical Service Corp., PO Box 35000, Louisville, KY 40232, (502)491-3440 [19282]

Display Technologies, 111-01 14th Ave., College Point, NY 11356, (718)321-3100 [25631]

Displaytech Inc., 2602 Clover Basin Dr., Longmont, CO 80503, (303)772-2191 [24346]

Disston Co., 7345-G W Friendly Ave., Greensboro, NC 27410-6252, (919)852-9220 [13666]

Distinctive Business Products Inc., 5328 W 123rd Pl., Alsip, IL 60803-3203, (708)371-6700 [20967]

DistribuPro Inc., 1288 McKay Dr., San Jose, CA 95131, (408)922-2600 [6213]

Distributing Inc., 1637 S 83rd St., West Allis, WI 53214, (414)774-4949 [13432]

Distribution Holdings Inc., 4 Triad Ctr., Ste. 800, Salt Lake City, UT 84180, (801)575-6500 [15111]

Distribution Plus Inc., 825 Green Bay Rd., Ste. 200, Wilmette, IL 60091, (847)256-8289 [10967]

Distribution Services Inc., Brandywine Ctr. 580, West Palm Beach, FL 33409, (561)688-0097 [3695]

Distribution Systems of America, 600 W John St., Hicksville, NY 11801, (516)465-0211 [3696]

Distribution Systems of America, 31 Grand Blvd. N, Brentwood, NY 11717, (516)952-1041 [3697]

Distributors Oil Co. Inc., 11441 Industriplex Blvd., Ste. 100, Baton Rouge, LA 70809-4268, (504)344-3314 [22203]

Distributors Warehouse Inc., PO Box 7239, Paducah, KY 42002-7239, (502)442-8201 [2548]

District Petroleum Products Inc., 1832 Milan Ave., Sandusky, OH 44870, (419)625-8373 [22204]

DIT-MCO International Corp., 5612 Brighton Ter., Kansas City, MO 64130, (816)444-9700 [8629]

Ditch Witch of Illinois Inc., 124 N Schmale Rd., Carol Stream, IL 60188, (630)665-5600 [7269]

Ditch Witch Sales Inc., PO Box 429, Sullivan, MO 63080, (573)468-8012 [7270]

Ditch Witch Trencher Incorporated of Florida, PO Box 490667, Leesburg, FL 34749-0667, (904)787-7607 [7271]

Dittmar Inc., 101 E Laurel Ave., Cheltenham, PA 19012, (215)379-5533 [19283]

Dittos, 1 5th St. E, Kalispell, MT 59901-4947, (406)752-7110 [20968]

Diversified Copier Products Inc., 9765 Clairemont Mesa Blvd., Ste. C, San Diego, CA 92124, (619)565-2737 [20969]

Diversified Data Products Inc., 1995 Highland Dr., Ste. D, Ann Arbor, MI 48108-2230, (734)761-7222 [6214]

Diversified Distributors, PO Box 41248, Charleston, SC 29423-1248, (803)760-0299 [15112]

Diversified Fastening, 501 Richings St., CharLes City, IA 50616-1838, (515)228-1162 [13667]

Diversified Foam Products Inc., 5117 Central Hwy., Pennsauken, NJ 08109, (609)662-1981 [22956]

Diversified Imports, 3215 Lind Ave. SW, Renton, WA 98055, (206)251-8099 [1652]

Diversified Investments Inc., 4311 Triangle St., Mc Farland, WI 53558, (608)838-8813 [23625]

Diversified Marine Products, 1914 Mateo St., Los Angeles, CA 90021, (213)624-5595 [18492]

Diversified Metals Inc., 49 Main St., Monson, MA 01057, (413)267-5101 [19933]

Diversified Ophthalmics Inc., PO Box 2530, Spokane, WA 99220-2530, (509)324-6364 [19284]

Diversified Ophthalmics, Inc., 250 McCullough St., Cincinnati, OH 45226-2145, (513)321-7988 [19285]

Divesco Inc., 5000 Hwy. 80 E, Jackson, MS 39208, (601)932-1934 [16833]

Divinci Ltd., 4220 Pinecrest Cir. W, Las Vegas, NV 89121-4924, (702)458-1349 [17397]

Divine Brothers Distributing Inc., PO Box 3445, Great Falls, MT 59403-3445, (406)453-5457 [1653]

Dixie Art Supplies Inc., PO Box 30650, New Orleans, LA 70190, (504)522-5308 [20970]

Dixie Auto Auction Inc., PO Box 1271, Grenada, MS 38901, (601)226-5637 [20623]

Dixie Bearings, Inc., 1005 S A St., Ft. Smith, AR 72901, (501)782-9128 [2549]

Dixie Bearings Inc., PO Box 93803, Cleveland, OH 44101, (216)881-2828 [2550]

Dixie Beverage Co., 2705 S Pleasant Valley Rd., Winchester, VA 22601, (540)667-1656 [1654]

Dixie Building Supplies Co., PO Box 31601, Tampa, FL 33631, (813)871-4811 [7272]

Dixie Chemical Co. Inc., PO Box 130410, Houston, TX 77219, (713)863-1947 [4373]

Dixie Craft & Floral Wholesale, 9070 McLaurin St., Bay St. Louis, MS 39520, (228)467-7261 [20971]

Dixie Electronics, 1900 Barnwell St., Columbia, SC 29201-2604, (803)779-5332 [5597]

Dixie Industrial Supply Co., 2100 The Oaks Pkwy., Belmont, NC 28012, (704)820-1000 [16834]

Dixie Industrial Supply Div., PO Box 1127, Belmont, NC 28012-1127, (704)482-5641 [16835]

Dixie International Co., 3636 Indianola Ave., Columbus, OH 43214, (614)262-0102 [2551]

Dixie Mill Inc., 901 Tchoupitoulas St., New Orleans, LA 70130, (504)525-6101 [15952]

Dixie News Co., 900 Atando Ave., Charlotte, NC 28206, (704)376-0140 [3698]

Dixie Oil Co. Inc., PO Box 1007, Tifton, GA 31793, (912)382-2700 [22205]

Dixie Parts and Equipment Co., PO Box 929, Sidney, OH 45365, (937)492-6133 [2552]

Dixie Pipe Sales Inc., PO Box 300650, Houston, TX 77230, (713)796-2021 [19934]

Dixie Produce and Packaging Inc., PO Box 23647, New Orleans, LA 70183-0647, (504)733-7500 [10968]

Dixie Store Fixtures and Sales Company Inc., 2425 1st Ave. N, Birmingham, AL 35203, (205)322-2442 [15476]

Dixieline Lumber Co., 3250 Sports Arena Blvd., San Diego, CA 92110, (619)224-4120 [7273]

Dixon Co.; William, 750 Washington Ave., Carlstadt, NJ 07072, (201)939-6700 [15953]

Dixon Lumber Company Inc., PO Box 907, Galax, VA 24333, (703)236-9963 [7274]

Dixon Medical Inc., 3445 Sexton Woods Dr., Atlanta, GA 30341-2622, (404)457-0602 [18776]

Dixon Muzzleloading Shop, 9952 Kunkels Mill Rd., Kempton, PA 19529, (610)756-6271 [13489]

Dixon Paper Co., 55 Madison Ave., Ste. 800, Denver, CO 80206, (303)329-6644 [22008]

Dixon Tom-a-Toe Co., 5051 Speaker Rd., Kansas City, KS 66106-1043, (913)321-0691 [11205]

Dixon Tom-A-Toe Cos., 1640 Power Ferry Rd., Marietta, GA 30067, (404)955-0947 [10969]

Dixons Bicycling Center Inc., 257 W Broad St., Athens, GA 30601-2810, (706)549-2453 [23626]

DJ Associates, Inc., 8411 S Zero St., Ft. Smith, AR 72903-7097, (501)452-3987 [13668]

D.J. Enterprises, Inc., PO Box 31366, Cleveland, OH 44131, (216)524-3879 [20533]

DJ Wholesale Building Material Distributors, 2575 Westside Pky., No. 800, Alpharetta, GA 30004-3852, (770)625-1700 [7966]

D.J.H. Inc., PO Box 1975, Hallandale, FL 33008-1975, (305)620-1990 [15477]

DJ's Alaska Rentals, Inc., 405 Boniface Pkwy., Anchorage, AK 99504, (907)333-6561 [15954]

DL Pet Supply, 2541 Hwy. 250 S, Norwalk, OH 44857, (419)668-3756 [27116]

D.M. Distributing Company Inc., 7976 Long Hill Rd., Pasadena, MD 21122-1053, (410)437-0900 [1655]

DMACS International Corp., 2 Perimeter Park S, 140 E Twr., Birmingham, AL 35243, (205)967-2153 [6215]

DMI Tile & Marble, 3012 5th Ave. S, Birmingham, AL 35233, (205)322-8473 [9867]

D.M.R. Distributors, 3500 SR 520 West, Bldg. A, Cocoa, FL 32926, (407)632-9065 [25632]

DMR International, 2263 SW 37 Ave., Miami, FL 33145, (305)661-8950 [25633]

DMS Systems Corp., PO Box 8049, Rocky Mount, NC 27804-1049, (252)985-2500 [6216]

DMV USA Inc., 1285 Rudy St., Onalaska, WI 54650-8580, (608)781-2345 [10970]

D.N. Motors Ltd., 531 Van Cortland Park, Yonkers, NY 10705, (914)476-7451 [2553]

DNB Engineering Inc., 3535 W Commonwealth Ave., Fullerton, CA 92833, (714)870-7781 [15955]

DNE World Fruit Sales Inc., 1900 Old Dixie Hwy., Ft. Pierce, FL 34946, (407)465-1110 [10971]

Do All Foreign Sales Corp., 254 N Laurel Ave., Des Plaines, IL 60016, (847)803-7350 [15956]

D.O. Inc., PO Box 1065, Gillette, WY 82716, (307)682-9049 [22206]

Do It Best Corp., PO Box 868, Ft. Wayne, IN 46801, (219)748-5300 [7275]

Do-It Corp., 501 N State St., Denver, IA 50622-0612, (319)984-6055 [23627]

Do-My Ceramics, PO Box 36, North Ferrisburg, VT 05473-0036, (802)425-2181 [26472]

DoAll Co., 254 N Laurel Ave., Des Plaines, IL 60016, (847)824-1122 [16836]

Dobkin Company, Inc.; W.W., 51 Benbro Dr., Cheektowaga, NY 14225, (716)684-1200 [9868]

Dobkin Company, Inc.; W.W., 801 E Hiawatha Rd., Syracuse, NY 13208, (315)478-5769 [9869]

Dobrow Industries, PO Box 2188, Muncie, IN 47307-0188, (765)284-1497 [26798]

Doc Freeman's, 1401 NW Leary Way, Seattle, WA 98107, (206)633-1500 [18493]

Dockters X-Ray Inc., 7515 18th Ave. NW, Seattle, WA 98117-5430, (206)784-7768 [18777]

Dockters X-Ray Inc., 7515 18th Ave. NW, Seattle, WA 98117-5430, (206)784-7768 [19286]

Doctor Computerized Systems, 100 Centerview Dr., Ste. 250, Birmingham, AL 35216-3749, (205)978-1088 [6217]

Doctor Ike's Home Center Inc., 4200 Interstate 35 N, Laredo, TX 78040, (956)723-8266 [7276]

Dr. Pepper/Seven Up, Inc., 5301 Legacy Dr., Plano, TX 75024, (972)673-7000 [10972]

Document Center, 111 Industrial Way Ste. 9, Belmont, CA 94002, (650)591-7600 [3699]

Document Solutions Inc., 500 Garden City Dr., Monroeville, PA 15146-1111, (412)373-6500 [20972]

Documentext, PO Box 1126, Kingston, NY 12402, (914)331-5807 [3945]

DocuSource Inc., 9346 DeSoto Ave., Chatsworth, CA 91311, (818)717-9790 [20973]

Dodge Chicago/IBT, 291 Frontage Rd., Burr Ridge, IL 60521, (630)325-7575 [5516]

Dodge Chicago/IBT, 4643 W 138th St., Crestwood, IL 60445, (708)396-1402 [15957]

Dodge Chicago Industrial Bearings, 8021 New Jersey Ave., Hammond, IN 46323, (219)844-5090 [16705]

Dodge City Cooperative Exchange Inc., PO Box 610, Dodge City, KS 67801, (316)225-4193 [2554]

Dodge City Implement Inc., PO Box 139, Dodge City, KS 67801, (316)227-2165 [520]

Dodge Company Inc., 165 Cambridge Park Dr., Cambridge, MA 02140, (617)661-0500 [25634]

Dodge & Son Inc.; Herman, 547 Library St., San Fernando, CA 91340-2523, (818)362-6771 [15113]

Dodson Wholesale Lumber Company Inc., PO Box 1851, Roswell, NM 88201, (505)622-3278 [7277]

Doerle Food Services Inc., PO Box 9230, New Iberia, LA 70562, (318)367-8551 [10973]

Dog Outfitters, Humboldt Industrial Park, 1 Maplewood Dr., PO Box 2010, Hazleton, PA 18201, (717)384-5555 [27117]

Dogloo Inc., 20455 Somma Dr., Perris, CA 92570-9567, (909)279-9500 [27118]

Dogroom Products, 368 Hempstead Ave., Hempstead, NY 11552, (516)483-8930 [27119]

Dohmen Co./Anoka; The F., 1101 Lund Blvd., Anoka, MN 55303, (612)656-2300 [19287]

Dohmen Co.; F., PO Box 9, Germantown, WI 53022, (414)255-0022 [14086]

Dokken Implement Co. Inc., 612 4th St. & Pine St., Nezperce, ID 83543, (208)937-2422 [521]

Dole and Bailey Inc., PO Box 2405, Woburn, MA 01888, (781)935-1234 [10974]

Dole Bakersfield Inc., 6001 Snow Rd., Bakersfield, CA 93308-9546, (805)664-6100 [10975]

Dole Fresh Vegetables Co., PO Box 1759, Salinas, CA 93902, (408)422-8871 [10976]

Dole Nut Co. Inc., PO Box 845, Orland, CA 95963, (530)865-5511 [10977]

Dolgencorp, 427 Beech St., Scottsville, KY 42164, (502)237-5444 [10978]

Dollar Computer Corp., 1809 E Dyer Rd., Ste. 304, Santa Ana, CA 92705, (949)975-0552 [6218]

Dollar Farm Products Co., 1001 Dothan Hwy., Bainbridge, GA 31717, (912)248-2750 [522]

Dolls By Jerri, 651 Anderson St., Charlotte, NC 28205, (704)333-3211 [26473]

Dolly Madison Bakery, 10343-A Julian Dr., Woodlawn, OH 45215, (513)771-0077 [10979]

Dolly Madison Cake Co., 4400 Dodds Ave., Chattanooga, TN 37407-3033, (423)867-9041 [10980]

Dolphin Acquisition Corp., 600 Townsend, San Francisco, CA 94103, (415)487-3400 [14087]

Dolphin Pools Inc., 6219 E 11th St., Tulsa, OK 74112-3121, (918)838-7670 [23628]

Dom-Ex Inc., 109 Grant St., PO Box 877, Hibbing, MN 55746, (218)262-6116 [7278]

Domecq Importers Inc., 355 Riverside Ave., Westport, CT 06880-4810, (203)637-6500 [1656]

Domestic Import Tile, 3650 South 300 West, PO Box 65663, Salt Lake City, UT 84115, (801)262-3033 [9870]

Domestic & International Technology, 115 West Ave., Jenkintown, PA 19046, (215)885-7670 [2555]

Dominion Electric Supply Co., 5053 Lee Hwy., Arlington, VA 22207, (703)536-4400 [8630]

Domsey Fiber Corp., 431 Kent Ave., Brooklyn, NY 11211, (718)384-6000 [4919]

Domus Corp., 9734 Hayne Blvd., New Orleans, LA 70127-1202, (504)242-5480 [9871]

Don and Co.; Edward, 2500 S Harlem Ave., North Riverside, IL 60546, (708)442-9400 [15478]

Don-Lin Jewelry Co. Inc., 39 Haskins St., Providence, RI 02903, (401)274-0165 [17398]

Don Overcast and Associates, 250 Spring St., Atlanta, GA 30303, (404)523-4082 [4920]

Donato; Janet, 883-93 Elton St., Brooklyn, NY 11208-5315, (718)649-1750 [2485]

Doneli Foods, Inc., 3104 Nebraska Ave., Fremont, NE 68025-2070, (402)986-1372 [10981]

Donico & Associates; J.P., 1754 West 24th St., Erie, PA 16502, (814)454-6000 [18778]

Donie Chair Co., 2380 N Indiana, Brownsville, TX 78521, (956)838-0005 [13093]

Donley Medical Supply Co., PO Box 83108, Lincoln, NE 68501, (402)474-3222 [19288]

Donley Seed Co., 2121 Cottage St., Ashland, OH 44805, (419)289-7459 [523]

Donnellson Implement Inc., PO Box 246, Donnellson, IA 52625, (319)835-5511 [524]

Donnybrook Building Supply Inc., PO Box 60509, Fairbanks, AK 99706, (907)479-2202 [7279]

Donovan Farmers Cooperative Elevator Inc., PO Box 159, Donovan, IL 60931, (815)486-7325 [17819]

Donovan Marine, 115 W South St., Albemarle, NC 28001, (704)983-5050 [18494]

Donovan Marine, 4757 S Loop E, Houston, TX 77033, (713)734-4171 [18495]

Donovan Marine Inc., 400 N Carrollton Ave., PO Box 19100, New Orleans, LA 70179, (504)488-5731 [18496]

Dooley Oil Company, Inc., PO Box 189, E Yellowstone Hwy., Evansville, WY 82636, (307)234-9812 [22207]

Dooley Oil Company, Inc., PO Box 370, Laramie, WY 82070, (307)742-5667 [22208]

Doonan Truck and Equipment Inc., PO Box 1286, Great Bend, KS 67530, (316)792-2491 [20624]

Door County Cooperative Inc., 92 E Maple St., Sturgeon Bay, WI 54235, (920)743-6555 [525]

Door Engineering Corp., PO Box 2378, Norfolk, VA 23501, (757)622-5355 [7280]

Doortown Inc., 2200 Lauder Rd., Houston, TX 77039-3112, (281)442-4200 [7281]

Dopar Support Systems Inc., 3011 W Grand Blvd., 322 Fisher Bldg., Detroit, MI 48202-3011, (313)871-0990 [6219]

Dopkin; Lee L., 2100 W Cold Spring Ln., Baltimore, MD 21209, (410)466-3500 [23396]

Dops, Inc., 116 Pates Dr., Ft. Washington, MD 20744-4841, (301)839-8650 [1657]

Doral Fabrics Inc., 191 Central Ave., East Farmingdale, NY 11735, (516)694-1570 [26019]

Doral Steel Inc., 1500 Coining Dr., Toledo, OH 43612, (419)476-0011 [19935]

Doran Co.; Bill, 619 W Jefferson St., Rockford, IL 61105, (815)965-8791 [14858]

Dorchester Farmers Cooperative, N Depot St., Dorchester, NE 68343, (402)946-2211 [17820]

Dorell Fabrics Co., 4900 District Blvd., Los Angeles, CA 90058, (213)585-5861 [26020]

Dorfman Auto Supply Inc., PO Box 611, Waverly, IA 50677-0611, (319)352-2180 [2556]

Dorfman-Pacific Company Inc., PO Box 213005, Stockton, CA 95213-9005, (209)982-1400 [4921]

Dorian International Inc., 2 Gannett Dr., White Plains, NY 10604, (914)697-9800 [24105]

Dorman Products Div., 1 Dorman Dr., Warsaw, KY 41095, (606)567-7000 [2557]

Dorr Fabrics Inc., PO Box 88, Guild, NH 03754-0088, (603)863-1197 [26021]

Dorsey Millwork Inc., 36 Railroad Ave., Albany, NY 12205, (518)489-2542 [15958]

Dorsey Oil Co.; B.A., PO Box 786, Nashville, GA 31639-0786, (912)686-3751 [22209]

Dosik International, 9519 Evergreen St., Silver Spring, MD 20901, (301)585-4259 [3700]

Dot Foods Inc., PO Box 192, Mt. Sterling, IL 62353, (217)773-4411 [10982]

Dot Line, 9420 Eton Ave., Chatsworth, CA 91311-5295, (818)631-9730 [22851]

Dothan Auto Auction Inc., 3664 S Oates St., Dothan, AL 36301, (334)792-1115 [20625]

Double A Provisions Inc., 64 Main St., Queensbury, NY 12804, (518)792-2494 [10983]

Double O Electronic Distributors, 9440 NE Halsey St., Portland, OR 97220-4580, (503)252-9500 [8631]

Double T Holding Co., 4421 NE Columbia Blvd., Portland, OR 97218, (503)288-6411 [7282]

Double-T Manufacturing Corp., PO Box 1371, 27139 CR-6, Elkhart, IN 46515, (219)262-1340 [7283]

Doubleday Brothers and Co., 1919 E Kilgore Rd., Kalamazoo, MI 49002, (616)381-1040 [20974]

Dougherty Hanna Resources Co., 6000 Harvard Ave., Cleveland, OH 44105, (216)271-2400 [7284]

Dougherty Lumber Co., 6000 Harvard Ave., Cleveland, OH 44105, (216)271-1200 [7285]

Doughten Films, Inc.; Russ, 5907 Meredith Dr., Des Moines, IA 50322, (515)278-4737 [25168]

Doughtie's Foods Inc., 2410 Wesley St., Portsmouth, VA 23707, (804)393-6007 [10984]

Douglas Brothers Produce Co., 648 Cowles St., Long Beach, CA 90813, (562)436-2213 [10985]

Douglas Model Distributors, 2065 East 3300 South, Salt Lake City, UT 84109-2630, (801)487-7752 [26474]

Douglas Northeast Inc., 2507 E 9th St., Texarkana, AR 71854, (870)773-3633 [10986]

Douglas Products and Packaging Co., 1550 E Old 210 Hwy., Liberty, MO 64068, (816)781-4250 [4374]

Douglas/Quikut, PO Box 29, Walnut Ridge, AR 72476-0029, (870)886-6774 [15114]

Douglas and Sons, Inc., 231 W Cedar St., Kalamazoo, MI 49007, (616)344-2860 [16837]

Douglas Stewart Co., 2402 Advance Rd., Madison, WI 53704, (608)221-1155 [6220]

Douglass Co.; J.R., PO Box 31075, Cincinnati, OH 45231, (513)931-4986 [24347]

Douron Inc., 30 New Plant Ct., Owings Mills, MD 21117, (410)363-2600 [21714]

Douron Incorporated Corporate Furniture, 30 New Plant Ct., Owings Mills, MD 21117, (410)363-2600 [13094]

Doussan Inc., PO Box 52407, New Orleans, LA 70152, (504)948-7561 [16838]

Doussard & Associates, Inc.; Ron, 6 Castle Pines Ct., Lake in the Hills, IL 60102, (847)854-6090 [3701]

Dove Wholesale, 4581 W Picacho, Las Cruces, NM 88005, (505)523-8668 [27120]

Dover Company Inc.; Bill L., PO Box 600, Jasper, TX 75951, (409)384-2441 [22210]

Dover Electric Supply Company Inc., 1631 S Du Pont Hwy., Dover, DE 19901, (302)674-0115 [8632]

Dover Handbag Corp., 20 W 33rd St., New York, NY 10001, (212)563-7055 [18389]

Dover Sales Co. Inc., PO Box 2479, Berkeley, CA 94702, (510)527-4780 [4375]

Dow Electronics Inc., 8603 Adamo Dr., Tampa, FL 33619, (813)626-5195 [8633]

Dow-Hammond Trucks Co., 720 G St., Modesto, CA 95354, (209)524-4861 [2558]

The Dowd Co., Tonkin-Symons Paper Div., 167 Klondike Ave., Fitchburg, MA 01420, (978)343-4861 [21715]

Dowler Enterprises Inc., RR 2, Box 226-1, Cole Camp, MO 65325-9803, (660)331-1744 [25635]

Dowling Inc.; J.H., 705 W Madison St., PO Box 308, Tallahassee, FL 32302-0308, (850)222-2616 [7286]

Down East Wholesalers Inc., 1 School St., Damariscotta, ME 04543, (207)563-3178 [26022]

Down Lite International, 106 Northeast Dr., Loveland, OH 45140, (513)677-3696 [15479]

Down River Equipment Co., 12100 W 52nd Ave., Wheat Ridge, CO 80033-2000, (303)467-9489 [23629]

Down River Home Health Supply, 3138 Biddle St., Riverview, MI 48192-5916, (734)285-3800 [18779]

Downard Hydraulics Inc., PO Box 1212, Princeton, WV 24740, (304)487-1492 [15959]

Downey Designs International Inc., 2265 Executive Dr., Indianapolis, IN 46241, (317)248-9888 [17399]

Downing Coal Co., 13 Pepperwood Ln., Cleveland, OH 44124-4701, (216)831-6750 [20534]

Downs Foods Co.; Tony, PO Box 28, St. James, MN 56081, (507)375-3111 [10987]

Downs Supply Co., PO Box 471010, Tulsa, OK 74147-1010, (918)252-5651 [9872]

Doyle Equipment Co., PO Box 1840, Cranberry Township, PA 16066-0840, (412)322-4500 [7287]

Doyles Wholesale, PO Box 2530, Hayden, ID 83835-2530, (208)772-7512 [26333]

Dozier Equipment Co., 770 South 70th St., Milwaukee, WI 53214, (414)443-0581 [15960]

DP Equipment Marketing Inc., 7595 E Gray Rd., No. 1, Scottsdale, AZ 85260, (602)948-2720 [6221]

DPC Inc., PO Box 149, Delphi, IN 46923, (765)564-3752 [507]

DPI-Epicurean Fine Foods, PO Box 5940, Mesa, AZ 85211-5940, (480)969-9333 [10988]

DPI Food Products Co., 8125 E 88th Ave., Henderson, CO 80640-8121, (303)301-1226 [10989]

DPI Southwest Distributing Inc., PO Box 25025, Albuquerque, NM 87125, (505)345-4488 [10990]

DPI Southwest Distributing Inc., PO Box 25025, Albuquerque, NM 87125, (505)345-4488 [10991]

DPI-Taylor Brothers, PO Box 5940, Mesa, AZ 85211-5940, (480)969-9333 [10988]

DPI-Taylor Brothers, PO Box 5940, Mesa, AZ 85211-5940, (602)834-6081 [10992]

DPM of Arkansas, 400 Mario Del Pero St., Booneville, AR 72927-0200, (501)675-4555 [10993]

Drago Supply Co. Inc., 740 Houston Ave., Port Arthur, TX 77640, (409)983-4911 [13669]

Drago Supply Company Inc., 740 Houston Ave., Port Arthur, TX 77640, (409)983-4911 [15961]

Drake America Div., 2 Gannett Dr., White Plains, NY 10604, (914)697-9800 [2559]

Drake Petroleum Company Inc., PO Box 72616, Elmwood Sta., Providence, RI 02907, (401)781-9900 [22211]

Drake's Salvage; Fred, 4195 Dupont Pky., Townsend, DE 19734, (302)378-4877 [2560]

Draper Energy Co. Inc., PO Box 419, Wilton, NH 03086-0419, (603)654-6400 [20535]

Draper Valley Farms Inc., PO Box 838, Mt. Vernon, WA 98273, (360)424-7947 [10994]

Drapery Hardware of Florida, 2147 NW 29th St., Ft. Lauderdale, FL 33311, (954)735-1046 [13670]

Drapery Stitch of Delphos, PO Box 307, 50 Summers Ln., Delphos, OH 45833, (419)692-3921 [15480]

Drayton Swimming Pool Supply, 4763 Dixie Hwy., Waterford, MI 48329-3523, (248)673-6734 [23630]

Dreisilker Electric Motors Inc., 352 Roosevelt Rd., Glen Ellyn, IL 60137, (630)469-7510 [8634]

Dremont-Levy Co., 365 Albany St., Boston, MA 02118, (617)423-5580 [21434]

Drescher Company Inc.; P., 200 Monarch Ln., Liverpool, NY 13088, (315)457-4911 [10995]

Dresco Reproduction Inc., 12603 Allard St., Santa Fe Springs, CA 90670, (562)863-6677 [25636]

Dresco Reproduction Inc., 12603 Allard St., Santa Fe Springs, CA 90670, (562)863-6677 [24348]

Dresser Industries Inc., PO Box 718, Dallas, TX 75221, (214)740-6000 [15962]

Drey and Co. Inc.; S.E., 9135 Harrison Park Ct., PO Box 26499, Indianapolis, IN 46226, (317)543-5640 [16839]

Dreyco Inc., 263 Veterans Blvd., Carlstadt, NJ 07072-2792, (201)896-9000 [2561]

Dreyer & Associates Inc., 4408 Village Oaks Trail, Atlanta, GA 30338-5726, (404)577-5376 [4922]

Dreyfus & Assoc., 305 Madison Ave., Ste. 966, New York, NY 10165-0026, (212)867-7700 [2562]

Dreyfus Corp. Allenberg Cotton Company Div.; Louis, PO Box 3254, Cordova, TN 38018-3254, (901)383-5000 [17821]

Dreyfus Corp.; Louis, PO Box 810, Wilton, CT 06897-0810, (203)761-2000 [17822]

DRG International Inc., 1167 U.S Hwy. 22, Mountainside, NJ 07092, (908)233-2075 [19289]

Dribeck Importers Inc., 1 Station Pl., PO Box 120 007, Stamford, CT 06912-0007, (203)388-2325 [1513]

Drilex Corporation, 10628 N Camino Rosas Nuevas, Tucson, AZ 85737-7081, (520)886-0956 [15963]

Drillers Service Inc., PO Box 1407, Hickory, NC 28603-1407, (704)322-1100 [25637]

Drillers Supply Inc., 6000 Brittmoore Rd., Houston, TX 77041, (713)466-7711 [15964]

Drillot Corporation, PO Box 97, Suwanee, GA 30024-0097, (404)932-7282 [15115]

Drinks Galore Inc., 1331 Jerome Ave., Bronx, NY 10452-3320, (212)681-0500 [1658]

Driscoll Grain Cooperative Inc., PO Box 208, Driscoll, TX 78351, (512)387-6242 [17823]

Driscoll Grain Cooperative Inc., PO Box 208, Driscoll, TX 78351, (512)387-6242 [10996]

Driscoll Leather Co. Inc., 714 S 15th St., Omaha, NE 68102-3103, (402)341-4307 [24727]

Driscoll Leather Company Inc., 714 S 15th St., Omaha, NE 68102-3103, (402)341-4307 [4923]

Drive Train Industries Inc., 3301 Brighton Blvd., Denver, CO 80216, (303)292-5176 [2563]

Drive Train Industries Inc., 3350 E Yellowstone, Casper, WY 82609, (307)266-4390 [2564]

Drivetrain Specialists, 1308 W 2nd St., Odessa, TX 79763, (915)333-3241 [2565]

Drogueria Betances, PO Box 368, Caguas, PR 00726, (787)746-0951 [19290]

Drogueria J.M. Blanco, PO Box 364129, San Juan, PR 00936-4929, (787)793-6262 [19291]

DRP Corp., PO Box 19689, Las Vegas, NV 89132-0689, (702)895-9033 [19448]

Drucker Associates, Inc., PO Box 36219, Grosse Pointe Woods, MI 48236, (313)882-8228 [2566]

Drug Center, Inc., GPO Box 3687, San Juan, PR 00936, (787)724-5115 [19292]

Drug Guild Distributors Inc., 350 Meadowland Pkwy., Secaucus, NJ 07094, (201)348-3700 [15116]

Drulane Co., PO Box 570, Farmington, WV 26571-0570, (304)825-6697 [15481]

Drulane/ Palmer Smith, PO Box 570, Farmington, WV 26571-0570, (304)825-6697 [15481]

Drummond Cooperative Elevator Inc., PO Box 56, Drummond, OK 73735, (580)493-2212 [526]

Drybranch Inc., 1 Commercial Ct., Plainview, NY 11803-1600, (516)576-7000 [23631]

DS America Inc., 5110 Tollview Dr., Rolling Meadows, IL 60008, (847)870-7400 [15965]

DS Design, 1157 Executive Cir., Ste. D, Cary, NC 27511, (919)319-1770 [6222]

D.S.A. Materials Inc., 517 W Johnson St., Jonesboro, AR 72403, (870)932-7461 [8635]

DsgnHaus, Inc., 1375 Kings Hwy., Ste. E, Fairfield, CT 06430, (203)367-1993 [6223]

DSi, 20A Oak Branch Dr., Greensboro, NC 27407-2145, (336)294-0141 [6224]

DSI Distributing, Inc., 9190 Corporation Dr., Indianapolis, IN 46256, (317)845-4400 [15117]

DSI Systems Inc., 9190 Corporation Dr., Indianapolis, IN 46256, (317)845-4400 [15117]

DSW Inc., PO Box 3817, Wilson, NC 27893, (919)291-0131 [20626]

DTC Tool Corp., 850 Mahler Rd., Burlingame, CA 94010, (650)697-1414 [15966]

DTK Computer Inc., 770 Epperson Dr., La Puente, CA 91748-1336, (626)810-0098 [6225]

Du Pont Co., 2929 Koapaka St., Honolulu, HI 96819, (808)833-4117 [21435]

Du-Wald Steel Corp., 1100 Umatilla St., Denver, CO 80204, (303)571-5530 [19936]

DuBarry International Inc., 10624 Southeastern, Ste. A-200, Henderson, NV 89052 [26799]

DuBell Lumber Co., Rte. 70 E, Medford, NJ 08055, (609)654-4143 [7288]

Dubl-Click Software Corp., 20310 Empire Blvd., Ste. A102, Bend, OR 97701, (541)317-0355 [6226]

Dublin Metal Corp., 6001 Tain Dr., No. 200, Dublin, OH 43017, (614)761-9502 [19937]

Dublin Yogurt Co., 9129 Haddington Ct., Dublin, OH 43017, (614)761-3415 [10997]

Dubois County Farm Bureau Cooperative, 901 Main St., Huntingburg, IN 47542, (812)683-2809 [527]

DuBois Elevator Co., 4886 E 450 N, Dubois, IN 47527, (812)678-2891 [528]

DuBois Fabrics, 5520 W 111th St., Oak Lawn, IL 60453, (708)499-2040 [26023]

DuBose and Son Co.; W.A., 207 N John Redditt Dr., Lufkin, TX 75904-2635, (409)632-3363 [529]

DuBose Steel Incorporated of North Carolina, PO Box 1098, Roseboro, NC 28382, (919)525-4161 [19938]

Duchess Royale Inc., 4350 S Winchester Ave., Chicago, IL 60609-3193, (773)651-5555 [15482]

Duchin Inc.; Gloria, PO Box 4860, Rumford, RI 02916-0860, (401)438-5400 [13347]

Duck Commander Company, Inc., 538 Mouth of Cypress Rd., West Monroe, LA 71291, (318)325-1189 [23632]

Duckett Truck Center Inc., Rte. 6, Box 580, Poplar Bluff, MO 63901-9806, (314)785-0193 [20627]

DuCoa, 115 Executive Dr., Highland, IL 62249, (618)654-2070 [20536]

DuCoa-Technical Products Group, 115 Executive Dr., Highland, IL 62249, (618)654-2070 [20536]

Dudek & Company, Inc.; R.C., 800 Del Norte Blvd., Oxnard, CA 93030, (805)988-4882 [8636]

Dudek & Company, Inc.; R.C., 2115 Old Oakland Rd., San Jose, CA 95131, (408)321-9011 [8637]

Duellman Electric Co., PO Box 771, Dayton, OH 45401, (937)461-8000 [8638]

Duferco Trading Corp., 100 Metro Park S, Laurence Harbor, NJ 08878-2001 [19939]

Duffco, PO Box 1513, Conway, NH 03818-1513, (603)356-7940 [10998]

Duffens Optical, 900 Lynn St., PO Box 631, Hannibal, MO 63401, (573)221-9200 [19293]

Duffens Optical, PO Box 897, Denver, CO 80201, (303)623-5301 [19294]

Duffy and Lee Co., 3351 SW 13th Ave., Ft. Lauderdale, FL 33315, (954)467-1288 [9873]

Dufour Editions, Inc., PO Box 7, Chester Springs, PA 19425-0007, (610)458-5005 [3702]

Dugan Equipment & Supply Co., PO Box 3040, Kansas City, KS 66103-0040, (913)236-4060 [14423]

Dugans Inc., 7841 S 180th St., PO Box 220, Kent, WA 98032, (425)251-9000 [23633]

Duggan Industries Inc., 3901 S Lamar St., Dallas, TX 75215, (214)428-8336 [19932]

Duhig and Co., 14275 Wicks Blvd., San Leandro, CA 94577, (510)352-6460 [23139]

Duhig and Co., 14275 Wicks Blvd., San Leandro, CA 94577, (510)352-6460 [19940]

Duke Energy Field Services Inc., 370 17th St Ste. 900, Denver, CO 80202, (303)595-3331 [22212]

Duke Scientific Corp., PO Box 50005, Palo Alto, CA 94303, (650)424-1177 [24349]

Duke Sports, PO Box 5355, Stateline, NV 89449-5355, (702)588-5052 [26024]

Duke University Press, Box 90660, Durham, NC 27708-0660, (919)687-3600 [3703]

Dukes Car Stereo Inc., 2833 S Dort Hwy., Flint, MI 48507-5213, (810)744-2500 [5598]

Duluth Plumbing Supply Co., PO Box 16329, Duluth, MN 55816-0329, (218)722-3393 [23140]

Dumans Custom Tailor Inc., 438 E Colfax Ave., Denver, CO 80203-1909, (303)832-1701 [4924]

Dumas Oil Co., PO Box 1296, Goldsboro, NC 27533-1296, (919)735-0571 [22213]

Dumes Salvage Terre Haute Compressed Steel Inc., PO Box 208, West Terre Haute, IN 47885-0208, (812)533-2147 [27013]

Dunavant Enterprises Inc., 3797 New Getwell Rd., Memphis, TN 38118, (901)369-1500 [17824]

Dunaway Supply Co., 211 Cherokee St., Longview, TX 75604, (903)759-4481 [7289]

Dunbar Doors and Millwork, 1316 Bonneville Ave., Snohomish, WA 98290, (360)568-0515 [27302]

Duncan Co., 425 NE Hoover, Minneapolis, MN 55413-2926, (612)331-1776 [16840]

Duncan-Edward Co., PO Box 14038, Ft. Lauderdale, FL 33302, (954)467-1461 [16841]

Duncan Equipment Co., PO Box 40, Duncan, OK 73533, (405)255-1216 [16842]

Duncan Supply Co. Inc., 910 N Illinois St., Indianapolis, IN 46204, (317)634-1335 [14424]

Dundee Citrus Growers Association, PO Box 1739, Dundee, FL 33838, (941)439-1574 [10999]

Dunken Distributing Inc., PO Box 1821, Twin Falls, ID 83303-1821, (208)733-3054 [9874]

Dunkirk Ice Cream Company, Inc., 1 Ice Cream Dr., Dunkirk, NY 14048, (716)366-5400 [11123]

Dunlap and Kyle Company Inc., PO Box 720, Batesville, MS 38606, (601)563-7601 [20628]

Dunlap Oil Company Inc., 759 S Haskell Ave., Willcox, AZ 85643, (602)384-2248 [22214]

Dunlaw Optical Laboratories, PO Box 3110, Lawton, OK 73502-3110, (580)355-8410 [19295]

Dunlop Aviation North America, 6573 Old Dixie Hwy., Ste. 120, Forest Park, GA 30297, (404)362-9900 [81]

Dunlop Tire Corp., PO Box 1109, Buffalo, NY 14240, (716)879-8200 [2567]

Dunn Sales; Skip, 162 Washington Ave., New Rochelle, NY 10801, (914)636-2200 [25638]

Dunns Sporting Goods Co. Inc., PO Box 631, Pevely, MO 63070, (314)479-4240 [23634]

Duo-Fast Carolinas Inc., PO Box 5564, Charlotte, NC 28225, (704)377-5721 [5839]

Duo-Fast Corp. North Central Sales Div., 200 Laura Dr., Addison, IL 60101, (708)543-7970 [13671]

Duo-Fast Northeast, 22 Tolland St., East Hartford, CT 06108, (860)289-6861 [13672]

Duplex Novelty Corp., 575 8th Ave., New York, NY 10018-3086, (212)564-1352 [26025]

Dupli-Fax Inc., 300 Commerce Sq. Blvd., Burlington, NJ 08016, (609)387-8700 [20975]

Duplin Wine Cellars, Hwy. 117 N, Rose Hill, NC 28458-9526, (910)289-3688 [1659]

Dupont de Nemours and Co.; E.I., 1007 Market St., Wilmington, DE 19898 [4376]

Dura Med Inc., 285 Southland Dr., Lexington, KY 40503-1934, (606)278-2858 [18780]

Dura Metals Inc., 620 28th Ave., Bellwood, IL 60104-1901, (708)547-7701 [19941]

Dura Sales Inc., RD 2, Box 81B, Tarentum, PA 15084, (724)224-7700 [7290]

Durable Packaging Corp., 3139 W Chicago Ave., Chicago, IL 60622, (773)638-4140 [15967]

Duradex Inc., 202 Main Ave., PO Box 1050, Clifton, NJ 07014, (973)773-0660 [21716]

Duraffourg Gem Company Inc.; Max, PO Box 568, Bedford, NY 10506-0568, (914)234-9784 [17400]

Duraline, 75 Hoffman Ln., Central Islip, NY 11722-5007, (516)234-2002 [8639]

Durand Equipment and Manufacturing Co., 5110 N Oak, Durand, MI 48429, (517)288-2626 [7291]

Durand International, PO Box 5001, Millville, NJ 08332, (609)825-5620 [13348]

Durastill Inc., PO Box 1570, Roswell, GA 30077, (404)993-7575 [25639]

Durham Boat Co. Inc., 220 Newmarket Rd., Durham, NH 03824-4203, (603)659-2548 [23635]

Durham Meat Co., 160 Sunol St., San Jose, CA 95126, (408)291-3600 [11000]

Durkin Hayes Publishing, 2221 Niagara Falls Blvd., Niagara Falls, NY 14304, (716)731-9177 [3704]

Durkopp Adler America Inc., 3025 Northwoods Pkwy., Norcross, GA 30071, (404)446-8162 [15968]

Duro Supply Co., 801 S Henry St., PO Box 188, Bay City, MI 48706, (517)894-2811 [23141]

Duromotive Industries, 241 41st St., Brooklyn, NY 11232-2811, (718)499-3838 [2568]

Durr-Fillauer Medical Inc., PO Box 244009, Montgomery, AL 36124-4009, (205)241-8800 [18781]

Durr Medical Corp., PO Box 165, Columbia, SC 29202, (803)791-5900 [19296]

Durr and Partners, 57 Punkhorn Pl., Mashpee, MA 02649, (508)477-5111 [6227]

Durrett-Sheppard Steel Co., 6800 E Baltimore St., Baltimore, MD 21224, (410)633-6800 [19942]

Durst Brokerage Inc., 135 E Algonquin Rd., Arlington Heights, IL 60005, (847)981-8880 [11001]

Durst Corp., PO Box 1252, Mountainside, NJ 07092-0252, (908)789-2880 [23142]

Duso Food Distributors, Rte. 52, Ellenville, NY 12428, (914)647-4600 [11002]

Dusty Strings Co., 3406 Fremont Ave. N, Seattle, WA 98103, (206)634-1656 [25169]

Dutch Gold Honey Inc., 2220 Dutch Gold Dr., Lancaster, PA 17601-1941, (717)393-1716 [11003]

Dutchess Beer Distributors, 5 Laurel St., Poughkeepsie, NY 12603, (914)452-0940 [1660]

Dutchess Quarry and Supply Company Inc., PO Box 651, Pleasant Valley, NY 12569, (914)635-8151 [7292]

Dutt and Wagner of Virginia Inc., PO Box 518, Abingdon, VA 24212-0518, (703)628-2116 [11004]

Dutton Co.; Andrew, 284 Bodwell St., Avon, MA 02322-1119, (508)586-4100 [15483]

Duvall Inc.; H.B., PO Box 70, Frederick, MD 21705-0070, (301)662-1125 [530]

DVH Co., PO Box 560604, Dallas, TX 75356-0604, (214)631-0200 [2569]

DW Distribution, PO Box 271023, Dallas, TX 75227, (214)381-2200 [7293]

DW Enterprises, 510 W 41st Ave., No. C, Anchorage, AK 99503, (907)561-8363 [24350]

Dwan and Company Inc., PO Box 96, Torrington, CT 06790, (860)489-3149 [1661]

DXP Enterprises Inc., 7272 Pinemont, Houston, TX 77040, (713)996-4700 [15969]

Dye Seed Ranch, Rte. 1, Box 99, Pomeroy, WA 99347, (509)843-3591 [531]

Dyer Auto Auction Inc., PO Box 115, Dyer, IN 46311, (219)865-2361 [20629]

Dyer and Co.; B.W., 106 Mine Brook Rd., Bernardsville, NJ 07924-2432, (908)204-9800 [11005]

Dyer Co.; H.G., 19 Old Bliss St., Rehoboth, MA 02769, (508)621-1622 [23143]

Dyer Lauderdale Co-op, PO Box 550, Dyersburg, TN 38025, (901)285-7161 [532]

Dyer Motor Co., PO Box 246, Dyer, TN 38330-0246, (901)692-2266 [20630]

Dykstra Food Service, 498 7 Mile Rd. NW, Comstock Park, MI 49321-9545, (616)784-1300 [11006]

Dyl-Chem Inc., PO Box 4096, New Bedford, MA 02741-4096, (508)997-1960 [4925]

Dyna Corp., 6300 Yarrow Dr., Carlsbad, CA 92009, (760)438-2511 [19297]

Dyna Group International Inc., 1661 S Sequin Ave., New Braunfels, TX 78130-3856, (830)620-4400 [13349]

Dyna Group International Inc., 1801 W 16th St., Broadview, IL 60153, (708)450-9200 [23636]

Dyna-Lube, 1056 E 425 N, Ogden, UT 84404, (801)782-0400 [22215]

Dyna Marketing, 10211 Foxrow, Ste. 101, Houston, TX 77064, (281)890-7107 [6228]

Dyna Marketing, 1425 W Pioneer Dr., Ste. 147, Irving, TX 75061, (972)259-2744 [6229]

Dynabit USA Inc., 501 E Kennedy Blvd., Ste. 750, Tampa, FL 33602-5200, (813)222-2050 [6230]

Dynacraft Co., 650 Milwaukee Ave., Algona, WA 98001, (253)351-3000 [20631]

Dynacraft Golf Products, Inc., 71 Malholm St., Newark, OH 43055, (740)344-1191 [23637]

Dynafluid Products, Inc., 1638 Production Rd., Jeffersonville, IN 47130, (812)288-8285 [15970]

DynAir Fueling Inc., 2000 Edmund Halley Dr., Reston, VA 20190, (703)264-9500 [22216]

Dynamic Classics Ltd., 230 5th Ave., New York, NY 10001, (212)571-0267 [23638]

Dynamic Computer Concepts, 8401 Corporate Dr., Ste. 460, Landover, MD 20785, (301)731-4393 [6231]

Dynamic Concepts Inc., 98 Sheffield Rd., Cranston, RI 02920-6040, (401)942-0381 [17401]

Dynamic Distributors, 9621 S Dixie Hwy., Miami, FL 33156, (305)665-5313 [7294]

Dynamic Engineers Inc., 2000 Dairy Ashford, No. 128, Houston, TX 77077, (281)870-8822 [8640]

Dynamic Foam Products Inc., PO Box 774942, Steamboat Springs, CO 80477-4942, (970)879-3631 [24728]

Dynamic International Company Inc., PO Box 640721, Kenner, LA 70064, (504)466-4703 [7295]

Dynamic Medical Equipment Ltd., 51 Rushmore St., Westbury, NY 11590, (516)333-1472 [19298]

Dynamic Reprographics Inc., 1002 W 12th St., Austin, TX 78703, (512)474-8842 [24351]

Dynamic Technology, 2416-A Over Dr., Lexington, KY 40510, (606)281-0045 [15971]

Dynamic Technology, 11584 Commonwealth Dr., Louisville, KY 40299-2340, (502)968-3603 [15972]

Dynamic Technology, 2608 Nordic Rd., Dayton, OH 45414, (937)274-3007 [16843]

Dynamic Technology, 2323 Crowne Point Dr., Cincinnati, OH 45241-5405, (513)793-4992 [16844]

E & B Beauty & Barber Supply, 1811 E Thayer Ave., Bismarck, ND 58501-4780, (701)223-7408 [14088]

E and B Beauty and Barber Supply, 1811 E Thayer Ave., Bismarck, ND 58501-4780, (701)223-7408 [24106]

E and B Electric Supply Co., 615 Strong Hwy., El Dorado, AR 71730, (870)862-8101 [8641]

E Big Inc., PO Box 385, Meridian, ID 83642-0385, (208)888-3606 [17402]

E-Corp, Inc., 6152 S Forest Ct., Littleton, CO 80121, (303)220-0250 [1662]

E and E Steel Company Inc., 2187 S Garfield Ave., City of Commerce, CA 90040, (213)723-0947 [19943]

E & G Auto Parts Inc., 211 W Long Ave., Du Bois, PA 15801-2105, (814)371-3350 [2570]

E-Heart Press, Inc., 3700 Mockingbird Ln., Dallas, TX 75205, (214)741-6915 [3705]

E & L Steel Co. Inc., 176 American Way, Madison, MS 39110, (601)853-4277 [19944]

E & M Ice Cream Distributors, 61 Hungerford Ter., Burlington, VT 05401, (802)862-6746 [11007]

E. M J Co, 5311 Clinton Dr., Houston, TX 77020, (713)672-1621 [19945]

E & R Sales Inc., 4800 Market Square Ln., Midlothian, VA 23112, (804)744-8000 [13350]

E-Y Laboratories Inc., 107 N Amphlett Blvd., San Mateo, CA 94401, (650)342-3296 [19299]

E-Z Mart Stores Inc., PO Box 1426, Texarkana, TX 75504, (903)838-0558 [11008]

E-Z Popcorn & Supply, 17151 SE Petrovitsky Rd., Renton, WA 98058-9610, (425)255-4545 [24204]

E-Z Serve Petroleum Marketing Co., 1824 Hillandale Rd., Durham, NC 27705-2650 [22217]

E.A. Martin Machinery Co., PO Box 988, Springfield, MO 65801-0988, (417)866-6651 [7653]

Eads Brothers Wholesale Furniture Co., PO Box 1546, Ft. Smith, AR 72902, (501)646-6617 [13095]

Eager Plastics Inc., 3350 W 48th Pl., Chicago, IL 60632-3000, (773)927-3484 [22957]

Eagle Beverage Co., PO Box 1492, Springfield, OH 45501, (513)322-2082 [1663]

Eagle Chemical Co., 125 Witman Rd., Reading, PA 19605, (215)921-2301 [4377]

Eagle Claw Fishing Tackle, 4245 E 46th Ave., Denver, CO 80216-3262, (303)321-1481 [23639]

Eagle of Cody Printing, PO Box 522, Cody, WY 82414-0522, (307)527-7523 [21717]

Eagle Communications Technology, 2443 Fair Oaks Blvd., Ste. 102, Sacramento, CA 95825, (916)481-9210 [5599]

Eagle Creek, 3055 Enterprise Ct., Vista, CA 92083-8347, (760)471-7600 [18390]

Eagle Distributing Co., PO Box 1286, Lumberton, NC 28359-1286, (919)738-8165 [1664]

Eagle Distributing Co. Inc., PO Box 27190, Knoxville, TN 37927, (423)637-3311 [1665]

Eagle Distributors Inc., 169 Kolepa Pl., Kahului, HI 96732-2433, (808)877-2520 [1666]

Eagle Distributors Inc., 2439 Albany St., Kenner, LA 70062-5243, (504)464-5991 [25170]

Eagle Electric Manufacturing Co., 112 Lake St S, Kirkland, WA 98033, (425)827-8401 [8642]

Eagle Family Foods, 61 Swift St., Waterloo, NY 13165, (315)539-9291 [24954]

Eagle Food Centers Inc., Rte. 67 & Knoxville Rd., Milan, IL 61264, 800-322-3143 [11009]

Eagle Foods Co., 3547 E 14th St., Ste. D, Brownsville, TX 78521-3242, (512)544-7721 [11010]

Eagle International, Inc., 520 Ralph St., Sarasota, FL 34242, (941)349-6124 [15973]

Eagle Milling Co., PO Box 15007, Casa Grande, AZ 85230-5007, (520)836-2131 [27121]

Eagle Optical, 205 E Boone Ave., Spokane, WA 99202-1707, (509)624-4565 [19300]

Eagle Pointe Inc., Rte. 2, Box 117, Huddleston, VA 24104-9643, (540)297-1274 [4926]

Eagle River Corp., 320 W 4th Ave., Anchorage, AK 99501-2321, (907)279-2401 [23640]

Eagle River Distributing, 120 Jack Frost Dr., Eagle River, WI 54521, (715)479-9060 [1667]

Eagle Sales Company Inc., PO Box 22968, Memphis, TN 38122-0968, (901)458-6133 [8643]

Eagle Supply Inc., PO Box 75305, Tampa, FL 33675, (813)248-4918 [7296]

Eagle Trophy, 32 Shannon Rd., Salem, NH 03079-1843, (603)893-6536 [17403]

Eagle Wholesale L.P., PO Box 742, Tyler, TX 75710, (903)592-4321 [11011]

Eaglecrafts Inc., 168 W 12th St., Ogden, UT 84404-5501, (801)393-3991 [26475]

Eakins Associates Inc., 67 E Evelyn Ave., Mountain View, CA 94041, (415)969-5109 [6232]

E.A.P. Co., PO Box 14, Keller, TX 76248, (817)498-4242 [6233]

Earlville Farmers Cooperative, 602 Railroad St., Earlville, IL 60518, (815)246-8461 [17825]

Early Tractor Co. Inc., PO Box 588, Blakely, GA 31723, (912)723-3595 [533]

Earnest Machine Products Co., 12502 Plaza Dr., Parma, OH 44130, (216)362-1100 [13673]

Earp Meat Company Inc., 6550 Kansas Ave., Kansas City, KS 66111, (913)287-3311 [11012]

Earth Brothers Ltd., PO Box 188, Proctorsville, VT 05153, (802)226-7480 [11013]

Earth Care Paper Inc., PO Box 14140, Madison, WI 53714-0140, (608)223-4000 [26800]

Earth Energy Technology and Supply Inc., PO Box 219, Marietta, OK 73448, (405)276-9455 [14425]

Earth Grains Company of Sacramento, 3211 6th Ave., Sacramento, CA 95817-0387, (916)456-3863 [11014]

Earth Waste Systems Inc., 29 Lund Rd, PO Box 187, Saco, ME 04072, (207)284-4516 [26801]

Earthgrains/Waldensian Bakerie, 320 E Main St., Valdese, NC 28690, (704)874-2130 [11015]

Earthworm Inc., 35 Medford St., Somerville, MA 02143-4211, (617)628-1844 [20976]

Earthworm Inc., 495 Ashford Ave., Ardsley, NY 10502, (914)693-0400 [7297]

EASI (Electronic Applications Specialists Inc.), 1250 Holden Ave., Milford, MI 48381, (248)685-8283 [8644]

East Alabama Lumber Co., PO Box 110, Lafayette, AL 36862, (334)864-9800 [7298]

East Central Cooperative Inc., PO Box 128, Cleveland, WI 53015, (920)693-8220 [534]

East Central Iowa Cooperative, PO Box 300, Hudson, IA 50643, (319)988-3257 [11016]

East Coast Connection Inc., 5016 Rte. 130 N, Delran, NJ 08075, (609)461-8003 [24729]

East Coast Embroidery Inc., 375 Waterman Ave., East Providence, RI 02914-0519, (401)434-9224 [4927]

East Coast Mill Sales Co., PO Box 580, Charlestown, MA 02129, (617)241-0440 [7299]

East Coast Tile Imports—East, Ludlow Industrial Park, Gate 4, Bldg. 261, State St., Ludlow, MA 01056, (413)589-0101 [9875]

East Coast Tile/Terrazzo, 420 S Neiman Ave., Melbourne, FL 32901, (407)723-4353 [9876]

East Coast Tile/Terrazzo, 450 Old Dixie Hwy., Vero Beach, FL 32960, (561)562-4164 [9877]

East Coast Tile/Terrazzo, 450 Old Dixie Hwy., Vero Beach, FL 32960, (561)562-4164 [7300]

East Continental Gems Inc., 580 5th Ave., New York, NY 10036, (212)575-0944 [17404]

East Distributors Ltd.; Ryan, 6325 Erdman Ave., Baltimore, MD 21205, (410)325-1298 [3706]

East Hampton Industries Inc., PO Box 5066, Ft. Lauderdale, FL 33310, (516)371-5553 [15484]

East Jordan Cooperative Co., PO Box 377, East Jordan, MI 49727, (616)536-2275 [2571]

East Jordan Cooperative Co., PO Box 377, East Jordan, MI 49727, (231)536-2275 [22218]

East Kentucky News Inc., 416 Teays Rd., PO Box 510, Paintsville, KY 41240, (606)789-8169 [3707]

East Providence Cycle Co. Inc., 414 Warren Ave., East Providence, RI 02914-3842, (401)434-3838 [23641]

East Side Beverage Co., 1260 Grey Fox Rd., Arden Hills, MN 55112, (612)482-1133 [1668]

East Side Lumberyard Supply, 1201 East University Ave., Urbana, IL 61801, (217)367-7000 [9878]

East Side Sporting Goods Co., 27427 Schoenherr Rd., Warren, MI 48093-6639, (810)755-5520 [23642]

East Texas Distributing Inc., 7171 Grand Blvd., Houston, TX 77054, (713)748-8120 [3708]

East Texas Gas Co., PO Box 660, Mineola, TX 75773, (903)592-3809 [22219]

East-West Center, 1601 East-West Rd., Honolulu, HI 96848-1601, (808)944-7145 [3709]

East West Connect Inc., 1862 Independence Sq., Atlanta, GA 30338-5150, (404)396-3145 [535]

East West Trading Co., PO Box 19188, Irvine, CA 92623-9188, (949)660-0888 [23643]

Easter-Owens Electric Co, 6522 Fig St., Arvada, CO 80004, (303)431-0111 [8645]

Easterday Janitorial Supply Co., 17050 Margay Ave., Carson, CA 90746, (310)762-1100 [4613]

Eastern Atlantic Company Inc., 111 Brook St., Scarsdale, NY 10583, (914)472-6464 [14089]

Eastern Auto Parts Company Inc., 795 Eastern Ave., Malden, MA 02148 [2572]

Eastern Bearings Inc., 158 Lexington St., Waltham, MA 02454, (781)899-3952 [2573]

Eastern Bearings Inc., 158 Lexington St., Waltham, MA 02454, (781)899-3952 [8646]

Eastern Book Co., 131 Middle St., Portland, ME 04101, (207)774-0331 [3710]

Eastern Butcher Block Corp., 25 Eagle St., Providence, RI 02908-5622, (401)273-6330 [13096]

Eastern Butcher Block Corp., 25 Eagle St., Providence, RI 02908-5622, (401)273-6330 [13097]

Eastern Data Paper, 135 Stevens Ave., Little Falls, NJ 07424, (973)256-4600 [20977]

Eastern Electric, PO Box 211088, West Palm Beach, FL 33421-1088, (561)640-3233 [15118]

Eastern Electric Supply Co., PO Box 1160, Rocky Mount, NC 27802, (252)442-5156 [8647]

Eastern Enterprises, 9 Riverside Rd., Weston, MA 02493, (781)647-2300 [25640]

Eastern Europe, Inc., 460 W 34th St., 12th Fl., New York, NY 10001, (212)947-8585 [536]

Eastern Farmers Co-op, PO Box A, Garretson, SD 57030, (605)594-3415 [382]

Eastern Farmers Coop, PO Box 266, Jasper, MN 56144, (507)348-3911 [537]

Eastern Fuels Inc., Hwy. 42 W, Ahoskie, NC 27910, (919)332-2037 [22220]

Eastern Furniture Distributors, 2424 State Rd., Bensalem, PA 19020, (215)633-8484 [13098]

Eastern Lift Truck Co., PO Box 307, Maple Shade, NJ 08052-0307, (856)779-8880 [15974]

Eastern Maine Healthcare, 489 State St., Bangor, ME 04401, (207)945-7000 [18782]

Eastern Moulding, Inc., 2370 Brentwood Rd., Columbus, OH 43209, (614)258-0207 [13099]

Eastern Ophthalmic Supply & Repair, PO Box 9666, Knoxville, TN 37940-0666, (865)579-3010 [19301]

Eastern Penn Supply Co., 700 Scott St., Wilkes Barre, PA 18705, (570)823-1181 [23144]

Eastern Petroleum Corp., PO Box 398, Enfield, NC 27823, (252)445-5131 [22221]

Eastern Pharmaceuticals, PO Box 299, Sunbury, NC 27979, (919)465-4405 [14090]

Eastern Refrigeration Co., 275 Old Hartford Rd., Colchester, CT 06415-0298, (860)859-0016 [14426]

Eastern Shore Seafood, PO Box 38, Mappsville, VA 23407, (804)824-5651 [11017]

Eastern States Components Inc., 108 Pratts Junction Rd., Sterling, MA 01564-2304, (978)422-7641 [8648]

Eastern Tool Warehouse Corp., 20 Fairfield Pl., West Caldwell, NJ 07006, (201)808-4637 [2574]

Eastern Wire Products, 498 Kinsley Ave., Providence, RI 02909, (401)861-1350 [19946]

Eastern Wood Products Company Inc., PO Box 1056, Williamsport, PA 17703-1056, (570)326-1946 [9879]

Eastes Distributing, PO Box 534, Grabill, IN 46741-0534, (219)627-2905 [6234]

Eastland Screen Prints Inc., 9425 Mathy Dr., Fairfax, VA 22031-4101, (703)250-2556 [4928]

Eastman-Cartwright Lumber Co., Hwy. 61 N, Lancaster, WI 53813, (608)723-2177 [7301]

Eastman Sign Co., 701 E Main St., Lewistown, MT 59457-1966, (406)538-2500 [13100]

Easton Iron and Metal Co. Inc., 1100 Bushkill Dr., Easton, PA 18042, (215)250-6300 [26802]

Easton Steel Service Inc., PO Box 599, Easton, MD 21601, (410)822-1393 [19947]

Easton Wholesale Co., PO Box 839, Easton, MD 21601, (410)822-0600 [18497]

Eastrade Inc., 609 5th Ave., New York, NY 10017, (212)752-8448 [17405]

Eastside Wholesale Supply Co., 6450 E 8 Mile Rd., Detroit, MI 48234, (313)891-2900 [9880]

Eastview Editions, PO Box 247, Bernardsville, NJ 07924, (908)204-0535 [3711]

Easy Gardener Inc., PO Box 21025, Waco, TX 76702-1025, (254)753-5353 [538]

Easy Shoe Distributors Inc., 2842 NE 187th St., Miami, FL 33180, (305)687-9576 [24730]

Eaton Corp., 1640 Monrovia Ave., Costa Mesa, CA 92627-4405, (949)642-2427 [82]

Eaton Corp. Golf Grip Div., PO Box 1848, Laurinburg, NC 28353, (919)276-6901 [23644]

Eaton; Daniel A., 1 Sheddhill Rd., Stoddard, NH 03464, (603)446-3535 [26026]

Eaton Equipment Corp., PO Box 250, Blasdell, NY 14219, (716)822-2020 [539]

Eaton Metal Products Co., 920 E C St., Casper, WY 82601, (307)234-0870 [22222]

Eaton Office Supply Company Inc., 180 John Glenn Dr., Amherst, NY 14226, (716)691-6100 [20978]

Eaton Steel Corp., 10221 Capital Ave., Oak Park, MI 48237, (248)398-3434 [19948]

Eau Claire Plumbing Supply Co., PO Box 166, Eau Claire, WI 54702-0166, (715)832-6638 [23145]

Ebbert's Field Seed Inc., 6840 N State 48, Covington, OH 45318, (937)473-2521 [540]

Ebbtide & Associates, 60 Red Bluff Rd., Okatie, SC 29910-3916, (803)524-7721 [15485]

Ebel Company Inc.; Fred C., 3101 N Causeway Blvd., Ste. D, Metairie, LA 70002-4831, (504)832-5000 [11018]

Ebeling & Reuss Co., 6500 Chapmans Rd., Allentown, PA 18106-9280, (215)776-7100 [13351]

Eber Brothers Wine and Liquor Corp., 155 Paragon Dr., Rochester, NY 14624-1167, (716)349-7700 [1669]

Eberle Sons Co.; C., 3222 Beekman St., Cincinnati, OH 45223, (513)542-7200 [11019]

Eberly Inc.; John A., PO Box 8047, Syracuse, NY 13217, (315)449-3034 [13674]

Ebinger Brothers Leather Co., 44 Mitchell Rd., Ipswich, MA 01938, (978)356-5701 [18391]

Ebisuzaki Fishing Supply, 92 Kalanianaole Ave., Hilo, HI 96720, (808)935-8081 [23645]

Eble Music Co., PO Box 2570, Iowa City, IA 52244, (319)338-0313 [3712]

Ebling Distribution, Inc., 711 E 14th St., North Kansas City, MO 64116, (816)842-7095 [9881]

ebm Industries, Inc., 100 Hyde Rd., Farmington, CT 06034, (860)674-1515 [15975]

ebm Papst Inc., 100 Hyde Rd., Farmington, CT 06034, (860)674-1515 [15975]

EBSCO Industries Inc. Western Region, 920 41st Ave., Santa Cruz, CA 95062, (408)475-5020 [4929]

Eby-Brown Company L.P., 280 Shuman Blvd., Naperville, IL 60566-7067, (630)778-2800 [26289]

E.C.A. Associates Press, PO Box 15004, Chesapeake, VA 23328, (757)547-5542 [3713]

ECCA America Inc., PO Box 330, Sylacauga, AL 35150, (205)249-4901 [4378]

Ecco Corp., 625 Spice Islands Dr., Ste. F, Sparks, NV 89431-7122, (702)329-9505 [20979]

E.C.F. Supply, 7553 NW 50th St., Miami, FL 33166, (305)477-5444 [9882]

Echo Spring Dairy Inc., 1750 W 8th Ave., Eugene, OR 97402, (541)342-1291 [11020]

Echter Ornaments Inc., 225 Beach 142nd St., Neponsit, NY 11694-1253, (718)639-3194 [11021]

Eck Supply Co., PO Box 85618, Richmond, VA 23285, (804)359-5781 [8649]

Eckart and Finard Inc., 80 Weston St., Hartford, CT 06120, (203)246-7411 [13675]

Eckart Supply Company Inc., 426 Quarry Rd., Corydon, IN 47112-8727, (812)738-3232 [8650]

Eckroat Seed Co., PO Box 17610, Oklahoma City, OK 73136, (405)427-2484 [541]

Eclyptic Inc., 136 W Orion St., Ste. 3, Tempe, AZ 85283-5602, (602)438-0799 [19302]

Eco Design Co., 1365 Rufina Circle, Santa Fe, NM 87502-2964, (505)438-3448 [21436]

EcoCycle Inc., PO Box 19006, Boulder, CO 80308, (303)444-6634 [21718]

Ecolab Inc. Food and Beverage Div., Ecolab Center, 370 Wabasha St., St. Paul, MN 55102, (612)293-2233 [4614]

Ecolab Inc. Institutional Div., Ecolab Center, 370 N Wabasha St., St. Paul, MN 55102, (612)293-2233 [4615]

Ecolab Inc. Professional Products Div., Ecolab Center, 370 N Wabasha St., St. Paul, MN 55102, (612)293-2233 [4379]

Ecolab Inc. Textile Care Div., Ecolab Center, 370 N Wabasha St., St. Paul, MN 55102, (612)293-2233 [4616]

Ecological Laboratories, 3314 Bertha Dr., Baldwin, NY 11510, (516)379-3441 [4380]

Ecology Detergents Inc., 237 West Ave., Stamford, CT 06902-5512, (203)324-0030 [14427]

Econ Equipment & Supplies Inc., 35350 Union Lake Rd., Harrison Township, MI 48045-3146, (810)791-4040 [18783]

Econo Trading Company, 500 S Independence Ave., Rockford, IL 61102, (815)968-5735 [13676]

Economical Wholesale Co., 6 King Philip Rd., Worcester, MA 01606, (508)853-3127 [3714]

Economy Builders Supply Inc., 3232 S 400 E, Salt Lake City, UT 84115-4102, (801)566-1500 [7302]

Economy Cash and Carry Inc., 1000 E Overland, El Paso, TX 79901, (915)532-2660 [11022]

Economy Distributors, 2370 N Flower St., Santa Ana, CA 92706, (714)542-2000 [27122]

Economy Electric Company Inc., 1158-1160 Hubbard, PO Box 299, Youngstown, OH 44501-0299, (330)744-4461 [8651]

Economy Foods, 333 7th Ave., Huntington, WV 25701-1927, (304)697-5280 [11023]

Economy Maintenance Supply Company Inc., PO Box 349, Fairfax Station, VA 22039, (703)461-7700 [8652]

Economy Office Furniture, 6300 N Sepulveda Blvd., Van Nuys, CA 91411-1112, (818)781-5552 [20980]

Economy Paper Company Inc., 1175 E Main St., PO Box 90420, Rochester, NY 14609, (716)482-5340 [21719]

Economy Paper Company Inc., 1175 E Main St., Rochester, NY 14601, (716)482-5340 [16845]

Economy Wholesalers, 4765 Bellevue St., Detroit, MI 48207, (313)922-0001 [11024]

Ecorse Sales and Machinery Inc., 75 Southfield, Ecorse, MI 48229, (313)383-2100 [15976]

EcoTech Recycled Products, 14241 60th St. N, Clearwater, FL 33760-2706, (813)531-5353 [20981]

ECR Sales & Service Inc., 1515 Western Ave., Las Vegas, NV 89102-2601, (702)385-0706 [20982]

ECS Marketing Services Inc., PO Box 70189, Bellevue, WA 98007-0189, (425)883-3420 [14428]

ECS Publishing Corporation, 138 Ipswich St., Boston, MA 02215, (617)236-1935 [3715]

ECW Enterprises Inc., 740 N Mary Ave., Sunnyvale, CA 94086, (408)245-5836 [6235]

Ed-Burt Corp., 400 1st Ave. N, Minneapolis, MN 55401-1715, (612)333-3156 [4930]

Ed Hommelsen, 4809 W 128th Pl., Alsip, IL 60803, (708)388-4344 [10032]

E.D. Packing Co., Rte. 3, Box 79, Lake City, SC 29560-9336, (803)389-7241 [11025]

Ed Wineland's Wholesale Pet Supplies, 3225 Eagle Dr., Greenwood, AR 72936, (501)996-0085 [27073]

Edcat Enterprises, 733 N Beach St., Daytona Beach, FL 32114, (904)253-2385 [19303]

EDCO Electronics Inc., 2209 American Ave., Hayward, CA 94545, (510)783-8900 [8653]

Edco Manufacturing Co., PO Box 5204, EK. Sta., Johnson City, TN 37602-5204, (423)926-6956 [27123]

Edcor Electronics, 7130 National Parks Hwy., Carlsbad, NM 88220, (505)887-6790 [8654]

Eddie's Tire Service Inc., Rte. 6, Box 12460, Berkeley Springs, WV 25411, (304)258-1368 [2575]

Edelsteins Better Furniture Inc., PO Box 3369, Brownsville, TX 78523, (956)542-5605 [13101]

Edelweiss Publishing Co., 110 Main St., PO Box 656, Nuremberg, PA 18241, (215)298-3437 [3716]

Eden Oil Company Inc., PO Box 1375, Reidsville, NC 27323, (336)349-8228 [22223]

Eden Valley Growers Inc., 7502 N Gowanda State, Eden, NY 14057, (716)992-9721 [11026]

Edgars Fabrics Inc., 261 5th Ave., New York, NY 10016, (212)686-2952 [26027]

Edgcomb Corp., 555 State Rd., Bensalem, PA 19020, (215)245-3300 [19949]

Edgcomb Metals Co., 555 State Rd., Bensalem, PA 19020, (215)245-3300 [20141]

Edgcomb Metals Co. New England Div., 385 W Hollis St., Nashua, NH 03061, (603)883-7731 [19950]

Edgerton Cooperative Farm Service Center, PO Box 126, Edgerton, MN 56128, (507)442-4571 [11027]

Edgerton Forge Inc., 257 E Morrison, Edgerton, OH 43517, (419)298-2333 [15977]

Edgewood Oil Co., PO Box 188, Edgewood, IA 52042-0188, (319)928-6437 [22224]

Edgewood Oil Inc., PO Box 188, Edgewood, IA 52042-0188, (319)928-6437 [22224]

Ediciones del Norte, PO Box A130, Hanover, NH 03755, 800-782-5422 [3717]

Ediciones Universal, 3090 SW 8th St., Miami, FL 33135, (305)642-3355 [3718]

Edison Liquor Corp., PO Box 609, Brookfield, WI 53045, (414)821-0600 [1670]

Edison Non-Stock Cooperative, PO Box 68, Edison, NE 68936, (308)927-3681 [542]

Edison West Liquor, 4454 Robertson Rd., Madison, WI 53714, (608)246-8868 [1671]

Edlis Inc., 327 Blvd. of Allies, Pittsburgh, PA 15222, (412)261-2862 [14091]

Edlo Sales and Engineering Inc., 407 Yorktown Road, Logansport, IN 46947, (219)753-0502 [15978]

EDM Business Interiors Inc., 7575 Empire Dr., No. 2, Florence, KY 41042, (606)371-0444 [20983]

Edmer Sanitary Supply Co. Inc., 519 E Meadow Ave., East Meadow, NY 11554, (516)794-2000 [4617]

Edmiston Brothers Inc., PO Box 371, Crockett, TX 75835, (409)544-2118 [11028]

Edmonson Wheat Growers Inc., PO Box 32, Edmonson, TX 79032, (806)864-3327 [17826]

Edmund Scientific Co., Industrial Optics Div., 101 E Gloucester Pike, Barrington, NJ 08007, (609)547-3488 [24352]

Edmunds & Co.; F.A., 6111 S Sayre Ave., Chicago, IL 60638, (773)586-2030 [26184]

Edmunds and Company Inc.; Frank A., 6111 S Sayre Ave., Chicago, IL 60638, (773)586-2772 [7303]

Edmunds and Company Inc.; Frank A., 6111 S Sayre Ave., Chicago, IL 60638, (773)586-2772 [27303]

Edmund's Dummy Company Inc., 362 Lakeside Dr., Foster City, CA 94404, (650)378-5159 [25641]

Edom Laboratories Inc., 860 Grand Blvd., Deer Park, NY 11729, (516)586-2266 [14092]

Edon Farmers Cooperative Association Inc., PO Box 308, Edon, OH 43518, (419)272-2121 [543]

Ed's Leather Co., 2603 S Lafayette St., Hwy. 18, Shelby, NC 28150, (704)482-8080 [27124]

EDS Refrigeration Inc., 2920 Girard Blvd. NE, Albuquerque, NM 87107-1935, (505)884-0085 [14429]

Edsung Foodservice Co., 1337 Mookaula, Honolulu, HI 96817-4308, (808)845-3931 [11029]

Edu-Tech Corp., 65 Bailey Rd., Fairfield, CT 06432, (203)374-4212 [3719]

Education Guide Inc., PO Box 421, Randolph, MA 02368, (781)961-2217 [3720]

Education People, Inc., Box 378, Chappaqua, NY 10514, (914)666-5423 [3721]

Educational Activities Inc., 1937 Grand Ave., Baldwin, NY 11510, (516)223-4666 [25171]

Educational Book Distributors, c/o Publishers Services, PO Box 2510, Novato, CA 94948, (415)883-3530 [3722]

Educational Coin Co., PO Box 3815, Kingston, NY 12401, (914)338-4871 [26476]

Educational Distributors of America, PO Box 1579, Appleton, WI 54913-1579, (920)734-5712 [13102]

Educational Geodesics Inc., 1971 Lou Ann Dr., New Braunfels, TX 78130-1213, (512)629-0123 [3723]

Educational Industrial Systems Inc., 140 E Dana St., Mountain View, CA 94041, (415)969-5212 [25172]

Educational Record Sales, Inc., 132 W 21st St., New York, NY 10011 [25173]

Educational Record & Tape Distributors of America, 61 Bennington Ave., Freeport, NY 11520, (516)867-3770 [25174]

Educational Technology Inc., 2224 Hewlett, Merrick, NY 11566-3692, (516)623-3200 [6236]

Educators Resource, Inc., 2575 Schillinger Rd., Semmes, AL 36575, (205)666-1537 [20984]

Edward Business Machines Inc., 524 Penn Ave., West Reading, PA 19611, (215)372-8414 [20985]

Edwards & Associates; John, 1 Loma Ln., Carmel Valley, CA 93924-9543, (408)659-7212 [23646]

Edwards & Co.; C.G., 272 Dorchester Ave., Boston, MA 02127, (617)268-4111 [18498]

Edwards Co.; Frank, 110 S 3rd W, Salt Lake City, UT 84110, (801)363-8851 [2576]

Edwards Fruit Co., PO Box 1687, Lakeland, FL 33802-1687, (813)682-8196 [11030]

Edward's Pet Supplies Co., 990 South 700 West, Salt Lake City, UT 84104, (801)972-3920 [27125]

Edwards Produce Co.; M and B, PO Box 661688, Miami Springs, FL 33266-1688, (305)324-6143 [11031]

Edwards Wood Products Inc. (Portola Valley, California), 14425 Liddicoat Dr., Los Altos Hills, CA 94022-1806, (650)493-6232 [25910]

Eerdmans Publishing Co.; William B., 255 Jefferson Ave. SE, Grand Rapids, MI 49503, (616)459-4591 [3724]

EESCO, A Division of WESCO Distribution, Inc., 3939 S Karlov Ave., Chicago, IL 60632, (773)376-8750 [8655]

EESCO Inc. Farrell-Argast Div., PO Box 26066, Indianapolis, IN 46226, (317)546-4041 [8656]

EEV, Inc., 4 Westchester Plaza, Elmsford, NY 10523, (914)592-6050 [18784]

EEV, Inc., 80 Post Rd., Buffalo, NY 14221, (716)626-9055 [5600]

Efficient Computer System, PO Box 2524, Hickory, NC 28603-2524, (704)328-2263 [6237]

Effingham Equity, PO Box 488, Effingham, IL 62401, (217)342-4101 [17827]

Efinger Sporting Goods Inc., 513 W Union Ave., Bound Brook, NJ 08805, (732)356-0604 [23647]

Efland Distributing Co., PO Box 26, Hwy. 70 W, Efland, NC 27243, 800-325-6463 [27126]

Egan and Co.; Bernard, 1900 Old Dixie Hwy., Ft. Pierce, FL 34946, (561)465-7555 [11032]

Egerstrom Inc., 10012 E 64th St., Kansas City, MO 64133, (816)358-3025 [11033]

Egerstrom-Kramer Inc., 10012 E 64th St., Kansas City, MO 64133, (816)358-3025 [11033]

Egger Steel Co., PO Box E, Sioux Falls, SD 57101, (605)336-2490 [19951]

Eggimann Motor and Equipment Sales Inc., 1813 W Beltline Hwy., Madison, WI 53713, (608)271-5544 [2577]

EGP Inc., 2715 Hwy. 44 W, Inverness, FL 34453, (352)344-1200 [20986]

EH Engineering Ltd., 3333 Cleveland Ave., No. 4, Lincoln, NE 68504, (402)466-6720 [8657]

Ehmer Inc.; Karl, 63-35 Fresh Pond Rd., Ridgewood, NY 11385, (718)456-8100 [11034]

Ehrhart Co.; T.F., 600 York St., Quincy, IL 62306, (217)222-9103 [14430]

Ehrke & Co.; A., 31100 Bainbridge Rd., Solon, OH 44139, (440)248-9400 [16846]

Eickoff Corp., PO Box 2000, Pittsburgh, PA 15230, (412)788-1400 [25642]

Eidai International, Inc., 2676 Waiwai Loop, Honolulu, HI 96819-1938, (808)836-0999 [24731]

Eide Industries Inc., 16215 Piuma Ave., Cerritos, CA 90703-1528, (310)402-8335 [15486]

Eikenhout and Sons Inc., 346 Wealthy St. SW, Grand Rapids, MI 49501-2862, (616)459-4523 [7304]

EIS Com-Kyl, 41444 Christy St., Fremont, CA 94538, (510)979-0070 [16847]

EIS, Inc., 3715 Northside Pkwy. Bldg. 100, Ste. 400, Atlanta, GA 30327, (404)355-1651 [8658]

Eisen Industries Inc., PO Box 2392, Beaumont, TX 77704, (409)838-1611 [20350]

Eisenberg Brothers Inc., PO Box 169, Camden, NJ 08101-0169, (609)964-5552 [21720]

Eisenberg International Corp., 948 Giswold Ave., San Fernando, CA 91340, (818)365-8161 [4931]

Eisenbrauns, PO Box 275, Winona Lake, IN 46590, (219)269-2011 [3725]

Eisner Bros., 75 Essex St., New York, NY 10002, (212)475-6868 [4932]

EIZO Nanao Technologies Inc., 5710 Warland Dr., Cypress, CA 90630, (310)431-5011 [6238]

E.K. Fasteners Inc., 15020 Marquardt Ave., Santa Fe Springs, CA 90670-5704, (562)404-2121 [13677]

EKCO International Metals Inc., 1700 Perrino Pl., Los Angeles, CA 90023, (213)264-1615 [26803]

EKD Computer Sales and Supplies Corp., PO Box 1300, Selden, NY 11784, (516)736-0500 [6239]

El Camino Resources International Inc., 21051 Warner Center Ln., Woodland Hills, CA 91367, (818)226-6600 [6240]

El Charro Mexican Foods, 1707 SE Main St., Roswell, NM 88201, (505)622-8590 [11035]

El Dorado Furniture Co., 1260 NW 72nd Ave., Miami, FL 33126, (305)592-5470 [13103]

El Encanto Inc., PO Box 293, Albuquerque, NM 87103, (505)243-2722 [11036]

El Galindo Inc., 1601 E 6th St., Austin, TX 78702, (512)478-5756 [11037]

El Grande Distributors Inc., PO Box 1136, Carlsbad, NM 88221-1136, (505)885-2425 [26290]

El Indio Shop, 3695 India, San Diego, CA 92103-4749, (619)299-0333 [11038]

El Mexicano Auto Salvage, 1200 Coors Blvd. SW, Albuquerque, NM 87121-3406, (505)242-2131 [2578]

El Paso Onyx Co. Inc., 1414 Common Dr., El Paso, TX 79936, (915)591-6699 [13352]

El Paso Saw and Belting Supply Co., 1701 Texas St., El Paso, TX 79901, (915)532-3677 [13678]

El Rancho Laundry Equipment, PO Box 1941, Taos, NM 87571-1941, (505)758-8729 [15119]

El Ray Distributing Company Inc., PO Box 750, Napa, CA 94559, (707)252-8600 [1672]

El Rey Stucco Co., 4100 1/2 Broadway Blvd. SE, Albuquerque, NM 87105, (505)873-1180 [7305]

El Toro Land and Cattle Co., PO Box G, Heber, CA 92249, (619)352-6312 [17828]

ELA Medical Inc., 2950 Xenium Ln. N, Ste. 120, Plymouth, MN 55441-2623, (612)935-2033 [18785]

Elan Chemical Co., 268 Doremus Ave., Newark, NJ 07105, (201)344-8014 [4381]

Elan Pharmaceuticals, 2 Thurber Blvd., Smithfield, RI 02917, (401)868-6400 [18786]

Elan-Polo Inc., 1699 S Hanley Rd., St. Louis, MO 63144, (314)645-3018 [24732]

Elan Technical Corp., 35 Kings Hwy. E, Fairfield, CT 06432, (203)335-2115 [24353]

Elberfeld Company Inc., PO Box 788, Logan, OH 43138, (740)385-5656 [13104]

Elberta Farmers Cooperative, Drawer B, Elberta, AL 36530, (205)986-8103 [544]

Elbow Lake Cooperative Grain, PO Box 68, Elbow Lake, MN 56531, (218)685-5331 [545]

Elburn Cooperative Co., PO Box U, Elburn, IL 60119, (630)365-6444 [17829]

Elchar Dog Bows, 5700 Old Heady Rd., Louisville, KY 40299, (502)267-5857 [27127]

Elco Manufacturing Company Inc., 39 W 19th St., New York, NY 10011-4225, (212)255-4300 [18392]

Elcotel Inc., 6428 Parkland Dr., Sarasota, FL 34243, (941)758-0389 [5601]

Elden Enterprises, PO Box 3201, Charleston, WV 25332-3201, (304)344-2335 [25175]

Elder Hosiery Mills Inc., PO Box 2377, Burlington, NC 27216, (910)226-2229 [4933]

Elder's Bookstore, 2115 Elliston Pl., Nashville, TN 37203, (615)327-1867 [3726]

Eldon Rubbermaid Office Products, 1427 William Blount Dr., Maryville, TN 37801-8249, (423)518-1600 [20987]

Eldorado Artesian Springs Inc., PO Box 445, Eldorado Springs, CO 80025-0445, (303)499-1316 [24955]

Eldorado Artesian Springs Inc., PO Box 445, Eldorado Springs, CO 80025-0445, (303)499-1316 [11039]

Eldridge Cooperative Co., 111 W Davenport St., Eldridge, IA 52748, (319)285-9615 [17830]

Electrex Inc., 108 E Sherman, Hutchinson, KS 67501, (316)669-9966 [8659]

Electric Car Distributors, 71415 Highway 111, Rancho Mirage, CA 92270, (760)346-5661 [23648]

Electric Fixture and Supply Co., PO Box 898, Omaha, NE 68101, (402)342-3050 [8660]

Electric Fuels Corp., PO Box 15208, St. Petersburg, FL 33733, (727)824-6600 [20537]

Electric Garage Supply Co., 204 N 9th St., Brainerd, MN 56401, (218)829-2879 [2579]

Electric Motor and Control Corp., 57 E Chestnut St., Columbus, OH 43215, (614)228-6875 [8661]

Electric Motor Engineering Inc., 25501 Arctic Ocean Dr., Lake Forest, CA 92630, (714)583-9802 [15979]

Electric Motor Repair Co., 700 E 25th St., Baltimore, MD 21218, (410)467-8080 [24107]

Electric Motor Repair & Sales, 1 Goodson St., Bristol, VA 24201, (540)669-9428 [8662]

Electric Motor Service, 2020 Division St., PO Box 1224, St. Cloud, MN 56302, (320)251-8691 [8663]

Electric Motor and Supply Inc., PO Box 152, Altoona, PA 16603, (814)946-0401 [8664]

Electric Motors Unlimited Inc., 1000 Jonathon Dr., Madison, WI 53701, (608)271-2311 [8665]

Electric Sales & Service of Savannah, PO Box 9661, Savannah, GA 31412-9661, (912)233-9663 [25176]

Electric Specialties Inc., 11536 W 4 A Rd., Plymouth, IN 46563, (219)936-5725 [2580]

Electric Supply Co., PO Box 6427, Raleigh, NC 27608, (919)834-7364 [8666]

Electric Supply Co. (Asheville, North Carolina), PO Box 2389, Asheville, NC 28802-2389, (704)255-8899 [8667]

Electric Supply Company of Fayetteville Inc., PO Box 2158, Fayetteville, NC 28302, (919)323-4171 [8668]

Electric Supply Co. (Raleigh, North Carolina), PO Box 6427, Raleigh, NC 27608, (919)834-7364 [8669]

Electric Supply Co. (Wilson, North Carolina), PO Box 1968, Wilson, NC 27894, (919)237-0151 [8670]

Electric Supply and Equipment Company Inc., 1812 E Wendover Ave., Greensboro, NC 27405, (336)272-4123 [8671]

Electric Switches Inc., PO Box 1868, Tehachapi, CA 93581, (661)823-7131 [8672]

Electrical Appliance Service Co., 1450 Howard St., San Francisco, CA 94103-2523, (415)777-0314 [15120]

Electrical Communications, 289 Scott, Memphis, TN 38112-3911, (901)324-8893 [8673]

Electrical Construction Co., PO Box 10286, Portland, OR 97210, (503)224-3511 [8674]

Electrical Controller Products Co., 3225 McKinney St., Houston, TX 77003, (713)222-9191 [8675]

Electrical Distributing Inc., PO Box 2720, Portland, OR 97208, (503)226-4044 [25177]

Electrical Distributors Inc., 74 Middlesex St., PO Box 8547, Lowell, MA 01853-8547, (978)454-7719 [8676]

Electrical Engineering and Equipment Co., 1201 Walnut St., Des Moines, IA 50309, (515)282-0431 [8677]

Electrical Equipment Co., 226 N Wilkonson Dr., Laurinburg, NC 28352-1747, (919)276-2141 [8678]

Electrical Equipment Co., 1440 Diggs Dr., Raleigh, NC 27603, (919)828-5411 [8679]

Electrical Insulation Suppliers Inc., 3715 Northside Pkwy. Bldg. 100, Ste. 400, Atlanta, GA 30327, (404)355-1651 [8658]

Electrical Materials Co., 1236 1st Ave., Ft. Dodge, IA 50501-4834, (515)573-7166 [23146]

Electrical Materials Inc., 796 San Antonio Rd., Palo Alto, CA 94306, (650)494-0400 [8680]

Electrical Power and Controls Inc., 2405 Mira Mar Ave., Long Beach, CA 90815, (310)498-6699 [8681]

Electrical Wholesale Supply Company Inc., PO Box 2147, Idaho Falls, ID 83403, (208)523-2800 [8682]

Electro Brand Inc., 5410 W Roosevelt, Chicago, IL 60601, (312)261-5000 [25178]

Electro-Line Inc., PO Box 1688, Dayton, OH 45401, (513)461-5683 [8683]

Electro-Matic Products Inc., 23409 Industrial Park, Farmington Hills, MI 48335, (248)478-1182 [8684]

Electro-Matic Products Inc., 23409 Industrial Park Ct., Farmington Hills, MI 48335, (248)478-1182 [15980]

Electro-Med Co. Inc., PO Box 18366, Louisville, KY 40261-0366, (502)459-6603 [18787]

Electro Media of Colorado, 5474 Marshall St., Arvada, CO 80002-3802, (303)423-1050 [8685]

Electro Rent Corp. Data Rentals/Sales Div., 6060 Sepulveda Blvd., Van Nuys, CA 91411-2501, (818)787-2100 [8686]

Electroglas Inc., 455 S 48th St Ste 102, Tempe, AZ 85281, (480)968-1110 [8687]

Electrograph Systems Inc., 175 Commerce Dr., Hauppauge, NY 11788, (631)436-5050 [6241]

Electrolarm Security Systems Inc., 1220 W Court St., Janesville, WI 53545-3537, (608)758-8750 [6413]

Electronic Arts Inc., 1450 Fashion Island Blvd., San Mateo, CA 94404, (650)571-7171 [6242]

Electronic Bus Systems of Nevada, PO Box 6150, Reno, NV 89513-6150, (702)746-3600 [20988]

Electronic Contracting Co., 2630 N 27th St., Lincoln, NE 68501, (402)466-8274 [8688]

Electronic Equipment Company Inc., 4027 NW 24th St., Miami, FL 33142-6715, (305)871-1500 [8689]

Electronic Fasteners Inc., PO Box 9182, Waltham, MA 02454, (617)890-7780 [13679]

Electronic Hardware Ltd, PO Box 15039, North Hollywood, CA 91615, (818)982-6100 [8690]

Electronic Hook-up, 195 E Main St., Milford, MA 01757, (508)478-3311 [8691]

Electronic Label Technology Inc., 708 W Kenosha, Broken Arrow, OK 74012, (918)258-2121 [6243]

Electronic Lighting Inc., 37200 Central Ct, Newark, CA 94560, (510)795-8555 [8692]

Electronic Maintenance Supply Co., 1230 W Central Blvd., Orlando, FL 32805, (407)849-6362 [8693]

Electronic Office Systems, 107 Fairfield Ave., Fairfield, NJ 07004-2402, (973)808-0100 [20989]

Electronic Product Tool, 10-6 Technology Dr., Setauket, NY 11733, (516)751-3333 [15981]

Electronic Security Integration, Inc., 68-46 Selfridge St., Forest Hills, NY 11375, (718)575-9493 [24535]

Electronic Security Services, 15050 Buck Ln., Upper Marlboro, MD 20772-7821, (301)449-3850 [24536]

Electronic Signage Systems Inc., 6489 Ridings Rd., Syracuse, NY 13206, (315)437-7556 [19781]

Electronic Specialties Inc., PO Box 248, Algona, IA 50511-0248, (515)295-7752 [8694]

Electronic Supply, 222 7th Ave., Huntington, WV 25701-1926, (304)523-6443 [15121]

Electronic Surplus Services, 900 Candia Rd., Manchester, NH 03109, (603)624-9600 [8695]

Electronic Tele-Communications Inc., 3605 Clearview Place, Atlanta, GA 30340-2178, (404)457-5600 [5602]

Electronic World Sales & Service, 27 S End Plaza, New Milford, CT 06776-4235, (860)355-9848 [25179]

Electronics 21 Inc., 5 Mall Terrace, Savannah, GA 31406-3602, (912)352-0585 [25180]

Electronics Discount World, 4935 Allison St., Arvada, CO 80002, (303)426-7772 [6244]

Electronics and Information Systems, PO Box 64525, St. Paul, MN 55164, (612)456-2222 [6245]

Electronics Supply Co., 4100 Main St., Kansas City, MO 64111, (816)931-0250 [8696]

Electrorep Energy Products Inc., 2121 Schuetz Rd., St. Louis, MO 63146, (314)991-2600 [8697]

Electrotex Inc., 2300 Richmond Ave., Houston, TX 77098, (713)526-3456 [8698]

Elem Corp., 225 W Trade St., Burlington, NC 27215, (919)228-8725 [4934]

Elevators Etc., 6802 Ringgold Rd., Chattanooga, TN 37412, (423)267-5438 [18788]

E.L.F. Software Co., 210 W 101 St., New York, NY 10025 [6246]

E.L.F. Software Distributors, 210 W 101 St., New York, NY 10025 [6246]

Elg Metals, Inc., PO Box 369, Mc Keesport, PA 15134, (412)672-9200 [26804]

ELG Metals Southern, Inc., PO Box 96166, Houston, TX 77213-6166, (281)457-2100 [26805]

Elgin Paper Co., 1025 N McLean Blvd., Elgin, IL 60120, (708)741-0137 [21721]

Elgin Salvage and Supply Company Inc., 464 McBride St., Elgin, IL 60120, (708)742-9500 [26806]

Elias Sales & Service, Inc.; T.J., 2716 E 31st St., Minneapolis, MN 55406, (612)721-1825 [15982]

Elish Paper Company Inc.; Harry, 407 Sette Dr., Paramus, NJ 07652, (201)262-1300 [21722]

Elite Computers and Software Inc., PO Box 756, Cupertino, CA 95015-0756, (408)257-8000 [6247]

Elite Consumer Products, 65 Grove St., Watertown, MA 02472, 800-457-4449 [23147]

Elite Denture Center, 2625 St. Johns Ave., Billings, MT 59102-4656, (406)652-6999 [18789]

Elite Supply Co., 323 E 8th Ave., Homestead, PA 15120, (412)461-9000 [14093]

Elixir Industries, 17925 S Broadway, Gardena, CA 90248, (213)321-1191 [14431]

Eliza Corporation, 100 Cummings Ctr., Ste. 350C, Beverly, MA 01915-6138, (978)921-2700 [5603]

Elizabethtown Distributing Co. Inc., PO Box 664, Elizabethtown, KY 42702-0664, (502)765-4117 [2581]

Elk River Trading Co., 5010 S 79 E Ave., Tulsa, OK 74145, (918)622-7655 [14094]

Elk Supply Company Inc., PO Box 1509, Clinton, OK 73601, (580)323-1250 [7306]

Elkhart Cooperative Equity Exchange, PO Box G, Elkhart, KS 67950, (316)697-2135 [11040]

Elkhart County Farm Cooperative, 806 Logan St., Goshen, IN 46526-0076, (219)533-4131 [22225]

Elkhart Farmers Cooperative Association Inc., PO Box 903, Elkhart, TX 75839, (903)764-2298 [546]

Elkhorn Valley Co., PO Box 466, Hooper, NE 68031, (402)654-3323 [17681]

Elki Corp., 2215 Merrill Creek Pkwy., Everett, WA 98203, (425)261-1002 [11041]

Elkins Inc.; Jerry, 1010 W Highway 66, Gallup, NM 87301-6845, (505)722-3878 [17406]

Ellenbecker Oil Co., 1514 Russell Ave., Cheyenne, WY 82001, (307)632-5151 [22226]

Ellett Brothers Inc., PO Box 128, Chapin, SC 29036, (803)345-3751 [13490]

Elliff Motors Inc., 1307 W Harrison St., Harlingen, TX 78550, (210)423-3434 [2582]

Elliot Electric Supply, 3804 South St., PO Box 630610, Nacogdoches, TX 75963, (409)569-7941 [8699]

Elliott Auto Supply Company Inc., 2855 Eagandale Blvd., St. Paul, MN 55121, (612)454-5184 [2583]

Elliott Aviation Inc., PO Box 100, Moline, IL 61266-0100, (309)799-3183 [83]

Elliott Equipment Company Inc., PO Box 401, Easton, MD 21601, (410)822-0066 [20632]

Elliott Manufacturing Company Inc., PO Box 11277, Fresno, CA 93772, (559)233-6235 [24108]

Elliott Office Products Inc., PO Box 235, Gardiner, ME 04345-0235, (207)582-4625 [20990]

Elliott Sales Corp., 2502 S 12th St., Tacoma, WA 98405, (253)383-3883 [23649]

Elliott Shoe Co., 3911 Western Ave., Knoxville, TN 37921-4452, (423)524-1722 [24733]

Ellis and Capp Equipment Co., 301 E 8th St., Greeley, CO 80631, (970)352-9141 [547]

Ellis Equipment Co. Inc., 701 S Main St., Logan, UT 84321-5402, (435)752-4311 [548]

Ellis and Everard Inc., 700 Galleria Pkwy., No. 350, Atlanta, GA 30339, (404)956-5360 [4382]

Ellis Inc., 1001 Commonwealth Ave., Boston, MA 02215, (617)782-4777 [2584]

Ellis Inc.; A.L., 278 Court, PO Box 6127, Plymouth, MA 02362-6127, (508)746-1941 [15487]

Ellis Paint Co., 3150 E Pico Blvd., Los Angeles, CA 90023, (213)261-9071 [21437]

Ellis Tanner Trading Co., 1980 Hwy. 602, Gallup, NM 87305-0636, (505)722-7776 [17407]

Ellsworth Builders Supply Inc., R.R. 4, Box 4, Ellsworth, ME 04605, (207)667-7134 [7307]

Ellsworth Farmers Union Cooperative Oil Co., 610 E Main St., Ellsworth, WI 54011, (715)273-4363 [549]

Ellsworth Supply Company Inc., 340 E Main St., Stratford, CT 06497-0328, (203)375-3317 [13680]

Ellsworth-William Cooperative Co., PO Box C, Ellsworth, IA 50075-0190, (515)836-4411 [17831]

Ellwood Quality Steels Co., 700 Moravia St., New Castle, PA 16101, (724)658-6502 [19952]

Elm Hill Meats Inc., PO Box 429, Lenoir City, TN 37771, (423)986-8005 [11042]

Elmco Distributors Inc., 30 Estling Lake Rd., Denville, NJ 07834-1907, (201)887-6600 [550]

Elmer's Distributing Co., E Hwy. 28, Morris, MN 56267, (320)589-1191 [1673]

Elmira Distributing, 374 Upper Oakwood Ave., Elmira, NY 14903, (607)734-6231 [1674]

Elmo Semiconductor Corp., 7590 N Glenoaks Blvd., Burbank, CA 91504-1052, (818)768-7400 [8700]

Elmore County Farms Exchange, 355 Queen Ann Rd., Wetumpka, AL 36092, (334)567-4321 [27128]

Elmore & Stahl Inc., 11 N Birch, Pharr, TX 78577, (956)787-2714 [11043]

Elmwood Beer Distributor, 2609 Elmwood Ave., Erie, PA 16508, (814)864-6112 [1675]

Elmwood Paint Center, 249 Academy Ave., Providence, RI 02908, (401)351-7200 [21438]

Elna Inc., 8220 Commonwealth Dr., Ste.202A, Eden Prairie, MN 55344, (612)941-5519 [26028]

Elser Oil Co., 461 Middle Rd., Sheridan, MT 59749, (406)842-5478 [22227]

Elsinore Ready-Mix Co., PO Box 959, Lake Elsinore, CA 92530, (909)674-2127 [7308]

Elson Import Export; Walter, 270 Park Side Ave., Brooklyn, NY 11226, (718)941-6670 [4935]

Eltrex Industries Inc., 65 Sullivan St., Rochester, NY 14605, (716)454-6100 [20991]

Elvee/Rosenberg Inc., 11 W 37th St., New York, NY 10018-6235, (212)575-0767 [17408]

Elwood Line Grain and Fertilizer Co., PO Box 127, Momence, IL 60954, (815)472-4842 [17832]

Ely Auto Dismantlers, PO Box 71, Ely, NV 89301-0071, (702)289-8242 [2585]

Ely & Walker, PO Box 1326, Lebanon, TN 37088-1326, (615)443-1878 [4936]

Emanuel Tire Co., 1300 Moreland Ave., Baltimore, MD 21216, (410)947-0660 [2586]

Embroidery Services Inc., 1530 Interstate Dr., PO Box 18040, Erlanger, KY 41018-0040, (606)283-6700 [4937]

Emco Inc., 2318 Arty Ave, PO Box 34549, Charlotte, NC 28208, (704)372-8281 [15983]

Emco Inc., 1310 Glenwood Ave., PO Box 3114, Greensboro, NC 27403, (919)272-3146 [2587]

EME Corp., 10 Central Pkwy., Ste. 312, Stuart, FL 34994-5903, (561)798-2050 [25181]

Emerald International Corp., 7310 Turfway Rd., No. 330, Florence, KY 41042, (606)525-2522 [20538]

Emerald Sunglass Co., 6925 216th St. SW, Ste. D, Lynnwood, WA 98036-7358, (425)776-1151 [19622]

Emerson Company Inc.; W. S., PO Box 10, Brewer, ME 04412-0010, (207)989-3410 [26029]

Emerson Hardwood Co., 2279 NW Front Ave., Portland, OR 97209, (503)227-4520 [7309]

Emerson Radio Corp., PO Box 430, Parsippany, NJ 07054-0430, (973)884-5800 [8701]

Emerson-Swan Inc., PO Box 783, Randolph, MA 02368, (781)986-2000 [23148]

Emery Air Charter Inc., PO Box 6067, Rockford, IL 61125, (815)968-8287 [15984]

Emery Distributors, 3800 Glover Rd., Easton, PA 18042, (215)258-3651 [26477]

Emery Pratt Co., 1966 W Main St., Owosso, MI 48867-1397, (517)723-5291 [3727]

Emery; Stuart, 261 Emery's Bridge Rd., South Berwick, ME 03908-1935, (207)384-2115 [2588]

Emery Waterhouse Co., PO Box 659, Portland, ME 04104, (207)775-2371 [13681]

Emit International Corp., PO Box 22238, Minneapolis, MN 55422-0238, (612)521-2246 [24734]

Emma Cooperative Elevator Co., 125 Lexington Ave., Sweet Springs, MO 65351-1302, (660)335-6355 [27129]

Emma Cooperative Elevator Co., 125 Lexington Ave., Sweet Springs, MO 65351, (660)335-6355 [551]

EMP Co-op Inc., 1519 Everson Rd., Woodburn, IN 46797, (219)632-4284 [17833]

EMP International Corp., PO Box 1226, Abingdon, VA 24210, (540)628-5970 [18790]

Empire Airgas, 1200 Sullivan St., Elmira, NY 14901, 800-666-6523 [16848]

Empire Airgas, 1200 Sullivan St., Elmira, NY 14901 [4383]

Empire Beef Company Inc., 171 Weidner Rd., Rochester, NY 14624, (716)235-7350 [11044]

Empire Bottle Company Inc., 4043 Maple Rd., Buffalo, NY 14226-1057, (716)832-5555 [25911]

Empire Comicsl, 1176 Mt. Hope Ave., Rochester, NY 14620, (716)442-0371 [3728]

The Empire Co., 6500 NE Halsey st., Portland, OR 97213-0250, (503)227-6433 [4938]

The Empire Company, Inc., 8181 Logistic Dr., Zeeland, MI 49464, (616)772-7272 [7310]

Empire Corporation, PO Box 1261, Burlington, VT 05402-1261, (802)862-5181 [4618]

Empire Distributing, 6100 Emmanuel Dr. SW, Atlanta, GA 30336, (404)349-1780 [1676]

Empire Distributors Inc., 8181 Logistic Dr., Zeeland, MI 49464, (616)772-7272 [7310]

Empire Distributors of NC Inc., 10 Walden Dr., Arden, NC 28704, (828)687-8662 [1677]

Empire/EMCO Inc., 4043 Maple Rd., Buffalo, NY 14226-1057, (716)832-5555 [25911]

Empire Equities Inc., 14735 SW Peachtree Dr., Tigard, OR 97224-1486 [19304]

Empire Fish Co., 11200 Watertown Plank Rd., Milwaukee, WI 53226, (414)259-1120 [11045]

Empire Generator Corp., PO Box 100, Thiensville, WI 53092-0100, (414)238-1311 [8702]

Empire Level Manufacturing Corp., 929 Empire Dr., Mukwonago, WI 53149, (262)368-2000 [13682]

Empire Machinery and Supply Co., 3550 Virginia Beach Blvd., Norfolk, VA 23501, (804)855-1011 [13683]

Empire N.A. Inc., 18284 N 1100th Ave., Cambridge, IL 61238-9364, (309)944-5321 [552]

Empire Office Machines Inc., 821 N Main St., Helena, MT 59601-3352, (406)442-8890 [20992]

Empire Paper Co., PO Box 479, Wichita Falls, TX 76307, (940)766-3216 [21723]

Empire Petroleum Inc., PO Box 4036, Toledo, OH 43609, (419)534-6025 [22228]

Empire Power Systems Inc., 2211 W McDowell Rd., Phoenix, AZ 85009-3074, (602)333-5600 [2589]

Empire Publishing Inc., PO Box 717, Madison, NC 27025, (336)427-5850 [3729]

Empire Recycling Inc., 15729 Crabbs Branch Way, Rockville, MD 20855, (301)921-9202 [26807]

Empire Refactory Sales Inc., 219 Murray St., Ft. Wayne, IN 46803, (219)456-5656 [16849]

Empire Sand and Gravel Company Inc., PO Box 1215, Billings, MT 59103, (406)252-8465 [7311]

Empire Sea Food Co. Inc., 1116 2nd Ave. N, Birmingham, AL 35203, (205)252-0344 [11046]

Empire Seafood, 1116 2nd Ave. N, Birmingham, AL 35203, (205)252-0344 [11046]

Empire Southwest L.L.C., PO Box 2985, Phoenix, AZ 85062-2985, (480)633-4300 [7312]

Empire Staple Co., 1710 Platte St., Denver, CO 80202, (303)433-6803 [13684]

Empire State Marble Manufacturing Corp., 207 E 110th St., New York, NY 10029-3202, (212)534-2307 [9883]

Empire State News Corp., 2800 Walden Ave., Cheektowaga, NY 14225, (716)681-1100 [3730]

Empire Wholesale Supply, 5119 Irving St., Boise, ID 83706-1207, (208)322-7889 [9884]

Empiregas Trucking Corp., R.R. 2, Box 80, Carthage, MO 64836-9617, (417)394-2670 [22229]

Emporium Specialties Company Inc., PO Box 65, Austin, PA 16720, (814)647-8661 [8703]

Empress International Ltd., 10 Harbor Park Dr., Port Washington, NY 11050, (516)621-5900 [11047]

Empress Linen Import Co., 16400 Ventura Blvd., Ste. 331, Encino, CA 91436-2123, (818)784-9511 [15488]

EMR Accessibilty, 6802 Ringgold Rd., Chattanooga, TN 37412, (423)267-5438 [18788]

EMSCO, 1230 W Central Blvd., Orlando, FL 32805, (407)849-6362 [8693]

EMSCO, 22350 Royalton Rd., PO Box 360660, Strongsville, OH 44136, (440)238-2100 [23650]

EMSCO, 12861 Rte. 30, North Huntingdon, PA 15642, (412)863-9480 [23651]

EMSCO Electric Supply Company Inc., 1101 W Sheridan St., Oklahoma City, OK 73106, (405)235-6331 [8704]

Emser International, 8431 Santa Monica Blvd., Los Angeles, CA 90069-4209, (213)650-2000 [15489]

EMT Electronics Inc., 1891 Grand Caillou Rd., Houma, LA 70363-7076, (504)879-2084 [8705]

Emtel Electronics Inc., 375 Vanderbilt Ave., Norwood, MA 02062-5007, (781)769-9500 [8706]

Emuge Corp., 104 Otis St., Northborough, MA 01532, (508)393-1300 [16850]

Emulex Corp., 3535 Harbor Blvd., Costa Mesa, CA 92626, (714)662-5600 [6248]

En Garde Health Products Inc., 7702-10 Balboa Blvd., Van Nuys, CA 91406, (818)901-8505 [14095]

En Pointe Technologies Inc., 100 N Sepulveda Blvd., 19th Fl., El Segundo, CA 90245, (310)725-5200 [6249]

Enco Manufacturing Co., 400 Nevada Pacific Hwy., Fernley, NV 89408 [15985]

Enco Materials Inc., PO Box 1275, Nashville, TN 37202, (615)256-3192 [19953]

Encore Broadcast Equipment Sales Inc., 2104 W Kennedy Blvd., Tampa, FL 33606-1535, (813)253-2774 [5604]

Encycle/Texas Inc., 5500 UpRiver Rd., Corpus Christi, TX 78407, (512)289-0035 [26808]

Encyclopaedia Britannica Educational Corp., 310 S Michigan Ave., Chicago, IL 60604, (312)347-7000 [3731]

Enderes Tool Co. Inc., PO Box 240189, Apple Valley, MN 55124, (612)891-1200 [13685]

Endolite North America Ltd., 105 Westpark Rd., Centerville, OH 45459, (937)291-3636 [18791]

Ener-Gee Sales Inc., 927 McCully St., Honolulu, HI 96826-2703, (808)949-1899 [24735]

Energy Answers Corp., 79 N Pearl St., Albany, NY 12207, (518)434-1227 [26809]

Energy Buyers Service Corp., PO Box 79265, Houston, TX 77279-9265, (713)464-5335 [22230]

Energy Group P.L.C., 701 Market St., Ste. 750, St. Louis, MO 63101, (314)342-7590 [20539]

Energy International Corp., 22226 Garrison St., Dearborn, MI 48124-2208, (313)563-8000 [14432]

Energy Plus, 4811 Miller Trunk Hwy., Duluth, MN 55811, (218)722-7818 [14433]

Energy and Process Corp., PO Box 125, Tucker, GA 30085, (770)934-3101 [19954]

EnergyNorth Propane Inc., 75 Regional Dr., Concord, NH 03301, (603)225-6660 [22231]

Enfield Industries Inc., PO Box 2530, Conway, NH 03818, (603)447-8500 [13105]

Enfield Overseas Trade Co., 17 W Forest Dr., Enfield, CT 06082, (860)749-8659 [15986]

Engan-Tooley-Doyle & Associates Inc., PO Box 829, Okemos, MI 48805-0829, (517)347-7970 [23652]

Engberg Janitorial Supply & Service, PO Box 222, Crosby, ND 58730-0222, (701)965-6803 [4619]

Engelhart Co.; H.C., 3811 N Pomona Rd., Tucson, AZ 85705-2421, (520)887-2277 [6250]

Engine Center Inc., 2351 Hilton, Ferndale, MI 48220, (248)399-0002 [15987]

Engine Distributors Inc., 332 S 17th St., Camden, NJ 08105, (609)365-8631 [15988]

Engine and Equipment Co., 20321 Susana Rd., Rancho Dominguez, CA 90220-5723, (310)604-9488 [15989]

Engine & Performance Warehouse Inc., 955 Decatur St., Unit D, Denver, CO 80204-3365, (303)572-8844 [2590]

Engine Service and Supply Co., 1902 N Grant, Odessa, TX 79761, (915)337-2386 [16851]

Engineered Components Inc., 404 Dividend Dr., Peachtree City, GA 30269, (404)487-7600 [8707]

Engineered Drives, 131 Lloyd St., Allentown, PA 18103, (215)264-9368 [2591]

Engineered Drives, Rte. 1, Dancehall Rd., Milton, PA 17847, (717)742-8751 [15990]

Engineered Equipment Co., PO Box 2707, Corona, CA 91718, (909)735-3326 [25643]

Engineered Equipment Co., 179 N Maple St., Corona, CA 92880, (909)735-3326 [7313]

Engineered Plastics Inc., 211 Chase St., PO Box 227, Gibsonville, NC 27249-0227, (336)449-4121 [22958]

Engineered Sales Inc., 18 Progress Pkwy., Maryland Heights, MO 63043, (314)878-4500 [15991]

Engineered Systems & Designs, Inc., 119A Sandy Dr., Newark, DE 19713, (302)456-0446 [24354]

Engineering and Equipment Co., PO Box 588, Albany, GA 31702, (912)435-5601 [23149]

Engineering Equipment Co., 1020 W 31st St., Ste. 125, Downers Grove, IL 60515, (630)963-7800 [15992]

Engineering Equipment Co., 1020 W 31st St., Downers Grove, IL 60515-5501, (630)963-7800 [24537]

Engle and Co.; Jack, PO Box 01705, Los Angeles, CA 90001, (213)589-8111 [19955]

Englefield Oil Co., 447 James Pkwy., Newark, OH 43055, (614)522-1310 [22232]

Englewood Electric, PO Box 2615, Kokomo, IN 46904-2615, (765)457-1136 [8708]

Englewood Electrical Supply, 3412 Boland Dr., South Bend, IN 46628-4302, (219)233-8233 [8709]

Englewood Electrical Supply/United Electric, 3939 S Karlov Ave., Chicago, IL 60632, (773)376-8750 [8655]

English Tanner Enterprises, PO Box 292638, Columbus, OH 43229-2638, (614)433-7020 [12696]

Englund Marine Supply, Foot of 15th St., Astoria, OR 97103, (503)325-4341 [18499]

Engs Motor Truck Co., 8830 E Slauson Ave., Pico Rivera, CA 90660, (213)685-9910 [20633]

Engs Motor Truck Co., 1550 S McCarran Blvd., Sparks, NV 89431, (702)359-8840 [2592]

Enos Home Oxygen Therapy Inc., PO Box 8756, New Bedford, MA 02742-8756, (508)992-2146 [18792]

Enos Home Oxygen Therapy Inc., PO Box 8756, New Bedford, MA 02742-8756, (508)992-2146 [19305]

Enraf Inc., 500 Century Plz. Dr., Houston, TX 77073, (281)443-4291 [25912]

Enrica Fish Books Inc., 814 Washington Ave. SE, Minneapolis, MN 55414, (612)623-0707 [3732]

Enrico Food Products Co. Inc., 6050 Court St. Rd., Syracuse, NY 13206, (315)463-2384 [11048]

Enright Co.; J.R., 4618 Leland St., Bethesda, MD 20815-6010, (301)654-1700 [25182]

Enron Liquid Fuels Co., 1400 Smith St., Houston, TX 77002, (713)654-6161 [22233]

Enron Power Services, PO Box 1188, Houston, TX 77251-1188, (713)853-6161 [22234]

Enslow Publishers, Inc., 40 Industrial Rd., Box 398, Berkeley Heights, NJ 07922-0398, (908)771-9400 [3733]

Enstrom Candies Inc., PO Box 1088, Grand Junction, CO 81502, (970)242-1655 [11049]

Enter-prices, 1240 S Hill St., Los Angeles, CA 90015, (213)746-2109 [17458]

Enterprise Computer Systems Inc., PO Box 2383, Greenville, SC 29602-2383, (864)234-7676 [6251]

Enterprise Oil Co., PO Box 366, Cartersville, GA 30120, (770)382-4804 [22235]

Entertainment Music Marketing Corp., 770-12 Grand Blvd., Deer Park, NY 11729, (516)243-0600 [25183]

Entre, 13400 Bishops Ln., No. 270, Brookfield, WI 53005, (414)821-1060 [6252]

Entree Corp., 8200 W Brown Deer Rd., Milwaukee, WI 53223, (414)355-0037 [11050]

Entrelec Inc., 1950 Hurd Dr., Irving, TX 75038-4312, (972)550-9025 [8710]

Entronic Industries Inc., PO Box 1370, Kingston, NY 12401, (914)338-5300 [8711]

Enumclaw Co.; Garrett, 803 Roosevelt Ave., Enumclaw, WA 98022, (206)825-2511 [15993]

Environetics, 1 Idexx, Westbrook, ME 04092, (207)856-0300 [24355]

Environment Ltd., 10865 Seaboard Loop, Houston, TX 77099, (281)983-0100 [13106]

Environmental Chemical Group Inc., PO Box 9, Rogers, TX 76569, (254)642-3444 [4384]

Environmental Control Inc., Rte. 20, Box 29-ECI, Santa Fe, NM 87501, (505)473-0982 [26810]

Environmental Interiors, 2595 Interstate Dr., Harrisburg, PA 17110-9602, (717)652-6060 [20993]

Envirosystems Equipment Company Inc., 4100 E Michigan St., Tucson, AZ 85714, (520)584-9001 [15994]

Envirotechnology Inc., PO Box 2681, Colorado Springs, CO 80901-2681, (719)633-9642 [25644]

Eoff Electric Co., PO Box 709, Salem, OR 97308, (503)371-3633 [8712]

Eon Labs Manufacturing, Inc., 227-15 N Conduit Ave., Laurelton, NY 11413, (718)276-8600 [19306]

EOTT Energy Operating L.P., PO Box 4666, Houston, TX 77210-4666, (713)993-5200 [22236]

EOTT Energy Partners L.P., 1330 Post Oak Blvd., Ste. 2700, Houston, TX 77056, (713)993-5200 [22237]

Epco-JKD Food Brokers Inc., 925 Pennsylvania Blvd., Feasterville, PA 19053, (215)322-9200 [11051]

EPI Technologies, Inc., 2111 Champlain St., Toledo, OH 43611, (419)727-0495 [26811]

Epic Inc., 150 Nassau St., New York, NY 10038, (212)308-7039 [24356]

Epicure Foods Inc., 2760 Bakers Industrial Dr., Atlanta, GA 30360-1230, (404)441-2227 [11052]

Epicurean International Inc., 229 Castro St., Oakland, CA 94607, (510)268-0209 [24109]

Epley Sales Co., 324 Murfreesboro Rd., Nashville, TN 37210, (615)254-7254 [24538]

Eppinger Manufacturing Co., 6340 Schaefer Rd., Dearborn, MI 48126, (313)582-3205 [23653]

EPPSCO Supply, 6914 Industrial Ave., El Paso, TX 79915-1108, (915)779-4800 [14434]

EPR Automotive Warehouse, 831 Gretna Blvd., Gretna, LA 70053-6939, (504)362-1380 [2593]

Epstein Co.; Harry J., 301 W 8th, Kansas City, MO 64105-1567, (816)421-4752 [13686]

Equality Screw Co. Inc., PO Box 1645, El Cajon, CA 92022, (619)562-6100 [13687]

Equality Trading, 17051 Malta Circle, Huntington Beach, CA 92649, (714)377-0125 [15995]

Equipment Corporation of America, PO Box 306, Coraopolis, PA 15108, (412)264-4480 [7314]

Equipment Inc., PO Box 1987, Jackson, MS 39215-1987, (601)948-3272 [15996]

Equipment and Parts Export Inc., 745 5th Ave., Ste. 1114, New York, NY 10151, (212)753-9730 [2594]

Equipment Rental, 4788 1st Ave. N, Duluth, MN 55803, (218)728-4441 [2595]

Equipment Sales Corp., 703 Western Dr., Mobile, AL 36607, (205)476-2220 [14435]

Equipment and Technology, Inc., PO Box 8766, Jacksonville, FL 32239, (904)744-3400 [15997]

Equipment Valve and Supply Inc., PO Box 722155, Houston, TX 77272-2155, (281)498-6600 [23150]

Equity Cooperative of Amery Inc., 319 S Keller Ave., Amery, WI 54001, (715)268-8177 [553]

Equity Cooperative Association, PO Box 340, Malta, MT 59538-0340, (406)654-2240 [22238]

Equity Cooperative Elevator Co., Main St., Sheyenne, ND 58374, (701)996-2231 [17834]

Equity Elevator and Trading Co., PO Box 69, Wood Lake, MN 56297, (507)485-3153 [17835]

Equity Grain and General Merchant Exchange, PO Box 46, Mullinville, KS 67109, (316)548-2222 [17836]

Equity Industries Corp., 5721 Bayside Rd., Virginia Beach, VA 23455, (757)460-2483 [15490]

Equity Supply Co., PO Box 579, Kalispell, MT 59901, (406)755-7400 [554]

Erb Equipment Company Inc., 200 Erb Industrial Dr., Fenton, MO 63026, (636)349-0200 [7315]

Erb Hardware Co. Ltd., PO Box 616, Lewiston, ID 83501, (208)746-0441 [13688]

Erb Lumber Co. Materials Distributors Div., 312 Mound St., Dayton, OH 45407, (937)294-1297 [7316]

Ergonomic Design Inc., 10650 Irma Dr Ste. 33, Northglenn, CO 80233, (303)452-8006 [20994]

Ergonomic Specialties Ltd., 954 N Du Page Ave., Lombard, IL 60148-1243, (630)268-1809 [13107]

Erickson Petroleum Corp., PO Box 1224, Minneapolis, MN 55440, (612)830-8700 [11446]

Erickson Wood Products, PO Box 61, Belmont, CA 94002, (415)591-5785 [27304]

Erickson's Decorating Products, Inc., 6040 N Pulaski Rd., Chicago, IL 60646, (773)539-7555 [21439]

Erickson's Flooring & Supply, 1013 Orchard St., Ferndale, MI 48220, (248)543-9663 [9885]

Erickson's Sheep Co., PO Box 1781, Billings, MT 59102, (406)259-1010 [17837]

Ericksons Super-Pros, Inc.; Vic, 1295 Ada Ave., Idaho Falls, ID 83402-2148, (208)524-6457 [23654]

Erie Beer Co., 812 W 14th St., Erie, PA 16501, (814)459-7777 [1678]

Erie Concrete Steel, 1301 Cranberry St., Erie, PA 16501, (814)453-4969 [19956]

Erie Concrete and Steel Supply Co., PO Box 10336, Erie, PA 16514, (814)453-4969 [19957]

Erie Crawford Cooperative, PO Box 312, Union City, PA 16438, (814)438-3881 [555]

Erie Industrial Supply Co., 931 Greengarden Rd., Erie, PA 16501-1525, (814)452-3231 [15998]

Erie Petroleum Inc., 1502 Greengarden Rd., Erie, PA 16502, (814)456-7516 [22239]

Erie Sand and Gravel Co., PO Box 179, Erie, PA 16512, (814)453-6721 [7317]

Erie Steel Products Inc., 2420 W 15th St., Erie, PA 16505, (814)459-2715 [19958]

Erie Stone Company Inc., 500 Erie Stone Dr., Huntington, IN 46750, (219)356-7214 [7318]

Erika-Record Inc., 20 Vanderhoof Ave., Rockaway, NJ 07866, (973)664-1750 [24110]

Eritech International, 4551 San Fernando Rd., Ste. 110, Glendale, CA 91204-1985, (818)244-6242 [6253]

ERM Recycling Inc./Crazy Bob's, 50 New Salem St., Wakefield, MA 01880-1906, (617)246-6767 [6254]

Ermco Inc., 2122 Kratky Rd., St. Louis, MO 63114-1704, (314)241-3334 [23151]

Ernest Paper Products, 2727 Vernon Ave., Vernon, CA 90058, (213)583-6561 [21724]

Ernest Telecom Inc., 6475 Jimmy Carter Blvd., Norcross, GA 30071, (404)448-7788 [5605]

ERS Distributors, Inc., 20 Midland Ave., Hicksville, NY 11801, (516)939-0060 [25184]

Ertel Products Inc., 1436 E 19th St., Indianapolis, IN 46218-4228 [2596]

Ervin Supply Corp. (Chattanooga, Tennessee), 3401 Ambrose Ave., Nashville, TN 37222, (423)899-2997 [10108]

Ervin Supply Corp. (Chattanooga, Tennessee), 1312 Chilhowee Ave., Knoxville, TN 37917, (423)899-2997 [10109]

Ervin Supply Corp. (Knoxville, Tennessee), 1599 Francisco Blvd. E, San Rafael, CA 94901-5503, (415)388-2750 [20722]

ERW International, Inc., PO Box 690, Barrington, IL 60011, (847)381-7972 [19307]

Erwin Distributing Co., 530 Monocacy Blvd., Frederick, MD 21701, (301)662-0372 [1679]

Escada Beaute Ltd., 1412 Broadway, New York, NY 10018, (212)852-5500 [14096]

Escalade Sports, PO Box 889, Evansville, IN 47706, (812)467-1200 [23742]

Esco Electric Supply Co., 820 N 2nd St., Philadelphia, PA 19123, (215)923-6050 [8713]

Esco Imports of Texas Inc., 1946 Shipman Dr., San Antonio, TX 78219, (210)271-7794 [26478]

ESCO Industries, 955 Grand Oak Dr., Howell, MI 48843, (517)546-6200 [2597]

Esco Supply Company Inc., 1234 San Francisco St., San Antonio, TX 78201, (210)736-4205 [23152]

Escondido Lumber & True Value, 310 S Quince, Escondido, CA 92025-4047, (760)745-0881 [7319]

ESD Co., 7380 Convoy Ct., San Diego, CA 92111, (619)636-4400 [8714]

ESI Computing, 468 Westford Rd., Carlisle, MA 01741, (978)369-8499 [6255]

ESI-Technologies Inc., The Rand Bldg., 7th Fl., Buffalo, NY 14203-2702, (716)852-8000 [6256]

Eskay Corp., 5245 Yeager Rd., Salt Lake City, UT 84116, (801)359-9900 [25913]

Eskew, Smith & Cannon, PO Box 1626, Charleston, WV 25326, (304)344-3414 [9886]

Esneault Inc., 3018 Galleria Dr., Metairie, LA 70001-2969, (504)833-6602 [23655]

Esojon International, Inc., 1871 Betmor Ln., Anaheim, CA 92805, (714)937-1575 [9887]

Espana General Importers, 1615 SW 8th St., Miami, FL 33135-3310, (305)856-4844 [13353]

Esprit International, PO Box 4025, Alameda, CA 94501-0425, (415)648-6900 [4939]

Espy Lumber Co., PO Box 5099, Hilton Head Island, SC 29938, (803)785-3821 [7320]

Essence Beauty Supply, 4118 Central Ave. SE, Ste. D, Albuquerque, NM 87108-1177, (505)268-9704 [14097]

Essex Electrical Supply Company Inc., 762 Western Ave., Lynn, MA 01905, (781)598-6200 [8715]

Essex Entertainment Inc., 95 Oser Ave., Ste. E, Hauppauge, NY 11788-3612 [25185]

Essex Grain Products Inc., 9 Lee Blvd., Frazer, PA 19355, (610)647-3800 [11053]

ESSROC Corp., 2 Oak Way, Berkeley Heights, NJ 07922, (908)771-0024 [7321]

ESSROC Corp., 3251 Bath Pike Rd., Nazareth, PA 18064, (610)837-6725 [7322]

Estrella Tortilla Factory & Deli Store, 1004 S Central Ave., Phoenix, AZ 85004-2732, (602)253-5947 [11054]

Esty Lumber, 441 Main St., Groveland, MA 01834, (978)374-0333 [7323]

Esty and Sons Inc.; Ralph A., 441 Main St., Groveland, MA 01834, (978)374-0333 [7323]

Etac USA Inc., 2325 Park Lawn Dr., Ste. J, Waukesha, WI 53186-2938, (414)796-4600 [18793]

Etac USA Inc., 2325 Park Lawn Dr., Waukesha, WI 53186-2938, (414)796-4600 [19308]

Etchomatic Inc., 179 Old Canal Dr., Lowell, MA 01851-2736, (781)893-2020 [8716]

ETD KroMar, 180 James Dr. E, St. Rose, LA 70087-9662, (504)467-5863 [3734]

ETD-West, 26545 Danti Ct., Hayward, CA 94545-3917, (650)349-7023 [3517]

Ethel M. Chocolates, Inc., 1 Sunset Way, Henderson, NV 89014, (702)458-8864 [11055]

Etheridge Produce, 3001 Barnsley Tr., Raleigh, NC 27604, (919)231-7546 [11056]

ETMA, 6640 185th Ave. NE, Redmond, WA 98052, (425)885-0107 [8717]

Etna Oil Company Inc., PO Box 429, Ottawa, IL 61350, (815)434-0353 [22240]

E.T.S. Distributing, 209 Bellefonte Ave., Lock Haven, PA 17745, (717)748-8419 [26479]

Eudora Garment Corp., PO Box B, Eudora, AR 71640, (870)355-8381 [4940]

Eugene Trading Inc., 3841 Broadway Pl., Los Angeles, CA 90037, (213)231-1918 [14098]

Eugene Welders Supply Co., PO Box 2330, Eugene, OR 97402, (541)344-1438 [16153]

Eureka Fisheries, 151 Starfish Way, Crescent City, CA 95531-4447, (707)464-3149 [11057]

Euro American Trading-Merchants Inc., 37 Centennial St., Collegeville, PA 19426-1847, (610)454-0854 [11058]

Euro Classic Distributors Inc., 9474 NW 13th St., Bay 76, Miami, FL 33172-2810, (305)591-3283 [15491]

Euro-Knit Corp., 1 Junius St., PO Box 179, Brooklyn, NY 11212, (718)498-0820 [26030]

EuroAmerican Brands LLC, 15 Prospect St., Paramus, NJ 07652, (201)368-2624 [11059]

Euroimport Co. Inc., PO Box 80624, Seattle, WA 98108-0624, (206)763-7303 [24736]

Europa Consulting, 10905 Ashford Ct., Upper Marlboro, MD 20772-2700, (301)627-8888 [6257]

European American Music Distributors Corp., PO Box 850, Valley Forge, PA 19482, (215)648-0506 [3735]

European Book Company Inc., 925 Larkin St., San Francisco, CA 94109, (415)474-0626 [3736]

European Crafts/USA, 3637 Cahuenga Blvd., Hollywood, CA 90068, (213)851-4070 [25186]

European Crafts/USA, 3637 Cahuenga Blvd., Hollywood, CA 90068, (213)851-4070 [15122]

European Kosher Provision, 21231 E Baltimore St., Baltimore, MD 21231-1403, (410)342-2002 [11060]

Eurostar Inc., 13425 S Figueroa St., Los Angeles, CA 90061, (310)715-9300 [24737]

Euroven Corp., 225 Industrial, Fredericksburg, VA 22408, (540)891-2481 [24111]

Evangel Publishing House, 2000 Evangel Way, PO Box 189, Nappanee, IN 46550-0189, (219)773-3164 [3737]

Evangeline Farmers Cooperative, 521 Lithcote Rd., Ville Platte, LA 70586, (318)363-1046 [17838]

Evans Co., 33 Eastern Ave., East Providence, RI 02914, (401)434-5600 [13689]

Evans Distributing Company Inc., PO Box 266, Marion, VA 24354, (703)783-4262 [1680]

Evans Electrical Supply Inc., 111435 Reiger Rd., Baton Rouge, LA 70809, (504)755-0066 [9297]

Evans Environmental Corp., 99 S East St., 4th Fl., Miami, FL 33131, (305)374-8300 [25187]

Evans Findings Company, Inc., 33 Eastern Ave., East Providence, RI 02914, (401)434-5600 [13689]

Evans Hydro, 18128 South Santa Fe Ave., Rancho Dominguez, CA 90220, (310)608-5801 [15999]

Evans Inc., 36 S State St., Chicago, IL 60603, (312)855-2000 [4941]

Evans Inc., 218 Pennsylvania Ave., Virginia Beach, VA 23462-2514, (757)399-3044 [14436]

Evans Inc.; J.D., 4000 N Cliff Ave., Sioux Falls, SD 57104, (605)336-2595 [7324]

Evans Oil Co., 520 Ave. F North, Bay City, TX 77414, (409)245-2424 [22241]

Evans Optical, PO Box 2030, Havre, MT 59501-2030, (406)265-1276 [19309]

Evans Pump Equipment Inc., 18128 South Santa Fe Ave., Rancho Dominguez, CA 90220, (310)608-5801 [15999]

Evans Systems Inc., PO Box 2480, Bay City, TX 77404-2480, (409)245-2424 [22242]

Evanston Wholesale Inc., PO Box 28, Evanston, WY 82931-0028, (307)789-3526 [1681]

Evansville Appliance Parts, 900 E Diamond Ave., Evansville, IN 47711, (812)423-8867 [15123]

Evansville Auto Parts Inc., 9000 N Kentucky Ave., Evansville, IN 47725-1396, (812)425-8264 [16000]

EVCO Wholesale Foods Co., 309 Merchant, Emporia, KS 66801, (316)343-7000 [11061]

Evelyn's Floral, 343 W Benson Blvd. No. 7, Anchorage, AK 99503, (907)561-7322 [14859]

Ever-Ready Oil Co., PO Box 25845, Albuquerque, NM 87125, (505)842-6120 [22243]

Everest and Jennings International Ltd., 3601 Rider Tr. S, Earth City, MO 63045, (314)512-7000 [19310]

Everett Anchor and Chain, PO Box 776, Everett, WA 98206, (206)682-3166 [19959]

Everett and Co.; R.B., PO Box 327, Houston, TX 77001, (713)224-8161 [7325]

Everett Square Sporting Goods, 427 Broadway, Everett, MA 02149-3435, (617)387-6530 [23656]

Evergreen Mills Inc., PO Box 548, Ada, OK 74820, (580)332-6611 [556]

Evergreen Nurseries, PO Box 2788, Honolulu, HI 96803-2788, (808)259-9945 [14860]

Evergreen Oak Electric Supply & Sales Co. Crest Lighting Studios Div., 13400 S Cicero, Crestwood, IL 60445, (708)597-4220 [8718]

Evergreen Oak Electric Supply and Sales Co. Evergreen Oak Div., 13400 S Cicero, Crestwood, IL 60445, (708)579-4220 [8719]

Evergreen Publishing & Stationery, 760 W Garvey Ave., Monterey Park, CA 91754, (626)281-3622 [3738]

Evergreen Scientific Inc., PO Box 58248, Los Angeles, CA 90058, (213)583-1331 [24357]

Everitt & Ray Inc., 1325 Johnson Dr., La Puente, CA 91745, (626)961-3611 [5]

Everpower Co., PO Box 2167 NMS, Niagara Falls, NY 14301-0167, (716)284-2809 [8720]

Everpure Inc., 660 N Blackhawk Dr., Westmont, IL 60559, (630)654-4000 [25645]

Evers Toy Store Inc., 204 1st Ave. E, Box 241, Dyersville, IA 52040-0241, (319)875-2438 [26480]

Everson Distributing Company, Inc., 280 New Ludlow Rd., Chicopee, MA 01020-4468, (413)533-9261 [11062]

Evil Empire, 2950 San Pablo Ave., Berkeley, CA 94702, (510)845-9851 [26415]

Evvan Importers Inc., 589 5th Ave., New York, NY 10017, (212)319-3100 [17409]

E.W. Tire & Service Centers, 718 Hope Hollow Rd., Carnegie, PA 15106-3627, (412)276-2141 [2598]

E.W.C. Supply Inc., 2336 S Main St., Elkhart, IN 46517, (219)293-9211 [23153]

Ewig Inc.; Carl F., 910 Oak Tree Rd., South Plainfield, NJ 07080, (908)756-3944 [25914]

Ewing Aquatech Pools Inc., 11414 Industriplex Blvd., Baton Rouge, LA 70809, (225)751-7946 [23657]

Ex-Cell-O North American Sales and Service Inc., 6015 Center Dr., Sterling Heights, MI 48312-2667, (810)939-1330 [16001]

Ex-Eltronics Inc., 137 Express St., Plainview, NY 11803, (516)351-5900 [8721]

Excalibur Cutlery & Gifts, PO Box 1818, Eugene, OR 97440, (541)484-4779 [15492]

Excel Corp., 4800 S Central, Chicago, IL 60638, (708)594-8887 [11063]

Excel Corp. DPM Foods Div., 1109 Chestnut St., Marysville, CA 95901, (530)742-2311 [11064]

Excel Electric Service Co., 2415 W 19th St., Chicago, IL 60608, (312)421-7220 [8722]

Excel Specialty Corp., 6335 N Broadway, Chicago, IL 60660-1401, (773)262-4781 [8723]

Excel Sports Science Inc., PO Box 1453, Eugene, OR 97440, (541)484-2454 [23521]

Excel Tanning Corp., 147 Palmer Ave., Mamaroneck, NY 10543, (914)381-0100 [18385]

Excel Tanning Corp., 715 Mamaroneck Ave., Mamaroneck, NY 10543, (914)381-0100 [18393]

Excellence Marketing, 7024 Tartan Curve, Eden Prairie, MN 55346, (612)949-9011 [8724]

Excelsior International Corp., PO Box 1268, Providence, RI 02901-1268, (401)737-7388 [17410]

Excelsior Manufacturing and Supply, 1465 E Industrial Dr., Itasca, IL 60143, (708)773-5500 [14437]

Exchange Lumber and Manufacturing Div., 15120 E Euclid Ave., Spokane, WA 99216-1801 [7326]

Execu-Flow Systems, Inc., 1 Ethel Rd., No. 106, Edison, NJ 08817, (732)287-9191 [19311]

Executive Business Machines, Inc., 2 Post Rd., Fairfield, CT 06430-6216, (203)254-8500 [6258]

Executive Coffee Service, 6239 E 15th St., Tulsa, OK 74112, (918)836-5570 [11548]

Executive Converting Corp., 4750 Simonton Rd., Dallas, TX 75244, (972)387-0500 [20995]

Executive Office Furniture Outlet, 1352 Reber St., Green Bay, WI 54301, (920)436-6820 [20996]

Executive Productivity Systems, PO Box 5539, Chesapeake, VA 23328, (757)547-0209 [6259]

Executone of Fort Wayne Inc., 3720 S Calhoun St., Ft. Wayne, IN 46807, (219)744-3365 [5606]

Executone Systems of St. Paul Inc., 30 W Water St., St. Paul, MN 55107, (612)292-0102 [5607]

Exhaust Specialties II, 700 SE Belmont St., Portland, OR 97214, (503)233-5151 [2599]

Exim Manufacturers Inc., 32 Garvies Point Rd., Glen Cove, NY 11542, (516)671-8200 [23923]

Exmart International, Inc., PO Box 408, Succasunna, NJ 07876-0408, (973)402-8600 [24112]

Exodus Computers, Inc., 70 East 3750 South, Salt Lake City, UT 84115, (801)265-8500 [6260]

Exotic Rubber and Plastics Corp., PO Box 395, Farmington, MI 48332, (810)477-2122 [16852]

Expanko Cork Co., PO Box 384, West Chester, PA 19380, (610)436-8300 [16853]

Experimental Applied Sciences, 555 Corp.orate Cir, Golden, CO 80401, (303)384-0080 [19312]

Expert Tile, Inc., 7795 Ellis Rd., Melbourne, FL 32904, (407)723-4301 [9888]

Exploration Resources Inc., 394 S Milledge Ave., Athens, GA 30605, (706)353-7983 [6261]

Exploration Supplies of Houma Inc., 9077 Park Ave., Houma, LA 70360, (504)851-1000 [16854]

Explosive Supply Company Inc., PO Box 217, Spruce Pine, NC 28777, (828)765-2762 [7327]

Expo Industries Inc., PO Box 26370, San Diego, CA 92196, (619)566-4343 [7328]

Export Consultant Service, 108 S Patton Dr., Coraopolis, PA 15108, (412)264-7877 [24358]

Export Consultants Corp., 250 Lackland Dr., No. 6, PO Box 308, Middlesex, NJ 08846, (732)469-0700 [84]

Export Contract Corp., PO Box 380039, Jacksonville, FL 32205-0539 [24113]

Export Division of Gordon E. Hansen Agency Inc., PO Box 98, Hampton, CT 06247, (860)455-9903 [2600]

Export of International Appliances, 8820 Monard Dr., Silver Spring, MD 20910-1815, (301)589-4610 [15124]

Export Oil Field Supply Company Inc., PO Box 770, Garden City, NY 11530, (516)227-2500 [22244]

Export Services Inc., PO Box 814432, Dallas, TX 75381, (972)243-8588 [6262]

Export USA, 2530 Lakefield Way, Sugar Land, TX 77479, (281)980-5370 [17411]

Express Fueling, 29120 Wick Rd., Romulus, MI 48174, (734)947-1811 [22634]

Express International Corp., PO Box 47, Flushing, NY 11352, (718)358-0200 [19313]

Express Optical Lab, 16-18 Bridge St., Brownsville, PA 15417-2310, (412)785-2160 [19314]

Expressive Art & Craft, 12455 Branford St., Unit 6, Arleta, CA 91331, (818)834-4640 [20997]

Exsaco Corp., PO Drawer 328, Alvarado, TX 76009, (817)783-2265 [23658]

EXSL/Ultra Labs Inc., 1767 National Ave., Hayward, CA 94545, (510)786-4567 [4385]

Extech Ltd., PO Box 659, Wilsonville, OR 97070, (503)682-7278 [18794]

Extend-A-Life Inc., 1010 S Arroyo Pkwy., Pasadena, CA 91105, (626)441-1223 [19315]

Extex Co., 2363 Boulevard Cir., Ste. 104, Walnut Creek, CA 94595, (510)988-1090 [23659]

Extrusions Inc., 2401 Main St., Ft. Scott, KS 66701, (316)223-1111 [19960]

Exxersource, 15000 Calvert St., Van Nuys, CA 91411, (818)787-6460 [23660]

Exxon Company USA, 17 Miles NW, La Barge, WY 83123, (307)276-6200 [22245]

Exxon Company U.S.A. Santa Ynez Unit, PO Box 5025, Westlake Village, CA 91359, (805)494-2000 [22246]

Eyak Aircraft, PO Box 87, Willow, AK 99688-0087, (907)495-6428 [85]

Eye Care Inc., 5858 Line Ave., Shreveport, LA 71106, (318)869-4443 [19316]

Eye Communication Systems Inc., 455 E Industrial Dr., Hartland, WI 53029, (414)367-1360 [22852]

Eye Kraft Optical Inc., PO Box 400, St. Cloud, MN 56302, (320)251-0141 [19317]

Eyeglass Shoppe, 508 Atkinson Dr., Honolulu, HI 96814, (808)949-1595 [19318]

Eyelet Enterprises Inc., 69 Tenean St., Boston, MA 02122-3401, (617)282-4700 [16002]

Eyemark Video Services, 310 Parkway View Dr., Pittsburgh, PA 15205, (412)747-4700 [25188]

EZ Nature Books, PO Box 4206, San Luis Obispo, CA 93403-4206, (805)528-5292 [3739]

Ezcony Interamerica Inc., 7620 NW 25th St., Ste. 4, Miami, FL 33122-1719, (305)599-1352 [8725]

Ezell-Key Grain Company Inc., PO Box 1062, Snyder, TX 79550, (915)573-9373 [557]

Ezell-Key Grain Company Inc., PO Box 1062, Snyder, TX 79550, (915)573-9373 [11065]

Ezon Inc., 1900 Exeter Rd., Germantown, TN 38138, (901)755-5555 [2601]

F & A Dairy California, 691 Inyo, Newman, CA 95360-9707, (209)862-1732 [11066]

F & A Food Sales Inc., 2221 Lincoln, PO Box 651, Concordia, KS 66901, (785)243-2301 [11067]

F and B Marketing Inc., 11920 W Silver Spring Dr., Milwaukee, WI 53225, (414)466-4620 [8726]

F-D-C Corp., PO Box 1047, Elk Grove Village, IL 60009-1047, (847)437-3990 [20998]

F & E Check Protector Co. Inc., 20 Rolfe Square, Cranston, RI 02910-2810, (401)738-9444 [20999]

F & E Sportswear Inc., 1230 Newell Pkwy., Montgomery, AL 36110-3212, (205)244-6477 [23661]

F and E Wholesale Food Service Inc., PO Box 2080, Wichita, KS 67201, (316)838-2400 [11068]

F and M Distributors Inc., 25800 Sherwood Ave., Warren, MI 48091, (734)758-1400 [19319]

F & M Electric Supply Co., 29 Federal Rd., Danbury, CT 06810-5014, (203)744-7445 [8727]

F and R International, 14611 Cypress Meadow Dr., Cypress, TX 77429, (281)251-4746 [22247]

F and R Oil Company Inc., PO Box 32756, Charlotte, NC 28232-2756, (704)333-6177 [22248]

F & R Sales Inc., 2101 S Dixie Rd., Dalton, GA 30720-7565, (706)226-8564 [4942]

F and S Alloys and Minerals Corp., 605 3rd Ave., New York, NY 10158, (212)490-1356 [19961]

F & S Co. Inc., 4500 Tower Rd. SW, Albuquerque, NM 87121-3424, (505)247-1451 [26481]

F & S Supply Company Inc., PO Box 373, Iola, KS 66749-0373, (316)365-3737 [8728]

F & W Rallye Engineering, 39W960 Midan Dr., Elburn, IL 60119, (630)232-6063 [2602]

F & W Welding Service Inc., 164 Boston Post Rd., Orange, CT 06477, (203)795-0591 [7329]

FABCO Equipment Inc., 11200 W Silver Spring Rd., Milwaukee, WI 53225, (414)461-9100 [558]

Fabco Industries, Inc., 8406 W Loop, No. 338, Odessa, TX 79764, (915)367-4988 [2603]

Fabel Inc.; Robert A., 92283 Highway 70, Vinton, CA 96135, (530)993-4647 [559]

Faber Brothers Inc., 4141 S Pulaski, Chicago, IL 60632, (773)376-9300 [23662]

Fabiano Brothers Inc., PO 469, Mt. Pleasant, MI 48858, (517)752-2186 [1682]

Fabiano Shoe Company Inc., 850 Summer St., Boston, MA 02127-1537, (617)268-5625 [24738]

Fabick Tractor Co.; John, 1 Fabick Dr., Fenton, MO 63026, (314)343-5900 [7330]

Fabric Art Inc., 3439 SW Dickinson St., Portland, OR 97219-7555, (503)224-1303 [4943]

Fabricated Plastics Inc., PO Box 1907, Morristown, NJ 07960-1907, (973)539-4200 [22959]

Fabricated Systems of Atlanta, 4620 S Atlanta Rd. SE, Smyrna, GA 30080, (404)792-1696 [14438]

Fabricating and Production Machinery Inc., PO Box 240, Sturbridge, MA 01566, (508)347-3500 [16003]

Fabricut Inc., PO Box 470490, Tulsa, OK 74147, (918)622-7700 [26031]

Fabsco Corp., 1745 W 124th St., Calumet Park, IL 60827, (708)371-7500 [13690]

FABTEX Inc., 111 Woodbine Ln., Danville, PA 17821, (570)275-7500 [15493]

Fabwel Inc., 1838 Middlebury St., Elkhart, IN 46516, (219)522-8473 [19962]

Facility Resource Inc. (Seattle, Washington), Seattle Design Ctr. 5701 6th Ave. S, Seattle, WA 98108, (206)764-7000 [13108]

Facit Div., Ahearn & Soper Co. Inc., 59 Chenell Dr., Concord, NH 03301-8541 [6263]

Factory Motor Parts, 5605 F St., Omaha, NE 68117-2820, (402)341-6318 [2604]

Factory Steel and Metal Supply Co., LLC, 14020 Oakland, Detroit, MI 48203, (313)883-6300 [19963]

Fadler Company Inc., PO Box 472306, Tulsa, OK 74147-2306, (918)627-0770 [11069]

Fadson International Company, PO Box 23036, Richfield, MN 55423, (612)861-7480 [14439]

Faella Co. Inc.; Don, 1271 Mineral Spring Ave., North Providence, RI 02904-4604 [25189]

Fagan Inc.; Ed, 769 Susquehanna Ave., Franklin Lakes, NJ 07417, (201)891-4003 [19964]

Fager Company Inc.; R.F., 2058 State Rd., Camp Hill, PA 17011, (717)761-0660 [23154]

Fail-Safe Lighting Systems Inc., 6721 W 73rd St., Bedford Park, IL 60638-6006 [8729]

Fain & Associates; Gary, PO Box 1370, Sand Springs, OK 74063 [23663]

Fair City Oil, PO Box 625, Franklinton, LA 70438, (504)839-4753 [22249]

Fair Company Inc.; R.E., 5601 Huberville Rd., Dayton, OH 45431, (937)253-1170 [2605]

Fair Inc., 2260 Terminal Rd., Roseville, MN 55113-2516, (612)379-0110 [24739]

Fairbank Reconstruction Corp., PO Box 170, Ashville, NY 14710, (716)782-2000 [11070]

Fairbanks Co., PO Box 1871, Rome, GA 30161, (706)234-6701 [13691]

Fairbury Winnelson Co., PO Box 419, Fairbury, NE 68352, (402)729-2215 [23155]

Fairchild Communications Services Co., 300 W Service Rd., Chantilly, VA 20151, (703)478-5888 [5608]

Fairclough and Sons Inc.; N.B., PO Box 69, Paterson, NJ 07513, (973)742-6412 [22250]

Fairco, Inc., 518 Gravier St., New Orleans, LA 70130, (504)524-0467 [11071]

Fairdale Farmers Cooperative Elevator Co., PO Box 102, Fairdale, ND 58229, (701)966-2515 [560]

Fairfax Trailer Sales Inc., 170 E Alton Ave., East Alton, IL 62024, (618)254-7411 [14440]

Fairfield Book Co., Inc., 42 Obtuse Rd. N, Brookfield Center, CT 06804, (203)775-0053 [3740]

Fairfield Book Service Co., 150 Margherita Lawn, Stratford, CT 06497, (203)375-7607 [3741]

Fairfield Line Inc., PO Box 500, Fairfield, IA 52556, (515)472-3191 [4944]

Fairfield Supply Co., 1675 S Sandusky, PO Box 429, Bucyrus, OH 44820, (419)562-4015 [2606]

Fairmont Roberts Dairy Co., 3805 Van Brunt Blvd., Kansas City, MO 64128, (816)921-7370 [12329]

Fairmont Supply Co., 90 W Chestnut St., Washington, PA 15301, (724)223-2200 [25646]

Fairmont Supply Co. (Washington, Pennsylvania), PO Box 501, Washington, PA 15301, (724)223-2200 [16855]

Fairmont Supply Co. Western Operations, 565 South 300 W, Price, UT 84501, (435)636-3100 [16856]

Fairmont Tamper, PO Box 415, Fairmont, MN 56031-0415, (507)235-3361 [13692]

Fairview-AFX Inc., 4932 S 83rd East Ave., Tulsa, OK 74145-6911, (918)664-8020 [8730]

Fairview Dairy Inc. & Valley Dairy, 3200 Graham Ave., Windber, PA 15963-2539, (814)467-5537 [11072]

Fairview True Value Hardware, 68 Violet Ave., Poughkeepsie, NY 12601-1521, (914)485-4700 [13693]

Fairway Foods, Inc., PO Box 1224, Minneapolis, MN 55440, (612)830-1601 [11073]

Fairway Foods, Inc., PO Box 1224, Minneapolis, MN 55440, (612)830-8700 [11446]

Fairway Foods Inc., PO Box 1224, Minneapolis, MN 55440, (612)830-1601 [11074]

Fairway Foods of Michigan Inc., 1230 48th Ave., Menominee, MI 49858, (906)863-5503 [11075]

Fairway Salvage Inc., 12428 Center St., South Gate, CA 90280-8052, (562)630-8766 [26812]

Fairwind Sunglasses Trading Company Inc., 8301 Biscayne Blvd., Miami, FL 33138, (305)758-0057 [19320]

Faithway Feed Company Inc., PO Box 995, Guntersville, AL 35976, (205)582-5646 [27130]

Falcon Industries Inc., PO Box 1971, Burlington, NC 27216, (336)229-1048 [26032]

Falcon Plumbing Inc., 2414 N Gilbert Rd., Mesa, AZ 85203-1302, (602)964-6622 [23156]

Falcon Products Inc., 9387 Dielman Industrial Dr., St. Louis, MO 63132, (314)991-9200 [13109]

Falcon Trading Co., 1055 17th Ave., Santa Cruz, CA 95062-3033, (831)462-1280 [11076]

Falcone and Italia Foods, 1361 NW 155th Dr., Miami, FL 33169, (954)467-8910 [11077]

Falgouts Refrigeration & Appliance Service, PO Box 10206, Sta. 1, Houma, LA 70363-0206, (504)873-8460 [14441]

Falk Corp., 4970 Joule St., Reno, NV 89502-4119, (702)856-6155 [16004]

Falk Supply Co., PO Box 1329, Hot Springs, AR 71902, (501)321-1231 [23157]

Falken Tire Corp., 10404 6th St., Rancho Cucamonga, CA 91730, (909)466-1116 [2607]

Fall City Boat Works, 3015 Upper River Rd., Louisville, KY 40207, (502)897-6521 [18500]

Fall River News Company, Inc., 144 Robeson St., Fall River, MA 02720-4925, (508)679-5266 [3742]

Fallah Enterprises, 11601 Seaboard Cir., Stanton, CA 90680-3427, (562)799-6642 [13354]

Fallani and Cohn, 415 Rte. 303, Tappan, NY 10983, (914)683-7631 [15494]

Falls Enterprises, 42 W 61st St., Chicago, IL 60621-3999, (773)684-6700 [21742]

Falls Welding & Fabricating, FWF Medical Products Div., 608 Grant St., Akron, OH 44311, (330)253-3437 [18795]

Falls Welding & Fabrication, Medical Products Div., 608 Grant St., Akron, OH 44311, (330)253-3437 [18795]

Falls Welding and Fabrication, Medical Products Div., 608 Grant St., Akron, OH 44311, (330)253-3437 [18795]

Fallsway Equipment Company Inc., PO Box 4537, Akron, OH 44310-0537, (216)633-6000 [16005]

Falmouth Supply Co. Inc., 12 Canapitsit Dr., East Falmouth, MA 02536-6211, (508)548-6000 [25190]

Familian Corp., 2750 S Towne Ave., Pomona, CA 91766-6205, (818)374-4200 [15125]

Familian Northwest Inc., PO Box 17098, Portland, OR 97217, (503)283-4444 [23158]

Familian Pipe and Supply, 7651 Woodman Ave., Van Nuys, CA 91402, (818)786-9720 [23159]

Familiar Northwest, PO Box 220, Minot, ND 58702-0220, (701)852-4411 [23160]

Family Clubhouse, Inc., 6 Chiles Ave., Asheville, NC 28803, (704)254-9236 [5041]

Family Life Productions, PO Box 357, Fallbrook, CA 92088-0357, (760)728-6437 [3743]

Family Reading Service, 1209 Toledo Dr., Albany, GA 31705, (912)439-2279 [3744]

Family Shoe Center, PO Box 911, Marion, VA 24354-0911, (540)783-5061 [24740]

Family Sweets Candy Co. Inc., 1010 Reed St., Winston-Salem, NC 27107-5446, (910)788-5068 [11078]

Famous Brands Distributors Inc., 2910 SW Topeka Blvd., Topeka, KS 66611, (785)267-6622 [1683]

Famous Enterprises Inc., PO Box 1889, Akron, OH 44309, (216)762-9621 [14442]

Famous Industries, PO Box 1420, Akron, OH 44309-1420, (216)535-1811 [23161]

Famous Manufacturing Co., PO Box 1889, Akron, OH 44309, (330)762-9621 [16006]

Famous Mart Inc., PO Box 220268, Charlotte, NC 28222, (704)333-5157 [4945]

Famous Smoke Shop Inc., 55 W 39th St., New York, NY 10018, (212)840-4860 [26291]

Famous Telephone Supply Inc., PO Box 28577, Akron, OH 44319, (330)762-8811 [5609]

Fancy Fare Distributors, 19-4 Freedom Park, Ste. 3, Bangor, ME 04401, (207)529-5879 [11079]

Fancy Feet Inc., 26650 Harding, Oak Park, MI 48237, (248)398-8460 [24741]

Fannon Petroleum Services Inc., PO Box 989, Alexandria, VA 22313, (703)836-1133 [22251]

Fantastic Foods Inc., 1250 N McDowell Blvd., Petaluma, CA 94954, (707)778-7801 [11080]

Fantasy Diamond Corp., 1550 W Carroll Ave., Chicago, IL 60607, (312)421-4444 [17412]

Fantec Inc., PO Box 45669, Baton Rouge, LA 70895-5669, (504)275-5900 [15126]

Far Corners Importers Ltd., 1006 Benstein, Ste. 105, Walled Lake, MI 48390, (248)669-7492 [13355]

Far East Restaurant Equipment Mfg. Co., 306 S Maple Ave., South San Francisco, CA 94080, (650)872-6585 [24114]

Far East Trading Company Inc., 3911 Old Lee Highway, Ste. 42A, Fairfax, VA 22030, (703)591-0993 [86]

Far-Mor Cooperative, 1433 Illinois St., Sidney, NE 69162, (308)254-5541 [22252]

Far-Vet Supply Co., 635 Prior Ave. N, St. Paul, MN 55104, (612)646-8788 [19322]

Fareway Wholesale, PO Box 70, Boone, IA 50036, (515)432-2623 [11081]

Fargo Glass and Paint Co., 1801 7th Ave. N, Fargo, ND 58102, (701)235-4441 [21440]

Fargo Manufacturing Company Inc., PO Box 2900, Poughkeepsie, NY 12603, (914)471-0600 [8731]

Fargo-Moorhead Jobbing Co., 1017 4th Ave. N, Fargo, ND 58107, (701)293-1521 [11082]

Faris Machinery Co., 5770 E 77th Ave., Commerce City, CO 80022, (303)289-5743 [7331]

Farm Boy Meats Inc., PO Box 996, Evansville, IN 47706, (812)425-5231 [11083]

Farm Equipment Company of Asheville Inc., PO Box 2745, Asheville, NC 28802, (704)253-8483 [561]

Farm Fresh Catfish Co., 1616 Rice-Mill Rd., PO Box 85, Hollandale, MS 38748, (601)827-2204 [11084]

Farm Fresh Foods Inc., 6534 Clara St., Bell Gardens, CA 90201, (562)927-2586 [11085]

Farm Fresh Inc., 7255 Sheridan Blvd., Arvada, CO 80003, (303)429-1536 [11086]

Farm Implement and Supply Company Inc., 520 W Mill, Plainville, KS 67663, (785)434-4824 [562]

Farm-Oyl Company Inc., 2333 Hampden Ave., St. Paul, MN 55114, (612)646-7571 [563]

Farm Service Company Inc., 1020 S 8th St., Council Bluffs, IA 51501, (712)323-7167 [564]

Farm Service Cooperative Inc., 2308 Pine St., Harlan, IA 51537, (712)755-3185 [565]

Farm Service Elevator Co., PO Box 933, Willmar, MN 56201, (612)235-1080 [17839]

Farm Service Inc., PO Drawer M, Hoxie, AR 72433, (870)886-7779 [566]

Farm Services Inc., PO Box 360, Vinton, IA 52349, (319)472-2394 [567]

Farmer and Co.; Leon, PO Drawer 1352, Athens, GA 30603, (706)353-1166 [1684]

Farmer Johns Packing Co., 222 S 9th Ave., Phoenix, AZ 85007-3103, (602)254-6685 [11087]

Farmer Office Products Inc., 3725 Reveille, Houston, TX 77087, (713)645-5666 [21000]

Farmers Co-op Elevator and Mercantile Association, PO Box 909, Dighton, KS 67839, (316)397-5343 [17840]

Farmers Coop Association of Jackson, Sherburn, Spring Lake & Trimont, PO Box 228, Jackson, MN 56143, (507)847-4160 [568]

Farmers Cooperative, PO Box 47, Dayton, IA 50530, (515)547-2813 [569]

Farmers Cooperative, 201 S 10th St., Ft. Smith, AR 72901, (501)783-8959 [570]

Farmers Cooperative Association, PO Box 3001, Gillette, WY 82717, (307)682-4468 [571]

Farmers Cooperative Association, PO Box 249, Vici, OK 73859, (580)995-4202 [572]

Farmers Cooperative Association, 110 River Rd., Akron, IA 51001, (712)568-2426 [587]

Farmers Cooperative Association, PO Box 2108, Broken Arrow, OK 74013, (918)251-5379 [573]

Farmers Cooperative Association, PO Box 1015, Port Gibson, MS 39150, (601)437-4281 [574]

Farmers Cooperative Association, PO Box 149, Canby, MN 56220, (507)223-7241 [22253]

Farmers Cooperative Association, 900 E Jefferson St., Siloam Springs, AR 72761, (501)524-6175 [575]

Farmers Cooperative Association, Kansas St. & Railroad, Brewster, KS 67732, (785)694-2281 [17841]

Farmers Cooperative Association, Hwy. 63 N, New Hampton, IA 50659, (515)394-3052 [576]

Farmers Cooperative Association, PO Box 187, Okarche, OK 73762, (405)263-7289 [577]

Farmers Cooperative Association, PO Box 1045, Manhattan, KS 66505-1045, (913)776-9467 [578]

Farmers Cooperative Association, PO Box 196, Meno, OK 73760, (580)776-2241 [579]

Farmers Cooperative Association, PO Box 220, Allen, NE 68710, (402)635-2312 [580]

Farmers Cooperative Association, Main St., Lindsay, NE 68644, (402)428-2305 [17842]

Farmers Cooperative Association, PO Box 390, Forest City, IA 50436, (515)582-2814 [581]

Farmers Cooperative Association, PO Box 608, Clinton, OK 73601, (580)323-1467 [17843]

Farmers Cooperative Association, 4th & Barnes, Alva, OK 73717, (405)327-3854 [582]

Farmers Cooperative Association, 808 Railroad St., Boyden, IA 51234, (712)725-2331 [22254]

Farmers Cooperative Association, E Country Rd., Columbus, KS 66725, (316)429-2296 [583]

Farmers Cooperative Association, 209 S Market St., Eldorado, OK 73537, (580)633-2274 [584]

Farmers Cooperative Association, 400 Walnut St., Laurens, IA 50554, (712)845-4566 [585]

Farmers Cooperative Association, PO Box 127, Brule, NE 69127, (308)287-2304 [17844]

Farmers Cooperative Association, PO Box 100, Milroy, MN 56263, (507)336-2555 [17845]

Farmers Cooperative Association, 105 Jackson St., Jackson, MN 56143, (507)847-4160 [17846]

Farmers Cooperative Association, PO Box 196, Meno, OK 73760, (580)776-2241 [11088]

Farmers Cooperative Association, Main St., Lindsay, NE 68644, (402)428-2305 [11089]

Farmers Cooperative Association (Brule, Nebraska), PO Box 127, Brule, NE 69127, (308)287-2304 [11090]

Farmers Cooperative Association (Okarche, Oklahoma), PO Box 187, Okarche, OK 73762, (405)263-7289 [4386]

Farmers Cooperative Association (York, Nebraska), Rte. 2 Box 3, York, NE 68467, (402)362-6691 [17847]

Farmers Cooperative Business Association, PO Box 38, Shelby, NE 68662, (402)527-5511 [586]

Farmers Cooperative (Carmen, Oklahoma), PO Box 100, Carmen, OK 73726, (580)987-2234 [17848]

Farmers Cooperative Co., 110 River Rd., Akron, IA 51001, (712)568-2426 [587]

Farmers Cooperative Co., PO Box 100, Carmen, OK 73726, (580)987-2234 [588]

Farmers Cooperative Co., 103 N Blanch, Manly, IA 50456, (515)454-2282 [589]

Farmers Cooperative Co., PO Box 186, Clear Lake, IA 50428, (515)357-5274 [590]

Farmers Cooperative Co., PO Box 127, Brookings, SD 57006, (605)692-6216 [591]

Farmers Cooperative Co., PO Box 505, Glidden, IA 51443, (712)659-2227 [592]

Farmers Cooperative Co., PO Box 70, Waverly, NE 68462, (402)786-2665 [593]

Farmers Cooperative Co., PO Box 157, Woolstock, IA 50599, (515)839-5532 [594]

Farmers Cooperative Co., 141 N Main, Paullina, IA 51046, (712)448-3412 [595]

Farmers Cooperative Co., 1303 9th Ave., Manson, IA 50563, (712)469-3388 [17849]

Farmers Cooperative Co., PO Box 248, Wolcott, IN 47995, (219)279-2115 [17850]

Farmers Cooperative Co., PO Box 308, Rudd, IA 50471, (515)395-2271 [596]

Farmers Cooperative Co., 445 S Main St., West Point, NE 68788, (402)372-5303 [597]

Farmers Cooperative Co., PO Box 278, Lost Nation, IA 52254, (319)678-2506 [598]

Farmers Cooperative Co., PO Box 192, Mondamin, IA 51557, (712)646-2411 [599]

Farmers Cooperative Co., PO Box 160, Pocahontas, IA 50574, (712)335-3575 [17851]

Farmers Cooperative Co., Washington & North, Remsen, IA 51050, (712)786-1134 [600]

Farmers Cooperative Co., PO Box 339, Readlyn, IA 50668-0339, (319)279-3396 [601]

Farmers Cooperative Co., 304 Ellsworth St., Dows, IA 50071, (515)852-4136 [17852]

Farmers Cooperative Co., PO Box 399, Alton, IA 51003, (712)756-4121 [602]

Farmers Cooperative Co., PO Box 35, Farnhamville, IA 50538, (515)544-3213 [603]

Farmers Cooperative Co., PO Box 179, Greenfield, IA 50849, (515)743-2161 [17853]

Farmers Cooperative Co., PO Box 186, Clear Lake, IA 50428, (515)357-5274 [11091]

Farmers Cooperative Co., PO Box 127, Brookings, SD 57006, (605)692-6216 [11092]

Farmers Cooperative Co., PO Box 192, Mondamin, IA 51557, (712)646-2411 [11093]

Farmers Cooperative Co., 304 Ellsworth St., Dows, IA 50071, (515)852-4136 [11094]

Farmers Cooperative Co., PO Box 399, Alton, IA 51003, (712)756-4121 [11095]

Farmers Cooperative Co. (Britt, Iowa), 368 Main Ave. N, Britt, IA 50423, (515)843-3878 [11096]

Farmers Cooperative Co. (Dike, Iowa), S Main St., Dike, IA 50624, (319)989-2416 [17854]

Farmers Cooperative Co. (Hinton, Iowa), PO Box 1046, Hinton, IA 51024, (712)947-4212 [17855]

Farmers Cooperative Company Inc., 111 N Weimer St., Ventura, IA 50482, (515)829-3891 [604]

Farmers Cooperative Co. (Milligan, Nebraska), PO Box 97, Milligan, NE 68406, (402)629-4275 [17856]

Farmers Cooperative Co. (Readlyn, Iowa), PO Box 339, Readlyn, IA 50668-0339, (319)279-3396 [17857]

Farmers Cooperative Co. (Woolstock, Iowa), PO Box 157, Woolstock, IA 50599, (515)839-5532 [17858]

Farmers Cooperative Compress, PO Box 2877, Lubbock, TX 79408, (806)763-9431 [17859]

Farmers Cooperative Dairy Inc., PO Box 685, Blakeslee, PA 18610, (570)454-0821 [11097]

Farmers Cooperative of El Campo, PO Box 826, El Campo, TX 77437, (409)543-6284 [17860]

Farmers Cooperative Elevator, PO Box 208, Ord, NE 68862, (308)728-3254 [605]

Farmers Cooperative Elevator, PO Box 348, Buffalo Center, IA 50424, (515)562-2828 [606]

Farmers Cooperative Elevator, Main St., Stockton, IA 52769, (319)785-4436 [607]

Farmers Cooperative Elevator, PO Box 67, Wakita, OK 73771, (580)594-2234 [608]

Farmers Cooperative Elevator, PO Box 38, Oslo, MN 56744, (218)695-2301 [17861]

Farmers Cooperative Elevator, PO Box 45, Thompson, IA 50478-0045, (515)584-2241 [609]

Farmers Cooperative Elevator, PO Box 67, George, IA 51237, (712)475-3347 [1087]

Farmers Cooperative Elevator, PO Box 67, Sharon, ND 58277, (701)524-1770 [17862]

Farmers Cooperative Elevator Association, PO Box 130, Crowell, TX 79227, (940)684-1234 [17863]

Farmers Cooperative Elevator Association, 401 Commercial St., Greenleaf, KS 66943, (785)747-2236 [610]

Farmers Cooperative Elevator Association, 1016 2nd Ave., Sheldon, IA 51201, (712)324-2548 [611]

Farmers Cooperative Elevator Association, 1016 2nd Ave., Sheldon, IA 51201, (712)324-2548 [11098]

Farmers Cooperative Elevator Co., PO Box 604, Rushford, MN 55971, (507)864-7733 [612]

Farmers Cooperative Elevator Co., PO Box 112, Winterset, IA 50273, (515)462-4611 [613]

Farmers Cooperative Elevator Co., PO Box 247, Cavalier, ND 58220, (701)265-8439 [17864]

Farmers Cooperative Elevator Co., PO Box 188, Ruthven, IA 51358, (712)837-5231 [614]

Farmers Cooperative Elevator Co., PO Box 200, Radcliffe, IA 50230, (515)899-2101 [615]

Farmers Cooperative Elevator Co., PO Box 518, Waukee, IA 50263, (515)987-4511 [616]

Farmers Cooperative Elevator Co., PO Box 150, Blairsburg, IA 50034, (515)325-6252 [17865]

Farmers Cooperative Elevator Co., 509 A Ave., Grundy Center, IA 50638, (319)824-5466 [617]

Farmers Cooperative Elevator Co., 533 Bradford St., Marble Rock, IA 50653, (515)397-2515 [618]

Farmers Cooperative Elevator Co., PO Box 1009, Dawson, MN 56232-1009, (320)769-2408 [17866]

Farmers Cooperative Elevator Co., N Main St., Rake, IA 50465, (515)566-3351 [619]

Farmers Cooperative Elevator Co., Hwy. 285, Arcadia, IA 51430, (712)689-2298 [620]

Farmers Cooperative Elevator Co., 3rd St. & Railroad Tracks, Echo, MN 56237, (507)925-4126 [17867]

Farmers Cooperative Elevator Co., PO Box 66, Plymouth, NE 68424, (402)656-3615 [621]

Farmers Cooperative Elevator Co., PO Box 316, Garden Plain, KS 67050, (316)535-2221 [17868]

Farmers Cooperative Elevator Co. (Buffalo Lake, Minnesota), PO Box 98, Ireton, IA 51027, (320)833-5981 [11099]

Farmers Cooperative Elevator Co. (Everly, Iowa), 701 N Main St., Everly, IA 51338, (712)834-2238 [17869]

Farmers Cooperative Elevator Co. Lake Lillian Div., Main St., Lake Lillian, MN 56253, (612)664-4121 [622]

Farmers Cooperative Elevator (Martelle, Iowa), 124 Morley Rd., Martelle, IA 52305, (319)482-3101 [17870]

Farmers Cooperative Elevator and Supply, 116 E 6th, Newkirk, OK 74647, (580)362-3376 [17871]

Farmers Cooperative Exchange, 109 South St., Pella, IA 50219, (515)628-4167 [623]

Farmers Cooperative Exchange, PO Box 188, Weatherford, OK 73096, (580)772-3334 [624]

Farmers Cooperative Exchange, PO Box 8, Otley, IA 50214, (515)627-5311 [625]

Farmers Cooperative Exchange, PO Box 158, Bessie, OK 73622, (580)337-6343 [626]

Farmers Cooperative Exchange, 804 1st Ave. NW, Rockford, IA 50468, (515)756-3611 [627]

Farmers Cooperative Exchange, 109 South St., Pella, IA 50219, (515)628-4167 [11100]

Farmers Cooperative Exchange (Elgin, Nebraska), PO Box 159, Elgin, NE 68636, (402)843-2223 [11101]

Farmers Cooperative Grain Association, 524 E Parallel St., Conway Springs, KS 67031, (316)456-2222 [628]

Farmers Cooperative Grain Association, 210 S Nebraska St., Waterville, KS 66548, (913)785-2555 [629]

Farmers Cooperative Grain Co., PO Box 12, Dalton City, IL 61925-0012, (217)874-2392 [17872]

Farmers Cooperative Grain and Seed, E 8th & Dewey Sts., Thief River Falls, MN 56701, (218)681-6281 [17873]

Farmers Cooperative Grain and Seed Co., PO Box 88, Lamoni, IA 50140, (515)784-3326 [630]

Farmers Cooperative Grain and Supply, PO Box 47, Burdett, KS 67523, (316)525-6226 [17874]

Farmers Cooperative Grain and Supply Co., 815 N Brown St., Minden, NE 68959, (308)832-2380 [631]

Farmers Cooperative Grain and Supply Co., PO Box 245, Rocky, OK 73661, (580)666-2440 [632]

Farmers Cooperative Grain and Supply Co., 815 N Brown St., Minden, NE 68959, (308)832-2380 [11102]

Farmers Cooperative Inc., 312-16 W 3rd St., Farmville, VA 23901, (804)392-4192 [633]

Farmers Cooperative Market, PO Box 187, Frisco City, AL 36445, (334)267-3175 [634]

Farmers Cooperative Mercantile Co., PO Box 350, Scribner, NE 68057, (402)664-2256 [205]

Farmers Cooperative Mill Elevator, 106 S Broadway Ave., Carnegie, OK 73015, (580)654-1016 [17875]

Farmers Cooperative (Odebolt, Iowa), 205 E 1st St., Odebolt, IA 51458, (712)668-2211 [17876]

Farmers Cooperative Oil of Balaton, PO Box 189, Balaton, MN 56115, (507)734-3331 [635]

Farmers Cooperative Oil Co., PO Box 310, Newman Grove, NE 68758, (402)447-6292 [636]

Farmers Cooperative Oil Co., Rte. 1, Parkin, AR 72373, (870)755-5418 [22255]

Farmers Cooperative Oil Company of Clara City, PO Box 717, Clara City, MN 56222, (320)847-2318 [22256]

Farmers Cooperative of Pilger, PO Box 326, Pilger, NE 68768-0326, (402)396-3414 [17877]

Farmers Cooperative Society, 390 E 5th St., Garner, IA 50438, (515)923-2695 [637]

Farmers Cooperative Society (Sioux Center, Iowa), 317 3rd St. NW, Sioux Center, IA 51250, (712)722-2671 [17878]

Farmers Cooperative Supply and Shipping Association, 136 E Elm St., West Salem, WI 54669, (608)786-1100 [638]

Farmers Cooperative Trading Co., PO Box 135, Mooreland, OK 73852, (580)994-5375 [639]

Farmers Cooperative Union, PO Box 159, Sterling, KS 67579, (316)278-2141 [640]

Farmer's Elevator Co-op, PO Box 67, Swanton, NE 68445, (402)448-2040 [17879]

Farmers Elevator Co., PO Box 158, Hutchinson, MN 55350, (612)587-4647 [18009]

Farmers Elevator Co., 434 1st St., Chappell, NE 69129, (308)874-2245 [17880]

Farmers Elevator Co., PO Box 399, Elk Point, SD 57025, (605)356-2657 [641]

Farmers Elevator Co., PO Box 346, Kingsley, IA 51028, (712)378-2888 [642]

Farmers Elevator Co., PO Box 37, Rock Valley, IA 51247, (712)476-5321 [17881]

Farmers Elevator Co., PO Box 175, Waverly, IL 62692, (217)965-4004 [643]

Farmers Elevator Co., 201 E Campbell, Ransom, IL 60470, (815)586-4221 [17882]

Farmers Elevator Co., Railroad Ave., Circle, MT 59215, (406)485-3313 [17883]

Farmers Elevator Co., 201 E Campbell, Ransom, IL 60470, (815)586-4221 [11103]

Farmers Elevator Company of Avoca, PO Box 157, Westbrook, MN 56183, (507)274-6141 [644]

Farmers Elevator Company of Manteno, PO Box 667, Manteno, IL 60950, (815)468-3461 [17884]

Farmers Elevator Co. Richey Div., PO Box 37, Richey, MT 59259, (406)773-5758 [17885]

Farmers Elevator Cooperative, 1204 Main St., Scranton, IA 51462, (712)652-3321 [645]

Farmers Elevator and Exchange Inc., PO Box 65, Wapello, IA 52653, (319)523-5351 [17886]

Farmers Elevator of Fergus Falls, 406 E Junius St., Fergus Falls, MN 56537, (218)736-2894 [17887]

Farmers Elevator Grain and Supply, 16-973 Rd. B, New Bavaria, OH 43548, (419)653-4132 [646]

Farmers Elevator Inc., Box 280, Temple, OK 73568, (580)342-6495 [17888]

Farmers Elevator and Supply Co., E Market St., Morrison, IL 61270, (815)772-4029 [17889]

Farmers Elevator Supply Co., 511 South Ctr., Clinton, MO 64735, (660)885-5578 [647]

Farmers Exchange, 115 Main St., Stevensville, MT 59870, (406)777-5441 [648]

Farmers Exchange Cooperative, PO Box 38, Lake Park, IA 51347, (712)832-3621 [649]

Farmer's Fur House, R.R.1, PO Box 28, Cayuga, ND 58013-9718, (701)427-5526 [17890]

Farmers Furniture Company Inc., 1851 Telefair, Dublin, GA 31021, (912)275-3150 [13110]

Farmers Gin Co., PO Box 217, Bells, TN 38006, (901)663-2996 [650]

Farmers Gin Company Inc., PO Box 295, Clinton, KY 42031, (502)653-2731 [17891]

Farmers Grain Co., PO Box 80, Palmer, IL 62556, (217)526-3114 [651]

Farmers Grain Company of Charlotte, R.R. 1, Chatsworth, IL 60921, (815)689-2673 [652]

Farmers Grain Company of Chestnut, 100 W Olive St., Chestnut, IL 62518, (217)796-3513 [17892]

Farmers Grain Company of Dorans, PO Box 715, Mattoon, IL 61938, (217)234-4955 [17893]

Farmers Grain Company Inc., PO Box 188, Kremlin, OK 73753-0188, (580)874-2219 [653]

Farmers Grain Company Inc., PO Box 477, Pond Creek, OK 73766, (580)532-4273 [17894]

Farmers Grain Company of Julesburg, PO Box 296, Julesburg, CO 80737, (970)474-2537 [17895]

Farmers Grain Cooperative, PO Box 9550, Ogden, UT 84409, (801)621-7803 [17896]

Farmers Grain Cooperative, PO Box 166, Colo, IA 50056, (515)377-2253 [654]

Farmers Grain Cooperative, PO Box 177, Walton, KS 67151, (316)837-3313 [655]

Farmers Grain Cooperative of Eureka, RR 1, Box 860, Eureka, IL 61530, (309)467-2355 [17955]

Farmers Grain Dealers Inc., PO Box 4887, Des Moines, IA 50306, (515)223-7400 [17897]

Farmers Grain Exchange, PO Box 990, Havre, MT 59501, (406)265-2275 [656]

Farmers Grain and Seed, PO Box 1568, Nyssa, OR 97913, (541)372-2201 [17898]

Farmers Grain and Supply Company Inc., 409 Main, Follett, TX 79034, (806)653-3561 [17899]

Farmers Grain and Supply Company Inc., Rte. 1, Star City, IN 46985, (219)595-7101 [657]

Farmers Grain Terminal, PO Box 1232, Tallulah, LA 71282, (318)574-0564 [17900]

Farmers Investment Company Inc., PO Box 316, Horse Cave, KY 42749, (502)786-2124 [20540]

Farmers Livestock Marketing Association, 84 Rte. 127, PO Box 435, Greenville, IL 62246, (618)664-1432 [17901]

Farmers Petroleum Cooperative Inc., 7373 W Saginaw Hwy., Lansing, MI 48909, (517)323-7000 [22257]

Farmers Shipping and Supply, PO Box 128, Edmore, ND 58330, (701)644-2271 [17902]

Farmers Soybean Corp., PO Box 749, Blytheville, AR 72316-0749, (501)763-8191 [17903]

Farmers Supply Cooperative-AAL, PO Box 1799, Greenwood, MS 38930, (601)453-6341 [658]

Farmers Supply Sales Inc., PO Box 1205, Kalona, IA 52247, (319)656-2291 [659]

Farmers Union Co-op, 600 W Broad St., PO Box 8, Blue Springs, NE 68318-0008, (402)645-3356 [17904]

Farmers Union Co-op, 600 W Broad St., Blue Springs, NE 68318-0008, (402)645-3356 [11104]

Farmers Union Cooperative, PO Box 729, Adams, WI 53910, (608)339-3394 [22258]

Farmers Union Cooperative Association, Rte. 1, Nora, NE 68961, (402)225-4177 [17905]

Farmers Union Cooperative Association, 131 S Nebraska St., Salem, SD 57058, (605)425-2691 [660]

Farmers Union Cooperative Association of Alcester and Beresford South Dakota, Rte. 3, Box 10-A, Beresford, SD 57004, (605)957-4141 [22259]

Farmers Union Cooperative Association of Howard County, PO Box 237, St. Paul, NE 68873, (308)754-4431 [661]

Farmers Union Cooperative Association (Mead, Nebraska), PO Box 154, Mead, NE 68041, (402)624-3255 [17906]

Farmers Union Cooperative Co., PO Box 135, Friend, NE 68359-0135, (402)947-4291 [17907]

Farmers Union Cooperative Elevator Co., PO Box 36, Wray, CO 80758, (970)332-4703 [17908]

Farmers Union Cooperative (Harvard, Nebraska), PO Box 147, Harvard, NE 68944, (402)762-3239 [11105]

Farmers Union Cooperative Oil Co., PO Box 1018, Luverne, MN 56156-2518, (507)283-9571 [662]

Farmers Union Elevator, PO Box 128, Buxton, ND 58218, (701)847-2646 [663]

Farmers Union Elevator Co., PO Box 390, Lindsborg, KS 67456, (785)227-3361 [17909]

Farmers Union Grain Cooperative, PO Box 8, Edgeley, ND 58433, (701)493-2481 [17910]

Farmers Union Oil Co., PO Box 398, Crookston, MN 56716-0398, (320)235-3700 [22260]

Farmers Union Oil Co., PO Box B, Maddock, ND 58348, (701)438-2861 [664]

Farmers Union Oil Co., PO Box 129, Lake Bronson, MN 56734, (218)754-4300 [22261]

Farmers Union Oil Co., PO Box 219, Ellendale, ND 58436, (701)349-3280 [22262]

Farmers Union Oil Co., PO Box 347, Menno, SD 57045, (605)387-5151 [665]

Farmers Union Oil Co., PO Box 67, Oslo, MN 56744, (218)695-2511 [666]

Farmers Union Oil Co., PO Box 67, Harvey, ND 58341, (701)324-2231 [22263]

Farmers Union Oil Co., Hwy. 2 and 19 W, Devils Lake, ND 58301, (701)662-4014 [22264]

Farmers Union Oil Co., 151 9th Ave. NW, Valley City, ND 58072, (701)845-0812 [22265]

Farmers Union Oil Co., PO Box 70, Climax, MN 56523, (218)857-2165 [22266]

Farmers Union Oil Co., PO Box U, Napoleon, ND 58561, (701)754-2252 [22267]

Farmers Union Oil Co., PO Box 129, Lake Bronson, MN 56734, (218)754-4300 [667]

Farmers Union Oil Co., PO Box 219, Ellendale, ND 58436, (701)349-3280 [22268]

Farmers Union Oil Co. (Crookston, Minnesota), PO Box 398, Crookston, MN 56716-0647, (218)281-1809 [668]

Farmers Union Oil Co. (Ellendale, North Dakota), PO Box 219, Ellendale, ND 58436, (701)349-3280 [17911]

Farmers Union Oil Co. (Great Falls, Montana), 1000 Snetter Ave., Great Falls, MT 59404, (406)453-2435 [4387]

Farmers Union Oil Company of Kenmare, PO Box 726, Kenmare, ND 58746, (701)385-4277 [669]

Farmers Union Oil Co. (Napoleon, North Dakota), PO Box U, Napoleon, ND 58561, (701)754-2252 [22269]

Farmers Union Oil Co. (Rolla, North Dakota), 104 W Main Ave., Rolla, ND 58367, (701)852-2501 [22270]

Farmers Union Oil Co. (Starbuck, Minnesota), 310 Wollan St., Starbuck, MN 56381, (320)239-2233 [670]

Farmers Union Oil Co. (Willmar, Minnesota), 721 W Litchfield Ave., Willmar, MN 56201, (612)235-3700 [671]

Farmers Union Oil Cooperative, 2006 E Broadway Ave., Bismarck, ND 58501, (701)223-8707 [22271]

Farmland Dairies Inc., 520 Main Ave., Wallington, NJ 07057, (973)777-2500 [12118]

Farmland Foods, 20 Carando Dr., Springfield, MA 01104, (413)781-5620 [11106]

Farmland Grain Div., 10100 N Executive Hills Dr., Kansas City, MO 64153, (816)459-3300 [17912]

Farmland Industries Inc. Union Equity Exchange Div., PO Box 3408, Enid, OK 73702, (580)233-5100 [17913]

Farmland Service Cooperative, PO Box 80, Gothenburg, NE 69138, (308)537-7141 [17914]

Farmstead Telephone Group Inc., 22 Prestige Park Circle, East Hartford, CT 06108, (860)282-0010 [5610]

Farmway Cooperative Inc., PO Box 568, Beloit, KS 67420, (785)738-2241 [672]

Farn Ltd.; Gary, 249 Pepes Farm Rd., Milford, CT 06460, (203)878-8900 [14099]

Farner Bocken Co., Hwy. 30 E, Carroll, IA 51401, (712)792-3503 [26292]

Farner Bocken Co., PO Box 716, Sioux City, IA 51102, (712)258-5555 [11107]

Farner & Co., 600 E Norfolk Ave., Norfolk, NE 68701, (402)371-2662 [11108]

Farnsworth Armored Inc., 2077 Kirby Pkwy., Memphis, TN 38119-5534, (901)753-4232 [20634]

Farr & Sons Co.; Asael, 274 21st St., Ogden, UT 84401, (801)393-8629 [11109]

Farrell Distributing, 5 Holmes Rd., South Burlington, VT 05403, (802)864-4422 [1685]

Farrell Imports Inc.; Patrick, 675 Anita St., Ste. C6, Chula Vista, CA 91911-4660, (619)482-1513 [18394]

Farriors Inc., 4545 Malsbary Rd., Cincinnati, OH 45242-5624 [4890]

Farris Enterprises, 1855 Sampson Ave., Corona, CA 91718, (909)272-3919 [25647]

Farwest Corrosion Control Co., 1480 W Artesia Blvd., Gardena, CA 90248-3215, (310)532-9524 [4388]

Farwest Equipment, Inc., 1802 Pike NW, Auburn, WA 98001, (253)833-2060 [673]

Farwest Steel Corp., PO Box 889, Eugene, OR 97440, (541)686-2000 [19965]

Fas-Co Coders Inc.orporated, 500 E Comstock Dr., Chandler, AZ 85225, (480)545-7500 [21001]

Fashion Bed Group, 5950 W 51st St., Chicago, IL 60638, (708)458-1800 [13111]

Fashion Slippers Import USA, PO Box 180, Stamford, CT 06904-0180, (203)324-2191 [24742]

Fashion Victim, 3651 Clearview Pl., Doraville, GA 30340-2129, (912)563-0111 [4946]

Fashions Inc. Jackson, PO Box 604, Jackson, MS 39205-0604, (601)353-4490 [4947]

Fasnap Corp., PO Box 1613, Elkhart, IN 46515, (219)264-1185 [13694]

Fast Multimedia U.S. Inc., 15029 Woodinville Redmond Rd. NE, Woodinville, WA 98072-6988, (425)354-2002 [6264]

Fast Track Communications Inc., 1270 Techwood Dr. NW, Atlanta, GA 30318, (404)870-6690 [5611]

Fastec Industrial, 23348 County Rd. 6, Elkhart, IN 46514, (219)262-2505 [13695]

Fastenal Co., 2001 Theurer Blvd., Winona, MN 55987-1500, (507)454-5374 [13696]

Fastener Controls Inc. (FASCON), 15915 Piuma Ave., Cerritos, CA 90703-1526, (562)860-1097 [13697]

Fastener Supply Co., 1340 Amble Dr., Charlotte, NC 28206, (704)596-7634 [13698]

Fasteners Inc., PO Box 80604, Seattle, WA 98108, (206)763-2275 [13699]

Fasteners & Metal Products Corp., 30 Thayer Rd., Waltham, MA 02454, (617)489-0414 [13700]

Fastlink Network Products, 90 S Spruce Ave., Ste. N, South San Francisco, CA 94080, (650)872-1376 [6265]

Fastner House, 4601 Honeywell Dr., Ft. Wayne, IN 46825-6270, (219)484-0702 [13701]

Faucet-Queens Inc., 401 Chaddick Dr., Wheeling, IL 60090, (847)541-7777 [13702]

Faucet-Queens Inc., 650 Forest Edge Dr., Vernon Hills, IL 60061, (847)821-0777 [13703]

Faulcon Industries, 133 Northeastern Blvd., Nashua, NH 03062-1917, (603)882-1293 [14100]

Fauver Co., 1500 E Avis Dr., Madison Heights, MI 48071, (734)585-5252 [16857]

Fawcett Boat Supplies Inc., 110 Compromise St., Annapolis, MD 21401, (410)267-8681 [18501]

Faxon Company Inc., 15 Southwest Pkwy., Westwood, MA 02090, (781)329-3350 [3745]

Faxon Engineering Company Inc., 467 New Park Ave., West Hartford, CT 06110, (860)236-4266 [16858]

Fay Electric Wire Corp., 752 N Larch Ave., Elmhurst, IL 60126-1522, (630)530-7500 [8732]

Fay Industries, PO Box 360947, Strongsville, OH 44136, (440)572-5030 [19966]

Fayette County Cooperative Inc., PO Box 448, Connersville, IN 47331, (317)825-1131 [674]

Fayetteville Automotive Warehouse, 226 Cool Spring, Fayetteville, NC 28301-5136, (910)483-6196 [2608]

F.B.F. Inc., 1925 N McArthur Blvd., Oklahoma City, OK 73127, (405)789-0651 [13491]

FDL Marketing Inc., 2040 Kerper Blvd., Dubuque, IA 52004, (319)588-5400 [11110]

FE. MA. Inc., 12 W 57th St., Ste. 1001, New York, NY 10019-3900, (212)438-8353 [24743]

FEA Industries, Inc., 1 N Morton Ave., Morton, PA 19070, (215)876-2002 [19323]

Feaster Foods Co., 11808 W Center Rd., Omaha, NE 68144-4397, (402)691-8800 [11111]

Feather Crest Farms Inc., 14374 E SH 21, Bryan, TX 77808, (979)589-2576 [11112]

Fedco Electronics Inc., PO Box 1403, Fond du Lac, WI 54936-1403, (920)922-6490 [8733]

Fedco Steel Corp., 785 Harrison Ave., Harrison, NJ 07029, (201)481-1424 [19967]

Federal Computer Corp., 2745 Hartland Rd., Falls Church, VA 22043, (703)698-7711 [6266]

Federal Corp., PO Box 26408, Oklahoma City, OK 73126, (405)239-7301 [14443]

Federal Express Aviation Services Inc., 2005 Corporate Ave., Memphis, TN 38132, (901)395-3830 [87]

Federal Fruit and Produce Co., 1890 E 58th Ave., Denver, CO 80216, (303)292-1303 [11113]

Federal Heating and Engineering Company Inc., 160 Cross St., Winchester, MA 01890, (781)721-2468 [22272]

Federal Pipe and Supply Co., 6464 E McNichols Rd., Detroit, MI 48212, (313)366-3000 [7332]

Federal Pipe and Supply Co., 6464 E McNichols Rd., Detroit, MI 48212, (313)366-3000 [7333]

Federal Plastics Corp., 715 South Ave., Cranford, NJ 07016, (908)272-5800 [22960]

Federal Screw Products Inc., 3917 N Kedzie Ave., Chicago, IL 60618, (773)478-5744 [13704]

Federal Signal Corp., 2645 Federal Signal Dr., University Park, IL 60466-3195, (708)534-3400 [8734]

Federal Systems Group Inc., 7799 Leesburg Pike, Falls Church, VA 22043-2413, (703)848-4747 [6267]

Federal Wholesale Company Inc., 734 Myron St., Hubbard, OH 44425, (330)534-1171 [15495]

Federal Wine and Liquor Co., PO Box 519, Kearny, NJ 07032, (973)624-6444 [1686]

Federated Foods Inc., 3025 W Salt Creek Ln., Arlington Heights, IL 60005, (847)577-1200 [11114]

Federated Foodservice, 3025 W Salt Creek Ln., Arlington Heights, IL 60005, (708)577-1200 [24115]

Federated Group, Inc., 3025 W Salt Creek Ln., Arlington Heights, IL 60005, (847)577-1200 [11115]

Federated Purchaser Inc., 268 Cliffwood Ave., Cliffwood, NJ 07721, (908)301-1333 [8735]

Federation Cooperative, 108 N Water St., Black River Falls, WI 54615, (715)284-5354 [675]

Federation of Ohio River Co-ops, 320 Outerbelt St., Ste. E, Columbus, OH 43213, (614)861-2446 [11116]

Fedor Steel Co., 2833 N Telegraph Rd., Monroe, MI 48162, (734)242-2940 [19968]

Fedway Associates Inc., PO Box 519, Kearny, NJ 07032, (973)624-6444 [1687]

Feed Products Inc., 1000 W 47th Ave., Denver, CO 80211, (303)455-3646 [676]

Feed-Rite Controls Inc., 3100 E Hennepin Ave., Minneapolis, MN 55413, (612)331-9100 [25648]

Feed Seed and Farm Supplies Inc., PO Box 536, Sylvania, GA 30467, (912)564-7758 [677]

Feenaughty Machinery Co., PO Box 13279, Portland, OR 97213, (503)282-2566 [7334]

Feeney; Karin, PO Box 36930, Albuquerque, NM 87176-6930, (505)255-8278 [17490]

Feesers Inc., PO Box 4055, Harrisburg, PA 17111, (717)564-4636 [11117]

Fegely Inc.; J., 1810 West High St., PO Box 619, Pottstown, PA 19464, (610)323-9120 [16859]

Fegley Oil Company Inc., PO Drawer A, Tamaqua, PA 18252, (717)386-4151 [22273]

Fehr Bros. Industries Inc., 895 Kings Hwy., Saugerties, NY 12477, (845)246-9525 [13705]

FEI America Inc., PO Box 72, Tualatin, OR 97062, (503)620-8640 [6268]

Feibelman & Krack, PO Box 8045, Cranston, RI 02920-0045, (401)943-6370 [17413]

Felder & Co.; W.D., PO Box 815, Lubbock, TX 79408, (806)763-6630 [17915]

Feldheim, Inc.; Philipp, 200 Airport Executive Park, Nanuet, NY 10954, (914)356-2282 [3746]

Feldman Glass Co., PO Box 406, Fair Haven Station, New Haven, CT 06513, (203)624-3113 [25915]

Feldmann Engineering & Manufacturing Company, Inc., 520 Forest Ave., Sheboygan Falls, WI 53085-2513, (920)467-6167 [678]

Feldstein and Associates Inc., 6500 Weatherfield Ct., Maumee, OH 43537, (419)867-9500 [13356]

Felicia Grace and Co., 63 Willow Ave., Larchmont, NY 10538-3640, (212)730-7004 [4948]

Felina Lingerie, 180 Madison Ave., No. 1506, New York, NY 10016-5201, (212)683-9205 [4949]

Felt Auto Supply, 645 S State, Salt Lake City, UT 84111-3819, (801)364-1977 [2609]

FEMCO Corp., 235 Arcadia St., Richmond, VA 23225-5611, (804)276-0011 [23664]

Fenders and More Inc., PO Box 2088, Brentwood, TN 37024-2088, (615)373-2050 [2610]

Fenton Brothers Electrical, 235 Ray Ave. NE, PO Box 996, New Philadelphia, OH 44663, (330)343-8858 [8736]

F.E.P. Inc., 5405 Boran Pl., Tampa, FL 33610, (813)621-6085 [3747]

Feralloy Corp., 8755 W Higgins Rd., Chicago, IL 60631, (312)380-1500 [19969]

Feralloy Corp. Birmingham Div., 1435 Red Hat Rd., Decatur, AL 35601-7588, (205)252-5605 [19970]

Feralloy Corp. Midwest Div., 12550 Stony Island Ave., Chicago, IL 60633, (773)646-4900 [19971]

Feralloy Corp./Western Div, 936 Performance Dr., Stockton, CA 95206, (209)234-0548 [19972]

Feralloy Processing Co, 6600 George Nelson Dr., Portage, IN 46368, (219)787-8773 [19973]

Ference Cheese Inc., 174 Weaverville Rd., No. A, Asheville, NC 28804, (828)658-3101 [11118]

Ferer and Sons Co.; Aaron, 909 Abbott Dr., Omaha, NE 68102, (402)342-2436 [19974]

Ferguson Cattle Co. Inc., PO Box 3286, Bozeman, MT 59772-3286, (406)586-1648 [17916]

Ferguson Electric Construction Company Inc., 333 Ellicott St., Buffalo, NY 14203, (716)852-2010 [8737]

Ferguson Enterprises, 4505 Triangle St., Mc Farland, WI 53558, (608)257-3755 [23162]

Ferguson Enterprises Inc., 6525 E 42nd St., Tulsa, OK 74145-4611, (918)628-1500 [14444]

Ferguson Enterprises, Inc., PO Box 2778, Newport News, VA 23609-0778, (757)874-7795 [14445]

Ferguson Enterprises Inc., 2700-A Yonkers Rd., Raleigh, NC 27604, (919)828-7300 [23163]

Ferguson Enterprises Inc., 250 Long Rd., King of Prussia, PA 19406-3099, (215)354-0575 [14446]

Ferguson Enterprises Inc., PO Box 2778, Newport News, VA 23609-0778, (804)874-7795 [23164]

Ferguson Manufacturing and Equipment Co., 4900 Harry Hines Blvd., Dallas, TX 75235, (214)631-3000 [7335]

Ferguson Metals, Inc., 3475 Symmes Rd., Hamilton, OH 45015, (513)860-6500 [19975]

Ferguson Steel Co., 2935 Howard St., Port Huron, MI 48060, (810)985-5178 [19976]

Ferguson Supply Co., 345 Pleasant St. SW, Grand Rapids, MI 49503, (616)456-1688 [23165]

Ferguson Tire Service Inc., 1139 Main St., Weirton, WV 26062, (304)748-5260 [2611]

Ferman Fabrics Centers, 43 W Hollis St., Nashua, NH 03060-3338, (603)889-0069 [26033]

Fermone Corporation Inc., 113 S 47th Ave., Phoenix, AZ 85043, (602)233-9047 [1358]

Ferodo America, 1 Grizzly Ln., Smithville, TN 37166-9979, (615)597-6700 [2612]

Ferranti Steel and Aluminum Inc., 722 Frelinghuysen Ave., Newark, NJ 07114, (973)824-8496 [19977]

Ferrara Food and Confections Inc., 195 Grand St., New York, NY 10013, (212)226-6150 [11119]

Ferrara Pan Candy Co., 7301 W Harrison St., Forest Park, IL 60130, (708)366-0500 [11120]

Ferrari North America Inc., 250 Sylvan Ave., Englewood Cliffs, NJ 07632, (201)816-2600 [2613]

Ferrellgas Partners L.P., 1 Liberty Plz., Liberty, MO 64068, (816)792-1600 [22274]

Ferrera and Sons Inc.; James, 135 Will Dr., Canton, MA 02021, (617)828-6150 [11121]

Ferrex International, Inc., 26 Broadway, 26th Fl., New York, NY 10004, (212)509-7030 [7336]

Ferriday Farm Equipment Company Inc., PO Box 712, Ferriday, LA 71334, (318)757-4576 [679]

Ferrin Cooperative Equity Exchange, 12805 Ferrin Rd., Carlyle, IL 62231, (618)226-3275 [680]

Ferro Co.; Michael, RR 1, Box 301, South Royalton, VT 05068-0301, (802)763-8575 [21002]

Ferro Foods Corp., 25 53rd St., Brooklyn, NY 11232, (718)492-0793 [11122]

Ferro Union Inc., 1000 W Francisco St., Torrance, CA 90502, (310)538-9900 [19978]

Fertility Technologies Inc., 313 Speen St., Natick, MA 01760, (508)653-3900 [18796]

Fertilizer by Shut-Gro, PO Box 97, Minnesota City, MN 55959, (507)689-2131 [371]

FES, PO Box 2306, York, PA 17405, (717)767-6411 [24116]

Fessenden Cooperative Association, PO Box 126, Fessenden, ND 58438, (701)547-3291 [17917]

Fessenden Hall Inc., 1050 Sherman Ave., Pennsauken, NJ 08110, (609)665-2210 [7337]

Fetco International Corp., PO Box 165, Randolph, MA 02368-0165, (617)871-2000 [13357]

Fetzer Company-Restaurateurs, 209 E Main St., Louisville, KY 40202, (502)583-2744 [24117]

Fetzer Vineyards, 4040 Civic Center Dr.Ste. 525, San Rafael, CA 94903, (415)444-7400 [1688]

Fewkes and Co.; Joseph T., 6 Springdale Rd., Cherry Hill, NJ 08003, (609)424-3932 [8738]

Fey Inc., 108 W Main, Ashley, ND 58413, (701)288-3471 [681]

FFP Operating Partners L.P., 2801 Glenda Ave., Ft. Worth, TX 76117-4391, (817)838-4700 [22275]

FFP Partners L.P., 2801 Glenda Ave., Ft. Worth, TX 76117-4391, (817)838-4700 [22276]

FFR Inc., 28900 Fountain Pkwy., Cleveland, OH 44139, (440)505-6919 [25649]

FGH Systems Inc., 2 Richwood Pl., Denville, NJ 07834, (973)625-8114 [16007]

FHC, 4711 N Lamon, Chicago, IL 60630-3896, (773)777-6100 [13113]

Fiamm Technologies, Cadillac, MI 49601, (616)775-1373 [2614]

Fiatallis North America Inc., 245 E North Ave., Carol Stream, IL 60188, (630)260-4000 [7338]

Fiber Glass West, 4604 Alawai Rd., No. 8, Waimea, HI 96796, (808)338-1162 [18502]

Fiber Optic Center Inc., 23 Center St., New Bedford, MA 02740-6322, (508)992-6464 [5612]

Fiberchem, Inc., 1415 Spar Ave., Anchorage, AK 99501, (907)274-5505 [7870]

Fiberglass Hawaii, Inc., 1377 Colburn St., Honolulu, HI 96817, (808)847-3951 [22961]

Fiberglass Representatives Inc., PO Box 1109, Antioch, CA 94509, (510)778-2200 [23166]

Fiberlay Inc., 2419 NW Market St., Seattle, WA 98107, (206)782-0660 [7339]

Fibertron Corp., 6400 Artesia Blvd., Buena Park, CA 90620, (714)670-7711 [5613]

Fibredyne Inc., 47 Crosby Rd., Dover, NH 03820, (603)749-1610 [23167]

Fibres International Inc., 1533 120th Ave. NE, Bellevue, WA 98005-2131, (206)762-8520 [26813]

FIC Corp., 12216 Parklawn Dr., Rockville, MD 20852, (301)881-8124 [8739]

FIC International Corp., 556 Commercial St., San Francisco, CA 94111, (510)463-1073 [22962]

Fidelity Paper Supply Inc., 901 Murray Rd., East Hanover, NJ 07936-2200, (973)748-3475 [21725]

Fidelity Sportswear Co., 167 Bow St., Everett, MA 02149, (617)389-7007 [4950]

Fidus Instrument Corp., 7400 Whitepine Rd., Richmond, VA 23237-2219, (804)275-1431 [8740]

Fiebiger and Son Inc.; Jim, 20909 Miami-Shelby Rd., Conover, OH 45317, (937)368-3880 [682]

Fiedler; John W., N5612 N Wall St., Spokane, WA 99205-6436, (509)487-7466 [15127]

Field and Associates Inc., 269 SE 5th Ave., Delray Beach, FL 33483, (561)278-0545 [17414]

Field Oil Inc., 136 W Rushton St., Ogden, UT 84401, (801)394-5551 [22277]

Field Tool Supply Co., 2358 N Seeley Ave., Chicago, IL 60647, (312)541-6500 [16008]

Fieldbrook Farms Inc., 1 Ice Cream Dr., Dunkirk, NY 14048, (716)366-5400 [11123]

Fieldcrest Fertilizer Inc., Rte. 3, Box 1-C, Madison, MN 56256, (612)598-7567 [683]

Fields and Co.; J.D., PO Box 218424, Houston, TX 77218, (281)558-7199 [7340]

Fields and Company of Lubbock Inc., 1610 5th St., Lubbock, TX 79408, (806)762-0241 [23168]

Fields Equipment Company Inc., PO Box 113, Winter Haven, FL 33880, (813)967-0602 [684]

Fiesta Book Co., PO Box 490641, Key Biscayne, FL 33149, (305)858-4843 [3748]

Fiesta Foods, 2570 Kiel Way, North Las Vegas, NV 89030-4153, (702)735-2198 [11124]

Fife Electric Co., 42860 9 Mile Rd., PO Box 8021, Novi, MI 48376-8021, (248)344-4100 [8741]

Figueroa International Inc., 239 N Causeway Blvd., Metairie, LA 70001-5452, (504)831-0037 [11125]

Fiji Wear Inc., 72 Suttle St., Durango, CO 81301-7978, (970)247-5581 [4951]

Filbert Corp., PO Box 161909, Altamonte Springs, FL 32716-1909, (407)862-1011 [24118]

Filbert Refrigeration, PO Box 161909, Altamonte Springs, FL 32716-1909, (407)862-1011 [24118]

Filco Inc., 1433 Fulton Ave., Sacramento, CA 95822, (916)739-6021 [15128]

File TEC, 7480 Lemhi, Boise, ID 83709, (208)377-5522 [6269]

Fillauer Inc., PO Box 5189, 2710 Amnicola Hwy., Chattanooga, TN 37406-0189, (423)624-0946 [18797]

Film Technologies International, Inc., 2544 Terminal Dr. S, St. Petersburg, FL 33712, (727)327-2544 [22853]

Filtemp Sales, Inc., PO Box 15860, Phoenix, AZ 85060, (602)243-4245 [16860]

Filter Fresh of Northern Virginia Inc., PO Box 3284, Merrifield, VA 22116, (703)207-9033 [15496]

Filter Supply Co., 1210 N Knollwood Cir., Anaheim, CA 92801, (714)527-8221 [2615]

Filtran Div., PO Box 328, Des Plaines, IL 60016, (708)635-6670 [2616]

Filtrex Inc., 1945 Alpine Way, Hayward, CA 94545, (510)783-3700 [25650]

Filut & Associates Inc.; R.J., 667 Old Shakopee Rd., Ste. 105, Minneapolis, MN 55438-5815, (612)942-6576 [23665]

Financial Commercial Security, 3655 Walnut St., Denver, CO 80205, (303)295-1066 [24539]

Finch-Brown Company Inc., PO Box 915, Boise, ID 83701-0915, (208)342-9345 [21003]

Finchers Findings Inc., PO Box 289, Medicine Lodge, KS 67104-0289, (316)886-5952 [4952]

Findley Welding Supply Inc., 1326 E 12th St., Erie, PA 16503, (814)456-5311 [16861]

Fine Associates, 1 Farragut Sq. S, Washington, DC 20006, (202)628-2610 [3749]

Fine Distributing Inc., 3225 Meridian Pkwy., Ft. Lauderdale, FL 33331-3503, (954)384-8005 [11126]

Fine-Line Products Inc., 738 10th Ave., PO Box 43, Grafton, WI 53024, (414)375-0000 [4953]

Fine Organics Corp., PO Box 2277, Clifton, NJ 07015, (973)472-6800 [16862]

Fine Wine Brokers Inc., 4621 N Lincoln Ave., Chicago, IL 60625, (773)989-8166 [1689]

Fine Wire Coil Company, 4130 E University Dr., Phoenix, AZ 85034, (602)437-9194 [8742]

Fineline Products, Inc., 1616 Grand Ave., Kansas City, MO 64108, (816)474-4593 [21004]

Fines Distributing Inc., 4000 Highlands Pkwy., Smyrna, GA 30082, (770)436-0411 [11127]

Finger Lakes Bottling Co., Wright Ave. Ext., Auburn, NY 13021, (315)253-6561 [1690]

Finger Lakes Livestock Exchange Inc., Rte. 5 & Rte. 20, Canandaigua, NY 14424, (716)394-1515 [17918]

Finger Office Furniture, 4001 Gulf Fwy., Houston, TX 77003, (713)225-1371 [13112]

Fingerle Lumber Co., PO Box 1167, Ann Arbor, MI 48106, (734)663-0581 [7341]

The Finishing Touch of KY, 109 A McArthur Ct., Nicholasville, KY 40356-9109, (859)885-4720 [17380]

FinishMaster Inc., 4259 40th St. SE, Kentwood, MI 49512, (616)949-7604 [2617]

Fink Baking Corp., 5-35 54th Ave., Long Island City, NY 11101, (718)392-8300 [11128]

Fink Brothers Inc., 1385 Broadway, New York, NY 10018, (212)921-5683 [4954]

Finn Distributing Co. Inc., PO Box 940, Wichita, KS 67201-0940, (316)265-1624 [15497]

Finnish National Distillers Inc., 30 Rockefeller Plz. 4300, New York, NY 10112, (212)757-4440 [1691]

Fiorano Design Center, 1400 Hempstead Turnpike, Elmont, NY 11003, (516)354-8453 [9889]

Fiorucci Foods USA Inc., 1800 Ruffin Mill Rd., Colonial Heights, VA 23834-5936, (804)520-7775 [11129]

Fircrest Pre-Fit Door Co., 3024 S Mullen St., Tacoma, WA 98409, (253)564-6921 [7342]

Fire Alarm Service Corp., 12226 Hazen Ave., Thonotosassa, FL 33592-9398, (813)986-5400 [24540]

Fire Appliance & Safety Co., Drawer 3648, Little Rock, AR 72203-3648, (501)455-2430 [24541]

Fire Boss of Louisiana Inc., 7905 Hwy. 90 W, New Iberia, LA 70560-7651, (318)365-6729 [24542]

Fire Brick Engineers Co., PO Box 341278, Milwaukee, WI 53234-1278, (414)383-6000 [7343]

Fire Command Company Inc., 475 Long Beach Blvd., Long Beach, NY 11561-2233, (516)889-1111 [24543]

Fire-Dex Inc., 780 S Progress Dr., Medina, OH 44256-1368, (330)723-0000 [25651]

Fire-Dex Inc., 780 S Progress Dr., Medina, OH 44256-1368, (330)723-0000 [4955]

Fire Equipment Inc., 88 Hicks Ave., Medford, MA 02155, (781)391-8050 [24544]

Fire Fighters Equipment Co., 3038 Lenox Ave., Jacksonville, FL 32254, (904)388-8542 [24545]

Fire Fighters Equipment Co., 3038 Lenox Ave., Jacksonville, FL 32254, (904)388-8542 [24119]

Fire Mountain Gems, 28195 Redwood Hwy., Cave Junction, OR 97523-9304, (541)592-2222 [17415]

Fire Spec Inc., PO Box 296, Raynham, MA 02767-0500, (508)279-0058 [24546]

Fire Systems Unlimited Inc., PO Box 190739, Hungry Horse, MT 59919-0739, (406)755-3473 [24547]

Fire-Tec Inc., 89 Prospect St., Manville, RI 02838-1013, (401)765-0213 [24548]

Fire Tech & Safety of Neng, PO Box 435, Winthrop, ME 04364-0435, (207)377-2800 [24549]

Firebird International, Inc., PO Box 751299, Petaluma, CA 94975, (707)769-9410 [7344]

Firecom Inc., 39-27 59th St., Woodside, NY 11377, (718)899-6100 [24550]

Fireman's Supply Inc., 6123 Airport Rd., Nampa, ID 83687-8567, (208)467-6729 [24551]

Fireplace Industries Inc., 4386 S Federal Blvd., Englewood, CO 80110-5311, (303)825-8600 [14447]

Fireside Distributors, 4013 Atlantic Ave., PO Box 41226, Raleigh, NC 27629-1226, (919)872-4434 [14448]

Fireside Distributors of Oregon, Inc., 18389 SW Boones Ferry Rd., Portland, OR 97224, (503)684-8535 [14449]

Fireside Office Products Inc., PO Box 2116, Bismarck, ND 58502-2116, (701)258-8586 [6270]

Firestone Plywood, 210 Miller Pl., Hicksville, NY 11801, (516)938-7007 [7345]

Firey Pet Supplies, 1065 W National, Unit 7, Sacramento, CA 95834, (916)928-7878 [27131]

First Aid Plus Inc., 4626 Illinois Ave., Louisville, KY 40213-1923, (502)499-9797 [18798]

First American Artificial Flowers Inc., Bradley Pkwy., Blauvelt, NY 10913, (914)353-0700 [14861]

First Automotive Inc., 103 S Dean, Bay City, MI 48706, (517)893-6521 [2618]

First Choice Food Distributors Inc., 6800 Snowden Rd., Ft. Worth, TX 76140, (817)551-5704 [11130]

First Choice Ingredients, 4208 San Saba Ct., Plano, TX 75074, (972)881-2794 [11131]

First Choice Tool Co., 1210 Progress St., PO Box 670, Sturgis, MI 49091, (616)651-7964 [13706]

First Class Business Systems Inc., PO Box 407, Seymour, IN 47274-2913, (812)522-3341 [6271]

First Coast Designs Inc., 7800 Bayberry Rd., Jacksonville, FL 32256-6815, (904)730-9496 [14862]

First Coast Pet Supply, 4549 St. Augustine Rd., No. 22, Jacksonville, FL 32207, (904)733-6400 [27132]

First Cooperative Association, 5057 Hwy. 3 W, Cherokee, IA 51012, (712)225-5400 [11132]

The First Delta Corporation, PO Box 188, Fairfield, CT 06430, (203)255-1969 [17817]

First Farmers Cooperative Elevator, PO Box 187, Cleghorn, IA 51014, (712)436-2224 [685]

First International Trading Company, 2231 South Pacific Ave., San Pedro, CA 90731, (310)514-8427 [16863]

First Line Marketing, Inc., 636 South Alaska, Seattle, WA 98108, (206)622-3335 [16864]

First National Trading Company Inc., 855 Avenue of the Americas, New York, NY 10016, (212)695-0610 [15498]

First Native American Corp., 7828 N 19th Ave., No. 11-12, Phoenix, AZ 85021-7029, (602)266-9889 [24744]

First Phillips Marketing Company Inc., 1 Acton Pl., Acton, MA 01720, (508)264-9034 [22963]

First Rep Associates, 16000 College Blvd., Lenexa, KS 66219, (913)599-3111 [25191]

First Service, Div. of Straightline Enterprises, Inc., 737 Southpoint Blvd., Ste. D, Petaluma, CA 94954 [23666]

First State Paper, Inc., 100 Paper Pl., New Castle, DE 19720, (302)656-6546 [21726]

First State Petroleum Services, RR 3 Box 156, Harrington, DE 19952, (302)398-9704 [22278]

First Supply Group, 6800 Gisholt Dr., Madison, WI 53708, (608)222-7799 [23169]

FirstMiss Fertilizer Inc., PO Box 1249, Jackson, MS 39215-1249, (601)948-7550 [686]

Fischer Inc.; Carl, 62 Cooper Sq., New York, NY 10003, (212)777-0900 [3750]

Fischer Lime and Cement Co., PO Box 18383, Memphis, TN 38181-0383, (901)363-4986 [7346]

Fiser Tractor and Equipment Co., 9700 Hwy. 5 N, Alexander, AR 72002, (501)847-3677 [687]

Fish Net Co., PO Box 462, Jonesville, LA 71343-0462, (318)339-9655 [23667]

Fisher Auto Parts, PO Box 148, Braceville, IL 60407, (815)237-2166 [2619]

Fisher Auto Parts Inc., 523 Edmunds, South Boston, VA 24592-3005, (804)572-3978 [2620]

Fisher Auto Parts Inc., 512 Greenville Ave., Staunton, VA 24401, (703)885-8905 [2621]

Fisher Auto Parts Inc. Manlove Div., PO Box 479, Seaford, DE 19973, (302)629-9185 [2622]

Fisher Auto Parts Professionals, 1830 SE 3rd Ave., Rochester, MN 55904-7922, (507)285-9976 [2623]

Fisher Bag Company Inc., 2301 S 200th St., Seattle, WA 98198-5571, (206)623-1966 [26034]

Fisher Brothers Steel Corp., PO Box 592, Englewood, NJ 07631, (201)567-2400 [19979]

Fisher Central Coast, 5949 S Eastern Ave., Los Angeles, CA 90040-4003, (805)962-5551 [11133]

Fisher Electric Motor Service, 2025 Wayne Haven St., Ft. Wayne, IN 46803, (219)493-0521 [2624]

Fisher Enterprises Inc., 2191 Hwy. 105, Boone, NC 28607-9210, (704)264-8827 [23668]

Fisher Farmers Grain and Coal Co., 1 Main St., Dewey, IL 61840, (217)897-1111 [17919]

Fisher Healthcare, 9999 Veterans Memorial Dr., Houston, TX 77038-2499, 800-640-0640 [24359]

Fisher Healthcare, 9999 Veterans Memorial Dr., Houston, TX 77038-2499 [19324]

Fisher Implement Co., PO Box 159, Albany, OR 97321, (541)926-1534 [688]

Fisher, Inc.; Marc J., 391 Broadway, 2nd Fl., New York, NY 10013-3510, (212)966-2534 [26035]

Fisher; Karen, 21 E Maple St., No. B, Hailey, ID 83333-8401, (208)788-4970 [4620]

Fisher Mills Inc., PO Box C-3765, Seattle, WA 98124, (206)622-4430 [11134]

Fisher Paper, PO Box 1720, Ft. Wayne, IN 46801, (219)747-7442 [21727]

Fisher Paper, PO Box 1720, Ft. Wayne, IN 46801, (219)747-7442 [21727]

Fisher Sand and Gravel Co., PO Box 1271, Midland, MI 48641-1271, (517)835-7187 [7347]

Fisher Scientific Co., 2000 Park Lane Dr., Pittsburgh, PA 15275-1126, (412)562-8300 [24360]

Fisher Scientific Co., 2000 Park Lane Dr., Pittsburgh, PA 15275, (412)490-8300 [19325]

Fisher Scientific International Inc., Liberty Ln., Hampton, NH 03842, (603)929-2650 [24552]

Fisher & Son Co. Inc., 237 E King St., Malvern, PA 19355, (215)644-3300 [689]

Fisher Steel and Supply Co., 259 Ottawa St., Muskegon, MI 49442-1008, (616)722-6081 [26814]

Fisheries Supply Co. Industrial Div., 1900 N Northlake Way, Seattle, WA 98103, (206)632-4462 [18503]

Fishermans Factory Outlet, 701 Dakota Ave., South Sioux City, NE 68776-2058, (402)494-6930 [23669]

Fisherman's Marine Supply, 901 N Columbia Blvd., Portland, OR 97217, (503)283-0044 [18504]

Fisher's Incorporated Painting Co., 2409 E 15th St., Cheyenne, WY 82001, (307)632-5096 [21441]

Fishery Products International, 18 Electronics Ave., Danvers, MA 01923, (978)777-2660 [11135]

Fishery Products International USA, 18 Electronics Ave., Danvers, MA 01923, (978)777-2660 [11136]

Fishing Hot Spots/FHS Maps, 2389 Air Park Rd., PO Box 1167, Rhinelander, WI 54501-1167, (715)365-5555 [3751]

Fit-All Sportswear Inc., 118 Fit-All Dr., PO Box 1428, Pilot Mountain, NC 27041, (336)368-2227 [4956]

Fitch Dustdown Co., 2201 Russell St., Baltimore, MD 21230-3198, (410)539-1953 [4621]

Fitch Dustdown Co., 2201 Russell St., Baltimore, MD 21230, (410)539-1953 [24120]

Fitch Industrial Welding Supply Inc., PO Box 2067, Lawton, OK 73501, (580)353-4950 [16865]

Fitchburg Hardware Company Inc., 692 N Main St., Leominster, MA 01453, (978)534-4956 [13707]

Fite Co.; Clifford D., PO Box 616, Cedartown, GA 30125, (770)748-5315 [11137]

Fite; Ted G., 6 Ardmore Mall, Ardmore, OK 73401-4363, (580)223-5820 [25652]

Fitness Corporation of America, PO Box 300, Linthicum Heights, MD 21090-0300, (410)859-3538 [23670]

Fitness Expo Inc., 4124 Vetarnes, Metairie, LA 70006, (504)887-0880 [23671]

Fitness Plus II, PO Box 3641, Bozeman, MT 59772, (406)585-9204 [11138]

Fitness Shop, 12012 SW Canyon Rd., Beaverton, OR 97005-2150, (503)641-8892 [23672]

Fitness Systems Inc., 7101 Sharondale Ct., PO Box 1544, Brentwood, TN 37024-1544, (615)661-5858 [23673]

Fitness Systems Inc., 5566 N Academy Blvd., Colorado Springs, CO 80918-3682, (719)594-6969 [23674]

Fitz Chem Corp., 757 Larch Ave., Elmhurst, IL 60126, (708)941-0410 [4389]

Fitzgerald Inc.; Albert F., 120 Commerce Way, Woburn, MA 01801, (781)935-7821 [9890]

Fitzgerald Ltd., 331 NE Mcwilliams Ct, Bremerton, WA 98311-2506, (360)792-1550 [690]

Fitzpatrick Electric Supply Co., PO Box 657, Muskegon, MI 49443-0657, (616)722-6621 [8743]

Fitzpatrick and Weller Inc., PO Box 490, Ellicottville, NY 14731, (716)699-2393 [7348]

Five Continent Enterprise Inc., PMB 4022, 5000 Birch St., Ste. 4000 W Tower, Newport Beach, CA 92660, (949)476-3649 [14101]

Five County Farmers Association, PO Box 758, Clarksdale, MS 38614, (601)627-7301 [691]

Five Foreign Auto Salvage, 601 Haines Ave. NW, Albuquerque, NM 87102-1225, (505)247-2227 [2625]

Five H Island Foods Inc., PO Box 19160, Honolulu, HI 96817, (808)848-2067 [11139]

Five JS Auto Parts Inc., 5404 Broadway Blvd. SE, Albuquerque, NM 87105-7422, (505)877-6270 [2626]

Five Star Trading Company, PO Box 11451, Bainbridge Island, WA 98110-5451, (206)842-6542 [13708]

Fixture Hardware Co., 4711 N Lamon, Chicago, IL 60630-3896, (773)777-6100 [13113]

Fixture-World, Inc., 1555 Interstate Dr., Cookeville, TN 38501, (931)528-7259 [24121]

Flack International, Inc.; Henry, PO Box 865110, Plano, TX 75086-5110, (972)867-5677 [4622]

Flagg Co.; R.M., PO Box 617, Bangor, ME 04401-0617, (207)945-9463 [24122]

Flaherty Company Inc.; L.H., 1577 Jefferson Ave. S, PO Box 7409, Grand Rapids, MI 49510, (616)245-9266 [2627]

Flame Spray Inc., PO Box 600510, San Diego, CA 92160, (619)283-2007 [4390]

Flamemaster Corp., PO Box 1458, Sun Valley, CA 91353, (818)982-1650 [21442]

Flanigan Farms, PO Box 347, Culver City, CA 90232, (310)836-8437 [11140]

Flannery Co., 13123 Aerospace Dr., Victorville, CA 92394 [3752]

Flash Clinic Inc., 9 E 19th St., 10th Fl., New York, NY 10003, (212)673-4030 [8744]

Flash Fireworks, RR 2, Box 102, St. Francis, KS 67756-9543, (785)734-2464 [26482]

Flask Chemical Corp., 13226 Nelson Ave., La Puente, CA 91746-1514, (626)336-6690 [4391]

Flato Electric Supply Co., PO Box 9317, Corpus Christi, TX 78469, (512)884-4555 [8745]

Flav-O-Rich Inc., 316 North 4th St., Campbellsville, KY 42718, (502)465-8119 [11141]

Flavtek Inc., 1960 Hawkins Cir., Los Angeles, CA 90001, (323)588-5880 [11142]

Flay-O-Rich Inc., 2537 Catherine St., Bristol, VA 24201, (540)669-5161 [11143]

F.L.D. Distributors Inc., 1 W 6th St., Medford, OR 97501-2704, (541)779-9491 [1692]

F.L.D./Empire Beverages, 1 W 6th St., Medford, OR 97501-2704, (541)779-9491 [1692]

Fleck Bearing, 3226 Blair Ave., St. Louis, MO 63107, (314)421-0919 [2976]

Fleet Distribution, Inc., 2696 Briarlake Rd. NE, PO Box 98074, Atlanta, GA 30329, (404)325-9214 [6272]

Fleet Parts Distributor, 1630 S Dupont Hwy., Dover, DE 19901, (302)674-5911 [2628]

Fleet Pride, 520 Lake Cook Rd., Bradley, IL 60915, (847)444-1095 [2629]

FLEET Specialties Co., PO Box 4575, Thousand Oaks, CA 91359, (818)340-8181 [8746]

Fleet Specialties Div., PO Box 4575, Thousand Oaks, CA 91359, (818)889-1716 [2630]

Fleet Wholesale, PO Box 971, Brainerd, MN 56401, (218)829-3521 [11144]

Fleetwood Paper Co., 2222 Windsor Ct., Addison, IL 60101, (630)268-9999 [21728]

Fleischli Oil Company Inc., PO Box 487, Cheyenne, WY 82003, (307)634-4466 [22279]

Fleischli Oil Company Inc., PO Box 158, Rock Springs, WY 82902, (307)362-6611 [22280]

Fleischli Oil Company Inc., PO Box 50097, Casper, WY 82605, (307)265-3300 [22281]

Fleischman Carpet Co., 19655 Grand River, Detroit, MI 48223, (313)534-9300 [9891]

Fleming, 91-315 Hanua St., Kapolei, HI 96707-1799, (808)682-7300 [11145]

Fleming Associates Inc.; J.S., 28 Lord Rd., Marlborough, MA 01752-4548, (508)460-0904 [14450]

Fleming Companies, Inc., 1700 South Laemie Ave., PO Box 490, Marshfield, WI 54449, (715)384-3191 [11146]

Fleming Companies, Inc., PO Box 1149, Superior, WI 54880, (715)392-8880 [11147]

Fleming Companies Inc., PO Box 26647, Oklahoma City, OK 73126-0647, (405)840-7200 [11148]

Fleming Companies Inc. Garland Div., PO Box 469012, Garland, TX 75046-9012, (972)840-4400 [11149]

Fleming Companies Inc. Heartland Div., PO Box 419796, Kansas City, MO 64141, (816)221-9200 [11150]

Fleming Companies Inc. Oklahoma City Div., 10 E Memorial Rd., Oklahoma City, OK 73114, (405)755-2420 [11151]

Fleming Companies Inc. Philadelphia Div., PO Box 935, Oaks, PA 19456, (215)935-5000 [11152]

Fleming Co.; T.J., 647 Southwest Blvd., Kansas City, KS 66103, (913)236-9000 [16866]

Fleming Foods, 1015 W Magnolia, Geneva, AL 36340, (205)684-3631 [11153]

Fleming Foods of Alabama Inc., PO Box 398, Geneva, AL 36340, (334)684-3631 [11154]

Fleming Foods of Ohio Inc., PO Box 207, Massillon, OH 44648, (216)879-5681 [11155]

Fleming Foods of Tennessee Inc., PO Box 448, Goodlettsville, TN 37070-0448 [11156]

Fleming Foodservice, PO Box 66, Cornelia, GA 30531, (706)778-2256 [11157]

Fleming/Gateway, 3501 Marshall St. NE, Minneapolis, MN 55418, (612)781-8051 [11158]

Fleming Sales Company Inc., 1020 W Fullerton Ave., Ste. B, Addison, IL 60101-4335, (630)627-4444 [692]

Flemington Block and Supply Inc., Hwy. 31, Flemington, NJ 08822, (908)782-2021 [7349]

Flemming and Associates Inc.; Tom, 10273 Yellow Circle Dr., Minnetonka, MN 55343, (612)933-2263 [11159]

The Fletcher-Terry Company, 225 Riverview Ave., Waltham, MA 02454, (781)647-5560 [13709]

Fleur de Paris, 5835 Washington Blvd., Culver City, CA 90232, (213)857-0704 [26036]

Fleurette California, 336 S Anderson St., Los Angeles, CA 90033, (213)269-5600 [4957]

Flex-a-Lite Consolidated, PO Box 580, Milton, WA 98354, (253)922-2700 [2631]

Flex-Foot Inc., 27412 Laguna Hills Dr., No. A, Aliso Viejo, CA 92656, (714)362-3883 [18799]

Flexbar Machine Corp., 250 Gibbs Rd., Central Islip, NY 11722-2612, (516)582-8440 [16009]

Flexi-Wall Systems, PO Box 89, Liberty, SC 29657, (864)843-3104 [15499]

Flexible Feat Sandals, 2344 County Rd. 225, Durango, CO 81301-7034, (970)247-4628 [24745]

Flexible Feat Sandals, 2344 County Rd. 225, Durango, CO 81301-7034, (970)247-4628 [4958]

Flexible Flyer Co., PO Box 1296, West Point, MS 39773, (601)494-4732 [26483]

Flexo-Printing Equipment Corp., 416 Hayward Ave. N, Oakdale, MN 55128, (651)731-9499 [25653]

Flexo-Printing Equipment Corp., 1298 Helmo Ave. N, Oakdale, MN 55128, (612)731-9499 [16010]

Flexstik Adheso Graphics, 625 Main St., Westbury, NY 11590, (516)333-3666 [6]

Flickinger Co., 3200 Bayshore Rd., Unit 3, Benicia, CA 94510, (707)747-9095 [16867]

Flight Deck U.S.A., 469 7th Ave., 10th Fl., New York, NY 10018, (212)695-1620 [5380]

Flight Products International, PO Box 1558, Kalispell, MT 59903-1558, (406)752-8783 [88]

Flihan Co.; Joseph, PO Box 4039, Utica, NY 13504, (315)452-5886 [24123]

Flinn Scientific, Inc., PO Box 219, Batavia, IL 60510-0219, (630)879-6962 [24361]

Flintex Marketing, Inc., 16420 Park Ten Pl., Ste. 540, Houston, TX 77084-5052, (281)578-0529 [22282]

Flirt Corp/Belldini, 1428 Maple Ave., Los Angeles, CA 90015-2526, (213)748-4442 [4959]

Flite Service, 9655 E 25th Ave., Unit 107, Aurora, CO 80010-1056, (303)363-6336 [11160]

Flitz International Ltd., 821 Mohr Ave., Waterford, WI 53185, (414)534-5898 [22283]

Flo-Pac Corp., 700 N Washington Ave., No. 400, Minneapolis, MN 55401, (612)332-6240 [4623]

Flo-Pac Pacific Div., 11690 Pacific Ave., Fontana, CA 92335-6960, (909)681-3747 [15500]

Flo-Products Co., 2305 Millpark Rd., Maryland Heights, MO 63043, (314)428-4000 [16868]

Floor Service Supply, 5860 88th St., Sacramento, CA 95828, (916)381-5034 [9892]

Floor Service Supply, 861 Auzerias Ave., San Jose, CA 95126, (408)280-0222 [9893]

Floor Supply Co., 1620 Spectrum Dr., Lawrenceville, GA 30043-5742, (404)513-1132 [9894]

Floor Supply Distributing Inc., PO BOX 3005, Spokane, WA 99220, (509)535-9707 [9895]

Flooring Distributors Inc., 3209 6th Ave. SW, Huntsville, AL 35805-3641, (205)536-3384 [9896]

Flooring Distributors Inc., 1100 Louisiana St., Ste. 5400, Houston, TX 77002-5218 [9897]

Floors, Inc., 108 N 28th St., Birmingham, AL 35203, (205)251-1733 [9898]

Floors, Inc., 981 Corporate Dr., S, Mobile, AL 36607, (205)471-4677 [9899]

Floors Northwest, 5515 E River Rd., No. 414, Minneapolis, MN 55421, (763)586-7070 [9900]

Floors Northwest Inc., 5515 E River Rd., No. 414, Minneapolis, MN 55421, (763)586-7070 [9900]

Flora-Dec Saes, Inc., 373 N Nimitz Hwy., Honolulu, HI 96817-5027, (808)537-6194 [14863]

Floral Acres Inc., PO Box 540939, Lake Worth, FL 33454-0939 [14864]

Floralife Inc., 120 Tower Dr., Burr Ridge, IL 60521, (630)325-8587 [14865]

Florence Turfgrass; Paul, 13600 Watkins Rd., Marysville, OH 43040, (937)642-7487 [14866]

Florexotica Hawaii, 826A Queen St., Honolulu, HI 96813, (808)842-5166 [14867]

Floribbean Wholesale Inc., 5151 NW 17th St., Margate, FL 33063, (954)968-4091 [11161]

Florida Bearings Inc., 3164 N Miami Ave., Miami, FL 33127, (305)573-8424 [16869]

Florida Bolt and Nut Co., 3875 Fiscal Ct., Riviera Beach, FL 33404, (561)842-2658 [13710]

Florida Bolt and Nut Co., 3875 Fiscal Ct., Riviera Beach, FL 33404, (561)842-2658 [13711]

Florida Classics Library, PO Drawer 1657, Port Salerno, FL 34992-1657, (561)546-9380 [3753]

Florida Clock & Supplies Inc., 9706 SE Hwy. 441, Belleview, FL 34420, (352)245-6524 [15501]

Florida Craft Wholesale, PO Box 3026, Weaverville, CA 96093-3026, (530)845-1822 [26484]

Florida Detroit Diesel-Allison North Inc., 5105 Bowden Rd., Jacksonville, FL 32216, (904)737-7330 [2632]

Florida Extruders International Inc., 2540 Jewett Ln., Sanford, FL 32771-1600, (407)323-3300 [19980]

Florida Hardware Co., 436 Cassat Ave., Jacksonville, FL 32254, (904)783-1650 [13712]

Florida Hardwood Floor Supply, 8506 Sunstate St., Tampa, FL 33634, (813)887-3064 [9901]

The Florida News Group, Ltd., PO Box 20209, West Palm Beach, FL 33416, (561)547-3000 [3754]

Florida Protective Coatings Consultants Inc., 250 Waymont Ct., Ste. 120, Lake Mary, FL 32746-6024, (407)322-1243 [21443]

Florida Seed Company Inc., 4725 Lakeland Commerce Pkwy., Lakeland, FL 33805, (863)669-1333 [693]

Florida Tile, 7029 Huntley Rd., Columbus, OH 43085, (614)436-2511 [9902]

Florie Corporation Turf Irrigation and Water Works Supply, 16012 N 32nd St., Phoenix, AZ 85032, (602)867-2040 [694]

Florig Equipment, 35 Industrial Pkwy., Woburn, MA 01801, (781)935-6462 [16011]

Florig Equipment, 775 Marconi Ave., Ronkonkoma, NY 11779, (516)467-2200 [16012]

Florig Equipment, 1611 Integrity Dr. E, Columbus, OH 43209, (614)443-5950 [8747]

Florig Equipment, 906 Ridge Pike, Conshohocken, PA 19428, (215)825-0900 [16013]

Florig Equipment, 113 Lyle Ln., Nashville, TN 37210, (615)242-2554 [16014]

Florig Equipment, 3202 Lanvale Ave., Richmond, VA 23230, (804)353-9966 [2633]

Florig Equipment of Buffalo, Inc., 188 Creekside Dr., Amherst, NY 14228, (716)691-9000 [16015]

Florig Equipment of Portland, Inc., 27 Washington Ave., Scarborough, ME 04074, (207)883-9751 [16016]

Florimex Inc., PO Box 260277, Tampa, FL 33685, (813)886-0470 [11162]

Florimex Worldwide Inc., 512 Bridge St., Danville, VA 24541, (804)792-7511 [14868]

Flotec-Town and Country, 293 Wright St., Delavan, WI 53115, (414)728-1543 [23170]

Flower Factory, 5655 Whipple Ave. NW, North Canton, OH 44720, (216)494-7978 [21005]

Flower Films & Video, 10341 San Pablo Ave., El Cerrito, CA 94530, (510)525-0942 [25192]

Flower Films and Video; 10341 San Pablo Ave., El Cerrito, CA 94530, (510)525-0942 [15129]

Flower Warehouse, 1308 Loagan, Costa Mesa, CA 92626, (714)545-0310 [14869]

Flowers Auto Parts Co., PO Box 1118, Hickory, NC 28603, (828)345-2133 [2634]

Flowers Industries Inc., PO Box 1338, Thomasville, GA 31799-1338, (912)226-9110 [11163]

Flowers School Equipment Company Inc., PO Box 70039, Richmond, VA 23255-0039, (804)288-8291 [13114]

Flower's Shellfish Distributors, 5 Carr Pl., Bayville, NY 11709, (516)628-1263 [11164]

Flowmatic Systems, 11611 SW 147th Ct., PO Box 1139, Dunnellon, FL 34432, (352)465-2000 [16017]

Flue-Cured Tobacco Cooperative Stabilization Corp., PO Box 12300, Raleigh, NC 27605, (919)821-4560 [26293]

Fluid-Air Components L.L.C., PO Box 55848, Portland, OR 97238, (503)254-9292 [16870]

Fluid-Dynamic Midwest Inc., 229 Wrightwood Ave., Elmhurst, IL 60126, (630)530-5500 [16018]

Fluid Engineering Inc., 2227 S Mission Rd., Tucson, AZ 85713, (520)623-9942 [5840]

Fluid-O-Tech International, Inc., 161 Atwater St., Plantsville, CT 06479, (860)620-0393 [23171]

Fluid Power Equipment, PO Box 1287, Mills, WY 82644, (307)472-6000 [16019]

Fluid Power Inc., 10451 Mill Run Circle, Ste. 40-D, Owings Mills, MD 21117, (410)646-1545 [16020]

Fluid Power Inc., 534 Township Line Rd., Blue Bell, PA 19422, (215)643-0350 [16021]

Fluid Power Inc., 135 Burgs Ln., York, PA 17406, (717)252-1535 [16022]

Fluid-Tech, Inc., 1226 Trapper Cir. NW, Roanoke, VA 24012-1138, (910)765-3955 [16023]

Flury & Co. Ltd., 322 1st Ave. S, Seattle, WA 98104-2506, (206)587-0260 [13358]

Flusche Supply Inc., Hwy. 25 S, Electra, TX 76360, (940)495-2166 [695]

Flute, 1500 S Western Ave., Chicago, IL 60608, (312)738-0622 [15664]

Fly Guard Systems Inc., PO Box 805, Sweet Home, OR 97386-0805, (541)367-1600 [4392]

Flying J Inc., PO Box 678, Brigham City, UT 84302, (435)734-6400 [22284]

Flying J Travel Plaza, 1920 Harrison Dr., Evanston, WY 82930, (307)789-9129 [22285]

Flying Phoenix Corp., PO Box 31, Riverton, WY 82501-0031, (307)856-0778 [9634]

Flying Phoenix Corp., PO Box 31, Riverton, WY 82501-0031, (307)856-0778 [26485]

Flynt Distribution Company Inc., 9171 Wilshire Blvd., No. 300, Beverly Hills, CA 90210, (310)858-7100 [3755]

Flytech Technology (USA) Inc., 1931 Hartog Dr., San Jose, CA 95131, (408)573-9113 [6273]

FM Systems, Inc., 3877 S Main St., Santa Ana, CA 92707, (714)979-3355 [5614]

Fmali Inc., 831 Almar Ave., Santa Cruz, CA 95060 [11165]

FMC Resource Management Corp., 14640 172nd Dr.SE, Monroe, WA 98272, (360)794-3157 [21006]

FMH Material Handling Solutions, Inc., 1054 Hawkins Blvd., El Paso, TX 79915, (915)778-8368 [16024]

FMH Material Handling Solutions, Inc., 4105 Globeville Rd., Denver, CO 80216, (303)292-5438 [16025]

FMI Hydrocarbon Co., 1615 Poydras St., New Orleans, LA 70112, (504)582-4899 [22286]

FMS Corp., 12637 Beatrice St., Los Angeles, CA 90066, (310)306-2800 [2919]

Foam Factory and Upholstery Inc., 7777 Sixteen Mile Rd., Sterling Heights, MI 48312, (810)795-3626 [22964]

Foam Products of San Antonio Inc., 1119 N Mesquite, San Antonio, TX 78202-1120, (210)228-0033 [22965]

Focus Carpet Corp., PO Box 608, Chatsworth, GA 30705, (706)695-5942 [9903]

Foehrkolb Inc.; Louis, 7901 Oceano Ave., Jessup, MD 20794, (410)799-4260 [11166]

Foell Packing Co., 3117 W 47th St., Chicago, IL 60632, (773)523-5220 [11167]

FOF Inc., 471 N Curtis Rd., Boise, ID 83706, (208)377-0024 [22287]

Foge Jensen Imports, PO Box 727, Napa, CA 94559-0727, (707)226-9123 [15502]

Folcomer Equipment Corporation, PO Box 340, Aberdeen, MD 21001, (410)575-6580 [7350]

Fold-A-Way Corporation, 307 New Venture Dr., Louisville, KY 40214, (502)366-2927 [7351]

Foldberger Foods Inc., 2815 Blaisdell Ave. S, Minneapolis, MN 55408, (612)872-6262 [11260]

Foley-Belsaw Co., 6301 Equitable Rd., Kansas City, MO 64120, (816)483-6400 [13713]

Foley Company Inc.; M.F., PO Box 3093, New Bedford, MA 02740, (508)997-0773 [11168]

Foley Equipment Co., 1550 S West St., Wichita, KS 67213, (316)943-4211 [696]

Foley Equipment Company Inc., 1550 S West St., Wichita, KS 67213, (316)943-4211 [7352]

Foley Holding Co., 3506 W Harry St., Wichita, KS 67213, (316)943-4237 [16026]

Foley Tractor Company Inc., 1550 S West St., Wichita, KS 67213, (316)943-4211 [696]

Foley Tractor Company Inc., 1550 S West St., Wichita, KS 67213, (316)943-4211 [7352]

Folkcraft Instruments, High & Wheeler Sts., PO Box 807, Winsted, CT 06098, (860)379-9857 [25193]

Folkcraft Instruments, High and Wheeler Sts., Winsted, CT 06098, (860)379-9857 [15130]

Follett Campus Resources, 2211 N West St., River Grove, IL 60171-1800, (708)583-2000 [3756]

Follett Corp., 2233 West St., River Grove, IL 60171-1895, (708)583-2000 [3757]

Follett Library Book Co., 1340 Ridgeview Dr., McHenry, IL 60050, (815)759-1700 [3758]

Follett Library Resources, 1340 Ridgeview Dr., McHenry, IL 60050, (815)455-1100 [3759]

Folloder Co., PO Box 19975, Houston, TX 77224-1975, (713)932-7171 [11169]

Follum Supply, 1880 E Centre St., Rapid City, SD 57701-4072, (605)343-3507 [4624]

Folsom Corp., 43 McKee Dr., Mahwah, NJ 07430, (201)529-3550 [23675]

Foltz Manufacturing and Supply Co., 65 E Washington St., Hagerstown, MD 21740, (301)739-1076 [13714]

Fones West, PO Box 6741, Denver, CO 80206, (303)393-7260 [5615]

Fontaine Fifth Wheel Co., 171 Cleage Dr., Birmingham, AL 35217, (205)856-1100 [2635]

Fontaine Industries Inc., 1500 Urban Ctr. Dr., No. 400, Birmingham, AL 35242-2566, (205)969-1119 [7353]

Fontaine Modification Co., 5325 Prosperity Dr., Springfield, OH 45502, (937)399-3319 [2636]

Fontana & Fontana Inc., PO Box 99, Indian Trail, NC 28079-0099, (704)882-1112 [4960]

FontHaus Inc., 1375 Kings Hwy., Ste. E, Fairfield, CT 06430, (203)367-1993 [6223]

Food Concepts Inc., 6601 Lyons Rd., Ste. C-12, Coconut Creek, FL 33073, (954)420-0882 [11533]

Food Country USA, Deadmore, Abingdon, VA 24210, (540)628-2562 [11170]

Food Equipment Specialists, 8181 Commerce Pk., Ste. 708, Houston, TX 77036-7403, (713)988-8700 [24124]

Food For Health, 3655 W Washington St., Phoenix, AZ 85009, (602)269-2371 [14102]

Food For Life Baking Co., PO Box 1434, Corona, CA 92878, (909)279-5090 [11171]

Food Gems Ltd., 84 23 Rockaway Blvd., Ozone Park, NY 11417, (718)296-7788 [11172]

Food Ingredients and Additives Group, 620 Progress Ave., Waukesha, WI 53186, (414)547-5531 [4393]

Food Lion Inc., PO Box 1330, Salisbury, NC 28145-1330, (704)633-8250 [11173]

Food Marketing Corp., 4815 Executive Blvd., Ft. Wayne, IN 46808-1150, (219)483-2146 [11174]

Food Masters Inc., 300 W Broad St., PO Box 1565, Griffin, GA 30224, (404)521-0780 [11175]

Food Match, Inc., 180 Duane St., New York, NY 10013, (212)334-5044 [11176]

Food Products, 8125 E 88th Ave., Henderson, CO 80640-8121, (303)301-1226 [10989]

Food Service Action Inc., 675 Village Square Dr., Stone Mountain, GA 30083, (404)296-2700 [11177]

Food Services of America, 4101 15th Ave. NW, Fargo, ND 58102-2830, (701)282-8200 [11178]

Food Services of America, 802 Parkway Ln., Billings, MT 59101, (406)245-4181 [11179]

Food Services of America Inc., 4025 Delridge Way SW, Seattle, WA 98106, (206)933-5000 [11180]

Food and Spirits Distributing Company Inc., PO Box 363127, San Juan, PR 00936, (787)788-7070 [1693]

Foodsales Inc., 14 Spring Mill Dr., Malvern, PA 19355, (215)644-8900 [11181]

FoodSalesWest Inc., 235 Baker St., Costa Mesa, CA 92626, (714)966-2900 [11182]

FoodScience Corp., 20 New England Dr., Ste. C-1504, Essex Junction, VT 05452, (802)863-1111 [11183]

FoodSource, Inc., PO Box 217, Smyrna, TN 37167, (615)459-2519 [11184]

Foot Loose Inc., PO Box 598, Irmo, SC 29063-0598, (803)772-3485 [24746]

Foothills Mill & Supply Inc., 6455 E 56th Ave., Commerce City, CO 80022, (303)287-2069 [7354]

For-Tek, 1400 Ironhorse Pk., North Billerica, MA 01862, (978)667-6011 [7355]

Forbes & Co., PO Box 750, Alexandria, VA 22313, (703)548-8833 [2637]

Forbes Distributing Co., PO Box 1478, Birmingham, AL 35201, (205)251-4104 [8748]

Forbes Implement Supply Inc.; Keith, 4825 White Oak Ave. SE, Iowa City, IA 52240, (319)351-8341 [697]

Forbes Seed & Grain, PO Box 85, Junction City, OR 97448, (541)998-8086 [698]

Forbex Corporation, 1167 Willis Ave., Albertson, NY 11507-1233, (516)625-4700 [9904]

Forbo America Inc., 1105 N Market St., Ste. 1300, Wilmington, DE 19801, (302)427-2139 [15503]

Forbo Industries Inc., PO Box 667, Hazleton, PA 18201, (717)459-0771 [9905]

Forbo Wallcoverings Inc., 3 Killdeer Ct., PO Box 457, Bridgeport, NJ 08014, (609)467-3800 [15504]

Forbo Wallcoverings Inc., 3 Killdeer Ct., Bridgeport, NJ 08014, (609)467-3800 [21444]

FORCE America Inc., 501 E Cliff Rd., Ste. 100, Burnsville, MN 55337, (612)707-1300 [16027]

Force America Inc., 420 NW Business Park Ln., Kansas City, MO 64150, (816)587-6363 [16028]

Force Electronics Inc., 606 Hawaii St., El Segundo, CA 90245, (213)772-1324 [8749]

Force Electronics Inc., 606 Hawaii St., El Segundo, CA 90245, (310)643-7676 [8750]

Force Electronics Inc. Texas Div., 3218 Beltline Rd., Ste. 510, Farmers Branch, TX 75234, (972)247-9955 [8751]

Force Machinery Company Inc., PO Box 3729, Union, NJ 07083, (908)688-8270 [16029]

Forcean Inc., 10338 Ilona Ave., Los Angeles, CA 90064, (213)551-1293 [18800]

Ford Audio-Video Systems Inc., 4800 W Interstate 40, Oklahoma City, OK 73128-1208, (405)946-9966 [25194]

Ford & Bailie, 20 Carleton Cir., PO Box 138, Belmont, MA 02478, (617)489-6635 [3760]

Ford Body Company Inc., 1218 Battleground Ave., PO Box 9354, Greensboro, NC 27429-0354, (336)272-1131 [20635]

Ford Brothers Wholesale Meats Inc., 9129 Rte. 219, West Valley, NY 14171, (716)592-9126 [11185]

Ford Distributing Co.; Leid, 948 May Ave., WalLa Walla, WA 99362, (509)525-8180 [22288]

Ford and Garland Inc., 1304 Locust St., Des Moines, IA 50309-2920, (515)288-6324 [25195]

Ford and Sons Inc.; C.D., PO Box 300, Geneseo, IL 61254, (309)944-4661 [699]

Ford Steel Co, PO Box 54, Maryland Heights, MO 63043, (314)567-4680 [19981]

Forderer Cornice Works Co., 269 Potrero Ave., San Francisco, CA 94103, (415)431-4100 [7356]

ForeFront Direct Inc., 25400 U.S Hwy 19 N, Ste. 285, Clearwater, FL 33763, (813)724-8994 [6274]

Foreign Candy Company Inc., 1 Foreign Candy Dr., Hull, IA 51239, (712)439-1496 [11186]

Foreign Car Parts Inc., 2390 5th Ave. S, St. Petersburg, FL 33712, (813)327-6161 [2638]

Foreign Car Parts Inc., 5214 Quesenberry Ln, Las Cruces, NM 88005-4812, (505)526-5883 [2639]

Foreign Exchange Ltd., 429 Stockton St., San Francisco, CA 94108, (415)677-5100 [20541]

Foreign Tire Sales Inc., 2204 Morris Ave., Union, NJ 07083, (908)687-0559 [2640]

Foreign Trade Marketing, 1279 Starboard Ln., Sarasota, FL 34242, (941)346-9900 [11187]

Foremost Athletic Apparel, 1307 E Maple Rd., Troy, MI 48083, (248)689-3850 [4961]

ForeSight Electronics Inc., 610 Palomar Ave., Sunnyvale, CA 94086, (408)732-7777 [8752]

Foresight Inc., 724 E 8th St., Sioux Falls, SD 57103-1633, (605)334-4387 [4625]

Foresight Partners, LLC, 209 W Main St., Boise, ID 83702, (208)336-7003 [11188]

Forest City-Babin Co., 5111 Richmond Rd., Cleveland, OH 44146, (216)292-2500 [7357]

Forest City Electric Supply, PO Box 297, Rockford, IL 61105-0297, (815)968-5781 [8753]

Forest City Electric Supply, PO Box 297, Rockford, IL 61105-0297, (815)968-5781 [8753]

Forest City Enterprises Inc., 1100 Terminal Twr., 50 Public Sq., Cleveland, OH 44113, (216)267-1200 [27305]

Forest City-North America Lumber, 26050 Richmond Rd., Cleveland, OH 44146, (216)292-5660 [7358]

Forest City Tool Co., 620 23rd St. NW, Hickory, NC 28601, (704)322-4266 [16030]

Forest City Trading Group Inc., PO Box 4209, Portland, OR 97208, (503)246-8500 [7359]

Forest Lumber Co., PO Box 101063, Pittsburgh, PA 15237, (412)367-2004 [7360]

Forest Medical Products Inc., PO Box 989, Hillsboro, OR 97123, (503)640-3012 [19326]

Forest Plywood Sales, 14711 Arteisa Blvd., La Mirada, CA 90638, (310)523-1721 [7361]

Forester Beverage Inc., Rte. 5, Box 2A, River Rd., North Wilkesboro, NC 28659-9805, (919)667-6272 [1694]

Forge Industries Inc., 4450 Market St., Youngstown, OH 44512, (330)782-8301 [16871]

Forged Vessel Connections Inc., PO Box 38421, Houston, TX 77238-8421, (713)688-9705 [16872]

Forgy Process Instruments Inc., 10785 Indian Head Industrial Blv, St. Louis, MO 63132, (314)423-6262 [23172]

Forklift Parts Mfg. Co. Inc., 1250 W 17th St., Long Beach, CA 90813, (562)437-0471 [15820]

Forlizzi Brothers, 114 New England Providence Center, Chelsea, MA 02150, (617)884-1858 [11189]

Forman Brothers Inc., 4235 Sheriff Rd. NE, Washington, DC 20019, (202)388-8400 [1906]

Forman Distributing Co., 7550 Accotink Park Rd., Springfield, VA 22150, (703)644-2425 [1695]

Forman Inc., 2036 Lord Baltimore Dr., Baltimore, MD 21244, (410)298-7500 [4626]

Forman Inc., 2036 Lord Baltimore Dr., Baltimore, MD 21244, (410)298-7500 [16873]

FORMation mg Inc., 15540 Rockfield Blvd. Ste.A, Irvine, CA 92618, (949)598-8890 [6275]

Forms and Supplies Inc., PO Box 18694, Memphis, TN 38181-0694, (901)365-1249 [21007]

Formtronix Inc., 2516 McHenry Dr., Silver Spring, MD 20904, (301)572-6902 [6276]

Fornaca Inc., 2400 National City Blvd., National City, CA 91950, (619)474-5573 [11190]

Forrer Supply Company Inc., PO Box 220, Germantown, WI 53022-0220, (414)255-3030 [23173]

Forrest-Keeling Nursery, Hwy. 79 S, Elsberry, MO 63343, (573)898-5571 [14870]

Forschner Group Inc., 1 Research Dr., Shelton, CT 06484-6226, (203)929-5391 [15505]

Forster Co.; John M., 300 Commerce Dr., Rochester, NY 14623, (716)334-0590 [2641]

Forsythe Ice Cream, 689 Cross Trail, Piqua, OH 45356, (937)773-6322 [11191]

Forsythe Technology Inc., 7500 Frontage Rd., Skokie, IL 60077, (847)675-8000 [6277]

Fort Collins Winnelson Co., 1616 Riverside Ave., Ft. Collins, CO 80524, (970)484-8161 [23174]

Fort Dodge Machine Supply Company Inc., PO Box 974, Ft. Dodge, IA 50501, (515)576-2161 [16031]

Fort Pitt Brand Meat Co., PO Box F, Evans City, PA 16033, (724)538-3160 [11192]

Fort Recovery Equity Exchange Co., 2351 Walbash St., Ft. Recovery, OH 45846-0307, (419)375-4119 [27133]

Fort Smith Winnelson Co., 1700 Towson Ave., PO Box 1299, Ft. Smith, AR 72902-1299, (501)783-5177 [23175]

Fort Wayne Fleet Equipment, 13710 Lower Huntington Rd., Roanoke, IN 46783, (219)493-1800 [2642]

Fort Worth Jet Center, 4201 N Main St., Ft. Worth, TX 76106, (817)625-4012 [22289]

Fort Worth Lumber Co., PO Box 969, Ft. Worth, TX 76101, (817)293-5211 [27306]

Forte Dupee Sawyer Co., 4 Mechanic St., Ste. 203, Natick, MA 01760-3460, (617)482-8434 [26037]

Forte Industrial Equipment Systems Inc., 6037 Commerce Ct., Mason, OH 45040, (513)398-2800 [16032]

Forte Industries, 6037 Commerce Ct, Mason, OH 45040, (513)398-2800 [16033]

Fortman's Paint & Glass, 1355 N 4th St., Laramie, WY 82072, (307)745-9469 [21445]

Fortmeyer's Inc., 4151 Goshen Rd., Ft. Wayne, IN 46818, (219)489-3511 [22290]

Fortress Press, PO Box 1209, Minneapolis, MN 55440, (612)330-3433 [3761]

Fortron/Source Corp., 47443 Fremont Blvd., Fremont, CA 94538, (510)440-0188 [16034]

Fortune Dogs Inc., 121 Gray Ave., Ste. 300, Santa Barbara, CA 93101, (805)963-8728 [4962]

Fortune Industries Inc., 2153 Eagle Pkwy., Ft. Worth, TX 76177-2311, (817)490-5700 [89]

Fortune Personnel Consultants of Springfield Inc., 180 Denslow Rd., Unit 4, East Longmeadow, MA 01028, (413)525-3800 [19327]

Forty Acres and A Mule Film Works, 124 DeKalb Ave., Brooklyn, NY 11217, (718)624-3703 [4963]

Fosburg & McLaughlin Inc., 615 Addison St., PO Drawer 2069, Berkeley, CA 94702, (510)845-8283 [16035]

Foss Co.; W.J., 380 Union St., No. LL24, West Springfield, MA 01089-4123, (413)737-0206 [16874]

Foster Associates Inc.; M., PO Box 585608, Dallas, TX 75258, (214)631-7732 [4964]

Foster Co.; L.B., 415 Holiday Dr., Pittsburgh, PA 15220, (412)928-3400 [16875]

Foster Company of St. Louis Inc.; John Henry, PO Box 5820, St. Louis, MO 63134, (314)427-0600 [16036]

Foster's Good Service Dairy, PO Box 129, Westerville, OH 43081, (614)891-6407 [11193]

Fotofolio Inc., 561 Broadway, New York, NY 10012, (212)226-0923 [21729]

Foundry Service Supply Inc., 7 Greenwood Pl., Baltimore, MD 21208, (410)486-6238 [16876]

Fountain Dispensers Co. Inc., 35 Greenwich St., Providence, RI 02907-2534, (401)461-8400 [14451]

Fountain Hijet, 1406 Sand Lake Rd., Orlando, FL 32809, (407)858-4822 [20663]

Fountain Lumber Co.; Ed, PO Box 904, Palos Verdes Estates, CA 90274-0904, (213)583-1381 [7362]

Four Circle Cooperative, PO Box 99, Bird City, KS 67731, (785)734-2331 [17920]

Four Corners Welding & Gas, 606 E Hwy. 66, Gallup, NM 87301, (505)722-3845 [19982]

Four M Parts Warehouse, 402 E Chambers, Cleburne, TX 76031-5626, (817)645-7222 [2643]

Four Seasons F.S. Inc., N 6055 State Rd. 40, Elk Mound, WI 54739, (715)835-3194 [17921]

Four Star Incentives Inc., 5617 Howard St., Niles, IL 60714, (847)647-7662 [25196]

Four States Industrial Distributors, PO Box 2896, Farmington, NM 87499-2896, (505)326-0472 [7363]

Four Wheeler Communications, 10 New Scotland Ave., Albany, NY 12208, (518)465-4711 [6278]

Fournier Rubber and Supply Co., 1341 Norton Ave., Columbus, OH 43212, (614)294-6453 [16877]

Fournier & Sons Seafoods; R., 9391 Fournier Ave., Biloxi, MS 39532-5419, (228)392-4293 [11194]

Fowler and Associates Inc.; R.W., 4730 Prince Edward Rd., Jacksonville, FL 32210-8118, (904)246-4886 [7364]

Fowler Brothers, 110 Gary Pl., San Rafael, CA 94912, (415)459-3406 [11195]

Fowler Company Inc.; Fred V., PO Box 66299, Newton, MA 02466, (617)332-7004 [24362]

Fowler Elevator Inc., PO Box L, Newtown, MO 64667, (660)794-5435 [17922]

Fowler Equity Exchange Inc., Hwy. 54 & Main St., Fowler, KS 67844, (316)646-5262 [17923]

Fowler Equity Exchange Inc., Hwy. 54 and Main St., Fowler, KS 67844, (316)646-5262 [11196]

Fowler Inc.; M.M., 4220 Neal Rd., Durham, NC 27705-2322, (919)596-8246 [22291]

Fowler and Peth Inc., PO Box 16551, Denver, CO 80216, (303)388-6493 [7365]

Fox Appliance Parts of Atlanta Inc., PO Box 16217, Atlanta, GA 30321-0217, (404)363-3313 [15131]

Fox Appliance Parts of Augusta Inc., PO Box 14369, Augusta, GA 30919, (706)737-3400 [15132]

Fox Appliance Parts of Columbus Inc., 2508 Cusseta Rd., PO Box 3158, Columbus, GA 31903, (706)687-2267 [15133]

Fox Appliance Parts of Macon Inc., 6357 Hawkinsville Rd., PO Box 13486, Macon, GA 31208-3486, (912)788-1793 [15134]

Fox Auctioneers Inc.; Michael, 3835 Naylors Ln., Baltimore, MD 21208, (410)653-4000 [16037]

Fox Co.; C.B., 220 Camp St., New Orleans, LA 70130, (504)588-9211 [17924]

Fox, Inc.; T.E., 960 Old Mounta, Statesville, NC 28687, (704)528-9162 [25197]

Fox International Inc.; Michael, 3835 Naylors Ln., Baltimore, MD 21208, (410)653-4000 [16038]

Fox Point Sportswear Inc., PO Box 1641, Waukesha, WI 53187-1641, (715)536-9461 [4965]

Fox River Foods Inc., 5030 Baseline Rd., Montgomery, IL 60538, (630)896-1991 [11197]

Fox River Mills, Inc., PO Box 298, Osage, IA 50461-0298, (515)732-3798 [4966]

Fox Sales Co.; Henry A., 4494 36th St. SE, Grand Rapids, MI 49512, (616)949-1210 [1696]

FOX Systems Inc., 3333 S Old U.S 23, Brighton, MI 48116, (810)227-4497 [6279]

Foxhome Elevator Co., PO Box 69, Foxhome, MN 56543, (218)643-6079 [700]

Foxley Grain, 814 N 5th St., PO Box 512, Clear Lake, IA 50428, (515)357-6131 [17925]

FoxMeyer Drug Co., PO Box 814204, Dallas, TX 75381, (972)446-9090 [19328]

FoxMeyer Drug Co. Carol Stream Div., 520 E North Ave., Carol Stream, IL 60188-2125, (630)462-6501 [19329]

FoxMeyer Drug Co. Slidell Div., PO Box 2677, Slidell, LA 70459, (504)646-1006 [14103]

FPC Foodservices, 321 E 5th St., Frederick, MD 21701, (301)663-3171 [11198]

F.R. Industries Inc., 557 Long Rd., Pittsburgh, PA 15235, (412)242-5903 [8754]

Fraenkel Wholesale Furniture Company Inc., PO Box 15385, Baton Rouge, LA 70895, (504)275-8111 [13115]

Fragments Inc., 107 Green St., New York, NY 10012, (212)226-8878 [17416]

Fragrance International Inc., 398 E Rayen Ave., Youngstown, OH 44505, (330)747-3341 [14104]

Frakco Inc., PO Box 566, Luverne, MN 56156, (507)283-4416 [23176]

Framers On Peachtree, 2351 Peachtree Rd. NE, Atlanta, GA 30305-4147, (404)237-2888 [15506]

Fran-TEC Computer, PO Box 261, Somerset, MA 02726-0261, (508)675-3950 [6280]

Francis Drilling Fluids Ltd., PO Box 1694, Crowley, LA 70526, (318)783-8685 [4394]

Franciscan Glass Co., 100 San Antonio Cir., Mountain View, CA 94040, (650)948-6666 [7366]

Franciscan Press, Quincy Univ., 1800 University, Quincy, IL 62301-2670, (217)228-5670 [3762]

Francisco Distributing, 5301 N Robin Ave., Livingston, CA 95334, (209)394-8001 [11199]

Franco-American Novelty Company Inc., 8400 73rd Ave., Glendale, NY 11385, (718)821-3100 [13359]

Franco; Carlos, 311 S Broadway, McAllen, TX 78501, (956)687-4662 [8755]

Franco Distributing Co. Inc., PO Box 927, Montgomery, AL 36102-0927, (205)834-3455 [26486]

Francosteel Corp., 345 Hudson St., New York, NY 10014, (212)633-1010 [19983]

Frank Brothers Flooring Distributors, PO Box 4141, Albany, NY 12204, (518)462-5375 [9906]

Frank Carroll Oil Co., 2957 Royal Palm Ave., Ft. Myers, FL 33901-6323, (941)334-2345 [22292]

Frank and Company Inc.; S.M., 1000 N Division St., PO Box 789, Peekskill, NY 10566, (914)739-3100 [26294]

Frank Distributing, 507 S Murray Ave., Anderson, SC 29624-1520, (864)225-7071 [1697]

Frank, Inc.; Sam, 15 Center St., Rutland, VT 05701, (802)773-7770 [26295]

Frank and Sons Inc.; A., 1501 Guilford Ave., Baltimore, MD 21202, (410)727-6260 [26038]

Frank & Thomas, Inc., 111 Smith Hines Rd., Thomas Centre, Ste. G, Greenville, SC 29607, (864)288-5050 [16039]

Frank Winne and Son Inc., 44 N Front St., Philadelphia, PA 19106, (215)627-8080 [26039]

Frankel Associates Inc., 1948 Troutman St., Ridgewood, NY 11385, (718)386-2455 [26040]

Frankel & Company Inc.; Lou, 68 Old Mill Rd., Greenwich, CT 06831-3047, (203)661-2370 [8756]

Frankel Metal Co., 19300 Filer Ave., Detroit, MI 48234, (313)366-5300 [26831]

Frankferd Farms, 318 Love Rd., No. 1, Valencia, PA 16059, (412)898-2242 [11200]

Frankfort Scrap Metal Company Inc., PO Box 344, Frankfort, KY 40602, (502)223-7607 [26815]

Franki Sales Co., 10 Wentworth Dr., Bedford, NH 03110, (603)472-6947 [8757]

Franklin Book Company, Inc., 7804 Montgomery Ave., Elkins Park, PA 19027, (215)635-5252 [3763]

Franklin Cigar and Tobacco Company Inc., PO Box 1151, Franklin, LA 70538, (318)828-3208 [26296]

Franklin County Grain Grower Inc., PO Box 32, Preston, ID 83263, (208)852-0384 [701]

Franklin Electric Company Inc. (Atlantic City, New Jersey), 1810 Baltic Ave., Atlantic City, NJ 08401, (609)345-6154 [8758]

Franklin Farmers Cooperative, PO Box 272, Decherd, TN 37324, (931)967-5511 [702]

Franklin Feed and Supply Co., 1977 Philadelphia Ave., Chambersburg, PA 17201, (717)264-6148 [703]

Franklin Industries Inc., 612 10th Ave. N, Nashville, TN 37203, (615)259-4222 [7367]

Franklin Iron and Metal Corp., PO Box 1857, Richmond, IN 47375, (765)966-8295 [26816]

Franklin Medical Products, 1320 Airport Rd., Montrose, CO 81401, (970)249-0677 [19330]

Franklin Quest Co., 2200 W Parkway Blvd., Salt Lake City, UT 84119, (801)975-1776 [6281]

Franklin Sports Industries Inc., PO Box 508, Stoughton, MA 02072, (781)344-1111 [23676]

Franklin Stores Inc.; Ben, PO Box 5938, Chicago, IL 60680, (630)462-6100 [26487]

Franklin Town Metals and Cores, 145 McVail St., Baltimore, MD 21229, (410)362-7470 [19984]

Frank's Auto Parts Co.; Johnny, 1225 Sawyer St., Houston, TX 77007, (713)869-6200 [2644]

Franks Inc.; M.E., 175 Strafford Ave., Ste. 230, Wayne, PA 19087, (610)989-9688 [11201]

Frank's Supply Company Inc., 3311 Stanford NE, Albuquerque, NM 87107, (505)884-0000 [7368]

Franz Optical Company Inc., 2041 E Burnside St., Gresham, OR 97030, (503)667-2303 [19331]

Fraser Steel Co., PO Box 160, Albertville, MN 55301-0160, (612)535-5616 [19985]

Fratzke Sales, Inc., 412 E 5th St., Winona, MN 55987-3921, (507)452-6973 [4967]

Fravert Services Inc., 133 W Park Dr., Birmingham, AL 35211, (205)940-7180 [8759]

Fraza Equipment Inc., 15725 E 12 Mile Rd., Roseville, MI 48066, (810)778-6111 [16040]

Fred Baker Firearms, 1925 N McArthur Blvd., Oklahoma City, OK 73127, (405)789-0651 [13491]

Frederick Fell Publishers, Inc., 2131 Hollywood Blvd., Hollywood, FL 33020, (954)925-0555 [3764]

Frederick Manufacturing Corp., 4840 E 12th St., Kansas City, MO 64127, (816)231-5007 [704]

Frederick Produce Company Inc., 321 E 5th St., Frederick, MD 21701, (301)663-3171 [11198]

Frederick Steel Co., 200 W North Bend Rd., Cincinnati, OH 45216, (513)821-6400 [19986]

Frederick Trading Co., 7901 Trading Ln., Frederick, MD 21705, (301)662-2161 [13715]

Fredericksburg Farmers Cooperative, 1905 Ivory Ave., Waverly, IA 50677, (319)352-1354 [705]

Frederickseal, Inc., 461 Straw Rd., Manchester, NH 03102, (603)668-0900 [16878]

Fredericksen Tank Lines, 850 Delta Ln., West Sacramento, CA 95691, (916)371-4655 [22293]

Fredonia Cooperative Association, PO Box 538, Fredonia, KS 66736, (316)378-2191 [17926]

Fredonia Cooperative Association, PO Box 538, Fredonia, KS 66736, (316)378-2191 [11202]

Fredrico Percussion, 152 Lancaster Blvd., Mechanicsburg, PA 17055, (717)766-1332 [25198]

Fredriksen and Sons Fire Equipment Company Inc., 760 Thomas Dr., Bensenville, IL 60106, (708)595-9500 [24553]

Free Service Tire Company Inc., 126 Buffalo St., Johnson City, TN 37601, (423)928-6476 [2645]

Free Shoe Shop, 217 W Main St., Union, SC 29379-2214, (864)427-3103 [24747]

Freeborn County Cooperative Oil Co., 226 E Clark St., Albert Lea, MN 56007, (507)373-3991 [22294]

Freeburg Sign & Lighting, 2326 5th Ave. N, Lewiston, ID 83501-1744, (208)746-0839 [25654]

Freed Appliance Distributing, 2969 Red Hawk Dr., Grand Prairie, TX 75052-7622, (817)478-5421 [15135]

Freeda Vitamins Inc., 36 E 41st St., New York, NY 10017, (212)685-4980 [14105]

Freedland Industries Corp., PO Box 278, Dearborn, MI 48121, (313)584-3033 [2646]

Freedman Company Inc.; Joseph, PO Box 3555, Springfield, MA 01101, (413)781-4444 [26817]

Freedman Seating Co., 4043 N Ravenswood, Chicago, IL 60613, (773)929-6100 [2647]

Freedman and Son Inc.; R., PO Box 1533, Green Island, NY 12183, (518)273-1141 [26818]

Freedman and Sons Inc.; S., 3322 Pennsy Dr., Landover, MD 20785, (301)322-5000 [21730]

Freeman Corp., 11103 Ripley Ct., Boise, ID 83704, (208)376-4341 [14452]

Freeman Manufacturing and Supply, 1101 Moore Rd., Avon, OH 44011, (440)934-1902 [16879]

Freeman Tobacco Warehouse, 439 E Office St., Harrodsburg, KY 40330, (606)734-2833 [26297]

Freeman's Car Stereo Inc., 6150 Brookshire Blvd., Charlotte, NC 28216-2410, (704)398-1822 [25199]

Freeport Marine Supply, 47 W Merrick Rd., Freeport, NY 11520, (516)379-2610 [18505]

Freeport Steel Co., PO Box 11453, Pittsburgh, PA 15238, (412)820-7040 [19987]

Freirich Food; Julian, 46-01 5th St., Long Island City, NY 11101, (718)361-9111 [11203]

Frejoth International Corp., 2050 N Durfee Ave., South El Monte, CA 91733, (626)443-8652 [19988]

Fremont Chemical Company Inc., 203 E Main St., Riverton, WY 82501, (307)856-6063 [4395]

Fremont Coin Co. Inc., 317 Fremont St., Las Vegas, NV 89101-5607, (702)382-1469 [17417]

Fremont Cooperative Produce Co., 540 W Main St., Fremont, MI 49412, (616)924-3851 [706]

Fremont Electric Company Inc., 744 N 34th St., Seattle, WA 98103, (206)633-2323 [2648]

French Dressing Inc., PO Box 971, Williston, VT 05495-0971, (802)658-1434 [24748]

French Gourmet Inc., 500 Kuwili St., Honolulu, HI 96817, (808)524-4000 [11204]

French Implement Company Inc., PO Box 187, Charleston, MO 63834, (573)649-3021 [707]

French Refrigeration Co., RR 1, Box 241, Norway, ME 04268-9709, (207)743-6573 [14453]

French Toast, 100 W 33rd St., New York, NY 10001, (212)594-4740 [4968]

French Transit Ltd., 398 Beach Rd., Burlingame, CA 94010, (650)548-9600 [14106]

Frenchman Valley Farmer's Cooperative, 143 Broadway Ave., Imperial, NE 69033, (308)882-4381 [17927]

Frenchman Valley Farmer's Cooperative, 143 Broadway Ave., Imperial, NE 69033, (308)882-4381 [708]

French's Athletics Inc., 1543 Harrison St., Batesville, AR 72501-7222, (870)793-8205 [23677]

Fresh Advantage, 5051 Speaker Rd., Kansas City, KS 66106-1043, (913)321-0691 [11205]

Fresh America Corp., 6600 LBJ Freeway, Ste. 180, Dallas, TX 75240, (972)774-0575 [11206]

Fresh Express, PO Box 298, Greencastle, PA 17225-1424, (717)597-1804 [11207]

Fresh Fish Company Inc., 8501 Page Blvd., St. Louis, MO 63114, (314)428-7777 [11208]

Fresh Fish Inc., 1116 2nd Ave. N, Birmingham, AL 35203, (205)252-0344 [11209]

Fresh Freeze Supply Inc., 2841 E St., Eureka, CA 95501, (707)442-8488 [11210]

Fresh Start Produce Sales, Inc., 5353 West Atlantic Ave., Delray Beach, FL 33484-8166, (561)496-7250 [11211]

FreshPoint Inc., 15305 Dallas Pkwy., Dallas, TX 75248, (972)392-8100 [11212]

FreshWorld Farms Inc., 6701 San Pablo Ave., Emeryville, CA 94608, (510)547-2395 [11213]

Fresno Distributing Co., PO Box 6078, Fresno, CA 93703, (559)442-8800 [8760]

Fresno Truck Center, 2727 E Central Ave., Fresno, CA 93725-2425, (209)486-4310 [20636]

Fretz Corp., 2001 Woodhaven Rd., Philadelphia, PA 19116, (215)671-8300 [15136]

Freund Can Co., 155 W 84th St., Chicago, IL 60620-1298, (312)224-4230 [25916]

Freund, Freund and Company Inc., 102 Franklin St., New York, NY 10013-2982, (212)226-3753 [15507]

Frey, Inc., 3880 Fourteen Mile Dr., Stockton, CA 95219-3809, (916)371-7914 [9907]

Frey Scientific, 100 Paragon Pky., Mansfield, OH 44903, (419)589-2100 [24363]

Frey the Wheelman Inc., 41-51 E Tupper St., Buffalo, NY 14203, (716)854-3830 [2649]

Frezzolini Electronics Inc., 5 Valley St., Hawthorne, NJ 07506-2084, (973)427-1160 [8761]

Frick Hog Buying & Trucking, PO Box 661, Yankton, SD 57078-0661, (605)665-6839 [17928]

Frick's Services Inc., PO Box 40, Wawaka, IN 46794, (219)761-3311 [17929]

Fried Brothers Inc., 467 N 7th St., Philadelphia, PA 19123, (215)627-3205 [13716]

Frieda's Inc., 4465 Corporate Center Dr., Los Alamitos, CA 90720, (714)826-6100 [11214]

Friedman Bag Company Inc., PO Box 866004, Los Angeles, CA 90086, (213)628-2341 [16880]

Friedman and Co., PO Box 8025, Savannah, GA 31412, (912)233-9333 [17418]

Friedman Electric Supply, 1321 Wyoming Ave., Exeter, PA 18643-1425, (717)654-3371 [8762]

Friedman Industries Inc., PO Box 21147, Houston, TX 77226, (713)672-9433 [19989]

Friedman Steel Company Inc., PO Box 430, Greenville, MS 38701, (601)378-2722 [19990]

Frieling USA Inc., 1812-A Center Park Dr., Charlotte, NC 28217, (704)357-1080 [15508]

Friend Bit Service Inc., RD 3, Smithfield, PA 15478, (412)564-2072 [25655]

Friend Tire Co., 11 Industrial Dr., Monett, MO 65708, (417)235-7836 [2650]

Friend Truck Equipment, Inc.; Matt, Hastings Industrial Park E, Bldg. SH66, PO Box 1083, Hastings, NE 68902-1083, (402)463-5675 [2651]

Friendly Distributors, 6501 Rainier Dr., Everett, WA 98201, (425)355-1900 [1698]

Friendly Frank's Distribution Inc., 3990 Broadway, Gary, IN 46408, (219)884-5052 [3765]

Friendship Press, 475 Riverside Dr., Rm. 860, New York, NY 10115, (212)870-2496 [3766]

Frigi-Cool Inc., PO Box 116968, Carrollton, TX 75007, (972)446-9497 [2652]

Frigi-Cool/RVAC Inc., PO Box 116968, Carrollton, TX 75007, (972)446-9497 [2652]

Frigid North Co., 3309 Spenard Rd., Anchorage, AK 99503-4503, (907)561-4633 [8763]

Frinks Greenhouses Inc., 418 W 13th St., Cedar Falls, IA 50613, (319)266-3517 [14871]

Frischkorn Distributors Inc., PO Box 1547, Washington, NC 27889-1547, (919)537-4169 [23177]

Frito-Lay Co., 7701 Legacy Dr., Plano, TX 75024, (972)334-7000 [11215]

Frito-Lay Inc., 35855 Stanley, Sterling Heights, MI 48312, (810)978-8770 [11216]

Frito-Lay Inc., 7491 Clyde Park Ave. SW, Wyoming, MI 49509-9708, (616)878-9579 [11217]

Fritz Company Inc., 1912 Hastings Ave., Newport, MN 55055, (612)459-9751 [11218]

Fritz Pet Products, 324 Towne E Blvd., Mesquite, TX 75149, (972)285-0101 [27134]

Fritz Pet Supply, PO Box 17040, Dallas, TX 75217-0040, (918)663-5991 [27135]

Fritzi of Utah, 1350 Calpac Ave., Spanish Fork, UT 84660-1805, (801)798-9811 [4969]

Frohman & Sons Inc.; L.H., 1580 N Northwest Hwy., Park Ridge, IL 60068-1444, (847)635-6520 [11219]

Fromm Electric Supply Corp., PO Box 15147, Reading, PA 19612-5147, (215)374-4441 [8764]

Fromm, Inc.; R.K., 3561 Copley Cir., PO Box 4224, Copley, OH 44321-0224, (330)666-6737 [16041]

Front Musical Literature; Theodore, 16122 Cohasset St., Van Nuys, CA 91406, (818)994-1902 [3767]

Front Street Fabrics Inc., PO Box 6084, Providence, RI 02940-6084, (401)728-4200 [26041]

Frontier, 35 York St., 11th Fl., Brooklyn, NY 11201, (718)855-3030 [17419]

Frontier Co-op Herbs, Box 299, Norway, IA 52318, (319)227-7996 [11220]

Frontier Cooperative Co., PO Box 379, David City, NE 68632, (402)367-3019 [17930]

Frontier Fasteners Inc., 12710 Market, Houston, TX 77015, (713)451-4242 [13717]

Frontier Hybrids, PO Box 177, Abernathy, TX 79311, (806)298-2595 [709]

Frontier Inc., PO Box 668, Wahpeton, ND 58074-0668, (701)642-6656 [710]

Frontier Inc., 730 Deere Dr., New Richmond, WI 54017, (715)246-6565 [711]

Frontier Inc., PO Box 668, Wahpeton, ND 58074-0668, (701)642-6656 [712]

Frontier Inc. (New Richmond, Wisconsin), 730 Deere Dr., New Richmond, WI 54017, (715)246-6565 [713]

Frontier Lumber Co., 1941 Elmwood Ave., Buffalo, NY 14207, (716)873-8500 [7369]

Frontier Network Systems Inc., 95 N Fitzhugh St., Rochester, NY 14614, (716)777-2562 [25200]

Frontier Texaco, 580 W Broadway, PO Box 1771, Jackson, WY 83001, (307)733-2168 [22295]

Frontier Trading Inc., PO Box 460, Roff, OK 74865, (580)456-7732 [714]

Frontier Truck Equipment and Parts Co., 7167 E 53rd Pl., Commerce City, CO 80022, (303)289-4311 [2653]

Frontier Water and Steam Supply Co., 366 Oak St., Buffalo, NY 14203, (716)853-4400 [23178]

Frontier Wholesale Co., PO Box 3928, Lubbock, TX 79452-3928, (806)744-1404 [7370]

Frontier Radio Inc., 3401 Sirius Ave. 18, Las Vegas, NV 89102-8313, (702)871-6166 [5616]

Frontier Radio Inc., 3401 Sirius Ave. 18, Las Vegas, NV 89102-8313, (702)871-6166 [8765]

Frost Engineering Service Co., PO Box 26770, Santa Ana, CA 92799-6770, (714)549-9222 [16042]

Frost Hardwood Lumber Co., PO Box 919065, San Diego, CA 92191-9065, (619)455-9060 [7371]

Frost Hardwood Lumber Co., PO Box 919065, San Diego, CA 92191-9065, (619)455-9060 [27307]

FRP Supplies Inc., 3 S Middlesex Ave., A, Cranbury, NJ 08512-3726, (201)288-7900 [7372]

Fruehauf Trailer Corp., 38600 Ford Rd., Westland, MI 48185, (734)729-6767 [20637]

Fruehauf Trailer Services, Inc., 38600 Ford Rd., Westland, MI 48185, (734)729-6767 [20637]

Fruit Distributors Inc., 129 S Central Ave., Lima, OH 45801, (419)223-8105 [11221]

Fruit a Freeze, 12919 Leyva St., Norwalk, CA 90650, (562)407-2881 [11222]

Fruit Growers Supply Co., 14130 Riverside Dr., Sherman Oaks, CA 91423, (818)986-6480 [715]

Fruita Consumers Cooperative, 1650 Hwys. 6 & 50, Fruita, CO 81521, (970)858-3667 [716]

F.S. Adams Inc., PO Box 73, Paloma, IL 62359, (217)455-2811 [717]

FS Cooperative Inc., PO Box 98, Amherst Junction, WI 54407, (715)824-3151 [718]

FSC Educational Inc., 223 S Illinois Ave., Mansfield, OH 44905, (419)589-8222 [3768]

FTC Corp., 31700 Bainbrook Rd., Westlake Village, CA 91361, (818)879-0229 [2654]

FTG Manufacturing, 4251 NE Port Dr., PO Box 266, Lees Summit, MO 64064, (816)795-7171 [23678]

Fuchs Copy Systems Inc., 12200 W Adler Ln., West Allis, WI 53214, (414)778-0210 [21008]

Fuchs Machinery Inc., 5401 F St., Omaha, NE 68117-2827, (402)734-1991 [16043]

Fuel South Company Inc., PO Box 572, Hazlehurst, GA 31539, (912)285-4011 [22296]

Fugitt Rubber & Supply Company, Inc., 1900 Thomas Rd., Memphis, TN 38134-6315, (901)525-7897 [16881]

Fuhrer Holdings Inc.; Frank, 3100 E Carson St., Pittsburgh, PA 15203, (412)488-8844 [1699]

Fuhrer Wholesale Co.; Frank B., 3100 E Carson St., Pittsburgh, PA 15203, (412)488-8844 [1700]

Fuji America Inc., 118 Bauer Dr., Oakland, NJ 07436, (201)337-1700 [23679]

Fuji Medical Systems USA Inc., 419 West Ave., Stamford, CT 06902-6300, (203)353-0300 [18801]

Fuji Medical Systems USA Inc., 419 West Ave., Stamford, CT 06902, (203)353-0300 [22854]

Fuji Natural Food Co., 515 S 1st St., Phoenix, AZ 85004-2503, (602)254-3890 [11223]

Fujii Associates, Inc., 120 E Burlington, La Grange, IL 60525, (708)354-2555 [3769]

Fujitsu Business Communication Systems Inc., 3190 E Miraloma Ave., Anaheim, CA 92806, (714)630-7721 [8766]

Fujitsu Computer Products of America Inc., 2904 Orchard Pkwy., San Jose, CA 95134-2009, (408)432-6333 [6282]

Fujitsu Network Switching of America Inc., 3055 Orchard Dr., San Jose, CA 95134, (408)432-1300 [6283]

Fukuda Denshi America Corp., 17725 NE 65th St., Bldg. C, Redmond, WA 98052, (425)881-7737 [18802]

Fukuda Denshi USA, Inc., 17725 NE 65th St., Bldg. C, Redmond, WA 98052, (425)881-7737 [18802]

Full Bore - Cycle Lines USA, 9515 51st Ave., Unit 12, College Park, MD 20740, (301)474-9119 [20638]

Full Bore - Cycle Lines USA, 9515 51st Ave., Unit 12, College Park, MD 20740, (301)474-9119 [2655]

Full Circle, Inc., PO Box 49, Madras, OR 97741, (541)475-2222 [719]

Full-Line Distributors, 1200 Airport Dr., Ball Ground, GA 30107, (404)409-8999 [5122]

Full Line Distributors, 2650 Button at Winnett Dr., Ste. E, Doraville, GA 30340 [4970]

Full Perspective Videos Services Inc., 150 S Mountain Ave., Montclair, NJ 07042, (973)746-0421 [25201]

Full Service Beverage Co., 2900 S Hydraulic St., Wichita, KS 67216-2403, (316)529-3777 [24956]

Fuller Associates Inc.; Arthur, PO Box 66, Newtown, CT 06470-0066, (203)426-7895 [25202]

Fuller Color Center Inc., 75 S Wells Ave., Reno, NV 89502-1334, (702)329-4478 [21446]

Fuller-O'Brien Paint Stores, 4500 Lois Dr., Anchorage, AK 99501, (907)261-9186 [21447]

Fuller-O'Brien Paint Stores, 4042 Pacific Ave., Ogden, UT 84405, (801)621-4633 [21448]

Fuller Oil Company Inc., PO Box 605, Fayetteville, NC 28302, (919)488-2815 [22297]

Fuller Paper Company Inc., 3700 Wm. Penn Hwy., Easton, PA 18042, (215)253-3591 [21731]

Fuller Supply Co., 1958 Turner NW, Grand Rapids, MI 49504, (616)364-8455 [23179]

Fuller Supply Co., 203 6th St., Montgomery, AL 36104 [27136]

Fuller Supply Co., Inc., 139 Southgate Rd., Dothan, AL 36301, (334)794-7812 [27137]

Fuller Supply Company Inc., 1010 N 24th St., Birmingham, AL 35203, (205)323-4431 [27138]

Fuller's Wholesale Electronics Inc., 713 Gladstone St., Parkersburg, WV 26101-5661, (304)428-2296 [8419]

Fullerton Metals Co., 3000 Shermer Rd., Northbrook, IL 60065-3002, (708)291-2400 [19991]

Fullwell Products Inc., 6140 Parkland Blvd., Cleveland, OH 44124-4187, (440)942-1200 [2656]

Fulton Corp., 303 8th Ave., Fulton, IL 61252, (815)589-3211 [13718]

Fulton, Mehring & Hauser Company, Inc., PO Box 2466, York, PA 17405-2466, (717)843-9054 [16882]

Fulton Paper Co., 334 Surburban Dr., Newark, DE 19711, (302)368-1440 [21732]

Fulton Paper Co., 1006 W 27th St., Wilmington, DE 19802, (302)594-0400 [21733]

Fulton Paper Company Inc., PO Box 43884, Atlanta, GA 30336-0884, (404)691-4070 [21734]

Fulton Radio Supply Co., PO Box 480, Jackson, MI 49204-0480, (517)784-6106 [8767]

Fulton Supply Co., 342 Nelson St. SW, PO Box 4028, Atlanta, GA 30313, (404)688-3400 [16883]

Fumoto Engineering of America, 12328 Northrup Way, Bellevue, WA 98005, (425)869-7771 [2657]

Funai Corp., 100 North St., Teterboro, NJ 07608, (201)288-2063 [25203]

Funco Inc., PO Box 241824, Omaha, NE 68124-5824, (402)734-0989 [23680]

Function Junction Inc., 306 Delaware St., Kansas City, MO 64105-1216, (816)471-6000 [15509]

Funderburk Company Inc.; G.A., PO Box 338, Jefferson, SC 29718-0338, (843)658-3405 [11224]

Funk Machine and Supply, 1805 Yolande Ave., Lincoln, NE 68521, (402)475-5477 [13719]

Funks Grove Grain Co., PO Box 246, McLean, IL 61754, (309)874-2771 [17931]

Funsten and Co.; B.R., 825 Van Ness Ave., Ste. 201, San Francisco, CA 94109-7837, (415)674-0530 [15510]

Furbay Electric Supply Co., PO Box 6268, Canton, OH 44706, (330)454-3033 [8768]

Furman Lumber Inc., PO Box 130, Nutting Lake, MA 01865, (978)670-3800 [7067]

Furnace & Duct Supply Co., 635 Elmwood Ave., Providence, RI 02907, (401)941-3800 [14454]

Furniture on Consignment Inc., 4911 S 72nd St., Omaha, NE 68127, (402)339-7848 [13116]

Furniture Consultants Inc., 11 W 19th St., New York, NY 10011, (212)229-4500 [21009]

Furniture Distributors Inc., PO Box 11117, Charlotte, NC 28220, (704)523-3424 [13117]

Furniture Makers Supply Co., PO Box 728, Lexington, NC 27292, (336)956-2722 [16884]

Fuses Unlimimted, 9248 Eton Ave., Chatsworth, CA 91311-5807, (818)786-8111 [90]

Futter Lumber Corp., PO Box 347, Rockville Centre, NY 11571, (516)764-4445 [7373]

Futura Adhesives & Chemicals, 795 Glendale Rd., Scottdale, GA 30079, (404)296-8288 [7]

Future Electronics Corporation, 41 Main St., Bolton, MA 01740, (978)779-3000 [8769]

Future Med, Inc., 654 E Capitol St. NE, Washington, DC 20002, (202)546-8036 [19332]

Future Metals Inc., 5400 NW 35th Ave., Ft. Lauderdale, FL 33309, (954)739-5350 [91]

Future Optics Inc., PO Box 1408, Jackson, TN 38302-1408, (901)424-5751 [19333]

Future Pro Inc., PO Box 486, Inman, KS 67546, (316)585-6405 [23681]

Future Tech International Inc., 7630 NW 25th St., Miami, FL 33122-1314, (305)477-6406 [6284]

FVB Enterprises, Inc., PO Box 126, Magnolia, NJ 08049, (609)435-1555 [26488]

FW Sales, Box 664, Coraopolis, PA 15108, (724)457-8333 [4971]

FWB Inc., 1555 Adams Dr., Menlo Park, CA 94025, (415)325-4392 [6285]

Fyda Freightliner Inc., 1250 Walcutt Rd., Columbus, OH 43228, (614)851-0002 [20639]

Fyr Fyter Inc., 10905-1 Gladiolus Dr., Ft. Myers, FL 33908, (941)481-5737 [24554]

G and B Oil Company Inc., PO Box 811, Elkin, NC 28621, (336)835-3607 [22298]

G & C Restaurant Equipment, 359 Elm St., Manchester, NH 03101, (603)627-1221 [24125]

G & E Parts Center, Inc., 1212 Bluff Rd., PO Box 1074, Columbia, SC 29202, (803)771-4346 [15137]

G and G Enterprises Inc., PO Box 1206, Laramie, WY 82073, (307)745-3236 [1701]

G and G Produce Company Inc., 5949 S Eastern Ave., City of Commerce, CA 90040, (213)727-1212 [11225]

G-III Apparel Group Ltd., 512 7th Ave., New York, NY 10018, (212)629-8830 [4972]

G and L Recycling Inc., 222 N Calverton Rd., Baltimore, MD 21223, (410)233-1197 [26819]

G. Leblanc Corp., 7001 Leblanc Blvd., Kenosha, WI 53141-1415, (262)658-1644 [25204]

G and M Oil Company Inc., HC 84, PO Box 6, Barbourville, KY 40906, (606)546-3909 [22299]

G-N Aircraft Inc., 1701 E Main St., Griffith, IN 46319, (219)924-7110 [92]

G & N Appliance Parts, 1525 S 4th Ave., Tucson, AZ 85713, (520)624-2102 [15138]

G & N Appliance Parts, 2742 W Mcdowell Rd, Phoenix, AZ 85009-1417, (602)269-6385 [15139]

G & N Distributors Inc., 6229 Vance Rd. 1, Chattanooga, TN 37421-2979, (423)892-2842 [15140]

G & O Paper & Supplies, PO Box 367, Lemmon, SD 57638-0367, (605)374-3697 [21735]

G-Riffco, 1011 Currie Ave. N, Minneapolis, MN 55403, (612)338-7355 [16044]

G & S Jewelry Manufacturing, 10016 Cochiti Rd. SE, Albuquerque, NM 87123, (505)293-7398 [17420]

G and S Motors Inc., 211 N I-70 Service Rd., St. Peters, MO 63376, (314)258-3298 [20640]

G & S Products Inc., PO Box 229, Ligonier, IN 46767-0229, (219)894-3620 [25205]

Gabler Inc.; H.C., PO Box 220, Chambersburg, PA 17201, (717)264-4184 [24275]

Gabor International Ltd.; Eva, 5775 Deramus St., Kansas City, MO 64120, (816)231-3700 [14107]

Gachassin Inc., PO Box 9068, New Iberia, LA 70562-9068, (318)369-7000 [4973]

Gachot & Gachot, Inc., 440 W 14th St., New York, NY 10014-1004, (212)675-2868 [11226]

Gaetano Food Distributor, 940 Forrester Way, Eugene, OR 97401, (541)344-6758 [11227]

Gaffey Inc., 9655 Alawhe Dr., Claremore, OK 74017-4366, (918)836-6827 [16045]

Gaffney-Kroese Electrical Supply Corp., 1697 Elizabeth Ave., Rahway, NJ 07065, (908)381-0500 [8770]

Gage Co., PO Box 658, Library, PA 15129-0658, (412)255-6904 [16885]

The Gage Co., 815 Main Ave., Hagerstown, MD 21740, (301)739-7474 [23180]

Gage Co. Central Div., 5420 W 84th St., Indianapolis, IN 46268, (317)872-8876 [16886]

Gage Co. Redlon and Johnson Plumbing Supply Div., PO Box 3554, Portland, ME 04104, (207)773-4755 [23181]

Gage Co. Westco Industrial Distribution, 166 Riverside Industrial Pkwy., Portland, ME 04103-1431, (207)774-5812 [16624]

Gage Food Products Co., 1501 N 31st Ave., Melrose Park, IL 60160, (708)338-1501 [11228]

Gaggenau USA Corp., 5551 McFadden Ave., Huntington Beach, CA 92649-1317 [15141]

Gagnons Reprographics Co., 308 9th Ave. S, Great Falls, MT 59405-4034, (406)727-2278 [6286]

Gahagen Iron and Metal Co., 4431 E 64th Ave., Commerce City, CO 80022, (303)288-6868 [26964]

Gahr Machine Co., 19199 St. Clair Ave., Cleveland, OH 44117-1090, (216)531-0053 [16046]

Gaines Electric Supply Co., 2501 Orange Ave., Long Beach, CA 90801, (562)595-8321 [8771]

Gainesville Industrial Supply, 280 High St. SW, PO Box 423, Gainesville, GA 30503, (404)536-1271 [2658]

Gainor Medical U.S.A. Inc., PO Box 353, McDonough, GA 30253-0353, (404)474-0474 [18803]

Gai's Northwest Bakeries Inc., PO Box 24327, Seattle, WA 98124, (206)322-0931 [11229]

Galan Enterprises, Inc., 2740 W Windrose Dr., Phoenix, AZ 85029, (602)993-3000 [26489]

Galaxie Hardware Publishers Inc., 5075 Nectar Way, Eugene, OR 97405, (541)345-1817 [6287]

Galaxy Liner Company Inc., 7546 W McNab Rd., North Lauderdale, FL 33068, (954)720-5384 [22966]

Galco Industrial Electronics, 26010 Pinehurst Dr., Madison Heights, MI 48071-4139, (248)542-9090 [8772]

Gale Force Compression Service, PO Box 1187, Enid, OK 73702, (580)233-2667 [5841]

Galesberg Cooperative Elevator Co., PO Box 115, Galesburg, ND 58035, (701)488-2216 [720]

Gallagher Co.; R.J., 7901 El Rio, Houston, TX 77054, (713)748-4501 [19992]

Gallagher Industrial Laundry, 151 McQuiston Dr., Battle Creek, MI 49015-1076, (616)965-5171 [4974]

Gallagher Steel Co., 19515 Mack Ave., Grosse Pointe, MI 48236, (313)884-0835 [19993]

Gallagher's Inc., 1450 Sheldon Rd., St. Albans, VT 05478, (802)524-5336 [17932]

Gallard-Schlesinger Industries Inc., 777 Zeckenderf Blvd., Garden City, NY 11530, (516)229-4000 [4396]

Galliher and Brother Inc.; W.T., PO Box 827, Springfield, VA 22150, (703)451-6500 [7374]

Galloup Co.; J.O., 130 N Helmer Rd., Battle Creek, MI 49015, (616)965-2303 [23182]

Gallup Sales Co. Inc., 530 E 66 Ave., Gallup, NM 87301-6028, (505)863-5241 [1702]

Gallup Welding Co., 903 W Wilson Ave., Gallup, NM 87301, (505)863-4882 [19994]

Galvin Flying Service Inc., 7149 Perimeter Rd., Seattle, WA 98108, (206)763-0350 [22300]

Gamble Co.; L.H., 3615 Harding Ave., Ste. 502, Honolulu, HI 96816-3735, (808)735-8199 [11230]

Gamblers General Store Inc., 500 S Main St., Las Vegas, NV 89101-6369, (702)382-9903 [26490]

Gambrinus Co., 14800 San Pedro, No. 310, San Antonio, TX 78232, (210)490-9128 [1703]

Gamco Education Materials, 325 N Kirkwood Rd., Ste. 200, St. Louis, MO 63122, (314)909-1670 [6726]

Gamco Manufacturing Co., PO Box 964, 422 Industrial Dr., Jamestown, TN 38556, (931)879-9712 [4975]

Games of Tennessee, 1220 W Jackson St., Shelbyville, TN 37160, (931)684-0100 [26491]

Games Unlimited, 2115 Murray Ave., Pittsburgh, PA 15217, (412)421-8807 [26492]

Gametree Inc., PO Box 6532, Boise, ID 83707-6532, (208)342-8281 [26493]

Gamma Inc., 3289 Mill Branch Rd., Memphis, TN 38116, (901)332-2944 [13118]

Gamtex Industries Inc., PO Box 308, Ft. Worth, TX 76101, (817)334-0211 [26820]

Gamzon Brothers Inc., 21 W 46th St., New York, NY 10036, (212)719-2550 [17421]

Ganahl Lumber Co., 1220 E Ball Rd., Anaheim, CA 92805, (714)772-5444 [7375]

Gander Mountain Inc., PO Box 1224, Minneapolis, MN 55440-1224, (612)862-2331 [23682]

Gani International Inc.; J., PO Box 713, Plaistow, NH 03865-0713, (603)382-7551 [25656]

Ganin Tire Company Inc., 1421 38th St., Brooklyn, NY 11218, (718)633-0600 [2659]

Ganin Tire Inc., 1421 38th St., Brooklyn, NY 11218, (718)633-0600 [2660]

Gann Company Inc.; E.C., 1621 196th Pl. SW, Lynnwood, WA 98036-7140, (425)774-4529 [26494]

Gannon Company Inc.; G.M., 3134 Post Rd., Warwick, RI 02886, (401)738-2200 [4397]

Gannsoft Publishing Co., 806 A Gillette Rd., Colville, WA 99114-9647, (509)684-7637 [6288]

Gans Tire Company Inc., PO Box 70, Malden, MA 02148-0001, (617)321-3910 [2661]

Ganson Engineering Inc., 18678 142nd Ave. NE, Woodinville, WA 98072, (425)489-2090 [6289]

Gant Food Distributors Inc., 1200 Carter Rd., Owensboro, KY 42301, (502)684-2382 [11231]

Gant Oil Co., PO Box 68, Walkertown, NC 27051, (336)595-2151 [22301]

G.A.R. International Corp., 3315 Commerce Parkway, Miramar, FL 33025, (954)704-9490 [7376]

Gar-Ron Plastics Corp., 5424 Pulaski Hwy., Baltimore, MD 21205, (410)483-1122 [22967]

Garan, Inc., 115 Dorsky St., Adamsville, TN 38310-2412, (901)632-3321 [4976]

Garber Brothers Inc., PO Box 296, Randolph, MA 02368, (617)341-0800 [11232]

Garbo Lobster Company Inc., PO Box 906, Stonington, CT 06378, (203)535-1590 [11233]

Garbose Metal Co., 770 Salisbury St., Apt. 416, Worcester, MA 01609-1167 [26821]

Garci Plastics Industries, 1730 W 38th Pl., Hialeah, FL 33012-7099, (305)558-8930 [15511]

Garco Wine, 4017 Folsom, St. Louis, MO 63110, (314)664-8300 [1704]

Garden Exchange Limited, 300 Keawe St., Hilo, HI 96720, (808)961-2875 [13720]

Garden Foods Products, 4844 Butterfield Rd., Hillside, IL 60162, (708)449-0171 [11234]

Garden Grove Nursery Inc., PO Box 80889, Phoenix, AZ 85060, (602)942-7500 [721]

Garden Grow Co, PO Box 280, Independence, OR 97351, (503)838-2811 [722]

Garden Island Motors Ltd., 3050 Hoolako St., Lihue, HI 96766, (808)245-6711 [20641]

Garden Spot Distributors, 438 White Oak Rd., New Holland, PA 17557, (717)354-4936 [11235]

Garden State Fireworks Inc., 383 Carlton Rd., PO Box 403, Millington, NJ 07946, (908)647-1086 [9635]

Garden State Tile Design Center, 231 Rte. 73, RD. 3, Berlin, NJ 08009, (609)753-0300 [9908]

Garden State Tile Distributors, 790 S Route 73, West Berlin, NJ 08091, (609)753-0300 [9909]

Garden State Tile Distributors, 1290 Rte. 130, Dayton, NJ 08810, (732)329-0860 [9910]

Garden State Tile Distributors, 5001 Industrial Rd., Rte. 34, Farmingdale, NJ 07727, (732)938-6663 [9911]

Garden State Tile Distributors, 790 S Route 73, West Berlin, NJ 08091, (609)753-0300 [7377]

Garden State Tile Distributors, Inc., 472 E Westfield Ave., Roselle Park, NJ 07204, (908)241-4900 [9912]

Garden Valley Coop., PO Box 38, Waumandee, WI 54622, (608)626-2111 [723]

Gardena Industrial Supply and Hardware Co., 17010 S Vermont, Gardena, CA 90247, (310)527-9500 [16887]

Gardena Recycling Center Inc., 1538 W 134th St., Gardena, CA 90249, (310)516-8195 [26822]

Gardenbolt International Corp., PO Box 39, Sayreville, NJ 08872-9998, (732)727-5800 [13749]

Gardener's Supply Co., 130 Intervale Rd., Burlington, VT 05401, (802)660-3506 [835]

Gardener's Supply Co., 128 Intervale Rd., Burlington, VT 05401, (802)660-3500 [14872]

Gardenview Eggs, PO Box 494, Reedsville, PA 17084, (717)667-2711 [11236]

Gardner and Benoit Inc., PO Box 30005, Charlotte, NC 28230, (704)332-5086 [24126]

Gardner Distributing Co., 6840 Trade Center Ave., Billings, MT 59101, (406)656-5000 [724]

Gardner Hardware Co., 515 Washington Ave. N, Minneapolis, MN 55401, (612)333-3393 [7378]

Gardner Inc., 1150 Chesapeake Ave., Columbus, OH 43212, (614)488-7951 [725]

Gardner Inc.; E.L., 1914 Forest Dr., Annapolis, MD 21401-4343, (410)266-8239 [7379]

Gardner and Meredith Inc., PO Box 4837, Chattanooga, TN 37405, (615)756-4722 [16047]

Gardner's Book Service, Inc., 4303 W Van Buren, No. 3, Phoenix, AZ 85043, (602)233-9424 [3770]

Gardners Good Foods Inc., 250 North St., White Plains, NY 10625, (914)335-2500 [11237]

Gardners Shoes Inc., 8513 Midlothian Tpke., Richmond, VA 23235-5123, (804)323-5979 [24749]

Gared Sports Inc., 1107 Mullanphy St., St. Louis, MO 63106, (314)421-0044 [23683]

Garialo; N.T., 480 W Beach St., Watsonville, CA 95076-4510, (408)724-1366 [10782]

Garick Corp., 13600 Broadway Ave., Cleveland, OH 44125, (216)581-0100 [27308]

Garka Mill Company Inc., 60 State Ave., Marysville, WA 98270, (206)659-8584 [7380]

Garment District Inc., 200 Broadway, Cambridge, MA 02139-1944, (617)876-5230 [4977]

Garment Inc.; Susan, 5601 Collins Ave., Apt. 1701, Miami Beach, FL 33140-2451, (305)272-6661 [4978]

Garmirian Company Inc.; H.K., 20 Jones St., New Rochelle, NY 10801, (914)645-0300 [4979]

Garner Meats Inc.; John, PO Box 625, Van Buren, AR 72957, (501)474-6894 [11238]

Garner Wholesale Merchandisers Inc., 305 Industrial Blvd., Greenville, NC 27835, (919)758-1189 [14108]

Garpac Corp., 462 Seventh Ave., New York, NY 10018, (212)760-0070 [4980]

Garrard County Stockyard, PO Box 654, Lancaster, KY 40444, (606)792-2118 [17933]

Garrett & Co., Inc., PO Box 57426, Murray, UT 84157 [23684]

Garrett Educational Corp., PO Box 1588, Ada, OK 74820, (580)332-6884 [3771]

Garrett III & Co. Inc.; J.W., 156 N Main St., Chase City, VA 23924-1610, (804)372-4555 [23685]

Garroutte Products, Bldg No. 5 Darrschool, Box 2930, Ponca City, OK 74602, (580)767-1622 [726]

Garston, Inc., 8 Parkridge Rd., Haverhill, MA 01835-6904, (978)374-0600 [25657]

Garston Sign Supplies, Inc., 110 Batson Dr., Manchester, CT 06040, (860)649-9626 [25658]

Gartner Refrigeration Inc., 2331 W Superior St., Duluth, MN 55806-1931, (218)722-4439 [14455]

Garton Ford Tractor Inc., PO Box 1849, Turlock, CA 95381, (209)632-3931 [727]

Garwood Implement and Supply Co., PO Box 428, Garwood, TX 77442, (409)758-3221 [17934]

Gary's Everfresh Products Inc., 1614 Dolwick Rd., Erlanger, KY 41018, (606)525-8228 [11239]

Gary's Machinery Inc., 1442 E Lincoln Ave., Orange, CA 92865-1934, (714)283-1900 [16888]

Gas & Electrical Equipment Co., PO Box 26763, Oklahoma City, OK 73126-0763, (405)528-3551 [25206]

Gas Equipment Distributors, 535 W Thompson Ln., No. B, Nashville, TN 37211, (615)242-1377 [15142]

Gas Equipment Supply Co., 1125 Satellite Blvd., Ste. 112, Suwanee, GA 30024, (770)813-1199 [22302]

Gas Technics of Ohio, 14788 York Rd., North Royalton, OH 44133, (440)237-8770 [16889]

Gaskins; Carlton J., 357 W Main St., Lake City, SC 29560-2315, (803)394-8830 [14456]

Gaspro, 2305 Kam Hwy., Honolulu, HI 96819, (808)842-2222 [18804]

Gass Horse Supply, 476 Main St., Orono, ME 04473-0476, (207)866-2075 [17935]

Gass Sales Stables, 476 Main St., Orono, ME 04473-0476, (207)866-2075 [17935]

Gassmon Coal and Oil Company Inc., Bronx Pl. & E 132nd St., Bronx, NY 10454, (212)369-7700 [20542]

Gaston Dupre Inc., 12455 Kerran St., Ste. 200, Poway, CA 92064-6855, (858)486-1101 [11951]

Gaston Sealey Company Inc., PO Box 428, Fairmont, NC 28340, (919)628-6761 [728]

Gate City Beverage Distributors, PO Box 8458, San Bernardino, CA 92412, (909)799-1600 [1705]

Gate City Equipment Company Inc., 2000 Northfield Ct., Roswell, GA 30076-3825, (404)475-1900 [22303]

Gate Group USA, Inc., 75 Varick St., New York, NY 10013, (212)966-8995 [22855]

Gate Petroleum Co., PO Box 23627, Jacksonville, FL 32241, (904)737-7220 [11240]

Gately Communication Company Inc., 501 Industry Dr., Hampton, VA 23661-1314, (757)826-8210 [5617]

Gately Communications Company Inc., 501 Industry Dr., Hampton, VA 23661-1314, (757)826-8210 [8773]

Gates/Arrow Distributing Inc., 39 Pelham Ridge Dr., Greenville, SC 29615 [6290]

Gates Arrow Distributing Inc., 39 Pleham Ridge Dr., Greenville, SC 29615, (843)234-0736 [8774]

Gates Co. Inc.; B., 1010 Pamela Dr., Euless, TX 76040, (817)267-8755 [23183]

Gates/FA Distributing Inc., 39 Pelham Ridge Dr., Greenville, SC 29615, (803)234-0736 [6291]

Gates InterAmerica, 3609 N 29th Ave., Hollywood, FL 33020, (954)926-7510 [16890]

Gateswood Software Inc., 222 S Rainbow, No. 111, Las Vegas, NV 89128, (702)363-7700 [6292]

Gateway Appliance Distributing Co., 19204 68th S, Kent, WA 98032, (253)872-7838 [15143]

Gateway Auto Parts, Rte. 20, PO Box 9, Huntington, MA 01050, (413)667-3101 [2662]

Gateway Co-Op, PO Box 125, Galva, IL 61434, (309)932-2081 [17936]

Gateway Distributing Co., 120 26th St., Ogden, UT 84401, (801)394-8839 [11241]

Gateway Distributors Inc., 3634 Village Ave., Norfolk, VA 23502-5600, (757)857-5931 [9913]

Gateway Foods Inc., 1637 St. James St., La Crosse, WI 54602, (608)785-1330 [11242]

Gateway Foods of Pennsylvania Inc., PO Box 478, Huntingdon, PA 16652, (814)643-2300 [11243]

Gateway Foods of Twin Ports Inc., PO Box 1149, Superior, WI 54880, (715)392-8880 [11147]

Gateway Seed Co., 510 Bittner St., St. Louis, MO 63147, (314)381-8500 [729]

Gateway Software Corp., PO Box 367, Fromberg, MT 59029, (406)668-7661 [6293]

Gateway Supply Co., 1401 E Higgins Rd., Elk Grove Village, IL 60007, (847)956-1560 [23184]

Gateway Supply Company Inc., PO Box 56, Columbia, SC 29202, (803)771-7160 [23185]

Gateway Tire Company Inc., 4 W Crescentville Rd., Cincinnati, OH 45246, (513)874-2500 [2663]

Gateway Tire Company Inc., 4 W Crescentville Rd., Cincinnati, OH 45246, (513)874-2500 [24276]

Gattas Company Inc.; Fred P., 5000 Summer Ave., Memphis, TN 38122, (901)767-2930 [15512]

GATX Corp., 500 W Monroe St., Chicago, IL 60661-3676, (312)621-6200 [23478]

GATX Terminals Corp., 500 W Monroe, Chicago, IL 60661, (312)621-6200 [22304]

Gatzke Farms Inc., Hwy. 22, PO Box 247, Montello, WI 53949-0247, (608)297-2193 [11244]

Gaucho Foods Inc., PO Box 307, Westmont, IL 60559, (630)241-3663 [11245]

Gauntlett Agency Ltd., 76 Amaral St., Riverside, RI 02915-2205, (401)434-3355 [25659]

Gavilanes Books from Indoamerica, PO Box 850286, New Orleans, LA 70185, (504)837-5806 [3772]

Gavlick Machinery Corporation, 100 Franklin St., PO Box 370, Bristol, CT 06011-0370, (860)589-2900 [16048]

Gay Johnson's Inc., PO Box 1829, Grand Junction, CO 81502, (970)245-7992 [2664]

Gayla Industries Inc., PO Box 920800, Houston, TX 77292, (713)681-2411 [26495]

Gayle Oil Company Inc., PO Drawer 100, Gueydan, LA 70542, (318)536-6738 [22305]

Gaylon Distributing Inc., 10310 S Dolfield Rd., Owings Mills, MD 21117-3510, (410)363-6600 [8775]

Gaylord Brothers, PO Box 4901, Syracuse, NY 13221-4901, (315)457-5070 [25207]

Gaylord Cash & Carry, 860 N Center Ave., Gaylord, MI 49735-1510, (517)732-8200 [11246]

Gaylord Manufacturing Co., PO Box 547, Ceres, CA 95307, (209)538-3313 [8776]

Gazaway & Associates; Jerry, 1703 S 6th St., Marshalltown, IA 50158, (515)752-7589 [23686]

Gazelle Athletics, PO Box 1011, The Dalles, OR 97058-9011, (541)298-4277 [23687]

GBC Technologies Inc., 6365 Carlson Dr., Ste. F, Eden Prairie, MN 55346, (612)947-1000 [6294]

GBS Corp., PO Box 2340, North Canton, OH 44720, (330)494-5330 [21736]

GC Thorsen Inc., 1801 Morgan St., Rockford, IL 61102-1209, (815)968-9661 [8777]

GCF Inc., 105 Dorothy St., Buffalo, NY 14206, (716)823-9900 [19995]

GCM Corp., 1329 Warwick Ave., Warwick, RI 02888-5030, (401)463-5262 [21449]

GCM International, 6140 W Quaker St., Orchard Park, NY 14127-2639, (716)662-4441 [10249]

GCR Rose Truck Tire Center, 17051 I-35 N, Schertz, TX 78154, (210)533-7138 [2665]

GCR Truck Tire Center, 4160 Reardon Rd., Forest, WI 54012, (608)846-2494 [2666]

G.D.E., Inc., 2715 E Saturn St., Brea, CA 92821-6705, (714)528-6880 [8778]

GE Capital Information Technology Solutions, 220 Girard St., Gaithersburg, MD 20884-6004, (301)258-2965 [6295]

GE Machine Tool Services, PO Box 32036, Louisville, KY 40232, (502)969-3126 [16049]

GE Supply, 2 Corporate Dr., PO Box 861, Shelton, CT 06484-0861, (203)944-3000 [8779]

Gear Clutch & Joint, 124 E Broadway, Lubbock, TX 79403, (806)763-5329 [2667]

Gear Motions Inc., 1750 Milton Ave., Syracuse, NY 13209, (315)488-0100 [16891]

Gear & Wheel Corp., 1965 Stan Home Way, Orlando, FL 32804, (407)843-1900 [2668]

Geary Pacific Corp., 1908 N Enterprise St., Orange, CA 92865, (714)279-2950 [14457]

GEC Alsthom Balteau, Inc., 300 W Antelope Rd., Medford, OR 97503, (541)826-2113 [8780]

Geddie; Thomas E., 314 Faulk St., Athens, TX 75751, (903)675-2424 [730]

Gee; Donald & Rema, 1349 Commanche Dr., Las Vegas, NV 89109-3112, (702)735-9637 [17422]

Geer Tank Trucks Inc., PO Drawer J, Jacksboro, TX 76458, (940)567-2677 [22306]

Gehlhausen Paint Wholesalers Inc., 520 N Main St., Evansville, IN 47711, (812)428-5444 [21450]

Gehman Feed Mill Inc., 44 N 3rd St., Denver, PA 17517, (215)267-5585 [731]

Gehr Industries, 7400 E Slauson Ave., Los Angeles, CA 90040-3308, (213)728-5558 [16050]

Geib Industries Inc., 3220 Wolf Rd., Franklin Park, IL 60131, (847)455-4550 [16892]

Geiger Bros., Mount Hope Ave., PO Box 1609, Lewiston, ME 04241, (207)755-5000 [3773]

Geis Building Products Inc., PO Box 622, Brookfield, WI 53008-0622, (414)784-4250 [7381]

Gelber Industries, 1001 Cambridge Dr., Elk Grove Village, IL 60007-2453, (708)437-4500 [16051]

Gell and Co.; Jack, 5700 Federal Ave., Detroit, MI 48209, (313)554-2000 [19334]

Gem East Corp., 2124 2nd Ave., Seattle, WA 98121, (206)441-1700 [17423]

GEM Electronics, 34 Hempstead Turnpike, Farmingdale, NY 11735, (516)249-6996 [8781]

Gem Enterprises, Inc., 12 E Broadway, Derry, NH 03038-2410, (603)432-1920 [17424]

Gem Equipment Inc., PO Box 149, Twin Falls, ID 83303-0149, (208)733-7272 [732]

Gem Furniture Co. Inc., 711 Westminster St., Providence, RI 02903-4016, (401)831-9737 [13119]

Gem Guides Book Co., 315 Cloverleaf Dr., No. F, Baldwin Park, CA 91706-6510, (626)855-1611 [3774]

Gem-La Jewelry Inc., 964 Mineral Spring Ave., North Providence, RI 02904-4933, (401)724-3150 [17425]

Gem Platinum Manufacturing Co., 48 W 48th St., New York, NY 10036, (212)819-0850 [17426]

Gem State Distributors Inc., PO Box 2499, Pocatello, ID 83206-2499, (208)237-5151 [26298]

Gem State Paper and Supply Co., PO Box 469, Twin Falls, ID 83303-0469, (208)733-6081 [21737]

Gemaire Distributors Inc., 2151 W Hillsboro Blvd., Ste. 400, Deerfield Beach, FL 33442 [14458]

Gemcarve, 1116 17th St. W, Billings, MT 59102-4130, (406)259-9622 [17427]

Gemini Cosmetics, 1380 Greg St., Ste. 234, Sparks, NV 89431-6072, (702)359-3663 [14109]

Gemini Cosmetics, 1380 Greg St., Ste. 234, Sparks, NV 89431-6072, (702)359-3663 [19335]

Gemini Enterprises Inc., 16920 Kuykendahl, Ste. 228, Houston, TX 77068, (281)583-2900 [22307]

Gemini Ex-Im, 11310 Riverview Dr., Houston, TX 77077, (281)497-0045 [15144]

Gemini Manufacturing Inc., Hwy. 67 N, Walnut Ridge, AR 72476, (870)886-5512 [23688]

Gemini Sound Products Corp., 8 Germak Dr., Carteret, NJ 07008-1102, (732)969-9000 [25208]

Gemmex Intertrade America Inc., PO Box 3274, West McLean, VA 22103-3274, (703)893-9601 [11247]

GemTek Enterprises Inc., 983 Cranston St., Cranston, RI 02920, (401)946-6760 [17428]

Genal Strap Inc., 31-00 47th Ave., Long Island City, NY 11101, (718)706-8700 [17429]

Genalco Inc., 333 Reservoir St., Needham Heights, MA 02494, 877-436-2526 [7382]

Gene Labs Inc., 6638 Meadowlark Dr., Indianapolis, IN 46226-3608, (317)547-3840 [6296]

Gene Schick Co., 3544 Arden Rd., Hayward, CA 94545-3921, (650)589-7850 [15145]

Genealogical Sources Unlimited, 407 Ascot Ct., Knoxville, TN 37923-5807, (423)690-7831 [3775]

Generac Corp., PO Box 8, Waukesha, WI 53187, (414)544-4811 [8782]

General Air Service and Supply Company Inc., 1105 Zuni St., Denver, CO 80204, (303)892-7003 [16052]

General Auto Parts Inc., 384 King Rd., Tiverton, RI 02878-2721, (401)624-6687 [2669]

General Auto Sales Company Inc., PO Box 177, Claremont, NH 03743-0177, (603)542-9595 [2670]

General Automation Inc., 17731 Mitchell N, Irvine, CA 92623, (949)250-4800 [6297]

General Automation Manufacturing Inc., 35444 Mound Rd., Sterling Heights, MI 48310, (810)268-0300 [16053]

General Automotive Supply, 414 E 75th St., New York, NY 10021, (212)737-3000 [2189]

General Beer Distributors, 6169 Mckee Rd., Madison, WI 53701, (608)271-1234 [1706]

General Beverage Sales Co., PO Box 44326, Madison, WI 53744, (608)271-1234 [1707]

General Biomedical Service Inc., 1900 25th St., Kenner, LA 70062, (504)468-8597 [18805]

General Brokerage Co., 600-604 E 9th, Los Angeles, CA 90015-1820, (213)627-9032 [11248]

General Business Machines Inc., PO Box 637, Brunswick, ME 04011-0637, (207)725-6333 [21010]

General Communications, 2171 Ralph Ave., Stockton, CA 95206-3625, (209)462-6059 [5618]

General Distributing Co., PO Box 16070, Salt Lake City, UT 84116, (801)531-7895 [1708]

General Distributors Inc., PO Box 11343, 800 E Indianapolis, Wichita, KS 67202, (316)267-2255 [9914]

General Drug Co., PO Box 1110, Mishawaka, IN 46546-1110 [19336]

General Electric Co. Marine and Industrial Engines Div., 1 Neumann Way, No. S158, Cincinnati, OH 45215, (513)552-5370 [16054]

General Electric Supply, 684 Robbins Dr., Troy, MI 48083-4563, (248)588-7300 [8783]

General Equipment and Supplies Inc., PO Box 2145, Fargo, ND 58107, (701)282-2662 [7383]

General Fabrics Co., PO Box 6084, Providence, RI 02940-6084, (401)728-4200 [26041]

General Fasteners Company Inc., 11820 Globe St., Livonia, MI 48150-1180, (313)591-9500 [13721]

General Floor, 1720 Bayberry Rd., Bensalem, PA 19020, (215)633-7373 [9915]

General Genetics Inc., 13811 Cypress Ave., Sand Lake, MI 49343-9639, (616)636-8876 [17937]

General Glass Company Inc., PO Box 3066, Charleston, WV 25331, (304)925-2171 [7384]

General Handling Systems Inc., 701 E Plano Pkwy., Plano, TX 75074-6758, (972)424-9339 [16055]

General Heating and Cooling Co., 820 Atlantic Ave., North Kansas City, MO 64116, (816)471-1466 [14459]

General Imaging Corp., 7151 Savannah Dr., Newburgh, IN 47630-2184, (812)853-9294 [18806]

General Industrial Tool and Supply Inc., 12540 Sherman Way, North Hollywood, CA 91605, (818)983-0520 [16056]

General Injectables and Vaccines Inc., PO Box 9, Bastian, VA 24314, (540)688-4121 [19337]

General Iron Industries Inc., 1909 N Clifton Ave., Chicago, IL 60614, (773)327-9600 [26823]

General Machinery Company Inc., PO Box 606, Birmingham, AL 35201, (205)251-9243 [5842]

General Materials Inc., PO Box 824, Jackson, MI 49204, (517)784-3191 [7385]

General Medical Corp., PO Box 27452, Richmond, VA 23261, (804)264-7500 [18807]

General Medical Publishers, 318 Lincoln Blvd., No. 117, Venice, CA 90291, (213)392-4911 [3776]

General Merchandise Services Inc., PO Box 700, Bellefontaine, OH 43311, (513)592-7025 [14110]

General Metal and Abrasives Co., PO Box 74037, Romulus, MI 48174-0037, (734)595-7300 [20011]

General Metals of Tacoma Inc., 1902 Marine View Dr., Tacoma, WA 98422, (206)572-4000 [26824]

General Microsystems Inc. (Bellevue, Washington), 3220 118th Ave. SE, Ste. 100, Bellevue, WA 98005-4198, (425)644-2233 [6298]

General Mill Supplies Inc., PO Box 23587, New Orleans, LA 70183, (504)736-0404 [23186]

General Mills Inc., 500 W Walnut St., Johnson City, TN 37604, (423)928-3137 [11249]

General Mills Operations, 500 W Walnut St., Johnson City, TN 37604, (423)928-3137 [11249]

General Motors Corporation - Harrison Div., 200 Upper Mountain Rd., Lockport, NY 14094-1896, (716)439-2011 [14460]

General Music Corp., 1164 Tower Ln., Bensenville, IL 60106, (630)766-8230 [25209]

General Office Interiors, 1071 Springfield Rd., Union, NJ 07083, (908)688-9400 [13120]

General Office Products Co., 2050 Old Hwy. 8, New Brighton, MN 55112, (612)639-4700 [21011]

General Parts Corp., 7 Emory Pl., Knoxville, TN 37917, (615)525-6191 [2671]

General Parts, Inc., PO Box 19268, Shawnee, KS 66214, (913)248-4200 [2672]

General Parts Inc., PO Box 26006, Raleigh, NC 27611, (919)573-3000 [2673]

General Pipe and Supply Company Inc., PO Box 13185, Memphis, TN 38113, (901)774-7000 [23187]

General Plumbing Supply Company of Maryland Inc., 1829 Edison Hwy., Baltimore, MD 21213, (410)276-5200 [23188]

General Polymers Div., 12001 Toepfer Rd., Warren, MI 48089, (810)755-1100 [22968]

General Potato and Onion Inc., PO Box 630, Stockton, CA 95201, (209)464-4621 [11250]

General Produce Company Ltd., PO Box 308, Sacramento, CA 95812-0308, (916)441-6431 [11251]

General Sales Co., 15-17-19 E Court St., Cincinnati, OH 45202, (513)621-2075 [26496]

General Steel Corp., 3344 E 80th St., Cleveland, OH 44127, (216)883-4200 [19996]

General Steel Fabricators, 927 Schifferdecker, Joplin, MO 64801, (417)623-2224 [19997]

General Steel Warehouse Inc., PO Box 2037, Lubbock, TX 79408, (806)763-7327 [19998]

General Supply and Paper Co., 1 George Ave., Wilkes Barre, PA 18705-2511, (717)823-1194 [21738]

General Supply and Paper Co., 1 George Ave., Wilkes Barre, PA 18705-2511, (717)823-1194 [16057]

General Supply of Yakima Inc., PO Box 2217, Yakima, WA 98907-2217, (509)248-1241 [4627]

General Tire Inc., 2550 Lukens Ln., Carson City, NV 89706, (775)882-3454 [2674]

General Tool and Supply Co., 2705 NW Nicolai St., Portland, OR 97210-1818, (503)226-3411 [13722]

General Tool & Supply Co., 5614 7th Ave. S, PO Box 80904, Seattle, WA 98108, (206)762-1500 [16893]

General Toys of Los Angeles, 522 E 4th St., Los Angeles, CA 90013, (213)687-4929 [26497]

General Trading Company Inc., 455 16th St., Carlstadt, NJ 07072, (201)935-7717 [11252]

General Trading House, PO Box 2617, Butler, PA 16003, (412)282-4528 [7421]

General Truck Body Co., 1919 10th St. NW, Roanoke, VA 24012, (540)362-1861 [2675]

General Truck Parts and Equipment Co., 3835 W 42nd St., Chicago, IL 60632, (773)247-6900 [2676]

General Truck Sales Corp., PO Box 8557, South Charleston, WV 25303, (304)744-1321 [20642]

General Waste Products Inc., PO Box 6690, Evansville, IN 47713-1038, (812)423-4267 [26825]

General Wholesale Co., 1271-A Tacoma Dr., Atlanta, GA 30318, (404)351-3626 [1709]

General Wine Co., 373 Victor Ave., Highland Park, MI 48203, (313)867-0521 [1710]

Generic Computer Products Inc., PO Box 790, Marquette, MI 49855, (906)226-7600 [6299]

Generic Distributors L.P., 1611 Olive St., Monroe, LA 71201, (318)388-8850 [19338]

Generic Systems Inc., PO Box 153, Perrysburg, OH 43552, (419)841-8460 [8784]

Genes Appliance Parts Inc., 788 Gorham St., Lowell, MA 01852-4636, (978)453-2896 [15146]

Genesee Ceramic Tile Distribution, Michigan Design Ctr., 1700 Stuty Dr., Ste. 108, Troy, MI 48084, (248)637-3272 [9916]

Genesee Ceramic Tile Distributors, 1307 N Belsay Rd., Burton, MI 48509, (810)743-2000 [9917]

Genesee Ceramic Tile Distributors, 24701 Telegraph Rd., Southfield, MI 48034, (248)354-3550 [9918]

Genesee Ceramic Tile Distributors, 43220 Merrill Rd., Sterling Heights, MI 48314, (810)254-4744 [9919]

Genesee Ceramic Tile Distributors, 24260 Indoplex, Farmington Hills, MI 48335, (248)478-3958 [9920]

Genesee Ceramic Tile Distributors, 459 36th St. SE, Grand Rapids, MI 49548, (616)243-5811 [9921]

Genesee Natural Foods, Rd. 2, Box 105, Genesee, PA 16923, (814)228-3200 [11253]

Genesee Reserve Supply Inc., PO Box 20619, Rochester, NY 14602-0619, (716)292-7040 [7386]

Genesee Union Warehouse Company Inc., PO Box 67, Genesee, ID 83832, (208)285-1141 [17938]

Genesis Associates Inc., 128 Wheeler Rd., Burlington, MA 01803-5170, (781)270-9540 [8785]

Genesis Manufacturing, Inc., PO Box 252, Albertville, AL 35950, (205)878-1003 [15513]

Genesis Medical Equipment, 3909 Beecher Rd., Flint, MI 48532-3602, (810)733-6322 [18808]

Genesis Safety Systems Inc., 7 Doig Rd., Wayne, NJ 07470, (973)696-9400 [24555]

Genesis Technologies Inc., PO Box 3789, Eagle, CO 81631, (970)328-9515 [15147]

Genesis Telecom Inc., 1235 North Loop W, Ste. 100, Houston, TX 77008, (713)868-5415 [5619]

Genetic Leaders International, 193 Woodburn Pl., Advance, NC 27006-9456, (910)998-3958 [17939]

Geneva Corp., PO Box 21962, Greensboro, NC 27420, (910)275-9936 [7387]

Geneva Elevator Co., PO Box 49, Geneva, IA 50633, (515)458-8145 [733]

Gennett Lumber Co., PO Box 5088, Asheville, NC 28813-5088, (828)253-3626 [7388]

Genny USA Inc., 650 5th Ave., New York, NY 10019, (212)245-4860 [4981]

Gensco, Inc., 1824 Ship Ave., Anchorage, AK 99501, (907)274-6507 [14461]

Gensco, Inc., 2270 NE Argyle, Portland, OR 97213, (503)288-7473 [14462]

Gensco, Inc., 3350 Pipebend Pl. NE, Salem, OR 97301, (503)585-1743 [14463]

Gensco, Inc., 921 SE Armour Rd., Bend, OR 97702, (541)388-1547 [14464]

Gensco Inc., 4402 20th St. E, Tacoma, WA 98424, (253)922-3003 [14465]

Gensco, Inc., 1703 6th Ave. S, Seattle, WA 98134, (206)682-7591 [14466]

Gensco, Inc., 11155 120th NE, Kirkland, WA 98033, (425)822-9644 [14467]

Gensco, Inc., 2501 River Rd., Yakima, WA 98902, (509)248-6226 [14468]

Gensco, Inc., 1630 Division, Bellingham, WA 98226, (206)676-8874 [14469]

Gensco, Inc., 2913 Marvin Rd. NE, Olympia, WA 98516, (206)491-8393 [19999]

Gensia Sicor Inc., 19 Hughes, Irvine, CA 92618, (949)455-4700 [18809]

Genuine Auto Parts Co., 415 W Main St., Rochester, NY 14608, (716)235-1595 [2677]

Genuine Parts Co., 2999 Circle 75 Pkwy., Atlanta, GA 30339, (770)953-1700 [2678]

Genuine Parts Company of West Virginia Inc., PO Box 670, Wheeling, WV 26003, (304)233-0300 [2679]

Genuine Rose Inc., 1031 S Broadway, No. 934, Los Angeles, CA 90015-4006, (213)747-4120 [4982]

Genzink Steel, 40 E 64th St., Holland, MI 49423, (616)392-1437 [20000]

Genzink Steel, 40 E 64th St., Holland, MI 49423, (616)392-1437 [20001]

GEO Drilling Fluids Inc., 1431 Union Ave., Bakersfield, CA 93305, (805)325-5919 [4398]

Geo-Hex, 2126 N Lewis Ave. 2, Portland, OR 97227-1708, (503)288-4805 [26498]

Geo-Synthetics, Inc., 428 N Pewaukee Rd., Waukesha, WI 53188, (414)524-7979 [26042]

GeoCHEM Inc., PO Box 838, Renton, WA 98057-0838, (425)227-9312 [22969]

George Co.; Edward, 12650 Springfield S, Alsip, IL 60803, (708)371-0660 [7389]

George Co.; Edward, 12650 S Springfield Ave., Alsip, IL 60803, (708)371-0696 [7390]

George Co. Inc.; William, 1002 Mize Ave., Lufkin, TX 75901-0102, (409)634-7738 [11254]

George H. International Corp., 5705 W Fort St., Detroit, MI 48209, (313)842-6100 [734]

George Inc.; Al, PO Box 3604, Lafayette, LA 70502, (337)233-0626 [16058]

George Malvese and Company Inc., PO Box 295, Hicksville, NY 11802, (516)681-7600 [983]

George Washington University Press, Academic Center, Rm. T-308, Washington, DC 20052, (202)676-5116 [3777]

Georgetown Energy Inc., 2104 N Austin Ave., Georgetown, TX 78626, (512)863-8607 [7391]

Georgetown Unimetal Sales, 1901 Roxborough Rd., No. 220, Charlotte, NC 28211, (704)365-2205 [20002]

Georgia Business Solutions, 2010 Huntcliff Dr., Lawrenceville, GA 30043-6357, (404)513-9280 [6300]

Georgia Crown Distributing, 255 Villanova Dr., Atlanta, GA 30336, (404)344-9550 [1711]

Georgia Crown Distributing Co., PO Box 7908, Columbus, GA 31908, (706)568-4580 [1712]

Georgia Fabrics Inc., 1430 Broadway, New York, NY 10018, (212)391-2550 [26043]

Georgia Flush Door Sales Inc., PO Box 43008, Atlanta, GA 30315-6008, (404)524-0223 [7392]

Georgia Impression Products Inc., 4215 Wendell Dr., Ste. H, Atlanta, GA 30336, (404)691-1230 [13121]

Georgia Lighting Supply Co., 530 14th St., Atlanta, GA 30318, (404)875-4754 [8786]

Georgia Marble Co., 1201 Roberts Blvd.B, No. 100, Kennesaw, GA 30144-3619, (404)421-6500 [7393]

Georgia Mountain Water Inc., PO Box 1243, Marietta, GA 30061, (404)928-9971 [24957]

Georgia-Pacific Corp. Distribution Div., PO Box 105605, Atlanta, GA 30348, (404)521-4000 [7394]

Georgia Steel and Chemical Co., 10810 Guilford Rd., Ste. 104, Annapolis Junction, MD 20701-1118, (301)317-5502 [18810]

Georgies Ceramic & Clay Co., 756 NE Lombard St., Portland, OR 97211-3562, (503)283-1353 [26499]

Georgino and Sons Inc.; Patsy, PO Box 300, Penfield, PA 15849, (814)637-5301 [16894]

Geotronics of North America Inc., 911 Hawthorn Dr., Itasca, IL 60143, (708)285-1400 [24364]

Geraghty Industrial Equipment Inc., 4414 11th St., Rockford, IL 61109, (815)397-4450 [16059]

Gerber Agri-Export Inc., 1640 Powers Ferry Rd., Bldg. 29, Ste. 200, Marietta, GA 30067, (404)952-4187 [11255]

Gerber Cheese Company Inc., 175 Clearbrook Rd., Elmsford, NY 10523-1109 [11256]

Gerber and Company Inc.; J., 11 Penn Plz., New York, NY 10001-2057, (212)631-1200 [20003]

Gerber Inc.; Max, 2293 N Milwaukee Ave., Chicago, IL 60647, (773)342-7600 [23189]

Gerber Metal Supply Co., 40-50 Montgomery St., Hillside, NJ 07205, (908)964-1955 [26826]

Gerber Plumbing Fixtures Corp., 4600 W Touhy Ave., Lincolnwood, IL 60712, (847)675-6570 [23190]

Gerber Radio Supply Co., 128 Carnegie Row, Norwood, MA 02062, (781)329-2400 [8787]

Gerhardt's Inc., PO Box 10161, New Orleans, LA 70181-0161, (504)733-2500 [2680]

Gerhardt's International, Inc., PO Box 36334, Houston, TX 77236, (713)789-8860 [16060]

Geriatric Medical & Surgical, 395 3rd St., Everett, MA 02149, (617)387-5936 [18811]

Gering; David, 2020 3rd St. N, Nampa, ID 83687-4425, (208)466-9003 [24127]

Gerlach Beef Inc., 841 Washington, New York, NY 10014-1307, (212)255-4750 [11257]

Gerlach Oil Company Inc., PO Box 364, Abilene, TX 79604, (915)692-1293 [22308]

German Implement Co.; L.E., 624 W Spring St., Princeville, IL 61559, (309)385-4316 [735]

German's Outdoor Power Equipment, 624 W Spring St., Box 218, Princeville, IL 61559, (309)694-3700 [736]

Gerrard Steel of Illinois, 25th Ave. & Main St., Melrose Park, IL 60160, (708)681-9190 [20004]

Gerrity Company Inc., 90 Oak St., Newton Upper Falls, MA 02464, (617)244-1400 [7395]

Gershow Recycling, PO Box 526, Medford, NY 11763, (516)289-6188 [26827]

Gerson Company Inc., 6100 Broadmoor St., Shawnee Mission, KS 66202, (913)262-7400 [17430]

Gessler Publishing Company, Inc., 15 E Salem Ave., Roanoke, VA 24011, (540)345-1429 [3778]

Gesswein and Co.; Paul H., 255 Hancock Ave., Bridgeport, CT 06605, (203)366-5400 [16061]

Gestetner Corp., PO Box 10270, Stamford, CT 06904-2270, (203)625-7600 [21012]

Getaway Sailing, 2701 Boston St., Baltimore, MD 21224, (410)342-3110 [18506]

Getchell Brothers Inc., 1 Union St., Brewer, ME 04412, (207)989-7335 [11258]

Gettel and Co., 91 N Caseville Rd., Pigeon, MI 48755, (517)453-3332 [737]

Getty Petroleum Marketing Inc., 125 Jericho Tpke., Jericho, NY 11753, (516)338-6000 [22309]

Getty Realty Corp., 125 Jericho Tpke., Jericho, NY 11753, (516)338-6000 [22310]

Getz Bros. & Company Inc., 150 Post St., Ste. 500, San Francisco, CA 94108-4707, (415)772-5500 [16062]

Getzen Co., 530 S Highway H, PO Box 440, Elkhorn, WI 53121, (414)723-4221 [25210]

Geviderm Inc., 3003 W Olive Ave., Burbank, CA 91505, (818)841-3003 [14111]

GF Office Furniture Ltd., 916 Merchandise Mart, Chicago, IL 60654, (312)836-1750 [21013]

GFG Foodservice Inc., PO Box 14489, Grand Forks, ND 58208-4489, (701)795-5900 [11259]

GFI America Inc., 2815 Blaisdell Ave. S, Minneapolis, MN 55408, (612)872-6262 [11260]

GFT USA Corp., 11 W 42nd St., 19th Fl., New York, NY 10036-8002, (212)265-2788 [4983]

Ghia Corp., 15870 River Rd., Guerneville, CA 95446-9288, (415)282-2832 [25660]

Ghiselli Brothers, 625 Du Bois St., No. A-B, San Rafael, CA 94901-3944, (415)282-7303 [11261]

G.I. Industries, 195 W Los Angles Ave., Simi Valley, CA 93065, (805)529-5871 [26828]

GIA, PO Box 3274, West McLean, VA 22103-3274, (703)893-9601 [11247]

Giancola Exports, Inc.; D.J., 4317 E Genesee St., PO Box 4, Syracuse, NY 13214, (315)446-1002 [4628]

Giant Refining Co., Interstate 40, Exit 39, Jamestown, NM 87347, (505)722-3833 [22311]

Gibb Co.; Clark R., 5251 W 73rd St. J, Minneapolis, MN 55439-2206, (612)831-4890 [6301]

Gibble Oil Company Inc., PO Box 1270, Cushing, OK 74023, (918)225-0189 [22312]

Gibbons Inc.; J.T., 649 Papworth Ave., Metairie, LA 70005, (504)831-9907 [11262]

Gibbons and LeFort Inc., PO Box 758, Thibodaux, LA 70302, (504)447-9338 [22313]

Gibbs Wire and Steel Co., PO Box 520, Southington, CT 06489, (203)621-0121 [20005]

Gibraltar Steel Corp., PO Box 2028, Buffalo, NY 14219-0228, (716)826-6500 [20006]

Gibraltar Steel Products, 635 S Park Ave., Buffalo, NY 14210, (716)826-6500 [20007]

Gibson Co.; C.R., 32 Knight St., Norwalk, CT 06856, (203)847-4543 [13360]

Gibson Dot Publications, PO Box 117, Waycross, GA 31502-0117, (912)285-2848 [3779]

Gibson Farmers Cooperative, PO Box 497, Trenton, TN 38382, (901)855-1891 [738]

Gibson Group Inc., PO Box 8028, Cincinnati, OH 45208, (513)871-9966 [21739]

Gibson McIlvain Co.; J., PO Box 222, White Marsh, MD 21162, (410)335-9600 [7396]

Gibson Overseas Inc., 2410 Yates Ave., Los Angeles, CA 90040-1918, (323)832-8900 [15514]

Gibson Wine Company Inc., 1720 Academy, Sanger, CA 93657, (209)875-2505 [1713]

Gidden Distributing, PO Box 449, Temple, TX 76503, (254)773-9933 [1714]

Gideon Distributing Inc., 5355 Ohio St., PO Box 3645, Beaumont, TX 77704, (409)833-3361 [1715]

Gierston Tool Company Inc., 382 Upper Oakwood Ave., PO Box 2247, Elmira, NY 14903, (607)733-7191 [16063]

Gifford-Brown Inc., PO Box 698, Des Moines, IA 50303-0698, (515)243-1257 [25211]

Gigatec (U.S.A.) Inc., PO Box 4705, Portsmouth, NH 03802, (603)433-2227 [6302]

Giglio Distributing Company Inc., PO Box 4046, Beaumont, TX 77704, (409)838-1654 [1716]

Gilbert Co.; A.L., PO Box 38, Oakdale, CA 95361, (209)847-1721 [739]

Gilbert Company Inc.; S.L., 40 E 34th St., New York, NY 10156-2031, (212)686-5145 [4984]

Gilbert Foods Inc., 7251 Standard Dr., Hanover, MD 21076, (410)712-6000 [11263]

Gilbert Lumber/IFCO Systems, PO Box 216, Smithville, OH 44677, (330)669-2726 [25917]

Gilbert Pipe and Supply Co.; A.A., 4037 Mansfield Rd., Shreveport, LA 71103, (318)425-2447 [23191]

Gilbert and Richards Inc., 70 State St., North Haven, CT 06473, (203)239-4646 [16064]

Gilbert & Son Shoe Company, 149 S Daniel Morgan Ave., Spartanburg, SC 29306-3211, (864)582-8049 [24750]

Gilco Meats Inc., 1111 Greenwood Rd., Baltimore, MD 21208, (410)484-3900 [11264]

Giles Farmers Cooperative Inc., PO Box 295, Pulaski, TN 38478, (931)363-2563 [740]

Giles and Ransome Inc., 2975 Galloway Rd., Bensalem, PA 19020, (215)639-4300 [16065]

Gillespie Oil Company Inc., 706 W Sandusky Ave., Bellefontaine, OH 43311, (937)599-2085 [2681]

Gillette Air Inc., 2000 Airport Rd., Rm 5, Gillette, WY 82716-8105, (307)686-2900 [93]

Gillies Coffee Co., PO Box 320206, Brooklyn, NY 11232-1005, (718)499-7766 [11265]

Gillmore Security Systems Inc., 26165 Broadway Ave., Cleveland, OH 44146-6519, (440)232-1000 [24556]

Gills Automotive Inc., 275 Rimmon St., Manchester, NH 03102-3714, (603)623-7193 [14470]

Gilman Industrial Exports, Inc., 98A Fairport Village Landing, Fairport, NY 14450, (716)425-0310 [24365]

Gilmou Inc.; Doug, RRNo. 1, Box 15A, Barnet, VT 05821, (802)633-2575 [17940]

Gilvins Boots & Shoes, 3838 S Madison Ave., Indianapolis, IN 46227-1310, (317)783-3210 [24751]

Gim Tree Manufacturing, 6950 NW 37th Ave., Miami, FL 33147-6514, (305)693-7873 [4906]

Ging and Co., PO Box 248, Farina, IL 62838, (618)245-3333 [17941]

Gingery Publishing; David J., PO Box 75, Fordland, MO 65652, (417)890-1965 [3780]

Ginsbergs Institutional Food Service Supplies Inc., Rte. 66, PO Box 17, Hudson, NY 12534, (518)828-4004 [11266]

Ginseng Co., PO Box 970, Simi Valley, CA 93062, (805)520-7500 [14112]

Ginseng Up Corp., 392 5th Ave., Rm. 1004, New York, NY 10018-8114, (212)696-1930 [24958]

Giordano International; Michael, 7 W 36th St., New York, NY 10018, (212)239-1800 [17431]

Girardi Distributors Corp., PO Box 967, Athol, MA 01331, (978)249-3581 [1717]

Girindus Corp., 34650 U.S Hwy. 19 N, No. 208, Palm Harbor, FL 34684-2156, (813)781-8383 [4399]

Girzen, Res., 9508 Locust Hill Dr., Great Falls, VA 22066, (703)757-9123 [19339]

Gita Sporting Goods, Ltd., 12600 Steele Creek Rd., Charlotte, NC 28273-3770, (704)588-7550 [24752]

Gita Sports Ltd., 12600 Steele Creek Rd., Charlotte, NC 28273-3770, (704)588-7550 [24752]

Giumarra Brothers Fruit Company, Inc., PO Box 21218, Los Angeles, CA 90021-1218, (213)627-2900 [11267]

Give Something Back Inc., 7303 Edgewater Dr., Oakland, CA 94621, (510)635-5500 [21014]

Givenchy Corp., 19 E 57th St., New York, NY 10022-2508, (212)931-2550 [4985]

G.J. Chemical Company Inc., 370-376 Adams St., Newark, NJ 07114, (201)589-1450 [4400]

GJ Sales Co., 209 Nooseneck Hill Rd., West Greenwich, RI 02817-2277, (401)397-6122 [7397]

GKM Enterprises Inc., 5059 Lankershi Blvd., North Hollywood, CA 91601-4224, (818)762-2846 [22856]

GKR Industries, Inc., 13653 S Kenton Ave., Crestwood, IL 60445, (708)389-2003 [21740]

Glacier Seafoods, 7930 King St., Anchorage, AK 99518-3058, (907)258-1234 [11268]

Glacier Studio, PO Box J, Browning, MT 59417, (406)338-2100 [22857]

Glacier Water Services Inc., 2261 Cosmos Ct., Carlsbad, CA 92009, (760)930-2420 [24128]

Glade and Grove Supply Inc., PO Drawer 760, Belle Glade, FL 33430, (561)996-3095 [741]

Glamour Glove Corp., 44-02 23rd St., Long Island City, NY 11101-5000, (718)361-9881 [4986]

GL&V/Celleco Inc., 1000 Laval Blvd., Lawrenceville, GA 30043, (404)963-2100 [16066]

Glant Pacific Co., PO Box C-3637, Seattle, WA 98124, (206)628-6222 [26829]

Glant Pacific Iron and Metal Co., PO Box C-3637, Seattle, WA 98124, (206)628-6232 [26830]

Glantz & Son; N., 650 Seco Rd., Monroeville, PA 15146, (412)372-8110 [25661]

Glasco Electric Co., 712 E 18th St., Kansas City, MO 64108-1705, (816)421-7020 [9285]

Glaser and Son Inc.; H., PO Box 5977, Holliston, MA 01746, (508)429-8381 [4987]

Glasgow Cooperative Association, 102 2nd St., Glasgow, MO 65254, (816)338-2251 [742]

Glasgow Distributors Inc., PO Box 146, Glasgow, MT 59230-0146, (406)228-8277 [1718]

Glasparts Inc., PO Box 30116, Portland, OR 97294-3116, (503)254-9694 [2682]

Glass Co., Inc.; The John M., 7504 Crews Dr., PO Box 26189, Lawrence, IN 46226, (317)547-0727 [16895]

Glass Crafters of Manhasset, Inc., 398 Interstate Ct., Sarasota, FL 34240 [13361]

Glass Crafters Stain Glass Supply, 398 Interstate Ct., Sarasota, FL 34240 [13361]

Glass Depot, 3235 Rosetta Place Dr., No. 2, South Bend, IN 46628-3448, (219)291-5150 [7398]

Glass Specialty Inc., 2439 S Main St., Box 737, Bloomington, IL 61701, (309)827-8087 [2683]

Glaze Inc., 11-B Jane Pl., Edison, NJ 08820, (908)755-2233 [13362]

Glaze Supply Company Inc., PO Box 1443, Dalton, GA 30720, (706)278-3663 [8788]

Glazer's of Iowa, 4401 NW 112th St., Urbandale, IA 50322, (515)252-7173 [1719]

Glazer's Wholesale Drug Co. Inc., 14860 Landmark Blvd., Dallas, TX 75240, (972)702-0900 [1720]

Gleeson Inc., PO Box 7449, Louisville, KY 40257-0449, (502)895-4880 [23689]

Glen Mills Inc., 395 Allwood Rd., Clifton, NJ 07012-1704, (973)777-0777 [24366]

Glen Rose Meat Services Inc., PO Box 58146, Vernon, CA 90058, (213)589-3393 [11269]

Glenco Hosiery Mills Inc., PO Box 1200, Cowpens, SC 29330-1200, (864)463-3295 [4988]

Glencourt Inc., 2800 Ygnacio Valley Rd., Walnut Creek, CA 94598, (925)944-4444 [11270]

Glencraft Lingerie Inc., 38 E 32nd, New York, NY 10016-5591, (212)689-5990 [4989]

Glendale Envelope Co., 807 Air Way, Glendale, CA 91201, (818)243-2127 [21741]

Glenn-Mar Marine Supply, Inc., 6870 142nd Ave. N, Largo, FL 33771, (813)536-1955 [18507]

Glenray Communications, PO Box 40400, Pasadena, CA 91114-7400, (626)797-5462 [25212]

Glenray Productions, Inc., PO Box 40400, Pasadena, CA 91114-7400, (626)797-5462 [25212]

Glen's Peanuts and Grains Inc., 1668 N M 88, Portales, NM 88130-9670, (505)276-8201 [17942]

Glentex Corp., 417 5th Ave., New York, NY 10016, (212)686-4424 [4990]

GLF/SAE, 125 Blaze Industrial Pky., Berea, OH 44017-8004, (440)239-2015 [13723]

Glidden Paint & Wallcovering, 4900 Jefferson St. NE, No. B, Albuquerque, NM 87109, (505)883-7339 [21451]

Gliers Meats Inc., 533 W 11th St., PO Box 1052, Covington, KY 41011, (606)291-1800 [11271]

Gliers Specialty Hams, 533 W 11th St., PO Box 1052, Covington, KY 41011, (606)291-1800 [11271]

Gligorea Livestock, PO Box 6628, Sheridan, WY 82801-7102, (307)674-7600 [17943]

Glindmeyer Distributors Co., PO Box 19003, New Orleans, LA 70119, (504)486-6646 [15148]

Global Access Entertainment Inc., 212 NW 4th Ave., Hallandale, FL 33009-4015, (954)458-7505 [25213]

Global Access Entertainment Inc., 212 NW 4th Ave., Hallandale, FL 33009-4015, (954)458-7505 [15149]

Global Bakeries, Inc., 13336 Paxton St., Pacoima, CA 91331-2339, (818)896-0525 [11272]

Global Beverage Co., PO Box 25107, Rochester, NY 14625, (716)381-3560 [24959]

Global Computer Corp., 11 Harbor Park Dr., Port Washington, NY 11050, (516)625-6262 [6303]

Global Directions Inc., PO Box 470098, San Francisco, CA 94147-0098, (415)982-8811 [3781]

Global Expediting and Marketing Co., PO Box 611, Avondale Estates, GA 30002, (404)296-2839 [16896]

Global Exports, Inc., 11 Orchard Hill Dr., Manalapan, NJ 07726, (732)308-0767 [23192]

Global Fastener Inc., 10634 Control Place Dr., Dallas, TX 75238-1310, (214)340-6068 [13724]

Global Forestry Management Group, PO Box 10167, Portland, OR 97296, (503)228-1950 [27309]

Global House, PO Box 993, Sanford, NC 27331, (919)776-2391 [16067]

Global Importing Inc., 20 Polk St., Johnston, RI 02919-2321, (401)232-2700 [17432]

Global Marketing Concepts, PO Box 19444, Charlotte, NC 28219, (704)398-2352 [7399]

Global Metrics Inc., 519 J. Marine View Ave., Belmont, CA 94002-0843, (650)592-2722 [2684]

Global Motorsport Group Inc., 16100 Jacqueline Court, Morgan Hill, CA 95037, (408)778-0500 [2685]

Global Optics Inc., 1255 Ontario Rd., Green Bay, WI 54311, (920)432-1502 [19340]

Global Petroleum Corp., 800 South St., Waltham, MA 02454, (617)894-8800 [22314]

Global Products, PO Box 93, Winterset, IA 50273, (515)462-3186 [26500]

Global Products Company, 3221 Rosemead Place, Rosemead, CA 91770, (626)288-5353 [16068]

Global Steel Trading Inc., 1199 E 5000N Rd, Bourbonnais, IL 60914, (815)936-4500 [20008]

Global Telecommunications, PO Box 2928, Winchester, VA 22604-2128, (540)667-6898 [5620]

Global Tile, 9797 W 151st St., Orland Park, IL 60462, (708)460-1600 [9922]

Global Titanium Inc., 19300 Filer Ave., Detroit, MI 48234, (313)366-5300 [26831]

Global Tropical, 91 Brooklyn Terminal Market, Brooklyn, NY 11236, (718)763-4603 [11273]

Globe Business Furniture Inc., 520 Royal Pky., Nashville, TN 37214-3645, (615)889-4722 [21015]

Globe Business Products, PO Box 50826, Indianapolis, IN 46250, (317)841-9322 [13123]

Globe Business Resources Inc., 1925 Greenwood Ave., Cincinnati, OH 45246, (513)771-4242 [13122]

Globe Electric Supply Company, Inc., 33-70 10th St., PO Box 6258, Long Island City, NY 11106, (718)932-1820 [8789]

Globe-Hamburg, Import/Export, 3170 Durham Rd., Hamburg, NY 14075, (716)627-3427 [8790]

Globe Inc., 6363 Hwy. 7, St. Louis Park, MN 55416, (612)929-1377 [23193]

Globe Industrial Supply Inc., PO Box 50826, Indianapolis, IN 46250, (317)841-9322 [13123]

Globe Iron Construction Company Inc., PO Box 2354, Norfolk, VA 23501, (804)625-2542 [20009]

Globe Machinery and Supply Co., 4060 Dixon St., Des Moines, IA 50313, (515)262-0088 [16897]

Globe Machinery and Supply Co., 4060 Dixon St., Des Moines, IA 50313, (515)262-0088 [16069]

Globe Motorist Supply Company Inc., 121-123 E 3rd St., Mt. Vernon, NY 10550, (914)668-6430 [2686]

Globe Seed and Feed Company Inc., PO Box 445, Twin Falls, ID 83303, (208)733-1373 [743]

Globe Trends Inc., PO Box 461, Chatham, NJ 07928, (973)984-7444 [11274]

Globemaster Inc., 9714 Old Katy Rd., Houston, TX 77055, (713)464-8256 [13725]

Globil Inc., PO Box 50456, 2350 Hemmert Ave., Idaho Falls, ID 83405-0456, (208)522-5121 [1721]

Globus Industries, PO Box 173, Holmdel, NJ 07733, (732)671-8310 [8791]

Glorybee Foods Inc., PO Box 2744, Eugene, OR 97402, (541)689-0913 [11275]

Glosser and Sons Inc.; M., 72 Messenger St., Johnstown, PA 15902, (814)533-2800 [20010]

Gloucester County Packing Co., Evergreen & Glassboro, Woodbury, NJ 08096-7178, (609)845-0195 [11276]

Glove Wagon Enterprises, Inc., 705 Knollwood Cir., Ft. Collins, CO 80524-1585, (970)490-1316 [4991]

Glover Equipment Inc., PO Box 405, Cockeysville, MD 21030, (410)771-8000 [13124]

Glover Oil Company Inc., 3109 S Main St., Melbourne, FL 32902-0790, (407)723-7461 [22315]

Glover Wholesale Inc., PO Box 484, Columbus, GA 31902, (706)324-3647 [11277]

GLS Corp., 723 W Algonquin Rd., Arlington Heights, IL 60006, (847)437-0200 [7400]

GLS Thermoplastic Elastomers Div., 833 Ridgeview Dr., McHenry, IL 60050, (815)385-8500 [22970]

Glucksman & Associates; Barry, 31 Algonquin Dr., Warwick, RI 02888-5301, (401)463-9933 [17433]

GM International Inc., PO Box 1346, Elkhart, IN 46515, (219)295-1080 [13726]

GM Service Parts Operations, 6060 W Bristol Rd., Flint, MI 48554, (734)635-5412 [2687]

GMA Industries Inc., PO Box 74037, Romulus, MI 48174-0037, (734)595-7300 [20011]

GMI Photographic Inc., 125 Schmitt Blvd., Farmingdale, NY 11735, (516)752-0066 [22858]

GMM Van Dock Distributors, 484 Main St., West Chicago, IL 60185-2864, (630)231-5770 [2694]

GMP, 3111 Old Lincoln Hwy., Trevose, PA 19053-4996, (215)357-5500 [5621]

GMP, 3111 Old Lincoln Hwy., Trevose, PA 19053-4996, (215)357-5500 [8792]

GMR Division MNH, 1199 Harlem Rd., Buffalo, NY 14227-1700, (716)652-4547 [14113]

GMS Corp., 1680 Carolina Dr., Elk Grove Village, IL 60007-2926, (847)985-9419 [18395]

GNI Group Inc., PO Box 220, Deer Park, TX 77536-0220, (281)930-0350 [4401]

Gnieweks Trophies Inc.; Hank, 21925 Michigan Ave., Dearborn, MI 48124-2379, (313)278-1130 [23690]

Gnomon, Inc., 1601 Fairview Dr., Carson City, NV 89701, (775)885-2305 [3782]

Gnomon Press, PO Box 475, Frankfort, KY 40602-0475, (502)223-1858 [3783]

GNS Foods Inc., 2109 E Division St., Arlington, TX 76011, (817)795-4671 [11278]

Go Fly A Kite Inc., PO Box AA, East Haddam, CT 06423, (860)873-8675 [26501]

Go/Sportsmen's Supply Inc., 1535 Industrial Ave., Billings, MT 59104, (406)252-2109 [23691]

Goble's Flower Farm, RR2 BOX 200, Kula, HI 96790, (808)878-6079 [14873]

Godbee Medical Distributors, PO Box 7, Jemison, AL 35085-0007, (205)755-1771 [18812]

Godbee Medical Distributors, 324 Montevallo Rd., Alabaster, AL 35007, (205)664-4455 [18813]

Godby Products Inc., 7904 Rockville Rd., Indianapolis, IN 46214, (317)271-8400 [14471]

Goddard Industries Inc., PO Box 165, Worcester, MA 01613-0765, (508)852-2435 [16898]

The Godfrey Group Inc., PO Box 90008, Raleigh, NC 27675-0008, (919)544-6504 [25662]

Godwin Company, Inc., 1175 W 16th St., Indianapolis, IN 46202, (317)637-3325 [16070]

Godwin Oil Company Inc., PO Box 150, Wilmington, NC 28402, (910)762-0312 [22316]

Goedecke Company Inc.; Vernon L., 4101 Clayton Ave., St. Louis, MO 63110, (314)652-1810 [7401]

Goedecke Inc.; Otto, PO Box 387, Hallettsville, TX 77964, (512)798-3261 [17944]

Goes Lithographing Co., 42 W 61st St., Chicago, IL 60621-3999, (773)684-6700 [21742]

Goetz Energy Corp., PO Box A, Buffalo, NY 14217, (716)876-4324 [22317]

GOEX International Inc., 423 Vaughn Rd. W, Cleburne, TX 76031, (817)641-2261 [22318]

Goff Custom Spring Inc., 410 Township Rd. 219, Bellefontaine, OH 43311 [13727]

Goforth Electric Supply Inc., PO Box 270, Gainesville, GA 30503, (404)536-3361 [8793]

Gold Bug, 4999 Oakland, Denver, CO 80239-2719, (303)371-2535 [4992]

Gold Coast Beverage Distributors, 3325 NW 70th Ave., Miami, FL 33122, (305)591-9800 [1722]

Gold Coast Distributors Inc., 837 Robinwood Ct., Traverse City, MI 49686, (616)929-7003 [1723]

Gold Coast Marine Distribution, 640 SW Flagler Dr., Ft. Lauderdale, FL 33335, (954)463-8281 [18508]

Gold Eagle Co., 4400 S Kildare Ave., Chicago, IL 60632, (773)376-4400 [2688]

Gold-Eagle Cooperative, PO Box 280, Goldfield, IA 50542-0280, (515)825-3161 [744]

Gold Father's, 3830 E Flamingo Rd., Ste. C-1, No. 173, Las Vegas, NV 89121, 800-642-2545 [17434]

Gold Father's Jewelry, Inc., 3830 E Flamingo Rd., Ste. C-1, No. 173, Las Vegas, NV 89121, 800-642-2545 [17434]

Gold Findings Company Inc., 55 W 47th, New York, NY 10036-2834, (212)354-7816 [17435]

Gold Key Electronics Inc., PO Box 186, Goffstown, NH 03045, (603)625-8518 [8794]

Gold Medal Bakery Inc., 21 Penn St., Fall River, MA 02724, (508)674-5766 [11279]

Gold Medal Products Co., 10700 Medallion Dr., Cincinnati, OH 45241-4807, (513)769-7676 [25663]

Gold & Reiss Corp., 254 Bay Ridge Ave., Brooklyn, NY 11220-5801, (718)680-2600 [7402]

Gold Rush Wrecking, PO Box 729, Osburn, ID 83849-0729, (208)784-9795 [2689]

Gold & Silver Exchange, 6101 Menaul Blvd. NE, Albuquerque, NM 87110-3319, (505)884-9230 [17436]

Gold Star Dairy, 6901 I-30, Little Rock, AR 72209, (501)568-6237 [11280]

Goldberg Company Inc., PO Box 4590, Glen Allen, VA 23058-4590, (804)228-5700 [15150]

Goldberg & Co., Inc.; H. E., 9050 M. L. King Way S, Seattle, WA 98118, (206)722-8200 [17945]

Goldberg Models Inc.; Carl, 4734 W Chicago, Chicago, IL 60651-3322, (773)626-9550 [26502]

Goldberg and Solovy Food Inc., 5925 S Alcoa Ave., Vernon, CA 90058, (213)581-6161 [11281]

Golden Bear Services Inc., 10511 E Tanglewood Rd., Franktown, CO 80116-9439, (303)688-5655 [6304]

Golden Belt Cooperative Association Inc., PO Box 138, Ellis, KS 67637, (785)726-3115 [17946]

Golden Boy Pies Inc., 4945 Hadley St., Overland Park, KS 66203-1329, (913)384-6460 [11282]

Golden Capital Distributors, 6610 Cabot Dr., Baltimore, MD 21226, (410)360-1300 [11283]

Golden Crown Corp., PO Box 820, Coeur D Alene, ID 83816-0820, (208)667-5689 [27139]

Golden Eagle of Arkansas Inc., 1900 E 15th St., Little Rock, AR 72202, (501)372-2800 [1724]

Golden Eagle Distributors, PO Box 27506, Tucson, AZ 85726, (520)884-5999 [1725]

Golden Electronics Inc., 951 Aviation Pky., Morrisville, NC 27560, (919)467-2466 [8795]

Golden Fleece, 469 7th Ave., 10th Fl., New York, NY 10018, (212)695-1620 [5380]

Golden Gem Growers Inc., PO Drawer 9, Umatilla, FL 32784, (352)669-2101 [24960]

Golden Goose, 39 Main St., Bar Harbor, ME 04609-1845, (207)288-9901 [4993]

Golden-Lee Book Distributors, Inc., 399 Thornall St., Ste. 3, Edison, NJ 08837-2238, (732)857-6333 [3784]

Golden Light Equipment Co., PO Box 9005, Amarillo, TX 79105, (806)373-4277 [24129]

Golden Needles Knitting and Glove Co. Monte Glove Div., PO Box 803, Wilkesboro, NC 28697, (919)667-5102 [4994]

Golden Neo-Life Diamite International, 3500 Gateway Blvd., Fremont, CA 94538, (510)651-0405 [14114]

Golden Peanut Co. De Leon Div., PO Box 226, De Leon, TX 76444, (254)893-2071 [11284]

Golden Poultry Company Inc., PO Box 2210, Atlanta, GA 30301, (404)393-5000 [11285]

Golden Pride International, PO Box 21109, West Palm Beach, FL 33416-1109, (561)640-5700 [11286]

Golden Products Co., 6101 Washington Blvd., Culver City, CA 90232-7470, (310)815-8283 [4629]

Golden Spike Equipment Co., 1352 W Main St., Tremonton, UT 84337, (435)257-5346 [745]

Golden State Containers Inc., 6817 E Acco St., Los Angeles, CA 90040-1901, (213)887-4266 [25918]

Golden State Flooring, 1015 North Market Blvd., No. 2, Sacramento, CA 95834, (916)928-0400 [9924]

Golden State Flooring, 240 Littlefield Ave., South San Francisco, CA 94080-6902, (650)872-0500 [9923]

Golden State Flooring Sacramento, 1015 North Market Blvd., No. 2, Sacramento, CA 95834, (916)928-0400 [9924]

Golden State Foods Corp., 1391 Progress Rd., Suffolk, VA 23434-2154, (757)538-8068 [11287]

Golden State Foods Corp., 18301 Von Karman Ave., No. 1100, Irvine, CA 92612-1009, (714)252-2000 [24961]

Golden State Medical Supply Inc., 27644 Newhall Ranch Rd., Unit 40, Valencia, CA 91355-4017, (661)295-8101 [19341]

Golden State Models, 21050 Questhaven Rd., Escondido, CA 92029, (760)744-7523 [26503]

Golden State Trading Co., 888 Brannan, Ste. 278, San Francisco, CA 94103-4928, (415)621-4653 [13363]

Golden Sun Feeds Inc. Danville Div., 621 485th Ave., Searsboro, IA 50242 [746]

Golden West Pipe & Supply Co., 11700 S Woodruff Ave., Downey, CA 90241-5630, (562)803-4321 [23194]

Goldfarb Electric Supply Company Inc., PO Box 3319, Charleston, WV 25333, (304)342-2153 [8796]

Goldin Industries Inc., PO Box 2909, Gulfport, MS 39505-2909, (601)896-6216 [20012]

Goldman Associates Inc., 10515 Liberty Ave., St. Louis, MO 63132, (314)428-3000 [13364]

Goldman Brothers Inc., PO Box 23345, Honolulu, HI 96823-3345 [4995]

Goldman Co.; H.R., 3350 N Durango Dr., Apt. 1101, Las Vegas, NV 89129-7271 [17437]

Goldman Paper Co.; G.B., 2201 E Allegheny Ave., Philadelphia, PA 19134, (215)423-8600 [21743]

Goldmar Sales Corp., Box 6398, Baltimore, MD 21230, (410)727-3922 [747]

Goldmark Plastic Co., Nassau Terminal Rd., New Hyde Park, NY 11040, (516)352-4373 [22971]

Goldner Company Inc.; Herman, 7777 Brewster Ave., Philadelphia, PA 19153, (215)365-5400 [23195]

Goldsmith Chemical and Metal Corp.; D.F., 909 Pitner Ave., Evanston, IL 60202, (847)869-7800 [20013]

Goldsmiths Inc., 151 N Main St., Wichita, KS 67202, (316)263-0131 [21016]

Goldsmiths Inc., 151 N Main St., Wichita, KS 67202, (316)263-0131 [13125]

Goldthwaites of Texas, Inc., 6000 N O'Connor Blvd., Irving, TX 75039, (972)910-0764 [748]

Goldthwaites of Texas Inc., 1401 Foch St., Ft. Worth, TX 76101, (817)332-1521 [749]

Golf Training Systems Inc., 3400 Corporate Way, Ste. G, Duluth, GA 30096, (404)623-6400 [23692]

Golf Ventures, 2101 E Edgewood Dr., Lakeland, FL 33803, (941)665-5800 [23693]

Golombeck Inc.; Morris J., 960 Franklin Ave., Brooklyn, NY 11225, (718)284-3505 [11288]

Gomoljak Block, 1841 McGuckian St., Annapolis, MD 21401, (410)263-6744 [7403]

Gonsalves Inc.; Arthur J., 165 Main St., North Reading, MA 01864, (508)644-1988 [26504]

Gonzalez International Inc., 28 Allegheny Ave., Ste. 1212, Baltimore, MD 21204, (301)321-1577 [16071]

Gooch Brake and Equipment Co., 506-12 Grand Blvd., Kansas City, MO 64106, (816)421-3085 [2690]

Good Apple, PO Box 2649, Columbus, OH 43216-2649, (614)357-3981 [3785]

Good Earth Farm, Inc., 55 Pleasant Hill Rd., Freeport, ME 04032, (207)865-9544 [14874]

Good Floral Distributors, Grove St. Extension, Houlton, ME 04730, (207)532-2040 [14875]

Good Food Inc., 4960 Horseshoe Pke., Box 160, Honey Brook, PA 19344, (610)273-3776 [11289]

Good Health Natural Foods Inc., 81 Scudder Ave., Northport, NY 11768, (631)261-2111 [11290]

Good Karma Publishing Inc., 202 Main St., PO Box 511, Ft. Yates, ND 58538, (701)854-7459 [3786]

Good News Communications, Inc., 3554 Strait St. E, Atlanta, GA 30340, (404)454-9445 [3787]

Good News Productions, International, PO Box 222, Joplin, MO 64802, (417)782-0060 [25214]

Good-O-Beverage Co., 1801 Boone Ave., Bronx, NY 10460, (718)328-6400 [24962]

Good Seed and Grain Company Inc., PO Box 157, Hamburg, IA 51640, (712)382-1238 [17947]

Good Sports Inc., PO Box 840, Manchester, CT 06040, (860)647-0880 [4996]

Good Time Clock Shop, 1141 Mt. Zion Rd., Bucyrus, OH 44820, (419)562-9118 [13416]

Goodall Rubber Co., 790 Birney Hwy., Aston, PA 19014-1443 [16899]

Goodell's Refrigeration, 801 E 4th St., Ste. 22, Gillette, WY 82716-4061, (307)686-7676 [14472]

Goode's Welding Inc., 926 E Mcgaffey St., Roswell, NM 88201, (505)622-3490 [20014]

Goodhue Elevator Association Cooperative, PO Box 218, Goodhue, MN 55027, (612)923-4496 [17948]

Goodin Co., 2700 N 2nd St., Minneapolis, MN 55411, (612)588-7811 [23196]

Gooding Livestock Community Co.; Lee'Mark W, 822 Ambassador Dr., Henderson, NV 89015-9629 [17949]

Gooding Rubber Co. (La Grange, Illinois), 411 E Plainfield Rd., La Grange, IL 60525, (708)354-2270 [16900]

Gooding Seed Co., PO Box 57, Gooding, ID 83330, (208)934-8441 [750]

Gooding and Shields Rubber Co., 4915 Campbell's Run Rd., Pittsburgh, PA 15205-1320, (412)257-5880 [24277]

Goodland Cooperative Equity Exchange Inc., PO Box 998, Goodland, KS 67735, (913)899-3681 [17950]

Goodman and Co. Inc.; C., 75 Spruce St., PO Box 2777, Paterson, NJ 07509, (973)278-1303 [26044]

Goodman; C.R., 2906 Cavitt, Bryan, TX 77801, (409)822-9460 [1726]

Goodman Inc.; Harry, 203 Tremont St., Springfield, MA 01101, (413)785-5331 [21744]

Goodman Knitting Company Inc., 300 Manley St., Brockton, MA 02303, (508)588-7200 [4997]

Goodmans Design Interior, 4860 Pan American Fwy. NE, Albuquerque, NM 87107, (505)889-0195 [21017]

Goodson Farms Inc., PO Box 246, Balm, FL 33503, (813)634-6679 [11291]

Goodwear Shoe Co. Inc., 144 Duane St., New York, NY 10013-3808, (212)233-6813 [24753]

Goodwin Machinery Co., 3115 Central St. N, Knoxville, TN 37917-5192, (423)546-0841 [7404]

Goodwin Refrigeration Co. Inc., 2410 Reliance Ave., Apex, NC 27502-7048, (919)387-5797 [14473]

Goody-Goody Liquor Store Inc., 10301 Harry Hines Blvd., Dallas, TX 75220, (214)350-5806 [1727]

Goodyear Tire Rubber Co., 3151 S Vaughn Way, Ste. 410, Aurora, CO 80014, (303)695-2413 [16901]

Goodyear Tire & Rubber Co., 300 S Salem Church Rd., York, PA 17404-5537 [2691]

Goomies, 2815 Junipero Ave., Ste. 110, Signal Hill, CA 90806-2111, (562)985-0076 [17593]

Goorland & Mann, Inc., 825 N Union St., Wilmington, DE 19805, (302)655-1514 [4630]

Gopher Bearing, 2490 Territorial Rd., St. Paul, MN 55114, (612)645-5871 [2692]

Gopher Electronics Co., 222 E Little Canada Rd., St. Paul, MN 55117, (651)490-4900 [8797]

Gopher News Co., 9000 10th Ave. N, Minneapolis, MN 55427-4322, (612)546-5300 [3788]

Gor-den Industries Inc., 50 Commerce Pkwy., Buffalo, NY 14224, (716)675-5600 [2693]

Gordon Brothers Corp., 40 Broad St., Ste. 11, Boston, MA 02109, (617)422-6218 [17438]

Gordon & Co.; Alan, 6517 N May, Oklahoma City, OK 73116-4811, (405)848-1688 [17439]

Gordon Co.; Len, 7215 Bermuda Rd., Las Vegas, NV 89119-4304, (702)361-0600 [22972]

Gordon Food Company Inc., PO Box 41534, Memphis, TN 38174, (901)523-0077 [11292]

Gordon Food Service Inc., PO Box 1787, Grand Rapids, MI 49501, (616)530-7000 [11293]

Gordon Rubber and Packing Company Inc., PO Box 298, Derby, CT 06418, (203)735-7441 [24278]

Gordon Waste Company Inc., PO Box 389, Columbia, PA 17512, (717)684-2201 [26832]

Gorence Mobile Marketing Distribution, 484 Main St., West Chicago, IL 60185-2864, (630)231-5770 [2694]

Gorton Communications Inc., 190 London Dairy Tpke., Hooksett, NH 03106, (603)622-9219 [5622]

Gorton & Co., Inc.; Slade, 225 Southampton St., Boston, MA 02118, (617)442-5800 [11294]

Gorton and Company Inc.; Slade, 225 Southampton St., Boston, MA 02118, (617)442-5800 [11295]

Goshen Sash and Door Co., PO Box 517, Goshen, IN 46527, (219)533-1146 [27310]

Gosiger Inc., 108 McDonough St., Dayton, OH 45402, (937)228-5174 [16072]

Gospel Light Publications, 2300 Knoll Dr., Ventura, CA 93003, (805)644-9721 [3789]

Gospel Light Publications, PO Box 3875, Ventura, CA 93006, (805)644-9721 [3790]

Gospel Publishing House, 1445 Boonville Ave., Springfield, MO 65802, (417)831-8000 [3791]

Goss Supply Co., 620 Marietta St., PO BOX 2580, Zanesville, OH 43702-2580, (740)454-2571 [16902]

Gotham Distributing Corp., 2324 Haverford Rd., Ardmore, PA 19003, (215)649-7565 [25215]

Gotham Sales Co., 150 Morris Ave., Springfield, NJ 07081, (973)912-8412 [25216]

Gothic Energy Corp., 6120 S Yale Ave., No. 1200, Tulsa, OK 74136-4241, (918)749-5666 [22319]

Gould Athletic Supply, 3156 N 96th St., Milwaukee, WI 53222-3499, (414)871-3943 [23694]

Gould Paper Corp., 11 Madison Ave., New York, NY 10010, (212)301-0000 [21745]

Goulds Sports Textiles Inc., 220 E Lafayette St., Lagrange, IN 46761-1907, (219)463-7506 [4998]

Goulet Supply Company Inc., 381 Elm St., Manchester, NH 03101, (603)669-2170 [23197]

Gourmet Award Foods, PO Box 12579, Albany, NY 12212-2579, (518)456-1888 [11296]

Gourmet Award Foods Tree of Life Inc., 2050 Elm St. SE, Minneapolis, MN 55414-2531 [11297]

Gourmet Regency Coffee Inc., 5500 Cottonwood Lane, Prior Lake, MN 55372, (612)226-4100 [11298]

Gourmet Specialties, 21001 Cabot Blvd., Hayward, CA 94545, (510)887-7322 [11299]

Gourmet Wine & Spirits, 4445 Walzem St., San Antonio, TX 78218, (210)654-1123 [1728]

Government Electronic Systems Div., Marne Hwy., Moorestown, NJ 08057, (609)722-4900 [5623]

Government Micro Resources Inc., 7203 Gateway Ct., Manassas, VA 20109-7313, (703)330-1199 [6305]

Government Technology Services Inc., 4100 Lafayette Center Dr., Chantilly, VA 20151, (703)502-2000 [6306]

GOYA Foods Inc., 1900 NW 92nd Ave., Miami, FL 33172, (305)592-3150 [24963]

GPOD of Idaho, PO Box 514, Shelley, ID 83274, (208)357-7646 [11300]

GPrime Ltd., 1790 Broadway, New York, NY 10019-1412, (212)765-3415 [25217]

GPX Inc., 108 Madison St., St. Louis, MO 63102, (314)621-3314 [8798]

GPX Inc., 108 Madison St., St. Louis, MO 63102, (314)621-3314 [15151]

GPX Inc. (St. Louis, Missouri), 108 Madison St., St. Louis, MO 63102, (314)621-3314 [25218]

Grabarczyk Associates, 578 San Remo Cir., Inverness, FL 34450, (352)344-1449 [15515]

Grabber Southeast, 3050 NW 60th St., Ft. Lauderdale, FL 33309-2249, (954)971-4730 [7405]

Grace and Co. Grace Dearborn Div.; W.R., 4636 Somerton Rd., Trevose, PA 19053-6742, (267)438-1800 [25664]

Grace Inc.; V.F., 605 E 13th Ave., Anchorage, AK 99501, (907)272-6431 [14115]

Gracewood Fruit Co., PO Box 370, Vero Beach, FL 32961, (561)567-1151 [11301]

Graco Fertilizer Co., PO Box 89, Cairo, GA 31728, (912)377-1602 [751]

Graebers Lumber Co., 218 Lincoln Hwy., Fairless Hills, PA 19030, (215)946-3000 [7406]

Graeffs Eastside Drugs; Mike, 8506 E Mill Plain Blvd., Vancouver, WA 98664-2011, (206)694-3353 [18814]

Graf Creamery Co., N 4051 Creamery St., PO Box 49, Zachow, WI 54182-0049, (715)758-2137 [11302]

Grafalloy Corp., 1020 N Marshall Ave., El Cajon, CA 92020, (619)562-1020 [23695]

Grafix Plastic, 19499 Miles Rd., Cleveland, OH 44128, (216)581-9050 [22973]

Gragnon Wholesale, 625 Weeks, New Iberia, LA 70560-5544, (318)364-6611 [11303]

Graham Blue Print Co., PO Box 1307, Little Rock, AR 72203-1307, (501)376-3364 [25665]

Graham Co.; Mike, 5505 Osuna Rd. NE, Ste. F, Albuquerque, NM 87109-2542, (505)884-4653 [17440]

Graham/Davis, Inc., PO Box 941177, Houston, TX 77094-8177, (281)558-8662 [8799]

Graham Grain Co., 200 Voorhees St., Terre Haute, IN 47802, (812)232-1044 [17951]

Graham-Hardison Hardwood Inc., PO Box 344, Linden, TN 37096, (931)589-2143 [27311]

Graham Radio Inc., 505 Main St., Reading, MA 01867, (781)944-4000 [25219]

Graham Services Inc., 180 James Dr. E, St. Rose, LA 70087-9662, (504)467-5863 [3734]

Graham Services Inc., 180 James Dr. E, St. Rose, LA 70087, (504)467-5863 [3792]

Graham Sporting Goods Burlington, 2535 S Church St., Burlington, NC 27215-5203, (910)226-5574 [4999]

Graico International, 5062 W Plano Pwky., No. 300, Plano, TX 75093-4409, (972)931-7272 [752]

Grail Foundation of America, 2081 Partridge Ln., Binghamton, NY 13903, (607)723-5163 [3793]

Grain Growers Cooperative (Cimarron, Kansas), PO Box 508, Cimarron, KS 67835, (316)335-5101 [17952]

Grain Land Co-op, Hwy. 22, Minnesota Lake, MN 56068, (507)462-3315 [17953]

Grain Land Cooperative, PO Box 65, Blue Earth, MN 56013, (507)526-3211 [17954]

Grain Processing Corp., 1600 Oregon St., Muscatine, IA 52761, (319)264-4265 [753]

Grain Storage Corp., Monroe & 2nd St., Sturgis, KY 42459, (502)333-5506 [754]

Grainger, Inc., 35 Corporate Cir., Albany, NY 12203, (518)869-1414 [16073]

Grainger, Inc., 1938 Elm Tree Dr., Nashville, TN 37210 [8800]

Grainger Inc., 800 W Willard St., Muncie, IN 47302, (765)741-8100 [8803]

Grainger Inc., 834 Riverside Dr., Asheville, NC 28806, (828)258-8986 [8801]

Grainger Inc.; W.W., 100 Grainger Pkwy., Lake Forest, IL 60045, (847)535-1000 [8802]

Grainger Industrial Supply, 800 W Willard St., Muncie, IN 47302, (765)741-8100 [8803]

Grainland, Rte. 1, Box 860, Eureka, IL 61530, (309)467-2355 [11304]

Grainland Cooperative, RR 1, Box 860, Eureka, IL 61530, (309)467-2355 [17955]

Grainland Cooperative, RR 1, Box 860, Eureka, IL 61530, (309)744-2218 [17956]

Gramex Corp., 11966 St. Charles Rock Rd., Bridgeton, MO 63044, (314)739-8300 [5000]

Granada Electronics Corp., 485 Kent Ave., Brooklyn, NY 11211, (718)387-1157 [8804]

Granada Systems Design Inc., 1886 Rte. 52, Hopewell Junction, NY 12533, (914)221-1617 [5624]

Granary Books, Inc., 307 Seventh Ave., 1401, New York, NY 10001, (212)337-9979 [3794]

Grand Blanc Cement Products, PO Box 585, Grand Blanc, MI 48439, (810)694-7500 [7407]

Grand Forks Equipment Inc., 5101 Gateway Dr., Grand Forks, ND 58203, (701)746-4436 [755]

Grand Haven Steel Products, 1605 Marion Ave., Grand Haven, MI 49417, (616)847-7793 [20015]

Grand Light and Supply Co., PO Box 9402, New Haven, CT 06534, (203)777-5781 [8805]

Grand Prairie Cooperative, PO Box 10, Sadorus, IL 61872, (217)598-2312 [17957]

Grand Rapids Sash and Door, PO Box E, Grand Rapids, MI 49501, (616)784-0101 [7408]

Grand River Cooperative Inc., 225 John St., Markesan, WI 53946, (920)398-2301 [756]

Grand River Meat Center, 8428 Grand River, Detroit, MI 48204-2234, (313)898-6743 [11305]

Grand Stage Co., Inc., 630 W Lake St., Chicago, IL 60661, (312)332-5611 [25666]

Grand Transformers Inc., 1500 Marion Ave., Grand Haven, MI 49417, (616)842-5430 [8806]

Grand Traverse Forging and Steel, 2465 N Aero Pk. Ct., Traverse City, MI 49686, (231)947-4931 [20019]

Grandma Brown's Beans Inc., PO Box 230, Mexico, NY 13114-0230, (315)963-7221 [11306]

Grandma's Bake Shoppe, 201 S 5th St., PO Box 457, Beatrice, NE 68310, (402)223-2358 [11307]

Grandoe Corp., PO Box 713, Gloversville, NY 12078, (518)725-8641 [23696]

Grandview Hatchery & Locker Plant, 716 10th Ave., Belle Fourche, SD 57717-1509, (605)892-3866 [17958]

Grange Supply Company Inc., NW 355 State St., Pullman, WA 99163, (509)332-2511 [757]

Granger Farmers Cooperative Creamery Association, PO Box 67, Granger, MN 55939, (507)772-4433 [11308]

Granger Lumber-Hardware, Inc., 1180 Lane Ave. S, Jacksonville, FL 32205-6234, (904)781-4116 [7409]

Granite City Electric Supply Co., 19 Quincy Ave., Quincy, MA 02169, (617)472-6500 [8807]

Granite City Ready Mix Inc., PO Box 1305, St. Cloud, MN 56302, (320)252-4324 [7410]

Granite City Ready Mix Inc., PO Box 1305, St. Cloud, MN 56302, (320)252-4324 [7411]

Granite Microsystems, Inc., PO Box 579, Mequon, WI 53092, (414)242-8800 [6307]

Granite Rock Co., PO Box 50001, Watsonville, CA 95077, (831)768-2000 [7412]

Granite Seed, 1697 West 2100 North, Lehi, UT 84043, (801)768-4422 [758]

Granite State Office Supplies, Inc., 6 Augusta National Ctr., Bedford, NH 03110-6132, (603)669-8179 [21018]

Grant & Associates, LLC; R.B., 30 Lower College Rd., Kingston, RI 02881-1316, (401)782-8077 [21746]

Grant Manufacturing & Equipment Co., 4009 W 49th St., Tulsa, OK 74107, (918)446-4009 [2695]

Grant and Sons Inc.; William, 130 Fieldcrest Ave., Raritan Center, Edison, NJ 08837, (732)225-9000 [1729]

Grant Truck Equipment Co., 1828 NW 4th St., Oklahoma City, OK 73106-2611, (405)236-1494 [2696]

Grantham Distributing Company Inc., 2685 Hansrob Rd., Orlando, FL 32804, (407)299-6446 [1730]

Granton Shoe Imports, 524 Riverdale Dr., Glendale, CA 91204, (818)507-8449 [24754]

Grapevine, 59 Maxwell Ct., Santa Rosa, CA 95401, (707)576-3950 [11309]

Graphco, 6563 Cochran Rd., Cleveland, OH 44139-3901, (440)248-1700 [25667]

Graphic Arts Center Publishing Co., PO Box 10306, Portland, OR 97210, (503)226-2402 [3795]

Graphic Arts Systems Inc., 19499 Miles Rd., Cleveland, OH 44128, (216)581-9050 [22973]

Graphic Arts Systems Inc., 19499 Miles Rd., Cleveland, OH 44128, (216)581-9050 [22974]

Graphic Controls, 189 Van Rensselear St., PO Box 1271, Buffalo, NY 14240-1271, (716)853-7500 [21747]

Graphic Media, 13916 Cordary Ave., Hawthorne, CA 90250, (310)679-0653 [25668]

Graphic Papers Inc., 2070 Poydras St., New Orleans, LA 70112, (504)525-5686 [21748]

Graphic Resources Corp., 12311 Industry St., Garden Grove, CA 92840, (714)891-1003 [6308]

Graphic Sciences Inc., 7515 NE Ambassador Pl, Portland, OR 97220, (503)460-0203 [16903]

Graphic Systems Inc., 301 Commerce Dr., Moorestown, NJ 08057-4208, (609)234-7500 [25669]

Graphic Systems Inc. (Memphis, Tennessee), 2127 Thomas Rd., Memphis, TN 38134-5615, (901)372-3762 [21019]

Graphline, Inc., 5701 NW 94th Ave., Tamarac, FL 33321, (954)722-3000 [25670]

Grasmick Lumber Company Inc.; Louis J., 6715 Quad Ave., Baltimore, MD 21237, (410)325-9663 [7413]

Grassland Dairy Products Inc., PO Box 160, Greenwood, WI 54437, (715)267-6182 [11310]

Grassland Equipment, 892-898 Troy-Schenectady Rd., Latham, NY 12110, (518)785-5841 [759]

Grassland West, 908 Port Dr., Clarkston, WA 99403-1845, (509)758-9100 [760]

Grattan & Sons Inc.; Dave, 16147 Montoya St., PO Box 2264, Irwindale, CA 91706-1147, (626)969-1703 [13728]

Grave and Son Inc.; F.D., PO Box 1626, New Haven, CT 06506, (203)624-9893 [26299]

Graveline Electronics Inc., 16415 NW 67th Ave., Miami Lakes, FL 33014, (305)824-9000 [5625]

Graves Automotive Supply, 645 W Holt Blvd., Ontario, CA 91762, (909)984-2401 [2697]

Graves Fire Protection, PO Box 451, Lunenburg, MA 01462, (978)345-0165 [24557]

Graves Import Co. Inc., 1911 21st Ave. S, Nashville, TN 37212-3833, (615)269-3475 [24755]

Graves Oil & Butane Co., 105 Dale St. SE, Albuquerque, NM 87101, (505)877-3753 [20016]

Gray Industrial Investments Inc., 77 E Palantine Rd., Prospect Heights, IL 60070, (847)537-7700 [16074]

Gray Machinery Co., 77 E Palantine Rd., Prospect Heights, IL 60070, (847)537-7700 [16074]

Gray Sales Co. Inc., PO Box 38, Somerville, MA 02143-0001, (617)625-6200 [6309]

Gray Storage and Dryer Company Inc., Hwy. 129 N, Ocilla, GA 31774, (912)468-9451 [17959]

Graybar Electric Company Inc., 1871 Old Okeechobee Rd., West Palm Beach, FL 33409-4138, (561)683-3801 [8808]

Graybar Electric Company Inc., 220 Industrial Blvd., Naples, FL 34104-3704, (941)643-4000 [8809]

Graybar Electric Company Inc., 1740 Fortune Ct., Lexington, KY 40509, (859)299-3787 [8810]

Graybar Electric Company Inc., 717 S Good Latimer, Dallas, TX 75226-1815, (214)939-0844 [8811]

Graybar Electric Company Inc., 655 S H St., San Bernardino, CA 92410-3417, (714)889-1051 [8812]

Graybar Electric Company Inc., PO Box 970709, Quail Heights, FL 33197, (305)232-1530 [8813]

Graybar Electric Company Inc., PO Box 7231, St. Louis, MO 63177, (314)727-3900 [8814]

Graybow-Daniels Co., 205 10th Ave. N, Plymouth, MN 55441, (612)797-7000 [23198]

Grayco Products, 1025 Old Country Rd., Westbury, NY 11590, (516)997-9200 [16904]

Grayline Housewares, 455 Kehoe Blvd., Carol Stream, IL 60188, (708)682-3330 [20017]

Graymont Cooperative Association Inc., PO Box 98, Graymont, IL 61743, (815)743-5321 [761]

Grays Harbor Equipment Inc., 401 S F St., Aberdeen, WA 98520, (206)532-8643 [16075]

Grays Petroleum Inc., PO Box 1010, De Queen, AR 71832, (870)642-2234 [22320]

Gray's Wholesale Inc., 513 State, PO Box 466, Clayton, NY 13624, (315)686-3541 [26300]

Graywell Equipment Corp., 50 Pond Rd., PO Box 464, Oakdale, NY 11769, (516)563-2880 [2698]

GRE America Inc., 425 Harbor Blvd., Belmont, CA 94002, (415)591-1400 [5626]

Great American Floor Care Center, 2318 Adams Ave., Huntington, WV 25704-1320, (304)429-3565 [15152]

Great American Wearhouse, 6750-H Jones Mill Ct., Norcross, GA 30092, (404)447-4660 [5001]

Great Bay Paper Co., 1900 Monkton Rd., Monkton, MD 21111, (410)329-3808 [21749]

Great Bear Spring Co., 777 W Putnam Ave., Greenwich, CT 06830, (203)531-4100 [24964]

Great Bend Cooperative Association, PO Box 68, Great Bend, KS 67530, (316)793-3533 [17960]

Great Brands of Europe Inc., 208 Harbor Dr., Stamford, CT 06902-7441, (203)425-1700 [24965]

Great Central Steel Co., 9801 S 76th Ave., Bridgeview, IL 60455, (708)599-8090 [20018]

Great Eastern Pet Supply, 1546 Decatur St., Ridgewood, NY 11385, (718)381-7300 [27140]

Great Falls Business Services, 9514 Georgetown Pike, Great Falls, VA 22066-2616, (703)759-3024 [21200]

Great Falls Paper Co., 600 2nd St. S, PO Box 269, Great Falls, MT 59405, (406)453-7671 [21750]

Great Falls Paper Co., 600 2nd St. S, Great Falls, MT 59405, (406)453-7671 [16905]

Great Graphic Originals, 1297 McD Dr., Dover, DE 19901, (302)734-7600 [5002]

Great Health, 2663 Saturn St., Brea, CA 92821-6703, (714)996-8600 [11311]

Great Lake Distributors, 1717 W Beltline Hwy., Ste. 102, Madison, WI 53713, (608)274-3123 [8815]

Great Lakes Air Systems Inc., 1154 E Lincoln, Madison Heights, MI 48071, (248)546-9191 [4631]

Great Lakes Airgas Inc., 10 W 4th St., Waterloo, IA 50701, (319)233-3540 [16681]

Great Lakes Area Distributing, PO Box 599, Bay City, MI 48707, (517)892-9042 [26505]

Great Lakes Electronics Supply Div., 4560 W Dickman Rd., Battle Creek, MI 49015, (616)963-6282 [8816]

Great Lakes Fastener, Inc., 125 Blaze Industrial Pky., Berea, OH 44017-8004, (440)239-2015 [13723]

Great Lakes Forge, Inc., 2465 N Aero Pk. Ct., Traverse City, MI 49686, (231)947-4931 [20019]

Great Lakes Marketing Inc., 2236G Bluemound Rd., Waukesha, WI 53186-2919, (414)798-6800 [11312]

Great Lakes Orthopedics Inc., 13601 Pioneer Trl, Eden Prairie, MN 55347-2613, (612)920-1520 [18815]

Great Lakes Peterbilt Inc., 5900 Southport Rd., Portage, IN 46368-6407, (219)763-7227 [20643]

Great Lakes Power Lift, 2006 Tobsal Ct., Warren, MI 48091, (810)759-5500 [2699]

Great Lakes Power Products, 5727 Old Boonville Hwy., Evansville, IN 47715, (812)422-4893 [18509]

Great Lakes Power Products, 2006 Tobsal Ct., Warren, MI 48091, (810)759-5500 [2699]

Great Lakes Power Products, 7455 Tyler Blvd., Mentor, OH 44060-8389, (440)951-5111 [18510]

Great Lakes Power Products, 340 Bilmar Dr., Pittsburgh, PA 15205, (412)937-0076 [2700]

Great Lakes Power Service, 2006 Tobsal Ct., Warren, MI 48091, (810)759-5500 [2699]

Great Lakes Sales, Inc., 4203 Roger B. Chaffee, Grand Rapids, MI 49548, (616)538-3840 [9925]

Great Lakes Sales, Inc., 11873 Belden, Livonia, MI 48150, (734)425-6227 [9926]

Great Lakes Technologies Corp., PO Box 51415, Kalamazoo, MI 49005-1415, (616)385-2200 [22859]

Great Northern Distributors, Inc., 935 N Washington Ave., Scranton, PA 18501, (717)342-8159 [3796]

Great Northern Products Ltd., PO Box 7622, Warwick, RI 02887, (401)821-2400 [11313]

Great Northern Video, 31 Industrial Park Dr., Ste. 9, Concord, NH 03301-8522, (603)228-0412 [25220]

Great Northwest Bicycle Supply, 2335 NW Savier St., Portland, OR 97210-2513, (503)226-0696 [23697]

The Great Organization Inc., 15125 N Hayden Rd., Ste. 120, Scottsdale, AZ 85260-2548, (480)998-1522 [7414]

Great Outdoors Publishing Co., 4747 28th St. N, St. Petersburg, FL 33714, (813)525-6609 [3797]

Great Plains, 5445 27th St., Moline, IL 61265, (309)764-8365 [7415]

Great Plains Co-op, PO Box 137, Benedict, NE 68316, (402)732-6622 [17961]

Great Plains Stainless Inc., 1004 N 129 E Ave., Tulsa, OK 74116, (918)437-5400 [20020]

Great Planes Model Distributors Co., 1608 Interstate Dr., Champaign, IL 61821, (217)398-6300 [26506]

Great Scott Services Ltd., 36 S College St., PO Box 1414, Danville, IL 61834-1414, (217)442-1143 [21751]

Great Southern Industries Inc., PO Box 5325, Jackson, MS 39216, (601)948-5700 [21752]

Great Southwest Sales, 3311 81st St., Lubbock, TX 79423, (806)792-9981 [11314]

Great West Truck and Auto Inc., PO Box 3697, Kingman, AZ 86402, (520)757-7936 [2701]

Great Western Airgas Inc., 2584 U.S Hwy. 6 and 50, Grand Junction, CO 81505, (303)243-1944 [16906]

Great Western Meats, 437 W Kaley St., Orlando, FL 32806, (407)841-4270 [11315]

Great Western Meats Inc., PO Box 568366, Orlando, FL 32856, (407)841-4270 [11316]

Great Western Pet Supply, 2001 N Black Cnyn Hwy., Phoenix, AZ 85009, (602)255-0166 [27141]

Great Western Products Inc., PO Box 466, Hollywood, AL 35752, (256)259-1079 [11317]

Great Western Recycling Industries Inc., 521 Barge Channel Rd., St. Paul, MN 55107, (651)224-4877 [26833]

Great Western Steel Co., 2310 W 58th St., Chicago, IL 60636, (312)434-5800 [20021]

Great Woods Fine Furniture, 25 Eagle St., Providence, RI 02908-5622, (401)273-6330 [13096]

Greater Lansing Auto Auction Inc., PO Box 359, Dimondale, MI 48821-0359, (517)322-2444 [20644]

Greater Mobile Auto Auction Div., 1400 Lake Hearn Dr. NE Ste. D, Atlanta, GA 30319-1464, (678)649-9800 [2702]

Greaves Company Inc., PO Box 99267, Seattle, WA 98199, (206)284-0660 [16076]

Greeff Company Inc.; R.W., 777 W Putnam Ave., Greenwich, CT 06830, (203)532-2900 [19342]

Greeff Fabrics Inc., 261 5th Ave., New York, NY 10016, (212)683-4800 [26045]

Greeley Elevator Co., 700 6th St., Greeley, CO 80631, (970)352-2575 [17962]

Greeley Publishing Co., PO Box 1138, Greeley, CO 80632, (970)352-0211 [3798]

Green Acre Farms Inc., PO Box 319, Sebastopol, MS 39359, (601)625-7432 [11318]

Green Associates; Dale, PO Box 263, Alamo, CA 94507-0263, (510)837-0355 [23698]

Green Bay Supply Company Inc., 2331 Topaz Dr., Hatfield, PA 19440, (215)822-1844 [20022]

Green and Co.; Carl, 3351 O'Brian Rd. SW, Grand Rapids, MI 49504, (616)453-1046 [16907]

The Green Company, Inc., 15550 W 109th St., Lenexa, KS 66219-1308, (913)888-8880 [17441]

Green and Company Inc.; A.A., 3330 NW 125th St., Miami, FL 33167, (305)685-7751 [11319]

Green Connection Inc., 804 E 15th Ave., Anchorage, AK 99501, (907)276-7836 [14876]

Green Gate Books, PO Box 934, Lima, OH 45802, (419)222-3816 [3799]

Green Leaf Distributors, Inc., 6500 New Venture Gear Dr., East Syracuse, NY 13057-1259, (518)459-3507 [27142]

Green Leaf Press, PO Box 880, Alhambra, CA 91802-0880, (626)281-7221 [3800]

Green/Line Equipment Inc., John Deere Rd., Farina, IL 62838, (618)245-6591 [762]

Green Manufacturing Company Inc., PO Box 26, Terrell, TX 75160, (972)524-1919 [2703]

Green Market Services Co., 1105 W Chestnut St., Brockton, MA 02301, (508)587-8661 [24756]

Green Meadow Auto Salvage, Inc., 7313 Green Meadow Dr., Helena, MT 59601-9381, (406)458-9204 [2704]

Green Mountain Florist Supply, State Hwy. 2, Montpelier, VT 05602, (802)223-7600 [14877]

Green Mountain Foam Products, RR 1, BOX 8000, Underhill, VT 05489-9801, (802)899-4668 [25671]

Green Mountain Tractor Inc., PO Box 229, Middlebury, VT 05753, (802)388-4951 [763]

Green Point Inc., 221 Green Point Rd., Brewer, ME 04412-9721, (207)989-3903 [2705]

Green Seed Co., 1730 NE Expy., Atlanta, GA 30329, (404)633-2778 [764]

Green Seed Co., 1080 Highway 29 N, Athens, GA 30601-1124, (706)548-7333 [17963]

Green Team of San Jose, 1333 Oakland Rd., San Jose, CA 95112-1364, (408)283-8500 [26834]

Green Top Sporting Goods Inc., PO Box 1015, Glen Allen, VA 23060, (804)550-2188 [23699]

Green Valley Seed, PO Box 185, Canfield, OH 44406, (330)533-4353 [765]

Green Valley Turf Farms, PO Box 185, Canfield, OH 44406, (330)533-4353 [765]

Green Velvet Sod Farms, 3640 Upper Bellbrook Rd., Bellbrook, OH 45305, (937)848-2501 [766]

Greenburg & Hammer, 24 W 57th St., New York, NY 10019, (212)246-2836 [26046]

Greene Beverage Company Inc., PO Box 1699, Tuscaloosa, AL 35406, (205)345-6950 [1731]

Greene Equipment Co., PO Box 565, Halifax, PA 17032, (215)834-6161 [2706]

Greene Farmers Cooperative, PO Box 430, Greeneville, TN 37744, (423)638-8101 [767]

Greene Rubber Company Inc., 20 Cross St., Woburn, MA 01801-5606, (781)937-9909 [24279]

Greenebaum Inc.; M.H., PO Box 6192, Parsippany, NJ 07054, (973)538-9200 [11320]

The Greenhouse, PO Box 4627, Kailua Kona, HI 96745-4627, (808)329-1979 [14878]

Greenleaf Distribution Inc., PO Box 54959, Santa Clara, CA 95056, (408)653-0222 [6310]

Greenleaf Produce, 1955 Jerrold Ave., San Francisco, CA 94124-1603, (415)647-2991 [11321]

Greenleaf Wholesale Florist, 3712 Edith Blvd. NE, PO Box 6364, Albuquerque, NM 87107-2218, (505)344-2331 [14879]

Greenleaf Wholesale Florists, PO Box 537, Brighton, CO 80601, (303)659-8000 [14880]

Greenpages Inc., 33 Badgers Island W, Kittery, ME 03904, (207)439-7310 [6311]

Green's/Pine Avenue Beer Distibuting, 3030 Pine Ave., Erie, PA 16504, (814)453-2094 [1732]

Greensboro Pipe Company Inc., 3102 Randleman Rd., Greensboro, NC 27406, (919)275-9156 [16908]

Greenstreak Inc., PO Box 7139, St. Louis, MO 63177, (636)225-9400 [22975]

Greenstreak Plastic Products, PO Box 7139, St. Louis, MO 63177, (636)225-9400 [22975]

Greenstreak Plastic Products, PO Box 7139, St. Louis, MO 63177, (314)225-9400 [22976]

GreenTek Inc., 1600 NW Washington Blvd., Grants Pass, OR 97526, (541)471-7111 [16077]

Greentree Productions Inc., 200 Lake St., Burlington, VT 05401, (802)865-0502 [22860]

Greenville Health Corp., 701 Grove Rd., Greenville, SC 29605, (864)455-6220 [18816]

Greenville Tile Distributors, 5500 Augusta Rd., Greenville, SC 29605, (803)277-3586 [9927]

Greenwich Instruments USA, 11925 Ramah Church Rd., Huntersville, NC 28078, (704)875-1922 [6312]

Greenwich Propane Inc., 255 Field Point Rd., Greenwich, CT 06830, (203)869-4388 [19106]

Greenwich Trading Co., 22 South St., Norwalk, CT 06854, (203)853-0041 [18511]

Greenwood Mills Inc., PO Box 1017, Greenwood, SC 29648, (864)229-2571 [5003]

Greenwood Mills Marketing Co., 111 W 40th St., New York, NY 10018, (212)398-9200 [26047]

Greenwood Supply Company Inc., PO Box 3069, Greenwood, SC 29648-3069, (864)229-2501 [8817]

Greer Appliance Parts Inc., 1018 S Rockford, PO Box 4563, Tulsa, OK 74159-0563, (918)587-3346 [15153]

Greer Industries Inc., PO Box 14249, Ft. Worth, TX 76117-0249, (817)222-1414 [8818]

Greg Orchards & Produce Inc., 4949 N Branch Rd., Benton Harbor, MI 49022-0000, (616)944-1414 [11322]

Gregco Inc., PO Box 810, Powell, TN 37849, (423)947-7500 [23700]

Gregg Company Ltd., 15 Dyatt Pl., Hackensack, NJ 07601, (201)489-2440 [23479]

Gregg Manufacturing Co., 143 Tuttle Ave., Fredericktown, OH 43019-1029, (740)694-4926 [15516]

Gregory Inc.; E.Z., PO Box 44268, Madison, WI 53744-4268, (608)271-2324 [14116]

Gregory Livestock, 1109 Felton Ave., Gregory, SD 57533-1145, (605)835-9408 [17964]

Gregory and Sons Inc.; J.J., 77 Highland Ave., East Providence, RI 02914, (401)434-7700 [7416]

Greg's Cookies Inc., 4500 1st Ave. N, Birmingham, AL 35222, (205)595-4627 [11323]

Greno Industries Inc., P.O. Box 542, Schenectady, NY 12301, (518)393-4195 [16909]

Gresham Petroleum Co., PO Box 690, Indianola, MS 38751, (662)887-2160 [22321]

Grey Eagle Distributors Inc., 2340 Millpark Dr., Maryland Heights, MO 63043, (314)429-9100 [1733]

Greylock Electronics Distributors, 763 Ulster Ave. Mall, Kingston, NY 12401, (914)338-5300 [8819]

Greystone Peripherals Inc., 130-A Knowles Dr., Los Gatos, CA 95030, (408)866-4739 [6313]

Grier and Sons Co.; R.D., 317 Railroad Ave., Salisbury, MD 21802, (410)749-4131 [16910]

Gries Seed Farms Inc., 2348 N 5th St., Fremont, OH 43420, (419)332-5571 [768]

Griffin and Brand Produce Sales Agency Inc., PO Box 833, Hereford, TX 79045, (806)364-1610 [11324]

Griffin & Brand Sales Agency, Inc., PO Box 833, Hereford, TX 79045, (806)364-1610 [11325]

Griffin Container and Supply Co., PO Box 916, Salinas, CA 93902, (408)422-6458 [21753]

Griffin-Holder Co., PO Box 511, Rocky Ford, CO 81067, (719)254-3363 [11326]

Griffin Manufacturing, Box 1928, Muskogee, OK 74402, (918)687-6311 [11327]

Griffin Refrigeration Inc., 80 Eastway, Reading, MA 01867-1107, (781)942-1522 [14474]

Griffin Wood Company Inc., PO Box 669, Marion, AL 36756, (334)683-9073 [27312]

Griffith Inc.; R.C., 1004 First Ave., Council Bluffs, IA 51501, (712)322-7331 [7417]

Griggs Inc.; Jack, PO Box 547, Exeter, CA 93221, (209)592-3154 [22322]

Griggs Paint Co., 3635 S 16th St., Phoenix, AZ 85040-1319, (602)243-3293 [21452]

Grimes Oil Company Inc., 165 Norfolk St., Boston, MA 02124, (617)825-1200 [22323]

Grimsley Oil Company Inc., PO Box 520, Avon Park, FL 33825, (941)453-3550 [22324]

Grimstad, Inc.; J.M., 6203 Chancellor Dr., Cedar Falls, IA 50613, (319)277-8550 [16078]

Grimstad Inc.; J.M., 1001 S 84th St., PO Box 14517, Milwaukee, WI 53214, (414)258-5200 [16079]

Grimstad, Inc.; J.M., 2251 Hutson Rd., Green Bay, WI 54303, (920)429-2040 [4402]

Grimstad, Inc.; J.M., 1100 Zane Ave. N, Minneapolis, MN 55422, (612)544-6100 [4403]

Grimstad, Inc.; J.M., 4792 Colt Rd., Rockford, IL 61125, (815)874-6666 [4404]

Grinders Clearing House Inc., 13301 E 8 Mile Rd., Warren, MI 48089, (810)771-1500 [16080]

Grinnell Door Inc. (GS & D), 315 North Ave. Mt. Clemens, MI 48043, (810)463-8667 [7418]

Grinnell Sash & Door Inc. (GS & D), 315 North Ave., Mt. Clemens, MI 48043, (810)463-8667 [7418]

Grinnell Supply Sales Co, 1600 E Orangethorpe Ave., Fullerton, CA 92831, (714)773-1166 [16911]

Grinnell Supply Sales Co., 1930 Warren St., North Kansas City, MO 64116, (816)474-0500 [23199]

Grismer Tire Co., PO Box 337, Dayton, OH 45401, (937)224-9815 [2707]

Grist Mill Co., 21340 Hayes Ave., PO Box 430, Lakeville, MN 55044, (612)469-4981 [11328]

Griswold and Company Inc.; S.T., PO Box 849, Williston, VT 05495, (802)658-0201 [7419]

Grocers Specialty Co., 5200 Shelia St., Commerce, CA 90040, (213)726-2601 [11329]

Grocers Supply Co., 4310 Stout Field N Dr., Indianapolis, IN 46241-4002, (317)243-6000 [11330]

Grocers Supply Company Inc., PO Box 14200, Houston, TX 77221, (713)747-5000 [11331]

Grocers Wholesale Co., 105 Embarcadero, Oakland, CA 94606-5138, (415)826-1235 [11332]

Grocery Supply Co., PO Box 638, Sulphur Springs, TX 75483-0638, (903)885-7621 [11333]

Grocery Supply Co., Inc., 2330 Roosevelt Ave., San Antonio, TX 78210, (210)533-1281 [11334]

Grocery Supply Company - Southeast, PO Box 17209, Pensacola, FL 32522, (850)438-9651 [11335]

Groff Meats Inc., 33 N Market St., Elizabethtown, PA 17022-2039, (717)367-1246 [11336]

Grogan's Healthcare Supply Inc., 1016 S Broadway, Lexington, KY 40504, (606)254-6661 [18817]

Grogan's, Inc., 1016 S Broadway, Lexington, KY 40504, (606)254-6661 [19343]

Groomingdales, 53 Middleburg Ln., Orchard Park, NY 14127, (716)826-5797 [27273]

Gross Electric Inc., PO Box 352377, Toledo, OH 43635-2377, (419)537-1818 [8820]

Gross and Hecht Trucking Corp., 35 Brunswick Ave., Edison, NJ 08818, (732)572-1500 [2708]

Gross and Janes Co., PO Box 26113, Fenton, MO 63026, (314)241-9170 [23480]

Gross-Medick-Barrows Inc., PO Box 12727, El Paso, TX 79913, (915)584-8133 [22861]

Gross-Yowell and Company Inc., 3720 Franklin Ave., Waco, TX 76710, (254)754-5475 [7420]

Grossenburg Implement Inc., HC 59, Box 1, Winner, SD 57580, (605)842-2040 [769]

Grosslein Beverages Inc., 13554 Tungsten St. NW, Anoka, MN 55303, (612)421-5804 [1734]

Grossman Iron and Steel Co., 5 N Market St., St. Louis, MO 63102, (314)231-9423 [20023]

Grosz; Leland, PO Box 472, Garrison, ND 58540-0152, (701)337-5438 [770]

Groth Corp., PO Box 15293, Houston, TX 77220-5293, (713)675-6151 [16912]

Group One Capital Inc., 1610 Des Peres Rd., Ste. 395, St. Louis, MO 63131, (314)821-5100 [14117]

Group One Ltd., 80 C Ln., Farmingdale, NY 11735, (516)249-1399 [5627]

Group Publishing, Inc., 1515 Cascade Ave., PO Box 481, Loveland, CO 80539, (970)669-3836 [3801]

Group W Video Sources, 310 Parkway View Dr., Pittsburgh, PA 15205, (412)747-4700 [25188]

Grove City Farmers Exchange Co., 3937 Broadway, Grove City, OH 43123, (614)875-6311 [771]

Grover Brothers Equipment Inc., 1500 N Main St., Hattiesburg, MS 39401-1911, (601)545-3505 [14475]

Grover Industries Inc., PO Box 79, Grover, NC 28073, (704)937-7434 [26048]

Grower Shipper Potato Co., PO Box 432, Monte Vista, CO 81144-0432, (719)852-3569 [11337]

Growers Cooperative Inc., PO Box 2196, Terre Haute, IN 47802, (812)235-8123 [772]

Growers Fertilizer Corp., PO Box 1407, Lake Alfred, FL 33850, (813)956-1101 [773]

Growers Ford Tractor Co., 8501 NW 58th St., Miami, FL 33166, (305)592-7890 [774]

Growers Marketing Service Inc., PO Box 2595, Lakeland, FL 33806, (941)644-2414 [11338]

Growers Precooler Inc., 2880 Lust Rd., Apopka, FL 32703, (407)889-4000 [11339]

Grower's Produce Corp., 380 3rd St., Oakland, CA 94607, (510)834-5280 [11340]

Growmark, 1701 Towanda Ave., Bloomington, IL 61701, (309)557-6000 [775]

Growmark, PO Box 2500, Bloomington, IL 61702-2500, (217)423-9738 [776]

GROWMARK Inc., 1701 Towanda Ave., Bloomington, IL 61701, (309)557-6000 [17965]

GRS Industrial Supply Co., 405 Grandville Ave. NW, Grand Rapids, MI 49503, (616)458-3601 [16913]

Gruen Export Co., 6310 N Port Washington Rd., PO Box 17287, Milwaukee, WI 53217, (414)964-4880 [17966]

Gruener Sales Inc., 1830 Kelso St., Flint, MI 48503, (810)744-3141 [2709]

Gruner & Company, Inc., 1350 Avenue Of The Americas, Ste. 804, New York, NY 10019-4702, (212)868-1484 [5004]

Gryphon House, Inc., 10726 Tucker St., PO Box 207, Beltsville, MD 20704-0207, (301)595-9500 [3802]

GSC Enterprises Inc., PO Box 638, Sulphur Springs, TX 75483-0638, (903)885-7621 [11341]

GSC Enterprises Inc., PO Box 638, Sulphur Springs, TX 75483-0638, (903)885-0829 [11342]

GSI Corp., 6399 Amp Dr., Clemmons, NC 27012, (336)766-7070 [21021]

GSI, Inc., PO Box 129, Trussville, AL 35173, (205)655-8299 [13492]

GSK Products Inc., 3422 W Wilshire, Ste. 13, Phoenix, AZ 85009, (602)278-6046 [14118]

GSL Enterprises Inc., 3113 Olu St., Honolulu, HI 96816-1425, (808)735-1800 [5005]

GT Interactive Software Corp., 417 5th Ave., Rm. 789, New York, NY 10016-2204, (212)726-6500 [6314]

GT Interactive Software Corp. Value Products Div., 2300 Berkshire Ln., N, Minneapolis, MN 55441-3606, (612)509-7600 [6315]

GT Sales and Manufacturing Inc., PO Box 9408, Wichita, KS 67277, (316)943-2171 [16914]

GTA Aviation Inc., 2730 E Sky Harbor Blvd., Phoenix, AZ 85034, (602)273-7704 [22325]

GTE Supply, 5615 Highpoint Dr., Irving, TX 75038, (972)751-4100 [5628]

GTH Holdings, Inc., PO Box 2617, Butler, PA 16003, (412)282-4528 [7421]

GTI, 7615 Golden Triangle Dr., Eden Prairie, MN 55344, (480)820-7680 [6316]

GTR Truck Equipment, Division of Grand Traverse Rubber Supply, 2098 M 37 S, Traverse City, MI 49684, (616)943-9640 [2710]

GTS Scientific Inc., PO Box 7555, Gaithersburg, MD 20898-7555, (301)929-1444 [18818]

Guaranteed Business Services Inc., 7 N Main St., West Hartford, CT 06107-1918, (860)521-4949 [6317]

Guard All Chemical Company Inc., PO Box 445, Norwalk, CT 06856, (203)838-5515 [22326]

Guardian Automotive, 6145 D Wall St., Sterling Heights, MI 48312, (810)979-2114 [2162]

Guardian Book Co., 8464 Brown St., Ottawa Lake, MI 49267, (734)856-1765 [3803]

Guarnieri Co.; Albert, 1133-71 E Market St., Warren, OH 44483, (216)394-5636 [21754]

Guernsey Farms Dairy, 21300 Novi Rd., Northville, MI 48167-9701, (248)349-1466 [11343]

Guerrero; Rick, 201 Hindry Ave., Inglewood, CA 90301-1519, (310)410-4907 [179]

Guest Supply Inc., PO Box 902, 720 U.S Hwy. 1, Monmouth Junction, NJ 08852-0902, (908)246-3011 [24130]

Guidelines Inc., 26076 Getty Dr., Laguna Niguel, CA 92677, (949)582-5001 [3804]

Guido Inc.; Gino, PO Box 17207, San Antonio, TX 78217, (210)828-9911 [7422]

Guido Lumber Company Inc., PO Box 790908, San Antonio, TX 78279-0908, (210)344-8321 [7423]

Guiffre Distributing Co.; Tony, 6839 Industrial Rd., Springfield, VA 22151-4289, (703)642-1700 [1735]

The Guild, 2634 Georgia Ave. NW, Washington, DC 20001-3852, (202)745-0417 [5006]

Guilfoil and Associates Inc.; T.V., 333 Pulaski St., Syracuse, NY 13204, (315)474-8771 [25919]

Guilford of Maine Textile Resources, 5300 Corporate Grove Dr. SE, No., Grand Rapids, MI 49512-5512, (616)554-2250 [26049]

Guinness America Inc., 6 Landmark Sq., Stamford, CT 06901, (203)359-7100 [1736]

Guinness Import Co., 6 Landmark Sq., Stamford, CT 06901, (203)323-3311 [1737]

Gulbenkian Swim Inc., 70 Memorial Plz., Pleasantville, NY 10570, (914)747-3240 [23701]

Gulbransen Inc. Crystal Products, 2102 Hancock St., San Diego, CA 92110, (619)296-5760 [25221]

Gulbranson Equipment Inc., Rte. 2, Park Rapids, MN 56470, (218)732-9744 [777]

Gulf Bolt & Supply, 403 E Brazos, PO Box 2112, Victoria, TX 77901, (512)575-6441 [13729]

Gulf Central Corp., 7819 Professional Pl., Tampa, FL 33637, (813)985-3185 [15154]

Gulf Central Seafoods Inc., 155 5th St., Biloxi, MS 39530, (228)436-6346 [11344]

Gulf Coast Auto Auction Inc., 6005 24th St. E, Bradenton, FL 34203, (941)756-8478 [20645]

Gulf Coast Electric Supply Company Inc., PO Box 9588, Houston, TX 77261-9588, (713)222-9086 [8821]

Gulf Coast Marine Supply Inc., 501 Stimrad Rd., Mobile, AL 36610, (205)452-8066 [18512]

Gulf Coast Software & Systems, 549 E Pass Rd., Ste. M, Gulfport, MS 39507-3261, (228)896-8217 [6318]

Gulf Coast Sportswear Inc., PO Box 1498, Lake Jackson, TX 77566, (409)297-7552 [5007]

Gulf Enterprises, 4333 Washington Ave., New Orleans, LA 70185, (504)822-0785 [9928]

Gulf Go-Fers Inc., 2136 Corporation Blvd., Naples, FL 34109-2053, (941)591-1353 [11345]

Gulf King Marine, 322 Huff St., Aransas Pass, TX 78336-5619, (512)758-3223 [18513]

Gulf Marine and Industrial Supplies, 401 St. Joseph St., New Orleans, LA 70130, (504)525-6252 [11346]

Gulf Materials Recycling Corp., PO Box 96166, Houston, TX 77213-6166, (281)457-2100 [26805]

Gulf Oil L.P., PO Box 9151, Chelsea, MA 02150-2337, (617)889-9000 [22327]

Gulf Pacific Rice Company Inc., 12010 Taylor Rd., Houston, TX 77041-1222, (713)464-0606 [11347]

Gulf Pool Equipment Co., PO Box 790462, San Antonio, TX 78279-0462, (210)341-9103 [23702]

Gulf Reduction Div., PO Box 611, Houston, TX 77001, (713)926-1705 [20543]

Gulf South Forest Products, Inc., PO Box 39299, Ft. Lauderdale, FL 33339-9299, (954)565-8355 [27313]

Gulf South Medical Supply Inc., 426 Christine Dr., Ridgeland, MS 39157, (601)856-5900 [18819]

Gulf States Optical Labs Inc., PO Box 60023, New Orleans, LA 70160-0023, (504)834-1646 [19344]

Gulf States Toyota Inc., PO Box 40306, Houston, TX 77040, (713)744-3300 [2711]

Gull Industries Inc., PO Box 24687, Seattle, WA 98124, (206)624-5900 [22328]

Gully Tri-Coop Association, PO Box 29, Gully, MN 56646, (218)268-4185 [778]

Gun Parts Corp., 226 Williams Ln., West Hurley, NY 12491, (914)679-2417 [13504]

The Gun Room Press, 127 Raritan Ave., Highland Park, NJ 08904, (732)545-4344 [4129]

Gun South Inc., PO Box 129, Trussville, AL 35173, (205)655-8299 [13492]

Gun Traders Inc., 512 Muldoon Rd., Anchorage, AK 99504-1508, (907)337-6522 [23703]

Gunderland Marine Supply, Inc., 1221 Cantwell Ln., PO Box 9758, Corpus Christi, TX 78407, (512)882-4231 [18514]

Gunderson Oil Co., 6339 Hwy. 44, Cuba, NM 87013, (505)289-4040 [22329]

Guns Of Yesteryear, 3936 Chattanooga Rd., Tunnel Hill, GA 30755, (706)673-2506 [13493]

Gunter Jr. & Associates; Guy T., 174 14th St. NW, Atlanta, GA 30318-7802, (404)874-7529 [15155]

Gunther and Co.; Albert, 1201 Desoto Rd., Baltimore, MD 21223, (410)644-0926 [7424]

Gunton Corp., 26150 Richmond Rd., Bedford Heights, OH 44146, (216)831-2420 [7425]

Guptons Sporting Goods Inc., 324 S Garnett St., Henderson, NC 27536-4538, (919)492-2311 [23704]

Gurley's Georgia Carpet, 15 Morrison Blvd., Bristol, VA 24201, (540)466-2061 [9929]

Gusmer Co.; A., PO Box 846, Cranford, NJ 07016, (908)272-9400 [16081]

Gusmer Enterprises Inc., 27 North Ave. E, Cranford, NJ 07016, (908)272-9400 [16915]

Guss Cleaning & Supply, 240 Wyant Ln., Hamilton, MT 59840-9371, (406)363-4427 [4632]

Gussoff-Reslow & Associates, 250 Spring St. NW, Ste. 12N104B, Atlanta, GA 30303-1101, (404)221-0261 [5008]

Gusto Brands Inc., PO Box 278, Lagrange, GA 30241, (706)882-2573 [1738]

Guterman International Inc., 603 Pleasant St., Paxton, MA 01612-1305, (508)852-8206 [23705]

Guthrie-Linebaugh-Coffey, Inc., 202 Oak Knoll Rd., New Cumberland, PA 17070-2837, (717)767-6991 [9930]

Guttman Oil Co., Speers Rd., Belle Vernon, PA 15012, (724)483-3533 [22330]

Guttmann Corp.; Victor, 95 Madison Ave., New York, NY 10016, (212)689-1899 [26050]

Guyan Machinery Company Inc., PO Box 150, Chapmanville, WV 25508-0150, (304)855-4501 [16916]

GWS Automotive and Truck Equipment Sales Inc., 2813 Agate St., Bakersfield, CA 93304, (805)832-3860 [2712]

GWS Supply, Inc., 2375 W Nordale Dr., Appleton, WI 54914, (920)739-6066 [16917]

Gyles; Janis, PO Box 1827, Pueblo, CO 81002-1827, (719)542-4325 [24558]

Gym Source, 40 E 52nd St., New York, NY 10022, (212)688-4222 [23706]

Gypsum Wholesalers Inc., 3334 Walters Rd., Syracuse, NY 13209, (315)451-5322 [7426]

H-A Distributors Inc., 1942 West St., Annapolis, MD 21401-3931, (410)266-0818 [25222]

H A Foodservice-HAFSCO, 47 Railroad Ave., West Haven, CT 06516, (203)933-5636 [24131]

H and D Steel Service Inc., 9960 York Alpha Dr., North Royalton, OH 44133, (440)237-3390 [20024]

H & D Transmission, 31-40 Whitestone Pkwy., Flushing, NY 11354, (718)961-9666 [2713]

H. and E. Brothers Inc., 14021 Amargosa Rd., Victorville, CA 92392, (760)241-7540 [13730]

H Enterprises International Inc., 120 S 6th St., Ste. 2300, Minneapolis, MN 55402, (612)340-8849 [19345]

H and F Food Products Inc., 321 Ramsdell Ave., Buffalo, NY 14216, (716)876-4345 [11348]

H & H Beauty & Barber Supply, 815 W South, Benton, AR 72015, (501)776-0237 [14119]

H and H Computers, 3400 Bradshaw Rd., Ste. A2, Sacramento, CA 95827, (916)362-4884 [6319]

H & H Distributing, 5949 Jackson, Ann Arbor, MI 48103, (734)662-1931 [27143]

H & H Distributing Inc., 550 E Amity Rd., Boise, ID 83705-5206, (208)345-4086 [7427]

H and H Distributors Inc., 4015 Washington Rd., McMurray, PA 15317, (412)621-8444 [2714]

H & H Equipment Inc., 611 Fairbanks St., Anchorage, AK 99501-3744, (907)277-9432 [6320]

H & H Foodservice, 304 S Vine, PO Box 494, West Union, IA 52175-0494, (319)422-3846 [11349]

H and H Meat Products Company Inc., PO Box 358, Mercedes, TX 78570, (210)565-6363 [11350]

H & H Products Co., PO Box 607668, Orlando, FL 32860, (407)299-5410 [24966]

H & H Sales Company, Inc., PO Box 686, Huntertown, IN 46748-0686, (219)637-3177 [2715]

H and H Sales Inc., RR 4, Box 36, Thief River Falls, MN 56701-9007, (218)681-1788 [26507]

H-H of Savannah, Inc., 2501 E President St., Savannah, GA 31404, (912)236-8284 [1739]

H & J Leather Finishing, 312 N Perry, Johnstown, NY 12095-1211, (518)762-7775 [18396]

H and L Marine Woodworking Inc., 2965 Harcourt St., East Rancho Dominguez, CA 90221, (310)638-8746 [18515]

H & M Distributing, PO Box 1633, Pocatello, ID 83204-1633, (208)233-6633 [24967]

H & M Distributing Inc., 167 Eastland Dr., PO Box 314, Twin Falls, ID 83303-0314, (208)733-1145 [26301]

H and N Fish Co., 2390 Jerrold Ave., San Francisco, CA 94124, (415)821-6637 [11351]

H n' M Associates Inc., 4520 E West Hwy., Ste. 300, Bethesda, MD 20814-3347, (301)776-9222 [11352]

H & R General Painting, PO Box 90570, Anchorage, AK 99509, (907)243-0728 [21453]

H & W Sport Monticello Inc., 1500 N Main St., No. 104, Monticello, KY 42633-2046, (606)348-6259 [23707]

H2O, 3000 South 300 West, Salt Lake City, UT 84115-3407, (801)486-9388 [23708]

HA-LO, 3628 Walnut Hills Rd., Cleveland, OH 44122, (216)292-2595 [5009]

Ha-Lo Marketing, 3628 Walnut Hills Rd., Cleveland, OH 44122, (216)292-2595 [5009]

Ha-Lo Marketing, 3628 Walnut Hills Rd., Cleveland, OH 44122, (216)292-2595 [5010]

HAACO Inc., PO Box 7190, Madison, WI 53707, (608)221-6200 [779]

HAAKE, 53 W Century Rd., Paramus, NJ 07652, (201)265-7865 [24367]

Haas Outdoors Inc., PO Box 757, West Point, MS 39773, (601)494-8859 [5011]

Haasco Inc., 27 U.S Hwy. 41 S, Henderson, KY 42420, (270)826-8808 [16918]

Habbersett Sausage Inc., PO Box 146, Folcroft, PA 19032, (610)532-9973 [11353]

Habegger Corp., 4995 Winton Rd., Cincinnati, OH 45232, (513)681-6313 [14476]

Haber Fabrics Corp., 1720 E Hwy. 356, Irving, TX 75060, (972)579-7451 [26051]

Habhegger Company Inc.; E.O., 460 Penn St., Yeadon, PA 19050-3017, (610)622-1977 [22331]

Habitat Softwear, PO Box 2086, Montrose, CO 81402, (970)249-3333 [5012]

Habot Steel Company Inc., 1180 Fahs St., York, PA 17404, (717)848-6080 [20025]

Habys Sales Candy Co., PO Box 1612, Castroville, TX 78009-9402, (512)538-3164 [11354]

Hach Co., PO Box 389, Loveland, CO 80539, (970)669-3050 [25672]

Hachik Distributors Inc., 2300 Island Ave., Philadelphia, PA 19142, (215)365-8500 [23709]

Hacker Art Books Inc., 45 W 57th St., New York, NY 10019, (212)688-7600 [3805]

Hackett Co.; J. Lee, 23550 Haggerty Rd., Farmington, MI 48335-2636, (313)478-0200 [16082]

Hackler Livestock; G.A., 3880 W Franklin Rd., Meridian, ID 83642-5442, (208)888-1732 [17967]

Hackney Co.; H.T., PO Box 238, Knoxville, TN 37901, (423)546-1291 [11355]

Hadco Inc., PO Box 97, Suwanee, GA 30024, (404)932-7282 [15156]

Haddad Electronic Supply Inc., PO Box 2707, Fall River, MA 02722-2707, (508)679-2596 [5629]

Haddon House Food Products Inc., PO Box 907, Medford, NJ 08055, (609)654-7901 [11356]

Hadfield Sport Shops Inc., 96 Webster Square Rd., Berlin, CT 06037-2327, (860)828-6391 [23710]

Hadley Braithwait Co., 2519 11th St., Columbus, NE 68601-5723, (402)564-7279 [11357]

Hadley Corp.; Raymond, 89 Tompkins St., Spencer, NY 14883, (607)589-4415 [11358]

Hadley Cos., 11001 Hampshire Ave. S, Bloomington, MN 55438, (612)943-8474 [3806]

Hadley Office Products Inc., 399 S River Dr., Wausau, WI 54402-1326, (715)842-5651 [21022]

Hadlock Paint Co., 7273 Victor-Pittsford Rd., PO Box 376, Victor, NY 14564, (716)924-8420 [21454]

Hadon Security Company Inc., PO Box 247, SR-82, Langley, OK 74350, (918)782-2709 [2716]

Hadro Aluminum & Metal Corp., 4001 G St., Philadelphia, PA 19124, (215)427-0100 [20026]

Hafele America Co., PO Box 4000, Archdale, NC 27263, (910)889-2322 [13731]

Haffner X-Ray Company Inc., PO Box 344, Noblesville, IN 46060-0344, (317)773-5171 [18820]

Hagale Industries Inc., 601 E South St., Ozark, MO 65721, (417)581-2351 [5013]

Hagan & Stone Wholesale, Hwy. 163 N, PO Box 158, Tompkinsville, KY 42167-0158, (270)487-6138 [780]

Hager Companies, 139 Victor St., St. Louis, MO 63104, (314)772-4400 [13732]

Hager Lumber Company Inc.; T.W., PO Box 912, Grand Rapids, MI 49509, (616)452-5151 [7428]

Hager Lumber Company Inc.; T.W., PO Box 912, Grand Rapids, MI 49509, (616)452-5151 [27314]

Hagerman and Company Inc., PO Box 139, Mt Zion, IL 62549, (217)864-2326 [6321]

Hagerty Brothers Co., PO Box 1500, Peoria, IL 61655, (309)699-7251 [16919]

Haggard and Stocking Associates Inc., 5318 Victory Dr., Indianapolis, IN 46203, (317)788-4661 [16920]

Haggard and Stocking Associates Inc., 5318 Victory Dr., Indianapolis, IN 46203, (317)788-4661 [16083]

Haggerty Lumber, PO Box 187, Walled Lake, MI 48390, (248)624-4551 [7429]

Hahn Automotive Warehouse Inc., 415 W Main St., Rochester, NY 14608, (716)235-1595 [2717]

Hahn Bros. Inc., PO Box 407, Westminster, MD 21158, (410)848-4200 [11359]

Hahn and Phillips Grease Company Inc., PO Box 130, Marshall, MO 65340, (660)886-9688 [17968]

Hahn Supply Inc., 2101 Main St., Lewiston, ID 83501, (208)743-1577 [23200]

Hahn Systems, PO Box 42427, Indianapolis, IN 46242-0427, (317)243-3796 [7430]

Hahn Watch & Jewelry Co., 102-30 66th Rd., Apt. 11H, Forest Hills, NY 11375-2090 [17442]

Hahnaman-Albrecht Inc., 1318 E State St., Rockford, IL 61104-2228, (815)288-7330 [17969]

Hahns of Westminster, 440 Hahn Rd., Westminster, MD 21157, (410)848-4200 [11360]

Haider; Raymond, 407 12th St. NW, Mandan, ND 58554-1932, (701)663-7236 [17970]

Haig Lighting & Electric, 34001 Groesbeck Hwy., Clinton Township, MI 48035, (810)791-2380 [8822]

Haik's Inc., 1240 E Trafficway, PO Box 709, Springfield, MO 65801-0709, (417)866-4391 [26052]

Haines & Company, Inc.; J.J., 6950 Aviation Blvd., Glen Burnie, MD 21061-2531, (410)760-4040 [9931]

Haines & Company, Inc.; J.J., 422 Business Ctr. Bldg. Z2630, Montgomery Ave., Oaks, PA 19456-0410, (215)666-1007 [9932]

Haines & Co.; J.J., 3283 Hwy. 70 W, Goldsboro, NC 27530-9567 [9933]

Hair Depot Beauty Consultants, 315 16th St. SW, Minot, ND 58701-3518, (701)852-1008 [14120]

Haitai America Inc., 7227 Telegraph Rd., Montebello, CA 90640, (562)923-3945 [11361]

Hajoca Corp., 127 Coulter Ave., Ardmore, PA 19003, (215)649-1430 [23201]

Hal-Hen Company Inc., 14-33 31st Ave., Long Island City, NY 11106, (718)392-6020 [18821]

Halasz from Dallas, 3775 West Bay, Dallas, TX 75214, (214)826-1422 [2718]

Halbro America, 885 Warren Ave., East Providence, RI 02914, (401)438-2727 [23711]

HALCO, 600 Green Ln., Union, NJ 07083, (908)289-1000 [24132]

Haldeman-Homme Inc., 430 Industrial Blvd., Minneapolis, MN 55413, (612)331-4880 [16921]

Hale & Associates; Robert, 7523 Avenue J, Norfolk, VA 23513-4638, (757)583-7001 [25223]

Hale Brothers Inc., 530 E Main St., Morristown, TN 37814, (615)586-6231 [11362]

Hale Center Wheat Growers Inc., PO Drawer F, Hale Center, TX 79041, (806)839-2426 [781]

Hale-Halsell Co., PO Box 582898, Tulsa, OK 74158, (918)835-4484 [11363]

Hale Industries Inc., 2038 S Cole Rd., Boise, ID 83709-2815, (208)322-0203 [24133]

Hale Trailer Brake & Wheel, PO Box 3305, Allentown, PA 18106-0305, (610)395-0371 [2719]

Halebian; Michael, 557 Washington Ave., Carlstadt, NJ 07072, (201)935-3535 [9934]

Haletky; Gerald E., 673 Black Brook Rd., Goffstown, NH 03045-2911, (603)774-5120 [25673]

Haley and Company Inc.; Caleb, 14 Fulton Fish Market, New York, NY 10038, (212)732-7474 [11364]

Haleyville Drapery Manufacturing, PO Box 695, Haleyville, AL 35565-9201, (205)486-9257 [15517]

Halferty and Sons Inc.; H.H., PO Box 298, Smithville, MO 64089, (816)532-0221 [782]

Halifax Floral Co., Inc., 395 Promenade St., Providence, RI 02908, (401)751-4333 [14881]

Hall Balloon Co., 2610 W 6th Ave., Pine Bluff, AR 71601-3796, (870)535-0426 [26508]

Hall Div.; Howard, 777 W Putnam Ave., Greenwich, CT 06830, (203)532-2900 [19346]

Hall Electric Supply Co., Inc. (HESCO), PO Box 124, Arlington, MA 02476-0984, (781)438-3800 [15157]

Hall Enterprises; Robert J., 2881 Heckman Rd., Uniontown, OH 44685-9003, (330)699-6155 [26509]

Hall Group Inc., 215 S Highway Ave., De Land, IL 61839, (217)664-3346 [6322]

Hall Inc.; Bob, 5600 SE Crane Hwy., Upper Marlboro, MD 20772, (301)627-1900 [1740]

Hall Inc.; Melville B., 3001 Spruce, St. Louis, MO 63103, (314)371-7000 [8823]

Hall-Mark Electronics Corp., 11333 Pagemill Rd., Dallas, TX 75243, (214)343-5000 [6323]

Hall; Melanie J., 3926 E Raines Rd., Memphis, TN 38118-6936, (901)260-2200 [16096]

Hall & Reis, Inc., 16 Short Hill Rd., Forest Hills, NY 11375-6074, (718)458-2567 [7431]

Hall Research Technologies, 3613 W Macarthur Blvd., Ste. 600, Santa Ana, CA 92704-6846, (714)641-6607 [6324]

Halliday Sand and Gravel Co., 8340 Calkins Rd., Houghton Lake, MI 48629, (517)422-3463 [7432]

Halliday-Smith Inc., 1st St. & Holiday Dr., Cairo, IL 62914, (618)734-0447 [1741]

Hallidie Machinery Company Inc., PO Box 3536, Seattle, WA 98124, (206)583-0600 [16084]

Hallmark Building Supplies Inc., 6060 N 77th St., Milwaukee, WI 53218-1293, (414)464-9990 [7433]

Hallmark Models, Inc., 4822 Bryan St., Dallas, TX 75204, (214)821-2550 [26510]

Hallmarkets International Ltd., 1415 Midway Dr., Alpine, CA 91901, (619)445-1999 [21023]

Hallock Coin Jewelry, 2060 W Lincoln Ave., Anaheim, CA 92801-5301, (714)956-2360 [17443]

Hallock Cooperative Elevator Co., 310 S Atlantic St., Hallock, MN 56728, (218)843-2624 [17971]

Hallock Cooperative Elevator Co., 310 S Atlantic St., Hallock, MN 56728, (218)843-2624 [11365]

Hallogram Publishing, 14221 E 4th Ave., Aurora, CO 80011, (303)340-3404 [6325]

Hallsmith-Sysco Food Services, 380 S Worcester St., Norton, MA 02766, (508)285-6361 [11366]

Hallwood Group Inc., 3710 Rawlans St., Ste. 1500, Dallas, TX 75219, (214)528-5588 [26053]

Halo Distributing Co., PO Box 7370, San Antonio, TX 78207-0370, (210)735-1111 [1742]

Halpin Equipment Corp.; Tim, 5670 NW 78th Ave., Miami, FL 33166, (305)591-3164 [2720]

Halron Oil Company Inc., PO Box 2188, Green Bay, WI 54306, (414)437-0466 [22332]

Halsey Company Inc.; W.L., PO Box 6485, Huntsville, AL 35824, (256)772-9691 [11367]

Halsey Seed Co., 2059 State Rt. 96, Trumansburg, NY 14886-9129, (607)387-7303 [783]

Halstad Elevator Co., PO Box 87, Halstad, MN 56548, (218)456-2135 [17972]

Halted Specialties Co., 3500 Ryder Ave., Santa Clara, CA 95051, (408)732-1573 [6326]

Halton Co., 4421 NE Columbia Blvd., Portland, OR 97218, (503)288-6411 [7434]

Halton System Inc., 80 Pine Tree Industrial Pkwy., Portland, ME 04102-1443, (207)774-7447 [25845]

Ham and McCreight Inc., PO Box 1046, Temple, TX 76503-1046, (254)778-4747 [23202]

Hamakor Judaica Inc., PO Box 48836, Niles, IL 60714-0836, (847)966-4040 [3807]

Hamamatsu Photonic Systems, PO Box 6910, Bridgewater, NJ 08807, (908)231-0960 [22862]

Hamburg, 3104 Farber Dr., Champaign, IL 61821, (217)352-7911 [1743]

Hamburg Brothers, 40 24th St., Pittsburgh, PA 15222, (412)227-6200 [15158]

Hamel Spanish Book Corp.; Bernard H., 10977 Santa Monica Blvd., Los Angeles, CA 90025, (310)475-0453 [3808]

Hamilton Appliance Parts Inc., 1832 McCalla Ave., Knoxville, TN 37915-1419, (423)525-0418 [15159]

Hamilton County Farm Bureau, PO Box 1106, Noblesville, IN 46060, (317)773-0870 [784]

Hamilton Electric Works Inc., 3800 Airport Blvd., Austin, TX 78722, (512)472-2428 [8824]

Hamilton Elevator Company Inc., PO Box 177, Campus, IL 60920, (815)567-3311 [17973]

Hamilton Equipment Inc., 567 S Reading Rd., Ephrata, PA 17522, (717)733-7951 [785]

Hamilton Inc.; David, 250 Spring St., Atlanta, GA 30303, (404)681-2752 [5014]

Hamilton Marine, PO Box 227, Searsport, ME 04974, (207)548-6302 [18516]

Hamilton Medical Inc., PO Box 30008, Reno, NV 89520-3008, (702)858-3200 [18822]

Hamilton Medical Inc., PO Box 30008, Reno, NV 89520-3008, (702)858-3200 [19347]

Hamilton-Parker, Co., 1865 Leonard Ave., PO Box 15217, Columbus, OH 43219, (614)358-7800 [9935]

Hamler Industries, 5811 Tacony St., Philadelphia, PA 19135, (215)535-7530 [4405]

Hammer-Johnson Supply Inc., 12 S White St., Athens, TN 37303, (423)745-2880 [7435]

Hammer Lumber Company Inc., PO Box 2550, Eugene, OR 97402, (541)687-1400 [7436]

Hammer's Plastic Recycling Corp., 10252 Hwy. 65, Iowa Falls, IA 50126-8823, (515)648-5073 [26940]

Hammett Co.; J.L., PO Box 9057, Braintree, MA 02184, (781)848-1000 [21024]

Hammill and Gillespie Inc., PO Box 104, Livingston, NJ 07039, (201)994-3650 [20544]

Hammond Candy Co, 2530 W 29th Ave., Denver, CO 80211, (303)455-2320 [11368]

Hammond Computer Inc., 70 E 3750 S, Salt Lake City, UT 84115, (801)265-8500 [6327]

Hammond Electronics, 1000 Fairway Blvd., Columbus, OH 43213-2521, (614)237-2504 [25224]

Hammond Electronics Inc., 1230 W Central Blvd., Orlando, FL 32805, (407)849-6060 [8825]

Hammond Sheet Metal Company Inc., 119 Cass Ave., St. Louis, MO 63102, (314)241-5922 [14477]

Hammons Products Co., PO Box H, Stockton, MO 65785, (417)276-5181 [11369]

Hamon Inc.; Gerard, PO Box 758, Mamaroneck, NY 10543, (914)381-4649 [3809]

Hampshire Furniture Co., 673 Black Brook Rd., Goffstown, NH 03045-2911, (603)774-5120 [25673]

Hampshire Furniture Co., 673 Black Brook Rd., Goffstown, NH 03045-2911, (603)774-5120 [24134]

Hampton Affiliates Inc., 9600 SW Barnes Rd., Ste. 200, Portland, OR 97225, (503)297-7691 [7437]

Hampton-Haddon Marketing Corp., 230 2nd Ave., Waltham, MA 02454, (781)290-4700 [21025]

Hampton House, 100 Furniture Pkwy., Norwalk, OH 44857, (419)668-4461 [13126]

Hampton Lumber Sales Co., 9600 SW Barnes Rd., Ste. 200, Portland, OR 97225, (503)297-7691 [7438]

Hampton Vision Center, 10 Depot Sq., Hampton, NH 03842, (603)926-2722 [19348]

Hana Hou Corp., PO Box 3174, Honolulu, HI 96801-3174, (808)533-1944 [5015]

Hana Tropicals, PO Box 247, Hana, HI 96713, (808)248-7533 [14914]

Hanco Corp., 3650 Dodd Rd., Eagan, MN 55123-1305, (612)456-5600 [2721]

Hancock Fabrics Inc., PO Box 2400, Tupelo, MS 38803-2400, (662)842-2834 [26054]

Hancock House Publishers, 98231 Harrison Ave., X-1, Blaine, WA 98231, (360)538-1114 [3810]

Hancock Lumber Inc., PO Box 299, Casco, ME 04015, (207)627-4400 [27315]

Handelsman Co.; Hanco M., 1323 S Michigan Ave., Chicago, IL 60605, (312)427-0784 [15518]

Handi-Ramp Inc., 1414 Armour Blvd., Mundelein, IL 60060, (847)816-7525 [16085]

Handicapped Driving Aids of Michigan Inc., 3990 2nd St., Wayne, MI 48184, (734)595-4400 [18823]

Handleman Co., 500 Kirts Blvd., Troy, MI 48084-4142, (248)362-4400 [25225]

Handleman Co., PO Box 7045, Troy, MI 48084-4142, (248)362-4400 [3811]

Handling Systems Inc., 2659 E Magnolia St., Phoenix, AZ 85034-6923, (602)275-2228 [16086]

Handy Care, 15900 Crenshaw Blvd., No. 1377, Gardena, CA 90249, (562)634-3937 [19349]

Handy Company Inc.; John T., PO Box 309, Crisfield, MD 21817, (410)968-1772 [11370]

Handy Hardware Wholesale Inc., PO Box 12847, Houston, TX 77217, (713)644-1495 [13733]

Hanes Converting Co., 500 N McLin Creek Rd., Conover, NC 28613, (828)464-4673 [26055]

Hanes Fabrics Co., PO Box 457, Conover, NC 28613, (704)464-4673 [26056]

Hanessian Mercantile Co., PO Box 2079, Nogales, AZ 85628-2079, (520)287-3211 [15160]

Haney Shoe Store Inc., PO Box 4400, Omaha, NE 68104-0400, (402)556-2022 [24757]

Hanford's Inc., PO Box 32666, Charlotte, NC 28232-2666, (704)375-2528 [13365]

Hankes Crafts, 215 N Galbraith, Box 6, Blue Earth, MN 56013-1964, (507)526-3110 [26511]

Hankins Lumber Company, Inc., PO Box 1397, Grenada, MS 38902-1397, (662)226-2961 [7439]

Hanks Seafood Company Inc., PO Box 70, Easton, MD 21601, (410)822-4141 [11371]

Hanley Company Inc., 641 W Main St., Sun Prairie, WI 53590, (608)837-5111 [786]

Hanley Paint Company Inc., 1400 N Solano Dr., Las Cruces, NM 88001, (505)527-0482 [21479]

Hanley Sales Inc.; Pat, PO Box 1035, Fergus Falls, MN 56538-1035, (218)736-6958 [5016]

Hanna Resin Distribution Inc.; M.A., PO Box 428, Lemont, IL 60439, (708)972-0505 [22977]

Hanna Rubber Co., 1511 Baltimore Ave., Kansas City, MO 64108, (816)221-9600 [24280]

Hannan Supply Co., PO Box 270, Paducah, KY 42002-0270, (502)442-5456 [8826]

Hannays, 1708 Central Ave. NE, Minneapolis, MN 55413, (612)781-7411 [18517]

Hanover Compression, 12001 N Houston Rosslyn, Houston, TX 77086, (281)447-8787 [22333]

Hanover Sales Co., 1550 York Ct., Hanover, PA 17331-9803, (717)632-6000 [11372]

Hanover Warehousing, Box 888, Winston-Salem, NC 27102, (919)723-1615 [11373]

Hans Metals, Inc., 94-170 Leokane St., Waipahu, HI 96797, (808)676-4797 [26835]

Hansco Technologies, Inc., 17 Philips Pkwy., Montvale, NJ 07645, (201)391-0700 [16087]

Hansen Agency Inc.; Gordon E., PO Box 98, Hampton, CT 06247, (860)455-9903 [2600]

Hansen Caviar Co., 93 D S Railroad Ave., Bergenfield, NJ 07621, (201)385-6221 [11374]

Hansen & Co., 244-246 Old Post Rd., Southport, CT 06490, (203)259-7337 [23712]

Hansen Electrical Supply, PO Box 604, Framingham, MA 01704-0604, (508)872-4353 [8827]

Hansen-Kinney Company Inc., PO Box 1203, Great Falls, MT 59403-1203, (406)727-6660 [21455]

Hansen Machine Co., 13040 Greenly St., Holland, MI 49424, (616)399-8880 [20027]

Hansen and Peterson Inc., PO Box 345, Burlington, WA 98233, (206)755-9011 [787]

Hansens Hobbies & Supplies, 471 Mullan Tr., Gold Creek Stage Stop, Gold Creek, MT 59733, (406)288-3436 [26557]

Hanser Automotive Co., 430 S Billings Blvd., Billings, MT 59101, (406)248-7795 [2722]

Hanser's Pick A Part Inc., 430 S Billing Blvd., Billings, MT 59101-9364, (406)248-6073 [2723]

Hansful Trading Company Inc., 1 W 28th St., New York, NY 10001, (212)696-1833 [8828]

Hansmeier and Son Inc., Main St., Bristol, SD 57219, (605)492-3611 [788]

Hanson Aggregates West, Inc., 1900 W Garvy Ave. S, Ste. 200, West Covina, CA 91790, (626)856-6700 [7440]

Hanson Tire Service Inc., R.R. 2, Box A-1, Le Roy, MN 55951, (507)324-5638 [2724]

Happy Acres Pet Supply, 41903 Savage Rd., Belleville, MI 48111, (734)699-0318 [27144]

Happy Feet Plus, 18837 U.S 19 N, Clearwater, FL 33764, (727)538-1111 [24758]

Happy Feet Plus, 18837 U.S 19 N, Clearwater, FL 33764, (813)539-7006 [5017]

Happy Harry's Healthcare Inc., 311 Ruthar Dr., Newark, DE 19711, (302)454-3390 [18824]

Happy Refrigerated Services, 900 Turk Hill Rd., Fairport, NY 14450, (716)388-0300 [11375]

Happy Shirts Inc., 1320 Liona St., Honolulu, HI 96814-2352, (808)949-7575 [5018]

Happy Valley Clothing Co., PO Box 168, Glen Arm, MD 21057-0168, (410)592-3500 [5019]

Har-Tru Corp., 12932 Salem Ave., Hagerstown, MD 21740, (301)739-3077 [23713]

Hara and Company Ltd.; T., 51 Makaala St., Hilo, HI 96720, (808)935-5425 [11376]

Harbor Distributing Co., 1515 E 4th St., Little Rock, AR 72202-2808, (501)372-0185 [1744]

Harbor Distributing Co., 2824 E 208th, Long Beach, CA 90810-1101, (310)632-5483 [1745]

Harbor Enterprises Inc., PO Box 389, Seward, AK 99664, (907)224-3190 [22334]

Harbor Fuel Company Inc., PO Box 270, Oyster Bay, NY 11771-0270, (516)676-2500 [22335]

Harbor Packaging Inc., 13100 Danielson St., Poway, CA 92064, (858)513-1800 [21026]

Harbor Sales Company, 1000 Harbor Ct., Sudlersville, MD 21668-1818 [7441]

Harbor Sales Co., 1000 Harbor Ct., Sudlersville, MD 21668-1818 [27316]

Harbor Tool Supply Inc., 20 SW Park Ave., Westwood, MA 02090, (781)329-4432 [16088]

Harco, 557 S Douglas St., El Segundo, CA 90245-4891, (310)643-9400 [13734]

Harco Distributing Co., PO Box 913, Stuttgart, AR 72160, (870)673-4071 [17974]

Harco Electronics Inc., PO Box 1136, Aberdeen, MD 21001, (410)575-6885 [8829]

Harcourt Brace Professional Publishing, 525 B St., Ste. 1900, San Diego, CA 92101-4495, (619)699-6716 [3812]

Harcourt Equipment, PO Box 115, Harcourt, IA 50544, (515)354-5331 [789]

Hard Hat Inc., 711 Leitchfield Rd., Owensboro, KY 42303-0350, (502)926-7000 [23714]

Hard Times Vending Inc., RR, Box 59, Tripp, SD 57376-0059, (605)935-6251 [24135]

Hardco, Inc., 3305 S Hwy. 79, Rapid City, SD 57701, (605)342-7860 [9936]

Hardeman Fayette Farmers Cooperative, PO Box 277, Somerville, TN 38068, (901)465-3655 [790]

Harder Paper and Packaging Inc., 5301 Verona Rd., Madison, WI 53711, (608)271-5127 [21755]

Hardesty Welding Supply Div., PO Box 6136, Evansville, IN 47719-0136, (812)425-5288 [16922]

Hardie Export; James, 5931 E Marginal Way S, Seattle, WA 98134, (206)763-1550 [7442]

Hardin Clothing Co. Inc.; J.M., PO Box 138, Calhoun City, MS 38916-0138, (601)628-5311 [5020]

Hardin Marine Inc., 1280 S Anaheim Blvd., Anaheim, CA 92805-6201, (714)956-9100 [18518]

Harding and Lawler Inc., PO Box 580, Orange, TX 77630, (409)883-4371 [7443]

Harding Metals Inc., Rte. 4, Northwood, NH 03261, (603)942-5573 [26836]

Harding Metals Inc., Rte. 4, Northwood, NH 03261, (603)942-5573 [26837]

Harding's Inc., PO Box 187, Lowell, IN 46356, (219)696-8911 [7444]

Hardin's-Sysco Food Services Inc., 4359 B.F. Goodrich Blvd., Memphis, TN 38118, (901)795-2300 [11377]

Hardlines Marketing Inc., PO Box 23080, Milwaukee, WI 53223, (414)351-4700 [13735]

Hardware Distribution Warehouses Inc., 6900 Woolworth Rd., Shreveport, LA 71129, (318)686-8527 [13736]

Hardware Distributors Inc., 2580 Getty St., Muskegon, MI 49444, (616)733-2641 [13737]

Hardware Imagination, 5329 W Crenshaw, Tampa, FL 33634, (813)882-0322 [7445]

Hardware Imagination, 4300 NW 37th Ave., Miami, FL 33142, (305)635-3300 [13738]

Hardware Imagination, 603 Landstreet Rd., Orlando, FL 32824, (407)855-2282 [7446]

Hardware Knowledge Group Inc., 448 E El Camino Real, Sunnyvale, CA 94087, (408)733-5454 [6328]

Hardware & Marine Co. of Alabama, 1875 N Conception St. Rd., Mobile, AL 36610, (334)452-3423 [18519]

Hardware Specialties Co., 3419 11th Ave. SW, Seattle, WA 98134, (206)624-5785 [13739]

Hardware Specialty Company Inc., 48-75 36th St., Long Island City, NY 11101, (718)361-9393 [13740]

Hardware and Supply Company of Chester Inc., PO Box 678, Chester, PA 19016-0678, (610)876-6116 [16923]

Hardware Supply Company Inc., 940 Chestnut, PO BOX 240, Terre Haute, IN 47808-0240, (812)232-9474 [13741]

Hardware Wholesalers Inc., PO Box 868, Ft. Wayne, IN 46801, (219)748-5300 [7275]

Hardwood Flooring & Finishes, 6831 Keating, Lincolnwood, IL 60646, (847)982-0665 [9937]

Hardwoods of Morganton Inc., PO Box 1099, Morganton, NC 28655-1099, (828)437-0761 [7447]

Hardy and Company Inc.; James G., 352 7th Ave., Ste. 1223, New York, NY 10001, (212)689-6680 [15519]

Hardy Cooperative Elevator Co., PO Box 8, Hardy, IA 50545, (515)824-3221 [17975]

Hardy Cooperative Elevator Co., PO Box 8, Hardy, IA 50545, (515)824-3221 [11378]

Hardy Corp., 711 W 103rd St., Chicago, IL 60628, (773)779-6600 [7448]

Hardy & Son; Joseph T., 425 Old Airport Rd., New Castle, DE 19720, (302)328-9457 [7449]

Hardy Turquoise Co., PO Box 1598, Apache Junction, AZ 85217-1598, (520)463-2371 [17444]

Harf Inc., 31 Church Rd., Hatfield, PA 19440, (215)822-0624 [25674]

Harken Inc., PO Box 80150, Billings, MT 59108-0150, (406)252-1207 [14478]

Harker's Distribution Inc., 801 6th St., SW, Le Mars, IA 51031, (712)546-8171 [11379]

Harley Industries Inc., PO Box 470203, Tulsa, OK 74147-0203, (918)492-9706 [16924]

Harley Metals Recycling Co., 3315 E Washington Blvd., Los Angeles, CA 90027, (213)264-0646 [26838]

Harlow International, 2307 North Champlain St., Arlington Heights, IL 60004, (847)870-0198 [2725]

Harman Appliance Sales, 334 N 115th St., Omaha, NE 68154-2523, (402)334-1883 [15161]

Harmonia Mundi U.S.A. Inc., 2037 Granville Ave., Los Angeles, CA 90025, (310)559-0802 [25226]

Harmony Agri Services, 25 2nd St. NE, Harmony, MN 55939, (507)886-6062 [791]

Harmony Co-op, 212 S Division St., Colby, WI 54421, (715)223-2306 [17976]

Harmony Country Cooperatives, PO Box 407, Colby, WI 54421, (715)223-2306 [792]

Harmony Enterprises America, 7 Backus Ave., Ste. 1515, Danbury, CT 06810-7427, (203)748-3411 [18825]

Harmony International Corporation, 3337 Kraft Ave. SE, Grand Rapids, MI 49512, (616)949-6342 [15162]

Harnack Co., 6015 S Main St., Cedar Falls, IA 50613, (319)277-0660 [793]

Harney County Farm Supply Co., 53 E Industrial St., Burns, OR 97720, (541)573-2031 [794]

Harold Implement Company Inc., 1101 N Missouri, Corning, AR 72422, (870)857-3931 [4406]

Harold Import Company Inc., 140 LeHigh Ave., Lakewood, NJ 08701, (732)367-2800 [15520]

Harold Jewelry Inc., 96 Bowery 5th Fl., New York, NY 10013-4727, (212)695-4905 [17445]

Harold's Tire and Auto, 709 Liberty Dr., Easley, SC 29640, (843)859-3741 [2726]

Harpel's Inc., 701 Cumberland, Lebanon, PA 17042, (717)272-6687 [21027]

Harper & Associates, PO Box 838, Allen, TX 75002, (972)727-6283 [23715]

Harper Distributing Company Inc., PO Box 6325, Florence, KY 41022, (606)283-1001 [22336]

Harper San Francisco, 353 Sacramento St., Ste. 500, San Francisco, CA 94111, (415)477-4400 [3813]

Harrell Co.; Hollis, PO Box 89, Hazlehurst, MS 39083, (601)894-4856 [13742]

Harrington Co., PO Box 3178, Butte, MT 59702-3178, (406)494-3200 [24136]

Harrington Corp., PO Box 10335, Lynchburg, VA 24506, (804)845-7094 [23203]

Harrington Industrial Plastics Inc., 14480 Yorba Ave., Chino, CA 91710, (909)597-8641 [22978]

Harrington Produce, 1207 S Harwood, Dallas, TX 75201-6190, (214)747-8701 [11380]

Harrington Tools Inc., 4316 Alger St., Los Angeles, CA 90039, (323)245-2142 [13743]

Harris Appliance Parts Company Inc., 110 Hwy. 29 N Bypass, PO Box 1867, Anderson, SC 29622, (864)225-7433 [15163]

Harris Chemical Group Inc., 399 Park Ave., 32nd Fl., New York, NY 10022, (212)750-3510 [4407]

Harris & Co.; William H., 320 Monroe Ave., Memphis, TN 38103-2720, (901)527-2558 [24759]

Harris Corp., 4393 Digital Way, Mason, OH 45040, (513)459-3700 [5630]

Harris Corporation, 330 Twin Dolphin Dr., Redwood City, CA 94065-1421, (650)594-3000 [5631]

Harris Corp.; Dub, 2301 Tubeway Ave., City of Commerce, CA 90040, (213)722-3344 [21028]

Harris County Oil Company Inc., 3325 W 11th St., Houston, TX 77008, (713)861-8115 [22337]

Harris Discount Supply, 7506 Melrose Ln., A, Oklahoma City, OK 73127-5163, (405)341-6963 [18826]

Harris Electric Inc., 4020 23rd Ave. W, Seattle, WA 98199, (206)282-8080 [8830]

Harris Enterprises Inc., 12111 W Markham St., No. 14-174, Little Rock, AR 72211-2734, (501)225-6350 [18827]

Harris Industrial Gases Inc., 8475 Auburn Blvd., Citrus Heights, CA 95610, (916)725-2168 [16089]

Harris Lamps, 3757 S Ashland, Chicago, IL 60609-2130, (773)247-7500 [13127]

Harris Marcus Furniture, 3757 S Ashland, Chicago, IL 60609-2130, (773)247-7500 [13127]

Harris Marcus Furniture, 3757 S Ashland, Chicago, IL 60609-2130, (773)247-7500 [13127]

Harris Marcus Group, 3757 S Ashland, Chicago, IL 60609-2130, (773)247-7500 [13127]

Harris Oil Co.; Bob, PO Box 691, Cleburne, TX 76031, (817)641-9749 [22338]

Harris Pump and Supply Co., 603 Parkway View Dr., No. 6, Pittsburgh, PA 15205-1412, (412)787-7867 [16090]

Harris Semiconductor, 3031 Tisch Way Ste. 800, San Jose, CA 95128, (408)985-7322 [8831]

Harris & Stearns, 910 W Cass St., PO Box 2459, Tampa, FL 33601, (813)253-0111 [26057]

Harris Supply Company Inc., 36 Central Pl., Wellsville, NY 14895, (716)593-5811 [16925]

Harris Supply Company Inc., 36 Central Pl., Wellsville, NY 14895, (716)593-5811 [23204]

Harris-Teller, Inc., 7400 S Mason Ave., Chicago, IL 60638, (708)496-2100 [3814]

Harris Tire Co., PO Box 888, Troy, AL 36081, (205)566-2691 [2727]

Harris Tire Co., 4355 Industrial Dr., Jackson, MS 39209, (601)948-7401 [2728]

Harris Truck Equipment Co.; Jay Dee, PO Box 189, Tremonton, UT 84337, (801)257-3333 [20646]

Harris Welco, 1051 York Rd., PO Box 69, Kings Mountain, NC 28086, (704)739-6421 [20028]

Harris Welding Supply, 8475 Auburn Blvd., Citrus Heights, CA 95610, (916)725-2168 [16089]

Harrison Company Inc., PO Box 72179, Bossier City, LA 71172-2179, (318)747-0700 [11381]

Harrison Livestock Co.; B.H., 903 Butler Ferry Rd., Bainbridge, GA 31717, (912)246-5344 [17977]

Harrison Oil Co., 16 E Martin Luther King St., Muskogee, OK 74403, (918)682-8861 [22339]

Harrison Piping Supply Co., 38777 Schoolcraft Rd., Livonia, MI 48150, (734)464-4400 [23205]

Harrison Poultry Inc., PO Box 550, Bethlehem, GA 30620, (404)867-7511 [11382]

Harrison Supply Co., 800 Passaic Ave., East Newark, NJ 07029, (973)483-4494 [7450]

Harrison Wholesale Products Inc., 108 Kingswood Ct., Cherry Hill, NJ 08034-1332, (609)344-6801 [27145]

Harrold Engineering Group, PO Box 385, Manhattan, KS 66502, (785)776-0550 [795]

Harrowood Books, 3943 N Providence Rd., Newtown Square, PA 19073, (610)353-5585 [3815]

Hart Beverage Co., 400 W Colonial Dr., South Sioux City, NE 68776, (402)494-3023 [24968]

Hart Co. Inc.; Edward R., 437 McGregor NW, Canton, OH 44706, (330)452-4055 [9938]

Hart Equipment Company Inc., PO Box 1187, Madisonville, KY 42431, (502)821-4645 [24559]

Hart Furniture Company Inc. (Siler City, North Carolina), Hwy. 64 E, Siler City, NC 27344, (919)742-4141 [13128]

Hart-Greer Ltd., 3313 1st Ave. N, Birmingham, AL 35222-1203, (205)320-0095 [15164]

Hart Seed Co.; Charles C., PO Box 9169, Wethersfield, CT 06129-0169, (860)529-2537 [796]

Hartford Distributors Inc., 131 Chapel Rd., Manchester, CT 06040, (860)643-2337 [1746]

Hartford Music Co., 100 Albert E Brumley Pkwy., Powell, MO 65730, (417)435-2225 [3596]

Hartford Provision Co., 159 Main St., Stamford, CT 06904, (203)324-6194 [11383]

Hartford Provision Co., 159 Main St., Stamford, CT 06904, (203)324-6194 [11384]

Hartley Manufacturing Inc., PO Box 398, Ravenswood, WV 26164, (304)273-5931 [26839]

Hartman Hide and Fur Company Inc., PO Box 518, Detroit Lakes, MN 56502, (218)847-5681 [17978]

Hartman & Sons Equipment; Lee, 3236 Cove Rd. NW, Roanoke, VA 24017-2804, (540)366-3493 [25227]

Hartman-Spreng Co., 26 W 6th St., Mansfield, OH 44901, (419)524-7211 [8832]

Hartmann of Florida, 1774 Executive Rd., Winter Haven, FL 33884, (863)325-8222 [8833]

Hartnett Co.; The C.D., 300 N Main, Weatherford, TX 76086-3245, (817)594-3813 [11385]

Hartnett Co. Food Service Div.; C.D., 4151 Blue Mound Rd., Ft. Worth, TX 76106, (817)625-8921 [11386]

Hartog Foods Inc., 529 5th Ave., New York, NY 10017, (212)687-2000 [11387]

Hartsburg Grain Co., PO Box 80, Hartsburg, IL 62643, (217)642-5211 [17979]

Hartsook Equipment & Pump Services, 1640 W 18th St., Cheyenne, WY 82001, (307)634-4489 [22340]

Hartwell Medical Corp., 6352 Corte Del Abeto, Ste. J, Carlsbad, CA 92009-1408, (760)438-5500 [19350]

Hartz Group Inc., 667 Madison Ave., New York, NY 10021, (212)308-3336 [27146]

Hartz Seed Company Inc.; Jacob, 901 N Park Ave., Stuttgart, AR 72160, (501)673-8565 [17980]

Hartzell Acquisition Corp., 13405 15th Ave. N, Plymouth, MN 55441, (612)553-8200 [13129]

Hartzler's Inc. Exporters, PO Box 661625, Arcadia, CA 91066, (626)796-6606 [18828]

Harvard Apparatus, Inc., 84 October Hill Rd., Holliston, MA 01746 [18829]

Harvard Associates Inc., 10 Holworthy St., Cambridge, MA 02138-4519, (617)492-0660 [6329]

Harvest House Publishers, Inc., 1075 Arrowsmith St., Eugene, OR 97402, (541)343-0123 [3816]

Harvest Land Cooperative Inc., PO Box 516, Richmond, IN 47375, (765)962-1527 [797]

Harvest Productions (E.B.M.), PO Box 2225, Kokomo, IN 46904-2225, (765)455-2112 [25228]

Harvest Publications, 2002 S Arlington Heights Rd., Arlington Heights, IL 60005, (847)228-1471 [3817]

Harvest States Cooperatives. Canton Div., PO Box 236, Canton, SD 57013, (605)987-2791 [798]

Harvest States Cooperatives Line Elevator Div., PO Box 432, Montevideo, MN 56265, (320)269-6531 [17981]

Harvest States Soybean Processing, PO Box 3247, Mankato, MN 56001, (507)625-7911 [17982]

Harvey Chevrolet Corp., PO Box 972, Radford, VA 24141, (703)639-3923 [2729]

Harvey Industries Inc., 43 Emerson Rd., Waltham, MA 02454, (617)899-3500 [7451]

Harvey Lumber Company Inc., 234 Primrose St., Haverhill, MA 01830, (508)372-7727 [7452]

Harvey Titanium Ltd., 1330 Colorado Ave., Santa Monica, CA 90404-3478, (310)829-0021 [20029]

Harvin Choice Meats Inc., PO Box 939, Sumter, SC 29150, (803)775-9367 [11388]

Harvin Foods Inc., 620 A St., Wilmington, DE 19801, (302)984-9500 [11389]

Harwell & Associates Inc. Chemical Div., 6507 E 42nd St., Tulsa, OK 74145, (918)622-1212 [4408]

Harwell Fabrics, Inc., 2030 W Quail Ave., Phoenix, AZ 85027-2610, (602)271-0045 [26058]

Harwick Standard Distribution Corporation, 60 S Seiberling, Akron, OH 44305, (330)798-9300 [4409]

Hascall Steel Company Inc., 4165 Spartan Industrial Dr. SW, Grandville, MI 49418, (616)531-8600 [20030]

Hashimoto Nursery, PO Box 525, Pahoa, HI 96778, (808)965-9522 [14882]

Haskel International, Inc., 100 E Graham Pl., Burbank, CA 91502, (818)843-4000 [16091]

Haskell Associates Inc., RR 5, Box 5, Augusta, ME 04330, (207)623-2393 [19473]

Hasley & Associates; Norvel, PO Box 936, Greensboro, GA 30642, (706)467-3328 [23716]

Hasley Recreation and Design Inc., PO Box 936, Greensboro, GA 30642, (706)467-3328 [23716]

Hassenfritz Equipment Co.; Tom, 1300 W Washington, Mt. Pleasant, IA 52641, (319)385-3114 [799]

Hassenfritz Equipment Co.; Tom, 1300 W Washington, Mt. Pleasant, IA 52641, (319)385-3114 [800]

Hasson-Bryan Hardware Co., 114 W Main, Morristown, TN 37814, (423)586-2283 [13744]

Hata Company Ltd.; S., 938 Austin Ln., Honolulu, HI 96817-4532, (808)841-0941 [26059]

Hatch Grinding Co., 320 S Lipan St., Denver, CO 80223, (303)744-7114 [2730]

Hatfield and Company Inc., 206 S Town East Blvd., Mesquite, TX 75149, (972)288-7625 [16926]

Hatfield Quality Meats Inc., PO Box 902, Hatfield, PA 19440, (215)368-2500 [11390]

Hathaway Paper Co., S Oak Ln., PO Box 1618, Waynesboro, VA 22980, (540)949-8285 [21756]

Hatley Lumber Co. Inc., 601 Emmonsville Rd., PO Box 82, Hatley, WI 54440-0082, (715)446-3311 [7453]

Hattenbach Co., 1929 E 61st St., Cleveland, OH 44103, (216)881-5200 [7454]

Hattiesburg Grocery Co., PO Box 350, Hattiesburg, MS 39403-0350, (601)584-7544 [11391]

Haubrich Enterprises Inc., 1901 Seminary Rd., Quincy, IL 62301-1484, (217)223-1183 [1747]

Hauck; Donald, PO Box 1914, Minot, ND 58702-1914, (701)839-7595 [17983]

Hauff Co.; H.F., 1801 Presson Pl., Yakima, WA 98903, (509)248-0318 [801]

Hauff Sporting Goods Co. Inc., 1120 Capitol Ave., Omaha, NE 68102-1113, (402)341-7011 [23717]

Hauler & Wade Associates Inc., PO Box 868, Mentor, OH 44061-0868, (440)951-7155 [26512]

Hauptly Construction and Equipment Company Inc., PO Box 225, Dunkerton, IA 50626-0225, (319)822-4205 [7455]

Hauser Company; M.L., PO Box 6174, Clearwater, FL 33758-6174, (813)855-5465 [16092]

Hausman Corp., 2842 Rand Rd., Indianapolis, IN 46241, (317)844-6044 [7456]

Hautly Cheese Company Inc., 5130 Northrup Ave., St. Louis, MO 63110, (314)772-9339 [11392]

HAVE Inc., 309 Power Ave., Hudson, NY 12534, (518)828-2000 [25229]

Haverhill Cooperative, PO Box 50, Haverhill, IA 50120, (515)475-3221 [17984]

Havice Inc.; James F., 5 Industrial Park Rd., Lewistown, PA 17044, (717)242-1427 [14121]

Haviland Agricultural Inc., 4160 Ten Mile Rd., Sparta, MI 49345, (616)887-8333 [4410]

Haviland Products Co., 421 Ann St. NW, Grand Rapids, MI 49504, (616)361-6691 [4411]

Havre Distributors Inc., 935 1st St., Havre, MT 59501-3705, (406)265-6212 [1748]

Hawaii Hardware Company Ltd., 550 Kilauea Ave., Hilo, HI 96720, (808)935-3795 [13745]

Hawaii ID Apparel, 930-C Austin Ln., Honolulu, HI 96817, (808)848-5400 [5021]

Hawaii Instrumentation, Inc., 822 Halekauwila St., Honolulu, HI 96813, (808)531-3595 [24560]

Hawaii Martial Art Supply, 1041 Maunakea St., Honolulu, HI 96817-5130, (808)536-5402 [23718]

Hawaii Modular Space Inc., 91-252 Kauhi St., Kapolei, HI 96707-1803, (808)682-5559 [7457]

Hawaii Plastics Corp., 570 Dillingham Blvd., Honolulu, HI 96817, (808)841-3358 [26060]

Hawaii Protea Corp., Haleakala Hwy., Kula, HI 96790, (808)878-2525 [14883]

Hawaii; Scott, 1212 Kona, Honolulu, HI 96814-4303, (808)591-2921 [24760]

Hawaiian Ceramic Tile, 703 Lower Main St., Wailuku, HI 96793, (808)242-1511 [9939]

Hawaiian Distributor Ltd., 96-1282 Waihona St., Pearl City, HI 96782, (808)456-3334 [11393]

Hawaiian Flour Mills Inc., PO Box 855, Honolulu, HI 96808, (808)545-2111 [11423]

Hawaiian Fluid Power, 803 Ahua St., Honolulu, HI 96819, (808)833-4516 [16093]

Hawaiian Greenhouse, Inc., PO Box 1, Pahoa, HI 96778, (808)965-8351 [14884]

Hawaiian Grocery Stores Ltd., 80 Sand Island Excess Rd., Honolulu, HI 96819, (808)839-5121 [11394]

Hawaiian Housewares, Ltd., 99-1305 Koaha Pl., Aiea, HI 96701, (808)453-8000 [15521]

Hawaiian Iles Distributors, 2839 Mokumoa St., Honolulu, HI 96819, (808)833-2244 [11428]

Hawaiian Isles Distributors, 843 Leilani St. No. A, Hilo, HI 96720, (808)935-7176 [26302]

Hawaiian Isles Distributors, 851 Eha St., Wailuku, HI 96793, (808)244-9019 [26303]

Hawaiian Natural Water Company Inc., 98-746 Kuahao Pl., Pearl City, HI 96782-3125, (808)832-4550 [24969]

Hawaiian Sunglass Co., 1200 College Walk No. 112, Honolulu, HI 96817, (808)945-3134 [19351]

Hawera Inc., PO Box 402, South Elgin, IL 60177-0402, (630)653-3044 [16094]

Hawk Electronics, 5718 Airport Fwy., Ft. Worth, TX 76117, (817)429-0432 [5632]

Hawk Electronics Inc., PO Box 1027F, Wheeling, IL 60090, (847)459-4030 [8834]

Hawk Flour Mills Inc., 639 Grammes Ln., Allentown, PA 18104, (215)435-8068 [11395]

Hawker Pacific Inc., 11240 Sherman Way, Sun Valley, CA 91352, (818)765-6201 [94]

Hawkeye Building Supply Co., PO Box 1343, Sioux City, IA 51102, (712)277-4001 [7458]

Hawkeye Seed Company Inc., 900 2nd St. SE, Cedar Rapids, IA 52401, (319)364-7118 [27147]

Hawkeye Seed Company Inc., 900 2nd St. SE, Cedar Rapids, IA 52401, (319)364-7118 [802]

Hawkins Auto Parts, PO Box 740, Calhoun City, MS 38916-0740, (601)628-5168 [2731]

Hawkins Chemical Inc., 3100 E Hennepin Ave., Minneapolis, MN 55413-2923, (612)331-6910 [16095]

Hawkins Fabrics, 111 Woodside Ave., Gloversville, NY 12078, (518)773-9550 [5022]

Hawkins Machinery Inc., 1475-89 Thomas St., Memphis, TN 38107, (901)525-5746 [7459]

Hawkinson, 149 Seegers, Elk Grove Village, IL 60007, (847)228-6222 [9940]

Hawley Industrial Supplies Inc., 1020 Fairfield Ave., Bridgeport, CT 06605, (203)366-4541 [13746]

The Haworth Press Inc., 10 Alice St., Binghamton, NY 13904-1580, (607)722-5857 [3818]

Hawthorne Machinery Inc., PO Box 708, San Diego, CA 92112, (619)674-7000 [2732]

Hawthorne Machinery Inc. Hawthorne Power Systems Div., PO Box 708, San Diego, CA 92112, (619)674-7000 [803]

Hay-A-Bar Dry Ice Wholesaler, 3207 S Grand Traverse St., Flint, MI 48507, (810)234-4155 [11396]

Hay Greenhouses, Inc.; Alexander, 75 Oakwood Ave., North Haledon, NJ 07508, (973)427-1193 [14885]

Hay Land and Livestock Inc., PO Box 52, Pinedale, WY 82941-0052, (307)367-4522 [17985]

Hayden Company Inc.; C.W., 306 Rodman Rd., Auburn, ME 04211-1030, (207)783-2054 [16927]

Hayden-Murphy Equipment Co., 9301 E Bloomington Fwy., Minneapolis, MN 55420, (612)884-2301 [7460]

Hayes Associates; Marvin, PO Box 10, Samburg, TN 38254, (901)538-2166 [11397]

Hayes & Lunsford Motor Repair, 226 Hilliard Ave., Asheville, NC 28801, (828)252-4785 [8835]

Hayes Medical Inc., 1115 Windfield Way, El Dorado Hills, CA 95762, (916)355-7100 [19352]

Hayes and Sons; John, PO Box 6184, Wolcott, CT 06716, (203)879-4616 [11398]

Haynes Manuals Inc., PO Box 978, Newbury Park, CA 91319, (805)498-6703 [2733]

Hays Distributing Corp., 1461 Elliott Ave. W, Seattle, WA 98119-3176, (206)284-7004 [26513]

Hayward Cooperative, PO Box 337, Hayward, MN 56043, (507)373-6439 [804]

Hayward Distribution Center, 31300 Medallion Dr., Hayward, CA 94544, (510)487-3000 [26304]

Haywin Textile Products Inc., PO Box 229013, Brooklyn, NY 11222-9013, (718)384-0317 [15522]

Haywood Builders Supply Inc., PO Box 187, Waynesville, NC 28786, (704)456-6051 [7461]

Hazard and Sons Inc.; L.A., 1695 Overhead Rd., Derby, NY 14047, (716)627-2364 [23206]

HAZCO Services Inc., PO Box 2635, Dayton, OH 45401, (513)293-2700 [24368]

Hazle Park Packing Co., 260 Washington Ave., West Hazleton, PA 18201, (570)455-7571 [11399]

Hazlett Company Inc.; T.R., 11950 Baltimore Ave., Beltsville, MD 20705, (301)419-0033 [7462]

Hazra Associates, Inc., 2996 Burnbrick Rd., PO Box 397, Bath, OH 44210, (330)659-4055 [18830]

HB Distributors, 8741 Shirley Ave., Northridge, CA 91324, (818)701-5100 [5633]

HB Distributors, 8741 Shirley Ave., Northridge, CA 91324, (818)701-5100 [8836]

HB Instruments, 53 W Century Rd., Paramus, NJ 07652, (201)265-7865 [24369]

HBG Export Corp., 454 S Anderson Rd., B.T.C. 506, Rock Hill, SC 29730, (803)329-2128 [22979]

H.C. Shaw Co., PO Box 31510, Stockton, CA 95213, (209)983-8484 [480]

HC Supply, PO Box 4748, Roanoke, VA 24015, (540)342-5327 [7463]

hci Coastal Chemical Co., LLC, PO Box 820, Abbeville, LA 70511-0820, (337)898-0001 [4412]

HCI Corp./International Marketing Services, 10 E Washington St., PO Box 936, Lexington, VA 24450-0936, (540)463-1095 [18831]

HCI Great Lakes Region, 4801 S Austin, Chicago, IL 60638, (773)586-2000 [4413]

HCIA Inc., 300 E Lumbard St., Baltimore, MD 21202, (410)576-9600 [3819]

HD Communications Inc., 15635 W McNichols Rd., Detroit, MI 48235, (313)838-5860 [5634]

H.E. Butt Grocery Co. San Antonio Distribution/Manufacturing Center, 4710 N Pan Am Expwy., San Antonio, TX 78218, (210)662-5000 [11400]

Head and Engguist Equipment L.L.C., PO Box 52945, Baton Rouge, LA 70892, (504)356-6113 [7464]

Heads & Threads Co., 2727 Shermer Rd., Northbrook, IL 60062-7708 [13747]

Heads and Threads Div., 2727 Shermer Rd., Northbrook, IL 60062, (847)564-1100 [13748]

Heads and Threads International, LLC, PO Box 39, Sayreville, NJ 08872-9998, (732)727-5800 [13749]

Heafner Company Inc.; J.H., PO Box 837, Lincolnton, NC 28092, (704)735-3003 [2734]

Heafner Tires & Products, 712 N Main St., Mauldin, SC 29662-1918, (864)675-9600 [2735]

Health Care Services, Inc., 342 4th Ave., Huntington, WV 25701, (304)525-9184 [19353]

Health Food Distributors, 1893 Northwood Dr., Troy, MI 48084, (248)362-4545 [14122]

Health and Leisure Mart Inc., 1516 W Mound St., Columbus, OH 43223, (614)274-3640 [23719]

Health Services Corporation of America, PO Box 1689, Cape Girardeau, MO 63702-1689, (573)334-7711 [19354]

Health Systems Technology Corp., 11701 Yates Ford Rd., Fairfax Station, VA 22039-1507, (703)978-2084 [6330]

Healthcare Press, PO Box 4784, Rollingbay, WA 98061, (206)842-5243 [3820]

Healthcare Services International, 6679 Rutledge Dr., Fairfax Station, VA 22039, (703)425-1546 [18832]

HealthComm Inc., 5800 Soundview Dr., PO Box 1729, Gig Harbor, WA 98335, (253)851-3943 [24970]

HealthComm Inc., 5800 Soundview Dr., Gig Harbor, WA 98335, (253)851-3943 [11401]

HealthComm International Inc., PO Box 1729, Gig Harbor, WA 98335, (253)858-6500 [14123]

HealthStyles, Inc., 201 Santa Monica Blvd., Ste. 400, Santa Monica, CA 90401, (310)451-9476 [19355]

HealthTech International Inc., 1237 S Val Vista Dr., Mesa, AZ 85204, (602)396-0660 [23720]

Heap Lumber Sales Company Inc., 11136 Manchester Rd., St. Louis, MO 63122, (314)966-3640 [7465]

Heard Optical Co., PO Box 1448, Long Beach, CA 90801-1448, (562)595-4461 [19356]

Hearing Aid Centers of America, PO Box 3055, Kalamazoo, MI 49003-3055, (616)324-0301 [18833]

Hearn Kirkwood, 7251 Standard Dr., Hanover, MD 21076, (410)712-6000 [11402]

Hearn Paper Company Inc., 556 N Merdian Rd., Youngstown, OH 44509, (330)792-6533 [21757]

Hearne Produce Co.; William P., PO Box 1975, Salisbury, MD 21802, (410)742-1552 [11403]

Heart of America Bolt, 5185 Merriam Dr., Shawnee Mission, KS 66203-2122, (913)384-0242 [13750]

Heart of Iowa Coop., 229 E Ash St., Roland, IA 50236, (515)388-4341 [11404]

Heart of Iowa Cooperative, 229 E Ash St., Roland, IA 50236, (515)388-4341 [805]

Heart Seed, PO Box 313, Fairfield, WA 99012, (509)283-2322 [806]

Heartland Co-op, 2829 Westown Pkwy., No. 350, West Des Moines, IA 50266, (515)225-1334 [807]

Heartland Co-op (Trumbull, Nebraska), PO Box 73, Trumbull, NE 68980, (402)743-2381 [17986]

Heartland Cooperative Inc., PO Box 432, Crawfordsville, IN 47933, (317)362-6700 [808]

Heartland Distributors, Inc., 111 N Telegraph Rd., Monroe, MI 48162, (734)241-8565 [26305]

Heartland Paper Co., 808 W Cherokee St., Sioux Falls, SD 57104, (605)336-1190 [21758]

Heartline, 905 Early St., Santa Fe, NM 87501-4237, (505)983-6777 [17446]

Heat Inc., 9 Flagstone Dr., Hudson, NH 03051, (603)889-0104 [14479]

Heat-N-Glo Fireplaces, 6665 W Hwy. 13, Savage, MN 55378, (612)985-6000 [14480]

Heatbath Corp., PO Box 2978, Springfield, MA 01102, (413)543-3381 [16928]

Heatilator Inc., 1915 W Saunders St., Mt. Pleasant, IA 52641, (319)385-9211 [7466]

Heating-Cooling Distributors Inc., 757 E Murry St., Indianapolis, IN 46227-1139, (317)791-4234 [14481]

Heating and Cooling Supply Inc., 3980 Home Ave., San Diego, CA 92105, (619)262-7543 [14482]

Heating Oil Partners, PO Box 431, Norwich, CT 06360, (860)887-3525 [22341]

Heating Specialties of New Hampshire, 25 Pond St., PO Box 621, Nashua, NH 03061, (603)882-2726 [14483]

Heaton Co.; G.A., 6595 Highway 49N, Mariposa, CA 95338, (209)377-8227 [17447]

Heatwave Supply Inc., 6529 E 14th St., Tulsa, OK 74112, (918)838-9841 [23207]

Heavy Machines Inc., 3926 E Raines Rd., Memphis, TN 38118-6936, (901)260-2200 [16096]

Heavy Parts International, 19651 Bruce B. Downs Blvd., Tampa, FL 33647, (813)991-7001 [2736]

Hebard and Associates Inc.; R.W., 825 3rd Ave., New York, NY 10022, (212)421-4590 [20031]

Heberer Equipment Company Inc., 505 S Railway St., Mascoutah, IL 62258, (618)566-2166 [809]

Hebes Motor Co., 2226 W 800 S, Sterling, ID 83210-0022, (208)328-2221 [2737]

Hecht Inc.; William, 508 Bainbridge St., Philadelphia, PA 19147, (215)925-6223 [25675]

Hecht Manufacturing Co., 8645 N Dean Cir., River Hills, WI 53217-2038, (414)271-4650 [5023]

Heckett Multiserv Div., PO Box 1071, Butler, PA 16003, (724)283-5741 [26840]

Heckler and Koch Inc., 21480 Pacific Blvd., Sterling, VA 20166-8903, (703)450-1900 [13494]

Heckman Metals Co., 220 Demeter St., Palo Alto, CA 94303, (650)324-9666 [26841]

Hector Farmers Elevator, 141 Ash Ave. E, Hector, MN 55342, (320)848-2273 [17987]

Hector Turf, 1301 NW 3rd St., Deerfield Beach, FL 33442, (305)429-3200 [810]

Hedahl's Auto Parts, PO Box 1038, Bismarck, ND 58502-1038, (701)223-8393 [2738]

Hedahl's Automotive Center, Hwy. 10 E & Jackson Ave., Detroit Lakes, MN 56501, (218)847-1355 [2739]

Heddinger Brokerage Inc., PO Box 65037, West Des Moines, IA 50265, (515)222-4458 [11405]

Hedlund Fabrics and Supply Co., 1710 E Washington St., Phoenix, AZ 85034, (602)252-6058 [26061]

Hedrick Beechcraft Inc., 8402 Nelms Rd., Houston, TX 77061, (713)567-5000 [95]

Heeren Brothers, Inc., 1020 Hall St. SW, Grand Rapids, MI 49503, (616)452-8641 [11406]

Heetco Inc., PO Box 188, Lewistown, MO 63452, (573)497-2295 [22342]

Heetco Inc. Kansas Div., 1853 E 1450 Rd., PO Box 886, Lawrence, KS 66044, (785)843-4655 [22343]

Heffner Brothers Co., PO Box 226, Hawthorn, PA 16230, (814)365-5311 [22344]

Heidelberg Distributing Co., 912 3rd St., Perrysburg, OH 43551, (419)666-9782 [1749]

Heidema Brothers Inc., A-5496 144th Ave., Holland, MI 49423, (616)396-6551 [20647]

Heidtman Steel Products Inc., PO Box 1793, Toledo, OH 43603, (419)691-4646 [20032]

Heights Pump & Supply, 1359 Clarhill Rd., Laurel, MT 59044, (406)628-4755 [24370]

Heigl Adhesive Sales, 7634 Washington Ave., Eden Prairie, MN 55344 [8]

Heikkinen Productions Inc., 1410 W Michigan Ave., Ypsilanti, MI 48197-5129, (734)485-4020 [5024]

Hein and Co., Inc.; William S., 1285 Main St., Buffalo, NY 14209, (716)882-2600 [3821]

Heineken USA Inc., 50 Main St., White Plains, NY 10606, (914)681-4100 [1750]

Heines Custom Draperies, 27223 Hwy. Blvd., Katy, TX 77450-1040, (281)391-3103 [15523]

Heinold Hog Market Inc., PO Box 375, Kouts, IN 46347, (219)766-2211 [17988]

Heirloom Bible Publications, PO Box 780189, Wichita, KS 67278-0189, (316)267-3211 [3822]

Heitmann; Chester, 504 E Railroad St., Cut Bank, MT 59427-3018, (406)873-2051 [17989]

Heitz Service Corp., 34-11 62nd St., Woodside, NY 11377, (718)565-0004 [22863]

Helen of Troy Ltd., 1 Helen of Troy Plz., El Paso, TX 79912-1148, (915)779-6363 [14124]

Helen of Troy Texas Corp., 1 Helen of Troy Plz., El Paso, TX 79912-1148, (915)779-6363 [14125]

Helena Chemical Company Hughes, PO Box 427, Hughes, AR 72348, (870)339-2363 [811]

Helena Wholesale Inc., 202 York St., Helena, AR 72342-3333, (501)338-3421 [11407]

Helicoflex Co., PO Box 9889, Columbia, SC 29290, (803)783-1880 [16929]

Helix Ltd., 310 S Racine St., Chicago, IL 60607, (312)421-6000 [22864]

Hella Inc., PO Box 2665, Peachtree City, GA 30269-0665, (770)631-7500 [2740]

Hellam Hosiery Company Inc., 198 Beaver St., Hellam, PA 17406, (717)755-3831 [5025]

Helland and Long Implement Co., PO Box 246, Belmond, IA 50421, (515)444-3011 [812]

Hellenbrand Water Conditioners Inc., 404 Moravian Valley Rd., PO Box 187, Waunakee, WI 53597, (608)849-3050 [25676]

Heller Co.; E.P., 21 Samson Ave., Madison, NJ 07940-2261, (973)377-2878 [16097]

Hellman Produce Inc.; J., 1601 E Olympic Blvd., No. 200, Los Angeles, CA 90021-1942, (213)627-1093 [11408]

Helman Corporation, PO Box 56387, Atlanta, GA 30343-0387, (404)688-8231 [5026]

The Helman Group Ltd., 1701 Pacific Ave., No. 280, Oxnard, CA 93033, (805)487-7772 [15524]

Helmbold Inc.; Fritz, 12 Industrial Park Rd., Troy, NY 12180-6197, (518)273-0810 [11409]

Helmet House Inc., 26855 Malibu Hills Rd., Calabasas Hills, CA 91301, (818)880-0000 [23721]

Helms Candy Company Inc., 3001 Lee Hwy., Bristol, VA 24201-8315, (540)669-2612 [11410]

Helpern Inc.; Joan & David, 1935 Revere Beach Pkwy., Everett, MA 02149-5945, (617)387-5005 [24761]

Helsel-Jepperson Electric Inc., 197th & Halsted Sts., Chicago Heights, IL 60411, (708)756-5600 [8837]

HemaCare Corp., 4954 Van Nuys Blvd., Sherman Oaks, CA 91403, (818)986-3883 [19357]

Hemisphere International, 3415 Eastern Ave., Grand Rapids, MI 49508, (616)247-1444 [26062]

Hemmelgran and Sons Inc., PO Box 169, Coldwater, OH 45828, (419)678-2351 [11411]

Hempstead County Farmers Association, 1400 E 3rd St., Hope, AR 71801, (870)777-5729 [813]

Henbest & Associates; Jen, PO Box 459, Oconomowoc, WI 53066 [23722]

Henco Inc., 1025 W 25th St., Norfolk, VA 23517-1014, (757)625-5361 [24762]

Henderson Auctions, PO Box 336, Livingston, LA 70754, (504)686-2252 [7530]

Henderson Auctions Inc., PO Box 336, Livingston, LA 70754, (225)686-2252 [24137]

Henderson and Baird Hardware Company Inc., 1100 Sycamore St., Greenwood, MS 38930, (601)453-3221 [15165]

Henderson Brothers Stores, PO Box 3289, Bakersfield, CA 93385, (661)322-5011 [2276]

Henderson and Co.; J.L., 2533 Peralta St., Oakland, CA 94607-1795, (510)839-1900 [15525]

Henderson Steel Corp., PO Box 3760, Meridian, MS 39303, (601)484-3000 [20033]

Henderson Wheel and Warehouse Supply, 1825 S 300 W, Salt Lake City, UT 84115, (801)486-2073 [2741]

Hendrix Technologies Inc., 20 Gilbert Ave., Ste. 101, Smithtown, NY 11787, (516)361-5021 [21029]

Henig Furs Inc., 4135 Carmichael Rd., Montgomery, AL 36106-3668, (205)277-7610 [5027]

Henkel Corp. Chemicals Group, 5051 Estecreek Rd., Cincinnati, OH 45232-1446, (513)482-3000 [4414]

Henley Paper Co., 8400 Triad Dr., Greensboro, NC 27409, (919)668-0081 [21639]

Hennepin Cooperative Seed Exchange Inc., 8175 Lewis Rd., Golden Valley, MN 55427, (612)545-7702 [17990]

Hennessy Ingredients; Ron, 1709 Pennsylvania Ave., Augusta, GA 30904, (706)736-7104 [11412]

Henry Corp.; E.P., PO Box 615, Woodbury, NJ 08096, (609)845-6200 [7467]

Henry Doneger Associates Inc., 463 7th Ave., New York, NY 10018, (212)564-1266 [5028]

Henry Farmers Cooperative Inc., 1211 W Wood, No. 1058, Paris, TN 38242, (901)642-1385 [814]

Henry J. Easy Pak Meats, 4460 W Armitage Ave., Chicago, IL 60639, (773)227-5400 [11413]

Henry J. Meat Specialties, 4460 W Armitage Ave., Chicago, IL 60639, (773)227-5400 [11413]

Henry Radio Inc., 2050 S Bundy Dr., Los Angeles, CA 90025, (310)820-1234 [25230]

Henry Radio Inc., 2050 S Bundy Dr., Los Angeles, CA 90025, (310)820-1234 [8838]

Henry Schein Inc. Dental Div., 135 Duryea Rd., Melville, NY 11747, (516)843-5500 [18834]

Henry Service Co., PO Box 79, Cambridge, IL 61238, (309)937-3369 [22345]

Henry Tile Co.; Robert F., 119 45th Pl. N, PO Box 11329, Birmingham, AL 35222, (205)592-8615 [9941]

Henry Tile Co.; Robert F., 919 Bell St., PO Box 2230, Montgomery, AL 36102-2230, (334)269-2518 [9942]

Henry's Foods Inc., PO Box 1057, Alexandria, MN 56308, (320)763-3194 [11414]

Henry's Hickory House Inc., PO Box 2823, Jacksonville, FL 32203, (904)354-6839 [11415]

Henry's Homemade Ice Cream, 2909 W 15th St., Plano, TX 75075, (972)612-9949 [11416]

Henry's Tackle L.L.C., PO Drawer 1107, Morehead City, NC 28557, (252)726-6186 [23723]

Hensley and Co., 4201 N 45th Ave., Phoenix, AZ 85031, (602)264-1635 [1751]

HEPA Corp., 3071 E Coronado St., Anaheim, CA 92806, (714)630-5700 [14484]

Heraa Inc., PO Box 591, Veguita, NM 87062-0591, (505)864-6935 [17991]

Heral Enterprises Inc., PO Box 193666, Little Rock, AR 72219-3666, (501)568-2090 [15166]

Herald House/Independence Press, PO Box 1770, Independence, MO 64055, (816)252-5010 [3823]

Herald Press, 616 Walnut Ave., Scottdale, PA 15683, (724)887-8500 [3824]

Herald Wholesalers Inc., 20830 Coolidge, Oak Park, MI 48237, (248)398-4560 [13751]

Herb's Seafood, 112 School House Rd., Mt. Holly, NJ 08060-9601, (609)267-0276 [11417]

Herc-U-Lift Inc., 5655 Hwy. 12 W, PO Box 187, Maple Plain, MN 55359-0187, (612)479-2501 [16098]

Herco Products Corp.; Ryan, PO Box 588, Burbank, CA 91503, (818)841-1141 [22980]

Hercules/CEDCO, 1300 Morrical Blvd., Findlay, OH 45840, (419)425-6400 [2742]

Hercules Industries, 1310 W Evans Ave., Denver, CO 80223, (303)937-1000 [20034]

Hercules Sales, Inc., 1465 Durham Hwy., PO Box 1057, Roxboro, NC 27573, (919)597-2275 [15526]

Hercules Tire and Rubber Co., 1300 Morrical Blvd., Findlay, OH 45840, (419)425-6400 [24281]

Hercules Tire & Rubber Products, 477 Main St., Sanford, ME 04073, (207)324-4211 [2743]

Hercules Vacu-Maid, 3686 S Schwieder Ln., Idaho Falls, ID 83406, (208)522-9666 [4633]

Hereford Grain Corp., PO Box 910, Hereford, TX 79045-0910, (806)364-3755 [17992]

Here's Fred Golf Co., 13627 Beach Blvd., Jacksonville, FL 32246, (919)223-3136 [23724]

Heritage FS Inc., PO Box 318, Gilman, IL 60938, (815)265-4751 [815]

Heritage F.S. Inc., PO Box 339, Gilman, IL 60938, (815)265-4751 [22346]

Heritage House Wines, 809 Jefferson Hwy., Jefferson, LA 70121, (504)837-6464 [1752]

Heritage Industries, 4605 Spring Rd., Cleveland, OH 44131-1021, (216)398-8776 [13752]

Heritage Lace Inc., PO Box 328, Pella, IA 50219, (515)628-4949 [15527]

Heritage Manufacturing Inc., 4530 NW 135th St., Opa Locka, FL 33054, (305)685-5966 [13495]

Heritage Marketing Inc., PO Box 225, Commack, NY 11725-0225, (516)499-9380 [11418]

Heritage Paper Company Inc., 4011 Morton St., Jacksonville, FL 32217, (904)737-6603 [21759]

Heritage Propane Partners, L.P., 8801 S Yale Ave., Ste. 310, Tulsa, OK 74137, (918)492-7272 [22347]

Heritage Wafers Ltd., 850 Vermont, Ripon, WI 54971, (920)748-7716 [11419]

Herkimer Cooperative Business Association, 317 Brenecke, Bremen, KS 66412, (785)744-3226 [17993]

Herman; Jeffrey, PO Box 704, Chepachet, RI 02814, (401)461-3156 [25677]

Herman-Norcross AG Services, 406 Pacific Ave. S, Herman, MN 56248, (612)677-2251 [1071]

Hermann Associates Inc., 1405 Indiana St., San Francisco, CA 94107, (415)285-8486 [24561]

Hermann Associates Inc., 1405 Indiana St., San Francisco, CA 94107, (415)285-8486 [21030]

Hermann Implement Inc., PO Box 69, Wanamingo, MN 55983-0069, (507)824-2256 [816]

Herman's Inc., PO Box 4748, Rock Island, IL 61204, (309)788-9568 [5029]

Hermes Consolidated Inc., 1600 Broadway Ste. 2300, Denver, CO 80202, (303)894-9966 [22348]

Hermes Machine Tool Company Inc., 5 Gardner Rd., Fairfield, NJ 07004, (973)227-9150 [16099]

Hermetic Aircraft International Corp., 100 Corporate Dr., Holtsville, NY 11742, (516)758-4242 [96]

Hermitage Electric Supply Corp., PO Box 24990, Nashville, TN 37202-4990, (615)843-3300 [15167]

Hermitage Publishing Co., PO Box 310, Tenafly, NJ 07670, (201)894-8247 [3825]

Hern Marine, 7341 Dixie Hwy., Fairfield, OH 45014, (513)874-2628 [18520]

Herndon Company Inc.; J.E., 100 Industrial Dr., Kings Mountain, NC 28086, (704)739-4711 [26842]

Heroes World Distribution, Inc., 1639 Rte. 10 E, Parsippany, NJ 07054, (973)984-8776 [3826]

Herregan Distributors Inc., 2128 NE Broadway, Des Moines, IA 50313, (515)265-9807 [9943]

Herregan Distributors, Inc., 3695 Kennebec, Eagan, MN 55122, (612)452-7200 [9944]

Herregan Distributors Inc., 1446 Taney, North Kansas City, MO 64116, (816)221-3355 [9945]

Herregan Distributors, Inc., 13412 Industrial Rd., Omaha, NE 68137, (402)330-4445 [9946]

Herregan Distributors Inc., 9340 N 107 St., Milwaukee, WI 53224, (414)354-1810 [9947]

Herreid Livestock Market, PO Box 67, Herreid, SD 57632-0067, (605)437-2265 [17994]

Herring & Co.; T.L., PO Box 3186, Wilson, NC 27895-3186, (919)291-1141 [11420]

Herr's and Bernat Inc., 70 Eastgate Dr., Danville, IL 61832, (217)442-4121 [26514]

Herr's Inc., 70 Eastgate Dr., Danville, IL 61832, (217)442-4121 [26063]

Hershey Foods Corp., PO Box 810, Hershey, PA 17033-0810, (717)534-6799 [11421]

Herzog Supply Inc.; C., 1915 Main St., East Worcester, NY 12064, (607)397-8292 [23208]

Herzogs Auto Parts Inc., 2301 Julia, New Orleans, LA 70119-7534, (504)827-2886 [2744]

Hesco Parts Corp., PO Box 3008, Louisville, KY 40201, (502)589-9600 [2745]

Hess; Charles, La Porte Rd., RR No. 2, Box 6830, Morrisville, VT 05661, (802)888-4078 [2746]

Hess and Company Inc.; John R., PO Box 3615, Cranston, RI 02910-0615, (401)785-9300 [4415]

Hess Hair Milk Laboratories Inc., PO Box 17100, St. Paul, MN 55117-0100, (612)488-7262 [25678]

Hesselbein Tire Company Inc., 3004 Lynch St., Jackson, MS 39209, (601)352-3611 [2747]

Hester Industries Inc. Pierce Foods Div., PO Box 2140, Winchester, VA 22604, (703)667-7878 [11422]

Hesters/McGlaun Office Supply Co., PO Box 3098, Lubbock, TX 79452, (806)766-8888 [21031]

Hettinger Cooperative Equity Exchange, Railroad Right of Way, Hettinger, ND 58639, (701)567-2408 [17995]

Hettinger-Mobridge Candy & Tobacco, PO Box 549, Hettinger, ND 58639-0549, (701)567-2440 [26306]

Heuer Time and Electronics Corp., 960 S Springfield Ave., Springfield, NJ 07081, (973)467-1890 [17448]

Hewitt Brothers Inc., PO Box 147, Locke, NY 13092, (315)497-0900 [817]

Hewlett-Packard Co. International, 3495 Deer Creek Rd., Palo Alto, CA 94304, (650)857-2032 [6331]

Hews Company Inc., 190 Rumery St., South Portland, ME 04106, (207)767-2136 [7468]

Heyboer Transformers Inc., 17382 Hayes St., Grand Haven, MI 49417, (616)842-5830 [8839]

HFM Foodservice, PO Box 855, Honolulu, HI 96808, (808)545-2111 [11423]

HG International Corporation, PO Box 51513, Durham, NC 27717, (919)489-4840 [23725]

HGS Power House, Inc., 7 W Albany St., Huntington Station, NY 11746, (516)423-1348 [818]

H.H. West Co., 505 N 22nd St., Milwaukee, WI 53233, (414)344-1000 [21032]

HHS USA Inc., 1733 H St., No. 330-705, Blaine, WA 98230-5107, (360)354-6515 [13366]

Hi Country Wire and Telephone Ltd., 6275 Simms Ave., Arvada, CO 80004, (303)467-9143 [5635]

Hi-Fashion Cosmetics Inc., 70 Herbert Ave., Closter, NJ 07624, (201)767-5755 [14126]

Hi Grade Meats Inc., 2160 SW Temple, Salt Lake City, UT 84115-2530, (801)487-5818 [11424]

Hi-Jac Corporation, PO Box 132, Ft. Payne, AL 35967-0132, (205)845-0461 [15528]

Hi-Line Electric Co., 2121 Valley View Ln., Dallas, TX 75234, (972)247-6200 [8840]

Hi-Line Fertilizer Inc., Main St., Hingham, MT 59528, (406)397-3194 [819]

HI Line Wholesale Co., 80 U.S Hwy. 2 E, Wolf Point, MT 59201-1942, (406)653-1313 [26307]

Hi Lo Table Manufacturing Inc., 915 W Cherry, PO Box 945, Chanute, KS 66720, (316)431-7140 [13130]

HI-Pac Ltd., PO Box 25038, Honolulu, HI 96825-0038, (808)395-0388 [11425]

Hi-Tec Industrial Supply, 3226 Blair Ave., St. Louis, MO 63107, (314)421-0919 [2976]

Hi-Tec Sports USA Inc., 4801 Stoddard Rd., Modesto, CA 95356, (209)545-1111 [24763]

HI-Tech Optical Inc., 3157 Christy Way, Saginaw, MI 48603-2226, (517)799-9390 [19358]

Hi-Way Products Inc., 500 Ash St., Ida Grove, IA 51445, (712)364-3763 [20035]

HIA Inc., 4275 Forest St., Denver, CO 80216, (303)394-6040 [820]

Hiawatha Grain Co., 4111 Central Ave. NE, No. 212, Columbia Heights, MN 55421, (612)789-5270 [17996]

Hibbard Aviation, 1825 Karin Dr., Carson City, NV 89706, (775)884-3555 [20648]

Hibdon Tire Center Inc., 828 SE 29th St., Oklahoma City, OK 73129, (405)632-5521 [2748]

Hibel Studio; Edna, PO Box 9967, Riviera Beach, FL 33419, (561)848-9633 [13367]

Hickel Investment Co., PO Box 101700, Anchorage, AK 99510, (907)343-2400 [25679]

Hickenbottom and Sons Inc., 301 Warehouse Ave., Sunnyside, WA 98944, (509)837-4100 [11426]

Hickey and Associates, 3 Clarendon Ave., Brockton, MA 02301, (508)559-5130 [6332]

Hickman & Willey, Inc., PO Box 146, Selbyville, DE 19975, (302)436-8533 [22349]

Hickman, Williams and Co., 17370 Laurel Park Dr. N, Ste. 330, Livonia, MI 48152, (734)462-1890 [20036]

Hickman, Williams and Co., Black Products Div., 13513 S Calumet Ave., Chicago, IL 60827-1834, (773)468-9700 [20037]

Hickory Auto Parts Inc., PO Drawer 729, Hickory, NC 28603, (704)322-1325 [2749]

Hickory Farms Inc., PO Box 219, Maumee, OH 43537, (419)893-7611 [11427]

Hickory Tech-Enterprise Solutions, 2920 Centre Pointe Dr., Roseville, MN 55113, (651)634-1800 [5636]

Hicks Equipment, 4444 W Bristol Rd., Flint, MI 48507, (810)733-6191 [8841]

Hicks Inc., PO Box 232, Luverne, AL 36049, (205)335-3311 [23726]

Hicks Oil and Hicks Gas Inc., PO Box 98, 202 N Rte. 54, Roberts, IL 60962, (217)395-2281 [22350]

Hickson's Office Supplies Co., 17 E Wheeling St., Washington, PA 15301, (412)222-0140 [21033]

Hidden Villa Ranch, PO Box 34001, Fullerton, CA 92834, (714)680-3447 [11741]

HIE Holdings, Inc., 2839 Mokumoa St., Honolulu, HI 96819, (808)833-2244 [11428]

Higdon Grocery Company Inc.; Ira, E Industrial Area, Cairo, GA 31728, (912)377-1272 [11429]

Higginbotham-Bartlett Co., PO Box 6880, Lubbock, TX 79493-6880, (806)793-8662 [7469]

Higgins Lumber Co.; J.E., 6999 Southfront Rd., Livermore, CA 94550, (925)245-4300 [7470]

Higgins Lumber Co.; J.E., 4734 E Jensen Ave., Fresno, CA 93725, (209)264-1771 [7471]

Higgins Lumber Co.; J.E., 13290 Paxton St., Pacoima, CA 91331, (818)890-2228 [7472]

Higgins Lumber Co.; J.E., 3612 Kurtz St., San Diego, CA 92110-4432, (760)686-8690 [7473]

Higgins Lumber Co.; J.E., 939 W Boone, Santa Maria, CA 93454, (805)928-8325 [7474]

Higgins Lumber Co.; J.E., PO Box 4124, Concord, CA 94524, (925)674-9300 [27317]

Higgins Productions, Inc.; Alfred, 15500 Hamner Dr., Los Angeles, CA 90077-1805, (818)762-3300 [25231]

Higgins Purchasing Group, 625 Market St., San Francisco, CA 94105, (415)908-0700 [13131]

High Country Kitchens, 7001 W Colfax Ave., Lakewood, CO 80215-4108, (303)233-6782 [15168]

High Country Sales Inc., 4110 High Country Rd., Colorado Springs, CO 80907-4319, (719)598-9200 [1753]

High Frequency Technology Company Inc., 172-D Brook Ave., Deer Park, NY 11729, (516)242-3020 [5637]

High Grade Beverage, PO Box 7092, North Brunswick, NJ 08902, (732)821-7600 [1754]

High Grade Beverage, PO Box 7092, North Brunswick, NJ 08902, (732)821-7600 [11430]

High Life Sales Co., 1325 N Topping, Kansas City, MO 64120, (816)483-3700 [1755]

High Mountain Distributing, 801 Ronan St., Ste. 4, Missoula, MT 59801, (406)721-7704 [27148]

High Performance Distributors, 1755 Mission Rd., South San Francisco, CA 94080, (650)755-3350 [2750]

High Plains Cooperative, PO Box 520, Kimball, NE 69145, (308)235-4655 [17997]

High Plains Cooperative Association, 405 E 4th St., Colby, KS 67701, (785)462-3351 [821]

High Point Oil Co., 3520 E 96th St., Ste. 11, Indianapolis, IN 46240-3734, (317)844-8886 [22351]

Highland Auto and Truck Inc., 1536 N Indiana St., Los Angeles, CA 90063, (323)268-1311 [2751]

Highland Auto and Truck Inc., 1536 N Indiana St., Los Angeles, CA 90063, (323)268-1311 [2752]

Highland Distributing Co., 213 Blount, Fayetteville, NC 28302, (919)483-4168 [1756]

Highland Exchange Service Co-op, PO Box K, Waverly, FL 33877, (813)439-3661 [11431]

Highland Laundry Co., 504-506 Pleasant St., Holyoke, MA 01040, (413)534-7391 [5030]

Highland Mills Inc., PO Box 33775, Charlotte, NC 28233, (704)375-3333 [5031]

Highland Stone Hall, 4845 Oakland St., Denver, CO 80239-2721, (303)371-1112 [11594]

Highmore Auction, PO Box 504, Highmore, SD 57345-0245, (605)852-2211 [17998]

Highsmith Inc., W5527 Hwy. 106, PO Box 800, Ft. Atkinson, WI 53538-0800, (920)563-9571 [25232]

Highsmith Inc., W5527 Hwy. 106, Ft. Atkinson, WI 53538-0800, (920)563-9571 [13132]

Hightower Oil and Petroleum Company Inc., PO Box 36, Plumerville, AR 72127, (501)354-4780 [22352]

Highway Agricultural Services Inc., PO Box 153, Le Center, MN 56057, (612)357-2245 [822]

Highway Auto Parts Inc., 5 Lake Dr., West Greenwich, RI 02817, (401)397-3000 [2753]

Highway Equipment and Supply Co., 1016 W Church St., Orlando, FL 32854, (407)843-6310 [16100]

Highway Metal Services Inc., 4735 W 150th St., Cleveland, OH 44135, (216)676-1500 [20038]

Hike A Bike, 621 Loma Prieta Dr., Aptos, CA 95003, (408)688-5411 [23727]

Hilfiger USA Inc.; Tommy, 25 W 39th St., New York, NY 10018, (212)840-8888 [5032]

Hilites; K.C., Avenida De Luces, Williams, AZ 86046, (520)635-2607 [8842]

Hill Brothers Chemical Co., 1675 N Main St., Orange, CA 92867, (714)998-8800 [4416]

Hill City Wholesale Company Inc., PO Box 10245, Birmingham, AL 35202, (804)847-6641 [21760]

Hill and Co., Inc.; Geo. W., PO Box 787, Florence, KY 41022-0787, (606)371-8423 [823]

Hill and Co., Inc.; O.S., PO Box 2170, East Liverpool, OH 43920, (330)386-6440 [20649]

Hill Floral Products, 2117 Peacock Rd., Richmond, IN 47374, (765)973-6600 [14886]

Hill; Gary A., 3516 Neal Dr., Knoxville, TN 37918-5229, (423)922-8314 [18835]

Hill Grain Co. Inc.; C.F., 116 Aisne St., Bartlett, TX 76511, (254)527-3311 [17999]

Hill and Griffith Co., 1262 State Ave., Cincinnati, OH 45204, (513)921-1075 [20545]

Hill and Son Co.; Fred, 2101 Hornig Rd., Philadelphia, PA 19116, (215)698-2200 [13133]

Hill and Son Co.; Fred, 2101 Hornig Rd., Philadelphia, PA 19116, (215)698-2200 [16101]

Hill Steel & Builders Supplies, 6110 Birch Rd., Flint, MI 48507, (810)232-6194 [20039]

Hillandale Farms Inc. of Pennsylvania, 12481 Rte. 6, Corry, PA 16407-9537, (814)664-9681 [11432]

The Hillcraft Group, 6800 Grant Ave., Cleveland, OH 44105, (216)441-5500 [21761]

Hillcrest Food Service Co., 2695 E 40th St., Cleveland, OH 44115, (216)361-4625 [21762]

Hillcrest Foods Inc., 2300 Louisiana St., Lawrence, KS 66046, (785)843-0023 [11433]

Hiller Corp.; Herbert S., 401 Commerce Pt., Harahan, LA 70123, (504)736-0008 [24562]

Hiller Investments Inc., PO Box 91508, Mobile, AL 36691-1508, (334)432-5570 [24563]

Hillger Oil Company Inc., PO Box 1989, Las Cruces, NM 88005, (505)526-8481 [22353]

Hillman Fastener, 10590 Hamilton Ave., Cincinnati, OH 45248, (513)851-4900 [13753]

Hillman International Brands, Ltd., 1441 Seamist Dr., Houston, TX 77008, (713)869-5441 [1757]

Hillmer's Luggage & Leather, 115 SE 6th Ave., Topeka, KS 66603-3564, (785)233-2314 [18397]

Hills Beaver Creek Coop Farm Service, PO Box 69, Beaver Creek, MN 56116, (507)673-2388 [824]

Hills Beaver Creek Cooperative Farm Service, 3rd & Summit Ave., Hills, MN 56138, (507)962-3221 [825]

Hills Office Supply Co. Inc., 490 Main St., Pawtucket, RI 02860-2914, (401)723-1240 [21034]

Hill's Pet Nutrition Inc., PO Box 148, Topeka, KS 66601, (913)354-8523 [27149]

Hillsboro Equipment Inc., PO Box 583, Hillsboro, WI 54634, (608)489-2275 [826]

Hillsdale Cooperative Elevator, PO Box 265, Hillsdale, IL 61257, (309)658-2218 [18000]

Hillsdale Paper Co., 4880 Hills & Dales Rd. NW, Canton, OH 44708, (330)477-3411 [21763]

Hillsdale Sash and Door Co, PO Box 629, Wilsonville, OR 97070, (503)682-1000 [27318]

Hillside Coffee of California Holding Co., PO Box 223200, Carmel, CA 93922, (408)633-6300 [11434]

Hillside Dairy Inc., 2600 W 11th, Pueblo, CO 81003, (719)544-7898 [11435]

Hilltop Beer Distributing, 4535 Buffalo Rd., Erie, PA 16510, (814)899-6157 [1758]

Hilmar Cheese Company Inc., PO Box 910, Hilmar, CA 95324, (209)667-6076 [11436]

Hilo Farmer's Exchange, 318 Kinoole St., Hilo, HI 96720, (808)935-6697 [14887]

Hilton Equipment Corp., 9336 Civic Center Dr., Beverly Hills, CA 90210, (310)278-4321 [13134]

Hilton, Gibson, and Miller Inc., PO Box 1237, Newburgh, NY 12551, (914)562-0353 [11437]

Hiltons Tent City Inc., 272 Friend St., Boston, MA 02114-1801, (617)227-9104 [23728]

HIM Mechanical Systems Inc., 90 1st St., Bridgewater, MA 02324-1054, (508)697-5000 [14485]

Himark Enterprises Inc., 497 Pinehurst Ct., Roslyn, NY 11576-3070, (516)273-3300 [13135]

Himber's Books, PO Box 41509, Eugene, OR 97404-0367, (541)686-8003 [3827]

Himex International Inc., PO Box 745, Ellicott City, MD 21041-0745, (410)247-7718 [24764]

Hinckley and Schmitt Bottled Water Group, 6055 S Harlem Ave., Chicago, IL 60638, (773)586-8600 [11438]

Hinely Aluminum Inc., 3645 Southside Industrial Pkwy., Ste. 101, Atlanta, GA 30354, (404)361-1944 [20040]

Hines Inc.; Angus I., 1426 Holland Rd., Suffolk, VA 23434, (757)539-2358 [22354]

Hines Nut Co., 2404 Canton, Dallas, TX 75226-1803, (214)939-0253 [11439]

Hinkle Metals and Supply Company Inc., PO Box 11441, Birmingham, AL 35202, (205)326-3300 [20041]

Hinojosa Parts Warehouse, 1416 Roosevelt, Brownsville, TX 78521-3110, (956)546-4513 [2754]

Hinrichs; E. Louis, PO Box 1090, Lompoc, CA 93438-1090, (805)736-7512 [3828]

Hinshaw Supply Company of California, 145 11th St., San Francisco, CA 94103, (415)431-2376 [14486]

Hintz Fire Equipment Inc., PO Box 2492, Fargo, ND 58108-2492, (701)237-6006 [24564]

Hipp Wholesale Foods Inc., PO Box 1145, North Platte, NE 69103, (308)532-0791 [11440]

Hirsch Pipe & Supply Co., 32107 Alipaz, San Juan Capistrano, CA 92675-3616, (949)493-4591 [23209]

Hirschfield Sons Co.; H., 1414 N Madison St., Bay City, MI 48708, (517)895-5571 [26843]

Hirschmann Corp., 123 Powerhouse Rd., Roslyn Heights, NY 11577, (516)484-0500 [16102]

Hirsh Precision Products Inc., 6420 Odell Pl, Boulder, CO 80301, (303)530-3131 [2755]

Hirshfield's, Inc., 725 2nd Ave. N, Minneapolis, MN 55405, (612)377-3910 [21456]

Hirst Imports, 1080 Metropolitan Ave., Oklahoma City, OK 73108-2032, (405)949-9393 [1759]

Hirt Jr., Co.; R., 3000 N Chrysler Dr., Detroit, MI 48207, (313)831-2020 [11441]

Hirten Company Inc.; William J., 6100 17th Ave., Brooklyn, NY 11204, (718)256-4801 [13368]

Hisco, 488 Regal Row, Ste. 102, Brownsville, TX 78521, (956)542-0843 [8843]

Hisco, 10863 Rockwall Rd., Dallas, TX 75238-1213, (214)343-8730 [8844]

Hisco, 6650 Concord Pk. Dr., Houston, TX 77040, (713)934-1700 [8845]

Hispania Trading Corporation, 5715 Manchester Ave., St. Louis, MO 63110, (314)781-1500 [25680]

Hispanic Books Distributors, Inc., 1665 W Grant Rd., Tucson, AZ 85745, (520)882-9484 [3829]

Hitachi America Ltd., 50 Prospect Ave., Tarrytown, NY 10591-4698, (914)332-5800 [25233]

Hitachi America Ltd., 200 Sierra Point Pkwy., Brisbane, CA 94005, (650)244-7900 [8846]

Hitachi America Ltd. Electron Tube Div., 3850 Holcomb Bridge Rd., Ste. 300, Norcross, GA 30092, (404)409-3000 [8847]

Hitachi Data Systems Corp., PO Box 54996, Santa Clara, CA 95054, (408)970-1000 [6333]

Hitachi Data Systems Corp., 750 Central Expy., Santa Clara, CA 95050, (408)970-1000 [6334]

Hitachi Home Electronics (America) Inc. Visual Technologies Div., 3890 Steve Reynolds Blvd., Norcross, GA 30093, (770)279-5600 [15169]

Hitachi Inverter, 608 Mossycup Oak Dr., Plano, TX 75025, (972)527-5313 [8848]

Hitachi Maxco Ltd., 1630 Albritton Dr., Kennesaw, GA 30144, (404)424-9350 [16930]

Hitachi Medical Systems America Inc., 1959 Summit Commerce Park, Twinsburg, OH 44087-2371, (330)425-1313 [6335]

Hitachi Power Tools USA Ltd., 3950 Steve Reynolds, Norcross, GA 30093, (770)925-1774 [13754]

Hitchcock Distributing Inc., 2901 W Arkansas, Durant, OK 74701-4847, (580)924-3350 [1760]

Hite Co., 1245 Benner Pike, State College, PA 16801-7324, (814)237-7649 [8849]

Hite Co., PO Box 1754, Altoona, PA 16603-1754, (814)944-6121 [8850]

Hitron Systems Inc., 3170 El Camino Real, Santa Clara, CA 95051, (408)261-2695 [6336]

Hiway 30 Auto Salvage, 960 Sunset Strip, Mountain Home, ID 83647-0118, (208)587-4429 [2756]

Hixon Manufacturing and Supply, 1001 Smithfield Dr., Ft. Collins, CO 80524, (970)482-0111 [16103]

HJV Inc., 742 S Division Ave., Grand Rapids, MI 49503-5111, (616)241-1602 [6337]

HK Laundry Equipment Inc., 530 Main St., Armonk, NY 10504, (914)273-5757 [4634]

H.L. Gage Sales Inc., PO 5170, Albany, NY 12205, (518)456-8871 [2757]

H.M. Terry Company Inc., PO Box 87, Willis Wharf, VA 23486, (757)442-6251 [12708]

HM Water Technologies Inc., PO Box 793, Barnegat, NJ 08005, (609)698-2468 [4417]

HMA/International Business Development Ltd., P.O Box 38602, Greensboro, NC 27438, (336)282-4773 [11442]

HNSX Supercomputers Inc., 305 Foster St., Littleton, MA 01460-2004, (978)742-4690 [6338]

Ho Imports, Inc., 3663 14 Mile Rd., Cedar Springs, MI 49319-9418, (616)696-3080 [26515]

Hoag Enterprises, Inc., PO Box 4406, Springfield, MO 65807, (417)883-8300 [22865]

Hoban Foods Inc., 1599 E Warren Ave., Detroit, MI 48207, (313)831-7900 [11443]

Hobart Arc Welding Systems, 11933 Woodruff Ave., Downey, CA 90241-5601, (714)521-7514 [16104]

Hobart Corp., 701 S Ridge Ave., Troy, OH 45373-0815, (513)332-3000 [16105]

Hobart Sales & Services, 76 Amaral St., Riverside, RI 02915-2205, (401)434-3355 [25659]

Hobbies of Huntsville, Book Villa, 1207 Countess Rd. NE, Huntsville, AL 35810-6337, (205)881-3910 [26516]

Hobbs Implement Company Inc., E Church St. Ext., Edenton, NC 27932, (919)482-7411 [827]

Hobby Book Distributors, 3150 State Line Rd., North Bend, OH 45052, (513)353-3390 [3830]

Hobby Crafts, 24 Eugene ONeill Dr., New London, CT 06320, (860)447-0315 [26517]

Hobby House Inc., 7407 Avon Ln., Chesterland, OH 44026-2901, (216)781-3210 [26518]

Hobby Lobby International Inc., 5614 Franklin Pike Cir., Brentwood, TN 37027-4324, (615)373-1444 [26519]

Hobby Stores Distributing Inc., 333 Park Ave., East Hartford, CT 06108, (860)282-7080 [26520]

HobbyGame Distributors Inc., 2433 W Sherwin Ave., Chicago, IL 60645-1427, (847)674-5075 [26521]

Hobbyquest Marketing, 62 White St., Red Bank, NJ 07701, (732)842-6082 [26522]

Hobbytyme Distributors, 64 C Oakland Ave., East Hartford, CT 06108, (860)528-9854 [26523]

Hobgood Electric & Machinery Company, Inc., PO Box 3073, Columbia, SC 29203, (803)754-8700 [8851]

Hoboken Wood Flooring Corp., Adirondack Div., 22 Kairnes St., Albany, NY 12205, (518)459-0277 [9948]

Hoboken Wood Flooring Corp., 70 Demarest Dr., Wayne, NJ 07470-6702, (973)694-2888 [15529]

Hoboken Wood Floors, 70 Dermerast Dr., Wayne, NJ 07470, (973)694-2888 [9949]

Hoboken Wood Floors, 181 Campanelli Pkwy., Stoughton, MA 02072, (781)341-2881 [9950]

Hoch & Selby Company, Inc., 809 NE 25th Ave., Portland, OR 97232, (503)234-6476 [26064]

Hockenberg Equipment Co., 2611 Sunset Rd., Des Moines, IA 50321-1146, (515)255-5774 [24138]

Hockman Lewis Ltd., 200 Executive Dr., West Orange, NJ 07052, (973)325-3838 [16106]

Hockstein Inc.; David, 8600 Ashwood Dr., Capitol Heights, MD 20743-3720, (301)336-6600 [9951]

Hocott Implement Company Inc., 1105 S 7th, Raymondville, TX 78580, (956)689-2481 [828]

Hoder-Rogers Inc., 885 Warren Ave., East Providence, RI 02914-1423, (401)438-2725 [97]

Hodgin Supply Company Inc., PO Box 2160, Greensboro, NC 27402, (910)275-8561 [7475]

Hoeckel Co.; C.F., PO Box 11519, Denver, CO 80211-0519, (303)433-7481 [21035]

Hoegemeyer Hybrids Inc., 1755 Hoegemeyer Rd., Hooper, NE 68031, (402)654-3399 [18001]

Hoegemeyer Hybrids Inc., 1755 Hoegemeyer Rd., Hooper, NE 68031, (402)654-3399 [11444]

Hoekstra Truck Equipment Company, Inc., 260 36th St. SE, PO Box 2246, Grand Rapids, MI 49501, (616)241-6664 [2758]

Hofert Co.; J., PO Box 51330, Sparks, NV 89435, (775)331-4000 [13369]

Hoffman Brothers, 5290 N Pearl St., Rosemont, IL 60018, (847)671-1550 [16107]

Hoffman Co.; H., 7330 W Montrose Ave., Chicago, IL 60634, (708)456-9600 [24565]

Hoffman Company Inc.; Rube P., 25792 Obero Dr., Mission Viejo, CA 92691, (714)770-2922 [26065]

Hoffman Cooperative Oil Association, PO Box 275, Hoffman, MN 56339, (612)986-2061 [829]

Hoffman Distributing Co., 2100 Resource Dr., Birmingham, AL 35242-2940, (205)991-3599 [26066]

Hoffman Inc.; A.H., PO Box 266, Lancaster, NY 14086, (716)684-8111 [14888]

Hoffman International Inc., 300 S Randolphville Rd, Piscataway, NJ 08855, (732)752-3600 [7476]

Hoffman and Reed Inc., 915 Shanklin Ave., Trenton, MO 64683, (816)359-2258 [830]

Hoffmann Aircraft Inc., 427 Cr. 125, Texico, NM 88135-9776, (505)389-5505 [98]

Hoffmeyer Co., 1600 Factor Ave., San Leandro, CA 94577, (510)895-9955 [2759]

Hog Inc., RR 2 Box 8, Greenfield, IL 62044-9603 [831]

Hogan and Associates Inc.; T.J., 34272 Doreka Ave., Fraser, MI 48026, (810)296-5160 [2760]

Hohner, Inc./HSS, PO Box 15035, Richmond, VA 23227, (804)515-1900 [25234]

Hoist Liftruck Manufacturing, 6499 W 65th St., Bedford Park, IL 60638, (708)458-2200 [16108]

Hoke Controls, 1 Madison St., No. B, East Rutherford, NJ 07073-1605, (973)812-0682 [16931]

Holberg Industries Inc., 545 Steamboat Rd., Greenwich, CT 06830, (203)661-2500 [11445]

Holcomb's Education Resource, PO Box 94636, Cleveland, OH 44101-4636, (216)341-3000 [21036]

Holcomb's Education Resource, PO Box 94636, Cleveland, OH 44101-4636, (216)341-3000 [21037]

Holden, Inc.; John W.W., 628 Union Ave., Providence, RI 02909, (401)944-1515 [19359]

Holden's Foundation Seeds Inc., PO Box 839, Williamsburg, IA 52361, (319)668-1100 [832]

Holden's Foundation Seeds L.L.C., PO Box 839, Williamsburg, IA 52361, (319)668-1100 [832]

Holdrege Seed and Farm Supply Inc., PO Box 530, Holdrege, NE 68949-0530, (308)995-4465 [833]

Holga Inc., 7901 Woodley Ave., Van Nuys, CA 91406, (818)782-0600 [21038]

Holiday Cos., PO Box 1224, Minneapolis, MN 55440, (612)830-8700 [11446]

Holiday Stores Inc., 4567 W 80th St., Bloomington, MN 55437, (612)830-8700 [11447]

Holiday Wholesale Inc., PO Box 177, Wisconsin Dells, WI 53965, (608)254-8321 [26308]

Holladay Color Center, 2291 E Murray-Holladay Rd., Holladay, UT 84117, (801)277-2604 [21457]

Holladay Surgical Supply Co., 2551 Landmark Dr., Winston-Salem, NC 27103-6717, (910)760-2111 [18836]

Holladay Surgical Supply Co., 2551 Landmark Dr., Winston-Salem, NC 27103-6717, (910)760-2111 [19360]

Holland Co.; M., 400 Skokie Blvd., Northbrook, IL 60062, (847)272-7370 [22981]

Holland Corp.; J. Henry, PO Box 5100, Virginia Beach, VA 23455, (757)460-3300 [20042]

Holland Southwest International Inc., PO Box 330249, Houston, TX 77233, (713)644-1966 [7477]

Hollandale Marketing Association, PO Box 70, Hollandale, MN 56045, (507)889-4421 [11448]

Hollandia Gift and Toy Co., PO Box 549, Princess Anne, MD 21853-0340, (410)651-3818 [26524]

Hollar Company Inc., PO Box 407, Gadsden, AL 35902, (205)547-1644 [22355]

Hollar and Greene Produce, PO Box 3500, Boone, NC 28607, (828)264-2177 [11449]

Hollar and Greene Produce Co., Inc., PO Box 3500, 230 Cabbage Row, Boone, NC 28607-3500, (704)264-2177 [11450]

Hollinger Corp., PO Box 8360, Fredericksburg, VA 22404-8360 [21764]

Hollingsworths' Inc., 1175 SW 30th St., Ontario, OR 97914, (541)889-7254 [834]

Hollins Enterprises, PO Box 148, Alpha, OH 45301-0148, (937)426-3503 [20813]

Holloway Brothers Tools Inc., PO Box 3055, Wilmington, DE 19804-0055, (302)322-5441 [16109]

Holloway Brothers Tools Inc., PO Box 3055, Wilmington, DE 19804-0055, (302)322-5441 [16110]

Holloway Corp., 2501 Front St., Philadelphia, PA 19148, (215)879-9550 [23210]

Holly Sea Food Inc., 414 Towne Ave., Los Angeles, CA 90013-2125, (213)625-2513 [11451]

Holmes A-One Inc., 2105 Morrie Ave., Cheyenne, WY 82001-3922, (307)632-6431 [7478]

Holmes Distributors Inc., 293 Target Industrial Cir., Bangor, ME 04401, (207)942-7357 [8852]

Holmes Limestone Co., PO Box 295, Berlin, OH 44610, (216)893-2721 [20546]

Holmes Plumbing and Heating Supply Inc., PO Box 460, Kearney, NE 68848-0460, (308)234-1922 [23211]

Holmes Protection Inc., 701 Callowhill, Philadelphia, PA 19123, (215)923-1500 [24566]

Holmes Smokehouse Inc.; S and D, PO Box 1166, Rosenberg, TX 77471, (281)342-3749 [11452]

Holmes Timber Company Inc., Rte. 2, Box 244, Johnston, SC 29832, (803)275-4755 [27319]

Holmgangers Press, Shelter Cove, 95 Carson Ct., Whitethorn, CA 95589, (707)986-7700 [3831]

Holmquist Grain and Lumber Co., 200 N Logan Ave., PO Box 127, Oakland, NE 68045, (402)685-5641 [18002]

Holo-Krome Co., PO Box 330635, West Hartford, CT 06110, (860)523-5235 [13755]

Holoubek Inc., W 238 N 1800, Waukesha, WI 53188-1198, (414)547-0500 [5033]

Holox Ltd., 1885 Broadway, Macon, GA 31201-2903, (912)746-6211 [16111]

Holstein Paper & Janitorial Supply, 12 Music Fair Rd., Owings Mills, MD 21117, (410)363-0400 [21765]

Holsten Import Corp., 75 N Saw Mill River Rd., Ste. C, Elmsford, NY 10523, (914)345-8900 [1761]

Holston Builders Supply Company Inc., 645 E Main St., Kingsport, TN 37660, (615)247-8131 [7479]

Holston Distributing Co., 310 Lafcox Dr., Johnson City, TN 37604, (423)928-6571 [1762]

Holston Gases Inc., PO Box 27248, Knoxville, TN 37927, (423)573-1917 [22356]

Holston Steel Services, 300 Piedmont Ave., Bristol, VA 24201, (540)466-6000 [20043]

Holt and Bugbee Co., PO Box 37, Tewksbury, MA 01876, (508)851-7201 [9952]

Holt Company of Texas, PO Box 207916, San Antonio, TX 78220-7916, (210)648-1111 [7480]

Holt Cos., PO Box 207916, San Antonio, TX 78220-7916, (210)648-1111 [7480]

Holt Distributors, Inc., 865 E Loockerman St., Dover, DE 19901-7419, (302)674-0666 [21766]

Holt Electric Inc., 1515 Walnut Ridge Dr., Hartland, WI 53029, (262)369-7100 [8853]

Holt Electric Motor Co., 5225 W State St., Milwaukee, WI 53208, (414)771-6600 [8854]

Holten Meat Inc., 1682 Sauget Business Blvd., East St. Louis, IL 62206, (618)423-8400 [11453]

Holthouse Brothers, 4373 State, Rte. 103, Willard, OH 44890, (419)935-0151 [11454]

Holtzman Office Furniture Co., 2155 E 7th St., Los Angeles, CA 90023, (323)266-5700 [21039]

Holyrood Cooperative Grain and Supply Co., 200 E Santa Fe St., Holyrood, KS 67450, (913)252-3233 [18003]

Holzberg Communications, Inc., Box 322, Totowa, NJ 07511, (973)389-9600 [5638]

Holzberg, Inc., Box 322, Totowa, NJ 07511, (973)389-9600 [5638]

Holzmueller Corp., 1000 25th St., San Francisco, CA 94107, (415)826-8383 [8855]

Homa Co., PO Box 5425, Parsippany, NJ 07054, (201)887-6500 [11455]

Homax Oil, 605 S Poplar St., Casper, WY 82601, (307)237-5800 [22357]

Home-Bound Medical Care Inc., 2165 Sticer Cove, Ste. 1, Memphis, TN 38134, (901)386-5082 [18837]

Home Crafts, Inc., 760 Railroad Ave., West Babylon, NY 11704, (516)669-0141 [14487]

Home Diagnostics Inc., 2300 NW 55th Ct., Ft. Lauderdale, FL 33309, (954)677-9201 [18838]

Home Edco Home Care, 100 Dowd, Bangor, ME 04402-1156, (207)942-6505 [18839]

Home Entertainment Distributors, 250 Turnpike St., Canton, MA 02021-2747, (781)821-0087 [25235]

Home & Farm Center Inc., RR, Box 4490, Rutland, VT 05701, (802)773-3877 [15170]

Home Fasions Distributor, 655 Post Rd., Wells, ME 04090, (207)646-3437 [15530]

Home & Garden Innovations, 130 Intervale Rd., Burlington, VT 05401, (802)660-3506 [835]

Home Interiors and Gifts Inc., 4550 Spring Valley Rd., Dallas, TX 75244-3705, (972)386-1000 [15531]

Home Lumber Company Inc., PO Box 1037, Hazard, KY 41702, (606)436-3185 [7481]

Home Medical Supply Inc., 265 West 1230 North, Provo, UT 84604-2546, (801)374-8101 [18840]

Home/Office Communications Supply, 430 Woodruff Rd., No. 300, Greenville, SC 29607, (803)297-6340 [5639]

Home Oil Co., PO Box 608, Osceola, AR 72370, (870)563-6573 [22358]

Home Oil Company of Sikeston Inc., PO Box 810, Sikeston, MO 63801, (314)471-5141 [22359]

Home Oil and Gas Company Inc., PO Box 397, Henderson, KY 42419-0397, (502)826-3925 [22360]

Home Reverse Osmosis Systems, RR 1, Peru, IL 61354, (815)339-6300 [23212]

Home Safety Products, 2534 Washington Blvd., Baltimore, MD 21230-1407, (410)646-3470 [25236]

Home Service Oil Company Inc., 6910 Front St., Barnhart, MO 63012, (314)464-5266 [22361]

HomeBase Inc., 3345 Michelson Dr., Irvine, CA 92612-0650, (949)442-5000 [15532]

Homelite, Inc., 14401 Carowinds Blvd., Charlotte, NC 28241, (704)588-3200 [7482]

HomeReach Inc., 404 E Wilson Bridge Rd., No. G-H, Worthington, OH 43085, (614)786-7060 [18841]

Homespun Hosiery, 115 Industrial Park Rd., Lincolnton, NC 28092, (704)735-3754 [5463]

Homestead Book Co., 6101 22nd Ave. NW, Seattle, WA 98107, (206)782-4532 [3832]

Homier Distributing Inc., 84 Commercial Rd., Huntington, IN 46750-8800, (219)356-9477 [13756]

Hommer Lumber Co.; J.H., Rte. 253, Glasgow, PA 16644, (814)687-4211 [7483]

Hondo Boots, 6425 Boeing Dr., Ste. C3, El Paso, TX 79925-1052, (915)778-9481 [24765]

Hondo Guitar Co., PO Box 30819, Charleston, SC 29417, (803)763-9083 [25237]

Hone Oil Co., 2004 Wall Ave., Ogden, UT 84401, (801)394-2649 [22362]

Honey Bee Fashions, 3912 S Broadway Pl., Los Angeles, CA 90037, (213)231-3333 [5034]

Honey Fashions Ltd., 417 5th Ave., New York, NY 10016, (212)686-4424 [5035]

Honeywell H.P.G., 11953 Challenger Ct., Moorpark, CA 93021, (805)531-0001 [99]

Honeywell Protection Services, 6707 Carnegie, Cleveland, OH 44103, (216)361-6585 [24567]

Honeywell Sensing and Control, 11 W Spring, Freeport, IL 61032-4353, (815)235-6847 [8856]

Honolulu Aquarium & Pet Supplies, 94-486 Ukee St., Waipahu, HI 96797, (808)676-3646 [27150]

Honolulu Optical, 1450 Ala Moana Blvd., Ste. 2250, Honolulu, HI 96814-4665, (808)536-3959 [19361]

Honolulu Wholesale Jewelry Exchange, 1525 Kalakaua Ave., Honolulu, HI 96826, (808)942-7474 [17449]

Honor Snack Inc., 6846 S Canton Ave., Ste. 110, Tulsa, OK 74136, (918)496-2666 [11456]

Honsador Inc., 91-151 Malakole Rd., Ewa Beach, HI 96706, (808)682-2011 [7484]

Hoogovens Aluminium Corp., PO Box 2127, Secaucus, NJ 07096, (201)866-7776 [20044]

Hooleon Corp., 411 S 6th St Ste B, Cottonwood, AZ 86326, (520)634-7515 [6339]

Hooper Electronics Supply, 1917 6th St., PO Box 1787, Meridian, MS 39301, (228)432-0584 [8857]

Hoopers Candies, 4632 Telegraph Ave., No. 4632, Oakland, CA 94609-2022, (510)654-3373 [11457]

Hoople Farmers Grain Co., PO Box 140, Hoople, ND 58243, (701)894-6116 [18004]

Hoosier Company Inc., PO Box 681064, Indianapolis, IN 46268, (317)872-8125 [7485]

Hoosier Oil Inc., PO Box 458, Jasper, IN 47547, (812)482-3191 [22363]

Hoosier Screen Printer Inc., 6336 Travis Rd., Greenwood, IN 46143-8625, (317)422-8231 [5036]

The Hoover Co., 101 E Maple St., North Canton, OH 44720, (330)499-9200 [15171]

Hoover Instrument Service Inc., 401 N Home Rd., Mansfield, OH 44906, (419)529-3226 [24371]

Hoover Tractor and Engine Co., 224 N East St., Woodland, CA 95695, (530)662-8612 [836]

Ho'Owaiwia Farms, RR 1, Box 199A, Papaikou, HI 96781, (808)964-5222 [14889]

Hope Cooperative Creamery, PO Box 117, Hope, MN 56046, (507)451-2029 [11458]

Hope Group, PO Box 840, Northborough, MA 01532-0840, (508)393-7660 [16112]

Hopewell Valley Specialties, 1360 Clifton Ave., No. 331, Clifton, NJ 07012-1343, (609)275-7426 [11459]

Hopkins-Carter Company Inc., 3701 NW 21st St., Miami, FL 33142, (305)635-7377 [18521]

Hopkins-Gowen Oil Company Inc., 402 W Main St., Folkston, GA 31537, (912)496-2331 [22364]

Hopkins Sporting Goods Inc., 10000 Hickman Rd., Des Moines, IA 50325-5326, (515)270-0132 [23729]

Hopkinsville Elevator Co., PO Box 767, Hopkinsville, KY 42241, (502)886-5191 [11460]

Hopkinsville Milling Company Inc., PO Box 669, Hopkinsville, KY 42241-0669, (502)886-1231 [11461]

Hopper and Son Inc.; Ora B., 302 S 30th St., Phoenix, AZ 85034, (602)273-1338 [7486]

Hopper Specialty West, Inc., 2824 Vassar NE, Albuquerque, NM 87107, (505)884-1939 [16932]

Hopson Broker Inc.; Thomas R., PO Box 7295, Marietta, GA 30065, (404)578-2400 [7487]

Horizon, 5214 S 30th St., Phoenix, AZ 85040, (602)276-7700 [837]

Alphabetic Index

Horizon Business Systems, 2 Townsend W, Nashua, NH 03063-1277, (603)882-8471 [6340]

Horizon Distribution Inc., 226 S 1st St., Yakima, WA 98901, (509)453-3181 [13757]

Horizon High Reach, Inc., 222 Bergen Tpk., Ridgefield Park, NJ 07660, (201)440-6002 [7488]

Horizon High Reach Inc., 222 Bergen Tpk., Ridgefield Park, NJ 07660, (201)440-6002 [7489]

Horizon Impex, 430 Armor Cir. NE, Atlanta, GA 30324, (404)892-5544 [5037]

Horizon Medical Inc., 324 State St., St. Paul, MN 55107-1608, (612)298-0843 [18842]

Horizon Micro Distributors, 7180 SW Sandburg St., Portland, OR 97223, (503)684-5544 [6341]

Horizon Publishers & Distributors, Inc., 50 South 500 West, Bountiful, UT 84011-0490, (801)295-9451 [3833]

Horizon Trading Company, 1510 H St. NW, 5th Fl., Washington, DC 20005, (202)783-4455 [13136]

Horizon USA Data Supplies Inc., 4955 Energy Way, Reno, NV 89502-4105, (702)826-4392 [6342]

Horizon West Draperies, 4613 Palm Dr., La Canada, CA 91011-2012, (213)589-6242 [15533]

Horizons Marketing Group Inc., W 62 N 228 Washington Ave., Cedarburg, WI 53012, (414)375-1140 [4635]

Horizons Publishers and Dstbrs, PO Box 490, Bountiful, UT 84010, (801)295-9451 [3834]

Hormel Foods International Corp., 1 Hormel Pl., Austin, MN 55912, (507)437-5478 [11462]

Horn Co.; E.T., 16141 Heron Ave., La Mirada, CA 90638, (714)523-8050 [4418]

Horn EB Replacement Service, 429 Washington St., Boston, MA 02108-5278, (617)542-7752 [15534]

Horn EB Replacement Service, 429 Washington St., Boston, MA 02108-5278, (617)542-7752 [17450]

Horn Plastics Inc., 4207 12th Ave. NW, PO Box 5312, Fargo, ND 58105-5312, (701)282-7447 [22982]

Horn Seed Company Inc., 1409 NW Expy., Oklahoma City, OK 73118, (405)842-6607 [838]

Horner Electric Inc., 1521 E Washington St., Indianapolis, IN 46201, (317)639-4261 [16113]

Horner Equipment of Florida Inc., 5755 Power Line Rd., Ft. Lauderdale, FL 33309, (305)944-3851 [23730]

Horner Flooring Company Inc., S Maple Ave., PO Box 380, Dollar Bay, MI 49922, (906)482-1180 [9953]

Horns Inc., 8101 Grand Ave., Billings, MT 59106-1901, (406)652-0550 [13370]

Hornung's Pro Golf Sales Inc., PO Box 1078, Fond du Lac, WI 54935, (920)922-2640 [23731]

Horpestad Ranch Inc., PO Box 93, Lavina, MT 59046-0093, (406)636-4831 [18005]

Horrigan & Associates; E.C., 4509 Taylor Ln., Warrensville Heights, OH 44128, (216)831-8090 [16114]

Horsehead Resource Development Company Inc., 110 East 59th St., New York, NY 10022, (212)527-3003 [20547]

Horsepower Control System, 906 Lydia, Kansas City, MO 64106, (816)471-6362 [2761]

Horton Distributing Co.; Lew, PO Box 5023, Westborough, MA 01581, (508)366-7400 [23732]

Horton's Downeast Foods Inc., PO Box 430, Waterboro, ME 04087, (207)247-6900 [11463]

Horton's Smoked Seafoods, PO Box 430, Waterboro, ME 04087, (207)247-6900 [11463]

Hosey and Port Sales Corp., PO Box 275, Medfield, MA 02052-0275, (508)359-4115 [15172]

Hoshino U.S.A. Inc., 1726 Winchester Rd., Bensalem, PA 19020, (215)638-8670 [25238]

Hosiery Sales Inc., 10 E 34th St., New York, NY 10016, (212)889-2220 [5038]

Hosokawa Micron International Inc., 780 3rd Ave. Ste. 3201, New York, NY 10017, (212)826-3830 [16115]

Host Apparel Inc., 1430 Broadway, New York, NY 10018, (212)302-0800 [5039]

Hot Products, Inc.com, 7625 E Redfield Rd., Scottsdale, AZ 85260, (480)368-9490 [26525]

Hotho & Co., 916 Norwood, Ft. Worth, TX 76107, (817)335-1833 [3835]

Hotsy Cleaning Systems, 2428 W Central Ave., Missoula, MT 59801-6464, (406)549-5447 [25681]

Hotsy Corp., PO Box 3867, Englewood, CO 80155, (303)792-5200 [23213]

Houff Co.; Roy, 6200 S Oak Pk. Ave., Chicago, IL 60638, (312)586-8118 [14890]

Hougen Manufacturing Inc., PO Box 2005, Flint, MI 48501, (810)732-5840 [16116]

Houghton Chemical Corp., PO Box 307, Allston, MA 02134, (617)254-1010 [4419]

Houk Co. Inc.; Clarence H., 1650 E Main St., Rochester, NY 14609, (716)482-5880 [11464]

Houles USA Inc., 8584 Melrose Ave., Los Angeles, CA 90069, (310)652-6171 [26067]

House of Bianchi Inc., 181 Canal St., Lawrence, MA 01840-1802, (781)391-6111 [5040]

House of Carpets, Inc., 3737 Gateway W, El Paso, TX 79932, (915)562-9521 [9954]

House of Ceramics Inc., 1011 N Hollywood St., Memphis, TN 38108, (901)324-3851 [13371]

House of Clean Inc., PO Box 1203, Bozeman, MT 59771-1203, (406)587-5012 [4636]

House For Sports Inc., 4411 Common St., Lake Charles, LA 70605-4507, (318)477-0348 [23733]

House of Glass Inc., PO Box 228, Aberdeen, SD 57402-0228, (605)225-2010 [21458]

House of Guitars Corp., 645 Titus Ave., Rochester, NY 14617, (716)544-3500 [25239]

House-Hasson Hardware Inc., 3125 Waterplant Rd., Knoxville, TN 37914, (931)525-0471 [13758]

House of Hubcaps, PO Box 6038, Great Falls, MT 59406-6038, (406)761-3288 [2762]

House of Lloyd Inc., 11901 Grandview Rd., Grandview, MO 64030, (816)966-2222 [13372]

House Of Batteries, 16512 Burke Ln., Huntington Beach, CA 92647, (714)375-0222 [8858]

House of Pets Supplies, PO Box 185190, Ft. Worth, TX 76181, (817)595-0808 [27151]

House of Plastic Inc., 329 W 14 Mile Rd., Clawson, MI 48017-1926, (248)549-3400 [19362]

House of Raeford Farms, 405 W Burr Oak, Athens, MI 49011, (616)729-5411 [11465]

House of Representatives Inc., 228 Willis Rd., Sudbury, MA 01776, (978)443-4818 [6343]

House of Rock Inc., 1725 Merriam Ln., Kansas City, KS 66106, (913)432-5990 [839]

House of Schwan Inc., PO Box 782950, Wichita, KS 67278, (316)636-9100 [1763]

House of Wines Inc., 6500 Chillum Pl. NW, Washington, DC 20012-2136, (202)882-3333 [1764]

Housen and Co. Inc.; G., PO Box 687, Keene, NH 03431-0687, (603)357-4171 [1765]

Houseware Warehouse Inc., PO Box 1330, Edgewater, FL 32132-1330, (904)423-7848 [15535]

Houston Foods Co., 3501 Mount Prospect Rd., Franklin Park, IL 60131, (847)957-9191 [11466]

Houston Harvest Gift Products LLC, 3501 Mount Prospect Rd., Franklin Park, IL 60131, (847)957-9191 [11466]

Houston Moneycreek Cooperative, PO Box 775, Houston, MN 55943, (507)896-3121 [840]

Houston Peterbilt Inc., 10200 N Loop E, Houston, TX 77029, (713)495-6323 [2763]

Houston Stained Glass Supply, 2002 Brittmoore Rd., Houston, TX 77043-2209, (713)690-8844 [7490]

Houston-Starr Co., 300 Brushton Ave., Pittsburgh, PA 15221, (412)242-6000 [7491]

Houston Texaco Oil Co.; Harry, 215 NW Texas St., Idabel, OK 74745, (580)286-3066 [22365]

Houston Trane, 10555 Westpark Dr., Houston, TX 77042, (281)530-4000 [14488]

Houston Wholesale Electronics Inc., 5205 Telephone Rd., Houston, TX 77087 [8859]

Houston Wiper and Mill Supply Co., PO Box 24962, Houston, TX 77229-4962, (713)672-0571 [26844]

Houston Wire and Cable Co., 10201 N Loop E, Houston, TX 77028, (281)609-2200 [8860]

Hoven Inc.; Thompson Center, 6015 Benjamin Rd., 332, Tampa, FL 33634, (813)886-9328 [26526]

H.O.W. Train Distribution, 400 Industrial Dr., Omro, WI 54963, (920)685-2200 [26527]

Howard-Arnold Inc., 47 Railroad Ave., West Haven, CT 06516, (203)933-5636 [24131]

Howard Corp.; H.H., 4837 S Kedzie Ave., Chicago, IL 60632, (773)254-0400 [20045]

Howard County Equity Cooperative Inc., PO Box 489, Elma, IA 50628, (515)393-2260 [841]

Howard Electric Co., 4801 Bellevue Ave., Detroit, MI 48207-1394, (313)923-0430 [8861]

Howard Enterprises Inc., 545 Calle San Pablo, Camarillo, CA 93012-8550, (805)383-7444 [5640]

Howard Hall International, 777 W Putnam Ave., Greenwich, CT 06830, (203)532-2900 [19346]

Howard Invitations and Cards, PO Box 2009, Hazleton, PA 18201-0675, (717)875-3571 [21767]

Howard Sales Inc., 5742 W 79th St., Indianapolis, IN 46278, (317)872-8300 [21768]

Howard Tire Service Inc., 120 El Camino Real, Belmont, CA 94002, (415)592-3200 [2764]

Howden Fan Co., 1 Westinghouse Plz., HyDe Park, MA 02136, (617)361-3700 [16117]

Howe Company Inc.; George J., PO Box 269, Grove City, PA 16127, (724)458-9410 [11467]

Howell Co.; R.B., 6030 NE 112th Ave., Portland, OR 97220-1012, (503)227-3125 [26528]

Howell Corp., 1500 Howell Buliding 1111 Fanni, Houston, TX 77002-6923, (713)658-4000 [22366]

Howell Petroleum Products Inc., 499 Van Brunt St., Brooklyn, NY 11231, (718)855-4400 [22367]

Howland Electric Wholesale Co., PO Box 4338, El Monte, CA 91734, (818)444-0503 [8862]

Howmedica Mountain States, Inc., 1182 W 2450 S, No. A, Salt Lake City, UT 84119-8510, (801)484-8244 [18843]

Howtek Inc., 21 Park Ave., Hudson, NH 03051, (603)882-5200 [6344]

Hoxie Implement Company Inc., 933 Oak Ave., Hoxie, KS 67740, (785)675-3201 [842]

HP Marketing Co., 7340 S Alton Way, Ste. G, Englewood, CO 80112, (303)804-9566 [25240]

HP Products, 4220 Saguaro Trl., Indianapolis, IN 46268, (317)298-9950 [4637]

HPF L.L.C., 3275 Sunset Ln., Hatboro, PA 19040, (215)442-0960 [14127]

HPG Industries Inc., PO Box 1001, Palm Beach, FL 33480-1001, (561)712-8842 [7492]

HPM Building Supply, 380 Kanoelehua Ave., Hilo, HI 96720, (808)935-0875 [13759]

HPM Building Supply, 380 Kanoelehua Ave., Hilo, HI 96720, (808)966-5466 [27320]

HPS, Inc., 8020 Zionsville Rd., PO Box 68536, Indianapolis, IN 46268-0536, (317)875-9000 [22866]

HPS Inc., 8020 Zionsville Rd., Indianapolis, IN 46268, (317)875-9000 [21040]

HPS Office Systems, 8020 Zionsville Rd., Indianapolis, IN 46268, (317)875-9000 [21041]

HPS Printing Products, 8020 Zionsville Rd., PO Box 68536, Indianapolis, IN 46268-0536, (317)875-9000 [22866]

HPS Printing Products, 8020 Zionsville Rd., Indianapolis, IN 46268, (317)875-9000 [21042]

HRD International, 148 Clarkson Executive Park, Ballwin, MO 63011, (314)230-5004 [11468]

HRS Corp., 5009 Cleveland St., Virginia Beach, VA 23462-2503, (757)490-2446 [14489]

H.S. Industrial Equipment, 55 Mushroom Blvd., Rochester, NY 14623, (716)424-4800 [16933]

HSB Computer Laboratories, 34208 Aurora Rd., Ste. 207, Cleveland, OH 44139, (440)498-1356 [6345]

HSO Corp., 9595 153rd Ave. NE, Redmond, WA 98052, (425)822-1966 [18844]

HSS Group, PO Box 310, San Pedro, CA 90732, (310)547-1181 [18522]

Hsu's Ginseng Enterprises Inc., T6819 Hwy. W, PO Box 509, Wausau, WI 54402-0509, (715)675-2325 [11469]

HT & T Co., PO Box 4190, Hilo, HI 96720-0190, (808)933-7700 [20650]

HT and T Company, PO Box 4190, Hilo, HI 96720-0190, (808)933-7700 [2765]

http://www.swpaper.comm, PO Box 21270, Wichita, KS 67208-7270, (316)838-7755 [21944]

Hub City Distributors Inc., PO Box 5124, Trenton, NJ 08648, (609)844-9600 [1766]

Hub City Foods Inc., PO Box 490, Marshfield, WI 54449, (715)384-3191 [11470]

Hub Grain Company Inc., HCR 1, Box 62, Friona, TX 79035, (806)265-3215 [18006]

Hub Inc., PO Box 125, Tucker, GA 30085, (770)934-3101 [19954]

Hub/Industrial Mill Supply Co., 8813 Grow Dr., Pensacola, FL 32514, (850)484-8202 [16934]

Hub Material Co., PO Box 526, Canton, MA 02021, (781)821-1870 [8863]

Hub Tool and Supply Inc., PO Box 11647, Wichita, KS 67202, (316)265-9608 [16118]

Hubb; William, PO Box 7072, Incline Village, NV 89452-7072, (702)832-0102 [17451]

Hubbard-Hall Inc., 563 S Leonard St., Waterbury, CT 06708, (203)756-5521 [4420]

Hubbard Implement Inc., Hwy. 65 N, Hubbard, IA 50122, (515)864-2226 [4421]

Hubbard Industrial Supply Co., 901 W 2nd St., Flint, MI 48502, (810)234-8681 [16119]

Hubbard Milling Co., PO Box 8500, Mankato, MN 56002, (507)388-9400 [27152]

Hubbard Paint and Wallpaper, Rte. 28, Hyannis, MA 02601, (508)775-1568 [21459]

Hubbard Peanut Company Inc., PO Box 94, Sedley, VA 23878, (757)562-4081 [11471]

Hubbard Pipe and Supply Inc., PO Drawer 1570, Fayetteville, NC 28302, (910)484-0187 [23214]

Hubbard Printing Equipment, 22C Worldfair Dr., Somerset, NJ 08873, (732)271-8200 [25682]

Hubbard Wholesale Lumber Corp.; A.P., PO Box 14100, Greensboro, NC 27415, (336)275-1343 [27321]

Hubbell Mechanical Supply Co., PO Box 3813, GS, Springfield, MO 65808, (417)865-5531 [14490]

Huber Brewing Co., Inc.; Joseph, 1208 14th Ave., PO Box 277, Monroe, WI 53566, (608)325-3191 [1767]

Hubert Co., 9555 Dry Fork Rd., Harrison, OH 45030-1906, (513)367-8600 [11472]

Hubert Distributors Inc., 1200 Auburn Rd., Pontiac, MI 48342, (810)858-2340 [1768]

Huckleberry People Inc., 1021 Waverly St., Missoula, MT 59802, (406)721-6024 [11473]

Hudgins Inc.; T.F., PO Box 920901, Houston, TX 77292, (713)682-3651 [16935]

Hudson Company, PO Box 646, Winchester, KY 40392-0646, (606)744-7040 [7493]

Hudson Cos., 89 Ship St., Providence, RI 02903-4218, (401)274-2200 [7494]

Hudson Distributing Inc.; Mike, PO Box 808033, Petaluma, CA 94975-8033, (707)763-7388 [11474]

Hudson Glass Company Inc., 219 N Division St., Peekskill, NY 10566-2700, (914)737-2124 [7495]

Hudson Home Health Care Inc., 72 Pane Rd., Newington, CT 06111-5521, (860)667-4871 [18845]

Hudson Liquid Asphalts, Inc., 30 Shipyard St., Providence, RI 02903, (401)781-8200 [7496]

Hudson News Co., 1305 Paterson Plank Rd., North Bergen, NJ 07047, (201)867-3600 [3836]

Hudson Paper Co., 1341 W Broad St., Stratford, CT 06497, (203)378-0123 [21769]

Hudson Valley Paper Co., PO Box 1988, Albany, NY 12201, (518)471-5111 [21770]

Hudson Valley Tile Co., 470 Central Ave., Albany, NY 12206-2213, (518)489-8989 [9955]

Huesing Corp.; A.D., PO Box 3880, Rock Island, IL 61204, (309)788-5652 [24971]

Huet & Associates; Pat, 15657 Marble Rd., Northport, AL 35475, (205)339-5518 [23734]

Huff Paper Co., Rte. 322 & Creek Pkwy., Boothwyn, PA 19061, (610)497-5100 [21771]

Huffaker's Inc., PO Box 790290, San Antonio, TX 78279, (210)344-8373 [13760]

Huffman Equipment Co., Rte. 1, Palestine, TX 75801, (903)729-6951 [843]

Hughes-Calihan Corp., 4730 N 16th St., Phoenix, AZ 85016, (602)264-9631 [21043]

Hughes Company Inc. of Columbus, PO Box 280, 1200 W James St., Columbus, WI 53925, (920)623-2000 [24139]

Hughes Company Inc.; R.S., PO Box 25061, Sunnyvale, CA 94086, (408)739-3211 [24568]

Hughes Golf Inc.; Art, 1044 Ruritan Blvd., Chesapeake, VA 23324-3646, (804)443-5820 [23735]

Hughes-Peters Inc., 5030 Oaklawn Dr., Cincinnati, OH 45227-1484, (513)351-2000 [8864]

Hughes Supply Inc., 4915 Commercial Dr., Huntsville, AL 35816, (205)830-6986 [23215]

Hughes Supply Inc., PO Box 2273, Orlando, FL 32802, (407)841-4755 [23216]

Hugo Neu-Proler Co., 901 New Dock St., Terminal Island, CA 90731, (213)775-6626 [20046]

Hugo-Neu-Schnitzen East, 1 Jersey Ave., Jersey City, NJ 07302, (201)333-4300 [26845]

Hull Cooperative Association, PO Box 811, Hull, IA 51239, (712)439-2831 [11475]

Hull Lift Truck Inc., 28747 U.S 33 W, Elkhart, IN 46516, (219)293-8651 [16120]

Hultgren Implement Inc., PO Box 239, Ida Grove, IA 51445, (712)364-3105 [844]

Humac Engineering and Equipment Inc., PO Box 581519, Minneapolis, MN 55458, (612)541-0567 [7497]

Humboldt Industries, Inc., Humboldt Industrial Pk., Hazleton, PA 18201-9798, (717)384-5555 [27153]

Humboldt Petroleum Inc., PO Box 131, Eureka, CA 95502, (707)443-3069 [22368]

Humco Holding Group Inc., 7400 Alumax Dr., Texarkana, TX 75501, (903)831-7808 [4422]

Humke Co.; Ken R., PO Box 5128, Portland, OR 97208, (503)222-9741 [13761]

Hummelstein Iron and Metal Inc., PO Box 1580, Jonesboro, AR 72403, (870)932-8361 [26846]

Humphrey Company Inc.; P.D., 590 Main Rd., Tiverton, RI 02878, (401)624-8414 [7498]

Humphreys Coop Tipton Location, 500 S Broadway, Tipton, OK 73570, (580)667-5251 [18007]

Humphries Decorative Fabrics; Gabe, 330 N Neil St., Champaign, IL 61820, (217)352-5318 [26068]

Humpty Dumpty Potato Chip Co., PO Box 2247, Portland, ME 04116-2247, (207)883-8422 [11476]

Hundley Brokerage Company Inc., 613 River Dr., PO Box 838, Marion, IN 46952-0838, (765)662-0027 [11477]

Hundman Lumber Do-it Center Inc., 1707 Hamilton Rd., Bloomington, IL 61704, (309)662-0339 [7499]

Hungates Inc., 102 Hungate Dr., Greenville, NC 27858-8045, (919)756-9565 [26529]

Hunsdon; Vernon, RFD 2, Box 801, Chester, VT 05143-9801, (802)875-3624 [18008]

Hunt & Associates; Robert W., 2828 W Lake Sammamish Pkwy. SE, Bellevue, WA 98008-5645, (425)746-4186 [6346]

Hunt Cleaners Inc., PO Box 12, Cozad, NE 69130-0012, (308)784-3366 [4638]

Hunt Co., 4883 Powderhorn Ln, Westerville, OH 43081-4427, (614)891-7089 [26530]

Hunt Co.; C.P., 2406-10 Webster St., Oakland, CA 94604, (510)444-1333 [2766]

Hunt Co.; C.P., 2406-10 Webster St., Oakland, CA 94604, (510)444-1333 [2767]

Hunt Company Inc., 1600 Paramount Dr., Waukesha, WI 53186, (262)513-0800 [8865]

Hunt Electric Supply Co., 1600 Paramount Dr., Waukesha, WI 53186, (262)513-0800 [8865]

Hunt and Sons Inc., 5750 S Watt Ave., Sacramento, CA 95829, (916)363-5555 [22369]

Hunt Wesson Inc., 1351 Williams Ave., Memphis, TN 38104, (901)726-6929 [11478]

Huntco Steel Inc., PO Box 10507, Springfield, MO 65808, (417)881-6697 [20047]

Hunter Co., Inc., 3300 W 71st Ave., Westminster, CO 80030-5303, (303)427-4626 [18398]

Hunter and Company Inc., 1734 Tully Circle NE, Atlanta, GA 30329, (404)633-2661 [26069]

Hunter and Company of North Carolina, PO Box 2363, High Point, NC 27261, (336)883-4161 [15536]

Hunter Farms, 7303 Orr Rd., Charlotte, NC 28213, (704)596-3001 [11479]

Hunter Grain Co., PO Box 97, Hunter, ND 58048, (701)874-2112 [845]

Hunter The Typewriter Man, 314 S Federal Blvd., Riverton, WY 82501-4730, (307)856-3240 [21044]

Hunter Trading Corporation, PO Box 166, Westport, CT 06881, (203)254-7030 [27322]

Hunter, Walton and Company Inc., PO Box 525, South Plainfield, NJ 07080, (908)769-0099 [11480]

Hunters Inc., PO Box 17508, Honolulu, HI 96817, (808)841-8002 [21045]

Huntington County Farm Cooperative, PO Box 388, Huntington, IN 46750, (219)356-8110 [846]

Huntington Steel and Supply Company Inc., PO Box 1178, Huntington, WV 25714, (304)522-8218 [20048]

Huntington Wholesale Furniture Company Inc., 740 8th Ave., Huntington, WV 25715, (304)523-9415 [13137]

Huntleigh Technology Inc., 40 Christopher Way, Eatontown, NJ 07724-3327, (732)446-2500 [18846]

Huntleigh Technology Inc., 227 Rte. 33 E, Manalapan, NJ 07726, (732)446-2500 [19363]

Huntsville Beverage Co., 2327 Meridian St., Huntsville, AL 35811, (205)536-8966 [1769]

Huntsville/Redstone Paper Co., PO Box 3368, Huntsville, AL 35810, (256)851-2100 [21772]

Alphabetic Index

Huntsville/Redstone Paper Co., PO Box 3368, Huntsville, AL 35810, (205)851-2100 [16936]

Hunzicker Brothers Inc., PO Box 25248, Oklahoma City, OK 73125, (405)239-7771 [8866]

Hurley Chicago Company Inc., 12621 S Laramie Ave., Alsip, IL 60803-3225, (708)388-9222 [25683]

Huron Steel Company Inc., PO Box 34367, Detroit, MI 48234, (313)366-6400 [20049]

Huron Valley Steel Corp., 41000 Huron River Dr., Belleville, MI 48111, (734)697-3400 [20050]

Hurst Lumber Company Inc., 104 E Hurst Blvd., Hurst, TX 76053, (817)282-2519 [7500]

Hurst Office Suppliers Inc., 257 E Short St., Lexington, KY 40507, (606)255-4422 [21046]

Hurst Supply, PO Box 580490, Tulsa, OK 74158, (918)835-4441 [7501]

Hurwitz Brothers Iron and Metal Company Inc., PO Box 5, Buffalo, NY 14220, (716)823-2863 [20051]

Husch and Husch Inc., PO Box 160, Harrah, WA 98933, (509)848-2951 [847]

Huser-Paul Company Inc., 3636 Illinois Rd., Ft. Wayne, IN 46804, (219)432-0557 [26309]

Hush Puppies Co., 9341 Courtland Dr., Rockford, MI 49351, (616)866-5500 [24766]

Huskers Coop., PO Box 1129, Columbus, NE 68601, (402)563-3636 [11481]

Husky Food Products of Anchorage, 6361 Nielson Way, Ste. 116, Anchorage, AK 99518-1715, (907)563-1836 [11482]

Huss Implement Co., PO Box 68, La Motte, IA 52054, (319)773-2231 [848]

Huston Distributors Inc., Coopertown Rd., Delanco, NJ 08075, (609)764-1500 [23736]

Hutch & Son Inc., 300 N Main St., Evansville, IN 47711-5416, (812)425-7201 [8867]

Hutchings Brokerage Co., PO Box 11487, Mobile, AL 36671, (205)457-7641 [11483]

Hutchins Manufacturing Co., 49 N Lotus Ave., Pasadena, CA 91107, (818)792-8211 [16121]

Hutchinson & Associates, Inc.; Roger J., PO Box 194, Troy, MO 63379 [23737]

Hutchinson Coop Elevator, PO Box 158, Hutchinson, MN 55350, (612)587-4647 [18009]

Hutchinson Health Care Services, 803 E 30th Ave., Hutchinson, KS 67502-4341, (316)665-0528 [18847]

Hutchs TV and Appliance, 50 E Main St., Lehi, UT 84043-2142, (801)768-3461 [15173]

Hutson Enterprises, Inc.; D.H., PO Box 429, Waxhaw, NC 28173-0429, (704)843-2251 [23738]

Huttig Sash & Door Co., 2059 Shawano Ave., PO Box 10975, Green Bay, WI 54307-0975, (920)499-2117 [7502]

Hutton Communications Inc., 2520 Marsh Ln., Carrollton, TX 75006-2282, (972)417-0100 [5641]

HVAC Sales and Supply Co., 3940 Senator St., Memphis, TN 38118, (901)365-1137 [14491]

HVC Inc., 4600 Dues Dr., Cincinnati, OH 45246, (513)874-9261 [4423]

HVL Technical Services Inc., PO Box 36266, Birmingham, AL 35236-6266, (205)822-2940 [6347]

HWC Distribution Corp., 10201 N Loop E, Houston, TX 77028, (713)609-2100 [8868]

Hyatt Graphic Supply Co., 910 Main St., Buffalo, NY 14202, (716)884-8900 [25684]

Hyatt's Graphic Supply Company, Inc., 910 Main St., Buffalo, NY 14202, (716)884-8900 [25684]

Hybco USA, 333 S Mission Rd., Los Angeles, CA 90033-3718, (213)269-3111 [11484]

Hyde Marine Inc., 28045 Ranney Pkwy., Westlake, OH 44145-1188, (440)871-8000 [25685]

Hyde Products, Inc., 28045 Ranney Pkwy., Westlake, OH 44145-1188, (440)871-8000 [25685]

Hydra-Power, Inc., 14630 28th Ave. N, Minneapolis, MN 55447, (612)559-2930 [16122]

Hydra-Power Systems Inc., 12135 Esther Lama Dr., Ste. G, El Paso, TX 79938-7728, (915)860-9919 [16123]

Hydradyene Hydraulics Inc., 2537 I-85 S, Charlotte, NC 28208, (704)392-6185 [16124]

Hydradyne Hydraulics, 2537 I-85 S, Charlotte, NC 28208, (704)392-6185 [16125]

Hydraquip Corp., 1119 111th St., Arlington, TX 76011, (972)660-7230 [16126]

Hydraquip Corp., PO Box 925009, Houston, TX 77292-5009, (713)680-1951 [16127]

Hydraquip Corp., 618-A W Rhapsody, San Antonio, TX 78216, (210)341-8896 [16128]

Hydraulic and Air Controls, PO Box 28208, Columbus, OH 43228, (614)276-8141 [16129]

Hydraulic Controls Inc., 4700 San Pablo Ave., Emeryville, CA 94608, (510)658-8300 [16130]

Hydrite Chemical Co., PO Box 0948, Brookfield, WI 53008-0948, (414)792-1450 [4424]

Hydro-Abrasive Machining Inc., 8831 Miner St., Los Angeles, CA 90002, (323)587-1342 [16131]

Hydro Agri North America Inc., 100 N Tampa St., No. 3200, Tampa, FL 33602, (813)222-5700 [849]

Hydro Dyne Inc., PO Box 443, Massillon, OH 44648, (330)832-5076 [16132]

Hydro-Power Inc., PO Box 2181, Terre Haute, IN 47802-0181, (812)232-0156 [16133]

Hydro-Scape Products, Inc., 5805 Kearny Villa Rd., San Diego, CA 92123, (619)560-6611 [850]

Hygrade Food Products, 8400 Executive Ave., Philadelphia, PA 19153-3806, (215)365-8700 [11485]

Hynes Industries Inc., PO Box 2459, Youngstown, OH 44509, (216)799-3221 [20052]

Hyperbaric Oxygen Therapy Systems Inc., 3224 Hoover Ave., National City, CA 91950-7224, (619)336-2022 [18848]

HyperGlot Software Company Inc., PO Box 10746, Knoxville, TN 37939-0746, (423)558-8270 [6348]

Hyperox Technologies, 2180 Garnet Ave., Ste. 2-G5, San Diego, CA 92109, (619)490-0193 [23739]

Hyster MidEast, 3480 Spring Grove Ave., Cincinnati, OH 45223, (513)541-0401 [16134]

Hyster New England, Inc., 358 Second Ave., Waltham, MA 02451, (781)890-7950 [16135]

Hyundai Motor America, PO Box 20850, Fountain Valley, CA 92728-0850, (714)965-3000 [20651]

I-90 Auto Salvage & Sales, Munich & Vienna, Butte, MT 59701, (406)723-5711 [2768]

I-O Corp., 2256 South 3600 West, Salt Lake City, UT 84119-9965, (801)973-6767 [6349]

I Play, 6 Chiles Ave., Asheville, NC 28803, (704)254-9236 [5041]

I See Optical Co., 44 W Church St., Blackwood, NJ 08012, (609)227-9300 [19364]

I. Wanna Distribution Company Inc., 2540 Shader Rd., Orlando, FL 32804, (407)292-0299 [11486]

The Iams Co., 7250 Poe Ave., Dayton, OH 45414-2572, (937)898-7387 [27154]

IBA Protection Services, 701 E Hyde Park Blvd., Inglewood, CA 90302-2507, (310)674-7000 [24569]

Iberia Tile, 4221 Ponce De Leon Blvd., Coral Gables, FL 33146, (305)446-0222 [9956]

Iberia Tile, 1711 N Powerline Rd., Pompano Beach, FL 33069, (954)978-8453 [9957]

Iberia Tiles Inc., 2975 NW 77th Ave., Miami, FL 33122, (305)591-3880 [9958]

IBS Co., 18834 SE 42nd St., Issaquah, WA 98027-9366, (425)643-1917 [24778]

IBT Inc., PO Box 2982, Shawnee Mission, KS 66201, (913)677-3151 [16136]

IBT Inc., 4323 Woodson, Woodson Terrace, MO 63134, (314)428-4284 [16137]

ICC Instrument Company Inc., 1483 E Warner Ave., Santa Ana, CA 92705, (714)540-4966 [16138]

ICE Export Sales Corp., 36 Maple Ave., PO Box 11, Manhasset, NY 11030, (516)365-0011 [7503]

Ice Systems & Supplies Inc., 163 E Mount Gallant Rd., Rock Hill, SC 29730-8977, (803)324-8791 [14492]

ICEE Distributors Inc., 1513 Swan Lake Rd., Bossier City, LA 71111-5335, (318)746-4895 [14493]

ICEE-USA Corp., 4701 Airport Dr., Ontario, CA 91761-7817, (909)467-4233 [24972]

ICF Gropu Showroom, 920 Broadway, New York, NY 10010 [13138]

ICG, 30481 Whipple Rd., Union City, CA 94587, (510)471-7000 [6350]

Ichikoh America Inc., 41650 Gardenbrook Rd., Ste. 120, Novi, MI 48375-1319, (248)380-7878 [2769]

Ichikoh Manufacturing Inc., 6601 Midland, Shelbyville, KY 40065, (502)633-4936 [15537]

ICI Dulux Paint Centers, 74-5599 Alapa St., Kailua Kona, HI 96740, (808)329-2766 [21460]

ICI Dulux Paints, 404-406 S Adams St., Peoria, IL 61602, (309)673-3761 [21461]

ICI Dulux Paints, 6100 Garfield Ave., Commerce, CA 90040, (323)727-2000 [21462]

ICI Fluoropolymers, PO Box 15391, Wilmington, DE 19850-5391, (302)363-4746 [4425]

ICI Paints, 925 Euclid Ave., Cleveland, OH 44115, (216)344-8000 [21463]

Icicle Seafoods Inc. Port Chatham Div., 4019 21st Ave. W, Seattle, WA 98107, (206)783-8200 [11487]

ICL Inc., 25902 Towne Centre Dr., Foothill Ranch, CA 92610, (949)855-5505 [6351]

Ico Rally Corp., PO Box 51350, Palo Alto, CA 94303, (650)856-9900 [8869]

Icon Office Solutions, PO Box 649, Exton, PA 19341-0649, (215)296-8600 [21047]

ICS-Executone Telecom Inc., 125 Highpower Rd., Rochester, NY 14623, (716)427-7000 [5642]

ICS Intercounty Supply, 255 S Regent St., Port Chester, NY 10573, (914)939-4350 [23217]

I.D. Foods, Inc., 1121 S Claiborne Ave., New Orleans, LA 70125, (504)523-6882 [11488]

IDA Inc., PO Box 13347, Memphis, TN 38113-0347, (901)757-8056 [7504]

Idaho Barber & Beauty Supply Inc., PO Box 8044, Boise, ID 83707-2044, (208)376-0821 [14128]

Idaho Coin Galleries, 302 Main Ave. N, Twin Falls, ID 83301-5956, (208)733-8593 [17452]

Idaho Livestock Auction Co., PO Box 2187, Idaho Falls, ID 83403-2187, (208)522-7211 [18010]

Idaho Outdoor Equipment, PO Box 8005, Boise, ID 83707-2005, (208)342-3063 [26070]

Idaho Souvenir, 8004 Woodlark, Boise, ID 83709, (208)362-9300 [13373]

Idaho Supreme Potatoes Inc., PO Box 246, Firth, ID 83236-0246, (208)346-6841 [11489]

IDE-Interstate Inc., 1500 New Horizon Blvd., Amityville, NY 11701, (516)957-8300 [14129]

Ideal American Dairy, PO Box 4038, Evansville, IN 47711, (812)424-3351 [11490]

Ideal Appliance Parts Inc., PO Box 7007, Metairie, LA 70010-7007, (504)888-4232 [15174]

Ideal Chemical and Supply Co., 4025 Air Park St., Memphis, TN 38118, (901)363-7720 [4426]

Ideal Computer Services Inc., 113 Rickenbacker Cir., Livermore, CA 94550, (925)447-4747 [6352]

Ideal Division, 3200 Parker Dr., St. Augustine, FL 32095, (904)829-1000 [13762]

Ideal Foreign Books, Inc., 132-10 Hillside Ave., Richmond Hill, NY 11418, (718)297-7477 [3837]

Ideal Foreign Books Inc., 132-10 Hillside Ave., Richmond Hill, NY 11418, (718)297-7477 [3838]

Ideal Machinery and Supply Co., 109 E Main St., Plainville, CT 06062, (860)747-1651 [16139]

Ideal Optics Inc., 4000 Cumberland Parkway Blvd., Ste. 500, Atlanta, GA 30339, (404)432-0048 [19365]

Ideal Pet Supplies, 8 Baldorioty St., PO Box 83, Naguabo, PR 00718, (787)874-4000 [27155]

Ideal Sales and Distributing Company Inc., 6811 E Slausen Ave., City of Commerce, CA 90040, (213)726-8031 [2770]

IDEAL Scanners & Systems, Inc., 11810 Parklawn Dr., Rockville, MD 20852, (301)468-0123 [21048]

Ideal Supply Co., 445 Communipaw Ave., Jersey City, NJ 07304, (201)333-2600 [23218]

Ideal Tile Co., Mt. Laurel, Inc, 1316 Rte. 73, Mt. Laurel, NJ 08054, (609)722-9393 [9959]

Ideal Wine & Spirits Co., Inc., 3890 Mystic Valley Pkwy., Medford, MA 02155, (781)395-3300 [1770]

Idec, 1175 Elko Dr., Sunnyvale, CA 94089, (408)747-0550 [8870]

Idek North America, 1 Ivy Brook Blvd., Ste. 120, Ivyland, PA 18974, (215)957-6543 [6354]

IDG, 3950 Virginia Ave., Cincinnati, OH 45227, (513)271-0618 [16937]

IDM Satellite Division Inc., 311 F St., ChuLa Vista, CA 91910, (619)422-1155 [5643]

IDN-ACME, Inc., PO Drawer 13748, New Orleans, LA 70185, (504)837-7315 [24570]

IDS, PO Box 799, St. Joseph, MI 49085-0799, (616)428-8400 [18856]

IEEI, 110 Agate Ave., Newport Beach, CA 92662, (949)673-2943 [6353]

I.E.F. Corp., PO Box 1088, Spanaway, WA 98387, (253)535-5289 [14891]

IEI Investments Inc., 1630 N Meridian St., Indianapolis, IN 46202-1496, (317)926-3351 [16938]

I.F. Optical Co. Inc., 2812 W Touhy Ave., Chicago, IL 60645, (773)761-8969 [19366]

Ifeco Inc., 1776 Commerce Ave., Boise, ID 83705-5309, (208)344-3574 [24140]

IGA Inc., 8725 W Higgins Rd., Chicago, IL 60631, (312)693-4520 [11491]

IGC Energy Inc., 1630 N Meridian St., Indianapolis, IN 46202-1496, (317)926-3351 [16939]

IGI, 85 Old Eagle School Rd., PO Box 383, Wayne, PA 19087, (610)687-9030 [22370]

IGI Div., 85 Old Eagle School Rd., PO Box 383, Wayne, PA 19087, (610)687-9030 [22370]

iGo, 9393 Gateway Dr., Reno, NV 89511-8910, (775)746-6140 [8871]

IHC Services Inc., 1624-E Cross Beam Dr., Charlotte, NC 28217, (704)357-1211 [7505]

IIRI International Inc., 120 Webster St., Pawtucket, RI 02861-1086, (401)272-8600 [5042]

Iiyama North America, Inc., 1 Ivy Brook Blvd., Ste. 120, Ivyland, PA 18974, (215)957-6543 [6354]

IJ Co., PO Box 51890, Knoxville, TN 37950-1890, (423)970-3200 [11492]

IJ Co. Tri-Cities Div., 2722 S Roan St., Johnson City, TN 37601-7588 [11493]

I.J. Cos., PO Box 51890, Knoxville, TN 37950-1890, (423)970-7800 [11494]

I.J.K. Sales Corp., 935 Cliffside Ave., North Woodmere, NY 11581, (516)791-9129 [18399]

IKO Notions, 4945 Lima St., Denver, CO 80239, (303)371-0660 [26071]

Ikon Office Solutions, PO Box 5615, Greenville, SC 29606, (864)281-5400 [21049]

Ikon Office Solutions, 12100 SW Garden Pl., Portland, OR 97223, (503)620-2800 [21050]

IKON Office Solutions Inc., PO Box 834, Valley Forge, PA 19482-0834, (610)296-8000 [21051]

IKR Corporation, 17 S Briar Hollow Ln., Ste. 202, Houston, TX 77027, (713)627-3520 [16140]

Ilani Shoes Ltd., 47 W 34th St., New York, NY 10001, (212)947-5830 [24767]

Ilani Shoes Ltd., 47 W 34th St., New York, NY 10001, (212)947-5830 [5043]

Ilapak Inc., 105 Pheasant Run, Newtown, PA 18940, (215)579-2900 [16141]

ILHWA, 91 Terry St., Belleville, NJ 07109, (973)759-1996 [11495]

Illco Inc., PO Box 1330, Aurora, IL 60507, (708)892-7904 [14494]

Illini F.S. Inc., 1509 E University St., Urbana, IL 61802, (217)384-8300 [22371]

Illinois Agricultural Association, 1701 Towanda Ave., Bloomington, IL 61701, (309)557-2111 [851]

Illinois Auto Electric Co., 656 County Line Rd., Elmhurst, IL 60126, (630)833-4300 [16142]

Illinois Blueprint Corp., 800 SW Jefferson Ave., Peoria, IL 61605, (309)676-1306 [25686]

Illinois Carbide Tool Co., 1322 Belvidere Rd., Waukegan, IL 60085, (847)244-1110 [16143]

Illinois Fruit and Produce Corp., 1 Quality Ln., Streator, IL 61364, (815)673-3311 [11496]

Illinois News Service, 1301 SW Washington St., Peoria, IL 61602, (309)673-4549 [4000]

Illinois Oil Products Inc., 321 24th St., Rock Island, IL 61201, (309)786-4474 [22372]

Illinois Roses Ltd., PO Box 184, Pana, IL 62557, (217)562-2421 [14795]

Illmo Rx Service Inc., PO Box 14520, St. Louis, MO 63178, (314)434-6858 [19367]

Illycaffe Espresso USA Inc., 15455 N Greenway Hayden Loop, Ste. 7, Scottsdale, AZ 85260-1611, (602)951-0468 [11497]

Ilva USA Inc., 10 Bank St., White Plains, NY 10606, (914)428-6010 [20053]

IM/EX Port Inc., 4417 Provens Dr., Akron, OH 44319, (330)896-3056 [16144]

Im-Pruv-All, 2660 US Highway 50 E, Carson City, NV 89701, (775)883-1314 [2771]

IMA Tool Distributors, 280 Midland Ave., Saddle Brook, NJ 07663-6404, (201)791-8787 [13763]

Image Industries Inc., PO Box 5555, Armuchee, GA 30105, (706)235-8444 [26847]

Image Processing Solutions, 500 W Cummings Park, Woburn, MA 01801-6503, (781)932-9644 [6355]

Imagetech RICOH Corp., 192 Nickerson St., No. 200, Seattle, WA 98109, (206)298-1600 [21052]

Imagex Inc., 6845 Elm St., No. 305, McLean, VA 22101, (703)883-2500 [6356]

Imagination & Co., 1575 Cattleman Rd., Sarasota, FL 34232, (941)371-5238 [7506]

Imaging Concepts Inc., 8237 Hermitage Rd., Richmond, VA 23228-3031, (804)261-1921 [18849]

Imaging Technologies, 2120 Rittenhouse, Des Moines, IA 50321, (515)953-7306 [21053]

Imar Industries Inc., 13108 Greenwood Rd., Minnetonka, MN 55343-8693, (612)938-2352 [5044]

IMCO Recycling Inc., 5215 N O'Connor Blvd., No. 940, Irving, TX 75039, (972)869-6575 [26848]

Imex Corp., 4846 Cranswick, Houston, TX 77041, (713)467-6899 [5045]

Imge Guided Technologies, Inc., 5710 B Flatiron Pky., Boulder, CO 80301, (303)447-0248 [6357]

Imlay City Total Oil Inc., 15750 N East St., Lansing, MI 48906, (517)372-2220 [22373]

Imlers Poultry, 3421 Beale Ave., Altoona, PA 16601-1311, (814)943-5563 [11498]

Impact Christian Books Inc., 332 Leffingwell Ave., Ste. 101, Kirkwood, MO 63122, (314)822-3309 [3839]

Imperia Foods Inc., 234 St. Nicholas Ave., South Plainfield, NJ 07080, (908)756-7333 [11499]

Imperial Beverage Co., 4124 Manchester, Kalamazoo, MI 49001-3275, (616)382-4200 [1771]

Imperial Commodities Corp., 17 Battery Pl., New York, NY 10004-1102, (212)837-9400 [11500]

Imperial Delivery Service Inc., 303 Smith St., East Farmingdale, NY 11735, (516)752-2255 [3840]

Imperial Display Co., 1049 Main St., Wheeling, WV 26003-2704, (304)233-0711 [26531]

Imperial Distributors Inc., 33 Sword St., Auburn, MA 01501, (508)756-5156 [14130]

Imperial Foods, Inc., PO Box 217, Smyrna, TN 37167, (615)459-2519 [11184]

Imperial Frozen Foods Company Inc., 45 N Station Plz., Great Neck, NY 11022, (516)487-0670 [11501]

Imperial Pet Products, PO Box 157, Walnutport, PA 18088, (215)377-8008 [27156]

Imperial Pools Inc., Cornfield Rd., Buxton, ME 04093, (207)929-4800 [23740]

Imperial Toy Corp., 2060 E 7th St., Los Angeles, CA 90021, (213)489-2100 [26532]

Imperial Trading Co., PO Box 23508, New Orleans, LA 70183-0508, (504)733-1400 [26310]

Imperial Wax and Chemical Company Inc., 2065 Robb Rd., Walnut Creek, CA 94596-6246, (925)825-9121 [23741]

Impex International, PO Box 214067, Auburn Hills, MI 48321, (248)852-4032 [16940]

Implant Dynamic, 37724 Hills Tech Dr., Farmington Hills, MI 48331-3416, (248)489-4290 [18850]

Implement Sales Company Inc., 1574 Stone Ridge Dr., Stone Mountain, GA 30083, (770)368-8648 [852]

Implement Sales LLC, 1574 Stone Ridge Dr., Stone Mountain, GA 30083, (770)368-8648 [852]

Impo International Inc., PO Box 639, Santa Maria, CA 93456, (805)922-7753 [5046]

ImpoGlaztile, 2852 W 167th St., PO Box 220, Markham, IL 60426-0220, (708)333-1800 [9960]

Import Export Management Service Inc., 2205 Royal Lane, Dallas, TX 75229, (972)620-9545 [21054]

Import Leather Inc., PO Box 1070, Exeter, NH 03833, (603)778-8484 [18400]

Import Ltd., 5249 N 35th St., Milwaukee, WI 53209, (414)461-1240 [17453]

Import Tile Co., 611 Hearst Ave., Berkeley, CA 94710, (510)843-5744 [9961]

Import Warehouse Inc., PO Box 29102, Dallas, TX 75229-0102, (972)241-4818 [13374]

Import Wholesale Co., 11351 Harry Hines Blvd., Dallas, TX 75229, (972)247-3772 [17454]

Imported Books, 2025 W Clarendon Ave., PO Box 4414, Dallas, TX 75208, (214)941-6497 [3841]

Importmex, 4 Harness Ct., Ste. 101, Baltimore, MD 21208-1352, (410)484-9996 [13375]

Imports International, 3670 Rosalinda Dr., Reno, NV 89503-1813, (702)786-5820 [13139]

Imports Wholesale, 3900 Paradise Rd., Ste. V, Las Vegas, NV 89109-0930, (702)369-1040 [5047]

Impression Technology Inc., 4270 Dow Rd., Ste. 213, Melbourne, FL 32934, (407)254-8700 [6358]

Impulse Merchandisers Inc., PO Box 77030, Baton Rouge, LA 70879-0809, (504)752-4800 [2772]

IMR Corp., PO Box 1690, Harvey, LA 70059-1690, (504)362-9888 [24768]

Imrex Company Inc., 307 E Shore Rd., Great Neck, NY 11023, (516)466-5210 [6359]

IMS Systems, Inc., 12081-B Tech Rd., Silver Spring, MD 20904, (301)680-0006 [25241]

IMT Corp., 330 Greco Ave., Ste. 103, Coral Gables, FL 33146-1800, (305)441-7680 [16145]

IMT Inc., 2313 North Shore Rd., Bellingham, WA 98226, 800-248-1752 [16146]

Imtra Corp., 30 Samuel Barnet Blvd., New Bedford, MA 02745, (508)995-7000 [18523]

In Products Inc., 4601 W 47th St., Chicago, IL 60632-4801, (773)585-9779 [15538]

InaCom Corp., 10810 Farnam Dr., Omaha, NE 68154, (402)392-3900 [6360]

InaCom Information Systems, 393 Inverness Dr. S, Englewood, CO 80112-5816, (303)754-5004 [6361]

Inagra, Inagra, Inc., PO Box 5153, New Britain, PA 18901-0939, (215)230-3476 [862]

Inaqua International, 3180 NW 72nd Ave., Miami, FL 33122-1316, (941)377-1889 [25687]

Inca Corp., 1648 W 134th St., Gardena, CA 90249, (310)808-0001 [8872]

Incentive Associates Inc., 6803 W 64th St., Ste. 114, Shawnee Mission, KS 66202, (913)722-2848 [15539]

InControl Solutions, 8285 SW Nimbus Ave Ste. 148, Beaverton, OR 97008, (541)574-4802 [6362]

Incorporated Business Interiors Inc., 2271 W 205th St., Ste. 101, Torrance, CA 90501, (310)257-0200 [13140]

Ind-Co Cable TV Inc., PO Box 3799, Batesville, AR 72503-3799, (870)793-4174 [8873]

Indeck Power Equipment Co., 1111 Willis Ave., Wheeling, IL 60090, (708)541-8300 [16147]

Independent Bakers' Cooperative, 300 Washington St., Chicago, IL 60606, (312)726-4606 [11502]

Independent Distribution Services Inc., 3000 Waterview Ave., Baltimore, MD 21230, (410)539-3000 [15175]

Independent Distributors of America Inc., 100 1st St., Lemont, IL 60439, (708)972-1919 [24141]

Independent Drug Co., 235 Northeast Ave., Tallmadge, OH 44278-1492, (330)633-9411 [19368]

Independent Foundry Supply Co., 6463 E Canning St., Los Angeles, CA 90040, (323)725-1051 [16941]

Independent Pet Co-op, Attn: Rick Newton, 10466 Tomkinson Dr., Scotts, MI 49088, (616)327-2257 [27157]

Independent Photocopy Inc., 14455 Jefferson Davis Hwy., Woodbridge, VA 22191, (703)494-5356 [21055]

Independent Publishers Group Inc., 814 N Franklin St., Chicago, IL 60610, (312)337-0747 [3842]

Independent Rental, Inc., 2020 S Cushman St., Fairbanks, AK 99701, (907)456-6595 [853]

Independent Steel Co., PO Box 472, Valley City, OH 44280-0472, (216)225-7741 [20054]

Independent Telephone Network Inc., 8741 Shirley Ave., Northridge, CA 91324, (818)701-5100 [5644]

Index 53 Optical, St. Stephen, PO Box 1111, St. Cloud, MN 56302, (320)252-9380 [19369]

India Hand Arts, 150 W Queen Ln., PO Box 12271, Philadelphia, PA 19144-0371, (215)848-4040 [5048]

Indian Den Traders, 1208 E Hwy. 66, Gallup, NM 87301-6513, (505)722-4141 [17455]

Indian Industries Inc., PO Box 889, Evansville, IN 47706, (812)467-1200 [23742]

Indian Mission Jewelry, PO Box 230, Prewitt, NM 87045-0230, (505)876-2721 [17456]

Indian Trade Center Inc., 3306 E Hwy. 66, Gallup, NM 87301, (505)722-6666 [17457]

Indiana Auto Auction Inc., PO Box 8039, Ft. Wayne, IN 46898, (219)489-2776 [20652]

Indiana Botanic Gardens, 3401 W 37th Ave., Hobart, IN 46342, (219)947-2912 [11503]

Indiana Carbon Company Inc., 3164 N Shadeland Ave., Indianapolis, IN 46226, (317)547-9621 [21056]

Indiana Concession Supply Inc., 2402 Shadeland Ave., Indianapolis, IN 46219, (317)353-1667 [11504]

Indiana Farm Systems Inc., PO Box 277, Russiaville, IN 46979, (765)883-5557 [854]

Indiana Oxygen Co., PO Box 78588, Indianapolis, IN 46278-0588, (317)290-0003 [16942]

Indiana Recreation Equipment & Design, Inc., 127 S Main St., PO Box 510, Monticello, IN 47960, (219)583-6483 [23743]

Indiana Seed Co., PO Box 1745, Noblesville, IN 46060, (317)773-5813 [855]

Indiana Soft Water Service Inc., 6901 E 38th St., Indianapolis, IN 46226, (317)925-6484 [15176]

Indiana Supply Corp., 3835 E 21st St., Indianapolis, IN 46218, (317)359-5451 [14495]

Indiana Supply Corp., 3835 E 21st St., Indianapolis, IN 46218, (317)359-5451 [16943]

Indiana Tees, 7260 Winton Dr., Indianapolis, IN 46268, (317)387-8600 [5049]

Indiana Wholesalers Inc., PO Box 5245, Evansville, IN 47716, (812)476-1373 [15540]

Indianapolis Auto Auctions Inc., 2950 E Main St., Plainfield, IN 46168-2723, (317)298-9700 [20578]

Indianapolis Belting & Supply, 8900 E 30th St., Indianapolis, IN 46219, (317)898-2411 [16148]

Indianapolis Coca-Cola Bottling Company Inc., 5000 W 25th St., Speedway, IN 46224, (317)243-3771 [24973]

Indianapolis Coca-Cola Bottling Company Inc./Richmond Div., 1700 Dana Pkwy., Richmond, IN 47374, (765)966-7687 [24974]

Indianapolis Fruit Company, Inc., 4501 Massachusetts Ave., Indianapolis, IN 46218, (317)546-2425 [11505]

Indianapolis Materials Recycling Facility, 832 Langsdale Ave., Indianapolis, IN 46202, (317)926-5492 [26849]

Indianapolis Welding Supply Inc., 315 W McCarty St., Indianapolis, IN 46225, (317)632-2446 [16944]

INDIV, PO Box 1275, Springfield, MO 65801, (417)862-2673 [863]

Indmar Products Industrial Div., 5400 Old Millington Rd., Millington, TN 38053, (901)353-9930 [18524]

Indresco, Inc., PO Box 650, Pine Brook, NJ 07058-0650, (914)969-6681 [16945]

Indurall Coatings Inc., PO Box 2371, Birmingham, AL 35201, (205)324-9588 [21464]

Indus-Tool, 300 N Elizabeth St., 2N, Chicago, IL 60607, (312)226-2473 [8874]

Indus-Tool Inc; Go For It Products; Yates & Bird; Motloid., 300 N Elizabeth St., 2N, Chicago, IL 60607, (312)226-2473 [318]

Indus-Tool Inc., 300 N Elizabeth St., 2N, Chicago, IL 60607, (312)226-2473 [2773]

Indusco, Ltd., 210 Midstream, Brick, NJ 08724, (732)899-2660 [8875]

Industrial Adhesives Inc., PO Box 2489, Eugene, OR 97402, (541)683-6677 [4427]

Industrial Battery Engineering Inc., 9121 De Garmo Ave., Sun Valley, CA 91352, (818)767-7067 [8876]

Industrial Belt & Transmissions, 4061 McCollum Ct., PO Box 32215, Louisville, KY 40232, (502)456-6100 [16149]

Industrial Belting & Transmission, Inc., 4061 McCollum Ct., PO Box 32215, Louisville, KY 40232, (502)456-6100 [16149]

Industrial Communications Co., G 12157 N Saginaw, Clio, MI 48420-1036, (810)686-4990 [5645]

Industrial Development & Procurement, 4000 Town Center, Ste. 480, Southfield, MI 48075, (248)358-5383 [16150]

Industrial Disposal Co., 1423 S Jackson St., Louisville, KY 40208-2777, (502)638-9000 [26850]

Industrial Distribution Group, Inc., 2500 Royal Pl., Tucker, GA 30084-3035, (770)243-9000 [16946]

Industrial Distributors, PO Box 1061, Lewiston, ME 04243-1061, (207)782-4116 [7507]

Industrial Electrics Inc., 1018 Arnold St., Greensboro, NC 27405-7102, (919)275-9111 [8877]

Industrial Electronic Supply Inc., 2321 Texas Ave., Shreveport, LA 71103, (318)222-9459 [8878]

Industrial Engineering Equipment Co., PO Box 4770, Davenport, IA 52808, (319)323-3233 [16553]

Industrial Environmental Products Inc., 4035 Nine-Mcfarland Dr., Alpharetta, GA 30022, (404)475-3993 [4428]

Industrial Fasteners Corp., 7 Harbor Park Dr., Port Washington, NY 11050, (516)484-4900 [13764]

Industrial Fuel Co., 25 1st Ave., NE, Hickory, NC 28601, (828)324-7887 [22374]

Industrial Fumigant Co., 19745 W 159th Street, PO Box 1200, Olathe, KS 66062, (913)782-7600 [856]

Industrial Gas and Supply Co., 518 Alabama St., Bristol, TN 37620, (615)968-1536 [16947]

Industrial Liaison Inc., 17835 Sky Park Cir. C, Irvine, CA 92614, (949)261-7079 [18525]

Industrial Management Systems Corp., PO Box 107, Worthington, CO 43085, (614)258-2580 [7508]

Industrial Material Corp., 7701 Harborside Dr., Galveston, TX 77554, (409)744-4538 [20055]

Industrial Metal Processing Inc., PO Box 578, Lyman, SC 29365-0578, (864)233-2747 [20056]

Industrial Metals of the South Inc., PO Box 10507, New Orleans, LA 70112, (504)586-9191 [20057]

Industrial Motor Supply Inc., PO Box 4128, Harrisburg, PA 17111-0128, (717)564-0550 [7509]

Industrial Municipal Equipment Inc., PO Box 369, West Islip, NY 11795-0369, (516)567-9000 [16151]

Industrial Paper Corp., 300 Villanova Dr. SW, Atlanta, GA 30336, (404)346-5800 [21773]

Industrial Paper & Plastic Products Company Inc., 240 Austin Rd., Waterbury, CT 06705, (203)753-2196 [21774]

Industrial Parts Distributors Inc., 522 Locust St., Kansas City, MO 64106, (816)471-8049 [2774]

Industrial Pipe & Steel, 9936 Rush, South el Monte, CA 91733-2637, (626)443-9467 [16152]

Industrial Plastics Inc., 740 S 28th St., Washougal, WA 98671, (253)835-2129 [22983]

Industrial Power Sales Inc., 8461 Garvey Dr., Raleigh, NC 27616, (919)876-6115 [13765]

Industrial Products Co., 105 Boswell St., Mt. Pleasant, TN 38474, (931)379-3227 [7510]

Industrial Rubber Products Co., PO Box 2348, Charleston, WV 25328, (304)344-1791 [24282]

Industrial Safety Supply Co., 176 Newington Rd., West Hartford, CT 06107, (860)233-9881 [16948]

Industrial Safety Supply Co. Interex Div., 176 Newington Rd., West Hartford, CT 06110, (860)233-9881 [24571]

Industrial Sales Company Inc., PO Box 2148, Wilmington, NC 28402, (919)763-5126 [23219]

Industrial Service Co., PO Box 2164, Providence, RI 02905-0164, (401)467-6454 [22867]

Industrial Services of America Inc., PO Box 32428, Louisville, KY 40232, (502)368-1661 [25688]

Industrial Soap Co., 2930 Market St., St. Louis, MO 63103, (314)241-6363 [4639]

Industrial Solvents Corp., 411 Theodore Fremd Ave., Rye, NY 10580, (914)967-7771 [4429]

Industrial Source, PO Box 2330, Eugene, OR 97402, (541)344-1438 [16153]

Industrial Steel and Machine Sales, 2712 Lackland Dr., Waterloo, IA 50702, (319)296-1816 [20058]

Industrial Steel Service Center, 1700 W Cortland Ct., Addison, IL 60101, (630)543-0660 [20059]

Industrial Steel Warehouse Inc., PO Box 3207, Longview, TX 75606, (903)759-4454 [20060]

Industrial Steel and Wire Co., 1901 N Narragansett, Chicago, IL 60639, (312)804-0404 [16949]

Industrial Supplies Co., 1225 Cottman Ave., Philadelphia, PA 19111, (215)742-6200 [16950]

Industrial Supply Co., 322-328 N 9th St., PO Box 179, Terre Haute, IN 47808-0179, (812)234-1569 [16951]

Industrial Supply Co., 12905 Hwy. 55, Plymouth, MN 55441, (612)559-0033 [16952]

Industrial Supply Co., 1408 Northland Dr., Ste. 103, Mendota Heights, MN 55120, (651)405-1526 [16953]

Industrial Supply Co., 1100 W Russell Ave., Sioux Falls, SD 57104, (605)336-3471 [16954]

Industrial Supply Co., 1635 South 300 West, Salt Lake City, UT 84130, (801)484-8644 [16154]

Industrial Supply Co., 3109 E Voorhees St., Danville, IL 61834, (217)446-5029 [16955]

Industrial Supply Company Inc. (Salt Lake City, Utah), PO Box 30600, Salt Lake City, UT 84130, (801)484-8644 [16956]

Industrial Supply Corp., 326 Ohio, Waynesboro, VA 22980-4516, (540)946-4500 [16957]

Industrial Supply Corp., PO Box 6356, Richmond, VA 23230, (804)355-8041 [16958]

Industrial Supply Solutions, Inc., 1531 S Main St., Salisbury, NC 28144, (704)636-4241 [2775]

Industrial Supply Solutions, Inc., PO Box 1866, Charleston, WV 25327, (304)346-5341 [16155]

Industrial Tool Products Inc., 919 N Central Ave., Wood Dale, IL 60191, (630)766-4040 [16156]

Industrial Tools and Abrasives Inc., PO Box 71809, Chattanooga, TN 37407, (423)266-1265 [16959]

Industrial Tractor Co., 6870 Phillips Hwy., PO Box 17309, Jacksonville, FL 32245, (904)296-5000 [857]

Industrial Trade and Development Co., 620 San Francisco Ave., Long Beach, CA 90802, (562)432-4583 [13376]

Industrial Transmission Inc., N Green St. Ext, Greenville, NC 27834, (919)752-1353 [2776]

Industrial Transmission Inc., 305 Friendship Dr., Greensboro, NC 27409, (919)668-3200 [2777]

Industrial Transmissions Inc., 576 Griffith Rd., Charlotte, NC 28217, (704)525-9423 [17022]

Industrial Tube & Steel, 29 Ormsbee Ave., Westerville, OH 43081, (614)899-0657 [20061]

Industrial Tube and Steel Corp., 1303 Home Ave., Akron, OH 44310, (330)633-8125 [20062]

Industrial Uniform Company Inc., 906 E Waterman St., Wichita, KS 67202-4732, (316)264-2871 [5050]

Industrial Video Systems Inc., PO Box 6083, Ashland, VA 23005-6083, (804)798-0557 [25242]

Industrial Vision Corp., 1976 Arsenal St., St. Louis, MO 63118, (314)892-9995 [19370]

Industrial and Wholesale Lumber Inc., 4401 N 25th Ave., Schiller Park, IL 60176, (847)678-0480 [7511]

Industrial Wiper & Paper, 200 Spruce St., PO Box 505679, Chelsea, MA 02150, (617)884-5550 [21775]

Industry-Railway Suppliers Inc., 811 Golf Ln., Bensenville, IL 60106, (630)766-5708 [23481]

Infant To Teen Headwear, 112 W 34th St., New York, NY 10120-0093, (212)564-7196 [5051]

Infincom Inc., 1702 W 3rd St., Tempe, AZ 85281, (602)894-6200 [21057]

Infinite Solutions Inc., 3000 Miller Ct. W, Norcross, GA 30071, (770)449-4033 [6363]

Infinity Data Systems, 1801 Clearview Pkwy., Metairie, LA 70001-2451, (504)455-8973 [6364]

Infinity Paper Inc., 51 Haddonfield Rd., Ste. 120, Cherry Hill, NJ 08002-4801, (856)665-5500 [21776]

Info-Mation Services Co., 3035 Directors Row, Bldg. B, No. 12, Memphis, TN 38131-0416, (901)332-5770 [6365]

Info Systems Inc., 590 Century Blvd., Wilmington, DE 19808, (302)633-9800 [6366]

Infocase Inc., 2437 Williams Ave., Cincinnati, OH 45212, (513)396-6744 [18401]

Infolab Inc., PO Box 1309, Clarksdale, MS 38614, (601)627-2283 [19371]

Infomax Inc., 5757 Ranchester Dr., No. 1900, Houston, TX 77036-1510, (713)776-1688 [6367]

Information Analysis Inc., 11240 Waples Mill Rd., Ste. 400, Fairfax, VA 22030, (703)383-3000 [6368]

Information Management Inc., 8110 E 32nd St. N, Ste. 150, Wichita, KS 67226-2616, (316)267-3163 [6369]

Information Processing Center, 454 N Phillippi St., Boise, ID 83706-1426, (208)377-3256 [21058]

Information Sales and Marketing Company Inc., PO Box 2772, Covington, LA 70434, (504)892-6700 [19372]

InfoSource Inc., 6947 University Blvd., Winter Park, FL 32792, (407)677-0300 [6370]

Infotel, 6990 US Rte. 36 E, Fletcher, OH 45326, (937)368-2650 [6371]

Infra Metals, 5208 24th Ave., Tampa, FL 33619, (813)626-6005 [20063]

Infra Metals, PO Box 1247, Hallandale, FL 33008-1247, (954)454-9505 [20064]

Ingardia Brothers Inc., 2120 Placentia Ave., Costa Mesa, CA 92627, (714)645-1365 [11506]

Ingham Publishing, Inc., 5650 1st Ave., N, PO Box 12642, St. Petersburg, FL 33733-2642, (727)343-4811 [3843]

Ingraham Corp.; George, 4605 Stonegate Industrial Bldg., Stone Mountain, GA 30083-1908, (404)296-0804 [8879]

Ingram Book Co., 1125 Heil Quaker Blvd., La Vergne, TN 37086, (615)793-5000 [25243]

Ingram Book Group Inc., 1 Ingram Blvd., La Vergne, TN 37086, (615)793-5000 [3844]

Ingram Co.; G.A., 12600 Newburgh Rd., Livonia, MI 48150-1002, (313)591-1515 [18851]

Ingram Entertainment, 30525 Huntwood Ave., Hayward, CA 94544-7019, (510)785-3730 [25244]

Ingram Entertainment, 12600 SE Highway 212 Bldg. B, Clackamas, OR 97015-9081, (503)281-2673 [25245]

Ingram Entertainment, 1430 Bradley Ln., No. 102, Carrollton, TX 75007, (972)245-6088 [25246]

Ingram Entertainment, 1224 N Post Oak Rd., Houston, TX 77055, (713)681-9951 [25247]

Ingram Entertainment Inc., 11103 E 53rd Ave., Denver, CO 80239, (303)371-8372 [25248]

Ingram Industries Inc., PO Box 23049, Nashville, TN 37202, (615)298-8200 [6372]

Ingram International Films, 7900 Hickman Rd., Des Moines, IA 50322, (515)254-7000 [25249]

Ingram Micro Inc., 1600 E St. Andrew Pl., Santa Ana, CA 92704, (714)566-1000 [6373]

Ingram Micro Inc., 1759 Wehrle Dr., Williamsville, NY 14221, (716)633-3600 [6374]

Ingram Paper Co., PO Box 60003, City of Industry, CA 91716, (818)854-5400 [21777]

Ingram Video, 7319 Innovation Blvd., Ft. Wayne, IN 46818, (219)489-6046 [25250]

Ingredient Resource Corp., 2401 Lower Hunters, Louisville, KY 40216, (502)448-4480 [858]

Inland Associates Inc., PO Box 940, Olathe, KS 66051, (913)764-7977 [6375]

Inland Detroit Diesel/Allison, PO Box 5942, Carol Stream, IL 60197-5942, (630)871-1111 [2778]

Inland Detroit Diesel-Allison Inc., 13015 W Custer Ave., Butler, WI 53007, (414)781-7100 [2779]

Inland Empire Equipment Inc., 1762 S Sycamore Ave., Rialto, CA 92376, (909)877-0657 [16157]

Inland Fruit and Produce Company Inc., PO Box 158, Wapato, WA 98951, (509)877-2126 [11507]

Inland Industries Inc., PO Box 15999, Shawnee Mission, KS 66285-5999, (913)492-9050 [16158]

Inland Leidy Inc., 2225 Evergreen St., Baltimore, MD 21216, (410)889-6600 [4430]

Inland Newspaper Machinery Corp., PO Box 15999, Shawnee Mission, KS 66285-5999, (913)492-9050 [16159]

Inland Northwest Distributors Inc., 5327 Southgate Dr., Billings, MT 59101, (406)248-2125 [9962]

Inland NW Services Inc., PO Box 1101, Lewiston, ID 83501-1101, (208)746-2557 [21059]

Inland Plywood Co., 375 Cass Ave., Pontiac, MI 48342, (248)334-4706 [7512]

Inland Seafood Corp., 1222 Menlo Dr., Atlanta, GA 30318, (404)350-5850 [11508]

Inland Steel Industries Inc., 30 W Monroe St., Chicago, IL 60603, (312)346-0300 [20065]

Inland Supply Inc., 109 Plum St., Syracuse, NY 13204, (315)471-6171 [23220]

Inland Truck Parts, 5678 NE 14th St., Des Moines, IA 50313, (515)265-9901 [2780]

Inland Truck Parts, 1313 S Young Ave., Wichita, KS 67209, (316)945-0255 [2781]

Inland Truck Parts, 3380 Mike Collins Dr., Eden Prairie, MN 55344, (651)454-1100 [2782]

Inland Truck Parts, 1620 Troost Ave., Kansas City, MO 64108, (660)471-3154 [2783]

Inland Truck Parts, 115 N 16th St., Billings, MT 59101, (406)248-7340 [2784]

Inland Truck Parts, 2300 Palmer, Missoula, MT 59802, (406)728-7413 [2785]

Inland Truck Parts, 704 E 8th St., North Platte, NE 69101, (308)532-4188 [2786]

Inland Truck Parts, 9944 S 136th St., Omaha, NE 68138, (402)331-1222 [2787]

Inland Truck Parts, 1330 Deadwood Ave., Rapid City, SD 57702, (605)348-4344 [2788]

Inlet Distributors, 4142 Kingston Dr., Anchorage, AK 99504-4441, (907)337-0963 [1772]

Inlite Corp., 939 Grayson St., Berkeley, CA 94710, (510)849-1067 [8880]

Inman Associates Inc.; Paul, PO Box 1600, Farmington Hills, MI 48333, (248)626-8300 [11509]

Inmed Corp., 2450 Meadowbrook Pkwy., Duluth, GA 30096-4635, (404)623-0816 [18852]

Innoland Inc., 11166 Downs Rd., Pineville, NC 28134-8445, (704)588-0519 [26533]

INOTEK Technologies Corp., 11212 Indian Tr., Dallas, TX 75229, (972)243-7000 [8881]

Inotek Technologies Corp., 11212 Indian Trl., Dallas, TX 75229, (972)243-7000 [16160]

Inouye Lei Flowers, Inc., 3222 Ala Laulani St., Honolulu, HI 96818, (808)839-0064 [14892]

Inovonics Co, 2100 Central Ave., Boulder, CO 80301, (303)939-9336 [8882]

Input Automation Inc., 3155 Fujita St., Torrance, CA 90505, (310)539-3598 [21060]

Inside Source, 100 Industrial Rd., San Carlos, CA 94070, (415)508-9101 [13141]

Insight Direct, 8123 S Hardy Dr., Tempe, AZ 85284-1106, (520)333-3000 [6376]

Insight Electronics Inc., 9980 Huennekens St., San Diego, CA 92121, (619)677-3100 [8883]

Insonic Technology, Inc., 1240 S Hill St., Los Angeles, CA 90015, (213)746-2109 [17458]

InSport International Inc., 1870 NW 173rd Ave., Beaverton, OR 97006, (503)645-3552 [5052]

Installation Telephone Services Inc., 3920 Grape St., Denver, CO 80207, (303)355-3330 [5646]

Institute for Childhood Resources, 268 Bush St., San Francisco, CA 94104, (415)864-1169 [26534]

Institution Food House Inc., PO Drawer 2947, Hickory, NC 28603-2947, (828)323-4500 [11510]

Institution Food House Inc., PO Box 1368, Hickory, NC 28603-1368, (828)328-5301 [11511]

Institutional Contract Sales, PO Box 4092, Manchester, NH 03108-4092, (603)432-2129 [13142]

Institutional Distributors Inc., 2742 Hwy. 25 N, PO Box 520, East Bernstadt, KY 40729, (606)843-2100 [11512]

Institutional Distributors, Inc., 417 Welshwood Dr., Nashville, TN 37211, (615)832-9198 [11513]

Institutional Equipment Inc., 4557 W 100 S, New Palestine, IN 46163-9624, (317)541-0021 [23744]

Institutional Jobbers, PO Box 51890, Knoxville, TN 37950-1890, (423)970-3200 [11492]

Institutional Linen Supply, 367 Simmonsville Ave., Apt. 3310, Johnston, RI 02919-6041, (401)233-2144 [26072]

Institutional Sales Associates, PO Box 8938, Houston, TX 77249, (713)692-7213 [11514]

Institutional Wholesale Co., 25 S Whitney Ave., Cookeville, TN 38501, (615)526-9588 [11515]

Instrument Engineers, 12335 World Trade Dr., Ste. 7A, San Diego, CA 92128-3783, (858)673-3644 [24372]

Instrument Sales-East, 24037 Acacia, Redford, MI 48239, (313)535-5252 [24373]

Insular Lumber Sales Corp., 280 Middlefield Rd., Washington, MA 01223-9414, (413)623-6657 [7513]

Insulectro Corp., 20362 Windrow Dr., Lake Forest, CA 92630-8138, (949)587-3200 [8884]

Intcomex, 2980 NW 108 Ave, Miami, FL 33172, (305)477-6230 [6377]

Intec Video Systems Inc., 23301 Vista Grande, Laguna Hills, CA 92653, (949)859-3800 [24572]

Intech Corp., 250 Herbert Ave., Closter, NJ 07624, (201)767-8066 [16960]

Intech EDM Electrotools, 2001 W 16th St., Broadview, IL 60153, (708)681-6110 [8885]

Intech Power-Core, 250 Herbert Ave., Closter, NJ 07624, (201)767-8066 [16960]

Intedge Industries Inc., 1875 Chumley Rd., Woodruff, SC 29388, (864)969-9601 [24142]

Integral Kitchens, 6419 N McPhearson, Laredo, TX 78044, (956)724-4521 [9963]

Integral Kitchens, 6419 N McPhearson, Laredo, TX 78044, (956)724-4521 [7514]

Integral Marketing Inc., 5000 Philadelphia Way, Ste. A, Lanham, MD 20706-4417, (301)731-4233 [8886]

Integral Systems Inc., 2730 Shadelands Dr., No. 101, Walnut Creek, CA 94598-2515, (510)939-3900 [6378]

Integrated Electronics Corp., 420 E 58th Ave., Denver, CO 80216, (303)292-5537 [9552]

Integrated Medical Inc., 8100 S Akron St., Ste. 320, Englewood, CO 80112-3508, (303)792-0069 [19373]

Integrated Medical Systems, 2717 19th Pl. S, Birmingham, AL 35209-1919, (205)879-3840 [18853]

Integrated Orbital Implants Inc., 12526 High Bluff Dr., No. 300, San Diego, CA 92130, (619)792-3565 [19374]

Integrated Process Equipment Corp., 911 Bern Ct. Ste. 110, San Jose, CA 95112, (408)436-2170 [16161]

Integrated Sensor Solutions, 625 River Oaks Pkwy, San Jose, CA 95134, (408)324-1044 [2789]

Integrated Systems Inc., 1904 SE Ochoco St., Portland, OR 97222, (503)654-7886 [16162]

Integrated World Enterprises, 8350 NW 66th St., Miami, FL 33166, (305)591-7797 [859]

Integrity Steel Co, 6300 Sterling Dr N, Sterling Heights, MI 48312, (810)826-3700 [20066]

Intel Corp., PO Box 58119, Santa Clara, CA 95052, (408)765-8080 [6379]

Intel Corp., 5200 NE Elam Young Pkwy, Hillsboro, OR 97124, (503)696-8080 [8887]

Intelligence Technology Corp., PO Box 671125, Dallas, TX 75367, (214)250-4277 [8888]

Intelligent Computer Networks, 613 Woodridge, Woodstock, GA 30188, (404)516-8445 [6380]

Intelligent Electronics Inc., 411 Eagleview Blvd., Exton, PA 19341, (610)458-5500 [6381]

Intelligent Electronics Inc. Advanced Systems Div., 411 Eagleview Blvd., Exton, PA 19341, (215)458-5500 [6382]

Intelligent Systems Corp., 4355 Shackleford Rd., Norcross, GA 30093, (770)381-2900 [6383]

Intelliphone Inc., 191 Chandler Rd., Andover, MA 01810, (978)688-4070 [5647]

Inter-Act Inc., 1030 E Baseline Rd., Ste. 148, Tempe, AZ 85283-3717, (480)730-6688 [25251]

Inter-American Trading, PO Box 12254, Seattle, WA 98102, (206)328-2575 [25689]

Inter-City Paper Co., PO Box 1401, Minneapolis, MN 55440, (612)228-1234 [21778]

Inter-County Bakers, 1110 Rte. 109, Lindenhurst, NY 11757, (516)957-1350 [11516]

Inter-Ocean Industries Inc., 1140 Ave. of the Amer, New York, NY 10036, (212)921-1700 [5648]

Inter-Pacific Corp., 2257 Colby Ave., Los Angeles, CA 90064, (310)473-7591 [24769]

Inter-Tel Integrated Systs Inc., 7300 W Boston St., Chandler, AZ 85226, (480)961-9000 [8889]

Inter-Tel Technologies, Inc., 10160 Linn Station Rd., Louisville, KY 40223, (502)426-2000 [5649]

Inter-Tel Technologies Inc., 4909 E McDowell Rd Ste 106, Phoenix, AZ 85008, (602)231-5151 [8890]

Interact Computers Systems Inc., PO Box 15084, Asheville, NC 28813, (828)254-9876 [6384]

InterACT Systems Inc., PO Box 15084, Asheville, NC 28813, (828)254-9876 [6384]

Interactive Medical Technologies Ltd., 7348 Bellaire Ave., North Hollywood, CA 91605-4301, (310)312-9652 [18854]

Interamerican Motor Corp., PO Box 3939, Chatsworth, CA 91313-3939, (818)775-5028 [2790]

Interatech, 4455 Twain Ave., Ste. F, San Diego, CA 92120, (619)528-1984 [6385]

Interceramic Inc., 2333 S Jupiter Rd., Garland, TX 75041, (214)503-5500 [9964]

Interchange Corp., 117 Garth Rd., Ste. 1A, Scarsdale, NY 10583, (914)472-7881 [860]

Intercoastal Tile, 5189 NW 15th St., Margate, FL 33063-3714, (954)971-5294 [9965]

Intercon, Inc., 501 A Upland Ave., Upland, PA 19015, (215)874-2100 [2791]

Interconsal Associates Inc., 544 E Weddell Dr., No. 9, Sunnyvale, CA 94089-2113, (408)745-0161 [4431]

Intercontinental Importers Inc., PO Box 411, Southfield, MI 48037, (248)355-1770 [5053]

Intercontinental Industries, 710 Kakoi St., Honolulu, HI 96819-2016, (808)836-1595 [5054]

Intercontinental Trade Development, PO Box 10838, Rockville, MD 20849-0838, (301)921-8200 [18855]

Interdonati, Inc.; H., PO Box 262, Cold Spring Harbor, NY 11724, (516)367-6613 [19375]

Interface Data Inc., 14 Heritage Rd., Billerica, MA 01821-1108, (781)938-6333 [6386]

Interface Systems Inc., 5855 Interface Dr., Ann Arbor, MI 48103, (734)769-5900 [6387]

Interior Design Nutritionals, 75 W Center St., Provo, UT 84601, (801)345-9000 [14131]

Interior Enterprises Inc., 101 W Grand Ave., Chicago, IL 60610, (312)527-3636 [21061]

Interior Fuels Co., PO Box 70199, Fairbanks, AK 99707, (907)456-1312 [22375]

Interior Plant Designs, Ltd., 5333 A St., Anchorage, AK 99518, (907)563-2535 [14893]

Interior Services Inc., 1360 Kemper Meadow Dr., Cincinnati, OH 45240, (513)851-0933 [21062]

Interior Services Inc., 1360 Kemper Meadow Dr., Cincinnati, OH 45240, (513)851-0933 [13143]

Interior Specialties of the Ozarks, 1314 N Nias, Springfield, MO 65808, (417)865-5447 [9966]

Interior Supply Inc., 481 E 11th Ave., Columbus, OH 43211, (614)424-6611 [7515]

Interior Systems Contract Group Inc., 28000 Woodward, Royal Oak, MI 48067-1051, (248)399-1600 [13144]

Interior Systems and Installation Inc., 15534 W Hardy, Ste. 100, Houston, TX 77060, (281)820-2600 [13145]

Interior Tropicals, Inc., 275 Market St.,Ste. 531, Minneapolis, MN 55405-1626 [14894]

Interiors By Loette, 409 S 8th St. 101, Boise, ID 83702-7136, (208)345-8598 [26073]

Interknit Inc., 645 Harrison St., 4th Fl., San Francisco, CA 94107, (415)882-4680 [5055]

Interlectric Corp., 1401 Lexington Ave., Warren, PA 16365, (814)723-6061 [16961]

Intermarket Imports Inc., PO Box 39, Guilderland Center, NY 12085-0039, (518)869-3223 [16163]

Intermetra Corp., 10100 NW 116th Way, Ste. 14, Miami, FL 33178, (305)889-1194 [8891]

Intermountain Beverage Company, PO Box 429, Pocatello, ID 83204-0429, (208)237-4711 [1773]

Intermountain Distributing Co., PO Box 1772, Billings, MT 59103-1772, (406)245-7744 [1774]

Intermountain Farmers Association, 1147 W 2100 S, Salt Lake City, UT 84119, (801)972-2122 [861]

Intermountain Irrigation, 350 N Interchange, Dillon, MT 59725, (406)683-6571 [23221]

Intermountain Lea Findings Co., 1064 East 300 South, Salt Lake City, UT 84102-2513, (801)355-3737 [24770]

Intermountain Lea Findings Co., 1064 East 300 South, Salt Lake City, UT 84102-2513, (801)355-3737 [5056]

Intermountain Lumber Co., PO Box 65970, Salt Lake City, UT 84165-0970, (801)486-5411 [7516]

Intermountain Piper Inc., 301 N 2370 W, Salt Lake City, UT 84116, (801)322-1645 [100]

Intermountain Resources, 3856 Hwy. 88 East, Mena, AR 71953, (501)394-7893 [23745]

Intermountain Scientific Corp., PO Box 380, Kaysville, UT 84037-0380, (801)547-5047 [24374]

Intermountain Specialty Coatings, 1021 W 24th St., Ogden, UT 84401, (801)394-3489 [21465]

Intermountain Trading Company Ltd., 1455 5th St., Berkeley, CA 94710-1337, (510)526-3623 [11517]

Intermountain Wholesale Hardware Inc., 4990 Dahlia St., Denver, CO 80216, (303)288-4040 [20653]

Intermountain Wood Products, 1948 S West Temple, Salt Lake City, UT 84115, (801)486-6859 [27323]

Internal Sound Communications, 10500 Chicago Dr., No. 80, Zeeland, MI 49464-9185, (616)772-4875 [8892]

International Advertising Gifts, 710 E San Ysidro Blvd., Ste B, San Ysidro, CA 92173, (619)428-5475 [13377]

International Agricultural Associates, Inc., PO Box 5153, New Britain, PA 18901-0939, (215)230-3476 [862]

International Air Leases Inc., PO Box 522230, Miami, FL 33152, (305)889-6000 [101]

International Airline Support Group Inc., 3030 SW 42nd St., Ft. Lauderdale, FL 33312-6809, (305)593-2658 [102]

International Armament Corp., 10 Prince St., Alexandria, VA 22314, (703)739-1560 [13500]

International Baking Co., 737 N Great SW Pkwy., Arlington, TX 76011-5426, (817)640-5284 [11518]

International Baking Co., 5200 S Alameda St., Vernon, CA 90058, (213)583-9841 [11519]

International Book Centre, 2007 Laurel St., PO Box 295, Troy, MI 48099, (248)879-8436 [3845]

International Book Distributors Ltd., 24 Hudson St., Kinderhook, NY 12106, (518)758-1755 [3846]

International Brake Industries Inc., 1840 McCullough St., Lima, OH 45801, (419)227-4421 [2792]

International Brands West, 915 Shelly St., Springfield, OR 97477, (541)726-5561 [1775]

International Bullion and Metal Brokers Inc., 49 W 24th St., New York, NY 10010, (212)929-8800 [17459]

International Business Equipment, 1402 S Minnesota Ave., Sioux Falls, SD 57105-1716, (605)335-1050 [21063]

International Business Machines Corp. EduQuest, PO Box 2150, Atlanta, GA 30327, (404)238-3100 [6388]

International Business & Management Institute, PO Box 3271, Tustin, CA 92781-3271, (949)552-8494 [3847]

International Cellulose Inc., 3110 W 28th St., Chicago, IL 60623, (773)847-8000 [26851]

International Components Corp., 420 N May St., Chicago, IL 60622-5888, (312)829-7101 [8893]

International Components Corp., 175 Marcus Blvd., Hauppauge, NY 11788, (631)952-9595 [11520]

International Computer and Office Products Inc., 108 E Ponce de Leon, No. 210, Decatur, GA 30030, (404)373-3683 [6389]

International Consulting & Contracting Services, PO Box 21202, Lansing, MI 48909, (517)393-3999 [7517]

International Contract Furnishings Inc., 920 Broadway, New York, NY 10010 [13138]

International Cultural Enterprises Inc., 1241 Darmouth Ln., Deerfield, IL 60015, (847)945-9516 [25252]

International Cultured Pearl & Jewelry Co., 71 W 47th, New York, NY 10036-2878, (212)869-5141 [17460]

International Dairy Queen Inc., 7505 Metro Blvd., Minneapolis, MN 55439, (612)830-0200 [24143]

International Data Acquisition and Control Inc., PO Box 397, Amherst, NH 03031, (603)673-0765 [6390]

International Decoratives Company Inc., PO Box 777, Valley Center, CA 92082, (760)749-2682 [14895]

International Diagnostic Systems Corp., PO Box 799, St. Joseph, MI 49085-0799, (616)428-8400 [18856]

International Dinghy Shop, 334 S Bayview Ave., PO Box 431, Amityville, NY 11701, (516)264-0005 [18491]

International Division, Inc., PO Box 1275, Springfield, MO 65801, (417)862-2673 [863]

International Domestic Development Corp., 4511 Bragg Blvd., Fayetteville, NC 28303, (919)864-5515 [18857]

International Engine Parts Inc., 8950 Lurline Ave., Chatsworth, CA 91311, (818)882-8803 [103]

International Eyewear Inc., PO Box 32308, Baltimore, MD 21282-2308, (410)486-8300 [19376]

International Farmers Grain, 460 W 34th St., 12th Fl., New York, NY 10001, (212)947-8585 [536]

International Food and Beverage Inc., 8635 W Sahara Ave., No. 433, Las Vegas, NV 89117-5859, (702)858-8800 [11521]

International Forest Products Corp., 1 Boston Pl., 35th Fl., Boston, MA 02108, (617)723-3455 [21779]

International Healthcare Products, 4222 S Pulaski Rd., Chicago, IL 60632, (773)247-7422 [18858]

International Hi-Tech Trading Corp., PO Box 7579, Burbank, CA 91510, (818)841-5453 [2793]

International Historic Films Inc., PO Box 29035, Chicago, IL 60609, (773)927-9091 [25253]

International Importers Inc., 2761 N 29th Ave., Hollywood, FL 33020, (954)920-6344 [17461]

International Importers Inc., 5221 S Millard Ave., Chicago, IL 60632, (773)581-5511 [8894]

International Imports Inc., 38741 Long St., Harrison Township, MI 48045-2140, (248)349-8900 [5057]

International Industries Corporation, 880 E Main St., Spartanburg, SC 29302-2000, (864)597-1414 [11522]

International Industries Inc., 915 Hartford Tpke., Shrewsbury, MA 01545-4148, (508)842-0393 [5058]

International Industries Inc., PO Drawer D, Gilbert, WV 25621, (304)664-3227 [7518]

International Lease Finance Corp., 1999 Avenue of the Stars, 39th Fl., Los Angeles, CA 90067, (310)788-1999 [104]

International Machine Tool Ltd., 2461 N Clybourn Ave., Chicago, IL 60614, (773)871-5282 [16164]

International Male, 741 F St., San Diego, CA 92101, (619)544-9900 [5059]

International Marine Fuels Inc., 2121 3rd St., San Francisco, CA 94107, (415)552-9340 [22376]

International Marine Industries, PO Box 3609, 221 Third St., Newport, RI 02840-0990, (401)849-4982 [23746]

International Marine Publishing Co., PO Box 545, Blacklick, OH 43004, 800-722-4726 [3848]

International Market Entry Management Co., 5825 Glenridge Dr., Ste. 1-126, Atlanta, GA 30328, (404)256-4244 [24638]

International Marketing Association Ltd., 10821 Lakeview, Lenexa, KS 66219-1327, (913)599-5995 [5060]

International Marketing Specialists Inc., 4108 McAlice Ct., Plano, TX 75093, (972)758-7226 [16165]

International Marketing Systems Ltd., PO Box 806, Fargo, ND 58107, (701)237-4699 [864]

International Medcom, 7497 Kennedy Rd., Sebastopol, CA 95472, (707)823-0336 [16166]

International Mill Service Inc., 1155 Business Center Dr., No. 200, Horsham, PA 19044, (215)956-5500 [26852]

International MultiFoods Corp., PO Box 17387, Denver, CO 80217, (303)662-7100 [24182]

International Oceanic Enterprises Inc. of Alabama, PO Box 767, Bayou la Batre, AL 36509, (334)824-4193 [12764]

International Office Systems Inc., 2740 W 80th St., Minneapolis, MN 55431, (612)456-9999 [21064]

International Optical Supply Co., 5027 South 300 West, Salt Lake City, UT 84107-4707, (801)269-1119 [19377]

International Organic Products Inc., PO Box 2737, Laurel, MD 20709, (301)470-1160 [14132]

International Paper Co. CDA Distributors Div., 3940 Olympic Blvd., No. 250, Erlanger, KY 41018, (859)282-5600 [22001]

International Paper Co. McEwen Lumber Co., PO Box 950, High Point, NC 27261, (919)472-1900 [7519]

International Parts Inc., 12677 Silicon Dr., San Antonio, TX 78249-3412, (210)694-4313 [6391]

International Periodical Distributors, 674 Via De La Valle, Ste. 200, Solana Beach, CA 92075, (858)481-5928 [3849]

International Petroleum Corp., 105 S Alexander St., Plant City, FL 33566, (813)754-1504 [26853]

International Piecework Controls Co., PO Box 1909, Edison, NJ 08818-1909, (732)225-8844 [15177]

International Pizza Co., 801 Dye Mill Rd., Troy, OH 45373, (937)335-2115 [11523]

International Playthings Inc., 75 Lackawanna Ave., Parsippany, NJ 07054-1078, (201)831-1400 [26535]

International Procurement Services, Inc., 300 Wildwood St., Woburn, MA 01801, (781)932-0820 [7520]

International Projects Inc., PO Box 397, Holland, OH 43528, (419)865-6201 [23747]

International Purchasers, Inc., PO Box 308, Reisterstown, MD 21136, (301)833-6400 [7521]

International Restaurant Equipment Company Inc., PO Box 35497, Los Angeles, CA 90035, (323)933-1896 [24144]

International Screw & Bolt, 7500 New Horizon Blvd., Amityville, NY 11701, (631)225-6400 [13766]

International Seeds, Inc., PO Box 168, Halsey, OR 97348, (541)369-2251 [865]

International Service Co., International Service Building, 333 4th Ave., Indialantic, FL 32903, (321)724-1443 [3850]

International Service Group, 3000 Langford Rd., Ste. 700, Norcross, GA 30071, (404)447-8777 [18011]

International Specialized Book Services, 5804 NE Hassalo St., Portland, OR 97213-3644, (503)287-3093 [3851]

International Surgical Systems, PO Box 16538, Phoenix, AZ 85011-6538, (602)277-2000 [18859]

International Tape Products Co., 901 Murray Rd., East Hanover, NJ 07936, (973)748-7870 [21065]

International Telecom Systems Inc., 8004 Split Oak Dr., Bethesda, MD 20817-6953, (301)718-9800 [5650]

International Television Corp., 9119 DeSoto Ave., Chatsworth, CA 91311, (213)467-7148 [8895]

International Tile & Marble, Ltd., 828 Principal, Chesapeake, VA 23320, (757)549-0055 [9967]

International Tile & Marble Ltd., 11761 Rock Landing Dr., Newport News, VA 23606, (757)873-1343 [9968]

International Tile and Supply Corp., 1288 S La Brea Ave., Los Angeles, CA 90019, (213)931-1761 [15541]

International Trade Group, 5726 Monticello Ave., Dallas, TX 75206, (214)827-0246 [18860]

International Trade Management, 6411 Lake Athabaska Place, San Diego, CA 92119, (619)697-3112 [6399]

International Trade & Telex Corp., 2621 E 20th, PO Box 91291, Long Beach, CA 90809, (213)435-3492 [19378]

International Trading Co., 3100 Canal St., Houston, TX 77003, (713)224-5901 [11524]

International Trading & Investment, 5159 Tilly Mill Rd., Atlanta, GA 30338, (404)451-1396 [13146]

International Typewriter Exchange, 1229 W Washington, Chicago, IL 60607, (312)733-1200 [21066]

International Waters, 989 Ave. of the Americas, 15th Fl., New York, NY 10018-5410, (212)564-3099 [5061]

International Wealth Success Inc., 24 Canterbury Rd., Rockville Centre, NY 11570, (516)766-5919 [3852]

International Wine and Spirits, 2536 Springfield Ave., Union, NJ 07083, (908)686-0800 [1516]

Internet Communication Corp., 7100 E Belleview Ave., Greenwood Village, CO 80111, (303)770-7600 [6392]

Interroyal Hospital Supply Corp., 168 Canal St., Ste. 600, New York, NY 10013, (212)334-0990 [18861]

Interstate Battery System of Dallas Inc., 12770 Merit Dr., No. 400, Dallas, TX 75251, (972)991-1444 [8896]

Interstate Bearing Co., 2501 E 80th St., Bloomington, MN 55425-1319, (612)854-0836 [2794]

Interstate Bearing Technologies, 244-A W Pioneer Rd., Fond du Lac, WI 54936, (920)921-8816 [2795]

Interstate Bingo Supplies Inc., RR 1 Box 28, Jamaica, VT 05343-9701, (802)874-4269 [26536]

Interstate Brands Corp., 6301 N Broadway, St. Louis, MO 63147-2802, (314)385-1600 [11525]

Interstate Brands Corp. Cotton Brothers Baking Co., 3400 Macarthur Dr., Alexandria, LA 71302, (318)448-6600 [11526]

Interstate Brands Corp. Dolly Madison Cakes Div., PO Box 419627, Kansas City, MO 64141-6627, (816)561-6600 [11527]

Interstate Chemical Co., 2797 Freeland Rd., Hermitage, PA 16148, (724)981-3771 [4432]

Interstate Commodities Inc., PO Box 607, Troy, NY 12180, (518)272-7212 [18012]

Interstate Companies of Louisiana, PO Box 3358, Baton Rouge, LA 70821, (504)387-5131 [21067]

Interstate Co., 2601 E 80th St., Minneapolis, MN 55425-1378, (612)854-2044 [16962]

Interstate Copy Shop, 1516 N Bennett St., Silver City, NM 88061-6522, (505)538-9530 [21068]

Interstate Detroit Diesel Inc., 2501 E 80th St., Minneapolis, MN 55425, (612)854-5511 [16167]

Interstate Distributors Inc., 4101 Blue Ridge, Norcross, GA 30071, (404)476-0103 [24145]

Interstate Distributors Inc., 199 Commander Shea Blvd., North Quincy, MA 02171, (617)328-9500 [3853]

Interstate Electric Supply, 1330 Courtland, Roanoke, VA 24012, (540)982-2500 [8897]

Interstate Electronics, Inc., Airport Plz., Hwy. 36, Hazlet, NJ 07730-1701, (732)264-3900 [25254]

Interstate Equipment Co., 1604 Salisbury Rd., Statesville, NC 28677, (704)873-9048 [7522]

Interstate Glass Distributors, 300 Unser Blvd. NW, Albuquerque, NM 87101, (505)836-2361 [7523]

Interstate Payco Seed Co., PO Box 338, West Fargo, ND 58078, (701)282-7338 [866]

Interstate Periodical Distributors Inc., 201 E Badger Rd., Madison, WI 53713, (608)271-3600 [3854]

Interstate Petroleum Products Inc., 3635 Dunbury Rd., Brewster, NY 10509, (914)279-5625 [22377]

Interstate Restaurant Equipment Corp., 37 Amoskeag St., Manchester, NH 03102, (603)669-3400 [24146]

Interstate Steel Co., 401 E Touhy Ave., Des Plaines, IL 60017, (847)827-5151 [20067]

Interstate Steel Supply Co, 1800 Byberry Rd., Philadelphia, PA 19116, (215)673-0300 [20068]

Interstate Steel Supply Co., 1800 E Byberry Rd., Philadelphia, PA 19116, (215)673-0300 [20069]

Interstate Supply, 9258 Bond St., Overland Park, KS 66214, (913)894-2663 [9969]

Interstate Supply Co., 2330 NW 10th, Oklahoma City, OK 73107-5616, (405)525-0041 [9970]

Interstate Supply Co., 4445 Gustine Ave., St. Louis, MO 63116, (314)481-2222 [9971]

Interstate Welding Sales Corp., 1801 Marinette Ave., Marinette, WI 54143, (715)732-7950 [16168]

Interstate Welding Sales Corp., 1801 Marinette Ave., Marinette, WI 54143, (715)732-7950 [16963]

Interstate Wholesale Inc., 5500 W 14th St., Sioux Falls, SD 57106-0206, (605)336-0999 [17462]

Intersystems of Delaware, 93 Mason St., Greenwich, CT 06830, (203)629-1400 [22984]

Intertech Services, 200 E 57th St., Apt. 5L, New York, NY 10022, (718)260-3715 [26074]

Intertile Distributors, Inc., 3651 Park Rd., Benicia, CA 94510, (707)745-4300 [9972]

Intertile Distributors, Inc., 2021 N Fine Ave., Fresno, CA 93727, (209)454-5000 [9973]

Intertile Distributors, Inc., PO Box 2106, Oakland, CA 94621-0006, (510)351-4600 [9974]

Intertrade, Inc., 29444 Northwestern Hwy., Ste. 600, Southfield, MI 48034, (248)356-1800 [13147]

Intertrade Ltd., 4700 N River Blvd. NE, Cedar Rapids, IA 52411, (319)378-3500 [105]

Interwest Home Medical Inc., 235 E6100 S, Salt Lake City, UT 84107, (801)261-5100 [18862]

Interwest Medical Equipment Distributors Inc., 235 E 6100 S, Salt Lake City, UT 84107-7349, (801)261-5100 [18863]

Interwest Safety Supply Inc., PO Box 31, Provo, UT 84603, (801)375-6321 [24573]

Interworld, 4161 Ingot St., Fremont, CA 94538, (510)226-6080 [4640]

inTEST Corp., 2 Pin Oak Ln., Cherry Hill, NJ 08003, (609)424-6886 [24375]

Intexco Inc., 7270 NW 12th St., Ste. 555, Miami, FL 33126-1927, (305)592-7063 [11528]

Intile Designs, Inc., 3750 Wow Rd., Corpus Christi, TX 78413, (512)855-9848 [9975]

Intile Designs Inc., PO Box 55645, Houston, TX 77255, (713)468-8400 [7524]

Intimate Fashions Inc., PO Box 375, Woodmere, NY 11598-0375, (212)686-1530 [5062]

Intoximeters Inc., 8110 Lackland Rd., St. Louis, MO 63114, (314)429-4000 [24376]

Intraco Corp., 530 Stephenson Hwy., Troy, MI 48083-1131, (248)585-6900 [2796]

Intrade, Inc., PO Box 10997, Southport, NC 28461-0997, (910)457-1935 [8898]

Intramar Inc., 10497 Town & Country Way, Ste. 225, Houston, TX 77024, (713)984-2791 [16169]

Intraoptics Inc., 1611 Owen Dr., Ste. C, Fayetteville, NC 28304-3400, (910)323-9797 [19379]

Intrepid Enterprises Inc., PO Box 1298, Harvey, LA 70059, (504)348-2870 [7525]

Intrepid Systems Inc., 16000 Sky Cliff Dr., Brookfield, WI 53005-2870, (414)790-0080 [6393]

Intromark Inc., 217 9th St., Pittsburgh, PA 15222, (412)238-1300 [26537]

Intruder Alert Security, 410 E Kennedy, Lakewood, NJ 08701, (732)363-4105 [24574]

Inventory Conversion Inc., 102 Tide Mill Rd., Ste. 6, Hampton, NH 03842, (603)926-0300 [6394]

Investrade Import & Export, 1040 Woodrow, Wichita, KS 67203, (316)265-9630 [16170]

IOA Data Corp., 383 Lafayette St., New York, NY 10003, (212)673-9300 [6395]

IOB Distributors, PO Box 142307, Austin, TX 78714-2307, (512)835-9648 [6396]

Ion Tech Inc., 2330 E Prospect Rd., Ft. Collins, CO 80525, (970)221-1807 [16171]

Ion Technologies Corp., 4815 Para Dr., Cincinnati, OH 45237-5009, (513)641-3100 [16172]

Ionics, Incorporated, 65 Grove St., Watertown, MA 02472, 800-457-4449 [23147]

Iowa Export Import Trading Co., 512 Tuttle St., Des Moines, IA 50309, (515)245-2464 [867]

Iowa Machinery and Supply Company Inc., 1711 2nd Ave., Des Moines, IA 50314, (515)288-0123 [16173]

Iowa Office Supplies Inc., PO Box 1386, Storm Lake, IA 50588, (712)732-4801 [21069]

Iowa Office Supply Inc., PO Box 1386, Storm Lake, IA 50588, (712)732-4801 [21070]

Iowa Oil Co., PO Box 712, Dubuque, IA 52001, (319)583-3563 [22378]

Iowa Paint Manufacturing Company Inc., PO Box 1417, Des Moines, IA 50305, (515)283-1501 [21466]

Iowa River Farm Service Inc., PO Box 99, Toledo, IA 52342, (515)752-4274 [868]

Iowa River Farm Service Inc., PO Box 99, Toledo, IA 52342, (515)752-4274 [868]

Iowa Soybean Association, 4554 114th St., Urbandale, IA 50322-5410, (515)223-1423 [18013]

Iowa Veterinary Supply Co., 124 Country Club Rd., PO Box 638, Iowa Falls, IA 50126, (515)648-2529 [27158]

Iowa Veterinary Supply Co., PO Box 518, Iowa Falls, IA 50126, (515)648-2529 [869]

IPC Information Systems Inc., 350 Sansome St Ste. 640, San Francisco, CA 94104, (415)788-6500 [8899]

IPD Co., Inc., 11744 NE Ainsworth Cir., PO Box 20339, Portland, OR. 97220, (503)257-7500 [2797]

IPE Trade Inc., 704 Hillwood Dr., PO Box 1250, Daphne, AL 36526, (205)626-3128 [870]

IPS of California, 70 Glenn Way, San Carlos, CA 94070, (650)592-1742 [16174]

IPX, 103 Indian Trail Rd., Oak Brook, IL 60521, (630)323-1223 [17463]

IQ Holdings Inc., 16212 State Hwy. 249, Houston, TX 77086, (281)444-6454 [14133]

IQ Products Co., 16212 State Hwy. 249, Houston, TX 77086, (281)444-6454 [2798]

IQ2000, 15402 Vantage Pky., No. 318, Houston, TX 77032, (281)447-1000 [6397]

Irby Co.; Stuart C., 3418 Washington, Vicksburg, MS 39180-5060, (601)638-3262 [8900]

Irby Co.; Stuart C., PO Box 1819, Jackson, MS 39215-1819, (601)969-1811 [16964]

Ireland Alloys Inc., PO Box 369, Mc Keesport, PA 15134-0369 [26854]

Ireland Coffee and Tea Inc., PO Box 1103, Pleasantville, NJ 08232, (609)646-7200 [11529]

Irex Corp., PO Box 1268, Lancaster, PA 17608, (717)397-3633 [7526]

Irish Books & Media, Inc., Franklin Business Center, 1433 Franklin Ave. E, Minneapolis, MN 55404-2135, (612)871-3505 [3855]

Iron Age Corp., Robinson Plz. 3, Ste. 400, Pittsburgh, PA 15205, (412)787-4100 [24771]

Iron City Distributing Company Inc., 2670 Commercial Ave., Mingo Junction, OH 43938, (614)598-4171 [1776]

Iron and Metals Inc., 5555 Franklin St., Denver, CO 80216, (303)292-5555 [26855]

Iron Mike's Welding & Fab, 1535 N Dort Hwy., Flint, MI 48506, (810)234-2996 [20070]

Iroquois Manufacturing Company, Inc., 596 Richmond Rd., Hinesburg, VT 05461, (802)482-2155 [2799]

Irr Supply Centers Inc., 908 Niagra Falls Blvd., North Tonawanda, NY 14120, (716)692-1600 [23222]

Irrideco International Corp., PO Box 1615, Englewood Cliffs, NJ 07632, (201)569-3030 [871]

Irv Seaver Motorcycles, 607 W Katella Ave., Orange, CA 92867, (714)532-3700 [2800]

Irvin-Alan Fabrics, PO Box 2248, Grand Rapids, MI 49501-2248, (616)459-4600 [26075]

Irvin-Alan Fabrics, 11875 Kemper Springs Dr., Forest Park, OH 45240, (513)825-8866 [26076]

Irving Materials Inc., 8032 N State Rd. 9, Greenfield, IN 46140, (317)326-3101 [7527]

Irwin International Inc., PO Box 4000, Corona, CA 91718, (909)372-9555 [106]

Irwin Sales, PO Box 2096, Baytown, TX 77522-2096, (281)424-7651 [26077]

ISC/BioExpress, 420 N Kays Dr., Kaysville, UT 84037, (801)547-5047 [18864]

ISC/BioExpress, 420 N Kays Dr., Kaysville, UT 84037, (801)547-5047 [19380]

Iseri Produce Co.; Thomas, PO Box 250, Ontario, OR 97914-0250, (541)889-5337 [11530]

ISHK Book Services, PO Box 1062, Cambridge, MA 02238, (781)289-5798 [3856]

Island Classic Automotive Inc., 750 E Sample Rd., Bldg. 7, Bay 4, Pompano Beach, FL 33064, (954)941-0400 [20654]

Island Cycle Supply Co., 425 Washington Ave. N, Minneapolis, MN 55401-1316, (612)333-7771 [23748]

Island Import and Export Co., 1020 Kristin Ct., St. Paul, MN 55110, (612)481-9663 [24772]

Island Instruments, Inc., 46-444 Kuneki St., Kaneohe, HI 96744, (808)235-7544 [25255]

Island-Northwest Distributing, Inc., N 2003 Waterworks, Spokane, WA 99212, (509)535-1601 [9976]

Island Pacific Distributors, Inc., PO Box 22189, Honolulu, HI 96826, (808)955-1126 [24575]

Island Snow Hawaii Inc., PO Box 364, Kailua, HI 96734-0364, (808)926-1815 [5063]

Island Spring & Drive Shaft Co., 7309 Grand Ave., Pittsburgh, PA 15225, (412)264-6714 [16965]

Island Style, PO Box 50458, Jacksonville Beach, FL 32240, (904)246-7182 [23749]

Island Tee Shirt Sales Inc., 29-D Hunter Rd., Hilton Head Island, SC 29926-3715, (803)681-4133 [5064]

Ison Equipment Inc., Hwy. 8 E, Monico, WI 54501, (715)487-5583 [16175]

Israel Aircraft Industries International, 50 W 23rd St., New York, NY 10010, (212)620-4400 [107]

Isspro Inc., 2515 NE Riverside Way, Portland, OR 97211, (503)288-4488 [2801]

Isspro Inc., PO Box 11177, Portland, OR 97211, (503)288-4488 [16176]

Isuzu Diesel of North America, 41280 Bridge St., Novi, MI 48375-1301, (248)426-4200 [2229]

Isuzu Motors America Inc., 13340 183rd St., #6007, Cerritos, CA 90703-8748 [20655]

Ital Fashion Inc., 1307 Santee, Los Angeles, CA 90015-2524, (213)748-8164 [5065]

Italgrani Elevator Co., 7900 Van Buren Ave., St. Louis, MO 63111, (314)638-1447 [18014]

Italian Sausage Inc., 8 Brightwater Dr., Savannah, GA 31410-3301, (912)354-8884 [11531]

Itasca Moccasin, PO Box 288, Lake George, MN 56458-0228, (218)266-3978 [24894]

ITBR, Inc., 2 Cielo Center, 3rd Fl., 1250 Capital of Texas Hwy. S, Austin, TX 78746, (512)329-2170 [5651]

ITC Electronics, 2772 W Olympic Blvd., Los Angeles, CA 90006-2631, (310)370-6211 [8901]

ITC Inc., 6 N Park Dr., Ste. 105, Hunt Valley, MD 21030, (410)825-2920 [21780]

ITC International, 96 N 3rd St., Ste. 680, San Jose, CA 95112, (408)292-7000 [8902]

Itco Tire Co., PO Box 641, Wilson, NC 27893, (919)291-8900 [2802]

Itco Tire Co., 485 Stafford Umberger Rd., Wytheville, VA 24382, (540)228-4353 [2803]

ITE Distributing, 1229 W Washington Blvd., Chicago, IL 60607, (312)733-1200 [21071]

ITEC Enterprises Inc., 2955 Hartley Rd., Ste. 205, Jacksonville, FL 32257, (904)262-5066 [6398]

Items Galore Inc., PO Box 1828, Warren, MI 48090-1828, (810)774-4800 [5066]

Items International Airwalk Inc., PO Box 951, Altoona, PA 16603-0951, (814)943-6164 [24773]

ITG, Inc., PO Box 1777, Victoria, TX 77902, (512)573-4378 [23482]

ITG Laboratories Inc., 702 Marshall St., Ste. 280, Redwood City, CA 94063, (650)361-1891 [19381]

ITI Interamericana Trade Inc., 9201 SW 76 Ter., Miami, FL 33173, (305)596-6288 [5067]

ITM, 6411 Lake Athabaska Place, San Diego, CA 92119, (619)697-3112 [6399]

ITM, Inc., 6386 Corley Rd., Norcross, GA 30071, (404)446-0925 [2804]

ITOCHU International Inc., 335 Madison Ave., New York, NY 10017, (212)818-8000 [11532]

ITP Business Communications, PO Box 866, Hickory, NC 28603-0866, (704)322-6261 [21072]

Itron Inc., PO Box 15288, Spokane, WA 99215, (509)924-9900 [6400]

It's Coffee Lovers Time, Inc., 6601 Lyons Rd., Ste. C-12, Coconut Creek, FL 33073, (954)420-0882 [11533]

ITS Corp., 10160 Linn Station Rd., Louisville, KY 40223, (502)426-2000 [5649]

ITS/Intertrade Scientific, Inc., 176 Bolton Rd., Vernon, CT 06066, (860)871-0401 [16177]

ITTCO Sales Co., Inc., 181 Remington Blvd., Ronkonkoma, NY 11779-6939, (516)737-6800 [2805]

Iuka Cooperative Inc., PO Box 175, Iuka, KS 67066, (316)546-2231 [18015]

I.V. Therapy Associates, 4055 Faber Pl. Dr., No. 105, Charleston, SC 29405, (803)747-0847 [19382]

IVA Manufacturing Co., PO Box 148, Iva, SC 29655, (864)348-6151 [5226]

Ivanco Inc., 218 Greenacres Rd., Ft. Walton Beach, FL 32547, (850)862-9001 [5652]

Ivars Sportswear Inc., PO Box 2449, Burlington, NC 27216-2449, (910)227-9683 [5068]

Iverson P.C. Warehouse Inc., 1420 Spring Hill Rd., Ste. 570, McLean, VA 22102-3029, (703)749-1200 [6401]

Ives Business Forms Inc., 1009 Camp St., New Orleans, LA 70130, (504)561-8811 [21073]

IVI Corp., 265 Oak St., Pembroke, MA 02359, (781)826-3195 [16178]

Ivystone Group, 528 Trestle Pl., Downingtown, PA 19335, (610)873-1040 [15542]

The IXL Group, Bernie, MO 63822, (573)293-5341 [13767]

Izenco Inc., 501 W 172nd St., South Holland, IL 60473, (708)596-3600 [24774]

Izod Lacoste, 200 Madison Ave., New York, NY 10016-3903, (212)502-0349 [5069]

Izumi International, Inc., 1 Pelham Davis Circle, Greenville, SC 29615, (864)288-8001 [16179]

Izuo Brothers Ltd., PO Box 1197, Honolulu, HI 96807-1197, (808)591-8488 [23750]

J and B Distributing Co., PO Box 1240, Verona, VA 24482-1240 [1790]

J and B Foam Fabricators Inc., PO Box 144, Ludington, MI 49431-0144, (616)843-2448 [23751]

J & B Import Ltd. Inc., 294 Columbia St., Fall River, MA 02721-1322, (508)679-2710 [24775]

J & B Importers Inc., 11925 SW 128th St., Miami, FL 33186-5207, (305)238-1866 [23752]

J and B Meats Corp., PO Box 69, Coal Valley, IL 61240, (309)799-7341 [11534]

J and B Meats Corp., PO Box 69, Coal Valley, IL 61240, (309)799-7341 [11535]

J and B Supply Inc., PO Box 10450, Ft. Smith, AR 72917, (501)649-4915 [14496]

J & B Tackle Company Inc., 25 Smith Ave., Niantic, CT 06357-3229, (860)739-7419 [23753]

J & B Wholesale Co., 39 Grovers, Winthrop, MA 02152, (617)846-2188 [5070]

J and B Wholesale Distribution, PO Box 212, St. Michael, MN 55376, (612)497-3913 [11536]

J & E Feed Distributors Inc., 1509 N Main St., Muskogee, OK 74401, (918)687-7111 [872]

J & E Fishing Supplies Inc., 2295 N King St., Honolulu, HI 96819-4505, (808)847-4327 [23754]

J & F Steel Corporation, 2424 Oakton St., Evanston, IL 60202-2796, (847)866-2100 [20071]

J & H Berge, Inc., 4111 S Clinton Ave., South Plainfield, NJ 07080, (908)561-1234 [24377]

J and H Oil Co., PO Box 9464, Wyoming, MI 49509, (616)534-2181 [22379]

J & J Cleaning Service, RR 62, Box 3121A, Livingston, MT 59047, (406)222-6231 [4641]

J & J Computer Resources, 6092 US Hwy. 49, Hattiesburg, MS 39401-6033, (601)544-6092 [6402]

J & J Distributors, 1028 Donaldson, San Antonio, TX 78228, (210)734-6165 [24576]

J & J Distributors Inc., 9461 E Washington, Indianapolis, IN 46229-3085, (317)899-2530 [25690]

J and J Food Service Inc., PO Box 1370, Meadville, PA 16335, (814)336-4435 [11537]

J & J Shoe Co., PO Box 792, Brinkley, AR 72021-0792, (870)734-2360 [24776]

J & J Steel and Supply Co., PO Box 1886, Odessa, TX 79760, (915)332-4351 [22380]

J and J Steel and Supply Co., PO Box 1886, Odessa, TX 79760, (915)332-4351 [20072]

J & J Supply, Inc., 2510 White Settlement Rd., Ft. Worth, TX 76107, (817)335-5536 [21467]

J & J Supply, Inc., 120 E Main St., Shawnee, OK 74801-6906, (405)878-0729 [18865]

J & K Distributors, 512 E Kirby Ave., Muncie, IN 47303, (765)289-0722 [25920]

J & K Distributors, 451 Defense Hwy., Annapolis, MD 21401 [4642]

J & L Book Co., PO Box 1300, Spokane, WA 99213, (509)535-3360 [3857]

J & L Livestock, 200 N Phillips Ave., Sioux Falls, SD 57104, (605)338-6232 [18016]

J & L Medical Supply Corp., PO Box 24067, Tempe, AZ 85285-4067, (602)967-9203 [18866]

J and L Strong Tool Co., 1251 E 286th St., Cleveland, OH 44132, (216)289-2450 [16180]

J & M Construction, 1014 S Market St., Wilmington, DE 19801, (302)995-2819 [7528]

J & M Industries, Inc., 1014 S Market St., Wilmington, DE 19801, (302)995-2819 [7528]

J & M Industries Inc., 6803 W 64th St., Ste. 320, Shawnee Mission, KS 66202-4178, (913)362-8994 [6403]

J & M Sportswear Inc., PO Box 23550, Shawnee Mission, KS 66223-0550, (913)897-5400 [5071]

J & M Wholesale Distributors, 70 1/2 Commonwealth Ave., Bristol, VA 24201, (540)669-4833 [26538]

J-Mark, 2790 Ranchview Ln., Minneapolis, MN 55447, (612)559-3300 [2806]

J and R Bottling and Distribution Co., 820 S Vail Ave., Montebello, CA 90640, (213)685-8387 [24975]

J and R Bottling and Distribution Co., 820 S Vail Ave., Montebello, CA 90640, (213)685-8387 [11538]

J & R Industries Inc., PO Box 4221, Shawnee Mission, KS 66204-0221, (913)362-6667 [21468]

J & R Mercantile Ltd., PO Box 5052, Gallup, NM 87305-5049, (505)722-6015 [18017]

J-Snell & Co., Inc., 156 Mendell St., San Francisco, CA 94124, (415)206-7700 [21074]

J & V Vending Wholesale, RR 155A Lover's Lane, Salmon, ID 83467, (208)756-3166 [26311]

J and V Vending Wholesale, RR 155A Lover's Ln., Salmon, ID 83467, (208)756-3166 [26312]

J.A. Apparel Corp., 650 5th Ave., 27th Fl., New York, NY 10019, (212)586-9140 [5072]

J.A. Optronics, 7337 Old Alexandria Ferry Rd., Clinton, MD 20735-1832, (301)868-5316 [19383]

Jabo Supply Corp., PO Box 238, Huntington, WV 25707, (304)736-8333 [23223]

JaCiva's Chocolate and Pastries, 4733 SE Hawthorne, Portland, OR 97215, (503)234-8115 [11539]

Jack Berman, 1101 Warson Rd., St. Louis, MO 63132, (314)997-5900 [13643]

Jack & Co.; K.L., 145 Warren Ave., Portland, ME 04103-1103, (207)878-3600 [18526]

Jack and Jill Ice Cream, 3100 Marwin Ave., Bensalem, PA 19020, (215)639-2300 [11540]

Jack Jochim, Jr., PO Box 488, Biloxi, MS 39533, (601)436-4697 [26283]

Jack LLC; Judith, 392 5th Ave., New York, NY 10018, (212)695-4004 [17464]

Jack Spratt Woodwind Shop, 11 Park Ave., Old Greenwich, CT 06870-0277, (203)637-1176 [15178]

Jacklin Seed Co., PO Box 218, Nezperce, ID 83543, (208)937-2481 [873]

Jacklin Seed Co., 1490 Industrial Way SW, Albany, OR 97321, (541)928-3677 [874]

Jacklin Seed Simplot Turf & Horticulture, 5300 W Riverbend Ave., Post Falls, ID 83854-9499, (208)773-7581 [875]

Jacklin Steel Supply Co., 2410 Aero Park Dr., Traverse City, MI 49686, (616)946-8434 [20073]

Jack's Bean Co., PO Box 327, Holyoke, CO 80734, (970)854-3702 [11541]

Jacks Fragrances, 1953 Canterbury Dr., Las Vegas, NV 89119-6102, (702)795-0564 [25691]

Jacks Original Pizza, 401 W North Ave., Little Chute, WI 54140, (920)788-7320 [11542]

Jack's Salvage & Auto Parts Inc., 625 Metacom Ave., Bristol, RI 02809-5131, (401)253-3478 [2807]

Jack's Tack International Distributors, 12607 Southeastern Ave., Indianapolis, IN 46259-1151, (317)862-6842 [5073]

Jackson Associates Inc.; Bill, PO Box 801867, Dallas, TX 75380-1867, (972)233-8954 [13148]

Jackson Coca-Cola Bottling Co., PO Box 2397, Jackson, MS 39225-2397, (601)355-6487 [24976]

Jackson Hole Distributing, PO Box 7503, Jackson, WY 83001, (307)733-5609 [1777]

Jackson Iron and Metal Co., PO Box 1327, Jackson, MI 49204-1166, (517)787-1731 [20074]

Jackson-Jennings Farm Bureau Cooperative, PO Box 304, Seymour, IN 47274, (812)522-4911 [22381]

Jackson Paper Company Inc., 197 N Gallatin St., Jackson, MS 39207, (601)360-9620 [21781]

Jackson Produce Co., 3226 McKelvey Rd., Bridgeton, MO 63044, (314)291-1080 [11543]

Jackson Supply Co., 1012 NE 3rd, Amarillo, TX 79107, (806)373-1888 [4643]

Jackson Supply Co., 1012 NE 3rd, Amarillo, TX 79107, (806)373-1888 [24147]

Jackson Welding Supply, 1421 W Carson St., Pittsburgh, PA 15219, (412)391-4500 [16181]

Jackson Wholesale Co., PO Box 634, Jackson, KY 41339, (606)666-2495 [11544]

Jackson Wholesale Company Inc.; Paul, PO Box 1020, Roseburg, OR 97470, (541)672-7771 [11545]

JacksonLea, 75 Progress Ln., Waterbury, CT 06705, (203)753-5116 [16966]

Jacksonville Candy Company Inc., 218 Woodrow St., Jacksonville, TX 75766, (903)586-8334 [11546]

Jacksonville Mechanical Supply Inc., 618 Richlands Hwy., Jacksonville, NC 28540, (252)455-8328 [16967]

Jacksonville Sound and Communications Inc., 5021 Stepp Ave., Jacksonville, FL 32216, (904)737-3511 [25256]

Jackster Inc., 670 Surf Ave., Stratford, CT 06497-6733, (203)378-4023 [5074]

Jaco Co., 4848 Ronson Ct., San Diego, CA 92111, (619)278-7743 [18867]

Jaco Electronics Inc., 145 Oser Ave., Hauppauge, NY 11788, (516)273-5500 [8903]

Jacob and Sons; M., PO Box 9069, Farmington Hills, MI 48333, (313)737-9440 [25921]

Jacobi Hardware Co., Inc., 721 Surry St., PO Drawer 3728, Wilmington, NC 28406, (919)763-1644 [18527]

Jacobi-Lewis Co., 622 S Front St., PO Box 1289, Wilmington, NC 28402, (910)763-6201 [24148]

Jacobi Sales Inc., Hwy. 150, Palmyra, IN 47164, (812)364-6141 [876]

Jacobi and Sons Inc.; Walter, PO Box 471, Belmont, CA 94002, (650)593-6815 [13149]

Jacobi and Sons Inc.; Walter, PO Box 471, Belmont, CA 94002, (650)593-6815 [13150]

Jacobs Iron and Metal Co., 3330 Pluto St., Dallas, TX 75212, (214)631-6740 [26856]

Jacob's Store Inc., 204 Centennial St., Carmine, TX 78932, (409)278-3242 [877]

Jacobs Supply Co.; Mylon C., PO Box 1469, Broken Arrow, OK 74013, (918)455-8811 [2808]

Jacobs Trading Co., 901 N 3rd St., Minneapolis, MN 55401, (612)349-2300 [15543]

Jacobson Capital Services Inc., 150 Croton Ave., Peekskill, NY 10566, (914)736-0600 [26078]

Jacobson Cattle Co., PO Box 874, Baker, MT 59313-0874, (406)778-3110 [18018]

Jacobson & Company Inc., 1079 E Grand St., Elizabeth, NJ 07207-0511, (908)355-5200 [7529]

Jacobson Computer Inc., 5610 Monroe St., Sylvania, OH 43560-2701, (419)885-0082 [6404]

Jacobus Co., 11815 W Bradley Rd., Milwaukee, WI 53224, (414)354-0700 [22382]

Jacobus Energy, 11815 W Bradley Rd., Milwaukee, WI 53224, (414)354-0700 [22382]

Jacoby Appliance Parts, 269 Main St., Hackensack, NJ 07601, (201)489-6444 [15179]

Jacon Fasteners and Electronics Inc., 9539 Vassar Ave., Chatsworth, CA 91311, (818)700-2901 [13768]

Jacques DuBois Perfume Inc., PO Box 4067, Ann Arbor, MI 48106, (734)769-5640 [14136]

Jade Electronics Distributors, 275 Andrews Rd., Trevose, PA 19053, (215)322-7040 [25257]

Jademar Corp., 10125 NW 116th Way, Ste. 10, Miami, FL 33178-1164, (305)488-5550 [8904]

Jaeckle Distributors, 3171 Rider Trl S, Bridgeton, MO 63045-1519, (314)344-9905 [9977]

Jaeckle Wholesale Inc., 2310 Daniels St., Madison, WI 53704-6706, (608)221-8400 [9978]

Jaftex Corp., 11 E 36th St., New York, NY 10016, (212)686-5194 [26079]

JaGee Corp., PO Box 9600, Ft. Worth, TX 76147, (817)335-5881 [18019]

Jagoe; Philip, 1536 Main Rd., Tiverton, RI 02878-4417, (401)624-9792 [26539]

Jaguar Cars, 555 MacArthur Blvd., Mahwah, NJ 07430-2327, (201)818-8500 [2809]

J.A.H. Enterprises, Inc., PO Box 336, Livingston, LA 70754, (504)686-2252 [7530]

Jahm Inc., 1155 E Whitcomb Ave., Madison Heights, MI 48071, (313)583-2710 [2810]

Jahn and Son Inc.; Henry R., 26 Broadway 20th Fl., New York, NY 10004, (212)509-7920 [16182]

Jain Publishing Co., PO Box 3523, Fremont, CA 94539, (510)659-8272 [3858]

Jalmar Press/Innerchoice Publishing, 24426 S Main St., No. 702, Carson, CA 90745, (310)816-3085 [3859]

Jalopy Jungle Inc., 7804 S Hwy. 79, Rapid City, SD 57701, (605)348-8442 [2811]

Jamco, 4309 Hilton NE, Albuquerque, NM 87110, (505)256-1092 [17465]

Jameco Electronics Inc., 1355 Shoreway Rd., Belmont, CA 94002, (650)592-8097 [8905]

James Agriculture Center Inc., PO Box 87, Neelyville, MO 63954, (573)989-3250 [878]

James and Company Inc.; E., 1725 W Division St., Chicago, IL 60622, (773)227-1881 [16968]

James Co.; Milton, 8411 Pulaski Hwy., Baltimore, MD 21237, (410)687-1700 [1292]

James Industries Inc., PO Box 407, Hollidaysburg, PA 16648, (814)695-5681 [26540]

James International Trading Company, 3215 Summit Dr., Birmingham, AL 35243, (205)879-0516 [25692]

James Oil Co., PO Box 328, Carlisle, IA 50047, (515)989-3314 [22383]

James River Coal Sales, Inc., 701 E Byrd St., Ste. 1100, Richmond, VA 23219, (804)780-3003 [20548]

James River Corporation of Connecticut, PO Box 6000, Norwalk, CT 06856, (203)854-2000 [21782]

James William Scott Corp., 10000 W 75th St., Ste. 200A, Shawnee Mission, KS 66204-2241, (913)384-0880 [6414]

Jamestown Distributors Inc., PO Box 348, Jamestown, RI 02835-0348, (401)423-2520 [18528]

Jamestown Implement Inc., PO Box 469, Jamestown, ND 58401, (701)252-0580 [879]

Jamestown Livestock Sales, RR 3, Jamestown, ND 58401-9803, (701)252-2111 [18020]

Jamesville Office Furnishing, 11309 Folsom Blvd., Ste. B, Rancho Cordova, CA 95742, (916)638-4050 [13151]

Jampro Antennas, Inc., 6340 Sky Creek Rd., Sacramento, CA 95828, (916)383-1177 [8906]

Jan-Mar Industries, PO Box 314, Hillsdale, NJ 07642, (201)664-3930 [25258]

Jane Co., 6901 Magda Dr., Osseo, MN 55369-5639, (612)533-6040 [6405]

Janesway Electronic Corp., 404 N Terrace Ave., Mt. Vernon, NY 10552, (914)699-6710 [8907]

Jani-Serv, 5500 W Howard St., Skokie, IL 60077-2699, (847)982-9000 [4644]

Janitor Supply Co., 1100 S Main St., Aberdeen, SD 57401-7030, (605)225-0444 [4645]

Janitor Supply Co., 1100 S Main St., Aberdeen, SD 57401-7030, (605)225-0444 [24149]

Janos Technology Inc., HCR 33, Rte. 35, Box 25, Townshend, VT 05353, (802)365-7714 [18868]

Jans Distributing Inc., 1807 W 47th Ave., Anchorage, AK 99517-3164, (907)243-5267 [26313]

Jansco Marketing Inc., 769 Plain St., Marshfield, MA 02050-2118, (781)837-4300 [26541]

Jansport Inc., PO Box 1817, Appleton, WI 54913, (920)734-5708 [5075]

Jantzen Inc., 101 Mountainview Dr., Seneca, SC 29678, (864)882-3393 [5076]

Janvey and Sons Inc.; I., 218 Front St., Hempstead, NY 11550, (516)489-9300 [4646]

JanWay Co., 11 Academy Rd., Cogan Station, PA 17728, (570)494-1239 [13378]

Japco Exports, 2472 SW Falcon Cir., Port St. Lucie, FL 34953, (561)878-6084 [27159]

Jarboe Sales Co., PO Box 580130, Tulsa, OK 74158, (918)836-2511 [1778]

Jardine Petroleum, 814 W 24th St., Ogden, UT 84401, (801)393-7930 [22384]

Jardine Petroleum Co., PO Box 510170, Salt Lake City, UT 84151-0170, (801)532-3211 [22385]

Jarett Industries Inc., 134 Brentwood, South Orange, NJ 07079-1141, (201)539-4410 [16969]

Jarnagin; C & D, 1012 Washington St., Corinth, MS 38834-4739, (601)287-4977 [26542]

Jarrell Distributors Inc., 2651 Fondren Dr., Dallas, TX 75206, (214)363-7211 [15180]

Jarritos Distributors, 1477 Lomaland Dr., Bldg. E, Ste. 7, El Paso, TX 79935, (915)594-1618 [24977]

Jarvis-Paris-Murphy Company Inc., PO Box 1848, Waco, TX 76703, (254)756-7261 [18021]

Jarvis Steel and Lumber Company Inc., 1030 E Patapsco Ave., Baltimore, MD 21225, (410)355-3000 [7531]

Jarvis Supply Co., PO Box 645, Winfield, KS 67156, (316)221-3113 [16183]

Jarvis Supply Co., 117 E Sherman, Hutchinson, KS 67501-7160, (316)221-3113 [2812]

Jasco Tile Company, Inc., 2345 Rte. 22, Center Island, Union, NJ 07083, (908)688-4900 [9979]

Jasmine Ltd., 8501 Maple Ave., Pennsauken, NJ 08109-3337, (609)665-7117 [24777]

Jasper County Farm Bureau Cooperative, PO Box 238, Rensselaer, IN 47978, (219)866-7131 [18022]

Jasper Engineering and Equipment Co., 3800 5th Ave. W, Hibbing, MN 55746-2816, (218)262-3421 [16970]

Jasper Farmers Elevator, PO Box 266, Jasper, MN 56144, (507)348-3911 [537]

Jasper Farmers Exchange Inc., 308 W Morrison Ave., Jasper, MO 64755, (417)394-2156 [880]

JATCO Inc., 725 Zwissig Way, Union City, CA 94587, (510)487-0888 [22985]

Jaunty Co., Inc., 1850 Beverly Blvd., Los Angeles, CA 90057, (213)413-3333 [15544]

Java City Inc., 717 W Del Paso Rd., Sacramento, CA 95834, (916)565-5500 [11547]

Java Dave's Executive Coffee Service, 6239 E 15th St., Tulsa, OK 74112, (918)836-5570 [11548]

Javatec Inc., State Rt. 684, Speedwell, VA 24374, (540)621-4572 [8908]

Javi Farm Inc., 425 E Moore Dr., Pharr, TX 78577-6309, (956)783-1112 [11549]

Jawd Associates Inc., 47-49 Little W 12th St., New York, NY 10014, (212)989-2000 [11550]

Jawz Inc., 501 Industrial Way, Fallbrook, CA 92028, (760)728-8380 [25693]

Jax International, 40 E Verdugo Ave., Burbank, CA 91502-1931, (707)584-7360 [21075]

Jay-Cee Sales and Rivet Inc., 32861 Chelsey Dr., Farmington, MI 48336, (248)478-2150 [13769]

Jay Instrument and Specialty Co., 555 N Wayne Ave., Cincinnati, OH 45215, (513)733-5200 [8909]

Jay-K Independent Lumber Corp., PO Box 378, New Hartford, NY 13413, (315)735-4475 [7532]

Jay Mar Sales Inc., 176 Chase River Rd., Waterbury, CT 06704-1408, (203)753-1815 [26543]

Jay Mart Wholesale, 1568 S Green Rd., Cleveland, OH 44121, (216)382-7600 [25259]

Jayark Corp., 300 Plaza Dr., Vestal, NY 13850-3647 [25260]

Jaydon Inc., PO Box 4990, Rock Island, IL 61201, (309)787-4492 [14134]

Jaydor Corp., 16 Bleeker St., Millburn, NJ 07041, (973)379-1234 [1779]

Jay's Indian Arts Inc., 2227 E 7th Ave., Flagstaff, AZ 86004, (520)526-2439 [17466]

Jay's Perfume Bar, PO Box 524, Marlboro, NJ 07746 [14135]

Jaytow International Inc., 82 Lake Shore Dr., Ste. 211, Rockaway, NJ 07866, (973)625-1197 [5843]

JB Junk & Salvage Inc., 2535 9th Ave. NW, Great Falls, MT 59404-5312, (406)454-1917 [2813]

JB Tile Co., PO Box 65217, Salt Lake City, UT 84165, (801)972-4444 [9980]

J.B. Wholesale, 289 Wagaraw Rd., Hawthorne, NJ 07506, (973)423-2222 [27160]

JBA Headers, 7149 Mission Gorge Rd., San Diego, CA 92120-1130, (619)229-7797 [2814]

JBL Professional, 8500 Balboa Blvd., Northridge, CA 91329, (818)894-8850 [25261]

JBM Associates Inc., PO Box 188, Foxboro, MA 02035-0188, (508)543-3611 [23755]

JBM Sales, 36 Moreau St., Stoughton, MA 02072-4022, (781)344-0573 [26080]

JC Industrial Motor Service Inc., 30121 Groesbeck Hwy., Roseville, MI 48066, (810)779-4663 [16184]

JC Paper, 650 Brennan St., PO Box 610460, San Jose, CA 95161-0460, (408)435-2700 [21783]

JC Produce Inc., PO Box 1027, West Sacramento, CA 95691, (916)372-4050 [11551]

J.C. Sales Company Inc., PO Box 1300, Anderson, IN 46015-1300, (765)644-8815 [26544]

J.C. Supply, 10030 Talley Lane, Houston, TX 77041, (281)448-8682 [8910]

JC Whitney & Co., 225 N Michigan Ave., Chicago, IL 60601, (312)431-6000 [2815]

JCA Technology Group, A TVC Company, 130 Industrial Dr., Chambersburg, PA 17201-0444, (717)263-8258 [25487]

JCA Technology Group, A TVC Company, 130 Industrial Dr., Chambersburg, PA 17201-0444, (717)263-8258 [15181]

JCG Corp., 501 Mokauea St. B, Honolulu, HI 96819-3232, (808)841-1882 [5077]

J.C.M.D. Inc., 498 7th Ave., New York, NY 10018, (212)594-3118 [5082]

JCS Enterprises, Inc., 99-061 Koaha Way, Aiea, HI 96701, (808)488-6195 [5078]

J.D. Products, PO Box 4067, Ann Arbor, MI 48106, (734)769-5640 [14136]

JDB Merchandising, PO Box 4032, St. Johnsbury, VT 05819, (802)748-1123 [2816]

JDK Enterprises Inc., 3948 Forest Oaks Ln., Mebane, NC 27302-9625, (919)563-5068 [5079]

JDL Technologies Inc., 5555 West 78th St., Ste. E, Edina, MN 55439, (612)946-1810 [6406]

JDM Data Systems Inc., PO Box 4219, Fall River, MA 02723-0402, (508)678-4904 [6407]

JDR Microdevices Inc., 1850 S 10th St., San Jose, CA 95112-4108, (408)494-1400 [6408]

JDS Fashions Inc., 601 Hansen Ave., Butler, PA 16001-5664, (724)282-8581 [5362]

JDS Industries Inc., 2704 W 3rd St., Sioux Falls, SD 57104-6210, (605)339-4010 [17467]

J.E. Hanger Incorporated of Georgia, PO Box 406, Alpharetta, GA 30009-0406, (770)442-9870 [19046]

Jealco International, Inc., 435 Jones Dr., Roswell, GA 30075, (404)998-2124 [16185]

Jeanie's Classics, 2123 Oxford St., Rockford, IL 61103-4160, (815)968-4544 [3860]

Jean's Dulcimer Shop and Crying Creek Publishers, Hwy. 32, PO Box 8, Cosby, TN 37722, (423)487-5543 [3861]

Jed Co.; Leonard, 1301 Covington St., Baltimore, MD 21230, (410)685-1482 [13770]

Jeff Bottling Company Inc., 1035 Bradley St., Watertown, NY 13601, (315)788-6751 [24978]

Jefferds Corp., Rte. 35 W, PO Box 757, St. Albans, WV 25177, (304)755-8111 [16186]

Jefferies Socks, PO Box 1680, Burlington, NC 27216-1680, (336)226-7315 [5080]

Jeffers Vet Supply, Old Airport Rd., West Plains, MO 65775, (417)256-3197 [27161]

Jeffers Vet Supply, PO Box 100, Dothan, AL 36302, (334)793-6257 [27162]

Jeffers Vet Supply, PO Box 100, Dothan, AL 36302, (334)793-6257 [19384]

Jefferson City Oil Company Inc., PO Box 576, Jefferson City, MO 65102-0576, (573)634-2025 [22386]

Jefferson County Farmco Coop., PO Box 359, Jefferson, WI 53549, (920)674-7000 [881]

Jefferson Farmers Cooperative, 106 Highway 92 South, PO Box 1429, Dandridge, TN 37725, (423)397-3434 [882]

Jeffress Business Services, 18834 SE 42nd St., Issaquah, WA 98027-9366, (425)643-1917 [24778]

Jeffrey's Seed Company Inc., PO Box 887, Goldsboro, NC 27530, (919)734-2985 [883]

Jeffrey's Steel Company Inc., PO Box 2763, Mobile, AL 36652, (334)456-4531 [20075]

Jelina International Ltd., 530 7th Ave., New York, NY 10018, (212)827-0228 [5081]

Jellyroll Productions, PO Box 255, Port Townsend, WA 98368, (360)385-1200 [3862]

Jemison Investment Company Inc., 320 Park Place Twr., Birmingham, AL 35203, (205)324-7681 [7533]

Jen-Mar Ltd., 498 7th Ave., New York, NY 10018, (212)594-3118 [5082]

Jenik Automotive Distributors Inc., 3385 Seneca Dr., Las Vegas, NV 89109-3136, (702)736-6556 [2817]

Jenkel Oil Company Inc., PO Box 25, Combined Locks, WI 54113, (920)739-6101 [22387]

Jenkins Co.; H.W., PO Box 18347, Memphis, TN 38181-0347, (901)363-7641 [27324]

Jenkins Gas and Oil Company Inc., PO Box 156, Pollocksville, NC 28573, (919)224-8911 [22388]

Jenkins Metal Corp. Hunting Classics Limited Div., PO Box 2089, Gastonia, NC 28053, (704)867-6394 [15545]

Jenkins Sons Company Inc.; J., 1801 Whitehead Rd., Baltimore, MD 21207, (410)265-5200 [17468]

Jenkins Trading Inc., PO Box 6059, Chelsea, MA 02150-0006, (617)387-7300 [3863]

Jenks & Son; W.S., 1933 Montana Ave., NE, Washington, DC 20002, (202)529-6020 [8911]

Jenne Distributors, 33665 Chester Rd., Avon, OH 44011-1307, (440)835-0040 [5653]

Jennings Implement Company Inc., Hwy. 54 & Hwy. 154, Curryville, MO 63339, (573)594-6493 [884]

Jennison Industrial Supply, PO Box 717, Bay City, MI 48707-0717, (517)895-5531 [13771]

Jensen Bridge and Supply Co., PO Box 151, Sandusky, MI 48471, (810)648-3000 [23224]

Jensen-Byrd Company Inc., PO Box 3708, Spokane, WA 99220, (509)624-1321 [13773]

Jensen-Byrd Company Inc., PO Box 3708, Spokane, WA 99220, (509)624-1321 [13772]

Jensen Distribution Services, PO Box 3708, Spokane, WA 99220, (509)624-1321 [13773]

Jensen Lloyd and Willis, 110 Dakota Ave. N, Huron, SD 57350-1630, (605)352-9309 [18023]

Jensen Tools Inc., 7815 S 46th St., Phoenix, AZ 85044, (602)453-3169 [8912]

Jensen Tools Inc., 7815 S 46th St., Phoenix, AZ 85044, (602)968-6231 [16187]

JEOL U.S.A. Inc., 11 Dearborn Rd., Peabody, MA 01960, (978)535-5900 [24378]

Jerabek Wholesalers, Inc.; Paul, 407 9th Ave. SE, Cedar Rapids, IA 52401, (319)365-7591 [1780]

Jerome Distribution Inc., PO Box 227, Dickinson, ND 58602-0227, (701)225-3187 [1781]

Jerome Wholesales Inc., PO Box 550, Devils Lake, ND 58301-0550, (701)662-5366 [1782]

Jerrine Company Inc., PO Box 53, Zumbrota, MN 55992, (507)732-7838 [885]

Jerry's Artarama Inc., 5325 Departure Dr., Raleigh, NC 27616-1835, (919)878-6782 [25694]

Jerry's At Misquamicut Inc., PO Box 371, Westerly, RI 02891-0371, (401)596-3155 [19385]

Jerry's Sport Center Inc., PO Box 121, Forest City, PA 18421-0121, (570)785-9400 [23756]

Jersey County Farm Supply Co., PO Box 367, Jerseyville, IL 62052, (618)498-5534 [886]

Jersey Model Distributors, 806 US Rte. 17, Ramsey, NJ 07446, (201)327-7911 [26545]

Jersey Truck Equipment Co., 5018 Industrial Rd., Wall, NJ 07719, (732)938-6688 [2818]

Jess Implements Inc.; Jim, PO Box 788, Coulee City, WA 99115, (509)632-5547 [887]

Jet Equipment and Tools, PO Box 1349, Auburn, WA 98071, (206)351-6000 [108]

Jet Wine and Spirits Inc., PO Box 1113, Manchester, NH 03105-1113, (603)669-5884 [1783]

Jeter Store Equipment, Inc.; Ken, 5124 Cliff Gookin Blvd., Tupelo, MS 38801-7001, (601)844-1192 [14497]

Jeter Systems Corp., 1560 Firestone Pkwy., Akron, OH 44301, (330)773-8971 [21076]

Jetfreeze Distributing, 2501 30th Ave., Gulfport, MS 39501, (228)864-1434 [11552]

Jethro Publications, 2105 Nighthawk Dr., Laramie, WY 82072-1900 [3864]

Jetmore Distributing, 3343 Merrick Rd., Wantagh, NY 11793, (516)826-1166 [15182]

Jetro Cash and Carry Enterprises Inc., 1506 132nd St., College Point, NY 11356, (718)649-8000 [11553]

JETT Supply Company Inc., PO Box 2400, Pueblo, CO 81005, (719)564-6791 [7534]

Jetzon Tire and Rubber Company Inc., 1050 Bethelem Pike, Box 249, Montgomeryville, PA 18936-0249, (215)643-2300 [2819]

Jewel Box Inc., 601 N Central Ave., Phoenix, AZ 85004-2126, (602)252-5777 [23757]

Jewel and Co., 9601 Apollo Dr., Largo, MD 20774, (301)925-6200 [5083]

Jewel Electric Inc., 225 Gladstone, Idaho Falls, ID 83401, (208)523-9862 [14628]

Jewel Paula-Ronn Records, PO Box 1125, Shreveport, LA 71163, (318)865-5318 [21077]

The Jewelers of Las Vegas, 2400 Western Ave., Las Vegas, NV 89102-4810, (702)382-7413 [17469]

Jewelmasters Inc., 3123 Commerce Pky., Miramar, FL 33025-3944, (561)655-7260 [17470]

Jewelry By Dyan & Eduardo, 2762 W Union Ave., Las Cruces, NM 88005-4313, (505)523-8031 [17471]

Jewelry Exchange Inc., 549 E Sahara Ave., Las Vegas, NV 89104-2730, (702)369-0669 [17472]

Jewelry Trend Inc., White Horse Sq., Box 56, Helen, GA 30545, (706)878-3080 [17473]

J.F. Bellini Co., 5550 Cameron St., Ste. A, Las Vegas, NV 89118-6221, (702)732-7275 [9721]

JFC International Inc., 540 Forbes Blvd., South San Francisco, CA 94080, (415)873-8400 [11554]

JFK Enterprises, No. 2 Schenkers Dr., Suite A, Kenner, LA 70062, (504)464-1128 [27163]

JGL Inc., 1901 Beverly Blvd., Los Angeles, CA 90057-9906, (213)413-0220 [17474]

J.H. Service Company Inc., PO Box 65, Bellaire, OH 43906-0218, (740)983-2525 [8913]

JH Service Company Inc., PO Box 65, Elberfeld, IN 47613, (812)983-2525 [8914]

JHB International Inc., 1955 S Quince St., Denver, CO 80231, (303)751-8100 [26081]

Jideco of Bardstown Inc., 901 Withrow Ct., Bardstown, KY 40004, (502)348-3100 [2820]

Jiffy Foam, Inc., PO Box 3609, Newport, RI 02840, (401)846-7870 [14896]

Jiffy Metal Products Co., 5025 W Lake St., Chicago, IL 60644, (773)626-8090 [2821]

Jilnance Corp., PO Box 20534, Rochester, NY 14602, (716)235-1662 [3109]

Jilnance Corp., PO Box 20534, Rochester, NY 14602, (716)235-1662 [2822]

Jim Sales & Service, 804 S B St., Grangeville, ID 83530-1510, (208)983-1442 [24379]

Jimbo's Jumbos Inc., PO Box 465, Edenton, NC 27932, (919)482-2193 [18024]

Jimlar Corp., 160 Great Neck Rd., Great Neck, NY 11021, (516)829-1717 [24779]

Jimmy's Seaside Co., 1 Boston Fish Pier, Boston, MA 02110 [11555]

Jim's Beauty Supply, 302 Pearman Dairy Rd., Anderson, SC 29625, (864)224-0577 [14137]

Jim's Formal Wear Co., 1 Tuxedo Park, Trenton, IL 62293, (618)224-9211 [5084]

Jim's Supply Company Inc., PO Box 668, Bakersfield, CA 93302, (661)324-6514 [20076]

Jimson Novelties Inc., 28 E 18th St., New York, NY 10003, (212)477-3386 [13379]

Jinelle, 1031 S Broadway, No. 934, Los Angeles, CA 90015-4006, (213)747-4120 [4982]

Jirdon Agri Chemicals Inc., PO Box 516, Morrill, NE 69358, (308)247-2126 [14897]

JJ Gold International Inc., 20227 NE 15th Ct., North Miami Beach, FL 33179, (305)654-8833 [17475]

J.J.R. Enterprises Inc., 10491 Old Placerville Rd., No. 150, Sacramento, CA 95827, (916)363-2666 [21078]

JK Miami Corp., 27000 NW 5th Ave., Ste. 13, Miami, FL 33127-4144, (305)576-1578 [5085]

JK Sports, 1801 W Lincoln Ave., Fergus Falls, MN 56537, (218)739-5299 [5086]

JLA Distributors Inc., 5950 6th Ave. S, Ste. 204, Seattle, WA 98108-3305, (206)767-2777 [10348]

JLJ Inc., 2538 Addison Ave., No. E-1, Twin Falls, ID 83301-6749, (208)734-9089 [24577]

JLK Direct Distribution Inc., PO Box 231, Latrobe, PA 15650-0231, (724)539-5000 [16188]

J.M. Equipment Co., 819 S 9th St., Modesto, CA 95351, (209)522-3271 [16189]

JM Family Enterprises Inc., 100 Northwest 12th Ave., Deerfield Beach, FL 33442, (954)429-2000 [20656]

JM/Ontario Tees, 847 S Wanamaker, Ontario, CA 91761, (909)390-0711 [5087]

JM Smith Corp., PO Box 1779, Spartanburg, SC 29304, (864)582-1216 [19386]

JMD Beverages, 99-1269 Iwaena St., Aiea, HI 96701, (808)487-9985 [1784]

JML Sales Corp., 15326 E Valley Blvd., La Puente, CA 91744, (626)369-3778 [14898]

JMR Inc., 9775 SW Commerce Cir., 3C, Wilsonville, OR 97070-9602, (503)682-1416 [5088]

JNT Corporation, PO Box 1125, Newport News, VA 23601-0125, (757)599-0916 [5089]

JO-D Books, 81 Willard Terr., Stamford, CT 06903, (203)322-0568 [3865]

J.O. Spice Company Inc., 3721 Old Georgetown Rd., Baltimore, MD 21227, (410)247-5205 [11556]

Joannou Cycle Company Inc.; G., 151 Ludlow Ave., Northvale, NJ 07647, (201)768-9050 [23758]

Joe's Firestone Inc., 819 Hwy. 1 S, Greenville, MS 38701, (601)335-9221 [2823]

Joffe Lumber and Supply Company Inc., 18 Burns Ave., Vineland, NJ 08360, (609)825-9550 [7535]

Jog-A-Lite Inc., 18 High St., PO Box 125, Silver Lake, NH 03875, (603)367-4741 [23759]

Jogue Corp., 6349 E Palmer St., Detroit, MI 48211, (313)921-4802 [11557]

Johannsens Inc., PO Box 23, Augusta, GA 30903-0023, (706)722-0949 [24780]

John J. Hudson, Inc., 30 Shipyard St., Providence, RI 02903, (401)781-8200 [7496]

John Pearse Strings, PO Box 295, Center Valley, PA 18034, (610)691-3302 [25108]

Johnny's Crab Traps Inc., 10410 Chef Menteur Hwy., New Orleans, LA 70127-4216, (504)246-2325 [23760]

Johnsen Co.; Hans, 8901 Chancellor Row, Dallas, TX 75247, (214)879-1515 [23761]

Johnson and Associates Business Interiors Inc., 223 W Erie St., Chicago, IL 60610, (312)649-0074 [13152]

Johnson & Associates; Steve, 66 E Escalon, No. 108, Fresno, CA 93710, (559)431-0320 [14138]

Johnson Books, 1880 S 57th Ct., Boulder, CO 80301, (303)443-9766 [3866]

Johnson Brothers, 223 Basalt, PO Box 1836, Idaho Falls, ID 83403-1836, (208)523-8600 [13774]

Johnson Brothers Co. (St. Paul, Minnesota), 2341 University Ave., St. Paul, MN 55114, (612)649-5800 [1785]

Johnson Brothers Liquor Co., 4520 S Church Ave., Tampa, FL 33611-2201, (813)884-0451 [1786]

Johnson Brothers Wholesale Liquor, 2341 University Ave. W, St. Paul, MN 55114, (651)649-5800 [1787]

Johnson Brothers Wholesale Liquor Co., 2341 University Ave. W, St. Paul, MN 55114, (612)649-5800 [1788]

Johnson Camping Inc., PO Box 966, Binghamton, NY 13902, (607)779-2200 [23762]

Johnson Company Inc.; George T., 141 Middlesex Tpk., Burlington, MA 01803, (781)272-4900 [4647]

Johnson and Company Wilderness Products Inc., PO Box 2009, Bangor, ME 04402, (207)862-3373 [5090]

Johnson Controls, Inc., 1600 Wilson Way SE, Smyrna, GA 30082, (770)436-2677 [14498]

Johnson Cooperative Grain Co., PO Box 280, Johnson, KS 67855, (316)492-6210 [888]

Johnson Dairy Co., PO Box 28, Bloomington, IN 47402, (812)332-2126 [11558]

Johnson Distributing, Inc., 1021 3rd St. NW, Great Falls, MT 59404-2360, (406)453-6541 [2824]

Johnson Distributors Truck Equipment, 1021 3rd St. NW, Great Falls, MT 59404-2360, (406)453-6541 [2824]

Johnson-Doppler Lumber Co., 3320 Llewellyn Ave., Cincinnati, OH 45223-2467, (513)541-0050 [7536]

Johnson Electric NA Inc., 3 Kent Pl., Asheville, NC 28804, (828)285-0575 [8915]

Johnson Electric Supply Co., 1841 Eastern Ave., Cincinnati, OH 45202, (513)421-3700 [8916]

Johnson Garment Corp., 3115 S Maple Ave., PO Box 603, Marshfield, WI 54449-0603, (715)384-5272 [5091]

Johnson Hardware Company Inc., 1201 Pacific St., Omaha, NE 68103, (402)444-1650 [7537]

Johnson Heater Corp.; 970 Executive Pkwy., St. Louis, MO 63141-6302, (314)542-9494 [14499]

Johnson Heating Supply, 232 NE 9th Ave., Portland, OR 97232, (503)234-5071 [14500]

Johnson Inc.; R.N., PO Box 448, Walpole, NH 03608, (603)756-3321 [889]

Johnson Motor Sales Inc., 620 Deere Dr., New Richmond, WI 54017, (715)246-2261 [2825]

Johnson Oil Company of Gaylord, 507 Otesgo Rd., Gaylord, MI 49735, (517)732-2451 [22389]

Johnson Pipe and Supply Co., 999 W 37th St., Chicago, IL 60609, (773)927-2427 [23225]

Johnson RDO Communications Co., 660 Transfer Rd., St. Paul, MN 55114-1402, (612)645-6471 [8917]

Johnson Safari Museum; Martin and Osa, 111 N Grant Ave., Chanute, KS 66720, (316)431-2730 [17476]

Johnson Supply Co., 50 S East St., PO Box 449, Pensacola, FL 32501, (850)434-7103 [18529]

Johnson Supply Controls Center, 24 W Memicken Ave., Cincinnati, OH 45210, (513)651-4328 [8918]

Johnson Supply and Equipment Corp., 10151 Stella Link, Houston, TX 77025, (713)661-6666 [14501]

Johnson and Towers Inc., PO Box 4000, Mt. Laurel, NJ 08054, (609)234-6990 [2826]

Johnston Coca-Cola, PO Box 207, Rockwood, TN 37854, (615)354-1631 [3867]

Johnston Company Inc.; George L., 1200 Holden Ave., Detroit, MI 48202 [14502]

Johnston County Feed & Farm Supply, PO Box 217, Tishomingo, OK 73460-0217, (580)371-3607 [890]

Johnston Distributing Co., 6523 Merle Hay Rd., PO Box 345, Johnston, IA 50131-0345, (515)276-5485 [2827]

Johnston Elevator Co., 307 N McEwan, Clare, MI 48617-1454, (517)386-7271 [18025]

Johnston Florist Inc., 14179 Lincoln, North Huntingdon, PA 15642, (412)751-2821 [14899]

Johnston Industrial Supply Co., 1435 N Nias, Springfield, MO 65802-2236, (417)869-1887 [16190]

Johnston-Lawrence Co., PO Box 1759, Kilgore, TX 75663-1759, (903)984-1591 [22390]

Johnstone Supply, 3720 E Pikes Peak Ave., Colorado Springs, CO 80909-6569, (719)550-0123 [14503]

Johnstone Supply, 3061 Kingston Ct., Marietta, GA 30067, (404)768-7337 [14504]

Johnstone Supply, 6019 Goshen Springs Rd., Norcross, GA 30071, (770)446-0400 [14505]

Johnstown Axle Works Inc., 100 Iron St., Johnstown, PA 15906, (814)533-2910 [2828]

Joiner Foodservice, Inc., PO Drawer 2547, Harlingen, TX 78550, (956)423-2003 [21784]

Joiner Foodservice Inc., PO Drawer 2547, Harlingen, TX 78550-0589, (956)423-2003 [11559]

Joint Clutch and Gear Service Inc., 1325 Howard, Detroit, MI 48226, (734)641-7575 [2829]

Joint and Clutch Service Inc., PO Box 21089, Indianapolis, IN 46221, (317)634-2428 [2830]

Joint and Clutch Service Inc., PO Box 30282, Charlotte, NC 28230, (704)334-6883 [2831]

Joint Production Technology Inc., 15381 Hallmark Ct., Macomb, MI 48042, (810)786-0080 [16191]

Joissu Products Inc., 4627 L B Mcleod Rd., Orlando, FL 32811-6405, (407)648-8746 [26546]

Jolie Handbags/Uptown Ltd., 10 W 33rd St., New York, NY 10001, (212)736-6677 [18402]

Joliet Equipment Corp., PO Box 114, Joliet, IL 60434, (815)727-6606 [2832]

Jolley Industrial Supply Company Inc., 105-109 Agate Way, Sharon, PA 16146, (412)981-5400 [16971]

Jolly & Sons, Inc.; Jack, 513 Pleasant Valley Ave., Moorestown, NJ 08057, (609)234-4448 [23763]

Jomar Distributors Inc., 767 Waverly St., Framingham, MA 01702-8512, (508)620-8885 [14506]

Jonas Aircraft and Arms Company Inc., 225 Broadway, New York, NY 10005, (212)619-0330 [109]

Jonas Aircraft and Arms Company Inc., 225 Broadway, New York, NY 10005, (212)619-0330 [24578]

Jonathan Abad, 455 16th St., Carlstadt, NJ 07072, (201)935-7717 [11252]

Jonel Inc., 600 N Mcclurg Ct. #2505, Chicago, IL 60611, (312)454-1214 [14139]

Jones & Bartlett Publishers Inc., 40 Tall Pine Dr., Sudbury, MA 01776, (978)443-5000 [3868]

Jones Blair Co., PO Box 35286, Dallas, TX 75235, (214)353-1600 [21469]

Jones Business Systems Inc., 13715 Murphy Rd., Ste. D, Stafford, TX 77477-4900, (281)403-8500 [6409]

Jones-Campbell Co., 3766 Bradview Dr., Sacramento, CA 95827, (916)362-0123 [13153]

Jones Co.; J.M., 2611 N Lincoln Ave., Urbana, IL 61801, (217)384-2800 [11560]

Jones Company of Memphis Inc.; Grady W., 3965 Old Getwell Rd., Memphis, TN 38118, (901)365-8830 [16192]

Jones Co.; Shelby, 8800 Westchester Pike, Upper Darby, PA 19082, (610)446-6600 [24380]

Jones Dairy Farm Distributors, N2195 Jones Ave., Ft. Atkinson, WI 53538, (920)563-2486 [11561]

Jones Distributors Inc.; Bill, PO Box 97, Sandpoint, ID 83864-0097, (208)263-5912 [1789]

Jones Electric Company Inc.; G.E., 204 N Polk St., Amarillo, TX 79105, (806)372-5505 [2833]

Jones Hardware Company Inc., 115 E Independence St., Shamokin, PA 17872, (570)648-4631 [13775]

Jones Inc.; Charlie C., 4041 E Thomas Rd., Ste. 200, Phoenix, AZ 85018-7530, (602)272-5621 [2834]

Jones Inc.; Ken, 73 Chandler St., Worcester, MA 01609, (508)755-5255 [2835]

Jones & Lee Supply Co., 1501 Linden Ave., Knoxville, TN 37917-7817, (423)524-5566 [8919]

Jones of Little Rock Inc.; Grady W., PO Box 97, North Little Rock, AR 72115, (501)945-2394 [16193]

Jones-McIntosh Tobacco Company Inc., PO Box 245, Syracuse, NY 13206, (315)463-9183 [26314]

Jones Office Equipment; Al, 8636 Highacre Dr., Las Vegas, NV 89128-4808, (702)623-2003 [21079]

Jones Oil Company Inc.; John E., 1016 S Cedar St., Stockton, KS 67669, (785)425-6746 [22391]

Jones Oil Company Inc.; N.E., PO Box 5070, Texarkana, TX 75505, (903)838-8541 [22392]

Jones Potatoes Inc.; Rolland, PO Box 475, Rupert, ID 83350, (208)436-9606 [11562]

Jones Sales Group, PO Box 270506, Flower Mound, TX 75027, (817)224-9000 [5654]

Jones Sportswear Company Inc., 1630 2nd Ave. S, Birmingham, AL 35233-1705, (205)326-6264 [5092]

Jones; Susan Brese, 110 E Main St., Thomaston, GA 30286-2920, (706)647-2178 [5093]

Jones Tractor Company Inc., PO Box 4187, Spartanburg, SC 29303, (864)582-1245 [891]

Jonesboro Coca-Cola, PO Box 19189, Jonesboro, AR 72402, (870)932-6601 [24979]

Jonesboro Grocer Co., PO Box 1873, Jonesboro, AR 72403, (501)932-3080 [11563]

Jonesboro Winnelson Co., 804 Dee Str., PO Box 637, Jonesboro, AR 72403-0637, (501)932-4543 [16972]

Jonner Steel Industries, 6349 Strong, Detroit, MI 48211, (313)262-5700 [20077]

Jordan Brookes Company Inc.; E., PO Box 910908, Los Angeles, CA 90091-0908, (323)722-8100 [20078]

Jordan Fashions Corp., 1385 Broadway, New York, NY 10018-6002, (212)921-5560 [5094]

Jordan Graphics, PO Box 668306, Charlotte, NC 28266, (704)394-2121 [21785]

Jordan Inc.; Leslie, 1230 SW 1st Ave., Portland, OR 97204-3234, (503)295-1987 [5095]

Jordan Lumber and Supply Inc., PO Box 98, Mt. Gilead, NC 27306, (910)439-6121 [7538]

Jordan Meat and Livestock Company Inc., 1225 W 3300 S, Salt Lake City, UT 84119, (801)972-8770 [11564]

Jordan Research Corp., 6244 Clark Center Ave., No. 4, Sarasota, FL 34238, (941)923-9707 [2836]

Jordanos Inc., 550 S Patterson Ave., Santa Barbara, CA 93111, (805)964-0611 [11565]

Jordan's Foods, PO Box 4657, Portland, ME 04112-4657, (207)871-0700 [11566]

Jordan's Meats Inc., PO Box 588, Portland, ME 04112, (207)772-5411 [11567]

Jorgensen Co.; Earle M., 3050 E Birch St., Brea, CA 92821, (714)579-8823 [20079]

Jorgensen Laboratories Inc., 1450 N Van Buren Ave., Loveland, CO 80538, (970)669-2500 [27164]

Jorgensen Steel Co., 1900 Mitchell Blvd., Schaumburg, IL 60193, (708)307-6100 [20080]

Jo's Designs, PO Box 1930, Zephyr Cove, NV 89448-1930, (702)588-3100 [5096]

JOS Projection Systems Inc., 180 S Prospect Ave., Tustin, CA 92780-3617, (714)476-2222 [21080]

Joseph Co.; David J., PO Box 1078, Cincinnati, OH 45201, (513)621-8770 [26857]

Joseph Co., Ferrous Div.; David J., PO Box 1078, Cincinnati, OH 45201, (513)621-8770 [26858]

Joseph Co. International Div.; David J., PO Box 1078, Cincinnati, OH 45201, (513)621-8770 [26859]

Joseph Co. Municipal Recycling Div.; David J., PO Box 1078, Cincinnati, OH 45201, (513)621-8770 [26860]

Joseph Co. Nonferrous Div.; David J., PO Box 1078, Cincinnati, OH 45201, (513)621-8770 [26861]

Joseph Foodservice, PO Box 51890, Knoxville, TN 37950-1890, (423)970-3200 [11492]

Joseph Industries Inc., 10039 Aurora Hudson Rd., Streetsboro, OH 44241, (330)528-0091 [16194]

Joseph Orchard Siding Inc.; George F., PO Box 158, Wapato, WA 98951-0158, (509)966-2130 [21786]

Joseph's Clothing & Sporting Goods, PO Box 180, Fairfield, ME 04937-0180, (207)453-9756 [23764]

Josephson's Smokehouse and Dock, PO Box 412, Astoria, OR 97103, (503)325-2190 [24150]

Joshua Distributing Co., 9246 Trinity Dr., Lake In The Hills, IL 60102, (708)697-5600 [6410]

Josin Fabrics, 2501 N 85th St., Omaha, NE 68134, (402)393-5677 [26082]

Jovino Company, Inc.; John, 5 Center Market Pl., New York, NY 10013, (212)925-4881 [13496]

Joy Co.; Edward, 903 Canal St., Syracuse, NY 13217, (315)474-3360 [8920]

Joy Company Inc.; B. Frank, 5355 Kilmer Pl., Bladensburg, MD 20710, (301)779-9400 [8921]

Joy Enterprises, 1104 53rd Court S, West Palm Beach, FL 33407-2350, (561)863-3205 [13776]

Joy Enterprises, 1104 53rd Court S, West Palm Beach, FL 33407-2350, (561)863-3205 [19388]

Joy Enterprises, 1104 53rd Court S, West Palm Beach, FL 33407-2350, (561)863-3205 [19387]

Joy Optical Co., 1104 53rd Court S, West Palm Beach, FL 33407-2350, (561)863-3205 [13776]

Joy Optical Co., 1104 53rd Court S, West Palm Beach, FL 33407-2350, (561)863-3205 [19388]

Joyce Brothers Inc., PO Box 888, Winston-Salem, NC 27102, (910)765-6927 [11568]

Joyce International Inc., 156 W 56th St., Ste. 1604, New York, NY 10019-3800, (212)463-9044 [21081]

Joyce Media Inc., 2654 Diamond St., PO Box 848, Rosamond, CA 93560, (661)256-0149 [3869]

Joyce-Munden Co., PO Box 25025, Winston-Salem, NC 27114-5025, (336)765-0234 [5097]

Joyce Sportswear Co., 1400 Calcutta Ln., Naperville, IL 60563-2215, (630)883-9681 [5098]

Joyserv Company Ltd., 1751 Talleyrand Ave., Jacksonville, FL 32206, (904)358-4400 [20657]

JP Associates, 488 7th Ave., 4th Fl., New York, NY 10018, (212)563-6663 [5099]

JP Foodservice Inc., 9830 Patuxent Woods Dr., Columbia, MD 21046, (410)312-7100 [11569]

JP Foodservice Inc., 9830 Patuxent Woods Dr., Columbia, MD 21046, (410)312-7100 [11570]

JP International Imports & Exports, PO Box 68, Marysville, MI 48040-0068, (810)364-9300 [23765]

JPA Electronics Supply Inc., Park 80 W, Plaza 1, Saddle Brook, NJ 07663, (201)845-0980 [18530]

JR Distributors, 3041 Marwin Rd., Bensalem, PA 19020, (215)639-1455 [11571]

JR Electronics and Assembly Inc., 2125 S 48th St., Tempe, AZ 85282, (602)438-2400 [8922]

J.R. Simplot Co., PO Box 70013, 418 S 9th St., Ste. 308, Boise, ID 83707-2700, (208)672-2700 [18234]

JRB Corp of Lynchburg, PO Box 1240, Verona, VA 24482-1240 [1790]

JRE Computing, PO Box 762, Baldwinsville, NY 13027-0762, (315)635-5009 [6411]

J.R.M. Inc., 523 E Malone St., Sikeston, MO 63801, (314)471-9111 [21082]

J.R.N. Inc., 1342 Featherbed Ln., Venice, FL 34292, (941)485-7517 [17477]

JS Enterprises Inc., 1905 Main St., MiLes City, MT 59301-3724, (406)232-6662 [24151]

J.S. Screw Manufacturing Co., 7040 Laurel Canyon, North Hollywood, CA 91615, (818)983-1715 [13777]

J.S. Woodhouse Co., PO Box 1169, West Springfield, MA 01089, (413)736-5462 [892]

JSB Software Technologies PLC, 108 Whispering Pine Dr., Scotts Valley, CA 95066, (831)438-8300 [6412]

JT Beverage Inc., PO Box 1526, Jamestown, ND 58402-1526, (701)252-3040 [1791]

JT Racing Inc., 515 Otay Valley Rd., Chula Vista, CA 91911-6059, (619)421-2660 [5100]

JTG of Nashville, PO Box 158116, Nashville, TN 37215, (615)665-8384 [25262]

JTM Tile Distributing, Inc., 112 N Layfair Dr., Jackson, MS 39208, (601)932-8689 [9981]

JTS Enterprises Inc., 4600 Post Oak Pl., Ste. 153, Houston, TX 77027, (713)621-6740 [4433]

Jud Bacastow, 6740 Dorsey Rd., Elkridge, MD 21075, (410)379-5100 [12421]

Judd Paper Co., PO Box 669, Holyoke, MA 01041, (413)534-5661 [21787]

Judee K Creations Inc., 7623 Fulton, North Hollywood, CA 91605, (818)765-4653 [17478]

Judson Lumber Co., 321 W Bigelow Ave., Plain City, OH 43064, (614)873-3911 [7539]

Judson Lumber Co., 321 W Bigelow Ave., Plain City, OH 43064, (614)873-3911 [27325]

Judson Press, PO Box 851, Valley Forge, PA 19482-0851 [3870]

Juergens Produce and Feed Co., PO Box 1027, Carroll, IA 51401, (712)792-3506 [893]

Julius Kraft Company Inc., 7 Pulaski St., Auburn, NY 13021, (315)252-7251 [24579]

Junction City Distributing Company Inc., PO Box 186, Junction City, KS 66441, (785)238-6137 [1792]

Jung Foundation; C.G., 28 E 39th St., New York, NY 10016, (212)697-6433 [3871]

Jungkind Photo-Graphic Inc., PO Box 1509, Little Rock, AR 72203, (501)376-3481 [25695]

Junius Book Distributors, Inc., PO Box 385, Hillsdale, NJ 07642-0385, (201)664-0127 [4135]

Juno Chefs Inc., 230 49th St., Brooklyn, NY 11220-1708, (718)492-1300 [11572]

Juno Industries Inc., 4355 Drane Field Rd., Lakeland, FL 33811, (813)646-1493 [16973]

Jupiter Band Instruments Inc., PO Box 90249, Austin, TX 78709, (512)288-7400 [25263]

Jurins Distributing Co., 200 N 16th St., PO Box 19476, Sacramento, CA 95819, (916)448-2052 [24152]

Just Desserts Inc., 1970 Carroll Ave., San Francisco, CA 94124, (415)330-3600 [11573]

Just Drop, Inc., 1950 NW 93rd Ave., Miami, FL 33172, (305)594-2969 [8923]

Just Phones, 15333 Culver Dr., Ste. 445, Irvine, CA 92604, (949)559-1844 [5655]

Justin Seed Company Inc., PO Box 6, Justin, TX 76247, (940)648-2751 [894]

Justis Supply Company Inc., 821 E Main, Farmington, NM 87401, (505)325-0291 [16974]

Justlin Medical Inc., 21717 NE 161st St., Woodinville, WA 98072-7460, (425)861-4770 [18869]

JV Inc., PO Box 628, Clearfield, PA 16830, (814)765-7511 [22393]

JVC Professional Products Co., 41 Slater Dr., Elmwood Park, NJ 07407, (201)794-3900 [8924]

JVLNET By Electrolarm, 1220 W Court St., Janesville, WI 53545-3537, (608)758-8750 [6413]

JVLNET By Electrolarm, 1220 W Court St., Janesville, WI 53545-3537, (608)758-8750 [24153]

JWS Corp., 10000 W 75th St., Ste. 200A, Shawnee Mission, KS 66204-2241, (913)384-0880 [6414]

JWS Technologies Inc., 490 Stelton Rd., Piscataway, NJ 08854, (908)752-4500 [16195]

JZ Allied International Holdings Inc., 13207 Bradley Ave., Sylmar, CA 91342, (818)364-2333 [13778]

K-9 Specialists, 319-36 Mound Rd., Warren, MI 48092, (810)939-5960 [27165]

K and A Lumber Company Inc., 1001 W Mowry Dr., Homestead, FL 33030, (305)245-5312 [27326]

K and D Exports Imports Corp., 225 5th Ave., New York, NY 10010, (212)683-8670 [14900]

K and F Industries Inc. (Indianapolis, Indiana), PO Box 1206, Indianapolis, IN 46206, (317)783-2385 [20081]

K & I Transeau Co., 4518 Hickory Downs Rd., Houston, TX 77084-3520, (281)463-7128 [27166]

K & J Jewelry Manufacturing, 1521 24th Ave. S, No. A2, Grand Forks, ND 58201-6736, (701)746-6678 [17479]

K-K Distributors Inc., 517 Snake River Ave., Lewiston, ID 83501-2262, (208)746-0114 [1928]

K & K Pet Talk, 2901 Bartlett, Tucson, AZ 85741, (520)887-4926 [27167]

K and K Pet Talk, 2901 Bartlett, Tucson, AZ 85741, (520)887-4926 [19389]

K and K Recycling Inc., PO Box 58055, Fairbanks, AK 99711, (907)488-1409 [26862]

K & K Vet Supply, 3190 A American St., Springdale, AR 72765-1756, (501)751-1516 [27168]

K and K Vet Supply, 3190 A American St., Springdale, AR 72765-1756, (501)751-1516 [19390]

K & L Associates, Inc., 1710 Clavinia Ave., Deerfield, IL 60015, (847)948-9438 [11574]

K and L Feed Mill Corp., PO Box 52, North Franklin, CT 06254, (203)642-7555 [895]

K & L Marketing Inc., RR 1, Box 79B, Cummings, ND 58223-9774, (701)786-3476 [26547]

K & M Associates, PO Box 9567, Providence, RI 02940-9567, (401)461-4300 [17480]

K and M Metals Inc., 845 Alexander Ave., Tacoma, WA 98421, (253)863-6800 [20082]

K and N Meats, PO Box 897, Renton, WA 98057, (425)226-7300 [11575]

K & P Manufacturing, 950 W Foothill Blvd., Azusa, CA 91702, (626)334-0334 [23766]

K & R Distributors, 3123 Esch, Warren, MI 48091, (810)574-9292 [27169]

K & R Instruments Inc., 4315-B SW 34th St., Orlando, FL 32811-6419, (407)859-7740 [24381]

K Rep Sales, 2726 Shelter Island Dr., Ste. 237, San Diego, CA 92106, (619)457-9654 [6415]

K & S Distributors, 5817 Tibby Rd., Bensalem, PA 19020, (215)750-1381 [19391]

K & S Militaria Books, PO Box 9630, Alpine, TX 79831, (915)837-5053 [3872]

K & S Tole & Craft Supply, 1556 Florence, Aurora, CO 80010, (303)364-3031 [21083]

K-Swiss Inc., 31248 Oak Crest Dr., Westlake Village, CA 91361 [23767]

K & T Lamp & Shade Company Inc., 2860 State Rte. 121 N, Mayfield, KY 42066, (502)247-5762 [15546]

K-Tech Aviation, Inc., 5025 E Nebraska St., Tucson, AZ 85706, (520)747-4417 [110]

K-Tel International Inc., 2605 Fernbrook Ln. N, Minneapolis, MN 55447-4736, (763)559-6800 [25264]

K-Tel International (USA) Inc., 2605 Fernbrook Ln. N, Minneapolis, MN 55447, (612)509-9416 [15547]

K & W Tire Co., 735 N Prince St., Lancaster, PA 17603, (717)397-3596 [2837]

K2 Corp., 19215 Vashon Hwy. SW, Vashon, WA 98070, (206)463-3631 [23768]

Kabana Inc., 616 Indian School Rd., Albuquerque, NM 87102, (505)843-9330 [17481]

Kabat Textile Corp., 247 W 37th St., 10th Fl., New York, NY 10018, (212)398-0011 [26083]

Kable News Company Inc., 641 Lexington Ave., 6th Fl., New York, NY 10022, (212)705-4600 [3873]

Kacher Selections; Robert, 3015 V St. NE, Washington, DC 20018, (202)832-9083 [1793]

Kaelbel Wholesale Inc., 2501 SW 31st. St., Ft. Lauderdale, FL 33312, (305)797-7789 [11576]

Kagedo Inc., 520 1st Ave. S, Seattle, WA 98104-2804, (206)467-9077 [26084]

Kagiya Trading Co. Ltd. of America, PO Box 21052, Nashville, TN 37221, (615)298-1220 [13779]

Kahant Electrical Supply Co., Rte. 10, Dover, NJ 07801, (201)366-2966 [8925]

Kahn & Son, Inc.; Irvin, 6555 Guion Rd., Indianapolis, IN 46268, (317)328-8989 [9982]

Kahn & Son, Inc.; Irvin, 1205 E Washington, PO Box 6093, Louisville, KY 40206, (502)584-2306 [9983]

Kahn's Bakery Inc., 4130 Rio Bravo St., No. B100, El Paso, TX 79902-1002, (915)533-8433 [11577]

Kaiser Wholesale Inc., PO Box 1115, New Albany, IN 47150, (812)945-2651 [26315]

Kako International Inc., 0110 SW Curry St., Portland, OR 97201-4375, (503)222-4801 [18870]

Kalamazoo Dental Supply, 710 Gibson St., Kalamazoo, MI 49007, (616)345-0260 [18871]

Kalamazoo International, Inc., 70 Van Buren, PO Box 271, South Haven, MI 49090, (616)637-2178 [16196]

Kalamazoo Mill Supply Co., 1820 Lake St., Kalamazoo, MI 49001, (616)349-9641 [16975]

Kalamazoo Mill Supply Co., PO Box 2421, Kalamazoo, MI 49003, (616)349-9641 [20083]

Kalamazoo Steel Processing Inc., PO Box 169, Kalamazoo, MI 49004, (616)344-9778 [20084]

Kalbus Office Supply, PO Box 800, Nampa, ID 83653-0800, (208)466-4653 [21084]

Kaldor Fabricmaker USA Ltd.; John, 500 7th Ave., New York, NY 10018, (212)221-8270 [26085]

Kalispell Livestock Auction, PO Box 914, Kalispell, MT 59903-0914, (406)752-1448 [18026]

Kalthoff International, 550 E 4th St., Apt. 7, Cincinnati, OH 45202-3333, (513)794-3367 [6416]

Kalweit Sales Company Inc., 8100 Wayzata Blvd., Minneapolis, MN 55426, (612)595-9933 [26548]

Kamaaina Distribution, 99-1305 Koaha Pl., Aiea, HI 96701, (808)488-8758 [11578]

Kamaaina Distribution Co., 69 Railroad Ave., Hilo, HI 96720, (808)935-3774 [26316]

Kamaaina Vision Center Inc., 508 Atkinson Dr., Honolulu, HI 96814-4728, (808)949-1595 [19392]

Kaman Corp., PO Box 1, Bloomfield, CT 06002, (203)243-8311 [16197]

Kaman Industrial, 240 E Verdugo Ave., Burbank, CA 91502, (818)845-8571 [16976]

Kaman Industrial Technologies, 840 W 24th St., Ogden, UT 84401 [8926]

Kaman Industrial Technologies, 2601 S 24th St., Phoenix, AZ 85034, (602)273-1641 [16977]

Kaman Industrial Technologies Inc., 1332 Blue Hills Ave., Bloomfield, CT 06002, (203)243-8311 [111]

Kaman Industrial Technology, 1600 Commerce Ave., Boise, ID 83705-5307, (208)343-1841 [16198]

Kaman Music Corp., 20 Old Windsor Rd., PO Box 507, Bloomfield, CT 06002, (860)243-8353 [25265]

Kaman Music Corp. Los Angeles, 1215 W Walnut St., PO Box 5686, Compton, CA 90224-5686, (310)537-1712 [25266]

Kaman Music Corp. Los Angeles, 1215 W Walnut St., Compton, CA 90224-5686, (310)537-1712 [15183]

Kambach & Kettman Inc., 323 N Harrison St., Davenport, IA 52801-1301, (319)322-2122 [24781]

Kamen Supply Company Inc., 4705 Nome St., Denver, CO 80239, (303)371-1700 [23226]

Kamp Implement Co., PO Box 629, Belgrade, MT 59714, (406)388-4295 [896]

Kamuela Roses, Inc., 1124 Kohou St., Honolulu, HI 96817, (808)847-6748 [14901]

Kanabec Cooperative Association, 206 S Union St., Mora, MN 55051, (320)679-2682 [22394]

Kanawha Scales and Systems, Rte. 1, Box 254A, Parkersburg, WV 26101, (304)344-5925 [24382]

Kanawha Steel and Equipment Inc., PO Box 3203, Charleston, WV 25332, (304)343-8801 [20085]

Kane International Corp., 411 Theodore Fremd Ave., Rye, NY 10580, (914)921-3100 [11579]

Kane Steel Co., PO Box 829, Millville, NJ 08332, (609)825-2200 [20086]

Kane X-Ray Company Inc., 2134 Espey Ct., Ste. 12, Crofton, MD 21114-2437, (301)261-3645 [18872]

Kaneka Far West, Inc., 2290 Nugget Way, Eugene, OR 97403-2472, (541)687-8374 [21085]

Kanematsu U.S.A. Inc., 114 W 47th St., New York, NY 10036, (212)704-9400 [22395]

Kanematsu U.S.A. Inc., 114 W 47th St., New York, NY 10036, (212)704-9400 [26086]

Kangaroo Brand Inc., 7620 N 81st St., Milwaukee, WI 53223, (414)355-9696 [11580]

Kanorado Cooperative Association, Box 40, Kanorado, KS 67741, (785)399-2321 [18027]

Kansas Brick and Tile Company Inc., PO Box 450, Hoisington, KS 67544, (316)653-2157 [7540]

Kansas Brick and Tile Company Inc., PO Box 450, Hoisington, KS 67544, (316)653-2157 [7541]

Kansas City Auto Auction Inc., 3901 N Great Midwest, Kansas City, MO 64161, (816)452-4084 [20658]

Kansas City Auto Auction Inc., 3901 N Skiles, Kansas City, MO 64161, (816)452-4084 [2838]

Kansas City Aviation Center Inc., PO Box 1850, Olathe, KS 66063, (913)782-0530 [112]

Kansas City Bolt, Nut and Screw Co., 1324 W 12th St., Kansas City, MO 64101, (816)471-6979 [13780]

Kansas City Periodical Distributing Co., PO Box 14948, Shawnee Mission, KS 66285-4948, (913)541-8600 [3874]

Kansas City Rubber and Belting Co., 1815 Prospect Ave., Kansas City, MO 64127, (816)483-8580 [24283]

Kansas City Rubber and Belting Co., 1815 Prospect Ave., Kansas City, MO 64127, (816)483-8580 [16978]

Kansas City Salad Company Inc., 5252 Speaker Rd., Kansas City, KS 66106, (913)371-4466 [11581]

Kansas City Winnelson Co., 1529 Lake Ave., Kansas City, KS 66103, (913)262-6868 [23227]

Kansas Communications Inc., 8206 Marshall Dr., Lenexa, KS 66214, (913)752-9100 [5656]

Kansas Communications Inc., 8206 Marshall Dr., Lenexa, KS 66214, (913)752-9100 [8927]

Kansas Electric Supply Company Inc., 721 E 12th St., Hays, KS 67601, (785)625-2516 [8928]

Kansas Oxygen Inc., PO Box 3007, Hutchinson, KS 67504-3007, (316)665-5551 [16979]

Kansas Propane, 707 N Main St., South Hutchinson, KS 67505, (316)663-3338 [22396]

Kaough Distributing Company, Inc., 2601 Brocklyn Ave., PO Box 10087, Ft. Wayne, IN 46850, (219)432-5556 [9984]

Kaplan Lumber Company Inc., PO Box 340, St. Peters, MO 63376, (314)397-4471 [7542]

Kaplan-Simon Co., 115 Messina Dr., Braintree, MA 02184, (781)848-6500 [26087]

Kappel Wholesale Co.; William J., 535 Liberty Ave., Pittsburgh, PA 15222, (412)471-6400 [17482]

Kar Products, 461 N 3rd Ave., Des Plaines, IL 60016, (847)296-6111 [13781]

Kar Products, Inc., 1085 Telegraph, Reno, NV 89502, (702)786-0811 [16980]

Kardas/Jelinek Gemstones, 52 Fisher Rd., Great Falls, MT 59405-8114, (406)454-1138 [17483]

Kardex Systems Inc., PO Box 171, Marietta, OH 45750, (740)374-9300 [21086]

Karemor Independent Distributor, PO Box 271564, Nashville, TN 37227, (615)847-5273 [14140]

Karhu USA Inc., 550 Hinesburg Rd., Ste. 200, South Burlington, VT 05403-6542, (802)864-4519 [23769]

Karl Optometric Clinic, 1415 N Sanborn Blvd., Mitchell, SD 57301-1015, (605)996-2020 [19400]

Karla's Kreations Inc., 1561 N 158th Ave., Omaha, NE 68118-2310 [13380]

Karmily Gem Corp., 580 5th Ave., New York, NY 10036-4793, (212)354-1828 [17484]

Karn Meats Inc., 922 Taylor Ave., Columbus, OH 43219, (614)252-3712 [11582]

Karpen Steel Custom Doors & Frames, 181 Reems Creek Rd., Weaverville, NC 28787-8204, (828)645-4821 [7543]

Karpen Steel Products Inc., 181 Reems Creek Rd., Weaverville, NC 28787-8204, (828)645-4821 [7543]

Karp's BakeMark, 9401 Le Saint Dr., Fairfield, OH 45014, (513)870-0880 [11583]

Karr & Company, Inc.; Jean, 5656 3rd St. NE, Washington, DC 20011 [3875]

Karshner Ceramics Inc., 3109 Griggsview Ct., Columbus, OH 43221-4605 [26549]

Karthauser and Sons Inc., W147 N Fond du Lac Ave., Germantown, WI 53022, (414)255-7815 [14902]

Karumit Associates Ltd., PO Box 11831, Winston-Salem, NC 27116, (336)765-8989 [5101]

Karystal International Inc., 322 Market St., Warren, RI 02885-2609, (401)245-8766 [26088]

Kas-Tex Corp., 5899 Downey Rd., Vernon, CA 90058-3701, (323)588-7700 [26089]

Kasch Co.; M.W., 5401 W Donges Bay, 104N, Mequon, WI 53092, (414)242-5000 [26550]

Kaser Implement Inc., PO Box 327, Osborne, KS 67473, (785)346-2126 [897]

Kash 'N Gold Ltd., 1 Trade Zone Ct., Ronkonkoma, NY 11779, (516)981-1600 [5657]

Kasle Steel Corp., PO Box 33536, Detroit, MI 48232, (313)943-2500 [20087]

KasLen Textiles, 5899 Downey Rd., Vernon, CA 90058-3701, (323)588-7700 [26089]

Kasperek Optical Inc., 3620 Biddle St., Riverview, MI 48192-6559, (734)283-0844 [19393]

Kass Electronics Distributors Inc., 2502 W Township Line Rd., Havertown, PA 19083-5212, (215)449-2300 [8929]

Kass Industrial Supply Corp., 443 E Tremont Ave., Bronx, NY 10457, (718)299-6060 [13782]

Kast Fabrics Inc., 540 Preston Rd., PO Box 1660, Pasadena, TX 77501-1660, (713)473-4848 [26090]

Kataman Metals Inc., 770 Bonhomme St., Ste. 550, St. Louis, MO 63105, (314)863-6699 [20088]

Katcef Brothers Inc., 2404 A & Eagle Blvd., Annapolis, MD 21401, (410)224-2391 [1794]

Katcef Sales Inc., 1981 Moreland Pkwy., Annapolis, MD 21401, (410)268-7877 [25696]

Katch and Company Inc.; M., 503 Branner St., Topeka, KS 66607, (785)234-2691 [20089]

Kate-Lo Div., 701 N Berkshire Ln., Plymouth, MN 55441, (612)545-5455 [9985]

Kathryn Farmers Mutual Elevators Inc., PO Box 196, Kathryn, ND 58049, (701)796-7861 [18028]

Kato Radiator Diesel Systems, 2200 4th Ave., Mankato, MN 56001, (507)625-4118 [2839]

Katolight Corp., 3201 3rd Ave, Mankato, MN 56001, (507)625-7973 [8930]

Katy Industries Inc., 6300 S Syracuse Way, Ste. 300, Englewood, CO 80111-6723, (303)290-9300 [8931]

Katz Paper, Foil & Cordage Corp., 2900 1st Ave. S, Seattle, WA 98134, (206)624-2494 [21788]

Kauai Paint & Jalousie, 3196 Akahi St., Lihue, HI 96766, (808)245-6181 [21470]

Kauai Screen Print, 3116 Houlako St., Lihue, HI 96766-1432, (808)245-5123 [5102]

Kaufenberg Enterprises, 4301 S Valley View Blvd., Ste. 11, Las Vegas, NV 89103-4007, (702)891-0054 [5103]

Kauffman Tire Service Inc., 4847 Clark-Howell Hwy., College Park, GA 30349, (404)762-8433 [2840]

Kaufman Co. Inc.; Hal, 2545 Jackson Ave., Memphis, TN 38108, (901)458-3143 [22868]

Kaufman Grain Co., PO Box 96, Cissna Park, IL 60924, (815)457-2185 [18029]

Kaufman Inc.; P., 153 E 53rd St., 42nd Fl., New York, NY 10022, (212)292-2200 [26091]

Kaufman Seeds Inc., PO Box 398, Ashdown, AR 71822-0398, (870)898-3328 [898]

Kaufman Supply, PO Box 44984, Atlanta, GA 30336, (404)699-8750 [15184]

Kauphusman Inc.; F.W., 525 Steelhead Way, Boise, ID 83704-8374, (208)377-1600 [14507]

Kaw River Shredding Inc., PO Box 3010, Kansas City, KS 66103-0010, (913)621-2711 [20090]

Kaw Valley Company Inc., 116 - 30 S Kansas Ave., Topeka, KS 66603, (785)233-3201 [11584]

Kawasaki Motors Corporation U.S.A., PO Box 25252, Santa Ana, CA 92799-5252, (714)770-0400 [20659]

Kawasaki Motors Corporation U.S.A. Engine Div., PO Box 888285, Grand Rapids, MI 49588-8285, (616)949-6500 [2841]

Kay Automotive Graphics, PO Box 1000, Lake Orion, MI 48361, (810)377-4949 [2842]

Kay Chemical Co., 8300 Capital Dr., Greensboro, NC 27409-9790, (336)668-7290 [4648]

Kay Distributing Co., 1063 W Lincoln, Ionia, MI 48846-1457, (616)527-0120 [11585]

Kay Guitar Co., PO Box 26266, Indianapolis, IN 46226, (317)545-2486 [25267]

Kayboys Empire Paper Company Inc., 11 Azar Ct., Benson Business Ctr., Baltimore, MD 21227, (410)247-5000 [21789]

Kaye Brothers Inc., 590 NE 185th St., North Miami Beach, FL 33179, (305)653-2880 [11586]

Kaye Corp., 1910 Lookout Dr., North Mankato, MN 56003, (507)625-5293 [899]

Kaye Inc.; Richard W., 760 Market, San Francisco, CA 94102-2401, (415)781-0524 [17485]

Kaye Pearl Co., 4131 58th St., Woodside, NY 11377, (718)446-7720 [17486]

Kays Enterprises Inc., 13127 Trinity St., Stafford, TX 77477-4297, (713)780-0808 [5104]

Kazette Enterprises Inc., 5411 Coliseum Blvd., Ste. A, Alexandria, LA 71303-3521, (318)442-3593 [6417]

Kazi Publications, 3023 W Belmont Ave., Chicago, IL 60618, (773)267-7001 [3876]

Kazuhiro Ltd., 6747 Paper Birch Cove, Memphis, TN 38119, (901)755-1264 [25697]

K.B. Brothers Inc., 55 Franklin Ave., Brooklyn, NY 11205-1503, (212)924-0673 [26551]

KBC Bargain Center Inc., 4201 N Old State Rd. 3, Muncie, IN 47303-9512, (765)284-1000 [5105]

KBM Office Equipment Inc., 320 S 1st St., San Jose, CA 95113-2803, (408)938-2200 [13154]

KBM Workspace, 320 S 1st St., San Jose, CA 95113-2803, (408)938-2200 [13154]

KCG Communications Inc., 7076 S Alton Way, Ste. E, Englewood, CO 80112, (303)773-1200 [5658]

K.D. Farms, Inc., Kawela, Kaunakakai, HI 96748, (808)567-6024 [14903]

KD Lamp Co., 1910 Elm St., Cincinnati, OH 45210, (513)621-4211 [2843]

KD Sales Associates, 59 Bean Rd., Merrimack, NH 03054-2406, (603)429-1298 [5106]

KD Sales Inc., 2039 S Burdick St., Kalamazoo, MI 49001-3627, (616)344-2999 [26552]

KEA Electronics, 46759 Fremont Blvd., Fremont, CA 94538, (510)651-2600 [8932]

Kearney's Metals Inc., PO Box 2926, Fresno, CA 93745, (559)233-2591 [20091]

Kearns Associates, 2071 N Fairview Ln., Rochester Hills, MI 48306-3927 [24782]

Keathley-Patterson Electric Co., 4217 E 43rd St., North Little Rock, AR 72117, (501)945-7143 [8933]

Keddie Kreations of California, 11367 Sunrise Gold Cir., Ste. C-D, Rancho Cordova, CA 95742, (916)635-0113 [5107]

Keebler Co., 3875 Bay Center Pl, Hayward, CA 94545, (510)783-5754 [11587]

Keefe Supply Co., 10950 Lin Page Rd., St. Louis, MO 63132, (314)423-4343 [24154]

Keelor Steel Inc., 5101 N Boone Ave., Minneapolis, MN 55428, (612)535-1431 [20092]

Keen Compressed Gas Co., PO Box 15146, Wilmington, DE 19850-5146, (302)594-4545 [16981]

Keen Jewelers, 419 9th St., Huntington, WV 25701, (304)529-2514 [14141]

Keene Div., 10100 East Rd., Potter Valley, CA 95469, (707)743-1154 [25922]

Keene Div., 10100 East Rd., Potter Valley, CA 95469, (707)743-1154 [27327]

Keep It Simple Technology Inc., PO Box 2981, Gaithersburg, MD 20886-2981 [6418]

Keesler Inc.; C.C. and F.F., PO Box 299, Prospect Park, PA 19076, (215)534-0700 [16199]

Keeter Manufacturing, Inc., PO Box 1227, Sisters, OR 97759-1227, (541)967-8400 [2844]

Keeton Sales Agency Inc., 6908 Woodway Dr., Waco, TX 76712-6196, (254)776-6011 [26092]

Kehe Food Distributors Inc., 333 S Swift Rd., Addison, IL 60101, (630)953-2829 [11588]

Kehe Food Distributors Inc., 900 Schmidt Rd., Romeoville, IL 60446, (815)886-0700 [11589]

Keibler-Thompson Corp., 130 Entrance Way, New Kensington, PA 15068, (724)335-9161 [20093]

Keidel Supply Co., 2026 Delaware Ave., Cincinnati, OH 45212, (513)351-1600 [23228]

Keilson-Dayton Co., PO Box 1457, Dayton, OH 45401, (937)236-1070 [26317]

Keith Co.; Ben E., PO Box 2628, Ft. Worth, TX 76113, (817)877-5700 [11590]

Keith Distributors Inc., 1055 S Ballenger Hwy., Flint, MI 48532, (810)238-9104 [3877]

Keith Foods; Ben E., 3205 Broadway Blvd. SE, Albuquerque, NM 87101, (505)843-7766 [11591]

Keith-Sinclair Company Inc., PO Box 24770, Nashville, TN 37202-4770, (615)259-3601 [21471]

Keizer Associates, 55 Mississippi St., San Francisco, CA 94107, (415)621-0881 [16200]

Kelaty International Inc., 8020 Lefferts Blvd., Kew Gardens, NY 11415-1724, (917)617-8282 [9986]

Kellco & Associates, 635 N 7th St., Tooele, UT 84074, (435)882-5125 [15185]

Kelleigh Corporation, Export Dept., 10 E Athens Ave., Ste. 202, Ardmore, PA 19003, (610)642-9850 [16201]

Keller Grain and Feed Inc., 7977 Main St., Greenville, OH 45331, (937)448-2116 [18030]

Keller Group, 3041 65th St. Ste. 3, Sacramento, CA 95820-2021 [13155]

Keller Marine Service Inc., PO Box 0190, Port Trevorton, PA 17864, (717)374-8169 [18531]

Keller Oil Inc., PO Box 147, St. Marys, PA 15857, (814)781-1507 [22397]

Keller & Sons, PO Box 490, Quincy, IL 62306, (217)228-6700 [900]

Keller Supply Co., 3209 17th Ave. W, Seattle, WA 98119, (206)285-3300 [23229]

Keller Supply Co., 21017 77th Ave., S, Kent, WA 98032, (253)872-7575 [23770]

Kellermeyer Co., PO Box 3357, Toledo, OH 43607, (419)255-3022 [4649]

Kellerstrass Oil Co., 2450 Wall Ave., Ogden, UT 84401, (801)392-9516 [22398]

Kelley and Abide Company Inc., PO Box 13516, New Orleans, LA 70185, (504)822-2700 [11592]

Kelley Bean Co., Inc., PO Box 2488, Scottsbluff, NE 69363-2488, (308)635-2438 [11593]

Kelley-Clarke, 4845 Oakland St., Denver, CO 80239-2721, (303)371-1112 [11594]

Kelley-Clarke Inc., PO Box 5326, Culver City, CA 90231-5326, (310)641-0672 [11595]

Kelley Inc.; Jack B., 8101 SW 34th Ave., Amarillo, TX 79121, (806)353-3553 [22399]

Kelley Manufacturing Corp., 61501 Bremen Hwy., Mishawaka, IN 46544, (219)255-4746 [7544]

Kellner Co., Inc.; M.J., 4880 Industrial Dr., Springfield, IL 62704, (217)787-4070 [11596]

Kellogg Co., PO Box 14756, Memphis, TN 38114-0756, (901)743-0250 [11597]

Kellogg Marine, Inc., 129 Mill Rock Rd., PO Box 809, Old Saybrook, CT 06475-0809, (860)388-4277 [18532]

Kellogg Marine Supply Inc., 129 Mill Rock Rd., PO Box 809, Old Saybrook, CT 06475-0809, (860)388-4277 [18532]

Kelly Computer Supplies, 3584 Hoffman Rd. E, St. Paul, MN 55110-5375, (651)773-1109 [6419]

Kelly; Dennis, 226 W 5th St., Winner, SD 57580-1715, (605)842-1824 [18031]

Kelly Furniture Co.; F.S., 204 Beal Bldg., Duluth, MN 55802, (218)722-6301 [13156]

Kelly Paper Co., 1441 E 16th St., Los Angeles, CA 90021, (213)749-1311 [21790]

Kelly Pipe Co., 11700 Bloomfield Ave., Santa Fe Springs, CA 90670, (562)868-0456 [16982]

Kelly Springfield Tire, 6650 Ramsey St., Fayetteville, NC 28311, (910)488-9295 [2845]

Kelly Supply Company of Iowa, PO Box 1328, Grand Island, NE 68802, (308)382-5670 [16983]

Kelly Tractor Co., 8255 NW 58th St., Miami, FL 33166, (305)592-5360 [16202]

Kelly's Pipe and Supply Co., PO Box 14750, Las Vegas, NV 89114, (702)382-4957 [23230]

Kelman Inc.; Nathan H., 41 Euclid St., Cohoes, NY 12047, (518)237-5133 [26863]

Kelmar Corp., 201 Airport N, Ft. Wayne, IN 46825, (219)484-4141 [14508]

Keltech, Inc., 9285 N 32nd St., PO Box 405, Richland, MI 49083, (616)629-4814 [23231]

Keltech Inc., 9285 N 32nd St., Richland, MI 49083, (616)629-4814 [23232]

Keltner Enterprises Inc., 2829 S Scenic Ave., Springfield, MO 65807, (417)882-8844 [2846]

Kem Distributing Inc., 2604 Causton Bluff Rd., Savannah, GA 31404, (912)233-1176 [1795]

Kemeny Overseas Products Corporation, 233 S Wacker, Chicago, IL 60606, (312)663-5161 [20094]

Kemlite Company, Inc., PO Box 2429, Joliet, IL 60434, (815)467-8600 [7545]

Kemp Grain Company Inc., 405 W Walnut St., Lexington, IL 61753, (309)365-2241 [18032]

Kemp Hardware and Supply Co., PO Box 529, Paramount, CA 90723, (562)634-2553 [13783]

Kemper Enterprises Inc., 13595 Twelfth St., Chino, CA 91710, (909)627-6191 [25698]

Kemps Dairy Products Distributors, 825 Woodside Ave., Ripon, WI 54971, (920)748-2353 [11598]

Ken Dor Corp., 5721 W Ryan St., Franklin, WI 53132, (414)421-8484 [18533]

Ken-Mac Metals Inc., 17901 Englewood Dr., Cleveland, OH 44130, (440)234-7500 [20095]

Ken-Son Inc., PO Box 25487, Salt Lake City, UT 84125, (801)972-5585 [11599]

Kenan Oil Co., 100 Europa Dr., No. 450, Chapel Hill, NC 27514, (919)929-9979 [11600]

Kenclaire Electrical Agencies Inc., 714 Old Country Rd., Westbury, NY 11590, (516)333-7373 [8934]

Kenco, PO Box 1385, Raton, NM 87740-1385 [2847]

Kenco Distributors, Inc., 436 Atlas Dr., Nashville, TN 37211, (615)244-3180 [9987]

Kendall; Dale B., East Barnet Rd., Barnet, VT 05821, (802)633-2626 [18033]

Kendall Electric Inc., 131 Grand Trunk Ave., Battle Creek, MI 49015-2285, (616)963-5585 [8935]

Kendall-Grundy FS Inc., 4000 N Division St., Morris, IL 60450, (815)942-3210 [901]

Kendall Industrial Supplies Inc., 702 N 20th St., Battle Creek, MI 49015, (616)965-2211 [16984]

Kendall-Polyken, 1400 Providence Hwy., Norwood, MA 02062, (781)440-6200 [21957]

Kendallville Iron and Metal Inc., 243 E Lisbon Rd., PO Box 69, Kendallville, IN 46755, (219)347-1958 [26864]

Kendell Co, 740 Vintage Ave., Ontario, CA 91764, (909)987-0042 [19394]

Kenilworth Creations Inc., PO Box 9541, Providence, RI 02940-9541, (401)739-1458 [17487]

Kenilworth Steel Co, 106 E Market St Ste. 807, Warren, OH 44481, (330)373-1885 [20096]

Kenkingdon & Associates, 12813 Westbranch Ct., Houston, TX 77072, (281)495-3071 [8936]

Kenlin Pet Supply, 2225 NC152 E, China Grove, NC 28023, (704)857-8192 [27170]

Kenlin Pet Supply Inc., 301 Island Rd., Mahwah, NJ 07430, (201)529-5050 [27171]

Kennametal, 550 Virginia Dr., Ft. Washington, PA 19034, (215)654-5330 [16985]

Kennametal Inc. Metalworking-Systems Div., PO Box 231, Latrobe, PA 15650, (724)539-5000 [16203]

Kennedy Engine Co., 980 Motsie Rd., Biloxi, MS 39532, (228)392-2200 [2848]

Kennedy-Kuhn Inc., 1042 S Washington St., Van Wert, OH 45891, (419)238-1299 [902]

Kennedy Manufacturing Co., 520 E Sycamore, Van Wert, OH 45891-1377, (419)238-2442 [16986]

Kennedy Oil Company Inc., 1203 Courtesy Rd., High Point, NC 27260, (910)885-5184 [22400]

Kennedy; Rob E., 1334 S Las Vegas, Las Vegas, NV 89104-1103, (702)386-2998 [17488]

Kennedy Wholesale Inc., 205 W Harvard St., Glendale, CA 91204, (818)241-9977 [11601]

Kennel-Aire Inc., 3580 Holly Ln. N, #10, Plymouth, MN 55447-1269, (612)519-0521 [27172]

Kennesaw Fruit Juice Co., 1300 SW 1st Ct., Pompano Beach, FL 33065, (954)782-9800 [11602]

The Kenneth Smith Golf Club Co., 12931 W 71st St., Shawnee, KS 66216-2640, (913)631-5100 [23948]

Kennett Liquid Fertilizer Co., PO Box 528, Kennett, MO 63857, (573)888-5361 [903]

Kennewick Industrial and Electrical Supply Inc., 113 E Columbia Dr., Kennewick, WA 99336, (509)582-5156 [8937]

Kennewick Industry & Electric Supply, 113 E Columbia Dr., Kennewick, WA 99336-3799, (509)582-5156 [8938]

Kennewick Industry and Electric Supply, 113 E Columbia Dr., Kennewick, WA 99336-3799, (509)582-5156 [15186]

Kenney Distributors; J.F., 37 Beach St., Westerly, RI 02891-0471, (401)596-6760 [24155]

Kenney Machinery Corp., PO Box 681068, Indianapolis, IN 46268, (317)872-4793 [904]

Kenosha-Racine FS Cooperative, 4304 S Beaumont, Kansasville, WI 53139, (414)886-5613 [905]

Kenrick Company Inc.; R. G., G-3530 Flushing Rd., Flint, MI 48504, (810)733-7440 [16987]

Ken's Craft Supply, 54 Ashman Cir., Midland, MI 48640, (517)835-8401 [21087]

Kensington Cooperative Association, PO Box 128, Kensington, KS 66951, (785)476-2211 [906]

Kent, 650 36th St. SE, Wyoming, MI 49548, (616)241-5022 [1796]

Kent Distribution Inc., PO Box 908001, Midland, TX 79708, (915)563-1620 [22401]

Kent Electronics Inc., 1300 N Larch St., Lansing, MI 48906-4422, (517)487-6267 [25268]

Kentec Inc., 3250 Centerville Hwy., PO Box 390040, Snellville, GA 30039, (770)985-1907 [13784]

Kentec Medical Inc., 17871 Fitch, Irvine, CA 92614, (949)863-0810 [18873]

Kentucky Bearings Service, 1111 Majaun Rd., Lexington, KY 40511, (606)231-8288 [16988]

Kentucky Bearings Service, PO Box 35157, Louisville, KY 40232-5157, (502)636-2571 [2849]

Kentucky Bearings Service, 900 E 2nd St., Owensboro, KY 42303-3304, (270)684-9601 [2246]

Kentucky Buyers Co-op, 140 Venture Ct., Suite 1, Lexington, KY 40511, (859)253-9688 [907]

Kentucky Buying Cooperative Int., 140 Venture Ct., Suite 1, Lexington, KY 40511, (859)253-9688 [907]

Kentucky Buying Cooperative Int., 140 Venture Ct., Suite 1, Lexington, KY 40509, (606)253-9688 [19395]

Kentucky Dental Supply Co. Inc., PO Box 12130, Lexington, KY 40580-2130, (606)299-6291 [18874]

Kentucky Derby Hosiery, 314 S South St., PO Box 987, Mt. Airy, NC 27030-4450, (919)786-4134 [5108]

Kentucky Home Care Services, Inc., 790 N Dixie Ave., Ste. 500, Elizabethtown, KY 42701-2503, (502)737-2900 [18875]

Kentucky Indiana Lumber Company Inc., 227 E Lee St., Louisville, KY 40208, (502)637-1401 [7546]

Kentucky Mine Supply Co., PO Box 779, Harlan, KY 40831, (606)573-3850 [16989]

Kentucky Welding Supply, PO Box 638, Prestonsburg, KY 41653, (606)874-8001 [16990]

Kentuckyiana Music Supply Inc., PO Box 14124, Louisville, KY 40214, (502)361-4697 [25269]

Kenwal Products Corp., 8223 W Warren Ave., Dearborn, MI 48126, (313)739-1000 [20097]

Kenwal Steel Corp., 8223 W Warren Ave., Dearborn, MI 48126, (313)739-1000 [20097]

Kenway Distributors Inc., PO Box 14097, Louisville, KY 40214, (502)367-2201 [4650]

Kenwil Sales, 362 Industrial Park Rd., Madisonville, TN 37354-6133, (423)442-3954 [5109]

Kenwood Data Systems Inc., 918 10th St., Greeley, CO 80631-1118, (970)353-4555 [6420]

Kenwood USA Corp., PO Box 22745, Long Beach, CA 90801-5745, (310)639-9000 [25270]

Kenworth Sales Company Inc., PO Box 65829, Salt Lake City, UT 84165-0829, (801)487-4161 [20660]

Kenworth of Tennessee Inc., Spence Ln. & I-40 E, Nashville, TN 37210, (615)366-5454 [2850]

Kenyon, Inc.; Harry, 203 N Market St., Wilmington, DE 19801, (302)656-8288 [26318]

Kenyon Packing Co.; Lowell C., PO Box 328, Tulelake, CA 96134, (916)667-2225 [11603]

Kenzacki Specialty Papers Inc., 1500 Main St., Springfield, MA 01115, (413)736-3216 [21791]

Keo Cutters Inc., PO Box 717, Warren, MI 48089-1509, (810)771-2050 [16204]

Keomed Inc., 11515 K Tel Dr., Minnetonka, MN 55343-8845, (612)944-7306 [18876]

Kepcor Inc., 215 Bridge St., PO Box 119, Minerva, OH 44657, (330)868-6434 [9988]

Kerber Milling Co., 1817 E Main St., Emmetsburg, IA 50536, (712)852-2712 [908]

Kerman, Inc.; A.C., 1308-K N Magnolia Ave., El Cajon, CA 92020-1646, (619)440-4470 [23771]

Kermit Nolan Lumber Sales, 1200 Rialto Rd., PO Box 450, Yazoo City, MS 39194, (601)746-1661 [7547]

Kern & Sons; Jacob, Nicholas St., Lockport, NY 14094, (716)434-3577 [11604]

Kern Special Tools Company Inc., 140 Glen St., New Britain, CT 06051-2507, (860)223-0236 [8939]

Kerr Group Inc., 500 New Holland Ave., Lancaster, PA 17602-2104, (717)299-6511 [22986]

Kerr Pacific Corp., 811 SW Front St., No. 620, Portland, OR 97204, (503)221-1301 [11605]

Kerr Pump and Supply Inc., PO Box 37160, Oak Park, MI 48237, (248)543-3880 [16205]

Kervar Inc., 119-121 W 28th St., New York, NY 10001, (212)564-2525 [14904]

Kesler-Schaefer Auto Auction Inc., PO Box 53203, Indianapolis, IN 46253, (317)297-2300 [20661]

Kesseli Morse Company Inc., 242 Canterbury St., Worcester, MA 01603, (508)752-1901 [7548]

Kessler Industries Inc., 40 Warren St., Paterson, NJ 07524, (201)684-2130 [23233]

Kesterson Food Company Inc., PO Box 87, Paris, TN 38242, (901)642-5031 [24156]

Ketcham Forest Products Inc., PO Box 22789, Seattle, WA 98122, (206)329-2700 [27328]

Ketcham Lumber Company Inc., PO Box 22789, Seattle, WA 98122, (206)329-2700 [7549]

Kett Tool Co., 5055 Madison Rd., Cincinnati, OH 45227-1494, (513)271-0333 [13785]

Kettle Foods, PO Box 664, Salem, OR 97308, (503)364-0399 [11606]

Kettle-Lakes Cooperative, PO Box 305, Random Lake, WI 53075, (414)994-4316 [909]

Kevco Inc., 1300 S University Dr., Ft. Worth, TX 76107, (817)332-2758 [27329]

Key Boston Inc., 126 Grove St., Franklin, MA 02038, (508)528-4500 [15187]

Key Curriculum Press Inc., PO Box 2304, Berkeley, CA 94702, (510)595-7000 [3878]

Key Distribution, Inc., 7611-K Rickenbacker Dr., Gaithersburg, MD 20879, (301)258-8992 [8940]

Key-Duncan Wallcoverings, 1729 Research Dr., Louisville, KY 40299, (502)491-5080 [15548]

Key Electronics Inc., 46908 Liberty Dr., Wixom, MI 48393-3600, (248)489-5455 [8941]

Key Food Stores Cooperative Inc., 8925 Avenue D, Brooklyn, NY 11236, (718)451-1000 [11607]

Key Imports, 1621 Braman Ave., Ft. Myers, FL 33901, (941)337-0889 [17489]

Key Marketing Group, 7611-K Rickenbacker Dr., Gaithersburg, MD 20879, (301)258-8992 [8940]

Key Oil Co., PO Box 123, Houston, TX 77001, (713)222-2041 [16206]

Key Products Co., 2659 Windmill Pkwy., Henderson, NV 89014, (702)361-1220 [6421]

Key Sales Inc., 820 Packer Way, Sparks, NV 89431-6445, (702)359-3535 [24157]

Key Wholesale Building Products Inc., PO Box 1256, Mason City, IA 50401, (515)423-0544 [7550]

Keyboard Decals, 1029 Pennsylvania Ave., Hagerstown, MD 21742, (301)791-2880 [25271]

Keys Fitness Products Inc., 11220 Petal St., Dallas, TX 75238, (214)340-8888 [23772]

Keyston Brothers, 3929 S 500 W, Salt Lake City, UT 84123, (801)264-8282 [26093]

Keyston Brothers, 2381 E Winston Rd., Anaheim, CA 92806, (714)774-9110 [26094]

Keyston Brothers, 2801 Academy Way, Sacramento, CA 95815, (916)927-5851 [26095]

Keyston Brothers, 9669 Aero Dr., San Diego, CA 92123, (619)277-7770 [26096]

Keyston Brothers, 476 Hester St., San Leandro, CA 94577, (510)430-2771 [26097]

Keyston Brothers, 3012 W Windsor Ave., Phoenix, AZ 85009-1604, (602)233-2233 [26098]

Keyston Brothers, 1100 Scott Rd., Burbank, CA 91504-4237, (818)841-6015 [26099]

Keyston Brothers, 5252 E Home Ave., Fresno, CA 93727, (209)255-0435 [26100]

Keyston Brothers, 1833 Riverview Dr., Ste. B, San Bernardino, CA 92408-3035, (909)796-5391 [26101]

Keyston Brothers, 1501 Custer Ave., San Francisco, CA 94124, (415)285-5050 [26102]

Keyston Brothers, 3275 Edward Ave., Santa Clara, CA 95054, (408)988-8811 [26103]

Keyston Brothers, 1601 N California, Ste. 350, Walnut Creek, CA 94596-4115, (925)945-4949 [26104]

Keyston Brothers, 222 Bryant St., Denver, CO 80219-1637, (303)935-6795 [26105]

Keyston Brothers, 690-A Kakoi St., Honolulu, HI 96819-2014, (808)836-1941 [26106]

Keyston Brothers, 920 Avenue N, Grand Prairie, TX 75050-1918, (214)742-1875 [26107]

Keyston Brothers, 6823 Fulton St., Houston, TX 77022-4832, (713)692-2132 [26108]

Keyston Brothers, 1601 N California Blvd., Ste. 350, Walnut Creek, CA 94596-4115, (925)945-4949 [26109]

Keystone Aniline Corp., 2501 W Fulton St., Chicago, IL 60612, (312)666-2015 [4434]

Keystone Automotive Industries Inc., 700 E Bonita Ave., Pomona, CA 91767, (909)624-8041 [2851]

Keystone Automotive Operations Inc., 44 Tunkhannock Ave., Exeter, PA 18643, (570)655-4514 [2852]

Keystone Automotive Warehouse, 44 Tunkhannock Ave., Exeter, PA 18643, (570)655-4514 [2852]

Keystone Builders Supply Co., 1075 Buffalo Rd., Rochester, NY 14624-1814, (716)458-5442 [7551]

Keystone Builders Supply Co., 85 Palm St., Rochester, NY 14615, (716)458-5442 [7552]

Keystone Cement Co., PO Box A, Bath, PA 18014, (610)837-1881 [7553]

Keystone Chemical Supply Inc., PO Box 398, Wayne, MI 48184, (734)397-2600 [4435]

Keystone Cue & Cushion Inc., 2800 Dickerson Rd., Reno, NV 89503-4313, (702)329-5718 [23773]

Keystone Detroit Diesel Allison Inc., Cranberry Industrial, 11 Progress Ave., Zelienople, PA 16063, (412)776-3237 [2853]

Keystone Iron and Metal Company Inc., 4903 E Carson St., Pittsburgh, PA 15207, (412)462-1520 [20098]

Keystone Mills, 309 Martindale Rd., Ephrata, PA 17522, (717)354-4616 [910]

Keystone Office Supply Co. Inc., 52 Olneyville Sq., Providence, RI 02909, (401)421-7872 [21088]

Keystone-Ozone Pure Water Co., 1075 General Sullivan Rd., Washington Crossing, PA 18977, (215)493-2511 [24980]

Keystone Plumbing Sales Co., 225 W 7th Ave., Homestead, PA 15120, (412)462-8600 [23234]

Keystone Resources Inc., PO Box 807, Mars, PA 16046, (412)538-3940 [26865]

Keystone Steel Sales Inc., 400 Barretto St., Bronx, NY 10474, (718)542-8400 [20099]

Keystone STIHL, Inc., RR 4 Box 1572, Mifflintown, PA 17059-9556 [16207]

Keystone Tube Co., 13527 S Halsted St., Chicago, IL 60629, (708)568-0800 [20100]

Keystone Wire & Cable Company Inc., Northhampton Industrial Pk., 154 Railroad Dr., Ivyland, PA 18974, (215)322-2390 [8942]

Keystops Inc., PO Box 2809, Franklin, KY 42135, (502)586-8283 [22402]

Keywell Corp., 3075 Lonyo Ave., Detroit, MI 48209, (313)841-6800 [26866]

Keywest Wire Div., 250 E Virginia St., San Jose, CA 95112, (408)971-9473 [7554]

KG Engineering Inc., 7620 Delhi Ave., Las Vegas, NV 89129, (702)648-5711 [25699]

KG Specialty Steel Inc., 2001 Elizabeth St., North Brunswick, NJ 08902, (732)297-9500 [20101]

Kgs Steel, Inc., 4717 Centennial Blvd., Nashville, TN 37209, (615)460-4620 [20102]

Khalsa Trading Co. Inc., PO Box 36930, Albuquerque, NM 87176-6930, (505)255-8278 [17490]

Kia Motors America Inc., PO Box 52410, Irvine, CA 92619-2410, (714)470-7000 [20662]

Kibar Bearings, 165 Jordan Rd., Troy, NY 12180-8386, (518)283-8002 [16991]

KIC International, 4109 Fruit Valley Rd., Vancouver, WA 98660, (206)696-0561 [27330]

Kidde Safety, 1394 S 3rd St., Mebane, NC 27302, (919)563-5911 [24580]

Kiddie Academy International Inc., 108 Wheel Rd., Bel Air, MD 21015-6198, (410)515-0788 [21089]

Kido Brothers Exports, Inc., 1028 Heartland Dr., Nampa, ID 83686-8158, (208)372-3827 [11608]

KIE Supply Corp., 113 E Columbia Dr., Kennewick, WA 99336-3799, (509)582-5156 [8938]

Kiefaber Co.; W.H., PO Box 681188, Indianapolis, IN 46268-7188 [23235]

Kiel Brothers Oil Company Inc., PO Box 344, Columbus, IN 47202, (812)372-3751 [22403]

Kielty and Dayton Co., 23125 Bernhard St., Hayward, CA 94545, (510)732-9200 [21090]

Kiemle-Hankins Co., PO Box 507, Toledo, OH 43697-0507, (419)891-0262 [8943]

Kieser and Sons; Ellwood, 5201 Comly St., Philadelphia, PA 19135, (215)744-6666 [2854]

Kiesub Corp., 3185 S Highland Dr., Ste. 10, Las Vegas, NV 89109, (702)733-0024 [8944]

Kiewit Mining Group, Inc., 1000 Kiewit Plaza, Omaha, NE 68131, (402)342-2052 [20549]

Kights' Printing and Office Products, 8505 Baymeadows Rd., Jacksonville, FL 32256, (904)731-7990 [21091]

KII, Inc., 2429 Vauxhall Rd., Union, NJ 07083, (908)964-4040 [23236]

Kilburn and Company Inc.; J.C., 501 E Cedar St., Rawlins, WY 82301, (307)324-2721 [22404]

Kilgo Co. Inc.; A.L., 180 Sand Island Rd., Honolulu, HI 96819, (808)832-2200 [13786]

Kilpatrick Co.; Martin, PO Box 157, Wilson, NC 27894-0157, (919)291-8202 [23774]

Kilpatrick; Eddie, 644 N Blythe St., Gallatin, TN 37066-2226, (615)452-5488 [24279]

Kilpatrick Equipment Co., PO Box 35786, Dallas, TX 75235, (214)358-4346 [21092]

Kilpatrick Table Tennis Co.; Martin, PO Box 157, Wilson, NC 27894-0157, (919)291-8202 [23774]

Kim Imports Inc., 14840 Landmark Blvd., No. 310, Dallas, TX 75240, (972)385-7555 [17491]

Kim International Mfg., L.P., 14840 Landmark Blvd., No. 310, Dallas, TX 75240, (972)385-7555 [17491]

Kim Originals Inc., PO Box 825, Sedalia, MO 65302-0825, (660)826-2500 [14905]

Kimber Petroleum Corp., 545 Martinsville Rd., PO Box 860, Liberty Corner, NJ 07938, (908)903-9600 [22405]

Kimbet Leather, 2090 Chestnut St., North Dighton, MA 02764, (508)252-6805 [27173]

Kimbo Educational, 10 N 3rd Ave., PO Box 477, Long Branch, NJ 07740-0477, (732)229-4949 [25272]

Kimbrell Ruffer Lumber, PO Box 605, Meridian, MS 39302, (601)693-4331 [7555]

Kimmel Automotive Inc., 505 Kane St., Baltimore, MD 21224, (410)633-3300 [2855]

Kims Family Shoes Inc., 132 N Morley Ave., Nogales, AZ 85621-3116, (520)287-2249 [24784]

Kim's Processing Plant, 417 3rd St., Clarksdale, MS 38614-4425, (601)627-2389 [11609]

Kimsco Supply Co., PO Box 307, Hancock, ME 04640-0307, (207)422-3363 [21093]

Kinast Distributors Inc.; E., 9362 W Grand Ave., Franklin Park, IL 60131, (708)451-9300 [7556]

Kincaid Coal Co. Inc.; Elmer, Off Hwy. 25 E, Thorn Hill, TN 37881, (423)767-2600 [20550]

Kindel Co.; J.A., 605 N Wayne Ave., Cincinnati, OH 45215, (513)733-9600 [13157]

Kinder-Harris Inc., PO Box 1900, Stuttgart, AR 72160-1900, (501)673-1518 [8945]

Kinder Seed Co., 2202 Hangar Pl., No. 170, Allentown, PA 18109-9507 [911]

Kindt Collins Co., 12651 Elmwood Ave., Cleveland, OH 44111, (216)252-4122 [25700]

Kinetics Inc., PO Box 7426, Madison, WI 53707, (608)241-4118 [7557]

Kinetronics Corp., 1778 Main St., Sarasota, FL 34236, (813)388-2432 [22869]

King Arthur Flour Co., Box 1010, Norwich, VT 05055, (802)649-3881 [11610]

King Auto Parts Inc., 935 High St., Central Falls, RI 02863-1505, (401)725-1298 [2856]

King Bearing Div., 2641 Irving Blvd., Dallas, TX 75207, (214)631-3270 [2857]

King Cobra, 16112-A NW 13th Ave., Miami, FL 33169-5748, (305)625-0511 [18384]

King Co. Inc.; E.F., 640 Pleasant St., Norwood, MA 02062, (617)762-3113 [23775]

King Co.; R.M., 315 N Marks Ave., Fresno, CA 93706, (209)266-0258 [912]

King Cotton Foods, 8000 Centerview Pkwy., Ste. 500, Cordova, TN 38018, (901)942-3221 [11611]

King Electronics Distributing, 1711 Southeastern Ave., Indianapolis, IN 46201-3990, (317)639-1484 [8946]

King Fish Inc., 414 S Lake St., Burbank, CA 91502-2114, (213)849-1226 [11612]

King Fleet Group, 1406 Sand Lake Rd., Orlando, FL 32809, (407)858-4822 [20663]

King Food Service, 4215 Exchange Ave., Los Angeles, CA 90058-2604, (213)582-7401 [11613]

King Grain Company Inc., 120 N 1st St., Muleshoe, TX 79347, (806)272-4541 [18034]

King and Keeney Inc., 5515 W Smithfield Rd., Mc Keesport, PA 15135, (412)751-5210 [22492]

King Kitchens Inc., 6075 E Shelby Dr., Ste. 1, Memphis, TN 38141, (901)362-9651 [15188]

King Koil Sleep Product, PO Box 830067, San Antonio, TX 78283-0067, (972)225-4300 [15549]

King Lobster Connection, 7403 Princess View Dr., Ste. A, San Diego, CA 92102, (619)286-3617 [11614]

King Louie International Inc., 13500 15th St., Grandview, MO 64030-3000, (816)765-5212 [5110]

King Milling Co., PO Box 99, Lowell, MI 49331, (616)897-9264 [11615]

King Provision Corp., 9009 Regency Square Blvd., Jacksonville, FL 32211, (904)725-4122 [11616]

King Safe and Lock Company Inc., 8429 Katy Fwy., Houston, TX 77024, (713)465-2500 [24581]

King Salmon Inc., 4163 S Lowe, Chicago, IL 60609-2627, (773)927-3366 [11617]

King Sash and Door Inc., PO Box 787, Clemmons, NC 27012, (910)768-4650 [7558]

King & Son Inc.; T.A., PO Box 190, Jonesport, ME 04649-0190, (207)497-2274 [18534]

King Wire and Cable Corp., PO Box 300, Jamaica, NY 11431, (718)657-4422 [8947]

King Wire Inc., 1 Cable Pl., North Chicago, IL 60064, (847)688-1100 [8948]

Kingdom Co., PO Box 506, Mansfield, PA 16933, (717)662-7515 [25273]

Kingman Aero Services Inc., 5070 Flightline Dr., Kingman, AZ 86401, (520)757-1335 [22406]

King's Cage, 145 Sherwood Ave., Farmingdale, NY 11735, (631)777-7300 [27174]

Kings Food Service Professionals Inc.; J., 700 Furrows Rd., Holtsville, NY 11742, (631)289-8401 [11618]

Kings Foodservice, 404 Arlington Ave., Nashville, TN 37210, (615)244-4626 [11619]

King's Foodservice Inc., 2333 Old Frankfort Rd., Lexington, KY 40510-9615, (606)254-6475 [11620]

Kings Liquor Inc., 6659 Camp Bowie Blvd., Ft. Worth, TX 76116, (817)732-8091 [1797]

Kingston Oil Supply Corp., Foot of N Broadway, Port Ewen, NY 12466, (914)331-0770 [22407]

Kinnealey & Co.; T.F., 1000 Massachusetts Ave., Boston, MA 02118-2621, (617)442-1200 [11621]

Kinokuniya Publications Service of New York, 10 W 49th St., New York, NY 10020, (212)765-1465 [3879]

Kinray, Inc., 152-35 10th Ave., Whitestone, NY 11357, (718)767-1234 [14142]

Kinray Inc., 152-35 10th Ave, Whitestone, NY 11357, (718)767-1234 [19396]

Kipling Shoe Company Inc., PO Box 187, Milton, WV 25541-0187, (304)743-5721 [24785]

Kipp Brothers Inc., 240 S Meridian St., Indianapolis, IN 46225, (317)634-5507 [26553]

Kirby Company of Wichita, 1905 E Central Ave., Wichita, KS 67214-4304, (316)683-5673 [25701]

Kirby Forest Products; J., 15213 Louis Mill Dr., Chantilly, VA 20151, (703)378-6930 [7559]

Kirby Oil Co., 2026 E Front St., Tyler, TX 75702, (903)592-3841 [22408]

Kirby Risk Electrical Supply, PO Box 5089, Lafayette, IN 47903-5089, (317)448-4567 [8949]

Kirchhoff Distributing Co., 2000 15th Ave. S, PO Box 1686, Clinton, IA 52733-1686, (319)242-3919 [11622]

Kiri Trading Co. Ltd., 815 Myrtle Ave., Natchez, MS 39120, (601)442-3388 [5111]

Kirk Artclothes; Jennifer Sly, 648 E Huron St., Milford, MI 48381, (248)684-7374 [5112]

Kirk Paper Co., 7500 Amigos Ave., Downey, CA 90242, (562)803-0550 [21792]

Kirkbride Bible Co.; B.B., PO Box 606, Indianapolis, IN 46206, (317)633-1900 [3880]

Kirkhill Aircraft Parts Co., PO Box 3500, Brea, CA 92821, (714)524-5520 [113]

Kirkland Marine Co., 3506 Stone Way N, Seattle, WA 98103, (206)633-1155 [18535]

Kirsch Energy System, 146 Florence Ave., Hawthorne, NJ 07506, (973)423-4488 [14509]

Kirsch Fabric Corp., 830 Decatur Avenue North, Minneapolis, MN 55427, (612)544-9111 [26110]

Kirsch Fabrics Corp., 830 Decatur Ave. N, Minneapolis, MN 55427 [26111]

Kiss International, 965 Park Center Dr., Vista, CA 92083, (760)599-0200 [25702]

Kissen News Agency Inc., 672 Rt., 211 E, Middletown, NY 10940-1718, (914)692-5222 [3881]

Kist Livestock Auction Co., PO Box 1313, Mandan, ND 58554-7313, (701)663-9573 [18035]

Kitchen Distributors Maryland, 2221 Greenspring Dr., Timonium, MD 21093-3115, (410)252-6200 [15189]

Kitchen Specialties Inc., 7921A W Broad St., Ste. 133, Richmond, VA 23294, (804)965-0860 [15550]

Kitchens Inc. of Paducah, 905 Harrison St., Paducah, KY 42001-1827, (502)442-9496 [15551]

Kitchens of the Oceans Inc., 104 SE 5th Ct., Deerfield Beach, FL 33441, (954)421-2192 [11623]

Kitcher Corp., 806 River Rd., Charlestown, NH 03603, (603)542-8768 [18932]

Kitcor Corp., 9959 Glenoaks Blvd., Sun Valley, CA 91352, (818)767-4800 [24158]

Kitrick Management Company, Ltd., 175 Novner Dr., PO Box 15523, Cincinnati, OH 45215, (513)782-2930 [24383]

Kitsinian Jewelers, 6743 Odessa Ave., Van Nuys, CA 91406, (818)988-9961 [17492]

Kittredge Equipment Co., 2155 Columbus Ave., Springfield, MA 01104, (413)788-6101 [24159]

Kittrich Corp., 14555 Alondra Blvd., La Mirada, CA 90638-5602, (213)582-0665 [15552]

Kiva Direct Distribution Inc., 821 W San Mato, Santa Fe, NM 87505-9802, (505)982-1523 [1798]

Kivort Steel Inc., 380 Hudson, Waterford, NY 12188, (518)590-7233 [20103]

Kiwi Brands, 447 Old Swede Rd., Douglassville, PA 19518-1239, (610)385-3041 [14143]

Kiwi Fence Systems Inc., 1145 E Roy Furman Hwy., Waynesburg, PA 15370, (412)627-8159 [7560]

K.J. Electric Inc., 5894 E Molloy Rd., Syracuse, NY 13211, (315)454-5535 [8950]

KK Motorcycle Supply, 431 E 3rd St., Dayton, OH 45401, (937)222-1303 [2858]

Klabin Marketing, 2067 Broadway, New York, NY 10023, (212)877-3632 [14144]

Klabin Marketing, 2067 Broadway, New York, NY 10023, (212)877-3632 [19397]

Klam International, 1234 Broadway, New York, NY 10001, (212)244-6990 [7561]

Klarman Sales Inc., 8 Cloverwood Rd., White Plains, NY 10605, (914)949-5130 [13787]

Klaus Companies, 8400 N Allen Rd., Peoria, IL 61615, (309)691-4840 [15190]

Klear-Knit Sales Inc., 64 Post Rd., W, Westport, CT 06880, (203)221-8650 [5113]

Kleberg County Farmers Cooperative, Rte. 1, Kingsville, TX 78363, (512)592-2621 [913]

Klee Wholesale Company, Inc., 408 Ridgeway Ave., Falmouth, KY 41040, (606)654-5744 [26319]

Kleeko Enterprises, 1907 S Cypress, Wichita, KS 67207, (316)682-9333 [14510]

Kleen Supply Co., 423 25th St., Galveston, TX 77550, (409)762-0140 [4651]

Kleenaire Corp., 2117 Jefferson St., Stevens Point, WI 54481, (715)344-2602 [14511]

Klein Brothers Ltd., PO Box 609, Stockton, CA 95201, (209)948-6802 [18036]

Klein News Co.; George R., 5131 Post Rd., Dublin, OH 43017-1160, (216)623-0370 [3882]

Klein Steel Service Inc., 811 West Ave., Rochester, NY 14611, (716)328-4000 [20104]

Klein's Allsports Distributors, 1 Crossgates Mall Rd., Albany, NY 12203, (518)464-1495 [23776]

Klein's Booklein, 108 N Grand Ave., PO Box 968, Fowlerville, MI 48836, (517)223-3964 [3883]

Klemer and Wiseman, 2301 S Broadway, Los Angeles, CA 90007, (213)747-0307 [26112]

Klemme Cooperative Grain Co., PO Box 250, Klemme, IA 50449, (515)587-2161 [914]

Klempner Bros. Inc., PO Box 4187, Louisville, KY 40204-0187, (502)585-5331 [26867]

Klenosky Co.; S., 543 Metropolitan Ave., Brooklyn, NY 11211, (718)782-7142 [21472]

Kleptz Aluminum Building Supply Co., 1135 Poplar St., Terre Haute, IN 47807, (812)238-2946 [7562]

KLF, Inc., 359 E Park Dr., Harrisburg, PA 17111-2727, (717)564-4040 [11624]

KLH Industries Inc., 703 Hwy. 80 W, Clinton, MS 39056, (601)924-3600 [8951]

KLH Research and Development Corp., PO Box 1085, Sun Valley, CA 91353, (818)767-2843 [15191]

Klinge Corp., PO Box 3608, York, PA 17402, (717)840-4500 [14512]

Klingelhofer Corp., PO Box 1098, Mountainside, NJ 07092, (908)232-7200 [16208]

Klinger Paint Co., Inc., 333 5th SE, PO Box 1945, Cedar Rapids, IA 52406, (319)366-7165 [21473]

Klinker; Norman, RR 1, Box 184, Fairfield, MT 59436-9713, (406)467-2945 [18037]

Klitzner and Son Inc.; B., PO Box 1357, Rocky Mount, NC 27802, (252)442-5740 [24786]

Klockner Namasco Corp., 5775 Glenridge Dr., Bldg. C, Ste. 110, Atlanta, GA 30328, (404)267-8800 [20213]

Klockner Namasco Corp., 5775 Glenridge Dr. NE, No. C, Atlanta, GA 30328-5380 [20105]

Klosterman Bakery Outlet, 2655 Courtright, Columbus, OH 43232, (614)338-8111 [11625]

Klosterman Baking Co. Inc., 4760 Paddock Rd., Cincinnati, OH 45229-1004, (513)242-1004 [11626]

Klosterman Company Inc.; John C., 901 Portage St., Kalamazoo, MI 49001, (616)381-0870 [26320]

Kluge, Finkelstein & Co., 6325 Woodside Ct., Columbia, MD 21046, (410)720-5300 [11627]

Kluyskens Company Inc.; Gerard, 295 5th Ave., New York, NY 10016, (212)685-5710 [19398]

Kmart Corp., 3100 W Big Beaver Rd., Troy, MI 48084, (248)643-1000 [15553]

Kmart Trading Services, Inc., 3100 W Big Beaver Rd., Troy, MI 48084, (248)643-1733 [26113]

KMC Corp., 2670 Commercial Ave., Mingo Junction, OH 43938, (740)598-4171 [1799]

KMG Chemicals Inc., 10611 Harwin Dr., Houston, TX 77036, (713)988-9252 [4436]

K.M.H. Equipment Co., 12565 Emerson Dr., Brighton, MI 48116-8562, (248)446-9002 [7563]

KMS Inc., 1135 N Washington St., Wichita, KS 67214-3058, (316)634-0441 [26554]

The KMW Group Inc., PO Box 888615, Grand Rapids, MI 49588-8615, (616)957-1950 [19041]

Knape and Vogt Manufacturing Co., 2700 Oak Industrial Dr., Grand Rapids, MI 49505-6083, (616)459-3311 [7564]

Knapp Company Inc.; R.S., PO Box 234, Lyndhurst, NJ 07071, (201)438-1500 [24384]

Knapp Shoes of Tucson Inc., 1835 S Alvernon Way, Tucson, AZ 85711-7602, (520)745-4643 [24787]

Knapp Supply Company Inc., PO Box 2488, Muncie, IN 47307-0488, (765)288-1893 [23237]

Knapp Supply & Equipment Co., PO Box 99, Casper, WY 82602-0099, (307)234-7323 [24160]

Knaubs Bakery, 218 Dew Drop Rd., York, PA 17402-4610, (717)741-0861 [11628]

Knauss and Son Inc.; E.W., 625 E Broad St., Quakertown, PA 18951, (215)536-4220 [11629]

KNB Computer Werx Inc., 1717 Dell Ave., Campbell, CA 95008-6904, (408)341-0570 [6422]

Knecht Home Lumber Center Inc., 320 West Blvd., Rapid City, SD 57701, (605)342-4840 [7565]

Knecht Home Lumber Center Inc., 320 West Blvd., Rapid City, SD 57701, (605)342-4840 [27331]

Knese, Inc.; Henry, 22-44 119th St., College Point, NY 11356, (718)353-9300 [16209]

Knievel's Inc., R.R. 1, Box 71, Ewing, NE 68735, (402)485-2598 [915]

Knight Corp., PO Box 332, Ardmore, PA 19003, (215)853-2161 [16992]

Knight Distributing Company Inc., 2150 Boggs Rd., Ste. 370, Duluth, GA 30096, (770)623-2650 [14145]

Knight Electronics Inc., 10940 Alder Cir., Dallas, TX 75238, (214)341-8631 [8952]

Knight Marketing Corp., 251 N Comrie Ave., PO Box 290, Johnstown, NY 12095, (518)762-4591 [4652]

Knightstown Elevator Inc., PO Box 65, Knightstown, IN 46148, (765)345-2181 [18038]

Knit-Rite Inc., PO Box 410208, Kansas City, MO 64141-0208, (816)221-5200 [18877]

Knitting Machine and Supply Company Inc., 1257 Westfield Ave., Clark, NJ 07066, (732)382-9898 [16210]

Knives & Things, 3343 Hollins Ferry Rd., Baltimore, MD 21227, (410)242-0069 [13846]

Knobel & Son Inc.; John, 3010 Wheatland Terr., Freeport, IL 61032-2996, (815)232-4138 [1800]

Knobler International Ltd., 225 5th Ave., New York, NY 10010-1101, (212)679-5577 [13381]

Knogo North America Inc., 350 Wireless Blvd., Hauppauge, NY 11788, (516)232-2100 [15192]

Knoll Motel, 1015 N Main St., Barre, VT 05641, (802)479-3648 [4653]

Knopp Inc., 1307 66th St., Emeryville, CA 94608, (510)653-1661 [8953]

Knott's Wholesale Foods Inc., 125 N Blakemore, Paris, TN 38242-4283, (901)642-1961 [11630]

Knowles Produce and Trading Co., W 2189 County Trunk Y, Lomira, WI 53048, (920)583-3747 [916]

Knox Computer Systems Inc., 3860 Convoy St., Ste. 107, San Diego, CA 92111-3748, (619)502-1205 [6423]

Knox County Farm Bureau Cooperative Association, PO Box 301, Vincennes, IN 47591, (812)882-6380 [917]

Knox Industrial Supplies Inc., 1600 E McFadden Ave., Santa Ana, CA 92705, (714)972-1010 [13788]

Knox Tile & Marble, 3032 Commerce St., Dallas, TX 75226-2581, (972)243-6100 [9989]

Knoxville Beverage Co., PO Box 51628, Knoxville, TN 37950-1628, (423)637-9411 [1801]

Knudson Manufacturing Inc., 10401 W 120th Ave., Broomfield, CO 80021, (303)469-2101 [16211]

Knutson Distributors, 15 Mill Dam Rd., Huntington, NY 11743, (516)673-4144 [18536]

Knutson Farms Inc., 16406 78th St. E, Sumner, WA 98390-2900, (253)863-5107 [14906]

KOA Speer Electronics Inc., PO Box 547, Bradford, PA 16701, (814)362-5536 [8954]

Koa Trading Co., 2975 Aukele St., Lihue, HI 96766, (808)245-1866 [11631]

Koba Nurseries & Landscaping, 41-709 Mokulama St., Waimanalo, HI 96795, (808)259-5954 [14907]

Kobayashi Farm & Nursery, PO Box 525, Captain Cook, HI 96704, (808)328-9861 [14908]

Kobelco Welding of America Inc., 7478 Harwin Dr., Houston, TX 77036-2008, (713)974-5774 [7566]

KOBOLD Instruments Inc., 1801 Parkway View Dr., Pittsburgh, PA 15205, (412)788-2830 [24385]

Kobrand Corp., 134 E 40th St., New York, NY 10016, (212)490-9300 [1802]

Kobrin Builders Supply Inc., 1401 Atlanta Ave., Orlando, FL 32806, (407)843-1000 [7567]

Koch Agriculture Company Inc. Agri Service Div., PO Box 450, Arapahoe, NE 68922-0450, (308)962-7790 [201]

Koch-Bailey & Associates, 302 W 5400 S, Ste. 109, Salt Lake City, UT 84107-8232, (801)261-5802 [15554]

Koch-Bailey Associates, 302 W 5400 S, Ste. 109, Salt Lake City, UT 84107-8232, (801)261-5802 [15554]

Koch-Bailey and Associates, 9226 N 5th Ave., Phoenix, AZ 85021, (602)870-9429 [15555]

Koch Filter Corp., PO Box 3186, Louisville, KY 40201-3186, (502)634-4796 [25703]

Koch International, 2 Tri Harbor Ct., Port Washington, NY 11050-4617, (516)484-1000 [25274]

Koch Resources Inc., PO Box 176, Crystal Bay, NV 89402-0647, (702)831-8213 [26555]

Koen Book Distributors, Inc., 10 Twosome Dr., PO Box 600, Moorestown, NJ 08057, (609)235-4444 [3884]

Koen Co.; U., 3112 Jessica St., Metairie, LA 70003, (504)944-2471 [25704]

Koenig Fuel & Supply Co., 500 East Seven Mile Rd., Detroit, MI 48203, (313)368-1870 [22409]

Koerner and Company Inc.; John E., PO Box 10218, New Orleans, LA 70181, (504)734-1100 [11632]

Kohl Building Products, 1047 Old Bernville Rd., Reading, PA 19605, (610)926-8800 [7568]

Kohl Grocer Company Inc.; N., PO Box 729, Quincy, IL 62306, (217)222-5000 [11633]

Kohl Sales; Walter A., 4022 Lake Ave., Lockport, NY 14094-1116, (716)433-3903 [20664]

Kohler Oil and Propane Co., 8956 Burnside Rd., Brown City, MI 48416, (810)346-2606 [22410]

Kohlmyer Supply Co., 5000 Grove Ave., Lorain, OH 44055-3612, (440)277-8288 [15837]

Koike America Inc., 635 W Main St., Arcade, NY 14009, (716)492-2400 [16212]

Kojemi Corp., PO Box 795, Syosset, NY 11791-0795, (516)921-5250 [20106]

Kokomo Grain Company Inc., 239 N Mill St., Greentown, IN 46936, (765)457-7536 [18039]

Kolb-Lena Cheese Co., 3990 N Sunnyside Rd., Lena, IL 61048, (815)369-4577 [11634]

Kold Temp Refigeration Inc., PO Box 6387, Reno, NV 89503-6387, (702)323-0070 [14513]

Kolda Corp., 16770 Hedgecroft, Ste. 708, Houston, TX 77060, (281)448-8995 [16213]

Koldkist-Beverage Ice Company Inc., 955 N Columbia Blvd., Bldg. C, Portland, OR 97217, (503)285-2800 [24981]

Koley's Medical Supply Company Inc., 505 Crown Point Ave., Omaha, NE 68110, (402)455-4444 [19399]

Kolon America Inc., 350 5th Ave., No. 5211, New York, NY 10118-0110, (212)736-0120 [5114]

Kolstad Company Inc., 8501 Naples St. NE, Blaine, MN 55449-6702, (612)633-8451 [20665]

Komac Paint Center, 119 Cole Shopping Ctr., Cheyenne, WY 82001, (307)635-5714 [21474]

Komac Paint Center, 215 W Broadway, Farmington, NM 87401, (505)325-7837 [21475]

Komatsu America Industries Corp., 199 E Thorndale Ave., Wood Dale, IL 60191, (708)860-3000 [16214]

Kombi Ltd., 102 Great Hill Rd., Naugatuck, CT 06770, (203)723-7441 [5115]

Komer and Co., 2528 W Pembroke Ave., Hampton, VA 23661, (757)247-6651 [21476]

Komerex Industries, Inc., 4401 Edison St., Houston, TX 77009, (713)691-6399 [16215]

Komori America Corp., 5520 Meadowbrook Industrial Ct., Rolling Meadows, IL 60008, (708)806-9000 [16216]

Komp Equipment Company Inc., PO Box 1489, Hattiesburg, MS 39403-1489, (601)582-8215 [16217]

Komp Equipment Company Inc., PO Box 1489, Hattiesburg, MS 39403-1489, (601)582-8215 [4437]

Kona Farmers Coop, PO Box 309, Captain Cook, HI 96704-0309, (808)328-2411 [11635]

Kona Marine Supply, 74-425 Kealakehe Pkwy., No. 8, Kailua Kona, HI 96740, (808)329-1012 [18537]

Koncor Forest Products Co., 3501 Denali St., Anchorage, AK 99503, (907)562-3335 [27332]

Konex Corp., 270 N Smith Ave., Corona, CA 92880, (909)371-1200 [8955]

Konica Business Machines U.S.A. Inc., 500 Day Hill Rd., Windsor, CT 06095, (860)683-2222 [21094]

Konica Business Technologies, Inc., 500 Day Hill Rd., Windsor, CT 06095, (860)683-2222 [21094]

Konica Quality Photo East, PO Box 2011, Portland, ME 04104-5008, (207)883-7200 [22870]

Konica U.S.A. Inc., 440 Silvan Ave., Englewood Cliffs, NJ 07632, (201)568-3100 [22871]

KoolaBrew Inc., 271 Calabash Rd. NW, Calabash, NC 28467, (919)579-6711 [13382]

Koolies Ice Cream, 3324 W Pierson Rd., Flint, MI 48504, (810)787-2140 [11636]

Koons Steel Inc., PO Box 476, Parker Ford, PA 19457, (610)495-9100 [20107]

Koontz Equipment Co.; Don, 6946 Lilac Rd., Plymouth, IN 46563, (219)936-4847 [7569]

Koontz-Wagner Electric Company Inc., 3801 Voorde Dr., South Bend, IN 46628, (219)232-2051 [8956]

Kopecky & Co.; J. M., PO Box 24271, Omaha, NE 68124-0271, (402)331-9408 [14514]

Kopecky & Yates Inc., PO Box 24271, Omaha, NE 68124-0271, (402)331-9408 [14514]

Kopke Jr. Inc.; William H., 3000 Marcus Ave., New Hyde Park, NY 11040, (516)328-6800 [11637]

Koplewitz; Jane, PO Box 4392, Burlington, VT 05406, (802)862-6336 [17493]

Koplik and Sons Inc.; Perry H., 505 Park Ave., 3rd Fl., New York, NY 10022, (212)752-2288 [26868]

Korbel and Bros. Inc.; F., 13250 River Rd., Guerneville, CA 95446, (707)887-2294 [1803]

Korber and Co.; J., PO Box 30548, Albuquerque, NM 87190, (505)884-4652 [2859]

Koremen Ltd., 2146 U.S 41, Schererville, IN 46375, (219)865-1455 [23238]

Korg U.S.A. Inc., 316 S Service Rd., Melville, NY 11747, (516)333-9100 [25275]

Kornfeld-Thorp Electric Co., PO Box 2904, Kansas City, KS 66110, (913)321-7070 [8957]

Kornish Distributors Co., 672 Rt. 211 E, Middletown, NY 10940-1718, (914)692-4321 [3885]

Kornylak Corp., 400 Heaton St., Hamilton, OH 45011, (513)863-1277 [16218]

Korol Co.; Leon, 2050 E Devon Ave., Elk Grove Village, IL 60007, (708)956-1616 [21793]

Korte Brothers Inc., 620 W Cook Rd., Ft. Wayne, IN 46825-3324, (219)745-4941 [7570]

Korvan Industries Inc., 270 Birch Bay Lynden Rd., Lynden, WA 98264, (360)354-1500 [918]

Kory Mercantile Company, 148 N Morley Ave., Nogales, AZ 85621-3116, (520)287-2550 [5116]

Kostelecky's Fiberglass, RR 2, Box 46, Jamestown, ND 58401-9505, (701)252-6725 [2860]

Kova Fertilizer Inc., 1330 N Anderson St., Greensburg, IN 47240, (812)663-5081 [919]

Koval Marketing Inc., 11208 47th Ave. W, Mukilteo, WA 98275, (425)347-4249 [15556]

Kovalsky-Carr Electric Supply Company Inc., 208 St. Paul St., Rochester, NY 14604-1188, (716)325-1950 [8958]

Kowalski Sausage Company Inc., 2270 Holbrook Ave., Hamtramck, MI 48212, (313)873-8200 [11638]

Koyo Corporation of USA, 47771 Halyard St., Plymouth, MI 48170, (734)454-4107 [16219]

Kozak Distributors, 520 E Hunting Park Ave., Philadelphia, PA 19124-6009, (215)426-1870 [21794]

Kozel and Son Inc.; J., 1150 Scottsville Rd., Rochester, NY 14624, (716)436-9807 [20108]

KPK Truck Body Manufacturing and Equipment Distributing Company Inc., 3045 Verdugo Rd., Los Angeles, CA 90065, (213)221-9167 [2861]

K.R. International, 14106 W 69th St., Shawnee, KS 66216, (913)268-6112 [11639]

Kraco Enterprises Inc., 505 E Euclid Ave., Compton, CA 90224, (213)774-2550 [2862]

Kraft Chemical Co., 1975 N Hawthorne Ave., Melrose Park, IL 60160, (708)345-5200 [21477]

Kraft Food Ingredients, 8000 Horizon Center Blvd., Memphis, TN 38133-5197, (901)381-6500 [11640]

Kraft Foods Inc. Distribution, Sales, Service Div., 1601 Ogletown Rd., Newark, DE 19711-5425, (302)453-7000 [11641]

Kraft Foodservice Inc., 800 Supreme Dr., Bensenville, IL 60106-1107, (708)595-1200 [11642]

Kraft General Foods Group. Kraft Food Service, PO Box 324, Deerfield, IL 60015, (847)405-8500 [11643]

Kraft Hardware Inc., 306 E 61st St., New York, NY 10021, (212)838-2214 [15557]

Kraft-Holleb, 800 Supreme Dr., Bensenville, IL 60106, (708)595-1200 [11644]

Kraft Korner Inc., 497 Eagle Truce, Cleveland, OH 44124-6113 [26556]

Kraft USA, 3692 West 2100 South, Salt Lake City, UT 84120-1202, (801)972-5904 [11645]

Kraftbilt Products, 6504 E 44th St., Tulsa, OK 74145-4614, (918)[25705]

Kragnes Farmers Elevator, 9749 21st St., N, Moorhead, MN 56560-7247, (218)233-4247 [18040]

Krall Optometric Professional LLC, 1415 N Sanborn Blvd., Mitchell, SD 57301-1015, (605)996-2020 [19400]

Kramer Beverage Company Inc., PO Box 1100, Pleasantville, NJ 08232, (609)645-2444 [1804]

Kramer Laboratories Inc., 8778 SW 8th St., Miami, FL 33174, (305)223-1287 [19401]

Kramer; L.C., 2525 E Burnside St., Portland, OR 97214, (503)236-1207 [26114]

Kramer Metals, 1760 E Slauson Ave., Los Angeles, CA 90058, (213)587-2277 [26869]

Kramer Scrap Inc., PO Box 588, Greenfield, MA 01302, (413)774-3103 [26870]

Kramig Company Inc.; R.E., 323 S Wayne Ave., Cincinnati, OH 45215, (513)761-4010 [7571]

Kranson Industries, 460 N Lindbergh Blvd., St. Louis, MO 63141-7808, (314)569-3633 [25923]

Krantor Corp., 120 E Industry Ct., Deer Park, NY 11729, (516)935-7007 [11646]

Kranz Automotive Supply, 300 Russell Blvd., PO Box 13300A, St. Louis, MO 63157, (314)776-3787 [2863]

Kranz Inc., 220 Decoven Ave., Racine, WI 53403 [4654]

Krasdale Foods Inc., 65 W Red Oak Ln., White Plains, NY 10604, (914)694-6400 [11647]

Krasdale Foods Inc., 65 W Red Oak Ln., White Plains, NY 10604, (914)694-6400 [11648]

Krause & Sons; M.P., 4956 S Monitor Ave., Chicago, IL 60638, (708)458-1600 [27175]

Krauss-Maffei Corp., PO Box 6270, Florence, KY 41022-6270, (606)283-0200 [25706]

Kravet Fabrics Inc., 225 Central Ave. S, Bethpage, NY 11714, (516)293-2000 [26115]

Kregel Publications & Bookstores, PO Box 2607, Grand Rapids, MI 49501-2607, (616)451-4775 [3886]

Kreher Steel Co., 812 Lexington Dr. Ste. 100, Plano, TX 75075-2357, (972)578-9116 [20109]

Kreher Steel Company Inc., 1550 N 25th Ave., Melrose Park, IL 60160, (708)279-0058 [20110]

Kreinik Manufacturing Company Inc., 3106 Timanus Ln., No. 101, Baltimore, MD 21241, (410)281-0040 [26116]

Krelitz Industries Inc., 800 N 3rd St., Minneapolis, MN 55401-1104, (612)339-7401 [19402]

Krema Nut Co., 1000 W Goodale Blvd., Columbus, OH 43212, (614)299-4131 [11649]

Kremer Marine, 1408 Cowan Rd., Gulfport, MS 39507, (228)896-1629 [18538]

Krentzman and Son Inc.; Joe, PO Box 508, Lewistown, PA 17044, (717)543-5635 [26871]

Krentzman Supply Co., Susquehanna St., Lewistown, PA 17044, (717)543-5635 [26872]

Krieg Consulting and Trading Inc.; A., 119 Maple Vale Dr., Woodbridge, CT 06525, (203)393-3672 [16220]

Krieger Associates; J., 1006 Sunset Ave., Clarks Summit, PA 18411, (570)585-2020 [25707]

Krieger Publishing Co., PO Box 9542, Melbourne, FL 32902-9542, (321)724-9542 [3887]

Krob and Co.; F.J., PO Box 159, Ely, IA 52227, (319)848-4161 [920]

Kroger Co., PO Box 305103, Nashville, TN 37230-5103, (615)871-2400 [11650]

Kroger Co. Dairy-Bakery Div., 1783 Ohio Pike, Amelia, OH 45102, (513)797-4900 [11651]

Kronheim and Co.; Milton S., 2900 V St. NE, Washington, DC 20018, (202)526-8000 [1805]

KR's Paint Shop, One Alii Molokai, Kaunakakai, HI 96748, (808)553-3744 [21478]

Kru-Kel Co. Inc., PO Box 71501, North Charleston, SC 29405, (803)744-2558 [14515]

Kruger Recycling Inc., 877 S Pearl St., Albany, NY 12202, (518)433-0020 [26873]

Kruger Trailer Inc., RR 1 Box 67, Georgetown, DE 19947, (302)856-2577 [16221]

The Kruse Company, 4275 Thunderbird Ln., Fairfield, OH 45014, (513)860-3600 [13789]

Kruse Inc., 104 Gallagherville Rd., PO Box 245, Downingtown, PA 19335, (610)925-5600 [20666]

Kryolan Corp., 132 9th St., San Francisco, CA 94103, (415)863-9684 [25708]

Kryptonics Inc., 740 S Pierce Ave., Louisville, CO 80027, (303)665-5353 [23777]

K's Distributors, 6801 Lockley Cir., Plano, TX 75074, (972)578-9116 [25709]

KS. Electronics L.L.C., 16406 N Cave Creek Rd., Phoenix, AZ 85032, (602)971-3301 [8959]

KS Group International, PO Box 19599, San Diego, CA 92159, (619)460-6355 [14146]

K's Merchandise Mart Inc., 3103 N Charles St., Decatur, IL 62526, (217)875-1440 [17494]

KSB Inc., 4415 Sarellen Rd., Richmond, VA 23231, (804)222-1818 [16222]

KSC Industries Inc., 8653 Ave.nida Costa Norte, San Diego, CA 92154, (619)671-0110 [15193]

KT Distributors, 10 Bridge St., Benton, ME 04901-3404, (207)453-2239 [11652]

KTS Services Inc., 5726 Corporate Ave., Cypress, CA 90630, (714)827-2200 [5659]

Kubota Inc., 4-1300 Kuhio Hwy., Kapaa, HI 96746, (808)822-4581 [1806]

Kubota Tractor Corp., PO Box 2992, Torrance, CA 90509-2992, (310)370-3370 [921]

Kuehl's Distributors, 3401 S 7th St., Lincoln, NE 68502, (402)423-2596 [11653]

Kuehn Company Inc.; J.W., 1504 Cliff Rd. E, Burnsville, MN 55337-1415, (612)890-4881 [16223]

Kuehn Company Inc.; Otto L., 160 Bishops Way, Brookfield, WI 53005, (414)784-1600 [11654]

Kuhlman and Co.; A., 3939 Woodward Ave., Detroit, MI 48201, (313)831-4050 [18878]

Kuhlman Corp., PO Box 714, Toledo, OH 43697-0714, (419)897-6000 [7572]

Kula Farm, 751E Pulehuiki Rd., Kula, HI 96790, (808)878-1046 [14909]

Kultur, White Star, Duke International Films Ltd.; Inc., 195 Hwy 36, West Long Branch, NJ 07764, (732)229-2343 [25276]

Kultur, White Star, Duke International Films Ltd. Inc., 195 Hwy 36, West Long Branch, NJ 07764, (732)229-2343 [15194]

Kulwin Electric Supply, PO Box 535001, Indianapolis, IN 46253-5001, (317)293-3363 [8960]

Kum Kee (USA) Inc.; Lee, 304 S Date Ave., Alhambra, CA 91803, (626)282-0337 [11655]

Kumho U.S.A. Inc., 14605 Miller Ave., Fontana, CA 92336-1695, (909)428-3300 [2864]

Kunau Implement Co., PO Box 39, Preston, IA 52069, (319)689-3311 [922]

Kunda and Sons Inc.; Watson, 349 S Henderson Rd., King of Prussia, PA 19406, (610)265-3113 [1807]

Kunkel Services Co., PO Box 708, Bel Air, MD 21014, (410)838-3344 [2865]

Kunz Oil Company Inc., 7900 Excelsior Blvd., Hopkins, MN 55343-3423, (612)920-9373 [22411]

Kunzler and Company Inc., PO Box 4747, Lancaster, PA 17604, (717)390-2100 [11656]

Kurian Reference Books; George, PO Box 519, Baldwin Place, NY 10505, (914)962-3287 [3888]

Kurman & Co.; S.J., 175 5th Ave., New York, NY 10010, (212)677-7664 [17495]

Kurtz Steel; James H., 18881 Sherwood, Detroit, MI 48234, (313)892-1212 [20111]

Kurtzman Book Sales, Inc., 1263 W Square Lake Rd., Bloomfield Hills, MI 48302 [3889]

Kustom Fit, 8990 S Atlantic, South Gate, CA 90280, (323)564-4481 [2866]

Kustom Tool Works Inc., 28310 Crocker Ave., Valencia, CA 91355, (805)295-8610 [16224]

Kuykendall's Press, 506 Chandler St., PO Box 627, Athens, AL 35612, (256)232-1754 [3890]

Kwal-Hanley Paint Co., 1400 N Solano Dr., Las Cruces, NM 88001, (505)527-0482 [21479]

Kwal-Howells Inc., PO Box 39-R, Denver, CO 80239, (303)371-5600 [21480]

Kwal-Howells Paint & Wallcovering, 390 N State St., Orem, UT 84057, (801)225-6630 [21481]

Kwal-Howells Paint & Wallcovering, 4285 S State St., Murray, UT 84107, (801)262-8466 [21482]

Kwal-Howells Paint & Wallcovering, 5640 S Redwood Rd., Salt Lake City, UT 84123, (801)967-8213 [21483]

Kwik-Affix Products, 5942 Richard St., Jacksonville, FL 32216, (904)448-1180 [15558]

Kwik Sew Pattern Company Inc., 3000 N Washington Ave., Minneapolis, MN 55411, (612)521-7651 [26117]

Kwik Ski Products, PO Box 465, Mercer Island, WA 98040, (425)228-4480 [23778]

Kwik Stop Car Wash Supply, 3802 Pine View Dr., Rapid City, SD 57702-6977, (605)341-1352 [4655]

Kwik-Way Corp., PO Box 340, Gratz, PA 17030-0340, (903)572-3435 [11657]

KYB Corporation of America, 140 N Mitchell Ct., Addison, IL 60101-1490, (708)620-5555 [2867]

Kyle Furniture Co.; R.H., PO Box 793, Charleston, WV 25323, (304)346-0671 [13158]

L-3 Communications Corp., 600 3rd Ave., New York, NY 10016, (212)697-1111 [5660]

L & B Pet Supplies, c/o Robert Elie, PO Box 738, Hwy. 1062, Loranger, LA 70446, (504)878-6241 [27176]

L-com Inc., 45 Beechwood Dr., North Andover, MA 01845, (978)682-6936 [8961]

L & D Appliance Corp., 11969 Telegraph Rd., Santa Fe Springs, CA 90670, (562)946-1105 [15195]

L H Ranch Bunk & Bisket & Hansens Hobby, 471 Mullan Tr., Gold Creek Stage Stop, Gold Creek, MT 59733, (406)288-3436 [26557]

L-K Industries Inc., PO Box 230305, Houston, TX 77223-0305, (713)926-2623 [22412]

L. Karp and Sons, 9401 Le Saint Dr., Fairfield, OH 45014, (513)870-0880 [11583]

L and L Concession Co., 1307 Maple Rd., Troy, MI 48084, (810)689-3850 [11658]

L & L Gas & Oil Inc., PO Box 754, Socorro, NM 87801, (505)835-1127 [22413]

L & L Implement Company Inc., PO Box 307, Yuma, CO 80759, (970)848-5482 [923]

L & L Insulation and Supply Co., PO Box 489, Ankeny, IA 50021-0489, (515)963-9170 [7573]

L and L Jiroch Distributing Co., 1180 58th St., Grand Rapids, MI 49509-9536, (616)530-6600 [26321]

L & L Lace, 218 S Binley Mountain Pkwy., Arab, AL 35016-1251, (205)586-6738 [26558]

L and L Nursery Supply Inc., PO Box 249, Chino, CA 91710, (909)591-0461 [924]

L & L Oil and Gas Service LLC, PO Box 6984, Metairie, LA 70009-6984, (504)832-8600 [22414]

L & L Pet Center, 14123 W Hardy, Houston, TX 77060 [27177]

L and L Products, 2700 Conneticut Ave. NW, Washington, DC 20008-5330, (202)483-1510 [6424]

L & L Shirt Shop, 5620 Fairview Ave., Boise, ID 83706-1167, (208)376-8881 [5117]

L & L Wine & Liquor Corp., 1410 Allen Dr., Troy, MI 48083-4001, (248)588-9200 [1808]

L & M Food Service, PO Box 2277, Laughlin, NV 89029-2277, (702)754-3241 [24161]

L and M Shape Burning Inc., PO Box 5289, Compton, CA 90224, (310)639-4222 [20112]

L. Powell Co./Generations for the 21st Century, PO Box 1408, Culver City, CA 90232-1408, (310)204-2224 [13159]

L & S Trading Co., 2311 Bobolink Cove, Memphis, TN 38134, (901)377-7655 [18403]

L and W Enterprises Inc., PO Box 190, Kearney, NE 68848-0190, (308)237-2185 [15196]

L and W Supply Corp., 125 S Franklin St., Chicago, IL 60606, (312)606-5400 [7574]

L-Z Truck Equipment Co., Inc., 1881 Rice St., Roseville, MN 55113, (612)488-2571 [2868]

La Barge Pipe and Steel, 901 N 10th St., St. Louis, MO 63101, (314)231-3400 [20113]

La Beau Brothers Inc., 295 N Harrison Ave., Kankakee, IL 60901, (815)933-5519 [20667]

La Belle Provence Ltd., 185 W Maple Rd., Birmingham, MI 48009, (248)540-3876 [13160]

La Boiteaux Co., PO Box 175708, Covington, KY 41017-5708, (606)578-0400 [21795]

La Cie. Ltd., 22985 NW Evergreen Pkwy., Hillsboro, OR 97124, (503)844-4500 [25924]

La Cite, 2306 Westwood Blvd., PO Box 64504, Los Angeles, CA 90064, (310)475-0658 [3891]

La Crosse Footwear, Inc., 1407 St. Andrew St., PO Box 1328, La Crosse, WI 54602, (608)782-3020 [24788]

La Crosse Plumbing Supply Co., 6800 Gisholt Dr., Madison, WI 53708, (608)222-7799 [23169]

La Crosse Truck Center Inc., 205 Causeway Blvd., PO Box 1176, La Crosse, WI 54602-1176, (608)785-0800 [20668]

LA Fads Inc., 1701 Pacific Ave., No. 280, Oxnard, CA 93033, (805)487-7772 [15524]

La Farge; Patricia Arscott, PO Box 762, Santa Fe, NM 87504-0762, (505)982-2912 [26118]

La Francis Associates; Mal, 59 Middlesex Tpke., No. 310, Bedford, MA 01730-1415, (781)275-2438 [13383]

L.A. Glo, 1662 S Long Beach Ave., Los Angeles, CA 90021, (213)746-4140 [5118]

La Grand Industrial Supply Co., PO Box 1959, Portland, OR 97207-1959, (503)224-5800 [24582]

L.A. Liquid Handling Systems, 15411 S Broadway St., Gardena, CA 90248, (213)321-8992 [16225]

La Madeleine Inc., 6060 N Central Expy., Dallas, TX 75206, (214)696-6962 [11659]

L.A. Marine Hardware, 345 N Beacon St., San Pedro, CA 90731, (310)831-9261 [18539]

La Parfumerie Inc., 750 Lexington Ave., 16th Fl., New York, NY 10022, (212)754-6666 [14147]

La Piccolina and Co. Inc., 2834 Franklin St., Avondale Estates, GA 30002, (404)296-1624 [11660]

La Plante Gallery Inc., 529 Adams St. NE, Albuquerque, NM 87108-1228, (505)265-2977 [13161]

La Playa Distributing Co., 32575 Industrial Dr., Madison Heights, MI 48071, (248)585-9630 [25292]

La Pointique International, PO Box 6504, Bellevue, WA 98008-0504, (206)575-8843 [18879]

La Porte County Cooperative, PO Box 160, La Porte, IN 46350, (219)362-2156 [18041]

La Reina Inc., 316 N Ford Blvd., Los Angeles, CA 90022, (213)268-2791 [11661]

La Salle County Farm Supply Co., 3107 N Ilinois, Rte. 23, Ottawa, IL 61350, (815)434-0131 [925]

La Salle Farmers Grain Co., PO Box 8, La Salle, MN 56056, (507)375-3468 [926]

L.A. Silver, 640 S Hill St., Booth H24, Los Angeles, CA 90014, (213)624-8669 [17496]

L.A. T Sportswear Inc., PO Box 926, Canton, GA 30114, (770)479-1877 [5119]

L.A. TRADE, 22825 Lockness Ave., Torrance, CA 90501, (310)539-0019 [6425]

La Vencedora Products, 3322 Fowler, Los Angeles, CA 90063-2510, (213)269-7273 [11662]

Laagco Sales, 2930 N San Fernando, Burbank, CA 91504, (818)843-2382 [21484]

Lab Safety Supply Inc., 401 S Wright Rd., PO Box 1368, Janesville, WI 53547-1368, (608)754-2345 [18880]

Labatt Food Service, PO Box 2140, San Antonio, TX 78297, (210)661-4216 [11663]

Labatt Institutional Supply Company Inc., PO Box 2140, San Antonio, TX 78297, (210)661-4216 [11664]

Labatt USA Inc., 23 Old King's Hwy. S, Darien, CT 06820, (203)750-6600 [1809]

LaBelle Time Inc., 65 NW 166 St., North Miami, FL 33169, (305)940-1507 [13384]

Labieniec & Associates; Paul, 28 Organ Hill Rd., Poughkeepsie, NY 12603, (914)462-1860 [23779]

Labinal, Inc., 881 Parkview Blvd., Lombard, IL 60148, (630)705-5700 [22987]

Labomed, Inc., 2921 S Lacienega Blvd., Culver City, CA 90232, (310)202-0814 [18881]

Laboratory & Biomedical Supplies Inc., 12625 High Bluff Dr., Ste. 311, San Diego, CA 92130-2054, (619)259-2626 [19403]

Laboratory Design and Equipment, 2615 Hwy. 160 W, Ft. Mill, SC 29715-8488, (803)548-0067 [13162]

Laboratory Supply Company, PO Box 9289, Louisville, KY 40209, (502)363-1891 [18882]

LABS, 12625 High Bluff Dr., Ste. 311, San Diego, CA 92130-2054, (619)259-2626 [19403]

LABSCO, PO Box 9289, Louisville, KY 40209, (502)363-1891 [18882]

Labsphere, Shaker St., North Sutton, NH 03260, (603)927-4266 [8962]

Lacey-Harmer Co, 4320 NW Saint Helens Rd., Portland, OR 97210, (503)222-9992 [8963]

Lachman & Son Inc.; S., PO Box 590, Odenton, MD 21113-0590, (410)551-2200 [26559]

LaCROIX Beverages Inc., 200 W Adams St., Ste. 2011, Chicago, IL 60606-5230, (312)683-0100 [24982]

Lacy Diversified Industries, 54 Monument Cir., Ste. 800, Indianapolis, IN 46204, (317)237-5400 [20671]

Lacy Ltd.; Alice, 1 Front St., Bath, ME 04530, (207)443-2319 [26560]

Lad Enterprises, Ltd., 1906 Great Falls Hwy., Lancaster, SC 29720, (803)285-2800 [21095]

Ladd, Inc.; Bob, 764 Scott St., Memphis, TN 38112, (901)324-8801 [927]

Lads Pet Supplies, 1701 Eden Evans Center Rd., Angola, NY 14006-9728, (716)947-4293 [27178]

Ladshaw Explosives Inc., 393 Landa St., New Braunfels, TX 78130, (830)625-4789 [9636]

Lady Baltimore Foods Inc., 1601 Fairfax Trafficway, Kansas City, KS 66115, (913)371-8300 [11665]

Lady Iris Cosmetic Company Inc., 93-B S Railroad Ave., Bergenfield, NJ 07621-1724, (201)384-3200 [14148]

Laethem Farm Service Co., 5040 Center St., Fairgrove, MI 48733, (517)693-6172 [928]

Lafarge Concrete, PO Box 726, San Marcos, TX 78667, (512)353-7733 [7575]

Lafarge Corp., PO Box 4600, Reston, VA 22096, (703)264-3600 [7576]

Lafayette Auto Electric, 102 Windsor Trl., Pelham, AL 35124-2848, (205)347-2264 [8964]

Lafayette Drug Company Inc., 220 N University Ave., Lafayette, LA 70502, (318)233-9041 [14149]

Lafayette Electronics Supply Inc., PO Box 4549, Lafayette, IN 47903, (765)447-9660 [8965]

Lafayette Electronics Supply Inc., PO Box 4549, Lafayette, IN 47903, (765)447-9660 [15197]

Lafayette Steel Co., 3600 N Military St., Detroit, MI 48210, (313)894-4552 [20114]

Laforza Automobiles Inc., PO Box 461077, Escondido, CA 92046 [2869]

LaFrance Equipment Corp., PO Box 333, Elmira, NY 14902, (607)733-5511 [24583]

Lagomarsino's, 3810 Transport St., Ventura, CA 93003, (805)644-2201 [1480]

Lagomarsino's Inc., 3810 Transport St., Ventura, CA 93003 [1810]

LaGrange Products Inc., 5656N Wayne St., PO Box 658, Fremont, IN 46737, (219)495-3025 [25925]

Lahr Co.; W.E., PO Box 8158, St. Paul, MN 55108-0158, (612)644-6448 [2870]

Lainiere De Picardie Inc., 180 Wheeler Ct., Ste. 4, Langhorne, PA 19047, (215)702-9090 [22988]

Laird Plastics Inc., 1400 Centrepark, Ste. 500, West Palm Beach, FL 33401, (561)684-7000 [22989]

Lake Aircraft Inc., PO Box 5336, Laconia, NH 03247-5336, (603)524-5868 [114]

Lake Andes Farmers Cooperative Co., PO Box 217, Lake Andes, SD 57356, (605)487-7681 [929]

Lake Andes Farmers Cooperative Co., PO Box 217, Lake Andes, SD 57356, (605)487-7681 [11666]

Lake Benton Farmers Elevator Inc., 110 W Lincoln Ave., Lake Benton, MN 56149, (507)368-4603 [930]

Lake Beverage Corp., 900 John St., West Henrietta, NY 14586-9797, (716)427-0090 [1811]

Lake Business Products, 38322 Apollo Pkwy., Willoughby, OH 44094, (440)953-1199 [21096]

Lake County Farm Bureau Cooperative Association Inc., PO Box C, Crown Point, IN 46307-0975, (219)663-0018 [22415]

Lake County Office Equipment Inc., 1428 Glen Flora Ave., Waukegan, IL 60085, (708)662-5393 [21097]

Lake Crescent Inc., 33-00 Broadway, Ste. 202, Fair Lawn, NJ 07410, (201)794-3500 [22990]

Lake Erie Distributors, 22 Simon Ave., Lackawanna, NY 14218-1015, (716)822-0949 [1812]

Lake Erie Supply, Inc., 2420 W 15th, Erie, PA 16505-4514, (814)453-6625 [7577]

Lake Instruments & Wholesale Corp., Box 329, South Haven, MI 49090, (616)637-3678 [26561]

Lake Martin Living, 375 Windy Wood, Alexander City, AL 35010, (256)329-2460 [3892]

Lake Preston Cooperative Association, 106 2nd Ave. NW, Lake Preston, SD 57249, (605)847-4414 [18042]

Lake Region Cooperative Oil Association, PO Box 728, Maple Lake, MN 55358, (320)963-3137 [22416]

Lake Region Pack Association, Box 1047, Tavares, FL 32778, (352)343-3111 [11667]

Lake States Lumber, 312 S Chester Street, PO Box 518, Sparta, WI 54656, (608)269-6714 [7578]

Lake States Lumber, 2104 E 5th Street, Ste., Superior, WI 54880, (715)398-2975 [7579]

Lake States Lumber, 899 Grossman Road, PO Box 408, Schofield, WI 54476, (715)359-9111 [7580]

Lake States Lumber Inc., PO Box 310, Aitkin, MN 56431, (218)927-2125 [7581]

Lake Steel Inc., PO Box 31748, Amarillo, TX 79120-1748, (806)383-7141 [20115]

Lake Tahoe Supplies, PO Box 7007, Incline Village, NV 89450-7007, (702)831-6395 [4656]

Lake Welding Supply Co., 363 Ottawa St., Muskegon, MI 49442, (231)722-3773 [16226]

Lakeland Auto Auction Inc., PO Box 90007, Lakeland, FL 33804, (941)984-1551 [20669]

Lakeland Engineer Equipment Co., 5735 Lindsay St., Minneapolis, MN 55422, (612)544-0321 [8966]

Lakeland Enterprises, Inc., 3809 Broadway, Lorain, OH 44052, (440)233-7266 [2871]

Lakeland FS, Inc., PO Box 50, Shelbyville, IL 62565, (217)774-3901 [931]

Lakeland Sand and Gravel Inc., PO Box 137, Hartstown, PA 16131, (814)382-8178 [20551]

Lakeland Wholesale Grocery, 1292 S Crystal, Benton Harbor, MI 49022-1808, (616)926-6644 [11668]

Lakeside Harvestore Inc., 2400 Plymouth St., New Holstein, WI 53061, (920)898-5702 [7582]

Lakeside Mills Inc., 716 W Main St., Spindale, NC 28160, (704)286-4866 [11669]

Lakeside Nonferrous Metals Co., PO Box 957, Oakland, CA 94607, (510)444-5466 [26874]

Lakeside Oil Company Inc., PO Box 23440, Milwaukee, WI 53223-0440, (414)445-6464 [22417]

Lakeside Spring Products, 422 N Griffin St., Grand Haven, MI 49417, (616)847-2706 [13790]

Lakeside Supply Company Inc., 3000 W 117th St., Cleveland, OH 44111, (216)941-6800 [23239]

Lakey Mouthpieces; Claude, PO Box 2023, Redmond, WA 98073, (425)861-5920 [25277]

LAM Electrical Supply Company, Inc., PO Box 429, Rte. 17M, Goshen, NY 10924-0429, (914)294-5469 [8967]

Lamanuzzi and Pantaleo, PO Box 296, Clovis, CA 93613, (209)299-7258 [11670]

Lamar Wholesale and Supply Inc., 7135 N Lamar St., Austin, TX 78752, (512)453-2852 [8968]

Lambert's Coffee Services, PO Box 181252-125, Memphis, TN 38181-1252, (901)365-7626 [11671]

Lambright's Inc., PO Box 71, Lagrange, IN 46761, (219)463-2178 [932]

Lamb's Office Products, PO Box 191, Beaumont, TX 77703-5256, (409)838-3703 [21098]

Lambs Yacht Center, 3376 Lakeshore Blvd., PO Box 7038, Jacksonville, FL 32210, (904)384-5577 [18540]

Laminates Unlimited Inc., PO Box 25036, Oklahoma City, OK 73125-0036, (405)239-2646 [22991]

Lamination Services Inc., 4040 Willow Lake Blvd., Memphis, TN 38175, (901)794-3032 [16227]

Lamons Beaumont Bolt & Gasket, PO Box 1710, Beaumont, TX 77704, (409)838-6304 [16993]

Lamont Grain Growers Inc., Main St., Lamont, WA 99017, (509)257-2206 [18043]

Lamp Glow Industries Inc., 819 Pickens Industrial, Marietta, GA 30062, (404)514-1441 [8969]

Lampert Yards Inc., 1850 Como Ave., St. Paul, MN 55108, (612)645-8155 [7583]

Lamport and Brother; Alexander, 7346 Creek View Ct., West Bloomfield, MI 48322-3515, (313)962-5303 [26119]

Lampson Tractor and Equipment Company Inc., PO Box 85, Geyserville, CA 95441, (707)857-3443 [933]

LamRite West Inc., 13000 Danice Pkwy., Strongsville, OH 44136, (440)238-7318 [13385]

Lanahan Sales, 10325 SW 57th Pl., Portland, OR 97219-5704, (503)244-6451 [24789]

Lanahan Sales, 10325 SW 57th Pl., Portland, OR 97219-5704, (503)244-6451 [5120]

Lance Construction Supplies Inc., 4225 W Ogden Ave., Chicago, IL 60623, (773)522-1900 [7584]

Land, Air & Sea Tool Corp., 5760 NW 72nd Ave., Miami, FL 33166, (305)592-5501 [13791]

Land-N-Sea Distribution East, 2968A Ravenswood Rd., Ft. Lauderdale, FL 33335, (954)792-5436 [18541]

Land-N-Sea Distribution West, 5900 Youngquist Rd., Ft. Myers, FL 33908, (941)433-5686 [18542]

Land-N-Sea—Norfolk, 1340 Azalea Garden Rd., Norfolk, VA 23502, (757)853-7658 [18543]

Land O Lakes Inc., 2001 Mogadore Rd., Kent, OH 44240-7274, (330)678-1578 [11672]

Land O Lakes Inc., W Hwy. 4, Luverne, MN 56156-0189, (507)283-4421 [11673]

Land Rover North America Inc., PO Box 1503, Lanham Seabrook, MD 20706, (301)731-6523 [2872]

Land & Sea Products, 3106 NW 3 Mile Rd., Grand Rapids, MI 49544, (616)791-0331 [25926]

Landers-Segal Color Co., 305 W Grand Ave., Montvale, NJ 07645, (973)779-5001 [21485]

Landew Sawdust Inc., 190 Clifford St., Newark, NJ 07105, (973)344-5255 [27333]

Landfill Alternatives Inc., PO Box A.H., Elburn, IL 60119, (630)365-2480 [26875]

Landis Rail Fastening Systems Inc., PO Box 638, Los Altos, CA 94022, (650)948-3557 [23483]

Landiseed International, Ltd., PO Box 25690, Portland, OR 97298-0690, (503)203-6956 [934]

Landman Co. Inc.; Carl, 200 Arlington Way, Menlo Park, CA 94025, (415)821-6710 [11674]

Landmark Co-Op Inc., PO Box 606, New Philadelphia, OH 44663, (216)339-1062 [935]

Landmark Supply Company Inc., N 58 W 6181 Columbia Rd., Cedarburg, WI 53012, (414)375-2909 [936]

Landrum News Agency—Cincinnati Div., 7115 Dillward Ave., Cincinnati, OH 45216, (513)821-5552 [3893]

Landrum News Agency Inc., 4100 Fisher Rd., Columbus, OH 43228, (614)272-0388 [3894]

Landsberg Co.; Kent H., 1640 S Greenwood Ave., Montebello, CA 90640, (213)726-7776 [21796]

Landsman International Inc., 18071 Biscayne Blvd., North Miami Beach, FL 33160, (305)931-1090 [11675]

Landvest Development Corp., 2828 Emerson Ave. S, Minneapolis, MN 55408, (612)870-0801 [7585]

Landwerlen Leather Co. Inc., PO Box 731, Indianapolis, IN 46206-0731, (317)636-8300 [24790]

Lane Fire Service; Donald, 230 Dolloff Ave., Peru, ME 04290, (207)562-4268 [24584]

Lane Ltd., 2280 Mountain Industrial Blvd., Tucker, GA 30084, (404)934-8540 [26322]

Lane and McClain Distributors Inc., 2062 Irving Blvd., Dallas, TX 75207, (214)748-7669 [24162]

Lane Office Furniture Inc., 116 John St., New York, NY 10038, (212)233-4100 [21099]

Lang Percussion, 325 Gold St., Ste. 1, Brooklyn, NY 11201-3040, (212)228-5213 [25278]

Lang and Washburn Electric Inc., 185 Creekside Dr., Amherst, NY 14228, (716)691-3333 [8970]

Lange Co.; Tom, 2031 Penn Ave., Pittsburgh, PA 15222-4417, (412)566-1700 [11676]

Langer Equipment Company Inc., 1400 W Chestnut St., Virginia, MN 55792, (218)749-4700 [20670]

Langer Inc.; David, PO Box 2080, Beverly Hills, CA 90213, (213)466-2225 [6426]

Langford Tool & Drill, 1125 Washington Ave. S, Minneapolis, MN 55405, (612)332-8571 [13792]

Langley Company Inc.; Frank P., PO Box 744, Buffalo, NY 14226-0744, (716)691-7575 [23240]

Langley Optical Company Inc., 8140 Marshall Dr., Lenexa, KS 66214, (913)492-5379 [19404]

Langley Press, Inc., 821 Georgia St., Key West, FL 33040, (305)294-3156 [3895]

Langlois Stores Inc., 3000 Henry St., Muskegon, MI 49441-4016, (616)733-2528 [15559]

Langstadt Electric Supply Co., 1524 W Civic St., Appleton, WI 54911, (920)733-3791 [8971]

Lanham Hardwood Flooring Co., 4704 Pinewood Rd., Louisville, KY 40218, (502)969-1345 [9990]

Lanier Worldwide Inc., 2300 Parklake Dr. NE, Atlanta, GA 30345, (404)496-9500 [21100]

Lankford-Sysco Food Services Inc., PO Box 477, Pocomoke City, MD 21851, (410)632-3271 [11677]

Lankhorst Distributors Inc., 11583 K Tel Dr., Hopkins, MN 55343-8845, (612)933-4876 [26562]

Lannans Paint & Decorating Ctr., 184 E Burkitt St., Sheridan, WY 82801, (307)674-8491 [21486]

Lano Equipment Inc., 3021 W 133rd St., Shakopee, MN 55379, (612)445-6310 [937]

Lans Sons Co.; William, 201 Wheeler Ave., South Beloit, IL 61080, (815)389-2241 [26876]

Lansa USA Inc., 1520 Kensinton Rd., Ste. 110, Oak Brook, IL 60523, (630)472-1234 [6427]

Lansdowne-Moody Company Inc., 8445 E Fwy., Houston, TX 77029, (713)672-8366 [938]

Lansing Company Inc., 36 E Platt Dr., Lansing, IA 52151, (319)538-4211 [26120]

Lansing Corp.; Ted, 8501 Sanford Dr., Richmond, VA 23228, (804)266-8893 [7586]

Lansing Wholesale, 622 E Grand River Ave., Lansing, MI 48906-5338, (517)485-7121 [6939]

Lantec Inc., 3549 N University Ave., Ste. 325, Provo, UT 84604, (801)375-7050 [6428]

Lantev, 460 Kent Ave., Brooklyn, NY 11211, (718)599-1900 [11678]

Lanz Inc., 8680 Hayden Pl., Culver City, CA 90232, (310)558-0200 [5121]

Lapeer County Cooperative Inc., 155 S Saginaw St., Lapeer, MI 48446, (313)664-2907 [18044]

Lapham-Hickey Steel Corp., PO Box 57, St. Louis, MO 63166, (314)535-8200 [20116]

Lapham-Hickey Steel Corp., 5500 W 73rd St., Chicago, IL 60638, (708)496-6111 [20117]

Lapham-Hickey Steel Corp., 2585 W 20th Ave., Oshkosh, WI 54901, (920)233-8502 [20118]

Lapham-Hickey Steel Corp. Clifford Metal Div., 200 Corliss St., Providence, RI 02904, (401)861-4100 [20119]

Lapierre; Bill, 924 E Main St., Newport, VT 05855-1812, (802)334-8878 [21487]

Lapis Lazuli Jewelry Distributors, 860 Worcester Rd., Framingham, MA 01702-5260, (508)875-2836 [17497]

Lapure Water Coolers, 4219 Central Ave., St. Petersburg, FL 33713, (727)327-8764 [15198]

Laramie Tire Distributors, PO Box 28, Norristown, PA 19404-0028, (215)275-6480 [2873]

Larcan TTC, 1390 Overlook Dr., No.2, Lafayette, CO 80026, (303)665-8000 [5661]

Laredo Hardware Co., 401 Market St., Laredo, TX 78040, (956)722-0981 [13793]

LaRose, Inc.; S., 3223 Yanceyville St., PO Box 21208, Greensboro, NC 27420, (336)621-1936 [17498]

Larrabee Brothers Distributing Company Inc., PO Box 1850, 815 S Blosser Rd., Santa Maria, CA 93456, (805)922-2108 [1813]

Larriva Corp., 75 N Terrace Ave., Nogales, AZ 85621-3298, (602)287-5815 [13386]

Larry's News, Empire State Plz., Albany, NY 12223, (518)462-3765 [3896]

Larsen Associates Inc., 10855 W Potter Rd., Wauwatosa, WI 53226, (414)258-0529 [8972]

Larsen and Associates Inc.; Bill, PO Box 1194, Tacoma, WA 98401, (253)383-4444 [13387]

Larsen Co., Inc.; A. R., 15040 NE 95th St., Redmond, WA 98073-0088, (425)861-8868 [24163]

Larsen Cooperative Company Inc., 8290 Hwy. T, Larsen, WI 54947, (414)836-2113 [939]

Larsen International, Inc., 700 W Metro Park, Rochester, NY 14623, (716)272-7310 [4438]

Larson Co.; Gustave A., W233 N2869 Roundy Cir. W, PO Box 910, Pewaukee, WI 53072, (262)542-0200 [14516]

Larson Co.; J.H., 700 Colorado Ave. S, Minneapolis, MN 55416, (763)545-1717 [8973]

Larson Distributing Company Inc., PO Box 16189, Denver, CO 80216, (303)296-7253 [9991]

Larson Electrical Co.; J.H., 700 Colorado Ave. S, Minneapolis, MN 55416, (763)545-1717 [8973]

Larson Fabrics, Inc., 11820 Mayfield, PO Box 51384, Livonia, MI 48151, (734)522-1080 [26121]

Las Cruces Leather Co., 745 E Lohman Ave., Las Cruces, NM 88001-3372, (505)523-0388 [18404]

Las Vegas Discount Golf and Tennis Inc., 2701 Crimson Canyon Dr., Las Vegas, NV 89128-0803 [23780]

LaSalle Paper and Packaging Inc., 105 S 41st Ave., No. 2, Phoenix, AZ 85009-4627, (602)484-7337 [21797]

Lascco Fish Products, 778 Kohler, Los Angeles, CA 90021, (213)622-0724 [11679]

Laser Logic Inc., 2190 Paragon Dr., San Jose, CA 95131, (408)452-1284 [21101]

Laser Magnetic Storage International Co., 4425 Arrowswest Dr., Colorado Springs, CO 80907, (719)593-7900 [21102]

Laser Optics, 738 S Perry Ln., Ste. 17, Tempe, AZ 85281, (602)267-0682 [19252]

Laser Resale Inc., 54 Balcom Rd., Sudbury, MA 01776, (978)443-8484 [24386]

Laser-Scan Inc., 45635 Willow Pond Plz., Sterling, VA 20164, (703)709-9306 [6429]

Laser Technologies and Services Inc., 1155 Phenixville Pike, No. 106, West Chester, PA 19380, (215)692-9756 [21103]

LaserCard Systems Corp., 2644 Bayshore Pkwy., Mountain View, CA 94043, (650)969-4428 [6430]

LaserTone Inc., 8 Fairfield Dr., North Little Rock, AR 72120-1816, (501)834-6557 [6431]

Lasley and Sons Inc.; Walter, PO Box 168, Stratford, TX 79084-0168, (806)753-4411 [940]

Lasonic Electronics Corp., 1827 W Valley Blvd., Alhambra, CA 91803, (626)281-3957 [15199]

Last Gasp of San Francisco, 777 Florida, San Francisco, CA 94110, (415)824-6636 [3897]

The Last Straw Inc., 444 Bayview Ave., Inwood, NY 11096-1702, (516)371-2727 [26563]

Lasting Impressions Inc., Box 22065, Dept. LH, Orlando, FL 32830, (407)263-6883 [17499]

LAT Sportswear, Inc., 1200 Airport Dr., Ball Ground, GA 30107, (404)409-8999 [5122]

Lata Export and Import, 1114 S Main St., Los Angeles, CA 90015, (213)749-4378 [17500]

Latah County Grain Growers Inc., PO Box 9086, Moscow, ID 83843, (208)882-7581 [18045]

Latah Distributors Inc., 220 W Morton St., Moscow, ID 83843-2004, (208)882-4021 [1814]

Latham Seed Co., 131 180th St., Alexander, IA 50420, (641)692-3258 [18046]

Lathrop's Shooters Supply Inc., 5146 E Pima St., Tucson, AZ 85712, (520)321-3878 [13476]

Latin Percussion Inc., 160 Belmont Ave., Garfield, NJ 07026, (973)478-6903 [25279]

Latin Trading Corp., 539 H St., Ste. B, Chula Vista, CA 91910-7505, (619)427-7867 [3898]

Latina Niagara Importing Co., 2299 Millitary Rd., Tonawanda, NY 14150, (716)693-9999 [11680]

Latina Trading Corp., 226 Cannon Blvd., Staten Island, NY 10306-4256, (718)351-1400 [11681]

Latona's Food Importing Corp., PO Box 10, Wood Ridge, NJ 07075-0010, (973)916-5646 [11682]

Latrobe Brewing Company Inc., 119 Jefferson St., Latrobe, PA 15650, (412)537-5545 [1815]

Latshaw Enterprises Inc., PO Box 7710, Wichita, KS 67277, (316)942-7266 [941]

Laube Technology Inc., P.O Box 6079, Camarillo, CA 93011, (805)388-1050 [16994]

Laufen International Inc., PO Box 570, Tulsa, OK 74101-0570, (918)428-3851 [9992]

Laughery Valley AG Co-Op Inc., 336 N Buckeye, Osgood, IN 47037, (812)689-4401 [942]

Laughlin China Co.; Homer, Harrison St., Newell, WV 26050-1299, (304)387-1300 [15560]

Laun-Dry Supply Company Inc., 3800 Durazno St., El Paso, TX 79905, (915)533-8217 [4657]

Laundry Textile Co., 2450 Ave. E SW, Winter Haven, FL 33880-0841, (941)294-2718 [26122]

Laurel Center, PO Box 583, Laurel, MS 39441, (601)428-4364 [7587]

Laurel Farms, PO Box 7405, Studio City, CA 91614, (213)650-1060 [11683]

Laurel Grocery Company Inc., PO Box 4100, London, KY 40741, (606)843-9700 [11684]

Laurel Valley Oil Co., State Rte. 800, Stillwater, OH 44679, (740)922-2312 [22418]

Laurel Valley Oil Co., State Rte. 800, Stillwater, OH 44679, (740)922-2312 [22419]

Laurel Vending Inc., 15 Nashua St., Greensburg, PA 15601, (412)834-4635 [24983]

Lauren Footwear Inc.; Ralph, 120 E 56th St., New York, NY 10022, (212)308-3805 [24791]

Lauren Hosiery Div.; Ralph, 1 Rockefeller Plz., New York, NY 10020-2002, (212)957-2000 [5123]

Laurence Company Inc.; C.R., 2503 E Vernon Ave., Los Angeles, CA 90058, (213)588-1281 [16228]

Lavanture Plastic Extrusion Technologies, PO Box 2088, Elkhart, IN 46515, (219)264-0658 [22992]

LaVanture Products Co., PO Box 2088, Elkhart, IN 46515, (219)264-0658 [2874]

LaVayne Distributors, 457 W Line St., Calhoun, GA 30701, (706)625-4959 [5124]

Lavdas Jewelry Ltd., 3671 E 12 Mile Rd., Warren, MI 48092, (810)751-8275 [17501]

Lavery Appliance Co.; S.K., 1003 Farmington Ave., West Hartford, CT 06107-2103, (860)523-5271 [15200]

Laves Jewelry Co., 2900 W Anderson Ln., Ste. F, Austin, TX 78757, (512)452-6491 [17336]

Lavetan and Sons Inc.; L., PO Box 389, York, PA 17405, (717)843-0931 [26877]

Lavin Candy Company Inc., 4989 S Catherine St., Plattsburgh, NY 12901, (518)563-4630 [11685]

Lavitt Mills Inc.; Paul, PO Box 1507, Hickory, NC 28602, (704)328-2463 [5125]

Lavro Inc., 16311 177th Ave. SE, Monroe, WA 98272-1942, (206)794-5525 [23781]

Law Cypress Distributing, 5883 Eden Park Pl., San Jose, CA 95138, (408)363-4700 [6432]

Law Distributors, 14415 S Main St., Gardena, CA 90248, (213)321-3275 [3899]

Law Office Information Systems Inc., 105 N 28th St., Van Buren, AR 72956-5005, (501)471-5581 [25280]

Lawes Coal Company Inc., PO Box 258, Shrewsbury, NJ 07702, (732)741-6300 [943]

Lawn and Golf Supply Company Inc., 647 Nutt Rd., Phoenixville, PA 19460, (215)933-5801 [944]

Lawn Hill Cooperative, PO Box 68, New Providence, IA 50206, (515)497-5291 [945]

Lawrence County Exchange, PO Box 487, Moulton, AL 35650, (256)974-9213 [18047]

Lawrence Electric Co.; F.D., 3450 Beekman St., Cincinnati, OH 45223, (513)542-1100 [8974]

Lawrence Eyewear, 115 Edwin Rd., Ste. 2, South Windsor, CT 06074-2413, (860)289-4465 [19405]

Lawrence Photo-Graphic Inc., 1211 Cambridge Cir. Dr., Kansas City, KS 66103, (913)621-1211 [22872]

Lawrence Photo & Video, PO Box 4406, Springfield, MO 65807, (417)883-8300 [22865]

Lawrence Plate Glass Co., PO Box 567, Lawrence, MA 01842, (978)683-7151 [7588]

Lawrin Lighting, Inc., PO Box 2128, Columbus, MS 39704-2128, (601)289-1711 [15561]

Lawson Products Inc., 1666 E Touhy Ave., Des Plaines, IL 60018, (847)827-9666 [16995]

Lawson Seafood Company Inc., 15 Rudds Ln., Hampton, VA 23669, (804)722-6211 [11686]

Lawson and Son; E.T., PO Box 249, Hampton, VA 23669, (757)722-1928 [22420]

Lawson-Yates Inc., PO Box 65278, Salt Lake City, UT 84165-0278, (801)467-5491 [23241]

Lawsons Locksmithing, 237 Wilson St., Brewer, ME 04412-2033, (207)989-5104 [25710]

Lay International Consulting Services, 12826 Sanfield Dr., St. Louis, MO 63146, (314)532-0517 [14517]

Lay Packing Co., 400 E Jackson Ave., Knoxville, TN 37901, (423)546-2511 [11688]

Laymon Candy Company Inc., 276 East Commercial Rd., San Bernardino, CA 92408, (909)825-4408 [11687]

Layne and Myers Grain Co., PO Box 86, New Market, IN 47965, (765)866-0175 [18048]

Lays Fine Foods, 400 E Jackson Ave., Knoxville, TN 37901, (423)546-2511 [11688]

Layton Marketing Group Inc., 1845 Buerkle Rd., St. Paul, MN 55110-5246, (612)490-5000 [21488]

Lazartigue Inc.; J.F., 764 Madison Ave., New York, NY 10021, (212)249-9424 [14150]

Lazartigue Inc.; J.F., 764 Madison Ave., New York, NY 10021, (212)249-9424 [19406]

Lazy-Man, Inc., 616 Hardwick St., PO Box 327, Belvidere, NJ 07823, (908)475-5315 [15201]

L.B. Electric Supply Company Inc., 5202 New Utrecht Ave., Brooklyn, NY 11219, (718)438-4700 [8975]

L.B. Industries Inc., PO Box 2797, Boise, ID 83701, (208)345-7515 [2875]

LB Steel Plate Co., 1207 E 143rd St., East Chicago, IN 46312, (219)397-9224 [26878]

L.B.I. Company, 3950 South 500 West, Salt Lake City, UT 84123, (801)262-9087 [9993]

L.B.I. Company, 3950 South 500 West, Salt Lake City, UT 84123, (801)262-9087 [7589]

LBI Wallcovering, 3950 South 500 West, Murray, UT 84123, (801)262-6618 [21489]

LBK Distributors, 1710 S Wabash St., Wabash, IN 46992-4118, (219)563-3372 [23782]

LBK Marketing Corp., 7800 Bayberry Rd., Jacksonville, FL 32256-6818, (904)737-8500 [13388]

LBM Sales Inc., 304 Walnut St., PO Box 488, Fayetteville, NY 13066, (315)637-5147 [11689]

LBM Sales Inc., 1307 Military Rd., Buffalo, NY 14217, (716)873-7251 [11690]

LCD Systems Corp., 43150 Osgood Rd., Fremont, CA 94539-5629, (510)353-1913 [8976]

LCI Corp., PO Box 16348, Charlotte, NC 28297-8804, (704)394-8341 [16229]

LCI Ltd., PO Box 4900, Jacksonville Beach, FL 32240-9000, (904)241-1200 [4439]

L.C.I. Process Division, PO Box 16348, Charlotte, NC 28297-8804, (704)394-8341 [16230]

LCR Corp., 6232 Siegen Ln., Baton Rouge, LA 70809, (504)292-9915 [23242]

LDC Corporation of America, 7 E Glenolden Ave., Glenolden, PA 19036, (610)586-0986 [18883]

LDI, Ltd., 54 Monument Cir., Ste. 800, Indianapolis, IN 46204, (317)237-5400 [20671]

LDI MFG Co., Inc., PO Box 400, Logansport, IN 46947-0400, (219)722-3124 [14518]

Le Creuset of America Inc., PO Box 575, Yemassee, SC 29945, (803)943-4308 [15562]

Le Roy Cooperative Association Inc., PO Box 248, Le Roy, KS 66857, (316)964-2225 [18049]

Le Roy Farmers Cooperative Creamery Association, PO Box 306, Le Roy, MN 55951, (507)324-5361 [946]

Le Roy Farmers Cooperative Grain and Stock Co., PO Box 120, Le Roy, MN 55951, (507)324-5605 [947]

LEA Book Distributors, 170-23 83rd Ave., Jamaica, NY 11432, (718)291-9891 [3900]

Lea County Livestock Marketing, PO Box 712, Lovington, NM 88260-0712, (505)396-5381 [18050]

Leach Company Inc.; W.W., 196 Bedford St., Fall River, MA 02720, (508)678-5238 [21490]

Leader Creek Marina, 536 E 48th Ave., Anchorage, AK 99503-7315, (907)561-8141 [18544]

Leader Instruments Corp., 380 Oser Ave., Hauppauge, NY 11788, (631)231-6900 [8977]

Leader Newspapers, PO Box 991, Glendale, CA 91209, (818)241-4141 [3901]

Leader Technologies Inc., 4590 MacArthur Blvd., Ste. 500, Newport Beach, CA 92660, (949)757-1787 [6433]

Leading Edge Products Inc., 10 Craig Rd., Acton, MA 01720-5405, (978)562-3322 [6434]

Leading Products Co., 614 Diez Y Ocho Ct. SE, Rio Rancho, NM 87124-2235, (505)892-5740 [4658]

LeadingSpect Corp., 1025 Segovia Cir., Placentia, CA 92870, (714)632-3599 [6435]

Leahy's Fuels Inc., PO Box 130, Danbury, CT 06813, (203)866-0738 [22421]

Leaman Co., 359 E Park Dr., Harrisburg, PA 17111-2727, (717)564-4040 [11624]

Leamco-Ruthco, PO Box 60050, Midland, TX 79711, (915)561-5837 [16231]

Lean Year Distributing Inc., 775 Milton St. N, St. Paul, MN 55104-1530, (612)487-3788 [26564]

Learning Materials Workshop, 274 N Winooski Ave., Burlington, VT 05401-3621, (802)862-8399 [26565]

The Learning Plant, PO Box 17233, West Palm Beach, FL 33416, (561)686-9456 [3902]

Lease Surgical Inc., 101 S Cleveland Ave., Sioux Falls, SD 57103-2034, (605)338-1033 [18884]

Lease Wholesale Plumbing Supply; A.L., PO Box 1600, Watsonville, CA 95077-1600, (831)724-1044 [23243]

Leasure & Associates Inc.; Ralph, 10555 Guilford Rd., Suite #113, Jessup, MD 20794-9110, (301)317-0070 [18885]

Leather Connection, 165 Classon Ave., Brooklyn, NY 11205, (718)783-1120 [18405]

Leather Loft Stores, PO Box 1070, Exeter, NH 03833, (603)778-8484 [18406]

The Leather Shop, 411 N Marion St., Ste. 1, Lake City, FL 32055, (904)752-7591 [5126]

Leatherman Tool Group Inc., PO Box 20595, 12106 NE Ainsworth Cl., Portland, OR 97220, (503)253-7826 [13794]

Leathertone Inc., PO Box 247, 153 Hamlet Ave., Woonsocket, RI 02895-0781, (401)765-2450 [22993]

Leavenworth Paper Supply Co., 521 S 2nd St., Leavenworth, KS 66048, (913)682-3861 [21798]

Lebanon Building Supply Co., 225 N 10th St., Lebanon, PA 17046, (717)272-4649 [7590]

Lebzelter and Son Co.; Philip, 300 N Queen St., Lancaster, PA 17603, (717)397-0372 [2876]

Lectorum Publications Inc., 111 8th Ave., Ste. 804, New York, NY 10011, (212)929-2833 [3903]

Ledford's Trading Post, 1833 12th Ave. NE, Hickory, NC 28601, (704)327-0055 [13497]

Ledgerwood-Herwig Associates Ltd., 119 S Easton Rd., Glenside, PA 19038-4525 [15202]

Ledo-Dionysus, PO Box 5708, Denver, CO 80217, (303)734-2400 [1816]

Ledu Corp., 36 Midland Ave., Port Chester, NY 10573, (914)937-4433 [8978]

Ledyard Company Inc., 1005 17th Ave., Santa Cruz, CA 95062, (408)462-4400 [24164]

Lee Brothers Corp., 1555 S Jefferson Ave., St. Louis, MO 63104, (314)773-6464 [14151]

Lee Cash & Carry, PO Box 630, Everett, WA 98206-0630, (425)259-6155 [11691]

Lee Co.; Henry, 3301 NW 125th St., Miami, FL 33167, (305)685-5851 [11692]

Lee Company Inc., PO Box 567, Terre Haute, IN 47807, (812)235-8156 [13163]

Lee Company Inc.; George G., 210 E 22nd St., PO Box 11105, Norfolk, VA 23517, (757)622-5733 [23244]

Lee Electric Company of Baltimore City, 600 W Hamburg St., Baltimore, MD 21230, (410)752-4080 [8496]

Lee Engineering Supply Company, Inc., 150 Plauche St., New Orleans, LA 70123, (504)733-3333 [16232]

Lee Equipment Co.; Ray, 910 N Date St., Plainview, TX 79072, (806)293-2538 [948]

Lee Flowers and Company Inc.; W., PO Box 1629, Lake City, SC 29560, (803)389-2731 [14910]

Lee F.S. Inc., 1129 Lee Center Rd., Amboy, IL 61310, (815)857-3535 [949]

Lee Jay Bed and Bath, 1 Federal St. #Hanify, Boston, MA 02110 [15563]

Lee Lumber and Building Materials Corp., 633 W Pershing Rd., Chicago, IL 60609, (773)927-8282 [7591]

Lee-Mar Aquarium and Pet Supplies, Inc., 2459 Dogwood Way, Vista, CA 92083, (760)727-1300 [27179]

Lee-Rowan Co., 900 S Highway Dr., Fenton, MO 63026, (314)343-0070 [25927]

Lee and Sons Inc.; W.S., PO Box 1631, Altoona, PA 16603, (814)696-3535 [11693]

Lee/Star Tire Co., Willow Brook Rd., Cumberland, MD 21502-2599, (301)777-6000 [2877]

Lee Supply Corp., 6610 Guion Rd., Indianapolis, IN 46268, (317)290-2500 [23245]

Lee Tennis, LLC, 2975 Ivy Rd., Charlottesville, VA 22903, (804)295-6167 [23783]

Lee Tennis Products, 2975 Ivy Rd., Charlottesville, VA 22903, (804)295-6167 [23783]

Lee Tomato Co., 140 Timberlawn Rd., Jackson, MS 39212-2329, (601)352-0821 [11694]

Lee Tractor Company Inc., PO Box 939, Kenner, LA 70063, (504)467-6794 [7592]

Lee Wholesale Floral Inc., 620 15th St., Lubbock, TX 79401, (806)765-8309 [14911]

Lee Wholesale Supply Company Inc., PO Box 299, New Hudson, MI 48165-0299, (248)437-6044 [7593]

Leeber Ltd. USA, 115 Pencader Dr., Newark, DE 19702-3322, (302)733-0998 [13389]

Leeco Steel Products Inc., 8255 S Lemont Rd., No. 100, Darien, IL 60561, (773)762-4800 [20120]

Leecom Data Systems, 5952 Royal Ln., Ste. 166, Dallas, TX 75230, (214)750-8000 [6436]

Leed Plastics Corp., 793 E Pico Blvd., Los Angeles, CA 90021-2105, (213)746-5984 [22994]

Leedal Inc., 4025 S Western Blvd., Chicago, IL 60609, (773)376-5900 [22873]

Leemon Oil Company Inc., 29120 Wick Rd., Romulus, MI 48174, (734)947-1811 [22634]

Leemon Oil Company Inc., 13507 Auburn Dr., Detroit, MI 48223, (313)272-6700 [22422]

Leemon Shores Oil, 13507 Auburn St., Detroit, MI 48223-3414, (313)776-2670 [22423]

Lees Office Equipment & Supplies, 170 W Granite St., Butte, MT 59701-9216, (406)782-8355 [21104]

Lee's Refrigeration, 2165 Wilder Ave., Helena, MT 59601-1503, (406)442-2712 [14519]

Lees Refrigeration, Div. of Hussmann Corp., 1713 Democrat St., Honolulu, HI 96819-3116, (808)847-3237 [14520]

Lees Refrigeration Sales & Service, 1713 Democrat St., Honolulu, HI 96819-3116, (808)847-3237 [14520]

Leese Flooring Supply, 63 San Rico Dr., Manchester, CT 06040, (860)649-7627 [9994]

Leeward Inc., 1121 Hempshire St., No. 135, Richardson, TX 75080, (972)690-9778 [18886]

Lefeld Implement Inc., 5228 State Rte. 118, Coldwater, OH 45828, (419)678-2375 [950]

Leff Electric Co.; H., 1163 E 40th St., Cleveland, OH 44114, (216)432-3000 [8979]

Leff Electronics Inc., 225 Braddock Ave., Braddock, PA 15104, (412)351-5000 [8980]

Leffelman and Sons Inc.; W.G., 340 N Metcalf Ave., Amboy, IL 61310, (815)857-2513 [951]

Leffler Inc.; Carlos R., PO Box 278, Richland, PA 17087, (717)866-2105 [22424]

Left Foot Ltd., 109 Tosca Dr., Stoughton, MA 02072-1505, (508)238-4686 [24792]

Lefton Co.; Geo Zolton, 3622 S Morgan St., Chicago, IL 60609, (773)254-4344 [15564]

Lefton Enterprises Inc., PO Box 219, East St. Louis, IL 62202, (618)274-4900 [26879]

Lefton Iron and Metal Co., 205 S 17th St., East St. Louis, IL 62207, (618)274-4900 [26880]

L.E.G. Inc., 501 S 9th St., Reading, PA 19602-2503, (610)374-4148 [11695]

Legal Books Distributing, 4247 Whiteside St., Los Angeles, CA 90063, (213)526-7110 [3904]

Legal Sportswear, 1450 Broadway, New York, NY 10018-2201, (212)398-2222 [5127]

Legal Star Communications, 10573 W Pico Blvd., Los Angeles, CA 90064, (310)275-8867 [25281]

Legend Computer Inc., 542 Lakeside Dr., Ste. 1, Sunnyvale, CA 94085-4005, (408)720-0818 [6437]

Legends of Racing Inc., 11820 Antebellum Dr., Charlotte, NC 28273, (704)543-9540 [26566]

Lehigh-Armstrong Inc., 202 Boston Rd., Billerica, MA 01862, (978)663-0010 [13795]

Lehigh Gas and Oil Co., 80-82 Broad St., Beaver Meadows, PA 18216, (717)455-5828 [22425]

Lehigh Oil Co., 1 Terminal Way, Norwich, CT 06360, (860)889-1311 [22426]

Lehigh Safety Shoe Co., 1100 E Main St., Endicott, NY 13760, (607)757-4800 [24793]

Lehleitner and Company Inc.; Geo H., 202 Crofton Rd., Kenner, LA 70062, (504)466-6678 [15565]

Lehman Co.; Charles, 14611 S Carmenita Rd., Norwalk, CA 90650-5228, (562)921-4424 [11696]

Lehman Paint Co. Inc., 112 S Canyon St., Carlsbad, NM 88220, (505)885-5330 [21491]

Lehmann Co. Inc.; Chester C., 1135 Auzerais St., San Jose, CA 95126, (408)293-5818 [8981]

Lehmann Company Inc.; Chester C., 1135 Auzerais St., San Jose, CA 95126, (408)293-5818 [8982]

Lehman's Commercial Service, 1501 Michigan St., Des Moines, IA 50314-3517, (515)243-1974 [14521]

Lehrhoff and Company Inc.; I., 50 Camptown Rd., Maplewood, NJ 07040, (973)374-5300 [15203]

Lehrkinds Inc., PO Box 399, Bozeman, MT 59771-0399, (406)586-2029 [1817]

Leibstone Associates, Inc.; William, 1776 N Pine Island Rd., Ste. 306, Plantation, FL 33322, (954)370-0855 [14257]

Leica Inc., 111 Deer Lake Rd., Deerfield, IL 60015, (847)405-0123 [24387]

Leich Div.; Charles, PO Box 869, Evansville, IN 47708, (812)428-6700 [19407]

Leico Industries Inc., 250 W 57th St., New York, NY 10107, (212)765-5290 [20121]

Leidy's Inc., 266 W Cherry Ln., PO Box 257, Souderton, PA 18964, (215)723-4606 [11697]

Leifheit Sales Inc., 1140 Broadway, No. 502, New York, NY 10001, (212)679-5260 [15566]

Leingang Siding and Window, PO Box 579, Mandan, ND 58554-0579, (701)663-7966 [7594]

Leisegang Medical Inc., 6401 Congress Ave., Boca Raton, FL 33487, (561)994-0202 [18887]

Leish; Bob, 4225 E Sahara Ave., Ste. 10, Las Vegas, NV 89104-6331, (702)641-5400 [25711]

Leisure Arts, Inc., PO Box 55595, Little Rock, AR 72215, (501)868-8800 [3905]

Leisure Components/SF Technology, 16730 Gridley Rd., Cerritos, CA 90703, (562)924-5763 [2878]

Leisure Crafts, PO Box 1650, Rancho Cucamonga, CA 91729, (909)948-8838 [25712]

Leisure Learning Products, PO Box 4869, Greenwich, CT 06830-8869, (203)531-8700 [26567]

Leisure-Lift, Inc., 1800 Merriam Ln., Kansas City, KS 66106, (913)722-5658 [18888]

Leisure-Lift Inc., 1800 Merriam Ln., Kansas City, KS 66106, (913)722-5658 [19408]

Leisure Time Products Inc., 2650 Davisson St., River Grove, IL 60171, (708)452-5400 [25713]

Leisurelife USA Inc., 5232 Buckhead Trail, Knoxville, TN 37919-8903, (865)558-6302 [23784]

LeJoy Uniforms Inc., 608 23rd St. S, Birmingham, AL 35233-2325, (205)252-8654 [18889]

LEK USA Inc., 333 Sylvan Ave., Englewood Cliffs, NJ 07632, (201)541-9310 [4440]

Lektro Inc., 1190 SE Flightline Dr., Warrenton, OR 97146, (503)861-2288 [115]

Leland Limited Inc., PO Box 382, Bedminster, NJ 07921, (908)668-1008 [23785]

Leland Paper Company Inc., PO Box 2148, Glens Falls, NY 12801-2148, (518)792-0949 [21105]

Lello Appliances Corp., 355 Murray Hills Pkwy., East Rutherford, NJ 07073, (201)939-2555 [15204]

LeMans Corp., PO Box 5222, Janesville, WI 53547-5222, (608)758-1111 [20672]

LeMare Medical Inc., PO Box 526743, Miami, FL 33172, (305)591-1152 [18890]

Leming Supply Inc., PO Box 4759, Lafayette, IN 47903-4759, (765)448-4553 [14522]

Lemke Cheese and Packaging Company Inc., PO Box 688, Wausau, WI 54402, (715)842-3214 [11698]

Lemma Wine Co., 120 E Market, Portland, OR 97204, (503)231-4033 [1818]

Lemmen Oil Co., 13 E Randall St., Coopersville, MI 49404, (616)837-6531 [22427]

Lemmon Livestock Inc., PO Box 477, Lemmon, SD 57638-0477, (605)374-3877 [18051]

Lemo USA, Inc., PO Box 2408, Rohnert Park, CA 94927-2408, (707)578-8811 [8983]

Lempco Industries Inc., 5490 Dunham Rd., Cleveland, OH 44137, (216)475-2400 [16996]

Lenco, Inc., 175 Quality Ln., Rutland, VT 05701-4995, (802)865-0604 [19409]

Lenco Inc., 42 Evergreen Ave., PO Box 979, Rutland, VT 05702-0979, (802)775-2505 [19410]

Lenore & Co.; John, 1250 Delevan Dr., San Diego, CA 92102-2437, (619)232-6136 [1819]

Lenover & Son Inc.; J.E., 13420 Wayne Rd., Livonia, MI 48150-1246, (734)427-0000 [9]

Lenox Junk Co., 1170 Massachusetts Ave., Dorchester, MA 02125, (617)288-2841 [20122]

Lens Co., 1350 S King St., Ste. 314, Honolulu, HI 96814-2008, (808)599-5454 [19411]

Lens Express Inc., 350 SW 12th Ave., Deerfield Beach, FL 33442, (954)421-5800 [19412]

Lensing Wholesale, Inc., PO Box 965, Evansville, IN 47706, (812)423-6891 [7595]

Lensland, 416 Waverly Ave., Mamaroneck, NY 10543, (914)381-4540 [19413]

Lenz Sports; Jerry, PO Box 4466, Victoria, TX 77903, (512)575-2378 [23786]

Lenzip Manufacturing Corp., 1900 W Kinzie St., Chicago, IL 60622, (312)829-1865 [26123]

Leo Distributors Inc., 3721 E Dupont Rd., Ft. Wayne, IN 46825, (219)484-0784 [7596]

Leo J. Distributors, 1000 Minnesota Ave., Duluth, MN 55802, (218)722-1757 [18545]

Leon Supply Company, Inc., PO Box 1437, Ogunquit, ME 03907-1437 [11699]

Leon Supply Company Inc., 160 Goddard Memorial Dr., Worcester, MA 01603-1260, (508)756-8768 [11700]

Leonard and Harral Packing Company Inc., PO Box 14514, San Antonio, TX 78214, (210)924-4403 [11701]

Leonard Inc.; Charles, 13130 S Normandie Ave., Gardena, CA 90249-2128, (310)715-7464 [20123]

Leonard Paper Company Inc., 725 N Haven St., Baltimore, MD 21205, (410)563-0800 [21799]

Leonard Refrigeration & Heating Sales & Service, 16119 Hubbell St., Detroit, MI 48235-4026, (313)838-2240 [14523]

Leonard Southwest Corp.; Harold, 600 Green Ln., Union, NJ 07083, (908)289-1000 [24132]

Leonard's Stone & Fireplace, 12200 S I 35 W, Burleson, TX 76028, (817)293-2204 [14524]

Leone Food Service Corp., 30660 Plymouth Rd., Livonia, MI 48150, (313)427-7650 [11702]

Leone's Animal Supply, 4352 William Penn Hwy., Rte. 22, Murrysville, PA 15668, (412)325-3030 [27180]

Leonhardt Company Inc.; W.L., 2218 W 2nd St., Santa Ana, CA 92703, (714)543-4858 [3113]

Leon's Molds, 1404 Memorial Dr., Waycross, GA 31501-1947, (912)285-1813 [16997]

Leppo Inc., 176 West Ave., Tallmadge, OH 44278, (330)633-3978 [7597]

Les Appel for Rex Lester Inc., 127 E 9th St., Los Angeles, CA 90015, (213)629-4539 [5128]

L.E.S. Distributing, 6015 Commerce Dr. No. 545, Irving, TX 75063-6025, (972)751-0488 [25282]

Lesco Corp. (Lansing, Michigan), PO Box 23098, Lansing, MI 48909, (517)394-1440 [25714]

LESCO Distributing, 51100 Bittersweet Rd., Granger, IN 46530-9140, (219)277-8001 [5662]

Lesco Distributing, 1203 E Industrial Dr., Orange City, FL 32763, (904)775-7244 [8984]

LESCO Inc., 20005 Lake Rd., Rocky River, OH 44116, (440)333-9250 [952]

Leshore Calgift Corp., 1006 Sunset Ave., Clarks Summit, PA 18411, (570)585-2020 [25707]

Leslie Company Inc.; Richard A., 7 Corporate Dr., Orangeburg, NY 10962-2615, (914)359-5200 [5129]

Leslie Paper Co. Chicago Div., 775 Belden Ave., Addison, IL 60101, (630)628-0400 [21800]

Lesman Instrument Co., 215 Wrightwood Ave., Elmhurst, IL 60126, (630)834-2200 [24388]

Lessco Products Inc., 529 Railroad Ave., South San Francisco, CA 94080, (650)873-8700 [21106]

Lestar Company Inc.; Kenneth O., PO Box 340, Lebanon, TN 37087, (615)444-2963 [12161]

Lester Company Inc.; Kenneth O., PO Box 340, Lebanon, TN 37087, (615)444-2963 [24165]

Letters N Logos Inc., 3375 SW 182nd Ave., Beaverton, OR 97006-3939, (503)642-1420 [5130]

Letts Equipment Div., 1111 Bellevue Ave., Detroit, MI 48207, (313)579-1100 [2879]

Levand Steel and Supply Corp., PO Box 24846, Los Angeles, CA 90024, (310)823-4453 [20124]

Level Export Corp., 1411 Broadway, RM 485, New York, NY 10018-3402, (212)354-2600 [26124]

Level Valley, 807 Pleasant Valley Rd., West Bend, WI 53095-9781, (414)675-6533 [11703]

Level Valley Creamery, Inc., 807 Pleasant Valley Rd., West Bend, WI 53095-9781, (414)675-6533 [11703]

Levin and Company Inc.; M., 326 Pattison Ave., Philadelphia, PA 19148, (215)336-2900 [11704]

Levin and Company of Tonawanda, Inc.; Louis, PO Box 6601, Buffalo, NY 14240-6601, (716)692-1395 [26881]

Levin-Liston and Associates Inc., PO Box 350, Delmar, NY 12054, (518)439-9985 [13487]

Levin and Sons Co.; J., 7610 W Chicago Ave., Detroit, MI 48204, (313)834-6920 [4659]

Levine Books & Judaica; J., 5 W 30th St., New York, NY 10001, (212)695-6888 [3906]

Levine & Co.; L, 1899 River Rd., Cincinnati, OH 45204, (513)471-5900 [20125]

Levinson Associates Inc.; Harold, 1 Enterprise Pl., Hicksville, NY 11801, (516)822-0068 [26323]

Levinson Steel Co., 110 Riossler Rd., Ste. 300C, Pittsburgh, PA 15220-1014, (412)572-3400 [20126]

Levis Paper Company Inc.; J.J., 12-18 Methuen, Lawrence, MA 01840, (978)682-0712 [21801]

Levi's Womenswear, 1411 Broadway, New York, NY 10018-3403, (212)354-5970 [5131]

Levonian Brothers Inc., PO Box 629, Troy, NY 12180, (518)274-3610 [11705]

Levor and Company Inc.; G., PO Box 866, Gloversville, NY 12078, (518)725-3185 [18052]

Levoy's, 2511 S Temple W, Salt Lake City, UT 84115, (801)481-7300 [5132]

Levy Co.; Charles, 1200 N North Branch St., Chicago, IL 60622, (312)440-4400 [3907]

Levy Home Entertainment, 4201 Raymond Dr., Hillside, IL 60162, (708)547-4400 [3908]

Levy Inc.; Frank, Denver Merchandise Mart, 451 E 58th Ave., Denver, CO 80216, (303)295-2286 [5133]

Levy, Inc.; Harris, 278 Grand St., New York, NY 10002-4488, (212)226-3102 [15567]

Levy Inc.; Victor H., 1355 S Flower St., Los Angeles, CA 90015, (213)749-8247 [17502]

Lewan and Associates Inc., PO Box 22855, Denver, CO 80222, (303)759-5440 [21107]

Lewis-Boyle Inc., 358 Second Ave., Waltham, MA 02451, (781)890-7950 [16135]

Lewis Brothers Bakeries Inc., 500 N Fulton Ave., Evansville, IN 47710, (812)425-4642 [11706]

Lewis Brothers Lumber Company Inc., PO Box 334, Aliceville, AL 35442, (205)373-2496 [7598]

Lewis Company Inc.; Dwight G., PO Box A, Hillsgrove, PA 18619, (717)924-3507 [7599]

Lewis Electronics Co., PO Box 100, Humboldt, TN 38343-0100, (901)784-2191 [8985]

Lewis-Goetz and Company Inc., 650 Washington Rd., No. 310, Pittsburgh, PA 15228, (412)341-7100 [24284]

Lewis Grocer Co., Hwy. 49 S, Indianola, MS 38751, (601)887-3211 [11707]

Lewis International, 55 E Palatine Rd., Prospect Heights, IL 60070, (847)537-6110 [953]

Lewis Manufacturing Co., PO Box 190, Woodland, NC 27897, (919)587-5221 [5134]

Lewis Marine Supply, 220 SW 32 St., PO Box 21107, Ft. Lauderdale, FL 33335, (954)523-4371 [18546]

Lewis Oil Co.; H.C., PO Box 649, Welch, WV 24801-0649, (304)436-2148 [22428]

Lewis Seed and Feed Co., 306 W Gertrude Ave., Drew, MS 38737-3228, (601)745-8543 [954]

Lewis-Simpson Ranch, PO Box 5, Robert Lee, TX 76945, (915)453-2555 [18053]

Lewis-Simpson Ranch, PO Box 5, Robert Lee, TX 76945, (915)453-2555 [18054]

Lewis Supply Company Inc., PO Box 220, Memphis, TN 38101, (901)525-6871 [16998]

Lewis Supply Company Inc., PO Box 24268, Richmond, VA 23224, (804)232-7801 [23246]

Lewisohn Sales Company Inc., PO Box 192, 4001 Dell Avenue, North Bergen, NJ 07047, (201)864-0300 [7600]

Lewiston AG Inc., R.R. 1, Lewistown, IL 61542, (309)547-3793 [955]

Lewiston Grain Growers, PO Box 467, Lewiston, ID 83501, (208)743-8551 [18055]

Lewiston Livestock Market Inc., PO Box 711, Lewiston, ID 83501-0711, (208)743-5506 [18056]

Lewiston Rubber & Supply Inc., PO Box 139, Lewiston, ME 04240-0139, (207)784-6985 [25715]

Lewiston Rubber and Supply Inc., PO Box 139, Lewiston, ME 04240-0139, (207)784-6985 [24389]

Lewistown Livestock Auction, PO Box 1190, Lewistown, MT 59457-1190, (406)538-3471 [18057]

Lex Computing and Management Corp., 1 Elm St., Keene, NH 03431, (603)357-3950 [6438]

Lexco Tile, 1616 S 108th St., West Allis, WI 53214, (414)771-2900 [9995]

Lexington Cooperative Oil Co., PO Box A, Lexington, NE 68850, (308)324-5539 [22429]

Lexington Steel Corp., 5443 W 70th Pl., Bedford Park, IL 60638, (708)594-9200 [20127]

Lexington Trotters and Breeders Association, PO Box 420, Lexington, KY 40585, (606)255-0752 [18058]

Lextron Inc., PO Box BB, Greeley, CO 80632, (970)353-2600 [27181]

Lexus Div., 19001 S Western Ave., Torrance, CA 90509, (310)328-2075 [2880]

LFS Inc., 851 Coho Way, Bellingham, WA 98225, (360)734-3336 [18547]

LI Tinsmith Supply Corp., 76-11 88 St., Glendale, NY 11385, (718)846-0400 [7601]

Lib-Com Ltd., 1150 Motor Pkwy., Central Islip, NY 11722, (516)582-8800 [13390]

Libbey Owens Ford Co., 500 E Louise Ave., Lathrop, CA 95330-9606, (209)858-5151 [7602]

Liberal Hull Co., 1600 W Pancake Blvd., Liberal, KS 67901, (316)624-2211 [22430]

Liberation Distributors, PO Box 5341, Chicago, IL 60680, (773)248-3442 [3909]

Liberto Inc.; R.J., PO Box 14027, Pittsburgh, PA 15239, (412)793-9500 [26882]

Liberty Business Systems Inc., PO Box 9887, Fargo, ND 58106-9887, (701)241-8504 [21108]

Liberty Distributors Inc., PO Box 48168, Wichita, KS 67201-8168, (316)264-7393 [15205]

Liberty Gold Fruit Co., PO Box 2187, South San Francisco, CA 94083, (650)583-4700 [11708]

Liberty Hobby, PO Box 922, Lakeland, FL 33802-0922, (941)688-5904 [26568]

Liberty Industries Inc., 555 Tibetts Wick Rd., Girard, OH 44420-1101, (330)539-4744 [27334]

Liberty Industries Inc., 133 Commerce St., East Berlin, CT 06023, (860)828-6361 [25716]

Liberty Iron and Metal Company Inc., PO Box 1391, Erie, PA 16503, (814)453-6758 [26883]

Liberty Leather Products Company Inc., 165 Classon Ave., Brooklyn, NY 11205, (718)783-1100 [18407]

Liberty Natural Products, 8120 SE Stark St., Portland, OR 97215, (503)256-1227 [14152]

Liberty Natural Products, 8120 SE Stark St., Portland, OR 97215, (503)256-1227 [19414]

Liberty Oil Company Inc., 2 Main St., Port Carbon, PA 17965, (717)622-3595 [22431]

Liberty Publishing Co. Inc., PO BOX 4248, Deerfield Beach, FL 33442, (954)360-9000 [3910]

Liberty Richter Inc., 1 Park 80 Olz. West, Saddle Brook, NJ 07663-5808, (201)843-8900 [11709]

Liberty Woods International, Inc., 1903 Wright Pl., Ste. 360, Carlsbad, CA 92008, (760)438-8030 [7603]

Library Book Selection Service, Inc., 2714 McGraw Dr., PO Box 277, Bloomington, IL 61704, (309)663-1411 [3911]

Library Corp., Research Park, Inwood, WV 25428, (304)229-0100 [6439]

Library Research Associates Inc., 474 Dunderberg Rd., Monroe, NY 10950, (914)783-1144 [3912]

Library Video Co., PO Box 580, Wynnewood, PA 19096, (610)645-4000 [25283]

Libros De Espania Y America, 170-23 83rd Ave., Jamaica, NY 11432, (718)291-9891 [3900]

Licht Company Inc.; J.C., 45 N Brandon Dr., Glendale Heights, IL 60139-2091, (630)351-0400 [21492]

Lichtman and Company Inc.; M., 4529 Crown Rd., Liverpool, NY 13088, (315)457-7711 [1820]

Liconix Industries Inc., 3611 164th St., Flushing, NY 11358-2003, (718)961-6008 [16999]

Liebherr-America Inc., PO Box Drawer O, Newport News, VA 23605, (757)245-5251 [7604]

Liebherr Construction Equipment Co., PO Box Drawer O, Newport News, VA 23605, (757)245-5251 [7605]

Liebherr Mining Equipment Co., PO Box O, Newport News, VA 23605, (757)245-5251 [7606]

Liebovich Brothers Inc., 2116 Preston St., Rockford, IL 61102, (815)987-3200 [20128]

Liechty Farm Equipment Inc., PO Box 67, Archbold, OH 43502, (419)445-1565 [956]

Life Care Medical Products, 70 Sea Ln., Farmingdale, NY 11735, (631)777-8899 [19534]

Life-Link International, PO Box 2913, Jackson, WY 83001, (307)733-2266 [23787]

Life-Tech Inc., PO Box 36221, Houston, TX 77236, (713)495-9411 [19415]

Life Unlimited, 800 N Ben Maddox, Ste. 204, Visalia, CA 93292, (209)733-1940 ´ [3913]

Lifecare Medical Inc., 42014 Veterans Ave., Hammond, LA 70403, (504)542-4343 [18676]

Lifeline Food Company Inc., 426 Orange St., Sand City, CA 93955, (831)899-5040 [11710]

Lifestyle International Inc., 110 S Enterprise Ave., Secaucus, NJ 07094, (201)863-2426 [18408]

Lifetime Books Inc., 2131 Hollywood Blvd., Hollywood, FL 33020, (954)925-0555 [3764]

Lifetime Hoan Corp., 1 Merrick Ave., Westbury, NY 11590, (516)683-6000 [15568]

Lift Truck Sales and Service Inc., 2720 Nicholson Rd., Kansas City, MO 64120, (816)241-6360 [16233]

Liftech Handling Inc., 6847 Elliott Dr., East Syracuse, NY 13057, (315)463-7333 [16234]

Light Creations, 260 S Main St., Fallon, NV 89406-3312, (702)423-8060 [22874]

Light House Electrical Suppliers Inc., 609 Andrew Ave., La Porte, IN 46350, (219)362-3171 [8986]

Light Impressions, PO Box 22708, Rochester, NY 14692-2708 [25284]

Light Wave Systems, 21029 Itasca St Ste. A-B, Chatsworth, CA 91311, (818)727-9900 [8987]

Lightbourn Equipment Co., PO Box 801870, Dallas, TX 75380, (972)233-5151 [2881]

The Lightbulb Shop, 7135 N Lamar St., Austin, TX 78752, (512)453-2852 [8968]

Lightening Oil Co., Philipsburg, MT 59858, (406)859-3164 [22432]

Lighting Parts Inc., 191 E Jefferson Blvd., Los Angeles, CA 90011, (213)233-8111 [8988]

Lightnin Fiberglass Co., PO Box 268, Kilauea, HI 96754, (808)828-1583 [23788]

Lightolier Inc. Norwich Div., 40 Wisconsin Ave., Norwich, CT 06360, (860)886-2621 [8989]

Lights Etc. Inc., 4510 N 16th St., Phoenix, AZ 85016, (602)230-8770 [8990]

Ligon Electric Supply Co., PO Box 5098, Winston-Salem, NC 27113, (919)723-9656 [8991]

Ligonier Ministries, Inc., 400 Technical Park, Ste. 150, Lake Mary, FL 32746, (407)333-4244 [25285]

Lil Brave Distributors Inc./Division of Plee-Zing Inc., 1640 Pleasant Rd., Glenview, IL 60025, (847)998-0200 [11711]

Liland Trade & Radiator Service Inc., 220 E 2nd, East Syracuse, NY 13057-2930, (315)432-0745 [2882]

Lill and Son Inc.; Frank, 656 Basket Rd., Webster, NY 14580, (716)265-0490 [16235]

Lillegard Inc., PO Box 1178, Wahpeton, ND 58074, (701)642-8424 [957]

Lilly Co.; Chas. H., 6000 E Marginal Way, Seattle, WA 98108, (206)762-1224 [958]

Lilly and Co. Pharmaceutical Div.; Eli, Lilly Corporate Ctr., Indianapolis, IN 46285, (317)267-2157 [19416]

Lilly Fasteners Inc.; Gary Kenneth, PO Box 6005, Newark, DE 19714-6005, (302)366-7640 [13796]

Lilyblad Petroleum Inc., PO Box 1556, Tacoma, WA 98401, (206)572-4402 [22433]

Limestone Detailers, 616 36th Ave. NE, Great Falls, MT 59404-1122, (406)453-3443 [25717]

Limestone Farmers Cooperative Inc., PO Box 429, Athens, AL 35611, (205)232-5500 [959]

Linco Distributors, 1037 Wray St., Knoxville, TN 37917-6452, (423)524-1476 [26324]

Lincoln Clutch and Brake Supply, 211 S 20th St., Lincoln, NE 68510, (402)475-1439 [2883]

Lincoln County Cooperative Oil Co., PO Box 190, Tyler, MN 56178, (507)247-5586 [22120]

Lincoln County Farmers Cooperative, 811 E Cherry St., Troy, MO 63379, (314)528-6141 [960]

The Lincoln Electric Co, 9804 Norwalk Blvd., Santa Fe Springs, CA 90670, (562)906-7700 [16236]

Lincoln Industries Inc., PO Box 80269, Lincoln, NE 68501, (402)421-7300 [3914]

Lincoln-Kaltek, PO Box 88390, Atlanta, GA 30338, (404)457-9448 [7607]

Lincoln Machine, 4317 Progressive Ave., Lincoln, NE 68504, (402)434-9140 [20129]

Lincoln Office Equipment Co., 2535 O St., Lincoln, NE 68510, (402)476-8833 [21109]

Lincoln Office Supply Company Inc., 7707 N Knoxville Ave., Peoria, IL 61614, (309)693-2444 [25928]

Lincoln Packing Co., 137 Newmarket Sq., Boston, MA 02118-2603, (617)427-2836 [11712]

Lincoln Part Supply Inc., 728 S 27th St., Lincoln, NE 68510-3105, (402)476-6908 [8992]

Lincoln Poultry and Egg Co., 2005 M St., Lincoln, NE 68510, (402)477-3757 [11713]

Lincoln Trading Co., 5925 Benjamin Center Dr., No. 113, Tampa, FL 33634-5239, (813)874-6620 [116]

Linde Gases of the Midwest Inc., 12000 Roosevelt Rd., Hillside, IL 60162, (708)449-9300 [17110]

Lindeco International Corp., 10600 NW 37th Ter., Miami, FL 33178, (305)477-4446 [2884]

Lindemann Produce Inc., 923 E Pacheco Blvd., Los Banos, CA 93635, (209)826-2442 [11714]

Lindemann Produce Inc., 300 E 2nd St., Ste. 1200, Reno, NV 89501, (775)323-2442 [11715]

Linden Tree Children's Records & Books, 170 State St., Los Altos, CA 94022, (650)949-3390 [3915]

Lindenmeyer Munroe, 240 Forbes Blvd., Mansfield, MA 02048, (508)339-6161 [21802]

Lindenmeyer Munroe, 468 Pepsi Rd., Manchester, NH 03109, (603)627-1320 [21803]

Lindenmeyer Munroe, 301 Veterans Blvd., Rutherford, NJ 07070-2706, (201)935-2900 [21804]

Lindenmeyer Munroe, 921 Riverside St., Portland, ME 04103, (207)878-0007 [21805]

Lindenmeyer Munroe, 3041 Industry Dr., Lancaster, PA 17603-4025, (717)393-2111 [21806]

Lindenmeyer Munroe, 921 Riverside St., Portland, ME 04103, (207)878-0007 [21807]

Lindenmeyr Munroe, 200 Riverpark Dr., Box 0129, North Reading, MA 01864-0129, (978)276-2300 [21808]

Lindenmeyr Munroe, PO Box 6033, Farmingdale, NY 11735, (718)520-1586 [21809]

Linder Electric Motors Inc., 308 Adrian St., Wausau, WI 54401-6107, (715)842-3725 [8993]

Linder Equipment Co., PO Box 1139, Tulare, CA 93275, (209)685-5000 [961]

Lindox Equipment Corp., 108 Randolph Rd., Newport News, VA 23601-4222, (757)599-4500 [24166]

Lindquist Industrial Supply Co., 13 Hamden Park Dr., Hamden, CT 06517, (203)497-1510 [17000]

Lindquist Investment Co., 3909 S Airport Rd., Ogden, UT 84405, (801)399-4532 [117]

Lindquist Steels Inc., PO Box 9718, Stratford, CT 06497, (203)377-2828 [20130]

Lindsay-Ferrari, 1057 Montague Expwy., Milpitas, CA 95035, (408)435-1300 [13164]

Lindsay Foods Inc., PO Box 04403, Milwaukee, WI 53204, (414)649-2500 [11716]

Lindsey Completion Systems, PO Box 2512, Odessa, TX 79760, (915)337-5541 [16237]

Line & Co.; R.Q., 803 E Rice St., 3rd Fl., Livestock Exchange Bldg., Sioux Falls, SD 57103, (605)336-3170 [18059]

Line Power Manufacturing Co., 329 Williams St., Bristol, VA, (540)466-8200 [20131]

Linear Industries Ltd, 1850 Enterprise Way, Monrovia, CA 91016, (626)303-1130 [17001]

Ling's International Books, 7531 Convoy Ct., San Diego, CA 92111, (619)292-8104 [3916]

Link Lumber Co.; C.J., PO Box 1085, Warren, MI 48090, (810)773-1200 [27335]

Linn Cooperative Oil Co., 325 35th St., Marion, IA 52302, (319)377-4881 [22434]

Linn; John, RR 2 Box 276, Richmond, VT 05477-0276, (802)434-4882 [18060]

Linox Gas Tech Inc., 12000 Roosevelt Rd., Hillside, IL 60162, (708)449-9300 [22592]

Linsey's Products Inc., 2140 Martin Luther King Jr. Dr., Atlanta, GA 30310, (404)696-3064 [14153]

Lintex Corp., 2609 Territorial Rd., St. Paul, MN 55114-1074, (612)646-6600 [18891]

Linton Livestock Market Inc., PO Box 365, Napoleon, ND 58561-0365, (701)254-4581 [18061]

Linvar Inc., 245 Hamilton St., Hartford, CT 06106, (860)951-3818 [25929]

Linvar Inc., 237 Hamilton St., Hartford, CT 06106, (860)951-3818 [24167]

Linvar LLC, 245 Hamilton St., Hartford, CT 06106, (860)951-3818 [25929]

Linwood; Mitchell, 1249 S Beretania St. B, Honolulu, HI 96814-1822, (808)539-9358 [24794]

The Lion Brewery, Inc., 700 N Pennsylvania, Wilkes Barre, PA 18702, (570)823-8801 [1821]

Lion Inc., 700 N Pennsylvania, Wilkes Barre, PA 18702, (570)823-8801 [1821]

Lion Notions Inc., 222 Harris Ct., PO Box 2468, South San Francisco, CA 94083-2468, (650)873-4692 [26125]

Lion Ribbon Company Inc., Rte. 24, Box 601, Chester, NJ 07930, (908)879-4700 [26126]

Lionel Lavallee Company Inc., PO Box 229, Haverhill, MA 01830, (978)374-6391 [11717]

Lipe-Rollway Corp. International Div., 7600 Morgan Rd., Liverpool, NY 13090, (315)457-6211 [17002]

Lipper International Inc., 230 5th Ave., New York, NY 10001, (212)686-6076 [15569]

Lippert International, PO Box 8766, Jacksonville, FL 32239, (904)744-3400 [15997]

Lipscomb and Co.; H.G., 621 Murfreesboro Rd., Nashville, TN 37210, (615)255-7401 [13797]

Lipsey's Inc., PO Box 83280, Baton Rouge, LA 70884, (225)755-1333 [13498]

Lipsitz and Company Inc.; M., PO Box 1175, Waco, TX 76703, (254)756-6661 [26884]

Liquid Town, 6802 McArdle, Corpus Christi, TX 78412, (512)991-7932 [1822]

Lisac's Inc., 2200 Yale Ave., Butte, MT 59701, (406)494-7056 [2885]

Lisk Lures, 915 Onslow Dr., Greensboro, NC 27408-7709, (336)299-7787 [23789]

Listening Library Inc., 1 Park Ave., Old Greenwich, CT 06870, (203)637-3616 [3917]

Lister-Petter Inc., 815 E 56 Hwy., Olathe, KS 66061-4914, (913)764-3512 [2886]

Liston Brick Company of Corona Inc., PO Box 1869, Corona, CA 91718, (909)277-4221 [20132]

Lit Refrigeration Co., 309 Union Ave., Memphis, TN 38103, (901)527-8445 [25718]

Litchfield Packaging Machinery Corp., PO Box 419, Morris, CT 06763, (860)567-2011 [16238]

Lite Brite Distributors, PO Box 142, 475 E Broadway, Trenton, IL 62293, (618)224-7314 [8994]

Lite-On Inc., 720 Hillview Dr., Milpitas, CA 95035, (408)946-4873 [6440]

Lite Source Inc., 4401 Eucalyptus Ave., Chino, CA 91710-9703, (909)597-8892 [13165]

Literal Books, 7705 Georgia Ave. NW, No. 102, Washington, DC 20012, (202)723-8688 [3918]

Littelfuse Inc., 800 E Northwest Hwy., Des Plaines, IL 60016, (847)824-1188 [8995]

Litter Distributing Co., 656 Hospital Rd., Chillicothe, OH 45601, (740)774-4600 [1823]

Litter Industries Inc., PO Box 297, Chillicothe, OH 45601, (740)773-2196 [1824]

Little Brass Shack Imports, 2708 N Armistead Ave., Hampton, VA 23666-1628, (757)766-1011 [13391]

Little Dania's Juvenile Promotions, 100 Paterson Plank Rd., Jersey City, NJ 07307, (201)659-2768 [3582]

Little River Marine Co., PO Box 986, Gainesville, FL 32602, (352)378-5025 [18548]

Little Rock Distributing Co., PO Box 3417, Little Rock, AR 72203, (501)490-1506 [1825]

Little Rock Drapery Co., 7501 Kanis Rd., PO Box 55003, Little Rock, AR 72215, (501)227-5900 [15570]

Little Rock Tool Service, Inc., 11600 Arch St., PO Box 164720, Little Rock, AR 72206-4720, (501)888-2457 [13798]

Little & Son; Michael, 191 Silk Farm Rd., Concord, NH 03302-1455, (603)225-6066 [21110]

Liuski International Inc., 6585 Crescent Dr., Norcross, GA 30071, (770)447-9454 [8996]

Livacich Produce Inc.; John, PO Box 70209, Riverside, CA 92513, (909)734-6060 [11718]

LIVE Entertainment Inc., 15400 Sherman Way, Van Nuys, CA 91406, (818)988-5060 [25286]

Living Systems Instrumentation, 156 Battery St., Burlington, VT 05401, (802)863-5547 [8997]

Livingston Apparel Inc., North Industrial Park, Livingston, AL 35470, (205)652-9566 [5135]

Livingston-Graham Inc., 1900 W Garvy Ave. S, Ste. 200, West Covina, CA 91790, (626)856-6700 [7440]

Livingston & Haven, Inc., 11616 Wilmar Blvd., Charlotte, NC 28273, (704)525-7910 [16239]

Livingston & Haven, Inc., 7523 Irmo Dr., Columbia, SC 29212 [16240]

Livingston & Haven, Inc., 316 Nancy Lynn Ln., Ste. 12B, Knoxville, TN 37919, (423)584-1124 [16241]

Livingston Service Co., 320 N Plum St., Pontiac, IL 61764, (815)844-7185 [962]

Liz and Co., 1441 Broadway, New York, NY 10018, (212)354-4900 [5136]

L.J. Technical Systems Inc., 85 Corporate Dr., Holtsville, NY 11742-2007, (516)234-2100 [6441]

LJO Inc., 401 Hamburg Tpk., Ste. 305, Wayne, NJ 07470, (973)956-6990 [24795]

LKG Industries Inc., PO Box 6386, Rockford, IL 61125, (815)874-2301 [8998]

LKS International Inc., 4001 W Devon Ave., Chicago, IL 60646, (773)283-6601 [24168]

LKS International Inc., 4001 W Devon Ave., Chicago, IL 60646, (773)283-6601 [14525]

Llewellyn Publications, PO Box 64383, St. Paul, MN 55164, (651)291-1970 [3919]

Llewellyn Supply, 507 N Figueroa St., Wilmington, CA 90744, (310)834-2508 [18549]

Lloyd F. McKinney Associates Inc., 25350 Cypress Ave., Hayward, CA 94544, (510)783-8043 [25287]

Lloyd Ltd.; Reston, PO Box 2302, Reston, VA 20195, (703)437-0003 [21493]

Lloyds Buying Service, 701 14th Ave. N, Greybull, WY 82426-1514, (307)765-4666 [18062]

Lloyd's Carnation, 357 IHE Pl., Kula, HI 96790, (808)878-6235 [14912]

Lloyd's Electronics, Inc., 2640 White Oak Cir., Aurora, IL 60504, (630)820-4800 [25469]

Lloyd's Refrigeration Inc., 3550 W Tompkins Ave., Las Vegas, NV 89103, (702)798-1010 [14526]

Lo-An Foods Inc., 6002 Benjamin Rd., Tampa, FL 33634, (813)886-3590 [11719]

Lob-Ster Inc., PO Box 2865, Plainfield, NJ 07062, (908)668-1900 [23790]

Lobel Chemical Corp., 100 Church St., Ste. 1608, New York, NY 10007-2682, (212)267-4265 [963]

Loboflor Bonar Flotex, 14286 Gillis Rd., Dallas, TX 75244, (972)788-2233 [9996]

Local Oil Company of Anoka Inc., 2015 7th Ave. N, Anoka, MN 55303, (612)421-4923 [22435]

Lockbourne Farmers Exchange Co., PO Box 11, Lockbourne, OH 43137, (614)491-0635 [964]

Lockhart Co., PO Box 1165, Pittsburgh, PA 15230, (412)771-2600 [27034]

Lockhart Co., PO Box 1165, Pittsburgh, PA 15230, (412)771-2600 [20133]

Lockney Cooperative Gin, PO Box 128, Lockney, TX 79241, (806)652-3377 [11720]

Locks Co., 2050 NE 151st St., North Miami, FL 33162, (305)949-0700 [24585]

Locks Co., 2050 NE 151st St., North Miami, FL 33162, (305)949-0700 [13799]

Lockwood Farmers Exchange Inc., 107 W 6th St., Lockwood, MO 65682, (417)232-4525 [965]

Loco Boutique, 150 Kaiulani Ave., Honolulu, HI 96815-3247, (808)922-7160 [5137]

Locoli Inc., 9119 Wicker Ave., PO Box 401, St. John, IN 46373-0401, (219)365-3125 [5138]

Locust Lumber Company Inc., PO Box 130, Locust, NC 28097, (704)888-4412 [7608]

Loda Poultry Company Inc., 551 E 400 North Rd., Loda, IL 60948, (217)386-2381 [11721]

Lodan West Inc., 1050 Commercial St., San Carlos, CA 94070, (650)592-4600 [8999]

Loeb Electric Co., 915 Williams Ave., Columbus, OH 43212, (614)294-6351 [9000]

Loef Company Inc., Box 80808, Athens, GA 30608-0808, (706)549-6700 [26885]

Loef Company Inc., Box 80808, Athens, GA 30608-0808, (706)549-6700 [26886]

Loeffler's Safety Shoes Inc., 959 Payne Ave., St. Paul, MN 55101-4003, (612)771-3833 [24796]

Loews Corp., 667 Madison Ave., New York, NY 10021-8087, (212)545-2000 [17503]

Loffler Business Systems Inc., 5707 Excelsior Blvd., Minneapolis, MN 55416, (612)925-6800 [9001]

Lofland Co., PO Box 35446, Dallas, TX 75235, (214)631-5250 [7609]

Loftin Business Forms Inc., 789 Gateway Center Way, San Diego, CA 92102, (619)262-0200 [21810]

Loftin Web Graphics, 789 Gateway Center Way, San Diego, CA 92102, (619)262-0200 [21810]

Loft's Seed Inc., 30 Southard Ave., Ste. 100, Farmingdale, NJ 07727-1213, (732)356-8700 [966]

Log Cabin Sport Shop, 8010 Lafayette Rd., Lodi, OH 44254, (330)948-1082 [13499]

Logan Corp., 555 7th Ave., Huntington, WV 25701, (304)526-4700 [25719]

Logan Inc., 653 Evans City Rd., Butler, PA 16001-8759, (724)482-4715 [11722]

Logan International Ltd., PO Box 1000, Boardman, OR 97818, (541)481-3070 [11723]

Logan and Whaley Company Inc., PO Box 1089, Marshall, TX 75671, (903)938-4377 [17003]

Logantex Inc., 1460 Broadway, New York, NY 10036, (212)221-3900 [26127]

LogEtronics Corp., 7001 Loisdale Rd., Springfield, VA 22150, (703)971-1400 [21111]

Logical Choice, 3118 Milton Rd., Charlotte, NC 28204, (704)535-8451 [6442]

Login Brothers Book Co., 1436 W Randolph St., Chicago, IL 60607, (312)432-7700 [3920]

Login Publishers Consortium, 1436 W Randolph, Chicago, IL 60607, (312)432-7650 [3922]

Logion Press, 1445 Boonville Ave., Springfield, MO 65802, (417)831-8000 [3791]

Logo Apparel, 5301 Everhart Rd., Corpus Christi, TX 78411, (512)855-7127 [5139]

Logo Designs, 5301 Everhart Rd., Corpus Christi, TX 78411, (512)851-9560 [5140]

Logo-Wear Inc., 717 W Freeport St., Broken Arrow, OK 74012-2406, (918)251-2140 [5141]

Logon Inc., 611 U.S Hwy 46 W, Hasbrouck Heights, NJ 07604-3120, (201)393-7600 [6443]

Logsdon Service Inc., PO Box 308, Wayland, MO 63472, (660)754-6417 [18063]

Lohr Structural Fasteners Inc., PO Box 1387, 2355 Wilson Rd., Humble, TX 77396, (281)446-6766 [13800]

Lohr Winery; J., 1000 Lenzen Ave., San Jose, CA 95126-2739, (408)288-5057 [1826]

LoJack of California Corp., 9911 W Pico Blvd., No. 1000, Los Angeles, CA 90035, (310)286-2610 [2887]

LoJack of New Jersey Corp., 12 Rte. 17 N, Paramus, NJ 07652, (201)368-8716 [24586]

LoJack of New Jersey Corp., 12 Rte. 17 N, Paramus, NJ 07652, (201)368-8716 [2888]

Lolo Sporting Goods Inc., 1026 Main St., Lewiston, ID 83501-1842, (208)743-1031 [23791]

Lomanco Inc., PO Box 519, Jacksonville, AR 72076, (501)982-6511 [14527]

Lomar Foods, PO Box 180, Des Moines, IA 50301, (515)244-3105 [11724]

Lombard Co.; F.W., 34 S Pleasant St., Ashburnham, MA 01430-0539, (978)827-5333 [13166]

Lombard Management Inc., 12015 Mora Dr., Unit 4, Santa Fe Springs, CA 90670, (562)944-9494 [2889]

Lombardini USA Inc., 2150 Boggs Rd., Duluth, GA 30026, (404)623-3554 [16242]

Londavia Inc., 399 Concord Tpke., Rte. 4, Barrington, NH 03825, (603)868-9900 [118]

London Bridge Trading Company Ltd., 3509 Virginia Beach Blvd., Virginia Beach, VA 23452-4421, (757)498-0207 [23792]

London Litho Aluminum Company Inc., 7100 N Lawndale Ave., Lincolnwood, IL 60645, (847)679-4600 [6444]

London Litho Aluminum Company Inc., 7100 N Lawndale Ave., Lincolnwood, IL 60712, (847)679-4600 [16243]

London's Farm Dairy, Inc., 2136 Pine Grove Ave., Port Huron, MI 48060, (810)984-5111 [11725]

Lone Elm Sales Inc., 9695 N Van Dyne Rd., Van Dyne, WI 54979, (920)688-2338 [11726]

Lone Star Company Inc., PO Box 2067, Jonesboro, AR 72402, (501)932-6679 [22436]

Lone Star Food Service Co., PO Box 2005, Austin, TX 78768-2005, (512)478-3161 [11727]

Lone Star Institutional Grocers, PO Box 28928, Dallas, TX 75228-0928, (214)357-1871 [11728]

Lone Star Produce Inc., 12450 Cutten Rd., Houston, TX 77066, (281)444-8596 [11729]

Long Equipment Co., 2009 Constitution Ave., Enid, OK 73703-2004, (580)237-2304 [967]

Long & Hansen Commission Co., 803 E Rice, Sioux Falls, SD 57101, (605)336-3640 [18064]

Long Inc.; Duncan, 2152 44th Dr., Long Island City, NY 11101-4710, (718)937-0701 [21112]

Long Inc.; E.W., 1102 Riverdale St., West Springfield, MA 01089-4607, (413)733-0808 [25288]

Long Island Transmission Corp., 495 Smith St., Farmingdale, NY 11735, (516)454-9000 [16244]

Long Lewis Inc., 430 N 9th St., Birmingham, AL 35203, (205)322-2561 [13801]

Long Lewis Inc., 430 N 9th St., Birmingham, AL 35203, (205)322-2561 [13802]

Long Machinery, PO Box 5508, Missoula, MT 59806, (406)721-4050 [968]

Long Machinery Inc., PO Box 5508, Missoula, MT 59806, (406)721-4050 [7610]

Long Machinery Inc. Lewiston, PO Box 1900, Lewiston, ID 83501, (208)746-3301 [969]

Long Motor Corp., PO Box 14991, Shawnee Mission, KS 66286-4991, (913)541-1525 [2890]

Long Trailer & Body Service, Inc., 5817 Augusta Rd., PO Box 5105, Sta. B, Greenville, SC 29606, (864)277-7555 [2891]

Long Wholesale Distributors Inc., 201 N Fulton Dr., Corinth, MS 38834-4621, (662)287-2421 [11730]

Long Wholesale Inc., PO Box 70, Meridian, MS 39301-0070, (601)482-3144 [11731]

Longhill Partners Inc., PO Box 237, Woodstock, VT 05091-0237, (802)457-4000 [17504]

Longhorn Liquors, Ltd., PO Box 5567, Arlington, TX 76005, (817)640-5555 [1827]

Longhorn Pet Supply, 6450 Clara, Ste. 100, Houston, TX 77041, (713)466-3999 [27182]

Longines-Wittnauer Watch Co., 145 Huguenot St., New Rochelle, NY 10802, (914)654-7200 [17660]

Longley Supply Company Inc., 2018 Oleander Dr., Wilmington, NC 28406, (919)762-7793 [23247]

Longman Publishing Group, 10 Bank St., White Plains, NY 10606-1951, (914)993-5000 [3921]

Longnecker Inc., 3707 Pacific Ave. SE, Olympia, WA 98501-2124, (360)459-3226 [23793]

Longo Distributors Inc., 355 Main St., Whitinsville, MA 01588-1860 [26325]

Longust Distributing Inc., 5333 S Kyrene Rd., Tempe, AZ 85283, (602)820-6244 [9997]

Longwear Hosiery Mill, PO Box 525, Hildebran, NC 28637-0525, (704)324-6430 [5142]

Loock & Company Inc.; R.J., 343 N Gay St., Baltimore, MD 21202-4837, (410)685-1771 [2892]

Look Company Inc.; O.W. and B.S., PO Box 504, Jonesport, ME 04649, (207)497-2353 [11732]

Lookout Beverages, PO Box 23448, Chattanooga, TN 37422, (423)899-3962 [1828]

Loomcraft Textiles Inc., 645 N Lakeview Pkwy., Vernon Hills, IL 60061, (847)680-0000 [15571]

Loomis Paint & Wallpaper Ctr, 35 Main St., Poultney, VT 05764-1106, (802)287-4009 [21494]

Loos and Dilworth Inc., 61 E Green Ln., Bristol, PA 19007, (215)785-3591 [4441]

Loppnow & Associates, 1420 NW Gilman Blvd., Ste. 2857, Issaquah, WA 98027, (425)392-3936 [9002]

LOR Inc., PO Box 647, Atlanta, GA 30301, (404)888-2750 [16245]

Lorbec Metals USA Ltd., 3415 Western Rd., Flint, MI 48506, (810)736-0961 [20134]

Lord Brothers & Higgins, PO Box 390, Seaford, DE 19973, (302)629-7093 [21811]

Lord Equipment Co., 1147 E C St., Casper, WY 82601, (307)265-4430 [22437]

Lord & Hodge, Inc., 362 Industrial Park Rd., Unit 4, PO Box 737, Middletown, CT 06457, (860)632-7006 [13803]

Lords Sausage, 411 Harvey St., Dexter, GA 31019, (912)875-3101 [11733]

Lore L. Ltd., 1631 S Nova Rd., Daytona Beach, FL 32119-1729, (904)756-0500 [7611]

Lorel Co., PO Box 570211, Houston, TX 77257, (713)464-0670 [21812]

Lorelei's Exotic Leis & Flower, PO Box 173, Makawao, HI 96768, (808)572-0181 [14913]

Lorenz & Jones Marine Distributors, Inc., 1920 SE Delaware Ave., Ankeny, IA 50021, (515)964-4205 [18550]

Loria & Sons Westchester Corp.; V., 1876 Central Park Ave., Yonkers, NY 10710, (914)779-3377 [25720]

Lorman Iron and Metal Co., PO Box 127, Ft. Atkinson, WI 53538, (920)563-2488 [26887]

Loroman Co., 95-25 149th St., Jamaica, NY 11430, (718)291-0800 [9003]

Lorraine Grain Fuel and Stock Co., PO Box 20, Lorraine, KS 67459-0020, (785)472-5271 [970]

Lors Medical Corp., PO Box 1718, Roanoke Rapids, NC 27870-7718, (919)537-0031 [18892]

Lory's West Inc., 314 S Beverly Dr., Beverly Hills, CA 90212, (310)551-1212 [17505]

Lory's West Inc., 314 S Beverly Dr., Beverly Hills, CA 90212, (310)551-1212 [17297]

Los Alamos Stationers, PO Box 620, Los Alamos, NM 87544-0620, (505)662-4229 [21113]

Los Altos PC Inc., PO Box 248, Los Altos, CA 94023-0248, (650)949-3451 [6445]

Los Amigos Tortilla Manufacturing Inc., 251 Armour Dr. NE, Atlanta, GA 30324-3979, (404)876-8153 [11734]

Los Angeles Carton Co., 5100 S Santa Fe Ave., Vernon, CA 90058, (213)587-1500 [21813]

Los Angeles Chemical Co., 4545 Ardine St., South Gate, CA 90280, (213)562-9500 [4442]

Los Angeles Freightliner, 1031 E Holt Ave., Ontario, CA 91761, (909)988-5511 [20673]

Los Angeles Nut House, 1601 E Olympic Blvd., Ste. 200, Los Angeles, CA 90021, (213)623-2541 [11735]

Los Angeles Paper Box and Board Mills. Paper Stock Div., PO Box 60830, Los Angeles, CA 90060-0830, (213)685-8900 [26888]

Los Angeles Rubber Co., PO Box 23910, Los Angeles, CA 90023-0910, (213)263-4131 [24285]

Losey and Company Inc., 3700 Hartley Ave., Easton, PA 18045-3757, (215)253-3511 [17004]

Lostant Hatchery and Milling Company Inc., PO Box 208, Lostant, IL 61334, (815)368-3221 [971]

Lotepro Corp., 115 Stevens Ave., Valhalla, NY 10595, (914)747-3500 [22438]

Lott Builders Supply Co., PO Box 269, Douglas, GA 31533, (912)384-1800 [7612]

Lott Builders Supply Co., PO Box 439, Douglas, GA 31534, (912)384-1800 [27336]

Lotus Cars USA Inc., 500 Marathon Pkwy., Lawrenceville, GA 30045-2800, (404)822-4566 [2893]

Lotus Group, 2411 Hamilton Mill Rd., Charlotte, NC 28270, (704)366-5505 [16246]

Lotus Light, PO Box 1008, Silver Lake, WI 53170, (414)889-8501 [25526]

Lotus Light Inc., PO Box 1008, Silver Lake, WI 53170, (414)889-8501 [19417]

Lotz Paper and Fixture Co.; F.W., 9710 Glenfield Ct., Dayton, OH 45458-9173, (937)223-7223 [21814]

Loui Michel Cie., 1927 W 139th St., Fl. 2, Gardena, CA 90249, (310)323-4567 [13392]

Louis Rich Co., 3704 Louis Rich Dr., Newberry, SC 29108, (803)276-5015 [11736]

Louis Steel Co.; Arthur, PO Box 518, Ashtabula, OH 44005-0518, (440)997-5545 [20135]

Louisiana Chemical Equipment Co., PO Box 65064, Baton Rouge, LA 70896-5064, (504)923-3602 [16247]

Louisiana Lift & Equipment, Inc., 6847 Greenwood Rd., PO Box 3869, Shreveport, LA 71119, (318)631-5100 [2894]

Louisiana Mill Supply, 109 N City Service Hwy., Sulphur, LA 70663, (318)625-2900 [17005]

Louisiana Mill Supply, 10093 Rayco Sandres Rd., Gonzales, LA 70737, (504)644-4100 [17006]

Louisiana Office Products, PO Box 23851, New Orleans, LA 70183-0851, (504)733-9650 [21114]

Louisiana Welding Supply Company Inc., 1931 Plank Rd., Baton Rouge, LA 70802, (504)343-9212 [16248]

Louisville Plate Glass Company Inc., 1401 W Broadway, Louisville, KY 40203-2059, (502)584-6145 [7613]

Louisville Tile Distributors, 650 Melrose Ave., Nashville, TN 37211-2161, (615)333-3196 [9998]

Louisville Tile Distributors, Inc., 2495 Palumbo Dr., Lexington, KY 40509-1116, (606)268-8373 [9999]

Louisville Tile Distributors Inc., 4520 Bishop Ln., Louisville, KY 40218, (502)452-2037 [10000]

Louisville Tile Distributors, Inc., 1417 N Cullen Ave., Evansville, IN 47715-2374, (812)473-0137 [10001]

Louisville Tile Distributors Inc., 4520 Bishop Ln., Louisville, KY 40218-4508, (502)452-2037 [7614]

Louisville Tile Distributors Inc., 1417 N Cullen Ave., Evansville, IN 47715-2374, (812)473-0137 [7615]

Lov-It Creamery Inc., 443 N Henry St., Green Bay, WI 54302-1838, (920)432-4383 [11737]

Love Bottling Co., PO Box 625, Muskogee, OK 74402, (918)682-3434 [24984]

Loveall Music Co., 3033 Kennedy Ln., Texarkana, TX 75503-2545, (903)794-3735 [25289]

Lovejoy Industries, Inc., 1761 Elmore St., Cincinnati, OH 45223, (513)541-1400 [20136]

Lovejoy Industries Inc., 10160 Philipp Pkwy., Streetsboro, OH 44241, (330)656-0001 [20137]

Loveland Industries, PO Box 1289, Greeley, CO 80632-1289, (970)356-8920 [972]

Loveline Industries Inc., 385 Gerard Ave., Bronx, NY 10451, (212)402-3500 [5143]

Loveman Steel Corp., PO Box 46430, Bedford Heights, OH 44146-0430, (440)232-6200 [20138]

Loving & Associates Inc., 409 W 78th St., Bloomington, MN 55420, (612)888-8227 [5144]

Loving; L.A., 409 W 78th St., Bloomington, MN 55420, (612)888-8227 [5144]

Lovotti Brothers, 1275 Vine St., Sacramento, CA 95814, (916)441-3911 [1829]

Lowe Inc.; Devan, 1151 Gault Ave. S, Ft. Payne, AL 35967, (205)845-0922 [20674]

Lowe Supply Co.; Bert, 5402 E Diana, Tampa, FL 33610-1926, (813)621-7784 [17007]

Lowell Corp., PO Box 158, Worcester, MA 01613-0158, (508)835-2900 [13804]

Lowell Packing Co., PO Box 220, Fitzgerald, GA 31750, (912)423-2051 [11738]

Lowes Home Centers Inc., PO Box 1111, North Wilkesboro, NC 28659-1111, (910)651-4000 [25290]

Lowe's Pellets and Grain Co., R.R. 4, Box 46, Greensburg, IN 47240, (812)663-7863 [18065]

Lowrance Electronics Inc., 12000 E Skelly Dr., Tulsa, OK 74128, (918)437-6881 [18551]

Lowry Computer Products Inc., Lowry Technology Park, Brighton, MI 48116, (810)229-7200 [6446]

Lowville Farmers Cooperative Inc., 5500 Shady Ave., Lowville, NY 13367, (315)376-6587 [973]

Lowy Group Inc., 4001 N Kingshighway Blvd., St. Louis, MO 63115, (314)383-2055 [10002]

Loyd Armature Works Inc., 4754 Center Park Blvd., San Antonio, TX 78218-4426, (210)599-4515 [9004]

Loyd LP Gas Co.; Bob, PO Box 367, Winters, TX 79567, (915)754-4555 [22439]

Loyd's Electric Supply Co., 117 E College St., PO Box 1169, Branson, MO 65616, (417)334-2171 [9005]

Lozars Total Screen Design, PO Box 520, Polson, MT 59860-0239, (406)883-9218 [5145]

LP Music Group, 160 Belmont Ave., Garfield, NJ 07026, (973)478-6903 [25291]

LPC, 1436 W Randolph, Chicago, IL 60607, (312)432-7650 [3922]

LPD Music International, 32575 Industrial Dr., Madison Heights, MI 48071, (248)585-9630 [25292]

LPKF Laser and Electronics, 28220 SW Boberg Rd., Wilsonville, OR 97070, (503)454-4200 [16249]

L.P.S. Records, Inc., 2140 St. Clair St., Bellingham, WA 98226-4016, (360)733-3807 [25293]

LRP Enterprises, 1275 Colusa Hwy., Ste. C, Yuba City, CA 95991, (530)743-4288 [14154]

LRP Enterprises, 1275 Colusa Hwy., Ste. C, Yuba City, CA 95991, (530)743-4288 [14169]

LSF, PO Box 1387, 2355 Wilson Rd., Humble, TX 77396, (281)446-6766 [13800]

L.S.I. Lectro Science Inc., 380 Stewart Rd., Wilkes Barre, PA 18706-1459, (570)825-1900 [9006]

LSI (Legacy Sports International LLC), 10 Prince St., Alexandria, VA 22314, (703)739-1560 [13500]

L.T. Plant, Inc., PO Box 609, Montville, NJ 07045, (973)882-9190 [11739]

LTD Dozier Inc., 869 Pickens Industrial Dr., Marietta, GA 30062-3100, (404)419-1920 [24170]

LTV Corp., PO Box 6778, Cleveland, OH 44101, (216)622-5000 [22440]

LU International, 500 N Highland Ave., Los Angeles, CA 90036-2020, (213)994-0878 [16250]

Luanka Seafood Co., 814 E Harrison St., PO Box 1086, Harlingen, TX 78551, (956)428-1862 [11740]

Lubbock Electric Co., 1108 34th St., Lubbock, TX 79405, (806)744-2336 [9007]

Luberski Inc., PO Box 34001, Fullerton, CA 92834, (714)680-3447 [11741]

Lubrichem Environmental Inc., 206 Valley Creek Rd., Elizabethtown, KY 42701, (502)491-6100 [22441]

Lucas Brothers Inc., 7700 Port Capital Dr., Baltimore, MD 21227, (410)799-7700 [21115]

Lucas Fluid Power Inc., 3528 Roger Chaffe Memorial Dr., Wyoming, MI 49548, (616)452-4560 [15818]

Lucas Industries Inc. Aftermarket Operations Div., 1624 Meijer Dr., Troy, MI 48084, (313)288-2000 [2895]

Lucas Tire Inc., 810 Neville St., Beckley, WV 25801, (304)253-3305 [2896]

Luce Candy Co., 3304 W Oceanfront, Newport Beach, CA 92663-3026, (213)221-4646 [11742]

Luce and Son Inc., 2399 Valley Rd., Reno, NV 89512, (702)785-7810 [1830]

Luce and Son Inc., 2399 Valley Rd., Reno, NV 89512, (775)785-7810 [1831]

Lucerne Textiles Inc., 519 8th Ave., New York, NY 10018, (212)563-7800 [26128]

Lucero Computer Products, 1320 Lincoln Rd., Idaho Falls, ID 83401, (208)524-0891 [6447]

Lucia Inc., PO Box 12129, Winston-Salem, NC 27107-3500, (919)788-4901 [5146]

Luckenbach and Johnson Inc., 1828 Tilghman St., Allentown, PA 18104, (610)434-6235 [9008]

Luckett Tobaccos Inc., 222 S 1st St., Louisville, KY 40202, (502)561-0070 [26326]

Lucky Distributing, PO Box 18000, Portland, OR 97218, (503)252-1249 [974]

Lucky Electric Supply, 325 Calhoun Ave. E, Memphis, TN 38126-3219, (901)525-0264 [9009]

Lucky Farmers Inc., PO Box 217, Woodville, OH 43469, (419)849-2711 [975]

Lucky Fruit and Produce Company Inc., 7735 Hill Rd., Granite Bay, CA 95746-6953, (916)446-7621 [11743]

Lucoral Company Inc., 26 W 46th St., New York, NY 10036, (212)575-9701 [9010]

Luden & Co., Inc.; J.J.W., Concord at Charlotte St., Charleston, SC 29403, (803)723-7829 [18552]

Ludlow Cooperative Elevator Company Inc., PO Box 155, Ludlow, IL 60949, (217)396-4111 [18066]

Ludlow Telephone Company Inc., 111 Main St., Ludlow, VT 05149-1025, (802)485-6012 [5663]

Luffeys Medical & Surgical Supplies, PO Box 4745, 2000 B Tower Dr., Monroe, LA 71211-4745, (318)388-4036 [19418]

Luggage America Inc., 1840 S Wilmington Ave., Compton, CA 90220-5118, (310)223-2990 [18409]

Lugo Hair Center Ltd., 20 Snyder Ave., Brooklyn, NY 11226, (718)284-0370 [14155]

Lumber Exchange Terminal Inc., 171 West St., Brooklyn, NY 11222, (718)383-5000 [7616]

Lumber Inc., PO Box 26777, Albuquerque, NM 87125, (505)823-2700 [7617]

Lumber Yards Inc., PO Box 27046, Tucson, AZ 85726, (520)747-5440 [27337]

Lumberman of Indiana, 849 Elston Dr., Shelbyville, IN 46176-1817, (317)392-4145 [7618]

Lumbermen's Inc., 4433 Stafford St., Grand Rapids, MI 49548, (616)538-5180 [7619]

Lumbermen's Merchandising Corp., 137 W Wayne Ave., Wayne, PA 19087, (215)293-7000 [7620]

Lumbermens Millwork and Supply Co., 2211 Refinery Rd., Ardmore, OK 73401-1666, (580)223-3080 [7621]

Lumberton Industries Inc., PO Box 443, Medina, OH 44258, (330)723-1700 [17008]

Lumberyard Supply Co., 5060 Manchester Ave., St. Louis, MO 63110, (314)533-7557 [7622]

Lumen Foods, 409 Scott St., Lake Charles, LA 70601, (318)436-6748 [11744]

Lun Fat Produce Inc., 227 Harrison Ave., Boston, MA 02111, (617)426-4045 [11745]

Lund Truck Parts Inc., PO Box 386, Tea, SD 57064-0386, (605)368-5611 [2897]

Lundahl Inc.; Warner T., 42-23 Francis Lewis Blvd., Bayside, NY 11361, (718)279-8586 [2898]

Luntz Corp., 237 E Tuscarawas St., Canton, OH 44702, (216)455-0211 [26889]

Lurie Associates; Fred, 777 NW 72nd Ave., Ste. 3AA9, Miami, FL 33126, (305)261-3682 [24797]

Lusk Metals and Plastics, PO Box 24013, Oakland, CA 94623, (510)785-6400 [20139]

Luter Packing Company Inc., PO Box 929, Laurinburg, NC 28353, (910)844-5201 [11746]

Lutheran Distributors Inc.; A.M., 1130 Lebanon Rd., West Mifflin, PA 15122, (412)461-3133 [1832]

Luther's Creative Craft Studios, 65 Innsbruck Dr., Buffalo, NY 14227-2703, (716)632-4741 [21116]

Luthier's Mercantile Int. Inc., 412 Moore Ln., Healdsburg, CA 95448, (707)433-1823 [25294]

Lutz News Co., 601 Abbott, Detroit, MI 48226-2556, (313)961-2615 [3923]

Luxor California Export Corp., 3659 India St., Ste. 200, San Diego, CA 92103, (619)692-9330 [11747]

Luxury Bath Showrooms, 31239 Mound Rd., Warren, MI 48090, (810)264-2561 [23116]

Luxury Liners, 14545 Valley View Ave., Ste. R, Santa Fe Springs, CA 90670, (562)921-1813 [18893]

Luxury Liners, 14545 Valley View Ave., Ste. R, Santa Fe Springs, CA 90670, (562)921-1813 [19419]

Luzerne Optical Labs, Ltd., 180 N Wilkes Barre Blvd., PO Box 998, Wilkes Barre, PA 18703-0998, (570)822-3183 [19420]

Luzo Food Service Inc., PO Box 50370, New Bedford, MA 02745, (508)993-9976 [24171]

LW Bristol Collection, PO Box 3397, Bristol, TN 37620, (423)968-7777 [5147]

LWR Inc., 2323 Memorial Ave., Lynchburg, VA 24501-2650, (804)528-2726 [5148]

Lyden Co., PO Box 1854, Youngstown, OH 44501, (330)744-3118 [22442]

Lyford Gin Association, PO Box 70, Lyford, TX 78569, (210)347-3541 [18067]

Lyk-Nu Inc., 1 Rotary Park Dr., PO Box 3390, Clarksville, TN 37043-3390, (931)647-0139 [4660]

Lykes Bros. Inc., PO Box 1690, Tampa, FL 33601, (813)223-3981 [11748]

Lyles-DeGrazier Co., PO Box 58263, Dallas, TX 75258, (214)747-3558 [17506]

Lyman Lumber Co., PO Box 40, Excelsior, MN 55331, (612)474-5991 [7623]

Lyman-Richey Corp., 4315 Cuming St., Omaha, NE 68131, (402)558-2727 [7624]

Lynch Enterprises Inc.; C.O., 2655 Fairview Ave. N, Roseville, MN 55113-2616, (612)331-3000 [24798]

Lynch Machinery Co., PO Box 1217, Havertown, PA 19083, (215)789-1210 [16251]

Lyncole XIT Grounding, 3547 Voyager St Ste. 104, Torrance, CA 90503, (310)214-4000 [9011]

Lynde Co., 3040 E Hennepin Ave., Minneapolis, MN 55413, (612)331-2840 [4443]

Lynde-Ordway Company Inc., PO Box 8709, Fountain Valley, CA 92728, (714)957-1311 [21117]

Lynn Ladder and Scaffolding Company Inc., PO Box 346, West Lynn, MA 01905, (617)598-6010 [7625]

Lynn Medical Instrument Co., PO Box 7027, Bloomfield Hills, MI 48302-7027, (248)338-4571 [18894]

Lynne Company Inc.; J.M., PO Box 1010, Smithtown, NY 11787, (516)582-4300 [15572]

Lynne Hosiery Mills Inc., 314 S South St., PO Box 987, Mt. Airy, NC 27030-4450, (919)786-4134 [5108]

Lynnwood Co., 8840 Elder Creek Rd., Unit B, Sacramento, CA 95828, (916)381-0293 [13393]

Lyntech Corp., 10177 S 77th East Ave., Tulsa, OK 74133-6802, (918)299-1321 [18895]

Lynton Group Inc., 9 Airport Rd., Morristown, NJ 07960, (973)292-9000 [119]

Lynwood Battery Manufacturing Co., 4505 E Washington Blvd., Los Angeles, CA 90040-1023, (213)263-8866 [2899]

Lyon County Cooperative Oil Co., 1100 E Main St., Marshall, MN 56258, (507)532-9686 [22443]

Lyons Equipment Co., PO Box 107, Little Valley, NY 14755, (716)938-9175 [7626]

Lyons Sawmill and Logging Equipment Co., 5445 NYS Route 353, PO Box 107, Little Valley, NY 14755, (716)938-9175 [27338]

Lyssy and Eckel Inc., PO Box 128, Poth, TX 78147, (830)484-3314 [976]

M & A Sales, 701 E Gude Dr., Rockville, MD 20850, (301)424-2500 [9012]

M & B Distributors, Inc., 3896 Virginia Ave., Cincinnati, OH 45227, (513)561-0060 [11749]

M-Bin International Imports, 3136 Norbrook Dr., Memphis, TN 38116, (901)398-6802 [18410]

M & E Marine Supply, Inc., PO Box 601, Rte. 130, Collingswood, NJ 08108, (609)858-1010 [18553]

M & E Sales - A Honeywell Business, 3303 Chestnut Ave., Baltimore, MD 21211, (410)889-2070 [24390]

M & F Foods, PO Box 5317, East Orange, NJ 07019-5317, (973)344-6700 [11750]

M-G Inc., 300 E Main St., Weimar, TX 78962, (409)725-8581 [977]

M & G Industries, 820 Greenleaf Ave., Elk Grove Village, IL 60007, (847)437-6662 [9013]

M & G Industries Inc., 85 Broadcommon Rd., Bristol, RI 02809, (401)253-0096 [9014]

M and H Sales and Marketing Inc., 155 White Plains Rd., Tarrytown, NY 10591, (914)524-9100 [14156]

M and L Industries Inc., 1210 St. Charles St., Houma, LA 70360, (504)876-2280 [978]

M & L Motor Supply Co., 1606 S Hastings Way, Eau Claire, WI 54701-4620, (715)832-1647 [2900]

M & L Trading Company, Inc., PO Box 263, Bothell, WA 98041, (425)481-3014 [11751]

M and M Chemical Products Inc., PO Box 27-56, Redwood City, CA 94063, (650)368-4900 [979]

M & M Chemical Supply Inc., PO Box 1467, Casper, WY 82602-1467, (307)473-8818 [4661]

M and M Chemical Supply Inc., PO Box 1467, Casper, WY 82602-1467, (307)473-8818 [4444]

M & M Distributors, 431 W 121st St., Anchorage, AK 99515-3364, (907)349-5941 [24172]

M and M Distributors Inc., PO Box 80077, Lansing, MI 48908, (517)322-9010 [1833]

M/M Electronic Products Ltd., 7 Corporate Dr., #117, North Haven, CT 06473-3258, (203)239-7099 [9015]

M and M Metals International Inc., 840 Dellway Ave., Cincinnati, OH 45229, (513)221-4411 [26890]

M & M News Agency, Civic Industrial Pk., PO Box 1129, La Salle, IL 61301, (815)223-2754 [3924]

M & M Sales & Equipment, 2639 Kermit Hwy., Odessa, TX 79763-2542, (915)332-1481 [17009]

M and M Supply Co., PO Box 548, Duncan, OK 73534-0548, (580)252-7879 [22444]

M and M Supply Co., PO Box 548, Duncan, OK 73534-0548, (580)252-7879 [16252]

M & M Vehicle Co., 530 N Jefferson, Mexico, MO 65265, (573)581-8188 [23794]

M & M Wholesale, 336 Willis St., Batesburg, SC 29006, (803)532-3101 [5149]

M & N Supply Corp., 30 Allen Blvd., Farmingdale, NY 11735-5612, (516)694-2230 [7627]

M & P Sales Inc., 3659 S Maryland Pkwy., Las Vegas, NV 89109-3001, (702)734-9595 [4662]

M & R Distributors Inc., 4232 S Saginaw St., Flint, MI 48507, (810)744-9008 [2901]

M and R International Inc., 15 Valley Dr., Greenwich, CT 06831, (203)625-0500 [21815]

M & R Sales & Service Inc., 1 N 372 Main St., Glen Ellyn, IL 60137, (630)858-6101 [26129]

M & R Sales & Supply Company Inc., 1 N 372 Main St., Glen Ellyn, IL 60137, (630)858-6101 [26129]

M & R Trading Inc., 514 W Maloney, Gallup, NM 87301-0687, (505)722-9020 [18068]

M-Tron Components Inc., 2110-1 Smithtown Ave., Ronkonkoma, NY 11779, (516)467-5100 [9016]

M & V Provision Company Inc., 146 N 6th St., Brooklyn, NY 11211-3201, (718)388-3440 [11752]

MA Laboratories Inc., 2075 N Capitol Ave., San Jose, CA 95132, (408)954-8886 [6448]

Maas-Hansen Steel Corp., PO Box 58364, Vernon, CA 90058, (213)583-6321 [20140]

Maats Enterprises, PO Box 4129, Philadelphia, PA 19144, (215)457-4134 [19421]

Mabis Healthcare Inc., 28690 N Ballard Dr., Lake Forest, IL 60045, (847)680-6811 [18896]

Mabon Business Equipment, 2965 Spaatz Rd., Monument, CO 80132, (970)481-2313 [3925]

Mac America, 200 Continental Blvd., El Segundo, CA 90245, (310)615-3080 [6449]

Mac Nuts of Hawaii, PO Box 833, Kealakekua, HI 96750, (808)328-7234 [11753]

Mac Papers Inc., PO Box 5369, Jacksonville, FL 32247, (904)348-3300 [21816]

Mac Supply Co., 16778 S Park Ave., South Holland, IL 60473, (708)339-2666 [7628]

Mac Thrift Clearance Center, 1201 S Holden, Greensboro, NC 27407, (919)852-1727 [21118]

MAC USA, 745 5th Ave., Ste. 1225, New York, NY 10151, (212)753-7015 [5160]

MacAlaster Bicknell Company Inc., 181 Henry St., New Haven, CT 06510, (203)624-4191 [24391]

MacAlaster Bicknell Company of New Jersey Inc., Depot & North Sts., Millville, NJ 08332, (609)825-3222 [4445]

Macalaster Bicknell Company of NJ, Inc., Depot & North Sts., PO Box 109, Millville, NJ 08332, (856)825-3222 [24392]

MacAlester Park Publishing Co., 7317 Cahill Rd., Minneapolis, MN 55439, (952)562-1234 [3926]

MacAllister Machinery Company Inc., PO Box 1941, Indianapolis, IN 46206, (317)545-2151 [7629]

MacArthur Co., 2400 Wycliff St., St. Paul, MN 55114, (612)646-2773 [7630]

Macauley's, Inc., 41554 Koppernick, Canton, MI 48187, (734)454-9292 [21288]

MacBean Inc.; Scottie, 660 High St., Worthington, OH 43085, (614)888-3494 [24173]

MacDonald Manufacturing; Stewart, 21 N Shafer St., Athens, OH 45701, (740)592-3021 [25295]

MacDonald and Owen Lumber, PO Box 238, Bangor, WI 54614, (608)486-2353 [7631]

MacGregor Sports and Fitness Inc., 8100 White Horse Rd., Greenville, SC 29611-1836, (864)294-5230 [23795]

Machine Drive, 8919 Rossash Rd., Cincinnati, OH 45236, (513)793-7077 [16253]

Machine Maintenance Inc., 2300 Cassens Dr., Fenton, MO 63026-2591, (314)487-7100 [7632]

Machine Service, Inc., 1000 Ashwaubenon St., Green Bay, WI 54303, (920)339-3000 [2902]

Machine Service Inc., 1954 S Stoughton Rd., Madison, WI 53716, (608)221-9122 [2903]

Machine Service, Inc., 4750 S 10th St., Milwaukee, WI 53221, (414)483-8338 [2904]

Machine Tool and Supply Corp., PO Box 1927, Jackson, TN 38302, (901)424-3400 [16254]

Machine and Welding Supply Co., PO Box 1708, Dunn, NC 28335, (910)892-4016 [16255]

Machinery and Equipment Sales, Inc., 3303 Chestnut Ave., Baltimore, MD 21211, (410)889-2070 [24390]

Machinery Sales Co., 4400 S Soto St., Los Angeles, CA 90058, (213)588-8111 [16256]

Machinery Systems Inc., 614 E State Pkwy., Schaumburg, IL 60173, (847)882-8085 [16257]

Macintosh Inc.; Dr., 36 Peddlers Village Shop, Newark, DE 19702-1582, (302)738-0334 [6450]

Mack-Chicago Corp., 2445 S Rockwell St., Chicago, IL 60608, (773)376-8100 [21817]

Mackay Industrial Sales Inc., 2131 Kalamazoo SE, Grand Rapids, MI 49507, (616)241-1671 [17010]

Macke Business Products, 55 Railroad St., Rochester, NY 14609, (716)325-4120 [13167]

Mackinaw Sales Inc., 2955 Crestwood Cir., East Lansing, MI 48823, (517)351-7210 [18554]

MacKinnon Paper Company Inc., PO Box 12, Mobile, AL 36601-0012, (205)666-8175 [21818]

MacLeod Group, 9309 Rayo Ave., South Gate, CA 90280, (213)567-7767 [26891]

MacMillan Bloedel Building Materials, 5895 Windward Pkwy., Ste. 200, Alpharetta, GA 30022, (404)740-7516 [7633]

Maco Vinyl Products Corp., 2900 Westchester Ave., Purchase, NY 10577-2551, (914)337-1600 [26130]

Macon Beauty Supply Co., PO Box 24690, Macon, GA 31212-4690, (912)474-2207 [14157]

Macon Iron and Paper Stock Company Inc., PO Box 506, Macon, GA 31202, (912)743-6773 [26892]

Macon Ridge Farmers Association, PO Box 428, Sicily Island, LA 71368, (318)389-5349 [18069]

Maconomy NE Inc., 33 Boston Post Rd. W, Ste. 310, Marlborough, MA 01752, (508)460-8337 [6451]

MacPherson's, 1351 Ocean Ave, Emeryville, CA 94608, (510)428-9011 [25721]

MacPherson's-Artcraft, 1351 Ocean Ave, Emeryville, CA 94608, (510)428-9011 [25721]

MacQueen Equipment Inc., 595 Aldine St., St. Paul, MN 55104, (612)645-5726 [16258]

MacRae's Indian Book Distributors, 1605 Cole St., PO Box 652, Enumclaw, WA 98022, (206)825-3737 [3927]

Macro Computer Products Inc., 2523 Product Ct., Rochester Hills, MI 48309, (248)853-5353 [6452]

Macsteel Service Centers USA - Edgcomb Metals Div., 555 State Rd., Bensalem, PA 19020, (215)245-3300 [20141]

Macuch Steel Products Inc., PO Box 3285, Augusta, GA 30914, (706)823-2420 [20142]

Macy Associates Inc., Mountain Rd., PO Box 40, Jaffrey, NH 03452, (603)532-7490 [21819]

Mad Bomber Co., 134 Windy Hill Ln., W2-1, Winchester, VA 22602, (540)662-8840 [5150]

Madaris Hosiery Mill, 1451 14th Ave. NE, Hickory, NC 28601-2729, (704)322-6841 [5151]

Maddalena Vineyard/San Antonio Winery, 737 Lamar St., Los Angeles, CA 90031, (323)223-1401 [1834]

Maddux Supply Co., c/o Tommy Joyner, 1512 Hooker Rd., Greenville, NC 27834-6323, (919)756-5506 [9017]

Made in Nature Inc., 1448 Industrial Ave., Sebastopol, CA 95472-4848, (707)535-4000 [11754]

Made-Rite Co., PO Box 3283, Longview, TX 75606, (903)753-8604 [24985]

Made Rite Potato Chip Company Inc., PO Box 1100, Bay City, MI 48706, (517)684-6271 [11755]

Madison Appliance Parts Inc., 1226 Williamson St., Madison, WI 53703, (608)257-2589 [15206]

Madison Bottling Co., 616 8th St., Madison, MN 56256, (320)598-7573 [1835]

Madison County Cooperative, PO Box 587, Canton, MS 39046, (601)859-1271 [980]

Madison County Cooperative Inc., PO Box 5345, Huntsville, AL 35814, (205)837-5031 [981]

Madison Dairy Produce Company Inc., PO Box 389, Madison, WI 53701, (608)256-5561 [11756]

Madison Electric Co., 31855 Van Dyke Ave., Warren, MI 48093-1047, (810)825-0200 [25296]

Madison Electric Co., 31855 Van Dyke Ave., Warren, MI 48093-1047, (810)825-0200 [15207]

Madison Farmers Elevator Co., PO Box F, Madison, SD 57042, (605)256-4584 [18070]

Madison Grocery Company Inc., PO Box 580, Richmond, KY 40476-0580, (606)623-2416 [11757]

Madison Landmark Inc., 254 W High St., London, OH 43140, (740)852-2062 [18071]

Madison Service Co., 900 Hillsboro Ave., Edwardsville, IL 62025, (618)656-3500 [982]

Madisonville Tire and Retreading Inc., PO Box 1593, 48 Fedeeral St., Madisonville, KY 42431, (502)821-2954 [2905]

Madrigal Audio Laboratories Inc., PO Box 781, Middletown, CT 06457, (860)346-0896 [25297]

MAG Innovision Inc., 2801 S Yale St., Santa Ana, CA 92704-5850, (714)751-2008 [6453]

Magazines Inc., 1135 Hammond St., Bangor, ME 04401, (207)942-8237 [3928]

Magee Marine Supply, 9946 Fancher Rd., Brewerton, NY 13029-9762, (315)676-2411 [18555]

Mager Scientific Inc., 1100 Baker Rd., PO Box 160, Dexter, MI 48130, (734)426-3885 [24393]

Magi Inc., Hwy. 97, Brewster, WA 98812, (509)689-2511 [11758]

Magic American Corp., 23700 Mercantile Rd., Beachwood, OH 44122, (216)464-2353 [4446]

Magic City Beverage Co., PO Box 1208, Minot, ND 58702-1208, (701)852-4031 [1836]

Magic Distributing, 1001 Orchard Lake Rd., Pontiac, MI 48341, (248)334-1730 [23796]

Magic Novelty Company Inc., 308 Dyckman St., New York, NY 10034, (212)304-2777 [17507]

Magic Refrigeration Co., 5423 S 99th East Ave., Tulsa, OK 74146-5726, (918)664-2160 [14528]

Magic Touch Enterprises, Inc., 836 Sox St., West Columbia, SC 29169-5028, (803)791-8516 [10003]

Magna Automotive Industries, 999 Central Ave., Woodmere, NY 11598-1205, (516)295-0188 [2906]

Magna Communications Inc., 30680 Montpelier Dr., Madison Heights, MI 48071-1800, (810)777-7999 [5664]

Magna Graphics, PO Box 1015, Lakeland, FL 33802-1015, (941)688-8515 [2907]

Magnamusic Distributors Inc., PO Box 338, Sharon, CT 06069-0338, (860)364-5431 [25298]

Magnamusic Distributors Inc., 74 Amenia Union Rd., Sharon, CT 06069, (860)364-5431 [15208]

Magness Huron Livestock Exchange, 560 7th St., NE, Huron, SD 57350, (605)352-8759 [18072]

MagneTek, Inc., 26 Century Blvd., Nashville, TN 37214, (615)316-5100 [9018]

Magnetic Technology, 290 W Madison St., Wytheville, VA 24382, (540)228-7943 [9019]

Magneto Diesel Injector Service Inc., 6931 Navigation Blvd., Houston, TX 77011, (713)928-5686 [2908]

Magnivision, 1500 S 66th Ave., Hollywood, FL 33023, (954)986-9000 [18897]

Magnolia Casket Co., PO Box 40105, Jacksonville, FL 32203, (904)384-0015 [24174]

Magnolia Chemical and Solvents Inc., PO Box 10278, New Orleans, LA 70181, (504)733-6600 [4447]

Magnolia Distributing Co., 249 N State Route 2, New Martinsville, WV 26155-2203, (304)455-2581 [1837]

Magnolia Liquor Lafayette Inc., 209 Lucille Ave., PO Box 3587, Lafayette, LA 70502, (318)233-9244 [1838]

Magnolia Marketing Co., PO Box 53333, New Orleans, LA 70153, (504)837-1500 [1839]

Magnum Corp., 32400 Telegraph Rd., No. 102, Bingham Farms, MI 48025, (810)433-1170 [17011]

Magnum Diversified Industries Inc., 279 Jenckes Hill Rd., Smithfield, RI 02917-1905, (401)942-5021 [20143]

Magnum Equipment Inc., 5817 Plauche St., New Orleans, LA 70123-4033, (504)733-5550 [14529]

Magnum Steel and Trading Inc., 5 E Main St., Hudson, OH 44236, (330)655-9365 [20144]

Magnum Tire Corp., 724 N 1st St., Minneapolis, MN 55401, (612)338-8861 [2909]

Magtrol Inc. (Tucson, Arizona), PO Box 85099, Tucson, AZ 85726, (520)622-7802 [9020]

Mahalick Corp., PO Box 604, Putnam Valley, NY 10579-0604, (914)963-1100 [25722]

Mahan Western Industries, Inc., 11333 Rojas Dr., El Paso, TX 79936 [5152]

Mahar Tool Supply Inc., PO Box 1747, Saginaw, MI 48605, (517)799-5530 [13805]

Maharam Fabric Corp., PO Box 6900, Hauppauge, NY 11788, (516)582-3434 [26131]

Mahaska Farm Service Co., PO Box 1040, Oskaloosa, IA 52577-1040, (515)672-2589 [18073]

Mahealani Farms Inc., PO Box 247, Hana, HI 96713, (808)248-7533 [14914]

Mahne Company Inc.; William P., 1920 S Vandeventer, St. Louis, MO 63103 [15573]

Mahoney's Garden Center, 242 Cambridge St., Winchester, MA 01890, (781)729-5900 [14915]

Mahoning Valley Supply Co., PO Box 5498, Poland, OH 44514-0498, (330)758-6601 [17012]

Mahowald; John G., PO Box 5157, Grand Forks, ND 58206-0157, (701)775-9231 [25723]

Maiale Metal Products, 1496 Hawthorne Rd., Grosse Pointe, MI 48236, (313)885-5540 [20145]

Maiden Music, PO Box 777, Trevilians, VA 23170, (540)967-0077 [25299]

Maier Inc.; Ernest, 4700 Annapolis Rd., Bladensburg, MD 20710, (301)927-8300 [7634]

Maier Manufacturing, 416 Crown Point Cir., Grass Valley, CA 95945-9389, (530)272-9036 [2910]

Maier Sporting Goods Inc.; Ray, 914 Main St., PO Box 1027, Duncan, OK 73534-1027, (580)255-7412 [5153]

Mailers Equipment Co., 20 Squadron Blvd., Ste. 380, New City, NY 10956, (914)634-7676 [6454]

Main Auction, 2912 Main St., Boise, ID 83702-4635, (208)344-8314 [13168]

Main Court Book Fair, 30 S 6th Ave., PO Box 109, Mt. Vernon, NY 10550, (914)664-1633 [3929]

Main Electric Supply Co., 6700 S Main St., Los Angeles, CA 90003-1541, (213)753-5131 [9021]

Main Line Book Company Inc., 1974 Sproul Rd., Ste. 400, PO Box 914, Broomall, PA 19008, (215)353-5166 [3930]

Main Line Equipment, Inc., 20917 Higgins Ct., Torrance, CA 90501-1723, (310)357-4450 [9022]

Main Line International Inc., 151 Ben Burton Cr., Bogart, GA 30622, (706)227-1800 [18898]

Main Office Machine Co., 613 Market St., Kirkland, WA 98033-5422, (206)282-0302 [5665]

Main Street and Main Inc., 5050 N 40th St., No. 200, Phoenix, AZ 85018-2163, (602)852-9000 [24175]

Main Street Produce Inc., 2165 W Main St., Santa Maria, CA 93454, (805)349-7170 [11759]

Main Tool Supply, 732 Commerce St., PO Box 204, Thornwood, NY 10594-0204, (914)769-7056 [17014]

Maine Battery Distributors, 261 Black Point Rd., Scarborough, ME 04074 [23797]

Maine Cottage Furniture Inc., PO Box 935, Yarmouth, ME 04096-1935, (207)846-1430 [13169]

Maine Distributing Co., 5 Coffey St., Bangor, ME 04401, (207)947-4563 [1840]

Maine Entrepreneurs Group, 19 Cottage St., Portland, ME 04103-4413, (207)772-8967 [17508]

Maine Equipment Company, Inc., RFD No. 2, Box 580, Bangor, ME 04401, (207)848-5738 [2911]

Maine Ladder & Staging Co., Inc., 13 Portland Rd., Box 899, Gray, ME 04039, (207)657-2070 [2912]

Maine Office Supply Co. Inc., 48 Quimby St., Biddeford, ME 04005-2308, (207)284-7782 [21119]

Maine Potato Growers Inc., PO Box 271, Presque Isle, ME 04769, (207)764-3131 [11760]

Maine Propane Distributors Inc., 1625 Hammond St., Bangor, ME 04401, (207)848-2456 [22445]

Maine Scrap Metal Inc., PO Box 326, Des Plaines, IL 60016-0326, (847)824-3175 [26893]

Maine Scrap Metal LLC, PO Box 326, Des Plaines, IL 60016-0326, (847)824-3175 [26893]

Maine Writers & Publishers Alliance, 12 Pleasant St., Brunswick, ME 04011, (207)729-6333 [3931]

Maines Paper and Food Service Inc., 12 Terrace Dr., PO Box 450, Conklin, NY 13748, (607)772-1936 [11761]

Maines Paper and Food Service Inc. Equipment and Supply Div., PO Box 438, Conklin, NY 13748-0438, (607)772-0055 [14530]

Mainline Supply Corp., 2 Gaines St., Binghamton, NY 13905, (607)772-1212 [10004]

Maintenance Engineering Corp., PO Box 1729, Houston, TX 77251, (713)222-2351 [4448]

Maintenance Warehouse/America Corp., PO Box 85838, San Diego, CA 92186, (619)452-5555 [13806]

Maisel Inc.; Skip, 510 Central Ave. SW, Albuquerque, NM 87102-3114, (505)242-6526 [17509]

Maisons Marques and Domaines USA Inc., 383 4th St., Ste. 400, Oakland, CA 94607, (510)286-2000 [1841]

Majega Records, 240 E Radcliffe Dr., Claremont, CA 91711, (909)624-0677 [25300]

Majesti Watch Company Inc., 70 W 36th St., New York, NY 10018, (212)239-0444 [17510]

Majestic Communications, 4091 Viscount, Memphis, TN 38118, (901)794-9494 [5666]

Majestic Glove Inc., 14660 NE N Woodinville Way, Ste. 100, Woodinville, WA 98072, (425)486-1606 [5154]

Majestic Penn State Inc., Comly & Caroline Rd., Philadelphia, PA 19154, (215)676-7600 [21120]

Majestic Steel Service Inc., 5300 Majestic Pkwy., Bedford Heights, OH 44146, (216)786-2666 [20146]

Majilite Corp., 1530 Broadway Rd., Dracut, MA 01826, (508)441-6800 [26132]

Majji Produce, Inc., 6170 Toledo, Detroit, MI 48209, (313)843-0660 [11762]

Major Appliances, 8687 SW 178th St., Miami, FL 33157-6031, (954)777-0079 [24176]

Major Brands, 6701 Southwest Ave., St. Louis, MO 63143, (314)645-1843 [1842]

Major Brands, 1502 Old Hwy. 40 W, Columbia, MO 65202, (573)443-3169 [1843]

Major Brands, 550 E 13th Ave., Kansas City, MO 64116, (816)221-1070 [1844]

Major Brands-Cape Girardeau, PO Box 818, Cape Girardeau, MO 63702-0818, (314)335-8079 [1845]

Major Medical Supply Co. Inc., 687 Laconia Rd., Belmont, NH 03220-3921, (603)267-7406 [18899]

Major Oil Inc., 3423 Money Rd., Montgomery, AL 36108, (205)263-5401 [22446]

Major-Sysco Food Services Inc., 136 Mariposa Rd., Modesto, CA 95354, (209)527-7700 [11763]

Majors Scientific Books Inc., PO Box 819074, Dallas, TX 75381-9074, (972)353-1100 [3932]

Majure Data Inc., 993 Mansell Rd., Roswell, GA 30076-1505, (404)587-3054 [6455]

Makita U.S.A. Inc., 14930 Northam St., La Mirada, CA 90638, (714)522-8088 [13807]

Malco Industries, 162 Eastern Ave., Lynn, MA 01902, (617)598-1990 [13808]

Malco Modes Inc., 1596 Howard St., San Francisco, CA 94103, (415)621-0840 [5155]

Malco Products Inc., Hwy. 55 & County Rd., No. 136, Annandale, MN 55302, (320)274-8246 [13809]

Maldaver Company Inc., 1791 Bellevue, Detroit, MI 48207, (313)579-2110 [2913]

Malden Mop and Brush Co., 162 Eastern Ave., Lynn, MA 01902, (617)598-1990 [13808]

Malik International Enterprises Ltd., Merchandise-Mart, PO Box 3194, Chicago, IL 60654, (773)334-6785 [15574]

Malin and Associates Inc.; N.J., PO Box 797, Addison, TX 75001-0797, (972)458-2680 [16259]

Malin Potato Cooperative Inc., E 4th, Merrill, OR 97633, (541)798-5665 [11764]

Malisani, Inc., PO Box 1195, Great Falls, MT 59403, (406)761-0108 [10005]

Mallard Oil Co., PO Box 1008, Kinston, NC 28503-1008, (919)393-8153 [22447]

Mallco Lumber and Building Materials Inc., PO Box 4397, Phoenix, AZ 85030, (602)252-4961 [7635]

Malletech/Marimba Productions Inc., 501 E Main St., Gurdon, AR 71743, (870)353-2525 [25301]

Mallin Brothers Company Inc., 3211 Gardner Ave., Kansas City, MO 64120, (816)483-1800 [26894]

Mallor Brokerage Co., 147-17 105th Ave., Jamaica, NY 11435-4917, (718)291-9300 [11765]

Mallory Inc., 550 Mallory Way, Carson City, NV 89701, (775)882-6600 [9023]

Mallory Pet Supplies, 740 Rankin Rd. NE, Albuquerque, NM 87107, (505)836-4033 [27183]

Malolo Beverages & Supplies, Ltd., 2815 Koapaka St., Honolulu, HI 96819, (808)836-2111 [24986]

Malolo Beverages and Supply Co., 2815 Koapaka St., Honolulu, HI 96819, (808)836-2111 [24986]

Malone & Hyde, 4701 Central, Monroe, LA 71203, (318)323-8717 [14158]

Malone and Hyde Inc., 1991 Corporate Ave., Memphis, TN 38132, (901)367-8200 [11766]

Malone and Hyde Inc. Lafayette Div., PO Box 91910, Lafayette, LA 70509, (318)236-3800 [11767]

Malone Products Inc., 3050 Classen Blvd., Norman, OK 73071, (405)321-5310 [11768]

Maloney, Cunningham & Devic, 1114 W Fulton St., Chicago, IL 60607, (312)666-4452 [11769]

Maloof & Co.; Joe G., 523 Commercial NE, PO Box 1086, Albuquerque, NM 87103-1086, (505)243-2293 [1846]

Maltby Company Inc., 11132-G Fleetwood St., Sun Valley, CA 91352, (818)768-4426 [4449]

Maltby Electric Supply Company Inc., 336 7th St., San Francisco, CA 94103, (415)863-5000 [9024]

Maltby's Golfworks; Ralph, 4820 Jacksontown Rd., Newark, OH 43056, (740)328-4193 [23798]

Malvese Equipment Company Inc., PO Box 295, Hicksville, NY 11802, (516)681-7600 [983]

Maly, 711 Windsor St., Sun Prairie, WI 53590, (608)837-6927 [10006]

Mama Rosa's Slice of Italy, 616 N Rampart, New Orleans, LA 70112-3538, (504)523-5546 [11770]

Mamiya America Corp., 8 Westchester Plz., Elmsford, NY 10523, (914)347-3300 [22875]

Man-I-Can Store Fixtures, Inc., 2519 Comanche Rd. NE, Albuquerque, NM 87107-4720, (505)881-2712 [13170]

Management Computer Systems Inc., 7301 N Shadeland Ave., No. B, Indianapolis, IN 46250-2023, (317)842-9696 [6456]

Management Supply Co., 2395 Research Dr., Farmington Hills, MI 48335-2630, (248)471-5500 [23248]

Management Techniques Inc., 760 Office Pkwy., Ste. 70, St. Louis, MO 63141, (314)994-9464 [6457]

Manassas Ice and Fuel Company Inc., 9009 Center St., Manassas, VA 20110-5486, (703)368-3121 [11771]

Manchester Equipment Company Inc., 160 Oser Ave., Hauppauge, NY 11788, (516)435-1199 [6458]

Manchester Manufacturing Acquisitions Inc., Gould St. Business Pk, Colebrook, NH 03576, (603)237-8383 [5156]

Manchester Manufacturing Inc., 8 Gould St., Colebrook, NH 03576-0119, (603)237-8383 [5157]

Manchester Medical Supply Inc., PO Box 300, Manchester, CT 06045-0831, (860)649-9015 [18900]

Manchester Wholesale Distributors, 64 Old Granite St., Manchester, NH 03101, (603)625-5461 [11772]

Manchester Wholesale Supply Inc., Hwy. 55E, PO Box 570, Manchester, TN 37355, (931)728-4011 [23249]

Mancini & Groesbeck, Inc., 164 East 3900 South, PO Box 57218, Salt Lake City, UT 84157-0218, (801)266-4453 [11773]

Mandala Corp., 1215 Reservoir Ave., Cranston, RI 02920-6009, (401)944-8070 [27184]

The Manderscheid Co., 624 W Adams St., Chicago, IL 60661, (312)782-8662 [17013]

Maneto Wholesale Flooring, Inc., 2509 Commercial NE, Albuquerque, NM 87102, (505)766-5161 [10007]

Mangelsen and Sons Inc.; Harold, 8200 J. St., Omaha, NE 68127, (402)339-3922 [13394]

Manhattan Brass and Copper Company Inc., PO Box 780145, Maspeth, NY 11378, (718)381-5300 [20147]

Manhattan Coffee Co., PO Box 14583, St. Louis, MO 63178, (314)731-2500 [11774]

Manhattan Distributing Co., 11675 Fairgrove Industrial Blvd., Maryland Heights, MO 63043, (314)567-1400 [1847]

Manhattan-Miami Corp., 5019 NW 165 St., Hialeah, FL 33014, (305)628-3630 [5158]

Manhattan Office Products Inc., 235 E 45th St., New York, NY 10017, (212)557-0123 [6459]

Manhattan Shirt Company-Winnsboro Distribution Center, 321 By-pass, Winnsboro, SC 29180, (803)635-4671 [5159]

Manhattan Wholesale Meat Company Inc., 209 Yuma St., Manhattan, KS 66502, (913)776-9203 [11775]

Mania-Testerion, 1220 Village Way, Santa Ana, CA 92705, (714)564-9350 [9025]

Manifatture Associate Cashmere USA Inc., 745 5th Ave., Ste. 1225, New York, NY 10151, (212)753-7015 [5160]

Manildra Milling Corp., 4210 Shawnee Mission, Shawnee Mission, KS 66205, (913)362-0777 [11776]

Manis Lumber Company Inc., 2 Riverside Industrial Park, Rome, GA 30161, (706)232-2400 [27339]

Mankato Business Products, 1715 Commerce Dr., North Mankato, MN 56003, (507)625-7440 [21121]

Mankato Iron and Metal Co., PO Box 3152, Mankato, MN 56002, (507)625-6489 [26895]

Mankato-Kasota Stone, 818 N Willow St., PO Box 1358, Mankato, MN 56002, (507)625-2746 [7636]

Manley Oil Co., 410 N Center St., Los Angeles, CA 90012, (213)628-5674 [22448]

Manlove Auto Parts, 117 E Market St., Georgetown, DE 19947-1405, (302)856-2507 [2914]

Mann and Company, Inc.; George, PO Box 9066, Providence, RI 02940, (401)781-5600 [4450]

Mann Edge Tool Co. Collins Axe Div., PO Box 351, Lewistown, PA 17044-0351, (717)248-9628 [13810]

Mann and Parker Lumber Co., 335 N Constitution Ave., New Freedom, PA 17349, (717)235-4834 [27340]

Mann U.V. Technology, Inc., 3217 Buncombe Rd., Greenville, SC 29609, (919)271-4036 [25724]

Manna Pro Corp. Denver Div., 4545 Madison St., Denver, CO 80216, (303)296-8668 [984]

Manneco, Inc., 600 S Cottage Ave., Independence, MO 64050, (816)833-3325 [13395]

Mannesmann Corp., 450 Park Ave., 24th Fl., New York, NY 10022, (212)826-0040 [16260]

Mannesmann Pipe and Steel Corp., 1990 Post Oak Blvd., No. 1800, Houston, TX 77056, (713)960-1900 [20148]

Manning Equipment Inc., PO Box 23229, Louisville, KY 40223, (502)426-5210 [2915]

Manning Grain Co., PO Box 217, Fairmont, NE 68354, (402)266-3701 [985]

Mannington Wood Floors, 1327 Lincoln Dr., High Point, NC 27260-9945, (336)884-5600 [10008]

Mannix World Imports Inc., 130 Commerce Way, Woburn, MA 01801, (781)935-4389 [26133]

Manoog Inc.; Charles, 9 Piedmont St., Worcester, MA 01610, (508)756-5783 [23250]

Manset Marine Supply Co., PO Box 709, Rockland, ME 04841, (207)596-6464 [18556]

Mansfield Bag & Paper Company Inc., 441 N Main St., PO Box 1414, Mansfield, OH 44902, (419)525-2814 [21820]

Mansfield Electric Supply Inc., 2255 Stumbo Rd., Mansfield, OH 44901, (419)529-2750 [9026]

Mansfield Oil Company of Gainesville Inc., 1025 Airport Pkwy. SW, Gainesville, GA 30506, (404)532-7571 [22449]

Mansfield Paper Company Inc., PO Box 1070, West Springfield, MA 01089, (413)781-2000 [21821]

Mansfield Typewriter Co., 1150 National Pkwy., Mansfield, OH 44906-1911, (419)529-6100 [21122]

Manson News Distributors, 1177 Avenue of the Americas, Ste. 36, New York, NY 10036-2714, (716)244-3880 [3933]

Manson Tool and Supply Co., 732 Commerce St., PO Box 204, Thornwood, NY 10594-0204, (914)769-7056 [17014]

Mantrose-Haeuser Company Inc., 1175 Post Rd. E, Westport, CT 06880, (203)454-1800 [21495]

Mantua Manufacturing Co., 7900 Northfield Rd., Walton Hills, OH 44146-5525, (440)232-8865 [13171]

Manu Reps Inc., 4710 W 73rd St., Indianapolis, IN 46268-2115, (317)298-0622 [25302]

Manufactured Rubber Products Inc., 4501 Tacony St., Philadelphia, PA 19124, (215)533-3600 [17015]

Manufacturers Representatives, 410 E 3rd St., Royal Oak, MI 48067, (248)546-3220 [7893]

Manufacturers Reserve Supply Inc., 16 Woolsey St., Irvington, NJ 07111-4089, (201)373-1881 [7637]

Manufacturers Steel Supply Company Inc., 400 Edwin St., St. Louis, MO 63103-2492, (314)371-5600 [20149]

Manufacturers Supplies Co., 4220 Rider Trail N, Earth City, MO 63045, (314)770-0880 [16261]

Manufacturing Distributors, 2444 Lycoming Creek Rd., Williamsport, PA 17701, (570)494-4770 [15209]

Manufacturing Sciences Corp., 804 Kerr Hollow Rd., Oak Ridge, TN 37830, (615)481-0455 [26896]

Manugistics Group Inc., 2115 E Jefferson St., Rockville, MD 20852-4999, (301)984-5000 [6460]

Manuscript Memories, PO Box F, Blacksburg, VA 24063-1020, (540)951-0467 [4070]

Manutec Inc., 2475 W Hampton Ave., Milwaukee, WI 53209, (414)449-3332 [20150]

Manware Inc., 1511 South 700 West, Salt Lake City, UT 84104, (801)972-1212 [13811]

Many Feathers Books & Maps, 2626 W Glenrose Ave., Phoenix, AZ 85017, (602)433-0616 [4062]

Many Feathers Books and Maps, 2626 W Indian School Rd., Phoenix, AZ 85017, (602)266-1043 [3934]

Manz, Jr.; Edward H., 2230 McCallie Ave., Chattanooga, TN 37404-3203, (423)698-1081 [5161]

Manzo Contracting Co., PO Box 341, Matawan, NJ 07747, (732)721-6900 [7638]

Map Link Inc., 30 S La Patera Ln. Unit #5, Santa Barbara, CA 93117, (805)692-6777 [3935]

Mapal Aaro, Inc., 4032 Dove Rd., Port Huron, MI 48060-1025, (810)364-8020 [16262]

Mapes and Sprowl Steel Ltd., 1100 E Devon Ave., Elk Grove Village, IL 60007, (708)364-0055 [20151]

Maple City Ice Co., 370 Cleveland Rd., Norwalk, OH 44857, (419)668-2531 [1848]

Maple Valley Cooperative, PO Box 68, Leigh, NE 68643, (402)487-2295 [11777]

Mapleton Grain Co., 111 N Front St., Mapleton, IA 51034, (712)882-2733 [18074]

MAPS, PO Box 10616, Portland, OR 97296-0616, (503)228-4972 [3949]

Mar Electronics Inc., 17201 Westfield Park Dr., Westfield, IN 46074-9537, (317)633-6699 [9027]

Mar and Sons Inc.; J, 119 Butterfield Rd., North Aurora, IL 60542-1313, (630)851-0814 [16263]

Mar Vista Lumber Co., 3860 Grandview Blvd., Los Angeles, CA 90066, (213)870-7431 [7639]

Maraj International, 494 Walleyford Dr., Berea, OH 44017, (440)891-3906 [6461]

Maran-Wurzell Glass and Mirror Co., 2300 E Slauson Ave., Huntington Park, CA 90255, (213)233-4256 [15575]

Maranatha, 710 Jefferson St., Ashland, OR 97520, (541)488-2747 [11778]

Maranatha Music, PO Box 31050, Laguna Hills, CA 92654, (714)248-4000 [25303]

Marantz Professional Products, 2640 White Oak Cir., Aurora, IL 60504, (630)820-4800 [25469]

Marathon Ashland Petroleum L.L.C., 539 S Main St., Findlay, OH 45840, (419)422-2121 [22450]

Marathon Boat Yard, 2059 Overseas Hwy., Marathon, FL 33050, (305)743-6641 [18557]

Marathon Codestar, 170 Knowles Dr., Ste. 212, Los Gatos, CA 95032, (408)366-9801 [6462]

Marathon Electric Manufacturing Corp., 417 Welshwood Dr., No. 201, Nashville, TN 37211, (615)834-3930 [9028]

Marathon Fuels, 29120 Wick Rd., Romulus, MI 48174, (734)947-1811 [22634]

Marathon International Group Inc., 170 Knowles Dr., Ste. 212, Los Gatos, CA 95032, (408)366-9801 [6462]

Marburn Stores Inc., 225 Walker St., CliffsiDe Park, NJ 07010, (201)943-0222 [15576]

Marc Sales Corp.; Ken, PO Box 188, Maspeth, NY 11378-0188, (718)386-4065 [9029]

Marcel Watch Corp., 200 Meadowlands Pkwy., Secaucus, NJ 07094-2302, (201)330-5600 [17511]

Marchand Contractors Specialties Inc.; R.J., 3515 Division St., Metairie, LA 70002, (504)888-2922 [7640]

Marcley Oil Inc., 614 Prairie St., Aurora, IL 60506, (708)892-3832 [22451]

Marco Business Products Inc., PO Box 250, St. Cloud, MN 56302, (320)259-3000 [6463]

Marco Marine Seattle, IMFS Div., 2300 W Commodore Way, Seattle, WA 98199, (206)285-3200 [18558]

Marco Polo Import & Export, 2685 S Dayton Way, Ste. 82, Denver, CO 80231-3972, (303)695-8782 [5162]

Marco Sales Inc., 1100 Macklind Ave., St. Louis, MO 63110, (314)768-4200 [14531]

Marco and Sons; R.B., 609 W Flagler St., Miami, FL 33130, (305)324-8308 [5163]

Marco Supply Company Inc., 812 Pocahantas Ave., Roanoke, VA 24012, (703)344-6211 [13812]

Marcom, 540 Hauer Apple Way, Aptos, CA 95003-9501, (831)768-8668 [5667]

Marcone Appliance Parts, 17300 Marquardt Ave., Cerritos, CA 90703, (626)289-3735 [15210]

Marcone Appliance Parts Center, 4410 Alamo Dr., Tampa, FL 33605, (813)247-4410 [15211]

Marcone Appliance Parts Center, 641 Monterey Pass Rd., Monterey Park, CA 91754, (213)283-7741 [15212]

Marcone Appliance Parts Center Inc., 2300 Clark Ave., St. Louis, MO 63103, (314)231-7141 [15213]

Marcus Brothers, 1755 McDonald Ave., Brooklyn, NY 11230-6906, (718)645-4565 [15577]

Margus, 104 SE 5th Ct., Deerfield Beach, FL 33441, (954)421-2192 [11623]

Marian Group Corp., PO Box 51898, Lafayette, LA 70505-1898, (318)233-9996 [5164]

Mariani Packing Company Inc., 320 Jackson St., San Jose, CA 95112, (408)288-8300 [11779]

Marie Sales; Gina, 43 Oak Grove Blvd., North Providence, RI 02911-2608, (401)232-0863 [17512]

Marie's Quality Foods, 1244 E Beamer, Woodland, CA 95776, (530)662-9638 [11780]

Marietta Ignition Parts Inc., PO Box 737, Marietta, OH 45750, (740)374-6746 [2916]

Marimon Business Machines Inc., 1500 N Post Oak, Ste. 100, Houston, TX 77055, (713)868-1262 [21123]

Marinco-AFI, 2655 Napa Valley Corporate Dr., Napa, CA 94558, (707)226-9600 [9030]

Marine Electric Co., 9804 James Cir. S, Minneapolis, MN 55431-2919, (612)881-0077 [23799]

Marine Equipment & Supply, 1401 Metropolitan Ave., PO Box 598, Thorofare, NJ 08086, (856)853-8320 [18559]

Marine & Industrial Supply, 8330 Harry Hines Blvd., Dallas, TX 75235, (214)631-2300 [18560]

Marine Optical Inc., 5 Hampden Dr., South Easton, MA 02375, (508)238-8700 [19422]

Marine Rescue Products Inc., PO Box 3484, Newport, RI 02840-0991, (401)847-9144 [18561]

Marine Specialty Company Inc., PO Box 1388, Mobile, AL 36633, (205)432-0581 [23251]

Marine Systems Inc., 116 Capital Blvd., Houma, LA 70360, (504)851-4990 [2917]

Marino Marble & Tile, 444 Graham Ave., Brooklyn, NY 11211, (718)389-2191 [10009]

Marinovich Trawl Co., PO Box 1416, Biloxi, MS 39533-1416, (228)436-6429 [18562]

Marion Fabrics Inc., PO Box 71, Burbank, CA 91503-0071, (818)567-0909 [26134]

Marion Iron Co., PO Box 345, Marion, IA 52302, (319)377-1529 [26897]

Marion Office Products Inc., 18 Airport Rd., Nashua, NH 03063-1714, (603)886-2760 [21124]

Marion Steel Co. Scrap Div., PO Box 1217, Marion, OH 43301-1217, (740)383-6068 [26898]

Mariotti Building Products Inc., 1 Louis Industrial Dr., Old Forge, PA 18518, (717)457-6774 [7641]

Maris Distributing Co., 3820 NE 49th Rd., Gainesville, FL 32609-1606, (352)378-2431 [1849]

Mark-Costello Co., 1145 Dominguez St., Ste. J, Carson, CA 90746, (310)637-1851 [16264]

Mark-It of Colorado LLC, 233 Milwaukee St., Denver, CO 80206, (303)377-9110 [23800]

Mark IV Pictures, 5907 Meredith Dr., Des Moines, IA 50322, (515)278-4737 [25168]

Mark Oil Company Inc., PO Box 32064, Charlotte, NC 28232, (704)375-4249 [22452]

Mark-Pack Inc., PO Box 305, Coopersville, MI 49404-0305, (616)698-0033 [21822]

Mark-Rite Distributing Corp., 4045 Vincennes Rd., Indianapolis, IN 46268 [21125]

Mark Seed Co., PO Box 67, Perry, IA 50220, (515)465-2122 [986]

Mark V Distributors Inc., 3093 Kennesaw St., Ft. Myers, FL 33916, (941)334-3511 [1850]

Mark VII Equipment Inc., 5981 Tennyson St., Arvada, CO 80003, (303)423-4910 [24177]

Marker USA, PO Box 26548, Salt Lake City, UT 84126-0548, (801)972-2100 [23801]

Market Actives, LLC, 8300 SW 71st Ave., Portland, OR 97223, (503)244-0166 [4451]

Market Equipment Company Inc., 1114 N Ruby St., Spokane, WA 99202-1737, (509)325-4526 [14532]

Market Share International Inc., 1230 S Main St., Gainesville, FL 32601, (352)372-9186 [11781]

Market Specialties, 536 Mariposa Rd., Modesto, CA 95352, (209)526-8511 [11782]

Marketex Computer Corp., 1601 Civic Center Dr., No. 206, Santa Clara, CA 95050, (408)241-3677 [6464]

MarketForce, Ltd., PO Box 3343, Palos Verdes Peninsula, CA 90274, (310)541-8679 [16265]

Marketing Group Inc. (Harvey, Illinois), 10 S Wacker Dr. Ste. 3500, Chicago, IL 60606-7407, (708)331-0200 [17513]

Marketing Performance Inc., 2147 Riverchase Office Rd., Birmingham, AL 35244, (205)982-1121 [11783]

Marketing Specialist Corp., 17855 Dallas Pkwy., Ste. 200, Dallas, TX 75287-6852, (972)349-6200 [11784]

Marketing Specialist Inc., 17855 Dallas Pkwy., Ste. 200, Dallas, TX 75287-6852, (972)349-6200 [11784]

Marketing Specialista, 2848 Coheatland Dr., Fargo, ND 58103, (701)235-8964 [11785]

Marketing Specialists - Southern California Div., 744 N Eckhuff St., Orange, CA 92868-1020, (714)939-6275 [11786]

Marketing Success, PO Box 2182, Ketchum, ID 83340-2182, (208)726-9728 [5165]

Marketor International Corp., PO Box 1721, Clackamas, OR 97015, (503)650-4788 [7642]

Marketware Corp., 101 Yesler Way, Ste. 101, Seattle, WA 98104-2595, (206)626-6100 [6465]

Markle Steel Co., PO Box 2346, Houston, TX 77252-2346, (713)225-1141 [20152]

Markley Strings, Inc.; Dean, 3350 Scott Blvd., No. 45, Santa Clara, CA 95054, (408)988-2456 [25304]

Markon Footwear Inc., 350 5th Ave., Ste. 1397, New York, NY 10118-1397, (212)947-0099 [24799]

Markos Wholesale Clothing Distributors, 127-129 S 3rd, La Crosse, WI 54601-3264, (608)784-8224 [5166]

Markovits and Fox, PO Box 611420, San Jose, CA 95161-1420, (408)453-7888 [20153]

Marks Co.; D.F., 8510 212th St. SE, Woodinville, WA 98072, (425)485-3802 [987]

Marks Paper Co., 1801 L and A Rd., Metairie, LA 70001, (504)832-1801 [21126]

Marks Paper Co., Inc., 1801 L & A Rd., Metairie, LA 70001, (504)832-1801 [21127]

Marks Pro Shop; Mike, 141 28th St. SE, Grand Rapids, MI 49548-1103, (616)245-7503 [23802]

Mark's Quality Meats, 6800 Dix St., Detroit, MI 48209-1269, (313)554-2500 [11787]

Marksman Products Inc., 5482 Argosy Ave., Huntington Beach, CA 92649-1039, (714)898-7535 [13501]

Markstein Beverage Co., 505 S Pacific St., San Marcos, CA 92069, (760)744-9100 [1851]

Markstein Beverage Company of Sacramento, 60 Main Ave., Sacramento, CA 95838, (916)920-9070 [1852]

Markuse Corp., 10 Wheeling Ave., Woburn, MA 01801, (617)932-9444 [15578]

Markwort Sporting Goods Co., 4300 Forest Park Ave., St. Louis, MO 63108-2884, (314)652-8935 [23803]

Marlboro Footworks Ltd., 60 Austin St., Newton, MA 02460, (617)969-7070 [24800]

Marlboro Footworks Ltd., 60 Austin St., Newton, MA 02460, (617)969-7070 [5167]

Marlen Trading Company Inc., 4101 Curtis Ave., Baltimore, MD 21226, (410)355-3300 [20154]

Marlenes Inc., 669 Hogan Rd., Bangor, ME 04401-3605, (207)945-9813 [5168]

Marley Mouldings Inc., PO Box 610, Marion, VA 24354, (540)783-8161 [7643]

Marlin Custom Embroidery, 5230 Kostoryz Rd., No. 19, Corpus Christi, TX 78415, (512)854-0906 [5169]

Marlin Distributors Inc., 91-312 Komohana St., Kapolei, HI 96707-1714, (808)682-4314 [26569]

Marlin Manufacturing & Distribution Inc.; R., 302 N Townsend, Santa Ana, CA 92703-3543, (714)547-3220 [13396]

Marlo Bags, 111 Marquardt Dr., Wheeling, IL 60090-6427, (847)215-1400 [18411]

Marmac Distributors Inc., 4 Craftsman Rd., East Windsor, CT 06088, (203)623-9926 [19423]

Marmelstein and Associates Inc., PO Box 1268, Jackson, NJ 08527, (908)363-5626 [11788]

Marmon Group, 15450 E Jefferson Ave., Grosse Pointe, MI 48230, (313)331-5100 [13813]

Marmon/Keystone Corp., PO Box 992, Butler, PA 16001, (724)283-3000 [20155]

Marnal Corp., 501 Industrial Park Dr., La Habra, CA 90631, (562)691-4443 [2918]

Marni International, 105 Campbell, No. 88, Kerrville, TX 78028, (512)895-1483 [21128]

Maroa Farmers Cooperative Elevator Co., PO Box 349, Maroa, IL 61756, (217)794-5533 [988]

Marquardt and Company Inc., 161 6th Ave., New York, NY 10013, (212)645-7200 [21823]

Marquart-Wolfe Lumber Company Inc., PO Box 9286, Newport Beach, CA 92658-9286, (714)966-0281 [7644]

Marquette Bottling Works Inc., 120 W Furnace St., Marquette, MI 49855, (906)225-1209 [3936]

Marquette Lumbermen's Warehouse Inc., PO Box 913, Grand Rapids, MI 49509-0913, (616)247-5100 [7645]

Marquis Corp., 596 Hoffman Rd., Independence, OR 97351-9601, (503)838-0888 [23804]

Marr Scaffolding Company Inc., 1 D St., Boston, MA 02127, (617)269-7200 [7646]

Mars Co.; W.P. and R.S., 215 E 78th St., Bloomington, MN 55420, (612)884-9388 [16266]

Marsch Enterprises, 8133 Old Seward Hwy., Anchorage, AK 99518, (907)522-8083 [25305]

Marsh Electronics Inc., 1563 S 101st St., Milwaukee, WI 53214, (414)475-6000 [9031]

Marsh Inc.; Paul, 654 Madison Ave., New York, NY 10021, (212)759-9060 [4452]

Marsh Kitchens Greensboro Inc., 2503 Greengate Dr., Greensboro, NC 27406-5242, (910)273-8196 [7647]

Marshal Glove & Safety Supply, PO Box 1346, Evansville, IN 47706-1346, (812)425-5167 [24801]

Marshall and Bruce Co., 689 Davidson St., Nashville, TN 37213, (615)256-3661 [25725]

Marshall Building Specialties Company Inc., 1001 E New York St., Indianapolis, IN 46202, (317)635-3888 [7648]

Marshall Building Supply, 4730 Wynn Rd., Las Vegas, NV 89103-5422, (702)871-4166 [7649]

Marshall Co.; A.J., 6635 Sterling Dr. S, Sterling Heights, MI 48312, (810)939-1600 [4663]

Marshall Co.; A.W., PO Box 16127, Salt Lake City, UT 84116, (801)328-4713 [11789]

Marshall Co.; John A., 10930 Lackman Rd., Lenexa, KS 66219-1232, (913)842-5368 [21129]

Marshall Co.; R.J., 26776 W 12 Mile Rd., Southfield, MI 48034, (248)353-4100 [4453]

Marshall Co.; R.J., 26776 W 12 Mile Rd., Southfield, MI 48034, (248)353-4100 [17016]

Marshall County Cooperative Association, PO Box 82, Warren, MN 56762, (218)745-5323 [22453]

Marshall Distributing Co., 2625 W 1100 S Directors Row, Salt Lake City, UT 84104, (801)973-8855 [11790]

Marshall Farmers Cooperative, 615 Ellington Pkwy., Lewisburg, TN 37091, (931)359-1558 [989]

Marshall Industries, 158 Gaither Rd., Mt. Laurel, NJ 08054, (609)234-9100 [9032]

Marshall Industries, 155 Passaic Ave., Ste. 410, Fairfield, NJ 07004-3502, (201)273-1515 [9033]

Marshall Industries, 100 Marshall Dr., Endicott, NY 13760, (607)785-2345 [9034]

Marshall Industries, 30700 Bainbridge Rd., Unit A, Solon, OH 44139, (440)248-1788 [9035]

Marshall Industries, 15260 NW Greenbaier Pkwy., Beaverton, OR 97006-5764, (503)644-5050 [9036]

Marshall Industries, 8504 Cross Park Dr., Austin, TX 78754, (512)837-1991 [9037]

Marshall Industries, 1551 N Glenville, Richardson, TX 75081, (972)705-0600 [9038]

Marshall Industries, 10681 Haddington, No. 160, Houston, TX 77043, (713)467-1666 [9039]

Marshall Industries, 2855 Cottonwood Pky., Ste. 220, Salt Lake City, UT 84121-7039, (801)973-2288 [9040]

Marshall Industries, 8214 154th Ave. NE, Redmond, WA 98052-3877, (425)486-5747 [9041]

Marshall and Johnson, 1146 N Central Ave., No. 396, Glendale, CA 91202, (818)243-5424 [24587]

Marshall Pottery Inc., 4901 Elysian Fields Rd., PO Box 1839, Marshall, TX 75671, (903)938-9201 [14916]

Marshall's Tile Co., 1970 N Holmes Ave., Idaho Falls, ID 83402, (208)523-4800 [10010]

Marshalltown Trowel Co., PO Box 738, Marshalltown, IA 50158, (515)753-0127 [7650]

Marshmallow Products Inc., 5141 Fischer Ave., Cincinnati, OH 45217-1157, (513)641-2345 [11792]

Marshmallow Products Inc., 9 W Mitchell Ave., Cincinnati, OH 45217-1525, (513)641-2345 [11791]

MarshmallowCone Co., 5141 Fischer Ave., Cincinnati, OH 45217-1157, (513)641-2345 [11792]

Marstan Industries Inc., 10814 Northeast Ave., Philadelphia, PA 19116, (215)969-0600 [24178]

Marta Cooperative of America, 15150 N Hayden Rd., Ste. 106, Scottsdale, AZ 85260, (602)443-0211 [15214]

Martec International, 910 Oak Tree Rd., South Plainfield, NJ 07080, (908)756-6222 [25930]

Martec International Trading, 910 Oak Tree Rd., South Plainfield, NJ 07080, (908)756-6222 [25930]

Martek International Inc., 5760 NW 72nd Ave., Miami, FL 33166, (305)592-5501 [13791]

Martek Ltd., Dept. LH, PO Box 15160, Charlotte, NC 28211, (704)364-7213 [13397]

Martensen Enterprises Inc., 1721 W Culver St., Phoenix, AZ 85007, (602)271-9048 [7651]

Martensen Enterprises Inc., 1721 W Culver St., Phoenix, AZ 85007, (602)271-9048 [17017]

Martexport Inc., 654 Madison Ave., Ste. 1409, New York, NY 10021, (212)935-0300 [15579]

Martha Weems Ltd., 8351 Leesburg Pike, Vienna, VA 22182, (703)827-9510 [13398]

Martin Bros. Distributing Co., Inc., 406 Viking Rd., PO Box 69, Cedar Falls, IA 50613-0069, (319)266-1775 [11793]

Martin Brothers International, PO Box 2230, Jacksonville, FL 32203, (904)353-4311 [26327]

Martin-Brower Co., 333 E Butterfield Rd., Lombard, IL 60148, (630)271-8300 [11794]

Martin Co.; E.A., 2222 E Kearngy St., PO Box 988, Springfield, MO 65803, (417)866-6651 [7652]

Martin Co.; E.A., PO Box 988, Springfield, MO 65801-0988, (417)866-6651 [7653]

Martin Enterprises Inc., 30000 Solon Rd., Solon, OH 44139, (440)248-7600 [20232]

Martin Forest Industries, PO Box 159, Healdsburg, CA 95448, (707)433-3900 [7217]

Martin Industries Inc., 301 E Tennessee St., PO Box 128, Florence, AL 35631, (256)767-0330 [15215]

Martin Instrument Co. (Burnsville, Minnesota), 11965 11th Ave. S, Burnsville, MN 55337-1404, (952)882-8222 [24394]

Martin and MacArthur, 1815 Kahai St., Honolulu, HI 96819, (808)845-6688 [7654]

Martin Millwork Inc., PO Box 2859, Springfield, MA 01101, (413)788-9634 [7655]

Martin News Agency Inc., 11325 Gemini Ln., Dallas, TX 75229, (972)501-5500 [3516]

Martin Oil Co., 528 N First St., Bellwood, PA 16617, (814)742-8438 [22454]

Martin Sons Inc.; Frank, PO Box 10, Ft. Kent Mills, ME 04744, (207)834-3171 [16267]

Martin Stationers, PO Box 3007, Idaho Falls, ID 83403, (208)529-0510 [21130]

Martin Tractor Company Inc., 1737 SW 42nd St., Topeka, KS 66609, (785)266-5770 [7656]

Martin Universal Design Inc., 4444 Lawton St., Detroit, MI 48208-2162, (313)895-0700 [13172]

Martindale Electric Co., PO Box 430, Cleveland, OH 44107-0430, (216)521-8567 [9042]

Martindale Feed Mill, PO Box 245, Valley View, TX 76272, (940)726-3203 [990]

Martinelli Inc.; John, 105 Avocado St., PO Box 3211, Springfield, MA 01101-3211, (413)732-4193 [11795]

Martinez; Gus, 205 W 3rd St., Roswell, NM 88201-4623, (505)623-4987 [21131]

Martini and Prati Wines Inc., 2191 Laguna Rd., Santa Rosa, CA 95401, (707)823-2404 [1853]

Martinsburg Farmers Elevator Co., PO Box 130, Martinsburg, MO 65264-0130, (573)492-6218 [18075]

Martinson-Nicholls, 4910 E 345th St., Willoughby, OH 44094-4609, (440)951-1312 [26135]

Martrex Alpha Corp., PO Box 1709, Minnetonka, MN 55345, (612)933-5000 [6466]

Martrex Inc., PO Box 1709, Minnetonka, MN 55345-3793, (612)933-5000 [4454]

Marubeni America Corp., 450 Lexington Ave., New York, NY 10017, (212)450-0100 [26136]

Marubeni International Electronics Corp., 790 Lucerne Dr., Sunnyvale, CA 94086, (408)727-8447 [6467]

Marubeni Solutions USA, Corp., 790 Lucerne Dr., Sunnyvale, CA 94086, (408)727-8447 [6467]

Maruri USA Corp., 21510 Gledhill St., Chatsworth, CA 91311, (818)717-9900 [13399]

Marus and Weimer, Inc., PO Box 749, Chagrin Falls, OH 44022, (440)247-3570 [23252]

Marval Industries Inc., 315 Hoyt Ave., Mamaroneck, NY 10543, (914)381-2400 [22995]

Marvel Group Inc., 3843 W 43rd St., Chicago, IL 60632, (773)523-4804 [21132]

Marvin Corp., 2911 Slauson Ave., Huntington Park, CA 90255, (213)585-5003 [7657]

Marvin Hayes Fish Co., PO Box 187, Samburg, TN 38254, (901)538-2166 [11796]

Marvin Land Systems, Inc., 12637 Beatrice St., Los Angeles, CA 90066, (310)306-2800 [2919]

Marvitec Export Corporation, 1475 NW 97th Ave., Miami, FL 33172, (305)593-1475 [16268]

Marwil Products Co., PO Box 287, Ft. Loramie, OH 45845-0287, (937)295-3651 [2920]

Mary Ann's Baking Co., 324 Alhambra Blvd., Sacramento, CA 95816, (916)441-4741 [11797]

Mary Fashion Manufacturing Company Inc., 380 W Main St., Bath, PA 18014, (610)837-6763 [5170]

Mary McFadden Couture, 240 W 35th St., New York, NY 10001-2506, (212)736-4078 [5180]

Maryland Clay Products, 7100 Muirkirk Rd., Beltsville, MD 20705, (301)419-2214 [7658]

Maryland Clay Products, 7100 Muirkirk Rd., Beltsville, MD 20705, (301)419-2214 [7659]

Maryland Historical Press, 9205 Tuckerman St., Lanham, MD 20706, (301)577-5308 [3937]

Maryland Hotel Supply Co., 701 W Hamburg St., Baltimore, MD 21230, (410)539-7055 [11798]

Maryland Import/Export, Inc., 4248 Cherry Valley Dr., Olney, MD 20832, (301)774-2960 [17514]

Maryland Industrial Inc., 28 Alco Pl., Baltimore, MD 21227-2004, (410)247-9117 [24802]

Maryland Industrial Inc., 28 Alco Pl., Baltimore, MD 21227-2004, (410)247-9117 [5171]

Maryland Leather Inc., 1012 Russell St., Baltimore, MD 21230, (410)547-6999 [18412]

Maryland News Distributing Co., 4000 Coolidge Ave., Baltimore, MD 21229, (301)536-4545 [3938]

Maryland Tile Distributors, 5621 Old Frederick Rd., Baltimore, MD 21228, (410)747-1416 [10011]

Maryland and Virginia Milk Producers Cooperative Association Inc., 1985 Isaac Newton Sq. W, Reston, VA 20190-5094, (703)742-6800 [11799]

Marysville Newspaper Distributor, 1117 Bancroft St., Port Huron, MI 48060, (810)984-5171 [3939]

Marysville Office Center, 116 S Main St., Marysville, OH 43040, (937)642-8893 [21133]

Maryville Wholesale Supply Inc., 1513 Monroe Ave., PO Box 4216, Maryville, TN 37802, (423)982-3630 [23458]

Maryville Wholesale Supply Inc., 1513 Monroe Ave., Maryville, TN 37802, (423)982-3630 [23253]

Mas-Tech International Inc., 29 Deer Run Dr., Randolph, NJ 07869-4334, (973)895-2200 [6468]

Masbeirn Corp., 5353 W Colfax Ave., Denver, CO 80214-1811, (303)232-6244 [19424]

Mascari & Associations; Charles, 32823 W 12 Mile Rd., Farmington Hills, MI 48334-3304, (248)399-0950 [11800]

Maschmedt and Associates, 12304 32nd Ave. NE, Seattle, WA 98125, (206)364-6304 [18563]

Masco Corp. Beacon Hill Showroom, 1 Design Center Pl., Boston, MA 02210, (617)482-6600 [13173]

Masco Fabrics Inc., 202 S 12th St., Birmingham, AL 35233, (205)322-3476 [26137]

Mascon Inc., 5 Commonwealth Ave., Woburn, MA 01801, (781)938-5800 [16269]

Mascon Inc., 5 Commonwealth Ave., Woburn, MA 01801, (781)938-5800 [16270]

Mascotech Forming Technologies, 690 W Maple, Troy, MI 48084, (248)362-1844 [20156]

Masda Corp., 22 Troy Rd., Whippany, NJ 07981, (973)386-1100 [15216]

Masda Corp. New England, 11 Rodgers Rd., Ward Hill, MA 01835, (978)373-3649 [15217]

Masek Distributing Inc., PO Box 130, Gering, NE 69341-0130, (308)436-2100 [2921]

Masek Sports Inc., PO Box 1089, Mills, WY 82644, (307)237-9566 [23805]

Mask-Off Corp., 582 Manville Rd., Woonsocket, RI 02895-5550, (401)232-0100 [17515]

Mason Co.; F.C., PO Box 318, St. Johns, MI 48879, (517)224-3291 [16271]

Mason Distributing Company, PO Box 183, Soda Springs, ID 83276-0183, (208)547-4516 [1854]

Mason Distributors, 5105 NW 159th St., Hialeah, FL 33014-6336, (305)624-5557 [19425]

Mason Glassware Co., PO Drawer A, Jane Lew, WV 26378, (304)884-7841 [15580]

Mason Supply Co., PO Box 83585, Columbus, OH 43203, (614)253-8607 [14533]

The Masonry Center, 1424 N Orchard, PO Box 7825, Boise, ID 83707, (208)375-1362 [7660]

Masonry Product Sales Inc., 410 N Alexander St., New Orleans, LA 70119, (504)486-4618 [7661]

Mass Hardware and Supply Inc., 170 High St., Waltham, MA 02454, (781)893-6711 [13814]

Massa Associates; Ronald A., 164 C.J. Cushing Hwy., Cohasset, MA 02025, (781)383-2100 [9043]

Massachusetts Export Corp., PO Box 823, Worcester, MA 01613-0823, (508)752-5496 [5172]

Massachusetts Gas and Electric Lighting Supply Co., 193 Friend St., Boston, MA 02101-4022, (617)926-4700 [9044]

Massachusetts Lumber Co., 1400 Ironhorse Pk., North Billerica, MA 01862, (978)667-6011 [7355]

Massachusetts Lumber Co., 929 Massachusetts Ave., Cambridge, MA 02139, (617)354-6000 [7662]

Massena Paper Company Inc., 345 E Orvis St., PO Box 28, Massena, NY 13662, (315)769-2433 [21824]

Massey Builders Supply Corp., 2303 Dabney Rd., Richmond, VA 23230, (804)355-7891 [7663]

Massey Coal Company Inc.; A.T., PO Box 26765, Richmond, VA 23261, (804)788-1800 [20552]

The Massey Company Inc., PO Box 26, Mt. Holly, NC 28120, (704)827-9661 [17018]

Massey Wood and West Inc., PO Box 5008, Richmond, VA 23220, (804)355-1721 [22455]

Massive Graphic Screen Printing, 2895 Broce Dr., Norman, OK 73072-2405, (405)364-3594 [5173]

Master Building Supply and Lumber Co., 10435 Reisterstown Rd., Owings Mills, MD 21117, (410)363-0500 [7664]

Master Cartridge Corp., PO Box 238, VilLa Rica, GA 30180-0238, (404)459-5116 [23806]

Master Cellars of Milwaukee, 3241 S 20th St., Milwaukee, WI 53215, (414)645-2900 [1525]

Master Cleaners Home Service, PO Box 1129, Helena, MT 59624-1129, (406)442-1964 [4664]

Master Feed and Grain Inc., Mulberry St., Conneautville, PA 16406, (814)587-3645 [991]

Master Industries Inc., PO Box 17808, Irvine, CA 92623-7808, (949)660-0644 [23807]

Master International Corp., PO Box 25662, Los Angeles, CA 90025, (310)452-1229 [9045]

Master Purveyors, PO Box 10063, Tampa, FL 33679-0063, (813)253-0865 [11801]

Master Tile, 7170 W 43rd St., Ste. 150, Houston, TX 77092, (713)331-3800 [10012]

Master Works International, 100 Dogwood Dr., Marietta, GA 30068-3301, (404)565-5220 [18901]

Masterchem Industries Inc., PO Box 368, Barnhart, MO 63012, (314)942-2510 [21496]

Mastercraft Inc., PO Box 326, Shipshewana, IN 46565, (219)768-4101 [13174]

Mastermans, PO Box 411, Auburn, MA 01501-0411, (508)755-7861 [18902]

Masterpiece Crystal, PO Drawer A, Jane Lew, WV 26378, (304)884-7841 [15580]

Masters Supply Inc., PO Box 34337, Louisville, KY 40232, (502)459-2900 [23254]

Mastoloni and Sons Inc.; Frank, 608 5th Ave., New York, NY 10020, (212)757-7278 [17516]

Matanuska Maid Dairy, 814 Northern Lights, Anchorage, AK 99503, (907)561-5223 [11802]

Matarazzo Brothers Company Inc., 290 4th St., Chelsea, MA 02150, (617)889-0516 [11803]

Matco Tools Corp., 4403 Allen Rd., Stow, OH 44224, (330)929-4949 [2922]

Material Handling Services Inc., 315 E Fullerton Ave., Carol Stream, IL 60188, (630)665-7200 [16272]

Material Sales Company Inc., 25885 W 8 Mile Rd., Redford, MI 48240-1047, (313)534-1320 [17019]

Material Service Corp., 222 N La Salle St., Chicago, IL 60601-1090, (312)372-3600 [7665]

Material Supply Inc., 255 Airport Rd., New Castle, DE 19720, (302)633-5600 [7666]

Materials Handling Equipment Corp., 7433 U.S Hwy. 30 E, Ft. Wayne, IN 46803, (219)749-0475 [16273]

Matex Products, Inc., 14812 Detroit Ave., Cleveland, OH 44107, (216)228-9911 [20157]

Matheny Motor Truck Co., 3rd St. & Anne St., Parkersburg, WV 26101, (304)485-4418 [2923]

Matheson Trucking Inc.; R.B., 10519 E Stockton Blvd., No. 125, Elk Grove, CA 95624, (916)685-2330 [2924]

Matheus Lumber Company Inc., 15800 Woodinville Redmond Rd. NE, PO Box 2260, Woodinville, WA 98072-2260, (206)284-7500 [7667]

Mathews Enterprises, 2345 Filbert St., Ste. 204, San Francisco, CA 94123, (415)563-1595 [17517]

Mathews; Manfred, 612 Civic Center Dr., Augusta, ME 04330-9439, (207)622-9400 [7668]

Mathews and Sons Inc.; G.D., 521 Medford St., Boston, MA 02129, (617)242-1770 [11804]

Mathewson Co.; George A., 415 Raymond Blvd., Newark, NJ 07105, (973)344-0081 [2925]

Mathias and Company Inc., PO Box 67, Petersburg, WV 26847, (304)257-1611 [11805]

Mathias Reprographics, 950 Penn Ave., Pittsburgh, PA 15222-3706, (412)281-1800 [25726]

Mathie Supply Inc., 4215 Portage St. NW, North Canton, OH 44720, (330)499-2575 [7669]

Matlow Company Inc., 333 Bridge St., Solvay, NY 13209, (315)488-3171 [26899]

Matrix Aviation Inc., 1701 S Hoover Rd., Wichita, KS 67209, (316)942-0844 [120]

Matt Friend Truck Equipment Inc., Hastings Industrial Park E, Bldg. SH66, Hastings, NE 68902-1083, (402)463-5675 [2926]

Matt-Son Inc., 28W005 Industrial Ave., Barrington, IL 60010, (847)382-7810 [23255]

Matthes and Associates, PO Box 50, Maryland Heights, MO 63043-9050, (314)569-3030 [11806]

Matthews and Associates Inc., 16000 Dallas Pkwy., No. 235, Dallas, TX 75248-1145, (972)385-3773 [22996]

Matthews Book Co., 11559 Rock Island Ct., Maryland Heights, MO 63043, (314)432-1400 [3940]

Matthews Brothers Wholesale Inc., PO Box 1186, Clarksburg, WV 26301, (304)624-7601 [22456]

Matthews Electric Supply Company Inc., 3317 5th Ave. S, Birmingham, AL 35201, (205)254-3192 [9046]

Matthews and Fields Lumber of Henrietta, 1230 Lehigh Station Rd., Henrietta, NY 14467, (716)334-5500 [7670]

Matthews Hinsman Co., 3821 Olive St., St. Louis, MO 63108-3488, (314)531-6554 [26138]

Matthews International Corp., Marking Systems Div., 6515 Penn Ave., Pittsburgh, PA 15206, (412)665-2500 [16274]

Matthews-McCoy, 11559 Rock Island Ct., Maryland Heights, MO 63043, (314)432-1400 [3940]

Matthews Medical Books, 11559 Rock Island Ct., Maryland Heights, MO 63043, (314)432-1400 [3940]

Matthews Paint Co., 8201 100th St., Kenosha, WI 53142-7739, (262)947-0700 [21497]

Mattingly Foods Inc., PO Box 2668, Zanesville, OH 43702-2668, (740)454-0136 [11807]

Mattingly Foods Inc., PO Box 2668, Zanesville, OH 43702-2668, (740)454-0136 [11808]

Mattos Inc., 4501 Beech Rd., Camp Springs, MD 20748, (301)423-1142 [21498]

Mattson Distributing Co.; Art, 11711 Fairview Ave., Boise, ID 83713, (208)375-4510 [25727]

Matz Paper Company, Inc., 14122 Aetna St., PO Box 195, Van Nuys, CA 91408-0195, (818)786-4153 [21825]

Maugansville Elevator and Lumber Company Inc., PO Box 278, Maugansville, MD 21767, (301)739-4220 [22457]

Maui Blooms, 300 Ohukoi Rd., Ste. C 304, Kihei, HI 96753, (808)874-0875 [14917]

Maui Potato Chip Factory, 295 Lalo Pl., Kahului, HI 96732-2915, (808)877-3652 [11809]

Maui and Sons Corp., PO Box 1251, Pacific Palisades, CA 90272-1251, (310)573-9499 [5174]

Maui Tropicals & Foliage, 1111 E Kuiaha Rd., Haiku, HI 96708, (808)572-9600 [14918]

Maumee Co., PO Box 621, Adrian, MI 49221-0621, (517)263-6791 [23808]

Mauney Hosiery Mills Inc., PO Box 1279, Kings Mountain, NC 28086, (704)739-3621 [5175]

Maurice Pincoffs Company Inc., PO Box 920919, Houston, TX 77292, (713)681-5461 [20158]

Maurice Sporting Goods, 1825 Shermer Rd., Northbrook, IL 60065, (847)480-7900 [23809]

Mauro Co.; A.G., 310 Alpha Dr., Pittsburgh, PA 15238, (412)782-6600 [13815]

Maury Farmers Cooperative, PO Box 860, Columbia, TN 38401, (931)388-0714 [992]

Mausner Equipment Company Inc., 651 Pierce Pl., East Meadow, NY 11554, (516)481-1600 [16275]

Mauston Farmers Cooperative, 310 Prairie St., Mauston, WI 53948, (608)847-5679 [993]

Mautino Distributing Company Inc., 500 N Richard St., Spring Valley, IL 61362, (815)664-4311 [1855]

Mautz Paint Co., PO Box 7068, Madison, WI 53707-7068, (608)255-1661 [21499]

Maverick Electric Supply Inc., 9239 King Arthur, Dallas, TX 75247-3609, (214)630-8191 [9047]

Maverick Ranch Lite Beef Inc., 5360 N Franklin St., Denver, CO 80216, (303)294-0146 [11810]

Maverick.com Inc., 117 S Cook St., Ste. 335, Barrington, IL 60010 [6469]

Max Nitzberg Inc., 11800 NW 102nd Rd., Medley, FL 33178, (305)883-8677 [5176]

Max Scrap Metals Inc., 21608 Nordhoff St., Chatsworth, CA 91311, (818)709-4100 [26900]

Maxam Corp., 1117 Maurice Rd., Broussard, LA 70518, (318)364-5536 [22458]

Maxcare International Inc., 1626 Delaware Ave., Des Moines, IA 50317, (515)265-6565 [19426]

Maxco Inc., PO Box 80737, Lansing, MI 48908, (517)321-3130 [20159]

Maxell Corporation of America, 22-08 Rte. 208 S, Fair Lawn, NJ 07410, (201)794-5900 [25306]

Maxey System Inc., 5910 Youree Dr., Ste. D, Shreveport, LA 71105-4255, (318)868-5422 [6470]

Maxi Switch Inc., 2901 E Elvira Rd., Tucson, AZ 85706, (520)294-5450 [6471]

Maxim Inc.; Mary, PO Box 5019, Port Huron, MI 48061-5019, (810)987-2000 [26570]

Maxima Electrical Sales Company Inc., PO Box 398, Shawnee Mission, KS 66201, (913)722-1591 [9048]

Maxim's Import Corp., 2719 NW 24th St., Miami, FL 33142, (305)633-2167 [11811]

Maximum Performance, 17551 E Tennessee Dr., Aurora, CO 80017, (303)368-4124 [6472]

Maxtec International Corp., 175 Wall St., Glendale Heights, IL 60139-1956, (773)889-1448 [9049]

Maxwell Microsystems Inc., 552 S 14th Ct, Brighton, CO 80601, (303)252-4561 [6473]

Maxwell Shoe Company Inc., PO Box 37, Readville, MA 02137, (617)364-5090 [24803]

May & Company Inc., PO Box 1111, Jackson, MS 39215-1111, (601)354-5781 [15218]

May Company Inc.; W.L., 1120 Southeast Madison St., PO Box 14368, Portland, OR 97214, (503)231-9398 [15219]

May Engineering Company Inc., 51 Washington Ave., Cranston, RI 02920-7828, (401)942-4221 [24179]

May Steel Corp., 100 Continental Dr., Columbus, WI 53925, (920)623-2540 [20160]

Mayar Silk Inc., 15 W 36th St., New York, NY 10018, (212)564-1380 [26139]

Mayco Fish Company Ltd., 2535 Jefferson Ave., Tacoma, WA 98402-1303, (253)572-3070 [11812]

Maycor Appliance Parts and Service Co., 240 Edwards St. SE, Cleveland, TN 37311, (423)472-3333 [15220]

Maye Hosiery Sales, 3408 Eastway Dr., Charlotte, NC 28205-6269, (704)537-5141 [24804]

Mayer Co.; Budd, 4429 Shores Dr., Metairie, LA 70006-2329, (504)885-6870 [11813]

Mayer Electric Co., 3405 4th Ave. S, Birmingham, AL 35222-2300, (205)583-3500 [9050]

Mayer Electric Supply Co., 3405 4th Ave. S, Birmingham, AL 35222-2300, (205)583-3500 [9050]

Mayer Electric Supply Co., PO Box 1328, Birmingham, AL 35201, (205)583-3500 [9051]

Mayer Electric Supply Company Inc., 3405 4th Ave. S, PO Box 1328, Birmingham, AL 35222, (205)583-3500 [9052]

Mayer-Hammant Equipment Inc., PO Box 733, Harvey, LA 70059, (504)368-4277 [9053]

Mayer Myers Paper Co., 1769 Latham St., Memphis, TN 38106, (901)948-5631 [21826]

Mayers Jewelry Company Inc., 2004 Grant St., Hollywood, FL 33020-3546, (954)921-1422 [17518]

Mayes Brothers Tool Manufacturing, 713 Clairmont Rd., Johnson City, TN 37605, (423)926-6171 [13816]

Mayes County Petroleum Products, 1600 N 11th St., Muskogee, OK 74401, (918)682-9924 [22459]

Mayfield Building Supply Co., PO Box 398, Arlington, TX 76010, (817)640-1234 [7671]

Mayfield & Co. Inc., 3101 W Clearwater Ave., Kennewick, WA 99336-2738, (509)735-8525 [23810]

Mayfield Lumber and Container Corp., PO Box 148, El Paso, TX 79942, (915)532-1483 [23811]

Mayfield Pool Supply L.L.C., PO Box 148, El Paso, TX 79942, (915)532-1483 [23811]

Mayfield Timber Co., PO Box 223, Toxey, AL 36921, (205)843-5543 [27341]

Mayflower Wines & Spirits, 3201 New Mexico Ave. NW, Washington, DC 20016, (202)363-5800 [1856]

Mayhew Steel Products, PO Box 88, Shelburne Falls, MA 01370, (413)625-6351 [13817]

Maynard Cooperative Co., PO Box 215, Maynard, IA 50655, (319)637-2285 [18076]

Mayo Seed Co.; D.R., PO Box 10247, Knoxville, TN 37939, (865)577-7568 [994]

Mays Chemical Co., 5611 E 71st St., Indianapolis, IN 46220, (317)842-8722 [19427]

Maytag Aircraft Corp., 6145 Lehman Dr., Ste. 300, Colorado Springs, CO 80918, (719)593-1600 [22460]

Maytag Corp., 403 W 4th St. N, Newton, IA 50208, (515)792-8000 [15221]

Maytown Shoe Manufacturing Company Inc., 1820 8th Ave., Altoona, PA 16602, (814)943-5343 [24805]

Maywood Cooperative Association, 103 Commercial St., Maywood, NE 69038, (308)362-4244 [995]

Maz Auto, 3800 San Pablo Ave., Emeryville, CA 94608-3814, (510)428-3950 [2927]

Mazda Motor of America Inc., PO Box 19734, Irvine, CA 92623, (714)727-1990 [20675]

Mazda North American Operations, 7755 Irvine Center Dr., Irvine, CA 92618, (714)727-1990 [20676]

Mazel Stores Inc., 31000 Aurora Rd., Solon, OH 44139, (440)248-5200 [25728]

Maznaim Publishers, 4304 12th Ave., Brooklyn, NY 11219, (718)438-7680 [3973]

Mazon Farmers Elevator, 604 South St., PO Box 361, Mazon, IL 60444, (815)448-2113 [996]

Mazon Farmers Elevator, 604 South St., Mazon, IL 60444, (815)448-2113 [11814]

Mazzei Injector Corp., 500 Rooster Dr., Bakersfield, CA 93307, (805)363-6500 [16276]

Mazzetta Co., 1990 St. Johns Ave., Highland Park, IL 60035 [11815]

MBI Inc., 1353 Arville St., Las Vegas, NV 89102-1608, (702)259-1999 [18903]

MBI Inc., 1353 Arville St., Las Vegas, NV 89102-1608, (702)259-1999 [19428]

MBI X-Ray & Medical Supply, 1353 Arville St., Las Vegas, NV 89102-1608, (702)259-1999 [18903]

MBL USA Corp., 601 Dayton Rd., Ottawa, IL 61350, (815)434-1282 [24286]

M.B.M. Corp., PO Box 800, Rocky Mount, NC 27802, (919)985-7200 [11816]

MBM Corp. (Charleston, South Carolina), PO Box 40249, Charleston, SC 29423-0249, (843)552-2700 [16277]

MBS/Net, Inc., 735 Beta Dr., Ste. C, Cleveland, OH 44143-2326, (440)461-7650 [6474]

MBS Textbook Exchange Inc., 2711 W Ash St., Columbia, MO 65203, (573)445-2243 [3941]

MBT International Inc., PO Box 30819, Charleston, SC 29417, (843)763-9083 [25307]

MC Industries, 1900 E Holland Ave., PO Box 1567, Saginaw, MI 48605-1567, (517)753-4405 [21846]

M.C. International, 455 Market St., Ste. 210, San Francisco, CA 94105, (415)836-6760 [19429]

MC Sales, 5070 Santa Fe St., San Diego, CA 92109, (858)490-5100 [26571]

Mc-U Sports, 822 W Jefferson St., Boise, ID 83702-5826, (208)342-7734 [23812]

McAbee Medical Inc., 1401 6th Ave. SE, Decatur, AL 35601-4200, (205)351-7747 [18904]

McAdams Pipe and Supply Co., PO Box 428, Muskogee, OK 74402, (918)682-1323 [22461]

McAlister Camera Co.; Don, 1454 W Lane Ave., Columbus, OH 43221, (614)488-1865 [22876]

McAllister Equipment Co., 12500 S Cicero Ave., Alsip, IL 60803, (708)389-7700 [7672]

McArthur Towels, Inc., 700 Moore St., Box 448, Baraboo, WI 53913, (608)356-8922 [15581]

McArthur Towels Inc., 700 Moore St., Baraboo, WI 53913, (608)356-8922 [15582]

McAuliffe Inc.; Howard, 15 Industrial Park Pl., Middletown, CT 06457-1501, (860)632-2678 [25308]

McBain Instruments, 9601 Variel Ave., Chatsworth, CA 91311, (818)998-2702 [24395]

McBax Ltd., 3501 Pearl St., Boulder, CO 80301, (303)442-6000 [22462]

McBee Grain and Trucking Inc., PO Box 74, Bluffton, OH 45817, (419)358-5931 [18077]

McBride and Associates Inc., PO Box 94090, Albuquerque, NM 87199-4090, (505)883-0600 [6475]

McBride Distributing Co., PO Box 1403, Fayetteville, AR 72702-0336, (501)521-2500 [1857]

McBride Distributing Inc.; J.B., 760 Iron St., Butte, MT 59701, (406)782-3034 [22463]

McBride Insulation Co., PO Box 358, Heyburn, ID 83336-0358, (208)678-9048 [7673]

McBroom Pool Products Inc., 2025 George Washington Memorial Hwy., Yorktown, VA 23692-4222, (757)874-1699 [23813]

McCabe Bait Company Inc., PO Box 190, Kennebunkport, ME 04046-0190, (207)967-2409 [23814]

McCabe Equipment Inc., PO Box 5550, Coralville, IA 52241-0550, (319)351-0828 [997]

McCabe's Quality Foods Inc., 17600 NE San Rafael St., Portland, OR 97230-5924, (503)256-4770 [11817]

McCall Fireworks Inc., PO Box 40, McAlester, OK 74502-0040, (918)423-3343 [26572]

McCall Oil and Chemical Co., 826 SW 15th Ave., Portland, OR 97205, (503)228-2600 [22464]

McCall Woodworks Inc., 861 Timber Ridge, Mc Call, ID 83638-5133, (208)634-2378 [13175]

McCallum Motor Supply Co., PO Box 216, Unionville, CT 06085, (860)677-2611 [2928]

McCann Construction Specialties Co., 543 Rohlwing Rd., Addison, IL 60101, (630)627-0000 [7674]

McCann Industries, Inc., 543 Rohlwing Rd., Addison, IL 60101, (630)627-0000 [7674]

McCarthy Drapery Company Inc., 909 Glencastle Way, Raleigh, NC 27606-3475, (919)834-1928 [15583]

McCarthy Steel Inc., PO Box 1887, Bakersfield, CA 93303, (805)324-6715 [20161]

McCarthy Tire Service, 987 Stony Battery Rd., Lancaster, PA 17603, (717)898-0114 [2929]

McCartney Carpet, 110 E Pioneer Park Rd., Westfield, WI 53964, (608)296-4444 [10013]

McCarty-Holman Company Inc., PO Box 3409, Jackson, MS 39207, (601)948-0361 [11818]

McCarty & Son; H.J., PO Box 1359, Newburyport, MA 01950-8357, (978)462-8111 [15584]

McCaughey Brothers, 500 Bay Flat Rd., Bodega Bay, CA 94923, (707)875-3935 [18564]

McCauley's Reprographics, Inc., 721 Gaffney Rd., Fairbanks, AK 99701, (907)452-8141 [24396]

McCausey Lumber Co., 32205 Little Mack, Roseville, MI 48066, (810)294-9663 [7675]

McChesney Co.; C.E., PO Box 236, Gladstone, IL 61437, (309)627-2374 [18078]

McClain Printing Co., PO Box 403, Parsons, WV 26287, (304)478-2881 [3942]

McClaskeys Wine Spirits & Cigars Distributor, 930 NW 14th Ave., Portland, OR 97209-2704, (503)224-3150 [1858]

McClendons Boot Store, 217 N Main St., McAlester, OK 74501-4650, (918)426-3291 [24806]

McClesky Mills Inc., Rhodes St., Smithville, GA 31787, (912)846-2003 [11819]

McClesky Mills Inc., 292 Rhodes St., Smithville, GA 31787, (912)846-2003 [18079]

McClintock and Bustad Inc., 25133 W Ave. Tibbitts, Valencia, CA 91355, (818)893-4609 [14534]

McClung Equipment Co., PO Box 1316, Mountain View, AR 72560, (870)269-3866 [998]

McComas Sales Co. Inc., 2315 4th St. NW, Albuquerque, NM 87102, (505)243-5263 [24180]

McComb Wholesale Paper Co., PO Box 463, McComb, MS 39649, (601)684-5521 [21827]

McComb Wholesale Paper Co., PO Box 463, McComb, MS 39649, (601)684-5521 [17020]

McCombs Supply Co., 815 S 26th St., Harrisburg, PA 17111, (717)558-7571 [15222]

McCombs Supply Company Inc., 346 N Marshall St., Lancaster, PA 17604, (717)299-3866 [15223]

McConkey and Company Inc.; J.M., PO Box 1690, Sumner, WA 98390, (253)863-8111 [14919]

McConnell and Sons Inc.; F., PO Box 417, New Haven, IN 46774, (219)493-6607 [11820]

McCord Auto Supply Inc., PO Box 743, Monticello, IN 47960, (219)583-4136 [2930]

McCorkle Cricket Farm Inc., PO Box 285, Metter, GA 30439-0285, (912)685-2677 [23815]

McCormick Beverage Co., PO Box 1346, Woodland, CA 95776-1346, (916)666-3263 [1859]

McCormick Co.; J.S., 650 Smiriges St., Ste. 1050, Pittsburgh, PA 15222-3907, (412)471-7246 [20553]

McCormick Distilling Company Inc., 1 McCormick Ln., Weston, MO 64098, (816)386-2276 [1860]

McCormick Refrigeration, 1600 Front St., Anniston, AL 36201, (205)831-2271 [14535]

McCoy Cattle Co.; M.W., PO Box 1781, Billings, MT 59103-1781, (406)248-7331 [18080]

McCoy and Company Inc.; Lawrence R., 100 Front St., Ste. 700, Worcester, MA 01608-1444, (508)368-7700 [7676]

McCoy and Company Inc.; Lawrence R., 100 Front St., No. 700, Worcester, MA 01608-1444, (508)798-7575 [27342]

McCoy and Son Inc.; J.B., PO Box 9256, Canton, OH 44711, (330)456-8261 [21828]

McCraken Livestock Inc., RR 2, Box 244, St. Albans, VT 05478-9802, (802)524-2991 [18081]

McCranie Motor and Tractor Inc., U.S Hwy. 41 S, Unadilla, GA 31091-0408, (912)627-3291 [999]

McCranie Motor and Tractor Inc. McCranie Implement Co., Hwy. 341 N, Hawkinsville, GA 31036, (912)892-9046 [1000]

McCray Lumber Co., 10741 Del Monte Ln., Overland Park, KS 66211, (913)341-6900 [7677]

McCrone Associates, PO Box 8439, Warwick, RI 02888-0597, (401)738-3115 [17519]

McCrudden Heating Supply, 523 Williamson, Youngstown, OH 44502, (330)744-4108 [14536]

McCubbin Hosiery Inc., 3B93 Apparel Mart, PO Box 585577, Dallas, TX 75258, (214)637-5224 [5177]

McCubbin Hosiery Inc., PO Box 24047, Oklahoma City, OK 73124-0047, (405)236-8351 [5178]

McCullagh Inc.; S.J., 245 Swan St., Buffalo, NY 14204, (716)856-3473 [11821]

McCullar Enterprises Inc., 1850 Gen. George Patton, Franklin, TN 37067, (615)371-1056 [24807]

McCullar Enterprises Inc., 1850 Gen. George Patton, Franklin, TN 37067, (615)371-1056 [5179]

McCullough Ceramic, 4801 Kellywood Dr., Glen Allen, VA 23060-3642, (804)747-8300 [10014]

McCullough Distributing Company, Inc., 5613-23 Tulip St., Philadelphia, PA 19124-1626, (215)288-9700 [2931]

McCullough Electric Co., 419 Ft. Pitt Blvd., Pittsburgh, PA 15219, (412)261-2420 [9054]

McCune Farmers Union Cooperative Association, PO Box 58, McCune, KS 66753, (316)632-4226 [1001]

McDaniels Sales Co., 16839 S US 27, Lansing, MI 48906, (517)482-0748 [15224]

McDATA Corp., 310 Interlocken Pkwy., Broomfield, CO 80021, (303)460-9200 [6476]

McDermott Co. Inc.; A.I., 2009 Jackson St., Oshkosh, WI 54901, (920)231-7080 [23256]

McDermott Corp.; Julian A., 1639 Stephen St., Flushing, NY 11385-5345, (718)456-3606 [24588]

McDermott Food Brokers Inc., PO Box 13300, Albany, NY 12212, (518)783-8844 [11822]

McDiarmid Controls Inc., 85579 Highway 99 S, Eugene, OR 97405, (541)726-1677 [9055]

McDonald Candy Company Inc., 2350 W Broadway St., Eugene, OR 97402, (541)345-8421 [11823]

McDonald Equipment Co., 37200 Vine St., Willoughby, OH 44094-6346, (440)951-8222 [9056]

McDonald Farms, Inc., 2313 Middle Rd., Winchester, VA 22601-2755, (540)662-1057 [11824]

McDonald Industries Inc., PO Box 88000, Seattle, WA 98138, (206)872-3500 [7678]

McDonald Livestock Co., 851 Arena Rd., West Fargo, ND 58078, (701)282-3206 [18082]

McDonald Lumber Company Inc., 126 Cedar Creek Rd., Fayetteville, NC 28302, (910)483-0381 [7679]

McDonald Supply Co.; A.Y., PO Box 1364, Joplin, MO 64801, (417)623-7740 [14537]

McDonald Supply Company Inc.; A.Y., PO Box 708, Dubuque, IA 52004-0708, (319)583-2558 [23257]

McDonald & Woodward Publishing, PO Box 10308, Blacksburg, VA 24062-0308, (540)951-9465 [3943]

McDonough Brothers, PO Box 249, Fairmont, WV 26555, (304)366-3279 [11825]

McDougall Company Inc.; John W., PO Box 90447, Nashville, TN 37209, (615)321-3900 [7680]

McDow & Sons Salvage; V.H., PO Box 208, Grafton, NH 03240-0208, (603)523-4555 [2932]

McElheney, Inc.; R.H., 16975 Westview Ave., South Holland, IL 60473, (708)596-3010 [27185]

McEllin Company, Inc., 17 Water St., Waltham, MA 02454, (781)647-9322 [10015]

MCF Systems Atlanta Inc., 5353 Snapfinger Woods, Decatur, GA 30035, (404)593-9434 [4665]

McFadden Inc.; Mary, 240 W 35th St., New York, NY 10001-2506, (212)736-4078 [5180]

McFadden Wholesale Company Inc.; F.B., 415 Railroad Ave., Rock Springs, WY 82901, (307)362-5441 [4666]

McFarlane Manufacturing Company Inc., PO Box 100, Sauk City, WI 53583-0100, (608)643-3321 [1002]

McFarling Foods Inc., 333 W 14th St., Indianapolis, IN 46202, (317)635-2633 [11826]

McGary Optical Co.; F.H., PO Box 675, Bangor, ME 04402-0675, (207)945-6429 [19430]

McGeary Grain Inc., PO Box 299, Lancaster, PA 17608, (717)394-6843 [18083]

McGee Eye Fashions Inc., 510 Commerce Park Dr., Marietta, GA 30060-2719, (404)422-0010 [19431]

McGee's Packing Co., Rte. J, Mexico, MO 65265, (573)581-4145 [11827]

McGehee & Associates; Thomas, PO Box 7331, Macon, GA 31209-7331, (912)471-0020 [6477]

McGill & Co.; P., 416 N Glendale Ave., Glendale, CA 91206-3398, (818)247-2552 [11828]

McGill Distributors, 1903 Longstreet St. N, Kingstree, SC 29556, (803)354-7404 [18565]

McGill Hose and Coupling Inc., PO Box 408, East Longmeadow, MA 01028, (413)525-3977 [17021]

McGinley Inc.; Wilson, 36th & Allegheny R. R., Pittsburgh, PA 15201, (412)621-4420 [1861]

McGinnis Farms Inc., 5610 McGinnis Ferry Rd., Alpharetta, GA 30022, (404)740-1874 [1003]

McGinnis Lumber Company Inc., PO Box 2049, Meridian, MS 39302, (601)483-3991 [7681]

McGlaun Office Supply Co.; Frank, PO Box 3098, Lubbock, TX 79452, (806)766-8888 [21031]

McGowan Electric Supply Inc., PO Box 765, Jackson, MI 49204, (517)782-9301 [9057]

McGraw-Curran Lumber Co., 1200 Rialto Rd., PO Box 450, Yazoo City, MS 39194, (601)746-1661 [7547]

McGraw Group Inc., 576 Griffith Rd., Charlotte, NC 28217, (704)525-9423 [17022]

McGraw Inc.; James, PO Box 85620, Richmond, VA 23285, (804)233-3071 [17023]

McGraw Inc.; James, PO Box 85620, Richmond, VA 23285, (804)233-3071 [16278]

McGuffy Company Inc.; Lynn, 18635 Telge Rd., Cypress, TX 77429-1362, (281)255-6955 [25729]

McGuire Bearing, 2611 BW 5th Ave., Eugene, OR 97402, (541)343-0820 [2933]

McGuire Bearing, 947 SE Market St., Portland, OR 97214, (503)238-1570 [2934]

McGuire Bearing, 5516 1st Ave. S, Seattle, WA 98108, (206)767-3283 [17024]

McGuire Bearing, 4230 E Mission Ave., Spokane, WA 99202-4407, (509)535-1511 [17025]

McGuire Furniture Co., 151 Vermont St., San Francisco, CA 94103-5020, (415)986-0812 [13176]

McGuire-Nicholas Co., Inc., PMB 170, 1175 Baker St., Ste. D13, Costa Mesa, CA 92626-4139, (213)722-6961 [17026]

McGuire Sun & Fitness Inc., 770 Tyvola Rd., Charlotte, NC 28217-3508, (704)522-9219 [23992]

McGuire Sun and Fitness Inc., 770 Tyvola Rd., Charlotte, NC 28217-3508, (704)523-2401 [23816]

McGuir Oil Company Inc., PO Box 2010, Bowling Green, KY 42101, (502)842-2188 [22465]

McIlvain Co.; Alan, 5th & Market St., Marcus Hook, PA 19061, (215)485-6240 [7682]

McIlvain Co.; T. Baird, 100 Filbert St., Hanover, PA 17331-9045, (717)630-0025 [7683]

McInerney-Miller Brothers Inc., 2001 Brewster St., Detroit, MI 48207, (313)833-4800 [11829]

McIntosh and Associates Inc.; Ron, 853 26th St., Santa Monica, CA 90403, (310)828-5694 [121]

McIntosh Cooperative Creamery, 245 State St., McIntosh, MN 56556, (218)563-2555 [11830]

McJunkin Appalachian Oil Field Supply Co., PO Box 513, Charleston, WV 25322, (304)348-5847 [22466]

McJunkin Corp., U.S 460 E, Princeton, WV 24740, (304)425-7594 [9058]

McJunkin Corp., PO Box 513, Charleston, WV 25322, (304)348-5211 [17027]

McKay Nursery Company Inc., PO Box 185, Waterloo, WI 53594, (920)478-2121 [14920]

McKee Brothers Inc., PO Box 490, Saddle River, NJ 07458-0490, (201)327-0850 [7684]

McKee Enterprises Inc., 1425 41st St. NW, Fargo, ND 58102-2822, (701)281-1600 [10016]

McKee Enterprises Inc., 2785 Hwy. 55, St. Paul, MN 55121, (612)454-1700 [10017]

McKee-Pitts Industrials Inc., 506 N 2nd St., Ft. Smith, AR 72901, (501)782-0373 [16279]

McKenney Supply Inc., 106 E Pleasure St., Searcy, AR 72143-7710, (501)268-8422 [14538]

McKenzie; C.D., PO Box 1552, Fallon, NV 89407-1552, (702)423-1599 [7685]

McKenzie Co.; P.C., PO Box 112638, Pittsburgh, PA 15241, (412)257-8866 [16280]

McKenzie Galleries and Commercial, 3200 W Dallas Ave., Houston, TX 77019-3803, (713)528-1561 [13177]

McKesson Drug, PO Box 27088, Salt Lake City, UT 84127-0088, (801)977-9500 [19432]

McKesson Drug Co., 1 Post St., San Francisco, CA 94104, (415)983-8300 [19433]

McKesson Drug Co., 1 Post St., San Francisco, CA 94104, (415)983-8300 [19434]

McKesson General Medical Corp., PO Box 27452, Richmond, VA 23228, (804)264-7500 [18905]

McKesson HBOC Inc., 1 Post St., San Francisco, CA 94104, (415)983-8300 [19435]

McKesson Health Systems, 1 Post St., San Francisco, CA 94104, (415)983-8300 [19436]

McKesson Pharmaceutical Inc., PO Box 1831, Phoenix, AZ 85001, (602)272-7916 [19437]

McKim Group, 225 Riverview Ave., Waltham, MA 02454, (781)647-5560 [13818]

McKittrick Company Inc.; Frank G.W., PO Box 929, North Chelmsford, MA 01863, (978)458-6391 [16281]

McKnight Sales Company Inc., 540 California Ave., PO Box 4138, Pittsburgh, PA 15202, (412)761-4443 [3944]

McLain Oil Company Inc., PO Box 1393, Lubbock, TX 79408, (806)762-0432 [22467]

McLane Company Inc., PO Box 6115, Temple, TX 76503-6115, (254)771-7500 [11831]

McLane Company Inc. High Plains, PO Box 5550, Lubbock, TX 79408-5550, (806)766-2966 [11832]

McLane Group Interntional L.P., 455 Market St., Ste. #210, San Francisco, CA 94105, (415)543-1455 [11833]

McLane Southwest, Inc., PO Box 6116, Temple, TX 76503-6116, (254)770-2800 [11834]

McLane Western, Inc., 2100 E Highway 119, Longmont, CO 80504, (303)682-7500 [11835]

McLaughlin Distributor; J.E., 155 Porter Pl., Rutland, VT 05701, (802)773-6258 [7686]

McLaughlin Industrial Distributors Inc., 7141 Paramount Blvd., Pico Rivera, CA 90660, (213)723-2411 [13819]

McLaughlin Livestock Auction, PO Box 559, Mc Laughlin, SD 57642-0559, (605)823-4821 [18084]

McLaughlin and Moran Inc., PO Box 20217, Cranston, RI 02920, (401)463-5454 [1862]

McLean County Service Co., 402 N Hershey Rd., Bloomington, IL 61701-1367, (309)662-9321 [1004]

McLean County Truck Company Inc., PO Box 102, Bloomington, IL 61702-0102, (309)662-1331 [20677]

McLean International Marketing Inc., PO Box 535, Mequon, WI 53092, (262)242-0958 [24589]

McLean International Marketing Inc., PO Box 535, Mequon, WI 53092, (414)242-0958 [17028]

McLeier Oil Inc., PO Box 2977, Kalamazoo, MI 49003-2977, (616)343-7677 [22468]

McLemore Wholesale and Retail Inc., PO Box 3409, Jackson, MS 39207, (601)948-0361 [11836]

McLendon Co., 1200 Dallas Trade Mart, Dallas, TX 75207, (214)748-1555 [11837]

McLendon Hardware Inc., 710 S 2nd St., Renton, WA 98055, (206)235-3555 [13820]

McLeod Mercantile Inc., Hwy. 287, Alder, MT 59710, (406)842-5495 [22469]

McLeod Mercantile Inc. Conoco, Jct. 84 and Hwy. 287, Norris, MT 59745, (406)685-3379 [22470]

McLeod Optical Company Inc., PO Box 6045, Providence, RI 02940-6045, (401)467-3000 [19438]

McLogan Supply, 711 S East St., Anaheim, CA 92805, (714)999-1194 [25730]

McLogan Supply, 2010 S Main, Los Angeles, CA 90007, (213)749-2262 [25731]

McLogan Supply, 7609 Convoy Ct., San Diego, CA 92111, (619)292-5664 [25732]

MCM Enterprise, PO Box 1001, Reno, NV 89504, (702)356-5601 [2935]

McMahon Foodservice Outlet, 2835 Madison Ave., Indianapolis, IN 46225-2405 [11838]

McMahon Paper Company Inc., PO Box 10162, Ft. Wayne, IN 46805, (219)422-3491 [21829]

McMann Loudan Farmers Cooperative, 15 East Ave., Athens, TN 37303-1619, (423)745-0443 [1005]

McMaster-Carr Supply Co. California, PO Box 54960, Los Angeles, CA 90054, (562)692-5911 [13821]

McMillan Conroy Machinery, PO Box 3069, Milford, CT 06460, (203)882-5301 [16282]

McMillan Sales Corp., 4801 E 46th, Denver, CO 80216, (303)399-8500 [23258]

McMillan-Shuller Oil Company Inc., PO Box 590, Fayetteville, NC 28302, (910)484-7196 [22471]

McMurray Co.; Charles, 2520 N Argyle, Fresno, CA 93727, (559)292-5751 [13822]

McMurray Printing Co., 175 Main, Brookville, PA 15825-1233, (814)849-5338 [25733]

McNabb Grain Co., PO Box 128, McNabb, IL 61335, (815)882-2131 [11839]

McNaughton-McKay Electric Company, 1011 E 5th Ave., Flint, MI 48501, (810)238-5611 [9059]

McNaughton-McKay Electric Company Inc., 1357 E Lincoln Ave., Madison Heights, MI 48071, (810)399-7500 [9060]

McNeil Marketing Co., 709 Vista Ter. Dr., Nampa, ID 83686, (208)466-7403 [1006]

McNichols Co., PO Box 30300, Tampa, FL 33630-3300, (813)289-4100 [20162]

McNutt Hosiery; Danny, Box 946, Ft. Payne, AL 35967, (205)845-4422 [5181]

McPhails Inc., PO Box 1789, Rohnert Park, CA 94927-1789, (707)769-9800 [15225]

McPherson & Co. Publishers, PO Box 1126, Kingston, NY 12402, (914)331-5807 [3945]

McQuade Distributing Company, Inc., 1150 Industrial Dr., Bismarck, ND 58501, (701)223-6850 [1863]

McQuade Distributing Company Inc., 1150 Industrial Dr., Bismarck, ND 58501, (701)223-6850 [1864]

McQueary Brothers Drug Co., PO Box 5955, Springfield, MO 65801, (417)869-2577 [18906]

McQuesten Company Inc.; Geo., 600 Iron Horse Park, North Billerica, MA 01862, (978)663-3435 [27343]

McQuiddy Office Designers Inc., 110 7th Ave. N, Nashville, TN 37203, (615)256-5643 [21134]

McRae Industries Inc., 402 N Main St., Mt. Gilead, NC 27306, (910)439-6147 [21135]

McWong International Inc.; M.W., 2544 Industrial Blvd., West Sacramento, CA 95691, (916)371-8080 [9061]

MD Foods Ingredients Inc., 2840 Morris Ave., Union, NJ 07083, (908)964-4420 [24181]

MDC Industries Inc., Collins St. & Willard St., PO Box 12730, Philadelphia, PA 19134-0730, (215)426-5925 [17029]

MDG Inc., PO Box 17387, Denver, CO 80217, (303)662-7100 [24182]

MDI Production, PO Box 61056, Honolulu, HI 96839, (808)988-6116 [25734]

MDR Corp., 101 Parsons Ave., Endicott, NY 13760, (607)754-2393 [21136]

M.E. Carter of Jonesboro Inc., PO Box 217, Jonesboro, AR 72403, (870)932-6668 [11840]

M.E. O'Brien and Sons Inc., 93 West St., Medfield, MA 02052-2043, (508)359-4200 [23817]

Mead Corp. Zellerbach Paper Co., 50 E Rivercenter Blvd., Ste. 700, Covington, KY 41011-1626 [21830]

Mead Pulp Sales Inc., Courthouse Plz. NE, Dayton, OH 45463, (937)222-6323 [21831]

Meade Hosiery; Elizabeth, PO Box 1031, Burlington, NC 27216-1031, (919)226-7216 [5182]

Meadow Gold Dairies, 420 Nora, Missoula, MT 59801-8057, (406)543-3173 [11841]

Meadow Gold Dairy, 4820 Forge Rd., Colorado Springs, CO 80907-3523, (719)599-8844 [11842]

Meadow Steel Products Div., 5110 Santa Fe Rd., Tampa, FL 33619, (813)248-1944 [7687]

Meadowbrook Distributing Corp., 550 New Horizons Blvd., Amityville, NY 11701-1166, (516)228-8200 [24987]

Meadows Company Inc.; Ben, PO Box 20200, Canton, GA 30114-1920, (404)455-0907 [1007]

Meares & Son Inc.; Ellis, PO Box 187, Fair Bluff, NC 28439-0187, (910)649-7521 [15226]

Meat Processors Inc., 2210 Hutson Rd., Green Bay, WI 54307-1327, (920)499-4841 [11843]

MEBCO Contractors Supplies, 757 Front St., Berea, OH 44017-1608, (440)234-5854 [13823]

Meca Sportswear Inc., Lincoln St., Ontario, WI 54651, (608)337-4436 [5183]

Mechanical Drives Co., 3015 Leonis Blvd., Los Angeles, CA 90058, (323)587-7901 [2936]

Mechanical Drives Inc., 1510 E 26th St., Chattanooga, TN 37401, (423)622-1153 [16283]

Mechanical Equipment Company Inc., PO Box 689, Matthews, NC 28106, (704)847-2100 [16284]

Mechanical Finishing Co., PO Box 1872, Meriden, CT 06450-1872, (203)235-4412 [16285]

Mechanical Refrigeration & AC, PO Box 3627, Little Rock, AR 72203-3627, (501)455-3590 [14539]

Mechanical Services of Orlando Inc., 9440 Sidney Hayes Rd., Orlando, FL 32824, (407)857-3510 [14540]

Mechanic's Auto Parts, Inc., 1041 Glassboro Rd., Ste. F1, Williamstown, NJ 08094-0741, (856)875-6700 [2937]

Mechanics Building Materials Inc., 82-40 73rd Ave., Glendale, NY 11385, (718)381-6600 [7688]

Med-Co., 13540 Lake City Way, Seattle, WA 98125, (206)367-3128 [19189]

Med Con Ltd., 8621 Barefoot Industrial Rd., Raleigh, NC 27613, (919)783-6116 [19037]

Med Dent Service Corp., 25 Falmouth Rd., Falmouth, ME 04105-1841, (207)781-2293 [18907]

Med-Lab Supply Company Inc., 923 NW 27th Ave., Miami, FL 33125, (305)642-5144 [18908]

Med-Tech Inc., 32035 Edward Ave., Madison Heights, MI 48071-1419, (248)589-3109 [18909]

Med-X International, Inc., PO Box 101, Tenafly, NJ 07670, (201)387-8556 [19439]

Medal, Inc., 330 Vine Ave., Sharon, PA 16146, (724)342-6839 [13824]

Medalist America Turfgrass Seed Co., 1490 Industrial Way SW, Albany, OR 97321 [1008]

Medallion Carpets, 2434 Polvorosa Ave., San Leandro, CA 94577, (510)351-8104 [10018]

Medallion Carpets, 1583 Enterprise Blvd., West Sacramento, CA 95691, (916)372-8500 [10019]

Medart Inc., 124 Manufacturers Dr., Arnold, MO 63010-4727, (636)282-2300 [12843]

Meddev Corp., 2468 Embarcadero Way, Palo Alto, CA 94303-3313, (650)494-1153 [18910]

Medeiros Optical Service, 1118 Fort St. Mall, Honolulu, HI 96813-2707, (808)536-8243 [19440]

Medek Inc.; George M., 216 W 36th St., Boise, ID 83714-6531, (208)343-4343 [4667]

Medesto News Co., 1324 Coldwell Ave., Modesto, CA 95350-5702, (209)577-5551 [3514]

Medfax Corp., 1838 Gold Hill Rd., Ft. Mill, SC 29715, (803)548-1502 [6478]

Medford Co-operative Inc., PO Box 407, Medford, WI 54451-0407, (715)748-2056 [18085]

Medi-Globe Corp., 6202 S Maple Ave., Tempe, AZ 85283-2861, (602)897-2772 [18911]

Medi Inc., 75 york Ave., Randolph, MA 02368, (617)961-1232 [19441]

Medi Inc. - School Health Div., 75 York Ave., PO Box 302, Randolph, MA 02368, (781)961-1232 [18912]

Media Communications Corp., 3251 Old Lee Hwy., No. 412, Fairfax, VA 22030, (703)385-3430 [22877]

Media Concepts Inc., 559 49 St. S, St. Petersburg, FL 33707, (727)321-2122 [25309]

Media Recovery Inc., PO Box 1407, Graham, TX 76450, (940)549-5462 [6479]

Medica International Ltd., 360 N Michigan Ave., Ste. 2001, Chicago, IL 60601, (312)263-1117 [1009]

Medical Advisory Systems Inc., 8050 Southern Maryland Blvd., Owings, MD 20736, (410)257-9504 [19442]

Medical Business Systems Corp., 735 Beta Dr., Ste. C, Cleveland, OH 44143-2326, (440)461-7650 [6474]

Medical Devices Inc., 12211 Old Shelbyville Ra., Ste. C, Louisville, KY 40243, (502)244-5200 [18913]

Medical Dynamics Inc., 99 Inverness Dr.E, Englewood, CO 80112, (303)790-2990 [19443]

Medical Electronics Sales & Service, 338 N 16th St., Phoenix, AZ 85006-3706, (602)252-5891 [18690]

Medical Electronics Sales and Service, 338 N 16th St., Phoenix, AZ 85006-3706, (602)252-5891 [19444]

Medical Equipment Repair Services Inc., 6092 Clark Center Ave., Sarasota, FL 34238, (941)921-2584 [18914]

Medical Equipment Resale, Inc., 45031 Grand River, PO Box 7006, Novi, MI 48376-7006, (248)380-7951 [18915]

Medical Equipment Resale, Inc., 45031 Grand River, PO Box 7006, Novi, MI 48376-7006, (248)380-7951 [18915]

Medical Equipment Resale Inc., 45031 Grand River, Novi, MI 48376-7006, (248)380-7951 [19445]

Medical Imaging Inc., PO Box 4023, Camp Verde, AZ 86322-4023, (602)943-4759 [18916]

Medical Imaging Services Inc., 800 Central Ave., Jefferson, LA 70121-1305, (504)733-9729 [18917]

Medical International Inc., PO Box 166, Spring Lake, NJ 07762, (732)974-1550 [18918]

Medical Manager Sales and Marketing Inc., 500 Clyde Ave., Mountain View, CA 94043-2218, (415)969-7047 [6480]

Medical Marketing Inc., 1771 South 900 West, No. 50, Salt Lake City, UT 84104-1700, (801)977-0168 [18919]

Medical Mart Inc., 465-G S Herlong Ave., Rock Hill, SC 29732, (803)366-5544 [18920]

Medical Procedures Inc., 2223 Eastern Ave., Baltimore, MD 21231-3112, (410)522-3451 [18921]

Medical Scientific Service, 11004 Los Arboles Ave. NE, Albuquerque, NM 87112-1721, (505)298-6639 [18922]

Medical Specialists Company Inc., 7770 Iliff Ave., Ste. D, Denver, CO 80231-5326, (303)750-2002 [18923]

Medical Specialists Company Inc., 7770 Iliff Ave., Ste. D, Denver, CO 80231-5326, (303)750-2002 [19446]

Medical Specialties Company Inc., 58 Norfolk Ave., South Easton, MA 02375-0600, (508)238-8590 [19447]

Medical Supplies Inc., 146 Kennedy Memorial Dr., Waterville, ME 04901-5133, (207)873-6151 [18924]

Medina Farmers Exchange Co., 320 S Court St., Medina, OH 44256, (216)723-3607 [1010]

Medina Landmark Inc., 241 S State St., Medina, OH 44256, (216)723-3208 [1011]

MediQuip International, 1865 Summit Ave., Ste. 600, Plano, TX 75074, (972)423-1600 [18925]

Medler Electric Co., 1313 Michigan Ave., Alma, MI 48801, (517)463-1108 [9062]

Medley Hotel and Restaurant Supply Co., PO Box 328, Albany, GA 31702, (912)432-5116 [24183]

Medply, PO Box 2488, White City, OR 97503, (541)826-3142 [27344]

MEE Material Handling Equipment, 11721 W Carmen Ave., Milwaukee, WI 53225, (414)353-3300 [16286]

Meeder Equipment Co., PO Box 3459, Alhambra, CA 91803, (818)289-3746 [22472]

Meenan Oil Company L.P., 6900 Jericho Tpke., Ste. 310, Syosset, NY 11791, (516)364-9030 [22473]

Mees Distributors, 645 S Broadway, Lexington, KY 40508, (606)252-4545 [10020]

Mees Distributors, 1541 West Fork Rd., Cincinnati, OH 45223, (513)541-2311 [10021].

Mees Distributors, 5193 Sinclair Rd., Columbus, OH 43229, (614)844-5830 [10022]

Mees Distributors, 2425 Stanley, Dayton, OH 45404, (937)224-1506 [10023]

Mees Tile and Marble Inc., 4536 Poplar Level Rd., Louisville, KY 40213, (502)969-5858 [10024]

Mega Cabinets Inc., 113 Albany Ave., Amityville, NY 11701-2632, (516)789-4112 [7689]

Mega Company, 2501 K St. NW, Ste. 9C, Washington, DC 20037, (202)338-2112 [2939]

MEGA HAUS Hard Drives, 2201 Pine Dr., Dickinson, TX 77539-4764, (281)534-3919 [6481]

Mega Hertz, 6940 S Holly Circle, Ste. 200, Englewood, CO 80112, (303)779-1717 [25310]

Mega Systems Chemicals Inc, 450 N McKemy Ave., Chandler, AZ 85226, (602)437-9105 [4455]

Mega Systems Chemicals Inc., 450 N McKerry Ave., Chandler, AZ 85226, (602)437-9108 [4456]

Meherrin Agricultural and Chemical Co., PO Box 200, Severn, NC 27877, (919)585-1744 [1012]

Mehrer Drywall Inc., 2657 20th Ave. W, Seattle, WA 98199, (206)282-4288 [7690]

MEID, 325 N Jackson Ave., PO Box 1893, Mason City, IA 50401, (515)423-8931 [18388]

Meidlinger Inc.; H.E., 18 14th St. S, Fargo, ND 58103-1620, (701)237-5240 [24184]

Meier Inc.; Walter, 12555 W Wirth St., Brookfield, WI 53005, (414)783-7100 [11844]

Meier Metal Servicenters Inc., 1471 E 9 Mile Rd., Hazel Park, MI 48030, (810)645-5090 [20163]

Meier Transmission Ltd., 1845 E 40th St., Cleveland, OH 44103, (216)881-0444 [9063]

Meijer Inc., 2929 Walker NW, Grand Rapids, MI 49504, (616)453-6711 [11845]

Meis Seed and Feed Co., PO Box 1406, Le Mars, IA 51031, (712)546-4131 [1013]

Meisel Music Inc., PO Box 90, Springfield, NJ 07081-0090, (973)379-5000 [25311]

Meisel Stringed Instruments Inc., PO Box 90, Springfield, NJ 07081-0090, (973)379-5000 [25311]

Mel Farr Automotive Group Inc., 24750 Greenfield Rd., Oak Park, MI 48237, (248)967-3700 [20678]

Mel Pinto Imports Inc., 2860 Annandale Rd., Falls Church, VA 22042-2149, (703)237-4686 [23818]

Melan International Trading, 5943 Peacock Ridge Rd., Rancho Palos Verdes, CA 90275-3406, (213)544-4109 [9064]

Melchs Food Products Inc., PO Box 278, Medina, OH 44258-0278, (330)253-8612 [11846]

Melco Embroidery Systems, 1575 W 124th Ave., Westminster, CO 80234, (303)457-1234 [16287]

Melco Inc., 4626 N 15th St., Philadelphia, PA 19019, (215)324-0213 [4872]

Melges; Gregory N., 8640 Riverwood Cir., New London, MN 56273-9710, (320)796-2421 [23819]

Melhado Co.; George, 10 Merchant St., Sharon, MA 02067, (781)784-5550 [26328]

MELIBRAD, PO Box 19689, Las Vegas, NV 89132-0689, (702)895-9033 [19448]

Melin Tool Company Inc., 3370 W 140th St., Cleveland, OH 44111, (216)251-7471 [16288]

Mellen Parts Company Inc., 126 Renaissance Pkwy., Atlanta, GA 30308, (404)876-4331 [2940]

Mello Smello, 5100 Hwy. 169 N, Minneapolis, MN 55428-4028, (612)504-5400 [13400]

Mellobuttercup Ice Cream Co., 400 S Douglas St., PO Box 324, Wilson, NC 27894, (919)243-6161 [11847]

Mellon Patch, PO Box 414, Mountain View, AR 72560-0414, (870)269-3354 [26573]

Mellott Estate Inc.; H.B., 100 Mellott Dr., Ste. 100, PO Box 25, Warfordsburg, PA 17267, (301)678-2000 [7691]

Melman-Moster Associates, Inc., 361 Clinton Ave., Wyckoff, NJ 07481, (201)847-0100 [3946]

Melo Envelope Company Inc., 525 W 52nd St., New York, NY 10019, (212)315-4700 [21832]

Melody Farms Inc., 31111 Industrial Rd., Livonia, MI 48150, (734)525-4000 [11848]

Melody Gloves Inc., 171 Madison Ave., New York, NY 10016-5110, (212)683-6878 [5184]

Melrose Appliance Inc., 424 Main St., Melrose, MA 02176-3842, (781)665-5310 [25312]

Melster Candies Inc., Madison St., PO Box 47, Cambridge, WI 53523, (608)423-3221 [11849]

Melton Book Company Inc., PO Box 140990, Donelson, TN 37214-0990, (615)391-3917 [3947]

Melton Steel Corp., 7204 Navigation Blvd., Houston, TX 77011, (713)928-5451 [20164]

Melvin Village Marina Inc., PO Box 165, Melvin Village, NH 03850-0165, (603)544-3583 [18566]

Members Service Corp., 1085 W Morse Blvd., Winter Park, FL 32789, (407)647-6600 [5668]

Memory Technologies Texas Inc., PO Box 13166, Austin, TX 78711, (512)451-2600 [6482]

Memphis Chemical Janitorial Supply Inc., PO Box 70512, Memphis, TN 38107, (901)521-1612 [4668]

Memphis Communications Corporation, PO Box 41735, Memphis, TN 38174-1735, (901)725-9271 [5669]

Memphis Ford New Holland Inc., 3849 Getwell Rd., Memphis, TN 38118, (901)362-9200 [1014]

Memphis Furniture Manufacturing Co., 3119 S Perkins Rd., Memphis, TN 38118-3239, (901)525-3765 [26140]

Memphis Group Inc., 3900 Willow Lake Blvd., Memphis, TN 38118, (901)362-8600 [122]

Memphis Import Company Inc., 648 Riverside Dr., Memphis, TN 38103, (901)526-4185 [23820]

Memphis Pool Supply Co. Inc., 2762 Getwell Rd., Memphis, TN 38118-1846, (901)365-2480 [23821]

Memphis Serum Company Inc., PO Box 16203, Memphis, TN 38186-0203, (901)332-4694 [18926]

Memtek Products/Memorex Audio & Video, 10100 Pioneer Blvd., Ste. 110, Santa Fe Springs, CA 90670, (562)906-2800 [25313]

Memtek Products/Memorex Audio, Video, CDR's, & Computer Peripherals, 10100 Pioneer Blvd., Ste. 110, Santa Fe Springs, CA 90670, (562)906-2800 [25313]

Menard Electronics Inc., 6451 Choctaw Dr., Baton Rouge, LA 70805, (504)355-0323 [9065]

Menchaca Brick & Tile Co., 3613 W Hwy. 83, Harlingen, TX 78552, (956)428-6956 [10025]

Menco Corp., PO Box 1300, Springfield, IL 62705, (217)544-7485 [2941]

Mendez & Co. Inc., PO Box 3348, San Juan, PR 00936-3348, (787)793-8888 [1865]

Mendocino Coast Produce, Inc., 543 N Franklin St., Ft. Bragg, CA 95437-3211, (707)964-3539 [11850]

Mendocino Sea Vegetable Co., PO Box 1265, Mendocino, CA 95460, (707)937-2050 [11851]

Mendon Leasing Corp., 362 Kingsland Ave., Brooklyn, NY 11222, (718)391-5300 [2942]

Mendota Farm Cooperative Supply Inc., PO Box 407, Mendota, IL 61342, (815)539-6772 [18086]

Menlo Tool Company Inc., PO Box 5127, Warren, MI 48090-5127, (810)756-6010 [18927]

Menominee Tribal Enterprises, PO Box 10, Neopit, WI 54150, (715)756-2311 [7692]

Menomonie Farmers Union Cooperative, PO Box 438, Menomonie, WI 54751, (715)232-6200 [1015]

Menoni and Mocogni Inc., 2160 Old Skokie Valley, Highland Park, IL 60035-0128, (847)432-0518 [7693]

Mentor Lumber and Supply Company Inc., 7180 N Center St., Mentor, OH 44060, (440)255-9145 [7694]

Mequon Distributors Inc., PO Box 366, Thiensville, WI 53092, (262)242-3600 [7695]

Mer Communications Systems Inc., 420 Fifth Ave., New York, NY 10118-2702, (212)719-5959 [5670]

Mer-Roc F.S. Inc., PO Box 129, Aledo, IL 61231, (309)582-7271 [27186]

Mercantile Buyer's Service Inc., 4715 N 32nd St., PO Box 090528, Milwaukee, WI 53209-0528, (414)445-4440 [21500]

Mercantile Sales Company Inc., 1141 S 7th St., St. Louis, MO 63104, (314)421-1676 [23822]

Mercedes-Benz of North America Inc., 1 Mercedes Dr., Montvale, NJ 07645, (201)573-0600 [20679]

Mercer's Dix Equipment, 21588 Dix-Toledo Rd., Trenton, MI 48183, (734)676-9637 [7696]

Merchandise International, 2604 NE Industrial Dr., Ste. 230, North Kansas City, MO 64116, (816)842-6500 [9066]

Merchant du Vin Corp., 18436 Cascade Ave., S, No. 140, Tukwila, WA 98188-4729, (206)322-5022 [1866]

Merchants Cash Register Co., 4422 Roosevelt Rd., Hillside, IL 60162, (708)449-6650 [21137]

Merchants Coffee Co., PO Box 50654, New Orleans, LA 70150, (504)581-7515 [11852]

Merchants Co., PO Box 1351, Hattiesburg, MS 39403-1351, (601)583-4351 [11853]

Merchants Distributors Inc., PO Box 2148, Hickory, NC 28603, (704)323-4100 [11854]

Merchant's Grain Inc., PO Box 398, Selma, NC 27576, (919)965-2303 [18087]

Merchants Grocery Co., PO Box 1268, Culpeper, VA 22701, (540)825-0786 [11855]

Merchants Inc., 9073 Euclid Ave., Manassas, VA 20110-5306, (703)368-3171 [2943]

Merchants Information Solutions Inc., 415 S Brandon St., Seattle, WA 98108, (206)763-1010 [21138]

Merchants Overseas Inc., 41 Bassett St., Providence, RI 02903-4633, (401)331-5603 [17520]

Merchants Overseas Inc., 41 Bassett St., Providence, RI 02903-4633, (401)331-5603 [17521]

Merck-Medco Managed Care Inc., 100 Summit Ave., Montvale, NJ 07645, (201)358-5400 [19449]

Mercury Air Center, 655 S Rock Blvd., Reno, NV 89502, (775)858-7300 [22474]

Mercury Air Group Inc., 5456 McConnell Ave., Los Angeles, CA 90066, (310)827-2737 [22475]

Mercury Beauty Company Inc., 9600 Lurline Ave., Chatsworth, CA 91311, (818)998-1811 [14159]

Mercury Communication Services, Inc., 1263 Record Crossing, Dallas, TX 75235, (214)637-4900 [5671]

Mercury Communication Services, Inc., 8711 Burnet Rd., Ste. E-56, Austin, TX 78758, (512)467-7227 [5672]

Mercury Computer Systems, 2105 S Bascom Ave Ste. 130, Campbell, CA 95008, (408)371-2733 [6483]

Mercury International Trading Corp., PO Box 222, North Attleboro, MA 02761-0222, (508)699-9000 [24808]

Mercury Waste Solutions Inc., 302 N Riverfront Dr., Ste. 100A, Mankato, MN 56001, (507)345-0522 [26901]

Mercy National Purchasing Inc., 55 Shuman Blvd., Naperville, IL 60563-8469, (708)355-5500 [18928]

Mercy National Purchasing Inc., 55 Shuman Blvd., Naperville, IL 60563-8469, (630)355-5500 [18929]

Mercy National Purchasing Inc., 55 Shuman Blvd., Naperville, IL 60563-8469, (708)355-5500 [19450]

Mercy Resource Management, Inc., 55 Shuman Blvd., Naperville, IL 60563-8469, (630)355-5500 [18929]

Meredith and Meredith Inc., 2343 Farm Creek Rd., Toddville, MD 21672, (410)397-8151 [11856]

Meredith Stained Glass Center, Inc., 1115 E West Hwy., Silver Spring, MD 20910, (301)650-8572 [25735]

Merfish Plumbing Supply Co.; N., PO Box 1937, Houston, TX 77251-1937, (713)869-5731 [23259]

Merfish Supply Co.; N., PO Box 1937, Houston, TX 77251-1937, (713)869-5731 [23259]

Meriden Cooper Corp., 112 Golden Street Pk., Meriden, CT 06450, (203)237-8448 [17030]

Meridian Aerospace Group Ltd., 3796 Vest Mill Rd., Winston-Salem, NC 27103, (919)765-5454 [123]

Meridian International Co., PO Box 6224, Libertyville, IL 60048, (847)362-3325 [24590]

Meridian Mattress Factory Inc., PO Box 5127, Meridian, MS 39301, (601)693-3875 [13178]

Meridian National Corp., 805 Chicago St., Toledo, OH 43611, (419)729-3918 [20165]

Meridian Synapse Corporation, 12020 Synapse Valley, No. 100, Reston, VA 20191, (703)318-0464 [18930]

Meridian Veterinary Products, PO Box 3593, Chapel Hill, NC 27515, (919)833-8119 [27187]

Merisel Inc., 200 Continental Blvd., El Segundo, CA 90245-0984, (310)615-3080 [6484]

Merisel Inc. Macamerica Div., 631 River Oaks Pkwy., San Jose, CA 95134, (408)434-0433 [6485]

Merisel Inc. Merisel World Class Distribution, 2010 NW 84th Ave., Miami, FL 33122, (305)591-6800 [6486]

Merit Fasteners Corp., 2510 County Rd., Hwy. 427, Longwood, FL 32750, (407)331-4815 [13825]

Merit Industries, PO Box 1448, Dalton, GA 30722-1448, (706)695-7581 [10026]

Merit Insulation Inc., PO Box 27500, Albuquerque, NM 87125-7500, (505)242-2681 [7697]

Merit Marketing Inc., 5773 Arrowhead Dr., Ste. 204, Virginia Beach, VA 23462-3203, (757)490-9396 [5185]

Merit Metal Products Corp., 242 Valley Rd., Warrington, PA 18976, (215)343-2500 [23260]

Merit USA, 620 Clark Ave., Pittsburg, CA 94565, (925)432-6900 [20166]

Meriwether Publishing, Ltd., 885 Elkton Dr., Colorado Springs, CO 80907-3576, (719)594-4422 [3948]

Merkel Donohue Inc., 200 South Ave., Rochester, NY 14604-1807, (716)325-7696 [21139]

Merkert Enterprises Inc., 500 Turnpike St., Canton, MA 02021, (781)828-4800 [11857]

Mermaid Water Services, 1801 Pewaukee Rd., Waukesha, WI 53188, (414)547-1862 [25736]

Merriam-Graves Corp., 1361 Union St., West Springfield, MA 01089, (413)781-6550 [18931]

Merriam-Graves Corp., 806 River Rd., Charlestown, NH 03603, (603)542-8768 [18932]

Merrill Co., 601 1st Ave. SW, Spencer, IA 51301, (712)262-1141 [2944]

Merrill Distributing, Inc., PO Box 707, Merrill, WI 54452-0707, (715)536-4551 [11858]

Merrimac Boyce Fabrics, 1303 Corporate Dr., High Point, NC 27263, (336)434-6060 [26141]

Merrimac Petroleum Inc., 444 W Ocean Blvd., Ste. 1106, Long Beach, CA 90802-4519, (562)983-9350 [22476]

Merrimack Jewelers Inc., 356 Daniel Webster Hwy., Merrimack, NH 03054-4131, (603)424-3434 [17522]

Merrimack Valley Distributing Company Inc., PO Box 417, Danvers, MA 01923, (978)777-2213 [1867]

Merrimack Valley Wood Products Inc., 1 B St., Derry, NH 03038, (603)432-8845 [7698]

Merritt Machine Inc., 2124 Snowhill Dr., Mt. Airy, NC 27030, (336)789-1600 [20167]

Merritt Marine Supply, 2621 NE 4th St., Pompano Beach, FL 33064, (954)946-5350 [18567]

Merritts Auto Salvage, 532 Hwy. 95, Weiser, ID 83672-5720, (208)549-1076 [2945]

Merrymeeting Corp., US Rte. 1, PO Box 372, Woolwich, ME 04579-0372, (207)442-7002 [23823]

Mersch-Bacher Associates Inc., 810 S Cincinnati Ave., Tulsa, OK 74119, (918)587-1500 [6621]

Merschman Inc., PO Box 67, West Point, IA 52656, (319)837-6111 [1016]

Mervis Industries Inc., PO Box 827, Danville, IL 61834, (217)442-5300 [20168]

Merz and Company Inc.; F.O., PO Box 430, Cowpens, SC 29330, (864)463-4200 [13401]

Mesa Microwave Inc., 2243 Verus St Ste. G, San Diego, CA 92154, (619)423-0705 [9067]

Mesa Optical, 1225 N 23rd St., Ste. 103, Grand Junction, CO 81501, (970)241-9166 [19451]

Mesa Sprinkler Inc., 201 W Juanita, Mesa, AZ 85210, (602)964-8888 [1017]

Mesabi Radial Tire Co., 18th St. at 5th Ave. E, Hibbing, MN 55746, (218)263-6865 [2946]

MESCO, 1401 Metropolitan Ave., PO Box 598, Thorofare, NJ 08086, (856)853-8320 [18559]

Meshekow Brothers Inc., 527 W 7th St., No. 704, Los Angeles, CA 90014, (213)623-7177 [5186]

Meskin and Davis Inc., 14400 Woodrow Wilson, Detroit, MI 48238, (313)869-4006 [26142]

Messer Distributing Co., 4401 NW 112th St., Urbandale, IA 50322, (515)252-7173 [1719]

Messina and Zucker Inc., 295 5th Ave., New York, NY 10016, (212)889-3750 [15585]

Mestre Equipment Co.; F.W., 5101 NW 79th Ave., Miami, FL 33166, (305)592-2090 [7699]

MET International, 212 Garret Ridge, Peachtree City, GA 30269, (770)487-6780 [6487]

Metabran Co., 94-501 Kau St., Waipahu, HI 96797, (808)676-6111 [1868]

Metagenics Inc., 971 Calle Negocio, San Clemente, CA 92673, (714)366-0818 [14160]

Metal Alloy Corp., PO Box 18060, River Rouge, MI 48218, (313)843-7700 [26902]

Metal Commodities Inc., 721 Emerson, No. 695, St. Louis, MO 63141, (314)434-3600 [6488]

Metal Industries Inc., 4314 State Route 209, Elizabethville, PA 17023-8438, (717)362-8196 [7700]

Metal Management Aerospace, Inc., 500 Flatbush Ave., Hartford, CT 06106, (860)522-3123 [26903]

Metal Management Inc., 500 N Dearborn St., Ste. 405, Chicago, IL 60610, (312)645-0700 [20169]

Metal Recovery Systems Inc., 665 St. Cyr Rd., St. Louis, MO 63137, (314)388-3600 [26904]

Metal Service and Supply Inc., 916 Harrison St., Indianapolis, IN 46202, (317)634-8720 [20170]

The Metal Store, 14506 Industrial Ave. S, Maple Heights, OH 44137, (216)663-0458 [20171]

Metal Store of Cleveland Inc., 14506 Industrial Ave. S, Maple Heights, OH 44137, (216)663-0458 [20171]

MetalCenter Inc., PO Box 60482, Los Angeles, CA 90060, (213)582-2272 [20172]

Metalink Corp., PO Box 1329, Chandler, AZ 85244, (480)926-0797 [9068]

Metallurg International Resources, 6 E 43rd St., Fl. 12, New York, NY 10017-4609, (212)835-0200 [20173]

Metalmart Inc., 12225 Coast Dr., Whittier, CA 90601, (562)692-9081 [20174]

Metals Engineering Co., PO Box 237, Monroe, CT 06468, (203)268-7325 [20175]

Metals USA Inc., 3 Riverway, Ste. 600, Houston, TX 77056, (713)965-0990 [20176]

Metalsco Inc., 2388 Schuetz Rd., Ste. A40, St. Louis, MO 63146, (314)997-5200 [26905]

Metalwest, 1774 W 2800 S, Ogden, UT 84401, (801)399-5700 [20177]

Metamora Elevator Co., State Rte. 120, Metamora, OH 43540, (419)644-4711 [1018]

Metamorphous Advances Product Services, PO Box 10616, Portland, OR 97296-0616, (503)228-4972 [3949]

Metaresearch Inc., 9220 SW Barbur Blvd., Ste. 119, Portland, OR 97219, (503)248-4131 [16289]

MetaSystems Design Group Inc., 2000 N 15th St., No. 103, Arlington, VA 22201, (703)243-6622 [5673]

Metech International Inc., 120 Mapleville Main St., Mapleville, RI 02839, (401)568-0711 [26906]

Methanex Methanol Co., 1237 Merrit Dr., Ste. 1237, Dallas, TX 75240, (972)702-0909 [22477]

Methods and Equipment Associates, 24860 Hathaway Dr., Farmington Hills, MI 48335, (248)442-2773 [16290]

Metric Metal, 4239 Monroe St., Toledo, OH 43606, (419)473-2481 [20265]

Metric & Multistandard Components Corp., 120 Old Saw Mill River Rd., Hawthorne, NY 10532, (914)769-5020 [17031]

Metrix South Inc., 6501 NW 12th Ave., Ft. Lauderdale, FL 33309-1109, (954)979-5660 [2947]

Metro Builders Supply Inc., 5313 S Mingo, Tulsa, OK 74145-8102, (918)622-7692 [15227]

Metro Crown International, PO Box 12238, Kansas City, MO 64152, (660)879-5514 [124]

Metro Export and Import Co., 1140 Broadway, Ste. 902, New York, NY 10001, (212)481-9077 [5187]

Metro Foods Inc., PO Box 688, Olive Branch, MS 38654-0688, (601)895-8880 [11859]

Metro Group Inc., 401 W 900 S, Salt Lake City, UT 84101, (801)328-2051 [26907]

Metro-Jasim, Inc., 39 Lloyd St., New Hyde Park, NY 11040, (516)248-1177 [125]

Metro Marketing Co., PO Box 3031, Woburn, MA 01888, (781)933-3311 [5188]

Metro Marketing Inc., 2851 E Las Hermanas St., East Rancho Dominguez, CA 90221, (310)898-1888 [15586]

Metro Metals Northwest, 5611 NE Columbia Blvd., Portland, OR 97218-1237, (503)287-8861 [26908]

Metro/North, 1199 Amboy Ave., Edison, NJ 08837, (732)205-0088 [9069]

Metro Recycling Co., 2424 Beekman St., Cincinnati, OH 45214, (513)251-1800 [21833]

Metro Recycling Co. Imagination Store Co., 2424 Beekman St., Cincinnati, OH 45214, (513)471-6060 [26909]

Metro Refrigeration Supply, Inc., 2050 Sigman Rd. NW, Conyers, GA 30012, (770)922-8606 [14541]

Metro Refrigeration Supply, Inc., 685 Thornton Way, Lithia Springs, GA 30122, (770)948-8400 [14542]

Metro Refrigeration Supply, Inc., 3061 Kingston Ct., Marietta, GA 30067, (770)953-0022 [14543]

Metro/Thebe, Inc., 2851 E Las Hermanas St., East Rancho Dominguez, CA 90221, (310)898-1888 [15586]

Metro Tile & Marble, Inc., 5455 Shirley St., Naples, FL 34109-1848, (941)598-4060 [10027]

Metrolina Greenhouses Inc., 16400 Huntersville Concord Rd., Huntersville, NC 28078, (704)875-1371 [14921]

Metron Steel Corp., 12900 S Metron Dr., Chicago, IL 60633, (773)646-4000 [20178]

Metropolis Metal Spinning and Stamping Inc., 4551 Furman Ave., Bronx, NY 10470, (718)325-5650 [13826]

Metropolitan AC & Refrigeration, PO Box 422, Everett, MA 02149-0003, (617)389-4300 [14544]

Metropolitan Diesel Supply Co., 18211 Weaver Ave., Detroit, MI 48228, (313)272-6370 [2948]

Metropolitan Marketing Inc., 3890 W Northwest Hwy., Ste. 500, Dallas, TX 75220-5167, (214)330-5088 [11860]

Metropolitan Medical Inc., 360-4 McGhee Rd., Winchester, VA 22603, 800-336-0318 [18933]

Metropolitan Mining Co., 58-30 57th St., Maspeth, NY 11378, (718)894-5025 [26910]

Metropolitan Poultry and Seafood Co., 1920 Stanford Ct., Landover, MD 20785-3219, (301)772-0060 [11861]

Metropolitan X-Ray Sales Inc., 24558 Michigan Ave., Dearborn, MI 48124-1711, (313)278-7373 [18934]

Metrotek Industries Inc., 12525 6th St. East, Treasure Island, FL 33706-2939, (727)547-8307 [9070]

Metz Baking Co., 981 Division St., Sharon, PA 16146-2884, (724)346-3103 [11862]

Metz Baking Co., PO Box 1475, Watertown, SD 57201, (605)886-5832 [11863]

Metz Baking Co., PO Box 448, Sioux City, IA 51102, (712)255-7611 [11864]

Metz Beverage Company Inc., 302 N Custer St., Sheridan, WY 82801, (307)672-5848 [1869]

Metz Beverage Company Inc., 302 N Custer St., Sheridan, WY 82801, (307)672-5848 [1870]

Meunier Electronics Supply Inc., 3409 E Washington St., Indianapolis, IN 46201, (317)635-3511 [9071]

Mexican Art Imports, 3103 E Van Buren, Phoenix, AZ 85008, (602)275-9552 [13402]

Mexican Marketplace, 1414 Maclovia, PO Box G, Santa Fe, NM 87505, (505)471-8020 [6993]

Meyda Tiffany, One Meyda Fine Pl., 55 Oriskany Blvd., Yorkville, NY 13495, (315)768-3711 [15587]

Meyer Company Inc.; William F., PO Box 37, Aurora, IL 60507-0037, (630)851-4441 [23261]

Meyer Co.; O.E., PO Box 479, Sandusky, OH 44871-0479, (419)625-3054 [17032]

Meyer Corp.; Mary, PO Box 275, 1 Teddy Bear Lane, Townshend, VT 05353-0275, (802)365-7793 [26574]

Meyer Diamond Company Inc.; Henry, 400 Madison Ave., New York, NY 10017, (212)644-1114 [17523]

Meyer Equipment Inc., PO Box 393, Lisbon, ND 58054, (701)683-4000 [1019]

Meyer Inc.; Frances, 104 Coleman Blvd., Savannah, GA 31408-9540, (912)748-5252 [13403]

Meyer Laminates Inc., 1264 La Quinta Dr., Rm. 4B, Orlando, FL 32809, (407)857-6353 [27345]

Meyer Oil Co., PO Box 2004, Cleona, PA 17042, (717)273-8544 [22478]

Meyer Plastics Inc., PO Box 20902, Indianapolis, IN 46220-4816, (317)259-4131 [22997]

Meyer Seed Co., 600 S Caroline St., Baltimore, MD 21231, (410)342-4224 [1020]

Meyer and Son of Sullivan Inc.; L.W., PO Box 37, Sullivan, WI 53178, (414)593-2244 [1021]

Meyer Tomatoes, PO Box 606, King City, CA 93930, (408)385-4047 [11865]

Meyer Vegetables, PO Box 1117, Nogales, AZ 85628-1117, (520)761-4119 [11866]

Meyer West, PO Box 8250, Stockton, CA 95208, (209)473-2966 [1022]

Meyers Medical Inc., 1112 Baywater Dr., West Columbia, SC 29170-3119, (803)791-7436 [18935]

Meyers; Tom, RD 3, Box 316, Ford City, PA 16226, (412)763-2422 [27188]

Meystel Inc., 4666 S Halsted St., Chicago, IL 60609 [5189]

MFA Agriservice, PO Box 312, Lebanon, MO 65536, (417)532-3174 [1023]

MFA Inc., 201 Ray Young Dr., Columbia, MO 65201-3599, (573)874-5111 [1024]

M.F.A. Oil Co., Box 774, Lees Summit, MO 64063, (816)524-3466 [22479]

M.G. West, 180 Hubbell St., San Francisco, CA 94107, (415)861-4800 [13179]

MGA Entertainment, 16730 Schoenborn St., North Hills, CA 91343-6122, (818)894-2525 [26575]

MGA Research Corp., PO Box 71, 1290 Main Rd., Akron, 07400, 14001, (716)542-5515 [16291]

MGD Enterprises, PO Box 412, Midwest, WY 82643-0412, (307)437-9216 [17524]

MGM Optical Laboratory, 621 Ave. De Diego, Puerto Nuevo, PR 00920, (787)781-6299 [19452]

MH Associates Ltd., 712 38th St. N, Fargo, ND 58102-2961, (701)282-7877 [23824]

M.H. Equipment Corp., 309 NE Rock Island Ave., PO Box 528, Peoria, IL 61651-0528, (309)686-4030 [16292]

MH World Trade Corp., 140 E 45th St., 23rd Fl., New York, NY 10017, (212)808-0810 [26143]

Mia Shoes Inc., 258 Chapman Rd., Ste. 100, Newark, DE 19702, (302)454-8500 [24809]

Miami Aviation Corp., 14980 NW 44th Ct., Opa Locka, FL 33054, (305)688-0511 [126]

Miami-Luken Inc., 265 S Pioneer Blvd., Springboro, OH 45066, (513)743-7775 [19453]

Miami Robes International, 19401 W Dixie Hwy., Miami, FL 33180-2214, (305)940-3377 [5190]

Miami Valley Steel Service Inc., 201 Fox Dr., Piqua, OH 45356, (937)773-7127 [20179]

Michael Foods Inc., 5353 Wayzata Blvd., Ste. 324, Minneapolis, MN 55416, (612)546-1500 [11867]

Michael Foods Refrigerated Distribution Cos., 5353 Wayzata Blvd. No. 324, Minneapolis, MN 55416, (612)546-1500 [11868]

Michael Fox Auctioneers Inc., 3835 Naylors Ln., Baltimore, MD 21208, (410)653-4000 [16038]

Michael Supply Company Inc., 301 East St. S, Talladega, AL 35160-2452, (205)362-6144 [15228]

Michaud Distributors, 92 Perry Rd., Bangor, ME 04401, (207)989-0747 [11869]

Michaud Distributors, 5 Lincoln Ave., Scarborough, ME 04074, (207)885-9473 [11870]

Michel Company Inc.; R.E., 1991 Mooreland Pkwy., Annapolis, MD 21401, (410)267-7500 [14545]

Michel Company Inc.; R.E., 10820 Guilford Rd., Annapolis Junction, MD 20701, (301)604-3747 [14546]

Michel Company Inc.; R.E., 2509 Schuster Dr., Cheverly, MD 20784, (301)322-4700 [14547]

Michel Company Inc.; R.E., 150-8 Airport Dr., Westminster, MD 21157, (410)876-9144 [14548]

Michel Company Inc.; R.E., 1918 Tucker, Burlington, NC 27215, (919)228-1304 [14549]

Michel Company Inc.; R.E., 4141 Barringer Dr., Charlotte, NC 28217, (704)523-5515 [14550]

Michel Company Inc.; R.E., 2200 Sullivan, Greensboro, NC 27405, (910)274-3844 [14551]

Michel Company Inc.; R.E., 309 W 9th St., Greenville, NC 27834, (919)758-0088 [14552]

Michel Company Inc.; R.E., 1310 Hodges St., Raleigh, NC 27604, (919)821-5700 [14553]

Michel Company Inc.; R.E., 4461 Sunset Ave., Rocky Mount, NC 27804, (919)937-2089 [14554]

Michel Company Inc.; R.E., 410 Haled St., Winston-Salem, NC 27127, (910)724-7000 [14555]

Michel Company Inc.; R.E., Bldg. 14E, Bound Brook, NJ 08805, (732)560-0560 [14556]

Michel Company Inc.; R.E., 827 New York Ave., Trenton, NJ 08638, (609)599-4535 [14557]

Michel Company Inc.; R.E., 749 N Delsea Dr., Vineland, NJ 08360, (609)691-8448 [14558]

Michel Company Inc.; R.E., 116 Hawley Ave., Syracuse, NY 13203, (315)474-6007 [14559]

Michel Company Inc.; R.E., 3412 S Ridge St. E, Ashtabula, OH 44004, (440)993-7881 [14560]

Michel Company Inc.; R.E., 4260 Lake Park Rd., Youngstown, OH 44512, (330)782-6600 [14561]

Michel Company Inc.; R.E., 929 E Highland St., Allentown, PA 18103, (215)434-6054 [14562]

Michel Company Inc.; R.E., 1807 9th Ave., Altoona, PA 16602, (814)942-6600 [14563]

Michel Company Inc.; R.E., 5384 Enterprise Ave., Bethel Park, PA 15102, (412)835-5500 [14564]

Michel Company Inc.; R.E., 1028 Morton Ave., Chester, PA 19013, (215)872-9420 [14565]

Michel Company Inc.; R.E., 1302 Myrtle, Erie, PA 16501, (814)453-6664 [14566]

Michel Company Inc.; R.E., RD 6, Box 518, Woodward Rd., Greensburg, PA 15601, (412)836-7646 [14567]

Michel Company Inc.; R.E., 803 S 26th St., Harrisburg, PA 17111, (717)564-7565 [14568]

Michel Company Inc.; R.E., 511 W Roseville Rd., Lancaster, PA 17604, (717)393-1790 [14569]

Michel Company Inc.; R.E., 10 Leonburg Rd., Mars, PA 16046, (412)776-0736 [14570]

Michel Company Inc.; R.E., 177 Mercer St., Meadville, PA 16335, (814)724-8046 [14571]

Michel Company Inc.; R.E., 845 Williams Ln., Reading, PA 19604, (215)929-3373 [14572]

Michel Company. Inc.; R.E., 405 Gilligan St., Scranton, PA 18508, (717)963-7881 [14573]

Michel Company Inc.; R.E., 2420 Commercial Blvd., State College, PA 16801, (814)234-1134 [14574]

Michel Company Inc.; R.E., 140 W Berkeley St., Uniontown, PA 15401, (412)438-4506 [14575]

Michel Company Inc.; R.E., 2250 Manor Ave., Upper Darby, PA 19082, (215)853-4570 [14576]

Michel Company Inc.; R.E., 915 Eastern Rd., Warrington, PA 18976, (215)343-2004 [14577]

Michel Company Inc.; R.E., 322 W Towne Rd., West Chester, PA 19380, (215)692-2966 [14578]

Michel Company Inc.; R.E., 1240 W Mark, York, PA 17404, (717)845-2681 [14579]

Michel Company Inc.; R.E., 830 N Lincoln St., Arlington, VA 22201, (703)524-8336 [14580]

Michel Company Inc.; R.E., 604 Henry Ave., Charlottesville, VA 22903, (804)977-4311 [14581]

Michel Company Inc.; R.E., 45 Sealtergood Dr., Christiansburg, VA 24073, (540)381-0700 [14582]

Michel Company Inc.; R.E., 131 Industrial Dr., Fredericksburg, VA 22408, (540)891-1534 [14583]

Michel Company Inc.; R.E., 26 Pleasant Hill Rd., Harrisonburg, VA 22801, (540)433-7848 [14584]

Michel Company Inc.; R.E., 3116 Oddfellows Rd., Lynchburg, VA 24501, (804)528-4441 [14585]

Michel Company Inc.; R.E., 9098 Owens Ct., Manassas Park, VA 20111, (703)330-0771 [14586]

Michel Company Inc.; R.E., 2742 Gallows Rd., Vienna, VA 22180, (703)698-6244 [14587]

Michel Company Inc.; R.E., 2735 Ellsmore Ave., Norfolk, VA 23513, (757)855-2011 [14588]

Michel Company Inc.; R.E., 401 5th St., Petersburg, VA 23803, (804)862-3535 [14589]

Michel Company Inc.; R.E., 3900 Garwood, Portsmouth, VA 23701, (757)465-2516 [14590]

Michel Company Inc.; R.E., 1714 W Cary St., Richmond, VA 23220, (804)358-9145 [14591]

Michel Company Inc.; R.E., 2419 Shenandoah Ave., Roanoke, VA 24017, (540)344-1666 [14592]

Michel Company Inc.; R.E., PO Box 56, US Rte. 13, Tasley, VA 23441, (757)787-8731 [14593]

Michel Company Inc.; R.E., 2609 Dean Dr., Virginia Beach, VA 23452, (757)463-7131 [14594]

Michel Company Inc.; R.E., 129 Kingsgate Pkwy., Williamsburg, VA 23185, (757)229-0028 [14595]

Michel Company Inc.; R.E., 130 Dye Dr., Beckley, WV 25801, (304)255-2222 [14596]

Michel Company Inc.; R.E., 1904 Bigley Ave., Charleston, WV 25302, (304)345-3303 [14597]

Michel Company Inc.; R.E., 716 30th St., Huntington, WV 25702, (304)529-1054 [14598]

Michel Company Inc.; R.E., 1089 Maple Dr., Morgantown, WV 26505, (304)598-3729 [14599]

Michel Company Inc.; R.E., 41 41st. St., Wheeling, WV 26003, (304)232-4540 [14600]

Michel Company Inc.; R.E., 1 R.E. Michel Dr., Glen Burnie, MD 21060, (410)760-4000 [14601]

Michelle International, Ltd., 6622 Eastside Dr. NE, No. 31, Browns Point, WA 98422-1175, (253)924-0844 [127]

Michelle Textile Corp., 7523 Little Ave., Ste. 210, Charlotte, NC 28226-8170, (704)544-5520 [26144]

Michelle's Family Bakery, 4321 41st St., Brentwood, MD 20722-1513, (301)985-6050 [11871]

Michiana Micro Inc., 61045 US Hwy. 31, South Bend, IN 46614-5020, (219)291-1196 [6489]

Michiana News Service, Inc., 2232 S 11th St., Niles, MI 49120, (616)684-3013 [3950]

Michigan Agricultural Commodities, PO Box 96, Blissfield, MI 49228, (517)486-2171 [18088]

Michigan Airgas, 311 Columbus Ave., Bay City, MI 48706, (517)894-4101 [17033]

Michigan Church Supply Company Inc., PO Box 279, Mt. Morris, MI 48458, (810)686-8877 [3951]

Michigan Glass Lined Storage Inc., 3587 W Tupperlake Rd., Lake Odessa, MI 48849, (616)374-8803 [1025]

Michigan Glove Company Inc., 12751 Capital St., Oak Park, MI 48237-3113, (248)543-6191 [5191]

Michigan Hardwood Distributors, 30691 Wixom Rd., Wixom, MI 48393, (248)669-0790 [10028]

Michigan Industrial Hardwood Co., PO Box 612, Whiting, IN 46394, (219)659-4255 [7701]

Michigan Industrial Piping Supply Company Inc., PO Box 282, Wyandotte, MI 48192, (313)285-2161 [23262]

Michigan Industrial Shoe Co., 25477 W 8 Mile Rd., Detroit, MI 48240, (313)532-0902 [24810]

Michigan Livestock Exchange, 6400 Bentley Rd., Williamston, MI 48895-9641, (517)337-2856 [18089]

Michigan Lumber Co., 1919 Clifford St., Flint, MI 48503, (810)232-4108 [7702]

Michigan Paper Recyling Corp., 1440 Oxford Rd., Grosse Pointe Woods, MI 48236-1818, (810)468-0600 [26911]

Michigan Peat Div., PO Box 3006, Houston, TX 77253, (713)522-0711 [18090]

Michigan Retail Packaging, 1688 Gover Pky., Mt. Pleasant, MI 48858, (517)772-9416 [21834]

Michigan State Seed Co., 717 N Clinton, Grand Ledge, MI 48837, (517)627-2164 [1026]

Michigan State University Press, 1405 S Harrison Rd., Ste. 25, East Lansing, MI 48823-5202, (517)355-9543 [3952]

Michigan Sugar Co., PO Box 1348, Saginaw, MI 48605, (517)799-7300 [11872]

Michigan Supply Co., PO Box 17069, Lansing, MI 48901, (517)484-6444 [23263]

Michigan Tractor and Machinery Co., 24800 Novi Rd., Novi, MI 48375, (248)349-4800 [7703]

Mickey's Mobile Metal Mending, 100 7th St., Alamogordo, NM 88310, (505)437-6437 [20180]

Mickeys Sales Co., 2601-09 Strong, Kansas City, KS 66106, (913)831-1493 [23825]

Mickler's Floridiana, Inc., PO Box 621450, Oviedo, FL 32762-1450, (407)365-6425 [3953]

Micro Bio-Medics Inc., 846 Pelham Pkwy., Pelham Manor, NY 10803, (914)738-8400 [19454]

Micro Central Inc., 8998 Route 18 N, Old Bridge, NJ 08857, (732)360-0300 [6490]

Micro Chef Inc., 2200 Huntington Dr., Plano, TX 75075, (972)985-4757 [11873]

Micro-Coax Communications Inc., 206 Jones Blvd., Pottstown, PA 19464, (610)495-0110 [9072]

Micro-Coax, Inc., 206 Jones Blvd., Pottstown, PA 19464, (610)495-0110 [9072]

Micro Comm Inc., 2612 Cameron, Mobile, AL 36607, (205)476-4872 [5674]

Micro-Comp Industries Inc., 1271 Oakmead Pkwy., Sunnyvale, CA 94086-4035, (408)733-2000 [9073]

Micro Computer Centre, 11745 Bricksome Ave., Baton Rouge, LA 70816-2369, (504)293-2733 [6491]

Micro Ear Technology Inc., PO Box 59124, Minneapolis, MN 55459-0124, (612)934-3001 [18936]

Micro Integrated Communications Corp., 3270 Scott Blvd., Santa Clara, CA 95054, (408)980-9565 [6492]

Micro K Systems Inc., 15874 E Hamilton Pl., Aurora, CO 80013, (303)693-3413 [6493]

Micro Metrology Inc., 9553 Vassar Ave., Chatsworth, CA 91311, (818)993-4971 [16293]

Micro-Pace Computers Inc., PO Box 6990, Champaign, IL 61826-6990, (217)356-1884 [6494]

Micro Star, 2245 Camino Vida Roble, No. 100, Carlsbad, CA 92009-1502, (760)931-4949 [6495]

Micro Switch/Honeywell, 11 W Spring, Freeport, IL 61032-4353, (815)235-6847 [8856]

Micro Symplex Corp., 2623 S 21st St., Phoenix, AZ 85034, (602)244-0080 [6496]

Micro-Trains Line Co., PO Box 1200, Talent, OR 97540-1200, (541)535-1755 [26576]

Micro-Tron Inc., 2918 Bridgeford Rd., Omaha, NE 68124-2515, (402)392-1856 [6497]

Microage, 219 1st Ave., Jamestown, ND 58401, (701)252-1835 [6498]

MicroAge Inc., PO Box 1920, Tempe, AZ 85282, (602)968-3168 [6499]

MicroCAD Technologies Inc., 1805 E Dyer Rd., Ste. 212, Santa Ana, CA 92705, (949)756-0588 [5887]

MicroCAD Technologies Inc., 1805 E Dyer Rd., Santa Ana, CA 92705, (714)756-0588 [6500]

Microchip Technology Inc., 2355 W Chandler Blvd., Chandler, AZ 85224-6199, (480)786-7200 [9074]

Microcomputer Cable Company Inc., 12200 Delta Dr., Taylor, MI 48180, (734)946-9700 [9075]

Microcomputer Company of Maryland Inc., 7668 Bel Air Rd., Baltimore, MD 21236, (410)668-2600 [6501]

Microfibres Inc., 1 Moshassuck St., Pawtucket, RI 02860, (401)725-4883 [26145]

Microform Systems Inc., 16803 Industrial Pkwy., Lansing, MI 48906, (517)323-3231 [21140]

Micrographics, PO Box 125, Waterloo, WI 53594-0125, (920)478-2889 [6502]

Microhelp Inc., 728 Thimble Shoals Blvd., No. E, Newport News, VA 23606-2574, (757)873-6707 [6503]

Microlink Enterprises Inc., 13731 E Proctor Ave., City of Industry, CA 91746, (626)330-9599 [6504]

Micronetics Inc. Information Management Systems, 14148 Magnolia Blvd., Sherman Oaks, CA 91423, (818)784-6890 [6505]

Microphor, 452 E Hill Rd., Willits, CA 95490, (707)459-5563 [23264]

Micropigmentation Devices Inc., 450 Raritan Center Pkwy., Edison, NJ 08837, (732)225-3700 [18982]

Micropoint Inc., 1280 L'Avinda Ave., Mountain View, CA 94043, (650)968-5511 [21141]

Micros of South Florida Inc., 852 S Military Trail, Deerfield Beach, FL 33442, (954)421-3184 [21142]

Micros-to-Mainframes Inc., 614 Corporate Way, Valley Cottage, NY 10989, (914)268-5000 [6506]

Microsearch Inc., 10515 Harwin Dr., Ste. 100, Houston, TX 77074, (713)988-2818 [6507]

Microsoft Corp., 1 Microsoft Way, Redmond, WA 98052-6399, (425)882-8080 [6508]

Microstar Computer Technology Inc., 13401 Brooks Dr., Baldwin Park, CA 91706, (626)337-9770 [6509]

MicroTech Conversion Systems, 2 Davis Dr., Belmont, CA 94002, (650)596-1900 [6510]

MICROTECH Systems Inc., 11940 SW Pacific Hwy., Ste. A, Tigard, OR 97223-6444, (503)620-9715 [6511]

Microtech-Tel Inc., 4985 Ironton St., Denver, CO 80239, (303)373-4444 [5675]

Microunited, 2200 E Golf Rd., Des Plaines, IL 60016, (847)699-5000 [6512]

Microware Inc., PO Box 55068, Portland, OR 97238-5068, (503)644-1296 [6513]

Microwave Oven Company of Oregon, 2114 SE 9th Ave., PO Box 14309, Portland, OR 97214-0309, (503)236-6140 [25314]

Mid-AM Building Supply Inc., 100 W Sparks, Moberly, MO 65270, (660)263-2140 [7704]

Mid-America Airgas Inc., PO Box 1117, Bowling Green, KY 42102-1117, (502)842-9486 [17034]

Mid-America Appliance Center, 2745 Belmont Blvd., Salina, KS 67401-7600, (785)825-8925 [25315]

Mid-America Auto Auction, 3515 Newburg Rd., Louisville, KY 40218, (502)454-6666 [20680]

Mid-America Dairymen Inc. Brown Swiss, PO Box 2553, Rapid City, SD 57709-2553 [11874]

Mid-America Dairymen Inc. Southern Div., 3253 E Chestnut Expwy., Springfield, MO 65802, (417)865-7100 [11875]

Mid-America Export Inc., 9650 E Colfax Ave., Aurora, CO 80010-5010, (303)364-3800 [15588]

Mid-America Footwear Co., 2700 Purdue Dr., Oklahoma City, OK 73128-5802, (405)681-5560 [24811]

Mid-America Industrial Equipment Co., 1601 N Corrington, Kansas City, MO 64120, (816)483-5000 [16294]

Mid-America Information Systems Inc., 908 Black Partridge, McHenry, IL 60050, (815)344-3564 [6514]

Mid-America Power Drives, 30 N 25th St., Ft. Dodge, IA 50501-4336, (515)955-7711 [17035]

Mid-America Power Drives, 420 NW Business Park Ln., Kansas City, MO 64150, (816)587-6363 [16028]

Mid-America Power Drives, 1601 Airport Rd., Waukesha, WI 53188, (414)896-3500 [16295]

Mid America Ribbon & Supply Co., 5710 Northwood Dr., Minneapolis, MN 55436-2054, (612)929-1656 [6515]

Mid-America Tile, 1650 Howard St., Elk Grove Village, IL 60007, (847)439-3110 [10029]

Mid-America Tile, 1412 Joliet Rd., Romeoville, IL 60446, (630)972-1500 [10030]

Mid-America Tile, Inc., 108 Terrace Dr., Mundelein, IL 60060, (847)566-5566 [10031]

Mid-America Tile L.P., 4809 W 128th Pl., Alsip, IL 60803, (708)388-4344 [10032]

Mid-America Wine Co., 3705 N Kenmore, Chicago, IL 60613, (773)327-7160 [1871]

Mid American Growers, Rte. 89, Granville, IL 61326, (815)339-6831 [14922]

Mid-Ark Salvage Pool Inc., 703 Hwy. 64 E, Conway, AR 72032, (501)796-2812 [2949]

Mid Atlantic Accessories, 4809 Lindstrom Dr., Charlotte, NC 28226-7905, (704)543-1828 [5192]

Mid Atlantic Foods Inc., 1842 Broad St., PO Box 367, Pocomoke City, MD 21851-9647, (410)957-4100 [11876]

Mid-Atlantic Marketing Inc., 966 Hungerford Dr., Ste. 31, Rockville, MD 20850-1714, (301)738-9270 [25316]

Mid-Atlantic Park & Playground Concepts, PO Box 710, Tunkhannock, PA 18657-0710, (570)836-8037 [23826]

Mid-Atlantic Snacks Inc., PO Box 232, York, PA 17405, (717)792-3454 [11877]

Mid-Atlantic Spa Distributors, 2611 Philmont Ave., Huntingdon Valley, PA 19006-5301, (215)947-8644 [23827]

Mid-Atlantic STIHL, Inc., 5017 Neal Rd., PO Box 2507, Durham, NC 27705, (919)383-7411 [16296]

Mid-Carolina Electric Supply Company, Inc., 1003 E Main, Rock Hill, SC 29730, (803)324-2944 [9076]

Mid-Central/Sysco Food Services Inc., PO Box 820, Olathe, KS 66061, (913)829-5555 [11878]

Mid-City Automotive Warehouse Inc., 3450 N Kostner Ave., Chicago, IL 60641, (773)282-9393 [2950]

Mid City Hardware, 130 W 25th St., New York, NY 10001, (212)807-8713 [4669]

Mid-City Iron and Metal Corp., 2104 E 15th St., Los Angeles, CA 90021, (213)747-4281 [20181]

Mid Columbia Producers Inc., PO Box 344, Moro, OR 97039, (503)565-3737 [18091]

Mid Continent Aircraft Corp., PO Box 540, Hayti, MO 63851, (314)359-0500 [128]

Mid-Continent Fire & Safety, Inc., 2909 S Spruce St., PO Box 16689, Wichita, KS 67216-6689, (316)522-0900 [24591]

Mid-Continent Paper Co., 4700 S Palisade, Wichita, KS 67217, (316)522-3494 [21964]

Mid-East Manufacturing Inc., 7694 Progress Cir., Melbourne, FL 32904, (407)724-1477 [25317]

Mid-East Materials Co., 25611 Colleen, Oak Park, MI 48237, (248)968-0043 [20182]

Mid-Iowa Cooperative (Beaman, Iowa), PO Box 80, Beaman, IA 50609, (515)366-2740 [18092]

Mid-Kansas Cooperative Association, PO Box D, Moundridge, KS 67107, (316)345-6328 [1027]

Mid-Lakes Distributing Inc., 1029 W Adams St., Chicago, IL 60607, (312)733-1033 [14602]

Mid-Michigan Regional Health Systems, 4005 Orchard Dr., Midland, MI 48640-6102, (517)839-3398 [18937]

Mid Michigan Trailer & Truck Equipment, Inc., 327 Lansing Rd., PO Box 427, Potterville, MI 48876, (517)645-8011 [2951]

Mid-Mountain Foods Inc., PO Box 129, Abingdon, VA 24210, (540)628-3105 [11879]

Mid Mountain Wholesale, 1308 1/2 Boulder Ave., Helena, MT 59601-3569, (406)449-7080 [26146]

Mid Pac Lumber, PO Box 31267, Honolulu, HI 96820-1267, (808)836-8111 [23265]

Mid-Penn Magazine Distributors, 935 N Washington Ave., Scranton, PA 18509-2924 [3954]

Mid-Plains Communications Systems Inc., 7520 Elmwood Ave., Middleton, WI 53562, (608)836-1912 [5676]

Mid-South Appliance Parts Inc., PO Box 193458, Little Rock, AR 72219-3458, (501)376-8351 [15229]

Mid-South Building Supply of Maryland Inc., 5640 Sunnyside Ave., Beltsville, MD 20705, (301)513-9000 [7705]

Mid-South Engine Systems Inc., 2063 Bonn St., Harvey, LA 70058, (504)347-2470 [18568]

Mid-South Malts/Memphis Brews Inc., 2537 Broad Ave., Memphis, TN 38112, (901)324-2739 [1872]

Mid South Marketing Inc., 285 German Oak Dr., Cordova, TN 38018, (901)755-8488 [25318]

Mid-South Metals Co., PO Box 96, Greenville, NC 27835, (919)752-5027 [26912]

Mid-South Oxygen Company Inc., 1385 Corporate Ave., Memphis, TN 38116, (901)396-5050 [17036]

Mid-South Supply Corp., 2417 S Wabash, Chicago, IL 60616-2306, (312)842-8282 [21501]

Mid-State Automotive, 915 N Cherry, Knoxville, TN 37917-7012, (423)523-5123 [2952]

Mid-State Bolt and Nut Company Inc., PO Box 2039, Columbus, OH 43216, (614)253-8631 [13827]

Mid-State Distributing, 2600 Bell Ave., Des Moines, IA 50321-1118, (515)244-7231 [9077]

Mid-State Distributors, 1201 Sheffler Dr., Chambersburg, PA 17201-6004, (717)263-2413 [3955]

Mid State Distributors Inc., PO Box 5886, Columbia, SC 29250, (803)771-6100 [1873]

Mid-State Industries Ltd., 1105 Catalyn St., Schenectady, NY 12303, (518)374-1461 [7706]

Mid-State Industries LLC, PO Box 68, Arcola, IL 61910, (217)268-3900 [20183]

Mid-State Periodicals Inc., 2516 W Schneidman Dr., PO Box 3455, Quincy, IL 62305, (217)222-0833 [3956]

Mid-State Potato Distributors Inc., 4302 W Airport Rd., Plant City, FL 33567-2489, (813)752-8866 [11880]

Mid State Power and Equipment Inc., PO Box 389, Columbus, WI 53925, (920)623-4020 [1028]

Mid States Classic Cars, 835 W Grant St., Hooper, NE 68031, (402)654-2772 [2953]

Mid States Concession Supply, 1026 S Burlington Dr., Muncie, IN 47302, (765)289-5505 [11881]

Mid-States Industrial Div., 907 S Main St., Rockford, IL 61105, (815)962-8841 [23266]

Mid States Paper/Notion Co., 810 Cherokee Ave., Nashville, TN 37207, (615)226-1234 [14161]

Mid-States Supply Company Inc., 1716 Guinotte Ave., Kansas City, MO 64120, (816)842-4290 [23267]

Mid-States Wool Growers Cooperative, 9449 Basil Western Rd., Canal Winchester, OH 43110, (614)837-9665 [1029]

Mid Valley Dairy Inc., PO Box 2898, Fairfield, CA 94533, (707)864-0502 [12625]

Mid-Valley Supply Co., 1912 S 1st St., Ironton, OH 45638, (614)532-3500 [17037]

Mid-West Crafts Inc., PO Box 367, Whitley City, KY 42653-0367, (606)376-5152 [26577]

Mid-West Golf Inc., PO Box 404, Westfield, IN 46074-0404, (317)896-3443 [5193]

Mid-West Materials Inc., 3687 Shepard Rd., PO Box 345, Perry, OH 44081, (440)259-5200 [20184]

Mid West Oil Ltd., PO Box 1681, Enid, OK 73702, (580)237-0299 [22480]

Mid-West Paper Products Co., 1237 S 11th St., Louisville, KY 40210, (502)636-2741 [21835]

Mid-West Steel Supply Co., 1328 N 2nd St., Minneapolis, MN 55411, (612)333-6868 [20185]

Mid-Wood Inc., 12818 E Gypsy Lane Rd., Bowling Green, OH 43402, (419)352-5231 [18093]

Midamar Corp., PO Box 218, Cedar Rapids, IA 52406, (319)362-3711 [11882]

MidAmerican Metals Company Inc., 519 E Third St., Owensboro, KY 42303, (502)926-3515 [2954]

Midark Optical, 23908 I-30, Ste. A, Alexander, AR 72002, (501)847-0271 [19455]

MIDCO International, 908 W Fayette Ave., PO Box 748, Effingham, IL 62401, (217)342-9211 [25319]

MIDCO International, 1926 Silver St., Garland, TX 75042, (972)272-8399 [25320]

Midco International Inc. (Effingham, Illinois), PO Box 748, Effingham, IL 62401, (217)342-9211 [25737]

Middle Tennessee Utility District, P.O Box 670, Smithville, TN 37166, (615)597-4300 [15230]

Middlefield Optical Company, Inc., 14561 Old State Rd., PO Box 1079, Middlefield, OH 44062, (440)632-0107 [19456]

Middleground Golf Inc., PO Box 612, Leitchfield, KY 42755-0612, (270)259-5510 [23828]

Middleville Apparel Co., 227 Spring St., PO Box 9, Middleville, MI 49333, (616)795-3341 [4796]

Midland 66 Oil Company Inc., 1612 Garden City Hwy., Midland, TX 79701, (915)682-9404 [22481]

Midland Aluminum Corp., 4635 W 160th St., Cleveland, OH 44135, (216)267-8044 [20186]

Midland Bean Co., PO Box 484, Dove Creek, CO 81324, (303)677-2215 [18094]

Midland Bottling Co., 1422 S 6th, St. Joseph, MO 64501-3638, (816)232-8477 [1874]

Midland Co-Op Inc., PO Box 560, Danville, IN 46122, (317)745-4491 [1030]

Midland Computers, 5699 W Howard St., Niles, IL 60714-4011, (847)588-2130 [6516]

Midland Cooperative Inc., 101 Main St., Axtell, NE 68924, (308)263-2441 [1031]

Midland Cooperative Inc., 101 Main St., Axtell, NE 68924, (308)743-2424 [11883]

Midland Cooperative Inc. Wilcox Div., PO Box 188, Wilcox, NE 68982, (308)478-5231 [18095]

Midland Groceries Michigan Inc., PO Box 570, Muskegon, MI 49443, (616)722-3151 [11884]

Midland Grocery Co., PO Box 125, Westville, IN 46391, (219)785-4671 [11885]

Midland Hospital Supply Inc., PO Box 2685, Fargo, ND 58108, (701)235-4451 [18938]

Midland Implement Co., PO Box 30358, Billings, MT 59107-0358, (406)248-7771 [1032]

Midland Iron and Steel Co., 3301 4th Ave., Moline, IL 61265, (309)764-6723 [26913]

Midland Lock & Safe Service, 1408 N Big Spring, Midland, TX 79701-2754, (915)682-4202 [24592]

Midland Marketing Cooperative, Inc., PO Box 639, Hays, KS 67601-0639, (785)628-3221 [18096]

Midland Medical Supply Co., 4850 Old Cheney Rd., Lincoln, NE 68516, (402)423-8877 [19457]

Midland Reclamation Co., RR 2 Box 100, Dow, IL 62022-9613, (618)885-5494 [23484]

Midland Steel, 1615 Dublin Rd., Midland, MI 48642, (517)631-6466 [20187]

Midland Steel Warehouse Co., 1120 Leggett Ave., Bronx, NY 10474, (718)328-4600 [20188]

Midland Suppliers Inc., 4804 Superior St., Lincoln, NE 68504-1441, (402)466-4000 [9078]

Midmarch Arts Press, 300 Riverside Dr., New York, NY 10025, (212)666-6990 [3957]

Midnight Sun Boat Company, Inc., 201 N Bragaw St., Anchorage, AK 99508, (907)279-3925 [18569]

Midor Ltd., N 3503 County T, PO Box 168, Elroy, WI 53929-9605, (608)462-8275 [1033]

Midpac Lumber Company Ltd., 1001 Ahua St., Honolulu, HI 96819, (808)836-8111 [7707]

Midsouth Electric Corp., PO Box 276, Austell, GA 30168-0276, (404)941-0110 [25321]

Midstate Beverage Inc., 5200 Franklin Ave., Waco, TX 76710-6924, (254)753-0305 [1875]

Midstate Mills Inc., PO Box 349, Newton, NC 28658, (704)464-1611 [11886]

Midtown Electric Supply, 157 W 18th, New York, NY 10011-4101, (212)255-3388 [9079]

Midtown Packing Company Inc., 2276 12th Ave., New York, NY 10027, (212)866-9150 [11887]

Midvale Industries Inc., 6310 Knox Industrial Dr., St. Louis, MO 63139-3092, (314)647-5604 [16297]

Midway Inc., 220 Sandusky St., Monroeville, OH 44847, (419)465-2551 [2955]

Midway Motor Supply Core Supplier, 68 W Sheffield, Pontiac, MI 48340, (248)332-4755 [2956]

Midway Oil Co., PO Box 4540, Rock Island, IL 61204, (309)788-4549 [22482]

Midway Parts Inc., 708 E Highway 212, Gettysburg, SD 57442-1814, (605)765-2466 [2957]

Midway Trading, Inc., PO Box 2128, Reston, VA 20195, (703)471-4020 [2958]

Midwest Action Cycle, 251 Host Dr., Lake Geneva, WI 53147-4607, (262)249-0600 [20681]

MidWest Air Motive Corp., PO Box 1014, Bismarck, ND 58502-1014, (701)663-7747 [129]

Midwest Athlete, 402 Church St., Ottumwa, IA 52501-4213, (515)682-2144 [5194]

Midwest Auto Parts Distributors Inc., PO Box 8158, St. Paul, MN 55108-0158, (612)644-6448 [2959]

Midwest Beverage Company Inc., 14200 E Moncrieff Pl., Aurora, CO 80011, (303)371-0832 [1876]

Midwest Bolt and Supply Inc., 405 E 14th Ave., North Kansas City, MO 64116, (816)842-7880 [13828]

Midwest Chemical and Supply Inc., 340 E 56th Ave., Denver, CO 80216, (303)293-2122 [4670]

Midwest Cleaning Systems Inc., E. 1st St., Alcester, SD 57001, (605)934-1711 [4671]

Midwest Coca-Cola Bottling Co. Rhinelander, PO Box 1108, Rhinelander, WI 54501, (715)362-3131 [24988]

Midwest Coil Processing, 720 E 111th St., Chicago, IL 60628, (312)468-2121 [20189]

Midwest Consolidated Cooperative, PO Box 129, Cyrus, MN 56323-0129, (612)795-2714 [1034]

Midwest Coop., PO Box 366, Quinter, KS 67752, (785)754-3348 [11888]

Midwest Cooperative, PO Box 366, Quinter, KS 67752, (785)754-3348 [1035]

Midwest Cooperatives, PO Box 787, Pierre, SD 57501, (605)224-5935 [18097]

Midwest Distributing Inc., Rte. 1, PO Box 39, Linden, IN 47955, (765)339-7283 [1036]

Midwest Distributors, PO Box 5224, Kansas City, KS 66119 [3958]

Midwest Electric Inc., PO Box 1198, Sioux City, IA 51102-1198, (712)252-4574 [15231]

Midwest Environmental Safety Supply, 1817 Gardner Rd., Broadview, IL 60153, (708)343-6766 [25738]

Midwest Farmers Cooperative, PO Box 65, Hospers, IA 51238, (712)752-8421 [1037]

Midwest Farmers Cooperative, PO Box 65, Hospers, IA 51238, (712)752-8421 [11889]

Midwest Floors, 2714 Breckenridge Indct., St. Louis, MO 63144, (314)647-6060 [10033]

Midwest Greeting Card Distributor, 2443 Burl Ct., Mc Farland, WI 53558, (608)838-6018 [21836]

Midwest Industrial Coatings Inc., 6667 W Old Shakopee Rd., Ste. 101, Bloomington, MN 55438, (612)942-1840 [21502]

Midwest Labs, 1450 N Dayton, Chicago, IL 60622, (773)261-3131 [19458]

Midwest Labs, Inc., 117 Salem St., PO Box 519, Indianola, IA 50125, (515)961-6593 [19459]

Midwest Lens, 14304 W 100 St., Lenexa, KS 66215, (913)894-1030 [19460]

Midwest Library Service, 11443 St. Charles Rock Rd., Bridgeton, MO 63044-2789, (314)739-3100 [3959]

Midwest Machinery, 12500 S Dupont Ave., Burnsville, MN 55337, (952)890-8880 [16441]

Midwest Machinery, 12500 S Dupont Ave., Burnsville, MN 55337, (612)890-8880 [16298]

Midwest Marine Supply Co., 24300 E Jefferson Ave., St. Clair Shores, MI 48080, (810)778-8950 [18570]

Midwest Medical Supply Company Inc., 13400 Lakefront Dr., Bridgeton, MO 63044, (314)291-2900 [19461]

Midwest Metallics L.P., 135 S LaSalle St., Ste. 3600, Chicago, IL 60603-4110, (708)594-7171 [20190]

Midwest Metals Inc., PO Box 4050, Davenport, IA 52808, (319)324-5243 [20191]

MidWest Micro, 6910 U.S Rte. 36 E, Fletcher, OH 45326, (937)368-2650 [6517]

Midwest Music Distributors, 5024 Montgomery Rd., Cincinnati, OH 45212, (513)631-8318 [25322]

Midwest Office Furniture and Supply Company Inc., 987 SW Temple, Salt Lake City, UT 84101, (801)359-7681 [21143]

Midwest Oil Co., 615 E 8th St., Sioux Falls, SD 57103, (605)336-3337 [22483]

Midwest Optical Laboratories, Inc., PO Box 842, Dayton, OH 45401, (937)878-6667 [19462]

Midwest Plastics Supply Inc., 2248 S Mead, Wichita, KS 67211, (316)267-7511 [22998]

Midwest Pool Distributors Inc., 7607 Murphy Dr., Middleton, WI 53562, (608)831-5957 [23829]

Midwest Refrigeration Supply Inc., 4717 F St., Omaha, NE 68117, (402)733-4900 [5844]

Midwest Refrigeration Supply Inc., 4717 F St., Omaha, NE 68117, (402)733-4900 [16299]

Midwest Sales Company of Iowa Inc., 1700 W 29th St., Kansas City, MO 64108, (816)753-0586 [7708]

Midwest Sales and Service Inc., 917 S Chapin St., South Bend, IN 46601-2829, (219)287-3365 [25323]

Midwest Sales and Service Inc., 917 S Chapin St., South Bend, IN 46601, (219)287-3365 [15232]

Midwest Sports Cards, 7190 University Ave. NE, Minneapolis, MN 55432-3100, (612)572-1770 [26578]

Midwest Telephone Inc., 883 S Lapeer Rd., Ste. 102, Lake Orion, MI 48362, (248)693-7775 [5677]

Midwest Tile, 200W Industrial Lake Dr., Lincoln, NE 68528, (402)476-2542 [10034]

Midwest Tile, 1421 Locust St., Des Moines, IA 50309, (515)283-1242 [10035]

Midwest Tile Supply Co., 4515 S 90th St., Omaha, NE 68127-1313, (402)331-3800 [10036]

Midwest Truck and Auto Parts Inc., 4200 S Morgan St., Chicago, IL 60609-2517, (312)225-1550 [2960]

Midwest Truck Equipment Inc., 825 N Main, Paris, IL 61944, (217)465-8785 [20682]

Midwest Veneer Company, 21168 Pke. 136, Louisiana, MO 63353, (573)754-4072 [7709]

Midwest Veterinary Supply Inc., 11965 Larc Industrial Blvd., Burnsville, MN 55337, (612)894-4350 [27189]

Midwest Vision Distributors Inc., Hwy. 23 E, Box 1167, St. Cloud, MN 56301, (612)252-6006 [18939]

Midwest Visual Equipment Co., 6500 N Hamlin Ave., Chicago, IL 60645, (312)478-1250 [25324]

Midwest Wrecking Co., PO Box 3757, Edmond, OK 73083, (405)478-8833 [2961]

Miedema Produce, Inc., 5005 40th Ave., Hudsonville, MI 49426, (616)669-9420 [11890]

Miesel/SYSCO Food Service Co., PO Box 33579, Detroit, MI 48232-5579, (734)397-7990 [12679]

Mifax-New Hampshire, 30 Liscette Dr., Salem, NH 03079, (603)898-5631 [21144]

Mighty Distributing System of America Inc., 650 Engineering Dr., Norcross, GA 30092, (770)448-3900 [2962]

Mikan Theatricals, 86 Tide Mill Rd., Hampton, NH 03842, (603)926-2744 [25739]

Mikara Corp., 3109 Louisiana Ave., Minneapolis, MN 55427, (612)546-9500 [14162]

Mikara Corp., 3109 Louisiana Ave., Minneapolis, MN 55427, (612)546-9500 [24185]

Mike-Sell's Inc., 333 Leo St., Dayton, OH 45404, (937)228-9400 [11891]

Mike Sell's Indiana Inc., 5767 Dividend Rd., Indianapolis, IN 46277, (317)241-7422 [11892]

Mike-Sell's Potato Chip Co., 333 Leo St., Dayton, OH 45404, (513)228-9400 [11893]

Mikes Computerland, PO Box 1120, Lebanon, VA 24266-1120, (540)889-5738 [6518]

Mike's Refrigeration Inc., 209 Highway 52 E, Velva, ND 58790-7347 [14603]

MIL-Pack Inc., 1380 Welsh Rd., Montgomeryville, PA 18936, (215)628-8085 [9080]

Mil-Spec Supply Inc., 21119 Superior St., Chatsworth, CA 91311, (818)700-1001 [9081]

Milam Optical Co. Inc.; J.S., PO Box 700, Nashville, TN 37202-0700, (615)242-3372 [19463]

Milan Farmers Elevator, PO Box 32, Milan, MN 56262, (320)734-4435 [18098]

Milan Farmers Elevator, PO Box 32, Milan, MN 56262, (320)734-4435 [11894]

Milano Brothers International Corp., 378 SW 12th Ave., Deerfield Beach, FL 33442-3106, (305)420-5000 [9082]

Milart Ceramics Inc., 26164 Westfield, Redford, MI 48239-1841, (313)937-2780 [25740]

Milchap Products, PO Box 27286, Milwaukee, WI 53227, (414)321-3111 [7710]

Mile Hi Frozen Food Co., 4770 E 51st, Denver, CO 80216, (303)399-6066 [11895]

Mile High Equipment Co., 11100 E 45th Ave., Denver, CO 80239, (303)371-3737 [24186]

Miles Farm Supply Inc., PO Box 22879, Owensboro, KY 42304, (502)926-2420 [1038]

Miles Treaster and Associates, 3480 Industrial Blvd., West Sacramento, CA 95691, (916)373-1800 [13180]

Milford Enterprises, Inc., 950 Glenmore Ave., Brooklyn, NY 11208, (718)277-6913 [10037]

Milgray Electronics Inc., 220 Rabro Dr., Hauppauge, NY 11788-4232, (516)420-9800 [9083]

Milhem & Brothers; Attea, 1509 Clinton, Buffalo, NY 14206-3008, (716)822-1665 [26329]

Military Industrial Supply Co., 1720 Main St., Ste. 1, Palm Bay, FL 32905, (321)952-8877 [130]

Milk Marketing Inc., PO Box 5530, Akron, OH 44334-0530, (216)826-4730 [11896]

Milk Products Holdings Inc., 3645 Westwind Blvd., Santa Rosa, CA 95403, (707)524-6700 [11897]

Mill City Music Record Distribution, Inc., 3820 E Lake St., Minneapolis, MN 55406, (612)722-6649 [25325]

Mill Contractor and Industrial Supplies, Inc., 7522 Pendleton Pke., Indianapolis, IN 46226, (317)545-6904 [7711]

Mill Creek Lumber and Supply Co., 6974 E 38th St., Tulsa, OK 74145-3203 [7712]

Mill-Log Equipment Company Inc., PO Box 8099, Coburg, OR 97408, (503)485-2203 [16300]

Mill Steel Co., PO Box 8827, Grand Rapids, MI 49518, (616)949-6700 [20192]

Mill Supplies Corp., PO Box 12120, Lansing, MI 48901-2120, (517)372-6610 [17038]

Mill Supplies Inc., 5105 Industrial Rd., PO Box 11286, Ft. Wayne, IN 46825-5266, (219)484-8566 [17039]

Mill Supply Corp., PO Box 12216, Salem, OR 97309, (503)585-7411 [2963]

Mill Waste Recovery Inc., PO Box 145, Brokaw, WI 54417, (715)675-5572 [26914]

Millard Metal Service Center, PO Box 9054, Braintree, MA 02184-9054, (617)848-1400 [20193]

Millbrook Distribution Services, PO Box 790, Harrison, AR 72602-0790, (870)741-3425 [14163]

Millbrook Distributors Inc., Rte. 56, Leicester, MA 01524, (508)892-8171 [14164]

Millbrook Sales & Service Co., 3060 Madison Ave. SE, Wyoming, MI 49548-1273, (616)241-0157 [5678]

The Millcraft Group, 6800 Grant Ave., Cleveland, OH 44105, (216)441-5500 [21837]

Millcraft Paper Co., 6800 Grant Ave., Cleveland, OH 44105, (216)441-5500 [21837]

Millcraft Paper Co., 6800 Grant Ave., Cleveland, OH 44105, (216)441-5505 [21838]

Mille Lacs Agriculture Services Inc., 10 1st St., Pease, MN 56363, (320)369-4220 [1039]

Miller Bearings Inc., 1635 N Magnolia Ave., Ocala, FL 34475, (352)732-4141 [17040]

Miller Bearings Inc., 17 S Westmoreland Dr., Orlando, FL 32805, (407)425-9078 [2964]

Miller Bearings Inc., 3210 Power Ave., Jacksonville, FL 32207, (904)737-9919 [2965]

Miller Bearings Inc., 6681 NW 82nd Ave., Miami, FL 33166, (305)593-1724 [2966]

Miller Bearings Inc., 1132 53rd Court N, West Palm Beach, FL 33407, (561)863-5111 [2967]

Miller Bearings Inc., 17 S Westmoreland Dr., Orlando, FL 32805, (407)425-9078 [17041]

Miller Brands, 31281 Wiegman Rd., Hayward, CA 94544-7809, (510)489-1919 [1877]

Miller Brands of the East Bay, 31281 Wiegman Rd., Hayward, CA 94544-7809, (510)489-1919 [1560]

Miller-Brands-Milwaukee L.L.C., 1400 N 113th St., Wauwatosa, WI 53226, (414)258-2337 [1878]

Miller Bros. Lumber Company Inc., 4918 W Lawrence Ave., Chicago, IL 60630-3883, (773)283-3460 [7713]

Miller Brothers Giant Tire Service Inc., PO Box 3965, Cayce, SC 29033, (803)796-8880 [2968]

Miller and Company Inc., 500 Hooper Dr., Selma, AL 36701, (205)874-8271 [7714]

Miller Corp.; C.C., PO Box 396, Morrisville, VT 05661-0396, (802)888-3670 [18099]

Miller of Dallas Inc., 2730 Irving Blvd., Dallas, TX 75207, (214)630-0777 [1879]

Miller Distributing, 43 E 5th St., Yuma, AZ 85364, (520)783-2136 [22484]

Miller Distributing Ft. Worth, PO Box 3062, Ft. Worth, TX 76113, (817)877-5960 [1880]

Miller Electric Co. (Omaha, Nebraska), 2501 St. Marys Ave., Omaha, NE 68105, (402)341-6479 [9084]

Miller Funeral Home Inc., 507 S Main Ave., Sioux Falls, SD 57104-6813, (605)336-2640 [25741]

Miller Hardware Co., 2 Necessity Ave., Harrison, AR 72601, (501)741-3493 [13829]

Miller and Hartman Inc., PO Box 81784, Lancaster, PA 17608, (717)397-8261 [11898]

Miller and Hartman South Inc., PO Box 218, Leitchfield, KY 42755-0218, (502)444-7246 [11899]

Miller Inc.; Herman, 2525 Arizona Biltmore Circle, No. 142, Phoenix, AZ 85016-2146, (602)955-3779 [13181]

Miller Inc.; Luther P., PO Box 714, Somerset, PA 15501, (814)445-6569 [22485]

Miller Industrial Tools Inc., 20315-19 Nordhoff St., Chatsworth, CA 91311, (818)983-1805 [16301]

Miller-Jackson Co., PO Box 26226, Oklahoma City, OK 73126, (405)235-8426 [5679]

Miller Livestock Sales Co., PO Box 237, Bassett, NE 68714-0237, (402)853-2461 [18100]

Miller Lumber Inc.; William T., PO Box 873, Camden, SC 29020, (803)432-6041 [7715]

Miller Lumber Industries Inc., PO Box 207, Montross, VA 22520, (804)472-2040 [7716]

Miller Machinery Corp., PO Box 668, Killingworth, CT 06419, (860)663-3511 [16302]

Miller Machinery and Supply Co., 127 NE 27th St., Miami, FL 33137, (305)573-1300 [24187]

Miller Machinery and Supply Company of Tampa, PO Box 4039, Jacksonville, FL 32201-4039, (813)623-3553 [4457]

Miller Mechanical Specialties, PO Box 1613, Des Moines, IA 50306, (515)243-4287 [24397]

Miller Metal Service Corp., 2400 Bond St., University Park, IL 60466, (708)534-7200 [20194]

Miller Office Pavillion; Herman, 2900 E Robinson St., Orlando, FL 32803, (407)895-5159 [21145]

Miller Oil Co., 1000 E City Hall Ave., Norfolk, VA 23504, (757)623-1682 [22486]

Miller Refrigeration Supply Co., 2915 N Jackson Hwy., Sheffield, AL 35660-3434, (205)381-6000 [14604]

Miller Safety Products, 1209 Orville Ave., Kansas City, KS 66102-5114, (913)321-4955 [24812]

Miller Safety Products, 1209 Orville Ave., Kansas City, KS 66102-5114, (913)321-4955 [5195]

Miller Sales Co.; Simon, 1218 Chestnut St., Philadelphia, PA 19107, (215)923-3600 [21839]

Miller Sellner Implement Inc., Hwy. 4 S, Sleepy Eye, MN 56085, (507)794-2131 [1040]

Miller Stockyards; A.E., N Main, Delphos, OH 45833, (419)695-1851 [18101]

Miller Supply Inc.; Bud, PO Box 5738, Ft. Wayne, IN 46895-5738, (219)482-3778 [14605]

Miller Tire Co. Inc., 3801 N Broadway Ave., Muncie, IN 47303, (765)282-4322 [2969]

Miller Tire Distributors, 3822 N Broadway Ave., Muncie, IN 47303, (765)282-7405 [2970]

Miller Tire Service Inc., PO Box 883, Columbia, SC 29203-6436, (803)252-5675 [2971]

Miller Welding Supply Company Inc., 1635 W Spenser St., Appleton, WI 54912, (920)734-9821 [16303]

Miller Wholesale Electric Supply Co., Inc.—Morristown Division, PO Box 337, Morristown, NJ 07963-0337, (973)538-1600 [9085]

Miller Workplace Resources; Herman, 2900 E Robinson St., Orlando, FL 32803, (407)895-5159 [21145]

Miller's Adaptive Technologies, 2023 Romig Rd., Akron, OH 44320, (330)753-9799 [19464]

Miller's Bakery Inc., 1415 N 5th St., Milwaukee, WI 53212, (414)347-2300 [11900]

Miller's Interiors Inc., PO Box 1116, Lynnwood, WA 98046, (425)743-3213 [10038]

Millers Rents & Sells, 2023 Romig Rd., Akron, OH 44320, (330)753-9799 [19464]

Millers Rents & Sells, 5410 Warner Rd., Cleveland, OH 44125, (216)642-1447 [19465]

Miller's Supply, PO Box 938, Anniston, AL 36202, (205)237-5415 [23268]

Millers Wholesale, Inc., PO Box 1070, Battle Creek, MI 49016-1070, (616)965-0518 [25742]

Millersburg Tire Service Inc., 7375 State Rte. 39 E, Millersburg, OH 44654, (330)674-1085 [2972]

Milligan News Co., Inc., 150 N Autumn St., San Jose, CA 95110, (408)298-3322 [3960]

Milligan-Spika Co., 463 Roland Way, PO Box 14006, Oakland, CA 94621, (510)562-6667 [17042]

Milliken & Co., 419 Skyline Dr., Elkhorn, NE 68022, (402)289-1029 [10039]

Millitrade International Inc., 6245 S Central Ave., Phoenix, AZ 85040, (602)276-2400 [20195]

Millman Lumber Co., 9264 Manchester Rd., St. Louis, MO 63144, (314)968-1700 [7717]

Mills Alloy Steel Co., 10160 Phillips Pkwy., Streetsboro, OH 44241, (330)656-0001 [20196]

Mills Communication Inc., 210 Pennsylvania Ave., Westminster, MD 21157-4343, (410)876-8600 [9086]

Mills Farmers Elevator, 14 Main Ave. S, New York Mills, MN 56567, (218)385-2366 [1041]

Mills, Inc.; Aladin, 1320 NW 163rd St., Miami, FL 33169, (305)624-8787 [10040]

Mills Inc.; Glen, 395 Allwood Rd., Clifton, NJ 07012-1704, (973)777-0777 [16304]

Mills and Lupton Supply Co., PO Box 1639, Chattanooga, TN 37401, (423)266-6171 [9087]

Mills Wilson George Inc., 1847 Vanderhorn Dr., Memphis, TN 38134, (901)373-5100 [16305]

Millstone Service Div., 20320 80th Ave. S, Kent, WA 98032, (206)575-1243 [11901]

Milner Document Products Inc., 5125 Peachtree Industrial Blvd., Norcross, GA 30092-3027, (770)263-5300 [21146]

Milrank Knitwear Inc., 9731 Sinclair Cir., Garden Grove, CA 92844-3247, (213)773-2588 [5196]

Milroy and Company Inc.; W.H., 29 Washington Ave., Hamden, CT 06518, (203)248-4451 [7718]

Miltan Export Corp., 47 Walker St., New York, NY 10013, (212)334-0202 [26147]

MILTCO Corp., PO Box 1321, Harrisburg, PA 17105, (717)541-8130 [3961]

Miltex International Inc., 7012 Union Ave., Cleveland, OH 44105-1330, (216)645-8390 [26148]

Milton's Foodservice Inc., 3501 Old Oakwood Rd., Oakwood, GA 30566, (404)532-7779 [12162]

Milton's Institutional Foods, Old Oakwood Rd., Oakwood, GA 30566-2802, (404)532-7779 [11902]

Milvan Packaging Company Inc., 31090 San Antonio St., Hayward, CA 94544-7904, (510)793-7918 [22999]

Milwaukee Appliance Parts Company Inc., 3455 N 124th St., Brookfield, WI 53005, (414)781-0111 [15233]

Milwaukee Biscuit, 6200 N Baker Rd., Milwaukee, WI 53209, (414)228-8585 [11903]

Milwaukee Stove and Furnace Supply Company Inc., 5070 W State St., Milwaukee, WI 53208, (414)258-0300 [14606]

Mimbres Valley Farmers Association Inc., 811 S Platinum St., Deming, NM 88030, (505)546-2769 [1042]

MIMICS Inc., PO Drawer 606, Angel Fire, NM 87710, (505)377-3955 [6519]

Mims Meat Company Inc., PO Box 24776, Houston, TX 77015, (713)453-0151 [11904]

Minami International Corp., 4 Executive Plz., Yonkers, NY 10701, (914)969-7555 [13404]

Mindis Acquisition Corp., 1990 Defor Ave., Atlanta, GA 30318, (404)332-1750 [26915]

MindWorks Corp., PO Box 60325, Sunnyvale, CA 94088-0325, (408)730-2100 [6520]

Mine and Mill Supply Co., 2500 S Combee Rd., Lakeland, FL 33801, (863)665-5601 [20197]

Mine Supply Co., PO Box 1330, Carlsbad, NM 88220, (505)887-2888 [17043]

Minfelt Wholesale Company Inc., PO Box 127, Syracuse, NY 13211, (315)455-5541 [7719]

Mingledorffs Inc., 6675 Jones Mill Ct., Norcross, GA 30092, (404)446-6311 [14607]

Mingo Cooperative Grain Co., 116 Misner, Mingo, Colby, KS 67701, (785)462-2033 [429]

Mini-Micro Supply Company Inc., 4900 Patrick Henry Dr., Santa Clara, CA 95054, (408)327-0388 [6521]

Miniat Inc.; Ed, 945 W 38th St., Chicago, IL 60609, (773)927-9200 [11905]

Minier Cooperative Grain Co., PO Box 650, Minier, IL 61759, (309)392-2424 [18102]

Mining Construction Supply, 1780 E Benson Hwy., Tucson, AZ 85714, (520)889-1100 [13830]

Minkin Chandler Corp., 13501 Sanders Ave., Detroit, MI 48217, (313)843-5900 [26916]

Minn-Kota AG Products Inc., PO Box 175, Breckenridge, MN 56520, (218)643-8464 [18103]

Minneapolis Equipment Co., 520 2nd St., SE, Minneapolis, MN 55414, (612)378-0111 [7720]

Minneapolis Glass Co., 14600 28th Ave. N, Plymouth, MN 55447, (612)559-0635 [7721]

Minneapolis Northstar Auto Auction Inc., 4908 Valley Industl Blvd. N, Shakopee, MN 55379, (612)445-5544 [20683]

Minneapolis Rusco Inc., 9901 Smetana Rd., Minnetonka, MN 55343-9003, (612)942-0641 [7722]

Minneola Cooperative Inc., PO Box 376, Minneola, KS 67865, (316)885-4235 [18104]

Minnesota Chemical Co., 2285 Hampden Ave., St. Paul, MN 55114, (612)646-7521 [4458]

Minnesota Clay Co. USA, 8001 Grand Ave., Minneapolis, MN 55420-1128, (612)884-9101 [26579]

Minnesota Conway, 4565 W 77th St., Edina, MN 55435-5009, (612)893-0798 [24593]

Minnesota Cultivated Wild Rice Council, 1306 W County Rd. F, Ste. 109, St. Paul, MN 55112, (612)638-1955 [11906]

Minnesota Electrical Supply Co., PO Box 997, Willmar, MN 56201, (612)235-2255 [9088]

Minnesota Mining & Manufacturing Co., 3M Center, St. Paul, MN 55144-1000, (612)737-6501 [21147]

Minnesota Mining & Manufacturing Co. Do-It-Yourself Div., 3M Center, Bldg. 223-4S-02, St. Paul, MN 55144-1000, (612)733-2931 [17044]

Minnesota Produce Inc., 2801 Wayzata Blvd., Minneapolis, MN 55405, (612)377-6790 [11907]

Minnesota Supply Co., 6470 Flying Cloud Dr., Eden Prairie, MN 55344, (612)941-9390 [16306]

Minnesota Western Inc., 921 Parker St., Berkeley, CA 94710, (510)848-2600 [25326]

Minnetonka Mills Inc., 810 1st St. S, Hopkins, MN 55343, (612)935-2663 [26149]

Minolta Corp., 101 Williams Dr., Ramsey, NJ 07446, (201)825-4000 [22878]

Minolta Corp., 11150 Hope St., Cypress, CA 90630, (714)895-6633 [22879]

Minooka Grain Lumber and Supply Co., PO Box 100, Minooka, IL 60447, (815)467-2232 [7723]

Minot Builders Supply Association, Hwy. 2 & 52 W, Minot, ND 58701, (701)852-1301 [7724]

Minster Farmers Cooperative Exchange Inc., PO Box 100, Minster, OH 45865, (419)628-2367 [18105]

Minter-Weisman Co., 1035 Nathan Ln. W, Plymouth, MN 55441-5081, (612)545-3706 [11908]

Minton-Jones Co., 1859-I Beaver Ridge Cir., Norcross, GA 30071, (770)449-4787 [13182]

Minton's Lumber and Supply Co., 455 W Evelyn Ave., Mountain View, CA 94041, (650)968-9201 [7725]

Mintzer Brothers Inc., PO Box 955, Rutland, VT 05702, (802)775-0834 [7726]

Minyard Food Stores Inc., 777 Freeport Pkwy., Coppell, TX 75019, (972)393-8700 [11909]

Minyard Food Stores Inc. Carnival Food Stores, PO Box 518, Coppell, TX 75019, (972)393-8700 [11910]

MIRA Inc., 87 Rumford Ave., Waltham, MA 02454, (617)894-2200 [18940]

Mirabile Beverage Company Inc., 710 E Main St., Norristown, PA 19401, (215)275-0285 [1881]

Miracle Computers Inc., 780 Montague Expwy., Ste. 202, San Jose, CA 95131, (408)435-8177 [6522]

Miracle Exclusives, Inc., PO Box 8, Port Washington, NY 11050, (516)621-3333 [15234]

Miracle Playground Sales, 27537 Commerce Ctr., Ste. 105, Temecula, CA 92590, (909)695-4515 [23830]

Miracle Recreation of Minnesota Inc., 2175 Brooke Ln., Hastings, MN 55033, (612)438-3630 [23831]

Mirage Rug Imports, 18924 S Laurel Park Rd., Rancho Dominguez, CA 90220, (310)669-8533 [10041]

Miramar Trading International Inc., 400 Foam St., Ste. 210, Monterey, CA 93940, (831)655-5450 [1882]

Mirassou Sales Co., 3000 Aborn Rd., San Jose, CA 95135, (408)274-4000 [1883]

Mirly Truck Center Inc., PO Box 9, Advance, MO 63730-0009, (573)722-3574 [2973]

Miroglio Textiles U.S.A. Inc., 1430 Broadway, New York, NY 10018, (212)382-2020 [26150]

Mirror Lite Co., PO Box 358, Rockwood, MI 48173-0358, (734)379-9828 [13405]

Misaba Steel Products Inc., 3213 S Saginaw Rd., Midland, MI 48640, (517)496-2720 [20198]

Misco Industries Inc., 155 N Market St., Ste. 125, Wichita, KS 67202-1802, (316)265-6641 [22487]

Misco Shawnee Inc., 2200 Forte Ct., Maryland Heights, MO 63043, (314)739-3337 [10042]

Misco Shawnee Inc., 2200 Forte Ct., Maryland Heights, MO 63043, (314)739-3337 [15589]

Miss Elliette Inc., 10829 Central Ave., South El Monte, CA 91733-3309, (213)585-2222 [5197]

Miss Kings Kitchen Inc, The Original Yahoo! Baking Co., 5302 Texoma Pkwy., Sherman, TX 75090-2112, (903)893-8151 [11911]

Miss Rubber & Specialty, 715 E McDowell Rd., Jackson, MS 39204-5908, (601)948-2575 [17059]

Missco Corporation of Jackson, 2510 Lakeland Ter., #100, Jackson, MS 39216, (601)948-8600 [13183]

Mission Janitorial Supplies, 9292 Activity Rd., San Diego, CA 92126, (858)566-6700 [4672]

Mission Lumber Co., 2210 Kansas City Rd., Olathe, KS 66061, (913)764-4243 [7727]

Mission Paint & Glass, PO Box 4665, Missoula, MT 59806-4665, (406)549-7802 [21503]

Mission Produce Inc., PO Box 5267, Oxnard, CA 93031-5267, (805)981-3650 [11912]

Mission Service Supply, PO Drawer 2957, West Monroe, LA 71294-2957, (318)397-2755 [25327]

Mission Valley Ford Trucks Sales Inc., PO Box 611150, San Jose, CA 95161, (408)436-2920 [2974]

Mississippi Safety Services Inc., PO Box 1379, Clinton, MS 39060, (601)924-7815 [24594]

Mississippi School Supply Co., 2510 Lakeland Ter., No. 100, Jackson, MS 39216, (601)987-8600 [21148]

Mississippi School Supply Co./MISSCO Corp., 2510 Lakeland Ter., No. 100, Jackson, MS 39216, (601)987-8600 [21148]

Mississippi Serum Distributors, 165 Wilmington St., PO Box 8776, Jackson, MS 39284-8776, (601)372-8434 [18941]

Mississippi Tool Supply Co., Hwy. 25 S, PO Box 204, Golden, MS 38847, (601)454-9245 [24595]

Mississippi Tool Supply Co., Hwy. 25 S, Golden, MS 38847, (601)454-9245 [24398]

Mississippi Valley Equipment Co., 1198 Pershall Rd., St. Louis, MO 63137, (314)869-8600 [7728]

Mississippi Valley STIHL, Inc., 3023 W Farmington Rd., Peoria, IL 61604, (309)676-1304 [16307]

Missoula Gold & Silver Exchange, 2020 Brooks St., Missoula, MT 59801-6646, (406)728-5786 [17525]

Missoula Hearing, 601 S Orange St., Missoula, MT 59801-2611, (406)549-1951 [18942]

Missouri Archaeological Society Inc., PO Box 958, Columbia, MO 65205, (573)882-3544 [3962]

Missouri Archaeological Society Inc., PO Box 958, Columbia, MO 65205, (573)882-3544 [3963]

Missouri Conrad Liquors, 1200 Taney, Kansas City, MO 64116-4413, (816)421-1145 [1884]

Missouri Export Trading Company, 1845 E Blaine, Springfield, MO 65803, (417)865-9283 [16308]

Missouri Petroleum Products, 1620 Woodson Rd., St. Louis, MO 63114, (314)991-2180 [22488]

Missouri Pipe Fittings Co., 400 Withers Ave., St. Louis, MO 63147, (314)421-0790 [23269]

Missouri Power Transmission, 1801 Santa Fe Pl., Columbia, MO 65202-1935, (573)474-1446 [2975]

Missouri Power Transmission, 3226 Blair Ave., St. Louis, MO 63107, (314)421-0919 [2976]

Missouri Swine Export Federation, 6235 Cunningham Dr., Rte. 11, Columbia, MO 65202, (573)445-8375 [18106]

Missouri Valley Electric Co., PO Box 419640, Kansas City, MO 64141, (816)471-5306 [9089]

Mister Remo of California Inc., 1801 Flower Ave., Duarte, CA 91010-2932, (626)357-3867 [5198]

Mistra, Inc., 22 42nd St. NW, Ste. A, Auburn, WA 98001, (253)852-3111 [25766]

Mitcham Industries Inc., PO Box 1175, Huntsville, TX 77342, (409)291-2277 [24399]

Mitchell Distributing Co., PO Box 32156, Charlotte, NC 28232, (704)376-7554 [7729]

Mitchell Hardware Co., Rte. 47, Delsea Dr., PO Box 96, Hurffville, NJ 08080, (856)589-1135 [23270]

Mitchell Home Medical, 4811 Carpenter Rd., Ypsilanti, MI 48197, (734)572-0203 [18943]

Mitchell-Hughes Co., PO Box 747, Wofford Heights, CA 93285, (760)376-4430 [16309]

Mitchell Inc.; E. Stewart, PO Box 2799, Baltimore, MD 21225, (410)354-0600 [7730]

Mitchell Industrial Tire Co., PO Box 71839, Chattanooga, TN 37407, (615)698-4442 [2977]

Mitchell Manufacturing, Hagens Division, 3150 W Havens, Box 82, Mitohell, SD 57301, (605)996-1891 [23832]

Mitchell Mogal Inc., 25 Hempstead Gardens Dr., West Hempstead, NY 11552, (516)564-1894 [13406]

Mitchell Orthopedic Supply Inc., PO Box 634, Brentwood, TN 37024-0634, (615)377-6900 [18944]

Mitchell-Powers Hardware, PO Box 2048, Bristol, TN 37621, (931)764-1153 [13831]

Mitchell Products; Allen, 1155 Industrial Ave., Oxnard, CA 93030-7407, (805)487-8595 [11913]

Mitchell Supreme Fuel Co., 532 Freeman St., Orange, NJ 07050, (201)678-1800 [22489]

Mitchell's Decorative Hardware, Rte. 47, Delsea Dr., PO Box 96, Hurffville, NJ 08080, (856)589-1135 [23270]

Mitchellville Cooperative, 101 S Center Ave., Mitchellville, IA 50169, (515)967-4288 [1043]

Mitee-Bite Products Inc., PO Box 430, Center Ossipee, NH 03814, (603)539-4538 [16310]

Mitek Industries Inc., PO Box 7359, St. Louis, MO 63177, (314)434-1200 [16311]

MITO Corp., 54905 County Rd. 17, Elkhart, IN 46516, (219)295-2441 [25328]

MITO Corp., 54905 County Rd. 17, Elkhart, IN 46516, (219)295-2441 [15235]

Mitscher Company Inc.; R.W., 9515 Main St., Clarence, NY 14031, (716)759-2350 [9090]

Mitsuba Corp., 1925 Wright Ave., La Verne, CA 91750, (909)392-2000 [6523]

Mitsubishi Electronics America Inc., PO Box 6007, Cypress, CA 90630, (714)220-2500 [25329]

Mitsubishi International Corp., 520 Madison Ave., New York, NY 10022, (212)605-2000 [26151]

Mitsubishi Intl Corp./Foods Div, 333 S Hope St Ste. 2500, Los Angeles, CA 90071, (213)687-2800 [11914]

Mitsubishi Motor Sales of America Inc., 6400 Katella Ave., Cypress, CA 90630-5208, (714)372-6000 [20684]

Mitsui and Company (U.S.A.) Inc., 200 Park Ave., New York, NY 10166, (212)878-4000 [20199]

Mitsui & Co. (USA), Inc. Seattle Branch, 1001 4th Ave., Ste. 3950, Seattle, WA 98154, (206)223-5604 [16312]

Mitsui Comtek Corp., 12980 Saratoga Ave., Saratoga, CA 95070, (408)725-8525 [6524]

Mitsui Foods, Inc., 35 Maple St., Norwood, NJ 07648-0409, (201)750-0500 [11915]

Mitsumi Electronics Corp., 5808 W Campus Cir. Dr., Irving, TX 75063, (972)550-7300 [6525]

Mitutoyo/MTI Corp., 965 Corporate Blvd., Aurora, IL 60504, (630)978-5385 [24400]

Mix Bookshelf, 6400 Hollis St., No. 12, Emeryville, CA 94608, (510)653-3307 [3964]

Mixon Fruit Farms Inc., PO Box 25200, Bradenton, FL 34206, (941)748-5829 [11916]

Mize Farm & Garden Supply, 625 Wesinpar, Johnson City, TN 37604, (423)928-2188 [27190]

Mizen International, Inc., 1603 Greenmount St., Rockford, IL 61107, (815)968-9700 [16313]

Mizutani USA, 31012 Huntwood Ave., Hayward, CA 94544, (510)487-2100 [13832]

MJL Corp., 1 Brozzini Court No. 1A, Greenville, SC 29615, (864)234-5992 [16314]

MK Health Food Distributors, 7180 Lampson Ave., Garden Grove, CA 92841-3914, (714)995-8858 [14165]

MKM Electronic Components Inc., 997 Palmr Ave., Mamaroneck, NY 10543-2409, (914)939-3940 [9091]

MKM Inc., 543 Newfield Ave., Stamford, CT 06905-3302, (203)324-3055 [18945]

MKS Industries Inc., 5801 Court St. Rd., PO Box 4948, Syracuse, NY 13221, (315)437-1511 [7731]

M.L. Sandy Lumber Sales Company Inc., PO Box 1535, Corinth, MS 38834-1535, (601)286-6087 [27346]

M.L. Wildey & Co., 2738 N Pleasantburg Dr., Greenville, SC 29609, (864)232-7996 [14053]

MLH and Associates, 1942 Mt. Shasta Dr., San Pedro, CA 90732, (310)519-9158 [6526]

MLT International Inc., PO Box 338, Line Lexington, PA 18932-0338, (215)699-5313 [17045]

MMB Music Inc., 3526 Washington Ave., St. Louis, MO 63103-1019, (314)427-5660 [25330]

MMC Metrology Lab Inc., 4989 Cleveland St., Virginia Beach, VA 23462, (804)456-2220 [24401]

MMI Inc., PO Box 305, Southfield, MI 48037, (248)358-1940 [18946]

MMRF Inc., PO Box 7049, Charlotte, NC 28241-7049, (704)588-5558 [15236]

MNP Fastener Distribution Group, 1500 W Bryn Mawr, Itasca, IL 60143, (217)621-1502 [13833]

Moates Sport Shop Inc.; Bob, 10418 Hull St., Midlothian, VA 23112, (804)276-2293 [13502]

Mobile Automotive Diagnostic, 309 Boston Rd., North Billerica, MA 01862-2621, (978)667-1934 [2978]

Mobile Beer & Wine Co., 966 N Beltline Hwy., Mobile, AL 36607-1109, (205)471-3486 [1885]

Mobile Communications of Gwinnett, 885 Cripple Creek Dr., Lawrenceville, GA 30043-4402, (404)963-3748 [5680]

Mobile Cycle Center, 5373 Halls Mill Rd., Mobile, AL 36619, (205)666-2650 [23833]

Mobile Data Shred Inc., 1744 W Burnett Ave., Louisville, KY 40210-1740, (502)778-8266 [21840]

Mobile Fleet Service of Spokane, 216 N Dyer Rd., Spokane, WA 99212-0830, (509)535-3311 [14608]

Mobile Paint Distributors, 4775 Hamilton Blvd., PO Box 717, Theodore, AL 36582, (205)443-6110 [21504]

Mobile Pen Company Inc., 2575 Schillinger Rd., Semmes, AL 36575, (205)666-1537 [20984]

Mobile Power and Hydraulics, 1721 S 7th St., St. Louis, MO 63104, (314)231-9522 [16315]

Moccasin Tipi, 1703 Acacia Dr., Colorado Springs, CO 80907-4811, (719)590-7668 [24813]

Modec Inc., 4725 Oakland St., Denver, CO 80266, (303)373-2696 [16316]

Model Rectifier Corp., 80 Newfieldn Ave., Edison, NJ 08837, (732)248-0400 [26580]

Modemsplus Inc., 3815 Presidential Pkwy., Atlanta, GA 30340, (404)458-2232 [5681]

Modern Builders Supply, 3684 Community Rd., Brunswick, GA 31520, (912)265-5885 [10043]

Modern Builders Supply, 116 Central Junction Dr., Savannah, GA 31405, (912)234-8224 [10044]

Modern Business Machines Inc., 505 N 22nd St., Milwaukee, WI 53233, (414)344-1000 [21149]

Modern Distributing Co., 1610 N Topping Ave., Kansas City, MO 64120, (816)231-8500 [1044]

Modern Door and Hardware Inc., PO Box 1930, Cordova, TN 38018-1930, (901)757-1300 [7732]

Modern Equipment Sales and Rental Co., 7667 Pulaski Hwy., Baltimore, MD 21237-2669, (410)918-9770 [7733]

Modern Group Ltd., PO Box 710, Bristol, PA 19007, (215)943-9100 [16317]

Modern Information Systems, PO Box 5479, Grand Forks, ND 58206-5479, (701)772-4844 [21150]

Modern Kitchen Center Inc., 5050 County Rd. 154, Glenwood Springs, CO 81601-9320, (970)945-9194 [7734]

Modern Mass Media Inc., PO Box 950, Chatham, NJ 07928, (973)635-6000 [25331]

Modern Mass Media Inc., PO Box 950, Chatham, NJ 07928, (973)635-6000 [15237]

Modern Material Handling Co., PO Box 5658, Greenville, SC 29606-5658, (864)242-9990 [17046]

Modern Methods Inc., PO Box 907, Owensboro, KY 42301, (502)685-5128 [7735]

Modern Options, 1930 Fairway Dr., San Leandro, CA 94577, (510)895-8000 [21595]

Modern Overseas, Inc., 311 California St., San Francisco, CA 94111, (415)392-1531 [14166]

Modern Paint & Wallpaper Inc., 899 Brighton Ave., Portland, ME 04102-1005, (207)772-4431 [21505]

Modern Supply Company Inc., 1202 W Summit St., Ponca City, OK 74601, (405)765-2524 [23271]

Modern Supply Company Inc., PO Box 22997, Knoxville, TN 37933-0997, (423)966-4567 [15238]

Modern Supply Company Inc. (Knoxville, Tennessee), PO Box 22997, Knoxville, TN 37933-0997, (615)966-4567 [23272]

Moderne Cabinet Shop, 2304 River Dr. N, Great Falls, MT 59401-1331, (406)453-4711 [7736]

Modernfold of Florida, Inc., PO Box 451206, Ft. Lauderdale, FL 33345, (954)747-7400 [7737]

Modernfold of Florida Inc., PO Box 451206, Ft. Lauderdale, FL 33345, (954)747-7400 [27347]

Modi Rubber Ltd., 10560 Main St., Fairfax, VA 22030, (703)273-0123 [2979]

Modular Mining Systems Inc., 3289 E Hemisphere Loop, Tucson, AZ 85706-5028, (520)746-9127 [6527]

Moes Marine Service, 2022 W Wind Rd., Oshkosh, WI 54901, (920)231-2799 [18571]

Moews Seed Company Inc., Hwy. 89 S, Granville, IL 61326, (815)339-2201 [18107]

Moffatt Hay Co., 2216 Smedley Rd., Carlsbad, NM 88220, (505)236-6392 [18108]

Moffett Co. Inc.; J.W., 11329 Oldfield Dr., Carmel, IN 46033-3777, (317)848-1171 [14609]

Moffett Co.; Preston I., PO Box 2870, Winchester, VA 22604, (540)662-7724 [1886]

Moffitt Oil Company Inc., 9000 Emmott, Ste. A, Houston, TX 77040, (713)896-4300 [22490]

Mohawk Dairy, 260 Forest Ave., Amsterdam, NY 12010, (518)842-4940 [11917]

Mohawk Distilled Products L.P., 11900 Biscayne Blvd., No. 600, North Miami, FL 33181-2726, (305)893-3394 [1887]

Mohawk Farms Inc., 112 Holmes Rd., Newington, CT 06111, (860)666-3361 [11918]

Mohawk Finishing Products Inc., 4715 State Hwy. 30, Amsterdam, NY 12010-7417, (518)843-1380 [21506]

Mohawk Machinery Inc., 10601 Glendale Rd., Cincinnati, OH 45215, (513)771-1952 [16318]

Mohawk Marketing Corp., PO Box 62229, Virginia Beach, VA 23466-2229, (757)499-8901 [25332]

Mohawk Rubber Sales of N.E. Inc., 65A Industrial Park Rd., Hingham, MA 02043, (781)741-6000 [24287]

Mohr Vinyl & Carpet Supplier, 1510 Rockwell Dr., Midland, MI 48642, (517)837-6647 [10045]

Molay Supply Inc., 801 1st Ave. N, Birmingham, AL 35203, (205)322-4321 [15239]

Mole Hole, 7309 W 12th St., Little Rock, AR 72204-2408, (501)663-4379 [5199]

Mole-Richardson Co., 937 N Sycamore Ave., Hollywood, CA 90038-2384, (323)851-0111 [25333]

Molls Inc., 1509 S Telegraph, Bloomfield Hills, MI 48302, (248)334-4242 [13834]

Molly Corp., 103 N Village Rd., Ogunquit, ME 03907, (207)646-5908 [23485]

Molo Oil Co., PO Box 719, Dubuque, IA 52004, (319)557-7540 [22491]

MOM/Modern Office Machines, PO Box 5615, Greenville, SC 29606, (864)281-5400 [21049]

Momeni Inc., 36 E 31st St., New York, NY 10016, (212)532-9577 [10046]

Momentum Metals Inc., PO Box 814045, Dallas, TX 75381, (972)241-1242 [20200]

Mom's Food Co., 1308 Potrero Ave., South El Monte, CA 91733-3013, (626)444-4115 [11919]

Mon-Dak Chemical Inc., PO Box 1187, Washburn, ND 58577, (701)462-8588 [4459]

Mon Valley Petroleum Inc., 5515 W Smithfield Rd., Mc Keesport, PA 15135, (412)751-5210 [22492]

Monahan Co.; Thomas, 202 N Oak St., Arcola, IL 61910, (217)268-4955 [27348]

Monahan Paper Co., 175 2nd St., Oakland, CA 94607, (510)835-4670 [21841]

Monahan Paper Co., 175 2nd St., Oakland, CA 94607, (510)835-4670 [17047]

Monarch Beverage Inc., PO Box 18434, Las Vegas, NV 89114-8434, (702)731-1040 [1888]

Monarch Brass and Copper Corp., PO Box S, New Rochelle, NY 10802, (914)235-3000 [13835]

Monarch Ceramic Tile, 3361 Columbia NE, Albuquerque, NM 87107, (505)881-0971 [10047]

Monarch Ceramic Tile, 3635 N 124th St., Milwaukee, WI 53205, (262)781-3110 [10048]

Monarch Ceramic Tile Inc., PO Box 853058, Mesquite, TX 75185 [10049]

Monarch Cermaic Tile, Inc., 5545 W Latham, Ste. 1, Phoenix, AZ 85043, (602)352-0301 [10050]

Monarch Electric Company Inc., PO Box CN40004, Fairfield, NJ 07004, (973)227-4151 [9092]

Monarch Hosiery Mills Inc., PO Box 1205, Burlington, NC 27216, (919)584-0361 [5200]

Monarch Industries Incorporated U.S.A., 9201 Pennsylva Ave. S, Ste. 12, Bloomington, MN 55431, (612)884-0226 [16319]

Monarch Knit and Sportswear Inc., 122 E Washington Blvd., Los Angeles, CA 90015, (213)746-5800 [5201]

Monarch Luggage Company Inc., 5 Delavan St., Brooklyn, NY 11231, (718)858-6900 [18413]

Monarch Machine and Tool Company Inc., PO Box 810, Pasco, WA 99301-0810, (509)547-7753 [13836]

Monarch Steel Co., 2464 Clybourn Ave., Chicago, IL 60614, (773)929-2050 [20201]

Monarch Steel Company Inc., 4389 Martin Ave., Cleveland, OH 44127, (216)883-8001 [20202]

Monarch Tile, 15000 N Hayden Rd., No. 400, Scottsdale, AZ 85260, (602)991-2626 [10051]

Monarch Tile, 5225 Phillips Hwy., Jacksonville, FL 32207, (904)733-0727 [10052]

Monarch Tile, 93 Weldon Pkwy., Maryland Heights, MO 63043, (314)569-5956 [10053]

Monarch Tile, 4375 S Valley View, Ste. A, Las Vegas, NV 89103, (702)252-0999 [10054]

Monarch Tile, 143 W Rhapsody, San Antonio, TX 78216, (210)341-2521 [10055]

Monarch Tile Inc., PO Box 853058, Mesquite, TX 75185 [10049]

Monarch Toilet Partition, 200 Buffalo Ave., Freeport, NY 11520-4732, (516)379-2700 [13184]

Monarch Wine Company of Georgia, 6300 Powers Ferry Rd., NW, No. 600-147, Atlanta, GA 30339-2946, (404)622-4661 [1889]

Mondovi Cooperative Equity Association Inc., 735 E Main St., Mondovi, WI 54755, (715)926-4212 [1045]

Monel Distributors, 2770 NW 24th St., Miami, FL 33142, (305)635-7331 [11920]

Money Machinery Co.; Joe, 4400 Lewisburg Rd., Birmingham, AL 35207, (205)841-7000 [16320]

Money Saver, 67 Leo Dr., Gardner, MA 01440-1228, (978)632-9500 [24814]

Monfort Electronic Marketing, 6136 S Belmont St., Indianapolis, IN 46217-9761, (317)872-8877 [9093]

Monfort Inc., PO Box G, Greeley, CO 80632, (970)353-2311 [11921]

Monfort International Sales Corp., PO Box G, Greeley, CO 80632, (303)353-2311 [11922]

Monfort-Swift Support Centers, PO Box G, Greeley, CO 80632, (970)353-2311 [11923]

Monica Elevator Co., 19213 N Main St., Princeville, IL 61559, (309)385-4938 [18109]

Monico Alloys Inc., 2301 E 15th St., Los Angeles, CA 90021, (213)629-4767 [20203]

Moniteq Research Labs, Inc., 7640 Fulerton Rd., Springfield, VA 22153-2814, (703)569-0195 [24596]

Moniteq Research Labs Inc., 7640 Fulerton Rd., Springfield, VA 22153-2814, (703)569-0195 [9094]

Monje Forest Products Co., 10800 SW Herman Rd., Ste. A, Tualatin, OR 97062-8033, (503)692-0758 [7738]

Monogram Sanitation Co., 800 W Artesia Blvd., PO Box 9057, Compton, CA 90224, (310)638-8445 [23273]

Monroe and Associates Inc., 1870 W Bitters, San Antonio, TX 78248, (210)493-5700 [11924]

Monroe City Feed Mill Inc., PO Box 126, Monroe City, IN 47557, (812)743-5121 [1046]

Monroe Distributing Co., 3010 University Dr. NW, Huntsville, AL 35816-3134, (205)536-0622 [25334]

Monroe Foods, 102 E Grove St., Monroe, MI 48162, (734)243-5660 [11925]

Monroe Hardware Co., 101 N Sutherland Ave., Monroe, NC 28110, (704)289-3121 [13837]

Monroe Insulation & Gutter Company Inc., 100 Ontario St., East Rochester, NY 14445-1340, (716)385-3030 [7739]

Monroe Lawrence Farm Bureau Cooperative, 1305 W Bloomfield Rd., Bloomington, IN 47403, (812)332-4471 [1047]

Monroe Oil Company Inc., PO Box 1109, Monroe, NC 28111, (704)289-5438 [22493]

Monroe Tractor and Implement Company Inc., PO Box 370, Henrietta, NY 14467, (716)334-3867 [20685]

Monroe Truck Equipment Inc., 1051 W 7th St., Monroe, WI 53566, (608)328-8127 [2980]

Monroeville Co-op Grain, 82 Townsend Ave., Norwalk, OH 44857, (419)465-2583 [18110]

Monsieur Touton Selections, LTD, 129 W 27th St. 9th Flr., New York, NY 10001, (212)255-0674 [1890]

Monson Chemicals Inc., 154 Pioneer Dr., Leominster, MA 01453, (508)534-1425 [4460]

Monsour's Inc., 112 N Elm St., Pittsburg, KS 66762, (316)231-6363 [11926]

Montage Foods Inc., 885 Providence Rd., Scranton, PA 18508, (717)347-2400 [11927]

Montana International Lvstk, 4385 Wylie Dr., Helena, MT 59601-9567, (406)227-5208 [18111]

Montana Leather Co. Inc., PO Box 394, Billings, MT 59103-0394, (406)245-1660 [25743]

Montana Naturals Int'l. Inc., 19994 U.S Highway 93 N, Arlee, MT 59821, (406)726-3214 [11928]

Montana Pollen & Herb, 19994 U.S Highway 93 N, Arlee, MT 59821, (406)726-3214 [11928]

Montana Scale Co. Inc., 1207 13th Ave. E, Polson, MT 59860-3620, (406)883-4697 [24402]

Montana Scale Company Inc., 1207 13th Ave. E, Polson, MT 59860-3620, (406)883-4697 [24188]

Montana Truck Parts, PO Box 123, Milltown, MT 59851-0123, (406)258-6221 [2981]

Monte Vista Cooperative Inc., E Hwy. 160, Monte Vista, CO 81144, (719)852-5181 [1048]

Monterey Chemical Co. Inc., PO Box 35000, Fresno, CA 93745-5000, (559)499-2100 [4461]

Montero International, Inc., 11016 Myrtle St., Downey, CA 90241, (562)862-0116 [6528]

Montezuma Cooperative Exchange, PO Box 98, Montezuma, KS 67867, (316)846-2231 [18112]

Montfort Publications, 26 S Saxon Ave., Bay Shore, NY 11706-8993, (631)665-0726 [3965]

Montgomery Beverage Co., 3181 Selma Hwy., Montgomery, AL 36108-5003, (205)284-0550 [1891]

Montgomery Building Materials, 919 Bell St., Montgomery, AL 36104-3003, (205)269-2518 [10056]

Montgomery Div., 17191 Chrysler Fwy., Detroit, MI 48203, (313)891-3700 [22494]

Montgomery Farmers Cooperative, Guthrie Hwy. 79, Clarksville, TN 37040, (931)648-0637 [1049]

Montgomery GMC Trucks Inc., PO Box 8187, Springfield, MO 65801, (417)869-0990 [20686]

Montgomery Hosiery Mill Inc., PO Box 69, Star, NC 27356, (919)428-2191 [5202]

Montgomery Seed, 255 Dexter Ave., Montgomery, AL 36104, (205)265-8241 [27191]

Montgomery Truck and Trailer Sales, PO Box 8187, Springfield, MO 65801, (417)869-0990 [20686]

Monticello Grain Company Inc., 420 W Marion St., Monticello, IL 61856, (217)762-2163 [18113]

Monticello Sports Inc., 100 W 1st St., Monticello, IA 52310-1519, (319)465-5429 [23834]

Montopolis Supply Co., 255 Bastrop Hwy., Austin, TX 78741-2399, (512)385-3270 [7740]

Montour Metals Inc., 5458 Steubenville Pike, No. 1st Fl., McKees Rocks, PA 15136-1412, (724)695-8990 [19834]

Montour Oil Service Co., 112 Broad St., Montoursville, PA 17754, (717)368-8611 [22495]

Montoya/MAS International Inc., 502 Palm St., No. 21, West Palm Beach, FL 33401, (561)832-4401 [25744]

Montrose Hardwood Company Inc., PO Box 278, Montross, VA 22520, (804)493-8021 [7741]

Monumental Paper Co., 8261 Preston Ct, Jessup, MD 20794-9681, (410)945-1370 [21842]

Monumental Supply Company Inc., 401 S Haven St., Baltimore, MD 21224, (410)732-9300 [23274]

Moodie Implement Co., 3701 U.S Hwy. 14, Pierre, SD 57501-5747, (605)224-1631 [1050]

Moody Co.; J.A., Phoenixville Pike, Malvern, PA 19355, (215)647-3810 [18572]

Moody Creek Produce Inc., PO Box 329, Sugar City, ID 83448, (208)356-9447 [11929]

Moody Institute of Science, 820 N LaSalle Blvd., Chicago, IL 60610, (312)329-4000 [25335]

Moody and Sons Inc.; M.D., 4652 Phillips Hwy., Jacksonville, FL 32207, (904)737-4401 [7742]

Moog Louisville Wholesale, 1421 W Magazine, Louisville, KY 40203-2063, (502)583-7795 [2982]

Mook & Blanchard Wholesale Library Books, 546 S Hofgaarden, La Puente, CA 91744, (626)968-6424 [3966]

Moon Distributors Inc., 2800 Vance St., Little Rock, AR 72206, (501)375-8291 [1892]

Moonachie Co., 1 Graphic Place, PO Box 393, Moonachie, NJ 07074, (201)641-2211 [17048]

Moonbeam Publications, Inc., 836 Hastings St., Traverse City, MI 49686-3441, (231)922-0533 [3967]

Mooney Cattle Co. Inc., 4801 Umatilla Ave., Boise, ID 83709-6142, (208)362-5091 [18114]

Mooney General Paper Co., 1451 Chestnut Ave., Hillside, NJ 07205, (973)926-3800 [21843]

Mooney General Paper Co., 1451 Chestnut Ave., Hillside, NJ 07205, (973)926-3800 [17049]

Mooney Process Equipment Co., 3000 E 14th Ave., Columbus, OH 43219-2355 [23275]

Moonlight Products Inc., PMB 392, 5663 Balboa Ave., San Diego, CA 92111-2705, (619)625-0300 [24403]

Moore Brothers Div., 1725 69th St., Sacramento, CA 95819, (916)454-9353 [17050]

Moore Brothers Inc., PO Box 1108, Cheraw, SC 29520, (803)537-5211 [5203]

Moore Co., PO Box 4564, Portland, OR 97214, (503)234-5000 [25336]

MOORE Co., 333 SE 2nd Ave., Portland, OR 97214, (503)234-5000 [15240]

Moore Discount Inc., 101 & 107 S White St., Athens, TN 37303, (423)745-6070 [15241]

Moore Drums Inc., 2819 Industrial Ave., Charleston, SC 29405, (803)744-7448 [22496]

Moore Drums Inc., 2819 Industrial Ave., Charleston, SC 29405, (803)744-7448 [17051]

Moore Equipment Co.; R.W., PO Box 25068, Raleigh, NC 27611, (919)772-2121 [1051]

Moore; Florence, PO Box 31151, Billings, MT 59107-1151, (406)652-1585 [26152]

Moore Food Distributors Inc., 9910 Page Blvd., St. Louis, MO 63132, (314)426-1300 [11930]

Moore-Handley Inc., 3140 Pelham Pkwy., Pelham, AL 35124, (205)663-8011 [11931]

Moore, Inc.; A.E., State St., Millsboro, DE 19966, (302)934-7055 [4673]

Moore Industries Inc., PO Box 311, Bradley, IL 60915, (815)932-5500 [19466]

Moore Medical Corp., PO Box 1500, New Britain, CT 06050, (860)826-3600 [19467]

Moore Oil Company Inc., PO Box 460, Manning, SC 29102, (803)435-4376 [22497]

Moore Oil Company Inc.; Lee, PO Box 9, Sanford, NC 27331, (919)775-2301 [22498]

Moore; Robert J., 2824 Bransford Ave., Nashville, TN 37204-3102, (615)297-5745 [25337]

Moore Sales Co., 11 Gilbert Rd., Burkburnett, TX 76354, (940)569-1463 [25338]

Moore-Sigler Sports World Inc., PO Box 6612, Shreveport, LA 71136-6612, (318)686-1880 [23835]

Moore Supply Co., PO Box 448, Conroe, TX 77305, (409)756-4445 [23276]

Moore Supply Co., 4332 W Ferdinand St., Chicago, IL 60624-1017, (312)235-4400 [14610]

Moore's Quality Snack Foods Div., PO Box 1909, Bristol, VA 24203, (540)669-6194 [11932]

Moore's Wholesale Tire Sales, 88 Railroad Ave. Exit, Albany, NY 12205, (518)446-9027 [2983]

Moorhead and Company Inc., PO Box 8092, Van Nuys, CA 91409-8092, (818)873-6640 [11933]

Moorhead and Company Inc., PO Box 8092, Van Nuys, CA 91409, (818)873-6640 [4462]

Mor-Rad Foodservice, 315 Hoohana St., Kahului, HI 96732, (808)877-2017 [11934]

Morazan, 104 Open Buckle Rd., Vaughn, MT 59487-9514 [18115]

More Mobility, 333 W Blaine St., McAdoo, PA 18237, (717)929-1456 [19468]

More; Ruth, 960 W Owens Ave., Las Vegas, NV 89106-2516, (702)646-6463 [14167]

The Morehouse Group, Inc., PO Box 1321, Harrisburg, PA 17105, (717)541-8130 [3968]

Morehouse Publishing Div., PO Box 1321, Harrisburg, PA 17105, (717)541-8130 [3968]

Moreira Tile, 1297 Kaumualii St., Honolulu, HI 96817, (808)845-6461 [10057]

Moreland Hosiery, PO Box 3245, Clearwater, FL 33767-8245, (813)585-9795 [5204]

Moreland Wholesale Co., Inc., 1812 Snyder Ave., Cheyenne, WY 82001, (307)638-8592 [11935]

Morelle Products Ltd., Philippe ADEC and Equipment, 209 W 38th St., New York, NY 10018, (212)391-8070 [5205]

Morgan Agency; J.R., 2540 E Thomas Rd., Phoenix, AZ 85016, (602)912-9801 [9095]

Morgan Distribution Inc., PO Box 2003, Mechanicsburg, PA 17055, (717)697-1151 [7743]

Morgan Engineering Systems Inc., 947 E Broadway, Alliance, OH 44601, (216)823-6130 [7744]

Morgan Forest Products, PO Box 20369, Columbus, OH 43220-0369, (614)457-3390 [7745]

Morgan Grain and Feed Co., PO Box 248, Morgan, MN 56266, (507)249-3157 [18116]

Morgan Graphic Supply, 224 Townsend St., San Francisco, CA 94107, (415)777-2850 [16321]

Morgan Lumber Company Inc., PO Box 309, Hwy. 74 West, Marshville, NC 28103, (704)624-2146 [7746]

Morgan Lumber Sales Company Inc., PO Box 20369, Columbus, OH 43220-0369, (614)457-3390 [7745]

Morgan Recreational Supply, 7263 Victor Pittsford Rd., Box F, Victor, NY 14564, (716)924-7188 [18573]

Morgan and Sampson Pacific, PO Box 3013, Los Alamitos, CA 90720, (714)220-4900 [14168]

Morgan Scientific, Inc., 151 Essex St., Haverhill, MA 01832-5564, (978)521-4440 [18947]

Morgan Tire and Auto Inc., 2021 Sunnydale Blvd., Clearwater, FL 33765, (727)441-3727 [2984]

Morgan Wholesale Feed; Fred, 700 W Johnson Ave., Terre Haute, IN 47802, (812)232-9613 [1052]

Morgan-Wightman Supply Company, 10199 Woodfield Ln., St. Louis, MO 63132, (314)995-9990 [7747]

Morgan-Wightman Supply Inc. Indiana, 3250 N Post Rd., Indianapolis, IN 46226, (317)895-9595 [7748]

Morgan's Auto Parts, 415 Airport Rd. No. B, New Castle, DE 19720, (302)322-2229 [2985]

Morgantown Tire Wholesalers, 111 Maple St., Morgantown, KY 42261, (502)526-5570 [2986]

Morgen Manufacturing Co., PO Box 160, Yankton, SD 57078, (605)665-9654 [7749]

Morin Steel, 4 Stone Rd., Alfred, ME 04002, (207)324-2112 [20204]

Morley Murphy Co., PO Box 19008, Green Bay, WI 54307-9008, (920)499-3171 [9096]

Morley Sales Company Inc., 809 W Madison St., Chicago, IL 60607, (312)829-1125 [11936]

Moroney, Inc.; James, 243-47 N 63rd St., Philadelphia, PA 19139, (215)471-5300 [1893]

Morpol Industrial Corporation Ltd., 7071 Orchard Lake Rd., Ste. 320, West Bloomfield, MI 48322, (248)855-9320 [16322]

Morrey Distributing Co., 1850 E Lincoln Way, Sparks, NV 89434-8944, (702)352-6000 [1894]

Morris Associates; William, PO Box 709, Asheville, NC 28802-0709, (704)255-7721 [18948]

Morris Co.; The Robert E., 17 Talcot Notch Rd., Farmington, CT 06032, (203)678-0200 [16323]

Morris Co.; S.G., 699 Miner Rd., Cleveland, OH 44143, (440)473-1640 [16324]

Morris Co.; S.G., 27439 Holiday Ln., Perrysburg, OH 43551, (419)874-8716 [16325]

Morris Co.; S.G., 699 Miner Rd., Highland Heights, OH 44143, (440)473-1640 [16326]

Morris Co.; Walter F., 425 Turnpike St., Canton, MA 02021, (617)828-5300 [23277]

Morris Cooperative Association, PO Box 150, Morris, MN 56267, (612)589-4744 [1053]

Morris Environmental T-Shirts; Jim, PO Box 18270, Boulder, CO 80308, (303)444-6430 [5206]

Morris Grain Company Inc., Rte. 3, Morris, MN 56267, (320)589-4050 [1054]

Morris Novelty Inc., 523 Main St., Pawtucket, RI 02860-2944, (401)728-3810 [26581]

Morris Oil Inc., 409 S High School Ave., Columbia, MS 39429, (601)736-2634 [22499]

Morris Rothenberg and Son Inc., 25 Ranick Rd., Smithtown, NY 11788, (631)234-8000 [23836]

Morris Scrap Metal Inc., PO Box 460, Sherman, MS 38869, (601)844-6441 [26917]

Morris Tile Distributors, 9132 Gaither Rd., Gaithersburg, MD 20877, (301)670-4222 [10058]

Morris Tile Distributors, 2525 Kenilworth Ave., Tuxedo, MD 20781, (301)773-7000 [10059]

Morris Tile Distributors Inc., 2525 Kenilworth Ave., Hyattsville, MD 20781, (301)772-2820 [10060]

Morris Tile Distributors Inc., 1890 Woodhaven, Philadelphia, PA 19116, (215)969-3400 [10061]

Morris Tile Distributors of Norfolk, Inc., 1339 Ingleside Rd., Norfolk, VA 23502-1914, (757)855-8017 [10062]

Morris Tile Distributors of Richmond, 2280 Dabney Rd., Richmond, VA 23230-3344, (804)353-4427 [10063]

Morris Tile Distributors of Roanoke, Inc., 3610 Aerial Way Dr. SW, Roanoke, VA 24018-1508, (540)343-4100 [10064]

Morrison Farms Popcorn, RR 1, Box 50A, Clearwater, NE 68726-9720, (402)887-5335 [11990]

Morrison Industrial Equipment Co., 1825 Monroe Ave. NW, Grand Rapids, MI 49505, (616)361-2673 [16327]

Morrison Industries Inc., PO Box P, Grand Rapids, MI 49501, (616)361-2673 [17052]

Morrison Petroleum Company Inc., 2600 S & 1710 W St., Woods Cross, UT 84087, (801)295-5591 [22500]

Morrison Supply Co., PO Box 70, Ft. Worth, TX 76101, (817)870-2227 [23278]

Morrisonville Farmers Cooperative, PO Box 17, Morrisonville, IL 62546, (217)526-3123 [18117]

Morristown Electric Wholesalers Co., 1601 W Andrew Johnson, Morristown, TN 37814-3734, (423)586-5830 [9097]

Morristown Electrical Supply Co., PO Box 337, Morristown, NJ 07963-0337, (973)538-1600 [9085]

Morrow County Grain Growers Inc., Hwy. 207, Lexington, OR 97839, (541)989-8221 [18118]

Morrow Equipment Company L.L.C., PO Box 3306, Salem, OR 97302-0306, (503)585-5721 [16328]

Morrow Snowboards Inc., 599 Menlo Dr., No. 200, Rocklin, CA 95765-3708 [23837]

Morse Co.; M.K., PO Box 8677, Canton, OH 44711, (330)453-8187 [13838]

Morse Distribution Inc., PO Box 490, Bellingham, WA 98227, (360)734-2400 [17053]

Morse Enterprises Inc., 108 S Stanton, El Paso, TX 79901, (915)533-2746 [24815]

Morse Industries Inc., PO Box 1779, Kent, WA 98035, (253)852-1399 [20205]

Morse Parker Motor Supply, 809 High St., Portsmouth, VA 23704-3333, (757)393-4051 [2987]

Morse Products Mfg., 12960 Bradley Ave., Sylmar, CA 91342-3829, (818)367-5951 [24606]

Morse Typewriter Company Inc., 131 Eileen Way, Syosset, NY 11791-5302, (516)364-1616 [21151]

Morse Wholesale Inc.; J.D., 6841 Hawthorn Park Dr., Indianapolis, IN 46220-3908, (317)849-7815 [26582]

Morse Wholesale Paper Company Inc., 3302 Canal St., Houston, TX 77003, (713)223-8361 [21844]

Mortemp Inc., PO Box 24967, Seattle, WA 98124, (206)767-0140 [14611]

Morton Company Inc.; J.P., PO Box 741188, Los Angeles, CA 90004, (213)487-1440 [17526]

Morton Supply Inc., 1724 S 1st St., Yakima, WA 98901, (509)248-3500 [9098]

Morweco Steel Co., 2911 N 20th St., Philadelphia, PA 19132-1536 [20206]

Mosaic Tile, 10911 Trade Rd., Richmond, VA 23236 [10065]

Mosaic Tile Co., 7890 Backlick Rd., Springfield, VA 22150, (703)451-8805 [10066]

Mosebach Electric and Supply Co., 1315 Ridge Ave., Pittsburgh, PA 15233-2102, (412)322-5000 [9099]

Mosehart-Schleeter Company, Inc., 4404 Directors Row, PO Box 8, Houston, TX 77092, (713)686-8601 [26153]

Moser Lumber Inc., 300 E 5th Ave., Ste. 430, Naperville, IL 60563-3182, (630)420-3000 [7750]

Moses Lake Steel Supply Inc., PO Box 1122, Moses Lake, WA 98837, (509)765-1741 [20207]

Mosey's Inc., 4 Mosey Dr., Bloomfield, CT 06002, (203)243-1725 [11937]

Moshofsky Enterprises, PO Box 2107, Lake Oswego, OR 97035-0034, (503)292-8861 [7751]

Moshy Brothers Inc., 127 W 25th St., New York, NY 10001, (212)255-0613 [3969]

Mosier Fluid Power of Indiana Inc., 9851 Park Davis Dr., Indianapolis, IN 46236-2393, (317)895-6200 [24404]

Mosier Fluid Power of Ohio Inc., 2495 Technical Dr., Miamisburg, OH 45342, (937)847-9846 [17054]

Moskowitz Brothers, 5300 Vine St., Cincinnati, OH 45217, (513)242-2100 [26918]

Moss Co.; Roscoe, PO Box 31064, Los Angeles, CA 90063, (213)261-4185 [7752]

Moss Dynamics, 1050 St. John St., Easton, PA 18042, (215)253-9385 [2988]

Moss Enterprises Inc., 137 Boyson Rd., Hiawatha, IA 52233-1205, (319)393-4048 [6529]

Motif Designs, Inc., 20 Jones St., New Rochelle, NY 10801, (914)633-1170 [21507]

Motion Ind., PO Box 764, East Windsor, CT 06088-0764, (860)292-6091 [2989]

Motion Industries, 80 Access Rd., Warwick, RI 02886-1002, (401)736-0515 [2990]

Motion Industries, 7701 N 67th St., Milwaukee, WI 53223, (414)365-8780 [17055]

Motion Industries, 7130 Packer Dr., Wausau, WI 54401, (715)848-2994 [2991]

Motion Industries, Atlantic Tracy Div., 190 Rand Rd., Portland, ME 04102-1408, (207)854-9721 [17056]

Motion Industries, Inc., 2222 Nordale Dr., Appleton, WI 54911, (920)731-4121 [2992]

Motion Industries Inc., 1605 Alton Rd., PO Box 1477, Birmingham, 26300, 35210, (205)956-1122 [17057]

Motion Pictures Enterprises, PO Box 276, Tarrytown, NY 10591, (212)245-0969 [25339]

Motivaction Inc., 9800 Shelard Pkwy., Ste. 300, Minneapolis, MN 55441-6453, (612)544-7200 [25340]

Motivatit Seafoods Inc., PO Box 3916, Houma, LA 70361-3916, (504)868-7191 [11938]

Motloid Co., 300 N Elizabeth St., 2N, Chicago, IL 60607, (312)226-2454 [19469]

Motloid Company, 300 N Elizabeth St., 2N, Chicago, IL 60607, (312)226-2454 [9100]

Moto America Inc., 613 Lillington St. E, Angier, NC 27501-9661, (919)893-6647 [20687]

Motor Master Products, 1307 Baltimore St., Defiance, OH 43512-1903, (419)782-7131 [2993]

Motor Parts & Bearing Co., 221 S Main, Bolivar, TN 38008-2705, (901)658-5263 [2994]

Motor Parts and Supply Inc., 750 Abbott Ln., Colorado Springs, CO 80905, (719)632-4276 [2995]

Motor Products Company Inc., 733 N 5th Ave., PO Box 3640, Knoxville, TN 37917-6722, (423)525-5321 [2996]

Motor Sound Corp., 541 Division St., Campbell, CA 95008, (408)374-7900 [5682]

Motorbooks International, 729 Prospect Ave., PO Box 1, Osceola, WI 54020-0001, (715)294-3345 [3970]

Motorcycle Stuff Inc., PO Box 1179, Cape Girardeau, MO 63701, (573)243-1111 [2997]

Motorola Communications, 430 N George, York, PA 17404-2750, (717)843-6764 [5683]

Motorola Inc. Communications and Electronics Div., 8325 Lenexa Dr., Ste. 150, Lenexa, KS 66214-1695, (913)492-6060 [5684]

Motorola MIMS. VLSI Tech Center, 4625 S Ash Ave Ste 12, Tempe, AZ 85282, (480)820-0885 [9101]

Mott Equity Exchange, 509 Country Rd., Mott, ND 58646, (701)824-3296 [13839]

Mott Meat Company, Inc., HWY B, PO Box 19, Rockville, MO 64780, (660)598-2365 [11939]

Mott Media L.L.C., 112 E Ellen St., Fenton, MI 48430-2115, (810)714-4280 [3971]

Mottahedeh and Co., 225 5th Ave., New York, NY 10010, (212)685-3050 [15590]

Moulinex Appliances Inc., 7 Reuten Dr., Closter, NJ 07624, (201)784-0073 [15242]

Moultrie Grain Association, Rte. 1, Box 147, Arthur, IL 61911, (217)543-2157 [18119]

Moultrie-Shelby FS Inc., PO Box 50, Shelbyville, IL 62565, (217)774-3901 [931]

Mound City Industries Inc., 1315 Cherokee St., St. Louis, MO 63118-3206, (314)773-5200 [11940]

Mound Steel Corp., 25 Mound Park Dr., Springboro, OH 45066, (513)748-2937 [20208]

Mt. Eden Floral Co., 531 E Evelyn Ave., Mountain View, CA 94041, (650)903-5020 [14923]

Mount Eden Nursery Co., 531 E Evelyn Ave., Mountain View, CA 94041, (650)903-5020 [14923]

Mt. Ellis Paper Company Inc., Gateway International Park, Wembly Rd., Box 4083, New Windsor, NY 12553, (914)567-1100 [21845]

Mt. Ellis Paper Company Inc., Gateway International Park, New Windsor, NY 12553, (914)567-1100 [17058]

Mt. Horeb Farmers Coop., 501 W Main, Mt. Horeb, WI 53572, (608)437-5536 [11941]

Mt. Kisco Truck & Auto Parts, 135 Kisco Ave., Mt. Kisco, NY 10549, (914)666-3155 [2998]

Mt. Kisco Truck & Fleet Supply, 135 Kisco Ave., Mt. Kisco, NY 10549, (914)666-3155 [2998]

Mt. Kisco Truck and Fleet Supply, 135 Kisco Ave., Mt. Kisco, NY 10549, (914)666-3155 [2999]

Mount Pleasant Hardware Inc., 249 Academy Ave., Providence, RI 02908-4144, (401)351-7200 [21508]

Mount Pleasant Seafood Co., 1 Seafood Dr., Mt. Pleasant, SC 29464, (843)884-4122 [11942]

Mount Pulaski Farmers Grain, PO Box 77, Mt. Pulaski, IL 62548, (217)792-5711 [18120]

Mt. Union Cooperative Elevator, PO Box 57, Mt. Union, IA 52644, (319)865-1450 [18121]

Mt. Union Cooperative Elevator, PO Box 57, Mt. Union, IA 52644, (319)865-1450 [11943]

Mount Vernon Auto Parts, 8351 Richmond Hwy., Alexandria, VA 22309, (703)780-3445 [3000]

Mountain Aire Medical Equipment, 3975 Interpark Dr., Colorado Springs, CO 80907-5067, (719)592-0333 [18949]

Mountain Ark Trading Co., 1601 Pump Station Rd., Fayetteville, AR 72701, (501)442-7191 [11944]

Mountain Cable Industries Inc., 16026 W 5th Ave., Golden, CO 80401-5518, (303)279-2825 [9102]

Mountain Food Products, 570 Brevard Rd., Asheville, NC 28806, (828)255-7630 [11945]

Mountain High Technology Inc., PO Box 5690, Steamboat Springs, CO 80477, (970)879-7063 [6530]

Mountain Imaging Inc., 1109 S Plaza Way 274, Flagstaff, AZ 86001-6317, (520)774-0027 [18950]

Mountain Lakes Distributors, 10 Romaine Rd., Mountain Lakes, NJ 07046, (973)263-1979 [26583]

Mountain Marketing, 716 SW 28th St., Pendleton, OR 97801, (541)276-7866 [25341]

Mountain Muffler, 1605 Hwy. 201 N, PO Box 374, Mountain Home, AR 72653-0374, (870)425-8868 [3001]

Mountain People's Warehouse, 12745 Earhart Ave., Auburn, CA 95602, (530)889-9531 [11946]

Mountain People's Warehouse Inc., 12745 Earhart Ave., Auburn, CA 95602, (530)889-9531 [11947]

Mountain Sales & Service Inc., 6759 E 50th Ave., Commerce City, CO 80022-4618, (303)289-5558 [14612]

Mountain Service Corp., 15503 Lee Hwy., Bristol, VA 24201-8431, (540)669-9555 [26584]

Mountain Service Distributors, 40 Lake St., PO Box 520, South Fallsburg, NY 12779-0520, (914)434-5674 [26330]

Mountain Shades Distributing Co., PO Box 609, Vail, CO 81658-0609, (970)949-6301 [23838]

Mountain State Muzzleloading Supplies, Inc., RR 2, Box 154-1, Williamstown, WV 26187, (304)375-7842 [13503]

Mountain States Medical Inc., 5220 Pinemont Dr., Salt Lake City, UT 84123-4607, (801)261-2255 [18951]

Mountain States Microfilm Inc., PO Box 8304, Boise, ID 83707-2304, (208)336-2720 [21152]

Mountain States News Distributor, 106 N Link, PO Box 2105, Ft. Collins, CO 80524, (970)221-2330 [3512]

Mountain States Pipe and Supply Co., PO Box 698, Colorado Springs, CO 80903, (719)634-5555 [23279]

Mountain States Sporting Goods, PO Box 25863, Albuquerque, NM 87125-0863, (505)243-5515 [23839]

Mountain States Supply Inc., 184 W 3300 S, Salt Lake City, UT 84115, (801)484-8885 [23280]

Mountain Sun Organic Juices, 18390 Highway 145, Dolores, CO 81323, (970)882-2283 [11948]

Mountain Supply Co., 2101 Mullan Rd., Missoula, MT 59801, (406)543-8255 [23281]

Mountain Systems Inc., 966 W Main St., Ste. 8, Brooksfield Sq., Abingdon, VA 24210, (540)676-2093 [6531]

Mountain Tile, 585 West Maple, PO Box 465, Pocatello, ID 83204-0465, (208)232-6696 [10067]

Mountain View Coop., 110 Main St. W, Dutton, MT 59433-9686, (406)476-3690 [1055]

Mountain View Supply Inc., PO Box 252, Billings, MT 59103-0252, (406)259-4493 [24189]

Mountain West Paint Distributor, 5080 S 1600 W, Ogden, UT 84405, (801)393-3333 [21509]

Mountain West Printing and Publishing Ltd., 1150 W Custer Pl, Denver, CO 80223, (303)744-3313 [3972]

Mountainland Supply Co., 1505 W 130 S, Orem, UT 84058, (801)224-6050 [23282]

Mounthood Beverage Co., 3601 NW Yeon Ave., Portland, OR 97210, (503)274-9990 [1895]

Mourad & Associated International Trade, PO Box 633, Rosemead, CA 91770, (626)572-9134 [18952]

Mouser Electronics, 2401 Hwy. 287 N, Mansfield, TX 76063, (817)483-6828 [9103]

Moustrak Inc., 503 N Division St., No. 2, Carson City, NV 89703-4104, (702)884-1925 [6532]

Movie Star Inc., 136 Madison Ave., New York, NY 10016, (212)679-7260 [5207]

Moviola/J & R Film Company, Inc., 1135 N Mansfield Ave., Hollywood, CA 90038, (213)467-3107 [22880]

Movsovitz and Sons of Florida Inc., PO Box 41565, Jacksonville, FL 32203, (904)764-7681 [11949]

Moweaqua Farmers Cooperative Grain Co., PO Box 146, Moweaqua, IL 62550, (217)768-4416 [18122]

Moyer and Son Inc., PO Box 198, Souderton, PA 18964, (215)723-6001 [1056]

Moynihan Lumber, PO Box 509, Beverly, MA 01915-4223, (978)927-0032 [7753]

Mozel Inc., 4003 Park Ave., St. Louis, MO 63110, (314)865-3115 [4463]

Moznaim Publishing Corp., 4304 12th Ave., Brooklyn, NY 11219, (718)438-7680 [3973]

MP Productions Co., 6301 Murray St., Little Rock, AR 72209, (501)562-7425 [25342]

MP-Tech Inc., 1724-B Armitage Ct., Addison, IL 60101, (708)916-9510 [20209]

MPBS Industries, 2820 E Washington Blvd., Los Angeles, CA 90023, (323)268-8514 [16329]

MPC Educational Systems Inc., 27 Fulton St., New Haven, CT 06512, (203)469-6481 [25343]

MPL Industries, Inc., 12900 Preston Rd., LB 18, Dallas, TX 75230, (972)233-0757 [20210]

MPS Multimedia Inc., 451 Victory Ave., Ste. 1, South San Francisco, CA 94080, (650)872-7100 [6533]

MQ Power Corp., 18910 Wilmington Ave., Carson, CA 90749, (310)537-3700 [7754]

Mr. Dell Foods, Inc., 300 W Major St., PO Box 494, Kearney, MO 64060, (816)903-4644 [11950]

M.R. Equipment Co., Inc., 1828 NW 4th St., Oklahoma City, OK 73106-2611, (405)236-1494 [2696]

Mr. Hardwood Distributors, 210 Commerce Way, Jupiter, FL 33458, (561)746-9663 [10068]

Mr. Hardwoods, 210 Commerce Way, Jupiter, FL 33458, (561)746-9663 [15591]

Mr. Hardwoods, Inc., 210 Commerce Way, Jupiter, FL 33458, (561)746-9663 [10068]

Mr. Hub Cap, 499 W San Carlos St., San Jose, CA 95110, (408)294-4304 [3002]

Mr. Logo Inc., 302 Shelley St., Ste. 5, Springfield, OR 97477-5903, (541)744-1575 [5208]

Mr. Paperback Publisher News, 2224 S 11th St., Niles, MI 49120-4410, (616)684-1551 [3974]

MR Supply Inc., PO Box 3106, Huntington, WV 25702-0106, (304)529-4168 [14613]

MRC Polymers Inc., 1716 W Webster Ave., Chicago, IL 60614, (312)276-6345 [26919]

M.R.D. Products Inc., 1415 U.S Hwy. 19, Holiday, FL 34691-5646, (813)934-3108 [26920]

MRK Technologies Ltd., 3 Summit Park Dr., No. 300, Independence, OH 44131, (216)520-4300 [6534]

MRL, Inc., 7640 Fulerton Rd., Springfield, VA 22153-2814, (703)569-0195 [24596]

MRL Industries, 19500 Nugget Blvd., Sonora, CA 95370, (209)533-1990 [9104]

MRR Traders, Ltd., 69 Inner Belt Rd., Somerville, MA 02143, (617)666-5939 [1896]

MRS Industries Inc., PO Box 773, Rocky Hill, CT 06067-0773, (860)828-9624 [18953]

Mrs. Leeper's Pasta, Inc., 12455 Kerran St., Ste. 200, Poway, CA 92064-6855, (858)486-1101 [11951]

MS Rubber Co., 715 E McDowell Rd., Jackson, MS 39204-5908, (601)948-2575 [17059]

MSC Industrial Direct Inc., 75 Mckess Rd., Melville, NY 11747, (516)812-2000 [17060]

MSC Industrial Supply Co., 151 Sunnyside Blvd., Plainview, NY 11803, (516)349-7100 [13840]

MSC Industrial Supply Company Inc., 75 Mckess Rd., Melville, NY 11747, (516)812-2000 [17060]

MSIS Semiconductor Inc., 2372 Qume Dr.Ste. B, San Jose, CA 95131, (408)944-6270 [9105]

MSM Solutions, 9427 F St., Omaha, NE 68127, (402)592-4300 [11952]

MTH Corp., 5 Northern Blvd., Amherst, NH 03031-2302, (603)886-0011 [23000]

MTI Corp., 965 Corporate Blvd., Aurora, IL 60504, (630)978-5390 [24405]

MTS Safety Products, Hwy. 25 S, PO Box 204, Golden, MS 38847, (601)454-9245 [24595]

MTS Wireless Components, 562 Captain Nevelle Dr., Waterbury, CT 06705, (203)759-1234 [24190]

Mucci; Patrick J., 31902 Groesbeck Hwy., Fraser, MI 48026-3914, (810)296-6118 [26585]

Muehlstein and Company Inc.; H., PO Box 5445, Norwalk, CT 06856-5445, (203)855-6000 [23001]

Mueller Bean Co., 254 Main St., Sunfield, MI 48890, (517)566-8031 [17685]

Mueller Bean Co., 254 Main St., Sunfield, MI 48890, (517)566-8031 [11953]

Mueller Co.; Charles H., 7091 N River Rd., New Hope, PA 18938, (215)862-2033 [14924]

Mueller Feed Mill Inc., PO Box 730, Martin, SD 57551, (605)685-6611 [1057]

Mueller Sales Inc., PO Box 930323, Wixom, MI 48393-0323, (248)348-2942 [23283]

Mueller Telecommunications Inc., 7334 S Alton Way, Bldg. 14, Ste. J, Englewood, CO 80112, (303)773-3575 [5685]

Muench Woodwork Company Inc., 2701 Jackson Ave., South Chicago Heights, IL 60411, (708)754-2108 [27349]

Muffin Town Inc., 17 Walden, Winthrop, MA 02152-2708, (617)846-1565 [11954]

Muir-Roberts Company Inc., PO Box 328, Salt Lake City, UT 84110, (801)363-7695 [11955]

Mulach Steel Corp., 100 Leetsdale Industrial Dr., Leetsdale, PA 15056, (412)257-1111 [20211]

Mulder Refrigeration, 1109 S Commerce Ave., Sioux Falls, SD 57103, (605)338-1897 [14614]

Mulgrew Oil Co., 85 Terminal, Dubuque, IA 52001, (319)583-7386 [22501]

Muller and Company Inc.; L.P., 1 S Executive Pk., Charlotte, NC 28287, (704)552-5204 [26154]

Mulligan Sales Inc., PO Box 90008, City of Industry, CA 91714, (818)968-9621 [11956]

Mullis Petroleum Co., PO Box 517, Bedford, IN 47421, (812)275-5981 [22502]

Multi Communication Systems, 30731 W 8 Mile Rd., Livonia, MI 48152-1363, (248)478-5256 [9106]

Multi-Craft Plastics, Inc., 240 N Broadway, Portland, OR 97227, (503)288-5131 [23002]

Multi-Grow Investments Inc., 9831 Oakwood Cir., VilLa Park, CA 92861-1221, (909)627-7676 [14925]

Multi-Line Industries Inc., 124 Commerce St., Bowdon, GA 30108-1505, (404)854-4049 [5209]

Multi Vision Optical, 202 Professional Bldg., PO Box 229, Wheeling, WV 26003, (304)232-9820 [19470]

Multicraft Inc., 3233 E Van Buren St., Phoenix, AZ 85008, (602)244-9444 [25745]

Multicraft Inc., 4701 Lakeside Ave. E, Cleveland, OH 44114-3805, (216)791-8600 [25746]

Multifacet Industrial Supply Company Inc., PO Box 207, Burlington, NJ 08016, (609)386-6900 [17061]

Multifocal Rx Lens Lab, 216 Valley Hill Rd., Riverdale, GA 30274, (404)478-2121 [19471]

Multifoods Specialty Distribution, PO Box 173773, Denver, CO 80217-3774 [11957]

Multigraphics Inc., 431 Lakeview Ct., Mt. Prospect, IL 60056-6048, (847)375-1700 [21153]

Multimedia Pacific Inc., 1725 Kalani St., Honolulu, HI 96819, (808)842-0077 [5686]

Multisports Inc., 4660 Pine Timbers St., Houston, TX 77041, (713)460-8188 [23840]

Muncer and Associates Inc.; J.B., 4041 Batton NE, Ste. 210, North Canton, OH 44720, (330)494-3355 [6535]

Mundy Enterprises, Inc.; K.C., 4 Florence Ct., Jackson, NJ 08527-2913, (732)574-3202 [3003]

Munnell & Sherrill Inc., PO Box 13249, Portland, OR 97213, (503)281-0021 [17062]

Munro and Co., PO Box 1157, Hot Springs, AR 71902, (501)262-1440 [24816]

Munsell Livestock, PO Box 1408, MiLes City, MT 59301-1408, (406)232-1644 [18123]

Muntz Electrical Supply Co.; Jack H., 1211 23rd Ave., Rockford, IL 61104, (815)968-8866 [9107]

Muntz Electrical Supply Co.; Jack W., 1211 23rd Ave., Rockford, IL 61104, (815)968-8866 [9284]

Muralo Company Inc., PO Box 455, Bayonne, NJ 07002, (201)437-0770 [21510]

Murata of America Inc., PO Box 667609, Charlotte, NC 28266, (704)394-8331 [16330]

Murata Business Systems Inc., 6400 International Pkwy., Ste. 1500, Plano, TX 75093-8213, (972)403-3300 [21154]

Murata Erie North America Inc. State College Div., 1900 W College Ave., State College, PA 16801, (814)237-1431 [9108]

Murdock Companies Inc., PO Box 2775, Wichita, KS 67201, (316)262-0401 [9109]

Murdock Co.; M.F., 310 Water St., Akron, OH 44308, (330)535-7105 [17064]

Murdock Electric and Supply Co., PO Box 2775, Wichita, KS 67201, (316)262-0401 [17063]

Murdock, Inc.; G.A., 1200 Division Ave. S, PO Box 465, Madison, SD 57042-0465, (605)256-9632 [23284]

Murdock Inc.; H.E., 88 Main St., Waterville, ME 04901-6602, (207)873-7036 [17527]

Murdock Industrial Inc., 310 Water St., Akron, OH 44308, (330)535-7105 [17064]

Murken Products Inc.; Frank, PO Box 1083, Schenectady, NY 12301, (518)381-4270 [24288]

Murphy Co., 455 W Broad St., Columbus, OH 43215-2795, (614)221-7731 [22881]

Murphy Door Specialties Inc.; Don, 10390 Chester Rd., Cincinnati, OH 45215, (513)771-6087 [7755]

Murphy Elevator Company Inc., 128 E Main St., Louisville, KY 40202, (502)587-1225 [16331]

Murphy's Tile & Marble, 4208 Henry S Grace Fwy., Wichita Falls, TX 76302, (940)767-1861 [10069]

Murray Biscuit Co., LLC (Division of Keebler Co.), 933 Louise Ave., Charlotte, NC 28204, (704)334-7611 [11958]

Murray Lighting Inc., PO Box 1544, Denton, TX 76201, (817)387-9571 [15243]

Murray; Thomas W., PO Box 214, Dover, DE 19903, (302)736-1790 [3004]

Murry's Inc., 8300 Pennsylvania Ave., Upper Marlboro, MD 20772-2673, (301)420-6400 [11959]

Muscle Shoals Mack Sales Inc., PO Box 535, Tuscumbia, AL 35674, (205)383-9546 [20688]

Muscle Shoals Mack Sales Inc., PO Box 535, Tuscumbia, AL 35674, (256)383-9546 [16332]

Musco Olive Products Inc., 17950 Via Nicolo, Tracy, CA 95376, (209)836-4600 [11960]

Music City Record Distributors Inc., PO Box 22773, Nashville, TN 37202, (615)255-7315 [25344]

Music Distributors Inc., 6413 Midway Rd., #B, Haltom City, TX 76117-5347, (817)831-2982 [25345]

Music Emporium Record Co., 3100 23rd Ave., Meridian, MS 39301, (601)483-5991 [25346]

Music Industries Inc., 99 Tulip Ave., Ste. 101, Floral Park, NY 11001, (516)352-4110 [25347]

Music Industries Inc., 99 Tulip Ave., Ste. 101, Floral Park, NY 11001, (516)352-4110 [15244]

Music People Inc., PO Box 270648, West Hartford, CT 06127-0648, (860)236-7134 [25348]

Music People Inc., PO Box 270648, West Hartford, CT 06127-0648, (860)236-7134 [9110]

Music for Percussion, Inc., 170 NE 33rd St., Ft. Lauderdale, FL 33334, (954)563-1844 [3975]

Music Sales Corp., 257 Park Ave. S, 20th Fl., New York, NY 10010, (212)254-2100 [3976]

Music Sales International, 7466 James Dr., Middleburg Heights, OH 44130, (440)243-5115 [25349]

Musolf Distributing Inc.; Lon, 985 Berwood Ave., St. Paul, MN 55110-5144, (612)631-8586 [10070]

Musolf Distributing Inc.; Lon, 7452 Washington Ave., Eden Prairie, MN 55344, (612)946-1332 [10071]

Musser Forests Inc., PO Box 340, Indiana, PA 15701, (412)465-5686 [14926]

Musson Rubber Co., PO Box 7038, Akron, OH 44306-0038, (330)773-7651 [10072]

Mustad and Son Inc.; O., PO Box 838, Auburn, NY 13021, (315)253-2793 [23841]

Mustang Fuel Corp., 2000 Classen Ctr No. 800, Oklahoma City, OK 73106, (405)557-9400 [22503]

Mustang Industrial Equipment Co., PO Box 15713, Houston, TX 77020, (713)675-1552 [16333]

Mustang Power Systems, 7777 Washington Ave., Houston, TX 77007, (713)861-0777 [3005]

Mustang Publishing Co., PO Box 770426, Memphis, TN 38177, (901)684-1200 [3977]

Mustang Tractor and Equipment Co., PO Box 1373, Houston, TX 77251, (713)460-2000 [1058]

Mustela USA, N19 W6727 Commerce Ct., Cedarburg, WI 53012, (414)377-6722 [14169]

Mustela USA, N19 W6727 Commerce Ct., Cedarburg, WI 53012, (414)377-6722 [19472]

MuTech Corp., 85 Rangeway Rd., North Billerica, MA 01862-2105, (781)935-1770 [6536]

Mutual Distributing Co., 2233 Capital Blvd., PO Box 26446, Raleigh, NC 27611, (919)828-3842 [1897]

Mutual Distributors Inc., PO Box 330, Lakeland, FL 33802, (941)688-0042 [11961]

Mutual Manufacturing and Supply Co., 3300 Spring Grove Ave., Cincinnati, OH 45225, (513)541-2330 [14615]

Mutual Pipe and Supply Inc., PO Box 55627, Indianapolis, IN 46205, (317)923-2581 [23285]

Mutual Sales Corp., 2447 W Belmont Ave., Chicago, IL 60618, (773)935-9440 [16334]

Mutual Sales Inc., 1650 Turnpike St., North Andover, MA 01845-6222, (508)685-7067 [26586]

Mutual Services of Highland Park, 1393 Half Day Rd., Highland Park, IL 60035, (847)432-0027 [13841]

Mutual Trading Co. Inc., 431 Crocker St., Los Angeles, CA 90013, (213)626-9458 [11962]

Mutual Truck Parts Co., 2000-04 S Wabash Ave., Chicago, IL 60616, (312)225-3500 [3006]

Mutual Wheel Co., 2345 4th Ave., Moline, IL 61265, (309)757-1200 [3007]

Mutual Wholesale Co., 2800 N Andrews Ave. Ext., Pompano Beach, FL 33069, (954)973-4300 [11963]

Mutual Wholesale Co., PO Box 330, Lakeland, FL 33802, (863)688-0042 [11964]

Muzak, 383 E Grand Ave., South San Francisco, CA 94080-1913, (650)871-1900 [25350]

Muzak, 100 Sebethe Dr., Cromwell, CT 06416-1032, (860)635-3236 [25351]

MVR Auto Refinishing Supplies, 891 Alua, No. B3, Wailuku, HI 96793, (808)242-8175 [21511]

MVR Auto Refinishing Supplies, 891 Alua, No. B3, Wailuku, HI 96793, (808)242-8175 [3008]

M.W. Manufacturers Inc., PO Box 136, Tupelo, MS 38802, (601)842-7311 [7756]

Myco Plastics, 1550 5th St. SW, Winter Haven, FL 33880, (941)299-7580 [3009]

Mycogen Plant Sciences. Southern Div., 3600 Columbia St., Plainview, TX 79072-9327, (806)744-1408 [1059]

Mycogen Seeds, 5501 Oberlin Dr., San Diego, CA 92121-1718, (619)453-8030 [1060]

Mycogen Seeds, 103 Tomaras Ave., Savoy, IL 61874, (217)373-5300 [1061]

Myer Brothers Implements Inc., 2740 N Columbus St., Ottawa, IL 61350-1096, (815)433-4461 [1062]

Myer Co.; Milton D., Rothesay Ave., Carnegie, PA 15106, (412)279-9151 [26587]

Myers Associates Inc.; Vic, PO Box 3586, Albuquerque, NM 87190-3586, (505)884-6878 [6537]

Myers Associates; Vic, 7800 S Elati, Ste. 210, Littleton, CO 80120, (303)730-7313 [6538]

Myers Associates; Vic, 4645 S Lakeshore Dr., Ste. 18, Tempe, AZ 85282, (602)345-6449 [6539]

Myers Associates; Vic, 1935 S Main St., Ste. 539, Salt Lake City, UT 84115, (801)467-1795 [6540]

Myers Equipment Corp., 8860 Akron-Canfield Rd., Canfield, OH 44406, (330)533-5556 [3010]

Myers Furnace Supply Co., 1020 Duquesne Blvd., Duquesne, PA 15110, (412)469-1010 [14616]

Myers Group Inc.; J.B., 1020 Duquesne Blvd., Duquesne, PA 15110, (412)469-1010 [14616]

Myers Inc., 610 W Main St., Lexington, IL 61753, (309)365-7201 [1063]

Myers Industries Inc., 1293 S Main St., Akron, OH 44301, (330)253-5592 [3011]

Myers Industries Inc. Myers Tire Supply, PO Box 1029, Akron, OH 44309, (330)253-5592 [3012]

Myers and Son Inc.; John H., 1285 W King St., York, PA 17405, (717)792-2500 [7757]

Myers and Sons Inc.; D., 4311 Erdman Ave., Baltimore, MD 21213, (410)522-7500 [24817]

Myerson Candy Co.; Ben, 928 Towne Ave., Los Angeles, CA 90021, (213)623-6266 [1898]

Myles Inc.; J.E., 310 Executive Dr., Troy, MI 48083-4587, (248)583-1020 [16335]

Myles Inc.; J.E., 310 Executive Dr., Troy, MI 48084, (313)583-1020 [17065]

Myrmo and Sons Inc., PO Box 3215, Eugene, OR 97403, (541)747-4565 [7758]

Myron L Co., 6115 Corte del Cedro, Carlsbad, 24895, 92009-1516, (760)438-2021 [24406]

N & L Inc., 5525 Cameron St., Las Vegas, NV 89118-2206, (702)362-4230 [7759]

N Pool Patio Ltd., PO Box 495, North Chatham, MA 02650-0495, (508)945-1540 [23842]

N Squared Inc., 4003D Green Briar Dr., Stafford, TX 77477, (281)240-3322 [24407]

N.A. Marketing Inc., RR 5, Box 5, Augusta, ME 04330, (207)623-2393 [19473]

N.A. Marketing Inc., RR 5, Box 5, Augusta, ME 04330, (207)623-2393 [19474]

Nabisco Foods. Phoenix Confections Div., 170 34th St., Brooklyn, NY 11232-2304, (718)768-7900 [11965]

Nabo Industries, 31 Cornelia St., New York, NY 10014, (212)645-6942 [18574]

Nackard Wholesale Beverage Co.; Fred, 4900 E Railhead Ave., Flagstaff, AZ 86001, (602)526-2229 [1899]

Nackard Wholesale Beverage Co.; Fred, 4900 E Railhead Ave., Flagstaff, AZ 86001, (602)526-2229 [1900]

Nacol Jewelry; C.S., 3703 Twin City Hwy., Port Arthur, TX 77642, (409)962-8522 [17528]

NACSCORP, 528 E Lorain St., Oberlin, OH 44074-1294, (440)775-7777 [3978]

Nada Concepts Inc., 771 NE Harding St., Minneapolis, MN 55413, (612)623-4436 [18954]

Nadel and Sons Toy Corp., 915 Broadway, New York, NY 10010, (212)254-1677 [26588]

Nagel Paper & Box Co., 1900 E Holland Ave., PO Box 1567, Saginaw, MI 48605-1567, (517)753-4405 [21846]

Naggar; Albert, 1407 Broadway, New York, NY 10018, (212)575-1851 [5210]

Nagy Sales Corp.; Tom, PO Box 464, Goshen, IN 46527, (219)262-4479 [24597]

Nailite International Inc., 1251 NW 165th St., Miami, FL 33169, (305)620-6200 [7760]

Najarian Music Company Inc., 269 Lexington St., Waltham, MA 02452, (781)899-2200 [3979]

Nakagawa Painting, Inc.; James, Waialo Rd., Hanapepe, HI 96716, (808)335-6412 [21512]

Nakai Trading Co., 8605 Central Ave. NW, Albuquerque, NM 87121-2102, (505)836-1053 [17529]

Nakamichi America Corp., 955 Francisco St., Torrance, CA 90502-1202, (310)538-8150 [25352]

Nalco Chemical Co., 6991 E Camelback Rd., Scottsdale, AZ 85251-2436, (480)941-3915 [4464]

Nalley Cos., 87 W Paces Ferry Rd., Atlanta, GA 30305, (404)261-3130 [3013]

Nally & Haydon Inc., Springfield Rd., Bardstown, KY 40004, (502)348-3926 [7761]

Nalpak Video Sales, Inc., 1937-C Friendship Dr., El Cajon, CA 92020, (619)258-1200 [16336]

Namasco, PO Drawer 450469, Houston, TX 77245, (713)433-7211 [20212]

Namasco Corp., 5775 Glenridge Dr., Bldg. C, Ste. 110, Atlanta, GA 30328, (404)267-8800 [20213]

Namasco Div., PO Box 446, Middletown, OH 45042, (513)422-4586 [20214]

Name Game, 95 S Main St., Memphis, TN 38103-2910, (901)527-3688 [5211]

Name Place, 5301 Everhart Rd., Corpus Christi, TX 78411, (512)854-9923 [5212]

Nana Development Corp., 1001 E Benson Blvd., Anchorage, AK 99508, (907)265-4100 [22504]

Nanbren-Compsol Ltd., 1056 N Tustin Ave., Anaheim, CA 92807, (714)632-5010 [6541]

Nance Corp., PO Box 29828, Richmond, VA 23242-9828, (804)784-5266 [16337]

Nance Frazer Sales Co., 111 Overton St., Hot Springs, AR 71901, (501)623-8201 [2082]

Nankang USA Inc., 300 W Artesia Blvd., Compton, CA 90220-5530, (310)604-8760 [3014]

Nannette, 112 W 34th, New York, NY 10120-0093, (212)967-7800 [5213]

Nannicola Wholesale Co., Inc., 1417 Youngstown Rd. SE, Warren, OH 44484-4247, (330)393-8888 [25747]

Nanny Goat Productions, PO Box 845, Laguna Beach, CA 92652, (714)494-7930 [3980]

NanoMaterials, Inc., 9 Preston Dr., Barrington, RI 02806, (401)433-7022 [4465]

Nansemond Ford Tractor Inc., 3750 Pruden Blvd., Suffolk, VA 23434, (757)539-0248 [1064]

Nantucket Inc., PO Drawer 429, Kinston, NC 28501, (919)523-7001 [5214]

Napa Auto Parts (Burlington, Vermont), 703 Pine St., Burlington, VT 05401-0506, (802)864-4568 [13842]

Napa Pipe Corp., 1025 Kaiser Rd., Napa, CA 94558, (707)257-5000 [20215]

Napa Valley Beverage Co., 5160 Fulton Dr., Suisun City, CA 94585-1639, (707)864-1741 [2020]

NAPCO, 755 Gray Dr., PO Box 729, Springdale, AR 72764, (501)751-7155 [4677]

NAPCO & LBK Marketing Corp., 7800 Bayberry Rd., Jacksonville, FL 32256-6815, (904)737-8500 [14927]

Napco Steel Inc., 1800 Arthur Dr., West Chicago, IL 60185, (630)293-1900 [20216]

Naples Rent-All and Sales Company Inc., 2600 Davis Blvd., Naples, FL 34104, (941)774-7117 [7762]

Napoleon Livestock Auction, PO Box 3, Napoleon, ND 58561-0003, (701)754-2216 [18124]

Napoli Foodservices Inc., 13623 Barrett Office Dr., Ballwin, MO 63021-7802, (314)821-3553 [11966]

Naporano Iron and Metal Co., PO Box 5158, Newark, NJ 07105, (201)344-4570 [26921]

Nappco Fastener Co., 11260 Hempstead Rd., PO Box 55586, Houston, TX 77255-5586, (713)688-2521 [9111]

Napsac Reproductions, Rte. 4, Box 646, Marble Hill, MO 63764, (573)238-4273 [3981]

Nar Inc., 585 Riverside St., Portland, ME 04103-1032, (207)797-8240 [4674]

Nardini Fire Equipment Company of North Dakota, PO Box 9707, Fargo, ND 58106-9707, (701)235-4224 [24598]

Nardone Bakery Pizza Co., 420 New Commerce Blvd., Wilkes Barre, PA 18706-1445, (717)825-3421 [11967]

Narragansett Trading Co. Ltd., PO Box 7322, Warwick, RI 02886-8545, (401)884-2985 [17530]

Nasco-Catalog, 901 Janesville Ave., Ft. Atkinson, WI 53538-0901, (920)563-2446 [26589]

Nasco Inc., 2100 Old Hwy. 8, St. Paul, MN 55112-1802, (612)780-2000 [16338]

Nasco West, PO Box 3837, Modesto, CA 95352-3837, (209)545-1600 [18955]

Nash Finch/Bluefield, PO Box 949, Bluefield, VA 24605, (540)326-2654 [11968]

Nash Finch Co., Hwy. 72 W, Lumberton, NC 28358, (919)739-4161 [11969]

Nash Finch Co., PO Box 1418, St. Cloud, MN 56302, (320)251-3961 [11970]

Nash Finch Co., 1425 Burdick Expwy. W, Minot, ND 58701-4255, (701)852-0365 [11971]

Nash Finch Co., 1402 W 2nd St., Liberal, KS 67901, (316)624-5655 [11972]

Nash Finch Co., PO Box 355, Minneapolis, MN 55440-0355, (612)832-0534 [11973]

Nashua Corp., 11 Trafalgar Sq., 2nd Fl., Nashua, NH 03063-1995, (603)880-2323 [21155]

Nashua Wallpaper & Paint Co., 129 W Pearl St., Nashua, NH 03060-3304, (603)882-9491 [21513]

Nashville Auto Auction Inc., 1450 Lebanon Rd., Nashville, TN 37210, (615)244-2140 [20689]

Nashville Pet Products Center, 2621 Cruzen St., Nashville, TN 37211, (615)242-2223 [27192]

Nashville Sash and Door Co., PO Box 40780, Nashville, TN 37204-0780, (615)254-1371 [7763]

Nashville Sporting Goods Co., 169 8th Ave. N, Nashville, TN 37203-3717, (615)259-4241 [23843]

Nashville Steel Corp., 7211 Centennial Blvd., Nashville, TN 37209, (615)350-7933 [20217]

Nason Automotive, 1007 Market St., Wilmington, DE 19898, (302)774-6950 [21514]

Nassifs Professional Pharmacy, PO Box 778, North Adams, MA 01247-0778, (413)663-3845 [18956]

Nataraj Books, 7073 Brookfield Plz., Springfield, VA 22150, (703)455-4996 [3982]

Natchez Coca-Cola Bottling Co., 191 Devereaux Dr., Natchez, MS 39120, (601)442-1641 [24989]

Natchez Electric Supply, 3051 Lynch, Jackson, MS 39209-7334, (601)352-5068 [9112]

Natchez Equipment Company Inc., PO Drawer A, Natchez, MS 39121, (601)445-9097 [20690]

Natco Food Service Merchants, PO Box 52209, New Orleans, LA 70152-2209, (504)525-7224 [11974]

Natcom International, 1944 Scudder Dr., Akron, OH 44320, (330)867-6774 [19475]

Nathan Segal and Company Inc., 2100 W Loop 610 S, Houston, TX 77027, (713)621-2000 [18125]

Nation Wide Die Steel and Machinery Co., PO Box 639, De Soto, MO 63020, (314)586-7979 [16339]

Nation Wide Paper Co., 6901 Scott Hamilton Dr., Little Rock, AR 72209, (501)565-8421 [21847]

National Airmotive Corp., PO Box 6069, Oakland, CA 94614, (510)613-1000 [131]

National Ammonia Co., 735 Davisville Rd., 3rd Fl., Southampton, PA 18966, (215)322-1238 [4525]

National Art Supply, 2021 Forest Ave., Kansas City, MO 64108, (816)842-6700 [25748]

National Association of College Stores Inc., 528 E Lorain St., Oberlin, OH 44074-1298, (440)775-7777 [3983]

National Audio Company Inc., PO Box 3657, Springfield, MO 65808, (417)863-1925 [25353]

National Barricade Co, 6518 Ravenna Ave NE, Seattle, WA 98115, (206)523-4045 [9113]

National Beauty Inc., 3109 Louisiana Ave., Minneapolis, MN 55427, (612)546-9500 [14162]

National Beverage Company Inc., 310 Back St., Thibodaux, LA 70301, (504)447-4179 [1901]

National Beverage Corp., 1 N University Dr., #400A, Plantation, FL 33324, (954)581-0922 [24990]

National Book Network Inc., 4720 Boston Way, Lanham, MD 20706-4310, (301)459-3366 [3984]

National Braille Press Inc., 88 St. Stephen St., Boston, MA 02115, (617)266-6160 [3985]

National Bushing and Parts Company Inc., PO Box 7007, St. Cloud, MN 56302, (320)251-3221 [3015]

National Business Furniture Inc., PO Box 514052, Milwaukee, WI 53203-3452, (414)276-8511 [13185]

National Candy, 15925 NW 52 Ave., Miami, FL 33014, (305)625-8888 [11975]

National Capital Flag Co. Inc., 100 S Quaker Ln., Alexandria, VA 22314-4526, (703)751-2411 [13407]

National Catholic Reading Distributor, 997 Macarthur Blvd., Mahwah, NJ 07430, (201)825-7300 [3615]

National Compressed Gases Inc., 24 McDermott Rd., North Haven, CT 06473, (203)624-5144 [17066]

National Compressed Steel Corp., PO Box 5246, Kansas City, KS 66119, (913)321-3358 [20218]

National Distributing Co., 4901 Savarese Circle N, Tampa, FL 33634, (813)885-3200 [1902]

National Distributing Co., 3601 Silver Star Rd., Orlando, FL 32808, (407)298-2300 [1903]

National Distributing Co., 6256 N W St., Pensacola, FL 32505, (850)476-1118 [1904]

National Distributing Co., 9423 N Main St., Jacksonville, FL 32218, (904)751-0090 [1905]

National Distributing Company, Inc., 4235 Sheriff Rd. NE, Washington, DC 20019, (202)388-8400 [1906]

National Distributing Company Inc., PO Box 44127, Atlanta, GA 30336, (404)696-9440 [1907]

National Distributing Co. Inc., 441 SW 12th Ave., Deerfield Beach, FL 33442 [1908]

National Distributing Company Inc., PO Box 27227, Albuquerque, NM 87125, (505)345-4492 [1909]

National Distributing Inc., 116 Wallace Ave., South Portland, ME 04106, (207)773-1719 [1910]

National Distributors Inc., 116 Wallace Ave., South Portland, ME 04106, (207)773-1719 [24991]

National Dry Goods, 1200 Trumbull Ave., Detroit, MI 48216-1941, (313)961-3656 [5215]

National Electric Supply Co., 702 Carmony Rd. NE, Albuquerque, NM 87107-4134, (505)345-3577 [15245]

National Electrical Supply Corp., 1 Corporate Dr., Holtsville, NY 11742-2006, (516)654-5533 [9114]

National Electro Sales Corp., 7110 Gerald Ave., Van Nuys, CA 91406-3711, (818)781-0505 [9115]

National Electronic Service Co., 6904-06 4th St. NW, Washington, DC 20012, (202)882-2216 [25354]

National Enzyme Co., PO Box 128, Forsyth, MO 65653, 800-825-8545 [11976]

National Equipment Co., 3401 E Truman Rd., Kansas City, MO 64127, (816)262-8200 [13186]

National Equipment Corp., 322 Bruckner Blvd., Bronx, NY 10454, (212)585-0200 [16340]

National Equipment Development Corp., PO Box 244, Newtown Square, PA 19073, (215)353-7272 [6542]

National Foods, 600 Food Center Dr., Bronx, NY 10474-7037, (718)842-5000 [11977]

National Hardware and Supplies, 5311 N Kedzie Ave., Chicago, IL 60625, (773)463-1470 [9116]

National Heritage Sales Corp., PO Box 1956, Cleburne, TX 76033-1956, (817)477-5324 [11978]

National Impala Association, 2928 4th Ave., PO Box 968, Spearfish, SD 57783, (605)642-5864 [3016]

National Impressions Corp., 1450 E Indian School Rd., Ste. 106, Phoenix, AZ 85014-4954, (602)230-5999 [25749]

National Industrial Hardware Inc., 462 N 4th St., Philadelphia, PA 19123, (215)627-1091 [16341]

National Industrial Lumber Co., 489 Rosemont Rd., North Jackson, OH 44451, (330)538-3386 [7764]

National Keystone Mizzy Tridynamics, 616 Hollywood Ave., Cherry Hill, NJ 08002, (609)663-4700 [19476]

National Learning Corp., 212 Michael Dr., Syosset, NY 11791, (516)921-8888 [3986]

National Lumber Co., 24595 Groesbeck Hwy., Warren, MI 48089, (313)775-8200 [7765]

National Manufacturing, Inc., 811 Atlantic, North Kansas City, MO 64116-3918, (816)221-8990 [7766]

National Material L.P., 1965 Pratt Blvd., Elk Grove Village, IL 60007, (847)806-7200 [20219]

National Medical Excess, 733 Brush Ave., Bronx, NY 10465-1839, (914)665-2777 [18957]

National Medical Excess, 144 E Kingsbridge Rd., Mt. Vernon, NY 10550, (914)665-2777 [19477]

National Metal Processing Inc., 6440 Mack Ave., Detroit, MI 48207, (313)571-4100 [20220]

National Mine Service Co. Mining Safety and Supply Div., PO Box 310, Indiana, PA 15701, (412)349-7100 [7767]

National Mine Service Inc., PO Box 310, Indiana, PA 15701, (724)349-7100 [24599]

National Oil and Gas Inc., PO Box 476, Bluffton, IN 46714, (219)824-2220 [22505]

National Oil Well Inc., 555 N Center St., Casper, WY 82601-1946 [16342]

National Optical Co. Inc., PO Box 4746, Monroe, LA 71211-4746, (318)387-2121 [19478]

National Paint Distributors, 25822 Schoolcraft, Detroit, MI 48239, (313)537-4500 [21515]

National Paint Distributors, 6280 Broad St., Pittsburgh, PA 15206, (412)361-8770 [21516]

National Patent Development Corp., 9 West 57th St., New York, NY 10019, (212)826-8500 [21517]

National Plastics Corp., 4th & Gaskill Ave., Jeannette, PA 15644, (412)523-5531 [9117]

National Potteries Corp., 7800 Bayberry Rd., Jacksonville, FL 32256, (904)737-8500 [13408]

National Propane Corp., PO Box 35800, Richmond, VA 23235-0800 [22506]

National Propane SGP Inc., PO Box 35800, Richmond, VA 23235-0800 [22507]

National Rubber Footwear Inc., 310 N Colvin St., Baltimore, MD 21202-4808, (410)752-0910 [24818]

National Rubber Footwear Inc., 310 N Colvin St., Baltimore, MD 21202-4808, (410)752-0910 [5216]

National Safety Apparel Inc., 3865 W 150th St., Cleveland, OH 44111, (216)941-1111 [24600]

National Safety Associates Inc., PO Box 18603, Memphis, TN 38181, (901)366-9288 [23286]

National Sales Engineering, 35455 Schoolcraft Rd., Livonia, MI 48150, (734)591-3030 [16343]

National Sanitary Supply Co. Portland Div., 2690 SE Mailwell Dr., Milwaukie, OR 97222-7316, (503)234-0210 [4675]

National Seed Co., 5300 Katrine Ave., Downers Grove, IL 60515, (630)963-8787 [1065]

National Specialty Services Inc., 556 Metroplex Dr., Nashville, TN 37211, (615)833-7530 [19479]

National Stock Sign Co., PO Box 5145, Santa Cruz, CA 95063-5145, (408)476-2020 [25750]

National Supermarkets, PO Box 23528, New Orleans, LA 70183, (504)733-6610 [11979]

National Switchgear Systems, 649 Franklin St., Lewisville, TX 75057, (972)420-0149 [9118]

National Systems Corp., 414 N Orleans St., Ste. 501, Chicago, IL 60610, (312)855-1000 [6543]

National Temperature Control Centers Inc., 13324 Farmington Rd., Livonia, MI 48150, (734)525-3000 [14617]

National Titanium Corp., 2187 S Garfield Ave., Los Angeles, CA 90040, (213)728-7370 [20221]

National Trading Co. Inc., PO Box 2773, Providence, RI 02907-0773, (401)861-1660 [21156]

National Tube Supply Co, 925 Central Ave., University Park, IL 60466, (708)534-2700 [20222]

National Welders Supply Company Inc., PO Box 31007, Charlotte, NC 28231, (704)333-5475 [17067]

National Welding Supply of Algona, PO Box 496, Algona, IA 50511, (515)295-7261 [17068]

National Wholesale, 1404 Rome Rd., Baltimore, MD 21227, (410)242-8313 [25355]

National Wine and Spirits Corp., PO Box 1602, Indianapolis, IN 46206-1607, (317)636-6092 [3017]

Nationwide Advertising Specialty Inc., PO Box 928, Arlington, TX 76004-0928, (817)275-2678 [13409]

Nationwide Beef Inc., 219 N Green St., Chicago, IL 60607, (312)829-4900 [11980]

Nationwide Ladder & Equipment Company Inc., 180 Rockingham Rd., Windham, NH 03087, (603)434-6911 [7768]

Nationwide Ladder and Equipment Company Inc., 180 Rockingham Rd., Windham, NH 03087, (603)434-6911 [16344]

Nationwide Papers Div., 1 Champion Plz., Stamford, CT 06921, (203)358-7000 [21848]

Natrol, Inc., 21411 Prairie St., Chatsworth, CA 91311, (818)739-6000 [14170]

Nat's Garden Produce, Inc., 7200 S Kimbark Ave., PO Box 19176, Chicago, IL 60619, (773)643-3121 [11981]

Nattinger Materials Co., PO Box 4007, Springfield, MO 65808, (417)869-2595 [7769]

Naturade Inc., 14370 Myford Rd, Irvine, CA 92606, (949)573-4800 [14171]

Natural Energy Unlimited Inc., 108 Royal St., New Orleans, LA 70130, (504)525-6887 [11982]

Natural Meat Specialties, 6331 Brightstar Dr., Colorado Springs, CO 80918, (719)548-1735 [11983]

Natural Ovens of Manitowoc Inc., PO Box 730, Manitowoc, WI 54221-0730, (920)758-2500 [11984]

Natural Resources, 6680 Harvard Dr., Sebastopol, CA 95472, (707)823-4340 [11985]

Natural Sales Network, Inc., 19290 S Harbor Dr., Ft. Bragg, CA 95437-5722, (707)964-1261 [11986]

Naturalizer, PO Box 1749, Ponce, PR 00733-1749, (787)259-7208 [24819]

Naturegraph Publishers Inc., PO Box 1047, Happy Camp, CA 96039, (530)493-5353 [3987]

Nature's Best, PO Box 2248, Brea, CA 92822-2248, (714)441-2378 [11987]

Nature's Gate Herbal Cosmetics, 9200 Mason, Chatsworth, CA 91311, (818)882-2951 [14172]

Nature's Herbs, 600 E Quality Dr., American Fork, UT 84003, (801)763-0700 [14173]

Naturipe Berry Growers, PO Box 1630, Watsonville, CA 95077-1630, (408)722-2430 [11988]

Naturo Co., 4250 E Washington, Los Angeles, CA 90023, (213)268-7291 [25751]

Naughton Plumbing Sales, Inc., 1140 W Prince Rd., Tucson, AZ 85705, (602)293-2220 [23287]

Naughton Plumbing Sales Inc., 1140 W Prince Rd., Tucson, AZ 85705, (602)293-2220 [23288]

Nautica Enterprises Inc., 40 West 57th St., New York, NY 10019, (212)541-5757 [5217]

Nautica International Inc., 40 West 57th St., 7th Fl., New York, NY 10019, (212)541-5990 [5218]

Nautical & Industrial Supply Inc., 2536 SE Clayton St., Stuart, FL 34997, (561)283-4010 [18575]

Navajo Manufacturing Co., 5801 Logan St., AW8, Denver, CO 80216, (303)292-3090 [17531]

Navarre Corp., 7400 49th Ave. N, New Hope, MN 55428, (612)535-8333 [6544]

Navasky & Company Inc.; Charles, PO Box 728, Philipsburg, PA 16866, (814)342-1160 [5219]

Navatron Communications, Inc., 33305 W 7 Mile, Livonia, MI 48152, (248)442-2233 [24530]

NavPress, 7899 Lexington Dr., Colorado Springs, CO 80920, (719)548-9222 [3988]

Naz-Dar Cincinnati, 3905 Port Union Rd., Fairfield, OH 45014-2203, (513)870-5706 [25752]

Nazarene Publishing House, PO Box 419527, Kansas City, MO 64141, (816)931-1900 [3989]

NBC Truck Equipment Inc., 28130 Groesbeck Hwy., Roseville, MI 48066, (810)774-4900 [3018]

NBN, 4720 Boston Way, Lanham, MD 20706-4310, (301)459-3366 [3984]

NC Machinery Co., PO Box 3562, Seattle, WA 98124-3562, (425)251-9800 [16345]

NC Plus Hybrids Coop., 3820 N 56th, Lincoln, NE 68504, (402)467-2517 [18126]

NCD, 6100 Hollywood Blvd., Hollywood, FL 33024, (954)967-2397 [6545]

NCS Assessments, 5605 Green Circle Dr., Minnetonka, MN 55343, (612)939-5000 [6546]

NCS Healthcare, 3200 E Reno Ave., Del City, OK 73115-6603, (405)670-2939 [18958]

NCS Healthcare, 3200 E Reno Ave., Del City, OK 73115-6603, (405)670-2939 [19480]

NCUBE, 1825 NW 167th Pl, Beaverton, OR 97006, (503)629-5088 [6547]

Ne-Mo's Bakery Inc., 416 N Hale Ave., Escondido, CA 92029, (760)741-5725 [11989]

NEA Professional Library, PO Box 2035, Annapolis Junction, MD 20701 [3990]

Neal's Gauging Trains, 86 Tide Mill Rd., Hampton, NH 03842, (603)926-9031 [26590]

Neapco Inc., Queen St. & Bailey St., Pottstown, PA 19464, (610)323-6000 [3019]

Nebraska Book Company Inc., PO Box 80529, Lincoln, NE 68501, (402)421-7300 [3991]

Nebraska Golf Discount Inc., 724 N 109th Ct., Omaha, NE 68154-1718, (402)493-5656 [23844]

Nebraska Iowa Supply Co., 1160 Lincoln St., Blair, NE 68008, (402)426-2171 [22508]

Nebraska Machinery Co., 401 N 12th St., Omaha, NE 68102, (402)346-6500 [7770]

Nebraska Medical Mart II, 720 E 23rd St., Fremont, NE 68025, (402)727-4270 [18959]

Nebraska Popcorn, Inc., RR 1, Box 50A, Clearwater, NE 68726-9720, (402)887-5335 [11990]

Nebraska Wine & Spirits Inc., 4444 S 94th St., Omaha, NE 68127-1209, (402)339-9444 [1911]

NEC America Inc., 14040 Park Center Rd., Herndon, VA 20171, (703)834-4000 [5687]

NEC America Inc. Data and Video Communications Systems Div., 110 Rio Robles, San Jose, CA 95134-1899, (408)433-1200 [6548]

NEC Business Communication Systems East Inc., 5890 Enterprise Pkwy., East Syracuse, NY 13057-2924, (315)446-2400 [5688]

NEC Technologies Inc., 1250 N Arlington Heights Rd., Ste. 500, Itasca, IL 60143-1248, (630)775-7900 [6549]

Necessary Organics Inc., 1 Nature's Way, New Castle, VA 24127-0305, (540)864-5103 [1066]

NECX Inc., 4 Technology Dr., Peabody, MA 01960, (978)538-8000 [9119]

NEDCO Supply, 4200 W Spring Mountain Rd., Las Vegas, NV 89102-8748, (702)367-0400 [9120]

Neece Paper Company Inc., 1307 Hadtner St., Williamsport, PA 17701, (717)323-4679 [21849]

Neely Coble Company Inc., PO Box 100347, Nashville, TN 37224, (615)244-8900 [20691]

Neely Industries, 2704 W Pioneer Pkwy., Arlington, TX 76013, (817)226-2500 [10]

Neely TBA, 6940 Clinton, Houston, TX 77020, (713)675-0924 [3020]

Neff Athletic Lettering Co., 645 Pine St., Greenville, OH 45331, (513)548-3194 [5220]

Neff Co., 112 N Main St., Avon, IL 61415, (309)465-3184 [1067]

Neff Engineering Co., PO Box 8604, Ft. Wayne, IN 46898, (219)489-6007 [17069]

Nefouse Brothers Distributing Co., 4320 Delemere Ct., Royal Oak, MI 48073-1810, (248)549-5554 [23845]

Nehawka Farmers Coop., PO Box 159, Nehawka, NE 68413, (402)227-2715 [11991]

Nehawka Farmers Cooperative, PO Box 159, Nehawka, NE 68413, (402)227-2715 [18127]

Neil Parts Distribution Corp., 1900 Route 112, Medford, NY 11763-0787, (516)758-1144 [3021]

Neill-LaVielle Supply Co., 1711 S Floyd St., Louisville, KY 40208, (502)637-5401 [13843]

Neill-LaVielle Supply Co., 1711 S Floyd St., Louisville, KY 40208, (502)637-5401 [17070]

Neil's Automotive Service, Inc., 167 E Kalamazoo, Kalamazoo, MI 49007, (616)342-9855 [3022]

Neil's Automotive Service, Inc., 62915 Red Arrow Hwy., Hartford, MI 49057, (616)621-2434 [3023]

Neiman Brothers Company Inc., 3322 W Newport Ave., Chicago, IL 60618, (312)463-3000 [11992]

Neiman Marcus Co., 1618 Main St., Dallas, TX 75201, (214)741-6911 [5221]

Neita Product Management, PO Box 1479, White River Junction, VT 05001, (802)765-4011 [16346]

Neithart Meats Inc., 12301 Gladstone Ave., Sylmar, CA 91342-5319, (818)361-7141 [11993]

Nekoosa Corp., PO Box 129, Nekoosa, WI 54457, (715)886-3800 [17071]

Nelco Sewing Machine Sales Corp., 164 W 25th St., New York, NY 10001, (212)924-7604 [15246]

Nelson Company Inc.; Walter E., 5937 N Cutter Cir., Portland, OR 97217, (503)285-3037 [4676]

Nelson-Dunn Inc., 940 S Vail Ave., Montebello, CA 90640-5420, (323)724-3705 [17072]

Nelson Electric Supply Co., 526 N Main St., Tulsa, OK 74103, (918)583-1212 [9121]

Nelson Electric Supply Company Inc., 926 State St., Racine, WI 53401, (414)637-7661 [9122]

Nelson Hawaiian, Ltd., 2080 S King No. 203, Honolulu, HI 96826, (808)941-3844 [19481]

Nelson Holland Inc., 5330 N 16th St., Phoenix, AZ 85016-3204, (602)264-1841 [24601]

Nelson-Jameson Inc., PO Box 647, Marshfield, WI 54449-0647, (715)387-1151 [16347]

Nelson Laboratories L.P., 4001 N Lewis Ave., Sioux Falls, SD 57104-5544, (605)336-2451 [1068]

Nelson Leasing Inc., PO Box 993, Willmar, MN 56201, (320)235-2770 [3024]

Nelson-Ricks Creamery Co., 314 W 3rd S, Salt Lake City, UT 84101, (801)364-3607 [11994]

Nelson Roanoke Corp., 7901 Trading Ln., Frederick, MD 21701-3275 [13844]

Nelson-Roanoke Div., 7901 Trading Ln., Frederick, MD 21701-3275 [13845]

Nelson; Todd, 2301 Highway 95, Council, ID 83612-5233, (208)253-6052 [18128]

Nelson Wholesale Corp., PO Box 16348, Mobile, AL 36616-0348, (334)479-1471 [24191]

Nelsons, 248-250 Main St., Gloucester, MA 01930, (978)283-5675 [5222]

Nemaha County Cooperative Association, PO Box 204, Seneca, KS 66538, (785)336-2153 [1069]

Nemo Tile Company, Inc., 177-02 Jamaica Ave., Jamaica, NY 11432, (718)291-5969 [10073]

Nemo Tile Company, Inc., 277 Old Country Rd. E, Hicksville, NY 11801, (516)935-5300 [10074]

Nemo Tile Company, Inc., 48 E 21st St., New York, NY 10010, (212)505-0009 [10075]

Neo Fabrics, Inc., 5650 Hayne Blvd., PO Box 26789, New Orleans, LA 70126, (504)241-4020 [26155]

Neo Fabrics, Inc., 1506 Corporate Dr., Shreveport, LA 71107, (318)424-4129 [26156]

Neon Co., 858 DeKalb Ave. NE, Atlanta, GA 30307, (404)873-6366 [25753]

Neopost, 1345 Valwood Pkwy., Ste. 310, Carrollton, TX 75006, (972)243-2421 [25754]

Neostyle Eyewear Corp., 2605 State St., San Diego, CA 92103, (619)299-0755 [19482]

Neowa F.S. Inc., PO Box 127, Maynard, IA 50655, (319)637-2281 [18129]

Neptune Polarized Sunglasses, PO Box 837, Kailua Kona, HI 96745, (808)329-6338 [19483]

Ner Tamid Book Distributors, PO Box 10401, Riviera Beach, FL 33419, (561)686-9095 [3992]

Nero Systems, Inc., 21331 Valley Forge Cir., King of Prussia, PA 19406, (610)783-5724 [25755]

Nesco Electrical Distributors Inc., PO Box 1484, Tupelo, MS 38802, (601)840-4750 [9123]

Neshaminy Valley Natural Foods Distributor, Ltd., 5 Louise Dr., Ivyland, PA 18974-1525, (215)443-5545 [11995]

Ness Company Inc., PO Box 667, York, PA 17405, (717)792-9791 [3025]

Ness Trading Co., 5730 Natural Bridge Ave., St. Louis, MO 63120, (314)381-4900 [3026]

Nesson Meat Sales, PO Box 11207, Norfolk, VA 23517, (804)622-6625 [11996]

Nesson Sales, 408 E 18th St., Norfolk, VA 23504, (757)662-3208 [26591]

Nestle Carnation Food Service Co., 800 N Brand Blvd., Glendale, CA 91203, (818)549-6000 [11997]

Nestor Sales Co., PO Box 1650, Pinellas Park, FL 33780, (813)535-6411 [16348]

Nethercott's Optical, 1641 Cara Loop, Anchorage, AK 99515, (907)345-6112 [19484]

Netherland Typewriter, 51 North St., Presque Isle, ME 04769, (207)769-2691 [21157]

Netterville Lumber; Fred, PO Box 857, Woodville, MS 39669, (601)888-4343 [7771]

Network Access Corp. (Pittsburgh, Pennsylvania), 7805 McKnight Rd., Ste. 206, Pittsburgh, PA 15237, (412)369-9790 [5689]

Network Center, 70 East 3750 South, Salt Lake City, UT 84115, (801)265-8500 [6260]

Network Marketing L.C., 853 Broken Sound Pkwy. NW, Boca Raton, FL 33487-3694, (561)994-2090 [14174]

Networks 2000, 1201 Tourmaline St., San Diego, CA 92109, (619)488-8753 [6550]

Neubert Millwork Co., 1901 Lee Blvd., North Mankato, MN 56003, (507)387-1105 [7772]

Neuman Distributors, 903 Moralis, San Antonio, TX 78207, (210)225-4123 [11998]

Neuman Distributors, Inc., 250 Moonacahie Rd., Moonachie, NJ 07074, (201)941-2000 [14175]

Neuman Distributors Inc., 175 Railroad Ave., Ridgefield, NJ 07657-2312, (201)941-2000 [19485]

Neuman Health Services Inc., 175 Railroad Ave., Ridgefield, NJ 07657-2312, (201)941-2000 [19486]

NeuroCom International Inc., 9570 SE Lawnfield Rd., Clackamas, OR 97015, (503)653-2144 [19487]

Neutron Industries Inc., 7107 N Black Canyon Hwy., Phoenix, AZ 85021, (602)864-0090 [4466]

Neuwirth Co., 225 5th Ave., New York, NY 10010, (212)685-6420 [15592]

Nevada Beverage Co., PO Box 93538, Las Vegas, NV 89193, (702)739-9474 [1912]

Nevada Business Systems Inc., 4041 S Industrial Rd., Las Vegas, NV 89103, (702)733-4008 [21158]

Nevada Cash Register Inc., PO Box 1566, Las Vegas, NV 89101-1566, (702)382-9200 [21159]

Nevada Food Service, 3550 S Procyon Ave., Las Vegas, NV 89103, (702)876-3606 [11999]

Nevada Illumination Inc., 2901 S Highland Dr. Bldg.3E, Las Vegas, NV 89109-1081, (702)735-8975 [9124]

Nevada Office Machines Inc., 1072 Matley Ln., Reno, NV 89502-2177, (702)329-2870 [21160]

Neville Chemical Co., 2800 Neville Rd., Pittsburgh, PA 15225-1496, (412)331-4200 [4467]

Neville Optical Inc., PO Box 2250, Westover, WV 26502-2250, (304)291-1087 [19488]

Nevitt; Stephen L., 210 Bonnyvale Rd., Brattleboro, VT 05301-8521, (802)257-4442 [17532]

New AG Center Inc., 25516 S Rte. 45, Monee, IL 60449, (815)469-5688 [1070]

New Age Distributing Co., 1000 E Markham St., Little Rock, AR 72201, (501)374-5015 [24992]

New Age Water Technology, 4515 N Hallmark Pkwy., San Bernardino, CA 92407, (909)384-7111 [25756]

New American Electric Distributors, Inc., 578 Perry St., Trenton, NJ 08618, (609)394-1860 [9125]

New American T-Shirt, 500 Alakawa St., No. 114, Honolulu, HI 96817-4576, (808)842-4466 [5223]

New Belgium Brewing Co, 500 Linden St., Ft. Collins, CO 80524, (970)221-0524 [1913]

New City Optical Company Inc., 1107-1109 Wilso Dr., Desoto Business Park, Baltimore, MD 21223, (301)646-3500 [19489]

New City Optical Company Inc., 5819 Ward Ct., Virginia Beach, VA 23455, (757)460-0939 [19490]

New City Shoes Inc., 29 W 56th St., New York, NY 10019, (212)262-9494 [24820]

New Concepts Books & Tapes Distributors, 9722 Pine Lake, PO Box 55068, Houston, TX 77055, (713)465-7736 [3993]

New Cooperative Company Inc., PO Box 607, Dillonvale, OH 43917, (614)769-2331 [12000]

NEW Cooperative Inc., PO Box 818, Ft. Dodge, IA 50501, (515)955-2040 [18130]

New DEST Corp., 4180 Business Ctr. Dr., Fremont, CA 94538, (510)249-0330 [9126]

New Energy Distributing, PO Box 87, Dyersville, IA 52040, (319)875-8891 [14618]

New Energy Distributors, PO Box 87, Dyersville, IA 52040, (319)875-2445 [23289]

New England CR Inc., 4 Liberty Ln. W, Hampton, NH 03842-1704, (603)246-4210 [26922]

New England Door Corp., 15 Campanelli Cir., Canton, MA 02021-2480, (978)443-5131 [7773]

New England Frozen Foods Inc., 1 Harvest Ln., Southborough, MA 01772, (508)481-0300 [12001]

New England Industrial Supply Company Inc., 210 Broadway, Everett, MA 02149, (617)389-2888 [21850]

New England Pet Supply, 3 Ledgeview Dr., Westbrook, ME 04092, (207)761-5687 [27193]

New England Pottery Co., 1000 Washington St., Rte. 1, Foxboro, MA 02035, (508)543-7700 [13410]

New England Propane Inc., 255 Field Point Rd., Greenwich, CT 06830, (203)869-4388 [19106]

New England Recycling Company Inc., 36 Garden St., Stamford, CT 06902, (203)327-9778 [26923]

New England Sand and Gravel Co., PO Box 3248, Framingham, MA 01701, (508)877-2460 [7774]

New England Serum Co., U.S. Rte. 1, PO Box 128, Topsfield, MA 01983, (978)887-2368 [27194]

New England Serum Co., U.S. Rte. 1, Topsfield, MA 01983, (978)887-2368 [19491]

New England Variety Distributors, 34 Industrial Park Rd., Niantic, CT 06357, (860)739-6291 [24993]

New England Variety Distributors, PO Box 804, Niantic, CT 06357, (860)739-6291 [12002]

New England Wholesale Drug Co., 1150 W Chestnut St., Brockton, MA 02301, (508)559-1550 [14176]

New England Wine & Spirits, 29 Ciro Rd., PO Box 660, North Branford, CT 06471-0660, (203)488-7155 [1914]

New Era Cap Company Inc., 8061 Erie Rd., Derby, NY 14047, (716)549-0445 [5224]

New Era Factory Outlet, 20 Orchard St., New York, NY 10002, (212)966-4959 [5225]

New Era Media Supply, 4440-A Commerce Cir., Atlanta, GA 30336, (404)691-4260 [22882]

New Fashion Inc., PO Box 148, Iva, SC 29655, (864)348-6151 [5226]

New Hampshire Distributor Inc., PO Box 267, Concord, NH 03302-0267, (603)224-9991 [1915]

New Hampshire Optical Co., 40 Terrill Park Dr., PO Box 1375, Concord, NH 03301, (603)225-7121 [19492]

New Hampshire Tile Distributors, Sheep Davis Rd., Rte. 106, Pembroke, NH 03275, (603)225-4075 [10076]

New Hampshire Tobacco Corp., 130 Northeastern Blvd., Nashua, NH 03062, (603)882-1131 [26331]

New Hampshire Tobacco Corp., 130 Northeastern Blvd., Nashua, NH 03060, (603)882-1131 [26332]

New Haven Body, Inc., 395 State St., PO Box 474, North Haven, CT 06473, (203)248-6388 [3027]

New Haven Filter Co., PO Box 16, New Haven, MO 63068, (573)237-3081 [3028]

New Horizon FS Inc., 655 Liberty Way, Anamosa, IA 52205, (319)462-3563 [22509]

New Horizons Ag Services, 406 Pacific Ave. S, Herman, MN 56248, (612)677-2251 [1071]

New Horizons FS Inc., PO Box 447, North Liberty, IA 52317, (319)626-8555 [22510]

New Horizons Meats and Dist., L.L.C., 2842 Massachusetts Ave., Cincinnati, OH 45225, (513)681-2850 [12003]

New Horizons Supply Cooperative, 770 Lincoln Ave., Fennimore, WI 53809, (608)822-3217 [1072]

New Hosiery, PO Box 21176, Chattanooga, TN 37424-0176, (423)845-5101 [5227]

New Jersey Art Drafting, 926 Haddonfield Rd., Cherry Hill, NJ 08002-2745, (609)779-7979 [25757]

New Jersey Book Agency, 59 Leamoor Dr., PO Box 144, Morris Plains, NJ 07950, (973)267-7093 [3994]

New Jersey Semiconductor Products Inc., 20 Stern Ave., Springfield, NJ 07081, (201)376-2922 [9127]

New Leaf Distributing Co., 401 Thornton Rd., Lithia Springs, GA 30122, (770)948-7845 [3995]

New Leaf Distributors Inc., 401 Thornton Rd., Lithia Springs, GA 30122, (770)948-7845 [3996]

New Man Barber & Beauty Supply, 12717 Lomas Blvd. NE, Albuquerque, NM 87112-6268, (505)293-8808 [14177]

New Mexico Beauty & Barber Supply, 1009 W 2nd St., Roswell, NM 88201-3009, (505)622-4311 [14178]

New Mexico Fire Works Inc., 137 Carlito Rd. NW, Albuquerque, NM 87107-6011, (505)344-5869 [26592]

New Mexico International Trade & Development, 4007 Comanche NE, Albuquerque, NM 87110, (505)264-1995 [21161]

New Mexico Mattress Co. Inc., 4015 Menaul Blvd. NE, Albuquerque, NM 87110-2935, (505)888-3533 [13187]

New Mexico Orthopedic Supplies, 4821 Central Ave. NE, Albuquerque, NM 87108-1226, (505)255-8673 [18960]

New Mexico Salvage Pool, 7705 Broadway Blvd. SE, Albuquerque, NM 87105-7455, (505)877-2424 [3029]

New Mexico School Products Co., PO Box 2126, Albuquerque, NM 87103-2126, (505)884-1426 [21162]

New Options on Waste Inc., 877 S Pearl St., Albany, NY 12202, (518)433-0033 [15593]

New Process Development, PO Box 462, Milltown, NJ 08850, (732)390-8893 [6551]

New Process Steel Corp., 5800 Westview Dr., Houston, TX 77055, (713)686-9631 [20223]

New Resource Inc., 106 Longwinter Dr., Norwell, MA 02061, (617)871-2020 [25356]

New Resource Inc., 106 Longwinter Dr., Norwell, MA 02061, (617)871-2020 [15247]

New Richmond Farmers Union Cooperative Oil Co., PO Box 188, New Richmond, WI 54017, (715)246-2125 [22511]

New Testament Christian Press, PO Box 1694, Media, PA 19063, (215)544-2871 [3997]

New United Distributors, 6917 Carnegie Ave., Cleveland, OH 44103, (216)881-4070 [21518]

New World Acquisition Inc., PO Box 731, Jackson, MI 49204, (517)787-1350 [22512]

New World Research Corp., 50 Broad Street, Suite 412, New York, NY 10004, (212)509-9091 [3030]

New World Technology Inc., 2541 Welland Ave. SE, Ste. A, Atlanta, GA 30316-4135, (404)243-6166 [18679]

New World Wines, 2 Henry Adams St., Ste. M58, San Francisco, CA 94103, (415)863-2220 [1916]

New York Enterprises, 32 W 30th, New York, NY 10001-4308, (212)725-5889 [5228]

New York Fastener Corp., 599 Industrial Ave., Paramus, NJ 07652, (201)265-8770 [9128]

New York Motorcycle, Ltd., 222-02 Jamaica Ave., Queens Village, NY 11428, (718)479-7777 [20692]

New York Notions/Craft Supply Corp., 3800 W 42nd St., Chicago, IL 60632, (773)247-2121 [26593]

New York Twist Drill Inc., 5368 E Rockton Rd., South Beloit, IL 61080 [17073]

New York Wire Co., 152 N Main St., Mt. Wolf, PA 17347, (717)266-5626 [20224]

Newark Electronics Corp., 2021 E Hennepin Ave., Ste. 338, Minneapolis, MN 55413-2725, (612)331-6350 [9129]

Newark Farmers Grain Co., 203 N Johnson St., Newark, IL 60541, (815)695-5141 [18131]

Newark Newsdealers Supply Company Inc., CN 910, Harrison, NJ 07029, (973)482-1500 [3998]

Newark Wire Cloth Co., 351 Verona Ave., Newark, NJ 07104, (973)483-7700 [20225]

Newark Wire Cloth Inc., 351 Verona Ave., Newark, NJ 07104, (973)483-7700 [20225]

Newborn Enterprises Inc., PO Box 1713, Altoona, PA 16603, (814)944-3593 [3999]

Newcomb Company Inc. Newcomb Associates, 6438 University Dr., Huntsville, AL 35806, (256)837-3233 [24408]

Newcomb Sportswear Inc.; Tony, 1824 Linwood Blvd., Oklahoma City, OK 73106-2626, (405)232-0022 [5229]

Newcomer Oil Corp., 101 E Cherry St., Elizabethtown, PA 17022, (717)367-1138 [22513]

Newell Company Inc.; C.A., 9877 40th S, Seattle, WA 98118, (206)722-0800 [10077]

Newell Office Products, 2514 Fish Hatchery Rd., Madison, WI 53713-2407, (608)257-2227 [21163]

Newell Oil Company Inc., PO Box 390, Alpine, TX 79831-0390, (915)837-3322 [22514]

Newell Paper Co., PO Box 631, Meridian, MS 39301, (601)693-1783 [21851]

Newell P.R. Ltd., PO Box 3379, Carolina, PR 00984-3379, (787)769-8885 [15594]

Newell Recycling Company Inc., PO Box 830808, San Antonio, TX 78283-0808, (210)227-3141 [26924]

Newells Bar & Restaurant Supply, Inc., 3110 Railroad Ave., Redding, CA 96001, (530)244-3980 [24192]

Newhouse Printers Supply Inc., 5737 E Cork St., Kalamazoo, MI 49001, (616)381-9500 [25758]

Newman Lumber Co., PO Box 2580, Gulfport, MS 39505-2580, (601)832-1899 [7775]

Newmans Inc., 1300 Gazin St., Houston, TX 77020, (713)675-8631 [17074]

The News Group, III, 1301 W Washington St., Peoria, IL 61602, (309)673-4549 [4000]

The News Group - Rocky Mount, 2 Great State Ln., Rocky Mount, NC 27803, (919)443-3124 [4001]

NewSoft America Inc., 47470 Seabridge Dr., Fremont, CA 94538, (510)445-8600 [6552]

Newsom Oil Company Inc., 1503 W 10th St., Roanoke Rapids, NC 27870, (919)537-3587 [22515]

Newsom Seeds, 14 Derwood Cir., Rockville, MD 20850, (301)762-2096 [1073]

NewSound, LLC, 81 Demerritt Place, Waterbury, VT 05676, (802)244-7858 [25357]

NewSound L.L.C., PO Box 669, Waterbury, VT 05676, (802)244-7858 [15248]

Newsouth Athletic Co., PO Box 604, Dallas, NC 28034-0604, (704)922-1557 [5230]

NEWSouth Distributors, PO Box 61297, Jacksonville, FL 32236, (904)783-2350 [4002]

Newton Appliance Sales & Service, PO Box 292, Newton, GA 31770-0292, (912)734-5554 [15249]

The Newton Group, Inc., PO Box 900, Newton, IA 50208 [19493]

The Newton Group, Inc. - Newton Lab, 623 N 19th Ave. E, Newton, IA 50208-1839 [19494]

Newton Manufacturing Co., 1123 1st Ave. E, Newton, IA 50208, (515)792-4121 [13411]

Newtown Appliance Sales & Services, 98-723 Kuahao Pl. B., Pearl City, HI 96782-3103, (808)488-1614 [15250]

Nezbeda Tile, Inc., 2995 E Aukele St., Lihue, HI 96766, (808)245-1765 [10078]

Nezbeda Tile Inc., 2995 E Aukele St., Lihue, HI 96766, (808)245-1765 [7776]

Nezperce Rochdale Company Inc., PO Box 160, Nezperce, ID 83543, (208)937-2411 [22516]

NFZ Products Inc., 3343 Hollins Ferry Rd., Baltimore, MD 21227, (410)242-0069 [13846]

NGE Inc., 2937 Tanager Ave., Los Angeles, CA 90040, (213)685-8340 [14619]

NHC Inc., 1503 W 10th St., Roanoke Rapids, NC 27870, (252)537-3587 [22517]

N.H.F. Musical Merchandise Corp., 9244 Commerce Hwy., Pennsauken, NJ 08110, (609)663-8900 [25358]

NHK Intex Corp., 1325 Remington Rd., Schaumburg, IL 60173, (708)843-7277 [20693]

Ni-Co. Sales Company Inc., PO Box 578, Georgiana, AL 36033-0578, (205)376-2296 [5231]

Niagara County News Company Inc., 70 Nicholls St., Lockport, NY 14094-4899, (716)433-6466 [4003]

Niagara Drinking Waters Inc., 17842 Cowen St., Irvine, CA 92614, (949)863-1400 [24994]

Niagara Foods Inc., PO Box 177, Middleport, NY 14105, (716)735-7722 [12004]

Niagara Medical, 707 Lowell Ave., Erie, PA 16505 [19495]

Nice Computer Designers, 4118 S 500 W, Salt Lake City, UT 84123, (801)261-3300 [6553]

Nice Computer Inc., 4118 S 500 W, Salt Lake City, UT 84123, (801)261-3300 [6553]

Nice Time & Electronics Inc., 1140 Broadway, Ste. 808, New York, NY 10001, (212)481-0251 [17533]

Nicewonger Co., 901 W Evergreen Blvd., Vancouver, WA 98660-3034, (206)699-4747 [24193]

Nicholas and Co., PO Box 45005, Salt Lake City, UT 84145-5005, (801)531-1100 [12005]

Nichols Companies of South Carolina, PO Box 827, Florence, SC 29503, (803)667-0096 [12006]

Nichols and Company Inc.; Austin, 156 East 46th St., New York, NY 10017, (212)455-9400 [1917]

Nichol's Farm Supply Inc., PO Box 118, Nichols, SC 29581, (843)526-2105 [1074]

Nichols Fleet Equipment, 2919 8th Ave., PO Box 72638, Chattanooga, TN 37407, (423)622-7528 [3031]

Nichols Foodservice Inc., PO Box 729, Wallace, NC 28466, (910)285-3197 [12007]

Nichols Motorcycle Supply, Inc., 4135 W 126th St., Alsip, IL 60803, (708)597-3346 [20694]

Nichting Company Inc.; J.J., 1342 Pilot Grove Rd., Pilot Grove, IA 52648, (319)469-4461 [1075]

Nickels Supply, 686 Rocky Branch Rd., Blountville, TN 37617-5636, (423)323-5738 [24821]

Nickerson Lumber and Plywood Inc., 7875 Willis Ave., Panorama City, CA 91402, (818)983-1127 [7777]

Nick's Junk Inc., PO Box 3392, Casper, WY 82602-3392, (307)265-5833 [3032]

Nicolet Imaging Systems, 8221 Arjons Dr., Ste. F, San Diego, CA 92126-4394, (619)635-8600 [24602]

NIDI Northwest Inc., 15209 NE 95th St., Redmond, WA 98052-2562, (425)861-6434 [6554]

NIDI Technologies, 15209 NE 95th St., Redmond, WA 98052-2562, (425)861-6434 [6555]

Nido, Inc.; Rafael J., PO Box 11978, Carparra Heights, San Juan, PR 00922, (787)251-1000 [10079]

N.I.E. International Inc., 3000 E Chambers St., Phoenix, AZ 85040, (602)470-1500 [6556]

Niehaus Lumber Co., PO Box 667, Vincennes, IN 47591, (812)882-2710 [7778]

Nielsen Co. Inc.; E.A., 1700 W 12th St., Kansas City, MO 64101, (816)421-0633 [7779]

Nielsen Oil and Propane Inc., 660 S Main St., West Point, NE 68788, (402)372-5485 [22518]

NIENEX Inc., 3000 E Chambers St., Phoenix, AZ 85040, (602)470-1500 [6557]

Night Owl Security Inc., 855 Brightseat Rd., Landover, MD 20785, (410)461-6300 [24603]

Nightblaster, 350 N Wheeler St., Ft. Gibson, OK 74434-8965, (918)683-9514 [9160]

Nightingale Medical Equipment Services Inc., 6161 Stewart Rd., Cincinnati, OH 45227, (513)271-5115 [19496]

Nihon Kohden America Inc., 2601 Campus Dr., Irvine, CA 92612, (714)250-3959 [18961]

Nikiforov, Inc.; George, 200 Park Ave. S, Ste. 514, New York, NY 10003, (212)473-4555 [14620]

Nikko America Inc., 2801 Summit Ave., Plano, TX 75074, (972)422-0838 [26594]

Nikon Inc., 1300 Walt Whitman Rd., Melville, NY 11747, (631)547-4200 [22883]

Nikzak, 6924 Valjean Ave., Van Nuys, CA 91406, (818)901-9031 [3033]

Niles Color Center, 7652 Milwaukee Ave., Niles, IL 60714, (847)967-9585 [21519]

Nimax Inc., 9275 Carroll Park Dr., San Diego, CA 92121-3234, (619)452-2220 [6558]

Nimbus Water Systems, Inc., 288 Distribution St., San Marcos, CA 92069, (760)591-0211 [25759]

Nine West Group, 5001 Kingsley Dr., Cincinnati, OH 45227-1114 [24822]

Nippan Shuppan Hanbai, 1123 Dominguez St., Ste. K, Carson, CA 90746, (310)604-9701 [4004]

Nippon Electric Glass America Inc., 650 E Devon, Itasca, IL 60143, (630)285-8500 [7780]

Nippon Steel Chemical Corporation of America, 345 Park Ave., New York, NY 10154, (212)486-7150 [4468]

Nippondenso of Los Angeles Inc., 3900 Via Oro Ave., Long Beach, CA 90810, (310)834-6352 [3034]

Nisbet Co.; E.P., PO Box 35367, Charlotte, NC 28235, (704)332-7755 [22519]

Nisbet Oil Co., PO Box 35367, Charlotte, NC 28235, (704)332-7755 [22519]

Niser Ice Cream, 16 E 11th, Newport, KY 41071-2137, (606)431-7556 [12008]

Nissan Motor Corporation U.S.A., PO Box 191, Gardena, CA 90248-0191, (310)532-3111 [20695]

Nissan Motor Corporation U.S.A. Infiniti Div., PO Box 191, Gardena, CA 90248, (310)719-5253 [20696]

Nissen Baking Co.; John J., 75 Quinsigamond Ave., Worcester, MA 01610-1893, (508)791-5571 [12009]

Nissen and Company Inc., 9508 Rush St., South el Monte, CA 91733, (213)723-3636 [7781]

Nissho Iwai American Corp., 1211 Avenue of the Americas, New York, NY 10036-8880, (212)704-6500 [20226]

Nitches Inc., 10280 Camino Sante Fe., San Diego, CA 92121, (619)625-2633 [5232]

Nitefighter International, 18 High St., PO Box 125, Silver Lake, NH 03875, (603)367-4741 [23759]

Nitek Metal Service Inc., 212 Apache Dr., Jackson, MS 39212, (601)373-4010 [20227]

Nittany Beverage Co., 139 N Patterson, State College, PA 16801-3757, (814)238-3031 [1918]

Nittany Oil Co., 321 N Front St., Philipsburg, PA 16866, (814)342-0210 [22520]

Nitterhouse Concrete Product Inc., PO Box N, Chambersburg, PA 17201, (717)264-6154 [7782]

Nitterhouse Masonry Products, LLC, PO Box 692, Chambersburg, PA 17201, (717)267-4500 [7783]

Nitto Tires, 10805 Holder St., Ste. 175, Cypress, CA 90630, (714)236-1863 [3035]

Niver Western Wear Inc., 1221 Hemphill St., Ft. Worth, TX 76104, (817)336-2389 [5233]

Nixon Power Services Co., 297 Hill Ave., Nashville, TN 37210, (615)244-0650 [9130]

NJ Rivet Co., 1785 Haddon Ave., Camden, NJ 08103-3007, (609)963-2237 [13847]

NJCT Corp., 775 Passaic Ave., West Caldwell, NJ 07006, (973)575-7500 [24194]

NK Lawn & Garden Co., PO Box 300, Tangent, OR 97389, (541)928-2393 [1076]

NKK Electronics America Inc., 450 Park Ave., New York, NY 10022-2605 [25359]

N.K.S. Distributors Inc., PO Box 758, New Castle, DE 19720, (302)322-1811 [1919]

NLS Animal Health, 11407 Cronhill Dr., Ste. D-W, Owings Mills, MD 21117, (410)581-1800 [27195]

NM Bakery Service Co., 310 San Pedro Dr. SE, Albuquerque, NM 87108-3033, (505)255-5225 [12010]

NMC Corp., 477 Madison Ave., Ste. 701, New York, NY 10022, (212)207-4560 [15251]

Nobel/Sysco Food Services Co., PO Box 5566, Denver, CO 80217, (303)458-4000 [12011]

Noble and Associates, 7136 S Yale, Ste. 311, Tulsa, OK 74136, (918)493-5015 [25760]

Noble Distributors Inc., 251 E University Dr., Phoenix, AZ 85004, (602)495-1852 [25360]

Noble Earth Inc., 331 NE Mcwilliams Ct, Bremerton, WA 98311-2506, (360)792-1550 [690]

Nobles County Cooperative Oil Co., PO Box 278, Worthington, MN 56187-0278, (507)376-3104 [22521]

NOCO Energy Corp., 2440 Sheridan Dr., Tonawanda, NY 14150, (716)614-6226 [22522]

Noe-Equal Hosiery Corporation, 207 S Payson St., Baltimore, MD 21223, (410)945-0900 [5234]

Noel Corp., 1001 S 1st St., Yakima, WA 98901, (509)248-4545 [24995]

Noel's Automotive Warehouse, 605 S Gallatin, PO Box 3487, Jackson, MS 39207, (601)948-4381 [3036]

Noerenberg's Wholesale Meats Inc., PO Box 23241, Milwaukee, WI 53223, (414)365-3553 [12012]

Noffsinger Manufacturing Co., PO Box 488, Greeley, CO 80632, (970)352-0463 [20228]

Noftz Sheet Metal, 2737 Penn Ave., Pittsburgh, PA 15222, (412)471-1983 [20229]

Nokia Display Products Inc., 123 Second St., Sausalito, CA 94965, (415)331-4244 [5690]

Nokia Inc., 2300 Valley View Ln., Ste. 100, Irving, TX 75062, (817)355-9070 [6559]

Nokomis Equity Elevator Co., 301 E State St., Nokomis, IL 62075, (217)563-8612 [18132]

Nolan Glove Company Inc., 131 W 33rd St., New York, NY 10001, (212)564-3266 [5235]

Nolan Scott Chatard L.L.C., 403 Allegheny Ave., Towson, MD 21204, (410)296-7262 [7784]

Noland & Associates, Inc.; Tim J., 10005 Trailridge Dr., Shreveport, LA 71106 [23846]

Noland Co., 80 29th St., Newport News, VA 23607, (757)928-9000 [23290]

Noland Co., 4700 Zenilworth Ave., Hyattsville, MD 20781, (301)779-8282 [23291]

Noland Co., Hwy. 5, Mechanicsville, MD 20659, (301)884-8141 [23292]

Noland Co., 5511 Nicholson Ln., Rockville, MD 20852, (301)881-4225 [23293]

Noland Co., 8849 Brookville Rd., Silver Spring, MD 20910, (301)588-0223 [23294]

Noland Co., 6607 Wilson Blvd., Falls Church, VA 22044, (703)241-5000 [14621]

Noland Co., 10512 Balls Ford Rd., Manassas, VA 20108, (703)369-5531 [14622]

Noland Co., 6601 Lee Hwy., Warrenton, VA 20186, (540)347-6660 [14623]

Nolarec Industries, Inc., Pinehurst Rd., PO Box 1065, Aberdeen, NC 28315, (919)944-7187 [15595]

Noleen Racing Inc., 17525 Alder St., Ste. 16, Hesperia, CA 92345-5005, (760)246-5000 [3037]

Nolo Press/Folklaw Inc., 950 Parker St., Berkeley, CA 94710, (510)549-1976 [4005]

Nolt's Ponds Inc., PO Box 40, Silver Spring, PA 17575, (717)285-5925 [27196]

Nomura America Corp., 60 E 42nd St., New York, NY 10165, (212)867-6684 [26157]

Nomura and Company Inc., 40 Broderick Rd., Burlingame, CA 94010, (415)692-5457 [18133]

Non-Ferrous Processing Corp., 551 Stewart Ave., Brooklyn, NY 11222, (718)384-5400 [20230]

Nonesuch Foods, 197 Rte. 1, Scarborough, ME 04074, (207)883-1440 [12013]

Noodle Head Network, 107 Intervale Ave., Burlington, VT 05401, (802)862-8675 [22884]

Noon Hour Food Products Inc., 660 W Randolph, Chicago, IL 60661, (312)782-1177 [12014]

Noonoo Rug Company Inc., 100 Park Plaza Dr., Secaucus, NJ 07094, (201)330-0101 [15596]

Nor-Cal Beverage Company Inc., PO Box 1823, West Sacramento, CA 95691, (916)372-0600 [12015]

Nor-Cal Produce Inc., PO Box 980188, West Sacramento, CA 95798-0188, (916)373-0830 [12016]

Nor-Del Productions Ltd., PO Box 93262, Rochester, NY 14692, (716)292-5550 [4006]

Nor-Joe Cheese Importing, 505 Frisco Ave., Metairie, LA 70005, (504)833-9240 [12017]

Nor-Mar Sales Company Inc., 20835 Nordhoff St., Chatsworth, CA 91311, (818)700-8804 [13848]

Nor-Mon Distributing Inc., 1134 SE Stark, Portland, OR 97214, (503)234-6215 [15252]

Norandex, Inc., 1133 S Gordon, Wichita, KS 67213, (316)942-7417 [7785]

Norandex, Inc., 10 Adams Dr., Williston, VT 05495, (802)864-0900 [7786]

Norandex Inc., 8450 S Bedford Rd., Macedonia, OH 44056, (330)468-2200 [7787]

Norandex/Reynolds Distribution Co., 8450 S Bedford Rd., Macedonia, OH 44056, (330)468-2200 [7788]

Norandex Sales Co., 2215 West 2200 South, Salt Lake City, UT 84119, (801)908-8747 [7789]

Norbest Inc., PO Box 1000, Midvale, UT 84047, (801)566-5656 [12018]

Norby Lumber Company Inc., PO Box 329, Madera, CA 93639, (209)674-6712 [27350]

Norco Inc., PO Box 15299, Boise, ID 83715, (208)336-1643 [4469]

Norcostco Inc., 3203 N Hwy. 100, Minneapolis, MN 55422, (612)533-2791 [25761]

Norden Inc., 4620 Churchill St., St. Paul, MN 55126-5829, (612)481-9092 [24823]

Nordic Computers, 5060 Commercial Cir Ste. A, Concord, CA 94520, (925)687-3050 [6560]

Nordic Delights Foods Inc., 72 Water St., Lubec, ME 04652, (207)733-5556 [12019]

Nordic Needle, Inc., 1314 Gateway Dr. SW, Fargo, ND 58103, (701)235-5231 [26158]

Nordic Products Inc., 2215 Merrill Creek Pky., Everett, WA 98203, (425)261-1000 [15597]

Nordic Wholesale Distributors Inc., 1021 W Oak, Kissimmee, FL 34741, (407)859-8508 [5236]

Nordica USA Inc., 1 Sportsystem Plz., Bordentown, NJ 08505, (609)291-5800 [23847]

Nordlie Inc., 262 E Montcalm St., Detroit, MI 48201, (313)963-2400 [14928]

Nordstrom Inc., 1501 5th Ave., Seattle, WA 98101-1603, (206)628-2111 [5237]

Nordstroms, 25513 480th Ave., Garretson, SD 57030-9340, (605)594-3910 [3038]

Nored Cotton Co.; W.H., PO Box 1009, Greenwood, MS 38935-1009, (601)453-3772 [18134]

Norfield Industries, PO Box 459, Chico, CA 95927-0459, (530)891-4214 [7790]

Norfolk Bearing & Supply Co., 3512 Princess Anne Rd., PO Box 12825, Norfolk, VA 23502, (757)853-3691 [17075]

Norfolk Iron and Metal Co., PO Box 1129, Norfolk, NE 68702-1129, (402)371-1810 [20231]

Norfolk Paint, 1373 Ingleside Rd., Norfolk, VA 23502, (757)853-4371 [21380]

Norfolk Wire and Electronics Inc., 5301 Cleveland St., Virginia Beach, VA 23462, (757)499-1100 [5691]

Noritake Company Inc., 75 Seaview Dr., Secaucus, NJ 07094-1806, (201)319-0600 [15598]

Noritsu America Corp., PO Box 5039, Buena Park, CA 90622, (714)521-9040 [22885]

Normad Fastener Company Inc., 2442 Rosemead Blvd., South el Monte, CA 91733, (626)443-0276 [13849]

Norman Equipment Company Inc., 9850 S Industrial Dr., Bridgeview, IL 60455, (708)430-4000 [16349]

Norman, Fox & Co., PO Box 58727, Vernon, CA 90058, (323)583-0016 [4470]

Norman Supply, PO Box 1811, Idaho Falls, ID 83403, (208)522-6994 [23295]

Norman Supply Co., PO Box 26048, Oklahoma City, OK 73126, (405)235-9511 [23296]

Normans Inc., 86 S Division St., Battle Creek, MI 49017, (616)968-6136 [12020]

Normark Corp., 10395 Yellow Circle Dr., Minnetonka, MN 55343, (612)933-7060 [23848]

Norpac Fisheries, Inc., 3140 Ualena St., Ste. 205, Honolulu, HI 96819, (808)528-3474 [12021]

Norpac Fisheries Inc., 3140 Valena St., Ste. 205, Honolulu, HI 96819, (808)528-3474 [12022]

Norpac Food Sales Inc., 4350 SW Galewood St., Lake Oswego, OR 97035, (503)635-9311 [12023]

Norrick Petroleum, 3919 E McGalliard Rd., Muncie, IN 47303, (765)284-7374 [22523]

Norris Co.; Garland C., PO Box 28, Apex, NC 27502, (919)387-1059 [21852]

Norris Co.; Garland C., PO Box 28, Apex, NC 27502, (919)387-1059 [17076]

Norris Co.; Walter, 5530 Milton Pkwy., Rosemont, IL 60018, (847)671-7410 [17077]

Norse Motors Inc., 255 Lafayette St., London, OH 43140, (614)852-1122 [3039]

Norseland Inc., 1290 E Main St., Stamford, CT 06902, (203)324-5620 [12024]

Norseworthy and Wofford Inc., PO Box 336, Weiner, AR 72479, (870)684-2271 [1077]

Norstan Inc., 5101 Shady Oak Rd., Minnetonka, MN 55343-5715, (612)352-4500 [5692]

Norstar Consumer Products Company Inc., 206 Pegasus Ave., Northvale, NJ 07647, (201)784-8155 [14179]

Nortel Federal Systems, 2400 Lakeside Blvd., Richardson, TX 75082, (972)301-7000 [5693]

Nortex Wholesale Nursery Inc., 1300 W Brown, Wylie, TX 75098, (972)442-5451 [14929]

North 54 Salvage Yard, PO Box 387, Alamogordo, NM 88311-0387, (505)437-4188 [3040]

North American Aqua Inc., 18008 State St., Vandalia, MI 49095, (616)476-2092 [25762]

North American Book Dealers Exchange, PO Box 606, Cottage Grove, OR 97424, (541)942-7455 [4007]

North American Cylinders Inc., PO Box 128, Citronelle, AL 36522, (205)866-2400 [3041]

North American Fur Producers New York Inc., 1275 Valley Brook Ave., Lyndhurst, NJ 07071-3519, (201)933-3366 [18135]

North American Investment Services, PO Box 35733, Albuquerque, NM 87176-5733, (505)888-0561 [17534]

North American Parts Inc., 10589 Main St., PO Box 392, Clarence, NY 14031, (716)759-8351 [23849]

North American Plywood Corp., 351 Manhattan Ave., Jersey City, NJ 07307-4441, (201)420-0440 [7791]

North American Security, 4138 E Ponce De Leon Ave., Clarkston, GA 30021-1818, (404)294-7222 [24604]

North American Shoe Co. Inc., 895 Warren Ave., East Providence, RI 02914-1423, (401)434-1177 [24824]

North American Treasures, PO Box 4338, Helena, MT 59604-4338, (406)227-8256 [17535]

North American Vision Services, 59 Hanse Ave., Freeport, NY 11520, (516)546-7507 [19497]

North American Watch Corp., 125 Chubb Ave., Lyndhurst, NJ 07071, (201)460-4800 [17536]

North American Wire Products, 30000 Solon Rd., Solon, OH 44139, (440)248-7600 [20232]

North Atlantic Communications Inc., 48 South Mall, Plainview, NY 11803, (516)756-9000 [5694]

North Atlantic Communications Inc., 207 Newtown Rd., Plainview, NY 11803, (516)756-9000 [9131]

North Atlantic Engineering Co., 15 Spencer St., Newton, MA 02465, (617)964-6180 [9132]

North Atlantic Seafood Inc., 4746 Dodge, San Antonio, TX 78217, (210)655-4746 [12449]

North Atlantic Services Inc., 39 Angus Ln., Greenwich, CT 06831-4402, (203)661-9249 [19498]

North Auburn Cash Market, 584 N Auburn Rd., Auburn, ME 04210-9803, (207)783-7378 [23850]

North Branch Flooring, 2415 W Barry Ave., Chicago, IL 60618, (312)935-3400 [10080]

North Brothers Co., 3250 Woodstock Rd. SE, Atlanta, GA 30316, (404)627-1381 [7792]

North Caddo Cooperative Inc., PO Box 669, Hinton, OK 73047, (405)542-3212 [1078]

North Carolina Equipment, PO Box 431, Raleigh, NC 27602, (919)833-4811 [7793]

North Carolina Mutual Wholesale Drug Co., PO Box 411, Durham, NC 27702, (919)596-2151 [19499]

North Castle Produce Inc., 911 N Broadway, North White Plains, NY 10603, (914)683-5771 [12025]

North Central Book Distributors, N57 W13636 Carmen Ave., Menomonee Falls, WI 53051, (262)781-3299 [4008]

North Central Commodities, Inc., PO Box 13055, Grand Forks, ND 58208-3055, (701)746-7436 [18136]

North Central Cooperative Association, 825 E 250 N, Warsaw, IN 46580-7869, (219)267-5101 [22524]

North Central Cooperative Elevator, PO Box 313, Clarion, IA 50525, (515)532-2881 [18137]

North Central Cooperative Inc., 2055 S Wabash St., Wabash, IN 46992, (219)563-8381 [1079]

North Central Farm Service Inc., PO Box 337, Hampton, IA 50441-0337, (515)456-2571 [18138]

North Central Grain Coop., PO Box 8, Bisbee, ND 58317, (701)656-3263 [12026]

North Central Grain Cooperative, PO Box 8, Bisbee, ND 58317, (701)656-3263 [1080]

North Central Optical Co., 3682 29th St., Grand Rapids, MI 49512, (616)949-8988 [19500]

North Coast Distributing, Inc., 26565 Miles Rd., Warrensville Heights, OH 44128, (216)292-6911 [13850]

North Coast Electric Co., 110 110th NE, Ste. 616, Bellevue, WA 98004-5840, (425)454-1747 [9133]

North Coast Sea Foods Inc., 12-14 Fargo, Boston, MA 02210-1915, (617)345-4400 [12027]

North Country Equipment Inc., 3603 Hwy. 2 W, Grand Rapids, MN 55744, (218)326-9427 [16350]

North Country Marketing Ltd., 9915 N 170th Ave., Hugo, MN 55038, (612)433-4600 [23851]

North East Auto-Marine Terminal Inc., 403 Port Jersey Blvd., Jersey City, NJ 07305, (201)432-7335 [20697]

North East Kingdom Sales, Inc., PO Box 550, Barton, VT 05822-0296, (802)525-4774 [18139]

North Electric Supply Inc., 1290 N Opdyke Rd., Auburn Hills, MI 48326, (313)373-1070 [9134]

North Farm Cooperative, 204 Regas Rd., Madison, WI 53714, (608)241-2667 [12028]

North Idaho Distributing Inc., PO Box 2530, Hayden, ID 83835-2530, (208)772-7512 [26333]

North Iowa Cooperative Elevator, PO Box 1275, Mason City, IA 50401, (515)423-5311 [1081]

North Pacific Dental, Inc., PO Box 1548, Woodinville, WA 98072-1548, (425)487-3157 [18692]

North Pacific Group, Inc., PO Box 3915, Portland, OR 97208, (503)231-1166 [7794]

North Pacific Lumber Co., PO Box 3915, Portland, OR 97208, (503)231-1166 [7794]

North Pacific Supply Co. Inc., 16250 SE Evelyn St., Clackamas, OR 97015-9515, (503)656-2940 [25361]

North Penn Equipment, 903 Lambson Ln., New Castle, DE 19720, (302)654-1990 [3042]

North Pittsburgh Systems Inc., 4008 Gibsonia Rd., Gibsonia, PA 15044-9311, (724)443-9600 [5695]

North Providence Auto Salvation, 940 Smithfield Rd., Providence, RI 02904-2911, (401)353-6720 [3043]

North Riverside Venture Inc., 50 Technology Park, Norcross, GA 30092, (404)446-5556 [3044]

North Shore Recycled Fibers, 53 Jefferson Ave., Salem, MA 01970, (978)744-4330 [26925]

North Shore Sportswear Company Inc., Dickson St., Glen Cove, NY 11542, (516)671-4390 [5238]

North Shore Supply Company Inc., PO Box 9940, Houston, TX 77213, (713)453-3533 [20233]

North Star Distributors, 2210 Hewitt Ave., Everett, WA 98201, (425)252-9600 [24996]

North Star Distributors, 2210 Hewitt Ave., Everett, WA 98201, (425)252-9600 [12029]

North Star Glove Co., PO Box 1214, Tacoma, WA 98401, (253)627-7107 [5239]

North Star Recycling Co., 7650 Edinborough Way, Edina, MN 55435, (952)367-3500 [20234]

North Star Sales Co., 5401 Fairbanks St., Ste. 3, Anchorage, AK 99518-1261, (907)561-1164 [15253]

North Star Water Conditioning, 1890 Woodlane Dr., Woodbury, MN 55125, (612)738-5839 [25763]

North Star Water Conditioning, 1890 Woodlane Dr., Woodbury, MN 55125, (612)738-5839 [23297]

North State Garment Company Inc., PO Box 215, Farmville, NC 27828, (919)753-3266 [5240]

North State Metals Inc., 468 Oakgrove Cloverhill Ch. Rd., Lawndale, NC 28090, (704)538-1452 [20235]

North States Steel Corp., 811 Eagle Dr., Bensenville, IL 60106, (708)595-5500 [20236]

North Texas Bolt, Nut & Screw, Inc., 1502 109th St., Grand Prairie, TX 75050-1903, (972)647-0608 [13851]

North Valley Distributing, 945 Merchant, PO Box 493789, Redding, CA 96049-3789, (530)222-1500 [9135]

North Warehouse Inc., 6181 Taylor Dr., Flint, MI 48507-4665, (810)767-5167 [5241]

North West Quality Innovations, 18050 Skyland Cir, Lake Oswego, OR 97034-6452, (503)636-1887 [24825]

Northampton County Seed, PO Box 51, Bath, PA 18014, (610)837-6311 [1082]

Northampton Farm Bureau Cooperative, 300 Bushkill St., Tatamy, PA 18085, (610)258-2871 [1083]

NorthCenter Foodservice Corp., PO Box 2628, Augusta, ME 04338-2628, (207)623-8451 [12030]

Northcoast Business Systems Inc., 8000 Hub Park, Cleveland, OH 44125, (216)642-7555 [21164]

Northeast Airgas Inc., PO Box 1647, Salem, NH 03079-1142, (603)890-4600 [17078]

Northeast Cooperative, PO Box 160, Wisner, NE 68791, (402)529-3538 [22525]

Northeast Cooperative, 445 S Main St., West Point, NE 68788, (402)372-5303 [18140]

Northeast Cooperatives, PO Box 8188, Brattleboro, VT 05304-8188, (802)257-5856 [12031]

Northeast Engineering Inc., 124 Trumbull Rd., Manhasset, NY 11030, (516)365-9633 [24409]

The Northeast Group, Inc., PO Box 127, Westwood, MA 02090-0127, (781)461-0880 [25362]

Northeast Group Inc., 4 Arlington Rd., Needham, MA 02494, (781)449-4223 [15254]

Northeast Hide & Fur Corp., RR 1, Box 890, Waterboro, ME 04087-9606, (207)247-4444 [18141]

Northeast Industrial Components Co., PO Box 868, Bristol, RI 02809, (401)253-2555 [17079]

Northeast Interior Systems Inc., PO Box 809, Clifton Park, NY 12065, (518)371-4080 [13188]

Northeast Louisiana Heating & Air Distributing, 504 N 17th St., Monroe, LA 71201-6440, (318)325-2040 [14624]

Northeast Mississippi Coca-Cola Bottling Co., PO Box 968, Starkville, MS 39760, (662)323-4150 [24997]

Northeast Scale Company Inc., 2 Priscilla Ln., Auburn, NH 03032-1739, (603)622-0080 [24410]

Northeast Steel and Machine Products, PO Box 9007, Forestville, CT 06010-9007, (860)589-2700 [17080]

Northeast Texas Farmers Cooperative Inc., PO Box 489, Sulphur Springs, TX 75482, (903)885-3143 [18142]

Northeast Tire of Maine, 1178 Hammond St., Bangor, ME 04401, (207)945-4517 [3045]

Northern Arizona News Co., 1709 N East St., Flagstaff, AZ 86004-4910, (520)774-6171 [3513]

Northern Auto Supply Co., 1906 N Peach Ave., Marshfield, WI 54449, (715)384-2124 [3046]

Northern Beverage, 250 Anton St., Coeur D Alene, ID 83815, (208)765-8100 [1920]

Northern California Beverage Company Inc., 2286 Stone Blvd., West Sacramento, CA 95691-4050, (916)372-0600 [24998]

Northern Chemical/Janitor Sply, 6110 NW Grand Ave., Glendale, AZ 85301, (623)937-1668 [24195]

Northern Coop Services (Lake Mills, Iowa), 107 W Main St., Lake Mills, IA 50450, (515)592-0011 [22526]

Northern Distributing Co., PO Box 315, Glens Falls, NY 12801, (518)792-3112 [1921]

Northern Eagle Beverages Inc., PO Box 827, Oneonta, NY 13820, (607)432-0400 [1922]

Northern Electronics Automation, PO Box 4760, Manchester, NH 03108-4760, (603)669-6080 [9136]

Northern Electronics Automation, PO Box 4760, Manchester, NH 03108-4760, (603)669-6080 [9137]

Northern Equipment Company Inc., 1 Timber Trail Dr. SE, Ada, MI 49301-9300, (616)531-5000 [7795]

Northern Indiana Supply Company Inc., PO Box 447, Kokomo, IN 46903, (765)459-4151 [17081]

Northern Industrial Supply Inc., 2800 E Holland Ave., Saginaw, MI 48601, (517)753-2414 [17082]

Northern Industries Inc., 4677 W Cal Sag Rd., Crestwood, IL 60445, (708)371-1300 [20237]

Northern Jersey Reserve Supply Co., PO Box 440, Elmwood Park, NJ 07407, (201)796-3000 [7796]

Northern Lakes Co-op Inc., 304 W 1st St., Hayward, WI 54843, (715)634-3211 [1084]

Northern Laminate Sales Inc., 11 Industrial Way, Atkinson, NH 03811-2194, (603)894-5804 [23003]

Northern League Sportscards, 858 Kirkwood Mall, Bismarck, ND 58504-5752, (701)223-4672 [26595]

Northern Machine Tool Co., 761 Alberta Ave., Muskegon, MI 49441-3002, (616)755-1603 [16351]

Northern Ohio Lumber and Timber Co., 1895 Carter Rd., Cleveland, OH 44113, (216)771-4080 [7797]

Northern Ohio Lumber and Timber Co., 1895 Carter Rd., Cleveland, OH 44113, (216)771-4080 [27351]

Northern Plains Distributing, PO Box 1921, Fargo, ND 58107-1921, (701)293-6868 [25363]

Northern Plumbing & Heating Supply, 404 Stephenson Ave., Escanaba, MI 49829-2734, (906)786-5252 [23298]

Northern Power Technologies, PO Box 2063, Rapid City, SD 57709, (605)342-2520 [9138]

Northern Seed Service, Star Rte. Box 45, Conrad, MT 59425, (406)627-2327 [1085]

Northern Steel Corp., 364 E Ave., Oswego, NY 13126, (315)343-1374 [20238]

Northern Sun, 2916 E Lake St., Minneapolis, MN 55406-2065, (612)729-2001 [13412]

Northern Telecom Inc., 1771 E Flamingo Rd., Ste. B100, Las Vegas, NV 89119, (702)733-3800 [9139]

Northern Truck Equip. Corp., 47213 Schweigers Cir., PO Box 1104, Sioux Falls, SD 57101-1104, (605)543-5206 [20698]

Northern Truck Equip. Corp., 47213 Schweigers Cir., Sioux Falls, SD 57101-1104, (605)543-5206 [16352]

Northern Video Systems Inc., 4465 Granite Dr., Ste. 700, Rocklin, CA 95677, (916)630-4700 [25364]

Northern Virginia Beverage Co., 6605 Springfield Ctr., Box 5266, Springfield, VA 22150, (703)922-9190 [1923]

Northern Wind, Inc., PO Box M40144, New Bedford, MA 02740, (508)997-0727 [12032]

Northern Wire & Cable, PO Box 2248, Oshkosh, WI 54903, (920)235-0022 [7872]

Northland Corp., PO Box 265, La Grange, KY 40031, (502)222-2536 [7798]

Northland Cranberries Inc., PO Box 8020, Wisconsin Rapids, WI 54495-8020, (715)424-4444 [12033]

Northland Electric Supply Co., PO Box 1275, Minneapolis, MN 55440, (612)341-6100 [9140]

Northland Equipment Company, Inc., 306 W State St., Janesville, WI 53546, (608)754-6608 [3047]

Northland Hub Inc., PO Box 73800, Fairbanks, AK 99707, (907)456-4425 [12034]

Northland Industrial Truck Company Inc., 6 Jonspin Rd., Wilmington, MA 01887, (978)658-5900 [20699]

Northland Industrial Truck Company Inc., 6 Jonspin Rd., Wilmington, MA 01887, (978)658-5900 [16353]

Northland Marketing, Inc., 1131 Westrac Dr., Ste. 107, PO Box 9948, Fargo, ND 58106-9948, (701)232-7220 [12035]

Northland Press, PO Box 1389, Flagstaff, AZ 86002, (520)774-5251 [4009]

Northland Publishing, PO Box 1389, Flagstaff, AZ 86002, (520)774-5251 [4009]

Northland Publishing Company, PO Box 1389, Flagstaff, AZ 86002, (520)774-5251 [4010]

Northland Sports Inc., PO Box 5009, Minot, ND 58702-5009, (701)857-1187 [23852]

Northmont Sand and Gravel Co., PO Box 185, Englewood, OH 45322, (937)836-1998 [20554]

Northpoint Trading Co. Inc., 5113 Pacific Hwy. E, No. 11, Tacoma, WA 98424, (253)922-2020 [27197]

Northridge Lumber Company Inc., 18537 Parthenia St., Northridge, CA 91324, (818)349-6701 [7799]

Northrup King Co., 7500 Olson Memorial Hy, Golden Valley, MN 55427, (612)593-7333 [1086]

Northstar Distributors, 10395A Democracy Ln., Fairfax, VA 22030, (703)591-0897 [1924]

Northstar Steel and Aluminum Inc., PO Box 4886, Manchester, NH 03108, (603)668-3600 [20239]

Northville Industries Corp., 25 Melville Park Rd., Melville, NY 11747, (516)293-4700 [22527]

Northway Acres Craft Supply, 9198 Brewerton Rd., PO Box 709, Brewerton, NY 13029, (315)699-5931 [21165]

Northway Acres Craft Supply, 9198 Brewerton Rd., Brewerton, NY 13029, (315)699-5931 [21166]

Northwest Arkansas Paper Co., 755 Gray Dr., PO Box 729, Springdale, AR 72764, (501)751-7155 [4677]

Northwest Blueprint and Supply, 13450 Farmington Rd., Livonia, MI 48150, (734)525-1990 [13413]

Northwest Bottling Co., 7523 15th Ave. NW, Seattle, WA 98117-5410, (425)251-0800 [24999]

Northwest Coast Trading Company, 1546 NE 89th St., Seattle, WA 98115, (206)524-2307 [23853]

Northwest Designs Ink Inc., 12870 NE 15th Pl., Bellevue, WA 98005-2212, (425)454-0707 [5242]

Northwest Diesel & Refrigeration Services, 601 Apollo Ave. NE, St. Cloud, MN 56304-0213, (320)252-6141 [14625]

Northwest Distribution Services Inc., PO Box 277, Emmett, ID 83617, (208)365-1445 [24196]

Northwest Electrical Supply, 30 S Main, Mt. Prospect, IL 60056-3224, (847)255-3706 [9141]

Northwest Farm Food Cooperative, 1370 S Anacortes St., Burlington, WA 98233-3038, (360)757-4225 [27198]

Northwest Farm Food Cooperative, 1370 S Anacortes St., Burlington, WA 98233-3038, (360)757-4225 [12036]

Northwest Foods, 1311 Lowe Ave., Bellingham, WA 98226, (206)647-2195 [12037]

Northwest Futon Co., PO Box 14952, Portland, OR 97214, (503)224-3199 [13189]

Northwest Grain, PO Box 128, St. Hilaire, MN 56754, (218)964-5252 [18143]

Northwest Grain Growers, Inc., PO Box 310, Walla Walla, WA 99362, (509)525-6510 [18144]

Northwest Graphic Supply Co., 4200 E Lake St., Minneapolis, MN 55406-2265, (612)729-7361 [25764]

Northwest Graphics, 4200 E Lake St., Minneapolis, MN 55406-2265, (612)729-7361 [25764]

Northwest Iowa Co-op, PO Box 67, George, IA 51237, (712)475-3347 [1087]

Northwest Iowa Cooperative, PO Box 218, Ashton, IA 51232, (712)724-6171 [18145]

Northwest Iowa Cooperative, 206 S Main St., PO Box 67, George, IA 51237-0067, (712)724-6171 [1088]

Northwest Meats Inc., 2615 E N St., Tacoma, WA 98421-2203, (253)383-3688 [12038]

Northwest Oil Company Inc., PO Box 1505, Fayetteville, AR 72702, (501)521-1573 [22528]

Northwest Parts & Equipment, PO Box 1205, Eagle, ID 83616-1205, (208)375-1500 [132]

Northwest Pipe Fittings Inc., 33 S 8th St. W, Billings, MT 59103, (406)252-0142 [23299]

Northwest Ribbon Recycling and Supplies, 8175 SW Nimbus Ave., Beaverton, OR 97008-6414, (503)641-5156 [26926]

Northwest Tobacco and Candy Inc., PO Box 4215, Fayetteville, AR 72702-4215, (501)442-8121 [26334]

Northwest Truck and Trailer Sales Inc., PO Drawer 2511, Billings, MT 59103, (406)252-5667 [20700]

Northwest Vet Supply Inc., PO Box 1841, Enid, OK 73702-1841, (580)234-5839 [27199]

Northwest Wholesale, 910 Automation Way, Medford, OR 97504, (541)779-4313 [25365]

Northwest Wholesale Distributors, 11427 SE Foster Rd., Portland, OR 97266-4041, (503)232-7114 [15255]

Northwest Wholesale Inc., PO Box 1649, Wenatchee, WA 98807, (509)662-2141 [1089]

Northwest Wood Products Inc., PO Box 377, Mill City, OR 97360, (503)897-2391 [7800]

Northwestern Bottle Co., 460 N Lindbergh Blvd., St. Louis, MO 63141-7808, (314)569-3633 [25945]

Northwestern Drug Co., 1101 Lund Blvd., Anoka, MN 55303, (612)656-2300 [19287]

Northwestern Equipment Supply, 635 Gilman St., Berkeley, CA 94710-1330, (510)527-4080 [16354]

Northwestern Supply Co., PO Box 426, St. Cloud, MN 56302, (320)251-0812 [1090]

Northwestern Systems, PO Box 1701, Great Falls, MT 59403-1701, (406)727-4881 [25765]

Northwood Cooperative Elevator, PO Box 227, Northwood, IA 50459, (515)324-2753 [18146]

Northwood Equipment Inc., PO Box 148, Northwood, IA 50459, (515)324-1154 [1091]

Northwood Equity Elevators, PO Box 380, Northwood, ND 58267, (701)587-5291 [18147]

Northwood Meats Inc., Hwy. 65 N, Northwood, IA 50459, (515)324-2483 [12039]

Norton Metal Products Inc., 1350 Lawson Rd., Ft. Worth, TX 76131-2723, (817)232-0404 [20240]

Norton Petroleum Corp., 290 Possum Park Rd., Newark, DE 19711, (302)731-8220 [22529]

Norvac Electronics Inc., PO Box 277, Beaverton, OR 97075-0277, (503)644-1025 [9142]

Norvel Hasley and Associates, PO Box 936, Greensboro, GA 30642, (706)467-3328 [23854]

Norvell Electronics Inc., 2251 Chenault Dr., Carrollton, TX 75006-5031, (214)233-0020 [9143]

Norwood Auto Parts Co., 624 Broadway, Long Branch, NJ 07740-4007, (732)222-3833 [3048]

Norwood Products Co., 3202 Railroad, Oscoda, MI 48750-0333, (517)739-9852 [23855]

Notari Sales Co.; John, 6715 Masonic Dr., Alexandria, LA 71301-2114, (318)442-0004 [12040]

Notini and Sons Inc.; Albert H., PO Box 299, Lowell, MA 01853, (508)459-7151 [26335]

Notions Marketing Corp., PO Box 7392, Grand Rapids, MI 49510, (616)243-8424 [26159]

Nott-Atwater Co, PO Box 13365, Spokane, WA 99213, (509)922-4522 [16355]

Nott Co.; Frank H., PO Box 27225, Richmond, VA 23261, (804)644-8501 [26927]

Noury and Sons Ltd., 5 Sampson St., Saddle Brook, NJ 07663-5911, (201)867-6900 [15599]

Nova Clutch Inc., 39 Front St., Brooklyn, NY 11201-1063, (718)858-8282 [3049]

Nova International Inc., 3401 K St. NW, Ste. 201, Washington, DC 20007, (202)338-4009 [13190]

Nova-Net Communications Inc., 58 Inverness Dr. E, Englewood, CO 80112, (303)799-0990 [9144]

Nova Science Inc., 9101 E Gelding Dr., Scottsdale, AZ 85260, (480)860-4447 [9145]

Nova Steel Processing Inc., 315 Park Ave., Tipp City, OH 45371, (937)667-6255 [20241]

Nova Technology Inc., 7135 Shady Oak Rd., Eden Prairie, MN 55344-3516, (612)944-6785 [6561]

Nova Vista Industries Inc., PO Box 731, Jackson, MI 49204, (517)787-1350 [22530]

Novakovich Enterprises, 3940 Alitak, Anchorage, AK 99515, (907)344-3230 [22531]

NovaQuest InfoSystems, 19950 Mariner Ave., Torrance, CA 90503, (310)214-4200 [6562]

Novartis Nutrition Corp., PO Box 370, Minneapolis, MN 55440, (612)925-2100 [12041]

Novartis Seeds Inc., PO Box 4188, Boise, ID 83704-4188, (208)322-7272 [1092]

Novartis Seeds Inc. (Golden Valley, Minnesota), 7500 Olson Memorial Hwy., Golden Valley, MN 55427, (612)593-7333 [1093]

Novel-Tees Wholesale, 959 East 3300 South, Salt Lake City, UT 84106, (801)484-6769 [26596]

Novellus Systems Inc., 4000 N 1st St., San Jose, CA 95134, (408)943-9700 [9146]

Novelty Advertising Co., 1148 Walnut St., Coshocton, OH 43812, (740)622-3113 [4011]

Novelty Cord and Tassel Company Inc., 107-20 Ave. D, Brooklyn, NY 11236-1911, (718)272-8800 [15600]

Novelty Machine and Supply Company Inc., 901 5th St., Sioux City, IA 51102, (712)255-0114 [17083]

Novelty Poster Co., 26 Clinton Ave., Valley Stream, NY 11580, (516)561-1378 [13414]

Novelty Poster Co., 26 Clinton Ave., Valley Stream, NY 11580, (516)561-1378 [13415]

Novo Nordisk North America Inc., 405 Lexington Ave., Ste. 6200, New York, NY 10017, (212)867-0123 [19501]

Novo Nordisk Pharmaceuticals Inc., 100 Overlook Ctr., No. 200, Princeton, NJ 08540, (609)987-5800 [19502]

Now Pet Products, 320 Berkshire Rd., Vermilion, OH 44089, (440)967-6560 [27200]

Now Products, 1141 Mt. Zion Rd., Bucyrus, OH 44820, (419)562-9118 [13416]

Nowak Dental Supplies Inc., PO Box 1489, Chalmette, LA 70044-1489, (504)944-0395 [18962]

Noyes and Son Inc.; J.C., PO Box 17382, Covington, KY 41017-0382, (606)431-4743 [12042]

NPA West Inc., 780 Chadbourne Rd., Ste. A, Suisun City, CA 94585, (707)421-1234 [6563]

N.R.F. Distributors, Inc., PO Box 2467, Augusta, ME 04338-2467, (207)622-4744 [10081]

N.R.G. Enterprises, Inc., 22 42nd St. NW, Ste. A, Auburn, WA 98001, (253)852-3111 [25766]

N.R.G. Enterprises Inc., 22 42nd St. NW, Ste. A, Auburn, WA 98001, (253)852-3111 [23300]

Nsa Independent Distributor, 585 Hoy Rd., Madison, MS 39110, (601)856-3236 [25767]

NSC International, PO Box 21370, Hot Springs, AR 71902, (501)525-0133 [21167]

NTC/Contemporary Publishing Group, 4255 W Touhy Ave., Lincolnwood, IL 60646-7975, (847)679-5500 [4012]

NTE Electronics Inc., 44 Farrand St., Bloomfield, NJ 07003, (973)748-5089 [9147]

Nu-Dimension Beauty Supply Inc., 10101 SW Arctic Dr., Beaverton, OR 97005, (503)643-0129 [14180]

Nu Horizons Electronics Corp., 70 Maxess Rd., Melville, NY 11747, (516)226-6000 [9148]

Nu-Look Fashions Inc., 5080 Sinclair Rd., Columbus, OH 43229, (614)885-4936 [5243]

Nu Skin Enterprises Inc., 75 W Center St., Provo, UT 84601, (801)345-6100 [19503]

Nu Skin International Inc., 75 W Center St., Provo, UT 84601, (801)345-1000 [14181]

Nu-Way Concrete Forms Inc., 4190 Hofmeister Ave., St. Louis, MO 63125, (314)544-1214 [7801]

Nu-Way Supply Company Inc., PO Box 182600, Utica, MI 48318-9004, (810)731-4000 [23301]

Nuclear Associates, 100 Voice Rd., Carle Place, NY 11514, (516)741-6360 [18963]

NUCO Industries Inc., 110 Schmitt Blvd., Farmingdale, NY 11735, (516)752-8600 [4678]

Nudo Products Inc., 2508 S Grand E, Springfield, IL 62703, (217)528-5636 [17084]

Nueces Tile Sales, 4516 S Padre Island Dr., Corpus Christi, TX 78411, (361)854-3166 [10082]

Nueske Hillcrest Farm Meats, RR 2, PO Box D, Wittenberg, WI 54499-0904, (715)253-2226 [12043]

Nugget Distributors Inc., PO Box 8309, Stockton, CA 95208, (209)948-8122 [12044]

Nulaid Foods Inc., 200 W 5th St., Ripon, CA 95366, (209)599-2121 [12045]

Numatics Inc./Microsmith Div, 7741 E Gray Rd Ste 5, Scottsdale, AZ 85260, (480)443-4773 [16356]

Number One International, 1775 S Redwood Rd., Salt Lake City, UT 84104, (801)975-5900 [3050]

Numeridex Inc., 241 Holbrook Dr., Wheeling, IL 60090, (847)541-8840 [6564]

Numrich Gunparts Corp., 226 Williams Ln., West Hurley, NY 12491, (914)679-2417 [13504]

Nunez Seafood, PO Box 126, Lafitte, LA 70067, (504)689-2389 [12046]

Nunn Electric Supply Corp., 105-19 Polk St., Amarillo, TX 79189, (806)376-4581 [9149]

Nurnberg Thermometer Co., PO Box 590, Rockville Centre, NY 11571, (516)766-7619 [24411]

NutraSource Inc., PO Box 1856, Auburn, WA 98071-1856, (206)467-7190 [12047]

Nutri-Fruit Inc., PO Box 338, Sumner, WA 98390, (425)643-4489 [25000]

NutriCology Inc., PO Box 55907, Hayward, CA 94544, (510)487-8526 [12048]

Nutrition For Life International Inc., 9101 Jameel Rd., Houston, TX 77040, (713)460-1976 [14182]

Nutrition International Co., PO Box 50632, Irvine, CA 92619-0632, (714)854-4855 [14183]

Nutrition Medical Inc., 5500 Wayzata Blvd., Ste. 800, Minneapolis, MN 55416-1249, (612)551-9595 [14184]

NWCS Inc., 7006 27th St. W, No. E, Tacoma, WA 98466-5281, (253)566-8866 [9150]

NY Apparel, 350 5th Ave., Ste. 826, New York, NY 10118, (212)465-8053 [5244]

N.Y. Sun Control, 4700 Vestal Pky. E, Vestal, NY 13850, (607)723-3066 [8087]

NYC Liquidators Inc., 158 W 27th St., New York, NY 10001-6216, (212)675-7400 [25366]

Nylander and Sorenson Inc., 2173 Blossom St., Dos Palos, CA 93620, (209)392-2161 [1094]

Nyle Home Health Supplies Inc., 72 Center St., Brewer, ME 04412, (207)989-4335 [25768]

Nyle International Corp., PO Box 1107, Bangor, ME 04401, (207)942-4851 [18964]

Nylen Products Inc., 1436 E 19th St., Indianapolis, IN 46218-4228 [3051]

NYMA Inc., 7501 Greenway Ctr. Dr., 1200, Greenbelt, MD 20770, (301)345-0832 [6565]

Nyssa Cooperative Supply Inc., 18 N 2nd St., Nyssa, OR 97913, (503)372-2254 [1095]

Nystrom Co., 3333 Elston Ave., Chicago, IL 60618, (773)463-1144 [4013]

O/E Automation Inc., 3290 W Big Beaver Rd., Troy, MI 48084, (248)643-2035 [6566]

O Henry Inc., 6920 W Market St., Greensboro, NC 27419-1805, (910)294-0630 [21168]

O-Rings Inc., PO Box 65675, Los Angeles, CA 90065, (323)343-9500 [17085]

O2 Emergency Medical Care Service Corp., 5950 Pine Tree Dr., West Bloomfield, MI 48322-1412, (734)661-0581 [18965]

Oak Distributing Company Inc., 5600 Williams Lake Rd., Waterford, MI 48329-3571, (248)674-3171 [1925]

Oak Paper Products Company Inc., 3686 E Olympic Blvd., Los Angeles, CA 90023, (213)268-0507 [21853]

Oakbrook Custom Embroidery, 960 Bacons Bridge Rd., Summerville, SC 29485-4108, (803)875-0790 [5245]

Oakes Oil Co., PO Box 160, Laceys Spring, AL 35754, (205)881-3310 [22532]

Oakland Carbide Engineering, 1232 51st Ave., Oakland, CA 94601-5602, (510)532-7669 [16780]

Oakton Distributors Inc., PO Box 1425, Elk Grove Village, IL 60007, (847)228-5858 [15256]

Oakville Feed and Grain Inc., PO Box 68, Oakville, IA 52646, (319)766-4411 [1096]

Oarsman Sportswear, 1530 Interstate Dr., PO Box 18040, Erlanger, KY 41018-0040, (606)283-6700 [4937]

OASIS Corp., 265 N Hamilton Rd., PO Box 13150, Columbus, OH 43213-0150, (614)861-1350 [25769]

Oasis Drinking Waters Inc., 1506 N Clinton St., Santa Ana, CA 92703, (714)554-6000 [25001]

Oasis Imaging Products, 1617 Southwood Dr., Nashua, NH 03063-1801, (603)880-3991 [25770]

Oberlin College Press-Field Magazine-Field Translation Series-Field Poetry Series-Field Editions, Oberlin College, 10 N Professor St., Oberlin, OH 44074, (440)775-8408 [4014]

O'Brien and Co., 3302 Harlan Lewis Rd., Bellevue, NE 68005, (402)291-3600 [12049]

O'Brien & Sons Inc.; M.E., 93 West St., Medfield, MA 02052-2043, (508)359-4200 [23856]

O'Brien Steel Service, PO Box 5699, Peoria, IL 61601, (309)671-5800 [20242]

Obrig Hawaii Contact Lens Lab, 1481 S King, Honolulu, HI 96814, (808)949-2020 [19504]

OCE-Bruning Inc., 6300 S Syracuse Way, Ste. 350, Englewood, CO 80111-2017, (303)779-6970 [25771]

OCE-USA Inc., 840 Croskys Office Pk., Fairport, NY 14450-3513, (716)425-4330 [25772]

OCE-USA Inc., 5450 N Cumberland Ave., Chicago, IL 60656, (773)714-8500 [21169]

Ocean Crest Seafoods Inc., PO Box 1183, Gloucester, MA 01930, (978)281-0232 [12050]

Ocean Floor Abalone, 1075 Reed Ave., San Diego, CA 92109, (858)271-5676 [12051]

Ocean Interface Company Inc., 21221 Commerce Point Dr., Walnut, CA 91789-3056, (909)595-1212 [6567]

Ocean Mist Farms, 10855 Cara Mia Pkwy., Castroville, CA 95012, (831)633-2144 [12052]

Ocean Originals, 3701 Wow Rd., Corpus Christi, TX 78413, (512)852-0252 [5246]

Ocean Pacific Apparel Corp., 3 Studebaker, Irvine, CA 92618-2013, (949)580-1888 [5247]

Ocean Pacific Sunwear Ltd., 3 Studebaker, Irvine, CA 92602, (949)580-1888 [5248]

Ocean Products Research, Inc., Rte. 645, Diggs, VA 23045, (804)725-3406 [18576]

Ocean Springs Distributors Inc., 14369 Oneal Rd., Gulfport, MS 39503, (228)832-6685 [4015]

Ocean State Yacht Brokerage and Marine Services, 801 Oaklawn Ave., Cranston, RI 02920-2819, (401)946-2628 [18577]

Oceana Ltd., 1811 VA St., PO Box 6691, Annapolis, MD 21401, (410)269-6022 [18578]

Oceana Publications Inc., 75 Main St., Dobbs Ferry, NY 10522, (914)693-8100 [4016]

Oceanex Services International, Inc., 16115 Park Row, Ste. 120, Houston, TX 77084, (281)579-0808 [22533]

Ocheyedan Cooperative Elevator Association, Box 69, Ocheyedan, IA 51354, (712)758-3621 [18148]

Ochs Inc., PO Box 361, Otis, KS 67565, (785)387-2361 [1097]

Ochterbeck Distributing Company Inc., 2405 Jackson St., Houston, TX 77004, (713)659-4922 [3052]

O'Connell Wholesale Lumber Co.; John J., PO Box 1250, Cedar Rapids, IA 52406, (319)366-5396 [7802]

O'Connor Company, Inc., PO Box 2253, Wichita, KS 67201, (316)263-3187 [14626]

O'Connor Company, Inc., 1250 Saline, North Kansas City, MO 64116, (816)471-4011 [14627]

O'Connor Distributing Company Inc., 9030 Directors Row, Dallas, TX 75247, (214)631-0151 [25367]

O'Connor Engineering Laboratories, 100 Kalmus Dr., Costa Mesa, CA 92626, (714)979-3993 [22886]

O'Connor and Raque Office Products Co., PO Box 1689, Louisville, KY 40201, (502)589-5900 [21170]

O'Connor Truck Sales Inc., H St & Hunting Park Av, Philadelphia, PA 19124, (215)744-8500 [3053]

Ocotillo Lumber Sales Inc., 3121 N 28th Ave., Phoenix, AZ 85017, (602)258-6951 [7803]

Ocotillo Lumber Sales Inc., 3121 N 28th Ave., Phoenix, AZ 85017, (602)258-6951 [27352]

OCT Equipment Inc., 7100 SW 3rd Ave., Oklahoma City, OK 73128, (405)789-6812 [7804]

O'Day Equipment Inc., PO Box 2706, Fargo, ND 58108, (701)282-9260 [22534]

Odeen International, Inc., 506 Cherry Rd., Memphis, TN 38117, (901)682-6910 [4471]

Odell Brewing Co., 800 E Lincoln Ave., Ft. Collins, CO 80524, (970)498-9070 [1926]

Odell Hardware Company Inc., PO Box 20688, Memphis, TN 38101-0140, (919)299-9121 [13852]

Odessa Trading Company Inc., PO Box 277, Odessa, WA 99159, (509)982-2661 [18149]

Odessa Trading Company Inc., PO Box 277, Odessa, WA 99159, (509)982-2661 [12053]

Odessa Union Warehouse Co-op, PO Box 247, Odessa, WA 99159-0247, (509)982-2691 [18150]

Odom Corp., PO Box 24627, Seattle, WA 98124, (206)623-3256 [1927]

Odom Northwest Beverages, 517 Snake River Ave., Lewiston, ID 83501-2262, (208)746-0114 [1928]

O'Donnell Co. Inc.; Roy J., 2256 S Delaware St., Denver, CO 80223-4138, (303)778-7575 [15257]

Odyssey Jewelry Inc., 1920 Westminster St., Providence, RI 02909-2802, (401)421-2230 [17537]

OEM Parts Center Inc., 110 S Sherman St., Spokane, WA 99202-1529, (509)838-3525 [3054]

Of Distinction, Inc. - The Silk Plant Co., 2110 W 98 St., Bloomington, MN 55431-2506, (612)888-5654 [14930]

Off the Dock Seafood Inc., 2224 Southern St., Memphis, TN 38104, (901)276-8784 [12054]

Off Price World, 4201 N Old State Rd. 3, Muncie, IN 47303-9512, (765)284-1000 [5105]

Off Road Specialty, 4866 Fenton St., Boise, ID 83714-1411, (208)376-3974 [3055]

Offenhauser Sales Corp., PO Box 32218, Los Angeles, CA 90032, (213)225-1307 [3056]

Office America Inc., PO Box 2430, Glen Allen, VA 23058-2430, (804)747-9964 [21171]

Office Club Inc., 1631 Challenge Dr., Concord, CA 94520, (510)689-2582 [21172]

Office Depot Inc., 2200 Old GermanTown Rd., Delray Beach, FL 33445, (561)278-4800 [21173]

Office Depot Inc. Business Services Div., 3366 E Willow St., Signal Hill, CA 90806, (562)490-1000 [21174]

Office Environments Inc., 11415 Granite St., PO Box 411248, Charlotte, NC 28241, (704)714-7200 [21175]

Office Equipment Co., 200 2nd St., Havre, MT 59501-3415, (406)265-9611 [21176]

Office Equipment Sales, 5319 W 25th St., Cicero, IL 60804, (708)652-1222 [21177]

Office Equipment Service, PO Box 16, Huron, SD 57350-0016, (605)352-8243 [21178]

Office Equipment Service Inc., 5520 Shelby Oaks Dr., Memphis, TN 38134, (901)388-4637 [21179]

Office Express, 164 Mushroom Boulevard, Rochester, NY 14623-6462, (716)424-1500 [21180]

Office Furniture & Design Center Inc., 2323 Cleveland Ave., Ft. Myers, FL 33901-3541, (941)337-1212 [21181]

Office Furniture Warehouse Inc., 1625 Cobb Pkwy. SE, Marietta, GA 30062, (404)988-0091 [13191]

Office Interiors Inc., 33 Chubb Way, Branchburg, NJ 08876, (908)231-1600 [21182]

Office Machine & Furniture Inc., PO Box 2881, Fargo, ND 58108-2881, (701)223-6250 [21183]

Office Manager, Inc., 143 Log Canoe Cir., Stevensville, MD 21666, (410)643-8000 [6568]

Office to Office Inc., 1474 Alameda St., St. Paul, MN 55117, (612)489-6113 [21184]

Office Pavilion/MBI Systems Inc., 1201 Mercer St., Seattle, WA 98109-5512, (206)343-5800 [18966]

Office Pavillion, 9850 16th St. N, St. Petersburg, FL 33716-4210, (813)577-2300 [13192]

Office Pavillion/National Systems Inc., 6315 McDonough Dr., Norcross, GA 30093-1208, (404)447-6650 [21185]

Office Planning Group Inc., 1809 S Eastern Ave., Las Vegas, NV 89104-3933, (702)798-5000 [21186]

Office Planning Group Inc., 11330 Sunrise Park Dr., Ste. B, Rancho Cordova, CA 95742, (916)638-2999 [13193]

Office Resources Inc., PO Box 1689, Louisville, KY 40201, (502)589-5900 [21187]

Office Stop Inc., 55 E Galena, Butte, MT 59701, (406)782-2334 [21188]

Office System Inc., PO Box 977, Bismarck, ND 58502-0977, (701)223-6033 [21189]

Office Systems Co., PO Box 9000, Sioux City, IA 51102, (712)277-7000 [21190]

Office Systems of Texas, 104 Lockhaven Dr., Houston, TX 77073, (281)443-2996 [21191]

Officeland of the N.H. Seacoast, 180 Lafayette Rd., North Hampton, NH 03862-0541, (603)964-1115 [21192]

Officers Equipment Co., PO Box 633, Stafford, VA 22554, (703)221-1912 [5249]

OfficeScapes Business Furniture, 9900 E 51st Ave., Denver, CO 80238, (303)574-1115 [21193]

OfficeScapes & Scott Rice, 9900 E 51st Ave., Denver, CO 80238, (303)574-1115 [21193]

OffiSource, PO Box 258, Jackson, MS 39205, (601)352-9000 [21194]

Offutt Co.; R.D., PO Box 7160, Fargo, ND 58106-7160, (701)237-6062 [1098]

Offutt Co.; R.D., 1650 Governors Rd., Casselton, ND 58012, (701)347-4403 [1099]

Ogden Aviation Services, Philadelphia Airport, TWA Hangar, Philadelphia, PA 19153, (215)492-2880 [24197]

Ogden Services Corp., 2 Penn Plz., New York, NY 10121, (212)868-6000 [22535]

Ogle & Co.; Jack, 1131 Poplar Pl.,S, Seattle, WA 98144, (206)324-3425 [16357]

Ogle Service Co., PO Box 138, Amboy, IL 61310, (815)857-3535 [1100]

Ohigro Inc., Gillette Rd., PO Box 196, Waldo, OH 43356, (614)726-2429 [1101]

Ohio Agriculture and Turf Systems Inc., 666 Redna Terr., Cincinnati, OH 45215, (513)771-2699 [1102]

Ohio Alloy Steels Inc., PO Box 1286, Youngstown, OH 44501, (216)743-5137 [20243]

Ohio Auto Rebuilders Supply, Inc., 2389 Refugee Pk., Columbus, OH 43207-2173, (614)443-0526 [3057]

Ohio Belt & Transmission, 300 N Westwood, PO Box 404, Toledo, OH 43697, (419)535-5665 [16358]

Ohio Brake & Clutch, 1460 Wolf Creek Trl., PO Box 325, Sharon Center, OH 44274, (216)781-0805 [17086]

Ohio Business Machines Inc., 1728 St. Claire Ave., Cleveland, OH 44114, (216)579-1300 [21195]

Ohio Calculating Inc., 20160 Center Ridge Rd., Cleveland, OH 44116, (216)333-7310 [21196]

Ohio Desk Co., 1122 Prospect Ave., Cleveland, OH 44115, (216)623-0600 [21197]

Ohio Farmers Inc., 2700 E 55th, Cleveland, OH 44104, (216)391-9733 [12055]

Ohio Kitchen and Bath, 19000 Miles Ave., Cleveland, OH 44128, (216)587-1222 [15601]

Ohio Light Truck Parts Co., 217 W 3rd St., Dover, OH 44622, (330)364-1881 [3058]

Ohio Machinery Co., 3993 E Royalton Rd., Broadview Heights, OH 44147, (440)526-6200 [7805]

Ohio Overseas Corp., 520 Madison Ave., Toledo, OH 43604, (419)241-4334 [16359]

Ohio Pipe and Supply Company Inc., 14615 Lorain Ave., Cleveland, OH 44111, (216)251-2345 [23302]

Ohio Pipe Valves and Fittings Inc., 3900 Trent Ave., Cleveland, OH 44109, (216)631-6000 [17087]

Ohio Pool Equipment Supply Co., 22350 Royalton Rd., PO Box 360660, Strongsville, OH 44136-3826, (440)238-2800 [23857]

Ohio Seed Company Inc., 8888 Parsons Rd., Croton, OH 43013-9731, (614)879-8366 [1103]

Ohio Steak and Barbecue Co., 3880 Lockbourne Rd., Columbus, OH 43207-4215, (614)491-3245 [12056]

Ohio Tile & Marble Co., 3809 Spring Grove Ave., Cincinnati, OH 45223, (513)541-4211 [10083]

Ohio Tile and Marble Co., 3809 Spring Grove Ave., Cincinnati, OH 45223, (513)541-4211 [7806]

Ohio Transmission Corp., 666 Parsons Ave., Columbus, OH 43206, (614)444-2172 [5845]

Ohio Truck Equipment, Inc., 4100 Rev Dr., Cincinnati, OH 45232, (513)541-4700 [3059]

Ohio Valley-Clarksburg Inc., PO Box 6295, Wheeling, WV 26003, (304)242-9526 [19505]

Ohio Valley Flooring, 5555 Murray Rd., Cincinnati, OH 45227, (513)561-3399 [10084]

Ohio Valley Sound Inc., 20 E Sycamore St., Evansville, IN 47713, (812)425-6173 [9151]

Ohio Valley Supply Co., 3512 Spring Grove Ave., Cincinnati, OH 45223, (513)681-8300 [7807]

OHM Electronics Inc., 746 Vermont Ave., Palatine, IL 60067, (847)359-5500 [9281]

Ohsman and Sons Co., 400 8th St. SE, PO Box 1196, Cedar Rapids, IA 52406, (319)365-7546 [18151]

Oil-Dri Corp., PO Box 200-A, Ochlocknee, GA 31773, (912)574-5131 [22536]

Oil Equipment Supply Corp., 3120 W Morris St., Indianapolis, IN 46241, (317)243-3120 [22537]

Oil Marketing Company Inc., PO Box 1709, Tahlequah, OK 74465, (918)456-9805 [22538]

Oil Recycling Inc., PO Box 46, Rosemount, MN 55068, (612)480-8825 [26928]

Oilfield Pipe and Supply Inc., 1730 S 11th St., St. Louis, MO 63104-3475, (314)231-0404 [20244]

Oils of Aloha, 66935 Kaukonahua Rd., PO Box 685, Waialua, HI 96791, (808)637-5620 [18152]

Oilseeds International Ltd., 855 Sansome, Ste. 100, San Francisco, CA 94111-1507, (415)956-7251 [12057]

Oilworld Supply Co., PO Box 55301, Houston, TX 77255, (713)681-9777 [22539]

O.K. Auto Parts, 1730 W Michigan St., Duluth, MN 55806, (218)722-6233 [3060]

OK Distributing Company Inc., 208 NW 132nd St., Oklahoma City, OK 73114-2306, (405)751-8833 [15258]

O.K. Distributing Company Inc., PO Box 1252, Williston, ND 58802-1252, (701)572-9161 [26336]

O.K. Electric Supply Co., PO Box 998, Perth Amboy, NJ 08862, (908)826-6100 [9152]

O.K. Grain Co., Box 156, Litchfield, IL 62056, (217)324-6151 [18153]

OK Hafens Tire Store Inc., 505 W Lake Mead Dr., Henderson, NV 89015-7015, (702)564-5312 [3061]

Okaw Buildings Inc., PO Box 144A, Arthur, IL 61911, (217)543-3371 [7808]

Okaya U.S.A. Inc., 400 Kelby St., 16th Fl., Ft. Lee, NJ 07024, (201)224-6000 [20245]

Okhai-Moyer Inc., PO Box 2668, Huntington, WV 25726, (304)523-9433 [21198]

OKI Semiconductor, 785 N Mary Ave., Sunnyvale, CA 94086, (408)720-1900 [9153]

OKI Systems Inc., 4665 Interstate Dr., Cincinnati, OH 45246, (513)874-2600 [16360]

OKI Systems Ltd., 4665 Interstate Dr., Cincinnati, OH 45246, (513)874-2600 [16360]

Oki Trading, Ltd.; T., 2722 Waiwai Loop, Honolulu, HI 96819, (808)834-2722 [7809]

Okie Dokie Services, PO Box 668, Ketchum, ID 83340-0668, (208)726-3196 [4679]

Oklahoma Leather Products Inc., 500 26th St., NW, Miami, OK 74354, (918)542-6651 [18414]

Oklahoma Rig and Supply Company Inc., PO Box 249, Muskogee, OK 74402, (918)687-5441 [17088]

Oklahoma Upholstery Supply Co., 706 N Villa, Oklahoma City, OK 73107, (405)235-2597 [26160]

Oklahoma Upholstery Supply Co., 1427 E 4th St., PO Box 50186, Tulsa, OK 74120, (918)585-5727 [26161]

Okleelanta Corp., PO Box 86, South Bay, FL 33493, (407)996-9072 [12058]

Olathe Boot Co., 705 S Kansas Ave, Olathe, KS 66061, (913)764-5110 [24826]

Olbro Wholesalers, 45 Park Ln., Rochester, NY 14625, (716)381-9521 [12059]

Old Dominion, 2409 Garnett Ct., Vienna, VA 22180-6908, (703)204-2918 [12060]

Old Dominion Export-Import Co. Inc., 2409 Garnett Ct., Vienna, VA 22180-6908, (703)204-2918 [12060]

Old Dominion Grain Corp., P. O. Box 18, West Point, VA 23181, (804)843-2922 [18154]

Old Dutch Bakery Inc., PO Box 319, Blandon, PA 19510, (215)926-1311 [12061]

Old Dutch Foods Inc., 2375 Terminal Rd., Roseville, MN 55113-2577, (612)633-8810 [12062]

Old Home Foods Inc., 370 University Ave., St. Paul, MN 55103, (651)228-9035 [12063]

Old Master, 65 N Congress St., PO Box 379, York, SC 29745, (803)684-6853 [23922]

Old Masters Products Inc., 3791 2nd Ave., Los Angeles, CA 90018, (323)291-0677 [10085]

Old Masters Products Inc., 7023 Valjean Avenue, Van Nuys, CA 91406, (818)785-8886 [10086]

Old Saltbox Publishing House Inc., 40 Felt St., Salem, MA 01970, (978)741-3458 [4017]

Old South Distributors Company Inc., 216 N Main St., Winchester, KY 40391-1516, (606)744-6666 [1929]

Old Sutler John, PO BOx 174 Westview Station, Binghamton, NY 13905, (607)775-4434 [26597]

Old World Bakery, 6210 Eastern Ave., Baltimore, MD 21224, (410)633-6690 [12064]

Old World Industries, Inc., 4065 Commercial Ave., Northbrook, IL 60062, (847)559-2000 [4472]

Old World Trading Co., 4065 Commercial Ave., Northbrook, IL 60062, (847)559-2000 [4472]

Olds Seed Co.; L.L., PO Box 7790, Madison, WI 53707, (608)249-9291 [1104]

Oldsmobile Div., 920 Townsend St., Lansing, MI 48921, (517)377-5000 [3062]

Olean Wholesale Grocery Cooperative Inc., PO Box 1070, Olean, NY 14760, (716)372-2020 [12065]

Olender and Company Inc.; P., 27000 Wick Rd., Taylor, MI 48180-3015, (313)921-3310 [12066]

Oley Distributing Co., 920 N Main, PO Box 4660, Ft. Worth, TX 76106-9421, (817)625-8251 [1930]

Olflex Wire and Cable Inc., 30 Plymouth St., Fairfield, NJ 07004-1697, (201)575-1101 [9154]

Olhausen Billiard Manufacturing, Inc., 12460 Kirkham Ct., Poway, CA 92064, (858)486-0761 [23858]

Olhausen Pool Table Manufacturing, 12460 Kirkham Ct., Poway, CA 92064, (858)486-0761 [23858]

Olicom USA Inc., 350 Park Pl., Chagrin Falls, OH 44022-4456, (216)247-0024 [6569]

Oliger Seed Co., 89 Hanna Pkwy., Akron, OH 44319-1166, (330)724-1266 [1105]

Olin Corp., PO Box 4500, Norwalk, CT 06856-4500, (203)356-2000 [4473]

Olinde and Sons Company Inc.; B., 9536 Airline Hwy., Baton Rouge, LA 70815, (504)926-3380 [1931]

Olinger Distributing Co., 9951 Heddon Rd., Evansville, IN 47711-9660, (812)867-7481 [1932]

Olinger Distributing Co., 5337 W 78th St., Indianapolis, IN 46268, (317)876-1188 [1933]

Oliver Peoples Inc., 8600 Sunset Blvd., Los Angeles, CA 90069-0290, (310)657-5475 [19506]

Oliver Stores Inc., 399 Lewiston Rd., Ste. 100, New Gloucester, ME 04260, (207)926-4123 [7810]

Oliver Supply Co., PO Box 430297, Pontiac, MI 48343-0297, (248)682-7222 [4680]

Oliver Supply Co., PO Box 430297, Pontiac, MI 48343-0297, (248)682-7222 [24198]

Oliver Worldclass Labs, 44834 S Grimmer Blvd., Fremont, CA 94538, (707)747-1537 [4018]

Olivetti Office USA Inc., PO Box 6945, Bridgewater, NJ 08807, (908)526-8200 [21199]

Ollesheimer & Son Inc.; Louis T., 605 E 12 Mile Rd., Madison Heights, MI 48071, (248)544-3900 [7811]

Olsen Audio Group Inc., 7845 E Evans Rd., Scottsdale, AZ 85260, (480)998-7140 [15259]

Olsen-Fennell Seeds, Inc., PO Box 15028, Salem, OR 97309, (503)371-2940 [1106]

Olson Inc.; Kenneth P., 7600 W 27th St., Ste. 213, St. Louis Park, MN 55426-3163, (612)478-9854 [5250]

Olson-Kessler Meat Company Inc., PO Box 9175, Corpus Christi, TX 78469, (512)853-6291 [12067]

Olton Grain Cooperative Inc., PO Drawer M, Olton, TX 79064, (806)285-2638 [18155]

Olympia Gold Inc., 11540 Wiles Rd., Ste. 2, Coral Springs, FL 33076, (954)345-6991 [17538]

Olympia International, 1840 S Wilmington Ave., Compton, CA 90220-5118, (310)223-2990 [18409]

Olympia Sports, 745 State Circle, PO Box 1941, Ann Arbor, MI 48106-1941, (734)761-5135 [23859]

Olympian Oil Co., 260 Michele Ct., South San Francisco, CA 94080, (415)873-8200 [22540]

Olympic Flooring Distributors Inc., 1000 Kieley, Cincinnati, OH 45217, (513)242-6500 [10087]

Olympic Industries Inc., PO Box 1832, Hobbs, NM 88241-1832, (505)393-8048 [23004]

Olympic Steel Inc., 5096 Richmond Rd., Bedford, OH 44146, (216)292-3800 [20246]

Olympic Steel Inc. Chicago Div., 1901 Mitchell Blvd., Schaumburg, IL 60193, (708)437-8980 [20247]

Olympic Steel Inc. Eastern Steel and Metal Div., 1 Eastern Steel Rd., Milford, CT 06460, (203)878-9381 [20248]

Olympic Steel Inc. Juster Steel Div., 625 Xenium Ln. N, Minneapolis, MN 55441, (612)544-7100 [20249]

Olympus America Inc., 2 Corporate Center Dr., Melville, NY 11747-3157, (516)844-5000 [22887]

Omaha Steaks Foodservice, 11030 O St., Omaha, NE 68137-2346, (402)597-8106 [12068]

Omaha Steaks International, 11030 O St., Omaha, NE 68137-2346, (402)597-8106 [12068]

Omaha Steaks International, PO Box 3300, Omaha, NE 68103, (402)331-1010 [12069]

Omaha Vaccine, PO Box 7228, Omaha, NE 68107, (402)731-9600 [27201]

Omega Optical Co., 13515 N Stemmons Fwy., Dallas, TX 75234, (972)241-4141 [19507]

Omega Optical, Inc., 3 Grove St., Brattleboro, VT 05301, (802)254-2690 [17089]

Omega Produce Company Inc., PO Box 277, Nogales, AZ 85628, (602)281-0410 [12070]

Omega Products Corporation, 360-10 Knickerbocker Ave., Bohemia, NY 11716, (516)563-7217 [13853]

Omega Publications, PO Box 4130, Medford, OR 97501, (541)826-4512 [4019]

Omega Publications, Inc., 256 Darrow Rd., New Lebanon, NY 12125, (518)794-8181 [4020]

Omega Refrigerant Reclamation Corp., 12504 E Whittier Blvd., Whittier, CA 90602, (310)698-0991 [25773]

Omega Tool, 360-10 Knickerbocker Ave., Bohemia, NY 11716, (516)563-7217 [13853]

Omicron Electronics, 11240 E 9 Mile Rd., Warren, MI 48089, (810)757-8192 [6570]

Omni Group Inc., PO Box 398, Timonium, MD 21094, (410)296-0113 [24605]

Omni Services Inc., 25 Union St., Worcester, MA 01608, (508)799-2746 [17090]

Omni USA Inc., 7502 Mesa Rd., Houston, TX 77028, (713)635-6331 [1107]

Omni-X Inc., 2751 W Mansfield Ave., Englewood, CO 80110, (303)789-3575 [16361]

Omnibooks, 456 Vista Del Mar, Aptos, CA 95003-4832, (408)688-4098 [4021]

Omnichron, 1438 Oxford St., Berkeley, CA 94709, (510)540-6455 [25774]

OmniFax, PO Box 80709, Austin, TX 78708-0709, (512)719-5566 [21200]

Omnifax Danka Co., 449 S 48th St., Ste. 103, Tempe, AZ 85281, (602)894-6688 [21201]

Omnigraphics Inc., 615 Griswold, Detroit, MI 48226, (313)961-1340 [4022]

Omnimedical Inc., 3700 E Columbia St., No. 100, Tucson, AZ 85714-3412 [18967]

Omnirax, PO Box 1792, Sausalito, CA 94966, (415)332-3392 [13194]

OmniSource Corp., 3101 Maumee Ave., Ft. Wayne, IN 46803, (219)422-5541 [26929]

OmniSource Lima Div., PO Box 5248, Lima, OH 45802, (419)227-3411 [26930]

Omnitrition, PO Box 111640, Carrollton, TX 75011-1640, (972)417-9200 [12071]

Omnitron International, Inc., PO Box 111640, Carrollton, TX 75011-1640, (972)417-9200 [12071]

Omnium Corp., 711 Keller Ave. S, Amery, WI 54001, (715)268-8500 [6571]

On the Beach, Inc., 203 W M.L. King Jr. Blvd., Los Angeles, CA 90037-1013, (213)234-9033 [5251]

On-Gard Systems Inc., 2323 Delgany St., Denver, CO 80202, (303)825-5210 [18968]

On Spot Janitor Supplies & Repair, 5308 4th St. NW, Albuquerque, NM 87107-5206, (505)343-0215 [4681]

Onan Indiana, 5125 Beck Dr., Elkhart, IN 46514, (219)262-4611 [9155]

One Source Distributors, 6154 Nancy Ridge Dr., San Diego, CA 92121-3223, (619)452-9001 [9156]

One Source Home and Building Centers, PO Box 99, North Little Rock, AR 72115, (501)372-8100 [7812]

One Stop Distributing, 225 Gladstone, Idaho Falls, ID 83401, (208)523-9862 [14628]

One Valley Bank of Huntington, PO Box 7938, Huntington, WV 25779, (304)522-8281 [25368]

One Workplace L. Ferrari LLC, 1057 Montague Expressway, Milpitas, CA 95035, (408)263-1001 [13195]

O'Neal Metals Co., PO Box 71900, Chattanooga, TN 37407, (423)867-4820 [20250]

O'Neal Steel Inc., PO Box 2623, Birmingham, AL 35202, (205)599-8000 [20251]

O'Neal Steel Inc. Evansville, 1323 Burch Dr., Evansville, IN 47711, (812)867-8700 [20252]

O'Neal Steel Inc. (Waterloo, Iowa), PO Box 1798, Waterloo, IA 50704, (319)235-6521 [20253]

O'Neill Div., PO Box 758, VilLa Rica, GA 30180, (770)459-1800 [26162]

Oneonta Trading Corp., PO Box 549, Wenatchee, WA 98801, (509)663-2631 [12072]

Onkyo USA Corp., 200 Williams Dr., Ramsey, NJ 07446, (201)825-7950 [25369]

Only Hearts Ltd., 15 E 32nd St., New York, NY 10016, (212)689-7808 [5252]

Only Once Inc., 266 Pine St., Burlington, VT 05401-4751, (802)863-2302 [5253]

Ontario Air Parts Inc., 15042 Whittram Ave., Fontana, CA 92335, (909)829-3031 [133]

Ontario Stone Corp., 34301 Chardon Rd., Ste. 5, Willoughby Hills, OH 44094, (216)631-3645 [7813]

Ontario Supply Corp., 100 N Mohawk, Cohoes, NY 12047-1707, (518)237-4723 [9157]

Onyx Petroleum Inc., 441 EE Butler Pkwy., Gainesville, GA 30506, (770)536-0068 [22541]

Oogenesis Inc., 66-249 Kam Hwy., Haleiwa, HI 96712, (808)637-4580 [5254]

Oomphies Inc., 5 Franklin St., Lawrence, MA 01840-1106, (978)682-5268 [24827]

Operations Technology Inc., Lambert Rd., PO Box 408, Blairstown, NJ 07825, (908)362-6200 [9158]

Operator Interface Technology, 650 Weaver Park Rd., Longmont, CO 80501, (303)684-0094 [6572]

Ophthalmic Instrument Co. Inc., 178 Page St., Stoughton, MA 02072, (781)341-5010 [19508]

OPICO, PO Box 849, Mobile, AL 36601, (334)438-9881 [1108]

Opler Sales Company Inc.; Jack, 2715 Avalon Ave., Muscle Shoals, AL 35661, (205)381-3242 [21854]

Oppenheimer Corp. Golbon, 877 W Main St., Boise, ID 83702, (208)342-7771 [12073]

Opperman Co., Inc.; Matthew, 5713 SW 150th Ave., Miami, FL 33193, (305)383-3929 [13854]

Opportunities for Learning, Inc., 941 Hickory Ln., PO Box 8103, Mansfield, OH 44901-8103, (419)589-1700 [4023]

Optech Inc., 41 Keenan St., PO Box 228, West Bridgewater, MA 02379, (508)583-3010 [19509]

Optek Inc., PO Box 42276, Mesa, AZ 85274-2276, (602)233-0888 [19510]

OPTEX Morse, Inc., 12960 Bradley Ave., Sylmar, CA 91342-3829, (818)367-5951 [24606]

Optex USA Inc., 365 Van Ness Way, Ste. 510, Torrance, CA 90501, (310)212-7271 [24607]

Optibal Co., 5 Allison Dr., Cherry Hill, NJ 08003-2309, (609)596-5757 [14185]

Optical Advantage, 8009 34th Ave. S, No. 125, Minneapolis, MN 55425, (612)854-6109 [6573]

Optical Associates, PO Box 189, Albany, OR 97321-0058, (541)926-6077 [19511]

Optical Cable Corp., PO Box 11967, Roanoke, VA 24022-1967, (540)265-0690 [9159]

Optical Center Laboratory Inc., 930 E Lewiston Ave., Ferndale, MI 48220-1451, (248)548-6210 [19512]

Optical Laboratory of New Bedford, PO Box H-3101, New Bedford, MA 02741, (508)997-9779 [19513]

Optical Laser Inc., 5702 Bolsa Ave., Huntington Beach, CA 92649-1169, (714)379-4400 [6574]

Optical Measurements Inc., 1900 E 14 Mile Rd., Madison Heights, MI 48071-1545, (248)588-8084 [19514]

Optical One, Inc., PO Box 489, Youngstown, OH 44502, (330)743-8518 [19515]

Optical Plastics, PO Box 4115, Clackamas, OR 97015, (503)655-4787 [19516]

Optical Suppliers Inc., 99-1253 Halawa Valley St., Aiea, HI 96701, (808)486-2933 [19517]

Optical Supply, 1526 Plainsfield NE, Grand Rapids, MI 49505, (616)361-6000 [19518]

Options International Inc., 913 18th Ave. S, Nashville, TN 37212, (615)327-8090 [25370]

Optique Paris Miki, 2134 Kalakaua Ave., Honolulu, HI 96815, (808)922-4310 [19519]

Optronics Inc., 350 N Wheeler St., Ft. Gibson, OK 74434-8965, (918)683-9514 [9160]

ORA Electronics, 9410 Owensmouth Ave., PO Box 4029, Chatsworth, CA 91313, (818)772-4433 [5696]

Oracle Corp. USA Div., 500 Oracle Pkwy., Redwood City, CA 94065, (650)506-7000 [6575]

Oral Logic Inc., 7000 Hwy. 2 E, Minot, ND 58701, (701)852-5906 [14186]

Orange Bakery Inc., 17751 Cowan Ave., Irvine, CA 92614, (949)863-1377 [12074]

Orange Blossom, PO Box 149056, Austin, TX 78714-9056, (512)444-0571 [17371]

Orange Distributors Inc., 4573 Dardanelle Dr., Orlando, FL 32808, (407)295-2217 [21855]

Orange Motor Company Inc., 799 Central Ave., Albany, NY 12206, (518)489-5414 [3063]

Orbex Inc., 4444 Ball Rd. NE, Circle Pines, MN 55014-1820, (612)333-1208 [23860]

Orbilt Compressors, Inc., 140 Mendel Dr. SW, Atlanta, GA 30336, (404)699-1521 [14629]

Orbit Fluid Power Co., 301 W 25th St., PO Box 886, Stuttgart, AR 72160, (870)673-2584 [16362]

Orbit Industries Inc. Clarkesville Garment Div., 2320 Perimeter Park Dr., Ste. 101, Atlanta, GA 30341-1317, (706)754-2151 [5255]

Orbital Trading Co., PO Box 2342, Culver City, CA 90230, (213)301-4705 [16363]

Orca Oil Company, Inc., 100 Ocean Dock Rd., Cordova, AK 99574, (907)424-3264 [22542]

Orcal Inc., 701 N Hariton Ave., Orange, CA 92856, (714)997-4780 [23861]

Orchard Yarn and Thread Company Inc./Lion Brand Yarn Co., 34 W 15th St., New York, NY 10011, (212)243-8995 [26163]

Orchid Plantation, Inc., 14-4970 Kaimu-Kapoho Rd., Pahoa, HI 96778, (808)965-6295 [14931]

Orchid Uniform Retail Sales, 501 N Meridian Ave., Ste. 104, Oklahoma City, OK 73107-5701, (405)947-2388 [5256]

Orders Distributing Company Inc., PO Box 17189, Greenville, SC 29606, (803)288-4220 [10088]

Ordway Sign Supply, 16540 Gaulet, Van Nuys, CA 91406, (818)908-9666 [25775]

Ore-Cal Corp., 634 S Crocker St., Los Angeles, CA 90021-1002, (213)680-9540 [12075]

Oreck Floorcare Center, 15261 E Mississippi Ave., Aurora, CO 80012-3747, (303)751-7133 [25776]

Oregon Educational Computing Consortium, 707 13th St. SE, Ste. 260, Salem, OR 97301, (503)588-1343 [6576]

Oregon Educational Technology Consortium, 707 13th St. SE, Ste. 260, Salem, OR 97301, (503)588-1343 [6576]

Oregon Equipment Co. Inc., 110 E 2nd St., The Dalles, OR 97058-1704, (541)296-2915 [15260]

Oregon Floral Distributors, 1130 Anderson Ln., Springfield, OR 97477, (541)746-8497 [14932]

O'Reilly Automotive Inc., 233 S Patterson Ave., Springfield, MO 65801, (417)862-6708 [3064]

Oremco Inc., 261 Madison Ave., New York, NY 10016, (212)867-4400 [20555]

Oren Van Aman Company Inc., PO Box 5266, Ft. Wayne, IN 46895, (219)625-3844 [17091]

Orenco Systems Inc., 814 Airway Ave., Sutherlin, OR 97479, (541)459-4449 [16364]

OREPAC Millwork Products, 13971 Norton Ave., Chino, CA 91710, (909)627-4043 [7814]

Organ Literature Foundation, 45 Norfolk Rd., Braintree, MA 02184-5918, (781)848-1388 [4024]

Organic Dyestuffs Corp., PO Box 14258, East Providence, RI 02914, (401)434-3300 [4474]

Organization Systems Inc., 750 Old Main St., Rocky Hill, CT 06067, (860)257-9322 [6577]

Orgill Brothers and Co., 2100 Latham St., Memphis, TN 38109, (901)948-3381 [13855]

Orgill Inc., 2100 Latham St., Memphis, TN 38109, (901)948-3381 [13855]

Orian Rugs Inc., Hwy. 81 N, Anderson, SC 29621, (864)224-0271 [10089]

Orient Book Distributors, PO Box 100, Livingston, NJ 07039, (973)746-3874 [4025]

Orient Express, 814 Branch Ave., Providence, RI 02904-1707, (401)751-7056 [17539]

Oriental Furniture Warehouse, 9030 W Sahara Ave., Ste. 132, Las Vegas, NV 89117-5826, (702)255-4056 [13196]

Original Appalachian Artworks Inc., PO Box 714, Cleveland, GA 30528, (706)865-2171 [26598]

Original Chili Bowl Inc., PO Box 470125, Tulsa, OK 74147, (918)628-0225 [12076]

Original Design Silk Screen Co., RR 1, Box 89, North Woodstock, NH 03262-9710, (603)745-6277 [26164]

Original Designs Inc., 44 40 11th, Long Island City, NY 11101-5105, (718)706-8989 [17540]

Original Marketing Concepts Ltd., 6955 Washington Ave. S, Minneapolis, MN 55439-1506, (612)941-2530 [25371]

Original Mink Oil Inc., PO Box 20191, Portland, OR 97220, (503)255-2814 [4475]

Origlio Inc.; Antonio, 2000 Bennett Rd., Philadelphia, PA 19116, (215)698-9500 [1934]

Orion Food Systems, PO Box 780, Sioux Falls, SD 57101, (605)336-6961 [12077]

Orion Group (USA), Ltd., 4826 Rio Vista Ave., San Jose, CA 95129, (408)554-1685 [20254]

Orkin Lawn Care, 2170 Piedmont Rd. NE, Atlanta, GA 30324, (404)888-2777 [14933]

Orlando Yamaha, 9334 E Colonial Dr., Orlando, FL 32817-4130, (407)273-3579 [20701]

Orleans Commissions Sales, PO Box 55, Orleans, VT 05860, (802)754-8533 [18156]

Orleans Materials and Equipment Company Inc., PO Box 26307, New Orleans, LA 70186, (504)288-6361 [20255]

Ornamental Tile and Design Center, 11450 Overseas Hwy., Marathon, FL 33050, (305)743-6336 [10090]

OroAmerica Inc., 443 N Varney St., Burbank, CA 91502, (818)848-5555 [17541]

Orr Safety Corp., PO Box 16326, Louisville, KY 40256-0326, (502)774-5791 [24608]

Orr-Sysco Food Services Co.; Robert, PO Box 305137, Nashville, TN 37230-5137, (615)350-7100 [24199]

ORRCO, Inc., PO Box 147, Orrville, OH 44667, (330)683-5015 [27202]

Orrefors Inc., 140 Bradford Dr., Berlin, NJ 08009, (609)768-5400 [15602]

Orrell's Food Service Inc., 9827 S NC Hwy. 150, Linwood, NC 27299-9461, (336)752-2114 [12078]

Orrville Pet Products, PO Box 147, Orrville, OH 44667, (330)683-5015 [27202]

Orscheln Farm and Home Supply Inc., 339 N Williams, Moberly, MO 65270, (660)263-4335 [1109]

Orsen-Porter-Rockwell International, 888 Brannan St., No. 2105, San Francisco, CA 94103, (415)558-8994 [18415]

Ortho-Care Southeast Inc., 632-D Matthews Mint Hill Rd., Matthews, NC 28105-2797, (704)845-2690 [18969]

Ortho-Tex Inc., 10408A Gulfdale, San Antonio, TX 78216, (210)490-3340 [19520]

Orton Industries Inc., PO Box 620130, Atlanta, GA 30362-2130, (404)986-9999 [9161]

Osage Cooperative Elevator, PO Box 358, Osage, IA 50461, (515)732-3768 [1110]

Osage Cooperative Elevator, PO Box 358, Osage, IA 50461, (515)732-3768 [12079]

Osakagodo America Inc., 600 3rd Ave., New York, NY 10016, (212)867-0678 [4476]

O'San Products Inc., PO Box 468, Camilla, GA 31730, (912)336-0387 [12080]

Osbon Medical Systems Ltd., 6585 City W Pkwy., Eden Prairie, MN 55344, (952)947-9410 [19079]

Osborn Brothers Inc., PO Box 649, Gadsden, AL 35907, (205)547-8601 [12081]

Osborn Machinery Company Inc., 424 N 4th St., Clarksburg, WV 26301, (304)624-5636 [13856]

Osborne Distributing Company Inc., PO Box 2100, Vernon, TX 76384, (817)552-7711 [1111]

OSCA Inc., PO Box 80627, Lafayette, LA 70598, (318)837-6047 [4477]

Oscars Wholesale Meats Company Inc., 250 W 31st, Ogden, UT 84401-3836, (801)394-6472 [12082]

OSG Tap and Die Inc., 676 E Fullerton Ave., Glendale Heights, IL 60139, (708)790-1400 [17092]

Osgood Machinery Inc., 800 Commerce Pkwy. W, Lancaster, NY 14086-1738, (716)684-7700 [16365]

Osgood SM Company Inc., 6513 City W Pky., Eden Prairie, MN 55344-3248, (612)937-2045 [14630]

Oshman's Sporting Goods Inc., 2302 Maxwell Ln., Houston, TX 77023, (713)928-3171 [23862]

Oshtemo Hill Inc., 2050 Turner NW, Grand Rapids, MI 49504-2046, (616)363-6854 [7815]

Osmonics, Aquamatic, 2412 Grant Ave., Rockford, IL 61103, (815)964-9421 [23303]

Osmonics, Inc., 5951 Clearwater Dr., Minnetonka, MN 55343-8995, (612)933-2277 [25777]

O.S.S. Publishing Co., 517 S Main St., Lima, OH 45802, (419)227-1818 [4026]

Ossoff Leather, 40 Endicott, Peabody, MA 01960-3122, (978)532-0707 [18416]

OST Inc. (Fremont, California), 41786 Christy St., Fremont, CA 94538, (510)440-0841 [24609]

Ost and Ost Inc., 1265 W Laurel Blvd., Pottsville, PA 17901, (717)622-4330 [3065]

Osterbauer Compressor Services, 5041 Santa Fe Ave., Los Angeles, CA 90058, (323)583-4771 [5846]

Ostrow Textile L.L.C., PO Box 10550, Rock Hill, SC 29731, (803)324-4284 [15603]

O'Sullivan Distributor Inc.; John P., 4047 Market Pl., Flint, MI 48507, (810)733-7090 [1935]

Oswald Supply Company Inc.; H.C., 120 E 124th St., New York, NY 10035, (212)722-7000 [23304]

Otagiri Mercantile Company Inc., 475 Ecceles Ave., South San Francisco, CA 94080, (650)871-4080 [15604]

Otake Instrument Inc., 1314 S King St., Ste. 615, Honolulu, HI 96814-1941, (808)592-8933 [18970]

Other Publishers, PO Box 35, Barrytown, NY 12507, (914)758-5840 [4027]

Otis Distributors, 4224 Airport Rd., Cincinnati, OH 45226, (513)321-6847 [24200]

Ottavino Corp.; A., 80-60 Pitkin Ave., Ozone Park, NY 11417, (718)848-9404 [7816]

Ottawa Cooperative Association Inc., 302 N Main St., Ottawa, KS 66067, (785)242-5170 [18157]

Ottawa Cooperative Association Inc., 302 N Main St., Ottawa, KS 66067, (785)242-5170 [1112]

Ottawa Electric Inc., 1051 Jackson St., Grand Haven, MI 49417, (616)733-2828 [9162]

Ottawa River Steel Co., 805 Chicago St., Toledo, OH 43611, (419)729-1655 [20256]

Ottenbergs Bakery, 655 Taylor NE, Washington, DC 20017-2063, (202)529-5800 [12083]

Otter Recycling, 570 Otter St., Bristol, PA 19007, (215)788-9327 [20257]

Otto Dental Supply Company Inc., 1010 Front St., Conway, AR 72032-4306, (501)327-9511 [18971]

Otto's Paint & Supply Co., 917 E 16th St., Cheyenne, WY 82001, (307)634-3549 [21520]

Ouachita Fertilizer Div., PO Box 4540, Monroe, LA 71211-4540, (318)388-0400 [1113]

OUR Designs Inc., PO Box 17404, Covington, KY 41017-0404, (606)282-5500 [25778]

Ourrison Inc., PO Box 5266, Cheyenne, WY 82003-5266, (307)632-5628 [1936]

Outdoor Equipment Co., 17485 N Outer Forty Dr., Chesterfield, MO 63005-1322, (314)532-6622 [1114]

Outdoor Outfitters of Wisconsin Inc., 705 Elm St., Waukesha, WI 53186, (414)542-7772 [24412]

Outdoor Research Inc., 2203 1st Ave. S, Seattle, WA 98134-1424, (206)467-8197 [23863]

Outdoor Sports Headquarters Inc., 967 Watertower Ln., Dayton, OH 45449, (937)865-5855 [23864]

Outer Bay Trading Co., 186 Porters Point Rd., PO Box 125, Colchester, VT 05446, (802)864-7628 [14934]

Outokumpu Metals (USA) Inc., 129 Fairfield Way, Bloomingdale, IL 60108, (708)307-1300 [20258]

Ouzunoff & Associates, 74 E Rocks Rd., Norwalk, CT 06851, (203)847-3285 [9163]

Oved Corp., 4143 NW 132nd St., Miami, FL 33054, (305)688-5865 [26599]

Oved Corp., 4143 NW 132nd St., Miami, FL 33054, (305)688-5865 [26165]

Over and Back Inc., 200 13th Ave., Ronkonkoma, NY 11779, (516)981-1110 [15605]

Overcast and Associates; Don, 250 Spring St., Atlanta, GA 30303, (404)523-4082 [5257]

Overhead Door Company Inc., 34 N Lakewood, Tulsa, OK 74158, (918)838-9901 [7817]

Overhill Farms, PO Box 6017, Inglewood, CA 90312-6017, (310)641-3680 [12084]

Overland West Press, PO Box 17507, Portland, OR 97217, (503)289-4834 [4028]

Overseas Capital Corp., 3615 Euclid Ave., Cleveland, OH 44115, (216)881-1322 [4478]

Overtons Sports Center, Inc., 111 Red Banks Rd., Greenville, NC 27835, (919)355-7600 [18579]

Owen Distributors Inc., 295 S Eastern Ave., PO Box 2445, Idaho Falls, ID 83403-2445, (208)524-1880 [13197]

Owen Manufacturing Company Inc.; Charles D., PO Box 457, 875 Warren Wilson Rd., Swannanoa, NC 28778, (704)298-6802 [15606]

Owenby Co., 5775 Murphy Hwy., Blairsville, GA 30512, (706)745-5531 [5258]

Owens Electric Supply Companies Inc., PO Box 3427, Wilmington, NC 28406, (910)791-6058 [9164]

Owens Electric Supply Inc., PO Box 3427, Wilmington, NC 28406, (910)791-6058 [25372]

Owens Electric Supply Inc., PO Box 3427, Wilmington, NC 28406, (910)791-6058 [15261]

Owens Forest Products, 2320 E 1st St., Duluth, MN 55812, (218)723-1151 [27353]

Owens Inc.; Arnold, PO Box 3697, Bloomington, IL 61702-3697, (309)828-7750 [22543]

Owens and Minor Inc., PO Box 27626, Glen Allen, VA 23060-7626, (804)747-9794 [18972]

Owens and Minor Inc. Augusta Div., 777 Lewiston Rd., Grovetown, GA 30813, (706)738-2571 [19521]

Owensboro Electric Supply, 1200 Moseley St., PO Box 1628, Owensboro, KY 42303, (502)684-0606 [9165]

Owensboro Supply Company Inc., PO Box 2029, Owensboro, KY 42302, (502)683-8318 [17093]

Ownbey Enterprises Inc., PO Box 1146, Dalton, GA 30722, (706)278-3019 [22544]

Owsley and Sons Inc., Gold Hill Rd. & I-77, Ft. Mill, SC 29715, (803)548-3636 [16366]

Oxbow Carbon International Inc., 1601 Forum Pl., West Palm Beach, FL 33401, (561)697-4300 [20556]

Oxbow Corp., 1601 Forum Pl., West Palm Beach, FL 33401, (561)697-4300 [22545]

Oxford of Burgaw Co., PO Box 109, Columbia, SC 29202-0109 [5259]

Oxford Industries Inc. Renny Div., 1001 6th Ave., New York, NY 10018, (212)556-5341 [5260]

Oxford Metal Products, 2629 Belgrade, Philadelphia, PA 19125-3899, (215)739-5000 [13198]

Oxford Recycling Inc., 2400 W Oxford Ave., Englewood, CO 80110, (303)762-1160 [7818]

OxTech Industries Inc., PO Box 8, Oxford, NJ 07863-0008, (908)453-2151 [13857]

Oxygen Co. Inc., 2205 Perl Rd., Richmond, VA 23230-2007, (804)673-6500 [18973]

Ozark Automotive Distributors Inc., 233 S Patterson Ave., Springfield, MO 65802, (417)862-6708 [3066]

Ozark Co-op Warehouse, PO Box 1528, Fayetteville, AR 72702, (501)521-4920 [12085]

Ozer; Jerome S., 340 Tenafly Rd., Englewood, NJ 07631, (201)567-7040 [4029]

Ozotech, Inc., 2401 Oberlin Rd., Yreka, CA 96097, (530)842-4189 [25779]

Oztex Inc., 7717 SW Nimbus Ave., Beaverton, OR 97008-6402, (503)644-2485 [5261]

P-80 Systems, 3310 5th Ave., Charleston, WV 25312, (304)744-7322 [6578]

P & B Enterprises Inc., PO Box 887, Mt. Holly, NC 28120-0887, (704)827-8406 [23865]

P & B Truck Accessories, 2122 S Stoughton Rd., Madison, WI 53716, (608)222-4499 [3067]

P & D Hobby Distributors, 31902 Groesbeck Hwy., Fraser, MI 48026, (810)296-6116 [26600]

P and E Inc., 709 Two Mile Pkwy., Goodlettsville, TN 37072-2315, (615)327-1210 [3068]

P & F Distributors Inc., PO Box 354, Lewiston, ID 83501-0354, (208)743-5901 [1937]

P-G Products Inc., 2831 Stanton Ave., Cincinnati, OH 45206, (513)961-5500 [3069]

P & K Athletics Inc., Hwy. 2, Cut Bank, MT 59427, (406)873-5242 [23866]

P & W Industries, Inc., PO Box 1550, Mandeville, LA 70470, (504)892-2461 [26931]

Pabco Fluid Power Co., 361 W Morley Dr., Saginaw, MI 48601, (517)753-6100 [16367]

Pabco Fluid Power Co., 7830 N Central Dr., Westerville, OH 43081-9671, (614)548-6444 [16368]

Pabco Fluid Power Co., PO Box 691007, Cincinnati, OH 45269, (513)941-6200 [16369]

Pabco Inc., PO Box 219, Perham, MN 56573-0219, (218)346-6660 [9166]

Pablo Don Cigar Co., 3025 Las Vegas Blvd. S, Las Vegas, NV 89109-1920, (702)369-1818 [26337]

Pac Aero, 120 S Weber Dr., Chandler, AZ 85226-3216, (602)365-2610 [134]

Pac States Electric Wholesalers, 757 E Washington Blvd., Los Angeles, CA 90021-3092, (213)749-7881 [9167]

Pac-West Inc., 2303 N Randolph St., Portland, OR 97227, (503)288-0218 [7819]

Pacasa, PO Box 104, New Hampton, IA 50659-0104, (515)394-4686 [5262]

PACCAR Inc. Parts Div., 750 Houser Way N, Renton, WA 98055, (425)251-7400 [3070]

PACCAR International, 777 106th Ave. NE, PO Box 1518, Bellevue, WA 98009, (425)828-8872 [3071]

PACCAR Leasing Corp., PO Box 1518, Bellevue, WA 98009, (425)455-7400 [3072]

Paccar Technical Ctr., 1261 Farm To Market Rd., Mt. Vernon, WA 98273, (360)757-8311 [3073]

Pace Electronics Inc., PO Box 6937, Rochester, MN 55903-6937, (507)288-1853 [9168]

Pace Fish Company Inc., PO Box 3365, Brownsville, TX 78523, (210)546-5536 [12086]

Pace Oil Company Inc., PO Box 827, Magee, MS 39111, (601)849-2492 [22546]

Pacesetter Steel Service Inc., PO Box 100007, Kennesaw, GA 30144, (770)919-8000 [20259]

Pacheco; James A., 648 S St., Raynham, MA 02767, (508)822-4792 [12087]

Pacific Abrasive Supply Co., 7100 Village Dr., Buena Park, CA 90621, (714)994-2040 [17094]

Pacific Airgas Inc., 3591 N Columbia Blvd., Portland, OR 97217-7463, (503)283-2294 [16370]

Pacific American Commercial Co., PO Box 3742, Seattle, WA 98124, (206)762-3550 [7820]

Pacific Beverage Company Inc., 5305 Ekwill St., Santa Barbara, CA 93111, (805)964-0611 [25002]

Pacific Books, 2573 Treasure Dr., Santa Barbara, CA 93105, (805)687-8340 [4030]

Pacific Clay Brick Products Inc., 14741 Lake St., Lake Elsinore, CA 92530, (909)674-2131 [7821]

Pacific Coast Air Tool and Supply Inc., 4560 Carter Ct., Chino, CA 91710, (909)627-0948 [135]

Pacific Coast Brush Company Inc., 11690 Pacific Ave., Fontana, CA 92335-6960, (909)681-3747 [15500]

Pacific Coast Building Products Inc., PO Box 160488, Sacramento, CA 95816, (916)444-9304 [7822]

Pacific Coast Cement Corp., PO Box 4120, Ontario, CA 91761-1067, (909)390-7600 [7823]

Pacific Coast Chemical Co., 2424 4th St., Berkeley, CA 94710, (510)549-3535 [21521]

Pacific Coast Fruit Co., 201 NE 2nd Ave., Portland, OR 97232-2984, (503)234-6411 [12088]

Pacific Coast Micro Inc., P. O. Box 18265, Irvine, CA 92623, (714)993-0471 [6579]

Pacific Coast One-Stop, 45 W Easy St., Simi Valley, CA 93065-1601, (818)709-3640 [25373]

Pacific Coca-Cola Tacoma, 3333 S 38th St., Tacoma, WA 98409, (253)474-9567 [4031]

Pacific Combustion Engineering Inc., 5520 Alhambra Ave., Los Angeles, CA 90032, (323)225-6191 [24413]

Pacific Commerce Company Inc., PO Box 3110, Wilsonville, OR 97070, (503)570-0200 [12089]

Pacific Criticare Inc., 91-340 Komohana St., Kapolei, HI 96707-1737, (808)671-5090 [18974]

Pacific Dataport Inc., 692 Mapunapuna St., Honolulu, HI 96819-2031, (808)833-3135 [5697]

Pacific Design Center, 8687 Melrose Ave., West Hollywood, CA 90069, (310)657-0800 [13199]

Pacific Detroit Diesel Allison Co., 5061 N Lagoon Ave., Portland, OR 97217, (503)283-0505 [16371]

Pacific Drapery Co., 3801 30th, San Diego, CA 92104-3609, (619)295-6031 [15607]

Pacific Dualies, Inc., 13637 Cimarron Ave., Gardena, CA 90249, (310)516-9898 [3074]

Pacific Electrical Supply, 1906 Republic Ave., San Leandro, CA 94577-4221, (510)483-0931 [9169]

Pacific Exports, PO Box 3113, San Dimas, CA 91773, (949)599-4424 [24414]

Pacific Fibers, Inc., 33 E Ashland Ave., Phoenix, AZ 85004, (602)254-9452 [16372]

Pacific Fibre and Rope Company Inc., PO Box 187, Wilmington, CA 90748, (310)834-4567 [17095]

Pacific Flooring Supply, 965 Detroit Ave., Ste. C, Concord, CA 94518, (925)682-5697 [10091]

Pacific Flooring Supply, 4220 Hubbard St., Emeryville, CA 94608, (510)654-0485 [10092]

Pacific Flooring Supply, 1308 Kansas Ave., Modesto, CA 95351, (209)522-5937 [10093]

Pacific Flooring Supply, 5042 Westside Rd., Redding, CA 96001, (530)244-3832 [10094]

Pacific Flooring Supply, 1527 North C St., Sacramento, CA 95814, (916)442-0491 [10095]

Pacific Flooring Supply, 770 Tennessee St., San Francisco, CA 94107, (415)826-4375 [10096]

Pacific Flooring Supply, 2754 Teepee Dr., Ste E, Stockton, CA 95205, (209)463-6842 [10097]

Pacific Floral Exchange, Inc., 16-685 Milo St., PO Box 1989, Keaau, HI 96749, (808)966-7427 [14935]

Pacific Fluid Systems Corp., 1925 NW Quimby Ave., Portland, OR 97209, (503)222-3295 [16373]

Pacific Fluids Systems Inc., PO Box 835, West Sacramento, CA 95691, (916)372-0660 [16374]

Pacific Fruit Processors Inc., 12128 Center St., South Gate, CA 90280-8048, (213)774-6000 [12090]

Pacific Grain Products, Inc., PO Box 2060, Woodland, CA 95776, (530)662-5056 [12091]

Pacific Group International, 2633 S Dupont, Ste. A, Anaheim, CA 92806, (714)634-4171 [13417]

Pacific Handy Cutter Inc., PO Box 10869, Costa Mesa, CA 92627, (714)662-1033 [17096]

Pacific Hardware & Specialties Inc., 7625 McKinley E, Tacoma, WA 98404-1764, (253)473-5670 [13858]

Pacific Hide and Fur Depot Inc., PO Box 1549, Great Falls, MT 59403-1549, (406)761-8801 [20260]

Pacific Hide & Leather Company, Inc., 14000 S Broadway, Los Angeles, CA 90061, (562)321-6730 [18417]

Pacific Home Furnishings, 98-735 Kuahoa Pl., Pearl City, HI 96782, (808)487-3881 [15608]

Pacific Industrial Supply Company Inc., PO Box 24045, Seattle, WA 98124, (206)682-2100 [17097]

Pacific Interface, 99-1285-B6 Hala Valley, Aiea, HI 96701, (808)488-3363 [6580]

Pacific International Marketing Co., 1300 W Olympic Blvd., No. 307, Los Angeles, CA 90015, (213)381-2826 [23867]

Pacific Intertrade Corporation, 4165 Thousand Oaks Blvd., Ste. 301, Westlake Village, CA 91362, (805)495-5239 [15262]

Pacific Lumber and Shipping Co., 1301 5th Ave. Ste. 3131, Seattle, WA 98101, (206)682-7262 [27354]

Pacific Machinery Inc., 3651 Lala Rd., Lihue, HI 96766, (808)245-4057 [16375]

Pacific Machinery Inc., 94-025 Farrington Hwy., Waipahu, HI 96797, (808)677-9111 [1115]

Pacific Machinery Inc., 456 Kalanianole Ave., Hilo, HI 96720, (808)961-3481 [7824]

Pacific Machinery and Tool Steel Co., 3445 NW Luzon St., Portland, OR 97210-1694, (503)226-7656 [20261]

Pacific Magtron Inc., 1600 California Cir., Milpitas, CA 95035, (408)956-8888 [9170]

Pacific Mat, 757 Highland Dr., Seattle, WA 98109-3550, (206)282-3770 [10202]

Pacific Metal Co., 3400 SW Bond Ave., Portland, OR 97201, (503)227-0691 [20262]

Pacific Model Distributing Inc., 7317 Somerset Blvd., Paramount, CA 90723-0346, (562)630-5222 [26601]

Pacific Mountain Book Associates, 3882 S Newport Way, Denver, CO 80237, (303)758-0494 [4032]

Pacific Mutual Door Co., 1525 W 31st St., Kansas City, MO 64108, (816)531-0161 [7825]

Pacific North Equipment Co., PO Box 8000, Seattle, WA 98138, (253)872-3500 [7826]

Pacific Northern, 100 W Harrison St., Seattle, WA 98119, (206)282-4421 [22547]

Pacific Northwest Books Co., PO Box 314, Medford, OR 97501, (541)664-5205 [4033]

Pacific O.E.M. Supply, 3500 W Garry Ave., Santa Ana, CA 92704, (714)688-5795 [18580]

Pacific Packaging Products Inc., PO Box 697, Wilmington, MA 01887, (978)657-9100 [21856]

Pacific Paint Center, Inc., 2865 Ualena St., Honolulu, HI 96819, (808)836-3142 [21522]

Pacific PreCut Produce Inc., PO Box 26428, San Jose, CA 95159, (408)998-0773 [12092]

Pacific Radio Exchange Inc., 969 N La Brea Ave., Hollywood, CA 90038, (213)969-2035 [9171]

Pacific Rim Telecommunications Inc., 1153 E 72nd Ave., Anchorage, AK 99518, (907)349-4933 [5698]

Pacific Salmon Company Inc., 3407 E Marginal Way S, Seattle, WA 98134, (206)682-6501 [12093]

Pacific Sea Food Company Inc., 15501 SE Piazza, Clackamas, OR 97015-9145, (503)657-1101 [12094]

Pacific Southwest Sales Company Inc., 4600 District Blvd., Vernon, CA 90058, (213)582-6852 [9172]

Pacific Southwest Seed and Grain Inc., PO Box 5540, Yuma, AZ 85366, (520)782-2571 [18158]

Pacific Steel Inc., 1700 Cleveland Ave., National City, CA 91950, (619)474-7081 [26932]

Pacific Steel and Recycling, Short & Gaylord St., Butte, MT 59701, (406)782-0402 [20263]

Pacific Steel and Supply Corp., 2062 W 140th, San Leandro, CA 94577, (510)357-0340 [7827]

Pacific STIHL, Inc., 11096 Midway, Chico, CA 95926, (530)343-1657 [16376]

Pacific Supply, 4310 Westside Rd., Redding, CA 96001-3747, (916)246-1191 [7828]

Pacific Supply Co., 900 Arlee Pl., Anaheim, CA 92805, (714)778-3313 [3075]

Pacific Terminals Ltd., PO Box 81126, Seattle, WA 98108, (206)762-2933 [4034]

Pacific Trade Group, 94-527 Puahi St., Waipahu, HI 96797, (808)671-6735 [1435]

Pacific Trade Wind Inc., PO Box 42601, Portland, OR 97242-0601, (503)234-0355 [5263]

Pacific Trading, 13501 N Railway Dr., Oklahoma City, OK 73114, (405)755-6680 [26602]

Pacific Utility Equipment Co., PO Box 23009, Portland, OR 97281, (503)620-0611 [16377]

Pacific Wine Co., 2701 S Western Ave., Chicago, IL 60608, (773)247-8000 [1938]

Pacini Wines, 3001 S State, Ste. 34, Ukiah, CA 95482, (707)468-0950 [1939]

Packaged Software Solutions Inc., PO Box 87931, Canton, MI 48187, (734)453-6845 [6581]

Packaging Concepts Corp., 12910 Woodburn Dr., Hagerstown, MD 21742, (301)733-5771 [12095]

Packaging Concepts and Design, 800 E Mandoline, Madison Heights, MI 48071, (248)585-3200 [21857]

Packers Distributing Co., 1301 E Commercial, Springfield, MO 65803, (417)866-7230 [12096]

Packers Engineering and Equipment Company Inc., 6720 N 16th St., Omaha, NE 68112, (402)451-1252 [17098]

Packet Engines, 11707 East Sprague #101, Spokane, WA 99206, (509)777-7000 [6582]

Packing Seals and Engineering Company Inc., 3507 N Kenton Ave., Chicago, IL 60641, (773)725-3810 [23305]

Packings & Insulations Corp., PO Box 6364, Providence, RI 02940-6364, (401)421-8090 [7829]

Packtronics Inc., 7200 Huron River Dr., Dexter, MI 48130-1099, (734)426-4646 [25374]

Pacon Machines Corp., PO Box 1236, Madison, CT 06443-1236, (203)245-1940 [16378]

Pacor Inc., PO Box 29278, Philadelphia, PA 19125-0278, (215)978-7100 [7830]

Padco Companies, Inc., 2220 Elm St. SE, Minneapolis, MN 55414, (612)378-7270 [21523]

Padco Inc., 2220 Elm St. SE, Minneapolis, MN 55414, (612)378-7270 [21523]

Paddington Corp., 1 Parker Plz., Ft. Lee, NJ 07024, (201)592-5700 [1940]

Paddock Seating Co., 1527 Madison Rd., Cincinnati, OH 45206, (513)961-1821 [13200]

Paddock Swimming Pool Co., 15120 Southlawn Ln., No. C, Rockville, MD 20850-1323, (301)424-0790 [23868]

Padnos Iron and Metal Co.; Louis, PO Box 1979, Holland, MI 49422-1979, (616)396-6521 [26933]

Padre Island Screen Printing, 3728 Wow Rd., Corpus Christi, TX 78413, (512)851-0700 [5264]

Padre Island Supply, 9830 S Padre Island Dr., Corpus Christi, TX 78418, (512)937-1473 [18581]

PAFCO Truck Bodies Inc., 1954 E Washington St., East Peoria, IL 61611, (309)699-4613 [3076]

Page Foam Cushion Products Inc., 850 Eisenhower Blvd., Johnstown, PA 15904, (814)266-6969 [13201]

Page Inc.; T.H., 6600 France Ave. S, Ste. 162, Minneapolis, MN 55435-1802, (612)920-7221 [18975]

Page Seed Co., 1-A Greene St., Greene, NY 13778, (607)656-4107 [1116]

Pagel Safety Inc., N51 W13251 Brahm Ct., Menomonee Falls, WI 53051, (414)783-3595 [24610]

Pagel Safety Inc., W229N1687 Westwood Dr., Ste. E, Waukesha, WI 53186-1174, (414)544-8060 [24611]

PAGG Corp., 425 Fortune Blvd., Milford, MA 01757, (508)478-8544 [6583]

Paging Plus Co., PO Box 25019, Glendale, CA 91225, (818)242-6444 [5699]

Paging Products Group, 1500 Gateway Blvd., Boynton Beach, FL 33426, (561)739-2000 [5700]

Paging Wholesalers, 1210 S Brand Blvd., Glendale, CA 91204-2615, (818)240-5640 [5701]

Pagoda Trading Co., 8300 Maryland Ave., St. Louis, MO 63105, (314)854-4000 [24828]

Paige Electric Company L.P., PO Box 368, Union, NJ 07083-0368, (908)687-7810 [9173]

Paige International, 3166 Tennyson St. NW, Washington, DC 20015-2360, (202)244-6406 [6584]

The Paint Bucket, 1051 W Holt Blvd., Ontario, CA 91762, (714)983-2664 [21524]

Paint Dept., PO Box 22737, Billings, MT 59104-2737, (406)245-5585 [21525]

Paint & Equipment Supply, 3400 Hwy. 30 W, Pocatello, ID 83201-6071, (208)232-8665 [21526]

Paint & Glass Supply Company Inc., 301 4th St., Devils Lake, ND 58301-2411, (701)662-4976 [21527]

The Paint Store, PO Box 1365, Casper, WY 82602-1365, (307)234-6454 [21528]

Paint Supply Co., 3504 S Grand Ave., St. Louis, MO 63118, (314)773-3223 [21529]

Paint West Decor Center, 1606 West 3500 South, West Valley City, UT 84119, (801)972-9380 [21530]

Painter's Choice, 43 North 700 East, St. George, UT 84770, (435)673-6222 [21531]

Pair Electronics Inc., 107 Trade St., Greenville, NC 27834-6851, (919)756-2291 [9174]

PairGain Technologies Inc., 14402 Franklin Ave., Tustin, CA 92780, (714)832-9922 [9175]

Paisano Publications, PO Box 3000, Agoura Hills, CA 91376, (818)889-8740 [5265]

Pak-Mor Manufacturing Co., PO Box 14147, San Antonio, TX 78214, (210)923-4317 [20702]

Pako Steel Inc., 2424 State Rd., Bensalem, PA 19020, (215)639-7256 [20202]

Pal Productions Inc., 1685 Lakewood Dr., Troy, OH 45373-9508, (937)890-6200 [26603]

Palacios Processors, 9 8th St., Palacios, TX 77465, (512)972-3932 [12097]

Paladin Press, PO Box 1307, Boulder, CO 80306, (303)443-7250 [4036]

Palagonia Italian Bread, 508 Junius St., Brooklyn, NY 11212-7126, (718)272-5400 [12098]

Palay Display Industries Inc., 2307 S Washington St., Grand Forks, ND 58201-6347, (701)775-0606 [13202]

Palay Display Industries Inc., 5250 W 73rd St., Minneapolis, MN 55439, (612)835-7171 [13203]

Palco Electronics, 18676 Eureka Rd., Southgate, MI 48195-2925, (734)283-1313 [9176]

Palermo Supply Company Inc., 71 N Washington Ave., Bergenfield, NJ 07621, (201)387-1141 [23306]

Palermo's Frozen Pizza, 800 W Maple, Milwaukee, WI 53204-3524, (414)643-0919 [12099]

Palex, PO Box 216, Smithville, OH 44677, (330)669-2726 [25917]

Palisades Beach Club, 1936 Mateo, Los Angeles, CA 90021, (213)623-9233 [5266]

Pallet Recycling Center Inc., PO Box 19638, Indianapolis, IN 46219, (317)351-2204 [25931]

Pallian & Co., PO Box 1704, Wells, ME 04090, (207)646-1600 [14936]

Palm Brothers Inc., 2727 Nicollet Ave., Minneapolis, MN 55408, (612)871-2727 [24201]

Palm Pool Products Inc., 32620 Dequindre Rd., Warren, MI 48092-1062, (313)537-5550 [23869]

Palmer Candy Co., PO Box 326, Sioux City, IA 51102, (712)258-5543 [12100]

Palmer-Donovan Manufacturing, 312 Mound St., Dayton, OH 45407, (937)461-1203 [7831]

Palmer News Inc., PO Box 1400, Topeka, KS 66601, (785)234-6679 [4037]

Palmer Pipe and Supply Inc., 1909 Garden City Hwy., Midland, TX 79702, (915)682-7337 [13859]

Palmer/Snyder Furniture Co., 400 N Executive Dr., Ste. 200, Brookfield, WI 53005, (414)351-2693 [13204]

Palmetto Ford Truck Sales Inc., 7245 NW 36th St., Miami, FL 33166, (305)592-3673 [3077]

Palmetto Tile Distributor, 316 Huger St., PO Box 42, Columbia, SC 29201, (803)771-4001 [10098]

Palmieri Associates, 369 Passaic Ave., Ste. 116, Fairfield, NJ 07004, (973)882-1266 [9177]

Palmieri Associates, 369 Passaic Ave., Ste. 116, Fairfield, NJ 07004, (973)882-1266 [15263]

Pam Oil Inc., PO Box 5200, Sioux Falls, SD 57117, (605)336-1788 [22548]

Pam Oil Inc., PO Box 5200, Sioux Falls, SD 57117-5200, (605)336-1788 [3078]

Pamas and Company Inc., 14 E Welsh Pool Rd., Exton, PA 19341, (215)524-1980 [7832]

Pameco, RR 1, Box 105H, Linn Creek, MO 65052, (573)346-5914 [14707]

Pameco Corp., 1000 Center Pl., Norcross, GA 30093-1725, (770)798-0700 [14631]

Pamida Inc., 8800 F St., Omaha, NE 68127, (402)339-2400 [12101]

Pampered Chef, 350 S Route 53, Addison, IL 60101, (708)261-8900 [15609]

PAMSCO Inc., PO Box 309, Longview, WA 98632, (425)423-3500 [4682]

Pan Am Distributing Inc., 2950 Thousand Oaks Dr., Ste. 23, San Antonio, TX 78247-3347, (210)225-3892 [7833]

Pan Am Sign Products, Inc., 2525 NW 75th St., Miami, FL 33147, (305)691-0581 [25780]

Pan Am Supply Company Inc., 2525 NW 75th St., Miami, FL 33147, (305)691-0581 [25780]

Pan American Frozen Food Inc., 1496 NW 23rd St., PO Box 420592, Miami, FL 33142-7625, (305)633-3344 [12102]

Pan American International, 3615 NW 20th Ave., Miami, FL 33142, (305)635-3134 [26604]

Pan American Papers Inc., 5101 NW 37th Ave., Miami, FL 33142, (305)635-2534 [21858]

Pana Bait Co., 284 N 2600 E Rd., Pana, IL 62557, (217)562-4122 [23870]

Pana Pacific Corp., 541 Division St., Campbell, CA 95008, (408)374-7900 [5702]

PanAm Sat Corp., 1 Pickwick Plz., Greenwich, CT 06830, (203)622-6664 [5703]

Panama Machinery and Equipment Co., PO Box 776, Everett, WA 98206, (206)682-3166 [13860]

Panasonic Broadcast and Television Systems Co., 1 Panasonic Way, Secaucus, NJ 07094, (201)348-7621 [15264]

Panasonic Copier Co., 1510 S Lewis St., Anaheim, CA 92805, (714)999-2500 [21202]

Panasonic Industrial Co., 2 Panasonic Way, Secaucus, NJ 07094, (201)348-7000 [9178]

PanaVise Products International, PO Box 584, Skokie, IL 60076, (847)674-9888 [13861]

Pancho's Mexican Foods Inc., 2881 Lamar Ave., Memphis, TN 38114, (901)744-3900 [12103]

Pande Cameron/Fritz and La Rue, 200 Lexington Ave., New York, NY 10016, (212)686-8330 [15610]

P&R Publishing, 1102 Marble Hill Rd., PO Box 817, Phillipsburg, NJ 08865, (908)454-0505 [4080]

Panhandle Trading Co., 5718 Westheimer Rd., Houston, TX 77057, (713)627-5400 [22549]

Panorama Casual, 605 E Main, Panora Plz., Panora, IA 50216-0604, (515)755-3966 [5267]

Panoramic Corp., 4321 Goshen Rd., Ft. Wayne, IN 46818, (219)489-2291 [18976]

Pantera International Corp., 320 5th Ave. N, New York, NY 10001, (212)279-1170 [18418]

Pantropic Power Products Inc., 8205 NW 58th St., Miami, FL 33166, (305)592-4944 [16379]

PanVera Corp., 545 Science Dr., Madison, WI 53711, (608)233-9450 [19522]

Paoku International Company Ltd., 1057 Shore Rd., Naperville, IL 60563, (630)369-5199 [6585]

Paoletti and Urriola Inc., 397 Court St., Elko, NV 89801-3157, (702)738-6005 [21203]

Paoli Farmers Cooperative Elevator Co., PO Box 5649, Paoli, CO 80746, (970)774-7234 [18159]

Pape Brothers Inc., 2300 Henderson Ave., Eugene, OR 97403 [7834]

Paper Center Inc., 154 Saint John St., Portland, ME 04102-3021, (207)774-3971 [21859]

Paper Corp., 1865 NE 58th Ave., PO Box 599, Des Moines, IA 50302, (515)262-9776 [21860]

Paper Corporation of the United States, 161 Ave. of the Amer., New York, NY 10013, (212)645-5900 [21861]

Paper Mart, 5631 Alexander, Commerce, CA 90040, (323)726-8200 [21862]

Paper Plus, 300 N Sherman St., PO Box 2677, York, PA 17405, (717)843-9061 [21893]

Paper Products Company Inc., 36 Terminal Way, Pittsburgh, PA 15219, (412)481-6200 [21863]

Paper Recovery Inc., 5222 Lovelock St., San Diego, CA 92110, (619)291-5257 [26934]

Paper Recycling International L.P., 3850 Holcomb Bridge Rd., No. 105, Norcross, GA 30092, (770)449-8688 [27036]

Paper Sales Corp., 4 Testa Pl., PO Box 1055, Norwalk, CT 06856, (203)866-5500 [21864]

Paper Service Company Inc., PO Box 970, 1419 N Riverfront Dr., Mankato, MN 56002, (507)625-7931 [21865]

Paper Stock of Iowa, PO Box 1284, Des Moines, IA 50305, (515)243-3156 [21866]

Paper Supply Co., PO Box 11823, Winston-Salem, NC 27116-1823, (336)759-9647 [4683]

Paperback Books, Inc., 4617 N Witchduck Rd., Virginia Beach, VA 23455, (757)456-0005 [3568]

Paperbacks for Educators, 426 W Front St., Washington, MO 63090-2103, (636)239-1999 [4038]

Papercraft Inc., 3710 N Richards St., PO Box 12615, Milwaukee, WI 53212, (414)332-5092 [21204]

Paperwork Products Co., 5 Eversley Ave., Norwalk, CT 06851, (203)866-2852 [21205]

Pape's Archery Inc., 250 Terry Blvd., PO Box 19889, Louisville, KY 40259-0889, (502)955-8118 [23871]

Papetti's Hygrade Egg Products Inc., 1 Papetti Plaza, Elizabeth, NJ 07206, (908)354-4844 [12104]

Papillon Agricultural Products Inc., PO Box 1161, Easton, MD 21601, (410)820-7400 [1117]

Pappy's Customs Inc., 244 E Main St., Kingsport, TN 37660-4302, (615)246-9594 [5268]

Par-Way Group, 107 Bolte Ln., St. Clair, MO 63077, (636)629-4545 [24202]

Par-Way/Tryson Co., 107 Bolte Ln., St. Clair, MO 63077, (636)629-4545 [24202]

Para-Pharm Inc., 1213 Main St., Willimantic, CT 06226-1907, (860)423-1661 [18977]

Paracca & Sons; Peter, 20254 Rte. 19, Evans City, PA 16033 [10099]

Paraclete Press, Southern Eagle Cartway, Brewster, MA 02631, (508)255-4685 [3670]

Paraco Gas Corp., 2975 W Chester Ave., Purchase, NY 10577, (914)696-4427 [22550]

Paradies and Co., 5950 Fulton Industrial, Atlanta, GA 30336, (404)530-2300 [4039]

Paradise Ceramics, Deviso Sur, No. 16, Aguada, PR 00602, (787)868-4981 [10100]

Paradise Flower Farms Inc., 352 Ihe Pl. No.B, Kula, HI 96790, (808)878-2591 [14937]

Paradise Manufacturing Company Inc., 2840 E 26th St., Los Angeles, CA 90023, (213)269-2106 [15611]

Paradise Optical Co., 848 S Beretania No. 100-A, Honolulu, HI 96813, (808)523-5021 [18978]

Paradise Optical Co., Pearlridge Center, Aiea, HI 96701, (808)488-6869 [19523]

Paradise Products Corp., 1080 Leggett Ave., Bronx, NY 10470-5605, (718)423-2601 [12105]

Paragon Fabrics Company Inc., 441 Broadway, New York, NY 10013, (212)226-8100 [26166]

Paragon Interiors Inc., 1614 Eisenhower Dr. N, Goshen, IN 46526-5381, (219)533-8641 [15612]

Paragon/Monteverde Food Service, 55 36th St., Pittsburgh, PA 15201, (412)621-2626 [12106]

Paragon Music Center Inc., 2119 W Hillsborough Ave., Tampa, FL 33603-1050, (813)876-3459 [25375]

Paragon Packaging Products Inc., 625 Beaver Rd., Girard, PA 16417, (814)774-9621 [21867]

Paragon Supply Co., 1180 Dundee Ave., Elgin, IL 60120, (708)742-8760 [23307]

Paragram Sales Co. Inc., 8455 -O Tyco Rd., Vienna, VA 22182, (703)356-0808 [6586]

Parallel PCs Inc., 1404 Durwood Dr., Reading, PA 19609, (215)670-1710 [6587]

Parallel Traders Inc., 8787 SW 132nd St., Miami, FL 33176, (305)235-7058 [14187]

Paramount Brands, Inc., 305 S Regent St., PO Box 351, Port Chester, NY 10573, (914)937-5007 [1941]

Paramount Computer, 1252 Diamond Way, Concord, CA 94520, (925)825-4046 [6589]

Paramount Export Co., 280 17th St., Oakland, CA 94612, (510)839-0150 [12107]

Paramount Feed and Supply Inc., 19310 W Longmeadow Rd., Hagerstown, MD 21742, (301)733-8150 [1118]

Paramount International, 92 Corporate Park, Ste. C-240, Irvine, CA 92606-5108, (949)252-8874 [6588]

Paramount Liquor Co., 400 N Rangeline, Columbia, MO 65201, (573)474-6702 [1942]

Paramount Manufacturing Co., 42885 Swan Lake Dr., Northville, MI 48167, (248)380-4927 [5269]

Paramount Sales Co., 548 Smithfield Ave., Pawtucket, RI 02860, (401)728-4400 [14188]

Paramount Sales Co., 548 Smithfield Ave., Pawtucket, RI 02860, (401)728-4400 [19524]

Paramount Technology, 1252 Diamond Way, Concord, CA 94520, (925)825-4046 [6589]

Paramount Uniform Rental Inc., 5421 Crestview Dr., Memphis, TN 38134-6415, (901)382-4411 [5270]

Parasoft Corp., 27415 Trabuco Cir., Mission Viejo, CA 92692, (714)380-9739 [6590]

Parco Foods LLC, 2200 W 138th St., Blue Island, IL 60406, (708)371-9200 [12108]

Parents Approved Video, 212 NW 4th Ave., Hallandale, FL 33009-4015, (954)458-7505 [25213]

Parfums de Coeur Ltd., 85 Old Kings Hwy. N, Darien, CT 06820, (203)655-8807 [14189]

Pargh Company Inc.; B.A., PO Box 23770, Nashville, TN 37202, (615)254-2500 [6591]

Paris Food Corp., 1632 Carman St., Camden, NJ 08105, (609)964-0915 [12109]

Paris Tire City of Montbello Inc.; Jim, 1150 E 58th Ave., Denver, CO 80216, (303)297-3600 [3079]

Paris Vienna, 3912 S Broadway Pl., Los Angeles, CA 90037, (213)231-0619 [5271]

Park Corporation, PO Box 1488, Green Valley, AZ 85622, (520)648-1630 [9179]

Park Farms Inc., 1925 30th NE, Canton, OH 44705, (330)455-0241 [12110]

Park Manufacturing Co., PO Box 634, Jamestown, TN 38556-0634, (931)879-5894 [5272]

Park Orchards Inc., 4428 Broadview Rd., Richfield, OH 44286, (216)659-6134 [12111]

Park Place Recreation Designs Inc., 4225 Woodburn Dr., San Antonio, TX 78218, (210)599-4899 [23872]

Park Supply Co. Inc., 1702 Hwy. 11 N, Picayune, MS 39466-2032, (601)798-1141 [15265]

Parkans International L.L.C., 5521 Armour Dr., Houston, TX 77020, (713)675-9141 [26935]

Parker Banana Company Inc., 1801 E Sahlman Dr., Tampa, FL 33605, (813)248-5448 [12112]

Parker Brothers and Company Inc., PO Box 107, Houston, TX 77001, (713)928-8400 [3080]

The Parker Company, 101 N 1st St., Decatur, IN 46733, (219)724-3141 [13862]

Parker Co.; Mitt, PO Box 1565, Forest Park, GA 30298-1565, (404)361-8600 [12113]

Parker Hannifin Corp. Fluidpower Sales Div., PO Box 3500, Troy, MI 48007-3500, (248)589-2400 [17099]

Parker Metal Goods Corp., PO Box 15052, Worcester, MA 01615-0052, (508)791-7131 [13863]

Parker Oil Company Inc., PO Box 120, South Hill, VA 23970, (804)447-3146 [22551]

Parker Steel Co., 4239 Monroe St., Toledo, OH 43606, (419)473-2481 [20265]

Parker-Tilton Co., PO Box 840, Scarborough, ME 04070, (207)883-3417 [12114]

Parker Tobacco Company, 636 Forest Ave., Maysville, KY 41056-0428, (606)564-5571 [26338]

Parks Company Inc.; Charles C., PO Box 119, Gallatin, TN 37066, (615)452-2406 [12115]

Parks Corp., One West St., Fall River, MA 02720, (508)679-5938 [21532]

Parks & History Association, Inc., PO Box 40060, Washington, DC 20016, (202)472-3083 [4040]

Parks Software Services Inc., PO Box 40763, Raleigh, NC 27629-0763, (919)872-9866 [6592]

Parkset Supply Ltd., 1499 Atlantic Ave., Brooklyn, NY 11213, (718)774-4060 [23308]

Parkside Candy Co., 3208 Main St., Buffalo, NY 14214, (716)833-7540 [12116]

Parkville Imports Inc., 1019 N Stadium Dr., Tempe, AZ 85281, (602)921-8485 [17542]

Parkway Automotive Warehouse, 640 W Brooks St., Ontario, CA 91762, (714)983-2651 [3081]

Parkway Drapery Co., 27209 W Warren, Dearborn Heights, MI 48127-1804, (313)565-7300 [15613]

Parkway Food Service Inc., PO Box 86, Greensburg, PA 15601, (412)837-6580 [12117]

Parkway Texaco, PO Box 159, Monticello, UT 84535-0159, (435)587-2215 [22076]

Parma Tile Mosaic & Marble, 29-10 14th St., Astoria, NY 11102-4119, (718)278-3060 [10101]

Parmalat USA, 520 Main Ave., Wallington, NJ 07057, (973)777-2500 [12118]

ParMed Pharmaceuticals Inc., 4220 Hyde Pk. Blvd., Niagara Falls, NY 14305, (716)284-5666 [19525]

Parnell-Martin Co., PO Box 30067, Charlotte, NC 28230, (704)375-8651 [23309]

Parnell Pharmaceuticals Inc., PO Box 5130, Larkspur, CA 94977-5130, (415)256-1800 [19526]

Parnell; Wayne, 1112 S Oak St., Broken Arrow, OK 74012-4959, (918)258-6000 [24829]

Parr Golf Car Company, Inc., 100 N Rockwell No. 76, Oklahoma City, OK 73127, (405)495-0585 [23873]

Parr Lumber Co., PO Box 989, Chino, CA 91708, (909)627-0953 [7835]

Parris Manufacturing Co., PO Box 338, Savannah, TN 38372-0338, (901)925-3918 [26605]

Parrish-Keith-Simmons Inc., PO Box 25307, Nashville, TN 37202, (615)244-4554 [16380]

Parry Corp., 925 S Main St., Akron, OH 44311, (330)376-2242 [16381]

Parshall Farmers Union Co-op Inc., PO Box 128, Parshall, ND 58770, (701)862-3113 [18160]

Parson Cos.; Jack B., PO Box 3429, Ogden, UT 84409, (801)731-1111 [7836]

Parsons Air Gas Inc. (Riverside, California), PO Box 5489, Riverside, CA 92517, (909)686-3481 [16382]

Parsons Paper Co.; Frank, 2270 Beaver Rd., Landover, MD 20785, (301)386-4700 [21868]

Particle Measuring Systems Inc., 5475 Airport Blvd., Boulder, CO 80301-2339, (303)547-7300 [24415]

Partners Book Distributing Inc., 2325 Jarco Dr., Holt, MI 48842, (517)694-3205 [4041]

Partners 4 Design Inc., 275 Market St., Ste. 109, Minneapolis, MN 55405-1622, (612)476-4444 [15266]

Parts Associates Inc., 12420 Plaza Dr., Cleveland, OH 44130, (216)433-7700 [13864]

Parts Depot Company L.P., PO Box 13785, Roanoke, VA 24037, (540)345-1001 [3082]

Parts Inc., PO Box 429, Memphis, TN 38101, (901)523-7711 [3083]

Parts Inc., 101 McNeeley Rd., PO Box 1119, Piedmont, SC 29673, (864)269-7278 [26936]

Parts Inc., PO Box 394, Heber City, UT 84032, (801)972-5293 [7837]

Parts Industries Corp., PO Box 429, Memphis, TN 38101, (901)523-7711 [1119]

Parts Now! Inc., 3517 W Beltline Hwy., Madison, WI 53713, (608)276-8688 [6593]

Parts Plus of Dearborn, PO Box 429, Memphis, TN 38101-0429, (901)582-3300 [3084]

Parts Warehouse Inc., 1901 E Roosevelt Rd., Little Rock, AR 72206, (501)375-1215 [3085]

PartsPort Ltd., 1801 Walthall Creek Dr., Colonial Heights, VA 23834, (804)530-1233 [6594]

Party Kits Unlimited Inc., PO Box 7831, Louisville, KY 40257-0831, (502)425-2126 [23874]

PAS Div., 10540 Ridge Rd., New Port Richey, FL 34654, (727)849-9240 [136]

Pascal Company Inc., PO Box 1478, Bellevue, WA 98009, (425)827-4694 [19527]

Pasch Optical Lab, 4589 W Morrison Rd., Denver, CO 80219, (303)922-7537 [19528]

Pasha Group Co., 802 S Fries St., Wilmington, CA 90744, (562)437-0911 [3086]

Paskesz Candies & Confectionery, 4473 1st Ave., Brooklyn, NY 11232, (718)832-2400 [12119]

Pasminco Inc., 70 St. George Ave., Stamford, CT 06905, (203)325-4232 [20266]

Pasqua Florist & Greenhouse, 659 Metacom Ave., Warren, RI 02885, (401)245-7511 [14938]

Passage Supply Co., PO Box 9037, El Paso, TX 79982, (915)778-9377 [14632]

Passaic Metal & Building Supplies Co., 5 Central Ave., PO Box 1849, Clifton, NJ 07015, (973)546-9000 [7838]

Passaic Metal Products, 5 Central Ave., PO Box 1849, Clifton, NJ 07015, (973)546-9000 [7838]

Passeggiata Press, Inc., 222 W B St., Pueblo, CO 81003-3404, (719)544-1038 [4042]

Passonno Paints, 500 Broadway, Watervliet, NY 12189, (518)273-3822 [21533]

Passport Furniture, PO Box 4750, Roanoke, VA 24015, (540)342-7800 [13205]

Pastian's Bakery, 3320 2nd St. NW, Albuquerque, NM 87107, (505)345-7773 [12959]

Pastorelli Food Products Inc., 162 N Sangamon St., Chicago, IL 60607, (312)666-2041 [12120]

P.A.T. Products Inc., 44 Central St., Bangor, ME 04401, (207)942-6348 [4479]

Patchis Yarn Shop; Peter, 174 Cross St., Central Falls, RI 02863-2907, (401)723-3116 [26167]

Patco Inc., 6955 Central Hwy., Pennsauken, NJ 08109, (609)665-5276 [14633]

Patented Products Inc., 513 Market St., Danville, OH 43014-0601, (740)599-6842 [15614]

Path Press Inc., PO Box 2925, Chicago, IL 60690-2925, (847)424-1620 [4043]

Pathfinder Press, 410 West St., New York, NY 10014, (212)741-0690 [4044]

Pathon Co., PO Box 443, Medina, OH 44258, (330)721-8000 [16383]

Pathtrace Systems Inc., 2143 Convention Center Way, Ste. 100, Ontario, CA 91764, (909)460-5522 [6595]

Pathway Book Service, 4 White Brook Rd., Gilsum, NH 03448, (603)357-0236 [4045]

Patio Production Inc., 4716 2nd St. NW, Albuquerque, NM 87107-4005, (505)344-5864 [13206]

Patnaude's Aquarium & Pet, 1193 Ashley Blvd., New Bedford, MA 02745, (508)995-0214 [27203]

Patrick and Co., 560 Market St., San Francisco, CA 94104, (415)392-2640 [21869]

Patrick Dry Goods Company Inc., 163 W 2nd S, Salt Lake City, UT 84101, (801)363-5895 [26168]

Patrick Electric Supply Co., 301 11th Ave. S, Nashville, TN 37203-4003, (615)242-1891 [9180]

Patrick Industries Inc., PO Box 638, Elkhart, IN 46515, (219)294-7511 [7839]

Patrick Lumber Company Inc., 828 SW 1st St., Portland, OR 97204, (503)222-9671 [7840]

Patriotic Fireworks Inc., 1314 S High School Rd., Indianapolis, IN 46241-3129, (317)243-7469 [13418]

Patron Transmission, 394 1st St., Hackensack, NJ 07601, (201)343-2200 [3087]

Patron Transmission, 75 Allen Blvd., Farmingdale, NY 11735, (516)293-8084 [17100]

Patrons Mercantile Cooperative, PO Box 230, Mt. Horeb, WI 53572, (608)437-5536 [1147]

Pat's Ceramics Tile Design Center, 1567 N Decatur Blvd., Las Vegas, NV 89108-1204, (702)646-6011 [26606]

Patten Corp., 10851 Bloomfield, PO Box 1129, Los Alamitos, CA 90720-1129, (562)598-6688 [16384]

Patten Inc.; H.I., 168 Eastern Ave., Lynn, MA 01902-1310, (781)592-4621 [24203]

Patten Industries Inc., 635 W Lake St., Elmhurst, IL 60126, (708)279-4400 [7841]

Patterson Brothers Meat Co., PO Box 710505, Dallas, TX 75371-0505, (214)821-3300 [12121]

Patterson Brothers Oil and Gas Inc., 141 S Pine St., Williamsville, IL 62693, (217)566-3328 [22552]

Patterson Dental Co., 1031 Mendota Heights Rd., St. Paul, MN 55120, (612)686-1600 [19529]

Patterson Oil Co., PO Box 898, Torrington, CT 06790, (860)489-1198 [22553]

Patterson Sales Associates, PO Box 13156, Savannah, GA 31416-0156, (912)598-0086 [21870]

Patterson Sales Associates, PO Box 13156, Savannah, GA 31416-0156, (912)598-0086 [17101]

Pattons Inc., 3201 South Blvd., Charlotte, NC 28209, (704)523-4122 [5847]

Paul Company Inc., 27385 Pressonville Rd., Wellsville, KS 66092-9119, (785)883-4444 [23875]

Paul-Son Gaming Supplies, Inc., 1700 Industrial Rd., Las Vegas, NV 89102, (702)384-2425 [26607]

Paulist Productions, 17575 Pacific Coast Hwy., Pacific Palisades, CA 90272, (310)454-0688 [22888]

Paulk Grocery; H.B., PO Box 637, Opp, AL 36467, (334)493-3255 [12122]

Paulk Grocery Inc.; H.B., PO Box 637, Opp, AL 36467, (334)493-3255 [12123]

Pauls Tops & Knobs, 7273 Old Pascagoula Rd., Theodore, AL 36582, (205)653-6881 [7842]

Paulsen Company Inc.; G., 27 Sheep Davis Rd., Pembroke, NH 03275, (603)225-9787 [4046]

Pavarini Business Communications Inc., 10032 NW46th St., Sunrise, FL 33351, (954)747-1298 [5704]

Paw Paw Wine Distributors, 816 S Kalamazoo, Paw Paw, MI 49079-9230, (616)657-5518 [1943]

The Pawley Co., PO Box 480585, Denver, CO 80248, (303)294-0115 [26169]

Pax Pacifica Ltd., 500 Alakawa St., No. 114, Honolulu, HI 96817-4576, (808)842-4466 [5223]

Paxton Co.; Frank, 6311 St. John Ave., Kansas City, MO 64114, (816)483-3007 [27355]

Paxton Company Inc., PO Box 12103, Norfolk, VA 23541, (757)853-6781 [18582]

Paxton Timber Co., PO Box 1227, Paxton, FL 32538, (850)834-2153 [27356]

Pay Cash Grocery Co., PO Box 469016, Garland, TX 75046-9016, (713)637-3550 [12124]

Payne & Dolan Inc. Muskego Site, PO Box 708, Waukesha, WI 53187, (414)662-3366 [7843]

Payne and Dolan Inc. State Sand and Gravel Co., PO Box 708, Waukesha, WI 53187, (414)662-3366 [7843]

Paynesville Farmers Union Cooperative Oil Co., 419 E Hoffman St., PO Box 53, Paynesville, MN 56362-0053, (320)243-3751 [22554]

P.B. and S. Chemical Inc., PO Box 20, Henderson, KY 42420, (502)827-3545 [4480]

PBD, Inc., 1650 Bluegrass Lake Pkwy., Alpharetta, GA 30004, (770)442-8633 [4087]

P.B.D. Inc., 1650 Bluegrass Lakes Pkwy., Alpharetta, GA 30004, (770)442-8633 [4047]

P.B.D. Worldwide Fulfillment Services, 1650 Bluegrass Lakes Pkwy., Alpharetta, GA 30004, (770)442-8633 [4047]

PBI Market Equipment Inc., 2667 Gundry Ave., Signal Hill, CA 90806, (562)595-4785 [16385]

PBM, Independence Mall E, Philadelphia, PA 19106, (215)922-4900 [5275]

PC Club Inc., 18537 E Gale Ave., City of Industry, CA 91748, (626)913-2582 [6596]

PC Drilling Control Co., 4932 Highway 169 N, Minneapolis, MN 55428-4026, (612)535-8377 [9181]

PC L.P., 500 Frank W Burr Blvd., Glenpointe Ctr., Teaneck, NJ 07666, (201)928-1212 [6597]

PC Professional Inc., 1615 Webster St., Oakland, CA 94612, (510)465-5700 [6598]

PC Service Source Inc., 2350 Valley View Ln., Dallas, TX 75234, (214)406-8583 [6599]

P.C. Solutions Inc., Entre', 13400 Bishops Ln., Ste. 270, Brookfield, WI 53005, (262)821-1060 [6600]

PC Wholesale Inc., 444 Scott Dr., Bloomingdale, IL 60108, (630)307-1700 [6601]

PCC Group Inc., 163 University Pkwy., Pomona, CA 91768, (909)869-6133 [6602]

PCE Inc., 468 Industrial Way W, Eatontown, NJ 07724, (732)542-7711 [9182]

PCI Foodservice, W226N767 Eastmound Dr., Ste. B2, Waukesha, WI 53186-1694, (414)781-6177 [12178]

PCI Rutherford Controls Intl. Corp., 2697 International Pkwy. 5, Ste. 100, Virginia Beach, VA 23452, (757)427-1230 [9183]

PCI Tech, 1103 Del Monte Ave., Monterey, CA 93940, (831)375-7700 [6603]

PCs Compleat Inc., 34 St. Martin Dr., Marlborough, MA 01752, (508)480-8500 [6604]

P.D. Music Headquarters Inc., PO Box 252, Village Sta., New York, NY 10014, (212)242-5322 [4048]

PD60 Distributors Inc., 5065 Avalon Ridge Pky., Norcross, GA 30071-4738, (770)446-0042 [15615]

PDM Adhesives Corp., 121 Bethea Rd., Ste. 307, Fayetteville, GA 30214, (770)461-9081 [13]

PDM Steel Service Centers Div., PO Box 310, Stockton, CA 95201-0310, (209)943-0513 [20267]

PDP Systems, 2140 Bering Dr., San Jose, CA 95131, (408)944-0301 [6605]

PDQ Air Service Inc., 3939 International, Columbus, OH 43219, (614)238-1912 [22555]

Peabody COALSALES Co., 701 Market St., St. Louis, MO 63101-1826, (314)342-7600 [20557]

Peabody Group, 701 Market St., St. Louis, MO 63101-1826, (314)342-3400 [20558]

Peabody Office Furniture Corp., 234 Congress St., Boston, MA 02110, (617)542-1902 [21206]

Peach Flying, 2216 N Broadway, Minot, ND 58701-1011, (701)852-4092 [137]

Peach State Ford Trucks Inc., I-85 Jimmy Carter Blvd., Norcross, GA 30091, (770)449-5300 [3088]

Peach State Truck Centers, I-85 Jimmy Carter Blvd., Norcross, GA 30091, (770)449-5300 [3088]

Peachey and Sons Inc.; A.J., RD 1, Box 101, Belleville, PA 17004, (717)667-2185 [12125]

Peachtree Fabrics Inc., 1400 English St., Atlanta, GA 30318, (404)351-5400 [26170]

Peachtree Fabrics Inc., 1480 Whipple Rd., Union City, CA 94587, (510)487-7799 [26171]

Peachtree Fabrics Inc., 18 Conneticut Dr. S, East Granby, CT 06026, (860)653-2188 [26172]

Peacock Alley, 650 Croswell Ave. SE, Grand Rapids, MI 49506-3004, (616)454-9898 [26608]

Peacock Alley Needlepoint, 650 Croswell Ave. SE, Grand Rapids, MI 49506-3004, (616)454-9898 [26608]

Peacock Co./Southwestern Cordage Co.; R.E., 3942 S Memorial Dr., Tulsa, OK 74145, (918)627-0206 [17102]

Peacock Radio & Wilds Computer Services, PO Box 2166, West Memphis, AR 72303-2166, (870)735-7715 [5705]

Peak Computer Solutions, 1426 Flower St., Glendale, CA 91201-2422, (818)240-0036 [6606]

Peak Distributing Co., 3636 South 300 West, Salt Lake City, UT 84115-4312, (801)261-3597 [12126]

Peak Technologies Inc. (Columbia, Maryland), 9200 Berger Rd., Columbia, MD 21046, (410)312-6000 [21207]

Peake Marketing Inc., 18808 SE Mildred Ave., Portland, OR 97267-6712, (503)653-1696 [6607]

Peakwon International Inc., 107 St. Francis St., No. 2411, Mobile, AL 36602, (205)433-4769 [18979]

Peanut Processors Inc., PO Box 160, Dublin, NC 28332, (910)862-2136 [12127]

Pearce Co., PO Box 1239, Mesa, AZ 85211, (602)834-5527 [1944]

Pearce Industries Inc., PO Box 35068, Houston, TX 77235-5068, (713)723-1050 [12386]

The Pearl Coffee Co., 675 S Broadway, Akron, OH 44311-1099, (330)253-7184 [12128]

Pearl Corp., PO Box 1111240, Nashville, TN 37211, (615)833-4477 [25376]

Pearl Equipment Co., 4717 Centennial Blvd., Nashville, TN 37209, (615)383-8703 [16387]

Pearl Paint Co., Inc., 2411 Hempstead Turnpike, East Meadow, NY 11554, (516)731-3700 [21534]

Pearl's Garden Center, PO Box 213, Captain Cook, HI 96704, (808)323-3009 [14939]

Pearl's Sports Center; Jack, 26 W Michigan, Battle Creek, MI 49017, (616)964-9476 [23876]

Pearlstine Distributors Inc., PO Box 72301, Charleston, SC 29415, (843)554-1022 [1945]

Pearse Pearson Co., 1370 Main St., Millis, MA 02054, (508)376-2947 [16388]

Pearsol Appliance Company, 3127 Main St., Dallas, TX 75226-1584, (214)939-0930 [15267]

Pearsol's Parts Center, 2319 Gilbert Ave., Cincinnati, OH 45206, (513)221-1195 [15268]

Pearson Electronics Inc., 1860 Embarcadero Rd., Palo Alto, CA 94303, (650)494-6444 [9184]

Pearson Inc.; Ronald Hayes, RR 1, Box 158, Deer Isle, ME 04627-9709, (207)348-2535 [17543]

Pearson Rug Manufacturing Co.; Billy D., 2240 Flint Hill Church Rd., Shelby, NC 28152, (704)434-9331 [10102]

Peatfield Industries, 11 Cozy Hollow Rd., Danbury, CT 06811, (203)743-7976 [26609]

Pechiney Corp., 475 Steamboat Rd., Greenwich, CT 06830, (203)661-4600 [20268]

Pechiney World Trade (USA) Inc., 475 Steamboat Rd., Greenwich, CT 06830, (203)622-8300 [20269]

Peck & Co.; S.A., 55 E Washington Blvd., Chicago, IL 60602-2103, (312)977-0300 [17544]

Peck-Polymers, PO Box 710399, Santee, CA 92072, (619)448-1818 [26610]

Peck Recycling Co., 3220 Deepwater Terminal Rd., Richmond, VA 23234, (804)232-5601 [26937]

Peck Recycling Co. Structural Steel Div., 3220 Deepwater Term Rd., Richmond, VA 23234, (804)291-3255 [26993]

Peck Road Ford Truck Sales Inc., 2450 Kella Ave., Whittier, CA 90601, (310)692-7267 [20703]

Peck's Petroleum Inc., PO Box 540, Boaz, AL 35957, (205)593-4286 [22556]

Peco Foods Inc., 3701 Kauloosa Ave., Tuscaloosa, AL 35405, (205)345-3955 [12129]

Pedersen's Ski and Sport, 1976 Candleridge Dr., Twin Falls, ID 83301-8304, (208)733-0367 [23877]

Pederson-Sells Equipment, 30 N 25th St., Ft. Dodge, IA 50501, (515)573-8129 [16389]

Pedley-Knowles and Co., 7303E Edgewater Dr., Oakland, CA 94621, (415)821-9580 [24612]

Pedroni Fuel Co., 385 E Wheat Rd., Vineland, NJ 08360, (609)691-4855 [22557]

Peebles Supply Div., 618 Bland Blvd., Newport News, VA 23602, (757)874-7400 [23310]

Peek Inc.; Walter D., 8 Wilson Dr., Rye, NY 10580-1216, (914)835-5945 [21871]

Peeler's Rug Co., 1224 Champion Ferry Rd., Gaffney, SC 29341, (864)489-3010 [10103]

Peenware International, 7171 Harwin Dr., Stes. 208-210, Houston, TX 77036, (713)266-0137 [13419]

Peer Light Inc., 301 Toland St., San Francisco, CA 94124-1145, (415)543-8883 [9185]

Peerless Coffee Co., 260 Oak St., Oakland, CA 94607, (510)763-1763 [12130]

Peerless Distributing Co., 21700 Northwestern Hwy., Southfield, MI 48075, (313)559-1800 [22558]

Peerless Electric Supply Co., 1401 Stadium Dr., Indianapolis, IN 46202, (317)635-2361 [9186]

Peerless Importers Inc., 16 Bridgewater St., Brooklyn, NY 11222, (718)383-5500 [1946]

Peerless Paper Mills Inc., 1122 Longford Rd., Oaks, PA 19456, (215)933-9015 [4684]

Peets Coffee and Tea Inc., PO Box 12509, Berkeley, CA 94712, (510)594-2100 [12131]

Pegler-Sysco Food Services Co., 1700 Center Park Rd., Lincoln, NE 68512, (402)423-1031 [12132]

Pehler Brothers, Inc., 700 S Clydesdale Dr., Arcadia, WI 54612, (608)323-3440 [1947]

PEI Genesis, 2180 Hornig Rd., Philadelphia, PA 19116, (215)673-0400 [9187]

Peiger Co.; J.J., 101-103 Market St., Pittsburgh, PA 15222, (412)281-3133 [26173]

Peine Inc., 103 N Main St., Minier, IL 61759, (309)392-2011 [1120]

Peirone Produce Co., E 524 Trent Ave., Spokane, WA 99202, (509)838-3515 [12133]

Pelican Paper Products Div., 3000 NE 30th Pl., 5th Fl., Ft. Lauderdale, FL 33306, (954)563-1224 [21872]

Pelican Plumbing Supply Inc., 139 Plantation Rd., Harahan, LA 70123, (504)733-6300 [15269]

Pelican Publishing Company Inc., PO Box 3110, Gretna, LA 70054, (504)368-1175 [4049]

Pella Windows and Doors Inc., 112 Alexandra Way, Carol Stream, IL 60188-2068, (630)682-4500 [7844]

Pellman Foods Inc., 122 S Shirk Rd., PO Box 337, New Holland, PA 17557, (717)354-8070 [12134]

Pells Radio Center, 415 N Mitchell, Cadillac, MI 49601-1838, (616)775-3141 [15270]

Pelreco Inc., 323 Pine Point Rd., Scarborough, ME 04074-8810, (207)282-3683 [14634]

Peltz Group Inc., PO Box 1799, Milwaukee, WI 53217, (414)449-3900 [26938]

Pem Press, 4 White Brook Rd., Gilsum, NH 03448, (603)357-0236 [4045]

Pemalot Inc., 1025 NW State Ave., Chehalis, WA 98532-1826, (206)748-8387 [24830]

Pen-Fern Oil Co., 640 Main Rd., Dallas, PA 18612, (717)675-5731 [22559]

Penachio Company Inc.; Nick, 240 Food Center Dr., Bronx, NY 10474, (718)842-0630 [12135]

Penberthy Lumber Co., 2011 E Carson St., Carson, CA 90810, (310)835-6222 [7845]

Pence Company Inc.; W.J., W 227 N880 Westmound Dr., Waukesha, WI 53186, (262)524-6300 [12136]

Pence International, Inc., 819 Cedar St., Springfield, OH 45503, (937)325-1813 [5273]

Penco Corp., PO Box 690, Seaford, DE 19973, (302)629-7911 [22560]

Penco Corp., PO Box 690, Seaford, DE 19973, (302)629-7911 [23311]

Pendleton Grain Growers Inc., 1000 Dorion SW, Pendleton, OR 97801, (541)276-7611 [18161]

Penfield Petroleum Products, 147 Peconic Ave., Medford, NY 11763, (516)758-3838 [22561]

Penfield Press, 215 Brown St., Iowa City, IA 52245, (319)337-9998 [4050]

Penguin Point Systems Inc., PO Box 975, Warsaw, IN 46581-0975, (219)267-3107 [12137]

Peninsula Bottling Company Inc., 311 S Valley St., Port Angeles, WA 98362, (206)457-3383 [25003]

Peninsula Bottling Company Inc., 311 S Valley St., Port Angeles, WA 98362, (360)457-3383 [12138]

Peninsula Engineering Group Inc., 1150 Morse Ave., Sunnyvale, CA 94089, (408)747-1900 [5706]

Peninsula Laboratories Inc., 601 Taylor Way, San Carlos, CA 94070, (650)592-5392 [19530]

Peninsula Supply Company Inc., PO Box 265, Newport News, VA 23607, (757)244-1496 [7846]

Peninsular Electric Distributors Inc., PO Box 2887, West Palm Beach, FL 33402, (561)832-1626 [9188]

Peninsular Electronic Distributors, PO Box 2887, West Palm Beach, FL 33402, (561)832-1626 [9189]

Peninsular Paper Company Inc., 5101 E Hanna Ave., Tampa, FL 33610, (813)621-3091 [21873]

Penmar Industries Inc., 1 Bates Ct., Norwalk, CT 06854, (203)853-4868 [21874]

Penn Color Inc., 400 Old Dublin Pike, Doylestown, PA 18901, (215)345-6550 [21535]

Penn Detroit Diesel, Rte. 222, Fleetwood, PA 19522, (215)944-0451 [3089]

Penn Detroit Diesel Allison Inc., 8330 State Rd., Philadelphia, PA 19136-2996, (215)335-0500 [3090]

Penn Distributors Inc., 401 Domino Ln., Philadelphia, PA 19128, (215)487-0300 [1948]

Penn-Jersey Paper Co., 2801 Red Lion Rd., Philadelphia, PA 19154, (215)671-9800 [21875]

Penn Machinery Company Inc.; H.O., 54 Noxon Rd., Poughkeepsie, NY 12603, (914)452-1200 [7847]

Penn Printed Shirts Corp., PO Box 516, Brooklyn, MI 49230-0516, (517)592-5642 [5274]

Penn Stainless Products Inc., PO Box 9001, Quakertown, PA 18951-9001, (215)536-3053 [20270]

Penn Telecom Inc., 2710 Rochester Rd., Ste. 1, Cranberry Twp, PA 16066-6546, (724)779-7700 [5707]

Penn Traffic Co., PO Box 4737, Syracuse, NY 13221-4737, (315)453-7284 [12139]

Penn Traffic Co. Riverside Div., Rte. 255 & Shaffer Rd., PO Box 607, Du Bois, PA 15801, (814)375-3663 [12140]

Penna Dutch Co., 408 N Baltimore Ave., Mt. Holly Springs, PA 17065-1603, (717)486-3496 [12141]

Pennfield Corp. Pennfield Farms-Poultry Meat Div., Rte. 22, Fredericksburg, PA 17026, (717)865-2153 [12142]

Pennington Seed Inc., PO Box 290, Madison, GA 30650, (706)342-1234 [1121]

Pennock Co., 3027 Stokley St., Philadelphia, PA 19129, (215)844-6600 [14940]

Pennsylvania Duth Candies, PO Box 3411, Shiremanstown, PA 17011-3411, (717)761-5440 [12879]

Pennsylvania Floor Coverings, 250 Seco Rd., Monroeville, PA 15146, (412)373-1700 [10104]

Pennsylvania Paper & Supply Co., 215 Vine St., PO Box 511, Scranton, PA 18501, (717)343-1112 [21876]

Pennsylvania Plywood & Lumber, 2590 Monroe St., York, PA 17404, (717)792-0216 [7848]

Pennsylvania Sewing Machine Co., 215 Vandale Dr., Houston, PA 15342-1250, (724)746-8800 [15271]

Pennsylvania State University Press, University Support Bldg. 1, Ste. C, University Park, PA 16802-1003, (814)865-1327 [4051]

Pennsylvania Steel Co., 1717 Woodhaven Dr., Bensalem, PA 19020, (215)633-9600 [20271]

Pennville Custom Cabinetry for the Home, 600 E Votaw, PO Box 1266, Portland, IN 47371, (219)726-9357 [7849]

Pennville Custom Cabinetry for the Home, 600 E Votaw, Portland, IN 47371, (219)726-9357 [27357]

PennWell Publishing Co., PO Box 1260, Tulsa, OK 74101, (918)835-3161 [4052]

Penny Curtiss Bakery, PO Box 486, Syracuse, NY 13211-0486, (315)454-3241 [12143]

Penobscot Paint Products Co., 31 Washington St., Bangor, ME 04401-6518, (207)945-3171 [21536]

Penrod Co., 2809 S Lynnhaven Rd.,No. 350, Virginia Beach, VA 23454-6714, (757)498-0186 [7850]

Pensacola Mill Supply Company Inc., 3030 N E St., Pensacola, FL 32501, (850)434-2701 [13865]

Penstan Supply, 850 Horner St., Johnstown, PA 15902 [23312]

Penstock, 6321 San Ignacio Ave., San Jose, CA 95119, (408)730-0300 [9190]

Pentacon Inc., 10375 Richmond Ave., Ste. 700, Houston, TX 77042, (713)860-1000 [13866]

Pentax Corp., 35 Inverness Dr. E, Englewood, CO 80112, (303)799-8000 [22889]

Pentecostal Publishing House, 8855 Dunn Rd., Hazelwood, MO 63042, (314)837-7300 [4053]

Penthouse Industries Inc., 84 N 9th St., Brooklyn, NY 11211, (718)384-5800 [15616]

Penton Overseas Inc., 2470 Impala Dr., Carlsbad, CA 92008-7226, (760)431-0060 [25377]

People's Coal Co., 75 Mill St., Cumberland, RI 02864, (401)725-2700 [20559]

Peoples Communitive Oil Cooperative, 211 Main St., Darlington, WI 53530, (608)776-4437 [22562]

Peoples Gas and Oil Company Inc., PO Drawer 8, Maxton, NC 28364, (910)844-3124 [22563]

Peoria County Service Co., R.R. 1, Edwards, IL 61528, (309)692-8196 [1122]

Pepin Distributing Co., 6401 N 54th St., Tampa, FL 33610, (813)626-6176 [1949]

Pepline/Wincraft, 1124 W 5th St., Winona, MN 55987, (507)454-5510 [13420]

Pepper Products, 3750 N IH 35, San Antonio, TX 78219-2222, (210)661-0940 [12144]

Pepsi; Buffalo Rock, PO Box 3218, Columbus, GA 31903-0218, (706)687-1240 [25004]

Pepsi-Cola Batavia Bottling Corp., 319 W Main St., Batavia, NY 14020, (716)343-7479 [25005]

Pepsi-Cola Co. of Daytona Beach, 860 Bellevue Ave., Daytona Beach, FL 32114-5106, (904)252-2507 [25006]

Pepsi-Cola Bottling Company of Denver, 3801 Brighton Blvd., Denver, CO 80216-3625, (303)292-9220 [25007]

Pepsi-Cola Bottling Company of La Crosse, PO Box 998, La Crosse, WI 54602-0998, (608)785-0450 [4054]

Pepsi-Cola Bottling Company of Luverne Inc., PO Box 226, Luverne, AL 36049, (334)335-6521 [25008]

Pepsi-Cola Bottling Company of Marysville Inc., 604 Center Dr., Marysville, KS 66508, (785)562-5334 [25009]

Pepsi-Cola Bottling Company of New Bern Inc., PO Box 12036, New Bern, NC 28561, (252)637-2193 [25010]

Pepsi-Cola Bottling Company of Rochester, 1307 Valley High Dr., Rochester, MN 55901, (507)288-3772 [25011]

Pepsi-Cola Bottling Company of Rockford, 4622 Hydraulic Rd., Rockford, IL 61125, (815)965-8701 [25012]

Pepsi-Cola Bottling Company of Salisbury, PO Box 2138, Salisbury, MD 21801, (410)546-1136 [25013]

Pepsi-Cola Bottling Company of Shreveport, 1501 Corporate Dr., Shreveport, LA 71107, (318)222-1201 [25014]

Pepsi-Cola Company of Jonesboro, 1301 Aggie Rd., Jonesboro, AR 72401, (870)932-6649 [25015]

Pepsi-Cola Company South, 4532 Hwy. 67, Mesquite, TX 75150, (214)324-8500 [25016]

Pepsi-Cola General Bottlers of South Bend, PO Box 1596, South Bend, IN 46634, (219)234-1311 [25017]

Pepsi-Cola General Bottlers of South Bend, PO Box 1596, South Bend, IN 46634, (219)234-1311 [12145]

Pepsi-Cola Northwest, 2300 26th Ave. S, Seattle, WA 98144, (206)323-2932 [12146]

Pepsi-Cola Ogdensburg Inc., 1001 Mansion Ave., Ogdensburg, NY 13669, (315)393-1720 [25018]

Pepsi-Cola Pittsfield, 1 Pepsi Cola Dr., Latham, NY 12110-2306, (518)445-4579 [25019]

Pepsi-Cola Pittsfield, 1 Pepsi Cola Dr., Latham, NY 12110-2306, (518)445-4579 [12147]

Pepsi-Cola of Salem, 3011 Silverton Rd. NE, Salem, OR 97303, (503)363-9221 [25020]

Pepsi-Cola of Washington, D.C. L.P., 3900 Penn Belt Pl., Forestville, MD 20747, (301)420-1166 [4055]

Peraldo Co. Inc.; L.W., PO Box 350, Winnemucca, NV 89446-0350, (702)623-2553 [1950]

Percura Inc., 19142 Mesa Dr., VilLa Park, CA 92861-1319 [23005]

Perdue Farms Grain Div., PO Box 1537, Salisbury, MD 21802, (410)543-3650 [18162]

Perdue Inc., 8443 Baymeadows Rd., Jacksonville, FL 32256-7440, (904)737-5858 [21208]

Pereira Inc.; Ed, 1725 Pontiac Ave., Cranston, RI 02920-4477, (401)397-4200 [17545]

Perennial Gardens, PO Box 770106, Eagle River, AK 99577, (907)688-2821 [14941]

Perez Farms Inc., 22001 E St., Crows Landing, CA 95313, (209)837-4701 [12148]

Perez Trading Company Inc., 3490 NW 125th St., Miami, FL 33167, (305)769-0761 [21877]

Perezi & Associates; K.M., 21007 NE 4th St., Redmond, WA 98053, (425)868-9249 [13867]

Perfect Fit Industries, Inc., 201 Cuthbertson St., PO Box 709, Monroe, NC 28110, (704)753-4161 [16390]

Perfect Measuring Tape Co., 1116 Summit St., Toledo, OH 43604, (419)243-6811 [24416]

Perfect Solution Multimedia Inc., 10032 San Pablo Ave., El Cerrito, CA 94530, (510)527-6908 [6608]

Perfection Bakeries Inc., 350 Pearl St., Ft. Wayne, IN 46802, (219)424-8245 [12149]

Perfection Distributing Co., 616 Lillian Way, Los Angeles, CA 90004-1108, (213)751-2345 [25781]

Perfection Equipment Co., 5100 W Reno, Oklahoma City, OK 73127, (405)947-6603 [20704]

Perfection Products Inc., 22672 Lambert St., Ste. 620, Lake Forest, CA 92630, (949)770-3489 [15617]

Perfection Type Inc., 1050 33rd Ave. SE, No. 1000, Minneapolis, MN 55414-2707, (612)917-8444 [16391]

Perferx Optical Co. Inc., PO Box 285, Dalton, MA 01226, (413)684-2550 [19531]

Performance Catamarans Inc., 1800 E Borchard Ave., Santa Ana, CA 92705-4694, (714)835-6416 [18583]

Performance Food Group Co., 6800 Paragon Pl., Ste. 500, Richmond, VA 23230, (804)285-7340 [12150]

Performance Medical Group, Inc., 803 Cajundome Blvd., Lafayette, LA 70506-2307, (318)237-1924 [18980]

Performance Northwest Inc., PO Box 23139, Portland, OR 97224, (503)624-0624 [12151]

Performance-Plus Distributing, 10651 E Bethany Dr., Ste. 100, Aurora, CO 80014, (303)671-8900 [25378]

Performance Products, 8000 Haskell Ave., Van Nuys, CA 91406, (818)787-7500 [3091]

The Performance Shop Inc., 747 Gaffney Rd., Fairbanks, AK 99701, (907)479-6125 [3092]

Perfumania, Inc., 11701 NW 101st Rd., Miami, FL 33178, (305)889-1600 [14190]

Perfumania Inc., 11701 NW 101 Street Rd., Miami, FL 33178, (305)889-1600 [19532]

Perfusion Services of Baxter Healthcare Corp., 16818 Via Del Campo Ct., San Diego, CA 92127, (619)485-5599 [19533]

Pericom Inc., 2271 Hwy. 33, Hamilton, NJ 08690, (609)895-0404 [6609]

Perigon Medical Dist. Corp., 70 Sea Ln., Farmingdale, NY 11735, (631)777-8899 [19534]

Perin Press, 226 E College Ave., Appleton, WI 54911, (920)735-6223 [4056]

Perine Co.; John, 820 S Adams, Seattle, WA 98108, (206)682-9755 [13868]

Periodical Services, 3231 F Ave., Gulfport, MS 39507, (228)864-6953 [4057]

Peripheral Land Inc., 47421 Bayside Pkwy., Fremont, CA 94538, (510)657-2211 [6610]

Peripheral Resources Inc., 2721 La Cienega Blvd., Los Angeles, CA 90034, (310)837-5888 [6611]

Peripheral Visions Inc., 27635 Covington Way SE, Kent, WA 98042-9120, (253)630-4045 [18981]

Perishable Distributors of Iowa Ltd., 2741 PDI Pl., Ankeny, IA 50021, (515)965-6300 [12152]

Perisol Technology Inc., 1148 Sonora Ct., Sunnyvale, CA 94086, (408)738-1311 [6612]

Perkins-Goodwin Company Inc., 300 Atlantic St., 5th Fl., Stamford, CT 06901-3522, (203)363-7800 [21878]

Perkins Inc.; Julian W., 40657 Butternut Ridge, Elyria, OH 44035, (216)458-5125 [22564]

Perkins Stationery, PO Box 3776, Sioux City, IA 51102-3776, (712)255-8892 [21209]

Perlow Steel Corp., 2900 S 25th Ave., Broadview, IL 60153, (708)865-1200 [20272]

Perm Inc., 7575 SW 134th St., Miami, FL 33156-6843, (305)591-2366 [17546]

Perma-Bound Books, E Vandalia Rd., Jacksonville, IL 62650, (217)243-5451 [4058]

Permalin Products Co., 109 W 26th St., New York, NY 10001-6806, (212)627-7750 [21879]

Permark, Inc., 450 Raritan Center Pkwy., Edison, NJ 08837, (732)225-3700 [18982]

Peroni Business Systems Inc., 388 Concord Rd., Billerica, MA 01821, (978)667-7200 [6613]

Perpall Enterprises; Michael E., 455 Quaker Ln., West Warwick, RI 02893-2114, (401)823-8500 [3093]

Perrier Group of America Inc., 777 W Putnam Ave., Greenwich, CT 06830, (203)531-4100 [25021]

Perrigo Inc., 204-216 Chapel St., New Haven, CT 06513, (203)787-0236 [23313]

Perry; Lynn, PO Box 867, Shelby, MT 59474-0867, (406)434-2040 [18163]

Perry Machinery Corp., 25 Mt. Laurel Rd., Hainesport, NJ 08036, (609)267-1600 [16392]

Perry and Son Inc.; C.J., 8401 Ridge Rd., Gasport, NY 14067, (716)772-2636 [1123]

Perry Supply Company Inc.; Roy L., 501 S 5th St., Phoenix, AZ 85004-2548, (602)254-4450 [18983]

Perry Supply Inc., PO Box 1237, Birmingham, AL 35201, (205)252-3107 [7851]

Perry Supply Inc., PO Box 1237, Birmingham, AL 35201, (205)252-3107 [7852]

Perry Videx, LLC, 25 Mt. Laurel Rd., Hainesport, NJ 08036, (609)267-1600 [16392]

Perryton Equity Exchange, PO Drawer 889, Perryton, TX 79070, (806)435-4016 [18164]

Perschon Paint & Wallcovering, 2468 S State St., South Salt Lake, UT 84115, (801)487-1061 [21537]

Persin and Robbin Jewelers, 24 S Dunton St., Arlington Heights, IL 60005, (847)253-7900 [17547]

Persinger Supply Co., PO Box 188, Prichard, WV 25555, (304)486-5401 [25782]

Persingers Inc., PO Box 1866, Charleston, WV 25327, (304)346-5341 [16155]

Persona Press, PO Box 14022, San Francisco, CA 94114-0022, (415)775-6143 [4059]

Persona Technologies Inc., 455 Valley Dr., Brisbane, CA 94005-1209 [9191]

Personal Workstations Inc., 3015 112th Ave. NE, Ste. 205, Bellevue, WA 98004, (425)828-4223 [6666]

Personally Yours, 3475 Nowlin Ln., Sparks, NV 89431-1371, (702)356-7001 [26174]

Perspectives, 352 Longview Dr., Lexington, KY 40503, (606)277-0521 [21538]

Perstorp Analytical Inc., 12101 Tech Rd., Silver Spring, MD 20904, (301)680-0001 [24417]

PerTronix Inc., 440 E Arrow Hwy., San Dimas, CA 91773-3340, (909)599-5955 [9192]

Perugina Brands of America, 299 Market St., Saddle Brook, NJ 07663, (201)587-8080 [12153]

Pervone, 790 Turnpike Ste. 202, North Andover, MA 01845, (508)725-5200 [6614]

Perz Feed & Delivery, 3607 W 400 N, La Porte, IN 46350, (219)326-6339 [27204]

Pestcon Systems Inc., 1808 Firestone Pky., Wilson, NC 27893-7991, (252)237-7923 [1124]

Pestorious Inc., R.R. 1, Albert Lea, MN 56007, (507)373-6758 [1125]

Pet Care Wholesale, 2341 Ampere Dr., Louisville, KY 40299-6411, (502)262-0220 [27205]

Pet Food Wholesale, Inc., 3160B Enterprise St., Brea, CA 92821, (714)254-1200 [27206]

Pet Food Wholesale Inc., 3160B Enterprise St., Brea, CA 92821, (714)254-1200 [12154]

Pet Life Foods Inc., PO Box 218, Hamilton, MI 49419-0218, (616)751-8277 [27207]

Pet Lift, 1192 Myrtal Ave., Brooklyn, NY 11221, (718)455-4907 [27208]

The Pet Pharmacy Inc., 1517 E 10th St., Alamogordo, NM 88310, (505)434-2556 [27209]

Pet Pro, 2313 American Ave., Hayward, CA 94545, (510)732-2781 [27064]

Pet Products Associates, Inc., PO Box 2558, Guaynabo, PR 00970-2558, (787)790-7387 [27210]

Pet Supply Warehouse, Roseytown Rd., Greensburg, PA 15601, (412)834-0500 [27211]

Pet World, 2833 W Ridge Rd., Rochester, NY 14626, (716)292-5786 [27212]

Petaluma Poultry Processors Inc., PO Box 7368, Petaluma, CA 94955, (707)763-1907 [12155]

Peter Pan of Hollywood Inc., 5430 Satsuma Ave., North Hollywood, CA 91601-2837, (213)877-9939 [12156]

Peterbilt of Knoxville Inc., 5218 Rutledge Pike, Knoxville, TN 37924, (615)546-9553 [3094]

Peterman & Company, Inc.; D.S., 110-114 N George St., PO Box 1664, York, PA 17401, (717)846-8823 [24831]

Peters Associates; George R., PO Box 850, Troy, MI 48099-0850, (248)524-2211 [25379]

Peters-De Laet Inc., 340 Harbor Way, South San Francisco, CA 94080, (650)873-9595 [9193]

Peters Office Equipment, 4124 Broadway, PO Box 1078, Galveston, TX 77553, (409)765-9403 [21210]

Petersburg Box and Lumber Inc., 1400 Southwest St., Petersburg, VA 23803, (804)732-8921 [27358]

Petersen Aluminum Corp., 1005 Tonne Rd., Elk Grove Village, IL 60007-4978, (847)228-7150 [20273]

Petersen-Arne, 3690 W 1st Ave., Eugene, OR 97402, (541)485-1406 [21211]

Petersen Products Co., 421 Wheeler, PO Box 340, Fredonia, WI 53021-0340, (414)692-2416 [23314]

Peterson-Biddick Co., PO Box 190, Wadena, MN 56482, (218)631-2954 [18334]

Peterson Business Systems Inc., 938 S Highway Dr., Fenton, MO 63026-2040, (314)343-1515 [21212]

Peterson Co.; Dale, 305 1st Ave., Milnor, ND 58060-4205, (701)427-9281 [26611]

Peterson Co.; Robert H., 14724 E Proctor Ave., City of Industry, CA 91746, (626)369-5085 [15618]

Peterson Distributing Co., 315 Railroad Ave., Riverton, WY 82501-3561, (307)856-3397 [1951]

Peterson Inc.; Darwin W., PO Box 16, Huron, SD 57350-0016, (605)352-8243 [21178]

Peterson Machine Tool Co., PO Box 278, Shawnee Mission, KS 66201, (913)432-7500 [16393]

Peterson Machinery Company Inc., 309 7th Ave. S, Nashville, TN 37203, (615)255-8606 [5848]

Peterson Oil Co., 55 East 680 South, Provo, UT 84606, (801)373-8620 [22565]

Peterson Paper Co., PO Box 254, Davenport, IA 52805-0254, (319)323-9946 [21880]

Peterson Spacecrafters, 938 S Hwy. Dr., Fenton, MO 63026, (314)343-7910 [21213]

Peterson Tractor Co., PO Box 5258, San Leandro, CA 94577, (510)357-6200 [7853]

Peterson's North Branch Inc., PO Box 218, North Branch, MN 55056, (612)674-4425 [1126]

Peterson's Rental, 2809 Vaughn Rd., Northwest Bypass, Great Falls, MT 59404, (406)771-7368 [19535]

Petillo Masterpiece Guitars, 1206 Herbert Ave., Ocean, NJ 07712, (732)531-6338 [25380]

Petri Baking Products, 18 Main, Silver Creek, NY 14136-1433, (716)934-2661 [12157]

Petro-Chem Equipment Co., PO Box 358, Baton Rouge, LA 70821, (504)292-8400 [16394]

Petrofina Delaware Inc., PO Box 2159, Dallas, TX 75201, (214)750-2400 [22566]

Petrolec Inc., PO Box 727, Clearfield, PA 16830-0727, (814)765-9603 [22567]

Petroleum Marketers Inc., PO Box 12203, Roanoke, VA 24023, (703)362-4900 [22568]

Petroleum Pipe and Supply Inc., PO Box 545, Carnegie, PA 15106, (412)279-7710 [20274]

Petroleum Products Corp., PO Box 2621, Harrisburg, PA 17105, (717)939-0466 [22569]

Petroleum Products Corporation North, 167 Willow Ave., Middleburg, PA 17842, (717)837-1724 [22570]

Petroleum Sales and Service Inc., 300 Ohio St., Buffalo, NY 14204, (716)856-8675 [22571]

Petroleum Service Co., PO Box 454, Wilkes Barre, PA 18703, (570)822-1151 [22572]

Petroleum Service Company Inc., PO Box 454, Wilkes Barre, PA 18703, (570)822-1151 [22572]

Petroleum Source and Systems Group Inc., PO Box 29399, Atlanta, GA 30359, (404)321-5711 [22598]

Petroleum World Inc., PO Box 307, Cliffside, NC 28024, (704)482-0438 [22573]

PetrolSoft Corp., 12780 High Bluff Drive, Ste., 270, San Diego, CA 92130, (619)259-9724 [6615]

Petron Oil Corp., 180 Gordon Dr., Lionville, PA 19353, (215)524-1700 [22574]

Petrotank Equipment Inc., 10709 E Ute St., Tulsa, OK 74116, (918)838-0781 [22575]

Petsche Company Inc.; A.E., 2112 W Division St., Arlington, TX 76012, (817)461-9473 [9194]

Petter Supply Co.; Henry A., PO Box 2350, Paducah, KY 42001, (270)443-2441 [17103]

Pettisville Grain Company Inc., PO Box 9, Pettisville, OH 43553, (419)446-2547 [1127]

Pettit and Sons, Box 22, Gays Mills, WI 54631, (608)735-4470 [23878]

Peugeot Citroen Engines, 150 Clove Rd., Little Falls, NJ 07424-2138, (201)438-5559 [3095]

Peysen Inc.; David, 1401 Oak Lawn Ave., Dallas, TX 75207-3613, (214)748-8181 [13207]

Peyton Meats Inc., PO Box 9066, El Paso, TX 79982, (915)858-6632 [12158]

Peyton's, PO Box 34250, Louisville, KY 40232, (502)429-4800 [21881]

Pez Candy Inc., 35 Prindle Hill Rd., Orange, CT 06477, (203)795-0531 [12159]

Pezrow Food Brokers Inc., 535 E Crescent Ave., Ramsey, NJ 07446, (201)825-9400 [12160]

Pfaff Pegasus of USA Inc., 7270 McGinnis Ferry Rd., Suwanee, GA 30024-1245, (404)623-1909 [16395]

Pfaff and Smith Builders Supply Co., PO Box 2508, Charleston, WV 25329, (304)342-4171 [7854]

Pfeiffer Hijet, 2424 28th St. SE, Grand Rapids, MI 49512, (616)949-7800 [3096]

PFG Lester, PO Box 340, Lebanon, TN 37087, (615)444-2963 [12161]

PFG Milton's, 3501 Old Oakwood Rd., Oakwood, GA 30566, (404)532-7779 [12162]

Pfizer Inc. Distribution Center, 230 Brighton Rd., Clifton, NJ 07012, (973)470-7700 [19536]

PFM Industries Inc., PO Box 57, Edmonds, WA 98020-0057, (425)776-3112 [26612]

PFS, PO Box 230765, Houston, TX 77223-0765, (713)923-6060 [12163]

PFT Of America Inc., 4857 W Van Buren St., Phoenix, AZ 85043, (602)269-9311 [7855]

PGL Building Products, PO Box 1049, Auburn, WA 98071, (253)941-2600 [7856]

Pharis Organization Inc., 111 Woodside Ave., Ridgewood, NJ 07450, (201)447-4451 [7857]

Pharm-Med Inc., 39023 Harper Ave., Clinton Township, MI 48036-3226, (810)468-1207 [18984]

Pharmacies In Medisav Homecare, 8820 Rogers Ave., Ft. Smith, AR 72903-5245, (501)452-2210 [18985]

Pharmacy Corporation of America, 1871 Lefthand Cir., Longmont, CO 80501, (303)626-7788 [19537]

PharMerica Inc., 175 Kelsey Ln., Tampa, FL 33619, (813)626-7788 [19538]

PharMerica Inc./PMSI, 175 Kelsey Ln., Tampa, FL 33619, (813)626-7788 [19538]

Phase II, 12410 N 28th Dr., Phoenix, AZ 85029-2433, (602)993-1130 [26613]

Phase II Distributors Inc., 13024 Chatsworth Rd., Moss Point, MS 39562-9566, (601)475-2400 [26614]

PHD, Inc., 29309 Clayton Ave., Wickliffe, OH 44092, (440)944-3500 [15272]

Phelans, 728 3rd Ave. SE, Cedar Rapids, IA 52401-1612, (319)363-9634 [15619]

Phenix Supply Co., PO Box 6963, Atlanta, GA 30315, (404)622-8136 [4685]

Phi Technologies Inc., 4605 N Stiles St., Oklahoma City, OK 73105, (405)521-9000 [25381]

Phibro Inc., 500 Nyala Farms, Westport, CT 06880-6262, (203)221-5800 [22576]

Phiebig Inc., Services to Libraries; Albert J., PO Box 352, White Plains, NY 10602-0352, (914)948-0138 [4060]

Phifer Wire Products Inc., PO Box 1700, Tuscaloosa, AL 35403-1700, (205)345-2120 [13208]

Philadelphia Fire Retardant Company Inc., PO Box 319, Haverford, PA 19041-0319, (610)527-1254 [7858]

Philadelphia Hide Brokerage, 1000 S Lenola Rd., Maple Shade, NJ 08052-1604, (609)439-0707 [18419]

Philadelphia Reserve Supply Co., 400 Mack Dr., Croydon, PA 19021, (215)785-3141 [7859]

Philadelphia Sign Company Inc., 707 W Spring Garden St, Palmyra, NJ 08065, (609)829-1460 [25783]

Philip Morris Products Inc., 2001 Walmsley Blvd., Richmond, VA 23234, (804)274-2605 [26339]

Philips and Co., PO Box 978, Columbia, MO 65205, (314)474-2800 [9195]

Philips Electronic Instruments Co., 85 McKee Dr., Mahwah, NJ 07430, (201)529-3800 [24418]

Philips Key Modules, 2001 Gateway Pl Ste. 650 W, San Jose, CA 95110, (408)453-7373 [9196]

Philips Medical Systems North America Co., PO Box 860, Shelton, CT 06484, (203)926-7674 [19539]

Phillip Metals Inc., PO Box 1182, Nashville, TN 37202, (615)271-3300 [20275]

Phillippe of California Inc., 10 W 33rd St., New York, NY 10001, (212)564-9191 [18420]

Phillips 66 Propane Inc., 756 Adams Bldg., Bartlesville, OK 74004, (918)661-3207 [22577]

Phillips Beverage Co., 25 Main St. SE, Minneapolis, MN 55414, (612)331-6230 [1952]

Phillips Brothers Lumber Company Inc., PO Box 1356, Brookhaven, MS 39601, (601)833-7461 [27359]

Phillips Company Inc.; Tom M., PO Box 207, Jasper, GA 30143, (706)692-2012 [22578]

Phillips Co.; Victor L., PO Box 4915, Kansas City, MO 64120, (816)241-9290 [7860]

Phillips, Day and Maddock Inc., 1800 E 30th St., Cleveland, OH 44114-4499, (216)861-5730 [7861]

Phillips Distributing Corp., PO Box 7725, Madison, WI 53707-7725, (608)222-9177 [1953]

Phillips Distribution Inc., 3000 E Houston, PO Box 200067, San Antonio, TX 78220, (512)227-2397 [4686]

Phillips Energy Inc., 989 S Airport Rd. W, Traverse City, MI 49684, (616)929-1396 [23879]

Phillips Hardware Co., PO Box 279, Cambridge, MD 21613, (410)228-4900 [22579]

Phillips Ice Service Inc., 438 State St., Bowling Green, KY 42101-1241, (502)843-8901 [14635]

Phillips Inc.; Ira, 310 N 3rd St., Gadsden, AL 35901, (256)547-0591 [22580]

Phillips Industries Inc., PO Box 1350, High Point, NC 27261, (910)882-3301 [26175]

Phillips and Jacobs Inc., 3991 Commerce Pkwy., Miramar, FL 33025, (954)432-1000 [25784]

Phillips Mushroom Farms, PO Box 190, Kennett Square, PA 19348, (610)444-4492 [12164]

Phillips Shoe Co. Inc.; Austin, 209 Terminal Ln., New Haven, CT 06519-1800, (203)777-5485 [24832]

Phillips Shoes, 115 Commercial Ave., Monterey, TN 38574, (931)839-3119 [24833]

Phillips and Son Inc.; Max, PO Box 202, Eau Claire, WI 54702-0202, (715)832-3431 [26939]

Phillips and Sons (Eau Claire, Wisconsin); Ed, PO Box 869, Eau Claire, WI 54701, (715)836-8600 [1954]

Phillips & Sons; Ed, 25 Main St. SE, Minneapolis, MN 55414, (612)331-6230 [1952]

Phillips and Sons; Ed, PO Box 869, Eau Claire, WI 54701, (715)836-8600 [1955]

Phillips & Sons of N.D.; Ed, PO Box 1978, Fargo, ND 58107, (701)277-1499 [1956]

Phillips and Temro Industries, 9700 W 7th St., Eden Prairie, MN 55344, (612)941-9700 [3097]

Phillipsburg Cooperative Association, PO Box 624, Phillipsburg, KS 67661, (785)543-2114 [22581]

Philosophical Research Society, Inc., 3910 Los Feliz Blvd., Los Angeles, CA 90027, (213)663-2167 [4061]

Phoenix Coal Sales of Florida Inc., 1401 Manatee Ave. W, Ste 520, Bradenton, FL 34205, (941)747-2630 [20524]

Phoenix Computer Associates Inc., 10 Sasco Hill Rd., Fairfield, CT 06430, (203)319-3060 [6616]

Phoenix Fuel Company Inc., 2343 N 27th Ave., Phoenix, AZ 85009, (602)278-6271 [22582]

Phoenix Group HI-TEC Corp., 600 Stewart St., Ste. 1728, Seattle, WA 98101-1217, (206)727-2286 [18986]

Phoenix Imports Ltd., 2925 Montclair Dr., Ellicott City, MD 21043, (410)465-1155 [1957]

Phoenix Inc., PO Box 676, Frederick, MD 21701-0676, (301)663-3151 [7862]

Phoenix Manufacturing Incorporated, PO Box 97, Nanticoke, PA 18634, (717)735-1800 [20705]

Phoenix Mapping Service, 2626 W Glenrose Ave., Phoenix, AZ 85017, (602)433-0616 [4062]

Phoenix Textile Corp., 13652 Lakefront Dr., Earth City, MO 63045, (314)291-2151 [26176]

Phoenix Wholesale Sporting Supplies Inc., 3500 E Lincoln Dr., No. 35, Phoenix, AZ 85018-1010, (602)620-3194 [23880]

Phone Land Inc., 4380 Malsbary Rd., Cincinnati, OH 45242-5644, (513)791-3000 [6617]

PhoneAmerica Corp., 70 W Lancaster Ave., Malvern, PA 19355, (215)296-2850 [5708]

Phoneby, 2755 Bristol St., No. 100, Costa Mesa, CA 92626-5985, (714)754-4000 [5709]

PHONEXPRESS Inc., 14 Industrial Rd., Fairfield, NJ 07004, (973)808-7000 [5710]

Photo-Cine Labs, 123 Grand Ave., Billings, MT 59101-6020, (406)252-3077 [22890]

Photo Control Corp., 4800 Quebec Ave. N, Minneapolis, MN 55428, (612)537-3601 [22891]

Photo Packaging West, 3100 NW Industrial St., Ste. 4, PO Box 10285, Portland, OR 97210-0285, (503)226-0369 [22915]

Photocomm Inc., 7681 E Gray Rd., Scottsdale, AZ 85260, (602)948-8003 [25785]

Photonics Management Corp., 360 Foothill Rd., Bridgewater, NJ 08807, (908)231-1116 [9197]

PhotoVision Inc., 3251 Progress Dr., Ste. B, Orlando, FL 32826, (407)382-2772 [18987]

Phylon Communications Inc., 47436 Fremont Blvd., Fremont, CA 94538, (510)656-2606 [9198]

Physician Sales and Service Inc., 4245 Southpoint Blvd., Ste. 300, Jacksonville, FL 32216-6187, (904)281-0011 [18988]

Physicians Optical Supply Inc., Box 31193, Omaha, NE 68101-1275, (402)558-5200 [19540]

Physicians Supply Co., 2650 S 1030 W, Salt Lake City, UT 84119-2469 [18989]

Physimetrics Inc., 111205 Alpharetta Hwy., Unit C-4, Roswell, GA 30076, (770)751-6322 [9199]

P.I., 1400 N Jefferson St., Unit A, Anaheim, CA 92807, (714)572-9195 [27214]

Piasa Motor Fuels Inc., PO Box 484, Alton, IL 62002, (618)254-7341 [22583]

Picanol of America Inc., PO Box 5519, Greenville, SC 29606, (803)288-5475 [16396]

Picatti Brothers Inc., PO Box 9576, Yakima, WA 98909, (509)248-2540 [9200]

Pick Systems, 1691 Browning, Irvine, CA 92606-4808, (949)261-7425 [6618]

Pickands Mather, Ltd., 1422 Euclid Ave., Ste. 1630, Cleveland, OH 44115, (216)694-5300 [20276]

Pickands Mathers Sales, Inc., 1422 Euclid Ave., Ste. 1630, Cleveland, OH 44115, (216)694-5300 [20276]

Pickens Electronics, PO Box 1178, Pocatello, ID 83204-1178, (208)233-1191 [21214]

Pickering Publications, 205 Crocus Ln., Asheville, NC 28803-3379, (828)684-7353 [4063]

A Pickle House, 1401 E Van Buren St., Phoenix, AZ 85006-3523, (602)257-1915 [13008]

Pick'n Save Warehouse Foods Inc., 11500 W Burleigh St., Wauwatosa, WI 53222, (414)453-7081 [12165]

Pickrel Brothers Inc., 901 S Perry St., Dayton, OH 45402, (937)461-5960 [23315]

Pickrell Cooperative Elevator Association, Main St., Pickrell, NE 68422, (402)673-3280 [18165]

Pickseed West, Inc., PO Box 888, Tangent, OR 97389, (541)926-8886 [1128]

Pico Products, Inc., 12500 Foothill Blvd., Lake View Terrace, CA 91342, (818)897-0028 [9201]

Picone Building Products, 180 Long Island Ave., Holtsville, NY 11742, (516)289-5490 [14636]

Pictorial Histories Publishing Co., 713 S 3rd W, Missoula, MT 59801, (406)549-8488 [4064]

PicturePhone Direct, 200 Commerce Dr., Rochester, NY 14623, (716)334-9040 [5711]

PID, Inc., PO Box 230, Augusta, ME 04332-0230, (207)623-8101 [16397]

Pied Piper Mills Inc., PO Box 309, Hamlin, TX 79520, (915)576-3684 [27213]

Piedmont Candy Co., PO Box 1722, Lexington, NC 27292, (704)246-2477 [12166]

Piedmont Clarklift Inc., PO Box 16328, Greenville, SC 29606, (864)297-1330 [16398]

Piedmont Distribution Centers, PO Box 7123, Charlotte, NC 28241, (704)588-2867 [15620]

Piedmont Mill Supply Co., 1531 S Main St., Salisbury, NC 28144, (704)636-4241 [2775]

Piedmont National Corp., PO Box 20118, Atlanta, GA 30325, (404)351-6130 [21882]

Piedmont Optical Co., Rte. 70 E off Airport Rd., PO Box 1470, Raleigh, NC 27602, (919)787-0151 [19541]

Piedmont Paper Company Inc., PO Box 5413, Asheville, NC 28813-5413, (704)253-8721 [21883]

Piedmont Propane Co., 100 Forsyth Hall Dr., Ste. E, Charlotte, NC 28273, (704)588-9215 [22584]

Piedmont Technology Group Inc., 830 Tyvola Rd. Ste. 104, Charlotte, NC 28217, (704)523-2400 [6619]

Pielet Brothers Scrap, Iron and Metal L.P., 135 S L Salle St., Chicago, IL 60603-4159, (708)594-7171 [20277]

Pierce Aluminum Company Inc., PO Box 100, Canton, MA 02021, (617)828-9005 [20278]

Pierce Box & Paper Corp., 1505 Kishwaukee St., Rockford, IL 61104, (815)963-1505 [21884]

Pierce Enterprises of Eagle Lake, Inc., PO Box 107, Eagle Lake, MN 56024-0107, (507)257-3331 [26615]

Pierce Inc.; Jack A., 3833 N Delaware St., Indianapolis, IN 46205-2647, (317)283-8279 [24834]

Pierre Shoes Inc., PO Box 2387, Woburn, MA 01888-0687, (781)933-6900 [24835]

Pierre's French Ice Cream Distributing Company of Akron, 1350 Kelly Ave., Akron, OH 44306, (216)724-5858 [12167]

Pierson Co.; J.W., 89 Dodd St., East Orange, NJ 07019, (201)673-5000 [22585]

Pietsch Aircraft Restoration & Repair, 2216 N Broadway, Minot, ND 58701-1011, (701)852-4092 [137]

Pifer, Inc., 1350 Indiantown Rd., Jupiter, FL 33458, (561)746-5321 [23881]

Piggly Wiggly Alabama Distributing Company Inc., 2400 J.T. Wooten Dr., Bessemer, AL 35020, (205)481-2300 [12168]

Piggott Tractor and Equipment Company Inc., PO Box 327, Piggott, AR 72454, (870)598-2221 [1129]

Piher International Corporation, 1640 Northwind Blvd., Libertyville, IL 60048-9634, (847)390-6680 [9202]

Pike County Cooperative, PO Box 937, McComb, MS 39648, (601)684-1651 [1130]

Pike Distributors Inc., 401 E John St., Newberry, MI 49868, (906)293-8611 [1958]

Pike Safe Co., 3655 Walnut St., Denver, CO 80205, (303)295-1066 [24539]

Pikes Peak Greenhouses, Inc., PO Box 7070, Colorado Springs, CO 80933, (719)475-2770 [14942]

Pikes Peak Wholesale Florist Inc., PO Box 7070, Colorado Springs, CO 80933, (719)475-2770 [14942]

Pikesville Lumber Co., 7104 Liberty Rd., Baltimore, MD 21207, (410)484-3800 [7863]

Pikotek, PO Box 260438, Lakewood, CO 80226, (303)988-1242 [17104]

Pilgrim Instrument & Controls, 38 Union St., East Walpole, MA 02032, (508)668-3500 [16399]

Pilgrim Way Press, 350 Pearl St., No. 1108, Eugene, OR 97401, (503)686-9594 [4065]

Pill Electric Supply Co.; Ralph, 307 Dorchester Ave., Boston, MA 02127, (617)269-8200 [9203]

Pilot Corporation of America, 60 Commerce Dr., Trumbull, CT 06611, (203)377-8800 [21215]

Pilottes Transport Refrigeration, PO Box 195, Swansea, MA 02777-0195, (508)673-4779 [14637]

Pimalco Inc., 6833 W Willis Rd. Ste. 5050, Chandler, AZ 85226, (520)796-1098 [20279]

Pinahs Company Inc., N8W22100 Johnson Dr., Waukesha, WI 53186, (262)547-2447 [12169]

Pinch a Penny Pool Patio, 32350 US 19 N, Palm Harbor, FL 34684, (813)785-8841 [23882]

Pincus Brothers Inc., Independence Mall E, Philadelphia, PA 19106, (215)922-4900 [5275]

Pine City Cooperative Association, 600 6th St., Pine City, MN 55063, (612)629-2581 [18166]

Pine Cone Lumber Company Inc., PO Box 61207, Sunnyvale, CA 94088, (408)736-5491 [7864]

Pine Grove Stable Inc., PO Box 803, North Scituate, RI 02857, (401)934-0097 [18196]

Pine Island Farmers Elevator Co., PO Box 1037, Pine Island, MN 55963, (507)356-8313 [18167]

Pine Lesser and Sons Inc., PO Box 1807, Clifton, NJ 07015, (973)478-3310 [26340]

Pine State Knitwear Co., PO Box 631, Mt. Airy, NC 27030, (919)789-9121 [5276]

Pine State Tobacco and Candy Co., PO Box 1080, Augusta, ME 04332-1080, (207)622-3741 [26341]

Pine Tree Lumber Co., 707 N Andreason Dr., Escondido, CA 92029, (760)745-0411 [7865]

Pine Valley Supply, 225 Gieger Rd., Philadelphia, PA 19115, (215)676-8100 [1131]

Pinetex, 108 W 39th St., Ste. 500, New York, NY 10018, (212)719-4999 [26177]

Pink Business Interiors Inc., 5825 Excelsior Blvd., St. Louis Pk., MN 55416, (612)915-3100 [10105]

Pinkney & Associates Inc., 7171 Commorse Cir. W, PO Box 32065, Minneapolis, MN 55432-0065, (763)571-2325 [9231]

Pinnacle Business Systems Inc., 100 S Baumann Ave., Edmond, OK 73034-5610, (405)359-0121 [6620]

Pinnacle Business Systems, Inc., 810 S Cincinnati Ave., Tulsa, OK 74119, (918)587-1500 [6621]

Pinnacle Distributing Co., 14200 E Moncrieff, Aurora, CO 80011, (303)371-5890 [1959]

Pinpoint Systems Inc., 4505 S Broadway, Englewood, CO 80110, (303)761-5227 [9204]

Pint Size Corp., 991287 Waiua Pl., Aiea, HI 96701, (808)487-0030 [12170]

Pinto Imports Inc.; Mel, 2860 Annandale Rd., Falls Church, VA 22042-2149, (703)237-4686 [23883]

Pioneer, 5440 Naiman Pkwy., Solon, OH 44139, (440)349-1300 [9205]

Pioneer Aluminum Inc., PO Box 23947, Los Angeles, CA 90023, (213)268-7211 [20280]

Pioneer Coatings Inc., 7265 Bethel St., Boise, ID 83704-9226, (208)377-0112 [21539]

Pioneer Dairy Inc., 214 Feeding Hills Rd., Southwick, MA 01077-9522, (413)569-6132 [12171]

Pioneer Electric Inc., 228 Mohonua Pl., Honolulu, HI 96819, (808)841-0107 [9206]

Pioneer Electronics USA Inc., 2265 E 220th St., Long Beach, CA 90810, (310)835-6177 [9207]

Pioneer Electronics (USA) Inc., PO Box 1720, Long Beach, CA 90801, (310)835-6177 [15273]

Pioneer Entertainment (USA) L.P., 2265 E 220th St., Long Beach, CA 90810, (310)835-6177 [6622]

Pioneer Equipment Inc., 3738 E Miami St., Phoenix, AZ 85040, (602)437-4312 [5849]

Pioneer Equipment Inc., 3738 E Miami St., Phoenix, AZ 85040, (602)437-4312 [16400]

Pioneer French Baking Company Inc., 512 Rose Ave., Venice, CA 90291, (310)392-4128 [12172]

Pioneer Growers Co-Op, PO Box 490, Belle Glade, FL 33430, (407)996-5561 [12173]

Pioneer Implement Corp., PO Box 1408, Pendleton, OR 97801, (541)276-6341 [1132]

Pioneer Industrial Corp., 400 Russell Blvd., St. Louis, MO 63104, (314)771-0700 [17105]

Pioneer Industries Inc., 11630 W 85th St., Lenexa, KS 66214, (913)888-6760 [5277]

Pioneer Laser Optical Products Div., 600 E Crescent Ave., Upper Saddle River, NJ 07458, (201)327-6400 [25382]

Pioneer Machinery, PO Box 9230, Richmond, VA 23227, (804)266-4911 [27360]

Pioneer Machinery, PO Box 9230, Richmond, VA 23227, (804)266-4911 [7866]

Pioneer Machinery Inc., PO Box 250, Lexington, SC 29071, (803)356-0123 [16401]

Pioneer Manufacturing Co., 4529 Industrial Pkwy., Cleveland, OH 44135, (216)671-5500 [21540]

Pioneer Mercantile Co., PO Box 1709, Bakersfield, CA 93302, (805)327-8545 [3098]

Pioneer Music Company Inc., PO Box 646, Chanute, KS 66720-0646, (316)431-2710 [9208]

Pioneer North America Inc., 2265 E 220th St., Long Beach, CA 90810, (310)835-6177 [25383]

Pioneer Photo Albums Inc., 9801 Deering Ave., Chatsworth, CA 91311-4304, (818)882-2161 [13421]

Pioneer Snacks Inc., 30777 Northwestern Hwy. Ste. 300, Farmington Hills, MI 48334, (248)862-1990 [12174]

Pioneer-Standard Electronics Inc., 4800 E 131st St., Cleveland, OH 44105, (216)587-3600 [9209]

Pioneer-Standard Electronics Inc., 9100 Gaither Rd., Gaithersburg, MD 20877, (301)921-3800 [6623]

Pioneer Steel Corp., 7447 Intervale St., Detroit, MI 48238, (313)933-9400 [20281]

Pioneer Steel and Tube Distributors, 1660 Lincoln St., Ste. 2300, Denver, CO 80264-2301, (303)289-3201 [20282]

Pioneer Wholesale Meat, 1000 W Carroll Ave., Chicago, IL 60607-1208, (312)243-6180 [12175]

Pipe Distributors Inc., PO Box 23237, Houston, TX 77228, (713)635-4200 [20283]

Pipe Valve and Fitting Co., PO Box 5806, Denver, CO 80217, (303)289-5811 [17106]

Pipeline Oil Sales Inc., 744 E South St., Jackson, MI 49203, (517)782-0467 [22586]

Piper Associates, 33 Marsh Rd., Needham, MA 02492, (781)449-1144 [9210]

Piper Sport Racks Inc., 1160 Industrial Rd., Ste. 8, San Carlos, CA 94070, (650)598-0858 [23884]

Piper Weatherford Co., 10755 Rockwall, Dallas, TX 75238-1219, (214)343-9000 [13869]

Piping Supply Company Inc., 3008 N Hickory St., Chattanooga, TN 37406, (615)698-8996 [17107]

Piqua Farmers Cooperative Association, PO Box 67, Piqua, KS 66761, (316)468-2535 [18168]

Piraeus International, 3909 Eastern Ave., Baltimore, MD 21224-4224, (410)675-4696 [25384]

Piramide Imports, PO Box 246, Manitou Springs, CO 80829-0246, (719)685-5912 [5278]

Piroutek; Daniel, HCR 1 Box6-A, Milesville, SD 57553, (605)544-3316 [18169]

Pirrone Produce, Inc.; Mike, 56825 Romeo Plank Rd., Macomb, MI 48042, (810)781-3303 [12176]

Pistoresi Distributing Inc., 325 Columbia, Omak, WA 98841, (509)826-5900 [1960]

Pitman Co.; Harold M., 721 Union Blvd., Totowa, NJ 07512, (973)812-0400 [25786]

Pitt-Des Moines Inc., 3400 Grand Ave., Pittsburgh, PA 15225, (412)331-3000 [20284]

Pittman International, 1400 N Jefferson St., Unit A, Anaheim, CA 92807, (714)572-9195 [27214]

Pittman International, 1400 N Jefferson St., Anaheim, CA 92807, (714)572-9195 [19542]

Pittsburgh Oakland Enterprises Inc., 377 McKee Pl., Pittsburgh, PA 15213, (412)683-9006 [12177]

Pittsburgh Plug and Products, PO Box H, Evans City, PA 16033, (412)538-4022 [23316]

Pittston Lumber and Manufacturing Co., 234 N Main St., Pittston, PA 18640, (717)654-3329 [7867]

Pivot Interiors, 2740 Zanker Rd., Ste. 100, San Jose, CA 95134-2116, (408)432-5600 [13209]

Pivot Rules Inc., 42 W 39th St., Fl. 9, New York, NY 10018, (212)944-8000 [5279]

Pixel U.S.A., 810 S Bascom Ave., San Jose, CA 95128-2605, (408)929-7218 [6624]

Pizza Commissary Inc., W226N767 Eastmound Dr., Ste. B2, Waukesha, WI 53186-1694, (414)781-6177 [12178]

Pizza Needs of Memphis Inc., 49 S Walnut Bend Rd., Cordova, TN 38018-7206, (901)372-4588 [12179]

PK Imports Inc., 1225 Broadway, Ste. 609, New York, NY 10001, (212)683-9350 [13422]

P.K. Morgan Instruments Inc., 151 Essex St., Haverhill, MA 01832-5564, (978)521-4440 [18947]

P.K. Safety Supply, 7303E Edgewater Dr., Oakland, CA 94621, (415)821-9580 [24612]

PL Preferred Products, PO Box 477, Ossipee, NH 03864-0477, (603)539-8013 [26178]

Plains Auto Refrigeration, 212 San Pedro SE, Albuquerque, NM 87108, (505)266-0055 [14638]

Plains Cotton Cooperative Association, 3301 E 50th St., Lubbock, TX 79408, (806)763-8011 [18170]

Plains Dairy Products, 300 N Taylor, Amarillo, TX 79107, (806)374-0385 [12180]

Plains Distribution Service, Inc., PO Box 3112, Fargo, ND 58108 [4066]

Plains Equity Exchange, PO Box 157, Plains, KS 67869, (316)563-7269 [18171]

Plainsco Inc., 15 N Kline St., Aberdeen, SD 57401, (605)225-7100 [15274]

Plakie Inc., PO Box 3386, Youngstown, OH 44512, (330)758-3500 [26616]

Plano International, 431 E South St., Plano, IL 60545-1601, (630)552-3111 [13870]

Plant and Flanged Equipment, 4000 85th Ave. N, Minneapolis, MN 55443, (612)424-8400 [23317]

Plant and Flanged Equipment, 4000 85th Ave. N, Minneapolis, MN 55443, (612)424-8400 [20285]

Plant Insulation Co., PO Box 8646, Emeryville, CA 94662, (510)654-7363 [7868]

Plant Maintenance Equipment, PO Box 48229, Seattle, WA 98148-0229, (206)242-5131 [4687]

Plant Service Co., 6th & Bingham, Pittsburgh, PA 15203, (412)381-4664 [17108]

Planters Cooperative Association, PO Box 8, Lone Wolf, OK 73655-0008, (580)846-9008 [1133]

Plaschem Supply & Consulting, 1415 Spar Ave., Anchorage, AK 99501, (907)274-5505 [7869]

Plaschem Supply & Consulting Inc., 1415 Spar Ave., Anchorage, AK 99501, (907)274-5505 [7870]

Plascom Trading Company, 2155 US Highway 1, Trenton, NJ 08648-4407, (609)587-9522 [23006]

Plasterer Equipment Company Inc., 2550 E Cumberland St., Lebanon, PA 17042, (717)867-4657 [1134]

Plastic Distributing Corp., Molumco Industrial Pk, Ayer, MA 01432, (508)772-0764 [23007]

Plastic Dress-Up Co., 11077 E Rush St., South El Monte, CA 91733, (626)442-7711 [13423]

Plastic Fabricators Inc., 555 Sherman Ave., Hamden, CT 06514, (203)288-2303 [23008]

The Plastic Man Inc., 3919 Renate Dr., Las Vegas, NV 89103-1804, (702)362-2113 [23009]

Plastic Piping Systems Inc., 3601 Tryclan Dr., Charlotte, NC 28217, (704)527-6494 [23010]

Plastic Recycling of Iowa Falls, Inc., 10252 Hwy. 65, Iowa Falls, IA 50126-8823, (515)648-5073 [26940]

Plastic Safety Systems, Inc., 2444 Baldwin Rd., Cleveland, OH 44120, (216)231-8590 [24613]

Plastic Sales Southern Inc., 6490 Fleet St., Los Angeles, CA 90040, (323)728-8309 [23011]

Plastic Supply Inc., 735 E Industrial Park Dr., Manchester, NH 03109-5640, (603)669-2727 [23012]

Plastic Supply Inc., 3448 Girard Ave., Albuquerque, NM 87107, (505)884-0507 [23013]

PlastiCom Industries Inc., 1011 W 45th Ave., Denver, CO 80211, (303)433-2333 [9211]

Plastoptics Inc., 2328 W Sinto Ave., Spokane, WA 99201-2948, (509)535-1529 [19543]

Plastruct Inc., 1020 S Wallace Pl., La Puente, CA 91748, (626)912-7017 [25787]

Plath North American; C., 214 Eastern Ave., Annapolis, MD 21403, (410)263-6700 [171]

Platinum Entertainment Inc., 2001 Butterfield Rd., Ste. 1400, Downers Grove, IL 60515, (630)769-0033 [25385]

Platt Electric Supply Inc., 10605 SW Allen Blvd., Beaverton, OR 97005, (503)641-6121 [9212]

Platt Hardin Inc., 7454 Harwin Dr., Houston, TX 77036-2008, (713)784-0613 [9213]

Plattsburgh Distributing, 215 Sharron Ave., Plattsburgh, NY 12901, (518)561-3800 [1961]

Platzer Company Inc.; Samuel, 31 W 47th St., New York, NY 10036, (212)719-2000 [17548]

Playboy Entertainment Group Inc., 9242 Beverly Blvd., Beverly Hills, CA 90210, (310)246-4000 [4067]

Player International; J.B., PO Box 30819, Charleston, SC 29417, (803)763-0220 [25386]

Player Piano Company Inc., 704 E Douglas, Wichita, KS 67202, (316)263-1714 [25387]

Playfield Industries Inc., Murray Industrial Blvd., PO Box 8, Chatsworth, GA 30705-0008, (404)695-4581 [23885]

Playmates Toys Inc., 611 Anton Blvd., Ste. 600, Costa Mesa, CA 92626-1904, (714)428-2000 [26617]

Playsafe Playground Systems of N.Y., 135 Freeman St., Brooklyn, NY 11222, (718)383-0791 [23886]

Plaza Fleet Parts, 1520 S Broadway, St. Louis, MO 63104, (314)231-5047 [3099]

Plaza Paint Co., 771 Roosevelt Ave., Carteret, NJ 07008, (732)969-8818 [21541]

Plaza Stationery & Printing Inc., 29-42 Northern Blvd., Long Island City, NY 11101, (718)784-7980 [21216]

Pleasant Co., PO Box 620998, Middleton, WI 53562-0998, (608)836-4848 [26618]

Pleasants Hardware Co., PO Box 5258, Winston-Salem, NC 27113-5258, (336)725-3067 [13871]

Plee-Zing Inc., 1640 Pleasant Rd., Glenview, IL 60025, (847)998-0200 [12181]

Plezall Wipers Inc., 9869 NW 79th Ave., Hialeah Gardens, FL 33016, (305)556-3744 [26179]

PLM Transportation Equipment Corp., 1 Market Plz., Ste. 800, Steuart Twr., San Francisco, CA 94105-1301, (415)974-1399 [16402]

Ploch Co.; A.J., PO Box 200658, San Antonio, TX 78220-0658, (210)661-2344 [22587]

Plotts Brothers, 462 Main St., PO Box 130, Royersford, PA 19468, (215)948-7220 [23318]

Plough Publishing House, Spring Valley Bruderhof, Rte. 381 N, Farmington, PA 15437-9506, (724)329-1100 [4068]

Plumb Supply Co., PO Box 4558, Des Moines, IA 50306, (515)262-9511 [23319]

Plumbers Supply Co., PO Box 33519, Indianapolis, IN 46203, (317)783-2981 [23320]

Plumbers Supply Co., PO Box 65987, Salt Lake City, UT 84165-0987, (801)261-1144 [23321]

Plumber's Supply Company Inc., 1000 E Main St., Louisville, KY 40206, (502)582-2261 [23322]

Plumbing Distributors Inc., PO Box 1167, Lawrenceville, GA 30046-1167, (404)963-9231 [23323]

Plunkett Optical Inc., PO Box 21, Ft. Smith, AR 72902-0021, (501)783-2001 [19544]

Plunkett Webster Inc., 2 Clinton Pl., New Rochelle, NY 10802-0251, (914)636-8770 [7871]

Plus Corporation of America, 80 Commerce Dr., Allendale, NJ 07401, (201)818-2700 [21217]

Plus Distributors Inc., 210 Airport Rd., Fletcher, NC 28732, (828)684-1992 [12182]

Plus Woman, 85 Laurel Haven Rd., Fairview, NC 28730-9642, (704)628-3562 [5280]

Pluswood Distributors, PO Box 2248, Oshkosh, WI 54903, (920)235-0022 [7872]

PLX Technology Inc., 390 Potrero Ave., Sunnyvale, CA 94086, (408)774-9060 [9214]

Ply-Gem Manufacturing Co., PO Box 189, Gloucester City, NJ 08030-0189, (609)546-0704 [25932]

Plyler Paper Stock Co., 102 Holly Dr., Hartsville, SC 29550-4912, (803)537-2921 [26941]

Plymouth Paper Company Inc., PO Box 188, Holyoke, MA 01041, (413)536-2810 [21885]

Plymouth Rock Associates, 28 Kristin Rd., Plymouth, MA 02360 [6625]

Plywood-Detroit Inc., 13250 Stephens Dr., Warren, MI 48089, (810)755-4100 [7873]

Plywood Discount Center, 1021 Arbor Ln., Glenview, IL 60025-3237, (773)478-2730 [7874]

Plywood Oshkosh Inc., PO Box 2248, Oshkosh, WI 54903, (920)235-0022 [13210]

Plywood Supply Inc., PO Box 82300, Kenmore, WA 98028, (206)485-8585 [7875]

Plywood Tropics USA Inc., 1 SW Columbia St., Portland, OR 97258, (503)222-1622 [7876]

PM AG Products Inc., 17475 Jovanna, Homewood, IL 60430, (708)206-2030 [1135]

PM Marketing, 109 Lake Ave., Ste. 18, Hilton, NY 14468-0613, (716)392-5110 [9215]

PMC of Indiana, PO Box 33803, Indianapolis, IN 46203, (317)353-6209 [21218]

PMC Machinery, Inc., 14600 Keel St., Plymouth, MI 48170-6004, (734)459-3270 [16403]

PMC Specialties Group, 3302 Ingleside Rd., Cleveland, OH 44122, (216)921-3848 [17109]

PMG International Inc., 1011 N Frio St., San Antonio, TX 78207, (210)226-6820 [4069]

PMH Associates, 9945 Wild Grape Dr., San Diego, CA 92131, (619)695-3878 [16404]

PMI-Eisenhart, 500 Waters Edge, Lombard, IL 60148, (630)620-7600 [12183]

PMI-Eisenhart St. Louis Div., 3171 Riverport Tech. Ct. Dr., Maryland Heights, MO 63043, (314)991-3992 [10321]

PMI-Eisenhart, St. Louis Div., 10430 Baur Blvd., St. Louis, MO 63132, (314)991-3992 [12184]

PMI-Eisenhart Wisconsin Div., PO Box 0948, Waukesha, WI 53187, (414)523-0300 [12185]

PMI Sales and Marketing Services Inc., 8967 Market St., Houston, TX 77029, (713)674-8735 [23324]

PML Inc., PO Box 570, Wilsonville, OR 97070, (503)570-2500 [19545]

PML Microbiologicals Inc., PO Box 570, Wilsonville, OR 97070, (503)570-2500 [19546]

PMX Industries Inc., 5300 Willow Creek Dr., Cedar Rapids, IA 52404-4303, (319)368-7700 [20286]

PNB Trading, Inc., 100 Stuyvesant Rd., Pittsford, NY 14534, (716)383-8149 [16405]

Pneumatic and Electric Equipment Co., 501 Garfield Ave., West Chester, PA 19380, (610)692-9270 [7877]

Pneumatrek, Inc., 3066 South 300 West, PO Box 15601, Salt Lake City, UT 84115, (801)486-2178 [16406]

PNR International Ltd., 1435 Joyce Ave., Palatine, IL 60067-5725, (847)934-1705 [16407]

Poag Grain Inc., PO Box 2037, Chickasha, OK 73023, (405)224-6350 [1136]

Pocahontas Foods USA Inc., PO Box 9729, Richmond, VA 23228, (804)262-8614 [12186]

Pocahontas Press Inc., PO Box F, Blacksburg, VA 24063-1020, (540)951-0467 [4070]

Pocahontas Welding Supply Co., 1319 Norfolk Ave., Ste., Roanoke, VA 24013, (540)344-0934 [16408]

Pocket Pool & Patio, 6220 Belleau Wood Ln., Sacramento, CA 95822-5922, (916)429-7145 [23887]

Poclain Hydraulics Inc., PO Box 801, Sturtevant, WI 53177, (262)554-6566 [16409]

Podell Industries Inc., 1930 E 65th St., Los Angeles, CA 90001, (213)955-2550 [5281]

Podgor Co. Inc.; Joseph E., 7055 Central Hwy., Pennsauken, NJ 08109-4699, (609)663-7878 [16410]

Poe Corp., 556 Perry Ave., Greenville, SC 29611-4852, (864)271-9000 [13872]

Pohang Steel America Corp., 2530 Arnold, No. 170, Martinez, CA 94553, (510)228-9720 [20287]

Pohle NV Center Inc., 9922 W Santa Fe Dr., Sun City, AZ 85351, (602)974-5859 [23888]

Pohlman Farms; Henry G., Henry St., Malinta, OH 43535, (419)256-7282 [18172]

Point Business Machines Inc., 1728 St. Claire Ave., Cleveland, OH 44114, (216)579-1300 [21195]

Point of Sale System Services Inc., 40 Jytek Dr., Leominster, MA 01453, (978)534-4445 [6626]

Point Sporting Goods Inc., 2925 Welsby Ave., Stevens Point, WI 54481, (715)344-4620 [23889]

Point Spring Co., 7307 Grand Ave., Pittsburgh, PA 15225-1043, (412)264-3152 [3100]

Pola Foods Inc., 2303 W Cermak, Chicago, IL 60608-3896, (773)254-1700 [12187]

Pola U.S.A. Inc., 251 E Victoria St., Carson, CA 90746, (310)527-9696 [14191]

Polar Electro Inc., 370 Crossways Park Dr., Woodbury, NY 11797-2050, (516)364-0400 [18990]

Polar Electro Inc., 370 Crossways Park Dr., Woodbury, NY 11797, (516)364-0400 [19547]

Polar Refrigeration & Restaurant Equipment, 6446 Homer Dr., Anchorage, AK 99518-1957, (907)349-3500 [14639]

Polar Supply Company Inc., 300 E 54th Ave., Anchorage, AK 99518-1230, (907)563-5000 [21542]

Polep Distribution Services Inc.; J., 705 Meadow St., Chicopee, MA 01013, (413)592-4141 [26342]

Polfus Implement Inc., 730 Deere Dr., New Richmond, WI 54017, (715)246-6565 [1137]

Polishers & Jewelers Supply Inc., PO Box 3448, Providence, RI 02909-0448, (401)454-2888 [17549]

Polk County Farmers Cooperative, PO Box 47, Rickreall, OR 97371, (503)623-2363 [1138]

Polk County Fertilizer Co., PO Box 366, Haines City, FL 33845, (941)422-1186 [1139]

Poll Electric Co.; H., 216 N Saint Clair St., Toledo, OH 43603, (419)255-1660 [9216]

Pollack Enterprises Inc.; Morton, 6500 Flotilla St., Los Angeles, CA 90040, (213)721-8832 [15275]

Pollack L.L.C.; J.O., 1700 W Irving Park Rd., Chicago, IL 60613-2559, (773)477-2100 [17550]

Pollard Co.; C.E., 13575 Auburn, Detroit, MI 48223, (313)837-6776 [20706]

Pollard Co.; C.E., 13575 Auburn, Detroit, MI 48223, (313)837-6776 [3101]

Pollard Company Inc.; Joseph G., 200 Atlantic Ave., New Hyde Park, NY 11040, (516)746-0842 [20288]

Pollard-Swain Inc., 218 E Meats Ave., Orange, CA 92856, (714)637-1531 [22588]

Pollock Corp.; Industrial Hwy., S Keim St., Pottstown, PA 19464, (610)323-5500 [26942]

Pollock Paper Distributors, PO Box 660005, Dallas, TX 75266-0005, (214)263-2126 [21886]

Pollock; Ralph, 12310 W Stark St., Portland, OR 97229, (503)644-8954 [12188]

Pollock Steel Corp.; Mayer, Industrial Hwy., S Keim St., Pottstown, PA 19464, (610)323-5500 [26943]

Polly-O Dairy, 856 64th St., Brooklyn, NY 11220, (718)361-9420 [12189]

Polo Ralph Lauren Corp., 650 Madison Ave., New York, NY 10022, (212)318-7000 [5282]

Polo-Ray Sunglass, Inc., 7596 Harwin Dr., Houston, TX 77036-1817, (713)975-8252 [19548]

Polson's Rock Shop, 2461 S Holmes Ave., Idaho Falls, ID 83404-6971, (208)529-8184 [17551]

Poly Processing Co., PO Box 4150, Monroe, LA 71211, (318)343-7565 [25933]

Polycoat Systems Inc., 5 Depot St., Hudson Falls, NY 12839, (518)747-0654 [7878]

Polyconcept USA, Inc., 69 Jefferson St., Stamford, CT 06902-4506, (203)358-8100 [9217]

Polycrystal Book Service, PO Box 3439, Dayton, OH 45401, (937)233-9070 [4071]

Polymer Plastics Corp., 645 National Ave., Mountain View, CA 94043, (650)968-2212 [23014]

Polyphase Corp., 16885 Dallas Pkwy., Ste. 400, Dallas, TX 75248, (972)732-0010 [1140]

Polysciences Inc., 400 Valley Rd., Warrington, PA 18976, (215)343-6484 [4481]

Polytag Paper, 2614 Pacific Hwy. E, Tacoma, WA 98424-1017, (253)922-5000 [21701]

Pomeco Corp., 2119 Wheeler, Ft. Smith, AR 72901, (501)785-1439 [14640]

Pomerantz Diversified Services Inc., PO Box 1284, Des Moines, IA 50305, (515)243-3156 [21887]

Pomeroy Grain Growers Inc., PO Box 220, Pomeroy, WA 99347, (509)843-1694 [18173]

Pomona Valley News Agency Inc., 10736 Fremont Ave., Ontario, CA 91762-3909, (909)591-3885 [4072]

Pompeian Inc., 4201 Pulaski Hwy., Baltimore, MD 21224, (410)276-6900 [12190]

Pomps Tire Service Inc., 1123 Cedar St., Green Bay, WI 54301, (920)435-8301 [3102]

Pond Brothers Peanut Company Inc., PO Box 1370, Suffolk, VA 23439-1370, (757)539-2356 [12191]

Pond International Inc., 1559 Hidden Valley Rd., Sandy, UT 84092-5724, (801)571-4365 [18174]

Ponderosa Paint Stores, 3040 West 3500 South, West Valley City, UT 84119, (801)966-1491 [21543]

Pontiac Livestock Sales, Rte. 116 E, Pontiac, IL 61764, (815)844-6951 [18175]

Ponto Associates; , 12816 NE 125th Way, Kirkland, WA 98034, (425)821-2996 [9218]

Pool Doctor, 101 E Linden, Burbank, CA 91502, (818)841-6161 [23890]

Pool Fact, Inc., PO Box 816639, Hollywood, FL 33081-0639 [23891]

Pool Water Products, 2334 Havenhurst, Dallas, TX 75234, (972)243-6006 [23892]

Pool Water Products, 17872 Mitchell Ave., Ste. 250, Irvine, CA 92614, (949)756-1666 [23893]

Pool Water Products, 12849 Windfern, Houston, TX 77064, (281)894-7071 [23894]

Poole Equipment Co.; Gregory, 4807 Beryl Rd., Raleigh, NC 27606, (919)828-0641 [7879]

Poolmaster Inc., 770 W Del Paso Rd., Sacramento, CA 95834, (916)567-9800 [23895]

Poore Brothers Distributing Inc., 3500 S Lacometa, Goodyear, AZ 85338, (602)925-0731 [12192]

Poore Brothers Inc., 3500 S Lacometa, Goodyear, AZ 85338, (602)925-0731 [12193]

Poorman-Douglas Corp., 10300 SW Allen Blvd., Beaverton, OR 97005, (503)350-5800 [6627]

Pope Distributing Co., PO Box 979, Coats, NC 27521, (919)897-6171 [5283]

Popes Parts Inc., PO Drawer 740, Thibodaux, LA 70302, (504)446-8485 [3103]

Poppers Supply Co., 340 SE 7th Ave., Portland, OR 97214, (503)239-3792 [12194]

Pop's E-Z Popcorn & Supply Co., 17151 SE Petrovitsky Rd., Renton, WA 98058-9610, (425)255-4545 [24204]

Poritzky's Wholesale Meats and Food Services, 6 John Walsh Blvd., Peekskill, NY 10566, (914)737-2154 [12195]

Pork Packers International, PO Box 158, Downs, KS 67437, (785)454-3396 [12196]

Port Cargo Service Inc., 5200 Coffee Dr., New Orleans, LA 70115, (504)891-9494 [12197]

Port Electric Supply Corp., 248-264 3rd St., Elizabeth, NJ 07206, (908)355-1900 [9219]

Port Everglades Steel Corp., PO Box 5768, Ft. Lauderdale, FL 33310, (954)942-9400 [20289]

Port Huron Electric Motor, 321 Court St., Port Huron, MI 48060, (810)985-7197 [9220]

Port Plastics Inc., 16750 Chestnut St., La Puente, CA 91747, (626)333-7678 [23015]

Port Stockton Food Distributors Inc., PO Box 30, Stockton, CA 95201, (209)948-1814 [12505]

Port Supply, 500 Westridge Dr., Watsonville, CA 95076, (831)728-4417 [18584]

Porta-Bote International, 1074 Independence Ave., Mountain View, CA 94043, (650)961-5334 [18585]

Porta-Lung Inc., 7854 Logan St., Denver, CO 80229-5810, (303)288-7575 [14641]

Porteous Fastener Co., 22795 S Utility, Carson, CA 90745, (310)549-9180 [13873]

Porter Cable, 3949 E Guasti Rd., Apt. A, Ontario, CA 91761-1549, (626)333-3566 [13874]

Porter Distributing Co., PO Box 187, Mitchell, SD 57301-0187, (605)996-7465 [1962]

Porter Office Machine Corp., PO Box 119, North Conway, NH 03860-0119, (603)356-2222 [21219]

Porter Oil Company Inc., 306 S Motel Blvd., Las Cruces, NM 88005, (505)524-8666 [22589]

Portland Bottling Co., 1321 NE Couch St., Portland, OR 97232, (503)230-7777 [12198]

Portland Distributing Co., PO Box 2812, Kirkland, WA 98083-2812 [1963]

Portland Merchandise Corp., 350 W 31st St., 4th Fl., New York, NY 10001, (212)239-8650 [5284]

Portland News Co., 10 Southgate Rd., Scarborough, ME 04074, (207)883-1300 [4073]

Portland Optical Company Inc., 2041 E Burnside St., Gresham, OR 97030, (503)667-2303 [19331]

Portland State University, School of Extended Studies, Continuing Education Press, PO Box 1394, Portland, OR 97207-1394, (503)725-4891 [4074]

Portman Hobby Distributors, 851 Washington St., Peekskill, NY 10566, (914)737-6633 [26619]

Portmeirion USA, 91 Great Hill Rd., Naugatuck, CT 06770, (203)723-1471 [15621]

Portolano Products Inc., 32 W 39th St., New York, NY 10018, (212)719-4403 [5285]

Portsmouth Paper Co., PO Box 600, Portsmouth, NH 03802-0600, (603)436-1910 [4688]

Pos-A-Traction Inc., 2400 S Wilmington Ave., Compton, CA 90224-8010, (310)637-8600 [3104]

POS Systems Company Inc., 10027 S 51st St., Ste. 102, Phoenix, AZ 85044, (480)598-8000 [6628]

Poseidon Adventure Inc., 3301 Lancaster Pike, Ste. 5A, Wilmington, DE 19805-1436, (302)656-2326 [23896]

Posey County Farm Bureau Cooperative Association Inc., PO Box 565, Mt. Vernon, IN 47620, (812)838-4468 [1141]

POSitive Software Co., 2600 N Columbia Center Blvd., Richland, WA 99352, (509)735-9194 [6629]

Posner Sons Inc.; S., 950 3rd Ave., New York, NY 10022, (212)486-1360 [21888]

Post Familie Vineyards and Winery, Rte. 1, Box 1, Altus, AR 72821, (501)468-2741 [1964]

Post Marine, 65 River St., New Rochelle, NY 10801, (914)235-9800 [18586]

Post Yacht Supplies, PO Box 571, Manasquan, NJ 08736-0571, (732)892-2214 [18587]

Postalia Inc., 1980 University Ln., Lisle, IL 60532-2152, (708)241-9090 [21220]

Postema Sales Co. Inc., 3396 Chicago Dr. SW, Grandville, MI 49418-1086, (616)532-6181 [15276]

Posters Please Inc., 37 Riverside Dr., New York, NY 10023, (212)787-4000 [13424]

Postville Farmers Cooperative, PO Box 520, Postville, IA 52162, (319)864-7234 [1142]

Potash Import and Chemical Corp., 201 E 42nd St., New York, NY 10017, (212)697-4994 [4482]

Potential Industries Inc., 922 E E St., Wilmington, CA 90744, (310)549-5901 [26944]

Potomac Adventist Book Center, 12004 Cherry Hill Rd., Silver Spring, MD 20904-1985, (301)572-0700 [4075]

Potomac Adventist Book Center, 8400 Carroll Ave., Takoma Park, MD 20912, (301)439-3547 [4076]

Potomac Industrial Trucks Inc., 800 Ritchie Rd., Capitol Heights, MD 20743, (301)336-1700 [16411]

Potomac Rubber Company Inc., 9011 Hampton Overlook, Capitol Heights, MD 20743, (301)336-7400 [24289]

Potomac Steel and Supply Inc., 7801 Loisdale Rd., Springfield, VA 22150, (703)550-7300 [20290]

Potter Distributing Inc., 4037 Roger B. Chaffee, Grand Rapids, MI 49548, (616)531-6860 [14642]

Potter Distributing Inc., 4037 Roger B. Chaffee, Grand Rapids, MI 49548, (616)531-6860 [15277]

Potter-Roemer, 3100 S Susan St., Santa Ana, CA 92704, (714)430-5300 [24614]

Potter-Webster Co., 130 SE 7th Ave., Portland, OR 97214, (503)232-8146 [3105]

Pottery Art Studio Inc., 4510 Killam Ave., Norfolk, VA 23508-2047, (757)489-7417 [25788]

Pottery Manufacturing and Distributing Inc., 18881 S Hoover St., Gardena, CA 90248-4284, (310)323-7754 [13425]

Pottery Manufacturing and Distributing Inc., 18881 S Hoover St., Gardena, CA 90248-4284, (310)323-7754 [15622]

Pottstown Truck Sales Inc., 1402 W High St., Pottstown, PA 19464, (215)323-8100 [20707]

Poultry Health, PO Box 40028, Jacksonville, FL 32203 [27215]

Poultry Specialties Inc., PO Box 2061, Russellville, AR 72811, (501)968-1777 [12199]

Pound International Corp., 1221 Brickell, No. 1480, Miami, FL 33131, (305)530-8702 [14192]

Pounds Motor Company Inc., PO Box 770248, Winter Garden, FL 34777, (407)656-1352 [1143]

Pow Wow Indian Jewelry, 1821 W Hwy. 66 Ave., Gallup, NM 87301-6805, (505)863-4426 [17552]

Powell Co./Generations for the 21st Century; L., PO Box 1408, Culver City, CA 90232-1408, (310)204-2224 [13211]

Powell Company Inc.; W.J., PO Box 1308, Thomasville, GA 31799, (912)226-4331 [12200]

Powell Co.; L., PO Box 1408, Culver City, CA 90232-1408, (310)204-2224 [15623]

Powell Distributing Company Inc., PO Box 17160, Portland, OR 97217-0160, (503)289-5558 [22590]

Powell Electronics Inc., PO Box 8765, Philadelphia, PA 19101, (215)365-1900 [9221]

Powell Tool Supply Inc., PO Box 1854, South Bend, IN 46634-6709, (219)289-4811 [16412]

Powell Wholesale Lumber Co., PO Box 65, Waynesville, NC 28786, (704)926-0848 [7880]

Power Chemical Company Inc., 375 Rider Ave., Bronx, NY 10451, (212)292-4320 [4483]

Power Drive & Equipment, 3333 Locust St., St. Louis, MO 63103, (314)533-3401 [3106]

Power Drive, Inc., 4401 W Esthner, Wichita, KS 67209, (316)942-4227 [3107]

Power Drives and Bearings Div., 801 S 20th St., Omaha, NE 68108, (402)344-7323 [16413]

Power Drives, Inc., 8031 Pence Rd., PO Box 25427, Charlotte, NC 28229, (704)568-7480 [3108]

Power Equipment Co., PO Box 20534, Rochester, NY 14602, (716)235-1662 [3109]

Power Equipment Co., PO Box 2311, Knoxville, TN 37901, (615)577-5563 [7881]

Power Equipment Company, 2373 S Kinnickinnic Ave., Milwaukee, WI 53207, (414)744-3210 [15278]

Power Equipment Corp., 1005 E Marshall St., Wytheville, VA 24382, (540)228-7371 [9222]

Power Industries, 926 Kaiser Dr., Napa, CA 94558-6206, (707)252-7333 [3110]

Power Lift Corp., 8314 E Slauson Ave., Pico Rivera, CA 90660, (562)949-1000 [16414]

Power Machine Service, 44 Buck Shoals Rd., No. F3, Arden, NC 28704, (828)684-8044 [9223]

Power Machinery Center, 3450 E Camino Ave., Oxnard, CA 93030, (805)485-0577 [16415]

Power/mation Inc., 1310 Energy Ln., St. Paul, MN 55108, (651)605-3312 [9224]

Power Motive Corp., 5000 Vasquez Blvd., Denver, CO 80216, (303)355-5900 [20708]

Power Plastics Inc., 2031 Karbach, Houston, TX 77092, (713)957-3695 [23016]

Power Products Service, 465 Hwy. 182, Morgan City, LA 70380-5107, (504)395-5224 [22591]

Power Pumps Inc., 2820 Seaboard Ln., Long Beach, CA 90805, (562)531-3333 [16416]

Power & Pumps Inc., 3402 SW 26th Ter., No. B-11, Ft. Lauderdale, FL 33312-5071, (954)563-5627 [3111]

Power & Pumps, Inc., 400 Pittman St., PO Box 2153, Orlando, FL 32801, (305)843-7400 [16417]

Power Sewing, 95 5th Ave., San Francisco, CA 94118, (415)386-0440 [4077]

Power Solutions, PO Box 877489, Wasilla, AK 99687, (907)229-0567 [9225]

Power-Sonic Corp., PO Box 5242, Redwood City, CA 94063, (650)364-5001 [9226]

Power Supply Inc., PO Box 1989, Houston, TX 77251, (713)674-3700 [9227]

Power & Telephone Supply Company Inc., 8017 Pinemont, Ste. 200, Houston, TX 77040-6519, (713)462-6447 [5712]

Power and Telephone Supply Company Inc., 2673 Yale Ave., Memphis, TN 38112, (901)324-6116 [5713]

Power & Telephone Supply Company Inc., 3107 SW 61st St., Des Moines, IA 50321, (515)244-4375 [5714]

Power & Telephone Supply Company, Inc., 1645 North Pkwy., Jackson, TN 38301, (901)423-0071 [9228]

Power & Telephone Supply Company, Inc., 3414 Henson Rd., Knoxville, TN 37921, (423)588-7570 [9229]

Power & Telephone Supply Company, Inc., 2950 Greensboro St. Extension, Lexington, NC 27292, (704)249-0256 [5715]

Power & Telephone Supply Company, Inc., 3412 Ambrose Ave., Nashville, TN 37207, (615)226-0321 [5716]

Power & Telephone Supply Company, Inc., 987 Ehlers Rd., Neenah, WI 54956, (920)725-5454 [9230]

Power & Telephone Supply Company, Inc., 16666 SW 72nd, Bldg. 12, Portland, OR 97224, (503)620-4909 [5717]

Power & Telephone Supply Company, Inc., Rte. 272, Reamstown, PA 17567, (717)336-4991 [5718]

Power Tool & Machinery, 2506 S Orchard St., Boise, ID 83705-3799, (208)336-1551 [16418]

Power Torque, 1741 Rudder Industrial Park Dr., Fenton, MO 63026, (314)343-2250 [3112]

PowerData Corp., 500 108th Ave. NE, Bellevue, WA 98004, (425)637-9960 [6630]

Powerline Oil Co., PO Box 2108, Santa Fe Springs, CA 90670-9883, (562)944-6111 [22119]

Powerline Publishing Co., 3600-K S Congress Ave., Boynton Beach, FL 33426, (561)732-8111 [3499]

Powers Candy Company Inc., PO Box 4338, Pocatello, ID 83205-4338, (208)237-3311 [12201]

Powers Candy & Nut Co., 6061 N Freya, Spokane, WA 99207-4910, (509)489-1955 [12202]

Powers Distributing Company Inc., 3700 Giddings Rd., Lake Orion, MI 48359-1306, (248)393-3700 [1965]

Powers Products Co., 1003 E Lincolnway St., Cheyenne, WY 82001, (307)632-5521 [7882]

PowerSolutions for Business, 1920 S Broadway, St. Louis, MO 63104, (314)421-0670 [6631]

Powertron Battery Co., 2218 W 2nd St., Santa Ana, CA 92703, (714)543-4858 [3113]

Powertronics Inc., 7171 Commorse Cir. W, PO Box 32065, Minneapolis, MN 55432-0065, (763)571-2325 [9231]

Powmet Inc., 2625 Sewell St., Rockford, IL 61109, (815)398-6900 [26945]

Powr-Lite Electric Supplies, 1333 Magnolia Ave., Bowling Green, KY 42104-3050, (502)842-1694 [9232]

Pozzi-Ginori Corporation of America, 41 Madison Ave., 6th Fl., New York, NY 10010, (212)213-6884 [15635]

Pozzolanic Northwest Inc., 7525 SE 24th St., Ste. 630, Mercer Island, WA 98040, (206)232-9320 [7883]

PPG Industries, Inc., 500 Oakridge Turnpike, Oak Ridge, TN 37830, (423)483-3524 [21544]

PPI Del Monte Tropical Fruit Co., 800 Douglas Rd., Coral Gables, FL 33134, (305)520-8400 [12203]

Practical Computer Inc., 1200 Mohawk Blvd., Springfield, OR 97477-3349, (541)726-7775 [6632]

Practical Cookbooks, 145 Malcolm Ave. SE, Minneapolis, MN 55414, (612)378-9697 [4078]

Prairie Belle Clothing Exports, 5243 Horton, Mission, KS 66202, (913)722-0732 [5286]

Prairie Farms Dairy Inc. Fort Wayne Div., PO Box 10419, Ft. Wayne, IN 46852, (219)483-6436 [12204]

Prairie Farms Dairy Inc. Ice Cream Specialties Div., PO Box 19766, St. Louis, MO 63144, (314)631-8171 [12205]

Prairie Farms Dairy Supply Inc., 1800 Adams St., Granite City, IL 62040, (618)451-5600 [24205]

Prairie Land Cooperative, PO Box 99, Windom, MN 56101, (507)831-2527 [1144]

Prairie Land Cooperative, PO Box 67, Jeffers, MN 56145-0067, (507)628-5566 [1145]

Prairie Land Cooperative Co., PO Box 309, Hubbard, IA 50122, (515)864-2266 [1146]

Prairie Livestock L.L.C., Barton Ferry Rd., West Point, MS 39773, (601)494-5651 [18176]

Prairie Tool Co., 110 Prairie Tool Dr., Prairie du Chien, WI 53821-2027, (608)326-6111 [16419]

Prasek's Hillje Smokehouse, Rte. 3, Box 18, El Campo, TX 77437, (409)543-8312 [12206]

Prassel Lumber Company Inc., PO Box 8549, Jackson, MS 39284, (601)922-0130 [7884]

Pratt Audio Visual and Video, 200 3rd Ave., SW, Cedar Rapids, IA 52404-5717, (319)363-8144 [9233]

Pratt Co.; Emery, 1966 W Main St., Owosso, MI 48867-1397, (517)723-5291 [4079]

Pratt & Co.; L.F., 117 Huxley Rd. No. D, Knoxville, TN 37922-3113, (423)522-0100 [6633]

Pratt & Dudley Building Materials, 1002 University Pl., Augusta, GA 30903, (706)724-7755 [7885]

Pratt Medical Inc., 404 N 4th, Olathe, CO 81425, (970)323-5616 [5287]

Prawn Seafoods Inc., 6851 NW 32nd Ave., Miami, FL 33147-6656, (305)691-2435 [12207]

Praxah Gas Tech Inc., 12000 Roosevelt Rd., Hillside, IL 60162, (708)449-9300 [22592]

Praxair Distribution, Inc., 4030 W Lincoln St., Phoenix, AZ 85009-5398, (602)269-2151 [16420]

Praxair Distribution/W. Div., 767 Industrial Rd., San Carlos, CA 94070, (650)592-7304 [16421]

Praxair Gas Tech, 12000 Roosevelt Rd., Hillside, IL 60162, (708)449-9300 [17110]

PRC-DeSoto International Inc. Semco Application Systems, PO Box 1800, Glendale, CA 91209, (818)247-7140 [4484]

Precept Business Products Inc., 1050 Northfield Ct., Ste. 400, Roswell, GA 30076, (404)410-4080 [21221]

Precise Industries, Inc., PO Box 10, Ardara, PA 15615-0010, (412)864-3900 [21222]

Precise International/Wenger, 15 Corporate Dr., Orangeburg, NY 10962, (914)365-3500 [24042]

Precision Aluminum and Sawing Service Inc., PO Box 2278, Huntington Park, CA 90255, (213)583-0021 [20291]

Precision Bearing, 1144 27th Ave. SW, Cedar Rapids, IA 52404, (319)365-5276 [17111]

Precision Bearing Co., 2050 Delaware, Des Moines, IA 50317, (515)265-9811 [3114]

Precision Bearing Co., 1919 Cornhusker Hwy., Lincoln, NE 68521-1878, (402)474-7700 [17112]

Precision Bearing Co., 2503 S 13th St., Norfolk, NE 68701, (402)371-6777 [17113]

Precision Built Parts, 1819 Troost Ave., Kansas City, MO 64108, (816)471-1552 [3115]

Precision Door Hardware, 223 Basalt, PO Box 1836, Idaho Falls, ID 83403-1836, (208)523-8600 [13774]

Precision Fitting & Gauge Co., 1001 Enterprise Ave., Ste. 14, Oklahoma City, OK 73128, (405)943-4786 [23325]

Precision Fitting & Gauge Co., 1214 S Joplin, Tulsa, OK 74112, (918)834-5011 [23326]

Precision Industrial Distributors Inc., 5151 Oceanus Dr., Huntington Beach, CA 92649, (714)379-1380 [17114]

Precision Industries, 909 Broadway, West Burlington, IA 52655, (319)753-6233 [16422]

Precision Industries Inc., 4611 S 96th St., Omaha, NE 68127, (402)593-7000 [3116]

Precision Instruments Inc., 801 S Rancho Dr., Ste. 3B, Las Vegas, NV 89106-3860, (702)382-8899 [18991]

Precision Metals Inc., 5265 N 124th St., Milwaukee, WI 53225, (414)781-3240 [20292]

Precision Optical Co., PO Box 280423, East Hartford, CT 06128-0423, (860)289-6023 [19549]

Precision Optical Laboratory, PO Box 68, Gallaway, TN 38036-0068, (901)867-2991 [19550]

Precision Propeller Service Inc., 4777 Aeronca St., Boise, ID 83705-5055, (208)344-5161 [138]

Precision Speed Instruments Inc., PO Box 27400, Phoenix, AZ 85061, (602)973-1055 [17115]

Precision Sports Surfaces Inc., PO Box 55, Charlottesville, VA 22902-0055, (804)971-9628 [23897]

Precision Steel Warehouse Inc., 3500 N Wolf Rd., Franklin Park, IL 60131, (847)455-7000 [20293]

Precision Technology Inc. (Norwood, New Jersey), 50 Maple St., Norwood, NJ 07648, (201)767-1600 [18992]

Precision Tool and Supply, 7510 Lawndale, Houston, TX 77012, (713)923-9381 [16423]

Precision Type Inc., 47 Mall Dr., Commack, NY 11725-5717, (516)864-0167 [6634]

Predot Company Inc., 3923 Euphrosine, New Orleans, LA 70125-1308, (504)822-2952 [5288]

Preferred Brokerage Co., 3627 Mattox, No. 4, El Paso, TX 79925-3629, (915)772-8559 [12208]

Preferred Brokerage Co., 1131 University Blvd. NE, Ste. H, Albuquerque, NM 87102-1701, (505)842-5996 [12209]

Preferred Carpets, 2600 Lakeland Rd., Dalton, GA 30721-4907, (706)277-2732 [10106]

Preferred Distributors Inc., PO Box 458, Tewksbury, MA 01876-0458, (978)851-9900 [26620]

Preferred Meats Inc., PO Box 565854, Dallas, TX 75356, (214)565-0243 [12210]

Preferred Products Inc., PO Box 59294, Minneapolis, MN 55459-0294, (612)448-5252 [12211]

Preferred Products Inc., 11095 Viking Dr., Eden Prairie, MN 55344-7223, (612)996-7400 [12212]

Preiser Scientific, 94 Oliver St., PO Box 1330, St. Albans, WV 25177-1330, (304)727-2902 [24419]

Premier Beverage, PO Box 592248, Orlando, FL 32859, (407)240-4631 [1966]

Premier Beverage, PO Box 1630, Pensacola, FL 32597, (850)433-3151 [1967]

Premier Beverage, 8221 Eagle Palm Dr., Riverview, FL 33569-8893, (813)623-6161 [1968]

Premier Cooperative, PO Box 230, Mt. Horeb, WI 53572, (608)437-5536 [1147]

Premier Distributors, 2600 Prairie Rd., Eugene, OR 97402-9747, (541)688-6161 [1969]

Premier Farnell Corp., PO Box 94884, Cleveland, OH 44101-4884, (216)391-8300 [9234]

Premier Food Brokerage Inc., 6 Way Rd., Middlefield, CT 06455, (860)349-7040 [12213]

Premier Food Marketing Inc., 6 Way Rd., Middlefield, CT 06455, (860)349-7040 [12213]

The Premier Group, 5200 Lawrence Pl., Hyattsville, MD 20781, (301)277-3888 [26621]

Premier Inc. (Greenwich, Connecticut), Greenwich Office Park One, Greenwich, CT 06831, (203)622-5800 [14193]

Premier Industrial Corp., PO Box 94884, Cleveland, OH 44101, (216)391-8300 [3117]

Premier Manufactured Systems, 17431 N 25th Ave., Phoenix, AZ 85023, (623)931-1977 [25789]

Premier Manufactured Systems, 17431 N 25th Ave., Phoenix, AZ 85023, (602)931-1977 [23327]

Premier Medical Supplies Inc., 4566 Emery Indstl Pkwy, Cleveland, OH 44128-5702, (216)831-2777 [18993]

Premiere AVD Corp., 274 Jamie Ln., Wauconda, IL 60084, (847)526-1800 [25388]

Premium Beverage Company Inc., 922 N Railroad St., Opelika, AL 36801, (205)745-4521 [1970]

Premium Cigars International Ltd., 15651 N 77th St., Scottsdale, AZ 85260, (602)922-8887 [26343]

The Premium Connection, 6165 S Pecos, Las Vegas, NV 89120, (702)434-6900 [15624]

Premium Distributors Incorporated of Washington, D.C. L.L.C., 3350 New York Ave. NE, Washington, DC 20002, (202)526-3900 [1971]

Premium Oil Co., 2005 S 300 W, Salt Lake City, UT 84115, (801)487-4721 [22593]

Prenssas Int'l Steel, 5208 24th Ave., Tampa, FL 33619, (813)626-6005 [20063]

Prentiss Manufacturing Company Inc., PO Box 360, Booneville, MS 38829, (601)728-4446 [5289]

Prentke Romich Co., 1022 Heyl Rd., Wooster, OH 44691, (330)262-1984 [5719]

PrePeeled Potato Co., 1585 S Union, Stockton, CA 95206-2269, (209)469-6911 [12214]

Prepress Supply, 18433 Amistad St., Fountain Valley, CA 92708, (714)965-9542 [22892]

Presbyterian & Reformed Publishing Co., 1102 Marble Hill Rd., PO Box 817, Phillipsburg, NJ 08865, (908)454-0505 [4080]

Prescott Inc.; Everett J., 191 Central St., Gardiner, ME 04345, (207)582-1851 [23328]

Prescotts Inc., PO Box 609, Monument, CO 80132-0609, (719)481-3353 [18994]

Preservative Paint Company Inc., 5410 Airport Way S, Seattle, WA 98108, (206)763-0300 [21545]

President Baking Co., Inc., 933 Louise Ave., Charlotte, NC 28204, (704)334-7611 [11958]

President Baking Co., Inc., PO Box 218, North Little Rock, AR 72115, (501)372-2123 [12215]

President Global Corp., 6965 Aragon Cir., Buena Park, CA 90620, (714)994-2990 [12216]

Presidio Press Inc., 505B San Marin Dr., Novato, CA 94945-1340, (415)898-1081 [4081]

Presser Co.; Theodore, Presser Pl., Bryn Mawr, PA 19010, (610)525-3636 [4082]

Pressotechnik Ltd., 4250 Weaver Pkwy., Warrenville, IL 60555-3924, (630)543-4400 [16424]

Pressure Service Inc., 2361 S Plaza Dr., Rapid City, SD 57702, (605)341-5154 [4689]

Prestige Marble & Tile Co., 22 E Merrick Rd., Freeport, NY 11520, (516)223-4100 [10107]

Prestige Packaging Inc., 6190 Regency Pkwy No. 312, Norcross, GA 30071-2345, (404)448-1422 [23017]

Presto Paper Company Inc., 292 5th Ave., No. 501, New York, NY 10001-4513, (212)243-3350 [21889]

Preston Corp.; J.A., PO Box 89, Jackson, MI 49204-0089, (517)787-1600 [18995]

Preston Fuels; John, PO Box 369, Ossipee, NH 03864-0369, (603)539-2807 [15279]

Preston Leather Products, 44 Mitchell Rd., PO Box 594, Ipswich, MA 01938-0594, (978)356-5701 [18421]

Preston Premium Wines, 502 E Vineyard Dr., Pasco, WA 99301, (509)545-1990 [1972]

Preventive Electrical Maintenance Co., PO Box 517, Marrero, LA 70073-0517, (504)341-3816 [9235]

Prewitt Cattle Co., 815 3rd St. Ne, Sidney, MT 59270-4717, (406)482-5251 [18177]

PRI Automation Inc., 1250 S Clearview Ave Ste 104, Mesa, AZ 85208, (480)807-4747 [9236]

Price Brothers Equipment Co., PO Box 3207, Wichita, KS 67201-3207, (316)265-9577 [1148]

Price/Costco Inc., 999 Lake Dr., Issaquah, WA 98027, (425)313-8100 [10851]

Price Direct Sales; Don, PO Box 751, Elizabethton, TN 37644-0751, (423)283-0109 [5290]

Price Engineering Company, Inc., N8 W22577 Johnson Dr., Waukesha, WI 53186, (262)547-2700 [17116]

Price Inc.; Albert E., PO Box 607, Bellmawr, NJ 08031, (609)933-1111 [13426]

Price Milling Co., PO Box 398, Russellville, AR 72801, (501)968-1662 [1149]

Price Modern Inc., 2604 Sisson St., Baltimore, MD 21211, (410)366-5500 [13212]

Price and Pierce International Inc., PO Box 971, Stamford, CT 06904-0971, (203)328-2000 [21890]

Price Stern Sloan Inc., 345 Hudson St., New York, NY 10014, (212)477-6100 [4083]

Price Turf Equipment Inc.; Howard, 18155 Edison Ave., Chesterfield, MO 63005, (314)532-7000 [1150]

Pricing Dynamics, 21 Dale St., Methuen, MA 01844, (978)685-5655 [12217]

Priddy's General Store, PO Box 1215, Sophia, WV 25921, (304)683-3906 [27216]

Pride Chemical, Inc., 224 State St., Ste. 2, Portsmouth, NH 03801-4035, (603)436-7489 [4570]

Priester Supply Company Inc., 701 107th St., Arlington, TX 76011, (817)640-6363 [9237]

Prima International, 3350 Scott Blvd., #7, Santa Clara, CA 95054-3108, (408)727-2600 [6635]

Primark Tool Group, 715 E Gray St., 3rd Fl., Louisville, KY 40212-1615, (502)635-8100 [13875]

Primary Image Inc., PO Box 781207, Orlando, FL 32878-1207, (407)382-7100 [6636]

Primary Industries (USA) Inc., EAB Plz., Uniondale, NY 11556, (516)794-1122 [20294]

Primary Steel, Inc., PO Box 341, Memphis, TN 38101, (901)948-0395 [20347]

Primary Steel Inc., PO Box 1716, Middletown, CT 06457, (860)343-5111 [20295]

Primavera Distributing, 3401 Ambrose Ave., Nashville, TN 37222, (423)899-2997 [10108]

Primavera Distributing, 1312 Chilhowee Ave., Knoxville, TN 37917, (423)899-2997 [10109]

Primax Inc., 10 Fox Hollow Rd., Old Saybrook, CT 06475, (860)399-5293 [6637]

Prime Alliance Inc., 1803 Hull Ave., Des Moines, IA 50309, (515)264-4110 [23018]

Prime Care Medical Supplies Inc., 30-68 Whitestone Expwy, Flushing, NY 11354, (718)353-3311 [18996]

Prime Coatings, 875 West 2600 South, Salt Lake City, UT 84119, (801)972-1436 [21546]

Prime Label Div., 3626 Stern Ave., St. Charles, IL 60174, (630)443-3626 [16425]

Prime Natural Health Laboratories Inc., 910 E Sandhill Ave., Carson, CA 90746-5308, (310)515-5774 [14194]

Prime Poultry Corp., 24 Chesterton St., Boston, MA 02119, (617)442-0707 [12218]

Prime Resources Corp., 1100 Boston Ave., Bridgeport, CT 06610, (203)331-9100 [13427]

Prime Systems, 9888 Bissonet, Houston, TX 77036, (713)270-1586 [6638]

Primeco Inc. Southeast Div., PO Box 36217, Charlotte, NC 28236, (704)348-2600 [13876]

Primeon, 25 Burlington Mall Rd., Burlington, MA 01803-4100, (781)685-2000 [6639]

Primesource, 1650 Magnolia Dr., Cincinnati, OH 45215, (513)563-6700 [25790]

Primesource, 1650 Magnolia Dr., Cincinnati, OH 45215, (513)563-6700 [22893]

PrimeSource Corp., 4350 Haddonfield Rd., No. 222, Pennsauken, NJ 08109, (609)488-4888 [25791]

PrimeSource Inc., 1881 Langley Ave., Irvine, CA 92614-5623, (949)250-2002 [7886]

Primrose Oil Company Inc., PO Box 29665, Dallas, TX 75229, (972)241-1100 [22594]

Primus Electronics Corp., 18424 S I-55 W Frontage Rd., Joliet, IL 60435-9654, (815)436-8945 [5720]

Primus Inc., 3110 Kettering Blvd., Dayton, OH 45439, (937)294-6878 [23329]

Prince Corp., 8351 E County Rd. H, Marshfield, WI 54449, (715)384-3105 [1151]

Prince of Peace Enterprises Inc., 3536 Arden Rd., Hayward, CA 94545, (510)887-1899 [12219]

Prince Street Technologies Ltd., 1450 W Ave., PO Drawer 2530, Cartersville, GA 30120, (770)606-0507 [10110]

Princess House Inc., 470 Miles Standish Blvd., Taunton, MA 02780, (508)823-0713 [15625]

Princeton Book Company Publishers, PO Box 831, Hightstown, NJ 08520, (609)426-0602 [4084]

Princeton Lipids, 1 Research Way, Princeton, NJ 08540, (609)734-8457 [4485]

Pringle Meats Inc., 216 7th St., Oakland, CA 94607-4493, (510)893-7400 [12220]

Prins/Basic Waste Systems Inc., 45 Bunker Hill Rd., Industrial Park, Charlestown, MA 02129, (781)396-1177 [26946]

Prins Grain Co., R.R. 1, Holland, MN 56139, (507)347-3131 [18178]

Prinsburg Farmers Cooperative, PO Box 56, Prinsburg, MN 56281-0056, (320)978-8100 [1152]

Print Gallery Inc., 29203 Northwestern Hwy., Southfield, MI 48034, (248)356-5454 [13428]

The Print Machine Inc., 1003 Laurens Rd., Greenville, SC 29607-1918, (864)271-4770 [6640]

Printed Matter Inc., 77 Wooster St., New York, NY 10012, (212)925-0325 [4085]

Printers Supply of Indiana Inc., PO Box 886, Indianapolis, IN 46206, (317)263-5298 [16426]

Printers Xchange Inc., 2839 Galahad Dr., Atlanta, GA 30345, (404)321-3762 [16427]

Prinz Grain and Feed Inc., PO Box 265, West Point, NE 68788, (402)372-2495 [18179]

Prior Inc.; John, 1600 Stewart Ave., Westbury, NY 11590, (516)683-1020 [3118]

Priority Healthcare Corp., 250 Technology Park, No. 124, Lake Mary, FL 32746-6232, (407)869-7001 [19551]

Priscilla Gold Seal Corp., 25 Charlotte Ave., Hicksville, NY 11801, (718)852-2500 [12221]

Pritchard Paint and Glass Co., PO Box 30547, Charlotte, NC 28230, (704)376-8561 [21547]

Private Eyes, 390 5th Ave., New York, NY 10018-8104, (212)760-2455 [19552]

Private Eyes Sunglasses Shop, 390 5th Ave., New York, NY 10018-8104, (212)760-2455 [19552]

Privilege Auto Parts, 95 Privilege Rd., Woonsocket, RI 02895-0779, (401)766-8456 [3119]

Priz Co., 4032 Transport St., Palo Alto, CA 94303, (650)493-8600 [24420]

PRN Pharmaceutical Services Inc., 8351 W Rockville Rd., Indianapolis, IN 46234, (317)273-1552 [19553]

Pro-Ag Chem Inc., PO Box 579, Chickasha, OK 73023, (405)224-2254 [1153]

Pro AG Farmers Co-op, PO Box 155, Miltona, MN 56354, (218)943-4001 [1154]

Pro Air Inc., 28731 CR-6, Elkhart, IN 46514, (219)264-5494 [14643]

Pro/Am Music Resources, Inc., 63 Prospect St., White Plains, NY 10606, (914)948-7436 [4086]

Pro-Chem Corp., 9536 Ann St., Santa Fe Springs, CA 90670, (562)946-9210 [20296]

Pro-Chem Ltd. Inc., 409 S Schultz Rd., Long Grove, IA 52756, (319)355-6666 [18997]

Pro Cooperative, PO Box 322, Gilmore City, IA 50541, (515)373-6532 [1155]

Pro Ed, 20235 Bahama, Chatsworth, CA 91311, (818)718-6782 [14196]

Pro-Fac Cooperative Inc., PO Box 682, Rochester, NY 14603-0682, (716)383-1850 [12222]

Pro-Flo Products, 30 Commerce Rd., Cedar Grove, NJ 07009, (973)239-2400 [23330]

Pro Form and File, PO Box 1370, Bucksport, ME 04416-1370, (207)469-2401 [21223]

Pro-Line Corp., 2121 Panoramic Cir., Dallas, TX 75212, (214)631-4247 [14195]

Pro-Mark Corp., 10707 Craighead Dr., Houston, TX 77025, (713)666-2525 [25389]

Pro-Mark Corp., 10707 Craighead Dr., Houston, TX 77025, (713)666-2525 [15280]

Pro-Med Supplies Inc., PO Box 201331, Bloomington, MN 55420-6331, (612)884-1518 [18998]

Pro Plastics Inc., 1190 Sylvan St., Linden, NJ 07036, (908)925-5555 [23019]

PRO Sports Products, 2438 W Anderson Ln., Austin, TX 78757, (512)451-7141 [23898]

Pro Systems, Inc., 420 Lake Nepessing, Lapeer, MI 48446, (810)667-0749 [6641]

Pro Systems Inc., 1020 Crews Rd., Ste. L, Matthews, NC 28105, (704)849-0400 [6642]

Pro-Tect Computer Products, PO Box 1002, Centerville, UT 84014-5002, (801)295-7739 [6643]

Pro-Visions Pet Specialty Enterprises Div., Checkerboard Sq., St. Louis, MO 63164, (314)982-1000 [27217]

PROACT, 2600 Garden Rd., No. 410, Monterey, CA 93940, (831)656-1470 [12223]

Probe Technology Corp., 2424 Walsh Ave., Santa Clara, CA 95051, (408)980-1740 [16428]

Probe Technology Inc., 10159 J St., Omaha, NE 68127, (402)593-9800 [6644]

Probst Supply Co., 366 W Center St., Marion, OH 43302, (614)383-6071 [23331]

Process Equipment Inc., 26569 Corporate Ave., Hayward, CA 94545, (510)782-5122 [16429]

Process Supplies & Accessories, Inc., 6700 Baum Drive, Ste. 18, Knoxville, TN 37919, (423)588-0392 [17117]

Processed Plastic Co., 1001 Aucutt Rd., Montgomery, IL 60538, (630)892-7981 [26622]

Processors Equipment & Hardware, 1605 Mono Dr., Modesto, CA 95355, (209)524-1404 [17118]

Procise Corp., PO Box 1011, Issaquah, WA 98027-1011, (425)392-0270 [6645]

ProCoil Corp., 5260 S Haggerty Rd., Canton, MI 48188, (734)397-3700 [20297]

Procon Products, 910 Ridgely Rd., Murfreesboro, TN 37129, (615)890-5710 [16430]

ProCraft, 11422 Grissom, Dallas, TX 75229-2352, (972)247-0677 [22824]

Proctor Co.; Stanley M., 2016 Midway Ave., Twinsburg, OH 44087, (216)425-7814 [16431]

Prodata Computer Marketing Corp., 2333 Western Ave., Seattle, WA 98121-1683, (206)441-4090 [6646]

Prodata Systems Inc., 2333 Western Ave., Seattle, WA 98121, (206)441-4090 [6647]

ProDiesel, 922 Main St., Nashville, TN 37206, (615)227-2242 [3120]

Produce Distributors Co., 1918 Wilson St., Jackson, MS 39202, (601)969-3133 [12224]

Producers Cooperative Association, 1800 N Hwy. 6, Bryan, TX 77806, (409)778-6000 [1156]

Producers Cooperative Association of Girard, PO Box 323, Girard, KS 66743, (316)724-8241 [18180]

Producers Livestock Association, 5909 Cleveland Ave., Columbus, OH 43231, (614)890-6666 [18304]

Producers Livestock Marketing Association, PO Box 540477, North Salt Lake, UT 84054, (801)292-2424 [18181]

Producers Rice Mill Inc., PO Box 461, Stuttgart, AR 72160, (870)673-4444 [12225]

Producers Tape Service-All Media, 395 E Elmwood, Troy, MI 48083, (248)585-8273 [9238]

Producers Tractor Co., 614 E Cypress St., Brinkley, AR 72021, (870)734-2231 [1157]

PRODUCT4, 1 Insurance Center Plz., St. Louis, MO 63141, (314)434-1999 [6648]

Production Arts Lighting Inc., 7777 West Side Ave., North Bergen, NJ 07047, (201)758-4000 [9239]

Production Carbide and Steel, PO Box 987, Warren, MI 48090, (313)755-2240 [20298]

Production Machinery Inc., 9000 Yellow Brick Rd., Baltimore, MD 21237, (410)574-2110 [16432]

Production Services Atlanta Inc., 2000 Lakewood Way Bldg. 4, Atlanta, GA 30315, (404)622-1311 [22894]

Production Supply Co., 4342 Michoud Blvd., New Orleans, LA 70129, (504)254-0505 [20299]

Production Supply Co., 4342 Michoud Blvd., New Orleans, LA 70129, (504)254-0505 [20300]

Production Tool Supply, PO Box 987, Warren, MI 48089, (810)755-7770 [17119]

Production Tool Supply of Jackson, PO Box 963, Jackson, MI 49204-0963, (517)787-5300 [17120]

Products Corp. of North America, Inc., 6726 SW Burlingname Ave., Portland, OR 97219-2126, (503)244-0701 [12226]

Proferas Pizza Bakery Inc., 1130 Moosic St., Scranton, PA 18505, (717)342-4181 [12227]

Professional Auto Parts, 605 S Gallatin, PO Box 3487, Jackson, MS 39207, (601)948-4381 [3036]

Professional Aviation Associates Inc., 4694 Aviation Pkwy., Ste. K, Atlanta, GA 30349, (404)767-0282 [139]

Professional Book Distributors, Inc., 1650 Bluegrass Lake Pkwy., Alpharetta, GA 30004, (770)442-8633 [4087]

Professional Book Service, PO Box 835, Horsham, PA 19044-0835, (215)674-8040 [4088]

Professional Computer Systems, 849 E Greenville Ave., Winchester, IN 47394, (765)584-2288 [6649]

Professional Dental Technologies Inc., 633 Lawrence St., Batesville, AR 72501, (870)698-2300 [19554]

Professional Education & Products Inc., 20235 Bahama, Chatsworth, CA 91311, (818)718-6782 [14196]

Professional Electronics Inc., 3855 Hughes Ave., 2nd Fl., Culver City, CA 90232, (310)287-1400 [6650]

Professional Housewares Distributors Inc., 29309 Clayton Ave., Wickliffe, OH 44092, (440)944-3500 [15272]

Professional Marketers Inc., 500 Waters Edge, Lombard, IL 60148, (630)620-7600 [12228]

Professional Media Service Corp., 19122 S Vermont Ave., Gardena, CA 90248, (310)532-9024 [25390]

Professional Medical Services Inc., 175 Kelsey Ln., Tampa, FL 33619, (813)626-7788 [19555]

Professional Ophthalmic Labs Inc., 3772 Peters Creek Rd. Ext., Roanoke, VA 24005, (540)345-7303 [19556]

Professional Optical, 255 Haywood St., Asheville, NC 28801, (704)252-2172 [19557]

Professional Optical Supply, PO Box 1930, Dallas, TX 75204, (214)826-5610 [19558]

Professional Paint Supply, 5610 Singer Blvd. NE, Albuquerque, NM 87109, (505)344-0000 [21548]

Professional Salon Concepts Inc., 48 Meadow Ave., Joliet, IL 60436, (815)744-3384 [14197]

Professional Salon Services, 16 Stafford Ct., Cranston, RI 02920-4464, (401)463-5353 [14198]

Professional Salon Services, 16 Stafford Ct., Cranston, RI 02920-4464, (401)463-5353 [24206]

Professional Telecommunication Services Inc., 2119 Beechmont Ave., Cincinnati, OH 45230, (513)232-7700 [5721]

Professional's Library, 2763 Townsend Rd., Watkins Glen, NY 14891-9581, (914)724-3000 [4089]

Proficient Food Co., 9408 Richmond Pl., Rancho Cucamonga, CA 91730, (909)484-6100 [24207]

PROFITsystems Inc., 422 E Vermijo Ave., No. 100, Colorado Springs, CO 80903-3702, (719)471-3858 [6651]

Progas Service Inc., PO Box 278, Ft. Madison, IA 52627, (319)372-1062 [22595]

Programart Corp., 124 Mount Auburn St., Cambridge, MA 02138, (617)661-3020 [6652]

Programma Incorporated, 1697 Forestview Dr., Bethel Park, PA 15102-1933 [6653]

Progress Electrical Supply Co., 21750 Coolidge Hwy., Oak Park, MI 48237, (248)541-8300 [9240]

Progressive Companies Inc., PO Box B, Spirit Lake, IA 51360, (712)336-1750 [12229]

Progressive Concepts Inc., 5718 Airport Fwy., Ft. Worth, TX 76117, (817)429-0432 [5722]

Progressive Distributors, PO Box 295, Winthrop, ME 04364, (207)377-2251 [14199]

Progressive Farmers Cooperative, 1221 Grant St., De Pere, WI 54115, (920)336-6449 [1158]

Progressive Marketing, 8026 Vantage, San Antonio, TX 78230-4733, (210)525-9171 [12230]

Progressive Marketing, 2980-A Enterprise St., Brea, CA 92821, (714)528-2072 [9241]

Progressive Produce Co., PO Box 911231, Los Angeles, CA 90091-1231, (323)890-8100 [12231]

Progressive Tire, 3000 35th Ave. N, Birmingham, AL 35207, (205)841-3336 [3121]

Progressive Tire Group, 950 Businesss Park Rd., Wisconsin Dells, MI 53094 [3122]

Progressive Wholesale Supply Co., 2445 Northline Industrial Dr., Maryland Heights, MO 63043-3308, (314)567-5131 [14644]

Projexions Video Supply, 1333 Logan Circle, Atlanta, GA 30318, (404)872-6247 [25391]

Proler International Corp., 4265 San Felipe, No. 900, Houston, TX 77027, (713)675-2281 [26947]

Prolerized Schiabo-Neu Co., 1 Linden Ave., E, Jersey City, NJ 07305, (201)333-3131 [26948]

ProMark, 7625 Hayvenhurst Ave., Unit 28, Van Nuys, CA 91406, (818)904-9390 [9242]

Promatek Medical Systems Inc., 1851 Black Rd., Joliet, IL 60435, (815)725-6766 [18999]

Prometex International Corp., PO Box 42404, Houston, TX 77042, (713)789-6562 [14200]

Promicro Systems, 229 Broadway, Yankton, SD 57078-4211, (605)665-4448 [21224]

Promotional Sales Co., 2301 S Broadway, Los Angeles, CA 90007-2715, (213)749-5015 [26180]

Promotions Plus, 112 N University Dr., Ste. L-126, Fargo, ND 58102, (701)236-7774 [13429]

ProNet Inc., 6340 LBJ Frwy., Dallas, TX 75240-6402, (972)687-2000 [5723]

Propane Equipment Corp., 11 Apple St., Tinton Falls, NJ 07724, (908)747-3795 [22596]

Propane/One Inc., PO Box 38, Oakland City, IN 47660, (812)749-4411 [22597]

Proper Tighe Marine, PO Box 537, Danville, CA 94526-0537 [18588]

Propet USA, Inc., 25612 74th Ave. S, Kent, WA 98032, (253)854-7600 [24836]

ProSource Inc., 1550 San Remo Ave., Miami, FL 33136, (305)740-1000 [24208]

Prospect Energy Inc., PO Box 112, Mt. Sterling, IL 62353, (217)773-3969 [20560]

Prosper Farmers Cooperative Elevator, PO Box 226, Harwood, ND 58042, (701)282-4094 [1159]

Prosper Shevenell and Son Inc., PO Box 667, Dover, NH 03820, (603)742-5636 [24837]

Prosperity & Profits Unlimited, PO Box 416, Denver, CO 80201-0416, (303)575-5676 [3489]

Prosperity Tool Corp., 2006 National Guard Dr., Plant City, FL 33567, (813)752-6602 [13877]

Prosteel Service Centers Inc., PO Box 5067, Delanco, NJ 08075, (609)461-8300 [20301]

Protech Communications, 3119 Lear Drv., Burlington, NC 27215, (336)222-0000 [5724]

Protech Safety Equipment, PO Box 400128, Cambridge, MA 02140-0002, (908)862-1550 [24615]

Protection Co-op Supply, PO Box 338, Protection, KS 67127, (316)622-4619 [18182]

Protein Databases Inc., 405 Oakwood Rd., Huntington Station, NY 11746, (516)673-3939 [24421]

Protein Foods Inc., PO Box 1545, Gainesville, GA 30503, (404)534-3514 [12232]

Proteus International Trading Co., PO Box 93, Winterset, IA 50273, (515)462-3186 [26500]

Protocol Systems Inc., 8500 SW Creekside Pl, Beaverton, OR 97008-7107, (503)526-8500 [19559]

Proton Corp., 13855 Struikman Rd., Cerritos, CA 90703, (562)404-2222 [25392]

Provico Inc., PO Box 579, Botkins, OH 45306, (513)693-2411 [27218]

Providence Casket Co., 1 Industrial Cir., Lincoln, RI 02865-2611, (401)726-1700 [25792]

Provident Music Group, 741 Cool Springs Blvd., Franklin, TN 37067, (615)261-6500 [4090]

Provo Craft Inc., 285 East 900 South, Provo, UT 84606, (801)377-4311 [26181]

Proxycare Inc., 4700 SW 51st St., Ste. 215, Ft. Lauderdale, FL 33314-5500, (954)791-5400 [19560]

Pruden Packing Company Inc., 1201 N Main St., Suffolk, VA 23434, (757)539-6261 [12233]

Prudential Builders Center, PO Box 3088, Spokane, WA 99220, (509)535-2401 [15281]

Prudential Building Materials, 171 Milton St., Dedham, MA 02026-0994, (617)329-3232 [7887]

Prudential Distributors Inc., PO Box 3088, Spokane, WA 99220, (509)535-2401 [15282]

Prudential Metal Supply Corp., 171 Milton St., Dedham, MA 02026, (781)329-3232 [7888]

Pruitt; Richard, 1212 S Rainbow Blvd., Las Vegas, NV 89102-9009, (702)870-8995 [13213]

Prybil Enterprises, PO Box 6, North Liberty, IA 52317-0006, (319)626-2333 [14645]

Pryor & Associates; Roger, 412 N Berry Pine Rd., Rapid City, SD 57702-1857, (605)343-4628 [25793]

Pryor Novelty Co., Inc., 1991 Hwy. 52, PO Box 4, Tuscumbia, MO 65082-0004, (573)369-2354 [13430]

P.S. Energy Group Inc., PO Box 29399, Atlanta, GA 30359, (404)321-5711 [22598]

PSDI, 1401 E Gartner, Naperville, IL 60540, (630)369-1680 [6654]

PSDI, 5215 N O'Connor Blvd., Ste. 1055, Irving, TX 75039, (972)402-8255 [6655]

PSDI, 19800 MacArthur Blvd., Ste. 1050, Irvine, CA 92612-2439 [6656]

PSDI, 100 Crosby Dr., Bedford, MA 01730, (781)280-2000 [6657]

PSDI, 151 W Passaic St., Rochelle Park, NJ 07662, (201)909-3765 [6658]

PSDI, 300 Vanderbilt Motor Pky., Ste. 200, Hauppauge, NY 11788, (516)951-4113 [6659]

PSDI, 2014 Sierra Dr., Fredericksburg, VA 22405-2786, (540)231-8660 [6660]

PSDI, 20 University Rd., Cambridge, MA 02138, (617)661-1444 [6661]

PSI Resources Inc., 1000 E Main St., Plainfield, IN 46168, (317)839-9611 [9243]

PSNC Propane Corp., PO Box 1398, Gastonia, NC 28053, (704)864-6731 [22599]

Psoul Company Inc., 384 Kingston Ave., Brooklyn, NY 11225, (718)756-9620 [5291]

PTC International, 401 E Pratt St., Ste. 2235, Baltimore, MD 21202-3003, (301)546-3966 [19000]

Pubco Corp., 3830 Kelley Ave., Cleveland, OH 44114, (216)881-5300 [5292]

Public Auction Yards, PO Box 1781, Billings, MT 59103-1781, (406)245-6447 [18183]

Public Software Library, PO Box 35705, Houston, TX 77235, (713)665-7017 [6662]

Publishers Associates, PO Box 140361, Irving, TX 75014-0361, (972)681-0361 [4091]

Publishers Distributing Co., 6922 Hollywood Blvd., 10th Fl., Los Angeles, CA 90028, (213)860-6070 [4092]

Publishers Distribution Service, 6893 Sullivan Rd., Grawn, MI 49637, (616)276-5196 [3466]

Publishers Group West Inc., 4065 Hollis St., Emeryville, CA 94608, (510)658-3453 [4093]

Publishers Group West Inc., 1700 4th St., Berkeley, CA 94710, (510)528-1444 [4094]

The Publishers Mark, PO Box 6300, Incline Village, NV 89450, (702)831-5139 [4095]

Publishers Supply Inc., 26 Keewaydin Dr., Ste. C, Salem, NH 03079-2898, (603)898-9898 [25794]

Publishing Center for Cultural Resources, 50 W 29th St., No. 7E, New York, NY 10001-4205, (212)260-2010 [4096]

Publix Office Supplies, Inc., 1301 International Pky., Woodridge, IL 60517-4956, (312)226-1000 [21225]

Puck Implement Co., Hwy. 141, Manning, IA 51455, (712)653-2574 [1160]

Puckett Machinery Co., PO Box 3170, Jackson, MS 39207, (601)969-6000 [7889]

Pueblo Chemical and Supply Co., PO Box 1279, Garden City, KS 67846, (316)275-6127 [4486]

Pueblo Fruits Inc., 5821-G Midway Park Blvd. NE, Albuquerque, NM 87109-5823, (505)344-2554 [12234]

Puget Sound Audio, 5105 N 46th, Tacoma, WA 98407, (253)759-4701 [25393]

Puget Sound Data Systems Inc., 10236 E Riverside Dr., Bothell, WA 98011-3709, (425)488-0710 [6663]

Puget Sound Instrument Co. Inc., 4611 11th Ave. NW, Seattle, WA 98107-4613, (206)789-1198 [25394]

Puget Sound Manufacturing Co., 1123 St. Paul Ave., Tacoma, WA 98421-2404, (253)572-5666 [7890]

Puget Sound Pipe and Supply Inc., 7816 S 202nd St., Kent, WA 98032, (253)796-9350 [20302]

Pugh & Associates, Inc.; C.L., 21510 Drake Rd., Cleveland, OH 44136, (440)238-1777 [9244]

Pugh & Associates, Inc.; C.L., 2144 Riverside Dr., Columbus, OH 43221, (614)486-9678 [9245]

Pugh & Associates, Inc.; C.L., 4838 Boomer Rd., Cincinnati, OH 45247, (513)662-8373 [9246]

Pulaski Chase Cooperative, PO Box 79, Pulaski, WI 54162, (920)822-3235 [1161]

Pulaski County Farm Bureau Cooperative, PO Box 346, Winamac, IN 46996, (219)946-6671 [1162]

Pulaski Equipment Co., Inc., 10600 Maybelline Dr., North Little Rock, AR 72117, (501)945-4121 [1163]

Pullen Inc.; Norman W., PO Box 10600, Portland, ME 04104-0600, (207)772-2211 [17553]

PullRite/Pulliam Enterprise Inc., 13790 E Jefferson Blvd., Mishawaka, IN 46545, (219)259-1520 [3123]

Pulmonary Data Service, PO Box 400, Louisville, CO 80027, (303)666-8100 [19561]

Pulsar Data Systems Inc., 4500 Forbes Blvd., No. 400, Lanham, MD 20706, (301)459-2650 [6664]

Pumilite-Salem Inc., PO Box 5348, Salem, OR 97304-0348, (503)585-1323 [7891]

Pump Engineering Co., 9807 Jordan Cir., Santa Fe Springs, CA 90670, (562)946-6864 [17121]

Pump Systems Inc., 15000 Bolsa Chica Rd., Huntington Beach, CA 92649, (714)898-0313 [17122]

Pumps, Parts and Service Inc., PO Box 7788, Charlotte, NC 28241, (704)588-1338 [16433]

Punch It Distributing Inc., 2690 Niles Rd., St. Joseph, MI 49085-3313, (616)429-9696 [26623]

Puratex Co., 6714 Wayne Ave., Pennsauken, NJ 08110-1699, (609)663-1050 [4487]

Purcell & Associates, 7 Crow Canyon Ct., Ste. 200, San Ramon, CA 94583, (510)855-9910 [12235]

Purchased Parts Group, 13599 Merriman Rd., Livonia, MI 48150, (734)422-7900 [13878]

Purchasing Support Services, 1 Town Ctr., West Amherst, NY 14228, (716)688-1994 [21226]

Purdy Electronics Corp., 720 Palomar Ave., Sunnyvale, CA 94086, (408)523-8200 [9247]

Pure Beverage Inc., 3902 E 16th St., Ste. B, Indianapolis, IN 46201-1538, (317)375-9925 [4097]

Pure Line Seeds Inc., PO Box 8866, Moscow, ID 83843, (208)882-4422 [1164]

Pure Sealed Dairy, 5031 Bass Rd., Ft. Wayne, IN 46808, (219)432-3575 [12236]

Pure Water Centers, 1155 Chest Dr., No. 109, Foster City, CA 94404 [15283]

Pure Water Centers, Inc., 2419 N Black Canyon Hwy., Ste. 10, Phoenix, AZ 85009, (602)254-6323 [15284]

Pure Water International Inc., 4350 NE 5th Terr., Oakland Park, FL 33334, (954)561-3155 [25795]

Pureflow Ultraviolet, Inc., 1750 Spectrum Dr., Lawrenceville, GA 30043-5744, (770)277-6330 [23332]

Purity Cylinder Gases Inc., PO Box 9390, Grand Rapids, MI 49509-0390, (616)532-2375 [16434]

Purity Dairies, Inc., PO Box 100957, Nashville, TN 37224-0957 [12237]

Purity Minonk Baking Co., 447 Oak, Minonk, IL 61760-1309, (309)432-2612 [12238]

Purity Products Inc., 4001 Washington Blvd., Baltimore, MD 21227, (410)242-7200 [1973]

Purity Products Inc. (Baltimore, Maryland), 4001 Washington Blvd., Baltimore, MD 21227, (410)242-7200 [25022]

Purity Wholesale Grocers Inc., 5400 Broken Sound Blvd. Ste. 100, Boca Raton, FL 33487-3594, (561)994-9360 [12239]

Puro Corporation of America, PO Box 10, Maspeth, NY 11378, (718)326-7000 [25023]

Puro Filter Co., 15151 S Prairie Ave., Lawndale, CA 90260, (213)937-1308 [25796]

Purolator Products, 3 Miracle Mile, Elmira, NY 14903-1031, (607)737-8011 [3124]

Purple Frog Software, PO Box 13928, Gainesville, FL 32604, (352)336-7208 [6665]

Purvis Bearing Service, 1315 S 7th St., Corsicana, TX 75110, (903)874-4721 [3125]

Purvis Bearing Service, 2413-17 Franklin Ave., Box 797, Waco, TX 76708, (254)753-6477 [3126]

Purvis Bearings, 3000 Airport Fwy., Ft. Worth, TX 76111, (817)831-4581 [17123]

Pusan Pipe America Inc., 9615 Norwalk Blvd., No. B, Santa Fe Springs, CA 90670-2931, (310)692-0600 [20303]

Putnam Auto Sales, PO Box 157, Letcher, SD 57359-0157, (605)248-2648 [3127]

Putnam Truck Parts, PO Box 157, Letcher, SD 57359-0157, (605)248-2648 [3127]

Putt-Putt Golf & Games, 2280 Lakeland Dr., Flowood, MS 39208-9592 [23899]

PWI Technologies, 3015 112th Ave. NE, Ste. 205, Bellevue, WA 98004, (425)828-4223 [6666]

PYA/Monarch Chain Distribution, PO Box 1004, Greenville, SC 29602, (864)295-8199 [12240]

PYA/Monarch Inc., PO Box 1328, Greenville, SC 29602, (803)676-8600 [12241]

PYA/Monarch Inc. Schloss and Kahn, U.S Hwy. 80 W, Montgomery, AL 36108, (205)288-3111 [4690]

Pyramid Agri-Products International, Rte. 3, Box 33-A, Larned, KS 67550, (316)285-7211 [18184]

Pyramid Art Supply, 100 Paragon Pky., Mansfield, OH 44903, (419)589-1900 [20838]

Pyramid Studios, 10 State St., Ellsworth, ME 04605, (207)667-3321 [17554]

Pyramid Supply Inc., PO Box 76239, Oklahoma City, OK 73147, (405)232-7628 [9248]

Pyrenees French Bakery Inc., PO Box 3626, Bakersfield, CA 93385, (661)322-7159 [12242]

Q Perfumes, 1965 Tubeway Ave., City of Commerce, CA 90040, (213)728-3434 [14201]

Q-Snap Corp., PO Box 68, Parsons, TN 38363-0068, (901)847-7155 [26624]

Q-T Foundations Company Inc., 385 Chestnut St., Norwood, NJ 07648, (201)750-8100 [5293]

Q-T Foundations Company Inc., 385 Chestnut St., Norwood, NJ 07648, (201)750-8100 [5294]

Q-T Intimates, 385 Chestnut St., Norwood, NJ 07648, (201)750-8100 [5293]

Q U.S.A, 15 E Salem Ave., Roanoke, VA 24011, (540)345-1429 [3778]

Q.A. Products Inc., 1301 Mark St., Elk Grove Village, IL 60007, (708)595-2390 [12243]

QA Technologies Inc., 222 S 72nd St., Ste. 301, Omaha, NE 68114, (402)391-9200 [6667]

QCA Inc., 2832 Spring Grove Ave., Cincinnati, OH 45225, (513)681-8400 [25395]

QCU Inc., 3056 Palm Ave., Warehouses 2 & 3, Ft. Myers, FL 33901, (941)332-2205 [13431]

QCU Inc., 3056 Palm Ave., Warehouses 2 & 3, Ft. Myers, FL 33901, (941)332-2205 [13431]

QED, 3560 S Valley View Blvd., Las Vegas, NV 89103-1812, (702)871-4108 [9249]

Q.E.D. Exports, PO Box 15005, Riverside, RI 02915, (401)433-4045 [12244]

Q.E.P. Co. Inc., 1081 Holland Dr., Boca Raton, FL 33487, (561)994-5550 [27361]

Q.I.V. Systems Inc., 4242 Woodcock Dr., Ste. 101, San Antonio, TX 78228, (210)736-4126 [6668]

QMI Inc., 4133 Pioneer Dr., Walled Lake, MI 48390, (248)855-3466 [25396]

Q.P.C., Inc., 3865 W 150th St., Cleveland, OH 44111, (216)941-1111 [24600]

QSN Manufacturing Inc., 101 Frontier Wy., Bensenville, IL 60106, (708)616-1500 [13879]

QSound Ltd., 875 Stanton Rd., Burlingame, CA 94010-1403, (213)876-6137 [25397]

Quad County Cooperative, PO Box 4, Exeter, NE 68351, (402)266-5951 [18185]

Quaglino Tobacco and Candy Company Inc., 2400 S Claiborne Ave., New Orleans, LA 70125, (504)561-0101 [26344]

Quail Ridge Press Inc., PO Box 123, Brandon, MS 39043, (601)825-2063 [4098]

Quaker City Hide Co., 25 Washington Ln., Ste. 6A, Wyncote, PA 19095-1400, (215)886-2400 [18186]

Quaker City Hide Co., 25 Washington Ln., Ste. 6A, Wyncote, PA 19095-1400, (215)886-2400 [18187]

Quaker City Motor Parts Co., PO Box 5000, Middletown, DE 19709, (302)378-9834 [3128]

Quaker City Paper & Chemical, Rte. 26, Ocean View, DE 19970, (302)539-4373 [21891]

Quaker City Paper and Chemical, Rte. 26, Ocean View, DE 19970, (302)539-4373 [21892]

Quaker City Paper Co., 300 N Sherman St., PO Box 2677, York, PA 17405, (717)843-9061 [21893]

Quaker City Paper Co., 300 N Sherman St., York, PA 17405, (717)843-9061 [17124]

Quaker Oats Co. International Foods Div., PO Box 9001, Chicago, IL 60604-9001, (312)222-7111 [12245]

Qualis Inc., 4600 Park Ave., Des Moines, IA 50321, (515)243-3000 [19562]

Qualitas Trading Co., 2029 Durant Ave., Berkeley, CA 94704, (510)848-8080 [6669]

Qualiton Imports Ltd., 24-02 40th Ave., Long Island City, NY 11101, (718)937-8515 [25398]

Quality Art, 200 E 52nd St., Boise, ID 83714, (208)672-0530 [21227]

Quality Bakery Co., 1105 Schrock Rd., No. 300, Columbus, OH 43085, (614)846-2232 [12246]

Quality Bakery Products Inc., 888 Las Olas Blvd., Ste. 700, Ft. Lauderdale, FL 33301-2272, (954)779-3663 [12247]

Quality Banana Inc., 3196 Produce Row, Houston, TX 77023-5814, (713)921-4161 [12248]

Quality Beverage Inc., PO Box 671, Taunton, MA 02780, (508)822-6200 [1974]

Quality Beverage Limited Partnership, PO Box 671, Taunton, MA 02780, (508)822-6200 [1974]

Quality Books Inc., 1003 W Pines Rd., Oregon, IL 61061, (815)732-4450 [4099]

Quality Brands Inc., 226 Dover Rd., Glen Burnie, MD 21060, (410)787-5656 [1975]

Quality Business Forms Inc., 5097 Nathan Ln., Minneapolis, MN 55442, (612)559-4330 [21228]

Quality Care Pharmaceuticals Inc., 3000 W Warner Ave., Santa Ana, CA 92704, (714)754-5800 [19563]

Quality Control Consultants, 3087 Bellbrook Center Dr., Memphis, TN 38116-3506, (901)396-2916 [19001]

Quality Croutons Inc., 825 W 37th Pl., Chicago, IL 60609, (773)927-8200 [12249]

Quality First Greetings Corp., 10500 American Rd., Cleveland, OH 44144, (216)252-7300 [21894]

Quality Foods Inc., PO Box 4908, Little Rock, AR 72214, (501)568-3141 [12250]

Quality Foods Inc., PO Box 4908, Little Rock, AR 72214, (501)568-3141 [12251]

Quality King Distributors Inc., 2060 9th Ave., Ronkonkoma, NY 11779, (631)737-5555 [14202]

Quality Meat Company Inc., 340 North Ave., Grand Junction, CO 81501, (970)242-1872 [12252]

Quality Meats and Seafood Inc., PO Box 337, West Fargo, ND 58078, (701)282-0202 [12253]

Quality Mill Supply Company Inc., PO Box 508, Columbus, IN 47201, (812)379-9585 [17125]

Quality Monitor Systems, 1950 Victor Pl., Colorado Springs, CO 80915-1501, (719)596-2187 [19002]

Quality Oil Company L.P., PO Box 2736, Winston-Salem, NC 27102, (919)722-3441 [22600]

Quality Oil Company L.P., PO Box 2736, Winston-Salem, NC 27102, (336)722-3441 [22601]

Quality Paper & Plastic Corp., PO Box 8981, Albuquerque, NM 87108-8981, (505)262-1722 [23020]

Quality Petroleum Corp., PO Box 3889, Lakeland, FL 33802-3889, (941)687-2682 [22602]

Quality Pets, Inc., 1501 S Agnew, Oklahoma City, OK 73108, (405)272-1091 [27219]

Quality Resources, 1 Water St., White Plains, NY 10601, (914)761-9600 [4100]

Quality Sew & Vac, 224 W 3rd St., Grand Island, NE 68801-5916, (308)382-7310 [15626]

Quality Sew and Vac, 224 W 3rd St., Grand Island, NE 68801-5916, (308)382-7310 [15285]

Quality Sound Enterprise Inc., 833 Bragg Blvd., Fayetteville, NC 28301-4507, (910)483-1212 [25399]

Quality Tile Corp., 2541 Boston Rd., Bronx, NY 10467, (718)653-0830 [10111]

Quality Truck Bodies & Repair, Inc., Firestone Pkwy., PO Box 1669, Wilson, NC 27893, (919)291-5795 [3129]

Quality Window & Door, 27888 County Rd. 32 W, Elkhart, IN 46517, (219)674-0867 [7892]

Quantum Labs Inc., 9851 13th Ave. N, Minneapolis, MN 55441-5003, (612)545-1984 [19003]

Quarex Industries Inc., 47-05 Metropolitan Ave., Ridgewood, NY 11385, (718)821-0011 [12254]

Que Tenga Buena Mano, PO Box 762, Santa Fe, NM 87504-0762, (505)982-2912 [26118]

Queen City Home Health Care Inc., 10780 Reading Rd., Cincinnati, OH 45241-2531, (513)681-8811 [19004]

Queen City Wholesale Inc., PO Box 1083, Sioux Falls, SD 57101, (605)336-3215 [12255]

Queen City Wholesale Inc., PO Box 1083, Sioux Falls, SD 57101, (605)336-3215 [12256]

Queen Oil & Gas, Mayhill 66, Hwy. 82, Mayhill, NM 88339, (505)687-3605 [22603]

Queen Shebra Co., 1421 62nd St., Brooklyn, NY 11219, (718)837-2800 [5295]

Queens City Distributing Co., PO Box 186, Bridgeville, PA 15017-0186, (412)257-4120 [23900]

Queens Decorative Wallcoverings Inc., 83-59 Smedley St., Jamaica, NY 11435, (718)523-4323 [15627]

Queensboro Steel Corp., PO Box 1769, Wilmington, NC 28402, (919)763-6237 [20304]

Quement Electronics, 1000 S Bascom Ave., San Jose, CA 95150, (408)998-5900 [9250]

Quest Electronic Hardware Inc., 6400 Congress Ave., Ste. 200, Boca Raton, FL 33487, (561)546-6200 [9251]

Quick Cable Corporation, 3700 Quick Dr., Franksville, WI 53126-0509, (262)824-3100 [9252]

Quick-Rotan Inc., 120 S La Salle St., #1450, Chicago, IL 60603-3403 [15286]

Quickcom, 2437 Williams Ave., Cincinnati, OH 45212, (513)396-6744 [18401]

Quickshine of America Inc., 277 Fairfield Dr., Fairfield, NJ 07004, (973)227-4011 [4488]

Quickshot Technology Inc., 10423 Valley Blvd., No. N, El Monte, CA 91731, (626)444-3697 [6670]

Quigley Corp., Landmark Bldg., 10 S Clinton St., Doylestown, PA 18901, (215)345-0919 [19564]

Quigley Sales and Marketing and Associates, 410 E 3rd St., Royal Oak, MI 48067, (248)546-3220 [7893]

Quikservice Steel Co., 515 Madison St., Muskogee, OK 74403, (918)687-5307 [20305]

Quill Corp., 100 Shelter Rd., Lincolnshire, IL 60069, (847)634-6690 [21229]

Quill, Hair & Ferrule, 1 Greengate Park Rd., Columbia, SC 29223, (803)788-4499 [21549]

The Quilt Digest Press — A division of NTC/Contemporary Publishing Group, 4255 W Touhy Ave., Lincolnwood, IL 60646-1933, (847)679-5500 [4101]

Quiltworks, 1055 E 79th St., Bloomington, MN 55420-1417, (612)854-1460 [26182]

Quimby Co. Inc.; Edward H., PO Box 918, Dover, NH 03820-0918, (603)742-3515 [21230]

Quimby Corp., 1603 NW 14th Ave., Portland, OR 97209, (503)221-1100 [17126]

Quimby Corp., 1603 NW 14th Ave., Portland, OR 97209, (503)221-1100 [16435]

Quimby-Walstrom Paper Co., PO Box 1806, Grand Rapids, MI 49501, (616)784-4700 [21895]

Quinn Coffee Co., 1455 E Chestnut Expwy., Springfield, MO 65802, (417)869-5523 [12257]

Quinn Coffee Co., 1455 E Chestnut Expwy., Springfield, MO 65802, (417)869-5523 [12257]

Quinn Electric Supply Co., 2724 Keith St. NW, Cleveland, TN 37312, (423)472-4547 [9253]

Quinsig Automotive Warehouse Inc., 13 Quinsigamond Ave., Worcester, MA 01608, (508)756-3536 [3130]

Quintal Farms, PO Box 462, Kurtistown, HI 96760, (808)966-7370 [14943]

Quintana Sales, 2411 Camino De Vida, Santa Fe, NM 87505-6428, (505)471-1053 [22895]

Quintel/Consort Watch Co., 44 Century Dr., Wheeling, IL 60090, (847)541-3333 [17555]

Quisenberrys Inc., PO Box 40, Vale, OR 97918-0040, (541)473-3932 [5296]

Quite Specific Media Group Ltd., 260 5th Ave., New York, NY 10001, (212)725-5377 [4102]

Quitman County Farmers Association, PO Box 160, Marks, MS 38646, (601)326-2391 [1165]

Qumax Corp., 1746 Junction Ave., No. E, San Jose, CA 95112-1018, (408)954-8040 [6671]

Quogue Sinclair Fuel Inc., PO Box 760, Hampton Bays, NY 11946, (516)726-4700 [22604]

Quorum Corp., PO Box 510, Hurricane, WV 25526, (304)743-9699 [21231]

R5 Trading International Inc., PO Box 3355, Princeton, NJ 08543, (609)951-9512 [19005]

R & B Orthopedics Inc., 7000 Hampton Center, Ste. G, Morgantown, WV 26505-1705, (304)598-0416 [19006]

R & B Service Co., 8524 Vineyard Ridge Rd. NE, Albuquerque, NM 87122-2620, (505)822-0829 [14646]

R/C Henry Company Inc., 3600 Chamberlain Ln., Ste. 342, Louisville, KY 40241, (502)339-0172 [26625]

R-Computer, 30 Golf Club Rd., Pleasant Hill, CA 94523, (925)798-4884 [6672]

R and D Industries Inc., 1824 130th Ave. NE, No. 2, Bellevue, WA 98005, (425)881-8490 [6673]

R and D Industries Inc., 10807 E Montgomery Dr., Ste. 7, Spokane, WA 99206, (509)924-9082 [6674]

R and D Products, PO Box 2365, Ft. Oglethorpe, GA 30742-2365, (706)867-4550 [4691]

R & E Supply Inc., PO Box 2010, Hot Springs National Park, AR 71914, (501)623-2541 [14647]

R & F Auto Sales, Rd. 3, Box 331, Seaford, DE 19973, (302)629-2587 [20709]

R & H Wholesale Supply, Inc., 1655 Folsom St., San Francisco, CA 94103, (415)863-0404 [24616]

R & J Apparel Distributors, 130 Penn Am Dr., Quakertown, PA 18951, (215)536-3633 [5297]

R. Johns Ltd., PO Box 149056, Austin, TX 78714-9056, (512)444-0571 [17371]

R-K Market, PO Box 940, Belfield, ND 58622-0940, (701)575-4354 [19007]

R & L Data Systems Inc., 1616 E 17th St., Idaho Falls, ID 83404-6366, (208)529-3785 [6675]

R & L Electronics, 1315 Maple Ave., Hamilton, OH 45011, (513)868-6399 [1575]

R and L Supply Co-op, 300 Vine St., Reedsburg, WI 53959, (608)524-6419 [1166]

R & R CB Distributors Inc., 245 Fletcher Ave., Waterloo, IA 50701-2304, (319)232-6282 [25400]

R & R Distributors, 2727-7 Clydo Rd., Jacksonville, FL 32207, (904)730-7700 [27220]

R and R Electronic Supply Co., PO Box 1860, Lubbock, TX 79408, (806)765-7727 [9254]

R & R Hardwood Floors, 5125 W Gage St., Boise, ID 83706, (208)377-5563 [10112]

R & R Mill Company, PO Box 187, Smithfield, UT 84335-0187, (435)563-3333 [15287]

R and R Plumbing Supply Corp., 170 Chandler St., Worcester, MA 01609-2924, (508)757-4543 [23333]

R and R Provision Co., PO Box 889, Easton, PA 18042, (215)258-5366 [12258]

R & R Sales Inc., 944 Dorchester Ave., Boston, MA 02125-1219, (617)265-0440 [7894]

R and R Salvage Inc., 1329 William St., Buffalo, NY 14206, (716)856-3608 [26949]

R & R Scaffold Erectors, Inc., 1150 E 68th Ave., Anchorage, AK 99518, (907)344-5427 [7895]

R & R Technical Bookfinders Inc., 1224 W Littleton Blvd., Littleton, CO 80120, (303)794-4518 [4103]

R & R Uniforms, 350 28th Ave. N, Nashville, TN 37209, (615)320-1000 [5364]

R & R Wood Products, 601 E Karcher Rd., Nampa, ID 83687-8281, (208)467-2406 [13214]

R Ruetz, PO Box 517, Racine, WI 53401, (414)637-7447 [13550]

R & S Sales Co. Inc., 21 Pleasant Valley Ln., Westport, CT 06880-2731, (203)226-1709 [24838]

R and S Steel Co., 4600 N Wabash, Ste. A, Denver, CO 80216, (303)321-9660 [20306]

R Squared Inc., 11211 E Arapahoe Rd., Englewood, CO 80112, (303)790-6090 [6849]

R & T Enterprises Inc., PO Box 727, Bridgeport, WV 26330-0727, (304)622-5546 [23901]

R & W Distribution Inc., 87 Bright St., Jersey City, NJ 07302, (201)333-1540 [4104]

R and W Supply Inc., PO Box 270, Littlefield, TX 79339, (806)385-4447 [17127]

R and W Technical Services Ltd., 7324 Southwest Fwy., Ste. 1000, Arena Tower, Houston, TX 77074-2079, (713)995-4200 [6676]

R.A.B. Holdings Inc., 444 Madison Ave., New York, NY 10022, (212)688-4500 [12259]

RABCO Equipment Corp., 1145 State Hwy. 33, Farmingdale, NJ 07727, (732)938-7200 [21232]

Racal-Chubb Security Systems Inc., 903 N Bowser, No. 250, Richardson, TX 75081, (972)690-4691 [24526]

Race Street Foods Inc., PO Box 28385, San Jose, CA 95159-8385, (408)294-6161 [12260]

RACER Computer Corp., 3000 E Chambers St., Phoenix, AZ 85040, (602)304-2424 [6677]

Racetrac Petroleum Inc., 300 Technology Ct., Smyrna, GA 30082, (770)431-7600 [22605]

Racewear Designs Inc., 340 Coogan Way, El Cajon, CA 92020, (619)442-9651 [5298]

Racine Elevator Co., PO Box 37, Racine, MN 55967, (507)378-2121 [22606]

Racine Vineyard Products, 1439 Junction Ave., Racine, WI 53403, (414)634-7300 [1976]

Racing Champions Corp., 800 Roosevelt Rd., Bldg. C., Ste. 320, Glen Ellyn, IL 60137, (630)790-3507 [26626]

Rack Service Company Inc., 2601 Newcomb, Monroe, LA 71211, (318)322-1445 [14203]

Rack Service Company Inc., 2601 Newcomb, Monroe, LA 71211, (318)322-1445 [19565]

Raco Industrial Corp., 2100 S Wolf Rd., Des Plaines, IL 60018, (847)298-8600 [16436]

Raco Manufacturing Inc., 61 E Longden Ave., Arcadia, CA 91006-5170, (213)723-9955 [23902]

Racom Products Inc., 5504 State Rd., Cleveland, OH 44134-2299, (216)351-1755 [5726]

RAD Graphics, 1427 Melody Ln., Chattanooga, TN 37412-1119, (423)867-3542 [6678]

Rad Oil Company Inc., 287 Bowman Ave., Purchase, NY 10577-2517, (914)253-8945 [22607]

Rada Manufacturing Co., PO Box 838, Waverly, IA 50677, (319)352-5454 [15628]

Radak Electronics, 1637 E Isaacs Ave., WalLa Walla, WA 99362, (509)529-0090 [5727]

Radandt Sons Inc.; Fred, 1800 Johnston Dr., Manitowoc, WI 54220, (920)682-7758 [7896]

Radar Electric, 704 SE Washington, Portland, OR 97214, (503)232-3404 [9255]

Radar Electric, 168 Western Ave. W, Seattle, WA 98119, (206)282-2511 [9256]

Radar, Inc., 168 Western Ave. W, Seattle, WA 98119, (206)282-2511 [9256]

Radar Marine Electronics, 16 Squalicum Mall, Bellingham, WA 98225, (206)733-2012 [18589]

Radcom, Inc., 12323 W Fairview Ave., Milwaukee, WI 53226, (414)771-6900 [5728]

Raden and Sons Inc.; G., 3215 Lind Ave. SW, Renton, WA 98055, (425)251-9300 [1977]

Radford Co., PO Box 2688, Oshkosh, WI 54903, (414)426-6200 [7897]

Radio City Automotive, 65 Main St., Lewiston, ME 04240, (207)782-1705 [25401]

Radio City Inc., 65 Main St., Lewiston, ME 04240-7738, (207)782-1705 [25402]

Radio Communications Co., 1282 Mountain Rd., Glen Allen, VA 23060-4033, (804)266-8999 [5729]

Radio Communications Co., PO Box 68, Cary, NC 27512-1328, (919)467-2421 [25403]

Radio Communications Co., 2131 N Towne Ln. NE, Cedar Rapids, IA 52402-1913, (319)393-7150 [5730]

Radio Communications Company Inc., PO Box 6630, Roanoke, VA 24017-0630, (540)342-8513 [5731]

Radio Holland U.S.A., 8943 Gulf Fwy., Houston, TX 77017, (713)943-3325 [18590]

Radio Research Instrument, 584 N Main St., Waterbury, CT 06704-3506, (203)753-5840 [9257]

Radio Resources and Services Corp., 814 A Light St, Baltimore, MD 21230, (410)783-0737 [5732]

Radio Resources and Services Corp., 814 A Light St, Baltimore, MD 21230, (410)783-0737 [9258]

Radiology Resources Inc., 20 Aegean Dr., Ste. 8, Methuen, MA 01844-1580, (781)935-4470 [19008]

Radiology Services Inc., PO Box 72, Georgetown, MA 01833-0072, (978)352-2050 [19009]

Radios Knobs Speakers & Things, 314 W Walton Blvd., Pontiac, MI 48340-1041, (248)334-2549 [25066]

RadioShack Corp., 100 Throckmorton St., Ste. 1800, Ft. Worth, TX 76102, (817)415-3700 [7890]

Radium Cooperative Co., Rte. 2, Radium, KS 67550, (316)982-4364 [18188]

Radium Cooperative Co., Rte. 2, Radium, KS 67550, (316)982-4364 [12261]

Radix Wire Co., 26260 Lakeland Blvd., Cleveland, OH 44132, (216)731-9191 [9260]

Radnor Alloys Inc., PO Box 269, Wayne, PA 19087, (215)687-3770 [20307]

RadServ Inc., 21540 Plummer St., Chatsworth, CA 91311-4103 [19010]

Radways Dairy, 29 Jefferson Ave., New London, CT 06320, (203)443-8921 [12262]

Rae Mel Sales Inc., 661 Akoakoa St., Kailua, HI 96734, (808)682-4466 [25404]

RAE Products and Chemical Inc., 11630 S Cicero Ave., Alsip, IL 60803, (708)396-1984 [4489]

Rafferty-Brown Steel Co., PO Box 18927, Greensboro, NC 27419, (336)855-6300 [20308]

Rafters Recreational Footwear, 16 Oakway Ctr., Eugene, OR 97401-5612, (541)485-2070 [24703]

Rag Man Inc., 14676 SE 82nd Dr., Clackamas, OR 97015, (503)657-5694 [26950]

Ragan Inc.; Brad, PO Box 240587, Charlotte, NC 28224, (704)521-2100 [3131]

Ragland Co.; C.B., PO Box 40587, Nashville, TN 37204, (615)259-4622 [12263]

Ragu Foods Co., 1135 E Artesia Blvd., Carson, CA 90746-1602, (818)760-0800 [12264]

Rah Rah Sales Inc., Drawer 1170, Irmo, SC 29063-1170, (803)781-9729 [5299]

Rahn Industries, Inc., 7720 Maie Ave., Los Angeles, CA 90001-2693, (213)588-1291 [3132]

Rail Europe Group, 500 Mamaroneck Ave., Harrison, NY 10528, (914)682-2999 [6679]

Rail Europe Holding, 500 Mamaroneck Ave., Harrison, NY 10528, (914)682-2999 [6680]

Rails Co., 101 Newark Way, Maplewood, NJ 07040, (201)763-4320 [23486]

Railway Services International, 38 Sheffield Rd., Gansevoort, NY 12831, (518)584-9407 [23487]

Rainbo Baking Co., 1916 N Broadway, Box 16, Oklahoma City, OK 73103, (405)524-8454 [12265]

Rainbo Baking Co., 4104 Leeland, Houston, TX 77023-3014, (713)237-0001 [12266]

Rainbo Baking Co., 303 E 4th, Pueblo, CO 81003-3313, (719)543-3725 [12267]

Rainbow Balloons Inc., 59 Waters Ave., Everett, MA 02149-2026, (617)389-1144 [26627]

Rainbow Distributing, Inc., 2718 N Paulina, Chicago, IL 60614, (773)929-7629 [14204]

Rainbow Inc. (Pearl City, Hawaii), 98-715 Kuahao Pl., Pearl City, HI 96782, (808)487-6455 [12268]

Rainbow Natural Foods, 15965 E 32nd Ave., Aurora, CO 80011, (303)373-1144 [12269]

Rainbow Paper Company, Inc., 2404 Hwy.14, PO Box 9985, New Iberia, LA 70562-9985, (318)369-9007 [21896]

Rainbow Photography, 213 E Grand Ave., Laramie, WY 82070-3639, (307)742-7597 [22896]

Rainbow Publishers, PO Box 261129, San Diego, CA 92196-1129, (619)271-7600 [4105]

Rainbow Raster Graphics, 2212 Greenwich Ln., Knoxville, TN 37932, (423)691-5080 [6681]

Rainbow Rug Inc., 74 Old Airport Rd., Sanford, ME 04073, (207)324-6600 [10113]

Rainbow Sales Distributing, 1637 S 83rd St., West Allis, WI 53214, (414)774-4949 [13432]

Rainbow Sports, 610 Cave Mill Rd., Bowling Green, KY 42104-4682, (502)782-5411 [23903]

Rainbow Trading Company Inc., 5-05 48th Ave., Long Island City, NY 11101, (718)784-3700 [13215]

Rainforest Inc., 420 5th Ave. Fl 26, New York, NY 10018-2729, (212)695-3195 [5300]

Rainhart Co., PO Box 4533, Austin, TX 78765, (512)452-8848 [19011]

Rainsoft Water Conditioning Co., 2080 Lunt Ave., Elk Grove Village, IL 60007, (847)437-9400 [25797]

Rainsweet, PO Box 6109, Salem, OR 97304, (503)363-4293 [12270]

Rair Systems, 7006-B S Alton Way, Englewood, CO 80112, (303)779-9888 [24247]

Raj India Trading Corp. Inc., PO Box 2644, Everett, WA 98203-0644, (425)257-0759 [5301]

Rajala Lumber Co., PO Box 578, Deer River, MN 56636, (218)246-8277 [7898]

Raketty Co.; A.E., PO Box 18555, Seattle, WA 98118, (206)722-5119 [26345]

RAL Corp., 24 Dunning Rd., Middletown, NY 10940-1819, (914)343-1456 [23334]

Raleigh Cycle of America, 22710 72nd S, Kent, WA 98032-1926, (425)656-0126 [23904]

Raleigh Hardware Co., PO Box 1183, Beckley, WV 25802, (304)253-7348 [13880]

Rally Products, Inc., 109 Hillside Ave., Londonderry, NH 03053, (603)434-2123 [19566]

Rally Products Inc., PO Box 702468, Tulsa, OK 74170-2468, (918)446-1006 [5302]

Ralston Purina Co., Golden Products Div., 300 Airport Rd., Cape Girardeau, MO 63701, (573)334-6618 [27221]

Ralston Purina/Pet Products, 4555 York St., Denver, CO 80216, (303)295-0818 [12271]

Ram Graphics Inc., PO Box 114, Alexandria, IN 46001, (765)724-7212 [5303]

Ram Meter Inc., 1903 Barrett Rd., Troy, MI 48084, (248)362-0990 [9261]

Ram Motors and Controls Inc., PO Box 629, Leesport, PA 19533-0629, (215)376-7102 [3133]

Ram Threading Co., 2640 Crockett, Beaumont, TX 77701, (409)833-2658 [13881]

Ram Tool and Supply Co., PO Box 320979, Birmingham, AL 35232, (205)591-2527 [13882]

Ram Turbos Inc., 2300 N Miami Ave., Miami, FL 33137, (305)576-4550 [3134]

Ramacom Inc., PO Box E, Norman, OK 73070-7005, (405)360-2666 [6682]

Ramallah Inc., 880 Hanna Dr., American Canyon, CA 94589, (707)649-0900 [15629]

Ramclif Supply Co., 1212 East Mason Avenue, York, PA 17403, (717)854-5534 [17128]

Ramer & Associates, Inc.; H., 41 Dunn St., Laguna Niguel, CA 92677, (949)249-2107 [4106]

RAMM Global, 50 Abele Rd., Ste. 1005, Bridgeville, PA 15017, (412)221-3700 [12272]

RAMM Metals Inc., 50 Abele Rd., Ste. 1005, Bridgeville, PA 15017, (412)221-3700 [12272]

RAMM Metals Inc., 50 Abele Rd., Ste. 1005, Bridgeville, PA 15017, (412)221-3700 [12273]

Ramsey Seed, Inc., 205 Stockton St., Manteca, CA 95336, (209)823-1721 [1167]

Ramson's Imports, 5159 Sinclair Rd., Columbus, OH 43229, (614)846-4447 [13433]

Ramy Seed Co., 1329 N Riverfront St., Mankato, MN 56001, (507)387-4091 [1168]

Rancilio Associates, PO Box 28869, St. Louis, MO 63123, (314)845-0202 [9262]

Rand International Leisure Products Ltd., 51 Executive Blvd., Farmingdale, NY 11735, (516)249-6000 [23905]

Rand & Jones Enterprises Co., Inc., 137 Wickham Dr., Williamsville, NY 14221, (716)632-2180 [16437]

Rand-Scot Inc., 401 Linden Center Dr., Ft. Collins, CO 80524, (970)484-7967 [19567]

Randall Brothers Inc., PO Box 1678, Atlanta, GA 30371, (404)892-6666 [7899]

Randall Farmers Cooperative Union, PO Box 95, Randall, KS 66963, (785)739-2312 [18189]

Randall Foods Inc., PO Box 2669, Huntington Park, CA 90255, (213)587-2383 [12274]

Randall-Graw Company Inc., PO Box 3119, La Crosse, WI 54602, (608)784-6228 [17129]

Randall Inc.; H.G., PO Box 221, Tomah, WI 54660, (608)372-4539 [18190]

Randall Tile Company, Inc., PO Box 69, Phenix City, AL 36868-0069, (205)298-0327 [10114]

Randall's Lumber, 315 Paseo Del Pueblo Sur, Taos, NM 87571 [7900]

Randazzo's Fruit Market #2, 49800 Hayes Rd., Macomb, MI 48044, (810)566-8700 [12275]

Randolph Distributing Corp., 31399 Farimount Blvd., Cleveland, OH 44124-4810, (216)883-0360 [13216]

Randolph, Hale & Matthews, PO Box 828, Clarksville, TN 37041-0828, (931)647-2325 [9263]

Randolph & Rice, 1213 McGavock St., Nashville, TN 37203, (615)255-5601 [9264]

Randolph Slaughter Co., PO Box 556, Laredo, TX 78042, (956)722-2252 [12276]

Random House Inc., 201 E 50th St., New York, NY 10022, (212)572-2120 [26628]

Randy's Frozen Meats, 1910 NW 5th St., Faribault, MN 55021-4606, (507)334-7177 [12277]

Range Paper Corp., PO Box 970, Virginia, MN 55792, (218)741-7644 [21897]

Rangel Distributing Co., PO Box 8192, Shawnee Mission, KS 66208, (913)262-4945 [5733]

Rangen Inc., PO Box 706, Buhl, ID 83316-0706, (208)543-6421 [18191]

Rangen Inc., PO Box 706, Buhl, ID 83316, (208)543-6421 [12278]

Ranger Communications Inc., 401 W 35th St., No. B, National City, CA 91950-7909, (619)259-0287 [5734]

Raniville Company Inc.; F., PO Box 888283, Grand Rapids, MI 49588-8283, (616)957-3200 [17130]

Rank America Inc., 5 Concourse Pkwy Ste. 2400, Atlanta, GA 30328, (404)392-9029 [16438]

Ransdell Surgical Inc., PO Box 34518, Louisville, KY 40232-4518, (502)584-6311 [19012]

Ransdell Surgical Inc., PO Box 4517, Louisville, KY 40204-0517, (502)584-6311 [19568]

Ransom County Implement Inc., PO Box 393, Lisbon, ND 58054, (701)683-4000 [1019]

Ransom Distributing Co., PO Box 2010, Sparks, NV 89432 [4107]

Rapac Network International, 291 S Van Brunt St., Englewood, NJ 07631, (201)871-9300 [3135]

Rapasadi Sons; Isadore A., N Peterboro, Canastota, NY 13032, (315)697-2216 [12279]

Rapers of Spencer Inc., 1109 N Salisbury Ave., Spencer, NC 28159-1832, (336)760-1512 [26629]

Rapid Air Corp., 4601 Kishwaukee St., Rockford, IL 61109, (815)397-2578 [16439]

Rapid City Beauty & Barber Supply, PO Box 7685, Rapid City, SD 57709-7685, (605)342-0435 [14205]

Rapid Controls Inc., PO Box 8390, Rapid City, SD 57709-8390, (605)348-7688 [17131]

Rapid Disposal Services Inc., 115 Churchill Ave., Somerset, NJ 08873-3443, (732)469-3117 [26951]

Rapid Industrial Plastics Co., 13 Linden Ave. E, Jersey City, NJ 07305, (201)433-5500 [23021]

Rappahannock Seafood Company Inc., PO Box 816, Kilmarnock, VA 22482-0816, (804)435-1605 [12280]

Rare Coins, 44 W 1st St., Reno, NV 89501-1402, (702)322-4166 [17556]

Raritan Computer Inc., 400 Cottontail Ln., Somerset, NJ 08873, (732)764-8886 [6683]

Raritan Computer Inc., 400 Cottontail Ln., Somerset, NJ 08873, (732)764-8886 [6684]

Raritan Supply Co., 301 Meadow Rd., Edison, NJ 08817-6082, (732)985-5000 [23335]

Rasco Supply Company Ltd., PO Box 25, Lihue, HI 96766-0025, (808)245-5356 [9265]

Rashid Sales Co., 191 Atlantic Ave., Brooklyn, NY 11201, (718)852-3295 [25405]

Rashti and Company Inc.; Harry J., 112 W 34th St., Ste. 921, New York, NY 10120-0101, (212)594-2939 [5304]

Rasmark Display Fireworks Inc., PO Box 1702, Bozeman, MT 59771-1702, (406)587-9060 [26630]

Rasmussen Equipment Co., 3333 W 2100 S, Salt Lake City, UT 84119-1197, (801)972-5588 [7901]

Raster Graphics Inc., 3025 Orchard Pkwy., San Jose, CA 95134, (408)232-4000 [21233]

Raub Radio and Television Co., 5909 Carrollton Ave., Indianapolis, IN 46220, (317)251-1595 [25406]

Raufeisen Enterprises, 513 31st St., Rock Island, IL 61201, (309)794-1111 [17132]

Rausch Naval Stores Company Inc., PO Box 4085, New Orleans, LA 70178, (504)833-3754 [4490]

Rave Associates, 6071 Jackson Rd., Ann Arbor, MI 48103-9504, (734)761-7702 [1978]

Rave Computer Association Inc., 36960 Metro Ct., Sterling Heights, MI 48312, (810)939-8230 [6685]

Rawson and Company Inc., PO Box 924288, Houston, TX 77292-4288, (713)684-1400 [24422]

Rax Works Inc., PO Box 2078, Del Mar, CA 92014-1378, (619)578-4430 [23906]

Ray-Carroll County Grain Growers Inc., PO Box 158, Richmond, MO 64085, (816)776-2291 [1169]

Raybro Electric Supplies, Inc., Utility Div., 1012-1020 Ellamea Ave., PO Box 1351, Tampa, FL 33601-4012, (813)227-9277 [9266]

Rayco Car Electronics Inc., 160 Boston Tpke., Shrewsbury, MA 01545-3601, (508)757-8388 [25407]

Raycomm Telecommunications Inc., 1230 S Parker Rd., Denver, CO 80237, (303)755-6500 [5735]

Raylon Corp., 345 Morgantown Rd., PO Box 91, Reading, PA 19603, (610)376-4871 [14206]

Raylon Corp., 527 N White Horse Pike, Somerdale, NJ 08083, (609)435-6850 [14207]

Raylon Corp., 2528 Monroeville Blvd., Monroeville, PA 15146, (412)823-1047 [14208]

Raylon Corp., 3619 Walnut St., Harrisburg, PA 17109, (717)652-7851 [14209]

Raymond Equipment Company Inc., 3816 Bishop Ln., Louisville, KY 40218-2906, (502)966-2118 [7902]

Raymond Jewelers, 695 Haddon Ave., Collingswood, NJ 08108-3722, (609)854-5186 [17557]

Raymond Oil Co., PO Box 142, Huron, SD 57350, (605)352-8711 [22608]

Raymond Oil Company Inc., 1 Main Pl., No. 900, Wichita, KS 67202, (316)267-4214 [22609]

Raymond Sales Corp., PO Box 130, Greene, NY 13778-0130, (607)656-2311 [16440]

Ray's Beaver Bag, 727 Las Vegas Blvd. S, Las Vegas, NV 89101, (702)386-8746 [13434]

Rays Beverage Co., 4218 N Coronado Ave., Stockton, CA 95204-2328, (209)466-6883 [1979]

Ray's Food Service, 12601 SE Highway 212, PO Box 919, Clackamas, OR 97015, (503)655-1177 [12746]

Ray's Hobby, 190 Buttonwoods Ave., Warwick, RI 02886-7541, (401)738-4908 [26631]

Ray's Wholesale Meat, 2113 S 3rd Ave., Yakima, WA 98903-1413, (509)575-0729 [12281]

Ray's Workshop, 1750 E 27th Ave., Anchorage, AK 99508-4017, (907)277-2101 [21550]

Rayside Truck & Trailer, 2983 S Military Tr., West Palm Beach, FL 33415, (561)965-7950 [3136]

Raytex Fabrics Inc., 469 7th Ave., New York, NY 10018, (212)268-6001 [26183]

Raytheon Aircraft Services, PO Box 51830, Indianapolis, IN 46251, (317)241-2893 [140]

Rayvern Lighting Supply Company Inc., 7901 Somerset Blvd., Ste. C, Paramount, CA 90723, (562)634-7020 [9267]

RB Royal Industries Inc., 442 Arlington Ave., Fond du Lac, WI 54935, (920)921-1550 [23336]

RB Rubber Products Inc., 904 NE 10th Ave., McMinnville, OR 97128, (503)472-4691 [15630]

RB & W Corp., 800 Mogadore Rd., Kent, OH 44240-7535, (330)673-3446 [13883]

RBC Tile & Stone, 1820 Berkshire Ln. N, Plymouth, MN 55441, (612)559-5531 [10115]

RBC Tile and Stone, 1820 Berkshire Ln. N, Plymouth, MN 55441, (612)559-5531 [7903]

RBI Corp., 101 Cedar Ridge Dr., Ashland, VA 23005, (804)550-2210 [3137]

RBM Company Inc., PO Box 12, Knoxville, TN 37901, (423)524-8621 [22610]

RC International, 11222 I St., Omaha, NE 68137-1296, (402)592-2102 [14210]

RC Sports Inc., 9910 Lakeview Ave., Lenexa, KS 66219-2502, (913)894-6040 [23907]

R.C.A. America, 25 E Front St., Ste. 700, Keyport, NJ 07735, (732)335-1474 [7904]

RCF Inc., Altlanta Gift Mart, 230 Spring St. NW, Ste. 1127, Atlanta, GA 30303, (404)688-0304 [13435]

RCH Distributors Inc., 3140 Carrier, Memphis, TN 38116, (901)345-3100 [1170]

RCI Custom Products, 5615 Fishers Ln., Rockville, MD 20852-5200, (301)984-2202 [25408]

RCI Systems Inc., 5615 Fishers Ln., Rockville, MD 20852-5200, (301)984-2202 [25408]

R.C.P. Block and Brick Inc., PO Box 579, Lemon Grove, CA 91946, (619)460-7250 [7905]

RCP Inc., 813 Virginia St. E, Charleston, WV 25301, (304)343-5135 [21234]

RDC Communications Inc., 19 Dupont Ave., South Yarmouth, MA 02664-1203, (508)394-2405 [5544]

RDO Equipment Co., PO Box 7160, Fargo, ND 58109-7160, (701)237-6062 [1171]

RDO Equipment Co., 12500 S Dupont Ave., Burnsville, MN 55337, (952)890-8880 [16441]

RDO Equipment Co., PO Box 1069, Riverside, CA 92502, (909)682-5353 [1172]

Re-Mark Co., 2444 Cavell Ave. S, Minneapolis, MN 55426-2318, (612)545-7744 [25409]

Re-Neva Inc., 935 S Rock Blvd., Sparks, NV 89431, (775)352-2510 [21551]

Rea International Corp., 1414 Randolph Ave., Avenel, NJ 07001, (732)382-7100 [9268]

Read-Ferry Company Ltd., 22 Wilkins Ave., Haddonfield, NJ 08033, (609)795-5510 [16442]

Read Optical Inc., 414 Yellowstone Ave., Pocatello, ID 83201-4532, (208)234-4160 [19569]

Reade Advanced Materials, PO Box 15039, Riverside, RI 02915-0039, (401)433-7000 [4491]

Readers Wholesale Distributors Inc., PO Box 2407, Houston, TX 77252-2407, (713)224-8300 [10116]

Reading Crane and Engineering Co., 11 Vanguard Dr., Reading, PA 19606-3765, (610)582-7203 [16443]

Reading Feed and Grain Inc., 313 S Ann St., Reading, MI 49274, (517)283-2156 [1173]

Readmore Inc., 22 Cortlandt St., New York, NY 10007, (212)349-5540 [4108]

Ready Made Sign Co., 480 Fillmore Ave., Tonawanda, NY 14150, (716)695-7300 [25798]

Real Sales; Paul A., 1507 Mission St., South Pasadena, CA 91030, 800-722-0558 [25410]

Real Veal Inc., N 8155 American St., Ixonia, WI 53036, (414)567-8989 [1174]

RealCom Office Communications Inc., 2030 Powers Ferry, No. 580, Atlanta, GA 30339, (404)859-1100 [5736]

Really Right Stuff Co., PO Box 6531, Los Osos, CA 93412, (805)528-6321 [22897]

Rebco West/Vistawall, 9272 Hyssop Dr., Rancho Cucamonga, CA 91730-6108, (909)481-6144 [20309]

Rebel and Associates Inc.; Albert, PO Box 712548, Los Angeles, CA 90071-7548, (909)594-9515 [16444]

Rebel Oil Company Inc., 1900 W Sahara Ave., Las Vegas, NV 89102, (702)382-5866 [22611]

ReCellular Inc., 1580 E Elsworth Rd., Ann Arbor, MI 48108-2417, (313)327-7200 [5737]

Recife Importing & Exporting Inc., 2260 State St., Hamden, CT 06517, (203)624-3503 [14648]

RECO, 24 NE 51st, Oklahoma City, OK 73105, (405)236-1511 [14649]

Reco Crane Inc., PO Box 10296, New Orleans, LA 70181, (504)733-6881 [7906]

Reco International Corp., 150 Haven Ave., Port Washington, NY 11050, (516)767-2400 [4109]

Recognition Systems Inc., 30 Harbor Park Dr., Port Washington, NY 11050, (516)625-5000 [25799]

Record Technology Inc., 486 S Dawson Dr., No. 45, Camarillo, CA 93012-8049, (805)484-2747 [25411]

Recovered Classics, PO Box 1126, Kingston, NY 12402, (914)331-5807 [3905]

Recreation Supply Co., Box 2757, Bismarck, ND 58502-2757, (701)222-4860 [23908]

Recreational Sports and Imports Inc., PO Box 1587, Idaho Falls, ID 83403, (208)523-5721 [25412]

Recycle America Northern California, 800 77th Ave., Oakland, CA 94621, (510)638-4327 [26952]

Recycle Metals Corp., Allenwood Rd., Conshohocken, PA 19428, (215)828-5553 [26953]

Recycled Auto Parts of Brattleboro Inc., R.R. 6, Brattleboro, VT 05301, (802)254-9034 [3138]

Recycled Wood Products, PO Box 3517, Montebello, CA 90640, (213)727-7211 [1175]

Recycling Industries Inc., 9780 S Meridian Blvd., Ste. 180, Englewood, CO 80112, (303)790-7372 [26954]

Recycling Services Inc., 725 44th Ave. N, Minneapolis, MN 55412, (612)522-6558 [26766]

Red Apple Food Marts Inc., 5218 Milford Rd., East Stroudsburg, PA 18301, (717)588-9391 [12282]

Red Apple Supermarkets, 823 11th Ave. (57th), New York, NY 10019, (212)956-5770 [12283]

Red Ball Medical Supply Inc., PO Box 7316, Shreveport, LA 71137-7316, (318)424-8393 [19013]

Red Bud Industries Inc., 200 B and E Industrial Dr., Red Bud, IL 62278, (618)282-3801 [20310]

Red Devil Inc., 2400 Vauxhall Rd., Union, NJ 07083, (908)688-6900 [13884]

Red Diamond Inc., PO Box 2168, Birmingham, AL 35201, (205)254-3138 [12284]

RED Distribution, 79 5th Ave., 15th Fl., New York, NY 10003-3034, (718)740-5700 [25413]

Red Gaskins and Co.; J., 357 W Main St., Lake City, SC 29560-2315, (803)394-8830 [24209]

Red Giant Oil Co., PO Box 247, Council Bluffs, IA 51502, (712)323-2441 [22612]

Red-Kap Sales Inc., PO Box 1078, Schenectady, NY 12301, (518)377-6431 [22613]

Red Mill Farms Inc., 290 S 5th St., Brooklyn, NY 11211-6214, (718)384-4887 [12285]

Red River Barbeque and Grille, PO Box 1342, Wexford, PA 15090-1342, (412)366-9200 [12286]

Red River Electric & Refrigeration Supply, 810 Crossland Ave., Clarksville, TN 37040-3765, (931)552-6580 [14650]

Red Rock Distributing Co., PO Box 82336, Oklahoma City, OK 73148, (405)677-3371 [22614]

The Red Shed, 1006 James Madison Hwy., Warrenton, VA 20186-7820, (703)439-8988 [13481]

Red Spot Paint Varnish Co., PO Box 418, Evansville, IN 47703-0418, (812)428-9100 [21552]

Red Star Bio Products, 433 E Michigan St., Milwaukee, WI 53202, (414)221-6333 [12287]

Red Star Yeast and Products, A Division of Universal Foods Corp., 433 E Michigan St., Milwaukee, WI 53202, (414)221-6333 [12287]

Red Steer Glove Co., PO Box 7167, Salem, OR 97303-0034, (503)463-6227 [5305]

Red Stone Inc., 114 Ashaway Rd., Westerly, RI 02891-1437, (401)596-5283 [3139]

Red Trolley Co., 1643 10th St., Santa Monica, CA 90404, (310)450-0400 [12288]

Red Wing Products Inc., PO Box 68, Kellyville, OK 74039-0068, (918)247-6162 [9269]

Red Wing Shoe Store, 1014 Harlow Rd., Springfield, OR 97477-1141, (541)344-2323 [24839]

Reda Sports Express, PO Box 68, Easton, PA 18044, (215)258-5271 [23909]

Redburn Tire, 3801 W Clarendon Ave., Phoenix, AZ 85019, (602)272-7601 [3140]

Redco Lighting & Maintenance, 145 Waterman Ave., East Providence, RI 02914, (401)434-5511 [9270]

Reddi-Made Foods Inc., 5302 E Diana St., Tampa, FL 33610, (813)623-3333 [12289]

Reddish Supply; Phil, 11725 Royalton Rd., North Royalton, OH 44133, (440)582-4333 [25414]

Reddy Ice Company Inc., 4444 Vine St., Riverside, CA 92507, (909)683-1730 [12290]

Redel, PO Box 2408, Rohnert Park, CA 94927-2408, (707)578-8811 [8983]

Redfield Livestock Auction Inc., PO Box 356, Redfield, SD 57469, (605)472-2360 [18192]

Redhawk Industries Inc., PO Box 25322, Portland, OR 97298, (503)297-7072 [27362]

REDI-FROZ, 6500 S US Hwy. 421, Westville, IN 46391-9420, (219)237-5111 [12291]

Redington USA Inc., 65 Industrial Way, Wilmington, MA 01887, (978)988-7500 [6686]

Redlake County Co-op, PO Box 37, Brooks, MN 56715, (218)698-4271 [22615]

Redlake Imaging Corp., 18450 Technology Dr., Ste A, Morgan Hill, CA 95037-5450, (408)779-6464 [22898]

Redlands Auto Parts, 402 W Stuart Ave., Redlands, CA 92374-3138, (949)793-2101 [3141]

Redline Healthcare Corp., 8121 10th Ave. N, Golden Valley, MN 55427, (612)545-5757 [19014]

Redline Healthcare Corp., 8121 10th Ave. N, Golden Valley, MN 55427, (612)545-5757 [19570]

RedMax Komatsu Zenoah America Inc., 4344 Shackleford Rd., Norcross, GA 30093, (770)381-5147 [1176]

Red's/Fisher Inc., 8801 Exchange Dr., Orlando, FL 32809-7970, (407)857-3930 [12292]

Red's Market Inc., 8801 Exchange Dr., Orlando, FL 32809-7970, (407)857-3930 [12293]

Reds Office Supply, PO Box 1131, Hamilton, MT 59840-1131, (406)363-2242 [21235]

Redwing Book Company, Inc., 44 Linden St., Brookline, MA 02446, (617)738-4664 [4110]

Redwood Empire Inc., PO Box 1300, Morgan Hill, CA 95038, (408)779-7354 [7907]

Redwood Valley Co-op Elevator, PO Box 393, Redwood Falls, MN 56283, (507)637-2914 [18193]

Redwood Vintners, 12 Harbor Dr., PO Box 685, Black Point, Novato, CA 94948, (415)892-6949 [1980]

Redy Inc., 1233 E Sahara Ave., Las Vegas, NV 89104, (702)734-4801 [14211]

Reebok International Ltd., 100 Technology Center Dr., Stoughton, MA 02072, (781)401-5000 [24840]

Reebok International Ltd. Reebok Metaphors, 4 W 58th St., New York, NY 10019, (212)755-2610 [24841]

Reece Oil Co., PO Box 3195, Terre Haute, IN 47803-0195, (812)232-6621 [22616]

Reece Supply Company of Dallas, 3308 Royalty Row, Irving, TX 75062, (972)438-3131 [25800]

Reed Distributors, PO Box 1704, Lewiston, ME 04241-1704, (207)784-1591 [4692]

Reed Equipment Co., 1551 Stimson St., Stockton, CA 95206, (209)983-0100 [1177]

Reed Export, Inc.; Charles H., 894 Main St, PO Box 596, Norwell, MA 02061, (781)659-1555 [10117]

Reed Inc.; Schweichert, PO Box 245, Midlothian, VA 23113-0245, (804)794-5402 [17558]

Reed Manufacturing Co., 1425 W 8th St., Erie, PA 16502, (814)452-3691 [17133]

Reed Optical Co. Inc.; Fred, PO Box 94150, Albuquerque, NM 87199-4150, (505)265-3531 [19571]

Reed Publications, Inc.; Thomas, 13 B St., South Boston, MA 02127, (617)268-5500 [4111]

Reeder Distributors Inc., PO Box 8237, Ft. Worth, TX 76124-0237, (817)429-5957 [22617]

Reeds Seeds Inc., PO Box 230, Chillicothe, MO 64601, (816)646-4426 [1178]

Reedsville Cooperative Association, 305 N 6th St., Reedsville, WI 54230, (920)754-4321 [1179]

Reedy International Corp., 25 E Front St., Keyport, NJ 07735, (732)264-1777 [4693]

Reeled Tubing Inc., 206 Gunther Ln., Belle Chasse, LA 70037, (504)393-7880 [22618]

Rees Ceramic Tile; Cynthia, 454 E Jericho Tpke., Huntington Station, NY 11746, (516)673-8453 [10118]

Reese Chemical Co., 10617 Frank Ave., PO Box 1957, Cleveland, OH 44106, (216)231-6441 [14212]

Reese Chemical Co., 10617 Frank Ave., Cleveland, OH 44106, (216)231-6441 [19572]

Reese Farmers Inc., 9715 Saginaw, Reese, MI 48757, (517)868-4146 [18194]

Reese Pharmaceutical Co., PO Box 1957, Cleveland, OH 44106, (216)231-6441 [19573]

Reeve Aleutian Airways Inc., 4700 W Intl. Airport Rd., Anchorage, AK 99502-1091, (907)243-1112 [141]

Reeves Audio Visual Systems Inc., 227 E 45th St., 15th Fl, New York, NY 10017, (212)573-8652 [25415]

Reeves Peanut Company Inc., PO Box 565, Eufaula, AL 36027, (205)687-2756 [12294]

Reeves Photo Sales Inc., 4440-A Commerce Cir., Atlanta, GA 30336, (404)691-4260 [22882]

Reeve's Refrigeration & Heating Supply, PO Box 546, Minot, ND 58702-0546, (701)838-0702 [14651]

Reeves Southeastern Corp., PO Box 1968, Tampa, FL 33601, (813)626-3191 [7908]

Reeves-Wiedeman Co., 14861 W 100 St., Lenexa, KS 66215, (913)492-7100 [23337]

Refco IDG., 730 Main St., PO Box 8, Boylston, MA 01505-0008, (508)869-2106 [17134]

Refractory Products Co., 770 Tollgate Rd., Elgin, IL 60123, (708)697-2350 [14652]

Refrigeration & Air-Conditioning Maintenance Co., PO Box 43477, Las Vegas, NV 89116-1477, (702)642-3224 [14653]

Refrigeration Contractors Inc., PO Box 661, Gresham, OR 97030-0163, (503)257-8668 [14654]

Refrigeration and Electric Supply Co., 1222 Spring St., Little Rock, AR 72202, (501)374-6373 [15288]

Refrigeration Equipment Co., 820 Atlantic Ave., North Kansas City, MO 64116, (816)471-1466 [14655]

Refrigeration Heating Inc., 345 19th St. N, PO Box 989, Fargo, ND 58107-0989, (701)232-7070 [14656]

Refrigeration Sales Corp., 3405 Perkins Ave., Cleveland, OH 44114, (216)881-7800 [14657]

Refrigeration Sales Inc., PO Box 928, Jackson, MI 49204-0928, (517)784-8579 [14658]

Refrigeration Suppliers Inc., 412 Aberdeen Rd., Hampton, VA 23661-1324, (757)622-7191 [14659]

Refrigeration Supply Co., 907 Barry Pl. NW, Washington, DC 20001-2298, (202)462-2600 [14660]

Refrigeration Supply Inc., 8110 Eager Rd., St. Louis, MO 63144, (314)644-5500 [13217]

Refron Inc., 38-18 33rd St., Long Island City, NY 11101, (718)392-8002 [14661]

Regal Bag Corp., PO Box 8, Newburgh, NY 12551-0008, (914)562-4922 [18422]

Regal Fruit Co., 215 W 4th, PO Box 428, Tonasket, WA 98855, (509)486-2158 [12295]

Regal Plastic Supply Co., 111 E 10th Ave., North Kansas City, MO 64116, (816)421-6290 [23022]

Regal Plastic Supply Co. Kansas City Div., 1500 Burlington, Kansas City, MO 64116-3815, (816)471-6390 [23023]

Regal Plastic Supply Inc., PO Box 59977, Dallas, TX 75229, (972)484-0741 [23024]

Regal Shearing, 39 W 960 Midan Dr., Elburn, IL 60119, (630)232-6063 [18423]

Regal Steel Supply Inc., PO Box 1050, Stockton, CA 95201, (209)943-3223 [20311]

Regal Supply & Chemical Co., 1801 Texas Ave., PO Box 1955, El Paso, TX 79950, (915)542-1831 [21898]

Regan Co.; Steve, 4215 South 500 West, Murray, UT 84123, (801)268-4500 [1180]

Regency Collection Inc., 200 Northridge Dr., Acworth, GA 30101, (770)529-4270 [17559]

Regency Collection Inc., 2880 Holcomb Bridge Rd., Ste. 544, Alpharetta, GA 30022, (770)650-8420 [17560]

Regent Book Co., 101A, Rte. 46 W, Saddle Brook, NJ 07663, (201)368-2208 [4112]

Regent Sports Corp., 45 Ranick Rd., Hauppauge, NY 11788-4208, (516)234-2800 [23910]

Region Oil Div., PO Box 828, Dover, NJ 07802-0828, (973)366-3100 [22619]

Regional Communications Inc., PO Box 144, Paramus, NJ 07653-0144, (201)261-6600 [5738]

Regional Home Care Inc., 125 Tolman Ave., Leominster, MA 01453-1912, (978)840-0113 [19015]

Regional Supply Inc., 3571 S 300 W, Salt Lake City, UT 84115, (801)262-6451 [23025]

Rehab Equipment Co., PO Box 17374, Winston-Salem, NC 27116-7374, (919)765-6630 [19574]

Rehab Medical Equipment Inc., PO Box 1869, Collegedale, TN 37315-1869, (423)899-8172 [19016]

Rehab Specialties, 308 E 6th St., Erie, PA 16507, (814)454-2863 [19575]

The Rehab Tech Center, Rehab Institute of Pittsburgh, 6301 Northumberland St., Pittsburgh, PA 15217, (412)521-9000 [19576]

Rehab Technology of Colorado, 5855 Stapleton Dr. N, Ste. A150, Denver, CO 80216, (303)322-6544 [19577]

R.E.I. Glitter, 21851 Sherman Way, Canoga Park, CA 91303-1941, (818)887-9300 [21236]

Reichenbach Fireworks, 815 High Ridge Dr., Billings, MT 59105-5337, (406)248-1150 [26632]

Reichman, Crosby, Hays Inc., 3150 Carrier, Memphis, TN 38116, (901)345-2200 [17135]

Reico Distributors Inc., 6790 Commercial Dr., Springfield, VA 22151, (703)256-6400 [7909]

Reid Enterprises; Desmond A., 33 Lafayette Ave., Brooklyn, NY 11217, (718)625-4651 [4113]

Reid Tool Supply Co., 2265 Black Creek Rd., Muskegon, MI 49444, (616)777-3951 [17136]

Reif Carbide Tool Company, Inc., 11055 E 9 Mile Rd., PO Box 862, Warren, MI 48090, (810)754-1890 [16445]

Reif Oil Co., 911 Osborn St., Burlington, IA 52601-5023, (319)752-9809 [22620]

Reilly-Benton Company Inc., 1645 Tchoupitoulas St., New Orleans, LA 70152, (504)586-1711 [18591]

Reilly Dairy and Food Co., PO Box 19217, Tampa, FL 33686, (813)839-8458 [12296]

Reily Electrical Supply Inc., 3011 Lausat St., Metairie, LA 70001, (504)835-8888 [9271]

Reinalt-Thomas Corp., 14631 N Scottsdale Rd., Scottsdale, AZ 85254, (602)951-1938 [3142]

Reinauer Petroleum Co., 3 University Plz., #606, Hackensack, NJ 07601, (201)489-9700 [22621]

Reinders, Inc., PO Box 825, Elm Grove, WI 53122-0825, (262)786-3300 [1181]

Reiner & Company, Inc.; John, 601 Commercial Ave., Carlstadt, NJ 07072, (201)460-9444 [16446]

Reiner Enterprises, 9683 Sycamore Trace Ct., Cincinnati, OH 45242, (513)527-4949 [23338]

Reinhart Food Service Inc., PO Box 2859, La Crosse, WI 54602-2859, (608)782-2660 [12297]

Reinhart Institutional Foods Inc., PO Box 2859, La Crosse, WI 54602-2859, (608)782-2660 [12297]

Reinhart Institutional Foods Inc. Milwaukee Div., PO Box 395, Oak Creek, WI 53154-0395, (414)761-5000 [12298]

Reis Environmental Inc., 11022 Linpage Pl., St. Louis, MO 63132, (314)426-5603 [24617]

Reisen Lumber and Millwork Co., 1070 Morris Ave., Union, NJ 07083, (908)354-1500 [7910]

Reiser and Co.; Robert, 725 Dedham St., Canton, MA 02021, (617)821-1290 [15289]

Reising and Co.; G., 70 La Prenda, Millbrae, CA 94030-2119, (650)259-0700 [14944]

Reisman Corp.; H., 377 Crane St., PO Box 759, Orange, NJ 07051, (973)677-9200 [4492]

Reisner Corp.; William, 33 Elm St., Clinton, MA 01510, (508)365-4585 [26955]

Reiss Coal Co.; C., PO Box 688, Sheboygan, WI 53082-0688, (920)457-4411 [20561]

Reiter Dairy, 10456 S State Rte. 224, Findlay, OH 45839, (419)423-2341 [12299]

Reitman Industries, 10 Patton Dr., West Caldwell, NJ 07006, (201)228-5100 [1981]

Relay Specialties Inc., 17 Raritan Rd., Oakland, NJ 07436, (201)337-1000 [9272]

Relco Corp., 10600 Mastin St., Overland Park, KS 66212, (913)894-9090 [3143]

Relco Engineers, 13303 E Rosecrans Ave., Santa Fe Springs, CA 90670, (562)404-7574 [21553]

Reliable Architectural Metals Co., 9751 Erwin, Detroit, MI 48213, (313)924-9750 [7911]

Reliable Architectural Products, 9751 Erwin, Detroit, MI 48213, (313)924-9750 [7912]

Reliable Automotive of Kansas Inc., 10600 Mastin, Overland Park, KS 66212, (913)894-9090 [3144]

Reliable Battery Co., 550 Springfield Rd., San Antonio, TX 78219-1881, (512)737-2288 [9273]

Reliable Belt & Transmission, 1120 Cherry, Toledo, OH 43608, (419)248-2695 [3145]

Reliable Chevrolet Inc., 3655 S Campbell St., Springfield, MO 65807, (417)887-5800 [20710]

Reliable Fabrics Inc., PO Box 6176, Chelsea, MA 02150, (617)387-5321 [15631]

Reliable Fire Equipment Co., 12845 S Cicero Ave., Alsip, IL 60803, (708)597-4600 [24618]

Reliable Glass Co., 9751 Erwin, Detroit, MI 48213, (313)924-9750 [7912]

Reliable Paper & Supply Company Inc., 13 Water St., PO Box 666, Claremont, NH 03743-0666, (603)542-2161 [21899]

Reliable Tire Co., PO Box 560, Camden, NJ 08101, (609)365-6500 [3147]

Reliable Tire Co., 2420 Greenleaf Ave., Elk Grove Village, IL 60007-5510, (847)593-0090 [3146]

Reliable Tire Distributors Inc., PO Box 560, Camden, NJ 08101, (609)365-6500 [3147]

Reliable Tire Distributors Inc., PO Box 560, Camden, NJ 08101, (609)365-6500 [24290]

Reliance Bedding Corp., 3437 D St., Philadelphia, PA 19134-2540, (215)739-9900 [13218]

Reliance Electric Co., 78 Crosby St., Bangor, ME 04401-6838, (207)989-1634 [9274]

Reliance Group of Michigan, 23920 Freeway Park Dr., Farmington Hills, MI 48335, (248)478-6620 [21900]

Reliance Paper Co., 1404 W 12th St., Kansas City, MO 64101, (816)471-8338 [21901]

Reliance Sheet and Strip Co., 2301 W 10th St., Antioch, CA 94509, (510)706-1061 [20312]

Reliance Steel and Aluminum Co., PO Box 60482, Los Angeles, CA 90060, (213)582-2272 [20313]

Reliance Steel Co., 2537 E 27th St., Los Angeles, CA 90058, (323)583-6111 [20314]

Reliance Trailer Manufacturing Inc., 7911 Redwood Dr., Cotati, CA 94931, (707)795-0081 [20711]

Reliance Wine & Spirits, 4677 S 83rd East Ave., Tulsa, OK 74145-6901, (918)664-3347 [1982]

Reliv' International Inc., PO Box 405, Chesterfield, MO 63006-0405, (636)537-9715 [14213]

Reliv' World Corp., PO Box 405, Chesterfield, MO 63005, (314)537-9715 [12300]

RELM Communications Inc., 7707 Records St., Indianapolis, IN 46226, (317)545-4281 [5739]

REM Electronics Supply Company Inc., PO Box 831, Warren, OH 44482, (330)373-1300 [9275]

REM Sales Inc., 34 Bradley Park Rd., East Granby, CT 06026, (203)653-0071 [16447]

Remar; Irving, 22 Anson Rd., Portland, ME 04102-2202, (207)772-8007 [17561]

Rembrandt Lamps, 3757 S Ashland, Chicago, IL 60609-2130, (773)247-7500 [13127]

Rembrandt Lamps, 3757 S Ashland, Chicago, IL 60609, (773)247-7500 [15632]

Remco Business Systems Inc., 3000 Parston Dr., Forestville, MD 20747, (301)420-0800 [21237]

Remedpar Inc., 101 Old Stone Bridge Rd., Goodlettsville, TN 37072-3201, (615)859-1303 [19017]

Remixer Contracting Inc., PO Box 5090, Tyler, TX 75712, (512)258-8318 [7913]

Remy Amerique Inc., 1350 Ave. of the Amer., New York, NY 10019, (212)399-0200 [1983]

Renaissance Ceramic Tile, 1250 Easton Rd., Horsham, PA 19044, (215)674-4848 [10119]

Renaissance Drywall and Construction Supplies Inc., 821 Sivert Dr., Wood Dale, IL 60191, (708)766-1222 [7914]

Renaissance Stoneworks, 8111 NW 2nd Ct., Coral Springs, FL 33071, (954)971-9122 [7915]

Renault Telephone Supplies, 66-67 69th St., Middle Village, NY 11379, (718)894-9404 [5740]

Renco Corp., 30 Rockefeller Plz., New York, NY 10112, (212)541-6000 [20315]

Renfrow Tile Distributing Company, Inc., PO Box 9388, Charlotte, NC 28204, (910)275-7607 [10120]

Renick and Company Inc., 1500 N Post Oak Dr., No. 180, Houston, TX 77055, (713)684-5930 [6687]

Renishaw Inc., 623 Cooper Ct., Schaumburg, IL 60173, (847)843-3666 [19018]

Renken Distributing; M., 24 Glen Carran Cir., Sparks, NV 89431-5830, (702)355-8001 [25801]

Renkus-Heinz Inc., 17191 Armstrong Ave., Irvine, CA 92614, (949)250-0166 [25416]

Renner & Associates; E.J., 1375 W Alameda Ave., Denver, CO 80223, (303)744-3631 [7916]

Reno Auto Wrecking Inc., 2429 W 4th St., Reno, NV 89503-8807, (702)329-8671 [3148]

Reno Brake Inc., PO Box 7452, Reno, NV 89510-7452, (702)322-8635 [21554]

Reno Game Sales Inc., 4750 Longley Ln., Ste. 105, Reno, NV 89502, (702)829-2080 [26633]

Reno Jet Center, 655 S Rock Blvd., Reno, NV 89502, (775)858-7300 [22474]

Reno; Mary Ann, 9340-46 N May Ave., Oklahoma City, OK 73120, (405)755-4033 [5306]

Reno; Richard H. & Mary Ann, 9340-46 N May Ave., Oklahoma City, OK 73120, (405)755-4033 [5306]

Ren's Clearfield Paint & Glass, 426 N Main St., Clearfield, UT 84015, (801)776-2190 [21555]

Renzi Brothers Inc., 948 Bradley, Watertown, NY 13601-1209, (315)788-5610 [12301]

Rep Associates Inc., 5209 Point Fosdick Dr. NW, Ste. 206, Gig Harbor, WA 98335-1728, (253)851-8098 [15290]

Repete Corp., PO Box 900, Sussex, WI 53089, (414)246-4541 [16448]

Replacement Hardware Manufacturing Inc., 500 W 84th St., Hialeah, FL 33014, (305)558-5051 [7917]

Representative Sales Co., 6111 S Sayre Ave., Chicago, IL 60638, (773)586-2030 [26184]

Repro Technology Inc., PO Box 357, Conroe, TX 77305, (936)539-4419 [25802]

ReproCAD Inc., 1100 Kings Hwy. E, Fairfield, CT, (203)332-4700 [6688]

Reptron Electronics Inc., 179 Witmer Rd., Horsham, PA 19044, (215)855-0925 [9276]

Reptron Electronics Inc., 14401 McCormick Dr., Tampa, FL 33626-3046, (813)854-2351 [9277]

Republic Alloys Inc., 419 Atando Ave., Charlotte, NC 28206, (704)375-5937 [26956]

Republic Automotive, 2550 W 5th Ave., Denver, CO 80204-4803, (303)534-6133 [3149]

Republic Automotive Parts Inc., 500 Wilson Pike Cir., Ste. 115, Brentwood, TN 37027-3225, (615)373-2050 [3150]

Republic Beverage Co., 9835 Genard Rd., Houston, TX 77041, (713)690-8888 [1984]

The Republic Companies, PO Box 3807, Davenport, IA 52805, (319)322-6204 [9278]

Republic Electric, PO Box 3807, Davenport, IA 52805, (319)322-6204 [9278]

Republic Group, 5801 Lee Highway, Arlington, VA 22207, (703)533-8555 [9279]

Republic Jewelry & Coin Co., 212 Center St., Auburn, ME 04210-6150, (207)782-9492 [17562]

Republic Supply Co. (Dallas, Texas), 5646 Milton St., Ste. 800, Dallas, TX 75206, (214)987-9868 [22622]

Republic Tobacco L.P., 2301 Ravine Way, Glenview, IL 60025, (847)832-9700 [26346]

Republic Tobacco L.P., 5100 N Ravenswood Ave., Chicago, IL 60640, (312)728-1500 [26347]

Rero Distribution Co., Inc., 2005 Brighton Henrietta Townline Rd., Rochester, NY 14623, (716)424-7376 [9280]

R.E.S. Associates, PO Box 9520, Warwick, RI 02889, (401)738-0715 [7918]

Resaca Inc., PO Box 3691, Brownsville, TX 78520, (956)546-5525 [12302]

Resco Inc., 5252 Sherman St., Denver, CO 80216, (303)296-2222 [6940]

Research Biochemicals Inc., 1 Strathmore Rd., Natick, MA 01760, (508)651-8151 [4493]

Research Books, Inc., 38 Academy St., PO Box 1507, Madison, CT 06443, (203)245-3279 [4114]

Research Environmental Industries, 2777 Rockefeller Ave., Cleveland, OH 44115, (216)623-8383 [26957]

Research Seeds Inc., PO Box 1393, St. Joseph, MO 64502, (816)238-7333 [1182]

Reser's Fine Foods Inc., PO Box 8, Beaverton, OR 97075, (503)643-6431 [12303]

Reserve Industries Corp., 20 1st Plz., No. 308, Albuquerque, NM 87102, (505)247-2384 [7919]

Reserve Iron and Metal L.P., 4431 W 130th St., Cleveland, OH 44135, (216)671-3000 [20316]

Reserve Supply of Central New York Inc., PO Box 362, Syracuse, NY 13206, (315)463-4557 [7920]

Resilite Sports Products Inc., PO Box 764, Sunbury, PA 17801, (570)473-3529 [23911]

Resin Management Corp., 2307 N 36th St., Tampa, FL 33605, (813)242-4444 [4494]

Resource Electronics, Inc., 746 Vermont Ave., Palatine, IL 60067, (847)359-5500 [9281]

Resource Electronics Inc., PO Box 408, Columbia, SC 29202, (803)779-5332 [9282]

Resource Net International, PO Box 2967, Shawnee Mission, KS 66201, (913)451-1213 [21902]

Resource Net International, PO Box 1337, Harrisburg, PA 17105, (717)564-9761 [21903]

Resource Publications Inc., 160 E Virginia St., No. 290, San Jose, CA 95112-5876, (408)286-8505 [4115]

Resource Trading Co., PO Box 1698, Portland, ME 04104, (207)772-2299 [12304]

ResourceNet International, W 232 N 2950 Roundy Cir. E, PO Box 550, Pewaukee, WI 53072-4034, (262)549-9400 [22003]

ResourceNet International (Cincinnati, Ohio), 4510 Reading Rd., Cincinnati, OH 45229, (513)641-5000 [22004]

ResourceNet International (Shawnee Mission, Kansas), 50 E River Center Blvd., Ste. 700, Covington, KY 41011, (606)655-2000 [21904]

Respiratory Homecare Inc., 40 E Broad St., Cookeville, TN 38501-3210, (931)528-5894 [19019]

Respironics Colorado Inc., 1401 W 122nd Ave., Westminster, CO 80234, (303)457-9234 [19578]

Restaurant Design & Development, 2885 Aurora Ave., Ste. 7, Boulder, CO 80303-2251, (303)449-9331 [14662]

Reston Lloyd Ltd., PO Box 2302, Reston, VA 20195, (703)437-0003 [21556]

Restonic Carolina Inc., 3100 Camden Rd., Fayetteville, NC 28306-3260, (919)425-0131 [13219]

Resyn Corp., 1540 W Blanke St., Linden, NJ 07036, (908)862-8787 [23026]

Retail Service Company Inc., PO Box 1216, Portland, ME 04104, (207)839-2516 [13220]

Retailers Supply Co., 380 Freeport Blvd., No. 22, Sparks, NV 89431-6263, (775)356-8156 [21905]

Retif Oil and Fuel Inc., PO Box 58349, New Orleans, LA 70158-8349, (504)349-9000 [22623]

Reuben's Bottle Shop, 107 W Stassney, Austin, TX 78745, (512)442-8395 [1985]

Reuben's Wines & Spirits, 107 W Stassney, Austin, TX 78745, (512)442-8395 [1985]

Reuther Material Co., PO Box 106, North Bergen, NJ 07047, (201)863-3550 [7921]

Rev-A-Shelf, Inc., 2409 Plantside Dr., Louisville, KY 40299, (502)499-5835 [15633]

Revco Products, Inc., 7221 Acacia Ave., Garden Grove, CA 92841-3908, (714)891-6688 [3151]

Revels Tractor Company Inc., PO Box 339, Fuquay Varina, NC 27526, (919)552-5697 [1183]

Revels Tractor Company Inc., PO Box 339, Fuquay Varina, NC 27526, (919)552-5697 [1184]

Revere Electric Supply Co., 2501 W Washington Blvd., Chicago, IL 60612, (312)738-3636 [9283]

Revere Electrical Supply Co., 1211 23rd Ave., Rockford, IL 61104, (815)968-8866 [9284]

Revere Elevator Company Inc., Main St. & Railrd Track, Revere, MN 56166, (507)752-7341 [18195]

Revere Mills Inc., 7313 N Harlem Ave., Niles, IL 60714, (847)647-7070 [15634]

Revere Products, 4529 Industrial Pkwy., Cleveland, OH 44135, (216)671-5500 [7922]

Reverse & Company, 745 Sunset Cliffs Blvd., Ste. 1001, San Diego, CA 92107, (619)223-5015 [5307]

Rew Material Inc., PO Box 3360, Kansas City, KS 66103, (913)236-4004 [7923]

Rex Auto Parts, 1233 Gordon Park Rd., Augusta, GA 30901, (706)722-7526 [3152]

Rex Carriers, 29120 Wick Rd., Romulus, MI 48174, (734)947-1811 [22634]

Rex Chemical Corp., 2270 NW 23rd St., Miami, FL 33142, (305)634-2471 [4694]

Rex International, 815 Western Ave. No. 2 & 3, Glendale, CA 91201, (818)242-2899 [23912]

Rex Lumber Co. (Acton, Massachusetts), 840 Main St., Acton, MA 01720-5804, (978)263-0055 [7924]

Rex Mid-South Service, PO Box 30169, Memphis, TN 38130-0169, (901)332-2229 [13221]

Rex Oil Company Inc., PO Box 1050, Thomasville, NC 27360, (919)472-3000 [22624]

Rex Playground Equipment Inc., PO Box 75141, Oklahoma City, OK 73147-0141, (405)942-2880 [23913]

Rex Supply Co., PO Box 266, Houston, TX 77001, (713)222-2251 [16449]

Rexall Co., 6111 Broken Sound Pkwy. NW, Boca Raton, FL 33487-3625, (561)241-9400 [14214]

Rexall Co., 6111 Broken Sound Pkwy. NW, Boca Raton, FL 33487-3625, (561)241-9400 [19579]

Rexall Managed Care, 851 Broken Sound Pkwy. NW, Boca Raton, FL 33487, (561)241-9400 [14215]

Rexall Sundown Inc., 4031 Northeast 12th Terr., Ft. Lauderdale, FL 33334, (561)241-9400 [14216]

Rexel Glasco, 712 E 18th St., Kansas City, MO 64108-1705, (816)421-7020 [9285]

Rexel Inc., 150 Alhambra Cir., Ste. 900, Coral Gables, FL 33134, (305)446-8000 [9286]

Rexel Inc. (Coral Gables, Florida), 150 Alhambra Circle, Ste. 900, Coral Gables, FL 33134, (305)446-8000 [9287]

Rexel-Summers, 1424 Natchitoches St., West Monroe, LA 71292-3751, (318)325-9696 [9288]

Rexel-Summers, 1424 Natchitoches St., West Monroe, LA 71292-3751, (318)325-9696 [9289]

Rexel-Taylor, 1709 SE 3rd Ave., Portland, OR 97214, (503)233-5321 [9290]

Reynold S. Smith Marketing Inc., 9427 F St., Omaha, NE 68127, (402)592-4300 [11952]

Reynolds Aluminum Supply, 3900 Pinson Valley Pkwy., Birmingham, AL 35217, (205)853-7100 [20317]

Reynolds Aluminum Supply Co., 6603 W Broad St., Richmond, VA 23230, (804)281-2000 [20318]

Reynolds Industries Inc. (Watertown, Massachusetts), 33 Mount Auburn St., Watertown, MA 02472, (617)924-4650 [22625]

Reynolds Manufacturing Co., 1 Paramount Dr., PO Box 98, Bourbon, MO 65441, (573)732-4411 [5308]

Reynolds Metals Co. Construction Products Div., PO Box 27003, Richmond, VA 23261, (804)281-2000 [7925]

Reynolds Polymer Technology, 607 Hollingsworth St., Grand Junction, CO 81505, (970)241-4700 [7926]

The Reynolds and Reynolds Co., 24800 Denso Dr., Ste. 140, Southfield, MI 48034, (248)353-8500 [6689]

Reynolds & Sons Inc., 12 Monroe Ctr., Grand Rapids, MI 49503, (616)456-7161 [23914]

Reynolds and Sons Inc.; A.T., PO Box K, Kiamesha Lake, NY 12751, (914)794-7040 [25024]

Reynolds Tire and Rubber Div., 1421 38th St., Brooklyn, NY 11218, (718)633-0600 [3153]

RF Ltd. Inc., PO Box 1124, Issaquah, WA 98027-1124, (425)222-4295 [5741]

RF Management Corp., 95 Madison Dr., Morristown, NJ 07960, (973)292-2833 [19020]

RF Power Products Inc., 1007 Laurel Oak Rd., Voorhees, NJ 08043, (609)627-6100 [9291]

RF Technology, Inc., 16 Testa Pl., South Norwalk, CT 06854, (203)866-4283 [5742]

RG Group Inc., PO Box 2824, York, PA 17405, (717)846-9300 [17137]

RGA Tire Shop, 9 Ledge Rd., Pelham, NH 03076, (603)898-9077 [3154]

RGH Enterprises Inc., 2300 Edison Blvd., Twinsburg, OH 44087, (330)963-6996 [19021]

RGH Enterprises Inc., 2300 Edison Blvd., Twinsburg, OH 44087, (330)963-6996 [19580]

R.H. Bailey Seeds, Inc., PO Box 13517, Salem, OR 97309, (503)362-9700 [270]

Rhapsody Film Inc., 30 Charlton St., New York, NY 10014, (212)243-0152 [25417]

Rheas Crafts, 1914 111th St., Lubbock, TX 79423-7203, (806)795-2655 [21238]

Rhee Bros. Inc., 9505 Berger Rd., Columbia, MD 21046, (410)381-9000 [12305]

Rheinpfalz Imports Ltd., PO Box 49, Underhill Center, VT 05490-0049, (802)899-3905 [1986]

Rhermaltite Insulating Glass, PO Box 707, Rockford, IL 61105-0707, (815)394-1400 [7140]

Rheuban Associates, 3180 S Ocean Dr., No. 606, Hallandale, FL 33009, (954)454-9787 [3155]

RHM Fluid Power Inc., 375 Manufacturers Dr., Westland, MI 48186, (734)326-5400 [16450]

RHO-Chem Div., PO Box 6021, Inglewood, CA 90301, (213)776-6233 [4695]

Rhoades Wine Group, Inc., PO Box 985, Plainfield, IN 46168, (317)839-2504 [1987]

Rhoads Co.; D.W., 133 Cannell Dr., Somerset, PA 15501, (814)445-6531 [23339]

Rhoads Mills Inc., PO Box 24, Selinsgrove, PA 17870-0024, (717)374-8141 [1185]

Rhoda Brothers-Steel & Welding, 131 S Union St., Lima, OH 45801, (419)228-7121 [20319]

Rhode Island Distributing Co., PO Box 1437, Coventry, RI 02816, (401)392-3390 [1988]

Rhode Island Publications Society, 1445 Wampanoag Trail, No. 203, Riverside, RI 02915-1000, (401)272-1776 [4116]

Rhode Island Tack Shop Inc., PO Box 803, North Scituate, RI 02857, (401)934-0097 [18196]

Rhode Island Tile/G & M Co., 55 Industrial Rd., Cranston, RI 02920, (401)942-6700 [10121]

Rhode Island Wholesale Jewelry, PO Box 19758, Johnston, RI 02919, (401)943-5980 [17563]

Rhodes Corp.; P.J., 1016 Railroad Ave., Novato, CA 94945-2510, (415)892-0022 [12306]

Rhodes Oil Co., PO Box 557, Cape Girardeau, MO 63701, (573)334-7733 [22626]

Rhodes Supply Company Inc., Hwy. 303 S, Rte. 3, Mayfield, KY 42066-9725, (502)382-2185 [7927]

Rhone Company Inc.; George D., 109-27 West St., Coleman, TX 76834, (915)625-4141 [13885]

RHS Inc., PO Box 394, 2005 W Oregon, Hiawatha, KS 66434, (785)742-2949 [1186]

RI Business Equipment Co. Inc., 1021 Waterman Ave., East Providence, RI 02914-1314, (401)438-9593 [21239]

Ri-Mat Enterprises Inc., PO Box 606, San Gabriel, CA 91776, (626)287-9793 [13436]

RI Refrigeration Supply Co., 199 Branch Ave., Providence, RI 02904-2739, (401)421-8422 [14663]

RI Roof Truss Co. Inc., 45 River Ave., Johnston, RI 02919-6815, (401)942-7658 [7928]

RIA International, 123 Columbia Tpke. 104, Florham Park, NJ 07932, (973)301-2011 [14217]

Rialto Inc., 784 S San Pedro St., Los Angeles, CA 90014, (213)689-9096 [5309]

Rib River Valley Cooperative, PO Box 215, 409 Pine St., Marathon, WI 54448, (715)443-2241 [1187]

Riback Supply Company Inc., 2412 Business Loop 70 E, Columbia, MO 65201, (573)875-3131 [23340]

Ribbons Pasta Co., 823 Yale Ave., Ste. C, Seattle, WA 98109, (206)623-7552 [12307]

Ribelin Sales Inc., PO Box 461673, Garland, TX 75046, (214)272-1594 [4495]

Riccar America Co., 1800 E Walnut Ave., Fullerton, CA 92831, (714)669-1760 [15291]

Ricci; Robert, 30 Roosevelt Trail, Windham, ME 04062-4350, (207)892-2635 [24210]

Rice Aircraft Inc., 350 Motor Pkwy., Hauppauge, NY 11788, (516)435-1500 [142]

Rice Electronics Inc., PO Box 1481, Morgan City, LA 70381-1481, (504)385-5950 [5743]

Rice Electronics LP, PO Box 1481, Morgan City, LA 70381-1481, (504)385-5950 [5743]

Rice Growers Association of California, 1620 E Kentucky Ave, Woodland, CA 95776, (530)662-3235 [12308]

Rice of Kansas City Inc.; Scott, PO Box 412027, Kansas City, MO 64141, (816)221-6025 [21240]

Rice Lake Farmers Union Cooperative, PO Box 448, Rice Lake, WI 54868-0448, (715)234-8191 [1188]

Rice Lake Products Inc., PO Box 146, Minot, ND 58702, (701)857-6363 [25803]

Rice Oil Company Inc., 34 Montague City Rd., Greenfield, MA 01302, (413)772-0227 [22627]

Rice Tire Co.; Donald B., 909 East St., Frederick, MD 21701, (301)662-0166 [3156]

Rice Welding Supply Co., 10141 Market St., Houston, TX 77029, (713)674-2012 [17138]

Riceland Foods Inc., PO Box 927, Stuttgart, AR 72160, (870)673-5500 [12309]

RiceTec Inc., PO Box 1305, Alvin, TX 77512, (281)331-5655 [12310]

Rich Brothers Co., PO Box 1185, Sioux Falls, SD 57101-1185, (605)336-3344 [26634]

Rich Metals Co., PO Box 3491, Davenport, IA 52802, (319)322-0975 [26958]

Rich Planned Foods, 1821 Ivystone Dr., Richmond, VA 23233-4215, (804)266-7468 [12311]

Rich Products Corp. Food Service Div., PO Box 245, Buffalo, NY 14240, (716)878-8000 [12312]

Richard Beauty Supply, 4250 Normandy Court, Royal Oak, MI 48073, (248)549-3350 [14218]

Richard Distributing Co., 1601 Commercial NE, Albuquerque, NM 87102-1572, (505)247-4186 [1989]

Richard Electric Supply Company Inc., 7281 NW 8th St., Miami, FL 33126, (305)266-8000 [9292]

Richard-Ewing Equipment Co. Inc., 27121 Parklane Dr., Sioux Falls, SD 57106-8000, (605)368-2528 [4696]

Richard-Ginori 1735, Inc., 41 Madison Ave., 6th Fl., New York, NY 10010, (212)213-6884 [15635]

Richard The Thread, 8320 Melrose, West Hollywood, CA 90069, (213)852-4997 [26185]

Richard Tucker, 155 Dow St., Ste. 402, Manchester, NH 03101, (603)666-7030 [13263]

Richard's American Food Service, 14323 W College Ave., Muskego, WI 53150, (262)679-1617 [12313]

Richards Co.; S.P., 1012 McDermott Rd., Metairie, LA 70001-6226, (504)834-3540 [21241]

Richards Co.; S.P., PO Box 1266, Smyrna, GA 30081, (770)436-6881 [21242]

Richards and Conover Steel Co., 6333 St. John Ave., Kansas City, MO 64123, (816)483-9100 [20320]

Richards International; Lyle, 1 Cabot Pl., Stoughton, MA 02072, (781)344-1994 [24842]

Richards Machine and Cutting Tools Inc., PO Box 471, Gretna, LA 70054, (504)368-1004 [16451]

Richards Machinery Company Inc.; L.L., PO Box 516, Butler, WI 53007-0516, (414)771-3120 [16452]

Richards Manufacturing Company Inc., 725 Ionia SW, Grand Rapids, MI 49503, (616)247-0965 [23341]

Richards Products Inc., PO Box 9000, Ft. Lauderdale, FL 33340, (954)978-0313 [14219]

Richards Quality Bedding, 702 Hall SW, Grand Rapids, MI 49503-4899, (616)241-2481 [13222]

Richardson Brands Co., 6330 Manor Ln., Miami, FL 33143, (305)667-3291 [12314]

Richardson Dana Div., 165 Presumpscot St., Portland, ME 04103, (207)773-0227 [7929]

Richardson Electronics, Ltd., 40W267 Keslinger Rd., Lafox, IL 60147-0393, (630)208-2787 [9293]

Richardson Electronics, Ltd., 40W267 Keslinger Rd., PO BOX 393, Lafox, IL 60147-0393, (630)208-2200 [9294]

Richardson Seeds Inc., PO Box 60, Vega, TX 79092, (806)267-2379 [1189]

Richardson & Sons Distributors, 3631 Hwy. 231, Panama City, FL 32401, (850)785-6124 [7930]

Richardson Sports Inc., 3490 W 1st Ave., Eugene, OR 97402, (541)687-1818 [23915]

Richardson Trident Co, 405 N Plano Rd., Richardson, TX 75081, (972)231-5176 [20321]

Richardson's Educators Inc., 2014 Lou Ellen Ln., Houston, TX 77018, (713)688-2244 [4117]

Richey Design Ltd.; William, 20 Main St., Camden, ME 04843-1704, (207)236-4731 [17564]

Richey Electronics Inc., 7441 Lincoln Way, Garden Grove, CA 92841, (714)898-8288 [9295]

Richfood Holdings Inc., PO Box 26967, Richmond, VA 23261-6967, (804)746-6000 [12315]

Richfood Inc., PO Box 26967, Richmond, VA 23261-6967, (804)746-6000 [12316]

Richland Ltd., PO Box 489, Spring Green, WI 53588, (608)588-7779 [3157]

Richlund Enterprises, 608 3rd St., Kentwood, LA 70444, (504)229-3252 [15292]

Richlund Sales Inc., 608 3rd St., Kentwood, LA 70444, (504)229-3252 [15292]

Richman Sons Inc.; S.D., 2435 Wheatsheaf Ln., Philadelphia, PA 19137, (215)535-5100 [26959]

Richman's Ice Cream Div., Rte. 40 and Kings Hwy., Woodstown, NJ 08098, (609)769-0350 [12317]

Richmond Electric Supply Co., PO Box 10, Richmond, IN 47374, (765)962-6543 [9296]

Richmond Foundry Inc., 8500 Sanford Dr., Richmond, VA 23228, (804)266-4244 [23342]

Richmond Machinery and Equipment Inc., PO Box 6588, Richmond, VA 23230, (804)359-4048 [7931]

Richmond Office Supply, 816 E Main St., Richmond, VA 23219-3306, (804)644-4025 [21243]

Richmond Optical Co., PO Box 4377, Hayward, CA 94540, (510)783-1420 [19581]

Richter Fertilizer Co., Hwy. 100, Pleasant Hill, IL 62366, (217)285-4475 [1190]

Richton International Corp., 211 Sheffield St., Mountainside, NJ 07092-2302, (973)966-0104 [1191]

Rickard Metals Inc., 1707 S Grove Ave., Ontario, CA 91761, (909)947-4922 [20322]

Rickett Grain Co., PO Box 32, Forest City, IL 61532, (309)597-2331 [18197]

Ricketts Bag Corporation, PO Box 15085, Tampa, FL 33684, (813)876-2474 [21664]

Rickreall Farms Supply Inc., PO Box 67, Rickreall, OR 97371, (503)623-2366 [1192]

Rickwood Radio Service of Tennessee, 1830 Air Lane Dr., Nashville, TN 37210-3817, (615)889-3270 [25418]

Rico Industries Inc., 1712 S Michigan Ave., Chicago, IL 60616, (312)427-0313 [18424]

Ricom Electronics Ltd., PO Box 17882, Milwaukee, WI 53217-0882, (414)357-8181 [6690]

Ridco Inc., 2707 Mt. Rushmore Rd., PO Box 5600, Rapid City, SD 57701-5600, (605)343-2226 [17565]

Ridge Auto Parts Company Inc., 714 S Thomas Rd., Ft. Wayne, IN 46804, (219)456-6913 [3158]

Ridge Co., PO Box 2859, South Bend, IN 46680, (219)234-3143 [3159]

Ridgeland Chetek Cooperative, PO Box 155, Ridgeland, WI 54763, (715)949-1165 [1193]

Ridgeview Inc., PO Box 8, Newton, NC 28658, (704)464-2972 [5310]

Ridgewood Corp., PO Box 716, Mahwah, NJ 07430, (201)529-5500 [23343]

Ridout Lumber Cos., 125 Henry Farr Dr., Searcy, AR 72143, (501)268-0386 [27363]

Ridout Plastics Inc., 5535 Ruffin Rd., San Diego, CA 92123, (619)560-1551 [23027]

Riedel Crystal of America Inc., 24 Aero Rd., Bohemia, NY 11716, (516)567-7575 [15636]

Rieger Medical Supply Co., 3111 E Central Ave., Wichita, KS 67214-4816, (316)684-0589 [19022]

Rieger's Ceramics Arts & Crafts, 1321 4th Ave. E, PO Box 572, Mobridge, SD 57601-0572, (605)845-2995 [26635]

Rieke Equipment Co. Inc.; Ernie, 3311 Merriam Ln., Kansas City, KS 66106, (913)432-1600 [7932]

Riekes Equipment Co., 6703 L St., Omaha, NE 68131, (402)593-1181 [16453]

Riemeier Lumber Company Inc., 1150 Tennessee Ave., Cincinnati, OH 45229-1010, (513)242-3788 [7933]

Riffel & Sons Inc.; C., 1253 S Water, Saginaw, MI 48601-2560, (517)752-8365 [1990]

Riggins Oil Co.; L.S., 3938 S Main Rd., Vineland, NJ 08360, (609)825-7600 [22628]

Riggs Supply Co., 320 Cedar St., Kennett, MO 63857, (573)888-4639 [13886]

Riggs Wholesale Supply, Hwy. 60 E, Poplar Bluff, MO 63901-9150, (573)785-5746 [7934]

Riggsbee Hardware & Industrial Supply, 1120 Sampson, Houston, TX 77003-3932, (713)224-6734 [13887]

Right Stuff Inc., 24 Ray Ave., Ste. 103, Burlington, MA 01803-4760 [24843]

Right of Way Equipment Co., 5500 Hillsborough Rd., Raleigh, NC 27606, (919)851-1750 [1194]

Rihm Motor Co., 2108 University Ave., St. Paul, MN 55114, (612)646-7833 [20712]

Riley and Geehr Inc., 2205 Lee St., Evanston, IL 60202-1597, (847)869-8100 [23028]

Riley Sales Inc., 1719 Romano Dr., Plymouth Meeting, PA 19462, (610)279-4500 [11]

Riley and Son Inc.; W.H., PO Box 910, North Attleboro, MA 02761, (508)699-4651 [22629]

Riley-Stuart Supply Co., 601 Western Dr., Mobile, AL 36607, (205)471-4361 [7935]

Riley's Electrical Supply, 111435 Reiger Rd., Baton Rouge, LA 70809, (504)755-0066 [9297]

Rim and Wheel Service Inc., 1014 Gest St., Cincinnati, OH 45203, (513)721-6940 [3160]

Rimfire Imports, Inc., 831-106 Eha St., Wailuku, HI 96793, (808)242-6888 [12318]

Rinella Beverage Co., 915 Tower Rd., Mundelein, IL 60060, (847)949-7777 [1991]

Rinella and Company Inc.; A.J., Broadway Menands Regional Market, Albany, NY 12204, (518)465-4581 [12319]

Ringhaver Equipment Co., PO Box 30169, Tampa, FL 33630, (813)671-3700 [16454]

Ring's Coal Co., 51 Main St., Yarmouth, ME 04096, (207)846-5503 [20562]

Rio Contract Sewing, 1009 E Miracle Mile, Box 3961, McAllen, TX 78502, (956)630-2761 [4809]

Rio Farmers Union Cooperative, PO Box 246, Rio, WI 53960, (920)992-3114 [18198]

Rio Grande Co., PO Box 17227, Denver, CO 80217, (303)825-2211 [7936]

Rio Grande, Neutec, Sonic Mill, West Coast, 7500 Bluewater Rd. NW, Albuquerque, NM 87121-1962, (505)839-3000 [17331]

Rio Grande Trading Co., 1441 W 46th Ave., No. 8, Denver, CO 80211, (303)433-5700 [14220]

Rippey Auto Parts Company Inc., 117 E 6th St., Columbia, TN 38401, (931)388-0723 [3161]

Rippey Farmers Cooperative, Perseville St., Rippey, IA 50235, (515)436-7411 [1195]

Ris Paper Company Inc., 7300 Turfway Rd., Ste. 540, Florence, KY 41042, (606)746-8700 [21906]

Rish Equipment Co., PO Box 330, Bluefield, WV 24701, (304)327-5124 [7937]

Rising Sun Import Parts Inc., 8983 Mira Mesa Blvd., San Diego, CA 92126, (619)693-0044 [3162]

Risser Oil Corp., 2865 Executive Dr., Clearwater, FL 33762, (813)573-4000 [22630]

Rita Selections Ltd., 8208 Mt. Nido Rd., Las Vegas, NV 89117-5224, (702)364-2284 [26636]

Ritchie Grocer Co., PO Box 71, El Dorado, AR 71730, (870)863-8191 [12320]

Ritchie and Page Distributing Company Inc., 292 3rd St., Trenton, NJ 08611, (609)392-1146 [1992]

Rite in the Rain Paper, 2614 Pacific Hwy. E, Tacoma, WA 98424-1017, (253)922-5000 [21701]

Rite Way Barber & Beauty Supplies, 5818 McClellan Blvd., Anniston, AL 36206, (205)820-1124 [14221]

Rite Way Oil and Gas Company Inc., PO Box 27049, Omaha, NE 68127-0049, (402)331-6400 [22631]

Rittenhouse Book Distributors, Inc., 511 Feheley Dr., King of Prussia, PA 19406, (215)277-1414 [4118]

Ritter Engineering Co., 100 Williams Dr., Zelienople, PA 16063, (724)452-6000 [23344]

Ritter Equipment Co.; E., 116 Hwy. 63 W, Marked Tree, AR 72365, (870)358-2555 [1196]

Ritter Sysco Food Services Inc., 640 Dowd Ave., Elizabeth, NJ 07207, (908)558-2700 [12321]

Rittner Products Inc., PO Box 301, Rochester, MI 48307, (248)651-1333 [7938]

Rival/Pollenex, 800 E 101 Terr., Ste. 100, Kansas City, MO 64131, (816)943-4100 [14222]

Rivard International Corp., 10979 Reed Hartman Hwy., Ste. 200, Cincinnati, OH 45242-2855, (513)984-8821 [7939]

Rivard's Quality Seeds Inc., PO Box 303, Argyle, MN 56713, (218)437-6638 [18199]

River City Enterprises, PO Box 9365, Peoria, IL 61612, (309)688-3223 [23029]

River City Petroleum Inc., 840 Delta Ln., West Sacramento, CA 95691, (916)371-4960 [22632]

River City Steel and Recycling Inc., PO Box 240580, San Antonio, TX 78224-0580, (210)924-1254 [26960]

River Country Cooperative, 1080 W River St., Chippewa Falls, WI 54729, (715)723-2828 [1197]

River Park, Inc., 21953 Protecta Dr., Elkhart, IN 46516, (219)295-8780 [25419]

River Petroleum Inc.; James, PO Box 7200, Richmond, VA 23221, (804)358-9000 [22633]

River Spring Cooperative, PO Box 87, Old Fort, OH 44861, (419)992-4223 [18200]

River Springs Cooperative Association, 8419 N State Rte. 19, Green Springs, OH 44836, (419)639-2242 [27222]

River Trading Co., 3300 Bass Lake Rd., No. 220, Brooklyn Center, MN 55429, (612)561-9206 [20563]

River Valley Cooperative, PO Box 30, Watertown, WI 53094, (414)262-6760 [1198]

Rivers Body Co., Inc., 10626 General Ave., PO Box 6009, Jacksonville, FL 32236, (904)781-5622 [3163]

Riverside Bearing, 3226 Blair Ave., St. Louis, MO 63107, (314)421-0919 [2976]

Riverside Book and Bible House, 1500 Riverside Dr., PO Box 370, Iowa Falls, IA 50126, (515)648-4271 [4119]

Riverside Chemical Company Inc., PO Box 197, 811 River Rd., North Tonawanda, NY 14120, (716)692-1350 [4496]

Riverside Communications, 653 Commercial Rd., Ste. 8, Palm Springs, CA 92262-6264, (760)322-5556 [5744]

Riverside Distributors, PO Box 370, Iowa Falls, IA 50126-0370, (515)648-4271 [4120]

Riverside Drives Inc., 4509 W 160th St., PO Box 35166, Cleveland, OH 44135, (216)362-1211 [3164]

Riverside Foods, 2520 Wilson, Two Rivers, WI 54241, (920)793-4511 [12322]

Riverside Group Inc., 7800 Belfort Pkwy., Jacksonville, FL 32256, (904)281-2200 [7940]

Riverside Homemade Ice Cream, 409 Marion Cardington Rd. W, Marion, OH 43301, (740)389-1013 [12323]

Riverside Liquors & Wine, 17 Connor Ave., Mt. Morris, NY 14510, (716)658-4701 [1993]

Riverside Paper Company Inc., 5770 NW 36th Ave., Miami, FL 33142, (305)633-5221 [21907]

Riverside Potatoes Inc., 23611 Adams Point Rd., PO Box 535, Merrill, OR 97633, (541)798-5184 [12324]

Riverside Recycling Inc., PO Box 17166, Louisville, KY 40217, (502)634-8531 [26961]

Riverside Scrap Iron, PO Box 5288, Riverside, CA 92517, (909)686-2120 [26962]

Riverside Seafoods Inc., 2520 Wilson, Two Rivers, WI 54241, (920)793-4511 [12322]

Rivertex Company, Inc., 401 Broadway, New York, NY 10013, (212)925-1410 [26186]

Riverton Coal Co., 1520 Kanawha Blvd., Charleston, WV 25311, (304)739-4136 [20564]

Riverview FS Inc., PO Box 5127, Rockford, IL 61125-0127, (815)332-4956 [1199]

Riviana Foods Inc., PO Box 2636, Houston, TX 77252-2141, (713)529-3251 [12325]

Riviera Tile Inc., 4515 North Expy., Brownsville, TX 78520, (956)350-4545 [10122]

Rizzoli International Inc., 300 Park Ave. S, New York, NY 10010, (212)387-3400 [4121]

R.J. Marketing, Ltd., 1010 Rockville Pike, Ste. 607, Rockville, MD 20852, (301)251-0330 [9298]

R.J. Marketing, Ltd., 3523 W Crown Ave., Philadelphia, PA 19114, (215)637-3429 [9299]

RJM Sales, Associates, Inc., 1739 Chestnut St., Glenview, IL 60025, (847)486-9133 [13888]

RKA Petroleum Companies, L.L.C., 29120 Wick Rd., Romulus, MI 48174, (734)947-1811 [22634]

RKB Enterprises Inc., PO Box 659, Portland, ME 04104-5020 [23345]

RKR Corp., 4600 Grape St., Denver, CO 80216, (303)321-7610 [17139]

RLB Food Distributors L.P., 2 Dedrick Pl., West Caldwell, NJ 07007, (973)575-9526 [12326]

RLI Corp., 9025 N Lindbergh Dr., Peoria, IL 61615, (309)692-1000 [19582]

RLP Inc., PO Box 37889, Phoenix, AZ 85069-7889, (602)943-0625 [19023]

RMC Foods, Inc., PO Box 338, St. George, UT 84771, (435)673-3583 [12327]

RMC Inc., PO Box 1109, Harrisonburg, VA 22801, (540)434-5333 [23346]

RMP Enterprises Inc., La Fonda Hotel, 100 E San Francisco St., Santa Fe, NM 87501, (505)983-5552 [17566]

RMT Engineering, Inc., 9779 Business Park Dr., Ste. I, Sacramento, CA 95827-1715, (916)366-0261 [9300]

RNM Specialty Co., PO Box 542, Bethpage, NY 11714, (516)933-1940 [13437]

R.O. Systems International, 1914 W Mission Rd., Ste. H, Escondido, CA 92029, (760)747-3100 [25804]

Ro-Vic Inc., PO Box 1140, Manchester, CT 06045-1140, (860)646-3322 [4697]

Roa Distributors, 341 E Liberty St., Lancaster, PA 17603, (717)295-9023 [21908]

Roach and Smith Distributors, Inc., 1005 S Montana St., Butte, MT 59701, (406)782-9158 [1994]

Road Machinery Co., 716 S 7th St. (85034), PO Box 4425, Phoenix, AZ 85030, (602)252-7121 [25805]

Road Rescue Inc., 1133 Rankin St., St. Paul, MN 55116, (612)699-5588 [3165]

Road Runner Pet Supplies, 403 Middle San Pedro, Espanola, NM 87532, (505)753-6196 [27223]

Road-Runner Tire Service, 33960 Old Willamette Hwy. S, Eugene, OR 97405, (541)744-2000 [3166]

Road Tested Recycled Auto Parts Inc., 4544 Woodson Rd., St. Louis, MO 63134-3704, (314)427-3900 [3167]

Roak's Seven-Acre Greenhouses, 963 Washington Ave., Portland, ME 04103, (207)772-5523 [14945]

Roane-Barker Inc., PO Box 2880, Greenville, SC 29602-2880, (864)234-0598 [19024]

The Roane Co., 14141 Arbor Pl., Cerritos, CA 90703, (562)404-3464 [10123]

The Roane Co., 6160 Marindustry Dr., San Diego, CA 92121-9663, (619)455-9663 [10124]

The Roane Co., 3537 E Corona Ave., Phoenix, AZ 85040-2841, (602)268-1441 [10125]

The Roane Co., 3955 W Mesa Vista Ave., No. A8, Las Vegas, NV 89118-2339, (702)736-1811 [10126]

The Roane Co., 14141 Arbor Pl., Cerritos, CA 90703, (562)404-3464 [27364]

Roanoke Distributing Company Inc., PO Box 4210, Roanoke, VA 24015-0210, (540)342-3105 [1995]

Roatan International Corporation, 20 West 38th St., 4th Floor, New York, NY 10018, (212)768-7538 [21244]

Robbins Auto Parts Inc., 110 Washington St., Dover, NH 03820, (603)742-2880 [3168]

Robbins Livestock Auction, PO Box 17004, Missoula, MT 59808-7004, (406)728-3052 [18201]

Robbinsdale Farm and Garden Pet Supply Inc., 7301 32nd Ave. N, Minneapolis, MN 55427-2835, (612)559-7166 [27224]

Robco Corp., 4842 Park Glen Rd., Minneapolis, MN 55416-5702, (612)920-8966 [23916]

Robco International Corporation/Advanced Technology International, PO Box 707, Oak Park, IL 60303, (708)524-1880 [17140]

Robela Knit Shop Ltd., 250 N Main St., Mt. Holly, NC 28120, (704)827-7246 [5311]

Robern Golfwear Inc., 166 Whitney Ln., Richboro, PA 18954-1080 [5312]

Robern Skiwear Inc., 350 5th Ave., New York, NY 10118, (212)563-7040 [5313]

Robert Allen Fabrics Inc., 55 Cabot Blvd., Mansfield, MA 02048, (508)339-9151 [26187]

Robert Distributors Inc.; Roland J., PO Box 70, Burnside, LA 70738, (504)644-4886 [22635]

Robert-James Sales Inc., PO Box 7999, Buffalo, NY 14225-7999, (716)874-6300 [20323]

Robert Manufacturing Company Inc., 1055 E 35th St., Hialeah, FL 33013, (305)691-5311 [18425]

Roberts Auto Parts; Fred, 320 Main, Arcade, NY 14009-1115, (716)492-5114 [3169]

Roberts Brothers Inc., PO Box 109, Shawboro, NC 27973, (919)232-2798 [18202]

Roberts and Brune Co., 939 Broadway, PO Box 5100, Redwood City, CA 94063, (650)366-3833 [17141]

Roberts Colonial House Inc., 570 W armory Dr., PO Box 308, South Holland, IL 60473, (708)331-6233 [23030]

Roberts Co.; D.B., 54 Jonspin Rd., Wilmington, MA 01887, (978)658-7000 [9301]

Roberts Co.; D.B., 1100 Valwood Pkwy., Ste. 108, Carrollton, TX 75006, (972)466-3666 [9302]

Roberts Co.; D.B., 3 Town Line Cir., Rochester, NY 14623, (716)475-0070 [9303]

Roberts Co. Inc., 180 Franklin St., Framingham, MA 01701, (508)875-8877 [4122]

Roberts and Company Inc.; F.L., 93 W Broad St., Springfield, MA 01105, (413)781-7444 [22636]

Roberts Dairy Co., PO Box 1435, Omaha, NE 68101, (402)344-4321 [12328]

Roberts Dairy Co., 3805 Van Brunt Blvd., Kansas City, MO 64128, (816)921-7370 [12329]

Roberts and Dybdahl Inc., Box 1908, Des Moines, IA 50306, (515)283-7100 [7941]

Roberts Foods Inc., 1615 W Jefferson St., Springfield, IL 62702, (217)793-2633 [12330]

Roberts-Hamilton Co., 800 Turners Crossroads S, Golden Valley, MN 55416, (612)544-1234 [23347]

Roberts-Hamilton Co., Div. of Hajoca Corp., 800 Turners Crossroads S, Golden Valley, MN 55416, (612)544-1234 [23347]

Roberts Inc.; M.L., 8 Industrial Ln., Johnston, RI 02919, (401)421-0600 [17567]

Roberts Industries Inc.; J.H., 3158 Des Plaines Ave., Des Plaines, IL 60018, (708)699-0080 [20324]

Roberts International, Inc., 200 Office Park Dr., Ste. 215, Birmingham, AL 35223, (205)879-0033 [7942]

Roberts Manufacturing Inc., 120 West 300 South, American Fork, UT 84003-2646, (801)756-6016 [13223]

Roberts Motor Co., 550 NE Columbia Blvd., Portland, OR 97211, (503)240-6282 [20713]

Roberts Motor Co., 550 NE Columbia Blvd., Portland, OR 97211, (503)240-6282 [16455]

Roberts Oxygen Company Inc., PO Box 5507, Rockville, MD 20855, (301)948-8100 [19025]

Roberts Paper Co., PO Box 1029, 100-104 Lincoln, Amarillo, TX 79105, (806)376-9814 [21909]

Roberts Seed Co., PO Box 206, Tangent, OR 97389, (541)926-8891 [1200]

Roberts and Sons Inc.; Frank, R.R. 2, Box 81, Punxsutawney, PA 15767, (814)938-5000 [7943]

Robertshaw Uni-Line North America, PO Box 2000, Corona, CA 91718-2000, (909)734-2600 [14664]

Robertson Distributing, PO Box 748, Norfolk, NE 68702-0748, (402)371-1891 [1996]

Robertson Heating Supply Co., 500 W Main St., Alliance, OH 44601, (330)821-9180 [23348]

Robertson Optical Labs, Inc., 1812 Washington St., Columbia, SC 29202, (803)553-3365 [19583]

Robertson Supply Inc., PO Box R, Nampa, ID 83653-0057, (208)466-8907 [23349]

Robin Seed Co.; Clyde, 3670 Enterprise Ave., Hayward, CA 94545, (510)785-0425 [1201]

Robins Brokerage Co., PO Box 1506, Salt Lake City, UT 84110, (801)974-0500 [12331]

Robin's Food Distribution Inc., PO Box 617637, Chicago, IL 60661, (312)243-8800 [12332]

Robins L.L.C.; A.K., 4030 Benson Ave., Baltimore, MD 21227, (410)247-4000 [24211]

Robinson Barbecue Sauce Company Inc., 942 Madison St., Oak Park, IL 60302, (708)383-1333 [12333]

Robinson Brick Co., PO Box 5243, Denver, CO 80217, (303)783-3000 [7944]

Robinson Co.; Frank L., 1150 S Flower St., Los Angeles, CA 90015, (213)748-8211 [5314]

Robinson Fin Machines Inc., 13670 Hwy. 68 S, Kenton, OH 43326-9302, (419)674-4152 [14665]

Robinson Iron and Metal Company Inc., 2735 Brooks St., Houston, TX 77020, (713)227-2376 [26963]

Robinson Lumber Company Inc., 4000 Tchoupitoulas St., New Orleans, LA 70115, (504)895-6377 [7945]

Robinson Lumber Company Inc., 4000 Tchoupitoulas St., New Orleans, LA 70115, (504)895-6377 [27365]

Robinson Manufacturing Company Inc., 798 S Market St., Dayton, TN 37321, (423)775-2212 [5315]

Robinson Steel Company Inc., 4303 Kennedy Ave., East Chicago, IN 46312, (219)398-4600 [20325]

Robinson Wholesale Inc., PO Box 338, Genoa City, WI 53128-0338, (414)279-2320 [23917]

Robinson's Woods, 1057 Trumbull Ave., Unit N, Girard, OH 44420, (330)759-3843 [21245]

Robison & Associates; Jerry, PO Box 17509, Fountain Hills, AZ 85269, (602)471-1411 [23918]

Robison Distributors Co., PO Box 2309, Salt Lake City, UT 84110, (801)486-3511 [10127]

Robnet Inc., 3701 Commerce Dr., Baltimore, MD 21227, (410)247-7273 [13889]

Robroy Industries, Hwy. 49 E, Rte. 1, Box 1, Avinger, TX 75630, (903)562-1341 [9304]

Robstown Hardware Co., PO Box 831, Robstown, TX 78380, (512)387-2564 [1202]

Robzens Inc., 240 River St., Scranton, PA 18505-1182, (717)344-1141 [12334]

Rocamar Services Inc., 12764 NW 9th Terrace, Miami, FL 33182, (305)221-7121 [23350]

Rocco Building Supplies Inc., PO Box 1860, Harrisonburg, VA 22801-9500, (540)434-1371 [7946]

Rochester Drug Cooperative Inc., PO Box 1670, Rochester, NY 14603, (716)271-7220 [19584]

Rochester Electronics Inc., 10 Malcolm Hoyt Drive, Newburyport, MA 01950, (978)462-9332 [9305]

Rochester Imports Inc., PO Box 1380, Seneca, SC 29679-1380, (864)882-5642 [26637]

Rochester Instrument Systems Inc., 255 N Union St., Rochester, NY 14605-2699, (716)263-7700 [9306]

Rochester Liquor Corp., PO Box 20596, Rochester, NY 14602-0596, (716)586-4911 [1997]

Rochester Midland Corp., PO Box 1515, Rochester, NY 14603, (716)336-2200 [4698]

Rock Candy Inc., 1401 W 8th St., Los Angeles, CA 90017-4302, (213)483-8570 [5316]

Rock Hill Coca-Cola Bottling Co., PO Box 2555, Rock Hill, SC 29732, (803)328-2406 [25025]

Rock Island North, 38 Hamilton Dr., Ignacio, CA 94949, (415)883-2375 [12335]

Rock Lumber and Supply Co.; Glen, PO Box 2545, Fair Lawn, NJ 07410, (201)796-4500 [7947]

Rock Mirrors Inc., 130 Ferry Ave., Oaklyn, NJ 08107, (609)962-6720 [13438]

Rock River Lumber and Grain Co., 406 Washington St., Prophetstown, IL 61277, (815)537-5131 [1203]

Rock River Provision Company Inc., 3309 W Rock Falls Rd., Rock Falls, IL 61071, (815)625-1195 [12336]

Rock Springs Casper Coca-Cola Bottling Co., PO Box 939, Rock Springs, WY 82902, (307)382-2233 [25026]

Rock Valley Oil and Chemical Company Inc., 1911 Windsor Rd., Loves Park, IL 61111, (815)654-2400 [22637]

Rockbridge Farmers Cooperative, 645 Waddell St., Lexington, VA 24450, (703)463-7381 [1204]

Rocket Jewelry Box Inc., 125 E 144th St., Bronx, NY 10451-5435, (212)292-5370 [17568]

Rocket Supply Corp., Hwy. 115 & Hwy. 54, Roberts, IL 60962, (217)395-2281 [20714]

Rocket World Trade Enterprise, 118 W 137th St., Ste. 1b, New York, NY 10030, (212)281-6898 [5850]

Rocketline, 42 W 61st St., Chicago, IL 60621-3999, (773)684-6700 [21742]

Rockford Bolt & Steel Co., 126 Mill St., Rockford, IL 61101-1491, (815)968-0514 [13890]

Rockford Industrial Welding Supply Inc., 4646 Linden Rd., Rockford, IL 61109-3300, (815)226-1900 [17142]

Rockford Industrial Welding Supply Inc., 4646 Linden Rd., Rockford, IL 61109-3300, (815)226-1900 [16456]

Rockingham Cooperative Farm Bureau, 101 Grace St., Harrisonburg, VA 22801, (540)434-3856 [1205]

Rockingham Electrical Supplies Inc., 187 River Rd., Newington, NH 03801, (603)436-2310 [9307]

Rockland Boat, Inc., 20 Park Dr., Rockland, ME 04841, (207)594-8181 [18592]

Rockland Industries Inc., 1601 Edison Hwy., Baltimore, MD 21213, (410)522-2505 [26188]

Rockland Marine Corp., 79 Mechanic St., Rockland, ME 04841, (207)594-7860 [18593]

Rockland Tire and Service Co., 109 Rte. 59, Monsey, NY 10952, (914)356-7100 [3170]

Rockmount of Arkansas, 17 N 2nd, Ft. Smith, AR 72901-1103, (501)782-4545 [5317]

Rockmount Ranch Wear Manufacturing Co., PO Box 481025, Denver, CO 80248, (303)629-7777 [5318]

Rocknel Fastener Inc., 5309 11th St., PO Box 5087, Rockford, IL 61125-5087, (815)873-4000 [13891]

Rockview Farms Inc., PO Box 668, Downey, CA 90241, (562)927-5511 [12337]

Rockville Fabrics Corp., 225 W 34th St., No. 1509, New York, NY 10122, (212)563-2050 [26189]

Rockville Fuel and Feed Company Inc., 14901 Southlawn Ln., Rockville, MD 20850, (301)762-3988 [7948]

Rockwell, 3323 Paterson Plank Rd., North Bergen, NJ 07047, (201)865-2228 [7949]

Rockwell and Son; H., PO Box 197, Canton, PA 17724, (717)673-5148 [1206]

Rockwood Chemical Co., PO Box 34, Brawley, CA 92227, (760)344-0916 [1207]

Rocky Mountain Conveyor and Equipment, 6666 E 47th Avenue Dr., Denver, CO 80216-3409, (303)333-5778 [16457]

Rocky Mountain Food Factory Inc., 2825 S Raritan St., Englewood, CO 80110, (303)761-3330 [12338]

Rocky Mountain Instrument Co, 106 Laser Dr., Ste. 1, Lafayette, CO 80026, (303)651-2211 [19585]

Rocky Mountain Lasers and Instruments Inc., 3975 E 56th Ave., Ste. A-1, Commerce City, CO 80022-3662, (303)898-5277 [24423]

Rocky Mountain Machinery Co., PO Box 26737, Salt Lake City, UT 84126, (801)972-3660 [7950]

Rocky Mountain Marketing Services Inc., 10885 E 51st Ave., Denver, CO 80239, (303)371-9770 [12339]

Rocky Mountain Natural Meats Inc., 2351 E 70th Ave., Denver, CO 80229, (303)287-7100 [12340]

Rocky Mountain Recycling, 4431 E 64th Ave., Commerce City, CO 80022, (303)288-6868 [26964]

Rocky Mountain Salon Consolidated, 1413 Gold Ave., Bozeman, MT 59715-2410, (406)586-2792 [14223]

Rocky Mountain Wine & Spirits, 14200 E Moncrieff Pl., Aurora, CO 80011, (303)371-0832 [1876]

Rockys II Inc., 615 N Wenatchee Ave., Wenatchee, WA 98801-2059, (509)663-7973 [23919]

Rod Co. Inc.; A.J., 5011 Navigation Blvd., Houston, TX 77011, (713)921-6111 [17143]

Rodan Inc., 5821 Citrus Blvd., Harahan, LA 70123, (504)734-2640 [6691]

RoData Inc., 247 Fort Pitt Blvd., 4th Fl., Pittsburgh, PA 15222, (412)316-6000 [5745]

Rodda Paint Co., 12000 SW Garden Pl., Portland, OR 97223, (503)521-4300 [21557]

Roddis Lumber and Veneer Company Inc., PO Box 1446, San Antonio, TX 78295-1446, (210)226-1426 [7951]

Rodefeld Company Inc., 96 W Main St., Richmond, IN 47374, (765)966-1571 [3171]

Roden Electrical Supply Co., 170 Mabry Hood Rd., Knoxville, TN 37923, (615)546-8755 [9308]

Rodgers International Trading Inc., 16716 Wanda Ct. SE, No. 1, Yelm, WA 98597, (206)458-2203 [12341]

Rodi Automotive Inc., 13 Harbor Park Dr., Port Washington, NY 11050, (516)484-9500 [3172]

Rodico Inc., 18 Park Way, Upper Saddle River, NJ 07458, (201)327-6303 [25934]

Rodon Foods, 1333 West 7900 South, West Jordan, UT 84088-9438, (801)566-0616 [12342]

Rodriguez Festive Foods Inc., PO Box 4369, Ft. Worth, TX 76164-0369, (817)624-2123 [12343]

Rodriguez Inc.; R.A., 20 Seaview Blvd., Port Washington, NY 11050-4618, (516)625-8080 [17144]

Rods Indiana Inc., PO Box 369, Butler, IN 46721, (219)868-2172 [13892]

Rodwell Sales, 3640 Concord Rd., York, PA 17402-8629, (717)848-2732 [15637]

Roe-Comm Inc., 1400 Ramona Ave., Kalamazoo, MI 49002-3638, (616)327-1045 [9309]

Roebic Laboratories Inc., 25 Connair Rd., Orange, CT 06477, (203)795-1283 [4497]

Roeden Inc., PO Box 50050, Henderson, NV 89016-0050, (702)798-2800 [17569]

Roeder Implement Company Inc., 1010 Skyline Dr., Hopkinsville, KY 42240, (502)886-3994 [1208]

Roeder Implement Inc., 2550 Rockdale Rd., Dubuque, IA 52003, (319)557-1184 [1209]

Roekel Co., PO Box 2220, Zanesville, OH 43702, (740)452-5421 [23351]

Roethele Building Materials Inc., 3100 Wells St., Ft. Wayne, IN 46808, (219)482-9591 [7952]

Roga International Div. Export-Import Marketing, 413 E 1st St., PO Box 6026, Rome, GA 30162, (706)295-5181 [15638]

Roger Gimbel Accessories Inc., 350 Fifth Ave., Ste. 2101, New York, NY 10118, (212)273-9200 [18447]

Rogers Brothers Wholesale Inc., 470 E Brooks St., Galesburg, IL 61401, (309)342-2127 [12344]

Rogers Co.; B.W., PO Box 1030, Akron, OH 44309, (330)315-3100 [17145]

Rogers Decorative Fabrics; Miles, 690 Miami Cir., Ste. 500, Atlanta, GA 30324 [26190]

Rogers Electric; Charles, 12745 Prospect, Dearborn, MI 48126-3653, (313)581-2611 [9310]

Rogers Electric Supply; Chas., 12745 Prospect, Dearborn, MI 48126-3653, (313)581-2611 [9310]

Rogers Electric Supply Co., 701 Jackson St., Sioux City, IA 51102, (712)252-3251 [9311]

Rogers Group Inc. Louisville, 12808 Townepark Way, Louisville, KY 40243-2312, (502)244-7060 [7953]

Rogers Heritage Trust; Will, W Will Rogers Blvd., PO Box 157, Claremore, OK 74018, (918)341-0719 [4123]

Rogers Iron and Metal Corp., PO Box 1806, Rogers, AR 72757, (501)636-2666 [26965]

Rogers Kitchens Inc., 130 Chestnut St., Norwich, CT 06360-4552, (860)886-0505 [13224]

Rogers Lumber International, 846 South EE Wallace Blvd., PO Box 1795, Ferriday, LA 71334, (318)757-4508 [8157]

Rogers Machinery Company Inc., PO Box 230429, Portland, OR 97281, (503)639-0808 [16458]

Rogers Pool Supply, Inc., 1826 Brooks Rd. E, Memphis, TN 38116-3608, (901)345-1470 [23920]

Rogue Aggregates Inc., PO Box 4430, Medford, OR 97501, (541)664-4155 [7954]

Rohde and Schwarz Inc., 4425 Nicole Dr., Lanham Seabrook, MD 20706, (301)459-8800 [9312]

Rohtstein Corp., PO Box 2129, Woburn, MA 01888, (781)935-8300 [12345]

Rol-Lift Corp., 12300 Amelia Dr., Houston, TX 77045, (713)434-3400 [3173]

Roland Corporation U.S., 7200 Dominion Cir., Los Angeles, CA 90040, (213)685-5141 [25420]

Roland Digital Group, 15271 Barranca, Irvine, CA 92618-2201, (714)975-0560 [6692]

Roland Foods, 2421 Schuster Dr., Cheverly, MD 20781, (301)322-5444 [12346]

Roland Machinery Co., PO Box 2879, Springfield, IL 62708, (217)789-7711 [7955]

Roldan Products Corp., 13545 Barrett Pkwy. Dr., Ste. 302, Ballwin, MO 63021, (314)822-7222 [15293]

Rolet Food Products Co., 70 Scott Ave., Brooklyn, NY 11237, (718)497-0476 [12347]

Roll and Hold Warehousing and Distribution, 1745 165th St., Hammond, IN 46320, (219)853-1125 [20326]

Roll-Rite Corp., 26265 Research Rd., Hayward, CA 94545, 800-345-9305 [16459]

Rolla Cooperative Equity Exchange, PO Box 196, Rolla, KS 67954, (316)593-4335 [18203]

Rolla Cooperative Grain Co., 116 Front St. S Box 177, Rolla, ND 58367, (701)477-5612 [18204]

Rolled Steel Co., 2525 Arthur Ave., Elk Grove Village, IL 60007, (847)981-8370 [20327]

Rolled Steel Products Corp., 2187 S Garfield Ave., Los Angeles, CA 90040, (213)723-8836 [20328]

Roller Derby Skate Corp., 311 W Edwards St., Litchfield, IL 62056, (217)324-3961 [23921]

Rolls Battery Engineering Inc., PO Box 671, Salem, MA 01970, (508)745-3333 [18594]

Roloff Manufacturing Corp., PO Box 7002, Kaukauna, WI 54130-7002, (920)766-3501 [18595]

Rolyn Inc., 189 Macklin St., Cranston, RI 02920, (401)944-0844 [17570]

Roma Chain Manufacturing, 21 SE 1st Ave., Ste. 300, Miami, FL 33131, (305)374-1169 [17571]

Roma Enterprises, 3281 Turgot Circle, Cincinnati, OH 45241, (513)769-5363 [25421]

Roma Food Enterprises Inc., 45 Stanford Rd., Piscataway, NJ 08854, (908)463-7662 [12348]

Roma Tile Co., Inc., 306 Wolf St., Syracuse, NY 13208, (315)471-7856 [10128]

Romac Export Management Corp., 2242 S Hobart Blvd., Los Angeles, CA 90018-2149, (213)734-2922 [15639]

Roman Inc., 555 Lawrence Ave., Roselle, IL 60172, (630)529-3000 [13439]

Romanelli and Son Inc., PO Box 544, Lindenhurst, NY 11757, (516)454-7500 [22638]

Romano Brothers Beverage Co., 7575 S Kostner Ave., No. 100, Chicago, IL 60652-1141, (773)767-9500 [1998]

Romanoff Corp.; Maya, 1730 W Greenleaf Ave., Chicago, IL 60626-2412, (773)465-6909 [15640]

Romanoff International Supply Corp., 9 Deforest St., Amityville, NY 11701, (631)842-2400 [17572]

Romar Industries Inc., 3149-B Haggerty Rd., Walled Lake, MI 48390, (248)669-7080 [9313]

Rome Cable Corp., 421 Ridge St., Rome, NY 13440, (315)337-3000 [9314]

Rome Paper Co., 1 E 16th St., PO Box 313, Rome, GA 30161, (706)234-8208 [21910]

Romeo & Sons, 100 Romeo Ln., Uniontown, PA 15401-2337, (724)438-5561 [12349]

Romic Chemical Corp., 2081 Bay Rd., East Palo Alto, CA 94303, (415)324-1638 [26966]

Ronald Hayes Pearson Inc., RR 1, Box 158, Deer Isle, ME 04627-9709, (207)348-2535 [17573]

Ronco, 84 Grand Island Blvd., Tonawanda, NY 14150, (716)879-8136 [9317]

Ronco, 595 Sheridan Dr., Tonawanda, NY 14150, (716)873-0760 [5746]

Ronco Communications and Electronics, 84 Grand Island Blvd., Tonawanda, NY 14150, (716)873-0760 [9315]

Ronco Communications and Electronics Inc., 595 Sheridan Dr., Tonawanda, NY 14150, (716)873-0760 [5746]

Ronco Power Systems Inc., 84 Grand Island Blvd., Tonawanda, NY 14150, (716)873-0760 [9316]

Ronco Specialized Systems Inc., 84 Grand Island Blvd., Tonawanda, NY 14150, (716)879-8136 [9317]

Ronlee Apparel Co., 165 Chubb Ave., Lyndhurst, NJ 07071, (201)507-5300 [5319]

Rons Office Equipment Inc., 127 W 4th St., Roswell, NM 88201-4709, (505)622-0756 [21246]

Ron's Produce Company Inc., 4504 S Country Club Rd., Tucson, AZ 85714-2046, (520)294-3796 [12350]

Ron's Steel Sales, 846 South St., Biddeford, ME 04005, (207)499-2736 [20329]

Rood Utilities, PO Box 216, Auburn, NY 13021, (315)252-7204 [14666]

Roofers Supplies Inc., PO Box 126, Bergenfield, NJ 07621, (201)384-4224 [7956]

Roofing Distributing Company Inc., 4401 Appleton St., Cincinnati, OH 45209, (513)871-4100 [7957]

Roofing Supply Inc., PO Box 90100, Anchorage, AK 99509-0100, (907)349-3123 [7958]

Roofing Wholesale Company Inc., 1918 W Grant St., Phoenix, AZ 85009, (602)258-3794 [7959]

Roosevelt Co.; W.A., PO Box 1208, La Crosse, WI 54602-1208, (608)781-2000 [14667]

Roosevelt Paper Co., One Roosevelt Dr., Mt. Laurel, NJ 08054, (856)303-3470 [21911]

Rooster Products International Inc., 8154 Bracken Creek, San Antonio, TX 78266, (210)651-5288 [13893]

Rooster Products International Inc./McGuire-Nicholas, 8154 Bracken Creek, San Antonio, TX 78266, (210)651-5288 [13893]

Root Brothers Manufacturing and Supply Co., 10317 S Michigan St., Chicago, IL 60628, (773)264-5000 [17146]

Root Corp., 152 N Main St., Mt. Wolf, PA 17347, (717)266-5626 [20224]

Root, Neal and Company Inc., PO Box 101, Buffalo, NY 14240, (716)824-6400 [9318]

Roots & Fruits Cooperative Produce, 451E Industrial Blvd. NE, Minneapolis, MN 55413-2930, (612)722-3030 [12351]

Roppel Industries Inc., 829 Logan St., Louisville, KY 40204, (502)581-1004 [3174]

Rorer West Inc., 655 Spice Island Dr., Sparks, NV 89431, (702)353-4100 [19586]

Rorke Data Inc., 9700 W 76th St., Eden Prairie, MN 55344-3714, (612)829-0300 [6693]

Rosamond Cooperative, PO Box 37, Rosamond, IL 62083, (217)562-2363 [18205]

Rosanna Imports Inc., 1239 S King St., Seattle, WA 98144-2024, (206)325-8883 [15641]

Rosanna Inc., 1239 S King St., Seattle, WA 98144-2024, (206)325-8883 [15641]

Rosario Candy Inc., 1150 Lyon Rd., Batavia, IL 60510, (630)584-4677 [26348]

Rosas Computer Co., 326 S Enterprise Pkwy., Corpus Christi, TX 78405, (512)289-5991 [6694]

Rose Brand Textile Fabrics, 75 9th Ave., New York, NY 10011, (212)242-7554 [26191]

Rose Brand-Theatrical Fabrics Fabrications and Supplies, 75 9th Ave., New York, NY 10011, (212)242-7554 [26191]

Rose Brothers Inc., PO Box 319, Lingle, WY 82223, (307)837-2261 [1210]

Rose Caster Co., 12402 Hubbell St., Detroit, MI 48227, (313)272-8200 [13894]

Rose City Awning Co., 1638 NW Overton St., Portland, OR 97209, (503)226-2761 [26192]

Rose Goldsmith; H.M., 801 Scalp Ave., Johnstown, PA 15904-3314, (814)266-9430 [17574]

Rose Hill Distribution Inc., 81 Rose Hill Rd., Branford, CT 06405, (203)488-7231 [12352]

Rose Inc.; Clare, 72 West Ave., Patchogue, NY 11772, (516)475-1840 [1999]

Rose Industries Inc. (Houston, Texas), PO Box 7887, Houston, TX 77270, (713)880-7000 [20330]

Rose Metal Processing, 2902 Center St., Houston, TX 77007, (713)880-7000 [26967]

Rose Metal Products Inc., PO Box 3238, Springfield, MO 65808, (417)865-1676 [20331]

Rose Metal Recycling Inc., 2902 Center St., Houston, TX 77007, (713)880-7000 [26967]

Rose Products and Services Inc., 545 Stimmel Rd., Columbus, OH 43223, (614)443-7647 [4699]

Rosebar Tire Shredding Inc., PO Box 924, Cedar Rapids, IA 52406-0924, (319)472-5271 [24291]

Rosebud Coal Sales Co., 1000 Kiewit Plaza, Omaha, NE 68131, (402)342-2052 [20549]

Rosebud Farmers Union Cooperative Associates Inc., PO Box 24 A, Gregory, SD 57533, (605)835-9656 [1211]

Rosebud Farmers Union Cooperative Associates Inc., PO Box 24 A, RR 2, Gregory, SD 57533, (605)835-9656 [22639]

Rosedale Fabricators/Ampco, Hwy. 1 N, Rosedale, MS 38769-0608, (601)759-3521 [21247]

Roselli's Wholesale Foods Inc., 33069 Groesbeck Hwy., Fraser, MI 48026, (810)296-9780 [12353]

Rosemont Pharmaceutical Corp., 301 S Cherokee St., Denver, CO 80223, (303)733-7207 [19587]

Rosemount Office Systems, Inc., 21785 Hamburg Ave., Lakeville, MN 55044-9035, (612)469-4416 [21248]

Rosenau Equipment Co., Hwy. 281 N, Carrington, ND 58421, (701)652-3144 [1212]

Rosenblum's World of Judaica, Inc., 2906 W Devon Ave., Chicago, IL 60659, (773)262-1700 [4124]

Rosen's Diversified Inc., PO Box 933, Fairmont, MN 56031, (507)238-4201 [4498]

Rosen's Inc., PO Box 933, Fairmont, MN 56031, (507)238-4201 [1213]

Rosenstein and Co., 413 N Cedar St., Mishawaka, IN 46545, (219)255-9639 [26193]

Rose's Stores Inc., PO Drawer 947, Henderson, NC 27536, (919)430-2100 [5320]

Rosetta Oil Inc., Rockledge & Robbins, Rockledge, PA 19046, (215)379-4400 [22640]

Rosetta Oil Inc., 1463 Lamberton Rd., Trenton, NJ 08611, (609)393-6899 [22641]

Rosetta Oil Inc. Duck Island Terminal, 1463 Lamberton Rd., Trenton, NJ 08611, (609)393-6899 [22642]

Rosholt Farmers Cooperative Elevator Co., PO Box 16, Rosholt, SD 57260, (605)537-4236 [18206]

Rosing; William, 4850 Diamond Dr., Colorado Springs, CO 80918, (719)591-1606 [5321]

Ross and Company International; Mark, PO Box 410506, San Francisco, CA 94141-0506, (415)285-5500 [12354]

Ross Corp., PO Box 2577, Eugene, OR 97402, (541)689-5031 [7960]

Ross-Erikson, 8471 Warwick Dr., Desert Hot Springs, CA 92240-1124 [4125]

Ross-Frazer Supply Co., 8th & Monterey, St. Joseph, MO 64503, (816)279-2731 [13895]

Ross Island Sand and Gravel Co., PO Box 82249, Portland, OR 97282-0249, (503)239-5504 [7961]

Ross Supply Company Inc., 3015 S Valley Ave., PO Box 1087, Marion, IN 46952, (765)664-2384 [23352]

Ross-Willoughby Co., PO Box 182054, Columbus, OH 43218-2054, (614)486-4311 [16460]

Rossignol Ski Co., PO Box 298, Williston, VT 05495, (802)863-2511 [24844]

Roswell Livestock Auction Co., PO Box 2041, Roswell, NM 88202-2041, (505)622-5580 [18207]

Roswell Winnelson Co., 223 E 3rd St., Roswell, NM 88201-6219, (505)623-8700 [14668]

Roswell Wool LLC, 212 E 4th St., Roswell, NM 88201, (505)622-3360 [18208]

Rota Systems Inc., PO Box 361, Derby, KS 67037-0361, (316)788-4531 [19588]

Rotary Corp., PO Box 947, Glennville, GA 30427, (912)654-3433 [1214]

Rotelle Inc., PO Box 370, West Point, PA 19486, (215)699-5300 [12355]

Roth Distributing Co., 11300 W 47th St., Minnetonka, MN 55343-8849, (952)933-4428 [15294]

Roth Distributing Co., 15845 E 32nd Ave., Ste. 2A, Aurora, CO 80011, (303)373-9090 [15295]

Roth Novelty Co., 333 N Pennsylvania Ave., Wilkes Barre, PA 18702, (717)824-9994 [25834]

Rothenberg and Schloss Inc., 6100 Broadmoor St., Mission, KS 66202-3229 [14224]

Rothenbuhler Engineering, 2191 Rhodes Rd., PO Box 708, Sedro Woolley, WA 98284-0708, (360)856-0836 [5747]

Rothman & Co.; Fred B., 1285 Main St., Buffalo, NY 14209, (716)882-2600 [3821]

Roto-Litho Inc., 1827 E 16th St., Los Angeles, CA 90021, (213)749-7551 [21912]

Rotometals Inc., 980 Harrison St., San Francisco, CA 94107, (415)392-3285 [18596]

Rott-Keller Supply Co., PO Box 390, Fargo, ND 58107-0390, (701)235-0563 [3175]

Round Butte Seed Growers Inc., PO Box 117, Culver, OR 97734, (541)546-5222 [1215]

Roundy's Foods, 4501 Peters Rd., Evansville, IN 47711, (812)423-8034 [12356]

Roundy's, Inc., 23000 Roundy Dr., Pewaukee, WI 53072-4095, (262)953-7999 [12357]

Roundy's Inc., 1100 Prosperity Rd., Lima, OH 45801, (419)228-3141 [12358]

Roundy's Inc. Eldorado Div., PO Box 411, Eldorado, IL 62930, (618)273-2671 [12359]

Roundy's Inc. Lima Div., 1100 Prosperity Rd., Lima, OH 45801, (419)228-3141 [12360]

Roundy's Westville Div., PO Box 125, Westville, IN 46391, (219)785-4671 [12361]

Rous Inc.; R.J., 4366 W Ogden Ave., Chicago, IL 60623, (773)521-3663 [12362]

Route 16 Grain Cooperative, 301 E State St., Nokomis, IL 62075, (217)563-8612 [18209]

Rouzee Green Company Inc.; The John, 65 N Congress St., PO Box 379, York, SC 29745, (803)684-6853 [23922]

Rovac Inc., 3055 Old Hwy. 8, Minneapolis, MN 55418-2500, (612)779-9444 [6695]

Rowenta Inc., 196 Boston Ave., Medford, MA 02155, (781)396-0600 [15296]

Rowland Co., 4900 N 20th St., PO Box 12278, Philadelphia, PA 19144, (215)455-4900 [17147]

Rowland Equipment, Inc., 2900 NW 73rd St., Miami, FL 33147, (305)691-9280 [3176]

Rowland Nursery Inc., 7402 Menaul NE, Albuquerque, NM 87110, (505)883-5727 [1216]

Rowley-Schlimgen Inc., 1020 John Nolen Dr., Madison, WI 53713-1428, (608)257-0521 [21249]

Royal Alaskan Sales, 3418 W 80th Ave., Anchorage, AK 99502-4421, (907)243-2106 [24845]

Royal Arts & Crafts, 768 James P Brawley Dr. NW, Atlanta, GA 30318-5243, (404)881-0075 [26638]

Royal Auto Supply Inc., 300 Enterprise Ln., Colmar, PA 18915, (215)643-7670 [3177]

Royal Beauty & Barber, 120 Baxter Ave. NW, PO Box 787, Knoxville, TN 37901, (865)637-0611 [14225]

Royal Brass and Hose, PO Box 51468, Knoxville, TN 37950-1468, (423)558-0224 [13896]

Royal Carpet Distribution, Inc., 20750 Hoover Rd., Warren, MI 48089, (810)756-2400 [10129]

Royal Centurian, Inc., 100 W Sheffield Ave., Englewood, NJ 07631, (201)568-0830 [14669]

Royal Chain Inc., 2 W 46th Ave., New York, NY 10036, (212)382-3340 [17575]

Royal Crown Beverage Co., 553 N Fairview Ave., St. Paul, MN 55104, (612)645-0501 [25027]

Royal Crown Bottling Company Inc., 2801 W 47th Pl., Chicago, IL 60632-2035, (630)229-0101 [25028]

Royal Cup Inc., PO Box 170971, Birmingham, AL 35217-0971, (205)849-5836 [12363]

Royal Doulton USA Inc., 700 Cottontail Ln., Somerset, NJ 08873, (732)356-7880 [15642]

Royal Essence Ltd., 380 Mountain Rd., No. 1814, Union City, NJ 07087-7335, (201)864-0450 [14226]

Royal Floor Mats, 5951 E Firestone Blvd., South Gate, CA 90280, (562)928-3381 [10130]

Royal Foods Distributors Inc., 215 Blair Rd., Woodbridge, NJ 07095, (732)636-0900 [12364]

Royal Fuel Co., PO Drawer 517, Oneida, TN 37841, (423)569-8900 [20565]

Royal Fuel Corp., 101 Lions Dr., Barrington, IL 60010, (708)304-4330 [22643]

Royal Golf, Inc., 32 Garvies Point Rd., Glen Cove, NY 11542, (516)671-8200 [23923]

Royal Golf Inc., 32 Garvies Point Rd., Glen Cove, NY 11542, (516)671-8200 [23924]

Royal Hawaiian Creations, 500 Alakawa St., No. 102-C, Honolulu, HI 96817-4576, (808)847-3663 [5322]

Royal Hill Co., 130 S Trade Center Pkwy., Conroe, TX 77385-8215, (409)273-3500 [2000]

Royal Inc.; H.M., PO Box 28, Trenton, NJ 08601, (609)396-9176 [20566]

Royal Industries, 538 N Milwaukee Ave., Chicago, IL 60622, (312)733-4920 [21913]

Royal Merchandise Corp. Royal Sales Div., PO Box 140035, Bath Beach Sta., Brooklyn, NY 11214-0035, (718)946-5947 [26640]

Royal Metals Company Inc., 120 Mokauea, Honolulu, HI 96819, (808)845-3222 [20332]

Royal Paper Corp., 185 Madison Ave., New York, NY 10016, (212)684-1200 [21914]

Royal Prestige of Missouri Inc., 3470 Hampton Ave. No. 206, St. Louis, MO 63139, (314)481-9888 [15643]

Royal Products Corp., PO Box 5026, Denver, CO 80217-5026, (303)778-7711 [26639]

Royal Publications, Inc., 790 W Tennessee Ave., Denver, CO 80223, (303)778-8383 [4126]

Royal Radio Sales & Service, 612 N Main St., Royal Oak, MI 48067-1834, (248)548-8711 [25422]

Royal Rubber and Manufacturing Co., 5951 E Firestone Blvd., South Gate, CA 90280, (562)928-3381 [10130]

Royal Sales, PO Box 140035, Bath Beach Sta., Brooklyn, NY 11214-0035, (718)946-5947 [26640]

Royal Seafoods Inc., PO Box 1347, Wharf 2, Monterey, CA 93942, (408)373-7920 [12365]

Royal Seeds Inc., PO Box 1393, St. Joseph, MO 64502, (816)238-0990 [1217]

Royal Sovereign Corp., 100 W Sheffield Ave., Englewood, NJ 07631, (201)568-0830 [14669]

Royal Stones Corp., 1212 Avenue of the Americas, Ste. 2301, New York, NY 10036-1601, (212)944-2211 [17576]

Royal Supply Inc., PO Box 629, Elyria, OH 44036-0629, (440)322-5411 [16461]

Royal Textile Mills Inc., PO Box 250, Yanceyville, NC 27379-0250, (919)694-4121 [5323]

Royal Toy Distributors Inc., PO Box 3202, Stamford, CT 06905-0202, (203)853-9513 [26641]

Royal Wine Co., 420 Kent Ave., Brooklyn, NY 11211, (718)384-2400 [2001]

Royalite Co., 101 Burton St., Flint, MI 48503, (810)238-4641 [9319]

Royalty Carpet Mills Inc., 17111 Red Hill Ave., Irvine, CA 92614-5877, (714)474-4000 [10131]

Royce, Inc., 723 Hickory Ln., Berwyn, PA 19312-1438, (215)873-9444 [21250]

Royce Industries Inc., 125 Rose Feiss Blvd., Bronx, NY 10454, (718)292-2024 [9320]

Royce International Inc., 1 Sound Shore Dr., Greenwich, CT 06830-7251, (203)625-2660 [24846]

Roye; Gene, 756 S Spring St., Los Angeles, CA 90014-2949, (213)629-9031 [5324]

Roy's Welding & Wrought Iron, 28 Mcdonald Rd., Alamogordo, NM 88310, (505)434-1696 [20333]

Rozin Optical Export Corp., 33-01 38th Ave., Long Island City, NY 11101, (718)786-1201 [19589]

RP Sales, Inc., 23735 Research Dr., Farmington Hills, MI 48335-2625, (313)937-3000 [9321]

RPC Video Inc., 384 Route 909, Verona, PA 15147, (412)828-1414 [25423]

RPL Supplies Inc., 280 Midland Ave., Saddle Brook, NJ 07663, (201)794-8400 [22899]

RPM Inc., 2628 Pearl Road, PO Box 777, Medina, OH 44258, (330)273-5090 [7962]

RPV Distributors, 580 W Lambert, Ste. K, Brea, CA 92821, (714)671-1270 [26642]

RRS Div., PO Box 40, Salem, VA 24153, (540)387-1151 [12802]

RRT Empire Returns Corp., 4545 Morgan Pl., Liverpool, NY 13090-3521, (315)455-7080 [26968]

R.S. Hughes Company Inc., PO Box 25061, Glendale, CA 91221, (818)563-1122 [12]

RSB Tile, Inc., 495 Route 208, Monroe, NY 10950, (914)783-6167 [10132]

RSB Tile Inc., 495 Route 208, Monroe, NY 10950, (914)783-6167 [7963]

R.S.B.I. Aerospace Inc., 3606 NE Independence, Lees Summit, MO 64063, (816)246-4800 [143]

RSC Electronics Inc., PO Box 1220, Wichita, KS 67201, (316)267-5213 [9322]

RSL Trading Company, Inc., 2494 Bayshore Blvd., Ste. 250, Dunedin, FL 34698, (813)736-6770 [16462]

R.S.R. Electronics Inc., 365 Blair Rd., Avenel, NJ 07001, (732)381-8777 [9323]

RSR Group Florida, Inc., 4405 Metric Dr., Winter Park, FL 32792, (407)677-1000 [13505]

RSR Group Texas, Inc., 1450 Post & Paddock Rd., Grand Prairie, TX 75053, (972)602-3131 [13506]

RSR Wholesale Guns Inc., 21 Trolley Cir., PO Box 60679, Rochester, NY 14606, (716)426-4380 [13507]

RSR Wholesale Guns Inc., 4405 Metric Dr., Winter Park, FL 32792, (407)677-4342 [13508]

RSR Wholesale Guns Midwest, Inc., 8817 W Lynx Ave., Milwaukee, WI 53225, (414)461-1111 [13509]

RSR Wholesale Guns Midwest Inc., 8817 W Lynx Ave., Milwaukee, WI 53225, (414)461-1111 [23925]

RSR Wholesale Guns South Inc., 4405 Metric Dr., Winter Park, FL 32792, (407)677-1000 [13505]

RSR Wholesale Guns Texas, Inc., 1450 Post & Paddock Rd., Grand Prairie, TX 75053, (972)602-3131 [13506]

RSR Wholesale Guns West, Inc., 4700 Aircenter Cir., PO Box 71540, Reno, NV 89502, (702)827-2111 [13510]

RSR Wholesale South Inc., 4405 Metric Dr., Winter Park, FL 32792, (407)677-1000 [13511]

RST Reclaiming Co. Inc., 66 River Rd. B, Hudson, NH 03051-5225, (603)595-8708 [21251]

RT Computers Inc., 1673 Rogers Ave., San Jose, CA 95112, (408)437-3063 [6696]

RTC Manufacturing, 1011 S Bowen Rd., Arlington, TX 76013-2292, (817)461-8101 [17577]

RTI, 486 S Dawson Dr., No. 45, Camarillo, CA 93012-8049, (805)484-2747 [25411]

RTI Technologies, Inc., PO Box 3099, York, PA 17402-0099, (717)840-0678 [14670]

RTM Inc., 13177 Ramona Blvd., Ste. F, Irwindale, CA 91706, (626)813-2630 [6697]

Ru-Mart Metal Specialties, 767 Hartford Ave., Johnston, RI 02919, (401)421-3055 [17578]

Ru-Mart Metal Specialties, 767 Hartford Ave., Johnston, RI 02919, (401)421-3055 [17579]

Rubber and Accessories Inc., PO Box 777, Eaton Park, FL 33840, (863)665-6115 [17148]

Rubber Plus Inc., PO Box 50430, Knoxville, TN 37950-0430, (865)588-2981 [24292]

Rubenstein Supply Co., 2800 San Pablo Ave., Oakland, CA 94608-4529, (510)444-6614 [23353]

Rubenstein Supply Co., 96 Woodland Ave., San Rafael, CA 94901, (415)454-1174 [23354]

Rubenstein & Ziff Inc., 1055 E 79th St., Minneapolis, MN 55420-1460, (612)854-1460 [26194]

Rubin Brothers Company Inc., 5600 Bucknell Dr. SW, Atlanta, GA 30336, (404)349-6900 [10133]

Rubin Brothers Company Inc., PO Box 5750, Harrisburg, PA 17110, (717)234-7071 [17149]

Rubin and Co.; J., 305 Peoples Ave., Rockford, IL 61104, (815)964-9471 [20334]

Rubin Inc., 120 25th St., Ogden, UT 84401-1302, (801)394-8946 [23926]

Rubin, Jack and Sons Inc., PO Box 3005, Compton, CA 90223, (310)635-5407 [20335]

Rubin Steel Co., 1430 Fruitville Pke., Lancaster, PA 17601, (717)397-3613 [20336]

Rubino Brothers Inc., PO Box 1110, Stamford, CT 06904, (203)323-3195 [26969]

Rubins Stone House, 36 NE 1st St., Ste. 335, Miami, FL 33132-2403, (305)374-5816 [17580]

Ruby Metal Traders Inc., 12303 Edwina Blvd., Houston, TX 77045, (713)433-0044 [26970]

Rucker Fuller Co., 1057 Montague Expressway, Milpitas, CA 95035, (408)263-1001 [13195]

Rudd Equipment Co., PO Box 32427, Louisville, KY 40232-2427, (502)456-4050 [7964]

Rude Corp.; R.T., 129 W 53rd Ave., Anchorage, AK 99518-1602, (907)563-9994 [15297]

Rudel Machinery Company Inc., 25 South St., Hopkinton, MA 01748, (508)497-0942 [16463]

Rudis Bakery, 3640 Walnut, Boulder, CO 80301-2500, (303)447-0495 [12366]

Rudisill Enterprises Inc., PO Box 190, Gastonia, NC 28053, (704)824-9597 [2002]

Rue Plastics Inc., 2999 Yorkton Blvd., St. Paul, MN 55117, (612)481-9000 [23031]

Rueb Associates Inc.; John, 250 Beechwood Dr., Boise, ID 83709-0944, (208)345-8265 [18210]

Rueff Lighting Co., 523 E Broadway, Louisville, KY 40202, (502)583-1617 [9324]

Ruff and Co. Business Furniture Div.; Thomas W., 911 S Orlando, Maitland, FL 32751, (407)628-2400 [13225]

Ruff and Company of Florida Inc.; Thomas W., 3201 Commerce Pkwy., Miramar, FL 33025, (954)435-7300 [21252]

Ruff and Co.; Thomas W., 1114 Dublin Rd., Columbus, OH 43215, (614)487-4000 [21253]

Ruffridge Johnson Equipment Company Inc., 3024 4th St. SE, Minneapolis, MN 55414, (612)378-9558 [7965]

The Rug Barn Inc., PO Box 1187, Abbeville, SC 29620, (864)446-2123 [15644]

Rugby Building Products, 2575 Westside Pky., No. 800, Alpharetta, GA 30004-3852, (770)625-1700 [7966]

Rugby Building Products Inc., 1335 S Main, PO Box 728, Greensburg, PA 15601, (412)834-5706 [7967]

Rugby Building Products, Inc., 2829 Awaawaloa St., Honolulu, HI 96819, (808)833-2731 [7968]

Rugby Building Products Inc., 1335 S Main, Greensburg, PA 15601, (412)834-5706 [27366]

Rugby Farmers Union Elevator Co., 105 E Dewey St., Rugby, ND 58368-0286, (701)776-5214 [18211]

Rugby USA Inc., 570 Lake Cook Rd., Deerfield, IL 60015, (847)405-0850 [27367]

Rugg Manufacturing Company Inc., PO Box 507, Greenfield, MA 01302, (413)773-5471 [1218]

Ruidoso Paint Center Inc., PO Box 848, Ruidoso, NM 88355-0848, (505)257-7447 [21558]

Ruklic Screw Company Inc.; J.P., PO Box 1608, Homewood, IL 60430, (708)798-8282 [13897]

Ruland's Used Office Furnishings, 215 North 16th St., Sacramento, CA 95814, (916)441-0706 [13226]

RuMar Manufacturing Corp., PO Box 193, Mayville, WI 53050, (920)387-2104 [20337]

Rumbold and Kuhn Inc., PO Box 26, Princeville, IL 61559, (309)385-4846 [18212]

Rundle-Spence Manufacturing Co., PO Box 510008, New Berlin, WI 53151, (414)782-3000 [23355]

Runge Paper Co., Inc., 2201 Arthur Ave., Elk Grove Village, IL 60007, (708)593-1788 [21915]

Running Strong Inc., 506 E Juanita Ave. 1, Mesa, AZ 85204-6544, (602)545-0068 [5325]

Running W Cattle Co., 4385 Wylie Dr., Helena, MT 59601-9567, (406)227-5208 [18111]

Rupp Oil Company Inc., PO Box 457, Bay City, MI 48707, (517)684-5993 [22644]

Rural Serv Inc., PO Box 870, Fremont, OH 43420, (419)332-6468 [18213]

Rush Company Inc.; J D, 5900 E Lerdo Hwy., Shafter, CA 93263, (661)392-1900 [20338]

Rush County Farm Bureau Cooperative, 627 W 3rd St., Rushville, IN 46173, (317)932-3921 [1219]

Rushin Upholstery Supply, Inc., 2600 Welch, Little Rock, AR 72206, (501)376-3194 [26195]

Rushmore Health Care Products, 821 Mount Rushmore Rd., Rapid City, SD 57701-3602, (605)341-2273 [19026]

Rushwin Publishing, c/o James Gibson, Manager, PO Box 1150, Buna, TX 77612, (409)423-2521 [4127]

Russ Doughten Films Inc., 5907 Meredith Dr., Des Moines, IA 50322, (515)278-4737 [15298]

Russel Metals-Bahcall Group, 975 N Meade St., PO Box 1054, Appleton, WI 54912-1054, (920)734-9271 [20339]

Russell Associates Inc., 5755 Rio Vista Dr., Clearwater, FL 33760-3114, (727)532-4545 [25806]

Russell Co.; T.J., PO Box 544, Bristol, RI 02809-0544, (401)253-2882 [4708]

Russell Corp. Knit Apparel Div., PO Box 272, Alexander City, AL 35010, (256)329-4000 [5326]

Russell; Herbert A., RR 8C54, Box 240, Nye, MT 59061, (406)328-6296 [18214]

Russell Petroleum Corp., PO Box 250330, Montgomery, AL 36125, (334)834-3750 [22645]

Russell Stover Candies, 4900 Oak Street, Kansas City, MO 64112, (816)842-9240 [12367]

Russell Stover Candies, 4900 Oaks St., Kansas City, MO 64112, (816)842-9240 [12368]

Russells Ice Cream, 2575 South 300 West, Salt Lake City, UT 84115-2908, (801)484-8724 [12369]

Russica Book & Art Shop Inc., 799 Broadway, New York, NY 10003, (212)473-7480 [4128]

Russo Farms Inc., 1962 S East Ave., Vineland, NJ 08360, (609)692-5942 [12370]

Rust Wholesale Company Inc., PO Box 230, Greensburg, IN 47240, (812)663-7394 [12371]

Rustic Creations, 118 Main St., PO Box 174, Streetman, TX 75859, (903)599-3181 [13227]

Rutgers Book Center, 127 Raritan Ave., Highland Park, NJ 08904, (732)545-4344 [4129]

Ruth Corp., PO Box 220, Holland, OH 43528, (419)865-6555 [16464]

Ruth Farmers Elevator Inc., 4600 Ruth Rd., Ruth, MI 48470, (517)864-3391 [18215]

Rutherford Controls Inc., 2697 International Pkwy., Ste. 100, Virginia Beach, VA 23452, (757)427-1230 [24619]

Rutherford Controls Inc., 2697 International Pkwy. 5, Ste. 100, Virginia Beach, VA 23452, (757)427-1230 [9183]

Rutherford Controls Int'l., 2697 International Pkwy., Ste. 100, Virginia Beach, VA 23452, (757)427-1230 [24619]

Rutherford Farmers Cooperative, 210 Sanbyrn Dr., Murfreesboro, TN 37130, (615)893-6212 [1220]

Rutland News Co., PO Box 1211, Rochester, NY 14603-1211 [4130]

Rutland Tool and Supply Company Inc., 2225 Workman Mill Rd., PO Box 997, Whittier, CA 90601, (562)566-5010 [16465]

Ruxer Ford, Lincoln, Mercury Inc., 123 Place Rd., Jasper, IN 47546, (812)482-1200 [20715]

RVS Controls Co., 380 Lapp Rd., Malvern, PA 19355, (610)889-9910 [17150]

RW Electronics Inc., 206 Andover St., Andover, MA 01810, (508)475-1303 [9325]

R.W. Sales, Inc., 635 N Fairview Ave., St. Paul, MN 55104-1785, (612)646-2710 [9326]

Rx Medical Services Corp., 888 E Las Olas Blvd., Ste. 210, Ft. Lauderdale, FL 33301, (954)462-1711 [19590]

Rx Rocker Corp., 3541 Old Conejo Rd., Ste. 101, Newbury Park, CA 91320, (805)499-0696 [19027]

Ryall Electric Supply Co., 2627 W 6th Ave., Denver, CO 80204, (303)629-7721 [9327]

Ryan and Co.; Connor F., PO Box 818, Southport, CT 06490-0818, (203)259-5133 [25424]

Ryan Company Inc.; W.E., 2325 N American, Philadelphia, PA 19133-3308, (215)427-3030 [12372]

Ryan Co.; Johnnie, 3084 Niagara St., Niagara Falls, NY 14303, (716)282-1606 [25029]

Ryan Cooperative Inc., PO Box 39, Ryan, IA 52330, (319)932-2101 [1221]

Ryan Equipment Co., Inc., 749 Creel Dr., Wood Dale, IL 60191, (708)595-5711 [20340]

Ryan Jewelry; Susan, 3715 Espejo St. NE, Albuquerque, NM 87111-3430, (505)294-5275 [17581]

Ryan's Pet Supplies, 3411 S Central Ave., Phoenix, AZ 85040, (602)276-5267 [27225]

Ryan's Wholesale Food Distributors, PO Box 30838, Billings, MT 59107, (406)657-1400 [12373]

Ryder Aviall Inc., PO Box 549015, Dallas, TX 75354-9015, (214)353-7000 [144]

Ryen, Re Associates, 585 Seminole St., Oradell, NJ 07649, (201)261-7450 [4131]

Ryerson Coil Processing Co., 5101 Boone Ave., N, Minneapolis, MN 55428, (612)535-1431 [20341]

Ryerson and Son Inc.; Joseph T., PO Box 8000, Chicago, IL 60680, (773)762-2121 [20342]

Ryerson and Son Inc., Ryerson Plastics Div.; Joseph T., PO Box 8000, Chicago, IL 60680, (773)762-2121 [23032]

Ryerson-Thypin - Div. of Ryerson Tull, 45 Saratoga Blvd., Ayer, MA 01432-5216, (978)784-2800 [20343]

Ryerson Tull Inc., 2621 West 15th Pl., Chicago, IL 60608, (773)762-2121 [20344]

Ryerson Tull Inc., PO Box 34275, Seattle, WA 98124, (206)242-3400 [20345]

Rykoff & Co.; S.E., PO Box 13489, Phoenix, AZ 85002, (602)352-3300 [12374]

Rykoff & Co.; S.E., PO Box 10007, Portland, OR 97210, (503)224-3553 [21916]

Rykoff-Sexton Distribution Div., 9755 Patuxent Woods Dr., Columbia, MD 21046-2286 [12375]

Rykoff-Sexton Inc., 9755 Patuxent Woods Dr., Columbia, MD 21046-2286 [12376]

Rykoff-Sexton Inc., 11711 N Creek Pkwy. S, No. D107, Bothell, WA 98011-8808, (206)281-4900 [24212]

Rykoff-Sexton Manufacturing L.L.C., 737 Terminal St., Los Angeles, CA 90021, (213)622-4131 [12377]

Rymer Foods Inc., 4600 S Packers Ave., Chicago, IL 60609, (773)927-7777 [12378]

Ryobi America Corp., 5201 Pearman Dairy Rd., Anderson, SC 29625, (803)226-6511 [1222]

S & C Importing, PO Box 420, Sun Valley, ID 83353, (208)726-4316 [2003]

S and D Coffee Inc., 300 Concord Pky. S, Concord, NC 28027, (704)782-3121 [12379]

S & D Industrial Supply Inc., PO Box 50252, Amarillo, TX 79159-0252 [4700]

S & F Associates Inc., PO Box 5996, Portland, OR 97228-5996, (503)288-6876 [23927]

S and G Trading Co., 7110 Newberry Dr., Columbia, MD 21044, (301)531-3911 [26643]

S & H Co., 101 Kappa Dr., Pittsburgh, PA 15238-2809 [26349]

S and H Tractor Co., PO Box 729, Guymon, OK 73942, (580)338-2519 [1223]

S I Metals, N5820 Johnson Rd., Portage, WI 53901, (608)742-9039 [20346]

S and I Steel Supply Div., PO Box 341, Memphis, TN 38101, (901)948-0395 [20347]

S and J Chevrolet Inc., PO Box 186, Cerritos, CA 90703, (562)924-1676 [9328]

S & L International, 875 Waimanu St., No. 610, Honolulu, HI 96813, (808)591-1336 [24847]

S & L Monograms and Embroidery, 9808 Santa Fe Dr., Overland Park, KS 66212-4564 [5327]

S & L Sales Co., Inc., 2165 Industrial Blvd., Waycross, GA 31503, (912)283-0210 [4132]

S and M Equipment Company Corp., PO Box 9230, Richmond, VA 23227, (804)266-4911 [7969]

S and M Food Service Inc., 12935 Lake Charles Hwy., Leesville, LA 71446, (318)537-3588 [12380]

S & M Lumber Co., 424 W Main St., Flushing, MI 48433, (810)659-5681 [7970]

S and M Lumber Co., 424 W Main St., Flushing, MI 48433, (810)659-5681 [27368]

S & M Produce, 42 S Water Mark, Chicago, IL 60608, (312)829-0155 [12381]

S & N Sales, 13 West Ln., Dearborn, MI 48124, (734)425-8277 [12382]

S & O Industries Inc., PO Box 3466, New Hyde Park, NY 11040, (516)487-9070 [26196]

S & P Whistle Stop, 3216 Spangle St., Canandaigua, NY 14424, (716)396-0160 [26644]

S & R Inc., PO Box 9275, Fargo, ND 58106-9275, (701)241-7960 [21254]

S and R Metals Inc., 2070 Randolph St., Huntington Park, CA 90255, (213)583-8904 [20348]

S & S, 2750 Maxwell Way, Fairfield, CA 94533, (707)426-6666 [27226]

S & S Appliance Service Co., 601 Graymont Ave. N, Birmingham, AL 35203-2523, (205)324-1673 [15299]

S and S Automotive Inc., 740 N Larch Ave., Elmhurst, IL 60126, (708)279-1600 [13898]

S/S Electronics Inc., 1412 44th St. NW, Fargo, ND 58108-3067, (701)281-3855 [15300]

S & S Firearms, 74-11 Myrtle Ave., Glendale, NY 11385, (718)497-1100 [13512]

S and S Inc., 21300 St. Clair Ave., Cleveland, OH 44117, (216)383-1880 [21917]

S. and S. Machinery Co., 140 53rd St., Brooklyn, NY 11232, (718)492-7400 [16466]

S and S Meat Company Inc., 637 Prospect Ave., Kansas City, MO 64124, (816)241-4700 [12383]

S & S Variety Beverages Inc., 905 Caldwell Ave., Tiffin, OH 44883 [25030]

S and S Worldwide Inc., PO Box 513, Colchester, CT 06415-0513, (860)537-3451 [25807]

S and S Worldwide Inc., PO Box 513, Colchester, CT 06415, (860)537-3451 [26645]

S & T Jewelers, 631 S Hill St., No. A, Los Angeles, CA 90014-1712, (213)623-1121 [17582]

S-T Leather Co., 2135 S James Rd., Bay F, Columbus, OH 43232, (614)235-1900 [18216]

S & W Distributors Inc., PO Box 14689, Greensboro, NC 27415, (336)272-7394 [4133]

S & W Farm Equipment, PO Box 82182, Portland, OR 97282-0182, (503)234-0278 [1224]

S & W Investments, 1600 Kentucky St. 2, Bellingham, WA 98226-4701, (206)676-0793 [5328]

S & W Supply Company Inc., 300 E 8th, Hays, KS 67601, (785)625-7363 [1225]

SA-SO, 1025 Post and Paddock Rd., Grand Prairie, TX 75050, (214)647-1525 [24620]

Saab Aircraft of America Inc., 21300 Ridgetop Cir., Sterling, VA 20163, (703)406-7200 [145]

Saab Cars USA Inc., 4405-A International Blvd., Norcross, GA 30093, (770)279-0100 [20716]

Saag's Products Inc., PO Box 2078, San Leandro, CA 94577, (510)352-8000 [12384]

Sabel Industries Inc., PO Drawer 4747, Montgomery, AL 36103, (334)265-6771 [26971]

Sabel Steel Service, PO Drawer 4747, Montgomery, AL 36103, (205)265-6771 [20349]

Saber Enterprises Inc., 9520 Padgett St., Ste. 216, San Diego, CA 92126-4452, (619)271-1523 [24424]

Sabin Robbins Paper Co., 106 Circle Freeway Dr., Cincinnati, OH 45246, (513)874-5270 [21918]

Sabina Farmers Exchange Inc., PO Box 7, Sabina, OH 45169, (937)584-2411 [1226]

Sabol and Rice Inc., PO Box 25957, Salt Lake City, UT 84125-0957, (801)973-2300 [14671]

Sabrett Food Products, 50 Colden St., Jersey City, NJ 07302, (201)434-7062 [12385]

Sabus Group, 1737 Aleutian St., Anchorage, AK 99508-3276, (907)277-4232 [6698]

Saccani Distributing Co., 2600 5th St., Sacramento, CA 95818-2899, (916)441-0213 [25031]

Sack Company Inc.; J. R., 1632 Leonard NW, Grand Rapids, MI 49504, (616)453-5757 [17151]

Sack Company Inc.; Stanley, 30 Barber Pond Rd., Bloomfield, CT 06002, (203)242-6228 [26972]

Sacks Electrical Supply Co., 711 Johnston St., Akron, OH 44306, (330)253-2141 [9329]

Sacks International Inc.; M., PO Box 1048, Akron, OH 44309-1048, (330)762-9385 [24293]

S.A.C.M. Textile Inc., Hwy. 29, Lyman, SC 29365, (864)877-1886 [16467]

Saco Steel Company Inc., PO Box 187, Saco, ME 04072, (207)284-4516 [26973]

Sacramento Bag Manufacturing Co., PO Box 1563, Sacramento, CA 95812, (916)441-6121 [21919]

Sacramento Sky Ranch Inc., PO Box 22610, Sacramento, CA 95822, (916)421-7672 [146]

Sadco Inc., PO Box 250547, Montgomery, AL 36125-0547, (205)288-5100 [15301]

Sadd Laundry and Dry Cleaning Supplies, 1359 Colburn St., Honolulu, HI 96817, (808)841-3818 [4701]

Saddle Brook Controls, 280 Midland Ave., Saddle Brook, NJ 07663, (201)791-0233 [17152]

Sadek Import Company Inc.; Charles, 125 Beachwood Ave., New Rochelle, NY 10802, (914)633-8090 [15645]

Sadisco of Florence, PO Box 6525, Florence, SC 29502, (843)669-1941 [3178]

Sadoff and Rudoy Industries, PO Box 1138, Fond du Lac, WI 54936, (920)921-2070 [26974]

Sadowsky and Son Inc.; G.A., PO Drawer D, Dickinson, ND 58601, (701)225-2713 [22646]

Saeco USA, 280 Midland Ave., Bldg. M-1, Saddle Brook, NJ 07663, (201)791-2244 [24103]

Saelens Beverages Inc., PO Box 669, Galesburg, IL 61402-0669, (309)787-4546 [2004]

Saettele Jewelers Inc., 8182 Maryland Ave. 205, St. Louis, MO 63105, (314)725-8182 [17583]

SAF-T-GARD International, Inc., 205 Huehl Rd., Northbrook, IL 60062, (847)291-1600 [17153]

Safa Enterprises Co., Inc., 6803 S Western Ave., No. 409, Oklahoma City, OK 73139, (405)631-0453 [12386]

Safari Museum Press, 111 N Grant Ave., Chanute, KS 66720, (316)431-2730 [17476]

Safari Press Inc., 15621 Chemical Ln., Ste. B, Huntington Beach, CA 92649, (714)894-9080 [4134]

Safe Stride Non-Slip USA Inc., PO Box 250093, West Bloomfield, MI 48325, (248)661-9176 [4499]

Safeguard Abacus, 226 Mary St., Reno, NV 89509-2719, (702)323-3592 [21920]

Safeguard International, Inc., PO Box 884, Chester, PA 19016, (215)876-2800 [24621]

Safesport Manufacturing Co., 1100 W 45th Ave., Denver, CO 80211, (303)433-6506 [23928]

Safety Flare Inc., 2803 Richmond Dr. NE, Albuquerque, NM 87107, (505)884-2274 [24622]

Safety Flare Inc., 2803 Richmond Dr. NE, Albuquerque, NM 87107, (505)884-2274 [24623]

Safety House, PO Box 1076, Lake Charles, LA 70601, (318)436-7538 [26975]

Safety Industries Inc., 1st and K Aves., PO Box 1137, Mc Gill, NV 89318, (702)235-7766 [3179]

Safety-Kleen, Southwest, 1340 W Lincoln St., Phoenix, AZ 85007, (602)258-6155 [26976]

Safety Optical, 2110 Congress Pkwy., PO Box 828, Athens, TN 37303, (423)745-9420 [19591]

Safety Service Co., 835 Fesslers Pkwy., Nashville, TN 37210, (615)244-2853 [3180]

Safety Signals Systems Inc., PO Box 5098, Lynnwood, WA 98046, (425)775-1557 [9330]

Safety Truck Equipment Inc., 669 Market St., Paterson, NJ 07513, (973)684-3668 [3181]

Safety West, 15200 Don Julian Rd., La Puente, CA 91745, (626)968-9444 [17154]

Safetywear, 1121 E Wallace, Ft. Wayne, IN 46803-2555, (219)456-3535 [5329]

Safeway Tire Co., 4623 Superior Ave., Cleveland, OH 44103, (216)881-1737 [3182]

Saffron Supply Co., 325 Commercial St., Salem, OR 97301, (503)581-7501 [13899]

Safier's Inc., 8700 Harvard Ave., Cleveland, OH 44105, (216)341-8700 [12387]

Safina Office Products, 5803 Sovereign, Ste. 214, Houston, TX 77036, (713)981-6153 [21255]

SAFLINK Corp., 2502 Rocky Point Dr., Tampa, FL 33607, (813)636-0099 [6699]

Sage Creek Refining Co., 339 Carmon Ave., Lovell, WY 82431-1603 [22647]

Sagebrush Sales Inc., PO Box 25606, Albuquerque, NM 87125, (505)877-7331 [7971]

Sager Electronics Inc., 60 Research Rd., Hingham, MA 02043, (617)749-6700 [9331]

Sager Midern Computer Inc., 18005 Cortney Ct., City of Industry, CA 91748, (626)964-8682 [6700]

Sager Spuck Statewide Supply Company Inc., PO Box 918, Albany, NY 12201-0918, (518)436-4711 [17155]

Sago Imports Inc., 1140 Broadway, Ste. 707, New York, NY 10001, (212)685-2580 [17584]

Sahlein Music Co.; J.M., 1859 Sabre St., Hayward, CA 94545, (510)293-0388 [25158]

Sahuaro Petroleum-Asphalt Company Inc., 1935 W McDowell Rd., Phoenix, AZ 85009, (602)252-3061 [7972]

Sailing Inc., 5401 N Marginal Rd., Cleveland, OH 44114 [18597]

Sailor Corporation of America, 121 Bethea Rd., Ste. 307, Fayetteville, GA 30214, (770)461-9081 [13]

The Sailor's Supply, 231 E Beach Dr., Panama City, FL 32401, (850)769-5007 [18598]

Saint Aepan's Press & Book Distributors, Inc., PO Box 385, Hillsdale, NJ 07642-0385, (201)664-0127 [4135]

St. Albans Commission Sales, RR 2, Box 244, St. Albans, VT 05478, (802)524-2991 [18217]

St. Angsar Mills Inc., PO Box 370, St. Ansgar, IA 50472-0370, (515)736-4520 [18218]

St. Angsar Mills Inc., PO Box 370, St. Ansgar, IA 50472-0370, (515)736-4520 [12388]

St. Charles County Cooperative Co., 5055 N Hwy. 94, St. Charles, MO 63301-6431, (314)258-3805 [27227]

St. Clair Service Co., PO Box 489, Belleville, IL 62222-0489, (618)233-1248 [1227]

St. Francis Mercantile Equity Exchange, PO Box 545, St. Francis, KS 67756, (913)332-2113 [1228]

St. Hilaire Cooperative Elevators, PO Box 128, St. Hilaire, MN 56754, (218)964-5252 [18143]

St. Joe Communications Inc., PO Box 1007, Port St. Joe, FL 32456, (904)227-7272 [5748]

St. John Grain Growers Inc., PO Box 6, St. John, WA 99171, (509)648-3316 [18219]

St. John's Food Service, Inc., 4 Louise St., St. Augustine, FL 32095, (904)824-0493 [12389]

St. Jude Medical Inc., 1 Lillehei Plz., St. Paul, MN 55117, (612)483-2000 [19028]

St. Louis Beverage Co., PO Box 765, Ottawa, IL 61350-0765, (815)433-0365 [2005]

St. Louis Business Forms Inc., 1571 Senpark Dr., Fenton, MO 63026, (314)343-6860 [21256]

St. Louis Coke and Foundry, 2817 Hereford St., St. Louis, MO 63139, (314)772-7500 [17156]

St. Louis Music Supply Co., 1400 Ferguson Ave., St. Louis, MO 63133, (314)727-4512 [25425]

St. Louis Ostomy Distributors Inc., PO Box 6520, Holliston, MA 01746-6520, (508)535-3535 [19029]

St. Louis Paper and Box Co., PO Box 8260, St. Louis, MO 63156-8260, (314)531-7900 [21921]

St. Louis Paper and Box Co., PO Box 8260, St. Louis, MO 63156, (314)531-7900 [17157]

Saint Louis Restaurant Steaks Inc., 9216 Clayton Rd., St. Louis, MO 63124, (314)993-6600 [12390]

St. Louis Screw and Bolt Co., 6900 N Broadway, St. Louis, MO 63147, (314)389-7500 [23356]

St. Louis Trimming, 9601-03 Dielman Rock Island Dr., St. Louis, MO 63132, (314)432-1131 [26197]

St. Martin Oil and Gas Inc., 2040 Terrace Hwy., St. Martinville, LA 70582, (318)394-3163 [22648]

St. Paul Appliance Center Inc., 7618 Lyndale Ave. S, Minneapolis, MN 55423-4028, (612)861-5960 [15302]

St. Paul Bar/Restaurant Equipment, 655 Payne Ave., St. Paul, MN 55101, (612)774-0361 [24213]

St. Paul Feed and Supply Inc., PO Box 67, St. Paul, OR 97137, (503)633-4281 [1229]

St. Pete Auto Auction Inc., 14950 Roosevelt Blvd., Clearwater, FL 33762-3501, (813)531-7717 [20717]

S.A.K. Industries, PO Box 725, 148 E Olive Ave., Monrovia, CA 91016, (626)359-5351 [13228]

Sakash Company Inc.; John, 433 Romans Rd., Elmhurst, IL 60126, (630)833-3940 [17158]

Sakata Seed America, Inc., 18095 Serene Dr., Morgan Hill, CA 95037, (408)778-7758 [1230]

Sakata U.S.A. Corp., 651 Bonnie Ln., Elk Grove Village, IL 60009, (708)593-3211 [9332]

Saladmaster Inc., 912 113th St., Arlington, TX 76011, (817)633-3555 [15646]

Salado Cattle Co., PO Box 38, Salado, TX 76571, (254)947-5132 [18220]

Salasnek Fisheries Inc., 12301 Conant St., Detroit, MI 48212, (313)368-2500 [12391]

Salazar International, Inc., 23800 Commerce Park, Beachwood, OH 44122, (216)464-2420 [3183]

Salco Inc., 1420 Major St., Salt Lake City, UT 84115-5306, (801)487-7841 [15647]

Saleff & Son New York Pastry; Richard, 807 Rennard Cir., Philadelphia, PA 19116-2921, (215)698-0525 [12392]

Salem Coca-Cola Bottling Co., 23 S Broadway, Salem, NH 03079, (603)898-5916 [25032]

Salem Farm Supply Inc., Rte. 22, Salem, NY 12865, (518)854-7424 [1231]

Salem Optical Co. Inc., 915 Brookstown Ave., Winston-Salem, NC 27101, (919)725-4286 [19592]

Salem Refrigeration Company Inc., 600 Aureole St., Winston-Salem, NC 27107-3250, (910)784-8815 [14672]

Salem Sales Associates, 2407 Central Ave., PO Box 9323, Charlotte, NC 28205, (704)375-3328 [16468]

SalePoint Inc., 9909 Huennekens St., San Diego, CA 92121-2929, (858)546-9400 [6701]

Sales Corporation of Alaska, 355 E 76th Ave., Ste. 104, Anchorage, AK 99518, (907)522-3057 [12393]

Sales Force Companies Inc., 180 Hansen Ct., Wood Dale, IL 60191-1114, (630)787-2600 [12394]

Sales Force of Fargo, 2848 Coheatland Dr., Fargo, ND 58103, (701)235-8964 [11785]

Sales Force of Omaha, 8642 F St., Omaha, NE 68127, (402)331-1666 [12395]

Sales International, 17922 Star of India Ln., Carson, CA 90746, (310)538-5725 [16469]

Sales Mark Alpha One Inc., 6400 International Pkwy., Plano, TX 75093, (972)349-1100 [12396]

Sales and Marketing Services Inc., PO Box 815, Columbia, MD 21044, (410)799-7040 [19030]

Sales Results, 1192 Clubview Blvd. S, Columbus, OH 43235, (614)885-4127 [12397]

Sales Systems Ltd., 700 Florida Ave., Portsmouth, VA 23707, (757)397-0763 [13900]

Salina Coffee House Inc., PO Box 1277, Salina, KS 67402-1277, (785)823-6394 [12611]

Salina Supply Co., 302 N Santa Fe, Salina, KS 67401, (785)823-2221 [23357]

Salinas Tile Sales Co., 1 Spring St., Salinas, CA 93901-3616, (408)424-8046 [10134]

Salinas Tile Sales, Inc., 1830 California St., Sand City, CA 93955, (408)899-5377 [10135]

Salinger Electric Co., 1020 Livernois Rd., Troy, MI 48083, (248)585-8330 [9333]

Salks Hardware & Marine Inc., 2524 W Shore Rd., Warwick, RI 02886-3848, (401)739-1027 [18599]

Sally Beauty Company Inc., PO Box 490, Denton, TX 76202, (940)898-7500 [14227]

Sally's Flower Shop, 333 Main St., Winooski, VT 05404, (802)655-3894 [14946]

Salman, 2425 W Commonwealth, Fullerton, CA 92833, (714)994-0990 [13229]

Salman Inc., 2425 W Commonwealth, Fullerton, CA 92833, (714)994-0990 [13229]

Salomon Co.; Paul R., 5000 Grand River St., Detroit, MI 48208, (313)894-2323 [18600]

Salomon North America Inc., 9401 SW Nimbus Ave., Beaverton, OR 97008-7145, (503)548-7001 [23929]

Salon Associates, 956 W Webster, Chicago, IL 60616, (773)348-8460 [14228]

Salt Lake Optical Inc., 315 E 3rd St. S, PO Box 297, Salt Lake City, UT 84111, (801)328-4791 [19593]

Saltillo Tile Co., 110 Este Es Rd., Taos, NM 87571, (505)751-0977 [7973]

Salton/Maxium Housewares Inc., 550 Business Center Dr., Mt. Prospect, IL 60056, (847)803-4600 [15648]

Salvors Inc., 200 Greene St., Key West, FL 33040, (305)325-7106 [17585]

Sam Farm Inc.; A., PO Box 591, Dunkirk, NY 14048, (716)366-6666 [12398]

Sam Yanen Ford Sales Inc., PO Box 534, Moundsville, WV 26041, (304)845-4244 [3184]

Samara Brothers, Inc., 240 Mill Rd., Edison, NJ 08817, (908)287-3939 [5330]

Sambito; William B., 179 Main St., Colebrook, NH 03576-1216, (603)237-5705 [21257]

Sammons Preston, 4 Sammons Ct., Bolingbrook, IL 60440, (630)226-1300 [19031]

Sampo Corporation of America, 5550 Peachtree Industrial Blvd., Norcross, GA 30071, (770)449-6220 [6702]

Sampson-Bladen Oil Co., PO Box 367, Elizabethtown, NC 28337, (919)862-3197 [22649]

Sampson Steel Corp., PO Box 2392, Beaumont, TX 77704, (409)838-1611 [20350]

Sam's Gourmet, 1577 N Laurel Ave., Upland, CA 91786-2216, (714)986-1908 [12399]

Sam's Ice Cream Inc., 2912 Broadway Blvd. SE, Albuquerque, NM 87101, (505)764-9524 [12400]

Sams Inc.; L.L., 1201 Industrial Blvd., Cameron, TX 76520, (254)752-9751 [13230]

Samsel Supply Co., 1285 Old River Rd., Cleveland, OH 44113, (216)241-0333 [7974]

Samson Hardware & Fairbanks, 100 N Turner St., Fairbanks, AK 99701, (907)452-3110 [13901]

Samson Technologies Inc., 575 Underhill Blvd., PO Box 9031, Syosset, NY 11791, (516)364-2244 [5749]

Samson's Novelty Company Inc., 37 Riverside Dr., Auburn, ME 04210-6870, (207)782-2929 [26646]

Samsung Electronics America Inc., 105 Challenger Rd., Ridgefield Park, NJ 07660, (201)229-4000 [25426]

Samsung Opto-Electronics America Inc., 40 Seaview Dr., Secaucus, NJ 07094, (201)902-0347 [22900]

Samuel Specialty Metals Inc., 4 Essex Ave., Bernardsville, NJ 07924-2265, (201)884-2222 [20351]

Samuel-Whittar Inc., 20001 Sherwood Ave., Detroit, MI 48234, (313)893-5000 [20567]

Samuels Glass Co., PO Box 1769, San Antonio, TX 78296, (210)227-2481 [7975]

Samuels Jewelers, 320 W Kimberly Rd., Davenport, IA 52806-5995, (319)391-4362 [17586]

Samuels Recycling Co., PO Box 8800, Madison, WI 53708, (608)241-7191 [26977]

Samuels Recycling Co. Green Bay Div., PO Box 10917, Green Bay, WI 54307, (920)494-3451 [20352]

Samuels Recycling Co. Janesville Div., 1753 Beloit Ave., Janesville, WI 53546, (608)756-2555 [26978]

Samuels Tile, 223 Nepperhan Ave., Yonkers, NY 10701, (914)423-0880 [10136]

San Antonio Brake and Clutch Service Inc., PO Box 976, San Antonio, TX 78294, (210)226-0254 [3185]

San Diego Beverage and Cup Inc., 5310 Riley St., San Diego, CA 92110, (619)297-2600 [25033]

San Diego Marine Exchange, 2636 Shelter Island Dr., San Diego, CA 92106, (619)223-7159 [18601]

San Esters Corp., 55 E 59th St., Fl. 19, New York, NY 10022-1112, (212)972-1112 [4500]

San Francisco Center for Visual Studies, 49 Rivoli St., San Francisco, CA 94117, (415)664-4699 [4136]

San Francisco Mart, 1355 Market St., San Francisco, CA 94103, (415)552-2311 [13231]

San Jacinto Foods, 314 S Fannin, Amarillo, TX 79106-6799, (806)374-4202 [12401]

San Joaquin Beverage Co., PO Box 1138, Stockton, CA 95201, (209)948-9400 [2006]

San Joaquin Lumber Co., PO Box 71, Stockton, CA 95201, (209)465-5651 [7976]

San Joaquin Sulphur Company Inc., PO Box 700, Lodi, CA 95241, (209)368-6676 [4501]

San Joaquin Supply Company Inc., PO Box 7737, Fresno, CA 93747, (209)251-8455 [4702]

San Joaquin Valley Hay Growers Association, PO Box 1127, Tracy, CA 95378-1127, (209)835-1662 [1232]

San Jose Surgical Supply Inc., 902 S Bascom Ave., San Jose, CA 95128, (408)293-9033 [19032]

San Luis Sourdough, 3580 Sueldo St., San Luis Obispo, CA 93401, (805)544-7687 [12402]

San Saba Pecan, Inc., 2803 W Wallace, San Saba, TX 76877, (915)372-5727 [12403]

Sanborn Cooperative Grain Co., 309 W 1st St., Sanborn, IA 51248, (712)729-3205 [1233]

Sanborn Farmers Elevator, PO Box 67, Sanborn, MN 56083, (507)648-3851 [18221]

Sanborn Farmers Elevator, PO Box 67, Sanborn, MN 56083, (507)648-3851 [12404]

Sanborn's Paint Spot Inc., 12 Terrill St., Rutland, VT 05701-4155, (802)775-7159 [21559]

Sanchez Fine Jewelers, PO Box 848, Jackson, WY 83001-0848, (307)733-9439 [17587]

Sand and Gravel Co.; J.P., PO Box 2, Lockbourne, OH 43137, (614)497-0083 [7977]

Sand Livestock Systems Inc., PO Box 948, Columbus, NE 68601, (402)564-1211 [1234]

Sand Mountain Shoe Co., PO Box 447, Sharon, TN 38255-0447, (901)456-2580 [24848]

Sand Seed Service Inc., Hwy. 143 N, Marcus, IA 51035, (712)376-4135 [1235]

Sandaga, 1231 Broadway, New York, NY 10001, (212)532-6820 [17588]

Sander Supply Co.; Joseph, 3720 14th Ave., Brooklyn, NY 11218-3608, (718)438-4223 [5331]

Sanders Co., PO Box 25758, Baltimore, MD 21224-0458, (410)288-6974 [7978]

Sanders Company Inc.; George T., 10201 W 49th Ave., Wheat Ridge, CO 80033, (303)423-9660 [23358]

Sanderson Safety Supply Co., 1101 SE 3rd Ave., Portland, OR 97214, (503)238-5700 [24624]

Sanderson and Sons North America Ltd.; Arthur, 285 Grand Ave., Englewood, NJ 07631, (201)894-8400 [15649]

Sandler Foods, 1224 Diamond Spring Rd, Virginia Beach, VA 23455, (804)464-3551 [24214]

Sandler Medical Services, 1244 6th Ave., Des Moines, IA 50314-2715, (515)244-4236 [19033]

Sandridge Foods Corp., 133 Commerce Dr., Medina, OH 44256, (330)725-2348 [12405]

Sandridge Gourmet Salads, 133 Commerce Dr., Medina, OH 44256, (330)725-2348 [12406]

Sands, Taylor and Wood Co., Box 1010, Norwich, VT 05055, (802)649-3881 [11610]

Sandstrand Corp., 4400 Ruffin Rd., PO Box 85757, San Diego, CA 92186-5757, (619)627-6501 [47]

Sandusco Inc., 11012 Aurora Hudson Rd., Streetsboro, OH 44241, (330)528-0410 [25427]

Sandusco Inc., 11012 Aurora Hudson Rd., Streetsboro, OH 44241, (330)528-0410 [9334]

Sandusky Distributing Co., 11012 Aurora Hudson Rd., Streetsboro, OH 44241-1029, (330)528-0410 [25428]

Sandusky Electrical Inc., 1516 Milan Rd., Sandusky, OH 44870, (419)625-4915 [9335]

Sandusky Industrial Supply, 2000 Superior St., Box 2190, Sandusky, OH 44870, (419)626-4467 [3186]

Sandy Lumber Sales Company Inc.; M.L., PO Box 1535, Corinth, MS 38835-1535, (662)286-6087 [7979]

Sandy Supply Co., PO Box 299, Wooster, OH 44691, (330)262-1730 [22650]

Sanel Auto Parts Inc., PO Box 1254, Concord, NH 03301, (603)225-4100 [3187]

Sanfilippo Co.; John B., 16435 I-Hwy., 35 N, Selma, TX 78154-1200, (210)651-5300 [12407]

Sanford and Associates Inc.; Gene, PO Box 37589, Phoenix, AZ 85069-7589, (602)997-6886 [12408]

Sanford Process Corp., 65 North Ave., Natick, MA 01760, (508)653-7860 [16470]

Sanford Shirt Co., 529 W 29th St., Baltimore, MD 21211-2916, (410)235-8338 [5332]

Sanford Tile Co., 5506 Wares Ferry Rd., Montgomery, AL 36117, (334)272-4498 [10137]

Sangamon Co., PO Box 410, Taylorville, IL 62568, (217)824-2261 [13440]

Sangray Corporation, 2318 Lakeview Ave., PO Box 2388, Pueblo, CO 81004, (719)564-3408 [13441]

Sani-Clean Distributors Inc., 585 Riverside St., Portland, ME 04103, (207)797-8240 [4703]

Sanofi Beaute Inc., 40 W 57th St., New York, NY 10019-4001, (212)621-7300 [14229]

Sanrio Inc., 570 Eccles Ave., South San Francisco, CA 94080, (650)952-2880 [13442]

Sanson Co., 4000 Orange Ave., Cleveland, OH 44115, (216)431-8560 [12409]

Sanson and Rowland Inc., PO Box 5768, Philadelphia, PA 19120, (215)329-9263 [13902]

Santa Barbara Instrument Group Corp., 147 Castilian Dr., Ste. A, Goleta, CA 93117-5598, (805)969-1851 [22901]

Santa Clara Tile Supply, 1129 Richard Ave., Santa Clara, CA 95050, (408)727-9050 [10138]

Santa Fe Communications, 9640 Legler, Lenexa, KS 66219, (913)492-8288 [25429]

Santa Fe Pet and Vet Supply, 2801 Cerrillos Rd., Santa Fe, NM 87505-2311, (505)988-2237 [27228]

Santa Fuel Inc., 154 Admiral St., PO Box 1141, Bridgeport, CT 06601-1141, (203)367-3661 [22651]

Santa Maria Tire Inc., PO Box 6007, Santa Maria, CA 93456, (805)928-2501 [3188]

Santa Rosa Bearing, 1100 Santa Rosa Ave., Santa Rosa, CA 95403, (707)545-7904 [3189]

Santanna Banana Co., 12th & Kelker, Harrisburg, PA 17105, (717)238-8321 [12410]

Santoni and Co.; V., PO Box 1236, Woodland, CA 95776-1346, (530)666-4447 [2007]

Santucci-Trigg Sales Co., 1195 NW 119th St., Miami, FL 33168, (305)685-7781 [12411]

Sanyo Sales and Supply (USA) Corp., 900 N Arlington, Itasca, IL 60143-1477, (630)775-0404 [25430]

SAP America, Inc., 3999 W Chester Pike, Newtown Square, PA 19073, (610)661-1000 [6703]

Saphrograph Corp., 4910-12 Ft. Hamilton Pkwy., Brooklyn, NY 11219, (718)331-1233 [4137]

Sapp Brothers Petroleum Inc., PO Box 37305, Omaha, NE 68137, (402)895-1380 [22652]

Sapporo U.S.A. Inc., 666 3rd Ave., 82th Fl., New York, NY 10017, (212)922-9165 [2008]

Sara Lee Corp., 3 1st National Plz., Chicago, IL 60602-4260, (312)726-2600 [12412]

Sarah's Attic Inc., PO Box 448, Chesaning, MI 48616, (517)845-3990 [13443]

Saratoga Specialties, 200 Wrightwood, Elmhurst, IL 60126-1113, (708)833-3810 [12413]

Sarco Inc., PO Box 893, Voorhees, NJ 08043, (609)795-0699 [17159]

Sarco Inc., 1402 Auburn Way N, PMB 393, Auburn, WA 98002-3309, (206)441-5977 [24215]

Sarco Inc., 2416 2nd Ave., Seattle, WA 98121-1425, (206)441-5977 [15303]

SARCOM Inc., 8405 Pulsar Pl., Columbus, OH 43240, (614)854-1000 [6704]

Sargent-Sowell Co., 1025 Post and Paddock Rd., Grand Prairie, TX 75050, (214)647-1525 [24620]

Sargent-Welch Scientific Co., 911 Commerce Ct., Buffalo Grove, IL 60089-2362, (708)459-6625 [24425]

Sargento Foods Inc., 1 Persnickety Pl., Plymouth, WI 53073, (920)893-8484 [12414]

Sargento Foods Inc., 1 Persnickety Pl, Plymouth, WI 53073, (920)893-8484 [12415]

Sargento Specialty Foods Inc., 1 Persnickety Pl., Plymouth, WI 53073, (920)893-8484 [12414]

Saria International Inc., 1200 Industrial Rd, Unit 2, San Carlos, CA 94070, (650)591-1440 [13903]

Saroff & Company Inc.; Sam, 223 Yuma, Manhattan, KS 66502-6235, (785)776-4846 [12416]

Sarreid Ltd., PO Box 3548, Wilson, NC 27895-3548, (919)291-1414 [13232]

Sartori Food Corp., 107 Pleasant View Rd., PO Box 258, Plymouth, WI 53073, (920)893-6061 [12417]

Sartori Foods, 107 Pleasant View Rd., PO Box 258, Plymouth, WI 53073, (920)893-6061 [12417]

Sartorius Sports Ltd., 175 W Main St., Avon, CT 06001-3670, (860)677-5540 [24849]

Sashco Inc., 1232 Monte Vista Ave., Ste. 4, Upland, CA 91786-8213, (909)949-3082 [7980]

Sasser Lumber Company Inc., PO Box 606, La Grange, NC 28551, (919)566-3121 [7981]

Sassounian Inc., 404 W 7th, Ste. 614, Los Angeles, CA 90014-1613, (213)627-1206 [17589]

Sat-Pak Inc., 1492 N 6th St., Redmond, OR 97756, (541)923-0467 [9336]

Satanta Cooperative Grain, PO Box 99, Satanta, KS 67870, (316)649-2230 [18222]

Satellite Information Systems Co., 7464 Arapahoe Rd., Ste. B-17, Boulder, CO 80303, (303)449-0442 [6705]

Sathers Inc., PO Box 28, Round Lake, MN 56167, (507)945-8181 [12418]

Satori Herbal-Business Development Labs, 825 W Market, Salinas, CA 93901, (408)475-6154 [12419]

Satterlund Supply Co., 26277 Sherwood Ave., Warren, MI 48091, (810)755-9700 [23359]

Sattex Corp., PO Box 2593, White City, OR 97503-0593, (541)826-8808 [4502]

Saturn Satellite System, Inc., DBA Saturn Distributing, 1199 Main St., Jackson, KY 41339, (606)666-8881 [9337]

Sauder and Rippel Inc., Rte. 51, Minonk, IL 61760, (309)432-2531 [1236]

Saunco Air Technologies, PO Box 178, Hickman, CA 95323, (209)874-2357 [14673]

Saunders & Associates; Keifer, 785 S Commerce St., Jackson, MS 39201-5618, (601)352-0737 [12420]

Saunders Oil Company Inc., 1200 W Marshall St., Richmond, VA 23220, (804)358-7191 [7982]

Saunders Supply Company Inc., PO Box 2278, Suffolk, VA 23432, (757)255-4531 [7983]

Saunier-Wilhelm Co., 3216 5th Ave., Pittsburgh, PA 15213-3026, (412)621-4350 [23930]

Saurer Textile Systems Charlotte, 4200 Performance Rd., Charlotte, NC 28214, (704)394-8111 [16471]

Sausalito Craftworks, PO Box 1792, Sausalito, CA 94966, (415)332-3392 [17590]

Sav-T Spot, PO Box 1020, Roseburg, OR 97470, (541)672-7771 [11545]

Savage Inc., 2968 Niagara Falls Blvd., North Tonawanda, NY 14120, (716)692-2208 [20718]

Savage Universal Corp., 550 E Elliot Rd., Chandler, AZ 85225, (480)632-1320 [22902]

Saval Foods, 6740 Dorsey Rd., Elkridge, MD 21075, (410)379-5100 [12421]

Savannah Communications, 11 Minus Ave., PO Box 7328, Savannah, GA 31418, (912)964-1479 [5750]

Savannah Communications, 11 Minus Ave., Savannah, GA 31418, (912)964-1479 [9338]

Savannah Distributing Company Inc., PO Box 1388, Savannah, GA 31402, (912)233-1167 [2009]

S.A.V.E. Half Price Books for Libraries, 303 N Main St., PO Box 30, Schulenburg, TX 78956, (409)743-4147 [4138]

Save On Software, PO Box 1312, Wilkes Barre, PA 18703-1312, (717)822-9531 [6706]

Savin Corp., PO Box 10270, Stamford, CT 06904-2270, (203)967-5000 [21258]

Savoir Technology Group Inc., 254 E Hacienda Ave., Campbell, CA 95008, (408)379-0177 [9339]

Savol Bleach Co., 15 Village St., East Hartford, CT 06108-3924, (203)282-0878 [4503]

Savoye Packaging Corp., 2050 S 10th St., San Jose, CA 95112-4112, (408)745-0614 [20353]

Saw Mill Auto Wreckers, 12 Worth St., Yonkers, NY 10701, (914)968-5300 [3190]

Sawing and Shearing Services Inc., 13500 Western Ave., Blue Island, IL 60406, (708)388-9955 [20354]

Sawnee Refrigeration & Welding Supply, Inc., PO Box 207, Cumming, GA 30028-0207, (770)889-2295 [14674]

Sawtooth Builders, 312 4th St., Ithaca, NY 14850 [10139]

Sawtooth Technologies Inc., 1007 Church St., Ste. 402, Evanston, IL 60201, (847)866-0870 [6707]

Sawyer and Company Inc.; J.E., PO Box 2177, Glens Falls, NY 12801, (518)793-4104 [13904]

Sawyer Gas Co., 7162 Phillips Hwy., Jacksonville, FL 32256, (904)296-8600 [22653]

Saxon Paper Co., 3005 Review Ave., Long Island City, NY 11101-3239, (718)937-6622 [21922]

Saxonburg Ceramics Inc., PO Box 688, Saxonburg, PA 16056, (412)352-1561 [17160]

Saxonville USA, 96 Springfield Rd., Charlestown, NH 03603, (603)826-5719 [7984]

Saxony Sportswear Co., 2301 W Allegheny Ave., Philadelphia, PA 19132, (215)227-0400 [5333]

Saybeck Inc., 1045 Airport Blvd., South San Francisco, CA 94080, (415)588-3088 [22654]

Sayers Computer Source, 1150 Feehanville Dr., Mt. Prospect, IL 60056, (708)391-4040 [6708]

Sazerac Company Inc., PO Box 52821, New Orleans, LA 70152-2821, (504)831-9450 [2010]

SB Developments Inc., PO Box 205, Milan, MI 48160-0205, (734)439-1231 [23360]

Sbar's, Inc., 14 Sbar Blvd., Moorestown, NJ 08057, (609)234-8220 [26647]

SBC/Sporto Corp., 2 Midway St., Boston, MA 02210, (617)345-8800 [24850]

SBM Drilling Fluids, 15810 Park Ten Pl., Ste. 300, Houston, TX 77084, (281)578-2919 [22655]

SBM Industries Inc., 1865 Palmer Ave., Larchmont, NY 10538, (914)833-0649 [9340]

S.C. Farm Bureau Marketing Association, 724 Knox Abbott Dr., Cayce, SC 29033, (803)796-6700 [18223]

SC and T International Inc., 7625 E Redfield Rd., Scottsdale, AZ 85260, (480)368-9490 [26525]

Scales Air Compressor Corp., 110 Voice Rd., Carle Place, NY 11514, (516)248-9096 [5851]

Scales Company Inc.; R.H., 240 University Ave., Westwood, MA 02090-2393, (781)320-0005 [3191]

Scallan Supply Co., 3950 Virginia Ave., Cincinnati, OH 45227, (513)271-0618 [16937]

Scana Propane Supply Inc., PO Box 640, Sumter, SC 29151-0640, (803)778-1981 [22656]

Scanning Technologies Inc., 2314 Durwood, Little Rock, AR 72207, (501)663-6912 [6709]

ScanSource Inc., 6 Logue Court, Ste. G, Greenville, SC 29615, (864)288-2432 [6710]

ScanSteel Service Center Inc., PO Box 2667, Clarksville, IN 47131, (812)284-4141 [20355]

Scantek Inc., 916 Gist Ave., Silver Spring, MD 20910, (301)495-7738 [24426]

Scarborough Auto Parts Inc., 40 Holmes Rd., Scarborough, ME 04074-9565, (207)883-4161 [3192]

Scariano Brothers Inc., PO Box 26009, New Orleans, LA 70186, (504)733-5033 [12422]

Scatena York Company, 2000 Oakdale Ave., San Francisco, CA 94124, (415)285-6600 [14675]

S.C.B. Distributors, 15608 S New Century Dr., Gardena, CA 90248, (310)532-9400 [4139]

Scenery Unlimited, 7236 W Madison St., Forest Park, IL 60130, (708)366-7763 [26648]

Scepter Industries Inc., R.R. 1, Box 551, Bicknell, IN 47512, (812)735-2500 [26979]

Schachter and Company Inc.; Leo, 579 5th Ave., New York, NY 10017, (212)688-2000 [17591]

Schadler and Sons Inc.; John, PO Box 1068, Clifton, NJ 07014, (973)777-3600 [25431]

Schaedler Brothers Inc., PO Box 2008, Harrisburg, PA 17105-2008, (717)233-1621 [9341]

Schaedler/Yesco Distribution, PO Box 2008, Harrisburg, PA 17105-2008, (717)233-1621 [9341]

Schaefer's Cold Storage, 9820 D St., Oakland, CA 94603, (510)632-5064 [12423]

Schaefer's Meats Inc., 9820 D St., Oakland, CA 94603, (510)632-5064 [12423]

Schaeperkoetter Store Inc., PO Box 37, Mt. Sterling, MO 65062, (573)943-6321 [6711]

Schafer Company Inc., 101 N 1st St., Decatur, IN 46733, (219)724-3141 [13862]

Schapero Co. Inc.; Eric, 98 Union Park St., Boston, MA 02118, (617)423-2842 [24851]

Scharpfs Twin Oaks Builders Supply Co., PO Box 887, Eugene, OR 97440, (541)342-1261 [7985]

Schawbel Corp., 529 Main St., Boston, MA 02129-1101, (617)241-7400 [14230]

Schecter and Sons, Inc.; Nathan, B & Lippincott St., Philadelphia, PA 19134, (215)634-2400 [13444]

Scheidelman Inc., 1201 Thorn St., Utica, NY 13502, (315)732-6186 [12424]

Scheidt Inc.; Bruno, 71 W 23rd St., New York, NY 10010, (212)741-8290 [12425]

Schein Pharmaceutical Inc., 100 Campus Dr., Florham Park, NJ 07932, (973)593-5500 [19594]

Scheinert & Son Inc.; Sidney, PO Box 527, 404 Midland Ave., Saddle Brook, NJ 07663, (201)791-4600 [13905]

Schelle Cellular Group Inc., 100 West Rd., Ste. 404, Baltimore, MD 21204-2331, (410)825-4211 [5751]

Schenck Co.; E.E., 2204 N Clark St., Portland, OR 97227, (503)284-4124 [26198]

Schenck Foods Company Inc., PO Box 2298, Winchester, VA 22604, (703)869-1870 [12426]

Schenck Trebel Corp., 535 Acorn St., Deer Park, NY 11729, (631)242-4010 [24427]

Scheppers Distributing; N.H., 1736 Southridge Dr., Jefferson City, MO 65109-2046, (573)636-4831 [2011]

Scherer Companies Inc., 5131 Post Rd., Dublin, OH 43017, (614)792-0777 [4239]

Scherer Laboratories Inc., 2301 Ohio Dr., Ste. 234, Plano, TX 75093, (972)612-6225 [19595]

Scherer Truck Equipment, Inc., 6105 NW River Park Dr., Kansas City, MO 64150, (816)587-0190 [3193]

Scherer Truck Equipment, Inc., 2670 Auburn Rd., Auburn Hills, MI 48326, (248)853-7277 [3194]

Schermerhorn Brothers Co., PO Box 668, Lombard, IL 60148, (630)627-9860 [25935]

Schetky Northwest Sales Inc., PO Box 20041, Portland, OR 97220-0041, (503)287-4141 [20719]

Schiavone and Sons Inc.; Michael, 234 Universal Dr., North Haven, CT 06473, (203)777-2591 [26980]

Schieffelin and Somerset Co., 2 Park Ave., New York, NY 10016, (212)251-8200 [2012]

Schiffer Wholesale Hardware; Leslie, 34 Ludlow St., New York, NY 10002, (212)677-7530 [24625]

Schildwachter and Sons Inc.; Fred M., 1400 Ferris Pl., Bronx, NY 10461, (212)828-2400 [22657]

Schillers Photo Graphics, 9420 Manchester Rd., St. Louis, MO 63144-2678, (314)968-3650 [22903]

Schilling Brothers Inc., R.R. 2, Mattoon, IL 61938, (217)234-6478 [1237]

Schilling Paper Co., 1500 Opportunity Rd. NW, Rochester, MN 55901, (507)288-8940 [21923]

Schilling TV Inc., 215 4th St., Pittsfield, MA 01201-4810, (413)443-9235 [25432]

Schillinger Associates Inc., 2297 E Boulevard, Kokomo, IN 46902-2453, (765)457-7241 [9342]

Schinner Co.; A.D., 4901 W State St., Milwaukee, WI 53208, (414)771-4300 [21924]

Schlachter Co. Inc.; Edward J., 9930 Commerce Park Dr., Cincinnati, OH 45246, (513)860-0700 [12427]

Schlafer Iron and Steel Co., 1950 Medbury Ave., Detroit, MI 48211, (313)925-8200 [26981]

Schlafer Supply Company Inc., PO Box 999, Appleton, WI 54912, (414)733-4433 [13906]

Schleicher and Schuell Inc., 10 Optical Ave., Keene, NH 03431, (603)352-3810 [24428]

Schleifer and Son Inc.; H., 352 7th Ave., New York, NY 10001, (212)564-5639 [5334]

Schluckbier Inc.; Jerry, 2760 Industrial Row, Troy, MI 48098, (248)280-0844 [14947]

Schlueter Company Inc., PO Box 548, Janesville, WI 53547, (608)755-5455 [24216]

Schmalenberge; Jacob, PO Box 39, Hebron, ND 58638-0039, (701)878-4948 [18224]

Schmann Auto Parts, 701 Clairton Blvd., Pittsburgh, PA 15236, (412)655-3434 [3195]

Schmid Motor Inc.; Don, PO Box 789762, Wichita, KS 67278-9762, (316)522-2253 [20720]

Schmidt Laboratories, PO Box 1264, St. Cloud, MN 56302, (320)255-9787 [19596]

Schmidt Machine Co., 7013 State Hwy. 199, Upper Sandusky, OH 43351, (419)294-3814 [1238]

Schmuckal Oil Co., 1516 Barlow, Traverse City, MI 49686, (231)946-2800 [22658]

Schnaible Service and Supply Company Inc., 231 Chestnut St., PO Box 1453, Lafayette, IN 47902-1453, (765)742-0280 [4704]

Schneider Company Inc.; J.R., 849 Jackson St., Benicia, CA 94510, (707)745-0404 [25808]

Schneider Corp., 285 Oser Ave., Hauppauge, NY 11788, (631)761-5000 [19597]

Schneider Dairy, 726 Frank, Pittsburgh, PA 15227-1210, (412)881-3525 [12428]

Schneider Optics Inc., 285 Oser Ave., Hauppauge, NY 11788, (631)761-5000 [19597]

Schneider Sales Inc.; Arthur, 1788 Ellsworth Industrial Blvd., Atlanta, GA 30318-3748, (404)350-2550 [24852]

Schnieber Fine Food Inc., 2510 S 64th Ave., Omaha, NE 68106, (402)558-5728 [12429]

Schnieber Fine Food Inc., 2500 State Fair Park Dr., Lincoln, NE 68504, (402)466-3663 [12430]

Schnitzer Steel Products, PO Box 10047, Portland, OR 97296, (503)286-5771 [26982]

Schoeller Textil USA Inc., RR 3 Box 9D, Newport, VT 05855, (802)334-5081 [26199]

Schoenhof's Foreign Books Inc., 486 Green St., Cambridge, MA 02139, (617)547-8855 [4140]

Scholarly Publications, 14601 Bellaire Blvd., Ste. 60, Houston, TX 77083, (281)504-4646 [4141]

Scholium International, Inc., PO Box 1519, Port Washington, NY 11050, (516)767-7171 [4142]

Scholl Forest Industries, 502 N Water, Corpus Christi, TX 78471, (361)883-1144 [7986]

Scholl Forest Products Inc., PO Box 40458, Houston, TX 77240-0458, (713)329-5300 [7987]

Scholl Oil & Transport Co., PO Box 148, Holyoke, CO 80734-0148, (970)854-3300 [25433]

Scholl Oil and Transport Co., PO Box 148, Holyoke, CO 80734-0148, (970)854-3300 [15304]

School Book Service, 3650 Coral Ridge Dr., Ste. 112, Coral Springs, FL 33065, (954)341-7207 [4143]

School Specialties Inc., 1000 N Bluemound Dr., Appleton, WI 54914, (920)734-5712 [13233]

School Specialty Inc., 5800 NE Hassalo St., Portland, OR 97213, (503)281-1193 [21259]

School Stationers Corp., 1641 S Main St., Oshkosh, WI 54901, (920)426-1300 [21925]

Schoonmaker Service Parts Co., PO Box 621, Petaluma, CA 94953-0621, (707)763-8100 [16472]

Schorin Company Inc., 1800 Penn Ave., Pittsburgh, PA 15222, (412)281-0650 [21926]

Schorr Insulated Glass Inc.; Norm, 6322 Easton Rd., Pipersville, PA 18947, (215)766-2707 [7988]

Schott Distributing Co., 5245 W 6th St., Goodview, Winona, MN 55987-1250, (507)452-5772 [2013]

Schrader-Bridgeport International, 500 S 45th St. E, Muskogee, OK 74403, (918)687-5427 [3196]

Schrafel Paper Corp.; A.J., PO Box 788, Floral Park, NY 11002-0788, (516)437-1700 [21927]

Schram & Associates; Mike, PO Box 201, Geneva, IL 60134 [23931]

Schreiber Inc.; E., 580 5th Ave., New York, NY 10036, (212)382-0280 [17592]

Schroeder Optical Company Inc., PO Box 12100, Roanoke, VA 24022-2100, (540)345-6736 [19598]

Schroeder's Book Haven, 104 Michigan Ave., League City, TX 77573, (281)332-5226 [4144]

Schroth Inc.; Emil A., PO Box 496, Farmingdale, NJ 07727, (908)938-5015 [20356]

Schuco Inc., 1720 Sublette Ave., St. Louis, MO 63110-1927, (314)726-2000 [19034]

Schukei Chevrolet Inc., PO Box 1525, Mason City, IA 50401, (515)423-5402 [3197]

Schulte Paint, PO Box 461, Florissant, MO 63032-0461, (314)381-3830 [21560]

Schultz Sav-O Stores Inc., PO Box 419, Sheboygan, WI 53082-0419, (920)457-4433 [12431]

Schultz Seed Co.; J.M., PO Box 211, Dieterich, IL 62424, (217)925-5212 [18225]

Schultz Snyder Steele Lumber Co., 2419 Science Pkwy., Lansing, MI 48909, (517)349-8220 [7989]

Schultz Snyder Steele Lumber Co., 2419 Science Pkwy., Lansing, MI 48909, (517)349-8220 [27369]

Schultz and Sons; H., 777 Lehigh Ave., Union, NJ 07083, (908)687-5400 [4705]

Schumacher and Seiler Inc., 15 W Aylesbury Rd., Timonium, MD 21093-4142, (410)561-2461 [23361]

Schumacher Wholesale Meats Inc., 1114 Zane Ave. N, Golden Valley, MN 55422, (612)546-3291 [12432]

Schuster Electronics Inc., 11320 Grooms Rd., Cincinnati, OH 45242-1480, (513)489-1400 [9343]

Schutte and Koerting Div., 2233 State Rd., Bensalem, PA 19020, (215)639-0900 [15305]

Schutte Lumber Company Inc., 3001 Southwest Blvd., Kansas City, MO 64108, (816)753-6262 [7990]

Schutte Lumber Company Inc., 3001 Southwest Blvd., Kansas City, MO 64108, (816)753-6262 [27370]

Schuyler-Brown FS Inc., PO Box 230, Rushville, IL 62681, (217)322-3306 [1239]

Schuylkill Haven Casket Co., PO Box 179, Schuylkill Haven, PA 17972, (717)385-0296 [25809]

Schwab Warehouse Center Inc.; Les, PO Box 667, Prineville, OR 97754, (503)447-4136 [3198]

Schwan Wholesale Co., 221 S 3rd St., PO Box 710, Devils Lake, ND 58301-0710, (701)662-4981 [12433]

Schwartz and Benjamin Inc., 100 Marine Blvd., Lynn, MA 01901, (781)595-5600 [24853]

Schwartz and Benjamin Inc., PO Box 831, Lynn, MA 01903, (781)595-5600 [5335]

Schwartz & Co.; Arthur, 234 Meads Mountain Rd., Woodstock, NY 12498, (914)679-4024 [4145]

Schwartz Co.; Louis J., 17 Wellington Pl., Amityville, NY 11701, (631)691-8889 [13234]

Schwartz Shoes Inc.; Jack, 155 Avenue of the Americas, New York, NY 10013, (212)691-4700 [5336]

Schwartzman Co., 2905 N Ferry St., Anoka, MN 55303, (612)421-1187 [26983]

Schwarz Paper Co., PO Box 82266, Lincoln, NE 68501, (402)477-1202 [21260]

Schwarz Service Co., 603 Main St., Ruma, IL 62278, (618)282-2028 [15306]

Schweigers, Inc., 47213 Schweigers Cir., PO Box 1104, Sioux Falls, SD 57101-1104, (605)543-5206 [20698]

Schwinn Cycling and Fitness, 340 W Crossroads Pky., Ste. B, Bolingbrook, IL 60440-4939, (630)231-5340 [23932]

Sci-Rep Inc., 9512 Lee Hwy. A, Fairfax, VA 22031-2303, (703)385-0600 [9344]

Science and Spirit Resources, Inc., 171-B Rumford St., Concord, NH 03301, (603)226-3328 [4146]

Scientific Anglers, 3M Ctr., Bldg. 223-4NE-513, St. Paul, MN 55144-1000, (651)733-4751 [23933]

Scientific Brake and Equipment Co., 702 Dickerson Rd., PO Box 1023, Gaylord, MI 49735, (517)732-7507 [3199]

Scientific Brake and Equipment Co., 314 W Genesee Ave., PO Box 840, Saginaw, MI 48602, (517)755-4411 [3200]

Scientific and Business Minicomputers Inc., 7076 Peachtree Blvd., No. 200, Norcross, GA 30071, (770)446-0404 [6712]

Scientific Equipment Co., 15 Kent Rd., Aston, PA 19014, (610)358-2855 [24429]

Scientific & Medical Publications of France Inc., 100 E 42nd St., Ste. 1510, New York, NY 10017, (212)983-6278 [4147]

Scion Steel Co., 23800 Blackstone Rd., Warren, MI 48089, (810)755-4000 [20357]

Scissors and Shears, 849 Roger Williams Ave., Rumford, RI 02916-2145, (401)434-4694 [14231]

SCMS Inc., 10201 Rodney St., Pineville, NC 28134, (704)889-4508 [9345]

Scofield Company Inc.; George, 3601 Taylor Way, Tacoma, WA 98421-4307, (253)272-8314 [7991]

Sconza Candy Co., 919 81st Ave., Oakland, CA 94621-2511, (510)568-8137 [12434]

Scope Imports Inc., 8020 Blankenship Dr., Houston, TX 77055, (713)688-0077 [5337]

Scope Office Services Inc., 1510 S Lewis St., Anaheim, CA 92805, (714)999-2500 [21261]

Scorpio Music Inc., 2500 E State St., Trenton, NJ 08619, (609)890-6000 [25434]

Scotland Yard, 1001 Columbia St., Newport, KY 41071, (606)581-0140 [27229]

Scotland Yard, 1001 Columbia St., Newport, KY 41071, (606)581-0140 [19599]

Scotsco Inc., 13101 SE 84th Ave., Clackamas, OR 97015-9733, (503)777-4726 [16473]

Scott Associates; L.S., 78-03 226th St., A, Flushing, NY 11364-3624, (212)695-2536 [5338]

Scott Cooperative Association, PO Box 340, Scott City, KS 67871, (316)872-5823 [1240]

Scott County Cooperative, PO Box 248, Forest, MS 39074, (601)469-1451 [1241]

Scott Drug Co., PO Box 34649, Charlotte, NC 28234, (704)375-9841 [19600]

Scott Electronics, 4040 Adams St., Lincoln, NE 68504-1996, (402)466-8221 [9346]

Scott Farm Service Inc., N Commercial St., Winchester, IL 62694, (217)742-3125 [1242]

Scott Foam & Fabrics, Inc., 2790 Broad, PO Box 820371, Memphis, TN 38112, (901)324-3800 [26200]

Scott-Hourigan Co., 511 S Lincoln Ave., York, NE 68467-4211, (402)362-7711 [1243]

Scott Industrial Systems Inc., PO Box 1387, Dayton, OH 45401, (937)233-8146 [17161]

Scott Laboratories Inc., PO Box 4559, Petaluma, CA 94955-4559, (707)765-6666 [2014]

Scott Lumber Co., 253 N Lincoln Ave., Bridgeport, OH 43912, (740)635-2345 [7992]

Scott Machinery Co., 4055 South 500 West, Salt Lake City, UT 84123, (801)262-7441 [16474]

Scott and Muscatine's Service Co., PO Box 609, Walcott, IA 52773, (319)284-6293 [18226]

Scott Paper, Inc., Hazlettville Rd., PO Box 7010 C, Dover, DE 19903, (302)678-2600 [21928]

Scott Seed Co., PO Box 849, New Albany, IN 47150, (812)945-0229 [1244]

Scott and Sons Co.; O.M., 14111 Scottslawn Rd., Marysville, OH 43041, (937)644-0011 [1245]

Scott Stainless Steel, 6201 W Howard St., Niles, IL 60714, (847)647-1000 [20358]

Scott Truck and Tractor Company Inc., PO Box 4948, Monroe, LA 71211, (318)387-4160 [1246]

Scott Water Treatment, 100 W Main St., Fair Bluff, NC 28439, (910)649-7581 [23363]

Scottco Service Co., PO Box 7729, Amarillo, TX 79114, (806)355-8251 [23362]

Scottish Connection, PO Box 94, Lincoln, NH 03251-0094, (603)745-3958 [5339]

Scotts Inc., 100 W Main St., Fair Bluff, NC 28439, (910)649-7581 [23363]

Scott's Market Equipment Inc., RR 1, Box 275, Marsing, ID 83639-9525, (208)888-3886 [14676]

Scotty's Foods Inc., 5037 SE Powell Blvd., Portland, OR 97206, (503)777-5484 [12435]

Scotty's Hardware Inc., 1931 Lake Tahoe Blvd., PO Box 7737, South Lake Tahoe, CA 96150, (530)541-3601 [13907]

Scotty's Inc., 5300 N Recker Hwy., Winter Haven, FL 33882, (941)299-1111 [7993]

The Scoular Co., 2027 Dodge St., Omaha, NE 68102, (402)342-3500 [18227]

SCR Inc., PO Box 1607, Lake Oswego, OR 97035, (503)968-1300 [7994]

SCR Inc., PO Box 1607, Lake Oswego, OR 97035, (503)968-1300 [27371]

Scranton Equity Exchange Inc., PO Box 127, Scranton, ND 58653, (701)275-8221 [7995]

Scranton Sales Co., 1027 Jefferson Ave., Scranton, PA 18510, (717)346-0718 [23364]

Scrap Corporation of America, 12901 S Stony Island Ave., Chicago, IL 60633, (312)646-1800 [26984]

Screen Industry Art Inc., 214 Industrial Dr., Soddy-Daisy, TN 37379, (423)332-6190 [16475]

Screen (USA), 5110 Tollview Dr., Rolling Meadows, IL 60008, (847)870-7400 [25810]

Scriptex Enterprises Ltd., 575 Corporate Dr., Mahwah, NJ 07430, (201)825-1100 [21262]

Scripts For All Reasons, c/o Bill McDonnell, Silver Spring, MD 20902, (301)598-8584 [5340]

Scrivner Inc., PO Box 26030, Oklahoma City, OK 73126, (405)841-5500 [12436]

Scrivner Inc. Buffalo Div., 1 Scrivner St., Cheektowaga, NY 14227-2721, (716)668-7200 [12437]

Scrivner of New York, 1 Scrivner Dr., Cheektowaga, NY 14227, (716)668-7200 [12438]

Scrivner of North Carolina Inc., PO Box 565, Warsaw, NC 28398, (919)293-7821 [12439]

Scrivner of Pennsylvania Inc., 1100 N Sherman St., York, PA 17402-2131, (717)755-1976 [12440]

Scruggs & Associates Inc., 542 Central Ave., Laurel, MS 39440-3955, (601)649-0383 [6713]

Scruggs Equipment Company Inc., 1940 Channel Ave., PO Box 13284, Memphis, TN 38113, (901)942-9312 [3201]

SCS Cases Inc., 7420 Unity Ave. N, Ste. 210, Brooklyn Park, MN 55443, (612)391-7600 [25936]

Sculli Brothers Inc., 1114-18 S Front St., Philadelphia, PA 19147, (215)336-1223 [12441]

Scullin Oil Co., PO Box 350, Sunbury, PA 17801, (717)286-4519 [22659]

SDA Security Systems, Inc., 2054 State St., San Diego, CA 92101, (619)239-3473 [24626]

SDI Technologies Inc., PO Box 2001, Rahway, NJ 07065-0901, (732)574-9000 [9347]

SDRS, 303 Higuera, San Luis Obispo, CA 93401-1002, (805)543-3636 [25462]

Sea Coast Distributors, Inc., 105 Wartburg Ave., Copiague, NY 11726, (516)842-2338 [18602]

Sea Containers America Inc., 1155 Ave. of the Amer., New York, NY 10036, (212)302-5055 [18603]

Sea Harvest Packing Co., PO Box 818, Brunswick, GA 31521, (912)264-3212 [12442]

Sea K. Fish Company Inc., PO Box 2040, Blaine, WA 98230, (360)332-5121 [12443]

Sea Level Products International, 2815 Junipero Ave., Ste. 110, Signal Hill, CA 90806-2111, (562)985-0076 [17593]

Sea-Pac Inc., PO Box 2707, Gardena, CA 90247, (310)324-3835 [16476]

Sea-Pac Sales Co., PO Box 3846, Seattle, WA 98124-3846, (206)223-5353 [10140]

Sea Recovery, PO Box 2560, Gardena, CA 90247, (310)327-4000 [23365]

Sea View Fillet Company Inc., 16 Hassey St., New Bedford, MA 02740, (508)994-1233 [12444]

SEA Wire & Cable Inc., 451 Lanier Rd., Madison, AL 35758, (205)772-9616 [9348]

Seaboard Automotive Inc., 721 Blackhorse Pike, Blackwood, NJ 08012, (609)227-2252 [3202]

Seaboard Corp., 200 Boylston St., Chestnut Hill, MA 02467, (617)332-8492 [12445]

Seaboard Industrial Supply, 151 N 3rd St., Philadelphia, PA 19106-1914, (215)627-5652 [16477]

Seaboard Manufacturing Co., 2010 Atlantic Hwy., Warren, ME 04864, (207)273-2718 [18604]

Seaboard Marine, 2947 W 5th St., Oxnard, CA 93030 [18605]

Seaboard Seed Co., PO Box 117, Bristol, IL 60512, (630)553-5800 [1247]

Seabrook Wallcoverings Inc., 1325 Farmville Rd., Memphis, TN 38122, (901)320-3500 [15650]

Seacoast Gallery, PO Box 1077, Wells, ME 04090-1077, (207)646-2359 [25811]

Seafood Express, 248 Chunns Cove Rd., Asheville, NC 28805, (704)252-1779 [12446]

Seafood Marketing, 814 E Harrison, PO Box 1086, Harlingen, TX 78551, (956)440-8840 [12447]

Seafood Producers Cooperative, 2875 Roeder Ave., Bellingham, WA 98225, (206)733-0120 [12448]

Seafood Wholesalers Inc., 4746 Dodge, San Antonio, TX 78217, (210)655-4746 [12449]

Seaford and Sons Lumber; C.A., 127 Buck Seaford Rd., Mocksville, NC 27028, (336)751-5148 [7996]

Seaforth Mineral and Ore Company Inc., 3690 Orange Pl., No. 495, Cleveland, OH 44122-4483, (216)292-5820 [4504]

Seago Distributing Co., 800 Airport Rd., Rockingham, NC 28379-4708, (919)997-5676 [2015]

Seago Export, PO Box 1894, Summerville, SC 29484, (843)875-2808 [7997]

Seagram Classics Wine Co., 2600 Campus Dr., Ste. 160, San Mateo, CA 94403, (650)378-3800 [2016]

Seagull Software Systems Inc., 2520 Northwinds Pkwy., Ste. 250, Alpharetta, GA 30004, (770)521-1445 [6714]

Sealand Power Industries, Inc., 568 E Elizabeth Ave., PO Box 1400, Linden, NJ 07036-0004, (908)486-7600 [18606]

Sealaska Corp., 1 Sealaska Plz., Ste. 400, Juneau, AK 99801-1276, (907)586-1512 [27372]

Sealaska Timber Corp., 2030 Sea Level Dr., Ste. 202, Ketchikan, AK 99901, (907)225-9444 [27373]

Sealed Air Corp., Park 80 E, Saddle Brook, NJ 07663, (201)791-7600 [21929]

Sealey Optical Co., 3611 Maryland Ct., C-3370, Richmond, VA 23233, (804)747-8700 [19601]

Sealts Co.; J.M., PO Box 300, Lima, OH 45802, (419)224-8075 [12450]

Sealy Mattress Georgia, 1705 Rockdale Industrial Blvd., Conyers, GA 30012-3937, (404)483-3810 [13235]

Seaman Grain Inc., PO Box 93, Bowersville, OH 45307, (513)453-2343 [1248]

Seaman Mill Supplies Co., 1317 Chester St., Reading, PA 19601, (215)376-5711 [17162]

Seaman Paper Co.; Patrick, 2000 Howard St., Detroit, MI 48216, (313)496-3131 [21930]

Seaman-Patrick Paper Co., 2000 Howard St., Detroit, MI 48216, (313)496-3131 [21931]

Seamans Supply Company Inc., PO Box 4540, Manchester, NH 03108-4540, (603)669-2700 [9349]

Seashore Food Distributors, 1 Satt Bl Railroad Ave., Rio Grande, NJ 08242-1652, (609)886-3100 [12451]

Seashore Supply Company Inc., PO Box 1286, Ocean City, NJ 08226-7286 [23366]

Seasia, 4601 6th Ave. S, Seattle, WA 98108-1716, (206)624-6380 [12452]

Seaside Supply Stores, 803 S Palos Verdes, San Pedro, CA 90731-3719, (310)831-0251 [18607]

Seatile Distributors, 4311 N Monroe St., Tallahassee, FL 32303, (850)562-2888 [10141]

Seatronics Inc., PO Box 1138, Auburn, WA 98071, (253)939-6060 [24627]

Seattle Box Co., 23400 71st Pl. S, Kent, WA 98032-2994, (206)854-9700 [25937]

Seattle Fish Co., 6211 E 42nd Ave., Denver, CO 80216, (303)329-9595 [12453]

Seattle Iron and Metals Corp., 601 S Myrtle St., Seattle, WA 98108-3424 [26985]

Seattle Kitchen Design Inc., 10002 Holman Rd. NW, Seattle, WA 98177-4921, (206)782-4900 [13236]

Seattle Kitchen Design Inc., 10002 Holman Rd. NW, Seattle, WA 98177-4921, (206)782-4900 [27374]

Seattle Marine Industrial Division, 2121 W Commodore, Seattle, WA 98199-0098, (206)285-5010 [18608]

Seattle Orthotics Group, 26296 Twelve Trees Ln NW, Poulsbo, WA 98370, (360)697-5656 [6715]

Seattle Ship Supply, PO Box 70438, Seattle, WA 98107-0438, (206)283-7000 [18609]

Seaway Distributors, Rte. 12, Box 128, Alexandra Bay, NY 13607, (315)482-9903 [12454]

Seaway Foods Co., 2223 Velp Ave., Green Bay, WI 54303-6529, (920)434-1636 [12455]

Seaway Importing Co., 8800 F St., Omaha, NE 68127-1507, (402)339-2400 [25435]

Seawind International, 5375 Avenida Encinas, Ste. A, Carlsbad, CA 92008, (760)438-5600 [12456]

Sebastian Equipment Company Inc., 1801 Joplin St., Joplin, MO 64802, (417)623-3300 [16478]

Sebastian Inc.; Paul, PO Box 1544, Jackson, NJ 08527-0358 [14232]

SEC International, PO Box 32, Cambridge, MA 02139-0001, (617)354-9600 [6716]

SECOM, 3402 Oakcliff Rd., Ste. B-4, Atlanta, GA 30340, (404)455-0672 [9384]

Second Chance Golf Ball Recyclers Inc., 1943 SE Airport Rd., Stuart, FL 34996-4016, (561)223-3730 [23934]

Second City Systems Inc., 28427 N Ballard Dr. No. D, Lake Forest, IL 60045, (847)362-2700 [21263]

Secor Elevator Company Inc., PO Box 79, Secor, IL 61771, (309)744-2218 [12457]

Secor Elevator Copmany Inc., RR 1, Box 860, Eureka, IL 61530, (309)744-2218 [17956]

Securaplane Technologies L.L.C., 10800 N Mavinee Dr., Tucson, AZ 85737, (520)297-0844 [24628]

Security Consultants, 6726 Arlington, Jacksonville, FL 32211, (904)724-2740 [24629]

Security Data Group, 6726 Arlington, Jacksonville, FL 32211, (904)724-2740 [24629]

Security Engineers, 8403 Benjamin Rd., Ste. C, Tampa, FL 33634-1204, (813)854-2078 [24630]

Security Engineers Systems Inc., 8403 Benjamin Rd., Ste. C, Tampa, FL 33634-1204, (813)854-2078 [24630]

Security Forces Inc., PO Box 36607, Charlotte, NC 28236-6607, (704)334-4751 [9350]

Security Silver and Gold Exchange, PO Box 1774, Boise, ID 83701-1774, (208)343-5050 [17594]

Security Supply Corp., Maple Ave., Selkirk, NY 12158, (518)767-2226 [23367]

SecurityLink Corp., 125 Frontage Rd., Orange, CT 06477, (203)795-9000 [24631]

SED International, Inc., 4916 N Royal Atlanta Rd., Tucker, GA 30085, (770)491-8962 [6717]

Sedalia Implement Company Inc., 2205 S Limit, Sedalia, MO 65301, (660)826-0466 [1249]

Sedmak; Louie, PO Box 51007, Casper, WY 82605-1007, (307)472-1904 [7998]

See First Technology Inc., 18809 Cox Ave., Ste. 100, Saratoga, CA 95070, (408)866-8928 [6718]

Seed Corp. of America, 4764 Hollins Ferry Rd., Arbutus, MD 21227, (410)247-3000 [1250]

Seed Research of Oregon, 27630 Llewellyn Road, Corvallis, OR 97333, (541)757-2663 [1251]

Seed Resource Inc., 1401 W 6th St., Tulia, TX 79088, (806)995-3882 [18228]

Seedex Distributors, Inc., 9110 Waterville-Swanton, Waterville, OH 43566, (419)878-8561 [1252]

Seeds, Inc., PO Box 866, Tekoa, WA 99033, (509)284-2848 [1253]

Seedway, 1734 Railroad Pl., Hall, NY 14463, (716)526-6391 [1254]

Seedway, Inc., 1734 Railroad Pl., Hall, NY 14463, (716)526-5651 [1255]

Seegott Inc., 1675 D Holmes Rd., Elgin, IL 60123, (847)468-6300 [4505]

Seeler Industries Inc., 1 Genstar Ln., Joliet, IL 60435-2668, (815)740-2645 [4506]

Seelye Plastics Inc., 9700 Newton Ave., Bloomington, MN 55431, (612)881-2658 [17163]

Sees & Faber-Berlin Inc., 1611 Grove Ave., Jenkintown, PA 19046-2303, (215)887-4899 [16479]

Sega of America Inc., 650 Townsend St., Ste. 575, San Francisco, CA 94103-5646 [26649]

Segal, Alpert, McPherson & Associates, 28831 Telegraph Rd., Southfield, MI 48034-1949, (248)258-6100 [25436]

Segel and Son Inc., PO Box 276, Warren, PA 16365, (814)723-4900 [26986]

Seghers Better Technology, 3114 Emery Cir., Austell, GA 30168, (770)739-4205 [16480]

Seghers Dinamec Inc., 3114 Emery Cir., Austell, GA 30168, (770)739-4205 [16480]

Segue Ltd., 119 W 40th St., Fl 22, New York, NY 10018-2500, (212)869-8526 [5341]

Segura Products Corp., 406 Fulton St., Middlesex, NJ 08846-1527, (732)968-2295 [19602]

Sehman Tire Service Inc., PO Box 889, Franklin, PA 16323, (814)437-7878 [3203]

Seibel & Stern Corp., 12 W 34th, New York, NY 10120-0093, (212)563-0326 [5342]

Seibert Equity Cooperative Association, PO Box 196, Seibert, CO 80834, (970)664-2211 [1256]

Seifert Farm Supply, PO Box 54, Three Oaks, MI 49128, (616)756-9592 [1257]

Seika Machinery, Inc., 3528 Torrance Blvd., Ste. 100, Torrance, CA 90503, (310)540-7310 [16481]

Seiko Corporation of America, 1111 MacArthur Blvd., Mahwah, NJ 07430, (201)529-5730 [17595]

Seiko Time West, 840 Apollo St., Ste. 100, El Segundo, CA 90245, (310)640-3308 [17596]

Seikosha America Inc., 111 Canfield Ave., No. Bld-A-14, Randolph, NJ 07869-1114, (201)327-7227 [6719]

Sejin America Inc., 2004 Martin Ave., Santa Clara, CA 95050, (408)980-7550 [6720]

Sekisui TA Industries Inc., 7089 Belgrave Ave., Garden Grove, CA 92841, (714)898-0344 [17164]

Sel-Leb Marketing, Inc., 495 River St., Paterson, NJ 07524, (973)225-9880 [14233]

Sel-Tronics, Inc., 9475 Lottsford Rd., Landover, MD 20785, (301)341-2700 [9351]

Selby Furniture Hardware Company Inc., 321 Rider Ave., Bronx, NY 10451, (718)993-3700 [13908]

Select Copy Systems of Southern California Inc., 6229 Santos Diaz St., Irwindale, CA 91706, (626)334-0383 [21264]

Select Foods Inc., PO Box 3097, Hayward, CA 94540, (510)785-1000 [12458]

Select-O-Hits Inc., 1981 Fletcher Creek Dr, Memphis, TN 38133, (901)388-1190 [25437]

Select Robinson Paper Co., 160 Fox St., Portland, ME 04101, (207)773-2973 [21932]

Select Sales, 7750 W 78th St., Bloomington, MN 55439, (612)941-9388 [6721]

Select Sales Inc., 7750 W 78th St., Bloomington, MN 55439, (612)941-9388 [6722]

Select Security Inc., 800 Seahawk Cir., Ste. 134, Virginia Beach, VA 23452-7814, (757)468-3700 [24632]

Select Wines & Spirits Co., 2200 S 13th St., Milwaukee, WI 53215-2774, (414)643-5444 [2017]

Selective Books Inc., PO Box 984, Oldsmar, FL 34677-0984, (813)891-6451 [4148]

Selectware Technologies, Inc., PO Box G, Bridgeport, MI 48722-0617, (248)477-7340 [6723]

Selene Export Company, 406 Fulton St., Middlesex, NJ 08846-1527, (732)968-2295 [19602]

Self Service Grocery, PO Box 277, Collinsville, VA 24078, (540)647-3452 [12459]

Self; William, Statesboro Mall, Hwy. 80 E, Statesboro, GA 30458, (912)764-2226 [5343]

Self's, Inc., 721 E Mount Vernon, Wichita, KS 67211, (316)267-1295 [10142]

Self's, Inc., 2720 S Austin, Springfield, MO 65807, (417)886-3332 [10143]

Sellers Oil Co., PO Box 1907, Bainbridge, GA 31717, (912)246-0646 [22660]

Sellers Process Equipment Co., 394 E Church Rd., Ste. A, King of Prussia, PA 19406-2694, (610)279-2448 [16482]

Sellers Tile Distributors, 109 Booker Ave., Albany, GA 31701-2541, (912)435-7474 [10144]

Sellers Tractor Company Inc., PO Box 1940, Salina, KS 67402-1940, (913)823-6378 [1258]

Selma Oil Mill Inc., PO Box 632, Selma, AL 36702-0632, (334)875-3310 [1259]

Selsi Company Inc., PO Box 10, Midland Park, NJ 07432-0010, (201)612-9200 [24430]

Sema Inc., 360 Industrial Ln., Birmingham, AL 35211, (205)945-8612 [19035]

Semcor Equipment & Manufacturing Corp., 18 Madison, Keyport, NJ 07735-1117, (732)264-6080 [13909]

Semi-Gas Systems Inc., 625 Wool Creek Dr., San Jose, CA 95112, (408)971-6500 [4507]

Semi Systems Inc., 7949 E Tacoma Dr., Ste. 101, Scottsdale, AZ 85260, (602)922-0040 [24431]

Semispecialists of America Inc., 226 Sherwood Ave., Farmingdale, NY 11735, (516)293-2710 [9352]

Semispecialists of America Inc., 226 Sherwood Ave., Farmingdale, NY 11735, (516)293-2710 [9353]

Semix Inc., 4160 Technology Dr., Fremont, CA 94538, (510)659-8800 [3204]

Semler Inc.; Arnold A., 11347 Vanowen St., North Hollywood, CA 91605, (818)760-1000 [5752]

Semler Industries Inc., 3800 N Carnation St., Franklin Park, IL 60131, (847)671-5650 [25812]

Semmelmeyer-Corby Co., 5432 Highland Park Dr., St. Louis, MO 63110, (314)371-4777 [17165]

Senco of Florida Inc., 1602 N Goldenrod Rd., Orlando, FL 32807-8345, (407)277-0412 [13910]

SenDel Wheel, 300 W Artesia Blvd., Compton, CA 90220-5530, (310)604-8760 [3014]

Seneca Beverage Corp., PO Box 148, Elmira, NY 14902, (607)734-6111 [2018]

Seneca News Agency Inc., 800 Pre-Emption Rd., Geneva, NY 14456-0631, (315)789-3551 [4149]

Seneca Paper, 5786 Collett Rd., Farmington, NY 14425-9536, (716)424-1600 [21933]

Seneca Plumbing and Heating Supply Company Inc., 192-196 Seneca St., Buffalo, NY 14204, (716)852-4744 [23368]

Seneca Supply and Equipment Co., Rte. 13 & Dryden Rd., Ithaca, NY 14850, (607)347-4455 [7999]

Senesac Inc., PO Box 592, Fowler, IN 47944, (765)884-1300 [1260]

Senex Harvest States, PO Box 387, Mcville, ND 58254, (701)322-4317 [12460]

Senior Engineering Company Inc. Industrial Products, 4810 N 124th St., Milwaukee, WI 53225-3601, (414)353-3112 [14340]

Senior Flexonics Inc. Dearborn Industrial Products Div., PO Box 307, Westmont, IL 60559, (815)886-1140 [17166]

Sennett Steel Corp., 1200 E 14 Mile Rd., Madison Heights, MI 48071, (734)585-6040 [20359]

Senor's Q Inc., 11719 E Ashlan Ave., Sanger, CA 93657-9326, (209)275-0780 [5344]

Senrenella Enterprises Inc., 7911 Amherst Ave., St. Louis, MO 63130, (314)863-9249 [18229]

Sentai Distributors International, 8839 Shirley Ave., Northridge, CA 91324, (818)886-3113 [26650]

Sentex Corp., 1920 Lafayette St., Ste. F, Santa Clara, CA 95050, (408)364-0112 [9354]

Sentinel Alarm Service, 6726 Arlington, Jacksonville, FL 32211, (904)724-2740 [24629]

Sentrol Inc., 12345 SW Leveton Dr., Tualatin, OR 97062, (503)691-4052 [9355]

Sentry Alarm, Inc., 707 Hickory Farm Ln., Appleton, WI 54914-3032, (920)739-9559 [24633]

Sentry Group, 900 Linden Ave., Rochester, NY 14625, (716)381-4900 [24634]

Sentry/Liberty Hardware Distributors Inc., 2700 River Rd., Des Plaines, IL 60018, (847)699-2323 [13911]

Sentry Technology Corp., 350 Wireless Blvd., Hauppauge, NY 11788, (516)232-2100 [24635]

Sentry Watch Inc., 1705 Holbrook, Greensboro, NC 27404, (919)273-8103 [24636]

Seow Company Inc.; Anthony, PO Box 1284, Orem, UT 84057, (801)225-6612 [19603]

Sepco Bearing and P.T. Group, 6618 E Hwy. 332, Freeport, TX 77541, (409)233-4491 [17167]

Sepco-Industries Inc., PO Box 1697, Houston, TX 77251, (713)937-0330 [16483]

Sepher-Hermon Press, 1153 45th St., Brooklyn, NY 11219, (718)972-9010 [4150]

Sepia Interior Supply, PO Box 82519, Kenmore, WA 98028, (425)486-3353 [8000]

September Enterprises Inc., PO Box 980804, Houston, TX 77098, (713)520-0359 [22661]

Sequence (USA) Co. Ltd., 151 E Rosemary St., Ste. 240, Chapel Hill, NC 27514, (919)918-7990 [21561]

Sequoia Floral International, 3245 Santa Rosa Ave., Santa Rosa, CA 95407, (707)525-0780 [14948]

Sequoia Paint, 700 Baker St., Bakersfield, CA 93305, (805)323-7948 [21562]

Sequoia Wholesale Florist Inc., 3245 Santa Rosa Ave., Santa Rosa, CA 95407, (707)525-0780 [14948]

Serconia Press, 30 St. Marks Pl., Brooklyn, NY 11217, (718)875-7731 [4151]

Serendipity Communications, Inc., 4703 Rose St., Houston, TX 77007, (713)863-9900 [25438]

Serendipity Couriers, Inc., 470 Du Bois St., San Rafael, CA 94901-3911, (415)459-4000 [4152]

Serendipity Couriers Inc., 470 Du Bois St., San Rafael, CA 94901-3911, (415)459-4000 [4153]

Seret & Sons Inc., 149 E Alameda St., Santa Fe, NM 87501-2117, (505)988-9151 [13237]

Sergeant's Pet Products Inc., 1 Central Park Plz., No. 700, Omaha, NE 68102-1693, (402)595-7000 [27230]

Sermel Inc., PO Box 359, Indianola, IA 50125-0359, (515)961-4222 [19604]

Serson Supply Inc., 3701 W 49th St., Chicago, IL 60632, (773)847-6210 [17168]

SerVaas Inc., 1000 Waterway Blvd., Indianapolis, IN 46202, (317)636-1000 [24294]

Servall Co., 2501 S Cedar St., Lansing, MI 48910-3137, (517)487-9550 [15307]

Servall Co., 6761 10 Mile Rd., Center Line, MI 48015, (810)754-1818 [15308]

Servall Co., 1834 E 55th St., Cleveland, OH 44103, (216)431-4400 [15309]

Servall Products Inc., 199-205 Westwood Ave., Long Branch, NJ 07740, (732)222-0083 [21934]

Servant Publications, PO Box 8617, Ann Arbor, MI 48107, (734)761-8505 [4154]

Servco Pacific Inc., PO Box 2788, Honolulu, HI 96803, (808)521-6511 [3205]

Server Technology Inc., 521 E Weddell Dr., Ste. 120, Sunnyvale, CA 94089, (408)745-0300 [9356]

Service Brokerage Inc., PO Box 18316, Shreveport, LA 71138, (318)688-1400 [12461]

Service Central, Inc., 1629 Palolo Ave., Honolulu, HI 96816, (808)735-9575 [21563]

Service Distributing, 8397 Paris St., Lorton, VA 22079, (703)339-6886 [2019]

Service Drug of Brainerd Inc., 218 W Washington St., Brainerd, MN 56401-2922, (218)829-3664 [19036]

Service Electric Supply Inc., 15424 Oakwood Dr., Romulus, MI 48174, (734)229-9100 [9357]

Service Engineering Co., 8621 Barefoot Industrial Rd., Raleigh, NC 27613, (919)783-6116 [19037]

Service Keystone Supply, 47 W Park Rd., Roselle, IL 60172, (630)351-3838 [8001]

Service Motor Parts, 2741 Turnpike Industrial Dr., Middletown, PA 17057, (717)939-1344 [3206]

Service Office Supply Corp., PO Box 2, Getzville, NY 14068, (716)691-3511 [21265]

Service Oil Company Inc., PO Box 446, Colby, KS 67701, (785)462-3441 [22662]

Service Oil Inc., 1718 E Main, West Fargo, ND 58078, (701)277-1050 [22663]

Service Packaging Corp., 3701 Highland Park NW, North Canton, OH 44720-4535, (330)499-0872 [21935]

Service Plus Distributors Inc., 1900 Frost Rd. Ste. 101, Bristol, PA 19007, (215)785-4466 [13912]

Service Steel Aerospace Corp., PO Box 2333, Tacoma, WA 98401, (253)627-2910 [20360]

Service Supply, 2400 N Walnut Rd., PO Drawer 2090, Turlock, CA 95380, (209)667-1072 [12462]

Service Supply Systems Inc., PO Box 749, Cordele, GA 31015, (912)273-1112 [23369]

Service Tire Co., 2737 W Vernor Hwy., Detroit, MI 48216, (313)237-0050 [3207]

Service Unlimited, PO Box 304, Mendon, MI 49072, (616)463-2958 [3208]

Services Group of America Inc., 4025 Delridge Way SW, Ste. 500, Seattle, WA 98106, (206)933-5000 [12463]

Servidio Beverage Distributing Co., 5160 Fulton Dr., Suisun City, CA 94585-1639, (707)864-1741 [2020]

Servidyne System, PO Box 93846, Atlanta, GA 30377-0846 [14677]

SERVISTAR Corp., PO Box 1510, Butler, PA 16003-1510, (412)283-4567 [8002]

Servsteel Inc., 214 Westbridge Dr., Morgan, PA 15064, (412)221-8600 [17169]

S.E.S. Inc., 1400 Powis Rd., West Chicago, IL 60185, (630)231-4840 [8003]

Sessions Company Inc., PO Box 311310, Enterprise, AL 36331, (334)393-0200 [12464]

Sessions Specialty Co., 5090 Styers Ferry Rd., Lewisville, NC 27023-9634, (919)722-7163 [4508]

Sessler Inc., 111 Hwy. 99 N, Eugene, OR 97402, (503)686-0515 [26987]

Setco Solid Tire and Rim, 2300 SE Washington St., Idabel, OK 74745, (580)286-6531 [3209]

Setko Fasteners Inc., 26 Main St., Bartlett, IL 60103, (708)837-2831 [13913]

Seton Name Plate Co., PO Box 3092, Branford, CT 06405, (203)315-1181 [25600]

Setton's International Foods Inc., 85 Austin Blvd., Commack, NY 11725, (516)543-8090 [12465]

Seven D Wholesale, PO Box 67, Gallitzin, PA 16641-0067, (814)886-8151 [8004]

Seven Hills Book Distributors Inc., 1531 Tremont St., Cincinnati, OH 45214, (513)471-4300 [4155]

Seven Paint and Wallpaper Co.; John, 3070 29th St. SE, Grand Rapids, MI 49512, (616)942-2020 [21564]

Seven Star Productions, PO Box 17126, Long Beach, CA 90807, (562)633-1777 [25439]

Seven-Up Baltimore Inc., PO Box 244, Gladwyne, PA 19035, (610)834-6551 [25034]

Seven-Up Dayton Div., 3131 Transportation Rd., Dayton, OH 45404, (937)236-0333 [25035]

Seven-Up Royal Crown, 5151 Fischer Ave., Cincinnati, OH 45217, (513)242-5151 [25036]

Seven-Up Salem, 2561 Pringle Rd. SE, Salem, OR 97302-1531, (503)585-2822 [25037]

Seventh Generation, Inc., 1 Mill St., Box A26, Burlington, VT 05401-1530, (802)658-3773 [21936]

Seventh Generation Wholesale, Inc., 1 Mill St., Box A26, Burlington, VT 05401-1530, (802)658-3773 [21936]

Severn Peanut Company Inc., PO Box 710, Severn, NC 27877, (919)585-0838 [12466]

Seville Watch Corp., 587 5th Ave., New York, NY 10018, (212)355-3450 [17597]

Sewell Hardware Company Inc., 528 Clematis St., West Palm Beach, FL 33401, (561)832-7171 [13914]

Sewing Center Supply Co., 9631 NE Colfax St., Portland, OR 97220-1232, (503)252-1452 [15310]

Sewing Machines Distributors, 1292 Foster Rd., Las Cruces, NM 88001, (505)522-8717 [16484]

Sewon America Inc., 2 University Plz., Ste. 202, Hackensack, NJ 07601, (201)343-1166 [4509]

Sexauer Company Inc., PO Box 58, Brookings, SD 57006-0058, (605)692-6171 [18230]

Sexauer Inc.; J.A., 531 Central Park Ave., Scarsdale, NY 10583, (914)472-7500 [23370]

Seybold Co., 107 Northeast Dr., Loveland, OH 45140-7145, (513)683-8553 [4706]

Seymour Livestock Trucking, 2809 S Montana St., Butte, MT 59701-3122, (406)723-5255 [18231]

Seymour of Sycamore Inc., 917 Crosby Ave., Sycamore, IL 60178, (815)895-9101 [21565]

SF Services Inc., 824 N Palm St., North Little Rock, AR 72114-5134, (501)945-2371 [27231]

SFI-Gray Steel Services Inc., 3510 Maury St., Houston, TX 77009, (713)225-0899 [20361]

SFK Steel Inc., 3130 N Palafox St., Pensacola, FL 32522, (850)434-0851 [20362]

S.G. & B. Inc., 8075 Reading Rd., Ste. 408, Cincinnati, OH 45237-1417, (513)761-2600 [13238]

SG Supply Co., 12900 S Throop St., Calumet Park, IL 60643, (708)371-8800 [23371]

SG Wholesale Roofing Supply Inc., PO Box 1464, Santa Ana, CA 92702, (714)568-1900 [8005]

SGA Sales and Marketing Inc., 155 White Plains Rd. Tarrytown, NY 10591, (914)694-4090 [12467]

Shachihata Incorporated USA, 3305 Kashiwa St., Torrance, CA 90505, (310)530-4445 [21266]

Shafmaster Company Inc., PO Box 1070, Exeter, NH 03833, (603)778-8484 [18426]

Shaheen Brothers Inc., PO Box 897, Amesbury, MA 01913, (978)688-1844 [12468]

Shaheen Carpet Mills, PO Box 167, Resaca, GA 30735-0167, (706)629-9544 [10145]

Shaheen Carpet Mills, PO Box 167, Resaca, GA 30735-0167, (706)629-9544 [15651]

Shaheen Paint and Decorating Company, Inc., 1400 St. Paul St., Rochester, NY 14621, (716)266-1500 [21566]

Shaklee Corp., 444 Market St., San Francisco, CA 94111, (415)954-3000 [14234]

Shaklee Distributor, 3440 Lynngate Cir., Birmingham, AL 35216, (205)823-2340 [12469]

Shaklee Distributor, 15123 Woodland Dr., Monroe, MI 48161, (734)242-0712 [12470]

Shakour Inc.; R.G., 254 Turnpike Rd., Westborough, MA 01581, (508)366-8282 [14235]

Shamash and Sons; S., 42 W 39th St., 12th Fl., New York, NY 10018, (212)840-3111 [26201]

Shamrock Auto Parts Inc., 2560 E 4th St., Reno, NV 89512-0867, (775)329-1606 [3210]

Shamrock Custom Truck Caps, Inc., 1820 N Black Horse Pke., Williamstown, NJ 08094, (609)629-1411 [3211]

Shamrock Farms Creamery, 2434 E Pecan Rd Fl 2, Phoenix, AZ 85040, (602)243-3244 [12471]

Shamrock Foods Co., 2228 N Black Canyon Hwy., Phoenix, AZ 85009, (602)272-6721 [12472]

Shane's Shoe, 1200 S Charles St., Baltimore, MD 21230, (410)539-4709 [24854]

Shank Spring Design Inc., 540 South St., Piqua, OH 45356, (937)773-0116 [13915]

Shankle Co. Inc.; Earle, 5200 46th Ave., Hyattsville, MD 20781, (301)699-8500 [3212]

Shankles Hosiery Inc., 804 Gault Ave. N, Ft. Payne, AL 35967-2725, (205)845-6161 [5345]

Shanks Co.; L.P., PO Box 1068, Crossville, TN 38557-1068, (931)484-5155 [12473]

Shannon Brothers Tile, 1309 Putnam Dr., Huntsville, AL 35816, (205)837-6520 [10146]

Shapco Inc., 640 Wheeling Rd., Wheeling, IL 60090-5707, (847)229-1435 [15652]

Shared Service Systems Inc., 1725 S 20th St., Omaha, NE 68108, (402)536-5300 [19605]

Shared Technologies Cellular Inc., 1 International Pl., Boston, MA 02110, (617)536-9152 [5753]

Shari Candies Inc., 1804 N 2nd St., Mankato, MN 56001, (507)387-1181 [12474]

Sharion's Silk Flower Outlet, 905 Lovers Lane Rd. SE, Calhoun, GA 30701-4633, (706)625-5519 [14949]

Sharon Piping and Equipment Inc., 2188 Spicer Cove, Memphis, TN 38134, (901)385-7015 [20363]

Sharp Brothers Seed Co., PO Box 140, Healy, KS 67850, (316)398-2231 [1261]

Sharp Communication, 3403 Governors Dr. SW, Huntsville, AL 35805-3635, (205)533-2484 [5754]

Sharp Co.; William G., 414 NE 11th, PO Box 10106, Amarillo, TX 79116-1106, (806)376-4440 [10147]

Sharp Oil Company Inc., PO Box 2645, Anthony, NM 88021, (505)882-2512 [22664]

Sharp Products International, Inc., PO Box 4339, Wallingford, CT 06492-4050, (203)284-2627 [17170]

Sharp and Son Inc., 10242 59th Ave. S, Seattle, WA 98178, (425)391-5646 [1382]

Sharp Wholesale Corp., 73-09 88th St., Glendale, NY 11385, (718)459-0756 [15311]

Sharpe; Cliff, PO Box 1282, Londonderry, NH 03053-1282, (603)432-7394 [13239]

Sharpe Inc.; M.E., 80 Business Park Dr., Armonk, NY 10504, (914)273-1800 [4156]

Sharut Furniture Co., 220 Passaic St., Passaic, NJ 07055, (973)473-1000 [13240]

Shaub Ellison Co., 1121 Court C, Tacoma, WA 98402, (253)272-4119 [3213]

Shaw Auto Parts Inc., PO Box 4729, Pocatello, ID 83205-4729, (208)232-5952 [3214]

Shaw Lumber Co., 217 Como Ave., St. Paul, MN 55103, (612)488-2525 [8006]

Shaw Publishers; Harold, 2375 TelStar Dr., Ste. 160, Colorado Springs, CO 80920, (719)590-4999 [4157]

Shaw-Ross International Inc., 1600 NW 163rd St., Miami, FL 33169, (305)625-6561 [2021]

Shawano Equity Cooperative Inc., 660 E Seward St., Shawano, WI 54166, (715)526-3197 [1262]

Shawnee Garment Manufacturing Co., 1 American Way, Shawnee, OK 74801, (405)273-0510 [5346]

Shawneetown Feed and Seed, 12778 U.S. Hwy. 61, Jackson, MO 63755, (573)833-6262 [1263]

Shaws-Healthtick, 1542 NE Weidler St., Portland, OR 97232-1411, (503)288-4226 [19606]

Shealy Electrical Wholesalers Incorporated Co., PO Box 48, Greenville, SC 29602, (803)242-6880 [9358]

Shear Associates Inc.; Ted, 1 West Ave., Larchmont, NY 10538, (914)833-0017 [12475]

Shearer Industrial Supply Co., PO Box 1272, York, PA 17405, (717)767-7575 [16485]

Shears Construction L.P., 1600 N Lorraine St., Hutchinson, KS 67501, (316)662-3307 [8007]

Sheats Supply Services, Inc., 6121 E 30th St., Indianapolis, IN 46219-1002, (317)542-1070 [16486]

Sheehy Inc.; Charles D., PO Box 105, Avon, MA 02322, (508)583-7612 [23372]

Sheffield Furniture Corp., 2100 E 38th St., Los Angeles, CA 90058, (323)232-4161 [13241]

Shehan-Cary Lumber Co., PO Box 19770, St. Louis, MO 63144, (314)968-8600 [8008]

Shehan-Cary Lumber Co., PO Box 19770, St. Louis, MO 63144, (314)968-8600 [27375]

Shelby Electric Company Inc., 112 EH. Crump Blvd. E, Memphis, TN 38101, (901)948-1545 [9359]

Shelby Grain and Feed Co., PO Box 49, Shelby, OH 44875, (419)342-6141 [1264]

Shelby Industries Inc., PO Box 308, Shelbyville, KY 40066, (502)633-2040 [3215]

Shelby Industries Inc., PO Box 88, La Follette, TN 37766, (423)562-3361 [22665]

Shelby-Skipwith Inc., PO Box 777, Memphis, TN 38101, (901)948-4481 [14678]

Shelby Supply Company Inc., PO Box 9050, Shelby, NC 28151-9050, (704)482-6781 [9360]

Sheldon and Company Inc.; H.D., 19 Union Sq. W, New York, NY 10003, (212)924-6920 [24217]

Sheldons', Inc., 626 Center St., Antigo, WI 54409-2496, (715)623-2382 [23935]

Shell Lake Cooperative, 331 Hwy. 63, Shell Lake, WI 54871, (715)468-2302 [22666]

Shelley Company Inc.; John G., 16 Mica Ln., Wellesley Hills, MA 02481, (781)237-0900 [14]

Shelley Tractor and Equipment Co., 8015 NW 103rd St., Hialeah, FL 33016-2201, (305)821-4040 [8009]

Shell's Bags Hats, PO Box 1701, Lahaina, HI 96761, (808)669-8349 [13445]

Shelly Electric Inc., PO Box 5104, Potsdam, NY 13676, (315)265-3400 [9361]

Shelmar Food, PO Box 277, Montrose, CA 91021-0277, (213)585-0972 [12476]

Shelter Super Store Corp., 4100 Dixon St., Des Moines, IA 50313-3944, (515)266-2419 [27376]

Shelton Clothing Inc., 2524 County Rd. 87, Moulton, AL 35650-5544, (205)974-9079 [5347]

Shelton Winair Co., 740 River Rd., Shelton, CT 06484, (203)929-6319 [14679]

Shelving Inc., PO Box 215050, Auburn Hills, MI 48321-5050, (248)852-8600 [25938]

Shelving Inc., PO Box 215050, Auburn Hills, MI 48321-5050, (248)852-8600 [9361]

Shenandoah Foods, Inc., 4048 Valley Pike, Winchester, VA 22604, (540)869-6300 [12477]

Shen's Books and Supplies, 821 S 1st Ave., Arcadia, CA 91006-3918, (626)445-6958 [4158]

Shepher Distributors and Sales Corp., 2300 Linden Blvd., Brooklyn, NY 11208, (718)649-2525 [26651]

Shepherd Electric Company Inc., 7401 Pulaski Hwy., Baltimore, MD 21237, (410)866-6000 [9362]

Shepherd Electric Supply Company Inc., PO Box 27, Goldsboro, NC 27533, (919)735-1701 [9363]

Shepherd Machinery Co., PO Box 6789, Los Angeles, CA 90022, (213)723-7191 [8010]

Shepherd Products Co., 8080 Moors Bridge Rd., No. 103, Portage, MI 49024-4074, (616)324-3017 [23033]

Shepherd's Auto Supply Inc., 1001 Williamson SE, Roanoke, VA 24034, (540)344-6666 [3216]

Shepler International Inc., 14206 Industry Rd., Houston, TX 77053, (713)433-5938 [8011]

Shepler Refrigeration Inc., PO Box 12146, Portland, OR 97212-0146, (503)282-7255 [14680]

Shepler's Equipment Company Inc., 9103 E Almeda Rd., Houston, TX 77054, (713)799-1150 [8012]

Sher Distributing Co., 8 Vreeland Ave., Totowa, NJ 07512, (973)256-4050 [4159]

Sher and Mishkin Inc., PO Box 430, Phoenixville, PA 19460-0430, (215)683-8771 [26202]

Sherburn Electronics Corp., 175 Commerce Dr., Hauppauge, NY 11788, (631)231-4300 [9364]

Sheriar Books, 807 34th Ave S, North Myrtle Beach, SC 29582, (843)272-1339 [4160]

Sheridan Optical Co., 108 Clinton Ave., PO Box 8, Pitman, NJ 08071, (609)582-0963 [19607]

Sherman Business Forms, Inc., 55 Tanners Rd., Great Neck, NY 11020-1628, (516)773-0142 [21937]

Sherman Business Forms Inc., 55 Tanners Rd., Great Neck, NY 11020-1628, (516)773-0142 [21267]

Sherri-Li Textile Inc., PO Box 6471, Providence, RI 02940-6471, (401)831-9742 [26203]

Sherron Broom & Associates, 1011 Hardy St., PO Box 1308, Hattiesburg, MS 39403-1308, (601)544-0853 [6724]

Sherwin Williams Paint Co., 1604 S Commerce St., Las Vegas, NV 89102, (702)382-4994 [21567]

Sherwin Williams Paint Co., 3905 E 2nd St., Casper, WY 82609, (307)235-0106 [21568]

Sherwin Williams Paint Co., 1706 Stillwater Ave., Cheyenne, WY 82009-7361, (307)638-8781 [21569]

Sherwin Williams Paint Co., 1281 Coffeen Ave., Sheridan, WY 82801, (307)672-5821 [21570]

Sherwin Williams Paint Co., 929 Grand Ave., Billings, MT 59102, (406)245-7155 [21571]

Sherwin Williams Paint Co., 1920 Harrison Ave., Butte, MT 59701, (406)782-0491 [21572]

Sherwin Williams Paint Co., 1700 N Montana Ave., Helena, MT 59601, (406)442-2300 [21573]

Sherwin Williams Paint Co., 405 W Idaho St., Kalispell, MT 59901, (406)752-5588 [21574]

Sherwin Williams Paint Co., 601 Main St., MiLes City, MT 59301, (406)232-3267 [21575]

Sherwin Williams Paint Co., 1428 S Reserve St., Missoula, MT 59801-4758, (406)543-5970 [21576]

Sherwood Corp. (La Mirada, California), 2346 E Walnut Ave., Fullerton, CA 92831, (714)870-5100 [25440]

Sherwood Food Distributors, 16625 Granite Rd., Maple Heights, OH 44137, (216)662-8000 [12478]

Sherwood Promotions Inc., 1335 S Chillicothe Rd., Aurora, OH 44202, (330)562-9330 [25813]

Shestokas Distributing Inc., 12970 McCarthy Rd., Lemont, IL 60439, (312)229-8700 [2022]

Shetakis Distributing Co.; Jim L., PO Box 14987, Las Vegas, NV 89114-4987, (702)735-8985 [24219]

Sheyenne Publishing Co., PO Box 449, Valley City, ND 58072-0449, (701)845-0275 [21268]

Shiau's Trading Co., 67-21 Fresh Meadow Ln., Flushing, NY 11365, (718)539-8276 [13446]

Shibamoto America, Inc., 2395 Pleasantdale Rd., No. 1, Doraville, GA 30340, (404)446-9232 [16487]

Shields Harper and Co., 5107 Broadway, Oakland, CA 94611, (510)653-9119 [22667]

Shields Soil Service Inc., 1009 County Rd., Ste. 3000 N, Dewey, IL 61840, (217)897-1155 [1265]

Shiflet and Dickson Inc., PO Box 815, Gastonia, NC 28053-0815, (704)867-7284 [25441]

Shil La Art Gems, Inc., 50 W 47th, Rm. 204, New York, NY 10036-8682, (212)719-1298 [17598]

Shima American Corp., 945 Larch Ave., Elmhurst, IL 60126, (630)833-9400 [17171]

Shimano American Corp., 1 Holland Dr., Irvine, CA 92618, (949)951-5003 [23936]

Shimano American Corp. Fishing Tackle Div., 1 Holland Dr., Irvine, CA 92618, (949)951-5003 [23937]

Shimaya Shoten Ltd., 710 Kohou St., Honolulu, HI 96817, (808)845-6691 [12479]

Shin-Etsu Silicones of America Inc., 1150 Damar Dr., Akron, OH 44305-1066, (330)630-9860 [4510]

Shingle & Gibb Co., Moorestown West Corp., 845 Lancer Dr., Moorestown, NJ 08057, (609)234-8500 [17172]

Shipley Oil Co., 550 E King St., York, PA 17405, (717)848-4100 [22668]

Shipley-Phillips Inc., PO Box 1047, Tucumcari, NM 88401, (505)461-1730 [22669]

Shipman Elevator Co., PO Box 349, Shipman, IL 62685, (618)836-5568 [18232]

Shipman Printing Industries Inc., PO Box 157, Niagara Falls, NY 14302, (716)731-3281 [21938]

Shippers Supply Corp., 2428 Crittenden Dr., Louisville, KY 40217, (502)635-6368 [4707]

Shiprock Trading Post, PO Box 906, Shiprock, NM 87420-0906, (505)368-4585 [17599]

Ships Wheel Brand Corp., PO Box 544, Bristol, RI 02809-0544, (401)253-2882 [4708]

Shirts Unlimited, 1181 Rock Blvd., Sparks, NV 89431-0933, (702)359-8755 [17600]

Shoe Barn, PO Box 92, Cecilia, KY 42724-0092, (502)862-4482 [24855]

Shoe Corp. of Birmingham, 1415 1st Ave. S, Birmingham, AL 35233, (205)326-2800 [24856]

Shoe Corporation of Birmingham Inc., 1415 1st Ave. S, Birmingham, AL 35233, (205)326-2800 [24856]

Shoe Corp. of Birmingham Inc., 2320 1st Ave. N, Birmingham, AL 35203-4302, (205)326-2800 [5348]

Shoe Flair, 108 Business Cir., Thomasville, GA 31792-3962, (912)226-8375 [24857]

Shoe Shack Inc., 47 Bridge St., East Windsor, CT 06088-0472, (860)623-3279 [24858]

Shoemaker of Indiana, Inc., 711 S Main St., South Bend, IN 46601-3009, (219)288-4661 [14681]

Shoemakers Candies Inc., PO Box 3345, Santa Fe Springs, CA 90670, (562)944-8811 [12480]

Shoes To Boot Center, 184 Deanna Dr., Lowell, IN 46356-2403, (219)696-4323 [26664]

Shoes To Boot Inc., PO Box 573, Lancaster, KY 40444, (606)792-4150 [24859]

Shohet Frederick of New Hampshire Inc., 159 Frontage Rd., Manchester, NH 03103-6013, (603)434-3050 [13916]

Shojin Natural Foods, PO Box 247, Kealakekua, HI 96750-0247, (808)322-3651 [12481]

Shokai Far East Ltd., 9 Elena Ct., Peekskill, NY 10566-6352, (914)736-5531 [9365]

Shollmier Distribution Inc., 312 Time Saver, Harahan, LA 70123, (504)733-8662 [14682]

Shook Builder Supply Co., PO Box 1790, Hickory, NC 28603, (704)328-2051 [13917]

Shook and Fletcher Insulation Co., PO Box 380501, Birmingham, AL 35238, (205)991-7606 [17173]

Shook and Fletcher Supply of Alabama Inc., 1041 11th Ct. W, Birmingham, AL 35204, (205)252-5157 [8013]

Shop Tools Inc., 892 Commercial, Palo Alto, CA 94303-4905, (650)494-8331 [13918]

ShopKo Stores Inc., PO Box 19060, Green Bay, WI 54307-9060, (920)429-2211 [12482]

Shopper's Food Warehouse Corp., 4600 Forbes Blvd., Lanham, MD 20706, (301)306-8600 [12483]

Shore Distributors Inc., PO Box 2017, Salisbury, MD 21802-2017, (410)749-3121 [14683]

Shore Imports Inc., PO Box 476, Weston, MA 02493-0003, (781)891-6363 [24860]

Shore Point Distributing Co., PO Box 275, Adelphia, NJ 07710, (732)308-3334 [2023]

Shores Marine, 24910 Jefferson, St. Clair Shores, MI 48080, (810)778-3200 [18610]

Shores Oil, 29120 Wick Rd., Romulus, MI 48174, (734)947-1811 [22634]

Shorewood Packaging of California Inc., 5900 Wilshire Blvd., No. 530, Los Angeles, CA 90036-5013, (213)463-3000 [21939]

Shorewood Packaging Company of Illinois Inc., 1300 W Belmont Ave., Ste. 504, Chicago, IL 60657-3242, (847)934-5579 [21940]

Shorr Paper Products Inc., PO Box 6800, Aurora, IL 60504, (630)978-1000 [21941]

Shorts Wholesale Supply Co., 404 State Rte. 125, Brentwood, NH 03833, (603)772-6355 [8014]

Shoshone Sales Yard Inc., PO Box 276, Shoshone, ID 83352-0276, (208)886-2281 [18233]

Showa Denko America Inc., 489 5th Ave., Fl. 18, New York, NY 10017-6105, (212)210-8730 [20364]

Showcase Kitchens and Baths Inc., 222 S Central Ave., Ste. 800, St. Louis, MO 63105-3509, (314)644-3105 [23373]

The Showroom, 331 Rio Grande St., Ste. 101, Salt Lake City, UT 84101-3802, (801)467-1213 [26204]

Showroom Seven, 498 Swaitu Ave., 24th Fl., New York, NY 10018, (212)643-4810 [5349]

Showroom Seven, 498 Swaitu Ave., 24th Fl., New York, NY 10018, (212)643-4810 [5350]

Showscan Entertainment Inc., 3939 Landmark St., Culver City, CA 90232, (310)558-0150 [25442]

Showstopper Exhibits Inc., 17 E Cary St., Richmond, VA 23219, (804)643-4011 [25814]

Shredded Products Corp., 700 Commerce Rd., Rocky Mount, VA 24151, (540)489-7599 [26988]

Shredex Inc., 49 Natcon Dr., Shirley, NY 11967, (516)345-0300 [21269]

Shtofman Company Inc., PO Box 4758, Tyler, TX 75712, (903)592-0861 [24861]

Shube Manufacturing Inc., 600 Moon SE, Albuquerque, NM 87123, (505)275-7677 [17601]

Shulman and Son Co.; I., 197 E Washington Ave., Elmira, NY 14901, (607)733-7111 [26989]

Shumway Seedsman; R.H., PO Box 1, Graniteville, SC 29829, (803)663-9771 [1266]

Shur-Line Inc., PO Box 285, Lancaster, NY 14086, (716)683-2500 [21577]

Shur-Lok Corp., PO Box 19584, Irvine, CA 92623, (949)474-6000 [13919]

Shurail Supply Inc., 9124 Grand Ave. S, Bloomington, MN 55420, (952)884-8266 [14684]

Shurfine International Inc., 2100 N Mannheim Rd., Northlake, IL 60164, (708)236-7100 [12484]

Shurfine International Inc., 2100 N Mannheim Rd., Northlake, IL 60164, (708)681-2000 [12485]

Shurflo, 12650 Westminster Ave., Santa Ana, CA 92706-2100, (714)554-7709 [25939]

Shuster Corp., 4 Wright St., New Bedford, MA 02740, (508)999-3261 [17174]

Shuster's Builders Supply Co., 2920 Clay Pike, Irwin, PA 15642, (412)351-0979 [8015]

Shutters Inc., 12213 Illinois Rt. 173, Hebron, IL 60034, (815)648-2494 [8016]

Shuttle Computer International, 40760 Encyclopedia Cir, Fremont, CA 94538, (510)623-8816 [6725]

Si-Tex Marine Electronics Inc., 11001 N Roosevelt Blvd., No. 800, St. Petersburg, FL 33716, (813)576-5995 [9366]

Siano Appliance Distributors Inc., 5372 Pleasantview Rd., Memphis, TN 38128, (901)382-5833 [15312]

Sibco Enterprises Incorporated, 87 Wedgemere Rd., Stamford, CT 06905, (203)322-4891 [3217]

Sibley Industrial Tool Co., 21938 John R, Hazel Park, MI 48030, (248)547-6942 [9367]

Siboney Learning Group, 325 N Kirkwood Rd., Ste. 200, St. Louis, MO 63122, (314)909-1670 [6726]

Sico Co., 15 Mount Joy St., Mt. Joy, PA 17552, (717)653-1411 [22670]

Sid Tool Company Inc., 151 Sunnyside Blvd., Plainview, NY 11803, (516)349-7100 [16488]

Sidener Supply Co., PO Box 28446, St. Louis, MO 63146, (314)432-4700 [25815]

Sidney Auto Wrecking Inc., RR 8C89, Box 5178, Sidney, MT 59270, (406)482-1406 [3218]

Sidney Furs Inc.; Robert, 150 W 30th St., Fl. 16, New York, NY 10001-4003, (212)279-4046 [5351]

Sidneys Department Store & Uniforms, Inc., 550-560 Broad St., Augusta, GA 30901-1420, (706)722-3112 [5352]

Siegel Oil Co., 1380 Zuni St., Denver, CO 80204, (303)893-3211 [22671]

Siegels Inc., PO Box 984, Evansville, IN 47706-0984, (812)425-2268 [5353]

Siemens Audio Inc., 450 Lexington Ave., New York, NY 10017, (212)949-2324 [25443]

Siemens Automotive Corp., PO Box 217017, Auburn Hills, MI 48326, (248)253-1000 [3219]

Siemens Energy and Automation Inc., 3 Hutton Center Dr., Santa Ana, CA 92707-5707, (714)979-6600 [9368]

Siemens Energy and Automation Inc. Electrical Apparatus Div., 3203 Woman'sClubDr. 202, Raleigh, NC 27612, (919)782-0904 [9369]

Sierra, PO Box 899, Brisbane, CA 94005, (650)871-8775 [12486]

Sierra Airgas Inc., PO Box 19252, Sacramento, CA 95819, (916)454-9353 [22672]

Sierra Alloys Company Inc., 5467 Ayon Ave., Irwindale, CA 91706, (626)969-6711 [20365]

Sierra Building Supply, Inc., PO Box 10, Soulsbyville, CA 95372, (209)532-3447 [8017]

Sierra Chemical Co, PO Box 50730, Sparks, NV 89435, (775)358-0888 [4511]

Sierra Concepts Corp., 9912 S Pioneer Blvd., Santa Fe Springs, CA 90670, (562)949-8311 [16489]

Sierra Craft Inc., 18825 E San Jose Ave., City of Industry, CA 91748, (626)964-2395 [23374]

Sierra Detroit Diesel Allison Inc., 1755 Adams Ave., San Leandro, CA 94577-1001, (510)526-0521 [3220]

Sierra Meat Company Inc., PO Box 2456, Reno, NV 89505, (702)322-4073 [12487]

Sierra Optical, 4757 Morena Blvd., San Diego, CA 92117-3462, (619)490-3490 [19608]

Sierra Pacific, 510 Salmar Ave., Campbell, CA 95008, (408)374-4700 [23938]

Sierra Pacific Steel Inc., PO Box 6024, Hayward, CA 94540-6024, (510)785-4474 [20366]

Sierra Point Lumber and Plywood Co., 601 Tunnel Ave., San Francisco, CA 94134, (415)468-5620 [8018]

Sierra Point Lumber and Plywood Co., 601 Tunnel Ave., San Francisco, CA 94134, (415)468-5620 [27377]

Sierra Roofing Corp., PO Box 3041, Reno, NV 89505, (702)323-0747 [8019]

Sierra Scales, 539 Ideal Ct., Reno, NV 89506-9604, (702)972-3760 [24432]

Sierra Seafood Co., PO Box 235, Oakhurst, CA 93644, (209)683-3479 [12488]

Sietec Inc., 320 Westway, Ste. 530, Arlington, TX 76018-1099, (817)468-3377 [19609]

Siferd-Hossellman Co., PO Box 450, Lima, OH 45802-0450, (419)228-1221 [3221]

Sig Cox Inc., 1431 Greene St., Augusta, GA 30901, (706)722-5304 [23375]

SIGCO Sun Products Inc., 90 N 8th St., Breckenridge, MN 56520, (218)643-8467 [1267]

Sigel Liquor Stores Inc., 2960 Anode Ln., Dallas, TX 75220, (214)350-1271 [2024]

Siggins Co., 512 E 12th Ave., North Kansas City, MO 64116, (816)421-7670 [16490]

Sigma America, 6024 Mission St., Daly City, CA 94014, (650)992-1820 [19610]

Sigma Corporation of America, 15 Fleetwood Ct., Ronkonkoma, NY 11779, (516)585-1144 [22904]

Sigma Data Inc., 26 Newport Rd., New London, NH 03257-4565, (603)526-7100 [6727]

Sigma Electronics Inc., 5935 E Washington Blvd., Los Angeles, CA 90040-2412, (213)721-2662 [5755]

Sigma Food Distributing, 25523 Seaboard Lane, Hayward, CA 94545-3209, (510)785-1492 [12489]

Sigma International Inc., 333 16th Ave. S, St. Petersburg, FL 33701, (727)822-1288 [12490]

Sigma-Tau Pharmaceuticals Inc., 800 S Frederick Ave., Gaithersburg, MD 20877, (301)948-1041 [19611]

Sign of the Crab Ltd., 3756 Omec Cir., Rancho Cordova, CA 95742, (916)638-2722 [23376]

Signal Electronic Supply, 589 New Park Ave., West Hartford, CT 06110-1334, (860)233-8551 [9370]

Signal Equipment Inc., PO Box 3866, Seattle, WA 98124, (206)324-8400 [9371]

Signal Vision, Inc., 27002 Vista Ter., Lake Forest, CA 92630, (949)586-3196 [9372]

Signalcom Systems Inc., 1499 Bayshore Hwy., Ste. 134, Burlingame, CA 94010-1708, (650)692-1056 [5756]

Signaltone, Cadillac, MI 49601, (616)775-1373 [2614]

Signature Apparel, PO Box 3639, Brockton, MA 02304-3639, (508)587-2900 [5354]

Signature Books Inc., 564 West 400 North, Salt Lake City, UT 84116, (801)531-1483 [4161]

Signature Housewares Inc., 671 Via Alondra, Ste. 801, Camarillo, CA 93012, (805)484-6666 [15653]

Signature Services Corp., 2705 Hawes St., Dallas, TX 75235, (214)353-2661 [25816]

Signcaster Corp., 9240 Grand Ave. S, Minneapolis, MN 55420, (952)888-9507 [23034]

Signs of All Kinds, 200 W Main St., Rockville, CT 06066, (860)875-9293 [25817]

Sigo Press/Coventure, PO Box 1435, Ft. Collins, CO 80522-1435, (978)740-0113 [4162]

Silber Knitwear Corp., 1635 Albany Ave., Brooklyn, NY 11210-3513, (718)377-5252 [5355]

Sile Distributors Inc., 7 Centre Market Pl., New York, NY 10013, (212)925-4111 [13513]

Silent Hoist and Crane Co., 841-877 63rd St., Brooklyn, NY 11220, (718)238-2525 [16491]

Silhouette Optical Ltd., 266 Union St., Northvale, NJ 07647, (201)768-8600 [19612]

Silicon Valley Electronics International, 7220 Trenton Pl., Gilroy, CA 95020, (408)842-7731 [6728]

Silicon Valley Technology Inc., PO Box 1408, San Jose, CA 95109-1408, (408)934-8444 [6729]

Siliconix Inc., PO Box 54951, Santa Clara, CA 95056, (408)988-8000 [3222]

Silk and Morgan Inc., 33866 Woodward Ave., Birmingham, MI 48009-0914, (248)644-4411 [14950]

Silke Communications Inc., 680 Tyler St., Eugene, OR 97402-4530, (541)687-1611 [5757]

Silky's Sportswear, RR 2 Box 1125, Mifflintown, PA 17059-9315, (717)567-6396 [5356]

Silliter/Klebes Industrial Supplies Inc., 13 Hamden Park Dr., Hamden, CT 06517, (203)497-1500 [17175]

Silo International Inc., 60 E 42nd St., New York, NY 10165, (212)682-4331 [8020]

Silton USA Corp., 64-68 185th St., Fresh Meadows, NY 11365, (718)445-8832 [19613]

Silver Blue Associated Ltd., 320 5th Ave., New York, NY 10001, (212)563-5858 [18427]

Silver Blue Associated Ltd., 320 5th Ave., New York, NY 10001, (212)563-5858 [18428]

Silver Bow News Distributing Company Inc., 219 E Park St., Butte, MT 59701, (406)782-6995 [4163]

Silver City, 607 S Hill St., No. 946, Los Angeles, CA 90014, (213)689-1488 [17602]

Silver Dust Trading Inc., 120 W Highway 66, Gallup, NM 87301-6226, (505)722-4848 [17603]

Silver Foods Corp., 2935 St. Xavier, Louisville, KY 40212-1936, (502)778-1649 [12491]

Silver Lake Cookie Co., 141 Freeman Ave., Islip, NY 11751-1420, (516)581-4000 [12492]

A Silver Lining Inc., PO Box 477, Boothbay Harbor, ME 04538-0477, (207)633-4103 [17604]

Silver Loom Associates, 271-80 Grand Central Pky., No. 80, Floral Park, NY 11005-1209, (212)684-2350 [10148]

Silver Ray, 6908 Central Ave. SE, Albuquerque, NM 87108-1855, (505)265-0444 [17605]

Silver Sage, 402 W 5050 N, Provo, UT 84604-5650, (801)571-6599 [14236]

Silver Springs Farm Inc., 640 Meeting House Rd., Harleysville, PA 19438-2247, (215)256-4321 [12493]

Silver State Roofing Materials, 1434 Industrial Way, Gardnerville, NV 89410-5726, (702)782-7663 [8021]

Silver State Welding Supply Inc., 3560 Losee Rd., North Las Vegas, NV 89030, (702)734-2182 [16492]

Silver Sun Wholesale Inc., 2011 Central Ave. NW, Albuquerque, NM 87104-1403, (505)246-9692 [17606]

SilverPlatter Information Inc., 100 River Ridge Rd., Norwood, MA 02062, (781)769-2599 [6730]

Silvers Inc., 151 W Fort St., Detroit, MI 48232, (313)963-0000 [13242]

SilverSource, 2118 Wilshire Blvd., No. 1155, Santa Monica, CA 90403, (310)828-8922 [17607]

Silverstate Co., 325 E Nugget Ave., Sparks, NV 89431, (702)331-3400 [2025]

Silvestri Corporation Inc.; Fitz and Floyd, 501 Corporate Drive, Lewisville, TX 75057, (972)918-0098 [15654]

Simco Sales Service of Pennsylvania, 3100 Marwin Ave., Bensalem, PA 19020, (215)639-2300 [12494]

Sime Health Ltd., 1200 6th Ave. S, Seattle, WA 98134, (206)622-9596 [14237]

Simione and Associates, Inc.; Bill, 5 Krey Blvd., Rensselaer, NY 12144, (518)283-0126 [23939]

Simmons Gun Specialty Inc., 20241 W 207th, Spring Hill, KS 66083, (913)686-3939 [13514]

Simmons Hosiery Mill Inc., 391 10th Ave. NE, Hickory, NC 28601-3833, (704)327-4890 [5357]

Simmons-Huggins Supply Co., 425 M.L. King, San Angelo, TX 76902, (915)655-9163 [23377]

Simmons Lumber Company Inc., PO Box 418, Booneville, AR 72927, (501)675-2430 [8022]

Simmons Mattress Factory Inc.; W., 11030 E Artesia Blvd., Cerritos, CA 90701, (562)865-0294 [13243]

Simmons Sporting Goods Company Inc., 2001 2nd Ave. N, Bessemer, AL 35020-4948, (205)425-4720 [23940]

Simmons Yarn & Rug Co., 835 Poplar Springs Church Rd., Shelby, NC 28152, (704)484-8691 [10149]

Simon Resources Inc., 2525 Trenton Ave., Williamsport, PA 17701, (717)326-9041 [26990]

Simon & Sons; Joseph, 2200 E River St., Tacoma, WA 98421, (253)272-9364 [26991]

Simons Millinery Mart, 128 S 17th St., Philadelphia, PA 19103, (215)569-9511 [5358]

Simple Wisdom Inc., 775 S Graham St., Memphis, TN 38111, (901)458-4686 [14238]

Simplex Chemical Corp., 6 Commercial St., Sharon, MA 02067, (781)784-8484 [4709]

Simplot AgriSource, PO Box 70013, 418 S 9th St., Ste. 308, Boise, ID 83707-2700, (208)672-2700 [18234]

Simpson Buick Co., 8400 E Firestone Blvd, Downey, CA 90241, (310)861-1261 [20721]

Simpson Equipment Corp., PO Box 2229, Wilson, NC 27894, (919)291-4105 [3223]

Simpson Industries Inc., 47603 Halyard Dr., Plymouth, MI 48170-2429, (248)540-6200 [16493]

Simpson Norton Corp., 4420 Andrews, Ste. A, North Las Vegas, NV 89031, (702)644-4066 [1268]

Simpson Norton Corp., PO Box 1295, Goodyear, AZ 85338, (623)932-5116 [1269]

Simpson Strong-Tie Company Inc., 4637 Chabot Dr., Pleasanton, CA 94588, (510)460-9912 [8023]

Simpson's Inc., 2 Dracut St., Lawrence, MA 01843, (978)683-2417 [8024]

Sims Brothers Inc., PO Box 1170, Marion, OH 43301-1170, (740)387-9041 [26992]

Sims Metal America - Structural Steel Div., 3220 Deepwater Term Rd., Richmond, VA 23234, (804)291-3255 [26993]

Simsim Inc., 192 Worcester Rd., Natick, MA 01760, (508)655-6415 [6731]

Simsmetal USA Corp., 600 S 4th St., Richmond, CA 94804, (510)412-5300 [26994]

Simsmetal USA Corp. C and C Metals Div., 11320 Dismantle Ct., Rancho Cordova, CA 95742, (916)635-8750 [20367]

Sinar-Bron Inc., 17 Progress St., Edison, NJ 08820, (908)754-5800 [22905]

Sinbad Sweets Inc., 2585 N Larkin Ave., Fresno, CA 93727, (209)298-3700 [12495]

Sinclair Imports Inc., 2775 W Hwy. 40, PO Box 707, Verdi, NV 89439, (702)345-0600 [23941]

Sinclair Lumber Co., PO Box 729, Laurinburg, NC 28352, (919)276-0371 [8025]

Sinclair Oil Corp., PO Box 30825, Salt Lake City, UT 84130, (801)524-2700 [22673]

Sinclair Oil Corp. Eastern Region, 3401 Fairbanks Ave., Kansas City, KS 66106, (913)321-3700 [22674]

Sinclair Produce Distributing, PO Box 432, Glasgow, MT 59230-0432, (406)228-2454 [2026]

Sinclair & Rush, Inc., 13515 Barrett Pkwy. Dr., Ste. 155, Ballwin, MO 63021-5870 [23942]

Singer Equipment Company Inc., PO Box 13668, Reading, PA 19612, (610)929-8000 [24220]

Singer Hosiery Mills Inc., PO Box 758, Thomasville, NC 27360, (919)475-2161 [5359]

Singer Optical Co. Inc., PO Box 3557, Evansville, IN 47734-3557, (812)423-1179 [19614]

Singer Products Export Company Inc., PO Box 484, Hartsdale, NY 10530-0484, (914)722-0400 [16494]

Singer Products Export Company Inc., 250 E Hartsdale Ave., Hartsdale, NY 10530, (914)722-0400 [3224]

Singer Sewing Co., PO Box 1909, Edison, NJ 08818-1909, (732)225-8844 [15313]

Singer Sewing Inc., 304 Park Ave. S, 11th Fl., New York, NY 10010-5339, (212)632-6700 [25444]

Singer Steel Co., 1 Singer Dr., Streetsboro, OH 44241-0279, (330)562-7200 [20368]

Singer Steel Inc., PO Box 3528, Enid, OK 73702, (580)233-0411 [20369]

Singer Textiles Inc., 55 Delancy St., New York, NY 10002, (212)925-4109 [26205]

Singing Poppe's, Inc., 8055 N 24th Ave., No. 104-105, Phoenix, AZ 85021-4865, (602)249-2617 [21270]

Single Point of Contact Inc., 20914 Bake Pkwy., Ste. 110, Lake Forest, CA 92630-2174, (949)599-9037 [5758]

Sinton Dairy Foods Co. Inc., PO Box 578, Colorado Springs, CO 80901, (719)633-3821 [12496]

Sintrigue, 385 Chestnut St., Norwood, NJ 07648, (201)750-8100 [5293]

Sioux Honey Association, PO Box 388, Sioux City, IA 51102-0388, (712)258-0638 [12497]

Sioux Preme Packing Co., PO Box 255, Sioux Center, IA 51250-0255, (712)722-2555 [12498]

Sioux Valley Cooperative, PO Box 965, Watertown, SD 57201, (605)886-5829 [22675]

Sioux Veneer Panel Co., PO Box 488, Payette, ID 83661-0488, (208)344-8358 [8026]

Siouxland Ophthalmics Lab Inc., 415 E 9th St., Sheldon, IA 51201, (712)324-4352 [19615]

Siperstein Freehold Paint, PO Box 298A, Rd. 1, Englishtown, NJ 07726, (732)780-2000 [21578]

Siperstein, Inc.; N., 326 S Washington Ave., Bergenfield, NJ 07621, (201)385-4800 [21579]

Siperstein, Inc.; N., 372 New Brunswick Ave., Fords, NJ 08863, (732)738-8300 [21580]

Siperstein, Inc.; N., 119 Rte. 46 West, Lodi, NJ 07644, (973)777-7100 [21581]

Siperstein, Inc.; N., 415 Montgomery St., Jersey City, NJ 07302, (201)867-0336 [21582]

Siperstein MK Paint, 935 Rte. 22 West, North Plainfield, NJ 07060, (908)756-0089 [21583]

Siperstein West End, 128 Broadway, Long Branch, NJ 07740, (732)542-6142 [21584]

Siperstein's Middletown, 549 Highway 35, Red Bank, NJ 07701, (732)842-6000 [21585]

Sipes Co.; Howe K., 249 Mallory Ave. E, Memphis, TN 38109-2598, (901)948-0378 [5360]

Sirak & Sirak Associates, 20 Davenport Rd., Montville, NJ 07045-9184, (973)299-0085 [4164]

Sirco International Corp., 13337 South St., Cerritos, CA 90703-7300 [18429]

Siri Office Equipment Inc., PO Box 2555, Reno, NV 89505-2555, (702)323-2776 [21271]

Siroflex of America Inc., 14658 Plummer, Van Nuys, CA 91402, (818)892-8382 [23378]

Sirsi Corp., 101 Washington St. SE, Huntsville, AL 35801-4827, (205)922-9820 [6732]

SIS Human Factor Technologies Inc., 55C Harvey Rd., Londonderry, NH 03053-7414, (603)432-4495 [13244]

Sisco Equipment Rental and Sales Inc., 3506 W Harry St., Wichita, KS 67213, (316)943-4237 [16495]

Sisco Products Inc., PO Box 549, Buford, GA 30518-0549, (404)945-2181 [14685]

Siskin Steel and Supply Company Inc., PO Box 1191, Chattanooga, TN 37401-1191, (423)756-3671 [20370]

Sita Tile Distributors, Inc., 523 Dunmore Pl., Capitol Heights, MD 20743, (301)336-0450 [10150]

Site Concepts, PO Box 9309, Chesapeake, VA 23321-9309, (757)547-3553 [23943]

Sitek Inc., 30 Lowell Rd., Hudson, NH 03051-2800, (603)889-0066 [6733]

Sitler's Electric Supply Inc., PO Box 542, 213-19 N Iowa, Washington, IA 52353, (319)653-2128 [9373]

Six Robblees Inc., PO Box 3703, Seattle, WA 98124, (206)767-7970 [3225]

Six States Distributors, 247 W 1700 S, Salt Lake City, UT 84115, (801)488-4666 [3226]

Six States Distributors Inc., 4432 Franklin Blvd., Eugene, OR 97403, (541)747-9944 [3227]

SJA Industries Inc., 1357 Kuehner Dr., Simi Valley, CA 93063, (805)527-8899 [15314]

SJL Beverage Co., 901 N Belcrest, Springfield, MO 65802, (417)866-8226 [2027]

SJL Liquor Co., 901 N Belcrest, Springfield, MO 65802, (417)866-8226 [2027]

SJS Products/Jamcor Corp., 6261 Angelo Ct., Loomis, CA 95650, (916)652-7713 [9374]

sjs X-Ray Corp., PO Box 148, Mt. Pleasant, SC 29465-0148, (843)884-8943 [19038]

SK Food International, Inc., PO Box 1236, Wahpeton, ND 58074, (701)642-3929 [12499]

SK Hand Tool Corp., 3535 W 47th St., Chicago, IL 60632, (773)523-1300 [13920]

Skaggs Automotive Inc., 110 S Sherman St., Spokane, WA 99202-1529, (509)838-3529 [3228]

Skane Ltd., 125 High St., Farmington, ME 04938, (207)778-9508 [5361]

SKC Communication Products Inc., 8320 Hedge Lane Ter., Shawnee Mission, KS 66227, (913)422-4222 [9375]

Skechers U.S.A. Inc., 228 Manhattan Beach Blvd., Ste. 200, Manhattan Beach, CA 90266, (310)318-3100 [24862]

Skeels and Co.; Robert, 19216 S Laurel Park Rd., Compton, CA 90220, (310)639-7240 [13921]

Skelton and Skinner Lumber Inc., PO Box 810, Greencastle, IN 46135-0810, (765)653-9705 [8027]

SKF Textile Products Inc., PO Box 977, Gastonia, NC 28053, (704)864-2691 [26206]

S.K.H. Management Co., PO Box 1500, Lititz, PA 17543-7025, (717)626-4771 [12500]

Ski America Enterprises Inc., PO Box 1140, Pittsfield, MA 01202-1140, (413)637-9810 [4165]

Skidmore Sales & Distributing Company, Inc., 9889 Cincinnati Dayton Rd., West Chester, OH 45069, (513)772-4200 [12501]

Skillers Workwear USA, Inc., 601 Hansen Ave., Butler, PA 16001-5664, (724)282-8581 [5362]

Skinner Baking Co.; James, 4657 G St., Omaha, NE 68117-1410, (402)558-7428 [12502]

Skinner Company Inc.; S.P., 91 Great Hill Rd., Naugatuck, CT 06770, (203)723-1471 [15655]

Skinner Corp., 1009 N Lanier Ave., Lanett, AL 36863, (205)644-2136 [13245]

Skinner Nursery Inc., 7415 SW 22nd Ct., Topeka, KS 66614-6070, (785)478-0123 [14951]

Skip Dunn Sales, 162 Washington Ave., New Rochelle, NY 10801, (914)636-2200 [24221]

Skipper Bills Inc., E7915 E Sprague Ave., Spokane, WA 99212-2938, (509)928-1000 [23944]

Skipper Heating and Air Conditioning, 3524 Green St., Muskegon, MI 49444-3812, (231)739-4444 [14686]

Skipper Heating, Air Conditioning & Fireplace Showroom, 3524 Green St., Muskegon, MI 49444-3812, (231)739-4444 [14686]

Skipper Shop, PO Box 519, Puerto Real, PR 00740, (787)863-5530 [18611]

Skips Ameritone Paint Center, 512 S Boulder Hwy., Henderson, NV 89015-7512, (702)565-9591 [21586]

Skis Dynastar Inc., Hercules Dr., PO Box 25, Colchester, VT 05446-0025, (802)655-2400 [23945]

SKL Company Inc., 511 Victor St., Saddle Brook, NJ 07663-6118, (201)845-5566 [17608]

Sklar Instrument Company Inc., 889 S Matlack St., West Chester, PA 19382, (610)430-3200 [19039]

Skokie Valley Beverage Co., 199 Shepard Ave., Wheeling, IL 60090, (847)541-1500 [2028]

SKR Distributors, 195 Thatcher St., Bangor, ME 04401, (207)945-9550 [8028]

Sky Brothers Inc., PO Box 632, Altoona, PA 16603, (814)946-1201 [12503]

Sky Knob Technologies LLC, 53 W Main, Hancock, MD 21750-1630, (301)678-5129 [6734]

Sky-Reach Inc., 53643 Grand River, PO Box 129, New Hudson, MI 48165, (248)437-1783 [8029]

Skyland Hospital Supply Inc., PO Box 51970, Knoxville, TN 37950-1970, (423)546-2524 [19040]

Skyline Designs, 1090 John Stark Hwy., Newport, NH 03773, (603)542-6649 [13246]

Skyline Designs, 1090 John Stark Hwy., Newport, NH 03773, (603)542-6649 [24222]

Skyline Distributing Co., PO Box 2053, Great Falls, MT 59403-2053, (406)453-0061 [15656]

Skyline Supply Company Inc., 71 Park Ln., Brisbane, CA 94005, (415)468-4200 [21272]

Skytron, PO Box 888615, Grand Rapids, MI 49588-8615, (616)957-1950 [19041]

Skyway Luggage Co., 30 Wall St., Seattle, WA 98121, (206)441-5300 [18430]

Slack Chemical Company, Inc., PO Box 30, Carthage, NY 13619-0030, (315)493-0430 [4512]

Slakey Brothers Inc., PO Box 15647, Sacramento, CA 95852, (916)329-3750 [8030]

Slane Hosiery Mills Inc., PO Box 2486, High Point, NC 27261, (919)883-4136 [5363]

Slaughter Industries, PO Box 551699, Dallas, TX 75355-1699, (214)342-4900 [8031]

Slavin and Sons Ltd.; M., 31 Belmont Ave., Brooklyn, NY 11212, (718)495-2800 [12504]

Slawson Communications, Inc., 165 Vallecitos de Oro, San Marcos, CA 92069, (760)744-2299 [4166]

Slay Industries Inc., 1441 Hampton Ave., St. Louis, MO 63139, (314)647-7529 [18235]

SLC Technologies Inc., 12345 S Leventon Dr., Tualatin, OR 97062, (503)691-7270 [24637]

Slick 50 Corp., 1187 Brittmoore Rd., Houston, TX 77043, (713)932-9954 [22676]

Slife and Associates; Robert M., 2754 Woodhill Rd., Cleveland, OH 44104, (216)791-3500 [16496]

Slingman Industries, 5 Shirley Ave., PO Box 6870, Somerset, NJ 08875, (732)249-3500 [3229]

Slip-Not Belting Corp., PO Box 89, Kingsport, TN 37662, (423)246-8141 [17176]

Slippers International Inc., PO Box 505602, Chelsea, MA 02150-5602, (617)884-3752 [24863]

SLM Power Group Inc., PO Box 9156, Corpus Christi, TX 78469, (512)883-4358 [3230]

Sloan and Company Inc., 15 Tobey Village, Pittsford, NY 14534-1727, (716)385-4004 [23379]

Sloan Electric Co, 1480 Simpson Way, Escondido, CA 92029, (760)745-5276 [9376]

Sloan Implement Company Inc., PO Box 80, Assumption, IL 62510-0080, (217)226-4411 [1270]

Sloan International, Inc., 2950 E Flamingo Rd., Las Vegas, NV 89121, (702)896-3955 [25818]

Sloan Miyasato, 2 Henry Adams St., San Francisco, CA 94103-5016, (415)431-1465 [13247]

Slocum & Sons Co., 25 Industry, West Haven, CT 06516, (203)932-3688 [2029]

The Slosman Corp., PO Box 3019, Asheville, NC 28802, (828)274-2100 [26207]

SLS Arts, Inc., 5524 Mounes St., New Orleans, LA 70123, (504)733-1104 [25819]

Slusser Wholesale Inc., PO Box 2439, Idaho Falls, ID 83403-2439, (208)523-0775 [26652]

SM Building Supply Coompany, Inc., 2140 Amnicola Hwy., Chattanooga, TN 37406, (423)622-3333 [8032]

SMA Equipment Inc., 5230 Wilson St., Riverside, CA 92509, (909)784-1444 [8033]

Small Apparel Co.; Horace, 350 28th Ave. N, Nashville, TN 37209, (615)320-1000 [5364]

Small Appliance Repair Inc., 1500 Albany Ave., Hartford, CT 06112-2113, (860)246-7424 [15315]

Small Changes Inc., 316 Terry Ave. N, PO Box 19046, Seattle, WA 98109, (206)382-1980 [4167]

Small Press Distribution Inc., 1341 7th St., Berkeley, CA 94710, (510)524-1668 [4168]

Small Talk Inc., 10489 St. Rd. 37 N, Elwood, IN 46036, (765)552-2007 [27232]

Small World Toys, PO Box 3620, Culver City, CA 90231-3620, (310)645-9680 [26653]

Smart & Final Foodservice, PO Box 30, Stockton, CA 95201, (209)948-1814 [12505]

Smarter Security Systems, Inc., 5825 Glenridge Dr., Ste. 1-126, Atlanta, GA 30328, (404)256-4244 [24638]

Smarter Security Systems Inc., 5825 Glenridge Dr., Atlanta, GA 30328, (404)256-4244 [9377]

SMARTEYE Corp., 2002, Ste.phenson Hwy., Troy, MI 48083-2151, (248)589-3382 [9378]

SMC Electrical Products Inc., PO Box 880, Barboursville, WV 25504, (304)736-8933 [9379]

Smeed Communication Services, PO Box 2099, Eugene, OR 97402, (541)686-1654 [15316]

Smeed Sound Service Inc., PO Box 2099, Eugene, OR 97402-0036, (541)686-1654 [5759]

Smellkinson Sysco Food Services Inc., 8000 Dorsey Run Rd., Jessup, MD 20794, (410)799-7000 [24223]

Smethurst & Sons; William, 344 Eastern Ave., Malden, MA 02148, (781)322-3210 [10151]

SMH (US) Inc., 35 E 21st St., New York, NY 10010, (212)271-1400 [17609]

Smith Abrasives, Inc., 1700 Sleepy Valley Rd., Hot Springs, AR 71901, (501)321-2244 [13922]

Smith Associates; Bernie, 7122 Ambassador Rd., Baltimore, MD 21244-2715, (410)298-0100 [25445]

Smith Associates; Jay, 840 Hinckley Rd., Ste. 221, Burlingame, CA 94010, (650)652-7800 [13923]

Smith Beverages, PO Box 1206, Laramie, WY 82073, (307)745-3236 [1701]

Smith Bros. Food Service Inc., PO Box 410, Port Washington, WI 53074-0410, (414)284-5577 [12506]

Smith Brothers of Dudley Inc., PO Box 10, Dudley, NC 28333, (919)735-2764 [22677]

Smith Brothers Farms Inc., 27441 68th Ave. S, Kent, WA 98032, (206)852-1000 [12507]

Smith Brothers Food Service Inc., 815 Sunset Rd., PO Box 410, Port Washington, WI 53074-0410, (414)284-5577 [12508]

Smith Brothers Office Environments Inc., PO Box 2719, Portland, OR 97208, (503)226-4151 [21273]

Smith Ceramics, 268 Main St., Bangor, ME 04401-6404, (207)945-3969 [26654]

Smith-Claypool; Shirley, PO Box 188, Opp, AL 36467-0188, (205)493-4551 [24864]

Smith Co.; A and B, PO Box 1776, Pittsburgh, PA 15230, (412)858-5400 [24433]

Smith Co.; Harold E., 3630 Concord Rd., York, PA 17402-8629, (717)397-2874 [16497]

Smith and Co.; R.W., PO Box 26160, San Diego, CA 92196, (619)530-1800 [25820]

Smith Crown Co., 1993 South 1100 East, Salt Lake City, UT 84106-2316, (801)484-5259 [25446]

Smith Detroit Diesel, 8 Glendale Ave., Sparks, NV 89431, (702)359-1713 [3231]

Smith Detroit Diesel Allison Inc., PO Box 27527, Salt Lake City, UT 84127, (801)262-2631 [3232]

Smith Distributing Co., PO Box 252, Anniston, AL 36202-0252, (205)237-2895 [23946]

Smith Distributors; Laurence, 3044 E Commerce Rd., Midland, MI 48642, (517)835-7313 [15657]

Smith Drug Co., PO Box 1779, Spartanburg, SC 29304, (864)582-1216 [19616]

Smith Drug Co.; C.D., PO Box 789, St. Joseph, MO 64502, (816)232-5471 [14239]

Smith Electronics; Larry, 1619 Broadway, Riviera Beach, FL 33404-5627, (561)844-3592 [18612]

Smith Enterprises Inc.; P., PO Box 3162, West Columbia, SC 29171-3162, (803)791-5155 [23947]

Smith Family Corp.; The Miles, 2705 5th St., Ste. 5, Sacramento, CA 95818, (916)442-1292 [12509]

Smith Floor Covering, 3106 Essex Path, Hendersonville, NC 28791-1869, (704)252-1038 [10152]

Smith Floor Covering Distributors, 1118 Smith St., PO Box 2826, Charleston, WV 25330, (304)344-2493 [10153]

Smith Glass Co.; L.E., PO Box 963, Mt. Pleasant, PA 15666, (412)547-3544 [15658]

Smith Group Inc.; E.J., PO Box 7247, Charlotte, NC 28241-7247, (704)394-3361 [1271]

Smith Hardware Company Inc., 515 N George St., Goldsboro, NC 27530, (919)735-6281 [13924]

Smith Hardwood Floors, 1115 S 10th, Ft. Smith, AR 72901, (501)783-2850 [10154]

Smith-Holden Inc., 99 Corliss St., Providence, RI 02904, (401)331-0742 [19042]

Smith Inc.; Del Cher, 8440 Ashland Ave., Pensacola, FL 32534, (850)474-0119 [12510]

Smith Inc.; Kenneth, 12931 W 71st St., Shawnee, KS 66216-2640, (913)631-5100 [23948]

Smith Kitchen Specialties; W.H., 129 Winfield Rd., St. Albans, WV 25177-1500, (304)727-2952 [15317]

Smith-Koch Inc., 886 Tryens Rd., Aston, PA 19014, (610)459-1212 [16498]

Smith Lumber Co.; G.W., 720 W Center St., Lexington, NC 27292, (336)249-4941 [8034]

Smith; Merle B., 161 Tower Dr., Unit I, Burr Ridge, IL 60521, (630)325-0770 [10155]

Smith Motor Sales, PO Box 692050, San Antonio, TX 78269-2050, (210)223-4281 [3233]

Smith; Nicholas, 2343 W Chester Pike, Broomall, PA 19008, (215)353-8585 [26655]

Smith Oil Co.; Glenn, 4 W Martin Luther King St., Muskogee, OK 74401, (918)682-2212 [22678]

Smith Oil Company Inc., PO Box 1719, Clinton, OK 73601, (580)323-2929 [22679]

Smith Packing Company Inc., PO Box 446, Utica, NY 13503-0446, (315)732-5125 [12511]

Smith Packing Corp.; H., PO Box 189, Blaine, ME 04734, (207)425-3421 [12512]

Smith Pipe and Steel Co., 735 N 19th Ave., Phoenix, AZ 85009, (602)257-9494 [20371]

Smith Potato Inc., Farm Rd. 145 E, PO Box 467, Hart, TX 79043, (806)938-2166 [12513]

Smith Provision Company Inc., 2251 W 23rd St., Erie, PA 16506, (814)459-4974 [12514]

Smith-Sheppard Concrete Company Inc., Tennille Rd., PO Box 855, Sandersville, GA 31082, (912)552-2594 [8035]

Smith & Son Fish; Luther, 1023 S Sea Shore Dr., Atlantic, NC 28511-9702, (919)225-3341 [12515]

Smith & Sons Co.; Dale T., 12450 S State, Draper, UT 84020-9510, (801)571-3611 [12516]

Smith and Sons Foods Inc., PO Box 4688, Macon, GA 31213-5799, (912)745-4759 [12517]

Smith and Sons Inc.; Jess, 2905 F St., Bakersfield, CA 93301, (805)325-7231 [18236]

Smith Southside Feed and Grain Inc., PO Box 446, Bowling Green, KY 42101, (502)529-5651 [18237]

Smith Sporting Goods Inc.; L.L., 2328 W Royal Palm Rd., Phoenix, AZ 85021-4937, (602)995-2424 [23949]

Smith-Thompson Co., 9433 E 51st St., Ste. F, Tulsa, OK 74145, (918)665-6044 [17177]

Smith-Thompson Inc., PO Box 2249, Amarillo, TX 79105, (806)372-6751 [17178]

Smith Tractor and Equipment Co., PO Box 2990, Tacoma, WA 98401-2990, (206)922-8718 [8036]

Smith Turf & Irrigation Co., 4355 Golf Acres Dr., Charlotte, NC 28208, (704)393-8873 [1272]

Smith Two-Way Radio Inc., 520 N College Ave., Fayetteville, AR 72701-3401, (501)443-2222 [5760]

SmithChem Div., 84 Dayton Ave., Passaic, NJ 07055, (201)779-5001 [21587]

Smithey Recycling Co., PO Box 19050, Phoenix, AZ 85005-9050, (602)252-8125 [26995]

Smithfield Companies Inc., 311 County St., No. 203, Portsmouth, VA 23704, (804)399-3100 [12518]

Smithfield Ham Products Co. Inc., 401 N Church St., PO Box 487, Smithfield, VA 23430-0487, (757)357-2121 [12519]

Smiths Industries, 148 East Ave., Ste. 2-I, Norwalk, CT 06851-5726 [147]

Smiths Sons Co.; F.X., 372-374 North St., PO Box 38, McSherrystown, PA 17344-0038, (717)637-5232 [26350]

Smith's Sons Inc.; Leroy E., 4776 Old Dixie Hwy., Vero Beach, FL 32967, (407)567-3421 [12520]

SMO Inc., 6355 Crain Hwy., La Plata, MD 20646, (301)934-8101 [22680]

Smoky Mountain Coal Corp., 9040 Executive Park Dr., Knoxville, TN 37923, (423)694-8222 [20568]

Smoky Mountain Distributors, 7 Roberts Rd., Asheville, NC 28803, (828)274-3606 [2030]

SMP Enterprises Inc., 99-1366 Koaha Pl., Aiea, HI 96701, (808)487-1129 [26656]

S.M.S. Distributors, 451 Beech Ave., PO Box 150, Woodbury Heights, NJ 08097, (609)853-5919 [14687]

SMS International Marketing Co., 68-46 Selfridge St., Forest Hills, NY 11375, (718)575-9493 [24535]

SMW Systems Inc., 9828 S Arlee Ave., Santa Fe Springs, CA 90670, (562)949-7991 [16499]

Smyrna Truck Body & Equipment, Inc., 2158 Atlanta St., Smyrna, GA 30080, (404)433-0112 [3234]

Smyth-Despard Company Inc., 800 Broad St., PO Box 4789, Utica, NY 13504-4789, (315)732-2154 [16500]

SNA Inc., 436 Atwells Ave., Providence, RI 02909-1031, (401)274-1110 [19043]

SNACC Distributing Co., 2105 Central Ave., Cincinnati, OH 45214, (513)723-1777 [12521]

Snak King Corp., 16150 E Stephens St., City of Industry, CA 91745, (626)336-7711 [12522]

Snap-on Tools Corp., PO Box 1410, Kenosha, WI 53141-1410, (414)656-5200 [13925]

Snap Products Inc., PO Box 2967, Houston, TX 77252-2967, (713)546-4000 [3235]

Snavely Forest Products Inc., PO Box 9808, Pittsburgh, PA 15227, (412)885-4000 [8037]

Snell; V.A., 5620 Snell Dr., San Antonio, TX 78219, (210)661-7300 [27233]

Snipes Webb Trailer & Livestock Co., 5100 Broadway Blvd. SE, Albuquerque, NM 87105-7416, (505)877-2471 [18238]

Snokist Growers, PO Box 1587, Yakima, WA 98907, (509)453-5631 [12523]

Snow Filtration Co., 6386 Gano Rd., West Chester, OH 45069-4809, (513)777-6200 [17179]

Snow & Stars Corp., 18 Delaine St., Providence, RI 02909-2429, (401)421-4134 [17610]

Snowbelt Insulation Company Inc., 664 County Rd., East Fairfield, VT 05448-9725, (802)827-6171 [8038]

S.N.S. International Trading, 9910 Harwin Dr., Houston, TX 77036, (713)789-9847 [13447]

Snyder Paper Corp., PO Box 758, Hickory, NC 28603, (828)328-2501 [21942]

Snyder Wholesale Inc., 1107 David Ln., PO Box 869, Blytheville, AR 72316-0869, (870)763-7341 [12524]

Snyder Wholesale Tire Co., PO Box 2280, Wintersville, OH 43952-0280, (740)264-5543 [25447]

Soave Enterprises L.L.C., 3400 E Lafayette St., Detroit, MI 48207, (313)567-7000 [26996]

Soccer House Inc., 803 W Coliseum Blvd., Ft. Wayne, IN 46808-3611, (219)482-3919 [23950]

Soccer Plus Inc., 161 Main St., Wethersfield, CT 06109-2339, (860)563-6263 [23951]

Society of Petroleum Engineers, 222 Palisades Creek Dr., Richardson, TX 75080, (972)952-9393 [4169]

Sockyard Company Inc., 366 5th Ave., No. 510, New York, NY 10001, (212)947-6295 [5365]

SOCO-Lynch Corp., 10747 Patterson Pl., Santa Fe Springs, CA 90670-4043, (323)269-0191 [4513]

Socoloff Health Supply Inc., 6665 Corners Industrial, Ste. C, Norcross, GA 30092-3661, (404)448-8541 [19617]

Sodak Distributing Co., 1710 N M Ave., Sioux Falls, SD 57104-0274, (605)336-3320 [2031]

Sodak Gaming Inc., 5301 S Hwy. 16, Rapid City, SD 57701, (605)341-5400 [25821]

Soderburg Optical Services, 230 Eva St., St. Paul, MN 55164, (612)291-1400 [19618]

S.O.E. Ltd., 259 Radnor-Chester Rd., Ste. 210, Radnor, PA 19087, (610)971-6653 [14240]

Sofco-Mead Inc., PO Box 2023, Scotia, NY 12302, (518)374-7810 [12525]

Soffe; M.J., 919 Filley St., Lansing, MI 48906, (517)321-4220 [23952]

Soft-As-A-Grape Inc., 328 Marion Rd., Wareham, MA 02571-1452, (508)548-6159 [5366]

Soft Solutions, 6999 Dublin Blvd., Ste. B, Dublin, CA 94568, (925)803-1358 [6735]

Softcell Inc., 307 Hempstead Ave., Fairfield, IA 52556-2810, (515)693-4828 [6736]

SoftKey International, 500 Redwood Blvd., Novato, CA 94947-6921 [6737]

SoftKlone Distributing Corp., 327 Office Plaza Dr., No. 100, Tallahassee, FL 32301, (904)878-8564 [6738]

Softouch Company Inc., 1167 NW 159th Dr., Miami, FL 33169-5807, (954)920-9117 [5367]

Software Associates Inc., 860 Broad St., Emmaus, PA 18049, (215)967-1846 [6739]

Software and Electrical Engineering, 248 Walnut St., Willimantic, CT 06226-2322, (860)456-2022 [6740]

Software Export Corporation, PO Box 32, Cambridge, MA 02139-0001, (617)354-9600 [6716]

Software Spectrum Inc., PO Box 479501, Garland, TX 75047-9501, (214)840-6600 [6741]

Software Technology Inc., 1621 Cushman Dr., Lincoln, NE 68512, (402)423-1440 [6742]

Softworks Development Corp., PO Box 579, Mequon, WI 53092, (414)242-8800 [6307]

Softworks Development Corp., PO Box 579, Mequon, WI 53092, (414)242-8800 [6743]

SOGEM-Afrimet Inc., 1212 6th Ave., New York, NY 10036, (212)764-0880 [20372]

Soil Shield International, 40780 Fremont Blvd., Fremont, CA 94538, (510)490-6600 [15659]

Soil Stabilization Products Company Inc., PO Box 2779, Merced, CA 95344, (209)383-3296 [4514]

Sokkia Corp., PO Box 2934, Overland Park, KS 66211, (913)492-4900 [8039]

Sokol Electronics Inc., 121 E Baltimore St., Hagerstown, MD 21740-6103, (301)791-2562 [6744]

Sol-Pro Inc., PO Box 1781, Tacoma, WA 98401-1781, (253)627-4822 [26997]

Sola International Inc., 2420 Sand Hill Rd. Ste. 200, Menlo Park, CA 94025, (650)324-6868 [19619]

Solair Inc., 3380 SW 11th Ave., Ft. Lauderdale, FL 33315, (954)523-9999 [148]

Solar Electric Specialites Co., 1210 Hornann Dr. SE, Lacey, WA 98503, (360)438-2110 [14324]

Solar Graphic Inc., 3337 22nd Ave. S, St. Petersburg, FL 33712, (813)327-4288 [15660]

Solar Pacific Inc., PO Box 5475, Kent, WA 98064-5475, (253)854-8664 [25822]

Solares Florida Corp., 7625 NW 54th St., Miami, FL 33166, (305)592-0593 [16501]

Solgar Vitamin and Herb Co., PO Box 330, Lynbrook, NY 11563, (516)599-2442 [14241]

Solinger and Associates, 1 E Delaware Pl., Ste. 208, Chicago, IL 60611-1452, (312)951-1011 [15318]

Solis America Inc., 1919 Stanley St., Northbrook, IL 60062-5324, (847)310-6357 [14242]

Solman Distributors Inc., 59 York St., Caribou, ME 04736-2227, (207)493-3389 [2032]

Soloman Metals Corp., Rte. 1-A N, 580 Lynnway, Lynn, MA 01905, (781)581-7000 [26998]

Solomon M. Casket Company of Rhode Island, 31 Slater Rd., Cranston, RI 02920-4467, (401)463-5860 [25823]

Solotken and Company Inc.; J., PO Box 1645, Indianapolis, IN 46206, (317)638-5566 [26999]

Soltex International Inc., 50 Commerce Ctr., Greenville, SC 29615-5814, (864)234-0322 [26208]

Soltis & Co., Inc.; A.R., 34443 Industrial Dr., Livonia, MI 48150, (734)522-1957 [16502]

Solutions, 1330 Russ Ln., McMinnville, OR 97128-5659, (503)472-9017 [6745]

Solutions and Cleaning Products, 208 W Brundage St., Sheridan, WY 82801, (307)672-1846 [4710]

Solutions and Cleaning Products, 208 W Brundage St., Sheridan, WY 82801, (307)672-1846 [24224]

SOM Publishing, School of Metaphysics, World Headquarters, Windyville, MO 65783, (417)345-8411 [4170]

Somers Lumber and Manufacturing Inc., PO Box 87, Union Grove, NC 28689, (704)539-4751 [8040]

Somersault Ltd., PO Box 1771, New York, NY 10016, (212)213-4774 [17611]

Somerset Pharmaceuticals Inc., 5215 W Laurel St., Tampa, FL 33607-1728, (813)288-0040 [19620]

Somerville Co.; Thomas, 4900 Sixth St. NE, Washington, DC 20017, (202)635-4321 [23380]

Somerville Co.; Thomas, 25 Gwynns Mill Ct., Owings Mills, MD 21117, (410)363-1322 [23381]

Somerville Co.; Thomas, 15901 Somerville Dr., Rockville, MD 20855, (301)948-8650 [23382]

Somerville, Co.; Thomas, 1300 Continental Dr., Abingdon, MD 21009-2334, (410)676-6400 [23383]

Somerville Co.; Thomas, 2349 Solomon's Island Rd., Annapolis, MD 21401, (410)266-6022 [23384]

Somerville Co.; Thomas, 11002 Cathal Rd., Berlin, MD 21811, (410)641-5020 [23385]

Somerville Co.; Thomas, PO Box 2247, York, PA 17405, (717)848-1545 [23386]

Somerville Co.; Thomas, 425 Nelson St., Chambersburg, PA 17201, (717)264-9300 [23387]

Somerville Co.; Thomas, 9825 Lee Hwy., Fairfax, VA 22030, (703)273-4900 [23388]

Somerville Co.; Thomas, 3703 Price Club Blvd., Midlothian, VA 23112, (804)745-6400 [23389]

Somerville Co.; Thomas, 824 Professional Place W, Chesapeake, VA 23320, (757)436-2323 [23390]

Somerville Co.; Thomas, 105 Fairfax, Martinsburg, WV 25401, (304)263-4981 [14688]

Sommer Advantage Food Brokers, 2056 Central Ave., Albany, NY 12205, (518)452-1834 [12526]

Sommer Brothers Seed Co., PO Box 248, Pekin, IL 61554, (309)346-2127 [1273]

Sommer Electric Corp., 818 3rd St., NE, Canton, OH 44704, (330)455-9454 [9380]

Sommer Inc.; John, 31 Pamaran Way, Novato, CA 94949, (415)884-2091 [12527]

Sommer and Maca Industries Inc., 5501 W Ogden Ave., Cicero, IL 60804-3507, (773)242-2871 [16503]

Sona Enterprises, 7828 Somerset Blvd., Ste. D, Paramount, CA 90723, (562)633-3002 [13926]

Sona & Hollen Foods Inc., 3712 Cerritos Ave., Los Alamitos, CA 90720-2481, (562)431-1379 [12528]

Sondras Beauty Supply, 1407 Broad St., Providence, RI 02905-2807, (401)781-1916 [14243]

Songtech International Inc., 46560 Fremont Blvd., #109, Fremont, CA 94538, (510)770-9051 [6746]

Sonics and Materials Inc., 53 Church Hill Rd., Newtown, CT 06470, (203)270-4600 [16504]

Sonin Inc., 301 Fields Ln., Ste. 201, Brewster, NY 10509, (845)277-4646 [13927]

Sonnen Mill Valley BMW, 1599 Francisco Blvd. E, San Rafael, CA 94901-5503, (415)388-2750 [20722]

Sontek Industries Inc., 20 Pond Park Rd., Hingham, MA 02043-4327, (781)749-3055 [19044]

Sony Corp. Business and Professional Products Group, Sony Dr., Park Ridge, NJ 07656, (201)930-1000 [25448]

Sony Magnescale America Inc., 20381 Hermana Cir., Lake Forest, CA 92630, (949)770-8400 [24434]

Sony Magnescale America Inc., 20381 Hermana Cir., Lake Forest, CA 92630, (949)770-8400 [25449]

Sony Precision Technology, 20381 Hermana Cir., Lake Forest, CA 92630, (949)770-8400 [24434]

Sony Precision Technology America, Inc., 20381 Hermana Cir., Lake Forest, CA 92630, (949)770-8400 [25449]

Sooner Airgas Inc., 2701 W Reno, Oklahoma City, OK 73108, (405)235-8621 [17180]

Sooner Pipe Inc., PO Box 1530, Tulsa, OK 74101, (918)587-3391 [22681]

Sooner Pipe and Supply Corp., PO Box 1530, Tulsa, OK 74101, (918)587-3391 [22681]

SOR Inc., 14685 W 105th St., Lenexa, KS 66215-5964, (913)888-2630 [9381]

Sorce, Inc., 2495 Walden Ave., Cheektowaga, NY 14225-4717, (716)681-3780 [10156]

Sorcerer Lures, 822 E 2nd St., Duluth, MN 55805, (218)723-8130 [23953]

Sorceror Distributors, 10118 Kinross Ave., Silver Spring, MD 20901, (301)681-8060 [26657]

Sorem and Associates; L.S., 7825 Telegraph Rd., Bloomington, MN 55438-1133, (612)934-0996 [12529]

Sormani Calendars, PO Box 6059, Chelsea, MA 02150-0006, (617)387-7300 [3863]

Sorrell Interiors, 2341 Recreation Dr., West Bloomfield, MI 48324, (810)683-6030 [15661]

SOS Alarm, 3273 Bittle Rd., Medford, OR 97504, (541)772-6668 [24639]

SOS Gases Inc., 1100 Harrison Ave., Kearny, NJ 07032, (201)998-7800 [4515]

Sosnick and Son; J., 258 Littlefield Ave., South San Francisco, CA 94080, (650)952-2226 [12530]

Soukup Brothers Mechanical Inc., 3328 S Highland Dr., Las Vegas, NV 89109-3427, (702)796-1600 [14689]

Soule Steam Feed Works, PO Box 5757, Meridian, MS 39302, (601)693-1982 [16505]

Soule Steam Feed Works, PO Box 5757, Meridian, MS 39302, (601)693-1982 [16506]

Soult Wholesale Co., PO Box 1112, Clearfield, PA 16830, (814)765-5591 [8041]

Sound Advice, 1180 Scenic Dr., Shelby, NC 28150-3239, (704)482-6456 [25450]

Sound Around Inc., 1600 63rd St., Brooklyn, NY 11204, (718)236-8000 [25451]

Sound Around Inc., 1600 63rd St., Brooklyn, NY 11204, (718)236-8000 [15319]

Sound Com Corp., 227 Depot St., Berea, OH 44017, (440)234-2604 [25452]

Sound Engineering, 12933 Farmington Rd., Livonia, MI 48150-4202, (734)522-2910 [5761]

Sound Floor Coverings Inc., 18375 Olympic Ave. S, Tukwila, WA 98188, (206)575-1181 [10157]

Sound Ford Inc., 750 S Rainier Ave., Renton, WA 98055, (425)235-1000 [20723]

Sound Limited Inc., 1246 Blue Lakes Blvd. N, Twin Falls, ID 83301-3307, (208)733-2123 [9382]

Sound Marketing Concepts, 3854 S Peach Way, Denver, CO 80237-1256, (303)758-4303 [9383]

Sound Optical, PO Box 1798, Tacoma, WA 98401, (253)474-0610 [19621]

Sound Warehouse Inc., 516 Elm St., Manchester, NH 03101-2511, (603)668-4979 [3236]

Sound Words Communications, Inc., 1000 S 84th St., Lincoln, NE 68510, (402)483-4541 [25453]

Sounds Write Productions, Inc., 6685 Norman Ln., San Diego, CA 92120, (619)697-6120 [25454]

Source Books, 20341 Sycamore Dr., PO Box 794, Trabuco Canyon, CA 92678, (949)858-1420 [4171]

Source Management Inc., 2460 W 26th Ave., Ste. 370-C, Denver, CO 80211, (303)964-8100 [21274]

Source Technologies Inc., 2910 Whitehall Park Dr., Charlotte, NC 28273, (704)969-7500 [21275]

Souris River Telephone Mutual Aid Cooperative, PO Box 2027, Minot, ND 58702, (701)852-1151 [5762]

South Alabama Brick, 230 Ross Clark Cir. NE, Dothan, AL 36303-5843, (334)794-4173 [10158]

South Asia Books, PO Box 502, Columbia, MO 65205, (573)474-0116 [4172]

South Atlantic Distributing Co., PO Box 1071, Skyland, NC 28776-1071, (704)665-1832 [26658]

South Atlantic Forest Products Inc., 15010 Abercorn Expwy., Savannah, GA 31419, (912)925-1100 [27378]

South Bay Foundry, Inc., 9444 Abraham Way, Santee, CA 92071-2853, (619)596-3825 [20373]

South Bay Growers Inc., PO Box 1207, Clewiston, FL 33440-1207, (561)996-2085 [12531]

South Bay Leather Corp., 3065 Beyer Blvd., Ste. B-101, San Diego, CA 92154, (619)428-7535 [18431]

South Bend Supply Company Inc., PO Box 1996, South Bend, IN 46634, (219)232-1421 [17181]

South Border Imports, Inc., 6925 216th St. SW, Ste. D, Lynnwood, WA 98036-7358, (425)776-1151 [19622]

South Carolina Distributors Inc., 1406 Cherokee Falls Rd., Cherokee Falls, SC 29702, (803)839-2766 [26659]

South Carolina Tees Inc., PO Box 66, Columbia, SC 29202, (803)256-1393 [5368]

South Cedar Greenhouses, 23111 Cedar Ave. S, Farmington, MN 55024-8017, (612)469-3202 [14952]

South Central Co-op, PO Box E, Fairfax, MN 55332, (507)426-8263 [1274]

South Central Co-op, 118 N Meyers Ave., Lacona, IA 50139, (515)534-4071 [1275]

South Central Company Inc., 2685 N National, Columbus, IN 47201, (812)376-3343 [23391]

South Central Cooperative, 310 Logan St., Holdrege, NE 68949, (308)995-8626 [18239]

South Central Pool Supply, Inc., 4310 Hessmer Blvd., Metairie, LA 70002, (504)887-2240 [23954]

South Central Pool Supply, Inc., 149 Distribution Dr., Birmingham, AL 35209, (205)945-9110 [23955]

South Central Pool Supply, Inc., 4800 Southridge, No. 20, Memphis, TN 38141, (901)367-4884 [23956]

South Central Pool Supply, Inc., 1305 N Hills Blvd., No. 105/106, North Little Rock, AR 72114, (501)771-1422 [23957]

South Central Pool Supply, Inc., 9802 Widmer, Lenexa, KS 66215, (913)888-6633 [23958]

South Central Pool Supply, Inc., 10801 Millington Ct., Cincinnati, OH 45242, (513)891-6977 [23959]

South Central Pool Supply, Inc., 2469 Bransford Ave., Nashville, TN 37204, (615)297-1616 [23960]

South Central Pool Supply, Inc., 2235-39 Hwy. 80, W, Jackson, MS 39204, (601)948-7277 [23961]

South Central Pool Supply, Inc., 320 Quapah Ave., N, Oklahoma City, OK 73107, (405)943-1700 [23962]

South Central Pool Supply, Inc., 3691 S 73rd Ave., Tulsa, OK 74145, (918)663-9101 [23963]

South Central Pool Supply, Inc., 4460 South Blvd., Charlotte, NC 28209, (704)522-7946 [23964]

South Central Pool Supply, Inc., 5821A Midway Park, NE, Albuquerque, NM 87109, (505)345-3535 [23965]

South Central Pool Supply, Inc., 9230 Neils Thompson Dr., Ste. 108, Austin, TX 78758-7647, (512)835-4200 [23966]

South Central Pool Supply, Inc., 9307 Millsview Rd., Houston, TX 77070, (281)469-9696 [23967]

South Central Pool Supply, Inc., 11225 Gordon Rd., No. 102, San Antonio, TX 78216, (210)545-6161 [23968]

South Central Pool Supply, Inc., 11140 Leadbetter Rd., Ashland, VA 23005, (804)798-2507 [23969]

South Central Pool Supply, Inc., 12 Parkwood Dr., Hopkinton, MA 01748-1660, (508)435-2321 [23970]

South China Import Inc., 42 W 29th St., New York, NY 10001, (212)689-3688 [24065]

South Coast Recycling Inc., 4560 Doran St., Los Angeles, CA 90039-1006, (213)245-5133 [27000]

South Dakota Livestock Sale, PO Box 164, Watertown, SD 57201-0164, (605)886-4804 [18240]

South Dakota Wheat Growers Association, PO Box 1460, Aberdeen, SD 57401, (605)225-5500 [18241]

South Gateway Tire Co., 65 Market St., Shreveport, LA 71101-2826, (318)222-8415 [3237]

South Jersey X-Ray Supply Co., 8015 Rte. 130 S, Delran, NJ 08075, (609)461-4261 [19045]

South Kentucky Trucks Inc., PO Box 1369, Somerset, KY 42502, (606)679-4321 [3238]

South King Kirby, 635 SW 150th, Seattle, WA 98166, (206)244-6440 [25824]

South Lake Apopka Citrus Growers Association, PO Box 8, Oakland, FL 34760, (954)656-2881 [12532]

South Main Metal Building, 4900 S Main St., Roswell, NM 88201, (505)623-8842 [20374]

South Omaha Supply, 3310 H St., Omaha, NE 68107, (402)731-3100 [18242]

South Pacific Wholesale, PO Box 249, East Montpelier, VT 05651, (802)223-1354 [17612]

South Pier Fish Co., PO Box 5310, Wakefield, RI 02880, (401)783-6611 [12533]

South Shore Produce Co., 216 Riviera Dr. W, Massapequa, NY 11758-8523, (516)799-2223 [12534]

South States, Inc, 6900 Woolworth Rd., Shreveport, LA 71129, (318)686-8527 [13736]

South-Tex Treaters Inc., PO Box 60480, Midland, TX 79711, (915)563-2766 [16507]

South Texas Implement Co., PO Box 35, Taft, TX 78390, (512)528-2535 [1276]

South Texas Lumber Co., 1308 Avenue E, Ozona, TX 76943, (915)392-2634 [8042]

South West New Mexico Communications, Inc., 665 Watson Ln., Las Cruces, NM 88005, (505)524-0202 [5763]

South Wool, PO Box 616, Stockbridge, MA 01262-0616, (413)298-4286 [5369]

Southampton Brick & Tile, Inc., 1540 North Hwy., Southampton, NY 11968, (516)283-8088 [10159]

Southard Supply Inc., 234-6 N 3rd St., Columbus, OH 43215, (614)221-3323 [23392]

Southchem Inc., PO Box 1491, Durham, NC 27702, (919)596-0681 [4516]

Southeast Cooperative Service Co., Hwy. 25 S, Advance, MO 63730, (573)722-3522 [18243]

Southeast Cooperative Service Co., Hwy. 25 S, Advance, MO 63730, (573)722-3522 [1277]

Southeast Dairy Products, 3803 Columbus Dr. E, PO Box 5088, Tampa, FL 33675-5088, (813)621-3233 [12535]

Southeast Frozen Food Co., 18770 NE 6th Ave., Miami, FL 33179, (305)652-4622 [12536]

Southeast Pet, 8005 2nd Flags Dr., SW, Austell, GA 30168, (404)948-7600 [27234]

Southeast Toyota Distributors Inc., 100 NW 12th Ave., Deerfield Beach, FL 33442, (305)429-2000 [20724]

Southeast Wholesale Equipment Distributors Inc., 4400 Zenith St., Metairie, LA 70001-1208, (504)888-2700 [14690]

Southeastern Access Control, PO Box 1968, Tampa, FL 33601, (813)626-3191 [7908]

Southeastern Access Control, PO Box 1968, Tampa, FL 33601, (813)626-3191 [8043]

Southeastern Adhesive Co., PO Box 2070, Lenoir, NC 28645, (704)754-3493 [23035]

Southeastern Colorado Coop., 408 S 1st St., Holly, CO 81047, (719)537-6514 [12537]

Southeastern Colorado Cooperative, 408 S 1st St., Holly, CO 81047, (719)537-6514 [1278]

Southeastern Communications, 3402 Oakcliff Rd., Ste. B-4, Atlanta, GA 30340, (404)455-0672 [9384]

Southeastern Construction Inc., PO Box 203, Avon, MA 02322, (781)767-2202 [8044]

Southeastern Equipment Company Inc., PO Box 536, Cambridge, OH 43725, (614)432-6131 [8045]

Southeastern Industries Inc., PO Box 809, Reidsville, NC 27320, (910)349-6243 [27001]

Southeastern Mills Inc., PO Box 908, Rome, GA 30161, (706)291-6528 [12538]

Southeastern Optical Corp., PO Box 12700, Roanoke, VA 24027, (540)989-8644 [19623]

Southeastern Paper Group, Wadsworth Industrial Pk., PO Box 6220, Spartanburg, SC 29304, (864)574-0440 [21943]

Southeastern Skate Supply of Virginia Inc., PO Box 12448, Roanoke, VA 24025, (540)342-7871 [23971]

Southeastern Supply Company Inc., PO Box 516, Indianapolis, IN 46206, (317)359-9551 [8046]

Southern Agriculture Insecticides Inc., PO Box 218, Palmetto, FL 34220, (813)722-3285 [1279]

Southern Apparel Corp., E 3rd Ext., Robersonville, NC 27871, (919)795-3031 [5370]

Southern Apparel Corp., 12420 73rd Ct. W, Largo, FL 33773, (813)536-8672 [5371]

Southern Architectural Systems, Inc., 10038 Talley Ln., PO Box 40223, Houston, TX 77240-0223, (713)462-6379 [8047]

Southern Automotive Inc., 597 N Saginaw St., Pontiac, MI 48342, (810)335-5555 [3239]

Southern Belting & Transmission, 218 Ottley Dr. NE, Atlanta, GA 30324, (404)875-1655 [16508]

Southern Belting & Transmissions, 6021 Coca Cola Blvd., Columbus, GA 31907, (706)561-6946 [17182]

Southern Beverage Company Inc., PO Box 1349, Jackson, MS 39215, (601)969-5550 [25038]

Southern Book Service, 5154 NW 165th St., Palmetto Lakes Industrial Pk., Hialeah, FL 33014-6335, (305)624-4545 [3572]

Southern Business Communications Inc., 3175 Corners North Ct., Norcross, GA 30071, (770)449-4088 [6747]

Southern Business Systems Inc., 4945 American Way, Memphis, TN 38118, (901)368-0044 [21276]

Southern California Air-Conditioning Distributors, 16900 E Chestnut St., La Puente, CA 91748, (626)854-4500 [14691]

Southern California Airgas Inc., 4007 Paramount Blvd., No. 100, Lakewood, CA 90712-4138, (310)329-7517 [17183]

Southern California Pipe and Steel Co., 12711 E Imperial Hwy., Santa Fe Springs, CA 90670, (562)868-1734 [8048]

Southern California Tees, 5201 6th St., Carpinteria, CA 93013, (805)684-0252 [5372]

Southern California Trophy Co., 2515 S Broadway, Los Angeles, CA 90007-2729, (213)623-3166 [13448]

Southern Carbide Specialists Inc., 901 N Highland Ave., PO Box 69, Quitman, GA 31643-0069, (912)263-8927 [13928]

Southern Commercial Machines, 2256 N Wakefield St., No. 100, Arlington, VA 22207-3529, (703)528-5202 [25825]

Southern Company Inc., PO Box 343, Williamsburg, VA 23187-0343, (757)229-2311 [22682]

Southern Contracts, 1608 Ridgeland Rd. W, Mobile, AL 36695-2720, (205)343-4777 [6748]

Southern Copy Machines, 495 Hawthorne Ave., Ste. 106, Athens, GA 30606-2503, (706)353-0229 [21277]

Southern Cross and O'Fallon Building Products Co., PO Box 907, O Fallon, MO 63366, (314)272-6226 [13929]

Southern Cross and O'Fallon Building Products Co., PO Box 907, O Fallon, MO 63366, (314)240-6226 [8049]

Southern Data Systems Inc., 6758 Shiloh Rd. E, Alpharetta, GA 30005-8364 [6749]

Southern Distributing, 3212 Milledgeville Rd., Augusta, GA 30909, (706)736-5526 [25455]

Southern Distributors Corp., 4730 Wynn Rd., Las Vegas, NV 89103-5422, (702)871-4166 [7649]

Southern Distributors Inc., 818 Perry St., Richmond, VA 23224-2230, (804)231-1128 [15662]

Southern Electric Service Company, Inc., 2225 Freedom Dr., Charlotte, NC 28208, (704)372-4832 [9385]

Southern Electric Supply Company Inc., 7401 W Ellis Rd., Melbourne, FL 32904, (407)768-0223 [9386]

Southern Electric Supply Company Inc., 301 46th Ct., Meridian, MS 39301, (601)693-4141 [9387]

Southern Electronics Corp., 4916 N Royal Atlanta Rd., Tucker, GA 30085, (770)491-8962 [6717]

Southern Electronics Supply, Inc., 1909 Tulane Ave., New Orleans, LA 70112, (504)524-2345 [9388]

Southern Farm and Home Center, PO Box 1566, Hattiesburg, MS 39403, (601)582-3545 [1280]

Southern Filters Inc., 284 Snow Dr., Birmingham, AL 35209, (205)942-5817 [17184]

Southern Flooring Distributors, PO Box 30337, Charlotte, NC 28230-0337 [10160]

Southern Flooring Distributors, 2008 Brengle Ave., Orlando, FL 32808, (407)578-7448 [10161]

Southern Flooring Distributors, 6675 Jimmy Carter Blvd., Norcross, GA 30071, (404)237-9276 [10162]

Southern Flooring Distributors, 727 Lakeside Dr., Mobile, AL 36693, (205)666-1587 [10163]

Southern Flooring Distributors, 1001 S Dupre St., New Orleans, LA 70125, (504)821-2211 [10164]

Southern Floral Co., 1313 W 20th, Houston, TX 77008-1639, (713)880-1300 [14953]

Southern Fluid Power, 2900 Dodds Ave., Chattanooga, TN 37407, (423)698-5888 [17185]

Southern Foods Inc., 117 Mitch McConnell Way, PO Box 1657, Bowling Green, KY 42102-1657, (270)843-1121 [12539]

Southern Gourmet Products Inc., 15925 NW 52nd Ave., Miami Lakes, FL 33014, (305)625-8888 [10881]

Southern Hardware Company Inc., PO Box 2508, West Helena, AR 72390-0508, (501)572-6761 [13930]

Southern Hardware and Supply Company Ltd., PO Box 1792, Monroe, LA 71210, (318)387-5000 [17186]

Southern Highland Accordions & Dulcimers Ltd., 1010 S 14th St., Slaton, TX 79364, (806)828-5358 [25456]

Southern Holdings Inc., 4801 Florida Ave., New Orleans, LA 70126, (504)944-3371 [27002]

Southern Ice Equipment Distributor, 4217 W Northside Dr., No. B, Jackson, MS 39213, (601)923-3332 [16509]

Southern Illinois Lumber Co., 204 W Main St., Fairfield, IL 62837, (618)842-3733 [8050]

Southern Illinois Wholesale Company Inc., Rte. 2, Box 234-A, Carterville, IL 62918, (618)985-3767 [2033]

Southern Importers Inc., PO Box 8579, Greensboro, NC 27419, (336)292-4521 [14954]

Southern Industrial Corp., 9009 Regency Square Blvd., Jacksonville, FL 32211, (904)725-4122 [24225]

Southern Interiors Inc., 2541 Farrisview Blvd., Memphis, TN 38118-1502, (901)363-7357 [15663]

Southern Leather Co., PO Box 6, Memphis, TN 38101, (901)525-1200 [24866]

Southern Leather Co., PO Box 6, Memphis, TN 38101, (901)774-0400 [5373]

Southern Lighting and Supply Company Inc., PO Box 16960, Memphis, TN 38116, (901)345-2871 [9389]

Southern Livestock Supply Co. Inc., 7333 Town S Ave., Baton Rouge, LA 70808-4141, (225)769-5811 [1281]

Southern LNG Inc., PO Box 2563, Birmingham, AL 35202, (205)325-7410 [22683]

Southern Machinery Company Inc., PO Box 110768, Nashville, TN 37222-0768, (615)832-3365 [16510]

Southern Metals Company Inc., PO Box 668923, Charlotte, NC 28266, (704)394-3161 [27003]

Southern Micro Instruments, 1700 Enterprise Way, Ste. 112, Marietta, GA 30067, (770)956-0343 [19624]

Southern Minnesota Machinery Sales Inc., 210 South St., Dodge Center, MN 55927, (507)374-6346 [16511]

Southern Motorcycle Supply, 3670 Ruffin Rd., San Diego, CA 92123-1810, (858)560-5005 [3240]

Southern Nevada Auto Parts Inc., 2221 Losee Rd., North Las Vegas, NV 89030-4106, (702)642-1333 [3241]

Southern Nevada T.B.A. Supply Inc., 1701 Las Vegas Blvd S, Las Vegas, NV 89104, (702)732-2382 [3242]

Southern New Mexico Office Machines, PO Box 940, Mesilla Park, NM 88047-0940, (505)525-1322 [21278]

Southern Office Furniture Distributors Inc., PO Box 49009, Greensboro, NC 27419, (919)668-4195 [21279]

Southern Optical Co., 103 J & L Dr., PO Box 8006, Goldsboro, NC 27530-8006, (919)735-2084 [19625]

Southern Optical Co., PO Box 2227, Greenville, SC 29602, (864)232-6762 [19626]

Southern Optical, Inc., PO Box 21328, Greensboro, NC 27420, (919)272-8146 [19627]

Southern Power Inc., 2001 Oak Mountain Dr., Pelham, AL 35124, (205)664-2001 [3243]

Southern Produce Inc., 1100 Pleasantville Dr., Houston, TX 77029-3232, (713)678-9000 [12540]

Southern Prosthetic Supply, PO Box 406, Alpharetta, GA 30009-0406, (770)442-9870 [19046]

Southern Prosthetic Supply Co., PO Box 406, Alpharetta, GA 30009, (770)442-9870 [19628]

Southern Publishers Group, Inc., 3918 Montclair Rd., Ste. 108, PO Box 130460, Birmingham, AL 35213, (205)870-9834 [4173]

Southern Pump and Filter Inc., 2883 Directors Cove, Memphis, TN 38131-0398, (901)332-4890 [25826]

Southern Pump and Filter Inc., 2883 Directors Cove, Memphis, TN 38131-0398, (901)332-4890 [16512]

Southern Pump and Tank Co., PO Box 31516, Charlotte, NC 28231, (704)596-4373 [16513]

Southern Refrigeration Corp., 2026 Salem Ave., Roanoke, VA 24027, (703)342-3493 [14692]

Southern Rubber Company Inc., PO Box 7039, Greensboro, NC 27417-0039, (919)299-2456 [17187]

Southern Sash Sales and Supply Co., PO Box 471, Sheffield, AL 35660, (205)383-3261 [8051]

Southern Scrap Material Company Ltd., PO Box 12388, Pensacola, FL 32582, (850)438-3197 [27004]

Southern Scrap Material Company Ltd., PO Box 26087, New Orleans, LA 70186, (504)942-0340 [27005]

Southern Seafood Co., 7901 Oceano Ave., Jessup, MD 20794, (410)799-5641 [12541]

A Southern Season, Eastgate Shopping Center, Chapel Hill, NC 27514, (919)929-7133 [12542]

Southern Specialty Corp., 5334 Distributor Dr., Richmond, VA 23225-6104, (804)232-5164 [8052]

Southern States Cooperative Inc., PO Box 26234, Richmond, VA 23260, (804)281-1000 [1282]

Southern States Cooperative Inc., PO Box 26234, Richmond, VA 23260, (804)281-1000 [1283]

Southern States Frederick Cooperative Inc., PO Box 694, Frederick, MD 21705, (301)663-6164 [1284]

Southern States Industrial Sales, PO Box 885, Paris, TN 38242-0885, (901)642-0885 [15320]

Southern States Lumber Company Inc., PO Box 265, Laurens, SC 29360, (864)984-4531 [8053]

Southern States Madisonville Cooperative, 1001 Pride Ave., Madisonville, KY 42431, (502)821-3325 [18244]

Southern Store Fixtures Inc., 275 Drexel Rd. SE, Bessemer, AL 35022, (205)428-4800 [8054]

Southern Tea Co., 1267 Cobb Industrial Dr., Marietta, GA 30066, (770)428-5555 [12543]

Southern Territory Associates, PO Box 13519, Arlington, TX 76094, (817)861-9644 [4174]

Southern Tile Distributors Inc., 1328 Canton Rd., Marietta, GA 30066, (404)423-0858 [10165]

Southern Tile Distributors Inc., 1814 Mt. Zion Rd., Morrow, GA 30260, (404)961-6179 [10166]

Southern Valley Co-op, 301 W Mabel St., Mankato, MN 56001, (507)625-7077 [22684]

Southern Watch Inc., 1239 Broadway, Ste. 1406, New York, NY 10001, (212)689-3995 [17613]

Southern Wholesale Co., PO Box 410368, Charlotte, NC 28241-0368, (704)588-0930 [1565]

Southern Wholesale Co., PO Box 5151, Rome, GA 30162-5151, (706)235-8155 [19629]

Southern Wholesalers Inc., 418 S Glenwood Ave., Dalton, GA 30720, (706)278-1583 [23393]

Southern Wine Co., 2614 3rd, Tuscaloosa, AL 35401-1024, (205)752-2596 [2034]

Southern Wine & Spirits, 1600 NW 163rd St., Miami, FL 33169-5641, (305)625-4171 [2035]

Southern Wine & Spirits, 1099 Rocket Blvd., Orlando, FL 32824, (407)855-7610 [2036]

Southern Wine & Spirits, 5210 16th Ave. S, Tampa, FL 33619, (813)623-1288 [2037]

Southern Wine & Spirits, 4500 Wynn Rd., Las Vegas, NV 89103, (702)876-4500 [2038]

Southern Wine & Spirits, 960 United Cir., Sparks, NV 89431, (702)355-4500 [2039]

Southern Wine and Spirits of America, 1600 NW 163rd St., Miami, FL 33169, (305)652-4171 [2040]

Southern Wine and Spirits of California Inc., 17101 Valley View Rd., Cerritos, CA 90701, (562)926-2000 [2041]

Southern Wisconsin News, 1858 Artisan Rd., Rte. 3, Edgerton, WI 53534, (608)884-2600 [4175]

Southford Garage Truck Equippers, Rte. Jct. 67 & 188, PO Box 174, Southbury, CT 06488, (203)264-5343 [3244]

Southland Carpet Supplies, 1450 N Wood Dale Rd., Wood Dale, IL 60191-1096 [10167]

Southland Carpet Supplies, 1450 N Wood Dale Rd., Wood Dale, IL 60191-1096, (630)227-1600 [10168]

Southland Distributors, 36 Sugar Loaf Rd. C., Hendersonville, NC 28792, (828)696-3535 [8055]

Southland Flooring Supplies Inc., 1450 N Wood Dale Rd., Wood Dale, IL 60191-1096, (630)227-1600 [10168]

Southland Flooring Supply, 6019 E 30th St., Indianapolis, IN 46219, (317)541-3333 [10169]

Southland Floors, Inc., 2701 NW 17th Ln., Pompano Beach, FL 33064-1561, (954)974-4700 [10170]

Southside Ford Truck Sales Inc., 810 W Pershing Rd., Chicago, IL 60609, (312)247-4000 [20725]

Southside Recycling Inc., 4076 Bayless Ave., St. Louis, MO 63125, (314)631-3400 [27006]

Southtowns Seafood & Meats, PO Box 1956, Blasdell, NY 14219-0156, (716)824-4900 [12544]

Southwark Metal Manufacturing Co., 1600 Washington Ave., Philadelphia, PA 19146, (215)735-3401 [20375]

Southwest Bingo Supply, 2112 2nd St. SW, Albuquerque, NM 87102-4513, (505)842-0022 [26660]

Southwest Book Co., 13003 H Murphy Rd., Stafford, TX 77477, (281)498-2603 [4176]

Southwest Business Furniture, 3110 McKinney, Houston, TX 77003, (713)227-4141 [13248]

Southwest Cookbook Distributors, Inc., PO Box 707, Bonham, TX 75418, (903)583-8898 [4177]

Southwest Cooperative Wholesale, 1821 E Jackson St., Phoenix, AZ 85034, (602)254-5644 [18245]

Southwest CTI Inc., 3625 W MacArthur Blvd., Ste. 311, Santa Ana, CA 92704-6849, (949)453-6200 [6750]

Southwest Distributing Inc., PO Box 25025, Albuquerque, NM 87125, (505)345-4488 [10990]

Southwest DoAll Industrial Supply, 514 Riverdale Dr., Glendale, CA 91204, (818)243-3153 [16514]

Southwest Electronics Inc., 12701 Royal Dr., Stafford, TX 77477, (281)240-5672 [9390]

Southwest Energy Distributors Inc., 415 N Grant Ave., Odessa, TX 79760, (915)332-1301 [22685]

Southwest Florida Auction Inc., PO Box 1646, Ft. Myers, FL 33902, (941)337-5141 [20726]

Southwest Grain Farm Marketing and Supply Div., PO Box 239, Lemmon, SD 57638, (605)374-3301 [22686]

Southwest Hallowell Inc., 637 S Rockford Dr., Tempe, AZ 85281, (602)966-3988 [16515]

Southwest Hide Co., 250 Beechwood Dr., Ste. 180, Boise, ID 83709-0944, (208)378-8000 [18246]

Southwest Import Co., 7047 Casa Loma, Dallas, TX 75214, (214)327-8006 [13449]

Southwest Modern Data Systems, 2816 NW 57th St., Ste. 101, Oklahoma City, OK 73112-7042, (405)842-6710 [6751]

Southwest Paper Company Inc., PO Box 21270, Wichita, KS 67208-7270, (316)838-7755 [21944]

Southwest Plywood and Lumber Corp., 11852 Alameda St., Lynwood, CA 90262-4019 [8056]

Southwest Specialties, PO Box 5407, San Clemente, CA 92674-5407, (949)492-3070 [12545]

Southwest Sporting Goods Co., PO Box 471, Arkadelphia, AR 71923-0471, (870)246-2311 [23972]

Southwest Stainless Inc., 8505 Monroe Ave., Houston, TX 77061, (713)943-3790 [20376]

Southwest Steel, 300 N 17th St., Las Cruces, NM 88001, (505)526-5412 [20377]

Southwest Steel Supply Co., 3401 Morganford Rd., St. Louis, MO 63116, (314)664-6100 [20378]

Southwest Wire Rope Inc., 1902 Federal Rd., Houston, TX 77015, (713)453-8518 [17188]

Southwestern Camera, 500 N Shepard, Houston, TX 77007, (713)880-0121 [22906]

Southwestern Ceramic, Tile & Marble Co., 999 Racheros Dr., No. A, San Marcos, CA 92069-3028, (619)298-3511 [10171]

Southwestern Ceramic, Tile & Marble Co., 999 Rancheros Dr., San Marcos, CA 92069-3028, (760)741-2033 [10172]

Southwestern Gold Inc., PO Box 9083, Albuquerque, NM 87119-9083, (505)881-3636 [17614]

Southwestern Irrigated Cotton Growers Association, PO Box 1709, El Paso, TX 79949, (915)581-5441 [18247]

Southwestern Jewelry & Gifts, 1117 S White Sands Blvd., Alamogordo, NM 88310-7251, (505)437-9828 [17615]

Southwestern Ohio Steel Inc., PO Box 148, Hamilton, OH 45012-0148, (513)896-2700 [20379]

Southwestern Suppliers Inc., 6815 E 14th Ave., PO Box 75069, Tampa, FL 33675-0069, (813)626-2193 [20380]

Southwestern Tobacco Co., 201 Price Rd., Lexington, KY 40511-1995, (606)253-2401 [26351]

Southwestern Wholesale Co. Inc., PO Box 18033, Shreveport, LA 71138-1033, (318)222-3184 [5374]

Southwire Co., 3555 W Washington St., Phoenix, AZ 85009, (602)233-1777 [17189]

Southworth-Milton Inc., 100 Quarry Dr., Milford, MA 01757, (508)634-3400 [1285]

Sovana, Inc., 4500 Fuller Dr., Ste. 426, Irving, TX 75038, (972)541-1100 [1286]

Sovereign Distributors, Inc., 3157 Fire Rd., Pleasantville, NJ 08232, (609)641-2770 [10173]

Soviet American Woolens, 475 Porterfield Rd., Porter, ME 04068 [26209]

Soyad Brothers Textile Corp., 24011 Hoover Rd., Warren, MI 48089, (810)755-5700 [5375]

Space Designs Inc., 2740 Zanker Rd., Ste. 100, San Jose, CA 95134-2116, (408)432-5600 [13209]

Space Page Inc., 16 Ketchum St., Westport, CT 06880-5908, (203)454-4150 [5764]

Spacecraft Components Corp., 14137 Chadrow Ave., Hawthorne, CA 90251-5027, (310)973-6400 [149]

SpaceLabs Medical Inc., PO Box 97013, Redmond, WA 98073, (425)882-3700 [19630]

SPADA Enterprises Ltd., 2711 SE Woodward St., Portland, OR 97202-1357, (503)234-9215 [12546]

Spadafore Distributing Co., 635 Filley St., Lansing, MI 48906, (517)485-4300 [2042]

Spahn and Rose Lumber Co., PO Box 149, Dubuque, IA 52004-0149, (319)582-3606 [8057]

Spainhower; Vic, 16680 S Beckman Rd., Oregon City, OR 97045-9302, (503)631-2291 [6752]

Spalding Cooperative Elevator Co., PO Box B, Spalding, NE 68665, (308)497-2266 [1287]

Spalding Holdings Corp., 425 Meadow St., Chicopee, MA 01021, (413)536-1200 [5376]

Spaman Jewellers; W.M., 112 W South, Kalamazoo, MI 49007-4711, (616)345-2073 [17616]

Spanish & European Bookstore Inc., 3102 Wilshire Blvd., Los Angeles, CA 90010, (213)739-8899 [4178]

SPAP Company International, PO Box 680, Huntington Beach, CA 92648, (714)960-0586 [4517]

SPAP Company LLC, PO Box 680, Huntington Beach, CA 92648, (714)960-0586 [4517]

Spar Medical Inc., 1606 Green Springs Hwy. S, Birmingham, AL 35205-4547, (205)252-2992 [19047]

Spar Tek Industries Inc., PO Box 17375, Portland, OR 97217, (503)283-4749 [16516]

Sparkomatic Corp., PO Box 277, Milford, PA 18337-0277, (717)296-6444 [25457]

Sparks Game & Toy Co., PO Box 2361, Pikeville, KY 41502-2361, (606)754-8069 [26661]

Sparlon Hosiery Mills Inc., 1600 SW 66th Ave., Pembroke Pines, FL 33023, (954)966-2050 [5377]

Sparrow-Star, 101 Winners Cir., Brentwood, TN 37024, (615)371-6800 [4179]

Spartan Distributors Inc., 487 W Division St., Sparta, MI 49345, (616)887-7301 [1288]

Spartan Iron Metal Company Inc., 826 N 3rd St., Philadelphia, PA 19123, (215)627-5344 [27007]

Spartan Lobster Traps Inc., 4 Walts Way, Narragansett, RI 02882-3438, (401)789-5350 [18613]

Spartan Oil Co., PO Box 710, Dover, NJ 07802-0710, (973)328-3434 [22687]

Spartan Pet Supply, 75 Modular Ave., Commack, NY 11725, (516)864-3222 [27235]

Spartan Petroleum Company Inc., PO Box 307, Cliffside, NC 28024-0307, (704)453-7351 [22688]

Spartan Sporting Goods Inc., 113 Appalachian Dr., Beckley, WV 25801-2201, (304)255-1434 [23973]

Spartan Stores Inc., PO Box 8700, Grand Rapids, MI 49518, (616)878-2000 [12547]

Spartan Stores Inc., PO Box 8700, Grand Rapids, MI 49518, (616)878-2000 [12548]

Spartan Supply Company Inc., 2600 Walker Rd., Chattanooga, TN 37421, (423)894-3007 [23588]

Spartan Tool Supply, 1660 Alum Creek Dr., Columbus, OH 43209-2709, (614)443-7607 [13931]

Spas Unlimited, 209 Mobile Ave., Trussville, AL 35173-1955 [23974]

Spatron Inc., 2468 Mariondale Ave., Los Angeles, CA 90032-3517, (323)227-6821 [9391]

Spaulding Brick Company Inc., 120 Middlesex Ave., Somerville, MA 02145, (617)666-3200 [8058]

Spaulding Brick Company Inc., 250 Station St., Cranston, RI 02910, (401)467-2220 [8059]

Spaulding Company Inc., 80-90 Hawes Way, Stoughton, MA 02072, (617)828-8090 [25458]

Spaz Beverage Co., 890 S Matlack, West Chester, PA 19382-4956, (215)696-6320 [25039]

SPC Corp., 26th St. & Penrose Ave., Philadelphia, PA 19145, (215)952-1501 [27008]

Speaker Company, Inc.; Guy, 14620 Martin Dr., Eden Prairie, MN 55344, (612)937-8705 [24435]

Speaks Oil Company Inc., PO Box 68, Camden, SC 29020, (803)432-3501 [22689]

Spear Oil Co., PO Box 128, Lapine, AL 36046, (205)537-4334 [22690]

Speartex Grain Co., PO Box 248, Spearman, TX 79081, (806)659-3711 [18248]

Special Care Medical Inc., PO Box 21564, Columbia, SC 29221-1564, (803)926-0161 [19048]

Special Fleet Service, 875 Waterman Dr., PO Box 990, Harrisonburg, VA 22801, (540)434-4488 [3245]

Special Mine Services Inc., PO Box 188, West Frankfort, IL 62896, (618)932-2151 [9392]

Special Promotion Co., 3655 N 2400 E, Layton, UT 84040, (801)771-3649 [26662]

Special Purpose Systems Inc., PO Box C-96078, Bellevue, WA 98009-9678, (425)451-8077 [6753]

Special-T-Metals Company Inc., 15850 W 108th St., Shawnee Mission, KS 66219-1340, (913)492-9500 [13932]

Specialized Marketing, 138 West St., Annapolis, MD 21401-2802, (410)267-0545 [21280]

Specialized Marketing, PO Box 809, Marshall, CA 94940, (510)420-1134 [12549]

Specialized Marketing, 138 West St., Annapolis, MD 21401-2802, (410)267-0545 [13249]

Specialized Sales and Service Inc., PO Box 968, Klamath Falls, OR 97601, (541)884-5103 [3246]

Specially Yours Inc., 3651 Joppa Ave. S, Minneapolis, MN 55416-4815, (612)927-4246 [13450]

Specialties Co., PO Box 266084, Houston, TX 77207, (713)644-1491 [24295]

Specialties of Surgery Inc., PO Box 560, Jenks, OK 74037-0560, (918)299-4970 [19049]

Specialty Box and Packaging Co., 1040 Broadway, Albany, NY 12204, (518)465-7344 [21945]

Specialty Building Products, Inc., 7505-C Veterans Pkwy., Columbus, GA 31909-2501, (706)327-0668 [10174]

Specialty Building Products Inc., 7505-C Veterans Pkwy., Columbus, GA 31909-2501, (706)327-0668 [8060]

Specialty Catalog Corp., 21 Bristol Dr., South Easton, MA 02375, (508)238-0199 [14244]

Specialty Chemical Company, Inc., PO Box 2606, Cleveland, TN 37320-2606, (423)479-9664 [4518]

Specialty Control Systems Inc., 100 E Nasa Rd. 1, Ste. 301, Webster, TX 77598, (281)332-0999 [9393]

Specialty Distribution, PO Box 1328, Greenville, SC 29602, (864)676-8600 [12550]

Specialty Distribution, 402 Staats Ave., PO Box 305, Maupin, OR 97037, (541)395-2553 [10175]

Specialty Distribution, PO Box 1004, Greenville, SC 29602, (864)295-8199 [12240]

Specialty Food Distributors, Inc., 4006 Airport Rd., Plant City, FL 33567-1124, (813)752-8558 [12551]

Specialty Grain Products Co., PO Box 3100, Omaha, NE 68103, (402)595-4000 [12552]

Specialty Hearse and Ambulance Sales Corp., 180 Dupont St., Plainview, NY 11803, (516)349-7700 [20727]

Specialty Hearse and Ambulance Sales Corp., 180 Dupont St., Plainview, NY 11803, (516)349-7700 [3247]

Specialty House Inc., 411 5th Ave., No. 700, New York, NY 10016, (212)532-0700 [5378]

Specialty Marketing Inc., PO Box 308, Mechanicsville, VA 23111-0308, (804)746-9683 [25459]

Specialty Merchandise Corp., 9401 De Soto Ave., Chatsworth, CA 91311-4991, (818)998-3300 [13451]

Specialty Metals, 2355 Tecumseh St., Baton Rouge, LA 70802, (504)358-0400 [20382]

Specialty Metals Industries, 42299 Winchester Rd., Temecula, CA 92590, (909)693-1300 [20381]

Specialty Metals and Minerals Inc., 2355 Tecumseh St., Baton Rouge, LA 70802, (504)358-0400 [20382]

Specialty Metals Supply Inc., 750 Ridgewood Rd., Ridgeland, MS 39157, (601)956-8555 [20383]

Specialty Pipe and Tube Co., PO Box 3116, Warren, OH 44485, (330)394-2512 [20384]

Specialty Products Inc., PO Box 565, Fairfield, AL 35064-0565, (205)785-1116 [17190]

Specialty Promotions Co., Inc., 6841 S Cregier Ave., Chicago, IL 60649, (773)493-6900 [4180]

Specialty Supply Co., 4364 Mangum St., Flowood, MS 39208, (601)936-4900 [9394]

Specialty Surgical Instrumentation Inc., 200 River Hills Dr., Nashville, TN 37210, (615)883-9090 [19050]

Specialty Vehicles Inc., 180 Dupont St., Plainview, NY 11803, (516)349-7700 [20727]

Specialty Vehicles, Inc., 16351 Gothard St., Ste. C., Huntington Beach, CA 92647, (714)848-8455 [20728]

Specialty Vehicles Inc., 16351 Gothard St., Ste. C., Huntington Beach, CA 92647, (714)848-8455 [3248]

Specialty World Foods Inc., 84 Montgomery St., Albany, NY 12207, (518)436-7603 [12553]

Spectacular Modes Inc., 2036-A NW 23rd Ave., Miami, FL 33142-7354, (305)634-7575 [5379]

Spectranetics Corp., 96 Talamine Ct., Colorado Springs, CO 80907, (719)633-8333 [19631]

Spectronic Instruments Inc., 820 Linden Ave., Rochester, NY 14625, (716)248-4000 [24436]

Spectronics Inc., 11230 NW Reeves St., Portland, OR 97229, (503)643-8030 [16517]

Spectrum, 1791 Hurstview Dr., Hurst, TX 76054-3430, (817)280-9898 [25460]

Spectrum Communications Corp., 1055 W Germantown Pike, Norristown, PA 19403-3912, (215)631-1710 [5765]

Spectrum Computer & Business Supplies, 205 Windward Dr., Ste. B, Ocean City, MD 21842-4830, (410)524-0528 [6754]

Spectrum Corp., PO Box 57, Rigby, ID 83442-0057, (208)745-8706 [25827]

Spectrum Data Products, 4003D Green Briar Dr., Stafford, TX 77477, (281)240-3322 [24407]

Spectrum Data Systems Inc., 1400 Lake Hearn Dr., Ste. 190, Atlanta, GA 30319-1464, (404)843-5560 [6755]

Spectrum Financial System Inc., 163 McKenzie Rd., Mooresville, NC 28115, (704)663-4466 [21281]

Spectrum Labs Inc., 301 W County Rd., Ste. E2, New Brighton, MN 55112, (612)633-0101 [4519]

Spectrum Labs Inc., PO Box 1685, Mesa, AZ 85211, (480)464-8971 [19632]

Spectrum Lighting/Sound & Beyond, 602 W 22nd St., Tempe, AZ 85282, (480)968-4334 [25828]

Spectrum Office Products Inc., 125 Mushroom Blvd., Rochester, NY 14692, (716)424-3600 [21289]

The Speech Bin, Inc., 1965 25th Ave., Vero Beach, FL 32960, (561)770-0007 [4181]

Speed Brite Inc., 1810 W Innes St., Salisbury, NC 28144-1766, (704)639-9771 [4711]

Speed Brite Inc., 1810 W Innes St., Salisbury, NC 28144-1766, (704)639-9771 [4711]

Speed-O-Motive, 12061 E Slauson Ave., Santa Fe Springs, CA 90670, (562)945-3444 [3249]

Speedimpex USA, Inc., 35-02 48th Ave., Long Island City, NY 11101, (718)392-7477 [4182]

Speen & Company Inc., PO Box 2408, Woburn, MA 01888-0708, (781)933-8490 [24867]

Speiser Pet Supplies, 7040 SW 21st Pl., Davie, FL 33317, (954)472-1404 [27236]

Spellbinders Inc., 257 S Water St., Kent, OH 44240-3525, (330)673-2230 [26663]

Spellman Hardwoods Inc., 4645 N 43rd Ave., Phoenix, AZ 85031, (602)272-2313 [8061]

Spelts-Schultz Lumber Company of Grand Island, PO Box 1447, Grand Island, NE 68802, (308)382-9656 [7102]

Spencer Chain Gear Co., 8410 Dallas Ave. S, Seattle, WA 98108-4423, (206)762-6767 [3250]

Spencer Companies Inc. (Huntsville, Alabama), PO Box 18128, Huntsville, AL 35804, (256)533-1150 [22691]

Spencer County Cooperative Associates Inc., PO Box 7, Chrisney, IN 47611, (812)362-7701 [1289]

Spencer Engine Inc., 1114 W Cass St., Tampa, FL 33606, (813)253-6035 [398]

Spencer Fruit Co., 1500 W Manning Ave., Reedley, CA 93654, (209)659-2055 [12554]

Spencer Industries, 1930 Rudkin Rd., Yakima, WA 98903, (509)248-0580 [17191]

Spencer Industries Inc., 8410 Dallas Ave., Seattle, WA 98108, (206)763-0210 [17192]

Spencer Industries Inc. Chain Gear Div., Chain Gear Div., 1229 S Orr, Seattle, WA 98108, (206)762-6767 [3251]

Spencer Industries Inc. (Seattle, Washington), 8410 Dallas Ave., Seattle, WA 98108, (206)763-0210 [150]

Spencer Products Co., 1859 Summit Commerce Park, Twinsburg, OH 44087-2370, (216)475-8700 [13933]

Sperry Instruments Inc.; A.W., PO Box 9300, Smithtown, NY 11787, (631)231-7050 [24437]

SPH Crane and Hoist Div., 2920 National Ct., Garland, TX 75041, (972)272-3599 [8062]

Sphar & Co., PO Box 849, New Albany, IN 47151-0849, (812)744-1671 [1290]

Spicers Paper Inc., 12310 E Slauson Ave., Santa Fe Springs, CA 90670, (562)698-1199 [21946]

Spiegel and Sons Oil Corp.; M., 10 E Village Rd., Tuxedo, NY 10987, (914)351-4701 [22692]

Spiewak, 469 7th Ave., 10th Fl., New York, NY 10018, (212)695-1620 [5380]

Spiewalk & Sons, Inc.; I., 469 7th Ave., 10th Fl., New York, NY 10018, (212)695-1620 [5380]

Spil Co.; Samuel, Box 220074, Charlotte, NC 28222, (704)364-3051 [17617]

Spinal Analysis Machine, 660 Middlegate Rd., Henderson, NV 89015-2608, (702)565-2633 [19051]

Spindler Co., 4430 Portage Rd., North Canton, OH 44720-7397, (330)499-2560 [12555]

Spinnaker Software, 500 Redwood Blvd., Novato, CA 94947-6921 [6737]

Spiral, 1500 S Western Ave., Chicago, IL 60608, (312)738-0622 [15664]

Spiral Binding Company Inc., PO Box 286, Totowa, NJ 07511, (973)256-0666 [21282]

The Spiral Collection, Inc., 1500 S Western Ave., Chicago, IL 60608, (312)738-0622 [15664]

Spirit Distributing Co., 5656 Morris Hill Rd., Boise, ID 83706, (208)378-0550 [2043]

Spirit II Distributing Inc., 5656 Morris Hill Rd., Boise, ID 83706, (208)378-0550 [2043]

Spitzer Electrical Co., 43 W 9th Ave., Denver, CO 80204, (303)629-7221 [3252]

Spivack's Antiques, 54 Washington, Wellesley, MA 02481, (781)235-1700 [13250]

SPL Associates Inc., PO Box 759, Williston, VT 05495-0759, (802)864-9831 [14693]

Splane Electric Supply, 8350 Haggerty Rd., Belleville, MI 48111-1667, (734)957-5500 [9395]

Splash Technology Inc., 555 Del Rey Ave., Sunnyvale, CA 94085, (408)328-6300 [21283]

SPMF, 100 E 42nd St., Ste. 1510, New York, NY 10017, (212)983-6278 [4147]

Spofford's Newspapers, 106 Summer St., Kennebunk, ME 04043, (207)985-7588 [4183]

Spoiled Rotten USA Inc., 305 E 140th St., Bronx, NY 10454, (718)993-7006 [5381]

Spokane Diesel Inc., E 6615 Mallon, Spokane, WA 99220, (509)535-3663 [3253]

Spokane Flower Growers, PO Box 53, Spokane, WA 99210, (509)624-0121 [14955]

Spokane Hardware Supply Inc., PO Box 2664, Spokane, WA 99220, (509)535-1663 [13934]

Spokane Machinery Company Inc., E 3730 Trent Ave., Spokane, WA 99202, (509)535-1576 [8063]

Spokane Seed Co., PO Box 11007, Spokane, WA 99211-1007, (509)535-3671 [18249]

Spokane Seed Co., PO Box 11007, Spokane, WA 99211-1007, (509)535-3671 [12556]

Spola Fibres International Inc., PO Box 1958, Passaic, NJ 07055, (973)471-7330 [26210]

Spong Trade Co., 4125 Landing Dr., Aurora, IL 60504, (630)851-1753 [20729]

Sport Design, 1 Commercial Ct., Plainview, NY 11803-1600, (516)576-7000 [23631]

Sport Obermeyer Ltd., 115 AABC, Aspen, CO 81611, (970)925-5060 [23975]

Sport Palace Wholesale, 3808 Rosecrans, No. 215, San Diego, CA 92110, (619)299-5236 [5382]

Sport Shop Inc., 8055 Airline Hwy., Baton Rouge, LA 70815-8108, (504)927-2600 [23976]

Sport Spectrum, 4421 Highway 58, Chattanooga, TN 37416-3012, (423)899-9238 [5383]

Sportcap Inc., 13401 S Main St., Los Angeles, CA 90061-1813, (310)538-3312 [5384]

Sportcap/Rivaltees, 99-061 Koaha Way, Aiea, HI 96701, (808)488-6195 [5078]

Sportif USA Inc., 1415 Greg St. No. 101, Sparks, NV 89431, (702)359-6400 [5385]

Sporting Dog Specialties Inc., 1989 Transit Way, Brockport, NY 14420-3007, (716)637-7508 [27237]

The Sporting House, PO Box 468, Vashon Island, WA 98070, (206)463-2563 [23977]

Sporting Image Inc., 1000 E Michigan Ave., Paw Paw, MI 49079, (616)657-5646 [5386]

Sportmaster Inc., 521 Madison Ave., Covington, KY 41011-1505, (606)431-3555 [23978]

Sports Cellar, 402 Sherman Ave., Coeur D Alene, ID 83814, (208)664-9464 [23979]

Sports Impressions Corp., 225 Windsor Dr., Itasca, IL 60143, (708)875-5300 [13452]

Sports Specialist Inc., 9559 Foley Ln., Foley, AL 36535-3723, (205)943-1901 [23980]

Sports Specialties Corp., 20001 Ellipse, Foothill Ranch, CA 92610, (949)768-4000 [5387]

Sportsarama Inc., PO Box 596, Sturgis, MI 49091-0596, (616)651-4991 [5388]

Sportscards & Comics Center, 184 Deanna Dr., Lowell, IN 46356-2403, (219)696-4323 [26664]

Sportsmans Inc., 414 Pierce St., Sioux City, IA 51101-1414, (712)255-0125 [23981]

Sportsprint Inc., 6197 Bermuda Rd., St. Louis, MO 63135, (314)521-9000 [5389]

Sportsware West, 415 E Figueroa St., Ste. A, Santa Barbara, CA 93101-1444, (805)962-7454 [23982]

SPOT Image Corp., 1897 Preston White Dr., Reston, VA 20191, (703)715-3100 [5766]

Spradling International Inc., 200 Cahaba Valley Pkwy. N, PO Box 1668, Pelham, AL 35124, (205)985-4206 [18432]

Spradling Originals, PO Box 96, 6841 Gadsen Hwy., Trussville, AL 35173-0096, (205)655-7404 [3254]

Sprague Devices Inc., 107 Eastwood Rd., Michigan City, IN 46360, (219)872-7295 [3255]

Sprague Energy Corp., 195 Hanover St., Ste. 1, Portsmouth, NH 03801-3771, (603)431-1000 [22693]

Sprague Energy Corp., 195 Hanover St., Ste. 1, Portsmouth, NH 03801-3771, (603)431-1000 [22694]

Sprawls Service and Sound, 856 York St. NE, Aiken, SC 29801-4022, (803)648-5885 [25461]

Sprayway Inc., 484 Vista Ave., Addison, IL 60101-4468, (630)628-3000 [4520]

Spreitzer Inc., PO Box 1288, Cedar Rapids, IA 52406, (319)365-9155 [8064]

SPRI Medical Products Corp. Ballert International Div., 642 Anthony Trl, Northbrook, IL 60062-2540, (847)272-7211 [19633]

Spring Arbor Distribution Company Inc., 1 Ingram Blvd., La Vergne, TN 37086-3629 [4184]

Spring and Buckley Inc., PO Box 1750, New Britain, CT 06050, (203)224-2451 [9396]

Spring Publishing, 299 E Quasset Rd., Woodstock, CT 06281-3308, (860)943-4093 [4185]

Spring Tree Corp., 28 Vernon St., No. 412, Brattleboro, VT 05301-3623, (802)254-8784 [12557]

Springfield Electric Supply Co., 718 N 9th St., Springfield, IL 62708, (217)788-2100 [9397]

Springfield Grocer Company Inc., PO Box 8500, Springfield, MO 65801, (417)883-4230 [12558]

Springfield Paper Co., PO Box 3336, Springfield, MO 65808, (417)862-5061 [21947]

Springfield Paper Specialties, Inc., 1754 Limekiln Pke., Ft. Washington, PA 19034, (215)643-2800 [21948]

Springfield Pepsi-Cola Bottling Co., PO Box 4146, Springfield, IL 62708, (217)522-8841 [25040]

Springfield Sugar and Products Co., PO Box 385, Windsor Locks, CT 06096, (860)623-1681 [12559]

Springs Industries Inc. Chesterfield Div., PO Box 111, Lancaster, SC 29721, (803)286-2491 [26211]

Sprint North Supply, 600 New Century Pkwy., New Century, KS 66031, (913)791-7000 [5767]

Sprite Industries, 1827 Capital St., Corona, CA 91718, (909)735-1015 [23394]

Spruill Oil Company Inc., 310 U.S Hwy. 13-17 S, Windsor, NC 27983, (252)794-4027 [22695]

Sprunger Corp., PO Box 1621, 2300 California Rd., Elkhart, IN 46515-1621, (219)262-2476 [17193]

SPS Company Inc., 6363 Hwy. 7, Minneapolis, MN 55416, (612)929-1377 [23395]

Spyder Active Sports Inc., 3600 Pearl St., Boulder, CO 80301, (303)449-0611 [5390]

Square Deal Recordings and Supplies, 303 Higuera, San Luis Obispo, CA 93401-1002, (805)543-3636 [25462]

Squeri FoodService, PO Box 14180, Cincinnati, OH 45250-0180, (513)381-1106 [12560]

Squibb-Taylor Inc., 10480 Shady Trail, No. 106, Dallas, TX 75220-2533, (214)357-4591 [22696]

Squire Supply Corp., PO Box 8086, Columbus, OH 43201, (614)291-4676 [14694]

Squires Timber Co., PO Box 549, Elizabethtown, NC 28337, (919)862-3533 [27379]

Squirrel Companies Inc., 1550 Bryant St., No. 830, San Francisco, CA 94103, (415)255-0119 [6756]

SR Distributing, PO Box 25957, Salt Lake City, UT 84125-0957, (801)973-4343 [25463]

S.R. & T.M. Gallagher, 1450 Sheldon Rd., St. Albans, VT 05478, (802)524-5336 [17932]

Sri Aurobindo Association, 2288 Fulton St., Ste. 310, Berkeley, CA 94704-1449, (650)848-1841 [4186]

SRS International, 367 Orchard St., Rochester, NY 14606-1040, (716)235-2040 [9398]

SSF Imported Auto Parts Inc., 466 Forbes Blvd., South San Francisco, CA 94080, (650)873-9280 [3256]

SSR Pump Co., PO Box 149, Michigan, ND 58259-9743, (701)259-2331 [3257]

SST Corp., PO Box 1649, Clifton, NJ 07012, (973)473-4300 [19634]

SST Sales Company Inc., 1302 Stratton Ave., Nashville, TN 37206, (615)262-7895 [5391]

S.T. and H. Oil Company Inc., 101 W Huron Ave., Bad Axe, MI 48413, (517)269-6447 [22697]

ST Laminating Corp., PO Box 1371, Elkhart, IN 46515, (219)262-4199 [25829]

St Lawrence Steel Corp., PO Box 2490, Streetsboro, OH 44241, (330)562-9000 [20385]

ST and T Communications Inc., 555 Iroquois St., Chickasaw, AL 36611, (334)457-1404 [5768]

Staab Battery Manufacturing Company Inc., 931 S 11th St., Springfield, IL 62703, (217)528-0421 [9399]

Stack; Al, 6100 4th Ave. S 281, Seattle, WA 98108-3234, (206)762-7607 [26665]

Stackpole Books, 5067 Ritter Rd., Mechanicsburg, PA 17055, (717)796-0411 [4187]

Stacoswitch Inc., 1139 W Baker St., Costa Mesa, CA 92626-4114, (714)549-3041 [9400]

Stacyville Cooperative Co., PO Box 217, Stacyville, IA 50476, (515)737-2348 [1291]

Stacyville Cooperative Creamery Association, 206 N Lawrence St., Stacyville, IA 50476, (515)737-2101 [12561]

Stadelman and Co.; Russell, PO Box 381767, Germantown, TN 38183-1767, (901)755-1391 [8065]

Staff, 116 N Blettner Ave., Hanover, PA 17331, (717)632-7455 [26666]

Stafford County Flour Mills Co., PO Box 7, Hudson, KS 67545, (316)458-4121 [4521]

Staflex/Harotex Co., PO Box 1106, Taylors, SC 29687-1106, (864)268-0613 [26212]

Stag/Parkway Inc., PO Box 43463, Atlanta, GA 30336, (404)349-1918 [20730]

Stage Inc., PO Box 9657, Knoxville, TN 37940, (615)577-5551 [15665]

Stage Rags, 150 S Water, Batavia, IL 60510, (630)879-5130 [4757]

Stahl Oil Company Inc., PO Box 773, Somerset, PA 15501, (814)443-2615 [22698]

Stahl's Bakery, 51021 Washington St., New Baltimore, MI 48047, (810)725-6990 [12562]

Stalling Inc., PO Box 4169, Lynchburg, VA 24502, (804)237-5947 [26352]

Stan Corporation of America, 447 Battery St., Ste. 300, San Francisco, CA 94111-3202, (415)677-0766 [6757]

Stancil Refrigeration Services Inc.; Bruce, RR 4, Box 534, Wilson, NC 27893-9432, (919)237-7959 [14695]

Stancorp Inc., PO Box 500, Girard, OH 44420-0500, (330)747-5444 [8066]

Standard Appliance Parts Corporation, 4814 Ayers St., PO Box 7199, Corpus Christi, TX 78415, (512)853-9823 [15321]

Standard Automotive Parts Corp., 25 West St., Lawrence, MA 01841-3497, (978)683-5731 [3258]

Standard Battery and Electric Co., PO Box 28, Waterloo, IA 50704, (319)235-1455 [3259]

Standard Beverage Corp., PO Box 968, Wichita, KS 67201, (316)838-7707 [2044]

Standard Building Products, 6550 Chase Rd., Dearborn, MI 48126, (313)846-0600 [8067]

Standard Commercial Corp., PO Box 450, Wilson, NC 27894-0450, (919)291-5507 [26353]

Standard Crown Distributing Co., PO Box 1077, Macon, GA 31202, (912)746-7694 [2045]

Standard Cycle and Auto Supply Co., 22 Rowley St., Winsted, CT 06098, (860)489-4183 [22699]

Standard Distributing Company Inc., 601 E Dodge St., Fremont, NE 68025, (402)721-9723 [2046]

Standard Distributing Company Inc. (Waterloo, Iowa), 2991 W Airline Cir., Waterloo, IA 50703, (319)234-7571 [2047]

Standard Drug Co., 1 CVS Dr., No. E, Woonsocket, RI 02895-0988, (401)765-1500 [19635]

Standard Duplicating Machines Corp., 10 Connector Rd., Andover, MA 01810, (508)470-1920 [21284]

Standard Electric Co., PO Box 5289, Saginaw, MI 48603-0289, (517)497-2100 [9401]

Standard Electric Supply Co., PO Box 651, Milwaukee, WI 53201-0651, (414)272-8100 [9402]

Standard Electric Time Corp., PO Box 320, Tecumseh, MI 49286, (517)423-8331 [24640]

Standard Electronics, 215 John Glenn Dr., Amherst, NY 14228, (716)691-3061 [9403]

Standard Equipment Co., 8411 Pulaski Hwy., Baltimore, MD 21237, (410)687-1700 [1292]

Standard Fruit and Vegetable Company Inc., PO Box 225027, Dallas, TX 75222-5027, (214)428-3600 [12563]

Standard Machine and Equipment Co., PO Box 1187, Uniontown, PA 15401, (412)438-0536 [16518]

Standard Marine Supply Co., Stock Island/Div., 1st & Maloney Ave., Key West, FL 33040, (305)294-2515 [18614]

Standard Marine Supply Co., 2nd & Alachua St., PO Box 477, Fernandina Beach, FL 32034, (904)261-3671 [18615]

Standard Marine Supply Corp., 120 N 20th St., PO Box 5001, Tampa, FL 33675, (813)248-2905 [18616]

Standard Meat Co., 700 Van Dorn, Lincoln, NE 68502-3342, (402)475-6328 [12564]

Standard Medical Imaging Inc., 9002 Red Branch Rd., Columbia, MD 21045, (410)997-1500 [19052]

Standard Metals Inc., 440 Ledyard St., Hartford, CT 06114, (860)296-5663 [20386]

Standard Motor Products Inc., 37-18 Northern Blvd., Long Island City, NY 11101, (718)392-0200 [9404]

Standard Parts Corp., 500 Commerce Rd., Richmond, VA 23224, (804)233-8321 [3260]

Standard Plumbing Supply Company Inc., 2100 W Cold Spring Ln., Baltimore, MD 21209, (410)466-3500 [23396]

Standard Publishing Co., 8121 Hamilton Ave., Cincinnati, OH 45231, (513)931-4050 [4188]

The Standard Register Co, 5743 Rostrata Ave., Buena Park, CA 90621, (714)521-0232 [21285]

Standard Roofings Inc., PO Box 1410, Tinton Falls, NJ 07724, (908)542-3300 [8068]

Standard Steel and Wire Corp., 2450 W Hubbard St., Chicago, IL 60612, (312)226-6100 [20387]

Standard Supplies Inc., 4 Meem Ave., Gaithersburg, MD 20877, (301)948-2690 [8069]

Standard Supply Co., 3424 S Main St., Salt Lake City, UT 84165, (801)486-3371 [25464]

Standard Supply Company Inc., Hwy. 66, Neptune, NJ 07753, (732)922-1200 [8070]

Standard Supply and Hardware Company Inc., PO Box 60620, New Orleans, LA 70160, (504)586-8400 [17194]

Standard Telecommunications Systems Inc., 175 Louis St., South Hackensack, NJ 07606, (201)641-9700 [5769]

Standard Textile Company Inc., 3130 Frederick Ave., Baltimore, MD 21229-3804, (410)233-4400 [15666]

Standard Tile Distributors of Springfield, Inc., 632 White St., Springfield, MA 01108-3221, (413)732-4191 [9732]

Standard Tube Sales Corp., PO Box 479, Marlborough, MA 01752, (508)481-7100 [20388]

Standard Wire & Cable Co., 1959 E Cashdan St., Rancho Dominguez, CA 90220, (310)609-1811 [9405]

Standfix Air Distribution Products - ACME, 214 Commercial St., Medina, NY 14103, (716)798-0300 [14696]

Standish Oil Co., PO Box 457, Bay City, MI 48707-0457, (517)846-6961 [22700]

Staneco Corp., 901 Sheehy Dr., Horsham, PA 19044, (215)672-6500 [9406]

Stanfields Inc., PO Box 245, Cheyenne, WY 82003-0245, (307)634-6921 [21286]

Stanford Grain Co., Main St., Stanford, IL 61774, (309)379-2141 [18250]

Stanford Lumber Company Inc., 2001 Rte. 286, Pittsburgh, PA 15239, (412)327-6800 [8071]

Stanford Paper Co., 1901 Stanford Ct., Landover, MD 20785, (410)772-1900 [21949]

Stange Co., 2324 Weldon Pkwy., St. Louis, MO 63146, (314)432-2000 [17618]

Stangel Co.; J.J., PO Box 280, Manitowoc, WI 54221-0280, (414)684-3313 [17195]

Stanion Wholesale Electric Company Inc., PO Drawer F, Pratt, KS 67124, (316)672-5678 [9407]

Stanis Trading Corp., PO Box 562, Shoreham, NY 11786, (516)744-1208 [19636]

Stanislaus Farm Supply Co., 624 E Service Rd., Modesto, CA 95358, (209)538-7070 [1293]

Stanislaus Imports Inc., 41 14th St., San Francisco, CA 94103, (415)431-7122 [26667]

Stanley Brothers Inc., 237 7th Ave., Huntington, WV 25701, (304)529-7114 [12565]

Stanley Home Products, PO Box 729, Great Bend, KS 67530, (316)792-1711 [14245]

Stanley-Lawrence Co., 2535 S Fairfax Ave., Culver City, CA 90232, (562)933-7136 [17619]

Stanley Roberts Inc., 65 Industrial Rd., Lodi, NJ 07644, (973)778-5900 [15667]

Stanline Inc., 2855 S Reservoir, Pomona, CA 91766, (909)591-0541 [10176]

Stano Components, PO Box 2048, Carson City, NV 89702-2048, (702)246-5281 [23983]

Stan's Frozen Foods, 2101 Columbia Dr. SE, Albuquerque, NM 87101, (505)247-3707 [12566]

Stan's Inc., 3533 E Jensen Rd., El Reno, OK 73036, (405)422-5375 [12567]

Stan's Smokehouse Inc., 3533 E Jensen Rd., El Reno, OK 73036, (405)422-5375 [12567]

Stan's Towing & Repair, Huckel Hill Rd., RR 1, Box 684, Vernon, VT 05354, (802)257-1032 [3261]

Stant Corp., 1620 Columbia Ave., Connersville, IN 47331-1696, (765)962-6655 [3262]

Stant Manufacturing Inc., 1620 Columbia Ave., Connersville, IN 47331, (765)825-3121 [14697]

Stanz Cheese Company Inc., PO Box 24, South Bend, IN 46624, (219)232-6666 [12568]

Staple Cotton Cooperative Association, PO Box 547, Greenwood, MS 38935, (601)453-6231 [18251]

Staples Business Advantage, 5399 Lancaster Dr., Cleveland, OH 44131, (216)351-5200 [21287]

Staples Business Advantage, 41554 Koppernick, Canton, MI 48187, (734)454-9292 [21288]

Staples Business Advantage, 125 Mushroom Blvd., Rochester, NY 14692, (716)424-3600 [21289]

Staples Office Products Inc., 100 Pennsylvania Ave., Framingham, MA 01701, (508)370-8500 [21290]

Staples, The Office Superstore Inc., 18300 Euclid St., Fountain Valley, CA 92708, (714)668-9523 [21291]

Star Beacon Products Co., 1104 Goodale Blvd., Columbus, OH 43212-3726, (614)294-4657 [25830]

Star Beam Inc., PO Box 471765, Tulsa, OK 74147, (918)664-2326 [9408]

Star Beam/Nightray Div. Gralco Corp., PO Box 471765, Tulsa, OK 74147, (918)664-2326 [9408]

Star Brite, 4041 SW 47 Ave., Ft. Lauderdale, FL 33314, (954)587-6280 [4712]

Star Com Computers, 585 Cypress Dr., Florence, AL 35630-1850, (205)766-7827 [6758]

Star Creation Inc., 1934 Westminster St., Providence, RI 02909, (401)421-9454 [13453]

Star Cutter Co., PO Box 376, Farmington, MI 48332-0376, (248)474-8200 [16519]

Star Distributors, 3543 Lamar Ave., Memphis, TN 38118, (901)363-5555 [2048]

Star Electric Supply Company Inc., PO Box 580640, Tulsa, OK 74158-0640, (918)835-7672 [9409]

Star of India Fashions, 1038 W Southern, Tempe, AZ 85282, (602)968-6195 [5392]

Star Industries Inc., 130 Lakeside Ave., Seattle, WA 98122-6538, (206)328-1600 [8072]

Star International Ltd., 3343 Dug Gap Rd., Dalton, GA 30720, (706)277-4410 [10177]

Star Jewelry Enterprises Inc., 1914 Westminster St., Providence, RI 02909-2802, (401)751-8335 [17620]

Star Micronics America Inc., 1150 King Georges Post Rd., Edison, NJ 08837, (732)572-9512 [6759]

Star Middle East USA Inc., 4801 Woodway Dr., Ste. 300 E, Houston, TX 77056, (713)871-1121 [16520]

Star Office Machines, PO Box 20215, Billings, MT 59104-0215, (406)259-0429 [21292]

Star Oil Company Inc., PO Box 610867, Port Huron, MI 48061-0867, (810)985-9586 [22701]

Star Products, 7015 Grand Blvd., Houston, TX 77054-2205, (713)747-1167 [13279]

Star Restaurant Equipment & Supplies, PO Box 1716, Bismarck, ND 58502-1716, (701)255-7729 [14698]

Star Sales Company of Knoxville, PO Box 1503, Knoxville, TN 37901, (865)524-0771 [26668]

Star Sales Company of Knoxville, PO Box 1502, Lake Oswego, OR 97035, (865)524-0771 [26213]

Star Sales and Distributing Co., PO Box 4008, Woburn, MA 01888, (617)933-8830 [8073]

Star Stainless Screw Co., PO Box 288, Totowa, NJ 07511, (201)256-2300 [13935]

Star Steel Supply Co., 24417 Groesbeck Hwy., Warren, MI 48089-4723 [14699]

Star Tubular Products Co., 4747 S Richmond St., Chicago, IL 60632, (773)523-8445 [23397]

Starboard Inc., 1714 E Blvd., Charlotte, NC 28203, (704)334-1677 [12569]

Starbuck Creamery Co., 101 E 5th St., Starbuck, MN 56381, (612)239-2226 [12570]

Starbuck Sprague Co., PO Box 1111, Waterbury, CT 06721, (203)756-8184 [9410]

Starbucks Corp., PO Box 34067, Seattle, WA 98124-1067, (206)447-1575 [12571]

StarchTech Inc., 720 Florida Ave., Golden Valley, MN 55426-1704, (612)545-5400 [25940]

Starfire Lumber Co., PO Box 547, Cottage Grove, OR 97424, (541)942-0168 [27380]

Stargel Office Systems Inc., 1220 Blalock Rd., Ste. 100, Houston, TX 77055, (713)461-5382 [21293]

Stark Candy Co., Division of New England Confectionery Co., 700 Hickory St., PO Box 65, Pewaukee, WI 53072, (414)691-0600 [12572]

Stark Carpet Corp., 979 3rd Ave., New York, NY 10022, (212)752-9000 [10178]

Stark Carpet Corp., 979 3rd Ave., New York, NY 10022, (212)752-9000 [15668]

Stark Co., 432 W Allegheny Arms, Philadelphia, PA 19133, (215)425-2222 [21950]

Stark Co., 432 W Allegheny Arms, Philadelphia, PA 19133, (215)425-2222 [17196]

Stark & Company Inc., 30301 Northwestern Hwy., Farmington Hills, MI 48334, (248)851-5700 [12573]

Stark and Company Inc., 30301 Northwestern Hwy., Farmington Hills, MI 48334, (248)851-5700 [12574]

Stark Electronics Inc., 401 Royalston Ave. N, Minneapolis, MN 55405, (612)372-3161 [9411]

StarKist Seafood/Heinz Pet Prd, 1054 Ways St., San Pedro, CA 90731, (310)519-2200 [12575]

Starks Sport Shop, 108 W Blackhawk, Prairie du Chien, WI 53821, (608)326-2478 [23984]

Starlight Archery Inc., 21570 Groesbeck Hwy., Warren, MI 48089, (313)771-1580 [23985]

Starmac Group, 627 Vassar Rd., Wenonah, NJ 08090, (856)582-4625 [5393]

Starr Display Fireworks Inc., 3805 52nd Ave. S, Fargo, ND 58104-5402, (701)469-2421 [26669]

StarTech International, 5575 Magnatron Blvd., San Diego, CA 92111, (619)457-0781 [6760]

Stash Distributing Inc., 2138 Fair, Chico, CA 95928-6746, (530)891-6000 [2049]

Stash Tea Co., PO Box 910, Portland, OR 97207, (503)684-4482 [12576]

Stat Surgical Center Inc., 291 Main St., Falmouth, MA 02540-2751, (508)548-1342 [19053]

STATCO Engineering and Fabricators Inc., 7595 Reynolds Cir., Huntington Beach, 24860, 92647, (714)375-6300 [20389]

State Beauty & Barbers Supply Co., PO Box 32786, Charlotte, NC 28232-2786, (704)845-2888 [14069]

State Beauty Supply, 1721 Logan Ave., Cheyenne, WY 82001-5005, (307)634-8984 [14246]

State Beauty Supply, 1522 Cerrillos Rd., Santa Fe, NM 87505-3550, (505)988-4152 [14247]

State Ceramic Tile, Inc., 23700 Aurora Rd., Bedford Heights, OH 44146, (440)439-3131 [10179]

State Electric Company Inc., PO Box 28589, St. Louis, MO 63146, (314)569-2140 [3263]

State Electric Supply, 2700 Rydin Rd., Ste. D, Richmond, CA 94804-5800, (510)836-1717 [9412]

State Electric Supply Co., PO Box 5397, Huntington, WV 25703, (304)523-7491 [9413]

State Electrical Supply Inc., 509 W Milwaukee St., Janesville, WI 53545, (608)752-9451 [9414]

State Fish Company Inc., 2194 Signal Pl., San Pedro, CA 90731, (310)832-2633 [12577]

State Gas and Oil Co., 110 Village Dr., State College, PA 16803, (814)237-4355 [22702]

State Janitorial Supply Co., 24 Maggies Way, Dover, DE 19901, (302)734-4814 [4713]

State Line Potato Chip Co., PO Box 218, Wilbraham, MA 01095-0218, (413)596-8331 [12578]

State Line Supply Co., 1333 E Main St., Bradford, PA 16701, (814)362-7433 [20390]

State Mutual Book & Periodical Service Ltd., 521 5th Ave., 17th Fl., New York, NY 10175, (212)292-4444 [4189]

State Optical Company, Inc., 1144 Fort St. Mall, Honolulu, HI 96813, (808)531-2761 [19637]

State Pipe and Supply Inc., PO Box 3286, Santa Fe Springs, CA 90670, (562)695-5555 [20391]

State Restaurant Equipment Inc., 3163 S Highland Dr., Las Vegas, NV 89109-1010, (702)733-1515 [24226]

State Salvage Company Inc., 22500 S Alameda St., Long Beach, CA 90810, (310)835-3849 [27009]

State Scale Co., Inc., 155 Bemis Rd., RFD No. 12, Manchester, NH 03102, (603)625-8274 [24438]

State Seal Co., 4135 E Wood St., Phoenix, AZ 85040, (602)437-1532 [17197]

State Service Systems Inc., 10405-B E 55th Pl., Tulsa, OK 74146-6599, (918)627-8000 [14248]

State Supply Co., 597 E 7th St., St. Paul, MN 55101, (612)774-5985 [23398]

Stateline Sports, PO Box 5511, West Lebanon, NH 03784-5511, (603)298-7078 [23986]

States Distributing, 100 E 5th St., PO Box 638, Brookport, IL 62910, (618)564-3377 [10180]

Statewide Electric Supply, 3560 S Valley View Blvd., Las Vegas, NV 89103-1812, (702)871-4108 [9249]

Statewide Floor Waxing Distributors, PO Box 718, Bangor, ME 04402-0718, (207)945-9591 [4714]

Stationers' Corporation of Hawaii Ltd., 708 Kanoelehua Ave., Hilo, HI 96720, (808)935-5477 [21294]

Stationers Inc. (Huntington, West Virginia), PO Box 2167, Huntington, WV 25722, (304)528-2780 [21295]

Stationers Inc. (Indianapolis, Indiana), 5656 W 74th St., Indianapolis, IN 46278, (317)298-0808 [21296]

Statler Body Works, 5573 Main St., Box D, Marion, PA 17235, (717)375-2251 [3264]

Staton Distributing Co.; Jim, 149 S Walnut Cir., Greensboro, NC 27409, (919)294-2714 [2050]

Statz and Sons Inc.; Carl F., PO Box 38, Waunakee, WI 53597, (608)849-4101 [1294]

Stauber Wholesale Hardware; E., 2105 Northwestern Ave., Waukegan, IL 60087-4149, (847)623-7740 [13936]

Staunton Food Inc., PO Box 569, Staunton, VA 24402, (540)885-1214 [12579]

Stavis Seafoods Inc., 7 Channel St., Boston, MA 02210, (617)482-6349 [12580]

Staz Food Services, 101 Alan Dr., Newark, DE 19711, (302)366-8990 [12581]

Steam Supply Co., PO Box 24703, Seattle, WA 98124, (206)622-4690 [17198]

Steam Way International Inc., 4550 Jackson St., Denver, CO 80216, (303)355-3566 [24227]

Steamboat International LLC, 7215 Bermuda Rd., Las Vegas, NV 89119-4304, (702)361-0600 [25831]

Steamboat International LLC, 7215 Bermuda Rd., Las Vegas, NV 89119, (702)361-0600 [23987]

Steel City Corp., PO Box 1227, Youngstown, OH 44501, (330)792-7663 [20392]

Steel City Milling Inc., 120 Victoria Rd., Youngstown, OH 44515, (216)793-3925 [12582]

Steel Co., 12500 Stoney Isle. Ave., Chicago, IL 60633, (773)646-3600 [20393]

Steel Engineers Inc., 716 W Mesquite Rd., Las Vegas, NV 89106, (702)386-0023 [20394]

Steel Inc., 6245 Clermont St., Commerce City, CO 80022, (303)287-0331 [20395]

Steel Industries Inc., 12600 Beech Daly Rd., Redford, MI 48239, (313)535-8505 [16521]

Steel Industries Inc., 12600 Beech Daly Rd., Detroit, MI 48239, (313)531-1140 [20396]

Steel Manufacturing and Warehouse Co., PO Box 02-5668, Kansas City, MO 64102, (816)842-9143 [20397]

Steel Partners L.P., 750 Lexington Ave., New York, NY 10022, (212)446-5217 [21297]

Steel and Pipe Supply Co., PO Box 1688, Manhattan, KS 66502, (785)537-2222 [20398]

Steel Services Inc., 7231 Forest Ave., No. 100, Richmond, VA 23226-3796, (804)673-3810 [20399]

Steel Suppliers Inc., PO Box 1185, Elkhart, IN 46515, (219)264-7561 [20400]

Steel Supply Co., PO Box 82579, Oklahoma City, OK 73148, (405)631-1551 [20401]

Steel Supply Co. (Rolling Meadows, Illinois), 5105 Newport Dr., Rolling Meadows, IL 60008, (847)255-2460 [20402]

Steel Warehouse Company Inc., PO Box 1377, South Bend, IN 46624, (219)236-5100 [20403]

Steel Yard Inc., PO Box 4828, Portland, OR 97208, (503)282-9273 [20404]

Steelco Inc., PO Box 3335, Salem, OR 97302, (503)581-2516 [20405]

Steele-Siman & Co., 803 E Rice St., Sioux Falls, SD 57103-0157, (605)336-0593 [18252]

Steeler Inc., 10023 Martin Lthr Kng Jr Way S, Seattle, WA 98178, (206)725-2500 [27381]

Steele's Sports Co., 5223 W 137th St., Brook Park, OH 44142, (216)267-5300 [23988]

Steelfab, 500 Marshall St., Paterson, NJ 07503, (973)278-0350 [3265]

Steelhead Inc., PO Box 21370, San Antonio, TX 78221-0370, (210)628-1066 [16522]

Steelmet Inc., PO Box 369, Mc Keesport, PA 15134, (412)672-9200 [26804]

Steepleton Tire Co., PO Box 90, Memphis, TN 38101, (901)774-6440 [3266]

Stefanelli Distributing, 1945 W Yale Ave., Fresno, CA 93705-4328, (559)233-7138 [2051]

Stein Distributing, 1013 Express Dr., Belleville, IL 62223, (618)398-2902 [22703]

Stein Distributing Co., PO Box 9367, Boise, ID 83707, (208)375-1450 [2052]

Stein Garden and Gifts, 5400 S 27th St., Milwaukee, WI 53221, (414)761-5404 [14956]

Stein Paint Co., 545 W Flagler St., Miami, FL 33130, (305)545-8700 [21588]

Stein Seal Company Inc., PO Box 316, Kulpsville, PA 19443, (215)256-0201 [151]

Stein World Inc., PO Box 9491, Memphis, TN 38109, (901)942-2441 [13251]

Steinberg Brothers Inc., PO Box 205, Amsterdam, NY 12010-0205, (212)246-0808 [19638]

Steiner Electric Co., 1250 Touhy Rd., Elk Grove Village, IL 60007-5302, (708)228-0400 [9415]

Steiner Inc.; S.S., 655 Madison Ave., New York, NY 10021, (212)838-8900 [18253]

Steinhardt & Hanson, Inc., 217-219 E Main St., PO Box 386, Madison, IN 47250, (812)265-4131 [21298]

Steinke Ranches Inc.; E.J., 5561 West 129 North, Idaho Falls, ID 83402-5254, (208)522-5159 [18254]

Stein's Inc., PO Box 248, Moorhead, MN 56561-0248, (218)233-2727 [4715]

Stella D'Oro Biscuit Company Inc., 184 W 237th St., Bronx, NY 10463, (718)601-9200 [12583]

Stella Products Co.; F.D., 7000 Fenkell Ave., Detroit, MI 48238, (313)341-6400 [24228]

Stelling Banjo Works Ltd., 7258 Banjo Ln., Afton, VA 22920, (804)295-1917 [25465]

Stem Brothers Inc., PO Box T, Milford, NJ 08848, (908)995-4825 [22704]

Stemmans Inc., PO Box 156, Carencro, LA 70520-0156, (318)234-2382 [19054]

Stephan Wood Products Inc., 605 Huron, PO Box 669, Grayling, MI 49738-0669, (517)348-5496 [27382]

Stephens Manufacturing Company Inc.; W. E., PO Box 190675, Nashville, TN 37219-0675, (615)255-1278 [5394]

Stephens; Stanley, 2565 Pearl Buck Rd., PO Box 2205, Bristol, PA 19007, (215)788-1515 [10181]

Stephenson Equipment Inc., 7201 Paxton St., Harrisburg, PA 17111, (717)564-3434 [8074]

Stepic Corp., 37-31 30th St., Long Island City, NY 11101, (718)784-2220 [19055]

Sterco New York Inc., 1380 N Jerusalem Rd., North Merrick, NY 11566-1011, (516)845-4525 [18433]

Sterett Supply Co., 4533 Baldwin, PO Box 5528, Corpus Christi, TX 78408-2709, (210)884-1661 [9416]

Steri-Systems Corp., PO Box 909, Auburn, GA 30011-0909, (404)963-1429 [19056]

Sterling Distributing Co., 4433 S 96th St., Omaha, NE 68127, (402)339-2300 [2053]

Sterling Publishing Co., Inc., 387 Park Ave. S, New York, NY 10016-8810, (212)532-7160 [4190]

Sterling Rubber and Plastics, 3190 Kettering Blvd., Dayton, OH 45439-1924, (937)298-0241 [24296]

Sterling Security Services Inc., 1018 S Van Buren St., Amarillo, TX 79101, (806)376-1193 [24641]

Sterling & Son; Clarence, 1014 W Main St., Crisfield, MD 21817, (410)968-1222 [18617]

Stern & Company, Inc.; Henry, 183 S Central Ave., Hartsdale, NY 10530, (914)761-4800 [9417]

Stern Corp.; Paul N., 1 Market St., Bldg. 25, Passaic, NJ 07055, (973)777-9422 [26214]

Stern Watch Agency Inc.; Henri, 1 Rockefeller Plz., New York, NY 10020, (212)581-0870 [17621]

Sterzing Food Co., 1819 Charles St., Burlington, IA 52601-2201, (319)754-8467 [12584]

Steuart Investment Co., 4646 40th NW, Washington, DC 20016, (202)537-8940 [12585]

Steuart Petroleum Co., 4646 40th NW, Washington, DC 20016, (202)537-8900 [22705]

Steuben County Farm Bureau Association Inc., 610 W Broad St., Angola, IN 46703, (219)665-3161 [27238]

Steven Hosiery Inc., 997 13th St. SW, Hickory, NC 28602-4914, (704)328-1046 [5395]

Steven Inc.; David G., 663 5th Ave., New York, NY 10022, (212)593-0444 [17622]

Steven Industries, Inc., 39 Avenue C, PO Box 8, Bayonne, NJ 07002, (201)437-6500 [21589]

Steven Smith/Stuffed Animals Inc., 330 E 89th St., Brooklyn, NY 11236, (718)272-2500 [26670]

Stevens Inc.; Gerald, 301 E LasOlas Blvd., Ft. Lauderdale, FL 33301, (954)713-5000 [14957]

Stevens International, PO Box 126, Magnolia, NJ 08049, (609)435-1555 [26488]

Stevens Ltd.; Michael, 712 5th Ave., Fl. 12, New York, NY 10019-4108, (212)947-5595 [18434]

Steves Electronics Service, 1621 E 11th St., Tulsa, OK 74120-4803, (918)582-0594 [25466]

Stewart Co.; Douglas, 2402 Advance Rd., Madison, WI 53718, (608)221-1155 [6761]

Stewart Co.; Jesse C., 360 Broadmoor Ave., Pittsburgh, PA 15228, (412)343-0600 [18255]

Stewart Crafts Inc., 905 Lovers Lane Rd. SE, Calhoun, GA 30701-4633, (706)625-5519 [14949]

Stewart Fastener Corp., 101 Southside Dr., Charlotte, NC 28217-1725, (704)527-4713 [13937]

Stewart Fastener and Tool, 101 Southside Dr., Charlotte, NC 28217-1725, (704)527-4713 [13937]

Stewart Lumber Co., 421 Johnson St. NE, Minneapolis, MN 55413, (612)378-1520 [8075]

Stewart & Stevenson, 2929 Vassar Dr. NE, Albuquerque, NM 87107, (505)881-3511 [3267]

Stewart & Stevenson, 1515 W Murray Dr., Farmington, NM 87401, (505)325-5071 [3268]

Stewart & Stevenson, 3919 Irving Blvd., Dallas, TX 75247, (214)631-5370 [3269]

Stewart & Stevenson, 5717 I-10 E, San Antonio, TX 78219, (210)662-1000 [16523]

Stewart and Stevenson Services Inc., PO Box 1637, Houston, TX 77251-1637, (713)868-7700 [3270]

Stewart and Stevenson Services Inc. Texas, PO Box 1637, Houston, TX 77251, (713)868-7700 [16524]

Stewart Supply Inc., 2369 Pecan Ct., Haltom City, TX 76117, (817)834-7313 [13938]

STI, 1621 Cushman Dr., Lincoln, NE 68512, (402)423-1440 [6742]

Sticht Company Inc.; Herman H., 57 Front St., Brooklyn, NY 11201-1038, (718)852-7602 [24439]

STIHL Northwest, PO Box 999, Chehalis, WA 98532, (360)748-8694 [16525]

STIHL Southeast, Inc., 2250 Principal Row, Orlando, FL 32837, (407)240-7900 [16526]

STIHL Southwest Inc., Hwy. 270 N, PO Box 518, Malvern, AR 72104, (501)332-2788 [16527]

Stiles Machinery Inc., 3965 44th St., Grand Rapids, MI 49512, (616)698-7500 [16528]

Stiller Distributors Inc., 833 Dyer, Cranston, RI 02920, (401)946-6600 [10182]

Stimpson Company Inc., 900 Sylvan Ave., Bayport, NY 11705, (516)472-2000 [13939]

Stimpson Productions; John, 11 California Ave., Framingham, MA 01701-8801, (508)626-0522 [22907]

Stimson Lane Wine and Spirits Ltd., PO Box 1976, Woodinville, WA 98072, (425)488-1133 [2054]

Stinnes Corp., 120 White Plains Rd., 6th Fl., Tarrytown, NY 10591-5522, (914)366-7200 [22706]

Stinnes Intercoal Inc., 605 3rd Ave., New York, NY 10158-0180, (212)986-1515 [20569]

Stinson, Inc.; C.F., 2849 Product Drive, Rochester Hills, MI 48309, (248)299-3800 [26215]

Stock Ltd.; Robert, 1370 Broadway, 14th Fl., New York, NY 10018-7302 [5396]

Stock Steel, PO Box 2610, Spokane, WA 99220, (509)535-6363 [20406]

Stockdale Ceramic Tile Center, Inc., 6301 District Blvd., Bakersfield, CA 93313-2143, (805)398-6000 [10183]

Stockman Supply Inc., 802 W Main Ave., West Fargo, ND 58078, (701)282-3255 [27239]

Stockmen's Livestock Exchange, PO Box 1209, Dickinson, ND 58602-1209, (701)225-8156 [18256]

Stockmen's Livestock Market, PO Box 280, Yankton, SD 57078-0280, (605)665-9641 [18257]

Stockton Feed and Milling Inc., PO Box 1446, Ft. Stockton, TX 79735, (915)336-3324 [1295]

Stockton Oil Co., PO Box 1756; Billings, MT 59103, (406)245-6376 [22707]

Stockton Service Corp., PO Box 508, Stockton, CA 95201-0508, (209)464-8333 [22708]

Stoelting Co., 620 Wheat Ln., Wood Dale, IL 60191-1109, (708)860-9700 [4191]

Stok Software Inc., 373 Smithtown Byp., No. 287, Hauppauge, NY 11788-2516, (718)699-9393 [6762]

Stokes Canning Co., 5590 High St., Denver, CO 80216, (303)292-4018 [12586]

Stokes Electric Co., 1701 McCalla Ave., Knoxville, TN 37915, (423)525-0351 [9418]

Stokes Equipment Co., 1001 Horsham Rd., Horsham, PA 19044, (215)672-6100 [16529]

Stokes-Shaheen Produce Inc., 477 Hawthorn St., Macon, GA 31201, (912)742-4517 [12587]

Stolls Medical Rentals Inc., 2500 E Main St., Waterbury, CT 06705-2803, (203)757-9818 [19057]

Stomel & Sons; Joseph H., 1 Stomel Plz., 33 Suffolk Rd., West Berlin, NJ 08091, (609)768-9770 [12588]

Stomel and Sons; Joseph H., 55 Corporate Dr., Hauppauge, NY 11788, (516)231-1852 [12589]

Stone Commodities Corp., 30 S Wacker Dr., Ste. 1300, Chicago, IL 60606, (312)454-3000 [12590]

Stone County Oil Company Inc., 101 N Commerce St., Crane, MO 65633, (417)723-5201 [22709]

Stone Electronic, 2062 SW 4th Ave., Ontario, OR 97914, (541)881-1338 [9419]

Stone Enterprises, 2570 Cloverdale Ave., No. C, Concord, CA 94518-2425, (510)582-4180 [5397]

Stone Heavy Vehicle Specialists Inc., PO Box 25518, Raleigh, NC 27611, (919)779-2351 [3271]

Stone Island; C.P., 85 5th Ave., 11 Fl., New York, NY 10003-3019, (212)366-9595 [5398]

Stone Medical Supply Corp., PO Box 1701, Mt. Vernon, NY 10551-1701, (516)783-6262 [19639]

Stone and Son Inc.; E.B., PO Box 550, Suisun City, CA 94585, (707)426-2500 [1296]

Stone Steel Corp., PO Box 2893, Baltimore, MD 21225, (410)355-4140 [20407]

Stonehill Group Inc., PO Box 6488, Manchester, NH 03108-5033, (603)626-1677 [5399]

Stones Inc., PO Box 974, Bainbridge, GA 31717, (912)246-2929 [18258]

Stoneway Electric Supply Co., N 402 Perry, Spokane, WA 99202, (509)535-2933 [9420]

Stoneway Electric Supply Co., 3665 Stoneway Ave. N, Seattle, WA 98103, (206)634-2240 [9421]

Stonington Cooperative Grain Co., PO Box 350, Stonington, IL 62567, (217)325-3211 [18259]

Stopol Inc., 31875 Solon Rd., Solon, OH 44139-3533, (440)498-4000 [23036]

Storage Equipment Company Inc., 1258 Titan Ave., Dallas, TX 75247, (214)630-9221 [25941]

Storage Equipment Company Inc., 1258 Titan Ave., Dallas, TX 75247, (214)630-9221 [24229]

Storage Solutions Inc., 12342 Hancock St., Carmel, IN 46032, (317)848-2001 [24230]

Storage Technology Corp., 2270 S 88th St., Louisville, CO 80028-4309, (303)673-5151 [6763]

StorageTek, 10260 SW Greenburg Rd Ste. 400, Portland, OR 97223, (503)293-3589 [6764]

Storck & Co.; M.A., PO Box 3758, Portland, ME 04104-3758, (207)774-7271 [26671]

Storm Pet Supply Inc., 625 Birkhead Ave., Owensboro, KY 42303, (502)926-4168 [27240]

Storm Products Co., 116 Shore Dr., Hinsdale, IL 60521-5819, (630)323-9121 [9422]

Storm Products Co., 3047 N 31st Ave., Phoenix, AZ 85017, (602)269-3485 [9423]

Storm Products Company Inc., 112 S Glasgow Ave., Inglewood, CA 90301, (310)649-6141 [9424]

Story Wright Printing, Shepherd & 3rd, Lufkin, TX 75901, (409)632-7727 [21299]

Stotler Grain Co., 1010 W Clark St., Champaign, IL 61821-3326, (217)356-9011 [18260]

Stottlemyer and Shoemaker Lumber Co., 2211 Fruitville Rd., Sarasota, FL 34237, (813)366-8108 [8076]

Stoudt Distributing Co., PO Box 4147, Longview, TX 75606, (903)753-7239 [2055]

Stouffer Foods Corp., PO Box 87008, 22800 Saui Ranch Pkwy., Yorba Linda, CA 92885, (714)282-4270 [12591]

Stover Broom, PO Box 1704, Lewiston, ME 04241, (207)784-1591 [15669]

Stover Greenlight Auto & Marine, Rte. 1, Junction 52 & N, Stover, MO 65078, (573)377-4621 [18618]

Stover Seed Company Inc., PO Box 21488, Los Angeles, CA 90021, (213)626-9669 [1297]

Stover Smith Electric Supplies Inc., PO Box 446, Laurel, MS 39441, (601)425-4791 [9425]

Stow Mills, PO Box 301, Chesterfield, NH 03443, (603)256-3000 [12592]

Stowers Machinery Corp., PO Box 14802, Knoxville, TN 37914, (615)546-1414 [8077]

Stowers Manufacturing Inc., PO Drawer A, Gadsden, AL 35904, (205)547-8647 [8078]

Strafco Inc., PO Box 600, San Antonio, TX 78292-0600, (210)226-0101 [3272]

Straight Talk Distributing, 75 Pasatiempo Dr., Santa Cruz, CA 95060-1440 [4192]

Strait and Lamp Lumber Company Inc., PO Box 718, Hebron, OH 43025, (614)861-4620 [8079]

Strasser Hardware Co.; A.L., 910 Southwest Blvd., Kansas City, KS 66103, (913)236-5858 [13940]

Strata Inc., 3501 Everett Ave., Everett, WA 98201-3816, (425)259-6016 [5770]

Stratcor Technical Sales Inc., 4955 Steubenville Pike, Pittsburgh, PA 15205, (412)787-4700 [20570]

Strategic Distribution Inc., 475 Steamboat Rd., Greenwich, CT 06830, (203)629-8750 [16530]

Strategic Products and Services Inc., 10810 Farnam Dr., Omaha, NE 68154, (402)392-3900 [6765]

Stratford Farmers Cooperative, PO Box 14, Stratford, WI 54484, (715)687-4443 [401]

Stratford Farmers Cooperative, PO Box 14, Stratford, WI 54484, (715)687-4136 [18261]

Stratford Grain and Supply Cooperative, 719 Commercial St., Stratford, IA 50249, (515)838-2410 [18262]

Stratham Hardware & Lumber Co., 17 Portsmouth Ave., Stratham, NH 03885-2520, (603)772-3031 [21590]

Stratham Tire Inc., 17 Portsmouth Ave., Stratham, NH 03885, (603)772-3783 [3273]

Strathman Sales Company Inc., 2127 SE Lakewood Blvd., Topeka, KS 66605-1188, (785)354-8537 [2056]

Stratton Electronics Inc., PO Box 4383, Missoula, MT 59806-4383, (406)728-8855 [9426]

Stratton Equity Cooperative, 98 Colorado Ave., Stratton, CO 80836, (719)348-5326 [1298]

Stratton Seed Co., PO Box 32, Stuttgart, AR 72160, (501)673-4433 [1299]

Stratton's Salads; Mrs., 380 Industrial Ln., PO Box 190187, Birmingham, AL 35219-0187, (205)940-9640 [12593]

Straub Brewery Company Inc., 303 Sorg, St. Marys, PA 15857-1537, (814)834-2875 [2057]

Straub and Co.; W.F., 5520 Northwest Hwy., Chicago, IL 60630, (773)763-5520 [12594]

Straus Frank Co., 1964 S Alamo St., San Antonio, TX 78204-1689, (210)226-0101 [3274]

Strauss Distributing, PO Box 191518, Little Rock, AR 72219, (501)565-0121 [2058]

Strauss Inc.; Herman, PO Box 6543, Wheeling, WV 26003, (304)232-8770 [27010]

Strawberry Hill Press, 3848 SE Division St., Portland, OR 97202-1641, (503)235-5989 [4193]

Strawn Merchandise Inc., 10966 Harry Hines Blvd., Dallas, TX 75220, (214)352-4891 [8080]

Strayer Products, PO Box 284, New Brighton, PA 15066-2020, (412)846-2600 [21300]

Stream International Inc., 275 Dan Rd., Canton, MA 02021, (781)821-4500 [6766]

Stream & Lake Tackle, 3305 Remembrance NW, Grand Rapids, MI 49544-2203, (616)791-2311 [23989]

Street Art Supply Dallas, 2270 Manana, Dallas, TX 75220, (972)432-0030 [21591]

Street Cars Inc., 7801 Mesquite Bend Dr., Ste. 110, Irving, TX 75063-6043, (972)230-7256 [24868]

Streett and Company Inc.; J.D., 144 Weldon Pkwy., Maryland Heights, MO 63043, (314)432-6600 [22710]

Streicher Mobile Fueling Inc., 2720 NW 55th Ct., Ft. Lauderdale, FL 33309, (954)739-3880 [22711]

Stretch and Sew Inc., PO Box 25306, Tempe, AZ 85285-5306, (602)966-1462 [26216]

Streva Distributing Co., 4512 W Admiral Doyle, New Iberia, LA 70560-9770, (337)369-3838 [2059]

Stribling Equipment Inc., PO Box 6038, Jackson, MS 39288, (601)939-1000 [1300]

Strickland Auto; Jewell, PO Box 2026, Wilmington, NC 28402-2026, (910)762-8533 [17199]

Strickland Beauty & Barber Supply Inc., 1245 N E St., San Bernardino, CA 92405, (909)888-1359 [14249]

Strictly Business Computer Systems Inc., PO Box 2076, Huntington, WV 25720, (304)529-0401 [6767]

Striker Products, 307 S Broadway, Pittsburg, KS 66762, (316)232-3111 [5400]

Stringfellow, Inc., 2710 Locust St., Nashville, TN 37207-4036, (615)226-4900 [3275]

Stringfellow Lumber Co., PO Box 1117, Birmingham, AL 35201, (205)731-9400 [8081]

Stripco Sales Inc., PO Box 248, Osceola, IN 46561, (219)256-7800 [20408]

Stripling Blake Lumber Co., PO Box 9008, Austin, TX 78766, (512)465-4200 [8082]

Striplings Tackle Co., PO Box 811, Waycross, GA 31502-0811, (912)283-8370 [23990]

STRO-WARE Inc., 6035 Bristol Pkwy., Culver City, CA 90230-6601, (310)575-1932 [6768]

Strober Building Supply Center Inc., 695 Wyoming Ave., Kingston, PA 18704, (717)287-5072 [8083]

Stroheim & Romann Inc., 31-11 Thomson Ave., Long Island City, NY 11101, (718)706-7000 [26217]

Strohmeyer and Arpe Co., 636 Morris Tpke., Short Hills, NJ 07078, (201)379-6600 [12595]

Strombecker Corp., 600 N Pulaski Rd., Chicago, IL 60624, (773)638-1000 [26672]

Stromberg; J. Edward, 6275 Harrison Dr., Ste. 6, Las Vegas, NV 89120-4022, (702)798-8970 [21301]

Stromberg Sales Company Inc., PO Box 22487, Indianapolis, IN 46222-0487, (317)638-0772 [9427]

Strong Tool Co., 1251 E 286th St., Cleveland, OH 44132, (216)289-2450 [13941]

Stroud Braided Rug Co., 2627 Rockford Rd., Shelby, NC 28152, (704)434-5098 [10184]

Structural Concepts Corp., 888 Porter Rd., Muskegon, MI 49441-5895, (616)846-3300 [24231]

Structural Materials Inc., 1401 NW 40th St., Fargo, ND 58102, (701)282-7100 [8084]

Struthers Industries Inc., 7633 East 63rd Plaza, Ste. 220, Tulsa, OK 74133, (918)582-1788 [22712]

Struve Distributing Company Inc., 276 West 100 South, Salt Lake City, UT 84101, (801)328-1636 [25832]

Struve Distributing Company Inc., 276 W 1st St., Salt Lake City, UT 84101, (801)328-1636 [24232]

Strygler Company Inc.; H.S., 595 Madison Ave., New York, NY 10022, (212)758-4100 [17623]

STS Truck Equipment and Trailer Sales, 6680 Manlius Center Rd., East Syracuse, NY 13057, (315)437-5406 [3276]

Stuart Medical Inc., Donohue & Luxor Rd., 1 Stuart Pl, Greensburg, PA 15601, (412)837-5700 [19058]

Stuart's Federal Fireplace, Inc., PO Box 252172, West Bloomfield, MI 48325-2172, (248)557-3344 [15670]

Stuart's Hospital Supply Co., 1 Stuart Plz., Greensburg, PA 15601, (412)271-3200 [19640]

Stuarts' Petroleum Co., 11 E 4th St., Bakersfield, CA 93307, (805)325-6320 [22713]

Stuck and Associates; Paul, PO Box 378070, Chicago, IL 60637-8070, (773)890-0700 [27011]

Stud Holdings Ltd., 1221 Brickell, No. 1480, Miami, FL 33131, (305)530-8702 [14192]

Studer Industrial Tool, PO Box 11343, Pittsburgh, PA 15238, (412)828-2470 [16531]

Studio Film & Tape Inc., 1215 N Highland Ave., Hollywood, CA 90038, (213)769-0900 [25467]

Studio Film & Tape Inc., 630 9th Ave., 8th Fl., New York, NY 10036, (212)977-9330 [22908]

Stull Enterprises Inc., PO Box 887, Concordville, PA 19331-0887, (610)459-8406 [1301]

Stull Industries Inc., 12155 Magnolia, Bldg. 5, Riverside, CA 92503, (909)343-2181 [3277]

Stultz Fluid Power, 190 Rand Rd., Portland, ME 04102, (207)828-4727 [16532]

Stulz-Sickles Steel Co., 929 Julia St., Elizabeth, NJ 07201, (908)351-1776 [20409]

Stump & Company Inc.; Weldon F., 1313 Campbell St., PO Box 3155, Toledo, OH 43607-0155, (419)243-6221 [16533]

Sturdevant Auto Supply, 100 Smith, Rock Rapids, IA 51246-1767, (712)472-3651 [3278]

Sturdevant Auto Supply, 505 E Main, Luverne, MN 56156-1905, (507)283-2371 [3279]

Sturdevant Auto Supply, 501 Broadway, Box 398, Wheaton, MN 56296, (320)563-8209 [3280]

Sturdvant Refrigeration/Air-Conditioning, 300 Hoohana St., Kahului, HI 96732-2966, (808)871-6404 [14700]

Sturgis Iron and Metal Company Inc., PO Box 579, Sturgis, MI 49091, (616)651-7851 [27012]

Sturgis Livestock Exchange, PO Box 1059, Sturgis, SD 57785-1059, (605)347-2575 [18263]

Stusser Electric Co., 660 S Andover St., Seattle, WA 98108, (206)623-1501 [9428]

Stusser Electric Co., 1606 130th Ave. NE, Bellevue, WA 98005, (425)454-3339 [9429]

Stusser Electric Co., 1815 Franklin St., Bellingham, WA 98225, (206)734-5500 [9430]

Stusser Electric Co., 917 N Wycoff Ave., Bremerton, WA 98312-3808, (206)373-5018 [9431]

Stusser Electric Co., 1104 132nd St. SW, Everett, WA 98204, (425)745-9666 [9432]

Stusser Electric Co., 310 E Olympia Ave., Olympia, WA 98501, (206)943-1900 [9433]

Stusser Electric Co., 21520 84th Place S, Kent, WA 98031, (253)395-3133 [9434]

Stusser Electric Co., 116 N 2nd Ave., Yakima, WA 98902, (509)453-0378 [9435]

Stusser Electric Co., 27929 SW 95th Ave. Ste. 701, Wilsonville, OR 97070, (503)639-4993 [9436]

Stusser Electric Co., 2290 Judson St., SE, Salem, OR 97302, (503)581-3711 [9437]

Stusser Electric Company, 411 E 54th Ave., Anchorage, AK 99518, (907)561-1061 [9438]

Stuttgart Industrial Service Inc., 1056 Old England Hwy., Stuttgart, AR 72160, (870)673-2801 [18264]

Stutz Candy Co., Inc., 400 S Warminster Rd., Hatboro, PA 19040-4015, (215)675-2630 [12596]

Stutz Co., 4450 W Carroll Ave., Chicago, IL 60624, (773)287-1068 [17200]

Style Asia Inc., 450 Barell Ave., Carlstadt, NJ 07072-2810, (201)532-5720 [13454]

Style Eyes of California, 833 W 16th St., Newport Beach, CA 92663, (949)548-5355 [19641]

Style Eyes Inc., 833 W 16th St., Newport Beach, CA 92663, (949)548-5355 [19641]

Style Master, 5020 Lincolnway E, PO Box 1330, Mishawaka, IN 46546, (219)255-9692 [20410]

Suarez and Co.; V., Rexco Industrial Park, PO Box 364588, Guaynabo, San Juan, PR 00901, (787)792-1212 [12597]

Suarez Food Distribution Co.; C.G., 355 N C.R. 427, Longwood, FL 32750-5440, (407)834-1300 [12598]

Suave Noble Creations Inc., PO Box 8272, New York, NY 10116-4651 [5401]

Subaru of America Inc., PO Box 6000, Cherry Hill, NJ 08034-6000, (609)488-8500 [20731]

Sublette Cooperative, Inc., Rte. 1, Box 56B, Copeland, KS 67837, (316)668-5615 [18265]

Sublette Farmers Elevator Co., PO Box 289, Sublette, IL 61367, (815)849-5222 [18266]

Subterranean Co., 265 S 5th St., PO Box 160, Monroe, OR 97456, (541)847-5274 [4194]

Suburban Manufacturing Co., PO Box 399, Dayton, TN 37321, (423)775-2131 [14701]

Suburban Ostomy Supply Company Inc., 75 October Hill Rd., Holliston, MA 01746, (508)429-1000 [19642]

Sues Young and Brown Inc., 5151 Commerce Dr., Baldwin Park, CA 91706-7890, (818)338-3800 [23991]

Sufrin Inc.; Adolph, 5770 Baum Blvd., Pittsburgh, PA 15206, (412)363-8000 [21302]

Sugar Creek Scrap, Inc., PO Box 208, West Terre Haute, IN 47885-0208, (812)533-2147 [27013]

Sugar Foods Corp., 950 3rd Ave., 21st Fl., New York, NY 10022-2705, (212)753-6900 [12599]

Sugar Records, PO Box 1181, Florissant, MO 63031, (314)837-4095 [25468]

Suhner Industrial Products Corporation, Hwy. 411 S, PO Box 1234, Rome, GA 30162-1234, (706)235-8046 [16534]

Suhner Manufacturing, Inc., Hwy. 411 S, PO Box 1234, Rome, GA 30162-1234, (706)235-8046 [16534]

Suisman and Blumenthal Inc., 500 Flatbush Ave., Hartford, CT 06106, (860)522-3123 [27014]

Suk Fashions, 747 Pittston, Allentown, PA 18103-3255, (215)435-4565 [5402]

Sukut Office Equipment Co., PO Box 1405, Williston, ND 58802-1405, (701)572-7676 [21303]

Sullco Inc., 40 Beach St., Ste. 105, Manchester, MA 01944, (978)526-4244 [24869]

Sullivan Candy & Supply, 1623 E 6th Ave., Hibbing, MN 55746-1433, (218)263-6634 [26354]

Sullivan Co. Inc.; C.B., 15 W Alice Ave., Hooksett, NH 03106, (603)624-4752 [14250]

Sullivan Dental Products Inc., 10920 W Lincoln Ave., West Allis, WI 53227, (414)321-8881 [19059]

Sullivan Inc., PO Box 703, Ulysses, KS 67880, (316)356-1219 [18267]

Sullivan Tile Distributors, 10 Railroad Ave., PO Box 485, West Haven, CT 06516, (203)934-2600 [10185]

Sullivan's, PO Box 5361, Sioux Falls, SD 57117-5361, (605)339-4274 [13455]

Sully Cooperative Exchange Inc., PO Box 250, Sully, IA 50251-0250, (515)594-4115 [18268]

The Sultan Co., 3049 Ualena St., No. 14, Honolulu, HI 96819-1942, (808)923-4971 [17624]

Sultan and Sons Inc., 650 SW 9th Ter., Pompano Beach, FL 33069, (954)782-6600 [15671]

Sumitok America Inc., 23326 Hawthorne Blvd., Ste. 360, Torrance, CA 90505, (310)378-7886 [3281]

Sumitomo Corporation of America, 345 Park Ave., New York, NY 10154, (212)207-0700 [20411]

Sumitomo Plastics America Inc., 900 Lafayette St., Ste. 510, Santa Clara, CA 95050-4967, (408)243-8402 [23037]

Summation Legal Technologies Inc., 100 Bush St., Ste. 2000, San Francisco, CA 94104, (415)442-0404 [6769]

Summers Fuel Inc., 28 Allegheny Ave., Ste. 1201, Baltimore, MD 21204, (410)825-8555 [20571]

Summers Hardware & Supply Co., 400 Buffalo St., PO Box 210, Johnson City, TN 37605-0210, (423)461-4700 [16535]

Summers Induserve Supply, 400 Buffalo St., PO Box 210, Johnson City, TN 37605-0210, (423)461-4700 [16535]

Summers Sales Company Inc.; Barney, 6226 Prospect Ave., Kansas City, MO 64130, (816)444-3474 [12600]

Summertime Potato Co., 2001 E Grand, Des Moines, IA 50317-5235, (515)265-9865 [12601]

Summertree Corp., 1380 Tulilp St., Ste. O, Longmont, CO 80501, (303)651-5226 [19060]

Summertree Medisales, 1380 Tulilp St., Ste. O, Longmont, CO 80501, (303)651-5226 [19060]

Summervilles Inc., PO Box 2094, Akron, OH 44309-2094, (330)535-3163 [21304]

Summit Aviation Inc., Summit Airport, Middletown, DE 19709, (302)834-5400 [152]

Summit Brick and Tile Co., PO Box 533, Pueblo, CO 81002-0533, (719)542-8278 [8085]

Summit Company, PO Box 23337, Louisville, KY 40223, (502)245-9764 [4522]

Summit Electric Supply Inc., PO Box 6409, Albuquerque, NM 87197-6409, (505)884-4400 [9439]

Summit Group, 150 Alhambra Cir., Ste. 900, Coral Gables, FL 33134, (305)446-8000 [9286]

Summit Handling Systems Inc., 11 Defco Park Rd., North Haven, CT 06473, (203)239-5351 [16536]

Summit Hats, 1120 Roberts St., Houston, TX 77003, (713)224-2683 [5403]

Summit Hats, 1120 Roberts St., Houston, TX 77003, (713)224-2683 [5404]

Summit Import Corp., 415 Greenwich St., New York, NY 10013-2099, (212)226-1662 [12602]

Summit Instruments Corp., 76 Woolens Rd., Elkton, MD 21921-1816, (410)398-7250 [19061]

Summit of New England, 386 Hill St., Biddeford, ME 04005, (207)283-1463 [3282]

Summit Pet Products, 400 Quaint Acres Dr., Silver Spring, MD 20904, (301)791-7138 [27241]

Summit Pet Products, 420 Chimney Rock Rd., Greensboro, NC 27409-9260, (910)665-0666 [27242]

Summit Trading Co., 4623 Old York Rd., Philadelphia, PA 19140 [19062]

Summit Wholesale, 38 Ganson Ave., PO Box 921, Batavia, NY 14021, (716)343-7022 [14702]

Summit Wholesale, 38 Ganson Ave., Batavia, NY 14021, (716)343-7022 [23399]

Summitville Atlanta, 8607 Roswell Rd., Atlanta, GA 30350, (404)587-1744 [10186]

Summitville Baltimore, 8 W Aylesbury Rd., Timonium, MD 21093, (410)252-0112 [10187]

Summitville Boardman, 631 Boardman Canfield Rd., Boardman, OH 44512, (330)758-0835 [10188]

Summitville Charlotte, 4618 South Blvd., Charlotte, NC 28209, (704)525-8453 [10189]

Summitville Fairfax, 6464 A General Green Way, Alexandria, VA 22312, (703)750-2660 [10190]

Summitville Orlando, 4210 L.B. McLeod, Ste. 101, Orlando, FL 32811, (407)849-5193 [10191]

Summitville Pompano, 1330 S Andrews Ave., Pompano Beach, FL 33069, (954)782-3522 [10192]

Summitville, USA, 1101 Lunt Ave., Elk Grove Village, IL 60007, (847)439-8820 [10193]

Sumter Machinery Company Inc., PO Box 700, Sumter, SC 29151-0700, (803)773-1441 [17201]

Sumter Wood Preserving Company Inc., PO Box 637, Sumter, SC 29151, (803)775-5301 [8086]

Sun America Corp., 770 Tyvola Rd., Charlotte, NC 28217-3508, (704)522-9219 [23992]

Sun Appliance Service Inc., 645 Griswold St., Ste. 3900, Detroit, MI 48226-4221, (313)531-3636 [25833]

Sun Aviation Inc., PO Box 18290, Raytown, MO 64133-8290, (816)358-4925 [153]

Sun Coast Imports, PO Box 559, Moose Lake, MN 55767, (218)485-4200 [26218]

Sun Coast Tile Distributors Inc., 2457 Fowler St., Ft. Myers, FL 33901, (941)334-3461 [10194]

Sun Company Inc., 1801 Market St., 10 Penn Ctr., Philadelphia, PA 19103-1699, (215)977-3000 [22714]

Sun Control Window Tinting and Shades, 4700 Vestal Pky. E, Vestal, NY 13850, (607)723-3066 [8087]

Sun Control Window Tinting and Shades, 4700 Vestal Pky. E, Vestal, NY 13850, (607)723-3066 [27383]

Sun Data Inc., PO Box 926020, Norcross, GA 30010, (770)449-6116 [6770]

Sun/Day Distributor Company, 1940 Railroad Dr., Sacramento, CA 95815-3514, (916)922-4370 [13456]

Sun Design Ltd., PO Box 35, Watertown, CT 06795-0035, (860)274-9830 [19643]

Sun Diamond Growers of California Mixed Nut Div., 16500 W 103rd St., Lemont, IL 60439, (630)739-3000 [10960]

Sun-Diamond Growers of California. Mixed Nut Div., 16500 W 103rd St., Lemont, IL 60439, (630)739-3000 [12603]

Sun Distributors L.P., 1 Logan Sq., Philadelphia, PA 19103, (215)665-3650 [16537]

Sun Down Foods, U.S.A., 291 Geary St., Ste. 407, San Francisco, CA 94102, (415)956-6600 [10539]

Sun Electrical Appliance Sales & Service, 4554 E Princess Anne Rd., Norfolk, VA 23502-1614, (757)855-3052 [15322]

Sun Fashion Designs Inc., PO Box 10745, Prescott, AZ 86304, (520)778-9585 [17625]

Sun & Fun Specialties Inc., PO Box 1406, Las Cruces, NM 88004-1406, (505)526-8906 [13457]

Sun Glo of Idaho Inc., PO Box 98, Rexburg, ID 83440, (208)356-7346 [12604]

Sun Hing Trading Company Inc., 16816 Johnson Dr., City of Industry, CA 91745, (626)330-0667 [13458]

Sun Imports Inc., PO Box 11618, Kansas City, MO 64138, (816)358-7077 [2060]

Sun Inc.; Bob, PO Box 2637, Honolulu, HI 96803-2637, (808)845-5999 [26673]

Sun International, 3700 Hwy. 421 N, Wilmington, NC 28401, (910)762-0278 [24440]

Sun International Trading Ltd., 3700 Hwy. 421 N, Wilmington, NC 28401, (910)762-0278 [24440]

Sun Medical Equipment and Supply Co., 1072 W 14th Mile Rd., Clawson, MI 48017, (248)280-2020 [19063]

Sun Moon Star, 1941 Ringwood Ave., San Jose, CA 95131, (408)452-7811 [5771]

Sun-Ni Cheese Co., 8738 W Chester Pike, Upper Darby, PA 19082-2618, (215)789-4340 [12605]

Sun Office Service, PO Box 19523, Austin, TX 78760, (512)444-3809 [12606]

Sun Pacific Industries, 15136 Valley Blvd., Ste. C, City of Industry, CA 91744, (626)855-9048 [25942]

Sun Pacific Trading Co. Inc., 3050 Ualena St. B, Honolulu, HI 96819-1914, (808)836-2168 [24870]

Sun Sales, California Mart, Ste. A-988, 110 E 9th St., Los Angeles, CA 90079, (213)489-9739 [17626]

Sun Shader International, Inc., 4601 10th Ave. N, Lake Worth, FL 33463-2203, (561)588-6887 [5405]

Sun States Beverage Co., 2480 Weaver Way, Doraville, GA 30340, (404)840-7178 [25041]

Sun Supply Corp., PO Box 149, Abilene, TX 79604, (915)673-2505 [9440]

Sun Valley Aviation Inc., PO Box 1085, Hailey, ID 83333-1085, (208)788-9511 [154]

Sun Valley Paper Stock Inc., 11166 Pendleton St., Sun Valley, CA 91352, (818)767-8984 [27015]

Sunbelt Beverage Company L.L.C., 4601 Hollins Ferry Rd., Baltimore, MD 21227, (410)536-5000 [2061]

Sunbelt Beverage L.L.C., 1115 N 47th Ave., Phoenix, AZ 85043-1801, (602)272-3751 [1486]

Sunbelt Data Systems Inc., 2629 NW 39th, Ste. 200, Oklahoma City, OK 73112, (405)947-7617 [6771]

Sunbelt Distributors Inc., 4494 Campbell Rd., Houston, TX 77041, (713)329-9988 [12607]

Sunbelt Food Sales, 1425 S 21st St., Ste. 102, Birmingham, AL 35205, (205)933-6833 [12608]

Sunbelt Publications, 1250 Fayette St., El Cajon, CA 92020, (619)258-4911 [4195]

Sunbelt Seeds Inc., PO Box 668, Norcross, GA 30091, (404)448-9932 [1302]

Sunbelt Supply Co., 8363 Market St. Rd., Houston, TX 77029, (713)672-2222 [17202]

Sunbelt Transformer Inc., PO Box 1500, Temple, TX 76503-1500, (254)771-3777 [9441]

Sunbrand Co., 3900 Green Industrial Way, Atlanta, GA 30341, (404)455-0664 [1303]

Sunburst Foods Inc., 1002 Sunburst Dr., Goldsboro, NC 27534, (919)778-2151 [12609]

Suncook Tanning Corp., PO Box 3009, Peabody, MA 01960, (978)532-0707 [18269]

Sundance Publishing, 234 Taylor St., PO Box 1326, Littleton, MA 01460, (978)486-9201 [4196]

Sunday School Publishing Board, 330 Charlotte Ave., Nashville, TN 37201, (615)256-2480 [4197]

Sunderland Motor Company Inc., PO Box 429, Jerseyville, IL 62052-0429, (618)498-2123 [20732]

Sundin Rand; Gloria, PO Box 133, Kennebunkport, ME 04046-0133, (207)967-4887 [13252]

Sundog Productions, 3809 Pickett Rd., Fairfax, VA 22031-3605, (703)978-0041 [5406]

Sundog Technologies, 4505 Wasatch Blvd. Ste. 340, Salt Lake City, UT 84124-4709, (801)424-0044 [6772]

Sundrop Inc., 29599 Old Hwy. 20, Madison, AL 35758, (256)772-8596 [25042]

Sundstrand Fluid Handling Corp., 14845 W 64th Ave., Arvada, CO 80007, (303)425-0800 [16538]

Suneel Alaska Corp., PO Box 1789, Seward, AK 99664-1789, (907)224-3120 [20572]

Sunfire Corporation, 150 Algerita Dr., San Antonio, TX 78230-4613, (210)340-9609 [12610]

Sunflower Restaurant Supply, PO Box 1277, Salina, KS 67402-1277, (785)823-6394 [12611]

Sunflower Restaurant Supply Inc., PO Box 1277, Salina, KS 67402-1277, (785)823-6394 [12612]

Sunflower University Press, 1531 Yuma, Box 1009, Manhattan, KS 66502-4228, (785)539-1888 [4198]

Sunfresh Inc., PO Box 400, Royal City, WA 99357, (509)346-9223 [12613]

Sunhopper Inc., PO Box 2551, Elizabethtown, KY 42702-2551 [14251]

Sunkist Growers Inc., 14130 Riverside Dr., Sherman Oaks, CA 91423, (818)986-4800 [12614]

Sunkist Growers Inc., PO Box 7888, Van Nuys, CA 91409-7888, (818)986-4800 [12615]

Sunkyong America Inc., 110 E 55th, 17th Fl., New York, NY 10022, (212)906-8100 [15323]

Sunland Steel Inc., 1004 N Hwy. 51, Truth Or Consequences, NM 87901, (505)894-7017 [20412]

Sunlight Foods Inc., 3550 NW 112th St., PO Box 680670, Miami, FL 33167, (305)688-5400 [12616]

Sunline USA Group Inc., Hwy. 29 N & Joe Brown Dr., PO Box 13206, Greensboro, NC 27415, (919)375-1143 [13942]

Sunlow Inc., 1071 Howell Mill Rd., Atlanta, GA 30318, (404)872-8135 [24233]

Sunny Group Inc., 2215 E Huntington Dr., Duarte, CA 91010, (626)303-2050 [6773]

Sunny International Inc., 8900 NW 33rd St., Miami, FL 33172, (305)591-3065 [13943]

Sunnyland Farms, Inc., PO Box 1275, Albany, GA 31702, (912)436-5654 [12617]

Sunny's Great Outdoors Inc., 7540 Washington Blvd., Ste. SS, Elkridge, MD 21075, (410)799-4900 [23993]

Sunnyside Auto Finance, 2424 W Montrose Ave., Chicago, IL 60618, (773)267-8200 [3283]

Sunnytech Inc., 500 Hollister Rd., Teterboro, NJ 07608, (201)288-8866 [6774]

Sunnyvale Lumber Inc., 870 W Evelyn Ave., Sunnyvale, CA 94086, (408)736-5411 [8088]

SunRace Technology (USA) Corp., 809 S Lemon Ave., Walnut, CA 91789, (909)468-2933 [6775]

Sunray Cooperative, PO Box 430, Sunray, TX 79086-0430, (806)948-4121 [1304]

Sunray Electric Supply Co., PO Box 489, Mc Keesport, PA 15134, (412)678-8826 [9442]

Sunridge Farms, 1055 17th Ave., Santa Cruz, CA 95062-3033, (831)462-1280 [11076]

Sunrise Cooperative Inc., 82 Townsend Ave., Norwalk, OH 44857, (419)668-3336 [1305]

Sunrise Glass Distributors, 916 4th St. SW, Albuquerque, NM 87101, (505)246-2997 [8089]

Sunseri's Inc., 2258 St. Claude Ave., PO Box 3127, Bywater Station, New Orleans, LA 70117, (504)944-6762 [15324]

Sunseri's Inc., 4500 I-10 Service Rd. S, Metairie, LA 70001, (504)888-3773 [15325]

Sunset Ice Cream Offices and Sales, 1849 Lycoming Creek Rd., Williamsport, PA 17701, (570)326-7475 [12618]

Sunset Industrial Parts, 16121 S Piuma Ave., Cerritos, CA 90701, (562)809-8300 [17203]

Sunset Models, Inc., 138 W Campbell Ave., Campbell, CA 95008, (408)866-1727 [26674]

Sunset Supply, 2411 S Hwy. 79, PO Box 2248, Rapid City, SD 57701, (605)342-5220 [13459]

Sunshine Cap Co., 1142 W Main, Lakeland, FL 33815-4362, (941)688-8147 [5407]

Sunshine Craft Supply, 9198 Brewerton Rd., PO Box 709, Brewerton, NY 13029, (315)699-5931 [21165]

Sunshine Dairy Foods Inc., 584 Coleman Rd., Middletown, CT 06457, (860)346-6644 [12619]

Sunshine Dairy Foods Inc., 801 NE 21st Ave., Portland, OR 97232, (503)234-7526 [12620]

Sunshine Golf, Inc., 13835 SW 77th Ave., Miami, FL 33158, (305)234-4448 [23994]

Sunshine Industries Inc., 1111 E 200th St., Cleveland, OH 44117, (216)383-9000 [13944]

Sunshine Market Inc., 1492 Hwy. 315, Wilkes Barre, PA 18702, (570)829-1392 [12621]

Sunshine Steel Enterprises Corp., 8265 Belvedere Ave., Sacramento, CA 95826, (916)451-7031 [20413]

SunSource, 5750 W Erie St., Chandler, AZ 85226, (602)254-8414 [17204]

SunSource Technology Services, 5390 E Ponce de Leon Ave., Ste. E, Stone Mountain, GA 30083, (770)491-6900 [16539]

Sunsweet Growers Inc., 901 N Walton Ave., Yuba City, CA 95993, (530)751-5203 [12622]

Suntuf USA, 2558 E 2980 S, Salt Lake City, UT 84109, (801)466-6919 [23038]

Sunwest Silver Co., 324 Lomas Blvd. NW, Albuquerque, NM 87102, (505)243-3781 [17627]

Supa Machinery Sales Inc., 2727 3 Mile Rd., PO Box 361, Franksville, WI 53126, (262)835-3400 [16540]

Super American Import, 5400 NW 161 St., Miami, FL 33014, (305)625-0772 [14958]

Super Food Services Inc., Kettering Box 2323, Dayton, OH 45429, (513)439-7500 [12623]

Super Glass Corp., 1020 E 48th St., Brooklyn, NY 11203, (718)469-9300 [15672]

Super-Nutrition Distributors Inc., 1500 Hempstead Tpke., No. 100, East Meadow, NY 11554-1558, (516)897-2480 [14252]

Super Parts Place, 605 S Gallatin, PO Box 3487, Jackson, MS 39207, (601)948-4381 [3036]

Super Rite Foods Inc., PO Box 2261, Harrisburg, PA 17110, (717)232-6821 [12624]

Super Shoe Stores Inc., PO Box 239, Cumberland, MD 21502, (301)759-4300 [24871]

Super Store Industries/Fairfield Dairy Division, PO Box 2898, Fairfield, CA 94533, (707)864-0502 [12625]

Super Stores Industries, PO Box 549, Lathrop, CA 95330, (209)858-2010 [12626]

Super Stores Industries, PO Box 549, Lathrop, CA 95330, (209)858-2010 [12627]

Super Valu Inc. - Midwest Region, 7400 95th St., PO Box 581908, Pleasant Prairie, WI 53158, (262)947-7290 [12628]

Super Valu Stores Inc., Industrial Park, Roberts Dr., Anniston, AL 36201, (205)831-1840 [12629]

Super Valu Stores Inc., 600 Selig Dr. SW, Atlanta, GA 30336, (404)699-3600 [12630]

Super Valu Stores Inc., PO Box 58506, Bismarck, ND 58502, (701)222-5600 [12644]

Super Valu Stores Inc., 1983 Tower Rd., Aurora, CO 80011, (303)361-0386 [12631]

Super Valu Stores Inc., 3900 NW 106th St., Des Moines, IA 50322, (515)278-0211 [12632]

Super Valu Stores Inc., 101 S Jefferson Ave., Hopkins, MN 55343, (612)932-4300 [12633]

Super Valu Stores Inc., 11016 E Montgomery Ave., Spokane, WA 99206, (509)928-7700 [12634]

Super Valu Stores Inc., 1525 East D. St., Tacoma, WA 98421, (253)593-3200 [12635]

Super Valu Stores Inc., 3900 106th St., Urbandale, IA 50322, (515)278-0211 [12636]

Super Valu Stores Inc. Ohio Valley, 1003 Belbrook Ave., Xenia, OH 45385, (937)374-7611 [12637]

Super Valu Stores Inc., Westpac Pacific Foods Div., PO Box 549, Lathrop, CA 95330, (209)858-2010 [12626]

Superb Cooking Products Co./Empire Comfort Systems, Inc., 918 Freeburg Ave., Belleville, IL 62222, (618)233-7420 [23995]

Superba Inc., 350 5th Ave., New York, NY 10118-0100, (212)594-2720 [5408]

Supercircuits Inc., 1 Supercircuits Plz., Leander, TX 78645, (512)260-0333 [22909]

Superfeet In-Shoe Systems Inc., 1419 Whitehorn St., Ferndale, WA 98248-8923, (206)384-1820 [24872]

SuperGrind Co., PO Box 538, Mentor, OH 44061, (440)257-6277 [17205]

Superide Air Suspensions, 2285 E Date Ave., Fresno, CA 93706-5477, (559)442-1500 [2228]

Superior Appliance Service Co., 1050 Scribner Ave. NW, Grand Rapids, MI 49504-4212, (616)459-3271 [15326]

Superior Auto Electric, 1847 Highland Ave., New Hyde Park, NY 11040-4049, (516)437-1267 [3284]

Superior Auto Sales Inc., 5201 Camp Rd., Hamburg, NY 14075, (716)649-6695 [20733]

Superior Auto Sales Inc., 5201 Camp Rd., Hamburg, NY 14075, (716)649-6695 [3285]

Superior Block and Supply Co., PO Box 57, Milldale, CT 06467-0057, (203)239-4216 [8090]

Superior Confections, 501 Industry Rd., Staten Island, NY 10314-3607, (718)698-3300 [12638]

Superior Cooperative Elevator Co., 603 Railroad St., Superior, IA 51363, (712)858-4491 [18270]

Superior-Deshler Inc., Main St., Davenport, NE 68335, (402)364-2125 [1306]

Superior Distributing Co., PO Box 107, Fostoria, OH 44830, (419)435-1938 [2062]

Superior Distributors, 333 N Pennsylvania Ave., Wilkes Barre, PA 18702, (717)824-9994 [25834]

Superior Div., 1610 N Calhoun St., Ft. Wayne, IN 46808, (219)422-5541 [27016]

Superior Electric Supply Co. (Elyria, Ohio), PO Box 509, Elyria, OH 44036, (216)323-5451 [9443]

Superior Epoxies & Coatings, Inc., 2527 Lantrac Ct., Decatur, GA 30035, (770)808-0023 [15]

Superior FomeBords Corp., 2700 W Grand Ave., Chicago, IL 60612, (773)278-9200 [16]

Superior Foods, 275 Westgate Dr., Watsonville, CA 95076, (408)728-3691 [12639]

Superior Group Inc., PO Box 6760, Radnor, PA 19087-8760, (610)964-2000 [17206]

Superior Insulated Wire Corp., 40 Washburn Ln., PO Box 658, Stony Point, NY 10980-0658, (845)942-1433 [9444]

Superior Linen Company Inc., PO Box 250, Hackensack, NJ 07601, (201)343-3300 [15673]

Superior Lumber Co., PO Box 250, Glendale, OR 97442, (503)832-1121 [27384]

Superior Manufacturing Co. (Santa Ana, California), 3133 W Harvard St., Santa Ana, CA 92704, (714)540-4605 [9445]

Superior Nut Company Inc., 225 Monsignor O'Brien Hwy., Cambridge, MA 02141, (617)876-3808 [12640]

Superior Pharmaceutical Co., 1385 Kemper Meadow, Cincinnati, OH 45240, (513)851-3600 [19644]

Superior Pool Products Inc., 4900 E Landon Dr., Anaheim, CA 92807, (714)693-8035 [23996]

Superior Products, PO Box 64177, St. Paul, MN 55164, (651)636-1110 [24234]

Superior Products, Inc., 7575 Washington Blvd., Baltimore, MD 21227, (410)799-1000 [10195]

Superior Products Manufacturing Co., 510 West County Rd. D, St. Paul, MN 55112, (651)636-1110 [24235]

Superior Products Manufacturing Company Hospitality Supply, PO Box 64177, St. Paul, MN 55164, (651)636-1110 [24234]

Superior Pump Exchange Co., 12901 Crenshaw Blvd., Hawthorne, CA 90250-5511, (310)676-4995 [3286]

Superior Supply Co., 2119 Wheeler, Ft. Smith, AR 72901, (501)785-1439 [14640]

Superior Supply Co., 14315 W 100 St., Lenexa, KS 66215, (913)888-4467 [14703]

Superior Supply Co., 2935 SW Van Buren, Topeka, KS 66611, (913)226-3571 [14704]

Superior Supply Co., 1420 S 6th St., St. Joseph, MO 64501, (816)233-9111 [14705]

Superior Supply Co., 1405 Illinois Ave., Columbia, MO 65203, (573)449-0806 [14706]

Superior Supply Co., RR 1, Box 105H, Linn Creek, MO 65052, (573)346-5914 [14707]

Superior Supply Co., 1020 Illinois, Joplin, MO 64801, (417)781-1520 [14708]

Superior Supply Company Inc., 215 Laura, Wichita, KS 67211, (316)263-6212 [14709]

Superior Tire Inc., 2320 Western Ave., Las Vegas, NV 89102, (702)384-2937 [3287]

Superior Tire Inc., 8577 Haven Ave., Rancho Cucamonga, CA 91730, (909)484-9497 [24297]

Superior Trading Co., 837 Washington St., San Francisco, CA 94108, (415)982-8722 [12641]

Superior Turf Equipment, 13212 E Indiana, Spokane, WA 99216, (509)926-8974 [23997]

Superior Water Systems, 13529 S Normandie Ave., Gardena, CA 90249, (310)532-0470 [25835]

Superior Wines and Liquors Inc., PO Box 165790, Kansas City, MO 64116-5790, (816)421-1772 [2063]

Superlearning, 450 7th Ave., Ste. 500, New York, NY 10213, (212)279-8450 [4199]

Supersafe, 1 Rotary Park Dr., PO Box 3390, Clarksville, TN 37043-3390, (931)647-0139 [4660]

Superscape Inc., 3945 Freedom Cir., Santa Clara, CA 95054, (408)969-0500 [6776]

Superscope Professional Products, 2640 White Oak Cir., Aurora, IL 60504, (630)820-4800 [25469]

Superscope Technologies, Inc./Marantz Professional, 2640 White Oak Cir., Aurora, IL 60504, (630)820-4800 [25469]

Supertek, 2231 Colby Ave., Los Angeles, CA 90064, (310)477-1481 [9446]

SUPERVALU, 3501 12th Ave. N, Fargo, ND 58102, (701)293-2100 [12642]

Supervalu, PO Box 1021, Quincy, FL 32353, (850)875-2600 [12651]

SUPERVALU Champaign Distribution Center, PO Box 9008, Champaign, IL 61826-9008, (217)384-2800 [12643]

SuperValu Inc., PO Box 58506, Bismarck, ND 58502, (701)222-5600 [12644]

SUPERVALU Inc., PO Box 990, Minneapolis, MN 55440, (612)828-4000 [12645]

SUPERVALU Inc. Charley Brothers Div., PO Box 1000, New Stanton, PA 15672, (412)925-6600 [12646]

SUPERVALU Inc. Food Marketing Div., PO Box 1198, Ft. Wayne, IN 46801-1198, (219)483-2146 [12647]

SuperValu International, 495 E 19th St., Tacoma, WA 98421, (253)593-3198 [12648]

Supervalu - Milton Div., PO Box 386, Milton, WV 25541, (304)743-9087 [12649]

SuperValu—New England, 2700 Plainfield Rd., Cranston, RI 02921, (401)942-4000 [12650]

SuperValu Quincy Div., PO Box 1021, Quincy, FL 32353, (850)875-2600 [12651]

Supply One Corp., 2601 W Dorothy Ln., Dayton, OH 45439, (937)297-1111 [23400]

The Supply Room Companies, Inc., 4103 W Clay St., Richmond, VA 23230-3307, (804)342-6060 [21305]

Supply Station Inc., PO Box 13219, Sacramento, CA 95813-3219, (916)920-2919 [13945]

Supplyline Inc., PO Box 915168, Longwood, FL 32791-5168, (407)843-5463 [6777]

SupplySource Inc., PO Box 3553, Williamsport, PA 17701, (717)327-1500 [21306]

Support Net Inc., 4400 W 96 St., Indianapolis, IN 46268, (317)735-0200 [6778]

SupportHealth Inc., 2204 Lakeshore Dr., Ste. 140, Birmingham, AL 35209, (205)802-1682 [19146]

Supra Alloys Inc., 351 Cortez Cir, Camarillo, CA 93012, (805)388-2138 [20414]

Supreme, 321 24th St., Rock Island, IL 61201, (309)786-4474 [22372]

Supreme Beverage Co. Inc., 3217 Airport Hwy., Birmingham, AL 35222-1259, (205)251-8010 [2064]

Supreme Oil Company Inc., PO Box 62, New Albany, IN 47151, (812)945-5266 [22715]

Surel International, Inc., 526 Garfield Ave., Ste. A, South Pasadena, CA 91030-2244 [9447]

Surfa-Shield Corp., 2360 Thompson Bridge Rd., Apt P6, Gainesville, GA 30501-1624 [13946]

Surface Sealing Inc., 235 E Dawson Rd., Milford, MI 48381-3211, (248)685-7355 [8091]

Surface Technology Corp., 15909 1/2 49th St. S, Gulfport, FL 33707, (813)323-0212 [15674]

Surfas Inc., 8825 National Blvd., Culver City, CA 90232, (310)559-4770 [24236]

Surfco Hawaii Inc., 98-723 Kuahao Pl., Pearl City, HI 96782, (808)488-5996 [23998]

Surge Components Inc., 1016 Grand Blvd., Deer Park, NY 11729, (631)595-1818 [9448]

Surgical Instrument Associates, 4220 Park Glen Rd., Minneapolis, MN 55416-4758, (612)922-4444 [19064]

Surgitec, 4325 Laurel, Ste. 103, Anchorage, AK 99508-5338, (907)562-7733 [19065]

Surner Heating Company Inc., 60 Shumway St., Amherst, MA 01002, (413)253-5999 [22716]

Surpless, Dunn & Co., 2150 W Lawrence Ave., Chicago, IL 60625-1496, (773)878-8300 [13947]

Surplus City USA Inc., PO Box 20425, Jackson, MS 39209-1425, (601)922-5120 [23999]

Surplus Office Equipment Inc., 295 Lincoln St., Manchester, NH 03103-3655, (603)668-9230 [21307]

Surratt Hosiery Mill Inc., 22872 NC Hwy. 8, Denton, NC 27239-8175, (336)859-4583 [5409]

Susquehanna Motor Company Inc., PO Box 55, West Milton, PA 17886, (717)568-6941 [20734]

Sussen Inc., 6000 Carnegie Ave., Cleveland, OH 44103, (216)361-1700 [3288]

Sussex Company Inc., PO Box J, Milford, DE 19963, (302)422-8037 [5410]

Sussman Co.; Frank, 28 N 3rd St., Philadelphia, PA 19106, (215)627-3221 [5411]

Sutey Oil CO., 2000 Holmes Ave., Butte, MT 59701, (406)494-2305 [22717]

Sutherland Farmers Cooperative, 201 1st St., Sutherland, IA 51058, (712)446-3335 [1307]

Sutherland Foodservice, Inc., PO Box 786, Forest Park, GA 30298, (404)366-8550 [12652]

Sutliff & Son; Norman, PO Box 1157, Kodiak, AK 99615, (907)486-5797 [18619]

Sutmyn America, 340 E Larkspur Ln., Tempe, AZ 85281, (480)970-5401 [6779]

Sutton-Garten Co., 901 N Senate Ave., Indianapolis, IN 46202, (317)264-3236 [17207]

Sutton Ranches, PO Box 33, Onida, SD 57564-0033, (605)258-2540 [18271]

Svendsen's Boat Works, 1851 Clement Ave., Alameda, CA 94501, (510)522-2886 [18620]

Svendsen's Marine Distribution, 1851 Clement Ave., Alameda, CA 94501, (510)522-7860 [18621]

Svetlana Electron Devices, Inc., 8200 S Memorial Pky., Huntsville, AL 35802, (205)882-1344 [17208]

SVI Systems Inc., 1520 W Altorfer Dr., Peoria, IL 61615, (309)692-1023 [25470]

S.W. Controls, Inc., 9200 Market Place, Cleveland, OH 44147, (440)838-4444 [24441]

SW Marketing Associates Inc., 10940 Alder Cir., Dallas, TX 75238, (214)341-8631 [8952]

Swaim Supply Company Inc., PO Box 2406, High Point, NC 27261, (919)883-7161 [23401]

Swam Electric Company Inc., 490 High, Hanover, PA 17331-2124, (717)637-3821 [9449]

Swaner Hardwood Company Inc., 5 W Magnolia St., Burbank, CA 91503, (213)849-6761 [8092]

Swanson Health Products, 1318 39th St. NW, Fargo, ND 58102, (701)277-1662 [14253]

Swanson, Inc., 1200 Park Ave., Murfreesboro, TN 37133, (615)896-4114 [21308]

Swanson-Nunn Electric Co., PO Box 508, Evansville, IN 47703-0508, (812)424-7931 [9450]

Swanson Sales and Service, 402 Main St., Truth or Consequences, NM 87901-2843, (505)894-7517 [21309]

Swansons Tire Company Inc., PO Box 1342, Oklahoma City, OK 73101, (405)235-8305 [3289]

Swanton Packing, Inc., PO Box 704, Swanton, VT 05488, (802)868-4469 [12653]

Swany America Corp., PO Box 867, Gloversville, NY 12078, (518)725-3333 [5412]

Swartz Supply Company Inc., 5550 Allentown Blvd., Harrisburg, PA 17112, (717)652-7111 [23402]

SWD Corp., PO Box 340, Lima, OH 45802-0340, (419)227-2436 [26355]

Swedes Sales, RR 1 Box 16, Raynesford, MT 59469, (406)735-4430 [17628]

Sween ID Products Inc., PO Box 8300, Mankato, MN 56002-8300, (507)386-4393 [24873]

Sweeney Brothers Tractor Co., 4001 38th St., S, Fargo, ND 58104-6903, (701)492-7300 [1308]

Sweeney & Co., 2330 Roosevelt Ave., San Antonio, TX 78210, (210)533-1281 [11334]

Sweeney Company Inc.; R.E., PO Box 1921, Ft. Worth, TX 76101, (817)834-7191 [8093]

Sweeney Seed Co., 488 Drew Park, King of Prussia, PA 19406 [1309]

Sweeper Corp., 2919 Mishawaka Ave., South Bend, IN 46615-2259, (219)288-1658 [25836]

Sweet Life Foods Inc., PO Box 385, Windsor Locks, CT 06096, (860)623-1681 [12654]

Sweet of Madison, Inc.; A.J., PO Box 8608, Madison, WI 53718, (608)222-8222 [12655]

Sweet Street Desserts, 722 Hiesters Ln., Reading, PA 19605, (215)921-8113 [12656]

Sweet Sue Kitchens, 106 Sweet Sue Dr., Athens, AL 35611, (205)232-4201 [12657]

Sweet Things Bakery, 1 Blackfield Dr., Tiburon, CA 94920, (415)388-8583 [12658]

Sweetman Construction Co., 1201 W Russell St., Sioux Falls, SD 57104, (605)336-2928 [8094]

Sweetwater Distributors Inc., 2300 Hoover Ave., Modesto, CA 95354, (209)521-2350 [2065]

Sweetwood Distributing Inc., PO Box 1859, Rapid City, SD 57709-1859, (605)342-9011 [2066]

Swensen's Inc., 200 Bullfinch Dr., No. 1000, Andover, MA 01810, (978)975-1283 [12659]

Swenson Imports, PO Box 70644, Seattle, WA 98107-0644, (206)784-7558 [24874]

Swenson Metal Salvage Inc., PO Box 363, Spanish Fork, UT 84660, (801)798-3548 [27017]

Swiff-Train Co., 2500 Agnes St., PO Box 9095, Corpus Christi, TX 78405, (361)883-1707 [10196]

Swiff-Train Co., 405 N "T" St., Harlingen, TX 78550, (956)428-6751 [10197]

Swiff-Train Co., 4650 S Pinemont, Ste. 100, Houston, TX 77047, (713)690-4472 [10198]

Swiff-Train Co., 3318 North Pan-Am Expressway, San Antonio, TX 78219, (210)227-2406 [10199]

Swiff-Train Co., 1304 E Rio Grande, Ste. 1, Victoria, TX 77901, (512)578-0286 [10200]

Swiff-Train Co., 2500 Agnes St., Corpus Christi, TX 78405, (512)883-1707 [15675]

Swift Co-op Oil Co., 1020 Atlantic Ave., Benson, MN 56215, (320)842-5311 [1310]

Swift-Eckrich, Inc., 600 Food Center Dr., Bronx, NY 10474-7037, (718)842-5000 [11977]

Swift Electric Supply Co., PO Box 4327, Union City, NJ 07087, (201)863-6457 [9451]

Swift Fulfillment Services, 290 Broadway, Lynbrook, NY 11563-3276, (516)593-1195 [4200]

Swift Instruments, Inc., 952 Dorchester Ave., Boston, MA 02125, (617)436-2960 [19645]

Swift Ltd.; S.A., PO Box 111, Waterville, ME 04903-0111, (207)872-2078 [17629]

Swift Lizard Distributors, PO Box A, New Mexico Tech, Socorro, NM 87801, (505)835-5200 [4201]

Swifty Oil Company Inc., PO Box 1002, Seymour, IN 47274, (812)522-1640 [22718]

Swimming Pool Supply Co., 5292 NW 111th Dr., Grimes, IA 50111-8731, (515)986-3931 [24000]

Swindal-Powell Co., PO Box 24428, Jacksonville, FL 32241-4428, (904)739-0100 [13253]

Swing Machinery and Equipment Company Inc., 106 W Rhapsody, San Antonio, TX 78216-3104, (210)342-9588 [17209]

Swire Coca-Cola USA, PO Box 794, Walla Walla, WA 99362, (509)529-0753 [12660]

Swiss Army Brands Inc., 1 Research Dr., Shelton, CT 06484, (203)929-6391 [15676]

Swiss Army Parfum, 15 Corporate Dr., Orangeburg, NY 10962, (914)365-3500 [24042]

Swiss Precision Instruments, PO Box 3135, Garden Grove, CA 92842-3135, (213)721-1818 [16541]

Switzer Petroleum Products, PO Box 860343, Plano, TX 75086, (972)423-0173 [22719]

Switzers Inc., 575 N 20th St., East St. Louis, IL 62205, (618)271-6336 [12661]

SWM Inc., 1978 Innerbelt Business Center Dr., St. Louis, MO 63114, (314)426-6677 [21951]

Swnteca, 79 N Industrial Pk., 510 North Ave., Sewickley, PA 15143, (412)749-5200 [15418]

Syban International Inc., PO Box 16132, Hooksett, NH 03106-6132, (603)645-6015 [155]

Sybron Chemicals Inc., PO Box 66, Birmingham, NJ 08011, (609)893-1100 [4523]

Sydney Supply Co., 176 Union Ave., Providence, RI 02909, (401)944-0200 [23403]

Sydnor Hydrodynamics Inc., 2111 Magnolia St., Richmond, VA 23261, (804)643-2725 [16542]

Sygma Network, 660 Detroit St., Monroe, MI 48162, (734)241-2890 [12662]

SYGMA Network of Ohio Inc., 4265 Diplomacy Dr., Columbus, OH 43228, (614)876-2500 [12663]

SYGMA Network of Pennsylvania Inc., 4000 Industrial Rd., Harrisburg, PA 17110, (717)232-3111 [12664]

Sygnet, PO Box 47953, Minneapolis, MN 55447, (612)473-0732 [16543]

Sylvan Ginsbury Ltd., 660 Kinderkamack Rd., Oradell, NJ 07649, (201)261-3200 [9452]

Sylvias Swimwear-Swim Shop, 14100 NE 20th St., Bellevue, WA 98007-3727, (425)747-1131 [5413]

Symantec Corp. Peter Norton Products Div., 2500 Broadway St., Santa Monica, CA 90404-3061, (310)453-4600 [6780]

Symbol Inc., 13030 S Kirkwood, Stafford, TX 77477, (281)240-7888 [5852]

Symco Group Inc., 3073 McCall Dr., Ste. 1, Atlanta, GA 30340-2831, (404)451-8002 [6781]

Symd Inc., 99-1253 Halawa Valley St., Aiea, HI 96701-3281, (808)486-2933 [19646]

Symphony Designs Inc., 810 Shames Dr., Westbury, NY 11590-1727, (212)695-2526 [5414]

Symphony Fabrics Corp., 229 W 36th St., New York, NY 10018, (212)244-6700 [26219]

Symtech Inc., PO Box 2627, Spartanburg, SC 29304, (864)578-7101 [16544]

Syncor International Corp., 20001 Prairie St., Chatsworth, CA 91311, (818)886-7400 [19066]

Syndee's Crafts Inc., PO Box 94978, Las Vegas, NV 89193, (702)361-7888 [26675]

Synergy Steel Inc., 1450 Rochester Rd., Troy, MI 48083, (248)583-9740 [20415]

Synnestvedt Co., 24550 W Hwy. 120, Round Lake, IL 60073, (847)546-4834 [14959]

Syracuse Banana Co., 2100 Park, Syracuse, NY 13208-1041, (315)471-2251 [12665]

Syracuse China Corp., PO Box 4820, Syracuse, NY 13221, (315)455-5671 [15677]

Syracuse Cooperative Exchange, PO Box 946, Syracuse, KS 67878, (316)384-5751 [18272]

Syracuse Cooperative Exchange, PO Box 946, Syracuse, KS 67878, (316)384-5751 [12666]

Syracuse Supply Co., PO Box 4814, Syracuse, NY 13221, (315)463-9511 [8095]

Syracuse University Press, 621 Skytop Rd., Ste. 110, Syracuse, NY 13244-5290, (315)443-5546 [4202]

Syrex, Inc., 211 Wellington Rd., Syracuse, NY 13214, (315)445-8008 [1311]

Syrvet, Inc., 16200 Walnut St., Waukee, IA 50263, (515)987-5554 [19067]

SYSCO/Alamo Food Services, Inc., PO Box 18364, San Antonio, TX 78218, (210)661-4581 [12667]

Sysco Corp., 1390 Enclave Pkwy., Houston, TX 77077-2099, (281)584-1390 [12668]

Sysco Food Service, 5900 Stewart Ave., Fremont, CA 94538-3134, (510)226-3000 [12687]

Sysco Food Service of Cincinnati Inc., 10510 Evendale Dr., Cincinnati, OH 45241, (513)563-6300 [12669]

SYSCO Food Service, Inc., 4753 S Union, Tulsa, OK 74107, (918)445-7772 [12670]

Sysco Food Service of Jamestown, PO Box 160, Jamestown, NY 14702-0160, (716)665-5620 [12671]

Sysco Food Service of Seattle Inc., PO Box 97054, Kent, WA 98064-9754, (206)622-2261 [12672]

SYSCO Food Services, PO Box 26004, Beaumont, TX 77720-6004, (409)892-3330 [12673]

SYSCO Food Services of Arkansas, Inc., PO Box 194060, Little Rock, AR 72219, (501)562-4111 [24237]

Sysco Food Services of Atlanta Inc., 2225 Riverdale Rd., College Park, GA 30349, (404)765-9900 [12674]

SYSCO Food Services of Atlantic City Inc., 100 Century Dr., Pleasantville, NJ 08232, (609)646-5300 [12675]

Sysco Food Services of Austin Inc., PO Box 149024, Austin, TX 78714, (512)388-8000 [12676]

Sysco Food Services of Beaumont Inc., PO Box 26004, Beaumont, TX 77720-6004, (409)892-3330 [12677]

Sysco Food Services-Chicago Inc., 250 Wieboldt Dr., Des Plaines, IL 60016, (847)699-5400 [12678]

SYSCO Food Services of Detroit, LLC, PO Box 33579, Detroit, MI 48232-5579, (734)397-7990 [12679]

SYSCO Food Services of Grand Rapids, 3700 Sysco Ct. SE, Grand Rapids, MI 49512, (616)949-3700 [12680]

Sysco Food Services of Houston Inc., PO Box 15316, Houston, TX 77220, (713)672-8080 [12681]

Sysco Food Services of Idaho Inc., 5710 Pan Am Ave., Boise, ID 83705, (208)345-9500 [24238]

SYSCO Food Services of Indianapolis Inc., P.O .Box 248, Indianapolis, IN 46206, (317)291-2020 [12682]

SYSCO Food Services Los Angeles Inc., 20701 E Currier Rd., Walnut, CA 91789-2904, (909)595-9595 [12683]

SYSCO Food Services of Minnesota Inc., 2400 County Rd. J, Mounds View, MN 55112, (612)785-9000 [12684]

Sysco Food Services of Philadelphia Inc., PO Box 6499, Philadelphia, PA 19145, (215)218-1600 [12685]

SYSCO Food Services of Portland, PO Box 527, Wilsonville, OR 97070, (503)682-8700 [12686]

Sysco Food Services of San Francisco, Inc., 5900 Stewart Ave., Fremont, CA 94538-3134, (510)226-3000 [12687]

SYSCO Food Services of South Florida, 555 NE 185 St., Miami, FL 33179, (305)651-5421 [12688]

Sysco Food Services of South Florida Inc., 555 NE 185th St., Miami, FL 33179, (305)651-5421 [12689]

SYSCO/Frost-Pack Food Services Inc., 3700 Sysco Ct. SE, Grand Rapids, MI 49512, (616)949-3700 [12680]

Sysco Intermountain Food Services Inc., PO Box 27638, Salt Lake City, UT 84127-0638, (801)972-5484 [12690]

SYSCO of Louisville, PO Box 32470, Louisville, KY 40232, (502)364-4300 [12691]

Syslink Computer Corp., 1025 S Placentia Ave., Fullerton, CA 92831, (714)871-8000 [6782]

Systel Business Equipment Inc., PO Box 35910, Fayetteville, NC 28303, (910)483-7114 [21310]

System Brunner USA Inc., 275 Edgemont Ter., Teaneck, NJ 07666, (201)907-0868 [17210]

System Solutions Technology Inc., 14100 Laurel Park Dr., Laurel, MD 20707, (301)725-6500 [6783]

Systematix Co., 1700 E Walnut Ave., Ste. B, Fullerton, CA 92831, (714)879-2482 [4524]

Systems House Inc., 1033 Rte. 46, Clifton, NJ 07013, (973)777-8050 [6784]

Systems Inc., PO Box 9713, New Haven, CT 06536-0713, (203)624-8600 [21311]

Systems Medical Co. Inc., PO Box 61, Owosso, MI 48867-0061, (517)725-9314 [19068]

Systems Solutions Inc., 2108 E Thomas Rd., Phoenix, AZ 85016-7758, (602)955-5566 [6785]

Systems Unlimited Inc., 3920 S Willow Ave., Sioux Falls, SD 57105, (605)334-8588 [21312]

Syverson Tile, Inc., 4015 S Western Ave., Sioux Falls, SD 57105-6540, (605)336-1175 [10201]

Szco Supplier Inc., PO Box 6353, Baltimore, MD 21230-0353, (410)547-6999 [15678]

T and A Industrial Distributors, 12550 Robin Ln., Brookfield, WI 53005-1398, (414)384-6000 [17211]

T & A Supply Co., 757 Highland Dr., Seattle, WA 98109-3550, (206)282-3770 [10202]

T and A Supply Co., 1105 Westlake Ave. N, Seattle, WA 98109, (206)282-3770 [15679]

T & A Trym-Tox, 757 Highland Dr., Seattle, WA 98109-3550, (206)282-3770 [10202]

T-Bone's Salvage and Equipment Inc., Box N, Bovina, TX 79009, (806)238-1614 [1312]

T & D Sporting Goods, PO Box 837, Pikeville, KY 41502-0837, (606)432-2153 [24001]

T & E Enterprises & Development, PO Box 240188, Anchorage, AK 99524, (907)563-5939 [27243]

T & E Timers Inc., 53 E 10 Mile Rd., Madison Heights, MI 48071-4202, (248)543-1156 [15327]

T & E Wholesale Outlet, 1019 S Craig Ave., Covington, VA 24426-2248, (540)962-0454 [13460]

T-Electra/TICA of Dallas Inc., 1127 Airport Circle S, Euless, TX 76040-6805, (817)267-5678 [9453]

T-Fal Corp., 25 Riverside Dr., Pine Brook, NJ 07058, (973)575-1060 [15680]

T-J Knit Enterprises Inc., 237 W 35th St., Ste. 806, New York, NY 10001-1905, (212)391-1700 [5415]

T & L Distributors Company Inc., 451 W 61st, Shreveport, LA 71106, (318)865-8072 [10203]

T & L Distributors Company Inc., 3201 Long Horn Blvd., Ste. 117, Austin, TX 78759, (512)832-0711 [10204]

T & L Distributors Company Inc., 4051 La Reunion Pkwy., Ste. 180, Dallas, TX 75212, (214)630-6101 [10205]

T & L Distributors Company Inc., PO Box 431709, Houston, TX 77243, (713)461-7802 [10206]

T & L Distributors Company Inc., 3453 N Panam Expy., Ste. 417, San Antonio, TX 78219-2340, (210)662-8200 [10207]

T & L Industries Co., 300 Quaker Ln., Ste. 7 (PMB 151), Warwick, RI 02886-6682, (401)884-1504 [3290]

T and L Supply Inc., 112 19th St., Wheeling, WV 26003, (304)233-3340 [23404]

T & M Inc., PO Box 627, Dunseith, ND 58329-0627, (701)244-5149 [2067]

T & R Beverage Control, 6680 N Government Way, Ste. 3, Coeur D Alene, ID 83815-7708, (208)667-2468 [24239]

T & R Dispensing Inc., 6680 N Government Way, Ste. 3, Coeur D Alene, ID 83815-7708, (208)667-2468 [24239]

T-Shirt City Inc., 12080 Mosteller Rd., Cincinnati, OH 45241-1529, (513)542-3500 [5416]

T-Shirt Factory & Odd Shop, 2630 1st Ave., Hibbing, MN 55746-2245, (218)262-4224 [5417]

T-Shirt Gallery and Sports, 5815 Weber Rd., Corpus Christi, TX 78413, (361)852-8992 [5418]

T-Shirts of Florida Inc., 4201 NE 12th Terrace, Oakland Park, FL 33334-4722, (954)564-4435 [5443]

T & T Distributors, 4448 Technology Dr., Fremont, CA 94538, (510)657-5220 [14254]

T & T Tile Distribution Inc., PO Box 5075, Winter Park, FL 32793-5075 [10208]

T-W Truck Equippers, Inc., 590 Elk St., Buffalo, NY 14210-2237, (716)683-2250 [3291]

Tab Business Systems Inc., 11960 Menaul Blvd. NE, Albuquerque, NM 87112-2422, (505)292-7887 [21313]

Tab Chemicals Inc., 4801 S Austin, Chicago, IL 60638, (773)586-2000 [4413]

Tab Electric Supply Inc., PO Box 12510, New Bern, NC 28562, (919)633-4929 [9454]

Tab Electric Supply Inc., PO Box 12510, New Bern, NC 28562, (252)633-4929 [9455]

Tab of Northern New England, 133 Spur Rd., Dover, NH 03820-9110, (603)749-4042 [21314]

TAB Products Co., 1400 Page Mill Rd., Palo Alto, CA 94304-1179, (650)852-2400 [13254]

Table Supply Co., 1513 Broadway NE, Albuquerque, NM 87102-1547, (505)224-9833 [24240]

Tabor City Lumber Inc., PO Box 37, Tabor City, NC 28463, (919)653-3162 [8096]

Tabor Grain Co., 4666 Faries Pkwy., Decatur, IL 62525, (217)424-5200 [18273]

Tacchini Apparel; Sergio, 1055 W Victoria St., Compton, CA 90220, (213)774-1746 [5419]

Tackle Craft, 1440 Kennedy Rd., Chippewa Falls, WI 54729, (715)723-3645 [24002]

Tackle Service Center, 246 E Washington St., Mooresville, IN 46158-1459, (317)831-2400 [24003]

TACO, 440 Fairmount Ave., Philadelphia, PA 19123, (215)629-0400 [13962]

Tacoa Inc., 385 5th Ave., Ste. 700, New York, NY 10016-2203, (212)889-5497 [17630]

Tacoma Fiberglass, 2406 Port of Tacoma Rd., Tacoma, WA 98422, (253)272-1258 [18622]

Taconite Oil Company Inc., 810 Hoover Rd., Virginia, MN 55792, (218)741-3350 [22720]

Tacony Corp., 1760 Gilsinn Ln., Fenton, MO 63026, (314)349-3000 [15328]

Tactical Business Services, 1260 W Northwest Hwy., Palatine, IL 60067-1897, (708)358-1638 [6786]

Tactilitics Inc., 4760 Walnut St. Ste. 105, Boulder, CO 80301, (303)442-7746 [19647]

Tadiran Electronic Industries Inc., 10 E 53rd St., New York, NY 10022-6102, (212)751-3600 [15329]

Taft Development Group, 4605 Macky Way, Boulder, CO 80303-6743, (303)494-4575 [6787]

Tailor-Made Signs, PO Box 5421, Pawtucket, RI 02862-5421, (401)331-0400 [13255]

Taintor Cooperative Co., 1380 Hwy. 63 S, Box 512, New Sharon, IA 50207, (515)637-4097 [18274]

Taitron Components Inc., 25202 Anza Dr., Santa Clarita, CA 91355, (805)257-6060 [9456]

Taiyo Inc., PO Box 31087, Honolulu, HI 96820-1087, (808)537-4951 [12692]

Taj Inc., 1050 Ala Moana Blvd., Ste. A7, Honolulu, HI 96814-4910, (808)592-1900 [5420]

Takahashi Trading Corp., 200 Rhode Island St., San Francisco, CA 94103, (415)431-8300 [15681]

Takitani Enterprises Inc.; K., 1162 Lower Main St., Wailuku, HI 96793, (808)244-3777 [25043]

Talays Inc., 34443 Schoolcraft, Livonia, MI 48150, (734)525-1155 [9458]

Talays Inc., 34443 Schoolcraft St., Livonia, MI 48150, (313)525-1155 [9457]

Talbert Trading Corp., 5 Quinsigamond Ave., Worcester, MA 01610, (508)752-5496 [5421]

TALCO Recycling Inc., 720 S Temescal St., Corona, CA 91718, (909)736-7040 [27018]

Talcup, Inc., 34443 Schoolcraft, Livonia, MI 48150, (734)525-1155 [9458]

Talk-A-Phone Co., 5013 N Kedzie, Chicago, IL 60625-4988, (773)539-1100 [5772]

Talladega Beverage Co., 928 N Railroad Ave., Opelika, AL 36801-4368, (205)358-0068 [2068]

Talladega Machinery and Supply Co., 301 N Johnson Ave., Talladega, AL 35160, (205)362-4124 [26220]

Talladega Machinery and Supply Company Inc., 301 N Johnson Ave., Talladega, AL 35160, (256)362-4124 [16545]

Talley Communications, 12866 Ann St., Bldg. 1, Santa Fe Springs, CA 90670, (562)906-8000 [5773]

Talley Electronics, 3137 Diablo Ave., Hayward, CA 94545, (415)783-2111 [5774]

Talley Electronics, 12866 Ann St., Bldg. 1, Santa Fe Springs, CA 90670, (562)906-8000 [5773]

Tallman Company Inc., 8642 Pardee Ln., Crestwood, MO 63126, (314)843-9119 [23405]

Talon Associates International, Inc., 1275 First Ave., Ste. 104, New York, NY 10021, (212)535-9580 [19069]

Tam Produce Inc., PO Box 6986, Fullerton, CA 92834-6986, (213)620-0650 [12693]

Tama-Benton Cooperative Co., PO Box 459, Dysart, IA 52224, (319)476-3666 [18275]

Tamara Imports, PO Box 47280, Dallas, TX 75247, (214)638-1889 [5422]

Tamarack Ltd., PO Box 70, Lanark, WV 25860, (304)255-6500 [19070]

Tamarkin Company Inc., 375 Victoria Rd., Youngstown, OH 44515, (330)792-3811 [12694]

Tamashiro Market Inc., 802 N King, Honolulu, HI 96817-4513, (808)841-8047 [12695]

Tamco Distributors Company Inc., 365 Victoria Rd., Youngstown, OH 44501, (330)792-2311 [14255]

Tamiami Range and Gun Distributors Inc., 2925 SW 8th St., Miami, FL 33135, (305)642-1941 [13515]

Tampa Appliance Parts Corp., 9840 Currie Davis Dr., Tampa, FL 33619, (813)623-3131 [15330]

Tampa Armature Works Inc., PO Box 3381, Tampa, FL 33601, (813)621-5661 [16546]

Tampa Rubber & Gasket Co., Inc., 22nd St. & Causeway Blvd., Tampa, FL, (813)247-3647 [24298]

Tampa Tile Center, 13670 Roosevelt Blvd., Clearwater, FL 33762, (813)573-5386 [10209]

Tampico Farmers Elevator Co., PO Box 187, Tampico, IL 61283, (815)438-6155 [1313]

Tamrock USA, 1 Driltech Dr., Alachua, FL 32615, (904)462-4610 [16547]

Tandy Corp., 100 Throckmorton St., Ste. 1800, Ft. Worth, TX 76102, (817)415-3700 [9259]

Taneum Computer Products Inc., 243 SW 41st St., Renton, WA 98055, (425)251-0711 [6788]

Tang Industries Inc., 1965 Pratt Blvd., Elk Grove Village, IL 60007, (708)806-7200 [20416]

Tanner Enterprises, Inc., PO Box 292638, Columbus, OH 43229-2638, (614)433-7020 [12696]

Tanner Forest Products Inc., 33 Vaughn Dr., Natchez, MS 39120-2019, (601)445-8206 [8097]

Tanner Grocery Company Inc.; C.M., PO Box 487, Carrollton, GA 30117, (404)832-6381 [12697]

Tanner Industries, Inc., 735 Davisville Rd., 3rd Fl., Southampton, PA 18966, (215)322-1238 [4525]

Tanner Trading Co.; Ellis, 1980 Hwy. 602, Gallup, NM 87305-0636, (505)722-7776 [17631]

Tapco USA, Inc., 5605 Pike Rd., Loves Park, IL 61111, (815)877-4039 [17212]

Tapesolutions, 649 S Vermont St., Palatine, IL 60067, (847)776-8880 [25943]

Tapeswitch Corp., 100 Schmitt Blvd., Farmingdale, NY 11735, (631)630-0442 [9459]

Tapetex Inc., 240 Commerce Dr., Rochester, NY 14623, (716)334-0480 [26221]

Taramax U.S.A., Inc., 600 Warren Ave., Spring Lake Heights, NJ 07762, (732)282-0300 [17632]

Tarantino Company Inc.; Lee Ray, PO Box 2408, South San Francisco, CA 94083, (650)871-4323 [12698]

Target Appliances, 6316 Reisterstown Rd., Baltimore, MD 21215-2309, (410)358-4433 [15331]

Target Distributing Co., 11730 Park Lawn Dr., Rockville, MD 20852, (301)770-9400 [25471]

Target Distributing Co., 11730 Parklawn Dr., Rockville, MD 20852, (301)770-9400 [15332]

Target Electronics Inc., 16120 Caputo Dr., Morgan Hill, CA 95037-5531, (408)778-0408 [9460]

Target Industries Inc., 1 Pleasant St., Cohasset, MA 02025, (781)383-6440 [19648]

Target Premiums Inc., 1075 Old Norcross Rd., Ste. E, Lawrenceville, GA 30045-3302, (404)972-5121 [15333]

Target Tire and Automotive Corp., 2221 Lejeune Blvd., Jacksonville, NC 28540, (919)353-4300 [3292]

Targun Plastics Co., 899 Skokie Blvd., Northbrook, IL 60062, (708)272-0869 [23039]

Tarheel Communications, 4611 Kimbro Rd., Hillsborough, NC 27278-9998, (919)644-2929 [25472]

Tari-Tan Ceramic Supply Inc., 3919 N Greenbrooke Dr. SE, Grand Rapids, MI 49512-5328, (616)698-2460 [26676]

Tarrant Distributors Inc., 9835 Genard Rd., Houston, TX 77041-7623, (713)690-8888 [2069]

Tarrant Service Agency, Inc., 2450 Valley Rd., Ste. 6, Reno, NV 89512-1609, (702)356-8141 [14710]

Tasco Insulations Inc., PO Box 1167, Youngstown, OH 44501, (330)744-2146 [8098]

Taser International Inc., 1314 Texas Ave., Ste. 1312, Houston, TX 77002, (713)224-0688 [1314]

Task-Force Batteries, 3596 Moline St., Ste. 101, Aurora, CO 80010-1422, (303)340-2727 [22910]

Taskforce Batteries, 3596 Moline St., Ste. 101, Aurora, CO 80010-1422, (303)340-2727 [22910]

Tasso Wallcovering, 1020 NW 6th St., Ste. H, Deerfield Beach, FL 33442-7711, (954)429-3883 [15682]

Tastee Apple Inc., 60810 County Rd. 9, Newcomerstown, OH 43832, (740)498-8316 [12699]

Tasty Foods/VCA, 5724 Hillside Ave., Cincinnati, OH 45233, (513)941-3342 [27244]

Tasty Mix Products, 88-90 Walworth St., Brooklyn, NY 11205, (718)855-7680 [12700]

Tasty Mix Quality Foods Inc., 88-90 Walworth St., Brooklyn, NY 11205, (718)855-7680 [12700]

Tate Builders Supply L.L.C., PO Box 18817, Erlanger, KY 41018, (606)727-1212 [8099]

Tate Engineering Systems, Inc., 1560 Caton Center Dr., Baltimore, MD 21227, (410)242-8800 [5853]

Tate Jr.'s Murray Auto Auction Inc.; Jim, Rte. 1, Almo, KY 42020, (502)753-8300 [20735]

Tate & Lyle Enterprises, Inc., 2801 Ponce De Leon Blvd., Ste. 1055, Coral Gables, FL 33134, (305)448-2845 [16548]

Tate-Reynolds Company Inc., 27 Commercial Blvd., Novato, CA 94949, (415)883-3591 [20736]

Tatung Company of America Inc., 2850 El Presidio St., Long Beach, CA 90810, (310)637-2105 [6789]

Tatung Company of America Inc. Marietta Div., 815 Allgood Rd., Marietta, GA 30062, (404)428-9090 [25473]

Tatung Science and Technology Inc., 1840 McCarthy Blvd., Milpitas, CA 95035, (408)383-0988 [21315]

Tauber Oil Co., PO Box 4645, Houston, TX 77210, (713)869-8700 [22721]

Tavdi Company, Inc., 300 County Rd., PO Box 298, Barrington, RI 02806, (401)245-2932 [16549]

Taxor Inc., 1201 W Foothill Blvd., Azusa, CA 91702, (626)969-2688 [17633]

Tay/Chem L.L.C., 3624 Melrose Dr., Raleigh, NC 27604-3815, (919)231-6668 [23040]

Tayloe Paper Co., PO Box 580880, Tulsa, OK 74158, (918)835-6911 [21952]

Taylor Brothers Wholesale Distributors Inc., PO Box 5940, Mesa, AZ 85211-5940, (480)969-9333 [10988]

Taylor Company Inc.; Nelson A., 66 Kingsboro Ave., Gloversville, NY 12078, (518)725-0681 [18623]

Taylor Co.; Jesse R., 405 S 10th St., Opelika, AL 36801, (334)745-5774 [18276]

Taylor Corp.; Jim, 133 Atlantic Dr., Maitland, FL 32751, (407)831-7800 [2070]

Taylor Dakota Distributors, 517 Airport Rd., Bismarck, ND 58504-6107, (701)223-2338 [14711]

Taylor Distributing Co.; J.J., PO Box 70098, North Dartmouth, MA 02747, (508)999-1266 [2071]

Taylor Distributing Miami Key-West; J.J., 3505 NW 107th St., Miami, FL 33167, (305)688-4286 [2072]

Taylor Distributors, 1651 S Rio Grande Ave., Orlando, FL 32805, (407)425-4145 [10210]

Taylor Distributors of Indiana, 2605 Alma Ave., Ft. Wayne, IN 46809-2956, (219)478-1551 [14712]

Taylor-Dunn Manufacturing Co., 2114 W Ball Rd., Anaheim, CA 92804, (714)956-4040 [16550]

Taylor Electric Supply Inc., 1709 SE 3rd Ave., Portland, OR 97214, (503)233-5321 [9290]

Taylor Feed & Pet Supply, 19 Smiley Ingram Rd., PO Box 1504, Cartersville, GA 30120-1504, (770)382-9665 [27245]

Taylor Fertilizers Co.; John, 841 W Elkhorn Blvd., Rio Linda, CA 95673, (916)991-4451 [1315]

Taylor & Francis, Inc., 325 Chestnut St., Ste. 800, Philadelphia, PA 19106 [4203]

Taylor Lumber and Treating Inc., PO Box 158, Sheridan, OR 97378, (503)291-2550 [8100]

Taylor-Made Office Systems Inc., PO Box 8026, Walnut Creek, CA 94596, (510)988-4000 [21316]

Taylor Optical Supplies Inc., 28 W Adams Ave., Ste. 1005, Detroit, MI 48226-1617, (313)962-6595 [19649]

Taylor-Parker Co., 1130 Kingwood Ave., Norfolk, VA 23502, (804)855-2041 [17213]

Taylor Publishing Co., PO Box 597, Dallas, TX 75221, (214)637-2800 [4204]

Taylor Rental Corp., PO Box 8000, New Britain, CT 06050, (860)229-9100 [1316]

Taylor Restaurant Equipment, 8307 Central Ave. NE, Albuquerque, NM 87108-2409, (505)255-9898 [24241]

Taylor Simkins Inc., 1235 Tower Trails, El Paso, TX 79907, (915)544-4252 [17214]

Taylor and Sledd Inc., PO Box 9729, Richmond, VA 23228, (804)262-8614 [12701]

Taylor and Sons Equipment Co., PO Box 40, Canal Winchester, OH 43110, (614)837-5516 [1317]

Taylor & Sons, Inc.; Robert, 381 W Ironwood Dr., South Salt Lake, UT 84115, (801)486-1335 [16551]

Taylor Sports & Recreation Inc., 136 Warm Springs Ave., Martinsburg, WV 25401, (304)263-7857 [24004]

Taylor Supply Co., 6530 Beaubien, Detroit, MI 48202, (313)872-0400 [23406]

Tayo's Tile Co., 12 Sunflower Ln., Peralta, NM 87042, (505)865-7179 [8101]

Tayters Distributing, 738 Main St., No. 250, Waltham, MA 02454, (781)893-2065 [12702]

Tayters Inc., 738 Main St., No. 250, Waltham, MA 02454, (781)893-2065 [12702]

Tayters Inc., 738 Main St., No. 250, Waltham, MA 02454, (781)893-2065 [12702]

Tazewell Farm Bureau Inc., PO Box 217, North Tazewell, VA 24630, (540)988-4131 [1318]

TBC Corp., PO Box 18342, Memphis, TN 38181-0342, (901)363-8030 [3293]

TBC Corp., PO Box 18342, Memphis, TN 38181-0342, (901)363-8030 [24299]

TBI, 6220 San Vivente Blvd., Los Angeles, CA 90048, (213)965-9511 [5423]

T.B.I. Corp., 700 E Industrial Park Dr., Manchester, NH 03109, (603)668-6223 [12703]

TBT Industries Inc., 838 Granada St., Socorro, NM 87801-4308, (505)835-3348 [13256]

TC Computers Inc., 5005 Bloomfield St., Jefferson, LA 70121, (504)733-0331 [6790]

TCB Inc., 1227 E Hennepin Ave., Minneapolis, MN 55414, (612)331-8880 [25944]

TCC Industries Inc., PO Box 684925, Austin, TX 78768, (512)708-5000 [13461]

TCI Aluminum, PO Box 2069, Gardena, CA 90247, (310)323-5613 [20417]

TCI Machinery Inc., 1720 Industrial Pke., PO Box 939, Gastonia, NC 28053, (704)867-8331 [16552]

TD Materials Inc., 2211 S Tubeway Ave., Los Angeles, CA 90040-1615, (213)232-6171 [156]

TDA Industries Inc., 122 E 42nd St., New York, NY 10168, (212)972-1510 [8102]

TDI Air Conditioning Appliances, 2600 E 5th St., Tyler, TX 75701, (903)597-8381 [15334]

TDK Corporation of America, 1600 Feehanville Dr., Mt. Prospect, IL 60056, (847)803-6100 [9461]

TDK Electronics Corp., 12 Harbor Park Dr., Port Washington, NY 11050, (516)625-0100 [25474]

TDK Electronics Corp., 12 Harbor Park Dr., Fl. 1, Port Washington, NY 11050, (516)625-0100 [9462]

TDK U.S.A. Corp., 12 Harbor Park Dr., Port Washington, NY 11050, (516)625-0100 [5775]

TD's Radio & TV, 316 W Main St., Norman, OK 73069-1311, (405)321-5210 [14713]

TEAC America Inc., 7733 Telegraph Rd., Montebello, CA 90640, (213)726-0303 [9463]

TEAC America Inc. Data Storage Products Div., PO Box 750, Montebello, CA 90640, (323)726-0303 [15335]

Teaching Aids Inc., 711 W 17th St., No. E-2, Costa Mesa, CA 92627, (949)548-9321 [6791]

Teague Industries Inc., 3445 County Rd. 154, McKinney, TX 75070, (972)516-0271 [9464]

Teague Refrigeration Service, PO Box 630, Deming, NM 88031-0630, (505)546-9691 [14714]

Teal Electric Company Inc., PO Box 1189, Troy, MI 48099, (810)689-3000 [9465]

Team Distributors Inc., PO Box 6069, Annapolis, MD 21401-0069, (410)263-0668 [24005]

Team Sporting Goods Inc., 2614 SW 17th St., Topeka, KS 66604-2670, (785)354-1794 [24006]

Team Up, PO Box 1115, Warrensburg, MO 64093, (660)747-3569 [4205]

Team Up Services, PO Box 382607, Duncanville, TX 75138, (972)709-7192 [4206]

Teaneck Graphics Inc., 197 Washington Ave., Carlstadt, NJ 07072, (201)438-2500 [13257]

TEC America Inc., 4401-A Bankers Cir., Atlanta, GA 30360, (770)449-3040 [25837]

TEC America Inc., 4401-A Bankers Cir., Atlanta, GA 30360, (770)449-3040 [24242]

TEC Industrial, PO Box 4770, Davenport, IA 52808, (319)323-3233 [16553]

Tec Laboratories Inc., PO Box 1958, Albany, OR 97321, (541)926-4577 [14256]

Tecan US Inc., PO Box 13953, Durham, NC 27709-3953, (919)361-5200 [19071]

Tech 101 Inc., 16812 Milliken Ave., Irvine, CA 92606, (949)261-5141 [6792]

Tech Aerofoam Products, Inc., 5242 Shawland, Jacksonville, FL 32254, (904)786-3840 [26222]

Tech-Aerofoam Products Inc., 3551 NW 116th St., Miami, FL 33167, (305)685-5993 [8103]

Tech Arts, 829 E Molloy Rd., Syracuse, NY 13211, (315)455-1003 [6793]

Tech Data Corp., 5350 Tech Data Dr., Clearwater, FL 33760, (813)539-7429 [6794]

Tech Distributing/Supply, 28300 Industrial Blvd., Hayward, CA 94545, (510)783-7085 [3294]

Tech Electro Industries Inc., 4300 Wiley Post Rd., Dallas, TX 75244-2131, (972)239-7151 [9466]

Tech Fire and Safety Co., 514 4th St., Watervliet, NY 12189, (518)274-7599 [24642]

Tech Fire and Safety Co., 514 4th St., Watervliet, NY 12189, (518)274-7599 [24243]

Tech Inc., PO Box 14310, Shawnee Mission, KS 66285-4310, (913)492-6440 [3295]

Tech Products, Inc., 5012 W Knollwood St., Tampa, FL 33634, (813)884-2503 [8104]

Techcom Systems Inc., 2051 Palmer Ave., Larchmont, NY 10538, (914)834-8007 [5776]

Teche Electric Supply Inc., PO Box 61640, Lafayette, LA 70596-1640, (318)234-7427 [9467]

Techexport, Inc., 1 North Ave., Burlington, MA 01803, (781)229-6900 [6795]

Techfarm Inc., 200 W Evelyn Ave., No. 100, Mountain View, CA 94041-1365, (408)720-7080 [6796]

Techline Studio Inc., 11225 Trade Center Dr., Ste. 150, Rancho Cordova, CA 95742, (916)638-1991 [13258]

Techlink Alaska, 1204 H St., Anchorage, AK 99501-4359, (907)276-6862 [6797]

Techmark Corporation, PO Box 375, Cheshire, CT 06410, (203)272-3559 [24442]

Techmart Computer Products, 1424 Odenton Rd., Odenton, MD 21113-0370, (410)674-8202 [21317]

Techmedia Computer Systems Corp., 37 Smith St., Englewood, NJ 07631-4067, (201)567-1583 [6798]

Techni-Tool, Inc., 1547 N Trooper Rd., PO Box 1117, Worcester, PA 19490-1117, (610)941-2400 [13948]

Technical Advisory Service, 5115 S Valley View Blvd., Las Vegas, NV 89118, (702)798-7926 [9468]

Technical Business Specialists Inc., 5720 E Washington St., Los Angeles, CA 90040, (323)727-0039 [6799]

Technical Devices Co., PO Box 26655, Salt Lake City, UT 84126, (801)972-5935 [9469]

Technical Marketing, Inc., 1776 N Pine Island Rd., Ste. 306, Plantation, FL 33322, (954)370-0855 [14257]

Technical Marketing Inc., 1776 N Pine Island Rd., Ste. 306, Plantation, FL 33322, (954)370-0855 [19650]

Technical Products Inc., 2416 Park Central Blvd., Decatur, GA 30035, (404)981-8434 [19072]

Technical Sales Inc., 433 Clyde Ave., Mountain View, CA 94043-2209, (650)969-6308 [3296]

Technical and Scientific Application Inc., 2040 W Sam Houston Parkway N, Houston, TX 77043, (713)935-1500 [6800]

Technical Telephone Systems Inc., 18 Worldsfair Dr., Somerset, NJ 08873, (732)560-9090 [5777]

Technicom Corp., 333 Cottonwood Dr., Winchester, VA 22603-3229, (540)432-9282 [5778]

TechniStar Corp., 1198 Boston Ave., Longmont, CO 80501, (303)651-0188 [16554]

Techno Steel Corp., 1207 Riverside Blvd., Memphis, TN 38106, (901)942-3770 [20418]

Technoland Inc., 1050 Stewart Dr., Sunnyvale, CA 94086, (408)992-0888 [6801]

Technology Specialists Inc., 303 2nd St., Ste. E, Annapolis, MD 21403-2545, (410)268-2300 [6802]

Technovance Corp., 956 W Hyde Park Blvd., Inglewood, CA 90302-3308, (310)674-5130 [3297]

TechQuest Inc., 3816 Bagley Ave., Culver City, CA 90232, (310)287-2444 [6803]

Techrepco Inc., PO Box 15608, Albuquerque, NM 87174-0608, (505)898-1727 [157]

Tecnica USA, Airport Rd., West Lebanon, NH 03784, (603)298-8032 [24875]

Tecot Electrical Supply Company Inc., PO Box 61, New Castle, DE 19720-0061, (302)421-3900 [9470]

Tedco Indus Inc., 3901 Washington Blvd., Baltimore, MD 21227, (410)247-0399 [26223]

Tee Pee Advertising Co., 155 Taft Ave., Pocatello, ID 83201-5108, (208)233-2388 [26677]

Tee Tile Distributors, Inc., 2140 Jonathan Dr., PO Box 461, Huntsville, AL 35804, (205)852-0025 [10211]

Teeco Products Inc., 16881 Armstrong Ave., Irvine, CA 92614, (714)261-6295 [22722]

Tees Dyes, 114 Old Colony Dr., Mashpee, MA 02649-2532, (781)643-8140 [5424]

Teeters Products Inc., 125 E 2nd St., Fletcher, OH 45326, (937)368-2376 [25838]

T.E.I./Texaco Bulk Services, 53 County Rd. 2AB, Cody, WY 82414, (307)527-7575 [12704]

Tejas Resources Inc., 105 Tejas Dr., Terrell, TX 75160, (972)563-1220 [20573]

Tek-Gear LLC, 637 S Broadway St Ste. B347, Boulder, CO 80303, (303)494-1116 [6804]

Tek-Matic, Inc., 7324 Forest Hills Rd., Loves Park, IL 61111, (815)282-1775 [17215]

Tekmatex Inc., PO Box 667429, Charlotte, NC 28266, (704)394-5131 [16555]

Teknis Corp., PO Box 3189, North Attleboro, MA 02761, (508)695-3591 [9471]

Teknor Apex Co., 505 Central Ave., PO Box 2290, Pawtucket, RI 02861, (401)725-8000 [24300]

Tekra Corp., 16700 W Lincoln Ave., New Berlin, WI 53151, (414)784-5533 [23041]

Tektronix Inc., PO Box 500, Beaverton, OR 97077, (503)627-7111 [6805]

Tektronix Inc. Logic Analyzer Div., 26600 SW Parkway Ave., Wilsonville, OR 97070, (503)627-7111 [6806]

Tekvisions Inc., 2350 W Mission Ln., Phoenix, AZ 85021, (602)943-6787 [6807]

Tel-Data Communications Inc., 8980 Blue Ash Rd., Cincinnati, OH 45242, (513)984-0749 [5779]

Tele-Measurements Inc., 145 Main Ave., Clifton, NJ 07014, (973)473-8822 [25475]

Tele Path Corp., 49111 Milmont Dr., Fremont, CA 94538-7347, (510)656-5600 [5780]

Tele-Vue Service Company Inc., 947 Federal Blvd., Denver, CO 80204, (303)623-3330 [6808]

Telebeep Wireless Inc., 504 Prospect Ave., Norfolk, NE 68701-4022, (402)371-2337 [9472]

Teleco Inc., 430 Woodruff Rd., No. 300, Greenville, SC 29607-3462, (803)297-4400 [5781]

Telecom Electric Supply Co., PO Box 860307, Plano, TX 75074, (214)422-0012 [9473]

Telecom Engineering Consultants Inc., 9400 NW 25th St., Miami, FL 33172, (305)592-4328 [5782]

Telecom Solutions Div., 2300 Orchard Pkwy., San Jose, CA 95131-1017, (408)433-0910 [6809]

Telecommunications Bank Inc., 302 Goodman St., Rochester, NY 14607, (716)442-2040 [5783]

Telecommunications Concepts Inc., 5554 Port Royal Rd., Springfield, VA 22151, (703)321-3030 [5784]

Telecomputer Inc., 17481 Mount Cliffwood Cir, Fountain Valley, CA 92708, (714)438-3993 [6810]

Telectron Inc., 3315 SW 11th Ave., Ft. Lauderdale, FL 33315, (954)832-0046 [9474]

Teledata Concepts Inc., 4421 N Dixie Hwy., Boca Raton, FL 33431, (561)367-1337 [9475]

Telelink Communications Co., 7111 Governors Cir., Sacramento, CA 95823, (916)424-5454 [5785]

Telemusica Co., 1888 Century Park E, Los Angeles, CA 90067, (310)284-6808 [25476]

Teleparts, Inc., 763-C Susquehanna Ave., Franklin Lakes, NJ 07417, (201)847-9509 [3298]

Telephony International Inc., 2351 Merritt Dr., Garland, TX 75041-6140, (972)423-6269 [5786]

Telesensory Corp., 520 Almanor Ave., Sunnyvale, CA 94086, (408)616-8700 [9476]

Telesystems Inc., 8626 I St., Omaha, NE 68127-1618, (402)339-0600 [5787]

Televan Sales Inc., 5451 Sylvia Ave., Dearborn Heights, MI 48125, (313)292-7150 [16556]

Television Technology Corp., 1390 Overlook Dr., No.2, Lafayette, CO 80026, (303)665-8000 [5661]

Telewire Supply, 94 Inverness Terrace E, Englewood, CO 80112, (303)799-4343 [5788]

Telmar Group Inc., 148 Madison Ave., New York, NY 10016, (212)460-9000 [6811]

Telogy Inc., 3885 Bohannon Dr., Menlo Park, CA 94025, (650)462-9000 [24443]

Telrad Telecommunications Inc., 135 Crossways Park Dr., Woodbury, NY 11797, (516)921-8300 [5789]

TEM Inc., 302 York, Gettysburg, PA 17325-1930, (717)334-6251 [13462]

Temp Glass, 291 M St., Perrysburg, OH 43551, (419)666-2000 [8105]

Temp Glass Southern, Inc., 1101 Fountain Pkwy., Grand Prairie, TX 75050, (972)647-4028 [8106]

Tempaco Inc., PO Box 547667, Orlando, FL 32803, (407)898-3456 [14715]

Tempco Contracting & Supply, PO Box 8305, Boise, ID 83707-2305, (208)376-0580 [8107]

Tempco Supplies Inc., 2034 S Southland Ave., Gonzales, LA 70737-4158, (504)647-3330 [14716]

Temperature Equipment Corp., 17725 Volbrecht Rd., Lansing, IL 60438, (708)418-0900 [14717]

Temperature Systems Inc., PO Box 9090, Madison, WI 53725-9090, (608)271-7500 [14718]

Temple Iron and Metal Company Inc., PO Box 805, Temple, TX 76503, (254)773-2700 [27019]

Temple Products of Indiana Inc., 4511 Pine Creek Rd., Elkhart, IN 46516, (219)294-3621 [3299]

Tempo Glove Manufacturing Inc., 3820 W Wisconsin Ave., Milwaukee, WI 53208-3154, (414)344-1100 [25839]

Ten Speed Press, PO Box 7123, Berkeley, CA 94707, (510)559-1600 [4207]

TENBA Quality Cases, Ltd., 50 Washington St., Brooklyn, NY 11201, (718)222-9870 [18435]

TENBA Quality Cases Ltd., 503 Broadway, New York, NY 10012-4401, (212)966-1013 [18436]

Teneff Jewelry Inc., W 510 Riverside Ave., Ste. 303, Spokane, WA 99201, (509)747-1038 [17634]

Tenenbaum Company Inc.; A., PO Box 15128, Little Rock, AR 72231, (501)945-0881 [27020]

Tenet Information Service Inc., 4885 South 900 East, Ste. 107, Salt Lake City, UT 84117-5746, (801)268-3480 [6812]

TENGASCO Inc., 4928 Humberg Dr., Ste. B-3, Knoxville, TN 37902-2609, (423)523-1124 [22723]

Tenneco Energy Resources Corp., PO Box 2511, Houston, TX 77252, (713)757-2131 [22724]

Tenneco Gas Marketing Co., PO Box 2511, Houston, TX 77252-2511, (713)757-2131 [22725]

Tennessee Building Products Inc., PO Box 40403, Nashville, TN 37204-0403, (615)259-4677 [8108]

Tennessee-Carolina Lumber Company Inc., PO Box 71855, Chattanooga, TN 37407-1855, (423)698-3381 [8109]

Tennessee Control-Equip Inc., 2044 E Magnolia Ave., Knoxville, TN 37917-8026, (865)522-5656 [14402]

Tennessee Dressed Beef Company Inc., PO Box 23031, Nashville, TN 37202, (615)742-5800 [12705]

Tennessee Electric Motor Co., PO Box 22839, Nashville, TN 37202, (615)255-7331 [9477]

Tennessee Farmers Cooperative, PO Box 3003, La Vergne, TN 37086, (615)793-8011 [1319]

Tennessee Florist Supply Inc., PO Box 3022, Knoxville, TN 37927, (423)524-7451 [14960]

Tennessee Mat Company Inc., PO Box 100186, Nashville, TN 37224, (615)254-8381 [17216]

Tennessee Shell Company, Inc., PO Box 609, Camden, TN 38320, (901)584-7747 [12706]

Tennessee Valley Electric Supply Co., 6210 Dividend St., Little Rock, AR 72209, (501)568-3627 [9478]

Tennessee Wholesale Drug Co., 200 Cumberland Bend, Nashville, TN 37228, (615)244-8110 [19651]

Tenneva Food and Supplies Inc., PO Box 1719, Bristol, VA 24201, (540)669-7126 [12707]

Tennis Factory, 2500 Wilson Blvd., Ste. 100, Arlington, VA 22201-3834, (703)522-2700 [24007]

Tennison Brothers Inc., PO Box 40126, Memphis, TN 38174-0126, (901)274-7773 [8110]

Tens of Charlotte Inc., 10201 Thomas Payne Cir, Charlotte, NC 28277, (704)846-2098 [19073]

Tepco Corp., Box 1160, Rapid City, SD 57709, (605)343-7200 [17217]

Tepper Electrical Supply Inc., 608 S Neil St., Champaign, IL 61820, (217)356-3755 [9479]

Terco Computer Systems, PO Box 1803, Lombard, IL 60148, (630)668-9999 [6813]

Terk Distributing, 4621 Maple St., Abilene, TX 79602, (915)695-3430 [2073]

Terk Distributing, PO Box 32148, Amarillo, TX 79120, (806)376-4183 [2074]

Terk Distributing, 1001 Pearl St., Odessa, TX 79761, (915)332-9183 [2075]

Term City Furniture & Appliance, 2255 Lamar, PO Box 14665, Memphis, TN 38114-0665, (901)452-6558 [13259]

Ternes Register System, 4851 White Bear Pkwy., St. Paul, MN 55110-3325, (612)633-2361 [16557]

Terra Haute Recycling, PO Box 1798, Terre Haute, IN 47808-1798, (812)232-1537 [27021]

Terra Industries Inc., 600 4th St., PO Box 6000, Sioux City, IA 51102-6000, (712)277-1340 [1320]

Terra International Inc., PO Box 6000, Sioux City, IA 51102-6000, (712)277-1340 [1321]

Terra Nova Press, 1309 Redwood Ln., Davis, CA 95616, (530)756-7417 [4208]

Terral-Norris Seed Company Inc., PO Box 826, Lake Providence, LA 71254, (318)559-2840 [18277]

Terral-Norris Seed Company Inc., PO Box 826, Lake Providence, LA 71254, (318)559-2840 [1322]

Terral Seed, Inc., PO Box 826, Lake Providence, LA 71254, (318)559-2840 [18277]

Terral Seed Inc., PO Box 826, Lake Providence, LA 71254, (318)559-2840 [1323]

Terralink International, 67 Wall St., Ste. 2411, New York, NY 10005, (212)923-5280 [5790]

Terramar Sports Worldwide Ltd., 10 Midland Ave., Port Chester, NY 10573, (914)934-8000 [5425]

Terre Company of New Jersey Inc., PO Box 1000, Clifton, NJ 07014, (973)473-3393 [1324]

Terre Hill Concrete Products, PO Box 10, Terre Hill, PA 17581, (717)445-3100 [8111]

Terrile Export & Import Corp., 20 E 46th St., Rm. 1003, New York, NY 10017-2417, (212)986-2930 [9480]

Terry Bros. Inc., PO Box 87, Willis Wharf, VA 23486, (757)442-6251 [12708]

Terry-Durin Company Inc., 407 7th Ave. SE, Cedar Rapids, IA 52406, (319)364-4106 [9481]

Terry Inc.; Jesse E., PO Box 67, Levittown, PA 19059-0067, (215)355-1000 [23407]

Terry Products Inc., Drawer 108, Kannapolis, NC 28082, (704)938-3191 [5426]

Terryberry Co., 2033 Oak Industrial Dr. NE, Grand Rapids, MI 49505-6011, (616)458-1391 [17635]

TES (USA) Corp., 1 World Trade Ctr., Ste. 1147, New York, NY 10048, (212)775-0555 [16558]

Tesco Distributors Inc., 300 Nye Ave., Irvington, NJ 07111, (973)399-0333 [14719]

Tescom, 15527 Ranch Rd. 620 N, Austin, TX 78717-5299, (512)244-6689 [9482]

Tesdell Refrigeration Supply Inc., 1800 Dixon St., No. H, Des Moines, IA 50316-2172, (515)288-3634 [14720]

Tesla Book Co., PO Box 121873, Chula Vista, CA 91912, (619)561-0341 [4209]

Tesoro Petroleum Corp., PO Box 17536, San Antonio, TX 78217, (210)828-8484 [22726]

Tesoro Petroleum Distributing Co., PO Box 23278, New Orleans, LA 70183, (504)733-6700 [22727]

Tesoro Petroleum Distributing Co., PO Box 23278, New Orleans, LA 70183, (504)733-6700 [22728]

Tessco Technologies Inc., 11126 McCormick Rd., Hunt Valley, MD 21031-1494, (410)229-1000 [5791]

TESSCO Technologies Inc., 11126 McCormick Rd., Hunt Valley, MD 21031-1494, (410)229-1000 [5792]

Tesserax Information Systems, 18796 Academy Cir., Huntington Beach, CA 92648, (714)841-0616 [6814]

The Test Connection Inc., 25 D Main St., Reisterstown, MD 21136, (410)526-2800 [24444]

Test Equipment Distributors, 1370 Piedmont, Troy, MI 48083, (734)524-1900 [24445]

Test Systems Inc., 217 W Palmaire Ave., Phoenix, AZ 85021, (602)861-1010 [9483]

Testor Corp., 620 Buckbee St., Rockford, IL 61104, (815)962-6654 [26678]

TET Incorporated, 806 18th St., Spirit Lake, IA 51360-1234, (712)338-6774 [5427]

Teters Floral Products Inc., PO Box 210, Bolivar, MO 65613, (417)326-7654 [14961]

TETKO Inc., 333 S Highland Ave., Briarcliff Manor, NY 10510, (914)941-7767 [26224]

Tetra Laval Convenience Food Inc., PO Box 358, Avon, MA 02322, (508)588-2600 [24244]

Tetra Laval Convenience Food Inc., PO Box 358, Avon, MA 02322, (508)588-2600 [16559]

Tetra Sales U.S.A., 201 Tabor Rd., Morris Plains, NJ 07950, (973)540-2000 [19652]

Tetra Technologies Inc., 25025 I-45 N, The Woodlands, TX 77380, (713)367-1983 [4526]

Teva Pharmaceutical USA, 650 Cathill Rd., Sellersville, PA 18960, (215)256-8400 [19653]

Tewes Company Inc.; George B., 323 S Date Ave., Alhambra, CA 91803, (818)281-6300 [17218]

Tewksbury Industries Inc., 860 East St., Tewksbury, MA 01876, (508)851-5946 [27022]

Tews Co., 6200 W Center St., Milwaukee, WI 53210, (414)442-8000 [8112]

Tex-Ag Co., PO Box 633, Mission, TX 78572, (956)585-4567 [4527]

Tex Isle Supply Inc., 10830 Old Katy Rd., Houston, TX 77043, (713)461-1012 [20419]

Tex-Mastic International Inc., PO Box 210309, Dallas, TX 75211-0309, (214)330-4605 [8113]

Texaco Additive Co., PO Box 27707, Houston, TX 77227-7707, (713)961-3711 [4528]

Texaco International Trader, Inc., 2000 Westchester Ave., White Plains, NY 10650, (914)253-4000 [22729]

Texaco Oil Co., 3511 NW Texas, Idabel, OK 74745, (580)286-3066 [22730]

Texaco Oil Trading and Supply Co., 2000 Westchester Ave., White Plains, NY 10650, (914)253-4000 [22729]

Texaco Trading and Transportation Inc., PO Box 5568, Denver, CO 80217, (303)861-4475 [22731]

Texas A & M University Press, Lewis St., Lindsey Bldg., 4354 TAMU, College Station, TX 77843-4354, (409)845-1436 [4210]

Texas Art Supply Co., PO Box 66328, Houston, TX 77006-6328, (713)526-5221 [25840]

Texas Book Co., 2601 King St., Greenville, TX 75401, (903)455-6937 [4211]

Texas Contractors Supply Co., 3221 Carpenter Fwy., Irving, TX 75062, (214)438-3323 [8114]

Texas Health Distributors, 840 Interchange Blvd., Austin, TX 78721, (512)385-3853 [12709]

Texas Hobby Distributors, 1516 Contour Dr., San Antonio, TX 78212, (210)824-9688 [26679]

Texas Kenworth Co., PO Box 560049, Dallas, TX 75356-0049, (214)920-7300 [3300]

Texas Leather Trim Inc., 2422 Blue Smoke Ct. S, Ft. Worth, TX 76105-1009, (817)535-5883 [18437]

Texas Mill Inc., 601 Foreman Rd., Orange, TX 77630-9082, (409)886-5686 [17219]

Texas Mill Inc., 905 W Cotton, Longview, TX 75604, (903)758-7005 [17220]

Texas Mill Inc., PO Box 167, Fairfield, TX 75840-0167, (512)446-7366 [17221]

Texas Mill Inc., 4801 Leopard St., Corpus Christi, TX 78408, (512)887-0000 [17222]

Texas Mill Supply Inc., 200 Union Bower Ct., Ste. 214, Irving, TX 75061, (972)554-1111 [13949]

Texas Mill Supply and Manufacturing Company Inc., 2413 Avenue K, Galena Park, TX 77547, (713)675-2421 [17223]

Texas Mining Co., PO Box 429, Brady, TX 76825-0429, (915)597-0721 [8115]

Texas Pipe and Supply Company Inc., 2330 Holmes Rd., Houston, TX 77051-1098, (713)799-9235 [20420]

Texas Plywood and Lumber Company Inc., PO Box 531110, Grand Prairie, TX 75053, (972)263-1381 [8116]

Texas Plywood and Lumber Company Inc., PO Box 531110, Grand Prairie, TX 75053, (972)263-1381 [27385]

Texas Recreation Corp., PO Box 539, Wichita Falls, TX 76307, (940)322-4463 [24008]

Texas Rubber Supply Inc., 2436 Irving Blvd., Dallas, TX 75207, (214)631-3143 [24301]

Texas Rubber Supply Inc., 2436 Irving Blvd., Dallas, TX 75207, (214)631-3143 [17224]

Texas Sales Co., PO Box 1826, El Paso, TX 79949, (915)772-1177 [15336]

Texas Screen Process Supply Co., 304 N Walton, Dallas, TX 75226, (214)748-3271 [25841]

Texas Staple Company Inc., 2422 Bartlett St., Houston, TX 77098, (713)524-8385 [13950]

Texas State Directory Press, 1800 Nueces St., Austin, TX 78701, (512)477-5698 [4212]

Texas Tees, 3815-C Jarrett Way, Austin, TX 78728-1214, (512)388-3530 [5428]

Texas Turbo Jet Inc., 7725 Waxwing Cir. W, Ft. Worth, TX 76137-1009 [158]

Texas-West Indies Co., PO Box 110, El Campo, TX 77437, (409)543-2741 [18278]

Texatek International, 7100 Regency Square Blvd., Ste. 168, Houston, TX 77036, (713)977-7200 [23042]

Texberry Container Corp., 1701 Crosspoint Ave., Houston, TX 77233, (713)796-8800 [23043]

Texhoma Wheat Growers Inc., PO Box 250, Texhoma, OK 73949, (405)827-7261 [1325]

Texo Corp., 2801 Highland Ave., Cincinnati, OH 45212, (513)731-3400 [4529]

Texpack USA Inc., 1001 S Bayshore Dr., Ste. 2402, Miami, FL 33131, (305)358-9696 [27023]

Texstyles Group Inc., 499 7th Ave., New York, NY 10018, (212)967-5113 [26225]

Textile Chemical Company Inc., PO Box 13788, Reading, PA 19612-3788, (610)926-4151 [4530]

Textile Import Corp., 135 W 50th St., No. 1910, New York, NY 10020, (212)581-2840 [26226]

Textiles South Inc., 10100 NW 116th Way, Miami, FL 33178, (305)887-9191 [16560]

Textron Automotive, 2100 Dove St., Port Huron, MI 48060, (810)989-3900 [3301]

Textronix Inc. Semiconductor Test Div., PO Box 500, Beaverton, OR 97077, (503)627-7111 [6815]

Texxon Enterprises Inc., 503 Bruce Ct., Ovilla, TX 75154-3603, (972)230-1630 [8117]

T.G. Sports Co., 13104 S Avalon Blvd., Los Angeles, CA 90061, (213)321-9714 [24013]

Thackeray Corp., 509 Madison Ave., Rm. 1714, New York, NY 10022-5501, (212)759-3695 [13951]

Thaler Oil Company Inc., 310 S Main St., Chippewa Falls, WI 54729, (715)723-2822 [22732]

Thalheimer Brothers Inc., 5550 Whitaker Ave., Philadelphia, PA 19124, (215)537-5200 [27024]

Thalner Electronic Labs Inc., 7235 Jackson Rd., Ann Arbor, MI 48103, (313)761-4506 [9484]

Thames America Trading Company Ltd., 714 Penny Royal Ln., San Rafael, CA 94903, (415)492-2204 [2076]

Thatcher Distributing Group, 5 Cotter Dr., New Brunswick, NJ 08901-1506, (732)246-1357 [4213]

Thau-Nolde Inc., 1884 Lackland Hill Pkwy., Ste. 9, St. Louis, MO 63146-3569, (314)531-6660 [19654]

Thayer Food Products Inc., 962 87th Ave., Oakland, CA 94621, (510)569-7943 [12710]

Thayer Inc., 225 5th St., PO Box 867, Benton Harbor, MI 49023-0867, (616)925-0633 [4716]

Thayer Inc., 225 5th St., Benton Harbor, MI 49023-0867, (616)925-0633 [24245]

THC Systems Inc., 395 N Service Rd No. 300, Melville, NY 11747, (516)753-3700 [15683]

the distributors, 702 S Michigan, South Bend, IN 46601, (219)232-8500 [4214]

Thego Corporation/Acme Marine Hoist, inc., 690 Montauk Hwy., Bayport, NY 11705, (516)472-3030 [18624]

Theis Company Inc.; H.W., PO Box 325, Brookfield, WI 53008-0325, (414)783-0500 [23408]

Theisen Farm and Home Stores, 4949 Chavenelle Rd., Dubuque, IA 52004-0146, (319)556-4738 [1326]

Theraquip Inc., PO Box 16327, Greensboro, NC 27416-0327, (910)665-1395 [19074]

Thermacote Welco Co., 1051 York Rd., PO Box 69, Kings Mountain, NC 28086, (704)739-6421 [20028]

Thermafil/Tulsa Dental Products, 5001 E 68th St., Ste. 500, Tulsa, OK 74136-3324, (918)493-6598 [19075]

Thermal Equipment Company Inc., RR 7, Box 1145, Thomasville, GA 31792-9541, (912)226-7110 [14721]

Thermal Supply Inc., 717 S Lander St., Seattle, WA 98134, (206)624-4590 [14722]

Thermal Tech, Inc., 2301 US Highway 2 E, Kalispell, MT 59901-2835, (406)755-3388 [8118]

Thermax Insulation Inc., 3103 Stinson Ave., Billings, MT 59102-1352, (406)656-1979 [8119]

Thermax Wire Corp., 3202 Linden Pl., Flushing, NY 11354-2823, (718)939-8300 [9485]

Thermion Technologies Inc., 130 E Crescent Ave., Mahwah, NJ 07430, (201)529-2275 [159]

Thermo Industries Inc., 4300 Golf Acres Dr., Charlotte, NC 28208, (704)394-7311 [14368]

Thermo King Atlanta Inc., PO Box 1305, Forest Park, GA 30298-1305, (404)361-4019 [15337]

Thermo King of Baltimore Inc., 7135 Standard Dr., Hanover, MD 21076-1320, (410)712-7200 [14723]

Thermo King of Chattanooga, PO Box 71826, Chattanooga, TN 37407-0826, (423)622-2159 [14724]

Thermo King of Nashville Inc., PO Box 101011, Nashville, TN 37224-1011, (615)244-2996 [14725]

Thermo King of Sioux Falls, 1709 N Cliff Ave., Sioux Falls, SD 57103-0145, (605)334-5162 [14726]

Thermwell Products Co. Inc., 150 E 7th St., Paterson, NJ 07524, (973)684-5000 [8120]

Thew Supply Company Inc.; W.E., PO Box 2426, Green Bay, WI 54306, (920)436-4520 [17225]

Thibaut Oil Company Inc., PO Box 270, Donaldsonville, LA 70346, (504)473-1300 [22733]

Thibodeau's Farms, 419 Buxton Rd., Saco, ME 04072, (207)283-3761 [12711]

Thiel Cheese Inc., N 7630 County Hwy. BB, Hilbert, WI 54129, (920)989-1440 [12712]

Thieme New York, 333 7th Ave., New York, NY 10001, (212)760-0888 [4215]

Thies and Sons Inc.; William, 1335 NE 26th St., Ft. Lauderdale, FL 33305, (954)566-1000 [2077]

Thigpen Distributing Inc., PO Box 888, Tifton, GA 31793, (912)382-1396 [1327]

Thigpen Pharmacy Inc., PO Box 760, Pikeville, NC 27863-0760, (919)242-5565 [19076]

Think and Tinker Ltd., PO Box 408, Monument, CO 80132, (719)488-9640 [16561]

Thinker's Press, PO Box 8, Davenport, IA 52805-0008, (319)323-7117 [4216]

Thinkware, 345 4th St., San Francisco, CA 94107, (415)777-9876 [6816]

Thistle Co.; R.F., PO Box 115, West Harwich, MA 02671-0115, (508)432-7133 [25477]

Thomas Brothers Ham Co., 1852 Gold Hill Rd., Asheboro, NC 27203, (910)672-0337 [12713]

Thomas Company Inc.; Frank R., PO Box 2587, Jackson, MS 39207-2587, (601)353-4793 [5429]

Thomas Hardware, Parts and Fasteners Inc., 1001 Rockland St., Reading, PA 19604-1596, (215)921-3558 [13952]

Thomas and Howard Company Inc., PO Box 23659, Columbia, SC 29224, (803)788-5520 [12714]

Thomas Industrial Products Company Inc., 11412 Cronhill Dr., Owings Mills, MD 21117, (410)356-0003 [24876]

Thomas; Johnny, 350 Avery Landing, Augusta, GA 30907-9749, (706)650-8613 [6817]

Thomas & Jones Sales Management, 808 Arapaho St., Cheyenne, WY 82009-4214, (307)632-5118 [18279]

Thomas Kitchens, Inc., 560 S Poplar St., Hazleton, PA 18201, (717)455-1546 [8121]

Thomas Meat Co., 2055 Nelson Miller Pky., Louisville, KY 40223-2185, (502)587-6947 [12715]

Thomas Nelson Inc., 501 Nelson Pl., Nashville, TN 37214-1000, (615)889-9000 [13463]

Thomas and Proetz Lumber Co., 3400 N Hall St., St. Louis, MO 63147, (314)231-9343 [8122]

Thomas Sales Company Inc., 9050 Hwy. 421, Colfax, NC 27235, (336)992-3545 [26680]

Thomas Scientific, PO Box 99, Swedesboro, NJ 08085, (856)467-2000 [24446]

Thomas Tile, 645 W Lake St., Addison, IL 60101, (630)543-9694 [10212]

Thomas Tile & Carpet Supply Co. Inc., 645 W Lake St., Addison, IL 60101, (630)543-9694 [10212]

Thomas-Walker-Lacey Inc., PO Box 1625, Canton, MS 39046, (601)859-1421 [12716]

Thompson Beauty Supply, 415 W 4th Ave., Bloomington, IN 47404, (812)339-1959 [14258]

Thompson-Clark-Gerritsen Co., 2120 Pewaukee Rd., Waukesha, WI 53188, (414)521-4300 [12717]

Thompson Company Inc., 1219 W North Front, Box 1466, Grand Island, NE 68802, (308)382-6581 [12718]

Thompson Company Inc.; W.B., PO Box 709, Iron Mountain, MI 49801, (906)774-6543 [3302]

Thompson and Cooke Inc., 4200 Kenilworth Ave., Bladensburg, MD 20710, (301)864-6380 [17226]

Thompson Dental Company Inc., PO Box 49, Columbia, SC 29202, (803)799-4920 [19077]

Thompson Distributing, PO Box 1702, Pocatello, ID 83204-1702, (208)232-2279 [2078]

Thompson Distributing Inc., 845 S Wyoming St., Butte, MT 59701-2970, (406)723-6528 [2079]

Thompson Farmers Cooperative Elevator Co., PO Box 327, Thompson, ND 58278, (701)599-2740 [1328]

Thompson Implement Co.; Joe, PO Box 370, Abernathy, TX 79311, (806)298-2541 [1329]

Thompson Implement Inc., PO Box 549, Olton, TX 79064, (806)285-2636 [1330]

Thompson and Johnson Equipment Company Inc., 6926 Fly Rd., East Syracuse, NY 13057, (315)437-2881 [16562]

Thompson Lacquer Company Inc., 2324 S Grand Ave., Los Angeles, CA 90007, (213)746-2290 [21592]

Thompson Mahogany Co., 7400 Edmund St., Philadelphia, PA 19136, (215)624-1866 [27386]

Thompson Office Equipment Company Inc., 5301 NW 9th Ave., Ft. Lauderdale, FL 33309-3119, (954)491-4500 [21318]

Thompson Oil Co., PO Box 589, Waynesboro, PA 17268, (717)762-3011 [22734]

Thompson Sales; Larry, 727 S Sherbrooke Cir., Mt. Carmel, TN 37645, (423)246-7894 [1331]

Thompson Silk Co.; Jim, 2100 Faulkner Rd., Atlanta, GA 30324, (404)325-5004 [26227]

Thompson & Son Inc.; Edwin L., 32 Billerica Rd., Chelmsford, MA 01824-3152, (978)256-8825 [5793]

Thompson Texaco, PO Box 159, Monticello, UT 84535-0159, (435)587-2215 [22076]

Thompson Tile Co., Inc., E 3900 Alki, PO Box 2944, Spokane, WA 99220, (509)535-2925 [10213]

Thompson Tile Co., Inc., 6700 Riverside Dr., Tukwila, WA 98188, (425)251-0575 [10214]

Thompson Tile Co., Inc., 4456 NW Yeon Ave., Portland, OR 97210-1430, (503)225-1273 [10215]

Thompson Tractor Company Inc., PO Box 10367, Birmingham, AL 35202, (205)841-8601 [8123]

Thompsons Inc., 1707 Broadway Ave., Boise, ID 83706-3803, (208)344-5179 [25842]

Thompson's State Beauty Supply, 415 W 4th Ave., Bloomington, IN 47404, (812)339-1959 [14258]

Thompson's Veterinary Supplies, 1340 N 29th Ave., Phoenix, AZ 85009, (602)258-8187 [27246]

Thoms-Proestler Co., 8001 TPC Rd., PO Box 7210, Rock Island, IL 61204-7210, (309)787-1234 [24246]

Thomson Company Inc.; Geo. S., PO Box 17, El Paso, TX 79999, (915)544-8000 [17227]

Thomson Corp., 7625 Empire Dr., Florence, KY 41042, (606)525-2230 [4217]

Thomson-CSF Inc., 99 Canal Center Plz., No. 450, Alexandria, VA 22314-1588, (703)838-9685 [9486]

Thomson National Press Co., 115 Dean Ave., Franklin, MA 02038, (508)528-2000 [16563]

Thomson Productions, PO Box 1225, Orem, UT 84059-1225, (801)226-0155 [25478]

Thor Electronics Corp., 321 Pennsylvania Ave., Linden, NJ 07036, (908)486-3300 [9487]

Thornburg Co. Inc.; C.I., PO Box 2163, Huntington, WV 25722, (304)523-3484 [23409]

Thornhill Oil Company Inc., 2920 Connett Ave., Ft. Wayne, IN 46802, (219)432-9407 [22735]

Thornton Industries, Inc., 5901 Courtesy Ln., Shreveport, LA 71108, (318)636-7450 [13953]

Thornton Wine Imports; J.W., PO Box 2289, Ketchum, ID 83340, (208)726-3876 [2080]

Thorpe Co.; B.K., PO Box 2547, Long Beach, CA 90806, (562)595-1811 [23410]

Thorpe Corp., PO Box 330403, Houston, TX 77233, (713)644-1247 [8124]

Thorpe Corp., PO Box 330407, Houston, TX 77233-3361, (713)641-3361 [8126]

Thorpe Distributing Co., 600 Clydesdale Tr., PO Box 337, Medina, MN 55340, (612)478-8502 [2081]

Thorpe Insulation Co., 2741 S Yates Ave., Los Angeles, CA 90040, (323)726-7171 [8125]

Thorpe Insulation Co., 215 S 14th St., Phoenix, AZ 85034, (602)258-6861 [17228]

Thorpe Livestock Inc., PO Box 1827, Aberdeen, SD 57401-1827, (605)225-2062 [18280]

Thorpe Products Co., PO Box 330407, Houston, TX 77233-3361, (713)641-3361 [8126]

Thorpe and Ricks Inc., PO Box 271, Rocky Mount, NC 27802-0271, (919)977-3151 [26356]

THP United Enterprises Inc., PO Box 1991, Milwaukee, WI 53201-1991, (262)523-6500 [8127]

Thrall Distribution Inc., PO Box 15190, Loves Park, IL 61111, (815)282-3100 [17229]

Threaded Fasteners, 358 St. Louis St., PO Box 2644, Mobile, AL 36652-2644, (205)432-0107 [13954]

Threadtex Inc., 1350 Ave. of the Americas, New York, NY 10019, (212)713-1800 [26228]

Three Continents Press, 222 W B St., Pueblo, CO 81003-3404, (719)544-1038 [4042]

Three Epsilon Inc., 6753 Jones Mill Ct, Ste. A, Norcross, GA 30092-4379, (404)452-7519 [24009]

Three Lakes Distributing Co., 111 Overton St., Hot Springs, AR 71901, (501)623-8201 [2082]

Three M Leisure Time, 4100 James Savage, Midland, MI 48642-5887, (517)496-3401 [24010]

Three Rivers Aluminum Co., 71 Progress Ave., Cranberry Township, PA 16066, (724)776-7000 [8128]

Three Rivers FS Co., PO Box 248, Earlville, IA 52041, (319)923-2315 [1332]

Three Sixty Services Inc., 12623 Newburgh Rd., Livonia, MI 48150, (734)591-9360 [25843]

Three States, 4001 Lakefront Ct., Earth City, MO 63045-1413 [14727]

Three States Supply Co., PO Box 646, Memphis, TN 38101, (901)948-8651 [14728]

Threshold Enterprises Ltd., 23 Janis Way, Scotts Valley, CA 95066, (408)438-6851 [14259]

Thrift Products Company Inc., 41 44th St. SE, Grand Rapids, MI 49548, (616)538-0930 [12719]

Thrifty Medical Supply Inc., 6815 NW 10th St., No. 4, Oklahoma City, OK 73127-4249, (405)787-3985 [19078]

Throttle Up Corp., 463 Turner Dr Ste. 104A, Durango, CO 81301, (970)259-0690 [9488]

Throwbot Inc., 955 Fee Dr., Sacramento, CA 95815, (916)923-0505 [3303]

Thruway Fasteners Inc., 2910 Niagara Falls Blvd., North Tonawanda, NY 14120, (716)694-1434 [13955]

Thruway Produce Inc., 99 West Ave., Lyndonville, NY 14098-9744, (716)765-2277 [12720]

Thunander Corp., PO Box 1428, Elkhart, IN 46515, (219)295-4131 [8129]

Thunder Mountain Dog Supplies, 1421 N Mullan Rd., Spokane, WA 99206-4051, (509)928-3677 [27247]

Thunderbird Silver Co., 4250 E Main St., Ste. 105E, Farmington, NM 87402-8635, (505)327-1696 [17636]

Thunderbird Steel Div., 4300 2nd St. NW, Albuquerque, NM 87107, (505)345-7866 [8130]

Thurmont Cooperative Inc., 36 Walnut St., Thurmont, MD 21788, (301)271-7321 [1333]

Thybony Wallcoverings Co., 3720 N Kedzie Ave., Chicago, IL 60618, (773)463-3005 [21593]

Thypin Stainless Steel, 125 Carson Rd., Birmingham, AL 35215, (205)663-1100 [20421]

Thypin Steel Co., 49-49 30th St., Long Island City, NY 11101, (718)937-2700 [20422]

Thypin Steel Company of New England Inc., 45 Saratoga Blvd., Ayer, MA 01432-5216, (978)784-2800 [20343]

Thyssen Incorporated N.A., 400 Renaissance Ctr., Detroit, MI 48243, (313)567-5600 [20423]

Thyssen Krupp Automotive, 9700 W 7th St., Eden Prairie, MN 55344, (612)941-9700 [3097]

Tianjin-Philadelphia Rug Co., 231 W Mount Pleasant, Philadelphia, PA 19119, (215)247-3535 [15684]

Tibbet Inc., PO Box 2266, Toledo, OH 43603, (419)244-9558 [21319]

TIC Industries Co., 15224 E Stafford St., City of Industry, CA 91744-4418, (626)968-0211 [25479]

TIC Industries Co., 15224 E Stafford St., City of Industry, CA 91744-4418, (626)968-0211 [15338]

Tichon Seafood Corp., PO Box 948, New Bedford, MA 02741, (508)999-5607 [12721]

Tidewater Companies Inc., PO Box 1116, Brunswick, GA 31521, (912)638-7726 [27387]

Tidewater Companies Inc., PO Box 1116, Brunswick, GA 31521-1116, (912)638-7726 [1334]

Tidewater Wholesalers Inc., 708 W Constance Rd., Suffolk, VA 23434, (757)539-3261 [4717]

TIE Systems Inc., 10975 Grandview Dr., Bldg 27, Overland Park, KS 66210, (913)344-0400 [5794]

Tiernay Metals Inc., 2600 Marine Ave., Redondo Beach, CA 90278, (310)676-0184 [20424]

Tiffin Farmers Cooperative, Inc., 585 S Seneca County Rd. 13, PO Box 576, Tiffin, OH 44883-0576, (419)447-0366 [1335]

Tiffin Farms Inc., 585 S Seneca County Rd. 13, PO Box 576, Tiffin, OH 44883-0576, (419)447-0366 [1335]

Tiger Enterprises, Columbia Falls Rd., Addison, ME 04606, (207)483-6000 [18625]

Tiger Machinery Co., 1600 Walcutt Rd., Columbus, OH 43228, (614)876-1141 [8131]

Tilcon Tomasso Inc., 909 Foxon Rd., PO Box 67, North Branford, CT 06471, (203)484-2881 [8132]

Tile America, 487 Federal Rd., Brookfield, CT 06804, (203)740-8858 [10216]

The Tile Barn, 1271 Rte. 22 E, Lebanon, NJ 08833, (908)236-9200 [10217]

The Tile Center, Inc., 1221 Reynolds St., Augusta, GA 30901-1050, (404)722-6804 [10218]

Tile City, c/o M & M Floor Covering, Inc., 359 E Park Ave., Chico, CA 95928-7125, (530)895-3455 [10219]

Tile City, c/o M & M Floor Covering, Inc., 2560 Creater Lake Hwy., Unit C, Medford, OR 97504-4167, (541)779-8453 [10220]

Tile City, 1355 Hartnell Ave., Redding, CA 96002, (530)221-0826 [10221]

Tile Club, 1655 Broadway St., Ste. 21, Chula Vista, CA 91911, (619)420-8801 [10222]

Tile Club, 2122 W Mission Rd., Escondido, CA 92029, (760)745-9123 [10223]

Tile Club, 1833 State College, Anaheim, CA 92806, (714)385-1717 [10224]

Tile Club, 1022 W Morena Blvd., San Diego, CA 92110, (619)276-0271 [10225]

Tile Club, 7129 Reseda Blvd., Reseda, CA 91335-4211, (818)345-2276 [10226]

Tile Club, 2122 W Mission Rd., Escondido, CA 92029, (760)745-9123 [8133]

Tile Collection, 4420 Edna Rd., San Luis Obispo, CA 93401, (805)549-0606 [10227]

The Tile Collection, Inc., 518 E Haley St., Santa Barbara, CA 93103-3108, (805)963-8638 [10228]

Tile Collections, 4420 Edna Rd., San Luis Obispo, CA 93401, (805)549-0606 [10227]

Tile Country Inc., 265 Rt. 22E, Green Brook, NJ 08812, (732)752-6622 [10229]

Tile Creations, 200 Bustleton Pke., Feasterville, PA 19053, (215)357-2400 [10230]

Tile Distributor Company Inc., 4421 Poplar Level Rd., Louisville, KY 40213, (502)456-2410 [10231]

Tile Distributor Company Inc., 4421 Poplar Level Rd., Louisville, KY 40213, (502)456-2410 [8134]

Tile Distributors Inc., 3002 N Nuygant, Portland, OR 97217, (503)286-6613 [10232]

Tile Distributors, Inc., 333 East College St., Florence, AL 35630, (256)766-1110 [10233]

Tile Expressions, 1420 Granite Ln., Modesto, CA 95351, (209)525-9337 [10234]

Tile For Less, 1640 Abilene, Aurora, CO 80012 [10235]

Tile Gallery Inc., Rte. 130 at Brooklawn Circle, Brooklawn, NJ 08030, (609)456-4777 [10236]

Tile Gallery Inc., 1500 Woodhaven Dr., Bensalem, PA 19020, (215)638-4130 [10237]

Tile Helper Inc., 3110 N River Rd., River Grove, IL 60171, (708)453-6900 [10238]

Tile Inc. of Fayetteville, 646 Winslow St., Fayetteville, NC 28306-1536, (919)484-2119 [10239]

Tile International, 319 Waverly Oaks Rd., Waltham, MA 02454, (781)899-8286 [10240]

Tile Mart, Inc., 1020 SE 14th St., Hialeah, FL 33010, (305)885-9804 [10241]

The Tile Place, 1604 Hwy. 35, Oakhurst, NJ 07755, (732)531-0500 [10242]

The Tile Place, 27 Englishtown Rd., Old Bridge, NJ 08857, (732)251-7711 [10243]

The Tile Place, 720 Rte. 70, Brick, NJ 08723, (732)477-4141 [10244]

The Tile Shop, 7505-C Veterans Pkwy., Columbus, GA 31909-2501, (706)327-0668 [10174]

Tile Warehouse, 74-5602D Alapa St., Kailua Kona, HI 96740, (808)329-8855 [10245]

Tile Wholesalers of Rochester, 470 Hollenbeck St., Rochester, NY 14621, (716)544-3200 [10246]

Tilers; J.R., 11125 S Leamington Ave., Alsip, IL 60803-6026, (708)425-2145 [10247]

Tilers—Pergo Shop; J.R., 11125 S Leamington Ave., Alsip, IL 60803-6026, (708)425-2145 [10247]

Tiles For Less, 1718 NE 122nd St., Portland, OR 97230, (503)252-4127 [10248]

Tiles International, 6140 W Quaker St., Orchard Park, NY 14127-2639, (716)662-4441 [10249]

Tiles Plus, 139-8 Westgate Parkway, Dothan, AL 36303, (205)671-4292 [10250]

Tileworks, 8481 Bash St., 1100, Indianapolis, IN 46250, (317)842-6641 [10251]

Tilia, Inc., 568 Howard St., 2nd Fl., San Francisco, CA 94105, (415)243-9890 [16564]

Tillinghast-Stiles Co., 850 Watermen Ave., East Providence, RI 02914, (401)434-2100 [26229]

Tilton & Sons, Inc.; Ben, 470 Bradford Rd., RR 2, Box 470, East Corinth, ME 04427, (207)285-3467 [18281]

Tilton; Sumner H., 66 Clinton St., Concord, NH 03301-2355, (603)225-6161 [18282]

Timber Crest Farms, 4791 Dry Creek Rd., Healdsburg, CA 95448, (707)433-8251 [12722]

Timber Products Co., PO Box 269, Springfield, OR 97477, (541)747-4577 [8135]

Timber Products Co. Medford, PO Box 1669, Medford, OR 97501, (541)773-6681 [27388]

Timberland Machines, 10A N Main St., Lancaster, NH 03584, (603)788-4738 [1336]

Timberline Feed Lot Inc., PO Box 1710, Worland, WY 82401-1710, (307)347-4388 [18283]

Timberline Instruments Inc., PO Box 20356, Boulder, CO 80308, (303)440-8779 [24447]

Timberwork Oregon Inc., PO Box 3955, Portland, OR 97208, (503)492-3089 [27389]

Timco Jewelers Corp., 59 Center St., Rutland, VT 05701, (802)773-3377 [17637]

Time Distribution Services Inc., 1271 Ave. of the Amer., New York, NY 10020, (212)522-8437 [4218]

Time Emergency Equipment, 2341 Avon Industrial Dr., Rochester Hills, MI 48309, (248)852-0939 [25844]

Time Equipment, 311 N Campbell, Rapid City, SD 57701, (605)348-2360 [3304]

Time Life Inc., 2000 Duke St., Alexandria, VA 22314-3414, (703)838-7000 [4219]

Time Oil Co., PO Box 24447, Seattle, WA 98124, (206)285-2400 [22736]

Time Out For Sports, 8840 Orchard Tree Ln., Baltimore, MD 21286-2143, (410)668-9160 [5430]

Time Products Inc., 701 Park Ave., Cranston, RI 02910-2104, (401)941-9100 [21320]

Time Saver Tool Corp., PO Box 4299, Hammond, IN 46324, (219)845-2500 [13956]

Time Service Inc., 245 23rd St., Toledo, OH 43624, (419)241-4181 [17638]

Time Systems Inc., 1434 Mishawaka Ave., South Bend, IN 46615-1226, (219)289-5733 [9489]

Time Warner and Sony Direct Entertainment, 1221 Avenue of the Americas, New York, NY 10020, (212)522-1212 [4220]

TimeSaving Services Inc., 8601 Dunwoody Pl., Ste. 348, Atlanta, GA 30350, (770)649-9499 [6818]

Timm Medical Systems, 6585 City W Pkwy., Eden Prairie, MN 55344, (952)947-9410 [19079]

Tims Cascade Style Chips, 1502 Pike St. NW, Auburn, WA 98001, (253)833-0255 [12723]

Tin-Nee-Ann Trading Co., 923 Cerrillos Rd., Santa Fe, NM 87504-0566, (505)988-1630 [17639]

Tindall Inc.; E.H., 357 Lawrence Station, Lawrenceville, NJ 08648, (609)587-5740 [18284]

Tinder Inc.; W.M., PO Box 2188, Manassas, VA 20110, (703)368-9544 [27390]

Tindle Mills Inc., PO Box 733, Springfield, MO 65801, (417)862-7401 [1337]

Tingue Brown and Company Inc., 535 N Midland Ave., Saddle Brook, NJ 07663-5521, (201)796-4490 [26230]

Tink Inc., 2361 Durham Dayton Hwy., Durham, CA 95938, (530)895-0897 [8136]

Tinley Performancewear, 5111 Santa Fe St., Ste. F, San Diego, CA 92109-1614, (619)581-2800 [5431]

Tipp Distributors Inc., 1477 Lomaland Dr., Bldg. E, Ste. 7, El Paso, TX 79935, (915)594-1618 [25044]

Tippecanoe Beverages Inc., 100 W Michigan St., PO Box 247, Winamac, IN 46996-0247, (219)946-6666 [2083]

Tippins Oil and Gas Company Inc., PO Box 98, Richmond, MO 64085, (816)776-5558 [22737]

Tipton Farmers Cooperative, 500 S Broadway, Tipton, OK 73570, (580)667-5251 [18007]

Tire Corral Inc., 800 Ash Ave., McAllen, TX 78501, (956)631-8473 [3305]

The Tire Rack Wholesale, 777 W Chippewa Ave., South Bend, IN 46614, (219)287-2316 [3306]

Tire Welder Inc., 3428 Pan America Fwy NE, Albuquerque, NM 87107-4741, (505)884-3550 [3307]

Tires Inc., 5951 Ames Ave., Omaha, NE 68104-2705, 800-228-2241 [3308]

Tires, Wheels, Etc. Wholesale Inc., 3910 Cherry Ave., No. 17038, Long Beach, CA 90807-3727, (310)981-2686 [3309]

Tires Wholesale Inc., 4540 E Hammer Ln., Las Vegas, NV 89115-1402, (702)644-5544 [3310]

Tisdale Used Auto Parts, PO Box 1213, Gardiner, ME 04345-1213, (207)582-7542 [3311]

Titan Industrial Corp., 555 Madison Ave., New York, NY 10022, (212)421-6700 [20425]

Titan Steel Co., 322 Miami St., Tiffin, OH 44883, (419)447-0442 [20426]

Titan Technologies Inc. (Albuquerque, New Mexico), 3202 Candelaria Rd. NE, Albuquerque, NM 87107, (505)884-0272 [3312]

Tite Co., 2896 Gant Quarters Cir., Marietta, GA 30068, (770)565-4580 [17]

Titgemeiers Feed, Inc., 701 Western Ave., Toledo, OH 43609, (419)243-3731 [1338]

Titleist Golf, 2819 Loker Ave. E, Carlsbad, CA 92008-6626, (760)745-1000 [24011]

Titus and Sons Inc.; F.D., 20420 Business Pkwy., Walnut, CA 91789-2938, (626)330-4571 [19655]

TJ Wholesale Distributor, 310 Wall St., Las Vegas, NV 89102, (702)598-1938 [26681]

T.J.T. Inc., PO Box 278, Emmett, ID 83617, (208)365-5321 [8137]

The TK Group, Inc., PO Box 867, Bountiful, UT 84011-0867, (801)298-8902 [9490]

TLC Beatrice International Holdings Inc., 9 W 57th St., No. 3910, New York, NY 10019, (212)756-8900 [12724]

TLD America, 812 Bloomfield Ave., Windsor, CT 06095, (860)688-9520 [160]

T.L.K. Industries Inc., 902 Ogden Ave., Superior, WI 54880, (715)392-6253 [17230]

T.L.K. Industries Inc., 902 Ogden Ave., Superior, WI 54880, (715)392-6253 [27025]

TMA Systems L.L.C., 6846 S Canton Ave., Ste. 510, Tulsa, OK 74136, (918)494-2890 [6819]

TMC Orthopedic Supplies Inc., 4747 Bellaire Blvd., Bellaire, TX 77401, (713)669-1800 [19656]

TML Associates Inc., PO Box 2235, Spartanburg, SC 29304-2235, (864)583-2678 [8138]

TMX, 12817 NE Airport Way, Portland, OR 97230, (503)254-2600 [20427]

TNT Insured Towing Auto Salvage, PO Box 8184, Boise, ID 83707-2184, (208)362-4418 [3313]

TNT Optical Supply, Inc., 8035 McDermitt Dr., Apt. 86, Davison, MI 48423-2970, (810)793-6261 [19657]

T.O. Haas Holding Co., PO Box 81067, Lincoln, NE 68501, (402)474-3211 [3314]

T.O. Haas Tire Company Inc., PO Box 81067, Lincoln, NE 68501, (402)473-1415 [3315]

To Market Two Markets Inc., 107 Lakemont Park Blvd., Altoona, PA 16602, (814)941-3090 [12725]

TOA Electronics, Inc., 601 Gateway Blvd., Ste. 300, South San Francisco, CA 94080, (650)588-2538 [9491]

Tobacco Alternative Inc., PO Box 678, Buffalo, NY 14207, (716)877-2983 [26258]

Tobacco Sales Company Inc., 2445 Santa Ana St., Dallas, TX 75228, (214)328-2821 [26357]

Tobacco Shop at Hyatt, 2424 Kalakaua Ave., Honolulu, HI 96815, (808)923-8109 [26358]

Tobacco Supply Company Inc., PO Box 726, Springfield, TN 37172-0726, (615)384-2421 [26359]

Tobe Turpen's Indian Trading Co., 1710 S 2nd St., Gallup, NM 87301, (505)722-3806 [13464]

Tober Industries Inc., 1520 Washington Ave., St. Louis, MO 63103, (314)421-2030 [24877]

Tocos America Inc., 1177 E Tower Rd., Schaumburg, IL 60173, (708)884-6664 [9492]

Today's Kids Inc., Hwy. 10 E, Booneville, AR 72927, (501)675-2000 [26682]

Todd; Robyn, 1495 Poleline Rd. E, Twin Falls, ID 83301-3588, (208)734-1488 [14260]

Todd Tractor Company Inc., PO Box 8, Seneca, KS 66538, (785)336-2138 [1339]

Todd Uniform Inc., 3668 S Geyer Rd., St. Louis, MO 63127, (314)984-0365 [5432]

Todd-Zenner Packaging, 6412 S 190th St., Kent, WA 98032, (425)251-9892 [21655]

Todd-Zenner Packaging, 20803 SW 105th St., Tualatin, OR 97062, (503)692-6992 [21953]

Todhunter Imports Ltd., 222 Lakeview Ave., Ste. 1500, West Palm Beach, FL 33401, (561)837-6300 [2084]

Todisco Jewelry Inc., 30-00 47th Ave., Long Island City, NY 11101, (212)997-1963 [17640]

Toggitt Ltd.; Joan, 140 Pleasant Hill Rd., Chester, NJ 07930-2136, (732)271-1949 [26231]

Tokico (USA) Inc., 17225 Federal Dr., Allen Park, MI 48101-3613, (313)336-5310 [3316]

Toland Enterprises Inc., 1751 South Ln., Mandeville, LA 70471, (504)893-9503 [10252]

Toledo Pickling and Steel Inc., 1149 Campbell St., PO Box 3395, Toledo, OH 43607, (419)255-1570 [20428]

Toledo Pickling and Steel Sales Inc., PO Box 3395, Toledo, OH 43607, (419)255-1570 [20429]

Toledo Tile, 2121 N Reynolds Rd., Toledo, OH 43615, (419)536-9321 [10253]

Tolman Computer Supply Group, 143 N 1200 E, Orem, UT 84097-5016, (801)576-1220 [6820]

Tom Cat Bakery, 43-05 10th St., Long Island City, NY 11101-6829, (718)786-4224 [12726]

Tom Thumb Glove Co., PO Box 640, Wilkesboro, NC 28697, (919)667-1281 [5433]

Toma International, PO Box 523, Santa Cruz, CA 95061, (831)990-0326 [1340]

Tomahawk Farms Inc., 603 S Wilson, Dunn, NC 28334, (919)892-6174 [12727]

Tomasco Mulciber Inc., 2001 Courtright Rd., Columbus, OH 43232-4210, (614)231-0075 [3317]

Tomba Communications and Electronics Inc., 718 Barataria Blvd., Marrero, LA 70072, (504)340-2448 [6821]

Tomchuck Insulators, 262 Old Hwy. 93, Ronan, MT 59864-9508, (406)676-3641 [23044]

Tomco Auto Products Inc., 4330 E 26th St., Los Angeles, CA 90023-4770, (213)268-4830 [3318]

Tomco Carburetor Company, 4330 E 26th St., Los Angeles, CA 90023-4770, (213)268-4830 [3318]

Tomen America Inc., 1285 Ave. of the Amer., New York, NY 10019, (212)397-4600 [20430]

Tomfoolery Serious Chocolate, Inc., 5362 Oceanus Dr., Ste. C, Huntington Beach, CA 92649, (714)903-6800 [12728]

Tomichi Studio, 390 5th Ave., New York, NY 10018-8104, (212)760-2455 [19552]

Tomra Maine, 80 Pine Tree Industrial Pkwy., Portland, ME 04102-1443, (207)774-7447 [25845]

Tom's Foods Inc., 2648 Byington Sloway Rd., Knoxville, TN 37931-3213, (423)690-8170 [12729]

Toms Sierra Company Inc., PO Box 759, Colfax, CA 95713, (530)346-2264 [22738]

Tom's Toasted Peanuts, 824 N Gloster, Tupelo, MS 38801-1949, (601)842-7537 [12730]

Toner Cable Equipment, Inc., 969 Horsham Rd., Horsham, PA 19044, (215)675-2053 [25480]

Toner Cable Equipment Inc., 969 Horsham Rd., Horsham, PA 19044, (215)675-2053 [15339]

Toner Sales Inc., 4290 Freeman Rd., Marietta, GA 30062-5640, (404)993-8805 [24012]

Toney Petroleum Inc., 508 S John St., Crawfordsville, IN 47933, (765)362-1800 [22739]

Toney Petroleum Inc., 508 S John St., Crawfordsville, IN 47933, (765)362-1800 [22740]

Tonkadale Greenhouses, 3739 Tonkawood Rd., Minnetonka, MN 55345-1445, (612)938-1445 [14962]

Tonnies Company Inc.; David F., 6520 W 110th St., Ste. 104, Shawnee Mission, KS 66211, (913)491-6200 [25481]

Tony Ingoglia Salami and Cheese Company Inc., PO Box 1501, West Sacramento, CA 95605-1501, (916)374-4000 [12731]

Tony's Fine Foods, PO Box 1501, West Sacramento, CA 95605-1501, (916)374-4000 [12731]

Too Goo Doo Farms Inc., 4693 Too Goo Doo Farm Rd., Yonges Island, SC 29449, (843)889-6468 [12732]

Tool Craft Inc., 767 Hartford Ave., Johnston, RI 02919, (401)521-9630 [17641]

Tool House Inc., PO Box 80759, Lincoln, NE 68501, (402)476-6673 [13957]

Tool King Inc., PO Box 366, Wheeling, IL 60090, (847)537-2881 [20431]

Tool Mart, 750 Citracado Pkwy., Escondido, CA 92025, (760)480-1444 [13958]

Tool Service Corp., PO Box 26248, Milwaukee, WI 53226, (414)476-7600 [16565]

Tool Steel Service Inc., 7333 S 76th Ave., Bridgeview, IL 60455, (708)458-7878 [20432]

Tool World, 1160 Air Way Blvd., El Paso, TX 79925, (915)779-5616 [13959]

Toole and Company Inc., PO Box 21322, Houston, TX 77226-1322, (713)691-2011 [23411]

Toolkraft Distributing, 352 Longhill St., Springfield, MA 01108, (413)737-7331 [16566]

Toolman Co., 721 Graywood Ave., Elkhart, IN 46516-5418, (219)295-0296 [13960]

Toolpushers Supply Co., PO Box 2360, Casper, WY 82602-2360, (307)266-0324 [8139]

Toombs Truck and Equipment Co., 1800 Walcutt Rd., Columbus, OH 43228-9612, (614)876-1181 [16567]

Top AG Inc., PO Box 284, Tipton, IN 46072, (317)675-8736 [1341]

Top Comfo Athletic Sox Inc., PO Box 10304, Lynchburg, VA 24506-0304, (804)237-2323 [5434]

Top Dog Ltd., 1510 Roper Mountain Rd., Greenville, SC 29615 [27248]

Top of Iowa Coop, PO Box 181, Joice, IA 50446, (515)588-3131 [18285]

Top Source Technologies Inc., 7108 Fairway Dr., No. 200, Palm Beach Gardens, FL 33418-3769, (561)775-5756 [3319]

Top Taste Bakery Inc., PO Box 297, Finley, ND 58230-0297, (701)524-1380 [12733]

Topco Associates Inc., 7711 Gross Point Rd., Skokie, IL 60077, (847)676-3030 [12734]

Topeka Seed and Stove Inc., PO Box 400, Topeka, IN 46571, (219)593-2494 [1342]

Topicz, 2121 Section Rd., PO Box 37289, Cincinnati, OH 45222, (513)351-7700 [26360]

Topline Corp., 13150 SE 32nd St., Bellevue, WA 98005-4436, (425)643-3003 [24878]

Toppan Printronics (USA) Inc., PO Box 655012, Dallas, TX 75265, (972)995-6575 [9493]

Topsville Inc., 11800 NW 102nd Rd., Medley, FL 33178, (305)883-8677 [5435]

Topworx, PO Box 37290, Louisville, KY 40233, (502)969-8000 [9494]

Torah Umesorah Publications, 5723 18th Ave., Brooklyn, NY 11204, (718)259-1223 [4221]

Toray Industries (America) Inc., 600 3rd Ave., 5th Fl., New York, NY 10016-1902, (212)697-8150 [4531]

Toray Industries Inc., 600 3rd Ave., New York, NY 10016-1902, (212)697-8150 [26232]

Toray Marketing and Sales (America) Inc., 140 Cypress Station Dr., Ste. 210, Houston, TX 77090, (281)587-2299 [19080]

Torello and Son Machine Co.; F., 206 Orange Ave., West Haven, CT 06516, (203)933-1684 [3320]

Torn and Glasser Inc., PO Box 21823, Los Angeles, CA 90021, (213)627-6496 [12735]

Tornos Technologies U.S. Corp., PO Box 325, Brookfield, CT 06804-0325, (203)775-4319 [16568]

Torosian Brothers, 492 Main St., Ft. Lee, NJ 07024, (201)944-5119 [10254]

Torque-A-Matic, 12822 E Indiana, Spokane, WA 99216, (509)928-0535 [17231]

Torque Drive, 317 S Park Ave., Warren, OH 44483, (330)399-1000 [3321]

Torrences Farm Implement, PO Box C, Heber, CA 92249, (760)352-5355 [1343]

Torres Hat Company, 216 Century Blvd., Laredo, TX 78040, (956)724-1473 [5436]

Torrington Supply Company Inc., PO Box 2838, Waterbury, CT 06723-2838, (203)756-3641 [23412]

TOSCO Marketing Co., 1500 Priest Dr., Tempe, AZ 85281, (602)728-8000 [22741]

Toshiba America Consumer Products Inc., 82 Totowa Rd., Wayne, NJ 07470, (973)628-8000 [9495]

Toshiba America Electronic Components Inc. Storage Device Div., 35 Hammond, Irvine, CA 92618, (949)457-0777 [6822]

Toshiba America Information Systems Inc. Network Products Div., PO Box 19724, Irvine, CA 92618-1697, (949)461-4840 [6823]

Toshiba America Medical Systems Inc., 2441 Michelle Dr., Tustin, CA 92780, (714)730-5000 [19081]

Toshiba America Medical Systems Inc., PO Box 2068, Tustin, CA 92780, (714)730-5000 [19658]

Toshiba Tungaloy America Inc., 1375 E Irving Park Rd., Itasca, IL 60143, (630)285-9500 [16569]

Toshin Trading Inc., PO Box 1226, Blythe, CA 92226, (760)922-4713 [1344]

Total Concepts Inc., 501 W Glenoaks Blvd., Glendale, CA 91202, (818)547-9476 [6824]

Total Electric Distributors Inc., 388 South Ave., Staten Island, NY 10303, (718)273-9300 [9496]

Total Information, 844 Dewey Ave., Rochester, NY 14613, 800-876-4636 [4222]

Total Office Interiors, PO Box 16010, Baltimore, MD 21218, (410)366-6000 [21954]

Total Orthopedic Div., 18978 Bonanza Way, Gaithersburg, MD 20879-1513, (301)840-9027 [19659]

Total Recall Corp., 50A S Main St., Spring Valley, NY 10977, (914)425-3000 [24643]

Total Safety Inc., 11111 Wilcrest Green., Ste. 425, Houston, TX 77017 [25846]

Total Supply, 1865 Beaver Ridge Cir., Norcross, GA 30071, (770)417-1806 [14729]

Total Supply, 5158 Kennedy Rd., Forest Park, GA 30297, (404)608-0062 [14730]

Total Supply, 4620 S Atlanta Rd. SE, Smyrna, GA 30080, (404)792-1696 [14731]

Total Supply Inc., 5158 Kennedy Rd., Ste. F, Forest Park, GA 30297, (404)608-0062 [14732]

Totem Food Products Co., 6203 S 194th, Kent, WA 98032-2127, (253)872-9200 [12736]

ToteVision, 969 Thomas St., Seattle, WA 98109-5213, (206)623-6000 [5795]

Tots Wear Company Inc., 235-239 Holliday St., Baltimore, MD 21202, (410)752-0134 [5437]

Totsy Manufacturing Co., Inc., 1 Bigelow St., Holyoke, MA 01040, (413)536-0510 [26683]

Totten Tubes Inc., 500 Danlee St., Azusa, CA 91702, (626)812-0220 [20433]

Touch Adjust Clip Co. Inc., 1687 Roosevelt Ave., Bohemia, NY 11716-1428, (516)589-3077 [17642]

Touch Flo Manufacturing, 75 E Palm Ave., Burbank, CA 91502, (818)843-8117 [23413]

Toudouze Inc., PO Box 7449, San Antonio, TX 78207-0449, (210)224-1891 [12737]

Tourbillon Farm, 401 Snake Hill Rd., North Scituate, RI 02857-9806, (401)934-2221 [18286]

Tout de Suite a la Microwave Inc., PO Box 60121, Lafayette, LA 70596-0121, (318)984-2903 [4223]

Tower Aviation Services, PO Box 2444, Oakland, CA 94614, (510)635-3500 [161]

Tower Equipment Company Inc., 385 Front St. N, Ste. 201, Issaquah, WA 98027-2929, (425)889-8886 [16570]

Tower Fasteners Company, Inc., 1690 N Ocean Ave., Holtsville, NY 11742-1823, (516)289-8800 [9497]

Tower-Flo, PO Box 58, Sterling, KS 67579, (316)278-3160 [24021]

Tower International Inc., 588 Saco Rd., Standish, ME 04084, (207)642-5400 [4224]

Tower Oil and Technology Co., 205 W Randolph St., Chicago, IL 60606, (312)346-0562 [22742]

Tower Paint Manufacturing, 620 W 27th St., Hialeah, FL 33010, (305)887-9583 [21594]

Tower Publishing Co., 588 Saco Rd., Standish, ME 04084, (207)642-5400 [4224]

Towle Manufacturing Co., 144 Addison St., East Boston, MA 02128-9115, (617)568-1300 [15685]

Towlift Inc., 1395 Valley Belt Rd., Cleveland, OH 44131, (216)749-6800 [16571]

Town and Country Coop., PO Box 250, Grafton, OH 44044, (440)926-2281 [1345]

Town & Country Pet Supply Inc., 6314 Arundel Cove Ave., Baltimore, MD 21226, (410)355-2400 [27249]

Town Pump Inc., 600 S Main St., Butte, MT 59701, (406)782-9121 [22743]

Town Square Books, 123 N 2nd St., PO Box 338, Stillwater, MN 55082, (612)430-2210 [4264]

Town Talk Cap Manufacturing Co., PO Box 58157, Louisville, KY 40268-0157, (502)933-7575 [5438]

Townsend-Strong Inc., PO Box 2802, Lubbock, TX 79401, (806)763-0491 [22744]

Townsend Supply Co., 120 Johnson St., Jackson, TN 38301, (901)424-4300 [9498]

TownTalk/Hostess, 1700 Island Ave., Pittsburgh, PA 15233, (412)231-2000 [12738]

Townzen Tile & Laminates, 13455 Puppy Creek, Springdale, AR 72762, (501)751-4043 [10255]

Toy Farmer Inc., RR 2, Box 5, Lamoure, ND 58458, (701)883-4430 [26684]

Toy Wonders Inc., 234 Moonachie Rd., Moonachie, NJ 07074, (201)229-1700 [26685]

The Toy Works, Inc., Fiddler's Elbow Rd., Middle Falls, NY 12848, (518)692-9665 [26686]

Toyo Trading Co., 13000 S Spring St., Los Angeles, CA 90061, (310)660-0300 [15686]

Toyo USA Inc., 1155 Dairy Ashford, Ste. 805, Houston, TX 77079, (281)496-4448 [22745]

Toyota Aviation U.S.A. Inc., 3250 Airflite Way, Long Beach, CA 90807, (562)490-6200 [162]

Toyota Motor Distributors Inc., 440 Forbes Blvd., Mansfield, MA 02048, (508)339-5701 [3322]

Toyota Motor Sales U.S.A. Inc., 19001 S Western Ave., Torrance, CA 90509, (310)618-4000 [20737]

Toyota Tsusho America Inc., 437 Madison Ave., New York, NY 10022, (212)418-0100 [20434]

T.R. Distributing, 7228 NW 79th Terr., Miami, FL 33166, (305)883-0697 [12739]

TR Systems, 2652 US Hwy. 41 W, Marquette, MI 49855-2257, (906)228-5757 [15340]

T.R. Trading Co., PO Box 310279, New Braunfels, TX 78131, (512)629-9203 [16572]

Trace Engineering, 5916 195th NE, Arlington, WA 98223, (253)435-8826 [3323]

Track 'N Trail, 4961-A Windplay Dr., El Dorado Hills, CA 95762, (916)933-4525 [5439]

Traco Industrial Corp., 461 W 126th, New York, NY 10027-2535, (212)865-7700 [14733]

The TRACOM Corporation, 8773 S Ridgeline Blvd., Ste. 101, Highlands Ranch, CO 80126, (303)470-4900 [4225]

Tracom Inc., 932 S Ayers Ave., Ft. Worth, TX 76103, (817)534-6566 [3324]

Tractor and Equipment Co., 1835 Harnish Blvd., Billings, MT 59101, (406)656-0202 [1346]

Tractor Place Inc., PO Box 689, Knightdale, NC 27545, (919)266-5846 [1347]

Tracy-Garvin Cooperative, PO Box 1098, Tracy, MN 56175, (507)629-3781 [1348]

Trade Am International Inc., 6580 Jimmy Carter Blvd., Norcross, GA 30071, (770)263-6144 [10256]

Trade America, 1862 Akron-Peninsula Rd., Akron, OH 44313, (330)923-5300 [16573]

Trade Corporation, PO Box 30277, Raleigh, NC 27622, (919)571-8782 [8140]

Trade Development Corporation of Chicago, 2049 Century Park E, Ste. 480, Los Angeles, 41400, 90067, (310)556-8091 [17232]

Trade Routes Ltd., 39 New York Ave. NE, Washington, DC 20002-3327, (202)371-0090 [5440]

Trade Supplies, 3188 E Slauson Ave., Vernon, CA 90058, (213)581-3250 [21955]

Tradearbed Inc., 825 3rd Ave., New York, NY 10022, (212)486-9890 [20435]

TradeCom International Inc., 32750 Solon Road, Ste. 9, Solon, OH 44139, (440)248-9116 [13961]

Trademark Dental Ceramics Inc., 1684 Barnett Shoals Rd., Athens, GA 30605-3007, (706)549-9960 [19082]

Tradequest International USA, PO Box 2759, Bristol, CT 06010, (860)589-1508 [6825]

Trader Vic's Food Products, PO Box 8603, Emeryville, CA 94662, (510)658-9722 [12740]

Tradeways Inc., 8 Music Fair Rd., No. A, Owings Mills, MD 21117, (410)664-7000 [13260]

Tradewinds International Inc., PO Box 9930, Savannah, GA 31412, (912)234-8050 [8141]

Tradewinds International Inc., 8548 W River Rd., Minneapolis, MN 55444-1311, (612)561-0009 [6826]

Tradex Corporation, PO Box 495188, Garland, TX 75049, (972)840-8805 [14734]

Tradex International, PO Box 495188, Garland, TX 75049, (972)840-8805 [14734]

Tradex International Corp., PO Box 8415, Newport Beach, CA 92660, (949)458-9808 [19083]

Tradex International Corp., 505 Northern Blvd., Great Neck, NY 11021, (516)829-3855 [20436]

Tradigrain Inc., 889 Ridge Lake Blvd., Memphis, TN 38120, (901)684-1496 [18287]

Traditional Quality Corp., 4498 Main St., Buffalo, NY 14226, (716)839-1018 [12741]

Trafalgar Square, PO Box 257, Howe Hill Rd, North Pomfret, VT 05053, (802)457-1911 [4226]

Traffic Control Service Inc., 1881 Betmor Ln., Anaheim, CA 92805, (714)937-0422 [24644]

Trags Distributors, 3023 Hancock St., Ste. C, San Diego, CA 92110, (619)688-1156 [26687]

Trailblazer Foods, PO Box 441, Fairview, OR 97024, (503)666-5800 [12742]

Trailer Craft, 1031 E 64th Ave., Anchorage, AK 99518, (907)563-3238 [3325]

Trails West Publishing, PO Box 1483, Great Falls, MT 59403, (406)453-6453 [21956]

Train Center Distributors, 506 S Broadway, Denver, CO 80209, (303)722-8444 [26688]

Trainor Grain and Supply Co., R.R. 2, Box 44, Wing Sta., Forrest, IL 61741, (815)832-5512 [18288]

Trak-Air/Rair, 7006-B S Alton Way, Englewood, CO 80112, (303)779-9888 [24247]

Trane Co, 3600 Pammel Creek, La Crosse, WI 54601, (608)787-2000 [14735]

Tranex Inc., 2350 Executive Cir, Colorado Springs, CO 80906, (719)576-7994 [9499]

Trans-Atlantic Co., 440 Fairmount Ave., Philadelphia, PA 19123, (215)629-0400 [13962]

Trans-Cal Industries Inc., 16141 Cohasset St., Van Nuys, CA 91406, (818)787-1221 [25847]

Trans-Global Sports Co., 13104 S Avalon Blvd., Los Angeles, CA 90061, (213)321-9714 [24013]

Trans-Tec Services Inc., 500 Frank W Burr Blvd., Teaneck, NJ 07666, (201)692-9292 [22746]

Trans West Communication Systems, PO Box 9069, Seattle, WA 98109-0069, (425)882-3140 [9500]

Trans World Company of Miami Inc., 2090 NW 13th Ave., Miami, FL 33142-7702, (305)545-5639 [12743]

Trans World Investments, Ltd., 1126 Pine Croft Dr., West Columbia, SC 29170, (803)794-5152 [15687]

Transamerican & Export News Co., 591 Camino de la Reina St., Ste. 200, San Diego, CA 92108-3192, (619)297-8065 [4227]

Transammonia Inc., 350 Park Ave., New York, NY 10022, (212)223-3200 [1349]

Transco Inc., PO Box 1025, Linden, NJ 07036, (908)862-0030 [25482]

Transco Industries Inc., PO Box 20429, Portland, OR 97294, (503)256-1955 [16574]

Transco Products Inc., 55 E Jackson Blvd., Chicago, IL 60604, (312)427-2818 [23488]

Transco South Inc., 418 Lafayette Rd., Hampton, NH 03842-2222, (603)926-6240 [21321]

Transcon Trading Company, Inc., 121 Dutchman Blvd., Irmo, SC 29063, (803)781-7117 [27250]

Transfer Print Foils, 1787 Pomona Rd., Ste. B, Corona, CA 91718, (949)753-1135 [20437]

Transit Mix Concrete Co., PO Box 1030, Colorado Springs, CO 80901, (719)475-0700 [8142]

Transit Mix Concrete Co., PO Box 1030, Colorado Springs, CO 80901, (719)475-0700 [20438]

Transit Services Inc., 69 McAdenville Rd., Belmont, NC 28012, (704)825-8146 [24448]

TransLogic Corp., 10825 E 47th Ave., Denver, CO 80239, (303)371-7770 [16575]

Transmedia Restaurant Company Inc., 750 Lexington Ave., 16th Fl., New York, NY 10022 [24248]

Transmission Engineering Co., PO Box 580, 1851 N Penn Rd., Hatfield, PA 19440, (215)822-6737 [3326]

Transmission Equipment Co., 134 S Turnpike Rd., Wallingford, CT 06492, (203)269-8751 [16576]

Transmission Equipment International Inc., 134 S Turnpike Rd., Wallingford, CT 06492, (203)269-8751 [16576]

Transmission Exchange Co., 1803 NE ML King Jr. Blvd., Portland, OR 97212, (503)284-0768 [3327]

Transmission and Fluid Equipment Inc., 6912 Trafalgar Dr., Ft. Wayne, IN 46803, (219)493-3223 [9501]

Transmission Products, Inc., 3024 Bells Rd., PO Box 24657, Richmond, VA 23234, (804)233-8351 [17233]

Transmission Products, Inc., 1519 11th St. NE, PO Box 5326, Roanoke, VA 24012, (540)344-2093 [17234]

TransMontaigne Product Services Inc., PO Box 1503, Fayetteville, AR 72702, (501)521-5565 [22747]

Transmudo Company Inc., 999 Brickell Ave., No. 1001, Miami, FL 33131-9044, (305)539-1205 [12744]

Transnational Motors Inc., PO Box 2008, Grand Rapids, MI 49501, (616)949-7570 [20738]

TransNet Corp., 45 Columbia Rd., Somerville, NJ 08876, (908)253-0500 [6827]

Transocean Coal Company L.P., 599 Lexington Ave., No. 2300, New York, NY 10022, (212)370-3600 [20574]

Transoceanic Trade, Inc., 2250 N Druid Hills Rd., Ste. 238, Atlanta, GA 30329, (404)633-8912 [22911]

Transparent Technology Inc., 520 Washington Blvd., No. 812, Marina Del Rey, CA 90292-5442, (310)215-8040 [6828]

Transply Inc., PO Box 7727, York, PA 17404-0727, (717)767-1005 [3328]

Transport Equipment, Inc., 637 Elmdale Rd., Toledo, OH 43609, (419)385-4641 [3329]

Transport Refrigeration of Sioux Falls, 4622 N Cliff Ave., Sioux Falls, SD 57104-0554, (605)332-3861 [14736]

TransPro Marketing, 21408 50th Dr. SE, Woodinville, WA 98072-8378, (425)485-6098 [6829]

Transtar Industries Inc., 7350 Young Dr., Walton Hills, OH 44146-5390, (216)232-5100 [3330]

Transtat Equipment, Inc., PO Box 593865, Orlando, FL 32859, (407)857-2040 [3331]

Transtech Industries Inc., 200 Centennial Ave., Piscataway, NJ 08855-1321, (732)981-0777 [4532]

Transupport Inc., 53 Turbine Way, Merrimack, NH 03054-4161, (603)424-3111 [16577]

Transworld Alloys Inc., 334 E Gardena Blvd., Gardena, CA 90248, (310)217-8777 [20439]

Transworld Metal USA Ltd., 335 Madison Ave., Rm 815, New York, NY 10017-4605, (212)750-8600 [20440]

Travers Tool Co., 128-15 26th Ave., Flushing, NY 11354, (718)886-7200 [13963]

Travers Tool Co., Inc., 128-15 26th Ave., PO Box 541550, Flushing, NY 11354-0108, (718)886-7200 [13964]

Travis Tile Sales, 3811 Airport Rd., Austin, TX 78722-1335, (512)478-8705 [10257]

Travis Tile Sales, 10542 Sentinel Dr., San Antonio, TX 78217-3822, (210)653-8372 [10258]

Trax Distributors, 16851 Vicory Blvd., No. 11, Van Nuys, CA 91406-5560, (818)902-0619 [25483]

Trax Farms Inc., RD 1, Box 68A, Rte. 88, Finleyville, PA 15332-9801, (412)835-3246 [12745]

Trax Inc., 1340 Perimeter Hwy. S, Atlanta, GA 30349, (770)996-6800 [8143]

Trayco Inc., PO Box 950, Florence, SC 29503, (803)669-5462 [23414]

Traylor Chemical and Supply Co., PO Box 547937, Orlando, FL 32854-7937, (407)422-6151 [1350]

TRC Industries Inc., 1777 Commerce Dr., Stow, OH 44224, (330)688-1583 [24302]

TRCA Electronic Division, 1429 Massaro Blvd., Tampa, FL 33619-3519, (813)623-3545 [5796]

Treacle Press, PO Box 1126, Kingston, NY 12402, (914)331-5807 [3945]

Treadway Electric Co., 3300 W 65th St., Little Rock, AR 72209, (501)562-2111 [9502]

Treadways Corp., 601 Gateway, Ste. 650, South San Francisco, CA 94080, (650)583-5555 [3332]

Trease Distributing Co.; Dan, 5600 S 5900 W, Hooper, UT 84315, (801)773-0450 [22748]

Treasure Chest Books, LLC, 451 N Bonita Ave., Tucson, AZ 85745, (520)623-9558 [4228]

Treasure State Seed, Inc., Box 698, Fairfield, MT 59436, (406)467-2557 [1351]

Treasure Valley X-Ray Inc., PO Box 7772, Boise, ID 83707-1772, (208)323-1968 [19084]

Treaty Co., PO Box 40, Greenville, OH 45331, (513)548-2181 [23415]

Tree Frog Trucking Co., 318 SW Taylor, Portland, OR 97204, (503)227-4760 [4229]

Tree of Life/Gourmet Award Foods, 12601 SE Highway 212, PO Box 919, Clackamas, OR 97015, (503)655-1177 [12746]

Tree of Life Inc., PO Box 410, St. Augustine, FL 32085, (904)824-8181 [12747]

Tree of Life Inc. Midwest, PO Box 2629, Bloomington, IN 47402, (812)333-1511 [12748]

Tree of Life Inc. Northeast, 2501 71st St., Box 852, North Bergen, NJ 07047, (201)662-7200 [12749]

Tree of Life Inc. Northwest, PO Box 88830, Seattle, WA 98188, (425)251-5220 [12750]

Tree of Life Inc. Southeast, 1750 Tree Blvd., PO Box 410, St. Augustine, FL 32085, (904)825-2240 [14261]

Tree of Life Inc. Southwest, 105 Bluebonnet Dr., Cleburne, TX 76031, (817)641-6678 [12751]

Trek Corp., 801 W Madison St., Waterloo, WI 53594, (920)478-4700 [15341]

Trelltex Inc., 5520 Armour Dr., Houston, TX 77020, (713)675-8590 [24303]

Trend Pacific Inc., 2580 Corporate Pl., Ste. F109, Monterey Park, CA 91754-7633, (323)266-8925 [15688]

Trenk and Sons; Joseph, 171 Thomas St., Newark, NJ 07114, (201)589-5778 [18289]

Trenton Iron and Metal Corp., 301 Enterprise Ave., Trenton, NJ 08638, (609)396-2250 [20441]

Trevarrow Inc., 1295 N Opdyke Rd., Auburn Hills, MI 48326-2648, (248)377-2300 [15342]

Trevose Electronics Inc., 4033 Brownsville Rd., Trevose, PA 19053, (215)357-1400 [25484]

TRI-Alaska, 7215 Foxridge Circle, No. 2, Anchorage, AK 99518, (907)561-1956 [14262]

Tri-Blue Kennel, 4013 County Line Rd., Southington, OH 44470, (330)889-3377 [27251]

Tri-Bro Supply Co., 232 Vestal Parkway W, Vestal, NY 13850, (607)748-8144 [23416]

Tri Central Co-op, PO Box 176, Ashkum, IL 60911, (815)698-2327 [18290]

Tri Citi Auto Warehouse, 6715 66th St. N, Pinellas Park, FL 33781-5035, (813)544-8856 [3333]

Tri City Electrical Supply Co., 1 E Hundred Rd., Chester, VA 23831-2608, (804)530-1030 [9503]

Tri-City Fuel and Heating Company Inc., PO Box 5708, West Columbia, SC 29171, (803)796-9172 [14737]

Tri-Color International, 9197 El Cortez Ave., Fountain Valley, CA 92708, (714)847-2191 [24014]

Tri-County Co-op, 107 Long Ave., Lost Nation, IA 52254, (319)678-2231 [1352]

Tri County Coors, PO Box 1053, Torrington, WY 82240-1053, (307)532-2932 [2085]

Tri-County Distributors, 1906 Harrison St., Evanston, IL 60201, (773)273-2160 [25848]

Tri-County Farmers Association, 416 E Cypress St., Brinkley, AR 72021, (870)734-4874 [1353]

Tri-County Truck Tops, Inc., Rtes. 62 & 25 PO Box 201, Algonquin, IL 60102, (847)658-7200 [3334]

Tri-Dee Distributors, 215 S 1st St., Mt. Vernon, WA 98273, (360)336-6131 [13261]

Tri E Distributors, PO Box 163, Nampa, ID 83653-0163, (208)466-7889 [13262]

Tri Lakes Petroleum, E 76 Mt. Branson, Branson, MO 65616, (417)334-3940 [22749]

Tri Lift, 180 Main St., New Haven, CT 06512, (203)467-1686 [16578]

Tri-Line Corp., 250 Summit Point Dr., Henrietta, NY 14467-9607, (716)874-2740 [5854]

Tri-Line Corp., 250 Summit Point Dr., Henrietta, NY 14467-9607, (716)377-3370 [16579]

Tri-Line Farmers Cooperative, PO Box 65, Clarkfield, MN 56223, (612)669-7501 [18291]

Tri-Lite Optical, 256 Burgen Blvd., West Paterson, NJ 07424, (201)337-1717 [19660]

Tri M Specialties, 554 Bailey Ln., Corvallis, MT 59828-9640, (406)961-4794 [24645]

Tri Marine International, 150 W 7th, San Pedro, CA 90731-3336, (310)548-6245 [12752]

TRI-New England, 73 Reservoir Park Dr., No. 6, Rockland, MA 02370, (781)871-7886 [14263]

Tri-Parish Communications Inc., 7530 E Industrial Dr., Baton Rouge, LA 70805-7517, (504)928-4151 [5797]

Tri-Parish Cooperative Inc., PO Box 89, Slaughter, LA 70777, (504)654-2727 [1354]

Tri-Power, Inc., 358 Milling Rd., Mocksville, NC 27028, (704)634-5348 [3335]

Tri-Power MPT, 1447 S Main St., Akron, OH 44301, (330)773-3307 [17235]

Tri-Quality Business Forms Inc., PO Box 2529, Eugene, OR 97402, (541)343-5755 [21322]

Tri River Foods Inc., PO Box 545, Bethel Park, PA 15102, (412)831-9090 [12753]

Tri-S Co., 2209 E Main St., Chattanooga, TN 37404, (423)698-8821 [24646]

Tri-Star Industrial Supply Inc., 10435 Baur Blvd., St. Louis, MO 63132, (314)997-0600 [16580]

Tri Star Seed Co., 20300 W 191st St., Spring Hill, KS 66083-8982, (913)780-6186 [1355]

Tri-State, 3 S Bedford St., Manchester, NH 03101-1111, (603)668-4840 [24249]

Tri-State Aluminum, PO Box 504, Toledo, OH 43697, (419)666-0100 [20442]

Tri-State Armature and Electrical Works Inc., PO Box 466, Memphis, TN 38101, (901)527-8412 [9504]

Tri-State Auction Company Inc., PO Box 772, West Fargo, ND 58078-0772, (701)282-8203 [3336]

Tri-State Bearing Co., 3418 E 25th St., Minneapolis, MN 55406, (612)721-2463 [3337]

Tri State Beauty Supply Inc., 5200 Overland Rd., Boise, ID 83705-2638, (208)345-1642 [14264]

Tri-State Breeders Cooperative, E 10890 Penny Ln., Baraboo, WI 53913, (608)356-8357 [27252]

Tri-State Breeders Cooperative, E 10890 Penny Ln., Baraboo, WI 53913, (608)356-8357 [27252]

Tri-State Brick and Tile Co., PO Box 31768, Jackson, MS 39286, (601)981-1410 [8144]

Tri-State Distributors Inc., PO Box 247, Royston, GA 30662-0247, (706)245-6164 [14738]

Tri State Electric Company Inc., PO Box 1107, Sioux Falls, SD 57101, (605)336-2870 [9505]

Tri State Electrical Supply Inc., PO Box 546, Michigan City, IN 46361-0546, (219)872-5551 [9506]

Tri-State Hobbycraft, 1 Trimont Ln., Apt. 750C, Pittsburgh, PA 15211-1225, (412)481-2100 [26689]

Tri-State Hospital Supply Corp., 8200 Utah, Merrillville, IN 46410, (219)942-6723 [19085]

Tri-State Insulation Co., PO Box 106, Miller, SD 57362, (605)853-2442 [8145]

Tri-State Iron and Metal Co., PO Box 775, Texarkana, AR 75504, (870)773-8409 [27026]

Tri-State Ladder & Scaffolding Company, Inc., 26 Colton St., Worcester, MA 01610, (508)754-3030 [3338]

Tri-State Lighting and Supply Company Inc., PO Box 327, Evansville, IN 47702-0327, (812)423-4257 [9507]

Tri-State Medical Supply Inc., 846 Pelham Pkwy., Pelham, NY 10803-2710, (516)420-1700 [19086]

Tri-State Optical Co. Inc., PO Box 30005, Shreveport, LA 71130-0005, (318)425-7432 [19661]

Tri-State Periodicals, Inc., 9844 Heddon Rd., PO Box 1110, Evansville, IN 47706, (812)867-7416 [4230]

Tri-State Police Fire Equipment Inc., 912 Broadway, East Providence, RI 02914-3718, (401)434-1892 [24647]

Tri-State Surgical Corp., 4353 N Mozart, Chicago, IL 60618, (773)267-8800 [19087]

Tri-State Truck and Equipment Inc., PO Box 1298, Billings, MT 59103, (406)245-3188 [8146]

Tri-State Vet & Pet Supply, 3300 Interstate Dr., Evansville, IN 47715-1781, (812)477-4793 [27253]

Tri State Veterinary Supply Co., 3300 Interstate Dr., Evansville, IN 47715-1781, (812)477-4793 [27253]

Tri State Warehouse Inc., PO Box 1719, Sioux Falls, SD 57101-1719, (605)336-1482 [3339]

Tri-State Wholesale Associated Grocers Inc., PO Box 971970, El Paso, TX 79997-1970, (915)774-6400 [12754]

TRI-Utah, 1155 N Industrial Park Dr., Orem, UT 84057, (801)226-1308 [14265]

Tri Valley Cooperative, PO Box 227, St. Edward, NE 68660, (402)678-2251 [1356]

Triad Machinery Inc., PO Box 301099, Portland, OR 97230, (503)254-5100 [8147]

Triangle Brass Manufacturing Co., PO Box 23277, Los Angeles, CA 90023, (323)262-4191 [13965]

Triangle Chemical Co., PO Box 4528, Macon, GA 31213, (912)743-1548 [4533]

Triangle Coatings, Inc., 1930 Fairway Dr., San Leandro, CA 94577, (510)895-8000 [21595]

Triangle Computer Corp., 50230 Pontiac Tr., Wixom, MI 48393, (248)926-0330 [6830]

Triangle Electric Supply Co., 3815 Durazno, El Paso, TX 79905, (915)533-5981 [9508]

Triangle Inc., 51 Fernwood Ln., Roslyn, NY 11576, (516)365-8143 [3340]

Triangle Industrial Sales, Inc., 3000 Town Ctr., No. 501, Southfield, MI 48075-1173, (248)352-6688 [16581]

Triangle Pacific Corp. Beltsville Div., 10500 Ewing Rd., Beltsville, MD 20705, (301)937-5000 [8148]

Triangle Paint, 1930 Fairway Dr., San Leandro, CA 94577, (510)895-8000 [21595]

Triangle Supply Company Inc., 12705 Bee St., Dallas, TX 75234, (972)620-1661 [23417]

Triarc Companies Inc., 280 Park Ave., New York, NY 10017, (212)451-3000 [12755]

Tribles of Maryland Inc., 901 Southern Ave., Oxon Hill, MD 20745-4359, (301)894-6161 [15343]

Tribune Co., 435 N Michigan Ave., Chicago, IL 60611, (312)222-9100 [4231]

Trick and Murray Inc., 300 W Lake Ave. N, Seattle, WA 98109, (206)628-0059 [21323]

Tricon Industries Inc. Electromechanical Div., 1600 Eisenhower Ln., Lisle, IL 60532-2167, (630)964-2330 [3341]

Triconic Labs Inc., 7 Canal St., Center Moriches, NY 11934, (516)878-2333 [19662]

Tricor Braun - Div. of Kranson, 460 N Lindbergh Blvd., St. Louis, MO 63141-7808, (314)569-3633 [25945]

Tricorp, Inc., PO Box 1009, Mobile, AL 36633-1009, (205)432-4800 [1357]

Trident International Ltd., PO Box 2128, Reston, VA 20195, (703)471-4020 [2958]

Trident Medical International, 7687 Winton Dr., Indianapolis, IN 46268, (317)870-4461 [19663]

TriGem Corp., 48400 Fremont Blvd., Fremont, CA 94538-6505, (510)770-8787 [6831]

Trillennium, 8 Carter Dr., Framingham, MA 01701-3003, (508)788-0330 [9509]

Trim-Pak Inc., 4135 Southstream Blvd., Charlotte, NC 28217-4523 [26233]

Trimble Company Inc.; William S., PO Box 154, Knoxville, TN 37901, (615)573-1911 [8149]

Trims II Inc., 4636 E Elwood St., Ste. 2, Phoenix, AZ 85040-1963, (480)966-1564 [26690]

Trinet Industries Inc., 19811 Colima Rd., No. 410, Walnut, CA 91789, (714)594-4676 [16582]

Trinidad Bean and Elevator Co., PO Box 128, Greeley, CO 80632-0128, (970)352-0346 [18292]

Trinidad/Benham, PO Box 29, Mineola, TX 75773, (903)569-2636 [12756]

Trinidad-Benham Corp., PO Box 378007, Denver, CO 80237, (303)220-1400 [18293]

Trinkle Sales Inc., 1010 Hadonfield Berlin Rd., Cherry Hill, NJ 08034, (856)988-9900 [9510]

Trioptics, Inc., PO Box 2138, Milwaukee, WI 53201, (414)481-9822 [19664]

Tripifoods Inc., PO Box 1107, Buffalo, NY 14240, (716)853-7400 [12757]

Triple Crown America Inc., 13 N 7th St., Perkasie, PA 18944, (215)453-2500 [4534]

Triple D Publishing Inc., 1300 S Dekalb St., Shelby, NC 28152, (704)482-9673 [4232]

Triple S Ranch Supply, 2635 SE Hwy 54, El Dorado, KS 67042-9347, (316)321-7514 [18294]

Tristate Electrical & Electronics Supply Company Inc./Uagemeyer N.V., 1741 Dual Hwy., PO Box 469, Hagerstown, MD 21741, (301)733-1212 [9511]

Tristate Electrical Supply Company Inc., 1741 Dual Hwy., PO Box 469, Hagerstown, MD 21741, (301)733-1212 [9511]

Tristate Electrical Supply Company Inc., 1741 Dual Hwy., Hagerstown, MD 21741, (301)733-1212 [9512]

TriTech Graphics Inc., 3348 Commercial Ave., Northbrook, IL 60062-1909, (847)564-7773 [6832]

Triton Electronics, 4700 Loyola Ln., Austin, TX 78723, (512)929-0073 [6833]

Triton Inc., 8255 Dunwoody Pl., Bldg. 17, Ste. 100, Atlanta, GA 30350, (770)992-7088 [22750]

Triton Marketing Inc., 8255 Dunwoody Pl., Atlanta, GA 30350, (404)992-7088 [12758]

Triton Marketing Inc., 8255 Dunwoody Pl., Bldg. 17, Ste. 100, Atlanta, GA 30350, (770)992-7088 [22750]

Triumph Motorcycles America Ltd., 403 Dividend Dr., Peachtree City, GA 30269, (404)631-9500 [3342]

Triumph Pet Industries, Inc., 7 Lake Station Rd., Warwick, NY 10990-3426, (914)469-5125 [27254]

Triumph Twist Drill Co., 1 Precision Plz., Crystal Lake, IL 60014, (815)459-6250 [16583]

TRM Copy Centers Corp., 5208 NE 122nd Ave., Portland, OR 97230-1074, (503)257-8766 [21324]

Troica Enterprise Inc., 241 5th Ave., Ste. 402, New York, NY 10016, (212)686-7777 [17643]

Trojan Pools, 25 Tivoli, Albany, NY 12207-1304, (518)434-4161 [24015]

Troll Associates of Memphis, 4600 Pleasant Hill Rd., Memphis, TN 38118, (901)365-4900 [4233]

Trompeter Co.; John F., 637 E Main St., Louisville, KY 40202, (502)585-5852 [26361]

Tronair Inc., S 1740 Eber Rd., Holland, OH 43528, (419)866-6301 [163]

Trophy Craft Source, 10001 3rd St., No. 7, Corpus Christi, TX 78404, (512)885-0500 [5441]

Trophy Nut Company, PO Box 199, Tipp City, OH 45371, (937)667-8478 [12759]

Trophy Products Inc., 9714 Old Katy Rd., Houston, TX 77055, (713)464-8256 [13966]

Tropical Fisheries, 1030 Basse Rd., San Antonio, TX 78212, (210)733-6258 [27255]

Tropical Gardens of Maui, Iao Valley Rd., Wailuku, HI 96793, (808)244-3085 [14963]

Tropical Hawaiian Products, PO Box 210, Keaau, HI 96749, (808)966-7435 [12760]

Tropical Music, 7091 NW 51st, Miami, FL 33166, (305)594-3909 [25485]

Tropical Music and Pro Audio, 7091 NW 51st, Miami, FL 33166, (305)594-3909 [25485]

Tropical Nut and Fruit, 11517-A Cordage St., Charlotte, NC 28273, (704)588-0400 [12761]

Trost Modelcraft Hobbies, 3129 W 47th St., Chicago, IL 60632-2901, (773)927-1400 [26691]

Trotter and Company Inc.; Nathan, PO Box 1066, Exton, PA 19341, (610)524-1440 [20443]

Troumbly Brothers Inc., PO Box 405, Taconite, MN 55786, (218)326-4815 [8150]

Trout-Blue Chelan, Inc., PO Box 669, Chelan, WA 98816, (509)682-2591 [12762]

Trout Inc., PO Box 669, Chelan, WA 98816, (509)682-2591 [12762]

Troutman Brothers, PO Box 73, Klingerstown, PA 17941, (717)425-2341 [22751]

Troxell Communications Inc., 4830 S 38th St., Phoenix, AZ 85040-2998 [25486]

Troxler World Trade Corp., 3008 Cornwallis Rd., PO Box 12057, Research Triangle Park, NC 27709, (919)549-8661 [19088]

Troy Belting Supply Co., 70 Cohoes Rd., Watervliet, NY 12189, (518)272-4920 [17236]

Troy Biologicals Inc., 1238 Rankin St., Troy, MI 48083-6004, (248)585-9720 [19665]

Troy BioSciences Inc., 113 S 47th Ave., Phoenix, AZ 85043, (602)233-9047 [1358]

Troy Elevator Inc., PO Box 190, Bloomfield, IA 52537, (515)675-3375 [18295]

Troy Top Soil Company Inc., 748 Hudson River Rd., Mechanicville, NY 12118-3802, (518)273-7665 [8151]

Troyer Foods Inc., 17141 State Rd., No. 4, PO Box 608, Goshen, IN 46526, (219)533-0302 [12763]

Tru-Care Health Systems Inc., 5004 N Portland Ave., Oklahoma City, OK 73112-6122, (405)949-9969 [19089]

Tru-Form Tool and Manufacturing Industries Inc., 14511 Anson Ave., Santa Fe Springs, CA 90670, (562)802-2041 [16584]

Tru-Part Manufacturing Corp., 232 Lothenbach Ave., St. Paul, MN 55118, (612)455-6681 [1359]

TruAl Inc., Rte. 1, Box 103, Lewisville, MN 56060, (507)435-4414 [1360]

Truck Body Manufacturing Company, Inc., 48 Hunter Ave., Johnston, RI 02919-4006, (401)351-0711 [3343]

Truck Enterprises Inc., PO Box 472, Harrisonburg, VA 22801, (540)433-2631 [20739]

Truck Equipment Boston, Inc., 316 N Beacon St., Brighton, MA 02135, (617)782-4320 [3344]

Truck Equipment Co., 511 N Channing Ave., St. Louis, MO 63103, (314)533-6200 [3345]

Truck Equipment Distributors, 2020 SW Blvd., Tulsa, OK 74107, (918)584-4733 [3346]

Truck Equipment Inc., 680 Potts Ave., Green Bay, WI 54304, (414)494-7451 [3347]

Truck Equipment Sales Inc., PO Box 1987, Dothan, AL 36302, (205)792-4124 [3348]

Truck Parts and Equipment Inc., 4501 Esthner St., Wichita, KS 67209, (316)942-4251 [3349]

Truck Pro, 818 Division, Evansville, IN 47711, (812)424-2900 [3350]

Truck Thermo King Inc., PO Box 898, Harrisonburg, VA 22801-0898, (540)434-7004 [14739]

Truckways Inc., PO Box 911, Mills, WY 82644-0911, (307)234-0756 [3351]

Truckwell of Alaska, 11221 Olive Ln., Anchorage, AK 99515, (907)349-8845 [3352]

True Blue Inc., 2601 W Commodore Way, Seattle, WA 98199-1231, (206)285-9480 [5442]

True Comp America Inc., 1264 S Bascom Ave., San Jose, CA 95128, (408)292-8889 [6834]

True Value Regional Distributor, 2150 Olympic St., Springfield, OR 97477, (541)726-8243 [13967]

True World Foods, Inc. of Alabama, PO Box 767, Bayou la Batre, AL 36509, (334)824-4193 [12764]

Truesdale Company Inc., 108 Holton St., Brighton, MA 02135, (617)782-5300 [4535]

Truex Associates, 4864 S Orange Ave., Orlando, FL 32806, (407)859-2160 [9513]

Truman Arnold Co., PO Box 1481, Texarkana, TX 75504, (903)794-3835 [22752]

Truman Farmers Elevator Co., PO Box 68, Truman, MN 56088, (507)776-2831 [1361]

Trumbull Industries Inc., PO Box 30, Warren, OH 44482-0030, (216)393-6624 [23418]

Trundle and Company Inc., 155 E 55th St., New York, NY 10022, (212)486-1011 [25045]

Trundle and Company Inc., 155 E 55th St., New York, NY 10022, (212)486-1011 [12765]

TruServ Corp., 8600 W Bryn Mawr Ave., Chicago, IL 60631-3505, (773)695-5000 [13968]

TRW. Inc, 11202 E Germann Rd., Queen Creek, AZ 85242, (480)987-4000 [3353]

TRW Replacement, 3717 Pipestone Rd., Dallas, TX 75212-6111, (214)637-2831 [3354]

Trym-Tex, Inc., 6032 N Cutter Cir., Ste. 400, Portland, OR 97217-3900, (503)233-1181 [10259]

Tryon Distributors, 136 E 36th St., Charlotte, NC 28206, (704)334-0849 [2086]

Tryon Mercantile Inc., 790 Madison Ave., New York, NY 10021, (212)570-4180 [17644]

Tryon Trading, Inc., PO Box 40, Tryon, NC 28782, (704)859-6999 [17237]

TSF Sportswear, 4201 NE 12th Terrace, Oakland Park, FL 33334-4722, (954)564-4435 [5443]

Tsigonia Paint Sales, 4117 Broadway, Astoria, NY 11103, (718)932-3664 [21596]

Tsuki's Hair Design, 1450 Ala Moana Blvd., Ste. 1241, Honolulu, HI 96814, (808)946-3902 [14266]

Tsumura International Inc., 300 Lighting Way, Secaucus, NJ 07096-1578, (201)223-9000 [14267]

TTI Inc., 2441 Northeast Pkwy., Ft. Worth, TX 76106, (817)740-9000 [9514]

T.T.S. Distributors, 116 Riveria St., San Marcos, TX 78666, (512)353-8725 [24016]

Tube City Inc., PO Box 2000, Glassport, PA 15045, (412)678-6141 [27027]

Tube Service Co., 9351 S Norwalk Blvd., Santa Fe Springs, CA 90670, (213)728-9105 [20444]

Tubelite Company, Inc., 4102 W Adams, Phoenix, AZ 85009, (602)484-0122 [9515]

Tubelite Company, Inc., 102 Semoran Commerce Pl., Apopka, FL 32703, (407)884-0477 [25849]

Tubesales, 175 Tubeway, Forest Park, GA 30297, (404)361-5050 [20445]

Tubular Products of Texas Inc., 4515 Brittmoore Rd., Houston, TX 77041, (713)937-3900 [17238]

Tubular Steel Inc., 1031 Executive Pkwy., St. Louis, MO 63141, (314)851-9200 [20446]

Tucker Company Inc.; M., 900 S 2nd St., Harrison, NJ 07029, (973)484-1200 [24250]

Tucker Company Inc.; M., 900 S 2nd St., Harrison, NJ 07029, (973)484-1200 [24251]

Tucker Library Interiors LLC, 155 Dow St., Ste. 402, Manchester, NH 03101, (603)666-7030 [13263]

Tuckers Tire & Oil Company Inc., 844 S Main, PO Box 1149, Dyersburg, TN 38025-1149, (901)285-8520 [3355]

Tucson Co-op Wholesale, 350 S Toole Ave., Tucson, AZ 85701, (520)884-9951 [12766]

Tucson Computer Products, 2850 W Camino De La Joya, Tucson, AZ 85741-9225, (520)297-6166 [6835]

Tucson Hobby Shop, 5250 E Pima St., Tucson, AZ 85712-3630, (520)326-8006 [26692]

Tuf-Nut Company Inc., 715 E Austin, Nevada, MO 64772, (417)667-8151 [5444]

Tufts Ranch Packing Shed, 27260 State, Hwy. 128, Winters, CA 95694-9701, (530)795-4144 [12767]

Tujay's Artist Dolls, 73 N Spring St., Concord, NH 03301-4203, (603)226-4501 [26693]

Tulare Pipe and Electric Supply Co., 800 W Inyo Ave., Tulare, CA 93274, (209)686-8307 [9516]

Tulco Oils Inc., 5240 E Pine St., Tulsa, OK 74115, (918)838-3354 [22753]

Tulia Wheat Growers Inc., PO Box 787, Dimmitt, TX 79027-0787, (806)995-4176 [1362]

Tull Metals Company Inc.; J.M., PO Box 4725, Norcross, GA 30091, (404)368-4311 [20447]

Tulnoy Lumber Inc., 1620 Webster Ave., Bronx, NY 10457, (718)901-1700 [8152]

Tulsa Automatic Music Co., 1218 W Archer St., Tulsa, OK 74127-8604, (918)584-4775 [26694]

Tulsa Bowling Supply Co., 3121 S Sheridan Rd., Tulsa, OK 74145-1102, (918)627-2728 [24017]

Tulsa Firearms Training Academy, 5949 S Garnett Rd., Tulsa, OK 74146-6825, (918)250-4867 [24018]

Tulsa Metal Processing Co., PO Box 4676, Tulsa, OK 74159, (918)584-3354 [20448]

Tumac Lumber Company Inc., 529 SW 3rd Ave., No. 600, Portland, OR 97204, (503)226-6661 [8153]

Tumbleweed Distributors, 6315 Doyle St., Emeryville, CA 94608, (650)428-9242 [12768]

Tung Pec Inc., 6965 Aragon Cir., Buena Park, CA 90620, (714)562-0848 [12769]

Tung Tai Trading Corp., 1325 Howard Ave., No. 611, Burlingame, CA 94010, (650)573-5705 [27028]

Tuong; Dam, 76 N Pauati St., Honolulu, HI 96817-5128, (808)531-6132 [12770]

Tupman Thurlow Company Inc., 40 Tower Ln., Avon, CT 06001-4222, (860)677-8933 [12771]

Turban Plus, 13692 Newhope St., Garden Grove, CA 92843-3712, (714)530-9590 [5445]

Turbana Corp., 550 Biltmore Way, Ste. 730, Coral Gables, FL 33134-5730, (305)445-1542 [12772]

Turbex Heat Transfer Corp., PO Box 10208, Westminster, CA 92685-0208, (714)996-3270 [14740]

Turbo Link International Inc., 1452 Crestview St., Clearwater, FL 33755, (813)442-2570 [24019]

Turf and Industrial Equipment Co., 2715 Lafayette St., PO Box 343, Santa Clara, CA 95052-0343, (408)727-5660 [1363]

Turf Merchants, 33390 Tangent Loop, Tangent, OR 97389, (541)926-8649 [1364]

Turf Products Corp., PO Box 1200, Enfield, CT 06083, (860)763-3581 [1365]

Turf-Seed, Inc., PO Box 250, Hubbard, OR 97032, (503)651-2130 [1366]

Turner Appliance, 1638 Tulip Dr., Indianapolis, IN 46227-5034, (317)788-9180 [15344]

Turner Dairy, PO Box 337, Paragould, AR 72450, (870)239-2143 [12773]

Turner Enterprises Inc., PO Box E, Americus, GA 31709, (912)924-0341 [13087]

Turner Marine Bulk Inc., 1 Elaine St., New Orleans, LA 70126-7100, (504)245-1089 [22754]

Turner Shellfish New Zealand Inc., PO Box 8919, Newport Beach, CA 92658, (949)622-6181 [12774]

Turner Sherwood Corp., PO Box 161038, Memphis, TN 38186-1038, (901)332-1414 [15345]

TurningPoint Systems Inc., 300 Rosewood Dr., Danvers, MA 01923-4515, (978)777-9991 [6836]

Turquoise World, 2933 San Mateo Blvd. NE, Albuquerque, NM 87110-3156, (505)881-6219 [17645]

Turtle and Hughes Inc., 1900 Lower Rd., Linden, NJ 07036, (908)574-3600 [9517]

Turtle Island Herbs Inc., 1705 14th St. Ste. 172, Boulder, CO 80302, (303)442-2215 [23419]

Turtle Plastics Co., 7450 A Industrial Pk., Lorain, OH 44053, (440)282-8008 [4718]

Tuscaloosa Electrical Supply Inc., 1616 25th Ave., Tuscaloosa, AL 35401, (205)759-5716 [9518]

Tuscaloosa Optical Dispensary, PO Box 1790, Tuscaloosa, AL 35403-1790, (205)752-2564 [19666]

Tuscan Dairy Farms Inc., 750 Union Ave., Union, NJ 07083, (908)686-1500 [12775]

Tuscan Dairy Farms Inc., 750 Union Ave., Union, NJ 07083, (908)686-1500 [12775]

Tuscan/Lehigh Dairies L.P., 750 Union Ave., Union, NJ 07083, (908)851-5180 [12776]

Tuscarora Corp., PO Box 912, Rocky Mount, NC 27802-0912, (252)443-7041 [24020]

Tusco Grocers Inc., 30 S Fourth St., PO Box 240, Dennison, OH 44621-0240, (740)922-2223 [12777]

Tuttle Co. Inc.; Charles E., 153 Milk St., 5th Fl., Boston, MA 02109-4809, (617)951-4080 [4234]

Tuttle Enterprises Inc., 934 N Industrial Park Dr., Orem, UT 84057-2804, (801)226-1517 [26695]

Tuxedo Junction Inc., 7105-7 Allentown Rd., Ft. Washington, MD 20744, (301)449-4465 [5446]

TVC Technology Group, 130 Industrial Dr., Chambersburg, PA 17201-0444, (717)263-8258 [25487]

TVM Professional Monitor Corp., 4260 E Brickell St., Ontario, CA 91761-1511, (909)390-8099 [6837]

TW Communication Corp., 81 Executive Blvd., Farmingdale, NY 11735, (516)753-0900 [5798]

TW Graphics Group, 7220 E Slauson Ave., Commerce, CA 90040, (323)721-1400 [25850]

TW Metals Co., 946 Kane, Toledo, OH 43612-1246, (419)476-7805 [20449]

TW Systems Ltd., 99-1434 Koaha Pl., Aiea, HI 96701, (808)486-2667 [4719]

Twin City Hardware Company Inc., 1010 N Dale St., St. Paul, MN 55117, (612)488-6701 [13969]

Twin City ICEE Inc., 8136 Cypress St., West Monroe, LA 71291-8290, (318)396-4266 [14741]

Twin City Implement Inc., 2123 Memorial Hwy., Mandan, ND 58554, (701)663-7505 [1367]

Twin City Manufacturing Co., PO Box 1797, Reidsville, NC 27323-1797, (912)763-2115 [5447]

Twin City Marble, 333 E 9th St., Texarkana, AR 71854, (870)772-3769 [10260]

Twin City Optical Inc., PO Box 267, Minneapolis, MN 55440, (612)546-6126 [19667]

Twin City Supply Company, 233 Harris Ave., Providence, RI 02903, (401)331-5930 [15346]

Twin City Tile, 34 State St., Brewer, ME 04412, (207)989-8060 [10261]

Twin County Grocers Inc., 145 Talmadge Rd., Edison, NJ 08818, (732)287-4600 [12778]

Twin County Service Co., PO Box 728, Marion, IL 62959, (618)993-5155 [1368]

Twin Falls Tractor and Implement Inc., 1935 Kimberly Rd., Twin Falls, ID 83301, (208)733-8687 [1369]

Twin Panda Inc./Katha Diddel Home Collection, 225 5th Ave., Ste. 804, New York, NY 10010, (212)725-6045 [15689]

Twin Valley Farmers Exchange Inc., 845 E Main St., Hegins, PA 17938, (717)682-3171 [12779]

Twinco Automotive Warehouse Inc., 4635 Willow Dr., Hamel, MN 55340, (612)478-2360 [4536]

Twinco Romax Inc., 4635 Willow Dr., Hamel, MN 55340, (612)478-2360 [3356]

Twinson Co., 1289-E Reamwood Ave., Sunnyvale, CA 94089-2234, (408)734-9558 [26696]

Two Left Feet, 7923 Norton Ave., West Hollywood, CA 90046, (415)626-5338 [24879]

Twomey Co., 1 State St., Smithshire, IL 61478, (309)325-7100 [18296]

T.W.P. Inc., 2831 10th St., Berkeley, CA 94710, (510)548-4434 [20450]

TWT Moulding Company Inc., PO Box 1425, Brownwood, TX 76804, (915)643-2521 [15690]

Twyman Templeton Company Inc., PO Box 44490, Columbus, OH 43204, (614)272-5623 [24648]

Tyco Adhesives, 1400 Providence Hwy., Norwood, MA 02062, (781)440-6200 [21957]

Tyler Equipment Corp., PO Box 544, East Longmeadow, MA 01028, (413)525-6351 [8154]

Tynan Equipment Co., 5926 Stockberger Pl., Indianapolis, IN 46241, (317)247-8474 [16585]

Tyndale House Publishers, 351 Executive Dr., PO Box 80, Wheaton, IL 60189, (630)668-8300 [25488]

Tyson Seafood Group, PO Box 79021, Seattle, WA 98119, (206)282-3445 [12780]

Tzetzo Brothers Inc., 1100 Military Rd., Buffalo, NY 14217, (716)877-0800 [12781]

U-Joints, Inc., 4220 Edith NE, Albuquerque, NM 87107, (505)345-2666 [3357]

U-Joints, Inc., 11213 Rojas, El Paso, TX 79926, (915)593-8215 [3358]

U and S Services Inc., 233 Fillmore Ave., No. 11, Tonawanda, NY 14150, (716)693-4490 [9519]

U.A.F. L.P., 6610 Anderson Rd., Tampa, FL 33634, (813)885-6936 [14964]

UAP Northwest, PO Box 506, Burlington, WA 98233, (360)757-6041 [1370]

Ubiquity Distributors, 607 Degraw St., Brooklyn, NY 11217, (718)875-5491 [4235]

UCG Energy Corp., 150 South East Pkwy., PO Box 682028, Franklin, TN 37068, (615)591-6200 [22755]

Uddeholm Corp., 4902 Tollview Dr., Rolling Meadows, IL 60008-3713, (708)577-2220 [20451]

Uddeholm Steel Corp., 9331 Santa Fe Springs Rd., Santa Fe Springs, CA 90670, (562)946-6503 [20452]

Udelson Equipment Co., 1400 Brookpark Rd., Cleveland, OH 44109, (216)398-7300 [16586]

UDL Laboratories, Inc., PO Box 2629, Loves Park, IL 61132-2629, (815)282-1201 [19668]

UETA Inc., 3407 Northeast Pkwy., San Antonio, TX 78212, (210)828-8382 [26362]

Ulbrich of California Inc., 5455 Home Ave., Fresno, CA 93727, (209)456-2310 [20453]

Ulbrich of Illinois Inc., 12340 S Laramie Ave., Alsip, IL 60803, (773)568-7500 [20454]

Ulery Greenhouse Co., PO Box 1108, Springfield, OH 45501, (937)325-5543 [14965]

Ullman Sails, 957 N Lime Ave., Sarasota, FL 34237, (941)951-0189 [18626]

Ulrich Chemical Inc., 3111 N Post Rd., Indianapolis, IN 46226-6566, (317)898-8632 [4537]

Ulster Linen Company, Inc., 148 Madison Ave., New York, NY 10016-6780, (212)684-5534 [15691]

Ulster Scientific Inc., PO Box 819, New Paltz, NY 12561, (914)255-2200 [19090]

Ultima, 345 E 103rd St., New York, NY 10029, (212)534-8921 [14742]

Ultima International Corp., 38897 Cherry St., Newark, CA 94560, (510)739-0800 [6838]

Ultimate Salon Services Inc., 2621 Ridgepoint Dr., No. 120, Austin, TX 78754, (512)926-9193 [14268]

Ultra Books, Inc., PO Box 945, Oakland, NJ 07436, (201)337-8787 [4236]

Ultra Hardware Products LLC, 1777 Hylton Rd., Dept. AWDD 2000, Pennsauken, NJ 08110, (856)663-5050 [13970]

Ultra Hydraulics Inc., 1110 Claycraft Rd., Ste. A, Columbus, OH 43230-6630, (614)759-9000 [17239]

Ultra Lens, 6611 NW 15th Way, Ft. Lauderdale, FL 33309, (954)975-8600 [19669]

Ultramar Diamond Shamrock Corp., 6000 N Loop 1604, W, San Antonio, TX 78249-1112, (210)592-2000 [22756]

Ultraseal International Inc., 1100 N Wilcox Ave., Los Angeles, CA 90038, (323)466-1226 [3359]

Ultrasource Inc., PO Box 237, Tallmadge, OH 44278-0237, (330)677-1929 [25851]

Ulysses Cooperative Supply Co., PO Box 947, Ulysses, KS 67880, (316)356-1241 [18297]

Uman Corp., 517 6th St. N, Texas City, TX 77590, (409)945-8353 [24880]

UMAX Computer Corp., 47470 Seabridge Dr., Fremont, CA 94538, (510)226-6886 [6839]

UMBRA U.S.A. Inc., 1705 Broadway, Buffalo, NY 14212 [15692]

UMI, 300 N Zeeb Rd., Ann Arbor, MI 48103, (734)761-4700 [22912]

Umpqua Dairy Products Co., PO Box 1306, Roseburg, OR 97470, (541)672-2638 [12782]

UMPQUA Technology Co., PO Box 63, Chesterfield, MO 63006 [4538]

Unarco Commercial Products, 8470 Belvedere Ave Ste. C, Sacramento, CA 95826, (916)381-7373 [24252]

Uncle Bens Inc., 5721 Harvey Wilson, Houston, TX 77020-8025, (713)674-9484 [12783]

Underwood Builders Supply Co., PO Box 1587, Mobile, AL 36633, (205)432-3581 [8155]

Underwood HVAC, Inc., 4450 Commerce SW, Atlanta, GA 30336, (404)691-1505 [14743]

Unelko Corp., 14641 N 74th St., Scottsdale, AZ 85260, (602)991-7272 [4539]

Unger Cattle Marketing; Randy J., PO Box 103, Watertown, SD 57201-0103, (605)882-1129 [18298]

Unger Co., 12401 Berea Rd., Cleveland, OH 44111, (216)252-1400 [21958]

Uni Distribution Co., 10 Universal City Plz., No. 400, Universal City, CA 91608, (818)777-1000 [25489]

Uni Distribution Co., 10 Universal City Plz., No. 400, Universal City, CA 91608, (818)777-1000 [15347]

Uni Filter Inc., 1468 S Manhattan Ave., Fullerton, CA 92831, (714)535-6933 [3360]

Uni-Flange Corp., 5285 Ramona Blvd., Jacksonville, FL 32205, (904)781-3628 [23420]

Uni-Marts Inc., 477 E Beaver Ave., State College, PA 16801-5690, (814)234-6000 [12784]

Uni-Patch, PO Box 271, Wabasha, MN 55981, (612)565-2601 [19670]

Uni-Steel Inc., G St. & Lexington St., Muskogee, OK 74403, (918)682-7833 [20455]

Uni-Steel Inc., PO Box 3528, Enid, OK 73702, (580)233-0411 [20456]

Unibri International, PO Box 7671, Algonquin, IL 60102, (847)458-7262 [17240]

Unicen Wastewater Treatment Co., PO Box 50001, Bellevue, WA 98015, (425)641-6168 [25852]

Unichem Industries Inc., 1 Bayberry Close, Piscataway, NJ 08854, (732)463-8442 [19671]

Unico Alloys Inc., 1555 Joyce Ave., Columbus, OH 43219, (614)299-0545 [20457]

Unicorn Books and Crafts, 1338 Ross St., Petaluma, CA 94954, (707)762-3362 [4237]

Unicorn International Inc., 7079 Depot St., Olive Branch, MS 38654-1603, (601)895-2921 [13264]

Unicover Corp., 1 Unicover Ctr., Cheyenne, WY 82008-0001, (307)771-3000 [26697]

Uniden America Corp., 4700 Amon Carter Blvd., Ft. Worth, TX 76155, (817)858-3300 [5799]

Uniform Center of Lansing Inc., 425 N Clippert St., Lansing, MI 48912, (517)332-2543 [5448]

Uniform House Inc., 1927 N Capitol Ave., Indianapolis, IN 46202-1219, (317)926-4467 [5449]

Unijax Div., 815 S Main St., Jacksonville, FL 32207-8140, (904)783-0550 [21959]

Unijax Div., 815 S Main St., Jacksonville, FL 32207-8140, (904)783-0550 [21959]

UniMark Group Inc., PO Box 229, Argyle, TX 76226, (817)491-2992 [12785]

Unimark Inc., 9910 Widmer Rd., Lenexa, KS 66215, (913)649-2424 [9520]

Unimast Inc., 9595 Grand Ave., Franklin Park, IL 60131, (708)451-1410 [20458]

Union Bearing & Transmission, 505 Bryant St., Denver, CO 80204-4809, (303)825-1540 [3361]

Union Butterfield Corp., PO Box 50000, Asheville, NC 28813, 800-222-8665 [13971]

Union Carbide Corp., IPX Services, Bldg. 82, Rm. 426, PO Box 8004, South Charleston, WV 25303, (304)747-7000 [16587]

Union Distributing Co., 4000 E Michigan St., Tucson, AZ 85714, (520)571-7600 [22757]

Union Elevator and Warehouse Co., PO Box 370, Lind, WA 99341, (509)677-3441 [18299]

Union Fertilizer Co., 4630 US Hwy. 60 E, Waverly, KY 42462-6900, (502)389-1241 [1371]

Union Grocery Company Inc., PO Box 327, New Albany, MS 38652, (601)534-5089 [12786]

Union Incorporated, 14522 Myford Rd., Irvine, CA 92606, (714)734-2200 [12787]

Union Oil Company of Maine, PO Box 2528, South Portland, ME 04106, (207)799-1521 [22758]

Union Oil Mill Inc., PO Box 1320, Greenwood, MS 38935-1320 [1372]

Union Paper Company Div., 10 Admiral St., Providence, RI 02908, (401)274-7000 [21960]

Union Paper Company Inc., 10 Admiral St., Providence, RI 02908, (401)274-7000 [21960]

Union Paper Company Inc., 10 Admiral St., Providence, RI 02908, (401)274-7000 [17241]

Union Produce Cooperative, PO Box 299, Ossian, IA 52161, (319)532-9381 [1373]

Union Seed Company Inc., PO Box 339, Nampa, ID 83653-0339, (208)466-3568 [18300]

Union Standard Equipment Co., 801 E 141st St., Bronx, NY 10454, (718)585-0200 [19672]

Union Supply Co., 3001 N Big Spring St., Ste. 200, Midland, TX 79705-5372, (915)684-8841 [23421]

Uniplex Software Inc., 10606 Shady Trl. Ste. 107, Dallas, TX 75220-2528, (972)753-6544 [6840]

UNIPRO Foodservice, Inc., 2500 Cumberland Pkwy. , No. 600, Atlanta, GA 30339, (770)952-0871 [12788]

Unipub, 4611-F Assembly Dr., Lanham, MD 20706-4391, (301)459-7666 [4238]

Uniq Distributing Corp., 909 N Nelson St., Ste. 60, Spokane, WA 99202-3729, (509)922-1009 [10262]

Uniq Distributing Group, 2020 Auiki St., Honolulu, HI 96819, (808)847-6767 [10263]

Unique Communications Inc., 3557 NW 53rd Ct., Ft. Lauderdale, FL 33309, (954)735-4002 [5800]

Unique Crafters Co., 10702 Trenton Ave., St. Louis, MO 63132, (314)427-5310 [13465]

Unique Industries Inc. (Philadelphia, PA), 2400 S Weccacoe Ave., Philadelphia, PA 19148, (215)336-4300 [13466]

Unique Sales, Inc., 1409 Hwy. 17, SurfsiDe Beach, SC 29575, (803)650-8989 [26698]

Uniquity, PO Box 10, Galt, CA 95632-0010, (209)745-2111 [19673]

Unirak Storage Systems, 26051 Michigan Ave., Inkster, MI 48141, (313)278-7600 [25946]

Unirex Inc., 9310 E 37th St. N, Wichita, KS 67226-2014, (316)636-1228 [164]

Unisorce Paper Co., PO Box 37190, Louisville, KY 40233-7190, (502)636-1341 [21961]

Unisource, 109 Lincoln Ave., PO Box 3395, Evansville, IN 47732, (812)422-1184 [21962]

Unisource, 2737 S Adams Rd., Rochester Hills, MI 48309, (248)853-9111 [21963]

Unisource, 4700 S Palisade, Wichita, KS 67217, (316)522-3494 [21964]

Unisource, 3587 Oakcliff Rd., Atlanta, GA 30340, (404)447-9000 [21965]

Unisource, PO Box 1129, Bangor, ME 04402-1129, (207)947-7311 [4720]

Unisource-Central Region Div., 1015 Corporate Square Dr., St. Louis, MO 63132, (314)919-1800 [21966]

UniSource Energy Inc., 245 W Rosevelt Rd., Bldg. 15, West Chicago, IL 60185, (630)231-7990 [22759]

Unisource International, International Plz., Ste. 2, Philadelphia, PA 19113, (610)521-3300 [21325]

Unisource Midwest Inc., PO Box 308001, Gahanna, OH 43230-8001, (614)251-7000 [21967]

Unisource Worldwide, 510 E Courtland St., Morton, IL 61550-9042, (309)263-6834 [21968]

Unisource Worldwide Inc., 7575 Brewster Ave., Philadelphia, PA 19153, (215)492-1776 [21969]

Unisource Worldwide Inc., PO Box 649, Exton, PA 19341-0649, (610)296-4470 [21970]

Unisource Worldwide Inc. Denver Div., 12601 E 38th Ave., Denver, CO 80239, (303)371-4260 [21971]

Unisource Worldwide Inc. (Southborough, Massachusetts), 9 Crystal Pond Rd., Southborough, MA 01772, (508)480-6000 [21972]

Unisource Worldwide Inc. West, 17011 Beach Blvd., Huntington Beach, CA 92647, (714)375-1650 [21973]

Unisteel Inc., PO Box 1090, Sterling Heights, MI 48311, (810)826-8040 [20459]

Unistrut Detroit Service Co., 4045 2nd St., Wayne, MI 48184, (734)722-1400 [20460]

Unistrut Fall Arrest Systems Inc., 3980 Varsity Dr., Ann Arbor, MI 48108-2226, (734)677-3380 [24649]

Unistrut Los Angeles, PO Box 3545, Santa Fe Springs, CA 90670, (562)404-9966 [20461]

Unistrut Northern California, 2057 West Ave. 140th, San Leandro, CA 94577, (510)351-4200 [20462]

Unitech Inc., PO Box 20639, Jackson, MS 39289-1639, (601)922-3911 [21326]

United-A.G. Cooperative Inc., PO Box 24887, Omaha, NE 68124-0887, (402)339-7300 [12789]

United Alloys Inc., PO Box 514599, Los Angeles, CA 90051, (323)264-5101 [20463]

United Art Distributors, 144 Mason NW, Grand Rapids, MI 49503, (616)459-6611 [25853]

United Auto Parts Inc., 301 W 1st, Mitchell, SD 57301-2514, (605)996-5585 [3362]

United Automatic Heating Supplies, 2125 Superior Ave., Cleveland, OH 44114, (216)621-5571 [14744]

United Automatic Heating Supplies, 133 N Summit St., Akron, OH 44304, (330)376-1011 [14745]

United Automatic Heating Supplies, 1087 N Meridian Rd., Youngstown, OH 44509, (330)793-7672 [14746]

United Automatic Heating Supplies, 399 Phillips Ave., Toledo, OH 43612, (419)478-4131 [14747]

United Automotive Supply Co., 2637 E 10 Mile Rd., Warren, MI 48091-6800, (248)399-3900 [3363]

United Beauty Equipment Co., 91 N Lowell Rd., Windham, NH 03087-1669, (603)434-8039 [14269]

United Beauty Equipment Co., 91 N Lowell Rd., Windham, NH 03087-1669, (603)434-8039 [24253]

United Beechcraft Inc., PO Box 51830, Indianapolis, IN 46251, (317)241-2893 [140]

United Beverage Inc., 2307 E Blanding Ave., Alameda, CA 94501, (510)748-0595 [12790]

United Beverage, Inc., 78 Regional Dr., Concord, NH 03301, (603)223-2323 [2087]

United Biomedical Inc., PO Box 377, Andover, KS 67002-0377, (316)733-5350 [19091]

United Builders Supply of Jackson Inc., PO Box 11367, Jackson, MS 39283-1367, (601)982-8421 [8156]

United Business Machines Inc., 91 Plaistow Rd., Plaistow, NH 03865, (603)382-3300 [21327]

United Candy and Tobacco Co., 7408 Tonnelle Ave., North Bergen, NJ 07047, (201)943-8675 [26363]

United Chemi-Con Inc., 9801 W Higgins Rd., Ste. 430, Rosemont, IL 60018-4725, (847)696-2000 [9521]

United Co-op, PO Box 37, Bigelow, MN 56117, (507)683-2731 [18301]

United Co-op Inc. (Hampton, Nebraska), PO Box 127, Hampton, NE 68843, (402)725-3131 [1374]

United Co-op Rushmore, PO Box 158, Rushmore, MN 56168, (507)478-4166 [1376]

United Container Corp., 1350 N Elston Ave., Chicago, IL 60622, (773)342-2200 [21974]

United Conveyor Corp., 2100 Norman Drive W, Waukegan, IL 60085, (847)473-5900 [16588]

United Cooperative Farmers Inc., 22 Kimball Pl., Fitchburg, MA 01420, (508)345-4103 [1375]

United Corporate Furnishings Inc., 1332 N Market Blvd., Sacramento, CA 95834, (916)553-5900 [13265]

United Dairymen of Arizona, PO Box 26877, Tempe, AZ 85285-6877, (480)966-7211 [12791]

United Distillers Group Inc., 6 Landmark Sq., Stamford, CT 06901, (203)359-7100 [2088]

United Distillers North America, 6 Landmark Sq., Stamford, CT 06901, (203)359-7100 [2089]

United Distributing Co., 101 N Kings Hwy., Cape Girardeau, MO 63701, (314)335-3341 [22760]

United Distributors Inc., 420 S Seneca St., Wichita, KS 67213, (316)263-6181 [25854]

United Distributors, Inc., 2627 Collins Springs Dr., Smyrna, GA 30080, (404)799-0333 [2090]

United Distributors, Inc., 20 Terry Ave., Burlington, MA 01803-2516, (781)272-6540 [10264]

United East Foodservice Supply Co., PO Box 1460, Woonsocket, RI 02895-0847, (401)769-1000 [24254]

United Electric Supply Co., 1530 Fairview, St. Louis, MO 63132-1344, (314)427-3333 [9522]

United Electric Supply Co. (Salt Lake City, Utah), 117 W 400 S, Salt Lake City, UT 84110, (801)363-4431 [9523]

United Electric Supply Inc., PO Box 10287, Wilmington, DE 19850, (302)322-3333 [9524]

United Engines, 7454 E 41st St., Tulsa, OK 74145, (918)627-8080 [3364]

United Engines Inc., 7255 Greenwood Rd., Shreveport, LA 71119, (318)635-8022 [3365]

United Engines Inc., PO Box 75079, Oklahoma City, OK 73147, (405)947-3321 [3366]

United Engines Inc., PO Box 75079, Oklahoma City, OK 73147, (405)947-3321 [16589]

United Envelope Co., 525 W 52nd St. 2nd Fl., New York, NY 10019, (212)315-4700 [21975]

United Export Import, Inc., 4113 Telegraph Rd., Ste. 227D, Bloomfield Hills, MI 48302, (248)644-6623 [20740]

United Exporters, 1095 Market St., Ste. 701, San Francisco, CA 94103, (415)255-9393 [19674]

United Fabrics, Inc., 9115 Pennsauken Hwy., Pennsauken, NJ 08110, (856)665-2040 [26234]

United Farmers Co-op, PO Box 158, Rushmore, MN 56168, (507)478-4166 [1376]

United Farmers Cooperative, PO Box 4, Lafayette, MN 56054, (507)228-8224 [1377]

United Farmers Cooperative, PO Box 4, Lafayette, MN 56054, (507)228-8224 [12792]

United Farmers Cooperative Inc., 408 James St., Stanton, IA 51573, (712)829-2117 [1378]

United Farmers Elevator Co., PO Box 47, Murdock, MN 56271, (320)875-2811 [18302]

United Farmers Mercantile Cooperative, 203 W Oak St., Red Oak, IA 51566, (712)623-2575 [18303]

United Fastener and Supply Co., 12565 E Slauson Ave., Whittier, CA 90606, (562)945-3302 [13972]

United Fire Equipment Co., 335 N 4th Ave., Tucson, AZ 85745, (520)622-3639 [24650]

United Fire Equipment Co., 335 N 4th Ave., Tucson, AZ 85745, (520)622-3639 [24255]

United Flooring Distributors Inc., 6201 Material Ave., Loves Park, IL 61111, (815)654-8383 [10265]

United Floral Supply Inc., PO Box 2518, North Canton, OH 44720, (330)966-9160 [14966]

United Food Service Inc., 1047 Broadway, Albany, NY 12204, (518)436-4401 [12793]

United Foods Inc., 10 Pictsweet Dr., Bells, TN 38006, (901)422-7600 [12794]

United Fruit and Produce Company Inc., 55 Produce Row, St. Louis, MO 63102, (314)621-9440 [12795]

United Grocers, Inc., PO Box 22187, Milwaukie, OR 97269, (503)833-1000 [12796]

United Hardware Distributing Co., 5005 Nathan Ln., Plymouth, MN 55442, (612)559-1800 [13973]

United Hardwood, L.L.C., 846 South EE Wallace Blvd., PO Box 1795, Ferriday, LA 71334, (318)757-4508 [8157]

United Heritage Corp., PO Box 1956, Cleburne, TX 76033-1956, (817)641-3681 [12797]

United Industrial Tire Inc., PO Box 689, Lebanon, IN 46052, (765)482-9603 [3367]

United Industries Inc., PO Box 58, Sterling, KS 67579, (316)278-3160 [24021]

United International Inc., PO Box 580, Charlestown, MA 02129, (617)241-0440 [8158]

United Iron and Metal Co., 2545 Wilkens Ave., Baltimore, MD 21223, (410)947-8000 [27029]

United Learning Inc., 6633 W Howard St., Niles, IL 60714, (847)647-0600 [25490]

United Light Co., 3959 Frankford Ave., Philadelphia, PA 19124, (215)289-1453 [9525]

United Liquors Corp., 4009 Airpark Cove, Memphis, TN 38188, (901)794-5540 [2091]

United Liquors Ltd., 1 United Dr., West Bridgewater, MA 02379, (508)588-2300 [2092]

United Magazine Company, 5131 Post Rd., Dublin, OH 43017, (614)792-0777 [4239]

United Magazine Company, 5131 Post Rd., Dublin, OH 43017, (614)792-0777 [4240]

United Magazine Co. Southern Michigan Division, 2571 Saradan, Jackson, MI 49202-1211, (517)784-7163 [4241]

United Manufacturers Service, 403 N Court St., Marion, IL 62959, (618)997-1375 [3368]

United Manufacturers Supplies Inc., 80 Gordon Dr., Syosset, NY 11791-4705, (516)496-4430 [13974]

United Marine Inc., 490 Northwind S River Dr., Miami, FL 33128, (305)545-8445 [18627]

United Meat Company Inc., 1040 Bryant St., San Francisco, CA 94103, (415)864-2118 [12798]

United Medical Supply Company Inc., 5117 NE Pkwy., Ft. Worth, TX 76106, (817)626-8261 [19675]

United Methodist Publishing House, 201 8th Ave. S, Nashville, TN 37203, (615)749-6000 [4242]

United Model Distributors Inc., 301 Holbrook Dr., Wheeling, IL 60090, (847)459-6700 [26699]

United Natural Foods, Inc., PO Box 999, Dayville, CT 06241, (860)779-2800 [12799]

United Noodles Inc., 2015 E 24th St., Minneapolis, MN 55404, (612)721-6677 [12800]

United Notions, PO Box 39486, Denver, CO 80239, (303)371-0660 [26235]

United Notions, 13795 Hutton Dr., Dallas, TX 75234, (972)484-8901 [26237]

United Notions, PO Box 814490, Dallas, TX 75381-4490, (972)484-8901 [26236]

United Notions & Fabrics, 13795 Hutton Dr., Dallas, TX 75234, (972)484-8901 [26237]

United Oil of the Carolinas, Inc., PO Box 68, Gastonia, NC 28053, (704)824-3561 [22761]

United Optical Co., PO Box 6400, Salt Lake City, UT 84106, (801)486-1001 [19676]

United Optical Corp., PO Box 1147, Shawnee, OK 74802-1147, (405)275-1228 [19677]

United Pacific Corp., 245 Roosevelt Rd., West Chicago, IL 60185, (630)231-6030 [24449]

United Pacific Pet L.L.C., 12060 Cabernet Dr., Fontana, CA 92337, (909)360-8550 [27256]

United Packaging Corp., 1136 Samuelson St., City of Industry, CA 91748, (626)968-0791 [23045]

United Paper Company Inc., 4101 Sarellen Rd., Richmond, VA 23231, (804)226-1936 [21976]

United Paper Company Inc., 4101 Sarellen Rd., Richmond, VA 23231 [17242]

United Pharmacal Co., 3705 Pear St., St. Joseph, MO 64502, (816)233-8800 [27257]

United Pharmaceutical & Medical Supply Co., 1338 W Fremont St., Stockton, CA 95203-2626, (510)568-5555 [19092]

United Pipe and Supply Company Inc., PO Box 2220, Eugene, OR 97402, (503)688-6511 [23422]

United Plumbing and Heating Supply Co., 9947 W Carmen Ave., Milwaukee, WI 53225, (414)464-5100 [23423]

United Plywood and Lumber Inc., PO Box 1088, Birmingham, AL 35201, (205)925-7601 [8159]

United Pride Inc., PO Box 84107, Sioux Falls, SD 57118-4707, (605)336-1558 [22762]

United Producers Consumers Cooperative, 1821 E Jackson St., Phoenix, AZ 85034, (602)254-5644 [1379]

United Producers, Inc., 5909 Cleveland Ave., Columbus, OH 43231, (614)890-6666 [18304]

United Receptacle, Inc., 14th St. & Laurel St., PO Box 870, Pottsville, PA 17901, (570)622-7715 [25855]

United Recycling Industries Inc., 1600 Harvester, West Chicago, IL 60185, (630)231-6060 [27030]

United Refrigeration Inc., 11401 Roosevelt Blvd., Philadelphia, PA 19154, (215)698-9100 [14748]

United Research Laboratories Inc., 1100 Orthodox St., Philadelphia, PA 19124, (215)288-6500 [19678]

United Restaurant Equipment, 2980 Jefferson St., PO Box 2223, Harrisburg, PA 17105-2223, (717)238-1214 [24256]

United Restaurant Equipment Co., PO Box 1460, Woonsocket, RI 02895-0847, (401)769-1000 [24254]

United Sales, 4731 W Jefferson Blvd., Los Angeles, CA 90016, (323)731-2424 [13315]

United Scale and Engineering Co., 16725 W Victor Rd., New Berlin, WI 53151, (414)785-1733 [25856]

United Scale and Engr. Corp., 1322 Russett Ct., Green Bay, WI 54313, (414)434-2737 [24450]

United School Bus Seat Services, 116 Depew Dr., Branson, MO 65616, (417)334-3100 [3369]

United Service Dental Chair, 5669 147th St. N, Hugo, MN 55038-9302, (612)429-8660 [19093]

United Service and Sales, 2808 S Main St., Salt Lake City, UT 84115, (801)485-5770 [1380]

United Services Association, 7025 Hickman Rd., Des Moines, IA 50322, (515)276-6763 [1381]

United Sewing Machine Distributing, 916 SW D Ave., Lawton, OK 73501-4531, (580)353-8800 [15348]

United Shoe Ornament Company Inc., 35 Tripoli St., Providence, RI 02909-5418, (401)944-3060 [24881]

United Sports Apparel Inc., 6850 Central Park, Lincolnwood, IL 60712 [5450]

U.S. Aircraft Industries International Inc., 30-A Field St., West Babylon, NY 11704, (516)420-0064 [165]

U.S. Amada Ltd., 7025 Firestone Blvd., Buena Park, CA 90621, (714)670-2121 [16590]

U.S. AudioTex L.L.C., 18 Crow Canyon Ct. Ste. 300, San Ramon, CA 94583, (925)838-7996 [6841]

U.S. Beverage Corp., PO Box 3364, Longview, TX 75606, (903)757-2168 [25046]

United States Check Book Co., PO Box 3644, Omaha, NE 68103, (402)345-3162 [21328]

U.S.-China Industrial Exchange Inc., 7201 Wisconsin Ave., Ste. 703, Bethesda, MD 20814, (301)215-7777 [19094]

U.S. Clinical Products, 2552 Summit Ave., No. 406, Plano, TX 75074, (214)424-6268 [19679]

United States Electric Co., 301 N 1st St., Springfield, IL 62702, (217)522-3347 [9526]

U.S. Equipment Co., 20580 Hoover Rd., Detroit, MI 48205, (313)526-8300 [16591]

U.S. Equipment Company Inc., 1810 W Venice Blvd., Los Angeles, CA 90006, (213)733-4733 [5855]

United States Exploration Inc., 1560 Broadway, Ste. 1900, Denver, CO 80202, (303)863-3550 [22763]

United States Export Co., 1693 Merchant St., Ambridge, PA 15003, (412)266-9300 [20741]

U.S. Export & Trading Company, Inc., 848 Harding St., Escondido, CA 92027, (760)743-8211 [14270]

U.S. Extrusion Tool and Die, 1110 Trumbull Ave., Girard, OH 44420, (330)759-2944 [16592]

U.S. Filter/Diversified Engineering, 8040 Villa Park Dr., Ste. 800, Richmond, VA 23228, (804)262-6600 [6842]

U.S. Food Service, 2800 NE 410, No. 105, San Antonio, TX 78218, (210)590-1322 [12801]

U.S. Foodservice Inc., 9830 Patuxent Woods Dr., Columbia, MD 21046, (410)312-7100 [24257]

U.S. Foodservice - RRS Div., PO Box 40, Salem, VA 24153, (540)387-1151 [12802]

U.S. Games Systems Inc., 179 Ludlow St., Stamford, CT 06902, (203)353-8400 [26700]

U.S. Global Resources, 10242 59th Ave. S, Seattle, WA 98178, (425)391-5646 [1382]

U.S. Home and Garden Inc., 655 Montgomery St., San Francisco, CA 94111, (415)616-8111 [1383]

U.S. Import Export Corp., 830 7th St., San Francisco, CA 94107, (415)863-7886 [12803]

U.S. Industrial Products Corp., 96-12 43rd Ave., Corona, NY 11368, (718)335-3300 [13975]

United States Industrial Supply, Inc., 417 Jeff Davis Hwy., Fredericksburg, VA 22401-3118, (703)373-8404 [9527]

U.S. Industrial Tool Supply, 15101 Cleat, Plymouth, MI 48170-6015, (734)455-3388 [13976]

U.S. International, 801 N Curtis Ave., Alhambra, CA 91801, (626)281-1804 [16593]

U.S. Line Co., 16 Union Ave., Westfield, MA 01085-2497, (413)562-3629 [24022]

U.S. Lock Corp., 77 Rodeo Dr., Brentwood, NY 11717, (631)243-3000 [24651]

U.S. Machinery, Inc., 1775 S West St., PO Box 13356, Wichita, KS 67213, (316)942-2120 [16594]

U.S. Manufacturing Corp., 2401 16th St., Port Huron, MI 48060, (810)984-4145 [3370]

U.S. Marketing Services, 7127 E Becker Ln. 63, Scottsdale, AZ 85254-5206, (602)998-2859 [5451]

United States Medical Corp., 7205 E Kemper Rd., Cincinnati, OH 45249-1030, (513)489-5595 [19095]

United States Medical Corp., 7205 E Kemper Rd., Cincinnati, OH 45249-1030, (513)489-5595 [19680]

U.S. Medical Supply Co., 3731 Northcrest Rd., Ste. 10, Atlanta, GA 30340-3416, (404)457-2677 [19096]

U.S. Metal Service Inc., 20900 Saint Clair Ave., Euclid, OH 44117, (216)692-3800 [20464]

U.S. Office Products Co., 1025 Thomas Jefferson St. NW, Ste. 600E, Washington, DC 20007, (202)339-6700 [21329]

U.S. Oil Company Inc., 425 S Washington St., Combined Locks, WI 54113, (920)739-6100 [3371]

United States Pharmaceutical Corp., 96 North 5th West, Ste. 200, Bountiful, UT 84010, (801)295-1000 [19681]

U.S. Printing Supply Co., 1618 Forbes Ave., Pittsburgh, PA 15219, (412)566-2244 [25857]

U.S. Products Inc., PO Box 1006, Orange, CT 06477-7006, (203)783-1468 [5452]

U.S. Pure Water Corp., 184 Bon Air Shopping Center, Greenbrae, CA 94904, (415)461-4040 [25858]

U.S. Recording Co., 9120 E Hampton Dr., Capitol Heights, MD 20743, (301)499-6700 [25491]

U.S. Rigging Supply Corp., 4001 W Carriage Dr., Santa Ana, CA 92704, (714)545-7444 [17243]

U.S. Ring Binder Corp., 6800 Arsenal St., St. Louis, MO 63139, (314)645-7880 [21330]

U.S. Safety Corp., 8101 Lenexa Dr., Lenexa, KS 66214, (913)599-5555 [19682]

U.S. Sugar Company Inc., PO Box 549, Buffalo, NY 14240, (716)828-1170 [12804]

U.S. Tire Recycling, 6322 Poplar Tent Rd., Concord, NC 28027-7580, (704)784-1210 [27031]

U.S. Tire Recycling Partners L.P., 6322 Poplar Tent Rd., Concord, NC 28027-7580, (704)784-1210 [27031]

United States Tobacco Sales and Marketing Co., 100 W Putnam Ave., Greenwich, CT 06830, (203)661-1100 [26364]

U.S. World Trade Corp., 111 SW 5th Ave., Ste. 1900, Portland, OR 97204, (503)275-4100 [18305]

United Stationers Inc., 2200 E Golf Rd., Des Plaines, IL 60016-1267, (847)699-5000 [21977]

United Steaks of America, 103 19th, Rock Island, IL 61201, (309)786-7757 [10403]

United Steel Associates Inc., 4501 Curtis Ave., Baltimore, MD 21226, (410)355-8980 [20465]

United Steel Service Inc., PO Box 149, Brookfield, OH 44403, (330)448-4057 [20466]

United Strategies Inc., 10810 Guilford Rd., Ste. 103, Annapolis Junction, MD 20701-1102, (301)417-7319 [6843]

United Suppliers Inc., PO Box 538, Eldora, IA 50627, (515)858-2341 [1384]

United Systems Software Inc., 955 E Javelina Ave Ste 106, Mesa, AZ 85204, (480)545-5100 [21978]

United Technical Products, 9947 W Carmen Ave., Milwaukee, WI 53225, (414)464-5100 [23423]

United Thread Mills Corp., 250 Maple Ave., Rockville Centre, NY 11570, (516)536-3900 [26238]

United Tile Company, Inc., 2350 Levy St., Shreveport, LA 71103-3656, (318)222-5150 [10266]

United Tile Company, Inc., 1505 Eraste Landry Rd., Lafayette, LA 70506, (318)234-2310 [10267]

United Tile of LaFayette, LLC, 1505 Eraste Landry Rd., Lafayette, LA 70506, (318)234-2310 [10267]

United Tire Distributors Inc., 3224 C Ave., Gulfport, MS 39507, (228)863-6193 [3372]

United Uniforms Inc., 15 Orange St., New Haven, CT 06510-3300, (203)624-8931 [5453]

United World Supply Co., 103 N Ben Jordan, Victoria, TX 77901-8628, (512)575-0464 [17244]

Unitex Inc., 5175 Commerce Dr., Baldwin Park, CA 91706 [26239]

Unity Grain and Supply Co., PO Box 229, Hammond, IL 61929, (217)578-3013 [18306]

Unity Manufacturing Co., 1260 N Clybourn Ave., Chicago, IL 60610, (312)943-5200 [3373]

Univar Corp., 6100 Carillon Pt., Kirkland, WA 98033, (425)889-3400 [4543]

Univelt Inc., PO Box 28130, San Diego, CA 92198-0130, (760)746-4005 [4243]

Universal Aqua, 10555 Norwalk Blvd., Santa Fe Springs, CA 90670, (562)944-4121 [25859]

Universal Athletic Services of Utah, PO Box 1629, Bozeman, MT 59771-1629, (406)587-1220 [24882]

Universal Blueprint Paper, 730 Great SW Pkwy., Atlanta, GA 30336-2338, (404)349-0600 [21979]

Universal Bowling and Golf Co., 619 S Wabash, Chicago, IL 60605, (312)922-5255 [24023]

Universal Brands Inc., 3325 NW 70th Ave., Miami, FL 33122, (305)591-9800 [1722]

Universal Card & Coin Center Inc., 18 Theresa Ave., Lewiston, ME 04240-4723, (207)774-6724 [26701]

Universal Case Company Inc./Designer Optical, 474 S Perkins, Memphis, TN 38117-3803, (901)767-8640 [19683]

Universal Coach Parts Inc., 105 E Oakton St., Des Plaines, IL 60018, (847)803-8900 [3374]

Universal Companies Inc. (Wichita, Kansas), PO Box 2920, Wichita, KS 67201, (316)832-0151 [22764]

Universal Cooperative Inc., 1300 Corporate Center Curve, PO Box 460, Eagan, MN 55121, (651)239-1000 [1385]

Universal Corp., PO Box 25099, Richmond, VA 23260, (804)359-9311 [26365]

Universal Fastener Co., 5930 Old Mt. Holly Rd., PO Box 668013, Charlotte, NC 28208, (704)392-5342 [13977]

Universal Forest Products, Inc., 2801 E Beltline, NE, Grand Rapids, MI 49505, (616)364-6161 [27391]

Universal Forms, Labels, and Systems, Inc., 2020 S Eastwood, Santa Ana, CA 92705, (714)540-8025 [21980]

Universal Industries Inc., 325 E Stahl Rd., Fremont, OH 43420, (419)334-9741 [25860]

Universal Industries Inc., 325 E Stahl Rd., Fremont, OH 43420, (419)334-9741 [8160]

Universal International Inc., 5000 Winnetka Ave. N, New Hope, MN 55428, (612)533-1169 [5454]

Universal Jewelers Inc., 6900 Central Ave. SE, Albuquerque, NM 87108-1855, (505)255-2225 [17646]

Universal Jewelers & Trading Co., 6900 Central Ave. SE, Albuquerque, NM 87108-1855, (505)255-2225 [17646]

Universal Joint Specialists Inc., PO Box 9605, Tulsa, OK 74157-0605, (918)585-5785 [3375]

Universal Leaf Tobacco Company Inc., PO Box 25099, Richmond, VA 23260, (804)359-9311 [26366]

Universal Lubricants Inc., PO Box 2920, Wichita, KS 67201-2920, (316)832-0151 [22765]

Universal Management Consultants Inc., 2017 Bainbridge Row Dr., Louisville, KY 40207, (502)895-9903 [14749]

Universal Marble and Granite Inc., 1954 Halethorpe Farms Rd., Ste. 500, Baltimore, MD 21227, (410)247-2442 [8161]

Universal Marine, 1 Venetian Dr., Portage Des Sioux, MO 63373, (314)899-0940 [18628]

Universal Marine Medical Supply Co., PO Box 199035, Brooklyn, NY 11219, (718)438-4804 [19684]

Universal Metal and Ore Company Inc., PO Box 187, Mt. Vernon, NY 10551, (914)664-0200 [27032]

Universal Metal Services Corp., 16655 S Canal St., South Holland, IL 60473, (708)596-2700 [20467]

Universal Paper Goods Co., 7171 Telegraph Rd., Los Angeles, CA 90040-3227, (213)685-6220 [21981]

Universal Paper and Packaging, PO Box 537, Appleton, WI 54912-0537, (920)731-4171 [21982]

Universal Percussion, 2773 E Midlothian Blvd., Struthers, OH 44471, (330)755-6423 [25492]

Universal Process Equipment Inc., 1180 Rte. 130 S, Robbinsville, NJ 08691, (609)443-4545 [16595]

Universal Process Equipment Inc., PO Box 338, Roosevelt, NJ 08555-0338, (609)443-4545 [4540]

Universal Products Enterprises, 1243 Bay Area, No. 1805, Houston, TX 77058, (281)480-2129 [19685]

Universal Sales Engineering Inc., 5060 E 62nd St., Indianapolis, IN 46220, (317)255-3181 [17245]

Universal Scrap Metals Co., 2500 W Fulton St., Chicago, IL 60612-2104, (312)666-0011 [27033]

Universal Security Instruments Inc., 7A Gwynns Mill Crt., Owings Mills, MD 21117, (410)363-3000 [24652]

Universal Semen Sales Inc., 2626 2nd Ave. S, Great Falls, MT 59405-3004, (406)453-0374 [18307]

Universal Service and Supply, 3605 W Twain Ave., Las Vegas, NV 89103-1901, (702)876-0333 [15349]

Universal Sewing Supply Inc., 1011 E Park Indus. Dr., St. Louis, MO 63130, (314)862-0800 [15350]

Universal Steel Co., 6600 Grant Ave., Cleveland, OH 44105, (216)883-4972 [20468]

Universal Supply Company Inc., 515 33rd St., Parkersburg, WV 26101, (304)422-3533 [23424]

Universal Tea Co., PO Box 910, Portland, OR 97207, (503)684-4482 [12576]

Universal/Univis Inc., 110 Frank Mossveig Dr., Attleboro, MA 02703, (508)226-9630 [19686]

Universe Publishing, 300 Park Ave. S, New York, NY 10010, (212)387-3400 [4121]

University of Alaska Press, Univ. of Alaska Fairbanks, Gruening Bldg., 1st Fl., PO Box 756240, Fairbanks, AK 99775-6240, (907)474-5831 [4244]

University Book Service, 2219 Westbrooke Dr., Columbus, OH 43228, (614)777-2336 [4245]

University Marketing Group, 62 Linden Ave., Apt. B, Branford, CT 06405-5205, (203)483-5761 [4246]

University Microfilms Inc., 300 N Zeeb Rd., Ann Arbor, MI 48103, (734)761-4700 [22912]

University of Missouri Press, 2910 LeMone Blvd., Columbia, MO 65201-8291, (573)882-7641 [4247]

University Motors Ltd., 60 S University Ave., Morgantown, WV 26505, (304)296-4401 [3376]

University Press of Colorado, PO Box 849, Niwot, CO 80544, (303)530-5337 [4248]

University Press of Kansas, 2501 W 15th St., Lawrence, KS 66049-3904, (785)864-4154 [4249]

University Press of Virginia, PO Box 400318, Charlottesville, VA 22904-4318, (804)924-3468 [4250]

University Products, Inc., PO Box 101, PO Box 101, Holyoke, MA 01041, (413)532-3372 [25493]

University Publishing Co., PO Box 80298, Lincoln, NE 68501, (402)476-2761 [13266]

University of Texas Press, PO Box 7819, Austin, TX 78713-7819, (512)471-7233 [4251]

University of Washington Press, PO Box 50096, Seattle, WA 98145-5096, (206)543-4050 [4252]

Unizone Inc., PO Box 27688, Tempe, AZ 85285-7688, (602)756-2806 [6844]

Unnex Industrial Corp., 1141 Broadway, 9th Fl., New York, NY 10001, (212)481-1900 [5455]

Unverferth Manufacturing Company Inc., PO Box 357, Kalida, OH 45853, (419)532-3121 [1386]

Up-Rad Inc., PO Box 289, Leonardtown, MD 20650-0289, (301)739-4556 [19097]

Upchurch Co.; Frank J., PO Box 669107, Charlotte, NC 28266, (704)394-4186 [17246]

UPCO Pet Vet Supply, 11200 Menaul St., Albuquerque, NM 87112, (505)292-6288 [27258]

The Upholstery Supply Co., 12530 W Burleigh Rd., Brookfield, WI 53005, (414)781-7490 [26240]

Upper Access Books, 1 Upper Access Rd., PO Box 457, Hinesburg, VT 05461, (802)482-2988 [4254]

Upper Access Books, PO Box 457, Hinesburg, VT 05461, (802)482-2988 [4253]

Upper Access Inc., 1 Upper Access Rd., PO Box 457, Hinesburg, VT 05461, (802)482-2988 [4254]

Upper Mississippi Valley Mercantile Co., 1607 Washington St., Davenport, IA 52804, (319)322-0896 [26702]

Upper Room, PO Box 189, Nashville, TN 37202-0189, (615)340-7200 [4255]

Upstart Publishing Company Inc., 155 N Wacker Dr., Chicago, IL 60606, (312)836-4400 [4256]

Uranus Impex Co., 5 Bank St., Manchester, CT 06040-5701, (860)645-1029 [5456]

Urban Ore Inc., 6082 Ralston Ave., Richmond, CA 94805, (510)235-0172 [8162]

Urban Wholesale, 329 Saint Francis St., Rapid City, SD 57701-5482, (605)343-0794 [4721]

Urethane Contractors Supply, 1425 Spar Ave., Anchorage, AK 99501, (907)276-7932 [8163]

Urken Supply Company Inc., 27 Witherspoon, Princeton, NJ 08540-3201, (609)924-3076 [15693]

U.R.M. Cash & Carry, 902 E Springfield, Spokane, WA 99202-2075, (509)489-4555 [12805]

U.R.M. Stores Inc., PO Box 3365, Spokane, WA 99220-3365, (509)467-2620 [12806]

Ursa Farmers Cooperative, 202 W Maple St., Ursa, IL 62376, (217)964-2111 [18308]

Urwiler Oil and Fertilizer Inc., Hwy. 20 N, Laurel, NE 68745, (402)256-3422 [1387]

US Airways Group Inc., 2345 Crystal Dr., Arlington, VA 22227, (703)872-5306 [166]

US Chemical Corporation, 300 N Patrick Blvd., Brookfield, WI 53045, (414)792-1555 [4541]

US Farathane Inc., 3905 Rochester Rd., Royal Oak, MI 48073, (248)585-1888 [3377]

US Food Service-Pittston Division, 13 Rutledge Dr., Pittston, PA 18640, (717)654-3374 [12807]

US FoodService Inc. Carolina Div., 125 Fort Mill Pkwy., Ft. Mill, SC 29715, (803)802-6000 [12808]

US Lighting & Electrical Supply, 417 Jeff Davis Hwy., Fredericksburg, VA 22401-3118, (703)373-8404 [9527]

US Office Products, Midwest District Inc., 4015 Papin St., St. Louis, MO 63110, (314)535-1414 [21331]

US Reflector, 144 Canterbury St., Worcester, MA 01603, (508)753-6373 [3378]

US TeleCenters, 745 Atlantic Ave., 9th Fl., Boston, MA 02111, (617)439-9911 [5801]

USA Datafax Inc., 1819 Firman Dr., Ste. 115, Richardson, TX 75081, (972)437-4791 [21332]

U.S.A. Floral Products, 1025 Thomas Jefferson NW, Ste. 300 E, Washington, DC 20007, (202)333-0800 [14967]

U.S.A. Marketing Alliance Inc., 8570 Jewel Ave. N, Stillwater, MN 55082, (612)426-2164 [1388]

USA Plastics Inc., 306A Mcknight Pk. Dr., Pittsburgh, PA 15237, (412)367-0594 [15694]

USA Test, Inc., 182 Village Rd., Roslyn Heights, NY 11577, (516)621-0012 [25494]

U.S.A. Woods International, PO Box 38507, Memphis, TN 38183, (901)753-7718 [8164]

USAP, 2295 Paseo de las Americas, Ste. 19, San Diego, CA 92154, (619)671-2398 [6845]

Usco Inc., PO Box 1160, Monroe, NC 28111, (704)289-5406 [23425]

User Friendly Software Hardware, PO Box 2888, LaGrange, GA 30241-2888, (706)883-8734 [6846]

USI Inc., 98 Fort Path Rd., Madison, CT 06443, (203)245-8586 [21333]

Uspar Enterprises Inc., 13404 S Monte Vista, Chino, CA 91710-5149, (909)591-7506 [9528]

Uster Imports, Inc.; Albert, 9211 Gaither Rd., Gaithersburg, MD 20877-1419, (301)258-7350 [12809]

Utah Wool Marketing Association, 855 South 500 West, Salt Lake City, UT 84101, (801)328-1507 [18309]

UTECO Inc., 8504 Sanford Dr., Richmond, VA 23228, (804)266-7807 [1389]

Utica Cooperative Grain Company Inc., PO Box 216, Utica, NE 68456, (402)534-2411 [18310]

Utica Cooperative Grain Company Inc., PO Box 216, Utica, NE 68456, (402)527-5511 [12810]

Utica Plumbing Supply Co., 332 Lafayette St., Utica, NY 13502, (315)735-9555 [23426]

Utikem Products, 225 Passaic St., Passaic, NJ 07055, (973)473-1222 [24024]

Utility Supply Co., 5929 E 15th St., Tulsa, OK 74112, (918)836-4645 [25861]

Utility Trailer Sales Co., PO Box 1510, Fontana, CA 92334, (909)428-8300 [3379]

Utility Trailer Sales Company of Arizona, 1402 N 22nd Ave., Phoenix, AZ 85009, (602)254-7213 [3380]

Utility Trailer Sales of Oregon Inc., PO Box 1190, Clackamas, OR 97015, (503)653-8686 [20742]

Utility Truck Equipment Sales, PO Box 15357, Boise, ID 83715, (208)384-5242 [3381]

Utter Company Inc., 955 W Pine St., Lexington, KY 40508-2431, (606)252-8834 [14750]

UV Process Supply Inc., 1229 W Cortland St., Chicago, IL 60614, (773)248-0099 [9529]

Uvalde Meat Processing, 508 S Wood, Uvalde, TX 78801, (512)278-6247 [12811]

Uvex Safety, 10 Thurber Blvd., Smithfield, RI 02917, (401)232-1200 [24653]

U.W. Provision Co., 2315 Evergreen Rd., Middleton, WI 53562-4244, (608)836-7421 [12812]

V-Labs Inc., 423 N Theard St., Covington, LA 70433, (504)893-0533 [12813]

V and M Cotton Co., PO Box 167, Inverness, MS 38753, (601)265-5801 [18311]

V-Tek Associates, 2092 Wilshire Dr., Marietta, GA 30064, (404)424-4043 [6847]

V & V Appliance Parts Inc., 27 W Myrtle Ave., Youngstown, OH 44507, (330)743-5144 [15351]

Vaagen Brothers Lumber Inc., 565 W 5th St., Colville, WA 99114, (509)684-5071 [8165]

Vacuum Center Central Michigan, G4099 S Saginaw St., Burton, MI 48529-1645, (810)742-8954 [15352]

Vacuum Pump Systems Inc., PO Box 1826, Gainesville, GA 30503-1826, (404)532-0260 [16596]

Vail Enterprises Inc., PO Box 765, New Castle, DE 19720, (302)322-5411 [23427]

Vair Corp., 9305 Gerwig Ln. Q-R, Columbia, MD 21046, (410)995-6000 [14751]

Val-Comm Inc., 249 Muriel St. NE, Albuquerque, NM 87123-2932, (505)292-7509 [9530]

Val Dere Co.; W.R., 712 S Hacienda Dr., No. 5, Tempe, AZ 85281-2949, (602)894-0980 [14752]

Valders Cooperative, PO Box 10, Valders, WI 54245, (414)775-4131 [18312]

Valdes Paint & Glass, 1008 Marquez Pl., Santa Fe, NM 87501, (505)982-4661 [21597]

Valdez, 7420 Sunset Blvd., Los Angeles, CA 90046, (213)874-9998 [25495]

Valdez, 7420 Sunset Blvd., Los Angeles, CA 90046, (213)874-9998 [15353]

Valencia Imports Co., 1020 Campus Dr. W, Morganville, NJ 07751, (732)972-7211 [24883]

Valenti Company Inc.; J.C., PO Box 11128, Tampa, FL 33680, (813)238-7981 [12814]

Valenti Inc.; F.M., 5 Bourbon St., Peabody, MA 01960-1339, (978)536-2666 [24654]

Valhalla Scientific Inc., 9955 Mesa Rim Rd., San Diego, CA 92121, (858)457-5576 [9531]

Valiac Inc., 208 College Crossing, Rolling Meadows, IL 60008-2155, (847)776-1010 [17247]

The Validation Group Inc., 1100 E Hector St., Ste. 415, Conshohocken, PA 19428 [19687]

Vallen Corp., PO Box 3587, Houston, TX 77253-3587, (713)462-8700 [24655]

Vallen Safety Supply Co., 12850 E Florence Ave., Santa Fe Springs, CA 90670, (562)946-0076 [19688]

Vallen Safety Supply Co., PO Box 3587, Houston, TX 77253, (713)462-8700 [17248]

Vallery Co.; William G., 209 W Loveland Ave. 102, Loveland, OH 45140-2933, (513)677-3339 [26703]

Vallet Food Service Inc., 1230 E 12th St., Dubuque, IA 52001, (319)588-2347 [12815]

Valley Appliance Parts Co., 719 Hamburg Tpke., Pompton Lakes, NJ 07442-1433, (973)835-2157 [15354]

Valley Athletic Supply Co. Inc., PO Box 995, Ft. Valley, GA 31030-0995, (912)825-3306 [24884]

Valley Auto Parts, 365 W Hwy. 14, Spearfish, SD 57783-9513, (605)642-4695 [3382]

Valley Auto and Truck Wrecking Inc., PO Box 586, Bakersfield, CA 93302, (805)831-8171 [3383]

Valley Best-Way Building Supply, PO Box 14024, Spokane, WA 99214-0024, (509)924-1250 [8166]

Valley Cities Supply Co., 9510 Rush St., South el Monte, CA 91733, (626)453-0020 [23428]

Valley Coin Laundry Equipment Co., Woods Bay, Bigfork, MT 59911, (406)837-6616 [4722]

Valley Communications, 730 N 16th Ave. 1, Yakima, WA 98902-1897, (509)248-0314 [5802]

Valley Controls & Supply Co., 3192 Hall Ave., Grand Junction, CO 81504-6036, (970)434-1374 [14753]

Valley Controls and Supply Co., 3192 Hall Ave., Grand Junction, CO 81504-6036, (970)434-1374 [14754]

Valley Convenience Products, 44 Drawbridge Dr., West Warwick, RI 02893-5580, (401)821-6073 [26367]

Valley Crest Tree Co., 24121 Ventura Blvd., Calabasas, CA 91302, (818)737-2600 [1390]

Valley Detroit Diesel Allison Inc., 425 S Hacienda Blvd., City of Industry, CA 91745-1123, (626)333-1243 [3384]

Valley Distributors, 15 11th St., Elkins, WV 26241, (304)636-1330 [2093]

Valley Distributors Inc., PO Box 548, Dillonvale, OH 43917, (740)769-2311 [2094]

Valley Distributors Inc., 534 Belgrade Rd., Oakland, ME 04963-0008, (207)465-2121 [2095]

Valley Distributors Inc., 880 E Front St., Fallon, NV 89406-8151, (702)423-3432 [2096]

Valley Electric Company Inc., PO Box 431, Manteca, CA 95337, (209)825-7000 [9532]

Valley Electric Supply Corp., PO Box 724, Vincennes, IN 47591, (812)882-7860 [9533]

Valley Farm Dairy Co., PO Box 78039, St. Louis, MO 63178-8039, (314)535-4004 [12816]

Valley Farm Inc., Hwy. 34 & Hwy. 61, Benkelman, NE 69021, (308)423-2515 [1391]

Valley Farmers Cooperative (Natchitoches, Louisiana), PO Box 2116, Natchitoches, LA 71457, (318)352-6426 [1392]

Valley Feed Mill Inc., 315 W Center St., Paris, TX 75460, (903)785-3501 [1393]

Valley Fertilizer and Chemical Company Inc., PO Box 816, Mt. Jackson, VA 22842, (540)477-3121 [1394]

Valley Fir and Redwood Co., 903 Morris Rd., Columbus, GA 31906, (706)687-9542 [8167]

Valley Foods, PO Box 50048, Santa Barbara, CA 93150, (805)565-1621 [12817]

Valley Ford Truck Sales, 5715 Canal Rd., Cleveland, OH 44125, (216)524-2400 [3385]

Valley Forge Leather Co., 314 Old Lancaster Rd., Merion Station, PA 19066, (610)668-2121 [18313]

Valley Forge Scientific Corp., 136 Greentree Rd., Oaks, PA 19456, (215)666-7500 [19098]

Valley Fruit, 12 Hoffer Rd., Wapato, WA 98951, (509)877-4188 [12818]

Valley Gun of Baltimore, 7719 Hartford Rd., Baltimore, MD 21234, (410)668-2171 [13516]

Valley Hardwood Inc., 5004 Nancy Cir., Huntsville, AL 35811, (205)852-6582 [1816]

Valley Industrial Trucks Inc., 1152 Meadowbrook St., Youngstown, OH 44512, (330)788-4081 [16597]

Valley Isle Produce Inc., PO Box 517, Kahului, HI 96732, (808)877-5055 [12819]

Valley Media Inc., PO Box 2057, Woodland, CA 95776, (530)661-6600 [25496]

Valley Motor Supply Inc., 101 2nd St., Havre, MT 59501-3507, (406)265-2231 [3386]

Valley National Gases, Inc., 1151 Findley St., Cincinnati, OH 45214, (513)241-5840 [16598]

Valley National Gases Inc., PO Box 6628, Wheeling, WV 26003-0900, (304)232-1541 [22766]

Valley Office Products Inc., 110 S Main St., Milbank, SD 57252-1807, (605)432-5536 [21334]

Valley Oil Co., PO Box 12249, Salem, OR 97309, (503)362-3633 [22767]

Valley Packing Service, 310 Walker St., Watsonville, CA 95076, (408)724-7551 [12820]

Valley Paint, 629 S State St., Salt Lake City, UT 84111, (801)595-1819 [21598]

Valley Pet Supply, 1029 Whipple Rd., Hayward, CA 94544, (510)489-3311 [27259]

Valley Sales Company Inc., PO Box 53, West Springfield, MA 01090-0053, (413)732-7754 [25497]

Valley Sales Company Inc., PO Box 429, Jamestown, ND 58402-0429, (701)252-3950 [2097]

Valley Sales Company Inc., PO Box 53, West Springfield, MA 01090-0053, (413)732-7754 [15355]

Valley Seed Co., PO Box 11188, Casa Grande, AZ 85230-1188, (520)836-8713 [18314]

Valley Supply Co., S Railroad & 11th St., Elkins, WV 26241, (304)636-4015 [23429]

Valley Tile Distributors, 1510 Southside Dr., PO Box 187, Salem, VA 24153, (540)387-0300 [10268]

Valley Tile & Marble, 1618 S San Gabriel Blvd., San Gabriel, CA 91776-3926, (626)572-0881 [10268]

Valley Vending Service Inc., PO Box 506, Martins Ferry, OH 43935, (614)633-3303 [26368]

Valley Vet Supply, PO Box 504, Marysville, KS 66508, (785)562-5106 [27260]

Valley View Vineyard, 1000 Upper Applegate Rd., Jacksonville, OR 97530, (541)899-8468 [2098]

Valley Vintners Inc., PO Box 4284, Ketchum, ID 83340-4284, (208)837-4413 [2099]

Valley Welders Supply Inc., 320 N 11th St., Billings, MT 59101, (406)256-3330 [17249]

Valley Welding Supply Co., 67 43rd St., Wheeling, WV 26003, (304)232-1541 [16599]

Valley Welding Supply Inc., PO Box 12609, Salem, OR 97309, (503)581-6400 [17250]

Valley-Western Distributors, Inc., 9666 Telstar Ave., El Monte, CA 91731, (626)443-1777 [10270]

Valley-Western Distributors, Inc., 4763 S Procyon, Las Vegas, NV 89103, (702)795-8284 [10271]

Valley-Western, Inc., 401 S Jay St., San Bernardino, CA 92410, (714)885-0286 [10272]

Valley-Western, Inc., 8060 Ajong Dr., San Diego, CA 92126, (619)578-6801 [10273]

Valley Wholesalers Inc., RR 5, Box 39, Winona, MN 55987-9700, (507)454-1556 [21983]

Val's Homemade Bagels Inc., PO Box 671, Clackamas, OR 97015, (503)656-2777 [12821]

Valtronics Engineering and Mfg, 6602 N 58th Dr., Glendale, AZ 85301, (623)937-0373 [9534]

Value Added Distribution Inc., 5458 Steubenvile Pike, No. 1st Fl., Mc Kees Rocks, PA 15136-1412, (412)695-1180 [20469]

Value City Furniture Div., 1800 Moler Rd., Columbus, OH 43207, (614)221-9200 [13267]

ValuNet Div., 2060 Craigshire Rd., St. Louis, MO 63146, (314)542-1956 [19099]

Vamac Inc., PO Box 11225, Richmond, VA 23230, (804)353-7996 [23430]

Van Arsdale-Harris Lumber, PO Box 34008, San Francisco, CA 94134, (415)467-8711 [8169]

Van Arsdale-Harris Lumber, PO Box 34008, San Francisco, CA 94134, (415)467-8711 [27392]

Van Ausdall and Farrar Inc., 1214 N Meridian St., Indianapolis, IN 46204, (317)634-2913 [21335]

Van Bebber Brothers Inc., PO Box 760, Petaluma, CA 94953, (707)762-4528 [20470]

Van Dam Brothers Co., 9753 East Ave., Lancaster, CA 93535, (805)946-1630 [12822]

Van Den Bosch Co.; John A., 509 E Washington Ave., Zeeland, MI 49464, (616)772-2179 [27261]

Van Dyke Supply Co., PO Box 278, Woonsocket, SD 57385, (605)796-4425 [25862]

Van Eerden Distribution Co., PO Box 3110, Grand Rapids, MI 49501-3110, (616)452-1426 [12823]

Van Emmerik Tool and Supply, 732 Commerce St., PO Box 204, Thornwood, NY 10594-0204, (914)769-7056 [17014]

Van Hala Industrial Co., 14812 Detroit Ave., Cleveland, OH 44107, (216)228-9911 [20157]

Van Hoose and Company Inc.; F.S., PO Box 1618, Paintsville, KY 41240, (606)789-5870 [8170]

Van Horn Company Inc.; Oliver H., 4100 Euphrosine St., New Orleans, LA 70150, (504)821-4100 [16600]

Van Horn Hybrids Inc., PO Box 380, Cerro Gordo, IL 61818, (217)677-2131 [18315]

Van Keppel Co.; G.W., PO Box 2923, Kansas City, KS 66110, (913)281-4800 [8171]

Van Leeuwen Pipe and Tube Corp., PO Box 40904, Houston, TX 77240, (713)466-9966 [23431]

Van Ness Water Gardens Inc., 2460 N Euclid Ave., Upland, CA 91784-1199, (909)982-2425 [14968]

Van Paper Co., 2107 Stewart Ave., St. Paul, MN 55116, (612)690-1751 [21984]

Van Ran Communications Services Inc., 3427 Oak Cliff Rd., No. 114, Doraville, GA 30340, (404)452-9929 [5803]

Van Roy Coffee Co., 2900 Detroit Ave., Cleveland, OH 44113, (216)771-1220 [12824]

Van Sant Equipment Corp., 185 Oberlin Ave., N, Lakewood, NJ 08701-4525, (732)363-5158 [17251]

Van Solkema Produce Inc., PO Box 308, Byron Center, MI 49315, (616)878-1508 [12825]

Van Son Holland Corporation of America, 92 Union St., Mineola, NY 11501, (516)294-8811 [25863]

Van Waters and Rogers, PO Box 34325, Seattle, WA 98124-1325, (425)889-3400 [4542]

Van Waters & Rogers, 6100 Carillon Pt., Kirkland, WA 98033, (425)889-3400 [4543]

Van Waters and Rogers Inc., PO Box 34325, Seattle, WA 98124-1325, (425)889-3400 [4544]

Van Waters and Rogers Inc., 3002 F St., Omaha, NE 68107, (402)733-3266 [22768]

Van Waters and Rogers Inc. Omaha, 3002 F St., Omaha, NE 68107, (402)733-3266 [4545]

Van Wingerden International Inc., 556 Jeffress Rd., Fletcher, NC 28732, (704)891-4116 [14969]

Van Woerkom; Jan, 701 Tobacco St., Lebanon, CT 06249-1633, (860)848-7535 [6848]

Van Zeeland Oil Company Inc., PO Box 208, Little Chute, WI 54140, (920)788-7980 [22769]

Van Zyverden Brothers, Inc., PO Box 550, Meridian, MS 39302-0550, (601)679-8274 [14970]

Van Zyverden, Inc., PO Box 550, Meridian, MS 39302-0550, (601)679-8274 [14970]

Vanadium Pacific Steel Co., 707 W Olympic Blvd., Montebello, CA 90640, (213)723-5331 [20471]

Vancol Industries Inc., 2460 W 26th Ave., No. 180C, Denver, CO 80211-0037, (303)455-6112 [12826]

Vandenberg Inc.; Jac, 100 Corporate Blvd., Yonkers, NY 10701-0811, (914)964-5900 [12827]

VanderHave USA, PO Box 338, West Fargo, ND 58078, (701)282-7338 [1395]

Vanderheyden Distributing Inc., PO Box 3685, South Bend, IN 46619-0685, (219)232-8291 [15356]

Vanee Foods Co., 5418 W McDermott Dr., Berkeley, IL 60163, (708)449-7300 [12828]

Vangard Technology, Inc., 11211 E Arapahoe Rd., Englewood, CO 80112, (303)790-6090 [6849]

Vanguard Distributors Inc., PO Box 608, Savannah, GA 31402, (912)236-1766 [24656]

Vanguard Imaging Corp., 55 Cabot Ct., Hauppauge, NY 11788, (516)435-2100 [4546]

Vanguard Petroleum Corp., 1111 N Loop W, Ste. 1100, Houston, TX 77008, (713)802-4242 [22770]

Vanguard Trading Services Inc., 22605 SE 56th St., No. 200, Issaquah, WA 98029-5289, (425)557-8250 [12829]

Vann Sales Co.; Hugh, PO Box 806, White Rock, SC 29177, (803)781-8266 [27262]

Van's Candy & Tobacco Service, PO Box 1105, Laramie, WY 82070, (307)745-4665 [12830]

Vans Pro Shop, 10001 W Bell Rd., Ste. 118, Sun City, AZ 85351-1284, (602)972-0171 [24025]

Van's Supply and Equipment Inc., 1018 Circle Dr., Green Bay, WI 54304, (920)499-5969 [1396]

Vansant Lumber, PO Box 50, Vansant, VA 24656, (540)935-4519 [8172]

Vantage Industries Inc., PO Box 43944, Atlanta, GA 30336, (404)691-9500 [10274]

Vantage Pools Inc., 1098 S 5th St., San Jose, CA 95112-3926, (408)275-6217 [24026]

Vantage Sales & Marketing, Inc., 12 Village Ct., Hazlet, NJ 07730, (732)739-3313 [4257]

VantageParts Inc., PO Box 20015, Portland, OR 97294-0015, (503)224-5904 [3387]

Variety Distributors Inc., 702 Spring St., Harlan, IA 51537, (712)755-2184 [15695]

Variety Distributors Inc., 702 Spring St., Harlan, IA 51537, (712)755-2184 [21336]

Variety Hosiery Mills, PO Box 446, Graham, NC 27253-2262, (919)226-6059 [5457]

Variety Sales, Inc., 426 S Cross St., PO Box 218, Youngsville, NC 27596-0218, (919)556-5630 [5458]

Variform Inc., PO Box 559, Kearney, MO 64060, (816)635-6400 [8173]

Varilease Corp., 8451 Boulder Ct., Walled Lake, MI 48390, (248)366-5380 [5804]

Varon and Associates Inc., 31255 Southfield Rd., Beverly Hills, MI 48025, (248)645-9730 [25864]

Varsity Sports Center Inc., 415 W Wall St., Griffin, GA 30223-2860, (404)228-2738 [24027]

Varta Batteries Inc., 300 Executive Blvd., Elmsford, NY 10523, (914)592-2500 [9535]

Vass U.S.A.; Joan, 485 7th Ave., No. 301, New York, NY 10018, (212)947-3417 [5459]

Vassilaros and Sons Inc.; J.A., 29-05 120th St., Flushing, NY 11354, (718)886-4140 [12831]

Vasso Systems, Inc., 159 Cook St., Brooklyn, NY 11206, (718)417-5303 [3388]

Vater Implement Inc., PO Box 749, Enid, OK 73702, (580)237-5051 [1397]

Vaughan and Bushnell Manufacturing, PO Box 390, Hebron, IL 60034-0390, (815)648-2446 [13978]

Vaughan & Bushnell Manufacturing Co., 225 Riverview Ave., Waltham, MA 02454, (781)647-5560 [13979]

Vaughan and Sons Inc., PO Box 17258, San Antonio, TX 78217, (210)352-1300 [8174]

Vaughn Lumber Co.; Emmet, PO Box 1747, Knoxville, TN 37901, (615)577-7577 [8175]

Vaughn Materials Company Inc., PO Box 679, Reno, NV 89504, (702)323-1381 [8176]

Vaughn Meat Packing Company Inc., 2117 Country Club Rd., PO Box 568, Greer, SC 29652, (803)877-0926 [12832]

VB Imports, 1111 Cedar Swamp Rd., Glen Head, NY 11545-2121, (516)626-9200 [1498]

VC Glass Carpet Co., 801 Logan St., Louisville, KY 40204, (502)584-5324 [10275]

VCI Home Video, 11333 E 60th Pl., Tulsa, OK 74146, (918)254-6337 [25498]

Veach Oil Co., Hwy. 37 & 146 W, Vienna, IL 62995, (618)658-2581 [22771]

Veazey Suppliers Inc., 214 Edwards Ave., Harahan, LA 70123-4215, (504)733-5234 [25499]

Veb Plastics Inc., 10748-A Tucker St., Beltsville, MD 20705, (301)937-5530 [23046]

VEC Inc., PO Box 3110, Grand Rapids, MI 49501-3110, (616)452-1426 [12833]

Vector Engineering Inc., 12438 Loma Rica Dr., Ste. C, Grass Valley, CA 95945, (530)272-2448 [24451]

Vector Industries Inc., 6701 90th Ave. N, Pinellas Park, FL 33782-4596, (813)541-6631 [8177]

Vector Security Systems Inc., 950 Windham Ct., Ste. 1, Boardman, OH 44512, (330)726-9841 [24657]

Vectra Fitness Inc., 15135 NE 90th St., Redmond, WA 98052, (425)867-1500 [24028]

Veeco Process Metrology, 2650 E Elvira Rd., Tucson, AZ 85706, (520)741-1297 [16601]

Veetronix Inc., 1311 West Pacific, PO Box 480, Lexington, NE 68850, (308)324-6661 [5805]

Vega Enterprises Inc., PO Box 4247, Las Vegas, NV 89127-0247, (702)642-8342 [26369]

Vegetarian Resource Group, PO Box 1463, Baltimore, MD 21203, (410)366-8343 [4258]

Vehicle Services/Commercial Truck & Van Equipment, Baltimore Pike & Marple Ave., Clifton Heights, PA 19018, (610)259-2260 [3389]

Vehicle Vibres Inc., 528 Barses, Hyannis, MA 02601-2760, (508)775-3623 [25500]

Vehrs Wine Inc., 1702 Rankin St., Missoula, MT 59802-1630, (406)543-6634 [2100]

Velda Farms, 5200 S Manhattan Ave., Tampa, FL 33611, (813)837-8555 [12834]

Vellano Brothers Inc., 7 Hemlock St., Latham, NY 12110, (518)785-5537 [25865]

Vena Inc.; John, 3301 S Galloway St., Unit 77, Philadelphia, PA 19148, (215)336-0766 [12835]

Vena Tech Corp., 910 University Pl., Ste. 8204, Evanston, IL 60201-3121, (847)866-1833 [25866]

Venada Aviation Inc., 685 Trade Center Dr., Las Vegas, NV 89119-3712, (702)897-1600 [167]

Vendor Supply of America Inc., PO Box 17387, Denver, CO 80217, (303)634-1400 [12836]

Vendor's Supply and Service Inc., 9350 James Ave. S, Bloomington, MN 55431, (612)881-8770 [25867]

Venice Convalescent Aids Medical Supply, 620 Cypress Ave., Venice, FL 34292, (941)485-3366 [19100]

Venture South Distributors, 1640 Kimberly Rd., Twin Falls, ID 83301-7323, (208)733-5705 [2101]

Venture Trading, PO Box 310, Nobleboro, ME 04555-0310 [5460]

Venture Vehicles Inc., 205 Pine St., Contoocook, NH 03229-2602, (603)746-6406 [24029]

Venturian Corp., 1600 2nd St. S, Hopkins, MN 55343, (612)931-2500 [3390]

Venus Knitting Mills Inc., 140 Spring St., Murray Hill, NJ 07974, (908)464-2400 [24030]

Venus Manufacturing Co., 707 E Curry Rd., Tempe, AZ 85281-1912, (602)894-0444 [8178]

Verby Company Inc.; H., 186-14 Jamaica Ave., Jamaica, NY 11423, (718)454-5522 [8179]

VerHalen Inc., PO Box 11968, Green Bay, WI 54307, (920)435-3791 [8180]

Veri-Best Bakers, PO Box 426, La Porte, IN 46352-0426, (219)398-4200 [12837]

Vermillion Elevator Co., PO Box 49, Vermillion, MN 55085, (612)437-4439 [18316]

Vermillion Wholesale Drug Company Inc., PO Box 1239, Opelousas, LA 70571-1239, (318)942-4976 [19689]

Vermont American Tool Co., 800 Woodside Ave., Fountain Inn, SC 29644-2029, (864)862-8000 [13980]

Vermont Flower Exchange, 47 Woodstock Ave., Rutland, VT 05701, (802)775-1836 [14971]

Vermont Hardware Company Inc., 180 Flynn Ave., PO Box 4509, Burlington, VT 05406-4509, (802)864-6835 [25501]

Vermont Optechs, PO Box 69, Charlotte, VT 05445-0069, (802)425-2040 [24452]

Vermont Pet Food & Supply, 2500 Williston Rd., South Burlington, VT 05403, (802)863-5597 [27263]

Vermont Pure Holdings Ltd., PO Box C, Randolph, VT 05060, (802)728-3600 [25047]

Vermont Whey Co., PO Box 2129, Milton, VT 05468, (802)527-7737 [12838]

Vermont Whey Co., PO Box 2129, Georgia, VT 05468-2129, (802)527-7737 [12839]

Vernitron Corp. AST Bearings Div., 115 Main Rd., Montville, NJ 07045, (973)335-2230 [3391]

Vernon Produce Co.; W.R., PO Box 4054, Winston-Salem, NC 27115-4054, (919)725-9741 [12840]

Veronica Foods Co., PO Box 2225, Oakland, CA 94621, (510)535-6833 [12841]

VersaTec, PO Box 2095, Tampa, FL 33601-2095, (813)251-2431 [13268]

Versatile Industrial Products, 1371-4 Church St., Bohemia, NY 11716, (631)567-8866 [18]

Versatile Vehicles, 12461 Rhode Island Ave., Savage, MN 55378, (952)894-1123 [24031]

Versatile Vehicles Inc., 12461 Rhode Island Ave., Savage, MN 55378, (952)894-1123 [24031]

Vertner Smith Co., 2300 Gault Pkwy., Louisville, KY 40233-4174, (502)361-8421 [2102]

Very Fine Resources Inc., 128 Parkville Ave., Brooklyn, NY 11230, (718)438-3191 [12842]

Vesco Oil Corp., PO Box 525, Southfield, MI 48037-0525, (810)557-1600 [22772]

Vestal Press Ltd., 4720 Boston Way, Lanham, MD 20706-4310, (301)797-4872 [4259]

Veterans Supply & Distributing Co., 3225 Caniff Ave., Hamtramck, MI 48212, (313)892-6660 [4723]

Veterinary Companies of America Inc., PO Box 148, Topeka, KS 66601-0148, (785)354-8523 [1398]

Veterinary Medical Supply, 950 Mack Todd Rd., Zebulon, NC 27597-9555, (919)772-3278 [27264]

Vetline Inc., 425 John Deere Dr., Ft. Collins, CO 80524, (970)484-1900 [27265]

Vets International Inc., PO Box 8595, Honolulu, HI 96830-0595, (808)926-2294 [27266]

VGC Corp., 5701 NW 94th Ave., Tamarac, FL 33321, (954)722-3000 [25670]

V.H. Associates Inc., PO Box 380, Cerro Gordo, IL 61818, (217)677-2131 [18317]

VHA Supply Co., 220 E Los Colinas, Irving, TX 75039, (972)830-0000 [19101]

Via West Interface Inc., 1228 E Prince Rd., Tucson, AZ 85719, (520)293-0771 [6850]

ViaGrafix Corp., 1 American Way, Pryor, OK 74361, (918)825-4844 [6851]

Viam Manufacturing Inc., 9440 Norwalk Blvd., Santa Fe Springs, CA 90670, (310)695-0651 [3392]

Vibrint Corp., 4185 Heather Way, Cumming, GA 30041-8925, (404)887-4551 [5461]

Vic Supply Co., 358 Romans Rd., Elmhurst, IL 60126, (708)833-0033 [4547]

Vickers International, PO Box 6187, Kokomo, IN 46904, (765)453-2419 [5462]

Vicki Lane Design, 303 S 5th, Springfield, OR 97477-7507, (541)726-0397 [13467]

Victor Business Systems Inc., 5300 E Raines Rd., Memphis, TN 38118, (901)363-6201 [21337]

Victor Machinery Exchange Inc., 251 Centre St., New York, NY 10013-3214, (212)226-3494 [17252]

Victor Sports, PO Box 208, Hinsdale, IL 60522, (708)352-1580 [24032]

Victorian Pearl, 1010 Waverly St., Eugene, OR 97401-5234, (541)343-1347 [26704]

Victor's House of Music, 762 Rt. 17 N, Paramus, NJ 07652, (201)444-9800 [25502]

Victory International Productions, 6191 Trinette Ave., Garden Grove, CA 92845-2744, (562)598-7208 [25503]

Victory Packaging, 800 Junction Ave., Plymouth, MI 48170, (734)459-2000 [21985]

Victory Seafood Processors Inc., 208 W Elina St., Abbeville, LA 70510, (318)893-9029 [12843]

Victory White Metal Co., 6100 Roland Ave., Cleveland, OH 44127, (216)271-1400 [17253]

Victs Computers Inc., 1245 Spacepark Way, Mountain View, CA 94043, (650)960-6811 [6852]

VID COM Distributing, 7622 Wornall, Kansas City, MO 64114, (816)363-3737 [9536]

VID COM Distributing, 7622 Wornall, Kansas City, MO 64114, (816)363-3737 [9537]

Vida Paint & Supply Co., PO Box 2706, Morgan City, LA 70380, (504)385-2884 [18629]

Vida Paint & Supply Co., 100 Bond St., Houma, LA 70360, (504)868-1005 [18630]

Vidalia Naval Stores Co., PO Box 1659, Vidalia, GA 30474, (912)537-8964 [8181]

Video Action, 708 W 1st St., Los Angeles, CA 90012, (213)687-8262 [25504]

Video Aided Instruction, Inc., 182 Village Rd., Roslyn Heights, NY 11577, (516)621-0012 [25494]

Video Aided Instruction Inc., 182 Village Rd., Roslyn Heights, NY 11577, (516)621-0012 [15357]

Video Communications, Inc., 11333 E 60th Pl., Tulsa, OK 74146, (918)254-6337 [25498]

Video Hi-Teck Inc., 303 Sunnyside Blvd., Plainview, NY 11803, (516)785-1200 [25505]

Video Products Distributors, 5 Burlington Sq., Fl. 3, Burlington, VT 05401, (802)860-0040 [9538]

Video Sentry Corp., 350 Wireless Blvd., Hauppauge, NY 11788, (516)232-2100 [24658]

Videomedia Inc., 175 Lewis Rd., No. 23, San Jose, CA 95111, (408)227-9977 [25506]

VideoTape Distributors Inc., 423 W 55th St., 3rd Fl., New York, NY 10019, (212)581-7111 [25507]

Vie Americas Inc., PO Box 958, Glastonbury, CT 06033, (860)659-1397 [4548]

Vierk Industrial Products, 3521 Coleman Ct., PO Box 1668, Lafayette, IN 47902, (765)447-0458 [23432]

Vihon Associates, 3620 Dekalb T Pkwy., Ste. 2013, Atlanta, GA 30340, (404)457-2970 [15358]

Viking, 295 E Industrial Park Dr., Manchester, NH 03109, (603)668-4545 [8182]

Viking Acoustical Corp., 21480 Heath Ave., Lakeville, MN 55044-9105, (612)469-3405 [21338]

Viking Cue Manufacturing, Inc., 2710 Syene Rd., Madison, WI 53713-3202, (608)271-5155 [24033]

Viking Distributing Company Inc., 1225 6th St., San Francisco, CA 94107, (415)626-3750 [17254]

Viking Distributing Company Inc., 685 Market St., Medford, OR 97504-6125, (541)773-4928 [15359]

Viking Distributors Inc., 1508 28th St., Gulfport, MS 39501, (228)868-1896 [10276]

Viking Formed Products, 23925 Reedy Dr., Elkhart, IN 46514, (219)262-9250 [17255]

Viking Materials Inc., 3225 Como Ave. SE, Minneapolis, MN 55414, (612)617-5800 [20472]

Viking Office Products Inc., 950 W 190th St., Gardena, CA 90248, (310)225-4500 [21339]

Viking Sewing Machines Inc., 31000 Viking Pkwy., Westlake, OH 44145, (440)808-6550 [26241]

Viking Supply Company Inc., 6319 Northwest Hwy., Chicago, IL 60631-1669, (773)775-5797 [9539]

Viking Technology Inc., 115 Industrial Park Rd., Lincolnton, NC 28092, (704)735-3754 [5463]

Viking Traders, Inc., 5 Cold Hill Rd. S, Ste. 18, Mendham, NJ 07945, (973)543-3211 [19102]

Viking Woodcrafts, Inc., 1317 8th St. SE, Waseca, MN 56093, (507)835-8043 [21599]

Viles and Associates Inc., 444 W 21st St., Tempe, AZ 85282, (602)437-0616 [12844]

Villa Lighting Supply Company Inc., 1218 S Vandeventer, St. Louis, MO 63110, (314)531-2600 [9540]

Villafane Inc.; Rene Ortiz, PO Box 2562, San Juan, PR 00902, (787)793-7141 [8183]

Village Electronics, PO Box 153, Southwest Harbor, ME 04679-0153, (207)244-7227 [25508]

Village Products, 10 Lamy Dr., Goffstown, NH 03045, (603)645-6060 [14755]

Villarreal Electric Company Inc., 1400 Lincoln St., PO Box 760, Laredo, TX 78040, (956)722-2471 [9541]

VillaWare Manufacturing Co., 1420 E 36th St., Cleveland, OH 44114, (216)391-6650 [15360]

Villeroy and Boch Tableware Ltd., 5 Vaughn Dr., Ste. 303, Princeton, NJ 08540, (609)734-7800 [15696]

Vilrore Foods Company Inc., 8220 San Lorenzo St., Laredo, TX 78041, (956)726-3633 [12845]

Vimco Concrete Accessories Inc., 300 Hansen Access Rd., King of Prussia, PA 19406, (215)768-0500 [8184]

Vina & Son Meat Distributors, 2020 NW 22nd St., Miami, FL 33142-7334, (305)545-6500 [12846]

Vincent Implements Inc., 8258 Hwy 45, Martin, TN 38237, (901)587-3824 [1399]

Vincent Jobbing Co., PO Box 144, Martin, TN 38237-0144, (901)587-2334 [24885]

Vincent Metal Goods, 455 85th Ave. NW, Minneapolis, MN 55433, (612)717-9000 [20473]

Vincent Metal Goods, PO Box 1165, Pittsburgh, PA 15230, (412)771-2600 [27034]

Vine Associates Inc.; George, 2380 Franklin Rd., Bloomfield Hills, MI 48302-0332, (248)858-2440 [5464]

Vine Trading Company, PO Box 537, Canaan, NH 03741-0537, (603)844-9613 [6853]

Vineland Electric CED/Supply, Inc., 301 Chestnut Ave., Vineland, NJ 08360-9549, (609)691-1267 [9542]

Vinson Supply Co., PO Box 702440, Tulsa, OK 74170-2440, (918)481-8770 [23433]

Vint & Associates; Keith, 15585 Graham St., Huntington Beach, CA 92649, (714)898-2318 [24034]

Vintage House Merchants, 1090 A Bailey Hill Rd., Eugene, OR 97402, (541)485-6868 [2103]

Vintage House Merchants, Inc., 624 NE Everett, Portland, OR 97232, (503)231-1020 [2104]

Vintage Petroleum Inc., 110 W 7th St., #2300, Tulsa, OK 74119-1029, (918)592-0101 [22773]

Vintage Sales Stables Inc., 3451 Lincoln Hwy. E, Paradise, PA 17562-9621, (717)768-8204 [18318]

Vintwood International Ltd., 40 Prospect St., Huntington, NY 11743, (516)424-9777 [2105]

V.I.P. Discount Auto Center, 12 Lexington St., Lewiston, ME 04240, (207)784-5423 [3393]

VIP Formal Wear Inc., 3801 S Wilmington St., Raleigh, NC 27603-3569, (919)772-7215 [5465]

VIP Sales Company Inc., 6116 S Memorial Dr., Tulsa, OK 74133, (918)252-5791 [12847]

Virginia Beach Beverages, 5700 Ward Ave., Virginia Beach, VA 23455, (757)464-1771 [25048]

Virginia Carolina Tools Inc., PO Box 3488, West Columbia, SC 29169, (803)791-8691 [16602]

Virginia City Furniture Inc., 3333 N Carson St., Carson City, NV 89706-0155, (702)883-3333 [13269]

Virginia Construction Supply Inc., PO Box 20368, Roanoke, VA 24018, (540)776-0040 [8185]

Virginia Food Service Group, PO Box 28010, Richmond, VA 23228, (804)266-0300 [12848]

Virginia Hardwood Co., 818 E Hammond Ln., Phoenix, AZ 85034, (602)252-6818 [10277]

Virginia Hardwood Co., PO Box 90, Monrovia, CA 91016, (626)358-4594 [8186]

Virginia Hardwood Co., 241 Lombard, Oxnard, CA 93030, (805)988-6017 [10278]

Virginia Hardwood Co., 8533 Production Ave., San Diego, CA 92121, (619)271-6890 [10279]

Virginia Hardwood Co., 1000 W Foothill Blvd., Azusa, CA 91702, (626)815-0540 [10280]

Virginia Imports, 881 S Pickett St., Alexandria, VA 22304, (703)823-1230 [2106]

Virginia Industrial Cleaners and Equipment Co., PO Box 6248, Roanoke, VA 24017-0248, (540)366-8311 [4724]

Virginia Materials, 3306 Peterson St., Norfolk, VA 23509, (757)855-0155 [16603]

Virginia Materials and Supplies, Inc., 3306 Peterson St., Norfolk, VA 23509, (757)855-0155 [16603]

Virginia Tile Co., 24404 Indoplex Cir., Farmington Hills, MI 48335-2526, (248)476-7850 [10281]

Virginia Tile Co., 6575 19 Mile Rd., Sterling Heights, MI 48314-2116 [10282]

Virginia Welding Supply Company Inc., PO Box 1268, Charleston, WV 25325, (304)346-0875 [17256]

Virginia West Uniforms Inc., 6601 Maccorkle Ave. SE, Charleston, WV 25304-2923, (304)925-0305 [5466]

Virginia Wholesale Co., 70 Commonwealth Ave., Bristol, VA 24201-3802, (540)669-4181 [12849]

Virgs Inc., 116 S Main St., Ishpeming, MI 49849-1820, (906)486-6671 [24886]

Vision Broadcasting Network, 1017 New York Ave., Alamogordo, NM 88310-6921, (505)437-6363 [22913]

Vision Plastic Wholesale, 3500 La Touche No. 110, Anchorage, AK 99508, (907)562-2845 [19690]

Vision Plastics USA, Inc., 3500 La Touche No. 110, Anchorage, AK 99508, (907)562-2845 [19690]

Vision Video, 2030 Wentz Church Rd., Box 540, Worcester, PA 19490, (610)584-1893 [25509]

Vista Bakery, Inc., PO Box 888, Burlington, IA 52601, (319)754-6551 [12850]

Vista Laboratories Inc., 3711 E Atlanta Ave., Phoenix, AZ 85040-2960, (602)257-8555 [19691]

Vista Manufacturing, 52864 Lillian St., Elkhart, IN 46514, (219)264-0711 [9543]

Vista Oil Co., PO Box 5127, McAllen, TX 78502, (210)381-0976 [22774]

Vista Trading Corp., 16800 Greenspoint Park Dr., Ste. 225 N, Houston, TX 77060, (281)876-8110 [18319]

Vistabooks Publishing, 0637 Blue Ridge Rd., Silverthorne, CO 80498, (970)468-7673 [4260]

Visual Aids Electronics, 202 Perry Pkwy., Ste. 5, Gaithersburg, MD 20877-2172, (301)680-8400 [5806]

Vita-Mix Corp., 8615 Usher Rd., Cleveland, OH 44138, (440)235-4840 [15361]

Vita-Plate Battery, Inc., PO Box 727, Port Clinton, OH 43452 [18631]

Vita Plus Corp., PO Box 259126, Madison, WI 53725-9126, (608)256-1988 [1400]

Vita Plus Industries Inc., 953 E Sahara Ave., Las Vegas, NV 89104, (702)733-8805 [14271]

Vital Image Technology Inc., 450 Portage Tr., Cuyahoga Falls, OH 44221, (330)940-3200 [6854]

Vitali Import Company Inc., 13020 Whittier Blvd., PO Box 4218, Whittier, CA 90602-3045 [25510]

Vitality Distributiors Inc., 940 NW 51st Pl., Ft. Lauderdale, FL 33309-3103, (954)771-0445 [14272]

Vitality Foodservice Inc., 400 N Tampa St., Ste. 1700, Tampa, FL 33602-4716, (813)783-6200 [25049]

The Vitamin Shoppe, 4700 Westside Ave., North Bergen, NJ 07047, (201)866-7711 [14273]

Vitamin Specialties Corp., 8200 Ogontz Ave., Wyncote, PA 19095, (215)885-3800 [14274]

Vitco Steel Supply Corp., PO Box 220, Posen, IL 60469, (708)388-8300 [20474]

Vitech America Inc., 2190 Nw 89 Pl., Miami, FL 33172-2419, (305)477-1161 [6855]

Vitex Foods Inc., 1821 E 48th Pl., Los Angeles, CA 90058, (213)234-4400 [12851]

Vitner Company Inc.; C.J., 4202 W 45th St., Chicago, IL 60632, (312)523-7900 [12852]

Vitra Seating Inc., 6560 Stonegate Dr., Allentown, PA 18106-9242, (215)391-9780 [21340]

Vitramon Inc., PO Box 544, Bridgeport, CT 06601, (203)268-6261 [9544]

Vitrano Co.; Tony, Maryland Wholesale Product Market, Jessup, MD 20794, (410)799-7444 [12853]

Vitriesse Glass Studio, 4 Andover Rd., PO Box 23, Weston, VT 05161, (802)824-6634 [17647]

Vitto Sheet Metal Inc.; Nicholas, 3426 Burnet Ave., Syracuse, NY 13206, (315)463-5550 [20475]

Vitus Electric Supply Co., PO Box 2789, Eugene, OR 97402-0316, (541)484-6333 [9545]

Viva Handbags Inc., 1803 S Hope St., Los Angeles, CA 90015, (213)748-3932 [18438]

Viva Vino Import Corp., 1021 1/2 Saville Ave., Eddystone, PA 19022, (215)872-1500 [2107]

Vivax Medical Corp., 139 Center St., PO Box 1400, Bristol, CT 06010, (860)589-8200 [19103]

Vivian Corp., PO Box 1266, Kingston, PA 18704, (717)288-0492 [8187]

Vivitar Corp., PO Box 2559, Newbury Park, CA 91319-8559, (805)498-7008 [22914]

Vlcek Corp.; Jerry K., 3760 Black Forest Ln., Yorba Linda, CA 92886, (714)970-1285 [16604]

VLP Holding Co., PO Box 4915, Kansas City, MO 64120, (816)241-9290 [8188]

VMC Inc., 1901 Oakcrest Ave., Ste. 10, St. Paul, MN 55113-2617, (612)636-9649 [24035]

VMC/USA, 7618 Slate Ridge Blvd., Reynoldsburg, OH 43068, (614)759-9800 [15697]

VMS Inc., 17600 S Williams St., No. 6, Thornton, IL 60476-1077, (708)877-2814 [4261]

VNA of Rhode Island Inc., 157 Waterman St., Providence, RI 02906-3126, (401)444-9770 [19104]

Vocational Marketing Services, 17600 S Williams St., No. 6, Thornton, IL 60476-1077, (708)877-2814 [4261]

Vodavi Technology Inc., 8300 E Raintree Dr., Scottsdale, AZ 85260, (480)443-6000 [9546]

Voell Machinery Company Inc., PO Box 2103, Waukesha, WI 53187, (262)786-6640 [16605]

Vogann Business Machines, 907 Willow Way, Deming, NM 88030-4446, (505)546-9183 [21341]

Vogel Tool & Die Corp., 1825 N 32nd, Stone Park, IL 60165-1003, (708)345-0160 [16606]

Vogel Tool and Die Corp., 1825 N 32nd, Stone Park, IL 60165-1003, (708)345-0160 [17257]

Vogue Bedding Co., 8937 National Blvd., Los Angeles, CA 90034, (213)870-5800 [13270]

Vogue Cuisine Inc., 3710 Grandview Blvd., Los Angeles, CA 90066-3110, (310)391-1053 [12854]

Voice It Worldwide Inc., 2643 Midpoint Dr.Ste. A, Ft. Collins, CO 80525, (970)221-1705 [6856]

VoiceWorld Inc., 11201 N 70th St., Scottsdale, AZ 85254, (480)922-5500 [5807]

Volcano Flowers & Greenery, PO Box 966, Volcano, HI 96785, (808)967-7450 [14972]

Volcano Press, Inc., PO Box 270, Volcano, CA 95689-0270, (209)296-3445 [4262]

Volcano Press Inc., PO Box 270, Volcano, CA 95689-0270, (209)296-3445 [4263]

Volkswagen of America Inc., 3800 Hamlin Rd., Auburn Hills, MI 48326, (313)340-5000 [20743]

Volkswagen of America Inc. Industrial Engine Div., 420 Barclay Blvd., Lincolnshire, IL 60069, (847)634-6000 [20744]

Volland Electric Equipment Corp., 75 Innsbruck Dr., Buffalo, NY 14227, (716)656-9900 [16607]

Voltgard, 205 Huehl Rd., Northbrook, IL 60062, (847)291-1600 [17153]

Volunteer Janitorial Supply Co., 2136 Hollywood Dr., Jackson, TN 38305-4323, (901)668-4005 [24036]

Volunteer Produce Co., 2015 Grand Ave., Knoxville, TN 37916-1207, (423)525-7078 [12855]

Volunteer Sales Co., PO Box 22087, Chattanooga, TN 37422-2087, (615)821-3575 [12856]

Volvo Cars of North America Inc., PO Box 913, Rockleigh, NJ 07647, (201)768-7300 [20745]

Volz Truck Equipment, Inc.; L.W., 1704 Rockwell Rd., Abington, PA 19001, (215)659-4164 [3394]

Von Housen Motors Inc., 1810 Howe Ave., Sacramento, CA 95825, (916)924-8000 [20746]

Voorhees Company Inc.; The Bill, 700 8th Ave. S, Nashville, TN 37203, (615)242-4481 [14756]

Voorhies Supply Company Inc., 401 W St. Peter St., New Iberia, LA 70560, (318)364-2431 [16608]

Vorberger Group Ltd., 409 Broad St., Sewickley, PA 15143, (412)741-1634 [20476]

Vorpahl, Inc.; W.A., PO Box 12175, Green Bay, WI 54307, (920)497-7200 [24659]

Vorys Brothers Inc., 834 W 3rd Ave., Columbus, OH 43212, (614)294-4701 [14757]

Voss Equipment Inc., 15241 Commercial Ave., Harvey, IL 60426, (708)596-7000 [16609]

Votech, Inc., 1675 D Holmes Rd., Elgin, IL 60123, (847)468-6300 [4505]

Voto Manufacturing Sales Company Inc., 500 N 3rd St., Steubenville, OH 43952, (740)282-3621 [17258]

Vowles Farm Fresh Foods, PO Box 2868, El Cajon, CA 92021, (619)448-2101 [12857]

Voyageur Press, Inc., 123 N 2nd St., PO Box 338, Stillwater, MN 55082, (612)430-2210 [4264]

Vreeken Enterprises Inc., 17151 SE Petrovitsky Rd., Renton, WA 98058-9610, (425)255-4545 [24204]

Vreeken Enterprises Inc., 17151 SE Petrovitsky Rd., Renton, WA 98058-9610, (425)255-4545 [24258]

VSS Inc., PO Box 2151, Manassas, VA 20108-0823 [6857]

V.T. Petroleum, 412 Metz Rd., King City, CA 93930, (408)385-4872 [22775]

Vuitton North America Inc.; Louis, 130 E 59th St., 10th Fl., New York, NY 10022, (212)572-9700 [18439]

VVP America Inc., 965 Ridgelake Blvd., Memphis, TN 38120, (901)767-7111 [15698]

VWR Scientific Products, 3745 Bayshore Blvd., Brisbane, CA 94005, (415)468-7150 [24453]

VWR Scientific Products Corp., 1310 Goshen Pkwy., West Chester, PA 19380, (610)431-1700 [24454]

VWR Scientific Products Corp., 1310 Goshen Pkwy., West Chester, PA 19380, (610)431-1700 [26242]

VWS Inc., 31000 Viking Pkwy., Westlake, OH 44145, (440)808-6550 [26241]

VWS Inc., 31000 Viking Pky., Cleveland, OH 44145-1019, (216)252-3300 [25511]

VZ Ltd., 945 W Wilshire, Oklahoma City, OK 73116, (405)843-8886 [19692]

W-B Supply Co., PO Drawer 2479, Pampa, TX 79066-2479, (806)669-1103 [22776]

W C L Co., PO Box 3588, La Puente, CA 91744-0588, (626)968-5523 [13981]

A and W Foods Inc., 16625 Granite Rd., Maple Heights, OH 44137, (216)662-8000 [12478]

W-L Research Inc., 8701 W US Hwy. 14, Evansville, WI 53536-8752, (608)882-4100 [18320]

W-P Milling Company Inc., 1119 S Cherokee St., Muskogee, OK 74402, (918)682-3388 [1401]

W & W Body, 219 Industrial Park South Blvd., Hwy. 31 S, Southside Industrial Park, Florence, SC 29505, (803)661-6339 [3395]

Wabash Elevator Co., PO Box 338, Uniontown, KY 42461, (502)822-4241 [18321]

Wabash Independent Oil Co., 707 E Fayette Ave., Effingham, IL 62401, (217)342-9755 [4725]

Wabash Power Equipment Co., 444 Carpenter, Wheeling, IL 60090, (847)541-5600 [22777]

Wabash Power Equipment Co., 444 Carpenter St., Wheeling, IL 60090, (847)541-5600 [9547]

Wabash Valley Service Co., 909 N Court St., Grayville, IL 62844, (618)375-2311 [1402]

W.A.C. Lighting, 615 South St., Garden City, NY 11530 [9548]

Wacker Chemical Corp., 460 McLaws Cir., Ste. 240, Williamsburg, VA 23185, (757)253-5663 [9549]

Wacker Chemicals (USA) Inc., 3301 Sutton Rd., Adrian, MI 49221-9397, (517)264-8791 [4549]

Waco Inc., PO Box 836, Sandston, VA 23150-0836, (804)222-8440 [20477]

Waco Meat Service Inc., PO Box 7249, Waco, TX 76714-7249, (817)772-5644 [12858]

Waco Sales Inc., 3603 N Main St., Wayland, MI 49348-1001, (616)792-2291 [24037]

WACO Scaffolding and Equipment Co., PO Box 318028, Cleveland, OH 44131-8028, (216)749-8900 [8189]

Wacom Technology Corp., 1311 SE Cardinal Ct., Vancouver, WA 98683, (360)750-8882 [25868]

Waddington Dairy, PO Box 550, Alloway, NJ 08001-0550, (609)935-2333 [12859]

Waddington/Richman Inc., PO Box 229, Woodstown, NJ 08098-0229, (609)769-0350 [12860]

Wade and Co.; R.M., PO Box 23666, Portland, OR 97223, (503)641-1865 [1403]

Wade Distributors, Inc., 1150 N Beltline Hwy., Mobile, AL 36617-1504, (205)476-1140 [10283]

Wade Distributors Inc., 1510 28th St., Gulfport, MS 39501, (228)822-2550 [8190]

Wades Dairy Inc., 1316 Barnum Ave., Bridgeport, CT 06610-2825, (203)579-9233 [12861]

Waechtersbach U.S.A., 4201 NE 34th St., Kansas City, MO 64117, (816)455-3800 [15699]

WAFAB International, 208 Lindbergh Ave., Livermore, CA 94550, (925)455-5252 [16610]

Waffle Book Co.; O.G., 897 13th St., PO Box 586, Marion, IA 52302, (319)373-1832 [4265]

Waggener Lumber Co., PO Box 430159, St. Louis, MO 63143-0259, (314)937-3618 [8191]

Wagman and Co.; N., 1450 Broadway, Ste. 3900, New York, NY 10018, (212)391-1700 [5467]

Wagner Appliance Parts Inc., 1840 E Race St., Allentown, PA 18103-9584, (215)264-0681 [15362]

Wagner Candy Co., 118 Joe Clifton Dr., Paducah, KY 42002, (502)442-6301 [12862]

Wagner-Electric of Fort Wayne Inc., 3610 N Clinton St., Ft. Wayne, IN 46805, (219)484-5532 [9550]

Wagner Enterprises Inc., 6015 Huntington Ct. NE, Cedar Rapids, IA 52402-1272, (319)393-3843 [5468]

Wagner Hardware Co., PO Box 607, Mansfield, OH 44901, (419)522-7811 [13982]

Wagner Hydraulic Equipment Co., 10528 Venice Blvd., Culver City, CA 90232-3308, (562)272-2091 [16611]

Wagner Livestock Auction, PO Box 548, Wagner, SD 57380-0548, (605)384-5551 [18322]

Wagner Mills Inc., PO Box 545, Schuyler, NE 68661, (402)352-2471 [18323]

Wagner Mills Inc., PO Box 545, Schuyler, NE 68661, (402)352-2471 [12863]

Wagner-Smith Co., PO Box 672, Dayton, OH 45401, (937)298-7481 [17259]

Wagner and Sons Inc.; John, 900 Jacksonville Rd., Ivyland, PA 18974-1778, (215)674-5000 [12864]

Wagners, 601 W Cook St., Wendell, NC 27591, (919)365-6669 [13468]

Wagners Formal Wear of Washington, PO Box 3851, Spokane, WA 99220-3851, (509)534-4481 [5469]

Wahl & Wahl of Iowa, Inc., 2711 Grand Ave., Des Moines, IA 50312, (515)244-5545 [21342]

Wahl and Wahl of Iowa Inc., 2711 Grand Ave., Des Moines, IA 50312, (515)244-5545 [21342]

Wahlborg-McCreary Inc., PO Box 920780, Houston, TX 77292, (713)684-0000 [3396]

Wahler Brothers, 2549 N Halsted, Chicago, IL 60614, (773)248-1349 [13983]

Waikiki Trader Corp., 99-061 Koaha Way, Aiea, HI 96701, (808)487-3663 [5470]

Wainoco Oil Corp., 10000 Memorial Dr., No. 600, Houston, TX 77024-3411, (713)688-9600 [22778]

The Wakanta Group, PO Box 144, Still River, MA 01467-0144, (978)772-3432 [6858]

Wakefern Food Corp., 600 York St., Elizabeth, NJ 07207, (908)527-3300 [12865]

Wakefern Food Corp., 600 York St., Elizabeth, NJ 07207, (908)527-3300 [12866]

Wakefield Oil Co., 311 S Virginia Ave., Roswell, NM 88201, (505)622-4160 [22779]

Wakely; Austin B., 611 Broad St., Altavista, VA 24517-1829, (804)369-4719 [6859]

Wal-Mart Stores Inc., 702 SW 8th St., Bentonville, AR 72716, (501)273-4000 [15700]

Walach Leather Splitting, 22 Pierpont St., Peabody, MA 01960-5663, (978)531-2040 [18440]

Walco International Inc., 520 S Main St., Grapevine, TX 76051, (817)601-6000 [27267]

Walco International Inc. Cody Div., PO Box 223, Cody, NE 69211, (402)823-4241 [1404]

Walczak Lumber Inc., PO Box 340, Clifford, PA 18413, (717)222-9651 [8192]

Waldeck Jewelers, 9817 Acoma Rd. SE, Albuquerque, NM 87123-3301, (505)299-2227 [17648]

Waldner Company Inc.; D., 125 Rte. 110, Farmingdale, NY 11735, (631)844-9300 [21343]

Waldo Brothers Co., 202 Southampton St., Boston, MA 02118, (617)445-3000 [8193]

Waldor Pump and Equipment, 9700 Humboldt Ave. S, Minneapolis, MN 55431, (612)884-5394 [25869]

Waldor Pump and Equipment, 9700 Humboldt Ave. S, Minneapolis, MN 55431, (612)884-5394 [23434]

Walgreen Co., 200 Wilmot Rd., Deerfield, IL 60015, (847)940-2500 [14275]

Waliga Imports and Sales Inc., 1467 Atwood Ave., Johnston, RI 02919-7704, (401)272-6777 [17649]

Walk Corp.; Benjamin, 511 Rte. 125, PO Box 627, Barrington, NH 03825-0627, (603)664-2400 [24887]

Walk Thru the Bible Ministries Inc., 61 Perimeter Park, PO Box 80587, Atlanta, GA 30366, (404)458-9300 [4266]

Walke Co.; Henry, 1415 E Bessemer Ave., Greensboro, NC 27405-7111, (919)275-9511 [17260]

Walker and Associates Inc., PO Box 1029, Welcome, NC 27374, (704)731-6391 [9551]

Walker and Associates Inc. (Welcome, North Carolina), 7129 Old Highway 52 N, Welcome, NC 27374, (336)731-6391 [5808]

Walker and Co., 435 Hudson St., New York, NY 10014-3941, (212)727-8300 [4267]

Walker Company, Inc.; J.F., 1180 58th Street, Wyoming, MI 49509, (616)261-6600 [12867]

Walker Co.; James, 7109 Industrial Rd., Baltimore, MD 21208, (410)486-3950 [17261]

Walker Component Group, 420 E 58th Ave., Denver, CO 80216, (303)292-5537 [9552]

Walker Distributors Inc., 413 W Chatham St., Cary, NC 27511, (919)467-1673 [12868]

Walker Distributors Inc.; Joe, 3522 SW 42nd Ave., Gainesville, FL 32608, (352)376-6524 [12869]

Walker Group Inc., PO Box 1029, Welcome, NC 27374, (336)731-6391 [9553]

Walker Inc.; M.S., 20 3rd Ave., Somerville, MA 02143, (617)776-6700 [2108]

Walker Machinery Co.; Cecil I., PO Box 2427, Charleston, WV 25329, (304)949-6400 [1405]

Walker River Pute Tribal Council, PO Box 220, Schurz, NV 89427-0220, (702)773-2306 [18324]

Walker and Son Inc.; P.G., PO Box 762, Springfield, MO 65801-0762, (417)862-1745 [17262]

Walker Vacuum Supply, 1400 S Van Buren St., Enid, OK 73703-7853, (580)234-1712 [15363]

Walker and Zanger Inc., 31 Warren Pl., Mt. Vernon, NY 10550-4527, (914)667-1600 [13271]

Walla Walla Farmers Co-op Inc., PO Box 928, WalLa Walla, WA 99362, (509)525-6690 [1406]

Walla Walla Grain Growers, Inc., PO Box 310, Walla Walla, WA 99362, (509)525-6510 [18144]

Wallace & Associates, 20 Fieldwood Pl., Newnan, GA 30263-1364, (404)251-5281 [24038]

Wallace Coast Machinery Co., 5225 7th St. E, Tacoma, WA 98424, (253)922-7433 [16612]

Wallace Company Inc., PO Box 1492, Houston, TX 77251-1492, (713)675-2661 [23435]

Wallace County Cooperative Equity Exchange, PO Box 280, Sharon Springs, KS 67758, (785)852-4241 [1407]

Wallace Grain Company Inc., PO Box 109, Sheridan, IN 46069-0109, (317)758-4434 [1408]

Wallace Hardware Co., PO Box 687, Morristown, TN 37815, (615)586-5650 [1409]

Wallace Inc.; Gary L., 12012 Manchester Rd., St. Louis, MO 63131, (314)822-8420 [25870]

Wallace Oil Co., 5370 Oakdale Rd., Smyrna, GA 30082, (404)799-9400 [22780]

Wallace Opticians Inc., 3040 Vine St., Lansing, MI 48912-4623, (517)332-8628 [19693]

Wallace Pump and Supply Company Inc., PO Box 157, Brundidge, AL 36010, (205)735-2338 [23436]

Wallace Sportswear, 460 Veterans Dr., Burlington, NJ 08016-3394, (609)387-3625 [5471]

Wallace Supply Co., PO Box 829, Vineland, NJ 08360, (609)692-4800 [23437]

Wallace's Old Fashion Skins Inc., 1512 McCurdy Rd., Florence, SC 29506, (803)665-5607 [12870]

Wallach's Poultry Farms, PO Box 144, Toms River, NJ 08754, (732)349-1694 [12871]

Wallbank Springs Inc.; P.J., 2121 Beard St., Port Huron, MI 48060, (810)987-2992 [13984]

Wallbaum Distributing; Dan, PO Box 199, Yankton, SD 57078-0199, (605)665-2436 [2109]

Wallcoverings, Ltd., 3654 Waialae Ave., Honolulu, HI 96816, (808)734-2177 [21600]

Wallock; John M., 616 Warwick Rd., Winchester, NH 03470, (603)239-8882 [3397]

Wallpaper Hawaii, Ltd., 3160 Waialae Ave., Honolulu, HI 96816, (808)735-2861 [21601]

Wallwork Inc.; W.W., PO Box 1819, Fargo, ND 58107, (701)476-7000 [20747]

Walman Optical Co., 801 12th Ave. N, Minneapolis, MN 55411, (612)520-6000 [19694]

Walmsley Marine Inc., 656 Metacom Ave., Warren, RI 02885-2316, (401)245-9069 [24039]

Walpeco, 1100 S 56th Ave., Hollywood, FL 33023, (954)983-4511 [1410]

Walsh Bros., PO Box 1711, Phoenix, AZ 85001, (602)252-6971 [21344]

Walsh Distribution Inc., 1702 Hampton Rd., Texarkana, TX 75503, (903)255-2300 [14276]

Walsh Healthcare Solutions, 1702 Hampton Rd., Texarkana, TX 75503, (903)255-2300 [14276]

Walston Co.; William H., 8216 Grey Eagle Dr., Upper Marlboro, MD 20772-2602, (301)967-3232 [8194]

Walters Cooperative Elevators Association, PO Box 7, Walters, OK 73572, (405)875-3344 [1411]

Walters Inc.; Dave, PO Box 946, Bemidji, MN 56601, (218)751-5655 [20748]

Walter's Meat Co., 8901 Wattsburg Rd., Erie, PA 16509, (814)825-4857 [12872]

Walters Optical Inc.; Wendel, 1624 Linwood Blvd., Oklahoma City, OK 73106-5026, (405)235-5301 [19695]

Walters Wholesale Electric Co., 2825 Temple Ave., Long Beach, CA 90806, (562)988-3100 [9554]

Walthers Inc.; Wm. K., PO Box 3039, Milwaukee, WI 53201, (414)527-0770 [26705]

Waltman's Inc., PO Box 3648, Modesto, CA 95352, (209)522-1001 [16613]

Walton Lumber Company Inc., Rte. 4, Mineral, VA 23117-9302, (540)894-5444 [8195]

Walton Manufacturing Co., 1912 Nancita Cir., Placentia, CA 92870-6737, (714)996-4111 [13272]

Walton Manufacturing Co., 1912 Nancita Cir., Placentia, CA 92870-6737, (714)996-4111 [13273]

Walton & Post, 8105 NW 77 St., Miami, FL 33166, (305)591-1111 [12873]

Walton Wholesale Corp., PO Box 38-1983, Miami, FL 33138, (305)757-0348 [10284]

Walton's Gold Diamond Co.; George, 4300 Old Seward Hwy., Anchorage, AK 99503-6034, (907)562-2571 [17650]

WAM Company Beverage, PO Box 1633, Pocatello, ID 83204-1633, (208)233-6633 [24967]

Wam Inc., 565 Canyon Rd., Wetumpka, AL 36093-1406, (205)262-8241 [5472]

Wamplers Farm Sausage, 781 Hwy 70 W, Lenoir City, TN 37771-9808, (423)986-2056 [12874]

Wang's International, Inc., 4250 E Shelby Dr., Memphis, TN 38118-7721 [21345]

Wang's International, Inc., 6135-A Northbelt Dr., Norcross, GA 30071, (404)622-0787 [21346]

Wang's International, Inc., PO Box 18447, Memphis, TN 38181-0447, (901)362-2111 [15701]

Wang's International Inc., 4250 E Shelby Dr., Memphis, TN 38118, (901)362-2111 [26706]

Wanke Cascade, 1030 West 2610 South, Salt Lake City, UT 84119-2434, (801)972-1391 [10285]

Wanke Cascade, 6330 N Cutter Cir., Portland, OR 97217, (503)289-8609 [10286]

Wapsie Valley Creamery Inc., Box 391, Independence, IA 50644, (319)334-7193 [12875]

Ward Egg Ranch Corp., 2900 Harmony Grove Rd., Escondido, CA 92029, (619)745-5689 [12876]

Ward Manufacturing Inc., 115 Gulick St., Blossburg, PA 16912, (717)638-2131 [20478]

Ward Technologies Inc., 5010 S Ash Ave, Tempe, AZ 85282, (480)831-5500 [16614]

Ward Thompson Paper Inc., PO Box 3839, Butte, MT 59702, (406)494-2777 [21347]

Ward and Van Scoy Inc., PO Box 359, Owego, NY 13827, (607)687-2712 [18325]

Warden Leathers Inc., PO Box 842, Gloversville, NY 12078, (518)725-6447 [18441]

Ward's, 4507 Davis St., Long Island City, NY 11101, (718)784-7632 [25871]

Ward's, 4507 Davis St., Long Island City, NY 11101, (718)784-7632 [25871]

Wards Cleaning & Supply, PO Box 176, Burley, ID 83318-0176, (208)678-5105 [4726]

Wards Cove Packing Co., PO Box C-5030, Seattle, WA 98105, (206)323-3200 [12877]

Ward's Natural Science Establishment Inc., PO Box 92912, Rochester, NY 14692-9012, (716)359-2502 [4268]

Wareco Service Inc., 400 W State St., Jacksonville, IL 62650, (217)245-9528 [22781]

Wareheim Air Brakes, 3100 Washington Blvd., Baltimore, MD 21230, (410)644-0400 [3398]

Warehouse Equipment Inc., 2500 York Rd., Elk Grove Village, IL 60007, (847)595-9400 [16615]

Warehouse Home Furnishing Distributors Inc., 1851 Telfair St., PO Box 1140, Dublin, GA 31040, (912)275-3150 [13274]

Warehouse Outlet Stores Inc., 95 Montgomery St., Paterson, NJ 07501-1117, (973)278-9702 [18442]

Warehouse Service Co., PO Box 666, Richmond, IN 47374, (765)962-4577 [3399]

Wargames West, 2434 Baylor SE, Albuquerque, NM 87106, (505)242-1773 [26707]

Warnaco Inc., 7915 Haskell Ave., Van Nuys, CA 91409, (818)782-7568 [5473]

Warner Book Distributors; W., 1763 Dutch Broadway, Elmont, NY 11003-5044, (718)949-5910 [4269]

Warner Candy Company Inc., 10507 Delta Pkwy., Schiller Park, IL 60176, (708)928-7200 [12878]

Warner-Elektra-Atlantic Corp., 111 N Hollywood Way, Burbank, CA 91505, (818)843-6311 [25512]

Warner Fertilizer Company Inc., PO Box 796, Somerset, KY 42502, (606)679-8484 [1412]

Warner Fruehauf Trailer Co., 5710 Dupont Pky., Smyrna, DE 19977, (302)653-8561 [3400]

Warner Manufacturing Co., 13435 Industrial Park Blvd., Minneapolis, MN 55441, (763)559-4740 [21602]

Warner Music Group, 75 Rockefeller Plz., New York, NY 10019, (212)484-6653 [25513]

Warner Press Inc., PO Box 2499, Anderson, IN 46018, (765)644-7721 [4270]

Warner's Parts Co.; Eddie, PO Box 110129, Nashville, TN 37222-0129, (615)254-1224 [25514]

Warrell Corp., PO Box 3411, Shiremanstown, PA 17011-3411, (717)761-5440 [12879]

Warren Associates, 290 Rickenbacker Cir., Ste. 400, Livermore, CA 94550, (925)449-9000 [9555]

Warren Cheese Plants, 415 Jefferson St., Warren, IL 61087-9768, (815)745-2627 [12880]

Warren Co. Inc.; E.R., PO Box 949, Kennebunk, ME 04043, (207)985-3154 [22782]

Warren Corp.; George E., 605 17th St., Vero Beach, FL 32960, (561)778-7100 [22783]

Warren Distributing Corp., PO Box 26628, Raleigh, NC 27611, (919)828-9100 [15364]

Warren Distributing Inc., 1750 22nd, Santa Monica, CA 90404-3921, (310)828-3362 [3401]

Warren Electric Co., 303 Commerce, Clute, TX 77531-5605, (409)265-9371 [9556]

Warren Electric Group, PO Box 67, Houston, TX 77001, (713)236-0971 [9557]

Warren Equipment Co., PO Box 2872, Beaumont, TX 77704, (409)838-3791 [24259]

Warren Farmers Cooperative, PO Box 1, Mc Minnville, TN 37110, (931)668-4151 [1413]

Warren Marine Supply Inc., 15 Read Ave., Warren, RI 02885-2213, (401)245-5333 [18632]

Warren of Stafford Corp. Fabric Merchandising Div., 46 E 61st St., New York, NY 10021-8008, (212)980-7960 [26243]

Warren Supply Co., 300 E 50th St. N, Sioux Falls, SD 57104-0690, (605)336-1830 [9558]

Warrenterprises Inc., 1102 Ave. B NW, Great Falls, MT 59404, (406)761-5428 [4727]

Warrington Group Ltd., Greenleaf Woods Dr., Portsmouth, NH 03801, (603)431-1515 [24888]

Warrior Asphalt Refining Corp., PO Box 40254, Tuscaloosa, AL 35404, (205)553-2060 [8196]

Warrior Inc., 825 S Dickerson Rd., Apt. 175, Goodlettsville, TN 37072-1738, (615)859-0026 [13469]

Warsaw Chemical Company Inc., PO Box 858, Warsaw, IN 46581, (219)267-3251 [25872]

Warshawsky and Co., 225 N Michigan Ave., Chicago, IL 60601, (312)431-6000 [2815]

Warwick Auto Parts Inc., 641 Warwick Ave., Warwick, RI 02888-2602, (401)781-2525 [21603]

Washburn-Garfield Corp., 100 Prescott St., Worcester, MA 01605, (508)753-7225 [23438]

Washer and Refrigeration Supply Company Inc., 716 2nd Ave., North, Birmingham, AL 35201, (205)322-8693 [15365]

Washington Avionics Inc., 8535 Perimeter Rd. S, Seattle, WA 98108-3802, (206)762-0190 [168]

Washington Belt & Drive, PO Box 58, Wenatchee, WA 98807-0058, (509)547-1661 [17263]

Washington Belt & Drive, 425 N Way, Box 387, Colville, WA 99114, (509)452-5669 [17264]

Washington Belt & Drive, 4201 Airport Way S, Seattle, WA 98108, (206)623-5650 [17265]

Washington Belt & Drive, PO Box 58, Wenatchee, WA 98801, (509)663-8591 [17266]

Washington Chain and Supply, PO Box 3645, Seattle, WA 98124, (206)623-8500 [18633]

Washington Chain and Supply Inc., PO Box 3645, Seattle, WA 98124, (206)623-8500 [18634]

Washington Compressed Steel Corp., 271 W Berkes St., Philadelphia, PA 19122, (215)427-2231 [27035]

Washington Electric Membership Cooperative, PO Box 598, Sandersville, GA 31082, (912)552-2577 [15366]

Washington Forge Inc., 28 Harrison Ave., Englishtown, NJ 07726, (732)446-7777 [15702]

Washington Loggers Corp., 3949 Iron Gate Rd., Bellingham, WA 98226, (206)734-3660 [27393]

Washington Marina Co., 1300 Maine Ave. SW, Washington, DC 20024, (202)554-0222 [18635]

Washington Natural Foods and Co., 2421 Schuster Ave., Cheverly, MD 20781, (301)595-3500 [12881]

Washington Shoe Company, 542 1st Ave. S, Seattle, WA 98104-2804, (206)622-8517 [5474]

Washington Tysons Golf Center, PO Box 9025, West McLean, VA 22102-0025, (703)790-8844 [24040]

Washita Refrigeration & Equipment Co., PO Box 577, Tishomingo, OK 73460-0577, (580)371-3112 [14758]

Washouse, 740 W Grant, Phoenix, AZ 85007, (602)258-9274 [8373]

Wasser Morton Co., 1450 Broadway, Ste. 1000, New York, NY 10018, (212)391-6669 [26244]

Wasserott's Medical Services Inc., PO Box 195, Luzerne, PA 18709-0195, (717)287-2176 [19696]

Wasserstrom Co., 477 S Front St., Columbus, OH 43215, (614)228-6525 [21348]

Waste Management Recycle America, 3850 Holcomb Bridge Rd., No. 105, Norcross, GA 30092, (770)449-8688 [27036]

Waste Recovery-Illinois, 2658 E Highway 6, Marseilles, IL 61341, (815)795-6676 [27037]

Waste Recovery Inc., 309 S Pearl Expwy., Dallas, TX 75201, (214)741-3865 [22784]

Waste Reduction Systems Inc., 12621 Featherwood Dr., No. 380, Houston, TX 77034-4902, (281)922-1000 [27038]

Watanabe Floral, Inc., 1607 Hart St., Honolulu, HI 96817, (808)848-1026 [14973]

Watanabe Floral, Inc., Lalamilo Farm Area, Lot 2, Kamuela, HI 96743, (808)885-7588 [14974]

Watches, 401 S Los Angeles St. 3, Los Angeles, CA 90013, (213)680-7733 [17651]

Water Products International, Inc., 6441 Topaz Ct, Ft. Myers, FL 33912-8311, (941)768-6100 [25873]

Water Safety Corporation of America, 320 Coney Island Dr., Sparks, NV 89431, (702)359-9500 [25874]

Water Source USA, 2929 N Prospect, Ste. 100, Colorado Springs, CO 80907, (719)630-0334 [4550]

Water-Vac Distributors-Rainbow, 649 Mckinney Rd., Mt. Airy, NC, (336)789-7979 [15367]

Water Warehouse, Etc., PO Box 123, Matawan, NJ 07747 [25050]

Water and Waste Water Equipment Co., PO Box 9405, Boise, ID 83707, (208)377-0440 [23439]

Water Works, 2513 Neudorf Rd., Clemmons, NC 27012, (336)766-3349 [25875]

Water Works and Industrial Supply Co., Inc., PO Box 585, Huntington, WV 25710, (304)525-7888 [17267]

Waterloo Service Company Inc., PO Box 300, Waterloo, IA 50704, (319)233-4232 [22785]

Watermark Association of Artisans Inc., Hwy. 158 E, Camden, NC 27921, (252)338-0853 [15703]

WaterPro Supplies Inc., 220 S Westgate Dr., Carol Stream, IL 60188, (708)665-1800 [23440]

Waters Edge Distributors Inc., PO Box 384, Ceda Indus, Charlestown, NH 03603, (603)826-3702 [24041]

Waters Truck and Tractor Company Inc., PO Box 831, Columbus, MS 39701, (601)328-1575 [3402]

The Watersmith Inc., 2513 Neudorf Rd., Clemmons, NC 27012, (336)766-3349 [25875]

Watertown Cooperative Elevator Association, 810 Burlington Northern, Watertown, SD 57201, (605)886-3039 [1414]

Watertown Livestock Auction, Inc., PO Box 256, Watertown, SD 57201-0476, (605)886-5052 [18326]

Wathena and Bendena Grain Company Inc., PO Box 249, Wathena, KS 66090, (785)989-3322 [1415]

Watkins & Associates; Steen, 390 Main St., No. 201, Woburn, MA 01801-4280, (781)932-6464 [6860]

Watkins Pharmaceutical & Surgical Supply, 1391 E Sherman Blvd., Muskegon, MI 49444, (616)739-7158 [19105]

Watkins System Inc., PO Box 4000, Concordville, PA 19331, (610)358-3400 [169]

Watmet Inc., 11 Montbleu Ct., Getzville, NY 14068-1326, (716)568-1556 [9559]

Watonwan Farm Services, Rte. 1, Box 4, Amboy, MN 56010, (507)674-3010 [1416]

Watonwan Farm Services Co., PO Box 68, Truman, MN 56088, (507)776-2831 [18327]

Watonwan Farm Services Co. Ormsby Div., PO Box 458, Ormsby, MN 56162, (507)736-2961 [18328]

Watseka Farmers Grain Company Cooperative, 228 W Walnut St., Watseka, IL 60970, (815)432-4169 [1417]

Watson Associates Inc.; Vivian, 316 Oak Lawn Design Plaza, 1444 Oak Lawn Ave., Dallas, TX 75207-3613, (214)651-0211 [13275]

Watson Company Inc.; J.C., PO Box 300, Parma, ID 83660, (208)722-5141 [12882]

Watson Company, Inc.; O.J., 5335 Franklin St., Denver, CO 80216-6213, (303)295-2885 [3403]

Watson Co.; Ray V., PO Box 4886, Baltimore, MD 21211, (410)467-0878 [3404]

Watson Electric Supply Co., 1012 N Raguet, Lufkin, TX 75901-8212, (409)634-3373 [9560]

Watson Electric Supply Co., PO Box 540297, Dallas, TX 75354-0297, (214)742-8441 [9561]

Watson Foodservice Inc., PO Box 5910, Lubbock, TX 79408, (806)747-2678 [12883]

Watson Inc.; Fannie, 2714 Riopelle St., Detroit, MI 48207, (313)831-4438 [13470]

Watson Lumber Co., PO Box 1177, Liberty, KY 42539, (606)787-6221 [8197]

Watson Truck and Supply Inc., PO Box 10, Hobbs, NM 88240, (505)397-2411 [3405]

Watters and Martin Inc., 3800 Village Ave., Norfolk, VA 23502, (757)857-0651 [13985]

Watts Regulator Co., Rte. 114 & Chestnut St., North Andover, MA 01845, (978)688-1811 [23441]

Watts/Taras Valve Corp., 815 Chestnut St., North Andover, MA 01845, (978)689-6157 [23442]

Waukegan Steel Sales Inc., 1201 Belvidere Rd., Waukegan, IL 60085, (847)662-2810 [20479]

Waukegan Steel Sales Inc., 1201 Belvidere Rd., Waukegan, IL 60085, (847)662-2810 [20480]

Waukesha Wholesale Foods Inc., 900 Gale St., Waukesha, WI 53186, (414)542-8841 [12884]

Waukon Equity Cooperative, 8th Ave. NW, Waukon, IA 52172, (319)568-3456 [1418]

Wausau Supply Co., PO Box 296, Wausau, WI 54402-0296, (715)359-2524 [8198]

Waverly Growers Cooperative, PO Box 287, Waverly, FL 33877, (941)439-3602 [12885]

Waxie Sanitary Supply, 9353 Waxie Way, San Diego, CA 92123, (619)292-8111 [4728]

Waxler Co., 565 Lakeview Pkwy., Vernon Hills, IL 60061, (847)816-0100 [12886]

Waxman Industries Inc., 24460 Aurora Rd., Bedford Heights, OH 44146, (216)439-1830 [23443]

Waxman Industries Inc. - Medal Div., 330 Vine Ave., Sharon, PA 16146, (724)342-6839 [13824]

Waxworks Inc., 325 E 3rd St., Owensboro, KY 42303, (270)926-0008 [25515]

WaxWorks/VideoWorks Inc., 325 E 3rd St., Owensboro, KY 42301, (502)926-0008 [25516]

Way-Point Avionics Inc., 2301 University Dr., No. 38, Bismarck, ND 58504-7595, (701)223-2055 [170]

Waymire Drum Company Inc., 9316 S Atlantic Ave., South Gate, CA 90280, (213)566-6103 [25517]

Waymouth Farms Inc., 5300 Boone Ave. N, New Hope, MN 55428, (612)553-5300 [12887]

Wayne Densch Inc., 2900 W 1st St., Sanford, FL 32771, (407)323-5600 [2110]

Wayne Distributing Co., 45 Sharpe Dr., Cranston, RI 02920, (401)463-7020 [2111]

Wayne Distributing Inc., PO Box 68530, Indianapolis, IN 46268-0530, (317)875-5024 [9562]

Wayne Fasteners Inc., 2611 Independence Dr., Ft. Wayne, IN 46808-1391, (219)484-0393 [13986]

Wayne Pipe and Supply Inc., PO Box 2201, Ft. Wayne, IN 46801, (219)423-9577 [23444]

Wayne Pipe and Supply Inc., PO Box 2201, Ft. Wayne, IN 46801, (219)423-9577 [23445]

Wayne Steel Co., PO Box 460, Elizabeth, NJ 07207, (908)354-7300 [20481]

Wayne Steel Co., Ray H. Morris Div., 30 Precision Ct., New Britain, CT 06051, (860)224-2678 [20482]

Wayne Tile Co., Rt. 23 N, Hamburg, NJ 07419, (973)875-7400 [10287]

Wayne Tile Co., 333 Rt. 46 W, Rockaway, NJ 07866, (973)625-3209 [10288]

Wayne Tile Co., 1459 Rte. 23 S, Wayne, NJ 07470, (973)694-5480 [10289]

Waytek Inc., PO Box 690, Chanhassen, MN 55317-0690, (612)949-0765 [9563]

WB Stores Inc., 35 Temple Pl., Boston, MA 02111, (617)426-8549 [13471]

WBH Industries, PO Box 98, Arlington, TX 76011, (817)649-5700 [13987]

W.B.R. Inc., PO Box 66001, Stockton, CA 95206, (209)983-0590 [8199]

W.C. Distributors Corp., 2887 Koapaka St., Honolulu, HI 96819, (808)836-3605 [26370]

WCI International Co., 3 Parkway Ctr., Pittsburgh, PA 15220, (412)928-0252 [15368]

WD-40 Co., 1061 Cudahy Pl., San Diego, CA 92110, (619)275-1400 [22786]

WD Industries Inc., PO Box 27100, Albuquerque, NM 87125-7100, (505)344-3441 [8200]

W.D. Trading Company Inc., 250 Beacham St., Everett, MA 02149, (617)389-5100 [12888]

WDI United Warehouse Inc., 10 Randolph St., Montgomery, AL 36101, (205)265-0728 [3406]

We Market Success Inc., 255 Colraid Ave., S W, Grand Rapids, MI 49548, (616)241-3476 [12889]

Weaks Martin Implement Co., PO Box 946, Mission, TX 78572, (210)585-1618 [1419]

Weaks Supply Co., 1424 Natchitoches St., West Monroe, LA 71292-3751, (318)325-9696 [9288]

Wear-Rite, PO Box 461, Florissant, MO 63032-0461, (314)381-3830 [21560]

Wearhouse, 616 N Chamberlain St., Terre Haute, IN 47803-9503, (812)234-1441 [24889]

Weatherford Enterprise of Flagstaff, 11705 N Hwy. 89, Flagstaff, AZ 86004, (520)526-3556 [27268]

Weatherhead Distributing Co., PO Box 306, Oakes, ND 58474-0306, (701)742-2685 [2112]

Weathertrol Supply Company Inc., 2600 East University Dr., Denton, TX 76209, (940)387-1778 [14759]

Weaver Co.; James A., PO Box 11268, Lancaster, PA 17605-1268, (717)393-0474 [12890]

WEB Machinery Co., PO Box 248, Jamestown, NY 14701, (716)488-1935 [16616]

Web Seal Inc., 15 Oregon St., Rochester, NY 14605-3094, (716)546-1320 [19]

WebAccess, 2573 Midpoint Dr., Ft. Collins, CO 80525, (970)221-2555 [6861]

Webb Bolt and Nut Co., 2830 Taft Ave., Orlando, FL 32804, (407)841-1844 [13988]

Webb Co.; F.W., 200 Middlesex Tpk., Burlington, MA 01803, (617)272-6600 [23446]

Webb Foods Inc.; Joseph, PO Box 1749, Vista, CA 92085, (760)599-6200 [12891]

Webb Inc.; Fred, PO Box 6084, Greenville, NC 27835, (919)758-2141 [18329]

Webber Cable and Electronics, 13477 12th St., Chino, CA 91710, (909)464-1526 [9564]

Webber Oil Co., PO Box 929, Bangor, ME 04402-0929, (207)942-5501 [22787]

Webbing Mills Co.; Elizabeth, PO Box 1168, Pawtucket, RI 02862-1168, (401)723-0500 [26245]

Webbs Appliance Service Ctr., 1519 Church St., Nashville, TN 37203-3004, (615)329-4079 [25518]

Webb's Oil Corp., 8223 Resevoir Rd., Roanoke, VA 24019-6939, (703)362-3796 [22788]

Weber Co.; H.J., 3140 W 25th St., Cleveland, OH 44109, (216)351-1200 [10290]

Weber Industries Inc., 84M New Hampshire Ave., St. Louis, MO 63123, (314)631-9200 [16617]

Weber Office Supply Inc., 412 E Main St., Riverton, WY 82501-4439, (307)856-4228 [21349]

Weber Piano Co., 40 Seaview Dr., Secaucus, NJ 07094, (201)902-0920 [25519]

Weber and Sons Inc., PO Box 104, Adelphia, NJ 07710, (908)431-1128 [21350]

Websource, 161 Ave. of the Americas, New York, NY 10013, (212)255-1600 [21351]

Webster Scale Inc., PO Box 127, Webster, SD 57274-0127, (605)345-3881 [24455]

Webster Watch Company Associates LLC, 44 E 32nd St., New York, NY 10016, (212)889-3560 [17652]

Webstone Company Inc., 703 Plantation St., Worcester, MA 01605, (508)852-5700 [23447]

WeCare Distributors Inc., PO Box 669047, Charlotte, NC 28266, (704)393-1860 [14277]

Wechsler Coffee Corp., 10 Empire Blvd., Moonachie, NJ 07074, (201)440-1700 [12892]

Wedco Inc., PO Box 1131, Reno, NV 89504, (702)329-1131 [9565]

Wedemeyer Electronic Supply Co., 2280 S Industrial Hwy., Ann Arbor, MI 48104, (734)665-8611 [9566]

Wedemeyers Bakery, 314 Harbor Way, South San Francisco, CA 94080, (650)873-1000 [12893]

Wedgwood U.S.A. Inc., PO Box 1454, Wall, NJ 07719, (908)938-5800 [15704]

Wedgworth's Inc., PO Box 2076, Belle Glade, FL 33430, (561)996-2076 [1420]

Wedin International Inc., Ball Screw Manufacturing and Repair, Inc., 1111 6th Ave., Cadillac, MI 49601, (231)779-8650 [13989]

Wedlo Inc., 1816 3rd Ave. N, Birmingham, AL 35203-3102, (205)322-4444 [17653]

Weed Chevrolet Company Inc., Rte. 413, Box 227, Bristol, PA 19007, (215)788-5511 [20749]

Weeke Wholesale Company Inc., 1600 N 89th St., Fairview Heights, IL 62208, (618)397-1900 [26371]

Weekend Exercise Co., Inc., 8960 Carroll Way, Ste. A, San Diego, CA 92121, (619)537-5300 [5475]

Weekley Auto Parts Inc., 7600 Gateway Dr., Grand Forks, ND 58203-9608, (701)772-2112 [3407]

Weeks Div., 330 N State St., Concord, NH 03301, (603)225-3379 [12894]

Weeks Div., 330 N State St., Concord, NH 03301, (603)225-3379 [12895]

Weems Brothers Seafood Co., 320 E Bayview Ave., Biloxi, MS 39530, (228)432-5422 [12896]

Weems & Plath, Inc., 214 Eastern Ave., Annapolis, MD 21403, (410)263-6700 [171]

Wegener Communications Inc., 11350 Technology Cir., Duluth, GA 30026, (404)623-0096 [5809]

Wegnar Livestock Inc.; Keith E., PO Box 543, Casselton, ND 58012-0543, (701)282-8582 [18330]

Wehle Electric Div., 475 Ellicott St., Buffalo, NY 14203, (716)854-3270 [9567]

Wehman Inc., PO Drawer W, Pleasanton, TX 78064, (210)569-2181 [22789]

Weider Health and Fitness Inc., 21100 Erwin St., Woodland Hills, CA 91367, (818)884-6800 [14278]

Weidner & Sons Publishing, Box 2178, Riverton, 11775, 08077, (856)486-1755 [4271]

Weigh-Tronix Inc., 19821 Cabot Blvd., Hayward, CA 94545, (510)264-1692 [24260]

Weil Brothers Cotton Inc., 4444 Park Blvd., Montgomery, AL 36116, (205)244-1800 [18331]

Weil and Co.; J., 5907 Clinton St., Boise, ID 83704, (208)377-0590 [12897]

Weil Inc.; Cliff, PO Box 427, Mechanicsville, VA 23116, (804)746-1321 [21352]

Weil Service Products Corp., PO Box 6127, Bloomingdale, IL 60108-6127, (773)528-6800 [22790]

Weil and Sons, Inc.; Joseph, 825 E 26th St., La Grange Park, IL 60526, (708)579-9595 [21986]

Weiland Associates, 1131 Rte. 31 S, Lebanon, NJ 08833, (908)735-9115 [12898]

Weiler Wilhelm Window and Door Co., 16900 Bagley Rd., Cleveland, OH 44130, (440)243-5000 [8201]

Weimer Bearing & Transmission Inc., 5368 Campbell Dr., No. W134, Menomonee Falls, WI 53052, (414)781-1992 [9568]

Weinberg Supply Company Inc.; E., 7434 W 27th St., Minneapolis, MN 55426-3104, (612)920-0888 [4729]

Weiner Steel Corp., 8200 E Slauson Ave., Pico Rivera, CA 90660-4321, (213)723-8327 [20483]

Weingart & Sons, 1251 Randall Ave., Bronx, NY 10474-6411, (718)589-1703 [13990]

Weingartner Company Inc.; Henry, 111 Brook St., Scarsdale, NY 10583, (914)472-6464 [20484]

Weinreich Co.; Charles, 300 S Mission Rd., Los Angeles, CA 90033, (213)268-2755 [27039]

Weinstein International Seafood Inc., 5738 Olson Hwy., Minneapolis, MN 55422, (612)546-4471 [12899]

Weinstein Supply Corp., Davisville & Moreland, Willow Grove, PA 19090, (215)657-0700 [23448]

Weintrob Brothers, 2036 11th Ave., Morgantown, WV 26505-8751, (304)296-4336 [24890]

Weiser Inc.; Samuel, PO Box 612, York Beach, ME 03910-0612, (207)363-4393 [4272]

Weiser Livestock Commission, PO Box 648, Weiser, ID 83672-0648, (208)549-0564 [18332]

Weisheimer Pet Supply, 1015 Taylor Rd., Blacklick, OH 43004, (614)864-2100 [27269]

Weiss Company Inc.; Max, 8625 W Bradley Rd., Milwaukee, WI 53224-2893, (414)355-8220 [16618]

Weiss Inc.; Harry, 870 5th Ave., No. 8F, New York, NY 10021-4953, (212)631-0684 [18443]

Weissman & Sons Inc.; Carl, PO Box 1609, Great Falls, MT 59403-1609, (406)761-4848 [21604]

Weissman and Sons Inc.; Carl, PO Box 1609, Great Falls, MT 59403, (406)761-4848 [13991]

Wel-Met Corp., 930 Wellington Ave., Cranston, RI 02910-3721, (401)467-3222 [17654]

Welbilt Corp., 2227 Welbilt Blvd., New Port Richey, FL 34655-5130, (727)375-7010 [15369]

Welco Gases Corp., 425 Avenue P, Newark, NJ 07105, (973)589-7895 [17268]

Weldco Inc., 1151 Findley St., Cincinnati, OH 45214, (513)241-5840 [16598]

Welded Products Inc., 1030 N Merrifield, Mishawaka, IN 46545, (219)255-9689 [20485]

Welders Equipment Company Inc., PO Box 2609, Victoria, TX 77902, (512)578-0307 [16619]

Welders Supply Inc., 430 S Industrial Blvd., Dallas, TX 75207, (214)748-4721 [17269]

Welding Equipment & Supply/All State Medical Gases, 255 Field Point Rd., Greenwich, CT 06830, (203)869-4388 [19106]

Welding Industrial Supply Inc., 2200 N Western Ave., Chicago, IL 60647, (773)384-7622 [17270]

Weldon Tool Co., 6030 Carey Dr., Cleveland, OH 44125, (216)642-5454 [16620]

Weldstar Co., PO Box 1150, Aurora, IL 60504, (708)859-3100 [17271]

Weldtube Inc., 5000 Stecker Ave., Dearborn, MI 48126, (313)584-6500 [20486]

Welker-McKee Supply Co. Division of Hajoca, 6606 Granger Rd., Cleveland, OH 44131, (216)447-0050 [23449]

Well Made Toy Manufacturing Co., 184-10 Jamaica Ave., Hollis, NY 11423, (718)454-1326 [26708]

Wellborn Paint Manufacturing Co., 215 Rossmoor Rd. SW, Albuquerque, NM 87105, (505)877-5050 [21605]

Wellman Inc., 1040 Broad St., Ste. 302, Shrewsbury, NJ 07702, (908)542-7300 [27040]

Wells & Associates; Kenyon, PO Box 429, Lexington, SC 29071-0429, (803)359-6020 [19107]

Wells Designs Inc.; Victoria, 2 Central St., Framingham, MA 01701-4163, (508)877-6722 [5476]

Wells Fargo Alarm Services Inc., 450 S 5th, Reading, PA 19602-2642, (215)372-8484 [24660]

Wells International, PO Box 189, Pearblossom, CA 93553, (805)944-2146 [12900]

Wells and Kimich Inc., PO Box 19216, Houston, TX 77224, (713)984-9993 [13276]

Wells Lamont Corp., 299A W Beacon, Philadelphia, MS 39350-3151, (601)656-2772 [5477]

Wells Lamont Corp., 6640 W Touhy Ave., Niles, IL 60714, (847)647-8200 [5478]

Wells and Wade Hardware, 201 S Wenatchee Ave., Wenatchee, WA 98801, (509)662-7173 [13992]

WellSpring Books, 325-A New Boston St., Woburn, MA 01801, (781)938-6001 [4273]

Welltep International Inc., 138 Palm Coast Pkwy. NE, No. 192, Palm Coast, FL 32137-8241, (904)445-7160 [4551]

Welsco Inc., PO Box 1058, North Little Rock, AR 72115-1058, (501)771-1204 [17272]

Wenatchee-Okanogan Cooperative Federation, PO Box 658, Wenatchee, WA 98807, (509)663-8585 [12901]

Wendell Farmers Elevator Co., PO Box 228, Wendell, MN 56590, (218)458-2127 [18333]

Wenger, 15 Corporate Dr., Orangeburg, NY 10962, (914)365-3500 [24042]

Wenger Manufacturing Inc., PO Box 130, Sabetha, KS 66534, (785)284-2133 [16621]

Wenger N.A., 15 Corporate Dr., Orangeburg, NY 10962, (914)365-3500 [24042]

Wensman Seed Co., PO Box 190, Wadena, MN 56482, (218)631-2954 [18334]

Wenzel Farm Sausage, E 29th, Marshfield, WI 54449-5313, (715)387-1218 [12902]

Werleins for Music, 3750 Veterans Blvd., Metairie, LA 70002, (504)883-5060 [25520]

The Wermers Co., 451 E 58th Ave., Ste. 3677, Denver, CO 80216, (303)295-1318 [5479]

Werner and Pfleiderer Corp., 663 E Crescent Ave., Ramsey, NJ 07446, (201)327-6300 [23047]

Werner & Son; Max, 1750 2nd Ave., New York, NY 10128-5361, (212)744-7373 [12903]

Werres Corp., 807 E South St., Frederick, MD 21701, (301)620-4000 [16622]

Werts Novelty Co., 1520 W 5th, Muncie, IN 47302-2103, (765)288-8825 [21987]

Wertz Candies; Allen, PO Box 1168, Chino, CA 91708, (909)613-0030 [12904]

Wesche Co., 10545 S Memorial, Tulsa, OK 74133, (918)583-7551 [13993]

Wesco Auto Parts, 1705 West Garvey N, West Covina, CA 91790, (562)692-9844 [3408]

Wesco Cedar Inc., PO Box 40847, Eugene, OR 97404-0161, (503)688-5020 [8202]

WESCO Distribution Inc., 4 Station Sq., Pittsburgh, PA 15219-1119, (412)454-2200 [9569]

Wesco Fabrics Inc., 4001 Forest St., Denver, CO 80216, (303)388-4101 [15705]

Wesco Financial Corp., 301 E Colorado Blvd., Ste. 300, Pasadena, CA 91101-1901, (626)585-6700 [20487]

Wesco Merchandising, 7101 E Slauson Ave., Los Angeles, CA 90040-3622, (213)269-0292 [14279]

Wesco Turf Inc., 2101 Cantu Ct., Sarasota, FL 34232, (941)377-6777 [1421]

Wescorp International Ltd., PO Box 1816, Salem, NH 03079-1144, (603)893-6202 [6862]

Wescosa Inc., PO Box 66626, Scotts Valley, CA 95066, (831)438-4600 [21353]

Wesley Electric and Supply Inc., 829 E Jefferson St., Louisville, KY 40206, (502)585-3301 [14760]

Wesley Ice Cream, 3717 King Hwy., Kalamazoo, MI 49001, (616)343-1291 [12905]

Wesley Press, Box 50434, Indianapolis, IN 46250, (317)570-5300 [4274]

Wesleyan Publishing House, Box 50434, Indianapolis, IN 46250, (317)570-5300 [4274]

Wesmac Enterprises, PO Box 606, Union, ME 04862-0606, (207)785-2636 [18636]

Wesson, Inc., PO Box 2127, Waterbury, CT 06722-2127, (203)757-7950 [22791]

West Agro Inc., 11100 N Congress Ave., Kansas City, MO 64153, (816)891-1600 [4552]

West Bay Resources Inc., 250 China Basin St., San Francisco, CA 94107, (415)957-9971 [27041]

West Bend Elevator Co., PO Box 49, West Bend, IA 50597-0049, (515)887-7211 [18335]

West Bend Elevator Inc., PO Box 408, West Bend, WI 53095, (414)334-2337 [1422]

West Bend Water Systems, 400 Washington St., West Bend, WI 53095, (414)334-6906 [25876]

West Carpenter Paint & Flooring, 124 Hall St., Concord, NH 03301-3442, (603)225-2832 [21606]

West Central Cooperative, 406 1st St., Ralston, IA 51459, (712)667-3200 [18336]

West Central Steel Inc., PO Box 1178, Willmar, MN 56201, (612)235-4070 [20488]

West Coast Beauty Supply, 5001 Industrial Way, Benicia, CA 94510, (707)748-4800 [14280]

West Coast Industries Inc., 3150 18th St., San Francisco, CA 94110, (415)621-6656 [13277]

West Coast Liquidators Inc., 2430 E Del Amo Blvd., Compton, CA 90220-6306, (310)537-9220 [5480]

West Coast Machine Tools, PO Box 88179, Seattle, WA 98138, (253)872-7540 [16623]

West Coast Paper Co., 23200 64th Ave. S, Kent, WA 98032, (206)623-1850 [21988]

West Coast Ship Chandlers Inc., 2665 Magnolia St., Oakland, CA 94607, (510)444-7200 [17273]

West Coast Shoe Co., PO Box 607, Scappoose, OR 97056, (503)543-7114 [24891]

West Coast Shoe Co., PO Box 607, Scappoose, OR 97056, (503)543-7114 [5481]

West Coast Tube and Pipe, 9165 Olema Ave., Hesperia, CA 92345, (760)956-8000 [19733]

West Coast Wire Rope and Rigging Inc., PO Box 5999, Portland, OR 97228, (503)228-9353 [17274]

West Coast Wire and Steel, 1027 Palmyrita Ave., Riverside, CA 92507-1701, (909)683-7252 [20489]

West Company; William H., 4509 Emerald St., Boise, ID 83706-2042, (208)344-1449 [8203]

West Equipment Company Inc., 1545 E Broadway St., Toledo, OH 43605, (419)698-1601 [8204]

West Implement Company Inc., PO Box 1389, Cleveland, MS 38732, (662)843-5321 [1423]

West L.A. Music, 11345 Santa Monica Blvd., West Los Angeles, CA 90025-3151, (310)477-1945 [25521]

West Liberty Oil Co., PO Box 147, MoscoW, IA 52760-0147, (319)627-2113 [22792]

West Lyon Cooperative Inc., PO Box 310, Inwood, IA 51240, (712)753-4528 [18337]

West Marine Corp., 120 Allied Dr., Dedham, MA 02026, (617)329-2430 [18637]

West Minerals Inc., 101 Tidewater Rd. NE, Warren, OH 44483, (330)372-1781 [22793]

West Nesbitt Inc., 59 Court St., Binghamton, NY 13901, (607)432-6500 [18338]

West Penn Laco Inc., 331 Ohio, Pittsburgh, PA 15209-2798, (412)821-3608 [17275]

West Penn Optical, 2576 W 8th St., Colony Plaza, Erie, PA 16505, (814)833-1194 [19697]

West Philadelphia Electric Supply Co., 5828 Market St., Philadelphia, PA 19139, (215)474-9200 [9570]

West; Reginald, RR 1, Box 1495, Franklin, VT 05457, (802)285-6600 [18339]

West Ridge Designs, 1236 NW Flanders, Portland, OR 97209, (503)248-0053 [18444]

West Side Distributors Ltd., 41839 Michigan Ave., Canton, MI 48188, (313)397-2500 [3409]

West Side Tractor Sales Inc., 1400 W Ogden Ave., Naperville, IL 60563, (708)355-7150 [1424]

West Tennessee Communications, 1295 US Hwy. 51, Bypass S, Dyersburg, TN 38024-9317, (901)286-6275 [5810]

West Tennessee Communications, 1295 US Hwy. 51, Bypass S, Dyersburg, TN 38024-9317, (901)286-6275 [9571]

West Texas Equipment Co., PO Box 61247, Midland, TX 79711, (915)563-1863 [1425]

West Texas News Co., 1214 Barranca Dr., El Paso, TX 79935-4601, (915)594-7586 [4275]

West Texas Wholesale Supply Co., PO Box 1020, Abilene, TX 79604, (915)677-2851 [23450]

West Union Corp., PO Box 3177, Memphis, TN 38173, (901)529-5700 [13994]

West Valley Farmers Inc., 2741 N Hwy. 99 W, McMinnville, OR 97128, (503)472-6154 [1426]

West Virginia Archery Supply, PO Box 9216, Charleston, WV 25309-0216, (304)768-6091 [24043]

West Virginia Ohio Motor Sales Inc., PO Box 71, Wheeling, WV 26003, (304)232-7515 [3410]

West Virginia Tractor Co., PO Box 473, Charleston, WV 25322, (304)346-5301 [8205]

West Wholesale, 800 NW 65th St., Ft. Lauderdale, FL 33309, (954)351-1117 [27270]

Westar Inc., 6031 S 58th St. C, Lincoln, NE 68516-3645, (402)421-2100 [24044]

Westbay Equipment Co., Rte. 4, Galesburg, IL 61401, (309)342-8112 [1427]

Westberg Manufacturing Inc., 3400 Westach Way, Sonoma, CA 95476, (707)938-2121 [24456]

Westbrook Pharmaceutical and Surgical Supply Co., 1910 Cochran Rd., Pittsburgh, PA 15220, (412)561-6532 [19698]

Westburgh Electric Inc., PO Box 1319, Jamestown, NY 14702-1319, (716)488-1172 [9572]

Westburne Supply Inc., PO Box 65013, Anaheim, CA 92815, (714)590-3000 [23451]

Westby Cooperative Creamery, 401 S Main St., Westby, WI 54667, (608)634-3181 [12906]

Westby Farmers Union Cooperative, 405 S Main St., Westby, WI 54667, (608)634-3184 [1428]

Westchester Marketing, 100 Corridor Park Dr., Monroe, OH 45050-1394 [5482]

Westco-BakeMark Las Vegas, 2570 Kiel Way, North Las Vegas, NV 89030, (702)642-4500 [12907]

Westco./DoAll Industrial Distribution, 166 Riverside Industrial Pkwy., Portland, ME 04103-1431, (207)774-5812 [16624]

Westco Food Service Co., 2570 Kiel Way, North Las Vegas, NV 89030, (702)642-4500 [12908]

Westcon Inc., 150 Main St., Eastchester, NY 10709, (914)779-4773 [5811]

Westcon Inc., 520 White Plains Rd., Tarrytown, NY 10591, (914)768-7180 [6863]

Westcott Worldwide, 11708 S Mayfield Ave., Worth, IL 60482, (708)389-7300 [10291]

WESTEC/PC Security Systems Inc., 950 Windham Ct., Ste. 1, Boardman, OH 44512, (330)726-9841 [24657]

Westech, PO Box 376, Igo, CA 96047-0376, (408)997-3547 [6864]

Westeel Inc.; W.S., 803 25th St. N, Fargo, ND 58102, (701)232-3201 [25947]

Western Aircraft Inc., 4444 Aeronca St., Boise, ID 83705-5090, (208)338-1800 [172]

Western Automation Inc., 23011 Moulton Pkwy., H-2, Laguna Hills, CA 92653, (714)859-6988 [14761]

Western Beef Inc., 47-05 Metropolitan Ave., Ridgewood, NY 11385, (718)417-3770 [12909]

Western Beverage Company Inc., PO Box 941, Taylors, SC 29687, (864)268-6036 [2113]

Western Book Distributors, 18 Virginia Gdns, Berkeley, CA 94702-1428, (510)849-0100 [4276]

Western Branch Diesel Inc., PO Box 7788, Portsmouth, VA 23707-0788, (757)673-7000 [16625]

Western Carolina Electrical Supply Co., PO Box 1530, Lenoir, NC 28645, (828)754-5311 [9573]

Western Carolina Optical Inc., PO Box 1596, Asheville, NC 28802-1596, (828)258-1706 [19699]

Western Cascade Equipment Co., 13456 SE 27th Pl., Bellevue, WA 98005-4211, (425)562-9400 [15370]

Western Cold Storage, 1505 W Lee Rd., Othello, WA 99344, (509)488-6677 [12910]

Western Component Sales Div., 20953 Devonshire St., Ste. 5, Chatsworth, CA 91311, (818)882-6226 [9574]

Western Dairy Products Inc., 3625 Westwind Blvd., Santa Rosa, CA 95403, (707)524-6770 [12911]

Western Dairymen Cooperative Inc., 1140 South 3200 West, Salt Lake City, UT 84104, (801)977-3000 [12912]

Western DataCom Company Inc., PO Box 45113, Westlake, OH 44145, (216)835-1510 [6865]

Western Depot, PO Box 3001, Yuba City, CA 95992-3001, (530)673-6776 [26709]

Western Design Tile, 9926 Horn Rd., Ste. I, Sacramento, CA 95827-1960, (916)366-8453 [10292]

Western Distributing Co., PO Box 5542, Denver, CO 80217, (303)292-1711 [2114]

Western Distributing Company Inc., PO Box 1969, Casper, WY 82602-1969, (307)265-8414 [2115]

Western Door and Sash Co., 4601 Malat St., Oakland, CA 94601, (510)535-2000 [8206]

Western Export Services, Inc., Export Management Center, 140 E 19th Ave., Ste. 201, Denver, CO 80203-1011, (303)302-5899 [12913]

Western Extralite Co., 1470 Liberty St., Kansas City, MO 64102, (816)421-8404 [9575]

Western Facilities Supply, Inc., PO Box 928, Everett, WA 98206-0928, (425)252-2105 [4730]

Western Facilities Supply Inc., PO Box 928, Everett, WA 98206-0928, (425)252-2105 [24261]

Western Family Foods Inc., PO Box 4057, Portland, OR 97208, (503)639-6300 [12914]

Western Farm Center, 21 W 7th St., Santa Rosa, CA 95401, (707)545-0721 [1429]

Western Farm Service/Cascade, PO Box 269, Tangent, OR 97389, (541)928-3391 [1430]

Western Farm Service Inc., 3705 West Beechwood, Ste. 101, Fresno, CA 93711, (209)436-0450 [1431]

Western Fastener Co., 7373 Engineer Rd., San Diego, CA 92111-1425, (619)292-5115 [13995]

Western Flag & Banner, PO Box 31151, Billings, MT 59107-1151, (406)652-1585 [26152]

Western Flat Rolled Steel, 141 S Western Coil Rd., Lindon, UT 84042, (801)785-8600 [20490]

Western Fluid Power, 4242 S Eagleson Rd., Unit 108, Boise, ID 83705, (208)362-2032 [16626]

Western Fluid Power, 3410 W 11th St., Eugene, OR 97402, (541)484-9666 [16627]

Western Fluid Power, 4309 NW St. Helens Rd., Portland, OR 97210, (503)228-6666 [16628]

Western Gold Thermoplastics Inc., 1769 Mount Vernon Ave., Pomona, CA 91768-3330, (213)235-3387 [27042]

Western Golf Inc., PO Box 970, Thousand Palms, CA 92276-0970, (760)343-1050 [24045]

Western Graphtec Inc., 11 Vanderbilt, Irvine, CA 92618, (714)454-2800 [6866]

Western Home Center Inc., 7600 Colerain Ave., Cincinnati, OH 45239, (513)931-6300 [8207]

Western Home Center Inc., 7600 Colerain Ave., Cincinnati, OH 45239, (513)931-6300 [27394]

Western Implement Co., 2919 North Ave., Grand Junction, CO 81504, (970)242-7960 [1432]

Western Iowa Cooperative, 150 Main St., Hornick, IA 51026, (712)874-3211 [18340]

Western Library Books, 560 S San Vicente Blvd., Los Angeles, CA 90048, (213)653-8880 [4277]

Western Livestock Inc., PO Box 850, Dickinson, ND 58602-0850, (701)225-8145 [18341]

Western MacArthur Co., 2855 Mandela Pkwy., Oakland, CA 94608, (510)251-2102 [8208]

Western Maryland Distributing, 101 Winston St., PO Box 33, Cumberland, MD 21502-2106, (301)722-8050 [2116]

Western Materials Inc., PO Box 430, Yakima, WA 98907, (509)575-3000 [8209]

Western Merchandisers Inc., PO Box 32270, Amarillo, TX 79120, (806)376-6251 [4278]

Western Micro Technology Inc., 6550 N Loop 1604 E, San Antonio, TX 78247-5004 [6867]

Western Micro Technology Inc., 254 E Hacienda Ave., Campbell, CA 95008, (408)379-0177 [9339]

Western Montana Scale Co. Inc., 1207 13th Ave. E, Polson, MT 59860-3620, (406)883-4697 [24402]

Western Nevada Supply Co., PO Box 1576, Sparks, NV 89432, (775)359-5800 [23452]

Western North Carolina Apple Growers, Rte. 9, PO Box 699, Hendersonville, NC 28792, (704)685-3232 [12915]

Western Office Equipment, PO Box 1822, Billings, MT 59103-1822, (406)245-3029 [21354]

Western Office Interiors, 5809 E Telegraph Rd., City of Commerce, CA 90040, (213)721-8833 [13278]

Western Pacific Data Systems Inc., 7590 Fay Ave., La Jolla, CA 92037, (619)454-0028 [6868]

Western Pacific Interior, 73-5564 Olowalu St., Kailua Kona, HI 96740, (808)329-6602 [10293]

Western Pacific Pulp and Paper, PO Box 4279, Downey, CA 90241, (562)803-4401 [27043]

Western Petroleum Co., 9531 W 78th St., Eden Prairie, MN 55344, (612)941-9090 [22794]

Western Photo Mount, 3100 NW Industrial St., Ste. 4, PO Box 10285, Portland, OR 97210-0285, (503)226-0369 [22915]

Western Photo Packaging, 3100 NW Industrial St., Ste. 4, PO Box 10285, Portland, OR 97210-0285, (503)226-0369 [22915]

Western Pioneer Inc., PO Box 70438, Seattle, WA 98107, (206)789-1930 [22795]

Western Pioneer Sales Co., 406 E Colorado St., Glendale, CA 91205, (213)245-7281 [25877]

Western Plains Machinery Co., PO Box 30438, Billings, MT 59107, (406)259-5500 [8210]

Western Power and Equipment Corp., 4601 NE 77th Ave., Ste. 200, Vancouver, WA 98662, (360)253-2346 [8211]

Western Power Sports, Inc., 5272 Irving St., Boise, ID 83706-1210, (208)376-8400 [3411]

Western Printing Co., PO Box 1555, Aberdeen, SD 57401, (605)229-1480 [21989]

Western Products Inc., 2001 1st Ave. N, Fargo, ND 58102-4120, (701)293-5310 [8212]

Western Purifier Water Purifier Co., PO Box 688, Woodland Hills, CA 91365-0688, (818)703-0444 [23453]

Western Radio Electronics Inc., PO Box 790, San Diego, CA 92112-0790, (619)268-4400 [9576]

Western Rubber and Supply Inc., PO Box 56117, Hayward, CA 94545, (510)441-6500 [17276]

Western Scrap Processing Co., PO Box 15158, Colorado Springs, CO 80935, (719)390-7986 [27044]

Western Seeds, PO Box 850, Burley, ID 83318, (208)678-2268 [1433]

Western Shower Door Inc., 4140 Business Center, Fremont, CA 94538, (510)438-0340 [8213]

Western Star Distributors, 325 N 2nd St., Lompoc, CA 93436, (805)736-1865 [26710]

Western States Equipment, 500 E Overland Rd., Meridian, ID 83642, (208)888-2287 [8214]

Western States Manufacturing Company, Inc., PO Box 3655, Sioux City, IA 51102, (712)252-4248 [3412]

Western States Oil Company Inc., 1790 S 10th St., San Jose, CA 95112, (408)292-1041 [22796]

Western States Petroleum Inc., 450 S 15th Ave., Phoenix, AZ 85007, (602)252-4011 [22797]

Western Stations Co., 2929 NW 29th, Portland, OR 97210, (503)243-2929 [22798]

Western Steel and Plumbing Inc., PO Box 774, Bismarck, ND 58502-0774, (701)223-3130 [23454]

Western Stockmen's Inc., 223 Rodeo Ave., Caldwell, ID 83605, (208)459-0777 [19700]

Western Tile Design Center, 1290 Diamond Way, Concord, CA 94520, (925)671-0145 [10294]

Western Tile Design Center (Dublin), 11825 Dublin Blvd., Dublin, CA 94568, (925)829-5544 [10295]

Western Tile Distributors, 3780 Santa Rosa Ave., Santa Rosa, CA 95407-8287, (707)585-1501 [10296]

Western Tile Distributors, 1290 Diamond Way, Concord, CA 94520, (925)671-0145 [10294]

Western Tile & Kitchen Design, 3780 Santa Rosa Ave., Santa Rosa, CA 95407-8287, (707)585-1501 [10296]

Western Tile Santa Rosa, Inc., 3780 Santa Rosa Ave., Santa Rosa, CA 95407-8287, (707)585-1501 [10296]

Western Tool Supply Inc., 2315 25th St. SE, Salem, OR 97302, (503)588-8222 [13996]

Western Toy and Hobby Inc., 160 West 21st South, Salt Lake City, UT 84115-1829, (801)486-5831 [26711]

Western Trading Post Inc., PO Box 9070, Denver, CO 80209-0070, (303)777-7750 [26712]

Western Truck Equipment Company Inc., PO Box 20723, Phoenix, AZ 85036, (602)257-0777 [3413]

Western United Electric Supply Corp., 1313 W 46th Ave., Denver, CO 80211, (303)455-2725 [9577]

Western Water Products, Inc., 6060 Enterprise Dr., Diamond Springs, CA 95619, (530)621-0255 [25878]

Western Wyoming Beverage Inc., PO Box 1336, Rock Springs, WY 82902, (307)362-6332 [25051]

Westex Automotive Corp., 40880 Encyclopedia Circle, Fremont, CA 94538-2470, (510)659-1700 [3414]

Westfield Decorator Fashions, PO Box 419, Westfield, IN 46074, (317)896-2521 [15706]

Westgate Building Materials, 1908 Modoc, Madera, CA 93637, (209)673-9118 [8215]

Westgate Enterprises Inc., 2118 Wilshire Blvd., No. 612, Santa Monica, CA 90403-5784, (310)477-5891 [9578]

Westgate Fabrics Inc., 1000 Fountain Pkwy., Grand Prairie, TX 75050, (972)647-2323 [26246]

Westgate Fabrics Inc., PO Box 539503, Grand Prairie, TX 75050-9503, (972)647-2323 [21607]

Westguard Inc., PO Box 616, Twinsburg, OH 44087, (330)963-6116 [24661]

Westinghouse Electical Supply, 100 Oakley Ave., Lynchburg, VA 24501-3237, (804)845-0948 [9579]

Westinghouse Electric Corp. Trading Co., 11 Stanwix St., Pittsburgh, PA 15222, (412)642-4141 [5812]

Westlake Inc., 40 N Water St., Lititz, PA 17543-1609, (717)626-0272 [3415]

Westland International Corp., 5000 Hwy. 80 E, Jackson, MS 39208, (601)932-7136 [9580]

Westland Seed, Inc., 1308 Round Butte Rd. W, Ronan, MT 59864, (406)676-4100 [1434]

Westmark Industries Inc., 6701 McEwan Rd., Lake Oswego, OR 97035, (503)620-0945 [16629]

Westmed Specialties Inc., 1420 20th St., NW, Ste. B, Auburn, WA 98001-3413, (206)431-8480 [19108]

Westmoreland Industrial Supply Co., RD 12, Greensburg, PA 15601, (412)242-3814 [17277]

Weston Woods Studio Inc., 265 Post Rd W, Westport, CT 06880, (203)226-3355 [25522]

Westport Corp., 331 Changebridge Rd., PO Box 2002, Pine Brook, NJ 07058, (973)575-0110 [18445]

Westreet Industries, 8901 Kelso Dr., Baltimore, MD 21221, (410)686-8400 [27045]

Westshore Glass Corp., PO Box 15216, Tampa, FL 33684-5216, (813)884-2561 [8216]

Westside Development Inc., PO Box 2110, Covington, KY 41012, (606)431-4252 [14762]

Westside Distributors, PO Box 649, South Gate, CA 90280, (213)566-5181 [12916]

Westside Tile Co., 6408 Depot Dr., Waco, TX 76712, (254)776-1122 [10297]

Westvaco Worldwide, 299 Park Ave., New York, NY 10171, (212)688-5000 [21990]

Westview Press, 5500 Central Ave., Boulder, CO 80301, (303)444-3541 [4279]

Westway Trading Corp., 7901 Xerxes Ave. S, Ste. 320, Minneapolis, MN 55431, (612)885-0233 [12917]

Westway Trading Corp., 365 Canal Pl., No. 2200, New Orleans, LA 70130, (504)525-9741 [12918]

Wesvic's Clothing and Shoe Brokers, Inc., PO Box 1379, Pembroke, GA 31321-1379, (912)653-2379 [24892]

Wetherbee and Co.; George C., 2566 E Grand Blvd., Detroit, MI 48211, (313)871-3200 [3416]

Wetherill Associates Inc., 1101 Enterprise Dr., Royersford, PA 19468, (610)495-2200 [3417]

Wetsel, Inc., PO Box 791, Harrisonburg, VA 22801, (540)434-6753 [1435]

Wetsel Inc., PO Box 791, Harrisonburg, VA 22801, (540)434-6753 [14975]

Wetterau Inc., Greene Dr., PO Box 427, Greenville, KY 42345, (502)338-2833 [12919]

Wetterau Inc., 600 Daugherty St., Scott City, MO 63780-0999, (573)264-3811 [12920]

Wetterau Inc. Northeast, 56 Milliken St., Portland, ME 04104, (207)797-5490 [12921]

Wetterau Inc. Providence Div., 2700 Plainfield Rd., Cranston, RI 02921, (401)942-4000 [12650]

Wetterau Inc. West Virginia Div., PO Box 386, Milton, WV 25541, (304)743-9087 [12649]

Wexler Meat Co., 963 W 37th St., Chicago, IL 60609-1436, (773)927-5656 [12922]

Weyerhaeuser Co. Recycling Business Div., Mail Stop CH CCB438, Tacoma, WA 98477, (253)924-3342 [27046]

Whalen Co., PO Box 1390, Easton, MD 21601, (410)822-9200 [4731]

Whalen Tire, 845 Nevada Ave., Butte, MT 59701, (406)723-6170 [3418]

Whalerknits, PO Box 4096, New Bedford, MA 02741-4096, (508)997-1960 [4925]

Whaley Pecan Company Inc., PO Drawer 609, Troy, AL 36081, (205)566-3504 [12923]

Wharton and Barnard Inc., PO Box 179, Milford, DE 19963, (302)422-4571 [3419]

Whatley Supply Co., 230 Ross Clark Cir. NE, Dothan, AL 36303-5843, (334)794-4173 [10158]

Whayne Supply Co., PO Box 35900, Louisville, KY 40232-5900, (502)774-4441 [1436]

Wheat International Communications Corp., 1890 Preston White Drive, Reston, VA 20191, (703)262-9100 [9581]

Wheatland Rock Shop, 1808 9th St., Wheatland, WY 82201-2143, (307)322-2192 [17655]

Wheaton Dumont Cooperative Elevator Inc., 1115 Broadway Ave., Wheaton, MN 56296, (612)563-8152 [18342]

Wheel City Inc., 244 Constitution Way, Idaho Falls, ID 83402-3541, (208)524-3193 [3420]

Wheel Masters Inc., PO Box 60910, Reno, NV 89506-0910, (775)972-7888 [3421]

Wheelabrator Air Pollution Control, 441 Smithfield St., Pittsburgh, PA 15222, (412)562-7300 [25879]

Wheelchair Pit-Stop, 28 E Decatur Ave., Pleasantville, NJ 08232, (609)645-1610 [19701]

Wheeler Brothers, 420 Santa Fe, Alva, OK 73717, (580)327-0141 [18343]

Wheeler Brothers, 420 Santa Fe, Alva, OK 73717, (580)327-0141 [12924]

Wheeler Brothers Grain Company Inc., PO Box 29, Watonga, OK 73772, (580)623-7223 [18344]

Wheeler Brothers Inc., PO Box 737, Somerset, PA 15501, (814)443-7000 [3422]

Wheeler Consolidated Inc., 1100 Hoak Dr., West Des Moines, IA 50265, (515)223-1584 [8217]

Wheelock Company Inc.; George F., PO Box 10544, Birmingham, AL 35202-0544, (205)251-5268 [14763]

Whelchel Co.; Harry J., PO Box 5022, Chattanooga, TN 37406, (423)698-4415 [1437]

Whisler Bearing Co., PO Box 1336, Rapid City, SD 57709-1336, (605)342-8822 [21608]

Whitaker Farmers Cooperative Grain Co., 7690 E 9000 N Rd., Grant Park, IL 60940, (815)465-6681 [18345]

Whitaker House, 30 Hunt Valley Cir., New Kensington, PA 15068-7069, (412)274-4440 [4280]

Whitaker Oil Co., PO Box 93487, Atlanta, GA 30377, (404)355-8220 [22799]

Whitby Pharmaceuticals Inc., PO Box 85054, Richmond, VA 23261-5054, (804)254-4400 [19702]

White Associates; Bob, PO Box 39104, Solon, OH 44139, (440)248-1317 [5813]

White Bear Equipment, Inc., 4 Anderson Dr., PO Box 5450, Albany, NY 12205, (518)438-4462 [3423]

White Brothers Inc., 24845 Corbit Pl., Yorba Linda, CA 92887, (714)692-3404 [3424]

White Cloud Grain Co., PO Box 276, Hiawatha, KS 66434, (913)595-3254 [1438]

White Coffee Corp., 18-35 38th St., Long Island City, NY 11105, (718)204-7900 [12925]

White Commercial Corp., 1101 E Ocean Blvd., Stuart, FL 34996, (561)283-2420 [12926]

White Co.; Brock, 2575 Kasota Ave., St. Paul, MN 55108, (612)647-0950 [8218]

White Co.; The C.E., PO Box 308, 417 N Kibler St., New Washington, OH 44854, (419)492-2157 [3425]

White Company Inc.; John R., PO Box 10043, Birmingham, AL 35202, (205)595-8381 [12927]

White and Company Inc.; L.N., 225 W 34th St., New York, NY 10122, (212)239-7474 [12928]

White Company Inc.; William D., 3427 Magnolia St., Oakland, CA 94608, (510)658-8167 [9582]

White County Farmers Cooperative, 271 Mayberry St., Sparta, TN 38583, (931)836-2278 [1439]

White Cross Corporation, Inc., 350 Theo Frend Ave., Rye, NY 10580, (914)921-0600 [19703]

White Dove International, PO Box 1000, Taos, NM 87571, (505)758-5400 [4281]

White Electric Supply Co., 427 S 10th St., Lincoln, NE 68508, (402)476-7587 [9583]

White Electric Supply Co. (Monroe City, Missouri), 215 N Main St., Monroe City, MO 63456, (314)735-4533 [9584]

White Feather Farms Inc., 800 W 17th St., Muncie, IN 47302, (765)288-6636 [12929]

White Fountain Supply Co.; Bob, 2211 S Saginaw St., Flint, MI 48503, (810)238-1231 [24262]

White Inc., 816 9th St. S, PO Box 3367, Great Falls, MT 59403-3367, (406)453-4307 [14764]

White Inc.; Billy D., PO Box 3466, Odessa, TX 79762, (915)362-0326 [3426]

White Inc.; H. Lynn, 8208 Nieman Rd., Lenexa, KS 66214, (913)492-4100 [15707]

White Mountain, 1930 Fairway Dr., San Leandro, CA 94577, (510)895-8000 [21595]

White Office Furniture and Interiors; J.C., 200 SW 12th Ave., Pompano Beach, FL 33069-3224, (305)785-3212 [21355]

White River Cooperative, PO Box 232, Washington, IN 47501, (812)254-4250 [1440]

White River Paper Company Inc., PO Box 455, White River Junction, VT 05001-0455, (802)295-3188 [21991]

White River Paper Company Inc., PO Box 455, White River Junction, VT 05001-0455, (802)295-3188 [17278]

White Rose Paper Co., 4665 Hollins Ferry Rd., Baltimore, MD 21227, (410)247-1900 [21992]

White Sewing Machine Co., PO Box 458012, Cleveland, OH 44145-8012, (216)252-3300 [15371]

White Star Machinery and Supply Company Inc., PO Box 1180, Wichita, KS 67201, (316)838-3321 [8219]

White Star Video, 195 Hwy. 36, West Long Branch, NJ 07764, (732)229-2343 [25523]

White Swan, Inc., 915 E 50th, Lubbock, TX 79404, (806)747-5204 [12930]

White Swan, Inc., 5330 Fleming Ct., Austin, TX 78744-1122, (512)447-4121 [12931]

White Swan, Inc., PO Box 948, Houston, TX 77001, (713)672-2279 [12932]

White Swan Ltd., 2527 Camino Ramon Ste. 200, San Ramon, CA 94583-4409 [1441]

White Water Manufacturing, 1700 Nebraska Ave., Grants Pass, OR 97527, (541)476-1344 [17279]

White and White Pharmacy Inc., PO Box 801, Grand Rapids, MI 49518-0801, (616)956-6100 [19704]

Whitebox Inc., 3585 Habersham, Tucker, GA 30084, (404)414-0301 [6869]

Whitehall Company Ltd., 750 Everett St., Norwood, MA 02062, (617)769-6500 [2117]

Whitehill Lighting and Supply Inc., 1524 N Atherton St., State College, PA 16801, (814)238-2449 [9585]

Whiteman Industries, 6850 Business Way, Boise, ID 83716-5522, (208)336-7650 [8220]

Whitenight; Delavan E., Rd. 6, Danville, PA 17821-9806, (717)275-5698 [12933]

White's Herring Tractor and Truck Inc., PO Box 3817, Wilson, NC 27893, (252)291-0131 [3427]

White's Inc., 4614 Navigation Blvd., Houston, TX 77011, (713)928-2632 [1442]

Whites Shoe Shop Inc., 4002 E Ferry Ave., Spokane, WA 99202, (509)487-7277 [24893]

Whiteside F.S. Inc., PO Box 79, Cambridge, IL 61238-0079, (815)772-2155 [22800]

Whiteville Oil Company Inc., PO Box 689, Whiteville, NC 28472, (919)642-3188 [22801]

Whitley Central Distributing Co., PO Box 436, Winner, SD 57580-0436, (605)842-1948 [2118]

Whitlock Group, 3900 Gaskins Rd., Richmond, VA 23233, (804)273-9100 [6870]

Whitman Candies/Panghurn Chocolates, 4900 Oak Street, Kansas City, MO 64112, (816)842-9240 [12367]

Whitman County Growers Inc., PO Box 151, Colfax, WA 99111, (509)397-4381 [18346]

Whitmor/Wirenetics, 27737 Hopkins Ave., Valencia, CA 91355, (661)257-2400 [9586]

Whitmor/Wirenetics, 27737 Hopkins Ave., Valencia, CA 91355, (661)257-2400 [9587]

Whitson and Co., 8107 Springdale Rd., Ste. 101, Austin, TX 78724-2437, (512)929-9600 [9588]

Whittaker, Clark and Daniels, 1000 Coolidge St., South Plainfield, NJ 07080, (908)561-6100 [4553]

Whittemore Cooperative Elevator, 502 Railroad, Whittemore, IA 50598, (515)884-2271 [18347]

Whitten Pumps Inc., 502 County Line Rd., Delano, CA 93215, (805)725-0250 [16630]

Whittenburg, Inc.; N.A., 80 NE 13th St., Miami, FL 33132, (305)373-7566 [26247]

Whittier-Ruhle Millwork, 80 N Main St., Wharton, NJ 07885-1633, (973)347-6100 [8221]

Whittington Wholesale Company Inc., PO Box 67, Tunica, MS 38676, (601)363-2411 [1443]

WHO Manufacturing Co, PO Box 1153, Lamar, CO 81052, (719)336-7433 [1444]

Whole Herb Co., 19800 8th St. E, PO Box 1203, Sonoma, CA 95476, (707)935-1077 [12934]

Whole Pie Company Ltd., PO Box 130, Middleton, WI 53562, (608)836-4600 [5483]

Wholesale Builder Supply Inc., 51740 Grand River Ave., Wixom, MI 48393-2303, (248)347-6290 [15372]

Wholesale Building Materials Co., 1701 Magoffin St., El Paso, TX 79901, (915)533-9721 [8222]

Wholesale Ceramic Tile, 2885 Immanuel Rd., Greensboro, NC 27407, (910)292-0130 [10298]

Wholesale Distributors of Alaska, 2548 N Post Rd., Anchorage, AK 99501-1757, (907)277-8584 [23455]

Wholesale Distributors of Alaska, 2548 N Post Rd., Anchorage, AK 99501-1757, (907)277-8584 [23456]

Wholesale Electric Supply Company of Houston Inc., PO Box 230197, Houston, TX 77223-0197, (713)748-6100 [9589]

Wholesale Electric Supply Company Inc. (Bowling Green, Kentucky), PO Box 2500, Bowling Green, KY 42102-2500, (502)842-0156 [9590]

Wholesale Electric Supply Company Inc. (Texarkana, Texas), PO Box 1258, Texarkana, TX 75504, (903)794-3404 [9591]

Wholesale Electronic Supply Inc., 2809 Ross Ave., Dallas, TX 75201, (214)969-9400 [9592]

Wholesale Electronics Inc., 123 W 1st Ave., PO Box 1011, Mitchell, SD 57301, (605)996-2233 [9593]

Wholesale Furniture Distributors, 7015 Grand Blvd., Houston, TX 77054-2205, (713)747-1167 [13279]

Wholesale Hardwood Interiors Inc., 1030 Campbellsville Bypass, PO Box 485, Campbellsville, KY 42719, (502)789-1323 [8223]

Wholesale Heating Supply Co., 135 Orchard Lake Rd., Pontiac, MI 48341, (313)338-6454 [14765]

Wholesale and Home Supply Company Inc., 4829 W Pico Blvd., Los Angeles, CA 90019, (213)263-2127 [13280]

Wholesale House, 503 W High St., Hicksville, OH 43526, (419)542-7739 [25524]

Wholesale Marine Supply Co. of Alaska, Inc., PO Box 102900, Anchorage, AK 99510-2900, (907)279-7754 [18638]

Wholesale Paint Center, Inc., PO Box 1526, Rocky Mount, NC 27802-1526, (919)446-6045 [21609]

Wholesale Produce Supply Company Inc., 752 Kasota Cir., Minneapolis, MN 55414, (612)378-2025 [12935]

Wholesale Supply Company Inc., 212 Linn St., PO Box 143, Yankton, SD 57078-0143, (605)665-7827 [26372]

Wholesale Supply Company Inc., PO Box 1948, Minot, ND 58702, (701)852-2753 [26373]

Wholesale Supply Group Inc., PO Box 4080, Cleveland, TN 37320-4080, (423)478-1191 [23457]

Wholesale Supply Group, Inc. Maryville Division, 1513 Monroe Ave., PO Box 4216, Maryville, TN 37802, (423)982-3630 [23458]

Wholesale T-Shirt Supply, 1352 N Illinois St., Indianapolis, IN 46202, (317)634-4423 [5484]

Wholesale Tire Company Auto Centers, PO Box 5430, Bay Shore, NY 11706-0307, (516)665-7100 [3428]

Wholesale Tire Inc., PO Box 1660, Clarksburg, WV 26302, (304)624-8465 [3429]

Wholey and Company Inc.; Robert, 1501 Penn Ave., Pittsburgh, PA 15222, (412)261-3693 [12936]

Who's Bags, 95 Montgomery St., Paterson, NJ 07501-1117, (973)278-9702 [18442]

Wichelt Imports Inc., N162 Hwy. 35, Stoddard, WI 54658, (608)788-4600 [26248]

Wichita Falls Nunn Electrical Supply, 1300-14 Indiana, Wichita Falls, TX 76301, (940)766-4203 [9594]

Wichita Recycling, 1300 Burk Rd., Wichita Falls, TX 76305, (940)322-1720 [27047]

Wichita Sheet Metal Supply Co., 1601 S Sheridan St., Wichita, KS 67213-1339, (316)942-9412 [14766]

Wickman Corp., 10325 Capital Ave., Oak Park, MI 48237, (248)548-3822 [16631]

Wiemuth and Son Company Inc., PO Box 3128, Terre Haute, IN 47803, (812)232-3384 [26374]

Wiens Tire; Ted, 1701 Las Vegas Blvd S, Las Vegas, NV 89104, (702)732-2382 [3242]

Wiers Farm Inc., PO Box 385, Willard, OH 44890, (419)935-0131 [12937]

Wiggins Airways Inc. Parts East, PO Box 250, Norwood, MA 02062, (617)762-5690 [173]

Wiggins Airways Inc. Parts East; E.W., PO Box 708, Norwood, MA 02062, (781)762-3500 [174]

Wiggins Concrete Products, Inc., 100 River St., Springfield, VT 05156-2909, (802)886-8326 [10299]

Wigglesworth Machine Co., PO Box 166, East Boston, MA 02128, (617)567-7210 [16632]

Wight Nurseries Inc., PO Box 390, Cairo, GA 31728, (912)377-3033 [14976]

Wigwam Inc., PO Box 288, Lake George, MN 56458-0228, (218)266-3978 [24894]

Wigwam Inc., PO Box 288, Lake George, MN 56458-0228, (218)266-3978 [5485]

Wilbanks Oil Company Inc., 110 Maple St., Cleburne, TX 76031, (817)645-2701 [22802]

Wilbert Vault of Aroostook, PO Box 127, Houlton, ME 04730, (207)532-6858 [25880]

Wilbro Inc., PO Box 400, Norway, SC 29113, (803)263-4201 [1445]

Wilbur Chocolate Company Inc., 517 Clearview Pky., Metairie, LA 70001-4626, (504)454-0124 [12938]

Wilbur-Ellis Co., 345 California St., 27th Fl., San Francisco, CA 94104-2606, (415)772-4000 [4554]

Wilbur-Ellis Co., 215 N Summer St., West Burlington, IA 52655-1191, (319)752-6324 [4555]

Wilbur-Ellis Co., 1200 Westlake Ave. N, Ste. 1000, Seattle, WA 98109, (206)284-1300 [18348]

Wilbur-Ellis Co. Southern Div., PO Box 1020, Edinburg, TX 78540, (956)383-4901 [1446]

Wilcher Associates, 13547 Ventura Blvd., I98, Sherman Oaks, CA 91423, (818)784-0474 [4282]

Wilco Farmers Inc., PO Box 258, Mt. Angel, OR 97362, (503)845-6122 [1447]

Wilco Supply, 5960 Telegraph Ave., Oakland, CA 94609-0047, (510)652-8522 [13997]

Wilcox Brothers Co., PO Box 86245, Pittsburgh, PA 15221-0245, (412)243-3604 [3430]

Wilcox Drug Company Inc., PO Box 391, Boone, NC 28607, (828)264-3615 [14281]

Wilcox Frozen Foods Inc., 2200 Oakdale Ave., San Francisco, CA 94124, (415)282-4116 [12939]

Wilcox Marine Supply Inc., PO Box 99, Mystic, CT 06355, (860)536-4206 [18639]

Wilcox Paper Co., 5916 Court St. Rd., PO Box 378, Syracuse, NY 13206-0378, (315)437-1496 [21993]

Wild Craft Herb, 831 Almar Ave., Santa Cruz, CA 95060, (831)423-7913 [12940]

Wild Game Inc., 2475 N Elston Ave., Chicago, IL 60647-2033, (773)278-1661 [12941]

Wild West Company Inc., 1400 N Rouse Ave., Bozeman, MT 59715-2941, (406)587-5133 [5486]

Wilderness Nursery, Box 6078-A, Palmer, AK 99645, (907)745-6205 [14977]

Wildflower Collection, 3359 Osceola St., Denver, CO 80212, (303)433-5346 [17656]

Wildflower Jewelry, 3359 Osceola St., Denver, CO 80212, (303)433-5346 [17656]

Wildhawk Inc., R.R. 2, Box 123, Warrens, WI 54666-9802, (608)378-4164 [1448]

Wildish Land Co., PO Box 7428, Eugene, OR 97401, (503)485-1700 [8224]

Wildish Sand and Gravel Co., PO Box 7428, Eugene, OR 97401, (541)485-1700 [8225]

Wildlife Lithographs, Inc., PO Box 403, Dixon, IL 61021, (815)284-3871 [13472]

Wildlife Publications, Inc., 1014 NW 14th Ave., Gainesville, FL 32601 [4283]

Wildman and Sons Ltd.; Frederick, 307 E 53rd St., No. 2, New York, NY 10022, (212)355-0700 [2119]

Wildwasser Sport U.S.A. Inc., PO Box 4617, Boulder, CO 80306, (303)444-2336 [18640]

Wildwood Natural Foods, 135 Bolinas Rd., Fairfax, CA 94930, (415)459-3919 [12942]

Wilf Corp.; Elias, 10234 S Dolfield Rd., Owings Mills, MD 21117, (410)363-2400 [10300]

Wilf Corp.; Elias, 12700 Townsend Rd., Philadelphia, PA 19154, (215)673-9161 [10301]

WILFARM L.L.C., 215 N Summer St., West Burlington, IA 52655-1191, (319)752-6329 [4556]

Wilfley and Sons Inc.; A.R., PO Box 2330, Denver, CO 80201, (303)779-1777 [16633]

Wilhelm Warehouse Company Inc.; Rudie, 2400 SE Mailwell Dr., Milwaukie, OR 97222, (503)653-1501 [12943]

Wilke International Inc., 15036 W 106th St., Lenexa, KS 66215-2052, (913)438-5544 [12944]

Wilkens-Anderson Co., 4525 W Division St., Chicago, IL 60651, (773)384-4433 [24457]

Wilkerson Fuel Company Inc., PO Box 2835, Rock Hill, SC 29731, (803)324-4080 [22803]

Wilkerson Jewelers, 222 S Main, Stuttgart, AR 72160-4355, (870)673-4441 [17657]

Wilkersons Pecans, 304 Eldridge St., Sylvester, GA 31791-1310, (912)776-3505 [12945]

Wilkie; Robert, PO Box 1491, Joshua Tree, CA 92252-0828, (760)366-3925 [4284]

Wilkins Supply Co.; M.P., PO Box 352918, Toledo, OH 43635-2918, (419)531-5574 [23459]

Wilkinson Supply Inc., PO Box 6066, Raleigh, NC 27628, (919)834-0395 [23460]

Wilkof Morris Steel Corp., PO Box 3095, North Canton, OH 44720, (330)456-3401 [20491]

Wilkoff and Sons Co.; S., 2700 E 47th St., Cleveland, OH 44104, (216)391-6600 [27048]

Wilks Tire and Battery Service, 428 N Broad St., Albertville, AL 35950, (256)878-0211 [3431]

Will-Du Page Service Co., 100 Manhattan Rd., Joliet, IL 60433, (815)740-2840 [18349]

Will Poultry Co., 1075 William St., Buffalo, NY 14206, (716)853-2000 [12946]

Willamette Electric Products Co., 810 N Graham St., Portland, OR 97227, (503)288-7361 [16634]

Willamette Graystone Inc., PO Box 7816, Eugene, OR 97401, (541)726-7666 [8226]

Willamette Seed Co., PO Box 21120, Keizer, OR 97307-1120, (503)926-8883 [1449]

Willar Corp., E 1212 Front, Spokane, WA 99202, (509)533-9911 [14767]

Willard Safety Shoe Co., 37455 Rhonswood Dr., Northville, MI 48167-9748, (248)471-4944 [24895]

Willco Sales and Services Inc., PO Box 320003, Fairfield, CT 06432, (203)366-3895 [25881]

Willco Wholesale Distributors, 1601 W 8th St., Muncie, IN 47302, (765)289-6606 [14768]

Willcox and Gibbs Inc. Consolidated Electric Supply, 4561 34th St., Orlando, FL 32811, (407)841-4860 [9595]

Wille Electric Supply Co., 101 S 7th St., Modesto, CA 95354, (209)527-6800 [9596]

Willets O'Neil Co.; A., 7200 Biscayne Blvd., Miami, FL 33179, (305)759-2424 [4732]

Willette Seed Farm Inc., 41721 160th St., Delavan, MN 56023, (507)854-3595 [1450]

William/Reid Ltd., PO Box 397, Germantown, WI 53022, (414)255-5420 [25882]

Williams Auto Parts, PO Box 1269, Decatur, AL 35602, (205)353-0811 [3432]

Williams Companies Inc., 1 Williams Ctr., Tulsa, OK 74172, (918)588-2000 [5814]

Williams and Company Inc., 901 Pennsylvania Ave., Pittsburgh, PA 15233, (412)237-2211 [20492]

Williams Co.; W.W., 835 W Goodale Blvd., Columbus, OH 43212, (614)228-5000 [16635]

Williams Detroit Diesel Allison, 2849 Moreland Ave., SE, Atlanta, GA 30315, (404)366-1070 [3433]

Williams Detroit Diesel Allison, 869 W Goodale, Columbus, OH 43212, (614)228-6651 [3434]

Williams Detroit Diesel Allison, 3325 Libby Rd., Lemoyne, OH 43441, (419)837-5067 [3435]

Williams Detroit Diesel Allison, 1835 S Hwy. 101, Greer, SC 29651, (864)877-0935 [3436]

Williams Detroit Diesel Allison, 2610 Augusta Rd., U.S 1 & I-26, West Columbia, SC 29169, (803)791-5910 [3437]

Williams Distributing Co., 658 Richmond NW, Grand Rapids, MI 49504-2036, (616)456-1613 [15373]

Williams Distributing Corp., 372 Pasco Rd., Springfield, MA 01119, (413)783-1266 [2120]

Williams Equipment Co., 14808 W 117th St., PO Box 3237, Olathe, KS 66063, (913)764-9326 [16636]

Williams Equipment and Supply Company Inc., 2425 S 3rd St., Memphis, TN 38109, (901)366-9195 [8227]

Williams Fertilizer Co.; Archie, PO Box 1176, Carbondale, IL 62901, (618)549-0541 [1451]

Williams Inc.; M.R., 235 Raleigh Rd., Henderson, NC 27536, (919)438-8104 [12947]

Williams Inc.; Ralph C., 429 Waynesburg Rd. SE, Canton, OH 44707, (330)452-6548 [17280]

Williams Inc.; T.O., 300 Wythe St., Portsmouth, VA 23704-5208, (757)397-0771 [12948]

Williams Industrial Products, Inc.; J.H., 6969 Jamesson Rd., PO Box 7577, Columbus, GA 31909, (706)563-9590 [13998]

Williams Industries Inc., 2849 Meadow View Rd., Falls Church, VA 22042, (703)560-5196 [8228]

Williams Investigation & SEC, PO Box 1313, Garden City, KS 67846-1313, (316)275-1134 [5815]

Williams Lawn Seed, Inc., PO Box 112, Maryville, MO 64468, (660)582-4614 [1452]

Williams Ltd.; Ernie, PO Box 737, Algona, IA 50511, (515)295-3561 [1453]

Williams; Lyle L., 22601 154th Ave., Box Elder, SD 57719-0184, (605)923-3133 [18350]

Williams Metals Company, 946 Kane, Toledo, OH 43612-1246, (419)476-7805 [20449]

Williams Oil Co., PO Box 220, Bridgeport, AL 35740, (205)495-2413 [22804]

Williams Oil Co.; A.T., PO Box 7287, Winston-Salem, NC 27109, (910)767-6280 [22805]

Williams Oil Company Inc.; J.H., PO Box 439, Tampa, FL 33601, (813)228-7776 [22806]

Williams Optical Laboratory Inc., PO Box 1246, Nashville, TN 37202, (615)256-6631 [19705]

Williams Paint & Coatings, 7680 N Government Way, Coeur D Alene, ID 83814-8753, (208)772-6243 [21610]

Williams Physicians and Surgeons Supplies, PO Box 27, Shreveport, LA 71161, (318)424-8186 [19706]

Williams Produce; Ron, 76 N Trenton, Tulsa, OK 74120-1602, (918)582-3908 [12949]

Williams Sales & Service; Jim, PO Box 873, New Town, ND 58763-0873, (701)627-3212 [24046]

Williams Steel and Supply Company Inc., 999 W Armour Ave., Milwaukee, WI 53221, (414)481-7100 [20493]

Williams Supply Inc., PO Box 2766, Roanoke, VA 24001, (540)343-9333 [9597]

Williams Tire Co.; Jack, PO Box 3655, Scranton, PA 18505, (717)457-5000 [3438]

William's Umbrella Co., 1255 Post Rd., Scarsdale, NY 10583, (914)472-2098 [13473]

Williams and Wells Corp., 100 State St., Moonachie, NJ 07074, (201)440-1800 [18641]

Williamson & Co., 9 Shelter Dr., Greer, SC 29650, (864)848-1011 [17281]

Williamson; Darcy, PO Box 717, Donnelly, ID 83615, (208)325-8606 [4285]

Williamson; Gary, PO Box 2800, Great Falls, MT 59401-3141, (406)761-0373 [21356]

Williamson Publishing Co., PO Box 185, Charlotte, VT 05445, (802)425-2102 [4286]

Williamsville Farmers Cooperative Grain Co., PO Box 169, Williamsville, IL 62693, (217)566-3321 [18351]

The Willing Group, 222 Saint Johns Ave., Yonkers, NY 10704-2717, (914)964-5800 [14282]

Willis Distribution Beauty Supply, 4600 Homer Ohio Ln., Groveport, OH 43125-9230, (614)836-0115 [14283]

Willis Music Co., 7380 Industrial Rd., Florence, KY 41042, (606)283-2050 [4287]

Willis Steel Corp., PO Drawer 149, Galesburg, IL 61401, (309)342-0135 [20494]

Williston Industrial Supply Corp., PO Box 2477, Williston, ND 58801, (701)572-2135 [22807]

Willmar Poultry Company Inc., PO Box 753, Willmar, MN 56201, (612)235-3113 [12950]

Willow Distributors Inc., PO Box 153169, Dallas, TX 75315-3169, (214)426-5636 [2121]

Willow Hill Grain Inc., PO Box 213, Willow Hill, IL 62480, (618)455-3201 [18352]

Willow Hill Grain Inc., PO Box 213, Willow Hill, IL 62480, (618)455-3201 [12951]

Willow Run Foods Inc., PO Box 1350, Binghamton, NY 13902, (607)729-5221 [12952]

Wills Co., 301 4th Ave. SE, Waseca, MN 56093-3067, (507)835-2670 [13474]

Wilmar Industries Inc., 303 Harper Dr., Moorestown, NJ 08057, (609)439-1222 [23461]

Wilmington Hospital Supply, PO Box 3516, Wilmington, NC 28406, (919)763-5157 [19707]

Wilmont Farmers Elevator Co., PO Box 219, Wilmont, MN 56185, (507)926-5141 [18353]

Wilsbach Distributors Inc., PO Box 6148, Harrisburg, PA 17112, (717)561-3760 [2122]

Wilshire Book Co., 12015 Sherman Rd., North Hollywood, CA 91605, (818)765-8529 [4288]

Wilson Audio Sales, 5972 Asberry Ct., Nashville, TN 37221, (615)646-4477 [25525]

Wilson Brothers Co., 212 Atlantic Ave. N, Thief River Falls, MN 56701-2059, (218)681-1880 [3439]

Wilson Capital Truck L.L.C.; Elliot, 8300 Ardwick-Ardmore Rd., Landover, MD 20785, (301)341-5500 [20750]

Wilson Co., PO Box 9100, Addison, TX 75001, (972)931-8666 [16637]

Wilson Co.; H., 555 W Taft Dr., South Holland, IL 60473, (708)339-5111 [9598]

Wilson Co.; Jim, PO Box 970, Cape Girardeau, MO 63702-0970, (314)334-4477 [3440]

Wilson Corp.; W.S., 24 Harbor Park Dr., Port Washington, NY 11050, (516)621-8800 [175]

Wilson Electric Supply Co., 680 2nd St., Macon, GA 31201-2848, (912)746-5656 [9599]

Wilson Foods Company L.L.C., 1811 W 1700 S, Salt Lake City, UT 84104, (801)972-5633 [12953]

Wilson Industries Inc., PO Box 1492, Houston, TX 77251, (713)237-3700 [22808]

Wilson Marketing & Sales, 202 Union St., PO Box 487, Westfield, MA 01086, (413)568-8181 [12954]

Wilson Nursery; Dave, 19701 Lake Rd., Hickman, CA 95323, (209)874-1821 [14978]

Wilson Optical Company Inc., 8990 Summerford Ln., El Paso, TX 79907, (915)859-3415 [19708]

Wilson Paper Co., 363 S Kellogg St., Galesburg, IL 61401, (309)342-0168 [21994]

Wilson Products Company Inc., 1811 W 1700 S, Salt Lake City, UT 84104, (801)972-5633 [12955]

Wilson Seeds Inc., PO Box 391, Harlan, IA 51537, (712)755-3841 [18354]

Wilson & Sons, 23264 SE 58th St., Issaquah, WA 98029-8906 [4289]

Wilson and Sons Inc.; W.A., 6 Industrial Park, Wheeling, WV 26003, (304)232-2200 [15708]

Wilson Supply Co., PO Box 94100, Oklahoma City, OK 73143, (405)677-3382 [22809]

Wilson Supply Inc., 4030 Howick St., Salt Lake City, UT 84107-1454 [1454]

Wilson Wholesale Sporting Goods; John, 3710 Liberty Dr. 1, Iowa City, IA 52240-1800, (319)338-6352 [24047]

Wilson's Appliance Co.; Charlie, 202 E Market St., Louisville, KY 40202-1218, (502)583-0604 [15374]

Wiltech Corp., PO Box 517, Longview, WA 98632, (425)423-4990 [21611]

Wilton Corp., 300 S Hicks Rd., Palatine, IL 60067, (847)934-6000 [16638]

Wilton Corp., PO Box 88839, Chicago, IL 60680, (847)934-6000 [17282]

Wilton Industries Inc., 2240 W 75th St., Woodridge, IL 60517, (630)963-7100 [12956]

Wilton Manufacturing Company Inc., PO Box 329, Ware, MA 01082-0329, (413)967-5811 [5487]

Wimmer Cookbook Distribution, 4210 B. F. Goodrich Blvd., Memphis, TN 38118, (901)362-8900 [4290]

Wimsatt Brothers Inc., PO Box 32488, Louisville, KY 40232, (502)458-3221 [8229]

Win Nelson Inc., 420 Byrd St., Little Rock, AR 72203, (501)376-1327 [23462]

Win Nelson Inc., 3110 Kettering Blvd., Dayton, OH 45439, (937)294-7242 [23463]

Winburn Tile, 1709 E 9th St., Little Rock, AR 72202, (501)375-7251 [10302]

Winburn Tile Supply, 1709 E 9th St., Little Rock, AR 72202, (501)375-7251 [10302]

Winchell's Donut Houses Operating Company L.P., 1800 E 16th St., Santa Ana, CA 92701, (714)565-1800 [12957]

Winchester Equipment Co., 620 Penn Ave., Winchester, VA 22601, (540)667-2244 [16639]

Winchester Hat Corp., 725 David Crockett, Winchester, TN 37398, (931)967-0686 [5488]

Winchester Optical, 758 Pre Emption Rd., Geneva, NY 14456, (315)789-3911 [19709]

Winchester Optical, 1219 W Southern Ave., PO Box 3248, Williamsport, PA 17701-0248, (717)323-7141 [19710]

Winchester Optical Company Inc., 1935 Lake St., Elmira, NY 14902, (607)734-4251 [19711]

Winchester Surgical Supply Co., PO Box 35488, Charlotte, NC 28235-5488, (704)372-2240 [19712]

Winchester Sutler, 270 Shadow Brook Ln., Winchester, VA 22603, (540)888-3595 [26713]

Winco Distributors Inc., PO Box 2401, Houston, TX 77252, (713)224-5361 [8230]

Wind-Dorf (USA) Inc., 11009 S Orange Blossom Trl, Orlando, FL 32837-9433, (407)438-3180 [8231]

Wind Line Sails, 1524 Glencoe Ave., Highland Park, IL 60035, (847)433-0551 [18642]

Windjammer Inc., 525 N Main, Bangor, PA 18013, (215)588-0626 [5489]

Windmoeller and Hoelscher Corp., 23 New England Way, Lincoln, RI 02865, (401)333-2770 [16640]

Windom Cooperative Association, 251 1st Ave. S, Windom, MN 56101, (507)831-2580 [1455]

Windom Sales Company Inc., PO Box 53, Windom, MN 56101, (507)831-2694 [18355]

Window Components Manufacturing, 3443 NW 107th St., Miami, FL 33167, (305)688-2521 [8232]

Window Headquarters Inc., 1459 E 13th St., Brooklyn, NY 11230-6603, (718)965-1200 [8233]

Windows Memory Corp., 920 Kline St., Ste. 100, La Jolla, CA 92037, (619)454-9701 [6871]

Windows of the World, 1855 Griffin Rd., Ste. A123, Dania, FL 33004, (954)921-8336 [15709]

Windsor Distributors Co., 19 Freeman St., Newark, NJ 07105, (973)344-5700 [9600]

Windsor Industries Inc. (Englewood, Colorado), 1351 W Stanford Ave., Englewood, CO 80110, (303)762-1800 [16641]

Windsor Rhodes Co., 593 Mineral Spring Ave., Pawtucket, RI 02860-3408, (401)722-9500 [26249]

Windsor Shade Tobacco Co., 158 Woodland St., Hartford, CT 06105, (860)522-1153 [26375]

The Wine Co., 2222 Elm St. SE, Minneapolis, MN 55414, (612)331-6422 [2123]

Wine Distributors Inc., 5800 Pennsylvania Ave., Maple Heights, OH 44137, (216)587-9463 [2124]

The Wine Enthusiast Companies, PO Box 39, Pleasantville, NY 10570, 800-356-8466 [15710]

The Wine Merchant, PO Box 401, Ardmore, PA 19003, (610)239-7400 [2125]

Wine Trends, Inc., 331 Tremorth Blvd., Broadview Heights, OH 44147, (440)526-0943 [2126]

Wine Warehouse, 6550 Washington Blvd., City of Commerce, CA 90040, (213)724-1700 [2127]

Winebow, Inc., 22 Hollywood Ave., Ste. C, Ho Ho Kus, NJ 07423, (201)445-0620 [2128]

Wines and Spirits International, 700 Anderson Hill Rd., Purchase, NY 10577, (914)253-3777 [2129]

Winesellers Ltd., 9933 N Lawler Ave., Ste. 355, Skokie, IL 60077, (847)679-0121 [2130]

Wink Davis Equipment Company Inc., 800 Miami Cir., Ste. 220, Atlanta, GA 30324, (404)266-2290 [4733]

Winkler Group, Ltd., 321 Veazie St., Providence, RI 02904-2120, (401)272-2885 [17658]

Winkler Inc., PO Box 68, Dale, IN 47523, (812)937-4421 [12958]

Winkler Store Fixtures Co., 1611 Westminster St., Providence, RI 02909-1808, (401)351-2124 [13281]

WINMED Products Co., PO Box 61556, Ft. Myers, FL 33906-1556, (941)791-4000 [19109]

Winn Inc., PO Box 1936, Huntington Beach, CA 92647, (714)842-1301 [24048]

Winnco Inc., PO Box 688, Weatherford, OK 73096, (580)772-3448 [22810]

Winnelson Inc., 3110 Kettering Blvd., Dayton, OH 45439, (937)294-7242 [23463]

Winners Circle Systems, 2618 Telegraph Ave., Berkeley, CA 94704, (510)845-4823 [6872]

Winneva Distributing Co. Inc., PO Box 250, Winnemucca, NV 89446-0250, (702)623-2118 [2131]

Winnie Walker Co., PO Box 61556, Ft. Myers, FL 33906-1556, (941)791-4000 [19109]

WINOCO Inc., PO Box 1765, Greeley, CO 80632-1765, (970)352-6722 [20495]

Winograd's Steel and Supply, PO Box 1765, Greeley, CO 80632-1765, (970)352-6722 [20495]

Winona River and Rail Inc., 1000 East 3rd St., Winona, MN 55987, (507)289-9321 [1456]

Winona Sales Inc., 412 E 5th St., Winona, MN 55987-3921, (507)452-6973 [4967]

Winrock Bakery Inc., 3320 2nd St. NW, Albuquerque, NM 87107, (505)345-7773 [12959]

Winston Brothers Iron and Metal Inc., 17384 Conant, Detroit, MI 48212, (313)891-4410 [27049]

Winston-Derek Publishers Group Inc., PO Box 90883, Nashville, TN 37209, (615)256-0201 [4291]

Winston Inc.; Harry, 718 5th Ave., New York, NY 10019, (212)245-2000 [17659]

Wintenna Inc., 911 Amity Rd., Anderson, SC 29621, (864)261-3965 [5816]

Winter Gardens Quality Foods, 304 Commerce St., New Oxford, PA 17350, (717)624-4911 [12960]

Winter Gardens Salad Co., 304 Commerce St., New Oxford, PA 17350, (717)624-4911 [12960]

Winter Harbor Fisheries, HC 1 Box 41c, East Jewett, NY 12424-9707, (516)477-1170 [12961]

Winter Haven Citrus Grower Association, PO Box 1874, Dundee, FL 33838-1874, (941)294-2959 [12962]

Winter Port Boot Shop, 264 State St., Brewer, ME 04412-1519, (207)989-6492 [24896]

Winter Wolff Inc., 131 Jericho Tpk., Jericho, NY 11753, (516)997-3300 [20496]

Winterbottom Supply Co., PO Box 507, Waterloo, IA 50704-0507, (319)233-6123 [14769]

Winters; Adam, Southard Ave., Peekskill, NY 10566-1830, (914)737-6464 [12963]

Winters Oil Co., PO Box 1637, Corsicana, TX 75151, (903)872-4166 [22811]

Winward Trading Company., PO Box 9833, San Rafael, CA 94912, (415)457-2411 [12964]

Wipeco Corp., 855 N Cicero Ave., Chicago, IL 60651, (773)261-0225 [15711]

Wire and Metal Separation Inc., 542 Southbridge St., Worcester, MA 01610, (508)752-5070 [27050]

Wire Supplies Inc., PO Box 277, Beech Grove, IN 46107, (317)786-4485 [9601]

Wireless Telecom Inc., 3025 S Parker Rd., Ste. 1000, Aurora, CO 80014-2931, (303)338-4200 [6873]

Wirenetics Co., 27737 Hopkins Ave., Valencia, CA 91355, (661)257-2400 [9586]

Wirenetics Co., 27737 Hopkins Ave., Valencia, CA 91355, (661)257-2400 [9587]

WirthCo Engineering Inc., 6519 Cecilia Cir., Bloomington, MN 55439, (612)941-9073 [3441]

Wirtz Corp., 680 N Lakeshore Dr., 16th Fl., Chicago, IL 60611, (312)943-7000 [2132]

Wis WetGoods Co., 607 S Arch St., Janesville, WI 53545, (608)755-4961 [2133]

Wisco Farm Cooperative, PO Box 753, Lake Mills, WI 53551, (920)648-3466 [12965]

Wiscomp Systems Inc., W266 N665 Eastmound Dr., Ste. 110, Waukesha, WI 53186, (414)544-5504 [6874]

Wisconsin Bearing, 7701 N 67th St., Milwaukee, WI 53223, (414)365-8780 [17055]

Wisconsin Bearing, 2222 Nordale Dr., Appleton, WI 54911, (920)731-4121 [2992]

Wisconsin Bearing, 695 Sullivan Dr., Fond du Lac, WI 54935, (920)923-7500 [17283]

Wisconsin Bearing, PO Box 5635, De Pere, WI 54115-5635, (920)437-6591 [3442]

Wisconsin Bearing, 206 Hood St., La Crosse, WI 54601, (608)785-1200 [16642]

Wisconsin Bearing, 2125 S Stroughton, Madison, WI 53716, (608)221-3328 [17284]

Wisconsin Bearing, 3669 Enterprise Dr., Sheboygan, WI 53083-2663, (920)467-2621 [17285]

Wisconsin Bearing, 7130 Packer Dr., Wausau, WI 54401, (715)848-2994 [2991]

Wisconsin Brake and Wheel Inc., 4700 N 124th St., Milwaukee, WI 53225, (414)536-2060 [3443]

Wisconsin Brick & Block Corp., 6399 Nesbitt Rd., Madison, Oahu, 53719-1817, (608)845-8636 [10303]

Wisconsin Distributors Inc., 2921 Syene Rd., Madison, WI 53713, (608)274-2337 [2134]

Wisconsin Drywall Distributors, 1015 Femrite Dr., Madison, WI 53701, (608)221-8636 [8234]

Wisconsin Lift Truck Corp., 3125 Intertech Drive, Brookfield, WI 53045, (262)781-8010 [16643]

Wisconsin Office Systems, 6531 N Sidney Place, Milwaukee, WI 53209-3215, (414)352-9700 [21357]

Wisconsin Packing Company Inc., PO Box 913, Butler, WI 53007-0913, (414)781-2400 [12966]

Wisconsin Paper and Products Co., PO Box 13455, Milwaukee, WI 53213-0455, (414)771-3771 [21995]

Wisconsin Steel and Tube Corp., PO Box 26365, Milwaukee, WI 53226, (414)453-4441 [20497]

Wisconsin Supply Corp., PO Box 8124, Madison, WI 53708-8124, (608)222-7799 [23464]

Wisconsin Toy Company Inc., 1107 Broadway, Ste. 1408, New York, NY 10010, (212)741-2125 [26714]

Wisconsin Wholesale Beer Distributor, 2805 E Washington Ave., Madison, WI 53701, (608)249-6464 [2135]

Wise El Santo Company Inc., PO Box 8360, St. Louis, MO 63132, (314)428-3100 [5490]

Wise Snacks Bryden Distributors, 100 W Lincoln Ave., Williamsport, PA 17701, (570)323-5150 [12967]

Wise & Son; Frank C., RR 120, Hallowell, ME 04347-0120, (207)623-2363 [5491]

Wise & Sons; A.B., 4544 Muhlhauser Rd., Hamilton, OH 45011, (513)874-9642 [12968]

Wise Wholesale Electronics, 1001 Towson, Ft. Smith, AR 72901-4921, (501)783-8925 [9602]

Wishek Livestock Market Inc., PO Box 401, Wishek, ND 58495-0401, (701)452-2306 [18356]

Wishing Well Video Distributing Co., PO Box 1008, Silver Lake, WI 53170, (414)889-8501 [25526]

Wishing Well Video Distributing Co., PO Box 1008, Silver Lake, WI 53170, (414)889-8501 [15375]

Wisner Manufacturing Inc., 1165 Globe Ave., Mountainside, NJ 07092, (908)233-4200 [16644]

Witch Equipment Company Inc., 343 N Bowen Rd., Arlington, TX 76012, (817)469-6096 [8235]

With Enterprises Inc., 4725 Lumber St. NE, Ste. 1, Albuquerque, NM 87109-2113, (505)889-3879 [4734]

Witherspoon Supply; Yandle, PO Box 31548, Charlotte, NC 28231, (704)372-2780 [14770]

Witmer Foods Inc., PO Box 3307, Lavale, MD 21502, (301)724-5950 [12969]

Witmer's Inc., PO Box 368, Columbiana, OH 44408, (330)427-2147 [1457]

Witt Co.; Eli, 1879 Forest Pkwy., Lake City, GA 30260-3674, (404)363-9110 [26376]

Witt Co.; The Eli, PO Box 1510, 8305 SE 58th Ave., Ocala, FL 34480, (352)245-5151 [12970]

Wittek Golf Supply Co., Inc., 3650 N Avondale, Chicago, IL 60618, (773)463-2636 [24049]

Wittichen Supply Company Inc., 1600 3rd Ave. S, Birmingham, AL 35233, (205)251-8500 [14771]

Wittigs Office Interiors, 2013 Broadway, San Antonio, TX 78215-1117, (512)270-0100 [21358]

Wittigs Office Interiors, 2013 Broadway, San Antonio, TX 78215-1117, (512)270-0100 [13282]

Wittnauer International, 145 Huguenot St., New Rochelle, NY 10802, (914)654-7200 [17660]

Wittock Supply Co., 2201 E Industrial Dr., Iron Mountain, MI 49801-1466, (906)774-4455 [23465]

Wiurth Adams Nut and Bolt, 10100 85th Ave. N, Maple Grove, MN 55369, (763)424-3374 [13999]

Wixson Brothers Equipment Co., PO Box 205, Fisher, AR 72429, (870)328-7251 [22812]

Wizard Equipment Corp., 920 Crooked Hill Rd., Brentwood, NY 11717, (631)231-6200 [8236]

WJS Enterprises Inc., PO Box 6620, Metairie, LA 70009, (504)837-5666 [21359]

W.L. Roberts Inc., 3791 Air Park, Memphis, TN 38118, (901)362-2080 [15376]

W.L.C. Ltd., PO Box 400, Calverton, NY 11933, (516)727-3535 [27271]

WMF of America, 85 Price Pkwy., Farmingdale, NY 11735, (631)293-3990 [15712]

WMF Hutschenreuther USA, 85 Price Pkwy., Farmingdale, NY 11735, (516)293-3990 [15713]

WMF Hutsehenrouther USA, 85 Price Pkwy., Farmingdale, NY 11735, (631)293-3990 [15712]

WMT Machine Tool Company Inc., 600 Hollister Rd., Teterboro, NJ 07608, (201)288-2400 [16645]

W.N.C. Pallet & Forest Products Company Inc., PO Box 38, Candler, NC 28715, (828)667-5426 [8237]

W.N.C. Pallet and Forest Products Company Inc., PO Box 38, Candler, NC 28715, (828)667-5426 [27395]

W.N.C. Tile Distributors, 508 Swannanoa River Rd., Asheville, NC 28805, (704)298-3251 [10304]

Wogaman Oil Co.; R.W., 425 S Barron St., Eaton, OH 45320, (513)456-4882 [22813]

Wolberg Electrical Supply Company Inc., 35 Industrial Park Rd., Albany, NY 12206, (518)489-8451 [9603]

Wolcott and Lincoln Inc., 4800 Main St., Kansas City, MO 64112, (816)753-6750 [18357]

Wolcott and Lincoln Inc., 4800 Main St., Kansas City, MO 64112, (816)753-6750 [12971]

Wolcotts Forms Inc., 15124 Downey Ave., Paramount, CA 90723, (310)630-0911 [21996]

Wolf Imports, 2700 Woodson Rd., Ste. 202, St. Louis, MO 63114-4828, (314)429-3439 [25527]

Wolf River Country Cooperative, 519 N Shawano St., New London, WI 54961, (920)867-2176 [1458]

Wolf and Sons Inc.; Charles, 1212 Avenue of the Americas, New York, NY 10036, (212)719-4410 [17661]

Wolf Warehouse Distributors, 312 E Market St., New Albany, IN 47150, (812)944-2264 [18643]

Wolfe Distributing Co., PO Box 711, Terrell, TX 75160, (972)563-6489 [2136]

Wolfe's Terre Haute Auto Auction Inc., 1601 Margaret Ave., Terre Haute, IN 47802, (812)238-1431 [20751]

Wolff Brothers Supply Inc., 6078 Wolff Rd., Medina, OH 44256, (330)725-3451 [23466]

Wolff Corp., 11204 W Greenfield, Milwaukee, WI 53214, (414)257-2555 [16646]

Wolff Shoe Co., 1705 Larkin Williams Rd., Fenton, MO 63026, (314)343-7770 [24897]

Wolfgang Candy Co. Inc.; D.E., 50 E 4th Ave., PO Box 226, York, PA 17405, (717)843-5536 [12972]

Wolfington Body Company Inc., PO Box 218, Exton, PA 19341, (610)458-8501 [20752]

Wolfpax Inc., PO Box 5214, Manchester, NH 03108-5214, (603)623-3326 [24898]

Wolfriver Country Cooperative, PO Box 320, Weyauwega, WI 54983, (414)867-2176 [22814]

Wolfstein International, Inc., 900 Wilshire Blvd., Ste 1530, Los Angeles, CA 90017, (213)689-9514 [12973]

Wolohan Lumber Co., PO Box 3235, Saginaw, MI 48605, (517)793-4532 [8238]

Wolpert Refrigeration Inc., 4962 Dixie Hwy., Saginaw, MI 48601-5452, (517)777-5270 [14772]

Wolverine Distributing, 305 S Fourth St., Basin, WY 82410, (307)568-2434 [4292]

Wolverine Metal Company Inc., 21870 Hoover Rd., Warren, MI 48089, (734)758-6100 [20498]

Wolverine Packing Co., 1340 Winder St., Detroit, MI 48207, (313)259-7500 [12974]

Wolverine Toy, Hwy. 10 E, Booneville, AR 72927, (501)675-2000 [26682]

Wolverine Tractor and Equipment, PO Box 19336, Detroit, MI 48219, (313)356-5200 [1459]

Wolverine X-Ray Sales and Service, 21277 Bridge St., Southfield, MI 48034, (810)352-8600 [19110]

Wolverton Farmers Elevator, PO Box 69, Wolverton, MN 56594, (218)995-2565 [18358]

Wolverton Pet Supply, 16020 Lowell Rd., Lansing, MI 48906, (517)321-7250 [27272]

Womack Machine, 8808 E Admiral Pl., Tulsa, OK 74115, (918)836-7763 [3444]

Womack Machine, 2010 Shea Rd., Dallas, TX 75235, (214)357-3871 [16647]

Womack Machine, 2300 Wirt Rd., Houston, TX 77055, (713)956-6400 [16648]

Womack Machine Supply, PO Box 35027, Dallas, TX 75235, (214)357-3871 [16649]

Wonalancet Co., 1711 Tulle Cir. NE, No. 104, Atlanta, GA 30329-2391, (404)633-4551 [26250]

Wonder Bread Thrift Store Inc., 5923 S 350 W, Murray, UT 84107, (801)268-8774 [12975]

Wonderful World of Imports, 1820 6th Ave. SE, Ste. U, Decatur, AL 35601-6044, (256)353-9610 [15377]

Wonderly Company Inc., 25 Cornell St., PO Box 1458, Kingston, NY 12401, (914)331-0148 [15714]

Wong's Advanced Technologies Inc., 3221 Danny Park, Metairie, LA 70002, (504)887-3333 [6875]

Wood Brothers and Halstead Lumber, 4098 N 35th Ave., Phoenix, AZ 85017, (602)269-3255 [25948]

Wood Co.; W.B., 150 Floral Ave., New Providence, NJ 07974, (908)771-9000 [21360]

Wood County Farm Supply, PO Box 56, Arpin, WI 54410, (715)652-3835 [1460]

Wood Feathers Inc., PO Box 17566, Portland, OR 97217, (503)289-8813 [8239]

Wood Floor Wholesalers, 5151 Convoy, Ste. B, San Diego, CA 92111, (619)467-9663 [10305]

Wood Floor Wholesalers, 1541 S Ritchey, Santa Ana, CA 92705, (714)542-9900 [10306]

Wood Flooring Distributors, 2341 Industrial Pkwy. W, Hayward, CA 94545, (510)293-3939 [10307]

Wood-Fruitticher Grocery, PO Box 610130, Birmingham, AL 35261-0130, (205)836-9663 [12976]

Wood Inc.; J.R., PO Box 545, Atwater, CA 95301, (209)358-5643 [12977]

Wood-N-Stuf, 520 W Sunset Rd., Ste. 1, Henderson, NV 89015-4117, (702)564-0178 [26715]

Wood & Plastics Industries, 2100 Universal Rd., Pittsburgh, PA 15235, (412)793-7483 [8240]

Wood Products Inc.; Stanley, 15248 Broadmoor, Shawnee Mission, KS 66223-3137, (913)681-2804 [25528]

Wood Supply Co.; Walter A., 4509 Rossville Blvd., Chattanooga, TN 37407, (423)867-1033 [17286]

Woodard and Company Inc.; P.L., PO Box 877, Wilson, NC 27894, (919)243-3541 [1461]

Woodburn Fertilizer Inc., PO Box 7, Woodburn, OR 97071, (503)981-3521 [1462]

Woodcrafters Lumber Sales, Inc., 212 NE 6th Ave., Portland, OR 97232, (503)231-0226 [4293]

Woodhaven Foods Inc., 1101 Market St., Philadelphia, PA 19107, (215)698-1200 [12978]

Woodhouse Co.; J.S., PO Box 1169, West Springfield, MA 01089, (413)736-5462 [1463]

Woodings-Verona Tool Works Inc., 3801 Camden Ave., Parkersburg, WV 26101 [14000]

Woodlawn Hardware, 4290 Katonah Ave., Bronx, NY 10470-2095, (718)324-2178 [17287]

Woodmansee Inc., PO Box 798, Bismarck, ND 58502-0798, (701)223-9595 [21361]

Woodpecker Truck and Equipment Inc., PO Box 1306, Pendleton, OR 97801, (503)276-5515 [20753]

Woodshill Pool, PO Box 843, Swanton, VT 05488, (802)868-7057 [24050]

Woodson & Bozeman Inc., PO Box 18450, Memphis, TN 38181-0450, (901)362-1500 [25529]

Woodson and Bozeman Inc., PO Box 18450, Memphis, TN 38181-0450, (901)362-1500 [15378]

Woodstocker Books, 234 Meads Mountain Rd., Woodstock, NY 12498, (914)679-4024 [4145]

Woodworker's Supply Inc., 1108 N Glenn Rd., Casper, WY 82601, (307)237-5528 [27396]

Woodworks, 108 S State St., Nampa, ID 83686-2630, (208)466-8823 [13283]

Woodwyk Inc.; Casey, PO Box 9, Hudsonville, MI 49426-0009, (616)669-1700 [12979]

Woody Tire Company Inc., 1606 50th St., Lubbock, TX 79412, (806)747-4556 [3445]

Woody's Big Sky Supply, Inc., 1221 Round Butte Rd. W, Ronan, MT 59864, (406)676-5726 [8241]

Wool Growers Central Storage Co., 212 E 4th St., Roswell, NM 88201, (505)622-3360 [18208]

Woolley Inc.; L.A., 620 Tifft St., Buffalo, NY 14220, (716)821-1200 [9604]

Woolson Spice Co., 1555 Kalani St., Honolulu, HI 96817, (808)847-3600 [4294]

Woolworth Corp., 233 Broadway, New York, NY 10279-0003, (212)553-2000 [15379]

Wooten Oil Co., PO Box 1277, Goldsboro, NC 27533, (919)734-1357 [22815]

Worad Inc., 299 Brooks St., Worcester, MA 01606-3308, (508)852-2693 [5817]

Word Entertainment, 3319 W End, Ste. 200, Nashville, TN 37203, (615)385-9673 [25530]

Word Records & Music, 3319 W End, Ste. 200, Nashville, TN 37203, (615)385-9673 [25530]

Word Systems Inc., 4181 E 96th St., Ste. 100, Indianapolis, IN 46240, (317)574-0499 [21362]

Word Technology Systems Inc., 12046 Lackland Rd., St. Louis, MO 63129, (314)434-9999 [21363]

Worden Co., 199 E 17th St., Holland, MI 49423, (616)392-1848 [13284]

Words Distributing Company, 7900 Edgewater Dr., Oakland, CA 94621, (510)553-9673 [4295]

Wordware Publishing Inc., 2320 Los Rios Blvd., Ste. 200, Plano, TX 75074, (972)423-0090 [4296]

Work Duds, 5215 S Laburnum Ave., Richmond, VA 23231-4432, (804)226-1366 [24899]

Workstation Technologies Inc., 75 Gilcrest Rd., Ste. 200, Londonderry, NH 30353, (603)425-1744 [6883]

Worland Livestock Auction Inc., PO Box 33, Worland, WY 82401-0033, (307)347-9201 [18359]

World Access Inc., 945 E Paces Ferry Rd., Ste. 2240, Atlanta, GA 30326, (404)231-2025 [5818]

World Buying Service Inc., PO Box 43369, Louisville, KY 40243, (502)245-1166 [9605]

World Candies Inc., 185 30th St., Brooklyn, NY 11232-1705, (718)768-8100 [12980]

World Carpets Inc., PO Box 1448, Dalton, GA 30722, (706)278-8000 [10308]

World Class Software Inc., 415 U.S 1, Ste. F, Lake Park, FL 33403-3585, (561)585-7354 [6876]

World Communications Inc., 10405 Baur Blvd., Ste. E, St. Louis, MO 63132-1908, (314)993-0755 [5819]

World Computer Corp., PO Box 217006, Auburn Hills, MI 48326-2722, (313)377-4840 [6877]

World Computer Inc., 3681 N Campbell Ave., Tucson, AZ 85719, (520)327-2881 [6878]

World Data Products Inc., 121 Cheshire Ln., Minnetonka, MN 55305, (612)476-9000 [6879]

World Data Products Inc., 121 Cheshire Ln., Minnetonka, MN 55305-1063, (612)476-9000 [6880]

World Finer Foods Inc., 300 Broadacres Dr., Bloomfield, NJ 07003, (973)338-0300 [12981]

World Food Tech Services, 153 Cherry St., Malden, MA 02148, (781)321-3750 [12982]

World Fuel Services Corp., 700 S Royal Poinciana Blvd., St, Miami Springs, FL 33166, (305)884-2001 [22816]

World Fuel Services Inc., 700 S Royal Poinciana Blvd., Ste. 800, Miami Springs, FL 33166, (305)883-8554 [176]

World-Net Microsystems Inc., PO Box 14010-513, Fremont, CA 94539-1410, (408)263-8088 [6881]

World Network Trading Corp., 7311 NW 12th St., Ste. 19, Miami, FL 33101, (305)762-4653 [18446]

World Products Inc., 19654 8th St. E, Sonoma, CA 95476, (707)996-5201 [9606]

World Source Trading Inc., 19 Beale St., Ste. 19A, Quincy, MA 02170-2702, (617)847-1616 [25531]

World Trade Network, Ltd., 16920 28th Ave. N, Minneapolis, MN 55447, (763)473-3825 [18644]

World Traders (USA) Inc., 98-05 67th Ave., Rego Park, NY 11374, (718)896-9560 [9607]

World Variety Produce Inc., 5325 S Soto St., PO Box 21127, Los Angeles, CA 90058-3624, (213)588-0151 [12983]

World Wen, Inc., 580 Lincoln Park Blvd., Ste. 255, Dayton, OH 45429, (937)298-3383 [6882]

World Wide Chemnet Inc., 2100 S Utica St., Tulsa, OK 74114, (918)749-9060 [4557]

World Wide Distributors Inc., 2730 W Fullerton, Chicago, IL 60647-3089, (773)384-2300 [25883]

World Wide Distributors Inc., 2730 W Fullerton, Chicago, IL 60647-3089, (773)384-2300 [24263]

World Wide Equipment Inc., PO Box 71, Prestonsburg, KY 41653, (606)874-2172 [20754]

World Wide Imports of Orlando Inc., 1511 S Lake Pleasant Rd., Apopka, FL 32703, (407)886-0090 [17662]

World Wide, Inc., PO Box 1224, Minneapolis, MN 55440, (612)830-8700 [11446]

World Wide Laser Service Corp., 1340 W San Pedro St., PO Box 1940, Gilbert, AZ 85299-1940, (602)892-8566 [16650]

World Wide Metric, Inc., 67 Veronica Ave., Somerset, NJ 08873, (732)247-2300 [23467]

World Wide Pictures, Inc., 1201 Hennepin Ave., Minneapolis, MN 55403, (612)338-3335 [25532]

World Wide Pictures Inc., 1201 Hennepin Ave., Minneapolis, MN 55403, (612)338-3335 [15380]

World Wide Wine and Spirit Importers Inc., 40 Oak St., Norwood, NJ 07648, (201)784-1990 [2137]

WorldCom Network Services Inc., PO Box 21348, Tulsa, OK 74121, (918)588-3210 [5820]

Worldwide Books, 1001 W Seneca St., Ithaca, NY 14850, (607)272-9200 [4297]

Worldwide Distributors Inc., PO Box 88607, Seattle, WA 98138-2607, (253)872-8746 [5492]

Worldwide Dreams LLC, 350 Fifth Ave., Ste. 2101, New York, NY 10118, (212)273-9200 [18447]

Worldwide Environmental Products Inc., 430 S Cataract Ave., San Dimas, CA 91773, (909)599-6431 [3446]

Worldwide Exporters Inc., 2600 Garden Rd., Ste. 202, Monterey, CA 93940, (408)648-8331 [9608]

Worldwide Manufacturing Inc., 12910 SW 89th Ct., Miami, FL 33176-5803, (305)235-5585 [15715]

Worldwide Media Service Inc., 1 Meadowlands Plaza, Ste. 900, East Rutherford, NJ 07073-2100, (201)332-7100 [4298]

Worldwide Medical, 1084 Flynt Dr., Bldg. A, Jackson, MS 39208, (601)932-1525 [19111]

Worldwide Wines, Inc., 155 Schoolhouse Rd., Cheshire, CT 06410, (203)272-2980 [2138]

Worldwide Wonders, PO Box 82086, Portland, OR 97282, (503)239-7004 [12984]

Wormell; L.C., 305 Bridgeton Rd., Westbrook, ME 04092, (207)829-5161 [18360]

Wormell Livestock; L.C., 305 Bridgeton Rd., Westbrook, ME 04092, (207)829-5161 [18360]

Worsley Oil Company of Wallace Inc., Hwy. 117 N, Wallace, NC 28466, (919)285-7125 [22817]

Worth Data, 623 Swift St., Santa Cruz, CA 95060, (831)458-9938 [9609]

Worthington Data Solutions Inc., 623 Swift St., Santa Cruz, CA 95060, (831)458-9938 [9609]

Worthington Industries Inc., 1205 Dearborn Dr., Columbus, OH 43085, (614)438-3210 [20499]

Worthington Steel Co., 1127 Dearborn Dr., Columbus, OH 43085, (614)438-3205 [20500]

WOS Inc., PO Box 10387, Green Bay, WI 54307-0387, (920)336-0690 [19713]

W.O.W. Distributing Company Inc., W 238 N 1777 Rockwood Dr., Waukesha, WI 53188, (414)547-2337 [2139]

Wrangler Power Products Inc., 1500 Willow Way, Prescott, AZ 86304 [3447]

Wren Electronics, Inc., 1605 NW 82nd Ave., Miami, FL 33122, (305)591-5888 [9610]

Wrenn Brungart, PO Box 410050, Charlotte, NC 28241, (704)587-1003 [16651]

WRG Corp., 143B SW 153rd St., PO Box 66557, Seattle, WA 98166, (206)242-9300 [177]

WRI Education, 968 Emerald St., No. 6700, PO Box 9359, San Diego, CA 92169-0359, (619)456-5278 [25533]

Wricley Nut Products Co., 110 Tasker St., Philadelphia, PA 19147-0095, (215)467-1106 [12985]

Wricley Nut Products Co. Edwards-Freeman Div., 441 E Hector St., Conshohocken, PA 19428, (215)828-7440 [12986]

Wright Brokerage Inc., 1815 Erle Rd., Mechanicsville, VA 23111-1505, (804)746-5294 [12987]

Wright and Co.; E.T., 1356 Williams St., Chippewa Falls, WI 54729 [24900]

Wright Co.; F.B., PO Box 770, Dearborn, MI 48121, (313)843-8250 [17288]

Wright Co.; William S., PO Box 1729, Nogales, AZ 85628-1729, (520)281-0951 [12988]

Wright Lorenz Grain Company Inc., PO Box 2420, Salina, KS 67402-2420, (913)827-3687 [18361]

Wright & McGill Co., 4245 E 46th Ave., Denver, CO 80216-3262, (303)321-1481 [23639]

The Wright One Enterprises Inc., 909 SE Everett Mall Way, Ste. B-200, Everett, WA 98208, (425)355-5005 [26716]

Wright; Ronald J., 48 Community Dr., Newport, VT 05855, (802)334-6115 [18362]

Wright Supplier, 14 Marlboro Ave., Brattleboro, VT 05301-3522, (802)254-4718 [3448]

Wright Tool Co., PO Box 1239, Troy, MI 48099, (248)643-6666 [3449]

Wright-Way Inc., 1605 Hwy. 201 N, PO Box 374, Mountain Home, AR 72653-0374, (870)425-8868 [3001]

Wright and Wilhelmy Co., 11005 E St., Omaha, NE 68137, (402)593-0600 [15381]

Wright Wisner Distributing Corp., 3165 Brighton Henrietta Town Lin, Rochester, NY 14623, (716)427-2880 [2140]

Writers & Books, 740 University Ave., Rochester, NY 14607, (716)473-2590 [4299]

wTe Corp., 7 Alfred Cir., Bedford, MA 01730, (781)275-6400 [27051]

WTE Recycling Corp., 7 Alfred Cir., Bedford, MA 01730, (781)275-6400 [27052]

WTI, 75 Gilcrest Rd., Ste. 200, Londonderry, NH 30353, (603)425-1744 [6883]

Wuite Traders International, PO Box 70608, Sunnyvale, CA 94086, (408)766-2717 [17663]

Wurzbach Company Inc.; William, 1939 International Blvd., Oakland, CA 94606, (510)261-0217 [14773]

Wurzburg Inc., PO Box 710, Memphis, TN 38101, (901)525-1441 [21997]

Wuu Jau Company Inc., PO Box 5062, Edmond, OK 73083, (405)359-5031 [24051]

WWF Paper Corp., 2 Bala Plz., Ste.200, Bala Cynwyd, PA 19004, (610)667-9210 [21998]

WWF Paper Corp., 1150 Lively Blvd., Elk Grove Village, IL 60007, (847)593-7500 [21999]

Wyatt-Quarles Seed Company Inc., PO Box 739, Garner, NC 27529, (919)772-4243 [1464]

Wyle Electronics, 15370 Barranca Pkwy., Irvine, CA 92618-2215, (949)753-9953 [9611]

Wyle Laboratories Electronics Marketing Group, 165 Technology, Irvine, CA 92618, (949)788-9953 [6884]

Wyle Systems, 165 Technology, Irvine, CA 92618, (949)788-9953 [6884]

Wylie and Son Inc., PO Box 100, Petersburg, TX 79250-0100, (806)667-3566 [1465]

Wyndmere Farmers Elevator Co., PO Box 67, Wyndmere, ND 58081, (701)439-2252 [1466]

Wynn and Graff Inc., 2613 Grandview Ave., Nashville, TN 37211, (615)255-0477 [26251]

Wynn and Graff Inc., 2401 Dutch Valley Rd., Knoxville, TN 37918, (423)688-3100 [26252]

Wynne Company Inc.; A.D., 710 Baronne St., New Orleans, LA 70113, (504)522-9558 [13285]

Wynn's International Inc., PO Box 14143, Orange, CA 92863, (714)938-3700 [14001]

Wyo-Ben Inc., PO Box 1979, Billings, MT 59103, (406)652-6351 [17289]

Wyoming Liquor Division, 1520 E 5th St., Cheyenne, WY 82002, (307)777-7120 [2141]

Wyoming Machinery Co., PO Box 2335, Casper, WY 82602, (307)472-1000 [8242]

Wyoming Machinery Co., 1700 Cutler Rd., Cheyenne, WY 82003, (307)634-1561 [8243]

Wyoming Periodical Distributors, 5734 Old W Yellowstone, Casper, WY 82604, (307)266-5328 [4300]

Wyoming Stationery Company of Casper, PO Box 19, Casper, WY 82602-0019, (307)234-2145 [21364]

X-Ray Industrial Distributor Corp., 338 Delawanna Ave., Clifton, NJ 07014, (201)773-9400 [24458]

X-Ray Industries Inc., 1961 Thunderbird St., Troy, MI 48084, (248)362-2242 [9612]

X-Ray Products Corp., PO Box 896, Atascadero, CA 93423-0896, (562)949-8394 [19112]

X-Ray SJS Corp., PO Box 148, Mt. Pleasant, SC 29465-0148, (843)884-8943 [19038]

X-S Beauty Supplies, 163 N Main St., Port Chester, NY 10573-3303, (914)937-8787 [14284]

Xander Co. Inc.; A.L., PO Box 98, Corry, PA 16407-0098, (814)665-8268 [16652]

Xcell International Corp., 644 Blackhawk Dr., Westmont, IL 60559, (630)323-0107 [12989]

Xcell International Corp., 646 Blackhawk Dr., Westmont, IL 60559, (630)323-0107 [15382]

Xebec Corp., 5612 Brighton Ter., Kansas City, MO 64130, (816)444-9700 [9613]

Xerographic Copier Services Inc., 231 E Rhapsody, San Antonio, TX 78216, (210)341-4431 [21365]

Xetal Inc., 3590 Oceanside Rd., Oceanside, NY 11572, (516)594-0005 [19714]

Xilinx Inc., 2100 Logic Dr., San Jose, CA 95124-3400, (408)559-7778 [9614]

XML Corp., PO Box 164305, Austin, TX 78716, (512)442-2522 [6885]

XNEX Inc., 900 N Lake Shore Dr., Ste. 1013, Chicago, IL 60611, (312)266-1808 [5493]

Xpedx, PO Box 1567, Chattanooga, TN 37401-1567, (423)698-8111 [22000]

xpedx, 775 Belden Ave., Addison, IL 60101, (630)628-0400 [21800]

Xpedx, 3940 Olympic Blvd., No. 250, Erlanger, KY 41018, (859)282-5600 [22001]

xpedx, PO Box 21767, Greensboro, NC 27420, (336)299-1211 [22002]

XPEDX, W 232 N 2950 Roundy Cir. E, PO Box 550, Pewaukee, WI 53072-4034, (262)549-9400 [22003]

xpedx, 4510 Reading Rd., Cincinnati, OH 45229, (513)641-5000 [22004]

Xpedx, 613 Main St., Wilmington, MA 01887, (978)988-7447 [17290]

Xpedx-Birmingham, PO Box 11367, Birmingham, AL 35202, (205)798-8380 [4558]

Xpedx/Carpenter Group, PO Box 2709, Grand Rapids, MI 49548, (616)452-9741 [22005]

Xpedx-Carpenter Group, 401 Fernhill Ave., Ft. Wayne, IN 46805, (219)482-4686 [22006]

Xpedx/Carpenter Group, PO Box 2709, Grand Rapids, MI 49548, (616)452-9741 [22007]

xpedx West Region, 55 Madison Ave., Ste. 800, Denver, CO 80206, (303)329-6644 [22008]

Xport Port Authority Trading Co., One World Trade Center, 34 N, New York, NY 10048, (212)435-8499 [4559]

XWW Alloys, Inc., 6200 N Telegraph Rd., Dearborn Heights, MI 48127, (313)274-0500 [16653]

XYZ Electronics Inc., 4700 N 600 W, McCordsville, IN 46055-9508, (317)335-2128 [6886]

Yaesu U.S.A. Inc., 17210 Edwards Rd., Cerritos, CA 90701, (562)404-2700 [25534]

Yaffe Iron and Metal Company Inc., PO Box 916, Muskogee, OK 74401, (918)687-7543 [20501]

Yahara Materials Inc., PO Box 277, Waunakee, WI 53597, (608)849-4162 [8244]

Yakima Hardware Co., 226 S 1st St., Yakima, WA 98901, (509)453-3181 [14002]

Yale/Chase Materials Handling, Inc., 2615 Pellissier Place, PO Box 1231, La Puente, CA 91749, (562)699-0501 [16654]

Yale Electric Supply Company Inc., 296 Freeport St., Dorchester, MA 02122, (617)825-9253 [9615]

Yale Farmers Cooperative, PO Box 128-127, Yale, SD 57386, (605)599-2911 [18363]

Yamada Distributors Ltd.; K., 2949 Koapaka St., Honolulu, HI 96819, (808)836-3221 [25949]

Yamaha Corporation of America, PO Box 6600, Buena Park, CA 90620, (714)522-9011 [25535]

Yamaha Corporation of America Band and Orchestral Division, 3445 E Paris Ave. SE, Grand Rapids, MI 49512-0899, (616)940-4900 [25536]

Yamaha Electronics Corporation USA, 6660 Orangethorpe Ave., Buena Park, CA 90620, (714)522-9105 [25537]

Yamaha Motor Corporation USA, PO Box 6555, Cypress, CA 90630, (714)761-7300 [20755]

Yamaha Systems Technology, 6600 Orangethorpe Ave., Buena Park, CA 90620-1396, (408)437-3133 [9616]

Yamashiro, Inc.; A., 746 Bannister St., Honolulu, HI 96819, (808)841-8726 [14979]

Yamato Corp., PO Box 15070, Colorado Springs, CO 80935-5070, (719)591-1500 [24459]

Yancey Machine Tool Co., 4110 SW Macadam Ave., Portland, OR 97201, (503)228-7259 [16655]

Yang Machine Tool Co., 4920 E La Palma Ave., Anaheim, CA 92807, (714)693-0705 [16656]

Yankee Book Peddler Inc., 999 Maple St., Contoocook, NH 03229, (603)746-3102 [4301]

Yankee Custom, Inc., 1271 Main St., Tewksbury, MA 01876, (978)851-9024 [3450]

Yankee Electronics Inc., 102 Maple St., Manchester, NH 03103, (603)625-9746 [9617]

Yankee Marketers Inc., PO Box 370, Middleton, MA 01949, (978)777-9181 [12990]

Yankee Paperback & Textbook Co., PO Box 18880, Tucson, AZ 85731, (520)325-7229 [4302]

Yankee Photo Products Inc., 4024 E Broadway, Ste. 1002, Phoenix, AZ 85040-8823, (602)437-8200 [22916]

Yankton Janitorial Supply, 1116 W 9th St., Yankton, SD 57078-3311, (605)665-6855 [4735]

Yankton Office Equipment, PO Box 604, Yankton, SD 57078-0604, (605)665-2289 [21366]

YAO Industries, 535 5th Ave., 33rd Fl., New York, NY 10017, (212)697-8686 [12991]

Yao Shih-Chin Corp., 535 5th Ave., 33rd Fl., New York, NY 10017, (212)697-8686 [12991]

Yarborough and Co., PO Box 308, High Point, NC 27261-0308, (919)861-2345 [14003]

Yarde Metals Inc., 71 Horizon Dr., Bristol, CT 06010, (860)589-2386 [20502]

Yardville Supply Co., PO Box 8427, Trenton, NJ 08650, (609)585-5000 [8245]

The Yarn Center, Rte. 2, Box 2691, Chatsworth, GA 30705, (706)695-3443 [26717]

Yarn Tree Designs, PO Box 724, Ames, IA 50010, (515)232-3121 [26253]

Yarnell Ice Cream Company Inc., 205 S Spring, Searcy, AR 72143-6730, (501)268-2414 [12992]

Yasutomo and Company Inc., 490 Eccles Ave., South San Francisco, CA 94080, (415)737-8888 [22009]

Yasutomo and Company Inc., 490 Eccles Ave., South San Francisco, CA 94080, (415)737-8888 [22009]

Yates & Bird, 300 N Elizabeth St., 2N, Chicago, IL 60607, (312)226-2412 [19715]

Yates and Bird, 300 N Elizabeth St., 2N, Chicago, IL 60607, (312)226-2412 [9618]

Yaun Company Inc., 17 Commercial Rd., Albany, NY 12205, (518)438-6433 [23468]

Ye Old Black Powder Shop, 994 W Midland Rd., Auburn, MI 48611, (517)662-2271 [13517]

Ye Olde Genealogie Shoppe, 9605 Vandergriff Rd., PO Box 39128, Indianapolis, IN 46239, (317)862-3330 [4303]

Yeager Hardware, 1610 E Main St., Van Buren, AR 72956, (501)474-5278 [10309]

Yearwoods Inc., PO Box 18350, Shreveport, LA 71138-1350, (318)688-1844 [24901]

Yeatman Architectural Hardware Inc., 8030 Holly Ave., Waldorf, MD 20601, (301)868-8850 [14004]

Yecies Inc.; Herman W., PO Box 688, Passaic, NJ 07055, (973)777-7200 [17291]

Yeck Antique Firearms, 579 Tecumseh St., Dundee, MI 48131, (734)529-3456 [13518]

Yeh Dah Ltd., 98-1805 Piki St., Aiea, HI 96701-1625, (808)487-7085 [17664]

Yell-O-Glow Corp., PO Box 6265, Chelsea, MA 02150-0007, 800-767-3225 [12993]

Yellow River Systems, 401 Broadway, Ste. 703, New York, NY 10013, (212)714-2789 [19113]

Yellowstone Paper Co., PO Box 1557, Billings, MT 59103-1557, (406)252-3488 [22010]

Yen Enterprises Inc., 1360 W 9th St., Cleveland, OH 44113-1254, (216)621-5115 [20503]

Yeomans Distributing Co., 1503 W Altorfer Dr., Peoria, IL 61615, (309)691-3282 [14774]

Yesco Ltd., 1960 Crossbeam Dr., Charlotte, NC 28217-2820, (704)357-6363 [26718]

Yezbak Enterprises, 108 N Beeson Blvd., Uniontown, PA 15401, (724)438-5543 [27397]

Yezbak Lumber Inc., 108 N Beeson Blvd., Uniontown, PA 15401, (412)438-5543 [8246]

Yingling Aircraft Inc., PO Box 9248, Wichita, KS 67277, (316)943-3246 [178]

Yoder Brothers Inc., 115 3rd St. SE, Barberton, OH 44203, (330)745-2143 [14980]

Yoder Oil Company Inc., PO Box 10, Elkhart, IN 46515, (219)264-2107 [22818]

Yoders Inc., PO Box 249, Grantsville, MD 21536-0249, (301)895-5121 [12994]

Yong's Watch & Clock Repair, 2700 State St. 13, Las Vegas, NV 89109-1604, (702)892-9776 [17665]

York Corrugating Co., PO Box 1192, York, PA 17405, (717)845-3511 [23469]

York Electrical Supply Co., PO Box 2008, Harrisburg, PA 17105-2008, (717)843-9991 [9619]

York Hannover Health Care Inc., 75 South Church Street, Pittsfield, MA 01201, (413)448-2111 [19716]

York International Corp., 160 Raritan Ctr. Pkwy., Ste. 6, Edison, NJ 08837, (732)469-5400 [14775]

York International Corp. Frick/Reco Div., 5692 E Houston St., San Antonio, TX 78220-1958, (210)661-9191 [14776]

York Novelty Import Inc., 10 W 37th St., New York, NY 10018, (212)594-7040 [17666]

York River Seafood Company Inc., PO Box 239, Hayes, VA 23072-9802, (804)642-2151 [12995]

York Tape and Label Co., PO Box 1309, York, PA 17405, (717)846-4840 [22011]

York Truck Center Inc., 55 S Fayette St., York, PA 17404, (717)792-2636 [20756]

Yorkshire Food Sales Corp., 2000 Plaza Ave., PO Box 148, New Hyde Park, NY 11040-0136, (516)328-1500 [12996]

Yorktown Industries Inc., 330 Factory Rd., Addison, IL 60101, (630)543-6110 [21367]

Yorktowne Inc., PO Box 231, Red Lion, PA 17356, (215)739-7700 [8247]

Yorktowne Kitchens, Distribution Center, 3405 Board Rd., York, PA 17402, (717)764-0699 [8248]

Yorktowne Kitchens, 2070 Bennett Ave., Lancaster, PA 17601, (717)291-1947 [8249]

Yorkville Sound Inc., 4625 Witmer Industrial Estate, Niagara Falls, NY 14305, (716)297-2920 [25538]

Yosemite Technologies, 2750 N Clovis Ave., Fresno, CA 93727, (209)292-8888 [6887]

Yost Office Systems, Inc., 675 E Anderson, Idaho Falls, ID 83401, (208)523-3549 [21368]

Younce and W.T. Ralph Lumber Company Inc.; J.W., 52 Younce Rd., PO Box 160, Pantego, NC 27860, (919)943-6166 [27398]

Young Co.; Behler, 3419 Lapeer Rd., Flint, MI 48503, (810)743-1160 [14777]

Young Co.; Behler, 929 Second St., Kalamazoo, MI 49001, (616)343-5504 [14778]

Young Co.; Behler, 1411 E High St., Jackson, MI 49203-3315, (517)789-7191 [14779]

Young Co.; Behler, 1244 E Carver St., Traverse City, MI 49684, (616)946-7391 [14780]

Young Co.; Behler, 3325 Enterprise, Saginaw, MI 48603, (517)799-4805 [14781]

Young Co.; Behler, 3100 W Main, Lansing, MI 48917, (517)371-1770 [14782]

Young Co.; Behler, 2440 S Industrial, Ann Arbor, MI 48104, (734)761-5511 [14783]

Young Co.; Behler, 1075 Golf Dr., Bloomfield, MI 48302, (248)335-6527 [14784]

Young Co.; Behler, 26444 Groesbeck Hwy., Warren, MI 48089, (810)779-1730 [14785]

Young Co.; Behler, 12920 Inkster Rd., Redford, MI 48239, (313)532-7990 [14786]

Young Company Inc.; A.R., PO Box 11135, Indianapolis, IN 46201, (317)263-3800 [3451]

Young Co.; William M., PO Box 10487, Wilmington, DE 19850, (302)654-4448 [8250]

Young Cos.; A.B., PO Box 90287, Indianapolis, IN 46290-0287, (317)844-7001 [16657]

Young Cos.; A.B., PO Box 90287, Indianapolis, IN 46290-0287, (317)844-7001 [17292]

Young Inc.; W.F., 111 Lyman St., Springfield, MA 01103, (413)737-0201 [19717]

Young Journal Inc.; Richard, 1096 E Newport Center Dr., Ste. 300, Deerfield Beach, FL 33442-7744, (954)426-8100 [6888]

Young Minds Inc., 1906 Orange Tree Ln., Ste. 220, Redlands, CA 92374-1350, (909)335-1350 [6889]

Young Oil CO., 1010 S Central Ave., Idabel, OK 74745, (580)286-5693 [22819]

Young Pecan Shelling Company Inc., PO Box 5779, Florence, SC 29502, (843)664-2330 [12997]

Young-Phillip Corporation, 6399 Amp Dr., Clemmons, NC 27012, (336)766-7070 [21021]

Young-Phillips Sales Co., 6399 Amp Dr., Clemmons, NC 27012, (910)766-7070 [25884]

Young Sales Corp., 1054 Central Industrial, St. Louis, MO 63110, (314)771-3080 [8251]

Young Steel Products Co., 17819 Foxborough Ln., Boca Raton, FL 33496, (330)759-3911 [20504]

Young Supply Co., 888 W Baltimore Ave., Detroit, MI 48202, (313)875-3280 [14787]

Young Supply North; Frank, 1913 Pickwick, Glenview, IL 60025, (847)657-7100 [14788]

Young and Vann Supply Co., PO Box 757, Birmingham, AL 35201, (205)252-5161 [17293]

Young Windows Inc., PO Box 387, Conshohocken, PA 19428, (610)828-5422 [3452]

Youngblood Oil Company Inc., PO Box 2590, Hendersonville, NC 28793, (704)693-6219 [22820]

Young's, 55 Cherry Ln., Souderton, PA 18964, (215)723-4400 [13286]

Young's Market Co., 2164 N Batavia, Orange, CA 92865, (714)283-4933 [2142]

Young's Market Co., 30740 Santana St., Hayward, CA 94544, (510)475-2278 [2143]

Young's: The Paint Place, 1421 W 2nd St., Roswell, NM 88201, (505)622-3251 [21612]

Ypsilanti Equity Elevator Company Inc., PO Box 287, Ypsilanti, ND 58497, (701)489-3379 [18364]

Yudkin & Associates; Samuel, A232 Woodber, 3636 16th St, NW, Washington, DC 20010, (202)232-6249 [4304]

Yukon Equipment, 2020 E Third Ave., Anchorage, AK 99501, (907)277-1541 [8252]

Yum Yum Donut Shops, Inc., 18830 E San Jose Ave., City of Industry, CA 91748, (626)964-1478 [12998]

Yuma Winnelson Co., PO Box 709, Yuma, AZ 85365, (520)341-1993 [23470]

Yves Saint Laurent Parfums Corp., 40 W 57th St., New York, NY 10019, (212)621-7300 [14285]

Z-Weigh Inc., 26469 Northline Rd., Taylor, MI 48180-4479, (313)846-2550 [24460]

Zabel Co.; C & W, PO Box 41, Leonia, NJ 07605-0041, (732)254-1000 [4305]

Zabin Industries Inc., 3957 S Hill St., Los Angeles, CA 90037, (213)749-1215 [26254]

Zachary Software Inc., 1090 Kapp Dr., Clearwater, FL 33755, (813)298-1181 [6890]

Zack Electronics, 1070 Hamilton Rd., Duarte, CA 91010-2742, (626)303-0655 [5821]

Zack Electronics Inc., 309 E Brokaw Rd., San Jose, CA 95112-4208, (408)324-0551 [9620]

Zack Trading, 2724 S Park Rd., Hallandale, FL 33009-3833, (954)983-9100 [17667]

Zacky Foods Co., 2000 N Tyler Ave., South el Monte, CA 91733, (818)443-9351 [12999]

Zagar Inc., 24000 Lakeland Blvd., Cleveland, OH 44132, (216)731-0500 [16658]

Zajac's Performance Seed, 33 Sicomac Rd., North Haledon, NJ 07508, (973)423-1660 [1467]

Zak Designs Inc., S 1604 Garfield Rd., Spokane, WA 99224, (509)244-0555 [15716]

Zakion; Robert, PO Box 677, Amesbury, MA 01913-0677, (978)388-0021 [21369]

Zaloudek Co.; Florein W., PO Box 187, Kremlin, OK 73753-0187, (580)874-2211 [1468]

Zamoiski Company Inc., 3000 Waterview Ave., Baltimore, MD 21230-3510, (410)539-3000 [15383]

Zamzow's Inc., 1201 Franklin Blvd., Nampa, ID 83687-6744 [1469]

Zanders Creamery Inc., 1214 Main, Cross Plains, WI 53528-9647, (608)798-3261 [13000]

Zanella Ltd., 681 5th Ave., New York, NY 10022, (212)371-2121 [5494]

Zanios Foods, 221 Airport Dr. NW, Albuquerque, NM 87101, (505)831-1411 [13001]

Zanios Foods Inc., PO Box 27730, Albuquerque, NM 87125-7730, (505)831-1411 [13002]

Zanker Road Resource Management Co., 575 Charles St., San Jose, CA 95112, (408)263-2385 [27053]

Zanotto Distributing Company Inc., 4117 NE Minnehaha St., Vancouver, WA 98661-1241, (360)693-6200 [26719]

Zapper Inc., 3131 Western Ave., Ste. 330, Seattle, WA 98121-1034, (425)822-7800 [9621]

Zappia Enterprises Inc., 173 Dingens St., Buffalo, NY 14206, (716)822-6850 [20757]

Zatarain's, PO Box 347, Gretna, LA 70054, (504)367-2950 [13003]

Zatkoff Seals and Packings Co., 23230 Industrial Park Dr., Farmington, MI 48335-2850, (248)478-2400 [17294]

ZDI Gaming Inc., 4117 NE Minnehaha St., Vancouver, WA 98661-1241, (360)693-6200 [26719]

Zeager Brothers Inc., 4000 E Harrisburg Pke., Middletown, PA 17057, (717)944-7481 [27399]

Zeb Pearce Cos., PO Box 1239, Mesa, AZ 85211-1239, (602)834-5527 [2144]

Zebra Pen Corp., 105 Northfield Ave., Edison, NJ 08837, (732)225-6310 [21370]

Zed Group Inc., IMC Box 6475, Chelsea, MA 02150, (617)889-2220 [16659]

Zee Medical Service Co., PO Box 849, Wolfeboro Falls, NH 03896-0849, (603)569-6284 [19114]

Zee Service Inc., 22 Corporate Park, Irvine, CA 92606-3112, (714)252-9500 [19718]

Zeeland Lumber and Supply Inc., 146 E Washington Ave., Zeeland, MI 49464, (616)772-2119 [8253]

Zeiger International Inc., 625 Prospect St., Trenton, NJ 08618, (609)394-1000 [26720]

Zeigler's Market, 315 N Ridgewood, US 1, Edgewater, FL 32132, (904)427-6136 [14981]

Zeiss Inc.; Carl, 1 Zeiss Dr., Thornwood, NY 10594, (914)747-1800 [24461]

Zekes Distributing Co., PO Box 145, Helena, MT 59624-0145, (406)442-7249 [2145]

Zeller Electric Inc., 4250 Hoffmeister Ave., St. Louis, MO 63125, (314)638-9641 [3453]

Zellerbach Co., 3131 New Mark Dr., Miamisburg, OH 45342, (937)495-6000 [22012]

Zenchiku Land and Cattle Co., 4600 Carrigan Ln., Dillon, MT 59725, (406)683-5474 [18365]

Zenith Supply Company Inc., 50 32nd St., Pittsburgh, PA 15201, (412)391-9570 [17295]

Zenobia Co., 3632 Kingsbridge Ave., Bronx, NY 10463-2339, (718)796-7700 [13004]

Zentao Corp., 650 N Edgewood Ave., Wood Dale, IL 60191-2615, (708)628-6780 [9622]

Zenter Enterprises Ltd., 53 Middleburg Ln., Orchard Park, NY 14127, (716)826-5797 [27273]

Zep Manufacturing Co., Springfield, 10 Fadem Rd., Springfield, NJ 07081, (973)379-6545 [4560]

Zephyr Egg Co., PO Box 9005, Zephyrhills, FL 33539-9005, (813)782-1521 [13005]

Zephyr Manufacturing Co., Inc., 201 Hindry Ave., Inglewood, CA 90301-1519, (310)410-4907 [179]

Zephyr Press, Inc., PO Box 66006, Tucson, AZ 85728-6006, (520)322-5090 [4306]

Zero 88 Inc., PO Box 14982, North Palm Beach, FL 33408, (561)842-2263 [9623]

Zero US Corp., Industrial Cir., Lincoln, RI 02865-2600, (401)724-4470 [21371]

Zeroid and Company Inc., 5500 Cherokee Ave., No. 120, Alexandria, VA 22312, (703)461-8383 [21372]

Zeroll Co., PO Box 999, Ft. Pierce, FL 34954, (561)461-3811 [15717]

Zeta Associates Inc., 10300 Eaton Pl., No. 500, Fairfax, VA 22030, (703)385-7050 [9624]

Zetex Inc., 47 Mall Dr., Ste. 4, Commack, NY 11725-5717, (516)543-7100 [9625]

Zeuschel Equipment Co., 2717 Breckenridge, St. Louis, MO 63144, [24462]

Zeuschel Equipment Co., 7824 Barton, Lenexa, KS 66214, (913)631-4747 [24463]

Zeuschel Equipment Co., 2717 Breckenridge Industrial Ct., St. Louis, MO 63144, (314)645-5003 [24464]

ZEXEL USA Corp., 625 Southside Dr., Decatur, IL 62521, (217)362-2300 [3454]

ZF Group NAO, 7310 Turfway Rd. No. 450, Florence, KY 41042, (606)282-4300 [18645]

ZF Industries Inc., 7310 Turfway Rd. No. 450, Florence, KY 41042, (606)282-4300 [18645]

Zidell Inc., 3121 SW Moody Ave., Portland, OR 97201, (503)228-8691 [18646]

Zidell Marine Corp., 3121 SW Moody Ave., Portland, OR 97201, (503)228-8691 [18646]

Ziegenbein Associates Inc., 200 Bishops Way, Brookfield, WI 53005, (414)785-1350 [9626]

Zieger and Sons Inc., 6215 Ardleigh St., Philadelphia, PA 19138, (215)438-7060 [14982]

Ziegler Repair, 925 Central, New Rockford, ND 58356, (701)947-2766 [14789]

Ziegler Steel Service Corp., 7000 Van Dini Blvd., Los Angeles, CA 90040, (213)726-7000 [8254]

Ziegler Tire and Supply Co., 4150 Millennium Blvd. SE, Massillon, OH 44646, (330)477-2747 [3455]

Ziegler's Bakers Supply and Equipment Corp., 6890 Kinne St., East Syracuse, NY 13057, (315)463-0060 [13006]

Ziegler's Bolt & Nut House, 4848 Corporate St. SW, Canton, OH 44706-1907, (330)478-2542 [14005]

Ziff Co., 180 Shrewsbury St., West Boylston, MA 01583 [17296]

Zilkoski's Auto Electric, 200 N 39th, Springfield, OR 97478-5746, (541)747-9213 [9627]

Zima Corp., PO Box 6010, Spartanburg, SC 29304, (864)576-5810 [16660]

Zimco Marine, 400 Washington St., PO Drawer AE, Port Isabel, TX 78578, (956)943-2762 [18647]

Zimmer & Associates; Jackson, PO Box 279, Oakley, UT 84055-0279, (801)486-3516 [19115]

Zimmer Machinery America Inc., PO Box 5561, Spartanburg, SC 29304, (864)463-4352 [16661]

Zimmer Machinery Corp., PO Box 5561, Spartanburg, SC 29304, (864)463-4352 [16661]

Zimmerman Dry Goods, 1656 Grand Ave., St. Paul, MN 55105-1804, (612)699-4273 [5495]

Zimmerman; Jerry, 253 Molasses Ln., Mt. Pleasant, SC 29464, (803)881-1223 [18648]

Zims Inc., 4370 South 300 West, Salt Lake City, UT 84107, (801)268-2505 [26721]

Zinc Positive Inc., PO Box 64157, Tacoma, WA 98464, (253)566-0869 [3456]

Zink Safety of Arkansas Inc., PO Box 15004, Little Rock, AR 72231-5004, (501)945-2666 [24662]

Zink Safety Equipment, 15101 W 110th St., Lenexa, KS 66219, (913)492-9444 [24663]

Zinsser & Co., Inc.; William, 173 Belmont Dr., Somerset, NJ 08875-1218, (732)469-8100 [21613]

Zip Dee Inc., 96 Crossen Ave., Elk Grove Village, IL 60007, (847)437-0980 [13287]

Znyx Corp., 48501 Warm Springs Blvd., Ste. 107, Fremont, CA 94539, (510)249-0800 [9628]

Zocchi Distributors, PO Box 5009, Holly Springs, MS 38634-5009 [26722]

Zodiac of North America, PO Box 400, Stevensville, MD 21666, (410)643-4141 [18649]

Zoeller Co., 3649 Cane Run Rd., PO Box 16347, Louisville, KY 40211-1961, (502)778-2731 [16662]

Zoltek Companies Inc. Equipment and Services Div., 400 Russell Blvd., St. Louis, MO 63104, (314)771-0700 [17105]

The Zondervan Corp., 5300 Patterson SE, Grand Rapids, MI 49530, (616)698-6900 [4307]

Zonic A and D Co., 50 W TechneCenter Dr., Milford, OH 45150, (513)248-1911 [24465]

Zonne Industrial Tool Co., 11945 Rivera Rd., Santa Fe Springs, CA 90670, (562)945-2951 [16663]

Zorbite Corp., 612 Meyer Ln., No. 8, Redondo Beach, CA 90278, (310)374-6465 [4561]

Zortec International Inc., 1321 Murfressboro Rd., Nashville, TN 37212, (615)361-7000 [6891]

Zucca Inc.; L.J., 760 S Delsea Dr., Vineland, NJ 08360-4464, (609)692-7425 [26377]

Zuckerman, Charles and Son Inc., PO Box 2037, Winchester, VA 22604, (540)667-9000 [20505]

Zuckerman-Honickman Inc., 191 S Gulph Rd., King of Prussia, PA 19406, (610)962-0100 [25950]

Zukerman and Sons Inc.; Sam, 1650 Smallman St., Pittsburgh, PA 15222, (412)261-0818 [13475]

Zumot and Son, 7710 Old Spring House Rd., McLean, VA 22102, (703)893-7233 [2146]

Zumpano Enterprises, Inc., 764 Miami Cir., NE, Ste. 100, Atlanta, GA 30324-5909, (404)233-2943 [10310]

Zumpano Enterprises, Inc., 119 Ben Burton Rd., Bogart, GA 30622, (404)549-5455 [10311]

Zumpano Enterprises, Inc., 7411 Tara Blvd., Jonesboro, GA 30236, (404)471-0666 [10312]

Zumpano Enterprises, Inc., 6354 Warren Dr., Norcross, GA 30093, (770)449-3528 [10313]

Zumpano Enterprises Inc., 6354 Warren Dr., Norcross, GA 30093, (770)449-3528 [8255]

Zuni Investment Co., 1380 Zuni St., Denver, CO 80204, (303)893-3211 [22821]

Zytronics Inc., 70 Tirrell Hill Rd., Bedford, NH 03110, (603)623-8888 [9629]

Zytronix Inc., 1208 Apollo Way Ste. 504, Sunnyvale, CA 94086, (408)749-1326 [6892]

Zzyzx Peripherals Inc., 5893 Oberlin Dr., Ste. 102, San Diego, CA 92121, (858)558-7800 [6893]